EL DORADO COUNTY LIBRARY
00588 2798

D0557270

The Film Encyclopedia

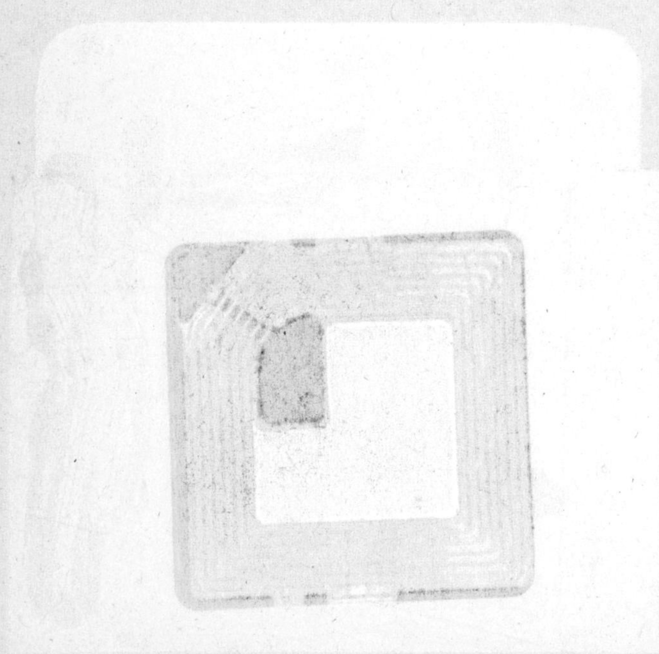

The Film Encyclopedia

THIRD EDITION

Ephraim Katz

Revised by Fred Klein and Ronald Dean Nolan

HarperPerennial
A Division of HarperCollins*Publishers*

Editor's Note:
In the first printing of this book, the entry about the well-known photographer and film director Morris Engel states that Mr. Engel died in 1986. This is inaccurate. Mr. Engel is very much alive and continues to thrive in New York City, the subject of his renowned films. He has recently completed an 80-minute video titled *Camellia,* and his classic film *Little Fugitive* was selected by the Library of Congress for inclusion in the National Film Registry in 1997.

For information address HarperCollins Publishers, Inc., 10 East 53rd Street, New York, NY 10022.

HarperCollins books may be purchased for educational, business, or sales promotional use. For information, please write: Special Markets Department, HarperCollins Publishers, Inc., 10 East 53rd Street, New York, NY 10022.

FIRST EDITION

Designed by George J. McKeon

Library of Congress Cataloging-in-Publication Data
Katz, Ephraim.
The film encyclopedia / Ephraim Katz. — 3rd ed. / revised by Fred Klein and Ronald Dean Nolan.
p. cm.
ISBN 0-06-273492-X
1. Motion pictures—Encyclopedias. I. Klein, Fred (Fred Merton) II. Nolan, Ronald Dean. III. Title.
PN1993.45.K34 1998
791.43'03—dc21 97-21745

---

00 01 02 ❖/RRD 10 9 8 7 6 5 4

Preface to the First Edition

This work is a one-man project. It has taken many years to compile, and its scope has gradually expanded far beyond the original plan, because of my desire to include in it much information that can be found elsewhere only in a wide variety of sources or that is treated sketchily in other works—to make it, in fact, the most comprehensive one-volume encyclopedia of world cinema ever published in the English language.

Every consideration has been given to the range and depth of material, even when this has meant the sacrifice of features that would make the book superficially attractive. Although the publishers and I would have liked to use photographs to enliven the text on one of the most visual of arts, we hope the reader will agree that their omission is preferable to the skimping on entries and information that the use of photographs would have necessitated. At my suggestion, the publishers have agreed to drop an entire category of subjects—the factual and critical survey of specific motion pictures. Even a modest sampling of the thousands of notable films would have added hundreds of pages to this already hefty volume and the selection would have been severely limited in both number of titles and information about them. We have, then, elected to disappoint the natural expectations of our audience rather than risk its protest with half-measures.

In the present volume I have concentrated on a broad range of entries about filmmakers and filmmaking with, I trust, a good balance of America, United Kingdom, and international subjects. Country by country, the history of major film industries is covered from its inception to the present day. Important film-related organizations and events are discussed; inventions, techniques, processes, equipment, and technical terms are explained in language that is at once precise and easy to follow. The numerous biographies of directors, producers, screenwriters, cinematographers, art directors, composers, film editors, stars, and featured players are sufficiently rich in personal and professional details (including, in most cases, day of birth and education) to please both the film scholar and the movie fan. Complete filmographies accompany the entries of most directors and of all major stars. The film credits of other personalities are extensive and carefully selected to represent their most important work.

Looking back on the years I have invested in this volume, perhaps my most sobering discovery was that an open-ended ratio exists between one unit of fact and multiple units of time. For every hour of actual writing time that went into the preparation of the encyclopedia, I must have spent ten hours of research—checking, cross-checking, and rechecking every fact in a great variety of sources in my own vast library and in outside facilities with film collections. I have tried, to the best of my abilities, to resolve conflicts between sources of information and to correct factual distortions that have been perpetuated in film literature over the years. But in a work of this size, a degree of oversight is inevitable, and I beg the indulgence of the reader if, after all, some errors have crept in.

As with any work of magnitude, this encyclopedia was seen into print with the aid of many people, and I am indebted to all of them. My grateful thanks to members of the combined Crowell and Harper & Row editorial staffs—particularly Nicholas Ellison, Bernard Skydell, Leland Lowther, and Patrick Barrett—who were always at hand with practical help, good advice, and gentle spurs. I owe a very special acknowledgment to James Daly, who, over several years of devoted, meticulous care to the manuscript as editor/copyeditor, gained an invaluable overview of the work and saved me from many slips and inconsistencies. For help in confirming a prodigious array of facts, I am indebted to Naomi Ben-Gur, Julie Guibord, and Louise Spence. Finally, an appreciation of my wife Helen, for loving encouragement, intelligent help in research, and, above all, forbearance during the long years the work played hob with our lives.

Ephraim Katz

Editor's Note

When we took on this assignment we were well aware of the prodigious work Mr. Katz and others had put into making *The Film Encyclopedia* the book of record on the international cinema. Fortunately, we were able to call on some of the same resources, as well as interesting new ones, to carry on the tradition. We decided right off there would be *no* entries eliminated—regardless of size constrictions. However, with so much happening, both technically and business-wise, we felt there should be a little less stress on private lives.

We were fortunate to have access to the rich field of information found in libraries from coast to coast—from New York's Lincoln Center Library for the Performing Arts (access to which was briefly blocked during the filming of the Academy Award scene in "In & Out") to the superb library at the Academy of Motion Picture Arts and Science in Los Angeles (where the silence was punctuated by the clatter of laptop computer keyboards) to the library at the University of California at Santa Barbara (visited with the help of a phony pass). We have been able to romance the Internet, as well as communicate with each other and friends (serving as helpful fact checkers), through a battery of home and office fax machines. And, both of us are blessed with the kind of irritating but retentive memory for film statistics that others reserve for baseball team records or Civil War battlefield strategies. This has been an eye-opening experience for us.

Fred Klein and Ronald Dean Nolen
Editors, *The Film Encyclopedia 3rd Edition*

Note to the Reader

The subjects of the encyclopedia are presented in alphabetical order. There is, therefore, no index, but the text is liberally cross-referenced to direct the reader to all entries that contain related or complementary information. The cross-references are indicated with the use of small capitals: BELUSHI; CLAPSTICKS; CINEMASCOPE.

In a biography the heading "FILMS" indicates that what follows is a complete list of credits, either for the professional capacity given in the biography after the person's name or for the function specified in the filmography itself. A partial listing is headed "FILMS INCLUDE." When it is not otherwise apparent, the national origin of a film, or the country in which it was produced, is shown by giving the country's name after the title, in parentheses and usually abbreviated.

A slash separating titles in the credits means that what follows is an alternate title, either in the same language as the original, in a second or third language for an international co-production, or for the release in a country other than that of origin. A slash used with country designations means that the film was a co-production of the two or more nations named.

Dates given with film titles are almost always the years of first release for general screening. For some films, however, the date reflects the year of a premiere (as when an American picture was screened near the end of a year to qualify it for the Academy Awards) or the year that the film was completed (as for some European films for which release dates could not be ascertained).

In some credits, a single film title is in most cases the title given the production in the country of origin. Whenever possible, original titles are given for pictures made in English, French, Spanish, Italian, and German. Titles of those made in less familiar languages (Swedish, Japanese, Russian, etc.) are those under which they have been released in the United States or in the United Kingdom. When no record of release in English-speaking countries is available, what is shown for a title in one of the unfamiliar languages is either a literal translation or the English rendering of an untranslatable title.

Abbreviations

Most of the abbreviations in the film credits, as for countries, are common enough to be self-explanatory. The list below identifies those that might not be readily apparent.

Alg.	Algeria	Gr.	Greece
Aus.	Austria	phot.	director of photography; cinematographer
Austral.	Australia	sc.	screenplay writer, scenarist
Br.	Brazil	supvr.	production supervisor
Can.	Canada	Sw.	Sweden
Eg.	Egypt	Switz.	Switzerland

The Film Encyclopedia

AAAA (Associated Actors and Artistes of America). The parent organization incorporating seven major unions and guilds representing actors and entertainers in the US, such as Actors Equity Association (AEA), the American Federation of Television and Radio Artists (AFTRA), the American Guild of Variety Artists (AGVA), and the Screen Actors Guild (SAG). Based in New York City, the "four A's" was organized in 1919 and is affiliated with the AFL-CIO. Membership is close to 200,000.

AADA. Commonly used abbreviation for the American Academy of Dramatic Arts, the oldest actors' training school in the English-speaking world. The Academy was founded in 1884 in New York City by Franklin Haven Sargent and was first known as the Lyceum Theatre School for Acting, later changing its name to the New York School for Acting, and finally to its present name. The curriculum emphasizes dramatic stage training but also includes classes in television and film. A West Coast campus of the AADA was founded in 1974, in Pasadena, Cal. Famous alumni of the school include Armand Assante, Lauren Bacall, Anne Bancroft, John Cassavetes, Hume Cronyn, Cecil B. De Mille, Danny De Vito, Colleen Dewhurst, Kirk Douglas, Nina Foch, Ruth Gordon, Jennifer Jones, Garson Kanin, Grace Kelly, Agnes Moorehead, Pat O'Brien, William Powell, Robert Redford, Edward G. Robinson, Rosalind Russell, Joseph Schildkraut, Annabella Sciorra, Spencer Tracy, Claire Trevor, Robert Walker, and Peter Weller.

A and B Editing. A method of editing that requires the use of two rolls of film in the preparation of a master print. By alternating pictures from one of the rolls with a blank LEADER from the other roll, DISSOLVES and other effects can easily be achieved. Both rolls have a common CUE MARK. Roll A contains all the scenes up to the first dissolve, followed by a strip of blank leader for the scene to be dissolved. Roll B contains a blank leader up to the first dissolve, followed by the scene into which the dissolve is to be made. Until the next dissolve is reached, roll B then contains the picture scenes, while roll A consists of a blank leader. The process of alternating blank leaders and scenes is continued until all dissolves, FADES, and other effects have been introduced. The system is also useful in eliminating visible splices in the editing of 16 mm film.

Abbott, Bud. Actor. *b.* William A. Abbott, Oct. 2, 1895, Asbury Park, N.J. *d.* 1974 of cancer. Snide straight man of the ABBOTT AND COSTELLO comedy team. The son of a circus couple, he grew up on Coney Island and at age 15 was Mickey-Finned and shanghaied aboard a ship bound for Norway. Unsuccessful at repeated attempts to break into show business, it was while he was working as a cashier at a Brooklyn theater in 1931 that a new career began for him when he was asked to substitute for comedian Lou Costello's ailing straight man. After the team split up in 1957, Abbott made a weak attempt at resuming his stage and TV career alone and with another partner. He suffered a series of strokes and spent his last years in retirement. See also ABBOTT AND COSTELLO; COSTELLO, LOU.

Abbott, Diahnne. Actress. Born in 1945, in New York City. Stately, voluptuous African-American actress in supporting and character parts. Formerly married to Robert DE NIRO, she appeared with him in *Taxi Driver*, *New York New York* (where she sang "Honeysuckle Rose"), and *The King of Comedy*.

FILMS INCLUDE: *Taxi Driver* 1976; *New York New York*, *Welcome to L.A.* 1977; *The King of Comedy* 1983; *Love Streams* 1984; *Jo Jo Dancer, Your Life Is Calling* 1986.

Abbott, George. Playwright, director, producer, screenwriter. Born on June 25, 1887, in Forestville, N.Y. *d.* 1995. *ed.* Rochester U.; Harvard. Legendary Broadway personality. Began his career as an actor in 1913. He later wrote numerous plays, often in collaboration, and directed and produced many others on Broadway. Several of his plays were adapted by others to the screen, including 'Broadway,' 'Coquette,' 'Lilly Turner,' 'Three Men on a Horse,' 'On Your Toes,' and 'The Boys From Syracuse.' He moved to Hollywood during the switch to sound, collaborated on the script of *All Quiet on the Western Front* (1930), and directed a number of films, usually supplying his own scripts. In 1931 he returned to the stage and subsequently directed only three films, two of them screen adaptations of his stage musicals, 'The Pajama Game' and 'Damn Yankees.' He also produced several films, including *Boy Meets Girl* (1938). Among the numerous hits he directed for the stage were 'Twentieth Century' (1932), 'Boy Meets Girl' (1935), 'Room Service' (1937), 'Pal Joey' (1940), 'On the Town' (1944), 'Where's Charley?' (1948), 'Call Me Madam' (1950), 'A Tree Grows in Brooklyn' (1951), 'Wonderful Town' (1953), 'The Pajama Game' (1954), 'Damn Yankees' (1955), 'Fiorello!' (1959), and 'A Funny Thing Happened on the Way to the Forum' (1962). In 1983, at the age of 95 (!) he directed and co-produced a Broadway revival of 'On Your Toes.' In 1993, at 105, he joined in festivities celebrating Broadway's 100th anniversary. Autobiography: *Mister Abbott* (1963).

FILMS (as director): *The Impostor* 1918; *Why Bring That Up?* (also dial., co-sc.), *Half-Way to Heaven* (also sc.) 1929; *Manslaughter* (also sc.), *The Sea God* (also sc.) 1930; *Stolen Heaven* (also sc.), *Secrets of a Secretary* (also sc.), *My Sin* (also sc.), *The Cheat* (also sc.) 1931; *Too Many Girls* (also prod.) 1940; *The Pajama Game* (co-dir., co-prod. with Stanley Donen; also co-sc. with Richard Bissell from their own stage musical) 1957; *Damn Yankees* (co-dir., co-prod. with Donen; also sc. from the stage musical he co-wrote with Douglass Wallop) 1958.

Abbott, L. B. Special effects technician. *b.* Lenwood Ballard Abbott, June 13, 1908, Pasadena, Calif., the son of a silent film cinematographer. *d.* 1985. Among Hollywood's leading trick photography experts. He won Oscars for *Dr. Doolittle* (1967), *Tora! Tora! Tora!* (1970), *The Poseidon Adventure* (1972), and *Logan's Run* (1976), as well as several Emmys for his TV work.

FILMS INCLUDE: *The Three Faces Of Eve, The Enemy Below, Peyton Place* 1957; *The Long Hot Summer, The Roots of Heaven, South Pacific, The Fly, The Young Lions* 1958; *The Diary of Anne Frank, Journey to the Center of the Earth* 1959; *From the Terrace, The Lost World, North to Alaska* 1960; *Voyage to the Bottom of the Sea* 1961; *Cleopatra* 1963; *The Agony and the Ecstasy, The Sound of Music* 1965; *Fantastic Voyage, Our Man Flint* 1966; *Doctor Doolittle, Valley of the Dolls* 1967; *The Detective, Planet of the Apes* 1968; *Butch Cassidy and the Sundance Kid, Hello Dolly!* 1969; *Patton, Tora! Tora! Tora!* 1970; *The Poseidon Adventure* 1972; *The Towering Inferno* 1974; *Logan's Run* 1976; *The Swarm* 1978; *When Time Ran Out* 1980.

Abbott and Costello. A highly successful comedy team of the 40s and early 50s. They first joined forces in 1931, with tall, slim Abbott playing straight man to short, chubby Costello, and soon were headliners on the vaudeville and burlesque circuit. They broke into radio in 1938 and the following year starred in the Broadway revue 'Streets of Paris.' Their first film, *One Night in the Tropics* (1940), was hardly noticed, but their next, *Buck Privates* (1941), grossed $10 million and firmly established the team. For the next decade they were included in every list of top-ten box-office grossers. In 1957, after more than 30 broad slapstick films and some success on television, the two broke up. Their reputation as a comedy team has not survived well, but their most famous routine, "Who's on First?," first performed on film in *The Naughty Nineties* (1945), is enshrined on a plaque in baseball's Hall of Fame. See also ABBOTT, BUD; COSTELLO, LOU.

FILMS: *One Night in the Tropics* 1940; *Buck Privates, In the Navy, Hold That Ghost, Keep 'Em Flying* 1941; *Ride 'Em Cowboy, Rio Rita, Pardon My Sarong, Who Done It?* 1942; *It Ain't Hay, Hit the Ice* 1943; *In Society, Lost in a Harem* 1944; *Here Come the Co-Eds, The Naughty Nineties, Abbott and Costello in Hollywood* 1945; *Little Giant, The Time of Their Lives* 1946; *Buck Privates Come Home, The Wistful Widow of Wagon Gap* 1947; *The Noose Hangs High, Abbott and Costello Meet Frankenstein, Mexican Hayride* 1948; *Africa Screams, Abbott and Costello Meet the Killer Boris Karloff* 1949; *Abbott and Costello in the Foreign Legion* 1950; *Abbott and Costello Meet the Invisible Man, Comin' Round the Mountain* 1951; *Jack and the Beanstalk, Lost in Alaska, Abbott and Costello Meet Captain Kidd* 1952; *Abbott and Costello Go to Mars, Abbott and Costello Meet Dr. Jekyll and Mr. Hyde* 1953; *Abbott and Costello Meet the Keystone Kops, Abbott and Costello Meet the Mummy* 1955; *Dance With Me Henry* 1956; *The World of Abbott and Costello* 1965 (compilation); *Entertaining the Troops* 1989 (archival footage).

Abel, Alfred. Actor. *b.* 1880, Leipzig, Germany. *d.* 1937. He worked as a forest warden, businessman, bank clerk, and designer before being discovered by Asta Nielsen in 1913. He was an outstanding performer in German films of the classical period, ranking with Emil Jannings, Conrad Veidt, and Werner Krauss. In the early 30s he directed three films.

FILMS INCLUDE: *Sodoms Ende* 1913(?); *Kameraden* 1919; *Sappho* 1921; *Dr. Mabuse der Spieler/Dr. Mabuse the Gambler, Die Flamme/Montmartre* 1922; *Die Buddenbrooks* 1923; *Metropolis* 1926; *L'Argent* (Fr.) 1928; *Narcose* (also dir.) 1929; *Dolly macht Karriere/Dolly's Way to Stardom* 1930; *Meine Frau die Hochstaplerin, Der Kongress tanzt/The Congress Dances* 1931; *Glückliche Reise* (dir. only) 1933; *Alles um eine Frau* (dir. only) 1935; *Kater Lampe* 1936; *Sieben Ohrfeigen* 1937; *Frau Sylvelin* 1938.

Abel, Walter. Actor. *b.* June 6, 1898, St. Paul, Minn. *d.* 1987. *ed.* AADA. On stage from 1919, he was an early interpreter of characters in plays of Eugene O'Neill. He played his first important film role in *Liliom* in 1930. After being miscast as d'Artagnan in the 1935 version of *The Three Musketeers,* he settled for a career as a competent character actor, in both light and dramatic roles. In the 60s he was president of the American National Theater and Academy.

FILMS INCLUDE: *The North Wind's Malice* 1920; *Liliom* 1930; *The Three Musketeers* 1935; *Fury* 1936; *Men with Wings* 1938; *Arise My Love* 1940; *Hold Back the Dawn, Skylark* 1941; *Holiday Inn, Wake Island* 1942; *Mr. Skeffington 1944*; *Kiss and Tell* 1945; *The Kid from Brooklyn, 13 Rue Madeleine* 1946; *That Lady in Ermine* 1948; *Night People* 1954; *Raintree County* 1957; *Mirage* 1965; *Zora* 1971; *Silent Night Bloody Night* 1974; *The Ultimate Solution of Grace Quigley/Grace Quigley* 1984.

above the line. That portion of a motion picture's budget which covers major expenditures incurred or negotiated before the actual shooting begins. These normally include fees for rights on original property (novel, play, short story, etc.), wages and expenses of the producer, the director, and the screenwriter, and salaries of the stars. These are the costliest items in a film's budget and are usually negotiable. Below-the-line expenditures include all other costs of production. They are usually fixed and comprise numerous items—payments to the remainder of the cast, wages of the technical crew, the use of technical equipment and studio facilities, travel and location expenses, etc.

Abraham, F(ahrid) Murray. Actor. Born on Oct. 24, 1939, in Pittsburgh, of Italian-Syrian origin. *ed.* University of Texas. Craggy, pockmarked, highly intense yet remarkably controlled character player of the American stage and screen. Trained for the stage with Uta Hagen at the Herbert Berghof, making his stage debut in Los Angeles in 1965 ('The Wonderful Ice Cream Suit') and in New York in 1966 ('The Fantasticks'). As a struggling actor, his television work included appearances on 'All in the Family' and Fruit Of The Loom commercials. He was still largely unknown when, at the age of 45, he won a best actor Academy Award for his complex virtuoso portrayal of composer Antonio Salieri in the film *Amadeus.* His subsequent film roles, however, offered far less rewarding opportunities. Subsequent stage credits have included 'Waiting for Godot' (1988).

FILMS INCLUDE: *They Might Be Giants* 1971; *Serpico* 1973; *The Prisoner of Second Avenue, The Sunshine Boys* 1975; *All The President's Men, The Ritz* 1976; *The Big Fix, Madman* (Isr.) 1978; *Scarface* 1983; *Amadeus* (as Salieri) 1984; *The Name of the Rose* (It./Fr./Ger.) 1986; *An Innocent Man, Russicum/The Third Solution* (It.), *Slipstream* (UK) 1989; *The Bonfire of the Vanities* 1990; *Cadence, Mobsters* 1991; *By the Sword, Last Action Hero, National Lampoon's Loaded Weapon I* 1993; *Jamila, Nostradamus, Surviving the Game* 1994; *Dillinger and Capone, Mighty Aphrodite* 1995; *Children of the Revolution, Fresh* (unbilled), *Looking For Richard* 1996.

Abrahams, Jim. Director, screenwriter, executive producer. Born on May 10, 1944, in Milwaukee. He was 26 and a private investigator in his native town when a chance meeting with childhood friends, David and Jerry ZUCKER, led to the trio's founding of the Kentucky Fried Theatre in Madison, Wisconsin. The show was a multimedia presentation that combined live improvisational skits with filmed and videotaped satirical material. They then moved on to Los Angeles, where their free-wheeling shenanigans provided the core for John Landis's *The Kentucky Fried Movie* (1977). Three years later the triumvirate scored a surprise box-office hit as the co-directors and co-screenwriters of *Airplane!,* a loony spoof of *Airport* and its sequels. Several other successful comedies followed, including the *Naked Gun* series, based on the team's short-lived TV series 'Police Squad!' (1982).

FILMS: *The Kentucky Fried Movie* (sc., act.) 1977; *Airplane!* (co-dir., co-sc.) 1980; *Top Secret!* (co-dir., co-sc.) 1984; *Ruthless People* (co-dir.) 1986; *Coming to America* (act.), *Big Business* (dir.), *The Naked Gun: From the Files of Police Squad!* (co-sc., co-exec. prod.) 1988; *Cry-Baby* (co-exec. prod.), *Welcome Home Roxy Carmichael* (dir.) 1990; *The Naked Gun 2½: The Smell of Fear* (co-exec. prod.), *Hot Shots!* (dir., co-sc.) 1991; *Hot Shots! Part Deux* (dir., co-sc.) 1993; *Naked Gun 33⅓: The Final Insult* 1994.

absolute film. An experimental film that attempts to create new reality by freeing images from their narrative function. In *Berlin: Symphony of a Great City* (1927) and *Melody of the World* (1929), Walter RUTTMANN assembled pieces of film to form a unity based on rhythm and psychological continuity rather than on conventional narrative continuity. The early films of BUÑUEL and COCTEAU qualify as absolute films, although they appear to have more of a narrative thread than other absolute films. See also ABSTRACT FILM; AVANT-GARDE.

abstract film. A film that attempts to communicate purely through visual expression, using nonrepresentational lines, patterns, shapes, and geometrical constructions to produce a psychological rather than a conscious impact on the viewer. Abstract films usually have no reference to concrete reality but may use real objects and actions within an abstract framework (like the repetitive shot of an old woman climbing stone steps in Fernand Léger's *Ballet mécanique*). The abstract film has its foundations in the work of Viking EGGELING and Hans RICHTER, German painters who began putting abstract lines and geometrical shapes on film in the early 1920s. Other leading abstract filmmakers in the 20s include Man RAY *(l'Étoile de Mer)* and Henri Chomette *(Five Minutes of Pure Cinema)*. Ralph Steiner made *H_2O*, a film of light patterns on water, in the 30s. Others active during that period were Lewis Jacobs and Len Lye. The 50s and 60s saw a revitalization of this form of cinema with works such as Ian Hugo's *Bells of Atlantis* and Francis Thompson's *N.Y., N.Y.,* the latter distorting the buildings of New York City into fantastic abstract shapes. The time paintings of Ed Emshwiller and the computer films of John Whitney are other examples of more recent experimentation with abstract film. See also AVANT-GARDE.

Abuladze, Tengiz. Director, screenwriter. Born on Jan. 31, 1924, in Georgia, USSR. A leading filmmaker of the Georgian branch of Soviet cinema. After graduating from the Tbilisi Railway School in 1943, he studied drama, then entered the Moscow Film Institute, where he was guided by Sergei YUTKEVICH and Mikhail ROMM. He directed several documentaries and fictional films with childhood friend and classmate Revaz Chkheidze (*b.* Dec. 8, 1926) before his solo debut in 1958. Their medium-length film *Magdan's Donkey* won a prize at Cannes in 1956. Abuladze won the Lenin Prize for his trilogy *The Plea, The Wishing Tree*, and *Repentance.* He usually writes or collaborates on his own scripts.

FILMS INCLUDE: *Dimitry Arakishvili* (doc.; co-dir.) 1955; *Our Palace* (doc.; co-dir.) 1953; *Magdan's Donkey* (co-dir.) 1955; *Someone's Else's Children/Stepchildren* 1958; *Me Grandma Iliko and Hillarion* 1963; *The Plea/The Entreaty* 1969; *A Necklace for My Beloved* 1972; *The Wishing Tree* 1977; *Repentance* 1987 (release delayed from 1984); *Hadji Murat* 1989.

Academy Awards. Annual awards of merit given since 1927 to film artists and technicians by the ACADEMY OF MOTION PICTURE ARTS AND SCIENCES, in the form of 13½-inch-high gold-plated statuettes known as OSCARS. Members of 13 art and craft branches select up to five nominees for awards in their particular area of specialty (actors select actors, directors select directors, editors select editors, etc.). The entire membership of more than 5,000 then votes in a secret ballot on the final winners in all categories.

The Academy Award ceremony is a glittering annual affair now brought into American homes via an enormously popular television broadcast, reaching one billion viewers in about 100 countries. Originally hosted by academy presidents, the ceremony soon came to be led by entertainers like Will Rogers, Jack Benny, Johnny Carson, and Billy Crystal. Beginning in 1940, Bob Hope hosted or co-hosted the event about 20 times.

Although still the most coveted film award, the aura of the Oscar has become increasingly tainted. Since the 1960s the voting system has been under fire by members of the industry and outside critics as being influenced more by publicity and sentiment than by actual quality and merit. The event has been derisively termed a popularity contest: Many of the voting members have been inactive in the industry for years and few get to see all the films they vote on. Studio block vote is also a consistent problem. Actor George C. Scott expressed his disdain by refusing to accept the best actor award he won in 1970 for his performance in *Patton.* Over the past two decades the Oscar ceremony has become a platform for political statements, on subjects ranging from treatment of Native Americans in the film industry to AIDS awareness and urban violence. Despite the varieties of dissent, the Academy Awards continue to carry weight in the economics of the film industry. A best picture award can be worth tens of millions of dollars more at the box office, and an individual Oscar can do wonders for a performer or filmmaker negotiating a salary.

ACADEMY AWARDS: WINNERS IN PRINCIPAL CATEGORIES

YEAR	BEST PICTURE	BEST DIRECTOR	BEST ACTOR	BEST ACTRESS
1927–28	*Wings*	Frank Borzage *Seventh Heaven*; Lewis Milestone *Two Arabian Knights*	Emil Jannings *The Last Command, The Way of All Flesh*	Janet Gaynor *Seventh Heaven, Street Angel, Sunrise*
1928–29	*The Broadway Melody*	Frank Lloyd *The Divine Lady*	Warner Baxter *In Old Arizona*	Mary Pickford *Coquette*
1929–30	*All Quiet on the Western Front*	Lewis Milestone *All Quiet on the Western Front*	George Arliss *Disraeli*	Norma Shearer *The Divorcee*
1930–31	*Cimarron*	Norman Taurog *Skippy*	Lionel Barrymore *A Free Soul*	Marie Dressler *Min and Bill*
1931–32	*Grand Hotel*	Frank Borzage *Bad Girl*	Wallace Beery *The Champ;* Fredric March *Dr. Jekyll and Mr. Hyde*	Helen Hayes *The Sin of Madelon Claudet*

YEAR	BEST PICTURE	BEST DIRECTOR	BEST ACTOR	BEST ACTRESS
1932–33	*Cavalcade*	Frank Lloyd *Cavalcade*	Charles Laughton *The Private Life of Henry VIII*	Katharine Hepburn *Morning Glory*
1934	*It Happened One Night*	Frank Capra *It Happened One Night*	Clark Gable *It Happened One Night*	Claudette Colbert *It Happened One Night*
1935	*Mutiny on the Bounty*	John Ford *The Informer*	Victor McLaglen *The Informer*	Bette Davis *Dangerous*
1936	*The Great Ziegfeld*	Frank Capra *Mr. Deeds Goes to Town*	Paul Muni *The Story of Louis Pasteur*	Luise Rainer *The Great Ziegfeld*
1937	*The Life of Emile Zola*	Leo McCarey *The Awful Truth*	Spencer Tracy *Captains Courageous*	Luise Rainer *The Good Earth*
1938	*You Can't Take It with You*	Frank Capra *You Can't Take It With You*	Spencer Tracy *Boys Town*	Bette Davis *Jezebel*
1939	*Gone With the Wind*	Victor Fleming *Gone With the Wind*	Robert Donat *Goodbye, Mr. Chips*	Vivien Leigh *Gone With the Wind*
1940	*Rebecca*	John Ford *The Grapes of Wrath*	James Stewart *The Philadelphia Story*	Ginger Rogers *Kitty Foyle*
1941	*How Green Was My Valley*	John Ford *How Green Was My Valley*	Gary Cooper *Sergeant York*	Joan Fontaine *Suspicion*
1942	*Mrs. Miniver*	William Wyler *Mrs. Miniver*	James Cagney *Yankee Doodle Dandy*	Greer Garson *Mrs. Miniver*
1943	*Casablanca*	Michael Curtiz *Casablanca*	Paul Lukas *Watch on the Rhine*	Jennifer Jones *The Song of Bernadette*
1944	*Going My Way*	Leo McCarey *Going My Way*	Bing Crosby *Going My Way*	Ingrid Bergman *Gaslight*
1945	*The Lost Weekend*	Billy Wilder *The Lost Weekend*	Ray Milland *The Lost Weekend*	Joan Crawford *Mildred Pierce*
1946	*The Best Years of Our Lives*	William Wyler *The Best Years of Our Lives*	Fredric March *The Best Years of Our Lives*	Olivia de Havilland *To Each His Own*
1947	*Gentleman's Agreement*	Elia Kazan *Gentleman's Agreement*	Ronald Colman *A Double Life*	Loretta Young *The Farmer's Daughter*
1948	*Hamlet*	John Huston *The Treasure of the Sierra Madre*	Laurence Olivier *Hamlet*	Jane Wyman *Johnny Belinda*
1949	*All the King's Men*	Joseph L. Mankiewicz *A Letter to Three Wives*	Broderick Crawford *All the King's Men*	Olivia de Havilland *The Heiress*
1950	*All About Eve*	Joseph L. Mankiewicz *All About Eve*	Jose Ferrer *Cyrano de Bergerac*	Judy Holliday *Born Yesterday*
1951	*An American in Paris*	George Stevens *A Place in the Sun*	Humphrey Bogart *The African Queen*	Vivien Leigh *A Streetcar Named Desire*
1952	*The Greatest Show on Earth*	John Ford *The Quiet Man*	Gary Cooper *High Noon*	Shirley Booth *Come Back, Little Sheba*
1953	*From Here to Eternity*	Fred Zinnemann *From Here to Eternity*	William Holden *Stalag 17*	Audrey Hepburn *Roman Holiday*
1954	*On the Waterfront*	Elia Kazan *On the Waterfront*	Marlon Brando *On the Waterfront*	Grace Kelly *The Country Girl*
1955	*Marty*	Delbert Mann *Marty*	Ernest Borgnine *Marty*	Anna Magnani *The Rose Tattoo*
1956	*Around the World in 80 Days*	George Stevens *Giant*	Yul Brynner *The King and I*	Ingrid Bergman *Anastasia*
1957	*The Bridge on the River Kwai*	David Lean *The Bridge on the River Kwai*	Alec Guinness *The Bridge on the River Kwai*	Joanne Woodward *The Three Faces of Eve*
1958	*Gigi*	Vincente Minnelli *Gigi*	David Niven *Separate Tables*	Susan Hayward *I Want to Live*
1959	*Ben-Hur*	William Wyler *Ben-Hur*	Charleton Heston *Ben-Hur*	Simone Signoret *Room at the Top*
1960	*The Apartment*	Billy Wilder *The Apartment*	Burt Lancaster *Elmer Gantry*	Elizabeth Taylor *Butterfield 8*
1961	*West Side Story*	Jerome Robbins and Robert Wise *West Side Story*	Maximilian Schell *Judgment at Nuremberg*	Sophia Loren *Two Women*
1962	*Lawrence of Arabia*	David Lean *Lawrence of Arabia*	Gregory Peck *To Kill a Mockingbird*	Anne Bancroft *The Miracle Worker*
1963	*Tom Jones*	Tony Richardson *Tom Jones*	Sidney Poitier *Lilies of the Field*	Patricia Neal *Hud*

YEAR	BEST PICTURE	BEST DIRECTOR	BEST ACTOR	BEST ACTRESS
1964	*My Fair Lady*	George Cukor *My Fair Lady*	Rex Harrison *My Fair Lady*	Julie Andrews *Mary Poppins*
1965	*The Sound of Music*	Robert Wise *The Sound of Music*	Lee Marvin *Cat Ballou*	Julie Christie *Darling*
1966	*A Man for All Seasons*	Fred Zinnemann *A Man for All Seasons*	Paul Scofield *A Man for All Seasons*	Elizabeth Taylor *Who's Afraid of Virginia Woolf?*
1967	*In the Heat of the Night*	Mike Nichols *The Graduate*	Rod Steiger *In the Heat of the Night*	Katharine Hepburn *Guess Who's Coming to Dinner?*
1968	*Oliver!*	Sir Carol Reed *Oliver!*	Cliff Robertson *Charly*	Katharine Hepburn *The Lion in Winter;* Barbra Streisand *Funny Girl*
1969	*Midnight Cowboy*	John Schlesinger *Midnight Cowboy*	John Wayne *True Grit*	Maggie Smith *The Prime of Miss Jean Brodie*
1970	*Patton*	Franklin J. Schaffner *Patton*	George C. Scott *Patton*	Glenda Jackson *Women in Love*
1971	*The French Connection*	William Friedkin *The French Connection*	Gene Hackman *The French Connection*	Jane Fonda *Klute*
1972	*The Godfather*	Bob Fosse *Cabaret*	Marlon Brando *The Godfather*	Liza Minnelli *Cabaret*
1973	*The Sting*	George Roy Hill *The Sting*	Jack Lemmon *Save the Tiger*	Glenda Jackson *A Touch of Class*
1974	*The Godfather Part II*	Francis Ford Coppola *The Godfather Part II*	Art Carney *Harry and Tonto*	Ellen Burstyn *Alice Doesn't Live Here Anymore*
1975	*One Flew Over the Cuckoo's Nest*	Milos Forman *One Flew Over the Cuckoo's Nest*	Jack Nicholson *One Flew Over the Cuckoo's Nest*	Louise Fletcher *One Flew Over the Cuckoo's Nest*
1976	*Rocky*	John G. Avildsen *Rocky*	Peter Finch *Network*	Faye Dunaway *Network*
1977	*Annie Hall*	Woody Allen *Annie Hall*	Richard Dreyfuss *The Goodbye Girl*	Diane Keaton *Annie Hall*
1978	*The Deer Hunter*	Michael Cimino *The Deer Hunter*	John Voight *Coming Home*	Jane Fonda *Coming Home*
1979	*Kramer vs. Kramer*	Robert Benton *Kramer vs. Kramer*	Dustin Hoffman *Kramer vs. Kramer*	Sally Field *Norma Rae*
1980	*Ordinary People*	Robert Redford *Ordinary People*	Robert De Niro *Raging Bull*	Sissy Spacek *Coal Miner's Daughter*
1981	*Chariots of Fire*	Warren Beatty *Reds*	Henry Fonda *On Golden Pond*	Katharine Hepburn *On Golden Pond*
1982	*Gandhi*	Richard Attenborough *Gandhi*	Ben Kingsley *Gandhi*	Meryl Streep *Sophie's Choice*
1983	*Terms of Endearment*	James L. Brooks *Terms of Endearment*	Robert Duvall *Tender Mercies*	Shirley MacLaine *Terms of Endearment*
1984	*Amadeus*	Milos Forman *Amadeus*	F. Murray Abraham *Amadeus*	Sally Field *Places in the Heart*
1985	*Out of Africa*	Sydney Pollack *Out of Africa*	William Hurt *Kiss of the Spider Woman*	Geraldine Page *The Trip to Bountiful*
1986	*Platoon*	Oliver Stone *Platoon*	Paul Newman *The Color of Money*	Marlee Matlin *Children of a Lesser God*
1987	*The Last Emperor*	Bernardo Bertolucci *The Last Emperor*	Michael Douglas *Wall Street*	Cher *Moonstruck*
1988	*Rain Man*	Barry Levinson *Rain Man*	Dustin Hoffman *Rain Man*	Jodie Foster *The Accused*
1989	*Driving Miss Daisy*	Oliver Stone *Born on the Fourth of July*	Daniel-Day Lewis *My Left Foot*	Jessica Tandy *Driving Miss Daisy*
1990	*Dances with Wolves*	Kevin Costner *Dances with Wolves*	Jeremy Irons *Reversal of Fortune*	Kathy Bates *Misery*
1991	*The Silence of the Lambs*	Jonathan Demme *The Silence of the Lambs*	Anthony Hopkins *The Silence of the Lambs*	Jodie Foster *The Silence of the Lambs*
1992	*Unforgiven*	Clint Eastwood *Unforgiven*	Al Pacino *Scent of a Woman*	Emma Thompson *Howards End*
1993	*Schindler's List*	Steven Spielberg *Schindler's List*	Tom Hanks *Philadelphia*	Holly Hunter *The Piano*

Year	Best Picture	Best Director	Best Actor	Best Actress
1994	*Forrest Gump*	Robert Zemeckis *Forrest Gump*	Tom Hanks *Forrest Gump*	Jessica Lange *Blue Sky*
1995	*Braveheart*	Mel Gibson *Braveheart*	Nicolas Cage *Leaving Las Vegas*	Susan Sarandon *Dead Man Walking*
1996	*The English Patient*	Anthony Minghella *The English Patient*	Geoffrey Rush *Shine*	Francis McDormand *Fargo*

Year	Supporting Actor	Supporting Actress	Foreign Language Film
1936	Walter Brennan *Come and Get It!*	Gale Sondergaard *Anthony Adverse*	
1937	Joseph Schildkraut *The Life of Emile Zola*	Alice Brady *In Old Chicago*	
1938	Walter Brennan *Kentucky*	Fay Bainter *Jezebel*	
1939	Thomas Mitchell *Stagecoach*	Hattie McDaniel *Gone With the Wind*	
1940	Walter Brennan *The Westerner*	Jane Darwell *The Grapes of Wrath*	
1941	Donald Crisp *How Green Was My Valley*	Mary Astor *The Great Lie*	
1942	Van Heflin *Johnny Eager*	Teresa Wright *Mrs. Miniver*	
1943	Charles Coburn *The More the Merrier*	Katina Paxinou *For Whom the Bell Tolls*	
1944	Barry Fitzgerald *Going My Way*	Ethel Barrymore *None but the Lonely Heart*	
1945	James Dunn *A Tree Grows in Brooklyn*	Anne Revere *National Velvet*	
1946	Harold Russell *The Best Years of Our Lives*	Anne Baxter *The Razor's Edge*	
1947	Edmund Gwenn *Miracle on 34th Street*	Celeste Holm *Gentleman's Agreement*	*Shoe Shine* (It.)
1948	Walter Huston *The Treasure of the Sierra Madre*	Claire Trevor *Key Largo*	*Monsieur Vincent* (Fr.)
1949	Dean Jagger *Twelve O'Clock High*	Mercedes McCambridge *All the King's Men*	*The Bicycle Thief* (It.)
1950	George Sanders *All About Eve*	Josephine Hull *Harvey*	*The Walls of Malapaga* (Fr./It.)
1951	Karl Malden *A Streetcar Named Desire*	Kim Hunter *A Streetcar Named Desire*	*Rashomon* (Jap.)
1952	Anthony Quinn *Viva Zapata!*	Gloria Grahame *The Bad and the Beautiful*	*Forbidden Games* (Fr.)
1953	Frank Sinatra *From Here to Eternity*	Donna Reed *From Here to Eternity*	No Award Given
1954	Edmond O'Brien *The Barefoot Contessa*	Eva Marie Saint *On the Waterfront*	*Gate of Hell* (Jap.)
1955	Jack Lemmon *Mister Roberts*	Jo Van Fleet *East of Eden*	*Samurai* (Jap.)
1956	Anthony Quinn *Lust for Life*	Dorothy Malone *Written on the Wind*	*La Strada* (It.)
1957	Red Buttons *Sayonara*	Miyoshi Umeki *Sayonara*	*The Nights of Cabiria* (It.)
1958	Burl Ives *The Big Country*	Wendy Hiller *Separate Tables*	*Mon Oncle* (Fr.)
1959	Hugh Griffith *Ben-Hur*	Shelley Winters *The Diary of Anne Frank*	*Black Orpheus* (Fr., filmed in Brazil)
1960	Peter Ustinov *Spartacus*	Shirley Jones *Elmer Gantry*	*The Virgin Spring* (Sw.)
1961	George Chakiris *West Side Story*	Rita Moreno *West Side Story*	*Through a Glass Darkly* (Sw.)
1962	Ed Begley *Sweet Bird of Youth*	Patty Duke *The Miracle Worker*	*Sundays and Cybele* (Fr.)
1963	Melvyn Douglas *Hud*	Margaret Rutherford *The V.I.P.'s*	*8½* (It.)
1964	Peter Ustinov *Topkapi*	Lila Kedrova *Zorba the Greek*	*Yesterday, Today, and Tomorrow* (It.)
1965	Martin Balsam *A Thousand Clowns*	Shelley Winters *A Patch of Blue*	*The Shop on Main Street* (Czech.)
1966	Walter Matthau *The Fortune Cookie*	Sandy Dennis *Who's Afraid of Virginia Woolf?*	*A Man and a Woman* (Fr.)
1967	George Kennedy *Cool Hand Luke*	Estelle Parsons *Bonnie and Clyde*	*Closely Watched Trains* (Czech.)
1968	Jack Albertson *The Subject Was Roses*	Ruth Gordon *Rosemary's Baby*	*War and Peace* (USSR)
1969	Gig Young *They Shoot Horses Don't They?*	Goldie Hawn *Cactus Flower*	*Z* (Fr./Alg.)
1970	John Mills *Ryan's Daughter*	Helen Hayes *Airport*	*Investigation of a Citizen Above Suspicion* (It.)
1971	Ben Johnson *The Last Picture Show*	Cloris Leachman *The Last Picture Show*	*The Garden of the Finzi-Continis* (It.)
1972	Joel Grey *Cabaret*	Eileen Heckart *Butterflies Are Free*	*The Discreet Charm of the Bourgeoisie* (Fr.)
1973	John Houseman *The Paper Chase*	Tatum O'Neal *Paper Moon*	*Day for Night* (Fr.)
1974	Robert De Niro *The Godfather Part II*	Ingrid Bergman *Murder on the Orient Express*	*Amarcord* (It.)
1975	George Burns *The Sunshine Boys*	Lee Grant *Shampoo*	*Dersu Uzala* (Jap./USSR)
1976	Jason Robards *All the President's Men*	Beatrice Straight *Network*	*Black and White in Color* (Ivory Coast/Fr.)
1977	Jason Robards *Julia*	Vanessa Redgrave *Julia*	*Madame Rosa* (Fr.)

YEAR	SUPPORTING ACTOR	SUPPORTING ACTRESS	FOREIGN LANGUAGE FILM
1978	Christopher Walken *The Deer Hunter*	Maggie Smith *California Suite*	*Get Out Your Handkerchiefs* (Fr.)
1979	Melvyn Douglas *Being There*	Meryl Streep *Kramer vs. Kramer*	*The Tin Drum* (W. Ger.)
1980	Timothy Hutton *Ordinary People*	Mary Steenburgen *Melvyn and Howard*	*Moscow Does Not Believe in Tears* (USSR)
1981	John Gielgud *Arthur*	Maureen Stapleton *Reds*	*Mephisto* (Hung.)
1982	Louis Gossett, Jr. *An Officer and a Gentleman*	Jessica Lange *Tootsie*	*Volvar a Empezar/To Begin Again* (Sp.)
1983	Jack Nicholson *Terms of Endearment*	Linda Hunt *The Year of Living Dangerously*	*Fanny and Alexander* (Sw.)
1984	Haing S. Ngor *The Killing Fields*	Peggy Ashcroft *A Passage to India*	*Dangerous Moves* (Switz.)
1985	Don Ameche *Cocoon*	Anjelica Huston *Prizzi's Honor*	*The Official Story* (Argent.)
1986	Michael Caine *Hannah and Her Sisters*	Dianne Wiest *Hannah and Her Sisters*	*The Assault* (Neth.)
1987	Sean Connery *The Untouchables*	Olympia Dukakis *Moonstruck*	*Babette's Feast* (Den.)
1988	Kevin Kline *A Fish Called Wanda*	Geena Davis *The Accidental Tourist*	*Pelle the Conqueror* (Den.)
1989	Denzel Washington *Glory*	Brenda Fricker *My Left Foot*	*Cinema Paradiso* (It.)
1990	Joe Pesci *GoodFellas*	Whoopi Goldberg *Ghost*	*Journey of Hope* (Switz.)
1991	Jack Palance *City Slickers*	Mercedes Ruehl *The Fisher King*	*Mediterraneo* (It.)
1992	Gene Hackman *Unforgiven*	Marisa Tomei *My Cousin Vinny*	*Indochine* (Fr.)
1993	Tommy Lee Jones *The Fugitive*	Anna Paquin *The Piano*	*Belle Epoque* (Sp.)
1994	Martin Landau *Ed Wood*	Dianne Wiest *Bullets Over Broadway*	*Burnt by the Sun* (Rus.)
1995	Kevin Spacey *The Usual Suspects*	Mira Sorvino *Mighty Aphrodite*	*Antonia's Line* (Neth.)
1996	Cuba Gooding Jr. *Jerry Maguire*	Juliette Binoche *The English Patient*	*Kolya* (Czech.)

Academy leader. A strip of film attached by the laboratory to the beginning and end of a RELEASE PRINT according to specifications set by the Academy of Motion Picture Arts and Sciences. The academy leader contains a descending sequence of numbers, as well as cue marks and other information, to guide a projectionist in threading the projector and changing over from one reel to the next. The leader not only protects the film itself from unnecessary handling but also permits the projector to gain full sound speed before the first image reaches the picture gate. Since 1965, a standard projection guidance system called the UNIVERSAL LEADER has largely replaced the academy leader. It was devised by the Society of Motion Picture and Television Engineers (SMPTE) for use both in motion picture theaters and in television transmission of motion pictures. See also ACADEMY MASK; ACADEMY STANDARDS.

Academy mask. A device that obstructs a portion of the aperture of a motion picture camera. It came into use after the introduction of sound, when it was realized that the sound track printed on the side of the film strip distorted the proportion of the standard 35 mm frame. The Academy of Motion Picture Arts and Sciences, after which the device was named, introduced the Academy mask in an effort to re-establish screen rectangularity at the then-standard aspect ratio of 1.33:1 (or 4:3). The area delineated by the mask is known as the Academy aperture. The Academy mask had outlived its purpose after the advent of the wide screen, when the question of standard screen rectangularity became, so to speak, "academic." See also ACADEMY LEADER; ACADEMY STANDARDS.

Academy of Motion Picture Arts and Sciences. A nonprofit organization established in 1927 to "improve the artistic quality of the film medium, provide a common forum for the various branches and crafts of the industry, foster cooperation in technical research and cultural progress, and pursue a variety of other stated objectives." It is best known, however, for its annual presentation of the ACADEMY AWARDS. Membership, now over 5,000, is by invitation only. Members are categorized according to several areas of film craftsmanship, including actors, administrators, art directors, cinematographers, directors, executives, film editors, composers, producers, public relations people, short-subject filmmakers, sound technicians, and writers. Presidents of the Academy over the years have included Walter Mirisch, Daniel Taradash, Gregory Peck, Arthur Freed, George Stevens, George Seaton, Charles Brackett, Jean Hersholt, Bette Davis, Walter Wanger, Frank Capra, Frank Lloyd, Conrad Nagel, William De Mille, Douglas Fairbanks, Sr., Karl Malden, and Arthur Hiller.

Academy standards. A set of technical requirements established by the Academy of Motion Picture Arts and Sciences to enforce standard practices throughout the film industry. They include the Academy aperture, the ACADEMY LEADER, and the ACADEMY MASK.

accelerated motion. A technical effect that makes people or objects appear to be moving at a faster-than-normal rate during projection. Popularly known as "fast motion," it is achieved by running the camera at a slower rate than the standard 24 frames per second.

Accelerated motion has been used for comic effect since the early days of film and was a standard device in Mack Sennett's comedies. It was used satirically by Eisenstein in *Old and New* (or *The General Line*) to depict bureaucrats jumping into action in the presence of a party functionary, and poetically by Georges Rouquier in *Farrébique* to show the blooming of flowers in a matter of seconds. The effect also has been widely used to speed up the pace of action and adventure films.

Silent films, shot at a rate of 16 frames per second, appear accelerated today because they are projected on modern equipment operating at 24 frames per second. The opposite effect is SLOW MOTION.

A.C.E. (American Cinema Editors). An honorary professional society founded in 1950 and dedicated to the promotion of better film-editing. Membership, by invitation only, is about 350. Based in West Hollywood, the society publishes a periodical, *The Cinemeditor,* and bestows an annual award, the "Eddie." Known by its full name, the Golden Eddie, the award recognizes achievement in filmmaking. A.C.E. also bestows two annual Career Achievement Awards to film editors and one annual Artistic Achievement Award for excellence in editing.

acetate base. A film support made of a slow-burning chemical substance. Since coming into use in the late 40s, it has gradually replaced the nitrate base, which had been a constant fire hazard in editing rooms and projection booths. Film coated on an acetate base is known as SAFETY FILM.

Achard, Marcel. Playwright, screenwriter, director. *b.* July 5, 1899, France. *d.* 1974 of diabetes. Before staging his first play in 1922, he was a teacher and journalist. After years of prolific work in the theater, highlighted by a number of hit "boulevard" comedies, he was elected to the French Academy (1959). His output includes numerous screenplays. He presided over the Cannes Film Festival in 1958 and 1959 and over the Venice Festival in 1960.

FILMS INCLUDE: As writer, alone or in collaboration—*Jean de la Lune* 1931; *Mistigri* 1932; *The Merry Widow* (US) 1934; *Folies-Bergère* (dial. of French version; US) 1935; *Mayerling* 1936; *L'Alibi, Gribouille/Heart of Paris* (story only) 1937; *Orage, L'Etrange M. Victor* 1938; *Untel Père et Fils/The Heart of a Nation, The Lady in Question* (story basis only; US) 1940; *L'Arlésienne, Félicie Nanteuil* 1942; *Les Petites du Quai aux Fleurs* 1943; *La Belle Aventure/Twilight* 1945; *Petrus* 1946; *Madame de. . . /The Earrings of Madame De* 1953; *La Garçonne* 1957; *La Femme et le Pantin/The Female* 1959; *Les Amours célèbres* 1961; *A Shot in the Dark* (play basis only, 'L'Idiot'; US/UK), *Patate/Friend of the Family* (play basis only) 1964. As director-writer—*Jean de la Lune* (remake) 1949; *La Valse de Paris/The Paris Waltz* 1950.

Acin, Jovan. Director, screenwriter. Born on May 23, 1941, in Belgrade, Yugoslavia. His first feature, *The Concrete Rose* (1975), so displeased the authorities that Acin was forced to leave the country. Years later, in annual reunions with friends and producers George Zecevic and Petar Jankovic, Acin reminisced about politics, life, and movie-watching in Yugoslavia in the 1950s. The result was the semi-autobiographical *Hey Babu Riba* (1986), which received wide distribution on the American art-house circuit.

FILMS: *The Concrete Rose* 1975; *Hey Babu Riba/Dancing on Water* (sc., dir.) 1986.

Ackerman, Bettye. See JAFFE, Sam.

Ackland, Joss. Actor. Born on Feb. 29, 1928, in London. Character player of the British stage, TV, and films. He made his stage debut in 1945 and his first screen appearance in 1950. In 1954, he abandoned acting to run a tea plantation in Central Africa. But he returned to England in 1957, soon joining the Old Vic, with which he toured Russia and the US. He has since appeared in numerous stage, screen, and TV productions, typically portraying characters of prominence, authority, and influence, often villainous. He starred as Perón in the London stage production of 'Evita.'

FILMS INCLUDE: *Seven Days To Noon* 1950; *Ghost Ship* 1952; *The Bridge* (Ger.) 1960, *Rasputin the Mad Monk* 1966; *Crescendo* 1969; *The House That Dripped Blood* 1970; *Villain* 1971; *The Happiness Cage/Mind Snatchers* 1972; *England Made Me, Hitler: The Last Ten Days* 1973; *The Black Windmill, The Little Prince, The Three Musketeers* 1974; *Royal Flash* 1975; *One of Our Dinosaurs Is Missing* 1976; *Who Is Killing the Great Chefs of Europe?/Too Many Chefs* 1978; *Saint Jack* 1979; *Rough Cut* 1980; *A Zed and Two Noughts* 1985; *Lady Jane* 1986; *White Mischief, The Sicilian* 1987; *It Couldn't Happen Here* 1988; *Lethal Weapon 2* 1989; *Dimenticare Palermo/To Forget Palermo* (It./Fr.), *The Hunt for Red October* 1990; *Bill & Ted's Bogus Journey, The Object of Beauty* 1991; *The Bridge, The Mighty Ducks, Once Upon a Crime* 1992; *Nowhere to Run* 1993; *Mad Dogs and Englishmen, Miracle on 34th Street, Mother's Boys, Nostradamus, The Princess and the Goblin* (v/o) 1994; *A Kid in King Arthur's Court* 1995; *D3 The Mighty Ducks 3, Surviving Picasso* 1996; *To the End of Time* 1997.

Ackland, Rodney. Screenwriter, playwright, actor. Born on May 18, 1908, in London. After studying drama and making his debut as an actor in 1924, he began writing for films and the stage in 1930. In addition to writing numerous plays and a number of screenplays for British films, he has directed one motion picture and played supporting parts in several. Autobiography: *The Celluloid Mistress; or the Custard Pie of Dr. Caligari* (1958).

FILMS INCLUDE: *The Skin Game* (act.) 1931; *Number Seventeen* (sc.) 1932; *The Case of Gabriel Perry* (act.) 1935; *Bank Holiday/Three on a Weekend* (sc.) 1938; *The Silent Battle/Continental Express* (sc.) 1939; *49th Parallel/The Invaders* (sc.) 1941; *Hatter's Castle* (sc.) 1942; *The Alibi* (act.) *Thursday's Child* (sc., dir.) 1943; *Love Story/A Lady Surrenders* (act.) 1944; *Wanted for Murder* (sc.) 1946; *Temptation Harbor* (sc.), *Bond Street* (sc.) 1947; *The Queen of Spades* (sc.) 1949.

Acord, Art. Actor. *b.* 1890, Stillwater, Okla. *d.* 1931. One of the few real cowpunchers to become a screen cowboy, he started out as a rodeo performer in Wild West shows. In 1909 he became a stuntman with the Bison Film Company of New Jersey in some of the earliest Western one-reelers. In 1914 he starred in Mutual two-reelers using the name Buck Parvin. Later he was billed as Art Acord or sometimes Art Accord. After WW I service in France, he became Universal's leading cowboy star of the 20s. He married and divorced actresses Edythe Sterling and Louise Lorraine. His film career ended with the coming of sound, and soon after he was arrested for bootlegging. He then went to Mexico with a rodeo but went broke there from gambling. In 1931 he was found dead in a Mexican hotel room, poisoned by cyanide. His death was ruled a suicide, but suspicions of murder were never entirely dismissed.

FILMS INCLUDE: *The Squaw Man* 1914; *Buckshot John, A Man Afraid of His Wardrobe* 1915; *The Battle of Life* 1916; *Cleopatra* (as Kephren, in Theda Bara vers.) 1917; *Headin' South* 1918; *The Moon Riders* (serial) 1920; *Winners of the West* (serial) 1921; *In the Days of Buffalo Bill* (serial) 1922; *The Oregon Trail* (serial) 1923; *Fighting for Justice* 1924; *The Call of Courage, The Circus Cyclone, Pals* 1925; *The Man From the West, The Set-Up, The Terror* 1926; *Hard Fists, Loco Luck, Spurs and Saddles* 1927; *Two Gun O'Brien* 1928; *The Arizona Kid, Fighters of the Saddle, Bullets and Justice, The White Outlaw* 1929.

Acres, Birt. Inventor, pioneer British filmmaker. *b.* July 23, 1854, Richmond, Va. *d.* 1918. Among his inventions: a camera with rapid-plate exposure (1893) and a primitive projector and movie camera (1894). In 1895 he made what is considered the first British film, recording the Oxford-Cambridge boat race. Collaborated with noted inventor and pioneer Robert W. PAUL.

FILMS INCLUDE: *Oxford-Cambridge Boat Race, The Derby, Inauguration of the Kiel Canal by Kaiser Wilhelm II* 1895; *Boxing Match, The Arrest of a Pickpocket* 1896; *Pierrot and Pierrette* 1897; *Briton vs. Boer* 1900.

acting, in cinema. Although an offshoot of the stage tradition, film acting gradually has evolved a style all its own. The performers in the earliest films of Lumière and Edison were ordinary people playing themselves; but then, with the development of the story film, the need for professional actors arose. Stage actors in the 1900s scorned the new raw medium, so most of the performers recruited for early film dramas were either amateurs or theater dropouts. They adopted a style of acting prevalent on the stage at the time—a declamatory technique characterized by bombastic delivery and exaggerated gestures.

In 1908, Film d'Art, the French film company, induced the Comédie-Française to allow the filming of some of its productions with the entire original casts, including such stage greats as Sarah BERNHARDT, Gabrielle RÉJANE, and Max DEARLY. The success of these productions, notably *The Assassination of the Duke de Guise,* helped remove the low-brow stigma from films but did little for the development of motion picture art. Gestures and movements that were perfectly valid on the stage were mercilessly exaggerated on film, and the result was often grotesque. However, the financial returns on these films encouraged imitators, especially in Italy and in the US, where Adolph ZUKOR soon launched his Famous Players in Famous Plays productions.

D. W. GRIFFITH is credited with being the first director to recognize the need for a new style of acting for the screen. He sensed that the size of the screen image and the camera's tendency to emphasize the slightest nuance required acting that was subtler and less stylized and concerned more with the *veracity* of an emotion than with its *projection.* As early as 1909, Griffith gathered a group of young actors and rehearsed them continually until he was able to achieve a new, restrained style of acting, which was to have a lasting influence on the development of the cinema.

There are basic differences in conditions under which actors perform on stage and on screen. Although the stage actor is able to build and sustain a characterization throughout one performance, the screen actor has both the advantage and disadvantage of film technique—short takes, out-of-continuity shooting, angle variance, and endless repetition of scenes until they are just right. The art of the screen actor, especially one who is typecast, is often further removed from that of his stage counterpart since the former usually does not assume a character's identity but rather presents a subtle variation of his own personality that is only slightly camouflaged under the different guises he assumes.

A stage actor must make certain adjustments when appearing in films. Although he does not have to memorize many lines or sustain a performance, he must be able to respond with a display of a given emotion at the time it is needed and without the benefit of building to it gradually. Since scenes in a film are shot out of continuity, he must have a firm grasp of the character he is portraying if the pieces of his performance are to match.

Most important, it is a great deal more difficult to fake an emotion on screen than on stage because of the closeness of the camera. The camera's ability to capture and magnify the smallest flicker of personality that flashes across an actor's face has led some theoreticians to say that what was needed in film was not acting but being. Certain directors feel that if this is the case they would rather use real people whose appearance and personality match those of the characters to be portrayed, thus hoping to achieve a stronger sense of reality.

The nonprofessional actor has been used extensively in European cinema, particularly in the Russian silent films of EISENSTEIN and PUDOVKIN. The latter called this use of nonprofessionals "typage." Though the practice has never been widely used, it reappears from time to time, notably in the Italian neorealistic films of Vittorio DE SICA and in the later films of Robert BRESSON.

The introduction of sound removed the last traces of stylization from film acting. The pantomimic exaggeration of gesture and movement, made necessary by the absence of verbal communication, was gone forever. Many of the silent era stars were unable to hold their own because of imperfections in diction and voice quality. Stage actors, whom producers began to import in large numbers, were successful to some degree, but many of them failed to make the transition because the screen demanded a more natural way of speaking than did the theater.

The contribution of acting to the total quality of a film varies from production to production. Certain directors, such as Clarence BROWN, Sidney FRANKLIN, and George CUKOR, have been known as "actors' directors" because they tended to rely heavily on the talent and personality of their performers. Others, such as Josef von STERNBERG and Alfred HITCHCOCK, tended to treat actors as just another element of their MISE-EN-SCÈNE. Since the advent of AUTEUR THEORY in the 50s, public opinion and critical thinking have swung toward the acceptance of the director as the primary force in the creation of a film, with a resulting devaluation of the role of the actor. However, many of the most talented directors since the 60s (beginning with Jean-Luc GODARD and François TRUFFAUT in France and continuing with John CASSAVETES, Robert ALTMAN, and Martin SCORSESE in the US) have achieved their results partly by relinquishing control to the improvisational skill of their performers.

No discussion of acting in cinema can be complete without mention of the star system, which has been central to Hollywood film production since audiences first fell in love with silent film actress Mary Pickford. Most movie stars (whether American or foreign) are known not for their ability to play different roles but for a consistent persona which carries over from film to film, accumulating associations that deepen its significance. The star's persona may be that of a hero, villain, or eccentric, but it must always be interesting to watch. Because popular movie stars are presumed to guarantee box-office receipts, they have wielded great power since the heyday of the studios. The decline of rigid studio control has only increased the power of a handful of movie stars—ensuring that many films are made as vehicles for a particular actor.

action. Movement before the camera, the visual development of events and situations in a narrative sense, including the interplay of characters and between characters and their surroundings.

"action!" The command given by a director—once camera and sound recorder are up to normal speed—to start the action in a scene.

action still. A still photograph blown up directly from the negative of a motion picture, in contrast to ordinary publicity stills which are shot during production with a still camera.

Actors' Equity Association (AEA). A union for actors in the legitimate theater, organized in 1913. National membership is about 39,000.

Actors Studio. A rehearsal group for professional actors, established in New York City in 1947 by Elia Kazan, Robert Lewis, and Cheryl Crawford. Lee Strasberg became its artistic director in 1949 and it soon became the center for advancing "the Method," a technique of acting inspired by Stanislavski's teachings. The Studio exerted considerable influence on the American theater and cinema of the 50s and nurtured the talents of such performers as Barbara Bel Geddes, Marlon Brando, Montgomery Clift, James Dean, Ben Gazzara, Julie Harris, Paul Newman, Jack Palance, Lee Remick, Rod Steiger, Eli Wallach, Shelley Winters, and Joanne Woodward. After Strasberg's death in 1982, artistic directors have included Ellen Burstyn, Al Pacino, and Frank Corsaro. Actors Studio West was founded in Los Angeles in 1966.

ACTT (Association of Cinematograph, Television and Allied Technicians). The British filmmakers' union. Founded in 1931, it is the only trade union in the world that operates its own film production unit, ACT Films.

actual sound. Sound whose source is either visible on the screen or implied by the action in a sequence, as distinguished from off-camera commentary such as narration.

acutance. The physical measurement of sharpness of a photographed image. A microdensitometer is used to measure the spatial rate of change of density across the image, thus defining its sharpness with scientific accuracy to verify an otherwise subjective judgment. It also helps to evaluate the quality of emulsions and lenses.

Adam, Ken. Art director, production designer. Born on Feb. 5, 1921, in Berlin. Came to England in 1934; studied architecture at London University and was an RAF pilot in WW II. He entered the film industry in 1947 as a draftsman on *This Was a Woman*, became an art director in the mid-50s and a production designer in the early 60s. His work has been known for its stylish inventiveness and sense of humor. Among his creations: the war room in *Dr. Strangelove* (1964) and the glittering interior of Fort Knox in *Goldfinger* (1964). He won an Oscar for the art direction of Kubrick's *Barry Lyndon* (1975) and *The Madness of King George* (1994), and has twice been nominated in the same category for *The Spy Who Loved Me* (1977) and *Addams Family Values* (1993).

FILMS INCLUDE: As Assistant Art Director—*Captain Horatio Hornblower* 1951; *The Crimson Pirate* 1952; *Helen Of Troy* 1956. As art director or production designer—*Around the World in 80 Days* (European sets) 1956; *Curse of the Demon* 1958; *The Trials of Oscar Wilde* 1960; *Dr. No, Dr. Strangelove, Sodom and Gomorrah* (It.) 1963; *Goldfinger* 1964; *Thunderball, The Ipcress File* 1965; *Funeral in Berlin* 1966; *You Only Live Twice* 1967; *Chitty Chitty Bang Bang* 1968; *Goodbye Mr. Chips* 1969; *The Owl and the Pussycat* 1970; *Diamonds Are Forever* 1971; *Sleuth* 1972; *The Last of Sheila* 1973; *Barry Lyndon* 1975; *The Seven-Per-Cent Solution* 1976; *The Spy Who Loved Me* 1977; *Moonraker* 1979; *Pennies from Heaven* (assoc. prod., visual consultant) 1981; *Agnes of God, King David* 1985; *Crimes of the Heart* 1986; *The Deceivers* 1988; *Dead Bang* 1989; *The Freshman* 1990; *Company Business, The Doctor* 1991; *Addams Family Values, Undercover Blues* 1993; *The Madness of King George* 1994; *Boys on the Side, Leaving Las Vegas* 1995; *Bogus* 1996; *In and Out* 1997.

Adams, Brooke. Actress. Born on Feb. 8, 1949, in New York City. *ed.* Dalton, NY High School for Performing Arts; Instit. of American Ballet; Lee Strasberg. Petite, perky leading lady of American TV and films. A stage performer from age six, she entered television as a teenager, appearing regularly in the short-lived series 'O.K. Crackerby' (1965–66). In feature films from the mid-70s, most notably as the center of the tragic love triangle in *Days of Heaven* (1978). TV roles in the 80s included several guest appearances on 'Moonlighting' (1985–89).

FILMS: *The Great Gatsby, The Lords Of Flatbush* 1974; *Car Wash* 1976; *Shock Waves/Death Corps/Almost Human* (release delayed from 1970) 1977; *Days of Heaven, Invasion of the Body Snatchers* 1978; *A Man a Woman and a Bank/A Very Big Withdrawal, Cuba* 1979; *Tell Me a Riddle* 1980; *Utilities* 1981; *The Dead Zone, Haunted* 1983; *Almost You* 1984; *Key Exchange* (reprising her Broadway role), *The Stuff* 1985; *Man on Fire* (It./Fr.) 1987; *The Unborn* 1991; *Gas Food Lodging* 1992; *My Boyfriend's Back, The Sandlot* 1993; *The Baby-Sitter's Club* 1995.

Adams, Donna. See REED, Donna.

Adams, Edie. Actress, singer. Born Elizabeth Edith Enke, on Apr. 16, 1927, Kingston, Pa. Glamorous blonde entertainer-comedienne of the American stage, TV, and films. A graduate of the Juilliard School of Music and the Columbia School of Drama, she entered show business via a TV talent show, later winning the titles Miss New York TV and Miss US TV. She gained popularity in the early 50s as a regular on the 'Ernie Kovacs Show' and in 1955 married Kovacs. She was widowed in 1962. In addition to making many TV and nightclub appearances, she starred on Broadway in 'Wonderful Town' (1953) and 'Li'l Abner' (Tony Award) (1956), in which she created the role of Daisy Mae. Her effervescence enlivened a number of films in the 60s, usually in secondary roles. In 1984 she portrayed Mae West in the TV biography 'Ernie Kovacs: Between the Laughter.'

FILMS: *The Apartment* 1960; *Lover Come Back* 1961; *Call Me Bwana, It's a Mad Mad Mad Mad World, Under the Yum Yum Tree* 1963; *Love With the Proper Stranger, The Best Man* 1964; *Made in Paris, The Oscar* 1966; *The Honey Pot* 1967; *Kovacs* (compilation doc.) 1971; *Up in Smoke* 1978; *Racquet* 1979; *The Happy Hooker Goes to Hollywood* 1980; *Boxoffice* 1982.

Adams, Julie. Actress. Born Betty May Adams, on Oct. 17, 1926, in Waterloo, Iowa. Leading lady of Hollywood second features. A secretary before breaking into films, she was first billed as Betty Adams before becoming Julie Adams. Married Ray DANTON.

FILMS INCLUDE: As Betty Adams—*The Dalton Gang, Red Hot and Blue* 1949. As Julie Adams—*Bright Victory, Hollywood Story* 1951; *Bend of the River, Horizons West, The Lawless Breed* 1952; *The Mississippi Gambler, Wings of the Hawk, The Man From the Alamo* 1953; *The Creature from the Black Lagoon* 1954; *Six Bridges to Cross, The Private War of Major Benson* 1955; *Away All Boats* 1956; *Slaughter on Tenth Avenue* 1957; *Gunfight at Dodge City* 1959; *The Underwater City* 1962; *Tickle Me* 1965; *The Valley of Mystery* 1967; *The Last Movie* 1971; *McQ* 1974; *The Wild McCullochs, Psychic Killer* 1975; *The Killer Inside Me* 1976; *Goodbye Franklin High* 1978; *The Fifth Floor* 1980; *Champions* (UK) 1984.

Adams, Maud. Actress. Born Maude Wikstrum, on Feb. 12, 1945, in Lulea, Sweden. Voluptuous leading lady who used a successful modeling career as a springboard into films and TV. Memorable in two James Bond extravaganzas, especially the title role in *Octopussy.*

FILMS INCLUDE: *The Boys In The Band* (bit) 1970; *The Christian Licorice Store* 1971; *The Girl in Blue, The Man With the Golden Gun* (her first James Bond movie) 1974; *Rollerball, Killer Force* 1975; *L'Uomo senza Pietà/The Merciless Man* 1977; *Tattoo* 1980; *Octopussy* (title role) 1983; *Hell Hunters* 1986; *Jane and the Lost City, The Women's Club* 1987; *Angel III: The Final Chapter* 1988; *La Nuit du serail, Pasion de Hombre/A Man of Passion* 1989.

Adams, Nick. Actor. *b.* Nicholas Adamshock, July 10, 1931, Nanticoke, Pa. *d.* 1968. *ed.* St. Peter's Coll. Played leads and supporting parts in many films of the 50s and 60s, often as a restive young man, but he was best known to American audiences as star of 'The Rebel' TV series. He was nominated for an Oscar as best supporting actor in *Twilight of Honor* (1963). His death was caused by an overdose of drugs he was taking for a nervous disorder.

FILMS INCLUDE: *Somebody Loves Me* 1952; *Mister Roberts, Picnic, Rebel Without a Cause* 1955; *No Time for Sergeants, Teacher's Pet* 1958; *The FBI Story, Pillow Talk* 1959; *Hell Is for Heroes, The Interns* 1962; *The Hook, Twilight of Honor* 1963; *The Young Lovers* 1964; *Young Dillinger, Die Monster Die!* 1965; *Frankenstein Conquers the World* (Jap.) 1966; *Fever Heat* 1968.

Addams, Dawn. Actress. *b.* Sept. 21, 1930, Felixstowe, England. *d.* 1985, of cancer. Educated in England, India, and the US. Came to Hollywood in 1950. Her undistinguished career was highlighted by a leading role in Chaplin's *A King in New York* (1957), after which she appeared in routine British and Continental films. At one time (1954–71) married to Italy's Prince Vittorio Massimo. After a second marriage to a businessman, she retired from the screen (and from a notorious succession of love affairs) and lived in Malta, then resettled in the US.

FILMS INCLUDE: In the US—*Night Into Morning* 1951; *Singin' in the Rain* (bit), *The Hour of 13, Plymouth Adventure* 1952; *Young Bess, The Moon Is Blue, The Robe* 1953; *Khyber Patrol* 1954. In Europe—*Secrets d'Alcove/Il Letto/The Bed* (Fr./It.) 1954; *Il Tesoro di Rommel/Rommel's Treasure* (It.) 1955;

A King in New York (UK) 1957; *The Silent Enemy* (UK) 1958; *L'Ile du Bout du Monde/Temptation* (Fr.) 1959; *The Two Faces of Dr. Jekyll/House of Fright* (UK), *Die tausend Augen des Dr. Mabuse/The 1000 Eyes of Dr. Mabuse* (Ger./Fr./It.) 1960; *Les Menteurs/The Liars* (Fr.) 1961; *Come Fly with Me* (US/UK) 1963; *Ballad in Blue/Blues for Lovers* (UK) 1965; *Where the Bullets Fly* (UK) 1966; *The Vampire Lovers* (UK) 1970; *The Vault of Horror* (UK) 1973.

Addinsell, Richard. Composer. *b.* Jan. 13, 1904, London. *d.* 1977. *ed.* Oxford. Composed many scores for stage and screen. He is best known for his "Warsaw Concerto" from the film *Dangerous Moonlight/Suicide Squadron* (1940).

FILMS INCLUDE: *Fire Over England* 1937; *Goodbye Mr. Chips* 1939; *Gaslight, Dangerous Moonlight/Suicide Squadron* 1940; *Blithe Spirit* 1945; *Under Capricorn* 1949; *Tom Brown's Schooldays, A Christmas Carol* 1951; *Encore* 1952; *Beau Brummel* 1954; *The Prince and the Showgirl* 1957; *A Tale of Two Cities* 1958; *The Waltz of the Toreadors* 1962; *Macbeth* 1963; *Life at the Top* 1965.

Addison, John. Composer. Born on Mar. 16, 1920, in West Chobham, England. *ed.* Wellington; Royal Coll. of Music. Prolific scorer of British films (from 1948), plays, ballets, and TV dramas. He won an Oscar in 1963 for *Tom Jones* and was again nominated in 1972 for *Sleuth.*

FILMS INCLUDE: *Seven Days To Noon* 1950; *Pool of London* 1951; *Private's Progress* 1955; *I Was Monty's Double* 1958; *Look Back in Anger* 1959; *The Entertainer* 1960; *A Taste of Honey* 1961; *The Loneliness of the Long Distance Runner* 1962; *Tom Jones* 1963; *The Loved One* 1965; *A Fine Madness* 1966; *The Honey Pot, Smashing Time* 1967; *The Charge of the Light Brigade* 1968; *Country Dance/Brotherly Love* 1970; *Luther* 1973; *Swashbuckler, The Seven-Per-Cent Solution* 1976; *A Bridge Too Far, Joseph Andrews* 1977; *Strange Invaders* 1983; *The Ultimate Solution of Grace Quigley/Grace Quigley* 1984; *Code Name: Emerald* 1985; *To Die For* 1989.

Adjani, Isabelle. Actress. Born on June 27, 1955, in Paris, to an Algerian father of Turkish ancestry and a German mother. At 12 she won a prize for recitation at school and began appearing in amateur stage productions and at 14 made her film debut during a summer vacation. She appeared in a second film two years later under similar circumstances, while continuing her high school education. By the time she graduated, she was appearing on French TV and in provincial stage productions. In 1972, with no previous formal training and just her limited acting experience, she became a member of the Comédie-Française and began drawing ecstatic rave notices from critics for her performances in plays by Molière, Lorca, and Giraudoux. She was called a phenomenon of her generation and the greatest young actress to grace the French stage in years. The Comédie offered her a 20-year contract, but she rejected it because it would have limited her outside opportunities, and instead accepted an invitation from François Truffaut to play the title role in his film *L'Histoire d'Adèle H./The Story of Adele H.* (1975).

She gave a mature, intricate, and altogether magnificent performance in the complex role as the tormented daughter of Victor Hugo who is consumed by her passion for a young British lieutenant, driving herself to madness in pursuing him to Nova Scotia and Barbados. She was hailed by many critics as the most extraordinary screen personality to come along since Jeanne Moreau. She was nominated for an Oscar and won several international awards for her work in that film and went on to become France's top female movie star. She was named best actress at Cannes in 1981 for *Possession* and *Quartet* and won César Awards for *Possession, L'Eté meurtrier* (1983), and *Camille Claudel* (1988). She also received the Berlin Festival best actress prize and a second Oscar nomination for her brilliant portrayal in the latter film as the sculptress who was the muse and the mistress of sculptor Auguste Rodin.

FILMS: *Le Petit Bougnat* 1969; *Faustine et le Bel Eté/Faustine and the Beautiful Summer* 1971; *La Gifle/The Slap* 1974; *L'Histoire d'Adèle H./The Story of Adele H.* 1975; *Le Locataire/The Tenant, Barocco* 1976; *Violette et François* 1977; *The Driver, Nosferatu Phantom der Nacht/Nosferatu the Vampyre* 1978; *Les Seours Brontë/The Brontë Sisters* (as Emily Brontë) 1979; *Clara et les Chic Types* 1980; *Possession, Quartet, L'Année prochaine si tout va bien* 1981; *Tout Feu tout Flamme/All Fired Up, Antonietta* 1982; *L'Eté meutrier/One Deadly Summer, Mortelle randonnée/Deadly Circuit* 1983; *Subway* 1985; *Maladie d'Amour, Ishtar* 1987; *Camille Claudel* (also co-prod.) 1988, *Lung Ta: Les cavaliers du vent* 1990; *Toxic Affair* 1993; *Queen Margot* 1994; *Diabolique* 1996.

Adler, Buddy. Producer. *b.* E. Maurice Adler, June 22, 1909, New York City. *d.* 1960. *ed.* Columbia; Pennsylvania U. Son of the famous elevator-shoe merchant, he wrote ads for his father's business, then short stories for magazines. In 1935 he began writing short subjects for MGM, one of which, *Quicker 'n a Wink* 1940, won an Academy Award. He was a lieutenant-colonel in the Army Pictorial Service in WW II. In 1947 he became producer for Columbia and in 1953 won an Academy Award for *From Here to Eternity.* He was named head of production for 20th Century-Fox in 1956, succeeding Darryl Zanuck. He died during preproduction work on *Cleopatra* (1963). He was married to Anita LOUISE.

FILMS INCLUDE: *The Dark Past* 1948; *A Woman of Distinction, No Sad Songs for Me* 1950; *Salome, From Here to Eternity* 1953; *Violent Saturday, Soldier of Fortune, Love Is a Many Splendored Thing, The Left Hand of God* 1955; *The Bottom of the Bottle, The Revolt of Mamie Stover, Bus Stop, Anastasia* 1956; *Heaven Knows Mr. Allison, A Hatful of Rain* 1957; *South Pacific, The Inn of the Sixth Happiness* 1958.

Adler, Luther. Actor. *b.* Lutha Adler, May 4, 1903, New York City. *d.* 1984. The descendant of a well-known theatrical family, he made his debut at five in 'Schmendrick' on the Yiddish stage. He remained basically a stage actor, but his infrequent films included some powerful, memorable character portrayals. His brother Jay (*d.* 1978) was also in occasional films, and his sister Stella (*d.* 1992) was a well-known stage personality and acting teacher. He was the second husband (1938–47) of Sylvia SIDNEY.

FILMS INCLUDE: *Lancer Spy* 1937; *Cornered* 1945; *Saigon, The Loves of Carmen, Wake of the Red Witch* 1948; *House of Strangers* 1949; *D.O.A., Under My Skin, Kiss Tomorrow Goodbye* 1950; *The Desert Fox, The Magic Face* (as Hitler in both), *M* 1951; *Hoodlum Empire* 1952; *The Tall Texan* 1953; *The Miami Story* 1954; *Crashout* 1955; *Hot Blood* 1956; *The Last Angry Man* 1959; *Cast a Giant Shadow* 1966; *The Brotherhood* 1968; *Crazy Joe* 1974; *The Man in the Glass Booth* 1975; *Voyage of the Damned* 1976; *The Three Sisters* (as Chebutykin) 1977; *Absence of Malice* 1981.

Adlon, Percy. Director, producer, screenwriter. Born on June 1, 1935, in Munich. *ed.* Munich University. After getting his start in German repertory theater and radio, he turned in the 70s to making television documentaries. His first full-length work for TV, *The Guardian and the Poet* (1978), garnered enough praise to allow him to direct and write his first feature, *Celeste* (1981), an account of Marcel Proust's last days. He gained international recognition with *Sugarbaby* (1985), as did Marianne Sagebrecht, the star of this unusual love story between an overweight woman and a subway conductor. Sagebrecht has starred in Adlon's subsequent films, which are distinguished by their humor and the inventiveness of their storylines and cinematic technique. Gentle in tone yet astute in their observations, his films are favorites on the art-house circuit. His wife Eleanore frequently collaborates as co-producer and co-screenwriter.

FILMS INCLUDE (as Director): *Celeste* (also sc.) 1981; *Letze Funf Tage/The Last Five Days* 1982; *Die Schaukel/The Swing* (also sc.) 1983; *Zuckerbaby/Sugarbaby* (also prod., sc., story) 1985; *Bagdad Cafe/Out of Rosenheim* (also co-prod., co-sc., story) 1987; *Rosalie Goes Shopping* (also co-sc., co-prod.) 1989; *Salmonberries* 1991; *Younger and Younger* 1993.

Adolfi, John G. Director. *b.* Feb. 19, 1888, New York City. *d.* 1933. Entered films around 1910 as an actor but soon after became a director. Turned out many films, mostly minor, during the silent era for Reliance, Fox, and other companies. Shortly after the advent of sound, he formed a partnership with George ARLISS and directed several of the famed actor's stagey film vehicles. Also credited as Jack Adolfi.

FEATURE FILMS: *A Man and His Mate, A Child Of God* 1915; *The Man Inside, Little Miss Happiness, The Ragged Princess, The Sphinx, Caprice of the Mountains, The Mischief Maker, Merely Mary Ann, A Modern Thelma* 1916; *A Modern Cinderella, A Small Town Girl, Patsy, A Child of the Wild* 1917; *The Heart of a Girl, Queen of the Sea, The Burden of Proof, The Woman the Germans Shot/The Cavell Case* 1918; *Who's Your Brother?* 1919; *The Amazing Woman, The Wonder Man, The Little 'Fraid Lady* 1920; *The Darling of the Rich* 1922; *The Little Red Schoolhouse* 1923; *What Shall I Do?, Chalk Marks* 1924; *The Scarlet West, Big Pal, Before Midnight, The Phantom Express* 1925; *The Checkered Flag* 1926; *Husband Hunters, What Happened to Father?* 1927; *The Devil's Skipper, The Little Snob, Prowlers of the Sea, The Midnight Taxi, Sinner's Parade* 1928; *Fancy Baggage, Evidence, The Show of Shows, In the Headlines* 1929; *Dumbbells in Ermine, Recaptured Love, Sinner's Holiday, College Lovers* 1930; *The Millionaire, Alexander Hamilton, Compromised* 1931; *The Man Who Played God, A Successful Calamity, Central Park* 1932; *The King's Vacation, The Working Man, Voltaire* 1933.

Adorée, Renée. Actress. *b.* Jeanne de la Fonte, Sept. 30, 1898, Lille, France. *d.* 1933. A circus performer from age five and later a chorine in Paris with the Folies-Bergère, she arrived in Hollywood in 1920. Played routine leads before gaining sudden stardom as John Gilbert's leading lady in *The Big Parade* (1925). Her first husband (1921–24) was actor Tom MOORE. Her career was cut short by tuberculosis, the cause of her death at 35.

FILMS INCLUDE: *l500 Reward* (Austral.) 1918; *The Strongest* 1920; *Made in Heaven* 1921; *Monte Cristo, West of Chicago, Honor First* 1922; *The Eternal Struggle* 1923; *A Man's Mate, Women Who Give, The Bandolero* 1924; *Excuse Me, Man and Maid, Parisian Nights, Exchange of Wives, The Big Parade* 1925; *The Black Bird, La Bohème, The Exquisite Sinner, Blarney, Tin Gods, The Flaming Forest* 1926; *The Show, Heaven on Earth, Mr. Wu, On Ze Boulevard, Back to God's Country* 1927; *The Cossacks, The Michigan Kid, Forbidden Hours, The Mating Call* 1928; *The Pagan, Tide of Empire* 1929; *Redemption, Call of the Flesh* 1930.

Adrian (Gilbert A. Adrian). Costume designer. *b.* Adrian Adolph Greenberg, Mar. 3, 1903, Naugatuck, Conn. *d.* 1959. Went to Hollywood after graduating from the New York School for Applied and Fine Arts. After designing several productions for Valentino and De Mille, he became chief costume designer for MGM, helping the "dream factory" glamorize such stars as Greta Garbo, Norma Shearer, Joan Crawford, and Jean Harlow. In 1942 he opened his own establishment, serving most major studios. He was married to Janet GAYNOR.

FILMS INCLUDE: *Her Sister from Paris, The Eagle* 1925; *Fig Leaves, Gigolo, The Volga Boatman* 1926; *The Angel of Broadway, Chicago, The Country Doctor, The Forbidden Woman, Vanity, The Wreck of the Hesperus* 1927; *The Blue Danube, The Mask of the Devil, Midnight Madness, Skyscraper, A Woman of Affairs* 1928; *The Bridge of San Luis Rey, Dynamite, The Godless Girl, The Kiss, The Last of Mrs. Cheyney, The Trial of Mary Dugan* 1929; *Anna Christie, The Divorcee, A Lady's Morals, Madam Satan, Our Blushing Brides* 1930; *A Free Soul, Private Lives* 1931; *Rasputin and the Empress, Red Dust, Strange Interlude, Smilin' Through, Grand Hotel* 1932; *Dinner at Eight, Today We Live* 1933; *Nana, The Painted Veil, The Merry Widow, Queen Christina, The Barretts of Wimpole Street* 1934; *China Seas, Broadway Melody of 1936, Naughty Marietta, Anna Karenina* 1935; *San Francisco, Rose Marie, Romeo and Juliet, The Great Ziegfeld, Camille* 1936; *Maytime* 1937; *Marie Antoinette* 1938; *Idiot's Delight, Ninotchka, The Wizard of Oz, The Women* 1939; *Boom Town, Pride and Prejudice, Waterloo Bridge, The Philadelphia Story* 1940; *Dr. Jekyll and Mr. Hyde, Ziegfeld Girl, Two-Faced Woman* 1941; *Keeper of the Flame, Woman of the Year* 1942; *They Got Me Covered* 1943; *Possessed* 1947; *Rope* 1948; *Lovely to Look At* 1952.

Adrian, Iris. Actress. Born Iris Adrian Hostetter, on May 29, 1913, in Los Angeles. Made her stage debut as a dancer in the Ziegfeld Follies after winning a 1929 beauty contest. Beginning in the early 30s she was a vivacious supporting player and occasional lead of some 100 Hollywood films. She typically played cheap, dumb blondes, talkative chorus girls, and gangsters' molls. Married former football star "Fido" Murphy.

FILMS INCLUDE: *Paramount On Parade* 1930; *Rumba* 1935; *A Message to Garcia, Gold Diggers of 1937* 1936; *Go West* 1940; *Road to Zanzibar* 1941; *Roxie Hart, To the Shores of Tripoli, Orchestra Wives* 1942; *Lady of Burlesque, His Butler's Sister, Action in the North Atlantic* 1943; *Shake Hands with Murder, Swing Hostess, The Woman in the Window* 1944; *The Stork Club* 1945; *The Paleface* 1948; *Always Leave Them Laughing* 1949; *Once a Thief* 1950; *My Favorite Spy* 1951; *The Fast and the Furious* 1954; *The Buccaneer* 1958; *Blue Hawaii* 1961; *The Errand Boy* 1962; *That Darn Cat* 1965; *The Love Bug, The Odd Couple* 1968; *The Apple Dumpling Gang* 1975; *The Shaggy D.A.* 1976; *Freaky Friday* 1977; *Herbie Goes Bananas* 1980.

advance. The distance between picture and sound gates on a projector, which must be taken into consideration when making sound prints. The sound track on a strip of film is always printed ahead of the corresponding picture so that sound and picture are synchronized during projection. The distance is 20 frames for 35 mm prints and 26 frames for 16 mm.

AEA. See ACTORS' EQUITY ASSOCIATION.

aerial image printer. See OPTICAL PRINTER.

Africa. Now the site of a diverse and innovative film industry, sub-Saharan Africa was slow to develop a cinema of its own. Until the 50s, filmmaking was limited to North Africa, particularly EGYPT, whose film industry (founded in the late 20s) has long dominated the Arab world. Other North African countries, notably Algeria and Tunisia, also directed their films principally to the Arab market. The 1953 film *Mourani* (Guinea), an adaptation of a traditional oral narrative, was the first work by a sub-Saharan African filmmaker. However, the most seminal work of African film was *Borom Sarret*, a 1963 short by Senegalese director Ousmane SEMBÈNE. Like much of his later work and that of other African directors, the film focused on class conflict and the after-effects of European colonialism in a newly independent country. In the decades since, African filmmakers have overcome the obstacles posed by widespread poverty and political instability to produce an impressive body of work.

Most of the continent's new cinema has emerged in France's former colonies in West Africa, aided by a tradition of government support for the arts and by financial support and training from France itself. Sembène (*Black Girl/La Noire de. . . ,* 1966; *Mandabi/The Money Order,* 1968; *Guelwaar,* 1992) and fellow Senegalese filmmaker Djibril Diop Mambéty (*Touki-Bouki,* 1973; *Hyenas*, 1992) are among the most prominent names in the industry, as are two directors from BURKINA FASO, Idrissa OUEDRAOGO (*Yam Daabo*, 1987; *Yaaba*, 1989) and Gaston KABORÉ (*Wend Kuuni*, 1981; *Zan Boko*, 1988). Med Hondo (*Soleil O*, 1969; *Sarraounia*, 1986) from Mauritania, Souleymane CISSÉ (*Cinq Jours d'une vie/Five Days in a Life*, 1972; *Yeelen/Brightness*, 1987) from Mali, and Safi Faye (*Letter From My Village/Kaddu beykat*, 1975; *Man Say Yay/I Your Mother*, 1980) from Senegal (the latter one of Africa's few women directors) are also major filmmakers. Other West African film-producing countries (most but not all of which are Francophone) include Ghana, Guinea, Guinea-Bissau, Ivory Coast, Niger, and Nigeria.

Southern Africa, particularly Zimbabwe and South Africa, has long been a favored location site for Western directors, who have usually brought their own cast and crew and done little to develop indigenous talent. Potential filmmakers here have not received as much financial and educational support from Britain (which formerly dominated most of the region) as France's former colonies have received from France. However, some enterprising filmmakers have arisen of late, notably Godwin Mawuru of Zimbabwe and Michael Hammon of South Africa. Kenya and Tanzania in East Africa are also producing films.

Despite continuing heavy competition in African theaters from Western film producers (particularly Hollywood), this continent has developed a unique and varied cinema, ranging in style from magical realism rooted in folklore to affectionate humor, pointed satire, and documentary authenticity. Though often bearing the traces of French influence, these films are utterly original. Many address persistent tensions in African life, most notably the conflicts between modernity and tradition, rural and urban lifestyles, and Western and indigenous influences. Critically acclaimed in Europe though still little known in the US, the films are showcased annually at African film festivals held in alternating years in Ouagadougou, Burkina Faso, and Carthage, Tunisia.

AFTRA (American Federation of Television and Radio Artists). A labor union that negotiates minimum wages, benefits, and working conditions for performers in television and radio. It is part of the AAAA and associated with the AFL-CIO.

Agar, John. Actor. Born on Jan. 31, 1921, in Chicago. Handsome but colorless leading man of Hollywood films, which he entered after service in WW II. Better known as the former husband (1946–49) of Shirley TEMPLE than for his film work, he failed to capitalize on an initial career opportunity in the films of John Ford and drifted into routine action pictures. His career was hampered by numerous arrests for drunken driving. Overcoming alcoholism, he retired from the screen to become an insurance salesman but returned in 1976 with a small role in *King Kong*, and has appeared in occasional films since.

FILMS INCLUDE: *Fort Apache* 1948; *Adventure in Baltimore, She Wore a Yellow Ribbon* 1949; *Sands of Iwo Jima, Breakthrough* 1950; *The Magic Carpet, Along the Great Divide* 1951; *Bait, The Golden Mistress* 1954; *Revenge of the Creature, Tarantula* 1955; *The Mole People* 1956; *Daughter of Dr. Jekyll* 1957; *Frontier Gun* 1958; *Journey to the Seventh Planet* 1962; *Law of the Lawless* 1964; *Johnny Reno* 1966; *The St. Valentine's Day Massacre* 1967; *The Undefeated* 1969; *Chisum* 1970; *Big Jake* 1971; *King Kong* 1976; *How's Your Love Life?* 1977; *Miracle Mile* 1989.

Age & Scarpelli. The Italian cinema's most famous screenwriting team. Age (born Agenore Incrocci, in 1919, in Brescia) and Scarpelli (born Furio Scarpelli, in 1919, in Rome), both began their careers writing for humor magazines. They started their partnership in the late 40s and for several years worked mainly on the popular 'Toto' comedies. They earned international recognition in 1958 for their contribution to Mario Monicelli's hilarious *Big Deal on Madonna Street* and were subsequently associated with many other hits. They wrote for all genres, including "spaghetti Westerns," but excelled most in comedy to which they brought a robust sense of humor, a knack for bright and lively dialogue, and a profound understanding of the contemporary Italian social scene. Their partnership dissolved in the early 80s.

FILMS INCLUDE: *I Due Orfanelli/The Two Orphans* (Age only) 1947; *Toto' cerca Casa* 1950; *Casa Ricordi/House of Ricordi, Casta Diva* 1954; *Il Bigamo/The Bigamist* 1956; *Padri e Figli/Fathers and Sons/The Tailor's Maid* 1957; *I Soliti ignoti/Big Deal on Madonna Street, Primo Amore* 1958; *La Grande Guerra/The Great War* 1959; *Il Mattatore/Love and Larceny, Risate di Gioia/The Passionate Thief, Tutti a Casa/Everybody Go Home!* 1960; *I Due Nemici/The Best of Enemies* 1961; *Il Commissario, Il Mafioso* 1962; *I Compagni/The Organizer, I Mostri/Opiate '67/15 From Rome, Sedotta e abbandonata/Seduced and Abandoned* 1963; *Casanova '70, L'Armata Brancaleone* 1965; *Signore e Signori/The Birds the Bees and the Italians, Il Buono il Brutto e il Cattivo/The Good the Bad and the Ugly* 1966; *Il Tigre/The Tiger and the Pussycat* 1967; *Dramma ella Gelosia/The Pizza Triangle* 1970; *In Nome del Popolo Italiano/In the Name of the Italian People* 1972; *Teresa la Ladra* 1973; *Romanzo popolare* 1974; *C'eravamo tanto amati/We All Loved Each Other So Much* 1975; *La Donna della Domenica/Sunday Woman* 1976; *I Nuovi Mostri* 1977; *Temporale Rosy* 1979; *La Terrazza* 1980; *Camera d'Albergo, Nudo di Donna/Portrait of a Woman Nude* 1981; *Spaghetti House* 1982; *Le Bal* (Scarpelli only), *Scherzo del Destino. . . /A Joke of Destiny* (Age only) 1983; *Un Ragazzo e una Ragazza* (Scarpelli only), *Le Bon Roi Dagobert* (Age only) 1984; *Maccheroni/Macaroni* (Scarpelli only) 1985; *I Soliti ignoti. . . vent'anni doppo/Big Deal on Madonna Street. . . Twenty Years Later* (Age only) 1986; *La Famiglia/The Family* (Scarpelli only) 1987; *Tempo di Uccidere/The Short Cut* (Scarpelli only), *Affetuose Lontananze* (Age only), *Una Botta di Vita/A Taste of Life* (Age only) 1989; *Luisa Carlo Lorenzo e. . . le Affetuose Lontananze* (Age only), *Il Viaggio di Capitan Fracasse* (Scarpelli only) 1990.

Agee, James. Film critic, screenwriter, novelist. *b.* 1910, Knoxville, Tenn. *d.* 1955. A Harvard graduate (he had edited *The Advocate* and was awarded the university's poetry prize), he published a volume of verse in 1934, then joined the staff of *Fortune* magazine as a feature writer. His highly acclaimed film reviews appeared throughout the 40s in *Time* and *Nation* and were subsequently published in book form as one of two volumes entitled *Agee on Film.* The other volume contains five film scripts that Agee wrote after moving to Hollywood in 1948. One of his three novels, *A Death in the Family,* was awarded a Pulitzer Prize in 1958. In 1963 it was turned into a film, *All the Way Home.*

FILMS: *The Quiet One* (narration and dial.) 1949; *The African Queen* (co-sc.) 1951; *Face to Face* ("The Bride Comes to Yellow Sky" episode) 1952; *The Night of the Hunter* 1955.

agent. A person authorized by another to act on his behalf. In the US and most other Western countries, actors, directors, writers, and other creative personnel in the theater, TV, and films, have been traditionally represented by agents, who negotiate contracts, wages, fees, benefits, and working conditions, usually in return for a percentage of the deal, normally 10 or 15 percent. In Hollywood, agents must be franchised by one or more of the talent unions or guilds to negotiate for their clients.

Agents have always provided an important link between talent and the film industry, but their importance and influence have greatly increased since the 50s, when Hollywood gradually phased out its roster of contract actors, directors, and writers. Studios and independent producers became more and more dependent on agents to provide them with the talent and literary properties needed for the production of each film, and many agents soon emerged as packagers of entire film productions who share in a film's profits in addition to the traditional percentage of the fees paid to the talent they represent. One of the leading agencies, MCA, became a virtual entertainment empire; another, William Morris, came to exert enormous influence on film and TV production. Many of Hollywood's top agents moved on into production, including Ted Ashley, Bill Dozier, Leland Hayward, Myron Selznick, and Jules Stein. Michael Ovitz, former head of Creative Artists Agency (CAA), and Jeff Berg, head of International Creative Management (ICM), regularly appear on lists of the most powerful people in Hollywood.

Agfacolor. A trichromatic film color process discovered in 1908 by the German chemists Fischer and Homolka for the Neue Photographische Gesellschaft. The Agfa Company made it commercially available in 1936 (reversible film) and in 1939 (negative film) as the first reliable subtractive process with couplers incorporated into the emulsion layers. The first film in Agfacolor was *Women Are the Best Diplomats* (Germany, 1940–41). See COLOR CINEMATOGRAPHY.

Agnew, Robert (Bobby). Actor. *b.* 1899, Louisville, Ky. *d.* 1983. Juvenile player and romantic lead of numerous Hollywood silents of the 20s. Retired shortly after the advent of sound.

FILMS INCLUDE: *The Valley of Doubt* 1920; *The Highest Law, The Passion Flower* 1921; *Without Fear, Clarence, Kick In* 1922; *Prodigal Daughters, Bluebeard's 8th Wife, The Marriage Maker, The Spanish Dancer* 1923; *Those Who Dance, Wine, Broken Barriers, Wine of Youth, Gold Heels* 1924; *Private Affairs, The Denial, The Great Love* 1925; *Racing Blood, The Taxi Mystery, Dancing Days* 1926; *Snowbound, She's My Baby, The College Hero, The Heart of Salome* 1927; *The Heart of Broadway, The Midnight Taxi* 1928; *Extravagance* 1930; *The Naughty Flirt* 1931; *Gold Diggers of 1933* 1933.

Agostini, Philippe. Director, director of photography. Born on Aug. 11, 1910, in Paris. In films as assistant cameraman from 1934, he later distinguished himself as one of France's leading cinematographers, collaborating with, among other directors, Bresson, Carné, Daquin, Grémillon, and Max Ophüls. He has been far less successful in his efforts as a director since the late 50s. Married actress Odette JOYEUX.

FILMS INCLUDE: As director of photography—*Itto* 1935; *Un Carnet de Bal* (co-phot.) 1937; *Les Deux Timides, Lettres d'Amour* 1942; *Les Anges du Péché/Angels of the Street, Douce/Love Story* 1943; *Les Dames du Bois de Boulogne/Ladies of the Park* (co-phot.) 1945; *Sylvie et le Fantôme/Sylvie and the Phantom, Les Portes de la Nuit/Gates of the Night* 1946; *Topaze* 1950; *Le Plaisir* (co-phot.) 1952; *Du Rififi chez les Hommes/Rififi* 1955. As director (complete)—*Ordinations* (short) 1954; *Le Naïf aux Quarante Enfants* (also co-sc.) 1958; *Tu es Pierre* (doc.), *Le Dialogue des Carmelites* (co-dir. with R. Bruckberger) 1960; *Rencontres* 1961; *La Soupe aux Poulets* 1963; *La Petite Fille è la Recherche du Printemps* 1971.

Agutter, Jenny. Actress. Born on Dec. 20, 1952, in Taunton, England. She trained as a ballet dancer, entered British films at the age of 12, and has since played leads and supporting roles in a number of film, stage, and TV productions in Britain and the US. She won an Emmy (best supporting actress) for her television role in 'The Snow Goose' (1971) and the British Academy Award (also best supporting actress) for the movie *Equus*.

FILMS INCLUDE: *East Of Sudan* 1964; *A Man Could Get Killed* 1966; *Gates to Paradise, Star!* 1968; *I Start Counting* 1969; *The Railway Children* 1970; *Walkabout* (Austral.) 1971; *Logan's Run* 1976; *The Eagle Has Landed, Equus* 1977; *China 9—Liberty 37/Clayton and Catherine* (It.) 1978; *Dominique, Sweet William, The Riddle of the Sands* 1979; *Amy, The Survivor, An American Werewolf in London* 1981; *Secret Places* 1984; *Dark Tower* 1988; *Darkman, Child's Play 2, King of the Wind* 1990; *Freddie as F.R.O.7.* (v/o) (UK) 1992.

AGVA (American Guild of Variety Artists). A union of the AFL-CIO, organized in 1939, for cabaret, circus, and other variety artists.

Aherne, Brian. Actor. *b.* May 2, 1902, King's Norton, England. *d.* 1986. A child actor from the age of eight, he resumed his stage career at 20 after studying architecture at Malvern College. He gained popularity in British silent films, then came to the US in 1931 to star in the Broadway production of 'The Barretts of Wimpole Street.' In Hollywood from 1933, he played many romantic leads, often typecast as a tweedy, pipe-smoking gentleman of the British school. He was nominated for an Oscar for *Juarez* (1939). An autobiography, *A Proper Job* (1969), discusses his long career and his short (1939–45) marriage to Joan FONTAINE.

FILMS INCLUDE: In the UK—*The Eleventh Commandment* 1924; *Safety First* 1926; *Shooting Stars, Underground* 1928; *The Constant Nymph* 1933. In the US—*Song of Songs* 1933; *Sylvia Scarlett* 1935; *Beloved Enemy* 1936; *The Great Garrick* 1937; *Merrily We Live* 1938; *Juarez* (as Emperor Maximilian), *Captain Fury* 1939; *The Lady in Question, Hired Wife, My Son My Son* 1940; *Smilin' Through, Skylark* 1941; *My Sister Eileen* 1942; *A Night to Remember, Forever and a Day, First Comes Courage* 1943; *The Locket* 1946; *Smart Woman* 1948; *I Confess, Titanic* 1953; *Prince Valiant* 1954; *The Swan* 1956; *The Best of Everything* 1959; *Susan Slade* 1961; *Rosie* 1967.

Aiello, Danny. Actor. Born on June 20, 1933, in New York City. Beefy, versatile, busy character lead and supporting player of Hollywood films of the 70s and 80s, typically in sympathetic roles, occasionally as a menace. He was 40 when he made his film debut in *Bang the Drum Slowly* (1973). Sixteen years later, he was nominated for an Academy Award as best supporting actor for *Do the Right Thing*. He has also appeared on the New York stage; his TV work was recognized with an Emmy Award in 1981.

FILMS: *Bang The Drum Slowly* 1973; *The Godfather Part II* 1974; *The Front* 1976; *Hooch* 1977; *Bloodbrothers, Fingers* 1978; *Defiance, Hide in Plain Sight* 1980; *Chu Chu and the Philly Flash, Fort Apache the Bronx* 1981; *Amityville II: The Possession* 1982; *Deathmask* 1983; *Old Enough, Once Upon a Time in America* 1984; *The Purple Rose of Cairo, Key Exchange, The Protector, The Stuff* 1985; *Radio Days, The Pick-Up Artist, Man on Fire* (It./Fr.), *Moonstruck* 1987; *The January Man, White Hot* 1988; *Do the Right Thing, Crack in the Mirror, Harlem Nights, Russicum/The Third Solution* (It.) 1989; *The Closer, Jacob's Ladder* 1990; *Once Around, Hudson Hawk, 29th Street* 1991; *Ruby, Mistress* 1992; *Me and the Kid, The Pickle* 1993; *The Professional, Ready to Wear* 1994; *2 Days in the Valley, City Hall, Two Much* 1996.

Aimée, Anouk. Actress. Born Françoise Sorya (Dreyfus), on Apr. 27, 1932, in Paris. The daughter of an actor and actress, she studied acting and dancing in France and England before making her film debut at 14. She first attracted attention in Cayatte's *Les Amants de Vérone/The Lovers of Verona* in a Juliet-like role especially created for her by poet-screenwriter Jacques Prévert. After a long succession of indifferent roles, her warm, feline, gracefully enigmatic personality finally blossomed in such films as Fellini's *La Dolce Vita* and *Ottó e Mezzo/8½*, Jacques Demy's *Lola,* and Claude Lelouch's *Un Homme et une Femme/A Man and a Woman* (1966). For her role in the latter film, she was nominated for an Oscar and won the British Academy Award as best foreign actress; she and co-star Jean-Louis Trintignant reprised their roles in the 1986 sequel. She was named best actress at Cannes for her performance in *Leap Into Void* (1980). Her first husband (1952–54) was director Nico PAPATAKIS. Her fourth marriage, to Albert FINNEY, also ended in divorce (1970–1978).

FILMS INCLUDE: *La Maison Sous La Mer* 1947; *Les Amants de Vérone/The Lovers of Verona* 1949; *The Golden Salamander* (UK) 1950; *Le Rideau cramoisi* 1951; *The Man Who Watched the Trains Go By/The Paris Express* (UK) 1952; *Les Mauvaises Rencontres* 1955; *Pot-Bouille* 1957; *Montparnasse 19/Modigliani of Montparnasse* 1958; *La Tëte contre les Murs, Les Dragueurs/The Chasers, The Journey* (US) 1959; *La Dolce Vita* (It./Fr.) 1960; *Le Farceur/The Joker, Lola, Il Giudizio Universale* (It.), *Sodoma e Gomorra/Sodom and Gomorrah* (It./Fr./US) 1961; *Otto e Mezzo/8½* (It.), *Les Grands Chemins/Of Flesh and Blood, Il Successo* (It./Fr.) 1963; *Le Voci bianche/ White Voices* (It./Fr.) 1964; *La Fuga* (It.) 1965; *Un Homme et une Femme/A Man and a Woman* 1966; *Justine* (US), *The Model Shop* (US) 1969; *The Appointment* (release delayed from 1969; US) 1970; *Si c'était à refaire/Second Chance* 1976; *Mon Premier Amour/My First Love* 1978; *Salto nel Vuoto/Leap Into Void* 1980; *Tragedia di un Uomo ridicolo/The Tragedy of a Ridiculous Man* 1981; *Qu'est-ce qui fait courir David* 1982; *Vive la Vie, Success Is the Best Revenge* (UK) 1984; *Flagrant Desire* 1985; *Un Homme et une Femme: 20 Ans déjà/A Man and a Woman: 20 Years Later* 1986; *Arrivederci e Grazie, La Table tournante* 1988; *Bethune: The Making of a Hero, Il y a des jours. . . et des lunes* 1990; *Ruptures* 1992; *Les Marmottes* 1993; *Ready to Wear* 1994.

Aitken, Harry E. Production executive, film pioneer. *b.* 1870, Waukesha, Wis. *d.* 1956. As a theater owner, he led a movement against the Edison Company, establishing Majestic Pictures in 1911. In 1912 he became president of the Mutual Film Corporation. The following year he lured D. W. GRIFFITH away from Biograph and helped finance and distribute *The Birth of a Nation* (1915). In the summer of 1915 he founded the Triangle Pictures Corporation, of which he was president until 1918. The company boasted the services of the top three creative talents of the American silent screen, D. W. Griffith, Thomas H. INCE, and Mack SENNETT. However, Aitken's ambitious production plans ended in failure, and in 1920 he retired from the film business.

Aitken, Spottiswoode. American actor. *b.* Frank Spottiswoode Aitken, 1869. *d.* 1933. Leading character player of silent films following long stage experience; memorable as Dr. Cameron in D. W. GRIFFITH's *The Birth of a Nation* (1915) and in several other Griffith films.

FILMS INCLUDE: *The Battle* 1911; *Home Sweet Home, The Old Maid, The Avenging Conscience, Liberty Belles* 1914; *The Birth of a Nation* 1915; *Intolerance, The Wharf Rat* 1916; *Captain Kidd, Jr., The White Heather, Her Kingdom of Dreams* 1919; *Nomads of the North, The White Circle* 1920; *Reputation, The Unknown Wife* 1921; *Man of Courage, The Trap, Manslaughter, Monte Cristo, The Price of Youth, The Young Rajah, A Dangerous Game* 1922; *Merry-Go-Round, Six Days* 1923; *Triumph, The Fire Patrol* 1924; *Accused, The Eagle, The Goose Woman* 1925; *The Power of the Weak* 1926; *God's Great Wilderness* (story only), *Roaring Fires* 1927.

Akerman, Chantal. Director, screenwriter, actress. Born in June, 1950, in Brussels, to working-class Jewish parents. *ed.* INSAS film school (Brussels); Université Internationale du Théâtre (Paris). Independent filmmaker noted for her minimalist narratives and static visual style. Inspired by Godard's *Pierrot le Fou,* she took on a variety of odd jobs to finance her first film, *Saute ma Ville/Blow Up My City* (1968), a black-and-white short that drew belated attention at the 1971 Oberhasen Festival. She spent much of 1972 in New York, living in the East Village, working as a cashier at a porno movie theater, among other occupations, and associating with the city's experimental filmmakers. She has since returned to the US periodically to get "re-energized" and engage in filmmaking projects, but has been working mostly in Europe. Her films, often dramatically vague and nearly plotless, typically seek to explore human emotion and character through unorthodox cinematic means. Although she is admired by serious critics, her films are barely accessible to general audiences.

FILMS: *Saute Ma Ville* (short) 1968; *L'Enfant aimé* (short) 1971; *Hotel Monterey, La Chambre* (short) 1972; *Le 15/18* (short; co-dir), *Hanging Out in Yonkers/Yonkers Hanging Out* 1973; *Je, tu, il, elles* 1974; *Jeanne Dielman 23 Quai du Commerce 1080 Bruxelles* 1975; *News from Home* 1976; *Les Rendez-vous d'Anna* 1978; *Dis-moi* (short) 1980; *Toute une Nuit* 1982; *Les Années 80/The Eighties/The Golden Eighties* 1983; *L'Homme à la Valise, J'ai Faim, J'ai Froid* (both shorts) 1984; *Golden Eighties* (not to be confused with the '83 film of the same title) 1986; *Seven Women Seven Sins* (Ger./Fr./US/ Aus./Belg.), *Histoires d'Amérique/American Stories, Les Ministères de l'art, Un jour Pina m'a demandé* 1988; *Window Shopping* 1992; *D'Est/From the East, Moving In* 1993; *Portrait of a Young Girl at the End of the 1960s in Brussels* 1994.

Akins, Claude. Actor. *b.* May 25, 1918, Nelson, Ga. *d.* 1994. *ed.* Northwestern. Character player of Hollywood films; typically a heavy, often in Westerns. A former salesman, he appeared in stock and on Broadway before entering films in the early 50s. Mellowing later in his career, he played kindlier roles in numerous episodes of TV series and in the 70s starred in the TV series 'Movin' On.'

FILMS INCLUDE: *From Here to Eternity* 1953; *The Caine Mutiny, The Human Jungle* 1954; *Johnny Concho* 1956; *The Lonely Man* 1957; *The Defiant Ones* 1958; *Rio Bravo, Porgy and Bess* 1959; *Comanche Station, Inherit the Wind* 1960; *Merrill's Marauders, How the West Was Won* 1962; *A Distant Trumpet, The Killers* 1964; *Return of the Seven* 1966; *Waterhole 3* 1967; *The Devil's Brigade* 1968; *The Great Bank Robbery* 1969; *Flap* 1970; *A Man Called Sledge* 1971; *Skyjacked* 1972; *Battle for the Planet of the Apes* 1973; *Timber Tramps* 1975; *Tentacles* (It.) 1977; *Little Mo* (orig. for TV) 1978; *Monster in the Closet* 1986; *The Curse* 1987; *Falling From Grace* 1992.

Akins, Zoë. Playwright, screenwriter. *b.* Oct. 30, 1886, Humansville, Mo. *d.* 1958. The author of many short stories for popular magazines and a number of plays that have been adapted for films. She spent the early 30s in Hollywood writing screenplays for pictures of appeal to women.

FILMS INCLUDE: From her stories or plays—*Déclassée, Daddy's Gone A-Hunting* 1925; *Her Private Life* 1929; *The Furies, Ladies Love Brutes* 1930; *Women Love Once, Girls About Town* 1931; *The Greeks Had a Word for Them* 1932;

Morning Glory 1933; *The Old Maid* 1939; *How to Marry a Millionaire* 1953; *Stage Struck* (remake of *Morning Glory*) 1958. As screenwriter—*Anybody's Woman, The Right to Love, Sarah and Son* 1930; *Christopher Strong* 1933; *Outcast Lady* 1934; *Lady of Secrets, Accused* 1936; *Camille* 1937; *The Toy Wife* 1938; *Desire Me* 1947.

Alazraki, Benito. Director. Born in 1923, in Mexico. He entered Mexican films in the mid-40s as producer and co-writer of Emilio Fernandez's *Enamorada* (1947). In 1955 he attracted worldwide attention with *Raices/The Roots,* a four-episode film about Mexican Indian life which he directed and co-scripted with Carlos Velo. The film won the International Critics Prize at the Cannes Film Festival of that year. Alazraki's subsequent films have been, however, far less significant, comprising mostly melodramas and horror films for popular consumption at the Mexican market.

FILMS INCLUDE: *Raices/The Roots* 1955; *Los Amantes* 1956; *Ladros de Niños* 1957; *Cafe Colón, Inferno de Almas, La Tijera d'Oro* 1958; *Muñecos Infernales/The Curse of the Doll People* 1960; *Espiritismo/Spiritism, Los Pistoleros* 1961; *The Time and the Touch* (made in the US, using pseudonym Carlos Arconti) 1962.

Alberghetti, Anna Maria. Singer, actress. Born on May 15, 1936, in Pesaro, Italy, of musician parents. At the age of 12 she made a European concert tour, at 14 her American debut at Carnegie Hall. The same year (1950) she made her screen debut in the film version of Gian-Carlo Menotti's opera *The Medium.* Retired from the screen after starring in the Broadway musical *Carnival* (1961), for which she won a Tony.

FILMS: *The Medium* 1950; *Here Comes the Groom* 1951; *The Stars Are Singing* 1953; *The Last Command* 1955; *10,000 Bedrooms, Duel at Apache Wells* 1957; *Cinderfella* 1960.

Alberini, Filoteo. Italian inventor, film pioneer. *b.* Mar. 14, 1865, Turin, Italy. *d.* 1937. In 1894 and 1895 he invented and developed the Cinetografo, or Kinetograph, an apparatus capable of recording, developing, and projecting animated motion pictures. In 1911 he invented the Auto-stereoscopio, a 70 mm stereoscopic process, one of the first efforts to create a wide-screen technique. The aspect ratio (2.52:1) was close to the dimensions of today's CINEMASCOPE (2.55:1), and the process was achieved by Alberini's Panoramica camera, which scanned the frames of 70 mm film. The process was used in his 1914 film *Il Sacco di Roma/The Sacking of Rome.* In 1928 he experimented with British film engineer Roy Hill on a wide-screen system involving double 35 mm frames running horizontally through the camera and the projector. Alberini was also active in film production and exhibition from 1901. He was co-founder, in 1904, of the Alberini e Santoni company, which turned out dozens of short subjects. In 1906 it was incorporated as Cines, one of Italy's major film-producing companies.

Alberni, Luis. Actor. *b.* 1887, Barcelona, Spain. *d.* 1962. A graduate of the University of Barcelona, he came to the US in his youth and soon began a simultaneous career on Broadway and in silent films. After the advent of sound, he became one of Hollywood's busiest character actors, typically playing an excitable Latin.

FILMS INCLUDE: *Little Italy* 1921; *The Bright Shawl* 1923; *The Santa Fe Trail* 1930; *Svengali, The Mad Genius* 1931; *Manhattan Parade, The Kid from Spain* 1932; *Topaze* 1933; *The Black Cat, The Count of Monte Cristo* 1934; *Roberta, In Caliente, The Gay Deception* 1935; *Anthony Adverse* 1936; *I'll Give a Million* 1938; *The Lady Eve, That Hamilton Woman* 1941; *Babes on Broadway* 1942; *A Bell for Adano* 1945; *What Price Glory* 1952.

Albers, Hans. Actor. *b.* Sept. 22, 1892, Hamburg, Germany. *d.* 1960. Recovering from wounds suffered during WW I, he began acting in light comedy, then in serious roles on the Berlin stage and in silent German films. He appeared with Max REINHARDT's Deutsches Theater in 1926–28 and soon thereafter became one of Germany's most popular screen performers. He played numerous romantic leads before gradually switching to character parts.

FILMS INCLUDE: *In Grossen Augenblick, Zigeunerblut* 1911; *Komödianten, Der Totentanz* 1912; *Lola Montez, Das Grand Hotel Babylon* 1919; *Die Marquise von O.* 1920; *Der falsche Dimitri* 1922; *Guillotine, Ein Sommernachtstraum/A Midsummer Night's Dream* 1924; *Eine Dubarry von Heute/A Modern Du Barry, Der Prinz und die Tänzerin/The Prince and the Ballet Dancer* 1926; *Rasputins Liebesabenteuer/Rasputin* 1928; *Asphalt* 1929; *Der blaue Engel/The Blue Angel* 1930; *Bomben auf Monte Carlo/Monte Carlo Madness* 1931; *Quick, Der Sieger/The Victor* 1932; *Gold, Peer Gynt* (title role) 1934; *Variété* 1935; *Münchhausen* (title role) 1943; *Und uber uns der Himmel/City of Torment* 1947; *Barbe-Bleue/Blue Beard* 1951; *Der letzte Mann* 1955; *Das Herz von St. Pauli* 1957; *Kein Engel ist so rein* 1960.

Albert, Eddie. Actor. Born Edward Albert Heimberger, on Apr. 22, 1908, in Rock Island, Ill. *ed.* U. of Minnesota. A former circus trapeze flier and veteran of radio and the stage, he made his film debut in 1938 and has since played numerous parts, mostly second leads. He specialized in hearty, slap-on-the-back types but occasionally he played heels. He starred in TV's successful series 'Green Acres.' Married the actress MARGO, 1945. Their son is actor Edward ALBERT. Eddie was nominated for Oscars for his roles in *Roman Holiday* (1953) and *The Heartbreak Kid* (1972).

FILMS INCLUDE: *Brother Rat* 1938; *Four Wives* 1939; *A Dispatch from Reuters* 1940; *Four Mothers, The Wagons Roll at Night* 1941; *Bombardier* 1943; *Smash-Up* 1947; *The Dude Goes West* 1948; *Actors and Sin, Carrie* 1952; *Roman Holiday* 1953; *Oklahoma!, I'll Cry Tomorrow* 1955; *Attack!, The Teahouse of the August Moon* 1956; *The Sun Also Rises, Orders to Kill* 1957; *The Roots of Heaven* 1958; *The Longest Day* 1962; *Captain Newman M.D.* 1963; *Seven Women* 1966; *The Heartbreak Kid* 1972; *McQ, The Longest Yard* 1974; *Escape to Witch Mountain, The Devil's Rain, Whiffs, Hustle* 1975; *Birch Interval, Moving Violation* 1976; *The Concorde—Airport '79/Airport '80. . . the Concorde* 1979; *Yesterday* (Can.) 1980; *Take This Job and Shove It* 1981; *Yes Giorgio* 1982; *Dreamscape* 1984; *Stitches* 1985; *Head Office* 1986; *Deadly Illusion* 1987; *The Big Picture* (cameo) 1989; *Body Language, Brenda Starr* 1992 (held from release since 1986).

Albert, Edward. Actor. Born on Feb. 20, 1951, in Los Angeles. *ed.* UCLA, Oxford. Leading man of Hollywood films and American TV. The son of actors Eddie ALBERT and MARGO, he made his screen debut at 14. As a young adult, he played an auspicious lead as Goldie Hawn's blind boyfriend in *Butterflies Are Free* but his subsequent big-screen roles were, on the whole, less rewarding. He is an exhibited photographer.

FILMS INCLUDE: *The Fool Killer* 1965; *Butterflies Are Free* 1972; *40 Carats* 1973; *Midway* 1976; *The Domino Principle, Un Taxi mauve* (Fr./It./Ire.) 1977; *The Greek Tycoon* 1978; *When Time Ran Out* 1980; *Galaxy of Terror* 1981; *Butterfly, The House Where Evil Dwells* 1981; *Ellie* 1984; *Getting Even/Hostage: Dallas* 1986; *The Rescue* 1988; *Mindgames, Fist Fighters* 1989; *The Ice Runner* 1993; *Guarding Tess* 1994.

Albertson, Frank. Actor. *b.* Feb. 2, 1909, Fergus Falls, Minn. *d.* 1964. Entered films in 1922 as a prop boy and developed into a light leading man and later a character player in scores of Hollywood productions.

FILMS INCLUDE: *The Farmer's Daughter* 1928; *Words and Music, Blue Skies, Salute* 1929; *Born Reckless, Men Without Women, So This Is London, Wild Company* 1930; *A Connecticut Yankee, The Brat* 1931; *Air Mail* 1932; *Rainbow Over Broadway* 1933; *Alice Adams, Ah Wilderness* 1935; *Fury, The Plainsman* 1936; *Room Service* 1938; *Bachelor Mother* 1939; *Man Made Monster, Father Steps Out* 1941; *Wake Island, The Man from Headquarters, City of Silent Men* 1942; *It's a Wonderful Life* 1946; *The Hucksters* 1947; *The Enemy Below* 1957; *The Last Hurrah* 1958; *Psycho* 1960; *Bye Bye Birdie* 1963.

Albertson, Jack. Actor. *b.* June 16, 1907, Malden, Mass. *d.* 1981. Character player of vaudeville, burlesque, Broadway, TV, and films. He won best supporting actor Academy Award for *The Subject Was Roses* (1968), in which he repeated his Tony Award–winning stage role. He won an Emmy for a supporting role in the 'Cher' TV show (1975) and a best actor Emmy for his co-star performance in the series 'Chico and the Man' (1976). His sister, Mabel Albertson (1901–82), also appeared on TV and in numerous films.

FILMS INCLUDE: *Next Time I Marry* 1938; *Strike Up The Band* 1940; *Miracle on 34th Street* 1947; *Top Banana* 1954; *The Harder They Fall* 1956; *Man of a Thousand Faces, Monkey on My Back* 1957; *Teacher's Pet* 1958; *Never Steal Anything Small* 1959; *Lover Come Back* 1961; *Period of Adjustment, Days of Wine and Roses* 1962; *How to Murder Your Wife* 1965; *The Flim Flam Man* 1967; *The Subject Was Roses* 1968; *Changes, Justine* 1969; *Rabbit Run* 1970; *Willy Wonka and the Chocolate Factory, A Time for Every Purpose, The Late Liz* 1971; *The Poseidon Adventure, Pickup on 101* 1972; *Dead and Buried* 1981.

Albright, Hardie. Actor. *b.* Hardy Albrecht, Dec. 6, 1903, Charleroi, Pa. *d.* 1975. Blond, blue-eyed leading man and supporting player of Hollywood films of the 30s and early 40s. The son of vaudevillians, he made his first stage appearance at the age of six. After drama studies at Carnegie Tech. and some art training at the Art Institute in Chicago, he joined Eva Le Gallienne's Civic Repertory Theatre and made his Broadway debut with the group in 1926. He played juvenile leads in many plays on Broadway and on the road before entering films in 1931. On the screen, he played leads, second leads, and eventually supporting roles in some 50 films, mostly minor productions at Fox, Warners, and other studios. He was teamed with Bette DAVIS in several of her early films. His Hollywood career ended in 1946, but he later appeared in an exploitative "sex education" film, *Mom and Dad* (1957) which was directed by William Beaudine. Albright taught drama at UCLA in 1962 and published several textbooks, including *Acting: The Creative Force* and *Stage Direction in Transition.* He died of congestive heart failure. His first wife (1934–40) was actress Martha Sleeper.

FILMS INCLUDE: *Young Sinners, Hush Money, Skyline, Heartbreak* 1931; *So Big, The Purchase Price, The Crash, Cabin in the Cotton, The Match King* 1932; *The Working Man/The Adopted Father, Song of Songs, Three-Cornered Moon* 1933; *The Ninth Guest, White Heat, Crimson Romance, The Scarlet Letter, The Silver Streak* 1934; *Ladies Love Danger, Calm Yourself, Red Salute* 1935; *Ski Patrol* 1940; *Flight From Destiny* 1941; *The Pride of the Yankees, The Loves of Edgar Allan Poe* 1942; *The Jade Mask* 1945; *Angel on My Shoulder* 1946; *Mom and Dad* 1957.

Albright, Lola. Actress. Born on July 20, 1925, in Akron, Ohio. She acted in bit dramatic parts while working as a switchboard operator and stenographer for a radio station and then became a photographer's model before being discovered by Hollywood. Film debut in *The Pirate* (1948). She was impressive in *Champion* (1949). After appearing in the successful 'Peter Gunn' TV series, she won critical acclaim for her performance as an aging stripper in the film *A Cold Wind in August* in 1961. She was married (1952–58) to Jack CARSON.

FILMS INCLUDE: *The Pirate, Easter Parade* 1948; *Champion* 1949; *The Good Humor Man* 1950; *Sierra Passage* 1951; *The Silver Whip* 1953; *The Magnificent Matador, The Tender Trap* 1955; *The Monolith Monsters* 1957; *A Cold Wind in August* 1961; *Kid Galahad* 1962; *Les Félins/Joy House* (Fr.) 1964; *Lord Love a Duck* 1966; *The Way West* 1967; *Where Were You When the Lights Went Out?, The Impossible Years, The Money Jungle* 1968.

Alcaine, Jose Luis. Cinematographer. Born on Dec. 26, 1938, in Tangier, Algeria (now Morocco). *ed.* Spanish Cinema School, Madrid. After starting out in commercials, he established himself in the 70s and 80s as one of Spain's leading cinematographers. Best known to US audiences for his work with director Pedro Almovodar on such films as *Tie Me Up! Tie Me Down!*

FILMS INCLUDE: *El Niño Es Nuestro* 1972; *Vera* 1973; *El Puente* 1977; *El Sur* 1983; *Rustlers' Rhapsody* (US) 1985; *Barbablú Barbablú/Bluebeard Bluebeard* 1987; *Women on the Verge of a Nervous Breakdown* 1988; *The Mad Monkey* 1989; *Atame!/Tie Me Up! Tie Me Down!, Ay Carmela!* 1990; *Belle Époque/The Age of Beauty* 1993.

Alcoriza, Luis. Director, screenwriter, actor. *b.* 1920, Badajóz, Spain. *d.* 1992. The son of show people, he started out in his teens as an actor on the European stage and later in Mexican films. In the late 40s he turned to screenwriting and soon became Luis BUÑUEL's favorite script collaborator. In the early 60s he began directing. He became a naturalized Mexican.

FILMS INCLUDE: As screenwriter—*El Gran Calavera/The Great Madcap* 1949; *Los Olvidados/The Young and the Damned* 1950; *La Hija del Engaño/Daughter of Deceit* 1951; *El/This Strange Passion* 1952; *El Rio y la Muerte/The River and Death* 1954; *La Mort en ce Jardin/Gina/Evil Eden/Death in the Garden* 1956; *La Fièvre mont á El Pao/Los Ambiciosos/Fever Mounts at El Pao/Republic of Sin* 1960; *El Angel Exterminador/The Exterminating Angel* 1962. As director-screenwriter—*Los Jovenès* 1961; *Tlayucan/The Pearly Tlayucan* 1962; *El Gangster* 1964; *Tarahumara* 1965; *Juego Peligroso* (co-dir.) 1966; *Preságio* 1974; *Las Fuerzas Vivas* 1975; *Terrór y Encajes Negros* 1986; *Lo Que Importa Es Vivír* 1989.

Alcott, John. *b.* ca. 1931, London. *d.* 1986, Cannes, France. British director of photography. He worked on several productions of the 60s as a focus puller before proving his ability with a number of scenes he shot for Stanley Kubrick's *2001: A Space Odyssey* (1968). He emerged in the early 70s as a superior cinematographer with two visually exquisite Kubrick films, *A Clockwork Orange* (1971) and *Barry Lyndon* (1975); the latter film won him an Oscar. He collaborated with Kubrick once more on *The Shining* (1980). He died of a heart attack after completing *No Way Out* (1987). The film was dedicated to him.

FILMS INCLUDE: *2001: A Space Odyssey* (addnl. phot. only) 1968; *A Clockwork Orange* 1971; *Little Malcolm and His Struggle Against the Eunuchs* 1974; *Barry Lyndon* 1975; *March or Die, Disappearance* (Can.) 1977; *Who Is Killing the Great Chefs of Europe?* 1978; *The Shining, Terror Train, Fort Apache the Bronx* 1980; *The Beastmaster* 1982; *Under Fire* 1983; *Greystoke: The Legend of Tarzan Lord of the Apes* 1984; *White Water Summer/Rites of Summer, No Way Out* 1987.

Alda, Alan. Actor, director, screenwriter. Born on Jan. 28, 1936, in New York City. *ed.* Fordham. Restrained, mannered, lightly sarcastic leading man of American stage, screen, and television. After preparing for the stage at the Cleveland Playhouse, he performed with the Second City improvisation troupe, then joined the cast of TV's satirical show 'This Was the Week That Was.' He scored his greatest success with the long-running TV series 'M*A*S*H' (1972–83), for which he won several Emmy Awards as best actor, best director, and best writer. He was also awarded the prestigious "Actor of the Year" Emmy in 1974. In films since the early 60s, he pleased the public and many critics with his debut as a big-screen director in 1981. He is the son of the late Robert ALDA.

FILMS (as actor): *Gone Are the Days* 1963; *Paper Lion* 1968; *The Extraordinary Seaman* 1969; *The Moonshine War* 1970; *The Mephisto Waltz* 1971; *To Kill a Clown* 1972; *Same Time Next Year, California Suite* 1978; *The Seduction of Joe Tynan* (also sc.) 1979; *The Four Seasons* (also dir., sc.) 1981; *Sweet Liberty* (also dir., sc.) 1986; *A New Life* (also dir., sc.) 1988; *Crimes and Misdemeanors* 1989; *Betsy's Wedding* (also dir., sc.) 1990; *Whispers in the Dark* 1992; *Manhattan Murder Mystery* 1993; *Canadian Bacon* 1994; *Everyone Says I Love You, Flirting with Disaster* 1996; *Murder at 1600* 1997.

Alda, Robert. Actor. *b.* Alphonso Giuseppe Giovanni Roberto D'Abruzzo, Feb. 26, 1914, New York City. *d.* 1986. *ed.* NYU. A barber's son, he was an architectural draftsman before breaking into show business as a vaudeville singer-entertainer. He later performed on radio and in burlesque, and in 1945 made his film debut portraying George Gershwin in Warner's biopic *Rhapsody in Blue.* As it later turned out, this first role would remain the most important in Alda's largely disappointing screen career. He was much more successful on the New York stage as the star of such Broadway productions as 'Guys and Dolls' (Tony Award), 'Harbor Lights,' and 'What Makes Sammy Run.' In the early 60s he settled in Rome and for the next two decades appeared in Italian films and European co-productions. He suffered a stroke in 1984 from which he never recovered. He was the father of actor Alan ALDA.

FILMS INCLUDE: *Rhapsody In Blue* (as George Gershwin) 1945; *Cinderella Jones, Cloak and Dagger* 1946; *The Beast With Five Fingers, The Man I Love, Nora Prentiss* 1947; *April Showers* 1948; *Tarzan and the Slave Girl* 1950; *Mr. Universe, Two Gals and a Guy* 1951; *La Donna più Bella del Mondo/Beautiful but Dangerous* (It.) 1955; *Imitation of Life* 1959; *The Devil's Hand, Force of Impulse, Il Sepolcro dei Re/Cleopatra's Daughter* (It./Fr.) 1961; *Toto e Peppino divisi a Berlino* (It.) 1962; *The Girl Who Knew Too Much* 1969; *Le Serpent/The Serpent* (Fr./Ger.) 1973; *House of Exorcism* (It.) 1975; *I Will I Will. . . for Now, Bittersweet Love* 1976; *Every Girl Should Have One* 1978; *The Squeeze* (It.) 1980.

Aldo, G. R. Director of photography. *b.* Aldo Graziati, Jan. 1, 1902, Scorze, Italy. *d.* 1953. Went to France at 19 to become an actor; appeared in one film, then went into still photography instead. Years later he become an assistant cameraman and by the late 40s had graduated to lighting cameraman. In 1947 he returned to Italy with the crew of a French production and stayed to become one of Italy's most distinguished postwar cinematographers. He lent some brilliant compositions and striking black-and-white images to films of Visconti, De Sica, and Orson Welles, among others. He died in an auto accident during the filming of Visconti's *Senso.*

FILMS INCLUDE: *La Chartreuse De Parme* (Fr./It.) 1947; *La Terra Trema* 1948; *Gli Ultimi Giorni di Pompei/The Last Days of Pompeii* 1949; *Miracolo a Milano/Miracle in Milan* 1951; *Othello* (co-phot.), *Umberto D* 1952; *Stazione Termini/Indiscretion of an American Wife, La Provinciale/The Wayward Wife* (US/It.) 1953; *Senso* (co-phot.) 1954.

Aldredge, Theoni V. Costume designer. Born Theoni Vachlioti, on Aug. 22, 1932, in Salonika, Greece. *ed.* American School, Athens; Goodman Memorial Theatre, Chicago. She began designing for the stage in 1950 and became established as a leading Broadway and Hollywood wardrobe stylist in the 60s. She won an Oscar for *The Great Gatsby* (1974) and Tony Awards for 'Annie' (1977) and 'Barnum' (1980). Her stage credits also include 'A Chorus Line' and '42nd Street.' Married to actor Tom Aldredge.

FILMS INCLUDE: *Girl Of The Night* 1960; *You're a Big Boy Now* 1966; *No Way to Treat a Lady, Uptight* 1968; *Last Summer* 1969; *I Never Sang for My Father* 1970; *The Great Gatsby* 1974; *Network* 1976; *Semi-Tough* 1977; *The Cheap Detective, The Eyes of Laura Mars, The Fury* 1978; *The Champ, The Rose* 1979; *Rich and Famous* 1981; *Annie, Monsignor* 1982; *Ghostbusters* 1984; *Moonstruck* 1987; *We're No Angels* 1989; *Stanley & Iris* 1990; *Other People's Money* 1991; *Addams Family Values* 1993; *Milk Money* 1994; *First Wives Club, The Mirror Has Two Faces* 1996.

Aldrich, Robert. Director, producer, *b.* Aug. 9, 1918, Cranston, R.I. *d.* 1983, of kidney failure. *ed.* U. of Virginia (Law and Economics). He went to Hollywood in 1941 and worked his way up from production clerk at RKO. He was a script clerk, then assistant to several directors (including Dmytryk, Milestone, Renoir, Wellman, Polonsky, Fleischer, Losey, and Chaplin), then production manager, and next associate producer. At the same time, he started writing and directing episodes for TV series ('The Doctor,' 'China Smith'). In 1953 he directed his first feature film, *The Big Leaguer.* In 1954 he established his own production company, Associates and Aldrich, and thereafter produced many of his own films. The financial success of *The Dirty Dozen* (1967) prompted him to acquire his own studio, but subsequent debacles forced him to sell it in 1973.

Aldrich seemed to have gained much of his dynamic quality from his TV experience and from working as assistant on such films as *The Southerner, G.I. Joe, Force of Evil,* and *Limelight.* His individual style was characterized by frantic motion within shots and in the progression of a sequence, often underlined by violence, brutality, and grotesque chaos. He won the Silver Award of the Venice Festival for *The Big Knife* in 1955, the Italian Critics Award for *Attack!* in 1956, and the best director award at the West Berlin Festival for *Autumn Leaves,* also in 1956. He served for a time as president of the Directors Guild of America. His daughter, Adell Aldrich (born on June 11, 1943, in Los Angeles), and his son, William McLaughry Aldrich (born on Oct. 17, 1944, in Los Angeles), both became filmmakers.

FILMS (as director): *The Big Leaguer* 1953; *World for Ransom* (also co-prod.), *Apache, Vera Cruz* 1954; *Kiss Me Deadly* (also prod.), *The Big Knife* (also prod.) 1955; *Autumn Leaves, Attack!* (also prod.) 1956; *The Garment Jungle* (replaced by Vincent Sherman, who got sole screen credit) 1957; *The Ride Back* (prod. only) 1957; *Ten Seconds to Hell* (also co-sc.) 1959; *The Last Sunset, Sodoma e Gemorra/Sodom and Gomorrah* (co-dir. with Sergio Leone; It./Fr./US) 1961; *What Ever Happened to Baby Jane?* (also prod.) 1962; *4 for Texas* (also prod., co-sc.) 1963; *Hush. . . Hush Sweet Charlotte* (also prod.) 1965; *The Flight of the Phoenix* (also prod.) 1966; *The Dirty Dozen* 1967; *The Legend of Lylah Clare* (also prod.), *The Killing of Sister George* (also prod.) 1968; *What Ever Happened to Aunt Alice?* (prod. only) 1969; *Too Late the Hero* (also prod., co-story, co-sc.) 1970; *The Grissom Gang* (also prod.) 1971; *Ulzana's Raid* 1972; *Emperor of the North Pole* 1973; *The Longest Yard* 1974; *Hustle* (also prod.) 1975; *Twilight's Last Gleaming* (US/Ger.), *The Choirboys* 1977; *The Frisco Kid* 1979; *. . . All the Marbles, The Angry Hills* 1981.

Alea, Tomás Gutiérrez. See GUTIÉRREZ ALEA, Tomás.

Aleandro, Norma. Actress. Born in 1941, in Argentina, into theatrical family. She began performing with her parents as a child and matured into one of Argentina's leading thespians. An outspoken liberal, she repeatedly clashed with her country's military junta and was forced to spend much of the late 70s and early 80s in exile, in Uruguay, then Spain. She returned to Buenos Aires in 1982 and resumed her starring career on stage and in films. She also performed on the New York stage. In 1985 she shared the best actress prize at Cannes for her powerful performance in *The Official Story,* an Oscar winner as best foreign language film. She was nominated for an Academy Award for *Gaby—A True Story* (1987). She collaborated on the screenplay of the Argentinian film *Los Herederos* and is the author of published short stories and poems.

FILMS INCLUDE: *La Historia Oficial/The Official Story/The Official Version* 1985; *Gaby—A True Story* (US) 1987; *Cousins* (US) 1989; *Cién Veces No Debo, Vital Signs* 1990; *One Man's War* (UK), *The Tombs/Las Tumbas* 1991; *Autumn Sun* 1996.

Alekan, Henri. Director of photography. Born on Feb. 10, 1909, in Paris, to parents of Bulgarian origin. Educated at Conservatoire des Arts et Métiers and Institut d'Optique. Became an assistant cameraman in 1925 and camera operator in 1928, working on such films as *Mademoiselle Docteur* (1937), *Drôle de Drame* (1937), and *Quai des Brumes* (1935). He escaped from prisoner-of-war camp in 1940 and joined the French Resistance. In 1941, he became director of photography, and he shot his first important film in 1945–46, René CLÉMENT's documentary *Le Bataille du Rail.* Alekan demonstrated his versatility during the same period by shooting Jean COCTEAU's elaborate costume fantasy, *La Belle et la Bête/Beauty and the Beast.* He is one of France's most reliable cinematographers, adapting his style to the needs of the script and the director and always capturing the essence of a location. He also directed a number of shorts, notably *L'Enfer de Rodin* (1958). More recently, he received renewed attention for his work with director Wim WENDERS in *Wings of Desire* (1987).

FILMS INCLUDE: *Les Petites Du Quai Aux Fleurs* 1944; *La Bataille du Rail/Battle of the Rails, La Belle et la Bête/Beauty and the Beast* 1946; *Les Maudits/The Damned* 1947; *Anna Karenina* (UK) 1948; *Une si Jolie Petite Plage/Riptide, Les Amants de Vérone/The Lovers of Verona* 1949; *La Marie du Port* 1950; *Juliette ou la Clef des Songes* 1951; *Le Fruit défendu/Forbidden Fruit* 1952; *Roman Holiday* (co-phot.; US) 1953; *Le Port du Désir/The House on the Waterfront* 1954; *Les Héros sont fatigués/Heroes and Sinners* 1955; *Austerlitz* (co-phot.), *Un Deux Trois Quatre!/Les Collants noirs/Black Tights* 1960; *Le Couteau dans la Plaie/Five Miles to Midnight* 1962; *Topkapi* (US) 1964; *Lady L* (US/Fr./It.) 1965; *Triple Cross* (UK/Fr.) 1966; *Mayerling* (UK/Fr.) 1968; *L'Arbre de Noël/The Christmas Tree* 1969; *Figures in a Landscape* (UK) 1970; *Soleil rouge/Red Sun* 1971; *L'Ombre et la Nuit* (release delayed from 1978) 1980; *The Territory* (Port./US) 1981; *Der Stand der Dinge/The State of Things* (Ger.), *La Truite/The Trout* 1982; *La Belle Captive/The Beautiful Prisoner* 1983; *Der Himmel über Berlin/Les Ailes du Désir/Wings of Desire* (Ger./Fr.) 1987; *Berlin Jerusalem, J'écris dans l'espace* 1989.

Alessandrini, Goffredo. Director. *b.* Sept. 9, 1904, Cairo, Egypt, of Italian parents. *d.* 1978. Started his film career in 1928 as assistant to director Alessandro BLASETTI. In 1930 he went to Hollywood to handle the Italian dubbing of MGM pictures. On his return to Italy in 1931, he turned to direction, and during Mussolini's regime, he directed several award-winning Fascist propaganda films. He emigrated to Egypt in 1952 but returned to Italy soon after. His output for the most part consisted of undistinguished but commercially successful films. He married Anna MAGNANI in 1936 (separated 1940).

FILMS: *La Diga Di Maghmod* (doc.) 1929; *La Segretaria Privata* 1931; *Seconda B* 1934; *Don Bosco* 1935; *Cavalleria* 1936; *Una Donna fra due Mondi/Between Two Worlds* 1937; *Luciano Serra—Pilota, La Vedova* 1938; *Abuna Messias* 1939; *Il Ponte di Vetro, Caravaggio* 1940; *Nozze di Sangue* 1941; *Giarabub, Noi Vivi/We the Living* 1942; *Chi l'ha Visto?, Lettere a Sottemente* 1943; *Furia* 1946; *L'Ebreo Errante/The Wandering Jew* 1947; *Lo Sparviero del Nilo* 1949; *Sangue sul Sagrato, Rapture* (also act.; US/It.) 1950; *Camicie Rosse/Anita Garibaldi* (completed by Francesco Rosi) 1952; *Opinione Pubblica* (supervision only) 1953; *Gli Amanti del Deserto* (supervision only) 1959.

Alexander, Ben. Actor. *b.* Nicholas Benton Alexander, May 26, 1911, Goldfield, Nev. *d.* 1969. A popular child actor in Hollywood silents from age four (his first directors were DE MILLE and GRIFFITH), he later played juveniles and eventually supporting parts in sound films. In the 30s he was well known as a radio announcer and in the 50s he re-emerged from obscurity as Jack Webb's patrol partner in TV's 'Dragnet' series. He later starred in 'Felony Squad.'

FILMS INCLUDE: *Each Pearl A Tear* 1916; *The Little American* 1917; *Little Orphan Annie, Hearts of the World* 1918; *The Better Wife, The Turn in the Road, The White Heather* 1919; *The Family Honor* 1920; *The Heart Line* 1921; *Boy of Mine, Penrod and Sam* 1923; *Pampered Youth, Flaming Love* 1925; *Scotty of the Scouts* (serial) 1926; *All Quiet on the Western Front* 1930; *Many a Slip* 1931; *Tom Brown of Culver* 1932; *Stage Mother* 1933; *Annapolis Farewell* 1935; *Hearts in Bondage* 1936; *Behind Prison Bars* 1937; *The Spy Ring* 1938; *Dark Command* 1940; *The Leather Pushers* 1940; *Dragnet* 1954; *Man in the Shadow* 1957.

Alexander, Jane. Actress. Born Jane Quigley, on Oct. 28, 1939, in Boston. *ed.* Sarah Lawrence; U. of Edinburgh. Highly acclaimed leading lady and supporting actress of the American stage, TV, and films. Memorable for her intense performances in both the Broadway (Tony Award, 1961) and screen (Oscar nomination) versions of 'The Great White Hope,' for her brilliant portrayal of Eleanor Roosevelt in the TV play 'Eleanor and Franklin,' and for a brief but striking role in the film *All the President's Men.* She received her second Academy-Award nomination for the latter, a third for her role in *Kramer vs. Kramer*, and a fourth for *Testament.* Married to director Edwin Sherrin, she is the mother of actor Jace Alexander. In 1993, she became chairwoman of the National Endowment for the Arts.

FILMS: *The Great White Hope* 1970; *A Gunfight* 1971; *The New Centurions* 1972; *All the President's Men* 1976; *The Betsy* 1978; *Kramer vs. Kramer* 1979; *Brubaker* 1980; *Night Crossing* 1982; *Testament* 1983; *City Heat* 1984; *Sweet Country* 1986; *Square Dance/Home Is Where the Heart Is* (also co-exec prod.) 1987; *Building Bombs, Glory* 1989.

Alexander, Jason. Actor. Born Jay Scott Greenspan on Sept. 23, 1959, in Newark, N.J. *ed.* Boston U. Neurotically urbane character actor of stage, television, and screen. Raised in Livingston, N.J., he spent much of his childhood taking voice lessons and learning Broadway scores. At 20 he gained his first Broadway role in 'Merrily We Roll Along.' Subsequent roles in 'Broadway Bound' and other plays followed; in 1989, he won a Tony for his performance in 'Jerome Robbins's Broadway.' He is best known for his role as New York every-nebbish, George Costanza, in TV's 'Seinfeld.' Married screenwriter Daena Alexander.

FILMS: *The Burning* 1981; *Brighton Beach Memoirs*, *The Mosquito Coast* 1986; *Pretty Woman, White Palace, Jacob's*

Ladder 1990; *I Don't Buy Kisses Anymore* 1992; *Coneheads, Down on the Waterfront* 1993; *Blankman, North, The Paper, The Return of Jafar* (v/o) 1994; *For Better or Worse* (also dir.) 1995; *Dunston Checks In, The Last Supper, Hunchback of Notre Dame* (v/o) 1996; *Love, Valour, Compassion* 1997.

Alexander, Ross. Actor. *b.* July 24, 1907. Brooklyn, N.Y. *d.* 1937, a suicide. On stage from age 16, he was groomed for stardom by Warners in the early 30s, but his career soon dwindled to leads in B pictures. He was married to actress Anne NAGEL.

FILMS INCLUDE: *The Wiser Sex* 1932; *Social Register, Flirtation Walk, Gentlemen Are Born* 1934; *A Midsummer Night's Dream* (as Demetrius), *Captain Blood, We're in the Money, Shipmates Forever* 1935; *Boulder Dam, China Clipper, Hot Money, I Married a Doctor* 1936; *Ready Willing and Able* 1937.

Alexandrov, Grigori. Director. *b.* Grigori Mormonenko, Feb. 23, 1903, Yekaterinburg, Russia. *d.* 1983. After a theatrical apprenticeship in his hometown and entertaining troops on the eastern front, he worked for two years as an actor at Sergei EISENSTEIN's theater in Moscow and followed when the maestro left to pursue films. For ten years he was Eisenstein's chief assistant, collaborating on scripts and aiding in the production of such films as *Strike* (1925), *The Battleship Potemkin* (1925), *Ten Days That Shook the World/October* (1927), and *Old and New/The General Line* (1929). In 1931 he accompanied Eisenstein on his trip to Europe, the US, and Mexico, assisting him in the production of the unfinished film *Que Viva Mexico.* In 1979 he completed editing an "official" version of the latter film.

In 1930, Alexandrov directed his first solo picture, a short subject called *Romance Sentimentale,* in Paris. In 1932 he directed a documentary, *The International.* His first important film was *Jolly Fellows* (1934), a lively musical comedy, also known as *Moscow Laughs, The Jazz Comedy,* and *The Shepherd of Abrau.* Borrowing heavily from Hollywood, not always successfully, this film is a welcome departure from the usually grim, politically oriented Soviet production. The leading role was played by Lyubov ORLOVA, the first star of Russian films, who appeared in all subsequent Alexandrov musicals and eventually became his wife. Alexandrov won international awards for *Spring* (1947), *Meeting on the Elbe* (1949), and *Glinka* (1952).

FILMS: *Romance sentimentale* (short; Fr.) 1930; *The International* (short) 1933; *Jazz Comedy/Jolly Fellows/Moscow Laughs* (also sc.) 1934; *The Circus* 1936; *Volga-Volga* (also sc.) 1938; *Tanya/The Bright Road* 1940; *A Family* 1943; *The Caspians* 1944; *Spring* 1947; *Meeting on the Elbe* 1949; *Glinka/Man of Music* (also co-sc.) 1952; *Man to Man* 1958; *Russian Souvenir* 1960; *Lenin in Poland* 1961; *Before October* 1965; *Lenin in Switzerland* (doc.) 1967; *Star and Lyra* 1973; *Que Viva Mexico* (official version; assoc dir., edit.) 1979.

Alexeieff, Alexander. (also **Alexandre**). Animator. *b.* Aug. 5, 1901, Kazan, Russia. *d.* 1982. Prepared for a military career, then went to Paris to study linguistics but eventually became an artist, book illustrator, stage designer, and film animator. He developed a "pin screen" method, involving the illumination of thousands of pinheads to produce a printlike effect in animated films, reminiscent of Seurat's pointillism technique of painting. From 1931 he collaborated with animator Claire Parker (*b.* 1907, Boston; *d.* 1980) who became his wife in 1941. They emigrated to the US in 1940 but returned to Paris in 1947. His major achievement was an animated interpretation of Mussorgsky's *Night on a Bare Mountain* (1933), a classic among animated films. He also won praise for the title sequence of Orson Welles's *The Trial* (1962). Worked mainly in France but occasionally in the US, Germany, and other countries. Made many animated commercials in addition to experimental and theatrical cartoons.

FILMS INCLUDE: *Une Nuit sur le Mont Chauve/Night on a Bare Mountain* 1933; *La Belle au Bois dormant* 1935; *Parade Chapeaux* 1936; *Les Oranges de Jaffa, Balatum* 1938; *En Passant* (US/Can.) 1943; *Masques* 1952; *Nocturne* (co-dir. with Georges Violet) 1954; *Cent pour Cent* 1957; *Anonyme, Automation* 1958; *Divertissement* 1960; *The Trial* (animated title sequence) 1962; *Le Nez* 1963; *L'Eau* 1966; *Tableaux d'une Exposition/Pictures at an Exhibition* 1972; *Trois Thèmes/Three Themes* 1980.

Algar, James. Director, screenwriter, producer. Born on June 11, 1912, in Modesto, Cal. *ed.* Stanford U. (M.A. in journalism). He joined Walt DISNEY productions as an animator in 1935 and spent his entire career with that establishment. After directing sequences for several major Disney features, he was assigned to direct many of the highly acclaimed "True-Life Adventure" nature features of the 50s, and when the series ended in 1960, he became a producer or co-producer of some of Disney's live-action features. He wrote many of his own scripts, alone or in collaboration, and shared in nine Academy Awards for his work. He also directed, produced, and wrote many episodes for the 'Wonderful World of Disney' TV series.

FEATURE FILMS: *Snow White and the Seven Dwarfs* (co-animator) 1938; *Fantasia* (dir. of "Sorcerer's Apprentice" sequence) 1940; *Bambi* (sequence dir.) 1942; *Victory Through Air Power* (WW II doc.; sequence dir.) 1943; *Ichabod and Mr. Todd* (co-dir.) 1949; *The Living Desert* (dir., co-sc.) 1953; *The Vanishing Prairie* (dir., co-sc.) 1954; *The African Lion* (dir., co-sc.) 1955; *Secrets of Life* (dir., sc.) 1956; *White Wilderness* (dir., sc.) 1958; *Jungle Cat* (dir., sc.), *Ten Who Dared* (assoc. prod.) 1960; *The Legend of Lobo* (dir., co-prod., co-sc.) 1962; *The Incredible Journey* (co-prod., sc.) 1963; *The Gnome-Mobile* (co-prod.) 1967; *Rascal* (Prod.) 1969; *The Best of Walt Disney's True-Life Adventures* (compilation film; dir., co-prod., co-sc.) 1975.

Allan, Elizabeth. Actress. *b.* Apr. 9, 1908, Skegness, England. *d.* 1990. She made her stage debut with the Old Vic in 1927, her film debut in *Alibi* (1931). A slender, delicate beauty, she appeared in several British films before going in 1933 to Hollywood, where she played ladylike heroines in a string of good and mediocre films. But her career suffered a sudden setback when she sued MGM for replacing her in a lead role in *The Citadel* (shot in England; released 1938). The studio barred her from any further work in Hollywood and she resettled in England, where she returned to the stage and occasional film appearances, mainly in supporting roles. She was popular on British TV in the late 50s. Retired in 1977, after the death of her agent-husband.

FILMS INCLUDE: In the UK—*Alibi, Michael and Mary* 1931; *Service for Ladies/Reserved for Ladies, The Lodger/The Phantom Fiend* 1932; *The Shadow* 1933; *Java Head* 1934. In the US—*Men in White* 1934; *David Copperfield, Mark of the Vampire, A Tale of Two Cities* 1935; *A Woman Rebels* 1936; *Camille, The Soldier and the Lady/Michael Strogoff, Slave Ship* 1937. In the UK—*Inquest* 1940; *Went the Day Well?/48 Hours* 1942; *The Great Mr. Handel* 1942; *He Snoops to Conquer* 1944; *No Highway/No Highway in the Sky* 1951; *Folly to Be Wise* 1952; *The Heart of the Matter* 1953; *Front Page Story* 1954; *Grip of the Strangler/The Haunted Strangler* 1958.

Alland, William. Producer, former actor. Born on Mar. 4, 1916, in Delmar, Del. Actor and stage manager with Orson Welles's Mercury Theater and assistant director of that company's radio series. He was dialogue director for the film *Citizen Kane* (1941), in which he appeared as the inquiring reporter and narrator. He also appeared in WELLES's *The Lady From Shanghai* and *Macbeth* (both 1948), among other films. In 1952 he became a producer, turning out many low-budget films, mostly in the science fiction genre, for Universal and other companies.

FILMS INCLUDE: (as producer) *The Black Castle, The Raiders* 1952; *It Came from Outer Space, The Lawless Breed* (also story) 1953; *The Creature from the Black Lagoon* 1954; *This Island Earth, Chief Crazy Horse, Revenge of the Creature* 1955; *The Mole People* 1956; *The Deadly Mantis* 1957; *The Lady Takes a Flyer, The Colossus of New York, The Space Children* 1958; *Look in Any Window* (also dir.) 1961; *The Lively Set* 1964; *The Rare Breed* 1966.

Allbritton, Louise. Actress. *b.* July 3, 1920, Oklahoma City, Okla. *d.* 1979. *ed.* U. of Oklahoma; Pasadena Playhouse. Vivacious blonde leading lady of Hollywood films, mainly Universal second features. Retired from the screen several years after her 1946 marriage to CBS-TV news correspondent Charles Collingwood.

FILMS INCLUDE: *Not a Ladies' Man, Who Done It?, Pittsburgh* 1942; *Fired Wife, Son of Dracula* 1943; *San Diego I Love You, Her Primitive Man* 1944; *Men in Her Diary* 1945; *Tangier* 1946; *The Egg and I* 1947; *Sitting Pretty, Walk a Crooked Mile* 1948; *The Doolins of Oklahoma/The Great Manhunt* 1949.

Allégret, Marc. French director. *b.* Dec. 22, 1900, Basel, Switzerland. *d.* 1973. *ed.* Ecole des Sciences Politiques (Paris; law). Brother of Yves ALLÉGRET and the nephew of André Gide. He accompanied Gide on his trip to Africa, recording it on film as the *Voyage au Congo* (1927), a short documentary that marked Allégret's first contribution to the cinema. He was assistant to Robert FLOREY and Augusto GENINA for several years; then, in 1931, he started a long career as a director. Allégret acquired a reputation as a competent and exacting master of film technique who handled scenes with an elegant touch. He was an excellent director of actors and was noted for his keen eye for new talent, having discovered or developed such stars as Simone Simon, Michèle Morgan, Jean-Pierre Aumont, Danièle Delorme, Gérard Philipe, Odette Joyeux, Jeanne Moreau, and Brigitte Bardot. His most important films were made in the 30s. His reputation declined considerably in the post-WW II period.

FEATURE FILMS: *Voyage au Congo* (medium-length doc.) 1927; *Le Blanc et le Noir* (completed for Robert Florey), *Les Amants de Minuit* (co-dir. with Augusto Genina), *Mam'zelle Nitouche* 1931; *La Petite Chocolatière, Fanny* 1932; *Lac aux Dames, L'Hôtel du Libre-Echange, Zou-Zou, Sans Famille* 1934; *Les Beaux Jours* 1935; *Sous les Yeux d'Occident/Razumov, Les Amants terribles, Aventure à Paris* 1936; *Gribouille/Heart of Paris, La Dame de Malacca* 1937; *Orage, Entrée des Artistes/The Curtain Rises* 1938; *Le Corsaire* 1939; *Parade en Sept Nuits* 1941; *L'Arlésienne* 1942; *Félicie Nanteuil* 1943; *Les Petites du Quai aux Fleurs* 1944; *La Belle Aventure/Twilight* 1945; *Lunegarde, Petrus* 1946; *Blanche Fury* (UK) 1947; *The Naked Heart/Maria Chapdelaine* (also sc.; UK/Fr.; filmed in Canada) 1950; *Blackmailed* (UK) 1951; *Avec André Gide* (full-length doc.), *La Demoiselle et son Revenant* 1952; *Julietta* 1953; *L'Amante di Paride/The Face That Launched a Thousand Ships/Loves of Three Queens* (also co-sc.; It.) 1954; *Futures Vedettes* (also co-sc.) *L'Amant de Lady Chatterley/Lady Chatterley's Lover* (also sc.) 1955; *En effeuillant la Marguerite/Please Mr. Balzac* (also co-sc.) 1956; *L'Amour est en Jeu* 1957; *Sois Belle et tais-toi/Be Beautiful but Shut Up* (also co-sc.), *Un Drôle de Dimanche* 1958; *Les Affreux* 1959; *Les Démons de Minuit* (co-dir. with Charles Gerard) 1961; *Les Parisiennes/Tales of Paris* ("The Tale of Sophie" episode) 1962; *L'Abominable Homme des Douanes* 1963; *Le Bal du Comte d'Orgel* (also co-sc.) 1970.

Allégret, Yves. Director. *b.* Oct. 13, 1907, Paris. *d.* 1987. Started in films as assistant to Augusto GENINA, Jean RENOIR, and brother Marc ALLÉGRET. He created several short subjects and commercials before directing his first feature film in 1940. His documentary short *The Girls of France* was presented at the 1939 New York World's Fair. After WW II he became established as a front-rank director, notably in the *film noir* genre, and achieved the pinnacle of his reputation in the late 40s, particularly with films starring Simone SIGNORET, who was his wife from 1944 to 1949. Their daughter is actress Catherine Allégret. Early in his career Allégret used the pseudonym Yves Champlain. He died just two months before he was scheduled to receive a Life Achievement César Award.

FEATURE FILMS: *Tobie Est Un Ange* (negative destroyed; never released) 1941; *Les Deux Timides/Jeunes Timides* 1942; *La Boîte aux Rêves* (also co-sc.) 1945; *Les Démons de l'Aube* 1946; *Dédée d'Anvers/Dedee* (also co-sc.) 1948; *Une si Jolie Petite Plage/Riptide* 1949; *Manèges/The Cheat* 1950; *Les Miracles n'ont lieu qu'une fois* 1951; *Les Sept Péchés capitaux/The Seven Deadly Sins* ("Lust" episode), *Nez de Cuir* (also sc.), *La Jeune Folle/Desperate Decision* 1952; *Les Orgueilleux/The Proud and the Beautiful* 1953; *Mam'zelle Nitouche* (also co-sc.) 1954; *Oasis* 1955; *La Meilleure Part* (also co-sc.) 1956; *Quand la Femme s'en mêle, Méfiez-vous Fillettes/Young Girls Beware* 1957; *La Fille de Hambourg/Port of Desire* 1958; *L'Ambitieuse* 1959; *La Chien de Pique* (also co-sc.) 1961; *Konga Yo* (full-length doc.; also co-sc.) 1962; *Germinal* (in Hung.) 1963; *Johnny Banco* (Ger./Fr./It.) 1967; *L'Invasion* 1970; *Orzowei* 1975; *Mords pas—on t'aime* (also co-sc.) 1976.

Allen, Corey. Actor, director, screenwriter. Born Alan Cohen, on June 29, 1934, in Cleveland. *ed.* UCLA. He began acting in college productions, making his professional film debut in 1954. Usually playing dashing but negative characters, he is best remembered as James Dean's drag-racing rival in *Rebel Without a Cause* (1955). He retired from acting in the early 60s, then turned to directing, mostly for TV. Won an Emmy for directing episodes of 'Hill Street Blues.'

FILMS INCLUDE: As actor—*The Bridges at Toko-Ri* 1954; *Rebel Without a Cause, Night of the Hunter* 1955; *Party Girl* 1958; *Private Property* 1960; *Sweet Bird of Youth, The Chapman Report* 1962. As director—*Erotic Adventures of Pinocchio* (also co-sc.) 1971; *Thunder and Lightning* 1977; *Avalanche* (also co-sc.) 1978.

Allen, Debbie. Actress, dancer, choreographer. Born on Jan. 16, 1950, in Houston, Tex. *ed.* Howard U. She performed in Broadway musicals before debuting in television and films in the late 70s. Making a strong impression as Lydia, the hard-driving dance teacher, in the film *Fame,* she repeated the role in the subsequent TV series, winning two Emmy Awards for choreography and a nomination for best actress. She gave a memorable straight dramatic performance in the film *Ragtime* and won a Tony for her starring role in the 1986 Broadway revival of 'Sweet Charity.' Her younger sister, Phylicia Rashad, was a regular on 'The Cosby Show'.

FILMS: *The Fish That Saved Pittsburgh* (also chor.) 1979; *Fame* 1980; *Ragtime* 1981; *Jo Jo Dancer, Your Life Is Calling* 1986; *Blank Check* 1994; *Forget Paris* (chor. only) 1995; *Amistad* (co-prod.) 1997.

Allen, Dede. Film editor. Born Dorothea Carothers Allen, in 1924, in Ohio. *ed.* Scripps College. She started out as a messenger girl at Columbia and worked her way up to sound cutter and assistant editor before getting her first important editing assignment from director Robert Wise in 1959. She has since worked on many important productions, including several with director Arthur Penn, and has acquired a reputation as one of the most creative film editors in American cinema. She has twice been nominated for Oscars as editor for *Dog Day Afternoon* (1975) and *Reds* (1981). She is married to news executive Stephen Fleischman.

FILMS INCLUDE: *Terror from the Year 5,000/Cage of Doom* 1958; *Odds Against Tomorrow* 1959; *The Hustler* 1961; *America America* 1963; *Bonnie and Clyde* 1967; *Rachel Rachel* 1968; *Alice's Restaurant* 1969; *Little Big Man* 1970; *Slaughterhouse Five* 1972; *Serpico* (co-edit.) 1973; *Night Moves, Dog Day Afternoon* 1975; *The Missouri Breaks* 1976; *Slap Shot* 1977; *The Wiz* 1978; *Reds* (also co-exec prod.) 1981; *Harry and Son, Mike's Murder* 1984; *The Breakfast Club* 1985; *Off Beat* (co-edit.) 1986; *The Milagro Beanfield War* (co-edit) 1988; *Let It Ride* (co-edit.) 1989; *Henry and June* 1990; *The Addams Family* 1991.

Allen, Fred. Comedian, humorist. *b.* John Florence Sullivan, May 31, 1894, Cambridge, Mass. *d.* 1956. *ed.* Boston U. He started in vaudeville, developed on the legitimate stage, and became a national institution on radio, in a series of popular comedy programs, for which he wrote his own witty lines. His wife, Portland Hoffa, was his partner in vaudeville and on radio for many years. His drawn face and baggy eyes became familiar to millions of filmgoers when he began appearing sporadically on the screen in the mid-30s. Autobiography: *Treadmill to Oblivion* (1954).

FEATURE FILMS: *Thanks A Million* 1935; *Sally Irene and Mary* 1938; *Love Thy Neighbor* 1940; *It's in the Bag* 1945; *We're Not Married, O. Henry's Full House* 1952.

Allen, Gracie. Comedienne. *b.* Grace Ethel Cecile Rosalie Allen, July 26, 1902, San Francisco. *d.* 1964. The daughter of vaudevillians, she began performing as a child. In 1922 she met George BURNS and together they formed the comedy team of Burns and Allen, of which she was the scatterbrained half. They married in 1926 and became popular in vaudeville and films and on radio and TV. Of some 20 feature films and many shorts, she made only two without her partner, *The Gracie Allen Murder Case* (1939) and *Mr. and Mrs. North* (1942).

FEATURE FILMS: *The Big Broadcast* 1932; *College Humor, International House* 1933; *Six of a Kind, We're Not Dressing, Many Happy Returns* 1934; *Love in Bloom, Big Broadcast of 1936, Here Comes Cookie* 1935; *Big Broadcast of 1937, College Holiday* 1936; *A Damsel in Distress* 1937; *College Swing/Swing Teacher Swing* 1938; *The Gracie Allen Murder Case, Honolulu* 1939; *Mr. and Mrs. North* 1942; *Two Girls and a Sailor* 1944.

Allen, Irving. Director, producer. *b.* Nov. 24, 1905, Poland. *d.* 1987. *ed.* Georgetown. Started his film career in 1929 as an editor. In the 40s he directed and produced several shorts, two of which won him Academy Awards, *Forty Boys and a Song* (1942) and *Climbing the Matterhorn* (1947). The low-budget feature films he directed during this period were less impressive and in the 50s he switched to producing, forming Warwick Films in Britain with Albert R. BROCCOLI.

FILMS INCLUDE: As director—*Strange Voyage, Avalanche* 1946; *High Conquest* 1947; *16 Fathoms Deep* 1948; *Slaughter Trail* 1951. As producer—*The Man on the Eiffel Tower* 1950; *New Mexico* 1951; *The Red Beret/Paratrooper 1953*; *Hell Below Zero* 1954; *A Prize of Gold, The Cockleshell Heroes* 1955; *Safari, Zarak* 1956; *Fire Down Below, Interpol/Pickup Alley* 1957; *Killers of Kilimanjaro* 1959; *The Trials of Oscar Wilde* 1960; *The Long Ships* 1964; *Ghengis Khan* 1965; *The Silencers* 1966; *The Ambushers* 1967; *Hammerhead* 1968; *The Desperadoes, The Wrecking Crew* 1969; *Cromwell* 1970.

Allen, Irwin. Director, producer, screenwriter. *b.* June 12, 1916, New York City. *d.* 1991. *ed.* CCNY; Columbia (journalism). Was a magazine editor, director and producer of a Hollywood radio show, and owner of an advertising agency before turning to film production in the early 50s. He specialized in grand-scale semidocumentary and nature films and later in science-fiction adventure and won a 1953 Academy Award for *The Sea Around Us.* He created and produced several successful science fiction TV series, including 'Lost in Space.' In the early 70s he produced two spectacular disaster films, *The Poseidon Adventure* and *The Towering Inferno*, notable for special effects and tremendous audience appeal.

FILMS INCLUDE (as producer-director-screenwriter): *Double Dynamite* (co-prod. only) 1951; *A Girl in Every Port* (co-prod. only) 1952; *The Sea around Us* 1953; *Dangerous Mission* (prod. only) 1954; *The Animal World* 1956; *The Story of Mankind* 1957; *The Big Circus* (prod., sc. only) 1959; *The Lost World* 1960; *Voyage to the Bottom of the Sea* 1961; *Five Weeks in a Balloon* 1962; *The Ambushers* (prod. only) 1967; *The Poseidon Adventure* (prod. only) 1972; *The Towering Inferno* (prod.; also dir. of action sequences) 1974; *The Swarm* (dir., prod. only) 1978; *Beyond the Poseidon Adventure* (dir., prod. only) 1979; *When Time Ran Out* (prod. only) 1980.

Allen, Jay Presson. Playwright, screenwriter, producer. Born Jay Presson on Mar. 3, 1922, in Fort Worth, Tex. The author of such hit plays as 'The Prime of Miss Jean Brodie' (1966), 'Forty Carats,' and 'Tru,' she also wrote a number of successful film scripts, alone or in collaboration. She created the TV series 'Family.' Married Lewis M. ALLEN.

FILMS: *Wives And Lovers* 1963; *Marnie* 1964; *The Prime of Miss Jean Brodie* (from her play; UK) 1969; *Cabaret, Travels With My Aunt* (UK) 1972; *Forty Carats* (from her play) 1973; *Funny Lady* 1975; *Just Tell Me What You Want* (from her novel; also co-prod.), *It's My Turn* (exec. prod. only) 1980; *Prince of the City* (also exec. prod.) 1981; *Deathtrap* (also exec. prod.) 1982; *Lord of the Flies* 1990; *Year of the Gun* 1991; *The Cemetery Club* (uncred.) 1992; *Copycat* (co-sc.) 1995.

Allen, Joan. Actress. Born on Aug. 20, 1956, in Rochelle, Ill. *ed.* East Illinois Univ. Versatile performer in leading and supporting roles on stage and screen. A founding member of Chicago's Steppenwolf Theater Company, she won a Tony for her Broadway debut in 'Burn This' (1987), then scored another hit with 'The Heidi Chronicles' (1989). Allen was nominated for the Academy Award two consecutive years as supporting actress for her riveting, "dead-on" performance as Pat Nixon in Oliver Stone's sweeping political epic *Nixon* (1995) and *The Crucible* (1996).

FILMS: *Compromising Positions* 1985; *Manhunter, Peggy Sue Got Married* 1986; *Tucker: The Man and His Dream* 1988; *In Country* 1989; *Ethan Frome, Searching for Bobby Fischer* 1993; *Mad Love, Nixon* 1995; *The Crucible* 1996; *The Ice Storm* 1997.

Allen, Karen. Actress. Born on Oct. 5, 1951, in Carrollton, Ill. *ed.* George Washington U.; U. of Maryland; Washington Theatre Laboratory; Lee Strasberg Theatre Institute. Skinny, wide-eyed, raspy-voiced, brunette leading lady of American stage, TV and films. She overcame temporary blindness, following a conjunctivitis condition, to begin a screen career in the late 70s that peaked with the feminine lead in the blockbuster *Raiders of the Lost Ark.*

FILMS INCLUDE: *National Lampoon's Animal House* 1978; *Manhattan, The Wanderers* 1979; *Cruising, A Small Circle of Friends* 1980; *Raiders of the Lost Ark* 1981; *Shoot the Moon, Split Image/Captured!* 1982; *Until September, Starman* 1984; *Terminus* (Fr./Ger./Hung.), *The Glass Menagerie* (as

Laura) 1987; *Backfire, Scrooged* 1988; *Animal Behavior* 1989; *Sweet Talker* (Austral.) 1990; *Malcolm X* 1992; *Ghost in the Machine, The Sandlot* 1993; *'Til There Was You* 1996; *The Terror* 1997.

Allen, Lewis. Director. *b.* Dec. 25, 1905, Shropshire, England. *d.* 1986. *ed.* Tettenhall Coll. A stage actor and director in the UK and the US before turning to films. After two years of apprenticeship with Paramount, he was given his first directorial assignment in 1943 and turned out an exciting ghost thriller, *The Uninvited.* His subsequent output was of variable quality but consistently entertaining and effective.

FILMS: *The Uninvited* 1943; *Our Hearts Were Young and Gay* 1944; *The Unseen, Those Endearing Young Charms* 1945; *The Perfect Marriage, The Imperfect Lady, Desert Fury* 1947; *So Evil My Love, Sealed Verdict* 1948; *Chicago Deadline* 1949; *Appointment With Danger, Valentino* 1951; *At Sword's Point* 1952; *Suddenly* 1954; *A Bullet for Joey, Illegal* 1955; *Another Time Another Place* 1958; *Whirlpool* (UK) 1959; *Decision at Midnight* 1963.

Allen, Lewis M. Producer. Born in 1922, in Berryville, Va. *ed.* Univ. of Virginia. The producer of such Broadway plays as 'I'm Not Rappaport,' he began his film career with an adaptation of the stage drama about heroin junkies, 'The Connection.' He has since specialized in unusual, artistically daring films, including both screen versions of the William Golding novel *Lord of the Flies*. Married screenwriter/producer/playwright Jay Presson ALLEN.

FILMS INCLUDE: *The Connection* 1961; *The Balcony* (exec. prod.), *Lord of the Flies* (UK) 1963; *Fahrenheit 451* (UK) 1966; *The Queen* (exec. prod.) 1968; *Fortune and Men's Eyes* 1971; *Never Cry Wolf* 1983; *1918* (exec. prod.) 1985; *On Valentine's Day* 1986 (exec. prod.); *End of the Line, O.C. and Stiggs, Swimming to Cambodia* (exec. prod. the latter two) 1987; *Miss Firecracker* (exec. prod.) 1989; *Lord of the Flies* (exec. prod.) 1990.

Allen, Nancy. Actress. Born on June 24, 1950, in New York City. *ed.* High School for the Performing Arts. Blonde, spunky leading lady and second lead of the American screen. A policeman's daughter, she was raised in Yonkers, where she began dancing as a child. As a teenager, she modeled in TV commercials and was soon drawn to acting. In 1979 she married Brian DE PALMA, the director of several of the films in which she was featured. They divorced in 1984.

FILMS: *The Last Detail* 1973; *Carrie* 1976; *I Wanna Hold Your Hand* 1978; *Home Movies, 1941* 1979; *Dressed to Kill* 1980; *Blow Out* 1981; *Strange Invaders* 1983; *The Buddy System, Forced Entry/The Last Victim, Not for Publication, The Philadelphia Experiment, Terror in the Aisles* 1984; *Sweet Revenge, Robocop* 1987; *Poltergeist III* 1988; *Limit Up* 1989; *Robocop 2* 1990; *Acting on Impulse, Robocop 3* 1993; *Les Patriotes* 1994.

Allen, Rex. Actor. Born on Dec. 31, 1922, in Wilcox, Ariz. Started in vaudeville, then sang on radio and starred in a traveling rodeo show before becoming a popular singing cowboy in Republic B films, often with sidekick Slim PICKENS and horse Koko. He starred in the TV series 'Frontier Doctor,' and narrated and sang for the sound track of several Disney films of the 60s. In 1973 narrated the Hanna-Barbera animated feature *Charlotte's Web.*

FILMS INCLUDE: *Arizona Cowboy, Under Mexicali Stars* 1950; *Thunder in God's Country* 1951; *The Last Musketeer* 1952; *The Old Overland Trail* 1953; *The Phantom Stallion* 1954; *Shadows of Tombstone* 1958; *For the Love of Mike* 1960; *The Legend of Lobo* (narr.) 1962; *The Incredible Journey* (narr.) 1963; *Swamp Country* 1966; *Charlie the Lonesome Cougar* (narr.) 1967; *Charlotte's Web* (narr.) 1973; *Legend of Cougar Canyon* (narr.) 1974.

Allen, Steve. Actor, songwriter, radio and TV entertainer. Born on Dec. 26, 1921, in New York City, to vaudeville comedians. A disc jockey before becoming established as a top-ranking radio and television personality. He has several books and short stories and hundreds of songs, but his film appearances are few. He is married to actress Jayne Meadows.

FILMS INCLUDE: *Down Memory Lane* 1949; *I'll Get By* 1950; *The Benny Goodman Story* (title role) 1956; *The Big Circus* (cameo) 1959; *College Confidential* 1960; *Warning Shot* 1967; *Where Were You When the Lights Went Out?* 1968; *The Comic* (as himself) 1969; *The Sunshine Boys* 1975; *Heartbeat* 1979; *Amazon Women on the Moon* 1987; *Great Balls of Fire!* (as himself) 1989; *The Player* (as himself) 1992; *Casino* 1995.

Allen, Woody. Actor, director, screenwriter, playwright, jazz clarinetist. Born Allen Stewart Konigsberg, on Dec. 1, 1935, in Brooklyn, N.Y. *ed.* NYU; CCNY. He began his career as a comedian, humorist, and playwright; he became one of America's most inventive and idiosyncratic filmmakers. A self-defined social misfit, the physically unprepossessing Allen started writing comedy material for television stars while still an adolescent. He also wrote jokes for newspaper columnists and contributed sketches for stage revues. In 1961 he reluctantly began performing his own material in Greenwich Village cafés. His special brand of cynical parody and devastating understatement was soon in demand on TV talk shows and at better nightclubs. Beginning in the 60s, he showed a gift for philosophical and literary humor in comic essays in *The New Yorker* and later in three books, *Getting Even*, *Without Feathers*, and *Side Effects*. The versatile performer also honed his skills as a jazz clarinetist, beginning a regular Monday night gig at Michael's Pub in New York that has continued for decades.

He broke into films in 1965 as both screenwriter and performer in *What's New, Pussycat?* The film featured Louise Lasser, who often appeared in his early movies and was his wife from 1966 to 1970. The following year he created a masterpiece of absurd low-keyed humor by the clever English dubbing of the sound track of a cheap Japanese film thriller, which he titled *What's Up, Tiger Lily?* For Broadway, he wrote two hits, 'Don't Drink the Water' and 'Play It Again, Sam,' both of which were later made into films. In 1969, he embarked on his career as an *auteur* when he directed, co-scripted, and starred in *Take the Money and Run*, a hilarious parody of crime films and documentaries. In the 70s, Allen directed, wrote, and acted in a string of highly successful comedies. Typically disjointed in continuity, these films contained many moments of comic brilliance, highlighted by self-effacing humor, inside jokes, and endless spoofs of filmmakers (Antonioni, Bergman, Eisenstein), movie conventions, authors, and philosophers.

In 1977, Allen scored his greatest critical and commercial success with *Annie Hall*, an account of a failed romance based on his own long-time relationship with frequent co-star Diane KEATON. The film fetched the best picture Oscar for that year as well as two personal Academy Awards for Allen, as director and co-screenwriter. The film was a turning point in Allen's career, revealing not only a more serious approach to comedy but also a greater maturity of ideas and a fuller command of film language and style. In 1978, he surprised his followers with his first straight drama, *Interiors,* an agonized, soul-searching, gloomy tale peopled by characters whose lives are ravaged by anxiety, self-doubt, and a myriad of other deeply felt emotions that had always been present in Allen's work but were hitherto swept under a carpet of laughs. The film earned him an Academy Award nomination as best director.

In *Manhattan* (1979) Allen returned to the self-confessional, autoanalytical format of *Annie Hall.* Again he played the Jewish intellectual nebbish bewildered by relationships with attractive shiksas and confounded by his own anxieties and neuroses. As in *Annie Hall*, the film's heroine was Diane Keaton. She would soon give way to a new lover and leading actress, Mia FARROW.

The intimately personal *Stardust Memories* (1980) was Allen's last film with United Artists; thereafter he began a long association with Orion Pictures. (He has also had long associations with such professional colleagues as co-writer Marshall Brickman and producers Jack Rollins and Charles Joffe.) *A Midsummer Night's Sex Comedy* (1982), a comic homage to Bergman, was his first in a long string of films with Mia Farrow. He experimented brilliantly with film technique in *Zelig* (1983), achieving remarkable results from the matching of newsreels and stills with live footage. He followed the Runyonesque *Broadway Danny Rose* (1984) with another excursion into technical invention with the charming bittersweet movieland fantasy *The Purple Rose of Cairo* (1985), for which he won the International Critics Prize at Cannes. Allen won hordes of new admirers but may have lost some old ardent fans with *Hannah and Her Sisters* (1986), an ambitious, intricate serio-comic family saga, for which he won an Academy Award for best screenplay.

Of Allen's subsequent films, *Crimes and Misdemeanors* (1989) received the most critical praise for its combination of dark drama and bittersweet comedy; it also netted Oscar nominations for director and screenplay. Other efforts, such as *Alice* (1990) and *Shadows and Fog* (1992), were less successful. However, he continued to experiment with cinematic form and to elicit strong performances, notably from Gena Rowlands in *Another Woman* (1988).

Allen has always been an intensely private individual, rarely doing publicity and avoiding Hollywood to stay near his home in New York. It was therefore ironic when he became the subject of a domestic scandal. At its center was his relationship with Mia Farrow, with whom he had adopted two children (Moses and Dylan Farrow) and had a biological son, Satchel Farrow (born in 1987 and named for the baseball pitcher Satchel Paige). The unmarried couple were famed for their closeness even as they carefully maintained their independence, living in separate apartments on opposite sides of Central Park.

In August 1992, the relationship came to a dramatic end when Allen filed for custody of their three children. The news turned to scandal when it was revealed that Allen had been having an affair with Soon-Yi Previn, one of Farrow's adopted children from a previous marriage to conductor Andre Previn. Though Soon-Yi was of college age and not related to Allen, the appearance of incest made front-page news across the nation and abroad.

FILMS: *What's New Pussycat?* (sc., act.) 1965; *What's Up Tiger Lily?* (co-sc., host/narr., assoc. prod.) 1966; *Casino Royale* (act.) 1967; *Don't Drink the Water* (play basis only), *Take the Money and Run* (dir., co-sc., act.) 1969; *Bananas* (dir., co-sc., act.) 1971; *Play It Again Sam* (sc. from own play, act.), *Everything You Always Wanted to Know About Sex but Were Afraid to Ask* (dir., sc., act.) 1972; *Sleeper* (dir., sc., act). 1973; *Love and Death* (dir., sc., act.) 1975; *The Front* (act) 1976; *Annie Hall* (dir., co-sc., act.) 1977; *Interiors* (dir., sc.) 1978; *Manhattan* (dir., sc., act.) 1979; *Stardust Memories* (dir., sc., act.) 1980; *Midsummer Night's Sex Comedy* (dir., sc. act.) 1982; *Zelig* (dir., sc., act.) 1983; *Broadway Danny Rose* (dir., sc., act.) 1984; *The Purple Rose of Cairo* (dir., sc.) 1985; *Hannah and Her Sisters* (dir., sc. act.) 1986; *Radio Days* (dir. sc., narr.), *King Lear* (US/Switz.; act.), *September* (dir, sc.), 1987; *Another Woman* (dir., sc.) 1988; *New York Stories* ("Oedipus Wrecks" episode; dir., sc., act.), *Crimes and Misdemeanors* (dir., sc.) 1989; *Alice* (dir., sc.) 1990; *Scenes from a Mall* (act.) 1991; *Shadows and Fog* (dir., sc., act.), *Husbands and Wives* (dir., sc., act.) 1992; *Manhattan Murder Mystery* (dir., sc., act.) 1993; *Bullets Over Broadway* (dir., co-sc.) 1994; *Mighty Aphrodite* (act., dir., sc.) 1995; *Everyone Says I Love You* (act., dir., sc.) 1996.

Alley, Kirstie. Actress. Born on Jan. 12, 1955, in Wichita, Kans. *ed.* Kansas State U.; U. of Kansas. High-strung brunette lead of Hollywood films of the 80s. She made her debut as the half-Vulcan Lt. Saavik in *Star Trek II*, then came to specialize in comic roles. Her television work included regular appearances in the series 'Masquerade'; from 1987 to 1993, she played hapless bar manager Rebecca Howe on 'Cheers,' a role that won her an Emmy in 1991. On screen, she is best known for the comedy *Look Who's Talking* and its sequels. Divorced from actor Parker Stevenson.

FILMS: *Star Trek II: The Wrath Of Khan* 1982; *Champions* (UK) 1983; *Blind Date, Runaway* 1984; *Summer School* 1987; *Shoot to Kill/Deadly Pursuit* 1988; *Look Who's Talking, Loverboy* 1989; *Madhouse, Look Who's Talking Too, Sibling Rivalry* 1990; *Look Who's Talking Now* 1993; *It Takes Two, Village of the Damned* 1995; *Sticks and Stones* 1996; *Nevada* 1997.

Allgood, Sara. Actress. *b.* Oct. 31, 1883, Dublin. *d.* 1950. With the Abbey Theatre from 1904. On the British screen, she repeated her greatest stage success playing Juno in Hitchcock's *Juno and the Paycock* (1930). In 1940 she went to Hollywood and played amiable character roles in many major films, typically as a kindly mother. She was nominated for a supporting actress Oscar for her role in *How Green Was My Valley* (1941).

FILMS INCLUDE: In Australia—*Just Peggy* 1918. In the UK—*Blackmail* 1929; *Juno and the Paycock* 1930; *The World, the Flesh and the Devil* 1932; *Irish Hearts/Nora O'Neale* 1934; *Peg of Old Drury, The Passing of the Third Floor Back* 1935; *Sabotage/The Woman Alone* 1936; *Storm in a Teacup* 1937; *On the Night of the Fire/The Fugitive* 1939. In the US—*That Hamilton Woman/Lady Hamilton, Dr. Jekyll and Mr. Hyde, How Green Was My Valley* 1941; *Roxie Hart, This Above All* 1942; *The Lodger, Jane Eyre, The Keys of the Kingdom* 1944; *The Spiral Staircase, Uncle Harry* 1945; *Cluny Brown* 1946; *Mourning Becomes Electra* 1947; *The Accused* 1948; *Challenge to Lassie* 1949; *Cheaper by the Dozen* 1950.

Alliance of Motion Picture and Television Producers. See AMPTP.

Allied Artists Pictures Corporation. An American film production company established in 1946 as Allied Artists Productions, a wholly owned subsidiary of Monogram Pictures. It was founded to handle Monogram's higher-budget films while Monogram went on producing B pictures under its own name. In 1953, Monogram itself became known as Allied Artists. The company did not enjoy great success until it released the Elvis Presley film *Tickle Me* in 1965. Allied Artists sold its production studio in 1967 and thereafter emphasized release of foreign films, such as *Belle de Jour* (1968). In the 70s, it returned to production of such films as *Papillon* and *The Man Who Would Be King*, but continued to be plagued by financial problems, leading to its bankruptcy filing in 1979 and its sale in 1980 to Lorimar Productions.

Allio, René. Director, screenwriter. Born in 1924, in Marseille, France. After winning recognition as a painter and an outstanding stage designer and director, he made his entry into films with an animated short, *La Meule/The Haystack* in 1962. He has since directed feature films distinguished for their originality and sincerity. He writes his own scripts.

FEATURE FILMS (as director-writer, sometimes in collaboration): *La Vieille Dame indigne/The Shameless Old Lady* 1964; *L'Une et l'Autre/The Other One* 1967; *Pierre et Paul* 1969; *Les Camisards* 1971; *Rude Journée pour la Reine* 1973; *Moi Pierre Rivière* 1976; *Retour à Marseille* 1980.

Allison, May. Actress. *b.* June 14, 1895, Rising Fawn, Ga. *d.* 1989. Blonde star of Hollywood silents. During the WW I years, she and Harold LOCKWOOD formed one of the earliest romantic teams of the American screen. She remained popular through the late 20s, when she retired to nurse her ailing second husband, *Photoplay* editor James Quirk. Quirk died in 1932. Her first husband had been actor Robert ELLIS.

FILMS INCLUDE: *A Fool There Was, David Harum, The Great Question, The End of the Road* 1915; *The River of Romance, Pidgin Island, Big Termaine, The Masked Rider* 1916; *The Promise, The Hidden Children* 1917; *Her Inspiration, Social Hypocrites* 1918; *Peggy Does Her Darnest, The Island of Intrigue, Almost Married* 1919; *Are All Men Alike? The Cheater* 1920; *Extravagance, Big Game, The Last Card* 1921; *The Woman Who Fooled Herself* 1922; *The Broad Road* 1923; *Flapper Wives* 1924; *I Want My Man, Wreckage* 1925; *The Greater Glory, Men of Steel, The City* 1926; *The Telephone Girl* 1927.

Allwyn, Astrid. Actress. *b.* Nov. 27, 1909, in South Manchester, Conn. *d.* 1978. Leggy blonde leading lady and supporting player of Hollywood films of the 30s and early 40s. Mostly in seductive, chilly "other woman" parts. Once married to actor Robert Kent.

FILMS INCLUDE: *Lady With A Past* 1932; *Bachelor Mother* 1933; *Beggars in Ermine, Mystery Liner, The White Parade* 1934; *Accent on Youth, One More Spring, Hands Across the Table, Way Down East* 1935; *Dimples, Stowaway, Star for a Night, Follow the Fleet* 1936; *International Crime* 1938; *Love Affair, Reno, Mr. Smith Goes to Washington* 1939; *The Lone Wolf Strikes* 1940; *No Hands on the Clock* 1941; *Hit Parade of 1943* 1943.

Allyson, June. Actress. Born Ella Geisman on Oct. 7, 1917, in the Bronx, N.Y. The daughter of a building superintendent, she began her career as a Broadway show girl and in the 30s was featured in several two-reel film shorts. After being featured in the Broadway musical *Best Foot Forward* (1941), she played the same part in the screen version (1943). Her husky voice and twinkling smile made her a favorite performer in many MGM musicals throughout the 40s, in many girl-next-door type of roles. During the 50s she switched to dramas, still playing "sweet" roles, often typecast as the devoted wife behind the successful husband. In 1955, however, she turned in a spine-chilling performance as a spiteful bitch of a wife in José Ferrer's *The Shrike.* Since 1960 she has occasionally ventured out of retirement for TV, stage, nightclub, film, and commercial appearances. She is the widow of actor-director Dick POWELL.

FILMS: *Best Foot Forward, Thousands Cheer, Girl Crazy* 1943; *Two Girls and a Sailor, Meet the People* 1944; *Music for Millions, Her Highness and the Bellboy* 1945; *The Sailor Takes a Wife, Two Sisters from Boston, Till the Clouds Roll By, The Secret Heart* 1946; *High Barbaree, Good News* 1947; *The Bride Goes Wild, The Three Musketeers, Words and Music* 1948; *Little Women, The Stratton Story* 1949; *The Reformer and the Redhead, Right Cross* 1950; *Too Young to Kiss* 1951; *The Girl in White* 1952; *Battle Circus, Remains to Be Seen* 1953; *The Glenn Miller Story, Executive Suite, Woman's World* 1954; *Strategic Air Command, The Shrike, The McConnell Story* 1955; *The Opposite Sex, You Can't Run Away From It* 1956; *Interlude, My Man Godfrey* 1957; *Stranger in My Arms* 1959; *They Only Kill Their Masters* 1972; *Blackout* (Can./Fr.) 1978.

Almendros, Nestor. Director of photography, director. *b.* Oct. 30, 1930, Barcelona, Spain. *d.* 1992. He began making amateur shorts while still a teenager, and after receiving a Ph.D. degree from the University of Havana (Cuba) he came to New York, where he studied cinematography and film editing at CCNY. Following further cinema studies at Rome's Centro Sperimentale di Cinematografia, he returned to the US and taught Spanish at Vassar. Shortly after the Castro takeover, Almendros went back to Cuba, where he directed documentaries from 1959 to 1961. Moving on to Paris, he worked for French TV and film shorts. In the mid-60s he began collaborating with Eric ROHMER and later with François TRUFFAUT and other directors of the French New Wave, soon gaining an international reputation as one of cinema's most gifted cinematographers. Thereafter he worked extensively in the US, where he won the Academy Award for *Days of Heaven* (1978). In that film, he achieved haunting and breathtaking effects through his characteristic use of natural light, based on intensive study of period art. He won the French César Prize for *The Last Metro* (1980). In 1984 he was decorated in France with the Chevalier (order Arts and Letters) of the Legion of Honor. In 1988 he co-directed, co-wrote, and co-produced *Nadie Escuchaba/Nobody Listened* (doc.), a documentary on oppression and human-rights violations in Cuba. Author: *A Man With a Camera* (1980), *Improper Conduct* (1984).

FILMS INCLUDE: *Nadja à Paris* (short) 1964; *Paris vu par. . . /Six in Paris* (Jean Douchet's and Eric Rohmer's episodes) 1965; *La Collectionneuse* 1967; *The Wild Racers* (co-phot.; US) 1968; *Gun Runner* (co-phot.; US), as John Nestor, *Ma Nuit chez Maud/My Night at Maud's, More* 1969; *L'Enfant sauvage/The Wild Child, Domicile Conjugal/Bed and Board* 1970; *Le Genou de Claire/Claire's Knee, Les Deux Anglaises et le Continent/Two English Girls* 1971; *Le Vallée/The Valley, L'Amour l'après-midi/Chloe in the Afternoon* 1972; *Poil de Carotte* 1973; *Cockfighter* (US) 1974; *L'Histoire d'Adèle H./The Story of Adele H., Maîtresse, Mes Petites Amoureuses/My Little Loves* 1975; *General Idi Amin Dada* (doc.) 1976; *Des Journées entières dans les Arbres, L'Homme qui aimait les Femmes/The Man Who Loved Women, La Vie devant soi/Madame Rosa* 1977; *La Chambre verte/The Green Room, Days of Heaven, Perceval le Gallois* 1978; *L'Amour en fuite/Love on the Run, Kramer vs. Kramer* (US) 1979; *The Blue Lagoon* (US), *Le Dernier Métro/The Last Metro* 1980; *Sophie's Choice* (US) 1982; *Pauline à la Plage/Pauline at the Beach, Vivement Dimanche!/ Confidentially Yours, Improper Conduct* (doc.; dir., sc. only) 1983; *Places in the Heart* (US) 1984; *Heartburn* 1986; *Nadine* 1987; *Imagine: John Lennon* (doc.), *Nadie Escuchaba/Nobody Listened* (doc.; dir., sc., prod. only) 1988; *New York Stories* ("Life Lessons" episode) 1989; *Billy Bathgate* 1991.

Almodóvar, Pedro. Director, screenwriter, actor, composer. Born Sept. 25, 1951, in Calzada de Calatrava, La Mancha, Spain. A leading figure in the new Spanish cinema. Formerly a telephone company employee and a contributor to underground magazines and comic books, he began dabbling in amateur film-making in 1974; his first film, *Dos Putas*, was shot in super-8. In the years that followed, he acted in avant-garde plays, sang with a rock band, and began publishing the "confessions" of fictional porn star Patty Diphusa. Several years later, he joined the professional ranks and by the late 80s became established as one of his country's internationally best known and most admired directors. Openly gay, he often creates characters who are homosexual or bisexual, and he has a special affinity for the confusions and desires of people who came of age in Spain after dictator Franco's death in 1975. Writing his own offbeat scripts, he is at his most effective with caustic, irreverent, shocking comedy. His *Women on the Verge of a Nervous Breakdown* (1988) was named best foreign film by the New York Critics and best young film at the European Film Awards. It won the best screenplay prize at Venice.

FILMS INCLUDE (complete from 1980): *Dos Putas, La Caida de Sodoma* 1974; *Sexo va Sexo viene* 1977; *Pepi, Luci, Bom y Otras Chicas del Montón/Pepi, Lucy, Bom and Other Girls on the Heap* (also sc.), *Salome* 1978; *Laberinto de Pasiones/Labyrinth of Passion* (also act., sc., prod. des.) 1980; *Entre Tinieblas/Dark Habits* (also sc., song) 1982; *Qué he hecho yo para merecer esto?/What Have I Done to Deserve This?* (also sc.) 1984; *Matador* (also act.) 1986; *La Ley del Deseo/Law of Desire* (also sc., composer, song) 1987; *Mujeres al Borde de un Ataque de Nervios/Women on the Verge of a Nervous Breakdown* (also sc.) 1988; *Atame!/Tie Me Up! Tie Me Down!* (also sc.) 1990; *High Heels* (sc.) 1991; *Kika* (sc.), *Mutant Action* (prod., dir., sc.) 1993; *The Flower of My Secret* (dir., sc.)1995.

Almond, Paul. Director, producer, screenwriter. Born on Apr. 26, 1931, in Montreal. *ed.* McGill (Montreal), Oxford. After completing his master's at Oxford, where he was president of the poetry society and editor of a literary magazine, he joined a British repertory company, then returned to Canada in 1954 as a TV director. He subsequently turned out television episodes in both countries, as well as in the US, then graduated to the big screen in the 60s.

FILMS INCLUDE (as director): *Backfire!* (UK) 1961; *7 Up* (incorporated in 1985 into Michael Apted's *7 Up/28 Up*) 1964; *Isabel* (also prod., sc.) 1968; *Acte du Coeur/Act of the Heart* (also prod., sc.) 1970; *Détour/Journey* (also prod., sc., ed.) 1972; *Final Assignment* 1980; *Ups and Downs* 1983; *Captive Hearts* 1987; *The Dance Goes On* 1992.

Alonso, Maria Conchita. Actress, singer. Born in 1957, in Cuba. Darkly exotic lead of Hollywood films from the mid-80s. Raised in Venezuela, where she became Miss Teenager of the World (1971) and Miss Venezuela (1975). Starred in soap operas in Latin TV market before she landed the plum role of an Italian immigrant, opposite Robin Williams, in Paul Mazursky's *Moscow on the Hudson.* In South America she is also a best-selling recording artist.

FILMS (in US): *Moscow On The Hudson* 1984; *Fear City* 1985; *A Fine Mess* 1986; *Touch and Go, Extreme Prejudice, The Running Man* 1987; *Colors* 1988; *Vampire's Kiss* 1989; *Predator 2* 1990; *McBain* 1991; *The House of the Spirits, Roosters* 1993; *Caught* 1996.

Alonzo, John A. Director of photography. Born in 1934, in Dallas, Tex. He is responsible for the cinematography of several sumptuous Hollywood productions beginning in the 70s, including *Chinatown* and *Close Encounters of the Third Kind.* In 1978 he directed a first film, *FM.*

FILMS INCLUDE: *Bloody Mama* 1970; *Vanishing Point, Harold and Maude* 1971; *Get to Know Your Rabbit, Sounder, Lady Sings the Blues, Pete 'n' Tillie* 1972; *Hit!, The Naked Ape* 1973; *Conrack, Chinatown* 1974; *The Fortune, Once Is Not Enough, Farewell My Lovely* 1975; *I Will I Will for Now, The Bad News Bears* 1976; *Black Sunday, Close Encounters of the Third Kind* (co-phot.) 1977; *The Cheap Detective, FM* (dir. only) 1978; *Norma Rae* 1979; *Tom Horn* 1980; *Back Roads, Zorro the Gay Blade* 1981; *Blue Thunder, Cross Creek, Scarface* 1983; *Runaway, Terror in the Aisles* 1984; *Out of Control* 1985; *Nothing in Common* 1986; *Overboard* 1987; *Physical Evidence, Steel Magnolias* 1989; *Internal Affairs, The Guardian, Navy SEALS* 1990; *HouseSitter, Cool World* 1992; *Meteor Man* 1993; *Clifford, Star Trek: Generations* 1994.

Alov, Alexander. Director. *b.* Sept. 6, 1923, Kharkov, Russia. *d.* 1983. A product of Moscow's Cinema Institute (graduated 1951), and a prominent representative of the postwar crop of Soviet directors. He directed several well-paced films in collaboration with Vladimir NAUMOV. Alov died during the production of *Bereg/River Bank.* The film went on to win the top Soviet award and represented the USSR at both Cannes and Venice.

FILMS (all co-directed with Vladimir Naumov): *Taras Schevchenko* (completed for Savchenko) 1951; *Restless Youth* 1954; *Pavel Korchagin* 1957; *The Wind* 1959; *Peace to Him Who Enters* 1961; *The Coin* 1963; *The Ugly Story/A Bad Joke/Nasty Incident* (release delayed from 1965) 1969; *The Flight* 1971; *The Curse of Mr. McKinley* 1975; *The Legend of Till Eulenspiegel* (in 2 parts) 1976–77; *Teneran–43* (in 2 parts; USSR/Switzerland) 1981; *Bereg/River Bank* 1984.

Altman, Robert. Director, screenwriter, producer. Born on Feb. 20, 1925, in Kansas City, Mo., of English-Irish-German descent. Maverick *auteur* whose quirky, multilayered films cast an astute and irreverent eye on American culture. The son of a successful insurance broker, he was educated in Jesuit schools before serving in WW II as a bomber pilot. After his discharge, he studied engineering at the University of Missouri and attempted a number of aborted business ventures, including a dog-tattooing machine of his own invention. At the same time, he began writing screen stories, and was able to sell one, in collaboration with George W. George, as a basis for Richard Fleischer's film *The Bodyguard* (1948). Another of their stories was reputedly used, uncredited, as part-basis for Edwin L. Marin's *Christmas Eve* (1947). Unsuccessful in his attempt to find employment in Hollywood, Altman went to work for an industrial films company in his hometown of Kansas City, and for several years developed skills in all aspects of filmmaking. Raising a tiny budget from local sources, he produced, wrote, and directed his first feature, *The Delinquents* (1957), an exploitation film about juvenile crime that he sold to United Artists at a handsome profit. After collaborating with George W. George on the bumpy compilation-documentary film *The James Dean Story* (1957), Altman found a niche in TV as the director of numerous episodes for such series as 'Bonanza' and 'Alfred Hitchcock Presents.'

A full decade elapsed before he returned to feature films (with *Countdown* in 1968) and another two yars before he asserted himself as a front-rank director with *M*A*S*H* (1970), an iconoclastic, furiously hectic antiwar black comedy, which won the Golden Palm at the Cannes Festival and the best screenplay Oscar (among a number of Oscar nominations, including best director). After the film's huge success at the box office, Altman was flooded by studio offers for big-budget productions, but he chose instead to direct *Brewster McCloud* (1970), a modest-scale whimsical allegory of limited marketability, made by his own newly formed production company, Lion's Gate Films. It was the start of a career-long chasm between the stubbornly individualistic Altman and the Hollywood establishment. His next few films, including *McCabe and Mrs. Miller* (1971), *Images* (1972), and *Thieves Like Us* (1974), garnered critical praise but failed to make an impact at the box office.

For the second (but not the last) time in his career, Altman came back from the Hollywood dead with *Nashville* (1975), a dazzlingly inventive mosaic of the American experience composed of the intricate interweaving of the stories of 24 archetypal characters. The film and Altman were nominated for Academy Awards and were named best film and best director by the New York Film Critics. Having regained Hollywood's trust, Altman quickly squandered his bankability on the bizarre *Buffalo Bill and the Indians* (1976). The next few efforts, including *Welcome to L.A.* (1976), *Three Women* (1977), and *A Wedding* (1978), were varied and interesting but again failed at the box office.

Later films, such as *Quintet* (a 1979 tale of a future ice age) and *Popeye* (a 1980 big-budget comic strip adaptation) failed to please either critics or audiences. Also working against him were his reputation for drinking (a habit he later quit) and for being arrogant, unpredictable, and difficult; one rumor told of a fist-fight with a studio executive who wanted to cut *Nashville*. Taking everything into consideration, the Hollywood establishment had written off Altman by the early 80s.

Living most of the time in Paris, Altman continued to work on theatrical adaptations, such as *Come Back to the Five and Dime Jimmy Dean Jimmy Dean* (1982) and *Secret Honor* (a 1984 monologue by an actor playing Richard Nixon). His cable miniseries *Tanner '88* (1988), a political satire, gained favorable notice, as did *Vincent and Theo* (1990), an evocative film about the artist Van Gogh. Then, in 1992, the maverick filmmaker surprised Hollywood yet again with *The Player*, his first major commercial and critical success since *Nashville*. A black comedy about a movie executive who kills a screenwriter, the film was enriched by cameo appearances from 66 celebrities (most memorably Bruce Willis and Julia Roberts) who agreed to work for scale for the legendary director. With perfect Altmanian irony, this scathing satire of Hollywood earned several Oscar nominations (including best director) and brought Altman back into Hollywood's embrace.

Following what he calls his "third comeback," Altman still refuses to march in step with the conventions of traditional American cinema. He has said, "Hollywood doesn't want to make the same pictures I do, and I'm too old to change," but he has shown that he can sometimes get Hollywood to see things his way. The success of *The Player* allowed him to make his next work, *Short Cuts* (1993), based on short stories by Raymond Carver. Like *Nashville*, it is a lengthy, complex film that interweaves the lives of nearly two dozen characters in creating a portrait of contemporary America. Thrice married, Altman is the father of six.

FILMS: *Christmas Eve* (story only, uncred.) 1947; *Bodyguard* (story only) 1948; *The Delinquents* (also prod., sc.), *The James Dean Story* (co-dir., co-prod. with George W. George) 1957; *Countdown* 1968; *Nightmare in Chicago* (expanded for theatrical release from the '64 TV movie *Once Upon a Savage Night*), *That Cold Day in the Park* 1969; *M*A*S*H, Brewster McCloud, Events* (act. only) 1970; *McCabe and Mrs. Miller* (also co-sc.) 1971; *Images* (also sc.; UK) 1972; *The Long Goodbye* 1973; *Thieves Like Us* (also co-sc.), *California Split* (also co-prod.) 1974; *Nashville* (also prod.) 1975; *Buffalo Bill and the Indians or Sitting Bull's History Lesson* (also prod., co-sc.) 1976; *Welcome to L.A.* (prod. only), *The Late Show* (prod. only), *Three Women* (also prod., sc.) 1977; *A Wedding* (also prod., co-sc.), *Remember My Name* (prod. only) 1978; *A Perfect Couple* (also prod., co-sc.), *Rich Kids* (exec. prod. only), *Quintet* (also prod., co-sc.), *H.E.A.L.T.H.* (also prod., sc.) 1979; *Popeye* 1980; *Endless Love* (act. only) 1981; *Before the Nickelodeon: The Early Cinema of Edwin S. Porter* (act. only), *Come Back to the Five and Dime Jimmy Dean Jimmy Dean* 1982; *Streamers* (also co-prod.) 1983; *Secret Honor* (also prod.) 1984; *Fool for Love, Jatszani Kell* (assoc. prod.) 1985; *Beyond Therapy* (also co-sc.), *O.C. and Stiggs* (also co-prod.), *Aria* ('Les Boréades' segment; also sc.; UK) 1987; *The Moderns* (assistance only) 1988; *Hollywood Mavericks* (act. only), *Vincent and Theo* 1990; *The Player* 1992; *Short Cuts* (also co-sc.) 1993; *Mrs. Parker and the Vicious Circle* (prod. only), *Ready to Wear* 1994; *Kansas City* (also sc.) 1996; *Wild Card* 1997.

Alton, John. Director of photography. Born on Oct. 5, 1901, in Hungary. Started his film career in 1924 as lab technician for MGM. In 1928 he became cameraman with Paramount. He later traveled to France and then to South America, where he stayed to direct, write and photograph several Spanish-language productions. He won an Argentine prize for best photography (1937), then returned to Hollywood. There he soon developed into one of the industry's most accomplished cinematographers. In 1951 he won an Academy Award (with Alfred Gilks) for best color photography, on *An American in Paris*. He has written several books on the art of photography, notably *Painting With Light*.

FILMS INCLUDE: *The Courageous Dr. Christian* 1940; *Atlantic City* 1944; *T-Men* 1947; *He Walked by Night, The Black Book/Reign of Terror, Border Incident* 1949; *Father of the Bride* 1950; *An American in Paris* (co-phot.), *The People Against O'Hara* 1951; *It's a Big Country* 1952; *Battle Circus* 1953; *The Big Combo* 1955; *Tea and Sympathy, The Teahouse of the August Moon, The Catered Affair* 1956; *Designing Woman* 1957; *The Brothers Karamazov* 1958; *Elmer Gantry, Twelve to the Moon* 1960.

Alton, Robert. Choreographer, director, *b.* Robert Alton Hart, Jan. 28, 1906, Bennington, Vt. *d.* 1957. Studied and danced with the Mordkin Ballet and Dramatic School in New York. Choreographed many Broadway musicals before branching out simultaneously into films in 1936. He thereafter directed the dance sequences of some of Hollywood's most glittering musicals. He also directed a number of Broadway plays and two so-so films.

FILMS INCLUDE: As choreographer—*Strike Me Pink* 1936; *You'll Never Get Rich, Two-Faced Woman* 1941; *The Harvey Girls, Ziegfeld Follies, Till the Clouds Roll By* 1946; *The Pirate, Easter Parade* 1948; *In the Good Old Summertime, The Barkleys of Broadway* 1949; *Annie Get Your Gun* 1950; *Show Boat* 1951; *Call Me Madam* 1953; *White Christmas, There's No Business Like Show Business, The Country Girl* 1954; *The Girl Rush* 1955. As director (complete)—*Merton of the Movies* 1947; *Pagan Love Song* 1950.

Alvarado, Don. Actor. *b.* José Paige, Nov. 4, 1904, Albuquerque, N.M. *d.* 1967. Also known professionally as Don Page. He got his first break as an extra in *Mademoiselle Midnight* (1924), after which his film roles grew rapidly in importance until he became established as a "Latin lover" type in many late silents and early talkies. He later began playing occasional character roles. Toward the end of the 30s, he worked briefly as assistant director.

FILMS INCLUDE: *The Pleasure Buyers, Satan In Sables* 1925; *The Night Cry, His Jazz Bride* 1926; *Loves of Carmen, The Monkey Talks* 1927; *Drums of Love, The Battle of the Sexes, The Scarlet Lady, The Apache* 1928; *Rio Rita, The Bridge of San Luis Rey* 1929; *The Bad One, Captain Thunder* 1930; *Beau Ideal, Reputation* 1931; *Bachelor's Affair, La Cucaracha* 1932; *Contraband, Black Beauty, Morning Glory* 1933; *Sweet Adeline, The Devil Is a Woman* 1935; *Rose of the Rancho* 1936; *Love Under Fire* 1937; *Cafe Society* 1939; *One Night in the Tropics* 1940; *The Big Steal* 1949.

Alvarado, Trini. Actress. Born in 1967 in New York City. Child actress in films beginning with *Rich Kids* at age 12. As Bette MIDLER's daughter in *Stella* (1990), she began the transition to adult roles. She has also worked in television and on the stage.

FILMS INCLUDE: *Rich Kids* 1979; *Times Square* 1980; *Mrs. Soffel* 1984; *Sweet Lorraine* 1987; *Stella* 1990; *The Babe* 1992; *Little Women* 1994; *The Perez Family* 1995; *The Frighteners* 1996.

Alvarez, Santiago. Director. Born on Mar. 8, 1919 in Havana, the son of Spanish immigrant grocers. *ed.* U. of Havana, Columbia U. (New York). During his student days in the US, he worked as a dishwasher in Brooklyn and as a coal miner in Pennsylvannia. Returning to Cuba in the early 40s, he joined the Communist Party and was arrested repeatedly for his underground activities against the Batista regime. Shortly after the Castro revolution, he was appointed to various posts at the Cuban Institute of Film Art and Industry (ICAIC), including chief of the newsreel division. In the early 60s, he began directing newsreels and documentaries, and before long became established as his country's leading cine-journalist. His films are noted for their audiovisual dynamics and polemic vigor. In 1983 he directed his first fiction feature, *Refugiados de la Cueva del Muerto* ("Refugees From the Death Cave").

FILMS INCLUDE: *Un Año De Libertad* (co-dir.) 1960; *Escambray* (co-dir.) 1961; *Forjadores de la Paz* 1962; *Ciclon/Hurricane, El Barbaro del Ritmo* 1963; *Solidaridad Cuba y Vietnam, Pedales sobra Cuba, Now* 1965; *Cerro Pelado* 1966; *La Guerra olvidada/Laos the Forgotten War, Hasta la Victoria siempre, Hanoi Martes 13* 1967; *La Hora de los Hornos, L.B.J.* 1968; *Despegue a las 18:00, 79 Primaveras/79 Springtimes of Ho Chi Minh* 1969; *Piedra sobre Piedra, El Sueño del Pongo* 1970; *La Estampida* 1971; *De America soy Hijo. . . y a Ella me debo* 1972; *El Tigre salto y mato. . . pero morira. . . morira/The Tiger Leaped and Killed but He Will Die He Will Die* 1973; *Los Cuatro Puentes* 1974; *Es Tiempo es el Viento, Morir por la Patria es vivir* 1976; *Mi Hermano Fidel* 1977; *El Gran Salto al Vacio* 1979; *La Guerra necessaria* 1980; *La Importancia Universal del Hueco* 1981; *A Galope sobre la Historia, Nova Sinfonia* 1982; *Refugiados de la Cueva del Muerto, Biografia di un Carnaval* 1983; *Gracias Santiago* 1984.

Alves, Joe. Production designer. Born on May 21, 1936, in San Leandro, Cal. *ed.* San Jose State, Chinaurd Institute (motion picture design), USC. The son of Portuguese immigrants, he began his career as an assistant animator at Disney in the 1950s. He worked as a theatrical set designer and television art director before rising to prominence in film, with a specialty in science fiction. In the course of his collaborations with director Steven Spielberg (beginning with *Sugarland Express*), he designed the shark in *Jaws* and the mother ship in *Close Encounters of the Third Kind* (the latter effort won the British Academy Award). He directed *Jaws 3-D*.

FILMS: *Torn Curtain* (asst. art dir.) 1966; *Winning* 1969; *Pufnstuf* 1970; *Sugarland Express* 1974; *Jaws* 1975; *Embryo* 1976; *Close Encounters of the Third Kind* 1977; *Jaws II* 1978; *Escape From New York* 1981; *Jaws 3-D* (dir. only) 1983; *Starman* (visual consultant, 2d-unit dir. only) 1984; *Everybody's All-American* 1988; *Freejack* (also assoc. prod., 2d-unit dir.) 1992; *Geronimo: An American Legend* 1993; *Drop Zone* 1994.

Alwyn, William. Composer. *b.* Nov. 7, 1905, Northampton, England. *d.* 1985. *ed.* Royal Academy of Music. A conductor and flutist, as well as an accomplished painter and poet, he wrote numerous symphonic works in addition to more than 100 film scores. He began composing for films in 1936, scoring many documentaries. From the early 30s, he scored many major feature films, notably for Carol REED.

FILMS INCLUDE: *The Future's In The Air* 1936; *They Flew Along/Wings and the Woman* 1941; *Squadron Leader X* 1942; *On Approval* 1943; *The Way Ahead* 1944; *The Rake's Progress/Notorious Gentleman* 1945; *I See a Dark Stranger/The Adventuress, Green for Danger* 1946; *Odd Man Out* 1947; *So Evil My Love* (co-mus.; US), *The Fallen Idol, The Winslow Boy* 1948; *The Rocking Horse Winner* 1949; *Madeleine, The Mudlark, State Secret/The Great Manhunt* 1950; *The Magic Box* 1951; *Mandy/Crash of Silence, The Crimson Pirate, The Card/The Promoter* 1952; *Million Pound Note/Man with a Million* 1953; *The Malta Story* 1954; *Svengali, Geordie/Wee Geordie* 1955; *I Accuse, A Night to Remember* 1958; *The Silent Enemy* 1959; *Swiss Family Robinson* 1960; *The Running Man* 1963.

Alyn, Kirk. Actor. Born on Oct. 8, 1910, in Oxford, N.J. A former Broadway chorus boy and vaudeville entertainer, he played bits and supporting roles in several minor films before attaining some popularity in the late 40s as the star of the serial *Superman* (1948). But after playing the hero of a few other serials, he drifted back into obscurity in the early 50s. He authored a book of memoirs, *A Job for Superman,* which he published privately. In 1977 he sued a comics publishing company and two film studios for $10 million for allegedly using his picture on an "obscene" plaque. The plaque showed him on a window ledge, attired in his Superman suit, with the words "Super Schmuck." Formerly (1943–49) married to actress-singer Virginia O'BRIEN, he is retired and lives alone in Arizona.

FILMS INCLUDE: Features—*My Sister Eileen, You Were Never Lovelier, Lucky Jordan* 1942; *Overland Mail Robbery, Pistol Packin' Mama, A Guy Named Joe* 1943; *Forty Thieves* 1944; *Sweet Genevieve, Little Miss Broadway, The Trap* 1947; *The Three Musketeers* 1948; *When Worlds Collide* 1951; *The Eddy Duchin Story* 1956; *Scalps* 1983; Serials—*Daughter of Don Q* 1946; *Superman* 1948; *Federal Agents vs. Underworld Inc.* 1949; *Radar Patrol vs. Spy King, Atom Man vs. Superman* 1950; *Blackhawk* 1952.

Amato, Giuseppe. Producer, director, screenwriter. *b.* Giuseppe Vasaturo, Aug. 24, 1899, Naples, Italy. *d.* 1964. Started as a stage and film actor and assistant director (1913–22), then turned to importing American films into Italy. He was a producer from 1932, and although he directed occasional pictures, his real contribution to film art was as producer, especially after 1943. Among the directors he helped establish was Vittorio DE SICA. He also collaborated on a number of scripts.

FILMS INCLUDE: As director—*Ma l'Amor mio non Muore* (also prod., sc.) 1938; *Malia* (also sc.) 1945; *Donne Proibite/Angels of Darkness* (also prod.) 1953; *Gli Ultimi Cinque Minuti* (also prod.) 1955. As producer—*Cinque a Zero* 1932; *I Grandi Magazzini* 1939; *Rose Scarlette, Melodie Eterne/Eternal Melodies* 1940; *La Cena delle Beffe* 1941; *Quattro Passi fra la Nuvole/Four Steps in the Clouds* (also co-sc.) 1942; *Campo de'Fiori/The Peddler and the Lady* (also sc.) 1943; *Natale al Campo/Escape Into Dreams* (also co-sc.) 1948; *Domani è troppo Tardi/Tomorrow Is Too Late, Francesco Giullare di Dio/Flowers of St. Francis* 1950; *Parigi èsempre Parigi* 1951; *La Presidentessa/Mademoiselle Gobette, Umberto D* 1952; *Nella Città l'Inferno/. . . And the Wild Wild Women* 1958; *Un Maledetto Imbroglio/The Facts of Murder* 1959; *La Dolce Vita* (co-prod.) 1960.

Ambler, Eric. Novelist, screenwriter. Born on June 28, 1909, in London. *ed.* U. of London. Worked as an engineer, then a stage actor and advertising copywriter before becoming a successful novelist. He had authored four novels by the time he first became associated with films as a script consultant for Alexander Korda, in 1938. In 1940 he joined the British army as a private, and after serving with a film combat unit in Italy, he was made assistant director of army cinematography in the British War Office, in charge of production of all educational and morale films. Following his discharge, with the rank of lieutenant colonel, he went to work for the Rank Organisation as a screenwriter. In addition to the many scripts he has since written directly for the screen, several of his novels have been adapted into films by others, notably *The Mask of Dimitrios, Journey Into Fear, Background to Danger* (originally *Uncommon Danger),* and *The Light of Day,* which provided the basis for the film *Topkapi.* Ambler's novels are typically suspense thrillers.

His spy stories influenced the trend for unglamorous surroundings and unheroic characters in modern espionage literature and films. He co-authored several crime novels with Charles Rodda under the common pseudonym of Eliot Reed. Ambler was nominated for an Oscar for his script for *The Cruel Sea* (1953). His second wife was Joan HARRISON, who produced Alfred Hitchcock's TV anthology series and collaborated on the scripts of several Hitchcock features.

FILMS INCLUDE (as screenwriter): *The Way Ahead* (also story) 1944; *The October Man* (also prod.) 1947; *The Passionate Friends/One Woman's Story* 1949; *The Clouded Yellow* 1950; *Encore, The Magic Box, The Card/The Promoter* 1951; *The Cruel Sea* 1953; *Lease of Life* 1954; *The Purple Plain* 1955; *Yangtse Incident/Battle Hell* 1957; *A Night to Remember* 1958; *The Wreck of the Mary Deare* (US) 1959; *Mutiny on the Bounty* (among several uncredited writers; US) 1962.

Ambrosio, Arturo. Producer, film pioneer. *b.* 1869, Turin, Italy. *d.* 1960. Founder of the Italian film industry. The owner of an optical equipment shop, he filmed and developed in his own lab the first Italian short documentary films (1904), then established the first Italian film studio in his own backyard (1905). His company, Film Ambrosio, produced documentary films of increasing length, then turned to the production of feature films, signing up such stars as Eleonora Duse and Alberto Capozzi and turning out such huge spectacles as *The Last Days of Pompeii* (1908). In 1911 he signed an exclusive contract with Gabriele d'Annunzio by which he acquired adaptation rights to all the poet's works. The same year he won first prize in the world's first film competition, held during the International Exposition in Turin. Following this, he went to Moscow to help establish the Czarist film industry. After WW I his new production company, U.C.I., produced huge, expensive, unsuccessful spectacles, among them *Theodora* (1919) and *La Nave* (1920). Between 1939 and 1943 he continued some film activity as a production manager; then he retired from moviemaking. Altogether, Ambrosio produced some 1,400 films.

Ameche, Don. Actor. *b.* Dominic Felix Amici, May 31, 1908, Kenosha, Wis. *d.* 1993. *ed.* Columbia (Loras) Coll.; Marquette; Georgetown; U. of Wisconsin. One of a barkeeper's eight children, he made his stage debut in stock while still at the University of Wisconsin (law) and was a radio personality for several years. Entered films in 1935 and quickly became one of the busiest stars in the 20th Century-Fox stable, playing leading roles in more than 40 films, mostly typecast as a bon vivant young-man-about-town. He is most closely identified with the title role in *The Story of Alexander Graham Bell* (1939), but the film that best capitalized on his dexterity with light comedy roles was Lubitsch's *Heaven Can Wait.* Also active on stage and TV. In 1975 he was reunited with his frequent screen partner, Alice FAYE, in a national tour of the musical 'Good News.' After a long absence, he made a sentimental big-screen comeback in the 80s, dapper as ever, winning a best supporting actor Oscar for *Cocoon* (1985). In 1988, he shared the best actor prize at Venice for *Things Change.*

FILMS: *Clive Of India, Dante's Inferno* 1935; *Sins of Man, Ramona, Ladies in Love* 1936; *One in a Million, Love Is News, Fifty Roads to Town, You Can't Have Everything, Love Under Fire* 1937; *In Old Chicago, Happy Landing, Josette, Alexander's Ragtime Band, Gateway* 1938; *The Three Musketeers* (as D'Artagnan), *Midnight, The Story of Alexander Graham Bell* (title role), *Hollywood Cavalcade* 1939; *Swanee River* (as Stephen Foster), *Lillian Russell, Four Sons, Down Argentine Way* 1940; *That Night in Rio, Moon Over Miami, Kiss the Boys Goodbye, The Feminine Touch, Confirm or Deny* 1941; *The Magnificent Dope, Girl Trouble* 1942; *Something to Shout About, Heaven Can Wait, Happy Land* 1943; *Wing and a Prayer, Greenwich Village* 1944; *It's in the Bag, Guest Wife* 1945; *So Goes My Love* 1946; *That's My Man* 1947; *Sleep My Love* 1948; *Slightly French* 1949; *Phantom Caravan* 1954; *Fire One* 1955; *A Fever in the Blood* 1961; *Rings Around the World* (doc.), *Picture Mommy Dead* 1966; *Suppose They Gave a War and Nobody Came, The Boatniks* 1970; *Won Ton Ton—The Dog Who Saved Hollywood* 1975; *Trading Places* 1983; *Cocoon* 1985; *Harry and the Hendersons* 1987; *Coming to America, Things Change, Cocoon: The Return* 1988; *Oddball Hall* 1990; *Oscar* 1991; *Folks!* 1992; *Homeward Bound: The Incredible Journey* (v/o) 1993; *Corrina, Corrina* 1994.

American Academy of Dramatic Arts. See AADA.

American Biograph, The. See BIOGRAPH.

American Cinema Editors. See A.C.E.

American Federation of Television and Radio Artists. See AFTRA.

American Film Institute. A private, nonprofit organization created in 1967 with the objective of "preserving the heritage and advancing the art of film in America." Headquartered in Washington, D.C. (with offices in New York City and Los Angeles), the AFI derives most of its funds from the National Endowment for the Arts and from contributions by the film and TV industry. Among its many ongoing projects is the preservation of thousands of old movie classics (housed in the National Film Collection at the Library of Congress), the publication of a complete catalog of all theatrical films ever made in America, and the provision of grants to promising filmmakers and guidance to film educators. The institute also operates the Center for Advanced Film and Television Studies, a lavish, well-equipped graduate film school in Los Angeles, Cal., where students are given an opportunity to make their own films and establish important contacts in the industry. Among the graduates are John Hancock, director of *Bang the Drum Slowly,* and Terrence Malick, director of *Badlands.*

Other AFI enterprises include the journal *American Film,* a small movie house in the Kennedy Center, and an annual televised ceremony, the Life Achievement Awards, honoring important screen personalities; the first award was presented to director John Ford in 1973. Since the 70s, the AFI has been the subject of controversy among film scholars and enthusiasts. Charges have been made of squandering funds on showy projects at the expense of the encouragement of research work and experimental film production. Directors of AFI have included George Stevens, Jr., and Jean Firstenberg.

American International Pictures (AIP). Releasing company founded in 1954 as American Releasing Corporation by James H. Nicholson and Samuel Z. ARKOFF; it was renamed American International Pictures in 1956. The company was known for releasing low-budget exploitation films in any genre that would sell—science fiction, horror, Westerns, hot-rod movies. Independent producers, most notably Roger CORMAN, delivered the films; Arkoff and Nicholson also co-produced many AIP films themselves. Beginning with *The House of Usher* in 1960, AIP began to distribute more expensive films in color and CinemaScope. Directed by Corman and starring Vincent Price, the feature also ushered in AIP's successful cycle of films based on the work of Edgar Allan Poe. The cycle of beach films beginning with *Beach Party* (1963) was also successful, as were the protest films beginning with *The Wild Angels* (1966).

Arkoff became AIP's president and chairman of the board after Nicholson's departure in 1972 to become an independent producer. In 1975, at the peak of the company's financial success, Arkoff announced that AIP would begin production of big-budget films. Movies from this later period include *The Island of*

Dr. Moreau (1977) and *The Amityville Horror* (1979). The new philosophy hurt the company's profits, and in 1979 AIP posted its first loss ever. That year, it merged with Filmways, which later merged with Orion.

American Museum of the Moving Image. Established in 1988, it is the only museum in the US devoted to the art history and technology of motion pictures, television, video and digital media. Located on part of the grounds but independent of the former ASTORIA STUDIOS (now Kaufman-Astoria Studios), it houses a collection of materials related to the production, marketing, and exhibition of films—costumes, props, technical apparatus, posters, and film merchandise. In addition, the museum sponsors exhibitions, screenings, and educational programs, all meant to explore film production and examine film's impact on culture and society. The museum's director is Rochelle Slovin.

American Mutoscope and Biograph Company. See BIOGRAPH.

American Society of Cinematographers. See A.S.C.

American Standards Association. See ASA.

Ames, Adrienne. *b.* Adrienne Ruth McClure, Aug. 3, 1907, Fort Worth, Tex. *d.* 1947. Charming leading lady and second lead of Hollywood films of the 30s, mainly in second features. She sometimes played decorative, elegant featured roles in larger-budget productions. Her third husband was actor Bruce CABOT. She died of cancer at 39.

FILMS INCLUDE: *Twenty-four Hours, Girls About Town* 1931; *Two Kinds of Women, Sinners in the Sun, Merrily We Go to Hell* 1932; *The Death Kiss, Broadway Bad, A Bedtime Story, Disgraced, The Avenger* 1933; *George White's Scandals, You're Telling Me* 1934; *Gigolette, Black Sheep, Harmony Lane* 1935; *Abdul the Damned* 1936; *City Girl, Fugitives for a Night* 1938; *The Zero Hour* 1939.

Ames, Leon. Actor. *b.* Leon Waycoff, Jan. 20, 1903, in Portland, Ind., to Russian immigrants. *d.* 1993. On stage from 1925 and in films beginning in 1932. Changed his name to Ames in 1935. He developed into one of the most reliable character actors, often in dapper or fatherly roles. In addition to some 100 films, he appeared in numerous TV episodes, memorably in the series 'Life With Father,' 'Frontier Judge,' 'Father of the Bride,' and 'Mr. Ed.' One of the founders of the Screen Actors Guild in 1933.

FILMS INCLUDE: *Quick Millions* 1931; *Murders in the Rue Morgue* 1932; *The Count of Monte Cristo* 1934; *Reckless* 1935; *Stowaway* 1936; *Mysterious Mr. Moto, Suez* 1938; *No Greater Sin* 1941; *Meet Me in St. Louis, Thirty Seconds Over Tokyo* 1944; *Weekend at the Waldorf, Yolanda and the Thief* 1945; *The Postman Always Rings Twice* 1946; *A Date With Judy, The Velvet Touch* 1948; *Little Women, Battleground, Ambush* 1949; *Crisis* 1950; *It's a Big Country* 1951; *Peyton Place* 1957; *From the Terrace* 1960; *The Absent-Minded Professor* 1961; *The Monkey's Uncle* 1965; *On a Clear Day You Can See Forever, Tora! Tora! Tora!* 1970; *Hammersmith Is Out* 1972; *The Meal* 1975; *Just You and Me Kid* 1979; *Testament* 1983; *Jake Speed, Peggy Sue Got Married* 1986.

Ames, Preston. Art director. *b.* 1905. *d.* 1983. For many years, one of Hollywood's top production designers. He shared Academy Awards for *An American in Paris* (1951) and *Gigi* (1958) and was nominated for several other Oscars.

FILMS INCLUDE: *The Hidden Eye* 1945; *Lady in the Lake* 1947; *That Midnight Kiss* 1949; *Crisis* 1950; *An American in Paris* 1951; *Brigadoon* 1954; *Kismet* 1955; *Lust for Life* 1956; *Gigi* 1958; *Bells Are Ringing, Home From the Hill* 1960; *All Fall Down, Jumbo* 1962; *The Unsinkable Molly Brown* 1964; *Airport, Brewster McCloud* 1970; *Lost Horizon* 1973; *Rooster Cogburn* 1975; *The Pursuit of D.B. Cooper* 1981.

Amfitheatrof, Daniele. Composer, conductor. *b.* Oct. 29, 1901, St. Petersburg, Russia, the son of a novelist and playwright. *d.* 1983. *ed.* Royal Acad. of Music (Rome). Appeared as conductor with symphony orchestras throughout Europe. In 1934, while still in Rome, he wrote the score for Max Ophüls's film *La Signora di Tutti.* In 1937 he emigrated to the US and for two years conducted the Minneapolis and the Boston symphony orchestras. In 1939 he went to Hollywood and was signed by MGM as a composer and conductor, although he was not given his first film to score until 1943.

FILMS INCLUDE: *La Signora di Tutti* (It.) 1934; *The Get-Away* 1941; *Lassie Come Home* 1943; *Cry Havoc, Days of Glory* 1944; *Guest Wife* 1945; *The Virginian, Suspense* 1946; *Smash-Up* 1947; *Letter From an Unknown Woman, Another Part of the Forest, An Act of Murder* 1948; *House of Strangers, The Fan* 1949; *The Desert Fox* 1951; *Human Desire* 1954; *Trial* 1955; *Heller in Pink Tights* 1959; *Major Dundee* 1965.

Amidei, Sergio. Screenwriter. *b.* Oct. 30, 1904, Trieste. *d.* 1981. Entered the Italian film industry in 1924 but worked in many other capacities before turning to screenwriting in 1938. It was not until after WW II that he emerged as one of Italy's leading scenarists, making an important contribution to the postwar neorealist movement through his collaborations with Roberto ROSSELLINI, Vittorio DE SICA, and others.

FILMS INCLUDE: *La Notte Delle Beffe* 1939; *Roma Città Aperta/Open City* 1945; *Paisà/Paisan, Sciuscia/Shoeshine* 1946; *Anni Difficili/Difficult Years* 1947; *Sotto il Sole di Roma/Under the Sun of Rome* 1948; *Stromboli* 1949; *Domenica d'Agosto/ Sunday in August* 1950; *Le Ragazze di Piazza di Spagna/Three Girls From Rome* 1952; *Villa Borghese/It Happened in the Park* 1953; *Picasso* (doc.; also prod.), *Angst/La Paura/Fear* (Ger./It.), *Secrets d'Alcove/Il Letto/The Bed* (Fr./It.) 1954; *Il Momento più Bello/The Most Wonderful Moment* 1957; *Il Generale Della Rovere/General Della Rovere* 1959; *Era Notte a Roma, Viva l'Italia* 1960; *Liolà/A Very Handy Man, La Vita Agra* 1964; *La Fuga* 1965; *Detenuto in Attesa di Giudizio/Why* 1971; *La più Bella Serata della Mia Vita* 1972; *Un Borghese Piccolo Piccolo* 1977; *Le Temoin* (Fr./It.) 1978; *Storie di Ordinaria Follia/Tales of Ordinary Madness* 1981; *La Nuit de Varennes* 1982.

Amiel, Jon. Director. Born in 1948, in London. A television director in Britain, he became known to audiences at home and in the US for the darkly comic, hallucinatory BBC miniseries 'The Singing Detective' (1986–87). His first feature film was *Queen of Hearts* (1989), which drew praise from critics for its gentle mix of comedy, fantasy, and drama in depicting the lives of an Italian family in England. He has since made films in America, beginning with *Tune in Tomorrow. . .* , based on Mario Vargas Llosa's novel *Aunt Julia and the Scriptwriter*.

FILMS INCLUDE: *Queen of Hearts* (UK) 1989; *Tune in Tomorrow. . .* 1990; *Sommersby* 1993; *Copycat* 1995.

Amis, Suzy. Actress. Born on Jan. 5, 1958, in Oklahoma City. *ed.* Actors Studio. Lead and second lead of Hollywood films beginning in the late 80s. A former model, publicized as "The Face of the Eighties." Married actor Sam Robards.

FILMS: *Fandango* 1985; *The Big Town* 1987; *Plain Clothes, Rocket Gibraltar, Twister* 1988; *Where the Heart Is* 1990; *The Ballad of Little Jo, Rich in Love, Two Small Bodies, Watch It* 1993; *Blown Away, Nadja* 1994; *The Usual Suspects* 1995; *Cadillac Ranch* 1997.

Amos, John. Actor. Born on Dec. 27, 1941, in Newark, N.J. *ed.* Colorado State University, Long Beach City College. Big, amiable supporting actor. He played football professionally and worked in social services and advertising before becoming a stand-up comedian and television comedy writer in the late 60s. He is best known for his TV roles, including the father in the sitcom 'Good Times' and the adult Kunta Kinte in the miniseries 'Roots,' but he has also provided dependable support in films since the 70s.

FILMS: *Vanishing Point, Sweet Sweetback's Baadasssss Song* 1971; *The World's Greatest Athlete* 1973; *Let's Do It Again* 1975; *Touched by Love* 1980; *The Beastmaster* 1982; *Dance of the Dwarfs* 1983; *American Flyers* 1985; *Coming to America* 1988; *Lock Up* 1989; *Die Hard 2, Two Evil Eyes/The Black Cat* (It.) 1990; *Ricochet* 1991; *Mac* 1993.

AMPTP (Alliance of Motion Picture and Television Producers, Inc.). An organization founded in 1924 by the major Hollywood studios for industry representation to the public, the government, etc., and to handle matters of common interest. It later took on the function of negotiating labor contracts for its members. Over the years it was expanded to include independent film producers and TV production companies. Originally named the Association of Motion Picture Producers, it was renamed the Association of Motion Picture and Television Producers in 1964 to reflect its merger with the Alliance of Television Film Producers. In 1975, two members of the Association, Paramount and Universal, left to form a new organization, the Alliance. In 1982, the Alliance and AMPTP merged to form the Alliance of Motion Picture and Television Producers.

Amy, George. Film editor, director. Born in October, 1903, in Brooklyn, N.Y. Began film editing at age 17. During the 30s and 40s worked on many major Warner Bros. productions, particularly for Michael CURTIZ, and won an Academy Award for Howard Hawks's *Air Force* (1943). He also directed several films, without much success. From the early 50s he worked mainly for TV.

FILMS INCLUDE: As editor—*Burn 'Em Up Barnes* 1921; *The Live Wire* 1925; *The Brown Derby* 1926; *Chinatown Charlie* 1928; *The Gorilla* 1930; *Cabin in the Cotton, Doctor X* 1932; *Footlight Parade, Gold Diggers of 1933, The Mystery of the Wax Museum* 1933; *Wonder Bar* 1934; *Captain Blood* 1935; *The Charge of the Light Brigade, The Green Pastures* 1936; *Kid Galahad* 1937; *Hollywood Hotel* 1938; *Dodge City, The Old Maid* 1939; *The Letter, Sante Fe Trail, The Sea Hawk, Virginia City* 1940; *Dive Bomber, The Sea Wolf* 1941; *Captains of the Clouds, Yankee Doodle Dandy* 1942; *Action in the North Atlantic* (co-edit.), *Air Force, This Is the Army* 1943; *Uncertain Glory* 1944; *Objective Burma* 1945; *Three Strangers* 1946; *Life With Father* 1947; *The Capture* 1950; *The Blue Veil* 1951; *Clash by Night* 1952; *A Lion Is in the Streets* 1953; *She Couldn't Say No* 1954. As director—*She Had to Say Yes* (co-dir. with Busby Berkeley) 1933; *Kid Nightingale* 1939; *Gambling on the High Seas, Granny Get Your Gun* 1940.

anaglyphic process. An early optical process permitting the projection of 3-D, or stereoscopic, films. It involves the printing of two superimposed images (anaglyphs) in primary colors, generally blue-green and red. When viewed by an audience wearing spectacles with filters of the same hues, the images are sorted out and a three-dimensional effect is achieved. The idea goes back to the 18th century. In the early 20s it was used in a series of 3-D Paramount shorts called Plastigrams and in the mid-20s by MGM's Audioscopiks. See also 3-D, STEREOSCOPIC CINEMA.

anamorphic lens. A lens especially designed to squeeze a wide image into a standard frame through distortion during photography. The image is opened out by a similar lens during projection, allowing such wide-screen processes as CINEMASCOPE and PANAVISION to be recorded on standard film stock. See also CHRÉTIEN, HENRI; WIDE-SCREEN PROCESSES.

Anders, Luana. American actress. Born in 1940. *d.* 1996. In Hollywood since her teens, she has played both leads and supporting roles, often in fringe, restricted-budget productions. She was most visible in the late 60s and 70s, in such films as *Easy Rider* and *Shampoo*.

FILMS INCLUDE: *Reform School Girl* 1957; *The Notorious Mr. Monks* 1958; *The Pit and the Pendulum* 1961; *Night Tide, The Young Racers, Dementia 13* 1963; *The Trip* 1967; *How Sweet It Is!* 1968; *That Cold Day in the Park, Easy Rider* 1969; *Sex and the College Girl* 1970; *B.J. Presents* 1971; *Greaser's Palace, When the Legends Die* 1972; *The Last Detail, The Killing Kind* 1973; *Shampoo* 1975; *The Missouri Breaks* 1976; *Goin' South* 1978; *Personal Best* 1982; *Irreconcilable Differences* 1984; *Movers and Shakers* 1985; *Border Radio* 1987; *You Can't Hurry Love* 1988; *Limit Up* (also co-sc. under pseudonym Lu Anders) 1989.

Anders, Merry. American actress. Born in 1932. Leading lady of mostly low-budget Hollywood films of the 50s and 60s, she co-starred in "How to Marry a Millionaire," among other TV series.

FILMS INCLUDE: *Belles On Their Toes, Les Miserables* 1952; *Titanic, How to Marry a Millionaire* 1953; *Three Coins in the Fountain, Phffft!* 1954; *All That Heaven Allows* 1955; *No Time to Be Young, The Desk Set, Death in Small Doses, The Dalton Girls* 1957; *Violent Road* 1958; *The Hypnotic Eye, Young Jesse James* 1960; *20,000 Eyes, The Gambler Wore a Gun* 1961; *Air Patrol, Beauty and the Beast* 1962; *House of the Damned, Police Nurse* 1963; *A Tiger Walks, The Quick Gun, The Time Travelers* 1964; *Raiders from Beneath the Sea, Tickle Me, Young Fury* 1965; *Women of the Prehistoric Planet* 1966; *Legacy of Blood* 1971.

Anderson, Eddie "Rochester." Actor. *b.* Sept. 18, 1905, Oakland, Cal. *d.* 1977. Raspy-voiced, banjo-eyed comedian of vaudeville, nightclubs, radio, TV, and films. His father was a blackface minstrel and his mother a former circus tightrope walker. He began his own show business career at 14 in a chorus line, then joined an all-black revue and formed a trio with a brother and a friend that toured the vaudeville circuit. He was a small-time entertainer who played bits and small roles in occasional films when he was hired by Jack BENNY in 1937 for a single performance on an Easter Sunday radio show. The success of the program led to a lifelong professional relationship between the two comedians, with Anderson playing Benny's manservant Rochester innumerable times on radio, on TV, and in films. On his own, Anderson played the lead role in the all-black cast of the film *Cabin in the Sky* (1943) and had featured parts in many other films.

FILMS INCLUDE: *What Price Hollywood?* 1932; *The Green Pastures, Show Boat, Three Men on a Horse* 1936; *Melody for Two* 1937; *Jezebel, Gold Diggers in Paris, You Can't Take It With You, Thanks for the Memory, Kentucky* 1938; *You Can't Cheat an Honest Man, Honolulu, Man About Town, Gone With the Wind* 1939; *Buck Benny Rides Again, Love Thy Neighbor* 1940; *Topper Returns, Kiss the Boys Goodbye, Birth of the Blues* 1941; *Tales of Manhattan, Star Spangled Rhythm* 1942; *The Meanest Man in the World, Cabin in the Sky* 1943; *Broadway Rhythm* 1944; *Brewster's Millions* 1945; *The Sailor Takes a Wife, The Show-Off* 1946; *It's a Mad Mad Mad Mad World* 1963.

Anderson, G(ilbert) M. ("Broncho Billy"). Director, actor, producer. *b.* Max Aronson, Mar. 21, 1882, Little Rock, Ark. *d.* 1971. Worked briefly as a traveling salesman, then went to New York in a futile search for a stage acting career and was working as a model when hired by the Edison studio to play the lead in an Edwin S. Porter one-reeler, *The Messenger Boy's*

Mistake (1902). The following year he played several roles in a Porter short that made film history, *The Great Train Robbery* (1903). Several months and a dozen acting roles later he joined Vitagraph, Edison's competitor, directing and acting in many one-reelers, including the successful *Raffles, the American Cracksman* (1905). He then moved on to the Selig Polyscope Company, where he wrote and directed several shorts.

In 1907, Anderson quit Selig to go into partnership with George K. Spoor. They established the ESSANAY company (S. and A.), then moved to California to produce a series of short comedies starring Ben Turpin, starting with *Ben Gets a Duck and Is Ducked* (1907).

Also in 1907, Anderson starred himself in the role of a cowboy called Broncho Billy in a highly successful two-reel Western, *The Bandit Makes Good.* Over the next seven years, he directed and starred in close to 400 Broncho episodes (the spelling was later changed to Bronco) at an average of one a week. Broncho Billy was one of the first recognizable characters in movie history. The continuing enthusiastic public response made Anderson one of the screen's first stars and certainly the first cowboy hero.

In 1911 Anderson launched the "Snakeville Comedy" series and the following year the "Alkali Ike" series. He then steered Essanay to the production of more costly ventures, including several Chaplin comedies (*The Pugilist, Carmen,* etc.). In 1916, when Chaplin left Essanay, Anderson sold his interest to Spoor and retired from the business. In 1920, after a string of failures as a Broadway producer, he attempted a comeback, directing several Stan Laurel shorts for Metro. That same year he went into permanent retirement as an actor, although he continued directing and producing for several more years. He was all but forgotten when, in 1957, he was honored by the Academy of Motion Pictures with a special Oscar "for his contributions to the development of motion pictures as entertainment."

FILMS INCLUDE (as actor and often also director, producer, and screenwriter): *The Messenger Boy's Mistake* 1902; *The Great Train Robbery* 1903; *The Life of an American Cowboy, Raffles the American Cracksman* 1905; *An Awful Skate, The Bandit Makes Good, The Bandit King, Western Justice* 1907; *A Tale of the West, A Mexican's Gratitude, The Indian Trailer, The Black Sheep, The Best Man Wins, The Heart of a Cowboy, Judgment, The Spanish Girl* 1909; *An Outlaw's Sacrifice, The Cowboy and the Squaw, Western Chivalry, The Flower of the Ranch, Away Out West, The Forest Ranger, The Desperado, Take Me Out to the Ball Game* (dir., sc. only), *Broncho Billy's Redemption, Under Western Skies, The Pony Express Rider, Pals of the Range, The Silent Message* 1910; *The Border Ranger, The Faithful Indian, Across the Plains, The Lucky Card, Broncho Billy's Adventure, The Cowboy Coward, The Outlaw and the Child* 1911; *Alkali Ike's Boarding House* (dir. only), *Broncho Billy Outwitted, The Smuggler's Daughter, An Indian's Friendship, Alkali Bests Broncho Billy* 1912; *Alkali Ike's Misfortunes* (dir. only), *The Three Gamblers, Broncho Billy's Oath* 1913; *The Calling of Jim Barton, The Good-for-Nothing, Broncho Billy's Indian Romance* 1914; *The Champion* (a bit in this Chaplin comedy), *Broncho Billy's Marriage, Broncho Billy's Vengeance, Andy of the Royal Mounted* 1915; *Broncho Billy and the Revenue Agent* 1916; *Humanity* 1917; *Naked Hands, The Son-of-a-Gun, Red Blood and Yellow* 1919; *Any Night* (prod. superv. only), *Ashes* (dir. only) 1922; *The Bounty Killer* (cameo) 1965.

Anderson, Dame Judith. Actress. *b.* Frances Margaret Anderson, Feb. 10, 1898, Adelaide, Australia. *d.* 1992. Made her stage debut in 1915 in Sydney and her first New York appearance in 1918. She gradually rose in stature to become one of the leading actresses of the contemporary stage, memorable for her performances as Lavinia Mannon in 'Mourning Becomes Electra' (1932), as Gertrude to John Gielgud's Hamlet (1936), as Lady Macbeth in 'Macbeth' (1937, 1941), and in the title role in 'Medea' (1947, 1949). In 1960 she was named Dame Commander of the British Empire.

Dame Judith made her first film appearance in 1933, in *Blood Money.* She appeared in many films, often in unsympathetic and at times sinister roles. Her most memorable film part is that of the housekeeper in Hitchcock's *Rebecca* (1940).

FEATURE FILMS: *Blood Money* 1933; *Rebecca, Forty Little Mothers* 1940; *Free and Easy, Lady Scarface* 1941; *All Through the Night, Kings Row* 1942; *Edge of Darkness, Stage Door Canteen* 1943; *Laura* 1944; *And Then There Were None* 1945; *The Diary of a Chambermaid, The Strange Love of Martha Ivers, Specter of the Rose* 1946; *Pursued, The Red House, Tycoon* 1947; *The Furies* 1950; *Salome* (as Queen Herodias) 1953); *The Ten Commandments* 1956; *Cat on a Hot Tin Roof* 1958; *Cinderfella* 1960; *Don't Bother to Knock/Why Bother to Knock* (UK) 1961; *Macbeth* (as Lady Macbeth opposite Maurice Evans; orig. shown on TV in 1960) 1963; *A Man Called Horse* 1970; *Inn of the Damned* (Austral.) 1974; *Star Trek III: The Search for Spock* 1984.

Anderson, Kevin. Actor. Born on Jan. 13, 1960, in Illinois. *ed.* Goodman School of Drama, Chicago. Handsome, talented lead of stage and screen. He first appeared in films as a friend of Tom Cruise in *Risky Business*, but rose to national attention through his work with Chicago's Steppenwolf Theater Company. He originated the part of the "wild child" Phillip in the company's production of Lyle Kessler's 'Orphans'; he went on to reprise the acclaimed performance in New York and London and in the 1987 screen version. Subsequent stage credits included the Broadway revival of 'Orpheus Descending'. He showed a flair for comedy playing a boorish yuppie in *The Night We Never Met*.

FILMS: *Risky Business* 1983; *Pink Nights* 1985; *Orphans, A Walk on the Moon* 1987; *Miles from Home* 1988; *In Country* 1989; *Liebestraum, Sleeping with the Enemy* 1991; *Hoffa* 1992; *The Night We Never Met, Rising Sun* 1993; *Balto* (v/o) 1995; *Eye of God, A Thousand Acres* 1997.

Anderson, Lindsay. Director, documentarist, writer, critic, theorist, actor. Born on Apr. 17, 1923, in Bangalore, India, the son of a Scottish major general. *d.* 1994. *ed.* Oxford. In 1947 he co-founded and became co-editor of *Sequence,* an influential film periodical advocating radical departures from traditional attitudes in British filmmaking. After the magazine went out of business in 1951, he continued his crusade in critical writings for *Sight and Sound, The Times* of London, *The Observer,* and *New Statesman.* Anderson also wrote a book, *Making a Film,* on the production of Thorold Dickinson's *Secret People,* and a number of essays assailing conformity in British films and calling for greater social consciousness and more relevant themes. Both as a writer and as a documentary filmmaker, he became a prime mover (with Karel Reisz, Tony Richardson, Gavin Lambert, and others) in the FREE CINEMA movement of the 50s.

Practicing what he preached, Anderson began making scathing, low-budget, industrially sponsored documentaries in 1948. He won an Oscar for his documentary short *Thursday's Children* (1954). In 1955–56 he ventured into mass-appeal production, directing five episodes of 'The Adventures of Robin Hood' for British TV, but he resumed pressing his ideas into practice in 1957 as a theater director ('Billy Liar,' etc.). In 1963 he made an impressive bow as a feature film director with the grim drama *This Sporting Life.* His film *If. . .* won the Golden Palm at the Cannes Film Festival. He also appeared in many films directed by others, most memorably as a schoolmaster in *Chariots of Fire* (1981). See also FREE CINEMA.

FILMS INCLUDE: *Meeting the Pioneers* (doc.) 1948; *Idlers at Work* (doc.) 1949; *The Pleasure Garden* (prod., act. only), *Three Installations* (doc.) 1952; *Wakefield Express* (doc.), *O Dreamland* (doc.) 1953; *Thursday's Children* (doc.; co-dir. with Guy Brenton), *Truck Conveyor* (doc.) 1954; *Green and Pleasant Land* (doc.), *Henry* (doc.), *The Children Upstairs* (doc.), *A Hundred Thousand Children* (doc.), *20 Pounds a Ton* (doc.), *Energy First* (doc.), *Foot and Mouth* (doc.), 1955; *Every Day Except Christmas* (doc.) 1957; *Let My People Go* (doc.; prod. only) 1961; *This Sporting Life* 1963; *The White Bus, The Singing Lesson* (in Poland) 1967; *Inadmissible Evidence* (act. only), *If. . .* (also co-prod.) 1968; *O Lucky Man!* (also act., co-prod.) 1973; *In Celebration* 1975; *Chariots of Fire* (act. only) 1981; *Britannia Hospital* 1982; *The Whales of August* (US) 1987; *Blame It on the Bellboy* (voice only) 1992.

Anderson, Maxwell. Playwright, screenwriter. *b.* Dec. 15, 1888, Atlantic, Pa. *d.* 1959. *ed.* Univ. of North Dakota; Stanford U. A teacher before turning to journalism (1918–24), he wrote many famous plays, some of which were turned into films, including: *What Price Glory, Saturday's Children, Elizabeth the Queen, Mary of Scotland, Winterset, Key Largo,* and *The Bad Seed.* Collaborated on several screenplays.

FILMS INCLUDE (as screenwriter, alone or in collaboration): *All Quiet on the Western Front* 1930; *Rain* 1932; *We Live Again/Resurrection* 1934; *So Red the Rose* 1935; *Joan of Arc* (from own play) 1948; *The Wrong Man* 1956.

Anderson, Michael. Director. Born on Jan. 30, 1920, in London, the son of prominent stage actor Lawrence Anderson. Educated in France, Germany, and Spain. Entered the motion picture industry as an errand boy at England's Elstree Studios. After a brief stint as an actor, he became assistant director (*Pygmalion, French Without Tears,* etc.) and unit production manager (*In Which We Serve*). After war service, he co-directed *Private Angelo* (1949), and has since directed steadily in both England and Hollywood. His two most successful films have been *Around the World in 80 Days* (1956) and *The Quiller Memorandum* (1966). His son, Michael Anderson, Jr. (*b.* Aug. 6, 1943, London), has been a film actor since boyhood; the son's career includes a performance in his father's film *Logan's Run.*

FILMS: *Private Angelo* (co-dir. with Peter Ustinov) 1949; *Waterfront* 1950; *Hell Is Sold Out* 1951; *Night Was Our Friend, Dial 17* (short; Fr.) 1952; *Will Any Gentleman?, The House of the Arrow* 1953; *The Dam Busters* 1954; *1984* 1955; *Around the World in 80 Days* (US) 1956; *Yangtse Incident/Battle Hell* 1957; *Chase a Crooked Shadow* 1958; *Shake Hands with the Devil* (also prod.), *The Wreck of the Mary Deare* (US) 1959; *All the Fine Young Cannibals* (US) 1960; *The Naked Edge* 1961; *Flight From Ashiya* (US/Jap.) 1963; *Wild and Wonderful* (US) 1964; *Operation Crossbow* 1965; *The Quiller Memorandum* 1966; *The Shoes of the Fisherman* (US) 1968; *Pope Joan* 1962; *Doc Savage: The Man of Bronze* (US), *Conduct Unbecoming* 1975; *Logan's Run* (US) 1976; *Orca* (US) 1977; *Bells/Murder by Phone* (Can.) 1980; *Second Time Lucky* 1984; *Separate Vacations* (Can.) 1986; *La Boutique de l'orfèvre/Jeweller's Shop, Millennium* 1989.

Anderson, Milo. Costume designer. *b.* 1912, Chicago. *d.* 1984. Educated in Los Angeles, she began designing for Goldwyn at age 20. Soon after, she joined Warner Bros., where she remained for two decades, creating the costumes for many of the studio's major films. She retired from films in the mid-50s to start a successful interior-decorating business.

FILMS INCLUDE: *The Kid from Spain* 1932; *Footlight Parade* 1933; *Captain Blood* 1935; *The Story of Louis Pasteur, Anthony Adverse, The Charge of the Light Brigade, Green Pastures* 1936; *Black Legion, The Prince and the Pauper, The Life of Emile Zola* 1937; *The Adventures of Robin Hood, Brother Rat* 1938; *Dodge City, Confessions of a Nazi Spy, The Roaring Twenties* 1939; *They Drive by Night, High Sierra* 1940; *They Died with Their Boots On* 1941; *Yankee Doodle Dandy, Gentleman Jim* 1942; *Action in the North Atlantic* 1943; *To Have and Have Not* 1944; *Mildred Pierce* 1945; *Three Strangers, Devotion, Night and Day* (co-des.), *Of Human Bondage* 1946; *Life with Father, Magic Town* 1947; *The Woman in White, Johnny Belinda* 1948; *The Fountainhead* 1949; *Stage Fright, Young Man with a Horn* 1950; *The Blue Veil* 1951; *So Big* 1953; *Miracle in the Rain* 1956.

Anderson, Richard. Actor. Born on Aug. 8, 1926, in Long Branch, N.J. Reliable second lead and supporting player of numerous Hollywood films and TV episodes. A busy contract player for MGM in the 50s, he was married for a time to a daughter of Norma Shearer. Gained a new audience in the 1970s playing government agent Oscar Goldman in two series, 'The Six Million Dollar Man' and 'The Bionic Woman.'

FILMS INCLUDE: *Twelve O'Clock High* 1950; *The Magnificent Yankee, Payment on Demand, Across the Wide Missouri* 1951; *Just This Once, Scaramouche* 1952; *The Story of Three Loves, Escape from Fort Bravo* 1953; *The Student Prince* 1954; *Hit the Deck* 1955; *Forbidden Planet, The Search for Bridey Murphy* 1956; *The Buster Keaton Story, Paths of Glory* 1957; *The Long Hot Summer, The Curse of the Faceless Man* (lead) 1958; *Compulsion* 1959; *The Wackiest Ship in the Army* 1960; *A Gathering of Eagles, Johnny Cool* 1963; *Seven Days in May* 1964; *Seconds* 1966; *The Ride to Hangman's Tree* 1967; *Tora! Tora! Tora!* 1970; *Doctors' Wives* 1971; *The Honkers, Play It As It Lays* 1972; *Black Eye* 1974; *The Player* 1992; *Gettysburg* 1993; *The Glass Shield* 1995.

Anderson, Robert. Playwright, screenwriter. Born on Apr. 28, 1917, in New York City. *ed.* Harvard. He achieved critical acclaim for his play 'Tea and Sympathy' (1953) and later wrote the screenplay for the film production. Married Teresa WRIGHT.

FILMS INCLUDE: *Tea And Sympathy* 1956; *Until They Sail* 1957; *The Nun's Story* 1959; *The Sand Pebbles* 1966; *I Never Sang for My Father* (from own play) 1970.

Andersson, Bibi. Actress. Born Birgitta Andersson, on Nov. 11, 1935, in Stockholm. A product of the Kungliga Dramatiska Teatern, the dramatic school that turned out such actresses as Greta Garbo and Ingrid Bergman, she was appearing on the stage at Malmö when discovered by Ingmar BERGMAN, who gave her a role in his film *Smiles of a Summer Night* (1955). She soon developed into one of the brightest talents in the Swedish cinema of the 50s and 60s, part of Bergman's brilliant stable of performers, especially adept at portraying the director's complex heroines. In 1958 she was awarded (with fellow performers Eva DAHLBECK and Ingrid THULIN) a Cannes Festival prize for her performance in Bergman's *Brink of Life.* In the mid-60s she began appearing in international films, including such American features as *The Kremlin Letter.* In the 70s, she appeared on the American stage and, after being arrested for tax evasion in her native country in 1976, made New York her home for a while. But in the 80s she returned to Sweden and to the cozier world of Scandinavian films. Divorced from director Kjell GREDE in 1973, she married Per Ahlmark, a former chairman of Sweden's Liberal party, in 1978.

FILMS INCLUDE: *Dum-bom* 1953; *Sir Arne's Treasure* 1954; *Smiles of a Summer Night* 1955; *The Seventh Seal* 1956; *Wild Strawberries* 1957; *The Magician, Brink of Life* 1958; *The Devil's Eye* 1960; *The Pleasure Garden* 1961; *Short Is the Summer, The Swedish Mistress* 1962; *All These Women* 1964;

The Island 1965; *My Sister My Love, Persona, Duel at Diablo* (US), *Le Viol/The Rape* (Fr./Sw.) 1967; *The Passion of Anna* 1969; *The Kremlin Letter* (US) 1970; *The Touch* (Sw./US) 1971; *Scenes From a Marriage* 1973; *Il pleut sur Santiago/It Is Raining on Santiago* (Fr./Bulg.) 1975; *Blondy* (Fr.) 1976; *I Never Promised You a Rose Garden* (US) 1977; *An Enemy of the People* (as Mrs. Stockman), *L'Amour en Question* (Fr.) 1978; *Quintet* (US), *The Concorde—Airport '79* (US), *Two Women* 1979; *Marmalade Revolution* 1980; *I Blush* 1981; *Exposed* (US), *Black Crows* 1983; *The Last Summer* 1984; *The Dark Side of the Moon* 1985; *Huomenna, Poor Butterfly* 1986; *Babette's Gastebud/Babette's Feast, Svart gryning* 1987; *Fordringsagare* 1989; *A Passing Season* 1992; *The Butterfly's Dream, Dreamplay* 1994.

Andersson, Harriet. Actress. Born on Jan. 14, 1932, in Stockholm. After starting as a music hall dancer, she made her film debut in 1949 in a minor crime melodrama, *While the City Sleeps.* Ingmar BERGMAN was so impressed when he saw her in *Trots/Defiance* 1952, that he wrote the script of *Monika* (1952) especially for her. She has since appeared in many of his films as well as those of other directors, including her husband, Jörn Donnor's, and is considered one of Sweden's most individual and spontaneous actresses. She won the best actress award in Venice for her performance in *To Love* (1964). She is no relation to Bibi Andersson.

FILMS INCLUDE: *While the City Sleeps* 1950; *Divorced* 1951; *U-Boat 39, Trots/Defiance, Monika/Summer With Monika* 1952; *Sawdust and Tinsel, The Naked Night* 1953; *A Lesson in Love* 1954; *Dreams, Smiles of a Summer Night* 1955; *Children of the Night* 1956; *Crime in Paradise* 1960; *Through a Glass Darkly* 1961; *Siska* 1962; *A Sunday in September* 1963; *All These Women, To Love, Loving Couples* 1964; *Adventure Starts Here* 1965; *The Deadly Affair* (UK), *People Meet and Sweet Music Fills the Heart, Stimulantia* 1967; *The Girls* 1968; *Anna* 1970; *Cries and Whispers* 1972; *The White Wall* 1975; *Cry of Triumph* 1977; *Linus La Sabina* 1979; *Fanny and Alexander* 1982; *Raskenstam—the Casanova of Sweden* 1983; *Sommarkvallar pa jorden* 1987; *Himmel og Helvede* 1988; *Blankt Vapen* 1990.

Andrejew (Andreyev), André. Art director, set designer. *b.* 1899, St. Petersburg, Russia. *d.* 1966. Trained as an architect, he put his talents to use first on the Berlin and Vienna stage, then in films. With his film décor, for Wiene's *Raskolnikow/Crime and Punishment* (1923), he established himself as one of Europe's foremost art directors. His overpowering, realistic sets often determined not only the atmosphere but the entire flow of major films by such directors as Pabst, Feyder, Duvivier, Clouzot, Reed, and Asquith.

FILMS INCLUDE: In Germany—*Raskolnikow/Crime and Punishment* 1923; *Du sollst nicht ehebrechen/Therese Raquin/ Shadows of Fear* 1928; *Die Buchse der Pandora/Pandora's Box* 1929; *Die letzte Kompanie* 1930; *Die Dreigroschenoper/The Threepenny Opera/The Beggar's Opera* 1931. In France—*Don Quichotte/Don Quixote* 1933; *L'Or dans la Rue* 1934; *The Beloved Vagabond* (UK), *Le Golem/The Golem, Mayerling* 1936; *La Symphonie fantastique* 1942; *Le Corbeau/The Raven* 1943. In the UK—*Anna Karenina, The Winslow Boy* 1948; *The Man Between* 1953. In the US—*Anastasia, Alexander the Great* 1956.

Andress, Ursula. Actress. Born on Mar. 19, 1936, in Bern, Switzerland. Statuesque "sex goddess" of international films. She went to Rome in her teens in search of a film career and landed in a string of quickie Italian productions in the mid-50s. Marlon Brando introduced her to a Paramount agent, but her first Hollywood sojourn was cut short by her reluctance to study English. A voluptuous beauty, she emerged as a popular star in a British production, the first James Bond movie, *Dr. No* (1962) and later played leads in films of many nations. Her ten-year marriage to actor John DEREK was wrecked by a highly publicized affair with Jean-Paul BELMONDO.

FILMS INCLUDE: *Le Avventure Di Giacomo Casanova/Sins Of Casanova* (bit.; It./Fr.), *Un Americano a Roma/An American in Rome* (bit; It.) 1954; *La Catena dell'Odio* (It.) 1955; *Dr. No* (UK) 1962; *Fun in Acapulco* (US), *4 for Texas* (US) 1963; *Nightmare in the Sun* (US) 1964; *She* (title role; UK), *What's New Pussycat?* (US/Fr.), *La Decima Vittima/The 10th Victim* (It./Fr.), *Les Tribulations d'un Chinois en Chine/Up to His Ears* (Fr./It.) 1965; *The Blue Max* (UK), *Once Before I Die* (US) 1966; *Casino Royale* (UK), *Le Dolci Signore/Anyone Can Play* (It.) 1967; *L'Etoile du Sud/The Southern Star* (Fr./UK) 1969; *Perfect Friday* (UK) 1970; *Soleil rouge/Red Sun* (Fr./It./Sp.) 1971; *L'Ultima Chance* (It.) 1973; *Loaded Guns* 1974; *Africa Express* (It.) 1975; *L'Infermiera* (It.), *40 Grada sotto le Lenzuola* (It.), *Scaramouche/The Loves and Times of Scaramouche* (as Napoleon's Josephine; It./Yug.) 1976; *Casanova e Compagni* (It.) 1978; *The Fifth Musketeer* (Aus.) 1979; *Clash of the Titans* (as Aphrodite; UK) 1981; *Mexico in Flames/Red Bells* (USSR/Mex./It.) 1982; *Liberté Egalité Choucroute* (as Marie Antoinette; Fr., It., Ger.), *Klassezämekunft* (Switz.) 1988; *Class Meeting* 1996.

Andrews, Anthony. Actor. Born on Dec. 1, 1948, in London. *ed.* Royal Masonic School, Herts. Boyishly handsome leading man of the British screen. He began his carrer in 1967 in regional stage and rose to popularity on TV in such series as 'Upstairs Downstairs,' 'Danger UXB,' and 'Brideshead Revisited,' and such TV movies as *Ivanhoe* (1982) and *The Scarlet Pimpernel* (1983).

FILMS INCLUDE: *Take Me High* 1973; *Percy's Progress/It's Not the Size That Counts* 1974; *Operation Daybreak/Price of Freedom 1976; Under the Volcano* 1984; *The Holcroft Covenant* 1985; *The Second Victory* 1986; *The Lighthorsemen* 1987; *Hanna's War* 1988; *Lost in Siberia* 1991.

Andrews, Dana. Actor. *b.* Carver Dana Andrews, Jan. 1, 1909, Collins, Miss. *d.* 1992. *ed.* Sam Houston State Teachers' Coll. The son of a minister and brother of actor Steve FORREST, he started out as a bookkeeper for Gulf Oil but was drawn to acting and hitchhiked to Los Angeles, hoping for a career in films. Instead, he worked at a gas station for several years while attending the Pasadena Playhouse and making the rounds of stage companies and film studios. He was finally signed by Sam Goldwyn and began playing secondary roles in Goldwyn and Fox films in 1940. His roles steadily grew in importance and in 1943 he drew excellent notices for his sensitive performance in William Wellman's *The Ox-Bow Incident* as a brooding victim of a lynching mob. His career reached its peak in the mid-40s with convincing roles in such films as *Laura* (1944), *A Walk in the Sun* (1946), *The Best Years of Our Lives* (1946), and *Boomerang* (1947). Without ever attaining a star's popularity, and despite a scarcity of good roles in subsequent years, Andrews remained a dependable, versatile, and more than competent leading man and supporting player in numerous productions over the next three decades. He also appeared in many television productions and from 1969 to 1972 starred in the daytime TV soap opera 'Bright Promise.'

FILMS: *Lucky Cisco Kid, Sailor's Lady, The Westerner, Kit Carson* 1940; *Tobacco Road, Belle Starr, Swamp Water* 1941; *Ball of Fire, Berlin Correspondent* 1942; *Crash Dive, The Ox-Bow Incident, The North Star/Armored Attack* 1943; *Up in Arms, The Purple Heart, Wing and a Prayer, Laura* 1944; *State Fair, Fallen Angel* 1945; *A Walk in the Sun, Canyon Passage, The Best Years of Our Lives* 1946; *Boomerang, Night Song, Daisy Kenyon* 1947; *The Iron Curtain, Deep Waters, No Minor Vices*

1948; *Britannia Mews/The Forbidden Street* (UK/US), *Sword in the Desert* 1949; *My Foolish Heart, Where the Sidewalk Ends, Edge of Doom* 1950; *Sealed Cargo, The Frogmen, I Want You* 1951; *Assignment Paris* 1952; *Elephant Walk, Duel in the Jungle* (UK/US), *Three Hours to Kill* 1954; *Smoke Signal, Strange Lady in Town* 1955; *Comanche, While the City Sleeps, Beyond a Reasonable Doubt* 1956; *Night of the Demon/Curse of the Demon* (UK), *Spring Reunion, Zero Hour* 1957; *The Fearmakers, Enchanted Island* 1958; *The Crowded Sky* 1960; *Madison Avenue* 1962; *In Harm's Way, The Satan Bug, Crack in the World, Brainstorm, Town Tamer, The Loved One, Battle of the Bulge, Berlino—Appuntamento per le Spie/Spy in Your Eye* (It.) 1965; *Johnny Reno* 1966; *Il Cobra/The Cobra* (It./Sp.), *Hot Rods to Hell, The Frozen Dead* (UK) 1967; *I Diamanti che Nessuno Voleva Rubare* (It.), *The Devil's Brigade* 1968; *Innocent Bystanders* (UK) 1972); *Airport 1975* 1974; *Take a Hard Ride* 1975; *The Last Tycoon* 1976; *Good Guys Wear Black, Born Again* 1978; *Good Guys Wear Black, The Pilot* 1979; *Prince Jack* 1984.

Andrews, Edward. Actor. *b.* Oct. 9, 1914, in Griffin, Ga. *d.* 1985. *ed.* U. of Virginia. Bespectacled, moon-faced character player of the American stage, TV, and films. The son of an Episcopal minister, he began his stage career at 12 and made his Broadway debut in 1935. Beginning in the mid-50s, he appeared in many films, sometimes as an amicable character but more often in a sinister or malicious role.

FILMS INCLUDE: *The Phenix City Story* 1955; *The Harder They Fall, Tea and Sympathy* 1956; *The Tattered Dress* 1957; *The Fiend Who Walked the West* 1958; *Elmer Gantry* 1960; *The Absent-Minded Professor, The Young Doctors* 1961; *Advise and Consent* 1962; *The Thrill of It All* 1963; *Good Neighbor Sam, Youngblood Hawke, Send Me No Flowers* 1964; *The Glass Bottom Boat* 1966; *The Trouble with Girls* 1969; *Tora! Tora! Tora!* 1970; *Avanti!* 1972; *Charley and the Angel* 1973; *Seniors* 1978; *Sixteen Candles, Gremlins* 1984.

Andrews, Harry. Actor. *b.* Nov. 10, 1911, Tonbridge, England. *d.* 1989. *ed.* Wrekin Coll. Rugged, square-jawed, imposing character actor of British, American, and international films, often in tough military roles. He had a distinguished stage career from 1933, especially in Shakespearean roles, before his film debut early in the 50s. On the screen, in key supporting parts, his presence often overshadowed the leading players. His son, David Andrews, is a TV director and former juvenile film actor.

FILMS INCLUDE: *The Red Beret/Paratrooper* 1952; *The Black Knight* 1954; *Alexander the Great* (as Darius; US), *Moby Dick* (US) 1956; *Saint Joan* 1957; *The Devil's Disciple* (UK/US), *Solomon and Sheba* (US) 1959; *I Due Nemici/The Best of Enemies* (It./UK), *Barabba/Barabbas* (as St. Peter; It.) 1962; *Nine Hours to Rama* (US/UK), *55 Days at Peking* (US), *Nothing but the Best* 1964; *The Agony and the Ecstasy* (US), *The Hill, Sands of the Kalahari* 1965; *Modesty Blaise, The Deadly Affair* 1966; *The Jokers, The Long Duel* 1967; *The Charge of the Light Brigade, The Night They Raided Minsky's* (US), *The Sea Gull* (US/UK) 1968; *The Battle of Britain* 1969; *Too Late the Hero* (US), *Country Dance/Brotherly Love, Entertaining Mr. Sloane, Wuthering Heights* 1970; *Nicholas and Alexandra* 1971; *Man of La Mancha* (US), *The Ruling Class* 1972; *The Mackintosh Man* 1973; *The Internecine Project* 1974; *Man at the Top* 1975; *The Blue Bird* (US/USSR), *Sky Riders* (US/Gr.), *The Passover Plot* (as John the Baptist; Isr./US) 1976; *The Prince and the Pauper/Crossed Swords, Equus* 1977; *The Medusa Touch, The Big Sleep, Death on the Nile, Watership Down* (voice only), *Superman* 1978; *S.O.S. Titanic* 1979; *Hawk the Slayer* 1980; *Mesmerized* (UK/Austral./NZ) 1984.

Andrews, Julie. Actress, singer. Born Julia Elizabeth Wells, on Oct. 1, 1935, in Walton-on-Thames, England. Highly popular musical star of the 60s. The daughter of show people, she began performing as a child and at age 12 made her London debut, singing operatic arias in the 'Starlight Roof' revue. Her New York stage debut in the imported production of 'The Boy Friend' (1954) was a turning point in her career. Two years later she created the part of Eliza Doolittle in 'My Fair Lady,' one of the most spectacular hits in Broadway history. After losing the part in the screen version to Audrey Hepburn, she scored a personal triumph by instead making her film debut in Walt Disney's *Mary Poppins* (1964), for which she won the best actress Academy Award. The following year she starred in *The Sound of Music,* one of the top-grossing films of all time. She was nominated for an Oscar for that film (and again, 17 years later, for *Victor/Victoria*). Her screen career faltered somewhat later in the 60s, but her popularity was revived early in the 70s via TV spectaculars and late in the decade with her appearance in the box-office hit *10.* It was one in a series of films made with her husband, director Blake EDWARDS, who she married in 1969 after her divorce from scenic designer Tony Walton. She has also written children's stories under the name Julie Edwards.

FILMS: *Rose of Bagdad* (voice only) 1952; *Mary Poppins, The Americanization of Emily* 1964; *The Sound of Music* 1965; *Torn Curtain, Hawaii* 1966; *The Singing Princess* (voice only), *Thoroughly Modern Millie* 1967; *Star!* 1968; *Darling Lili* 1970; *The Tamarind Seed* 1974; *10* 1979; *Little Miss Marker* 1980; *S.O.B.* 1981; *Victor/Victoria* 1982; *The Man Who Loved Women* 1983; *That's Life!, Duet for One* 1986; *A Fine Romance* (US/It.) 1992.

Andrews Sisters, The. A singing group comprising the three daughters of Norwegian-Greek parents, all born in Minneapolis: LaVerne, July 6, 1915 (*d.* 1967); Maxine (often Maxene), Jan. 3, 1918 (*d.* 1995); and Patricia (Patti or Patty), Feb. 16, 1920. They formed a harmony trio when quite young, won some amateur contests, and achieved national fame with their 1937 recording of "Bei Mir Bist Du Schoen." Their popularity reached a peak on radio, and throughout the 40s they appeared as themselves in a score of films. Maxine and Patti staged a brief nostalgic revival with a "borrowed" third sister early in the 70s, in a Broadway musical, 'Over Here.'

FILMS: *Argentine Nights* 1940; *Buck Privates, In the Navy, Hold That Ghost* 1941; *What's Cookin'?, Private Buckaroo, Give Out Sisters* 1942; *Always a Bridesmaid, How's About It?, Swingtime Johnny* 1943; *Follow the Boys, Moonlight and Cactus, Hollywood Canteen* 1944; *Make Mine Music* (voices only) 1946; *Road to Rio* 1947; *Melody Time* (voices only) 1948; *The Phynx* (Patti only, cameo) 1970.

Andrews, William. See FORREST, Steve.

Andriot, Lucien. Director of photography. *b.* Nov. 19, 1897, Paris. *d.* 1979. In Hollywood from the age of 19, he was behind the camera on numerous silent and sound films. He worked on some distinguished productions, but his prolific output also consisted of many routine B pictures. Active in TV from the early 50s until his retirement in 1966.

FILMS INCLUDE: *The Marked Woman* 1914; *M'Liss, Camille* 1915; *The Feast of Life, La Vie de Boheme* 1916; *The Pride of the Clan, The Poor Little Rich Girl* (co-phot.), *The Whip* 1917; *Lest We Forget* 1918; *The Man Who Lost Himself, A Connecticut Yankee in King Arthur's Court* 1920; *Shame* 1921; *Monte Cristo, A Fool There Was* 1922; *East of Broadway* 1924; *Gigolo* 1926; *Loves of Carmen* (co-phot.) 1927; *The Valiant, Christina* 1929; *The Golden Calf* 1930; *The Spy, Daddy Long Legs* 1931; *The Animal Kingdom* 1932; *Hallelujah I'm a Bum, Topaze, Bondage* 1933; *The Crime Doctor* 1934; *The Return of*

Peter Grimm 1935; *The Gay Desperado* 1936; *Cafe Metropole, On the Avenue* 1937; *The Lady in Question* 1940; *The Hairy Ape, The Sullivans* 1944; *The Southerner, And Then There Were None* 1945; *Diary of a Chambermaid* 1946; *New Orleans, Dishonored Lady* 1947; *Outpost in Morocco* 1949; *Borderline* 1950; *Home Town Story* 1951.

Angel, Heather. Actress. *b.* Feb. 9, 1909, Oxford, England. *d.* 1986. *ed.* London Polytechnic of Dramatic Arts. Delicate leading lady of Hollywood films of the 30s. She made her stage debut in 1926 at the Old Vic. After showing much promise in British films, she was brought to Hollywood by Fox films but, with some notable exceptions—like *Berkeley Square* (1933), *The Mystery of Edwin Drood* (1935), and *The Informer* (1935)—was entrusted primarily with undemanding roles. By the late 30s she was appearing in B pictures, including several in the "Bulldog Drummond" series, or playing second fiddle in A productions, memorably as the mother who drowns herself after her baby dies in Hitchcock's *Lifeboat* (1943). Her career came to a virtual halt in the mid-40s, but she later appeared in much TV, including regular roles as the housekeeper in the 'Peyton Place' and 'Family Affair' series. Married and divorced from screen actors Ralph FORBES and Henry WILCOXON, she witnessed the fatal stabbing of her third husband, director Robert B. SINCLAIR, by a prowler in 1970.

FILMS INCLUDE: In the UK—*City of Song/Farewell to Love* 1930; *The Hound of the Baskervilles* 1931; *Bill the Conqueror/The Man Who Won* 1932. In the US—*Pilgrimage, Berkeley Square, Charlie Chan's Greatest Case* 1933; *Orient Express, Romance in the Rain* 1934; *The Mystery of Edwin Drood, It Happened in New York, The Informer, The Three Musketeers* 1935; *The Last of the Mohicans, Daniel Boone* 1936; *Bulldog Drummond Escapes* 1937; *Bulldog Drummond in Africa* 1938; *Bulldog Drummond's Bride* 1939; *Kitty Foyle, Pride and Prejudice* 1940; *That Hamilton Woman, Suspicion* 1941; *The Undying Monster, Time to Kill* 1942; *Cry Havoc* 1943; *Lifeboat* 1944; *The Saxon Charm* 1948; *Alice in Wonderland* (voice only) 1951; *Peter Pan* (voice only) 1953; *Premature Burial* 1962.

Angeli, Pier. Actress. *b.* Anna Maria Pierangeli, June 19, 1932, Cagliari, Sardinia, Italy. *d.* 1971. Twin sister of Marisa PAVAN. Discovered for films by director Léonide MOGUY, who gave her the innocent adolescent lead in his Italian film *Domani é troppo Tardi/Tommorow Is Too Late* (1949) and in the sequal, *Domani é un altro Giorno* (1950), both dealing with the pains of adolescence and the need for sex education. After appearing in Fred Zinnemann's *Teresa* (1951), she enjoyed a modest career as a leading lady in Hollywood films, typically playing fragile, innocent heroines. But she had trouble adjusting to stardom and to her marriage (1954–58) to singer Vic Damone and she returned to Europe, where she later appeared in many forgettable productions. She died of an overdose of barbiturates at the age of 39.

FILMS INCLUDE: In Italy—*Domani é troppo Tardi/Tomorrow Is Too Late* 1949; *Domani é un altro Giorno* 1950. In the US—*Teresa, The Light Touch* 1951; *The Devil Makes Three* 1952; *The Story of Three Loves, Sombrero* 1953; *The Flame and the Flesh* 1954; *The Silver Chalice* 1955; *Somebody Up There Likes Me, Port Afrique* (US/UK) 1956; *The Vintage* 1957; *Merry Andrew* 1958. In Europe—*S.O.S. Pacific* (UK) 1959; *The Angry Silence* (UK) 1960; *Sodoma e Gomorra/Sodom and Gomorrah* (It./Fr./US) 1961; *L'Ammutinamento/White Slave Ship* (It./Fr.) 1962; *Banco a Bangkok/Shadow of Evil* (Fr./It.) 1964; *Berlino Appuntamento per le Spie/Spy in Your Eye* (It.), *Battle of the Bulge* (US; filmed in Spain) 1965; *Rey de Africa/One Step to Hell* (Sp./It./US), *Every Bastard a King* (Isr.) 1968; *Addio Alexandra/Love Me—Love My Wife* (It.) 1969; *Nelle Pieghe della Carne/In the Folds of the Flesh* (It.), *Octaman* (US) 1971.

Angelo, Jean. Actor. *b.* Jean Barthélémy, May 17, 1875, Paris. *d.* 1933. At 15 he joined Sarah BERNHARDT's stage company, becoming her protégé. He made his screen debut in the famous *L'Assassinat de Duc de Guise* (1908) and after WW I, during which he suffered combat injuries, he rose to prominence as the leading man of such French silent films as Feyder's *L'Atlantide* (1921) and Renoir's *Nana* (1926). He appeared in several talkies and died during the production of *Colomba* (1933).

FILMS INCLUDE: *L'assassinat de Duc de Guise* 1908; *Les Misérables, La Vendetta* 1913; *Expiation* 1918; *La Riposte* 1919; *L'Atlantide* 1921; *L'Aventurier* 1924; *Nana* 1926; *Marquita, La Fin de Monte Carlo* 1927; *La Vierge Folle, Chantage, La Ronde infernale* 1928; *Monte Cristo* 1929; *Mon Coeur incognito, L'Homme qui assassina* 1930; *L'Atlantide* (French version of Pabst's *Die Herrin von Atlantis*) 1932; *Colomba* 1933.

Angelopoulos, Theodoros. Director. Born on Apr. 27, 1935, in Athens, Greece. He practiced law briefly, after graduating from the University of Athens, but found himself drawn to the arts and began publishing essays, short stories, and poetry. Following compulsory military service, he went to Paris early in the 60s and enrolled at the Sorbonne as a literature student. But soon after he dropped out to attend IDHEC, the noted Paris film school. After an apprenticeship under Jean ROUCH at the Musée de l'Homme, he returned to Greece, where he became a film critic for a left-wing journal. His first attempt at professional directing, in 1965, was aborted by a dispute with the producer. It was not until 1968 that he turned out his first film, a half-hour documentary. His first fiction feature followed in 1970. Collaborating on his own scripts, Angelopoulos went on to assert himself as Greece's premier contemporary director. His films are typically structurally episodic and thematically ambiguous. *Traveling Players* (*Othassios,* 1975) was named best film by the British Film Institute. *Alexander the Great* (*O Megalexandros*) won the "Cinema 80 series" Golden Lion at the 1980 Venice Film Festival, and *Landscape in the Mist* shared the Silver Lion at Venice in 1988.

FILMS: *The Broadcast/The Transmission* (doc. short) 1968; *Reconstruction* 1970; *Days of '36* 1972; *The Traveling Players* 1975; *The Hunters/The Huntsmen* 1977; *Alexander the Great* 1980; *Athens* (doc.) 1982; *Voyage to Cythera* 1984; *L'Heritage de la chouette* (act. only), *Melissokomos Petheni—O Alles Mythos, Enas* (act. only), *O Melissokomos/The Beekeeper* 1986; *Landscape in the Mist* 1988; *The Suspended Step of the Stork* 1991; *Ulysses' Gaze* 1996.

Anger, Kenneth. Avant-garde filmmaker. Born in 1932, in Santa Monica, Cal. Though he grew up in Hollywood, learned tap-dancing alongside Shirley Temple, and appeared in several films (including Reinhardt's *Midsummer Night's Dream*) as a child, he turned against traditional filmmaking while still a boy. At nine he turned out his first short subject, *Who Has Been Rocking My Dream Boat?* He gradually developed into one of the standard-bearers of the American underground film movement. His films are characterized by provocative themes, violent atmosphere, mystic ritualism, the occult, and sexual exhibitionism. In *Fireworks* (1947), for example, a sailor's penis turns into an exploding Roman candle. Much of his work was done in Europe, mainly in France. Many of his films were abandoned during production and never exhibited. He is the author of *Hollywood Babylon* (first published in France in 1958), an exposé dealing with some of the more lurid aspects of the film capital. A followup volume, *Hollywood Babylon II*, was published in 1984.

FILMS INCLUDE: *Escape Episode* 1944–46; *Fireworks* 1947; *Puce Moment* 1949; *La Lune des Lapins* 1950; *La Jeune Homme et la Mort, Eaux d'Artifice* 1953; *Inauguration of the Pleasure Dome* 1954; *Thelema Abbey* 1955; *The Story of O* 1959–61; *Scorpio Rising* 1964; *Invocation of My Demon Brother* 1969; *Rabbit's Moon* 1971; *Lucifer Rising* 1973; *Lucifer Rising* (revised version) 1980; *He Stands in a Desert Counting the Seconds of His Life* (act. only) 1985; *Jonas in the Desert* 1993.

angle, camera. The camera's point of view when it is set up for shooting; the relative depth, height, or width at which an object or an action is photographed. The angle from which the camera views the subject determines not only what will be included in any particular shot but to a large extent *how* the audience will view it—from near or far, from above or below, subjectively or objectively, etc. The choice of camera angle thus affects not only the progression of the plot but also the aesthetic quality of a scene and the psychological attitude of the viewer.

Over the years, directors and cameramen have established a set of conventions regarding the technical, aesthetic, and psychological properties of the various camera angles. The *eye-level angle* is considered the most lifelike but least dramatic. It is supposed to provide the normal viewpoint and is usually shot from a height of four to six feet, with no distortion of vertical lines. The eye level of the performer, not the cameraman, determines camera height, and is especially crucial in close-up shots. Because of normal viewpoint, the eye-level shot is considered useful in establishing situations and providing audiences with a frame of reference.

In a *high-angle* shot the camera looks down on the subject. Technically, it may allow a director to cover much ground and action in deep focus. Such a shot will also tend to slow the action and to reduce the height of an object or a person by foreshortening. This last feature may produce psychological side effects, such as giving an audience a sense of superiority over screen characters or implying the subordination of any of the characters to surrounding persons or environment. In Murnau's *The Last Laugh,* for example, actor Emil JANNINGS is often shot from a high angle after his downfall, while earlier scenes depicting him as a proud doorman are shot mostly from a low-angle position.

In a *low-angle* shot the camera looks up at a subject. The effect is often highly dramatic, producing a powerful distortion of perspective and composition. It tends to speed up action and to attribute stature and strength to characters. The low-angle setup was dominant in Orson Welles's *Citizen Kane* to suggest the titanic dimension of the tycoon protagonist. To permit the frequent use of the low-angle, Welles had to build his sets complete with ceilings, and the omnipresence of ceilings in the background is one of the many unusual features of *Citizen Kane.* By merely shifting camera angles, a director can suggest not only the ups and downs in a character's fortune but also the attitude an audience should adopt toward any personality or action in the film.

The variety of camera angles is almost infinite. There are no strict rules regarding the exact position of the camera relative to the subject photographed. The eye-level, high, and low angles are just broad categories, as are the *sideview angle* (which tends to give an object added dimension), the so-called *"Dutch" angle* (which presents an object in a highly effective diagonal tilt), and the many other camera positions that have been discovered and utilized over decades of filmmaking.

Anhalt, Edward. Screenwriter. Born on Mar. 28, 1914, in New York City. *ed.* Columbia. Involved in prebroadcasting TV experimentation before turning to films as writer and associate producer. He collaborated with his wife, Edna (*b.* Apr. 10, 1914, N.Y.C.), on several films, including *Panic in the Streets* (1950), an original story that brought them a joint Academy Award. Anhalt won another Oscar for his screenplay of *Becket* (1964).

FILMS INCLUDE: *Avalanche* 1946; *Bulldog Drummond Strikes Back* 1947; *Panic in the Streets* 1950; *The Sniper* 1952; *The Member of the Wedding* 1953; *Not as a Stranger* 1955; *The Pride and the Passion* 1957; *The Young Lions* 1958; *The Young Savages* 1961; *Becket* 1964; *The Satan Bug, Boeing Boeing* 1965; *Hour of the Gun* 1967; *The Boston Strangler* 1968; *The Madwoman of Chaillot* 1969; *The Salzburg Connection* 1971; *Jeremiah Johnson* 1972; *Luther* 1974; *The Man in the Glass Booth* 1975; *Escape to Athena* 1979; *Green Ice* 1981; *The Right Stuff* 1983; *The Holcroft Covenant* 1985.

animal performers. Animal appeal has been used to advantage by the film industry since the early days of the cinema. A great many members of the animal kingdom of countless species and varieties have appeared on the screen, and some have even achieved the status of "stars." Among the best-known film animals have been the dogs Rin Tin Tin, Asta, Lassie, and Benji, the cat Rhubarb, the chimp Cheta, the mule Francis, the porpoise Flipper, the cross-eyed lion Clarence, and the horses Rex, Champion, and Trigger. More recently, Clyde the orangutan, Bart the bear, and Beethoven the dog have carried on the tradition. In Hollywood, animals are rented from neighboring ranches or from trainers who specialize in particular species or breeds.

Animal "acting" is achieved only after arduous training, great patience, clever cutting, and a variety of other special techniques. Animals are usually tricked into performing, often by the promise of an immediate reward of a bit of food. Some easily frightened animals are given tranquilizers. The easiest animals to train are dogs, especially German shepherds. Animals learn one trick at a time, and after many rehearsals they appear in short takes. Often, several look-alikes are used for the same role.

The actions of animals are mostly nondirectional. When Lassie is seen running toward an actor, she is actually running toward her trainer or master off screen. Shots of an animal's aimless movements are later edited to appear as a logical part of a film's action.

Enterprising publicists have been successfully exploiting an annual event known as the PATSY AWARDS, in which screen animals win recognition for their "performances" just as humans do with the Academy Awards.

animatics. Animated film or video used to draft or block out sequences of finished film. Widely used for planning TV commercials, it also substitutes for special effects shots in workprints until the final shots are done.

animation. The branch of filmmaking in which drawings or three-dimensional objects are photographed (or, rarely, drawn directly on film) so as to create the illusion of movement. The animated cartoon is the most common form of film animation, but equally legitimate forms are the puppet film, the silhouette film, and object animation (see STOP MOTION).

The fundamental distinction between live-action filming and animation is that, while in the former the action is filmed continuously at the rate of 24 frames per second, the latter is usually recorded by exposing the film frame by frame. In cartoon animation, drawings representing fractions of movements, each occupying 1/24 second, are shot one by one, so that when they are projected on a screen at the standard 24-frames-per-second speed they give the illusion of smooth, continuous movement. In puppet animation, slightly adjusted poses of movable puppets are photographed frame by frame, each adjusted pose also occupying 1/24 second. In silhouette animation, flat, jointed cut-out figures, laid out on glass plates, are adjusted slightly 24 times per second, frame by frame. Similarly, any object can be animated (object animation) by moving it fractionally and exposing the broken-up action frame by frame.

As with live-action filming, the first of the many considerations in the production process of an animated film is the script. The difference lies in the form of the script. Instead of the written script, which provides the basis for live-action filming, the animator relies on a storyboard. The storyboard tells the story graphically, showing the plot in pictures. A standard board may contain some 60 drawings, usually rough sketches in black pencil or charcoal. Three boards are usually needed to tell the story of a short, while as many as 30 may be required for a feature-length film.

Once the storyboard is deemed satisfactory by the story person who conceived it, the layout person who will plan the settings, and the director who bears overall responsibility for the production, it is photographed and photostatic blow-ups are distributed to all artists working on the film. The layout person, whose duties somewhat resemble those of the art director in live-action films, refines the drawn characters and provides them with appropriate backgrounds, props, and costumes. As the layouts are completed and approved by the director, tracings of them are made and given to the animators.

To a much greater extent than the live-action film, the animated cartoon depends on music and sound effects to make the action on the screen believable. Timing is of the essence, so that every movement is accompanied by the corresponding sounds. Unlike the sound track for live-action films, which is usually recorded simultaneously with action and sometimes postsynchronized, the sound track for an animated film is ideally recorded *before* most other phases of production begin. Every sound is recorded on a chart that becomes a guide for the visuals. The prerecorded sound track along with the chart go to the animator, who also gets an exposure sheet indicating the length of each scene, its musical tempo, and other essential information.

The animator, a skilled artist, outlines the scene by drawing the characters at key positions. He draws only the extreme phases of each movement—known as "key animation"—leaving the routine work of completing the interim phases to assistants known as "in-betweeners." The pencil drawings of each completed scene are sent to the camera department for line-test shooting and viewed by the director and the animator on a Moviola. If the results meet their approval, the drawings are sent to "clean-up," where the lines are put into final form.

By this time, the original layout of the complete scene has gone to the background department, where the proper environment for the cartoon characters is traced and painted by background artists, skilled stylists who give visual expression to the layout person's original conception. Like the character drawings, background drawings are submitted to the line test and put to final form.

Next, the drawings are traced by inkers on thin, transparent sheets of celluloid, called "cels." Painters then apply opaque water colors to the reverse side of the cels, according to a predetermined color scheme. Finally, the cels are checked for accuracy and color, cleaned, and sent along with the scene's background and exposure chart to the camera department for filming.

Animation developed considerably ahead of the invention of motion pictures. The urge to make drawings appear to move was present among artists since the dawn of history, judging by attempts at serial drawing of a wrestling match on an ancient Egyptian mural or the successive drawings of an athlete in motion on early Greek pottery. Animation was first attempted as a show with *ombres Chinoises,* shadows produced on a screen by silhouette puppets.

The first real precursor of film animation was the Belgian professor Joseph-Antoine PLATEAU, who in 1832 invented the PHENAKISTICOPE, the first device to produce an apparent moving picture from a series of drawings. The action was viewed through slits on revolving discs. Two years later, William G. Horner, an Englishman, described the Daedalum, or the "Wheel of the Devil," a prototype of the Zoetrope, a drum-shaped device for the viewing of action serially recorded on paper strips. Emile REYNAUD of France signaled a breakthrough in 1891 when he combined his PRAXINOSCOPE (invented 1877) with a projecting technique to become the first man to project animated drawings upon a screen in a presentation he called *Pantomimes Lumineuses.* He used carbon lights, mirrors, and revolving drums containing hand-colored pictures to project 15-minute shows at the Théâtre Optique in Paris to the accompaniment of mood music.

The invention of motion picture machinery opened unlimited horizons for animated films. In 1906, J. Stuart BLACKTON, an American, first applied the technique of stop-motion photography in producing the first cartoon on motion picture film, for VITAGRAPH, *Humorous Phases of a Funny Face.* In 1908, Emile COHL of France amazed early cinema audiences with a magical demonstration of little white match-stick figures dancing about against a black background, which he called *Fantasmagorie.* He created more than one hundred cartoons between 1908 and 1918 and is credited by the French with creating the first regular cartoon character, Fantoche. In the United States, meanwhile, in 1909, Winsor MCCAY, a cartoonist for the New York *Journal,* produced *Gertie the Dinosaur,* the first animated cartoon to be shown as part of a regular theatrical program. In 1918 he made the first feature-length animated film, *The Sinking of the Lusitania.*

By the end of WW I, the animated cartoon was gradually becoming an accepted form of screen entertainment, with such series as "The Katzenjammer Kids," "Krazy Kat," "Felix the Cat," and "Coco the Clown" leading the way. These films were crudely drawn but were already taking advantage of newly developing techniques, such as Earl Hurd's labor-saving method of "cel" animation, allowing the tracing of moving parts of characters on celluloid sheets without having to redraw the entire character and background for every frame of film.

During the 20s, animated cartoons became a regular part of the program in motion picture theaters, but the decade was lean in creativity or technical innovation. It was not until the coming of sound in 1928 that the screen cartoon really came into its own. For the next dozen or so years the art of film animation was dominated by the creative personality of Walt DISNEY with his "Silly Symphony" series (*Skeleton Dance,* etc.) and such immortal cartoon characters as Mickey Mouse, Donald Duck, Pluto, and Goofy. A master craftsman as well as a brilliant organizer and technical innovator, Disney streamlined cartoon production into a massive assembly-line studio operation, complete with conferences, storyboards, and a clearly defined division of labor. In the mid-30s Disney began turning out a series of successful feature-length cartoons, including *Snow White and the Seven Dwarfs, Pinocchio, Bambi,* and most notably *Fantasia.*

Other studios besides Disney produced animation during the 30s, 40s, and 50s. MGM housed a cartoon studio headed by Fred Quimby; its most popular characters, Tom and Jerry, were created by William Hanna and Joseph Barbera. Warner Bros.'s "Looney Tunes" and "Merrie Melodies" series featured such characters as Bugs Bunny, Porky Pig, and Daffy Duck. Warner Bros. animators included Chuck Jones, Tex Avery, and Friz Freleng. Other majors releasing animation included Universal ("Oswald the Rabbit"), Paramount ("Puppetoon" and "Noveltoon"), and Columbia ("Color Rhapsodies," 1934–49). Independent producers included Max Fleischer (best known for two features, *Gulliver's Travels* and *Hoppity Goes to Town*, and the 30s Popeye and Betty Boop shorts) and Walter Lantz ("Woody Woodpecker").

In 1941 a group of Disney animators went on strike and were eventually dismissed from their jobs. The group, including John Hubley, Bob Cannon, Stephen Bosustow, and Ernest Pintoff, formed UPA (United Productions of America) in 1943. In reaction to the naturalistic, representational graphic style and the sentimental theme of the Disney cartoon, UPA animators developed freer, more economical, contemporary art styles and whimsical, sophisticated themes that came to dominate screen animation in the 50s.

Among UPA's famous cartoon creations were Mr. Magoo, Gerald McBoing Boing, Christopher Crumpet, and Howdy Doody. The group's liberated graphic style has strongly influenced postwar animation in Western Europe as well as in such Eastern states as Poland, Czechoslovakia, and Yugoslavia, where film animation has rapidly been developing into a brilliant art form, surpassing in its inventiveness and modern style anything currently produced in the US or Western Europe. The situation is quite different in the Soviet Union and East Germany, where the graphic forms still tend to be traditional and didactic, consisting for the most part of faithfully representational children's fables.

Experimentation with nonrepresentational animation began in the early 20s by such artists of the European AVANT-GARDE as Viking Eggeling, Hans Richter, Walter Ruttmann, Fernand Léger, and Oscar Fischinger, and continued with direct drawing and painting on celluloid by Len Lye and Norman McLaren and the pinhead shadow films of Alexei Alexeieff.

The art of silhouette animation was pioneered in the 20s by Lotte Reiniger in Germany. Puppet animation owes much of its development to the works of the Soviet Ptushko, the Pole Starevitch, the Hungarian George Pal, and its most noted practitioner, the Czech Jirí Trnka.

By the 60s, rising costs and the collapse of the Hollywood studio system, among other factors, had drastically curtailed theatrical animation. Disney continued to produce features (*Sleeping Beauty, 101 Dalmatians*), albeit with more modest art direction than its earlier efforts. "Underground" styling emerged in adult-oriented features of the 60s and 70s, such as *Yellow Submarine* and Ralph Bakshi's films (most notably *Fritz the Cat*), while animators around the world continued to produce innovative shorts for art-house distribution. The same period saw a momentous expansion of animation made for television, generally aimed at children or offered in commercials, with far lower production values than the old theatrical cartoons.

Theatrical animation found its audience again in the 80s. A breakthrough came with the 1988 Disney release, *Who Framed Roger Rabbit*, which used the latest computer technology to combine animation and live action in a dazzling comic spectacle. The movie (which earned a special Oscar for director of animation Richard Williams) also featured "cameo" appearances by scores of famous cartoon characters and ushered the word "toon" (for cartoon character) into common currency. Following *Roger Rabbit* came a new series of Disney musical fairy tales—*The Little Mermaid*, *Beauty and the Beast*, *Aladdin, The Lion King, Pocahontas*—which featured innovations in color and animation technique, not to mention record-breaking box-office success. Don Bluth productions (another group of former Disney animators) released several ambitious features, including *The Land Before Time* and *An American Tail*. With the growing interest in animation, art houses have been more likely to program packages of animated shorts (*Animation Celebration*) and Japanese action features (*Akira*).

In addition to its more visible manifestations, animation has long been used in support of special effects shots in movies (for example, the "monster from the Id" in *Forbidden Planet*, 1956). This use of animation has expanded in recent years due to the rise of special effects blockbusters such as the *Star Wars* series and the refinement of COMPUTER ANIMATION, which can simulate objects, settings, and even people with growing authenticity. The animator is now as likely to manipulate computer-generated images as hand-drawn cels or table-top models. Most major studios of today are developing their own animation departments or enhancing their existing capabilities to include the latest animation technology, an area of filmmaking experiencing tremendous growth throughout the 90s.

animation camera. A camera equipped with a stop-motion motor so that it can photograph fractions of animation movement frame by frame. Mounted on an ANIMATION STAND, it can be moved vertically to vary the size of the photographed image or to create zoom effects.

animation stand. An inclusive term to describe the basic working unit of the animation photographer, comprising a camera, its mounting, and the elaborately constructed table on which the artwork is placed. Modern animation stands are equipped with computerized motion control systems for special effects shots, such as combining live-action and animated scenes.

animator. The artist who draws the key positions of a cartoon character's movements and is generally entrusted with the actual execution of the cartoon as conceived by the director and the layout person. Animators may also draw the images used in composite special effects shots, manipulate models in stop-motion animation, and generate images on computer.

animatronics. See PUPPETS.

Ankers, Evelyn. Actress. *b.* Aug. 17, 1918, Valparaiso, Chile, to British parents. *d.* 1985. *ed.* RADA. She appeared in British films before coming to the US. On the New York stage, then in numerous Hollywood pictures, mostly second features. She is best remembered for heroine roles in horror and action films. Among film buffs she is known as "Queen of the Horror Movies" or "The Screamer." Married Richard DENNING in 1942. At the time of her death, they resided in Haiku, on the Hawaiian island of Maui.

FILMS INCLUDE: In the UK—*Land Without Music/Forbidden Music, Rembrandt* 1936; *Fire Over England, Knight Without Armor, Over the Moon, Wings of the Morning* 1937; *Murder in the Family* 1938. In the US—*Hit the Road, Hold That Ghost, Burma Convoy, The Wolf Man* 1941; *The Ghost of Frankenstein, Eagle Squadron, Sherlock Holmes and the Voice of Terror, The Great Impersonation* 1942; *Captive Wild Woman, All by Myself, Son of Dracula, The Mad Ghoul, His Butler's Sister* 1943; *Ladies Courageous, Weird Woman, The Invisible Man's Revenge, Jungle Woman, Pardon My Rhythm, Pearl of Death* 1944; *The Frozen Ghost, The Fatal Witness* 1945; *Queen of Burlesque, The French Key, Black Beauty, Flight to Nowhere* 1946; *Last of the Redmen, The Lone Wolf in London* 1947; *Parole Inc.* 1948; *Tarzan's Magic Fountain* 1949; *The Texan Meets Calamity Jane* 1950; *No Greater Love* (Lutheran Church-sponsored film) 1960.

Annabella. Actress. Born Suzanne Georgette Charpentier, on July 14, 1909, in La Varenne-Saint-Hilaire, near Paris, a publisher's daughter. *d.* 1996. She began as a dancer and made her film debut at 16 with a small role in Abel Gance's *Napoléon* (1926). Several minor roles followed before she was chosen by René Clair to play the leads in *Le Million* (1931) and *Quatorze Juillet/July 14th* (1933). She became France's most celebrated young actress and in 1936 went to England, where she starred in three films, including Britain's first color production, *Wings of the Morning* (1937). She was then invited to Hollywood, but her accomplishments there were minor. Divorced from French actor Jean MURAT, she married Tyrone POWER in 1939. After their divorce in 1948, she returned to Europe and shortly after retired to her farm in the Pyrenees.

FILMS INCLUDE: In France—*Napoléon* 1927; *Maldone* 1928; *Le Million* 1931; *Paris-Mediterranée* 1932; *La Bataille, Quatorze Juillet/July 14th* 1933; *Veille d'Armes* (best actress prize at Venice Biennale), *L'Equipage/Flight Into Darkness, La Bandera/Escape From Yesterday* 1935. In the UK—*Wings of the Morning, Under the Red Robe, Dinner at the Ritz* 1937. In France—*La Citadelle du Silence/The Citadel of Silence* 1937; *Hôtel du Nord* 1938. In the US—*The Baroness and the Butler, Suez* 1938; *Bridal Suite* 1939; *Tonight We Raid Calais, Bomber's Moon* 1943; *13 Rue Madeleine* 1947. In France—*Dernier Amour* 1949. In Spain—*Don Juan* 1950.

Annakin, Ken. Director. Born on Aug. 10, 1914, in Beverley, England. A restless young man, he quit his job as an income tax clerk and emigrated successively to New Zealand, Australia, and the US. On returning to England, he became an automobile salesman and a journalist. He was disabled out of the RAF in 1941 with a case of amnesia and became an assistant cameraman. He worked in several capacities on documentary films before directing his first feature film in 1947. His career hit its peak in the 60s with such large-scale adventure films as *The Longest Day* and *Those Magnificent Men in Their Flying Machines*.

FEATURE FILMS: *Holiday Camp* 1947; *Miranda, Broken Journey, Here Come the Huggetts, Quartet* ("The Colonel's Lady" episode) 1948; *Vote for Huggett, The Huggetts Abroad, Landfall* 1949; *Double Confession, Trio* ("The Verger" and "Mr. Know-All" episodes) 1950; *Hotel Sahara* 1951; *The Planter's Wife/Outpost in Malaya, The Story of Robin Hood* 1952; *The Sword and the Rose* 1953; *You Know What Sailors Are, The Seekers/Land of Fury* 1954; *Value for Money* 1955; *Three Men in a Boat, Loser Takes All* 1956; *Across the Bridge* 1957; *Nor the Moon by Night/Elephant Gun* 1958; *Third Man on the Mountain* (US/UK) 1959; *The Swiss Family Robinson* (US/UK) 1960; *A Very Important Person/A Coming-Out Party, The Hellions* 1961; *Crooks Anonymous, The Longest Day* (British sequences only; US) 1962; *The Fast Lady, The Informers/Underworld Informers* 1963; *Those Magnificent Men in Their Flying Machines; or How I Flew From London to Paris in 25 Hours and 11 Minutes* (also co-sc.), *Battle of the Bulge* (US) 1965; *The Long Duel* (also prod.) 1967; *The Biggest Bundle of Them All* (US/It.) 1968; *Monte Carlo or Bust/Those Daring Young Men in Their Jaunty Jalopies* (also prod., co-sc.; UK/Fr./It.) 1969; *Call of the Wild* (UK/Ger./It./Fr./Sp.) 1972; *Paper Tiger* 1975; *The Fifth Musketeer/Behind the Iron Mask* 1977; *Cheaper to Keep Her* 1980; *The Pirate Movie* 1982; *The New Adventures of Pippi Longstocking* (also sc. co-prod.) 1988.

Annaud, Jean-Jacques. French director. Born on Oct. 1, 1943, in Draveil, France. A graduate of IDHEC, the Paris film school, he began his career as a director of educational films for the French army. He later turned out hundreds of TV commercials before making an auspicious debut as a feature director. His first film, *Black and White in Color,* shot in the Ivory Coast, won the Academy Award as best foreign film for 1977. His third film, *Quest for Fire,* an unusual portrait of humanity's Stone Age ancestors, was honored with French César Awards for best film and best director. He won another César, best foreign film, in 1986, for *The Name of the Rose,* and a third, for best director, in 1989, for *The Bear.* Also in that year he was honored with the French Academy's Cinema Prize for his cummulative work. Despite the honors, and his growing reputation as an original filmmaker, his output has been remarkably sparse.

FILMS: *La Victoire En Chantant/Noirs Et Blancs En Couleurs/Black And White In Color* (also sc.) (Ivory Coast/Fr.) 1977; *Je suis timide, mais je me soigne/Too Shy to Try* (sc. only) 1978; *Coup de Téte/Hothead* 1979; *La Guerre du Feu/Quest for Fire* (Fr./Can.) 1982; *The Name of the Rose* (It./Fr./W. Ger.) 1986; *L'Ours/The Bear* (also co-sc.) 1988; *The Lover* (dir., sc.) 1992; *Wings of Courage* (prod., sc.) 1995; *7 Years in Tibet* 1997.

Annekov, Georges. Costume designer. Born on June 1, 1901, in Petropavlovsk, Russia. Active in Soviet theater 1924, when he went to Germany, then to France. He created the costumes for many important French films. He also wrote two books, *En habillant les Vedettes* (*Dressing the Stars*) and *Max Ophüls,* the latter an account of his long association with that noted director, with whose work his own career is closely associated.

FILMS INCLUDE: In Germany—*Faust* 1926. In France—*Les Nuits Moscovites/Moscow Nights* 1935; *Mayerling* 1936; *Mademoiselle Docteur* 1937; *L'Eternel Retour/The Eternal Return* 1943; *La Symphonie pastorale* 1946; *La Chartreuse de Parme* (Fr./It.) 1948; *La Ronde* 1950; *Le Plaisir* 1952; *Madame de. . . /The Earrings of Madame De* 1953; *Lola Montès* 1955; *Montparnasse 19/Modigliani of Montparnasse* 1958.

Annis, Francesca. Actress. Born on May 14, 1944, in London. Trained for ballet, she switched to drama as a child. Played juvenile leads, then leads and supporting roles in British plays, TV, and films. Voluptuously built, she became the screen's first nude Lady Macbeth in Roman Polanski's 1971 movie version of the Shakespeare play.

FILMS INCLUDE: *The Cat Gang* 1958; *No Kidding/Beware of Children 1960; Cleopatra* (US/UK) 1963; *The Eyes of Annie Jones* (US/UK), *Flipper's New Adventure* (US), *Saturday Night Out* 1964; *Murder Most Foul, The Pleasure Girls* 1965; *Run with the Wind* 1966; *The Sky Pirate* (US), *The Walking Stick* 1970; *Macbeth* (as Lady Macbeth) 1971; *Penny Gold* 1973; *Stronger Than the Sun* 1980; *Krull* 1983; *Dune* 1984; *Under the Cherry Moon* 1986.

Ann-Margret. Actress, singer, dancer. Born Ann-Margaret Olsson, on Apr. 28, 1941, in Valsjobyn, Sweden. Brought to the US at five and raised in various Illinois towns, she first enjoyed the spotlight at 16, on 'Ted Mack's Amateur Hour' on TV. She later sang with the band of Northwestern University, which she attended for one year, then joined a combo and appeared in various night spots. She made her screen debut as Bette Davis's daughter in Capra's *Pocketful of Miracles* (1961). After a zestful performance in *Bye-Bye Birdie* (1963) she became popular with young audiences as a song-and-dance entertainer and for years was typecast in films as a teen-market sex kitten, a sort of female counterpart of Elvis Presley. In 1971, however, she surprised most critics and moviegoers with a sensitive and touching dramatic performance in Mike Nichols's *Carnal Knowledge,* and the film proved a turning point in her career. She was nominated for Oscars for her performances in that film and in *Tommy* (1975). Concurrent with her work in films, she has led a highly successful career as a star of TV specials and top Las Vegas nightclubs. Her career and very life were jeopardized in 1972 when she was accidentally thrown 22 feet from a platform during a performance in Lake Tahoe, but she recovered and resumed working within a year. She received critical kudos for her portrayal of Blanche in the TV-movie remake of *A Streetcar Named Desire* (1984). She authored *Exercises for the Tired Businessman* and, in 1994, *Ann-Margret: My Story*. She has been married since 1967 to TV actor Roger Smith, who is also her personal manager.

FILMS: *Pocketful of Miracles* 1961; *State Fair* 1962; *Bye-Bye Birdie* 1963; *Viva Las Vegas, Kitten with a Whip, The Pleasure Seekers* 1964; *Bus Riley's Back in Town, Once a Thief,*

The Cincinnati Kid 1965; *Made in Paris, Stagecoach, The Swinger, Murderers' Row* 1966; *Criminal Affair* (It.), *Il Tigre/The Tiger and the Pussycat* (It./US), *Il Profeta/The Prophet/Mr. Kinky* (It.) 1967; *Sette Uomini e un Cervello* (It./Arg.) 1968; *Rebus* (It./Sp./Monaco); *C.C. and Company, R.P.M.* 1970; *Carnal Knowledge* 1971; *The Train Robbers, Un Homme est Mort/The Outside Man* (Fr.) 1973; *Tommy* (UK) 1975; *Folies bourgeoises/The Twist* (Fr.) 1976; *Joseph Andrews* (UK), *The Last Remake of Beau Geste* 1977; *The Cheap Detective, Magic* 1978; *The Villain* 1979; *Middle Age Crazy* 1980; *The Return of the Soldier* (UK), *I Ought to Be in Pictures, Lookin' to Get Out* 1982; *Twice in a Lifetime* 1985; *52 Pick-Up* 1986; *A Tiger's Tale, A New Life* 1988; *Newsies* 1992; *Grumpy Old Men* 1993; *Grumpier Old Men* 1995.

Anouilh, Jean. Playwright, screenwriter, director. *b.* June 23, 1910, Bordeaux, France. *d.* 1987. Educated in law. Worked in advertising before entering the theater as an administrator. Since 1932 he wrote many noted plays, including 'L'Hermine' (his first), 'Antigone,' 'Medea,' 'The Waltz of the Toreadors' (filmed), and 'Becket' (filmed). His association with the cinema started during his advertising days when he worked on a number of commercials. Since 1936 he collaborated on the screenplays of several films and directed two. His daughter, Catherine Anouilh, is a stage and screen actress.

FILMS INCLUDE: As screenwriter, alone or in collaboration—*Les Dégourdis de la Onzième* 1936; *Vous n'avez rien à déclarer* 1937; *Cavalcade d'Amour, Les Otages* 1939; *Monsieur Vincent* 1947; *Anna Karenina* (UK) 1948; *Pattes blanches* 1949; *Caroline Chérie* 1951; *Le Chevalier de la Nuit* 1953; *La Mort de Belle/The Passion of Slow Fire* 1961; *La Ronde/Circle of Love* 1964. As director (complete)—*Le Voyageur sans Bagages* (also co-sc., from own play) 1944; *Deux Sous de Violettes* 1951.

Anschutz, Ottomar. German photographer, cinema pioneer. *b.* May 16, 1846, Leszno, Poland. *d.* 1907. Improving on the experiments of MUYBRIDGE, he developed, from 1882 on, various systems showing serial movement. His Tachyscope (1887) was an improved version of the ZOETROPE, with a series of pictures mounted on a large revolving disc. He next developed the Electrotachyscope (1889), a device for viewing a succession of photographs through illumination, approximating the effect of projection.

Ansco. An American film-manufacturing company established in 1890. Around 1896 it became active in the sale of projection equipment. It was eventually absorbed by the General Aniline and Film Company (GAF). Anscolor, no longer produced, was an integral tripack color-film process in use from 1941. Anscochrome, a reversal color-film process, is widely used in the production of 16 mm and 35 mm motion pictures.

Anspach, Susan. Actress Born on Nov. 23, 1939, in New York City. *ed.* Catholic U. of America. Slim, attractive leading lady of Hollywood films of the 70s following appearances in several off-Broadway plays. Often cast in offbeat roles, she has appeared in smaller films since, including the well-received comedy *Montenegro* (1981).

FILMS: *The Landlord, Five Easy Pieces* 1970; *Play It Again Sam* 1972; *Blume in Love* 1973; *Nashville* 1975; *The Big Fix* 1978; *Running* 1979; *Gas* (Can.), *Montenegro* (Swed./UK), *The Devil and Max Devlin* 1981; *Misunderstood* 1984; *Blue Monkey* 1987; *The Legend of Wolf Lodge/Into the Fire* (Can.) 1988; *Blood Red* 1989; *Back to Back, The Rutanga Tapes, Killer Instinct* 1990.

Anspaugh, David. Director. Born on Sept. 24, 1946, in Decatur, Ind. *ed.* Indiana U.; USC. A former school teacher, he began his directing career in TV, turning out many episodes for such TV series as 'Hill Street Blues' (Emmy Award), 'St. Elsewhere,' and 'Miami Vice.' He graduated to the big screen in the mid-80s.

FILMS: *Hoosiers* 1986; *Fresh Horses* 1988; *Hard Boiled* 1990; *Rudy* 1993; *Moonlight and Valentino* 1995.

Anstey, Edgar. Documentary producer-director, film critic. *b.* Harold Macfarlane Anstey, Feb. 16, 1907, Watford, England. *d.* 1987. One of the young filmmakers organized by John GRIERSON to form the British documentary movement in 1929. He was with the Empire Marketing Board Film Unit (1930–34), then organized the Shell Film Unit. In 1935 he became production director of "The March of Time" in London, then foreign editor of "The March of Time" in New York. During the war he produced many documentary films for the British government, then organized British Transport Films (1949) and became chairman of the British Film Academy (1956), president of the International Scientific Film Association (1959–62), governor of the British Film Institute (1964), and chairman of the Society of Film and Television Arts (1967). He was film critic for *The Spectator* (1941–46) and for the BBC (1946–49). Author: *The Development of Film Technique in Britain* (1948).

FILMS (as director): *Uncharted Waters* 1933; *Eskimo Village, Granton Trawler* 1934; *Housing Problems* (co-dir. with Arthur Elton) 1935; *Enough to Eat/Nutrition/Dinner Hour* 1936.

answer print. The first combined sound and picture print that is sent by the lab to a film producer for approval. Also known as "approval print" or "first-trial print," it is screened for close examination of light grading, color balance, fades, dissolves, and other printing standards. The lab makes any corrections required by the producer, and often several answer prints are made before the final approval is given. When the quality is accepted, the answer print then serves as the standard by which the subsequent release prints are prepared. See also RELEASE PRINT.

Antheil, George. Composer. *b.* June 8, 1900, Trenton, N.J. *d.* 1959. He began piano lessons at age six and later studied composition under Ernest Bloch. After a successful tour of Europe as a concert pianist in the early 20s he took up residence in Paris, turned to composing, and shocked contemporary audiences with his use of jazz rhythms and mechanical devices in symphonic music. His most famous work, *Ballet mécanique* (1924), an accompaniment to the experimental Fernand LÉGER film of that name, is a score that calls for such unorthodox instruments as mechanical pianos, airplane propellers, and electric bells. His later work was more traditional in orchestration and style. Returning to the US in the early 30s, he began composing for Hollywood films in 1935 while continuing his work for the concert hall.

FILMS INCLUDE: *Ballet Mécanique* 1924; *Once in a Blue Moon, The Scoundrel* 1935; *The Plainsman, Make Way for Tomorrow* 1937; *The Buccaneer* 1938; *Union Pacific* 1939; *Angels over Broadway* 1940; *Specter of the Rose* 1946; *Knock on Any Door, We Were Strangers* 1949; *In a Lonely Place, House by the River* 1950; *The Sniper* 1952; *The Juggler* 1953; *Not as a Stranger* 1955; *The Pride and the Passion* 1957.

Anthony, Joseph. Director, screenwriter, actor, dancer. *b.* Joseph Deuster, May 24, 1912, Milwaukee. *d.* 1993. *ed.* U. of Wisconsin; Pasadena Playhouse; Daykarhanova Drama School. A versatile stage and screen artist, he began collaborating on Hollywood film scripts in the mid-30s while pursuing a career as a stage actor. He made his Broadway acting debut in 1937, and in the early 40s he was Agnes De Mille's dancing partner in concerts and a film actor as well as a set designer. In 1948 he began a long and distinguished career as a Broadway director, his output highlighted by such productions as 'The Rainmaker,' 'The

Most Happy Fella,' 'The Best Man,' 'Under the Yum Yum Tree,' 'Rhinoceros,' 'Mary Mary,' and '110 in the Shade.' Meanwhile he continued acting on stage and TV. He made his first stab at directing films in 1956. In addition to a handful of films, he also directed the TV series 'Brenner.' He was author of the play 'A Ship Comes In' (1934).

FILMS INCLUDE: As screenwriter—*Crime and Punishment, One Way Ticket* 1935; *Lady of Secrets, And So They Were Married, Meet Nero Wolfe* 1936; *The Spellbinder* (story only) 1939. As actor—*Shadow of the Thin Man* 1941; *Joe Smith American* 1942. As director (complete)—*The Rainmaker* 1956; *The Matchmaker* 1958; *Career* 1959; *All in a Night's Work* 1961; *La Città Prigioniera/Conquered City/Captive City* (It.) 1962; *Tomorrow* 1972.

Antonelli, Laura. Actress. Born 1948 (?), in Pola, Italy (now Pula, Croatia). Delicately sensual leading lady of Italian films and European co-productions. She became known in the 70s for appearing in sex farces, but also worked with such respected directors as Claude CHABROL and Luchino VISCONTI. She won a David di Donatello Award as best supporting actress for her performance in Ettore SCOLA's *Passione d'Amore* (1981).

FILMS INCLUDE: *Le Spie Vengono Del Semifredo/I Due Mafiosi Dell'fbi/Dr. Goldfoot and the Girl Bombs* 1966; *La Rivoluzione sessuale* 1968; *Sledge/A Man Called Sledge* 1970; *Sans Mobile apparent/Without Apparent Motive* 1971; *Malizia/Malicious* 1973; *Mio Dio Come sona caduta in Basso!/Till Marriage Do Us Part* 1974; *L'Innocente/The Innocent, Divina Creatura/The Divine Nymph* 1976; *Mogliamante/Wifemistress* 1977; *Passione d'Amore/Passion of Love* 1981; *Tranches de Vie* (Fr.), *Grandi Magazzini, La Gabbia* 1985; *La Venexiana* 1986; *Rimini Rimini* 1987; *Roba da Ricchi* 1987; *L'Avaro* 1990.

Antonioni, Michelangelo. Director. Born on Sept. 29, 1912, in Ferrara, Italy. *ed.* U. of Bologna (business and economics). After experimenting with 16 mm films, writing film criticism for a local newspaper, and working for a bank, he went to Rome in 1939 to pursue cinema seriously. There he contributed articles to *Cinema,* the official film magazine of the Fascist party. In 1940 he briefly attended the Centro Sperimentale di Cinematografia, the famous Italian film school.

He made his first real contact with film production at 30, collaborating on the scripts of ROSSELLINI's *Una Pilota Ritorna* and Fulchignoni's *I Due Foscari* (both 1942), also working as assistant director on the latter film. That same year he went to France to assist Marcel Carné as the Italian representative of the French-Italian co-production *Les Visiteurs du Soir.* He began directing his first film, *Gente del Po,* a short documentary about Po River fishermen, in 1943 but could not complete it until 1947.

Antonioni then collaborated on the screenplay of De Santis's *Caccia Tragica* (1947). During the next three years he directed six short documentaries. In 1950, at 38, he finally directed his first feature film, *Cronaca di un Amore/Story of a Love Affair,* largely unnoticed, though it contained many elements that would crystallize into his highly individualistic and acclaimed style. During the next ten formative years, he directed four films—*I Vinti/The Vanquished, La Signora senza Camelie/Camille Without Camelias, Le Amiche/The Girl Friends,* and *Il Grido/The Outcry*—and also collaborated on the script of Fellini's *The White Sheik* (1952) and directed the "Tentato Suicidio" episode for the film *Amore in Città/Love in the City.* In 1960 he scored his first international triumph, *L'Avventura,* which marked the coming to maturity of his unique aesthetic and of his theme and camera style. The dominant theme of *L'Avventura,* of the next two units in Antonioni's so-called trilogy (*La Notte/The Night* and *Eclisse/Eclipse*), and of the subsequent *Deserto Rosso/The Red Desert* (1964), is the emotional barrenness of modern man—his futile search to assert himself in a technological world and his frustrating inability to communicate with others. Long, lingering shots follow his characters until their inner selves are revealed. By their leisurely immobility the shots suggest the overbearing pressure that time exerts upon human emotions. The surrounding physical world is also used to convey a state of mind and to express the strains of alienation and psychological agony. Antonioni's films are almost plotless, their narrative vagueness almost bordering on mystery. Interest centers on the female, with the male functioning as catalyst.

L'Avventura also marks the first appearance of Monica VITTI as an Antonioni antiheroine. She helped extend the appeal of his films to a wider audience and also seems to have stimulated the element of sensuality that appeared in the director's later films.

Antonioni's skill in manipulating time and space to express the metaphysical world of his characters found a new outlet with his first color film, *Red Desert,* in which he even had natural surroundings painted to serve the film's mood and psychological scheme. His next film, *Blow-Up* (1966), marked a considerable break with the past: it was set in England, used English dialogue, focused on a male protagonist, and proceeded at a brisk, jittery pace. But the element of mystery and ambiguity was still there, and relationships between characters were still tentative and enigmatic.

Antonioni's next film, *Zabriskie Point* (1970), was set in the American West. Then, after a long absence, Antonioni returned to his style of the 60s and to his preoccupation with the frustration and malaise of modern society with the international co-production *Professione: Reporter/The Passenger* (1975). Following a setback with *The Oberwald Mystery,* an undistinguished attempt, marred by experimentation with video techniques, to resurrect Cocteau's *The Eagle Has Two Heads,* Antonioni returned to more familiar ground with *Identification of a Woman* (1982). But his reputation rests mainly on his films of the early 60s, truly original works by one of the most remarkable creative artists of the postwar cinema.

FILMS: Documentary shorts—*Gente del Po* (also sc.) 1943–47; *N.U./Nettezza Urbana* (also sc.) 1948; *Superstizione* (also sc.), *L/Amorosa Menzogna* (also sc.) 1949; *Sette Canne un Vestito* (also sc.), *La Villa dei Mostri* (also sc.), *La Funivia del Faloria* (also sc.) 1950. Features—*Cronaca di un Amore/Story of a Love Affair* (also story, co-sc.) 1950; *I Vinti/The Vanquished* (also co-story, co-sc.), *La Signora senza Camelie/Camille Without Camelias* (also story, co-sc.), *L'Amore in Cittá/Love in the City* ("Tentato Suicidio" episode; also co-sc.) 1953; *Le Amiche/The Girl Friends* (also co-sc.) 1955; *Il Grido/The Outcry* (also story, co-sc.) 1957; *L'Avventura* (also story, co-sc.) 1960; *La Notte/The Night* (also story, co-sc.) 1961; *L'Eclisse/Eclipse* (also co-story, co-sc.) 1962; *Deserto Rosso/Red Desert* (also co-story, co-sc.) 1964; *I Tre Volti* ("Prefazione" episode) 1965; *Blow-Up* (also story, co-sc.; UK/It.) 1966; *Zabriskie Point* (also story, co-sc.; US) 1970; *Chung Kuo* (full-length doc.) 1972; *Professione: Reporter/The Passenger* (also co-sc.) 1975; *Il Mistero di Oberwald/The Oberwald Mystery* (also co-sc.) 1979; *Identificazione di una Donna/Identification of a Woman* (also co-sc.) 1982; *The Crew* 1990; *Volcanoes and Carnival* 1992; *Beyond the Clouds* (co-dir., co-sc.) 1996.

Anwar, Gabrielle. Actress. *b.* 1970, Leleham, England. This slim, engaging actress made her debut at the age of 15 in the BBC television series 'Hideaway.' Her feature film career began with a small role in the US/Yugoslavian comedy *Manifesto* (1988) which lead to the lead role in Disney's *Wild Hearts Can't Be Broken* (1991). She is perhaps best remembered for dancing a tango opposite Al PACINO in *Scent of a Woman* (1992).

FILMS: *Manifesto* (US/Yugos.) 1988; *If Looks Could Kill, Wild Hearts Can't Be Broken* 1991; *Scent of a Woman* 1992; *For Love or Money, The Three Musketeers* 1993; *Body Snatchers* 1994; *Things to Do in Denver When You're Dead* 1995; *Nevada* 1997.

Aoki, Tsuru. See HAYAKAWA, Sessue.

aperture. 1. The opening in a lens, usually formed by an adjustable iris, which controls the amount of light passing to and exposing the film. The aperture in the printing apparatus controls the passage of light to exposed film. 2. The opening in a camera or a projector that defines the area of each frame exposed or projected and at which each frame stops during exposure or projection.

Apfel, Oscar C. Director, actor. *b.* 1880(?), Cleveland. *d.* 1938. A veteran stage and opera producer-director, he entered the American film industry in 1911 as a director for Edison, Reliance, Selig, and other companies. He gained prominence in 1914–15, when he directed many prestigious feature-length productions for Lasky-Paramount, at times collaborating with C. B. DE MILLE. In 1916 he joined Fox and later worked for various small studios. His career declined in the 20s, when he turned out mainly routine melodramas, often for poverty-row producers. He directed his last film in 1927 and in the following year began a new Hollywood career as an actor, typically playing distinguished character roles.

FILMS INCLUDE: As director—*Aida* (co-dir. with J. Searle Dawley) 1911; *The Passer-By* 1912; *The Bells, Her Rosary, The Fight for Right* 1913; *The Squaw Man* (co-dir., co-prod., co-sc. with Cecil B. De Mille), *Brewster's Millions, The Call of the North* (co-dir. with De Mille), *The Man on the Box, The Master Mind, The Only Son, The Last Volunteer, Ready Money, Snobs, The Wild Olive, The Circus Man, The Ghost Breaker* 1914; *After Five, Kilmeny, The Rug Maker's Daughter, Peer Gynt* (also sc.), *The Broken Law* (also co-sc.), *The Little Gypsy, Cameo Kirby, The Soldier's Oath* 1915; *Man of Sorrow* (also sc.), *The Battle of Hearts* (also sc.), *The Man From Bitter Roots* (also sc.), *The End of the Trail* (also sc.), *Fighting Blood* (also sc.), *The Fires of Conscience* 1916; *The Hidden Children, The Price of Her Soul, A Man's Man* 1917; *The Turn of the Card, The Interloper, Tinsel, Merely Players, To Him That Hath, The Grouch* 1918; *Auction of Souls* (general release in 1922), *The Rough Neck, Phil-for-Short, Mandarin's Gold, Crook of Dreams, The Little Intruder, Bringing Up Betty, The Amateur Widow, The Oakdale Affair* (also prod.), *Me and Captain Kidd, The Steel King* (also prod.) 1919; *Ten Nights in a Bar Room* 1921; *The Man Who Paid, The Wolf's Fangs* (also prod.) 1922; *A Man's Man* (remake), *The Social Code, In Search of a Thrill* 1923; *The Heart of a Bandit, Trail of the Law* 1924; *Sporting Chance, The Thoroughbred, Borrowed Finery* 1925; *Midnight Limited, Somebody's Mother* (also sc.), *Perils of the Coast Guard, The Call of the Klondike, The Last Alarm, Race Wild* 1926; *Cheaters, When Seconds Count, Code of the Cow Country* 1927. As actor—*The Heart of Broadway, Romance of the Underworld* 1928; *True Heaven, Halfway to Heaven* 1929; *The Texan, Abraham Lincoln* (as Secretary of War Edwin Stanton), *The Spoilers, The Virtuous Sin, The Right to Love* 1930; *Inspiration, The Maltese Falcon, Huckleberry Finn, Five Star Final* 1931; *The Heart of New York, Shopworn, The World and the Flesh, I Am a Fugitive From a Chain Gang* 1932; *The Bowery, The World Changes, Only Yesterday* 1933; *The House of Rothschild* 1934; *Man on the Flying Trapeze* 1935; *And Sudden Death* 1936; *The Soldier and the Lady, History Is Made at Night, The Toast of New York* 1937.

"A" picture. A designation for a comparatively high-budget film or one that is expected to be a major audience attraction. It is usually exhibited at first-run theaters or presented as the main feature of a double bill. See also "B" PICTURE.

apple boxes. Boxes of varying sizes used on a set to elevate people or objects.

Apted, Michael. Director. Born on Feb. 10, 1941, in Aylesbury, England. *ed.* Cambridge (history and law). He entered British TV in 1963 and directed many series, teleplays, and documentaries. He assisted director Paul Almond on the documentary short *7 Up* (1963), a presentation of the lives and aspirations of several seven-year-old children; Apted went on to check on these individuals at ages 14, 21, 28, and 35, providing a unique record of growing up within the British class system. He turned to feature films in the early 70s, beginning with *Triple Echo*. Later also working in the US, he achieved his first big critical and commercial success with *Coal Miner's Daughter* (1980), a screen biography of country singer Loretta Lynn. In 1988 he scored another hit with *Gorillas in the Mist,* the story of ape zealot Dian Fossey.

FILMS: *Triple Echo* 1973; *Stardust* 1974; *The Squeeze* 1977; *Stronger Than the Sun* (orig. for TV) 1978; *Agatha* 1979; *Coal Miner's Daughter* 1980; *Continental Divide* 1981; *Kipperbang* 1982; *Gorky Park* 1983; *The River Rat* (exec. prod. only), *28 Up* (doc.; also co-prod.), *Bring on the Night* (doc.), *Spies Like Us* (act. only) 1985; *Critical Condition* 1987; *Gorillas in the Mist* 1988; *The Long Way Home* 1989; *Class Action* 1990; *35 Up* 1991; *Thunderheart, Incident at Oglala* (doc.), *Bram Stoker's Dracula* (co-exec. prod. only) 1992; *Blink, Moving the Mountain, Nell* 1994; *Extreme Measures* 1996.

aquarium. A colloquial term for the booth in which sound mixing is performed.

Arab film. See EGYPT.

Aragon, Manuel Gutierrez. Director. Born in Spain. Aragon's career ascended in the 70s with the liberalization of Spanish culture following the death of Generalissimo Franco. His forte is political commentary mixed with melodrama. *La Mitad Del Cielo* (1986), presently the only one of his films with an American distributor, is a trenchant piece of social criticism about class relations as expressed in a family's generational struggles.

FILMS INCLUDE: *Hable Mudita* 1973; *Camada Negra, Sonambulos* 1977; *El Corazon Del Bosque* 1978; *Demonios en el Jardin* 1982; *Feroz* 1983; *La Noche Mas Hermosa* 1984; *La Mitad Del Cielo/Half of Heaven* 1986; *Malaventura/Misadventure* 1988.

Arau, Alfonso. Mexican director and actor. Independent Mexican director who frequently produces, writes, edits, and acts in his films. His films show great range in both style and content, from the satiric social comment on illegal immigrants in the United States in *Wetback Power* (1980) to the sensual magical realism of *Like Water for Chocolate* (1992), which he produced and directed from a screenplay by his wife Laura Esquivel, based on her novel. The latter film was an art-house hit that brought him international recognition as a filmmaker, though he was already known as an actor in the US for his performances in adventure films such as *The Wild Bunch.*

FILMS INCLUDE: As actor (US)—*The Wild Bunch* 1969; *Scandalous John* 1971; *Posse* 1975; *Used Cars* 1980; *Romancing the Stone* 1984; *Three Amigos!* 1986; *Walker* 1987. As director (Mex.)—*The Barefoot Eagle* 1967; *Calzonzin Inspector* 1974; *Mojada Power/Wetback Power* 1980; *Chido*

Guan 1984; *Como Agua Para Chocolate/Like Water for Chocolate* (Mex.) 1992; *A Walk in the Clouds* 1995.

Arbuckle, Roscoe "Fatty." Comic actor, director, screenwriter. *b.* Roscoe Conkling Arbuckle, Mar. 24, 1887, Smith Center, Kans. *d.* 1933. Worked as a plumber's assistant before becoming a performer in carnivals and vaudeville. Baby-faced and amazingly agile for his heavy frame, he was hired in 1908 by the Selig Polyscope Company as an extra and appeared in many one-reel comedy films. In 1913 he joined Mack SENNETT's Keystone Cops and soon rose to stardom in a series of short comedies with such partners as Mabel Normand, Ford Sterling, Chester Conklin, and Charlie Chaplin. From 1916 he wrote and directed many of his own films, as well as some of those of other comics, and within a few years became one of Hollywood's most popular personalities. In 1917 he set up his own production company and gave Buster KEATON his career start.

In 1921, while Arbuckle was at the peak of success, his career was ruined by scandal. During a wild drinking party he threw at a San Francisco hotel, a starlet by the name of Virginia Rappe (the fiancée of Henry "Pathé" LEHRMAN, who directed some of Arbuckle's films) was seized by severe convulsions, allegedly after having been sexually assaulted by the 320-pound actor. A few days later she died of a ruptured bladder, and Arbuckle was charged with manslaughter. The case twice ended in a hung jury, and in a third trial he was acquitted. The press played up the sensational case, and much indignation was aroused in the public, who saw Hollywood as a modern Sodom. A frightened industry hurriedly set up the Hays Office to enforce self-regulation and censorship. Public opinion forced Arbuckle's retirement from the screen, and his films were banned and withdrawn from circulation. However, with the help of friends, he quietly returned to films as a director, using the pseudonym of William B. Goodrich and directing, among others, a Marion Davies vehicle and Eddie Cantor's first two films. But wanting to perform, he went to Europe on an abortive acting tour in 1932, only to return to the US disillusioned and brokenhearted. The following year he died in New York. A weak attempt at re-creating the Arbuckle scandal was made in the 1975 film *The Wild Party.* He was married to actress Minta DURFEE. They divorced in 1925.

FILMS INCLUDE: As actor—*The Sanitarium/The Clinic* 1910; *Help! Help! Hydrophobia! The Waiters' Picnic, A Bandit, For the Love of Mabel, Courage, Passions He Had Three, The Gangsters, The Noise from the Deep, Love and Courage, Mabel's New Hero, Mother's Boy, The Gypsy Queen, A Quiet Little Wedding, Fatty's Day Off, Fatty's Flirtation* 1913; *In the Clutches of the Gang, A Rural Demon, A Film Johnnie, Tango Tangles, His Favorite Pastime, A Suspended Ordeal, The Masquerader, The Rounders, The Knockout, The Sea Nymphs, Bathing Beauty* 1914; *Mabel and Fatty's Wash Day, The Little Teacher, Mabel and Fatty's Married Life* 1915; *The Round-Up, The Life of the Party* 1920; *Brewster's Millions, Gasoline Gus* 1921. As director-actor—*The Alarm* (co-dir. with Eddie Dillon), *The Sky Pirate* (co-dir. with Dillon), *Fatty and the Heiress* (co-dir. with Dillon), *Fatty's Gift* (co-dir. with Dillon), *A Brand New Hero* (co-dir. with Dillon), *Fatty's Debut* (co-dir. with Dillon), *Fatty Again, Leading Lizzie Astray* (co-dir. with Dillon), *Fatty's Jonah Day* (co-dir. with Dillon), *Fatty's Magic Pants* (co-dir. with Dillon), *Fatty's Wine Party* (co-dir. with Dillon) 1914; *Fatty and Minnie He-Haw* (co-dir. with Dillon), *Fatty's Faithful Fido* (co-dir. with Dillon), *That Little Band of Gold, When Love Took Wings, Fatty's New Role* (co-dir. with Dillon), *Fickle Fatty's Fall, Fatty and the Broadway Stars* (co-dir. with Dillon), *The Village Scandal* 1915; *Fatty and Mabel Adrift, He Did and He Didn't/Love and Lobsters, Bright Lights/The Lure of Broadway, His Wife's Mistake, The Other Man, The Waiter's Ball, His Alibi, A Cream Puff Romance/A Reckless Romeo* 1916; *The Butcher Boy, The Rough House, His Wedding Night, Oh Doctor! Fatty at Coney Island, A Country Hero* 1917; *Out West, The Bell Boy, Moonshine, Good Night Nurse, The Cook* 1918; *Love, A Desert Hero, Back Stage, The Hayseed* 1919; *The Garage* 1920. As director only (all but first film under pseudonym William Goodrich; all shorts unless noted otherwise)—*The Moonshiners* 1916; *The Movies, The Tourist, The Fighting Dude* 1925; *Cleaning Up, My Stars, Fool's Luck, His Private Life* 1926; *The Red Mill* (feature), *Special Delivery* (feature) 1927; *Won by a Neck, Up a Tree* 1930; *Smart Work, The Tamale Vendor, The Lure of Hollywood, Honeymoon Trio, Up Pops the Duke, The Back Page, Marriage Rows, Beach Pajamas* 1931; *Bridge Wives, It's a Cinch, Keep Laughing, Moonlight and Cactus, Niagara Falls, Gigolettes, Hollywood Luck, Anybody's Goat* 1932.

arc. A high-intensity lamp, usually operating on direct current, which produces light from the electronic flow between two electrodes. There are two main types: the carbon arc, in which the electrodes are made of carbon and require frequent adjustment, and the mercury and xenon arcs, in which the electrodes are contained in tubes filled with gas and require no adjustment. Carbon arcs are used in studios as well as in outdoor locations and are known for their capacity to simulate sunlight. Since their color temperature closely resembles that of daylight, they are often used as boosters for outdoor color shooting.

Arcand, Denys. Director. Born in 1941, in Deschambault, Quebec, Canada. A political and social activist from early youth, he constributed to the review *Parti Pris* before studying history at the University of Montreal. It was at the university that he directed his first film, the feature-length *Seul ou avec des autres* (1962), in collaboration with Denis Héroux and Stéphane Venne. In 1963, he joined the National Film Board for which he directed a number of documentary shorts, notably a trilogy about colonial Quebec. But his first full-length documentary, *On est au Coton* (1970), an exposé of the exploitation of textile workers, aroused a controversy that resulted in the shelving of the film until 1976. Moving on to fiction features in the 70s, Arcand gained respect for the quality of his work; but it wasn't until the late 80s that he made an international impact with *The Decline of the American Empire,* a witty, irreverent satire that won the International Critics Prize at Cannes in 1986. He made an even greater impression with *Jesus of Montreal,* an audacious, wickedly funny burlesque of contemporary life, for which he won the Jury Prize at Cannes in 1989.

FEATURE FILMS: *Seul Ou Avec D'autres* (co-dir.) 1962; *On est au Coton* (doc.) 1970; *Québec: Duplessis et aprés. . .* (doc.; also sc.), *La Maudite Galette* 1972; *Réjeanne Padovani* (also sc., ed.) 1973; *Gina* (also sc.) 1974; *Le Confort et l'Indifference* 1981; *Le Crime d'ovide plouffe* (also sc.) 1984; *Le Déclin de l'Empire Américain/The Decline of the American Empire* (also sc.) 1986; *Un Zoo la nuit/Night Zoo* (act. only) 1987; *Jésus de Montréal/Jesus of Montreal* (also sc., act.) (Can./Fr.) 1989; *Montréal Sextet* 1991; *Love and Human Remains* 1993; *Poverty and Other Delights* 1996.

Archainbaud, George. Director. *b.* May 7, 1890, Paris. *d.* 1959. With the European stage as actor and assistant stage manager before coming to Hollywood, where he began as assistant film director to Emile CHAUTARD in 1915. Within two years, he was directing on his own. His prolific output consists of films of all genres, but toward the end of his career his work was confined mostly to Westerns, including many HOPALONG CASSIDY films and Gene AUTRY vehicles. He also directed Western film series for TV.

FILMS INCLUDE: *As Man Made Her, Yankee Pluck, The Brand of Satan, The Iron Ring, A Maid Of Belgium, The*

Awakening 1917; *The Divine Sacrifice, The Trap, The Cross Bearer* 1918; *The Love Cheat, A Damsel in Distress* 1919; *What Women Want, The Wonderful Chance, Marooned Hearts, The Pleasure Seekers* 1920; *The Miracle of Manhattan, The Girl From Nowhere, Handcuffs or Kisses* 1921; *Evidence, Under Oath, One Week of Love* (also co-story) 1922; *Cordelia the Magnificent, The Common Law* (also co-story) 1923; *The Plunderer, The Mirage, For Sale, Single Wives, Christine of the Hungry Heart* 1924; *Enticement, What Fools Men, The Necessary Evil* 1925; *Men of Steel, Puppets, The Silent Lover* 1926; *Easy Pickings, Night Life* 1927; *The Tragedy of Youth, Ladies of the Night Club, Bachelor's Paradise, The Grain of Dust, George Washington Cohen* 1928; *The College Coquette, Broadway Scandals, The Broadway Hoofer* 1929; *Framed, Alias French Gertie, Shooting Straight, The Silver Horde* 1930; *The Lady Refuses, Three Who Loved* 1931; *Men of Chance, The Lost Squadron, State's Attorney, Thirteen Women, The Penguin Pool Murder* 1932; *The Big Brain, After Tonight* 1933; *Keep 'Em Rolling, Murder on the Blackboard* 1934; *Thunder in the Night* 1935; *My Marriage, The Return of Sophie Lang* 1936; *Hideaway Girl, Blonde Trouble, Thrill of a Lifetime* 1937; *Boy Trouble, Her Jungle Love, Campus Confessions, Thanks for the Memory* 1938; *Some Like It Hot, Night Work* 1939; *Untamed, Comin' Round the Mountain* 1940; *Hoppy Serves a Writ, The Kansan, Flying With Music* 1942; *The Woman of the Town* 1943; *Mystery Man, Alaska* 1944; *The Big Bonanza, Girls of the Big House* 1945; *The Devil's Playground, Fool's Gold, Unexpected Guest* 1946; *King of the Wild Horses, The Marauders* 1947; *False Paradise, The Dead Don't Dream, Silent Conflict* 1948; *Hunt the Man Down* 1950; *The Old West, Apache Country, Barbed Wire* 1952; *Winning of the West, On Top of Old Smoky, Last of the Pony Riders* 1953.

Archer, Anne. Actress. Born on Aug. 25, 1947, in Los Angeles. Striking brunette leading lady of American (and some British) films. In 1987 she received an Academy Award nomination in the supporting actress category as the beleaguered, ultimately triumphant wife in *Fatal Attraction.* Daughter of screen actor John ARCHER and actress Marjorie LORD. Married actor (and TV sports producer/director) Terry Jastrow.

FILMS: *The Honkers, Cancel My Reservation* 1972; *The All-American Boy* 1973; *Trackdown, Lifeguard* 1976; *Good Guys Wear Black, Paradise Alley* 1978; *Raise the Titanic!* (UK), *Hero at Large* 1980; *Green Ice* (UK) 1981; *Waltz Across Texas* (also co-story) 1982; *The Naked Face* (UK) 1984; *Too Scared to Scream* 1985; *The Check Is in the Mail* 1986; *Fatal Attraction* 1987; *Love at Large, Narrow Margin* 1990; *Eminent Domain* 1991; *Nails, Patriot Games* 1992; *Body of Evidence, Family Prayers, Short Cuts* 1993; *Clear and Present Danger, There Goes My Baby* 1994.

Archer, John. Actor. Born Ralph Bowman, on May 8, 1915, in Osceola, Nebr. *ed.* USC. Entered films in 1938 after winning a talent contest. He played leads in B pictures and supporting roles in A productions. He was credited under his real name in some of his early films. Divorced from actress Marjorie LORD, he is the father of Anne ARCHER.

FILMS INCLUDE: *Overland Stage Raiders* (as Ralph Bowman), *A Letter of Introduction* 1938; *Career* 1939; *Curtain Call* 1940; *Cheers for Miss Bishop* (as Ralph Bowman), *King of the Zombies* 1941; *Bowery at Midnight* 1942; *Hello Frisco Hello, Crash Dive, Guadalcanal Diary* 1943; *The Eve of St. Mark* 1944; *I'll Remember April* 1945; *The Lost Moment* 1947; *Colorado Territory, White Heat* 1949; *Destination Moon* 1950; *Sante Fe, My Favorite Spy* 1951; *The Big Trees, Rodeo* 1952; *The Stars Are Singing* 1953; *Emergency Hospital* 1956; *Affair in Reno, She Devil* 1957; *City of Fear* 1959; *Blue Hawaii* 1962; *Apache Rifles* 1964; *I Saw What You Did* 1965; *How to Frame a Figg* 1971.

archives, film. A film archive contains a variety of materials pertaining to motion pictures: cans of film, stills, scripts, documents, books, and periodicals on film subjects. Its principal function is to maintain a collection of important works for research, study, and exchange. The film archive faces many difficult problems: the perishability of film materials, especially of old prints having a flammable nitrate base; the high cost of prints; the limitations of storage space (an average film consists of ten reels); and, perhaps most important, the constant search for copies of precious classics lost through neglect and indifference.

The need for film archives was recognized early in the development of the cinema. In 1919 a small collection was started in Paris, but it was confined to newsreels and documentary films. It was not until 1935 that the first big step was taken with the establishment of the National Film Archive in London and the Museum of Modern Art film collection in New York. A year later the Cercle du Cinéma was launched in Paris by Henri LANGLOIS and Georges FRANJU. It was the forerunner of the now famous CINÉMATHÈQUE FRANÇAISE, which long possessed the largest film collection in the world. In 1938 these three archives joined with the newly formed Reichsfilmarchiv of Berlin and the film library of Moscow's School of Cinema (VGIK) in the formation of the International Federation of Film Archives, known by its French initials, FIAF, with headquarters in Paris.

Russia, represented by Gosfilmofond of Moscow, has accumulated vast archives (nearly 50,000 titles at last count), including many silent American movies not available in the US. Nearly 60 other countries, from Albania to Canada to India to Venezuela, also have national archives of titles, stills, and movie material.

In the US, the American Film Institute in Washington, D.C., has collected 24,000 film titles, housed at the Library of Congress or at other American archives. The Library of Congress has performed a vital service with the restoration of early American films from its paper print collection, prints originally filed with the library for copyright purposes. Other major American archives are those of the Museum of Modern Art, the George Eastman House (Rochester, N.Y.), the Pacific Film Archive (Berkeley, Cal.), and the Wisconsin Center for Film and Theater Research (Madison).

Ardant, Fanny. Actress. Born in 1949 in Monte Carlo. On stage following political-science studies, she played intense dramatic leads in many French films of the 80s. She has been a favorite of Truffaut, Lelouch, Resnais, and other leading French directors.

FILMS INCLUDE: *Les Chiens* 1979; *Les Uns et les Autres/The Ins and the Outs/Bolero, La Femme d'à Coté/The Woman Next Door* 1981; *La Vie est un Roman/Life Is a Bed of Roses; Vivement Dimanche!/Confidentially Yours, Benvenuta* 1983; *Un Amour de Swann/Swann in Love, L'Amour á Mort/Love Unto Death* 1984; *Les Enragés, L'Eté prochain/Next Summer* 1985; *Conseil de Famille/Family Business, Le Paltoquet, Mélo* 1986; *La Famiglia/The Family* (It./Fr.) 1987; *Paura e Amore/Fear and Love/Three Sisters* (It./Fr./W. Ger.), *Pleure pas my love* 1988; *Australia* 1989; *Afraid of the Dark, The Deserter's Wife* 1992; *Amok* 1993; *Col. Chabert* 1994; *Beyond the Clouds, Ridicule* 1996; *Pedale Douce* 1997.

Arden, Eve. Actress. *b.* Eunice Quedens, Apr. 20, 1912, Mill Valley, Calif. *d.* 1990. Caustic comedienne of the American stage, radio, TV, and films. She made her stage debut in stock at 16 and her first New York appearance in 'The Ziegfeld Follies' of 1934. Before starting a prolific screen career in 1937, she appeared in two isolated films as Eunice Quedens. In films she often played the warmhearted but acerbic friend of the heroine and enlivened many a production with her snappy barbs. At the height of her screen career in the 40s she averaged three films a year, but she is probably best known as the titular heroine, an English teacher, of the situation comedy series 'Our Miss Brooks' on radio (1948–56) and TV (1956–57), winning an Emmy Award for her work in the TV series. She later starred in the series 'The Eve Arden Show' (1957–58) and 'The Mothers-in-Law' (1967–69). She was nominated for an Oscar for best supporting actress for her performance in *Mildred Pierce* (1945). In 1975 she returned to film work after a decade-long absence. Divorced from literary agent Edward Bergen, she married actor Brooks West (ca. 1916–1984) in 1951. Autobiography: *Three Phases of Eve* (1985).

FILMS INCLUDE: As Eunice Quedens—*The Song of Love* 1929; *Dancing Lady* (bit) 1933; As Eve Arden—*Oh Doctor!, Stage Door* 1937; *Having Wonderful Time, Letter of Introduction* 1938; *Eternally Yours, At the Circus* 1939; *A Child Is Born, Slightly Honorable, No No Nanette, Comrade X* 1940; *Ziegfeld Girl, That Uncertain Feeling, Manpower, Whistling in the Dark* 1941; *Bedtime Story* 1942; *Let's Face It* 1943; *Cover Girl, The Doughgirls* 1944; *Pan-Americana, Mildred Pierce* 1945; *My Reputation, The Kid from Brooklyn, Night and Day* 1946; *Song of Scheherazade, The Unfaithful, The Voice of the Turtle* 1947; *One Touch of Venus* 1948; *My Dream Is Yours* 1949; *Tea for Two, Three Husbands* 1950; *Goodbye My Fancy 1951*; *We're Not Married* 1952; *The Lady Wants Mink* 1953; *Our Miss Brooks* (feature version of TV series) 1956; *Anatomy of a Murder* 1959; *The Dark at the Top of the Stairs* 1960; *Sergeant Deadhead* 1965; *The Strongest Man in the World* 1975; *Grease* 1978; *Under the Rainbow* 1981; *Pandemonium, Grease II* 1982.

Ardolino, Emile. Director. *b.* 1943, New York City. *d.* 1993. *ed.* Queens College. He started out as an actor with a touring company of 'The Fantasticks.' During the late 70s and early 80s he produced and directed the 'Dance in America' and 'Live From Lincoln Center' series for Public Television, winning an Emmy in 1979. Following a number of TV specials, he graduated to the big screen with an Oscar-winning feature-length documentary, *He Makes Me Feel Like Dancin'* (1983). He scored a commercial hit with his first fiction feature, *Dirty Dancing* (1987).

FILMS: *He Makes Me Feel Like Dancin'* (doc.; also prod.) 1983; *Dirty Dancing* 1987; *Chances Are* 1989; *Three Men and a Little Lady* 1990; *Sister Act* 1992; *The Nutcracker* 1993.

Ardrey, Robert. Screenwriter, playwright, novelist, writer on human behavior. *b.* Oct. 16, 1908, Chicago. *d.* 1980. He studied natural sciences at the University of Chicago and for two years lectured on anthropology. But he was drawn to drama and after some coaching by Thornton Wilder began writing plays, the first of which, 'Star Spangled,' was produced on Broadway in 1936. He wrote several other plays, including 'Thunder Rock,' and began writing screenplays for Hollywood films in the early 40s. He also wrote a couple of novels. But his best-known work is a series of nonfiction books on behavioral evolution which enjoyed mass popularity: *African Genesis* (1961), *The Territorial Imperative* (1966), and *The Social Contract* (1970).

FILMS INCLUDE: *They Knew What They Wanted* 1940; *A Lady Takes a Chance* 1943; *Thunder Rock* (play basis only; UK) 1944; *The Green Years* 1946; *Song of Love* 1947; *The Three Musketeers* 1948; *The Secret Garden, Madame Bovary* 1949; *Quentin Durward* 1955; *The Power and the Prize* 1956; *The Wonderful Country* 1959; *The Four Horsemen of the Apocalypse* 1962; *Khartoum* (UK) 1966.

Argentina. Feature film production in this Latin American country began in 1908 with *El Fusilamento de Dorrego/The Execution of Dorrego,* a historical epic with famous stage personalities, by the Italian immigrant Mario GALLO. But it was not until 1915, with the production of *Nobleza Gaucha,* that Argentine films became commercially successful. Between 1915 and 1927 the industry saw the establishment of several studios, and there was a steady improvement in technical proficiency. The dominant director of this era was José A. Ferreyra, whose many films, such as *El Tango de la Muerte, El Gaucho,* and *Viejita,* were extremely popular locally. Film production during the silent era reached an annual output of about a dozen features.

Sound infused new life into Argentine films because the Spanish-speaking world was eager for entertainment that spoke its language. Following the great success of Ferreyra's *Muñequitas Porteñas* (1931), the industry enjoyed continuous prosperity through the 30s, producing scores of comedies and melodramas for an ever-widening market. Commercial success encouraged producers to attempt more ambitious films, resulting in the appearance of more sophisticated directors, such as Luis Saslawsky, Mario Soffici, and Manuel Romero. During WW II, Mexico gained dominance in film production for the Spanish-speaking world. Under Perón's dictatorship the regime tried to expand the Argentine film industry but without much success; even though production reached 50 films annually, government policies did not favor artistic individuality or pure nonpropaganda entertainment. With few exceptions, such as Hugo DEL CARRIL's *Las Aguas Bajan Turbias* (1952), production was mediocre. The reputation of Argentine films in the early 60s rested chiefly on the talents of Leopoldo TORRE NILSSON, a director who rose to international prominence with such films as *The House of the Angel* (1957), *La Caida* (1959), *Fin de Fiesta/The Blood Feast/The Party Is Over* (1960), *Summerskin* (1961), and *The Eavesdroppers* (1964). Since the 70s, despite intensified political repressions, strict censorship, and one of the world's worst inflation spirals, young Argentine filmmakers have surprised the international film community again and again with a number of high-quality productions.

Argento, Dario. Director, screenwriter. Born in 1943, in Rome. The son of producer Salvatore Argento, he entered Italian films as a screenwriter, collaborating on several action adventures, including the internationally popular *C'era una Volta il West/Once Upon a Time in the West* (1968). He turned director in the late 60s and over the years has established a reputation as Italy's stylish master of cheap blood and gore.

FILMS INCLUDE (as director): *L'Uccello dalle Piume di Cristallo/The Bird With the Crystal Plumage* (also story, sc.) 1970; *Il Gatto a Nove Code/The Cat o'Nine Tails* (also co-story, sc.), *Quattro Mosche di Velluto Grigio/Four Flies on Grey Velvet* (also co-story, sc.) 1971; *Le Cinque Giornate* (also sc.) 1973: *Profondo Rosso/Deep Red* (also co-story) 1976; *Suspiria* (also sc., mus.) 1977; *Dawn of the Dead* (mus. only), *Inferno* (also sc.) 1979; *Tenebrae/Unsane* (also co-sc.) 1982; *Phenomena/Creepers* (also co-sc.) 1985; *Demoni/Demons* (prod., co-sc. only) 1985; *Demoni 2/Demons 2* (prod., co-sc. only), *Opera* (also co-sc.) 1987; *Due Occhi diabolici/Two Evil Eyes* ("The Black Cat" episode; also co-prod., co-sc.) 1990; *The Sect* (prod., sc.) 1991; *Innocent Blood* (act. only) 1992; *Trauma* (co-sc.) (It./US) 1993.

Arkin, Alan. Actor, director. Born on Mar. 26, 1934, in New York City. *ed.* Los Angeles City Coll. Started as a member of a folk-singing group, the Tarriers. He first attracted attention as a member of The Second City satirical group out of Chicago. An overnight critical sensation in his first Broadway appearance, in 'Enter Laughing' (Tony Award, 1963), he later appeared in

'Luv' and directed a number of plays, including the off-Broadway production of 'Little Murders' as well as the subsequent screen version (1971). Basically a comedian, at his best playing bumbling, loud comic types, he played a sensitive dramatic lead as a deaf-mute in *The Heart Is a Lonely Hunter* (1968). He was nominated for a best actor Oscar for this film, as well as for his screen-debut role in *The Russians Are Coming, the Russians Are Coming* (1966). He authored a children's book, *Tony's Hard Work Day* (1972) and a book about his involvement with yoga, *Halfway Through the Door: An Actor's Journey Towards the Self* (1975). Married actress Barbara Dana. His three sons (two from a previous marriage) Adam (*b.* Aug. 19, 1956, Brooklyn), Matthew, and Tony Arkin, have also appeared in films.

FEATURE FILMS (as actor): *The Russians Are Coming, the Russians Are Coming* 1966; *Woman Times Seven, Wait Until Dark* 1967; *Inspector Clouseau, The Heart Is a Lonely Hunter* 1968; *The Monitors, Popi* 1969; *Catch 22* 1970; *Little Murders* (also dir.) 1971; *Deadhead Miles, Last of the Red Hot Lovers* 1972; *Freebie and the Bean* 1974; *Rafferty and the Gold Dust Twins, Hearts of the West* 1975; *The Seven-Per-Cent Solution* (as Sigmund Freud) 1976; *Fire Sale* (also dir.) 1977; *The Magician of Lublin* (Isr./Ger.), *The In-Laws* (also exec. prod.), *Simon* 1980; *Improper Channels* (Can.), *Chu Chu and the Philly Flash, Full Moon High* 1981; *The Last Unicorn* (voice only), *Deadhead Miles* 1982; *The Return of Captain Invincible* (Austral./US) 1983; *Joshua Then and Now* (Can.), *Bad Medicine* 1985; *Big Trouble* 1986; *Coup De Ville, Edward Scissorhands, Havana* 1990; *The Rocketeer* 1991; *Glengarry Glen Ross* 1992; *Indian Summer* 1993; *Jerky Boys, Steal Big, Steal Little* 1995; *Mother Night* 1996; *Gattaca* 1997.

Arkoff, Samuel Z. Executive, producer. Born on June 12, 1918, in Fort Dodge, Iowa. *ed.* U. of Iowa; U. of Colorado; Loyola U. (law). Co-founder (with James H. Nicholson), with $3,000 of borrowed capital in 1954, and later chairman of the board, of AMERICAN INTERNATIONAL PICTURES (AIP), a company that became notorious for its low-budget exploitation films but gained some respectability by the late 60s. Co-produced many of the company's films with Nicholson. In 1979 he was honored on the occasion of a retrospective of AIP films at New York's Museum of Modern Art. After selling AIP to Filmways, he became chairman and president of the Samuel Z. Arkoff Company in 1980 and Arkoff International Pictures in 1981. His son, Louis S. Arkoff (*b.* Jan. 4, 1950, Los Angeles), a graduate of USC, entered films at 17 as a production assistant, later serving the family business as a producer and executive producer.

FILMS INCLUDE (as producer or executive producer): *Reform School Girl, Motorcycle Gang* 1957; *Terror From the Year 5000, Machine Gun Kelly, The Bonnie Parker Story* 1958; *House of Usher* 1960; *The Pit and the Pendulum* 1961; *Poe's Tales of Terror, The Premature Burial* 1962; *The Comedy of Terrors, The Raven, Operation Bikini, The Man With the X-Ray Eyes* 1963; *Muscle Beach Party* 1964; *How to Stuff a Wild Bikini, Beach Blanket Bingo, Dr. Goldfoot and the Bikini Machine* 1965; *Fireball 500* 1966; *Wild in the Streets* 1968; *De Sade* 1969; *Bloody Mama, The Dunwich Horror* 1970; *Wuthering Heights* 1971; *Blacula* 1972; *Dillinger* 1973; *Madhouse* 1974; *Hennessy, Return to Macon County* 1975; *The Food of the Gods, Futureworld, A Matter of Time* 1976; *Empire of the Ants, The Island of Dr. Moreau* 1977; *Force 10 from Navarone, Our Winning Season* 1978; *The Amityville Horror* 1979; *Underground Aces* 1981; *Up the Creek* 1984.

Arkush, Allan. Director. Born on Apr. 30, 1948, in New York City. *ed.* Franklin & Marshall; NYU Film School. Offbeat cult director from the Roger Corman school of shoestring-budget movies. He started out as an editor of trailers and has directed extensively for TV. He has also directed rock videos with such performers as Mick Jagger and Bette Midler. Can be glimpsed playing a cameo in pal Paul BARTEL's *Cannonball* (1976).

FILMS: *Hollywood Boulevard* (co-dir. with Joe Dante; also co-edit.) 1976; *Grand Theft Auto* (2nd-unit dir. only) 1977; *Deathsport* (co-dir. with Henry Suso) 1978; *Rock 'n' Roll High School* (also story) 1979; *Heartbeeps* 1981; *Get Crazy* 1983; *Caddyshack II* 1988.

Arlen, Harold. Composer, songwriter. *b.* Hyman Arluck, Feb. 15, 1905, Buffalo, N.Y. *d.* 1986. The son of a cantor, he sang in his father's synagogue, then, at 15, joined a trio, playing the piano. In 1927 he came to New York City, working as arranger, pianist, and singer. The following year his 'Get Happy' was sung in the '9:15 Revue' and he was on his way to a brilliant career as songwriter and composer. His Broadway shows include 'St. Louis Woman,' 'Vanities,' and 'House of Flowers.' His many popular songs include 'Stormy Weather,' 'It's Only a Paper Moon,' 'I Love a Parade,' 'That Old Black Magic,' and 'Blues in the Night.' He won an Academy Award in 1939 for 'Over the Rainbow' from *The Wizard of Oz.*

FILMS INCLUDE: *The Big Broadcast, Manhattan Parade* 1932; *Take a Chance* ('It's Only a Paper Moon') 1933; *Let's Fall in Love* 1934; *Strike Me Pink, The Singing Kid, Stage Struck* 1936; *Artists and Models* 1937; *Love Affair, Babes in Arms, The Wizard of Oz* ('Over the Rainbow'), *At the Circus* 1939; *Blues in the Night* 1941; *Rio Rita, Cairo, Star Spangled Rhythm* ('That Old Black Magic,' etc.) 1942; *Cabin in the Sky* ('Happiness Is Just a Thing Called Joe,' etc.), *The Sky's the Limit* ('One for My Baby,' etc.) 1943; *Here Come the Waves* ('Accentuate the Positive,' etc.) 1944; *Casbah* 1948; *My Blue Heaven* 1950; *A Star Is Born, The Country Girl* 1954; *Gay Purr-ee* 1962; *I Could Go On Singing* (UK) 1963; *The Swinger* 1966.

Arlen, Richard. Actor. *b.* Cornelius Richard Van Mattimore, Sept. 1, 1899, Charlottesville, Va. *d.* 1976. *ed.* U. of Pennsylvania. Brawny star of Hollywood films of the 20s who endured in lead roles and supporting parts well into the late 60s. A sportswriter, swimming coach, and a pilot with the Royal Canadian Flying Corps before his film debut in 1920, he was first billed as Van Mattimore. He played his first important role in 1923 and he achieved the peak of his career in two William Wellman films, *Wings* (1927) and *Beggars of Life* (1928), and in Victor Fleming's *The Virginian* (1929). He subsequently appeared in innumerable films, playing hero parts in B pictures and supporting roles in A productions. He married and divorced Jobyna RALSTON, his co-star in *Wings.*

FILMS INCLUDE: As Van Mattimore—*Ladies Must Lie* 1921; *The Green Temptation* 1922; *Quicksands, Vengeance of the Deep* 1923; *The Fighting Coward* 1924. As Richard Arlen—*Sally, In the Name of Love* 1925; *Padlocked, Behind the Front* 1926; *Rolled Stockings, The Blood Ship, Wings, She's a Sheik* 1927; *Feel My Pulse, Ladies of the Mob, Beggars of Life, Manhattan Cocktail* 1928; *The Man I Love, The Four Feathers, Thunderbolt, Dangerous Curves, The Virginian* 1929; *The Dangerous Paradise, The Light of Western Stars, The Border Legion, The Sea God, The Santa Fe Trail, Only Saps Work* 1930; *The Conquering Horde, Gun Smoke, The Lawyer's Secret, Touchdown!* 1931; *Wayward, Sky Bride, Guilty As Hell, Tiger Shark, The All American* 1932; *Island of Lost Souls, Song of the Eagle, College Humor, Three-Cornered Moon, Alice in Wonderland* (as the Cheshire Cat) 1933; *Come on Marines!* 1934; *Helldorado* 1935; *The Calling of Dan Matthews* 1936; *Secret Valley, The Great Barrier/Silent Barriers* (UK), *Artists and Models, Murder in Greenwich Village* 1937; *No Time to*

Marry, Call of the Yukon, Straight Place and Show 1938; *Mutiny on the Blackhawk, Legion of Lost Flyers* 1939; *The Devil's Pipeline* 1940; *Raiders of the Desert* 1941; *Submarine Alert* 1943; *The Lady and the Monster, Storm Over Lisbon* 1944; *The Big Bonanza* 1945; *When My Baby Smiles at Me* 1948; *Hurricane Smith 1952; Sabre Jet* 1953; *The Mountain* 1956; *Warlock* 1959; *The Best Man* 1964; *Apache Uprising* 1966; *Fort Utah* 1967; *Buckskin* 1968; *Sex and the College Girl* 1970; *Won Ton Ton—The Dog Who Saved Hollywood* (bit) 1976.

Arletty. Actress. *b.* Léonie Bathiat, May 15, 1898, Courbevoie, France. *d.* 1992. At 16 she worked in a factory and later became a secretary and model before appearing in music hall revues. She made her film debut in 1931 and rose to eminence in several Marcel CARNÉ films scripted by Jacques PRÉVERT. Her appearance in *Les Enfants du Paradis/Children of Paradise* (1945) is an image of beauty and femininity long to be remembered. Elegant and darkly mysterious, she subsequently divided her talents between films and the Paris stage. After the Liberation, she spent two months in jail as a collaborator, the consequence of a love affair with a German officer during the Occupation. From the early 60s she was nearly inactive, following an accident that left her temporarily blind. Author: *La Défense* (1971).

FILMS INCLUDE: *La Douceur D'aimer* 1930; *Un Chien qui rapporte* 1931; *Das schöne Abenteuer/La Belle Aventure* (Ger./Fr.) 1932; *Walzerkrieg/La Guerre de Valses* (Ger./Fr.) 1933; *Pension Mimosas* 1935; *La Garçonne* 1936; *Faisons un Rêve, Les Perles de la Couronne* 1937; *Hôtel du Nord* 1938; *Le Jour se lève/Daybreak, Fric-Frac, Circonstances atténuantes/Extenuating Circumstances* 1939; *Madame Sans-Gêne* 1941; *Les Visiteurs du Soir/The Devil's Own Envoy* 1942; *Les Enfants du Paradis/Children of Paradise* 1945; *Portrait d'un Assassin* 1949; *L'Amour Madame* 1951; *Le Grand Jeu/Flesh and the Woman, Huis clos/No Exit, L'Air de Paris* 1954; *Maxime, Un Drôle de Dimanche* 1958; *The Longest Day* (US) 1962; *Les Volets fermés* 1972.

Arling, Arthur E. Director of photography. Born on Sept. 2, 1906, in Missouri. *ed.* New York Inst. of Photography. Started as assistant cameraman for Fox in 1927, became second cameraman in 1931. He was camera operator on *Gone With the Wind* (1939). After WW II, in which he served as a naval lieutenant commander, he returned to films as director of photography. He shared an Academy Award with Charles ROSHER and Leonard Smith in 1946 for the cinematography of *The Yearling.*

FILMS INCLUDE: The Yearling (co-phot. 1946); *Captain from Castile* (co-phot.) 1948; *You're My Everything* 1949; *My Blue Heaven* 1950; *Call Me Mister* 1951; *Belles on Their Toes* 1952; *Love Me or Leave Me* 1955; *I'll Cry Tomorrow* 1956; *Pillow Talk* 1959; *Lover Come Back, The Story of Ruth* 1960; *The Notorious Landlady, Boys' Night Out* 1962; *The Secret Invasion* 1964; *Ski Party* 1965; *Once Before I Die* 1966.

Arliss, George. Actor *b.* George Augustus Andrews, Apr. 10, 1868, London. *d.* 1946. Made his London stage debut at 18. In 1902 an American tour brought him great success and he stayed for 20 years, to appear in many Broadway productions and films. He was particularly popular for his stage portrayals of such historical figures as Voltaire, Richelieu, Disraeli, and Alexander Hamilton, a specialty he was later to transfer to the screen.

In 1921 he made his first film appearance in *The Devil,* an adaptation of the Molnar play, in which he had appeared on Broadway in 1906. That same year he repeated another Broadway success in a silent film version of *Disraeli.* A sound version of the same film brought him an Academy Award for 1929–30. He authored two autobiographical books, *Up the Years From Bloomsbury* (1927) and *My Ten Years at the Studios* (1940). His wife, Florence (Montgomery) Arliss, appeared with him in several films. He retired from the screen in 1937 when she lost her sight. Their son was director Leslie ARLISS.

FILMS: In the US—*The Devil, Disraeli* 1921; *The Man Who Played God, The Ruling Passion* 1922; *Twenty Dollars a Week* 1924; *Disraeli* (sound remake) 1929; *The Green Goddess, Old English* 1930; *The Millionaire, Alexander Hamilton* 1931; *The Man Who Played God, A Successful Calamity* 1932; *The King's Vacation, The Working Man, Voltaire* 1933; *The House of Rothschild, The Last Gentleman* 1934; *Cardinal Richelieu* 1935. In the UK—*The Iron Duke* (as Wellington); *The Guv'nor/Mister Hobo, The Tunnel/Transatlantic Tunnel* 1935; *East Meets West, Man of Affairs, His Lordship* 1936; *Dr. Syn* 1937.

Arliss, Leslie. Director. *b.* Leslie Andrews, 1901, London. *d.* 1988. Son of George and Florence ARLISS. A critic and journalist, he collaborated on screenplays for British films from 1932, among them *Tonight's the Night* (1932), *Orders Is Orders* (1933), *Jack Ahoy* (1934), *Heat Wave* (1935), *Rhodes of Africa/Rhodes* (1936), *Pastor Hall* (1940), and *The Foreman Went to France/Somewhere in France* (1942). He began directing in 1941 and in the mid-40s turned out several popular melodramas, notably *The Man in Grey* (1943), *Love Story/A Lady Surrenders* (1944), and *The Wicked Lady* (1945), films that established James MASON, Stewart GRANGER, and Margaret LOCKWOOD as stars. He also directed a number of shorts. After 1955 he worked mostly in TV.

FEATURE FILMS: *The Farmer's Wife* (co-dir. with Norman Lee) 1941; *The Night Has Eyes* 1942; *The Man in Grey* (also co-sc.) 1943; *Love Story/A Lady Surrenders* (also co-sc.) 1944; *The Wicked Lady* 1945; *A Man About the House* (also co-sc.) 1947; *Idol of Paris* 1948; *Saints and Sinners* (also prod., co-sc.) 1949; *The Woman's Angle* (also co-sc.) 1952; *See How They Run* (also co-sc.), *Miss Tulip Stays the Night* 1955.

Armat, Thomas. Inventor. *b.* Oct. 26, 1866, Fredricksburg, Va. *d.* 1948. A Washington, D.C., real estate agent, he invented a variety of machines, including an oarlock for boats and an automatic car coupler for railroads. In 1894 he joined with another inventor, Charles Francis JENKINS, to develop the world's first motion picture projection machine utilizing an intermittent motion mechanism. The machine failed, however, and in the following year Armat alone assembled an improved version, employing a loop-forming device and the first practicable intermittent motion mechanism. In September 1895 he exhibited his invention, called the Phantoscope, at the Cotton States Exposition in Atlanta. The following year the Edison company agreed to manufacture the machine.

According to Armat it was decided that "for the purpose of adding prestige, the projector would be advertised as Edison's Vitascope." And so, on April 23, 1896, the Edison Vitascope made its bow, projecting Edison Company films on a New York music-hall screen, several months after LUMIÈRE had demonstrated his CINÉMATOGRAPHE in Paris, and with Armat himself acting as the projectionist. The era of screen projection had thus begun. Armat later sued both the Edison company and Biograph over patent rights but eventually joined with them to form the Motion Pictures Patent Company.

Armendariz, Pedro. Actor. *b.* May 9, 1912, Churubusco, Mexico. *ed.* in San Antonio, Tex., and at California Polytechnic Inst. *d.* 1963 of a self-inflicted gunshot wound after learning he had cancer. After working for a Mexican railroad and at a hotel, he had a brief stage career before entering Mexican films in 1935. He rapidly became Mexico's top film star, appearing in some 45 local films, many directed by Emilio FERNANDEZ. He won international recognition for his appearance in Fernandez's celebrated

Maria Candelaria (1943) and *The Pearl* (1945). European and American directors, notably Luis BUÑUEL and John FORD, sought his services, and his strong screen presence and virile personality were effectively used in a variety of roles in more than 75 films. His son, Pedro Armendariz, Jr., is also in films.

FILMS INCLUDE: *Rosario Bordertown, Maria Elena* 1935; *Mi Candidato* 1937; *El Indio* 1938; *Los Olvidados de Dios, La Reina del Rio* 1939; *La Isla de la Pasión/Passion Island, Simon Bolivar/The Life of Simon Bolivar* 1941; *Soy Puro Mexicano, Guadalajara* 1942; *Flor Sylvestre, Maria Candelaria* 1943; *Las Abandonadas, Bugambilia, El Corsaro Negro* 1944; *La Perla/The Pearl* 1945; *Enamorada* 1946; *The Fugitive* (US) 1947; *Fort Apache* (US) 1948; *Three Godfathers* (US), *We Were Strangers* (US), *Tulsa* (US), *La Malquerida* 1949; *Del Odio nace el Amor/The Torch/Bandit General* 1950; *El Bruto* 1952; *Lucrèce Borgia/Lucrezia Borgia/Sins of the Borgias* (Fr./It.), *Les Amants de Tolède/The Lovers of Toledo* (Fr./It./Sp.) 1953; *Border River* (US) 1954; *The Littlest Outlaw* (US/Mex.) 1955; *Diane* (US), *The Conqueror* (US), *Uomini e Lupi* (It.) 1956; *Manuela/Stowaway Girl* (UK), *Flor de Mayo/Beyond All Limits, The Big Boodle* (US) 1957; *La Cucaracha/The Bandit* 1958; *The Wonderful Country* (US) 1959; *Francis of Assisi* (US) 1961; *Arrivano i Titani/My Son the Hero* (as Cadmus, King of Thebes) 1962; *Captain Sinbad* (US), *From Russia With Love* (UK) 1963.

Armitage, George. Director, screenwriter. He got his start in the mailroom of 20th Century-Fox in 1965. He went on to serve as a television associate producer before joining Roger CORMAN's New World studio, where he scripted the youth-oriented fantasy *Gas-s-s-s* (1970), directed by Corman. Thereafter Armitage directed several modestly budgeted action pictures, always working from his own screenplays. After an 11-year absence from feature film directing, Armitage returned with *Miami Blues* (1990), produced by Jonathan DEMME.

FILMS INCLUDE: As director and screenwriter—*Private Duty Nurses* 1972; *Hit Man* 1973; *Vigilante Force* 1976; *Hot Rod* 1979; *Miami Blues* 1990.

Armstrong, Bess. Actress. Born on Dec. 11, 1953, in Baltimore. *ed.* Brown U. Leading actress in numerous film and television roles. Married producer John Fiedler.

FILMS INCLUDE: *The House of God* 1979; *The Four Seasons* 1981; *Jaws 3-D, High Road to China* 1983; *Nothing in Common* 1986; *Second Sight* 1989; *The Skateboard Kid* 1993; *Dream Lover* 1994.

Armstrong, Gillian. Director. Born on Dec. 18, 1950, in Melbourne, Australia. Trained in stage and costume design at the Swinburne Technical College, she directed a short, *The Roof Needs Mowing,* as part of a film class requirement. She then moved to Sydney, where she enrolled in 1973 in the Film and TV School, eeking out a living as a waitress. On the strength of three shorts—*100 a Day, Satdee Night,* and *Gretel*—she entered the film industry as an assistant director. She won a top award at the 1976 Sydney Film Festival for the hour-long featurette *The Singer and the Dancer* and international accolades for her first full-length feature, *My Brilliant Career.* The film about an independent young woman with literary aspirations in turn-of-the-century Australia won the British Critics' Award for best first feature and seven AFI Awards, including best film and best director; it also brought lead actress Judy DAVIS to worldwide attention. Armstrong has made some films in America, beginning with *Mrs. Soffel,* but these have not been as well received as her Australian work.

FEATURE FILMS: *The Singer And The Dancer* (also prod.) 1976; *My Brilliant Career* 1979; *Starstruck* 1982; *Mrs. Soffel* (US) 1984; *High Tide* 1987; *Fires Within* (US) 1991; *The Last Days of Chez Nous* 1992; *Little Women* 1994.

Armstrong, Louis. Musician, singer. *b.* July 4, 1900, New Orleans. *d.* 1971. One of the world's leading jazz performers, whose career spanned more than half a century, he was a virtuoso trumpet player and a singer with an inimitable raspy voice that radiated warmth and good cheer. His many worldwide tours earned him the unofficial title of "America's Ambassador of Goodwill." A capable all-around entertainer, he also appeared in a score of films, usually as himself, playing, singing, and clowning while repeatedly mopping his forehead with his trademark prop, a large white handkerchief. He wrote an autobiography, *Satchmo* (his nickname, short for "Satchelmouth"), in 1954, and in 1957 he was the subject of a 'CBS Reports' TV documentary, 'Satchmo the Great,' which was released as a feature film in some theaters.

FEATURE FILMS: *Ex-flame* 1930; *Pennies From Heaven* 1936; *Artists and Models* 1937; *Every Day's a Holiday, Dr. Rhythm, Going Places* 1938; *Cabin in the Sky* 1943; *Jam Session, Atlantic City, Hollywood Canteen* 1944; *New Orleans, Carnegie Hall* 1947; *A Song Is Born* 1948; *The Strip, Here Comes the Groom* 1951; *Glory Alley* 1952; *The Glenn Miller Story* 1954; *High Society* 1956; *Satchmo the Great* (doc.) 1957; *The Beat Generation, The Five Pennies* 1959; *Jazz on a Summer's Day* (doc.) 1960; *Paris Blues* 1961; *When the Boys Meet the Girls* 1965; *A Man Called Adam* 1966; *Hello Dolly!* 1969.

Armstrong, Robert. Actor. *b.* Donald R. Smith, Nov. 20, 1890, Saginaw, Mich. *d.* 1973. After studying law at the University of Washington, he acted in vaudeville and on the legitimate stage, making occasional bit appearances in films. In 1927, he began performing in films regularly. He soon became one of Hollywood's busiest character actors, appearing mostly in action pictures and usually cast in the role of a good tough guy, on either side of the law, both in leads and supporting parts. Perhaps best remembered as the white hunter who brings the ape to civilization in *King Kong* (1933). Retired in the early 60s after a long stint on TV.

FILMS INCLUDE: *The Silent Voice* 1915; *War and the Woman* 1917; *Boys Will Be Boys* 1921; *The Man Who Came Back* 1924; *New Brooms* 1925; *The Main Event* 1927; *The Leopard Lady, A Girl in Every Port, Square Crooks, The Cop, Celebrity, Show Folks, Ned McCob's Daughter* 1928; *The Shady Lady, The Woman from Hell, Big News, The Racketeer 1929*; *Be Yourself, Dumbbells in Ermine, Paid* 1930; *Iron Man, Suicide Fleet* 1931; *Panama Flo, The Lost Squadron, Radio Patrol, The Most Dangerous Game* 1932; *The Billion Dollar Scandal, King Kong, Blind Adventure, Son of Kong* 1933; *The Hell Cat, Kansas City Princess* 1934; *G-Men, Little Big Shot* 1935; *Public Enemy's Wife, Without Orders* 1936; *Three Legionnaires, The Girl Said No* 1937; *Man of Conquest* (as Jim Bowie) 1939; *Enemy Agent, Behind the News* 1940; *Citadel of Crime, Sky Raiders* (serial), *Dive Bomber* 1941; *My Favorite Spy, Gang Busters* (serial) 1942; *The Mad Ghoul* 1943; *Action in Arabia* 1944; *Blood on the Sun, Gangs of the Waterfront, Arson Squad* 1945; *Criminal Court* 1946; *Fall Guy, The Sea of Grass, The Fugitive* 1947; *The Paleface* 1948, *Mighty Joe Young* 1949; *Captain China* 1950; *Las Vegas Shakedown* 1955; *The Crooked Circle* 1957; *Johnny Cool* 1963; *For Those Who Think Young* 1964.

"Army-Navy Screen Magazine." A WW II newsreel series written and edited by GIs for GIs. Subtitled "a pictorial report from all fronts," it was a weekly compilation of footage shot by Signal Corps cameramen, with emphasis on the point of view of the enlisted man. Some segments reached such a high level of drama and poetry that critics compared it favorably to civilian newsreels and "The March of Time" series.

Arnaz, Desi. Musician, bandleader, actor. *b.* Desiderio Alberto Arnaz y de Acha III, Mar. 2, 1917, Santiago, Cuba. *d.* 1986. The only son of wealthy landowners, he arrived in the US at 16 as a poor refugee of the Batista revolution. He joined a Cuban combo, then formed his own band and became popular as a singing bongo player. In 1940 he married Lucille BALL, his co-star in *Too Many Girls,* his screen debut. A decade later they formed Desilu Productions and reaped a fortune from their long-running TV series 'I Love Lucy' as well as many other TV shows. After their 1960 divorce Miss Ball bought out her husband's share in the business and he became an independent TV producer. Their children, Desi Arnaz, Jr. (*b.* Desiderio Arnaz IV, Jan. 19, 1953, Los Angeles) and Lucie Arnaz (*b.* Lucy Désirée Arnaz, July 17, 1951, Los Angeles), are both TV and film performers. Autobiography: *A Book* (1976).

FILMS: *Too Many Girls* 1940; *Father Takes a Wife* 1941; *Four Jacks and a Jill* 1941–42; *The Navy Comes Through* 1942; *Bataan* 1943; *Cuban Pete* 1946; *Holiday In Havana* (also wrote songs) 1949; *The Long Long Trailer* 1954; *Forever Darling* 1956; *The Escape Artist* 1982.

Arness, James. Actor. Born James Aurness, on May 26, 1923, in Minneapolis. Brother of actor Peter GRAVES. *ed.* Beloit Coll. Recovering from severe wounds inflicted in the WW II Anzio landing, he joined a little theater group and supported himself as a real estate agent and advertising man. He made his screen debut in 1947, and for a couple of years was billed under his real surname, Aurness. As a supporting player, he found good roles hard to come by because of his huge frame (6' 6"), which dwarfed most leading men. His size was put to fearsome effect when he played the title role in the science-fiction thriller *The Thing*. He finally discovered his niche in television as the star of the long-running (20 seasons!) series 'Gunsmoke' (1955–75). In 1981–82 he played the title role in the police series 'McClain's Law.'

FILMS INCLUDE: *The Farmer's Daughter* 1947; *Battleground* 1949; *Wagonmaster* 1950; *The Thing, The People Against O'Hara* 1951; *Carbine Williams, Big Jim McLain, Horizons West* 1952; *Lone Hand, Hondo* 1953; *Them, Her Twelve Men* 1954; *Many Rivers to Cross, The Sea Chase* 1955; *Flame of the Islands, Gun the Man Down, The First Traveling Saleslady* 1956; *Alias Jesse James* (unbilled cameo as Matt Dillon) 1959.

Arnheim, Rudolf. Educator, psychologist, art and film theoretician. Born on July 15, 1904, in Berlin. *ed.* U. of Berlin. Associate editor of publications, International Institute of Educational Cinematography (League of Nations) Rome, 1933–39. He came to the US in 1940 and was naturalized in 1946. He served on the faculties of Sarah Lawrence and other American colleges and universities. He is the author of *Film* (1933), *Art and Visual Perception* (1954), *Film as Art* (1957), and *Picasso's Guernica* (1962).

His *Film as Art* contains the body of his cinema theory; it comprises a revision of *Film* and four essays published in the 30s. Its main thesis is that the peculiar virtues of film as art derive from the exploitation of inherent limitations of the medium, such as optical distortions; the limitations imposed by the frame, angle, and size of image, the absence of space-time continuum, etc.

Arno, Sig. Actor. *b.* Siegfried Aron, 1895, Hamburg, Germany. *d.* 1975. A leading comedian and character actor of German stage and screen, he played in many German films as Siegfried Arno before Hitler's ascent to power. After leaving Germany in 1933, he toured the Continent for several years, and toward the end of the decade he arrived in the US.. Here he launched a successful Hollywood career, playing many character roles, mostly comic. He also appeared in several Broadway productions, notably in 'Time Remembered' and 'Song of Norway.'

FILMS INCLUDE: In Germany—*Manon Lescaut* 1926; *Die Liebe der Jeanne Ney/The Love of Jeanne Ney* 1927; *Die Buchse ser Pandora/Pandora's Box, Das Tagerbuch einer Verlorenen/Diary of a Lost Girl* 1929; *Die vom Rummelplatz* 1930; *Schubert's Frühlingstraum, Keine Feier ohne Meyer, Die grosse Attraktion* 1931. In the US—*The Star Maker* 1939; *The Great Dictator* (bit), *The Mummy's Hand* 1940; *This Thing Called Love, It Started With Eve* 1941; *New Wine, Tales of Manhattan, The Palm Beach Story* 1942; *The Crystal Ball, His Butler's Sister* 1943; *Up in Arms* 1944; *A Song to Remember* 1945; *The Great Lover* 1949; *Nancy Goes to Rio, The Toast of New Orleans* 1950; *Diplomatic Courier* 1952; *The Great Diamond Robbery* 1954.

Arnold, Edward. Actor. *b.* Gunther Edward Arnold Schneider, Feb. 18, 1890, New York City, to German immigrants. *d.* 1956. Character star of Hollywood films. Grew up on New York's Lower East Side, where he made his first amateur stage appearance as Lorenzo in 'The Merchant of Venice.' In 1907 he appeared on the stage with Ethel Barrymore in 'Dream of a Summer Night.' In 1915 he was engaged by the Essanay studio in Chicago as a cowboy star and appeared in some 50 silent two-reel action pictures. He also played supporting roles in a number of social drama and comedy features, before returning to the stage in 1919. In 1932 he returned to the screen and became one of Hollywood's most versatile and convincing character actors, specializing in authoritative roles—judges, senators, uncompromising businessmen—as well as in roles of amiable scoundrels. In all, he appeared in some 150 pictures. Best remembered for his leading roles in *Diamond Jim* (1935) and *Sutter's Gold* (1936) and in Capra's *You Can't Take It with You* (1938) and *Mr. Smith Goes to Washington* (1939). Arnold was a president of the Screen Actors Guild.

FEATURE FILMS: *The Misleading Lady, Vultures Of Society, The Return Of Eve* 1916; *The Slacker's Heart* 1917; *Phil-for-Short, A Broadway Saint* 1919; *The Cost* 1920; *Okay America!, Three on a Match, Afraid to Talk/Merry-Go-Round, Rasputin and the Empress* 1932; *Whistling in the Dark, The White Sister, The Barbarian, Jennie Gerhardt, Her Bodyguard, The Secret of the Blue Room, I'm No Angel, Roman Scandals, The Life of Jimmy Dolan* 1933; *Madame Spy, Sadie McKee, Unknown Blonde, Thirty Day Princess, Hide-Out, Million Dollar Ransom, The President Vanishes, Wednesday's Child* 1934; *Biography of a Bachelor Girl, Cardinal Richelieu* (as Louis XIII), *The Glass Key, Diamond Jim* (as "Diamond" Jim Brady), *Crime and Punishment* (as Inspector Porfiry Petrovich), *Remember Last Night?* 1935; *Sutter's Gold* (as John Sutter, on whose California property the 1848 Gold Rush started), *Meet Nero Wolfe* (title role, as the Rex Stout detective), *Come and Get It* 1936; *John Meade's Woman, Easy Living, The Toast of New York* (as tycoon Jim Fisk), *Blossoms on Broadway* 1937; *The Crowd Roars, You Can't Take It with You* 1938; *Idiot's Delight, Let Freedom Ring, Man About Town, Mr. Smith Goes to Washington* 1939; *The Earl of Chicago, Slightly Honorable, Lillian Russell* (again as "Diamond" Jim Brady), *Johnny Apollo* 1940; *Meet John Doe, The Penalty, The Lady From Cheyenne, All That Money Can Buy* (as Daniel Webster), *Nothing but the Truth, Design for Scandal* 1941; *Johnny Eager, Eyes in the Night, The War Against Mrs. Hadley* 1942; *The Youngest Profession* 1943; *Standing Room Only, Janie, Kismet, Mrs. Parkington* 1944; *Main Street After Dark, The Hidden Eye, Week-End at the Waldorf* 1945; *Ziegfeld Follies, Janie Gets Married, Three Wise Fools, No Leave No Love* 1946; *The Mighty*

McGurk, Dear Ruth, My Brother Talks to Horses, The Hucksters 1947; *Three Daring Daughters, Big City, Wallflower* 1948; *Command Decision, John Loves Mary, Take Me Out to the Ball Game, Big Jack* 1949; *Dear Wife, The Yellow Cab Man, Annie Get Your Gun, The Skipper Surprised His Wife* 1950; *Dear Brat* 1951; *Belles on Their Toes* 1952; *City That Never Sleeps, Man of Conflict* 1953; *Living It Up* 1954; *The Houston Story, The Ambassador's Daughter, Miami Exposé* 1956.

Arnold, Jack. Director. *b.* Oct. 14, 1916, New Haven, Conn. *d.* 1992. *ed.* Ohio State; AADA. A former stage and screen actor, he directed and produced some 25 documentaries for government agencies and private industry before tackling feature films in the early 1950s, specializing in science-fiction and horror pictures. His output also included Westerns, dramas, and comedies.

FILMS: as director—*With These Hands* (full-length semi-doc. for ILGW Union; also co-prod.) 1950; *Girls in the Night, It Came from Outer Space, The Glass Web* 1953; *Creature from the Black Lagoon* 1954; *Revenge of the Creature, The Man from Bitter Ridge, Tarantula* 1955; *Red Sundown, Outside the Law* 1956; *The Incredible Shrinking Man, The Tattered Dress* 1957; *Man in the Shadow, The Lady Takes a Flyer, High School Confidential, The Space Children, Monster on the Campus* 1958; *No Name on the Bullet* (also co-prod.), *The Mouse That Roared* (UK) 1959; *Bachelor in Paradise* 1961; *A Global Affair, The Lively Set* 1964, *Hello Down There* 1969; *Black Eye* 1974; *Boss Nigger* (also co-prod.), *Games Girls Play* 1975; *The Swiss Conspiracy* 1977; *Into the Night* (act. only) 1985.

Arnold, John. Director of photography, inventor, film pioneer. Born on Nov. 16, 1889, in New York City. *ed.* Columbia (engineering). Started out in films with the engineering department of the Thomas Edison company. Later was instrumental in a variety of technical developments at Biograph and other pioneer film companies. A director of photography since 1915, he experimented with lighting and various effects and in the 20s distinguished himself as a truly outstanding cinematographer. He retired from active duty in 1929 to become president of the American Society of Cinematographers (1931–36) and head of the MGM camera department (1931–56).

FILMS INCLUDE: *Blue Jeans* 1918; *Satan Junior* 1919; *Blackmail* 1920; *Puppets of Fate* 1921; *Love in the Dark* 1922; *The Fog, Rouged Lips, The Social Code* 1923; *The Heart Bandit, Revelation, Sinners in Silk, The Beauty Prize* 1924; *The Big Parade, Bright Lights, Sally Irene and Mary* 1925; *Paris, Love Blindness* (co-phot.) 1926; *The Show, Mr. Wu* 1927; *Show People, Rose Marie, Garden of Eden, The Cardboard Lover* 1928; *The Broadway Melody* 1929; *Lust for Life* (some scenes only) 1956.

Arnold, Malcolm. Composer. Born on Oct. 21, 1921, in Northampton, England. *ed.* Royal College of Music and in Italy. Played the trumpet with the London Philharmonic Orchestra. Composed the ballet 'Homage to the Queen' for the 1953 coronation and many outstanding film scores, including the one for *The Bridge on the River Kwai,* which brought him an Academy Award.

FILMS INCLUDE: *The Sound Barrier/Breaking Through The Sound Barrier* 1952; *The Captain's Paradise* 1953; *Hobson's Choice* 1954; *I Am a Camera* 1955; *Trapeze* 1956; *Island in the Sun, The Bridge on the River Kwai* 1957; *The Key, The Roots of Heaven, The Inn of the Sixth Happiness* 1958; *The Angry Silence, Tunes of Glory* 1960; *The Lion* 1962; *The Chalk Garden* 1964; *The Heroes of Telemark* 1966; *David Copperfield* 1970.

Arnold, Tom. Comedian, actor. *b.* March 6, 1959, in Ottumwa, Ia. *ed.* Indian Hills Community College. Amusing, blue-collar stand-up comic turned character actor. After a well-publicized marriage to TV star Roseanne, followed by a bitter, equally public divorce, he parlayed a floundering television career into a successful film career out of his role opposite Arnold SCHWARZENEGGER in *True Lies* (1994).

FILMS: *Freddy's Dead: The Final Nightmare* 1991; *Hero* 1992; *Coneheads, Undercover Blues* 1993; *True Lies* 1994; *Nine Months* 1995; *Carpool, The Stupids, To Gillian on Her 37th Birthday* 1996; *Touch, McHale's Navy* 1997.

Arnoul, Françoise. Born Françoise Gautsch, on June 3, 1931, in Constantine, Algeria. Studied acting in Paris and made her film debut in *L'Epave* (1950). Diminutive, well-proportioned, vivacious, and talented, she was publicized in France early in her career as a "sex kitten" but was displaced by Brigitte Bardot. She has remained, however, a highly competent leading lady and supporting player in a wide range of roles.

FILMS INCLUDE: *L'Epave, Nous Irons à Paris, Quai De Grenelle/The Strollers* 1950; *Le Désir et l'Amour* 1951; *Le Fruit défendu/Forbidden Fruit* 1952; *Les Amants de Tolède/The Lovers of Toledo* (Fr./It./Sp.), *Dortoir des Grandes/Inside a Girls' Dormitory, Les Compagnes de la Nuit/Companions of the Night, La Rage au Corps/Tempest in the Flesh* 1953; *Secrets d'Alcôve/Il Letto/The Bed* (Fr./It.), *Le Mouton á Cinq Pattes/The Sheep Has Five Legs* 1954; *Napoléon, French Cancan/Only the French Can, Les Amants du Tage/Lover's Net* 1955; *Paris Palace-Hôtel/Paris Hotel* 1956; *Sait-on jamais?/No Sun in Venice* 1957; *La Chatte/The Cat* 1958; *La Morte-Saison des Amours/The Season for Love* 1961; *Les Parisiennes/Tales of Paris, Le Diable et les Dix Commandements/The Devil and the Ten Commandments, Vacances portugaises* 1962; *Compartiment tueurs/The Sleeping Car Murder* (cameo) 1965; *Le Dimanche de la Vie* 1966; *Le Petit Théâtre de Jean Renoir* 1971; *Violette et François, Dernière Sortie avant Roissy* 1977. *Bobo Jacco* 1979.

Arnshtam, Lev Oscarovich. Director. Born in 1905, in Dnepropetrovsk, Russia. A graduate of the Leningrad Conservatory, he gave up a promising career as a pianist to go into films. In 1931, KOZINTSEV and TRAUBERG put him in charge of the sound recording of *Alone.* In 1933 he collaborated on the screenplay of *Counterplan* and in 1934 turned out a compilation film with the co-operation of the Turkish government. In 1936 he directed his first fiction film, *Girl Friends/Three Women,* with the assistance of designer Moisei Levin. During WW II he directed *Zoya* (1944), a sensitive, poetic true story of the heroism of a young Soviet girl in the fight against the Nazis.

FILMS INCLUDE: *The Soviets Greet New Turkey* (compilation film) 1934; *Girl Friends/Three Women* (also sc.) 1936; *Friends* (also co-sc.) 1938; *Zoya* (also co-sc.) 1944; *Glinka/The Great Glinka* (also sc.) 1947; *Romeo and Juliet/The Ballet of Romeo and Juliet* (co-dir., co-sc. with Leonid Lavrovsky) 1955; *A Lesson in History* (co-dir., co-sc. with Hristo Piskov; USSR/Bulg.) 1957; *Five Days Five Nights* (also co-sc.; USSR/E. Ger.) 1961; *Sekret Upeshka/Bolshoi Ballet 67* (sc. only) 1965.

Aroma-Rama. A scenting system developed by inventor Charles Weiss and used to add a sense of smell to the documentary film *Behind the Great Wall* (1959). It competed with another process, SMELL-O-VISION, for the attention of audiences in Hollywood's desperate attempt in the 50s to regain customers lost to television. Unlike Smell-O-Vision, which piped odors into individual seats, the Oriental scents of Aroma-Rama were filtered into the auditorium through the air-conditioning system. Neither system proved popular, although technically they were both successful, and the idea of scenting films was promptly abandoned. The idea goes back to the 19th century, when a London theater was sprayed with scents to add atmosphere to a stage production. It was tried in a Pennsylvania motion picture theater as early as 1906 and was used in isolated theaters in 1929 to add "impact" to two early talkies, *Lilac Time* and *The Hollywood Revue.* John WATERS revived the idea of scented film with the more low-tech Odorama system used with *Polyester* (1981). In this system, audience members were handed scratch-and-sniff cards and cued when to sniff by a number on the screen.

Arquette, Patricia. Actress. *b.* April 8, 1968, in Chicago, Il. Fascinating and gripping leading lady of American films. She got her start in television series and quickly developed into a compelling, believable performer. Best known for her gutsy portrayal of 'Alabama' in the violent, ultra-hip action film *True Romance* and a sensitive, tender, critically lauded performance in *Ethan Frome* (both 1993). Her brothers Alexis and David and sister Rosanna ARQUETTE are also actors. She is married to actor Nicolas CAGE.

FILMS: *A Nightmare on Elm Street 3: Dream Warriors, Pretty Smart, Time Out* 1987; *Far North* 1988; *The Indian Runner* 1991; *Inside Monkey Zetterland* 1992; *Ethan Frome, Trouble Bound, True Romance* 1993; *Ed Wood, Holy Matrimony* 1994; *Beyond Rangoon* 1995; *Flirting with Disaster, Infinity, Night Watch, The Secret Agent* 1996; *Lost Highway* 1997.

Arquette, Rosanna. Actress. Born on Aug. 10, 1959, in New York City, into a Russian-French-Jewish show-business family. Petite, offbeat, sensual lead of Hollywood films of the 80s. The daughter of actor Lewis Arquette and granddaughter of comedian Cliff ("Charley Weaver") Arquette, she started an early career in children's theater. At 18, she began appearing in TV movies and two years later co-starred in the TV series 'Shirley.' She was nominated for an Emmy for her passionate performance in the TV movie (shown theatrically abroad) *The Executioner's Song* (1982) and in the same year won accolades for the title role in the TV remake of *Johnny Belinda.* Sparkling in comedy as she is compelling in dramatic roles, she scored a huge hit on the big screen in 1985 with *Desperately Seeking Susan.* Her siblings Alexis, David, and Patricia ARQUETTE are also actors.

FILMS: *More American Graffiti* 1979; *Gorp* 1980; *S.O.B.* 1981; *Baby It's You, Off the Wall* 1983; *Desperately Seeking Susan, The Aviator, Silverado, After Hours* 1985; *Eight Million Ways to Die, Nobody's Fool* 1986; *Amazon Women on the Moon* 1987; *Le Grand Bleu/The Big Blue* 1988; *New York Stories* ("Life Lessons" episode), *Black Rainbow* 1989; *Almost/Wendy Cracked a Walnut* (Austral.), *Flight of the Intruder* 1991; *The Linguini Incident* 1992; *Nowhere to Run, The Wrong Man* 1993; *Pulp Fiction* 1994; *Search and Destroy* 1995; *Gone Fishin'* 1996; *Crash* 1997.

Artaud, Antonin. Dramatist, theorist, actor, screenwriter. *b.* Antoine-Marie-Joseph Artaud, Sept. 4, 1896, Paris. *d.* 1948. A key figure in the French avant-garde, he is most closely identified with his ideas of the "Theater of Cruelty," which he expressed in the book *Le Théâtre et son Double.* (*The Theater and Its Double,* 1938). In this book, as well as in many essays, he also dealt with the theory and aesthetic of cinema. Artaud wrote a couple of scripts for avant-garde films and acted in a number of French productions, notably in the role of a young priest in Carl Dreyer's *The Passion of Joan of Arc.* Artuad was plagued by physical and mental hardships throughout his life. A victim of meningitis, he nearly died at age five. For the rest of his life he suffered from severe headaches and neurological pains, and later became addicted to drugs. After returning to Paris from a Mexican trip, he suffered a mental breakdown and was hospitalized in 1937. He was confined to asylums for most of his remaining years, gaining his final release in 1946.

FILMS INCLUDE: As screenwriter—*L'Etoile de Mer* 1926; *Le Coquille et le Clergyman/The Seashell and the Clergyman* 1927. As actor—*Fair divers* 1922; *Surcouf* 1924; *Le Juif errant* 1926; *Napoléon* (as Marat) 1927; *La Passion de Jeanne d'Arc/The Passion of Joan of Arc, L'Argent* 1928; *L'Opéra de Quat' Sous/The Threepenny Opera* (French version of Pabst's *Die Dreigroschenoper*) 1930; *Les Croix de Bois* 1932; *Mater Dolorosa* 1933; *Liliom* 1934; *Lucrèce Borgia* (as Savonarola), *Koenigsmark* 1936.

art director. Also called a production designer, this is the person on a film crew ultimately responsible for every aspect of film décor and set construction. His duties range from designing and preparing all studio and outdoor settings to the acquisition of all properties required by the script.

Probably the most underrated of cinema artists, the art director may dominate the visual quality of a film, and the caliber of his work often determines its mood and atmosphere. His is one of the most complex jobs in filmmaking. It requires knowledge of architecture and design, a good grasp of decorative and costume styles of all periods, graphic ability, business acumen, and a working knowledge of everything concerning film production, including photography, lighting, special effects, and editing.

The art director confers with the director and the producer to determine how a film should be interpreted visually, then proceeds to prepare detailed sketches of the suggested sets, at the proper scale and from approximate camera angles. In planning his sets, the art director must think not only in aesthetic terms but also in budgetary and technical ones. He must evaluate the cost of construction and allow for the shooting of each set from every possible angle. In carrying out his functions, he often is aided by a team consisting of a set decorator, a scenic artist, a construction manager, a property buyer, and a number of draftsmen.

Artistically, the art director provides a visual translation of the script. Everything that surrounds the action in front of the camera, in the foreground as well as in the background, is his responsibility, including the choice of costumes, which he coordinates with the costume designer. He is also responsible for the authenticity of architecture on location and may be required to supervise the construction of a fake building, a street, or a whole town.

Nowadays, the title "production designer" is usually given to the person in charge of a film's total visual design (formerly known as an art director). In modern terminology, art directors and set designers work under the supervision of the production designer.

Among the art directors (or production designers) whose skills have influenced cinema art are André Andrejew, Richard Day, Cedric Gibbons, Alfred Junge, Boris Leven, Lazare Meerson, William Cameron Menzies, Walter Rörig, Alexander Trauner, and Hermann Warm. In recent years, noted production designers have included Anton Furst, Polly Platt, Richard Sylbert, Dean Tavoularis, and Patrizia von Brandenstein.

art house. A theater specializing in the exhibition of quality films, either classic revivals or new films of limited box-office appeal. The International Confederation of Art Houses (CICAE) was established in Paris in 1955.

Arthur, George K. Actor. Born George Brest, on Apr. 27, 1899, in Aberdeen, Scotland. Entered films via the Shakespearean stage and became popular in England after appearing in the film *Kipps* (1921). He came to Hollywood in 1922 and stayed to enjoy a successful career as a light leading man and supporting player. In a marked departure from his usual sunny roles, he played the sad and dreamy hero of Josef von Sternberg's *The Salvation Hunters* in 1925. In 1927 he was teamed up with Karl DANE in *Rookies,* the first of a series of highly popular comedies in which the two actors co-starred through 1929. He retired in 1935 to go into business and, among other ventures, produced and distributed films.

FILMS INCLUDE: In the UK—*Kipps, A Dear Fool* 1921. In the US—*Madness of Youth, Hollywood* 1923; *Flames of Desire* 1924; *The Salvation Hunters, Lady of the Night, Her Sister from Paris, Lights of Old Broadway* 1925; *Irene, The Exquisite Sinner, Kiki, The Waning Sex, The Boob, The Boy Friend, Bardelys the Magnificent* 1926; *Rookies, The Gingham Girl, The Student Prince, Spring Fever* 1927; *Baby Mine, Circus Rookies, Detectives, Brotherly Love* 1928; *All at Sea, China Bound, The Last of Mrs. Cheyney* 1929; *Chasing Rainbows* 1930; *Oliver Twist* (as Toby Crackit) 1933; *Riptide* 1934; *Vanessa: Her Love Story* 1935.

Arthur, Jean. Actress. *b.* Gladys Georgianna Greene, Oct. 17, 1905, New York City. *d.* 1991. The daughter of a still photographer, she quit school at 15 to become a model and later an actress. She made her screen debut in 1923, playing a small role in John Ford's *Cameo Kirby* and for the next few years played routine ingenue and leading lady parts in numerous low-budget Westerns and some comedy shorts. Her unusual cracked, husky voice became an asset with the coming of sound. She was cast in better films and her roles improved, but not enough. In 1932 she quit films briefly for an unsuccessful Broadway stint. The turning point in her career came in 1935, in John Ford's *The Whole Town's Talking,* in which she first demonstrated her light comedy touch and the appeal of her girl-next-door personality. She went on to play a succession of fetching, vivacious, often oddball, unpretentious heroines. She reached the peak of her popularity in Frank CAPRA's social comedies of the late 30s. She was nominated for an Oscar for her performance in George STEVENS's *The More the Merrier* (1943). Stevens later called her "one of the greatest comediennes the screen has ever seen" and Capra described her as "my favorite actress." In the mid-40s, at the end of a long-lasting fight with Columbia boss Harry COHN, she was released from her contract commitments from that studio and returned to the screen only twice, making her last appearance in Stevens's classic Western *Shane* (1953). In 1950 she won critical acclaim for her appearance in a Broadway production of 'Peter Pan.' In 1956 she starred in a short-lived TV series, 'The Jean Arthur Show,' in which she played a lawyer. She later taught drama at Vassar and other colleges and made infrequent out-of-town stage appearances. Her second husband (1932–49) was singer-turned-producer Frank ROSS.

FEATURE FILMS: *Cameo Kirby, The Temple of Venus* (unbilled bit), 1923; *Biff Bang Buddy, Fast and Fearless, Bringin' Home the Bacon, Travelin' Fast, Thundering Romance* 1924; *Seven Chances* (bit), *Drug Store Cowboy, The Fighting Smile, A Man of Nerve, Tearin' Loose, Hurricane Horseman, Thundering Through* 1925; *Under Fire, Born to Battle, The Fighting Cheat, Double Daring, Lightning Bill, The Cowboy Cop, Twisted Triggers, The College Boob, The Block Signal* 1926; *The Masked Menace* (serial), *Husband Hunters, The Broken Gate, Horse Shoes, The Poor Nut, Flying Luck* 1927; *Wallflowers, Warming Up, Brotherly Love, Sins of the Fathers* 1928; *The Canary Murder Case, Stairs of Sand, The Greene Murder Case, The Mysterious Dr. Fu Manchu, The Saturday Night Kid, Half-Way to Heaven* 1929; *Street of Chance, Young Eagles, Paramount on Parade, The Return of Dr. Fu Manchu, Danger Lights, The Silver Horde* 1930; *The Gang Buster, Virtuous Husband, The Lawyer's Secret, Ex-Bad Boy* 1931; *Get That Venus, The Past of Mary Holmes* 1933; *Whirlpool, The Defense Rests, The Most Precious Thing in Life* 1934; *The Whole Town's Talking, Public Hero No. 1, Party Wire, Diamond Jim, The Public Menace, If You Could Only Cook* 1935; *Mr. Deeds Goes to Town, The Ex-Mrs. Bradford, Adventure in Manhattan, More Than a Secretary* 1936; *The Plainsman* (as Calamity Jane), *History Is Made at Night, Easy Living* 1937; *You Can't Take It With You* 1938; *Only Angels Have Wings, Mr. Smith Goes to Washington* 1939; *Too Many Husbands, Arizona* 1940; *The Devil and Miss Jones* 1941; *The Talk of the Town* 1942; *The More the Merrier, A Lady Takes a Chance* 1943; *The Impatient Years* 1944; *A Foreign Affair* 1948; *Shane* 1953.

artificial light. A source of light other than daylight or some natural phenomenon—firelight, moonlight, etc. In filmmaking the artificial source is usually supplied by electricity in the form of spotlights or floodlights. The use of artificial light for filming requires adjustments in exposure, since photographic materials are generally more sensitive to daylight than to artificial light. Thus, most films come in two speed ratings, one for daylight and one for artificial light.

Arvidson, Linda. American actress. *b.* 1884. *d.* 1949. The first wife of D. W. GRIFFITH, she played leads in many of his early films. Her book, *When the Movies Were Young* (1925, reprinted 1968), is an invaluable source of information about Griffith and his early work. She sometimes used the screen name Linda Griffith.

FILMS INCLUDE: *The Adventures of Dollie, Balked At the Altar, After Many Years, An Awful Moment, The Test Of Friendship, The Helping Hand* 1908; *The Cord of Life, Edgar Allan Poe, The Politician's Love Story, A Drunkard's Reformation, The Cricket on the Hearth, The Mills of the Gods, Lines of White on a Sullen Sea, Pippa Passes, The Day After* 1909; *The Rocky Road, The Converts, The Unchanging Sea,* 1910; *Fisher Folks, Enoch Arden* (also sc.) 1911; *The Scarlet Letter* 1913; *A Fair Rebel, The Wife* 1914; *The Gambler of the West* 1915; *Charity* 1916.

Arzner, Dorothy. Director. *b.* Jan. 3, 1900, San Francisco. *d.* 1979. *ed.* USC (pre-med studies). One of the few American women directors of the studio era, she made her first contact with movie personalities while waiting on tables in her father's small Hollywood café. She drove an ambulance in WW I, then worked on a newspaper. In 1919 she was hired by William De Mille as a stenographer in the script department of Famous Players and was later promoted to script clerk and film cutter and then to film editor. Her editing of the bullfight scenes in *Blood and Sand* (1922, starring Valentino) was so imaginative that director James CRUZE entrusted her with the editing of his famous *The Covered Wagon* (1923). She also wrote a number of scripts, alone or in collaboration, including Cruze's *Old Ironsides* (1926). In 1927, Paramount gave Miss Arzner her first directing assignment, *Fashions for Women.* She continued directing films until 1943 and produced WAC training films during WW II. Although she officially retired in the mid-40s, Arzner continued to be involved with cinema for many years. She taught film at the Pasadena Playhouse and UCLA (among her students was Francis Ford Coppola) and produced Pepsi commercials for her friend, Joan Crawford. Interest in her work revived during the 70s with the rise in feminist consciousness, although her films did not typically promote the cause of women's liberation. In 1975 she was paid a special tribute by the Directors Guild of America, of which she was the first woman member.

FILMS: *Fashions For Women, Ten Modern Commandments, Get Your Man* 1927; *Manhattan Cocktail* 1928; *The Wild Party* 1929; *Sarah and Son, Paramount on Parade* (co-dir, with many others), *Anybody's Woman* 1930; *Honor Among Lovers, Working Girls* 1931; *Merrily We Go to Hell* 1932; *Christopher Strong*

1933; *Nana* 1934; *Craig's Wife* 1936; *The Bride Wore Red* 1937; *Dance Girl Dance* 1940; *First Comes Courage* 1943.

ASA. American Standards Association. Beginning in 1930 this association established technical standards, known as the "ASA Standards," for motion pictures, still photography, and television, among them the ASA Ratings (see below). In 1966 it changed its names to the USA Standards Institute.

ASA Speed Rating. An internationally recognized rating, established by the ASA to indicate the emulsion speed of film. The film's sensitivity to light is rated as an ASA number, printed by the manufacturer on every package of film. This recommended number is used by the cameraman to calculate his exposure.

A.S.C. (American Society of Cinematographers). A professional association founded in 1919 by leading Hollywood cameramen "to advance the art of cinematography." Membership, by invitation only, numbers some 250 directors of photography as well as some associate members from allied crafts. The initials A.S.C. usually follow the name of a director of photography in the screen credits. The British counterpart is B.S.C. The A.S.C. publishes *The American Cinematographer.*

Ashby, Hal. Director, film editor. *b.* 1929, Ogden, Utah. *d.* 1988, of liver cancer. A product of a broken home, he experienced a severe personal crisis at age 12, when his father committed suicide. He later dropped out of high school, but eventually attended Utah State University. He married and divorced twice by age 21 (two more divorces followed later), when he hitchhiked to Los Angeles in 1950. After working for a while at Universal as a multilith operator, mimeographing scripts, he moved on to Republic, where he became an apprentice editor. Later, as assistant editor to Robert SWINK, he worked with William WYLER and George Stevens, among other directors. After becoming full editor in 1965, he collaborated mainly with Norman JEWISON, and won an Academy Award for editing that director's *In the Heat of the Night* (1967). Ashby turned out his first film as a director in 1970, and for the rest of the decade enjoyed a growing reputation for his skill, originality, and zest for the offbeat. His second film, *Harold and Maude,* initially ignored, became over the years an enormously popular cult movie. His third, *The Last Detail,* won him the admiration of serious critics. He reached the peak of his success with the post-Vietnam drama *Coming Home* (1978), an Academy Award nominee for best picture and best director. But after a lesser, if still considerable, achievement with *Being There* (1979), Ashby's career went into a decline from which it never recovered.

FILMS: As editor—*The Loved One* (co-edit.), *The Cincinnati Kid* 1965; *The Russians Are Coming, the Russians Are Coming* 1966; *In the Heat of the Night* 1967. As associate producer—*The Thomas Crown Affair* 1968; *Gaily Gaily* 1969. As director—*The Landlord* 1970; *Harold and Maude* (also cameo) 1971; *The Last Detail* 1973; *Shampoo* 1975; *Bound for Glory* 1976; *Coming Home* (also cameo) 1978; *Being There* (also edit., cameo) 1979; *Second Hand Hearts/The Hamster of Happiness* (also edit., release delayed from 1979) 1981; *Lookin' to Get Out, Let's Spend the Night Together* (Rolling Stones concert film) 1982; *The Slugger's Wife* (also cameo) 1985; *8 Million Ways to Die* 1986.

Ashcroft, Dame Peggy. Actress. *b.* Dec. 22, 1907, Croydon, England. *d.* 1991. Made her London stage debut in 1927, her New York stage debut in 1937. A distinguished Shakespearean interpreter, she appeared in occasional films. She was created Dame Commander of the British Empire in 1956. At age 77 she won an Academy Award as best supporting actress for her performance in *A Passage to India.*

FEATURE FILMS: *The Wandering Jew* 1933; *The Thirty-nine Steps* 1935; *Rhodes of Africa/Rhodes* 1936; *Quiet Wedding* 1940; *The Nun's Story* 1959; *Tell Me Lies, Secret Ceremony* 1968; *Three Into Two Won't Go* 1969; *Sunday Bloody Sunday* 1971; *Der Fussgänger/The Pedestrian* (Ger.) 1974; *Joseph Andrews* 1977; *Hullabaloo Over Georgie and Bonnie's Pictures* 1979; *A Passage to India* 1984; *When the Wind Blows* (voice only), *Madame Sousatzka* 1988; *She's Been Away* 1989.

Asher, William. Director. Born in 1919. Made his first film, a low-budget boxing drama, in collaboration with Richard QUINE, in 1948. He then directed for TV, returning briefly to feature films in 1957. Back in features again in the mid-60s, he started a vogue for silly, youth-oriented beach pictures, then went back to TV, where he was best known as producer-director of 'Bewitched' (starring his wife Elizabeth Montgomery). He returned to feature films again in the 80s.

FILMS: *Leather Gloves* (co-dir., co-prod. with Richard Quine) 1948; *The Shadow on the Window, The 27th Day* 1957; *Beach Party, Johnny Cool* (also prod.) 1963; *Muscle Beach Party* (also co-story), *Bikini Beach* (also co-sc.) 1964; *Beach Blanket Bingo* (also co-sc.), *How to Stuff a Wild Bikini* (also co-sc.) 1965; *Fireball 500* (also co-sc.) 1966; *Night Warning* 1983; *Movers and Shakers* 1984.

Asherson, Renée. Actress. Born Renée Ascherson, in 1920, in London. Made her stage debut in 1935, playing a walk-on part in John Gielgud's *Romeo and Juliet.* She had a rich theatrical career before her first film appearance, in Laurence Olivier's *Henry V* (1944). Her film appearances have been infrequent.

FILMS INCLUDE: *The Way Ahead/Immortal Battalion, Henry V* (as Princess Katharine) 1944; *The Way to the Stars/Johnny in the Clouds, Caesar and Cleopatra* 1945; *Once a Jolly Swagman/Maniacs on Wheels* 1948; *The Cure for Love, The Small Back Room* 1949; *Pool of London* 1950; *Malta Story* 1953; *The Day the Earth Caught Fire* 1962; *Rasputin the Mad Monk* (as the Tsarina) 1966; *Theatre of Blood* 1973; *Hell House Girls* 1975; *A Man Called Intrepid* 1979.

Ashley, Elizabeth. Actress. Born Elizabeth Ann Cole on Aug. 30, 1939, in Ocala, Fla. Versatile, intense leading lady of the American stage, TV, and films. She won a Tony Award for her very first Broadway performance, in 'Take Her She's Mine' (1961–62), and enjoyed great success in 1963 as the star of the stage comedy hit 'Barefoot in the Park.' She made her screen debut the following year in *The Carpetbaggers,* but in 1965, after appearing in two more films, she retired from acting for personal reasons. She returned to full activity in the early 70s and in 1974 received critical accolades for her strong portrayal of Maggie in the Broadway revival of Tennessee Williams's 'Cat on a Hot Tin Roof.' She has since appeared in film with greater regularity and become known as the eccentric Aunt Frieda on TV's 'Evening Shade.' She is divorced from actors James FARENTINO and George PEPPARD. Autobiography: *Actress—Postcards From the Road* (1978).

FILMS: *The Carpetbaggers* 1964; *Ship of Fools, The Third Day* 1965; *Hawaii* 1966; *The Marriage of a Young Stockbroker* 1971; *Paperback Hero* 1973; *Golden Needles* 1974; *Rancho Deluxe, 92 in the Shade* 1975; *The Great Scout and Cathouse Thursday* 1976. *Coma* 1978; *Windows* 1980; *Paternity* 1981; *Split Image* 1982; *Dragnet* 1987; *Dangerous Curves* 1988; *Vampire's Kiss* 1989.

Ashman, Howard. Lyricist, playwright, stage director. *b.* May 17, 1950, Baltimore. *d.* 1991. *ed.* Goddard College (B.A.), Indiana U. (M.A.). The son of an ice cream cone manufacturer, he came to New York to write plays, beginning with 'The Confirmation' in 1976, and also served as artistic director of the WPA Theatre (1977–82). Interested in writing lyrics, he embarked on a long-term collaboration with composer Alan MENKEN. Their first production was the musical 'God Bless You, Mr. Rosewater' (1979); Ashman directed and wrote the book and lyrics. In 1983, the collaborators enjoyed their first major commercial success with the Tony-nominated 'Little Shop of Horrors.' Based on the cult horror-comedy film by Roger CORMAN, it became off-Broadway's most lucrative musical and was in turn brought to the screen. After collaborating with Marvin HAMLISCH on the unsuccessful stage show 'Smile' (1986), Ashman reunited with Menken to write original songs for a series of Disney animated features. Marking a renaissance for Disney's fairy-tale genre, the films were greatly enhanced by the bright, hummable songs written in a pastiche of styles—calypso for *The Little Mermaid*'s 'Under the Sea' (Oscar winner, best song), French music-hall for *Beauty and the Beast*'s 'Be Our Guest.' The title song from the latter film won an Oscar for best song. Soon after the Oscar win for *The Little Mermaid*, Ashman announced to his collaborator that he was sick with AIDS. He lived to write the lyrics for half of the songs in *Aladdin* before succumbing to the illness. The lyrics for *Aladdin* were completed by Tim Rice, who won on Oscar with Menken for 'Whole New World.'

FILMS: *Little Shop of Horrors* 1986; *The Little Mermaid* (music dir., also co-prod.) 1989; *Beauty and the Beast* 1991; *Aladdin* (co-lyricist) 1992.

Ashton, John. Actor. Born on Feb. 22, 1948, Springfield, Mass. *ed.* USC. Beefy, moustached character player, memorable as the sour detective Taggart in *Beverly Hills Cop* and as a bounty hunter in *Midnight Run*.

FILMS INCLUDE: *Oh, God!* 1977; *Breaking Away* 1979; *Borderline* 1980; *Beverly Hills Cop* 1984; *King Kong Lives* 1986; *Beverly Hills Cop II, Some Kind of Wonderful* 1987; *Midnight Run, She's Having a Baby* 1988; *Curly Sue* 1991; *The Tommyknockers* 1993; *Little Big League, Trapped in Paradise* 1994.

ASIFA (Association Internationale du Film d'Animation). International body established in 1959 to encourage the development of animated films through co-operation and free exchange of ideas between nations. Among the member countries are the US, Russia, the UK, Canada, Japan, Belgium, Hungary, and Germany.

Asner, Edward. Actor. Born on Nov. 15, 1929, in Kansas City, Mo. *ed.* U. of Chicago. Gruff, balding, paunchy character player of the American stage, TV, and films. He made his professional debut in Chicago at 18, and after challenging Broadway in the 50s moved on to Hollywood, where he found ample employment in TV and films. He scored a huge success on the small screen in the role of boss Lou Grant in the comedy series 'The Mary Tyler Moore Show' (1970–77) and as the star of his own offshoot drama series 'Lou Grant' (1977–82). He won four Emmy Awards for his performance in these series and two additional Emmys for his roles in the miniseries 'Rich Man, Poor Man' and 'Roots.' An outspoken activist for liberal causes, Asner was the center of much controversy in the 80s, when he was accused by opponents of using his fame and his standing as president of the Screen Actors Guild (1981–85) to cause turmoil and dissent in the industry's labor relations.

FILMS: *Kid Galahad* 1962; *The Satan Bug, The Slender Thread* 1965; *The Venetian Affair, El Dorado, Gunn* 1967; *Change of Habit* 1969; *Halls of Anger, They Call Me Mister Tibbs* 1970; *Skin Game, The Todd Killings* 1971; *The Wrestler* 1974; *Gus* 1976; *Fort Apache the Bronx* 1981; *O'Hara's Wife* 1982; *Daniel* 1983; *Pinocchio and the Emperor of the Night* (voice only) 1987; *Moon Over Parador* (cameo) 1988; *Happily Ever After* (v/o) 1990; *JFK* 1991.

Asp, Anna. Production designer. Born in 1946, in Sweden. *ed.* Academy of Fine Arts and Dramatic Institute, Stockholm. Her impressive production designs have enhanced the work of Scandinavia's best known directors, including Ingmar BERGMAN, Andrei TARKOVSKY, and Bille AUGUST. She won an Oscar for Bergman's *Fanny and Alexander*.

FILMS INCLUDE (as art director or production designer): *Giliap* 1973; *Ansikte mot ansikte/Face to Face* 1976; *Hostsonaten/Autumn Sonata* (sets only) 1978; *Min Alskade* 1979; *Fanny and Alexander* 1982; *After the Rehearsal* 1984; *Offret-Sacrificatio/The Sacrifice* 1986; *Pelle Erobreren/Pelle the Conqueror* 1987; *Katinka* 1988.

aspect ratio. The width-to-height ratio of a printed motion picture frame or the image it projects on a screen. For some 50 years after the advent of cinema the standard ratio was 4:3, or 1.33:1. This shape, established in 1906 as an international standard, was considered ideal for composition and viewing comfort. However, experimentation with various screen shapes continued (Eisenstein, among others, toyed with the idea of a square screen), and during the 50s, with the advent of wide screens, a range of aspect ratios was introduced, from 1.65:1 to 2.55:1. More revolutionary screen shapes are still in the experimental stage. See also SCREEN; WIDE-SCREEN PROCESSES; CINEMASCOPE; CINERAMA.

Asquith, Anthony. Director. *b.* Nov. 9, 1902, London. *d.* 1968. *ed.* Oxford. The son of H. H. Asquith, Britain's Liberal prime minister (1908–16). In 1925 Asquith, nicknamed "Puffin," co-founded the Film Society, with Bernard Shaw, H. G. Wells, Julian Huxley, and others. He then went to Hollywood to study filmmaking and returned to England in 1926 to start his film career as assistant director, screenwriter, and editor. His first film, *Shooting Stars* (co-dir., 1928), was an exceptionally inventive silent film, noted for its bold cutting techniques and subtle continuity. He extended his experimentation to include the sound track in his first two sound films, *A Cottage on Dartmoor/Escaped from Dartmoor* (1930) and *Tell England* (co-dir., 1930), for which he gained a reputation as Hitchcock's equal.

Most of Asquith's subsequent work was divided between semidocumentaries and rather talky adaptations from drama and literature. At his best, he is a master of atmosphere and can extract the most from a dramatic situation. His *Pygmalion*, which he co-directed in 1938, is considered by many the best screen adaptation of Shaw to date, and his *The Importance of Being Earnest* (1952) catches most of the sparkle of Oscar Wilde's wit.

FEATURE FILMS: *Shooting Stars* (assoc. dir., sc. only), *Underground* (also sc.) 1928; *The Runaway Princess* 1929; *A Cottage on Dartmoor/Escaped From Dartmoor* 1930; *Tell England/The Battle of Gallipoli* (co-dir. with Geoffrey Barkas), *Dance Pretty Lady* 1931; *Lucky Number* 1933; *The Unfinished Symphony* 1934; *Moscow Nights/I Stand Condemned* 1935; *Pygmalion* (co-dir. with Leslie Howard) 1938; *French Without Tears* 1939; *Freedom Radio/The Voice in the Night, Quiet Wedding* 1940; *Cottage to Let/Bombsite Stolen* 1941; *Uncensored* 1942; *The Demi-Paradise/Adventure for Two, We Dive at Dawn, Welcome to Britain* (co-dir. with Burgess Meredith) 1943; *Fanny by Gaslight/Man of Evil* 1944; *The Way to the Stars/Johnny in the Clouds* 1945; *While the Sun Shines* 1947; *The Winslow Boy* 1948; *The Woman in Question/Five Angles on Murder* 1950; *The Browning Version* 1951; *The Importance of Being Earnest* (also sc.) 1952; *The Net/Project M–7/The Final Test* 1953; *The Young Lovers/Chance Meeting, Carrington V.C./Court-Martial* 1954; *Orders to Kill* 1958; *The Doctor's Dilemma, Libel* 1959; *The Millionairess* 1960; *Two Living One Dead* 1961; *Guns of Darkness* 1962; *The V.I.P.s, An*

Evening with the Royal Ballet (co-dir. with Anthony Havelock Allan) 1963; *The Yellow Rolls-Royce* 1964.

Assante, Armand. Actor. Born on Oct. 4, 1949, in New York City. *ed.* AADA. Darkly handsome, Latin-type leading man and supporting player of the New York stage, Hollywood films, and television.

FILMS: *The Lords of Flatbush* 1974; *Paradise Alley* 1978; *Prophecy* 1979; *Little Darlings, Private Benjamin* 1980; *Love and Money, I, the Jury* 1982; *Unfaithfully Yours* 1984; *Belizaire the Cajun* 1986; *The Penitent* 1988; *Animal Behavior* 1989; *Eternity, Q&A* 1990; *The Marrying Man* 1991; *The Mambo Kings, 1492, Hoffa* 1992; *Fatal Instinct* 1993; *Trial by Jury* 1994; *Judge Dredd* 1995; *Striptease* 1996.

assembly. In editing, the initial joining together of shots in proper continuity in an attempt to bring the film to a rough-cut stage. This involves a selection of takes, the elimination of unwanted footage, the trimming of scenes to a more or less desirable length, and the marking of transitions. See also EDITING; ROUGH CUT.

assistant cameraman. A member of a camera crew responsible for loading and unloading film, changing camera lenses, maintaining focus while the camera is in motion, keeping the camera in working order, and filling out camera reports. A full production crew includes at least one assistant cameraman. A second assistant cameraman is often on the payroll of large-budget productions. He relieves the first assistant of some of his simpler duties and is responsible for keeping the slate with the clapsticks ready for shooting.

assistant director. The director's right-hand man, he performs the function of a foreman on the set. The "A.D.," as he is frequently called, relieves the director of many routine responsibilities so that the director can concentrate on the creative aspects of his work. The A.D. is responsible for, among other things, the "call" (summoning the actors, crews, and logistical support to the right place at the right time). It is also his responsibility to keep the production moving on schedule and to maintain order and discipline on the set. It is his voice that pleads for "Quiet on the set!" and orders the camera operator to "Roll."

On the creative side, the assistant director is directly responsible for crowd scenes. Prior to the start of production, he breaks down the script for a shooting schedule, with special attention to bit players and extras. With the director's approval, he determines the number of extras to be used in any particular scene and hires them (usually from CENTRAL CASTING CORPORATION).

The assistant director often has one or two second assistants, known as "seconds."

assistant editor. The film editor's apprentice. His varied duties include keeping shot records, splicing film, cutting prints, labeling cans, and in general maintaining a schedule and order in the usually cramped cutting room.

assistant producer. A member of a production crew responsible for carrying out the producer's instructions. In the absence of the producer, he may perform on-location supervision and co-ordination duties.

Associated Actors and Artistes of America. See AAAA.

Associated British. British film production company. It was founded in 1930, with Pathé as its distributing arm. Its base of operations was London's Elstree Studios, the first British studios to turn out sound films. The company later came under the control of EMI (Electrical and Musical Industries).

associate producer. Nominally a producer's second-in-command, he often shares both creative and business responsibilities with the producer. Sometimes he is the actual producer of a film with the credited producer funtioning only as a figurehead.

Association of Cinematograph Television and Allied Technicians. See ACTT.

Association Internationale du Film d'Animation. See ASIFA.

Association of Motion Picture and Television Producers. See AMPTP.

Asta. A bouncy wirehaired fox terrier who shared the limelight with Myrna Loy and William Powell in MGM's "The Thin Man" feature series and barked his way to popularity through other Hollywood films of the 30s and early 40s. As is frequently the case with animal "stars," more than one dog played Asta over the years. A distant relative was recruited for the "Thin Man" TV series in the late 50s.

Astaire, Fred. Actor, dancer, choreographer. *b.* Frederick Austerlitz, May 10, 1899, Omaha, Neb. *d.* 1987. At the age of seven he started touring the vaudeville circuit with his sister Adele as a dancing partner. According to some sources, they appeared in 1915 in Mary Pickford's film *Fanchon the Cricket.* In 1917 they made their Broadway dancing debut in the musical 'Over the Top,' followed by their first big success, 'The Passing Show of 1918,' after which they became perennial favorites with Broadway and London audiences. After more stage hits, including 'Lady Be Good' (1924), 'Smiles' (1930), and 'The Band Wagon' (1931), the partnership was dissolved following Adele's marriage to Lord Charles Cavendish. Astaire was given a Hollywood screen test, resulting in the famous verdict: "Can't act. Slightly bald. Can dance a little." Nevertheless he got a small part opposite Joan Crawford in *Dancing Lady* (1933).

Shortly afterward, Astaire was paired with newcomer Ginger ROGERS, a partnership that was to last through ten films and produced some of the most magical moments in screen musical history. When Miss Rogers turned to dramatic roles, Astaire continued to dominate the musical film scene with such partners as Lucille Bremer, Rita Hayworth, Eleanor Powell, and Cyd Charisse. In 1946, with Gene Kelly fast becoming his heir apparent, Astaire announced his retirement, but two years later he replaced the ailing Kelly as Judy Garland's partner in *Easter Parade.* His comeback was triumphant.

Almost single-handedly, Fred Astaire restyled the song-and-dance film, leaving his graceful mark on all musical movies to come. His own films always included solo dance numbers in which he skillfully improvised in his free, easygoing style, charming audiences with his relaxed exuberance and sophistication. He also introduced many hit songs, written especially for his pleasant, if untrained, singing voice. He later proved to be a capable actor in his first dramatic role in *On the Beach* (1959). He subsequently abandoned song-and-dance parts for straight acting and was nominated for an Oscar as best supporting actor for his performance in *The Towering Inferno* (1974).

Astaire received a special Academy Award in 1949 for his contribution to films. In 1981 he was honored with the American Film Institute's Life Achievement Award. Autobiography: *Steps in Time* (1960).

FILMS: *Dancing Lady, Flying Down to Rio* 1933; *The Gay Divorcee* 1934; *Roberta, Top Hat* 1935; *Follow the Fleet, Swing Time* 1936; *Shall We Dance, A Damsel in Distress* 1937; *Carefree* 1938; *The Story of Vernon and Irene Castle* 1939; *Broadway Melody of 1940, Second Chorus* 1940; *You'll Never Get Rich* 1941; *You Were Never Lovelier, Holiday Inn* 1942; *The Sky's the Limit* 1943; *Yolanda and the Thief* 1945; *Ziegfeld Follies, Blue Skies* 1946; *Easter Parade* 1948; *The Barkleys of Broadway* 1949; *Three Little Words, Let's Dance* 1950; *Royal Wedding* 1951; *The Belle of New York* 1952; *The Band Wagon* 1953; *Daddy Long Legs* 1955; *Funny Face, Silk Stockings* 1957; *On the Beach* 1959; *The Pleasure of His Company* 1961; *The*

Notorious Landlady 1962; *Finian's Rainbow* 1968; *Midas Run* 1969; *That's Entertainment* (on-camera co-narr.), *The Towering Inferno* 1974; *That's Entertainment II* (on-camera co-narr.) 1976; *The Amazing Dobermans, Un Taxi mauve/The Purple Taxi* (Fr./It./Ire.) 1977; *Ghost Story* 1981; *George Stevens: A Filmmaker's Journey* (doc.; on-camera commentary) 1985.

Asther, Nils. Actor. *b.* Jan. 17, 1897, Malmö, Sweden. *d.* 1981. Suave, romantic star of European and Hollywood films. A graduate of the famed Royal Dramatic Theater, he entered films under the guidance of director Mauritz STILLER, Garbo's mentor. He appeared in Swedish and German productions before arriving in Hollywood in 1927. He was very popular during the waning years of the silent era, but his foreign accent limited his range after the advent of sound, and his stature diminished. He continued to play leads, however, and gave a memorable performance in Capra's *The Bitter Tea of General Yen* (1933). After an interlude in England in the mid-30s, he returned to Hollywood, where he was cast for the most part in low-budget programmers. He returned to Sweden in 1959. His second wife was actress Vivian Duncan.

FILMS INCLUDE: *The Wings* (Sw.) 1916; *Love's Crucible* (Sw.) 1922; *Finale der Liebe* (Ger.) 1925; *Die Drei Kuckucksuhren* (Ger.) 1926; *Topsy and Eva, Sorrell and Son* 1927; *The Blue Danube, The Cossacks, Laugh Clown Laugh, Loves of an Actress, The Cardboard Lover, Adrienne Lecouvreur, Our Dancing Daughters, Dream of Love* 1928; *Wild Orchids, The Single Standard* 1929; *The Sea Bat* 1930; *Letty Lynton, But the Flesh Is Weak* 1932; *The Right to Romance, The Bitter Tea of General Yen, If I Were Free* 1933; *Madame Spy, The Love Captive, The Crime Doctor* 1934; *Abdul the Damned* (UK) 1935; *The Night of January 16th* 1941; *Night Monster* 1942; *Mystery Broadcast* 1943; *The Man in Half Moon Street* 1944; *Son of Lassie* 1945; *That Man From Tangier* 1953; *When Darkness Falls* (Sw.) 1960; *Gudrun/Suddenly, a Woman!* (Den.) 1963.

astigmatism. A defect in a camera lens which causes an optical distortion by not allowing reflected rays of light to focus uniformly. This aberration is especially noticeable at the edges of a frame.

Astor, Gertrude. Actress. *b.* Nov. 9, 1887, Lakewood, Ohio. *d.* 1977. Tall, blonde leading lady and second lead of Hollywood silents and early talkies; later in scattered character roles. A stage actress in stock from age 13, she joined Universal in 1914 and remained with that studio through the mid-20s, later freelancing for various companies. She typically played vampy roles, often as the calculating "other woman." She was quite popular among fans and enjoyed the reputation of being one of Hollywood's most elegant and best-dressed women. She was a favorite of John Ford and appeared in many of his films through the early 60s. At one point in her career she played the trombone on a Mississippi showboat. She died on her 90th birthday.

FILMS INCLUDE: *The Devil's Pay Day, Bondage* 1917; *The Brazen Beauty* 1918; *The Wicked Darling* 1919; *The Branding Iron* 1920; *The Concert, Through the Back Door* 1921; *Beyond the Rocks, The Wall Flower, The Impossible Mrs. Bellew, The Kentucky Derby, You Never Know* 1922; *Alice Adams, The Ne'er-Do-Well, Rupert of Hentzau, Flaming Youth, The Wanters* 1923; *Secrets, Broadway or Bust, Daring Love, The Torrent, The Silent Watcher* 1924; *The Reckless Sex, The Charmer, The Verdict, Kentucky Pride, Satan in Sables, Stage Struck, Ship of Souls* 1925; *Kiki, The Boy Friend, Don Juan's Three Nights, The Strong Man, The Old Soak, The Country Beyond* 1926; *The Taxi Dancer, The Cat and the Canary, Shanghaied, The Irresistible Lover, Pretty Clothes, Ginsberg the Great, Uncle Tom's Cabin* 1927; *The Cohens and the Kellys in Paris, Rose-Marie, Stocks and Blondes* 1928; *Synthetic Sin, The Fall of Eve, Twin Beds, Frozen Justice, Untamed* 1929; *Be Yourself!, Dames Ahoy!* 1930; *Come Clean* (short; as Oliver Hardy's wife), *Hell Bound* 1931; *Western Limited* 1932; *I Have Lived 1933; Wine Women and Song* 1934; *Empty Saddles* 1936; *Misbehaving Husbands* 1940; *Hold Back the Dawn* 1941; *My Dear Secretary* 1948; *Father Makes Good* 1950; *Around the World in 80 Days* 1956; *All in a Night's Work* 1961; *The Man Who Shot Liberty Valance* 1962.

Astor, Mary. Actress. *b.* Lucille Vasconcellos Langhanke, May 3, 1906, Quincy, Ill. *d.* 1987. Delicately beautiful star of silent and sound films. Driven by a career-minded German-immigrant father, she entered a beauty contest at 14 and films at 15. After playing an assortment of small roles, she coasted to stardom in 1924 as John Barrymore's leading lady in *Beau Brummel.* She remained an important screen personality through the remainder of the silent era and through the 40s. Her off-screen adventures, including a stormy love affair with John Barrymore, four marriages, alcoholism, and attempted suicide, were popular subjects of Hollywood gossip. Her first husband, director Kenneth Hawks (brother of Howard Hawks), died in a 1930 plane crash while on a filming assignment. During a custody battle over her daughter in divorcing her second husband, a physician, in 1936, Miss Astor's personal diary was introduced in court, listing indiscretions that embarrassed many in the film community, and including a secret affair with playwright George S. KAUFMAN. The affair, Hollywood's most publicized scandal of the 30s, almost ruined her career, but she quickly returned to the screen, typically playing elegant, sophisticated, often bitchy women of the world. After 1949 she was seen in films only occasionally, in character parts. A heart condition kept her off the screen after 1965. She spent her final years confined to the Motion Picture Country Home. She authored two autobiographical volumes, *My Story* (1959) and *A Life on Film* (1971) and several moderately successful novels.

FILMS: *Sentimental Tommy* (bit, cut from final print), *The Beggar Maid* (2-reel art film) 1921; *The Young Painter* (2-reel art film), *The Man Who Played God, John Smith* 1922; *Second Fiddle, Success, The Bright Shawl, Hollywood* (cameo), *The Marriage Maker, Puritan Passions, The Rapids, Woman-Proof* 1923; *The Fighting Coward, Beau Brummel, The Fighting American, Unguarded Women, The Price of a Party, Inez from Hollywood* 1924; *Oh Doctor!, Enticement, Playing With Souls, Don Q Son of Zorro, The Pace That Thrills, Scarlet Saint* 1925; *High Steppers, The Wise Guy, Don Juan, Forever After* 1926; *The Sea Tiger, The Rough Riders, The Sunset Derby, Rose of the Golden West, No Place to Go, Two Arabian Knights* 1927; *Sailors' Wives, Dressed to Kill, Three-Ring Marriage, Heart to Heart, Dry Martini, Romance of the Underworld* 1928; *New Year's Eve, The Woman From Hell* 1929; *Ladies Love Brutes, The Runaway Bride, Holiday, The Lash/Adios* 1930; *The Royal Bed, Behind Office Doors, The Sin Ship, Other Men's Women, White Shoulders, Smart Woman* 1931; *Men of Chance, The Lost Squadron, A Successful Calamity, Those We Love, Red Dust* 1932; *The Little Giant, Jennie Gerhardt, The World Changes, The Kennel Murder Case, Convention City* 1933; *Easy to Love, Upper World, Return of the Terror, The Man With Two Faces, The Case of the Howling Dog* 1934; *I Am a Thief, Red Hot Tires, Straight From the Heart, Dinky, Page Miss Glory, Man of Iron* 1935; *The Murder of Dr. Harrigan, And So They Were Married, Trapped by Television, Dodsworth, Lady From Nowhere* 1936; *The Prisoner of Zenda, The Hurricane* 1937; *Paradise for Three, No Time to Marry, There's Always a Woman, Woman Against Woman, Listen Darling* 1938; *Midnight* 1939; *Turnabout, Brigham Young* 1940; *The Great Lie, The Maltese Falcon* 1941;

In This Our Life (unbilled cameo), *Across the Pacific, The Palm Beach Story* 1942; *Thousands Cheer, Young Ideas* 1943; *Blonde Fever, Meet Me in St. Louis* 1944; *Claudia and David* 1946; *Fiesta, Cynthia, Desert Fury, Cass Timberlane* 1947; *Act of Violence, Little Women, Any Number Can Play* 1949; *A Kiss Before Dying, The Power and the Prize* 1956; *The Devil's Hairpin* 1957; *This Happy Feeling* 1958; *Stranger in My Arms* 1959; *Return to Peyton Place* 1961; *Youngblood Hawke* 1964; *Hush Hush. . . Sweet Charlotte* 1965.

Astoria Studios. Movie production center opened on Sept. 20, 1920, in Astoria, Queens, New York. It was owned by Famous Players-Lasky, which later became Paramount. Numerous silent features (including all of D. W. Griffith's Paramount films) and early sound features (including the 1929 films *The Letter* and *The Cocoanuts*) were produced on the lot. From 1925, it was also the site of the Paramount Acting School. By the 30s, its exclusive association with Paramount ended, and it became an independent production center. During WW II, the War Department renamed it the US Army Pictorial Center and used it to produce war-related films, including "Army-Navy Screen Magazine." No further commercial features were made at the studio until after 1976, when it was revived by the Astoria Motion Picture and Television Center Foundation. Since then, numerous features, including *Thieves* (1977), *Arthur* (1981), and *Shadows and Fog* (1992) have been made at the studio. Since 1988, the Kaufman-Astoria studios (as they are now called) have also been the site of the AMERICAN MUSEUM OF THE MOVING IMAGE.

Astruc, Alexandre. Director. Born on July 13, 1923, in Paris. *ed.* Sorbonne (degrees in literature and law). A novelist and literary and film critic, he advanced the theory of *caméra-stylo* (camera-pen), which claimed for films a means of expression all its own, free of the "tyranny of the visual" and limitations of traditional storytelling concepts, "a means of writing just as flexible and subtle as the written language." He started in films as Marc Allégret's assistant on *Blanche Fury* (1947), then directed two amateur 16 mm films, *Aller et Retour* (1948) and *Ulysse ou les Mauvaises Rencontres* (1949), and collaborated on the scripts of Achard's *Jean de la Lune* (1948) and Pagliero's *La P. . . Respectueuse/The Respectful Prostitute* (1949) before becoming a full-fledged director.

Astruc's films show a conscious concern for style for its own sake. Influenced by the German cinema of the 20s, he selects his shots carefully, concentrating on camera angles and on framing and lighting, often at the expense of the human drama and theme. On the whole, his product as director falls short of his theoretical claims.

FEATURE FILMS: *Le Rideau Cramoisi/The Crimson Curtain* (medium length; also sc.) 1953; *Les Mauvaises Rencontres* 1955; *Une Vie/End of Desire* (also co-sc.) 1958; *La Proie pour l'Ombre* 1960; *L'Education sentimentale* 1962; *La Longue marche* 1966; *Flammes sur l'Adriatique* 1968; *Sartre par lui-même* (3-hour doc.; co-dir. with Michel Contat) 1976.

asynchronism. The opposite of synchronism, characterized by a discrepancy between the sound track and the visual image on the screen. It may occur accidentally, through editing errors, or may be used intentionally for artistic effect.

Early sound films tended to identify the source of sound visually, often resulting in an annoying redundancy. It was soon discovered, however, that important effects may be achieved by the independent manipulation of sight and sound, by divorcing the shown image from the corresponding sound track.

Ates, Roscoe. Actor. *b.* Jan. 20, 1892, Grange, Miss. *d.* 1962. Accumulated 15 years of concert (violin) and stage experience, including vaudeville, before entering films in 1929. He played comic parts in scores of Hollywood films, often as a sidekick to screen cowboys. Cured of a stutter in his childhood, he later used it for comic effect along with his rubber face and bulging eyes. He was married to actress Barbara Ray.

FILMS INCLUDE: *South Sea Rose* 1929; *The Big House, Billy the Kid* 1930; *Cimarron, The Champ* 1931; *Freaks* 1932; *Alice in Wonderland* 1933; *The People's Enemy* 1935; *God's Country and the Woman* 1937; *Gone With the Wind* 1939; *Chad Hanna* 1940; *Sullivan's Travels, Ziegfeld Girl* 1941; *The Palm Beach Story* 1942; *Colorado Serenade* 1946; *Inner Sanctum* 1948; *Abbott and Costello Meet the Keystone Kops* 1955; *Come Next Spring* 1956; *The Sheepman* 1958; *The Errand Boy* 1961.

Atherton, William. Actor. Born William Knight, on July 30, 1947, in Orange, Conn. Leading man and supporting player of the American stage and screen. While still a high school student he became the youngest member of the Long Wharf Theatre company in New Haven. He later gained a scholarship to the Pasadena Playhouse and continued his drama studies at Carnegie Tech, then came to New York and joined the national touring company of 'Little Murders.' He subsequently appeared in a number of New York plays, making his film debut in 1972. He specializes in playing obnoxious second villains, notably the priggish bureaucrat in *Ghostbusters* and the heartless reporter in *Die Hard*.

FILMS: *The New Centurions* 1972; *Class of '44* 1973; *The Sugarland Express* 1974; *The Day of the Locust, The Hindenburg* 1975; *Looking for Mr. Goodbar* 1977; *Ghostbusters* 1984; *Real Genius* 1985; *No Mercy* 1986; *Die Hard* 1988; *Die Hard 2, Grim Prairie Tales, Navy SEALS* 1990; *Oscar* 1991; *Chrome Soldiers* 1992; *The Pelican Brief* 1993; *Bio-Dome* 1996; *Hoodlum* 1997.

Atkins, Christopher. Actor. Born on Feb. 21, 1961, in Rye, N.Y. *ed.* Dennison U. Curly blond lead who rocketed to fame as the object of Brooke SHIELDS's innocent passion in *The Blue Lagoon,* his first film. Little else followed.

FILMS: *The Blue Lagoon* 1980; *The Pirate Movie* (Austral.) 1982; *A Night in Heaven* 1983; *Mortuary Academy* 1988; *Listen to Me* 1989; *Shakma* 1990; *Shoot* 1992; *It's My Party* 1996.

atmosphere. The dominant mood or emotional tone of a film, which may evoke a psychological response from a viewer through association with its physical action and background. Many elements contribute to a film's atmosphere, including locales, sets, lighting, pace, camera positions, and musical background. Directors such as Fritz Lang, Murnau, Renoir, von Sternberg, von Stroheim, and Welles are noted for their ability to create atmosphere.

In Hollywood jargon, the term is sometimes used to denote persons or objects in the background of a shot, such as passers-by or an early automobile. Among audio technicians the term denotes the transmission or reception of sound.

Attanasio, Paul. Screenwriter. *ed.* Harvard University, Harvard Law School, Cambridge, Mass. Talented, intelligent writer who started out as a TV critic for the *Washington Post.* After breaking into writing for television on the series 'Homicide: Life on the Streets,' he moved to writing for films, most notably the exquisite, Academy Award nominated screenplay for *Quiz Show* (1994).

FILMS: *Rapid Fire* 1992; *Disclosure, Quiz Show* 1994; *Donnie Brasco* 1997.

Attenborough, Sir Richard (Samuel). Actor, director, producer. Born on Aug. 29, 1923, in Cambridge, England, the son of a college administrator. He was drawn early to acting, began performing at 12, and made his professional stage debut in 1941 while still attending the Royal Academy of Dramatic Art (RADA). The following year he played a small but important part in Noël Coward's WW II film drama *In Which We Serve,* portraying a coward, a role in which he was to be typecast for some time. He subsequently played a variety of lead and character roles in numerous British and some Hollywood films. In 1959 he turned to producing, forming a partnership with actor-director-screenwriter Bryan Forbes. Their company, Beaver Films, was dissolved in 1964. While continuing his acting career, Attenborough made an impressive start as a director with *Oh What a Lovely War!* in 1969. Distinguising himself as a sincere and efficient, if not an inventive director, he achieved his greatest success with the mammoth labor-of-love production *Gandhi* (1982) for which he received Academy Awards for best film and best director, as well as many other international prizes. He described his 20-year obsession with the project in a book, *In Search of Gandhi* (1982). His subsequent big-budget epics have been less successful. Attenborough, who was knighted in 1976, is known as a workaholic, a dedicated activist in the service of wide-ranging organizations and causes. Among the many offices he holds are chairman of the Royal Academy of Dramatic Art, vice-president of the British Academy of Film and Television Arts, governor of the National Film School, chairman of the Actors' Charitable Trust, pro-chancellor of Sussex University, a director of the Chelsea Football Club, and a trustee of the Tate Gallery. On the business side, he is chairman of Goldcrest Film and TV, chairman of Capital Radio, and deputy chairman of Channel 4 TV. He married actress Sheila Sim in 1944. Their son and two daughters also act. Richard's younger brother, David Attenborough, is a wildlife expert, noted for his books and educational TV programs.

FILMS: As actor—*In Which We Serve* 1942; *Schweik's New Adventures* 1943; *The Hundred Pound Window* 1944; *Journey Together* 1945; *A Matter of Life and Death/Stairway to Heaven, School for Secrets/Secret Flight* 1946; *The Man Within/The Smugglers, Dancing with Crime, Brighton Rock/ Young Scarface* 1947; *London Belongs to Me/Dulcimer Street* 1948; *The Guinea Pig, The Lost People* 1949; *Boys in Brown, Morning Departure/Operation Disaster* 1950; *Hell Is Sold Out, The Magic Box* 1951; *The Gift Horse/Glory at Sea, Father's Doing Fine* 1952; *Eight O'Clock Walk* 1954; *The Ship That Died of Shame* 1955; *Private's Progress, The Baby and the Battleship* 1956; *Brothers in Law, The Scamp* 1957; *Dunkirk, The Man Upstairs, Sea of Sand/Desert Patrol* 1958; *Danger Within/ Breakout, Jet Storm, I'm All Right Jack, S.O.S. Pacific* 1959; *The Angry Silence* (also co-prod.), *The League of Gentlemen* 1960; *Only Two Can Play, All Night Long, The Dock Brief/Trial and Error* 1962; *The Great Escape* (US) 1963; *The Third Secret, Seance on a Wet Afternoon* (also co-prod.), *Guns at Batasi* 1964; *The Flight of the Phoenix* (US) 1965; *The Sand Pebbles* (US) 1966; *Doctor Dolittle* (US) 1967; *Only When I Larf, The Bliss of Mrs. Blossom* 1968; *The Magic Christian* 1969; *The Last Grenade, David Copperfield* 1970; *A Severed Head, 10 Rillington Place, Loot* 1971; *And Then There Were None/Ten Little Indians* 1974; *Brannigan* (UK/US), *Rosebud* (US), *Conduct Unbecoming* 1975; *The Chess Players* 1977; *The Human Factor* 1979; *Jurassic Park* 1993; *Miracle on 34th Street* 1994; *Hamlet* 1996. As producer—*Whistle Down the Wind* 1961; *The L-Shaped Room* (co-prod.) 1962. As director—*Oh What a Lovely War!* (also co-prod.) 1969; *Young Winston* 1972; *A Bridge Too Far* 1977; *Magic* 1978; *Gandhi* (also prod.) 1982; *A Chorus Line* 1985; *Cry Freedom* (also prod.) 1987; *Chaplin* 1992; *Shadowlands* (also co-prod.) 1993; *In Love and War* (also co-prod.) 1996; *The Lost World* 1997.

Atwill, Lionel. Actor. *b.* Mar. 1, 1885, Croydon, England. *d.* 1946. A veteran of the London stage (from 1904), he appeared in many Broadway productions of the 20s and in a number of silent films. He became a Hollywood fixture in the early 30s, when he began a long list of character portrayals in both lead and supporting roles, often as a crafty villain. Best remembered for his imposing appearances in horror films.

FILMS INCLUDE: *Eve's Daughter* 1918; *The Marriage Price* 1919; *The Eternal Mother* 1920; *Indiscretion* 1921; *The Silent Witness, Dr. X* 1932; *The Mystery of the Wax Museum, The Sphinx, Song of Songs, The Vampire Bat, Murders in the Zoo, The Secret of the Blue Room* 1933; *Nana, Beggars in Ermine, Stamboul Quest* 1934; *Mark of the Vampire, The Devil Is a Woman, Rendezvous, Captain Blood, Lives of a Bengal Lancer* 1935; *Absolute Quiet, The Last Train From Madrid, The Great Garrick* (as playwright Beaumarchais), *Lancer Spy* 1937; *Three Comrades, The Great Waltz* 1938; *Son of Frankenstein, The Three Musketeers* (as De Rochefort), *The Hound of the Baskervilles, The Gorilla, The Sun Never Sets, Balalaika* 1939; *The Mad Empress* (also production adviser), *Johnny Apollo, Boom Town* 1940; *Man Made Monster* 1941; *The Mad Doctor of Market Street, To Be or Not to Be, The Strange Case of Dr. Rx, The Ghost of Frankenstein, Cairo, Night Monster* 1942; *Captain America* (serial), *Sherlock Holmes and the Secret Weapon, Frankenstein Meets the Wolf Man* 1943; *Secrets of Scotland Yard, House of Frankenstein* 1944; *Crime Inc., House of Dracula* 1945; *Lost City of the Jungle* (serial), *Genius at Work* 1946.

Auberjonois, René. Actor. Born on June 1, 1940, in New York City, of French-Canadian descent. *ed.* Carnegie Mellon U. Versatile character player of Hollywood films beginning in the 60s. A respected stage and television actor, he won a Tony award for 'Coco' and has been nominated three times since, most recently for 'City of Angels.' He has also played regular roles in the TV series 'Benson' and 'Star Trek: Deep Space Nine.'

FILMS INCLUDE: *Lilith* 1964; *Petulia* 1968; *M*A*S*H*, *Brewster McCloud* 1970; *McCabe and Mrs. Miller* 1971; *Pete 'n' Tillie* 1972; *The Hindenburg* 1975; *The Big Bus, King Kong* 1976; *Eyes of Laura Mars* 1978; *Where the Buffalo Roam* 1980; *Police Academy 5: Assignment Miami Beach* 1988; *The Little Mermaid* (voice only) 1989; *The Player* 1992; *The Ballad of Little Jo* 1993; *Batman Forever* 1995.

Aubry, Cécile. Actress. Born Anne-Marie-José Bénard, on Aug. 3, 1929, in Paris. She was discovered by director Henri-Georges CLOUZOT, who made her an overnight star in his *Manon* (1949). Her mature body and childlike face made her an erotic predecessor of Brigitte Bardot. But after six more film performances she married a Moroccan prince (later divorced) and retired from films. She has since written and illustrated children's books and produced children's programs for French television.

FILMS INCLUDE: *Manon* 1949; *The Black Rose* (US) 1950; *Barbe-Bleu/Bluebeard* 1951; *Bonjour la Chance* 1954; *The Reluctant Thief* (It.) 1955.

Auclair, Michel. Actor. *b.* Vladimir Vujović, Sept. 14, 1922, Koblenz, Germany, to a Serbian father and a French mother. *d.* 1988. Had a successful stage career in France before entering films in 1945. He played a great variety of leading roles with considerable subtlety and sophistication. He appeared mostly in French films but also in many other European productions and one American film, *Funny Face* (1957).

FILMS INCLUDE: *La Belle et La Bête/Beauty and the Beast* 1946; *Les Maudits/The Damned, Eternel Conflit* 1947; *Manon, Singoalla* (Sw./Fr.) 1949; *Justice est faite/Justice Is Done* 1950; *Camicie Rosse/Anita Garibaldi* (It./Fr.), *La Fête a Henriette/Holiday for Henrietta* 1952; *Si Versailles m'etait conté/Royal Affairs in Versailles* 1953; *Quai des Blondes* 1954; *Bonnes à tuer/One Step to Eternity, Double Destin, Andrea*

Chenier (It./Fr.) 1955; *Funny Face* (US), *Les Fanatiques/A Bomb for a Dictator* 1957; *Une Fille pour l'Eté/A Mistress for the Summer* 1960; *Le Rendez-Vous de Minuit, L'Education sentimentale* 1962; *Symphonie pour un Massacre/Symphony for a Massacre* 1963; *Le Coeur fou* 1970; *Les Mariés de l'An Deux* 1971; *The Day of the Jackal* (UK/Fr.), *L'Impossible Objet/ Impossible Object* (Fr./UK/It.) 1973; *Les Guichets du Louvre/ Black Thursday* 1974; *Souvenirs d'en France/French Provincial* 1975; *Le Juge Fayard dit le Sheriff* 1977; *L'Amour en Question* 1978; *Le Coup de Sirocco, Le Toubib* 1979; *Trois Hommes à abbatre/Three Men to Destroy* 1980; *Le Bon Plaisir* 1984.

Auden, W. H. Poet, playwright. *b.* Wystan Hugh Auden, Feb. 21, 1907, London. *d.* 1973. In the 30s this famous poet showed deep interest in Britain's documentary movement and collaborated on several productions, writing the verse for such rhythmically paced documentary films as *Coal Face* and *Night Mail* (both 1936).

Audiard, Michel. Screenwriter, director. *b.* May 15, 1920, Paris. *d.* 1985. A former optician and racing cyclist, and later a journalist and novelist, he turned to screenwriting in the late 40s. He collaborated on many French films of the 50s and 60s, demonstrating a special flair for bright if shallow dialogue. He began directing in the late 60s and brought to his own films the same corrosive humor that had made his scripts popular. Abroad, his films remained best known for their unusually long titles. In the mid-70s he returned to scriptwriting for others, sometimes in collaboration with his son, Jacques Audiard.

FILMS INCLUDE: As screenwriter (scripts or dialogue or both, alone or in collaboration)—*Mission a Tangèr* 1949; *Le Passe-Muraille/Mr. Peek-a-Boo* 1951; *Des Dents longues, L'Ennemi public No. 1/The Most Wanted Man, Les Trois Mousquetaires/The Three Musketeers* 1953; *Gas-Oil* 1955; *Le Rouge est mis/Speaking of Murder, Retour de Manivelle/There's Always a Price Tag* 1957; *Les Misérables, Maigret tend un Piège/Inspector Maigret, Le Désordre et la Nuit/Night Affair, Les Grandes Familles/The Possessors* 1958; *Babette s'en va-t-en Guerre/Babette Goes to War* 1959; *La Française et l'Amour/Love and the Frenchwoman* 1960; *Un Taxi pour Tobrouk/Taxi for Tobruk* 1961; *Le Diable et les Dix Commandements/The Devil and the Ten Commandments, Un Singe en Hiver/A Monkey in Winter* 1962; *Mélodie en Sous-Sol/Any Number Can Win* 1963; *Cent Mille Dollars au Soleil/ Greed in the Sun, La Chasse à l'Homme/Male Hunt, Les Barbouzes/The Great Spy Chase* 1964; *Tendre Voyou/Tender Scoundrel* 1966; *Johnny Banco* 1967; *L'Incorrigible* 1975; *Le Corps de mon Ennemi, Le Grand Escogriffe* 1976; *L'Animal, Tendre Poulet/Dear Detective/Dear Inspector* 1977; *Le Cavaleur* 1979; *On a volé la Cuisse de Jupiter/Jupiter's Thigh, Pile ou Face/Head or Tails* 1980; *Garde à Vue/The Inquisitor* 1981; *On ne meurt que deux fois/He Died With His Eyes Open, La Cage aux Folles III ("Elles" se marient)/La Cage aux Folles 3: The Wedding* 1985. As director-screenwriter—*Faut pas prendre les Enfants du Bon Dieu pour des Canards sauvages/ Operation Leontine* 1968; *Une Veuve en Or* 1969; *Elle boit pas elle fume pas elle drague pas mais. . . elle cause!, Le Cri du Cormoran le Soir au-dessus des Jonques* 1970; *Le Drapeau noir flotte sur la Marmite* 1971; *Elle cause plus. . . elle flingue* 1972; *Vive la France!* (doc.) 1973; *Comment reussir dans la Vie quand on est con et pleurnichard* 1974.

audio. Pertaining to sound or dialogue, as distinguished from "video," which pertains to the visual elements.

audiovisual. Pertaining to both sound and sight. A term popular with educators to describe a variety of instructional aids, such as film, television, and slides.

Audran, Stéphane. Born Colette Suzanne Jeannine Dacheville, on Nov. 2, 1932, in Versailles, France. The favorite star and former wife of director Claude CHABROL. A radiant beauty, she has been adept at roles suggesting emotional upheaval and unsuspected strength beneath a deceiving façade of cool, detached sophistication. She won the best actress prize at the Berlin Festival for *Les Biches* (1968), the British Film Academy Award for *Just Before Nightfall* (1971) and *The Discreet Charm of the Bourgeoisie* (1972), and a César award for her performance in *Violette Nozière/Violette* (1978). She was also acclaimed for her performance in *Babette's Feast* (1987). Before marrying Chabrol in 1964, she was the wife of actor Jean-Louis TRINTIGNANT.

FILMS INCLUDE: *La Bonne Tisane/Kill or Cure* 1958; *Les Cousins/The Cousins* 1959; *Les Bonnes Femmes* 1960; *Les Godelureaux* 1961; *L'Oeil du Matin/The Third Lover, Le Signe du Lion/The Sign of Leo* 1962; *Landru/Bluebeard* 1963; *Le Tigre aime la Chair fraiche/The Tiger Likes Fresh Blood* 1964; *Paris vu par. . . /Six in Paris* 1965; *La Ligne de Démarcation* 1966; *Le Scandale/The Champagne Murders* 1967; *Les Biches* 1968; *La Femme infidèle* 1969; *Le Boucher, La Rupture/The Breakup, La Dame dans l'Auto avec des Lunettes et un Fusil/The Lady in the Car with Glasses and a Gun* 1970; *Juste avant la Nuit/Just Before Nightfall, Aussi Loin que l'Amour, Sans Mobile apparent/Without Apparent Motive* 1971; *Le Charme discret de la Bourgeoisie/The Discreet Charm of the Bourgeoisie, Un Meurtre est un Meurtre/A Murder Is a Murder* 1972; *Les Noces rouges/Wedding in Blood* 1973; *And Then There Were None/Ten Little Indians* (UK/Fr./Ger.) 1974; *The Black Bird* (US), *Vincent François Paul et les autres/Vincent François Paul and the Others* 1975; *E la Donna creo l'Amore* (It.), *Folies Bourgeoises* 1976; *Mort d'un Pourri, Silver Bears* (US), *Les Liens du Sang, Violette Nozière/Violette* 1977; *The Prisoner of Zenda* (US), *Eagle's Wing* (UK), *Le Soleil en face* 1979; *The Big Red One* (US) 1980; *Coup de Torchon/Clean Slate* 1981; *Le Choc, Mortelle Randonnée* 1982; *La Scarlatine* 1983; *Le Sang des Autres/The Blood of Others, Les Voleurs de la nuit* 1984; *La Cage aux folles III: "Elles" se marient, La Gitane, Poulet au Vinaigre/Cop au vin* 1985; *Babette's Gastebud/Babette's Feast, Les Predateurs de la nuit, Les Saisons du plaisir* 1987; *Manika* 1988; *Sons* 1989; *Jours tranquilles à Clichy/Quiet Days in Clichy, La Messe en si mineur* 1990; *Betty* 1992; *Maximum Risk* 1995.

Audry, Jacqueline. Director. *b.* Sept. 25, 1908, Orange, France. *d.* 1977. Started as a script girl in 1933, then became an assistant director working with Pabst, Delannoy, Ophüls, and others. She directed her first film, a short, *Les Chevaux du Vercors,* in 1943; her first feature, *Les Malheurs de Sophie,* in 1945. She has a penchant for psychological themes. Most of her scripts were written by Pierre Laroche, her husband. She died in a car accident. Her sister, Colette Audry (1906–1990), was a noted novelist, playwright, literary critic, and prize-winning screenwriter.

FILMS: *Les Chevaux Du Vercors* (short) 1943; *Les Malheurs de Sophie* 1946; *Sombre Dimanche* 1948; *Gigi* 1949; *Minne—L'Ingenue libertine/Minne* 1950; *Olivia/Pit of Loneliness* 1951; *La Caraque blonde* 1953; *Huis clos/No Exit* 1954; *Mitsou* 1956; *La Garçonne, C'est la Faute d'Adam* 1957; *L'Ecole des Cocottes* 1958; *Le Secret du Chevalier d'Eon* 1960; *Les Petits Matins, Cadavres en Vacances* 1961; *Soledad/Fruits amers* 1966; *Le Lis de Mer* 1971.

Auen, Signe. See OWEN, Seena.

Auer, John H. Director, producer. *b.* Aug. 3, 1906, Budapest. *d.* 1975. Educated in Vienna. Child actor in European films at age 12. After a brief career in business, he came to Hollywood in 1928 in search of work as a film director but first gained recognition in Mexico, where he directed several productions and won a special award from the Mexican government. From the mid-30s through the late 50s he directed and produced many routine Hollywood films for Republic and other studios. He went on to work in television.

FILMS (as director): In Mexico—*Una Vida per Otra* 1933; *Su Ultima Cancion, The Pervert, Rest in Peace* 1934. In the US—*Frankie and Johnnie, The Crime of Dr. Crespi* (also prod., story) 1935; *A Man Betrayed, Circus Girl, Rhythm in the Clouds* 1937; *Outside of Paradise, Invisible Enemy, A Desperate Adventure, I Stand Accused* (also co-prod.), *Orphans of the Street* 1938; *Forged Passport* (also co-prod.), *S.O.S. Tidal Wave, Smuggled Cargo* (also co-prod.), *Calling All Marines* 1939; *Thou Shalt Not Kill, Women in War, Hit Parade of 1941* 1940; *A Man Betrayed/Wheel of Fortune, The Devil Pays Off* 1941; *Pardon My Stripes, Moonlight Masquerade* (also co-prod.), *Johnny Doughboy* (also co-prod.) 1942; *Tahiti Honey* (also assoc. prod.), *Gangway for Tomorrow* (also prod.) 1943; *Seven Days Ashore* (also prod.), *Music in Manhattan* (also prod.) 1944; *Pan-Americana* (also prod., co-story) 1945; *Beat the Band, The Flame* (also prod.) 1947; *I Jane Doe* (also assoc. prod.), *Angel on the Amazon* (also assoc. prod.) 1948; *The Avengers* (also assoc. prod.), *Hit Parade of 1951* (also assoc. prod.) 1959; *Thunderbirds* (also assoc. prod.) 1952; *City That Never Sleeps* (also prod.) 1953; *Hell's Half Acre* (also prod.) 1954; *The Eternal Sea* (also assoc. prod.) 1955; *Johnny Trouble* (also prod.) 1957.

Auer, Mischa. Actor. *b.* Mischa Ounskowski, Nov. 17, 1905, St. Petersburg, Russia. *d.* 1967. Brought to the US in 1920 by his maternal grandfather, violinist Leopold Auer, from whom he took his stage name. Attended New York's Ethical Culture school, then turned to the theater. He was appearing in the play 'Magda' on Broadway when director Frank Tuttle offered him a part in the film *Something Always Happens* (1928). For several years he appeared in films in small parts, mostly as a villain. The turning point in his career came with his hilarious performance in Gregory La Cava's *My Man Godfrey* (1936), for which he was nominated for an Oscar. His long, sad face, bulging eyes, and droll accent enlivened many a production, and he became one of Hollywood's most popular supporting actors, typically in eccentric, comic roles. He appeared in some 60 American films before settling in Europe, where he played in many more.

FILMS INCLUDE: In the US—*Something Always Happens* 1928; *Marquis Preferred* 1929; *The Benson Murder Case* 1930; *The Unholy Garden, The Yellow Ticket, Delicious* 1931; *The Midnight Patrol, Scarlet Dawn* 1932; *Sucker Money* (lead), *Tarzan the Fearless, Cradle Song* 1933; *Viva Villa!, Stamboul Quest* 1934; *The Lives of a Bengal Lancer, Clive of India, The Crusades* 1935; *The Princess Comes Across, My Man Godfrey, Winterset* 1936; *Three Smart Girls, Top of the Town, Vogues of 1938, 100 Men and a Girl, It's All Yours* 1937; *Rage of Paris, You Can't Take It with You, Sweethearts* 1938; *East Side of Heaven, Unexpected Father* (lead), *Destry Rides Again* 1939; *Alias the Deacon, Spring Parade, Seven Sinners* 1940; *The Flame of New Orleans, Hold That Ghost, Hellzapoppin* 1941; *Around the World* 1943; *Lady in the Dark, Up in Mabel's Room* 1944; *A Royal Scandal, Brewster's Millions, And Then There Were None* 1945; *Sentimental Journey* 1946; *Sofia* 1948. In Europe—*Al Diavolo la Celebrità* (lead; It.), *Il Cielo e Rosso/The Sky Is Red* (It.) 1949; *Escalier de Service* (Fr.), *Futures Vedettes* (Fr.), *Frou-Frou* (Fr./It.), *Mr. Arkadin/Confidential Report* (Sp./Switz.) 1955; *Cette Sacrée Gamine/Mam'zelle Pigalle* 1956; *Montecarlo/The Monte Carlo Story* (It.), *Nathalie/The Foxiest Girl in Paris* (Fr.) 1957; *Tabarin* (Fr.) 1958; *Il Natale che Quasi non fu/The Christmas That Almost Wasn't* (It./US) 1965; *Drop Dead Darling!/ Arrivederci Baby!* (UK) 1966.

Auger, Claudine. Actress. Born on Apr. 26, 1942, in Paris. Sensual brunette leading lady of French and international films, following studies at the Paris drama conservatory. She is best known to English-speaking audiences as James Bond's love interest Domino in *Thunderball* (1965).

FILMS INCLUDE: *Le Testament D'orphée/Testament Of Orpheus* (as Minerva; Fr.) 1960; *A La Française/In the French Style* (Fr./US) 1963; *Die Lady/Games of Desire* (Ger./Fr.) 1964; *Yoyo* (Fr.), *Thunderball* (UK) 1965; *Triple Cross* (Fr./UK), *L'Homme de Marrakech/That Man George* (Fr./It./Sp.), *Operazione San Gennaro/Treasure of San Gennaro* (It./Fr./Ger.), *L'Arcidiavolo/The Devil in Love* (It.) 1966; *Jeu de Massacre/The Killing Game* (Fr.), *Le Dolci Signore/Anyone Can Play* (It.) 1967; *Il Padre di Famiglia/The Head of the Family* (It./Fr.) 1968; *Antefatto* (It.) 1971; *La Tarantola dal Ventre Nero/The Black Belly of the Tarantula* (It.) 1972; *Flic Story* (Fr.) 1975; *Emmenez-moi au Ritz* (Fr.) 1977; *Un Papillon sur l'Epaule/A Butterfly on the Shoulder* (Fr./Sp.) 1978; *Viaggio con Anita/Travels with Anita/Lovers and Liars* (It./Fr.), *L'Associé/The Associate* (Fr./Ger/) 1979; *Fantastica* (Can./Fr.) 1980; *Secret Places* (UK) 1985; *Il Frullo del Passero* (It./Fr.) 1988; *Desire* 1993.

August, Bille. Director, screenwriter, cinematographer. Born in 1948, in Denmark. An advertising photographer by training, he became a cinematographer after graduating from the Danish Film School in 1971. The films he photographed included *Karleken* (1980) and *The Grass Is Singing* (1981). Turning director in the late 70s, he soon became established as his country's leading filmmaker. He scored his first success with *Zappa* (1983) and a veritable hit with its sequel, the bittersweet *Twist and Shout* (1986), which became Denmark's all-time most popular film. He then achieved international recognition with *Pelle the Conqueror* (1987), a relentlessly bleak portrait of life on a turn-of-the century Scandinavian farm. The film won the Golden Palm at Cannes and an Oscar as best foreign language picture. He generally writes his own screenplays, though he also directed Ingmar Bergman's script for *The Best Intentions*, based on a memoir about Bergman's parents.

FEATURE FILMS: as director—*Honning Maane/In My Life* 1978; *Zappa* 1983; *Twist and Shout* 1985; *Pelle Erobreren/Pelle the Conqueror* (Den./Swed) 1987; *The Best Intentions* 1992; *The House of the Spirits* (also sc.) 1993; *Jerusalem* (also co-sc.) 1996; *Smilla's Sense of Snow* 1997.

August, Edwin. American actor, director. *b.* Edwin August Philip von der Butz, 1883. *d.* 1964. Handsome star of many D. W. Griffith early silents. He later played dashing heroes for other directors, and himself directed several films, but his career slowed considerably in the 20s, and he all but disappeared from the screen after the advent of sound.

FILMS INCLUDE: *A Child's Impulse, Simple Charity, The Fugitive* 1910; *His Daughter, Madame Rex, A Smile of a Child, The Revenue Man and the Girl* 1911; *The Eternal Mother, A Tale of the Wilderness, The Girl and Her Trust, The Lesser Evil, The Old Actor, The School Teacher and the Waif, The Sands of Dee* 1912; *In a Roman Garden* (also sc.), *The Actor, The Primitive Man* 1913; *The Romance of an Actor* 1914; *Evidence* (also dir., sc.), *Bondwomen* (also dir., sc.) 1915; *The Yellow Passport* (also dir., co-sc.), *The Social Highwayman* (also dir.), *The Perils of Divorce* (dir. only), *The Summer Girl* (dir. only) 1916; *A Broadway Scandal, The City of Tears, The Mortgaged Wife* 1918; *The Poison Pen* (dir. only) 1919; *The Idol of the North* 1921; *The Blonde Vampire* 1922; *Scandal Street* 1925; *Side Street* 1929; *Romance of the West* 1930; *The Magnificent Ambersons* 1942; *Over My Dead Body* 1943; *The Exile* 1947.

August, Joseph H. Director of photography. *b.* Apr. 26, 1890, Idaho Springs, Colo. *d.* 1947. A graduate of the Colorado

School of Mining. He entered films in 1911 as assistant cameraman for Thomas INCE and within a year became first cameraman. His illustrious career spanned the most important years of American film history, from its formative years through maturation. During the silent era he was the regular cinematographer of Reginald Barker and William S. Hart, among others, and after the arrival of sound he created memorable images for some of John FORD's most distinguished films, notably *The Informer* (1935). In 1918 he was among the founding members of the A.S.C. During WW II he served as a Navy commander in Iceland and the Pacific. He collapsed and died on the set during the production of the hauntingly elaborate *Portrait of Jennie* (released in 1949). His son, Joseph A. August, Jr., is a TV cameraman.

FILMS INCLUDE: *Lure Of The Violin* 1912; *The Disciple* 1915; *Between Men, Hell's Hinges, The Aryan, The Return of Drew Egan, Civilization* (co-phot.), *The Patriot* 1916; *Truthful Tulliver, The Gun Fighter, Wolf Lowry, The Silent Man* 1917; *Blue Blazes Rawden, Shark Monroe, Riddle Gawne, Branding Broadway* 1918; *Square Deal Sanderson, Wagon Tracks* 1919; *Sand* (co-phot.), *The Toll Gate* 1920; *The Whistle, White Oak* 1921; *Arabian Love* 1922; *Madness of Youth, The Temple of Venus* 1923; *The Vagabond Trail, Dante's Inferno* 1924; *Tumbleweeds, Lightnin', The Ancient Mariner* 1925; *The Road to Glory, Fig Leaves* 1926; *Two Arabian Knights* (co-phot.), *The Beloved Rogue* 1927; *Salute, The Black Watch* 1929; *Men Without Women* 1930; *Quick Millions* 1931; *The Brat* 1932; *Man's Castle* 1933; *No Greater Glory, Twentieth Century* 1934; *The Whole Town's Talking, The Informer* 1935; *Sylvia Scarlett, Mary of Scotland* 1936; *A Damsel in Distress, The Plough and the Stars* 1937; *Gunga Din, The Hunchback of Notre Dame* 1939; *All That Money Can Buy* 1941; *They Were Expendable* 1945; *Portrait of Jennie* 1949.

Aumont, Jean-Pierre. Actor. Born Jean-Pierre Philippe Salomons, on Jan. 5, 1909, in Paris. Charming, durable leading man of French, American, and international films. The son of a well-to-do proprietor of a chain of department stores and a former actress, he enrolled at 16 at the Paris Conservatory, made his stage debut in 1930, and his first film appearance in 1931. He became established as a stage star in Jean Cocteau's 'La Machine infernale' (1934) and was subsequently much in demand as a young lead in both plays and films. His career was interrupted during the early years of WW II, when he fought with the Free French forces in Tunisia, Italy, and France; he was awarded both the Legion of Honor and the Croix de Guerre. He arrived in the US in 1942 and after appearing in a West Coast stage production, he was assigned by MGM to play the lead in a film about the French Resistance, *Assignment in Brittany* (1943). He starred in several other routine Hollywood films, then returned to France. A tall, blond, blue-eyed Continental, he remained, however, popular with American audiences, and has since returned periodically to the US for stage, screen, and television appearances. Aumont has written several plays and in 1976 authored an autobiography, *Sun and Shadow.* His first wife was French film actress Blanche Montel; his second, Hollywood siren Maria MONTEZ, left him a widower. He was once engaged to Hedy LAMARR. He later married, divorced, then remarried actress Marisa PAVAN. His daughter by Montez, Tina Marquand (nee Maria-Christina Salomons), is a film actress. His brother is French film director François Villiers (*b.* François Salomons, 1920).

FILMS INCLUDE: *Jean de la Lune* 1931; *Dans les Rues/Song of the Street* 1933; *Lac aux Dames, Maria Chapdelaine* 1934; *Les Yeux noirs/Dark Eyes, L'Equipage/Flight Into Darkness* 1935; *Tarass Boulba, La Porte du Large/The Great Temptation* 1936; *Le Messager, Drôle de Drame/Bizarre Bizarre, Maman Colibri* 1937; *La Femme du Bout du Monde, Chéri-Bibi, La Belle Étoile, Hôtel du Nord* 1938; *Le Déserteur/Je t'attendrai/Three Hours* 1939; *Assignment in Brittany* (US), *The Cross of Lorraine* (US) 1943; *Heartbeat* (US) 1946; *Song of Scheherazade* (as Nikolai Rimski-Korsakov; US) 1947; *Siren of Atlantis* (US), *The First Gentleman* (UK) 1948; *Hans le Marin* (also sc.), *La Vie commence demain/Life Begins Tomorrow* (semidoc.), *L'Homme du Joie* 1950; *L'Amant de Paille, La Vendetta del Corsaro* (It.) 1951; *Lili* (US), *The Gay Adventure* (UK), *Koenigsmark, Moineaux de Paris* 1953; *Si Versailles m'était conté/Royal Affairs in Versailles, Charge of the Lancers* (US) 1954; *Napoléon, Mademoiselle de Paris 1955; Hilda Crane* (US) 1956; *John Paul Jones* (US) 1959; *The Enemy General* (US) 1960; *Una Domenica d'Estate* (It.), *The Devil at 4 O'Clock* (US) 1961; *Les Sept Péchés capitaux/Seven Capital Sins, Le Couteau dans la Plaie/Five Miles to Midnight* (Fr./It./US) 1962; *Carnival of Crime* (release delayed from 1961; US) 1964; *Castle Keep* (US) 1969; *Cauldron of Blood/Blind Man's Bluff* (release delayed from 1967; US/Sp.) 1971; *La Nuit americaine/Day for Night* 1973; *The Happy Hooker* (US), *Mahogany* (US), *Catherine & Cie./Catherine & Co., Le Chat et la Souris/Cat and Mouse* 1975; *Des Journées entières dans les Arbres* 1976; *Blackout* (Can./Fr.), *Two Solitudes* (Can.) 1978; *Something Short of Paradise* (US) 1979; *Allons z'Enfants* 1981; *Nana* (It./US), *La Java des ombres* 1983; *Le Sang des Autres/The Blood of Others* (Fr./Can.) 1984; *On a Volé Charlie Spencer!* 1986; *Sweet Country* (US) 1987; *A notré regrettable époux* 1988; *Becoming Colette* (Ger./US) 1992; *Jefferson in Paris* 1995; *The Proprietor* 1996.

Aurenche, Jean. Screenwriter. *b.* Sept. 11, 1904, Pierrelatte, France. *d.* 1992. Made his first contact with films about 1932, as director of commercials, then short documentaries. He started writing for the screen in 1936, working both alone and in collaboration with other writers, such as Anouilh, Achard, and Jeanson, but his best work was in collaboration with Pierre BOST. Beginning in 1943 they wrote scripts and dialogue for dozens of important French films, notably for director Claude AUTANT-LARA.

FILMS INCLUDE: Alone or in collaboration with various writers—*Les Dégourdis de la Onzième, L'Affaire du Courrier de Lyon/The Courier of Lyons* 1937; *Hôtel du Nord* 1938; *Madame Sans-Gêne* 1941; *Le Mariage de Chiffon, Lettres d'Amour* 1942; *Douce/Love Story* (first collaboration with Pierre Bost) 1943; *Sylvie et le Fantôme/Sylvie and the Phantom, La Symphonie pastorale 1946; Le Diable au Corps/Devil in the Flesh* 1947; *Au-delà des Grilles/La Mura di Malapaga/The Walls of Malapaga* 1948; *Occupe-toi d'Amélie/Oh Amelia!* 1949; *Dieu a besoin des Hommes/God Needs Men* 1950; *L'Auberge rouge/The Red Inn* 1951; *Jeux interdits/Forbidden Games, Les Sept Péchés capitaux/Seven Deadly Sins* 1952; *Les Orgueilleux/The Proud and the Beautiful, Mademoiselle Nitouche* 1953; *Destinées/Daughters of Destiny, Le Rouge et le Noir/The Red and the Black, Le Blé en Herbe/The Game of Love* 1954; *Gervaise, La Traversée de Paris/Four Bags Full, Notre-Dame de Paris/The Hunchback of Notre Dame* 1956; *En Cas de Malheur/Love Is My Profession, Le Joueur* 1958; *Le Jument verte/The Green Mare* 1959; *Vive Henri IV. . . Vive l'Amour* 1961; *Le Crime ne paie pas/Crime Does Not Pay* 1962; *Le Meurtrier/Enough Rope* 1963; *Les Amitiés particulières/This Special Friendship* 1964; *Is Paris Burning?* (US/Fr.) 1966; *Le plus Vieux Metièr du Monde/The Oldest Profession* 1967; *Les Patates* 1969; *Que la Fête commence/Let Joy Reign Supreme* 1975; *Le Juge et l'Assassin* 1976; *Coup de Torchon/Clean Slate, L'Etoile du Nord* 1982; *De guerre lasse, Fucking Fernand* 1987; *Le Palanquin des larmes* 1988.

Auric, Georges. Composer. *b.* Feb. 15, 1899, Lodève, France. *d.* 1983. France's ablest creator of film music, Auric started composing at 15 and went on to write prolifically for concert hall, ballet, stage, and screen. With Milhaud, Honneger, Poulenc, Durey, and Tailleferre, he was one of *Le Groupe des Six,* six composers who in the early 20s sought to carve out new musical directions. In 1924 he was among the Paris intellectuals who appeared in René Clair's avant-garde film *Entr'acte.*

Auric's first film score was for Jean Cocteau's experimental *Le Sang d'un Poète/The Blood of a Poet* (1930). His output encompassed nearly 100 film scores, including those for all of Cocteau's films, as well as for dozens of major films by such directors as Clair, Ophüls, Huston, Delannoy, Wyler, Cavalcanti, and Clouzot. His scores won awards at Cannes, Venice, and other film festivals. Some of his themes (such as that from *Moulin Rouge*) became popular songs. In 1962 he was named director of the Paris Opera.

FILMS INCLUDE: *Le Sang D'un Poète/The Blood of a Poet* 1930; *A nous la Liberté* 1931; *Lac aux Dames* 1934; *Gribouille/Heart of Paris, L'Alibi* 1937; *Orange, Entrée des Artistes/The Curtain Rises* 1938; *L'Eternel Retour/The Eternal Return* 1943; *La Belle Aventure/Twilight, Dead of Night* (UK) 1945; *Caesar and Cleopatra* (UK), *La Belle et la Bête/Beauty and the Beast, La Symphonie pastorale* 1946; *Hue and Cry* (UK), *It Always Rains on Sunday* (UK), *Les Jeux sont faits/The Chips Are Down* 1947; *Ruy Blas, L'Aigle à Deux Têtes/Eagle With Two Heads* 1948; *Les Parents terribles/The Storm Within, Passport to Pimlico* (UK), *Queen of Spades* (UK) 1949; *Orphée/Orpheus* 1950; *Caroline Chérie, The Lavender Hill Mob* (UK) 1951; *La P. . . respectueuse/The Respectful Prostitute* 1952; *Roman Holiday* (US), *Moulin Rouge* (US/UK), *Le Salaire de la Peur/The Wages of Fear* 1953; *Du Rififi chez les Hommes/Rififi, Lola Montès* 1955; *Gervaise, Le Mystère Picasso/The Mystery of Picasso* (doc.) 1956; *Celui qui doit mourir/He Who Must Die, Heaven Knows Mr. Allison* (US) 1957; *Bonjour Tristesse* (US) 1958; *Le Testament d'Orphée/The Testament of Orpheus* 1960; *Aimez-vous Brahms?/Goodbye Again* (Fr./US), *The Innocents* (UK) 1961; *Le Rendez-vous de Minuit, La Chambre ardente/The Burning Court* 1962; *The Mind Benders* (UK) 1963; *Therese and Isabelle* (US/Ger.) 1968; *L'Arbre de Noël/The Christmas Tree* 1969.

Aurthur, Robert Alan. Screenwriter, novelist. *b.* June 10, 1922, New York City. *d.* 1978. *ed.* U. of Pennsylvania. Served in the Marines during WW II and wrote *The History of the Third Marine Division.* A short-story writer and novelist, he wrote and produced several stage plays and dozens of quality dramas for TV and is credited with several screenplays. He directed his only film in 1969.

FILMS: (as screenwriter): *Edge of the City* (from his own TV play 'A Man Is Ten Feet Tall'), *Spring Reunion* (TV play basis only) 1957; *Warlock* 1959; *Lilith* (co-sc., uncredited) 1964; *Grand Prix* 1966; *For Love of Ivy* 1968; *The Lost Man* (also dir.) 1969; *All That Jazz* (also prod.) 1979.

Australia. As early as 1899 a fiction film was produced in Australia, *The Early Christian Martyrs,* by J. H. Perry, sponsored by the Salvation Army. Australia was the first country to produce a film longer than one reel, *The Story of the Kelly Gang,* in 1906; it was also one of the first countries to acquire sound equipment.

In the beginning, Australia was best known for the quality of its documentary films. During WW II the Commonwealth Film Unit was formed and became the most active documentary film producer in Australia, releasing some 50 films a year in association with the Australian National Film Board. Many of its films won awards in international film festivals.

Feature production, for many years, consisted mostly of collaborations with British or American companies who hired local crews and equipment but had creative control. Among the better-known films produced under such arrangements were *On the Beach* (1959) and *The Sundowners* (1960). Before the 70s, independently produced local features were rarely seen abroad, but efforts within the country were made to encourage quality film production for international consumption through the government-subidized Australian Film Development Corporation (AFDC). While the AFDC is no longer in existence, Australia has, with the encouragement and backing of the more recently developed Australian Film Commission, gone on to produce vital and award-winning films.

With the worldwide success of *"Crocodile" Dundee* (1986) and its ensuing sequel, Paul HOGAN was one of the more prominent Australian film figures, as a producer, director, writer, and actor. Yet as Hogan's popularity faded, the international film community was becoming more aware of the host of talented directors, writers, and actors that burst into prominence in the late 70s, 80s, and 90s, many of whom were lured to Hollywood. They include directors Gillian ARMSTRONG, whose *My Brilliant Career* (1979) garnered critical acclaim; Bruce BERESFORD, whose early career produced *Don's Party* (1976) and *Breaker Morant* (1979) to name a few, and led to the Academy Award winning *Tender Mercies* (1983) and *Driving Miss Daisy* (1989); Jane CAMPION, arguably one of the most intriguing and fiercely independent filmmakers to emerge in recent years with *Sweetie* (1989) and the Cannes and Academy Award winner *The Piano* (1993); Peter WEIR whose *Picnic at Hanging Rock* (1975) hinted at a versatility and sensitivity which eventually made *Dead Poets Society* a critical and box-office success; and Michael Rymer's *Angel Baby* (1996).

More recently, Baz Luhrman's *Strictly Ballroom* (1992), *Romeo and Juliet* (1996), Stephen Elliott's *The Adventures of Priscilla, Queen of the Desert* (1994), and Scott Hick's *Shine* (1996) provide proof of the diversity and creative force behind a thriving, respected film community. The latter film received seven Academy Award nominations including best picture and director, and a win for Australian actor Geoffrey Rush.

Austria. Despite the early availability of equipment and studios and the cultural environment, Austria has produced only occasional films, mostly mass-entertainment spectacles, such as operettas, musical biographies, and costume affairs set at the court of Emperor Franz-Josef.

Film production in Austria began in 1908 and reached a peak of sorts, in the early 30s, when such directors as Max Ophüls, Otto Preminger, and Willi Forst made films there. But throughout most of its history, the local film industry has been dominated by the more powerful studios of neighboring Germany. Recent production has been limited to a handful of feature films a year, mostly for the German-speaking market. A tiny government subsidy has done little to encourage the growth of the film industry and general public apathy has made Austria one of Europe's least film-minded nations.

Autant-Lara, Claude. Director. Born on Aug. 5, 1903, in Luzarches, France. The son of architect Edouard Autant, he also kept the surname of his mother, actress Louise Lara. She was forced into self-exile in England during WW I because of her strong pacifist stand and she took Claude with her. He spent several years in a London school before returning to France to take up art. At 16 he painted the sets for Marcel L'Herbier's film *Le Carnaval des Vérités* and continued for some years as a set decorator and costume designer for L'Herbier, Renoir, and other directors.

In 1923 he directed a short avant-garde film, *Fait Divers.*

He served as second assistant director that same year on René Clair's *Paris qui Dort* and again, in 1925, on *Le Voyage Imaginaire.* After directing a short documentary, *Vittel* (1926), he tackled a wide-screen experiment with the short *Construire un Feu* (1927), an avant-garde adaptation of a Jack London story. In 1930 he went to Hollywood to direct French versions of American films, notably those of Buster Keaton and Harry Langdon. On returning to France he directed several shorts.

It was not until 1933, 14 years after entering the industry, that he directed his first feature film, *Ciboulette.* Three more years passed before he was given another film to direct, *My Partner Mr. Davis/The Mysterious Mr. Davis* (UK, 1936). In 1937–39 he became involved in the production of three films, for which he was given screen credit as technical adviser but which he is said to have actually directed: *L'Affaire du Courrier de Lyon/The Courier of Lyons, Le Ruisseau,* and *Fric-Frac.*

Autant-Lara's career as a front-rank director actually began in 1942, when he turned out two elegant, entertaining films, *Le Mariage de Chiffon* and *Lettres d'Amour.* He then gained an international reputation with *Le Diable au Corps/Devil in the Flesh* (1946), almost 30 years after entering films. He is known for his atheist and leftist views, which are often expressed in his films in the form of audacious attacks on the bourgeoisie, the military, and the church—frequently in defiance of official pressure and censorship.

He has usually worked with the same production team: screenwriters Jean AURENCHE and Pierre BOST, cameraman Jacques Natteau, art director Max Douy, composer René Cloërec, and editor Madeleine Gug. His wife, Ghislaine, is a screenwriter, assistant director, and actress. *Gloria*, his last film to date, appeared in 1977.

FEATURE FILMS: *Ciboulette* 1933; *My Partner Mr. Davis/The Mysterious Mr. Davis* (UK) 1936; *L'Affaire du Courrier de Lyon/The Courier of Lyons* (co-dir. with Maurice Lehmann) 1937; *Le Ruisseau* (co-dir. with Lehmann) 1938; *Fric-Frac* (co-dir. with Lehmann) 1939; *Le Mariage de Chiffon, Lettres d'Amour* 1942; *Douce/Love Story* 1943; *Sylvie et le Fantôme/Sylvie and the Phantom* 1946; *Le Diable au Corps/ Devil in the Flesh* 1947; *Occupe-toi d'Amélie/Oh Amelia!* 1949; *L'Auberge rouge/The Red Inn* 1951; *Les Sept Péchés capitaux/Seven Deadly Sins* ("Pride" episode) 1952; *Le Bon Dieu sans Confession* 1953; *Le Rouge et le Noir, Le Blé en Herbe/The Game of Love* 1954; *Marguerite de la Nuit, La Traversée de Paris/Four Bags Full* 1956; *En Cas de Malheur/Love Is My Profession, Le Joueur* 1958; *La Jument verte/The Green Mare* 1959; *Les Régates de San Francisco, Le Bois des Amants* 1960; *Vive Henri IV. . . Vive l'Amour!, Le Comte de Monte Cristo/The Story of the Count of Monte Cristo* 1961; *Tu ne tueras point/Non Uccidere/Thou Shalt Not Kill* (Yug./Fr./It./Liecht.) 1962; *Le Meurtrier/Enough Rope, Le Magot de Joséfa* 1963; *Le Journal d'une Femme en Blanc/A Woman in White* 1965; *Le nouveau Journal d'une Femme en Blanc* 1966; *Le plus vieux Métier du Monde/The Oldest Profession* ("Paris Today" episode) 1967; *Le Franciscain de Bourges* 1968; *Les Patates* 1969; *Le Rouge et le Blanc* 1971; *Gloria* (also co-sc.) 1977.

automated dialogue replacement. See LOOPING.

Auteuil, Daniel. Actor. Born on Jan. 24, 1950, in Algeria. Accomplished leading man and humorous supporting player of French films of the 80s. The son of roving opera singers, he traveled extensively as a youth and began his career in musical comedy. Recipient of the British Academy Award as best supporting actor for *Jean De Florette* (1986) and France's Bourvil Prize in 1987. He dubbed in the baby's voice (originally provided by Bruce Willis) in the French version of *Look Who's Talking.* He is romantically involved with Emmanuelle BEART, his co-star in *Manon of the Spring* and *Un Coeur en Hiver.*

FILMS INCLUDE: *L'Agression/Act of Aggression* 1975; *La Nuit de St.-Germain de Prés, L'Amour violé/Rape of Love* 1977; *A Nous Deux* 1979; *La Banquière* 1980; *Les Hommes préférent Les Grosses/Men Prefer Fat Girls* 1981; *L'Indic* 1983; *P'tit Con* 1984; *L'Amour en Douce, Palace* 1985; *Le Paltoquet, Jean de Florette, Manon des Sources/Manon of the Spring* 1986; *Quelques Jours avec moi/A Few Days with Me* 1988; *Look Who's Talking* (Fr. version, voice only) 1989; *Romuald et Juliette/Mama There's a Man in Your Bed* 1989; *Lacenaire* 1990; *My Life Is Hell* 1991; *L'Elegant Criminel* 1992; *Ma Saison Preferee/My Favorite Season, Un Coeur en Hiver/A Heart in Winter* 1993; *Queen Margot, The Separation* 1994; *The Eighth Day, Les Voleurs* 1996.

auteur theory. The theory that the director is the "author" of a film. The reasoning that leads to this conclusion is that a film is a work of art, and since a work of art is stamped with the personality of its creator, it is the director, more than anyone else, who gives the film its distinctive quality. The term was first used in the early 60s by critic Andrew Sarris as a loose translation of the *politique des auteurs* notion, first promulgated in 1954 by François Truffaut while still a critic with *Cahiers du Cinéma.*

The debate over the artistic "authorship" of a film—a medium depending on the creative collaboration of many artists and craftsmen: producer, art director, editor, actors, etc.—goes back to the beginnings of cinema theory. Serious debate narrowed the field to the director and the screenwriter. Some argued that the screenplay could exist independently, while there would be no film without a scenario; others claimed that the same scenario directed by two directors would result in two entirely different films.

The debate was more appropriate to Hollywood, where studio control has often hampered individual expression, than to Europe, where directors traditionally have more nearly complete control over production. When the issue exploded on the pages of *Cahiers du Cinéma* in January 1954, it was used to undermine traditional philosophies of the French cinema. Unpretentious American films and forgotten American directors were resurrected, and a pantheon of *auteurs* was created of directors whose personalities dominated their films through a more or less consistent theme or style. Two main schools of *auteur* critics developed eventually, those who stress consistency of theme and those who are more concerned with a director's formal style, or his MISE-EN-SCÈNE.

Many critics have addressed the weaknesses of auteur theory, most notably its inattention to the collaborative nature of film. At its most extreme, auteur theory neglects the contributions of actors, screenwriters, cinematographers, production designers, and others. It also fails to address directors such as Michael Curtiz, the prolific Warner Bros. contract employee, who create excellent films without evidence of a strong "personal vision." Since 1970, critical approaches such as structuralism, semiology, and Marxism have deemphasized the "author" in favor of analysis of the film "text." Even so, auteur theory has had a lasting influence. In both scholarly and popular venues, the director is now often considered the closest thing to a film's creator, particularly when discussing films of high artistic worth.

Autry, Gene. Actor, singing cowboy, songwriter, producer. Born Orvon Gene Autry, on Sept. 29, 1907, on a ranch near Tioga, Tex. He was working as a railroad telegrapher at a junction in Oklahoma when Will Rogers heard him sing and encouraged him to go into show business. In 1928 he started singing on a local radio station and three years later starred in his own radio show and made his first recordings. In 1934 he made his first film appearance, singing briefly in a Ken Maynard Western, *In*

Old Santa Fe. This led to a lead role in the 13-chapter serial *Phantom Empire* and to his first starring role in a feature film, *Tumblin' Tumbleweeds* (1935). Autry, along with his comic sidekick Smiley BURNETTE and his horse Champion, went on to make dozens of Westerns for Republic.

Gaining fame as a singing cowboy, Autry led the popularity poll of Western stars for several years and is the only Western star to be listed among the ten top moneymakers in Hollywood films (1938–42). On the screen, Autry was a no-nonsense cowboy hero. His films typically were packed with action and thin on romance. In addition, his network radio show had a considerable following, and his recordings sold by the millions. Autry has written some 200 popular songs, including "Here Comes Santa Claus." During WW II he served as flight officer with the Air Transport Command. In his absence a young man named Roy ROGERS inherited the rank of Republic's King of the Cowboys. Undaunted, Autry went over to Columbia Pictures, then formed his own film production company, Gene Autry Productions. He is an astute businessman and his many business interests include a radio and TV chain, ranches, oil wells, a flying school, a music publishing company, and the California Angels baseball team. His Flying A Pictures has produced several TV series. Author: *Back in the Saddle Again* (1978).

FILMS INCLUDE: *In Old Santa Fe* 1934; *Phantom Empire* (serial), *Tumblin' Tumbleweeds, The Singing Vagabond* 1935; *The Singing Cowboy, Oh Susannah!, Boots and Saddles, Manhattan Merry-Go-Round, Springtime in the Rockies* 1937; *Rhythm of the Saddle* 1938; *In Old Monterey, South of the Border* 1939; *Shooting High, Melody Ranch, Rancho Grande* 1940; *Down Mexico Way, Ridin' on a Rainbow* (also song) 1941; *Cowboy Serenade* 1942; *Robin Hood of Texas* 1947; *Loaded Pistols* 1949; *Mule Train* 1950; *Texans Never Cry* 1951; *Apache Country* 1952; *On Top of Old Smoky, Last of the Pony Riders, Saginaw Trail, Winning of the West* 1953; *It's Showtime* 1976.

available light. A term used to describe natural light and especially the shooting of film in poor lighting conditions with whatever light source is available without the use of artificial light.

Avakian, Aram. Editor, director. *b.* Apr. 23, 1926, New York City, of Armenian descent. *d.* 1987. After graduating from Yale, he served in the Navy, then lived for several years in Paris, where he attended the Sorbonne. Returning to New York in 1953, he apprenticed for a still photographer, then joined CBS television in 1955, where through 1958 he edited Edward R. Murrow's famed news program 'See It Now.' His creative editing of *Jazz on a Summer's Day* (1959), an exciting filmed record of the 1958 Newport Jazz Festival, led to highly regarded editing assignments in fiction features. He also made the most from several opportunities to direct. He drew admiring reviews and an X rating for *End of the Road,* which included a graphically harrowing abortion scene. The film boasted a strong performance from Dorothy Tristan, Avakian's wife at the time. Later, his constant companion was ballerina Allegra Kent. From 1983 until shortly before his death of heart failure he headed the film program and taught directing and screenwriting at the State University College at Purchase, New York.

FILMS: As editor—*Jazz on a Summer Day* (doc.) 1959; *Girl of the Night* 1960; *The Miracle Worker* 1962; *Lilith* 1964; *Andy, Mickey One* 1965; *You're a Big Boy Now* 1966; *The Next Man* 1976; *Honeysuckle Rose* 1980. As director—*Lad: A Dog* 1962; *End of the Road* 1970; *Cops and Robbers* 1973; *11 Harrowhouse/Anything for Love* (UK) 1974.

Avalon, Frankie. Singer, actor. Born Francis Thomas Avallone, on Sept. 18, 1939, in Philadelphia. A trumpet prodigy at the age of nine, he turned to singing in his teens, later becoming a popular recording star. In films, he has played both light and dramatic lead parts, mostly in low-brow productions. In 1987 he was reteamed with Annette FUNICELLO in *Back to the Beach,* a nostalgic tribute to the "Beach Party" series that highlighted their careers in the 60s. Two of his eight children also appeared in that film.

FILMS INCLUDE: *Jamboree* 1957; *Guns of the Timberland; The Alamo* 1960; *Voyage to the Bottom of the Sea* 1961; *Panic in the Year Zero!* 1962; *Beach Party, The Castilian* (Sp.), *Drums of Africa, Operation Bikini* 1963; *Bikini Beach, Muscle Beach Party* 1964; *Beach Blanket Bingo, I'll Take Sweden, Sergeant Deadhead, How to Stuff a Wild Bikini, Mr. Goldfoot and the Bikini Machine* 1965; *Fireball 500* 1966; *The Million Eyes of Su-Muru* 1967; *Skidoo* 1968; *Horror House* 1970; *The Take* 1974; *Grease* 1978; *Back to the Beach* 1987; *Troop Beverly Hills* 1989.

avant-garde. A term encompassing the unorthodox and experimental in the arts. In films it has been applied to movements and individuals whose work constitutes a marked departure from conventional form and narrative content. It covers such diverse styles of expression as Dadaism, surrealism, futurism, expressionism, impressionism, abstract films, absolute films, pure cinema, underground films, trash cinema, midnight movies, and other noncommercial film movements. Among the features that have characterized many avant-garde films are the search for a pure poetic form free of narrative logic, disdain for visual realism, and a call for social action. In a stricter sense the term "avant-garde" applied to a movement in filmmaking which began simultaneously in Germany and France at the end of WW I and later spread in varying forms to the Soviet Union, the United States, and Great Britain.

Theoretically, the French movement had its roots in the writings of critic Ricciotto CANUDO, who in 1908 founded the Seventh Art Club in Paris, dedicated to the liberation of film art. Artistically, it was influenced by the works of Emile COHL (*La Course aux Potirons,* 1907) and Jean DURAND (*Onésime Horloger,* 1912).

The French avant-garde flourished between 1920 and 1930. One of its foremost exponents was critic Louis DELLUC, who pursued the creative use of light and rhythm and described cinema as "painting in movement." His *Fièvre* (1921) later influenced Jean VIGO and Marcel CARNÉ. Also influential was a group whose films were characterized by their literary aspiration and trick photography. It included Germaine DULAC (*La Fête espagnole,* 1919, etc.), Marcel L'HERBIER (*Eldorado,* 1922; *L'Inhumaine,* 1923, etc.), Jean EPSTEIN (*The Fall of the House of Usher,* 1928), and Dmitri KIRSANOV (*Menilmontant,* 1926, etc.), as well as several directors better known for their commercial ventures. The school of "pure cinema" was presented by Henri Chomette (*Cinq Minutes de Cinéma pur,* 1926), Jean GRÉMILLON (*Photogénie Mécanique,* 1924), Marcel DUCHAMP (*Anemic Cinema,* 1925), Eugène Deslaw (*La Marche des Machines,* 1928), and Ferdinand LÉGER (*Ballet mécanique,* 1924).

The surrealist branch of the French avant-garde included Luis BUÑUEL (*Un Chien Andalou,* 1928; *L'Age d'Or,* 1930), Jean Vigo (*A Propos de Nice,* 1930), Man RAY (*Emak Bakia,* 1927, etc.), and Jean COCTEAU (*The Blood of a Poet,* 1930).

The German avant-garde movement was led by four former abstract painters who sought further visual expression through film. Its pioneer was Viking EGGELING, who in 1919 turned out *Vertikal-Horizontale Messe,* a short abstract animated film. The following year he joined forces with Hans RICHTER to produce the *Vertikal-Horizontale Symphonie.* They lived together in Berlin and experimented with filmic manipulation of scroll paintings.

In 1921, while Eggeling continued to experiment with

scroll paintings in his *Diagonale Symphonie,* Richter began exploring the use of geometric shapes in motion by drawing directly on film. His efforts resulted in such abstract shorts as *Rythmus 21, 23,* and *25* (1921–25), and *Filmstudie* (1926). In 1928 he turned out a Dadaist comedy, *Vormittagspuck/Ghosts Before Breakfast.* During the same period, Walter RUTTMANN Produced his *Opus I, II, III,* and *IV* (1923–25), abstract rhythmic studies in animation. He is best known for his two experimental documentaries, *Berlin: Symphony of a Great City* (1927) and *Melody of the World* (1929), which through the use of rhythmic montage attempted symphonic visual organization.

Oskar FISCHINGER made a series of abstract films manipulating geometric shapes along a curve of changing patterns all of which were governed by the laws of music. Among them were *Studio No. 6, Studio No. 7, Studio No. 8,* etc., and *Komposition in Blau* (1933). Like Richter, Fischinger later went to the US and continued his experimentation with such films as *Rhapsody in Blue* and *Hungarian Rhapsody.* The famous German expressionist films of that period (*The Cabinet of Dr. Caligari, Nosferatu,* etc.), cannot be properly considered part of the avant-garde in the stricter sense of the term, despite their originality and unique contribution.

The Soviet avant-garde, always under political pressure, stayed clear of abstraction and total formalism but was noted for its esoteric experimentation and daring innovation. The two most influential avant-garde Russian filmmakers were Dziga VERTOV and Sergei EISENSTEIN. Vertov virtually created the principles of *cinéma vérité* with his Kino Pravda series (from 1922) and *Man With a Movie Camera* (1929). Eisenstein instituted the creative use of montage.

Lesser-known Russian experimenters included KOZINTSEV and TRAUBERG (*The Cloak,* 1926), KULESHOV (*The Extraordinary Adventures of Mr. West in the Land of the Bolsheviks,* 1924), and PROTAZONOV (*Aelita,* 1924).

British cinema saw only a limited manifestation of the avant-garde. Len LYE, the originator of a process of drawing directly on film stock, made short semi-abstract propaganda films for the GPO Film Unit (*Colour Box,* 1935; *Trade Tattoo,* 1937; *Musical Poster,* 1940, etc.). Norman MCLAREN, first to imprint sound track directly on film, experimented with a variation of abstract techniques in many of his 50 or so films. The documentary movement turned out some innovative samples of rhythmic montage in such films as Basil Wright's *Song of Ceylon* (1934) and *Night Mail* (1936).

Seeds of the American avant-garde were planted as early as 1921 with Charles Sheeler and Paul STRAND's *Manhattan,* a documentary about New York with titles from a poem by Walt Whitman. Paul FEJOS's *The Last Moment* (1927) was more truly experimental. But the first film to achieve true personal expression was *The Life and Death of 9413—A Hollywood Extra* (1928) directed by Robert Florey and shot by Gregg TOLAND. Other experimental ventures of that period include James Watson's expressionist version of *The Fall of the House of Usher* (1928), noted for the use of prismatic lenses and creative lighting; Ralph Steiner's *H_2O* (1929); and Herman Weinberg's *City Symphony* (1929), inspired by the work of the German Ruttmann.

Ralph Steiner and Elia KAZAN made *Pie in the Sky* (1934) in a junk yard; Lewis Jacobs made several short experimental films, including *Synchronization* (1934); and Mary Ellen Bute did a series of experimental animated films, including *Anitra's Dance* (1936), *Evening Star* (1937), and *Toccata and Fugue* (1940).

The avant-garde found renewed vigor in the 40s, especially in the films of Maya DEREN, whose *Meshes in the Afternoon* (1943) dominated the experimental style of the decade. Also influential were the psychosexual films of Kenneth ANGER, largely concerned with homosexuality, sado-masochism, and fetishism, like *Escape Episode* (1946), *Fireworks* (1947), and *Inauguration of the Pleasure Dome* (1954). The German Hans Richter, who settled in America, continued his activity in collaboration with Marcel Duchamps, Max Ernst, Fernand Léger, Man Ray, and other artists, creating *Dreams That Money Can Buy* (1946) and *8 × 8* (1957). Among the many other American filmmakers of the avant-garde during the same period are Gregory MARKOPOULUS, Curtis HARRINGTON (*On the Edge,* 1949), Ian Hugo (*Bells of Atlantis,* 1952), and John Whitney (*Variations,* 1941; and computer films in the 60s).

The mid-50s saw the gradual emergence of a new avant-grade movement, consciously concerned with film as a medium. Filmmakers of the so-called underground film movement typically used amateur equipment, including 8 mm (and later super-8) cameras, which gave their films a home-movie intimacy, and sought freedom from conventional reality in their disregard for established continuity principles. Arbitrary splices, shaky images from hand-held cameras, and grainy film were some of the nontechniques with which underground filmmakers made their personal statements. Among the better-known underground filmmakers who emerged in the 60s and 70s were Robert BREER, Jonas MEKAS, Stan BRAKHAGE, Stan van der Beek, Jack Smith (*Flaming Creatures* 1963), Bruce CONNER, Mike and George Kuchar, Bruce BAILLIE, Robert FRANK, Shirley CLARKE, Hillary Harris, Ed EMSHWILLER, Francis Thompson, Michael SNOW, Andy WARHOL (*Blow Job* 1964), and Yoko Ono (*Bottoms* 1966).

Energized by the anti-Vietnam war movement and the various social reforms that shook America in the 60s, the avant-garde of the 70s took on a decidedly political caste. This concern with making personal political statements was reflected in mainstream cinema as well as in the avant-garde, and segued into a new movement within the latter, that of self-revelation as a political statement. Carolee Schneemann's *Autobiographical Trilogy* (1967–78) and Jonas Mekas's *Walden* (1970) are representative of the period, which also included filmmakers Robert Huot and Andrew Noren.

Trash cinema flourished in the early 70s: films that followed a fairly conventional narrative, but flaunted the cheapness of the equipment used in their making and were often acted in an abrasive, ridiculous style as a parody of mainstream cinema. These films were inspired by the tawdry melodramas and the unintentionally amateurish films of such 50s directors as Ed Wood. John WATERS exemplifies the movement, from *Hag in a Black Leather Jacket* (1964) to *Polyester* (1981). His *Pink Flamingos* (1972) is one of the most widely viewed trash films ever made, thanks in large part to the advent of home VCRs several years later, a factor that has widened the audience for all alternative filmmaking. Trash cinema paved the way for midnight movies: intentionally "bad," often sexually explicit and/or comically violent films that for years were popular draws at drive-ins and art houses offering midnight screenings.

The 80s and 90s have seen the legitimization of the avant-garde as a viable field of study. Film courses centered on the avant-garde have sprung up at nearly every major university. With this sudden interest in what had previously been a niche market, the avant-garde has become a potentially moneymaking endeavor, and filmmakers working today do so with the knowledge that their work might possibly be viewed by mass audiences over time.

The escalating appreciation for the avant-garde has led to more lavishly produced efforts (such as Todd HAYNES's *Poison,* 1991) and a general absorption of elements of the avant-garde into both the mainstream cinema, as in the films of Spike LEE, and in music videos, one of the dominant forces in popular entertainment from the mid-80s.

The single greatest factor in the shaping of the avant-garde of the 80s and 90s has been the accessibility of handheld video cameras. Video films, infused with the spontaneity that the medium affords, are almost certainly the future of the movement.

Avant-garde filmmakers of the 80s and 90s include Peter WATKINS, Trinh T. Minh-ha, James BENNING, Ross McElwee, Godfrey REGGIO, Su Friedrich, Warren Sonbert, Yvonne RAINER, Michael Snow, Todd Haynes, and Sadie Benning.

Averback, Hy. Director, actor. Born ca. 1924, in Minneapolis. A comedy specialist with considerable radio and TV experience, he directed several films, mainly in the late 60s. He also appeared as an actor in three films. His television career was more prolific, comprising numerous shows and series episodes both as a performer and a director.

FILMS: As actor—*The Benny Goodman Story* 1956; *Four Girls in Town* 1957; *How to Succeed in Business Without Really Trying* 1967. As director—*Chamber of Horrors* (also prod.) 1966; *Where Were You When the Lights Went Out, I Love You Alice B. Toklas!, The Great Bank Robbery* 1969; *Suppose They Gave a War and Nobody Came* 1970; *Where the Boys Are* 1984.

Avery, Tex. Animator. *b.* Frederick Bean Avery, Feb. 26, 1907, Taylor, Tex. *d.* 1980. Entered film industry in 1930, working on the "Aesop's Fables" series. He later directed "Oswald the Rabbit" cartoons for Walter Lantz at Universal and was also one of the creators of BUGS BUNNY for Warner Bros. After collaborating on many conventional cartoons, he developed at MGM an animation style in the 40s noted for its violence and freewheeling, almost surrealistic, fantasy. Among his best-known characters are Chilly Willy the penguin, Droopy the dog, and Lucky Ducky. He exerted considerable influence on American animation, especially on the work of Friz Freleng, Chuck Jones, and Robert McKimson. From the late 50s he mostly made commercials.

CARTOONS INCLUDE: *Golddiggers of '49, Porky the Wrestler* 1936; *Uncle Tom's Bungalow, Daffy Duck and Egghead, Little Red Walking Hood* 1937; *The Penguin Parade, Daffy Duck in Hollywood, Cinderella Meets Fella* 1938; *A Day at the Zoo, Detouring America, Screwball Football* 1939; *Circus Today* 1940; *Haunted Mouse, Hollywood Steps Out, The Bug Parade* 1941; *Speaking of Animals Down at the Farm, The Blitz Wolf* 1942; *Red Hot Riding Hood* 1943; *Screwy Squirrel, Batty Baseball* 1944; *The Shooting of Dan Magoo, Swing Shift Cinderella* 1945; *Northwest Hounded Police, Henpecked Hoboes* 1946; *Uncle Tom's Cabana* 1947; *Lucky Ducky, The Cat That Hated People* 1948; *Señor Droopy, The House of Tomorrow* 1949; *Ventriloquist Cat* 1950; *Symphony in Slang, The Magical Maestro* 1951; *Rock-a-Bye Bear* 1952; *The Flea Circus, Dixieland Droopy* 1954; *Field and Scream* 1955; *Cat's Meow* 1956; *Polar Pests* 1958.

Avildsen, John G. Director, cinematographer, editor. Born on Dec. 21, 1935, Oak Park, Ill. *ed.* NYU. The son of a tool manufacturer, he began his working career as an advertising copywriter. After two years of military service as a chaplain's assistant, he worked as an assistant director on an independently made low-budget feature, *The Greenwich Village Story* (1963). He was an assistant director on *Black Like Me* (1964), assistant production manager on Arthur Penn's *Mickey One* (1965), and production manager on the shot-in-the-US Italo-French film *Una Moglia Americana/Run for Your Wife* (1965), 2nd-unit director on Otto Preminger's *Hurry Sundown* (1967), and associate producer and director of photography on the low-budget *Out of It* (1969). During these years of apprenticeship, he directed several shorts, including *Smiles* and *Light—Sound—Diffuse,* and made a number of commercials for advertising agencies. He launched his career as a feature director with two best-forgotten sex-oriented films, one a melodrama, the other a satire, then first drew critical attention with *Joe,* a tightly budgeted film about a hardhat bigot which became a surprise sleeper at the box office in 1970. After a string of disappointing films, he came up with another critical and commercial sleeper in *Rocky* (1976), for which he won an Academy Award as best director. *Rocky* also won the best picture Oscar and spawned a series of sequels, of which Avildsen directed *Rocky V*. In 1980, he scored another huge box-office hit with *The Karate Kid*. Avildsen executed his own cinematography on his early films and himself edited some of his later productions. He married actress Tracy Brooks Swope.

FEATURE FILMS (as director): *Turn On to Love* (also phot., co-edit.), *Sweet Dreams* (also phot.) 1969; *Guess What We Learned in School Today?* (also co-sc., phot., edit.), *Joe* (also phot.) 1970; *Okay Bill* (also sc., phot.), *Cry Uncle* (also phot.) 1971; *The Stoolie* (also co-phot.) 1972; *Save the Tiger* 1973; *The Inauguration Ball* (doc.) 1974; *W. W. and the Dixie Dancekings, Foreplay* (co-dir.) 1975; *Rocky* 1976; *Slow Dancing in the Big City* (prod., edit.) 1978; *The Formula* 1980; *Neighbors* 1981; *Traveling Hopefully* (doc.) 1982; *A Night in Heaven* (also edit.) 1983; *The Karate Kid* (also co-edit.) 1984; *The Karate Kid Part II* (also co-edit.) 1986; *Happy New Year* 1987; *For Keeps?* (also edit.) 1988; *Lean on Me* (also co-edit.), *The Karate Kid Part III* (also co-edit.) 1989; *Rocky V* (also co-edit.) 1990; *The Power of One* (also edit.) 1992; *8 Seconds* 1994.

Avnet, Jonathan Michael. Producer. Born on Nov. 17, 1949, in Brooklyn. *ed.* U. of Pennsylvania, Wharton School of Business, Sarah Lawrence. He won a directing fellowship at the American Film Institute but made his mark as a producer. With partners Steve Tisch and later Jordan Kerner, he has produced films ranging from the teen comedy *Risky Business* to the offbeat comedy-drama *Fried Green Tomatoes* (1992). He has also produced films for television, including the acclaimed drama of wife abuse, 'The Burning Bed' (1984).

FILMS INCLUDE: *Checkered Flag or Crash* (assoc. prod. only) 1977; *Coast to Coast* 1980; *Deal of the Century* (exec. prod. only) 1983; *Risky Business* 1983; *Less Than Zero* 1987; *Funny About Love, Men Don't Leave* (also second unit dir.) 1990; *Fried Green Tomatoes, The Mighty Ducks* 1992; *The War* 1994; *Up Close and Personal* 1996; *Red Corner* 1997.

Axel, Gabriel. Director. Born in 1920(?), in Denmark. Partly raised in France, he studied acting at the Danish National Conservatory, then performed on the stages of Copenhagen and Paris. He began directing films in the late 50s and for three decades remained one of his country's most dependable filmmakers. After years of toiling in relative anonymity, he burst upon the international scene with the delightful *Babette's Feast* (1987), an Oscar (and British Academy) winner as best foreign film.

FILMS INCLUDE: *Golden Mountains* 1957; *Crazy Paradise* 1962; *The Red Mantle/Hagbard and Signe* 1967; *Danish Blue* (doc.) 1968; *Babette's Feast* (also sc.) 1987; *Christian* (also sc.) 1989.

Axelrod, George. Screenwriter, playwright, director, producer. Born on June 9, 1922, in New York City. After some acting, WW II service, and ten years of writing radio and TV scripts (400 of them), he became famous as the author of two successful Broadway comedies, 'The Seven Year Itch' (1953) and 'Will Success Spoil Rock Hunter?' (1955). He later co-produced the plays 'Visit to a Small Planet' (1957) and his own 'Goodbye Charlie' (1965), also directing the latter. He wrote the novel,

Beggar's Choice (1947) and memoirs, *Where Am I Now When I Need Me?* (1971). Axelrod's association with films has been for the most part through screenplays, but he also has proved himself a capable director, especially skillful in his handling of actors. His stepson, Jonathan Axelrod (*b.* July 9, 1948, New York City), is also a screenwriter. His daughter, Nina Axelrod, is an actress.

FILMS (as screenwriter): *Phffft* 1954; *The Seven Year Itch* 1955; *Bus Stop* 1956; *Breakfast at Tiffany's* 1961; *The Manchurian Candidate* (also co-prod.) 1962; *Paris When It Sizzles* (also co-prod.) 1964; *How to Murder Your Wife* 1965; *Lord Love a Duck* (also prod., dir.) 1966; *The Secret Life of an American Wife* (also prod., dir.) 1968; *The Lady Vanishes* (UK) 1979; *The Holcroft Covenant* (UK) 1985; *The Fourth Protocol* 1987.

Aykroyd, Dan. Actor, screenwriter. Born Daniel Edward Aykroyd, on July 1, 1952, in Ottawa, Canada. A dropout from Ottawa's Carleton University, he worked as a train brakeman and surveyor before beginning a career as a comedian. He was an alumnus of the Toronto branch of the Second City comedy theater and Canadian TV by the time he arrived in New York in 1975. Within months, he embarked on the road to success as he started a fortuitous five-season stint as a regular member of NBC's comedy series 'Saturday Night Live.' He teamed up with longtime buddy John BELUSHI to entertain TV audiences with some of the show's most hilarious moments. They also appeared together in three films, most memorably in *The Blues Brothers* (1980). After Belushi's tragic death in 1982, Aykroyd continued in films, often collaborating on his own scripts. He scored a huge box-office hit with *Ghostbusters* (1984), in which he teamed up with another 'Saturday Night Live' veteran, Bill MURRAY. He showed an unexpected flair for drama as Jessica Tandy's son in *Driving Miss Daisy* (1989), a performance that earned him an Academy Award nomination for best supporting actor. Though his debut as a director with *Nothing But Trouble* (1991) was ill fated, he has continued to be a popular and inventive comic performer. In 1993, he returned to his 'Saturday Night Live' roots in *Coneheads*, based on a recurring sketch from the series. Married actress Donna DIXON. He is co-owner of the popular Hard Rock Café.

FILMS: *Love at First Sight* (Can.) 1977; *Mr. Mike's Mondo Video, 1941* 1979; *The Blues Brothers* (also co-sc.) 1980; *Neighbors* 1981; *It Came from Hollywood* (compilation film) 1982; *Trading Places, Doctor Detroit, Twilight Zone—The Movie* 1983; *Indiana Jones and the Temple of Doom, Ghostbusters* (also co-sc.), *Nothing Lasts Forever* 1984; *Into the Night, Spies Like Us* 1985; *Once More Saturday Night* (exec. prod. only) 1986; *Dragnet* (also co-sc.) 1987; *The Couch Trip, The Great Outdoors, Caddyshack II, My Stepmother Is an Alien* 1988; *Ghostbusters II* (also co-sc.), *Driving Miss Daisy* 1989; *Loose Cannons* (also song) 1990; *Masters of Menace, Nothing But Trouble* (also dir., sc.), *My Girl* 1991; *This Is My Life, Sneakers, Chaplin* 1992; *Coneheads* 1993; *Exit to Eden, My Girl 2, North* 1994; *Casper* (v/o), *Tommy Boy* 1995; *Feeling Minnesota, Getting Away with Murder, Rainbow, Sgt. Bilko* 1996; *Grosse Pointe Blank* 1997.

Aylmer, Sir Felix. Actor. *b.* Felix Edward Aylmer-Jones, Feb. 21, 1889, Corsham, England. *d.* 1979. *ed.* Oxford. Sagacious-seeming, distinguished-looking character player of British stage (from 1911) and screen (1930). Typically playing aristocrats and patriarchs, he also appeared in numerous Hollywood films. For many years he served as president of Britain's Actors Equity. He wrote a number of plays and adapted several plays of others for the movies. He was knighted in 1965. His son, David Aylmer (1933–1964), was also a stage and screen actor.

FILMS INCLUDE: *Escape* 1930; *The Lodger/The Phantom Fiend* 1932; *The Wandering Jew* 1933; *Evergreen* 1934; *The Iron Duke* 1935; *Rhodes of Africa/Rhodes, Tudor Rose/Nine Days a Queen* (as Edward Seymour), *As You Like It* (as Duke Frederick) 1936; *The Mill on the Floss, Dreaming Lips, Victoria the Great* (as Lord Palmerston) 1937; *The Citadel, Sixty Years a Queen* (again as Lord Palmerston) 1938; *Night Train to Munich/Night Train* 1940; *The Young Mr. Pitt* 1942; *The Demi-Paradise/Adventure for Two, The Life and Death of Colonel Blimp* 1943; *Mr. Emmanuel* (title role), *Henry V* (as the Archbishop of Canterbury) 1944; *The Way Ahead/Johnny in the Clouds, The Wicked Lady* 1945; *The Years Between* 1946; *Hamlet* (as Polonius) 1948; *Edward My Son, Christopher Columbus, Prince of Foxes* (US) 1949; *So Long at the Fair, Alice in Wonderland* 1950; *Quo Vadis* (US) 1951; *Ivanhoe* (US/UK) 1952; *Knights of the Round Table* (US/UK) 1954; *The Angel Who Pawned Her Harp* (lead) 1955; *Anastasia* (US) 1956; *Saint Joan* (as the Inquisitor; UK/US) 1957; *The Doctor's Dilemma, Separate Tables* (US) 1958; *The Mummy* 1959; *From the Terrace* (US), *Exodus* (US) 1960; *Macbeth* (on TV in 1960) 1963; *Becket* (as the Archbishop of Canterbury; UK/US), *The Chalk Garden* 1964; *Masquerade* 1965; *Decline and Fall* 1968.

Ayres, Agnes. Actress. *b.* Agnes Hinkle, Sept. 4, 1896, Carbondale, Ill. *d.* 1940. Star of the American silent screen, famous as Valentino's paramour in both *The Sheik* (1921) and *The Son of the Sheik* (1926). Her career began in Essanay shorts around 1915, reached a peak in the early 20s, when she starred in many silents, and ended with the coming of sound. She returned to the screen only once, for a bit in *Souls at Sea* (1937), and three years later died of a cerebral hemorrhage at age 44.

FILMS INCLUDE: *His New Job* (bit) 1915; *Motherhood, The Debt, The Defeat of the City* 1917; *One Thousand Dollars* 1918; *The Sacred Silence* 1919; *The Furnace, Go and Get It* 1920; *Forbidden Fruit, The Love Special, Too Much Speed, The Affairs of Anatol, The Sheik* 1921; *Bought and Paid For, Borderland, Clarence, A Daughter of Luxury, The Ordeal* 1922; *The Heart Raider, Racing Hearts, The Marriage Maker, The Ten Commandments* 1923; *Don't Call It Love, Bluff, The Guilty One, The Story Without a Name, When a Girl Loves, Worldly Goods* 1924; *Tomorrow's Love, Her Market Value, The Awful Truth, Morals for Men* 1925; *The Son of the Sheik* 1926; *Into the Night* 1928; *The Donovan Affair, Broken Hearted, Bye Bye Buddy* 1929; *Souls at Sea* (bit) 1937.

Ayres, Lew. Actor. Born Lewis Frederick Ayres III, on Dec. 28, 1908, in Minneapolis. *d.* 1996. *ed.* U. of Arizona (medicine). A big-band banjo, guitar, and piano player, he was spotted for a movie contract while playing at a Hollywood night club in 1928. Within a year he was Garbo's leading man in *The Kiss* and he gained international prominence in 1930 with his sensitive portrayal of a disillusioned young German soldier in Milestone's pacifist *All Quiet on the Western Front,* the best role of his career. But after this auspicious start, he was relegated for the most part to routine leads in B pictures. After an unsuccessful stab at directing (*Hearts in Bondage,* for Republic in 1936), he returned to lackluster roles in programmers, with the notable exception of Cukor's *Holiday* (1938). He subsequently returned to films, and was nominated for an Oscar for his performance in *Johnny Belinda* (1948), but appeared on the screen only occasionally after the early 50s.

In 1941, Ayres alienated America's moviegoers by declaring himself a conscientious objector and refusing to fight in WW II. He was shunned by the studios, and exhibitors refused to show his films. He later volunteered for noncombatant medical service and distinguished himself under fire. A deeply spiritual man and a student of comparative religion, he wrote, produced, and narrated the five-part documentary *Altars of the East* (1955), based on his own book. In 1976 he released a follow-up documentary, the 150-minute *Altars of the World,* which he personally directed, produced, photographed, and edited. He served on the US National Committee for UNESCO. Divorced from actresses Lola LANE (1931–33) and Ginger ROGERS (1934–41).

FILMS: *The Sophomore* (bit), *The Kiss* 1929; *All Quiet on the Western Front, Common Clay, East Is West, The Doorway to Hell* 1930; *Iron Man, Up for Murder, Many a Slip, The Spirit of Notre Dame, Heaven on Earth/Mississippi* 1931; *The Impatient Maiden, Night World, Okay America!* 1932; *State Fair, Don't Bet on Love, My Weakness* 1933; *Cross Country Cruise, Let's Be Ritzy, She Learned About Sailors, Servants' Entrance* 1934; *The Lottery Lover, Silk Hat Kid* 1935; *The Leathernecks Have Landed, Panic on the Air, Hearts in Bondage* (dir. only), *Shakedown, Lady Be Careful, Murder with Pictures* 1936; *The Crime Nobody Saw, The Last Train from Madrid, Hold 'Em Navy* 1937; *Scandal Street, King of the Newsboys, Holiday, Rich Man Poor Girl, Young Dr. Kildare, Spring Madness* 1938; *Ice Follies of 1939, Broadway Serenade, Calling Dr. Kildare, These Glamour Girls, The Secret of Dr. Kildare, Remember?* 1939; *Dr. Kildare's Strange Case, Dr. Kildare Goes Home, The Golden Fleecing, Dr. Kildare's Crisis* 1940; *Maisie Was a Lady, The People vs. Dr. Kildare, Dr. Kildare's Wedding Day* 1941; *Dr. Kildare's Victory, Fingers at the Window* 1942; *The Dark Mirror* 1946; *The Unfaithful* 1947; *Johnny Belinda* 1948; *The Capture* 1950; *New Mexico* 1951; *No Escape, Donovan's Brain* 1953; *Advise and Consent* 1962; *The Carpetbaggers* 1964; *The Biscuit Eater, The Man* 1972; *Battle for the Planet of the Apes* 1973; *End of the World* 1977; *Damien—Omen II* 1978; *Battlestar Galactica* 1979.

Azaria, Hank. Actor, comedian. *b.* April 25, 1964, in Forest Hills, NY. *ed.* Tufts University. After making his mark on the stand-up circuit, this funny, gifted character actor made the transition to feature films from television, notably his many voice characterizations in the popular animated series 'The Simpsons.' He is most recognizable as the outrageously wacky maid opposite Robin WILLIAMS in *The Birdcage* (1996). He is married to actress Helen HUNT.

FILMS: *Cool Blue, Pretty Woman* 1990; *Quiz Show* 1994; *Heat, Now and Then* 1995; *The Birdcage* 1996.

Azéma, Sabine. Actress. Born in Paris. *ed.* Paris Conservatoire. Female lead in French films. She twice won the César (the French Oscar) for *A Sunday in the Country* (1984) and *Mélo* (1986).

FILMS INCLUDE: *Le Chasseur de Chez Maxim's, La Dentellière/The Lacemaker* 1977; *La Vie est un roman/Life Is a Bed of Roses, L'Amour à Mort/Love Unto Death, Un Dimanche à la Campagne/A Sunday in the Country* 1984; *Melo* 1986; *Cinq jours en juin, Vanille Fraise, La Vie et rien d'autre/Life and Nothing But* 1989; *Trois Années* 1990.

Aznavour, Charles. Singer, actor, composer, songwriter. Born Shahnour Varenagh Aznavourian, on May 22, 1924, in Paris, the son of an Armenian cook. He started out as a dancer at age nine but gained fame and popularity in the late 50s as a sentimental, foggy-voiced singing star of haunting French *chansons,* many written by himself. A diminutive man (5' 3", 110 lbs.), he has nonetheless demonstrated a strong screen presence in a long string of French and international films since 1958. His most memorable role was the lead in Truffaut's *Shoot the Piano Player* (1960). He has also written scores and songs for a number of films. Autobiography: *Aznavour by Aznavour* (1972).

FILMS INCLUDE (as actor): *La Tëte contre les Murs, Les Dragueurs/The Chasers* 1959; *Le Testament d'Orphée/The Testament of Orpheus* (cameo, as himself), *Tirez sur le Pianiste/Shoot the Piano Player, Le Passage du Rhin/Tomorrow Is My Turn* 1960; *Un Taxi pour Tobrouk/Taxi for Tobruk* 1961; *Le Diable et les Dix Commandements/The Devil and the Ten Commandments, Le Rat d'Amerique, Les Quatre Vérités/Three Fables of Love* 1962; *Alta Infedeltà/High Infidelity* (It./Fr.) 1964; *La Métamorphose des Cloportes/Cloportes* 1965; *Paris au Mois d'Aoüt/Paris in the Month of August* (also co-song), *Le Facteur s'en va-t-en Guerre/The Postman Goes to War* 1966; *Candy* (US/Fr./It.) 1968; *The Adventurers* (US), *The Games* (UK) 1970; *The Blockhouse* (UK) 1973; *And Then There Were None/Ten Little Indians* (UK/Fr./It./Ger.) 1974; *Sky Riders* (US/Ger.), *Folies Bourgeoises* 1976; *Die Blechtrommel/The Tin Drum* (Ger./Fr./Yug./Pol.) 1979; *Qu'est-ce qui fait courir David?, Les Fantômes du Chapelier* 1982; *Edith et Marcel/Edith and Marcel* (also lyrics) 1983; *Viva la Vie* 1984; *Yiddish Connection* (also sc.) 1986; *Mangeclous, Migrations* 1988; *Il Maestro* 1989; *Les Annees Campagne 1991.*

B

Baarová, Lida. Actress. Born on May 12, 1910, in Prague. Leading lady of Czech, German, and Italian films of the 30s and early 40s, notorious for her romantic entanglement with Nazi propaganda minister Josef Goebbels. She was Czechoslovakia's top star and increasingly popular on the German screen when her relationship with Hitler's aide began in 1934. Their infatuation was so strong that she turned down an offer by Louis B. Mayer to star in Hollywood films. In 1938 Goebbels asked Hitler's permission to divorce his wife and marry the actress. Hitler not only rejected the request but ordered a ban of all of Baarová's films. Defying confinement to Germany, the actress escaped to Prague, where she resumed her career and became active in anti-Nazi espionage. In 1941, when the authorities barred her from the Czech screen, she went to Italy for several assignments. After the war, Baarová was jailed in Prague for nearly two years for her association with the Nazis. After her release, she moved to Italy, where she appeared in several films, including Fellini's *I Vitelloni* (1953). In 1960 she returned to Berlin as a stage actress, appearing in, among other plays, Rainer Werner's Fassbinder's 'The Bitter Tears of Petra von Kant' (1971).

FILMS INCLUDE: *The Career of Pavel Camrda* 1931; *Okénko* 1933; *Barcarolle* 1934; *Die Stunde der Versuchung*

1936; *Die Fledermaus, Patrioten, Panenstvi/Virginity* 1938; *Der Spieler* 1938; *Ohnivé Léto/A Fiery Summer* 1939; *Turbina* 1940; *La Fornarina* 1942; *Ti conosco Mascherina!* 1943; *Il Cappello de Prete* 1945; *Gli Amati di Ravello* 1950; *La Vendetta di una Pazza* 1951; *Carne inquieta/Restless* 1952; *I Vitelloni/The Young and the Restless/The Loafers* 1953; *Rhapsodia del Sangre* 1958.

Babenco, Hector. Director. Born Hector Eduardo Babenco on Feb. 7, 1946, in Buenos Aires. The son of Jewish immigrants from Poland and Russia, he left home at 17 and traveled extensively throughout Europe before turning to filmmaking. He worked as a house painter, salesman, freelance writer, and extra in spaghetti Westerns, then settled in Brazil. He drew worldwide attention with *Pixote,* for which he shared the Grand Prix at the Biarritz Film Festival, and won the Silver Leopard at Locarno. After receiving an Oscar nomination as the director of the American-Brazilian co-production *Kiss of the Spider Woman,* he was invited to direct in the US.

FILMS: *Rei da Noite/King of the Night* 1975; *Lucio Flavio—Passaqeioro da Agonia* 1979; *Pixote a Lei do mais fraco/Pixote* (also co-sc.) 1981; *Kiss of the Spider Woman* (US/Brz.) 1985; *Ironweed* (US) 1987; *Besame Mucho* (prod.) 1987; *At Play in the Fields of the Lord* (US) (dir., co-sc.) 1991.

Babochkin, Boris. Actor. *b.* Jan. 18, 1904, Saratov, Russia. *d.* 1975. A veteran of the Leningrad stage, he began playing minor roles in films in 1927 and won instant fame for his heroic portrayal of the title role in *Chapayev* (1934). He subsequently appeared effectively in many other films, even directing two, but never repeated his *Chapayev* triumph. He spent his final years working mainly in the theater as actor, director, and administrator, and teaching at Moscow's Cinema Institute.

FILMS INCLUDE: *Revolt* 1927; *Myatesh* 1929; *The Return of Nathan Becker* 1932; *Chapayev* 1934; *Podrugi/Girl-Friends/Three Women* 1936; *Drusya/Friends* 1938; *Chapayev Is with Us* 1941; *The Defense of Tsaritsin/Fortress on the Volga* 1942; *Actress, Invincible* 1943; *Native Fields* (also co-dir.) 1944; *Povest o Niestovom* (also dir.) 1947; *Story of a Real Man* 1948; *The Great Force* 1950; *Restless Youth* 1955; *Annushka* 1959; *Ivan Rybakov* 1961; *The Curse of Mr. McKinley* 1975.

Baby LeRoy. Child actor. Born LeRoy Winebrenner, on May 12, 1932, in Los Angeles. While still a toddler of one year plus, he made several heartwarming appearances in films, most notably with W. C. FIELDS. He plagued the child-hating Fields in four films and in return got his share of abuse. At the ripe age of four, Baby LeRoy retired from the screen. Among his adult professions has been merchant marine.

FILMS: *A Bedtime Story, Torch Singer, Tillie and Gus, Alice in Wonderland* 1933; *The Old-Fashioned Way, It's a Gift, Miss Fane's Baby Is Stolen, The Lemon Drop Kid* 1934; *It's a Great Life* 1936.

Baby Peggy. Child actress, author. Born Peggy Jean Montgomery, in 1918, in San Diego, Calif. Popular child star of the 20s; the Shirley Temple of her day. The daughter of a cowboy stuntman, she entered films at age three and before reaching ten starred in numerous two-reelers and more than a dozen features. Her popularity gradually diminished as she neared adolescence. In October of 1925, Baby Peggy left Hollywood to headline a vaudeville tour of the US and Canada for four years, returning to Hollywood in 1932 as Peggy Montgomery, coincidentally, a name also used by a silent film star. (See MONTGOMERY, Peggy). Since retiring from the screen in the late 30s, she has been a freelance journalist, a greeting card company executive, and a book-buyer for a university bookstore. In 1975 she authored, under her married name Diana Serra Cary, *The Hollywood Posse,* a book about the silver screen's cowboy extras and stuntmen. In 1979 she published *Hollywood Children: An Inside Account of the Child Star Era*. Her autobiography, *Whatever Happened to Baby Peggy?,* was published in 1996. Her first husband was actor Gordon Ayres.

FILMS INCLUDE: *Little Miss Hollywood, Peggy Behave* 1922; *The Darling of New York* 1923; *Captain January, Helen's Babies, The Law Forbids, The Family Secret* 1924; *April Fool* 1926; *Off His Base* 1933; *Eight Girls in a Boat* 1934; *Ah! Wilderness* 1936; *Having a Wonderful Time* 1938.

Baby Sandy. Child performer. Born Sandra Lee Henville, on Jan. 14, 1938, in Los Angeles. Cute little tot who brightened several Universal films of the late 30s and early 40s. She was popular enough to make the cover of *Life* magazine and in 1940 was chosen "Baby of the Year" by *Parents* magazine, but her "meteoric" career had faded before she reached her fifth birthday. Today she is a legal secretary.

FILMS INCLUDE: *East Side of Heaven, Unexpected Father/Sandy, Little Accident* 1939; *Sandy Is a Lady, Sandy Gets Her Man* 1940; *Sandy Steps Out, Bachelor Daddy, Melody Lane* 1941; *Johnny Doughboy* 1942.

baby spot. A small spotlight used to highlight a limited area or to illuminate a close-up of a subject. It uses a 500- or 750-watt lamp, mounted in a housing with a lens.

baby tripod. A short-legged tripod, also called a "shorty," for setting up a camera at a low angle.

Bacall, Lauren. Actress. Born Betty Joan Perske, on Sept. 16, 1924, in the Bronx, N.Y. *ed.* Julia Richman High School, Manhattan. After some training at the American Academy of Dramatic Arts, she played minor roles in several Broadway plays, then turned to modeling. In 1943, Mrs. Howard Hawks saw her photograph on the cover of *Harper's Bazaar* and told her Hollywood producer-director husband of her discovery. Within a month Miss Bacall had a Hollywood contract. In her Hollywood debut, she appeared with Humphrey BOGART in *To Have and Have Not* (1945). Both public and critics were highly impressed. James Agee wrote: "Lauren Bacall has cinema personality to burn. . . . She has a javelinlike vitality, a born dancer's eloquence of movement, a fierce female shrewdness, and a special sweet-sourness. With these faculties, plus a stone-crushing self-confidence and a trombone voice, she manages to get across the toughest girl. . . Hollywood has dreamed of in a long, long while."

Studio publicity dubbed her "The Look," because of the suggestive, come-on twinkle in her eye, and she was on her way to stardom at Warner Bros. In 1945 she married Bogart, with whom she later appeared in three more films, *The Big Sleep* (1946), *Dark Passage* (1947), and *Key Largo* (1948). Their on-screen relationship was characterized by such memorable provocative Bacall phrases as "If you want anything, all you have to do is whistle" (from *To Have and Have Not,* 1944). Their off-screen relationship was close and warm. When Bogart fell ill of cancer, she nursed him devotedly until his death in 1957. In 1961 she married Jason ROBARDS, Jr. (whom she later divorced). Bacall's relationship with Warner Bros. was much less cordial. After repeated rifts over roles she refused to play, the studio suspended her services and fined her. After 1950 she worked for 20th Century-Fox and other studios. In the late 60s she appeared successfully on Broadway in 'Cactus Flower.' In 1970 she won the Tony Award for her performance in Broadway's 'Applause,' a musical remake of the film *All About Eve.* She triumphed again on Broadway in 1981, in 'Woman of the Year.' She returned to the screen in 1974 after an eight-year absence and, in 1996, earned her first Academy Award nomination as supporting actress for her role as Barbra Streisand's mother in *The Mirror Has Two Faces*. Autobiography: *Lauren Bacall by Myself.* (1979)

FILMS: *To Have and Have Not* 1944; *Confidential Agent* 1945; *Two Guys from Milwaukee* (cameo), *The Big Sleep* 1946; *Dark Passage* 1947; *Key Largo* 1948; *Young Man with a Horn, Bright Leaf* 1950; *How to Marry a Millionaire* 1953; *Woman's World* 1954; *The Cobweb, Blood Alley* 1955; *Written on the Wind, Designing Woman* 1957; *The Gift of Love* 1958; *North West Frontier/Flame Over India* (UK) 1959; *Shock Treatment* 1964; *Sex and the Single Girl* 1965; *Harper* 1966; *Murder on the Orient Express* (UK/US) 1974; *The Shootist* 1976; *Health* 1979. *The Fan* 1981; *Appointment with Death* (UK), *Mr. North* 1988; *Tree of Hands* (UK) 1989; *Misery* 1990; *A Star for Two, All I Want for Christmas* 1991; *Ready To Wear* 1994; *The Mirror Has Two Faces, My Fellow Americans* 1996.

Bach, Barbara. Actress. Born on Aug. 27, 1946, in New York City. Sensual, voluptuous leading lady of European and American films, and international co-productions. Married Beatle Ringo Starr.

FILMS INCLUDE: *La Tarantola del Ventre nero/The Black Belly of the Tarantula* (It./Fr.) 1972; *L'Ultima Chance/Stateline Motel* (It.) 1973; *Wolf Larsen/The Legend of Seawolf* 1975; *The Spy Who Loved Me* (UK) 1977; *Force 10 From Navarone* (UK) 1978; *Jaguar Lives* (US) 1979; *Up the Academy* (US) 1980; *Caveman* (US), *The Unseen* (US) 1981; *Give My Regards to Broad Street* (UK) 1984.

Bacharach, Burt. Composer, songwriter, conductor, arranger. Born on May 12, 1928, in Kansas City, Mo. *ed.* McGill (Montreal); Tanglewood; Mannes School of Music; Music Academy of the West. The son of syndicated columnist Bert Bacharach, he studied music at Tanglewood and with Darius Milhaud in California and during the Korean War toured Army bases as a concert pianist in uniform. After his tour of duty he became an accompanist to such performers as Vic Damone, Polly Bergen, and Joel Grey and made the big time as the conductor-arranger of Marlene DIETRICH's worldwide concert tour. At the same time, he began composing songs and film scores and in 1968 wrote the musical 'Promises Promises' for Broadway. In 1969 he won two Oscars, for scoring the film *Butch Cassidy and the Sundance Kid* and for the song 'Raindrops Keep Fallin' on My Head' in that film. Other hit songs he wrote with lyricist Hal David include 'Alfie,' 'What the World Needs Now,' 'I'll Never Fall in Love Again,' 'What's New, Pussycat?,' and 'Do You Know the Way to San Jose?' His music is typically written in syncopated, offbeat rhythms and his songs are often too complicated for simple humming by an untrained voice. He has created several successful recordings and makes personal appearances as a nightclub composer-entertainer. Divorced from singer Paula Stewart, actress Angie DICKINSON, and Carole Bayer Sager, his lyricist on the Oscar-winning theme song 'Best That You Can Do' for *Arthur* (1981) and on subsequent films, as well as on the song 'On My Own,' one of the top hit singles of 1986.

FILMS INCLUDE: *Lizzie* (songs), *The Sad Sack* (title song) 1957; *The Blob* (song), *Country Music Holiday* (song) 1958; *Love in a Goldfish Bowl* (title song) 1961; *The Man Who Shot Liberty Valance* (song) 1962; *Wives and Lovers* (song) 1963; *A House Is Not a Home* (title song), *Send Me No Flowers* (title song) 1964; *Who's Been Sleeping in My Bed?* (song), *What's New Pussycat?* (score and songs) 1965; *Alfie* (title song; UK), *Made in Paris* (title song), *Promise Her Anything* (title song; UK); *After the Fox* (score; US/UK/It.) 1966; *Casino Royale* (score and songs; UK) 1967; *The April Fools* (title song), *Bob & Carol & Ted & Alice* (song, 'What the World Needs Now'), *Butch Cassidy and the Sundance Kid* (score, song, 'Raindrops Keep Fallin' on My Head') 1969; *The Boys in the Band* (song, 'The Look of Love,' sung by Bacharach himself) 1970; *Something Big* (score, title song) 1971; *Lost Horizon* (score, songs) 1973; *Arthur* (score, songs) 1981; *Night Shift* (score, songs) 1982; *Best Defense* (song) 1984; *Tough Guys* (song, 'They Don't Make Them Like They Used To'), *Baby Boom* (song, 'Everchanging Times') 1987; *Arthur 2 on the Rocks* (score, songs) 1988; *Grace of My Heart* (songs) 1996.

Bachelet, Jean. Director of photography. *b.* Oct. 8, 1894, in Azans, France. Deceased. In films from 1912 when he served as a newsreel photographer in Russia for the Gaumont film company. Became a director of photography in 1924. He was behind the camera in some 160 films, most notably those of Jean RENOIR during the latter's peak years, from the mid-20s to the mid-30s.

FILMS INCLUDE: *La Fille de l'Eau* 1924; *Nana* (co-phot.) 1926; *Charleston* (short) 1927; *La Petite Marchande d'Allumettes/The Little Match Girl, Tire-au-Flanc* 1928; *L'Arlésienne, La Petite Lise* 1930; *Crainquebille, Madame Bovary, Sans Famille* 1934; *Le Crime de Monsieur Lange, Les Bas-Fonds/The Lower Depths* 1936; *La Règle du Jeu/The Rules of the Game* 1939; *Nous les Gosses* 1941; *Tire-au-Flanc* (remake) 1950; *Les Mains sales/Dirty Hands* 1951; *La Rue des Bouches peintes* 1955.

background. The portion of a scene or of action behind the main scene or action (the FOREGROUND). It plays an important part in the overall composition of a shot and, if carefully staged, may contribute greatly to the continuity of the action and to an extended meaning of the theme. The background action in Wyler's *The Best Years of Our Lives* and Welles's *Citizen Kane,* made possible by deep-focus, was especially notable, often dominating the main action. More conventionally, the background is kept busy but is photographed somewhat out of focus so that it remains unobtrusive. Abbreviated "b/g."

background noise. Unintelligible voices and other sounds added to the sound track to increase the realism of a scene, as on a busy street or other locations noisy with people, traffic, etc. See also WILD SOUND.

backing. A large backdrop, usually a painting or a photograph, used on a studio set to simulate a view seen through a door or a window or as a substitute for a natural background on an exterior set.

back lighting. The illumination of a scene from behind the subject and toward the camera. It tends to produce a light fringe, increase contrast, and make the subject appear to stand out from the background, thus suggesting a third dimension. It is also used for such specific effects as adding sheen to hair.

back lot. An open-air area on studio property designated for the shooting of exteriors. It may consist of stark open spaces or include elaborate re-creations of background architecture, such as a typical Western street or a downtown intersection in a big city. Although the results often seem artificial, the use of a back lot can save a studio the cost and the time consumed by shooting on location.

back projection. The projection of film onto the back of a translucent screen, instead of the conventional method of projection onto the front of a reflecting screen. Since the projector is operated behind the screen and out of the way of the audience, this method has a distinct advantage in the presentation of films in small auditoriums or conference rooms. In addition, it permits the showing of films in a lighted room.

Back projection (also called rear projection or process photography) was once widely used in studio cinematography to simulate action. In this technique, the picture projected from behind the screen served as a background for the live action being photographed on the set. Thus, actors would sit in a mock car in the studio while street scenes raced past the window, projected from behind; the result would be the illusion of a moving vehicle. The result was less than perfect because of the unequal sharpness and illumination of the rear and front images. The technique has been largely replaced by FRONT PROJECTION and the BLUE SCREEN PROCESS (see also TRAVELING MATTE).

Back projection is sometimes still used for shots in which a previously photographed scene is combined with a matte painting of the surroundings. For example, film of a group of actors may be projected through a translucent hole in a painting of a spaceship. When a camera photographs the painting, it also re-photographs the actors, who appear to be glimpsed through the spaceship window.

backup schedule. A filming schedule prepared as an alternative to the regular schedule in the event that shooting cannot proceed according to plans. Exterior filming is often frustrated by the weather, and it is useful to have a backup schedule of interior shooting for a rainy day.

Backus, Jim. Actor. *b.* James Gilmore Backus, Feb. 25, 1913, Cleveland. *d.* 1989, of pneumonia. A graduate of the American Academy of Dramatic Arts in 1933, he was a veteran of stage, vaudeville, and radio by the time he began appearing regularly in films in 1949. Readily identifiable by his beaming expression and inimitable voice, he played character roles, both dramatic and comic, in scores of films and numerous TV shows. He also starred in several television series, including 'I Married Joan' (1952–55), 'Gilligan's Island' (1964–67), and 'Blondie' (1968–69). The latter co-starred his wife, Henny Backus (née Henriette Kay). He was perhaps most famous, however, as the offscreen voice of the cartoon character Mr. Magoo. He authored the books *Rocks on the Roof* and *What Are You Doing After the Orgy?* (co-written with Henny, 1962) and the autobiography *Only When I Laugh* (1965), as well as several TV and radio scripts. On his hospital deathbed, he spent his last two weeks collaborating with his wife on two humorous books about his battle with Parkinson's disease, *Backus Strikes Back* and *Forgive Us Our Digressions.*

FILMS INCLUDE: *The Pied Piper* 1942; *Easy Living, Father Was a Fullback, The Great Lover* 1949; *His Kind of Woman, M, Bright Victory* 1951; *Deadline USA, Pat and Mike, Don't Bother to Knock* 1952; *Above and Beyond, Androcles and the Lion* 1953; *The Human Jungle* 1954; *Rebel Without a Cause* 1955; *Meet Me in Las Vegas, The Great Man* 1956; *Man of a Thousand Faces* 1957; *Macabre* 1958; *Ice Palace* 1960; *Boys' Night Out, The Wonderful World of the Brothers Grimm* 1962; *The Wheeler Dealers, Johnny Cool, It's a Mad Mad Mad Mad World, Sunday in New York* 1963; *Advance to the Rear* 1964; *Billie* 1965; *Hurry Sundown* 1967; *Where Were You When the Lights Went Out?* 1968; *Hello Down There* 1969; *Myra Breckinridge* 1970; *Now You See Him Now You Don't* 1972; *Crazy Mama* 1975; *Pete's Dragon* 1977; *Good Guys Wear Black* 1978; *There Goes the Bride* (UK), *Angels' Brigade, C.H.O.M.P.S.* 1979; *Slapstick/Slapstick of Another Kind, Prince Jack* 1984.

Baclanova, Olga. Actress. *b.* 1899, Moscow. *d.* 1974. Started her stage career at 16 with the Moscow Art Theater. In 1923 she came to the US on a tour with a Soviet company and decided to stay. After a minor role in the film *The Dove* (1928), she played important parts in Josef von Sternberg's *The Docks of New York* and in *Street of Sin* (both also 1928) with Emil JANNINGS. Several leading roles followed, memorably the horror classic *Freaks,* in which she played an exotic trapeze artist who marries a midget for his money. She also appeared on Broadway and hosted a radio program in the late 30s.

FILMS INCLUDE: In the USSR—*Symphony of Love and Death* 1914; *Wanderer Beyond the Grave* 1915; *He Who Gets Slapped* 1916; *The Flowers Are Late* 1917. In the US—*The Dove, Street of Sin, Forgotten Faces, The Docks of New York, Three Sinners, The Man Who Laughs, Avalanche* 1928; *A Dangerous Woman, The Wolf of Wall Street, The Man I Love* 1929; *Are You There?, Cheer Up and Smile* 1930; *The Great Lover* 1931; *Freaks* 1932; *Billion Dollar Scandal* 1933; *Claudia* 1943.

Bacon, Irving. Actor. *b.* Sept. 6, 1893, St. Joseph, Mo. *d.* 1965. A character player in well over 200 Hollywood films and many more stage plays and TV programs. He was usually cast as a doleful simpleton in comic supporting roles and was most at home in rural surroundings.

FILMS INCLUDE: *Anna Christie* 1923; *California or Bust* 1927; *The Head Man* 1928; *Half Way to Heaven* 1929; *Street of Chance* 1930; *Million Dollar Legs* 1932; *It Happened One Night* 1934; *Private Worlds, Diamond Jim* 1935; *The Big Broadcast of 1937* 1936; *Seventh Heaven, Big City* 1937; *The Amazing Dr. Clitterhouse, Sing You Sinners* 1938; *Hollywood Cavalcade, The Oklahoma Kid, Gone With the Wind* 1939; *The Grapes of Wrath, Dr. Ehrlich's Magic Bullet, The Return of Frank James* 1940; *Meet John Doe, Tobacco Road, Western Union, Never Give a Sucker an Even Break* 1941; *Holiday Inn, Footlight Serenade* 1942; *Shadow of a Doubt, Action in the North Atlantic* 1943; *Since You Went Away* 1944; *Guest Wife* 1945; *Monsieur Verdoux* 1947; *State of the Union, Good Sam* 1948; *Wabash Avenue* 1950; *O. Henry's Full House* 1952; *The Glenn Miller Story, A Star Is Born* 1954; *Fort Massacre* 1958.

Bacon, Kevin. Actor. Born on July 8, 1958, in Philadelphia. *ed.* Manning Street Actor's Theatre, Philadelphia. Boyish, energetic, pug-nosed young lead of Hollywood films of the 80s and 90s. He has also appeared on the stage, winning an Obie Award for his performance in 'Forty Deuce' off-Broadway, and in TV movies. In 1996, Bacon directed his first film, *Losing Chase*, centering on the relationship between a woman challenged by mental illness and a young female student who spends a summer caring for her. The film starred his wife, actress Kyra SEDGWICK.

FILMS: *National Lampoon's Animal House* 1978; *Starting Over* 1979; *Hero at Large, Friday the 13th* 1980; *Only When I Laugh* 1981; *Diner, Forty Deuce* 1982; *Footloose* 1984; *Enormous Changes at the Last Minute* 1985; *Quicksilver* 1986; *White Water Summer, End of the Line, Planes Trains and Automobiles* 1987; *She's Having a Baby* 1988; *The Big Picture, Criminal Law* 1989; *Tremors, Flatliners* 1990; *Queens Logic, Pyrates, He Said/She Said, JFK* 1991; *A Few Good Men* 1992; *The Air Up There, The River Wild* 1994; *Apollo 13, Balto* (v/o), *Murder in the First* 1995; *Losing Chase* (dir. only), *Sleepers* 1996; *Perfect Picture* 1997.

Bacon, Lloyd. Director, actor. *b.* Jan. 16, 1890, San Jose, Calif. *d.* 1955. One of Hollywood's most prolific directors, he began as a stage actor, making his film debut in 1913 playing heavy roles in Lloyd Hamilton comedies. He later became the perfect foil to Charlie Chaplin in such comedies as *The Champion, In the Park, A Jitney Elopement, The Bank, The Tramp* (all 1915); *The Floorwalker, The Vagabond, Behind the Screen, The Rink,* and *The Fireman* (all 1916). After WW I service, he rejoined Chaplin at Mutual in 1918, then moved on to Triangle the following year. In 1919–20 he played supporting roles, and occasional leads, in a dozen feature films of various studios.

In 1921, Bacon became a director, turning out comedy shorts for Lloyd Hamilton and Mack Sennett, until 1926, when he directed his first feature. His first important film was *The Singing Fool* (1928) with Al Jolson, Hollywood's first full-dialogue production. Bacon soon established himself as a musical comedy specialist on the Warner Bros. lot, directing memorable musical extravaganzas made famous by the choreography of Busby Berkeley, including *42nd Street, Footlight Parade* (both 1933), *Wonder Bar* (1934), and *Gold Diggers of 1937* (1936). His fluid style also characterized the other types of films he directed, from breezy comedies to gutsy action dramas. In 1944 he moved over to 20th Century-Fox, where he did the bulk of his work for the remainder of his career. He was known for his prolific output, his solid craftsmanship, and his ability to direct actors. His experience with Sennett was evident in the precise timing of action in his many films, particularly the comedies.

FEATURE FILMS: *Broken Hearts of Hollywood, Private Izzy Murphy* 1926; *Finger Prints, White Flannels, The Heart of Maryland, A Sailor's Sweetheart, Brass Knuckles* 1927; *Pay As You Enter, The Lion and the Mouse, Women They Talk About, The Singing Fool* 1928; *Stark Mad, No Defense, Honky Tonk, Say It With Songs, So Long Letty* 1929; *The Other Tomorrow, She Couldn't Say No, A Notorious Affair, Moby Dick, The Office Wife* 1930; *Sit Tight, Kept Husbands, Fifty Million Frenchmen, Gold Dust Gertie, Honor of the Family* 1931; *Manhattan Parade, Fireman Save My Child, Alias the Doctor, The Famous Ferguson Case, Miss Pinkerton, Crooner, You Said a Mouthful* 1932; *42nd Street, Picture Snatcher, Mary Stevens M.D., Footlight Parade, Son of a Sailor* 1933; *Wonder Bar, A Very Honorable Guy, He Was Her Man, Here Comes the Navy, Six-Day Bike Rider* 1934; *Devil Dogs of the Air, In Caliente, Broadway Gondolier, The Irish in Us, Frisco Kid* 1935; *Sons o' Guns, Cain and Mabel, Gold Diggers of 1937* 1936; *Marked Woman, Ever Since Eve, San Quentin, Submarine D–1* 1937; *A Slight Case of Murder, Cowboy from Brooklyn, Racket Busters, Boy Meets Girl* 1938; *Wings of the Navy, The Oklahoma Kid, Indianapolis Speedway, Espionage Agent* 1939; *A Child Is Born, Invisible Stripes, Three Cheers for the Irish, Brother Orchid, Knute Rockne—All American* 1940; *Honeymoon for Three, Footsteps in the Dark, Affectionately Yours, Navy Blues* 1941; *Larceny Inc., Wings for the Eagle, Silver Queen* 1942; *Action in the North Atlantic* 1943; *The Sullivans, Sunday Dinner for a Soldier* 1944; *Captain Eddie* 1945; *Home Sweet Homicide, Wake Up and Dream* 1946; *I Wonder Who's Kissing Her Now* 1947; *You Were Meant for Me, Give My Regards to Broadway, Don't Trust Your Husband/An Innocent Affair* 1948; *Mother Is a Freshman, It Happens Every Spring, Miss Grant Takes Richmond* 1949; *Kill the Umpire, The Good Humor Man, The Fuller Brush Girl* 1950; *Call Me Mister, The Frogmen, Golden Girl* 1951; *The I Don't Care Girl, The Great Sioux Uprising, Walking My Baby Back Home* 1953; *The French Line, She Couldn't Say No* 1954.

Badal, Jean. Director of photography. Born János Badal, in 1927, in Budapest. He worked in the Hungarian film industry before leaving his country in the wake of the 1956 uprising. He settled in France, where he soon became established as a leading lighting cameraman.

FILMS INCLUDE: *Les Mauvais Coups/Naked Autumn* 1961; *Le Rendez-vous de Minuit, L'Education sentimentale* 1962; *Behold a Pale Horse* (US) 1964; *What's New Pussycat?* (US/Fr.) 1965; *Les Coeurs verts/Naked Hearts* 1966; *Playtime* (co-phot.) 1967; *La Fiancée du Pirate/A Very Curious Girl* 1969; *La Promesse de l'Aube/Promise at Dawn* (Fr./US) 1970; *Les Assassins de l'Ordre* 1971; *Projection privée/Private Projection* 1973; *Blondy* 1976; *Goodbye Emmanuelle* 1978.

Baddeley, Hermione. Actress. *b.* Hermione Clinton-Baddeley, Nov. 13, 1906, Broseley, England. *d.* 1986. A stage actress from the age of six, she made her London debut at 12 and played her first film role at 22. She appeared in numerous plays and many films, typically in ribald character roles. She was nominated for an Oscar for her performance in *Room at the Top* (1959). In the early 60s she began commuting across the Atlantic, appearing in both British and American stage, TV, and film productions. Memorable as Mrs. Naugatuck, the hard-drinking maid, in the TV series 'Maude.' Her sister, Angela Baddeley (*b.* Madeleine Angela Clinton-Baddeley, July 4, 1904, London. *d.* 1976), was also a successful stage actress but appeared rarely in films. Angela became familiar to US TV audiences as Mrs. Bridges, the cook, in the imported 'Upstairs Downstairs' TV series.

FILMS INCLUDE: *A Daughter in Revolt* 1926; *The Guns of Loos* 1928; *Caste* 1930; *Royal Cavalcade* 1935; *Kipps* 1941; *It Always Rains on Sunday, Brighton Rock/Young Scarface* 1947; *Quartet, No Room at the Inn* 1948; *Dear Mr. Prohack, Passport to Pimlico* 1949; *The Woman in Question* 1950; *Scrooge/A Christmas Carol* (as Mrs. Cratchit), *Tom Brown's School Days* 1951; *Time Gentlemen Please, The Pickwick Papers* 1952; *The Belles of St. Trinian's* 1954; *Room at the Top, Expresso Bongo* 1959; *Midnight Lace* (US) 1960; *The Unsinkable Molly Brown* (US), *Mary Poppins* (US) 1964; *Harlow* (as Marie Dressler, in Carol Lynley version; US), *Marriage on the Rocks* (US), *Do Not Disturb* (US) 1965; *The Happiest Millionaire* (US) 1967; *The Black Windmill* 1974; *C.H.O.M.P.S.* 1979. *The Secret of Nimh* (voice only) 1982.

Badger, Clarence. Director. *b.* June 8, 1880, San Francisco. *d.* 1964. A graduate of the Boston Polytechnic Institute and a former artist and newspaperman, he joined Mack SENNETT at Triangle-Keystone in 1915 as a continuity writer and within months began directing two-reel comedies for the studio. From the start, he felt uncomfortable with the frantic slapstick style typical of the Sennett product and he developed a series of gentler romantic comedies starring Gloria Swanson and Bobby Vernon. He left Sennett in 1917 and in the following year began directing features for Goldwyn. Several of these starred Will ROGERS. Through the early 30s, Badger directed numerous silent films and talkies for various studios, mainly romantic comedies that were noted for their charm and wit, including Clara Bow's famous *It* (1927). In 1940 he emigrated to Australia and retired.

FILMS: Shorts—*Gypsy Joe, His Wild Oats* (co-dir. with Ford Sterling), *A Social Cub, Haystacks and Steeples, The Danger Girl* 1916; *The Nick-of-Time Baby, Teddy at the Throttle, The Sultan's Wife, The Pullman Bride* 1917. Features—*A Modern Enoch Arden* (co-dir. with Charles Avery), *The Floor Below, The Venus Model, Friend Husband, Kingdom of Youth, A Perfect Lady* 1918; *Day Dreams, Sis Hopkins, Daughter of Mine, Leave It to Susan, Through the Wrong Door, Strictly Confidential, Almost a Husband, Jubilo* 1919; *Water Water Everywhere, The Strange Boarder, Jes' Call Me Jim, The Man Who Lost Himself, Cupid the Cowpuncher, Honest Hutch* 1920; *Guile of Women, Boys Will Be Boys, An Unwilling Hero, Doubling for Romeo, A Poor Relation* 1921; *Don't Get Personal, The Dangerous Little Demon, Quincy Adams Sawyer* 1922; *Your Friend and Mine, Red Lights, Potash and Perlmutter* 1923; *Painted People, The Shooting of Dan McGrew, One Night in Rome* 1924; *New Lives for Old, Eve's Secret, Paths to Paradise, The Golden Princess* 1925; *Hands Up, Miss Brewster's Millions, The Rainmaker, The Campus Flirt* 1926; *It, A Kiss in a Taxi, Senorita, Man Power, Swim Girl Swim, She's a Sheik* 1927; *Red Hair, The Fifty-Fifty Girl, Hot News, Three Week-Ends* 1928; *Paris* 1929; *No No Nanette, Murder Will Out, Sweethearts and Wives, The Bad Man* 1930; *The Hot Heiress, Woman Hungry, Party Husband* 1931; *When Strangers Marry* 1933; *Rangle River* (also prod.; Austral.) 1939; *That Certain Something* (also sc.; Austral. 1940).

Badham, John. Director, also producer. Born on Aug. 25, 1939, in Luton, England. *ed.* Yale School of Drama. In US from age two, he was raised in Alabama, naturalized in 1950, and educated at Yale (B.A., M.F.A. in drama). After a stint in the service, he entered films as a mail room clerk at Universal, eventually graduating to tour guide, casting director, and associate producer. Gaining experience behind the cameras in TV, he began directing features in the late 70s and soon became established as a superior craftsman, one of new Hollywood's most accomplished technicians. Brother to actress Mary Badham.

FILMS: *The Bingo Long Traveling All-Stars and Motor Kings* 1976; *Saturday Night Fever* 1977; *Dracula* 1979; *Who's Life Is It Anyway?* 1981; *Blue Thunder, WarGames* 1983; *American Flyers* 1985; *Short Circuit* 1986; *Stakeout* (also exec. prod.) 1987; *Disorganized Crime* (co-exec. prod. only) 1989; *Bird on a Wire* 1990; *The Hard Way* 1991; *Point of No Return, Another Stakeout* 1993; *Drop Zone* 1994; *Nick of Time* (also prod.) 1995.

Baer, Max. Boxer, actor. *b.* 1909, Omaha, Nebr. *d.* 1959. At the height of his popularity in the ring in the early 30s, he starred in a film opposite Myrna Loy. He became heavyweight champion of the world in 1934 and later appeared in occasional films. At one time married to actress Dorothy Dunbar. His brother Buddy Baer (*b.* Jacob Henry Baer, 1915. *d.* 1986) played giants in *Quo Vadis* (1951), *Jack and the Beanstalk* (1952), and other films. His son, Max Baer, Jr. (*b.* Dec. 4, 1937, Oakland, Calif.), appeared in 'The Beverly Hillbillies' TV series and in several movies, then turned producer and director of the films *Macon County Line* (prod., co-story, act. only; 1974), *The Wild McCullochs* (1975), *Ode to Billy Joe* (1976), and *Hometown USA* (1979).

FILMS INCLUDE: *The Prizefighter and the Lady* 1933; *The Navy Comes Through* 1942; *Ladies' Day* 1943; *Africa Screams, Bride for Sale* 1949; *Riding High* 1950; *Skipalong Rosenbloom* 1951; *The Harder They Fall* 1956; *Utah Blaine* 1957; *Once Upon a Horse* 1958.

baffle. Something that checks or reflects, as a shield or partition. 1. One or more sound-absorbing screens inside a loudspeaker designed to improve the fidelity of sound reproduction by preventing sound waves from bouncing back and forth. 2. A microphone attachment designed to accentuate high frequencies. 3. A portable wall, draped with sound-absorbing material, used in the studio to prevent reverberation in recording. Also known as a "baffle blanket." 4. A louvered shutter mounted on a studio lamp to help direct light and control its intensity.

Baggot, King. Director, actor. *b.* 1874, St. Louis, Mo. *d.* 1948. Coming to the movies from the stage, he was one of the first American film performers to be publicized by name, and he quickly developed into a popular star of silent adventure dramas. Virile and handsome, he appeared in more than 300 shorts and feature films, then turned to directing, making dozens of films, most of which have been lost. Among his best-known surviving films (as director) are the quality Western *Tumbleweeds* (1925), with William S. Hart, and *Lovey Mary* (1926), a Bessie Love vehicle. The former film, shot by Joseph AUGUST, contains some breathtaking action sequences. In the early 30s, Baggot, occasionally billed as King Baggott, returned to acting, in character roles.

FILMS INCLUDE: As actor—*The Scarlet Letter* 1911; *Lady Audley's Secret, Human Hearts, King the Detective and the Smugglers* 1912; *Dr. Jekyll and Mr. Hyde* (title role), *Ivanhoe* (title role), *The Anarchist, The Actor's Christmas, Love vs. Law* 1913; *Absinthe, Across the Atlantic* 1914; *The Marble Heart, The City of Terrible Night, The Corsican Brothers, The Suburban* 1915; *Half a Roque, The Man From Nowhere* 1916; *The Eagle's Eye* (serial), *Kildare of the Storm* 1918; *The Man Who Stayed at Home* 1919; *The Hawk's Eye* (serial), *The Cheater, The Dwelling Place of Light, The Forbidden Thing* 1920; *The Butterfly Girl* 1921; *The Thrill Chaser* 1923; *The Czar of Broadway, Once a Gentleman* 1930; *Sweepstakes* 1931; *Fame Street* 1932; *Mississippi* 1935; *Come Live with Me* 1941; *Tish* 1942. As director (features complete)—*Crime's Triangle* (also sc., act.) 1915; *Cheated Love, Luring Lips, Moonlight Follies, Nobody's Fool* 1921; *Kissed, Human Hearts, The Kentucky Derby, The Lavender Bath Lady, A Dangerous Game* 1922; *The Love Letter, The Town Scandal, Crossed Wires* (also co-story), *Gossip, The Darling of New York* (also co-story) 1923; *The Whispered Name, The Gaiety Girl, The Tornado* 1924; *Raffles the Amateur Cracksman, The Home Maker, Tumbleweeds* 1925; *Lovey Mary* 1926; *Perch of the Devil, The Notorious Lady, Down the Stretch* 1927; *The House of Scandal, Romance of a Rogue* 1928.

Bailey, John. Director of photography, cinematographer, director. Born on Aug. 10, 1942, in Moberly, Missouri. *ed.* U. of Santa Clara; Loyola; USC; U. of Vienna. A product of the University of Southern California's Film School, he began his career in the 70s, with low-budget productions. He emerged in the 80s as a highly proficient lighting cameramen, achieving impressive visual results with exterior as well as interior color cinematography of major films. He made his directorial debut in 1990 with the film version of Lily Tomlin's acclaimed one-woman performance piece, *The Search for Signs of Intelligent Life in the Universe*. Married film editor Carol LITTLETON.

FILMS INCLUDE: *Premonition* 1972; *End of August* 1974; *Legacy* 1976; *Boulevard Nights* 1979; *American Gigolo, Ordinary People* 1980; *Honky Tonk Freeway* 1981; *Cat People, That Championship Season* 1982; *Without a Trace, The Big Chill* 1983; *Racing with the Moon, The Pope of Greenwich Village* 1984; *Silverado, Mishima* 1985; *Brighton Beach Memoirs* 1986; *Light of Day, Swimming to Cambodia* 1987; *Vibes, The Accidental Tourist* 1988; *My Blue Heaven, The Search for Signs of Intelligent Life in the Universe* (also dir.), *A Brief History of Time* 1990; *Groundhog Day* 1993; *China Moon* (dir.), *Nobody's Fool* 1994; *Extreme Measures, Mariette in Ecstasy* (dir.) 1996.

Bailey, Pearl. Singer, actress. *b.* Mar. 29, 1918, Newport News, Va. *d.* 1990. A preacher's daughter, she started her career at 15, after winning an amateur contest, touring as a dancer, and singing and dancing with various bands. She made her legitimate stage debut in the Broadway musical, 'St. Louis Woman,' for which she received an award as the most promising newcomer of 1946. She won a Tony Award for the title role in the all-black production of Broadway's 'Hello Dolly!' in the late 60s. Best known as a jazz singer, she made sporadic film appearances. In 1971 she hosted her own TV variety show. In 1975 she announced her retirement from show business and was named to the US delegation to the UN. In her last years, she devoted much of her time to AIDS causes. Autobiography: *The Raw Pearl* (1968).

FILMS: *Variety Girl* 1947; *Isn't It Romantic?* 1948; *Carmen Jones* 1955; *That Certain Feeling* 1956; *St. Louis Blues* 1958; *Porgy and Bess* 1959; *All the Fine Young Cannibals* 1960; *The Landlord* 1970; *Norman. . . Is That You?* 1976.

Baillie, Bruce. Filmmaker. Born on Sept. 24, 1931, in Aberdeen, S. Dakota. *ed.* U. of Minnesota; U. of Calif. (Berkeley); London School of Film Technique. Among the leading voices of the contemporary American avant-garde film movement. His experimental works are noted for their vivid imagery and evocative lyricism. His themes often challenge the established social order.

FILMS INCLUDE: *On Sundays, Mr. Hayashi, the Gymnasts* 1961; *Everyman, Here I Am* 1962; *To Parsifal* 1963; *Mass for the Dakota Sioux* 1964; *Quixote* 1965; *Yellow Horse* 1965; *Tung, Castro Street, Still Life, Termination* 1966; *Quixote* (revised), *Valentin de las Sierras* 1967; *Quick Billy* 1970; *Roslyn Romance* 1971–84; *The Cardinal's Visit* 1981–86.

Bainter, Fay. Actress. *b.* Dec. 7, 1892, in Los Angeles. *d.* 1968. First appeared in stock at the age of five; made her Broadway debut in 1912. In 1934 she appeared in her first film, *This Side of Heaven.* In 1938 she was nominated for Academy Awards as both best actress (for *White Banners*) and best supporting actress (for *Jezebel*) and won in the latter category. The controversy resulting from the dual nomination led to changes in the Motion Picture Academy's rules. She was nominated again as best supporting actress for *The Children's Hour* (1962), her last and grimmest role. She was usually cast as an understanding mother or sympathetic matron.

FILMS INCLUDE: *This Side of Heaven* 1934; *Quality Street, Make Way for Tomorrow* 1937; *Jezebel, White Banners, The Shining Hour* 1938; *Daughters Courageous* 1939; *Young Tom Edison, A Bill of Divorcement, Our Town* 1940; *Babes on Broadway* 1941; *Woman of the Year, The War Against Mrs. Hadley, Journey for Margaret* 1942; *The Human Comedy, Presenting Lily Mars, Cry Havoc* 1943; *Dark Waters* 1944; *State Fair* 1945; *The Kid from Brooklyn, The Virginian* 1946; *The Secret Life of Walter Mitty* 1947; *June Bride* 1948; *The President's Lady* 1953; *The Children's Hour* 1962.

Baird, Leah. American actress, screenwriter. *b.* 1887. *d.* 1971. Star of early silent films. On stage from her early teens, she appeared with Douglas Fairbanks on Broadway in 'The Gentleman from Mississippi' (1908–10) before entering films with Vitagraph in New York. Some of her American films, typically domestic melodramas, were produced lavishly in Europe, many by her husband, Arthur Beck. She wrote several of the scripts of her films and after retiring from acting in 1925 continued writing screenplays for films starring other players. She returned to the screen for small roles in 1941.

FILMS INCLUDE: As actress—*Chumps, The Adventure of the Italian Model, All for a Girl, Adam and Eve* 1912; *A Soul in Bondage* (also sc.), *Ivanhoe,* (as Rebecca) *The Anarchist* 1913; *Absinthe, Neptune's Daughter* 1914; *The Lights of New York, The People vs. John Doe* 1916; *Sins of Ambition* 1917; *Wolves of Kultur* (serial), *Moral Suicide, Life of Honor* 1918; *Echo of Youth, The Volcano, The Capitol* 1919; *Cynthia of the Minute* 1920; *The Heart Line* 1921; *Don't Doubt Your Wife* (also story, sc.), *When the Devil Drives* (also story, sc.), *When Husbands Deceive* (also story, sc.) 1922; *Is Divorce a Failure?* (also sc.), *The Destroying Angel* (also sc.), *The Miracle Makers* (also story) 1923; *The Law Demands, The Radio Flyer* (both films are probably re-cut versions of the 1918 serial *Wolves of Kultur*) 1924; *The Unnamed Woman* 1925; *Lady Gangster* 1942. As screenwriter—*Barriers Burned Away, The Primrose Path* 1925; *The Shadow of the Law* (also co-prod.), *Devil's Island, The False Alarm, Spangles* 1926; *Stolen Pleasures, The Return of Boston Blackie* 1927; *Jungle Bride* (story only) 1933. *Manpower* 1941; *Lady Gangster, Kings Row* 1942; *Air Force, Watch on the Rhine* 1943; *The Last Ride* 1944; *Mildred Pierce* 1945; *My Reputation, Shadow of a Woman* 1946.

Baker, Carroll. Actress. Born on May 28, 1931, in Johnstown, Pa. The daughter of a traveling salesman, she left St. Petersburg (Fla.) Junior College after one year to join a dance company, then worked as an assistant in a magic act. Following a brief marriage to a furrier, she went to Hollywood and played a bit role in the film *Easy to Love* (1953). Discouraged, she left for New York, where she appeared in TV commercials and did a walk-on in Broadway's 'Escapade.' In 1954 she enrolled at the Actors Studio, where she met director Jack Garfein. They married the following year and divorced in 1969. Their daughter is actress Blanche Baker. She appeared in Robert Anderson's play 'All Summer Long' (1955), followed by several TV dramas. Hollywood took notice, and in 1956 she was cast by Warners in *Giant.* The same year she became famous as the thumb-sucking child-wife in *Baby Doll,* her best film role to date and one that gained her an Academy Award nomination. In the 60s, Hollywood producers groomed her to replace Marilyn Monroe as the screen's new sex goddess, but such exploitative films as *The Carpetbaggers* and *Harlow* did little to advance her career. In the late 60s she moved to Italy and began appearing in Italian and Spanish films. She made her London stage debut in 1977, in a production of Somerset Maugham's 'Rain.' In the 80s she was back in front of the cameras in the US. In 1982 she married actor Donald Burton. Autobiography: *Baby Doll.*

FILMS INCLUDE: *Easy to Love* 1953; *Giant, Baby Doll* 1956; *The Big Country* 1958; *But Not for Me, The Miracle* 1959; *Bridge to the Sun, Something Wild* 1961; *How the West Was Won* 1962; *Station Six—Sahara* (UK/Ger.) 1963; *The Carpetbaggers, Cheyenne Autumn* 1964; *Sylvia, The Greatest Story Ever Told, Mister Moses, Harlow* (as Jean Harlow) 1965; *The Bob Hope Vietnam Christmas Show* (doc.; distributed theatrically after initial showing on TV) 1966; *Jack of Diamonds* (US/Ger.) 1967; *L'Harem* (It./Fr./Ger.), *Il Dolce Corpo de Deborah/The Sweet Body of Deborah* (It./Fr.) 1968; *Orgasmo* (It./Fr.), *Paranoia* (It./Sp.) 1969; *Cosi Dolce. . . cosi Perversa* (It./Fr.) 1970; *In Fondo alla Piscina* (It./Sp.), *Captain Apache* (UK/Sp.) 1971; *Il Diavolo a Sette Facce/The Devil Has Seven Faces* (It.), *Il Coltello di Ghiaccio* (It./Sp.) 1972; *The Madness of Love* (It./Sp.), *Baba Yaga* (Sp.) 1973; *The Sky Is Falling* (Sp.) 1975; *The Flower with the Deadly Sting* (It.), *Domani saremo ricchi* (It./Ger.), *La Moglie vergine* (It.), *Zerschossene Träume/ L'Appât* (Aus./Ger./Fr.) 1976; *Andy Warhol's Bad, Cyclone* (Mex.) 1977; *The World Is Full of Married Men* (UK) 1979; *The Watcher in the Woods* 1980; *Star 80* 1983; *The Secret Diary of Sigmund Freud* 1984; *Native Son* 1986; *Ironweed* 1987; *Kindergarten Cop* 1990; *Gipsy Angel, Blonde Fist* (UK) 1991; *Cyberden* 1993; *The Game* 1997.

Baker, Diane. Actress. Born on Feb. 25, 1938, in Hollywood, Calif. *ed.* USC. The daughter of stage actress Dorothy Harrington, she made her screen debut as the heroine's sister in *The Diary of Anne Frank.* A pretty brunette, she subsequently played leads and second leads in a variety of Hollywood films. In the early 70s she tried the other side of the camera, directing a documentary film, *Ashyana,* which competed at the San Sebastian film festival. In the early 80s she tried her hand at producing.

FILMS: *The Diary of Anne Frank, Journey to the Center of the Earth, The Best of Everything* 1959; *The Wizard of Baghdad* 1960; *Hemingway's Adventures of a Young Man, The 300 Spartans* 1962; *Nine Hours to Rama, Stolen Hours, The Prize* 1963; *Straight-Jacket, Marine* 1964; *Mirage* 1965; *Sands of Beersheba* (Isr./US) 1966; *The Horse in the Gray Flannel Suit* 1968; *Krakatoa East of Java* 1969; *Baker's Hawk* 1976; *The Pilot* 1979; *Never Never Land* (prod. only) 1982; *The Silence of the Lambs* 1991; *The Closer* 1991; *Imaginary Crimes* 1994; *The Net* 1995.

Baker, George D. American director and screenwriter. A former illustrator and stage actor, director, and writer, he began his directorial career at Vitagraph, under the supervision of J. Stuart Blackton. Between 1910 and 1914 he directed a series of comedies starring John BUNNY and Flora FINCH. In these and subsequent romantic adventure dramas, he distinguished himself as an able craftsman and imaginative artist and is considered one of the most prominent directors of that early era. He wrote many of his own screenplays as well as some for films of other directors. He later became general director of the Metro company and continued directing through the mid-20s, when he departed from the Hollywood scene.

FILMS INCLUDE: *The New Stenographer, The Politician's Dream, Captain Barnacle's Courtship* 1911; *Chumps, Bunny All at Sea, The Troublesome Step-Daughters* 1912; *The Autocrat of Flapjack Junction, John Tobin's Sweetheart* 1913; *Love's Old Dream, Bunny Buys a Harem, Bunny's Birthday, Bunny's Mistake, Bunny's Scheme, Father's Flirtation, Pigs Is Pigs, The Honeymooners, Polishing Up, How Cissy Made Good* 1914; *The Dust of Egypt, A Price for Folly* 1915; *A Night Out, The Shop Girl, The Tarantula* (also sc.), *The Wager* (also story, sc.) 1916; *The White Raven* (also sc.), *The End of the Tour* (also sc.), *His Father's Son, Sowers and Reapers* (also sc.), *The Duchess of Doubt* (also sc.), *The Lifted Veil, Outwitted* 1917; *Revelation* (also co-sc.), *The Shell Game* (also sc.), *Toys of Fate, No Man's Land* (also titles superv., edit.), *The Demon* (also sc.), *In Judgment Of, The Return of Mary* (also sc.), *Hitting the High Spots* (also co-sc.) 1918; *Peggy Does Her Darnest* (also sc.), *Castle in the Air* (also sc.), *The Lion's Den* (also sc.) 1919; *The Cinema Murder, The Man Who Lost Himself* (also sc.), *Heliotrope* (also sc., edit.) 1920; *Buried Treasure* (also sc.), *Without Limit* (also sc.), *The Hunch, Proxies* (also sc.), *Garments of Truth* 1921; *Little Eva Ascends, I Can Explain, Don't Write Letters* (also sc.) 1922; *Slave of Desire* 1923; *Revelation* (also sc.) 1924.

Baker, Joe Don. Actor. Born on Feb. 12, 1936, in Groesbeck, Tex. *ed.* North Texas State Coll. Husky, squinty-eyed leading man and supporting player of the American stage, TV, and films. On the New York stage from 1963, he entered films in 1967 and gained popularity as the star of *Walking Tall* (1973), in which he portrayed a fearless sheriff. Later played similarly tough roles in many films, mostly in the low-budget action category, and as the star of the TV police series 'Eischied' (1979–80).

FILMS: *Cool Hand Luke* 1967; *Guns of the Magnificent Seven* 1969; *Adam at 6 A.M.* 1970; *Wild Rovers* 1971; *Welcome Home Soldier Boys, Junior Bonner* 1972; *Walking Tall, Charley Varrick* 1973; *The Outfit, Golden Needles* 1974; *Mitchell, Framed* 1975; *The Pack* 1977; *Wishbone Cutter, Checkered Flag or Crash, Speedtrap* 1978; *Wacko, Joysticks* 1983; *The Natural* 1984; *Fletch* 1985; *Getting Even* 1986; *The Living Daylights* (UK), *The Killing Time, Leonard Part 6* 1987; *Waxwork* 1988; *Criminal Law* 1989; *The Children* 1990; *Cape Fear* 1991; *The Distiguished Gentleman* 1992; *Reality Bites* 1994; *Congo, Panther, The Underneath* 1995; *Goldeneye, The Grass Harp* 1996.

Baker, Josephine. Singer, entertainer. *b.* June 3, 1906, St. Louis, Mo. *d.* 1975. The daughter of a washerwoman, she started her career at eight, singing in Harlem nightclubs, then became a Broadway chorine and went on to become a legend in Paris music halls and the highest-paid entertainer in Europe. At the height of her fame in the late 20s and 30s, she was also featured in a number of French films. She was decorated by the French government for her activities as entertainer and ambulance driver during WW II and for her work among refugees at the end of the war. In the 1950s she adopted a dozen orphans of various nationalities, an act of humanity that was later to lead her into debt.

FILMS: *La Folie du Jour* (short), *La Revue des Revues, La Sirène des Tropiques* 1927; *Zou-Zou* 1934; *Princesse TamTam/Moulin Rouge* 1935; *Fausse Alerte/The French Way* 1940; *An jedem Finger zehn* (Ger.) 1954.

Baker, Kathy. Actress. Born on June 8, 1950, in Midland, Tex. Compact, unadorned, talented leading lady of Hollywood films of the 80s. The daughter of Quakers, she was raised in Albuquerque, N.M., by a French mother and an American father, a college professor at Princeton and the Sorbonne. She started acting at age ten but dropped out of the theater department of the California Institute of the Arts and transferred to University of California, Berkeley, where she graduated with a degree in French. Giving up on acting, she married, divorced, and moved to Paris, where she studied cooking. Back in the US, she worked for a while as a chocolate seller and a pastry chef. But she kept being drawn to the stage and after a highly acclaimed performance in Sam Shepard's play 'Fool for Love' she began appearing in films with increasing success. The National Society of Film Critics named her best supporting actress for *Street Smart* (1987).

FILMS: *The Right Stuff* 1983; *Street Smart* 1987; *Permanent Record, A Killing Affair, Clean and Sober* 1988; *Jacknife, Dad* 1989, *Mister Frost* (Fr./UK), *Edward Scissorhands* 1990; *Article 99, Jennifer 8* 1992; *Mad Dog and Glory* 1993; *Lush Life, Major League II* 1994; *To Gillian on Her 37th Birthday* 1996; *Inventing the Abbotts* 1997.

Baker, Kenny. Actor, singer. *b.* Kenneth Laurence Baker, Sept. 30, 1912, Monrovia, Calif. *d.* 1985. A former nightclub singer, he enjoyed some popularity in the 30s as the regular vocalist and bumbling sidekick on the Jack Benny radio show and as the juvenile lead in some Hollywood musical films. Not to be confused with another Kenny Baker, a dwarf (*b.* Aug. 24, 1934, Birmingham, England), who played Artoo-Detoo (R2-D2) in *Star Wars* and its sequels, and appeared in such films as *The Elephant Man, Flash Gordon, Time Bandits, Amadeus,* and *Mona Lisa.*

FILMS INCLUDE: *Metropolitan* 1935; *King of Burlesque* 1936; *Turn Off the Moon, The King and the Chorus Girl, 52nd Street* 1937; *The Goldwyn Follies, Radio City Revels* 1938; *The Mikado, At the Circus* 1939; *Hit Parade of 1941* 1940; *Silver Skates, Doughboys in Ireland* 1943; *The Harvey Girls* 1946; *Calendar Girl* 1947.

Baker, Rick. Special effects makeup artist. Born Richard A. Baker on Dec. 8, 1950, in Binghamton, N.Y. His imaginative renditions of monsters, animals, and bodily transformations were crucial in the success of several blockbuster productions. After a stint as chief lab assistant to makeup artist Dick Smith, he went solo in 1972 and worked widely for American International, among other studios. He was responsible for aging Cicely Tyson in the TV-film 'The Autobiography of Miss Jane Pittman' (1974), but became best known for his effects in horror and fantasy films. Beginning with *Schlock* and continuing through *King Kong* and *Gorillas in the Mist,* he has made a sub-specialty of simulating apes, often playing gorillas himself onscreen. He won the first-ever Academy Award in the makeup category for *An American Werewolf in London* (1981) and an additional Oscar for *Harry and the Hendersons* (1987). He also did makeup for and appeared in the Michael Jackson video 'Thriller.'

FILMS INCLUDE: *Octaman* 1971; *The Thing with Two Heads* 1972; *The Exorcist, Schlock/The Banana Monster, Live and Let Die* 1973; *It's Alive* 1974; *Death Race 2000* 1975; *King Kong* 1976 (also act., title role); *Star Wars, Kentucky Fried Movie* (act. only) 1977; *The Fury, The Incredible Melting Man* 1978; *An American Werewolf in London* 1981; *Videodrome* (Can.) 1983; *Greystoke: The Legend of Tarzan Lord of the Apes* (also cost. des.), *Starman* (transformation scenes) 1984; *Into the Night* (act. only), *Cocoon* (consultant) 1985; *Ratboy* 1986; *Harry and the Hendersons* 1987; *Missing Link, Coming to*

America, Gorillas in the Mist (also assoc. prod.) 1988; *Gremlins 2: The New Batch* (also co-prod., f/x supervisor) 1990; *Batman Forever* 1995; *The Nutty Professor* 1996; *Men in Black, Waiting for Guffman* 1997.

Baker, Robert S. Producer, director. Born in 1916, in London. Entered British films in 1937 as assistant director. After returning from WW II service, he established his own production company, through which he directed a number of routine pictures and produced many more. His most profitable venture was as producer of the long-running TV series 'The Saint.'

FILMS (as director-producer): *Blackout* 1950; *13 East Street* 1952; *The Steel Key* 1953; *Passport to Treason* 1956; *Jack the Ripper* 1959; *The Siege of Sidney Street* 1960; *The Hellfire Club, The Treasure of Monte Cristo* 1961.

Baker, Roy Ward. Director, producer. Born in 1916, in London. *ed.* France and England. Entered British films as assistant director in 1934. After WW II service, which gave him the opportunity to direct documentaries, he became a director for Two Cities, turning out his first film in 1947. From 1951 to 1953 he directed several productions in Hollywood. A documentary-like approach lends credibility to many of his films, though many critics feel that his work lacks a personal style. In the late 60s he switched to themes of horror and science fiction. He has also directed many episodes for TV series, notably 'The Avengers.'

FEATURE FILMS: *The October Man* 1947; *The Weaker Sex* 1948; *Paper Orchid* 1949; *Morning Departure/Operation Disaster, Highly Dangerous* 1950; *The House in The Square/I'll Never Forget You* (UK/US) 1951; *Don't Bother to Knock* (US), *Night Without Sleep* (US) 1952; *Inferno* (US) 1953; *Passage Home* 1955; *Jacqueline, Tiger in Smoke* 1956; *The One That Got Away* 1957; *A Night to Remember* 1958; *The Singer Not the Song* (also prod.), *Flame in the Streets* (also prod.) 1961; *The Valiant* (co-dir. with Giorgio Capitani; UK/It.) 1962; *Two Left Feet* (also prod.) 1963; *Quatermass and the Pit/Five Million Years to Earth* 1967; *The Anniversary* 1968; *Moon Zero Two* 1969; *The Vampire Lovers, The Scars of Dracula* 1970; *Dr. Jekyll and Sister Hyde* 1971; *Asylum, The Vault of Horror* 1972; *And Now the Screaming Starts* 1973. *The Legend of the Seven Golden Vampires/The 7 Brothers Meet Dracula/Dracula and the Seven Golden Vampires* (UK/Hong Kong) 1974; *The Monster Club* 1980.

Baker, Sir Stanley. Actor. *b.* Feb. 8, 1927, Ferndale, Wales. *d.* 1976. Made his film debut as a teenager in 1943, then pursued a stage career before returning to the screen in the late 40s, following military service. Through a series of tough, tight-lipped character roles, he developed into a rugged, determined, working-class he-man star of British films, in partnership with Joseph LOSEY, then Cy ENDFIELD. In the 60s he also co-produced some of his own films. He was knighted by the Queen in 1976, just a month before his death of lung cancer at 49.

FILMS INCLUDE: *Undercover/Undercover Guerillas* 1943; *Obsession/The Hidden Room* 1948; *All Over the Town* 1949; *Your Witness/Eye Witness, Lilli Marlene* 1950; *Captain Horatio Hornblower* 1951; *The Cruel Sea, The Red Beret/Paratrooper, The Tell-Tale Heart* (short; as Edgar Allan Poe) 1953; *The Good Die Young, Hell Below Zero, The Beautiful Stranger/Twist of Fate, Knights of the Round Table* 1954; *Helen of Troy* (as Achilles; US/It.), *Alexander the Great* (US); *Richard III* (as Henry Tudor) 1955; *A Hill in Korea, Checkpoint* 1956; *Sea Fury, Violent Playground* 1958; *Blind Date/Chance Meeting, Jet Storm, The Angry Hills* 1959; *The Criminal/The Concrete Jungle, Yesterday's Enemy* 1960; *The Guns of Navarone, Sodoma e Gomorra/Sodom and Gomorrah* (It./Fr./US) 1961; *A Prize of Arms, Eva* (Fr./It.) 1962; *Zulu* (also co-prod.) 1964; *Sands of the Kalahari* (also co-prod.) 1965; *Robbery* (also co-prod.), *Accident* 1967; *Where's Jack?* (also prod.), *The Italian Job* 1969; *Popsy Pop/The Butterfly Affair* (Fr.), *The Games, The Last Grenade, Perfect Friday* 1970; *Una Lucertola con la Pelle di Donna/A Lizard in a Woman's Skin* (It./Fr.) 1971; *Innocent Bystanders* 1972; *Zorro* (Fr./It.), *Orzowei* (Fr.) 1975; *Petita Jimenez* (Sp.) 1976.

Bakshi, Ralph. Animation film director. Born on Oct. 26, 1938, in Haifa, Palestine (now Israel). The son of Jewish immigrants from Russia, he was raised in poverty in a Brooklyn slum neighborhood. After graduating from Manhattan's High School of Industrial Arts, he went to work as an animator with Terrytoons and among others inked such cartoon characters as Hekyll and Jekyll and Mighty Mouse. In 1965 he was appointed creative director of Terrytoons and the following year became president of Paramount's New York cartoon division. Shortly after, the department was disbanded and Bakshi began working independently. In the early 70s he delighted some critics and offended many others with a string of outrageous X-rated animated features that were noted for their frank coarseness and irreverent street humor and language. His animation/live action production *Coonskin* (1975), proved particularly abrasive and controversial. Its 1974 preview at the Museum of Modern Art was picketed by members of the Congress of Racial Equality. Bakshi was roughed up in the ensuing melee. Paramount promptly dropped plans to distribute the film. Bakshi often writes his own scripts, drawing liberally on his own rough experiences as a child. Mixing animation, background paintings, and live-action in various combinations, he developed a style all his own, technically innovative and strongly personal. *Cool World* represented his foray into big-budget movie-making, blending live-action and animated sequences in a futuristic setting that featured the character Holli Would, voiced by Kim BASINGER. Although his output and defiance have diminished in recent years, he remains an important independent voice in American animation.

FEATURE FILMS: *Fritz the Cat* (also sc.) 1972; *Heavy Traffic* (also sc.) 1973; *Coonskin* (also sc.) 1975; *Wizards* (also prod., sc.) 1977; *The Lord of the Rings* 1978; *American Pop* (also co-prod.) 1981; *Hey Good Lookin'* (also prod., sc.; release delayed from 1975) 1982; *Fire and Ice* (also co-prod.) 1983; *Cannonball Run II* (anim. only) 1984; *Cool World* 1992.

Baky, Josef von. German director. *b.* Mar. 23, 1902, Zombor, Hungary. *d.* 1966. A former film distributor, he entered film production as an assistant director and became a director in 1936. He is best known for *Münchhausen* (1943), an ambitious color production ordered by Goebbels to mark the 25th anniversary of UFA, the prestigious German production company.

FILMS: *Intermezzo* 1936; *Die Frau am Scheidewege, Die kleine und die grosse Liebe/Minor Love and the Real Thing* 1938; *Menschen vom Varieté, Ihr erstes Erlebnis/Her First Romance* 1939; *Der Kleinstadtpoet* 1940; *Annelie* 1941; *Münchhausen* 1943; *Via Mala* 1945; *Und über uns der Himmel/City of Torment* 1947; *Der Ruf/The Last Illusion, Die seltsame Geschichte des Brandner Kaspar* 1949; *Das doppelte Lottchen* 1950; *Der träumende Mund/Dreaming Lips* 1952; *Tagebuch einer Verliebten* 1953; *Hotel Adlon, Dunja* 1955; *Fuhrmann Henschel* 1956; *Robinson soll nicht sterben/The Girl and the Legend* 1957; *Die Frühreifen, Gestehen Sie Dr. Corda!/Confess Dr. Corda!, Stefanie* 1958; *Der Mann der sich verkaufte, Die ideale Frau, Marili* 1959; *Sturm im Wasserglas* 1960; *Die seltsame Gräfin* 1961.

Balaban, Barney. Motion picture executive, pioneer exhibitor. *b.* June 8, 1887, Chicago. *d.* 1971. The son of an immigrant grocer, he went to work at 12 as a Western Union messenger, later becoming chief clerk in a cold-storage company. In 1908 he opened a movie theater in Chicago with his brother Abe and a friend, Sam Katz. The venture soon grew into a prosperous, nationwide chain of theaters. In 1917, Balaban and Katz introduced ice-cooled refrigeration, a primitive air-conditioning system, to movie theaters. Balaban was elected president of Paramount Pictures in 1936, where he reorganized business procedures, thus saving the company from bankruptcy. He became Paramount's board chairman in 1964. Father of Burt BALABAN.

Balaban, Bob. Actor, also director. Born on Aug. 16, 1945, in Chicago. *ed.* Colgate; NYU. Small-framed, mercurial character player of the American screen, typically in intellectual roles. He joined the Second City satirical troupe while still in high school and later appeared in numerous plays, TV programs, and films. Having directed shorts and TV segments, he took a modest first step as a feature director with *Parents* (1989). Early in his career he was billed as Robert Balaban.

FILMS: *Midnight Cowboy, Me, Natalie* 1969; *The Strawberry Statement, Catch–22, Lovers and Other Strangers* 1970; *Making It* 1971; *Bank Shot* 1974; *Report to the Commissioner* 1975; *Close Encounters of the Third Kind* 1977; *Girlfriends* 1978; *Altered States* 1980; *Prince of the City, Absence of Malice, Whose Life Is It Anyway?* 1981; *In Our Hands* (doc.), *2010* 1984; *End of the Line* 1987; *Parents* (dir. only), *Dead-Bang* 1989; *Alice* 1990; *Little Man Tate* (uncredited) 1991; *Bob Roberts* 1992; *Amos and Andrew, For Love or Money* 1993; *The Last Good Time* (dir.) 1994; *Two Bits* 1995; *Waiting for Guffman* 1997.

Balaban, Burt. Director-producer. *b.* Mar. 6, 1922, Chicago. *d.* 1965. *ed.* Roanoke Coll. The son of Barney BALABAN. He gained film experience as a combat cameraman for the Marines in WW II. He produced and directed TV films before turning to features in the late 50s. His sparse output was routine, except for the tautly directed gangster melodrama *Murder Inc.* (1960).

FILMS: *Lady of Vengeance* 1957; *High Hell* 1958; *Murder Inc.* 1960; *Mad Dog Coll* 1961; *The Gentle Rain* (US/Braz.) 1966.

balance. 1. An essential quality of pictorial composition achieved through the disposition of the various elements making up a picture in an eye-pleasing arrangement. 2. The relative arrangement of sound sources, such as musical instruments, in recording the sound track of a film. 3. The harmonious co-ordination between key and filler lights.

balancing stripe. A narrow band sometimes placed on film on the edge opposite the magnetic stripe to balance the thickness of the stock, thus permitting even winding of the film onto a smooth roll.

Balázs, Béla. Film theoretician and aesthetician, director, screenwriter. *b.* Herbert Bauer, Aug. 4, 1884, Szeged, Hungary. *d.* 1949. After studying philosophy, he published novels, plays, poems, and literary criticism, as well as librettos for composer Béla Bartók, and directed early Hungarian silent films. He was in the forefront of Hungarian cultural life but was forced into exile in Austria and Germany for Communist activity in 1919. There he developed ideas about films as an autonomous art form, and from 1923 he published theoretical essays dealing in particular with the potentialities of montage, camera angle, the close-up, and sound.

In 1924, in his book *The Visible Man (Der Sichtbare Mensch),* he outlined the prospects of the medium: "Film is about to inaugurate a new direction in our culture. . . . Humanity is already learning the rich and colorful language of gesture, movement, and facial expression. This is not a language of signs as a substitute for words, like the sign-language of the deaf-and-dumb—it is the visual means of communication, without intermediary of souls clothed in flesh. Man has again become visible." In his book *Spirit of Film (Der Geist des Films,* 1930) he made an early plea for asynchronous sound.

In *Theory of Film* (first published in Moscow in 1945 as *The Art of Cinema),* Balázs discusses in philosophical and psychological depth the technical components of film: sound, dialogue, color, script, editing, camera manipulation, etc. He emphasizes the importance of theory in the understanding and enjoyment of the art and welcomes the development of an entirely new art form. He maintains that film could have been spawned only in an industrial civilization, that the universality of film is tied to economics, and that film is often used as an extension of the propaganda machinery of the state. Such Hegelian-Marxist notions tend to obscure his otherwise clear ideas of film function and technique.

For Balázs, camera angle is the "strongest means of characterization that the film possesses. . . . The camera carries the spectator into the film picture itself." His writings were a theoretical precursor of the *mise-en-scène,* the shot-in-depth notion, and its attendant psychological values. During his stay in Germany he collaborated on a number of screenplays, among them Pabst's *The Threepenny Opera.*

Upon Hitler's rise to power, Balázs left Vienna for the Soviet Union, where he taught film aesthetics at Moscow's State Film Institute from 1933 to 1945. After the war, he returned to Hungary and continued writing scripts and lecturing on film in his native land, as well as in Poland and Czechoslovakia. A film studio in Budapest is named after him.

FILMS INCLUDE: As director (in Hungary)—*Agyu es Harang* 1915; *Maki allast Vallal* 1916; *Obistos* 1917; *Sphynx* 1918; *A Megfagyottgyermek* 1921; *Das blaue Licht* (co-dir. with Leni Riefenstahl; Ger.) 1932; *Edes Mostoha* 1935; *Azurexpress* 1938; *Opiumkeringo* 1943. As screenwriter (in Germany)—*Die Abenteuer eines Zehnmarkscheines, Madame wünscht keine Kinder* 1926; *Dona Juana, Grand Hotel* 1927; *Narkose* 1929; *Sonntag des Lebens* (German version of Hollywood's *The Devil's Holiday*) 1930; *Die Dreigroschenoper/The Threepenny Opera* 1931; *Valahol Europabahn/Somewhere in Europe* (Hung.) 1947.

Balchin, Nigel. Novelist, screenwriter. *b.* Dec. 3, 1908, Potterne, Wiltshire, England. *d.* 1970. An honor graduate of Cambridge, he started out as a fruit grower and later recounted his experiences in the business in a series of satirical articles for *Punch,* which he eventually published in book form under the pseudonym Mark Spade. He began writing fiction in 1933 and became famous with his satire on wartime civil-service bureaucracy, *The Small Back Room* (1943). The novel was successfully adapted to the screen in 1948. He himself adapted his own psychological thriller *Mine Own Executioner* (1947) and wrote screenplays, alone or in collaboration, from material by other authors. During WW II he was a scientific adviser to the British Army Council.

FILMS INCLUDE: *Mine Own Executioner* (from own novel), *Fame Is the Spur* 1947; *The Small Back Room* (novel basis only) 1948; *Mandy/The Story of Mandy/The Crash of Silence* 1952; *Malta Story* 1953; *23 Paces to Baker Street* (US), *The Man Who Never Was* 1956; *The Blue Angel* (US) 1959; *Suspect/The Risk* 1960; *Circle of Deception, Barabba/Barabbas* (It.), *The Singer Not the Song* 1961; *Cleopatra* (collaborated on the initial script, later mostly discarded) 1963.

Balcon, Sir Michael. Producer, production executive. *b.* May 19, 1896, Birmingham, England. *d.* 1977. Started his film activity in 1919 as regional distributor. Also that year he founded, with Victor SAVILLE, Victory Motion Picture, a Birmingham-based company that turned out several industrial shorts for the Anglo-American Oil Company. In 1923 he produced his first feature, *Woman to Woman,* directed by Graham Cutts, on which he employed young Alfred HITCHCOCK as an art director, screenwriter, and assistant director. He later gave Hitchcock his first opportunity as a director. In 1924, Balcon and Cutts founded Gainsborough Pictures and acquired Islington studios. In 1931 he was appointed director of production for Gaumont-British and in 1936 for MGM-British. During these years he was behind the production of several important British films, including Hitchcock's early masterpieces and Flaherty's *Man of Aran.* During the years 1937–59 he served as director and chief of production for the Ealing Studios and was responsible for the famous Ealing comedies of the late 40s and early 50s. In 1959 he formed Bryanston Films, and in 1964, after a much publicized control battle, took over British Lion. He was knighted in 1948. His daughter, Jill Balcon (*b.* 1925), appeared in a number of films. His autobiography, *A Lifetime of Films,* was published in 1969.

FILMS INCLUDE: *Woman to Woman* (completed in 1923), *The White Shadow/White Shadows, The Passionate Adventure* 1924; *The Black Guard* 1925; *The Rat, The Lodger/The Case of Jonathan Drew* 1926; *The Pleasure Garden* (completed in 1926), *Easy Virtue* 1927; *The Constant Nymph, The Vortex* 1928; *Journey's End, Balaclava/Jaws of Hell* 1930; *The Ringer, The Ghost Train* 1931; *Hindle Wakes, Sunshine Susie/The Office Girl, Jack's the Boy* 1932; *Rome Express, The Good Companions, The Ghoul, Friday the Thirteenth* 1933; *The Constant Nymph, Waltzes From Vienna/Strauss' Great Waltz, Evergreen, Man of Aran, Chu-Chin-Chow* 1934; *Jew Süss/Power, The Iron Duke, The Man Who Knew Too Much, Bulldog Jack/Alias Bulldog Drummond, The 39 Steps* 1935; *The Tunnel/Transatlantic Tunnel, Rhodes of Africa/Rhodes, Tudor Rose/Nine Days a Queen, Secret Agent* 1936; *Sabotage/The Woman Alone, King Solomon's Mines* 1937; *A Yank at Oxford* 1938; *The Four Just Men/The Secret Four* 1939; *Return to Yesterday, The Proud Valley* 1940; *Ships With Wings, The Foreman Went to France/Somewhere in France, The Next of Kin, Went the Day Well?/48 Hours* 1942; *Nine Men* 1943; *Champagne Charlie* 1944; *Dead of Night, Pink String and Sealing Wax* 1945; *The Captive Heart* 1946; *Hue and Cry, Nicholas Nickleby, It Always Rains on Sunday* 1947; *Scott of the Antarctic, Passport to Pimlico, Whisky Galore!/Tight Little Island, Kind Hearts and Coronets* 1949; *The Blue Lamp* 1950; *Pool of London, The Lavender Hill Mob, The Man in the White Suit* 1951; *Secret People* (exec. prod.) 1952; *The Cruel Sea* (exec. prod.) 1953; *Lease of Life, The Divided Heart* (exec. prod.) 1954; *The Ladykillers* 1955; *The Long Arm/The Third Key* 1957; *Dunkirk* 1958; *The Scapegoat* 1959; *The Long and the Short and the Tall/Jungle Fighters* 1961; *Sammy Goin' South/A Boy Ten Feet Tall* (exec. prod.) 1963.

Balderston, John L. Screenwriter, playwright. *b.* Oct. 22, 1889, in Philadelphia. *d.* 1954. *ed.* Columbia. Trained as a journalist, he was a war correspondent (1914–18), then editor of *Outlook* magazine and London correspondent for the New York *World* before turning to play- and screenwriting. He specialized in horror and fantasy as well as romantic adventure scripts. Often wrote in collaboration.

FILMS: *Dracula* (play basis only), *Frankenstein* (play basis only) 1931; *The Mummy* 1932; *Berkeley Square* (from own play) 1933; *Mad Love, The Mystery of Edwin Drood, The Lives of a Bengal Lancer, The Bride of Frankenstein* 1935; *Beloved Enemy, The Last of the Mohicans, The Man Who Lived Again* 1936; *The Prisoner of Zenda* 1937; *Little Old New York* (story only), *Victory* 1940; *Scotland Yard, Smilin' Through* 1941; *Stand By for Action, Tennessee Johnson* 1942; *Gaslight* 1944; *Red Planet Mars* (co-sc., from own co-play), *I'll Never Forget You* (remake of *Berkeley Square*) 1951; *The Prisoner of Zenda* 1952; *Dracula* (play basis only) 1979.

Baldwin, Adam. Actor. Born on February 27, 1962, in Chicago. Muscular, innocent-faced young lead and supporting player of Hollywood films of the 80s and 90s.

FILMS: *My Bodyguard, Ordinary People* 1980; *D.C. Cab* 1983; *Reckless, Hadley's Rebellion* 1984; *Bad Guys, 3:15 The Moment of Truth* 1986; *Full Metal Jacket* 1987; *The Chocolate War, Cohen & Tate, Next of Kin* 1989; *Predator 2, Internal Affairs* 1990; *Guilty by Suspicion* 1991; *Radio Flyer, Poison Ivy, Where the Day Takes You* 1992.

Baldwin, Alec. Actor. Born Alexander Rae Baldwin III, on Apr. 3, 1958, in Amityville, N.Y. *ed.* George Washington U. (political science); NYU (drama). Star of Hollywood films. The second of six children, he was raised in Massapequa, Long Island, where his father taught high school. Had intended to become a lawyer and a politician, but was drawn to acting and trained at Lee Strasberg's Theatre. He began his professional career in New York, performing in the TV soap opera 'The Doctors' by day and on the stage, in Shakespeare's 'Midsummer Night's Dream,' by night. Having gained additional experience on TV ('Knots Landing,' etc.) and on the stage (an award-winning performance in a revival of 'Loot' among other roles), he made his film debut in 1987. Good-looking, gifted, and versatile, he rapidly joined the ranks of Hollywood's most sought-after screen personalities. In 1992, he gave up the chance to star in *Patriot Games*, the sequel to *The Hunt for Red October*, due to a schedule conflict that would have kept him from playing Stanley Kowalski in a Broadway revival of 'A Streetcar Named Desire.' Brother of actors William and Stephen BALDWIN and Daniel Baldwin. Married to actress Kim BASINGER, with whom he starred in *The Marrying Man* and *The Getaway*.

FILMS: *Forever Lulu* 1987; *She's Having a Baby, Beetlejuice, Married to the Mob, Talk Radio, Working Girl* 1988; *Great Balls of Fire!* (as Rev. Jimmy Swaggart) 1989; *The Hunt for Red October, Miami Blues, Alice* 1990; *The Marrying Man* 1991; *Prelude to a Kiss, Glengarry Glen Ross* 1992; *Malice* 1993; *The Getaway, The Shadow* 1994; *Ghosts of Mississippi, Heaven's Prisoners* (also co-exec. prod.), *The Juror* 1996; *The Edge* 1997.

Baldwin, Ruth Ann. Director and screenwriter. Little is known of this former journalist and pioneer woman director. In 1915, she became part of Carl Laemmle's Universal Studio, which featured other female directors like Lois Weber and Grace Cunard. That year she directed her first serial, *The Black Page*, and for the next six years wrote and directed a number of features and shorts, including a remarkable 13 pictures in 1917.

FILMS INCLUDE: *The Black Page* (ser.), *The Double Deal in the Park* (ser., also sc.), *An Arrangement with Fate* (ser., also sc.) 1915; *The Recoiling Vengeance* (also sc.) 1916; *The Butterfly* (also sc.), *Is Money All, It Makes a Difference* (also sc.), *The Black Mantilla, When Liz Lets Loose, The Women Who Could Not Pat* (also sc.), *The Rented Man* (also sc.), *A Soldier of the Legion* (also sc.), *The Storm Women* (also sc.), *A Wife on Trial, Three Women of France, Twixt Love and Desire* (ser., also sc.) *49–17* 1917; *The Mothers Call* 1918; *Broken Commandments* 1919; *The Devil's Ripple* 1920; *The Marriage of William Ashe* (also sc.) 1921; *Puppets of Fate* 1921.

Baldwin, Stephen. Actor. Born in 1966, in Massapequa, N.Y. Handsome, hip actor who followed in the footsteps of his older brothers Alec, William, and Daniel BALDWIN. He gained prominence as a Calvin Klein model before making his mark as an actor in the films *Last Exit to Brooklyn* (1989) and the provocative college-days-remembered *Threesome* (1994). He is at his best in tough, wise-guy roles, such as films like *The Usual Suspects* (1995).

FILMS: *The Beast, Homeboy* 1988; *Born on the Fourth of July, Last Exit to Brooklyn* 1989; *Crossing the Bridge* 1992; *Posse* 1993; *8 Seconds, Mrs. Parker and the Vicious Circle, Simple Twist of Fate, Threesome* 1994; *Under the Hula Moon, The Usual Suspects* 1995; *Bio-Dome, Crimetime* 1996.

Baldwin, William. Actor. Born in 1963, in Massapequa, N.Y. *ed.* SUNY Binghamton (political science). After working on Capitol Hill and appearing in print advertising, he debuted as a platoon soldier in *Born on the Fourth of July* and has since developed into an impish romantic lead. Brother of actors Alec, Daniel, and Stephen BALDWIN.

FILMS INCLUDE: *Born on the Fourth of July* 1989; *Flatliners, Internal Affairs* 1990; *Backdraft* 1991; *Three of Hearts, Sliver* 1993; *Fair Game, A Pyromaniac's Love Story* 1995; *Curdled* 1996.

Balfour, Betty. Actress. *b.* Mar. 27, 1903, London. *d.* 1979. Britain's most popular star of the silent era. On stage from age 11, she made her screen debut at 17 and gained great popularity playing the title role in *Squibs* (1921), one of the biggest box-office hits of the 20s. A blue-eyed curly blonde, she starred in numerous silents, mostly comedies. After the arrival of sound she eased into supporting roles. At the height of her career, many of Balfour's films were produced by her own company. Most of these films were directed by George PEARSON.

FILMS: *Nothing Else Matters* 1920; *Squibs, Mary Find-the-Gold* 1921; *Squibs Wins the Calcutta Sweeps, Mord Em'ly/Me and My Girl, Wee MacGregor's Sweetheart* 1922; *Squibs' Honeymoon, Squibs MP, Love Life and Laughter* 1923; *Reveille, A Sister of Six* 1924; *Satan's Sister, Somebody's Darling, Monte Carlo* (Fr.) 1925; *Blinkeyes, La Petite Bonne du Palace* (Fr.), *Sea Urchin, The Little People* 1926; *Croquette* (Fr.), *Le Diable au Coeur/The Little Devil May Care* (Fr.), *Die sieben Töchter der Frau Gyurkovics* (Ger.) 1927; *Paradise, Champagne, Monkeynuts* (Fr.), *A Little Bit of Fluff/Skirts, Die Regimentstochter/Daughter of the Regiment* (Ger.) 1928; *The Vagabond Queen, Bright Eyes* 1929; *The Nipper/The Brat, Raise the Roof* 1930; *Paddy the Next Best Thing* 1933; *Evergreen, My Old Dutch* 1934; *Brown on Resolution/Forever England/Born for Glory, Squibs* 1935; *Eliza Comes to Stay* 1936; *29 Acacia Avenue/The Facts of Love* 1945.

Balin, Mireille. Actress. *b.* July 20, 1911, Monte Carlo. *d.* 1968. A former high-fashion model, she became an internationally popular star of French films in the 30s. Most memorably as Dulcinea in Pabst's *Don Quixote,* opposite Fyodor Chaliapin in the title role, and as the femme fatale who caused the downfall of Jean Gabin in *Pépé le Moko,* a role later played by Hedy Lamarr in the American remake, *Algiers.* Retired in the mid-40s.

FILMS INCLUDE: *Vive la Classe* 1932; *Don Quichotte/Don Quixote, Le Sexe faible* 1933; *Marie des Angoisses* 1935; *Jeunes Filles de Paris* 1936; *Naples au Baiser de Feu/The Kiss of Fire, Pépé le Moko,* 1937; *Le Vénus de l'Or,* 1938; *Menaces, Macao l'Enfer du Jeu* 1940; *Dernier Atout* 1942; *Malaria* 1943; *La Dernière Chevauchée* 1947.

Ball, Lucille. Actress. *b.* Lucille Désirée Ball, Aug. 6, 1911, Celoron (outside Jamestown), N.Y. *d.* 1989. One of Hollywood's most delightful comic personalities, regarded by many as America's greatest television comedienne. The daughter of a pianist and a telephone lineman who died when she was three, she embarked on a show-business career at 15, when she went to Manhattan to study drama with John Murray Anderson. Discouraged by repeated attempts to make the chorus line on Broadway, she worked as secretary, waitress, and model. Exposure as the Chesterfield Cigarette Girl in 1933 helped her crash Hollywood as a Goldwyn Girl in *Roman Scandals,* an Eddie Cantor vehicle. She appeared in dozens of films over the next few years (11 in 1934 alone), mostly in bits and later in supporting, comic-relief roles. Gradually she established herself as Hollywood's foremost female clown, the feminine counterpart of Bob Hope and Red Skelton, with both of whom she frequently co-starred. But the movies never took full advantage of her talent.

On an RKO set in 1940, Miss Ball met Cuban bandleader Desi ARNAZ, and they married the following year. In the 50s, they packaged one of the most successful comedy shows in TV history, 'I Love Lucy' (1951–57), and a subsequent series of hour-long specials, 'The Lucy-Desi Comedy Hour' (1957–60). Their Desilu Productions soon developed into one of the world's largest TV concerns, controlling the same RKO studios where the two had once been under contract. After their divorce in 1960, Arnaz sold out his interest to Miss Ball, who became the president of Desilu, in charge of a business grossing more than $25 million annually. She eventually sold Desilu to Gulf and Western. She continued appearing on TV, in 'The Lucy Show' (1962–68), 'Here's Lucy' (1968–74), and 'Life With Lucy' (in 1986). In 1960 she starred briefly on Broadway in the musical 'Wildcat.' In 1961 she married nightclub comedian Gary Morton. Her children, Desi Arnaz, Jr. (*b.* Desiderio Arnaz IV, Jan. 19, 1953, Los Angeles) and Lucie Arnaz (*b.* Lucy Désirée Arnaz, July 17, 1951, Los Angeles), are both TV and film performers.

FILMS: *Broadway Thru a Keyhole* (bit), *Blood Money* (bit), *Roman Scandals* (bit) 1933; *Moulin Rouge* (bit), *Nana* (bit), *Bottoms Up* (bit), *Hold That Girl* (bit), *Bulldog Drummond Strikes Back* (bit), *The Affairs of Cellini* (bit), *Kid Millions* (bit), *Broadway Bill* (bit), *Jealousy* (bit), *Men of the Night, The Fugitive Lady* (bit) 1934; *Carnival, Roberta* (bit), *Old Man Rhythm* (bit), *Top Hat, I Dream Too Much* 1935; *Chatterbox, Follow the Fleet, Bunker Bean* 1936; *That Girl From Paris, Winterset* (bit), *Don't Tell the Wife, Stage Door* 1937; *Joy of Living, Go Chase Yourself, Having Wonderful Time, The Affairs of Annabel, Room Service, Next Time I Marry, Annabel Takes a Tour* 1938; *Beauty for the Asking, Twelve Crowded Hours, Panama Lady, Five Came Back, That's Right—You're Wrong* 1939; *The Marines Fly High, You Can't Fool Your Wife, Dance Girl Dance, Too Many Girls* 1940; *A Girl a Guy and a Gob, Look Who's Laughing* 1941; *Valley of the Sun, The Big Street, Seven Days' Leave* 1942; *Du Barry Was a Lady, Best Foot Forward, Thousands Cheer* (cameo) 1943; *Meet the People* 1944; *Without Love, Abbott and Costello in Hollywood* (cameo) 1945; *Ziegfeld Follies* (sketch), *The Dark Corner, Lover Come Back, Easy to Wed, Two Smart People* 1946; *Lured, Her Husband's Affairs* 1947; *Sorrowful Jones, Easy Living, Miss Grant Takes Richmond* 1949; *A Woman of Distinction* (unbilled cameo), *Fancy Pants, The Fuller Brush Girl* 1950; *The Magic Carpet* 1951; *The Long Long Trailer* 1954; *Forever Darling* 1956; *The Facts of Life* 1960; *Critic's Choice* 1963; *A Guide for the Married Man* (cameo) 1967; *Yours Mine and Ours* 1968; *Mame* 1974.

Ballard, Carroll. Director. Born on Oct. 14, 1937, in Los Angeles. *ed.* UCLA. He demonstrated a remarkable visual flair with his very first film, but his subsequent output has been curiously sparse.

FILMS: *Harvest* (prod.) 1967; *Star Wars* (cam. op.) 1977; *The Black Stallion* 1979; *Never Cried Wolf* 1983; *Nutcracker: The Motion Picture* 1986; *Wind* 1992; *Fly Away Home* 1996.

Ballard, Lucien. Director of photography *b.* May 6, 1908,

Miami, Okla. *d.* 1988. Part Cherokee Indian. *ed.* U. of Oklahoma; U. of Pennsylvania. Joined Paramount as a cutter and assistant cameraman, assisted Lee Garmes on *Morocco* (1930), and impressed director Josef von STERNBERG, who made him co-photographer on *The Devil Is a Woman* and director of photography on *Crime and Punishment* (both 1935). Ballard soon distinguished himself as a master of black-and-white interior photography and lighting and, in later years, of exciting Western outdoor color photography. He was married to actress Merle OBERON (1945–49) and photographed several of her films, notably *The Lodger* (1944).

FILMS INCLUDE: *Morocco* (addnl. phot. only) 1930; *The Devil Is a Woman* (co-phot.), *Crime and Punishment* 1935; *The King Steps Out, Craig's Wife* 1936; *The Devil's Playground, The Shadow* 1937; *Penitentiary* 1938; *The Undying Monster* 1942; *Bomber's Moon, Holy Matrimony* 1943; *The Lodger* 1944; *This Love of Ours* 1945; *Temptation* 1946; *Night Song* 1947; *Berlin Express* 1948; *Fixed Bayonets* 1951; *Don't Bother to Knock* 1952; *The Desert Rats, Inferno* 1953; *Prince Valiant* 1954; *The Magnificent Matador* 1955; *A Kiss Before Dying, The Killing, The King and Four Queens* 1956; *A Band of Angels* 1957; *Anna Lucasta, Al Capone* 1959; *The Rise and Fall of Legs Diamond, Pay or Die* 1960; *Ride the High Country* 1962; *The Caretakers, Wives and Lovers* 1963; *The Sons of Katie Elder, Boeing Boeing* 1965; *Nevada Smith* 1966; *Hour of the Gun* 1967; *Will Penny, The Party* 1968; *The Wild Bunch, True Grit* 1969; *The Hawaiians* (co-phot.), *The Ballad of Cable Hogue* 1970; *Arruza* (Mex.), *What's the Matter With Helen?* 1971; *Junior Bonner, The Getaway* 1972; *Thomasine and Bushrod* 1974; *Breakout* 1975; *Breakheart Pass, St. Ives, Drum, From Noon Till Three, Mikey and Nicky* (co-phot.) 1976; *Rabbit Test* 1978.

Ballhaus, Michael. Director of photography. Born on Aug. 5, 1935, in Berlin. One of the New German Cinema's most gifted cinematographers, a favorite of Rainer Werner FASSBINDER. He has been working in the US since the early 80s. He was nominated for an Oscar for *The Fabulous Baker Boys* (1989).

FILMS INCLUDE: In Germany—*Whity, Warnung vor einer heiligen Nutte/Beware of a Holy Whore* 1970; *Die Bitteren Tränen der Petra von Kant/The Bitter Tears of Petra von Kant* 1972; *Faustrecht der Freiheit/Fox and His Friends* 1974; *Mütter Kusters fahrt zum Himmel/Mother Kusters Goes to Heaven* 1975; *Satansbraten/Satan's Brew* (co-phot.), *Chineisisches Roulette/Chinese Roulette* 1976; *Bolweiser/The Stationmaster's Wife* 1977; *Eine Reise ins Licht/Despair* 1977; *Deutschland im Herbst/Germany in Autumn* (co-phot.), *Die Ehe der Maria Braun/The Marriage of Maria Braun* 1978; *Heller Wahn/Sheer Madness* 1982. In the US—*Baby It's You* 1983; *Heartbreakers* 1984; *Death of a Salesman* (orig. for TV), *After Hours* 1985; *The Color of Money* 1986; *The Glass Menagerie, Broadcast News* 1987; *The Last Temptation of Christ, Dirty Rotten Scoundrels, Working Girl* 1988; *The Fabulous Baker Boys* 1989; *GoodFellas, Postcards from the Edge* 1990; *Guilty By Suspicion, What About Bob?* 1991; *The Mambo Kings, Bram Stoker's Dracula* 1992; *The Age of Innocence* 1993; *I'll Do Anything, Quiz Show* 1994; *Outbreak* 1995; *Sleepers* 1996; *Air Force One* 1997.

Ballin, Hugo. Director. *b.* 1880, New York City. *d.* 1956. A celebrated portrait painter in his day, he was hired by Sam Goldwyn to create sets for such productions as John S. Robertson's *Baby Mine* and Allan Dwan's *Fighting Odds* (both 1917). He then turned to directing for Goldwyn and in the early 20s established his own production company, through which he directed a number of elaborate adaptations of literary classics, most of them starring his wife, Mabel Ballin. The venture wasn't financially successful and Ballin gave up on producing and directing in 1925. Two years later he was an art director on Gloria Swanson's *The Love of Sunya* (1927), then retired from films.

FILMS INCLUDE: *Thais* (co-dir. with Frank Crane) 1917; *The Splendid Sinner* 1918; *Pagan Love* (also prod., sc.) 1920; *East Lynne* (also prod., sc.), *The Journey's End* (also prod., sc.), *Jane Eyre* (also prod., sc.) 1921; *Other Women's Clothes* (also prod.), *Married People* (also prod., co-sc.) 1922; *Vanity Fair* (also prod., sc.) 1923; *The Prairie Wife* (also sc.), *The Shining Adventure* 1925.

Balsam, Martin. Actor. Born on Nov. 4, 1919, in New York City. A product of the Actors Studio and a veteran of stage and television, he has kept busy as a screen character actor since his debut in *On the Waterfront* (1954). He won an Academy Award as best supporting actor for *A Thousand Clowns* (1965) and a Tony Award for his stage role in 'You Know I Can't Hear You When the Water's Running.' Memorable as the ill-fated detective in Hitchcock's *Psycho.* His hundreds of TV appearances include a regular role as Archie Bunker's Jewish business partner in 'Archie Bunker's Place' (1979–81). Formerly married to actress Joyce Van Patten. Their daughter, Talia Balsam, is a budding film actress.

FILMS INCLUDE: *On the Waterfront* 1954; *12 Angry Men, Time Limit* 1957; *Marjorie Morningstar* 1958; *Al Capone, Middle of the Night* 1959; *Psycho, Tutti a Casa/Everybody Go Home!* (It./Fr.) 1960; *Ada, Breakfast at Tiffany's* 1961; *Cape Fear, La Città Prigioniera/Conquered City* (It.) 1962; *Who's Been Sleeping in My Bed?* 1963; *The Carpetbaggers, Seven Days in May* 1964; *Harlow, The Bedford Incident, A Thousand Clowns* 1965; *After the Fox* (US/UK/It.) 1966; *Hombre* 1967; *Me Natalie, Trilogy, The Good Guys and the Bad Guys* 1969; *Catch–22, Tora! Tora! Tora!, Little Big Man* 1970; *The Anderson Tapes, Confessione di un Commissario di Polizia al Procuratore della Republica* (It.) 1971; *The Man* 1972; *The Stone Killer, Summer Wishes Winter Dreams, I Consigliori* (It.) 1973; *The Taking of Pelham One Two Three, Murder on the Orient Express, Corruzione al Palazzo di Giustizia/Counselor at Crime* (It.) 1974; *Il Tempo degli Assassini* (It.), *Mitchell* 1975; *All the President's Men, Two-Minute Warning* 1976; *The Sentinel, Silver Bears* 1977; *Cuba* 1979; *The Salamander* (UK/US/It.) 1981; *The Goodbye People* 1984; *St. Elmo's Fire, Death Wish 3* 1985; *The Delta Force* 1986; *Private Investigations* 1987; *Due Occhi diabolici/Two Evil Eyes (The Black Cat)* (It.) 1990; *Cape Fear* 1991; *Innocent Prey* 1992; *Silence of the Hams* 1994.

Bancroft, Anne. Actress. Born Anna Maria Louise Italiano, on Sept. 17, 1931, in the Bronx, N.Y. *ed.* AADA; Actors Studio. Actress and dancer, beginning at age four, she started her professional career on TV in 1950, using the name Anne Marno, and made her motion picture debut in *Don't Bother to Knock* (1952). Hollywood kept her busy in a succession of B films until she returned to New York and appeared in 'Two for the Seesaw' (1958) opposite Henry Fonda, for which she received a Tony. The following year, she won the New York Drama Critics Award as well as another Tony for her performance in 'The Miracle Worker.' She repeated her performance with resounding success in the film version, winning the 1962 Academy Award for best actress. She played memorable roles in the British film *The Pumpkin Eater,* shared best actress prize at Cannes (1964), and also in *The Graduate* (1967) and *The Turning Point* (1977). She was Oscar-nominated for the latter, as well as for *Agnes of God* (1985). She was named best actress by the British Film Academy for her performance in *84 Charing Cross Road* (1987). After attending the American Film

Institute's Directing Workshop for Women, she first tried her hand at directing in 1976 with a film titled *The August*, but it was never released. The product of her next directorial effort, *Fatso*, was released in 1980 but met with only modest success. Married to comedy director, writer, and producer Mel BROOKS.

FILMS: *Don't Bother to Knock* 1952; *Tonight We Sing, Treasure of the Golden Condor, The Kid From Left Field* 1953; *Gorilla at Large, Demetrius and the Gladiators, The Raid* 1954; *New York Confidential, A Life in the Balance, The Naked Street, The Last Frontier* 1955; *Walk the Proud Land* 1956; *Nightfall, The Restless Breed, The Girl in Black Stockings* 1957; *The Miracle Worker* 1962; *The Pumpkin Eater* (UK) 1964; *The Slender Thread* 1965; *Seven Women* 1966; *The Graduate* 1967; *Young Winston* (as Lady Randolph Churchill; UK) 1972; *The Prisoner of Second Avenue, The Hindenburg* 1975; *Lipstick, Silent Movie* (unbilled cameo) 1976; *The Turning Point* 1977; *Fatso* (also dir., sc.), *The Elephant Man* (UK) 1980; *To Be or Not to Be* 1983; *Garbo Talks* 1984; *Agnes of God* 1985; *'Night Mother* 1986; *84 Charing Cross Road* 1987; *Torch Song Trilogy* 1988; *Bert Rigby You're a Fool* 1989; *Honeymoon In Vegas, Love Potion No. 9* 1992; *Mr. Jones* 1993; *Dracula: Dead and Loving It* (cameo), *Home for the Holidays, How to Make an American Quilt* 1995; *Sunchaser* 1996; *G.I. Jane* 1997.

Bancroft, George. Actor. *b.* Sept. 30, 1882, Philadelphia. *ed.* Annapolis. *d.* 1956. Began his stage career as a black-face entertainer in minstrel shows, then went on to the New York stage in dramas ('The Trail of the Lonesome Pine,' 'Paid in Full,' etc.) and in musical comedies.

In 1921, he made his screen debut in *The Journey's End*. His first film for Paramount, *Code of the West* (1925), brought him to the attention of director James Cruze, who cast him in *The Pony Express* (1925). Strongly built, he soon developed into one of the most accomplished heavies, with a smooth style of villainy that was especially effective as a pre-Cagney gangster in Josef von Sternberg's *Underworld* (1927) and *The Docks of New York* (1928). He was nominated for an Academy Award as best actor for *Thunderbolt* (1929). Also played tough "good guy" leads and supporting parts, memorably as the stagecoach driver in John Ford's *Stagecoach* (1939). In 1942 he retired to become a rancher. He was married to former actress Octavia Brooke.

FILMS INCLUDE: *The Journey's End* 1921; *The Prodigal Judge* 1922; *Driven, Code of the West, The Rainbow Trail, The Pony Express, The Splendid Road* 1925; *The Enchanted Hill, Sea Horses, The Runaway, Old Ironsides* 1926; *The Rough Riders, White Gold, Underworld, Too Many Crooks, Tell It to Sweeney* 1927; *The Showdown, The Dragnet, The Docks of New York* 1928; *The Wolf of Wall Street, Thunderbolt, The Mighty* 1929; *Ladies Love Brutes, Derelict* 1930; *Scandal Sheet, Rich Man's Folly* 1931; *The World and the Flesh, Lady and Gent* 1932; *Blood Money* 1933; *Elmer and Elsie* 1934; *Mr. Deeds Goes to Town, Wedding Present* 1936; *A Doctor's Diary, John Meade's Woman, Racketeers in Exile* 1937; *Submarine Patrol, Angels With Dirty Faces* 1938; *Stagecoach, Each Dawn I Die, Espionage Agent, Rulers of the Sea* 1939; *Green Hell, Young Tom Edison, When the Daltons Rode, North West Mounted Police, Little Men* 1940; *Texas* 1941; *The Bugle Sounds, Syncopation, Whistling in Dixie* 1942.

Band, Albert. Director, producer. Born on May 7, 1924, in Paris. Entered films in the mid-40s as a cutter at Pathé's Paris studios. He later became assistant to director John Huston, for whom he also wrote the adaptation for *The Red Badge of Courage* (1951). An independent producer-director of routine action films since the mid-50s, he operated out of Hollywood, then out of Rome, then back out of Hollywood again. He recently formed Albert Band International Productions. His son, Charles Band (b. 1952, Los Angeles), is also a producer and occasional director.

FILMS INCLUDE: *The Red Badge of Courage* (adapt.) 1951; *The Young Guns* (dir., prod.) 1956; *I Bury the Living* (dir., prod.) 1958; *Face of Fire* (dir. prod.) 1959; *La Leggenda di Enea/The Avenger* (co-prod.) 1962; *Massacro al Grande Canyon/Grand Canyon Massacre* (co-prod., co-sc.) 1963; *Gli Uomini dal Passo Pesante/The Tramplers* (co-dir., co-prod., co-sc.) 1966; *I Crudeli/The Hellbenders* (prod., co-sc.), *Escondido/A Minute to Pray a Second to Die/Dead or Alive* (prod., co-story) 1967; *Little Cigars* (prod.) 1973; *Dracula's Dog* (dir., co-prod.) 1978; *She Came to the Valley* (dir., co-prod., co-sc.) 1979. *Metalstorm: The Destruction of Jared-Syn* (co-exec. prod.) 1983; *Troll* (prod.), *Terrorvision* (prod.), *Ghost Warrior/Swordkill* (co-exec. prod.) 1986; *Ghoulies II* 1988; *Buy & Cell* (exec. prod.) 1989; *Robot Jox* (also prod.) 1990; *Joey Takes a Cab* 1991; *Doctor Mordrid: Master of the Unknown* (co-dir. with son Charles), *Honey, I Blew Up the Kid* (exec. prod.) 1992; *Prehysteria!* 1993.

Banderas, Antonio. Actor. Born in 1960 in Malaga, Spain. *ed.* School of Dramatic Art, Malaga. Well established as a leading man of the Spanish cinema, he came to international attention with his roles in Pedro Almodóvar's *Women on the Verge of a Nervous Breakdown* (1988) and *Tie Me Up! Tie Me Down!* (1990). In 1996, he married actress Melanie GRIFFITH in the wake of a much publicized 'final' break-up between Griffith and actor Don Johnson.

FILMS INCLUDE: *Laberinto de Pasiones/Labyrinth of Passion, Pestañas Postizas* 1982; *El Señor Galindez* 1983; *El Caso Almería, Los Zancos/The Stilts* 1984; *Casa Cerrado, La Cort de Faraón, Requiem por un Campesino Español* 1985; *27 Horas, Matador* 1986; *Así Como Habían Sido, La Ley del Deseo/The Law of Desire, El Placér de Matar/The Pleasure of Killing* 1987; *Baton Rouge, Mujeres al Borde de un Ataque de Nérvios/Women on the Verge of a Nervous Breakdown* 1988; *Si Te Dicen Que Caí* 1989; *Átame!/Tie Me Up! Tie Me Down!, Contra el Viento* 1990; *The Mambo Kings* 1992; *Philadelphia* 1993; *The House of Spirits, Interview with a Vampire, Of Love and Shadows* 1994; *Assassins, Desperado, Four Rooms, Miami Rhapsody, Never Talk to Strangers* 1995; *Evita, Two Much* 1996.

bank. A set of incandescent lamps mounted in a single reflector casing without a focusing lens. Used for general illumination of large areas. See also LIGHTING.

Bankhead, Tallulah. Actress. *b.* Jan. 31, 1903, in Huntsville, Ala. *d.* 1968. One of the American theater's most brilliant and legendary actresses, she was the daughter of the late Speaker of the House of Representatives William Brockman Bankhead. She received a strict convent education, but after winning a local beauty contest at the age of 15, she went to New York and made her stage debut at the Bijou Theater in 'Squab Farm.' After playing a variety of stage roles and two silent films, she went to London in 1923, and for the next seven years she was the toast of the town. Her tempestuous, quick-witted personality, uninhibited behavior, and her deep, raspy voice and explosive laughter won her admirers in the British as well as the American theater. In London she appeared in two British films, *His House in Order* and *A Woman's Law* (both 1928). Upon returning to the US in 1930, she resumed her stage career and signed a film contract with Paramount. Her film work was intermittent and on the whole less memorable than her stage work. She was cited by New York Film Critics for her performance in Hitchcock's *Lifeboat* (1944). Among her stage triumphs were 'The Little Foxes' (1939), 'The Skin of Our Teeth' (Drama

Critics Award, 1943), and 'Private Lives' (1947). Her sporadic TV appearances included the role of the villainous Black Widow in a 1967 episode of 'Batman.' She was married at one time to actor John Emery.

FILMS: *Who Loved Him Best?, When Men Betray, 30 a Week* 1918; *The Trap* 1919; *His House in Order* (UK), *A Woman's Law* (UK) 1928; *Tarnished Lady, My Sin, The Cheat* 1931; *Devil and the Deep, Thunder Below, Make Me a Star* (unbilled cameo), *Faithless* 1932; *Stage Door Canteen* 1943; *Lifeboat* 1944; *A Royal Scandal* 1945; *Main Street to Broadway* 1953; *Fanatic/Die! Die! My Darling!* (UK) 1965; *The Daydreamer* (voice only) 1966.

Banks, Leslie. Actor. *b.* June 9, 1890, West Derby, England. *d.* 1952. *ed.* Oxford. A distinguished stage actor and director from 1911, he toured England and the US, where he made his first important film appearance as the villain in *The Most Dangerous Game* (1932). Putting to advantage a tough appearance, the result of a disfiguring injury in WW I, he later played strong leads and character parts in many British films. He was also known as a gifted painter.

FILMS INCLUDE: *The Most Dangerous Game/The Hounds of Zaroff* (US) 1932; *Strange Evidence* 1933; *I Am Suzanne* (US), *The Night of the Party* 1934; *Sanders of the River, The Man Who Knew Too Much, The Tunnel/Transatlantic Tunnel* 1935; *Debt of Honor* 1936; *Wings of the Morning, Fire Over England, Farewell Again/Troopship,* 1937; *Jamaica Inn* 1938; *Busman's Honeymoon/Haunted Honeymoon, 21 Days/21 Days Together* (release delayed from 1937) 1940; *Ships With Wings* 1941; *Went the Day Well/48 Hours* 1942; *Henry V* 1945; *The Small Back Room* 1949; *Madeleine* 1950.

Banks, Monty. Director, actor. *b.* Mario Bianchi, 1897, Cesena, Italy. *d.* 1950. The son of a composer and bandleader, he was a comic dancer when he came to the US in 1914 to appear on the New York stage. He later went to Hollywood, where he advanced from minor roles in "Fatty" Arbuckle comedies to principal comic roles in silent two-reelers, some of which he directed himself. Typically, he played pudgy, wistful little guys, who inadvertently became heroes. He went to England in 1928, where he became a director but still played bit parts in many of his own films. After returning to the US in 1940, he directed one feature, Laurel and Hardy's *Great Guns* (1941), which was not very successful, and appeared as an actor in a couple of films. He was married to Gracie Fields.

FILMS INCLUDE: As actor (in the US)—*The Geezer of Berlin* 1918; *Too Much Johnson, Racing Luck* 1924; *Keep Smiling* (also prod., co-story) 1925; *Atta Boy* (also exec. prod.) 1926; *Play Safe* (also exec. prod., story), *Horse Shoes* (also exec. prod., co-story, co-sc.), *Flying Luck* (also exec. prod., co-story) 1927; *A Perfect Gentleman, Adam's Apple* (UK), *Weekend Wives* (UK) 1928; *Atlantic* (UK) 1929; *Blood and Sand* 1941; *A Bell for Adano* 1945. As director (in the UK)—*Cocktails* 1928; *Eve's Fall, The Compulsory Husband* (also act.) 1929; *Not So Quiet on the Western Front, Why Sailors Leave Home, Almost a Honeymoon* 1930; *Old Soldiers Never Die, What a Night!* 1931; *Tonight's the Night, Money for Nothing* 1932; *Heads We Go/The Charming Deceiver, You Made Me Love You* 1933; *Falling in Love/Trouble Ahead, The Girl in Possession* (also act.), *The Church Mouse* (also act.), *Father and Son* 1934; *Man of the Moment, No Limit* 1935; *Queen of Hearts, We're Going to Be Rich, Keep Smiling/Smiling Along* 1938; *Shipyard Sally* 1939; *Great Guns* (US) 1941.

Banky, Vilma. Actress. *b.* Vilma Lonchit, Jan. 9, 1898, Nagyrodog, near Budapest. *d.* 1992. Discovered in Europe by Samuel Goldwyn, she began her meteoric rise as a silent screen star in Hollywood in 1925. Graceful and ethereal, she had a spectacular career opposite such partners as Rudolph Valentino, Gary Cooper, and Ronald Colman but retired from the screen with the coming of sound. At the height of her fame, she was promoted by studio publicity as "The Hungarian Rhapsody." In 1927 she married Rod La Rocque, and they remained one of Hollywood's happiest couples until his death in 1969. An avid golfer, she was still teeing off well into her 80s.

FILMS INCLUDE: In Europe—*Im letzten Augenblick* (Austria/Hung.) 1920; *Galathea* (Hung.) 1921; *Das Auge des Toten* (Ger.), *Schattenkinder des Glücks* (Ger.) 1922; *Hotel Potemkin* (Aus.), *Das verbotene Land* (Aus.), *Der Zirkuskönig/Clown aus Liebe* (Aus.), *Das schöne Abenteuer/The Lady From Paris* (Ger.) 1924; *Das Bildnis* (Aus.), *Soll man heiraten?* (Ger.) 1925. In the US (complete)—*The Dark Angel, The Eagle, The Son of the Sheik, The Winning of Barbara Worth* 1926; *The Night of Love, The Magic Flame* 1927; *Two Lovers, The Awakening* 1928; *This Is Heaven* 1929; *A Lady to Love* (and German version, *Die Sehnsucht jeder Frau*) 1930. In Germany—*Der Rebell/The Rebel* 1932.

Bannen, Ian. Actor. Born on June 29, 1928, in Airdrie, Scotland. *ed.* Ratcliffe Coll., Leicestershire. A stage actor since the mid-40s, he has also played solid supporting parts and some leads in many British and occasional American films since the mid-50s. He was nominated for a best supporting actor Oscar for his role in *The Flight of the Phoenix* (1965).

FILMS INCLUDE: *Private's Progress, The Long Arm/The Third Key* 1956; *A Tale of Two Cities* 1958; *Carlton-Browne of the F.O./Man in a Cocked Hat* 1959; *Suspect/The Risk, The French Mistress, Macbeth* (as Macduff; made for US TV; later released theatrically) 1960; *Station Six—Sahara* (UK/Ger.) 1963; *Psyche 59* 1964; *Mister Moses* (US), *Rotten to the Core, The Hill, The Flight of the Phoenix* (US) 1965; *Penelope* (US) 1966; *The Sailor from Gibraltar* 1967; *Lock Up Your Daughters* 1969; *Too Late the Hero* (US) 1970; *La Spina Dorsale del Diavolo/The Deserter* (It./Yug.), *Jane Eyre, Fright* 1971; *The Offence/The Offense, The Mackintosh Man* 1973; *Identikit/The Driver's Seat* (It.), *Il Viaggio/The Voyage* (It.) 1974; *Bite the Bullet* (US), *From Beyond the Grave, Doomwatch* 1975; *Sweeney* 1977; *The Watcher in the Woods* 1980; *Eye of the Needle* 1981; *Night Crossing, Gandhi* 1982; *Gorky Park* (US) 1983; *The Prodigal* (US) 1984; *Defence of the Realm/Defense of the Realm, Lamb* 1986; *Hope and Glory* 1987; *The Courier* 1988; *Ghost Dad* (US), *The Big Man: Crossing the Line, George's Island* (Can.), *The Cherry Orchard* 1991; *Damage* 1992; *A Pin for a Butterfly* 1994; *Braveheart* 1995.

Bannerjee, Victor (Banerjee). Actor. Born on Oct. 15, 1946, in Calcutta, India. A child stage actor in India, he was well established in Indian films (some with Satyajit Ray) before his international breakthrough as Dr. Aziz in *A Passage to India* (1984). He helped to found India's Screen Extras Union.

FILMS INCLUDE: *The Chess Players* (Ind.) 1977, *A Passage to India* 1984; *The Home and the World* (Bengal) 1985; *Foreign Body* (UK) 1986; *World Within, World Without* 1991; *Bitter Moon* 1994.

Bannon, Jim. Actor. Born in 1911, in Kansas City, Mo. *ed.* Rockhurst Coll. A former college athlete and radio sportscaster, he entered films as a stuntman in 1940. In the mid-40s he played leads in low-budget action dramas, and in 1949 he took over as star of the "Red Ryder" Western series (he was the fourth Hollywood "cowboy" to play the role), then drifted into supporting parts and TV work. He was married to TV/film actress Bea Benaderet (*b.* Apr. 4, 1906, New York City; *d.* 1968). Their son, Jack Bannon (*b.* June 14, 1940) appeared on TV ('Lou Grant,' etc.) and occasional films.

FILMS INCLUDE: *The Soul of a Monster, The Missing Juror* 1944; *Tonight and Every Night, The Gay Señorita, I Love a Mystery* 1945; *The Devil's Mask, Renegades, The Unknown* 1946; *Framed, Johnny O'Clock, T-Men* 1947; *Dangers of the Canadian Mounties* (serial), *The Man from Colorado* 1948; *Ride Ryder Ride, The Fighting Redhead, The Cowboy and the Prizefighter* 1949; *Kill the Umpire* 1950; *Lawless Cowboys* 1951; *Jack Slade* 1953; *Chicago Confidential* 1955; *A Gathering of Eagles* 1963.

Banton, Travis. Costume designer. *b.* Aug. 18, 1894, Waco, Tex. *d.* 1958. *ed.* Columbia; Art Students League. A New York fashion designer before going to Hollywood in 1924 to work for Paramount. He gained a reputation for the daring designs of Marlene DIETRICH's costumes, which helped establish her unique sexuality, in Josef von Sternberg's pictures. At Paramount, he also designed the gowns for such glamour stars as Carole LOMBARD and Claudette COLBERT in films of Ernst LUBITSCH, Rouben Mamoulian, Mitchell Leisen, and other directors. He moved over to Fox in 1939 and ended his career as head stylist for Universal. Banton designed Mary PICKFORD's wedding dress when she married Douglas FAIRBANKS.

FILMS INCLUDE: *Poppy* 1917; *The Dressmaker from Paris* 1924; *The Grand Duchess and the Waiter* 1926; *Miss Brewster's Millions* 1927; *Doomsday* 1928; *The Wild Party, The Canary Murder Case* 1929; *Morocco, The Vagabond King* 1930; *Dishonored* 1931; *Shanghai Express, Blonde Venus, Dr. Jekyll and Mr. Hyde, Love Me Tonight, One Hour with You, Trouble in Paradise, A Farewell to Arms* 1932; *Design for Living, Song of Songs, Three-Cornered Moon* 1933; *Belle of the Nineties, The Scarlet Empress, Nana* 1934; *The Devil Is a Woman, The Gilded Lily, The Crusades, Hands Across the Table, The Lives of a Bengal Lancer, Ruggles of Red Gap* 1935; *Desire, The General Died at Dawn, My Man Godfrey* 1936; *Easy Living, High Wide and Handsome, Maid of Salem, Angel* 1937; *Intermezzo: A Love Story, Made for Each Other* 1939; *Lillian Russell, The Mark of Zorro, The Return of Frank James, Tin Pan Alley* 1940; *Blood and Sand, Charley's Aunt, The Great American Broadcast, Man Hunt, That Night in Rio, Western Union* 1941; *Scarlet Street, Song to Remember* 1945; *Magnificent Doll* 1946; *A Double Life* 1947; *The Paradine Case, Mourning Becomes Electra, Letter From an Unknown Woman* 1948; *Valentino* 1951.

Bara, Theda. Actress. *b.* Theodosia Goodman, July 29, 1890, Cincinnati. *d.* 1955. First appeared with stock companies and played a secondary role, billed as Theodosia de Coppet, in the 1908 Broadway production of Ferenc Molnar's 'The Devil.' She became an overnight sensation in her first starring role as a ruthless femme fatale in the film *A Fool There Was* (1915), based on a Kipling poem, 'The Vampire.' Although the daughter of a Cincinnati tailor, she was billed as a woman of mystic powers, born in the Sahara Desert, the love child of a French artist and his Egyptian mistress. Her name, so the publicity legend went, was an anagram of "Arab Death." She wore indigo make-up to emphasize her pallor; surrounded herself with symbols of death, such as human skulls, ravens, etc.; rode in a white limousine; was served by "Nubian slaves"; and received the press while stroking a serpent in a room permeated with incense. She was soon famous as The Vamp, and her command "Kiss me, my fool!," taken from a subtitle card of her first big film, became a popular phrase.

Between 1914 and 1919 she appeared in more than 40 films, playing such vamp roles as Carmen, Madame Du Barry, Salome, and Cleopatra, and also some nonvamp parts, notably Juliet to Harry Hilliard's Romeo and the kindhearted gypsy Esmeralda in *The Darling of Paris,* based on *The Hunchback of Notre Dame.* The unrestrained publicity eventually led to her downfall, as more sophisticated post–WW I audiences began to laugh at her absurdly exotic characterizations. In 1919 she left Hollywood for the Broadway stage. In 1926 she made her last screen appearance, in a comedy short, *Madame Mystery,* a parody of her former screen image co-directed by Stan LAUREL. She was never heard of afterward until her death from cancer. She had been married to Charles BRABIN.

FILMS: *A Fool There Was, The Kreutzer Sonata, The Clemenceau Case, The Devil's Daughter, Lady Audley's Secret, The Two Orphans, Sin, Carmen, The Galley Slave* 1915; *Destruction, The Serpent, Gold and the Woman, The Eternal Sappho, East Lynne, Under Two Flags, Her Double Life, Romeo and Juliet, The Vixen* 1916; *The Darling of Paris, The Tiger Woman, Her Greatest Love, Heart and Soul, Camille, Cleopatra, The Rose of Blood* 1917; *The Forbidden Path, Madame Du Barry, The Soul of Buddha, Under the Yoke, When a Woman Sins, Salome, The She-Devil* 1918; *The Light, When Men Desire, The Siren's Song, A Woman There Was, Kathleen Mavourneen, La Belle Russe, The Lure of Ambition* 1919; *The Unchastened Woman* 1925; *Madame Mystery* (short) 1926.

Baranovskaya, Vera. Actress. Born in Russia. *d.* 1935, in Paris. A favorite pupil of Stanislavsky, she was a major figure of the Moscow Art Theater when Pudovkin chose her to play the title role in his film *Mother* (1926). Her performance in that role and in his *The End of St. Petersburg* (1927) brought her international fame. She left the USSR in 1929 to pursue an acting career in Czechoslovakia, Germany, and France. Retired in 1933.

FILMS INCLUDE: *The Thief* 1916; *The Burden of Fate* 1917; *Giftgas/Poison Gas* (Ger.) 1929; *The Wolves* 1925; *Mother* 1926; *The End of St. Petersburg* 1927; *Ruts* 1928; *Such Is Life* (Czech.) 1929; *Die Galgentonitonischka, Tonka Sibenice* (both Czech.) 1930; *Leichtsinnige Jugend* (Ger.) 1931; *Monsieur Albert* (Fr.) 1932; *Les Aventures du Roi Pausole* (Fr.) 1933.

Baranski, Christine. Actress. Born on May 2, 1952, in Cheetowaga, N.Y. An accomplished stage actress ('The Real Thing'), she has appeared in several films, primarily in supporting roles.

FILMS INCLUDE: *Soup for One* 1982; *Lovesick* 1983; *Crackers* 1984; *9½ Weeks, Legal Eagles* 1986; *The Pick-Up Artist* 1987; *Reversal of Fortune* 1990; *Life with Mikey* 1993; *The Ref, The War* 1994; *Jeffrey, New Jersey Drive* 1995; *The Birdcage* 1996.

Barbeau, Adrienne. Actress. Born on June 11, 1945, in Sacramento, Calif. *ed.* Foothill Coll. Busty leading lady of the American stage, TV, and films. After her nomination for a Tony in 1972 for her performance in the Broadway musical 'Grease,' she joined the regular cast of the TV series 'Maude,' in which she played the title character's divorced daughter through 1978. She then ventured into feature films, typically in *The Cannonball Run.* In 1979 she married director John CARPENTER.

FILMS INCLUDE: *The Fog* 1980; *The Cannonball Run, Escape From New York* 1981; *Swamp Thing, Creepshow* 1982; *Back to School* 1986; *Cannibal Women in the Avocado Jungle of Death* 1989; *Due Occhi diabolici/Two Evil Eyes (The Black Cat)* (It.) 1990; *Double-Crossed* 1991; *Father Hood* 1993.

Barber, Frances. Actress. Born in 1957, in Wolverhampton, England. *ed.* Bangor U.; Cardiff U. Intriguing leading lady of the British stage, TV, and films. The daughter of a bookie and a cook, she was raised with six brothers in a working-class community. She started out in repertory, then joined the Royal Shakespeare Company for three years, making her London stage debut in 1985. First seen on the screen in 1982, she attracted international attention with *Sammy and Rosie Get Laid* (1987) and subsequently sustained audience interest with other unconventional roles. Nicknamed "Frankie."

FILMS: *The Missionary* 1982; *A Zed and Two Naughts* 1985; *White City* 1986; *Prick Up Your Ears, Castaway, Sammy and Rosie Get Laid* 1987; *We Think the World of You* 1988; *The Grasscutter, Chambre à Part/Separate Bedrooms, Duck* (short) 1989; *Young Soul Rebels* 1991; *Secret Friends* (US/UK) 1992.

Barbera, Joseph. Animator, producer. Born on Mar. 24, 1911, in New York City. *ed.* NYU American Inst. of Banking. An accountant and freelance magazine cartoonist before joining MGM as a story man in 1937. With William HANNA and producer Fred QUIMBY he created the cartoon characters of Tom and Jerry and produced more than 100 short films, starring their animated cat and mouse heroes, for which they won seven Academy Awards. In 1957, Hanna and Barbera left MGM and set up their own production company, Hanna-Barbera, a virtual factory turning out television cartoons at an astonishing rate through a computerized numbering system. Among their TV cartoon series are 'The Flintstones,' 'Top Cat,' 'Quick Draw MacGraw,' 'Yogi Bear,' 'Huckleberry Hound,' and 'Ruff and Reddy.' In the early 60s Hanna-Barbera expanded its output to feature films. In 1968, the company became a subsidiary of Taft, which was absorbed in 1988 by Great American Broadcasting, with Barbera as president.

CARTOONS INCLUDE (Academy Award winners are denoted AA): Shorts—*Yankee Doodle Mouse* (AA) 1943; *Mouse Trouble* (AA) 1944; *Quiet Please* (AA) 1945; *The Cat Concerto* (AA) 1946; *Kitty Foiled* 1947; *The Little Orphan* (AA), *Professor Tom* 1948; *The Two Mouseketeers* (AA) 1951; *Johann Mouse* (AA) 1952; *Mouse for Sale* 1955; *Life With Loopy* 1960; *Just a Wolf at Heart* 1962. Features—*Hey There It's Yogi Bear* (co-dir., co-prod., co-sc.) 1964; *The Man Called Flintstone* (co-dir. co-prod., co-story) 1966; *C.H.O.M.P.S.* (prod., story, co-sc.) 1979; *Heidi's Song* (co-prod., co-sc.) 1982; *Gobots: Battle of the Rocklords* (co-exec. prod.) 1986; *Jetsons: The Movie* (co-dir., co-prod.) 1990; *The Flintstones* (ex-prod, cameo) 1994.

Bardem, Juan Antonio. Director, screenwriter. Born on July 2, 1922, in Madrid. The son of an actor and actress, he was trained as an agricultural engineer and assigned by the Spanish Ministry of Agriculture to the department's cinema section in 1946. The following year he registered as a student with the Spanish Institute of Cinema Research and Experimentation (Instituto de Investigaciones Cinematográficas) but failed to impress the faculty with his film work and never received his diploma.

He supported himself by contributing cinema articles and criticism to Spanish magazines while he and a fellow student, Luis-Garcia BERLANGA, collaborated on several unproduced scripts. In 1948 they directed a short documentary film, *Paseo Sobre una Guerra Antigua.* A turning point in both their careers came about in 1951 when they wrote the screenplay for *Bienvenido, Mr. Marshall (Welcome, Mr. Marshall),* directed by Berlanga. The film enjoyed great success and gained European recognition for the hitherto unknown Spanish film industry. The same year the two men directed *Esa Pareja Feliz (That Happy Pair).* In 1953, Bardem wrote the screenplay for and directed his first solo film, *Cómicos (Comedians),* which was well received by international critics. This was followed in 1954 by *Felices Pascuas.*

Bardem's next two films established his reputation as one of the world's leading filmmakers. In these—*Muerte de un Ciclista/Death of a Cyclist/Age of Infidelity* (1955) and *Calle Mayor* (also known in the US as *The Lovemaker,* 1956)—he bitterly explores Spanish life under Franco's regime. These courageous films made him the idol of Spanish students and intellectuals but angered the authorities. He was arrested while shooting *Calle Mayor* and was still in a Spanish jail when *Death of a Cyclist* won the Critics' Award at Cannes. His next film, *La Venganza (The Vengeance,* 1958), was altered drastically by the censors and hence disappointed his admirers. Government control affected most of his subsequent output. In 1955, Franco censorship also terminated the film magazine *Objectivo,* which he had founded two years earlier.

In 1958, Bardem helped found and became president of a film production company, Uninci. He was responsible for the production of Buñuel's *Viridiana* (1961), the political repercussions of which caused an upheaval in the Spanish film industry: many lost their jobs, and Uninci's operations were drastically curtailed.

Bardem, who headed Spain's directors' guild, during the 70s is noted for his use both of the camera in probing social ills, and of the streets and villages as the unadorned settings for his films, and for his concern with themes and characters that reflect the troubled times under tyranny. He writes the screenplays for all his films, alone or in collaboration.

FEATURE FILMS (as director and writer or co-scripter): *Esa Pareja Feliz* (co-dir. with Luis-Garcia Berlanga) 1951; *Welcome Mr. Marshall* (co-scr) 1952; *Novio a la Vista* (co-dir. with Berlanga), *Cómicos* 1953; *Felices Pascuas* 1954; *Muerte di un Ciclista/Death of a Cyclist/Age of Infidelity* 1955; *Calle Mayor/The Lovemaker/Main Street* 1956; *La Venganza* 1958; *Sonatas* 1959; *A las Cinco de la Tarde* 1960; *Los Inocentes* 1962; *Nunca Pasa Nada* 1963; *Los Pianos Mecánicos/Les Pianos mécaniques/The Uninhibited* (Sp./Fr./It.) 1965; *El Ultimo Dia de la Guerra/The Last Day of the War* (Sp./It./US) 1969; *Variétés* 1971; *La Corrupción de Chris Miller/The Corruption of Chris Miller, L'Ile mysterieuse/The Mysterious Island of Captain Nemo* (co-dir. with Henri Colpi; Fr./Sp.), *Behind the Shutters* 1973; *El Podor del Deseo, Foul Play* 1976; *The Dog, El Puente* 1977; *Siete Dias de Enero/Seven Days in January* 1979; *The Warning* (Bulg./USSR/E. Ger.) 1982; *Adios, Peqeña* (act.) 1986; *Lorca, la Muerte de un Poeta* 1987.

Bardot, Brigitte. Actress. Born on Sept. 28, 1934, in Paris. The daughter of an industrialist, she studied ballet from early childhood. At 15 she posed for the cover of France's leading women's magazine, *Elle,* and her pouting child-woman image brought her to the attention of Roger VADIM, then assistant to director Marc Allégret. She and Vadim were married in 1952, divorced in 1957. In 1952 she made her film debut, in Jean Boyer's *Le Trou Normand/Crazy for Love,* and then played a variety of secondary roles, graduating to leads in 1955. In 1956 her appearance in Vadim's first film as director, *Et Dieu créa la Femme/And God Created Woman,* brought her international fame. The success of the film was astounding. Under her husband's guidance she emerged as a new type of sex symbol, a child of nature responding to the call of sensuality, a playful kitten to whom the supreme commandment is love. Box-office receipts the world over announced the birth of a new superstar; the greatest impact was in the US, where "BB" single-handedly brought French films out of the small art houses and into the major movie theaters.

The new Bardot "sex kitten" image was maintained in most of her subsequent films. Clad in a breakaway towel, nude, or in abbreviated underwear or bathing suits, she kept packing audiences in from Afghanistan to Zanzibar. Her private life became the subject of world interest and church condemnation. Transitory romances, marriages, and divorces (Vadim, Jacques CHARRIER, millionaire playboy Gunther Sachs) made world headlines. Since 1960, with her appearance in Clouzot's *La*

Vérité/The Truth, she has also been taken more seriously by critics as a capable actress. Still glamorous long after her retirement from the screen in the early 70s, Bardot remains a popular figure and the subject of frequent reports in French and foreign publications. In 1976 she established the Foundation for the Protection of Distressed Animals, a cause that has kept her visibly active ever since. In 1987 she raised $500,000 for the foundation by auctioning off her jewels. In 1985 she was awarded the French Legion of Honor. Among several books on her life and career is a famous treatise by Simone de Beauvoir, *Brigitte Bardot and the Lolita Syndrome* (1960).

FILMS: *Le Trou normand/Crazy for Love, Manina la Fille sans Voiles/The Girl in the Bikini* 1952; *Les Dents longues, Le Portrait de son Père* 1953; *Si Versailles m'était conté/Royal Affairs in Versailles, Act of Love/Un Acte d'Amour* (US/Fr.), *Tradita* (It.)/*Night of Love* 1954; *Le Fils de Caroline Chérie, Futures Vedettes, Doctor at Sea* (UK), *Frou-Frou* (It./Fr.), *Les Grandes Manoeuvres/The Grand Maneuver* 1955; *Helen of Troy* (US), *La Lumière d'en Face/The Light Across the Street, Cette Sacrée Gamine/Mam'zelle Pigalle, Mio Figlio Nerone/Nero's Mistress* (It./Fr.), *En effeuillant la Marguerite/Please Mr. Balzac, Et Dieu Créa la Femme/And God Created Woman, La Mariée est trop Belle/The Bride Is Much Too Beautiful* 1956; *Une Parisienne* 1957; *Les Bijoutiers du Clair de Lune/The Night Heaven Fell, En Cas de Malheur/Love Is My Profession* 1958; *La Femme et le Pantin/The Female, Babette s'en va-t-en Guerre/Babette Goes to War, Voulez-vous danser avec moi?/Come Dance With Me!* 1959; *Le Testament d'Orphée/The Testament of Orpheus* (cameo), *La Vérité/The Truth* 1960; *La Bride sur le Cou/Please Not Now!, Les Amours célèbres* 1961; *La Vie privée/A Very Private Affair, Le Repos du Guerrier/Love on a Pillow* 1962; *Le Mépris/Contempt* 1963; *Une Ravissante Idiote/A Ravishing Idiot* 1964; *Dear Brigitte* (cameo; US), *Viva Maria* 1965; *Masculin-Féminin/Masculine Feminine* (cameo) 1966; *A Coeur joie/Two Weeks in September* (Fr./UK) 1967; *Shalako* (UK), *Histoires extraordinaires/Spirits of the Dead* 1968; *Les Femmes* 1969; *L'Ours et la Poupée/The Bear and the Doll, Les Novices/The Novices* 1970; *Boulevard du Rhum/Rum Runner, Les Pétroleuses/The Legend of Frenchy King* 1971; *Don Juan 1973 ou Si Don Juan etait une Femme/Ms. Don Juan, L'histoire très bonne et très joyeuse de Colinot Trousse chemise* 1973.

Bare, Richard. Director, also screenwriter, producer. Born on Aug. 12, 1925, in Turlock, Calif. Directed routine Hollywood films and many short subjects from the late 40s to the late 50s, then produced and directed numerous TV films and series segments, including all 168 episodes of 'Green Acres.' Author: *The Film Director* (1971).

FILMS INCLUDE: *Smart Girls Don't Talk* 1948; *Flaxy Martin, The House Across the Street* 1949; *This Side of the Law, Return of the Frontiersman* 1950; *Prisoners of the Casbah* 1953; *Shoot-Out at Medicine Bend* 1957; *The Rebel Breed* 1960; *Wicked Wicked* (also prod., sc.) 1973.

Bari, Lynn. Actress. *b.* Marjorie Schuyler Fisher, Dec. 18, 1913, Roanoke, Va. *d.* 1989. She moved with her family to Los Angeles, when her stepfather, Rev. Robert Bitzer, became head of the Institute of Religious Science there. She appeared in school plays, then made her screen debut as a chorus dancer in *Dancing Lady* (1933). After several other extra spots and bit roles, she signed a long-term contract with Fox. She subsequently developed into a competent actress, playing second leads in some major features, often as the "other woman," and leading roles in numerous B pictures, including several Charlie Chan and Mr. Moto mysteries. She also starred in a couple of series on early TV. At the height of her career, she was publicized as "The Girl with the Million-Dollar Figure" and "The Woo Woo Girl." She was second only to Betty Grable as the choice of WW II GIs for the most popular pinup girl. Her second husband was producer Sid Luft (Judy Garland's third). In 1956, she went into semi-retirement after marrying a doctor and becoming his nurse. But she later reappeared sporadically in films and in the 70s toured with stage companies.

FILMS INCLUDE: *Dancing Lady* 1933; *Stand Up and Cheer* 1934; *The Man Who Broke the Bank at Monte Carlo* 1935; *Pigskin Parade* 1936; *Wee Willie Winkie, Lancer Spy, Love Is News, On the Avenue* 1937; *The Baroness and the Butler, Mr. Moto's Gamble, Battle of Broadway, Always Goodbye, I'll Give a Million, Meet the Girls, Speed to Burn, Sharpshooters* 1938; *The Return of the Cisco Kid, Chasing Danger, News Is Made at Night, Hotel for Women, Pack Up Your Troubles, Charlie Chan in City of Darkness* 1939; *City of Chance, Free Blonde and 21, Lillian Russell, Earthbound, Pier 13, Kit Carson* 1940; *Sleepers West, Blood and Sand, We Go Fast, Sun Valley Serenade, Moon Over Her Shoulder, The Perfect Snob* 1941; *Secret Agent of Japan, The Night Before the Divorce, The Falcon Takes Over, The Magnificent Dope, Orchestra Wives* 1942; *China Girl, Hello Frisco Hello* 1943; *The Bridge of San Luis Rey, Tampico* 1944; *Captain Eddie* 1945; *Shock, Home Sweet Homicide, Margie, Nocturne* 1946; *Man From Texas, The Spiritualist* 1948; *The Kid From Cleveland* 1949; *I'd Climb the Highest Mountain, On the Loose* 1951; *Has Anybody Seen My Gal?* 1952; *Francis Joins the WACs* 1954; *Abbott and Costello Meet the Keystone Cops* 1955; *The Women of Pitcairn Island* 1956; *Damn Citizen* 1958; *Trauma* 1962; *The Young Runaways* 1968.

Barish, Keith. Producer. Born in Los Angeles, Calif. After forming Keith Barish Productions in 1979, he entered the film world as executive producer of *Endless Love* (1981). Eclecticism has characterized his projects, which have ranged from literary dramas to light comedy and erotic melodramas. Former partner with Taft Broadcasting Company. He is also the founder and chairman of the trendy chain of restaurants Planet Hollywood.

FILMS INCLUDE: *Endless Love* (exec. prod.) 1981; *Sophie's Choice, Kiss Me Goodbye* 1982; *Misunderstood* (exec. prod.) 1984; *9½ Weeks* (exec. prod.), *Big Trouble in Little China* (exec. prod.) 1986; *Ironweed, Light of Day, The Monster Squad* (exec. prod.), *The Running Man* (exec. prod.) 1987; *The Serpent and the Rainbow* (exec. prod.) 1988; *Her Alibi* 1989; *Fire Birds* (exec. prod.) 1990; *The Fugitive* 1993.

Barker, Clive. Writer, director. Born in 1952 in Liverpool, England. Respected horror novelist and short-story writer who adapted and directed his own works after witnessing a series of unsatisfying adaptations by other directors. Like his writing, his films are noted for their horrific, ornate style.

FILMS INCLUDE: *Hellraiser* 1987; *Nightbreed* 1990; *Candyman, Hellraiser III: Hell on Earth, Sleepwalkers* 1992; *Candyman II: Farewell to the Flesh* (sc.), *Lord of Illusions* 1995.

Barker, Lex. Actor. *b.* Alexander Crichlow Barker, Jr., May 8, 1919, Rye, N.Y. *d.* 1973 of a heart attack. The son of a socially prominent family, he left Princeton University after two years to join a theatrical stock company. Entered films in 1945, playing a minor role in *Doll Face.* Virile and athletic, he was cast as Tarzan in five films between 1949 and 1953, the tenth actor to play the role. He next appeared in a series of Westerns and a variety of roles in minor films. After 1958 he appeared frequently in Italian and German adventure films and Westerns. He was particularly popular in Germany, where he starred in a series of American-frontier sagas based on the stories of Karl

May. Barker's most important role in Europe was in Fellini's *La Dolce Vita.* Among his five wives were actresses Arlene DAHL (1951–52) and Lana TURNER (1953–57).

FILMS INCLUDE: *Doll Face* 1945; *Two Guys From Milwaukee* 1946; *The Farmer's Daughter, Crossfire, Unconquered* 1947; *Mr. Blandings Builds His Dream House, The Velvet Touch* 1948; *Tarzan's Magic Fountain* 1949; *Tarzan and the Slave Girl* 1950; *Tarzan's Peril* 1951; *Tarzan's Savage Fury* 1952; *Tarzan and the She-Devil, Thunder Over the Plains* 1953; *The Yellow Mountain* 1954; *The Man from Bitter Ridge* 1955; *Away All Boats* 1956; *War Drums, The Deerslayer* 1957; *Captain Fuoco* (It.) 1958; *La Scimitarra del Saraceno/The Pirate and the Slave Girl* (It./Fr.) 1959; *La Dolce Vita* (It./Fr.) 1960; *Im Stahlnetz Dr. Mabuse/The Return of Dr. Mabuse* (Ger./Fr./It.) 1961; *Der Schatzim Silbersee/Treasure of Silver Lake* (Ger./Fr./Yug.) 1962; *Winnetou—I. Teil/Apache Gold* (Ger./Fr./It./Yug.) 1963; *Winnetou—II. Teil/Last of the Renegades* (Ger./Fr./It./Yug.), *Old Shatterhand/Shatterhand* (Ger./Fr./It./Yug.) 1964; *Victim Five/Code 7—Victim 5!* (UK), *24 Hours to Kill* (UK), *Winnetou—III. Teil/The Desperado Trail* (Ger./Yug.), *Die Hölle von Manitoba/A Place Called Glory* (Ger./Sp.) 1965; *Woman Times Seven* (US/Fr./It.) 1967; *Wenn du bei mir bist* (Ger.) 1970.

Barker, Reginald. Director. *b.* 1886, Bothwell, Scotland. *d.* 1937. Came to California at the age of ten. In 1901 he made his stage debut with a Burbank stock company. He began his screen career in 1913 as director of adventure shorts for Thomas INCE. He soon distinguished himself as an outdoor director, a pioneer of the Western genre at its best. Directed the early Westerns of William S. HART and subsequently a competent mixture of melodramas and action pictures.

FILMS: *The Wrath of the Gods* (co-dir.), *The Typhoon, The Bargain* 1914; *The Devil* (co-dir.), *On the Night Stage, The Reward, The Iron Strain, The Man From Oregon, The Coward, The Golden Claw, The Despoiler, The Italian* 1915; *The Conqueror, The Stepping Stone, The Bugle Call, The Market of Vain Desire, Civilization* (co-dir.), *Shell Forty-Three, The Thoroughbred, The Criminal, Jim Grimsby's Boy, Three of Many* 1916; *The Iced Bullet, Back of the Man, Sweetheart of the Doomed, Happiness, Paws of the Bear, A Strange Transgressor, Golden Rule Kate* 1917; *Madam Who, Carmen of the Klondike, Shackled, The Turn of the Wheel, The One Woman, The Hell Cat* 1918; *Shadows, The Brand, The Stronger Vow, The Crimson Gardenia, Flame of the Desert, The Girl From Outside, Bonds of Love* 1919; *Dangerous Days, The Woman and the Puppet, The Branding Iron* 1920; *Bunty Pulls the Strings* (also prod.), *Godless Men, Snowblind, The Old Nest, The Poverty of Riches* 1921; *The Storm* 1922; *Hearts Aflame, The Eternal Struggle, Pleasure Mad* 1923; *Women Who Give, Broken Barriers* 1924; *The Dixie Handicap, The Great Divide, The White Desert, When the Door Opened* 1925; *The Flaming Forest* 1926; *The Frontiersman, Body and Soul* 1927; *The Toilers* 1928; *The Rainbow, New Orleans, The Great Divide* (sound version), *The Mississippi Gambler* 1929; *Seven Keys to Baldpate, Hide-Out* 1930; *The Moonstone* 1934; *Women Must Dress, The Healer* 1935; *Forbidden Heaven* 1936.

Barker, Sir William G(eorge). Pioneer producer, director, cameraman of British films. *b.* 1867, London. *d.* 1951. He was a traveling salesman before entering films as a cameraman of early newsreels, including the historical *Queen Victoria's Diamond Jubilee* (1897). In 1901 he founded the Autoscope Company and in 1904 launched Ealing's first studio.

Barker's grand-scale productions, keen business sense, and daring publicity campaigns were instrumental in the early development of British films. In 1911 he paid stage actor Sir Herbert Tree £1,000 for one day of shooting on *Henry VIII,* then exhibited the film at select auditoriums at high admission prices. *Sixty Years a Queen* (1913) was an expensive tribute to the recently deceased Victoria. His most ambitious production was *East Lynne* (1913), a two-hour spectacle with many scenes, extravagant décor, and sweeping photography. His films, particularly his crime melodramas, were noted for their authentic atmosphere in re-creating life on the streets of London. He retired from screen activity in 1916.

FILMS INCLUDE: *Henry VIII, Princess Clementina, The Anarchist's Doom* 1911; *Jim the Fireman, The Last Round* 1912; *The Battle of Waterloo, Sixty Years a Queen, East Lynne, The Great Bank Robbery, The Great Bullion Robbery, Greater Love Hath No Man, In the Hands of London Crooks, London by Night* 1913; *As a Man Soweth, Brother's Atonement, The Fighting Parson, Lights of London, Younita* 1914; *Jane Shore* 1915.

Barkin, Ellen. Actress. Born on Apr. 16, 1954, in the Bronx, N.Y. *ed.* Hunter Coll. Sensual, versatile lead of the American stage, TV, and films, often in vulnerable roles. Following a stint in daytime soaps, she debuted as the only female lead in Barry Levinson's first film *Diner* and has since appeared in an eclectic range of roles, memorably the straight-backed attorney in *The Big Easy*. Divorced from actor Gabriel BYRNE, whom she had married in 1988 after co-starring with him in *Siesta*.

FILMS INCLUDE: *Diner, Tender Mercies* 1982; *Daniel, Eddie and the Cruisers* 1983; *The Adventures of Buckaroo Banzai, Harry and Son* 1984; *Enormous Changes at the Last Minute* 1985; *Desert Bloom, Down by Law* 1986; *The Big Easy, Siesta, Made in Heaven* (unbilled) 1987; *Sea of Love, Johnny Handsome* 1989; *Switch* 1991; *Man Trouble* 1992; *Mac, This Boy's Life, Into the West* 1993; *Bad Company* 1994; *Wild Bill* 1995; *The Fan, Mad Dog Time* 1996.

barn doors. Folding metal flaps mounted on the rims of a studio lamp or around the lamp of a spotlight to control the spread of light. They can be adjusted to direct a beam of light to avoid unwanted light spill and to shade portions of a subject from direct illumination.

Barnes, Binnie. Actress. Born Gitelle Gertrude Maude Barnes, on Mar. 25, 1905, in London. She worked as a milkmaid, nurse, chorus girl, and dance hostess before her screen debut in 1929, appearing mostly in comedy shorts. Made 26 two-reel comedies with Stanley Lupino (father of Ida Lupino) before playing her first prominent part in a feature, *A Night in Montmartre* (1931). Her big break came two years later in the role of Catherine Howard in *The Private Life of Henry VIII,* with Charles Laughton. An invitation to Hollywood followed and she appeared in dozens of films, typically as a vitriolic, wisecracking second lead, but also in many leading roles. After retiring from the screen in 1955, she came back in 1966, playing a nun in *The Trouble with Angels* and its 1968 sequel. She married Mike FRANKOVICH, production executive at Columbia pictures, in 1940.

FILMS INCLUDE: In the UK—*Phonofilm* 1929; *A Night in Montmartre* 1931; *Murder at Covent Garden* 1932; *Taxi to Paradise, Heads We Go/The Charming Deceiver, The Private Life of Henry VIII* (as Catherine Howard) 1933; *The Lady Is Willing, The Private Life of Don Juan* 1934. In the US—*There's Always Tomorrow* 1934; *Diamond Jim* (as Lillian Russell), *Rendezvous* 1935; *Sutter's Gold, Small Town Girl, The Last of the Mohicans, The Magnificent Brute* 1936; *Three Smart Girls, Breezing Home, Broadway Melody of 1938* 1937; *The Divorce of Lady X* (UK), *The Adventures of Marco Polo, Three Blind Mice, Holiday, Always Goodbye, Tropic Holiday, Gateway* 1938; *The Three Musketeers* (as Milady De Winter), *Wife*

Husband and Friend, Man About Town, Frontier Marshal, Daytime Wife 1939; *'Til We Meet Again* 1940; *This Thing Called Love, Tight Shoes, Skylark* 1941; *Call Out the Marines, New Wine, In Old California, I Married an Angel* 1942; *The Man From Down Under* 1943; *Up in Mabel's Room, The Hour Before Dawn, Barbary Coast Gent* 1944; *It's in the Bag, The Spanish Main* 1945; *The Time of Their Lives* 1946; *If Winter Comes* 1948; *My Own True Love, I Pirati di Capri/The Pirates of Capri* (It.), *La Strada Buia/Fugitive Lady* (It.) 1949; *Shadow of the Eagle* (UK) 1950; *Decameron Nights* (UK) 1953; *Malaga/Fire Over Africa* (UK) 1954; *The Trouble with Angels* 1966; *Where Angels Go Trouble Follows* 1968; *40 Carats* 1973.

Barnes, George. American director of photography. *b.* 1893. *d.* 1953. Entered films in 1919 with Thomas H. Ince and for a quarter of a century was responsible for the cinematography of many of Hollywood's most prestigious productions, both silents and talkies, black and white and color. He worked with such directors as Fred Niblo, King Vidor, Henry King, Clarence Brown, Frank Capra, Ernst Lubitsch, Raoul Walsh, Harry D'Arrast, Allan Dwan, Frank Borzage, Fritz Lang, Alfred Hitchcock, Robert Siodmak, Billy Wilder, and Cecil B. De Mille and helped shape the career of cinematographer Gregg TOLAND, who began as his assistant. Barnes was nominated for Academy Awards many times, and won an Oscar for the cinematography of Hitchcock's *Rebecca* (1940). His seven wives included Joan BLONDELL.

FILMS INCLUDE: *Vive La France!* (co-phot.) 1918; *The Haunted Bedroom* 1919; *Dangerous Hours, The False Road* 1920; *The Bronze Bell* 1921; *The Real Adventure, Peg o' My Heart, Dusk to Dawn* 1922; *Alice Adams, Desire, Conquering the Woman* 1923; *Janice Meredith, Yolanda* 1924; *Zander the Great* (co-phot.), *The Dark Angel, The Eagle* 1925; *Mademoiselle Modiste, The Son of the Sheik, The Winning of Barbara Worth* 1926; *The Night of Love, The Magic Flame, The Devil Dancer* 1927; *Sadie Thompson* (co-phot.), *Two Lovers, The Awakening, Our Dancing Daughters* 1928; *Bulldog Drummond* (co-phot.), *The Trespasser* (co-phot.), *Condemned* (co-phot.) 1929; *A Lady's Morals, Raffles, What a Widow!* 1930; *The Unholy Garden* (co-phot.) *Street Scene* 1931; *The Wet Parade, Blondie of the Follies, Sherlock Holmes* 1932; *Goodbye Again, Footlight Parade* 1933; *Dames, Flirtation Walk* (co-phot.) 1934; *Gold Diggers of 1935, In Caliente* (co-phot.), *Broadway Gondolier* 1935; *Cain and Mabel* 1936; *Black Legion, Marked Woman* 1937; *Jesse James* (co-phot.), *Stanley and Livingstone* 1939; *Rebecca, Devil's Island, Maryland* (co-phot.), *The Return of Frank James* (co-phot.) 1940; *Meet John Doe, That Uncertain Feeling, Unholy Partners, Remember the Day* 1941; *Rings on Her Fingers, Once Upon a Honeymoon* 1942; *Mr. Lucky* 1943; *Frenchman's Creek, Jane Eyre, None but the Lonely Heart* 1944; *The Spanish Main, Spellbound, The Bells of St. Mary's* 1945; *From This Day Forward, Sister Kenny* 1946; *Sinbad the Sailor* 1947; *Mourning Becomes Electra, The Emperor Waltz, Force of Evil* 1948; *Samson and Delilah* 1949; *Riding High* 1951, *The Greatest Show on Earth* (co-phot.) 1952; *The War of the Worlds* 1953.

Barnet, Boris. Director, actor. *b.* June 16, 1902, in Moscow. *d.* 1965, a suicide. At 15, served as a frontline medic in the Revolution; later was a boxer before joining the State Film School and becoming a member of the Kuleshov experimental workshop. He started his film career as an actor in Kuleshov's satire *The Extraordinary Adventures of Mr. West in the Land of the Bolsheviks* (1924), and later appeared in such films as *Storm Over Asia* (1928) and *A Living Corpse* (1929). His first directorial assignment was the serial *Miss Mend* (1926), which he co-directed with Fedor Ozep. Barnet's most successful silent film was the satirical comedy *The Girl with the Hat Box/When Moscow Laughs* (1927), and cinema historians consider *Okraina/Patriots/Outskirts* (1933) his best all-around film. In addition to their humor, Barnet's films reveal warmth and tenderness, an acute visual sensibility, good control of his actors, and a disciplined precision in editing. Following a string of poorly received films in the late 50s and early 60s, Barnet took his own life. He left behind a suicide note indicating that he seemed to have lost the ability to make good films, and with it the desire to live.

FILMS (as director): *Miss Mend* (co-dir. with Fedor Ozep; also co-sc., act.) 1926; *The Girl with the Hat Box/When Moscow Laughs, Moscow in October* (also act.) 1927; *The House on Trubyana Square* (also act.) 1928; *Production of Musical Instruments* (doc.), *The Piano* (doc.) 1930; *The Thaw/Anka* 1931; *Okraina/Patriots/Outskirts* (also co-sc.) 1933; *One and Ten* (co-dir.) 1934; *By the Bluest of Seas* 1936; *A Night in September* 1939; *Manhood* ('Fighting Film Album' No. 3) 1941; *A Priceless Head* ('Fighting Film Album' No. 10) 1942; *Men of Novgorod* 1943; *One Night/Dark Is the Night* (also act.) 1945; *The Scout's Exploit/Secret Agent* (also act.) 1947; *Pages of Life* 1948; *Bountiful Summer* 1951; *Concert of the Masters of Ukrainian Art* (doc.; also sc.) 1952; *Liana* (also co-sc.) 1955; *The Poet, The Wrestler and the Clown* (co-dir. with K. Yudin) 1957; *The Old Horseman* (release delayed from 1940), *Annushka* 1959; *Alenka* 1962; *Whistle Stop* (also co-sc.) 1963.

barney. A flexible cover, made of several layers of insulating materials, placed over a camera as a substitute for a blimp to dampen noise in sound recording or to protect the camera from extreme temperatures. See also BLIMP.

Baroncelli, Jacques de. Director. *b.* Jacques de Baroncelli-Javon, June 25, 1881, Boillargues, France. *d.* 1951. The son of a titled family, he was a journalist before entering film production. He was one of France's most prolific directors, turning out 76 films in a variety of genres between 1915 and 1947. His early films were noted for their elegance and were more interesting than his later ones. His son, Jean de Baroncelli, was the film critic of the Paris daily *Le Monde.*

FILMS INCLUDE: *La Maison de l'Espoir, La Nouvelle Antigone, Le Jugement de Salomon* 1916; *Une Vengeance, Le Roi de la Mer* 1917; *Le Scandale, Le Retour aux Champs* 1918; *Ramuntcho* 1919; *L'Héritage* 1920; *Le Père Goriot* 1921; *Roger-la-Honte* 1922; *Le Carillon de Minuit, La Légende de Soeur Béatrix Nêne* 1923; *Pêcheurs d'Islande* 1924; *Veille d'Armes* 1925; *Nitchevo* 1926; *Feu* 1927; *Le Duel* 1928; *La Tentation, La Femme et le Pantin* 1929; *L'Arlésienne* 1930; *Le Rêve, Brumes* 1931; *Le Dernier Choc* 1932; *Gitane* 1933; *Cessez le Feu/Cease Firing, Crainquebille* 1934; *Nitchevo* (sound remake), *Michel Strogoff* 1936; *La Belle Etoile, SOS Sahara* 1938; *L'Homme du Niger/Forbidden Love, Fausse Alerte/The French Way* 1940; *La Duchesse de Langlais/The Wicked Duchess* 1942; *Les Mystères de Paris* 1943; *Marie la Misère* 1945; *La Rose de la Mer* 1946; *Rocambole* (It.) 1947.

Barr, Byron. See YOUNG, Gig.

Barrault, Jean-Louis. Actor, stage director. *b.* Sept. 8, 1910, Vésinet, France. *d.* 1994. A pupil of Charles Dullin (drama) and Etienne Decroux (pantomime), he made his Paris stage debut in 1931 in 'Volpone.' Directed his first stage production in 1935 and made his film acting debut in Marc Allégret's *Les Beaux Jours* (1935). He went on to appear in many films, most memorably *Drôle de Drame/Bizarre Bizarre* (1937) and *Les Enfants du Paradis/Children of Paradise* (1945). But his screen activity was always secondary to his enormous contribution to the French theater, including acting and directing at the Comédie-Française (1940–46) and in his own stage company in partnership with his wife, Madeleine Renaud. In 1959 he was named director of the Théâtre de France but was removed from the post for siding with the students and workers during the May 1968 riots. He also served twice (1965–67, 1972–74) as director of the Théâtre des Nations and in 1974–81 was director of the Théâtre d'Orsay.

FILMS INCLUDE: *Les Beaux Jours* 1935; *Sous les Yeux d'Occident/Razumov, Un Grand Amour de Beethoven/The Life and Loves of Beethoven, Hélène* 1936; *Mademoiselle Docteur/Street of Shadows, Les Perles de la Couronne/The Pearls of the Crown, Drôle de Drame/Bizarre Bizarre* 1937; *Orage, Le Puritain, Altitude 3200/Youth in Revolt* 1938; *La Symphonie fantastique* (as composer Hector Berlioz), *Le Destin fabuleux de Désirée Clary/Mlle. Désirée* (as Napoleon) 1942; *Les Enfants du Paradis/Children of Paradise, La Part de l'Ombre/Blind Desire* 1945; *D'Homme à Hommes/Man to Men* 1948; *La Ronde* 1950; *Si Versailles m'était conté/Royal Affairs in Versailles* 1954; *Le Dialogue des Carmélites* 1960; *Le Testament du Docteur Cordelier* 1961; *The Longest Day* (US) 1962; *Chappaqua* (US) 1967; *La Nuit de Varennes* 1981.

Barrault, Marie-Christine. Born on Mar. 21, 1944, in Paris. Leading lady of the Paris stage and French TV and films. A niece of Jean-Louis Barrault, she trained with René Simon and later at the Paris Conservatoire and appeared in many stage and TV productions before making an impressive screen debut in Eric Rohmer's *Ma Nuit chez Maud/My Night at Maud's* (1969).

FILMS INCLUDE: *Ma Nuit chez Maud/My Night at Maud's* 1969; *Le Distrait/The Daydreamer* 1970; *Les Intrus* 1971; *L'Amour l'après-Midi/Chloe in the Afternoon* (bit) 1972; *Cousin Cousine, Du Côté des Tennis* 1976; *The Medusa Touch* (UK), *L'Etat sauvage, Perceval le Gallois* 1978; *Ma Chérie, Stardust Memories* (US) 1980; *Table for Five* (US) 1983; *Un Amour de Swann/Swann in Love, Pianoforte, Ein Liebe in Deutschland/A Love in Germany* (Ger./Fr.) 1984; *Le Jupon rouge* 1987; *Un Eté d'Orages* 1989; *Dames Galantes, L'Etat Sauvage/Savage State* 1990.

Barreto, Bruno. Director/screenwriter. Born in 1955 in Brazil. He was only 22 at the time of his first international hit, the sex comedy *Doña Flor and Her Two Husbands*. An independent voice, he has found his early success a hard act to follow. His ensuing output has failed to capture the popular and critical acclaim of his initial effort. In 1982, he Americanized *Doña Flor*'s screenplay with *Kiss Me Goodbye*. He has a child with Amy Irving, his leading lady in *A Show of Force*.

FILMS INCLUDE: *A Estrela sobe* 1974; *Doña Flor e Seus Dois Moridos/Doña Flor and Her Two Husbands* 1977; *Amada Amante* (dir. only) 1979; *Kiss Me Goodbye* (sc. from *Doña Flor and Her Two Husbands*) 1982; *Gabriela* 1983; *Alem Da Paixao* 1985; *Where the River Runs Black* (line prod.—Rio de Janeiro) 1986; *Romance de Empregada* (dir. only) 1988; *A Show of Force* (US) 1990; *Story of Fausta* 1992.

Barreto, Lima. Director. *b.* 1905, São Paulo, Brazil. *d.* 1982. An obscure documentary filmmaker before impressing international film circles with his poetic adventure film *O Cangaceiro/The Bandits* (1953), Brazil's best-known picture to date. Beautifully photographed to the accompaniment of a haunting melody, the film was received enthusiastically at the 1954 Cannes Festival. Barreto subsequently directed only one feature film.

FEATURE FILMS: *O Cangaceiro/The Bandits* 1953; *A Primeira Missa/The First Mass* 1961.

Barrie, Mona. Actress. *b.* Mona Smith on Dec. 18, 1909, in London. *d.* 1964. Educated in a convent in Sydney, Australia. Active on the Australian and British stage before arriving in Hollywood in 1933. She played some leads and many second leads, mostly in routine pictures of the 30s and 40s. Typically in ladylike roles.

FILMS INCLUDE: *Sleepers East* 1933; *Carolina, One Night of Love, Charlie Chan in London* 1934; *Mystery Woman* 1935; *King of Burlesque, A Message to Garcia, Love on the Run* 1936; *Mountain Justice, I Met Him in Paris* 1937; *Say It in French* 1938; *I Take This Woman* 1940; *When Ladies Meet, Never Give a Sucker an Even Break, Skylark* 1941; *Today I Hang, Road to Happiness, Syncopation, Cairo* 1942; *One Dangerous Night* 1943; *Storm Over Lisbon* 1944; *Just Before Dawn* 1946; *I Cover the Big Town, Cass Timberlane* 1947; *Strange Fascination* 1952; *Plunder of the Sun* 1953.

Barrie, Wendy. Actress. *b.* Margaret Jenkins, Apr. 18, 1912, Hong Kong. *d.* 1978. Daughter of a British attorney, she was educated in England and Switzerland. She made her London stage debut in 1930 and her British screen debut the following year. Brought to Hollywood on the strength of her performance as the sluttish Jane Seymour in Alexander Korda's *The Private Life of Henry VIII* (1933), she played leads in many productions of the 30s and early 40s, but her roles rarely did justice to her talent and looks. Her intimate association with mobster Bugsy Siegel, to whom she was engaged, hastened the demise of her Hollywood career. After retiring from the screen, she hosted one of TV's earliest talk shows and a syndicated radio program. She died alone in a nursing home at age 65.

FILMS INCLUDE: In the UK—*Collision* 1931; *Wedding Rehearsal* 1932; *The Private Life of Henry VIII* (as Jane Seymour) 1933. In the US—*It's a Small World, The Big Broadcast of 1936, Millions in the Air* 1935; *Love on a Bet, Speed, Ticket to Paradise, Under Your Spell* 1936; *Wings Over Honolulu, A Girl with Ideas, Dead End* 1937; *I Am the Law* 1938; *Pacific Liner, The Saint Strikes Back, Daytime Wife, The Hound of the Baskervilles, The Witness Vanishes* 1939; *The Saint Takes Over, Women in War, Men Against the Sky* 1940; *The Gay Falcon* 1941; *Eyes of the Underworld* 1942; *Forever and a Day* 1943; *It Should Happen to You* 1954. *The Moving Finger* 1963.

Barriscale, Bessie. American actress. *b.* 1884. *d.* 1965. Star of early silent films, typically romantic melodramas, she worked for Lasky, Triangle, and other studios, then established her own company. She was at her peak in the 1914–20 period, but could still be seen in occasional Hollywood productions as late as the mid-30s.

FILMS INCLUDE: *Eileen of Erin* 1913; *Rose of the Rancho, Ready Money* 1914; *The Cup of Life, The Devil, The Reward, The Mating, The Golden Claw, The Painted Soul* 1915; *Honor's Altar, The Sorrows of Love, The Payment, Home, Plain Jane* 1916; *The Hater of Men, Borrowed Plumage, Wooden Shoes* 1917; *Madam Who, Blindfolded, Patriotism, The White Lie, The Heart of Rachael* 1918; *A Trick of Fate, Josselyn's Wife, Her Purchase Price* 1919; *The Notorious Mrs. Sands, Life's Twist, The Broken Gate* 1920; *The Breaking Point* 1921; *Show Folks* 1928; *Secrets* 1933; *Beloved* 1934; *The Man Who Reclaimed His Head* 1935.

Barry, Don(ald) ("Red"). Actor, director. *b.* Donald Barry de Acosta, Jan. 11, 1912, Houston, Tex. *d.* 1980, a suicide by a self-inflicted shot. A football star in high school and at the Texas School of Mines, he turned to advertising, then to acting in stock, before making his film debut in 1933. His career seemed to go nowhere until 1940, when he starred in the serial *The Adventures of Red Ryder.* This led to a whole series of "Red Ryder" Western films featuring the character of Red Ryder with Barry as the hero and Tommy Cook as his little Indian friend. For several years he was voted one of the "Top Ten Money-Making Western Stars."

In 1949, Barry quit Republic to produce and star in his own productions but did not have much success. In 1954 he directed *Jesse James' Women,* in which he also starred. He later turned to playing character roles in non-Western films. He was married to actress Peggy Stewart.

FILMS INCLUDE (as actor): *This Day and Age* 1933; *Night Waitress* 1936; *The Woman I Love, Dead End* 1937; *The Crowd Roars, The Duke of West Point* 1938; *Calling Dr. Kildare, Only Angels Have Wings, Calling All Marines* 1939; *The Adventures of Red Ryder* (serial), *One Man's Law* 1940; *Death Valley Outlaws, The Phantom Cowboy* 1941; *Jessie James Jr., Remember Pearl Harbor* 1942; *Black Hills Express, The Sundown Kid* 1943; *The Purple Heart* 1944; *The Chicago Kid* 1945; *The Last Crooked Mile* 1946; *That's My Gal* 1947; *Madonna of the Desert* 1948; *Ringside, The Dalton Gang* 1949; *I Shot Billy the Kid* 1950; *Jesse James' Women* (also dir.) 1954; *I'll Cry Tomorrow* 1955; *Seven Men from Now* 1956; *Frankenstein 1970* 1958; *Warlock* 1959; *Walk on the Wild Side* 1962; *Twilight of Honor* 1963; *The Carpetbaggers* (bit), *Law of the Lawless* 1964; *Convict Stage* 1965; *Apache Uprising* 1966; *Fort Utah* 1967; *Bandolero!, Shalako* 1968; *Dirty Dingus Magee, Rio Lobo* (bit) 1970; *Junior Bonner* 1972; *Hustle, Blazing Stewardesses* 1975; *Orca, Seabo* 1977; *The Swarm* 1978; *Back Roads* 1980.

Barry, Gene. Actor. Born Eugene Klass, on June 14, 1921, in New York City. Leading man of routine Hollywood films of the 50s, following stage experience. Became popular on TV as the hero of the adventure series 'Bat Masterson' and 'Burke's Law.' In the early 70s he formed a production company with himself as producer and son, Michael, as director.

FILMS INCLUDE: *The Atomic City* 1952; *The Girls of Pleasure Island, The War of the Worlds, Those Redheads of Seattle* 1953; *Red Garters, Alaska Seas, Naked Alibi* 1954; *Soldier of Fortune, The Purple Mask* 1955; *Back From Eternity* 1956; *China Gate* 1957; *Thunder Road* 1958; *Maroc 7* 1968; *Subterfuge* 1969; *The Second Coming of Suzanne* (also exec. prod.) 1974; *Guyana—The Crime of the Century* (as Congressman Leo J. Ryan; Mex.) 1979; *A Cry For Love* 1980.

Barry, Iris. Film librarian. *b.* 1895, Birmingham, England. *d.* 1969. Educated in England and Belgium. Founding member of the London Film Society, 1925, then film critic of *The Spectator* and motion picture editor for the London *Daily Mail,* 1925–30. In 1932 she became librarian at the Museum of Modern Art in New York City; she was appointed the museum's film library curator in 1935 and director in 1947. In 1946 she was elected president of the International Federation of Film Archives. Author of books on film. Chevalier of the French Legion of Honor, 1949. Retired to France in 1950.

Barry, John. Composer. Born J. B. Prendergast in 1933, in York, England. A former rock 'n' roll trumpeter, he began working in films in the late 50s following his success as a composer-conductor-arranger of pop music. He gained plaudits for his dynamic scores for several James Bond films and won Academy Awards for the music of *Born Free* (1966), *The Lion in Winter* (1968), and *Out of Africa* (1985). Not to be confused with another John Barry (1936–79), a superior London-born art director who designed the sets for such films as *A Clockwork Orange* (1971), *The Little Prince* (1974), and *Superman* (1978), and won an Oscar for *Star Wars* (1977). He was married to Jane Birkin.

FILMS INCLUDE: *Beat Girl* 1959; *Dr. No* (arranged theme only), *The L-Shaped Room* 1962; *From Russia with Love, Zulu* 1963; *Seance on a Wet Afternoon, Goldfinger* 1964; *The Ipcress File, King Rat, The Knack, Mister Moses, Thunderball* 1965; *Born Free, The Quiller Memorandum, The Chase, The Wrong Box* 1966; *The Whisperers, You Only Live Twice* 1967; *Petulia, Boom!, The Lion in Winter* 1968; *Midnight Cowboy, On Her Majesty's Secret Service* 1969; *Monte Walsh, The Last Valley* 1970; *They Might Be Giants, Walkabout, Mary Queen of Scots* 1971; *Alice's Adventures in Wonderland* 1972; *A Doll's House* 1973; *The Man with the Golden Gun, The Dove* 1974; *The Day of the Locust* 1975; *Robin and Marian, King Kong* 1976; *The Deep, White Buffalo* 1977; *Moonraker, The Black Hole* 1979; *Somewhere in Time, Inside Moves* 1980; *Body Heat* 1981; *Hammett, Frances* 1982; *Octopussy* 1983; *The Cotton Club* 1984; *A View to a Kill, Jagged Edge, Out of Africa* 1985; *Peggy Sue Got Married* 1986; *The Living Daylights* 1987; *Dances with Wolves* 1990; *Chaplin* 1992; *Indecent Proposal, Ruby Cairo* 1993; *The Specialist* 1994; *Cry the Beloved Country, My Life, The Scarlet Letter* 1995.

Barrymore, Diana. Actress. *b.* Diana Blanche Barrymore Blythe, Mar. 3, 1921, New York City. *d.* 1960. The daughter of John Barrymore and poetess Michael Strange (Blanche Oelrichs), she was educated at private schools in France and the US, then attended the American Academy of Dramatic Arts. Acting debut in stock, 1938. Film debut, 1942. Her career was full of obstacles. Her autobiography, *Too Much, Too Soon* (1957), tells of her unhappy childhood, her unsuccessful marriages, her bouts with alcoholism, and her attempted suicides. The book was later turned into a movie, starring Dorothy Malone. In 1955, Miss Barrymore was voluntarily committed to a New York sanatorium. Upon her release the following year, she made an off-Broadway comeback in 'The Ivory Branch,' then went on the road with 'Cat on a Hot Tin Roof.'

FILMS: *Eagle Squadron, Between Us Girls, Nightmare* 1942, *Frontier Badmen, Fired Wife* 1943, *Ladies Courageous* 1944.

Barrymore, Drew. Actress. Born on Feb. 22, 1975, in Los Angeles. The daughter of John Barrymore, Jr. (John Drew Barrymore), she appeared in a commercial at nine months and made her movie debut at age four. She gained much popularity from an endearing performance in Steven Spielberg's *E.T.: The Extraterrestrial* and seemed assured of a bright future. But her prematurely adult lifestyle in the fast lane soon took its toll. She took her first alcoholic drink at nine, smoked marijuana at 11, and sniffed cocaine at 12. After an attempted suicide, she was confined to a rehabilitation clinic for a long stretch. She returned to the screen, however, in 1989, and revealed the tragic story of her tormented young life in a book, *Little Girl Lost.* She rebounded in the early 90s as an updated femme fatale, shedding her clothes (at 17) for a controversial cover of *Interview* magazine, and for her role in *Poison Ivy.* She appeared as Amy Fisher in one of three TV movies based on the notorious "Long Island Lolita."

FILMS: *Altered States* 1980; *E.T. The Extraterrestrial* 1982; *Firestarter, Irreconcilable Differences* 1984; *Cat's Eye* 1985; *See You in the Morning, Far From Home* 1989; *Poison Ivy, Doppelganger: The Evil Within* 1992; *Guncrazy, Wayne's World 2* 1993; *Bad Girls* 1994; *Batman Forever, Boys on the Side, Mad Love* 1995; *Everyone Says I Love You, Scream* 1996.

Barrymore, Ethel. Actress. *b.* Ethel Mae Blythe, Aug. 15, 1879, Philadelphia. *d.* 1959. The daughter of actors Maurice Barrymore (Herbert Blythe) and Georgiana Drew; the sister of actors John and Lionel Barrymore. Convent-educated, she made her stage debut at 15 with her uncle, John Drew, the foremost actor of his era. Played her first starring role on Broadway in 1900, in 'Captain Jinks of the Horse Marines.' True to the tradition of her illustrious family, she soon established herself as "the first lady of the American theater."

Miss Barrymore made her film debut in 1914, followed by

a variety of movie roles through 1919. Then, except for a remarkable performance as the Czarina in the film *Rasputin and the Empress* (1933), in which she appeared with her brothers, it became all theater for her until 1944, when she made a triumphant return to the screen, winning the best supporting actress Academy Award for her performance in *None but the Lonely Heart.* After that, she played many engaging character roles as the last surviving member of the "Fabulous Barrymores." She was nominated for Oscars for *The Spiral Staircase, The Paradine Case,* and *Pinky.* Known for her morbid sense of humor, her huge book collection, and her great love for baseball. A Broadway theater was named after her. Autobiography: *Memories* (1956).

FILMS: *The Nightingale* 1914; *The Final Judgement* 1915; *The Kiss of Hate, The Awakening of Helen Ritchie,* 1916; *The White Raven, The Call of Her People, The Greatest Power, The Lifted Veil, Life's Whirlpool, The Eternal Mother, An American Widow* 1917; *Our Mrs. McChesney* 1918; *The Divorcee* 1919; *Rasputin and the Empress* (as the Czarina) 1933; *None but the Lonely Heart* 1944; *The Spiral Staircase* 1946; *The Farmer's Daughter, Moss Rose, Night Song* 1947; *The Paradine Case, Moonrise* 1948; *Portrait of Jennie, The Great Sinner, That Midnight Kiss, The Red Danube, Pinky* 1949; *Kind Lady, The Secret of Convict Lake* 1951; *It's a Big Country, Deadline USA, Just for You* 1952; *The Story of Three Loves, Main Street to Broadway* 1953; *Young at Heart* 1955; *Johnny Trouble* 1957.

Barrymore, John. Actor. *b.* John Sidney Blythe, Feb. 15, 1882, Philadelphia. *d.* 1942. *ed.* Georgetown Academy; Seton Hall (N.J.); King's College (Wimbledon, England). The youngest of the "Fabulous Barrymores," he was the son of stage actors Maurice Barrymore (Herbert Blythe) and Georgiana Drew, the brother of Lionel and Ethel BARRYMORE, and the father of Diana BARRYMORE and John (Drew) BARRYMORE, JR. Defying the family tradition, John Barrymore started out as a cartoonist for a New York daily newspaper. But in 1903 he too followed that tradition and made his stage debut, in 'Magda.' Despite his late start, John soon surpassed the achievements of his sister and brother, becoming the most admired stage idol of his day with appearances in such plays as 'The Affairs of Anatol,' 'Peter Ibbetson,' and 'Redemption.' He reached his peak with an inspired interpretation of two Shakespearean roles, Richard III in 1920 and Hamlet in 1922.

John made his film debut in 1913. His silent films were primarily romantic dramas, comedies, and swashbuckling adventures. Even without the deployment of his magnificent voice, John Barrymore's performance was often the highlight of these mostly undistinguished pictures. His forceful yet restrained gestures, his almost playful bravura made even the poorest roles come to life. Although most successful with audiences in the role of the great lover, he preferred playing grotesque, tortured parts, such as his famous *Dr. Jekyll and Mr. Hyde* (1920), in which he accomplished the transformation from one characterization to another without the aid of makeup.

With the coming of sound Barrymore's wonderful voice combined with his Great Profile to make him a major box-office attraction. Hollywood studios rushed him from one lot to another in a race to exploit his reputation as a stage star. In his very first "talkie," the all-star production *Show of Shows,* he obliged by delivering a soliloquy from 'Richard III.' In his very last, 'Playmates,' he recited the "To be or not to be" soliloquy from 'Hamlet.'

Some of his early vehicles afforded Barrymore the opportunity to display his acting talent on the screen. But sound arrived too late to present him at his full glory. In his 50s, and already suffering from lapses of memory, he often resorted to reading his lines from cue cards. He had been a heavy drinker since his teens, and his handsome face was now showing signs of his roguish, reckless lifestyle. Compounding his problems was the memory of four unsuccessful marriages (one was to poetess Michael Strange, another to screen actress Dolores COSTELLO) and countless romantic scandals. He was a star in decline, frequently assigned roles that were nothing but parodies of his own painful state, portraying aging actors basking in the glory of their past.

John Barrymore wrote an early autobiography, *Confessions of an Actor* (1926) and the book *We Three* (1935) about himself, Ethel, and Lionel. His life story is the subject of Gene Fowler's *Good Night Sweet Prince* (1944). He is pictured admiringly, but not too favorably, in the tragic autobiography of his daughter Diana, *Too Much, Too Soon* (1957). In the film version of that book he is portrayed by another notorious screen rogue, Errol Flynn. He was later portrayed by Jack Cassidy in *W. C. Fields and Me* (1976).

FILMS: *An American Citizen, The Man from Mexico* 1914; *Are You a Mason? The Dictator, The Incorrigible Dukane* 1915; *Nearly a King, The Lost Bridegroom, The Red Widow* 1916; *Raffles the Amateur Cracksman* 1917; *On the Quiet* 1918; *Here Comes the Bride, The Test of Honor* 1919; *Dr. Jekyll and Mr. Hyde* (dual title role) 1920; *The Lotus Eater* 1921; *Sherlock Holmes* (title role) 1922; *Beau Brummel* (title role) 1924; *The Sea Beast* (as Captain Ahab of *Moby Dick* fame), *Don Juan* (title role) 1926; *When a Man Loves, The Beloved Rogue* (as François Villon) 1927; *Tempest* 1928; *Eternal Love, The Show of Shows* 1929; *General Crack, The Man From Blankley's, Moby Dick* (again as Ahab) 1930; *Svengali* (title role), *The Mad Genius* 1931; *Arsène Lupin* (title role), *Grand Hotel, State's Attorney, A Bill of Divorcement* 1932; *Rasputin and the Empress* (as a thinly veiled Prince Youssoupoff), *Topaze* (title role), *Reunion in Vienna* (as Archduke Rudolph von Hapsburg), *Dinner at Eight, Night Flight, Counsellor-at-Law* 1933; *Long Lost Father, Twentieth Century* 1934; *Romeo and Juliet* (as Mercutio) 1936; *Maytime, Bulldog Drummond Comes Back, Night Club Scandal, True Confession* 1937; *Bulldog Drummond's Revenge, Romance in the Dark, Bulldog Drummond's Peril, Marie Antoinette* (as Louis XV), *Spawn of the North, Hold That Co-Ed* 1938; *The Great Man Votes, Midnight* 1939; *The Great Profile* 1940; *The Invisible Woman, World Premiere, Playmates* 1941.

Barrymore, John, Jr. (a.k.a. **John Drew Barrymore**). Actor. Born John Blythe Barrymore, Jr., on June 4, 1932, in Beverly Hills, Calif. *ed.* St. John's Military Academy. The son of John BARRYMORE and screen actress Dolores COSTELLO, he hardly ever saw his celebrated father after his parents separated when he was 18 months old. He was educated at various private and public schools, including St. John's Military Academy. He made his film debut at 18 under the name John Barrymore, Jr., but soon ran afoul of the law and his own volatile temper and landed in jail a number of times, for speeding, drunken driving, and violent quarrels with his first wife, actress Cara WILLIAMS.

After being suspended for a year by Actors' Equity, he returned to films in 1958 as John Drew Barrymore, but the change in name was not accompanied by a change of image, nor did it result in an upgrading of the usually poor films in which he appeared. The following year he went to Europe and for several years played leads in low-budget Italian costume action pictures. In 1964 he returned to the US and before long found himself again in jail for possession of marijuana. In the late 60s he underwent a sudden change, left the Hollywood scene and withdrew from social contact altogether. He secluded himself in the California desert, where he has been leading the life of a recluse, practicing yoga and meditation. In the mid-70s he was back in circulation, playing occasional bits in films and on TV. He is the father of child actress Drew BARRYMORE.

FILMS INCLUDE: As John Barrymore, Jr.—*The Sundowners, High Lonesome* 1950; *Quebec, The Big Night* 1951; *Thunderbirds* 1953; *While the City Sleeps* 1956. As John Drew Barrymore—*High School Confidential, Never Love a Stranger* 1958; *Night of the Quarter Moon, I Cosacchi/The Cossacks* (It./Fr.) 1959; *Les Nuits de Raspoutine/L'Ultimo Zar/The Night They Killed Rasputin* (as Prince Youssoupoff, a role played by John Barrymore, Sr., in *Rasputin and the Empress), La Donna dei Faraoini/The Pharaohs' Woman* 1960; *La Guerra di Troia/The Trojan Horse* (as Ulysses; It./Fr.) 1961; *Il Conquistatore di Corinto/The Centurion* (It./Fr.), *Col Ferro e col Fuoco/Invasion 1700* (It./Fr./Yug.) 1962; *Roma Contro Roma/The War of the Zombies* (It.) 1963; *The Christine Keeler Affair* (UK) 1964; *This Savage Land* (orig. shown on TV in 1966) 1969; *Baby Blue Marine* (bit) 1976; *Nocturna* 1979; *Full Moon High* 1982.

Barrymore, Lionel. Actor, occasionally director and screenwiter. *b.* Lionel Blythe, Apr. 28, 1878, Philadelphia. *d.* 1954. *ed.* Gilmore School (London); St. Vincent's Academy (N.Y.); Seton Hall (N.J.); Arts Students League (N.Y.). The son of Maurice Barrymore (Herbert Blythe) and Georgina Drew; brother of Ethel and John BARRYMORE. Made his stage debut with his parents while still an infant but did not act professionally on a regular basis until his late teens. By 1900 he was a leading Broadway actor, often appearing with his uncle, John Drew. In 1903 he went to Paris as an aspiring artist but returned to the US and to acting in 1907.

The first Barrymore to appear in films and among the first legitimate stage stars to actively seek a screen career, he joined Biograph in 1909 and began playing leading roles in films two years later. He appeared in many of D. W. GRIFFITH's early films, including *The New York Hat, The Informer, The Musketeers of Pig Alley* (all 1912), and *Judith of Bethulia* (1914). He also wrote several scripts for Griffith, including *The Tender-Hearted Boy* (1913). In 1915 he appeared in the Pearl White serial *The Exploits of Elaine* and its sequel, *The Romance of Elaine,* and later played leading roles for various studios, occasionally also directing.

Barrymore continued appearing regularly on the Broadway stage until 1925, when he finally abandoned the theater completely to devote his talents exclusively to acting in films. In 1926 he signed with MGM, a studio with which he was associated for the remaining 27 years of his film career. He continued playing leading-man roles for several years but gradually moved into character parts and in the 30s and 40s became established as one of Hollywood's foremost character stars, dominating many a production with his strong presence. In all, he played some 250 screen roles of varied character and range. He won an Academy Award for his performance in *A Free Soul* (1931). In the late 30s and early 40s he was popularly identified with the role of Dr. Gillespie, which he played in all 15 films of the "Dr. Kildare" series. In 1938 he was partially paralyzed by a combination of arthritis and a leg injury but managed to continue his busy acting schedule even though confined to a wheelchair.

Barrymore authored a novel, *Mr. Cantonwine,* and a volume of memoirs, *We Barrymores* (1951). He had some success as a painter and etcher and composed orchestral music. His tone poem 'In Memoriam,' dedicated to his brother John, was performed by the Philadelphia Symphony in 1942. Several others of his musical works, including a symphony, were played in various concert halls. He was married twice, both times to actresses. His first wife (1904–23) was Doris Rankin, the second Irene Fenwick, who married him in 1923 and died in 1936.

FILMS INCLUDE (as actor): *Fighting Blood* (sc. only), *The Battle* 1911; *Friends, The Musketeers of Pig Alley, The One She Loved, Brutality, The New York Hat, The Informer, Gold and Glitter, My Hero, The God Within, The Burglar's Dilemma* 1912; *An Adventure in the Autumn Woods, Oil and Water, The Sheriff's Baby, The Wanderer, The Lady and the Mouse, Just Gold, Death's Marathon, The House of Discord* 1913; *Classmates, Judith of Bethulia, Strongheart, Men and Women, The Power of the Press, The Seats of the Mighty* 1914; *The Exploits of Elaine* (serial), *The Romance of Elaine* (serial), *Wildfire, A Modern Magdalen, The Flaming Sword, A Yellow Streak* 1915; *The Quitter, The Upheaval, The Brand of Cowardice* 1916; *His Father's Son, The Millionaire's Double, Life's Whirlpool* (also dir.) 1917; *The Copperhead, The Devil's Garden, The Master Mind* 1920; *The Great Adventure, Jim the Penman* 1921; *Boomerang Bill, The Face in the Fog* (as Boston Blackie) 1922; *The Enemies of Women, Unseeing Eyes, The Eternal City* 1923; *Decameron Nights* (UK/Ger.), *America* (as the infamous Captain Walter Butler), *Meddling Women, I Am the Man* 1924; *The Iron Man, Children of the Whirlwind, The Wrongdoers, The Splendid Road* 1925; *The Barrier, Brooding Eyes, The Lucky Lady, Paris at Midnight, The Bells, The Temptress* 1926; *The Show, Women Love Diamonds, Body and Soul, The Thirteenth Hour* 1927; *Sadie Thompson, Drums of Love, The Lion and the Mouse, West of Zanzibar, The River Woman* 1928; *Alias Jimmy Valentine, Confession* (short; dir. only), *Madame X* (dir. only), *His Glorious Night* (dir. only), *The Unholy Night* (dir. only) 1930; *Ten Cents a Dance* (dir. only), *A Free Soul, Guilty Hands, The Yellow Ticket, Mata Hari* 1931; *Broken Lullaby/The Man I Killed, Arsène Lupin, Grand Hotel, The Washington Masquerade* 1932; *Rasputin and the Empress* (as Rasputin), *Sweepings, Looking Forward, The Stranger's Return, Dinner at Eight, One Man's Journey, Night Flight, Christopher Bean, Should Ladies Behave?* 1933; *This Side of Heaven, Carolina, The Girl from Missouri, Treasure Island* (as Billy Bones) 1934; *David Copperfield* (as Dan Peggotty), *The Little Colonel, Mark of the Vampire, Public Hero No. 1, The Return of Peter Grimm* (title role), *Ah Wilderness!* 1935; *The Voice of Bugle Ann, The Road to Glory, The Devil Doll, The Gorgeous Hussy* (as Andrew Jackson) 1936; *Camille* (as Monsieur Duval), *A Family Affair* (as Judge Hardy in the film that initiated the "Andy Hardy" series, a role later played by Lewis Stone), *Captains Courageous, Saratoga, Navy Blue and Gold* 1937; *A Yank at Oxford, Test Pilot, You Can't Take It With You, Young Dr. Kildare* (as Dr. Gillespie in the first of 15 films in the "Dr. Kildare" series, all featuring Barrymore), *Let Freedom Ring, On Borrowed Time* 1940; *The Penalty, Lady Be Good* 1941; *Calling Dr. Gillespie, Tennessee Johnson* (as Congressman Thaddeus Stevens) 1942; *A Guy Named Joe* 1943; *Three Men in White, Since You Went Away* 1944; *The Valley of Decision* 1945; *Three Wise Fools, The Secret Heart, It's a Wonderful Life* 1946; *Duel in the Sun, Dark Delusion* 1947; *Key Largo* 1948; *Down to the Sea in Ships* 1949; *Malaya, Right Cross* 1950; *Bannerline* 1951; *Lone Star* 1952; *Main Street to Broadway* 1953.

Barsacq, Léon. Art director. *b.* Oct. 18, 1906, Crimea, Russia. *d.* 1969. After studies at the Paris School of Decorative Arts, he entered French films in 1931 as an assistant decorator, working with André ANDREJEW, among others. In 1938 he worked on his first film as an art director, collaborating on Jean Renoir's *La Marseillaise.* He went on to an illustrious career as one of France's most skillful art directors, a creative master of atmosphere. He co-designed the sets for Carné's *Les Enfants du Paradis/Children of Paradise* (1945) and worked on many of René CLAIR's films. His book *Le Décor de Film* was published posthumously in Paris in 1970.

Léon's brother, André Barsacq (*b.* Jan. 24, 1909, Crimea, Russia), also designed some sets for French films, including *L'Argent* (1928) and *Yoshiwara* (1937), but is primarily known as a stage designer and director. He also directed one film, *Le Rideau rouge* (1952).

FILMS INCLUDE: *La Marseillaise* (co-art dir.) 1938; *Lumière d'Eté* (co-art dir.), *Les Mystères de Paris* 1943; *Les Enfants du Paradis/Children of Paradise* (co-art dir.), *Boule de Suif* 1945; *L'Idiot/The Idiot* 1946; *Le Silence et d'Or* 1947; *Pattes blanches* 1949; *La Beauté du Diable/Beauty and the Devil* 1950; *Roma Ore 11/Rome 11 O'Clock* (It.), *Les Belles de Nuit/Beauties of the Night* 1952; *Le Grand Jeu* 1954; *Les Diaboliques/Diabolique, Les Grandes Manoeuvres/The Grand Maneuver* 1955; *The Ambassador's Daughter* (US) 1956; *Porte de Lilas/Gates of Paris, Pot-Bouille* 1957; *The Longest Day* (co-art dir.; US) 1962; *Symphonie pour un Massacre/Symphony for a Massacre* 1963; *Der Besuch/The Visit* (Ger./Fr./It./US) 1964; *Phèdre* 1969.

Bartel, Paul. Director, screenwriter, actor. Born on Aug. 6, 1938, in New York City. *ed.* UCLA. Fascinated by cinema from an early age, he first became involved in the medium at age 13, when he spent a summer at UPA, assisting in the creation of cartoons. As a student at UCLA, he turned out a number of animated and documentary shorts and won acting and playwriting awards. On a Fulbright scholarship, he then studied film directing at Rome's Centro Sperimentale di Cinnematografica. His graduation short, *Progetti,* was presented at the Venice Film Festival. Returning to the US, he started his professional career as an assistant director on training films at the Army Pictorial Center in Long Island City and later wrote and directed a monthly newsreel series in Spanish for the US Information Agency. As a Hollywood feature director from the early 70s, he exhibited technical skill and satirical talent, occasionally erratic, with a bend toward the offbeat and the outrageous, sometimes bordering on the lewd and even perverse. He sustained a parallel career as a pudgy, balding character actor in his own films and those of others, mainly close colleagues.

FEATURE FILMS: As director (complete)—*Private Parts* 1972; *Death Race 2000* 1975; *Cannonball* (also co.-sc., act.) 1976; *Eating Raoul* (also co-sc., act.) 1982; *Not for Publication* (also co-sc.) 1984; *Lust in the Dust* 1985; *The Longshot* 1986; *Scenes from the Class Struggle in Beverly Hills* (also act.) 1989. As actor (partial listing)—*Eat My Dust!* 1976; *Hollywood Boulevard, Grand Theft Auto, Mr. Billion* 1977; *Piranha* 1978; *Rock 'n' Roll High School* 1979; *Heartbeeps* 1981; *Trick or Treats, White Dog* 1982; *Heart Like a Wheel* 1983; *Into the Night, National Lampoon's European Vacation* 1985; *Chopping Mall/Killbots* 1986; *Amazon Women on the Moon* 1987; *Mortuary Academy* 1988; *Gremlins 2: The New Batch* (cameo), *Far Out Man* 1990; *The Pope Must Die/The Pope Must Diet* (UK) 1991; *Pucker Up and Bark Like a Dog, Desire and Hell at Sunset Motel* 1992; *Shelf Life* 1993; *Acting On Impulse* 1994; *The Jerky Boys, Red Ribbon Blues, The Usual Suspects* 1995; *Basquiat* 1996.

Barthelmess, Richard. Actor. *b.* May 9, 1895, New York City. *d.* 1963. The son of an actress, and himself in amateur dramatics at Trinity College (Hartford, Conn.), he was discovered in 1916 by a friend of the family, screen star Alla NAZIMOVA. Within several years he was one of Hollywood's leading stars, the hero of several prominent D. W. Griffith productions, notably *Broken Blossoms* (1919) and *Way Down East* (1920). His first wife (1920–27), actress Mary Hay, played a minor role in the latter film. Quietly handsome, both gentle and virile (he was described by co-star Lillian Gish as having "the most beautiful face of any man who ever went before the camera"), he proved to be an ideal Griffith hero. Their collaboration seemed to benefit both the director and the actor, but in 1920, Barthelmess left Griffith to form his own production company, Inspiration, with Henry KING as director.

The new association resulted almost immediately in a film role many consider to be Barthelmess's best—a country lad in *Tol'able David* (1921). His popularity continued throughout the remainder of the silent era, and in 1927–28, the Oscar's first year, he was nominated for the best acting Academy Award for his appearances in *The Noose* and *The Patent Leather Kid.* Barthelmess remained popular in the early sound era, but his films and his roles were gradually diminishing in importance. Eventually he began playing character roles, often as the heavy. He quit films in 1942 to join the Naval Reserve, and never returned to Hollywood. He lived in prosperous retirement on Long Island until his death of cancer at 68.

FILMS: *Gloria's Romance* (serial), *War Brides, Just a Song at Twilight* 1916; *The Moral Code, The Eternal Sin, The Valentine Girl, The Soul of a Magdalen, The Streets of Illusion, Bab's Diary, Bab's Burglar, For Valour, Nearly Married, The Seven Swans* 1917; *Sunshine Nan, Rich Man Poor Man, Hit-the-Trail Holiday, Wild Primrose* 1918; *The Hope Chest, Boots, The Girl Who Stayed Home, Three Men and a Girl, Peppy Polly, Broken Blossoms, I'll Get Him Yet, Scarlet Days* 1919; *The Idol Dancer, The Love Flower, Way Down East* 1920; *Experience, Tol'able David* 1921; *The Seventh Day, Sonny, The Bond Boy, Just a Song at Twilight* 1922; *Fury, The Bright Shawl, The Fighting Blade, Twenty-One* 1923; *The Enchanted Cottage, Classmates* 1924; *New Toys, Soul-Fire, Shore Leave, The Beautiful City* 1925; *Just Suppose, Ransom's Folly, The Amateur Gentleman, The White Black Sheep* 1926; *The Patent Leather Kid, The Drop Kick* 1927; *The Noose, The Little Shepherd of Kingdom Come/Kentucky Courage, Wheel of Chance, Out of the Ruins* 1928; *Scarlet Seas, Weary River, Drag, Young Nowheres, The Show of Shows* 1929; *Son of the Gods, The Dawn Patrol, The Lash/Adios* 1930; *The Finger Points, The Last Flight* 1931; *Alias the Doctor, Cabin in the Cotton* 1932; *Central Airport, Heroes for Sale* 1933; *Massacre, A Modern Hero, Midnight Alibi* 1934; *Four Hours to Kill* 1935; *A Spy of Napoleon* (UK) 1936; *Only Angels Have Wings* 1939; *The Man Who Talked Too Much* 1940; *The Spoilers, The Mayor of 44th Street* 1942.

Bartholomew, Freddie. Actor. *b.* Frederick Llewellyn, Mar. 28, 1924, London. *d.* 1992. Curly-haired, dimpled, angelic boy star of Hollywood films. Brought up by an aunt, Millicent Bartholomew, from whom he borrowed his surname. He was on the London stage from the age of three and, later, in a couple of British films. He was visiting the US with his aunt when he was offered the title role in the film *David Copperfield* (1935). He stayed in Hollywood, to become one of the most popular child actors of the 30s and early 40s. Refined and gentle-mannered despite a humble background, he used his good breeding and excellent diction to advantage in portraying boy-hero roles in Hollywood adaptations of adventure classics. He is most readily identified with the sissy role he played in *Little Lord Fauntleroy* (1936).

In 1937 he was involved in two court fights. In one, his parents were attempting to wrest him from his aunt's guardianship; in the other, his aunt tried to have him released from his MGM contract. Both attempts failed. In 1941 his career began to decline. Experiencing a progressive shrinkage of roles, he eventually retired from films. In the early 50s he hosted a daytime TV show, was an associate director of a New York TV station, and finally became an advertising executive. In the 70s he produced the daytime soap opera 'As the World Turns' for CBS.

FILMS: In the UK—*Toyland* 1930; *Fascination, Let's Go*

Naked 1931; *Lily Christine* 1932. In the US—*David Copperfield* (title role), *Anna Karenina* (as Garbo's son) 1935; *Professional Soldier, Little Lord Fauntleroy* (title role), *The Devil Is a Sissy, Lloyds of London* 1936; *Captains Courageous* 1937; *Kidnapped, Lord Jeff, Listen Darling* 1938; *Spirit of Culver, Two Bright Boys* 1939; *The Swiss Family Robinson, Tom Brown's Schooldays* 1940; *Naval Academy* 1941; *Cadets on Parade, A Yank at Eton, Junior Army* 1942; *The Town Went Wild* 1944; *Sepia Cinderella* 1947; *St. Benny the Dip* 1951.

Bartkowiak, Andrzej. Director of photography. Born in 1950, in Lodz, Poland. Trained at the Polish Film School, he came to the US in 1972 and shortly after began working in commercials and low-budget features. Working for Sidney Lumet and other major directors, he asserted himself in the 80s as a top-level lighting cameraman.

FILMS INCLUDE: *Deadly Hero* 1976; *Prince of the City* 1981; *Deathtrap, The Verdict* 1982; *Daniel, Terms of Endearment* 1983; *Garbo Talks* 1984; *Prizzi's Honor* 1985; *Power, The Morning After* 1986; *Nuts* 1987; *Twins* 1988; *Family Business* 1989; *Q & A* 1990; *Off and Running* 1991; *Hard Promises* 1992; *Guilty as Sin* 1993; *The Devil's Advocate* 1997.

Bartlett, Bonnie. Actress. See DANIELS, William.

Bartlett, Hall. Director, producer, screenwriter. *b.* Nov. 27, 1922, in Kansas City, Mo. *d.* 1993. *ed.* Yale. After WW II service with the Navy, he became involved in film production and formed his own company in 1952. His first project, a feature-length documentary, *Navajo* (1952), won a number of awards. His later fiction films were of varying quality. At one time (1966–71) married to Rhonda FLEMING. Author: *The Rest of Our Lives.*

FILMS (as director-producer-screenwriter): *Navajo* (prod. only) 1952; *Crazylegs* (prod., sc. only) 1953; *Unchained* 1955; *Drango* (co-dir. with Jules Bricken), *Zero Hour!* (dir., sc. only) 1957; *All the Young Men* 1960; *The Caretakers* 1963; *A Global Affair* (prod. only) 1964; *Sol Madrid* (prod. only) 1968; *Changes* 1969; *The Wild Pack/Sandpit General* 1972; *Jonathan Livingston Seagull* 1973; *The Sandpit Generals* 1975; *The Children of Sanchez* 1978.

Bartlett, Richard. Director. Born in 1925. Inventive end-of-studio-era director of genre films, primarily Westerns, for Universal. His final feature, *The Gentle People and the Quiet Land*, is a documentary about the Pennsylvania Amish.

FILMS INCLUDE: *The Silent Riders* 1954; *The Silver Star, The Lonesome Trail* 1955; *Two-Gun Lady, I've Lived Before* 1956; *Rock Pretty Baby, Joe Dakota, Slim Carter* 1957; *Money, Women and Guns* 1959; *The Gentle People and the Quiet Land* 1972.

Bartlett, Sy (Sydney S.). Screenwriter, producer. *b.* Sacha Baraniev, July 10, 1909, Nikolaiev, Russia. *d.* 1978. *ed.* Northwestern. In the US from age four, he was raised in Chicago. A journalist, he went to Hollywood in the early 30s and wrote many screenplays, adaptations, and original stories, alone and in collaboration. In 1956 he formed Melville Productions in partnership with Gregory PECK and later wrote and produced films for various studios. Once married to Alice WHITE and Ellen DREW.

FILMS INCLUDE: As screenwriter—*The Big Brain* 1933; *Kansas City Princess* 1934; *Boulder Dam* 1936; *Danger Patrol* 1937; *Cocoanut Grove* 1938; *Road to Zanzibar* 1941; *Two Yanks in Trinidad* 1942; *The Princess and the Pirate* 1944; *13 Rue Madeleine* 1947; *Down to the Sea in Ships* 1949; *12 O'Clock High* 1950; *Red Beret/Paratrooper* (adapt. only; UK) 1954; *Last Command* 1955; *The Big Country* 1958; *Beloved Infidel* 1959. As producer—*Pork Chop Hill* 1959; *The Outsider, Cape Fear* 1962; *A Gathering of Eagles* 1963; *Che* (also sc.) 1969.

Bartok, Eva. Actress. Born Eva Martha Szöke, on June 18, 1926, in Kecskemet, Hungary. Was first married at the age of 15. A Budapest stage actress, she made her film debut in 1947 in the Hungarian production *The Prophet of the Fields.* Producer Alexander Paal whisked her out of Communist Hungary, brought her to London, married her, and gave her her first break in his film *A Tale of Five Cities/A Tale of Five Women* (1951). After the picture's release she divorced Paal, later marrying and divorcing publicist William Wordsworth and German actor Curt JURGENS. Her private life, studded with actual and rumored romantic adventures, is more provocative than her acting career, which has consisted mostly of roles in undistinguished films under many flags. She retired from the screen in the mid-60s and settled in Indonesia. Autobiography: *Worth Living For* (1959).

FILMS INCLUDE: *The Prophet of the Fields* (Hung.) 1947; *A Tale of Five Cities/A Tale of Five Women* (UK) 1951; *The Crimson Pirate* (US), *The Venetian Bird/The Assassin* (UK) 1952; *Der letzte Walzer/The Last Waltz* (Ger.) 1953; *Front Page Story* (UK), *Viktoria und ihr Husar* (Ger.), *Orient Express* (It./Ger.) 1954; *Special Delivery* (US), *Djunga* (Ger.), *Break in the Circle* (UK) 1955; *The Gamma People* (UK), *Ohne Dich wird es Nacht* (Ger.) 1956; *Ten Thousand Bedrooms* (US) 1957; *Madeleine* (Ger.), *Der Arzt von Stalingrad* (Ger.) 1958; *Operation Amsterdam* (UK), *SOS Pacific* (UK) 1959; *Beyond the Curtain* (UK) 1960; *Sei Donne per l'Assassino/Blood and Black Lace* (It./Ger./Fr.) 1964; *Savina* (Isr.) 1966.

Barton, Charles T. Director. *b.* May 25, 1902, near San Francisco. *d.* 1981. A former stock, vaudeville, and film performer, he became a director the hard way, starting as a prop boy for director James Cruze. He later ran errands for director William WELLMAN, who eventually made him assistant director. In 1934 the diminutive Barton (5' 2", 112 lbs.) was given his first assignment as director. His output consisted mostly of routine light fare, including several Abbott and Costello comedies. From the early 60s he directed for TV.

FILMS: *Wagon Wheels* 1934; *Car 99, Rocky Mountain Mystery, The Last Outpost* (co-dir. with Louis J. Gasnier) 1935; *Timothy's Quest, Nevada, And Sudden Death, Rose Bowl, Murder with Pictures* 1936; *The Crime Nobody Saw, Forlorn River, Thunder Trail* 1937; *Born to the West, Titans of the Deep* 1938; *Behind Prison Gates, Five Little Peppers and How They Grew* 1939; *My Son Is Guilty, Five Little Peppers at Home, Island of Doomed Men, Babies for Sale, Out West with the Peppers, Five Little Peppers in Trouble, Nobody's Children* 1940; *The Phantom Submarine, The Big Boss, Richest Man in Town, Two Latins From Manhattan, Harmon of Michigan, Sing for Your Supper, Honolulu Lu* 1941; *Shut My Big Mouth, Tramp Tramp Tramp, Hello Annapolis, Sweetheart of the Fleet, Parachute Nurse, A Man's World, Lucky Legs, Spirit of Stanford, Laugh Your Blues Away* 1942; *Reveille With Beverly, Let's Have Fun, She Has What It Takes, What's Buzzin' Cousin?, Is Everybody Happy?* 1943; *Beautiful but Broke, Hey Rookie, Jam Session, Louisiana Hayride* 1944; *The Beautiful Cheat* (also prod.), *Men in Her Diary* (also assoc. prod.) 1945; *Smooth As Silk, White Tie and Tails, The Time of Their Lives/The Ghost Steps Out* 1946; *Buck Privates Come Home, The Wistful Widow of Wagon Gap* 1947; *The Noose Hangs High* (also prod.), *Abbott and Costello Meet Frankenstein, Mexican Hayride* 1948; *Africa Screams, Abbott and Costello Meet the Killer Boris Karloff, Free for All* 1949; *The Milkman* 1950; *Double Crossbones* 1951; *Ma and Pa Kettle at the Fair* 1952; *Dance with Me Henry* 1956; *The Shaggy Dog* 1959; *Toby Tyler* 1960; *Swingin' Along* 1962.

Barty, Billy. Actor. Born on Oct. 25, 1924, in Millsboro, Pa. *ed.* L.A. City Coll.; L.A. State U. Hollywood's most enduring and endearing midget, a 3-foot 9-inch, 80-pound concentration of energy and talent. He began performing at age three, and in the late 20s and early 30s played Mickey Rooney's kid brother in the "Mickey McGuire" series of comedy shorts. In feature films from 1933, he also pursued a busy career on TV from the early days of the medium. Active in the cause of advancing the rights of persons of small stature, he founded Little People of America in 1957 and the Billy Barty Foundation in 1975.

FILMS INCLUDE: *Gold Diggers of 1933, Footlight Parade, Roman Scandals* 1933; *Gift of Gab* 1934; *A Midsummer Night's Dream* 1935; *Nothing Sacred* 1937; *Pygmy Island* 1950; *The Clown* 1953; *The Undead* 1957; *Jumbo* 1962; *Roustabout* 1964; *Harum Scarum* 1965; *Pufnstuf* 1970; *The Day of the Locust* 1975; *The Amazing Dobermans, W.C. Fields and Me* 1976; *Foul Play* 1978; *Firepower* (UK) 1979; *Hardly Working, Under the Rainbow* 1981; *Night Patrol* 1984; *Legend* 1985; *Tough Guys* 1986; *Body Slam, Rumpelstiltskin* (title role) 1987; *Willow* 1988; *Lobster Man from Mars, UHF* 1989; *The Rescuers Down Under* (voice only) 1990; *Life Stinks, Digging Up Business* 1991.

Baryshnikov, Mikhail. Dancer, Actor. Born on Jan. 27, 1948, in Riga, Latvia, the son of an engineer and a dressmaker. A star dancer with the Kirov Ballet in Leningrad, he defected to the US in 1974 and joined the American Ballet Theatre, of which he eventually became the director. In 1978–79 he danced with George Balanchine's New York City Ballet. He was nominated for an Oscar as best supporting player for his very first film, *The Turning Point,* and gave another strong performance in *White Nights,* portraying a defecting Soviet ballet star whose plane force-lands in Russia. He made his Broadway debut as a dramatic actor in 'Metamorphosis' in 1989. Baryshnikov's name has been linked romantically to several Hollywood stars, including at one time Jessica LANGE, with whom he has a daughter.

FILMS: *The Turning Point* 1977; *That's Dancing!, White Nights* (also co-choreog.) 1985; *Dancers* (also choreog., co-prod.) 1987; *Company Business, The Cabinet of Dr. Ramirez* 1991.

Barzman, Ben. Screenwriter. *b.* Oct. 19, 1911, Toronto. *d.* 1989. Reed Coll. (Phi Beta Kappa) A journalist, novelist, and author of several musical revues, he began writing Hollywood screenplays in the early 40s. But his sojourn was soon cut short by blacklisting, in the wake of the House Un-American Activities Committee hearings on the film industry. He went into self-exile in Europe, where he collaborated on the films of fellow McCarthy-era victims Joseph LOSEY, Edward DMYTRYK, and Jules DASSIN. Also collaborated on some Hollywood scripts anonymously or under various pseudonyms before resurfacing legitimately in the early 60s. In 1949 he settled in France, where he remained for 30 years. In 1982, he was honored by a retrospective at the Paris Cinématheque and in 1985 was awarded the Order of Arts and Letters by the French government. One of his novels, *Echo X* (1960) is widely admired among science-fiction lovers.

FILMS INCLUDE: In the US—*True to Life* (co-story only) 1943; *Meet the People* (co-story only) 1944; *Back to Bataan* 1945; *Never Say Goodbye* 1946; *The Boy with Green Hair* 1948. In the UK—*Give Us This Day* 1949; *Imbarco a Mezzanotte/Stranger on the Prowl* (It.) 1952; *Celui qui doit mourir/He Who Must Die* (Fr.), *Time Without Pity* 1957; *Blind Date/Chance Meeting* 1959; *The Damned* 1961; *The Ceremony* (US/Sp.) 1963; *Der Besuch/The Visit* (Ger./Fr./It./US), *The Fall of the Roman Empire* (US) 1964; *The Heroes of Telemark* 1965; *The Blue Max* 1966; *L'Attentat/The French Conspiracy* (Fr./It.) 1972; *La Tête de Normande St. Onge/Normande* (Can.) 1976.

base. A transparent celluloid material coated with sensitized emulsion that acts as a support to the photographic image on film. Originally, film base material was composed of flammable nitrate. Nonflammable cellulose derivatives, notably acetate, are now widely used.

Basehart, Richard. Actor. *b.* Aug. 31, 1914, Zanesville, Ohio. *d.* 1984. The son of a local newspaper editor, he worked as a reporter and radio announcer before opting for a stage career in 1938. He made his Broadway debut in 1943 and in 1945 won the New York Drama Critics Award for his lead role in 'The Hasty Heart.' Hollywood responded with an invitation, and Basehart made his film debut in 1947. The following year he impressed critics with his acting in *He Walked by Night.* Using his talent discriminatingly, he successfully avoided the pitfalls of Hollywood stereotyping, selecting his roles carefully and returning occasionally to the stage. His versatility was tested by frequent appearances in European film productions, highlighted by his sensitive portrayal as The Fool in Fellini's *La Strada.* Among his other memorable roles were that of a man threatening suicide in *14 Hours* and that of Ishmael in *Moby Dick.* In the 60s he starred in the TV series 'Voyage to the Bottom of the Sea.' In 1951 he married actress Valentina CORTESA. In his later years, he used his marvelous resonant voice to advantage as the off-screen narrator of many documentaries. The morning after narrating the closing ceremonies of the 1984 Los Angeles Summer Olympics, he suffered a stroke from which he never recovered.

FILMS INCLUDE: *Repeat Performance, Cry Wolf* 1947; *He Walked by Night* 1948; *Roseanna McCoy, The Black Book/Reign of Terror, Tension* 1949; *Outside the Wall* 1950; *Fourteen Hours, The House on Telegraph Hill, Fixed Bayonets* 1951; *Decision Before Dawn* 1952; *Titanic, La Mano dello Straniero/The Stranger's Hand* (It.) 1953; *Avanzi di Galera/Jailbirds* (It./US), *Le Avventure di Cartouche/Cartouche* (It.), *La Strada* (It.), *The Good Die Young* (UK) 1954; *Il Bidone/The Swindle* (It./Fr.), *La Vena d'Oro* (It.), *The Golden Touch, Canyon Crossroads* 1955; *The Intimate Stranger/A Finger of Guilt* (UK), *Moby Dick* (as Ishmael) 1956; *Arrivederci Dimas* (It./Sp.), *Time Limit* 1957; *The Brothers Karamazov* (as Ivan Karamazov) 1958; *Jons und Erdme* (Ger.), *L'Ambitieuse* (Fr.) 1959; *Jovanka e le Altre/Five Branded Women* (It./Yug.), *Portrait in Black, Visa to Canton/Passport to China* (UK) 1960; *Hitler* (title role), *The Savage Guns* 1962; *Kings of the Sun* 1963; *The Satan Bug* 1965; *Un Homme qui me plait* 1969; *Chato's Land, Rage* 1972; *Mansion of the Doomed* 1976; *The Island of Dr. Moreau, The Great Bank Hoax* 1977, *Being There* 1979.

Basevi, James. Art director, special-effects expert. Born in 1890(?), in Plymouth, England. After WW I service with the British army, during which he rose from private to colonel, he spent some time in Canada, then went to Hollywood, where he became an art director for the newly created MGM in 1924. He designed the sets for many of MGM's late silent productions, usually in collaboration with Cedric GIBBONS, and during the switch to sound took charge of the studio's special-effects department. Among many other films, he helped create the famous earthquake sequence in *San Francisco* (1936). The following year he moved over to Fox, where he created the storm sequence that was the highlight of John FORD's *The Hurricane* (1937). In 1939 he returned to his original craft as an art director and subsequently designed, alone or in collaboration, many of Fox's most prestigious productions, including several other films of John Ford. He shared an Academy Award with William Darling for the art direction of *The Song of Bernadette* (1943).

FILMS INCLUDE (as art director, alone or in collaboration): *Confessions of a Queen, Fine Clothes* (color consultant only), *The Tower of Lies, The Big Parade, The Circle* 1925; *Dance Madness, The Temptress* 1926; *Wuthering Heights* 1939; *The Long Voyage Home* 1940; *Tobacco Road* 1941; *The Ox-Bow Incident, Heaven Can Wait, The Song of Bernadette* 1943; *Jane Eyre, The Lodger, The Purple Heart, The Sullivans* 1944; *The Keys of the Kingdom, Wilson* 1945; *Claudia and David, My Darling Clementine* 1946; *Captain From Castile, The Late George Apley* 1947; *Duel in the Sun, Fort Apache* 1948; *Three Godfathers, She Wore a Yellow Ribbon* 1949; *Wagonmaster* 1950; *Across the Wide Missouri, The People Against O'Hara* 1951; *Battle Circus, Island in the Sky* 1953; *East of Eden* 1955.

basher. A small, versatile studio lamp that can be used either as a floodlight or a spotlight. It can be held in the hand or mounted in a fixed position.

Basinger, Kim. Actress. Born on Dec. 8, 1953, in Athens, Ga. *ed.* Neighborhood Playhouse. Sensual, full-lipped, gorgeous blonde star of Hollywood films of the 80s. The daughter of a financier and a former model, she took up dancing at age two and later pursued singing, using the alias Chelsea. At 17, she left her hometown for New York, where she studied drama and posed for *Playboy.* She then began modeling and soon reached the top echelons of that profession. In 1977 she began appearing in TV series and movies, including a plum role in the small-screen version of *From Here to Eternity.* She made her feature debut in 1981 and thanks to her stunning good looks and some convincing performances rapidly soared to stardom. A vegetarian and environmentalist, she made headlines in 1989 when she bought an entire town in Georgia not far from her birthplace. She also appeared in the news when she lost a multimillion dollar lawsuit filed against her for backing out of an agreement to star in the controversial *Boxing Helena*, the story of a woman whose limbs are amputated by her love-obsessed captor. Married actor Alec BALDWIN, with whom she appeared in *The Marrying Man* and *The Getaway*.

FILMS: *Hard Country* 1981; *Mother Lode* 1982; *Never Say Never Again, The Man Who Loved Women* 1983; *The Natural* 1984; *Fool for Love* 1985; *9½ Weeks, No Mercy* 1986; *Blind Date, Nadine* 1987; *My Stepmother Is an Alien* 1988; *Batman* 1989; *The Marrying Man* 1991; *Final Analysis, Cool World* 1992; *The Getaway, Ready to Wear* 1994.

Basquette, Lina. Actress, dancer. Born Lena Baskette, on Apr. 19, 1907, in San Mateo, Calif. The stepdaughter of dance instructor Ernest Belcher and half sister of actress-dancer Marge CHAMPION. As a child ballerina, she was featured in the 1915 San Francisco World's Fair, then was signed by Universal to star in a series of shorts, the "Lena Baskette Featurettes," and to play child roles in feature films. She left the screen to concentrate on ballet and by age 16 was the *première danseuse* of the 'Ziegfeld Follies' (1923 edition). A sultry beauty, she gave up dancing to re-enter films in 1927, under the modified name Lina Basquette. But her screen career suffered from the entanglements of her marriage to Sam Warner, the "elder statesman" of the Warner Brothers family, in 1925. His death in 1927 was followed by court battles between herself and the Warners over his huge estate and the custody of their child. As a result of the strain, she attempted suicide several times.

This was the first of her six successive husbands, which were to include cameraman J. Peverell MARLEY and boxer Jack Dempsey's trainer. Her most important screen role was the lead in De Mille's *The Godless Girl* (1929). But most of her subsequent films were minor, including Buck Jones and Hoot Gibson Westerns. By the late 30s she was reduced to bit roles, and she soon retired. In 1943 a GI was sentenced to 20 years for raping her. She now lives in Pennsylvania, where she breeds championship Great Danes.

FILMS INCLUDE: *Shoes* 1916; *The Gates of Doom* 1917; *The Weaker Vessel* 1919; *Penrod* 1922; *Ranger of the North, Serenade* 1927; *The Noose, Wheel of Chance, Celebrity, Show Folks* 1928; *The Younger Generation, The Godless Girl, Come Across* 1929; *The Dude Wrangler* 1930; *Hard Hombre, The Arizona Terror, Goldie, Morals for Women* 1931; *Hello Trouble, The Midnight Lady, Phantom Express* 1932; *The Final Hour* 1936; *Ebb Tide* 1937; *The Buccaneer, Four Men and a Prayer* 1938; *A Night for Crime* 1943.

Bass, Saul. Animator, graphic designer, director. *b.* May 8, 1920, in New York City. *d.* 1996. *ed.* Art Students League; Brooklyn Coll. Worked for ten years as a freelance designer. In 1946 formed Saul Bass & Associates, Inc., in Los Angeles, through which he later revolutionized the style of feature film credits by introducing imaginatively drawn animation to replace the conventional listing of names in titles. His animated titles often suggest the theme and the mood of a film, functioning more like a prologue and epilogue rather than a mere cluttered printed foreword. Bass has also produced and directed TV commercials, animated shorts, and live documentaries, notably *The Searching Eye* (1963), *From Here to There* (1964), *Why Man Creates* (Academy Award, 1968), and *Phase IV* (1974).

FILM TITLE DESIGNS INCLUDE: *Carmen Jones, The Big Knife, The Seven Year Itch* 1955; *Saint Joan, The Man with the Golden Arm, Johnny Concho, Around the World in 80 Days* 1956; *The Pride and the Passion* 1957; *Cowboy, Bonjour Tristesse, Vertigo, The Big Country* 1958; *Anatomy of a Murder, North by Northwest* 1959; *Psycho, Ocean's 11, Exodus, Spartacus* 1960; *West Side Story* 1961; *Walk on the Wild Side, Advise and Consent* 1962; *Nine Hours to Rama, The Cardinal, It's a Mad Mad Mad Mad World* 1963; *Bunny Lake Is Missing* 1965; *Seconds, Grand Prix* 1966; *Broadcast News* 1987; *Big* 1988; *The War of the Roses* 1989; *GoodFellas* 1990; *Cape Fear* 1991; *The Age of Innocence* 1993.

Basserman(n), Albert. Actor. *b.* Sept. 7, 1867, Mannheim, Germany. *d.* 1952 in an air crash over the Atlantic. Studied chemistry but was drawn to the stage, working with the theater of Max REINHARDT between 1909 and 1915. Made his film debut in the German film *Der Andere* (1913), a variation of the Dr. Jekyll and Mr. Hyde story. He had achieved great prominence on the German stage and screen before being forced to flee the Nazi regime to Switzerland in 1933. In 1939 he arrived in Hollywood and played in a succession of character roles, typically as a wise, well-educated elderly European gentleman. He was nominated for an Academy Award for his supporting role in *Foreign Correspondent* (1940). In the late 40s he returned to Europe, where he spent his final years. His wife, Elsa, also appeared in some of his films.

FILMS INCLUDE: In Germany—*Der Andere, Der König* 1913; *Das Weib des Pharao/Loves of Pharaoh* 1921; *Lukrezia Borgia/Lucrecia Borgia* 1922; *Erdgeist/Earth Spirit* 1923; *Fräulein Else* 1929; *Dreyfus/The Dreyfus Case, Alraune* 1930; *Kadetten, 1914: Die letzte Tage vor dem Weltbrand/1914: The Last Days Before the War, Voruntersuchung/Inquest* 1931; *Ein gewisser Herr Gran* 1933; In France—*Le Héros de la Marne/Heroes of the Marne* 1938. In the US—*Dr. Ehrlich's Magic Bullet, Foreign Correspondent, Escape, A Dispatch From Reuters* 1940; *The Great Awakening/Captain of Koepenick, A Woman's Face, The Shanghai Gesture* 1941; *New Wine, Invisible Agent, Desperate Journey, The Moon and Sixpence, Once Upon a Honeymoon* 1942; *Reunion in France, Madame Curie* 1943; *Since You Went Away* 1944; *Rhapsody in Blue, The Searching Wind* 1946; *The Private Affairs of Bel Ami, Escape Me Never* 1947. In the UK—*The Red Shoes* 1948.

Bassett, Angela. Actress. Powerful, theatrically trained actress with a commanding yet endearing screen presence. She made a lasting impression on critics and audiences alike with her Oscar nominated performance as Tina Turner in the film biography *What's Love Got to Do With It*.

FILMS INCLUDE *Boyz N the Hood* 1991; *Malcolm X* (as Betty Shabazz) 1992; *What's Love Got to Do with It* 1993; *Strange Days, Vampire in Brooklyn, Waiting to Exhale* 1995; *Contact* 1997.

Batalov, Alexei. Actor, director. Born in 1928, in Vladimir, Russia. The nephew of veteran stage and screen actor Nikolai Batalov (1898–1937), he studied drama at the Moscow Art Theater School and performed with the Soviet Army Theater (1950–53), then with the Moscow Art Theater (1953–56). He was discovered by Soviet film director Josef HEIFITZ, who gave him a leading role in *A Big Family* (1954) and others of his films. In 1956 he played the same role in Donskoy's *Mother/1905* that his uncle had played in the Pudovkin version of 1926. Batalov's frank face and innocent smile made him an ideal incarnation of positive Soviet youth in many films. His strong performance in *The Cranes Are Flying* (1957) brought him international acclaim. He was named People's Artist of the USSR in 1976, then was appointed professor at the Film Actors Workshop at the Moscow Film Institute. He also directed occasionally.

FILMS INCLUDE (as actor): *Zoya* (bit), *A Big Family* 1954; *Mother/1905, The Rumiantsev Case* 1956; *The Cranes Are Flying* 1957; *My Beloved* 1958; *The Overcoat* (also dir.), *The Lady with the Dog* 1960; *Nine Days in One Year* 1962; *A Day of Happiness* 1963; *The Light of a Distant Star* 1965; *Three Fat Men* (also co-dir.) 1966; *The Living Corpse* 1969; *The Flight* 1971; *Igork* (dir. only) 1972; *A Very English Murder, Riki-Tiki-Tavi* 1973; *No Return* 1974; *Moscow Does Not Believe in Tears* 1980; *O Lyudiakh Atomakh* 1983.

Batchelor, Joy. Animator, producer. *b.* May 12, 1914, Watford, England. *d.* 1991. After art studies, she entered films in 1935 as a commercial artist. While working on the cartoon *Music Man* (1936) in a British studio, she met the Hungarian animator John HALAS. They married and in 1940 founded their own company, Halas-Batchelor Cartoon Films. During the war they made many information and propaganda cartoons for the British government and later produced hundreds of cartoons, commercials, and industrial, scientific, and promotional films. They produced the only feature-length British cartoon, *Animal Farm* (1954), which took three years to make. The work of their successful animation studio in Britain has been widely represented in international film festivals, winning many prizes and awards.

FILMS INCLUDE: *The Pocket Cartoon* 1941; *Handling Ships* 1945; *Robinson Charley* 1948; *Magic Canvas* 1951; *The Owl and the Pussycat* 1953; *Animal Farm* 1954; *History of the Cinema* 1956; *All Lit Up* 1957; *Dam the Delta* 1960; *For Better for Worse* 1961; *Automania 2000* 1963; *Ruddigore* 1966; *What Is a Computer?* 1970; and several cartoon series.

batch number. The serial number stamped by the manufacturer on packages of negative film to indicate that their emulsion was prepared at a single time. All negative film treated with the same emulsion mixture is said to be of one batch. Since each emulsion batch has distinct characteristics, care is taken by professional filmmakers to shoot all scenes in one sequence with stock of the same batch to avoid possible variations in emulsion speed, color sensitivity, etc.

Bates, Alan. Actor. Born on Feb. 17, 1934, in Allestree, Derbyshire, England. *ed.* RADA. Assertive, versatile leading man of stage and screen. Especially adept at offbeat roles. He made his stage debut in 1955, following service with the RAF. Has since appeared prominently on the London stage and Broadway as well as in a good number of films on either side of the Atlantic. He was nominated for a best actor Oscar for his performance in *The Fixer* (1968).

FILMS: *The Entertainer* 1960; *Whistle Down the Wind* 1961; *A Kind of Loving* 1962; *The Running Man* 1963; *The Caretaker/The Guest, Nothing but the Best* 1964; *Zorba the Greek* (US/Gr.) 1965; *Georgy Girl, Le Roi de Coeur/King of Hearts* (Fr./It.) 1966; *Far from the Madding Crowd* 1967; *The Fixer* (US) 1968; *Women in Love, Three Sisters* 1970; *The Go-Between* 1971; *A Day in the Death of Joe Egg* 1972; *L'Impossible Objet/The Impossible Object/Story of a Love Story* (Fr./UK) 1973; *Butley* 1974; *In Celebration, Royal Flash* 1975; *An Unmarried Woman* (US), *The Shout* 1978; *The Rose* (US) 1979; *Nijinsky* (as Sergei Diaghilev) 1980; *Quartet* 1981; *The Return of the Soldier, Britannia Hospital* 1982; *The Wicked Lady* 1983; *Duet for One* 1986; *A Prayer for the Dying* 1987; *We Think the World of You* 1988; *Force Majeure* (Fr.) 1989; *Mister Frost* (Fr./UK), *102 Boulevard Haussmann* (as Marcel Proust), *Hamlet* (as Claudius), *Docteur M./Club Extinction* 1990; *Secret Friends* (US/UK) 1992; *Silent Tongue* 1994; *Gentlemen Don't Eat Poets* 1997.

Bates, Barbara. Actress. *b.* Aug. 6, 1925, Denver. *d.* 1969. She was a ballet dancer and a model before her film debut in *Salome Where She Danced* (1945). Played supporting ingenue roles in A pictures and lead roles in B pictures before retiring in the late 50s. Her career hampered by ill health, she committed suicide by asphyxiation at age 43.

FILMS INCLUDE: *Salome Where She Danced, Lady on a Train, Strange Holiday, This Love of Ours* 1945; *A Night in Paradise* 1946; *Johnny Belinda, June Bride* 1948; *Adventures of Don Juan, The House Across the Street, The Inspector General* 1949; *Cheaper by the Dozen, Quicksand, All About Eve* 1950; *I'd Climb the Highest Mountain, The Secret of Convict Lake* 1951; *Belles on Their Toes, The Outcasts of Poker Flat* 1952; *The Caddy* 1953; *Rhapsody* 1954; *House of Secrets/Triple Deception* (UK), *Town on Trial* (UK) 1957; *Apache Territory* 1958.

Bates, Florence. Actress. *b.* Florence Rabe, Apr. 15, 1888, San Antonio, Tex. *d.* 1954. A lawyer and businesswoman, she became irresistibly attracted to acting and at the age of 47 enrolled at the Pasadena Playhouse school. She was a minor player on stage and in films when Hitchcock chose her to portray a key character role in *Rebecca* (1940), as the domineering employer of Joan Fontaine. She went on to play character parts in many other films, typically as a strong-willed dowager.

FILMS INCLUDE: *The Man in Blue* 1937; *Rebecca, Kitty Foyle* 1940; *The Devil and Miss Jones, The Chocolate Soldier* 1941; *We Were Dancing, The Moon and Sixpence* 1942; *They Got Me Covered, Heaven Can Wait, His Butler's Sister* 1943; *The Mask of Dimitrios, Since You Went Away, Kismet* 1944; *Tonight and Every Night, Saratoga Trunk* 1945; *Cluny Brown, The Diary of a Chambermaid, Claudia and David* 1946; *The Secret Life of Walter Mitty* 1947; *I Remember Mama, Winter Meeting* 1948; *A Letter to Three Wives, Portrait of Jennie, On the Town* 1949; *Lullaby of Broadway* 1951; *Les Miserables* 1952; *Main Street to Broadway* 1953.

Bates, Kathy. Actress. Born Kathleen Bates on June 28, 1948, in Memphis, Tenn. *ed.* Southern Methodist U. Intense, sympathetic star of stage and screen. Daughter of a foundry engineer and a housewife, she moved to New York to act in the early 70s and worked various odd jobs, including a singing waitress in the Catskills. She made her film debut in 1971 in *Taking Off* and her off-Broadway debut in 1976 in 'Vanities.' She came to prominence as a stage actress in 1983 with a Tony nomination as the suicidal daughter in ''night, Mother.' An Obie award for 'Frankie and Johnny in the Clair de Lune' followed in 1987. Her film roles were minor until Rob Reiner cast her as the psychopathic "Number One Fan" Annie Wilkes in *Misery* (1990), for which she won a best actress Academy Award. Since then, serio-comic roles in *Fried Green Tomatoes* (1991) and *Used People* (1992), among other films, have demonstrated her emotional range and versatility.

FILMS: *Taking Off* 1971; *Straight Time* 1978; *Come Back to the Five and Dime Jimmy Dean Jimmy Dean* 1982; *Two of a Kind* 1983; *Summer Heat* 1987; *My Best Friend Is a Vampire, Arthur 2: On the Rocks* 1988; *Signs of Life, High Stakes/Melanie Rose* 1989; *Men Don't Leave, Dick Tracy, White Palace, Misery* 1990; *At Play in the Fields of the Lord, Fried Green Tomatoes* 1991; *Shadows and Fog, Prelude to a Kiss, Used People* 1992; *A Home of Our Own* 1993; *Curse of the Starving Class, North* 1994; *Angus, Dolores Claiborne* 1995; *Diabolique, The War at Home* 1996.

bath. 1. A chemical solution in which film is immersed during processing. 2. The container in which these chemical solutions are placed.

Bathing Beauties. "Beautiful but dumb" beach belles used by Mack Sennett from 1916 to the early 20s as "sexy relief" from the crazy antics of his slapstick comedians. Over the years they numbered more than a hundred, and most of them slipped into oblivion. But some of these leggy girls became successful leading ladies in feature films, including Phyllis Haver, Marie Prevost, Marion (Marian) Nixon, Olive Borden, Juanita Hansen, Julia Faye, and Carole Lombard. One of them, Irene Lentz, became a top costume designer at MGM.

batteries. On outdoor locations, batteries are necessary as a power source for professional motion picture cameras and sound-recording equipment. Although modern transistorized sound recorders can operate for many hours with one small, self-contained battery, cameras and lighting equipment require large-capacity batteries.

Three types of batteries are used in motion picture production: the wet-cell battery, which has the advantage of being rechargeable but is too bulky to carry on remote expeditions; the nonrechargeable dry-cell battery, which is highly portable but has limited life; and the nickel-cadmium battery, which has long life, is resistant to high and low temperatures, and requires a minimum of maintenance.

Bauer, Yevgeni. Director. *b.* 1880(?), Russia. *d.* 1917 following an accident while scouting locations in the Crimea. A painter, he entered films in 1913 as set designer and director for the Pathé and Drankov studios in Moscow. One of the first Russian artists to devote his talents exclusively to the cinema, Bauer soon distinguished himself as one of the foremost directors of the czarist era. Given a free hand by producer Alexander Khanzhonkov, he directed many contemporary dramas that were to exert a lasting influence on the Soviet cinema. He made a star of Vera Kholodnaya and formed the acting style of the great Ivan Mozhukhin. In only four years of activity, he directed some 60 films.

FILMS INCLUDE: *K the Hunchback, Bloody Glory, Guilty Passion* 1913; *Freed Bird, Child of the Big City, Tears, Life in Death, Silent Witnesses, Armor of Death* 1914; *Song of Triumphant Love, Singed Wings, Children of the Century, Nation's Dignity, Resurrection, Irina Kirsanova* 1915; *Queen of the Screen, A Life for a Life, Griffon of an Old Warrior, Nina, Broken Chains, The Mysterious World* 1916; *The Alarm, Toward Happiness, The Lie, Puppet of Destiny, The Revolutionary, Death of a Swan, The King of Paris* 1917.

Baur, Harry. Actor. *b.* Apr. 12, 1880, Montrouge, France. *d.* 1943. A lion of the French cinema throughout the 30s, he began his acting career on the Paris stage in 1904. Except for occasional appearances in silent films, he was active mainly in the theater until the advent of sound. He then imposed his strong personality on many diverse roles, becoming one of the dominant actors of the European cinema of the era. Among his best remembered portrayals are those in *Samson, Les Misérables* (as Jean Valjean), *Un Grand Amour de Beethoven/The Life and Loves of Beethoven* (as the composer), *Crime et Châtiment/Crime and Punishment, Taras Boulba,* and *Volpone.* In 1942, Baur's Jewish wife was arrested in Paris. Baur himself was arrested in Berlin on charges of being an Allied agent. He was later sent to a French prison, where he was tortured by the Gestapo. In April 1943, several days after his release, he died mysteriously.

FILMS INCLUDE: *Shylock* (title role) 1910; *L'Ame du Bronze* 1918; *La Voyante* 1923; *David Golder, Les Cinq Gentlemen maudits, Le Juif polonais* 1931; *Criminel, Poil de Carotte* 1932; *La Tête d'un Homme, Le Trois Mousquetaires/The Three Musketeers, Cette Vieille Canaille* 1933; *Rothschild* (title role), *Les Misérables* (as Jean Valjean), *Les Nuits moscovites/Moscow Nights* 1934; *Moscow Nights/I Stand Condemned* (UK), *Golgotha, Crime et Châtiment/Crime and Punishment, Les Yeux noirs/Dark Eyes* 1935; *Samson, Le Golem/The Golem* (as Rudolph II, Emperor of Prague), *Paris, Nitchevo, Taras Boulba, Un Grand Amour de Beethoven/The Life and Loves of Beethoven* (as the composer), *Les Hommes nouveaux* 1936; *Un Carnet de Bal, Nostalgie/The Postmaster's Daughter, Les Secrets de la Mer rouge* 1937; *La Tragédie impériale/Rasputin* (as Rasputin), *Mollenard/Hatred, Le Patriote/The Mad Emperor* (as Russian Emperor Paul I) 1938; *L'Homme du Niger/Forbidden Love* 1940; *Volpone* (title role; release delayed from 1939), *L'Assassinat du Père Noël/Who Killed Santa Claus?, Péchés de Jeunesse* 1941; *Symphonie eines Lebens* (Aus./Ger.) 1942.

Bava, Mario. Director, director of photography. *b.* July 31, 1914, San Remo, Italy. *d.* 1980. The son of a sculptor, he entered Italian films as assistant cameraman, graduating to full cinematographer in the late 30s. While working for such directors as Monicelli, Soldati, Camerini, and Freda, he began directing shorts on his own. In 1959 he did some directing on *La Battaglia di Maratona/The Giant of Marathon,* but received credit only as director of photography. The following year he directed his first solo feature, and for a while he continued to do his own photography. Although his output consisted mainly of muscle epics and not-too-profound horror and science fiction films, he has become a cult figure among some critics who admire his visual style and his tongue-in-cheek exaggeration of the clichés of these genres. He often collaborated on his own scripts and sometimes hid behind pseudonyms, such as John M. Old or John Foam. His son, Lamberto Bava, is also a film director, specializing in stylish horror.

FEATURE FILMS (as director): *La Maschera del Demonio/Black Sunday* (also co-sc., co-phot.), *Gli Invasori/Erik the Conqueror/Fury of the Vikings* (also co-sc., co-phot.), *Ercole al Centro della Terra/Hercules in the Haunted World* (also co-sc., phot.) 1961; *Le Meraviglie di Aladino/The Wonders of Aladdin* (2nd-unit dir. only) 1962; *La Ragazza che Sapeva Troppo/Evil Eye* (also co-story, co-sc., phot.), *La Frusta e il Corpo/Night Is the Phantom/What!, I Tre Volti della Paura/Black Sabbath* (also co-sc.) 1963; *Sei Donne per l'Assassino/Blood and Black Lace* (also co-sc.) 1964; *La Strada per Fort Alamo/The Road to Fort Alamo, Terrore nello Spazio/Planet of the Vampires/Planet of Blood* (also co-sc.) 1965; *Operazione Paura/Kill Baby Kill* (also co-sc.), *Dr. Goldfoot and the Girl*

Bombs/Le Spie Vengono dal Semifreddo (US/It.) 1966; *I Coltelli del Vendicatore/Raffica di Coltelli/ Knives of the Avenger* (also co-sc.) 1967; *Diabolik/Danger: Diabolik* (also co-sc.) 1968; *Roy Colt e Winchester Jack, Il Rosso Segno della Follia/Un'Accetta per la Luna di Miele/Hatchet for a Honeymoon* (also co-sc., phot.) 1970; *Antefatto* (also sc., phot.) 1971; *Gli Orrori del Castello de Norimberga/Baron Blood* 1972; *Reazione a Catena, Quante Volte... Quella Notte/Four Times That Night* 1973; *Il Diavolo e il Morto* 1974; *Moses* (special effects only; UK/It.) 1976; *Shock, Baby Kong* 1977; *La Venere dell'Ille* 1979.

Baxter, Alan. Actor. *b.* Nov. 19, 1908, in East Cleveland, Ohio. *d.* 1976. *ed.* Williams Coll.; Yale (drama). After three years of professional stage experience, he made his Hollywood debut in 1935. Played leads in B pictures and supporting roles in better-quality productions. He eventually matured into character parts.

FILMS INCLUDE: *Mary Burns Fugitive* 1935; *The Trail of the Lonesome Pine, Big Brown Eyes, Parole* 1936; *The Last Gangster* 1937; *Gangs of New York* 1938; *Let Us Live, Each Dawn I Die, My Son Is a Criminal* 1939; *The Lone Wolf Strikes, Abe Lincoln in Illinois, Santa Fe Trail* 1940; *Bad Men of Missouri* (as Jesse James), *Shadow of the Thin Man, Rags to Riches* 1941; *Saboteur, Prisoner of Japan* 1942; *The Human Comedy, Behind Prison Walls* 1943; *Winged Victory* 1944; *The Prairie* 1947; *Close-Up* 1948; *The Set-Up* 1949; *The True Story of Jesse James* 1957; *The Restless Years* 1958; *The Mountain Road* 1960; *Judgment at Nuremberg* 1961; *This Property Is Condemned* 1966; *Welcome to Hard Times* 1967; *Paint Your Wagon* 1969; *Chisum* 1970; *Willard* 1971.

Baxter, Anne. Actress. *b.* May 7, 1923, Michigan City, Ind. *d.* 1985. The granddaughter of architect Frank Lloyd Wright, she was raised in Bronxville, N.Y., and attended private schools in New York City. She was only 11 when she took up acting with Maria OUSPENSKAYA and 13 when she made her Broadway debut in 'Seen but Not Heard.' Subsequent Broadway roles eventually led to a screen debut in 1940. A competent actress, she relied on natural charm more than on physical beauty to construct a career studded with interesting but only occasionally outstanding performances. She won a best supporting actress Oscar for *The Razor's Edge* (1946) and was nominated for another Academy Award for her portrayal of the ambitious, scheming young actress in *All About Eve* (1950). She worked for some of Hollywood's most illustrious directors, like Welles, Wilder, Milestone, Wellman, Hitchcock, Lang, and Mankiewicz, but her roles after the mid-50s were for the most part unrewarding. She was at one time (1946–53) married to John HODIAK. In 1961, she turned her back on the glamour of Hollywood and with her second husband (1960–68), Randolph Galt, went to live for several years on a cattle station in the Australian outback in primitive, isolated conditions. She told of the experience, the radical change in her life, and her final disillusionment, in *Intermission: A True Story* (1976), a book that met with high critical acclaim. In 1971 she took over from Lauren Bacall the role of Margo Channing in the Broadway production of 'Applause,' a musical based on *All About Eve.* Ironically, Baxter, who had played Eve in the film, was now portraying her rival, the established star represented on the screen by Bette Davis. The paths of the two stars seemed destined to cross once more. In 1983, Baxter replaced an ailing Davis in the TV series 'Hotel.' She stayed with the show until her death of a stroke at 62.

FILMS: *Twenty-Mule Team, The Great Profile* 1940; *Charley's Aunt, Swamp Water* 1941; *The Magnificent Ambersons, The Pied Piper* 1942; *Crash Dive, Five Graves to Cairo, The North Star/Armored Attack* 1943; *The Sullivans, The Eve of St. Mark, Guest in the House, Sunday Dinner for a Soldier* 1944; *A Royal Scandal* 1945; *Smoky, Angel on My Shoulder, The Razor's Edge* 1946; *Mother Wore Tights* (off-screen narrator), *Blaze of Noon* 1947; *Homecoming, The Walls of Jericho, The Luck of the Irish* 1948; *Yellow Sky, You're My Everything* 1949; *A Ticket to Tomahawk, All About Eve* 1950; *Follow the Sun* 1951; *The Outcasts of Poker Flat, My Wife's Best Friend, O. Henry's Full House* 1952; *I Confess, The Blue Gardenia* 1953; *Carnival Story* 1954; *Bedevilled, One Desire* 1955; *The Spoilers, The Come-on, The Ten Commandments* 1956; *Three Violent People* 1957; *Chase a Crooked Shadow* (UK) 1958; *Summer of the Seventeenth Doll/Season of Passion* (Austral./UK) 1959; *Cimarron* 1960; *Mix Me a Person* (UK), *Walk on the Wild Side* 1962; *The Family Jewels* (cameo) 1965; *Las Siete Magnificas/The Tall Women* (Sp./It./Aus.) 1966; *The Busy Body* 1967; *Fool's Parade, The Late Liz* 1971; *Little Mo* (orig. for TV) 1978; *Jane Austen in Manhattan* 1980.

Baxter, Jane. Actress. Born Feodora Forde, on Sept. 9, 1909, in Germany, to an English father and German mother. On the London stage from 1925, she played genteel leads in many British and some Hollywood films of the 30s.

FILMS INCLUDE: *Bed and Breakfast* 1930; *Down River* 1931; *Two White Arms* 1932; *The Constant Nymph* 1933; *We Live Again* (US), *Blossom Time, April Romance* 1934; *Enchanted April* (US), *The Clairvoyant, Royal Cavalcade* 1935; *The Man Behind the Mask* 1936; *The Ware Case* 1938; *Murder Will Out* 1939; *The Chinese Bungalow, The Chinese Den* 1940; *Ships with Wings* 1941; *The Flemish Farm* 1943; *Death of an Angel* 1952. *All Hallowe'en* (short) 1953.

Baxter, John. Director, producer. Born in 1896 in Foots Cray, Kent, England. A theater manager before entering films as an assistant director in 1932. In 1933 he became a director, and later producer-director, mostly of "quota quickies," the term for inexpensive films turned out in a rush to take advantage of British government subsidies to the national industry. Some of his films, however, like *Love on the Dole* (1941), were poetic although technically indifferent. They are noted for their warmth and sentiment. He also produced many films that he did not direct.

FILMS INCLUDE (as director): *Doss House, Song of the Plough* 1933; *Lest We Forget, Say It With Flowers, Music Hall, Floodtide* 1934; *The Small Man* 1935; *Men of Yesterday, Hearts of Humanity* 1936; *Song of the Road* 1937; *Secret Journey* 1939; *Old Mother Riley in Society, Crooks Tour* 1940; *Love on the Dole, The Common Touch* 1941; *Let the People Sing* 1942; *The Shipbuilders* 1943; *Dreaming* 1944; *The Grand Escapade* 1946; *Three Bags Full* 1948; *The Dragon of Pendragon Castle* 1950; *Judgment Deferred* 1952; *Ramsbottom Rides Again* 1956.

Baxter, Warner. Actor. *b.* Mar. 29, 1891, Columbus, Ohio. *d.* 1951. Raised in San Francisco by his widowed mother, he dropped out of high school to work as an office boy and later a salesman. Drawn to acting, he joined a stock company and quickly advanced from juvenile to leading man. He broke into films during WW I and played a variety of routine leads for the remainder of the silent era. His big break came with his very first sound film, *In Old Arizona* (1929), in which he portrayed the happy-go-lucky Mexican bandit Cisco Kid, a role for which he won the Academy Award and which he was to repeat twice in subsequent films. Ironically, he had been assigned to the role by default, following a car accident in which the intended star, actor-director Raoul Walsh, had lost an eye. Dashingly handsome and a competent actor with a resonant voice, Baxter was a popular romantic leading man throughout the 30s. Early in the 40s he suffered a nervous breakdown but continued playing leads in low-budget films, including the "Crime Doctor" detective series. He died of pneumonia following a lobotomy performed to relieve him of an arthritic condition. His second wife was screen actress Winifred Bryson.

FILMS INCLUDE: *Her Own Money* 1914; *All Woman* 1918; *Lombardi Ltd.* 1919; *The Love Charm, Cheated Hearts, First Love* 1921; *If I Were Queen* 1922; *In Search of a Thrill* 1923; *Alimony, Those Who Dance, The Female, The Garden of Weeds* 1924; *The Golden Bed, The Air Mail, The Awful Truth, A Son of His Father* 1925; *Mannequin, Miss Brewster's Millions, The Runaway, Aloma of the South Seas, The Great Gatsby* 1926; *The Coward, Drums of the Desert, Singed* 1927; *Tragedy of Youth, Three Sinners, Ramona, Craig's Wife, West of Zanzibar* 1928; *In Old Arizona, Thru Different Eyes, Romance of the Rio Grande* 1929; *Happy Days, The Arizona Kid, Renegades* 1930; *Doctors' Wives, Daddy Long Legs, The Squaw Man, The Cisco Kid, Surrender* 1931; *Man About Town, Six Hours to Live* 1932; *42nd Street, Penthouse* 1933; *Stand Up and Cheer, Broadway Bill* 1934; *One More Spring, Under the Pampas Moon, King of Burlesque* 1935; *The Prisoner of Shark Island, Robin Hood of El Dorado, The Road to Glory, White Hunter* 1936; *Slave Ship, Vogues of 1938, Wife Doctor and Nurse* 1937; *Kidnapped, I'll Give a Million* 1938; *The Return of the Cisco Kid, Barricade* 1939; *Earthbound* 1940; *Adam Had Four Sons* 1941; *Crime Doctor* 1943; *Lady in the Dark* 1944; *Just Before Dawn* 1946; *Prison Warden* 1949; *State Penitentiary* 1950.

Baye, Nathalie. Actress. Born on July 6, 1948, in Mainneville, France. Trained as a dancer, she came to New York at 17 to study classical ballet and modern dance, then toured the US with a dance company. Returning to France, she decided to take up acting and studied drama at the Paris Conservatory. She began appearing in films immediately after her 1972 graduation and for nearly two decades remained one of France's leading screen performers, an actress of intelligence, maturity, and wide range. She won César Awards as best actress for *Sauve qui peut (La Vie)* (1979) and *La Balance* (1982).

FILMS INCLUDE: *Two People* (bit; US), *La Nuit américaine/Day for Night* 1973; *La Gueule ouverte, La Gifle/The Slap* 1974; *La Jalousie* 1975; *Mado* 1976; *L'Homme qui aimait les Femmes/The Man Who Loved Women, Monsieur Papa* 1977; *La Chambre verte/The Green Room, Mon Premier Amour* 1978; *Sauve qui peut (La Vie)/Every Man for Himself/Slow Motion* 1979; *Une Semaine de Vacances/A Week's Vacation, La Provinciale/A Girl From Lorraine* 1980; *Beau-Père, Une Etrange Affaire, L'Ombre rouge* 1981; *Le Retour de Martin Guerre/The Return of Martin Guerre, La Balance* 1982; *Ja'i épousé une Ombre/I Married a Shadow* 1983; *Détective, Rive Droite Rive Gauche* 1984; *Le Neveu de Beethoven/Beethoven's Nephew* 1985; *Honeymoon* (US) 1987; *La Baule—Les Pins, Un Weekend Sur Deux/Every Other Weekend, Giocodi Massacro, The Man Inside* (US) 1990; *La Voix* 1992; *The Lie* 1993; *Arabian Knight* 1995.

Bayne, Beverly. Actress. *b.* Nov. 11, 1894, Minneapolis. *d.* 1982. Popular leading lady of Hollywood silents. She began her career with Essanay in Chicago, where she was soon teamed with one of the studio's leading stars, Francis X. BUSHMAN. They formed the first important love team of American films, the initiators of a tradition that was followed by such screen romantic partnerships as Ronald Colman and Vilma Banky, Charles Farrell and Janet Gaynor, and John Gilbert and Greta Garbo. Bayne and Bushman appeared in many films together, reaching a peak of popularity during 1916–18 at Metro. They were married in 1918 but kept their marriage a secret for fear of dampening fan interest in their on-screen love scenes. Their divorce in 1924 and the resultant dissolution of their screen partnership meant the end of Miss Bayne's starring career. In the early 30s she tried a comeback in films but finally retired from the medium in 1935. She continued acting in vaudeville and on the legitimate stage for another decade but gave up acting altogether in the late 40s and retired to Arizona.

FILMS INCLUDE: *The Loan Shark, A Good Catch, The Snare, Billy McGrath's Love Letters, The Magic Wand, The Penitent* 1912; *The Power of Conscience, Dear Old Girl, The Toll of the Marshes, The Stigma* 1913; *Through the Storm, One Wonderful Night, Under Royal Patronage* 1914; *The Great Silence, Graustark, Pennington's Choice* 1915; *The Great Secret* (serial), *Romeo and Juliet* (as Juliet), *Man and His Soul, A Million a Minute* 1916; *The Adopted Son, Red White and Blue Blood, Their Compact* 1917; *Social Quicksands, A Pair of Cupids, Poor Rich Man, With Neatness and Dispatch, Under Suspicion* 1918; *God's Outlaw, Daring Hearts* 1919; *Smiling All the Way* 1920; *Modern Marriage* 1923; *The Age of Innocence, Her Marriage Vow, The Tenth Woman* 1924; *Who Cares, Passionate Youth* 1925; *Once in a Lifetime* 1932; *As Husbands Go* 1934; *Seven Keys to Baldpate* 1935.

Bazin, André. Film critic and theorist. *b.* Apr. 8, 1918, Angers, France. *d.* 1958. France's most influential post–WW I film critic. Studied at a teachers' college but was refused a teaching post because of a stammer. During WW II he founded a cinema club, where he showed politically banned films in defiance of the German Occupation authorities. After the war he became film critic for *Le Parisien Liberé* and contributed articles to many other French publications. In 1947 he started a film periodical, *La Revue du Cinéma,* and in 1951 founded, with Jacques DONIOL-VALCROZE *Les Cahiers du Cinéma,* which grew, under Bazin's direction, into Europe's most influential film publication.

Some of the numerous articles Bazin wrote about film were assembled after his death into a four-volume work entitled *Qu'est-ce que Le Cinéma?.* (An abbreviated, one-volume English version, *What Is Cinema?,* was published in 1967 by the University of California Press.) The concept of objective reality as a fundamental quality of the filmic image is central to Bazin's theoretical work. He therefore considered documentary and scientific films as the purest examples of untampered reality, and the Italian neorealist movement as the most valid expression of filmic truth. He upheld *mise-en-scène* against *montage* because, to him, the former represented "true continuity" and reproduced situations more realistically, leaving the interpretation of a particular scene to the spectator rather than to the director's viewpoint through editing. Consistent with this view, Bazin also argued in support of the deep focus, the shot-in-depth, brought to the fore in Orson Welles's *Citizen Kane,* which enabled a scene to be shot with both foreground and background in full view, minimizing the need to break up a scene into a series of shots. Bazin's theoretical writings and support of the *politique des auteurs* (the *auteur* theory) greatly influenced the direction of the French *Nouvelle Vague* (New Wave), many of whose members (notably Godard, Truffaut, Chabrol, and Rohmer) developed as writers for *Cahiers du Cinéma* under Bazin's guidance. See also AUTEUR THEORY; CAHIERS DU CINÉMA; DEEP FOCUS; NOUVELLE VAGUE.

bazooka. In film terms, a device used to support lighting units on the catwalk of a film studio. Named after the portable rocket launcher of WW II fame, which in turn was named after the crude wind instrument made popular by comedian Bob Burns.

BCU. Big close-up. See EXTREME CLOSE-UP.

Beal, John. Actor. Born J. Alexander Bliedung, on Aug. 13, 1909, in Joplin, Mo. *d.* 1997. *ed.* U. of Pennsylvania. Clean-cut juvenile lead of Hollywood films of the 30s following brief exposure on the stage. He continued to play an assortment of leads and supporting roles in films through 1960, while frequently returning to the stage. As part of his WW II military service, he directed training films for the U.S.A.A.F. He was married to stage actress Helen Craig (*b.* 1912; *d.* 1986).

FILMS INCLUDE: *Another Language* 1933; *The Little Minister* 1934; *Les Miserables, Laddie, Break of Hearts* 1935; *We Who Are About to Die* 1936; *The Man Who Found Himself, Border Cafe, Madame X, Double Wedding, Danger Patrol* 1937; *Port of Seven Seas, I Am the Law, The Arkansas Traveler* 1938; *The Cat and the Canary* 1939; *The Great Commandment, Doctors Don't Tell* 1941; *Atlantic Convoy* 1942; *Edge of Darkness* 1943; *Key Witness* 1947; *Alimony, Chicago Deadline* 1949; *My Six Convicts* 1952; *Remains to Be Seen* 1953; *That Night, The Vampire* 1957; *The Sound and the Fury* 1959; *Ten Who Dared* 1960; *The Bride/The House That Cried Murder* 1973; *The Funhouse* 1981; *Amityville 3-D* 1983.

Beals, Jennifer. Actress. Born on Dec. 19, 1963, in Chicago. Slender, well-built leading lady of Hollywood films. A former fashion model, she made her screen debut in 1980 and attained popularity in *Flashdance* (1983).

FILMS INCLUDE: *My Bodyguard* (bit) 1980; *Flashdance* 1983; *The Bride* 1985; *Split Decisions, Layover, La Partita* 1988; *Vampire's Kiss, Sons* 1989; *Docteur M./Club Extinction, Blood and Concrete: A Love Story* 1990; *In the Soup* 1992; *Dear Diary, Mrs. Parker and the Vicious Circle* 1994; *Devil in a Blue Dress, Four Rooms* 1995.

Béart, Emmanuelle. Actress. Born in 1965, in Gassin, France, the daughter of French pop singing star Guy Béart. Raised by her mother in a tiny mountain town (population 22), she departed at 15 for a position as an au pair French tutor in Montreal, Canada, where she saw her first motion picture. She was encouraged to try film acting by director Robert ALTMAN, for whom she even screentested. An ethereal blonde beauty, she intrigued international audiences with her title role in Claude Berri's *Manon of the Spring* and was believably angelic in her Hollywood debut, *Date with an Angel.* She is romantically involved with Daniel AUTEUIL, her co-star in *Manon of the Spring* and *Un Coeur en Hiver*.

FILMS INCLUDE: *L'Amour en Douce* 1985; *Manon des Sources/Manon of the Spring* 1986; *Date with an Angel* (US) 1987; *Children of Chaos* 1989; *Il Vaggio Di Capitan Fracassa/Captain Fracassa's Journey* (It./Fr.) 1990; *Door on Your Left as You Leave the Elevator* 1991; *Ruptures, Un Coeur en Hiver/A Heart in Winter* 1993; *Belle Epoque, L'Enfer* 1994; *Mission: Impossible* 1996.

Beatles, The. This phenomenally successful rock music group exerted tremendous influence on the music, fashions, and lifestyles of young people the world over and played a decisive role in the development of an international subculture in the 60s. The group consisted of John Lennon (*b.* Oct. 9, 1940; *d.* 1980), Paul McCartney (*b.* June 18, 1942), Ringo Starr (*b.* Richard Starkey, July 7, 1940), and George Harrison (*b.* Feb. 25, 1943). All were born in Liverpool or its suburbs. The group enjoyed unprecedented success in youth concerts, TV specials, and many best-selling records. Its members were awarded the M.B.E. (Member of the Order of the British Empire) title by the Queen in 1964, in recognition of their international impact and the millions in foreign currency they brought into the British treasury. Lennon and McCartney composed hundreds of songs, many of which are held in high regard by serious musicologists. The group starred in several films before its dissolution in 1970. Individual members also appeared separately in other films. Starr directed a film, *Born to Boo* McCartney wrote the words and music ture, *All This and World War II* (1976). scores and songs for several films, notat (1973).

FILM APPEARANCES: Beatles as a *Day's Night* 1964; *Pop Gear/Go Go Mania* rock-concert footage), *Help!* 1965; *Yellow Subr* voices only) 1968; *What's Happening* (doc. about of the US), *Let It Be* (doc.) 1970; *The Day the Music* pilation film) 1977. Harrison alone—*Concert for B* (along with Ringo Starr) 1972; *Water* (unbill., along wi Starr) 1984; *Shanghai Surprise* (unbill.) 1986; Lennon a *How I Won the War* 1967; *Diaries Notes and Sketches* (a Mekas "film diary"; along with McCartney) 1970; *Supersta Film Concert* 1971; *Oh Calcutta!* 1972. McCartney alone—*T Family Way* (score only, UK) 1966; *Live and Let Die* (song only, UK) 1973; *Give My Regards to Broad Street* (act., sc., score, UK) 1984; Starr alone—*Candy* 1968; *The Magic Christian* 1970; *200 Motels* 1971; *Blindman* 1972; *Son of Dracula* (also prod.), *That'll Be the Day* 1974; *Lisztomania* 1975; *Sextette, The Last Waltz* (rock doc.) 1978; *The Kids Are Alright* (rock doc.) 1979; *Caveman* 1981.

Beaton, Sir Cecil. Photographer, designer. *b.* Jan. 14, 1904, London. *d.* 1980. *ed.* Harrow; Cambridge. The noted artist who gained fame as the photographer of British royalty and celebrities of the entertainment world (notably Greta Garbo), also authored and illustrated a number of books and designed the sets for numerous stage, opera, and ballet productions in London and New York. He created costumes for a number of films, winning an Academy Award for *Gigi* (1958) and for *My Fair Lady* (1964), on both of which he also served as overall production designer. He was knighted in 1972.

FILMS INCLUDE (as costume designer): *Beware of Pity* 1946; *An Ideal Husband, Anna Karenina* 1948; *Gigi* (also production designer) 1958; *The Doctor's Dilemma* 1959; *My Fair Lady* (also production designer) 1964; *On a Clear Day You Can See Forever* 1970.

Beatty, Ned. Actor. Born on July 6, 1937, in Louisville, Ky. Chubby, puff-jowled, versatile character player of Hollywood films beginning in the 70s, following extensive experience in regional theater. Has played key supporting roles in many important productions, starting with *Deliverance* (1972). He was nominated for a best supporting actor Oscar for *Network* (1976).

FILMS INCLUDE: *Deliverance, The Life and Times of Judge Roy Bean* 1972; *The Thief Who Came to Dinner, White Lightning, The Last American Hero* 1973; *W.W. and the Dixie Dancekings, Nashville* 1975; *All the President's Men, The Big Bus, Network, Silver Streak, Mikey & Nicky* 1976; *Exorcist II: The Heretic, The Great Bank Hoax* 1977; *Alambrista!/The Illegal, Gray Lady Down, Superman* 1978; *Promises in the Dark, 1941, American Success Company, Wise Blood* 1979; *Hopscotch, Superman II* 1980; *The Incredible Shrinking Woman* 1981; *The Toy* 1982; *Stroker Ace, The Ballad of Gregorio Cortez, Touched* 1983; *Restless Natives* (UK) 1985; *Back to School* 1986; *The Fourth Protocol* (UK), *Rolling Vengeance, The Trouble with Spies, The Big Easy* 1987; *Switching Channels, The Unholy, After the Rain/The Passage, Midnight Crossing, Shadows in the Storm, Purple People Eater* 1988; *Physical Evidence, Ministry of Vengeance, Time Trackers, Twist of Fate, Chattahoochee* 1989; *Big Bad John, Captain America, Repossessed* 1990; *A Cry in the Wild, Hear My Song* (UK/Ire.) 1991; *Prelude to a Kiss, Blind Vision* 1992; *Rudy* 1993; *The Legend of O. B. Taggart, Radioland Murders* 1994; *Just Cause* 1995.

Beatty, Robert. Actor. *b.* Oct. 19, 1909, Hamilton, Ont., *d.* 1992. *ed.* U. of Toronto. Worked as a cashier and sales- while gaining amateur experience on stage and radio. Later died at the Royal Academy of Dramatic Art in London and de both his London stage and British film debuts in 1938. ayed leads and character parts, mostly in rugged roles.

FILMS INCLUDE: *Murder in Soho* 1938; *Mein Kampf My Crimes* 1940; *Dangerous Moonlight/Suicide Squadron* 1941; *49th Parallel/The Invaders, One of Our Aircraft Is Missing* 1942; *San Demetrio London* 1943; *Appointment With Crime* 1946; *Odd Man Out* 1947; *Against the Wind* 1948; *Captain Horatio Hornblower, The Magic Box* 1951; *The Gentle Gunman* 1952; *Albert RN, Man on a Tightrope* 1953; *Out of the Clouds* 1954; *Tarzan and the Lost Safari, Something of Value* 1957; *The Shakedown* 1960; *The Amorous Mr. Prawn* 1962; *2001: A Space Odyssey* 1968; *Where Eagles Dare* 1969; *Pope Joan* 1972; *The Spikes Gang* 1974. *The Pink Panther Strikes Again* 1976; *The Spaceman and King Arthur/Unidentified Flying Oddball* 1979; *The Amateur* 1981; *Superman III* 1983.

Beatty, Warren. Actor, producer, director. Born Henry Warren Beaty, on Mar. 30, 1937, in Richmond, Va. With his older sister, Shirley MACLAINE, he started acting as a child in amateur productions directed by their mother, a drama coach. After a year at Northwestern University, he was a construction worker for a while before taking drama lessons with Stella Adler and starting a slow ascent on TV. After playing a lead role in 'Compulsion' in stock, he appeared on Broadway in William Inge's 'A Loss of Roses,' then made a good start in films, opposite Natalie Wood, in *Splendor in the Grass* (1961). His virile good looks and magnetic antihero personality appealed to young audiences, and his popularity reached a peak with his portrayal of Clyde Barrow in *Bonnie and Clyde* (1967), which he also produced. In 1978 he made an impressive directorial debut with *Heaven Can Wait,* which he co-directed with Buck Henry and co-wrote with Elaine May. He also co-produced and starred in this [illegible], which enjoyed considerable success at the box office and [illegible] nominated for an Oscar as best picture. The film also earn[illegible]eatty two Academy Award nominations, as best director [illegible]collaboration) and best actor. He won the directing Oscar th[illegible]ears later for *Reds* (1981), a sprawling political saga, in which he also starred as the idealist journalist John Reed. After several years of inactivity, Beatty met his Waterloo as the producer of the expensive box-office disaster *Ishtar* (1987). Undaunted, he made a healthy financial recovery with the blockbuster *Dick Tracy* (1990), which he produced and directed, with himself starring in the title role. Enigmatic and somewhat of a maverick in his work habits, he has also developed quite a reputation for his off-screen romantic exploits, which have involved some of the screen's best-looking women. He has also been actively involved in social issues and liberal politics. Married Annette BENING, whom he met while working on *Bugsy*.

FILMS: (as actor) *Splendor in the Grass, The Roman Spring of Mrs. Stone* 1961; *All Fall Down* 1962; *Lilith* 1964; *Mickey One* 1965; *Promise Her Anything, Kaleidoscope* 1966; *Bonnie and Clyde* (also prod.) 1967; *The Only Game in Town* 1970; *McCabe and Mrs. Miller, $* 1971; *Year of the Woman* (doc.) 1973; *The Parallax View* (1974); *Shampoo* (also prod., co-sc.), *The Fortune* 1975; *Heaven Can Wait* (also co-dir. with Buck Henry, co-prod., co-sc.) 1978; *Reds* (also dir., prod., co-sc.) 1981; *Ishtar* (also prod.) 1987; *Dick Tracy* 1990 (also dir., prod.); *Bugsy* (also co-prod.) 1991; *Love Affair* (also co-prod., co-sc.) 1994.

Beaudine, William. Director. *b.* Jan. 15, 1892, New York City. *d.* 1970. One of Hollywood's original old-timers, he entered films in 1909 as a combination handyman and property boy for D. W. Griffith. He worked in various capacities in the industry before becoming a director in 1915. Following numerous shorts, he began directing features in 1922 and soon gained a reputation as a capable director of light films with a special knack for handling child performers. As a result, he was assigned to direct two of Mary Pickford's films, *Little Annie Rooney* (1925) and *Sparrows* (1926). During his long and highly prolific career he turned out films in a wide variety of genres, from farces, musicals, and light romances to Westerns and melodramas, mainly in the medium- to low-budget category. Over a period of more than half a century he directed hundreds of films, grinding out several productions every year for various studios through the late 60s. He directed more than a dozen films in England from 1934 to 1937. From the early 40s he worked mainly for such poverty-row studios as PRC, Monogram, and Allied Artists, and was responsible for, among numerous other films, many East Side Kids and Bowery Boys comedies. In 1944 he directed a notorious sex-education picture, *Mom and Dad,* which depicted the actual birth of a baby and was bounced around the courts for years until it was finally released in 1957. But he later directed several religious dramas for the Protestant Film Commission. At the time of his death, at 78, he was Hollywood's oldest active director. He had also directed numerous episodes for TV series, including 70 'Lassie' installments. His son, William Beaudine, Jr. (*b.* Apr. 28, 1921, in Hollywood) has produced and directed, mainly for TV.

FILMS INCLUDE: *Almost a King* (also sc.) 1915; *A Bad Little Good Man* 1917; *Watch Your Step, Catch My Smoke, Heroes of the Street* 1922; *Her Fatal Millions, Penrod and Sam, The Printer's Devil, The Country Kid, Boy of Mine* 1923; *Daring Youth, Daughters of Pleasure, Wandering Husbands, A Self-Made Failure, Cornered, The Narrow Street* 1924; *A Broadway Butterfly, Little Annie Rooney* 1925; *That's My Baby, The Social Highwayman, Sparrows, The Canadian* 1926; *Frisco Sally Levy, The Life of Riley, The Irresistible Lover* 1927; *The Cohens and the Kellys in Paris, Heart to Heart, Home James, Do Your Duty, Give and Take* 1928; *Fugitives, Two Weeks Off, The Girl from Woolworth's, Wedding Rings* 1929; *Those Who Dance, Road to Paradise* 1930; *Father's Son, The Lady Who Dared, The Mad Parade, Penrod and Sam* (remake), *Misbehaving Ladies, Men in Her Life* 1931; *Three Wise Girls, Make Me a Star* 1932; *The Crime of the Century, Her Bodyguard* 1933; *The Old-Fashioned Way, Dandy Dick* (UK) 1934; *Two Hearts in Harmony* (UK), *Boys Will Be Boys* (UK), *Mr. Cohen Takes a Walk* (UK) 1935; *It's in the Bag* (UK), *Where There's a Will* (UK) 1936; *Said O'Reilly to McNab/Sez O'Reilly to McNab* (UK), *Take It from Me* (UK), *Feather Your Nest* (UK) 1937; *Torchy Gets Her Man* 1938; *Torchy Blane in Chinatown* 1939; *Misbehaving Husbands* 1940; *Federal Fugitives, Emergency Landing, Desperate Cargo* 1941; *Duke of the Navy, The Broadway Big Shot, The Panther's Claw, The Miracle Kid, Men of San Quentin, Gallant Lady, One Thrilling Night, Phantom Killer, Foreign Agent, The Living Ghost* 1942; *Clancy Street Boys, The Ape Man, Spotlight Scandals, Here Comes Kelly, The Mystery of the 13th Guest* 1943; *What a Man!, Voodoo Man, Hot Rhythm, Detective Kitty O'Day, Follow the Leader, Leave It to the Irish, Oh What a Night!, Shadows of Suspicion, Bowery Champs, Crazy Knights* 1944; *Fashion Model, Come Out Fighting, Blonde Ransom, Swingin' on a Rainbow, Black Market Babies* 1945; *The Shadow Returns, The Face of Marble, Don't Gamble With Strangers, Spook Busters, Below the Deadline, Mr. Hex* 1946; *Philo Vance Returns, Hard Boiled Mahoney, Too Many Winners, Killer at Large, News Hounds, Gas House Kids Go West, The Chinese Ring/The Red Hornet* 1947; *The Shanghai Chest, The Golden*

Eye, Kidnapped, Smugglers' Cove, The Feathered Serpent 1948; *Incident, Tuna Clipper, Forgotten Women, Trail of the Yukon, Tough Assignment* 1949; *Blue Grass of Kentucky, Blonde Dynamite, Jiggs and Maggie Out West, County Fair* 1950; *The Prince of Peace* (religious drama; co-dir. with Harold Daniels), *Bowery Battalion, Cuban Fireball, Ghost Chasers, Let's Go Navy!, Havana Rose* 1951; *Rodeo, Jet Job, Here Come the Marines!, The Rose Bowl Story, Yukon Gold* 1952; *Jalopy, Roar of the Crowd, Murder Without Tears* 1953; *Yukon Vengeance, Paris Playboys, Pride of the Blue Grass* 1954; *High Society* (a Bowery Boys comedy, not the Crosby-Sinatra musical of 1956), *Jail Busters* 1955; *Mom and Dad* (sex-education film; release delayed from 1944), *In the Money, Westward Ho the Wagons!* 1957; *Ten Who Dared* 1960; *Lassie's Great Adventure* (orig. made for TV) 1963; *Billy the Kid vs. Dracula, Jesse James Meets Frankenstein's Daughter* 1966.

Beaumont, Charles. Screenwriter. *b.* 1930, Chicago. *d.* 1967. A science-fiction enthusiast, he began writing fantasy stories in his early teens. At age 18 he went to Hollywood, where he inked cartoons, ran messages, and toiled at a variety of odd jobs while trying to break into screenwriting. He finally made it in the late 50s, but after writing only nine films he died as a consequence of spinal meningitis, which had afflicted him as a child.

FILMS: *Queen of Outer Space* 1958; *The Intruder* (also act.), *The Premature Burial, Burn Witch Burn/The Night of the Eagle, The Wonderful World of the Brothers Grimm* 1962; *The Haunted Palace* 1963; *The Seven Faces of Dr. Lao, The Masque of the Red Death* 1964; *Mister Moses* 1965.

Beaumont, Harry. Director. *b.* Feb. 10, 1888, Abilene, Kans. *d.* 1966. Left school at an early age to join a stock company and eventually came to New York to perform in vaudeville. He began appearing in Edison films in 1912 and over the next few years played both leads and supporting roles in many shorts and one or two serials. During that period he also collaborated on several scripts and made his debut as director in 1915. He joined Essanay late in 1916 and subsequently directed numerous films in a variety of genres for Goldwin, Fox, Metro, Warners, and MGM, among other studios. Technically efficient and always dependable, he reached the peak of his career in the 20s, when he was entrusted with the direction of such major films as *Main Street, The Gold Diggers, Babbitt,* and the prestigious John Barrymore vehicle *Beau Brummel.* In 1928 he directed *Our Dancing Daughters,* a silent "musical" on a grand scale, with Joan Crawford heading the cast and dancing the Charleston. The film's great success prompted MGM to assign him to direct their first sound musical film, *The Broadway Melody* (1929), which included a Technicolor sequence. Despite its technical defects, the film reaped tremendous rewards at the box office and an Academy Award as best picture for 1928–29. Beaumont continued directing for MGM through the late 40s, but his talkies were for the most part undistinguished, consisting chiefly of lightweight, run-of-the-mill productions.

FILMS: *The Call of the City* 1915; *The Truant Soul* 1916; *Skinner's Dress Suit, Skinner's Bubble, Skinner's Baby, Burning the Candle, Filling His Own Shoes* 1917; *Brown of Harvard, Thirty a Week* 1918; *Little Rowdy, Wild Goose Chase, A Man and His Money, Go West Young Man, One of the Finest, The City of Comrades, Heartsease, Lord and Lady Algy, Toby's Bow, The Gay Lord Quex* 1919; *The Great Accident, Dollars and Sense, Going Some, Stop Thief!, Officer 666* 1920; *The Fourteenth Lover, Glass Houses, The Ragged Heiress, Very Truly Yours, Seeing's Believing, The Five Dollar Baby* (also prod.), *Lights of the Desert, They Like 'Em Rough, June Madness* (also sc.), *Love in the Dark* (also prod.) 1922; *Crinoline and Romance, A Noise in Newboro, Main Street* (also edit.), *The Gold Diggers* 1923; *Beau Brummel, Don't Doubt Your Husband, Babbitt, The Lover of Camille, A Lost Lady* 1924; *Recompense, His Majesty Bunker Bean, Rose of the World* 1925; *Sandy, Womanpower* 1926; *One Increasing Purpose* 1927; *Forbidden Hours, Our Dancing Daughters* 1928; *A Single Man, The Broadway Melody, Speedway* 1929; *Lord Byron of Broadway* (co-dir. with William Nigh), *Children of Pleasure, The Floradora Girl, Our Blushing Brides, Those Three French Girls* 1930; *Dance Fools Dance, Laughing Sinners, The Great Lover, West of Broadway* 1931; *Are You Listening?, Unashamed, Faithless* 1932; *Made on Broadway, When Ladies Meet, Should Ladies Behave?* 1933; *Murder in the Private Car* 1934; *Enchanted April* 1935; *The Girl on the Front Page* 1936; *When's Your Birthday?* 1937; *Maisie Goes to Reno* 1944; *Twice Blessed* 1945; *Up Goes Maisie, The Show-Off* 1946; *Undercover Maisie* 1947; *Alias a Gentleman* 1948.

Beaumont, Hugh. Actor. *b.* Feb. 16, 1909, Lawrence, Kans. *d.* 1982. *ed.* U. of Chattanooga; USC. Leading man and second lead of Hollywood B pictures, whose roles included several portrayals of private eye Michael Shayne. On TV, he is best remembered as the father in the long-running (1957–63) series 'Leave It to Beaver.'

FILMS INCLUDE: *South of Panama* 1941; *Flight Lieutenant* 1942; *The Fallen Sparrow, The Seventh Victim* 1943; *Apology for Murder, Blood on the Sun, The Lady Confesses, Objective Burma!* 1945; *Blonde for a Day, The Blue Dahlia, Murder Is My Business* 1946; *The Guilt of Janet Ames, Three on a Ticket, Bury Me Dead* 1947; *The Counterfeiters* 1948; *The Last Outpost, Roaring City, Pier 23* 1951; *Night Without Sleep, Phone Call From a Stranger* 1952; *The Mississippi Gambler* 1953; *The Mole People* 1956; *Night Passage* 1957; *The Human Duplicators* 1965.

Beauregard, Georges de. Producer. *b.* Edgar Denys Nau de Beauregard, Dec. 23, 1920, Marseilles, France. *d.* 1984. After law studies and military training, he became a journali[illegible]d in 1947 founded a news agency. The following year he e[illegible] the film business as an exporter of French pictures. In 195[illegible]vent to Spain to start his career as producer. During his two-y[illegible]tay he exerted considerable influence on the revival of Spa[illegible]lm production. He later was co-producer of BARDEM's two best-known films, *Death of a Cyclist* (1955) and *Calle Mayor* (1956).

A daring, flamboyant businessman, Beauregard is credited with being the driving force behind the French NEW WAVE. Among his protégés were Jean-Luc Godard, Agnès Varda, Claude Chabrol, and Jacques Demy. In 1984, months before his death, he was awarded a special César prize for his contribution to the French film industry.

FILMS (as producer or co-producer) include: *Muerte di un Ciclista/Death of a Cyclist/Age of Infidelity* (Sp./Fr.) 1955; *Calle Mayor/The Lovemaker* (Sp./Fr.) 1956; *A Bout de Souffle/Breathless* 1960; *Lola, Une Femme est une Femme/A Woman Is a Woman, Léon Morin—Prêtre* 1961; *Cléo de 5 à 7/Cleo From 5 to 7, L'Oeil du Matin/The Third Lover* 1962; *Landru/Bluebeard, Le Petit Soldat* (release delayed from 1960), *Le Doulos/Doulos—The Finger Man, Les Carabiniers, Le Mépris/Contempt* 1963; *La Religieuse/The Nun, Pierrot le Fou* 1965; *La Ligne de Demarcation, Made in USA* 1966; *La Collectioneuse* 1967; *Le Crabe-Tambour* 1977; *Le Cheval d'Orgueil/Horse of Pride* 1980; *L'Honneur d'un Capitaine* 1982.

Beavers, Louise. Actress. *b.* Mar. 8, 1902, in Cincinnati. *d.* 1962. A minstrel show singer, she began her Hollywood career in the early 20s as the real-life maid of actress Leatrice Joy—and later was to enact the role of a maid in many films. She became one of Hollywood's most frequently employed black performers, but her considerable talent was wasted in a constant repetition of good-natured black mama roles, nearly always as a maid, housekeeper, or cook. She is best remembered for her powerful portrayal as a pancake maker à la Aunt Jemima in *Imitation of Life* (1934). She later won popularity with TV audiences in the title role in the 'Beulah' series (1952–53), one of television's earliest programs to star a black person. In 1976 she was inducted into the Black Filmmakers Hall of Fame.

FILMS INCLUDE: *Gold Diggers* 1923; *Uncle Tom's Cabin* 1927; *Coquette, Wall Street* 1929; *She Couldn't Say No* 1930; *Annabelle's Affairs* 1931; *What Price Hollywood* 1932; *She Done Him Wrong, Bombshell* 1933; *Imitation of Life* 1934; *Rainbow on the River, Bullets or Ballots* 1936; *Make Way for Tomorrow* 1937; *Brother Rat* 1938; *Made for Each Other* 1939; *No Time for Comedy* 1940; *Belle Starr, Shadow of the Thin Man* 1941; *Reap the Wild Wind, Holiday Inn* 1942; *Du Barry Was a Lady* 1943; *Jack London* 1944; *Delightfully Dangerous* 1945; *Lover Come Back* 1946; *Banjo* 1947; *Mr. Blandings Builds His Dream House, Good Sam* 1948; *The Jackie Robinson Story* 1950; *Never Wave at a WAC* 1952; *Tammy and the Bachelor* 1957; *The Goddess* 1958; *All the Fine Young Cannibals, The Facts of Life* 1960.

Becker, Harold. Director. He began his career in Britain, then turned out an intermittent succession of quality Hollywood films.

FILMS: *The Ragman's Daughter* (UK) 1972; *The Onion Field* 1979; *The Black Marble* 1980; *Taps* 1981; *Vision Quest* 1985; *The Boost* 1988; *Sea of Love* 1989; *Malice* 1993; *City Hall* (also co-prod.) 1995.

Becker, Jacques. Director. *b.* Sept. 15, 1906, Paris. *d.* 1960. His interest in films was stimulated by a meeting with King VIDOR, who offered him employment in the US as actor and assistant director. However, he remained in France and became assistant to Jean RENOIR, a friend of the family, during that director's peak period (1932–39). In 1934 he ventured briefly into independent production, co-directing with Pierre Prévert a short film, *Le Commissaire est Bon Enfant.* In 1935 he turned out a five-reeler, *Tête de Turc,* which he later refused to acknowledge as his. In 1939 he began shooting a feature film, *L'Or du Cristobal,* but walked out after three weeks, leaving the film to be finished by Jean Stelli. In 1942, after a year in a German prisoner-of-war camp, he began his career as director. His entire output consisted of only 13 films, but they include some of the most artistically and technically substantial in French cinema. He is one of the few Old Guard directors done honor by the New Wave, which reveres him for his masterpiece, the atmospheric period love story *Casque d'Or,* and also for his lesser films, such charming love tales as *Antoine et Antoinette* and *Edouard et Caroline,* in which he vividly depicts French social milieus through careful attention to background. His *Touchez pas au Grisbi,* a gangster film distinguished for its detailed action and penetration of character, exerted considerable influence on subsequent *série noire* French films. He was less successful with such commercial ventures as *Ali Baba,* which was dominated by Fernandel, and *Montparnasse 19,* a biographical sketch of the last years in the life of Modigliani. Becker's widow is French stage and screen actress Françoise Fabian (*b.* Michèle Cortès de Leone y Fabianera). He was the father of Jean BECKER.

FEATURE FILMS: *L'Or de Cristobal* (replaced by Jean Stelli; uncredited) 1939; *Dernier Atout* (also co-prod., co-sc.) 1942; *Goupi Mains rouges/It Happened at the Inn* (also co-sc.) 1943; *Falbalas/Paris Frills* (also co-sc.) 1945; *Antoine et Antoinette/Antoine and Antoinette* (also co-sc.) 1947; *Rendez-vous de Juillet* (also co-story, sc.) 1949; *Edouard et Caroline/Edward and Caroline* (also co-sc.) 1951; *Casque d'Or* (also co-sc., dial.) 1952; *Rue de l'Estrapade* 1953; *Touchez pas au Grisbi/Grisbi* (also co-sc.), *Ali Baba et les Quarante Voleurs/Ali Baba* (also co-sc.) 1954; *Les Aventures d'Arsène Lupin/The Adventures of Arsène Lupin* (also co-sc.) 1957; *Montparnasse 19/Modigliani of Montparnasse* (also co-sc.) 1958; *Le Trou/The Night Watch/The Hole* (also co-sc.) 1960.

Beckett, Scotty. Actor. *b.* Oct. 4, 1929, Oakland, Calif. *d.* 1968, a probable suicide. Began screen career at age three as a regular member of the Our Gang comedy troupe. In feature films, he gradually moved on from child roles to likable adolescents, memorably as the young Jolson in *The Jolson Story.* But his popularity waned when he reached maturity.

FILMS INCLUDE: *Gallant Lady* 1933; *Stand Up and Cheer, Whom the Gods Destroy* 1934; *Dante's Inferno* 1935; *Anthony Adverse, The Charge of the Light Brigade* 1936; *Conquest* 1937; *Marie Antoinette* 1938; *The Escape* 1939; *The Blue Bird, My Son My Son, My Favorite Wife* 1940; *Aloma of the South Seas* 1941; *Kings Row* 1942; *Ali Baba and the Forty Thieves, The Climax* 1944; *Junior Miss* 1945; *My Reputation, The Jolson Story* 1946; *Cynthia, Dangerous Years* 1947; *A Date With Judy* 1948; *Battleground* 1949; *Nancy Goes to Rio, Louisa* 1950; *Corky of Gasoline Alley* 1951; *Three for Jamie Dawn* 1956.

Bedelia, Bonnie. Actress. Born on March 25, 1952, in New York City. *ed.* School of the American Ballet, N.Y.; Hunter College, N.Y. Former TV and stage child actor and ballerina who made an auspicious adult acting debut as female race car driver Shirley Muldowney in *Heart Like a Wheel.* She graduated to leading and supporting roles in films and on TV, typified by her role as the sturdy wife in *Die Hard* and *Die Harder.*

FILMS INCLUDE: *The Gypsy Moths, They Shoot Horses Don't They?* 1969; *Lovers and Other Strangers* 1970; *The Strange Vengeance* 1972; *Get Back* 1973; *The Big Fix* 1978; *Heart Like a Wheel* 1982; *Death of an Angel* 1985; *The Boy Who Could Fly, Violets Are Blue* 1986; *The Stranger* 1987; *Die Hard, The Prince of Pennsylvania* 1988; *Fat Man and Little Boy* 1989; *Die Hard 2: Die Harder, Presumed Innocent* 1990; *Needful Things* 1993; *Speechless* 1994.

Bedford, Barbara. Actress. Born in 1900(?), in Prairie du Chien, Wis. Leading lady of Hollywood silents and early talkies. Later in supporting parts. She appeared typically in romantic melodramas and some Westerns, opposite such leading men as John Gilbert, Lon Chaney, Conrad Veidt, Tom Mix, and William S. Hart.

FILMS INCLUDE: *The Last of the Mohicans* 1920; *The Big Punch, Cinderella of the Hills* 1921; *Gleam O'Dawn, Arabian Love, Alias Julius Caesar, Arabia, The Power of Love* 1922; *Romance Land, Forbidden Love, The Spoilers, The Acquittal* 1923; *Women Who Give* 1924; *The Mad Whirl, Before Midnight, What Fools Men, Tumbleweeds* 1925; *Old Loves and New, The Sporting Lover, Devil's Dice* 1926; *Life of an Actress, The Notorious Lady, Mockery, The Girl From Gay Paree, A Man's Past, Backstage* 1927; *The Port of Missing Girls, Marry the Girl, The Cavalier, The Haunted House, The Broken Mask, Manhattan Nights, City of Purple Dreams, Bitter Sweets* 1928; *Brothers, The Heroic Lover* 1929; *The Love Trader, Tol'able David, Sunny, The Lash/Adios* 1930; *Desert Vengeance* 1931; *The Death Kiss* 1932; *Found Alive, A Girl of the Limberlost* 1934; *The World Accuses, The Keeper of the Bees* 1935; *Ring Around the Moon, Easy Money* 1936; *The Toy Wife, Three Comrades, Fast Company, Young Dr. Kildare* 1938; *Stronger Than Desire* 1939; *The Earl of Chicago* 1940; *Love Crazy, Whistling in the Dark* 1941; *Nazi Agent, Reunion in France* 1942; *Girl Crazy* 1943; *Meet the People* 1944.

Beebe, Ford. Director. *b.* Nov. 26, 1888, in Grand Rapids, Mich. *d.* 1978. In films from 1916, he started out as a screenwriter on low-budget Westerns and action pictures. In 1932 he began a long stint as an efficient and prolific director of B pictures and serials for Mascot, Columbia, Republic, and other small independents. Considering their low budgets, tight schedules, and simple-minded subject matter, many of his films turned out surprisingly well. Among numerous serials, he co-directed the popular fantasy serials *Flash Gordon's Trip to Mars* and *Buck Rogers.* In 1940, in an extreme departure from his regular fare, he co-directed the Beethoven Pastoral Symphony segment in Disney's *Fantasia.* He produced and wrote the scripts of some of his films. He ended his career as director-producer-writer of a string of 'Bomba, The Jungle Boy' films.

FILMS (as director; serials are indicated by "S"): *The Honor of the Range* (co-dir. with Leo Maloney) 1920; *The Last of the Mohicans* (S; co-dir. with B. Reeves Eason; also co-sc.), *The Shadow of the Eagle* (S; also co-sc.), *The Pride of the Legion/The Big Pay-Off* (also story) 1932; *Laughing at Life* (also sc.) 1933; *The Adventures of Rex and Rinty* (S; co-dir. with Eason), *Law Beyond the Range, The Man From Guntown* (also sc.) 1935; *Ace Drummond* (S; co-dir., with Cliff Smith), *Stampede* 1936; *Jungle Jim* (S; co-dir. with Smith), *Radio Patrol* (S; co-dir. with Smith), *Secret Agent X-9* (S; co-dir. with Smith), *Tim Tyler's Luck* (S), *Wild West Days* (S; co-dir. with Smith), *Westbound Limited* (also co-sc.), *Trouble at Midnight* (also co-sc.) 1937; *Flash Gordon's Trip to Mars* (S; co-dir. with Robert Hill), *Mars Attacks the World* (feature version of former serial), *Red Barry* (S; co-dir. with Alan James) 1938; *Buck Rogers* (S; co-dir. with Saul Goodkind), *The Phantom Creeps* (S; co-dir. with Goodkind), *The Oregon Trail* (S), *Oklahoma Frontier* (also sc.) 1939; *The Green Hornet* (S; co-dir. with Ray Taylor), *The Green Hornet Strikes Again* (S; co-dir. with John Rawlins), *Flash Gordon Conquers the Universe* (S; co-dir. with Taylor), *Junior G-Men* (S; co-dir. with Rawlins), *Winners of the West* (S; co-dir. with Taylor), *Fantasia* (co-dir. Pastoral Symphony sequence with Hamilton Luske and Jim Handley), *Son of Roaring Dan* 1940; *The Reluctant Dragon* (co-dir. with five others), *Riders of Death Valley* (S; co-dir. with Taylor), *Sea Raiders* (co-dir. with Rawlins), *Sky Raiders* (S; co-dir. with Taylor) 1941; *Don Winslow of the Navy* (S; co-dir. with Taylor), *Overland Mail* (S; co-dir. with Rawlins), *Arabian Nights* (2nd-unit dir. only), *Night Monster* (also prod.) 1942; *Frontier Badmen* (also prod.), *Son of Dracula* (prod., 2nd-unit dir. only) 1943; *The Invisible Man's Revenge* (also prod.), *Enter Arsène Lupin* (also prod.) 1944; *Easy to Look At* 1945; *My Dog Shep* (also sc.) 1946; *Six Gun Serenade* 1947; *Courtin' Trouble* (also sc.), *Shep Comes Home* (also sc.) 1948; *Bomba the Jungle Boy, The Dalton Gang* (also sc.), *Satan's Cradle* (also sc.), *Red Desert* (also sc.), *Bomba on Panther Island* (also sc.) 1949; *The Lost Volcano, Bomba and the Hidden City* 1950; *The Lion Hunters* (also sc.), *Elephant Stampede* (also sc.) 1951; *African Treasure, Wagons West, Bomba and the Jungle Girl* (also sc.) 1952; *Safari Drums* (also prod., sc.) 1953; *The Golden Idol* (also prod., sc.), *Killer Leopard* (also prod., sc.) 1954; *Lord of the Jungle* (also prod, sc.) 1956.

Beery, Noah. Actor. *b.* Jan. 17, 1884, Kansas City, Mo. *d.* 1946. Brother of actor Wallace BEERY, father of actor Noah BEERY, Jr. He started his stage career around 1900, some 16 years before making his first film appearance. On the screen, he soon established himself as king of the "bad guys," a lecherous scoundrel, a villain's villain, the heaviest of heavies. Among his most famous silent vehicles were *The Mark of Zorro, The Sea Wolf, The Dove,* many Zane Grey Westerns, and most of all *Beau Geste,* in which he portrayed the ruthless Sergeant Lejaune. The owner of a confident, resonant voice, he made a smooth transition to sound films and continued playing character roles, mainly in second features, until shortly before his death.

FILMS INCLUDE: *The Social Highwayman* 1916; *The Mormon Maid, The Hostage* 1917; *The Whispering Chorus, His Robe of Honor, Believe Me Xantippe, The Source, The Squaw Man* 1918; *The Red Lantern, Louisiana, The Valley of the Giants* 1919; *The Sea Wolf, The Mark of Zorro, The Mutiny of the Elsinore* 1920; *Bits of Life, The Call of the North* 1921; *Tillie, Wild Honey, The Crossroads of New York, Ebb Tide, Flesh and Blood, Omar the Tentmaker, I Am the Law* 1922; *The Soul of the Beast, Main Street, The Spoilers, The Destroying Angel, Quicksands, To the Last Man, The Call of the Canyon* 1923; *The Heritage of the Desert, The Fighting Coward, The Wanderer of the Wasteland, Lily of the Dust, The Female, North of 36* 1924; *East of Suez, Contraband, The Light of the Western Stars, Wild Horse Mesa, The Vanishing American, Lord Jim, The Spaniard, The Thundering Herd* 1925; *The Enchanted Hill, The Crown of Lies, Padlocked, Beau Geste, Paradise* 1926; *The Rough Riders, Evening Clothes, The Love Mart* 1927; *The Dove, Beau Sabreur, Two Lovers, Hellship Bronson* 1928; *Noah's Ark, Careers, The Four Feathers, The Isle of Lost Ships* 1929; *Under a Texas Moon, Murder Will Out, Golden Dawn, The Way of All Men, Renegades, Tol'able David, Mammy, Bright Lights* 1930; *The Millionaire, Riders of the Purple Sage, Homicide Squad* 1931; *The Big Stampede, The Kid from Spain* 1932; *She Done Him Wrong, The Woman I Stole* 1933; *Madame Spy, David Harum, Caravan* 1934; *Sweet Adeline* 1935; *King of the Damned* (UK) 1936; *Zorro Rides Again* (serial) 1937; *The Bad Man of Brimstone* 1938; *Mutiny on the Blackhawk* 1939; *The Adventures of Red Ryder* (serial) 1940; *Isle of Missing Men, Tennessee Johnson* 1942; *Salute to the Marines* 1943; *Barbary Coast Gent* 1944; *This Man's Navy* 1945.

Beery, Noah, Jr. Actor. *b.* Aug. 10, 1913 in New York City. *d.* 1994. *ed.* Harvard Military Academy. The son of Noah BEERY and the nephew of Wallace BEERY, he made his screen debut as a child in the silent *The Mark of Zorro* (1920) with his father and Douglas Fairbanks. He was educated at military academies between stock-company appearances with his father. His screen career consists mostly of supporting roles, appearing as second hero to such Western stars as Tom Mix, Johnny Mack Brown, and Buck Jones. (He married Jones's daughter, Maxine, in 1940.) He has also played character parts in dramas and comedies and lead roles in some low-budget pictures.

FILMS INCLUDE: *The Mark of Zorro* 1920; *Penrod* 1922; *Father and Son* 1929; *Heroes of the West* 1932; *Rustler's Roundup* 1933; *The Call of the Savage* 1935; *Ace Drummond* (serial), *Parole* 1936; *The Road Back* 1937; *Forbidden Valley* 1938; *Bad Lands, Only Angels Have Wings* 1939; *Of Mice and Men, Twenty-Mule Team, Passport to Alcatraz* 1940; *Sergeant York* 1941; *Gung Ho* 1943; *The Daltons Ride Again* 1945; *The Cat Creeps* 1946; *Red River* 1948; *The Doolins of Oklahoma* 1949; *Davy Crockett Indian Scout* 1950; *The Last Outpost, The Texas Rangers* 1951; *The Story of Will Rogers, The Cimarron Kid* 1952; *The Yellow Tomahawk* 1954; *White Feather* 1955; *The Fastest Gun Alive, Jubal* 1956; *The Spirit of St. Louis* 1957; *Inherit the Wind* 1960; *The Seven Faces of Dr. Lao* 1964; *Heaven with a Gun* 1969; *Little Fauss and Big Halsy* 1970; *Walking Tall* 1973; *The Spikes Gang* 1974; *Part 2 Walking Tall* 1975; *The Best Little Whorehouse in Texas* 1982.

Beery, Wallace. Actor. *b.* Apr. 1, 1885, Kansas City, Mo. *d.* 1949. The younger brother of Noah BEERY and uncle of Noah BEERY, Jr., in 1902, at 16, he joined the Ringling Bros. circus as assistant to the elephant trainer; two years later he was singing in New York musical variety shows. He then alternated between Broadway musicals and Kansas City stock until 1913, when he signed a film contract with Essanay and moved to Hollywood. He started his film career modestly, in a series of comedy shorts in which he impersonated Sweedie, a Swedish maid. After appearing in several one- and two-reelers with Keystone and Universal, he formed his own company and tried, unsuccessfully, to produce films in Japan. He then returned to Hollywood to play a wide array of villainous and comic roles in feature films. In 1916 he married Gloria SWANSON, his co-star in a series of SENNETT comedies. They divorced two years later.

With the advent of sound, Beery was able to shake off being typecast as a heavy and soon proved his great versatility in leading roles. His gross physique, gravel voice, rubbery face, crooked mouth, and mischievous twinkle added up to a most unlikely hero personality; yet he became one of the most popular performers of his time, often playing a lovable slob. Among his most memorable pictures were *The Big House, Grand Hotel, Dinner at Eight, Viva Villa!, The Mighty Barnum,* and *A Message to Garcia.* He was particularly adept at playing opposite youngsters and won the best actor Academy Award (in an unprecedented tie, with Fredric March) for his performance in *The Champ* (1931) with child-actor Jackie Cooper, with whom he later appeared in such films as *The Bowery* and *Treasure Island.* His ideal screen-mate was Marie DRESSLER (*Min and Bill, Tugboat Annie*). She was succeeded by Marjorie MAIN.

FILMS INCLUDE (talkies complete): *Sweedie the Swatter, The Plum Tree, Sweedie Learns to Swim, Sweedie at the Fair, The Fable of the Bush League Lover Who Failed to Qualify* 1914; *Sweedie's Suicide, Sweedie and Her Dog, Sweedie's Hopeless Love, Sweedie Goes to College, Sweedie in Vaudeville, The Slim Princess, The Broken Pledge* 1915; *A Dash of Courage* 1916; *Teddy at the Throttle, Cactus Nell, Patria* (serial), *The Little American* 1917; *Johanna Enlists* 1918; *The Unpardonable Sin, The Love Burglar, The Life Line, Soldiers of Fortune, Victory* 1919; *Behind the Door, The Virgin of Stamboul, The Mollycoddle, The Last of the Mohicans, The Roundup* 1920; *A Tale of Two Worlds, The Four Horsemen of the Apocalypse,* 1921; *The Rosary, Trouble, Robin Hood* (as King Richard the Lion-Hearted) 1922; *Bavu, The Drums of Jeopardy, the Flame of Life, Stormswept, Three Ages, White Tiger, Ashes of Vengeance, Drifting, The Spanish Dancer* (as King Philip IV), *The Eternal Struggle, Richard the Lion-Hearted* (title role) 1923; *Unseen Hands, The Sea Hawk, The Signal Tower, The Red Lily* 1924; *So Big, The Devil's Cargo, The Lost World, The Great Divide, Adventure, The Wanderer, The Pony Express, Rugged Water* 1925; *Behind the Front, Volcano, We're in the Navy Now, Old Ironsides* 1926; *Casey at the Bat, Fireman Save My Child, Now We're in the Air* 1927; *Wife Savers, Partners in Crime, The Big Killing, Beggars of Life* 1928; *Chinatown Nights, The River of Romance, Stairs of Sand* 1929; *The Big House, Billy the Kid, A Lady's Morals, Min and Bill, Way for a Sailor* 1930; *The Stolen Jools* (charity short), *The Secret Six, The Champ, Hell Divers* 1931; *Grand Hotel, Flesh* 1932; *Tugboat Annie, Dinner at Eight, The Bowery* 1933; *Viva Villa!* (as Pancho Villa), *Treasure Island* (as Long John Silver), *The Mighty Barnum* (as circus showman P. T. Barnum) 1934; *West Point of the Air, China Seas, O'Shaughnessy's Boy, Ah Wilderness!* 1935; *A Message to Garcia, Old Hutch* 1936; *Good Old Soak, Slave Ship* 1937; *The Bad Man of Brimstone, Port of Seven Seas, Stablemates* 1938; *Stand Up and Fight, Sergeant Madden, Thunder Afloat* 1939; *The Man From Dakota, Twenty-Mule Team, Wyoming* 1940; *The Bad Man, Barnacle Bill* 1941; *The Bugle Sounds, Jackass Mail* 1942; *Salute to the Marines* 1943; *Rationing, Barbary Coast Gent* 1944; *This Man's Navy* 1945; *Bad Bascomb* 1946; *The Mighty McGurk* 1947; *Alias a Gentleman, A Date with Judy* 1948; *Big Jack* 1949.

Begley, Ed. Actor. *b.* Edward James Begley, Mar. 25, 1901, Hartford, Conn., of Irish immigrant parents. *d.* 1970. At 11, after only five years of grammar school, he ran away from home to join a traveling carnival, then worked at an assortment of odd jobs and served in the US Navy before embarking on a show-business career as a radio announcer in 1931. In 1943 he made his Broadway stage debut, and in 1947 he created the Joe Keller role on Broadway in Arthur Miller's 'All My Sons,' directed by Elia Kazan. That same year he made his film debut in *Boomerang,* also directed by Kazan. From then on he was kept busy in a wide range of roles, on stage and in films.

After a brilliant characterization of William Jennings Bryan during 789 performances in Broadway's 'Inherit the Wind,' he took over the opposing role of Clarence Darrow from Paul Muni in 1955, playing it with equal brilliance. Begley appeared in some 12,000 radio shows, 250 television shows, a dozen Broadway plays, and 35 motion pictures. On the screen he usually played imposing heavy types, often a corrupt businessman or politician. Among his most impressive appearances were those in *Patterns* and *12 Angry Men,* in which he repeated earlier TV triumphs. Perhaps his finest portrayal came in *Sweet Bird of Youth* as Boss Finley, for which he won the 1962 Academy Award as best supporting actor. He was also comfortable in lighter fare, such as *The Unsinkable Molly Brown* (1964), in which he sang, danced, and clowned. Father of Ed BEGLEY Jr.

FILMS INCLUDE: *Boomerang* 1947; *Sitting Pretty, The Street with No Name, Sorry Wrong Number* 1948; *The Great Gatsby* 1949; *Backfire, Dark City, Convicted* 1950; *On Dangerous Ground* 1951; *Deadline U.S.A., The Turning Point, Lone Star* 1952; *Patterns* 1956; *12 Angry Men* 1957; *Odds Against Tomorrow* 1959; *The Green Helmet* 1961; *Sweet Bird of Youth* 1962; *The Unsinkable Molly Brown* 1964; *The Oscar* 1966; *Billion Dollar Brain, Warning Shot* 1967; *Hang 'Em High, Firecreek, Wild in the Streets* 1968; *The Monitors* 1969; *The Dunwich Horror, Road to Salina* 1970.

Begley, Ed, Jr. Actor. Born on Sept. 16, 1949, in Los Angeles. The son of character player Ed BEGLEY, he made his acting debut at 17 as a guest star in TV's 'My Three Sons.' He subsequently appeared in numerous films and TV shows, mainly in supporting parts. He was nominated twice for Emmy Awards for his regular role (1982–88) in the series 'St. Elsewhere.'

FILMS INCLUDE: *Now You See Him, Now You Don't* 1972; *Charley and the Angel* 1973; *Superdad* 1974; *Stay Hungry* 1976; *Citizen's Band/Handle With Care* 1977; *Blue Collar, Goin' South, The One and Only* 1978; *Hardcore, Battlestar Galactica, The In-Laws, The Concorde—Airport '79* 1979; *Buddy Buddy* 1981; *Cat People, Eating Raoul* 1982; *Get Crazy* 1983; *This Is Spinal Tap, Streets of Fire* 1984; *Transylvania 6–5000* 1985; *Amazon Women on the Moon* 1987; *The Accidental Tourist* 1988; *Scenes from the Class Struggle in Beverly Hills, She-Devil* 1989; *Meet The Applegates* 1991; *Even Cowgirls Get the Blues, Greedy, The Pagemaster, Renaissance Man* 1994; *Batman Forever* (unbilled cameo) 1995.

Behrman, S(amuel) N(athaniel). Playwright, screenwriter. *b.* June 9, 1893, Worcester, Mass. *d.* 1973. *ed.* Harvard (B.A.), Columbia (M.A.). A leading Broadway writer of witty comedy, biographer *(Duveen, Portrait of Max)*, and novelist *(The Burning Glass),* he also contributed original stories, adaptations, screenplays, and dialogues, alone or in collaboration, to many Hollywood films, including several Garbo vehicles.

FILMS INCLUDE: *The Sea Wolf, Liliom, Lightnin'* 1930; *The Brat, Surrender, Daddy Long Legs* 1931; *Tess of the Storm*

Country, Rebecca of Sunnybrook Farm 1932; *Hallelujah I'm a Bum, Queen Christina* 1933; *Anna Karenina, A Tale of Two Cities* 1935; *Parnell, Conquest* 1937; *The Cowboy and the Lady* 1938; *No Time for Comedy* (play basis only), *Waterloo Bridge* 1940; *Two-Faced Woman* 1941; *The Pirate* (play basis only) 1948; *Quo Vadis* 1951; *Gaby* 1956; *Me and the Colonel* (from his and Franz Werfel's play 'Jacobowsky and the Colonel') 1958; *Fanny* (partly based on the play he wrote with Josh Logan and Harold Rome) 1961.

Beineix, Jean-Jacques. Director. Born in 1946, in France. He entered films in 1970 as an assistant director and within several years began collaborating on screenplays. In 1977, he directed a short, *Le Chien de Monsieur Marcel,* which won first prize at the Trouville Festivals. He won international acclaim, a César Award and a number of festival prizes for his very first feature, the visually stunning thriller *Diva* (1981). His *Betty Blue* (1986) was nominated for an Oscar as best foreign language film.

FILMS: *Diva* (also co-sc., dial.) 1981; *La Lune dans le Caniveau/The Moon in the Gutter* (also co-sc.) 1983; *37.2 le Matin/Betty Blue* (also sc., co-prod.) 1986; *Le Grande Cirque* (act., prod.), *Roselyne et les Lions* (dir., prod., sc.) 1989; *Island of Pachyderms* 1992.

Belafonte, Harry. Singer, actor. Born Harold George Belafonte, Jr., on Mar. 1, 1927, in Harlem, New York City. He spent a good part of his poverty-stricken childhood in Jamaica, his father's birthplace. In 1944 he quit high school to join the Navy. After the war he worked at various manual jobs while attending the Dramatic Workshop in New York. In 1952 he started his professional career singing folk ballads and helping to popularize the calypso beat. Film debut in 1953 in *Bright Road.* That same year he won a Tony award for his performance in 'John Murray Anderson's Almanac' on Broadway. A handsome man with a velvet husky voice, he has made many successful concert tours, recordings, and TV appearances but has appeared only sporadically in films. In 1992, he considered a bid for a Democratic seat in the New York Senate. His daughter, Shari Belafonte-Harper (*b.* Sept. 22, 1954 in New York City), is a successful model and sometime actress in TV and films.

FILMS: *Bright Road* 1953; *Carmen Jones* 1955; *Island in the Sun* 1957; *The World the Flesh and the Devil, Odds Against Tomorrow* 1959; *King* (doc.), *The Angel Levine* 1970; *Buck and the Preacher* 1972; *Uptown Saturday Night* 1974; *Beat Street* (co-prod., co-mus. only) 1984; *Beetlejuice* (song) 1988; *First Look* 1989; *The Player* (cameo) 1992; *Ready to Wear* 1994; *White Man's Burden* 1995; *Kansas City* 1996.

Bel Geddes, Barbara. Actress. Born on Oct. 31, 1922, in New York City. The daughter of architect and stage designer Norman Bel Geddes. First stage appearance in 1940, a walk-on in 'The School for Scandal' in summer stock. She made her Broadway debut the following year as the ingenue in 'Out of the Frying Pan' and has since appeared in many plays, including 'The Moon Is Blue' (1951), 'Cat on a Hot Tin Roof' (1955), and 'Mary Mary' (1961). In 1945 she won a New York Drama Critics Award for her portrayal in 'Deep Are the Roots.' She made a strong impression with her first screen role in *The Long Night* (1947) and was nominated for a supporting actress Oscar for *I Remember Mama* (1948), but in spite of continued critical acclaim, her screen appearances have been few, partly as a consequence of the House Un-American Activities Committee hearings of the early 50s. Seen in many live TV plays in the early days of the medium, as well as in episodes of 'Alfred Hitchcock Presents,' she returned to the small screen in 1978, to play the role of Miss Ellie Ewing in 'Dallas.' She won an Emmy Award in 1980, and remained with the series for the duration of the 80s, taking a breather in 1984 to recuperate from a heart operation. Miss Bel Geddes also designed greeting cards and illustrated children books.

FILMS: *The Long Night* 1947; *I Remember Mama, Blood on the Moon* 1948; *Caught* 1949; *Panic in the Streets* 1950; *Fourteen Hours* 1951; *Vertigo* 1958; *The Five Pennies, Five Branded Women* 1959; *By Love Possessed* 1961; *Summer-tree, The Todd Killings* 1971.

Belgium. The physical and cultural proximity of this small country to both France and Holland has been a factor in the slow development of its film industry. The local market is not large enough to support regular feature film production, and Belgian filmmakers must produce their more ambitious projects jointly with other countries. Much of the French-speaking Belgian talent (for example, Chantal AKERMAN) has been assimilated into the film industry of France. As a result, Flemish-speaking films have been more prevalent in Belgium, and their appeal is limited to the Belgian-Dutch market. Feature film production has nevertheless proceeded on a limited scale since the mid-20s. Few Belgian feature films are of international significance, and they are rarely exhibited abroad. Documentary, art appreciation, and scientific films, mostly shorts, are the backbone of the Belgian film industry; many have won international awards. Foremost among the documentary directors is Henri STORCK. Feature director Jaco von Dormael (*Toto le Héros*, 1991) has received international acclaim.

Belita. Ice skater, dancer, actress. Born Gladys Lyne Jepson-Turner, on Oct. 25, 1923, in Garlogs, Hampshire, England. An expert skater from childhood, she was a featured attraction of an ice ballet before she reached 11. At 14 she starred in the London spectacle 'Opera on Ice.' The following year she toured the US, then starred for two years as headliner of the 'Ice Capades.' Hollywood presented her in a number of films, most of them with a skating or ballet background.

FILMS: *Ice Capades* 1941; *Silver Skates* 1943; *Lady Let's Dance* 1944; *Suspense* 1946; *The Gangster* 1947; *The Hunted* 1948; *The Man on the Eiffel Tower* 1949; *Never Let Me Go* 1953; *Invitation to the Dance, Silk Stockings* 1957; *The Terrace* 1964.

Bell, Marie. Actress. *b.* Marie-Jeanne Bellon-Downey, Dec. 23, 1900, Bégles, France *d.* 1985. She began as a dancer in England at 13. Later studied drama at the Paris Conservatory and in 1928 became a member of the Comédie-Française. She played supporting roles in French silent films from 1924, but came into her own with the advent of sound, playing many distinguished parts. Her two best-known films are Feyder's *Le Grand Jeu* 1934 and Duvivier's *Un Carnet de Bal* 1937. She was awarded the Legion of Honor by General de Gaulle for her activity in the French Resistance during WW II.

FILMS INCLUDE: *Paris* 1924; *La Valse de l'Adieu* 1926; *Madame Récamier* 1928; *Figaro* 1929; *La Nuit est à nous/The Night Is Ours* (Fr./Ger.), *L'Homme qui assassina* 1930; *La Chance* 1931; *L'Homme à l'Hispano* 1933; *Le Grand Jeu, Fédora, Polichè* 1934; *La Garçonne* 1936; *Pantins d'Amour, Un Carnet de Bal* 1937; *Lègion d'Honneur* 1938; *La Charrette fantôme/The Phantom Carriage* 1939; *Ceux du Ciel* 1940; *Vie privée* 1942; *Le Colonel Chabert* 1943; *La Bonne Soupe/Careless Love* 1964; *Vaghe Stelle dell'Orsa/Sandra* (It.) 1965; *Hotel Paradiso* (UK/US) 1966; *Les Volets clos* 1973.

Bell, Monta. Director, producer, screenwriter, film editor. *b.* Feb. 5, 1891, Washington, D.C. *d.* 1958. He started out as a newspaperman, eventually becoming an editor on the Washington *Herald.* He then spent two years producing, directing, and acting in stock. In Hollywood in the early 20s, he befriended Charlie CHAPLIN and in 1923 appeared as an actor in

Chaplin's *The Pilgrim* and was entrusted with the editing of another Chaplin film, *A Woman of Paris.* He became a director the following year and after turning out two films for Warner Bros. joined MGM, a studio with which he remained for several years. His most important assignment there was Greta GARBO's first American film, *The Torrent* (1926). His directorial style was much influenced by the work of Ernst LUBITSCH. In 1929, Bell was put in charge of production at Paramount's Astoria, N.Y., sound studios. Although he continued directing occasionally, he functioned chiefly as a producer and dialogue writer after 1932. Among the films he produced are *The Big Pond* (1930), *Applause* (assoc. prod.), *The Letter* (1931), *The Worst Woman in Paris* (1933), *Men in White* (1934), *West Point of the Air* (1935), and *Aloma of the South Seas, Birth of the Blues,* and *Beyond the Blue Horizon* (all 1941). At one time he was married to actress Betty Lawford.

FILMS (as director): *Broadway After Dark, How to Educate a Wife, The Snob* (also sc.) 1924; *Lady of the Night, Pretty Ladies, The King on Main Street* (also adapt.), *Lights of Old Broadway* 1925; *The Torrent/Ibanez's Torrent, The Boy Friend, Upstage* 1926; *After Midnight* (also story), *Man Woman and Sin* (also story) 1927; *Bellamy Trial* (also sc.) 1929; *Young Man of Manhattan, East Is West* 1930; *The Fires of Youth* (also story), *Up for Murder* (also story), *Personal Maid* (co-dir. with Lothar Mendes) 1931; *Downstairs* 1932; *The Worst Woman in Paris?* (also prod., story, sc.) 1933; *China's Little Devils* 1945.

Bell, Rex. Actor. *b.* George Francis Beldam, Oct. 16, 1905, Chicago. *d.* 1962. *ed.* U. of Iowa. A tall, handsome college football hero, he played leads and supporting parts in late silent and early sound Hollywood films, mostly romantic comedies and dramas. But it was as a Western star in the 30s that he enjoyed his greatest popularity. In 1931 he made headlines by eloping with the screen's famous "It" girl, Clara Bow. They married and settled down on a Nevada ranch. Bell retired from films in the early 40s and ran a store in Las Vegas. In 1954 he was elected lieutenant governor of Nevada, and in 1958 he made an unsuccessful bid for the governorship of the state.

FILMS INCLUDE: *The Cowboy Kid, Wild West Romance* 1928; *Salute, Joy Street, They Had to See Paris, Pleasure Crazed* 1929; *Harmony at Home, Lightnin', True to the Navy* 1930; *Forgotten Women, Law of the Sea* 1931; *From Broadway to Cheyenne, The Man from Arizona, Crashin' Broadway, Arm of the Law* 1932; *Fighting Texans, The Diamond Trail, The Fugitive, Rainbow Ranch* 1933; *Saddle Aces, Gunfire, Fighting Pioneer* 1935; *The Idaho Kid, Stormy Trails, West of Nevada, Too Much Beef* 1936; *Tombstone—The Town Too Tough to Die, Dawn on the Great Divide* 1942; *Lone Star* 1952; *The Misfits* 1961.

Bell, Tom. Actor. Born in 1932, in Liverpool, England. Gaunt, brooding leading man of the British stage, TV, and films. In regional repertory from age 15, he made his screen debut in 1960. Often seen in lean, mean roles, occasionally in leads, mainly in supporting parts. He portrayed Nazi monster Adolf Eichmann in the TV miniseries 'Holocaust' (1978).

FILMS INCLUDE: *The Criminal/The Concrete Jungle* 1960; *Payroll, The Kitchen* 1961; *H.M.S. Defiant/Damn the Defiant!, A Prize of Arms, The L-Shaped Room* 1962; *Ballad in Blue/Blues for Lovers, Sands of Beersheba* (Isr./US) 1965; *He Who Rides a Tiger* 1966; *In Enemy Country* (US), *The Long Day's Dying* 1968; *Lock Up Your Daughters* 1969; *All the Right Noises, Quest for Love* 1971; *Royal Flash* 1975; *The Sailor's Return* 1978; *Wish You Were Here, The Magic Toy Shop* 1987; *Resurrected* 1989; *The Krays* 1990; *Dark River, Let Him Have It, Prospero's Books* 1991; *Feast of July* 1995; *Preaching to the Perverted* 1997.

Bellamy, Earl. Director. Born on Mar. 11, 1917, in Minneapolis. *ed.* City College of Los Angeles. A veteran producer and director of successful TV series, he has also directed occasional low-budget films since the late 50s, mostly Westerns.

FILMS: *Seminole Uprising* 1955; *Blackjack Ketchum—Desperado* 1956; *Toughest Gun in Tombstone* 1958; *Stagecoach to Dancers' Rock* (also prod.) 1962; *Fluffy* 1965; *Gunpoint, Incident at Phantom Hill, Munster Go Home!* 1966; *Three Guns for Texas* ("No Bugle—One Drum" episode, orig. made for TV's 'Laredo' series) 1968; *Backtrack* (re-cut from various TV episodes) 1969; *Sidecar Races, Seven Alone, Part 2 Walking Tall, Against a Crooked Sky* 1975; *Sidewinder One* 1977; *Speedtrap* 1978; *Magnum Thrust* 1981.

Bellamy, Madge. Actress. *b.* Margaret Phillpot, June 30, 1900, Hillsboro, Tex. *d.* 1990. Popular star of Hollywood silents and early talkies. The daughter of the dean of literature at the University of Texas, she made her stage debut at five and took up acting seriously ten years later. As a screen personality from 1920, she projected sweet innocence and good breeding. She starred in several prestigious productions, such as *Lorna Doone* and John Ford's *The Iron Horse,* and she remains memorable for her role in the horror chiller *White Zombie,* but most of her vehicles were undistinguished and her career disintegrated by the mid-30s. Bellamy's 1928 marriage to a stockbroker lasted only four days. In 1943 she was given a six-month suspended sentence for shooting a boyfriend, lumber magnate A. Stanford Murphy, after he abruptly married another woman. In *Darling of the Twenties* (1990), an autobiography completed just before her death, she tells of her glory years and of her post-career days of lonely anonymity and abject poverty.

FILMS INCLUDE: *The Riddle Woman* 1920; *The Cup of Life, Blind Hearts, The Call of the North, Hail the Woman, Love Never Dies* 1921; *Lorna Doone, The Hottentot* 1922; *Are You a Failure?, The Soul of the Beast* 1923; *Love's Whirlpool, His Forgotten Wife, No More Women, The White Sin, Love and Glory, The Iron Horse* 1924; *A Fool and His Money, The Reckless Sex, Havoc, The Dancers, The Parasite, Wings of Youth, Lightnin', Lazybones, The Golden Strain* 1925; *Sandy, Black Paradise, Summer Bachelors, Bertha the Sewing Machine Girl* 1926; *Ankles Preferred, Colleen, The Telephone Girl, Silk Legs* 1927; *Soft Living, The Play Girl, Mother Knows Best* 1928; *Tonight at Twelve, Fugitives* 1929; *White Zombie* 1932; *Gordon of Ghost City* (serial), *Charlie Chan in London* 1934; *The Great Hotel Murder, The Daring Young Man* 1935; *Northwest Trail* 1945.

Bellamy, Ralph. Actor. *b.* June 17, 1904, Chicago. *d.* 1991. Directly out of high school, he began an intensive apprenticeship for a stage career—acting, directing, producing, designing sets, and handling props with 15 different traveling stock companies during a ten-year stint. In 1927 he started his own company, the Ralph Bellamy players. Two years later he made an inauspicious Broadway debut in a short-lived play. In Hollywood from the early 30s, he played leads in dozens of B pictures, including the title role in the "Ellery Queen" detective series. Concurrently, he became typecast as the "other man" who loses the girl to the hero in a string of sophisticated comedies, starting with *The Awful Truth* (1937). He was nominated for an Oscar for his performance in that film. After the mid-40s, he worked primarily on the stage, giving fine performances in such Broadway plays as 'Tomorrow the World,' 'State of the Union,' 'Detective Story,' and his most memorable achievement, the role of FDR in 'Sunrise at Campobello' (1958), for which he received many accolades, including the Tony and the New York Drama Critics awards. In 1960 he repeated the role in the film version. From the mid-40s he was seen only occasionally in films, in character parts. He was more active on TV, appearing both in series ('Men Against Crime,' 'The Eleventh Hour') and in specials. Between 1940 and 1960 he served on the State of California Arts Commission. He served four terms (1952–64) as president of Actors' Equity. In 1986 he was awarded an Honorary Oscar "for his unique artistry and his distinguished service to the profession of acting." Autobiography: *When the Smoke Hit the Fan* (1979).

FILMS INCLUDE: *The Secret Six, The Magnificent Lie, Surrender* 1931; *Forbidden, Rebecca of Sunnybrook Farm, Air Mail* 1932; *Second Hand Wife, Destination Unknown, The Picture Snatcher, Flying Devils, Ace of Aces* 1933; *Spitfire, This Man Is Mine* 1934; *Helldorado, Gigolette, Hands Across the Table* 1935; *Dangerous Intrigue, The Man Who Lived Twice* 1936; *Let's Get Married, The Awful Truth* 1937; *Fools for Scandal, Boy Meets Girl, Carefree* 1938; *Trade Winds, Let Us Live, Blind Alley* 1939; *His Girl Friday, Brother Orchid, Dance Girl Dance* 1940; several "Ellery Queen" films 1940–41; *Footsteps in the Dark, Affectionately Yours, Dive Bomber, The Wolf Man* 1941; *The Ghost of Frankenstein, Lady in a Jam* 1942; *Guest in the House* 1944; *Delightfully Dangerous, Lady on a Train* 1945; *The Court-Martial of Billy Mitchell* 1955; *Sunrise at Campobello* 1960; *The Professionals* 1966; *Rosemary's Baby* 1968; *Doctors' Wives* 1971; *Cancel My Reservation* 1972; *Oh God!* 1977; *Trading Places* 1983; *Disorderlies, Amazon Women on the Moon* 1987; *Coming to America, The Good Mother* 1988; *Pretty Woman* 1990.

Bellocchio, Marco. Director. Born on Nov. 9, in 1939, in Piacenza, Italy. The son of a lawyer and a schoolteacher, he had a strict Catholic upbringing in a bourgeois home. Having trained briefly as an actor, he interrupted his philosophy studies at Milan's University of the Sacred Heart to study directing at Rome's Centro Sperimentale film school and London's Slade School of Art. He directed several shorts and documentaries before making an auspicious debut as a feature director in 1965 with *I Pugni in Tasca/Fist in His Pocket,* an award winner at the Locarno Film Festival. The film, a powerful comment on social decadence symbolized through a sordid tale of incestuous relations among a family of epileptics, was made with a tiny budget, much of it borrowed from Bellocchio's own family. It immediately established Bellocchio as a major new talent in the Italian cinema. Bellocchio used his favorite dramatic device—a bourgeois family as a microcosm of society and its ills—once more in his second feature, *La Cina e vicina/China Is Near,* winner of both the Special Jury Prize (shared) and the International Critics Prize at the 1967 Venice Festival. The following year, however, he joined the extreme-left Communist Union and renounced fictional films for politically militant cinema. He became involved in the co-operative production of propaganda shorts and seemed lost to mainstream cinema. But he returned to features and his favorite anti-establishment allegorical themes with *Nel Nome del Padre/In the Name of the Father* (1971). His handling of *Salto nel Vuoto/Leap Into Void* resulted in the awarding of both the best actor and best actress prizes to the film's stars, Michel Piccoli and Anouk Aimée, at the 1980 Cannes Festival.

FEATURE FILMS: *I Pugni in Tasca/Fist in His Pocket* (also sc.) 1966; *La Cina e Vicina/China Is Near* (also story, co-sc.) 1967; *Amore e Rabbia/Vangelo '70* ("Discutiamo Discutiamo" episode; also act.) 1969; *Nel Nome del Padre/In the Name of the Father* (also story, sc.) 1971; *Sbatti il Monstro in Prima Pagina/Strike the Monster on Page One* 1972; *Marcia Trionfale/Victory March* (also co-sc.) 1976; *Les Yeux fertiles* (Fr./It.), *Il Gabbiano* (also co-sc.) 1977; *Salto nel Vuoto/Leap Into Void* (also story, co-sc.) 1980; *Gli Occhi la Bocca/The Eyes the Mouth* (also co-story co-sc.) 1982; *Enrico IV/Henry IV* (also co-sc.) 1984; *Il Diavolo in Corpo/Devil in the Flesh* (also co-sc.) 1986; *La Visione del Sabba* (dir., sc.) 1988; *La Condanna* 1991; *Il Sogne della Farfalla* 1994.

Belmondo, Jean-Paul. Actor. Born on Apr. 9, 1933, in Neuilly-sur-Seine, near Paris. The son of a sculptor. He studied drama at the Paris Conservatory and for several years performed on stage in the provinces before breaking into Paris theaters. He had appeared in supporting roles in nine films prior to his "overnight" rise to fame as the protagonist of Godard's first feature film, *À Bout de Souffle/Breathless* (1960), in which he played a sort of cross between Humphrey Bogart and James Dean, with a bit of James Cagney, Marlon Brando, and Jean Gabin thrown in. He soon became established as France's leading male star, an antiheroic screen incarnation of the New Wave's image of rebellious youth. His appealing sweet-and-sour personality made him popular with international audiences. In 1963 he was elected president of the French actor's union and published an autobiography, *Trente Ans et Vingt-Cinq Films (Thirty Years and Twenty-Five Films).* Although he has appeared indiscriminately in numerous French and international productions, good, mediocre, and bad, he has managed to remain a top screen star thanks to the winning combination of his acting talent and engaging personality. He heads his own production company, Cerito films.

FILMS INCLUDE: *Soi Belle et tais-toi/Be Beautiful but Shut Up, Les Tricheurs/The Cheaters, Drôle de Dimanche* 1958; *A Double Tour/Leda/Web of Passion, Ein Engel auf Erden/Angel on Earth* (Ger./Fr.) 1959; *Classe tous Risques/The Big Risk, À Bout de Souffle/Breathless, Moderato Cantabile, La Français et l'Amour/Love and the Frenchwoman, La Ciociara/Two Women* (It./Fr.), *Lettere di una Novizia/Rita* (It./Fr.) 1960; *La Viaccia/The Love Makers* (It./Fr.), *Léon Morin—Prêtre, Une Femme est une Femme/A Woman Is a Woman, Un nomée La Rocca,* 1961; *Cartouche, Un Singe en Hiver/A Monkey in Winter* 1962; *Le Doulos/Doulos—The Finger Man, L'Aîné de Ferchaux, Dragées au Poivre/Sweet and Sour* 1963; *L'Homme de Rio/That Man From Rio, Cent Mille Dollars au Soleil/Greed in the Sun, Week-End à Zuydcoote/Weekend at Dunkirk, Peau de Banane/Banana Peel, Echappement libre/Backfire, La Chasse à l'Homme/Male Hunt* 1964; *Pierrot le Fou, Les Tribulations d'un Chinois en Chine/Up to His Ears* 1965; *Paris brûle-t-il?/Is Paris Burning?* (Fr./US), *Tendre Voyou/Tender Scoundrel* 1966; *Casino Royale* (cameo; UK); *Le Voleur/The Thief of Paris* 1967; *Ho!* 1968; *Le Cerveau/The Brain, La Siréne du Mississippi/Mississippi Mermaid, Un Homme qui me plaît/Love Is a Funny Thing* 1969; *Borsalino* 1970; *Les Mariés de l'An Deux, Le Casse/The Burglars* 1971; *L'Héritier/The Inheritor, Docteur Popaul* 1972; *Le Magnifique, Stavisky* 1974; *L'Incorrigible, Peur sur la Ville/Night Caller* 1975; *L'Alpageur* (also exec. prod. co-sc.), *Le Corps de mon Ennemi* (also prod.) 1976; *L'Animal* 1977; *Flic ou voyou* 1979; *L'As des As* 1982; *Le Marginal* 1983; *Joyeuses Paques* (also prod.) 1984; *Hold-Up* 1985; *Le Solitaire* 1987; *Itinéraire d'un enfant gate* (also prod.) 1988; *Les Miserables* 1995.

below the line. See ABOVE THE LINE.

Belushi, James (Jim). Actor. Born on June 15, 1954, in Chicago. *ed.* DuPage Coll.; Southern Illinois U. Following in the footsteps of his older brother (and near lookalike), John BELUSHI, he performed with Chicago's Second City and reached Hollywood via television. He, too, would become (in 1983–85) a regular on NBC's 'Saturday Night Live.' Carving his own path after John's death, he proved himself a capable actor, playing leads and supporting roles, both comic and serious, in many films. Starred in Oliver STONE's futuristic TV mini-series 'Wild Palms' (1993).

FILMS: *Thief* 1981; *Trading Places* 1983; *The Man With One Red Shoe* 1985; *Salvador, About Last Night. . . , Jumpin' Jack Flash* (cameo), *Little Shop of Horrors* 1986; *Number One With a Bullet* (co-sc only), *The Principal, Real Men* 1987; *Red Heat* 1988; *Who's Harry Crumb?, K-9, Homer and Eddie* 1989; *Dimenticare Palermo/To Forget Palermo* (It./Fr.), *Taking Care of Business, Masters Of Menace* (cameo), *Mr. Destiny* 1990; *Only the Lonely, Curly Sue* 1991; *Once Upon a Crime, Diary of a Hitman, Traces of Red* 1992; *Canadian Bacon, Destiny Turns on the Radio, The Pebble and the Penguin* (v/o) 1995; *Jingle All the Way, Race the Sun* 1996.

Belushi, John. Actor. *b.* Jan. 24, 1949, Chicago, of Albanian descent. *d.* 1982. *ed.* U. of Michigan. Manic, outrageously funny star of American TV and films whose brief, spectacular career left its mark on the country's pop culture. An alumnus of Chicago's Second City comedy troupe (1971–72), he appeared in the 1973 off-Broadway revue 'Lemmings' before joining the original cast of the NBC TV series 'Saturday Night Live.' His absurd characterizations (a Samurai warrior and killer bee, among others) won him a devout cult following and an Emmy Award in 1977. He teamed with Dan AYKROYD to create the Blues Brothers duo for the show, a loving caricature of rhythm-and-blues stars, which later catapulted them into prominence in the popular movie, *The Blues Brothers*. Beefy and crass-featured, Belushi was ideally cast as the gross Bluto in his first film, *National Lampoon's Animal House* (1978), a crude parody of college life that became a huge box-office hit. He played another memorable role, as a lunatic fighter pilot, in Steven Spielberg's fiasco *1941* (1979). But his subsequent parts were far less rewarding. His meteoric rise and life in the fast lane were increasingly accompanied by booze and drugs. On March 5, 1982, he was found dead in a Beverly Hills hotel bungalow, the victim of a lethal dose of heroin and cocaine. His tragic story was told in Bob Woodward's best-selling *Wired* (1984) and its film adaptation (1989).

FILMS: *National Lampoon's Animal House, Goin' South* 1978; *Shame of the Jungle* (voice only for American re-edited vers. of '75 French-Belgian film *La Honte de la Jungle*), *Old Boyfriends, 1941* 1979; *The Blues Brothers* 1980; *Continental Divide, Neighbors* 1981.

Benaderet, Bea. See BANNON, Jim.

Benchley, Robert. Humorist, journalist, critic, screenwriter, actor. *b.* Sept. 15, 1889, Worcester, Mass. *d.* 1945. After graduating from Harvard in 1912 he did advertising and personnel work, then became associate editor of the New York *Tribune* Sunday magazine and later the editor of the Tribune *Graphic*. In 1918 he served as secretary of the federal Aircraft Board. After the war he was managing editor of *Vanity Fair,* then a columnist for the New York *World.* From 1920 to 1929 he was drama editor of *Life* and later became theater critic for *The New Yorker.*

Benchley's sophisticated wit found a delightful outlet in films. Between 1928 and 1945 he wrote and appeared in an outrageously funny series of short subjects in which he lectured on a variety of improbable topics, such as *The Sex Life of the Polyp, The Trouble with Husbands,* and *How to Take a Vacation.* He won an Academy Award for best short subject (comedy) for one of these ten-minute comedies, *How to Sleep* (1935). Made many appearances in feature films, usually as a bon vivant or a double-talking, amiable pest. He also collaborated on several screenplays. He was the father of author-screenwriter Nathaniel Benchley and grandfather of author-screenwriter Peter Benchley.

FILMS INCLUDE: Shorts (as actor-writer)—*The Treasurer's Report, The Sex Life of the Polyp* 1928; *Stewed Fried and Boiled* 1929; *Your Technocracy and Mine* 1933; *How to Sleep* 1935; *How to Behave, How to Vote, How to Become a Detective* 1936; *The Romance of Digestion, A Night at the Movies* 1937; *How to Figure Income Tax, Music Made Simple, The Courtship of a Newt, Mental Poise* 1938; *How to Sub-Let, Dark Magic, How to Eat, See Your Doctor* 1939; *That Inferior Feeling, Home Movies, The Trouble with Husbands* 1940; *Crime Control, The Forgotten Man, How to Take a Vacation* 1941; *Nothing but Nerves, Keeping in Shape* 1942; *My Tomato, No News Is Good News* 1943; *Boogie Woogie* 1945. Features (as actor): *The Sport Parade* 1932; *Headline Shooters, Dancing Lady* 1933; *Social Register* 1934; *Murder on a Honeymoon* (co-sc. only), *China Seas* 1935; *Piccadilly Jim* 1936; *Live Love and Learn* 1937; *Foreign Correspondent* (also dial.), *Hired Wife* 1940; *Nice Girl?, You'll Never Get Rich, Bedtime Story* 1941; *Take a Letter Darling, The Major and the Minor, I Married a Witch* 1942; *The Sky's the Limit, Flesh and Fantasy* 1943; *Song of Russia, See Here Private Hargrove, Practically Yours* 1944; *It's in the Bag, Weekend at the Waldorf, Kiss and Tell* 1945; *Road to Utopia, The Bride Wore Boots, Janie Gets Married* 1946.

Bender, Lawrence. Producer, actor. Born 1958, in the Bronx, N.Y. *ed.* University of Maine. Primarily known as producing partner to Quentin TARANTINO on such films as *Reservoir Dogs* (1992) and *Pulp Fiction* (1994), he began as an actor-dancer, appearing in mostly bit parts. After training at the American Film Institute, where he met Tarantino, he embarked on a producing career of mostly violent, over-the-top but brilliantly written and performed features. He was nominated for a best picture Academy Award for *Pulp Fiction*.

FILMS: As producer or executive producer—*Reservoir Dogs* (also act.) 1992; *Fresh, Killing Zoe, Pulp Fiction* (also act.) 1994; *Four Rooms* (also act.), *White Man's Burden* (also act.) 1995; *From Dusk Till Dawn* 1996.

Bendix, William. Actor. *b.* Jan. 4, 1906, New York City. *d.* 1964. The son of Max Bendix, conductor and violinist of the Metropolitan Opera Orchestra, he appeared in a Vitagraph film as a five-year-old child. Later played minor league baseball, managed a grocery store in Newark, N.J., and was with the New Jersey Federal Theater before joining the New York Theater Guild. Made his Broadway debut as an Irish cop in William Saroyan's 'The Time of Your Life' in 1939. He began a prolific Hollywood career in 1942 and was promptly nominated for a best supporting actor Academy Award for *Wake Island.* But despite a long succession of imposing film roles he remains best known to many for his weekly 'Life of Riley' show, first on radio, then on TV. Large-skulled and heavy jawed, he typically played either dumb and brutish or kindly but simple characters. His memorable films include his starring role in *The Hairy Ape* and *The Babe Ruth Story* and appearances in *Lifeboat* and *A Bell for Adano,* as well as his several appearances in Alan Ladd action vehicles.

FILMS INCLUDE: *Woman of the Year, Brooklyn Orchid, Wake Island, The Glass Key, Who Done It?* 1942; *Taxi Mister, China, Hostages, Guadalcanal Diary* 1943; *Lifeboat, The Hairy Ape, Greenwich Village, Abroad with Two Yanks* 1944; *It's in the Bag, A Bell for Adano, Don Juan Quilligan* 1945; *Sentimental Journey, The Dark Corner, The Blue Dahlia, Two Years Before the Mast* 1946; *Blaze of Noon, Calcutta, The Web, Where There's Life* 1947; *The Time of Your Life, The Babe Ruth Story* 1948; *A Connecticut Yankee in King Arthur's Court, The Life of Riley, Streets of Laredo, The Big Steal* 1949; *Johnny Holiday, Kill the Umpire* 1950; *Detective Story, Submarine Command* 1951; *A Girl in Every Port, Macao* 1952; *Dangerous Mission*

1954; *Crashout* 1955; *The Deep Six* 1958; *The Rough and the Smooth/Portrait of a Sinner* (UK) 1959; *Johnny Nobody* (UK) 1961; *Boys' Night Out* 1962; *For Love or Money* 1963; *Law of the Lawless* 1964; *Young Fury* 1965.

Benedek, Laslo (Laszlo). Director. *b.* Mar. 5, 1907, in Budapest. *d.* 1992. After psychiatry studies at the University of Vienna, he joined UfA in Berlin as assistant cameraman, then cameraman and assistant to producer Joe PASTERNAK, whom he followed to Vienna in 1933. Later he worked as film editor in France and screenwriter in England. In 1937 he came to the US, resuming his film career as editor, for MGM. He then worked in Mexico as screenwriter. Upon returning to Hollywood, he renewed his association with Pasternak, becoming associate producer of some of the latter's musical films. In 1948 he directed his first film, the musical *The Kissing Bandit,* with Frank Sinatra.

Benedek's career as a director was spotty, highlighted by only two important films, both produced by Stanley Kramer, *Death of a Salesman* (1951), which many critics panned for lack of filmic originality, attributing its success to the strength of the Miller play, and *The Wild One* (1954), with Marlon Brando and Lee Marvin, which has been highly praised both as a visual treat and as a social document. Retiring from active filmmaking in the mid-70s, he turned to teaching. He was the chairman of the graduate film program at NYU from 1976 to 1980, then taught film at the University of Pennsylvania and at the Film and TV Academy in Munich, Germany. He also served as production advisor to South Carolina Educational TV.

FILMS: *The Kissing Bandit* 1948; *Port of New York* 1949; *Death of a Salesman* 1951; *The Wild One, Bengal Brigade* 1954; *Kinder Mütter und ein General* (Ger.) 1955; *Affair in Havana* 1957; *Malaga/Moment of Danger* (UK) 1959; *Recours en Grâce* (Fr.) 1960; *Namu the Killer Whale* (also prod.) 1966; *Daring Game* 1968; *The Night Visitor* (Sw.) 1971; *Assault on Agathon* (UK/Ger.) 1975; *King Kong's Faust* (act. only) 1985.

Benegal, Shyam. Director. Born on Dec. 14, 1934, in Alwal, near Hyderabad, India. One of ten children of a still photographer, he made his first home movie at 12 with a hand-cranked camera and became enamored with the medium. He later founded a film society and became involved in drama during his studies at Osmania University, where he received a master's degree in economics. Arriving in Bombay on the false promise of a job, with only five rupees in his pocket, he endured hardships before securing a position as a copywriter with a large advertising agency. Eventually, he began scripting, then directing advertising shorts for the agency and during the next ten years turned out more than 250 commercials and some 30 documentaries. In 1969 he went to the US on a fellowship, observed the operations of New York's Children's Television Workshop, and was briefly engaged as an associate producer in a Boston TV station.

Benegal was 40 by the time he directed his first feature film, *The Seedling* (1974). Like many of his future films, it was set against a rural background, paced leisurely, shot austerely in attractive color, dealt with the theme of revolution against oppression, and depicted women with a compassionate understanding uncharacteristic of the traditional Indian cinema. Making his films in the popular Hindi, rather than regional dialect, Benegal rapidly gained a loyal following at home. His reputation abroad grew steadily as his films garnered top prizes at international film festivals.

FEATURE FILMS: *The Seedling* 1974; *Charandas the Thief, Night's End* 1975; *The Churning* 1976; *The Role, The Boon/The Sqae From the Sea* 1977; *Possessed/The Obsession/ Flight of Pigeons* 1978; *The Machine Age* 1981; *The Ascent/ Ascending Scale* 1982; *The Marketplace* 1983; *Trikal/Past Present Future* 1986.

Benigni, Roberto. Actor, screenwriter, director, comedian. Elastic-faced, wiry, and hilarious comic lead and supporting player of Italian and several American films from the 70s. One of Italy's most noted and beloved actors, he is most recognizable to American audiences as the zany, put-upon cab driver in Jim JARMUSCH's *Night on Earth* (1991) and the illegitimate offspring of the late Peter SELLERS's famous character in *Son of the Pink Panther* (1993). Having worked with many top international directors such as FELLINI and COSTA-GAVRAS, his films have found a growing American audience specifically on the art-house circuit. He is married to actress Nicoletta Braschi.

FILMS INCLUDE: In Italy except where noted—*Letti Selvaggi* 1978; *Chedo Asilo, Womanlight, I Giorni Cantati, Luna, Wild Beds* 1979; *Il Minestrone* 1980; *Il Pap'Occhio* 1981; *FFSS Cioe, Lieto Fine, Tu Mi Turbi* (also dir., sc.) 1983; *Non ci resta che piangere* (also dir., sc.) 1984; *Tuttobenigni* 1985; *Coffee and Cigarettes* (also sc.), *Down By Law* (US) 1986; *The Little Devil* (also dir., sc.) 1988; *La Voce della Luna* 1990; *Johnny Stecchino* (also sc.), *Night on Earth* (US) 1991; *Son of the Pink Panther* (US), *Faraway, So Close!* (Ger.) 1993; *The Monster* (also prod., dir.; US release 1996) 1995.

Bening, Annette. Actress. *b.* May 29, 1958, in Topeka, Kan. *ed.* San Francisco State University, American Conservatory Theatre. Bright, elegant, confident leading lady of the American stage and screen. After training at ACT, Bening won accolades and a Tony nomination for her performance in Tina Howe's 'Coastal Disturbances.' She made a rather inauspicious film debut in the comedy *The Great Outdoors* (1988) but quickly proved her ability to shine on the silver screen with her stunning performances in Milos Forman's *Valmont* (1989) and Stephen Frear's *The Grifters* (1990). She received a supporting actress Oscar nomination for the latter, confirming her talent as a solid, dependable performer. She is married to former Hollywood playboy, actor-director-producer Warren BEATTY, whom she met on the set of his film *Bugsy* (1991).

FILMS: *The Great Outdoors* 1988; *Valmont* 1989; *The Grifters, Postcards from the Edge* 1990; *Bugsy, Guilty By Suspicion, Regarding Henry* 1991; *Love Affair* 1994; *The American President, Richard III* 1995; *Mars Attacks!* 1996.

Benjamin, Richard. Actor, director. Born on May 22, 1938, in New York City. *ed.* High School of Performing Arts (N.Y.C.); Northwestern. Struggled along in stock and with touring companies before making his mark on Broadway in 'The Star-Spangled Girl' (1966). The following year he was cast in the TV series 'He and She' opposite Paula PRENTISS, his wife since 1961. He went on to become an important young Hollywood star as the protagonist of two Philip Roth novels, *Goodbye Columbus* and *Portnoy's Complaint.* He typically portrayed gawky, snide, urbane pseudo-intellectuals. With his acting career declining, he turned in the early 80s to directing, with some success. Not to be confused with another Richard (Dick) Benjamin (né Lightner), an actor who played supporting roles in several films of the 50s.

FILMS: As actor—*Goodbye Columbus* 1969; *Diary of a Mad Housewife, Catch–22* 1970; *The Marriage of a Young Stockbroker, The Steagle* 1971; *Portnoy's Complaint* 1972; *The Last of Sheila, Westworld* 1973; *The Sunshine Boys* 1975; *House Calls* 1978; *Love at First Bite, Scavenger Hunt* 1979; *The Last Married Couple in America, How to Beat the High Cost of Living, First Family, Witches' Brew* 1980; *Saturday the 14th* 1981. As director—*My Favorite Year* 1982; *Racing with the Moon, City Heat* 1984; *The Money Pit* 1986; *Little Nikita, My Stepmother Is an Alien* 1988; *Downtown, Mermaids* 1990;

Made in America 1993; *Milk Money* 1994; *Mrs. Winterbourne* 1996.

Bennet (also **Bennett), Spencer Gordon.** Director. *b.* Jan. 5, 1893, Brooklyn, N.Y. *d.* 1987. Started out in films in 1912 as a stuntman and bit actor in Edison action pictures. After a period of apprenticeship under director George B. SEITZ, he began directing serials in the early 20s. From the early 30s, also directed (and sometimes produced) low-budget features with an accent on action. His serials include the popular *Superman, Batman and Robin,* and *Captain Video.*

FILMS INCLUDE (serials are indicated by "S"): *Behold the Man* (modern episode) 1921; *Play Ball* (S), *The Green Archer* (S) 1925; *The Fighting Marine* (S and feature versions), *The House Without a Key* (S) 1926; *Hawk of the Hills* (S) 1927; *The Man Without a Face* (S), *The Terrible People* (S), *The Yellow Cameo* (S), *The Tiger's Shadow* (S) 1928; *The Black Book* (S; co-dir. with Thomas Storey) 1929; *Rogue of the Rio Grande* 1930; *The Last Frontier* (S) 1932; *Midnight Warning* 1933; *Night Alarm* 1934; *Calling All Cars, Rescue Squad, Western Courage, Lawless Riders* 1935; *Heroes of the Range, The Cattle Thief, The Unknown Ranger, The Fugitive Sheriff* 1936; *The Mysterious Pilot* (S), *The Rangers Step In* 1937; *Rio Grande* 1938; *Across the Plains* 1939; *Cowboy From Sundown* 1940; *Arizona Bound* 1941; *The Secret Code* (S), *They Raid by Night* 1942; *Secret Service in Darkest Africa* (S), *The Masked Marvel* (S), *Calling Wild Bill Elliott, Canyon City* 1943; *The Tiger Woman* (S), *Beneath Western Skies* 1944; *The Purple Monster Strikes* (S; co-dir. with Fred Brannon), *Lone Texas Ranger* 1945; *King of the Forest Rangers* (S; co-dir. with Brannon), *The Phantom Rider* (S; co-dir., with Brannon) 1946; *The Black Widow* (S; co-dir. with Brannon), *Brick Bradford* (S), *Son of Zorro* (S; co-dir. with Brannon) 1947; *Superman* (S; co-dir. with Thomas Carr), *Congo Bill* (S; co-dir. with Carr) 1948; *Adventures of Sir Galahad* (S), *Batman and Robin* (S) 1949; *Cody of the Pony Express* (S), *Atom Man vs. Superman* (S) 1950; *Captain Video* (S; co-dir. with Wallace Grissell), *Mysterious Island* (S) 1951; *Blackhawk* (S), *King of the Congo* (S; co-dir. with Grissell), *Son of Geronimo* (S), *Brave Warrior, Voodoo Tiger* 1952; *The Lost Planet* (S), *Savage Mutiny, Killer Ape* 1953; *Riding with Buffalo Bill* (S) 1954; *Adventures of Captain Africa* (S), *Devil Goddess, Perils of the Wilderness* (S) 1956; *Submarine Seahawk* 1959; *The Atomic Submarine* 1960; *The Bounty Killer, Requiem for a Gunfighter* 1965.

Bennett, Alan. Screenwriter, playwright. Born May 9, 1934, in Leeds, England. *ed.* Oxford. A former member of the British revue 'Beyond the Fringe,' which launched the careers of Dudley Moore and Peter Cook. He occasionally takes an acting role, but his primary vocation is as a writer. He is most adept at sketching the personal tribulations of complex men, such as murdered gay playwright Joe Orton in *Prick Up Your Ears.*

FILMS INCLUDE: *Pleasure at Her Majesty's* (act.) 1976; *Long Shot* (act.) 1978; *The Secret Policeman's Other Ball* (act.) 1981; *An Englishman Abroad, Return of the Jedi* (act.) 1983; *A Private Function* 1984; *Dreamchild* (act.), *The Insurance Man* 1985; *Prick Up Your Ears* 1987; *Little Dorrit* (act.) 1988; *102 Boulevard Haussmann* 1990; *The Madness of King George* 1994.

Bennett, Belle. Actress. *b.* 1891, Milaca, Minn. *d.* 1932. Talented star of silent films. A veteran of vaudeville and the legitimate stage, she entered films in 1916 and reached the peak of her screen career with her performances in Henry King's *Stella Dallas* (1925) and John Ford's *Mother Machree* (1928). She got rave reviews for her appearance on Broadway, opposite Tyrone Power, Sr., in 'The Wandering Jew' (1921). She was married to screen director Fred Windemere.

FILMS INCLUDE: *Mrs. Wiggs of the Cabbage Patch* 1914; *Mignon* 1915; *Sweet Kitty Bellairs* 1916; *Fires of Rebellion, The Charmer, The Bond of Fear, Ashes of Hope, Because of a Woman* 1917; *The Lonely Woman, The Last Rebel, The Atom* 1918; *The Mayor of Filbert* 1919; *Flesh and Spirit* 1922; *In Hollywood with Potash and Perlmutter* 1924; *His Supreme Moment, East Lynne, Playing with Souls, If Marriage Fails, Stella Dallas* 1925; *The Reckless Lady, The Lily* 1926; *The Fourth Commandment, Mother, The Way of All Flesh, Wild Geese, The Devil's Skipper, The Sporting Age* 1927; *Mother Machree, The Power of Silence, The Battle of the Sexes* 1928; *The Iron Mask, Molly and Me, My Lady's Past, Their Own Desire* 1929; *The Woman Who Was Forgotten, Courage, Recaptured Love* 1930; *The Big Shot* 1931.

Bennett, Bruce. Actor. Born Herman Brix, on May 19, 1909, in Tacoma, Wash. *ed.* U. of Washington. A champion shot-putter, he represented the US in the 1932 Olympic Games in Los Angeles. His athletic prowess attracted attention in Hollywood and he became the screen's eighth Tarzan in two independent-studio productions. He appeared in several other adventure films as Herman Brix before changing his screen name to Bruce Bennett in 1940. He subsequently played leads and supporting parts in a variety of films, often as the "other man." Memorable as a desperate prospector in John Huston's *The Treasure of the Sierra Madre.* After retiring from films he ventured in real estate.

FILMS INCLUDE: As Herman Brix—*Student Tour* 1934; *The New Adventures of Tarzan* (serial and feature versions) 1935; *Shadow of Chinatown* (serial), *Million Dollar Racket, Danger Patrol, Amateur Crook* 1937; *Hawk of the Wilderness* (serial), *Tarzan and the Green Goddess, The Lone Ranger* (serial) 1938. As Bruce Bennett—*My Son Is Guilty, The Man with Nine Lives, The Secret Seven, Before I Hang* 1940; *The Phantom Submarine, The Officer and the Lady* 1941; *Atlantic Convoy, Sabotage Squad* 1942; *The More the Merrier, Sahara* 1943; *Mildred Pierce, Danger Signal* 1945; *A Stolen Life* 1946; *The Man I Love, Nora Prentiss, Cheyenne, Dark Passage* 1947; *The Treasure of the Sierra Madre, Silver River, To the Victor* 1948; *The Younger Brothers, Task Force, Without Honor* 1949; *Mystery Street, The Second Face* 1950; *The Great Mission Raid, The Last Outpost, Angels in the Outfield* 1951; *Sudden Fear* 1952; *Strategic Air Command* 1955; *The Bottom of the Bottle, Love Me Tender* 1956; *Three Violent People* 1957; *The Alligator People* 1959; *The Fiend of Dope Island* 1961; *The Outsider* 1962; *Deadhead Miles* 1972; *The Clones* 1973.

Bennett, Charles. Screenwriter. *b.* Aug. 2, 1899, in Shoreham-by-Sea, England. *d.* 1995. A former actor, he began writing scripts and stage plays in the late 20s. Collaborated on the screenplays of several notable Hitchcock thrillers of the British period, then went to Hollywood. He also directed two films and wrote extensively for TV.

FILMS INCLUDE (alone or in collaboration): In the UK—*Blackmail* (from own play) 1929; *The Man Who Knew Too Much* (co-story) 1934; *The Thirty-Nine Steps, The Clairvoyant* 1935; *King of the Damned, Secret Agent, Sabotage, The Woman Alone* 1936; *Young and Innocent/The Girl Was Young, King Solomon's Mines* 1937. In the US—*The Young in Heart* 1938; *Balalaika* 1939; *Foreign Correspondent* 1940; *They Dare Not Love* 1941; *Joan of Paris, Reap the Wild Wind* 1942; *Forever and a Day* 1943; *The Story of Dr. Wassell* 1944; *Ivy, Unconquered* 1947; *Madness of the Heart* (also dir. in the UK), *Black Magic* 1949; *Kind Lady* 1951; *The Green Glove* 1952; *No Escape* (also dir.) 1953; *Dangerous Mission* 1954; *The Man Who Knew Too Much* (co-story) 1956; *The Story of Mankind* 1957; *The Big Circus* 1959; *The Lost World* 1960;

Voyage to the Bottom of the Sea 1961; *Five Weeks in a Balloon* 1962; *War Gods of the Deep* 1965.

Bennett, Compton. Director. *b.* Robert Compton-Bennett, on Jan. 15, 1900, Tunbridge Wells, England. *d.* 1974. Left school at 15. Was a bandleader, interior decorator, and freelance commercial artist before entering motion pictures as a film editor for Alexander KORDA and Sydney BOX in 1932. During 1939–41 he edited propaganda and instructional films for the British army. In 1942 he directed his first film, a documentary. Directed his first and best feature film, *The Seventh Veil,* in 1945. This successful romantic drama, starring James Mason and Ann Todd, resulted in an invitation in the late 40s to direct in Hollywood. After three American assignments, including the spectacular *King Solomon's Mines,* he returned to England, continuing as a film and TV director.

FILMS: *Find Fix and Strike* (doc.) 1942; *Men of Rochdale* (doc.) 1944; *Julius Caesar* (short), *The Seventh Veil* (1945); *The Years Between* 1946; *Daybreak* 1947; *My Own True Love* (US), *That Forsyte Woman/The Forsyte Saga* (US) 1949; *King Solomon's Mines* (US) 1950; *It Started in Paradise, So Little Time* 1952; *Desperate Moment, The Gift Horse/Glory at Sea* 1953; *After the Ball, That Woman Opposite, The Flying Scot/Mailbag Robbery* 1957; *Beyond the Curtain* 1960; *First Left Past Aden* (short) 1961; *How to Undress in Public Without Undue Embarrassment* 1965.

Bennett, Constance. Actress. *b.* Oct. 22, 1904, New York City. *d.* 1965. Daughter of matinee idol Richard BENNETT and sister of actresses Barbara (*b.* Aug. 13, 1906, Montreal; *d.* 1958) and Joan BENNETT, she was educated at private schools in New York and Paris. Impulsive and determined, she married at 16, but the marriage was annulled. Apart from a bit role at 12 in a film starring her father, she made her screen debut at 17 and soon developed into a popular leading lady of Hollywood silents. But she gave up acting in 1926, following her marriage to a steamship and railroad heir, and became an active member of the swinging international set. She returned to the screen in 1929 after her divorce and re-established herself as a leading star in talkies. Her husky voice and natural delivery of wisecracking lines became valuable assets in her specialty, the sophisticated comedy, but she also had her share of leads in sentimental melodramas and unabashed tearjerkers. In the early 50s she left films for the stage, mostly on the road. She also ventured into business with the Constance Bennett Cosmetics Company. Her five husbands included screen actor Gilbert ROLAND (1941–44). She died of a cerebral hemorrhage shortly after completing her only film of the 60s, *Madame X.*

FEATURE FILMS: *The Valley of Decision* (bit) 1916; *Reckless Youth, Evidence, What's Wrong with the Women?* 1922; *Cytherea, Into the Net* 1924; *The Goose Hangs High, Code of the West, My Wife and I, My Son, The Goose Woman, Sally Irene and Mary, Wandering Fires, The Pinch Hitter* 1925; *Married?* 1926; *This Thing Called Love* 1929; *Rich People, Son of the Gods, Common Clay, Three Faces East, Sin Takes a Holiday* 1930; *The Easiest Way, Born to Love, The Common Law, Bought* 1931; *Lady With a Past, What Price Hollywood, Two Against the World, Rockabye* 1932; *Our Betters, Bed of Roses, After Tonight* 1933; *Moulin Rouge, The Affairs of Cellini, Outcast Lady* 1934; *After Office Hours* 1935; *Everything Is Thunder* (UK), *Ladies in Love* 1936; *Topper* 1937; *Merrily We Live, Service De Luxe* 1938; *Topper Takes a Trip, Tail Spin* 1939; *Submarine Zone/Escape to Glory, Law of the Tropics, Two-Faced Woman* 1941; *Wild Bill Hickok Rides, Sin Town, Madame Spy* 1942; *Paris Underground* 1945; *Centennial Summer* 1946; *The Unsuspected* 1947; *Smart Woman, Angel on the Amazon* 1948; *As Young As You Feel* 1951; *It Should Happen to You* 1954; *Madame X* 1966.

Bennett, Enid. Actress. *b.* July 15, 1895, York, West Australia. *d.* 1969. Star of Hollywood silents. Arrived in the US during WW I with an Australian stage touring troupe, then settled in Hollywood, where she became a protégée of Thomas INCE. She reached her peak in the early 20s, when she played such heroines as Maid Marian opposite Douglas Fairbanks in Allan Dwan's *Robin Hood,* but retired from the screen soon after her marriage to director Fred NIBLO. She accompanied Niblo to Italy and assisted him on the direction of his famous *Ben-Hur* (1926). Later returned to the screen in occasional supporting roles. Her sister, Marjorie Bennett (1896?–1982) also appeared in numerous films.

FILMS INCLUDE: *The Battle of Gettysburg* 1914; *Princess of the Dark, Happiness, The Girl Glory, The Mother Instinct* 1917; *Naughty Naughty!,* 1917; *The Marriage Ring, The Biggest Show on Earth, The Vamp, Fuss and Feathers* 1918; *Happy Though Married, The Haunted Bedroom, Stepping Out* 1919; *The Woman in the Suitcase, Hairpins, Her Husband's Friend, Silk Hosiery* 1920; *Keeping Up With Lizzie* 1921; *Robin Hood* (as Maid Marian), *Scandalous Tongues, The Bootlegger's Daughter* 1922; *Strangers of the Night, The Bad Man, The Courtship of Miles Standish* 1923; *A Fool's Awakening, The Sea Hawk, The Red Lily* 1924; *A Woman's Heart* 1926; *The Wrong Mr. Wright* 1927; *Skippy, Waterloo Bridge, Sooky* 1931; *Intermezzo—A Love Story* 1939; *Strike Up the Band* 1940.

Bennett, Joan. Actress. *b.* Feb. 27, 1910, Palisades, N.J. *d.* 1990. The daughter of actor Richard BENNETT and actress Adrienne Morrison, and the sister of screen actresses Barbara and Constance BENNETT, she attended a boarding school in Connecticut and a finishing school in Versailles, France, before making a stage debut with her father in 'Jarnegan' (1928). That same year she went to Hollywood, played a minor role in the minor film *Power,* then emerged a star in *Bulldog Drummond,* opposite Ronald Colman, the following year. She continued a successful career, appearing in starring roles in many films, but she really came into her own after marrying producer Walter WANGER in 1940. It was under his supervision that she made some of her best films, particularly the four that were directed by Fritz Lang: *Man Hunt, The Woman in the Window, Scarlet Street,* and *The Secret Beyond the Door.*

Wanger was Miss Bennett's third husband. She had married first at 16, become a mother at 17, a divorcée at 18. Her second husband was producer-writer Gene MARKEY, whom she married in 1932 and divorced in 1937. In 1952, Wanger was arrested and jailed for several months after allegedly shooting and wounding Miss Bennett's agent, Jennings Lang, in a jealous rage. She and Wanger later divorced.

Originally a blonde, Miss Bennett became a brunette for a film in 1938 and kept her new hair color, which made her resemble Hedy Lamarr. Ironically, her second husband, Gene Markey, later married Miss Lamarr. In 1978 Miss Bennett married her fourth husband, movie-drama critic David Wilde.

Joan Bennett's roles varied widely, ranging from that of the selfish, plotting femme fatale in *The Woman in the Window* to a light, motherly role in the comedy *Father of the Bride,* opposite Spencer Tracy. She was at her best playing sensual, mercenary, ambitious women but is equally memorable as the desperate mother under the threat of a blackmailer in Max Ophüls's *The Reckless Moment.*

Miss Bennett appeared in several stage plays throughout the 50s and early 60s. In 1966–71 she starred in the TV daytime soap-shocker serial 'Dark Shadows' and in 1970 headed its cast in an offshoot feature film.

FILMS: *The Valley of Decision* (bit) 1916; *The Eternal City* (bit) 1923; *Power* 1928; *Bulldog Drummond, Three Live Ghosts, Disraeli, The Mississippi Gambler* 1929; *Puttin' on the*

Ritz, Crazy That Way, Moby Dick, Maybe It's Love, Scotland Yard 1930; *Doctor's Wives, Many a Slip, Hush Money* 1931; *She Wanted a Millionaire, Careless Lady, The Trial of Vivienne Ware, Week-Ends Only, Wild Girl, Me and My Gal* 1932; *Arizona to Broadway, Little Women* (as Amy) 1933; *The Pursuit of Happiness* 1934; *The Man Who Reclaimed His Head, Private Worlds, Mississippi, Two for Tonight, She Couldn't Take It, The Man Who Broke the Bank at Monte Carlo* 1935; *13 Hours by Air, Big Brown Eyes, Two in a Crowd, Wedding Present* 1936; *Vogues of 1938* 1937; *I Met My Love Again, The Texans, Artists and Models Abroad* 1938; *Trade Winds, The Man in the Iron Mask* (as Queen Maria Theresa), *The Housekeeper's Daughter* 1939; *Green Hell, The House Across the Bay, The Man I Married, The Son of Monte Cristo* 1940; *Man Hunt, She Knew All the Answers, Wild Geese Calling, Confirm or Deny* 1941; *Twin Beds, The Wife Takes a Flyer, Girl Trouble* 1942; *Margin for Error* 1943; *The Woman in the Window* 1944; *Nob Hill* 1945; *Scarlet Street, Colonel Effingham's Raid* 1946; *The Macomber Affair, The Woman on the Beach* 1947; *Secret Beyond the Door, Hollow Triumph/The Scar* 1948; *The Reckless Moment* 1949; *Father of the Bride, For Heaven's Sake* 1950; *Father's Little Dividend, The Guy Who Came Back* 1951; *Highway Dragnet* 1954; *We're No Angels* 1955; *There's Always Tomorrow, Navy Wife* 1956; *Desire in the Dust* 1960; *House of Dark Shadows* Autobiography: *The Bennett Playbill* 1970; *Gidget Gets Married* (TV movie), *The Eyes of Charles Sand* (TV movie) 1972; *Inn of the Damned* (unreleased) 1974; *Suspiria* (It.) 1977.

Bennett, Richard. Actor. *b.* May 21, 1873, Deacon's Mills, Ind. *d.* 1944. Father of actresses Barbara, Constance, and Joan BENNETT by his second wife, Broadway actress Adrienne Morrison. He made his stage debut in Chicago in 1891 and quickly rose to great prominence, becoming one of the leading matinee idols of his day. He appeared only occasionally in films, at first in leads and later in character roles. He also served as a technical director on a number of silent films.

FILMS INCLUDE (as actor): *Damaged Goods* 1914; *Philip Holden—Waster, And the Law Says, The Valley of Decision* 1916; *The Gilded Youth* 1917; *Secret Marriage* (sc. only), *The End of the Road* 1919; *R.S.V.P.* (tech. dir. only) 1921; *The Barnstormer* (tech. dir. only) 1922; *The Eternal City* 1923; *Youth for Sale* 1924; *Lying Wives* 1925; *The Home Towners* 1928; *Five and Ten, Bought, Arrowsmith* 1931; *This Reckless Age, No Greater Love, Madame Racketeer, Strange Justice, If I Had a Million* 1932; *Song of Songs* 1933; *Nana* 1934; *This Woman Is Mine* 1935; *The Magnificent Ambersons* 1942; *Journey Into Fear* 1943.

Bennett, Richard Rodney. Composer. Born on Mar. 29, 1936, in Broadstairs, England. He has written scores for British films since the age of 20.

FILMS INCLUDE: *Interpol/Pickup Alley* 1957; *Indiscreet* 1958; *The Mark* 1961; *Only Two Can Play* 1961; *Satan Never Sleeps* 1962; *Billy Liar* 1963; *The Nanny* 1965; *Far from the Madding Crowd* 1967; *Secret Ceremony* 1968; *The Buttercup Chain, Figures in a Landscape* 1970; *Nicholas and Alexandra* 1971; *Lady Caroline Lamb* 1972; *Murder on the Orient Express* 1974; *Permission to Kill* 1975; *Equus* 1977; *The Brink's Job* 1978; *Yanks* 1979; *The Jazz Singer* (song only) 1980; *The Return of the Soldier* 1982; *Enchanted April* 1991; *Four Weddings and a Funeral* 1994.

Benning, James. Director. Born in 1942 in Milwaukee, Wis. *ed.* U. of Wisconsin (B.S., mathematics; M.F.A., film and graphic arts). Avant-garde director who works almost exclusively in 16 mm and has drawn critical notice for his structuralist methods, including the combination of multiple texts in a single frame. He is known for works that may assume the form of autobiography and documentary but maintain the formal rigor of outright experimental projects. Father of video artist Sadie Benning.

FILMS INCLUDE: *Michigan Avenue* (co-dir.), *8½ x 11* (co-dir.) 1974; *The United States of America* (co-dir.), *9–1–75* 1975; *11 x 14* 1976; *One Way Boogie Woogie* 1977; *Grand Opera* 1978; *Him and Me* 1982; *American Dreams* 1984; *O Panama* 1985; *Landscape Suicide* 1986; *Used Innocence* 1988; *North on Evers* 1992.

Benny, Jack. Comedian. *b.* Benjamin Kubelsky, Feb. 14, 1894, Waukegan, Ill. *d.* 1974. His unpromising career as a violin player was interrupted by WW I, during which he discovered his knack for comedy while serving in the Navy. Returning to civilian life, he appeared in vaudeville, at first using the stage name Ben K. Benny.

Made his first film appearance in 1929 but gained stardom on radio and later repeated his success on TV. On the air and in films he was characterized as a self-deprecating, violin-playing, wisecracking miser, aided by black valet Eddie "Rochester" ANDERSON. Benny's comedy style was based on perfect timing and supreme use of the pause for milking laughs. Contrary to his professional image as a vain, selfish, and stingy man, Benny was in reality among the most generous and modest people in show business. He was married to radio performer Mary Livingstone (Sadye Marks) from 1927 until his death in 1974. Among his best film vehicles were *Charley's Aunt, To Be or Not to Be,* and *George Washington Slept Here.* Eternally "39," Benny died of cancer at 80, ending one of the most durable and influential careers in American comedy. His widow published a memoir, *Jack Benny,* in 1978.

FEATURE FILMS (not including unbilled cameos): *Hollywood Revue of 1929* 1929; *Chasing Rainbows, The Medicine Man* 1930; *Broadway Melody of 1936, Transatlantic Merry-Go-Round, It's in the Air* 1935; *The Big Broadcast of 1937* 1936; *College Holiday, Artists and Models* 1937; *Artists and Models Abroad* 1938; *Man About Town* 1939; *Buck Benny Rides Again, Love Thy Neighbor* 1940; *Charley's Aunt* 1941; *To Be or Not to Be, George Washington Slept Here* 1942; *The Meanest Man in the World* 1943; *Hollywood Canteen* 1944; *The Horn Blows at Midnight, It's in the Bag* 1945; *A Guide for the Married Man* 1967.

Benoit-Lévy, Jean. Director, producer. *b.* Apr. 25, 1888, Paris. *d.* 1959. Nephew of French film pioneer Edmond Benoit-Lévy. Entered films in 1910 as an assistant director and from 1920 on he directed and produced more than 400 information and educational films. He was active in League of Nations film affairs, was consultant on motion pictures to the French government, and was awarded the cross of the Legion of Honor for his work in educational films. He was artistic director on Jean EPSTEIN's first film, *Pasteur* (1922). He turned out many ballet films and full-length documentaries but was best known for his few feature films, including *La Maternelle, Itto,* and *La Mort du Cygne,* several of which he co-directed with Jean Epstein's sister, Marie Epstein.

In 1940, during WW II, he sought refuge in the US. From 1941 to 1946 he taught at the New School for Social Research (he had been a professor at the Ecole Nationale de Cinématographie in Paris). In 1946 he was appointed Director of Films and Visual Information for the United Nations, and in 1947 he became executive director of the UN Film Board. He resumed his private activity as producer-director in 1949, turning out March of Time and television films. In 1958 he created UNESCO's International Board of Cinema and Television. He wrote many essays on cinema and the books *Le Cinéma d'Enseignement et l'Education, Les Grandes Missions du*

Cinéma (The Art of the Motion Picture), and *L'Instruction Visuelle aux Etats-Unis.*

FEATURE FILMS (as director): *Pasteur* (artistic dir. only, assisting Jean Epstein) 1922; *Peau de Pêche* (co-dir. with Marie Epstein) 1925; *Le Nid, Le Voile sacré* 1926; *Ames d'Enfants* (co-dir. with Marie Epstein) 1928; *Maternité* (co-dir. with Marie Epstein) 1930; *Lé Petit Jimmy* (co-dir. with Marie Epstein), *Le Coeur de Paris* (co-dir. with Marie Epstein) 1931; *La Maternelle* (co-dir. with Marie Epstein) 1933; *Itto* (co-dir. with Marie Epstein) 1935; *Hélène* 1936; *La Mort du Cygne/Ballerina* 1937; *Altitude 3200/Youth in Revolt* 1938; *Feu de Paille/Fire in the Straw* 1940.

Benson, Robby. Actor. Born Robert Segal, on Jan. 21, 1956, in Dallas. The son of a writer (Jerry Segal) and a stage actress (Ann Benson), he began appearing in commercials at age three, played summer stock at five, and toured Japan with the musical 'Oliver' at eight. He was 12 when he made his Broadway debut in 'Zelda' and 14 when he began appearing in the TV soap opera 'Search for Tomorrow.' Blue-eyed and innocent-faced, he broke into films in 1972 and for a while specialized in portraying shy, soulful youngsters in tearful situations. Over time, he attempted tougher roles with middling success. In 1982 he married actress-rock singer Karla DeVito. He bounced back from open-heart surgery in 1984 to star in the 1986 TV series 'Tough Cookies,' and in 1988 directed his first film. He also co-wrote several screenplays with his father and taught film at USC. His career took yet a different turn when he supplied the voice of the Beast in the animated feature *Beauty and the Beast* (1991).

FILMS: *Jory* 1972; *Jeremy* 1973; *Lucky Lady* 1975; *Ode to Billy Joe* 1976; *One on One* (also co-sc.) 1977; *The End, Ice Castles* 1978; *Walk Proud* (also co-mus.) 1979; *Die Laughing* (also co-prod., co-sc., co-mus.), *Tribute* (Can.) 1980; *The Chosen* 1981; *Running Brave* (Can.) 1983; *Harry and Son* 1984; *City Limits* 1985; *Rent-a-Cop* 1988; *Crack in the Mirror/White Hot* (also dir.) 1989; *Modern Love* (also prod., sc.) 1990; *Beauty and the Beast* (voice only) 1991; *Invasion of Privacy* 1992.

Benson, Sally. Screenwriter, short-story writer. *b.* Sept. 3, 1900, St. Louis, Mo. *d.* 1972. A former bank teller, she began writing articles and reviewing films for the N.Y. *Morning Telegraph,* then, sometimes using the pen name Esther Evarts, contributed short stories to *The New Yorker.* Some of her most popular stories were collected into books, two of which, *Junior Miss* and *Meet Me in St. Louis,* became best-sellers and were made into successful films. She began writing scripts directly for the screen in the early 40s.

FILMS INCLUDE (alone or in collaboration): *Shadow of a Doubt* 1943; *Meet Me in St. Louis* (stories basis only) 1944; *Junior Miss* (stories basis only) 1945; *Anna and the King of Siam* 1946; *Come to the Stable* 1949; *Conspirator, No Man of Her Own* 1950; *The Farmer Takes a Wife* 1953; *Summer Magic* 1963; *Viva Las Vegas* 1964; *Signpost to Murder, Joy in the Morning* 1965; *The Singing Nun* 1966.

Benton, Robert. Director, screenwriter. Born on Sept. 29, 1932, in Waxahachie, near Dallas, Tex. *ed.* U. of Texas; Columbia. Intending to become an artist, he served a stint with the Army as a diorama painter before landing an assistant's position at the art department of *Esquire.* In 1958 he became the magazine's art director, a position he held through 1964, then a contributing editor through 1972. During that period, he co-authored *The IN and OUT Book* (1959), a tongue-in-cheek guide for city sophisticates, and *The Worry Book* (1962). He also wrote a children's book, *Little Brother No More* (1960), which was illustrated by painter Sally Rendigs, whom he would marry in 1964.

In 1961, Benton began a long and fruitful collaboration with David NEWMAN, first on special pop-culture projects at *Esquire* (among them the annual college issue and the Dubious Achievement Awards), then on *Extremism: A Non-Book* (1964) and the short-lived Broadway musical 'It's a Bird... It's a Plane... It's Superman' (1966). They next tackled the movies, making a fortuitous start with their original script for *Bonnie and Clyde* (1967), one of the most influential films of the 60s. It earned them a nomination for an Academy Award. Benton, who considers cinema an extention of painting, then ventured into directing, making his debut with *Bad Company* (1972), a highly regarded Civil War–era Western. In 1979 he scored a huge hit with the child-custody drama *Kramer vs. Kramer,* a box-office blockbuster and the winner of five Academy Awards (best picture, best director, best adapted screenplay, best actor, and best supporting actress). The film established him as one of Hollywood's most sought-after director-writers. But despite several intelligent efforts he was never able to repeat its commercial success. He did reap critical kudos, however, for *Places in the Heart* (1984), a Depression-era survival drama, for which he won an Oscar for best original screenplay and the Berlin Festival Silver Bear as best director. Largely shot on location in his Texan home town, the film echoes memories of Benton's ancestors and reflects the director's preoccupation with themes of friendship and family relations.

FILMS: As co-screenwriter—*Bonnie and Clyde* 1967; *There Was a Crooked Man* 1970; *What's Up Doc?, Oh! Calcutta!* 1972; *Superman* 1978. As director—*Bad Company* (also co-sc.) 1972; *The Late Show* (also sc.) 1977; *Kramer vs. Kramer* (also sc.) 1979; *Still of the Night* (also co-story, sc.) 1982; *Places in the Heart* (also sc.) 1984; *Nadine* (also sc.) 1987; *The House on Carroll Street* (co-exec. prod. only) 1988; *Billy Bathgate* 1991; *Nobody's Fool* 1994.

Berenger, Tom. Actor. Born on May 31, 1950, in Chicago. *ed.* U. of Missouri. Handsome, masculine star of Hollywood films. He started out in regional theater and off-off Broadway and appeared in daytime TV soaps before breaking into movies in the mid-70s. Memorable as the war-hardened Sgt. Barnes in 'Platoon,' for which he earned a best supporting actor Oscar nomination. He appeared as an amorous plumber on the final two episodes of the TV sitcom 'Cheers' (1993).

FILMS: *The Sentinel, Looking for Mr. Goodbar* 1977; *In Praise of Older Women* (Can.) 1978; *Butch and Sundance: The Early Days* (as Butch Cassidy) 1979; *The Dogs of War* (UK) 1980; *Oltre la Porta/Beyond the Door* (It.) 1982; *The Big Chill, Eddie and the Cruisers* 1983; *Fear City* 1984; *Rustler's Rhapsody* 1985; *La Sposa americana* (It.), *Platoon* 1986; *Someone to Watch Over Me* 1987; *Shoot to Kill/Deadly Pursuit, Betrayed, Last Rites* 1988; *Born on the Fourth of July, Major League* 1989; *The Field (UK), Love at Large, At Play in the Fields of the Lord* 1990; *Shattered* 1991; *Sniper, Sliver* 1993; *Chasers, Major League II* 1994; *Last of the Dogmen, The Substitute* 1995.

Berenson, Marisa. Actress. Born on Feb. 15, 1946 in New York City. Willowy leading lady of films of the 70s, following a successful modeling career. An active member of the international jet set, she is the grandniece of Bernard Berenson, the famed art historian and collector. Her father was a Boston diplomat and her mother is the Marchesa Cicciapouti di Guilliano through a second marriage. Her maternal grandmother was the noted couturiere Elsa Schiaparelli. She maintains homes in Manhattan and Beverly Hills but travels extensively, intermittently working in Europe. She authored a fashion book, *Dressing Up,* with photos by her sister Berry.

FILMS: *Morte a Venezia/Death in Venice* (It.) 1971;

Cabaret (US) 1972; *Barry Lyndon* (UK) 1975; *Casanova & Co./Some Like It Cool* (Ger./Aus./It./Fr.) 1977; *Killer Fish/ Deadly Treasure of the Piranha* (It./Bra.) 1979; *Naked Sun* (It./US) 1980; *S.O.B.* (US) 1981; *The Secret Diary of Sigmund Freud* (US), *La Tête dans le Sac* (Fr.), *L'Arbalète* (Fr.) 1984; *White Hunter Black Heart* (US) 1990.

Beresford, Bruce. Director. Born on Aug. 16, 1940, in Sydney, Australia. Obsessed by movies from childhood, he became involved in amateur film production during his philosophy studies at the University of Sydney. After graduation in 1961, he worked briefly in local advertising and TV, then sailed for London, where he tried a variety of odd jobs, including laboring in a factory and teaching at a girls' school. All the while, he kept trying to break into British films or TV but was denied a union card. Determined to work in film somehow, somwhere, he went in 1964 to East Nigeria, in quest of a position as a film editor. Returning to London in 1966 in the wake of political unrest in the African country, the now-experienced Beresford was hired as secretary to the British Film Institute's Production Board and later became the BFI's head of production. In a period of five years, he participated in one capacity or another in the production of nearly 100 documentary shorts and three feature-length films. Following the Australian government's decision to help finance the country's film Industry, Beresford returned to Sydney in 1971 and immediately began directing his first feature film. Based on a comic strip, *The Adventures of Barry McKenzie* (1972) was a broad, bawdy comedy that offered barely a clue to the talent behind the camera. It was panned by the critics, but loved by the Australian public, prompting a sequel. He fared much better with *Don's Party* (1976), an astute black comedy of Australian mores and politics, for which he was named best director at the Australian Film Award and by the American Film Institute. After confirming his growing skill with *The Getting of Wisdom* (1977), Beresford directed the film many consider his best and one of the greatest in the annals of Australian cinema. A stirring drama of cynical military politics during the Boer War, *Breaker Morant* (1980) won a slew of prizes, including best director at the Australian Film Awards and became Australia's biggest commercial hit. More than any film, it helped put Australia on the international movie map. Its success brought Beresord great prestige and paved his way to an international career. His work in Hollywood was highlighted by the crowning of his *Driving Miss Daisy* as best picture of 1989.

FEATURE FILMS: *The Adventures of Barry McKenzie* (also co-sc.) 1972; *Barry McKenzie Holds His Own* (also prod., co-sc.) 1974; *Side by Side* (UK) 1975; *Don's Party* 1976; *The Getting of Wisdom* 1977; *Money Movers* (also sc.) 1978; *Breaker Morant* (also co-sc.), *The Club* 1980; *Puberty Blues* 1981; *Tender Mercies* (US) 1983; *The Fringe Dwellers* (also co-sc.) 1984; *King David* (US) 1985; *Crimes of the Heart* (US) 1986; *Aria* ('Die Tote Stadt' segment; also sc.; UK) 1987; *Her Alibi* (US), *Driving Miss Daisy* (US) 1989; *Mister Johnson* (US) 1990; *Black Robe* (Can./Austral.) 1991; *Rich in Love* (US) 1993; *A Good Man in Africa, Silent Fall* 1994; *Curse of the Starving Class* (ex-prod.) 1995; *Last Dance* 1996; *Paradise Road* 1997.

Berg, Peter. Actor, screenwriter. Born 1964, in Chappaqua, N.Y. *ed.* Macalaster College in St. Paul, Minn. Charmingly boyish, attractive leading man of the American stage and screen. At his best when portraying the innocent boy next door, he won the hearts of many critics as the naïve straight man to Linda Fiorentino's wickedly funny con woman in John Dahl's modern noir classic *The Last Seduction* (1994). Moving effortlessly from films to television, he became a series regular on the hit hospital drama 'Chicago Hope.'

FILMS: *Slamdance* 1987; *Heart of Dixie, Miracle Mile, Shocker* 1989; *Full Fathom Five* 1990; *Crooked Hearts, Late for Dinner* 1991; *A Midnight Clear* 1992; *Aspen Extreme, Fire in the Sky* 1993; *The Last Seduction* 1994; *The Great White Hype* 1996; *Cop Land* 1997.

Bergen, Candice. Actress. Born on May 8, 1946, in Beverly Hills, Calif. Cool, striking, outdoor-type leading lady of Hollywood films. The daughter of ventriloquist Edgar BERGEN, she attended a high school in Switzerland and began modeling while still a student at the University of Pennsylvania. At 19 she dropped out of college, after two years, and shortly after made her screen debut playing a young lesbian in *The Group* (1966). Subsequent roles established her as a bright, dependable star. She was nominated for an Academy Award as best supporting actress for *Starting Over* (1979). Pursuing a parallel career as a photo-journalist, she wrote and photographed for leading national magazines and newspapers. Her work was exhibited in museums and prominent galleries. In 1980 she married French director Louis MALLE. They maintained a happy and successful marriage, he living part of the year in Paris, until his death in 1996. Bergen is perhaps best known now as the star of the TV sitcom 'Murphy Brown' (three Emmy awards). Autobiography: *Knock Wood* (1984).

FILMS: *The Group, The Sand Pebbles* 1966; *Vivre pour vivre/Live for Life, The Day the Fish Came Out* 1967; *The Magus* 1968; *The Adventurers, Getting Straight, Soldier Blue* 1970; *Carnal Knowledge, The Hunting Party, T.R. Baskin* 1971; *11 Harrowhouse* 1974; *The Wind and the Lion, Bite the Bullet* 1975; *The Domino Principle, A Night Full of Rain* 1977; *Oliver's Story* 1978; *Starting Over* 1979; *Rich and Famous* 1981; *Gandhi* 1982; *Stick* 1985.

Bergen, Edgar. Ventriloquist, actor. *b.* Edgar John Bergen, Feb. 16, 1903, Chicago. *d.* 1978. Father of Candice BERGEN. While still in high school he conceived the idea for his ventriloquist dummy, Charlie McCarthy, which cost $35 but soon helped pay his way through Northwestern University. After college he made the vaudeville circuit in the US and Europe, then got a start on radio with Rudy VALLEE.

Bergen and Charlie McCarthy appeared in a dozen film shorts for the Vitaphone company between 1933 and 1935. After their radio success, with the "younger" dummy Mortimer Snerd included, they appeared in feature films, reaching the height of their popularity in the late 30s. In 1937, Bergen won a special Academy Award for the creation of Charlie. After WW II, Bergen appeared mostly in nightclubs, and in 1956 he began hosting a daytime TV quiz show, 'Do You Trust Your Wife?' He later appeared in several films, sans dummies, in straight character roles. He bequeathed Charlie McCarthy to the Smithsonian Institution. He influenced many future puppeteers, including Jim HENSON, who dedicated *The Muppet Movie* (1979) to Bergen.

FILMS: *The Goldwyn Follies, Letter of Introduction* 1938; *You Can't Cheat an Honest Man, Charlie McCarthy Detective* 1939; *Look Who's Laughing* 1941; *Here We Go Again* 1942; *Stage Door Canteen* 1943; *Song of the Open Road* 1944; *Fun and Fancy Free* 1947; *I Remember Mama* 1948; *Captain China* 1949; *One-Way Wahine* 1965; *Don't Make Waves* 1967; *The Phynx* (cameo) 1970; *Won Ton Ton—The Dog That Saved Hollywood* (cameo) 1976; *The Muppet Movie* 1979.

Bergen, Polly. Actress, singer. Born Nellie Paulina Burgin, on July 14, 1930, in Knoxville, Tenn. A professional radio singer at age 14, she appeared in summer stock, light opera, and nightclubs before making her Hollywood debut in the early 50s. She supplied the romantic interest in a variety of films and in addition made numerous TV appearances as a game-show panelist, singer, and dramatic actress. Won an Emmy for her performance in TV's 'The Helen Morgan Story' in 1957. With her film career fading out in the late 60s, she turned to business and began promoting her own cosmetics line. She became chairman of the Polly Bergen and the Culinary companies and co-chairman of the National Business Council for the Equal Rights Amendment. She remained active in TV and in the late 80s returned to movies. Her first husband was screen actor Jerome Courtland. Author: *Polly's Principles* (1974).

FILMS INCLUDE: *At War with the Army, That's My Boy, Warpath* 1951; *The Stooge, Arena, Escape From Fort Bravo, Fast Company* 1953; *Cape Fear* 1962; *The Caretakers, Move Over Darling* 1963; *Kisses for My President* 1964; *A Guide for the Married Man* 1967; *Making Mr. Right* 1987; *Cry-Baby* 1990; *Dr. Jekyll and Ms. Hyde* 1995.

Berger, Helmut. Actor. Born Helmut Steinberger, on May 29, 1942, in Salzburg, Austria. The son of a hotelier-restaurateur, he decided on acting after graduating from high school and, thanks to his handsome features, was able to find occasional work on commercials in France and England, after supporting himself as a waiter, parking-lot attendant, and tour guide in Switzerland. Moving on to Italy, he was appearing as an extra in films when he caught the eye of director Luchino VISCONTI, who took charge of Berger's career and gave it a considerable boost with a leading role in *The Damned* (1969) as Martin, the neurotic heir to a steel fortune. Berger went on to play leads in many other Italian films and European co-productions, gaining prominence as an extremely good-looking leading man with considerable acting talent.

FILMS INCLUDE: *Le Streghe/The Witches* (Visconti episode) 1967; *I Giovani Tigri/The Young Tigers* 1968; *La Caduta degli Dei/Götterdämmerung/The Damned* 1969; *Das Bildnis des Dorian Gray/Dorian Gray* 1970; *Il Giardino dei Finzi-Contini/The Garden of the Finzi-Continis* 1971; *Ludwig* (title role), *Ash Wednesday* (US) 1973; *Reigen/Merry-Go-Round, El Clan de los Immorales/Order to Kill* 1974; *Gruppo di Famiglia in un Interno/Conversation Piece, The Romantic Englishwoman* 1975; *Salon Kitty/Madam Kitty* 1976; *Feroce, Paperback* (US) 1978; *Heroin* 1980; *Victory* 1983; *Tunnel* 1985; *Nie Im Leben/Never Ever* (also dir.), *The Godfather Part III* 1990; *Ludwig 1881* 1993.

Berger, Ludwig. Director. *b.* Ludwig Bamberger, Jan. 6, 1892, Mainz, Germany. *d.* 1969. *ed.* U. of Munich; U. of Heidelberg (Ph.D. in musicology). Produced and directed operas, ballets, and stage plays, often in collaboration with Max REINHARDT, before directing his first film in 1922. His film work was strongly influenced by his musical background and was noted for its search for an effective sound track, as well as for its civilized charm and decorative elegance. Filmed operettas were his forte, but he demonstrated considerable skill in other genres, like the British Arabian Nights fantasy *The Thief of Bag(h)dad* (1940), which he co-directed with Tim Whelan and Michael Powell. In 1928–30, he piloted several Hollywood productions that starred such imported personalities as Pola Negri, Emil Jannings, and Maurice Chevalier. Returning to Europe, Berger worked in Germany, France, Holland, and England until the outbreak of WW II. After the war he directed only one film but wrote screenplays for several others. He retired in the late 50s to operate a brasserie in Luxemburg.

FILMS: In Germany—*Der Richter von Zalamea* (also sc.) 1920; *Der Roman der Christine von Herre* (also sc.) 1921; *Das Spiel der Königin/Ein Glas Wasser* (also co-sc.), *Der verlorene Schuh/Cinderella* (also sc.) 1923; *Ein Walzertraum/The Waltz Dream* 1925; *Die Meistersinger von Nürnberg/Meistersinger* (also co-sc.) 1927; *Das brennende Herz/The Burning Heart* 1929. In the US—*The Woman from Moscow, Sins of the Fathers* 1928; *The Vagabond King, Playboy of Paris* (and French version, *Le Petit Café*) 1930. In Europe—*Ich bei Tag und Du bei Nacht* (Ger.) 1932; *Walzerkrieg/Waltz Time in Vienna/War of the Waltzes* 1933; *Pygmalion* (Holl.) 1937; *Trois Valses/Three Waltzes* (Fr.), *The Thief of Bag(h)dad* (co-dir. with Tim Whelan and Michael Powell; also co-sc.; UK, completed in the US) 1940; *Ballerina/Dream Ballerina* (Fr.) 1950.

Berger, Senta. Actress. Born on May 13, 1941, in Vienna. Sensuous leading lady of international films. Studied ballet, then trained for the stage at Vienna's Reinhardt Seminar. Has had a busy screen career since age 16, in Germany, Hollywood, and elsewhere.

FILMS INCLUDE: *Der Lindenwirtin vom Donaustrand* (Ger.) 1957; *Der brave Soldat Schwejk/The Good Soldier Schweik* (Ger.) 1960; *The Secret Ways* (US) 1961; *Das Testament des Dr. Mabuse/The Terror of Dr. Mabuse* (Ger.) 1962; *The Victors* (UK/US) 1963; *Major Dundee* (US), *The Glory Guys* (US) 1965; *Cast a Giant Shadow* (US), *Our Man in Marrakesh/Bang! Bang! You're Dead!* (UK), *Operazione San Gennaro/Treasure of San Gennaro (It./Fr./Ger.), The Quiller Memorandum* (UK/US) 1966; *Danse Macabre* (prod. only), *Peau d'Espion/How to Commit Murder* (Fr./It./Ger.), *The Ambushers* (US) 1967; *De Sade* (US/Ger.) 1969; *Quando le Donne aveano la Coda/When Women Had Tails* (It.) 1970; *Roma Bene* (It./Fr.), *Le Saut de l'Ange* (Fr.) 1971; *Sancorsiap* (It.), *Die Moral der Ruth Halbfass* (Ger.) 1972; *The Scarlet Letter* (as Hester Prynne) 1973; *Reigen/Merry-Go-Round* (Ger.) 1974; *La Padrona* (It.) 1975; *Signore e Signori Buonanotte* (It.), *Mitgift* (Ger.) 1976; *Das Chinesische Wunder* (Ger.), *Cross of Iron* (UK/Ger.) 1977; *Ritratto di Borghese in Nero/Nest of Vipers* (It.) 1978; *Le Due Vite di Mattia Pascal/The Two Lives of Mattia Pascal* (It./Fr./Ger.) 1985.

Bergere, Ouida. See RATHBONE, Basil.

Bergin, Patrick. Actor. Born in 1954, in Dublin, Ireland. Craggy leading man memorable as the obsessive villain in *Sleeping with the Enemy* (1991).

FILMS INCLUDE: *Mountains of the Moon* 1990; *Sleeping with the Enemy, Highway to Hell, Love Crimes* 1991; *Patriot Games* 1992; *Map of the Human Heart* 1993; *Soft Deceit* 1995.

Bergman, Alan and Marilyn. Lyricists, songwriters. He was born on September 11, 1925, in Brooklyn, N.Y. *ed.* University of North Carolina; UCLA. She was born Marilyn Keith on November 10, 1929, in New York City. *ed.* New York University. Extremely successful husband and wife songwriting team with several academy awards to their credit.

FILMS INCLUDE: *Any Wednesday* (lyr.), *Stop the World—I Want to Get Off* (addnl. material) 1966; *The Thomas Crown Affair* (lyr.) 1968; *Gaily, Gaily* (song), *The Happy Ending* (song), *John and Mary* (song) 1969; *Doctors' Wives* (lyr.), *Pieces of Dreams* (lyr.) 1970; *The African Elephant* (lyr.), *Le Mans* (lyr.), *Sometimes a Great Notion* (lyr.) 1970; *The Life and Times of Judge Roy Bean* (song), *Molly and Lawless John* (lyr.) 1972; *Forty Carats* (lyr.), *Breezy* (lyr.), *The Way We Were* (lyr.) 1973; *99 and 44/100% Dead* (lyr.) 1974; *Ode to Billy Joe* (lyr.) 1975; *From Noon to Three* (lyr.), *Harry and Walter Go to New York* (lyr.), *A Star Is Born* (lyr.) 1976; *The One and Only* (lyr.), *Same Time Next Year* (lyr.) 1978; *And Justice for All* (lyr.), *The Promise* (lyr.), *Starting Over* (lyr.) 1979; *A Change of Seasons* (lyr.) 1980; *Back Roads* (lyr.) 1981; *Author, Author!* (lyr.), *Best Friends* (score), *Tootsie* (lyr.), *Yes Giorgio* (lyr.) 1982; *The Man Who Loved Women* (lyr.), *Never Say Never Again* (lyr.), *Yentl* (lyr.) 1983; *Micki & Maude* (song) 1984; *Shy People* (song) 1987; *Big* (song), *The January Man* (lyr.) 1988; *Major League* (lyr.), *Shirley Valentine* (lyr.), *Welcome Home* (song) 1989; *Moonlight and Valentino, Sabrina* 1995.

Bergman, Andrew. Screenwriter, director. Born in 1945, in Queens, N.Y. After graduating magna cum laude from Harpur College and gaining a doctorate in history from the University of Wisconsin, he worked briefly as a publicist at United Artists. He turned to writing, specializing at first in film-related subjects: *We're in the Money* (1971), a study of Depression-era films, and *James Cagney* (1975), a biography. He also wrote two mystery novels and a Broadway comedy, 'Social Security.' He made his first contribution to the screen in 1974 as the writer of the original story and collaborator on the screenplay of Mel BROOKS's madly hilarious Western spoof *Blazing Saddles.* He made his debut as a director in 1981. He was replaced in the midst of production of *Big Trouble* (1985) by John Cassavetes. After developing a production company with producer Michael Lobell in the 1980s, he gained another chance to prove himself as a director in 1990 with *The Freshman*.

FILMS: *Blazing Saddles* (story, co-sc.) 1974; *The In-Laws* (story, sc.) 1979; *So Fine* (dir., story, sc.) 1981; *Oh God! You Devil* (story, sc.) 1984; *Fletch* (sc.) 1985; *Chances Are* (co-exec prod.) 1989; *The Freshman* (dir., sc.) 1990; *Soapdish* (co-sc.) 1991; *Honeymoon in Vegas* (dir., sc.) 1992; *Undercover Blues* (ex-prod. only) 1993; *It Could Happen to You, Little Big League* (ex-prod.), *The Scout* (co-sc.) 1994; *Striptease* 1996.

Bergman, Henry. Actor, assistant director. *b.* 1868, Sweden. *d.* 1946. After immigrating to the US, he made his first appearance in American films in 1914. In 1916 he started a long association with Charlie CHAPLIN, appearing in many of his films and later assisting him in directing. He figured prominently in most of Chaplin's films of the Mutual-First National-United Artists period.

FILMS INCLUDE (as actor): *The Melting Pot, A Million Dollars* 1915; *The Pawnshop, The Floorwalker, The Rink, Behind the Screen, In the Diplomatic Service* 1916; *Easy Street, The Cure, The Immigrant* (two roles), *The Adventurer* 1917; *A Dog's Life, Shoulder Arms* 1918; *Sunnyside, A Day's Pleasure* 1919; *The Kid* 1921; *Pay Day* 1922; *The Pilgrim, A Woman of Paris* 1923; *The Gold Rush* 1925; *The Circus* 1928; *City Lights* (also asst. dir.) 1931; *Modern Times* (also asst. dir.) 1936.

Bergman, Ingmar. Director. Born on July 14, 1918, Uppsala, Sweden. The son of a stern Lutheran pastor who eventually became chaplain to Sweden's royal family, he was raised under strict discipline, on occasion spending hours in a dark closet for infractions of his father's rigid ethical code. The traumatic experiences of his childhood were later to play a significant role in his work as a stage and film director. He fell in love with the theater at the age of five, after seeing his first play, and at the age of nine conjured up a toy theater under a table in his playroom. He became involved in stage production, as an actor and director, at the University of Stockholm, where he studied literature and art, and after graduation he became a trainee-director at a Stockholm theater. During that period he wrote a number of plays, novels, and short stories, most of which he failed to have produced or published. He entered the Swedish film industry in 1941 as a script doctor. His big opportunity came in 1944 when he was assigned to write the script for *Hets* (titled *Torment* in the US, *Frenzy* in the UK) for director Alf Sjöberg. The film became an international success and the following year Bergman was assigned his first film as director.

Bergman's early films are in themselves largely insignificant, but they are interesting from a film historian's point of view as works that contain the seeds of the director's artistic development and hint at greatness to come. They typically dealt with problems and frustrations of the young and the generation gap in Swedish society. Bergman's first important film was *Fängelse* (*The Devil's Wanton* in the US, *Prison* in the UK), released in 1949. It is the first complete Bergman work, drawn from his own original script, and it is imprinted with many of the expressive means that were to become identified as the director's personal style. The plot, dealing with events leading to a young prostitute's suicide, is dotted with references to God and Devil, Life and Death—philosophical and ethical questions that were to torment Bergman in many of his future films.

Another consistent Bergman theme—the psychology of women and their introspective inner world—began to emerge in his next film, *Törst* (*Three Strange Loves* in the US, *Thirst* in the UK). He later developed the theme further in such films as *Sommarlek/Illicit Interlude/Summer Interlude* (1951), *Kvinnors Väntan/Secrets of Women/Waiting Women* (1952), *Sommaren med Monika/Monika/Summer With Monika* (1953), *Kvinnodröm/Dreams/Journey Into Autumn* (1955), and *Sommarnattens Leende/Smiles of a Summer Night* (1955). The inner world of women remained an integral part of the Bergman theme in many other films, within the context of broader issues and personal concerns. A landmark in Bergman's development was *Gycklarnas Afton/The Naked Night/Sawdust and Tinsel* (1953), a film that reveals the director's maturation as a visual stylist as well as a philosophical artist. But Bergman remained an ignored director at home and virtually unknown abroad until *Sommarnattens Leende/Smiles of a Summer Night* (1955) and *Det Sjunde Inseglet/The Seventh Seal* (1957) catapulted him into fame as a new Scandinavian master by winning prizes at the Cannes Film Festival.

The Seventh Seal in particular, a film dealing allegorically and agonizingly with the philosophy and metaphysics of man's relationship to God and his encounters with the idea of Death, created a Bergman vogue in art theaters all over the world. His films began reflecting more and more his personal, inner world, his anguish and fears, his joys and hopes. He developed a team of players which grew into a virtual stock company, in his stage productions as well as in his films. Gunnar BJÖRNSTRAND and Max von SYDOW were his most notable male protagonists. The latter came to be identified over the years as Bergman's on-screen *alter ego,* an incarnation of the artist's torment and doubts. Actresses who played an important role in Bergman's screen dissertations include Bibi ANDERSSON, Harriet ANDERSSON (they are unrelated), Ingrid THULIN, and Liv ULLMANN. The latter lived with the director for many years and gave birth to his child. Gunnar FISCHER and later Sven NYKVIST were his regular cameramen, providing the visual boldness that was so necessary for his themes.

Another landmark film in Bergman's career was *Smultronstället/Wild Strawberries* (1957), which deals powerfully and profoundly with the subject of man's isolation, and like several others of the director's films uses a journey as a plot structure. The film marked a pinnacle in the international Bergman cult, after which his reputation went into an anticlimatic semidecline. The Bergman "trilogy" of the early 60s, which consisted of *Sasom i en Spegel/Through a Glass Darkly* (1961), *Nattvardsgästerna/Winter Light/The Communicants* (1963), and *Tystnaden/The Silence* (1963) met with mixed critical reaction, possibly because of the director's overly ambitious attempt to deal in physical film terms with the complex metaphysical question of the existence of God and the equally difficult-to-sustain phenomena of human isolation and alienation. Of the three films, *The Silence* fared best with critics and audiences. But Bergman enjoyed a significant resurrection of reputation with *Persona* (1966), a film that marked his departure from metaphysics toward the realm of human psychology. This renewed reputation was further enhanced by *Viskningar och Rop/Cries and Whispers* (1972).

The year 1976 was a traumatic one in the life of Ingmar Bergman. On January 30, while rehearsing Strindberg's 'Dance of Death' at Stockholm's Royal Dramatic Theater, he was arrested by two plainclothes policeman, booked like a common criminal, and charged with income-tax fraud. The impact of the event on Bergman was devastating. He suffered a nervous breakdown as a result of the humiliation and was hospitalized in a state of deep depression. Even though the charges were later dropped, Bergman was for a while inconsolate, fearing he would never again return to directing. He eventually recovered from the shock, but despite pleas by the Swedish prime minister, high public figures, and leaders of the film industry, he vowed never to work again in Sweden. He closed down his studio on the barren Baltic island of Faro and went into self-imposed exile abroad. In April of 1976 he visited Hollywood and announced plans to make films in the United States. His next was a German-American production, which he filmed in Munich. The film, *The Serpent's Egg* (1978), Bergman's first in English, deals with the collapse of the German currency and other events of the 20s that paved the way for Hitler's rise to power. It was followed by a British-Norwegian co-production *Autumn Sonata* (1978), in which for the first time he directed another famous Swede, Ingrid BERGMAN. Although he continued to operate from Munich, by mid-1978, Ingmar Bergman seemed to have overcome much of his bitterness toward his motherland. In July of that year he was back in Sweden, celebrating his 60th birthday on Faro and resuming his work as a director at Stockholm's Royal Dramatic Theater. To honor his return, the Swedish Film Institute launched a new Ingmar Bergman prize to be awarded annually for excellence in filmmaking.

In 1983, just when it seemed his career had gone years past its zenith, Bergman astonished the film world with what many consider one of his finest achievements. An intimately personal work, *Fanny and Alexander* offered a mature, sober reappraisal of the themes and soul-searching questions that preoccupied the director throughout his career. But the film was surprisingly mellow and accessible to a wider audience. Gone were the pessimism and anguish that characterized many of his earlier films. Instead, filmgoers found an exuberant affirmation of life, love, and faith, bathed in vivid colors—a hopeful summation of a cinema poet's lifelong inner conflict. *Fanny and Alexander* fared commercially well in the US, where it won Academy Awards for best foreign language film, best cinematography, best art direction, and best costume design. Bergman was nominated for best director. The film also shared the International Critics Prize at the 1983 Venice Festival. After the film's release, Bergman announced his retirement from filmmaking. Within a year he was back, however, with *After the Rehearsal,* a small-scale production originally made for TV that went on to receive theatrical distribution.

Ingmar Bergman, for years now a dominant figure in Swedish theater and cinema, is widely recognized as one of the leading film artists living today. He is among a select few directors who have consistently used the medium of cinema as a creative art of personal expression, and among an even smaller group that has been able to exercise near-complete freedom and total artistic control over its film product. He is the author of autobiography *The Magic Lantern* (1988) and film memoir *Images: My Life in Film* (1993). He wrote the novel *The Best Intentions* (1993), based on his parents' lives, and the screenplay for the 1992 film on the same subject.

FILMS: As screenwriter—*Hets/Torment/Frenzy* 1944; *Kvinna utan Ansikte/Woman Without a Face* 1947; *Eva* (story, co-sc.) 1948; *Medan Standen Sover/While the City Sleeps* (synopsis only) 1950; *Franskild/Divorced* (story, co-sc.) 1951; *Sista Paret Ut/The Last Couple Out* (story, co-sc.) 1956; *Lustgarden/Pleasure Garden* (co-sc.) 1961. As director-screenwriter—*Kris/Crisis* 1945; *Det Regnar pa var Kärlek/It Rains on Our Love* 1946; *Skep till Indialand/Frustration/The Land of Desire/A Ship to India* 1947; *Musik i Mörker/Night Is My Future, Hamnstad/Port of Call* 1948; *Fängelse/The Devil's Wanton/Prison, Törst/Three Strange Loves/Thirst* 1949; *Till Glädje/To Joy, Sant Händer inte Här/High Tension/This Can't Happen Here* 1950; *Sommarlek/Illicit Interlude/Summer Interlude* 1951; *Kvinnors Väntan/Secrets of Women/Waiting Women* 1952; *Sommaren med Monika/Monika/Summer with Monika, Gycklarnas Afton/The Naked Night/Sawdust and Tinsel* 1953; *En Lektion i Kärlek/A Lesson in Love* 1954; *Kvinnodrö/Dreams/Journey Into Autumn, Sommarnattens Leende/Smiles of a Summer Night* 1955; *Det Sjunde Inseglet/ The Seventh Seal, Smultronstället/Wild Strawberries* 1957; *Nära Livet/Brink of Life/So Close to Life, Ansiktet/The Magician/ The Face* 1958; *Jungfrukällan/The Virgin Spring, Djaäulens Öga/The Devil's Eye* 1960; *Sasom i en Spegel/Through a Glass Darkly* 1961; *Nattsvardsgästerna/Winter Light/The Communicants, Tystnaden/The Silence* 1963; *För Att Inte Talla om alla dessa Kvinnor/All These Women/Now About These Women* 1964; *Persona* 1966; *Stimulantia* ("Daniel" episode; also phot.) 1967; *Vargtimmen/Hour of the Wolf, Skammen/Shame/The Shame* 1968; *Riten/The Ritual/The Rite* (originally made for TV), *En Passion/The Passion of Anna/Passion* 1969; *Farö-Dokument/The Faro Documentary* (doc.) 1970; *Beröringen/The Touch* (Sw./US) 1971; *Viskningar och Rop/Cries and Whispers* 1972; *Scener ur ett Äktenskap/Scenes From a Marriage* (originally a TV series) 1973; *The Magic Flute* 1974; *Ansikte mot Ansikte/Face to Face* 1976; *Das Schlangenei/The Serpent's Egg* (Ger./US) 1977; *Herbstsonate/Autumn Sonata* (Ger./Nor./UK) 1978; *Farö-Dokument/Faro 1979* (doc.; also narr.; orig. for TV) 1979; *Aus dem Leben der Marionetten/From the Life of the Marionettes* (Ger.) 1980; *Fanny och Alexander/Fanny and Alexander* (Sw./Ger./Fr.) 1983; *Efter Repetitionen/After the Rehearsal* (orig. for TV) 1984; *The Best Intentions* (sc. only) 1992.

Bergman, Ingrid. Actress. *b.* Aug. 29, 1915. *d.* 1982. An orphan since early childhood, she was raised by relatives. After graduating from high school in 1933 she enrolled at Stockholm's Royal Dramatic Theater School. Within a year she was given the leading role in Swedish films and quickly became the most promising young actress on the Swedish screen. After her appearance in Gustaf Molander's *Intermezzo* in 1936, David O. SELZNICK invited her to Hollywood to star in a 1939 American version of the same film, opposite Leslie Howard and under the direction of Gregory Ratoff. The following year she made her Broadway debut in 'Liliom.'

Exuding radiance, strength, and vitality, she gained a popularity that increased with every screen appearance, through such career landmarks as *Casablanca, For Whom the Bell Tolls, Gaslight, Notorious,* and *Joan of Arc.* Her screen image, bolstered by studio publicity, of a wholesome, almost saintly woman, boomeranged in 1949 when she deserted her husband, Dr. Peter Lindstrom (a dentist she had married in 1937), and her daughter Pia (later a N.Y. TV arts critic), for Roberto ROSSELLINI.

They married in 1950 amid the clamor of public indignation. Their union, which produced a son and twin girls (one of whom is film actress Isabella ROSSELLINI) amounted to a near disaster professionally. The films he directed with her, even the much-heralded *Stromboli,* were neither critical nor commercial successes. Attacks by religious groups and women's clubs and even politicians—on the floor of the US Senate she was called

"Hollywood's apostle of degradation" and "a free-love cultist"—barred her from American films for seven years. She seemed well on her way to oblivion when, in 1956, her career was suddenly resurrected, first in Paris, where she appeared in Renoir's film *Elena et les Hommes/Paris Does Strange Things,* then in London, where she starred in the American production of *Anastasia.* The Academy Award she won for the latter film signified more than anything else Hollywood's forgiveness of her "sins." (She had won an Oscar for her appearance in *Gaslight,* in 1944.) After her marriage to Rossellini was annulled in 1958, she married Swedish stage producer Lars Schmidt. They divorced in 1975. Bravely battling cancer for the final eight years of her life, Bergman continued appearing in films and television. She won a third Oscar, this time as best supporting actress, for her portrayal of a simple-minded nurse in *Murder on the Orient Express* (1974) and was again nominated for an Academy Award as best actress for her role as a concert pianist in Ingmar BERGMAN's *Autumn Sonata* (1978), one of her most complex performances in what turned out to be her last feature film. Her final role was a portrait of Israel's Prime Minister Golda Meir in the TV movie 'A Woman Called Golda' (1981). Autobiography: *Ingrid Bergman My Story* (1980).

FILMS: In Sweden—*The Count From the Monk's Bridge* 1934; *Ocean Breakers/The Surf, Swedenhielms, Walpurgis Night* 1935; *On the Sunny Side, Intermezzo* 1936; *Die Vier Gesellen* (Ger.), *Dollar, A Woman's Face, One Single Night* 1938; *A Night in June* 1940. In the US—*Intermezzo: A Love Story* 1939; *Adam Had Four Sons, Rage in Heaven, Dr. Jekyll and Mr. Hyde* 1941; *Casablanca, Swedes in America* (2-reel doc.), *For Whom the Bell Tolls* 1943; *Gaslight* 1944; *Spellbound, Saratoga Trunk, The Bells of St. Mary's* 1945; *Notorious* 1946; *Arch of Triumph, Joan of Arc* 1948. In the UK—*Under Capricorn* 1949. In Italy—*Stromboli* 1949; *Europa '51/The Greatest Love* 1952; *Siamo Donne/We the Women* 1953; *Viaggio in Italia/The Lonely Woman* 1953; *Giovanna d'Arco al Rogo/Joan at the Stake* 1954. Internationally—*Angst/La Paura/Fear* (Ger./It.) 1954; *Elena et les Hommes/Paris Does Strange Things* (Fr./It.), *Anastasia* (US; filmed in the UK) 1956; *Indiscreet* (UK/US), *The Inn of the Sixth Happiness* (UK/US) 1958; *Goodbye Again/Aimez-vous Brahms?* (US/Fr.) 1961; *Der Besuch/The Visit* (Ger./Fr./It./US), *The Yellow Rolls-Royce* (UK) 1964; *Stimulantia* (Sw.) 1967; *Cactus Flower* (US) 1969; *A Walk in the Spring Rain* (US) 1970; *From the Mixed-Up Files of Mrs. Basil E. Frankweiler* (US) 1973; *Murder on the Orient Express* (UK/US) 1974; *A Matter of Time* (US/It.) 1976; *Herbstsonate/Autumn Sonata* (Ger./Nor./UK) 1978.

Bergner, Elisabeth. Actress *b.* Elisabeth Ettel, Aug. 22, 1897, Drohobycz, Poland (now Drogobych, Russia). *d.* 1986. *ed.* Vienna Conservatory. Made her stage debut in Zurich in 1919 and subsequently appeared in Vienna, Munich, Berlin, and on Broadway gaining an international reputation for her leading roles in plays directed by Max REINHARDT. Her film career began in 1923 and was closely linked to that of her husband (from 1933), Dr. Paul CZINNER, who directed most of her productions. She gained quite a following as the star of German films, but with Hitler's ascent to power she and Czinner moved to England in 1933, following virulent attacks on the Jewish Bergner in the Nazi press. She subsequently appeared in many London and Broadway plays and in several British and one American film. She became a British citizen in 1938. At the height of her career she was called by Alexander Woollcott "probably the ablest actress living today." She was nominated for an Oscar for her performance in *Escape Me Never* (1935). But her career after the early 40s was confined to occasional stage and film appearances. Memoirs: *Bewundert viel und gescholten.*

FILMS: In Germany—*Der Evangelimann* 1923; *Nju/Husbands or Lovers* 1924; *Der Geiger von Florenz/Impetuous Youth Liebe* 1926; *Donna Juana, Köulein Luise/Queen Louise* 1927; *Fräulein Else/Miss Else* 1929; *Ariane* (and English version, *The Loves of Ariane*) 1931; *Derträumende Mund/Dreaming Lips* 1932. In the UK—*Catherine the Great* 1934; *Escape Me Never* 1935; *As You Like It* 1936; *Dreaming Lips* 1937; *Stolen Life* 1939. In the US—*Paris Calling* 1942. In Germany—*Die Glückliche Jahre der Thorwalds* 1962. In the UK—*Cry of the Banshee* 1970. In Germany—*Strogoff/Courier to the Czar* 1968; *Der Fussgänger/The Pedestrian* (cameo) 1974; *Der Pfingstausflug* 1978; *Feine Gesellschaft* 1982.

Berke, William. Director, producer. *b.* Oct. 3, 1903. Milwaukee. *d.* 1958. Berke entered the film industry in 1920 as office boy and worked his way up to cameraman. Cataracts on both eyes forced him to quit photography and he became an independent producer. Produced many low-budget Westerns and after 1941 was producer-director of B pictures, mostly Westerns and action pictures.

FILMS INCLUDE (as director): *Bad Men of the Hills, Riders of the Northland* 1942; *Frontier Fury, The Fighting Buckaroo, Robin Hood of the Range, Silver City Riders, Minesweeper, Tornado* 1943; *The Girl in the Case, The Vigilantes Ride, Wyoming Hurricane, Dangerous Passage, Double Exposure, The Falcon in Mexico, The Last Horseman, The Navy Way, Sailor's Holiday, That's My Baby* 1944; *Betrayal From the East, Why Girls Leave Home, Dick Tracy* 1945; *Ding Dong Williams, Sunset Pass, The Falcon's Adventure* 1946; *Code of the West* (also prod.), *Renegade Girl* (also prod.), *Rolling Home* (also prod.), *Shoot to Kill* (also prod.) 1947; *Caged Fury, Waterfront at Midnight, Speed to Spare, Racing Luck, Jungle Jim* 1948; *Highway 13, Arson Inc., Skyliner, Zamba, The Treasure of Monte Cristo* (also sc.), *Deputy Marshal* (also sc.) 1949; *Gunfire* (also prod., sc.), *Mark of the Gorilla, Captive Girl, Pygmy Island, On the Isle of Samoa, Border Rangers* (also prod., sc.), *The Bandit Queen* (also prod.) 1950; *Danger Zone, Smuggler's Gold, FBI Girl, Savage Drums* (also prod.), *Fury of the Congo, Pier 23* (also prod.), *Roaring City* (also prod.) 1951; *The Jungle* (also prod.) 1952; *Valley of the Headhunters, The Marshal's Daughter* 1953; *Four Boys and a Gun, Street of Sinners* 1957; *Island Woman, Cop Hater* (also prod.), *The Mugger* (also prod.), *The Lost Missile* (also prod.) 1958.

Berkeley, Busby. Choreographer, director. *b.* William Berkeley Enos, Nov. 29, 1895, Los Angeles. *d.* 1976. The son of a stage director and a stage and film actress, he was nicknamed after Amy Busby, a Broadway star at the turn of the century. When he was three the family moved to New York, where he first went on stage at age five. He later attended a military academy, then worked for a shoe company. After WW I services as a field artillery lieutenant, he began playing bit roles on Broadway and directing in stock. By late 20s he had acquired a reputation as one of Broadway's top dance directors, with 21 musicals to his credit, including 'A Connecticut Yankee,' 'Rainbow,' and 'Sweet and Low.' In 1930 he was imported to Hollywood by Samuel Goldwyn to choreograph the musical numbers of several Eddie Cantor vehicles and Mary Pickford's only musical film, *Kiki.*

But it was at the Warner Bros. studios that the Berkeley legend began unfolding in 1933. With the studios' great technical facilities at his command, and his own inventive mind free to create at any expense, he overwhelmed Depression-era audiences with a larger-than-life dose of escapist entertainment in a lavish style that was to have lasting effect on the American musical film. The grandeur of his vision, the gaudy, vulgar, erotic, stupendous, inimitable extravaganza of his mass choreography, still appeals to audiences wherever his films are shown. Each of his lavish numbers employed dozens of girls at once in a spectacular array of rhythmic movement. One of these routines was described by a film critic as "kaleidoscopic patterns of female flesh, dissolving into artichokes, exploding stars, snowflakes, and the expanding leaves of water lilies."

However, it wasn't only the choreography that made Berkeley's dance numbers exciting. His use of the camera became progressively more inventive and daring—diagonal angles, incredible traveling shots, and impeccable rhythmic cutting. He invented a monorail to give his camera greater mobility and devised a technique of filming from directly above the action which has become known as the "Berkeley top shot." In his pursuit of the right perspective for some of his complex shots, he drilled holes through stage floors and bored through the ceilings of the Warners soundstage, causing an angry executive to exclaim, according to a *New York Times* article: "Jesus, now Berkeley's going through the roof!"

It was inevitable that Berkeley would go on to direct his own films after establishing such a reputation as a director of musical numbers in films directed by others. But he was only occasionally successful with his fuller creative control, expectedly with films that emphasized musical verve, such as *Gold Diggers of 1935, Babes in Arms,* and *For Me and My Gal.* He directed his last film in 1949 but continued staging musical numbers for films of others through the mid-50s. With the exception of one job of choreography early in the 60s, the eclipse of the musical genre brought about his forced retirement to his Palm Desert home, where he lived with his sixth wife. But the late 60s saw a resurgence of interest in Berkeley's career, especially after the re-release of some of his early films. He made numerous appearances on campuses, on speaking tours, and on TV. In 1970 he played a cameo part in the film *The Phynx.*

FILMS: As choreographer—*Whoopee* 1930; *Kiki, Palmy Days, Flying High* 1931; *Night World, Bird of Paradise, The Kid from Spain* 1932; *42nd Street, Gold Diggers of 1933, Footlight Parade, Roman Scandals* 1933; *Wonder Bar, Fashions of 1934, Twenty Million Sweethearts, Dames* 1934; *Go Into Your Dance, In Caliente, Stars Over Broadway* 1935; *Gold Diggers of 1937* 1936; *The Singing Marine, Varsity Show* 1937; *Gold Diggers in Paris* 1938; *Broadway Serenade* 1939; *Ziegfeld Girl, Lady Be Good, Born to Sing* 1941; *Girl Crazy* 1943; *Two Weeks With Love* 1950; *Call Me Mister, Two Tickets to Broadway* 1951; *Million Dollar Mermaid* 1952; *Small Town Girl, Easy to Love* 1953; *Rose Marie* 1954; *Billy Rose's Jumbo* 1962. As director—*She Had to Say Yes* (co-dir. with George Amy) 1933; *Gold Diggers of 1935, Bright Lights, I Live for Love* 1935; *Stage Struck* 1936; *The Go-Getter, Hollywood Hotel* 1937; *Men Are Such Fools, Garden of the Moon, Comet Over Broadway* 1938; *They Made Me a Criminal, Babes in Arms, Fast and Furious* 1939; *Strike Up the Band, Forty Little Mothers* 1940; *Blonde Inspiration, Babes on Broadway* 1941; *For Me and My Gal* 1942; *The Gang's All Here* 1943; *Cinderella Jones* 1946; *Take Me Out to the Ball Game* 1949.

Berkoff, Steven. Actor, playwright, theatrical director. Born in 1937 in London. Though most of his work is in the theater and is political in nature, he has also made a memorable movie villain in a diverse variety of films, such as the nefarious art/drug dealer in *Beverly Hills Cop*. He is the author of the book *I Am Hamlet* (1993).

FILMS INCLUDE: *A Clockwork Orange, Nicholas and Alexandra* 1971; *Barry Lyndon* 1975; *Outland* 1981; *Octopussy* 1983; *Beverly Hills Cop* 1984; *Rambo: First Blood Part II, Revolution* 1985; *Absolute Beginners, Under the Cherry Moon, Transmutations/Underworld* 1986; *Prisoner of Rio* 1988; *Streets of Yesterday* 1989; *The Krays* 1990; *My Forgotten Man* 1993; *Decadence* 1994; *Fair Game* 1995.

Berlanga, Luis Garcia. Director. Born June 12, 1921, in Valencia, Spain. Educated at Valencia U. and in Switerzerland. After serving in the Spanish Civil War and WW II, he enrolled in 1947 in the Spanish Institute of Cinema (IIEC). Collaborating with ex-schoolmate Juan BARDEM in 1951, he co-authored and co-directed a humorous feature film, *Esa Pareja Feliz/That Happy Pair.* That same year the two collaborated on the screenplay of *Bienvenido, Mr. Marshall/Welcome, Mr. Marshall.* Berlanga directed the film, which was exhibited to rave notices at the Cannes Festival. The success of this movie contributed considerably to the prestige of Spanish cinema. A liberal and an individualist, Berlanga continued on a course of personal expression despite harassment by the Spanish censors. His *Plácido* (1961) was nominated for an Academy Award as best foreign film. In 1977 he shocked audiences at the Valladolid Festival with *Life Size/Love Doll,* a film laden with sexual symbolism and injected with a large dose of eroticism.

FEATURE FILMS: *Esa Pareja Feliz/That Happy Pair* (co-dir., co-sc. with Juan Antonio Bardem) 1951; *Bienvenido Mr. Marshall/Welcome Mr. Marshall* (also co-sc.) 1952; *Novio a la Vista* (co-dir. with Bardem) 1953; *Los Gancheros* 1955; *Calabuch/The Rocket from Calabuch* (also co-story) 1956; *Los Jueves Milagro* ("Arrivederci Dimas" episode; also story, co-sc.) 1957; *Plácido* (also co-sc.) 1961; *Les Quates Vérités*/("El Lenador y la Muerte" episode) 1962; *El Verdugo/Not on Your Life* (also co-sc.) 1963; *Las Pirañas* (also co-sc.) 1967; *¡Vivan los Novios!* 1970; *Life Size/Love Doll* (also co-sc.) 1977; *La Escopeta Nacionál* (also co-sc.) 1978; *Moros y Cristianos* (also sc.) 1987.

Berle, Milton. Comedian. Born Milton Berlinger, on July 12, 1908, in New York City. At five he won a contest, impersonating Charlie Chaplin, and soon was playing children's parts for Biograph and other studios. With the encouragement of his mother, he and his sister toured the country in vaudeville. He made his New York stage debut at 12 in 'Floradora' and later appeared in several plays, including 'Life Begins at 8:40' and 'The Ziegfeld Follies.' He made his adult film debut in 1937 and went on to display his comic antics in a modest number of films, including some mildly amusing whodunits. His most successful medium has been TV, which he practically dominated between 1948 and 1956 to the point that he was nicknamed "Mr. Television" or, more endearingly, "Uncle Miltie." Author: *Out of My Trunk* (1945); *Earthquake* (1959).

FILMS INCLUDE: *The Perils of Pauline* (serial), *Tillie's Punctured Romance* 1914; *Easy Street* 1916; *Little Brother* 1917; *Humoresque, The Mark of Zorro* 1920; *Lena Rivers* 1925; *Sparrows* 1926; *New Faces of 1937* 1937; *Tall Dark and Handsome, Sun Valley Serenade* 1941; *Over My Dead Body, Margin for Error* 1943; *Always Leave Them Laughing* 1949; *The Bellboy, Let's Make Love* 1960; *It's a Mad Mad Mad Mad World* 1963; *The Loved One* 1965; *The Oscar* 1966; *The Happening, Who's Minding the Mint?* 1967; *Where Angels Go Trouble Follows, For Singles Only* 1968; *Can Hieronymous Merkin Ever Forget Mercy Humppe and Find True Happiness?* 1969; *Journey Back to Oz* (voice only) 1974; *Lepke* 1975; *Won Ton Ton—The Dog Who Saved Hollywood* (cameo) 1976; *The Muppet Movie* (voice only) 1979; *Broadway Danny Rose* 1984; *Driving Me Crazy* 1990.

Berlin, Irving. Composer, lyricist. *b.* Israel Baline, May 11, 1888, Temun (also spelled Tyumen), near Siberia, Russia, the son of a cantor. *d.* 1989. In the US from age five, he grew up on New York's Lower East Side and as a child sang on the streets for pennies. While working as a singing waiter in his teens, he began writing songs. The first published was 'Marie from Sunny Italy' (1907), and his first big hit was 'Alexander's Ragtime Band' (1911). He subsequently composed and wrote the lyrics for some 1,500 songs for his own music publishing house, for Broadway musicals, and for films. Although he could play and compose only in the key of F sharp (a gadget on his piano transposed keys mechanically), he became one of America's most celebrated composers. He received the Medal of Merit for his patriotic stage and screen musical *This Is the Army* and the Congressional Gold Medal for the song 'God Bless America.' He was also awarded the French Legion of Honor and in 1942 won an Oscar for the song 'White Christmas,' which he wrote for the film *Holiday Inn.* In 1986 he came out of a long, self-imposed seclusion to receive the Medal of Liberty from President Ronald Reagan on the 100th anniversary of the Statue of Liberty. Two years later his 100th birthday was celebrated in a gala benefit. When Berlin died at 101, someone recalled a quote by Jerome Kern: "Irving Berlin has no place in American music. He *is* American music."

FILMS INCLUDE: *The Jazz Singer* ('Blue Skies') 1927; *The Awakening* ('Marie,' etc.) 1928; *Coquette, Hallelujah!, The Cocoanuts* 1929; *Puttin' on the Ritz, Mammy* 1930; *Reaching for the Moon* 1931; *Kid Millions* 1934; *Top Hat* ('Cheek to Cheek,' etc.) 1935; *Follow the Fleet* ('Let's Face the Music and Dance,' etc.) 1936; *On the Avenue* ('This Year's Kisses,' etc.) 1937; *Carefree* ('Change Partners,' etc.), *Alexander's Ragtime Band* (numerous songs) 1938; *Second Fiddle* ('Back to Back,' etc.) 1939; *Louisiana Purchase* 1941; *Holiday Inn* ('White Christmas,' etc.) 1942; *This Is the Army* (also assoc. prod., act., sang 'Oh, How I Hate to Get Up in the Morning') 1943; *Blue Skies* 1946; *Easter Parade* ('Happy Easter,' etc.) 1948; *Annie Get Your Gun* 1950; *Call Me Madam* 1953; *White Christmas* ('Count Your Blessings,' etc.), *There's No Business Like Show Business* 1954; *Sayonara* (title song) 1957.

Berlin, Jeannie. Actress, screenwriter. Born November 1, 1949, in Los Angeles. Talented, appealing leading and character actress of the American stage and screen. Her first critical success as an actress came when she was cast as the bewildered, put-upon bride in *The Heartbreak Kid* (1972), directed by her mother, actress-screenwriter-director Elaine MAY. Nominated for a supporting actress Academy Award for the role, she made several other films before turning her attention more to the stage and screenwriting. In 1990 she wrote and starred opposite May in the New Age comedy-mystery *In the Spirit*, directed by Sandra Seacat.

FILMS: *The Baby Maker, Getting Straight, The Strawberry Statement* 1970; *Bone, The Heartbreak Kid, Portnoy's Complaint* 1972; *Sheila Levine Is Dead and Living in New York* 1975; *In the Spirit* (also sc.) 1990.

Berman, Pandro S. Producer. *b.* Mar. 28, 1905, in Pittsburgh. *d.* 1996. Educated in New York City. Son of Harry M. Berman, general manager of Universal, he made an early start in films as an assistant director for Tod Browning, Ralph Ince, Alfred Santell, and Mal St. Clair. Later he became chief film editor for RKO, then assistant to William Le Baron and David O. Selznick. He became a producer in 1931, first for RKO, then (in 1940) for MGM. He was responsible for several Fred Astaire–Ginger Rogers hits and for some of MGM's most prestigious motion pictures. His films are noted for their technical proficiency and their strong entertainment value. Retired in 1970. In the 1977 Oscar ceremony he received the honorary Irving G. Thalberg Memorial Award. His younger brother, Henry Berman (*b.* Jan. 1, 1914, Newcastle, Pa.), was a film editor who shared an Oscar for *Grand Prix* (1966).

FILMS INCLUDE: *Symphony of Six Million, Age of Consent* 1932; *Ann Vickers, Morning Glory* 1933; *The Gay Divorcee, Of Human Bondage, The Little Minister* 1934; *Roberta, Alice Adams, Top Hat* 1935; *Follow the Fleet, Mary of Scotland, Winterset, Swing Time* 1936; *Stage Door, A Damsel in Distress, Shall We Dance* 1937; *Room Service* 1938; *Gunga Din, The Hunchback of Notre Dame, The Story of Vernon and Irene Castle* 1939; *Ziegfeld Girl, Love Crazy* 1941; *Rio Rita, Somewhere I'll Find You* 1942; *Slightly Dangerous* 1943; *Dragon Seed, The Seventh Cross, National Velvet* 1944; *The Picture of Dorian Gray* 1945; *Undercurrent* 1946; *Sea of Grass, If Winter Comes* 1947; *The Three Musketeers* 1948; *Madame Bovary* 1949; *Father of the Bride* 1950; *Father's Little Dividend* 1951; *The Prisoner of Zenda, Ivanhoe* 1952; *The Knights of the Round Table, All the Brothers Were Valiant* 1953; *The Blackboard Jungle* 1955; *Bhowani Junction* 1956; *Tea and Sympathy, Something of Value* 1957; *The Brothers Karamazov, The Reluctant Debutante* 1958; *All the Fine Young Cannibals, Butterfield 8* 1960; *Sweet Bird of Youth* 1962; *The Prize* 1963; *A Patch of Blue* 1965; *Justine* 1969; *Move* 1970; *George Stevens: A Filmmaker's Journey* (doc.; appearance only) 1984.

Bern, Paul. Production executive, director, screenwriter. *b.* Paul Levy, Dec. 3, 1889, Wandsbek, Germany. *d.* 1932. In the US from childhood, he was educated at New York's public schools and at the American Academy of Dramatic Arts. Between 1911 and 1915 he was active in the theater as actor, stage manager, and producer. He started in films as a cutter, then a screenwriter and director. He wrote scripts for Lubitsch, von Sternberg, and other top directors and directed Pola Negri and Florence Vidor, among other famous stars. In 1926 he rose to the executive ranks of MGM as production assistant (actually producer) and story consultant to Irving G. THALBERG. He soon became Thalberg's closest associate and was entrusted with the supervision of all Greta GARBO pictures.

In July 1932, Bern married Jean HARLOW. At 42, he was exactly twice her age. Shortly after, he was found dead in his bathroom, a pistol at his side. Impotence was mentioned as the cause of the suicide.

FILMS INCLUDE: As director—*The North Wind's Malice* (co-dir. with Carl Harbaugh) 1920; *Head Over Heels* (co-dir. with Victor Schertzinger), *The Man with Two Mothers* 1922; *Open All Night, Worldly Goods* 1924; *Tomorrow's Love, The Dressmaker from Paris, Grounds for Divorce, Flower of Night* 1925. As screenwriter—*Women Men Forget* 1920; *Suspicious Wives* 1921; *The Christian, Lost and Found on a South Sea Island, The Wanters* 1923; *Name the Man, The Marriage Circle, Lily of the Dust, Vanity's Price* 1925; *The Great Deception, The Prince of Tempters* 1926; *The Beloved Rogue, Three Hours* 1927; *The Dove* 1928.

Bernard, Raymond. Director. *b.* Oct. 10, 1891, Paris. *d.* 1977. The son of novelist and playwright Tristan Bernard, he entered films as an actor, appearing in *Jeanne Doré* (1915), opposite Sarah Bernhardt, and some of Jacques Feyder's short comedies. In 1917 he began a durable career as a film director, starting out with adaptations of his father's works. His first important film was *Le Petit Café* (1919), scripted by his father and starring Max Linder. After several comedies, he turned to dramas, specializing in grand-scale epic and historic films, notably *Le Miracle des Loups* (1924) and the first sound version of *Les Misérables* (1934), starring Harry Baur and Charles Vanel. Bernard continued directing until the late 50s.

FILMS INCLUDE: *Le Ravin sans Fond* 1917; *Le Gentilhomme commerçant* 1918; *Le Petit Café* 1919; *Le Secret de Rosette Lambert* 1920; *La Maison vide* 1921; *Tripleplate* 1922; *Grandeur et Décadence* 1923; *Le Miracle des Loups/The*

Miracle of the Wolves 1924; *Le Joueur d'Echecs/The Chess Player* 1927; *Tarakanova* 1930; *Faubourg Montmartre, Les Croix de Bois/Wooden Crosses* 1932; *Les Misérables, Tartarin de Tarascon* 1934; *Amants et Voleurs* 1935; *Anne-Marie* 1936; *Le Coupable, Marthe Richard* 1937; *J'étais une Aventurière* 1938; *Les Otages/The Mayor's Dilemma* 1939; *Cavalcade d'Amour* 1940; *Un Ami viendra ce Soir/A Friend Will Come Tonight, Adieu Chérie* 1946; *Maya* 1950; *Le Cap de l'Espérance* 1951; *Le Jugement de Dieu* 1952; *La Dame aux Camelias, La Belle de Cadix* 1953; *Les Fruits de l'Eté/Fruits of Summer* 1955; *Le Septième Commandement* 1957; *Le Septième Ciel* 1958.

Bernardi, Herschel. Actor. *b.* Oct. 30, 1923, New York City. *d.* 1986. Burly Broadway star ('Fiddler on the Roof,' 'Zorba,' etc.), he also played occasional character parts in films. His voice was often used for cartoon characters in TV commercials, such as the Jolly Green Giant and Charlie the Tuna. Appeared in the TV series 'Peter Gunn' and 'Arnie.'

FILMS: *Green Fields* (in Yiddish) 1937; *Yankel the Blacksmith* (in Yiddish) 1939; *Stakeout on Dope Street, Murder by Contract* 1958; *The Savage Eye* 1960; *A Cold Wind in August, The George Raft Story* 1961; *Irma La Douce* 1963; *Love with the Proper Stranger* 1964; *The Man from Button Willow* (voice only) 1965; *Journey Back to Oz* (voice only) 1974; *No Deposit No Return, The Front* 1976.

Bernds, Edward. American director. Born in 1911. Started out as a sound technician in the early 30s. A director since the late 40s, he turned out many low-budget films for Columbia, Fox, and Allied Artists, among other studios, often writing his own scripts. His films include several installments in the "Blondie" and "Bowery Boys" series, as well as a couple of Three Stooges comedies. He also directed numerous Three Stooges shorts.

FILMS: *Blondie's Secret* 1948; *Blondie's Big Deal, Blondie Hits the Jackpot, Feudin' Rhythm* 1949; *Blondie's Hero, Beware of Blondie* 1950; *Gasoline Alley, Gold Raiders, Corky of Gasoline Alley* 1951; *Harem Girl* 1952; *Loose in London, Clipped Wings, Hot News, Private Eyes* 1953; *The Bowery Boys Meet the Monsters, Jungle Gents* 1954; *Bowery to Bagdad, Spy Chasers* 1955; *Dig That Uranium, World Without End, Navy Wife, Calling Homicide* 1956; *The Storm Rider, Reform School Girls* 1957; *Escape from Red Rock, Quantrill's Raiders, Space Master X–7, Queen of Outer Space, Joy Ride* 1958; *Alaska Passage, High School Hellcats, Return of the Fly* 1959; *Valley of the Dragons* 1961; *The Three Stooges Meet Hercules, The Three Stooges in Orbit* 1962; *Tickle Me* (co-sc. only) 1965.

Bernhard, Sandra. Actress. Born on June 6, 1955, in Flint, Mich. Talented, peculiar-looking comic performer. She moved with her family to Scottsdale, Arizona at age ten, and began her career at 19 as a standup comedian in Los Angeles, supplementing her income as a manicurist in Beverly Hills. Her big break came in 1977 when she was a regular on the Richard Pryor TV show. In films from 1981, she registered a memorable performance as an obsessed fan in *The King of Comedy* (1983), which made her a cult favorite. She has since written articles for leading magazines, recorded a first singing album, 'I'm Your Woman' (1985), and starred in a one-woman, off-Broadway show, 'Without You I'm Nothing' (1988), which later became a film. Recurring role on TV's 'Roseanne.' Author: *Confessions of a Pretty Lady* (1988), a collection of essays, short stories, and memoirs.

FILMS: *Cheech and Chong's Nice Dreams* 1981; *The King of Comedy* 1983; *Sesame Street Presents: Follow That Bird* 1985; *The Whoopee Boys, Track 29* (UK) 1988; *Heavy Petting* (doc.) 1989; *Without You I'm Nothing* (also co-sc.) 1990; *Hudson Hawk* 1991; *Inside Monkey Zetterland* 1993.

Bernhardt, Curtis (Kurt). Director. *b.* Apr. 15, 1899, Worms, Germany. *d.* 1981. *ed.* State School for Dramatic Arts (Frankfurt-am-Main). Active as an actor and producer on the Berlin stage, he began film directing in 1927, turning out several German films, including a Marlene Dietrich vehicle, *Three Loves,* and UFA's first talkie. He emigrated to France when the Nazis came to power, and from 1933 to 1939 he directed several French films, with time out for one British film. In 1940 he signed a Hollywood contract with Warner Bros., and went on to direct many films of all genres, for Warners, MGM, and others, specializing in melodramas. Inactive after the mid-60s.

FILMS: In Germany—*Qualen der Nacht* (also co-sc.), *Die Waise von Lowood* 1926; *Kinderseelen klagen an, Das Mädchen mit den fünf Nullen, Schinderhannes/The Prince of Rogues* (also co-sc.) 1927; *Das letzte Fort* 1928; *Die Frau nach der Mann sich sehnt/Three Loves* 1929; *Die letzte Kompanie/13 Men and a Girl* 1930; *Der Mann der den Mord beging* (and French version, *L'Homme qui assassina*) 1931; *Der Rebell/The Rebel* (co-dir. with Luis Trenker), *Der grosse Rausch* 1932; *Der Tunnel* (and French version, *Le Tunnel* also co-sc.) 1933. In France—*L'Or dans la Rue* 1934; *Carrefour/Crossroads* 1938; *Nuit de Décembre* 1939. In the UK—*The Beloved Vagabond* 1934. In the US—*My Love Came Back, Lady with Red Hair* 1940; *Million Dollar Baby* 1941; *Juke Girl* 1942; *Happy Go Lucky* 1943; *Conflict* 1945; *My Reputation, Devotion, A Stolen Life* 1946; *Possessed* 1947; *High Wall* 1948; *The Doctor and the Girl* 1949; *Payment on Demand* (also co-sc.), *Sirocco, The Blue Veil* 1951; *The Merry Widow* 1952; *Miss Sadie Thompson* 1953; *Beau Brummel* 1954; *Interrupted Melody* 1955; *Gaby* 1956; *Stephanie in Rio* (Ger.) 1960; *Damon and Pythias/Il Tirano di Siracusa* (US/It.) 1961; *Kisses for My President* (also prod.) 1964.

Bernhardt, Sarah. Actress. *b.* Henriette-Rosine Bernard, Oct. 25, 1844, Paris. *d.* 1923. This celebrated star of the French stage had a sporadic love-hate affair with early cinema. After her film debut in *Hamlet's Duel* in 1900, she declared she detested the medium; yet she consented to appear in another film, *Tosca,* in 1908. Upon seeing the results, she reportedly recoiled in horror, demanding that the negative be destroyed. Her next film appearance, in the Film d'Art production of *La Dame aux Camélias* (1911), was a critical and popular success, helping give cinema artistic dignity. The following year she made *Queen Elizabeth* in Britain. The receipts from this film's distribution in the US provided Adolph Zukor with the funds to found Paramount.

Bernhardt, at 69, was offered a fortune to make films with other companies, but stayed with Film d'Art, appearing in 1913 in *Adrienne Lecouvreur.* She appeared in two more pictures after losing a leg in 1915, *Jeanne Doré* (1915) and *Mères Françaises* (1917), both produced as WW I morale boosters. In 1923, when she was 79, her hotel room was turned into a studio so that she could appear in the film *La Voyante.* But her failing health halted production and she died before the film was completed. She was portrayed on the screen by Glenda Jackson in *The Incredible Sarah* (UK, 1976).

FILMS: *Le Duel d'Hamlet/Hamlet's Duel* 1900; *Tosca* 1908 (never released); *La Dame aux Camélias* 1911; *La Reine Elisabeth/Queen Elizabeth* 1912; *Adrienne Lecouvreur* (also sc.) 1913; *Jeanne Doré* 1915; *Mères Françaises/Mothers of France,* 1917; *La Voyante* (unfinished) 1923.

Bernsen, Corbin. Actor. Born on Sept. 7, 1954, in North Hollywood, Calif. *ed.* UCLA (B.A. theater arts; M.F.A. playwriting). The son of soap-opera queen Jeanne Cooper, he played small roles in films while still in college. Moving to New York in 1981, he supported himself as a carpenter and as a model for a cigarette company before joining the regular cast of the daytime TV serial 'Ryan's Hope.' He later co-starred in the series 'L.A. Law' and appeared sporadically in films. Married actress Amanda Pays.

FILMS INCLUDE: *Three the Hard Way* 1974; *Eat My Dust, King Kong* 1976; *S.O.B.* 1981; *Hello Again, Mace* 1987; *Bert Rigby You're a Fool, Major League, Disorganized Crime* 1989; *Shattered* 1991; *Frozen Assets* 1992; *Major League II, The New Age, Radioland Murders* 1994; *Tales from the Hood* 1995; *The Great White Hype* 1996.

Bernstein, Elmer. Composer. Born on Apr. 4, 1922, in New York City. *ed.* Juilliard; NYU. A former dancer, actor, painter, and concert pianist, he composed music for UN radio shows before entering films in the early 50s. As one of Hollywood's most prolific and versatile composers, he has scored numerous motion pictures and TV shows. His scores are noted for their zestful vibrance and full-bodied melodiousness. He won an Emmy for his scoring of TV's 'The Making of a President,' an Oscar for the original score of the film *Thoroughly Modern Millie* (1967), and multiple Oscar nominations. He has also composed vocal and chamber music. In film circles he is known as "Bernstein West" to distinguish him from "Bernstein East," New York's Leonard Bernstein.

FILMS INCLUDE: *Saturday's Hero* 1951; *Sudden Fear* 1952; *Robot Monster* 1953; *The Eternal Sea* 1955; *The Man with the Golden Arm, The Ten Commandments* 1956; *Sweet Smell of Success, The Tin Star* 1957; *Desire Under the Elms, God's Little Acre* 1958; *The Buccaneer, Some Came Running* 1959; *The Rat Race, From the Terrace, The Magnificent Seven* 1960; *By Love Possessed, The Comancheros* 1961; *Summer and Smoke, Walk on the Wild Side, Birdman of Alcatraz* 1962; *To Kill a Mockingbird, Hud, The Great Escape* 1963; *Love with the Proper Stranger, The Carpetbaggers* 1964; *The Hallelujah Trail, The Sons of Katie Elder* 1965; *Seven Women, Hawaii, Cast a Giant Shadow* 1966; *Thoroughly Modern Millie* 1967; *I Love You Alice B. Toklas* 1968; *True Grit, The Gypsy Moths* 1969; *The Liberation of L. B. Jones* 1970; *Doctors' Wives, Big Jake, See No Evil* 1971; *Cahill US Marshal* 1973; *McQ, Gold* (UK) *The Trial of Billy Jack* 1974; *Report to the Commissioner* 1975; *The Incredible Sarah* (UK), *The Shootist, From Noon Till Three* 1976; *Slap Shot* (music superv.) 1977; *National Lampoon's Animal House, Bloodbrothers* 1978; *Meatballs* (Can.), *Zulu Dawn* (UK), *The Great Santini/The Ace* 1979; *Airplane!* 1980; *Stripes, An American Werewolf in London, Honky Tonk Freeway, Heavy Metal* (Can.), *The Chosen* 1981; *Trading Places* 1983; *Ghostbusters* 1984; *Spies Like Us* 1985; *Legal Eagles* 1986; *Da, The Good Mother* 1988; *Slipstream* (UK), *My Left Foot* (UK) 1989; *The Field* (UK) 1990; *The Grifters* 1990; *Oscar, A Rage in Harlem, Rambling Rose, Cape Fear* (adaptation only) 1991; *The Babe, A River Runs Through It* 1992; *Lost in Yonkers, The Age of Innocence* 1993; *Canadian Bacon* 1994; *Devil in a Blue Dress, Frankie Starlight, Roommates, Search and Destroy* 1995; *Bulletproof* 1996; *Hoodlum* 1997.

Bernstein, Leonard. Composer, conductor, pianist. *b.* Aug. 25, 1918, Lawrence, Mass. *d.* 1990. *ed.* Harvard; Curtis Inst. of Music. He studied conducting with Fritz Reiner and Serge Koussevitzky. In 1942 he became assistant conductor of the New York Philharmonic and from 1957 to 1970 was the orchestra's principal conductor. He composed symphonies, ballets, a Mass, and many other compositions. His Broadway musicals include 'On the Town,' 'Wonderful Town,' 'Candide,' and 'West Side Story.' A leading figure in American music, his contribution to film was important but sparse.

FILMS: As composer—*On the Town* 1949; *On the Waterfront* 1954; *West Side Story* 1961; Personal appearances—*Satchmo the Great* 1958; *A Journey to Jerusalem* 1968.

Bernstein, Walter. Screenwriter. Born on Aug. 20, 1919, in Brooklyn, N.Y. *ed.* Dartmouth. After graduation, he wrote regularly for *The New Yorker* and during WW II he served as a roving reporter for the G.I. weekly *Yank.* After demobilization he returned to magazine writing, then headed for Hollywood. He was blacklisted by the industry in the wake of the House Un-American Activities Committee hearings after collaborating on only one screenplay, in 1948, and did not work again in films for a decade. In 1976 he wrote the script for *The Front,* a film that dealt with the blacklisting era. He has also written for TV. In 1980 he took a weak first stab at directing. Author: *Keep Your Head Down.*

FILMS (alone or in collaboration): *Kiss the Blood Off My Hands* (co-adapt. only) 1948; *That Kind of Woman* 1959; *Heller in Pink Tights, A Breath of Scandal, The Magnificent Seven* (uncredited) 1960; *Paris Blues* 1961; *Fail Safe* 1964; *The Train* 1965; *The Money Trap* 1966; *The Molly Maguires* 1970; *The Front* 1976; *Semi-Tough* 1977; *The Betsy* 1978; *An Almost Perfect Affair, Yanks* (UK) 1979; *Little Miss Marker* (also dir.) 1980; *The House on Carroll Street* 1988.

Berri, Claude. Director, producer. Born Claude Langmann, on July 1, 1934, in Paris, to Polish-Rumanian immigrants. A former furrier, then actor, he won a prize at Venice and a Hollywood Oscar for his first directing effort, the 1963 short *Le Poulet/The Chicken.* Graduating to feature films in the late 60s, he turned out a number of semiautobiographical, sentimental tragicomedies, flavored with the ethnic humor of his Jewish background. He writes his own scripts. Through his own production company, Renn Films, he began in 1979 to produce films of other directors, as well as his own. Among these were *Tess, L'Africain/The African, Banzai, L'Homme blessé, L'Ours/The Bear,* and *Valmont.* Although he continued directing intermittently, his reputation declined. In 1986, however, Berri revived his standing as a superior director with the delectable twin-film package *Jean de Florette* and *Manon of the Spring,* adapted from works by Marcel Pagnol. The former was named the year's best film by the British Film Academy.

FEATURE FILMS (as director-writer): *Les Baisers* (one episode), *La Chance et l'Amour* (one episode) 1964; *Le Vieil Homme et l'Enfant/The Two of Us* 1967; *Mazel Tov ou le Mariage/Marry Me! Marry Me!* (also act.) 1968; *Le Pistonneé/The Man With Connections* 1970; *Le Cinéma de Papa* (also act.) 1971; *Le Sex Shop* (also act.) 1972; *Le Male du Siècle/Male of the Century* (also act.) 1975; *La Première Fois* 1976; *Un Moment d'Egarement/In a Wild Moment* 1978; *Je vous aime* (also prod.) 1980; *Le Maître d'Ecole* (also prod.) 1981; *Tchao Pantin* (also prod.) 1983; *Jean de Florette, Manon des Sources/Manon of the Spring* 1986; *Hotel de France* (prod. only) 1987; *The Bear* (exec. prod.), *Valmont* (exec. prod.) 1989; *The Door on the Left as You Leave the Elevator* (exec. prod.), *Uranus* 1991; *Germinal* (also co-prod., co-sc.) 1993; *Queen Margot* 1994.

Berry, Halle. Actress. Born 1966, in Cleveland, Ohio. *ed.* Cuyahoga Community College. Lovely, endearing leading lady of American films. Before a recurring role on the long-running television series 'Knots Landing,' Berry was a model and former beauty queen. She stunned audiences and critics alike with her earnest, gritty portrayal of a dope fiend in Spike Lee's *Jungle Fever* (1991). Subsequent films roles have proven her to be a versatile and compelling actress as in the touching drama *Losing Isaiah* (1995) and a comic turn in *B.A.P.S.* (1997).

FILMS: *Jungle Fever, The Last Boy Scout, Strictly Business* 1991; *Boomerang* 1992; *Father Hood, The Program* 1993; *The Flintstones* 1994; *Executive Decision, Losing Isaiah* 1995; *Race the Sun, Girl 6, Rich Man's Wife* 1996; *B.A.P.S.* 1997.

Berry, John (Jack). Director. Born in 1917, in New York City. A vaudeville and stage actor from childhood, he directed and acted for Orson Welles's Mercury Theater before entering films in 1943, as assistant to Billy Wilder on *Double Indemnity.* He directed a number of films of varying quality, ranging from *From This Day Forward,* a soap opera with Joan Fontaine, to *Casbah,* a musical remake of *Pépé le Moko* and of *Algiers,* and such melodramas as *Tension* and *He Ran All the Way.* His Hollywood career was suddenly cut short by the House Un-American Activities Committee hearings in which he was identified as a Communist by director Edward DMYTRYK and others. Blacklisted by the industry, Berry directed a 16 mm documentary, *The Hollywood Ten* (1951), which was produced to raise funds for the defense of the hearings' victims. He then went to France, where he directed a number of commercially oriented entertainment films, and to London, where he directed avant-garde productions for the stage. He resumed directing in the US in the 70s but in the 80s was working again in France. He also acted in several films, including *Autour de Minuit/'Round Midnight* (Fr./US 1986), *Un Homme amoureux/A Man in Love* (Fr./It. 1987), and *Blancs Cassés* 1988.

FILMS: In the US—*Miss Susie Slagle's, From This Day Forward* 1946; *Cross My Heart* 1947; *Casbah* 1948; *Tension* 1949; *He Ran All the Way, The Hollywood Ten* (doc.) 1951. In France—*C'est arrive à Paris* (credited to Henri Lavoral) 1953; *Ça va barder* (also co-sc.), *Je suis un Sentimental* (also co-sc.) 1955; *Don Juan/Pantaloons* (also co-sc.) 1956; *Tamango* (also co-sc.), *Oh que Mambo!* 1958; *Maya* (US; filmed in India) 1966; *A tout casser/Breaking It Up* (also co-sc.) 1969. In the US—*Claudine* 1974; *Thieves* 1977; *The Bad News Bears Go to Japan* 1978; *Le Voyage à Paimpol* (also co-sc.) 1985; *Il y a maldonné* (also sc.) 1988.

Berry, Jules. Actor. *b.* Jules Paufichet, Feb. 9, 1883, Poitiers, France. *d.* 1951. A veteran of the Paris stage, he appeared in three silent films. But it was in the talkies that he emerged as a character star. He performed in more than 90 sound films between 1931 and 1951, sometimes in as many as 14 in one year. His imposing screen presence, enhanced by an incisive, often insidious, voice, made him a favorite with some of France's leading directors, especially Jean RENOIR, who used him in *Le Crime de M. Lange* (1936), and Marcel CARNÉ, who cast him as the villain in *Le Jour se Lève* (1939) and as the devil in *Les Visiteurs du Soir* (1942).

FILMS INCLUDE: *Tirez s'il vous plait* 1908; *Cromwell* 1911; *L'Argent* 1929; *Quick* (Ger./Fr.) 1932; *Le Crime de M. Lange/The Crime of Monsieur Lange, Le Mort en fuite, Rigolboche, Les Loups entre eux* 1936; *L'Homme à abattre, Arsène Lupin Détective* (title role) 1937; *Le Voleur de Femmes, Carrefour/Crossroads* 1938; *Accord final, L'Inconnue de Monte Carlo, Derrière la Façade/32 Rue de Montmartre, Le Jour se lève/Daybreak* 1939; *La Symphonie fantastique, Les Visiteurs du Soir/The Devil's Own Envoy* 1942; *Le Voyageur de la Toussaint* 1943; *Etoile sans Lumière/Star Without Light* 1946; *Rêves d'Amour* 1947; *Portrait d'un Assassin* 1949; *Les Maîtres Nageurs* 1950.

Bertini, Francesca. Actress. *b.* Elena Seracini Vitiello, Apr. 11, 1888, Florence, Italy. *d.* 1985. The daughter of a stage actress, she began a theatrical career in her teens and made her film debut in *La Dea del Mare* in 1907. She had her first success with *Il Trovatore* (1910) and emerged as an international star in 1915 with the film *Assunta Spina.* Featured as Italy's first screen diva, she became one of the main attractions of the early period of the Italian cinema, and women the world over imitated her style and manners. She reportedly signed a million-dollar contract with Fox in 1920 to star in Hollywood films. But the following year she married Swiss count Paul Cartier and announced her retirement from the screen. She later resurfaced sporadically, however, in a variety of European films. A documentary about her career by Giancalo Mignozzi, *The Last Diva,* was released in 1983. Autobiography: *Il Resto non conta* (1969).

FILMS INCLUDE: *La Dea del Mare* 1907; *Il Trovatore* 1910; *Ernani, Giulietta e Romeo/Romeo and Juliet, Tristano e Isotta/Tristan and Isolde, Francesca da Rimini, Re Lear/King Lear, Lorenzo il Magnifico* 1911; *Il Mercante di Venezia, La Rosa di Tebe, Idillio tragico* 1912; *La Gloria, Terra promessa, La Madre, Salome* 1913; *Eroismo d'Amore* 1914; *Assunta Spina, La Signora dalle Camelie/Camille* 1915; *La Perla del Cinema, Fedora, Odette* 1916; *Andreina* 1917; *La Tosca, Frou-Frou, Anima allegra, La Donna nuda* 1918; *La Contessa Sarah, Spiritismo, Beatrice* 1919; *Anima selvaggia* 1920; *Marion, La Giovinezza del Diavolo* 1921; *Conseulita* 1922; *Monte Carlo, Odette* 1928; *Possession* 1929; *Dora* 1943; *A Sud Niente di Nuovo* 1956; *Novecento/1900* 1976.

Bertolucci, Bernardo. Director. Born on Mar. 16, 1940, in Parma, Italy. One of the most accomplished directors of the contemporary Italian cinema. The son of poet and film critic Attilio Bertolucci, he began writing poetry as a child, and his work was published in periodicals before he was 12. Eight years later, while still a student at Rome University, he won a national poetry prize for his volume *In Search of Mystery.* While still in his teens he had developed a passion for the cinema and made several amateur 16 mm films. In 1961 he dropped out of college to become PASOLINI's assistant director on *Accattone!,* and the following year, barely 22, he directed his first film, *The Grim Reaper,* a somber affair that was a commercial disaster and made little impact on critics. He then spent two years preparing his second, *Before the Revolution,* a remarkably mature and intensely romantic exploration of turbulent youth. Despite stylistic flaws and Godard-like excesses, the film was widely hailed by critics in Europe and the USA, and it earned him the Max Ophüls Prize in France.

But the true milestone year in Bertolucci's career was 1970, when he turned out two outstanding films, the visually lovely *The Spider's Stratagem,* originally made for Italian TV, and a richly poetic, stunningly elegant, intricate, ambivalent, and completely personal adaptation of Alberto Moravia's novel *The Conformist.* Bertolucci, who believes that "cinema is the true poetic language," had applied his celluloid poesy mostly to political-human themes, but with *Last Tango in Paris* (1972) he moved into the realm of the purely human. The highly controversial film, which was condemned in the Italian courts as "obscene, indecent, and catering to the lowest instincts of the libido," became a worldwide box-office hit on the strength of its explicit sexuality and the presence of Marlon Brando in the leading role. It established Bertolucci as a commercially viable director as well as a highly gifted one. His next film, *1900* (1976), an epic covering 70 years of life and social conflict in the Emilia region of Italy, caused controversy not only because of its explicit sexuality and graphic violence but also because of its unusual length. The original cut, screened at the Cannes Festival, ran five and a half hours. After a heated dispute between the director and the film's producer, Alberto Grimaldi, it was considerably pared down. The next peak in Bertolucci's career was *The Last Emperor* (1987), a majestic epic that recreated, through dazzling color cinematography and with exquisite sets and costumes, the glory and doom of the final chapter in the history of China's royalty. The film won nine Academy Awards, including best picture, best director, and best adapted screenplay. Bertolucci's younger brother Giuseppe (*b.* Feb. 27, 1947, Parma), himself a filmmaker, collaborated on several of

Bernardo's films as an assistant or screenwriter. A cousin, Giovanni Bertolucci (*b.* June 24, 1940, Parma), is a producer.

FEATURE FILMS (as director-screenwriter): *La Commare Secca/The Grim Reaper* 1962; *Prima della Rivoluzione/Before the Revolution* 1964; *La Via del Petrolio* (3-part doc. on Italian oil operations in Iran) 1965–66; *Amore e Rabbia/Vangelo '70/Love and Anger* ("Il Fico Infruttuoso" episode), *C'era una Volta il West/Once Upon a Time in the West* (co-sc. only) 1967; *Partner* 1968; *La Strategia del Ragno/The Spider's Stratagem, Il Conformista/The Conformist* 1970; *I Poveri Morino Prima* (doc.) 1971; *Ultimo Tango a Parigi/Last Tango in Paris* 1972; *Novecento/1900* 1976; *La Luna* 1979; *La Tragedia di un Uomo ridiculo/The Tragedy of a Ridiculous Man* 1981; *The Last Emperor* (UK/It./China) 1987; *The Sheltering Sky* (also co-sc.)(US) 1990; *Little Buddha* 1994; *Stealing Beauty* 1996.

Besserer, Eugénie. Actress. *b.* 1870, Marseilles, France. *d.* 1934. Leading character player of American silents and early talkies. Convent-educated in Canada, she began a stage career in her teens. By the time she entered films in 1911 she was playing mature leads. Memorable in D. W. Griffith's *Scarlet Days, The Greatest Question,* and *Drums of Love,* and above all as Al Jolson's mother in Hollywood's first talkie, *The Jazz Singer.*

FILMS INCLUDE: *The Profligate* 1911; *Monte Cristo/The Count of Monte Cristo* 1912; *The Rosary* 1915; *The Crisis, The Garden of Allah* 1916; *The Curse of Eve* 1917; *The City of Purple Dreams, The Still Alarm, A Hoosier Romance, Little Orphan Annie* 1918; *Scarlet Days, The Greatest Question* 1919; *The Fighting Shepherdess, The Brand of Lopez, Forty-Five Minutes From Broadway* 1920; *Molly O, The Breaking Point, The Light in the Clearing, The Sin of Martha Queed* 1921; *Kindred of the Dust, June Madness, Penrod* 1922; *The Lonely Road, Her Reputation, Anna Christie* (as Marthy) 1923; *Bread, The Price She Paid* 1924; *Confessions of a Queen, Friendly Enemies, The Coast of Folly, The Circle, Bright Lights* 1926; *The Fire Brigade* 1926; *Flesh and the Devil, Wandering Girls, When a Man Loves, The Jazz Singer* 1927; *Two Lovers, Drums of Love, The Yellow Lily, Lilac Time* 1928; *Illusion, Madame X, The Bridge of San Luis Rey, Thunderbolt, Seven Faces* 1929; *A Royal Romance, In Gay Madrid* 1930; *To the Last Man* 1933.

Bessie, Alvah. Novelist, journalist, screenwriter. *b.* June 4, 1904, New York City. *d.* 1985. *ed.* Columbia. After publishing his first novel, *Dwell in the Wilderness,* in 1935, he became the book and drama editor of the *Brooklyn Daily Eagle,* where he got involved in union activities. In 1938 he joined the Abraham Lincoln Brigade and saw action in the Spanish Civil War. Upon returning to the US he published a book about his war experiences, *Men in Battle.* He wrote screenplays for Warner Bros. in the mid-40s before and after WW II service and was nominated for an Academy Award for the original story of the patriotic action film *Objective Burma* (1945). In 1947 he refused to affirm or deny membership in the Communist Party before the House Un-American Activities Committee and in 1950 was sentenced to prison for contempt of Congress as one of the HOLLYWOOD TEN. Studio blacklisting ended his career. He wrote a book about the affair, *Inquisition in Eden* (1965). After his release from prison, he supported himself as a publicist, book and film reviewer, and for a number of years as a $70-a-week stage manager at San Francisco's night club 'the hungry i.' The latter experience provided the basis for his book *One for My Baby.* In 1975 he authored *Spain Again,* a book about his collaboration as screenwriter and actor on a Spanish film, *España otra Vez.*

FILMS: *Northern Pursuit* 1943; *The Very Thought of You* 1944; *Objective Burma!* (orig. story only), *Hotel Berlin* 1945; *Smart Woman* 1948; *España otra Vez* (Sp.) 1973.

Besson, Luc. Director, screenwriter, producer. Born on March 18, 1959, in Paris. Popular French director whose sparse first film, *Le Dernier Combat*, established him as an imaginative stylist. His *La Femme Nikita* was hugely successful in American art houses, and was remade in the US as *Point of No Return* (1993).

FILMS INCLUDE: *Le Dernier Combat* 1984; *Subway* 1985; *The Big Blue* 1988; *La Femme Nikita* 1991; *The Professional* (dir., sc., prod.) 1994; *The Fifth Element* (also co-sc.) 1997.

Best, Edna. Actress. *b.* Mar. 3, 1900, Hove, Sussex, England. *d.* 1974. Gentle romantic lead, then character player of British and American films. She made her London stage debut at 17 in 'Charley's Aunt' and enjoyed her greatest success in 'The Constant Nymph' (1926). In 1928 she married Herbert MARSHALL. They appeared together in a number of plays in London and New York before their divorce in 1940. On the British screen from 1921, she went to Hollywood in 1939 and became an American citizen in 1950.

FILMS: In the UK—*Tilly of Bloomsbury* 1921; *A Couple of Down and Outs* 1923; *Sleeping Partners, Loose Ends, Escape, Beyond the Cities* 1930; *Michael and Mary, The Calendar/Bachelor's Folly* 1931; *The Faithful Heart/Faithful Hearts* 1932; *The Key* (US), *The Man Who Knew Too Much* 1934; *South Riding, Prison Without Bars* 1938. In the US—*Intermezzo, Escape to Happiness* 1939; *The Swiss Family Robinson, A Dispatch from Reuter's* 1940; *The Ghost and Mrs. Muir, The Late George Apley* 1947; *The Iron Curtain* 1948.

Best, Willie. Actor. *b.* May 27, 1916, Mississippi. *d.* 1962, of cancer. He started out with a traveling show in Southern California, entering films in the early 30s. For several years he was known by the name of the character he played, Sleep 'n Eat, a wide-eyed, easily frightened, dim-witted black man. He continued playing similar self-demeaning roles under his own name and typified (like Stepin Fetchit and Mantan Moreland) Hollywood's racist view of African-Americans in the 30s and 40s. He was also a busy performer in early television.

FILMS INCLUDE: *Feet First* 1930; *Up Pops the Devil* 1931; *The Monster Walks* 1932; *Little Miss Marker, Kentucky Kernels* 1934; *The Arizonian, The Littlest Rebel* 1935; *Murder on a Bridle Path, Thank You Jeeves* 1936; *Saturday's Heroes* 1937; *Merrily We Live, Blondie* 1938; *The Ghost Breakers* 1940; *High Sierra, Nothing but the Truth* 1941; *The Body Disappears, Whispering Ghosts, A-Haunting We Will Go* 1942; *Cabin in the Sky* 1943; *Home in Indiana, The Adventures of Mark Twain* 1944; *Hold That Blonde* 1945; *The Bride Wore Boots* 1946; *Suddenly It's Spring* 1947; *South of Caliente* 1951.

best boy. In film-set jargon, an assistant or apprentice, such as the assistant to the GAFFER or the KEY GRIP.

Bettger, Lyle. Actor. Born on Feb. 13, 1915, in Philadelphia. *ed.* AADA. Entered films in the early 50s, following acting experience in summer stock and on Broadway. Played a variety of supporting roles and eventually became typecast as a heavy, mostly in Westerns. Also in numerous TV programs.

FILMS INCLUDE: *No Man of Her Own, Union Station* 1950; *The First Legion* 1951; *Hurricane Smith, The Greatest Show on Earth* 1952; *All I Desire, Forbidden* 1953; *Carnival Story* 1954; *Destry, The Sea Chase* 1955; *The Lone Ranger* 1956; *Gunfight at the OK Corral* 1957; *Guns of the Timberland* 1960; *Town Tamer* 1965; *Johnny Reno, Nevada Smith* 1966; *Impasse* 1969; *The Hawaiians* 1970; *The Seven Minutes* 1971.

Betty Boop. A cartoon vamp created by Max Fleischer in the late 20s. Provocatively alluring and sexier than many live stars, she reigned supreme as the pinup girl of the animated world until killed by the Hays Office censors in 1935 for reasons of "immorality." The character was reportedly patterned after singer-actress Helen KANE. Her voice was dubbed by Mae Questel.

Bevan, Billy. Actor. *b.* William Bevan Harris, Sept. 29, 1887, Orange, Australia. *d.* 1957. After studies at the University of Sydney and stage experience with the Pollard Opera Company, he entered films in 1917, playing supporting roles in one- and two-reel comedies. Between 1920 and 1929 he starred in some 70 two-reel comedies for Mack SENNETT. His brush mustache became his trademark in most of these hilarious slapstick shorts, though he sometimes appeared without it, especially toward the end of his Sennett period. From 1928 till his retirement in 1952, he played bit parts and character roles in many feature productions.

FILMS INCLUDE: Shorts—*Let 'Er Go, The Quack Doctor* (also co-dir.), *It's a Boy, My Goodness* 1920; *Be Reasonable* 1921; *The Duck Hunter, Oh Daddy, Gymnasium Jim* 1922; *Nip and Tuck, Inbad the Sailor* 1923; *One Spooky Night, Wall Street Blues, Lizzies of the Field, The Cannon Ball Express* 1924; *Honeymoon Hardships, The Lion's Whiskers, Skinners in Silk, The Iron Nag, Butter Fingers, From Rags to Britches* 1925; *Circus Today, Fight Night, A Sea Dog's Tale, Hoboken to Hollywood, The Divorce Dodger* 1926; *Should Sleepwalkers Marry?, The Bull Fighter, The Golf Nut* 1927; *The Best Man, The Bicycle Flirt, His Unlucky Night, Caught in the Kitchen, Hubby's Latest Alibi, The Lion's Roar* 1928; *Foolish Husbands, Pink Pajamas* 1929. Features—*Love Honor and Behave* 1920; *A Small Town Idol* 1921; *The Crossroads of New York* 1922; *The Extra Girl* 1923; *The White Sin* 1924; *Easy Pickings* 1927; *Riley the Cop* 1928; *High Voltage* 1929; *The Sky Hawk, Journey's End* 1930; *Transatlantic* 1931; *The Silent Witness, Sky Devils, Payment Deferred* 1932; *Cavalcade, Luxury Liner, A Study in Scarlet, Alice in Wonderland* (as the Two of Spades) 1933; *The Lost Patrol, Caravan* 1934; *The Last Outpost, A Tale of Two Cities* 1935; *Dracula's Daughter, Lloyds of London* 1936; *Slave Ship, Another Dawn* 1937; *The Girl of the Golden West* 1938; *Captain Fury, We Are Not Alone* 1939; *The Earl of Chicago, The Long Voyage Home, Tin Pan Alley* 1940; *Dr. Jekyll and Mr. Hyde* 1941; *Counter-Espionage* 1942; *The Lodger* 1944; *The Picture of Dorian Gray* 1945; *Cluny Brown* 1946; *Moss Rose* 1947; *The Black Arrow* 1948; *Fortunes of Captain Blood* 1950.

Bevans, Clem. Actor. *b.* 1880, Cozaddale, Ohio. *d.* 1963. On stage in stock, vaudeville, and burlesque before going to Hollywood in 1935 to start a busy career as character actor. White-haired and weather-beaten, he played innumerable "Pop" parts, often against a rural or pioneer community setting.

FILMS INCLUDE: *Way Down East* 1935; *Rhythm on the Range, Come and Get It* 1936; *Big City* 1937; *Of Human Hearts* 1938; *Zenobia, Thunder Afloat* 1939; *Abe Lincoln in Illinois, Young Tom Edison, 20-Mule Team* 1940; *Sergeant York* 1941; *Saboteur, Captains of the Clouds, Tombstone, The Forest Rangers* 1942; *The Human Comedy* 1943; *Captain Eddie* 1945; *Gallant Bess, The Yearling* 1946; *Mourning Becomes Electra* 1947; *Relentless, The Paleface* 1948; *Portrait of Jennie, Streets of Laredo* 1949; *Harvey, Man in the Saddle* 1951; *Hangman's Knot* 1952; *The Stranger Wore a Gun* 1953; *Ten Wanted Men, The Kentuckian* 1955; *Davy Crockett and the River Pirates* 1956.

Bey, Turhan. Actor. Born Turhan Gilbert Selahettin Saultavey, on Mar. 30, 1920, in Vienna, of a Turkish father and Czech mother. He migrated to the US in the 30s and studied acting at Ben Bard's School of Dramatic Art and at the Pasadena Playhouse. In 1941 he began a Hollywood career that consisted initially of mysterious or villainous parts and later of exotic roles in a series of Arabian Nights type of films in which he co-starred with Maria Montez, Jon Hall, and Sabu. His popularity diminished in the late 40s with the decline of that genre, and his career was dealt a final blow by an extended period of military service. After returning to Hollywood in the early 50s, he produced a B picture, *Stolen Identity* (1953), appeared in another, then returned to Vienna to work as a photographer.

FILMS: *Footsteps in the Dark, Raiders of the Desert, Burma Convoy, Shadows on the Stairs, The Gay Falcon* 1941; *Bombay Clipper, Junior G-Men of the Air* (serial), *The Falcon Takes Over, A Yank on the Burma Road, Drums of the Congo, The Unseen Enemy, Danger in the Pacific, The Mummy's Tomb, Destination Unknown, Arabian Nights* 1942; *Adventures of Smilin' Jack* (serial), *White Savage, Background to Danger, The Mad Ghoul* 1943; *Ali Baba and the Forty Thieves, Follow the Boys, Dragon Seed, Bowery to Broadway, The Climax* 1944; *Frisco Sal, Sudan* 1945; *Night in Paradise* (as Aesop) 1946; *Out of the Blue* 1947; *The Amazing Mr. X/The Spiritualist, Adventures of Casanova, Parole Inc.* 1948; *Song of India* 1949; *Prisoners of the Casbah* 1953; *Stolen Identity* (prod. only) 1953.

Beymer, Richard. Actor, director. Born George Richard Beymer, on Feb. 21, 1939, in Avoca, Iowa. A child performer on a Los Angeles TV kiddie show at 12, he made his film debut at 14 in De Sica's *Stazione Termini/Indiscretion of an American Wife.* He matured from boy roles to juvenile leads, notably in *The Diary of Anne Frank* and *West Side Story,* but failed to click with audiences and gave up on Hollywood in 1963. He went to New York to study at the Actors Studio and the following year took part in the drive to register black voters in Mississippi. He made a documentary film of the event, which won a prize at the Mannheim (Germany) Festival. He later directed a fiction short, *A Very Special Day.* He presented his first feature film as director, *The Innerview,* at international festivals in 1974. In the 80s he returned to the screen twice in character roles; in 1990, he was a regular on the eerie David Lynch TV series 'Twin Peaks.'

FILMS INCLUDE (as actor): *Stazione Termini/ Indiscretion of an American Wife, So Big* 1953; *Johnny Tremain* 1957; *The Diary of Anne Frank* 1959; *High Time* 1960; *West Side Story* 1961; *Bachelor Flat, Five Finger Exercise, Hemingway's Adventures of a Young Man, The Longest Day* 1962; *The Stripper* 1963; *Free Grass/Scream Free* 1969; *The Innerview* (also dir., prod., sc., phot., edit.) 1974; *Cross Country* (Can.) 1983; *Silent Night, Deadly Night III: Better Watch Out!* 1989; *My Girl 2* 1994.

B.F.A. See BRITISH FILM ACADEMY.

BFI See BRITISH FILM INSTITUTE.

b/g. See BACKGROUND.

Biberman, Abner. Actor, director. *b.* Apr. 1, 1909, Milwaukee. *d.* 1977. *ed.* U. of Pennsylvania. A magazine writer, he turned to the stage, acting on Broadway and directing in stock. In Hollywood from the late 30s, he played character roles in a variety of films, often as a sly villain. During this period he was also an acting coach at Universal; Marilyn Monroe and Tony Curtis were among his pupils. In the mid-50s he took up directing, but his films were of little consequence and he finally found his niche as a TV director, turning out episodes for such series as 'Ben Casey,' 'The Virginian,' and 'Ironsides.' He was married to actress Joanna Barnes.

FILMS INCLUDE: As actor—*Gunga Din, The Rains Came, Another Thin Man, The Roaring Twenties, Balalaika* 1939; *His Girl Friday, Zanzibar* 1940; *This Woman Is Mine* 1941; *Broadway* 1942; *The Leopard Man* 1943; *The Bridge of San Luis Rey* 1944; *Salome—Where She Danced, Captain Kidd* 1945; *Viva Zapata!* 1952; *Knock on Wood, Elephant Walk, The Golden Mistress* 1954. As director—*The Looters, Running Wild* 1955; *The Price of Fear, Behind the High Wall* 1956; *Gun for a Coward, The Night Runner* 1957; *Flood Tide* 1958.

Biberman, Herbert J. Director, screenwriter, producer. *b.* Mar. 4, 1900, Philadelphia. *d.* 1971. *ed.* U. of Pennsylvania; Yale; and in Europe. Spent several years in the family's textile business before joining the Theater Guild as assistant stage manager in 1928. He soon became one of the company's leading directors. In 1935 he began a modest career as director, screenwriter, and sometimes co-producer of low-budget Hollywood films. In 1947 he made headlines when he refused to confirm or deny Communist party membership before the House Un-American Activities Committee. In 1950, as one of the HOLLYWOOD TEN, he was convicted of contempt of Congress and jailed for six months. He was identified as a Communist by Budd Schulberg, Edward Dmytryk, and others in the industry. His wife, since 1930, Gale SONDERGAARD, also refused to testify about her political affiliations, jeopardizing her career.

Blacklisted by the Hollywood studios, Biberman went on his own and directed *Salt of the Earth* (1954), a powerful drama about striking New Mexico miners and the deplorable conditions under which they lived. Actual miners and their families played the leading roles. The film was financed by a miners' union, but union projectionists abided by Hollywood's blacklist and refused to screen the film. It was shown—to rave reviews—in only one New York theater. The film enjoyed great success in Europe, where it was voted the year's best picture by the French Motion Picture Academy and won the top prize at Czechoslovakia's Karlovy Vary Film Festival. The film finally went into general US release in 1965. Biberman's last film, *Slaves* (1969), inspired by *Uncle Tom's Cabin,* was dismissed as old fashioned in technique by most American critics but hailed as a "beautiful" and "important" film in France.

FILMS: *One Way Ticket* (dir.) 1935; *Meet Nero Wolfe* (dir.) 1936; *King of Chinatown* (sc.) 1939; *The Master Race* (dir., sc.), *Action in Arabia* (sc.), *Together Again* (story) 1944; *Abilene Town* (prod.) 1946; *New Orleans* (co-prod., co-sc.) 1947; *Salt of the Earth* (dir.) 1954; *Slaves* (dir., co-sc.) 1969.

Bickford, Charles. Actor. *b.* Jan. 1, 1889, Cambridge, Mass. *d.* 1967. *ed.* MIT. A sailor and a civil engineer before entering show business in burlesque in 1914. Returning from WW I service, he switched to the legitimate stage and made his Broadway debut in 1919. In 1929 he joined the hundreds of stage performers lured to Hollywood by the advent of sound. At first he played romantic leads, memorably as Greta Garbo's seaman lover in *Anna Christie.* But he soon found his niche as a commanding character player, tackling supporting parts with a high level of intensity and dominating many a film with his powerful screen presence. Bickford co-authored a play. 'The Cyclone Lover' (1928), and wrote an autobiography, *Bulls, Balls, Bicycles, and Actors* (1965). He was nominated for an Oscar three times (for *The Song of Bernadette, The Farmer's Daughter,* and *Johnny Belinda*) but never won the award. Co-starred in 'The Virginian' TV series.

FILMS: *South Sea Rose, Dynamite* 1929; *Hell's Heroes, Anna Christie, The Sea Bat, River's End, Passion Flower* 1930; *The Squaw Man, Pagan Lady, East of Borneo, Men in Her Life* 1931; *Panama Flo, Scandal for Sale, Thunder Below, The Last Man, Vanity Street* 1932; *No Other Woman, Song of the Eagle, This Day and Age, White Woman* 1933; *Little Miss Marker, A Wicked Woman* 1934; *Under Pressure, A Notorious Gentleman, The Farmer Takes a Wife, East of Java* 1935; *Rose of the Rancho, Pride of the Marines, Red Wagon* 1936; *The Plainsman, High Wide and Handsome, Thunder Trail, Night Club Scandal, Daughter of Shanghai* 1937; *Gangs of New York, Valley of the Giants, The Storm* 1938; *Stand Up and Fight, Romance of the Redwoods, Street of Missing Men, Our Leading Citizen, One Hour to Live, Mutiny in the Big House, Thou Shalt Not Kill* 1939; *Of Mice and Men, Girl from God's Country, South to Karanga, Queen of the Yukon* 1940; *Riders of Death Valley* (serial), *Burma Convoy* 1941; *Reap the Wild Wind, Tarzan's New York Adventure* 1942; *Mr. Lucky, The Song of Bernadette* 1943; *Wing and a Prayer* 1944; *Captain Eddie, Fallen Angel* 1945; *The Farmer's Daughter, Duel in the Sun, The Woman on the Beach, Brute Force* 1947; *The Babe Ruth Story, Four Faces West, Johnny Belinda* 1948; *Command Decision, Roseanna McCoy* 1949; *Whirlpool, Guilty of Treason* (as Josef Cardinal Mindszenty), *Riding High* 1950; *Branded, Jim Thorpe—All American, The Raging Tide, Elopement* 1951; *A Star Is Born* 1954; *Prince of Players, Not as a Stranger, The Court-Martial of Billy Mitchell* 1955; *You Can't Run Away From It* 1956; *Mister Cory* 1957; *The Big Country* 1958; *The Unforgiven* 1960; *Days of Wine and Roses* 1962; *A Big Hand for the Little Lady* 1966.

Biehn, Michael. Actor. Born in 1957, in Anniston, Ala. Tough-but-vulnerable-looking young lead of American TV and films. At 18 he moved to Los Angeles, where he studied drama, making his professional debut at 20. He co-starred in the TV series 'The Runaways' (1978–79).

FILMS INCLUDE: *Coach* 1978; *Hog Wild* (Can.) 1980; *The Fan* 1981; *The Lords of Discipline* 1983; *The Terminator* 1984; *Aliens* 1986; *Rampage, The Seventh Sign, In a Shallow Grave* 1988; *The Abyss* 1989; *Navy Seals* 1990; *Timebomb* 1991; *K–2* 1992; *Tombstone* 1993; *Deadfall* 1994; *Jade* 1995; *The Rock* 1996.

big close-up. See EXTREME CLOSE-UP.

Bigelow, Kathryn. American director. Born in 1952. An exhibited painter, she switched careers after studies at Columbia University's graduate film school. She directed a 20-minute short, *Set-Up,* before venturing into features in the early 80s. Following the release of *Near Dark*, she was feted with a career retrospective by the Museum of Modern Art. In 1989 she married director James CAMERON.

FILMS: *Union City* (script supervisor) 1982; *Born in Flames* (act.)1982; *The Loveless* (co-dir., co-sc.) 1984; *Near Dark* (also co-sc.) 1987; *Blue Steel* (also co-sc.) 1990; *Strange Days* 1995.

Bikel, Theodore (Meir). Actor, singer. Born on May 2, 1924, in Vienna. Emigrated to Palestine (Israel) in his teens and made his stage debut in 'Tevye the Milkman,' at the Habimah Theater in Tel Aviv. Following studies at Britain's Royal Academy of Dramatic Art, he made his London stage debut in 1948 and his first New York appearance in 1955. Since the early 50s, starting with Huston's *The African Queen,* he has played character parts in many British and American films, typically portraying foreigners. In 1958 he was nominated for an Oscar for his performance in *The Defiant Ones.* Bikel is also an established folk singer and guitarist and an active participant in Democratic Party politics. He was president of Actors Equity from 1973 till 1982 and honorary president from 1982 on.

FILMS INCLUDE: *The African Queen* 1952; *Melba, Desperate Moment* 1953; *The Divided Heart, The Little Kidnappers* 1954; *The Colditz Story* 1955; *The Vintage, The Pride and the Passion, The Enemy Below* 1957; *Fraulein, The Defiant Ones, I Want to Live!* 1958; *The Angry Hills, The Blue Angel* 1959; *A Dog of Flanders* 1960; *My Fair Lady* 1964; *Sands of the Kalahari* 1965; *The Russians Are Coming the Russians Are Coming* 1966; *Sweet November* 1968; *My Side of the Mountain* 1969; *Darker Than Amber* 1970; *200 Motels* 1971; *The Little Ark* 1972; *Prince Jack* 1984; *Dark Tower* 1988.

Bill, Tony. Actor, producer, director. Born on Aug. 23, 1940, in San Diego. *ed.* Notre Dame (B.A., M.A.). He began his film career in 1963, playing Frank Sinatra's naïve kid brother in

Come Blow Your Horn and later portrayed pleasant but insipid juveniles and young leads in other Hollywood productions. In the early 70s he ventured into production, scoring a box-office hit with *The Sting* (1973). He made yet another successful transition in 1980, when he turned out his first film as a director, *My Bodyguard.* All along, he continued acting, in TV as well as in films.

FILMS INCLUDE: As actor—*Come Blow Your Horn, Soldier in the Rain* 1963; *None but the Brave, Marriage on the Rocks* 1965; *You're a Big Boy Now* 1967; *Never a Dull Moment, Ice Station Zebra* 1968; *Castle Keep* 1969; *Flap* 1970; *Shampoo* 1975; *Las Vegas Lady* 1976; *Heart Beat* 1980; *Pee-Wee's Big Adventure* 1985; *Less Than Zero* 1987. As producer—*Deadhead Miles* (co-prod) 1972; *Steelyard Blues* (co-prod.), *The Sting* (co-prod.) 1973; *Hearts of the West* 1975; *Harry and Walter Go to New York* (exec. prod.) 1976; *Boulevard Nights* (exec. prod.), *Going in Style* (co.-prod.) 1979; *The Little Dragons* (co-exec. prod., act.) 1980. As director—*My Bodyguard* 1980; *Six Weeks* 1982; *Five Corners* (also co-prod.) 1988; *Crazy People* 1990; *A Home of Our Own* 1993.

billing. The relative position in which an actor or actress is listed in a film's CREDITS. The order and type size of the billing is deemed important by many performers as a reflection of their status and prestige in the industry. Disagreement over billing has often led to bickering on the set and sometimes to a court battle.

bin. In films, a large receptacle used in cutting rooms to hold unwound film while assembling shots or when running film through a viewer without using a take-up spool. It is usually made of fiber or fitted with an inner cloth bag to minimize film abrasion. Often it is equipped with an overhanging wooden strip spiked with nails onto which pieces of film are hung during editing.

Bing, Herman. Actor. *b.* Mar. 30, 1889, Frankfurt, Germany. *d.* 1947, a suicide. A former circus clown, vaudevillian, and stage actor, he entered German films as an assistant to F. W. MURNAU and in the late 20s accompanied the master director to Hollywood. Here, he assisted Murnau on *Sunrise* (1927), then became a character comedian, turning on his heavy accent and excitable manner in numerous films of the 30s and early 40s. With his career declining, he shot himself.

FILMS INCLUDE: *A Song of Kentucky* 1929; *The Guardsman* 1931; *Dinner at Eight, The Bowery, Footlight Parade* 1933; *The Merry Widow, The Black Cat, Twentieth Century, The Mighty Barnum* 1934; *In Caliente, Hands Across the Table, Call of the Wild* 1935; *Rose Marie, The Great Ziegfeld, Dimples, Human Cargo, The King Steps Out* 1936; *Maytime* 1937; *Sweethearts, The Great Waltz, Bluebeard's Eighth Wife* 1938; *Bitter Sweet* 1940; *The Devil with Hitler* 1942; *Where Do We Go From Here?* 1945; *Night and Day* 1946.

Binoche, Juliette. Actress. Born in 1964 in Paris. Sweet, sensual lead who achieved international recognition in the film version of the Milan Kundera novel *The Unbearable Lightness of Being* (1988), as well as the late Krzysztof KIESLOWSKI's masterwork trilogy *Red* (1992)/*Blue* (1993)/*White* (1994). She gained prominence in the US for her tender performance in *The English Patient* (1996), receiving the Academy Award for best supporting actress.

FILMS INCLUDE: *Les Nanas, La Vie de Famille/Family Life* 1984; *Je vous salue, Marie/Hail Mary, Mon beau-frère a tué ma soeur, Rendez-vous* 1985; *Mauvais sang/Bad Blood* 1986; *Un Tour de manège, The Unbearable Lightness of Being* (US) 1988; *Wuthering Heights* (UK), *Damage, Red* 1992; *Blue* 1993; *White* 1994; *The English Patient, The Horseman on the Roof* 1996.

Binyon, Claude. Director, screenwriter. *b.* Oct. 17, 1905, Chicago. *d.* 1978. *ed.* U. of Missouri. A reporter for the Chicago *Herald-Examiner* and Hollywood city editor for *Variety,* he reputedly wrote the now-famous *Variety* headline about the 1929 stock market crash: "Wall Street Lays an Egg." He started working on screenplays and dialogues for Paramount in 1932 and subsequently turned out numerous scripts alone or in collaboration, many of them amusing sophisticated comedies. Between 1948 and 1953 he directed several films of mediocre quality, then returned to screenwriting, in which he was much more successful.

FILMS: As director (complete)—*The Saxon Charm* (also sc.) 1948; *Family Honeymoon* 1949; *Mother Didn't Tell Me* (also sc.), *Stella* (also sc.) 1950; *Aaron Slick from Punkin Crick* (also sc.), *Dreamboat* (also sc.) 1952; *Here Come the Girls* 1953. As screenwriter (alone or in collaboration; partial list)—*If I Had a Million* 1932; *Gambling Ship* (adapt. only) 1933; *The Gilded Lily, Mississippi, Accent on Youth, The Bride Comes Home* 1935; *Valiant Is the Word for Carrie* 1936; *I Met Him in Paris, True Confession* 1937; *Sing You Sinners* (also story) 1938; *Invitation to Happiness* 1939; *Too Many Husbands, Arizona* 1940; *You Belong to Me* 1941; *Take a Letter Darling, Holiday Inn* 1942; *Dixie, This Is the Army, No Time for Love* 1943; *And the Angels Sing* (story only) 1944; *Incendiary Blonde* 1945; *The Well-Groomed Bride* 1946; *Suddenly It's Spring* (also prod.) 1947; *My Blue Heaven* 1950; *Down Among the Sheltering Palms* 1953; *Woman's World* 1954; *Rally 'Round the Flag Boys!* 1958; *North to Alaska, Pepe* 1960; *Satan Never Sleeps* 1962; *Kisses for My President* 1964.

Biograph. 1. Trade name for an early projection apparatus first introduced publicly at New York's Olympia Music Hall on October 12, 1896. To distinguish it from a French projector of the same name patented in 1894 it was officially known as The American Biograph. The apparatus used nonperforated film of a much larger frame area than was customary at the time, resulting in a much sharper screen image but requiring very careful handling by the projectionist. Biograph's first projectionist was former cameraman Billy BITZER.

2. The abbreviated commonly used name for the American Mutoscope and Biograph Company, a corporation set up in 1896 to exploit the Biograph camera and projector after the men who became its heads—Elias Koopman, Henry Marvin, Herman Casler, and William K. L. Dickson—were refused a regular supply of films by the Edison Company. Biograph and Edison were engaged in bitter competition during the early years of the American cinema but later joined forces in the formation of the Motion Picture Patents Company, set up to block the encroachment of independent producers into the lucrative field. Biograph developed into one of the most active forces in the formative days of the American screen. Its studios on East 14th Street in New York City were the spawning ground of such directors as D. W. GRIFFITH and Mack SENNETT and of such stars as Mary PICKFORD, the GISH sisters, and of course "The Biograph Girl," Florence LAWRENCE. Griffith directed hundreds of films during his years with Biograph (1908–13). The company was dissolved in 1915 following antitrust action by the US Government.

biopic. A filmed biography. Commonly used in motion picture trade publications, the term is derived from the contraction of the words "biography" and "picture."

bioscope. A name given to several unrelated early inventions, such as Max SKLADANOWSKY's projector, developed in 1894 and first demonstrated in 1895; Georges DEMENY's camera, developed in 1893; and Robert W. PAUL's projector of 1896.

bipack. A filming process originally used in color photography but now virtually obsolete. It involves the simultaneous passage of two films through a camera or printer aperture. The two films are differently sensitized to yield a color separation upon simultaneous exposure. They are threaded with their emulsion sides touching and exposed as one, so that the focus is the same on both. More recently, with the standardization of monopack color films, the bipack color process is used solely for special effects, such as process matting and SUPERIMPOSITION. Cameras must be especially equipped to handle the simultaneous passage of the two films required by the system.

Birell, Tala. Actress. *b.* Natalie Bierl, Sept. 10, 1908, Vienna. *d.* 1959. Of German-Polish extraction. Blonde, blue-eyed star of the European stage, she was heralded into Hollywood films of the 30s as "another Garbo" but soon settled into routine leads, mostly in B pictures. In the 40s she retreated into supporting roles and by the end of the decade had retired from the screen. She returned to Europe, where she died behind the Iron Curtain.

FILMS INCLUDE: *Berge in Flammen/The Doomed Battalion* (Ger.), *Cape Forlorn* (UK) 1931; *Nagana* 1933; *The Captain Hates the Sea* 1934; *Let's Live Tonight, Air Hawks, Crime and Punishment* 1935; *The Lone Wolf Returns, The White Legion* 1936; *She's Dangerous* 1937; *Bringing Up Baby, Invisible Enemy, Josette* 1938; *Seven Miles from Alcatraz, The Song of Bernadette* 1943; *Women in Bondage, The Purple Heart, The Monster Maker, Till We Meet Again, Mrs. Parkington* 1944; *Frozen Ghost, The Power of the Whistler* 1945; *Dangerous Millions* 1946; *Philo Vance's Gamble, Song of Love* 1947; *Women in the Night* 1948; *Homicide for Three* 1949.

Birkin, Jane. Actress. Born on Dec. 14, 1946, in London. Former sex kitten of European co-productions. First attracted attention as one of the two romping nude models in Antonioni's *Blow-Up* (1966); she has since established herself as an actress of range. She has also been successful in France as a recording star and was the subject of the 1988 Agnes Varda documentary *Jane B. par Agnes V.* Formerly married to composer John BARRY. Mother of actress Charlotte Gainsbourg; sister of writer-director Andrew Birkin.

FILMS INCLUDE: *The Knack* (bit) 1965; *Kaleidoscope, Blow-Up* 1966; *La Piscine/The Swimming Pool, Slogan, Les Chemins de Katmandou* 1969; *Sex Power* 1970; *Romance of a Horsethief* 1971; *Trop jolie pour être Honnêtes* 1972; *Don Juan 1973/Si Don Juan était une Femme/Ms. Don Juan, Projection privée/Private Projection* 1973; *Le Mouton enragé/Love at the Top/The French Way, Dark Places* 1974; *Serieux comme le Plaisir, La Course et l'Echalote/The Wild Goose Chase, Sept Morts sur Ordonnance, Catherine & Cie./Catherine & Co.* 1975; *Je t'aime moi non plus, Le Diable au Coeur* 1976; *L'Animal* 1977; *Death on the Nile* 1978; *Mélancholie Baby* 1979; *Evil Under the Sun* 1982; *La Pirate* (Fr.), *L'Amour par Terre/Love on the Ground* 1984; *Dust, Le Neveu de Beethoven/Beethoven's Nephew* 1985; *La Femme De Ma Vie* 1986; *Comedie!* 1987; *Daddy Nostalgie* (also song) 1990; *La Belle Noiseuse, Thick as Thieves* (song only) 1991.

Biro, Lajos. Screenwriter, playwright. *b.* Lajos Blau, 1880, Nagyvarad, Hungary. *d.* 1948. As an influential liberal journalist in Budapest, he was appointed secretary of state at the Foreign Ministry during the 1918 October Revolution, but the ensuing political turmoil forced him to flee to Austria. A popular playwright and short-story writer in Vienna, he came to Hollywood in 1924 to conclude the sale of his play 'The Czarina' (1912) to Ernst LUBITSCH as the basis for the screenplay of *Forbidden Paradise* (1924). The same material was remade in 1945 as *A Royal Scandal.* Another of his plays, 'Hotel Imperial,' was adapted to the screen three times, twice (1927, 1939) under the same title and once for Billy WILDER's *Five Graves to Cairo* (1943). In addition to other original stories and plays, he also wrote screenplays directly for the screen, alone or in collaboration. In 1932 he moved to England, where he became screenwriter and executive director of Alexander KORDA's London Films.

FILMS INCLUDE: In the US—*Forbidden Paradise* (play basis only) 1924; *Eve's Secret* (co-play basis only) 1925; *The Silent Lover* (play basis only) 1926; *Hotel Imperial* (play basis only), *The Way of All Flesh* 1927; *The Last Command, The Yellow Lily, A Modern Du Barry, The Night Watch, The Haunted House, Adoration* 1928; *Women Everywhere* 1930. In the UK—*Service for Ladies* 1932; *The Private Life of Henry VIII* 1933; *Catherine the Great, The Private Life of Don Juan* 1934; *The Scarlet Pimpernel, Sanders of the River* 1935; *Knight Without Armour* 1937; *The Drum/Drums* 1938; *The Four Feathers* 1939; *The Thief of Bagdad* 1940; *An Ideal Husband* 1948.

Biroc, Joseph. Director of photography. Born on Feb. 12, 1903, in New York City. One of Hollywood's busiest and most gifted lighting cameramen of the post–WW II period. His career as a cinematographer began in the mid-40s, following military service, during which he recorded on film the Liberation of Paris for the Army Signal Corps. A versatile craftsman, he has proved himself equally proficient at black-and-white mood photography and glossy color productions. In the early 50s he shot Hollywood's first 3-D film, *Bwana Devil.* He is the favorite cameraman of Robert ALDRICH and is much in demand by other directors. He shared with Fred KOENEKAMP the Academy Award for the cinematography of *The Towering Inferno* (1974). The Society of American Cinematographers honored him with its Life Achievement Award in 1989.

FILMS INCLUDE: *It's a Wonderful Life* (co-phot.) 1946; *Magic Town* 1947; *Johnny Allegro* 1949; *Cry Danger* 1951; *Bwana Devil* (in 3-D), *The Glass Wall, The Tall Texan, Vice Squad, Donovan's Brain* 1953; *Down Three Dark Streets* 1954; *Nightmare, Attack!* 1956; *The Ride Back, The Garment Jungle, The Amazing Colossal Man* 1957; *Home Before Dark* 1958; *The FBI Story* 1959; *Ice Palace* 1960; *The Devil at 4 O'Clock* 1961; *Hitler, Sail a Crooked Ship* 1962; *Bye Bye Birdie, Toys in the Attic, Under the Yum Yum Tree* 1963; *Viva Las Vegas* 1964; *Hush Hush. . . Sweet Charlotte* 1965; *The Swinger, Flight of the Phoenix, The Russians Are Coming the Russians Are Coming* 1966; *Enter Laughing, Who's Minding the Mint?* 1967; *The Killing of Sister George, The Detective, Lady in Cement, The Legend of Lylah Clare* 1968; *What Ever Happened to Aunt Alice?* 1969; *Too Late the Hero* 1970; *The Organization, The Grissom Gang, Escape From the Planet of the Apes* 1971; *Ulzana's Raid* 1972; *Emperor of the North Pole* 1973; *Blazing Saddles, The Longest Yard, The Towering Inferno* (co-phot.) 1974; *Hustle* 1975; *The Duchess and the Dirtwater Fox* 1976; *The Choirboys* 1977; *Beyond the Poseidon Adventure* 1979; *Airplane!* 1980; *. . . All the Marbles* 1981; *Hammett, Airplane II: The Sequel* 1982.

Bischoff, Samuel. Producer. *b.* Aug. 11, 1890, Hartford, Conn. *d.* 1975. *ed.* Boston U. In films since 1923, starting as a producer of more than 100 short comedy films before joining Columbia in 1928 as production supervisor. In 1933 he joined Warner Bros. in the same capacity, later becoming a producer. Functioned as de facto producer on early Warners films although credited as assistant or associate producer. Has since produced many films for major studios and independently. Directed one film, *The Last Mile,* in 1932.

FILMS INCLUDE: *The Dark Horse* 1932; *Twenty Million Sweethearts* 1934; *The Charge of the Light Brigade* 1936; *Kid Galahad, San Quentin* 1937; *Angels with Dirty Faces* 1938; *The Oklahoma Kid, The Roaring Twenties* 1939; *They Dare Not Love, Texas* 1941; *A Night to Remember* 1943; *None Shall*

Escape 1944; *A Thousand and One Nights* 1945; *Pitfall* 1948; *Outpost in Morocco* 1949; *Sealed Cargo* 1951; *Macao, The Half-Breed* 1952; *South Sea Woman* 1953; *The Bounty Hunter* 1954; *A Bullet for Joey, The Phenix City Story* 1955; *Screaming Eagles* 1956; *Operation Eichmann* 1961; *The Strangler* 1964.

Bishop, Joey. Entertainer, actor. Born Joseph Abraham Gottlieb, on Feb. 3, 1918, in the Bronx, N.Y. Grew up in South Philadelphia, where he formed the Bishop Brothers Trio with two friends after graduating from high school. Had a modest career as nightclub comedian prior to Army service in WW II. In the early 50s he moved into the big time under the patronage of Frank SINATRA, whose famous "Rat Pack" he later joined. After exposure on the Jack Paar 'Tonight Show' he became a popular TV personality, starred in a situation comedy series, and for a while hosted his own talk show. Film appearances have been sporadic, mostly in comic supporting roles.

FILMS: *The Deep Six, The Naked and the Dead, Onionhead* 1958; *Ocean's Eleven, Pepe* 1960; *Sergeants Three* 1962; *Johnny Cool* 1963; *Texas Across the River* 1966; *A Guide for the Married Man, Who's Minding the Mint?, Valley of the Dolls* 1967; *The Delta Force* 1986; *Betsy's Wedding* 1990; *Ceremony, Mad Dog Time* 1996.

Bishop, Julie. Actress. Born Jacqueline Brown, on Aug. 30, 1914, in Denver. The daughter of a prominent banker and oilman, she began her film career in the silent era as a child star under the name Jacqueline Wells. After a four-year absence, during which she attended school and studied dance under Theodore Kosloff, she returned to the screen early in the 30s in Hal ROACH comedy shorts and soon matured into a young leading lady in serials and feature films. As Jacqueline Wells she played leads in many films of the 30s, mostly second features. When her career seemed to be leading nowhere, she switched studios and names in 1941 and began a new career at Warners as Julie Bishop. She retired in 1957. She is the mother of actress Pamela Shoop.

FILMS INCLUDE: As Jacqueline Wells—*Maytime, Children of Jazz, Bluebeard's Eighth Wife* 1923; *Captain Blood, Dorothy Vernon of Haddon Hall* 1924; *The Home Maker, The Golden Bed, Classified* 1925; *The Family Upstairs* 1926; *Clancy of the Mounted* (serial), *Tarzan the Fearless* (both feature and serial), *Tillie and Gus, Alice in Wonderland* 1933; *The Black Cat, Kiss and Make Up* 1934; *Coronado* 1935; *The Bohemian Girl* 1936; *Counsel for Crime, Paid to Dance* 1937; *Flight Into Nowhere, Highway Patrol, Spring Madness* 1938; *My Son Is a Criminal, Behind Prison Doors* 1939. As Julie Bishop—*The Nurse's Secret, International Squadron* 1941; *I Was Framed, Lady Gangster, Escape from Crime, The Hidden Hand* 1942; *The Hard Way, Action in the North Atlantic, Princess O'Rourke, Northern Pursuit* 1943; *Rhapsody in Blue, You Came Along* 1945; *Last of the Redmen, High Tide* 1947; *Sands of Iwo Jima* 1949; *Westward the Women* 1952; *Sabre Jet* 1953; *The High and the Mighty* 1954; *The Big Land* 1957.

Bishop, William. Actor. *b.* July 16, 1917, Oak Park, Ill. *d.* 1959. *ed.* West Virginia U. (law). Leading man and second lead of mostly routine Hollywood films, following radio, stock, and Broadway experience. Co-starred in the TV series 'It's a Great Life.' Died of cancer at age 42.

FILMS INCLUDE: *A Guy Named Joe* 1943; *Song of the Thin Man, The Romance of Rosy Ridge* 1947; *Adventures in Silverado, Port Said, Black Eagle, Coroner Creek* 1948; *Anna Lucasta* 1949; *Harriet Craig, The Killer That Stalked New York* 1950; *The Frogmen, The Texas Rangers, Lorna Doone* 1951; *Breakdown, The Raiders* 1952; *The Redhead From Wyoming* 1953; *Overland Pacific* 1954; *Top Gun* 1955; *The Boss* 1956; *The Phantom Stagecoach* 1957; *The Oregon Trail* 1959.

Bissell, Whit(ner). Actor. *b.* 1919, New York City. *d.* 1996. Versatile character player of Hollywood films since the mid-40s, often as prissy fussbudget or upright professional man. On stage from boyhood, he had an impressive lineup of Broadway credits before entering films. Also much on TV, notably as Woodrow Wilson in the 'Profiles in Courage' series.

FILMS INCLUDE: *Holy Matrimony* 1943; *Somewhere in the Night* 1946; *Brute Force, A Double Life* 1947; *Another Part of the Forest, That Lady in Ermine* 1948; *Side Street* 1949; *Convicted* 1950; *Red Mountain* 1951; *Devil's Canyon* 1953; *The Caine Mutiny, Riot in Cell Block 11, It Should Happen to You, Creature from the Black Lagoon* 1954; *The Desperate Hours, Not as a Stranger* 1955; *Invasion of the Body Snatchers* 1956; *Gunfight at the O.K. Corral* 1957; *The Defiant Ones* 1958; *The Black Orchid, Never So Few* 1959; *The Time Machine* 1960; *Birdman of Alcatraz, The Manchurian Candidate* 1962; *Hud* 1963; *Seven Days in May* 1964; *The Hallelujah Trail* 1965; *Five Card Stud* 1968; *Airport* 1970; *The Salzburg Connection, Pete 'n' Tillie* 1972; *Soylent Green* 1973; *Psychic Killer* 1975; *The Lincoln Conspiracy* 1977; *Casey's Shadow* 1978.

Bisset, Jacqueline. Actress. Born Winifred Jacqueline Fraser Bisset, on Sept. 13, 1944, in Weybridge, England, of Scottish-English-French parentage. A photographer's model at 18, she began playing sexy bit parts in British films in the mid-60s, then went to Hollywood, where she was groomed as a starlet and by 1970 was playing leading roles in international productions. By the end of the decade—her acting skills ripening along with her beauty—she was an established, bankable star. Early in her career she was billed as Jackie Bisset.

FEATURE FILMS: *The Knack. . . and How to Get It/The Knack* (bit) 1965; *Drop Dead, Darling/Arrivederci Baby, Cul de Sac* 1966; *Casino Royale, Two for the Road, The Capetown Affair* 1967; *The Sweet Ride, The Detective, Bullitt* 1968; *La Promesse/L'Echelle blanche/Secret World, The First Time* 1969; *Airport, The Grasshopper* 1970; *The Mephisto Waltz, Believe in Me* 1970; *Stand Up and Be Counted, The Life and Times of Judge Roy Bean* 1972; *The Thief Who Came to Dinner, La Nuit américaine/Day for Night, Le Magnifique/How to Destroy the Reputation of the Greatest Secret Agent, Murder on the Orient Express* 1974; *The Spiral Staircase, Der Richter und sein Henker/The Judge and His Hangman/End of the Game/ Deception* 1975; *La Donna della Domenica/The Sunday Woman, St. Ives* 1976; *The Deep* 1977; *Secrets* (release delayed from 1971), *Who Is Killing the Great Chefs of Europe?, The Greek Tycoon* 1978; *Amo non amo/I Love You, I Love You Not/Together* 1979; *When Time Ran Out* 1980; *Rich and Famous, Inchon* 1981; *Class* 1983; *Under the Volcano* 1984; *High Season* (UK) 1987; *La Maison de Jade* 1988; *Scenes From the Class Struggle in Beverly Hills* 1989; *The Maid, Wild Orchid* 1990; *Judgment in Stone* 1996; *End of Summer* 1997.

bit. A small speaking part in a film. Actors assigned such roles are called "bit players." See also SILENT BIT.

Bitzer, G. W. (Billy). Director of photography. *b.* Johann Gottlob Wilhelm Bitzer, Apr. 21, 1872, in Roxbury, Mass. *d.* 1944. A former silversmith, he joined the Magic Introduction Company, novelty entrepreneurs, in New York in 1894. When the company began exploiting William K. L. DICKSON's Mutoscope movie camera and projector, changing its name to the American Mutoscope and Biograph Company, Bitzer became its leading cameraman. At first he photographed news items and street scenes, but gradually the product evolved into story films. By 1909 the company had become known as BIOGRAPH, a name associated with the formative years of American cinema.

In 1908, Bitzer began a 16-year association with director

D. W. GRIFFITH, one of the most remarkable partnerships in the history of cinema. Except for a few early Griffith films, photographed by Arthur Marvin, and some of his last films, all the master's enormous output was photographed by Bitzer, including such classics as *The New York Hat* (1912), *Judith of Bethulia* (1914), *The Birth of a Nation* (1915), *Intolerance* (1916), and *Broken Blossoms* (1919). They worked together so closely that it is difficult to attribute to one or the other their technical contributions, such as the CLOSE-UP, the FADE, the IRIS, BACK LIGHTING, and the DOLLY. Bitzer's mechanical ingenuity enabled him to turn Griffith's ideas and discoveries into workable film techniques, and the front of his camera was always loaded with newly developed gadgets that were the envy of bewildered fellow cameramen.

Griffith's films owe much of their visual and aesthetic quality to Bitzer's camera work; yet their celebrated association came to a virtual end after 1920, when Griffith began using Bitzer only intermittently, in collaboration with other cameramen. By that time, both men were in a state of mental and financial depression and out of place in an industry that was quickly becoming a big, impersonal business. Bitzer went into semiretirement and in the 1930s was recruited by the Film Library of New York's Museum of Modern Art. He performed research on the old Biograph days and wrote autobiographical notes that were published in 1973 as a book of memoirs, *Billy Bitzer—His Story.* He died in California after a series of heart attacks.

FILMS INCLUDE: *William McKinley at Canton Ohio* 1896; *USS Maine, Havana Harbor* 1898; *Jim Jeffries-Tom Sharkey Fight, The Picturesque West* 1899; *Love in the Suburbs* 1900; *St. Louis Exposition* 1902; *American Soldier in Love and War, In the New York Subway, Pajama Girl, Wages of Sin* 1903; *Chicken Thief, Moonshiners* 1904; *The Great Jewel Mystery* (co-phot.), *Kentucky Feud, Pipe Dream, The Spirit of '76* 1905; *The Black Hand, Married for Millions, Masqueraders, Trial Marriages* 1906; *Dr. Skinum, Elopement, Fights of Nations, Hypnotist's Revenge* 1907; *The Yellow Peril, Caught by Wireless, When Knights Were Bold, A Zulu's Heart, Devil, Romance of a Jewess, After Many Years, The Taming of the Shrew* 1908; *The Honor of Thieves, The Sacrifice, The Hindoo Dagger, Tragic Love, Edgar Allan Poe, The Prussian Spy, The Violin Maker of Cremona, The Lonely Villa, In Old Kentucky, The Awakening, Pippa Passes* (co-phot.), *A Corner in Wheat, In Little Italy* 1909; *In Old California, The Man, Thou Shalt Not, Ramona, The Call to Arms, The Broken Doll, The Fugitive* 1910; *When a Man Loves, His Trust, The Italian Barber, Conscience, Three Sisters, The Lily of the Tenements, The Lonedale Operator, The Spanish Gypsy, Madame Rex, Enoch Arden, Fighting Blood, The Ruling Passion, Swords and Hearts, The Eternal Mother, The Awakening, The Battle* 1911; *A Tale of the Wilderness, For His Son, The Root of Evil, The Mender of Nets, The Girl and Her Trust, The Punishment, The Female of the Species, Lena and the Geese, An Indian Summer, A Man's Genesis, A Pueblo Legend, The Painted Lady, Musketeers of Pig Alley, The Informer, The New York Hat* 1912; *The Massacre, Oil and Water, Fate, The Wanderer, Death's Marathon* 1913; *Judith of Bethulia, The Battle at Elderbush Gulch, The Escape, Home Sweet Home, The Avenging Conscience* 1914; *The Birth of a Nation* 1915; *Intolerance* 1916; *Hearts of the World, The Great Love* 1918; *A Romance of Happy Valley, The Great Thing in Life, The Girl Who Stayed at Home, True Heart Susie, Scarlet Days, Broken Blossoms, The Greatest Question* 1919; *The Idol Dancer, The Love Flower, Way Down East* (co-phot.) 1920; *Orphans of the Storm* (co-phot.) 1922; *The White Rose* (co-phot.) 1923; *America* (co-phot.) 1924; *Drums of Love* (asst. cam.), *The Battle of the Sexes* (co-phot.) 1928; *Lady of the Pavements* (co-phot.) 1929.

Björk, Anita. Actress. Born on Apr. 25, 1923, in Tällberg, Sweden. She made her film debut in 1942, in Alf SJÖBERG's *The Road to Heaven,* but established herself as a screen actress of the first magnitude after her appearance in the title role of Sjöberg's *Miss Julie* nine years later. Critics hailed her performance as one of the most remarkable demonstrations of screen acting in film history. She also starred in Ingmar Bergman's *Secrets of Women* (1952), in several of the films of Molander and Mattsson, and in Nunnally Johnson's *Night People* (1954), an American film shot in Germany. She made several lesser films in Sweden and Germany and is among the leading performers of the Royal Dramatic Theater in Stockholm and of Swedish TV.

FILMS INCLUDE: *The Road to Heaven* 1942; *No Way Back, Woman Without a Face* 1947; *The Realm of Men* 1949; *The Quartet That Split Up* 1950; *Miss Julie* 1951; *Secrets of Women* 1952; *Night People* (US), *Die Hexe* 1954; *Song of the Scarlet Flower* 1956; *Married Life/Of Love and Lust, Guest at One's Own Home* 1957; *Lady in Black, The Phantom Carriage, Model in Red* 1958; *Good Friends and Faithful Neighbors* 1960; *Lady in White* 1962; *Square of Violence* (US/Yug.) 1963; *Loving Couples* 1964; *Adalen 31* 1969.

Björnstrand, Gunnar. Actor. *b.* Nov. 13, 1909, Stockholm. *d.* 1986. An actor's son, he tried his hand at various manual and white-collar jobs before deciding on an acting career in the early 30s. After playing a bit in a 1931 film, he joined the Royal Dramatic Theater School as a classmate of Ingrid Bergman. He developed into one of Sweden's finest stage and screen dramatic actors and won international recognition for his elegant portrayals in Ingmar BERGMAN's films.

FILMS INCLUDE: *The False Millionaire* 1931; *Panic* 1939; *An Adventurer* 1942; *Night in the Harbor* 1943; *Torment/Frenzy* 1944; *Sussie* 1945; *It Rains on Our Love* 1946; *Night Is My Future* 1947; *The White Cat* 1950; *Secrets of Women/Waiting Women* 1952; *The Naked Night/Sawdust and Tinsel* 1953; *A Lesson in Love* 1954; *Dreams/Journey Into Autumn, Smiles of a Summer Night, The Pawnshop* 1955; *Seventh Heaven* 1956; *The Seventh Seal, Wild Strawberries* 1957; *The Magician/The Face* 1958; *Crime in Paradise* 1959; *The Devil's Eye* 1960; *Through a Glass Darkly, Pleasure Garden* 1961; *My Love Is a Rose, Winter Light* 1963; *Loving Couples* 1964; *My Sister My Love* 1965; *Here's Your Life, Persona, The Sadist* 1966; *Hagbard and Signe/The Red Mantle, Stimulantia* 1967; *The Girls, Shame* 1968; *The Island* (It.), *The Ritual/The Rite* 1969; *The Pistol* 1974; *Face to Face* 1976; *Tabu/Taboo* 1977; *Autumn Sonata* 1978; *Fanny and Alexander* 1983.

Blaché, Alice. See GUY-BLACHÉ, Alice.

Blaché, Herbert. Director. Born in Brussels. Deceased. A former cameraman of early French films, he came to the US in 1907 with his wife, director Alice Guy (later Alice GUY-BLACHÉ or Alice Blaché). Here he became a director, turning out many American silent films through the late 20s.

FILMS INCLUDE: *A Prisoner in the Harem* (also sc.), *The Star of India* 1913; *Fighting Death, Hook and Hand, The Million Dollar Robbery, The Chimes* (filmed in the UK), *The Mystery of Edwin Drood* (filmed in the UK), *The Temptations of Satan* 1914; *The Shooting of Dan McGrew, Greater Love Hath No Man, Her Own Way, The Song of the Wage Slave Barbara Frietchie* 1915; *The Girl with Green Eyes, The Woman's Fight* 1916; *The Auction of Virtue, The Peddler* 1917; *The Silent Woman, Loaded Dice, A Man's World* 1918; *The Uplifters, Fools and Their Money, The Divorcee, The Man Who Stayed at Home, The Parisian Tigress, Satan Junior, The Brat* 1919; *Stronger Than Death, The Hope, The New York Idea* 1920; *Out of the Chorus, The Beggar Maid* (2-reel art film), *The Bashful Suitor*

(2-reel art film) 1921; *The Young Painter* (2-reel art film) 1922; *Fools and Riches, The Near Lady, Nobody's Bride, The Untamable, The Wild Party* 1923; *High Speed* 1924; *Head Winds, The Calgary Stampede, Secrets of the Night* 1925; *The Mystery Club* 1926; *Burning the Wind* (co-dir. with Henry MacRae) 1929.

Black, Karen. Actress. Born Karen Ziegler, on July 1, 1942, in Park Ridge, Ill. *ed.* Northwestern. A leading personality of the American cinema of the early 70s. Began acting in off-Broadway satirical revues. While struggling through the ups and downs of a fledgling stage career, she worked as a waitress and attended Lee Strasberg's classes at the Actors Studio. She finally made it to Broadway in 1965 in the chiller 'The Playroom.' Her performance was nominated for acting laurels by the Critics Circle. The play folded within a month, but it led to her first significant film role in *You're a Big Boy Now* (1967). After an impressive performance as an acid-tripping whore in *Easy Rider* (1969), she won the 1970 New York Film Critics Award as best supporting actress for her role as a simple-hearted waitress in *Five Easy Pieces.* The role also brought her a nomination for an Oscar. Although she continued playing offbeat leads in numerous films through the 80s, most of her appearances after the mid-70s were in low-budget, independent productions or foreign films. She married screenwriter L. M. Kit CARSON in 1975 and appeared with their son Hunter Carson in *Invaders from Mars* (1986).

FEATURE FILMS: *The Prime Time* 1960; *You're a Big Boy Now* 1967; *Hard Contract, Easy Rider* 1969; *Five Easy Pieces* 1970; *Drive He Said, A Gunfight, Born to Win* 1971; *Cisco Pike, Portnoy's Complaint* 1972; *The Pyx* (also wrote songs), *Little Laura and Big John, The Outfit* 1973; *Rhinoceros, The Great Gatsby, Airport 1975, Law and Disorder* 1974; *Owen* (UK), *The Day of the Locust, Nashville* 1975; *Crime and Passion/An Ace Up My Sleeve* (US/Ger.), *Family Plot, Burnt Offerings* 1976; *Controrapina/The Rip-Off/The Big Rip-Off/The Squeeze* (It.), *Capricorn One, In Praise of Older Women* (Can.) 1978; *Killer Fish/Deadly Treasure of the Piranha* (It./Braz.), *The Last Word* 1979; *The Grass Is Singing/Killing Heat* (UK/Sw.), *Separate Ways/Valentine, Chanel Solitaire* (UK/Fr.) 1981; *Come Back to the Five and Dime, Jimmy Dean, Jimmy Dean* 1982; *Can She Bake a Cherry Pie?, Growing Pains/Bad Manners* 1982; *Martin's Day* (Can.) 1984; *Savage Dawn* 1985; *Invaders from Mars, Cut and Run* (It.), *Flight of the Spruce Goose* 1986; *It's Alive III: Island of the Alive, Hostage* 1987; *The Invisible Kid* 1988; *Homer and Eddie* 1989; *Twisted Justice, Overexposed, The Children, Mirror Mirror, Zapped Again* 1990; *Caged Fear, Children of the Night, The Player* 1992; *The Trust* 1993; *Crimetime* 1996.

Black, Noel. American director. Born on June 30, 1940. Directed shorts and documentaries before making an impressive bid as feature film director in 1968 with the psychological thriller *Pretty Poison.* But his subsequent output has been meager.

FILMS: *Pretty Poison* 1968; *Cover Me Babe* 1970; *Jennifer on My Mind* 1971; *Mirrors* 1978; *A Man a Woman and a Bank* (Can.) 1979; *Private School* 1983; *Mischief/Heart and Soul* (exec. prod, sc.) 1985.

Blackman, Honor. Actress. Born in 1926, in London. Leading lady and supporting player of British films since the mid-40s. Achieved some popularity in the 60s as action-prone anthropologist Cathy Gale on TV ('The Avengers' series) and in films, memorably in the role of Pussy Galore in the James Bond film *Goldfinger.* She was later also in US films.

FILMS INCLUDE: *Fame Is the Spur* 1947; *Quartet* 1948; *Conspirator, So Long at the Fair* 1950; *Diplomatic Passport* 1955; *A Night to Remember* 1958; *A Matter of WHO* 1961; *Serena* 1962; *Jason and the Golden Fleece* 1963; *Goldfinger* 1964; *Life at the Top* 1965; *Moment to Moment* 1966; *A Twist of Sand, Shalako* 1968; *The Last Grenade, The Virgin and the Gypsy* 1970; *Something Big* 1971; *Fright* 1972; *Lola* 1973; *To the Devil a Daughter* 1976; *The Cat and the Canary* 1978.

Black Maria. The world's first film studio, built in 1893 by Thomas Alva Edison near his West Orange, N.J., laboratories. Designed by William K. L. DICKSON, it was a large, ugly structure covered with tar paper inside and out. Part of the roof could be removed to allow sunlight to reach the stage. The entire structure revolved on a track so it could follow the sun for shooting at all hours of the day. Edison's co-workers nicknamed it Black Maria after the slang term for a police van.

Blackmer, Sidney. Actor. *b.* July 13, 1895, Salisbury, N.C. *d.* 1973. He started playing minor parts in films in 1914 while awaiting his opportunity to make good on the New York stage. He made his Broadway debut in 1917 and later appeared in many plays, notably as Doc in 'Come Back, Little Sheba' (for which he received both the Tony and Donaldson awards) and as Boss Finley in 'Sweet Bird of Youth.' His film career gained prominence with the coming of sound. He started out in leads but soon settled into character parts, mostly as a polished heavy. In all he appeared in more than 100 pictures. He also portrayed Teddy Roosevelt more than a dozen times in plays and films. His first wife (1928–39) was actress Lenore ULRIC; his second (1942–73) actress Suzanne Kaaren.

FILMS INCLUDE: *The Perils of Pauline* (serial) 1914; *The Romance of Elaine* (serial) 1915; *Million Dollar Mystery* (serial) 1927; *A Most Immoral Lady, The Love Racket* 1929; *Strictly Modern, Sweethearts and Wives, Kismet* 1930; *Little Caesar, Woman Hungry, It's a Wise Child, The Lady Who Dared* 1931; *Cocktail Hour, Deluge* 1933; *The Count of Monte Cristo, The President Vanishes* 1934; *A Notorious Gentleman, The Little Colonel, Great God Gold* 1935; *The President's Mystery* 1936; *House of Secrets, This Is My Affair* (as President Theodore Roosevelt), *Wife Doctor and Nurse, Heidi, The Last Gangster, Charlie Chan at Monte Carlo, Thank You Mr. Moto* 1937; *In Old Chicago* (as General Philip Sheridan), *Straight Place and Show, Suez* 1938; *Trade Winds, It's a Wonderful World, Hotel for Women* 1939; *Maryland* 1940; *Cheers for Miss Bishop, Love Crazy, Ellery Queen and the Perfect Crime, The Feminine Touch* 1941; *Always in My Heart, The Panther's Claw, Nazi Agent, Quiet Please—Murder* 1942; *Murder in Times Square, In Old Oklahoma* (again as Teddy Roosevelt) 1943; *The Lady and the Monster, Buffalo Bill* (again as Teddy Roosevelt), *Wilson* 1944; *Duel in the Sun* 1947; *My Girl Tisa* (again as Teddy Roosevelt) 1948; *People Will Talk, Saturday's Hero* 1951; *The San Francisco Story, Washington Story* 1952; *The High and the Mighty* 1954; *The View from Pompey's Head* 1955; *High Society, Beyond a Reasonable Doubt* 1956; *Tammy and the Bachelor* 1957; *How to Murder Your Wife* 1965; *A Covenant with Death* 1967; *Rosemary's Baby* 1968.

Blackton, J(ames) Stuart. Pioneer director, producer, screenwriter, actor, and innovator. *b.* Jan. 5, 1875, Sheffield, England. *d.* 1941. In the US from the age of ten, he first worked as a journalist-illustrator for the New York *World.* Interviewing Thomas Alva Edison, he so impressed the inventor with his drawings that Edison suggested he allow some of them to be photographed by the Kinetograph camera. The result was a short film, *Blackton, The Evening World Cartoonist* (1896). Fascinated by the new medium, Blackton bought a Kinetoscope from Edison, went into partnership with a friend, Albert E. Smith, and exhibited films with it.

In 1897 they added a third partner, William T. Rock, and

the young partners converted the projector into a motion-picture camera and established the VITAGRAPH Company. They started film production in an open-air studio on the roof of the Morse Building at 140 Nassau Street, New York City. Their first film, *The Burglar on the Roof,* was about 50 feet long, with Blackton playing the leading role. In 1898, during the Spanish-American War, they produced *Tearing Down the Spanish Flag,* probably the world's first propaganda film. Smith operated the camera and Blackton was again the actor, tearing down the Spanish flag and raising the Stars and Stripes to the top of a flagpole.

Blackton and his partners continued filming fake and real news events, ranging from Spanish-American War footage to coverage of local fires and crimes in New York City. They constantly expanded their activities and soon moved into the world's first glass-enclosed studios, in Flatbush, Brooklyn. Blackton directed most of the production of this early period, including such story films as *A Gentleman of France* (1903) and *Raffles, the Amateur Cracksman* (1905), two milestones in the development of the American feature film.

Blackton pioneered the single-frame (one turn, one picture) technique in cinema animation, turning out a number of animated cartoons between 1906 and 1910, including the immensely successful *Humorous Phases of a Funny Face, The Haunted Hotel* (1906), and *The Magic Fountain Pen* (1907). He also introduced (in 1908, before Griffith) the CLOSE SHOT, a camera position between the close-up and the medium shot. Like Griffith, he emphasized film editing, setting his films apart from most of the products of this very early period. His film editing was especially noteworthy in his "Scenes of True Life" series, a realistic group of films he directed beginning in 1908.

Next to Griffith, Blackton was probably the most innovative and creative force in the development of the motion picture art, not only as the director of hundreds of films but also as organizer, producer, actor, and animator. He pioneered the production of two- and three-reel comedies and starred in one such series as a character called Happy Hooligan. Beginning in 1908, he also pioneered the American production of distinguished stage adaptations, including many Shakespeare plays and historical re-creations. When the output at Vitagraph became too heavy for one man to handle, he initiated the system (later to be adopted by Ince) of overseeing the work of several underling directors as production supervisor. In 1917 he left active work with Vitagraph and began independent productions. During WW I, he directed and produced a series of patriotic propaganda films, the most famous of which, and which he also wrote, was *The Battle Cry of Peace/A Call to Arms Against War* (1915), based on a hypothetical attack on New York City by a foreign invader.

Blackton later went to England, where he directed a number of costume pageants, two of them experiments in color. When Vitagraph was absorbed by Warner Bros. in 1926, Blackton retired. He lost his entire fortune in the 1929 crash and was forced to seek work on a government project in California. Later he was hired as director of production at the Anglo-American Film Company, where he worked until his death.

Between 1900 and 1915, Blackton was president of the Vitaphone Company, a manufacturer of record players. In 1915 he organized and became president of the Motion Picture Board of Trade, later known as the Association of Motion Picture Producers and Distributors of America. He was also publisher and editor of *Motion Picture Magazine,* one of America's first film-fan publications.

FILMS INCLUDE (as director unless otherwise stated): *The Burglar on the Roof, Tearing Down the Spanish Flag* (co-dir.) 1898; *Spot Filming of Windsor Hotel Fire in New York* 1899; *A Gentleman of France* 1903; *Raffles the Amateur Cracksman* 1905; *A Modern Oliver Twist, The San Francisco Earthquake, Humorous Phases of a Funny Face, The Haunted Hotel* 1906; *The Magic Fountain Pen, A Curious Dream* 1907; *Macbeth, Romeo and Juliet, Richard III* (prod.), *Salome, The Merchant of Venice, Antony and Cleopatra* (prod.), *Julius Caesar* (prod.), *Barbara Frietchie, The Viking's Daughter* 1908; *Napoleon—The Man of Destiny, Princess Nicotine or the Smoke Fairy* (a fantasy on the dreams of a pipe smoker; co-dir.), *Ruy Blas* (prod.), *Saul and David, Washington Under the American Flag* (prod.), *King Lear* (prod.), *Oliver Twist, Les Misérables, A Midsummer Night's Dream* (prod.) 1909; *The Life of Moses* (in five parts, each one reel long) 1909–10; *Elektra, Uncle Tom's Cabin, A Modern Cinderella* 1910; *The New Stenographer* (prod.) 1911; *Lincoln's Gettysburg Address* (co-dir. with James Young), *The Two Portraits, Cardinal Wolsey* (co-dir. with Lawrence Trimble), *The Lady of the Lake, As You Like It* (co-dir. with Young) 1912; *Love's Sunset* (prod.) 1913; *Love Luck and Gasoline* (sc.), *The Christian* (prod.) 1914; *The Battle Cry of Peace* (prod., sc.) 1915; *Whom the Gods Destroy* (co-sc.) 1916; *Womanhood, The Glory of a Nation* (co-dir. with William Earle, co-prod., co-story), *Within the Law* (prod.), *The Message of the Mouse, The Judgment House* (also prod, sc.) 1917; *The World for Sale, Wild Youth* (prod.), *Missing* (prod.) 1918; *Life's Greatest Problem* (also prod.), *The Common Cause* (also prod.), *A House Divided, The Moonshine Trail* 1919; *My Husband's Other Wife, Respectable by Proxy, The Blood Barrier* (also prod.), *Passers-By, Man and His Woman, The House of the Tolling Bell, Forbidden Valley* (also prod.) 1920; *The Glorious Adventure* (US/UK), *A Gypsy Cavalier* (UK) 1922; *The Virgin Queen* (UK), *On the Banks of the Wabash* 1923; *Let Not Man Put Asunder, Between Friends, The Clean Heart, The Beloved Brute, Behold This Woman* 1924; *The Redeeming Sin, Tides of Passion, The Happy Warrior* 1925; *Bride of the Storm, The Gilded Highway, Hell-Bent for Heaven, The Passionate Quest* 1926.

Blackwell, Carlyle. Actor. *b.* 1888, Troy, Pa. *d.* 1955. A former Broadway actor, he was among the earliest he-man stars of the American screen, appearing opposite such leading ladies as Mary Pickford and Mae Marsh. His importance had diminished considerably by 1920 and he spent the remaining decade of his film career in England. He retired from the screen shortly after the advent of sound. His son, Carlyle Blackwell, Jr. (1912–74), also appeared in films.

FILMS INCLUDE: In the US—*A Dixie Mother, Uncle Tom's Cabin* 1909; *The Indian Uprising at Santa Fe, A Bell of Penance, The Apache Renegade* 1912; *The Battle for Freedom, The Invaders, Perils of the Sea, The Struggle* 1913; *The Spitfire, Such a Little Queen, The Key to Yesterday, The Man Who Could Not Lose* (also dir.) 1914; *The High Hand, The Puppet Crown, The Secret Orchard, The Case of Becky* 1915; *The Clarion, His Brother's Wife, Sally in Our Alley, A Woman's Way, The Ocean Waif* 1916; *The Social Leper, The Crimson Dove, The Price of Pride, Youth, The Burglar, The Good for Nothing* (also dir.) 1917; *The Beautiful Mrs. Reynolds* (as Alexander Hamilton), *His Royal Highness* (also dir.), *Leap to Fame* (also dir.), *Stolen Orders, The Golden Wall, By Hook or Crook, The Road to France* 1918; *Love in a Hurry, Courage for Two, Three Green Eyes* 1919; *The Third Woman, The Restless Sex* 1920. In the UK—*The Virgin Queen* 1921; *Bulldog Drummond, The Beloved Vagabond* 1923; *Les Deux Gosses* (Fr.) 1924; *She* 1925; *The Wrecker* 1929; *The Hound of the Baskervilles* 1931.

Blades, Rubén. Actor, singer, musician. Born on July 16, 1948, in Panama City, Panama. *ed.* U. of Panama (law and political science); Harvard (L.L.M.). Formerly an attorney for

Panama's National Bank, he entered show business in 1975 as a legal advisor to a recording company. Before long, he began recording himself, soon emerging as a popular salsa vocalist and bandleader. In the early 80s he began appearing in films, first attracting wide notice in *Crossover Dreams* (1985), the story of an ambitious salsa singer. He subsequently played straight dramatic leads and supporting roles in nonmusical films. He was the subject of the documentary, *The Return of Ruben Blades* (1987) and has appeared occasionally in TV dramas.

FILMS INCLUDE: *When the Mountains Tremble* (semi-doc.; mus.), *The Last Fight* 1983; *Beat Street* (co-mus. only) 1984; *Crossover Dreams* (also co-sc.) 1985; *Critical Condition, Fatal Beauty* 1987; *The Milagro Beanfield War, Oliver & Company* (songs only) 1988; *Disorganized Crime, The Lemon Sisters, True Believer* (songs only), *Do the Right Thing* (songs only), *Chances Are* (songs only), 1989; *Q & A* (mus. only), *Mo' Better Blues, The Two Jakes, Predator 2* 1990; *Crazy from the Heart, The Super* 1991; *Color of Night* 1994; *The Devil's Own* 1997.

Blain, Gérard. Actor. Born on Oct. 23, 1930, in Paris. Youthful, innocent-faced leading man of French and Italian films; memorable as the sensitive hero of Chabrol's *Le Beau Serge* and *The Cousins* (both 1958). Beginning his career as an extra in Marcel Carné's *The Children of Paradise*, he suspended his acting career during World War II, but later resumed it, becoming publicized in the late 50s as "a French James Dean." He was seldom seen in the 60s but reappeared in the early 70s as a director. Emulating Robert BRESSON, he adopted a minimalist style of directing, characterized by a neutral, unemotive approach to themes of passionate humanity.

FILMS INCLUDE: As actor—*Avant le Déluge, Les Fruits sauvages* 1954; *Le Temps des Assassins/Deadlier than the Male, Crime et Châtiment/Crime and Punishment* 1956; *Giovani Mariti* (It.) 1957; *Les Mistons* 1958; *Le Beau Serge, Les Cousins/The Cousins* 1959; *Il Gobbo/The Hunchback of Rome* (It./Fr.), *I Delfini/The Dauphins* (It.), *Via Margutta/Run with the Devil* (It./Fr.) 1960; *L'Oro di Roma* (It.) 1961; *Hatari!* (US) 1962; *La Smania Addosso/The Eye of the Needle* (It./Fr.) 1963; *La Bonne Soupe/Careless Love* 1964; *Un Homme de trop/Shock Troops* 1967; *La Machine, Der Amerikanische Freund/The American Friend* (Ger./Fr.) 1977; *La Derelitta* (It./Fr.) 1983; *Pussière d'Ange/Angel Dust* 1987; *Jour après Jour, Natalia* 1988; *L'enfant de l'hiver* 1989. As director-screenwriter—*Les Amis* 1971; *Le Pélican* (also act.) 1973; *Un Enfant dans la Foule* 1976; *Un Second Souffle* 1978; *Le Rebelle* (also co-sc.) 1980; *Pierre et Djemila* (also co-sc.) 1987.

Blaine, Vivian. Actress, singer. *b.* Vivian Stapleton, on Nov. 21, 1921, in Newark, N.J. *d.* 1995. A former band and nightclub singer, she played pleasant, lively leads in Hollywood musicals and light films of the 40s, but it was on Broadway in 1950 that she scored her biggest triumph in 'Guys and Dolls.' She repeated her success on the London stage and re-created the role in the 1955 film version. She was formerly married (1959–61) to Milton Rackmil, president of Universal Pictures and Decca Records.

FILMS: *Thru Different Eyes, It Happened in Flatbush, Girl Trouble* 1942; *He Hired the Boss, Jitterbugs* 1943; *Greenwich Village, Something for the Boys* 1944; *Nob Hill, State Fair, Doll Face* 1945; *If I'm Lucky, Three Little Girls in Blue* 1946; *Skirts Ahoy!* 1952; *Main Street to Broadway* (cameo), *Guys and Dolls* 1955; *Public Pigeon No. 1* 1957; *Richard* (cameo) 1972; *The Dark* 1979; *I'm Going to Be Famous* 1981; *Parasite* 1982.

Blair, Betsy. Actress. Born Betsy Boger, on Dec. 11, 1923, in New York City. Following a stage career, she entered films in 1947. Although usually playing second leads, she won critical acclaim, an Oscar nomination, and the Cannes Festival Award for best actress in 1955 for her lead role in *Marty.* She later moved to Europe, where she starred in several films, including Bardem's *Calle Mayor/The Lovemaker,* and Antonioni's *Il Grido/The Outcry.* Formerly married to Gene KELLY (1940–57) and Karel REISZ (1963–69), she lives in London with her third husband, a physician.

FILMS: *The Guilt of Janet Ames* 1947; *A Double Life, Another Part of the Forest, The Snake Pit* 1948; *Mystery Street* 1950; *Kind Lady* 1951; *Marty* 1955; *Calle Mayor/The Lovemaker* (Sp.) 1956; *Il Grido/The Outcry* (It.), *The Halliday Brand* 1957; *I Delfini/The Dauphins* (It.) 1960; *Senilita* (It.) 1961; *All Night Long* (UK) 1962; *Mazel Tov ou le Marriage/Marry Me! Marry Me!* (Fr.) 1968; *A Delicate Balance* 1973; *Descente aux Enfers* 1986; *Betrayed* 1988.

Blair, Janet. Actress, singer. Born Martha Janet Lafferty, on Apr. 23, 1921, in Altoona (or Blair), Pa. She was a vocalist with a band before starting her film career with Columbia in 1941. The following year she played two of her best parts, in *Broadway* and *My Sister Eileen* (in the title role). She continued appearing in films throughout the 40s in gradually diminishing roles. In 1950 she left Hollywood and went on the road with a highly successful production of the musical 'South Pacific,' which played more than 1,200 performances over a period of two years. She later became a popular torch singer in nightclubs and on TV. She returned to films occasionally in the 60s. Co-starred with Henry Fonda in the TV series 'The Smith Family' (1971–72).

FILMS: *Three Girls About Town* 1941; *Blondie Goes to College, Two Yanks in Trinidad, Broadway, My Sister Eileen* 1942; *Something to Shout About* 1943; *Once Upon a Time* 1944; *Tonight and Every Night* 1945; *Tars and Spars, Gallant Journey* 1946; *The Fabulous Dorseys* 1947; *I Love Trouble, The Fuller Brush Man, The Black Arrow* 1948; *Public Pigeon No. 1* 1957; *Boys' Night Out, Night of the Eagle/Burn Witch Burn* (UK) 1962; *The One and Only Genuine Original Family Band* 1968; *Won Ton Ton—The Dog Who Saved Hollywood* (cameo) 1976.

Blair, Linda. Actress. Born on Jan. 22, 1959, in St. Louis. Juvenile player, then young lead of Hollywood films. A model for children's apparel at age five, she later appeared in TV commercials and made her film debut at 11. As a chubby 14-year-old, she startled audiences with a chilling performance as a possessed child in *The Exorcist* (1973), for which she was nominated for an Oscar as best supporting actress. Her transition to young adult roles was temporarily hampered by a flirtation with drugs and an encounter with the law in 1977 over the possession of cocaine. She went on, however, to appear in numerous films, mainly of the low-budget variety. An accomplished horsewoman offscreen, she competed under the name Martha McDonald.

FILMS INCLUDE: *The Way We Live Now* 1970; *The Sporting Club* 1971; *The Exorcist* 1973; *Airport 1975* 1974; *Exorcist II: The Heretic* 1977; *Wild Horse Hank* (Can.), *Roller Boogie* 1981; *Ruckus, Hell Night* 1981; *Chained Heat* 1983; *Savage Streets, Night Patrol* 1984; *Savage Island* 1985; *Grotesque* (also co-assoc. prod.) 1988; *Bad Blood* 1989; *Dead Sleep, Moving Target, Repossessed* 1990; *Fatal Blond* 1991.

Blake, Bobby. See BLAKE, Robert.

Blake, Robert (Bobby). Actor. Born Michael Gubitosi, on Sept. 18, 1933, in Nutley, N.J. Started out as child actor in the Our Gang shorts in the late 30s and early 40s, initially billed as Mickey Gubitosi. Under the name of Bobby Blake, he later appeared in Republic's "Red Ryder" Westerns as Little Beaver, and in many other features of the 40s and early 50s, notably as a Mexican boy in Huston's *The Treasure of the Sierra Madre.* After military service he returned to the screen in 1956 as Robert Blake, adult, but it wasn't until the late 60s that he made his mark as one of the two young murderers in *In Cold Blood* and in the title role in *Tell Them Willie Boy Is Here.* At his best in offbeat roles. A feisty, pugnacious young man off screen and on, he had to combat a drug habit and his own rebellious temper during a difficult transition to adult life. Popular as the star of the TV series 'Baretta' (1975–78), for which he won an Emmy Award as best actor in a series in 1975. He was married (1964–77) to actress Sondra Kerr.

FILMS INCLUDE: As Bobby Blake—*I Love You Again* 1940; *Andy Hardy's Double Life* 1942; *Slightly Dangerous* 1943; *The Big Noise, Woman in the Window* 1944; *Dakota, Pillow to Post, The Horn Blows at Midnight* 1945; *In Old Sacramento* 1946; *Humoresque, The Last Roundup, The Return of Rin Tin Tin* 1947; *The Treasure of the Sierra Madre* 1948; *The Black Rose* 1950; *Apache War Smoke* 1952; *Treasure of the Golden Condor* 1953; *The Rack* 1956. As Robert Blake—*Rumble on the Docks* 1956; *The Tijuana Story* 1957; *The Beast of Budapest, Revolt in the Big House* 1958; *Battle Flame* 1959; *The Purple Gang* 1960; *Town Without Pity* 1961; *The Connection* 1962; *PT–109* 1963; *The Greatest Story Ever Told* 1965; *This Property Is Condemned* 1966; *In Cold Blood* 1968; *Tell Them Willie Boy Is Here* 1969; *Un Uomo dalla Pelle Dura/Ripped-Off* (It.), *Corky/Looking Good* 1972; *Electra Glide in Blue* 1973; *Busting* 1974; *Coast to Coast* 1980; *Second-Hand Hearts/The Hamster of Happiness* 1981.

Blakely, Colin. Actor. *b.* Sept. 23, 1930, Bangor, Northern Ireland. *d.* 1987. One of Britain's finest character players, in films, on TV, and mainly on the stage. He became involved in amateur dramatics while working as a salesman in his family's sporting goods store. He was 27 by the time he began performing in regional theater and 29 when he made his London debut. In the early 60s he rose to prominence with the Royal Shakespeare and National Theatre companies and began establishing a reputation as an imposing, wide-ranging supporting player in films.

FILMS INCLUDE: *Saturday Night and Sunday Morning* 1960; *The Hellions* 1961; *This Sporting Life* 1963; *The Long Ships* 1964; *A Man for All Seasons, The Spy With a Cold Nose* 1966; *Charlie Bubbles* 1967; *Decline and Fall, The Vengeance of She* 1968; *Alfred the Great* 1969; *The Private Life of Sherlock Holmes* (as Dr. Watson) 1970; *Young Winston, Something to Hide* 1972; *The National Health/Nurse Norton's Affair* 1973; *Murder on the Orient Express* 1974; *Galileo* 1975; *The Pink Panther Strikes Again, Something to Hide, It Shouldn't Happen to a Vet* 1976; *Equus* (US) 1977; *The Big Sleep* 1978; *All Things Bright and Beautiful, Meetings with Remarkable Men* 1979; *Nijinsky, Loophole, The Dogs of War* 1980; *Evil Under the Sun* 1982; *Red Monarch* 1983.

Blakely, Susan. Actress. Born Sept. 7, 1948, in Frankfurt, Germany, where her father was stationed with the US Army. *ed.* U. of Texas. Shapely blonde leading lady of Hollywood films of the 70s; a former fashion model. Married producer Steve Jaffe. Initially billed as Susie Blakely.

FILMS: *Savages* 1972; *The Way We Were* 1973; *The Lords of Flatbush, The Towering Inferno* 1974; *Report to the Commissioner, Capone* 1975; *Dreamer, The Concorde—Airport '79* 1979; *Over the Top* 1987; *My Mom's a Werewolf, Dream a Little Dream* 1989; *Tout les Jours Dimanche* 1994.

Blakley, Ronee. Singer, actress. Born in 1946, in Stanley, Idaho. *ed.* Stanford U. A country-and-western singer and songwriter, she made an auspicious screen debut as an actress in Robert Altman's *Nashville* (1975), providing one of the highlights of the film in a moving part she had written herself. She was nominated for an Oscar for her performance and was heralded by critics as an important new screen talent. Earlier, in 1972, she had contributed songs to the film *Welcome Home Soldier Boys.*

FILMS INCLUDE: *Nashville* 1975; *The Private Files of J. Edgar Hoover, Renaldo and Clara, The Driver* 1978; *She Came to the Valley, Good Luck, Miss Wyckoff* 1979; *The Baltimore Bullet* 1980; *A Nightmare on Elm Street* 1984; *Return to Salem's Lot, Student Confidential* 1987; *Someone to Love* 1988.

Blanc, Mel. Voice specialist, musician. *b.* Melvin Jerome Blanc, June 30, 1892, San Francisco, to Frederik and Eva Katz Blanc, managers of a women's clothing business. *d.* 1989. He began his career as a musician with NBC radio and later played the violin, bass, and tuba with various bands. In 1937 he joined the cartoon department of Warner Bros. as a voice specialist and over the years supplied the off-screen voices of dozens of cartoon characters, including Bugs Bunny, Porky Pig, Daffy Duck, Tweety Pie, Sylvester, and the Road Runner. In all, he provided voices for some 3,000 cartoon shorts, enriching American pop jargon with phrases like "What's up, Doc?" "Th-th-th-th-that's all f-f-f-folks," and "I tawt I taw a puddy tat." He also performed regularly on radio and TV, and sporadically in films, in cameo roles. After Mel Blanc's death, his cartoon characters got their voices from his son, Noel Blanc. The latter was seriously injured in a 1991 helicopter accident, in which actor Kirk Douglas was also hurt.

FILMS INCLUDE: *Neptune's Daughter* 1949; *Champagne for Caesar* (voice only) 1950; *Kiss Me Stupid* 1964; *The Man Called Flintstone* (voices only); *The Phantom Tollbooth* (voices only) 1969; *Scalawag* 1973; *Journey Back to Oz* (voice only); *Bugs Bunny Superstar* (voices only) 1975; *Buck Rogers in the 25th Century* (voice only) 1979; *Strange Brew* (voice only) 1983; *Heathcliff: The Movie* (voice only) 1986; *Who Framed Roger Rabbit?* (voices only) 1988; *Jetsons: The Movie* (voice only) 1990.

Blanchar, Pierre. Actor. *b.* Pierre Blanchard, June 30, 1892, Philippeville, Algeria. *d.* 1963. *ed.* Paris Conservatory. He started a brilliant acting career in 1920, playing leading roles in numerous plays and in more than 120 French films, and reached the peak of his popularity in the 30s. Among his best portrayals is that of Raskolnikov in *Crime et Châtiment/Crime and Punishment* (1935). Other memorable performances in *Un Carnet de Bal, L'Atlantide,* and *La Symphonie pastorale.* He also directed two films, *Secrets* (1942) and *Un Seul Amour* (1943). His daughter, Dominique Blanchar (*b.* 1927, Paris), is also a stage and screen actress. She appeared in Antonioni's *L'Avventura,* among other films.

FILMS INCLUDE: *Papa Bon Coeur* 1920; *Jocelyn* 1922; *La Terre Promise, L'Arriviste* 1924; *Le Joueur d'Echecs/The Chess Player* 1927; *La Marche nuptiale* 1928; *Le Capitaine Fracasse* 1929; *L'Atlantide, Le Croix de Bois, La Couturière de Luneville, Mélo* 1932; *Cette Vieille Canaille* 1933; *Prinzessin Turandot* (Ger.) 1934; *Crime et Châtiment/Crime and Punishment* (as Raskolnikov), *Amants et Voleurs* 1935; *Le Coupable, Mademoiselle Docteur/Street of Shadows, L'Homme de nulle part/The Man From Nowhere/The Late Mathias Pascal, La Dame de Pique, Un Carnet de Bal, L'Affaire du Courrier de Lyon/The Courier of Lyons* 1937; *A Royal Divorce* (UK), *Les Bateliers de la Volga/The Volga Boatman, Le Joueur, L'Etrange M. Victor* 1938; *Nuit de Décembre* 1939; *L'Empreinte du Dieu/Two Women* 1940; *La Neige sur les Pas* 1941; *Pontacarral* 1942; *Secrets* (also dir.), *Un Seul Amour* (also dir.) 1943; *Le Bossu* 1944; *Patrie, La Symphonie pastorale* 1946; *Le Bataillon du Ciel/They Are Not Angels* 1947; *Aprés l'Amour* 1948; *Du*

Rififi chez les Femmes/Riff Raff Girls 1959; *Katia/Magnificent Sinner* 1960; *Le Monocle noir* 1961.

Blanchard, Mari. Actress. *b.* Mary Blanchard, Apr. 13, 1927, Long Beach, Calif. *d.* 1970, of cancer. *ed.* U. of California, Santa Barbara. Her childhood dancing career was interrupted by polio at the age of nine. She later modeled before entering films in 1951. Played leads in many low-budget films of the 50s. She starred in the TV series 'Klondike' (1960–61).

FILMS INCLUDE: *Mr. Music* (bit) 1950; *On the Riviera, Ten Tall Men* 1951; *Back at the Front* 1952; *Abbott and Costello Go to Mars, The Veils of Bagdad* 1953; *Rails Into Laramie* 1954; *Destry, Son of Sinbad, The Crooked Web, The Return of Jack Slade* 1955; *The Cruel Tower* 1956; *She Devil, Jungle Heat* 1957; *Machete, No Place to Land* 1958; *Don't Knock the Twist* 1962; *Twice Told Tales, McLintock!* 1963.

Blandick, Clara. Actress. *b.* June 4, 1880, on an American ship anchored in Hong Kong. *d.* 1962, a suicide. Following a successful stage career, she made her first film appearance in 1908, but became a screen regular only after 1929. She played dozens of supporting roles, typically as a mother. She is remembered best for her portrayal of Judy Garland's aunt (Auntie Em) in *The Wizard of Oz* (1939).

FILMS INCLUDE: *Wise Girls* 1929; *Sins of the Children, Romance, Tom Sawyer* 1930; *Daybreak, Huckleberry Finn, Murder at Midnight, Possessed* 1931; *Shopworn, The Wet Parade, Three on a Match* 1932; *The Bitter Tea of General Yen, Child of Manhattan, One Sunday Afternoon, Charlie Chan's Greatest Case, Three-Cornered Moon* 1933; *The Show-Off, Broadway Bill* 1934; *Princess O'Hara* 1935; *Hearts Divided, Anthony Adverse, The Gorgeous Hussy* 1936; *Her Husband's Secretary, A Star Is Born* 1937; *Crime Ring* 1938; *Huckleberry Finn* (remake), *The Wizard of Oz, Drums Along the Mohawk* 1939; *Swanee River, North West Mounted Police* 1940; *The Wagons Roll at Night, It Started with Eve, One Foot in Heaven* 1941; *Rings on Her Fingers* 1942; *Heaven Can Wait* 1943; *Can't Help Singing* 1944; *A Stolen Life* 1946; *Life with Father* 1947; *The Bride Goes Wild* 1948; *Key to the City, Love That Brute* 1950.

Blank, Les. Documentary director. Born in 1935, in Tampa, Fla. After graduating from Tulane with a B.A. in English and a master's degree in playwriting, he attended the USC film school and made a collaborative debut as a director in 1964. Specializing in ethnic and regional explorations of everyday life, he turned out many documentary and industrial films characterized by their humor and attention to detail. His best-known film, *Burden of Dreams* (1982), offers a revealing portrait of German director Werner Herzog during his obsessive filming of *Fitzcarraldo,* an epic about obsession. Several critics deemed Blank's documentary more intriguing than Herzog's feature. Winner of the American Film Institute Maya Deren award for lifetime achievement in independent filmmaking (1990).

FILMS INCLUDE: *Dizzy Gillespie* (co-dir.) 1964; *God Respects Us When We Work but Loves Us When We Dance* 1968; *The Blues Accordin' to Lightnin' Hopkins* 1969; *Spend It All* 1971; *Hot Pepper* 1973; *A Poem Is a Naked Person* 1974; *Chulas Fronteras* 1976; *Always for Pleasure* 1978; *Garlic Is as Good as Ten Mothers, Werner Herzog Eats His Shoe* 1980; *Burden of Dreams* 1982; *Sprout Wings and Fly* 1983; *In Heaven There Is No Beer?* 1984; *Cigarette Blues* 1985; *Gap-Toothed Woman* 1987; *J'ai été au bal* 1989; *Yum, Yum, Yum! A Taste of Cajun and Creole Cooking* 1990.

Blanke, Henry. Producer. *b.* Dec. 30, 1901, in Berlin-Steglitz, Germany, the son of a painter. *d.* 1981. In 1920 he joined the German production company UFA, and the following year became personal assistant to Ernst LUBITSCH. He accompanied Lubitsch to the US, assisting on the production of his films between 1922 and 1926. Blanke then briefly returned to Germany to act as production manager of Fritz Lang's *Metropolis.* He worked for Warner Bros. in Hollywood (1927–28), headed their production in Germany (1928–30), their foreign production in Hollywood (1930–31), and finally supervised their American output (1931–32). He became producer in 1933, turning out a great many important films on the Warners lot, often with the title of production supervisor under Hal B. WALLIS.

FILMS INCLUDE: *Female, Bureau of Missing Persons* 1933; *Fashions of 1934, Madame Du Barry* 1934; *The Story of Louis Pasteur, A Midsummer Night's Dream* 1935; *The Petrified Forest, Anthony Adverse, Green Pastures* 1936; *The Life of Emile Zola* 1937; *Jezebel, The Adventures of Robin Hood* 1938; *Juarez, The Old Maid* 1939; *The Sea Hawk* 1940; *The Maltese Falcon, The Great Lie* 1941; *The Gay Sisters* 1942; *The Constant Nymph, Old Acquaintance, Edge of Darkness* 1943; *The Mask of Dimitrios* 1944; *Roughly Speaking* 1945; *Deception, My Reputation, Of Human Bondage* 1946; *Cry Wolf, Deep Valley* 1947; *The Treasure of the Sierra Madre, Winter Meeting* 1948; *The Fountainhead, Beyond the Forest* 1949; *Lightning Strikes Twice, Come Fill the Cup* 1951; *The Iron Mistress* 1952; *So Big* 1953; *Phantom of the Rue Morgue, King Richard and the Crusaders* 1954; *The McConnell Story* 1955; *Serenade* 1956; *Too Much Too Soon* 1958; *The Nun's Story, The Miracle* 1959; *Ice Palace* 1960; *The Sins of Rachel Cade* 1961; *Hell Is for Heroes* 1962.

Blasetti, Alessandro. Director. *b.* July 3, 1900, Rome. *d.* 1987. After flirting briefly with screen acting and obtaining a law degree, he turned to journalism and film criticism. In his reviews and articles he campaigned relentlessly against the melodramas and epic spectacles that dominated the Italian screen, calling for a more socially relevant cinema. In 1928 he joined other young Italian film enthusiasts (including Alessandrini and Barbaro) in creating a filmmaking co-operative, Augustus, through which he turned out his first film, the experimental *Sole* (1929). His films throughout the 30s and early 40s elevated him (with Mario CAMERINI) to a leading position in the Italian cinema during the Fascist era. His celebrated *1860* (1934), depicting Garibaldi's conquest of Sicily as seen through the eyes of two peasants (played by nonprofessional actors), is a forerunner of the postwar neorealist movement. That same year his *Vecchia Guardia/Old Guard* put him at odds with the Mussolini regime. Important films during the war years were *La Corona di Ferro/The Iron Crown* (1941), a historical spectacle, and *Quattro Passi fra le Nuvole/Four Steps in the Clouds* (1942), a marvelously restrained tender romance which is widely acknowledged as an important forerunner of Italian neorealism.

Blasetti's importance diminished in the postwar years, though *Fabiola* and *Prima Communione/Father's Dilemma* won international awards and *Altri Tempi/Times Gone By* and *Tempi Nostri/Anatomy of Love* won some critical attention. He collaborated on the scripts of most of his films and appeared in some of them. Author: *Come nasce un Film* (1932); *Scritti sul Cinema* (1982); *Il Cinema che ho vissuto* (1982).

FILMS: *Sole* 1929; *Nerone* 1930; *Resurrectio, Terra Madre* 1931; *Assisi* (doc.), *Palio, La Tavola dei Poveri* 1932; *Il Caso Haller, L'Impiegata di Papa* 1933; *1860/Gesuzza la Sposa Garibaldina* 1934; *Vecchia Guardia/Old Guard, Aldebaran* (also act.) 1935; *La Contessa di Parma* 1937; *Caccia alla Volpe* (doc.) 1938; *Ettore Fieramosca, Abuna Messias* (doc.), *Retroscena* 1939; *Napoli e le Terre d'Oltremare* (unfinished doc.), *Un'Avventura di Salvator Rosa* 1940; *La Corona di Ferro/The Iron Crown, La Cena delle Beffe* 1941; *Quattro Passi fra le Nuvole/Four Steps in the Clouds* (also act.) 1942; *Nessuno torna indietro* 1943; *La Gemma Orientale di Papi* (doc.), *Il Duomo di Milano* (doc.), *Castel Sant'Angelo* (doc.), *Un Giorno nella Vita* 1946; *Fabiola* 1948; *Ippodromi all'Alba* (doc.), *Prima Communione/Father's Dilemma* 1950; *Miracolo a Ferrara* (doc.) 1951; *Altri Tempi/Times Gone By* 1952; *La Fiammata* 1953; *Tempi Nostri/Anatomy of Love* 1954; *Peccato che sia una Canaglia/Too Bad She's Bad* 1955; *La Fortuna di essere Donna/Lucky to Be a Woman* 1956; *Amore e Chiacchiere* 1957; *Europa di Notte/European Nights* 1959; *Io amo Tu ami/I Love—You Love* 1961; *Les Quatres Vérités/Three Fables of Love* ("The Tortoise and the Hare" episode; Fr./It.) 1962; *Liolà/A Very Handy Man* 1964; *Io Io Io. . . e gli Altri* 1965; *La Ragazza del Bersagliere* 1967; *Simon Bolivar, Venezia una Mostra per il Cinema* (doc.), 1969.

Blatt, Edward A. Director, playwright. *b.* Feb. 12, 1903, Russia. *d.* 1991. *ed.* Columbia. In the US from childhood, he wrote several stage plays (including 'Young Man With a Horn') and produced many others before joining Paramount as associate producer in 1932. In 1941 he joined Warners as dialogue director. In the mid-40s he directed three films, then returned to the stage, and eventually became involved also in TV production.

FILMS: *Between Two Worlds* 1944; *Escape in the Desert* 1945; *Smart Woman* 1948.

Blatty, William Peter. Novelist, screenwriter, producer, director. Born on Jan. 7, 1928, in New York City. *ed.* Georgetown; George Washington U.; Seattle U. After serving with the Air Force, he began his career as an editor for the US Information Agency, then served as a publicity director for USC and Loyola universities. He had his first novel published in 1959 and saw his first screenplay produced in 1963. But it wasn't until 1970 that he scored his first big commercial hit, with *The Exorcist,* a chilling novel of the supernatural that remained on the best-seller list for more than a year. He later produced and wrote the novel's 1973 screen adaptation, winning an Academy Award for the screenplay. He made an impressive debut as a director in 1980.

FILMS (as screenwriter): *The Man from the Diners Club* (also co-story) 1963; *A Shot in the Dark* 1964; *John Goldfarb Please Come Home* (from his own novel) 1965; *Promise Her Anything, What Did You Do in the War Daddy?* 1966; *Gunn* 1967; *The Great Bank Robbery* 1969; *Darling Lili* 1970; *The Exorcist* (from own novel; also prod.) 1973; *Exorcist II: The Heretic* 1977; *The Ninth Configuration* (from his own novel, *Twinkle Twinkle Killer Kane*; also dir., prod.) 1980; *Exorcist III* (also dir., from own novel *Legion*) 1990.

Blaustein, Julian C. Producer. *b.* May 30, 1913, in New York City. *d.* 1995. *ed.* Harvard. Joined Universal in 1935 as a reader and moved up to story editor the following year. After heading the story departments at Paramount and Selznick, and five years in the Army, he was appointed producer for Fox in 1949 and executive producer in 1951.

FILMS INCLUDE: *Broken Arrow, Mister 880* 1950; *The Day the Earth Stood Still* 1951; *Don't Bother to Knock, The Outcasts of Poker Flat* 1952; *Désirée* 1954; *The Racers* 1955; *Storm Center* 1956; *Cowboy, Bell Book and Candle* 1958; *The Wreck of the Mary Deare* 1959; *Two Loves* 1961; *The Four Horsemen of the Apocalypse* 1962; *Khartoum* 1966; *Three Into Two Won't Go* 1969.

blaxploitation films. A category of sensational, low-budget motion pictures made in the early 70s that featured tough African-American heroes in gritty urban settings. Typically crime thrillers laden with violence and sex, the films often employed black directors as well as actors. Examples included Melvin VAN PEEBLES's *Sweet Sweetback's Baadasssss Song* (1971), Gordon PARKS's *Shaft* (1971), and Gordon Parks, Jr.'s *Super Fly* (1972). See also EXPLOITATION FILMS, RACE MOVIES.

Blier, Bernard. Actor. *b.* Jan. 11, 1916, Buenos Aires, of French parents. *d.* 1989. He studied drama with Raymond Rouleau, and at the Paris Conservatory under Louis Jouvet. Appeared briefly on the stage, then made film debut in 1937. He was mobilized at the outbreak of WW II and shortly after was taken prisoner by the Germans. But he returned to stage and screen work in 1941. Portly and progressively balding, he played character leads and important supporting roles in scores of French and Italian films. His many awards include a Chevalier of the Legion of Honor. He was the father of director Bertrand BLIER.

FILMS INCLUDE: *Gribouille/Heart of Paris* 1937; *Altitude 3200/Youth in Revolt, Entrée des Artistes/The Curtain Rises, Hôtel du Nord* 1938; *Le Jour se lève/Daybreak, L'Enfer des Anges* 1939; *L'Assassinat du Père Noël/Who Killed Santa Claus?* 1941; *La Symphonie fantastique* 1942; *Carmen* (release delayed from 1943), *Seul dans la Nuit* 1945; *Messieurs Ludovic* 1946; *Quai des Orfèvres/Jenny Lamour* 1947; *Dedée d'Anvers/Dedee, D'Homme à Hommes/Man to Men* 1948; *L'Ecole buissonnière/Passion for Life, Les Casse-Pieds/The Spice of Life, Monseigneur* 1949; *La Souricière, Manèges/The Cheat* 1950; *Sans laisser d'Adresse* 1951; *Agence matrimoniale* 1952; *Il Letto/The Bed* (It./Fr.) 1953; *Avant le Deluge* 1954; *Le Dossier noir* 1955; *Crime et Châtiment/Crime and Punishment* 1956; *L'Homme à l'Imperméable/The Man in the Raincoat, Retour de Manivelle/There's Always a Price Tag* 1957; *Les Misérables* (as Javert), *La Chatte/The Cat, Les Grandes Familles/The Possessors, Sans Famille* 1958; *Marie-Octobre, La Grande Guerra/The Great War* (It./Fr.), *Archimède le Clochard/The Magnificent Tramp* 1959; *Il Gobbo/The Hunchback of Rome* (It./Fr.), *Crimen/And Suddenly It's Murder* (It./Fr.) 1960; *Le President, Le Cave se rebiffe/The Counterfeiters of Paris/Money Money Money, Arrêtez les Tambours/Women and War* 1961; *Le Septième Juré/The Seventh Juror, Germinal* 1962; *I Compagni/The Organizer* (It./Fr.) 1963; *La Bonne Soupe/Carless Love, Alta Infedeltà/High Infidelity* (It./Fr.), *Cent Mille Dollars au Soleil/Greed in the Sun, Il Magnifico Cornuto/The Magnificent Cuckold* (It./Fr.), *La Chasse à l'Homme/Male Hunt, Les Barbouzes/The Great Spy Chase* 1964; *Casanova/Casanova '70* 1965; *Lo Straniero/The Stranger* (It./Fr.), *Peau d'Espion/How to Commit Murder* 1967; *Mon Oncle Benjamin* 1969; *Catch Me a Spy* (UK/Fr.), *Homo Eroticus/Man of the Year* (It.) 1971; *Le Grand Blond avec une Chaussure noire/The Tall Blond Man With One Black Shoe* 1972; *La Main à couper* 1974; *Ce Cher Victor, Amici miei/My Friends* (It.) 1975; *Calmos/Femmes Fatales, Le Corps de mon Ennemi, Nuit d'Or* 1976; *Le Compromis* 1978; *Il Malato imaginario/The Hypochondriac* (It./Fr.), *Série noire* 1979; *Buffet froid* 1980; *Passione d'Amore* (It./Fr.) 1981; *Le Due Vite di Mattia Pascal/The Two Lives of Mattia Pascal* (It./Fr./Ger.) 1985; *Je hais les Acteurs/I Hate Actors!* 1986; *I Picari* 1987; *Paganini* (It.), *Una Botta di Vita/A Taste of Life* (It./Fr.) 1989.

Blier, Bertrand. Director. Born on March 14, 1939, in Paris. The son of actor Bernard BLIER, he entered films in 1960 as an assistant to John Berry, George Lautner, Christian-Jacques, Jean Delannoy, and Denys de la Patellière, among other directors. In 1962 he turned out his own first film, *Hitler. . . connais pas!,* a full-length documentary, *cinéma vérité*–style, exploring the views and lifestyles of contemporary French youth. He then returned to assisting others, contributing to scripts, and directing a short, *Le Grimace* (1966), before resuming as a feature director in 1967. It was not until 1974, however, that Blier first attracted wide attention to his work with *Les Valseuses/Going Places,* a cynical, frankly erotic "road movie" (the original title is a slang word for testicles) that was a huge box-office hit in France and later acquired cult status abroad. It was adapted from the director's own 1972 novel. Blier's preoccupation with the power of sex, and particularly the variations and conflicts in the sexual appetites and adequacies of men and women, continued with *Calmos/Femmes fatales* (1976) and *Préparez vos Mouchoirs/Get Out Your Handkerchiefs* (1978). The latter won a Hollywood Oscar as best foreign film. In the 80s Bertrand solidified his growing reputation as a technically polished director with a witty, if sardonic, insight into human relationships. He won a César for the screenplay of *Buffet froid* (1979) and a Special Jury Prize at Cannes for *Trop Belle pour toi/Too Beautiful for You* (1989).

FEATURE FILMS: *Hitler. . . connais pas!* 1962; *Si j'etais un Espion/Breakdown* 1967; *Les Valseuses/Going Places* 1974; *Calmos/Femmes Fatales* 1976; *Preparez vos Mouchoirs/Get Out Your Handkerchiefs* 1978; *Buffet froid* 1979; *Beau-Père* (from his own novel) 1981; *La Femme de mon Pote/My Best Friend's Girl* 1983; *Notre Histoire/Our Story* 1984; *Tenue du Soirée/Ménage* 1986; *Trop Belle pour toi/Too Beautiful for You* 1989; *Un, Deux, Trois Soleil* 1993; *Grosse Fatigue* 1994; *My Man* 1996.

blimp. A soundproof housing in which a camera is placed to prevent the noise of its mechanism from being picked up by the microphone during sound recording.

One of the first camera-noise-prevention devices was the soundproof booth, popular in Hollywood in the early 30s. However, the need to place the camera and its entire crew inside a glass-enclosed booth was done away with as quieter cameras were developed, making possible the use of noise-dampening covers, leading to the modern blimp and other soundproofing systems.

The typical blimp is aluminum or magnesium, lined with several layers of rubber and plastic foam. Most camera controls are extended through it so that the camera can be operated without opening the blimp.

Cameras built so that their normal casing will absorb mechanism noise are called "self-blimped" cameras. See also BARNEY.

Bloch, Robert. Novelist, screenwriter. *b.* Apr. 5, 1917, in Chicago. *d.* 1994. The prolific author of dozens of mystery, suspense, and science fiction novels and hundreds of short stories, he began writing screenplays in the early 60s, following the success of Hitchcock's *Psycho* (1960), which was based on one of his novels. His scripts, like his books, have been confined mainly to the mystery, suspense, and horror genres. He has also written prolifically for TV, including many episodes of the "Thriller" and "Alfred Hitchcock Presents" anthology series.

FILMS INCLUDE: *Psycho* (novel basis only) 1960; *The Couch, The Cabinet of Caligari* 1962; *Straight-Jacket* 1964; *The Night Walker, The Skull* (story basis only) 1965; *The Psychopath* (UK) 1966; *The Deadly Bees* (UK) 1967; *The Torture Garden* (from a collection of his own short stories; UK) 1968; *The House That Dripped Blood* (UK) 1971; *Asylum* (UK) 1972.

block-booking. A film industry business practice, now illegal, by which an exhibitor is compelled to buy sight unseen a whole line of mediocre and poor films along with the few features in which he is interested. The system enabled producers and distributors of good prestige films with big-name stars and strong box-office potential to unload blocks of feature films with weak-potential box-office returns onto exhibitors who would normally turn them down. The system, which spread from the US to Europe, came to a virtual halt in 1948 as a result of a court decision that forced the separation of the production and exhibition functions of the industry.

blocking. The working out of the composition of a scene, usually in the form of a general rehearsal of movements by actors as well as the setup and positioning of cameras, lights, and other technical equipment.

Blom, August. Director, actor. *b.* Dec. 26, 1869, Copenhagen. *d.* 1947. One of the founders and most important directors of the early Danish cinema. A former stage actor, he joined Nordisk as a bit player in 1908. He directed scores of films of all genres from 1910 to the mid-20s. Turned out several films a year, specializing in melodramatic, grand-scale productions. Wrote the screenplays for most of his own films. Among his many discoveries were Valdemar Psilander and Asta NIELSEN.

FILMS INCLUDE: *Life's Tempest, Robinson Crusoe, The White Slave, Dr. Jekyll and Mr. Hyde, Hamlet* 1910; *At the Prison Gates/Temptations of a Big City, A Lady's Diary, A Ballet Dancer's Love, The Prime of Life, A Dream of Death, The Power of Love, The Vampire Dancer* 1911; *The Governor's Daughter, The Black Chancellor, The Life of a Mother, Three Comrades, First Love, The Fugitives* 1912; *A Harvest of Tears, Paradise Lost, Atlantis, A Modern Jack the Ripper* 1913; *The Outcast's Return, Nemesis, Reformation, Pro Patria* 1914; *The Samaritan, Blind Fate, For His Country's Honor* 1915; *The Mysterious Companion* 1916; *The Maharajha's Favorite* 1917; *Lace, Via Crucis* 1918; *Prometheus/Bonds of Fate* 1919; *His Genius, The Vicar of Vejlby/Land of Fate* 1920; *Circus Lights, With All Might* 1924; *The Dragon* 1925.

Blondell, Joan. Actress. b. Aug. 30, 1909, New York City. d. 1979, of leukemia. The daughter of stage comic Eddie Blondell, one of the original Katzenjammer Kids, she spent her childhood touring the US, Europe, China, and Australia, performing in vaudeville numbers with her parents. At the age of 17 she joined a stock company in Dallas, Tex. After winning a Miss Dallas beauty contest, she came to New York, where she appeared in the Broadway productions of 'Tarnished' and 'The Trial of Mary Dugan,' and in the 'Ziegfeld Follies.' In 1929 she was teamed with another unknown, James CAGNEY, in the stage musical 'Penny Arcade.' The following year the production was transformed to the screen, with both performers, under the title *Sinners' Holiday.*

Miss Blondell remained in Hollywood, enjoying a tremendously productive career, both as a leading lady and as a second lead, typically playing cynical, wisecracking broads with hearts of gold. Her busiest years were the 30s, when she was known as a virtual workhorse at Warner Bros., appearing in as many as ten films a year. She spent most of the 50s on stage, then returned to films in character parts. Among her most memorable roles (she appeared in more than 80 films) was that of Aunt Sissy in *A Tree Grows in Brooklyn.* She was nominated for an Academy Award as best supporting actress for her performance in *The Blue Veil* (1951). She was twice nominated for Emmy Awards for her portrayal of Lottie, the saloon keeper in the series 'Here Come the Brides' (1968–70), one of her many TV portrayals. She was married three times, to cameraman George BARNES (1932–36), actor Dick POWELL (1936–44), and producer Mike TODD (1947–50). Author of a novel *Center Door Fancy* (1972), loosely based on her own life and career. Her sister, Gloria Blondell, also appeared in TV and films.

FILMS: *The Office Wife, Sinners' Holiday* 1930; *Illicit, Millie, My Past, God's Gift to Women, Other Men's Women, The*

Public Enemy, Big Business Girl, Night Nurse, The Reckless Hour, Blonde Crazy 1931; *Union Depot, The Greeks Had a Word for Them, The Crowd Roars, The Famous Ferguson Case, Make Me a Star, Miss Pinkerton, Big City Blues, Three on a Match, Central Park, Lawyer Man* 1932; *Broadway Bad, Blondie Johnson, Gold Diggers of 1933, Goodbye Again, Footlight Parade, Havana Widows, Convention City* 1933; *I've Got Your Number, He Was Her Man, Smarty, Dames, Kansas City Princess* 1934; *Traveling Saleslady, Broadway Gondolier, We're in the Money, Miss Pacific Fleet* 1935; *Colleen, Sons o' Guns, Bullets or Ballots, Stage Struck, Three Men on a Horse, Gold Diggers of 1937* 1936; *The King and the Chorus Girl, Back in Circulation, The Perfect Specimen, Stand-In* 1937; *There's Always a Woman* 1938; *Off the Record, East Side of Heaven, The Kid from Kokomo, Good Girls Go to Paris, The Amazing Mr. Williams* 1939; *Two Girls on Broadway, I Want a Divorce* 1940; *Topper Returns, Model Wife, Three Girls About Town* 1941; *Lady for a Night* 1942; *Cry Havoc* 1943; *A Tree Grows in Brooklyn, Don Juan Quilligan* 1945; *Adventure* 1946; *The Corpse Came C.O.D., Nightmare Alley, Christmas Eve* 1947; *For Heaven's Sake* 1950; *The Blue Veil* 1951; *The Opposite Sex* 1956; *Lizzie, This Could Be the Night, Desk Set, Will Success Spoil Rock Hunter?* 1957; *Angel Baby* 1961; *Advance to the Rear* 1964; *The Cincinnati Kid* 1965; *Ride Beyond Vengeance* 1966; *Waterhole #3* 1967; *Kona Coast, Stay Away Joe* 1968; *Big Daddy* (release delayed from 1965) 1969; *The Phynx* (cameo) 1970; *Support Your Local Gunfighter* 1971; *Won Ton Ton—The Dog Who Saved Hollywood* 1976; *Opening Night, Grease* 1978; *The Champ, The Glove* 1979; *The Woman Inside* (released 1981).

bloom. The treatment of a lens or any glass surface with a special transparent fluoride coating to reduce reflection.

Bloom, Claire. Actress. Born Claire Blume, on Feb. 15, 1931, in London. In 1940, at nine, she was brought to the US as a war evacuee during the London Blitz. She was returned to England in 1943 and enrolled in a drama school. After an appearance in a BBC radio play, she joined the Oxford Repertory Theatre at 15, and two years later, after having appeared in several Stratford-on-Avon productions, including 'Hamlet' as Ophelia, she made her film debut in *The Blind Goddess* in 1948. Achieved world fame as Terry in CHAPLIN's film *Limelight* (1952) and the same year joined the Old Vic, with which she later toured Canada and the US. She has since divided her time between the stage and films in the US, the UK, and on the Continent, consistently creating memorable, ladylike portrayals. Has also done considerable TV. Formerly married to actor Rod STEIGER (1959–69), stage producer Hilliard Elkins (1969–76), and novelist Philip Roth. Autobiography: *Limelight and After: The Education of an Actress* 1982.

FILMS: *The Blind Goddess* 1948; *Limelight* 1952; *Innocents in Paris, The Man Between* 1953; *Richard III* (as Lady Anne), *Alexander the Great* 1956; *The Brothers Karamazov* (as Katya) 1958; *Look Back in Anger, The Buccaneer* 1959; *Die Schachnovelle/Brainwashed/The Royal Game* (Ger.) 1960; *The Wonderful World of the Brothers Grimm, The Chapman Report* 1962; *Il Maestro di Vigevano* (It.), *The Haunting* 1963; *Alta Infedeltà/High Infidelity* (It./Fr.), *The Outrage* 1964; *The Spy Who Came in from the Cold* 1965; *Charly* 1968; *Three Into Two Won't Go, The Illustrated Man* 1969; *A Severed Head* 1970; *Red Sky at Morning* 1971; *A Doll's House* (as Nora) 1973; *Islands in the Stream* 1977; *Clash of the Titans* (as Hera) 1981; *Déja Vu* 1985; *Sammy and Rosie Get Laid* 1987; *Crimes and Misdemeanors* 1989; *The Princess and the Goblin* (v/o) 1994; *Mighty Aphrodite* 1995; *Daylight* 1996.

Bloom, Verna. Actress. Born on Aug. 7, 1939, in Lynn, Mass. *ed.* Boston U. After drama studies at the Uta Hagen-Herbert Berghof School, she appeared in stock, then in Denver repertory, finally landing on Broadway in 'Marat/Sade,' playing the role of Charlotte Corday. She made her screen debut in *Medium Cool* (1969) and subsequently played leads and supporting parts in a number of films.

FILMS INCLUDE: *Medium Cool* 1969; *The Hired Hand* 1971; *High Plains Drifter, Badge 373* 1973; *National Lampoon's Animal House* 1978; *Honkytonk Man* 1982; *After Hours, The Journey of Natty Gann* 1985; *The Last Temptation of Christ* (as the Virgin Mary) 1988.

bloop. A clicking noise caused by the passage of a soundtrack splice through reproduction equipment. Also, the opaque triangular patch applied to the splicing area or painted on it with blooping ink to silence that noise. This is often accomplished with a special blooping machine. The quick-drying blooping ink, incidentally, is also used for blacking out unwanted areas on film.

blooper. A special-effects device, usually a round, open tank, used on a set to stimulate water explosions and similar effects. It is operated pneumatically.

Blore, Eric. Actor. *b.* Dec. 23, 1887, London. *d.* 1959. After working as an insurance agent, he gained stage experience touring Australia and then appeared in many shows and revues in England. In the US from 1923, he played character roles in scores of Broadway plays and Hollywood films, often as a haughty waiter or petulant butler.

FILMS INCLUDE: *A Night Out and a Day In* (short; UK) 1920; *The Great Gatsby* 1926; *Laughter* 1930; *Tarnished Lady* 1931; *Flying Down to Rio* 1933; *The Gay Divorcee* 1934; *Diamond Jim, Top Hat* 1935; *Swing Time* 1936; *Quality Street, Shall We Dance?* 1937; *Swiss Miss* 1938; *Island of Lost Men* 1939; *The Lone Wolf Strikes* 1940; *Road to Zanzibar, The Lady Eve, Sullivan's Travels, The Shanghai Gesture* 1941; *The Moon and Sixpence* 1942; *Forever and a Day, Holy Matrimony* 1943; *San Diego I Love You* 1944; *Kitty* 1945; *Abie's Irish Rose* 1946; *The Lone Wolf in London* 1947; *Romance on the High Seas* 1948; *Love Happy* 1949; *Fancy Pants* 1950; *Bowery to Bagdad* 1955.

blow-up. The enlargement of a photographic image by an optical printing process. In movie use this is most commonly an enlargement from 16 mm stock to 35 mm prints.

Blue, Ben. Comic actor, dancer. *b.* Benjamin Bernstein, Sept. 12, 1901, Montreal, *d.* 1975. Sad-faced, rubber-limbed, deadpan mime, comedian, and dancer of the American stage, TV, and films. On stage and in vaudeville and New York musicals from age 15, he made his screen debut in 1926, appearing in a series of short subjects for Warner Bros., Hal Roach, and other studios. His later cameo appearances provided the comedy highlights of many features. He also performed regularly on TV and in nightclubs. In the 60s he operated his own club in Santa Monica but was forced to close it down in 1967 because of income tax trouble.

FEATURE FILMS: *The Arcadians* (UK) 1927; *College Rhythm* 1934; *Follow Your Heart, College Holiday* 1936; *Top of the Town, Turn Off the Moon, High Wide and Handsome, Artists and Models, Thrill of a Lifetime* 1937; *The Big Broadcast of 1938, College Swing, Coconut Grove* 1938; *Paris Honeymoon* 1939; *Panama Hattie, For Me and My Gal* 1942; *Thousands Cheer* 1943; *Broadway Rhythm, Two Girls and a Sailor* 1944; *Two Sisters From Boston, Easy to Wed* 1946; *My Wild Irish Rose* 1947; *One Sunday Afternoon* 1948; *It's A Mad Mad Mad Mad World* 1963; *The Russians Are Coming the Russians Are Coming* 1966; *A Guide for the Married Man, The Busy Body* 1967; *Where Were You When the Lights Went Out?* 1968.

Blue, Monte. Actor. *b.* Jan. 11, 1890, Indianapolis. *d.*

1963. Part Cherokee Indian. Brought up in an orphanage, he worked as a lumberjack, cowboy, and railway porter before being hired by D. W. GRIFFITH in 1915 as a combination script clerk, stuntman, and actor, on such productions as *The Birth of a Nation, Intolerance,* and *Orphans of the Storm.* After playing many roles as a simple outdoor youth, he rose to stardom, playing tough romantic leads throughout the 20s. His parts diminished in importance in later years, but he continued playing character roles into the 50s. Later worked for a circus. In all, he appeared in some 200 films.

FILMS INCLUDE: *The Birth of a Nation* (bit), *Ghosts* 1915; *Intolerance, The Microscope Mystery, The Matrimaniac* 1916; *Wild and Woolly, The Man from Painted Post, Hands Up!, Betrayed, The Ship of Doom* 1917; *Till I Come Back to You, Johanna Enlists, M'Liss, The Romance of Tarzan, The Squaw Man* 1918; *Pettigrew's Girl, In Mizzoura, Everywoman* 1919; *The Thirteenth Commandment, A Cumberland Romance, Something to Think About, Too Much Johnson* 1920; *The Kentuckians, A Perfect Crime, A Broken Doll, Moonlight and Honeysuckle, The Affairs of Anatol* 1921; *Peacock Alley, Orphans of the Storm* (as Danton), *My Old Kentucky Home, Broadway Rose* 1922; *Brass, The Tents of Allah, Main Street, The Purple Highway, Defying Destiny, Lucretia Lombard* 1923; *Loving Lies, Daughters of Pleasure, The Marriage Circle, How to Educate a Wife, Mademoiselle Midnight, Revelation, Her Marriage Vow, Being Respectable, The Lover of Camille, The Dark Swan/The Black Swan* 1924; *Recompense, Kiss Me Again, The Limited Mail, Red Hot Tires, Hogan's Alley* 1925; *The Man Upstairs, Other Women's Husbands, So This Is Paris, Across the Pacific* 1926; *Wolf's Clothing, The Brute, Bitter Apples, The Black Diamond Express, The Bush Leaguer, One-Round Hogan, Brass Knuckles* 1927; *Across the Atlantic, White Shadows in the South Seas* 1928; *Conquest, The Greyhound Limited, No Defense, From Headquarters, Skin Deep, Tiger Rose* 1929; *Isle of Escape, Those Who Dance* 1930; *The Flood* 1931; *The Stoker* 1932; *The Intruder* 1933; *Come on Marines!, The Last Round-Up* 1934; *The Lives of a Bengal Lancer, G-Men* 1935; *Undersea Kingdom* (serial), *Mary of Scotland, Desert Gold* 1936; *The Outcasts of Poker Flat, Souls at Sea* 1937; *The Great Adventures of Wild Bill Hickok* (serial), *Hawk of the Wilderness* (serial) 1938; *Dodge City, Juarez* 1939; *Geronimo, Mystery Sea Raider, A Little Bit of Heaven* 1940; *King of the Texas Rangers* (serial), *The Great Train Robbery* 1941; *Across the Pacific, Road to Morocco, The Palm Beach Story* 1942; *Edge of Darkness, Northern Pursuit, Mission to Moscow* 1943; *Passage to Marseille, The Mask of Dimitrios, The Conspirators* 1944; *San Antonio* 1945; *Cinderella Jones* 1946; *Possessed, Life with Father* 1947; *Silver River, Key Largo, Johnny Belinda* 1948; *South of St. Louis, Homicide* 1949; *Dallas* 1950; *Warpath* 1951; *Hangman's Knot* 1952; *The Last Posse* 1953; *Apache* 1954.

blue screen process. The most common method now used for creating TRAVELING MATTES, moving silhouettes that allow images to be combined in special effects shots. Actors or model objects are filmed in front of a brightly illuminated blue screen. The film is then re-photographed twice, each time with a different filter. The first filter turns all the blue to black, yielding a film of actors against a black background. The second filter turns the blue to white and blocks out other colors, yielding a film of the actors' silhouettes against a clear-white background. The latter film is used as a mask (or matte) to cover part of another film as it travels through the camera. By this means, moving silhouettes are created as unexposed "holes" in footage of a desired setting—for example, a cliffside in Africa. An OPTICAL PRINTER is then used to combine the film of the cliffside with the film of the actors moving against a black background. The image of the actors precisely fills in the "holes" in the cliffside footage; the finished product appears to show the actors walking on the cliffside.

The biggest drawback to the process is "blue spill," in which light from the blue screen reflects off the actors and contaminates the final image, creating a visible matte line. Innovations in lighting and processing of blue screen shots have reduced this problem.

Bluth, Don. American animator, director. *ed.* Brigham Young U. Leading contemporary animator. He started out in 1956 as an animator with the Walt Disney studios and later worked as animation director on such films as *Robin Hood* (1973), *The Rescuers* (1977), *Pete's Dragon* (1977), and *Xanadu* (1980). Establishing his own company in 1979, he turned to directing as well as producing his own animated films, at times under the aegis of Steven SPIELBERG. Recently he moved his work to Ireland, for its lower production costs and government support of the arts.

FILMS (as director): *The Secret of Nimh* (also prod., sc.) 1982; *An American Tail* (also co-prod., des.) 1986; *The Land Before Time* (also co-prod.) 1988; *All Dogs Go to Heaven* 1989; *Thumbelina, A Troll in Central Park* (v/o) 1994; *The Pebble and the Penguin* (v/o) 1995.

Blystone, John G. Director. *b.* Dec. 2, 1892, Rice Lake, Wis. *d.* 1938. *ed.* Univ. of Wisconsin. Entered the film industry in 1916 as a property man and during the 20s and 30s directed a number of motion pictures, mostly comedies but also some dramas and adventure films. He collaborated with Buster KEATON on the direction of *Our Hospitality* and directed two of LAUREL AND HARDY's better feature-length films, *Swiss Miss* and *Block-Heads,* his last productions.

FEATURE FILMS: *Friendly Husband* (also story), *Soft Boiled* (also co-story, sc.), *Our Hospitality* (co-dir. with Buster Keaton) 1923; *Ladies to Board, Oh You Tony!, Teeth, The Last Man on Earth* 1924; *Dick Turpin, The Lucky Horseshoe, The Everlasting Whisper, The Best Bad Man* 1925; *My Own Pal, Hard Boiled, The Family Upstairs, Wings of the Storm* 1926; *Ankles Preferred, Slaves of Beauty, Pajamas* 1927; *Sharp Shooters, Mother Knows Best* 1928; *Captain Lash, Thru Different Eyes, The Sky Hawk* 1929; *The Big Party, So This Is London, Tol'able David* 1930; *Mr. Lemon of Orange, Men on Call, Young Sinners* 1931; *Charlie Chan's Chance, She Wanted a Millionaire, Amateur Daddy, The Painted Woman, Too Busy to Work* 1932; *Hot Pepper, Shanghai Madness, My Lips Betray* 1933; *Coming Out Party, Change of Heart, Hell in the Heavens* 1934; *The County Chairman, Bad Boy* 1935; *Gentle Julia, Little Miss Nobody, The Magnificent Brute* 1936; *Great Guy, 23½ Hours Leave, Woman Chases Man, Music for Madame* 1937; *Swiss Miss, Block-Heads* 1938.

Blyth, Ann. Actress. Born Ann Marie Blyth, on Aug. 16, 1928, in Mt. Kisco, N.Y. After making her radio debut at five, she studied voice and later spent three years as a soprano with the San Carlo Opera Company. At 13 she appeared on Broadway, as the daughter of Paul Lukas in 'Watch on the Rhine,' and at 15 she was signed to a Hollywood contract. She first played juvenile roles (she was nominated for an Oscar as best supporting actress for her part as Joan Crawford's daughter in *Mildred Pierce*), and later female leads. Recovering from a back fracture she suffered in 1945, she appeared in dramas (most effectively in *Another Part of the Forest,* 1948) and adventure films as well as in several musical pictures, such as *The Great Caruso* and *The Student Prince,* which made use of her trained singing voice. She retired from the screen in 1957 but later appeared occasionally in light opera and in musical stage productions.

FILMS: *Chip Off the Old Block, The Merry Monahans, Babes on Swing Street, Bowery to Broadway* 1944; *Mildred Pierce* 1945; *Swell Guy, Brute Force, Killer McCoy* 1947; *A Woman's Vengeance, Another Part of the Forest, Mr. Peabody and the Mermaid* 1948; *Red Canyon, Top o' the Morning, Free for All* 1949; *Our Very Own* 1950; *The Great Caruso, Katie Did It, Thunder on the Hill, The Golden Horde, The House in the Square, I'll Never Forget You* 1951; *Sally and Saint Anne, One Minute to Zero, The World in His Arms* 1952; *All the Brothers Were Valiant* 1953; *Rose Marie, The Student Prince* 1954; *The King's Thief, Kismet* 1955; *Slander, The Buster Keaton Story, The Helen Morgan Story* (as singer Helen Morgan) 1957.

Blythe, Betty. Actress. *b.* Elizabeth Blythe Slaughter, Sept. 1, 1893, Los Angeles. *d.* 1972. *ed.* USC. Following some stage experience in Europe and on Broadway, she made her film debut in 1918 at the Brooklyn Vitagraph studios. She rapidly became a popular star and reached a peak of prestige after playing the title role in *Queen of Sheba* (1921). She played leads in numerous silent productions in Hollywood and several in England, notably the 1925 version of *She.* She made a smooth transition to talkies, but by that time she was playing supporting parts. She continued appearing regularly in films through the late 40s, and after a 15-year absence could be glimpsed briefly in the ballroom sequence of *My Fair Lady* (1964).

FILMS INCLUDE: *His Own People, Over the Top, A Game With Fate, Tangled Lives, The Green God, Miss Ambition* 1918; *Fighting Destiny, Beauty-Proof, The Man Who Won, Undercurrent* 1919; *The Third Generation, The Silver Horde, Nomads of the North* 1920; *The Truant Husband, Mother o' Mine, The Queen of Sheba* (title role) 1921; *Fair Lady, His Wife's Husband, How Women Love* 1922; *The Darling of the Rich, The Truth About Wives, Chu Chin Chow* (UK), *Sinner or Saint* 1923; *The Recoil, The Spitfire, In Hollywood with Potash and Perlmutter, The Breath of Scandal* 1924; *The Folly of Vanity, Percy, Speed, Le Puits de Jacob/A Daughter of Israel* (Fr.), *She* (UK) 1925; *Snowbound, A Million Bid, Eager Lips, The Girl From Gay Paree* 1927; *Domestic Troubles, Glorious Betsy, Sisters of Eve, Stolen Love* 1928; *Tom Brown of Culver* 1932; *Pilgrimage, Only Yesterday* 1933; *Ever Since Eve, The Scarlet Letter* 1934; *The Gorgeous Hussy* 1936; *Conquest* 1937; *Honky Tonk* 1941; *Where Are Your Children?* 1944; *Docks of New York* 1945; *Madonna of the Desert* 1948; *My Fair Lady* 1964.

Boam, Jeffrey. Screenwriter. Born on November 30, 1949, in Rochester, N.Y. *ed.* Sacramento State College, UCLA. Leading screenwriter of action-adventures that highlight male bonding.

FILMS INCLUDE: *Straight Time* (co-sc., asst. dir.) 1978; *The Dead Zone* (co-sc., assoc. pr.) 1983; *Innerspace* (co-sc., act.), *The Lost Boys* (so.-sc.) 1987; *Funny Farm* 1988; *Lethal Weapon 2, Indiana Jones and the Last Crusade* 1989; *Lethal Weapon 3* (co-sc.) 1992.

Boardman, Eleanor. Actress. *b.* Aug. 19, 1898, Philadelphia. *d.* 1991. She became known nationally as the Kodak Girl on publicity posters for Eastman Kodak. After gaining stage experience, she went to Hollywood and starred in silents and early talkies. She is best remembered for her leading role in *The Crowd,* directed by King VIDOR, whom she married and later divorced. Vidor also directed her in several other films. In 1940 she married director Harry d'Abbadie D'ARRAST.

FILMS INCLUDE: *The Stranger's Banquet* 1922; *Gimme, Souls for Sale, Vanity Fair, Three Wise Fools, The Day of Faith* 1923; *Wine of Youth, Sinners in Silk, The Turmoil, The Silent Accuser, So This Is Marriage, The Wife of the Centaur* 1924; *The Way of a Girl, Proud Flesh, Exchange of Wives, The Only Thing, The Circle* 1925; *Memory Lane, The Auction Block, Bardelys the Magnificent, Tell It to the Marines* 1926; *The Crowd, Diamond Handcuffs* 1928; *She Goes to War* 1929; *Mamba, Redemption* 1930; *The Great Meadow, The Flood, Women Love Once, The Squaw Man* 1931; *The Phantom President* 1932; *The Big Chance* 1933.

Bochner, Hart. Actor. Born on December 3, 1956, in Toronto, the son of actor Lloyd Bochner. *ed.* University of California, San Diego (English). Smoldering actor usually appearing as a romantic lead. He made his film debut at 20 opposite George C. Scott in the film adaptation of Hemingway's *Islands in the Stream*, but is best remembered for the TV miniseries 'War and Remembrance' and his role as a cowardly suit in *Die Hard*.

FILMS INCLUDE: *Islands in the Stream* 1976; *Breaking Away* 1979; *Terror Train* 1980; *Rich and Famous* 1981; *Supergirl, The Wild Life* 1984; *Making Mr. Right* 1987; *Apartment Zero, Die Hard, Teach 109* (short) 1988; *Fellow Traveller* 1989; *Mr. Destiny* 1990; *The Innocent* 1993; *PCU* (dir.) 1994; *High School High* (dir.) 1996.

Bode, Ralf D. American director of photography. Born in Berlin, Germany. *ed.* U. of Vermont, Yale. Having trained as an actor and director at Yale, he acquired field experience as a cinematographer for the US Army. He began his feature film career as a gaffer and lighting designer for director John G. Avildsen, making his debut as a lighting cameraman in the mid-70s. He quickly developed into one of Hollywood's most proficient and reliable cinematographers.

FILMS INCLUDE: *Foreplay* 1975; *Rocky* (2nd-unit phot.) 1976; *Saturday Night Fever* 1977; *Moment by Moment* (tech. adv.), *Slow Dancing in the Big City* 1978; *Rich Kids* 1979; *Coal Miner's Daughter, Dressed to Kill* 1980; *Raggedy Man* 1981; *A Little Sex* 1982; *Gorky Park* 1983; *Firstborn* 1984; *Violets Are Blue* 1986; *The Big Town, Critical Condition* 1987; *The Accused, Distant Thunder* 1988; *Cousins, Uncle Buck, The Long Way Home* 1989; *One Good Cop* 1991.

Bodeen, DeWitt. Screenwriter. *b.* July 25, 1908, Fresno, Calif. *d.* 1988. *ed.* UCLA. A former stage actor and occasionally a playwright, he was active in Hollywood as a story and screenwriter in the 40s. His later film collaborations were sporadic, but he wrote several books about film and screen personalities and contributed frequently to film periodicals.

FILMS INCLUDE: *Cat People* 1942; *The Seventh Victim* 1943; *The Curse of the Cat People, The Yellow Canary* 1944; *The Enchanted Cottage* 1945; *I Remember Mama* 1948; *Mrs. Mike* 1950; *The Girl in the Kremlin* (co-story) 1957; *12 to the Moon* 1960; *Billy Budd* (UK) 1962.

body frame. A metal bracket used to secure a hand-held camera to the operator's body during filming.

body makeup artist. According to Hollywood union regulations, the ordinary makeup artist, is allowed to apply cosmetics only from the top of the head to the apex of the breastbone and from the tips of the fingers to the elbows. All other areas of the body are the province of the body makeup artist.

Boehm, Karl Heinz (Karlheinz Böhm). Actor. Born on Mar. 16, 1927, in Darmstadt, Germany, the son of noted conductor Karl Boehm. *ed.* U. of Graz (philosophy). After pursuing a stage career, he made his film debut in 1952. He has appeared in German, Austrian, Italian, French, British, and American films, usually playing (with the exception of Mark Lewis in *Peeping Tom*) clean-cut, intelligent romantic leads. Became popular in the saccharine "Sissi" series opposite Romy SCHNEIDER, filmed in Austria.

FILMS INCLUDE: *Haus des Lebens* (Ger.), *Alraune* (Ger.) 1952; *Salto Mortale* (Ger.) 1953; *Die Hexe* (Ger.), *Die*

Goldene Pest/The Golden Plague (Ger.) 1954; *Sissi* (Aus.) 1956; *Sissi—die junge Kaiserin* (Aus.) 1957; *Sissi—Schicksalsjahre einer Kaiserin* (Aus). (Note: the three last films were re-cut, condensed into one, and released in the US in 1962 as *Forever My Love.* Boehm played the role of Emperor Franz Josef.), *Das Dreimäderlhaus/The House of the Three Girls* (as Franz Schubert; Ger.), *Le Passager clandestin* (Fr.) 1958; *Kriegsgericht/Court Martial* (Ger.), *La Paloma* (Ger.) 1959; *Peeping Tom* (UK), *Too Hot to Handle* (UK) 1960; *The Magnificent Rebel* (as Ludwig van Beethoven; made for US TV but released theatrically in Europe), *The Four Horsemen of the Apocalypse* (US), *The Wonderful World of the Brothers Grimm* (as Jacob Grimm; US), *La Croix des Vivants/Cross of the Living* (Fr.) 1962; *Rififi à Tokyo/Rififi in Tokyo* (Fr./It.), *Come Fly With Me* (US/UK) 1963; *The Venetian Affair* (US) 1967; *Effi Briest* 1974; *Faustrecht der Freiheit/Fox and His Friends* (Ger.), *Mother Kusters Goes to Heaven* 1975.

Boehm, Sydney. Screenwriter. *b.* Apr. 4, 1908, Philadelphia. *d.* 1990. *ed.* Lehigh. After working as a reporter for a newspaper and a wire service, he started writing for the screen in 1947. He won the Mystery Writers of America's Edgar Allan Poe Award for his screenplay of *The Big Heat* (1953). He later produced several motion pictures.

FILMS INCLUDE: *High Wall* 1948; *The Undercover Man, Side Street* 1949; *Mystery Street, Union Station* 1950; *When Worlds Collide* 1951; *The Atomic City, The Savage* 1952; *The Big Heat, Six Bridges to Cross* 1953; *The Raid, Rogue Cop, Black Tuesday* 1954; *Violent Saturday, The Tall Men* 1955; *Hell on Frisco Bay, The Bottom of the Bottle, The Revolt of Mamie Stover* 1956; *Harry Black and the Tiger* 1958; *A Woman Obsessed* (also prod.), *Seven Thieves* (also prod.) 1959; *One Foot in Hell* (also prod.) 1960; *Shock Treatment* 1964; *Sylvia* 1965; *Rough Night in Jericho* 1967.

Boetticher, Budd. Director. Born Oscar Boetticher, Jr., on July 29, 1916, in Chicago. *ed.* Ohio State. A varsity boxer and football player, he went to Mexico in the mid-30s, where he became a professional matador. Entered films through the "back door" as technical adviser on Mamoulian's *Blood and Sand* (1941) and stayed in Hollywood as a messenger, then assistant director on a number of productions. Made his debut as director in 1944 and for the next six years turned out routine low-budget pictures. His first important film was the semiautobiographical *The Bullfighter and the Lady* (1951). Then came more routine B pictures, and another bullfighting film, *The Magnificent Matador* 1965.

Between 1956 and 1960, Boetticher directed a cycle of Westerns that were to secure for him an enthusiastic following among connoisseurs of the genre both here and abroad. These films usually were produced by Harry Joe BROWN, written with Burt KENNEDY, and starred Randolph SCOTT, Brown's business partner. They were made on a medium budget and were commercially successful. The films are masculine affairs, involving confrontations between male antagonists constantly at odds with their world and always ready to deal with expected treachery. In 1960, Boetticher ventured into the gangster's world with his *The Rise and Fall of Legs Diamond,* a film called by critic Andrew Sarris "a minor classic."

That same year, just as he was becoming recognized and financially secure, Boetticher left Hollywood for Mexico with his Rolls-Royce and a beautiful wife to film a documentary about the career of a close friend, the great matador Carlos Arruza. Boetticher did not return to Hollywood for seven years. He tells the incredible story of this harrowing period in his book *When in Disgrace.* Obsessed with his documentary, he had turned down profitable Hollywood offers and suffered humiliation and despair to stay with his project—he had run out of money, divorced, spent seven days in jail and another week in an insane asylum, and nearly died, first of starvation and later of a severe lung ailment. In the meantime, Arruza, the hero of his film, was killed in an automobile accident, as was most of Boetticher's film crew. After returning to Hollywood in 1967, Boetticher began a new business association with Audie MURPHY. Murphy produced and Boetticher wrote and directed in Spain *A Time for Dying,* a film they hoped would rejuvenate both their careers. They had other projects in the planning stage when Murphy was killed in a plane crash in 1971. Boetticher wrote the story for Don Siegel's *Two Mules for Sister Sara* (1970). He appeared as an actor in *Tequila Sunrise* (1988).

FILMS: As Oscar Boetticher—*One Mysterious Night, The Missing Juror* 1944; *Youth on Trial, A Guy a Gal and a Pal, Escape in the Fog* 1945; *The Fleet That Came to Stay* 1946 (and other propaganda films made during his military service, 1946–47); *Assigned to Danger, Behind Locked Doors* 1948; *Black Midnight, Wolf Hunters* 1949; *Killer Shark* 1950. As Budd Boetticher—*The Bullfighter and the Lady* (also co-story), *The Sword of d'Artagnan, The Cimarron Kid* 1951; *Bronco Buster, Red Ball Express, Horizons West* 1952; *City Beneath the Sea, Seminole, The Man From the Alamo, Wings of the Hawk, East of Sumatra* 1953; *The Magnificent Matador* (also story) 1955; *The Killer Is Loose, Seven Men From Now* 1956; *The Tall T, Decision at Sundown* 1957; *Buchanan Rides Alone* 1958; *Ride Lonesome* (also prod.), *Westbound* 1959; *Comanche Station* (also prod.), *The Rise and Fall of Legs Diamond* 1960; *A Time for Dying* (also sc; release delayed from 1969), *Arruza* (doc.; also prod., co-sc.; release delayed from 1968) 1971; *My Kingdom For. . .* (doc., also sc.) 1985; *Tequila Sunrise* (act. only) 1988.

Bogarde, Dirk. Actor. Born Derek Jules Gaspard Ulric Niven van den Bogaerde, on Mar. 28, 1921, in London. *ed.* University Coll., Glasgow. The son of a Dutch-born art editor for the London *Times,* he worked as a scenic designer and commercial artist while studying acting. He made his debut at a small theater in 1939, and in that year appeared as an extra in the George Formby screen comedy *Come on George,* but it wasn't until he returned from WW II service that his stage career began in earnest. He was spotted in a London production and signed by the Rank studios on a film contract. After a slow start, his popularity picked up rapidly, and he played progressively more important roles in a wide range of films, from thrillers and comedies to costume melodramas. A subtle and sensitive actor, he was able to demonstrate a convincing versatility in many mediocre productions and was finally rewarded in the 1960s with complex roles that permitted him to display his talent, notably as a homosexual in distress in Basil DEARDEN's *Victim* (1961) and as a decadent valet in Joseph LOSEY's *The Servant* (1963). He won the British Film Academy Award as best British actor for the latter and for the subsequent *Darling* (1965). From the late 60s through the late 70s he starred in international productions. He surpassed all his previous accomplishments early in the 70s with a superb character portrayal in VISCONTI's *Death in Venice* (1971). In the late 70s he turned to writing. Memoirs: *A Postillion Struck by Lightning* (1977); *Snakes and Ladders* (1978); *An Orderly Man* (1983). Novels: *A Gentle Occupation* (1980); *Voices in the Garden* (1981); *West of Sunset* (1984). In 1990 he returned to the screen after a 12-year absence.

FILMS: *Come on George* (extra) 1939; *Dancing with Crime* (bit) 1947; *Esther Waters, Quartet, Once a Jolly Swagman* 1948; *Dear Mr. Prohack, Boys in Brown* 1949; *The Blue Lamp, So Long at the Fair, The Woman in Question* 1950; *Blackmailed* 1951; *Hunted/The Stranger in Between, Penny*

Princess, The Gentle Gunman 1952; *Appointment in London, Desperate Moment, They Who Dare* 1953; *Doctor in the House, The Sleeping Tiger, For Better for Worse, The Sea Shall Not Have Them* 1954; *Simba, Doctor at Sea, Cast a Dark Shadow* 1955; *The Spanish Gardener* 1956; *Ill Met by Moonlight/Night Ambush, Doctor at Large, Campbell's Kingdom* 1957; *A Tale of Two Cities* (as Sydney Carton), *The Wind Cannot Read* 1958; *The Doctor's Dilemma, Libel* 1959; *Song Without End* (as Franz Liszt; US), *La Sposa Bella/The Angel Wore Red* (It./US) 1960; *The Singer Not the Song, Victim* 1961; *H.M.S. Defiant/Damn the Defiant!, The Password Is Courage, We Joined the Navy* (cameo) 1962; *The Mind Benders, I Could Go On Singing, Doctor in Distress, The Servant* 1963; *Hot Enough for June/Agent 8¾, King and Country* 1964; *The High Bright Sun/McGuire Go Home!, Darling* 1965; *Modesty Blaise* 1966; *Accident, Our Mother's House* (UK/US) 1967; *Sebastian, The Fixer* (US, filmed in Hungary) 1968; *Oh! What a Lovely War, Justine* (US), *La Caduta degli Dei/Gotterdämmerung/The Damned* (It./Ger./Switz.) 1969; *Upon This Rock* (as Bonnie Prince Charlie; made for US TV; released theatrically in Europe) 1970; *Morte a Venezia/Death in Venice* (It./Fr.) 1971; *Le Serpent/The Serpent* (Fr./Ger.) 1973; *Il Portiere di Notte/The Night Porter* (It.) 1974; *Vollmacht zum Mord/Permission to Kill* (UK/Aus.) 1975; *Providence* (Fr.), *A Bridge Too Far* 1977; *Despair* (Ger.) 1978; *Daddy Nostalgie* (Fr.) 1990.

Bogart, Humphrey. Actor. Humphrey DeForest Bogart, *b.* Jan. 23, 1899, New York City. *d.* 1957. The son of a noted Manhattan surgeon and a successful magazine illustrator, he was sent to the Phillips Academy in Andover, Mass., in preparation for medical studies at Yale, but met with disciplinary problems and was expelled. When the US entered WW I, he joined the Navy. It was on board the vessel *Leviathan,* during a shelling, that he acquired the scarred and partly paralyzed upper lip that later accounted for his tight-set mouth and characteristic lisp.

After his discharge, Bogart approached a friend of the family, producer William A. Brady, for employment in the theater. He started out as an office boy and worked his way up to road company manager and stage manager. He also performed various chores at Brady's New York film studio, World Film Corporation. In 1920, while on the road, Bogart decided to switch to acting and for a while found the going rough. In a much-quoted Alexander Woollcott review of the play 'Swiftly' (1922), Bogart's acting is referred to as "what is usually and mercifully described as inadequate." But he went on to play indifferent stage roles, mostly romantic or callow juveniles, throughout the 20s.

Bogart took his first excursion to Hollywood in 1930, making his film debut in a ten-minute short, *Broadway's Like That.* He then played a succession of bland second-lead roles in feature films for Fox, Universal, Columbia, and other production companies. Dissatisfied, he kept shuttling to Broadway for additional stage roles. The year 1935 provided Bogart with his first important break, when he was cast as the baleful gangster Duke Mantee in the Broadway production of Robert E. Sherwood's 'The Petrified Forest.' Leslie Howard played the lead role of Alan Squier. When Warner Bros. acquired the film rights to the play and intended casting Edward G. Robinson in the Mantee role, Howard threatened to withdraw unless the role was given to Bogart. The studio gave in, *The Petrified Forest* (1936) proved a tremendous success, and Bogart was on his way to stardom.

The following five years were an intermediate stage in Bogart's career. Between 1936 and 1940 he appeared in no less than 28 feature films, mostly in standard gangster parts, often as the villain. He also appeared in two Westerns. Another turning point was 1941, the beginning of the "Bogey" legend. A screenwriter by the name of John HUSTON provided the impetus, with the script of *High Sierra* (in collaboration with W. R. Burnett), in which Bogart gave a remarkable performance as a gangster with soul. Later that year Huston, in his debut as a director, guided Bogart into his tour de force as the ruthless private eye Sam Spade in the excellent thriller *The Maltese Falcon.*

Bogart sustained a peak of popularity through such films as *Casablanca, The Big Sleep,* and *Key Largo.* On the set of *To Have and Have Not* he met and fell in love with—and later married—his co-star Lauren BACALL (his fourth wife; the other three, also actresses, had been Helen Menken, Mary Philips, and Mayo Methot). In 1947 he formed his own company, Santana Pictures, and in the following year he played one of his most memorable parts, again under the direction of Huston, as the greedy, paranoid prospector in *The Treasure of the Sierra Madre.* The 50s saw him extend his acting range as he had never done before with widely diverse roles in such films as *In a Lonely Place, The African Queen, The Caine Mutiny, Sabrina,* and *The Barefoot Contessa.* He won the Academy Award for his captivating performance in *The African Queen.* Shortly after the release of his last film, *The Harder They Fall,* in March 1956, Bogart underwent an operation for cancer of the esophagus. He died in his sleep at his Hollywood home on January 14, 1957.

The lonely, self-reliant, brooding, sardonic, skeptical, and cynical image of Bogart was resurrected in the 60s by millions of fans the world over and is still celebrated in a huge "Bogey" cult in the form of posters and retrospective film festivals. An unlikely movie star but a very credible antihero, he left a lasting mark on film history.

FILMS: *Broadway's Like That* (short), *A Devil with Women, Up the River* 1930; *Body and Soul, Bad Sister, Women of All Nations, A Holy Terror* 1931; *Love Affair, Big City Blues, Three on a Match* 1932; *Midnight* 1934; *The Petrified Forest, Bullets or Ballots, Two Against the World, China Clipper, Isle of Fury* 1936; *Black Legion, The Great O'Malley, Marked Woman, Kid Galahad, San Quentin, Dead End, Stand-In* 1937; *Swing Your Lady, Crime School, Men Are Such Fools, The Amazing Dr. Clitterhouse, Racket Busters, Angels with Dirty Faces* 1938; *King of the Underworld, The Oklahoma Kid, Dark Victory, You Can't Get Away with Murder, The Roaring Twenties, The Return of Doctor X, Invisible Stripes* 1939; *Virginia City, It All Came True, Brother Orchid, They Drive by Night* 1940; *High Sierra, The Wagons Roll at Night, The Maltese Falcon* 1941; *All Through the Night, The Big Shot, In This Our Life* (cameo), *Across the Pacific* 1942; *Casablanca, Action in the North Atlantic, Thank Your Lucky Stars, Sahara* 1943; *Passage to Marseille* 1944; *To Have and Have Not, Conflict* 1945; *Two Guys From Milwaukee* (cameo), *The Big Sleep* 1946; *Dead Reckoning, The Two Mrs. Carrolls, Dark Passage* 1947; *Always Together* (cameo), *The Treasure of the Sierra Madre, Key Largo* 1948; *It's a Great Feeling* (cameo), *Knock on Any Door, Tokyo Joe* 1949; *Chain Lightning, In a Lonely Place* 1950; *The Enforcer, Sirocco, The African Queen* 1951; *Road to Bali* (cameo), *Deadline—U.S.A.* 1952; *Love Lottery* (cameo), *Battle Circus* 1953; *Beat the Devil, The Caine Mutiny, Sabrina, The Barefoot Contessa* 1954; *We're No Angels, The Left Hand of God, The Desperate Hours* 1955; *The Harder They Fall* 1956.

Bogart, Paul. Director. Born on Nov. 21, 1919 in New York City. After WW II service with the USAAF, he entered show business in 1946 as a puppeteer-actor with the Berkeley Marionettes. In 1950 he joined NBC-TV as a stage manager and associate director. Two years later he became a freelance director and subsequently turned out scores of dramas, comedies, specials, and series segments, winning a number of awards in the process. His prolific TV work overshadowed his motion picture output, which began in the late 60s.

FILMS: *Marlowe* 1969; *Halls of Anger* 1970; *Skin Game* 1971; *Cancel My Reservation* 1972; *Class of '44* (also prod.) 1973; *Mr. Ricco* 1975; *The Three Sisters* 1977; *Oh God! You Devil* 1984; *Torch Song Trilogy* 1988; *The Sparrow* 1990.

Bogdanovich, Peter. Director, producer, screenwriter. Born on July 30, 1939, in Kingston, N.Y. Studied acting with Stella Adler and made several appearances with the American and the New York Shakespeare festivals. From 1959 directed plays off Broadway and in summer stock. In the early 60s wrote monographs of film directors for the Museum of Modern Art and later published books on the film work of Fritz Lang, John Ford, Allan Dwan, and Orson Welles, and wrote articles on film for *Esquire.* In 1966 he entered films as an assistant director and uncredited second-unit director and screenwriter on Roger Corman's *The Wild Angels.* He then directed additional sequences for a cheap Russian import titled here *Voyage to the Planet of Prehistoric Women,* and in 1968 he piloted his first movie, *Targets,* starring Boris Karloff. His next project, the documentary *Directed by John Ford,* was an American entry at the 1971 Venice Film Festival. The following year Bogdanovich made a big splash with audiences and critics alike with *The Last Picture Show,* a nostalgic black-and-white look at small-town America of the 50s.

An unabashed sentimentalist about things past and a film buff, Bogdanovich sees himself as the keeper of the flame kindled by such veteran Hollywood directors as HAWKS and FORD and initially felt little affinity with the new generation of American directors who emphasize camera technique over theme and atmosphere. In *What's Up Doc?* he tried to capture the zing of Hawk's madcap comedies of the 30s, and *Paper Moon* was to an extent a stab at reviving Ford's vision of rural America.

He was less successful with *Daisy Miller* and *At Long Last Love,* films he made as showcase vehicles for Cybill SHEPHERD, a former model who had become a personal as well as a professional favorite of Bogdanovich. They lived together following his legal separation from screenwriter-art director Polly PLATT, who designed the sets for his early films. Several of Bogdanovich's films were produced by The Directors' Company, a joint venture he created in partnership with two other *wunderkinder* of the new American cinema, William FRIEDKIN and Francis Ford COPPOLA. In 1976, Bogdanovich suffered a third flop in a row with *Nickelodeon,* a comedy about the cinema's silent era that was panned by most critics as an empty exercise in stylistics and virtually ignored by the ticket-buying public.

Bogdanovich enjoyed a mild comeback with *Saint Jack* (1979), an absorbing character study of a Singapore pimp in which the director himself appeared as a supporting player. But he suffered another setback with *They All Laughed* (1981), a film he was forced to distribute through his own Moon company, with disastrous commercial consequences. The financial debacle was accompanied by personal tragedy when Dorothy Stratten, a former Playboy Playmate of the Year and Bogdanovich's mistress, was gunned down by her jealous husband after completing a featured role in the film. The director paid her a loving tribute in his book *The Killing of the Unicorn: Dorothy Stratten 1960–1980* (1984). He married her younger half-sister, Louise Hoogstraten. During that time he also prepared a monograph of D. W. Griffith. Several years passed before Bogdanovich returned to filmmaking, with *Mask* (1985), a tender, moving portrait of a disfigured youth. It earned Cher, who played the youth's mother, a best actress prize at Cannes and went a long way toward resurrecting Bogdanovich's reputation as a leading American director. In 1986 he reorganized his company as Crescent Moon Productions. His *Texasville* (1990) was a disappointing sequel to *The Last Picture Show.* Author: *The Cinema of Orson Welles* (1961); *The Cinema of Howard Hawks* (1962); *The Cinema of Alfred Hitchcock* (1963); *Fritz Lang in America* (1967, revised 1981); *John Ford* (1968, revised 1978); *Allan Dwan: The Last Pioneer* (1971, revised 1981); *Pieces of Time* (1973, revised 1985); *The Killing of the Unicorn* (1984).

FILMS (as director-producer): *Voyage to the Planet of Prehistoric Women* (dir. addnl. sequences only) 1965; *Targets* (also sc.) 1968; *Directed by John Ford* (doc.; also sc.), *The Last Picture Show* (dir., co-sc. only) 1971; *What's Up Doc?* (also story) 1972; *Paper Moon* 1973; *Daisy Miller* 1974; *At Long Last Love* (also sc.) 1975; *Nickelodeon* (dir., co-sc. only) 1976; *Saint Jack* (dir. co-sc. only) 1979; *They All Laughed* (dir., sc. only) 1981; *The City Girl* (exec. prod. only) 1984; *Mask* (dir. only) 1985; *Illegally Yours* 1988; *Texasville* (also sc.) 1990; *The Thing Called Love* 1993; *The Substance of Fire* 1996.

Bogosian, Eric. Performance artist, actor, playwright, screenwriter. Born in 1953 in Woburn, Mass. *ed.* University of Chicago; Oberlin College, Ohio (drama). Archetypal New York one-man show who made his name on and off Broadway in a series of canny monologue plays that dissect 80s and 90s culture, including 'Funhouse,' 'Talk Radio,' and 'Sex, Drugs, Rock & Roll.' Appearing first in alternative films, he entered mainstream movies in director Oliver Stone's film version of *Talk Radio*, playing gonzo radio deejay Barry Champlain.

FILMS INCLUDE: *Born in Flames* (act.) 1982; *Special Effects* (act.) 1985; *Arena Brains* (short; act., sc.) 1987; *Talk Radio* (act., co-sc. with Oliver Stone) 1988; *Suffering Bastards* (act.) 1989; *Last Flight Out: A True Story* 1990; *Sex, Drugs, Rock & Roll* (act., sc.) 1991; *The Lion King* (v/o) 1994; *Arabian Knight, Dolores Claiborne, Under Siege 2: Dark Territory* 1995; *SubUrbia* (sc. only) 1997.

Böhm, Karlheinz. See BOEHM, Karl Heinz.

Bohringer, Richard. Actor. Born in 1942, in Paris, of Alsatian origin. Curly-haired leading player of French films of the 80s. He first became known internationally for his role in *Diva* (1981); he won Césars as best supporting actor for *L'Addition* (1984) and *Le Grand Chemin/The Grand Highway* (1987).

FILMS INCLUDE: *Le Dernier Métro/The Last Metro* 1980; *Diva, Les Uns et les autres/Bolero* 1981; *J'ai épousé une Ombre/I Married a Shadow* 1983; *L'Addition* 1984; *Péril en la Demeure/Peril/Death in a French Garden, Subway* 1985; *Le Paltoquet, Kamikaze* 1986; *Le Grand Chemin/The Grand Highway* 1987; *Les Saisons du Plaisir/The Seasons of Pleasure* 1988; *Aprés la Guerre* 1989; *The Cook the Thief His Wife and Her Lover, Marat* 1989; *Dames Galantes, Stan the Flasher* 1990.

Boisrond, Michel. Director. Born on Oct. 9, 1921, in Chateauneuf, France. After a long apprenticeship with such directors as Jean DELANNOY, Jean COCTEAU, and René CLAIR (he directed the second unit on the latter's *Les Grandes Manoeuvres*), he made his directorial debut in 1955 with the Brigitte Bardot comedy *Cette Sacrée Gamine.* He is considered a technically competent, always dependable director, with a sense of humor that sometimes borders on the vulgar.

FILMS: *Cette Sacrée Gamine/Mam'zelle Pigalle, C'est arrivé à Aden, Lorsque l'Enfant paraît* 1956; *Une Parisienne* 1957; *Faibles Femmes/Women Are Weak, Le Chemin des Ecoliers, Voulez-vous danser avec moi?/Come Dance With Me!* 1959; *La Française et l'Amour/Love and the French-woman*

("Virginity" episode) 1960; *Un Soir sur la Plage, Les Amours célèbres* 1961; *Les Parisiennes/Tales of Paris* ("The Tale of Antonia" episode), *Comment réussir en Amour* 1962; *Comment trouvez-vous ma Soeur?* 1963; *Cherche l'Idole, Comment epouser un Premier Ministre* 1964; *Atout Coeur à Tokyo pour OSS 117* 1966; *L'Homme qui valait des Milliards* 1968; *La Leçon particulière/The Tender Moment* 1969; *Du Soleil plein les Yeux* 1970; *On est toujours trop bon avec les Femmes* 1971; *Le Petit Poucet/Tom Thumb* 1972; *Dis-moi que tu m'aime* 1974; *Catherine & Cie./Catherine & Co.* 1975.

Boisset, Yves. Director. Born on Mar. 14, 1939, in Paris. A graduate of IDHEC, he worked as an assistant director to Robert HOSSEIN, Yves CIAMPI, and René CLÉMENT, among others, and directed several shorts before making his debut as a feature director in the late 60s. He quickly became recognized as a sure-handed filmmaker with a special knack for action-packed political and social thrillers. He usually collaborates on his own scripts.

FEATURE FILMS: *Coplan sauve sa Peau* 1968; *Cran d'Arret, Un Condé/The Cop* 1970; *Le Saut de l'Ange* 1971; *L'Attentat/The French Conspiracy* 1972; *R.A.S.* 1973; *Une Folle à tuer, Dupont la Joie/Rape of Innocence* 1975; *Le Juge Fayard dit le Sheriff, Un Taxi mauve/The Purple Taxi* 1977; *La Clé sur la Porte* 1978; *La Femme Flic* 1980; *Alloms z'Enfanats* 1981; *Espion lève-toi* 1982; *Le Prix du Danger* 1983; *Canicule/Dog Day* 1984; *Bleu comme l'Enfer* 1986; *Radio Corbeau* (also sc. adapt.) 1988; *La Travéstie* (also sc.) 1989; *Double Identity, La Tribu* (also sc. adapt.) 1991; *Le Nuit de Herrison* 1993; *The Dreyfuss Affair* 1994.

Boland, Mary. Actress. *b.* Jan. 28, 1880, Philadelphia. *d.* 1965. Convent-educated in Detroit. She followed her father's example and began acting in stock while still in her teens. She made her Broadway debut in 1905 and for a while excelled as a tragedienne, both on the stage and in early silent films. But it was as a comedienne that she would become famous in the theater of the 20s and in Hollywood films of the 30s, portraying with delectable abandon madcap wives and mothers of the scatterbrain variety, memorably opposite Charlie RUGGLES in *Ruggles of Red Gap* (1935) and in other films.

FILMS INCLUDE: *The Edge of the Abyss* 1915; *The Price of Happiness, The Stepping Stone* 1916; *Mountain Dew* 1917; *The Prodigal Wife* 1918; *The Perfect Lover* 1919; *His Temporary Wife* 1920; *Secrets of a Secretary* 1931; *The Night of June 13th, Evenings for Sale, Trouble in Paradise, If I Had a Million* 1932; *Mama Loves Papa, Three-Cornered Moon, The Solitaire Man* 1933; *Four Frightened People, Six of a Kind, Melody in Spring, Stingaree, Here Comes the Groom, Down to Their Last Yacht, The Pursuit of Happiness* 1934; *Ruggles of Red Gap, People Will Talk, The Big Broadcast of 1936, Two for Tonight* 1935; *Early to Bed, A Son Comes Home, Wives Never Know, College Holiday* 1936; *Marry the Girl, Danger—Love at Work, There Goes the Groom 1937*; *Artists and Models Abroad, Little Tough Guys in Society* 1938; *The Magnificent Fraud, The Women, Night Work* 1939; *He Married His Wife, New Moon, Pride and Prejudice* 1940; *In Our Time* 1944; *Nothing but Trouble* 1945; *Julia Misbehaves* 1948; *Guilty Bystander* 1950.

Boles, John. Actor. *b.* Oct. 27, 1895, Greenville, Tex. *d.* 1969. The son of a banker. He attended the University of Texas with the intention of studying medicine but became involved in theatrical activity on campus and decided on a stage career. After WW I service, which involved espionage activities in Germany, Bulgaria, and Turkey, he took voice lessons in New York and Paris and began a professional acting and singing career that culminated in the mid-20s on Broadway and in silent films. In Hollywood he rapidly developed into a popular romantic leading man. The demand for his services increased with the advent of sound, when his good looks were enhanced by his rich speaking and singing voice. Through the early 40s he kept busy playing a variety of leads in dramas, romantic comedies, and musical films.

FILMS INCLUDE: *So This Is Marriage* 1924; *Excuse Me* 1925; *The Love of Sunya* 1927; *The Shepherd of the Hills, We Americans, Fazil, Virgin Lips, Romance of the Underworld* 1928; *The Last Warning, The Desert Song, Scandal, Rio Rita* 1929; *Song of the West, Captain of the Guard, The King of Jazz* 1930; *One Heavenly Night, Resurrection, Seed, Frankenstein, Good Sport* 1931; *Careless Lady, Back Street, Six Hours to Live* 1932; *Child of Manhattan, My Lips Betray, Only Yesterday* 1933; *Beloved, Bottoms Up, I Believed in You, Stand Up and Cheer, The Life of Vergie Winters, Wild Gold, The Age of Innocence, The White Parade, Music in the Air* 1934; *Curly Top, Orchids to You, The Littlest Rebel* 1935; *Rose of the Rancho, A Message to Garcia, Craig's Wife* 1936; *As Good As Married, Stella Dallas, Fight for Your Lady* 1937; *She Married an Artist, Romance in the Dark, Sinners in Paradise* 1938; *Road to Happiness* 1941; *Between Us Girls* 1942; *Thousands Cheer* 1943; *Babes in Bagdad* 1952.

Boleslawski (also **Boleslawsky**), **Richard.** Director. *b.* Ryszard Srzednicki Boleslawsky, Feb. 4, 1889, Warsaw. *d.* 1937. *ed.* U. of Odessa. A stage actor from age 16, he studied and performed under Stanislavsky at the Moscow Art Theater. In 1914 he began appearing in Russian films and the following year made his debut as director. In 1918 he co-directed and acted in the Bolshevik propaganda film *Bread,* but in 1919 he returned to Poland to fight against the Bolsheviks as a cavalry officer. He was put in charge of the motion picture coverage of the Polish army campaigns and in 1920 compiled the film footage into a semidocumentary, *The Miracle of the Vistula.* The following year he went to Germany to act in Carl Dreyer's film *Die Gezeichneten/Love One Another* (1922) and after a stopover in France sailed for the US. Here he quickly became established as a successful director of Broadway plays and musicals and headed the Laboratory Theater, an experimental group.

In 1929 he joined the Broadway hegira to Hollywood with the advent of the talkies and within a year had moved up from dialogue director to feature film director. He directed a number of minor productions at Columbia and RKO before replacing Charles Brabin at the helm of MGM's prestigious *Rasputin and the Empress,* which starred the three famous Barrymores. At MGM, and later also at Fox, Boleslawski became associated with elegant, commercially attractive productions, notably an elaborate version of *Les Misérables,* starring Charles Laughton and Fredric March; the effervescent, sophisticated comedy *Theodora Goes Wild,* with Irene Dunne and Melvyn Douglas; and the exotic *The Garden of Allah,* with Marlene Dietrich and Charles Boyer. He died suddenly at 48 during the production of *The Last of Mrs. Cheyney* and the film was completed by George Fitzmaurice. Boleslawski was the author of *Six Lessons of Dramatic Art,* an analysis of the Stanislavsky method of acting, and of two autobiographical novels, which dealt with the East European phase of his life.

FILMS: In Russia—*Three Meetings* 1915; *Bread* (co-dir. with Boris Sukevich) 1918. In Poland—*Bohaterstwo Polskiego Skavto* 1919; *The Miracle of the Vistula* 1920. In the US—*Treasure Girl* (short), *The Grand Parade* (dir. musical numbers only), *The Last of the Lone Wolf* 1930; *The Gay Diplomat, Woman Pursued* 1931; *Rasputin and the Empress, Storm at Daybreak, Beauty for Sale* 1933; *Hollywood Party* (co-dir. with Allan Dwan and Roy Rowland, uncredited), *Fugitive Lovers, Men in White, Operator 13, The Painted Veil* 1934; *Clive of*

India, Les Misérables, O'Shaughnessy's Boy, Metropolitan 1935; *Three Godfathers, Theodora Goes Wild, The Garden of Allah* 1936; *The Last of Mrs. Cheyney* (completed by George Fitzmaurice) 1937.

Bolger, Ray. Actor, dancer. *b.* Raymond Wallace Bolger, Jan. 10, 1904, Dorchester, Mass. *d.* 1987. He was a bank clerk, vacuum-cleaner salesman, and accountant while taking dancing lessons and appearing in amateur shows. He made his professional debut in 1922 with a musical-comedy repertory company, touring small New England towns, and entered vaudeville in 1924, a dancing partner in "Sanford and Bolger, a Pair of Nifties." After several Broadway appearances, including 'George White's Scandals,' 'Life Begins at 8:40,' and 'On Your Toes,' he made his motion picture debut in *The Great Ziegfeld* (1936).

Bolger's acting, dancing, and comic talents were seldom used by Hollywood, although he will always be remembered for his part as the understuffed scarecrow in *The Wizard of Oz* and in the lead role of *Where's Charley?* (a musical version of 'Charley's Aunt,' in which he had also starred in a long-running Broadway production).

FILMS: *The Great Ziegfeld* 1936; *Rosalie* 1937; *Sweethearts* 1938; *The Wizard of Oz* 1939; *Sunny* 1941; *Four Jacks and a Jill* 1942; *Stage Door Canteen* 1943; *The Harvey Girls* 1946; *Make Mine Laughs, Look for the Silver Lining* 1949; *Where's Charley?* 1952; *April in Paris* 1953; *Babes in Toyland* 1961; *The Daydreamer* 1966; *The Entertainer* 1975; *Just You and Me Kid, The Runner Stumbles* 1979.

Bolkan, Florinda. Actress. Born Florinda Soares Bulcao, on Feb. 15, 1941, in Ceara, Brazil. The daughter of a poet-novelist who served in the national assembly and died when she was two and a half and an Indian mother, she banked on her proficiency in several languages to begin her working life in the public relations department of the Brazilian national airline in Rio. In 1965 she went to Paris, where she studied art at the Sorbonne for two years. During a vacation in Italy in 1967, she met Luchino VISCONTI, who recommended her to other directors, then gave her career a lift with the role of the prostitute in *The Damned* (1969). A tall, leggy brunette with an exquisitely etched face, she soon became a popular star in Europe and gained international prominence in the 70s with her performance in Vittorio DE SICA's *A Brief Vacation* (1973), in the role of a working wife whose view of life is transformed during a forced rest cure in the Italian Alps.

FILMS INCLUDE: *Candy* (US/Fr./It.), *Gli Intoccabili/Machine Gun MacCain, Metti una Sera a Cena/One Night at Dinner* 1968; *La Caduta degli Dei/Götterdämmerung/The Damned, Un Detective/Detective Belli* 1969; *Indagine su un Cittadino al di Sopra di ogni Sospetto/Investigation of a Citizen Above Suspicion* 1970; *The Last Valley, L'Anonimo Veneziano/The Anonymous Venetian, Una Lucertola con la Pelle di Donna/A Lizard in a Woman's Skin* 1971; *Incontro, Un Uomo da Rispettare/Hearts and Minds, Le Droit d'aimer/The Right to Love* 1972; *Una Breve Vacanza/A Brief Vacation* 1973; *Le Mouton enragé/Love at the Top/The French Way* (Fr.) 1974; *Royal Flash* (UK) 1975; *Assassination in Sarajevo/The Day That Shook the World* (Yug./Czech.) 1976; *Terrore, La Casa sul Lago* 1978; *Manaos* 1979; *Acqua e Sapone* 1984; *Some Girls* (US), *Prisoner of Rio* 1988.

Bologna, Joseph. Actor, screenwriter, playwright. Born on Dec. 30, 1936, in Brooklyn, N.Y. *ed.* Brown (art history). After a stint with the Marines, he directed and produced commercials for an advertising agency. With his wife (from 1965) and frequent collaborator, Renee Taylor (*b.* Mar. 19, 1945), he directed a short, *2*, that was shown at the 1966 New York Film Festival. They wrote and starred in the delightful Broadway comedy 'Lovers and Other Strangers' (1968), which they transferred successfully to the screen in 1970. They created and wrote the TV series 'Calucci's Dept.' and co-directed their first film in 1989.

FEATURE FILMS (as actor): *Lovers and Other Strangers* (co-sc. only, from own co-play) 1970; *Made for Each Other* (also co-sc.) 1971; *Cops and Robbers* 1973; *Mixed Company* 1974; *The Big Bus* 1976; *Chapter Two* 1979; *My Favorite Year* 1982; *Blame It on Rio, The Woman in Red* 1984; *Transylvania 6–5000* 1985; *It Had to Be You* (also co-dir., co-sc.) 1989; *Coupe De Ville* 1990; *Mutation* 1991; *Love Is All There Is* (also co-sc.) 1996.

Bolognini, Mauro. Director. Born on June 28, 1922, in Pistoia, Italy. *ed.* U. of Florence (architecture); Centro Sperimentale di Cinematografia (set design). He started out as an assistant director to Luigi ZAMPA and acquired additional experience in France, as assistant to Yves ALLÉGRET and Jean DELANNOY. A director since 1953, he first drew attention in international film circles with *Gli Innamorati/Wild Love* (1955). Many of his films have been commercially successful and several earned critical acceptance. He is a keen, optimistic observer of the Italian social scene but is sometimes guilty of stylistic self-indulgence. Several of his films were adapted from novels and scripts by PASOLINI. He shared an Award at Cannes for the screenplay of *Young Husbands* (1958).

FILMS: *Ci Troviamo in Galleria* 1953; *I Cavalieri della Regina* (also co-sc.) 1954; *La Vena d'Oro* (also co-sc.), *Gli Innamorati/Wild Love* 1955; *Guardia Guardia scelta Brigadiere e Maresciallo* 1956; *Marisa la Civetta* (also story, co-sc.) 1957; *Giovani Mariti/Young Husbands* (also co-sc.) 1958; *Arrangiatevi, La Notte Brava/On Any Street/Bad Girls Don't Cry* 1959; *Il Bell'Antonio, La Giornata balorda/From a Roman Balcony/A Crazy Day/Pickup in Rome* 1960; *La Viaccia/The Love Makers* 1961; *Senilità/Careless, Agostino* (also co-sc.) 1962; *La Corruzione* 1963; *La mia Signora* ("I miei Cari" and "Luciana" episodes), *La Donna è una cosa Meravigliosa* 1964; *Le Bambole/The Dolls* ("Monsignor Cupid" episode), *I Tre Volti* ("Amanti Celebri" episode), *Madamigella di Maupin* 1965; *Le Fate/The Queens* ("Queen Elena" episode) 1966; *Le Streghe/The Witches* ("Civic Sense" episode), *Le plus vieux Métier du Monde/The Oldest Profession* ("Roman Nights" episode; Fr./It./Ger.), *Arabella* 1967; *Capriccio all'Italiana* ("Perche?" and "La Gelosia" episodes), *Un Bellissimo Novembre/That Splendid November* 1968; *L'Assoluto Naturale* (also co-sc.) 1969; *Metello* (also co-sc.) 1970; *Bubù* (also co-sc.) 1971; *Imputazione di Omicidio per uno Studente* 1972; *Libera Amore Mio, Fatti di Gente Perbene/La Grande Bourgeoise* 1974; *Per le Antiche Scale/Down the Ancient Stairs* 1975; *Eredità Ferramonti* 1976; *La Signora degli Orrori/Black Journal, Gran Bolitto* 1977; *Dove vai in Vacanza?* ("Saro tutta per te" episode) 1978; *La Vera Storia della Signora delle Camelie/The True Story of Camille* (also co-prod., co-sc.) 1981; *Mosca Addio* 1987.

Bolt, Robert. Playwright, screenwriter, director. *b.* Aug. 15, 1924, in Sale, England. *d.* 1995. *ed.* Exeter; U. of Manchester. A former teacher. He had his first play produced on the London stage in 1958 and established a reputation two years later with 'A Man for All Seasons.' The play won the New York Drama Critics Award in 1962 and was made into an Academy Award–winning film in 1966. Bolt himself received an Oscar for the screenplay, his second in succession. He had won the award in 1965 for the screenplay of *Dr. Zhivago.* In 1972 he made his debut as a film director. He married actress Sarah MILES; he is the father of director Ben Bolt.

FILMS (as screenwriter): *Lawrence of Arabia* 1962; *Dr. Zhivago* 1965; *A Man for All Seasons* 1966; *Ryan's Daughter* 1970; *Lady Caroline Lamb* (also dir.) 1972; *The Bounty* 1984; *The Mission* 1986.

Bolton, Guy. Playwright, novelist, screenwriter. *b.* Nov. 23, 1885, Wilmington, Del. *d.* 1979. Studied architecture in London and Paris but turned to playwriting during WW I. Wrote numerous light plays and stage musicals alone or in collaboration with such writers as George Middleton, P. G. Wodehouse, Oscar Hammerstein II, and Fred Thompson. Among his plays or musicals are 'Leave It to Jane,' 'College Widow,' 'Lady Be Good,' 'Rio Rita,' 'Oh Kay!,' 'Girl Crazy,' 'Anything Goes,' and 'Anastasia.' He also wrote several novels and wrote and collaborated on many screenplays, both light and dramatic.

FILMS INCLUDE: Adapted by others from his plays, novels, or stories—*The Cave Girl* 1921; *Adam and Eva* 1923; *Sally, Secrets of the Night* (from 'The Nightcap'), *Wages for Wives* (from 'Chicken Feed') 1925; *Lady Be Good, Oh Kay!* 1928; *Sally* (remake), *Rio Rita* 1929; *The Cuckoos* (from 'The Ramblers'), *Top Speed* 1930; *Girl Crazy* 1932; *The Murder Man, The Dark Angel* 1935; *Rosalie* 1937; *Till the Clouds Roll By* 1946; *Words and Music* 1948; *Anything Goes, Anastasia* 1956. As screenwriter, alone or in collaboration—*Grounds for Divorce* (adapt.) 1925; *The Love Doctor* 1929; *The Love Parade* 1930; *The Lady Refuses, The Yellow Ticket, Transatlantic, Ambassador Bill, Delicious* 1931; *Careless Lady, The Devil's Lottery, The Woman in Room 13, The Painted Woman* 1932; *Pleasure Cruise* 1933; *The Lady Is Willing, Ladies Should Listen* 1934; *The Guv'nor/Mister Hobo* (UK), *The Morals of Marcus* 1935; *Week-End at the Waldorf* (adapt.) 1945; *Adorable Julia* (Aus./Fr.) 1962.

Bonanova, Fortunio. Actor, singer. *b.* Jan. 13, 1893, Palma de Mallorca, Spain. *d.* 1969. *ed.* Barcelona Inst.; U. of Madrid (law); Real Conservatory of Madrid; Paris Conservatory. At 17 he started his singing career as a baritone in Madrid, later appearing with the Paris Opera and touring Europe and Latin America. At 21 he produced, directed, and starred in the Spanish film *Don Juan.* He appeared on Broadway in 'Dishonored Lady' (1930) with Katharine Cornell, and made his US film debut in 1932. Memorable as the singing tutor in *Citizen Kane* (1941). He later played supporting, often comic, roles in many Hollywood films. He also wrote several operettas, five plays, and two novels.

FILMS INCLUDE: *Don Juan* (also prod., dir.; Sp.) 1924; *Careless Lady* 1932; *Tropic Holiday* 1938; *Citizen Kane, That Night in Rio, Blood and Sand* 1941; *Larceny Inc., The Black Swan* 1942; *For Whom the Bell Tolls, Five Graves to Cairo* 1943; *Ali Baba and the Forty Thieves, Mrs. Parkington, Double Indemnity, Going My Way* 1944; *A Bell for Adano* 1945; *Monsieur Beaucaire* 1946; *Fiesta, The Fugitive* 1947; *Adventures of Don Juan* 1948; *Whirlpool* 1949; *Nancy Goes to Rio* 1950; *September Affair* 1951; *The Moon Is Blue* 1953; *Kiss Me Deadly* 1955; *Jaguar* 1956; *An Affair to Remember* 1957; *Thunder in the Sun* 1959; *The Running Man* 1963.

Bond, Derek. Actor. Born on Jan. 26, 1919, in Glasgow, Scotland. Following a London stage debut in 1937, he served with the British Grenadier Guards in WW II and was awarded the Military Cross. Upon his release he was signed by the Rank organization and has since played leading roles in an assortment of British films. From 1984 to 1986 he served as president of British Actors Equity. He is the author of several books, including *Steady Old Man.*

FILMS INCLUDE: *The Captive Heart* 1946; *Nicholas Nickleby* (title role), *Uncle Silas, The Inheritance* 1947; *Broken Journey, The Weaker Sex* 1948; *Scott of the Antarctic, Christopher Columbus, Marry Me* 1949; *Tony Draws a Horse* 1950; *The Quiet Woman* 1951; *The Hour of 13, Distant Trumpet* 1952; *Trouble in Store* 1953; *Svengali* 1954; *The High Terrace* 1956; *Gideon's Day/Gideon of Scotland Yard 1958*; *The Hand* 1960; *Saturday Night Out* 1964; *Secrets of a Windmill Girl* 1965; *Press for Time* 1966; *When Eight Bells Toll* 1971; *Intimate Reflections* 1975; *Vanishing Army* 1976.

Bond, Ward. Actor. *b.* Apr. 9, 1903, Denver. *d.* 1960. He was a football player for the University of Southern California when John FORD selected him and fellow player John WAYNE to appear in an Annapolis film, *Salute* (1929). A three-way friendship developed between the director and the two young actors, who were cast as sidekicks in many of his films. Big and muscular, Bond appeared in supporting roles in some 200 films, sometimes as a brutal heavy, more often as a rugged but kind-hearted lawman or friend of the hero. He also played the starring role of the wagon master in the popular TV series 'Wagon Train.'

FILMS INCLUDE: *Salute, Words and Music* 1929; *Born Reckless, The Big Trail* 1930; *White Eagle* 1932; *Heroes for Sale, Unknown Valley* 1933; *The Poor Rich, It Happened One Night, Frontier Marshal, Here Comes the Groom, Broadway Bill, Fighting Rangers* 1934; *Devil Dogs of the Air, She Gets Her Man, Black Fury, Fighting Shadows* 1935; *Pride of the Marines, The Man Who Lived Twice, Legion of Terror* 1936; *Conflict, You Only Live Once, Night Key, Dead End* 1937; *The Amazing Dr. Clitterhouse, Submarine Patrol, Professor Beware, Gun Law* 1938; *Made for Each Other, Dodge City, Young Mr. Lincoln, Drums Along the Mohawk, The Oklahoma Kid, Gone With the Wind* 1939; *The Grapes of Wrath, The Long Voyage Home, Little Old New York, The Mortal Storm, Virginia City, Kit Carson, Santa Fe Trail* 1940; *Tobacco Road, Sergeant York, Manpower, The Shepherd of the Hills, The Maltese Falcon, Swamp Water* 1941; *Gentleman Jim* (as boxer John L. Sullivan), *Ten Gentlemen From West Point* 1942; *A Guy Named Joe, Hello Frisco Hello, Hitler Dead or Alive* (lead), *They Came to Blow Up America* 1943; *Tall in the Saddle, The Sullivans, Home in Indiana* 1944; *They Were Expendable, Dakota* 1945; *Canyon Passage, It's a Wonderful Life, My Darling Clementine* 1946; *The Fugitive, Unconquered* 1947; *Fort Apache, Tap Roots, Joan of Arc, Three Godfathers* 1948; *Riding High, Singing Guns, Kiss Tomorrow Goodbye, Wagonmaster* 1950; *Operation Pacific, The Great Missouri Raid, Only the Valiant* 1951; *The Quiet Man, On Dangerous Ground, Hellgate* 1952; *Blowing Wild* 1953; *Hondo, Johnny Guitar* 1954; *The Long Gray Line, Mister Roberts* 1955; *The Searchers, Pillars of the Sky* 1956; *The Halliday Brand, The Wings of the Eagles* 1957; *China Doll* 1958; *Alias Jesse James, Rio Bravo* 1959.

Bondarchuk, Sergei. Actor, director. *b.* Sergei Fyodorovich Bondarchuk on Sept. 25, 1920, in Belozersk, Ukraine. *d.* 1994. An amateur actor from early boyhood, he took part in semiprofessional productions in his teens and at seventeen enrolled at the Rostov drama school, where he was introduced to the Stanislavsky method. Following WW II service as front-line entertainer with various Red army theatrical ensembles, he enrolled at Moscow's All-Union State Institute of Cinematography, where he studied under GERASIMOV, PUDOVKIN, and Savchenko, among others. Made his screen debut in Gerasimov's *The Young Guard* (1948), playing a man twice his real age, and went on to become one of the Soviet cinema's most imposing screen personalities, notably in the title roles of *Taras Shevchenko* and *Othello.* His Desdemona in the latter film, actress Irina Skobtseva, subsequently became his wife.

Bondarchuk made an auspicious debut as director with

Fate of a Man/Destiny of a Man (1959), in which he also played the lead role. In an industry dominated by heroic propaganda themes, the film stands out for its unmitigated realism and sincere humanism in its treatment of lives in war. Bondarchuk spent several years preparing his next film, the four-part epic *War and Peace,* the most ambitious production in the annals of Soviet cinema. He cast himself in the plum role of Pierre. He followed this with another epic, the Italian-Soviet-British co-production of *Waterloo.* Twice decorated with the Order of Lenin, Bondarchuk was named People's Artist of the USSR in 1952 and Hero of Soviet Labor in 1980.

FILMS: As actor—*Young Guard, Michurin, Story of a Real Man* 1948; *The Path of Glory* 1949; *Cavalier of the Golden Star/Dream of a Cossack* 1950; *Taras Shevchenko* 1951; *Admiral Ushakov, The Ships from the Bastions* 1953; *This Must Not Be Forgotten* 1954; *The Grasshopper, The Unfinished Tale* 1955; *Othello, Ivan Franko* 1956; *Two from the Housing Block* 1957; *Pages from a Story* 1958; *The Soldiers Marched On* 1959; *Seriozha/A Summer to Remember, Era Notte a Roma/It Was a Night in Rome* (It.) 1960; *The Battle of Neretva* 1970; *Uncle Vanya* 1971; *The Peaks of Zelengore* (Yug.) 1976; *Father Serqius* (title role) 1978. As director—*Fate of a Man/Destiny of a Man* (also act.) 1959; *War and Peace* (also act.; in four parts: I. "Andrei Bolkonsky" 1966; II. "Natasha Rostova," 1966; III. "1812," 1967; IV. "Pierre Bezukov") 1967; *Waterloo* (also co-sc.) 1970; *They Fought for Their Country* (also co-sc., act.) 1975; *The Peaks of Zelengore* (Yug.) 1976; *The Steppe* (also sc., act.) 1978; *Red Bells/Mexico in Flames* 1982; *Boris Godunov* 1986 (also sc., act. in title role).

Bondi, Beulah. Actress. *b.* Beulah Bondy, on May 3, 1892, Chicago. *d.* 1981. She made her first stage appearance at the age of seven in a small-town production of 'Little Lord Fauntleroy.' After 24 years in stock and repertory, she finally made her Broadway debut, in 'One of the Family' (1925). Six years and several Broadway productions later, she appeared in the film *Street Scene,* then stayed in Hollywood to play scores of supporting roles in a wide variety of mature characterizations. A superlative actress, she was nominated for Oscars for her performances in the *Gorgeous Hussy* (1936) and *Of Human Hearts* (1938). Retired from films in the early 60s, but could still be seen on the stage and TV in the early 70s. She won an Emmy in 1977 for her role in 'The Waltons' TV series. She never married.

FILMS INCLUDE: *Street Scene, Arrowsmith* 1931; *Rain* 1932; *The Stranger's Return, Christopher Bean* 1933; *Finishing School, Registered Nurse* 1934; *The Good Fairy* 1935; *The Invisible Ray, The Trail of the Lonesome Pine, The Moon's Our Home, The Gorgeous Hussy* 1936; *Make Way for Tomorrow, Maid of Salem* 1937; *The Buccaneer, Of Human Hearts, Vivacious Lady, The Sisters* 1938; *On Borrowed Time, The Under-Pup, Mr. Smith Goes to Washington* 1939; *Remember the Night, Our Town* 1940; *Penny Serenade, The Shepherd of the Hills, One Foot in Heaven* 1941; *Tonight We Raid Calais, Watch on the Rhine* 1943; *Our Hearts Were Young and Gay, And Now Tomorrow* 1944; *The Southerner, Back to Bataan* 1945; *Sister Kenny, It's a Wonderful Life* 1946; *The Sainted Sisters, The Snake Pit* 1948; *So Dear to My Heart, The Black Book, The Life of Riley* 1949; *The Baron of Arizona, The Furies* 1950; *Lone Star* 1952; *Latin Lovers* 1953; *Track of the Cat* 1954; *Back From Eternity* 1956; *The Big Fisherman, A Summer Place* 1959; *The Wonderful World of the Brothers Grimm* 1962; *Tammy and the Doctor* 1963.

Bonham Carter, Helena. Actress. Born on May 26, 1966, in London. The great-granddaughter of H. H. Asquith, granddaughter of Lady Violet Bonham Carter, and grandniece of director Anthony Asquith, she was raised comfortably by her banker father and mother. Her delicate, classic features and ladylike manner more than made up for her inexperience when she entered films in the mid-80s. Her role in *A Room With a View* (1986) established her as a leading screen presence.

FILMS: *A Pattern of Roses* 1983; *Lady Jane* (as Lady Jane Grey), *A Room with a View* 1986; *Maurice, The Vision* 1987; *La Maschera/The Mask* 1988; *Francesco, Getting It Right* 1989; *Hamlet* (as Ophelia) 1990; *Where Angels Fear to Tread* 1991; *Howards End* 1992; *Mary Shelley's Frankenstein* 1994; *Mighty Aphrodite* 1995; *Twelfth Night* 1996; *Margaret's Museum* 1997.

Bonnaire, Sandrine. Actress. Born in 1967 in Clermont-Ferrand, France. After establishing herself in 1983 with her first film, *À Nos Amours*, she has developed into an important talent in French cinema. She won a César in 1985 for her performance in Agnés Varda's *Vagabond*.

FILMS INCLUDE: *À Nos Amours* 1983; *La Meilleur de la Vie, Tir à Vue* 1984; *Police, Sans toit ni loi/Vagabond* 1985; *La Puritaine* 1986; *Les Innocents, Jaune revolver* 1987; *Under Satan's Sun* 1987; *Peaux de vachés, Quelques jours avec moi/A Few Days With Me* 1988; *Monsieur Hire, La Révolution Française* 1989; *Captive of the Desert, Verso Sera* 1990; *La Ceremonie* 1996.

Bonnard, Mario. Actor, director, screenwriter. *b.* May 21, 1889, Rome. *d.* 1965. Among Italy's leading male stars of the pre–World War I period, he played suave, elegant seducers in many films after 1909. In 1917 he turned to directing, turning out Italian, French, and German films, mostly sentimental comedies and costume dramas.

FILMS INCLUDE: As actor—*Othello* 1909; *Santarellina* 1911; *Parsifal, Satanas* 1912; *Gli Ultimi Giorni di Pompei/The Last Days of Pompeii, Ma l'Amor mio non muore* 1913; *La Pantomima della Morte* 1915; *La Falena* 1916; *Don Juan* 1923. As director—*Pupilla nell'Ombra* (also act.), *I Promessi Sposi* (also act.), *Passa la Ruina* (also act.) 1919; *La Morte piagne* (also act.) 1920; *Il Tacchino* 1923; *Teodoro e Socio, Altro Io* (also act.) 1924; *Der Kampf ums Matterhorn* (co-dir. with Nunzio Malasoma; Ger.) 1928; *Der Sohn der weissen Berge* (Ger.) 1930; *Fra Diavoio* (Ger./It./Fr.) 1931; *Tre Uomini in Frak/L'Amore che Canta, Cinque a Zero, Pas des Femmes* (Fr.) 1932; *Il Trattato Scomparso* (also prod.) 1933; *Marcia Nuziale* 1934; *Milizia Territoriale* 1935; *Trenta Secondi d'Amore* 1936; *L'Albero di Adamo/Adam's Tree, Il Feroce Saladino* 1937; *Il Conte de Berchard, Jeanne Dore, Io suo Padre* 1938; *Frenesia/Frenzy, Papa per una Notte* 1939; *Il Ponte dei Sospiri, La Faniculla di Portici* (also story, sc.), *L'Uomo del Romanzo* (also sc.), *Marco Visconti* (also sc.) 1940; *Il Re si Diverte/The King's Jester, Rossini* (also co-sc.) 1941; *Avanti c'é Posto* 1942; *Campo di Fiori/The Peddler and the Lady, Una Distinta Famiglia* 1943; *Il Ratto delle Sabine* 1945; *Addio mia Bella Napoli!* 1946; *La Città Dolente* (also sc.) 1949; *Margherita da Cortona/Margaret of Cortona* (also co-sc.) 1950; *Stasera Sciopero* (also story), *L'Ultima Sentenza* (also sc.), *Il Voto* 1951; *I Figli non si Vendono* (also co-story, co-sc.), *Tormento del Passato* (also co-sc.) 1952; *Frine—Cortigiana d'Oriente* (also co-sc.) 1953; *Hanno Rubato um Tram* (also co-sc.) 1954; *La Ladra* (also co-story, co-sc.) 1955; *Mi permette Babbo!* 1956; *Gli Ultimi Giorni di Pompei/The Last Days of Pompeii, Gastone* (also co-sc.) 1959; *I Masnadieri* 1961.

booking. A contractual agreement between film distributor and theater owner for the exhibition of a film, stipulating where it is to be shown, the number of showings, the rental fee or percentage of receipts to be charged, etc.

boom. A counterbalanced extension device, usually a steel arm, used as a support for a camera or a microphone. A camera boom is a mobile, cranelike mount used to move a camera in and over the set to shoot continuous action or a series of related actions at more than one level or angle. See also BOOM SHOT; MICROPHONE BOOM.

boom man. The member of a production crew assigned to handle a MICROPHONE BOOM and associated equipment.

boom shot. A continuous single shot incorporating any number of camera levels and angles. Achieved through the use of a BOOM, this versatile shot permits the fluid filming of an entire sequence or even a whole film (as Hitchcock nearly did in *The Rope*) without breaking up the action into units of montage.

Boone, Pat. Singer, actor. Born Charles Eugene Boone, on June 1, 1934, in Jacksonville, Fla. *ed.* Columbia (magna cum laude). He was raised in Nashville, Tenn., where he sang on his own radio show at 17. His successful TV appearances on the 'Ted Mack Amateur Hour' and 'Arthur Godfrey's Talent Scouts' shows helped make him an immensely popular recording star during the latter half of the 50s, when his records sold by the millions. Religious, wholesome, and soft-spoken, he appealed to youngsters as well as to parents who felt uneasy about rock 'n' roll, Elvis Presley, and other phenomena of the 50s. After starring in several teen-oriented musical films, Boone began appearing also in nonsinging acting roles. A devout born-again Christian, he has authored several books that offer a religious approach to teen-age problems. His daughter, Debby Boone (*b.* Sept. 22, 1956, Hackensack, N.J.), is a successful pop singer.

FILMS: *Bernardine, April Love* 1957; *Mardi Gras* 1958; *Journey to the Center of the Earth* 1959; *All Hands on Deck* 1961; *State Fair, The Main Attraction* (UK) 1962; *The Yellow Canary* 1963; *Never Put It in Writing* (UK), *The Horror of It All* (UK), *Goodbye Charlie* 1964; *The Greatest Story Ever Told* 1965; *The Perils of Pauline* 1967; *The Cross and the Switchblade* 1970; *Matilda* (voice only) 1978; *Roger and Me* (doc.) 1988.

Boone, Richard. Actor. *b.* June 18, 1916, Los Angeles. *d.* 1981. He attended Stanford University and was a member of its boxing team before being expelled from the school for a minor offense. He worked for a while in the oil fields of southern California, then embarked unsuccessfully on careers as a prizefighter, a painter, and a short-story writer. After four years of WW II Navy service as a gunner, he prepared for the stage at New York's Actors Studio on the GI Bill and in 1947 made his Broadway debut in Judith Anderson's 'Medea.' In 1951 he made his motion picture debut in Milestone's *The Halls of Montezuma.*

Boone subsequently appeared in many films, typically as a tough guy, whether good or bad. Craggy-faced and menacingly lean, he was equally effective as a formidable heavy or a masterful good guy. He owed much of his popularity to television, on which he starred in such shows as 'Medic,' 'Have Gun Will Travel,' and 'The Richard Boone Show.' In 1968 he ventured into film production with *Kona Coast,* in which he also starred.

FILMS: *The Halls of Montezuma, Call Me Mister, The Desert Fox* 1951; *Return of the Texan, Red Skies of Montana/Smoke Jumpers, Kangaroo, Way of a Gaucho* 1952; *Man on a Tightrope, Vicki, The Robe, City of Bad Men, Beneath the 12-Mile Reef* 1953; *The Siege at Red River, Dragnet, The Raid* 1954; *Man Without a Star, Ten Wanted Men, Robber's Roost* 1955; *Battle Stations, Star in the Dust, Away All Boats* 1956; *Lizzie, The Tall T, The Garment Jungle* 1957; *I Bury the Living* 1958; *The Alamo* (as Sam Houston) 1960; *A Thunder of Drums* 1961; *Rio Conchos* 1964; *The War Lord* 1965; *Hombre* 1967; *Kona Coast* (also exec. prod.) 1968; *The Night of the Following Day, The Arrangement* 1969; *The Kremlin Letter, Madron* (US/Isr.) 1970; *Big Jake* 1971; *Against a Crooked Sky* 1975; *The Shootist* 1976; *The Big Sleep* (UK) 1978; *The Bushida Blade* (Jap.), *Winter Kills* 1979.

Boorman, John. Director. Born on Jan. 18, 1933, in Shepperton, near London. After an inauspicious start in the dry-cleaning business and writing occasional film reviews for a girl's magazine and for radio, he entered British television in 1955 as an assistant film editor. He worked his way up through provincial TV studios in the BBC, where he distinguished himself as an innovative documentary director. In 1962 he became head of the BBC documentary unit in Bristol. He made his debut as a feature director in 1965 with the lively *Catch Us If You Can/Having a Wild Weekend,* starring the pop group the Dave Clark Five. After additional work for the BBC, including a documentary on D. W. Griffith, Boorman came to the US to direct two features starring Lee Marvin, *Point Blank* and *Hell in the Pacific,* both of which reveal Boorman's skill at tight dramatic construction and sustained narrative pace. He returned briefly to England to direct *Leo the Last,* which won him the best director award at Cannes, then came back to the US to direct the harrowing survival drama *Deliverance,* which met with much critical and commercial success. It remains one of the most memorable films of the 70s. Boorman's next two films were resounding flops, but in the 80s he reasserted himself as a stimulating filmmaker and exciting visual stylist with a string of fine productions. Especially fascinating was *The Emerald Forest* (1985), a based-on-fact adventure about a father's search for his kidnapped boy, who is raised by Amazonian Indians in a primitive Brazil jungle. The boy was played by the director's son, Charley Boorman, who has appeared in several of his father's productions, as has Boorman's daughter, Katrine. Another daughter, Telsche Boorman, collaborated on several of his screenplays. Boorman was named best director by the National Society of Film Critics for *Hope and Glory* (1987). Boorman also received Oscar nominations for best film (as producer), best director, and best original screenplay for the film. He served as chairman of the National Film Studios of Ireland from 1975 to 1985 and as governor of the British Film Institute thereafter. He wrote *Money Into Light* (1985), a diary of the traumatic three years he spent making *The Emerald Forest* in the rain forests of Brazil. *Hope and Glory* (1987), his warm autobiographical film of the WW II British homefront, was nominated for several Oscars.

FEATURE FILMS: *Catch Us If You Can/Having a Wild Weekend* 1965; *Point Blank* (US) 1967; *Hell in the Pacific* (US) 1968; *Leo the Last* (also co-sc.) 1970; *Deliverance* (also prod.; US) 1972; *Zardoz* (also prod., sc.) 1974; *Exorcist II: The Heretic* (also co-prod.; US) 1977; *Long Shot* (act. only, as himself) 1978; *Excalibur* (also prod., co-sc.; Ireland/US) 1981; *Danny Boy* (exec. prod. only; Ireland) 1982; *The Emerald Forest* (also prod.; US) 1985; *Nemo/Dream One* (co-prod. only; Fr./UK) 1984; *Hope and Glory* (also prod., sc.) 1987; *Where the Heart Is* (also co-sc.) 1990; *Beyond Rangoon* (also co-prod.) 1995.

booster. 1. A dynamo used for raising the voltage of photoflood lamps, thus increasing the light output over and above their normal wattage. 2. A particularly strong developing solution added to the chemicals in the bath during processing.

booster light. A lamp, usually of the arc type, used during exterior daylight shooting to illuminate shadowy areas, thus improving shadow detail.

Booth, Adrian. Actress, singer. Born Virginia Mae Pound, on July 26, 1918, in Grand Rapids, Mich. She began in show business in the mid-30s as Ginger Pound, a vocalist with Roger Pryor's band. Changing her professional name to Lorna Gray, she entered films in 1938 and through the mid-40s played leads in numerous serials and low-budget action pictures for Columbia, Monogram, and Republic, occasionally making minor appearances in major movies. Hoping for a fresh start, she changed her name again to Adrian Booth in 1946, but still found herself competing with horses for the affection of cowboy stars of B-Westerns. She retired shortly after her 1949 marriage to actor David BRIAN.

FILMS INCLUDE: As Lorna Gray—*Adventure in Sahara, Red River Range* 1938; *The Lone Wolf Spy Hunt, Flying G-Man* (serial), *The Man They Could Not Hang, Mr. Smith Goes to Washington, The Stranger From Texas* 1939; *Bullets for Rustlers, Deadwood Dick* (serial), *Drums of the Desert* 1940; *Father Steps Out* 1941; *The Perils of Nyoka* (serial), *Ridin' Down the Canyon* 1942; *So Proudly We Hail, O My Darling Clementine* 1943; *Captain America* (serial), *The Girl Who Dared* 1944; *Fashion Model, Dakota* 1945. As Adrian Booth—*Daughter of Don Q* (serial), *Home on the Range, Valley of the Zombies* 1946; *Spoilers of the North, Along the Oregon Trail, Under Colorado Skies* 1947; *The Gallant Legion, The Plunderers* 1948; *The Hideout, The Last Bandit, Brimstone* 1949; *The Savage Horde* 1950; *Oh! Susanna, The Sea Hornet* 1951.

Booth, Edwina. Actress. *b.* Edwina Woodruff, Sept. 13, 1909, in Provo, Utah. *d.* 1991. After some stage experience, she played small parts in several Hollywood films, including *Manhattan Cocktail* (1928) and *Our Modern Maidens* (1929). She gained sudden fame after her appearance as the white goddess in *Trader Horn* (1931), but the following year she disappeared from public view. False rumors said she had died of jungle fever contracted in Africa while filming *Trader Horn.* Years later she was spotted as an employee at a Mormon temple in Hollywood.

FILMS INCLUDE: *Manhattan Cocktail* 1928; *Our Modern Maidens* 1929; *The Vanishing Legion* (serial), *Trader Horn* 1931; *The Last of the Mohicans* (serial), *Trapped in Tia Juana, The Midnight Patrol* 1932.

Booth, Karin. Actress. Born Katharine Hoffman, on June 20, 1919, in Minneapolis. A former photographer's model, she entered films in the early 40s as a Paramount contract player, billed as Katharine Booth. She then moved on to MGM, where she was slowly groomed to stardom. Renamed Karin Booth, she finally got ingenue leads in two Margaret O'Brien vehicles in 1947–48, before her contract was abruptly terminated. She was later reduced to playing leads in second features, mostly Westerns.

FILMS INCLUDE: As Katharine Booth—*Louisiana Purchase* 1941; *The Fleet's In, This Gun for Hire, Holiday Inn* 1942; *Swing Shift Maisie, Girl Crazy* 1943; *Marriage Is a Private Affair, Lost in a Harem* 1944; *Wonder Man, Abbott and Costello in Hollywood, Dangerous Partners* 1945; *Ziegfeld Follies, Easy to Wed* 1946. As Karin Booth—*The Unfinished Dance* 1947; *Big City* 1948; *My Foolish Heart* 1949; *State Penitentiary, The Cariboo Trail* 1950; *Cripple Creek* 1952; *Let's Do It Again* 1953; *Tobor the Great, Jungle Man-Eaters* 1954; *Seminole Uprising, Top Gun* 1955; *Badman's Country, The World Was His Jury* 1958; *Beloved Infidel* 1959.

Booth, Margaret (Maggie). Film editor. Born in 1898, in Los Angeles. She started her career in 1921 as an assistant editor at the Mayer studios and in the late 20s and early 30s ranked among the top cutters at MGM. In 1939 she was appointed MGM's supervising film editor, a position she held through 1968. She then resumed active cutting, working independently for various producers. She won an honorary Academy Award during the Oscar ceremony in 1977 for the quality of her cumulative work.

FILMS INCLUDE: *Why Men Leave Home* (co-edit.), *Husbands and Lovers* (co-edit.) 1924; *Fine Clothes* (co-edit.) 1925; *Memory Lane, The Gay Deceiver* 1926; *In Old Kentucky* (co-edit.) 1927; *The Enemy, Bringing up Father, The Mysterious Lady, A Lady of Chance* 1928; *The Bridge of San Luis Rey, Wise Girls* (also titles writer) 1929; *The Rogue Song, Redemption, The Lady of Scandal/The High Road, A Lady's Morals* 1930; *The Cuban Love Song, New Moon, Susan Lenox: Her Fall and Rise* 1931; *Lovers Courageous, Smilin' Through, The Son-Daughter, Strange Interlude* 1932; *Bombshell, The White Sister, Dancing Lady, Storm at Daybreak* 1933; *Riptide, The Barretts of Wimpole Street* 1934; *Reckless, Mutiny on the Bounty* 1935; *Romeo and Juliet* 1936; *Camille* 1937; *A Yank at Oxford* 1938; *The Owl and the Pussycat* (superv. edit.) 1970; *To Find a Man, Fat City* 1972; *The Way We Were* 1973; *Funny Lady* (superv. edit.), *The Sunshine Boys* (co-edit.), *The Black Bird* (co-edit.) 1975; *Murder by Death* 1976; *The Goodbye Girl* (superv. edit.) 1977; *California Suite* (superv. edit.), *The Cheap Detective* (superv. edit.; also assoc. prod.) 1978; *Chapter Two* (also assoc. prod.) 1979; *Annie, The Toy* (assoc. prod. only), *The Slugger's Wife* (exec. prod. only) 1985.

Booth, Shirley. Actress. *b.* Thelma Booth Ford, Aug. 30, 1907, in New York City. *d.* 1992. In amateur plays from the age of 12, she made her first professional appearance in 1923 in 'The Cat and the Canary' in Hartford, Conn., and her Broadway debut in 1925 in a supporting role in 'Hell's Bells,' alongside another newcomer, Humphrey Bogart. It was ten years before she was cast in her first important Broadway role, in 'Three Men on a Horse.' A leading part in 'My Sister Eileen' (1940) and a successful radio career were then followed by her biggest Broadway triumph, the role of frowzy Lola Delaney in 'Come Back, Little Sheba' (1950), for which she won the Tony Award and the New York Drama Critics Award. She repeated her triumph in the screen version of the same play, winning the Academy Award, the New York Film Critics Award, and the Cannes Festival acting award. She subsequently appeared in several other films, most notably in the role of Dolly Levi in *The Matchmaker* (the comedy on which the musical 'Hello Dolly!' was later based). She achieved wide popularity playing the title role in the TV series 'Hazel.'

FILMS: *Come Back, Little Sheba* 1952; *Main Street to Broadway* 1953; *About Mrs. Leslie* 1954; *The Matchmaker, Hot Spell* 1958.

Boothe, Powers. Actor. Born in 1949, in Snyder, Tex. *ed.* Southern Methodist U. Dynamic leading man and second lead of the American stage, TV, and films. He made his presence strongly felt in several movies of the 80s. But it was on TV that he fared best, memorably in the title role in the 'Philip Marlowe' series. He won an Emmy Award as best actor for his performance in the TV movie *Guyana Tragedy: The Story of Jim Jones* (1980).

FILMS INCLUDE: *Cruising* 1980; *Southern Comfort, Red Dawn, A Breed Apart* 1984; *The Emerald Forest* 1985; *Extreme Prejudice* 1987; *Stalingrad* 1990; *Rapid Fire* 1992; *Tombstone* 1993; *Blue Sky* 1994; *Bye Bye Love, Nixon, Sudden Death* 1995; *U-Turn* 1997.

Borau, José Luis. Director. Born in 1929, in Saragosa, Spain. *ed.* U. of Madrid (law). A cinema enthusiast from childhood, he began writing film criticism in 1953 and turned to directing after graduating from the Madrid Film Institute in 1961. In 1967 he founded his own company, El Imán, through which he produced many documentaries and TV programs as well as feature films. His output as a director, though relatively meager, is versatile and proficient. His political allegory, *Furtivos/Poaches* (1974), marked a turning point in the evolution of Spanish cinema. Beyond his own films, Borau exerted influence on contemporary Spanish films as a professor of screenwriting at the Madrid Film Institute (1965–70) and as a supportive producer who nurtured young filmmakers. Among other films, he produced and co-wrote the screenplay for Manuel Gutiérrez Aragón's notable *Camada negra* (1977).

FILMS (as director): *En el Rio* (diploma film) 1961; *Brandy el Sheriff de Losatumba/Brandy* 1964; *Crimen de Doble Filo/Double-Edged Crime* 1965; *Hay que matar a B/B Must Die* (also prod., co-sc.) 1974; *Furtivos/Poachers* (also prod., sc., act.) 1975; *La Sabina/The Sabina* (also prod., sc.; Sp./Sw.) 1979; *Rio abajo/On the Line* (also co-prod., co-sc.) 1984; *Tanta mia/My Dear Nanny* (also prod., co-sc.) 1986.

Borchers, Cornell. Actress. Born Cornelia Bruch, on Mar. 16, 1925, in Heydekrug, Germany. After attending medical school, she enrolled at a Berlin drama school in 1947 and two years later made her debut in German films. She appeared in several American films, most memorably in *The Big Lift,* opposite Montgomery Clift.

FILMS INCLUDE: *Martina* 1949; *Die tödlichen Träume, The Big Lift* (US) 1950; *Das Ewige Spiel, Schwarze Augen* 1951; *Haus des Lebens* 1952; *The Divided Heart* (UK) 1954; *Oasis* (Fr./Ger.), *Never Say Goodbye* (US) 1956; *Istanbul* (US) 1957; *Flood Tide* (US) 1958; *Das letzte Geheimnis* 1959.

Borden, Lizzie. Director, producer. Born Linda E. Borden on February 3, 1958, in Detroit, Mich. *ed.* Wellesley College, Mass. (fine arts). Independent filmmaker whose films explore women's place in American society. Her first film, *Born in Flames* (1982), was widely praised and gained much free publicity for its low budget of about $30,000. She is perhaps best known for *Working Girls* (1986), her unsparing look at middle-class prostitution.

FILMS INCLUDE: *Born in Flames* (also sc.), *King Blank* (ed. asst.) 1983; *Working Girls* (also sc., ed.) 1986; *Calling the Shots* (act.) 1988; *Love Crimes* 1992; *Erotique* (co-dir.) 1994.

Borden, Olive. Actress. *b.* Sybil Tinkle, July 14, 1906, Richmond. Va. *d.* 1947. Leading lady of Hollywood silents and early talkies. Convent-educated in Baltimore, she had entered films at 19 as a Mack SENNETT bathing beauty and broke into features in 1925 as Tom MIX's leading lady. Her star rose rapidly in films of John Ford, Howard Hawks, and Allan Dwan and sank even more rapidly with Hollywood's switch to sound. An exotic and extravagant star in her glory days, she failed to adjust to a life away from the studio lights and ended up on the Los Angeles Skid Row as an alcoholic. She died at 41 at a hotel for destitute women.

FILMS INCLUDE: *The Happy Warrior, The Overland Limited* 1925; *The Yankee Señor, My Own Pal, Yellow Fingers, Three Bad Men, Fig Leaves, The Country Beyond* 1926; *The Monkey Talks, The Secret Studio, The Joy Girl, Pajamas, Come to My House* 1927; *Sinners in Love, Gang War, Stool Pigeon, Virgin Lips* 1928; *The Eternal Woman, Half Marriage, Love in the Desert, Dance Hall* 1929; *Wedding Rings, Hello Sister, The Social Lion* 1930; *Hotel Variety* 1933.

Bordwell, David. Film scholar. Born in 1947. Critical trailblazer in field of film aesthetics termed "formalism" (after the Russian formalist poetic of the early 20th century), which focuses on the dynamic relation of narrative to the spectator's perception. This criticism examines the interworkings of the components of a film (sound, color, framing, camera movement) in the transmission of narrative meaning. Among his books are *The Classical Hollywood Cinema* (1967, Columbia University Press; with Janet Staiger and Kristen Thompson); *Narration in the Fiction Film* (1985, University of Wisconsin Press) and *Film Art* (4th ed., 1993). He is the Jacques Ledoux professor of film at the University of Wisconsin at Madison.

Borg, Veda Ann. Actress. *b.* Jan. 11, 1915, Boston. *d.* 1973. A New York model, she was signed to a Paramount contract after a secret test and made her film debut in 1936 in *Three Cheers for Love.* Her career was interrupted briefly in 1939 by an automobile crash after which her face was completely reconstructed by plastic surgery. She played occasional leads and scores of supporting roles through 1960, typically as a fallen woman, blonde gangster moll, or a friend of the heroine. For some reason, perhaps because she appeared in a great many obscure films, her name became a favorite quiz item among trivia and nostalgia buffs. Her second husband (1946–57) was director Andrew MCLAGLEN.

FILMS INCLUDE: *Three Cheers for Love* 1936; *The Singing Marine, Kid Galahad, San Quentin, Confession, It's Love I'm After, Alcatraz Island, Submarine D–1, Missing Witnesses* 1937; *She Loved a Fireman, Over the Wall* 1938; *Cafe Hostess, The Law Comes to Texas* 1939; *The Shadow* (serial), *Laughing at Danger, Glamour for Sale, Bitter Sweet, Behind the News* 1940; *The Penalty, The Pittsburgh Kid, Honky Tonk, The Corsican Brothers* 1941; *Duke of the Navy, About Face, Two Yanks in Trinidad, She's in the Army* 1942; *Something to Shout About, Murder in Times Square, Revenge of the Zombies* 1943; *Standing Room Only, Detective Kitty O'Day, Marked Trails, The Big Noise, Irish Eyes Are Smiling, The Falcon in Hollywood* 1944; *Jungle Raiders* (serial), *What a Blonde!, Fog Island, Rough Tough and Ready, Don Juan Quilligan, Scared Stiff, Dangerous Intruder, Love Honor and Goodbye, Mildred Pierce, Life with Blondie* 1945; *Avalanche, Accomplice, Wife Wanted* 1946; *The Pilgrim Lady, Big Town, The Bachelor and the Bobby-Soxer, Mother Wore Tights* 1947; *Julia Misbehaves, Blonde Savage* 1948; *Chicken Every Sunday, One Last Fling, Forgotten Women* 1949; *The Kangaroo Kid* 1950; *Aaron Slick From Punkin Crick, Hold That Line, Big Jim McLain* 1952; *A Perilous Journey, Mister Scoutmaster, Hot News, Three Sailors and a Girl* 1953; *You're Never Too Young, Guys and Dolls, I'll Cry Tomorrow, Love Me or Leave Me* 1955; *The Fearmakers* 1958; *Thunder in the Sun* 1959; *The Alamo* 1960.

Borgnine, Ernest. Actor. Born Ermes Effron Borgnino, on Jan. 24, 1917, in Hamden, Conn., to parents of Italian origin. He lived in Milan between the ages of two and seven, then attended school in New Haven, Conn., before joining the Navy in 1935. Discharged at the end of WW II, he studied acting at the Randall School of Dramatic Art in Hartford, then from 1946 to 1950 was a member of a theatrical group in Virginia. After some TV appearances, he made his film debut in *China Corsair* (1951). Stout, with a wide face, beady eyes, and gap teeth, he made a natural heavy, gaining attention as the sadistic sergeant in *From Here to Eternity* (1953) and as a menacing villain in *Bad Day at Black Rock* (1955).

In a surprising change of pace, Borgnine was given the title role of a kind, lonely butcher in *Marty* (1955). This part won him an Academy Award, the best actor honors at the Cannes Festival, the New York Film Critics Award, and the National Board of Review award. Following this triumph, he played a variety of film roles, rarely villainous. He played the hero of the popular TV series 'McHale's Navy,' the basis for a 1964 feature film of the same name, in which he starred. In the 70s and 80s he appeared in numerous low-budget films and TV movies and co-starred in the series 'Airwolf' (1984–86). His five marriages included actress Katy JURADO (1959–64) and singer Ethel MERMAN (briefly in 1964).

FILMS: *China Corsair, The Whistle at Eaton Falls, The Mob* 1951; *The Stranger Wore a Gun, From Here to Eternity* 1953; *Johnny Guitar, Demetrius and the Gladiators, The Bounty Hunter, Vera Cruz* 1954; *Bad Day at Black Rock, Marty, Run for Cover, Violent Saturday, The Last Command* 1955; *The Square Jungle, Jubal, The Catered Affair, The Best Things in Life Are Free* 1956; *Three Brave Men* 1957; *The Vikings, The Badlanders, Torpedo Run* 1958; *The Rabbit Trap, Summer of the Seventeenth Doll/Season of Passion* (Austral./UK) 1959; *Man on a String, Pay or Die* 1960; *Go Naked in the World, Il Re di Poggioreale* (It.), *Il Giudizio Universale* (It.), *Barabba/Barabbas* (It.) 1961; *I Briganti Italiani* (It.) 1962; *McHale's Navy* 1964; *The Flight of the Phoenix* 1965; *The Oscar* 1966; *The Dirty Dozen, Chuka* 1967; *The Legend of Lylah Clare, The Split, Ice Station Zebra* 1968; *The Wild Bunch* 1969; *Los Desperados/A Bullet for Sandoval* (Sp./It.), *The Adventurers, Suppose They Gave a War and Nobody Came* 1970; *Willard, Bunny O'Hare, Rain for a Dusty Summer, Hannie Caulder* (UK) 1971; *The Revengers, Un Uomo dalla Pelle Dura/Ripped-Off* (It.), *The Poseidon Adventure* 1972; *The Neptune Factor, Emperor of the North Pole* 1973; *Law and Disorder* 1974; *Sunday in the Country, The Devil's Rain, Hustle* 1975; *Natale in Casa di Appuntamento/Love By Appointment/Holiday Hookers* (It.), *Won Ton Ton—The Dog That Saved Hollywood* (cameo), *Shoot* (Can.) 1976; *The Greatest* (as Ali's trainer, Angelo Dundee), *The Prince and the Pauper/Crossed Swords* (UK) 1977; *Convoy* 1978; *Ravagers, The Double McGuffin, The Black Hole* 1979; *When Time Ran Out* 1980; *Super Fuzz/Super Snooper* (It./US), *Escape from New York, High Risk, Deadly Blessing* 1981; *Young Warriors* 1983; *Codename: Wildgeese* (It./Ger.) 1984; *Spike of Bensonhurst* 1988; *Turnaround, Laser Mission* 1989; *Any Man's Death, Moving Target* 1990; *Mistress* 1992; *The Wild Bunch* 1995; *All Dogs Go To Heaven* (v/o) 1996; *Gattaca, McHale's Navy* 1997.

Borgström, Hilda. Actress. *b.* Oct. 13, 1871, Stockholm. *d.* 1953. Trained for the ballet from age nine, she also studied drama at the Dance School of Stockholm's Royal Dramatic Theater. She began performing on the stage in her early teens and was an established leading lady by the time she made her screen debut in 1912. Starring in films of Sjöström and others, she rapidly emerged as one of the world's most admired screen actresses during the heyday of Swedish silent cinema. She later played supporting parts in scores of talkies, including an early Bergman film, through the 40s.

FILMS INCLUDE: *A Summer Tale, A Secret Marriage* 1912; *Lady Marion's Summer Flirtation, Ingeborg Holm/Give Us This Day* 1913; *Do Not Judge* 1914; *Brandsoldaten* 1916; *Fru Kristina* 1917; *Caroline Redivinaa* 1920; *The Phantom Carriage/Thy Soul Shall Bear Witness* 1921; *Flight from Paradise* 1924; *The Lady of the Camelias* 1925; *Giftas* 1926; *Adalens Poesi* 1928; *Värmlänningarna* 1932; *The Andersson Family* 1937; *A Woman's Face* 1938; *Bastard, A Crime* 1940; *The Fight Goes On* 1941; *Dangerous Roads, Flames in the Dark, Ride Tonight!* 1942; *Women in Prison, I Killed* 1943; *A Day Shall Dawn, Appassionata, The Invisible Wall, The Emperor of Portugal* 1944; *Royal Rabble, Mandragora* 1945; *Desire* 1946; *Music in Darkness/Night Is My Future, Banquet, Eva* 1948; *The Girl from the Gallery* 1949.

Boris, Robert. Director, screenwriter. Born on Oct. 12, 1945, in New York City. He turned to directing in 1984 after several contributions as a screenwriter.

FILMS: As screenwriter—*Electra Glide in Blue* 1972; *Some Kind of Hero* 1982; *Doctor Detroit* 1983. As director—*Oxford Blues* (also sc.) 1984; *Steele Justice* (also sc.) 1987; *Buy and Cell* 1989.

Borowczyk, Walerian. Animator, director. Born on Oct. 21, 1923 in Kwilcz, Poland. Studied painting at the Academy of Fine Arts in Kraków and exhibited frequently in Poland and abroad. In 1953 he won Poland's National Prize for his lithographic work. In 1955 he began designing posters for Polish films. Two years later he launched his career as animator, collaborating with Jan LENICA on several outstanding cartoons. In 1958 he made his first solo animated film, then went to France, where he soon became a leading animator. In 1966 he first ventured into the live-action field and has since directed a number of feature films.

Together with Lenica, Borowczyk is considered one of the greatest film cartoonists of this generation, among the few who approach the cartoon as a serious art form. An imaginative artist and an inventive filmmaker, he manifests strong individuality along with a ferocious, precise, cold, and almost violent style to match the macabre satire of his films. As a director of live-action features, his work was far less distinguished, and at times cheaply sensational.

FILMS INCLUDE: Animated shorts—*Once Upon a Time* (co-dir. with Jan Lenica), *Striptease* (co-dir. with Lenica) 1957; *Dom/House* (co-dir. with Lenica), *L'Ecole/School* 1958; *Terra Incognita, Le Magicien, Les Astronautes* (co-dir. with Chris Marker) 1959; *Boéte à Musique* (co-dir. with Lenica), *Solitude* (co-dir. with Lenica) 1961; *Le Concert de Monsieur et Madame Kabal* 1962; *L'Encyclopedie de Grand'maman en 13 Volumes, Holy Smoke, Renaissance* 1963; *Les Jeux des Anges* 1964; *Le Dictionnaire de Joachim* 1965; *Le Théâtre de Monsieur et Madame Kabal* (feature-length) 1967; *Le Phonographe* 1969. Live-action shorts—*Glowa* 1953; *Photographies vivantes, L'Atelier de Fernand Léger* 1954; *Jesien* 1956; *Gavotte, Diptique* 1967; *Une Collection particulière* 1973. Live-action features—*Mazepa* 1968; *Goto l'Ile d'Amour* 1969; *Blanche* 1971; *Contes immoraux* 1974; *La Bête/The Beast* 1975; *The Story of a Sin* 1975; *La Marge/The Margin/The Streetwalker* 1976; *Interno di un Convento/Interior of a Convent/Behind Convent Walls* 1978; *Les Héroines du Mal/Heroines of Evil/Three Immoral Women* 1979; *Lulu* 1980; *Dr. Jekyll et les Femmes/The Blood of Dr. Jekyll* 1981; *L'Art d'aimer/The Art of Love* 1983; *Emmanuelle 5* 1987; *Céremonie d'amour/Ceremony of Love* 1988.

Borradaile, Osmond H. Director of photography. Born on July 17, 1898, in Winnipeg, Manitoba, Canada. After university studies in British Columbia, he came to Hollywood and in 1915 started working in the camera department of Jesse L. Lasky Productions. After WW I service with the Canadian army, he joined Paramount's camera department in 1919. In 1929 he was transferred to Paris, and in 1930 he went to London, where he became a director of photography for the Alexander KORDA organization. Specializing in exterior photography, Borradaile was responsible as a second-unit cameraman for the African location footage of *Sanders of the River* (1935), for the exteriors of *The Private Life of Henry VIII* (1933) and *The Scarlet Pimpernel* (1934), and for the splendid outdoor sequences of such films as *Elephant Boy* (1937), *The Drum* (1938), *The Four Feathers* (1939), and *The Thief of Bagdad* (1940).

FILMS INCLUDE: *The Private Life of Henry VIII* (2nd unit) 1933; *The Scarlet Pimpernel* (2nd unit) 1934; *Sanders of the River* (co-phot.) 1935; *Elephant Boy* (2nd unit) 1937; *The Drum/Drums* (2nd unit) 1938; *The Four Feathers* (co-phot.), *The Lion Has Wings* 1939; *The Thief of Bagdad* (co-phot.) 1940; *The Overlanders* 1946; *The Macomber Affair* (US) 1947; *Bonnie Prince Charlie, Scott of the Antarctic, The Winslow Boy* (exteriors only) 1948; *I Was a Male War Bride* (US) 1949; *The Trap* (2nd unit; Can./UK) 1966.

Borzage, Frank. Director. *b.* Apr. 23, 1893, Salt Lake City, Utah. *d.* 1962. At 13 went to work in a silver mine but soon latched on to a touring stage company as a group boy and eventually an actor. In 1912 he arrived in Hollywood and began playing bit parts in INCE films. Before long, he was playing heavies and leads in dozens of Ince Westerns and Mutual comedies. By 1916 he was directing films for Universal. Most of his early efforts were quickie melodramas and Westerns in which he also starred. His first important film, *Humoresque* (1920), contained many of the elements that would characterize his work in years to come.

Along with Clarence BROWN, Borzage was Hollywood's great romanticist, an unabashed sentimentalist who told some of the screen's most beautiful love stories with warm, lyrical tenderness. He pioneered in the use of the soft focus, and the gauzed photography of his films, combined with a fluid, caressing camera movement, gave his lovers an idealized halo that contrasted sharply with the selfish, unfeeling world around them.

Dismissed by some film historians as a "gushy sentimentalist," Borzage was one of Hollywood's most original artists and one of the most consistent in style. His reputation reached its peak in the late silent and early sound era when he won Academy Awards as best director for *Seventh Heaven* (1927) and *Bad Girl* (1931). Among his other memorable films of the 20s and 30s are *Lazybones, Street Angel, The River, A Farewell to Arms, Man's Castle, No Greater Glory, Desire, History Is Made at Night, Three Comrades,* and *The Mortal Storm.* With several exceptions, Borzage's films of the 40s and 50s were the least interesting of his illustrious career.

FILMS: *That Gal of Burke's* (also act.), *Mammy's Rose* (co-dir. with James Douglass; also act.), *Life's Harmony* (co-dir. with Lorimer Johnston; also act.), *The Silken Spider* (also act.), *The Code of Honor* (also act.), *Nell Dale's Men Folks* (also act.), *The Forgotten Prayer* (also act.), *The Courtin' of Calliope Clew* (also act.), *Nugget Jim's Pardner* (also act.), *The Demon of Fear* (also act.), *Land o' Lizzards/Silent Shelby* (also act.), *Immediate Lee/Hair Trigger Casey* (also act.), *Enchantment* (also sc., act.), *The Pride and the Man* (also sc., act.), *Dollars of Dross* (also sc.) 1916; *Wee Lady Betty* (co-dir. with Charles Miller; also act.), *Flying Colors, Until They Get Me* 1917; *The Atom* (also act.), *The Gun Woman* (also act.) *Shoes That Danced, Innocent's Progress, An Honest Man, Society for Sale, Who Is to Blame?, The Ghost Flower, The Curse of Iku* (also act.) 1918; *Toton, Prudence of Broadway, Whom the Gods Would Destroy, Ashes of Desire* 1919; *Humoresque* 1920; *The Duke of Chimney Butte, Get-Rich-Quick Wallingford* 1921; *Back Pay, Billy Jim, The Good Provider, Hair Trigger Casey* (re-edited version of 1916's *Immediate Lee*; also act.), *Silent Shelby* (reissue of 1916's *Land o' Lizzards*), *The Valley of Silent Men, The Pride of Palomar* 1922; *The Nth Commandment, Children of the Dust, Age of Desire* 1923; *Secrets* 1924; *The Lady, Daddy's Gone a-Hunting, Lazybones, Wages for Wives, The Circle* 1925; *The First Year, The Dixie Merchant, Early to Wed, Marriage License?* 1926; *Seventh Heaven* 1927; *Street Angel* 1928; *The River, Lucky Star, They Had to See Paris* 1929; *Song o' My Heart, Liliom* 1930; *Doctors' Wives, Young As You Feel, Bad Girl* 1931; *After Tomorrow, Young America, A Farewell to Arms* 1932; *Secrets* (remake of 1924 film), *Man's Castle* 1933; *No Greater Glory, Little Man What Now?, Flirtation Walk* (also prod.) 1934; *Living on Velvet, Stranded, Shipmates Forever* 1935; *Desire, Hearts Divided* 1936; *Green Light, History Is Made at Night, Big City* 1937; *Mannequin, Three Comrades, The Shining Hour* 1938; *Disputed Passage* (also co-prod.) 1939; *Strange Cargo, The Mortal Storm* (also co-prod.) 1940; *Flight Command, Smilin' Through* 1941; *The Vanishing Virginian, Seven Sweethearts* 1942; *Stage Door Canteen, His Butler's Sister* (also co-prod.) 1943; *Till We Meet Again* (also prod.) 1944; *The Spanish Main* 1945; *I've Always Loved You* (also prod.), *Magnificent Doll* 1946; *That's My Man* (also prod.) 1947; *Moonrise* 1949; *China Doll* (also prod.) 1958; *The Big Fisherman* 1959.

Bosco, Philip. Actor. Born on Sept. 26, 1930, in Jersey City, N.J. Character lead and supporting player of the American stage, TV, and films. The son of a carnival operator, he was expelled from Catholic U. in Washington D.C., but returned to the school after Army service as a cryptographer, finally graduating at age 27 with a degree in drama. He subsequently appeared in numerous plays, mainly in the New York area, specializing in Shakespeare and the classics, although later portrayals, as in the comedy 'Lend Me a Tenor,' established his comedic talent (and won him a Tony). He made an isolated film appearance in 1968. It wasn't until the 80s that he asserted himself as a screen actor.

FILMS INCLUDE: *A Lovely Way to Die* 1968; *Trading Places* 1983; *The Pope of Greenwich Village* 1984; *Heaven Help Us, Flannagan/Walls of Glass* 1985; *The Money Pit, Children of a Lesser God* 1986; *Suspect, Three Men and a Baby* 1987; *Another Woman, Working Girl* 1988; *The Luckiest Man in the World, The Dream Team* 1989; *Blue Steel, Quick Change* 1990; *F/X 2, True Colors* 1991; *Shadows and Fog* 1992; *Angie, Milk Money, Nobody's Fool, Safe Passage* 1994; *It Takes Two* 1995; *My Best Friend's Wedding* 1997.

Bosé, Lucia. Actress. Born on Jan. 28, 1931, in Milan. A bakery worker, she was crowned Miss Italy in 1947. Made her film debut in De Santis's *Non c'è Pace tra gli Ulivi/Under the Olive Tree* (1950) and soon after demonstrated her ability to handle subtle psychological roles in Antonioni's *Cronaca di un Amore* and *La Signora senza Camelie.* She also figured prominently in Bardem's *Death of a Cyclist* and Buñuel's *Cela s'appelle l'Aurore* but retired from the screen in 1956 to marry the famous bullfighter Luis-Miguel Dominguin. Returned to films in the late 60s after their separation.

FILMS INCLUDE: *Non c'è Pace tra gli Ulivi/Under the Olive Tree* 1950; *Cronaca di un Amore/Story of a Love Affair* 1950; *Le Regazze di Piazza di Spagna/Three Girls from Rome, Roma Ore 11/Rome 11 O'Clock* 1952; *La Signora senza Camelie/The Lady Without Camelias* 1953; *Questa è la Vita/Of Life and Love, Sinfonia d'Amore, Muerta di un Ciclista/Death of a Cyclist/Age of Infidelity* (Sp.) 1954; *Cela s'appelle l'Aurore* (Fr.) 1956; *Le Testament d'Orphée/Testament of Orpheus* (cameo; Fr.) 1960; *Sotto il Segno dello Scorpione* 1968; *Fellini Satyricon* 1969; *Metello, Ciao Gulliver* 1970; *L'Ospite, Facce Nude* 1971; *Nathalie Granger* (Fr.), *Un Solo Grande Amore* 1972; *La Colonna Infame* 1973; *The Legend of Blood Castle* (Sp.) 1974; *Per le Antiche Scale/Down the Ancient Stairs* 1975; *Lumière* (Fr.) 1976; *Cronica de una Muerte anunciada* 1987; *L'Avaro/The Miser* 1990.

Bost, Pierre. Screenwriter, novelist, playwright. *b.* Sept. 5, 1901, Lasalle, France. *d.* 1975. He was the editor of French magazines and the author of several novels and plays before turning to writing screenplays in 1942. His best work was done in collaboration with screenwriter Jean AURENCHE, beginning in 1943. Together they created the scripts for many important French films, by such directors as René Clement, Claude Autant-Lara, and Jean Delannoy. Aurenche usually was responsible for the continuity of the plot and Bost for the dialogue. Among their best-known collaborations: *La Symphonie Pastorale, Le Diable au Corps/Devil in the Flesh* (1946); *Jeux interdits/Forbidden Games* (1952); *Le Rouge et le Noir/The Red and the Black* (1954); and *Gervaise* (1956). For a fuller list of credits see AURENCHE, Jean.

Bosustow, Stephen. Producer, animator. *b.* Nov. 6, 1911, Victoria, B.C., Canada. *d.* 1981. He won an art prize at the age of 11 and began working professionally at animation in the early 30s. He worked with Ub Iwerks on *Flip the Frog* in 1932 and with Walter Lantz in 1933 and joined Walt DISNEY as an animator-writer in 1934. In 1941 he led a rebellion of dissident artists against autocratic rule and artistic stagnation at the Disney studio and in the wake of the dispute resigned and joined Hughes

Aircraft as a design illustrator. In 1942 he formed his own company and among other animated films made a famous cartoon for President Franklin D. Roosevelt's re-election campaign, *Hell-Bent for Election* (1944). In 1945 he and several other disenchanted Disney artists formed UPA (UNITED PRODUCTIONS OF AMERICA), an independent animation company that allowed its artists great creative freedom and experimented with a wide variety of animation styles. While president of UPA he personally produced many of its cartoons, including Academy Award winners *Gerald McBoing Boing* (1951), *When Magoo Flew* (1954), and *Magoo's Puddle Jumper* (1956). He sold his share in the company in 1961 and formed Stephen Bosustow Productions, producers of educational shorts and travel documentaries. After his death the company was run by his sons, Ted Bosustow (*b.* Feb. 18, 1938) and Nick Bosustow (*b.* Mar. 28, 1940).

Boswell, Connee. Singer. *b.* Dec. 3, 1907, New Orleans. *d.* 1976. A highly popular radio and recording star, she began her career singing in a trio with her sisters Martha and Vet (Helvetia) on a local radio station. By the early 30s they were nationally famous and in 1935 they made a triumphant tour of Europe, including a command performance at Buckingham Palace. Soon after, the trio dissolved and Connee reached even greater fame and popularity on her own, appearing in concerts, films, and Broadway musicals and making many hit records, several as a duet with Bing Crosby. Her career was hampered from the start by crippling polio, which had partly paralyzed her at age four. Throughout her career she performed from a tall wheelchair, covered by a long gown, creating the illusion that she was standing. She died at 68 of cancer. Her last public appearance was in 1975, when she performed in Carnegie Hall with the Benny Goodman orchestra.

FILMS: *The Big Broadcast* 1932; *Moulin Rouge, Transatlantic Merry-Go-Round* 1934; *Artists and Models* 1937; *Kiss the Boys Goodbye* 1941; *Syncopation* 1942; *Swing Parade of 1946* 1946; *Senior Prom* 1958.

Bosworth, Hobart. Actor, director, screenwriter, producer. *b.* Aug. 11, 1867, Marietta, Ohio. *d.* 1943. He ran away to sea at the age of 12 and took to the stage at 18, making several starring appearances on Broadway by 1902, when he was forced to leave the stage after temporarily losing his voice. He started his film career in 1909, starring in the Selig Company's *In the Sultan's Power,* presumably the first dramatic film to be shot on the West Coast. He subsequently played in many Selig one-reelers and directed, produced, and wrote the screenplays for others. In 1913 he formed his own production company and directed the ambitious, seven-reel-long feature film *The Sea Wolf,* in which he also starred. After more than a decade as a leading Hollywood star, Bosworth began playing supporting roles during the 20s, often as a heavy. He remained active in films until he was 75. His first of two wives was actress Adele Farrington.

FILMS INCLUDE (as actor): *In the Sultan's Power, Up San Juan Hill* 1909; *Davy Crockett, The Courtship of Miles Standish, The Roman, Across the Plains* 1910; *The Profligate* 1911; *Monte Cristo/The Count of Monte Cristo, A Reconstructed Rebel* 1912; *Altar of the Aztecs, A Wise Old Elephant, The Sea Wolf* (as Wolf Larsen; also dir., prod., sc.) 1913; *The Valley of the Moon* (also dir., prod.), *John Barleycorn* (also dir., prod.), *Martin Eden* (also dir., prod., sc.), *An Odyssey of the North* (also dir., prod.), *Burning Daylight* (in two parts; also dir., prod.), *The Pursuit of the Phantom* (dir., prod., sc.), *The Country Mouse* (also dir., prod., sc.) 1914; *Buckshot John* (also dir., prod.), *Help Wanted* (also dir.), *The Scarlet Sin, Fatherhood* (also dir., sc., des.), *Colorado, The White Scar* (also prod., sc.) 1915; *The Target, The Yaqui, The Way of the World, Oliver Twist* (as Bill Sykes), *Joan the Woman* 1916; *A Mormon Maid, Unconquered, Freckles, The Little American, The Woman God Forgot* (as Hernando Cortez), *The Devil-Stone* 1917; *The Border Legion* 1918; *Behind the Door* 1919; *Below the Surface, The Brute Master* (also co-sc.) 1920; *The Foolish Matrons, The Cup of Life, Blind Hearts* (also prod.), *The Sea Lion* (also prod.) 1921; *White Hands, The Stranger's Banquet* 1922; *The Man Alone, Vanity Fair, Little Church Around the Corner, Rupert of Hentzau, The Common Law, The Eternal Three, In the Palace of the King* 1923; *Name the Man, Captain January, Bread, The Silent Watcher, Hearts of Oak, Sundown* 1924; *If I Marry Again, My Son, Chickie, Zander the Great, Winds of Chance, The Big Parade, The Golden Strain* 1925; *The Far Cry, The Nervous Wreck, Spangles* 1926; *Three Hours, Annie Laurie, The Blood Ship, The Chinese Parrot, My Best Girl* 1927; *Freckles, The Smart Set, After the Storm, Hangman's House, The Sawdust Paradise, A Woman of Affairs* 1928; *Eternal Love, General Crack* 1929; *Mammy, The Devil's Holiday, The Office Wife, Abraham Lincoln* (as Robert E. Lee), *Du Barry—Woman of Passion, Just Imagine, The Third Alarm* 1930; *Dirigible, Shipmates, This Modern Age, Fanny Foley Herself* 1931; *The Last of the Mohicans* (serial), *The Miracle Man, No Greater Love, County Fair, The Phantom Express* 1932; *Lady for a Day* 1933; *Whom the Gods Destroy, Music in the Air* 1934; *The Keeper of the Bees, The Crusades, Steamboat Round the Bend* 1935; *General Spanky* 1937; *The Secret of Treasure Island* (serial) 1938; *Law of the Tropics, One Foot in Heaven* 1941; *They Died With Their Boots On, Sin Town* 1942.

Botelho, Joao. Director, producer, screenwriter, critic. Born on May 11, 1949, in Lamego, Portugal. *ed.* National Conservatory School of Cinema, Portugal. Seminal force in development of modern Portuguese cinema. Originally a student in mechanical engineering, he switched to the Cinema School of the National Conservatory, and founded and edited a film journal, *M.* His film features exhibit a sharp political bent, particularly his 1988 adaptation of Charles Dickens's *Hard Times* (*Tempas Dificeis*). All have enjoyed wide exposure on the film festival circuit.

FILMS INCLUDE: *Alexandre e Rosa* (co-dir.) 1978; *Conversa Acabada* 1981; *Um Adeus Português/A Portuguese Goodbye* (dir., sc., prod., ed.) 1985; *Tempos Dificeis/Hard Times* (dir., sc, prod., ed.) 1988.

Bottoms, Timothy. Actor. Born on Aug. 30, 1950, in Santa Barbara, Calif. Juvenile lead, then leading man of Hollywood TV and films. The son of a high-school art teacher, he showed an early penchant for performing and at 17 toured Europe with his town's Madrigal Society. He made an auspicious, double-edged, motion-picture debut in 1971, playing the leads in both Dalton Trumbo's *Johnny Got His Gun* and Peter Bogdanovich's *The Last Picture Show.* He gave another memorable performance as a harassed law school freshman in James Bridges' *The Paper Chase* (1973). But his subsequent roles offered him scant opportunities to excel. His younger brothers, Joseph Bottoms (*b.* Apr. 22, 1954) and Sam Bottoms (*b.* Oct. 17, 1955) also play leads on TV and in movies.

FILMS INCLUDE: *Johnny Got His Gun, The Last Picture Show* 1971; *Love and Pain and the Whole Damn Thing, The Paper Chase* 1973; *The White Dawn, The Crazy World of Julius Vrooder* 1974; *Operation Daybreak/Seven Men at Daybreak/ Price of Freedom* 1975; *A Small Town in Texas* 1976; *Rollercoaster* 1977; *The Other Side of the Mountain—Part 2* 1978; *Hurricane* 1979; *The High Country* 1981; *The Tin Man* 1983; *Hambone and Hillie, The Census Taker* 1984; *In the Shadow of Kilimanjaro, Invaders from Mars* 1986; *The Drifter, Land of Faraway/Mio in the Land of Faraway* (USSR/Nor./Sw.)

1988; *Husbands Wives Money and Murder, Return From the River Kwai* 1989; *Istanbul: Keep Your Eyes Open* (Sw.), *Texasville, Picture This* (doc., co-prod. only) 1990; *Digger* 1993.

Boulanger, Daniel. Screenwriter, novelist, actor. Born in 1922, in France. Favorite script and dialogue writer of several directors of the French New Wave, particularly of Philippe de BROCA. Noted for his black humor and robust style. Boulanger has made occasional screen appearances as an actor, usually in heavy roles, in such films as *A Bout de Souffle/Breathless, Tirez sur le Pianiste/Shoot the Piano Player* (both 1960), *L'Oeil du Malin/The Third Lover* (1962), *La Mariée etait en Noir/The Bride Wore Black* (1968), *Domicile conjugal/Bed and Board* (1970), and *Toute une Vie/And Now My Love* (1974).

FILMS INCLUDE (as screenwriter, alone or in collaboration, and usually also dialogue writer): *Le Jeux de l'Amour/The Love Game* 1960; *Le Farceur/The Joker, La Récréation/Playtime, L'Amant de Cinq Jours/The Five Day Lover, Sept Péchés capitaux/Seven Capital Sins* (De Broca episode), *Cartouche* 1962; *L'Homme de Rio/That Man from Rio, Echappement libre/Backfire, Peau de Banane/Banana Peel* 1964; *Marie-Chantal contre le Docteur Kha* (dial. only), *Les Tribulations d'un Chinois en Chine/Up to His Ears* 1965; *La Vie de Château/A Matter of Resistance* (dial. only), *Tendre Voyou/Tender Scoundrel, Le Roi de Coeur/King of Hearts* (also act.) 1966; *Le Voleur/The Thief of Paris* (dial. only), *Un Homme de trop/Shock Troops* (dial. only), *La Route de Corinthe/Who's Got the Black Box?* 1967; *Histories extraordinaires/Spirits of the Dead* (Malle episode) 1968; *Le Diable par la Queue/The Devil by the Tail* 1969; *Les Caprices de Marie/Give Her the Moon* 1970; *Les Pétroleuses/The Legend of Frenchy King* 1971; *Une Femme fidèle* 1976; *La Menace* 1977; *Ils sont grands ces Petits* 1979; *Le Cheval d'Orqeuil/The Horse of Pride* 1980; *La Revolution Française/The French Revolution* 1989.

Boulting, John and Roy. Twin-brother director-producer team. Born on Nov. 21, 1913, in Bray, Buckinghamshire, England. John died in 1985. *ed.* McGill (Montreal). Together they founded Charter Films in 1937, each serving as producer on the films directed by the other. They separated only during WW II, when John served with the Royal Air Force Film Unit (for which he directed *Journey Together,* 1945) and Roy served with the Army Film Unit (*Desert Victory,* 1943; *Tunisian Victory,* 1944; and *Burma Victory,* 1945). In 1958 they were both appointed directors of British Lion Films. In 1971, Roy married actress Hayley MILLS, some 33 years his junior. They later divorced.

The brothers' earlier work, including *Pastor Hall, Thunder Rock, Seven Days to Noon, and The Magic Box,* was held in high regard by critics. Their later output was typically light comedy and farce.

FILMS: Roy directing (and John usually producing)—*The Landlady* (short), *Ripe Earth* (short), *Seeing Stars* (short), *Consider Your Verdict* (short) 1938; *Trunk Crime* 1939; *Inquest, Pastor Hall* 1940; *Dawn Guard* (short) 1941; *Thunder Rock, They Serve Abroad* (short) 1942; *Desert Victory* (doc.) 1943; *Tunisian Victory* (doc.; co-dir. with Frank Capra) 1944; *Burma Victory* (doc.) 1945; *Fame Is the Spur* 1947; *The Guinea Pig/The Outsider* (also co-sc.) 1948; *Single-handed/Sailor of the King, High Treason* (also co-sc.) 1951; *Josephine and Men* 1955; *Run for the Sun* (also co-sc.; US) 1956; *Brothers in Law* (also co-sc.), *Happy Is the Bride* (also co-sc.) 1957; *Carlton-Browne of the F.O./Man in a Cocked Hat* (co-dir., co-sc. with Jeffrey Dell) 1959; *A French Mistress* (also co-sc.) 1960; *The Family Way* (also co-adapt.) 1966; *Twisted Nerve* (also co-sc.) 1968; *There's a Girl in My Soup* 1970; *Soft Beds and Hard Battles/Undercovers Hero* (also co-sc.) 1974; *The Number* (US) 1979. John directing (and Roy usually producing)—*Journey Together* 1945; *Brighton Rock/Young Scarface* 1947; *Seven Days to Noon* 1950; *The Magic Box* 1951; *Private's Progress* (also co-sc.) 1956; *Lucky Jim* 1957; *I'm All Right Jack* (also co-sc.) 1959; *Heavens Above!* (also co-sc.) 1963; *Rotten to the Core* 1965. Roy and John co-directing—*Seagulls Over Sorrento/Crest of the Wave* (both also prod., Roy also sc.) 1954; *Suspect/The Risk* (both also prod.) 1960.

Bouquet, Michel. Actor. Born in 1926, in Paris. Outstanding character player of the French stage and screen. He hoped to become a doctor but quit school at age 15 to work as a baker's helper, then a bank clerk, after his father had been taken prisoner in WW II. A year later he began attending acting classes and within six months had made his debut on the Paris stage. He rapidly established a reputation as a superb actor in the theater, but the parallel film career he pursued from 1947 was much slower to develop. It was not until the 60s that he began playing on the screen the types of complex enigmatic roles in which he excels, particularly in the films of Claude CHABROL.

FILMS INCLUDE: *Monsieur Vincent* 1947; *Manon, Pattes blanches* 1949; *Deux Sous des Violettes* 1951; *La Tour de Nesle* 1955; *Le Piège* 1958; *Katia/Magnificent Sinner* 1960; *Les Amitiés particulières/This Special Friendship* 1964; *Le Tigre se parfume à la Dynamite/An Orchid for the Tiger,* 1965; *Lamiel, La Route de Corinthe/Who's Got the Black Box?* 1967; *La Mariée était en Noir/The Bride Wore Black* 1968; *La Femme infidèle, La Sirène du Mississippi/Mississippi Mermaid* 1969; *Borsalino, Un Condé/The Cop, La Rupture/The Breakup* 1970; *Juste avant la Nuit/Just Before Nightfall, L'Humeur vagabonde* 1971; *Malpertuis* (Belg./Fr.), *L'Attentat/The French Conspiracy* 1972; *Le Serpent/The Serpent, Il n'y a pas de Fumée sans Feu/Where There's Smoke, Le Complot, Défense de Savoir, Deux Hommes dans la Ville/Two Against the Law* 1973; *France Société anonyme, La Main a couper, Les Suspects* 1974; *Audelà de la Peur/Beyond Fear* 1975; *Le Jouet/The Toy* 1977; *La Raison d'Etat, L'Ordre et la Sécurité du Monde* 1978; *Les Misérables* (as Inspector Javert) 1982; *Poulet au Vinaigre/Cop au Vin* 1985; *Toto, The Heroes* 1991.

Bourgoin, Jean (also known as **Yves** or **Georges Bourgoin).** Director of photography. Born Jean-Serge Bourgoin, on Mar. 4, 1913, in Paris. Among France's leading cameramen and a specialist in color films, he spent several years in apprenticeship with such cameramen as Jean BACHELET and Christian MATRAS before coming into his own in 1937. He has since worked for such directors as Renoir, Tati, Becker, Yves Allégret, Cayatte, and Orson Welles.

FILMS INCLUDE: *La Vie est à nous* (co-phot.) 1937; *La Marseillaise* 1938; *Goupi Mains-Rouges* 1943; *Voyage surprise* 1946; *Dédée d'Anvers/Dedee* 1947; *Manèges/The Cheat, Justice est faite/Justice Is Done* 1950; *Nous sommes tous des Assassins/We Are All Murderers* 1952; *Avant le Déluge* 1954; *Mr. Arkadin/Confidential Report* 1955; *Mon Oncle* 1958; *Orfeu nègre/Black Orpheus* 1959; *The Counterfeit Traitor* (US), *Gigot* (US), *The Longest Day* (co-phot.; US) 1962; *Germinal* 1963; *Pas Question le Samedi/Impossible on Saturday* 1965; *Qui?* 1970; *La Chambre rouge* 1973.

Bourguignon, Serge. Director. Born on Sept. 3, 1928, in Maignelay, France. After studies at IDHEC from 1948–50, he worked briefly as assistant director, then began directing short documentaries. A journey to India and the Far East provided him with material for several short and medium-length films, one of which (*Le Sourire*) won him an award at the 1960 Cannes Festival. His very first feature film, *Les Diamanches de Ville d'Avray/Sundays and Cybèle,* won the Academy Award for best foreign language film in 1962.

FILMS: Shorts and documentaries—*Le Rhin Fleuve International* (co-dir.) 1952; *Médecin des Sols* 1953; *Démons et Merveilles de Bali, Borneo* 1954; *Sikkim Terre secrète* (doc.) 1956; *La Jeune Patriarche* 1957; *Marie Lumière* 1958; *Le Montreur d'Ombres, Etoile de Mer, Escale, Le Sourire* 1960; *Le Rançon* 1961. Feature films—*Les Dimanches de Ville d'Avray/Sundays and Cybèle* (also co-sc., act.) 1962; *The Reward* (also co-sc.; US) 1965; *A Coeur joie/Two Weeks in September* (also co-sc.; Fr.) 1967; *The Picasso Summer* (release delayed) 1969; *Mon Royaume pour un Cheval/My Kingdom for a Horse* (doc.; also sc., co-phot.) 1978.

Bourne, Mel. American art director, production designer. Born in Chicago. *ed.* Yale School of Drama. Specializing in urban motifs, he was responsible for the sets of some major films of Woody ALLEN and other directors. He created settings as diverse as the New York of *Fatal Attraction* and of *Manhattan.*

FILMS INCLUDE: *That Night* 1957; *The Miracle Worker* 1962; *Annie Hall* 1977; *The Greek Tycoon, Interiors* 1978; *Manhattan* 1979; *Stardust Memories* 1980; *Thief* 1981; *A Midsummer Night's Sex Comedy, Still of the Night* 1982; *Zelig* 1983; *Broadway Danny Rose, The Natural* 1984; *F/X, Manhunter* 1986; *Fatal Attraction* 1987; *Cocktail* (cons. only), *The Accused* 1988; *Rude Awakening* 1989; *Reversal of Fortune* (US) 1990; *The Fisher King* 1991; *Man Trouble* 1992; *Indecent Proposal* 1993; *Angie, Kiss of Death* 1994.

Bourvil. Actor. *b.* André Raimbourg, July 27, 1917, Petrot-Vicquemare, France. *d.* 1970. He was raised to be a farmer in the town of Bourville, from which he borrowed his professional name. After working as an apprentice to a baker, at the age of 20 he began performing as an amateur entertainer, reciting his own nonsensical lyrics at provincial gatherings. While appearing professionally in music hall shows, he was discovered by French radio and soon became a nationally popular comedian. His small frame and long nose were first seen on the screen in 1941. He then appeared in a great many French films, mostly in comic roles but sometimes in touching dramas, as he did in *Le Miroir à deux Faces/The Mirror Has Two Faces,* opposite Michele Morgan. In 1956 he won the best actor award at the Venice Festival for his tragicomic role as cab-driver-turned-black-marketer in Autant-Lara's *La Traversée de Paris/Four Bags Full* opposite Jean Gabin.

FILMS INCLUDE: *Croisières sidèrales* 1941; *La Ferme du Pendu* 1945; *Pas si Bête* 1947; *Blanc comme Neige* 1948; *Miquette et sa Mère/Miquette* 1949; *Le Rosier de Madame Husson/The Prize* 1950; *Le Passe-Muraille/Mr. Peek-A-Boo* 1951; *Le Trou Normand/Crazy for Love* 1952; *Les Trois Mousquetaires/The Three Musketeers* 1953; *Le Fils à la Patte* 1955; *La Traversée de Paris/Four Bags Full* 1956; *Les Misérables, Le Miroir à Deux Faces/The Mirror Has Two Faces, Un Drôle de Dimanche* 1958; *Le Chemin des Escoliers, La Jument verte/The Green Mare, Le Bossu* 1959; *Le Capitan* 1960; *The Longest Day* (US) 1962; *Les Bonnes Causes/Don't Tempt the Devil, Un Drôle de Paroissien/Thank Heaven for Small Favors, La Cuisine au Beurre/My Wife's Husband* 1963; *Le Corniaud/The Sucker, La Guerre secrète/The Dirty Game, Les Grandes Gueules/Wise Guys* 1965; *La Grande Vadrouille/Don't Look Now* 1966; *Le Cerveaú/The Brain, Monte Carlo or Bust/Those Daring Young Men in Their Jaunty Jalopies* (UK/Fr./It.), *L'Arbre de Noël/The Christmas Tree* 1969; *L'Etalon, Le Cercle rouge, Le Mur de l'Atlantique* 1970.

Bow, Clara. Actress. *b.* Aug. 25, 1905, Brooklyn, N.Y. *d.* 1965. The popular "It" girl of the Roaring 20s was the daughter of a Coney Island waiter and a mentally unstable mother. She spent her childhood in dire poverty, escaping drudgery at 16 by winning a movie-fan-magazine beauty contest and getting a bit role in a film as part of her prize. Other roles followed, mostly in low-budget productions, under contract to independent producer B. P. SCHULBERG. Her big break came in 1925, when Schulberg rejoined Paramount as staff producer, bringing her with him. Helped by the big studio's publicity machine and slick productions, she was molded into a symbol of the flapper age, a vibrant, liberated young woman of personal magnetism and boundless energy whose bobbed hair, cupid bow lips, and sparkling eyes came to represent the era.

Her popularity soared in 1927, when she starred in the film *It,* from a story and script by Elinor Glyn. She was thence known as the "It" girl, as the title became widely accepted as a term defining the unself-conscious attraction of the modern young woman—that "something extra" that separated her from the ordinary crowd. However, Bow's popularity was short-lived. Nasty rumors and scandals involving her romantic affairs, changing public tastes, and her own physical and mental fragility combined to end her career shortly after the advent of sound. In the late 20s she suffered several nervous breakdowns. In 1931 she eloped with cowboy star Rex BELL. They married and settled on his Nevada ranch. She made a faint try at a comeback but finally retired in 1933. Bell went on to become lieutenant governor of Nevada, but Bow was rarely at his side. She spent many of her post-movie years confined to various sanitariums.

FILMS: *Beyond the Rainbow* 1922; *Down to the Sea in Ships, Enemies of Women* (bit), *The Daring Years, Maytime* 1923; *Grit, Black Oxen, Poisoned Paradise, Daughters of Pleasure, Wine, Empty Hearts, This Woman, Black, Black Lightning, Helen's Babies* 1924; *Capital Punishment, The Adventurous Sex, My Lady's Lips, Parisian Love, Eve's Lover, Kiss Me Again, The Scarlet West, The Primrose Path, The Plastic Age, The Keeper of the Bees, Free to Love, The Best Bad Man, Lawful Cheaters, My Lady of Whims, The Ancient Mariner* 1925; *Two Can Play, Dancing Mothers, Fascinating Youth, The Runaway, The Shadow of the Law, Mantrap, Kid Boots* 1926; *It, Children of Divorce, Rough House Rosie, Hula, Wings, Get Your Man* 1927; *Red Hair, Ladies of the Mob, The Fleet's In, Three Week-Ends* 1928; *The Wild Party, Dangerous Curves, The Saturday Night Kid* 1929; *Paramount on Parade, True to the Navy, Love Among the Millionaires, Her Wedding Night* 1930; *No Limit, Kick In* 1931; *Call Her Savage* 1932; *Hoopla* 1933.

Bowers, John. Actor. *b.* Dec. 25, 1899, Garrett, Ind. *d.* 1936. Handsome leading man of Hollywood silents. Entered films in 1916 and starred in many productions, opposite some of the screen's most glamorous leading ladies, mainly in romantic and domestic dramas. His career declined sharply, however, with the advent of sound and after appearing in only two early talkies he could find no work in films. He became an alcoholic and at the age of 36 committed suicide by drowning. The manner and circumstances of his death provided the idea for the setting of the suicide scene in the film *A Star Is Born* (1937) and its subsequent remakes. He was at one time married to actress Marguerite DE LA MOTTE.

FILMS INCLUDE: *The Little Dutch Girl* 1915; *Madame X, The Eternal Grind, Destiny's Toy, Huld from Holland* 1916; *Darkest Russia, Maternity, The Divorce Game, Betsy Ross, Easy Money* 1917; *The Way Out, The Cabaret, Journey's End, Heredity, The Sea Waif* 1918; *Day Dreams, Sis Hopkins, The Pest, Daughter of Mine, Strictly Confidential* 1919; *The Loves of Letty, The Woman in Room 13, Out of the Storm, A Cumberland Romance* 1920; *Godless Men, Roads of Destiny, The Ace of Hearts, Bits of Life, The Sky Pilot, An Unwilling Hero, The Silent Call, The Poverty of Riches, The Night Rose* 1921; *The Golden Gift, The Bonded Woman, Affinities, Lorna*

Doone, Quincy Adams Sawyer 1922; *What a Wife Learned, The Woman of Bronze, Divorce, The Destroying Angel, The Barefoot Boy, Desire, Richard the Lion-Hearted* 1923; *When a Man's a Man, The White Sin, Code of the Wilderness, Empty Hearts, Those Who Dare* 1924; *So Big, Flattery, Confessions of a Queen, Daughters Who Pay, Chickie* 1925; *Hearts and Fists, The Danger Girl, Whispering Smith, Rocking Moon, Laddie, Pals in Paradise* 1926; *Jewels of Desire, Three Hours, The Heart of the Yukon, The Dice Woman, For Ladies Only, Ragtime, Heroes in Blue, The Opening Night* 1927; *Skin Deep* 1929; *Mounted Fury* 1931.

Bowers, William. Screenwriter, playwright. *b.* Jan. 17, 1916, Las Cruces, N.M. *d.* 1987. A former journalist, he arrived in Hollywood early in the 40s as correspondent for a news agency and stayed to write many scripts, alone or in collaboration, often with an accent on action or humor, sometimes a blend of both. He was nominated for Academy Awards for the screenplays of *The Gunfighter* (1950) and *The Sheepman* (1958). Appeared as a Senate committee chairman in *The Godfather, Part II* (1974).

FILMS INCLUDE: *My Favorite Spy* 1942; *Higher and Higher* 1943; *The Notorious Lone Wolf* (orig. story only), *Night and Day* 1946; *The Wistful Widow of Wagon Gap* (story only), *Something in the Wind, The Web* 1947; *Black Bart, Larceny, The Countess of Monte Cristo* 1948; *The Gal Who Took the West* 1949; *The Gunfighter* 1950; *The Mob* 1951; *Assignment Paris* 1952; *Split Second* 1953; *Tight Spot* 1955; *My Man Godfrey* 1957; *The Sheepman, The Law and Jake Wade, Imitation General* 1958; *Alias Jesse James* 1959; *Advance to the Rear* 1964; *Way... Way Out* 1966; *Support Your Local Sheriff* (also prod.) 1969.

Bowie, David. Singer, actor. Born David Robert Jones, on Jan. 8, 1947, in Brixton, South London, England. A magnetically paradoxical, fair-haired rock superstar who has made an impact in sporadic films. The son of a Soho wrestling club operator and a movie-theater usherette, he dropped out of high school at 16 and eked out a living as an advertising designer. His career as a performer rose in 1972, when he started making the rounds as Ziggy Stardust, an androgynous king of space rock. His recordings quickly soared in the charts, selling in the millions. He began appearing in films in the late 60s, but it was in 1976, playing the title role in Nicolas Roeg's *The Man Who Fell to Earth,* when his enigmatic personality first found its proper expression on the screen. In 1980, Bowie astounded critics with his performance in the Broadway production of 'The Elephant Man.' A self-admitted bisexual, he is the father of a son, Zowie Bowie. He is currently married to model Iman.

FILMS: *The Image* (short) 1967; *The Virgin Soldiers* (bit) 1969; *The Man Who Fell to Earth* 1976; *Schöner Gigolo—armer Gigolo/Just a Gigolo* (Ger.) 1978; *Radio On* (as himself) 1979; *Christiane F.* (as himself; Ger.) 1981; *Cat People* (theme lyrics written and performed only) 1982; *Ziggy Stardust and the Spiders From Mars* (concert film; release delayed from 1973), *The Hunger* (US), *Merry Christmas Mr. Lawrence* (UK/Jap./NZ), *The Snowman* (short) 1983; *Into the Night, Hero* (co-mus. only) 1985; *Absolute Beginners, Labyrinth* (also songs) 1986; *When the Wind Blows* (anim; co-songs only), *The Last Temptation of Christ* (as Pontius Pilate) 1988; *Imagine—John Lennon* (doc.) 1989; *The Linguini Incident, Twin Peaks: Fire Walk with Me* 1992; *Basquiat* 1996.

Bowie, Les. Special effects artist. *b.* 1913, England. *d.* 1979. Famed for his matte shot and mechanical expertise, he was a prolific and ingenious visual artist. Among his achievements was the creation of the world in *One Million Years B.C.* on a budget of only £1,100.

FILMS INCLUDE: *Great Expectations* 1946; *The Red Shoes* 1948; *The Haunted Strangler* (also cin.), *One Million Years B.C.* (prologue designer), *The Quiller Memorandum* 1966; *Mosquito Squadron* 1968; *The Assassination Bureau* 1969; *Dracula A.D. 1972* 1972; *Call Him Mr. Shatter, The Lifetaker* 1975; *To the Devil a Daughter* 1976; *Star Wars* 1977; *Superman* 1978.

Bowman, Lee. Actor. *b.* Dec. 28, 1914, Cincinnati. *d.* 1979. After university studies in the US and France, he attended the American Academy of Dramatic Arts and began a modest career as stage actor and radio singer. Tall, dark, and suave, he made his film debut in 1937 and played many romantic leads and second leads through the 40s, when he began devoting his energies mostly to the stage. His best-remembered film role was the lead opposite Susan Hayward in *Smash-Up* (1947). In the early 50s he starred in the TV series 'Ellery Queen.' After retiring from acting he became a special consultant to the Republican Campaign Committee and later to Bethlehem Steel, coaching politicians and business executives in the art of public speaking and on-camera techniques.

FILMS INCLUDE: *Internes Can't Take Money, I Met Him in Paris, The Last Train from Madrid, Sophie Lang Goes West* 1937; *Having Wonderful Time, A Man to Remember, Tarnished Angel, Next Time I Marry* 1938; *Love Affair, Fast and Furious, Dancing Co-Ed, The Great Victor Herbert* 1939; *Florian, Gold Rush Maisie, Wyoming, Third Finger Left Hand* 1940; *Buck Privates, Model Wife, Washington Melodrama, Design for Scandal* 1941; *Kid Glove Killer, We Were Dancing, Pacific Rendezvous, Tish* 1942; *Three Hearts for Julia, Bataan* 1943; *Cover Girl, Up in Mable's Room, The Impatient Years* 1944; *Tonight and Every Night, She Wouldn't Say Yes* 1945; *The Walls Came Tumbling Down* 1946; *Smash-Up* 1947; *My Dream Is Yours* 1949; *There's a Girl in My Heart, House by the River* 1950; *Youngblood Hawke* 1964.

Box, Betty. Producer. Born in 1920, in Beckenham, Kent, England. The sister of Sydney Box and wife of producer Peter Rogers (*Carry On, Sergeant; Carry On, Nurse;* etc.), she started out as an assistant to her brother on more than 200 propaganda and training films during WW II. Afterward continued with such films as *The Seventh Veil* (1945) and *The Years Between* (1946). In 1947 she was put in charge of production at the Islington Studios and has since produced numerous pictures.

FILMS INCLUDE: *Dear Murderer* 1947; *The Blind Goddess* 1948; *So Long at the Fair, The Clouded Yellow* 1950; *Appointment with Venus/Island Rescue* 1951; *The Venetian Bird/The Assassin* 1952; *A Day to Remember* 1953; *Doctor in the House* 1954; *Doctor at Sea* 1955; *Checkpoint* 1956; *A Tale of Two Cities* 1957; *The 39 Steps, Conspiracy of Hearts* 1960; *No Love for Johnnie* 1961; *Hot Enough for June/Agent 8¾* 1963; *Deadlier Than the Male* 1966; *Nobody Runs Forever, The High Commissioner* 1968; *Some Girls Do* 1969; *Doctor in Trouble* 1970; *Percy* 1971; *Percy's Progress/It's Not the Size That Counts* 1974.

Box, John. Art director. Born Jan. 27, 1920, in London. *ed.* London School of Architecture. In British films in various capacities since 1947, he came into his own in the 60s as a leading production designer of grand-scale films in Britain and the US, winning several Academy Awards (designated AA below).

FILMS INCLUDE: *Zarak* 1957; *The Inn of the Sixth Happiness* 1958; *Our Man in Havana* 1959; *The World of Suzie Wong* 1961; *Lawrence of Arabia* (AA) 1962; *Of Human Bondage* 1964; *Doctor Zhivago* (AA) 1965; *A Man for All Seasons* (BFA Award) 1966; *Oliver!* (AA, Moscow Festival Award) 1968; *The Looking Glass War* (prod.) 1970; *Nicholas and Alexandra* (AA) 1971; *Travels with My Aunt* 1972; *The*

Great Gatsby 1974; *Rollerball* 1975; *Sorcerer* 1977; *The Keep* 1983; *A Passage to India* 1984.

Box, Muriel and **Sydney.** British wife-husband screenwriter-director-producer team. Muriel (*b.* Muriel Baker, 1905, Tolworth, England) started out in 1927 as script girl for director Anthony Asquith. She wrote her first script, for the film *Alibi Inn,* in 1935. That same year she married Sydney (*b.* Apr. 29, 1907, Beckenham, Eng.; *d.* 1983). They teamed up to write dozens of one-act plays. In 1939, Sydney founded a motion picture company, which produced scores of propaganda and training films for the British government during WW II. After the war, he established himself as one of Britain's top producers and collaborated with his wife on the screenplays of most of his films. They shared an Oscar for the original script of *The Seventh Veil* (1945). In the early 50s, Muriel turned director, and Sydney continued as occasional co-scriptwriter. Their collaboration ended in 1958, when Sydney became a British TV executive. They divorced in 1969, and the following year Muriel married Lord Gardiner. In 1974 she published an autobiography, *Odd Woman Out.* Sydney was the brother of Betty Box.

FILMS INCLUDE: As screenwriters, Sydney producing—*The Seventh Veil* 1945; *The Years Between* 1946; *The Man Within/The Smugglers* (Muriel also co-prod.), *The Brothers, Daybreak, Dear Murderer* (Muriel also co-prod.), *Holiday Camp* 1947; *Quartet* (Sydney prod. only), *The Blind Goddess, Easy Money, Portrait from Life/The Girl in the Painting* (all co-sc. only) 1948; *Christopher Columbus* (co-sc. only) 1949; *The Astonished Heart* (Muriel only), *So Long at the Fair* (co-sc. only) 1950; *Deadlier Than the Male* (Sydney prod. only). Muriel directing (complete)—*The Happy Family/Mr. Lord Says No!* (also co-sc.) 1952; *A Prince for Cynthia* (short), *Street Corner, Both Sides of the Law* (also co-sc.) 1953; *To Dorothy a Son/Cash on Delivery, The Beachcomber* 1954; *Simon and Laura* 1955; *Eyewitness* 1956; *The Passionate Stranger/A Novel Affair* (also co-sc.) 1957; *The Truth About Women* (also prod.) 1958; *Subway in the Sky, This Other Eden* (Ire.) 1959; *Too Young to Love* 1960; *The Piper's Tune* 1962; *Rattle of a Simple Man* 1964.

box office. 1. The booth in a theater or other place of entertainment where tickets of admission are sold. 2. The gross receipts from the exhibition of a play, a film, or any other entertainment. 3. The potential profit of a show, as in "This film will be good box office."

As a center of a multimillion dollar industry, Hollywood has always been intensely conscious not only of box-office current receipts but also of the box-office potential of its producers, directors, and especially its actors. Many a star's future career has been determined by the extent of his or her popularity at the box office. For many years lists of leading box-office stars were published. For producers and directors there was the Champion of Champions poll, conducted among exhibitors on the basis of film receipts. There were even special lists compiled of top moneymaking Western stars, as well as a special survey of young potential stars.

Since it is difficult to determine to what extent any producer, director, or star contributes to the box-office popularity of any film, the validity of all these lists, whatever their worth, is at best doubtful. The one compilation that does deserve some attention is the master list of the all-time top moneymaking films, which throws some light on American public taste and preferences at the cinema box office.

Accompanying is a list of the top five moneymaking films from each of the last four decades, as of October 1996, according to *Variety.* The figures quoted reflect rental figures—that is, the monies paid to film distributors (usually studios) by film exhibitors (movie theaters or theater chains). They do not directly reflect gross box office receipts—the monies paid to theaters by moviegoers. These numbers cover only receipts from the US-Canada market and omit foreign market rentals. They also omit such lucrative sources of income as merchandising and sales to television and video.

ALL-TIME FILM RENTAL CHAMPIONS: 1960S–1990S

Film	Director	Studio	Total Film Rentals US & Canada
1990s			
1 *Jurassic Park* 1993	Steven Spielberg	Universal	380,000,000
2 *Forrest Gump* 1994	Robert Zemekis	Paramount	330,000,000
3 *The Lion King* 1994	Roger Allen/Rob Minkoff	Disney	315,000,000
4 *Independence Day* 1996	Roland Emmerich	Fox	300,000,000
5 *Home Alone* 1990	Chris Columbus	Fox	285,000,000
1980s			
1 *E.T. The Extra-terrestrial* 1982	Steven Spielberg	Universal	400,000,000
2 *Return of the Jedi* 1983	Richard Marquand	Fox	265,000,000
3 *Batman* 1989	Tim Burton	Warners	252,000,000
4 *Raiders of the Lost Ark* 1981	Steven Spielberg	Paramount	245,000,000
5 *Ghostbusters* 1984	Ivan Reitman	Columbia	240,000,000
1970s			
1 *Star Wars* 1977	George Lucas	Fox	193,777,000
2 *Jaws* 1975	Steven Spielberg	Universal	129,549,000
3 *Grease* 1978	Randal Kleiser	Paramount	96,300,000
4 *The Exorcist* 1973	William Friedkin	Warners	89,000,000
5 *The Godfather* 1972	Francis Ford Coppola	Paramount	86,275,000
1960s			
1 *The Sound of Music* 1965	Robert Wise	Fox	79,975,000
2 *Doctor Zhivago* 1965	David Lean	MGM/United Artists	60,964,000
3 *Butch Cassidy and the Sundance Kid* 1969	George Roy Hill	Fox	45,953,000
4 *Mary Poppins* 1964	Robert Stevenson	Disney	45,000,000
5 *The Graduate* 1968	Mike Nichols	Avco Embassy	44,091,000

Boyd, Russell. Director of photography. Born in 1944 in Australia. A superior craftsman, he was behind the camera of some of the finest Australian productions in the vintage years of the late 70s and early 80s. He also excelled on several American films. He won the British Academy Award for the cinematography of *Picnic at Hanging Rock* (1975).

FILMS INCLUDE: *Between Wars, The Man from Hong Kong* 1974; *Picnic at Hanging Rock* 1975; *Break of Day* 1976; *The Last Wave* 1977; *Dawn* 1978; *Chain Reaction* 1979; *Gallipoli, Starstruck* 1981; *Tender Mercies* (US), *The Year of Living Dangerously* 1982; *Phar Lap* 1983; *A Soldier's Story* (US), *Mrs. Soffel* (US) 1984; *Burke and Wills* 1985; *"Crocodile" Dundee* 1986; *High Tide* 1987; *The Rescue* 1988; *Confidence* 1989.

Boyd, Stephen. Actor. *b.* William Millar, July 4, 1928, Belfast. *d.* 1977. Rugged leading man of British, American, and international films. On stage since childhood, he came to Canada in 1946 and performed on radio and in summer stock. In 1950 he toured the US with a stock company and decided to stay but found the going rough and had to work as a cafeteria attendant for a living. He finally broke into films in England in 1955 and four years later achieved international fame as Messala in MGM's spectacle *Ben-Hur.* He subsequently starred in many American and European productions. In the early 70s he appeared mainly in bottom-budget Spanish films.

FILMS INCLUDE: *An Alligator Named Daisy* 1955; *The Man Who Never Was, A Hill in Korea* 1956; *Seven Waves Away/Abandon Ship, Island in the Sun* 1957; *Les Bijoutiers Du Clair De Lune/The Night Heaven Fell* (Fr./It.), *The Bravados* (US) 1958; *Woman Obsessed* (US), *The Best of Everything* (US), *Ben-Hur* (as Messala; US) 1959; *The Big Gamble* 1961; *The Inspector/Lisa* (UK/US), *Jumbo* (US) 1962; *The Fall of the Roman Empire* (US), *The Third Secret* 1964; *Genghis Khan* (US/UK/Ger.) 1965; *The Oscar* (US), *Fantastic Voyage* (US), *La Bibbia/The Bible* (as Nimrod; It./Us) 1966; *The Caper of the Golden Bulls* (US) 1967; *Assignment K, Shalako* 1968; *Slaves* (US) 1969; *Kill! Kill! Kill! Kill!* (Fr./Ger./It./Sp.) 1971; *Il Diavolo A Sette Facce/The Devil Has Seven Faces* (It.) 1972; *The Man Called Noon* 1973; *Impossible Love* (Sp.), *La Polizia Interviene—Ordine Di Uccidere* 1975; *Evil in the Deep* (US), *Potato Fritz* (Ger.) 1976; *The Squeeze* 1977.

Boyd, William (Bill). Actor, producer. *b.* June 5, 1895, Cambridge, Ohio. *d.* 1972. Shortly after his family moved to Oklahoma, both his parents died; he was forced to quit school and toiled in the state's oil fields. He later worked his way westward at an assortment of odd jobs (orange packer, laborer, and night watchman in California) while trying to break into movies.

He landed his first film role in 1919, as an extra in Cecil B. DE MILLE's *Why Change Your Wife?* (released 1920). He later became a favorite actor of De Mille, who gave him some of his best silent film roles, such as the lead in *The Volga Boatman* and the part of Simon of Cyrene in *King of Kings.* Ruggedly handsome, Boyd was a popular hero of many major films in the 20s, including Lewis Milestone's *Two Arabian Knights* and D. W. Griffith's *Lady of the Pavements.*

Boyd's popularity suffered in 1931 when a stage actor, also named William Boyd (he had also played some film parts), was involved in a gambling and liquor scandal. Earlier Boyd had tried to put a stop to the identity confusion by changing his name to Bill; eventually, when the stage actor died, he changed his name back to William. In film circles they still refer to the "Other Boyd" as William "Stage" Boyd (1890–1935), who appeared in such films as *The Locked Door* (1929), *Sky Devils* and *Painted Woman* (both 1932), and *Oliver Twist* (1933). To add to the confusion, a third Bill Boyd (1910–77), nicknamed "The Cowboy Rambler," starred in six musical Westerns as a singing cowboy, including *Raiders of the West* and *Rolling Down the Great Divide* (both 1942).

A new phase in Boyd's career began when he was chosen to star in the Western *Hop-a-Long Cassidy* in 1935. (The hyphens were later dropped and the name written Hopalong.) The film's success launched a series of productions based on the Clarence E. Mulford stories of the Wild West. Boyd, who had always been a poor rider, quickly adapted himself to the cowboy image and became an excellent horseman on a mount called Topper. Boyd's prematurely gray hair added dignity to the character, who didn't smoke, drink, or swear. He played 54 Cassidy episodes before producer Harry (Pop) Sherman dropped the series in 1943. Boyd then took over as producer and turned out 12 more episodes. He later acquired all rights to the Cassidy character, and when television came along, he made a fortune from exhibiting his old films, from the production of new ones, and from a variety of by-products tied in with the name of the western hero. Three of Boyd's four marriages ended in divorce. All four of his wives were film actresses: Ruth Miller (married 1921, later divorced), Elinor FAIR (1926–29), Dorothy Sebastian (1930–36), and Grace Bradley (from 1937).

FILMS INCLUDE: *Why Change Your Wife?* (extra) 1920; *Brewster's Millions, Moonlight and Honeysuckle, Exit the Vamp* 1921; *Bobbed Hair, Nice People, Manslaughter, The Young Rajah* 1922; *The Temple of Venus, Enemies of Children* 1923; *Changing Husbands, Tarnish, Feet of Clay* 1924; *Forty Winks, The Midshipman, The Road to Yesterday* 1925; *Steel Preferred, The Volga Boatman, Eve's Leaves, Her Man o' War, The Last Frontier* 1926; *Jim the Conqueror, Wolves of the Air, The Yankee Clipper, The King of Kings, Dress Parade, Two Arabian Knights* 1927; *The Night Flyer, Skyscraper, Power, The Cop* 1928; *Lady of the Pavements, The Leatherneck, High Voltage, The Flying Fool, His First Command* 1929; *Officer O'Brien* 1930; *The Painted Desert, Beyond Victory, The Big Gamble, Suicide Fleet* 1931; *Carnival Boat* 1932; *Lucky Devils, Emergency Call* 1933; *Hop-a-Long Cassidy, The Eagle's Broad, Bar 20 Rides Again* 1935; *Call of the Prairie, Three on the Trail, Heart of the West, Hop-a-Long Cassidy Returns, Federal Agent* 1936; *Borderland, North of the Rio Grande, Hopalong Rides Again, Texas Trail* 1937; *Partners of the Plains, Heart of Arizona, Pride of the West, Cassidy of Bar 20, In Old Mexico, The Frontiersman* 1938; *Range War, Law of the Pampas* 1939; *Santa Fe Marshal, The Showdown* 1940; *Doomed Caravan, Border Vigilantes, Wide Open Town* 1941; *Undercover Man, Lost Canyon* 1942; *Hoppy Serves a Writ, Border Patrol, False Colors* 1943; *Mystery Man, Forty Thieves, Texas Masquerade* 1944; *The Devil's Playground* 1946; *Unexpected Guest, Dangerous Venture, The Marauders* 1947; *The Dead Don't Dream, Sinister Journey, False Paradise* 1948; *The Greatest Show on Earth* (cameo) 1952.

Boyer, Charles. Actor. *b.* Aug. 28, 1897, Figeac, France. *d.* 1978. *ed.* Sorbonne (philosophy); Paris Conservatory (drama). Made both his stage and his film debut in 1920, but for the remainder of the decade developed primarily as a stage actor, a matinee idol Paris-style. In 1929–31 he made a tentative and not-too-successful stab at a Hollywood career, but after an auspicious interlude in Europe, he returned to Hollywood in 1934 to stay. This time he rapidly developed as one of the American screen's "great lovers," a celluloid personification of Gallic charm and romance. His tools in trade were a deep velvet voice, inviting eyes, and matchless bedroom elegance. A fine actor, as well as a lady's heartthrob, he played opposite some of Hollywood's most glamorous female stars of the 30s and 40s, from Garbo to Bergman.

During WW II, Boyer became active in cementing Franco-American cultural relations and in 1942 won a special Academy Award for establishing the French Research Foundation in Los Angeles. He later became an American citizen. From the early 50s he appeared in films on both sides of the Atlantic, in increasingly mature roles. He also made occasional stage appearances, most memorably in Shaw's 'Don Juan in Hell.' In 1951 he was a co-founder, with Dick Powell and David Niven, of Four Star Television and starred in many of the company's TV productions in the 50s and 60s. Boyer took his own life with an overdose of barbiturates just two days before his 81st birthday and two days after the death of his wife since 1934, British-born actress Pat (Patricia) Paterson. Their only child, Michael, committed suicide in 1965.

FILMS: In France—*L'Homme du Large* 1920; *Chantelouve* 1921; *Le Grillon du Foyer* 1922; *L'Esclave* 1923; *La Ronde infernale* 1927; *Le Capitaine Fracasse* 1929. In the US—*Le Procès du Mary Dugan* (French version of *The Trial of Mary Dugan*) 1929; *Revolte dans la Prison* (French version of *The Big House*) 1930. In Germany—*La Barcarolle d'Amour* (French version of *Brand in der Oper/Barcarole*) 1930; *Tumultes* (French version of *Stürme der Leidenschaft*) 1931. In the US—*The Magnificent Lie* 1931; *The Man from Yesterday, Red-Headed Woman* 1932. In Germany—*F.P. 1 ne répond plus* (French version of *F.P. 1 antwortet nicht*) 1932; *Moi et l'Impératrice* (French version of *Ich und die Kaiserin*), *The Only Girl/Heart Song* (English version of *Ich und die Kaiserin*) 1933. In France—*L'Epervier/Les Amoureux* 1933; *La Bataille* (and English version, *The Battle*), *Liliom* 1934. In the US—*Caravan* (and French version, *Carvane*) 1934. In France—*Le Bonheur* 1935. In the US—*Private Worlds, Break of Hearts, Shanghai* 1935; *Mayerling* (as Archduke Rudolph of Austria) 1936. In the US—*The Garden of Allah* 1936; *History Is Made at Night, Conquest/Maria Walewska* (as Napoleon), *Tovarich* 1937; *Algiers* (as Pepe le Moko) 1938. In France—*Orage* 1938. In the US—*Love Affair, When Tomorrow Comes* 1939; *All This and Heaven Too* 1940; *Back Street, Hold Back the Dawn, Appointment for Love* 1941; *Tales of Manhattan* 1942; *Untel Père et Fils/The Heart of a Nation* (narrator only; made in France in 1940 but completed and narration added in the US, where it was first shown), *The Constant Nymph, Flesh and Fantasy* 1943; *Gaslight, Together Again* 1944; *Confidential Agent* 1945; *Cluny Brown* 1946; *A Woman's Vengeance, Arch of Triumph* 1948; *The Thirteenth Letter, The First Legion* 1951; *The Happy Time* 1952; *Thunder in the East* 1953. Internationally—*Madame de. . . /The Earrings of Madame De* (Fr./It.), 1953; *Nana* (Fr./It.), *The Cobweb* (US) 1955; *La Fortuna di Essere Donna/Lucky to Be a Woman* (It./Fr.), *Paris-Palace Hôtel/Paris Hotel* (Fr./It.), *Around the World in 80 Days* (US) 1956; *Une Parisienne* (Fr./It.) 1957; *Maxime* (Fr.), *The Buccaneer* (US) 1958; *Fanny* (US) 1961; *The Four Horsemen of the Apocalypse* (US), *Les Démons de Minuit* (Fr.), *Adorable Julia* (Aus./Fr.) 1962; *Love Is a Ball* (US) 1963; *A Very Special Favor* (US) 1965; *How to Steal a Million* (US), *Paris brûle-t-il?/Is Paris Burning?* (Fr./US) 1966; *Casino Royale* (UK), *Barefoot in the Park* (US) 1967; *Le Rouble à Deux Faces/The Day the Hot Line Got Hot* (Fr./Sp.) 1968; *The April Fools* (US), *The Madwoman of Chaillot* (UK) 1969; *Lost Horizon* (US) 1972; *L'Empire d'Alexandre/Stavisky* (Fr./It.) 1974; *A Matter of Time* (US/It.) 1976.

Boyer, Jean. Director. *b.* Jan. 26, 1901, Paris. *d.* 1965. The son of noted singer and songwriter Lucien Boyer, and the brother of well-known female singer Lucienne Boyer, he started writing songs for musical films in 1930. He began writing screenplays in 1931 and directed his first film in 1932. One of France's most prolific directors, he turned out some 70 films, including several entertaining Fernandel comedies. Light, unpretentious, and geared for mass audiences, they never gained much attention outside France. He also directed Brigitte Bardot in her first film role, in *Le Trou Normand/Crazy for Love* (1952).

FILMS INCLUDE: *Monsieur Madame et Bibi* 1932; *Un Mauvais Garçon* (also sc.) 1936; *Prends la Route* 1937; *La Chaleur du Sein, Ma Soeur de Lai* (also sc.) 1938; *Noix de Coco, Circonstances atténuates/Extenuating Circumstances* (also co-sc.) 1939; *Miquette et sa Mère, Sérénade/Schubert's Serenade* 1940; *L'Acrobate, Romance de Paris* 1941; *Le Prince charmant, Boléro* 1942; *La Bonne Etoile* 1943; *La Femme fatale* 1945; *Les Aventures de Casanova/Loves of Casanova* 1947; *Mademoiselle s'amuse* (also sc.) 1948; *Tous les Chemins mènent à Rome* 1949; *Nouis irons à Paris, La Valse brillante, Le Rosier de Madame Husson/The Prize* 1950; *Le Passe-Muraille/Mr. Peek-A-Boo* (also co-sc.), *Nous irons à Monte Carlo/Monte Carlo Baby* 1951; *Le Trou Normand/Crazy for Love, Coiffeur pour Dames/The French Touch* 1952; *Femmes de Paris* 1953; *J'avais Sept Filles/My Seven Little Sins* (also co-adapt.) 1954; *La Madelon* 1955; *Le Couturier de ces Dames/Fernandel the Dressmaker* 1956; *Sénéchal le Magnifique/Senechal the Magnificent, Le Chômeur de Clochemerle* 1957; *Nina, Les Vignes du Seigneur* 1958; *Le Confident de ces Dames* 1959; *Coup de Bamboo* 1962; *Relaxe-toi Chérie* 1964.

Boyle, Lara Flynn. Actress. Born 1970, in Davenport, Iowa. *ed.* Chicago Academy of Arts. Composed, attractive young leading lady who found herself cast in a television miniseries while still in college. She has maintained a steady career in films since but is perhaps most recognized for her role in David Lynch's offbeat TV series 'Twin Peaks.'

FILMS: *Poltergeist III* 1988; *Dead Poets Society, How I Got Into College* 1989; *The Rookie* 1990; *The Dark Backward, Eye of the Storm* (Ger./US), *Mobsters* 1991; *Wayne's World, Where the Day Takes You* 1992; *Equinox, Red Rock West, The Temp* 1993; *Baby's Day Out, The Road to Wellville, Threesome* 1994; *The Big Squeeze* 1996; *Café Society, Farmer and Chase* 1997.

Boyle, Peter. Actor. Born on Oct. 18, 1933, in Philadelphia. A graduate of LaSalle College, he was a monk in the Christian Brothers order before coming to New York in search of an acting career in the early 60s. He appeared in several off-Broadway productions and was a member of the Second City satirical improvisation troupe, then began appearing on TV and in films in the late 60s. A bald, burly, but magnetic character player, he scored a personal triumph in the title role of *Joe* (1970) with a true-to-life portrayal of a redneck bigot and went on to portray a variety of other interesting characterizations in films of the 70s, in both leads and supporting roles. He was memorable in a 1977 TV special portraying Senator Joseph McCarthy.

FILMS: *The Virgin President* 1968; *Medium Cool* 1969; *Joe* (title role), *Diary of a Mad Housewife* 1970; *T. R. Baskin* 1971; *The Candidate* 1972; *Steelyard Blues, Slither, Kid Blue, The Friends of Eddie Coyle* 1973; *Crazy Joe* (title role; It.), *Young Frankenstein* (as the Monster) 1974; *Taxi Driver, Swashbuckler* 1976; *F.I.S.T., The Brink's Job* 1978; *Hardcore, Beyond the Poseidon Adventure* 1979; *Where the Buffalo Roam, In God We Trust* 1980; *Outland* 1981; *Hammett* 1982; *Yellowbeard* 1983; *Johnny Dangerously* 1984; *Turk 182!* 1985; *Surrender, Walker* 1987; *Red Heat* 1988; *The Dream Team* 1989; *Solar Crisis* (Jap.) 1990; *Shadow of the Wolf: Kickboxer II* 1991, *Honeymoon in Vegas, Nervous Ticks* 1992; *The Shadow* 1994; *Bulletproof Heart, While You Were Sleeping* 1995; *Milk and Money* 1996; *That Darn Cat* 1997.

Boyle, Robert. Art director, production designer. Born in 1910, in Los Angeles. *ed.* USC. Trained as an architect, he began appearing in films as an extra when his employers went bankrupt during the Depression. In 1933, he was hired as an assistant to art director Wiard IHNEN at Paramount, then worked for various studios as a sketch artist, draftsman, and assistant designer. He became a full-fledged art director in 1942 with *Saboteur,* a film by Alfred HITCHCOCK, a director he would serve several more times in the ensuing three decades.

FILMS INCLUDE: *Saboteur* 1942; *Flesh and Fantasy, Shadow of a Doubt* 1943; *Nocturne* 1946; *Ride the Pink Horse* 1947; *Another Part of the Forest* 1948; *Mystery Submarine* 1950; *It Came from Outer Space* 1953; *Chief Crazy Horse* 1955; *The Brothers Rico* 1957; *North by Northwest* 1959; *Cape Fear* 1962; *The Birds, The Thrill of It All* 1963; *Marnie* 1964; *The Reward* 1965; *The Russians Are Coming the Russians Are Coming* 1966; *How to Succeed in Business Without Really Trying, In Cold Blood* 1967; *The Thomas Crown Affair* 1968; *Gaily Gaily* 1969; *The Landlord* 1970; *Fiddler on the Roof* 1971; *Portnoy's Complaint* 1972; *Bite the Bullet* 1975; *Leadbelly, W. C. Fields and Me, The Shootist* 1976; *The Big Fix* 1978; *Winter Kills* 1979; *Private Benjamin* 1980; *Staying Alive* 1983; *Rhinestone* 1984; *Jumpin' Jack Flash* 1986; *Dragnet* 1987.

B picture. A low-budget film, usually shown on the lower half of a DOUBLE FEATURE program. Double bills began appearing regularly on American screens in 1932 and were the rule rather than the exception by 1935. The B picture phenomenon was spawned by the great demand for inexpensive entertainment during the Depression and the consequent need of Hollywood's big studios to keep their theater chains supplied with constant programming. There was little profit but also little risk in producing B pictures. While A PICTURES—that is, major productions on the top half of double bills—were exhibited on the basis of a percentage of the box-office take, B pictures were rented for a fixed flat rate, regardless of attendance. As the big studios gradually lost interest in the B picture, there ensued a proliferation of small independent studios—collectively known as Poverty Row, Gower Gulch, or the B-Hive—that specialized in the manufacture of B pictures for an unspectacular but nearly guaranteed profit. The leading B studios were Republic and Monogram, but there were many others, including such now-forgotten names as Grand National, Mascot, Producers Releasing Corporation (PRC), Tiffany, Sono Art-World Wide, Chesterfield, Victory, Invincible, Ambassador-Conn, Puritan, and Majestic.

The B studios cranked out their product at an astonishing rate, compensating for the meager profit outlook per picture by the sheer volume of their product. The typical B picture was a quickie made on a bargain-basement budget under coolie working conditions and on extremely tight shooting schedules that allowed directors little time for inspiration or invention. It was typically a genre picture with a formula concept, most often a crime melodrama or a Western, but many times a lowbrow comedy, a light romance, or a horror or science-fiction fantasy. On the whole, the B picture was treated by establishment critics with utter contempt, when it was reviewed at all, and indeed the great majority of the thousands of these cheaply made films that have been made over the years deserved to be ignored. Most were poorly scripted, sticking to formula plots, and standard direction, with phony cardboard backdrops and indifferent cinematography betraying their humble origins. However, from time to time the B picture factory turned out real little gems and even minor classics. Unsung directors like Val Lewton, Edgar G. Ulmer, André De Toth, Rudolph Maté, Roy Rowland, and, much later, Roger Corman, somehow managed to operate nobly within the B factory system and turn out many neat little films packed with action and atmosphere, and peopled with offbeat characters, elevating the formula through their inventiveness and craftsmanship.

The 1948 Supreme Court antitrust decision that forced the major studios to divest themselves of their theater chains, combined with the concurrent rise of television and the growing sophistication of movie audiences, signaled the end of the double feature and along with it the decline of the B picture. Low-budget movies continued to be made, as new B factories like Allied Artists and American International Pictures (AIP) emerged on the Hollywood scene. But the great B picture era that had produced millions of feet of celluloid waste but also many memorable unpretentious little films was all but gone by the early 50s.

Brabin, Charles J. Director. *b.* Apr. 17, 1883, Liverpool. *d.* 1957. He came to the US as a young man and gained some acting experience on the stage. In 1908 he joined the Edison company as a film actor, and three years later began directing films for Edison and various other companies. In 1919 he directed two of the last films of screen vamp Theda BARA, who became his wife in 1921. Brabin's work was held in high regard in the 20s. His independent production *Driven* (1923), a rural drama, was acclaimed a masterpiece by a number of contemporary critics. As a result of this and several other prestigious productions, he was chosen to direct the most ambitious project of the era, *Ben-Hur.* However, after many days of shooting and thousands of feet of disappointing rushes, Brabin was dropped by the newly formed MGM management and the assignment was turned over to Fred Niblo. Brabin sued the studio for half a million dollars in damages. In 1930 he was rehired by MGM and directed several films for the studio, including such thrillers as *The Beast of the City* and *The Mask of Fu Manchu* (both 1932). Unfortunately, Brabin's work history was to repeat itself. After starting on the prestigious *Rasputin and the Empress* (1933), starring all three Barrymores, he was removed by Irving Thalberg for inefficiency and replaced with Richard Boleslawski. In 1934, Brabin retired from films and moved to Manhattan, where he spent the rest of his years with his wife, until her death in 1955.

FILMS INCLUDE (complete from 1915): *The Awakening of John Bond* 1911; *The Man Who Disappeared* (serial), *The Midnight Ride of Paul Revere* 1914; *House of the Lost Court, The Raven* 1915; *That Sort, The Price of Fame* 1916; *Mary Jane's Pa, The Sixteenth Wife, The Secret Kingdom* (serial; co-dir. with Theodore Marston), *Babette, Persuasive Peggy, The Adopted Son, Red White and Blue Blood* 1917; *Breakers Ahead, Social Quicksands, A Pair of Cupids, The Poor Rich Man, Buchanan's Wife, His Bonded Wife* 1918; *Thou Shalt Not, Kathleen Mavourneen* (also sc.), *La Belle Russe* (also sc.) 1919; *While New York Sleeps, Blind Wives* (also sc.) 1920; *Footfalls* (also sc.) 1921; *The Broadway Peacock, The Lights of New York* (also story, sc.) 1922; *Driven* (also prod.), *Six Days* 1923; *So Big, Stella Maris* (also co-sc.) 1925; *Mismates, Twinkletoes* 1926; *Framed, Hard-Boiled Haggerty, The Valley of the Giants* 1927; *Burning Daylight, The Whip* 1928; *The Bridge of San Luis Rey* 1929; *The Ship from Shanghai, Call of the Flesh* 1930; *The Great Meadow, Sporting Blood* 1931; *The Beast of the City, New Morals for Old, The Washington Masquerade, The Mask of Fu Manchu* 1932; *The Secret of Madame Blanche, Stage Mother, Day of Reckoning* 1933; *A Wicked Woman* 1934.

Brabourne, Lord John. Producer. Born on Nov. 9, 1924, in London. Involved in the making of many fine British productions from the late 50s on. He has earned several Oscar nominations, most recently for *A Passage to India.*

FILMS INCLUDE: *Seven Thunders* (assoc. prod.) 1957; *Harry Black/Harry Black and the Tiger* 1958; *Sink the Bismarck* 1960; *H.M.S. Defiant/Damn the Defiant!* 1962; *Othello* 1965; *Dance of Death, Romeo and Juliet* 1968; *Tales of Beatrix Potter* 1971; *Murder on the Orient Express* 1974; *Death on the Nile* 1978; *The Mirror Crack'd* 1980; *Evil Under the Sun* 1982; *A Passage to India* 1984; *Little Dorrit* 1987.

Bracco, Lorraine. Actress. Born in 1955 in Brooklyn, N.Y. The daughter of a Fulton Market fishmonger, she began modeling at 16. After finishing high school, she went to Paris, where she spent ten years as a model and a disc jockey for Radio Luxembourg. She also produced a TV fashion special in 1983 and appeared in an obscure film, *Duo sur Canapé*. Returning to New York, she met and married actor Harvey KEITEL (now separated), accompanied him to acting classes, and began appearing in films, gaining instant recognition for her ability. Memorable as wiseguy wife Karen Hill in *GoodFellas*. Married Edward James OLMOS.

FILMS INCLUDE: *Duo sur Canapé* (Fr.) 1983; *Un Complicato Intrigo di Donne Vicoli e Delitti/Camorra* (It.) 1986; *The Pick-Up Artist, Someone to Watch Over Me* 1987; *Sing, The Dream Team, Sea of Love* 1989; *On a Moonlit Night, GoodFellas* 1990; *Switch, Talent for the Game* 1991; *Medicine Man, Radio Flyer, Traces of Red* 1992; *Being Human, Even Cowgirls Get the Blues* 1994; *The Basketball Diaries, Hackers* 1995.

Brach, Gérard. French screenwriter. Born in 1927 in Paris. He was a penniless newly divorced Parisian, just back from a sanatorium after a five-year recuperation from tuberculosis, when he met the equally broke Roman POLANSKI at a Paris party in 1963. The two became close friends and career-long script collaborators. Brach eventually became established as one of France's premier screenwriters, working in a variety of genres for many directors.

FILMS INCLUDE: *Aimez-vous les Femmes?/A Taste for Women* (dial. only), *Les Plus Belles Escroqueries du Monde/The Beautiful Swindlers* 1964; *Repulsion* (UK) 1965; *Cul-de-Sac* (UK) 1966; *Dance of the Vampires/The Fearless Vampire Killers* (UK/US), *Le Vieil Homme et l'Enfant/The Two of Us* 1967; *La Promesse/Secret World* 1969; *Che?/What?* (It./Fr.) 1973; *Le Locataire/The Tenant* 1976; *Le Point de Mire* 1977; *Tess* 1979; *Chère Inconnue/I Sent a Letter to My Love* 1980; *La Guerre du Feu/Quest for Fire* 1981; *L'Africain/The African, La Femme de Mon Pote/My Best Friend's Girl* 1983; *Les Favoris de la Lune/Favorites of the Moon* 1984; *Maria's Lovers* (US) 1985; *Pirates, The Name of the Rose* (It./Fr./Ger.), *Jean de Florette, Manon des Sources/Manon of the Spring* 1986; *Shy People* (US) 1987; *Frantic* (US) 1988; *Domino* (It.), *The Bear, Une vie suspendué* 1989; *Divertimenti nella casa privata* 1990.

Bracken, Eddie. Actor. Born Edward Vincent Bracken, on Feb. 7, 1920, in Astoria, Queens, N.Y. Educated at New York's Professional Children's School, he made an early start in show business, acting and singing on stage and in vaudeville and nightclubs before he reached ten. As a child he also appeared in four "Our Gang" comedy shorts and in six episodes of another comedy series, "The New York Kiddie Troopers," at Fox. Following several successful juvenile stints on Broadway and on tour, he was signed by Paramount, making his feature film debut in 1940. His comic talent and shy, befuddled, bumbling professional personality were put to good use in many light films, memorably in two superior Preston Sturges comedies, *The Miracle of Morgan's Creek* and *Hail the Conquering Hero* (both 1944). Bracken's film career declined sharply in the early 50s and he retired from the screen in 1953. He later appeared in many stage productions and TV programs but failed to sustain the popularity he had attained in films. He became involved in theatrical ventures as a producer but suffered a serious financial setback in the early 70s when his grandiose plan to create a chain of stock theaters collapsed in a disastrous fiasco, resulting in a $2 million loss.

FILMS: *Too Many Girls* 1940; *Life With Henry, Reaching for the Sun, Caught in the Draft* 1941; *The Fleet's In, Sweater Girl, Star Spangled Rhythm* 1942; *Young and Willing, Happy Go Lucky* 1943; *The Miracle of Morgan's Creek, Hail the Conquering Hero, Rainbow Island* 1944; *Bring on the Girls, Out of This World, Duffy's Tavern, Hold That Blonde* 1945; *Ladies' Man, Fun on a Weekend* 1947; *The Girl from Jones Beach* 1949; *Summer Stock* 1950; *Two Tickets to Broadway* 1951; *About Face, We're Not Married* 1952; *A Slight Case of Larceny* 1953; *Wild Wild World* (doc.; narrator only; It.), *Una Domenica d'Estate* (bit; It.) 1961; *Shinbone Alley* (voice only) 1971; *National Lampoon's Vacation* 1983; *Oscar* 1991; *Home Alone 2* 1992; *Baby's Day Out* 1994.

Brackett, Charles. Producer, screenwriter. *b.* Nov. 26, 1892, Saratoga Springs, N.Y. *d.* 1969. After graduating from Williams College in 1915, he studied law at Harvard, as had his father, who also served in the New York legislature. His studies were interrupted by World War I service in Europe, first as vice-consul in Nazaire, France, then as a second lieutenant with the American Expeditionary Forces. Upon his discharge, he returned to Harvard and in 1920 completed his law studies and also published his first novel, *The Council of the Ungodly.* For the next six years he practiced law but continued writing magazine articles and stories. His second novel, *Weekend* (1925), resulted in a post with *The New Yorker* as drama critic, a job he held until 1929. His other novels include *The Last Infirmity, American Colony,* and *Entirely Surrounded.* Hollywood began buying stories from Brackett in the early 20s.

In 1932 Brackett signed a contract as a staff writer with Paramount, but his first credit as a screenwriter did not come until 1935. After several indifferent collaborations, he was assigned by Paramount to work with Billy WILDER, then a young writer from Vienna. Their collaboration was successful from the start, resulting in some of the brightest Hollywood screenplays in the period 1938 to 1950. In 1943 they embarked upon their celebrated teamwork as producer (Brackett), director (Wilder), and screenwriter (both), which was to win them Academy Awards for *The Lost Weekend* (1945) and *Sunset Boulevard* (1950).

Brackett went on to produce many distinguished films, collaborating with other directors and screenwriters. In 1953 he won another Academy Award, as co-author of the screenplay of *Titanic.* He was president of the Academy of Motion Picture Arts and Sciences from 1949 to 1955.

FILMS: Based on his stories—*Tomorrow's Love* 1924; *Risky Business* 1926; *Pointed Heels* 1929; *Secrets of a Secretary* 1931; *Woman Trap* 1936. As screenwriter, in collaboration—*Enter Madame, College Scandal, The Last Outpost, Without Regret* 1935; *Rose of the Rancho, Piccadilly Jim, The Jungle Princess* (uncredited), *Wild Money* (uncredited), *Live Love and Learn* 1937; *Bluebeard's Eighth Wife* 1938; *Midnight, What a Life, Ninotchka* 1939; *Arise My Love* 1940; *Hold Back the Dawn* 1941; *Ball of Fire, The Major and the Minor* 1942. As producer-screenwriter—*Five Graves to Cairo* 1943; *The Lost Weekend* 1945; *To Each His Own* (also story) 1946; *The Emperor Waltz* (also co-story), *A Foreign Affair, Miss Tatlock's Millions* 1948; *Sunset Boulevard* 1950; *The Mating Season* 1951; *The Model and the Marriage Broker* 1952; *Niagara* (also co-story), *Titanic* (co-sc., also co-story) 1953; *The Girl in the Red Velvet Swing* (also co-story) 1955; *Teenage Rebel* 1956; *Journey to the Center of the Earth* 1959. As producer only—*The Uninvited* 1944; *Garden of Evil, Woman's World* 1954; *The Virgin Queen* 1955; *D-Day the Sixth of June, The King and I* 1956; *The Wayward Bus* 1957; *The Gift of Love, Ten North Frederick* 1958; *The Remarkable Mr. Pennypacker, Blue Denim* 1959; *High Time* 1960; *State Fair* 1962.

Brackett, Leigh. American novelist, screenwriter. *b.* 1915. *d.* 1978. She worked only sporadically in films, notably contributing screenplays for several major Howard Hawks productions, alone or in collaboration. As a novelist she specialized in science fiction and mystery.

FILMS: *The Vampire's Ghost* (story, sc.), *Crime Doctor's Manhunt* (sc.) 1945; *The Big Sleep* (co-sc.) 1946; *Rio Bravo* (co-sc.) 1959; *Gold of the Seven Saints* (co-sc.) 1961; *13 West Street* (novel basis only, *The Tiger Among Us*), *Hatari!* 1962; *El Dorado* (sc.) 1967; *Rio Lobo* (co-sc.) 1970; *The Long Goodbye* (sc.) 1973; *The Empire Strikes Back* (co-sc.) 1980.

Bradbury, Ray. Novelist, screenwriter. Born Ray Douglas Spaulding on August 22, 1920, in Waukegan, Ill. Prolific, acclaimed science-fiction writer who has dabbled in an eclectic assortment of films. A former newsboy, he published his first story at 21; three of his novels have become films (*The Illustrated Man, Fahrenheit 451, Something Wicked This Way Comes*). He (and co-writer John Huston) won an Oscar for the screenplay to *Moby Dick*.

FILMS INCLUDE: *The Beast from 20,000 Fathoms* 1953; *Moby Dick* (co-sc.) 1956; *Icarus Montgolfier Wright* (co-sc.) 1962; *An American Journey* (doc., also creative cons.) 1964; *Picasso Summer* (co-sc. as Douglas Spaulding) 1969; *Rich and Famous* (act. only) 1981; *Something Wicked This Way Comes* 1983; *The Fantasy Film World of George Pal* (doc., appearance only).

Bradbury, Robert North. American director. Born in 1885(?). A Western specialist, he directed numerous low-budget silent and sound horse operas for various Hollywood studios. Among the cowboy stars he directed was his son, Robert North Bradbury, Jr., who became popular as Bob STEELE. Jack HOXIE and, in the early 30s, John WAYNE were others. Bradbury wrote many of his own scripts.

FILMS INCLUDE: *The Iron Test* (serial, co-dir. with Paul Hurst) 1918; *The Faith of the Strong* 1919; *The Death Trap* (also sc.) 1920; *Things Men Do* (also sc.) 1921; *Riders of the Law* (also sc.) 1922; *The Forbidden Trail* (also sc., edit.), *Desert Rider, What Love Will Do, The Red Warning* 1923; *Wanted by the Law* (also sc.), *The Galloping Ace, The Phantom Horseman, Yankee Speed* (also sc.), *In High Gear* (also co-story, co-sc.) 1924; *Moccasins, Riders of Mystery, The Speed Demon, The Battler* (also sc.) 1925; *The Border Sheriff* (also sc.), *The Fighting Doctor, Davy Crockett at the Fall of the Alamo* 1926; *Sitting Bull at the Spirit Lake Massacre, The Mojave Kid* 1927; *Lightning Speed* (also story, sc.), *The Bantam Cowboy* (also story) 1928; *Son of the Plains* (also story, sc.) 1931; *The Man From Hell's Hinges* (also story, sc.) 1932; *Hidden Valley, Galloping Romeo* (also story) 1933; *Blue Steel* (also story, sc.) 1934; *Westward Ho!* 1935; *Cavalry* 1936; *Stars Over Arizona* (also prod.), *Danger Valley* (also prod.), *Trouble in Texas* 1937.

Bradbury, Robert North, Jr. See STEELE, Bob.

Bradna, Olympe. Actress. Born on Aug. 12, 1920, in Paris, backstage in the famous Olympia Theater, where her parents were presenting a dog act. A fourth-generation circus performer, she joined the family act at 18 months and later developed her own acrobatic dance routine. While still a teenager she was performing at the Folies-Bergère, and in 1934 she was included in the Folies troupe that toured the US. An attractive brunette, she soon found her way to Hollywood, where she enjoyed a minor career as a leading lady in the late 30s. She retired in 1941 to marry a California socialite.

FILMS INCLUDE: *Three Cheers for Love, College Holiday* 1936; *The Last Train from Madrid, Souls at Sea* 1937; *Stolen Heaven, Say It in French* 1938; *The Night of Nights* 1939; *South of Pago Pago* 1940; *Highway West, Knockout, International Squadron* 1941.

Brady, Alice. Actress. *b.* Nov. 2, 1892, New York City. *d.* 1939. The daughter of noted stage and film producer William A. Brady, she studied voice and began her stage career as a singer-actress in operettas, at first using the stage name Rose Marie. In her twenties she established herself as a fine dramatic performer on Broadway and in silent films, many of which were produced by her father's company. On the screen, she played romantic leads and was among the highest paid stars during the WW I era. But she became disenchanted with films in the early 20s and in 1924 returned to the stage. It wasn't until the 30s that she returned to the screen. By that time, she was cast mainly in character roles, ranging from screwball comedy to heavy drama. She was nominated for an Oscar for *My Man Godfrey* (1936) and won the best supporting actress Academy Award for her performance in *In Old Chicago* (1938). She died of cancer shortly after completing a key role in John Ford's *Young Mr. Lincoln* (1939).

FILMS INLCUDE: *As Ye Sow* 1914; *The Boss, The Cup of Chance, The Lure of Woman* 1915; *The Ballet Girl, Tangled Fates, Miss Petticoats, La Vie de Boheme* (as Mimi), *The Gilded Cage, Bought and Paid For* 1916; *A Hungry Heart, The Dancer's Peril, Darkest Russia, Maternity, The Divorce Game, Betsy Ross* (title role), *The Maid of Belgium, Her Silent Sacrifice* 1917; *Woman and Wife* (as Jane Eyre), *The Knife, The Spurs of Sybil, The Ordeal of Rosetta, The Whirlpool, The Death Dance* 1918; *The Indestructible Wife, Marie Ltd., Redhead, His Bridal Night* 1919; *The Fear Market, Sinners, The New York Idea* 1920; *Out of the Chorus, Little Italy, The Land of Hope, Dawn of the East, Hush Money* 1921; *Anna Ascends, Missing Millions* 1922; *The Leopardess, The Snow Bride* 1923; *When Ladies Meet, Broadway to Hollywood, Beauty for Sale, Stage Mother, Should Ladies Behave?* 1933; *The Gay Divorcee* 1934; *Gold Diggers of 1935, Lady Tubbs, Metropolitan* 1935; *The Harvester, My Man Godfrey, Go West Young Man* 1936; *Three Smart Girls, Mama Steps Out, 100 Men and a Girl* 1937; *In Old Chicago, Joy of Living, Goodbye Broadway* 1938; *Zenobia, Young Mr. Lincoln* 1939.

Brady, Scott. Actor. *b.* Gerald Tierney, Sept. 13, 1924, Brooklyn, N.Y. *d.* 1985, of respiratory failure. Younger brother of screen actor Lawrence TIERNEY. A lumberjack in his youth and a lightweight boxing champion during his service in the Navy, the husky, handsome Brady enrolled at a Beverly Hills drama school after his discharge in 1945. He made his film debut in 1948 and has played many tough-guy leading roles, mostly in Westerns and other low-budget productions. He was also seen much on TV, including the title role in the series 'Shotgun Slade' and a recurring part in 'Police Story.' Late in his career he played mainly character roles.

FILMS INCLUDE: *Canon City, He Walked by Night* 1948; *Undertow, The Gal Who Took the West* 1949; *Port of New York, Kansas Raiders, I Was a Shoplifter, Undercover Girl* 1950; *The Model and the Marriage Broker, Bronco Buster, Montana Belle, Untamed Frontier, Yankee Buccaneer, Bloodhounds of Broadway* 1952; *A Perilous Journey* 1953; *White Fire, Johnny Guitar, The Law vs. Billy the Kid* (as Billy), *El Alamein* 1954; *Gentlemen Marry Brunettes, The Vanishing American* 1955; *Mohawk, The Maverick Queen* 1956; *The Restless Breed, The Storm Rider* 1957; *Ambush at Cimarron Pass, Blood Arrow*

1958; *Battle Flame* 1959; *Operation Bikini* 1963; *John Goldfarb Please Come Home* 1964; *Black Spurs* 1965; *Castle of Evil, Destination Inner Space* 1966; *Red Tomahawk, Journey to the Center of Time, Fort Utah* 1967; *Arizona Bushwhackers* 1968; *Five Bloody Graves, Marooned, Satan's Sadists* 1969; *Cain's Way, Hell's Bloody Devils* 1970; *$* 1971; *The Loners* 1972; *Wicked Wicked* 1973; *The China Syndrome* 1979; *Dead Kids* (Austral./NZ) 1981; *Gremlins* 1984.

Braga, Sonia. Actress. Born in 1951, in Maringa, Parana, Brazil. Dark, petite, earthy, sensual leading lady of Brazilian and international films. Orphaned from her part-black realtor father at age eight, she helped support her part-Indian seamstress mother and her six siblings at 14, when she began appearing in a children's show on Brazilian TV. She first performed on the Sao Paolo stage at 17, later gaining attention in a local production of 'Hair.' Leading roles in TV soap operas led to early film appearances, a worldwide reputation as the sex symbol of Brazil and eventually an ongoing career in films.

FILMS INCLUDE: *The Main Road, A Moreninha, Captain Bandeira vs. Dr. Moura Brasil, Mestica, The Indomitable Slave, The Couple* 1970–76; *Dona Flor e seus Dois Maridos/Dona Flor and Her Two Husbands* 1977; *I Love You, The Lady on the Bus* 1981; *Gabriela* 1983; *Kiss of the Spider Woman* (US/Braz.) 1985; *The Milagro Beanfield War* (US), *Moon Over Parador* (US) 1988; *The Rookie* (US) 1990; *Roosters* 1993; *Tieta of Agreste, Two Deaths* 1996.

Brahm, John. Director. *b.* Hans Brahm, Aug. 17, 1893, Hamburg, Germany. *d.* 1982. Son of noted stage actor Ludwig Brahm, he worked as a stage director in Vienna, Berlin, and Paris for a dozen years before starting work in films as editor, screenwriter, and production supervisor in London. In 1935 he supervised the production of *Scrooge* and *The Last Journey.* The following year he made his debut as director with a remake of the Griffith classic *Broken Blossoms,* starring Emlyn Williams and Brahm's wife, Dolly Haas.

In 1937 he came to Hollywood, where he turned out several routine films before directing two taut, atmospheric melodramas, *The Lodger* and *Hangover Square* in the mid-40s. He returned to run-of-the-mill productions, however, and in 1956 he turned to TV, to direct some 150 television films during a ten-year span, including episodes for 'Thriller,' 'Alfred Hitchcock Presents,' and 'Twilight Zone.'

FILMS: *Broken Blossoms* (UK) 1936; *Counsel for Crime* 1937; *Penitentiary, Girls' School* 1938; *Let Us Live, Rio* 1939; *Escape to Glory/Submarine Zone* 1940; *Wild Geese Calling* 1941; *The Undying Monster* 1942; *Tonight We Raid Calais, Wintertime* 1943; *The Lodger, Guest in the House* 1944; *Hangover Square* 1945; *The Locket* 1946; *The Brasher Doubloon, Singapore* 1947; *Il Ladro di Venezia/The Thief of Venice* (It.) 1950; *The Miracle of Our Lady of Fatima, Face to Face* (co-dir. with Bretaigne Windust) 1952; *The Diamond Queen* 1953; *The Mad Magician, Die goldene Pest/The Golden Plague* (Ger.) 1954; *Vom Himmel gefallen/Special Delivery* (Ger./US), *Bengazi* 1955; *Hot Rods to Hell* 1967.

Brakhage, Stan. Director. Born on Jan. 14, 1933, in Kansas City, Mo. Among the most influential figures of the American avant-garde, he is a technical innovator and outspoken social observer. Adopted at three weeks from a home for unwed mothers, he led a nomadic childhood, tagging along on his mother's travels and bouncing back and forth from foster homes. At age ten he was singing soprano in church and, for a fee, at social functions. Throughout his childhood, he was an avid moviegoer. At 18, he got a scholarship to Dartmouth, but dropped out after three months following a nervous breakdown. He returned to his then-home in Denver and with several high school friends turned out his first film. His experimental films, mostly short, have often been concerned with the manipulation of light. His *Mothlight* (1963) was done without a camera by running pasted moth wings through an optical printer. Other favorite techniques of his include scratching directly on film and using optical distortions and superimpositions. His films (mostly 16 mm, some 8 mm) are often concerned with his personal life: *Wedlock House: An Intercourse* (1959) shows him making love to his bride on negative film, and *Window Water Baby Moving* (1959) is a graphic depiction of the birth of their first child. In *Sirius Remembered* (1959) he attempts through camera motion to "bring back to life" his dead pet dog.

Overcoming limitations of funds and resources, Brakhage poured out an astonishingly large number of long and short films in a wide range of themes and styles. A poet with a camera, he consistently endowed his prolific output with a pathfinder's zeal and innovative personal vision. Brakhage is also a highly regarded theorist and lecturer on film. His books include *Metaphors on Vision* (1963), *A Motion Picture Giving and Taking Book* (1971), *The Brakhage Lectures* (1972), *The Seen* (1975), and *The Brakhage Scrapbook* (1982).

FILMS INCLUDE: *Interim* 1951; *Unglassed Windows Cast a Terrible Reflection* 1953; *Desistfilm, The Extraordinary Child* 1954; *Reflections on Black, The Wonder Ring* 1955; *Nightcats* 1956; *Flesh of Morning, Daybreak* 1957; *Loving, Anticipation of the Night* 1958; *Cat's Cradle, Wedlock House: An Intercourse, Window Water Baby Moving, Sirius Remembered* 1959; *The Dead* 1960; *Blue Moses* 1962; *Mothlight* 1963; *Dog Star Man, The Art of Vision, Black Vision* 1965; *Scenes from Under Childhood* 1967; *Lovemaking* 1968; *The Horseman the Woman and the Moth, Eyes, Deus Ex, Sexual Meditations No. 1: Motel* 1970; *The Machines of Eden, The Act of Seeing With One's Own Eyes, Fox Fire Child Watch* 1971; *The Process, The Riddle of Lumen, The World Shadow* 1972; *Sincerity, The Women* 1973; *Aquarian, Flight, Hymn to Her, He Was Born, He Suffered, He Died, Star Garden, The Text of Light, The Stars Are Beautiful* 1974; *Traqoedia, Gadflies, Rembrandt, etc.* 1976; *Soldiers and Other Cosmic Subjects, The Domain of the Moment* 1977; *Duplicity, Nightmare Series, Purity and After* 1978; *Salome* 1980; *Garden of Earthly Delights* 1981; *Unconscious London, Strata* 1982; *Hell Spit Flexion* 1983; *Tortured Dust* 1984; *Invocation Maya Deren* (act. only) 1987; *I . . . Dreaming, Marilyn's Window* 1988.

Branagh, Kenneth. Actor, director. Born on Dec. 10, 1960, in Belfast, Northern Ireland. He moved with his family to England at age nine. After drama studies, he scored an instant triumph on the London stage in 'Another Country.' He later left the Royal Shakespeare Company to form his own Renaissance Theatre Company, for which he also directed and wrote. Critics pronounced him a major talent, comparing him to Laurence Olivier in his youth. In 1989 he astonished film audiences with a powerful production of *Henry V,* for which he was nominated for Academy Awards as both best actor and best director. The well-received *Much Ado About Nothing* (1993) continued to demonstrate his acumen at presenting Shakespeare to modern audiences. He is divorced from actress Emma THOMPSON.

FILMS (as actor): *High Season, A Month in the Country* 1987; *Henry V* (title role; also dir., adapt.) 1989; *Dead Again* (also dir.) 1991; *Peter's Friends* (also dir.), *Swing Kids* 1992; *Much Ado About Nothing* (also dir., adapt.) 1993; *Mary Shelley's Frankenstein* (also dir.) 1994; *Othello* (act.), *A Midwinter's Tale* (dir., sc. only) 1995; *Hamlet* (dir., act.), *Looking for Richard* 1996.

Brand, Neville. Actor. *b.* Aug. 13, 1921, Kewanee, Ill. *d.* 1992. Left high school and served in the US Army for ten years.

He was discharged in 1946 as the fourth most decorated GI of WW II. After drama studies in New York, he made his Hollywood film debut in *D.O.A.* (1949). His cruel but intelligent face made him one of Hollywood's leading heavies, though he occasionally played good-guy roles. He portrayed Al Capone twice, in *The George Raft Story* (1961) and in *The Scarface Mob* (1962). He also played a convincing lead role as a convict in *Riot in Cell Block 11* (1954). He starred in the TV series 'Laredo' (1965–67).

FILMS INCLUDE: *D.O.A.* 1949; *Where the Sidewalk Ends* 1950; *The Halls of Montezuma, Only the Valiant, The Mob* 1951; *Red Mountain, Kansas City Confidential* 1952; *Stalag 17, The Charge at Feather River, Gun Fury* 1953; *Return From the Sea, Riot in Cell Block 11* 1954; *The Prodigal, Bobby Ware Is Missing* 1955; *Mohawk, Raw Edge, Love Me Tender* 1956; *The Tin Star, The Way to the Gold* 1957; *Cry Terror* 1958; *Five Gates to Hell* 1959; *The Adventures of Huckleberry Finn* 1960; *The Last Sunset, The George Raft Story* 1961; *The Scarface Mob, Birdman of Alcatraz, Hero's Island* 1962; *That Darn Cat* 1965; *Three Guns for Texas* 1968; *The Desperadoes, Backtrack* 1969; *Tora! Tora! Tora!* 1970; *Cahill US Marshal, The Mad Bomber, The Deadly Trackers, Scalawag* 1973; *Psychic Killer* 1975; *Eaten Alive/Death Trap* 1977; *Five Days from Home* 1978; *The Ninth Configuration, Without Warning, Angels Brigade* 1980; *Evils of the Night* 1983.

Brandauer, Klaus Maria. Actor. Born on June 22, 1944, in Altaussee, Austria. A graduate of the Academy of Music and Dramatic Arts in Stuttgart, he became famous throughout the German-speaking world for his distinguished performances on the German and Austrian stage. He was virtually unknown elsewhere, however, when he stunned moviegoers with his extraordinary portrait of a moral coward in István Szabó's Hungarian-German film *Mephisto* (1981). Named best actor at Cannes for this performance, he went on to play character leads in many other international productions. He was nominated for an Academy Award as best supporting actor for *Out of Africa* (1985) and made an impressive debut as a film director in 1990. He married director-screenwriter Karin Müller.

FILMS INCLUDE: *The Salzburg Connection* (US) 1972; *Mephisto* (Hung./Ger.) 1981; *Never Say Never Again* (UK) 1983; *The Kindergarten* (USSR) 1984; *Redl Ezredes/Colonel Redl* (Hung./Ger./Aus.), *The Lightship* (US), *Out of Africa* (US) 1985; *Blue Velvet* (US), *Streets of Gold* (US) 1986; *Burning Secret* (UK/US/Ger.), *Hanussen* (Hung./Ger.) 1988; *La Revolution Française/The French Revolution* (as Danton; Fr./Ger./It./Can.) 1989; *Georg Elser/Seven Minutes* (also dir.; Ger./US), *The Russia House* 1990; *White Fang* 1991; *Becoming Collette* 1992; *Mario and the Magician* 1994.

Brandenstein, Patrizia von. Art director, production designer. One of Hollywood's leading craftspeople of the 80s, she won an Academy Award for the magnificent sets of *Amadeus* (1984). Earlier she was Oscar-nominated for *Ragtime* (1981).

FILMS INCLUDE: *Saturday Night Fever* (co-costumes only) 1977; *Girlfriends* 1978; *Ragtime* 1981; *Silkwood* 1983; *Amadeus* 1984; *A Chorus Line* 1985; *No Mercy* 1986; *The Untouchables* (visual consultant) 1987; *Betrayed, Working Girl* 1988; *State of Grace, Postcards from the Edge* 1990; *Billy Bathgate* 1991; *Leap of Faith, Sneakers* 1992; *Six Degrees of Separation* 1993; *The People vs. Larry Flynt* 1996.

Brando, Marlon. Actor. Born Marlon Brando, Jr., on Apr. 3, 1924, in Omaha, Nebr., son of a salesman and an actress in the local community playhouse. After being expelled from a Minnesota military academy, he attended the Dramatic Workshop in New York for one year and, following a season of summer stock on Long Island, made his Broadway debut in 1944 as Nels in 'I Remember Mama.' Two years later he was seen in two other Broadway plays, 'Truckline Cafe' and 'Candida,' and in Ben Hecht's salute to Israel, 'A Flag Is Born,' which starred Paul Muni.

In 1947, Brando exploded into Broadway stardom with his forceful portrayal of the screaming, cursing, scratching brute Stanley Kowalski in Tennessee Williams' 'A Streetcar Named Desire.' His naturalistic style of acting and his casual, mumbling delivery, under the guidance of Elia Kazan, also heralded the arrival of "the Method" as a fashionable style of acting. In the late 40s he became one of the early members of the Actors Studio, a workshop for professional actors.

In 1950, Brando brought his Actors Studio training and his magnetic, rebellious personality to the screen. In his film debut he played an embittered paraplegic in Stanley Kramer's *The Men.* (In preparation for his role, he spent a month in a hospital ward to gain firsthand experience in the rehabilitation of paraplegics.) He was nominated for a best actor Academy Award four successive years: for his performances in the film version of *A Streetcar Named Desire* (1951), for the title role of *Viva Zapata!* (1952), for his Marc Antony in *Julius Caesar* (1953), and for his portrayal of Terry Malloy in Kazan's *On the Waterfront* (1954). He won the Oscar for the 1954 effort and also received the New York Film Critics Award and the Cannes Film Festival prize.

Throughout the 50s Brando's charisma, both on and off screen, made him an artistic and social force. Young audiences acclaimed him as the rebellious, nonconforming prototype of the beat generation; older audiences often saw him as an antisocial menace, unkempt and unrestrained—but audiences and critics agreed that he was one of the most original and compelling personalities to appear on the screen in a long time.

In 1959, Brando founded his own production company, Pennebaker Productions, and produced, directed, and starred in *One-Eyed Jacks* (1961). In the 60s, unable to find proper roles and unwilling to co-operate with most directors, he played in a succession of unsuccessful movies that considerably weakened his professional and personal image. But he made a remarkable comeback in the early 70s with superb performances in two extremely diverse roles. His powerful portrayal in the title role of *The Godfather* brought him a second Oscar, which he refused to accept in protest against the plight of the American Indian. Yet he won another Oscar nomination as well as unanimous acclaim for his study of middle-age sexuality in Bernardo Bertolucci's controversial *Last Tango in Paris.* Although he chose to limit his screen appearances in size and frequency, and allowed his body to bloat to mammoth dimensions, reaching 300 pounds, Brando remained a charismatic film personality, capable of commanding huge fees even for cameo roles. For a while he commuted to locations from his principal home at Tetiaroa, an atoll near Tahiti. After a long absence, he returned to the screen in 1989, promptly gaining yet another Oscar nomination, this time as best supporting actor, for *A Dry White Season.* Many consider him the greatest actor the American screen has ever known. Brando's first two of three broken marriages were to actresses Anna KASHFI (1957–59) and Movita (Castenada 1960–68). In mid-1990, Brando's son by Kashfi, Christian, was arrested and charged with killing the abusive boyfriend of his pregnant half sister, Cheyenne. The latter twice attempted suicide when she was called to testify in the ensuing trial. His sister, Jocelyn Brando (*b.* Nov. 18, 1919, San Francisco) is a stage actress who makes occasional appearances in films.

FILMS: *The Men* 1950; *A Streetcar Named Desire* 1951;

Viva Zapata! 1952; *Julius Caesar* (as Marc Anthony) 1953; *The Wild One, On the Waterfront, Désirée* (as Napoleon) 1954; *Guys and Dolls* 1955; *The Teahouse of the August Moon* 1956; *Sayonara* 1957; *The Young Lions* 1958; *The Fugitive Kind* 1960; *One-Eyed Jacks* (also dir.) 1961; *Mutiny on the Bounty* 1962; *The Ugly American* 1963; *Bedtime Story* 1964; *Morituri/The Saboteur—Code Name Morituri* 1965; *The Chase, The Appaloosa* 1966; *The Countess from Hong Kong, Reflections in a Golden Eye* 1967; *Candy* 1968; *The Night of the Following Day, Queimada/Burn!* (It./Fr.) 1969; *The Nightcomers* (UK) 1971; *The Godfather, Ultimo Tango a Parigi/Last Tango in Paris* (It.) 1972; *The Missouri Breaks* 1976; *Superman* 1978; *Raoni* (doc.; narrator; Fr./Braz.), *Apocalypse Now* 1979; *The Formula* 1980; *A Dry White Season* 1989; *The Freshman* 1990; *Christopher Columbus: The Discovery* 1992; *Don Juan DeMarco* 1995; *The Island of Dr. Moreau* 1996.

Brandon, Henry. *b.* Heinrich von Kleinbach, June 18, 1912, Berlin, Germany. *d.* 1990. Evil-eyed character player of numerous Hollywood films. He arrived in the US as an infant and made his screen debut in 1934, portraying "the meanest man in Toyland" in a Laurel and Hardy comedy. In this and several other early films, he was billed as Harry Kleinbach. As Henry Brandon, he played a variety of menacing or exotic parts in scores of films. He was the animator's model for Captain Hook in Disney's 1953 feature *Peter Pan.* But he also had a distinguished parallel career portraying classic roles on the New York stage and played a wide range of parts on TV.

FILMS INCLUDE: *Babes in Toyland* 1934; *Killer at Large, The Garden of Allah* 1936; *Black Legion, Jungle Jim* (serial) 1937; *Spawn of the North* 1938; *Buck Rogers* (serial), *Beau Geste, Nurse Edith Cavell* 1939; *Drums of Fu Manchu* (serial; title role), *Dark Streets of Cairo, The Son of Monte Cristo* 1940; *Underground* 1941; *Edge of Darkness* 1943; *Joan of Arc, The Paleface* 1948; *The Fighting O'Flynn* 1949; *Cattle Drive* 1951; *Scarlet Angel, Hurricane Smith, Harem Girl* 1952; *Pony Express, Scared Stiff, The War of the Worlds* 1953; *Vera Cruz* 1954; *The Searchers* 1956; *Omar Khayyam* 1957; *Auntie Mame, The Buccaneer* 1958; *The Big Fisherman* 1959; *Two Rode Together* 1961; *Captain Sinbad* 1963; *So Long Blue Boy* 1973; *The Manhandlers* 1975; *Assault on Precinct 13* 1976; *To Be or Not to Be* 1983.

Brasselle, Keefe. Actor. *b.* Feb. 7, 1923, Elyria, Ohio. *d.* 1981. The son of a Hollywood hair stylist, he began performing with bands while still at high school, then worked in nightclubs and in vaudeville as a drummer, singer, and comedian. After WW II service with the Air Force, during which he staged two military shows, he made his film debut in a minor role in *Janie* (1944). He went on to play light leading roles in low-budget films and some supporting roles in major films. The highlight of his acting career was the title role in *The Eddie Cantor Story.* He later retired from the screen, founded Richelieu Productions, and produced several TV series. Author of the books *The Cannibals* and *The Barracudas,* both exposés of TV broadcasting. In 1971 he was arrested for "assault with intent to commit murder," after a shooting incident during a bar brawl, but the charges were later dropped.

FILMS INCLUDE: *Janie* 1944; *River Gang* 1945; *Railroaded* 1947; *Not Wanted* 1949; *Dial 1119* 1950; *A Place in the Sun, Bannerline* 1951; *It's a Big Country, Skirts Ahoy* 1952; *The Eddie Cantor Story* (title role) 1953; *Three Young Texans* 1954; *Mad at the World* 1955; *Battle Stations* 1956; *West of Suez/The Fighting Wildcats* (UK) 1957; *If You Don't Stop You'll Go Blind* 1977.

Brasseur, Claude. Actor. Born on June 15, 1936, in Paris. *ed.* Paris Conservatoire. The son of Pierre BRASSEUR and Odette JOYEUX, he began appearing in French films in the late 50s and has since played both leads and supporting roles in numerous productions. Also very active on the stage and in French TV.

FILMS INCLUDE: *Le Pays d'où je viens* 1956; *Rue des Prairies* 1959; *Pierrot la Tendresse, Les Yeux sans Visage/The Horror Chamber of Dr. Faustus* 1960; *La Bride sur le Cou/Please Not Now!, Les Menteurs/The Liars* 1961; *Les Enemies, Les Sept Péchés capitaux/Seven Capital Sins, Germinal, Le Caporal épinglé/The Elusive Corporal* 1962; *Dragées au Poivre/Sweet and Sour, Germinal 1963*; *Bande à part/Band of Outsiders, Peau de Banane/Banana Peel* 1964; *Du Rififi à Paname/The Upper Hand* 1966; *Un Homme de trop/Shock Troops* 1967; *Le Portrait de Marianne* 1970; *Une Belle Fille comme moi/Such a Gorgeous Kid Like Me* 1972; *Gli Eroi/The Heroes* (It.) 1973; *Les Seins de Glace/Icy Breasts* 1974; *L'Agression/Act of Aggression, Il faut vivre dangereusement* 1975; *Attention les Yeux!, Le Guepier, Un Elephant ça trompe enormement/Pardon Mon Affaire, Barocco, Le Grand Escogriffe* 1976; *Monsieur Papa, Nous irons tous au Paradis/We Will All Meet in Paradise* 1977; *L'Etat sauvage, Une Histoire simple/A Simple Story, L'Argent des Autres* 1978; *Si je suis comme ça c'est la Faute à Papa/Bye—See You Monday* (Can./Fr.), *Ils sont grands ces Petits* 1979; *La Boum, La Banquière* 1980; *Une Affaire d'Hommes, L'Ombre Rouge* 1981; *Josepha* 1982; *Le Léopard* 1984; *Palace, Détective, Les Loups entre eux* 1985; *Descente aux Enfers* 1986; *Radio Corbeau, L'Orchestre rouge* 1989; *Dancing Machine* 1990; *Dirty Like an Angel* 1991; *Le Souper* 1993; *Delit Mineur* 1994.

Brasseur, Pierre. Actor. *b.* Pierre-Albert Espinasse, Dec. 22, 1903, Paris. *d.* 1972. The son of an actress, he studied acting with Harry BAUR. Made his stage debut at 15 and his screen debut at 20. However, it wasn't until 1938, that he moved into the forefront of the French cinema with his role in Marcel Carné's *Quai des Brumes/Port of Shadows.* An imposing performer, superb at expressing irony and wit, he appeared in a great variety of roles in more than 80 films, achieving his best characterization in the screenplays of Jacques PRÉVERT. He was also a poet and wrote several plays and an autobiography, *Ma Vie envrac.* His son, from his marriage to Odette JOYEUX (divorced), is screen actor Claude BRASSEUR.

FILMS INCLUDE: *La Fille de l'Eau* 1924; *Madame Sans-Gêne* 1925; *Feu* 1928; *Mon Ami Victor* 1931; *Quick* (Ger.) 1932; *Le Sexe faible* 1933; *Caravane* (French version of *Caravan*; US) 1934; *Les Pattes de Mouche* 1936; *Mademoiselle ma Mère* 1937; *Claudine à l'Ecole/Claudine, Gosse de Riche, Giuseppe Verdi* (It.), *Quai des Brumes/Port of Shadows* 1938; *Frères corses/The Corsican Brothers, Dernière Jeunesse/Last Desire* 1939; *Les Deux Timides, Promesses à l'Inconnue* 1942; *Adieu Leonard, Lumière d'Eté* 1943; *Les Enfants du Paradis/Children of Paradise* 1945; *Jéricho, Les Portes de la Nuit/Gates of the Night, Pétrus, L'Arche de Noë/Noah's Ark* 1946; *Les Amants de Vérone/The Lovers of Verona* 1948; *Portrait d'un Assassin* 1949; *Souvenirs perdus* 1950; *Maitre après Dieu/Skipper Next to God, Barbe-Bleue/Bluebeard, Les Mains sales/Dirty Hands* 1951; *Le Plaisir* 1952; *Raspoutine* 1954; *Oasis, La Tour de Nesle, Napoléon* 1955; *Porte de Lilas/Gates of Paris* 1957; *Sans Famille, Les Grandes Familles/The Possessors* 1958; *La Loi/Where the Hot Wind Blows, La Tête contre les Murs* 1959; *Les Yeux sans Visage/The Horror Chamber of Dr. Faustus, Cartagine in Fiamme/Carthage in Flames* (It./Fr.), *Il Bell'Antonio* (It./Fr.), *Candide* (as Pangloss) 1960; *Les Amours célèbres* 1961; *Le Crime ne paie pas/Crime Does Not Pay* 1962; *Les Bonnes Causes/Don't Tempt the Devil* 1963; *Liolà/A Very Handy Man* (It./Fr.) 1964; *La Vie de Chateau/A Matter of Resistance, Un Mondo Nuovo/A Young World* (It./Fr.), *Le Roi de*

Coeur/King of Hearts 1966; *Les Oiseaux vont mourir aux Pérou/Birds in Peru* 1968; *Fortuna* (Isr.) 1969; *Les Mariés de l'An Deux* 1971; *La Sera piu bella della sua Vita* (It.) 1972.

Braunberger, Pierre. Producer. *b.* July 29, 1905, in Paris. *d.* 1990. After beginning in films as an actor at the age of 17, he was only 20 when he started a remarkable career as producer, exerting considerable influence on the development of French films from the avant-garde of the 20s to the New Wave of the 50s and 60s. Working with such directors as Clair, Renoir, Buñuel, Cavalcanti, Resnais, Godard, and Truffaut, he achieved a good balance between the artistic and commercial requirements of the cinema. Uncle of François REICHENBACH. Autobiography: *Pierre Braunberger, Producteur* (1987).

FILMS INCLUDE: *Nana* (also act.), *Voyage au Congo, Rien que les Heures* 1926; *Un Chien Andalou* 1928; *Tire-au-Flanc* 1929; *L'Age d'Or* 1930; *La Chienne* 1931; *Une Partie de Campagne* 1936; *Paris 1900* 1946; *Van Gogh* (short), *Guernica* (short) 1948; *La Course de Taureaux/Bullfight* (also dir.-sc.) 1951; *Moi un Noir* 1958; *Ein Engel auf Erden/Angel on Earth* (Ger./Fr.) 1959; *Tirez sur le Pianiste/Shoot the Piano Player* 1960; *Le Temps du Ghetto/The Witness* 1961; *Un Coeur gros comme ça/The Winner, La Dénonciation/The Immoral Moment, Vivre sa Vie/My Life to Live* 1962; *De l'Amour* 1965; *Un Homme et une Femme/A Man and a Woman* 1966; *Erotissimo* 1969; *On n'arrête pas le Printemps, Catch Me a Spy* (UK/Fr.), *La Cavale, Fantasia Chez Les Ploucs* 1971; *Elle Court, Elle Court la Banlieue* 1972; *Collections Privées, Les Héroînes du Mal* 1979; *Dionysos, Kusameikyu* (short) 1984; *Les Chévaliers de la table ronde* 1990.

Bray, John Randolph. Animator. *b.* Aug. 25, 1879, Detroit. *d.* 1978. *ed.* Alma Coll. (Mich.). Son of a clergyman, he began his career in New York as a cartoonist for the Brooklyn *Eagle* and national magazines. In 1910 he became one of the pioneers of American film animation when he produced his first animated cartoon, *The Dachshund and the Sausage.* He later created many more cartoons, including the "Colonel Heeza Liar" series, which lampooned President Theodore Roosevelt and launched the early careers of leading animators like Max and David FLEISCHER (Popeye), Paul TERRY (Terry Toons), and Walter LANTZ (Woody Woodpecker). But his most important contribution to the art of animation was the invention of the cel system, which revolutionized film animation by making the production of film cartoons much cheaper and speedier.

In 1917 he formed the Bray-Hurd Process Company to exploit this and other inventions with co-inventor Earl Hurd. During WW I, Bray began producing US Army training films and subsequently remained active in the production of documentaries and educational film strips as well as animated films. The Bray studios, now run by his grandson Paul, are still active in the production of documentaries. A special reception and retrospective exhibition of Bray's early films was held by the Museum of Modern Art in August of 1975. The guest of honor was Bray himself, age 96.

FILMS INCLUDE: *The Dachshund and the Sausage* 1910; *Colonel Heeza Liar Wins the Pennant* 1916; *How We Breathe* 1919; *Happy Hooldini* 1920; various "Colonel Heeza Liar" cartoons 1922–23; various cartoons in the series "Dinkey Doodle," "Unnatural History," and "Hot Dog Cartoons" 1925–27; *Bride of the Colorado* (doc.) 1927; *Father Nile* (doc.) 1931.

Brazil. Brazilian cynics have summed up the state of their vast homeland with a popular phrase: "Brazil is the country of the future and always will be." Like other huge untapped resources of this nation, fifth in the world in land area and eighth in population, the tremendous potential of its film industry has never been fully realized. Film production has never kept pace with the fantastic growth of audiences and increase of theaters; foreign exhibitors have been the main beneficiaries of the Brazilian public's increasing interest in the cinema.

Films first were shown in Rio de Janeiro in 1897, and by 1900 some newsreel footage was shot by local residents. An immigrant from Portugal, Antonio Leal, filmed the country's first documentary in 1903 and its first feature film, *Los Estranguladores,* in 1906. Feature film production proceeded subsequently in a haphazard manner in the big cities. The common denominator for most of these productions was their appeal to popular taste. Since much of the population was illiterate and could not read titles, efforts were made from the very start to somehow incorporate sound into films. As early as 1910, attempts were made to show musical films with "sound" by having actors behind the screen talk and sing to match their on-screen lip movements. Other methods were tried, the most successful of which came in 1920 when films were shown in synchronization with records. Film production increased in the 20s, reaching an annual average of 15 features.

The most important figure of the period and perhaps the entire history of Brazilian cinema was Humbert MAURO, who elevated the generally poor level of local production with such serious films as *Ganga Bruta* (1933). There were also some not too original attempts at films of the avant-garde. Adalbert Kememy directed *Sao Paulo: Sinfonia de una Metropoli* (1929), a direct derivative of Ruttmann's *Berlin: Symphony of a City,* and Mario Peixoto borrowed generously from Eisenstein and Pudovkin in directing *Limite* (1930). During the 30s the quantity of Brazilian film production suffered a great decline. To reach the country's millions of illiterates, studios equipped early to make sound films but sound caused production costs to soar, and many companies were forced to suspend production.

By 1940 the average annual feature output was reduced to one single film. The situation began to reverse around 1943, with production again averaging 10 to 15 feature films a year, but for the most part these were cheap, vulgar films, often built around the famous Rio Carnival, which appealed to common tastes. In 1949 a large production house, Vera Cruz Films, attempted to bring quality to its films by appointing a native son, Alberto CAVALCANTI, head of production at its studios. Cavalcanti, whose entire career had been molded abroad, tried hard—he imported key technicians, developed local talent, and chose authentic Brazilian themes as subjects for his films. But the experiment was on the whole unsuccessful. The only internationally important film to come out of the Vera Cruz studios during Cavalcanti's regime was Lima Barreto's famous *O Cangaceiro* (1953). Soon after this, Cavalcanti resigned his post and returned, disillusioned, to Europe.

The maturation of Brazilian cinema finally came in the 60s. The change was brought about largely by increased government attention to the needs of the industry. A national film institute was established (Instituto Nacional do Cinema, or INC). It initiated government subsidies and special bonuses to encourage quality production. It has also launched the INC Prize, the equivalent of the Hollywood Oscar, to reward outstanding talent in all branches of filmmaking, and in 1969 INC promoted the first Rio de Janeiro film festival. The institute publishes a number of serious film publications. The 60s also saw the emergence of a Cinema Nôvo, a New Wave movement of young filmmakers who have been turning out an increasing number of important films of social, cultural, and artistic merit. The outstanding figure in the movement was Glauber ROCHA. But increasing political restrictions and a growing complacency among young filmmakers combined to throw the Brazilian cinema back into stagnation in the 70s and 80s.

The major problem facing Brazilian filmmakers in the 90s is the gridlock between film exhibitors and the oppressive government. Under government law, exhibitors must show nationalistic films at least 140 days of the year, and are further restricted by laws mandating showings that are ultimately unprofitable.

Against the odds, several young filmmakers have managed to produce films of international significance since the 70s, including Bruno BARRETO (*Doña Flor and Her Two Husbands* 1977) and Hector BABENCO, who later made films in America.

Brazzi, Rossano. Actor. *b.* Sept. 18, 1916, in Bologna, Italy. *d.* 1994. After his parents were killed by the Fascists, he left law school (San Marco University, Florence) and turned to the stage. He made his film debut in 1939 and rapidly became one of the leading romantic stars on the Italian screen. After work with the resistance in Rome during WW II, he moved to Hollywood and made his first Hollywood appearance in *Little Women* (1949). It was not until 1954, in *The Barefoot Contessa,* that he established himself as a Hollywood star, specializing in Continental lovers and aristocrats. In the late 60s he resettled in Italy, reverting to character roles, occasionally also directing. Brazzi, who lives in Rome with his wife (from 1940), actress Lydia Bartalini, is a member-knight of the Sovereign Order of Paragonia, a medieval cult. In 1984 he was arrested for involvement in an arms-smuggling conspiracy.

FILMS INCLUDE: In Italy—*Ritorno* 1939; *Processo e Morte di Socrate, Kean, La Forza Bruta, La Tosca/The Story of Tosca* 1940; *Il Re si Diverte/The King's Jester* 1941; *Noi Vivi/We the Living, Una Signora dell'Ovest, I Due Foscari, La Gorgona* 1942; *Malia, La Resa di Titi/The Merry Chase, I Dieci Comandamenti/The Ten Commandments* 1945; *Aquila Nera, Furia, La Grande Aurora/The Great Dawn* 1946; *Eleonora Duse, Il Passatore/Bullet for Stefano, La Monaca di Monza, Il Diavolo bianco* 1947; *Little Women* (US), *Vulcano/Volcano* 1949; *Romanzo d'Amore* 1950; *La Vendetta di Aquila nera* 1951; *L'Inguista Condanna/Guilt Is Not Mine* 1952; *Il Fuco nelle Vene/La Chair et le Diable/Flesh and Desire* (It./Fr.) 1953; *Angela* 1954. In the US—*Three Coins in the Fountain, The Barefoot Contessa* 1954; *Summertime/Summer Madness* (US/UK), *Gli Ultimi Cinque Minuti* (It./Fr.) 1955; *Loser Takes All* (UK) 1956; *Timbuctu/Legend of the Lost* (It./US), *Interlude, The Story of Esther Costello* (UK/US) 1957; *South Pacific* 1958; *Count Your Blessings* 1959; *L'Assedio di Siracusa/Siege of Syracuse* (as Archimedes; It./Fr.), *Austerlitz* (as Lucien Bonaparte; Fr./It.) 1960; *Light in the Piazza, Rome Adventure, Les Quatre Vérités/Three Fables of Love* (Fr./It./Sp.) 1962; *L'Intrigo/Dark Purpose* (It./Fr./US) 1964; *La Ragazza in Prestito/Engagement Italiano* (It./Fr.), *The Battle of the Villa Fiorita* (US/UK) 1965; *The Christmas That Almost Wasn't* (also dir.; US/It.) 1966; *The Bobo* (UK), *Sept fois Femme/Woman Times Seven* (Fr./It./US) 1967; *Sette Uomini e un Cervello* (also dir. under pseudonym Edward Ross), *Rey de Africa/One Step to Hell* (Sp./It./US) 1968; *Krakatoa East of Java, The Italian Job* (UK), *Salvare la Faccia/Psychout for Murder* (also dir. under pseudonym Edward Ross; Arg./It.) 1969; *The Adventurers* 1970; *Detras de esa Puerta* (Mex./Guat.), *The Great Waltz* 1972; *Cappuucetto rosso Cenerentola. . . e voi ci credte* (also dir.), *House of Freaks/Frankenstein's Castle of Freaks* 1973; *Il Tempo degli Assassini, I Telefoni bianchi* 1976; *Maestro d'Amore/Master of Love* (It.) 1977; *The Final Conflict* 1981; *Fear City* 1984; *Formula for Murder* (It.) 1985; *Russicum/The Third Solution* (It.), *Michelangelo and Me* 1989.

Brdeçka, Jiři. Director and screenwriter of animated and fantasy films. Born Jiři Brneçka, on Dec. 24, 1917, in Hranice, Moravia, Czechoslovakia. *ed.* Charles U. (Prague; art history). Fascinated with American folklore, at 22 he wrote a parody of the Wild West, *Lemonade Joe,* which was made into a play and eventually, in 1964, into a film by Oldrich Lipsky. In 1943 he began working in films as an animator, but had to supplement his income as a book illustrator. In 1945, when Czech animation and puppetry began attracting worldwide attention under the leadership of Jiři TRNKA, Brdeçka began contributing imaginative screenplays and, later, his own animated films.

FILMS INCLUDE: As screenwriter—*The Resourceful Man and the S.S.* 1946; *The Emperor and the Nightingale/The Emperor and the Golem* 1948; *Song of the Prairie* 1949; *The Emperor's Baker* 1951; *Old Czech Legends* 1953; *A Midsummer Night's Dream* 1959; *That Cat* 1963; *Lemonade Joe* 1964; *Adele Hasn't Had Her Supper Yet* 1978. As director—*Love and the Dirigible* 1947; *How Man Learned to Fly/A Comic History of Aviation* 1958; *Look Out!* 1959; *Our Red Riding Hood* 1960; *Man Under Water, The Television Fan* 1961; *Reason and Emotion* 1962; *Gallina Vogelbirdae/The Grotesque Hen* 1963; *Minstrel's Song* 1964; *The Deserter* 1965; *Why Do You Smile Mona Lisa?* 1966; *Prague Nights* (one episode), *Power of Destiny, The Hand* 1968; *Aristotle* (co-dir.) 1971; *Mysterious Castle in the Carpathians* 1981.

breakaway. A prop or part of a set especially constructed of such lightweight material or in such a way that it will shatter or come apart easily with the slightest effort. Breakaways are widely used in action sequences, as when a shirt is torn off in a fight, a table is broken during a barroom brawl, etc., to achieve a realistic effect without endangering the actors or the stuntmen.

breakdown (or **breakdown script).** A detailed list of everything required for the shooting of a film, scene by scene and day by day. The breakdown is usually prepared by the assistant director, who rearranges separate elements of the shooting script and groups them, out of sequence, into such categories as exteriors and interiors, night or day shooting, sound or silent sequences, etc. All the shots intended to be filmed on one location are grouped together, as are sequences requiring certain props, costumes, special lighting or sound recording equipment, or the presence of extras or other short-term members of the cast. The breakdown helps the director plan his shooting schedule and prevents unforeseen omissions or needless duplications.

breathing. A rapid fluctuation of focus in a photographic image caused by a defective fluttering movement of the film in the camera GATE.

Brecher, Irving S. Screenwriter, director. Born on Jan. 17 1914, in New York City. After working as a reporter, he wrote comedy material for the Milton BERLE, Al JOLSON, and other radio shows. He started writing screenplays in 1937, mostly for comedies or musical films, including two MARX BROTHERS vehicles. He also directed three films.

FILMS INCLUDE: As screenwriter—*New Faces of 1937* 1937; *Fools for Scandal* 1938; *At the Circus* 1939; *Go West, Broadway Melody of 1940* 1940; *Shadow of the Thin Man* 1941; *Du Barry Was a Lady, Best Foot Forward* 1943; *Meet Me in St. Louis* 1944; *Yolanda and the Thief* 1945; *Summer Holiday* 1948; *The Life of Riley* (also dir., prod.) 1949; *Somebody Loves Me* (also dir.) 1954; *Cry for Happy* 1961; *Sail a Crooked Ship* (also dir.) 1962; *Bye Bye Birdie* 1963.

Brecht, Bertolt. Playwright, poet, screenwriter, *b.* Feb. 10, 1898, Augsburg, Germany. *d.* 1956. One of the most influential forces in 20th-century theater, he expressed only a moderate interest in the cinema. It is not widely known, however, that in addition to films based on his plays (notably Pabst's *Dreigroschenoper/The Threepenny Opera,* 1931), his contribution to the medium included several screenplays, alone or in collaboration, written expressly for films. In the early 40s he worked briefly in Hollywood, collaborating with Fritz Lang and

John Wexley on the script of *Hangmen Also Die,* the story of the Czech village of Lidice destroyed by the Nazis. He did not receive screen credit for this work. In 1947 he left the US to avoid being called to testify before the House Un-American Activities Committee. He went to Switzerland and finally settled in East Germany. Two of his plays, 'The Mother' and 'Mother Courage,' were filmed as they were performed on stage by the Berliner Ensemble, in 1958 and 1960 respectively. René Allio's *La Vieille Dame indigne/The Shameless Old Lady* (Fr., 1965) was based on a Brecht short story. Brecht's ideas on the art of film were presented in his book *On Cinema* (1930).

FILMS INCLUDE (as screenwriter): *Kuhle Wampe/ Whither Germany?* (for Slatan Düdow) 1932; *Hangmen Also Die* (for Fritz Lang; US) 1943; *Das Lied der Strome* (doc., for Joris Ivens) 1954; *Herr Puntila und sein Knecht Matti* (for Alberto Cavalcanti) 1955.

Breen, Richard L. Screenwriter. *b.* June 26, 1919, Chicago. *d.* 1967. *ed.* Fordham. He freelanced as a radio writer, then served in the Navy in WW II. Afterward he went to Hollywood, where he began a highly successful career as a screenwriter, both alone and in collaboration with Billy Wilder and Charles Brackett. In 1953 he won an Academy Award for his part in the screenplay of *Titanic.* He directed one film, *Stopover Tokyo* (1957).

FILMS: *A Foreign Affair, Isn't It Romantic?, Miss Tatlock's Millions* 1948; *Top o' the Morning* 1949; *Appointment with Danger, The Mating Season* 1951; *The Model and the Marriage Broker, O. Henry's Full House* 1952; *Niagara, Titanic* 1953; *Dragnet* 1954; *Pete Kelly's Blues, Seven Cities of Gold* 1955; *Stopover Tokyo* (also dir.) 1957; *The FBI Story* 1959; *Wake Me When It's Over* 1960; *State Fair* 1962; *Mary Mary, PT–109* 1963; *Captain Newman M.D.* 1964; *Do Not Disturb* 1965; *A Man Could Get Killed* 1966; *Tony Rome* 1967.

Breer, Robert. Avant-garde filmmaker. Born on Sept. 30, 1926, in Detroit. *ed.* Stanford. An abstract painter, he began expressing his art on film in Paris, in the early 50s. In 1959 he settled in New York, where he continued experimenting with abstract and free-form animation. He developed a style all his own, utilizing motion, rhythm, and sound in inventive, unexpected cadences and combinations. His later films often integrate fragments of still photography but seldom live-action cinematography. He has been teaching filmmaking at New York's Cooper Union since 1973.

FILMS INCLUDE: *Form Phases I* 1952; *Images by Images I, Un Miracle* 1954; *Motion Pictures, Cats* 1956; *Recreation I, Jamestown Baloos* 1957; *A Man and His Dog Out for Air, Par Avion* 1958; *Chutes de Pierres, Eyewash, Trailer* 1959; *Inner and Outer Space* 1960; *Blazes* 1961; *Pat's Birthday, Horse Over Tea Kettle* 1962; *Breathing* 1963; *Fist Fight* 1964; *Elevator* 1971; *Gulls and Buoys* 1972; *Fuuji, Rubber Cement* 1974; *Swiss Army Knife, Rats and Pigeons* 1981; *Trial Balloons* 1982.

Bregman, Martin. Producer. Born on May 18, 1931, in New York City; *ed.* Indiana U.; NYU. He began his career as business manager to such stars as Barbra STREISAND, Faye DUNAWAY, and Candice BERGEN. Began producing as an extension of his representation of Al PACINO. He helped establish and became chairman of New York City's Advisory Council for Motion Pictures, Radio, and TV. Married actress Cornelia Sharpe. His sons, Michael Scott Bregman and Christopher Bregman, have also been involved in films.

FILMS INCLUDE (as producer or co-producer): *Serpico* 1973; *Dog Day Afternoon* 1975; *The Next Man* (also co-story, act.) 1976; *The Seduction of Joe Tynan* 1979; *Simon* 1980; *The Four Seasons* 1981; *Venom* 1982; *Scarface* 1983; *Sweet Liberty* 1986; *Real Men* 1987; *A New Life* 1988; *Sea of Love* 1989; *Betsy's Wedding* 1990; *Whispers in the Dark* 1992; *Carlito's Way* 1993; *The Shadow* 1994; *Matilda* 1996; *Nothing to Lose* 1997.

Brejchová, Jana. Actress. Born on Jan. 20, 1940, in Prague. Lovely, spontaneous leading lady of postwar Czech cinema. A milkman's daughter, she entered films at 14 with no previous training or acting experience and went on to become her country's most popular screen star. Married to actor Vlastimil BRODSKY, she was the first wife of director Milos FORMAN. Her sister, Hana Brejchová, also starred in Czech films, including Forman's *Loves of a Blonde.*

FILMS INCLUDE: *Leaden Bread* 1954; *The Golden Spider* 1956; *The Puppies/Youngsters, The Wolf Trap, A Local Romance* 1957; *Desire* 1958; *Awakening* 1959; *Baron Prásil/ Baron Munchhausen* 1960; *Labyrinth of the Heart, People Behind the Camera* 1961; *Green Horizons* 1962; *Everyday Courage/Courage for Every Day* 1964; *Return of the Prodigal* 1966; *The Bride's Night, Marathon* 1967; *End of a Priest* 1968; *Diabolical Honeymoon* (also sc.) 1970; *Miss Golem* 1972; *Attempted Murder* 1973; *Sign Language* 1974; *The Young Man and the White Whale* 1978; *Escapes Home* 1980; *Zánik Samoty Berhof* 1983; *Killing with Kindness* 1989.

Bremer, Lucille. Dancer, actress. Born in 1923, in Amsterdam, N.Y. Raised in Philadelphia, she began taking dance lessons there at age seven and at 12 joined the corps de ballet of the Philadelphia Opera Company. At 16 she became a Rockette at New York's Radio City Music Hall and later danced in Manhattan nightclubs and in the chorus line of Broadway musicals. She was spotted by MGM musical producer Arthur FREED and after drama coaching at the studio made her film debut in 1944. An attractive and graceful redhead, she was groomed for stardom and became Fred ASTAIRE's dance partner in two productions. But her promising career never materialized. MGM dropped her in 1947 and she retired from the screen the following year. A mother of five, she operates a children's dress shop in La Jolla, Calif.

FILMS: *Meet Me in St. Louis* 1944; *Yolanda and the Thief* 1945; *Ziegfeld Follies, Till the Clouds Roll By* 1946; *Dark Delusion* 1947; *Adventures of Casanova, Ruthless, Behind Locked Doors* 1948.

Brennan, Eileen. Actress. Born on Sept. 3, 1935, in Los Angeles. *ed.* Georgetown U.; AADA. Caustic, light leading lady and supporting player of the American stage and screen, often in brassy, neurotic dame roles. The daughter of silent screen actress Jean Manahan, she got her big break in 1959 as the title star of the off-Broadway musical 'Little Mary Sunshine,' for which received glowing reviews and an Obie Award. She began appearing in films in 1967 and received national exposure the following year as a regular on TV's 'Laugh-In.' She was nominated for an Academy Award for her supporting role as the sarcastic Captain Doreen Lewis in the film *Private Benjamin* (1980) and won an Emmy when she repeated that role in the TV series (1981–83) that followed. Her career was disrupted in 1983, when she was severely injured in a car accident and for a while was confined to a wheelchair. But overcoming a dependency on prescription painkillers, she returned to the screen in 1985.

FILMS: *Divorce American Style* 1967; *The Last Picture Show* 1971; *Scarecrow, The Sting* 1973; *Daisy Miller* 1974; *At Long Last Love, Hustle* 1975; *Murder by Death, The Last of the Cowboys/The Great Smokey Roadblock* 1976; *The Last of the Cowboys* 1977; *FM, The Cheap Detective* 1978; *Private Benjamin* 1980; *The Funny Farm* (Can.), *Pandemonium* (cameo) 1982; *Clue* 1985; *Sticky Fingers, Rented Lips, The New*

Adventures of Pippi Longstocking 1988; *It Had to Be You* 1989; *Stella, Texasville, White Palace* 1990; *Joey Takes a Cab* 1991; *I Don't Buy Kisses Anymore* 1992; *Reckless* 1995; *Changing Habits* 1997; *Boy's Life 2* 1997.

Brennan, Walter. Actor. *b.* July 25, 1894, Swampscott, Mass. *d.* 1974. Trained in engineering, he chose acting as a career, appearing in vaudeville and stock and supporting himself as a lumberjack and bank clerk before enlisting for WW I service in 1917. In 1923 he arrived in Hollywood and broke into films as an extra and stuntman. He went on to become one of the screen's most versatile and best-known supporting players in character parts of astonishing range in well over 100 films. He was the first actor ever to win three Academy Awards: for best supporting actor in *Come and Get It* (1936), *Kentucky* (1938), and *The Westerner* (1940). He was nominated for yet another Oscar for *Sergeant York* (1941). He also starred in the TV series 'The Real McCoys,' 'Tycoon,' and 'The Guns of Will Sonnett.'

FILMS: *Tearin' Into Trouble, The Ridin' Rowdy* 1927; *The Ballyhoo Buster* 1928; *Smilin' Guns, The Lariat Kid, The Long Long Trail, One Hysterical Night* (as Paul Revere), *The Shannons of Broadway* 1929; *The King of Jazz* 1930; *Dancing Dynamite, Neck and Neck* 1931; *The Air Mail Mystery* (serial), *Law and Order, Texas Cyclone, Two-Fisted Law, All American* 1932; *Parachute Jumper, The Phantom of the Air* (serial), *Man of Action, Fighting for Justice, Sing Sinner Sing, Strange People, Silent Men, One Year Later* 1933; *Good Dame, Half a Sinner* 1934; *Northern Frontier, The Wedding Night, Law Beyond the Range, Bride of Frankenstein, Lady Tubbs, Man on the Flying Trapeze, Metropolitan, Barbary Coast, Seven Keys to Baldpate* 1935; *The Three Godfathers, These Three, The Moon's Our Home, Fury, The Prescott Kid, Come and Get It, Banjo on My Knee* 1936; *She's Dangerous, When Love Is Young, The Affair of Cappy Ricks, Wild and Woolly* 1937; *The Adventures of Tom Sawyer, The Buccaneer, The Texans, Mother Carey's Chickens, The Cowboy and the Lady, Kentucky* 1938; *The Story of Vernon and Irene Castle, They Shall Have Music, Stanley and Livingstone, Joe and Ethel Turp Call on the President* 1939; *Northwest Passage, Maryland, The Westerner* (as Judge Roy Bean) 1940; *Meet John Doe, Nice Girl?, Sergeant York, This Woman Is Mine, Swamp Water, Rise and Shine* 1941; *The Pride of the Yankees, Stand by for Action* 1942; *Slightly Dangerous, Hangmen Also Die, The North Star* 1943; *Home in Indiana, To Have and Have Not, The Princess and the Pirate* 1944; *Dakota* 1945; *A Stolen Life, Centennial Summer, Nobody Lives Forever, My Darling Clementine* 1946; *Driftwood* 1947; *Scudda-Hoo! Scudda-Hay!, Red River, Blood on the Moon* 1948; *The Green Promise, The Great Dan Patch, Brimstone, Task Force* 1949; *A Ticket to Tomahawk, Singing Guns, Curtain Call at Cactus Creek, The Showdown, Surrender* 1950; *Along the Great Divide, Best of the Badmen, The Wild Blue Yonder* 1951; *Return of the Texan, Lure of the Wilderness* 1952; *Sea of Lost Ships* 1953; *Drums Across the River, Four Guns to the Border* 1954; *Bad Day at Black Rock, The Far Country, At Gunpoint* 1955; *Come Next Spring, Goodbye My Lady, The Proud Ones* 1956; *The Way to the Gold, Tammy and the Bachelor, God Is My Partner* 1957; *Rio Bravo* 1959; *Shoot Out at Big Sag, How the West Was Won* 1962; *Those Calloways* 1965; *The Oscar* 1966; *The Gnome-Mobile, Who's Minding the Mint?* 1967; *The One and Only Genuine Original Family Band* 1968; *Support Your Local Sheriff!* 1969; *Smoke in the Wind* 1975.

Brenner, Albert. American art director, production designer. He designed outstanding sets for many major Hollywood productions and was nominated for Academy Awards for *The Sunshine Boys* (1975) and *The Turning Point* (1977).

FILMS INCLUDE: *The Hustler* 1961; *The Connection* 1962; *The Luck of Ginger Coffey* (Can.), *Fail Safe* 1964; *A Midsummer Night's Dream* 1966; *Point Blank* 1967; *Bullitt* 1968; *Monte Walsh* 1970; *Brother John, Summer of '42* 1971; *The Other* 1972; *Scarecrow* 1973; *Bank Shot* 1974; *The Sunshine Boys* 1975; *The Missouri Breaks* 1976; *The Goodbye Girl, The Turning Point* 1977; *Coma* 1978; *Only When I Laugh* 1981; *Max Dugan Returns* 1983; *Unfaithfully Yours, 2010* 1984; *Sweet Dreams* 1985; *The Morning After* 1986; *The Monster Squad* 1987; *The Presidio* 1988; *Beaches* 1989; *Pretty Woman* 1990; *The Program* 1993.

Brenon, Herbert. Director. *b.* Jan. 13, 1880, Dublin. *d.* 1958. The son of a London editor, he emigrated to the US at 16 and after briefly working as a call boy at a New York theater began acting and managing in stock, touring companies, and vaudeville. For a while he also operated a small motion picture theater in Johnstown, Pa. In 1909 he entered films as a screenwriter for Carl LAEMMLE's Imperial Company in New York and three years later made his debut as a film director. His success was immediate; within months he was hailed by critics as an important new talent. His prestige remained high throughout the silent era. He directed some of Hollywood's most glamorous stars and was often entrusted with big-budget productions by Fox, Paramount, and other studios. He also worked periodically in England and Italy.

Among Brenon's notable films were *Neptune's Daughter,* starring Annette Kellermann (Brenon was badly injured when a tank she swam in exploded); *The Two Orphans,* starring Theda Bara (and Brenon himself); *War Brides,* starring Alla Nazimova, which he considered his best; *Peter Pan,* starring Betty Bronson; *The Great Gatsby,* starring Warner Baxter; *Beau Geste,* starring Ronald Colman; and *Laugh Clown Laugh,* starring Lon Chaney. While the director was at the height of his fame, critics spoke with admiration of "the Brenon touch."

Brenon met the advent of the talkies with skepticism. In 1928 he spoke disparagingly of sound as a passing fad brought about by the inferiority of the current crop of silent films. He reluctantly switched to talkies when the fad proved permanent, but met with little success, and in 1934 went to England, where he continued to direct until his retirement in 1940.

FILMS: In the US—*All for Her* (also sc., act.), *The Clown's Triumph, Leah the Forsaken* (also sc.), *The Long Strike* (also sc., act.) 1912; *Kathleen Mavourneen* (also sc.), *The Angel of Death, Ivanhoe* (filmed in England; also sc., act. as Isaac of York), *The Anarchist, Time Is Money* (filmed in Germany; also sc., act.) 1913; *Absinthe* (filmed in France; also sc.), *Neptune's Daughter* (filmed in Bermuda; also act.), *Across the Atlantic* (filmed in England; also sc., act.) 1914; *The Heart of Maryland* (also sc., act.), *Kreutzer Sonata* (also sc.), *The Clemenceau Case* (also sc.), *The Two Orphans* (also sc., act.), *Sin* (also sc.), *The Soul of Broadway* (also sc.) 1915; *The Ruling Passion* (filmed in Jamaica; prod. sc. only), *The Marble Heart* (filmed in Jamaica; prod., sc. only), *A Daughter of the Gods* (also sc.), *The Missing Witness* (short; also act.), *The Bigamist* (short), *The Governor's Decision* (short), *War Brides* (also prod., co-sc.), *The Voice Upstairs* (short), *Bubbles* (short), *Love or an Empire* (short; also sc.) 1916; *The Eternal Sin* (also prod., adapt.), *The Lone Wolf* (also prod.), *The Fall of the Romanoffs* (also prod.) 1917; *Empty Pockets* (also prod.), *The Passing of the Third Floor Back* (also prod., co-sc.) 1918. In UK—*Victory and Peace/The Invasion of Britain* 1918; *Twelve-Ten* 1919. In Italy—*La Principessa Misteriosa/The Mysterious Princess, Beatrice* 1919; *Sorella contro Sorella/Sister Against Sister* 1920. In the US—*The Passion Flower* (also co-sc.), *The Sign on the Door* (also co-sc.), *The Wonderful Thing* (also co-sc.) 1921; *Any Wife, A Stage*

Romance, Shackles of Gold, Moonshine Valley (also co-sc.) 1922; *The Custard Cup, The Rustle of Silk, Sister Against Sister, The Woman with Four Faces, The Spanish Dancer* (also prod.) 1923; *Shadows of Paris, The Breaking Point, The Side Show of Life* (also prod.), *The Alaskan, Peter Pan* 1924; *The Little French Girl, The Street of Forgotten Men* 1925; *The Song and Dance Man, Dancing Mothers, Beau Geste, The Great Gatsby, God Gave Me Twenty Cents, A Kiss for Cinderella* 1926; *The Telephone Girl* (also prod.), *Sorrell and Son* (also sc.) 1927; *Laugh Clown Laugh* 1928; *The Rescue* 1929; *Lummox, The Case of Sergeant Grischa* 1930; *Beau Ideal, Transgression* 1931; *Girl of the Rio* 1932; *Wine Women and Song* 1933. In the UK—*Royal Cavalcade* (doc.), *Honors Easy* 1935; *Living Dangerously, Someone at the Door* 1936; *The Dominant Sex, Spring Handicap, The Live Wire* 1937; *Housemaster, Yellow Sands* 1938; *Black Eyes* 1939; *The Flying Squad* 1940.

Brent, Evelyn. Actress. *b.* Mary Elizabeth Riggs, Oct. 20, 1899, Tampa, Fla. *d.* 1975. Raised in Brooklyn, N.Y. In 1914, while still in high school, she began appearing as an extra in films produced at Fort Lee, N.J., initially billed as Betty Riggs. Gradually her roles improved and by 1916 she was playing leads. Among other early roles, she played the feminine lead opposite John Barrymore in *Raffles the Amateur Cracksman* (1917). She starred in several British pictures of the early 20s and after returning to Hollywood in 1922 soon rose to prominence in silents, notably as the star of Josef von STERNBERG's *Underworld* (1927) and *The Last Command* (1928). Her sultry good looks were put to best use in "vampy" or gang moll roles. She made a smooth transition to sound, but her roles and her films gradually diminished in quality and importance until her retirement in the late 40s.

FILMS INCLUDE: As Betty Riggs—*The Pit* 1914; *The Shooting of Dan McGrew* 1915. As Evelyn Brent—*The Lure of Heart's Desire, The Soul Market, The Spell of the Yukon, The Iron Woman* 1916; *Who's Your Neighbor?, Raffles the Amateur Cracksman* 1917; *Daybreak* 1918; *The Other Man's Wife, The Glorious Lady, Fool's Gold* 1919; *The Shuttle of Life* (UK), *The Law Divine* (UK) 1920; *Sonia* (UK) 1921; *The Spanish Jade* (filmed in Spain) 1922; *Held to Answer* 1923; *Loving Lies, The Plunderer, The Arizona Express, The Lone Chance, The Desert Outlaw, The Dangerous Flirt, My Husband's Wives, Silk Stocking Sal* 1924; *Midnight Molly, Forbidden Cargo, Alias Mary Flynn, Lady Robinhood, Smooth as Satin, Three Wise Crooks* 1925; *Queen o' Diamonds, The Imposter, The Jade Cup, Flame of the Argentine, Love 'Em and Leave 'Em* 1926; *Love's Greatest Mistake, Blind Alleys, Underworld, Women's Wares* 1927; *Beau Sabreur, The Last Command, The Showdown, A Night of Mystery, The Dragnet, His Tiger Lady, The Mating Call* 1928; *Interference, Broadway, Fast Company, Woman Trap, Why Bring That Up?, Darkened Rooms* 1929; *Slightly Scarlet, Framed, The Silver Horde, Madonna of the Streets* 1930; *Traveling Husbands, The Mad Parade, Pagan Lady* 1931; *High Pressure, Attorney for the Defense, The Crusader* 1932; *The World Gone Mad* 1933; *Home on the Range, The Nitwits* 1935; *Hopalong Cassidy Returns, The President's Mystery* 1936; *Jungle Jim* (serial), *Night Club Scandal, The Last Train from Madrid, Daughter of Shanghai* 1937; *Tip-Off Girls, Mr. Wong—Detective, The Law West of Tombstone* 1938; *The Mad Empress* (as Empress Eugenie) 1940; *Holt of the Secret Service* (serial), *Emergency Landing* 1941; *Westward Ho!* 1942; *The Seventh Victim* 1943; *Bowery Champs* 1944; *The Golden Eye* 1948.

Brent, George. Actor. *b.* George Brendan Nolan, Mar. 15, 1904, Shannonsbridge, Ireland. *d.* 1979. At age 11 he came to America to stay with relatives after the death of his parents, later returning to Ireland, where he started his acting career playing bit parts and walk-ons in Abbey Theatre productions. Because of his subversive activities during the Irish Rebellion, however, he was forced to flee the country and was smuggled aboard a freighter bound for Canada. After working at various odd jobs, he joined a stock company, with which he toured Canada for two years, then came to New York, where he began his American career with a stage company in the Bronx. He later appeared with several stock companies, forming three of his own. After appearing in a number of Broadway productions in the late 20s, he went to Hollywood to begin a 20-year-long film career as a gallant, romantic leading man. Gentlemanly and suave, and sporting a familiar pencil-thin mustache, he soon became established as one of Hollywood's most dependable, if least animated, leading men. He projected restrained virility opposite such screen idols as Greta Garbo, Ginger Rogers, Barbara Stanwyck, Myrna Loy, Olivia de Havilland, and especially Bette DAVIS, with whom he appeared in a succession of 11 Warner Bros. dramas of the late 30s and early 40s. He retired from the screen in the early 50s to run a horse-breeding ranch but returned for an isolated appearance in 1978. Among his six wives were actresses Ruth CHATTERTON (1932–34), Constance Worth (briefly in 1937), and Ann SHERIDAN (1942–43).

FILMS: *Under Suspicion, Once a Sinner, Fair Warning, The Lightning Warrior* (serial), *Charlie Chan Carries On, Ex-Bad Boy, Homicide Squad* 1931; *So Big, The Rich Are Always With Us, Week-End Marriage, Miss Pinkerton, The Purchase Price, The Crash, They Call It Sin* 1932; *Luxury Liner, 42nd Street, The Keyhole, Lilly Turner, Baby Face, Private Detective 62, Female, From Headquarters* 1933; *Stamboul Quest, Housewife, Desirable, The Painted Veil* 1934; *The Right to Live, Living on Velvet, Stranded, Front Page Woman, The Goose and the Gander, Special Agent, In Person* 1935; *Snowed Under, The Golden Arrow, The Case Against Mrs. Ames, Give Me Your Heart, More Than a Secretary* 1936; *God's Country and the Woman, Mountain Justice, The Go-Getter, Submarine D-1* 1937; *Gold Is Where You Find It, Jezebel, Racket Busters, Secrets of an Actress* 1938; *Wings of the Navy, Dark Victory, The Old Maid, The Rains Came* 1939; *The Fighting 69th, Adventure in Diamonds, Till We Meet Again, The Man Who Talked Too Much, South of Suez* 1940; *Honeymoon for Three, The Great Lie, They Dare Not Love, International Lady* 1941; *Twin Beds, In This Our Life, The Gay Sisters, You Can't Escape Forever, Silver Queen* 1942; *Experiment Perilous* 1944; *The Affairs of Susan* 1945; *My Reputation, The Spiral Staircase, Tomorrow Is Forever, Lover Come Back, Temptation* 1946; *Slave Girl, The Corpse Came C.O.D., Out of the Blue, Christmas Eve* 1947; *Luxury Liner, Angel on the Amazon* 1948; *Red Canyon, Illegal Entry, The Kid From Cleveland, Bride for Sale* 1949; *FBI Girl* 1951; *The Last Page, Montana Belle* 1952; *Tangier Incident, Mexican Manhunt* 1953; *Death of a Scoundrel* (bit) 1956; *Born Again* 1978.

Bresler, Jerry. Producer. *b.* Jerome S. Bresler, Apr. 13, 1908, Denver. *d.* 1977. *ed.* Swarthmore. Started in films as a production supervisor with a small company and later formed his own production group. Joined MGM as unit manager in the late 30s, working on the "Dr. Kildare" series and other films. After winning Academy Awards for producing the two-reeler *Heavenly Music* (1943) and the one-reeler *Stairway to Light* (1945), he became a producer of feature films, first for MGM, then for other companies, and finally as an independent.

FILMS INCLUDE: *Main Street After Dark, Bewitched* 1945; *The Web, The Arnelo Affair, Singapore* 1947; *Another Part of the Forest, An Act of Murder/Live Today for Tomorrow* 1948; *Abandoned/Abandoned Woman* 1949; *Convicted* 1950; *The Mob* 1951; *Assignment—Paris* 1952; *Lizzie* 1957; *The*

Vikings 1958; *Gidget Goes Hawaiian* 1961; *Diamond Head* 1963; *Major Dundee* 1965; *Casino Royale* (UK) 1967; *Pussycat Pussycat I Love You* 1970.

Bressart, Felix. Actor. *b.* 1890, Eydtkuhnen, East Prussia. *d.* 1949. Character comedian of the German stage (from 1914) and screen (from 1928), he was forced to leave the country after the Nazi rise to power in 1933. He first went to Switzerland, then, in 1937, came to the US, where two years later he started a busy career in Hollywood films. Typically he played an amiable, whimsical European, most memorably in *Ninotchka.*

FILMS INCLUDE: In Germany—*Liebe im Kuhstall* 1928; *Die Drei von der Tankstelle* 1930; *Der wahre Jakob, Nie wieder Liebe/No More Love* 1931; *Und wer kusst mich?* 1933. In the US—*Three Smart Girls Grow Up, Ninotchka* 1939; *Swanee River, The Shop Around the Corner, Edison the Man, Comrade X, Escape, Bitter Sweet* 1940; *Ziegfeld Girl, Blossoms in the Dust* 1941; *To Be or Not to Be, Crossroads, Iceland* 1942; *Above Suspicion* 1943; *Song of Russia, Greenwich Village, The Seventh Cross* 1944; *Without Love* 1945; *I've Always Loved You* 1946; *A Song Is Born* 1948; *Portrait of Jennie, Take One False Step* 1949.

Bresson, Robert. Director. Born on Sept. 25, 1907, in Bromont-Lamothe, France. Little is known about the early life of this reclusive, secretive genius of the French cinema, except that he turned to painting after graduating from high school, where he had excelled in Greek, Latin, and philosophy studies. He married at 19. In 1933 he made his entry into films as screenwriter on *C'était un Musicien.* The following year he directed a medium-length comedy, *Les Affaires publiques,* of which no print survives. He collaborated on several more scripts, including René Clair's *L'Air pur* (1939) before the outbreak of WW II. During the war he spent more than a year in a German prison, an experience he was later to incorporate into his film *A Man Escaped* (1956). Bresson prefers to dissociate himself from his early work in films and to regard his film career as really beginning with his first feature, *Les Anges du Péché* (1943).

Bresson occupies a unique place in French cinema. He cannot be classified with either the old guard or the New Wave but is highly respected by both for pursuing his own individual style, unperturbed by the cinema around him. "He expresses himself cinematographically as a poet would with his pen," Jean Cocteau said of him. "His cinema is closer to painting than to photography," says Truffaut. Others see in him a philosopher with a camera, an uncompromising Jansenist rigorously preoccupied with ideas of predestination and spiritual grace.

Above all, Bresson is the complete cinema stylist whose universe remains unchanged from film to film and whose personal signature is imprinted clearly on each and every one. Of all contemporary directors, he probably comes closest to the definition of an *auteur.* His films are tightly constructed to the exclusion of all but the bare essence of the material he intends to explore. Nothing is allowed to interfere with his basic theme either by addition or subtraction. What he does choose to show is presented with rigorous, almost fanatic, attention to detail. But the realism he achieves is not of the kind associated with documentary films. His concern is with truth beyond mere reality, and he discovers it not in the artifacts themselves but in the inner life of the characters who are surrounded by them.

A purist, Bresson resists being influenced by the tools of other arts. He rejects the conventional plot as "a novelist's trick" and most of the time employs nonprofessional or inexperienced actors. "Acting is for the theater, which is a bastard art," he says. To him, acting, like all other extraneous matters, is a hindrance rather than an aid in his search for inner truth. Unlike the theater, Bresson contends, "film can be a true art because in it the author takes fragments of reality and arranges them in such a way that their juxtaposition transforms them. . . . Each shot is like a word, meaning nothing by itself. . . .[It] is given its meaning by its context. . . . Acting has nothing to do with that. It can only get in the way. Films can be made only by bypassing the will of those who appear in them, using not what they do but what they are."

This emphasis on the relationship of images also accounts for the "flat" composition of Bresson's individual frames. "Painting," he says further, "taught me to make not beautiful images but necessary ones." The sound track, too, is used by Bresson not for effect but functionally, as another dimension of his universe, an extension of the world of his characters and nothing more. Bresson has made only ten feature films in nearly 30 years, yet he is one of the most discussed and revered figures in cinema today—creative, original, unique. In 1975 he published *Notes Sur le Cinématographe,* a book-size essay expressing his ideas on filmmaking. An English translation, *Notes on Cinematography,* was published in New York in 1977. He shared the Grand Prix de Création at the 1983 Cannes Festival for *L'Argent.*

FILMS: *Les Affaires publiques* (medium length) 1934; *Les Anges du Péché/Angels of the Streets* 1943; *Les Dames du Bois de Boulogne/Ladies of the Park* 1945; *Le Journal d'un Curé de Campagne/Diary of a Country Priest* 1951; *Un Condamné à Mort s'est échappé* (or *Le Vent souffle où il veut)/A Man Escaped* 1956; *Pickpocket* 1959; *Le Procès de Jeanne d'Arc/ The Trial of Joan of Arc* 1962; *Au Hasard Balthazar/ Balthazar* 1966; *Mouchette* 1967; *Une Femme douce* 1969; *Quatre Nuits d'un Rêveur/Four Nights of a Dreamer* 1971; *Lancelot du Lac/Lancelot of the Lake* (formerly known as *Le Graal/The Grail*) 1974; *Le Diable probablement/The Devil Probably* 1977; *L'Argent* 1983; *De Weg Naar Bresson* (act. only) 1984.

Brest, Martin. Director. Born in 1951, the Bronx, N.Y. While studying at the NYU Film School, he made an award-winning short, *Hot Dogs for Gauguin.* He was then accepted into the American Film Institute's fellowship program under whose auspices he turned out his first feature, *Hot Tomorrows.* After successfully helming his first commercial project, *Going in Style* (1979), he was assigned to direct the electronic-age thriller *War Games,* but was fired from the set following friction with the producers. He rebounded strongly, however, as the director of *Beverly Hills Cop* (1984), one of Hollywood's biggest box-office blockbusters. He was nominated for an Oscar for directing *Scent of a Woman* (1992), the film that finally brought Al Pacino his Oscar.

FEATURE FILMS: *Hot Tomorrows* (also prod., sc., edit.) 1978; *Going in Style* (also sc.) 1979; *Fast Times at Ridgemont High* (act. only) 1982; *Beverly Hills Cop* 1984; *Spies Like Us* (act. only), *Into the Night* (act. only) 1985; *Midnight Run* (also prod.) 1988; *Scent of a Woman* (also prod.) 1992.

Bretherton, Howard. Director. *b.* Feb. 13, 1896, Tacoma, Wash. *d.* 1969. Entered films in 1914 and within a dozen years had worked his way up from prop boy to director. With few exceptions, he directed low-budget films, mostly Westerns, including several William Boyd and Buck Jones vehicles. He gained a reputation as a competent editor, cutting most of his own films as well as scores of others, including William Wellman's *Heroes for Sale* (1933). Early in his career he was billed as H. P. Bretherton.

FILMS: *While London Sleeps* 1926; *Hills of Kentucky, The Black Diamond Express, The Bush Leaguer, One-Round Hogan, The Silver Slave* 1927; *Across the Atlantic, The Chorus Kid, Turn Back the Hours, Caught in the Fog* 1928; *The Redeeming*

Sin, From Headquarters, The Argyle Case, The Greyhound Limited, The Time the Place and the Girl 1929; *Second Choice, Isle of Escape* 1930; *The Match King* 1932; *Ladies They Talk About* (co-dir. with William Keighley) 1933; *Return of the Terror, El Cantante de Napoles* (in Spanish) 1934; *Dinky* (co-dir. with D. Ross Lederman), *Hop-a-Long Cassidy, The Eagle's Brood, Bar 20 Rides Again* 1935; *Call of the Prairie, The Leathernecks Have Landed, Three on the Trail, Heart of the West, The Girl From Mandalay, Wild Brian Kent, King of the Royal Mounted* 1936; *Secret Valley, It Happened Out West, Western Gold, County Fair* 1937; *Irish Luck, Wanted by the Police, Tough Kid* 1938; *Boys' Reformatory, Undercover Agent, Sky Patrol, Danger Flight, Navy Secrets* 1939; *Chasing Trouble, The Midnight Limited, The Showdown, On the Spot, Laughing at Danger, Up in the Air* 1940; *You're Out of Luck, Sign of the Wolf, In Old Colorado, Outlaws of the Desert, Twilight on the Trail* 1941; *West of Tombstone, Below the Border, Ghost Town Law, Down Texas Way, Riders of the West, West of the Law, Riders of the Prairie, Rhythm Parade, Dawn of the Great Divide* 1942; *Riders of the Rio Grande, Fugitive From Sonora, Bordertown Gunfighters, Wagon Tracks West, Beyond the Last Frontier, Whispering Footsteps* 1943; *Outlaws of Santa Fe, Hidden Valley Outlaws, Law of the Valley, The San Antonio Kid, The Girl Who Dared* 1944; *The Monster and the Ape* (serial), *Who's Guilty?* (serial; co-dir. with Wallace Grissell), *The Navajo Trail, The Big Show-Off, The Topeka Terror, Gun Smoke, Identity Unknown, Renegades of the Rio Grande* 1945; *The Trap* 1946; *Ridin' Down the Trail, Where the North Begins* 1947; *The Prince of Thieves, The Story of Life, Triggerman* 1948; *Whip Law* 1950; *Night Raiders* 1952.

Brialy, Jean-Claude. Actor, director. Born on Mar. 30, 1933, in Aumale, Algeria. The son of a high-ranking French Army officer, he graduated from the Conservatoire de Strasbourg, then went on stage in the provinces. In 1955 he arrived in Paris and was immediately cast in several short films made by his friends Jacques RIVETTE and Jean-Luc GODARD. He made his feature film debut in a supporting role in Jean Renoir's *Eléna et les Hommes/Paris Does Strange Things* (1956). After several more supporting roles, he gained sudden prominence as the lead in two Claude CHABROL films, *Le Beau Serge* (1958) and *Les Cousins/The Cousins* (1959). A confident actor of courtly manner, lively temperament, and often cynical screen personality, he developed into one of France's leading male performers of the 60s, a favorite of many New Wave directors. In 1961 alone he appeared in no fewer than 13 films. In the early 70s he began directing without curtailing his activity as an actor.

FILMS INCLUDE: As actor—*Eléna et les Hommes/Paris Does Strange Things* 1956; *Un Amour de Poche/Nude in His Pocket* 1957; *Christine, Le Beau Serge/Bitter Reunion* 1958; *Les Cousins/The Cousins, La Notte Brava* (It./Fr.), *Le Chemin des Ecoliers* 1959; *Le Bel Age, Paris nous appartient/Paris Belongs to Us* 1960; *Le Gigolo, Vanina Vanini* (It.), *Le Puits aux Trois Vérités/Three Faces of Sin, Une Femme est une Femme/A Woman Is a Woman, Les Amours célèbres, L'Education sentimentale* 1961; *La Chambre ardente/The Burning Court, Les Sept Péchés capiteaux/Seven Capital Sins, Le Diable et les Dix Commandements/The Devil and the Ten Commandments* 1962; *Le Glaive et la Balance/Two Are Guilty, Château en Suède/Nutty Naughty Chateau* 1963; *La Bonne Soupe/Careless Love, La Chasse à l'Homme/Male Hunt, Tonio Kröger* (Ger./Fr.), *La Ronde/Circle of Love, Un Monsieur de Compagnie/Male Companion* 1964; *La Mandragola/The Love Root* (It./Fr.) 1965; *Le Roi de Coeur/King of Hearts* 1966; *Le plus vieux Métier du Monde/The Oldest Profession, Un Homme de trop/Shock Troops* 1967; *La Mariée était en Noir/The Bride Wore Black* 1968; *Le Bal du Comte d'Orgel* 1970; *Le Genou de Claire/Claire's Knee* 1971; *Un Meurtre est un Meurtre/A Murder Is a Murder* 1972; *Le Fantôme de la Liberté* 1974; *Catherine & Cie./Catherine & Co.* 1975; *Le Juge et l'Assassin/The Judge and the Assassin, Les Oeufs brouillés, L'Année Sainte, Barocco* 1976; *Julie Pot de Colle, L'Imprecateur, Le Point de Mire* 1977; *Robert et Robert* 1978; *La Banguière* 1980; *Les Uns et les Autres/Bolero* 1981; *La Nuit de Varennes* 1982; *Le Démon dans l'Ile, Cap Canaille, Edith et Marcel/Edith and Marcel, Stella, La Crime* 1983; *Pinot Simple Flic* 1984; *Un Homme et une Femme: Vingt Ans déja/A Man and a Woman: 20 Years Later* (cameo) 1986; *Levy et Goliath, Grand Guignol, Le Grand Chemin/The Grand Highway* 1987; *Comédie d'Eté* 1989; *Ripoux Contre Ripoux/My New Partner 2, Faux Et Usage De Faux/Forgery and the Use of Forgeries, La Femme fardée, Ripoux contre Ripoux, S'en fout la mort* 1990. As director—*Eglantine* (also co-sc.) 1972; *Les Volets clos/Closed Shutters* (also co-sc.), *L'Oiseau rare* (also sc., act.) 1973; *Un Amour de Pluie/Loving in the Rain* (also co-sc.) 1974; *Les Malheurs de Sophie* (also co-adapt.) 1981; *Un Bon Petit Diable* (also co-sc.) 1983; *S'en Foi La Mort* 1989; *August* 1991; *Queen Margot* 1994.

Brian, David. Actor. *b.* Aug. 5, 1914, New York City. *d.* 1993. *ed.* CCNY. He worked as a doorman and chorus boy before drifting into vaudeville and nightclubs as a song-and-dance man. After WW II service with the Coast Guard he turned to the legitimate stage and then made his film debut in *Flamingo Road* in 1949, opposite Joan Crawford. For the next several years he played lead roles in Warner Bros. dramas, typically portraying strong or ruthless characters. In later Westerns he sometimes played powerful villains. He was a star of the early TV series 'Mr. District Attorney' and later the series 'The Immortal.' In 1949 he married actress Adrian BOOTH.

FILMS INCLUDE: *Flamingo Road, Beyond the Forest* 1949; *Intruder in the Dust, Breakthrough, The Great Jewel Robber, The Damned Don't Cry* 1950; *Inside Straight, Fort Worth, Inside the Walls of Folsom Prison* 1951; *This Woman Is Dangerous, Springfield Rifle, Million Dollar Mermaid* 1952; *A Perilous Journey, Ambush at Tomahawk Gap* 1953; *The High and the Mighty, Dawn at Socorro* 1954; *Timberjack* 1955; *Fury at Gunsight Pass* 1956; *Ghost of the China Sea* 1958; *The Rabbit Trap* 1959; *A Pocketful of Miracles* 1961; *How the West Was Won* 1962; *The Rare Breed, Castle of Evil* 1966; *The Destructors* 1968; *Childish Things* 1969; *The Seven Minutes* 1971.

Brian, Mary. Actress. Born Louise Byrdie Dantzler, on Feb. 17, 1908, in Corsicana, Tex. She entered films at 16 as Wendy in *Peter Pan* (1924) as a result of winning a "Miss Personality" prize in a Los Angeles beauty contest. She subsequently played "nice girl" romantic leads in numerous Hollywood silent and sound productions through the mid-30s, notably *Beau Geste* (1926), *The Virginian* (1929), *The Front Page,* (1931) and *The Man on the Flying Trapeze* (1935). In 1937 she retired to marry her second husband, the late film editor George Tomasini, then returned to low-budget films occasionally in the 40s. In 1953 she played the mother in the TV series 'Meet Corliss Archer.'

FILMS INCLUDE: *Peter Pan* (as Wendy) 1924; *The Air Mail, The Little French Girl, The Street of Forgotten Men, A Regular Fellow* 1925; *The Enchanted Hill, Paris at Midnight, Behind the Front, Brown of Harvard, Beau Geste* 1926; *Running Wild, High Hat, Man Power, Shanghai Bound, Two Flaming Youths* 1927; *Partners in Crime, Forgotten Faces, The Big Killing, Under the Tonto Rim, Someone to Love, Harold Teen, Varsity* 1928; *The Man I Love, The Marriage Playground, River of Romance, The Virginian* 1929; *The Kibitzer, Only the Brave,*

Burning Up, The Light of the Western Stars, The Social Lion, Only Saps Work 1930; *The Royal Family of Broadway, The Front Page, Gun Smoke, Homicide Squad* 1931; *It's Tough to Be Famous, Blessed Event, Manhattan Tower* 1932; *Hard to Handle, Girl Missing, The World Gone Mad, Song of the Eagle, Moonlight and Pretzels* 1933; *Shadows of Sing Sing, Ever Since Eve, Private Scandal, College Rhythm* 1934; *Charlie Chan in Paris, The Man on the Flying Trapeze* 1935; *Spendthrift, Killer at Large* 1936; *Navy Blues* 1937; *Calaboose, I Escaped From the Gestapo* 1943; *The Dragnet* 1947.

Brice, Fanny. Comedienne, singer. *b.* Fanny Borach, Oct. 29, 1891, New York City. *d.* 1951. While still in her early teens she began acting in light stage shows in Brooklyn. She later appeared in vaudeville and in Manhattan-based burlesque shows, first as a chorus girl, then as singer and dancer. Florenz Ziegfeld gave her her first big chance in his 1910 Follies. She subsequently starred in all but two of the 'Ziegfeld Follies' until 1923, gaining an enormous following for her singing and Brooklyn-dialect comedy. She later starred in 'The Music Box Revue' (1924–25) and in Broadway plays, including 'Fanny,' written especially for her. She was best known as radio's 'Baby Snooks.' She married gambler Nick Arnstein and producer Billy Rose.

She made only sporadic film appearances after her screen debut in *My Man* (1928). Her life story was the subject of the Broadway musical and the film *Funny Girl* (1968) and the sequel, *Funny Lady* (1975), in which she was portrayed by Barbra Streisand. Thinly disguised references to her life were also made in *Broadway Thru a Keyhole* (1933), starring Constance Cummings, and *Rose of Washington Square* (1939), starring Alice Faye.

FILMS: *Night Club, My Man* 1928; *Be Yourself!, The Man from Blankley's* 1930; *The Great Ziegfeld* 1936; *Everybody Sing* 1938; *Ziegfeld Follies* 1946.

Brickman, Marshall. Screenwriter, director. Born on Aug. 25, 1941, in Rio de Janeiro. *ed.* U. of Wisconsin. He was a vocalist and banjo player with the folk-singing groups The Tarriers and The Journeymen before entering TV as a writer for 'Candid Camera,' the 'Tonight Show,' and the 'Dick Cavett Show' (Emmy Award). His association with a Woody ALLEN special led to a screenwriting collaboration on three of the director's key films. They shared an Oscar for the script of *Annie Hall* (1977). Brickman himself turned to directing (with lesser distinction) in 1980.

FILMS INCLUDE: As screenwriter (in collaboration)—*Sleeper* 1973; *Annie Hall* 1977; *Manhattan* 1979; *For the Boys* 1991; *Intersection* 1994. As director-screenwriter—*Simon* 1980; *Lovesick* 1983; *The Manhattan Project* (also co-prod.) 1986.

Brickman, Paul. Screenwriter, director, producer. Born in Chicago. *ed.* Claremont Men's College, Calif. Screenwriter and director of varied domestic comedies and dramas. Formerly a camera assistant and story analyst at Columbia and Paramount, among other studios, he wrote his first screenplay for the early Jonathan Demme comedy *Citizens Band/Handle With Care* (1977). Difficult to categorize, his works are noteworthy for the turns they take on traditional genre forms, such as the teen film-turned-psychological comedy and satire *Risky Business* (1983).

FILMS INCLUDE: *The Bad News Bears in Breaking Training* (sc.), *Handle With Care/Citizen's Band* (assoc. prod., sc.) 1977; *Deal of the Century* (exec. prod., sc.), *Risky Business* (dir., sc.) 1983; *Men Don't Leave* (dir., sc.) 1990.

Bricusse, Leslie. Composer, lyricist, screenwriter. Born on Jan. 29, 1931, in London. *ed.* Cambridge. Working for the British stage and screen since the mid-50s, he acquired prominence in the late 60s with several large-budget British and American musical productions. Won Academy Awards for the song "Talk to the Animals" in the film *Doctor Dolittle* (1967) and lyrics for *Victor/Victoria* (1982), and was nominated for Oscars for the music and lyrics of *Goodbye Mr. Chips* (1969), *Scrooge* (1970), and *Willy Wonka and the Chocolate Factory* (1971).

FILMS INCLUDE: *Charley Moon* (sc., mus.) 1956; *Bachelor of Hearts* (co-sc.) 1958; *Goldfinger* (co-title song) 1964; *Stop the World I Want to Get Off* (co-sc., co-mus., co-lyrics), *Penelope* (lyrics, title song) 1966; *A Guide for the Married Man* (co-title song), *Doctor Dolittle* (sc., mus., lyrics) 1967; *Sweet November* (co-title song) 1968; *Goodbye Mr. Chips* (mus., lyrics) 1969; *Scrooge* (exec. prod., sc., mus., lyrics) 1970; *Willy Wonka and the Chocolate Factory* (lyrics) 1971; *Stop the World* (co-book, co-mus., co-lyrics) 1978; *Sunday Lovers* (sc., 'An Englishman's Home' episode) 1980; *Victor/Victoria* (lyrics) 1982; *Santa Claus* 1985; *That's Life!* (lyrics) 1986; *Home Alone* 1990; *Hook* 1991; *Tom & Jerry: The Movie* 1992.

bridge music. Music intended to accompany or enforce visual transitions.

Bridges, Alan. Director. Born on Sept. 28, 1927, in England. A veteran of many TV dramas for the BBC, he ventured into feature films in the mid-60s but continued working mainly in television. His film *The Hireling* won the grand prize at Cannes in 1973.

FILMS: *An Act of Murder* 1965; *Invasion* 1966; *The Lie* 1970; *Shelley* 1972; *The Hireling* 1973; *Out of Season* 1975; *Summer Rain* (Can.) 1976; *La Petite Fille en Velours bleu* (Fr.) 1978; *The Return of the Soldier* 1983; *The Shooting Party* 1985; *Secret Places of the Heart* 1991.

Bridges, Beau. Actor. Born Lloyd Vernet Bridges III, on Dec. 9, 1941, in Los Angeles. *ed.* UCLA; U. of Hawaii. The son of Lloyd BRIDGES and brother of Jeff BRIDGES, he appeared as a child in some films directed by his father's friends, but was more interested in a basketball career, for which he prepared at high school and during his two years in college. But his relatively short stature (5' 9") kept him away from professional athletics and diverted him back into films. In the late 60s he began to emerge as an all-American type of Hollywood leading man. In the late 80s he twice tried his hand at directing; in the 1990s he also established himself as a solid TV actor.

FILMS: *Force of Evil, No Minor Vices* 1948; *The Red Pony, Zamba* 1949; *The Explosive Generation* 1961; *Village of the Giants* 1965; *The Incident* 1967; *For Love of Ivy* 1968; *Gaily Gaily* 1969; *Adam's Woman* (Austral.), *The Landlord* 1970; *The Christian Licorice Store* 1971; *Hammersmith Is Out, Child's Play* 1972; *Your Three Minutes Are Up* 1973; *Lovin' Molly* 1974; *The Other Side of the Mountain* 1975; *One Summer Love/Dragonfly, Swashbuckler, Two-Minute Warning* 1976; *Greased Lighting, The Fifth Musketeer/Behind the Iron Mask* (as King Louis XIII; Aus.) 1977; *The Four Feathers* (TV movie shown theatrically abroad), *Something Light/Shimmering Light* (Austral.) 1978; *Norma Rae, The Runner Stumbles* 1979; *Silver Dream Racer* (UK) 1980; *Honky Tonk Freeway* 1981; *Night Crossing, Love Child* 1982; *Heart Like a Wheel* 1983; *The Hotel New Hampshire* 1984; *The Killing Time, The Wild Pair* (also dir.) 1987; *Seven Hours to Judgment* (also dir.) 1988; *The Iron Triangle, Signs of Life, The Fabulous Baker Boys* 1989; *Daddy's Dying. . . Who's Got the Will?, The Wizard* 1990; *Married to It* 1993; *Sidekick* 1993; *Jerry Maguire* (unbilled), *Losing Chase* 1996.

Bridges, James. Director, screenwriter, actor. *b.* Feb. 3, 1936, in Paris, Ark. *d.* 1993. *ed.* Arkansas Teachers Coll.; USC.

He started out as an actor, appearing in the late 50s in some 50 TV shows and such films as *Johnny Trouble* (1957), *Joy Ride* (1958), and *Faces* (1968). He turned to screenwriting in the mid-60s and made his debut as a director in 1970. Although his films varied in quality, nearly all effectively examined contemporary problems of young adults.

FILMS: As screenwriter—*The Appaloosa* (co-sc.) 1966; *The Forbin Project/Colossus: The Forbin Project* 1970; *Limbo/Women in Limbo/Chained to Yesterday* (co-sc.), *White Hunter, Black Heart* (co-sc.) 1990. As director—*The Baby Maker* (also sc.), *The Paper Chase* (also sc.) 1973; *9–30–55/September 30, 1955/24 Hours of the Rebel* (also sc.) 1977; *The China Syndrome* (also co-sc.) 1979; *Urban Cowboy* (also co-sc.) 1980; *Mike's Murder* (also sc.) 1984; *Perfect* (also prod., co-sc.) 1985; *Bright Lights, Big City* (also co-sc.) 1988.

Bridges, Jeff. Actor. Born on Dec. 4, 1949, in Los Angeles. The son of Lloyd BRIDGES and younger brother of Beau BRIDGES, he made his acting debut at eight, appearing in segments of the TV series 'Sea Hunt,' starring his father. After a stint in the Coast Guard Reserve and drama studies at New York's Herbert Berghof Studio, he made his adult film debut in 1970. He soon established himself as one of the American screen's most engaging personalities. A capable, versatile performer, he was nominated for Academy Awards as best supporting actor for *The Last Picture Show* (1971) and *Thunderbolt and Lightfoot* (1974) and as best actor for *Starman* (1984). Through his characters he explores the conflicts of the seemingly content American dreamer.

FILMS: *The Company She Keeps* 1951; *Halls of Anger, The Yin and Yang of Mr. Go* (never released) 1970; *The Last Picture Show* 1971; *Fat City, Bad Company* 1972; *Lolly Madonna XXX/The Lolly-Madonna Wars, The Last American Hero/Hard Driver, The Iceman Cometh* 1973; *Thunderbolt and Lightfoot* 1974; *Rancho Deluxe, Hearts of the West/Hollywood Cowboy* 1975; *Stay Hungry, King Kong* 1976; *Somebody Killed Her Husband* 1978; *Winter Kills* 1979; *Success/American Success/The American Success Company, Heaven's Gate* 1980; *Cutter's Way/Cutter and Bone* 1981; *Tron, The Last Unicorn* (voice only), *Kiss Me Goodbye* 1982; *Against All Odds, Starman* 1984; *Jagged Edge* 1985; *Eight Million Ways to Die, The Morning After* 1986; *Nadine* 1987; *Tucker: The Man and His Dream* 1988; *See You in the Morning, Cold Feet, The Fabulous Baker Boys* 1989; *Texasville* 1990; *The Fisher King* 1991; *American Heart, The Vanishing* 1993; *Blown Away* 1994; *Wild Bill* 1995; *The Mirror Has Two Faces, White Squall* 1996.

Bridges, Lloyd. Actor. Born on Jan. 15, 1913, in San Leandro, Calif. *ed.* UCLA. After stage experience in stock, he made his Broadway debut in the late 30s in a modern-dress version of *Othello.* In 1941 he was signed by Columbia and during the next four years appeared in some 25 low-budget films. Tall, blond, and rugged, he was used frequently in Westerns and action pictures, sometimes as a heavy. After he left Columbia and began freelancing in 1945, his roles and films improved and included many lead parts in B pictures and important parts in A pictures, such as his role as the calculating deputy sheriff in *High Noon.* He also starred in the popular underwater TV series 'Sea Hunt.' In the early 50s he was a key witness in the second round of hearings of the House Un-American Activities Committee after affirming his own past membership in the Communist party. His marriage, to actress Dorothy Simpson, produced three sons, two of whom, Beau and Jeff BRIDGES, are film personalities in their own right.

FILMS INCLUDE: *The Lone Wolf Takes a Chance, Here Comes Mr. Jordan, Two Latins From Manhattan* 1941; *Alias Boston Blackie, Shut My Big Mouth, Talk of the Town* 1942; *Sahara, Passport to Suez* 1943; *Louisiana Hayride, The Master Race* 1944; *A Walk in the Sun, Miss Susie Slagle's* 1945; *Abilene Town, Canyon Passage* 1946; *Ramrod* 1947; *16 Fathoms Deep* 1948; *Home of the Brave, Red Canyon, Calamity Jane and Sam Bass* 1949; *Colt 45, Rocketship XM, The White Tower, The Sound of Fury* 1950; *Three Steps North, Whistle at Eaton Falls* 1951; *High Noon, Plymouth Adventure* 1952; *The Kid From Left Field* 1953; *Pride of the Blue Grass* 1954; *Wichita* 1955; *The Rainmaker* 1956; *Ride Out for Revenge* 1957; *The Goddess* 1958; *Around the World Under the Sea* 1966; *Attack on the Iron Coast, Daring Game* 1968; *The Happy Ending* 1969; *Lost Flight* 1971; *To Find a Man/Sex and the Teenager* 1972; *Running Wild* 1973; *The Fifth Musketeer/Behind the Iron Mask* (as Aramis; Austria) 1977; *Bear Island* (UK/Can.), *Airplane!* 1980; *Airplane II: The Sequel* 1982; *Weekend Warriors* 1986; *The Wild Pair* 1987; *Tucker: The Man and His Dream* (bit) 1988; *Cousins, Winter People* 1989; *Joe Versus the Volcano* 1990; *Hot Shots!* 1991; *Honey I Blew Up the Kid!* 1992, *Hot Shots! Part Deux* 1993; *Blown Away* 1994; *The War at Home* 1996.

bridging shot. Any shot, such as a CUTAWAY or an INSERT, used in editing to cover a break in continuity.

Bright, John. Screenwriter. *b.* Jan. 1, 1908, Baltimore. *d.* 1989. *ed.* Lake Forest. He began his career at 13 as Ben Hecht's copy boy on the Chicago *Daily News.* He later became a crime reporter and at 19 published his first book, *Hizzoner Big Bill Thompson,* an unauthorized biography of Chicago's mayor. When the mayor sued him, he moved to Hollywood, where he began writing gangster stories with Kubec Glasmon, a Polish-born pharmacist who employed him as a soda jerk. Their novelette-length "Beer and Blood" became the basis for *The Public Enemy* (1931), a milestone in the American cinema's gangster genre and in the career of its star, James Cagney. Under contract to Warner Bros., the two collaborated on a number of other crime and action films in 1931–32. Bright then moved to Paramount. In 1933, rebelling against the low wages and poor working conditions of Hollywood writers, Bright and Glasmon were among the ten founders of the Screen Writers Guild (now the WRITERS GUILD OF AMERICA). A political activist with leftist leanings, Bright was blacklisted in 1951 after being named a Communist in testimony before the House Un-American Activities hearings. Returning to Hollywood from seven years of self-exile in Mexico, he wrote magazine articles and became a reader, story editor, and literary advisor for Bill COSBY's production company. He was instrumental in the company's filming of *Johnny Got His Gun* (1971), the antiwar film by Dalton TRUMBO, one of the HOLLYWOOD TEN.

FILMS INCLUDE: *The Public Enemy, Blonde Crazy, Smart Money* 1931; *Taxi, Union Depot, The Crowd Roars, Three on a Match, If I Had a Million* 1932; *She Done Him Wrong* 1933; *The Accusing Finger* 1936; *San Quentin* 1937; *Back Door to Heaven* 1939; *Glamour for Sale* 1940; *Broadway, Sherlock Holmes and the Voice of Terror* 1942; *I Walk Alone, Close-Up* 1948; *The Kid From Cleveland* 1949 *The Brave Bulls* 1951.

Bright, Richard. Actor. Born in Brooklyn, N.Y. Character actor of screen and television, often in calmly menacing roles. Accomplished Broadway and regional stage actor ('Short Eyes,' 'The Basic Training of Pavlo Hummel'), he has appeared in a variety of serious dramatic films, many set in New York and many with fellow New York-trained colleague AL PACINO. His most enduring role is as the omnipresent family associate Al Neri in the *Godfather* trilogy.

FILMS INCLUDE: *Odds Against Tomorrow* 1959; *Panic in Needle Park* 1971; *The Godfather, The Getaway* 1972; *Pat Garrett and Billy the Kid* 1973, *The Godfather Part II* 1974; *Rancho Deluxe* 1975, *Marathon Man* 1976; *Citizens Band,*

Looking for Mr. Goodbar 1977; *On the Yard, Hair* 1979; *The Idolmaker* 1980; *Vigilante* 1982; *Once Upon a Time in America, Crackers* 1984; *Crimewave* 1985; *Brighton Beach Memoirs, 52 Pick-up* 1986; *Red Heat* 1988; *The Godfather Part III* 1990.

Briley, John. Screenwriter. Born in 1925, in Kalamazoo, Mich. Long a resident of England, he contributed literate screenplays for a number of British films, winning an Oscar for *Gandhi* (1982). He also wrote novels, short stories, and plays.

FILMS INCLUDE: *Invasion Quartet* 1961; *Children of the Damned* 1964; *Situation Hopeless—But Not Serious* 1965; *Pope Joan* 1972; *That Lucky Touch* 1975; *The Medusa Touch* 1978; *Eagle's Wing* 1979; *Gandhi* 1982; *Enigma* 1983; *Marie* (US) 1985; *Tai-Pan* (US) 1986; *Cry Freedom* (also co-prod.) 1987; *Sandino* (Sp./Chile) 1990.

Brimley, Wilford. Actor. Born on Sept. 27, 1934, in Salt Lake City. Formerly a blacksmith, ranch hand, and racehorse trainer, he entered films in the late 60s as an extra and stuntman, moving on to supporting parts by the end of the decade. Playing increasingly significant roles, he developed in the 80s into one of Hollywood's most effective and reliable character actors. Typically seen as a heavily moustached, gruff old-timer or wise counselor. He co-starred in the TV series 'Our House.' Also billed as A. Wilford Brimley.

FILMS INCLUDE: *True Grit* 1969; *Lawman* 1971; *The China Syndrome, The Electric Horseman* 1979; *Brubaker, Borderline* 1980; *Absence of Malice* 1981; *The Thing* 1982; *10 to Midnight, Tender Mercies* 1982; *Harry and Son, The Hotel New Hampshire, The Stone Boy, The Natural, Country* 1984; *Cocoon, Remo Williams: The Adventure Begins* 1985; *American Justice* 1986; *End of the Line* 1987; *Cocoon: The Return* 1988; *Eternity* 1990; *The Firm, Hard Target* 1993; *Last of the Dogmen* 1995; *My Fellow Americans* 1996; *In and Out* 1997.

Brind, Tessa. See Brown, Vanessa.

Brissac, Virginia. Actress. *b.* 1895 (?) *d.* 1979. Character player of scores of Hollywood films, typically as a well-bred matron.

FILMS INCLUDE: *Honeymoon Limited* 1935; *Three Godfathers* 1936; *Artists and Models* 1937; *Jesse James, Dark Victory* 1939; *Little Old New York, Black Friday* 1940; *The Great Lie, The Little Foxes* 1941; *The Mummy's Tomb* 1942; *Phantom Lady* 1944; *A Tree Grows in Brooklyn* 1945; *Renegades* 1946; *Monsieur Verdoux, Captain From Castille* 1947; *The Snake Pit, An Act of Murder* 1948; *Mother Is a Freshman* 1949; *Harriet Craig* 1950; *Executive Suite, About Mrs. Leslie* 1954; *Rebel Without a Cause* 1955.

British Film Academy (B.F.A.). A professional society of filmmakers founded in Britain in 1946 for "the advancement of film." It grants annual awards for excellence in filmmaking and gives private showings of significant films. In 1959 it became part of the Society of Film and Television Arts.

British Film Institute (BFI). An organization founded in 1933 "to encourage the development of the art of the film, to promote its use as a record of contemporary life and manners, and to foster public appreciation and study of it from these points of view." Its best-known activity is the operation of the National Film Theatre, which regularly exhibits choice films, both new and of historical importance. It also includes the National Film Archive, which contains prints of rare films, a large film library, a huge still collection, a film distribution agency, and an information service. The institute, based in London, is subsidized partly by government funds and partly by membership fees. It publishes the highly regarded periodical *Sight and Sound*.

Britt, May. Actress. Born Maybritt Wilkens, on Mar. 22, 1933, in Lidingo, Sweden. The daughter of a postal service official, she was discovered by Carlo Ponti, who hired her for a film in Italy in 1952. She later appeared in several major American films but retired from the screen in 1960 after marrying Sammy Davis, Jr. (divorced). She returned to films in 1977.

FILMS INCLUDE: In Italy—*Le Infideli* 1952; *Cavalleria Rusticana/Fatal Desire, La Figlia del Corsaro nero, La Lupa* 1953; *Vergine moderna* 1954; *Ça va Barder!* (Fr.) 1955. In the US—*War and Peace* 1956; *The Young Lions, The Hunters* 1958; *The Tempest, The Blue Angel* 1959; *Murder Inc.* 1960; *Haunts/The Veil* 1977.

Britton, Barbara. Actress. *b.* Barbara Brantingham, Sept. 26, 1919, Long Beach, Calif. *d.* 1980. *ed.* Long Beach City Coll. Pleasantly pretty, she entered films in 1941, after some experience in college stage productions. She played routine leads in a variety of films from the mid-40s to the mid-50s, when she retired from the screen. She later appeared sporadically on Broadway, in stock, and dinner theaters, and starred in the TV series 'Mr. and Mrs. North' and the soap opera 'Date With Life.' But mostly she became familiar to TV audiences as a spokeswoman for Revlon cosmetics and a huckster on commercials for other products.

FILMS INCLUDE: *Secrets of the Wastelands, Louisiana Purchase* 1941; *The Fleet's In, Wake Island, Reap the Wild Wind* 1942; *So Proudly We Hail* 1943; *Till We Meet Again* (first lead), *The Story of Dr. Wassell* 1944; *Captain Kidd, The Great John L.* 1945; *The Virginian, They Made Me a Killer, The Return of Monte Cristo* 1946; *Gunfighters* 1947; *Albuquerque, The Untamed Breed* 1948; *I Shot Jesse James* 1949; *The Bandit Queen, Champagne for Caesar* 1950; *The Raiders* 1952; *Bwana Devil* 1953; *Dragonfly Squadron* 1954; *Ain't Misbehavin', Night Freight* 1955; *The Spoilers* 1956.

Brix, Herman. See Bennett, Bruce.

broad. A lighting unit designed to illuminate a relatively large area. Also known as a "broadside." A single broad uses a 500- or 750-watt lamp; a double broad may use two 1,000-watt lamps. Either is used as a general-purpose floodlight to illuminate backgrounds and minimize shadows.

Broca, Philippe de. Director. Born Mar. 15, 1933, Paris. A graduate of the Paris Technical School of Photography and Cinematography, he began as a cameraman on a 16 mm documentary shot in Africa. He later was assistant to directors Decoin, Lacombe, Chabrol, and Truffaut. Making his debut as director in the late 50s, he quickly moved away from his roots in the French New Wave and became identified with eccentric, irreverent comedies, made with gusto and technical skill. Many of them starred Jean-Pierre Cassel and later Jean-Paul Belmondo. De Broca's own production company, Fildebrol, is managed by his wife, Michèle. They have an adopted son, a Nepal native they took in while filming *Up to His Ears* on location.

FEATURE FILMS: (as director and co-screenwriter): *Les Jeux de l'Amour/The Love Game* 1960; *Le Farceur/The Joker, L'Amant de Cinq Jours/The Five Day Lovers* 1961; *Les Sept Péchés capitaux/Seven Capital Sins* ("Gluttony" episode; dir. only), *Cartouche* (also act.), *Les Veinards* ("La Vedette" episode) 1962; *L'Homme de Rio/That Man from Rio, Un Monsieur de Compagnie/Male Companion* 1964; *Les Tribulations d'un Chinois en Chine/Up to His Ears* 1965; *Le Roi de Coeur/King of Hearts* (also prod. but did not collaborate on script) 1966; *Le plus vieux Métier du Monde/The Oldest Profession* ('Mademoiselle Mimi' episode; dir. only) 1967; *Le Diable par le Queue/The Devil by the Tail* 1969; *Les Caprices de Marie/Give Her the Moon* 1970; *La Poudre d'Escampette/Touch and Go* 1971; *Chère Louise* 1972; *Le Magnifique/Comment détruire la Réputation du plus célèbre Agent Secrèt du*

Monde/How to Destroy the Reputation of the Greatest Secret Agent 1974; *L'Incorrigible/Incorrigible* 1975; *Julie Pot de Colle* (dir. only) 1977; *Tendre Poulet/Dear Inspector/Dear Detective* 1978; *Le Cavaleur/Practice Makes Perfect* 1979; *On a volé la Cuisse de Jupiter/Someone's Stolen the Thigh of Jupiter* 1980; *Psy* (dir. only) 1981; *L'African/The African* 1983; *Louisiane* (dir. only; Fr./Can.) 1984; *La Gitane/The Gypsy* 1986; *Chouans!* 1988; *Scheherazade* (also sc.) 1990; *The Green House* 1996.

Broccoli, Albert R. Producer. *b.* Apr. 5, 1909, in New York City. *d.* 1996. *ed.* CCNY. He was an agronomist before entering films in 1938 as assistant director with 20th Century-Fox. In the early 50s he went to England, where, with Irving ALLEN, he founded Warwick Pictures. He produced a large number of competent pictures but was most successful as co-producer with Harry SALTZMAN of the James Bond film series, including *Dr. No, From Russia with Love, Goldfinger,* and *Thunderball.* The Broccoli-Saltzman partnership dissolved in 1976, with Broccoli maintaining the rights to produce the lucrative Bond series through the company Eon Productions. Broccoli, who is known by the nickname "Cubby," was honored with the prestigious Irving G. Thalberg Award during the 1982 Oscar ceremonies.

FILMS INCLUDE: *Red Beret/Paratrooper* 1953; *Hell Below Zero, The Black Knight* 1954; *A Prize of Gold, The Cockleshell Heroes* 1955; *Safari, Zarak, Odongo, The Gamma People* 1956; *Fire Down Below, No Time to Die* 1957; *The Man Inside* 1958; *Killers of Kilimanjaro* 1959; *The Trials of Oscar Wilde* 1960; *The Hellions, Johnny Nobody* 1961; *Dr. No* 1962; *Call Me Bwana, From Russia with Love* 1963; *Goldfinger* 1964; *Thunderball* 1965; *You Only Live Twice* 1967; *Chitty Chitty Bang Bang* 1968; *On Her Majesty's Secret Service* 1969; *Diamonds Are Forever* 1971; *Live and Let Die* 1973; *The Man With the Golden Gun* 1974; *The Spy Who Loved Me* 1977; *Moonraker* 1979; *For Your Eyes Only* 1981; *Octopussy* 1983; *A View to a Kill* 1985; *The Living Daylights* 1987; *Licence to Kill* 1989; *Goldeneye* 1996.

Brocka, Lino. Director. Born in 1940, in San José, Nuevo Ecija, Philippines. *ed.* U. of the Philippines. The best known and most highly regarded contemporary Philippine filmmaker. The son of a fisherman and a schoolteacher, he converted to the Mormon religion after graduating from college and served briefly as a missionary in a leper colony on the Hawaiian island of Molokai. Returning to Manila, he began acting, directing, and writing for the stage and TV. He directed his first film in 1970, but it was in 1978 that he first attracted international attention at the Cannes Festival, with *Insiang* (1976). Brocka's films often carry a social message and are typically sympathetic to the poor and the working class. They are frequently politically controversial. His French co-production *L'Insoumis* (1989) mercilessly depicts the lawlessness and terror in the post-Marcos Philippines.

FILMS INCLUDE: *Wanted: Perfect Mother, Santiago* 1970; *Tubog sa Ginto* 1971; *Caena de Amor, Cherry Blossoms* 1972; *Villa Miranda, Stardom* 1973; *You Are Weighed in the Balance But Are Found Lacking* 1974; *Manila in the Claws of Light* 1975; *Insiang* 1976; *Inay* 1977; *Jaguar* 1979; *Bona* 1980; *Cain and Abel* 1982; *Bona* 1983; *Kapit sa Patalim/Bayan Ko* 1984; *Signed, Lino Brocka* (act. only) 1986; *Macho Dancer* 1988; *L'Insoumis/Fight for Us* (Fr./Philip.) 1989.

Brockwell, Gladys. Actress. *b.* 1894, Brooklyn, N.Y. *d.* 1929. Leading lady, then character star of Hollywood silents and a handful of early talkies. Typically played fallen women in romantic and domestic melodramas, mainly for Fox. Her career was cut short by injury sustained in an automobile accident. Complications led to her death.

FILMS INCLUDE: *The Typhoon* 1914; *A Man and His Mate, On the Night Stage, Double Trouble* 1915; *The Crippled Hand, The End of the Trail, The Fires of Conscience, Sins of Her Parent* 1916; *The Honor System, The Price of Her Soul, Her Temptation, The Soul of Satan, Conscience, For Liberty* 1917; *The Moral Law, The Bird of Prey, Kultur, The Strange Woman* 1918; *The Forbidden Room, Pitfalls of a Big City, The Divorce Trap, Chasing Rainbows, Broken Commandments* 1919; *Flames of the Flesh, White Lies, The Mother of His Children* 1920; *Paid Back, Oliver Twist* 1922; *Penrod and Sam, The Hunchback of Notre Dame, The Drug Traffic, The Darling of New York* 1923; *Unmarried Wives, The Foolish Virgin, So Big* 1924; *The Ancient Mariner, The Reckless Sex, Stella Maris, The Splendid Road* 1925; *Her Sacrifice, The Skyrocket, The Carnival Girl, Spangles, Twinkletoes* 1926; *Long Pants, Seventh Heaven, The Satin Woman, Man Woman and Sin* 1927; *Law and the Man, Lights of New York, My Home Town, The Woman Disputed* 1928; *From Headquarters, The Hottentot, The Argyle Case, The Drake Case* 1929.

Broderick, Matthew. Actor. Born on Aug. 21, 1962, in New York City. The son of character actor James Broderick (*b.* Mar. 7, 1930, Charlestown, N.H.; *d.* 1982) and writer Patricia Broderick, he began acting as a teenager, making his screen debut at 21. He won immediate popularity for his natural portrayal of a computer whiz-kid in *War Games* (1983) and went on to play other convincing parts. He also enjoyed early success on the stage, especially with his Broadway portrayals of Neil Simon's youthful alter ego in 'Brighton Beach Memoirs' (Tony Award) and 'Biloxi Blues.' After a number of years, Broderick returned to Broadway in 1996 to star in the revival of 'How to Succeed in Business Without Really Trying' for which he received the Tony Award for best actor in a Musical. In that same year, he helmed his first feature film, *Infinity*. He is married to actress Sarah Jessica PARKER.

FILMS: *Max Dugan Returns, War Games* 1983; *Ladyhawke, 1918* 1984; *On Valentine's Day, Ferris Bueller's Day Off* 1986; *Project X* 1987; *Biloxi Blues, Torch Song Trilogy* 1988; *Glory, Family Business* 1989; *Lay This Laurel, The Freshman* 1990; *Out on a Limb* 1992; *The Night We Never Met* 1993; *The Lion King* (voice only), *Mrs. Parker and the Vicious Circle, The Road to Wellville* 1994; *Arabian Knight* 1995; *The Cable Guy, Infinity* (also dir., co-prod.) 1996.

Brodie, Steve. Actor. *b.* John Stevens, Nov. 25, 1919, Eldorado, Kans. *d.* 1992. Rugged leading man and supporting player of numerous Hollywood films, mostly Westerns and action pictures, following some stage experience in stock.

FILMS INCLUDE: *Thirty Seconds Over Tokyo* 1944; *This Man's Navy* 1945; *A Walk in the Sun, Badman's Territory* 1946; *Code of the West, Crossfire, Out of the Past* 1947; *The Arizona Ranger, Bodyguard* 1948; *Rose of the Yukon, Home of the Brave, Massacre River* 1949; *Winchester '73, Kiss Tomorrow Goodbye* 1950; *The Steel Helmet, Only the Valiant, M* 1951; *Three for Bedroom C, Lady in the Iron Mask* 1952; *The Charge at Feather River, Donovan's Brain* 1953; *The Far Country* 1955; *Gun Duel in Durango* 1957; *Sierra Baron* 1958; *Three Came to Kill* 1960; *Of Love and Desire* 1963; *Roustabout* 1964, *The Wild World of Batwoman* 1966; *The Cycle Savages* (bit) 1969; *The Giant Spider Invasion* 1975; *Bobbie Jo and the Outlaw* (co-prod. only) 1976; *Wizard of Speed and Time* 1988.

Brodin(e), Norbert F. Director of photography. *b.* 1897, St. Joseph, Mo. *d.* 1970. *ed.* Columbia. Became involved with photography while working in a Los Angeles camera shop and served as US Army photographer during WW I. Entered films in 1919 as still photographer but within months graduated to assistant cameraman and finally director of photography. Gained a reputation for his outdoor photography and was one of Hollywood's first cameramen to use actual locations. Did some of his best work in the 40s for 20th Century-Fox. Switched to TV work in the early 50s. Changed his name from Brodin to Brodine in 1930.

FILMS INCLUDE: *Almost a Husband* (co-phot.), *The Gay Lord Quex* (co-phot.), *Toby's Bow* 1919; *Dollars and Sense, Stop Thief* 1920; *A Tale of Two Worlds, The Invisible Power* 1921; *Grand Larceny, Remembrance* 1922; *Pleasure Mad, Dulcy* 1923; *The Foolish Virgin, Black Oxen, The Sea Hawk, The Silent Watcher* 1924; *Winds of Chance, What Fools Men Are, The Splendid Road* 1925; *Paris at Midnight, The Eagle of the Sea* 1926; *The Romantic Age, Brass Knuckles* 1927; *The Lion and the Mouse* 1928; *Paris Bound, This Thing Called Love* 1929; *Rich People, The Divorcee, Let Us Be Gay, Holiday* 1930; *Pagan Lady, The Guardsman* 1931; *The Passionate Plumber, The Beast of the City* 1932; *Broadway to Hollywood, The Deluge* (both co-phot.) 1933; *Princess O'Hara, She Gets Her Man, The Affairs of Susan* 1935; *Libeled Lady* 1936; *Topper* 1937; *Swiss Miss, There Goes My Heart, Merrily We Live* 1938; *Captain Fury* 1939; *Of Mice and Men, One Million B.C.* 1940; *Road Show* 1941; *Lady for a Night* 1942; *The Dancing Masters* 1943; *The Bullfighters, The House on 92nd Street, Don Juan Quilligan* 1945; *Sentimental Journey, Somewhere in the Night* 1946; *Kiss of Death, Boomerang, 13 Rue Madeleine* 1947; *Sitting Pretty* 1948; *I Was a Male War Bride* (co-phot.), *Thieves' Highway* 1949; *Right Cross* 1950; *The Frogmen, The Desert Fox* 1951; *Five Fingers* 1952; *Captain Scarface* 1953.

Brodsky, Vlastimil. Actor. Born in 1920 in Czechoslovakia. A leading performer of postwar Czech stage and screen. He won the best actor prize at the 1975 Berlin Festival for the title role in the East German film *Jacob the Liar.* Married actress Jana BREJCHOVÁ.

FILMS INCLUDE: *The Stolen Frontier* 1947; *The Blood Mystery* 1953; *September Nights* 1957; *Between Heaven and Earth* 1958; *Five Out of a Million* 1959; *The Girl from the Moon* 1961; *That Cat, Transport From Paradise* 1963; *Everyday Courage/Courage for Every Day* 1964; *Tales from the First Republic* 1965; *People on Wheels, Closely Watched Trains, Never Strike a Woman Even with a Flower* 1966; *Capricious Summer, Crime in a Night Club, End of a Priest* 1968; *A Devilish Honeymoon* 1970; *Jakob der Lügner/Jacob the Liar* (E. Ger.) 1975.

Brolin, James. Actor. Born on July 18, 1940, in Los Angeles. *ed.* UCLA. He entered TV directly out of college, making his debut in the 'Bus Stop' series. He later appeared in other TV shows and won an Emmy Award for his portrayal of Robert Young's young assistant in the popular 'Marcus Welby, M.D.' series. Tall (6' 4"), dark, and handsome, he made his film debut in 1963 and went on to play leads and supporting roles, mostly in undistinguished productions. He impersonated Clark Gable, not too convincingly, in the film *Gable and Lombard* (1976). In the 80s he returned to television, where in addition to many TV movies he co-starred in the long-running series 'Hotel.'

FILMS INCLUDE: *Take Her She's Mine* 1963; *Goodbye Charlie* 1964; *John Goldfarb, Please Come Home, Dear Brigitte, Von Ryan's Express* 1965; *Fantastic Voyage* 1966; *Our Man Flint* 1967; *The Boston Strangler* 1968; *Skyjacked* 1972; *Westworld* 1973; *Gable and Lombard* (as Clark Gable) 1976; *The Car* 1977; *Capricorn One* 1978; *The Amityville Horror* 1979; *Night of the Juggler* 1980; *High Risk* 1981; *Pee-Wee's Big Adventure* (cameo) 1985; *Bad Jim* 1990; *Ted & Venus* 1991; *Gas Food Lodging* 1992; *Paper Hearts* 1994; *Mars Attacks!* 1996.

Bromberg, J. Edward. Actor. *b.* Dec. 25, 1903, Temesvar, Hungary. *d.* 1951. In the US from infancy, he worked at a variety of odd jobs before making his stage debut in 1926 in the Greenwich Village Playhouse. Ten years later he arrived in Hollywood, was signed to a 20th Century-Fox contract, and went on to play many sensitive character roles and occasional leads.

FILMS INCLUDE: *Under Two Flags, The Crime of Dr. Forbes, Sins of Man, Girls' Dormitory, Star for a Night, Reunion, Stowaway* 1936; *Seventh Heaven, Second Honeymoon* 1937; *Four Men and a Prayer, Suez, Sally Irene and Mary, Rebecca of Sunnybrook Farm* 1938; *Hollywood Cavalcade, Jesse James* 1939; *The Mark of Zorro, The Return of Frank James* 1940; *Invisible Agent, Life Begins at 8:30* 1942; *Lady of Burlesque, Son of Dracula, Phantom of the Opera* 1943; *The Missing Corpse, Salome Where She Danced, Easy to Look At* 1945; *Tangier, Cloak and Dagger* 1946; *Queen of the Amazons* 1947; *Arch of Triumph, A Song Is Born* 1948; *I Shot Jesse James* 1949; *Guilty Bystander* 1950.

Bron, Eleanor. Actress. Born in 1934, in London. Light character player of the British stage, TV, and films. She began her career with The Establishment revue in London and toured with the group in the US for two years in the early 60s. She is at her best in type caricatures.

FILMS INCLUDE: *Help!* 1965; *Alfie* 1966; *Two for the Road* (US/UK), *The Sailor fFrom Gibraltar, Bedazzled* 1967; *Thank You All Very Much, Women in Love* 1969; *Little Dorrit* 1988; *Black Beauty, A Little Princess* 1994.

Bronson, Betty. Actress. *b.* Elizabeth Ada Bronson, Nov. 17, 1906, Trenton, N.J. *d.* 1971. A bit player in films from age 16, she suddenly rocketed to stardom in 1924 when Sir James Barrie himself selected her to play the title role in the first film version of his play 'Peter Pan.' For a while, Paramount capitalized on her petiteness and spritely personality in a succession of elfin roles, hoping to build her up as a successor to Mary Pickford as "America's Sweetheart." But the changing public tastes soon forced her into more mature roles and her popularity quickly diminished. Still, she starred in many silent films and some early talkies before retiring from the screen in the early 30s to marry a wealthy Southerner. She returned once in 1937, in a Western starring Gene Autry but was not heard of again until the 1960s, when she re-emerged as a character actress.

FILMS: *Anna Ascends* (bit) 1922; *Java Head* 1923; *Peter Pan* 1924; *Are Parents People? Not So Long Ago, The Golden Princess* 1925; *Ben-Hur* (as the Virgin Mary), *A Kiss for Cinderella, Paradise, Everybody's Acting, The Cat's Pajamas* 1926; *Paradise for Two, Ritzy, Open Range, Brass Knuckles* 1927; *The Singing Fool, Companionate Marriage* 1928; *The Bellamy Trial, Sonny Boy, A Modern Sappho, One Stolen Night, The Locked Door* 1929; *The Medicine Man* 1930; *Lover Come Back* 1931; *The Midnight Patrol* 1932; *The Yodelin' Kid From Pine Ridge* 1937; *Pocketful of Miracles* 1961; *The Naked Kiss* 1964; *Blackbeard's Ghost* 1968; *Evel Knievel* 1971.

Bronson, Charles. Actor. Born Charles Bunchinsky (later Buchinski, then Buchinsky), on Nov. 3, 1920, in Ehrenfeld, Pa. One of 15 children of a Lithuanian coal miner, he was the only one to finish high school, but at 16 he went to work at the coal mines as did all his brothers. After WW II action as a tail gunner aboard a B-29 bomber, he went to Philadelphia, where he studied art and joined an acting company as a set designer and bit player. In 1949 he enrolled at the Pasadena Playhouse school and soon began playing supporting roles in Hollywood films and TV productions. Craggy-faced and toughly built, he was tagged from the start for brawny character parts and was often typecast as a punk, ethnic roughneck, or demented villain. But gradually his unique facial features and powerful physique helped him secure lead roles in B pictures (the title role in Corman's *Machine Gun Kelly,* etc.) and on TV ('Man With a Camera' series, 1958, etc.).

Bronson (he acquired the name in 1954) remained primarily a supporting player, however, until 1968, when he left Hollywood for Europe. Almost overnight he became a top-flight star, the biggest box-office draw in Paris, Rome, and Madrid. European audiences adored his toughness and animal magnetism. He became known in France as *le sacre monstre* and in Italy as *Il Brutto.* At the age of fifty he was suddenly a sex symbol, and one of the highest paid stars in international cinema. In 1971 he received a Golden Globe Award as the world's most popular actor. The following year he returned to the US to capitalize on his newly won status and has since starred in a number of Hollywood action features, most successfully in *Death Wish* (1974) and its sequels. Bronson's second wife (1968–90) was the late Jill IRELAND, who appeared with him in no fewer than 15 films. He is the father of seven.

FILMS: As Charles Buchinski or Buchinsky—*You're in the Navy Now/USS Teakettle, The People Against O'Hara, The Mob* 1951; *Red Skies of Montana, My Six Convicts, The Marrying Kind, Pat and Mike, Diplomatic Courier, Bloodhounds of Broadway* 1952; *House of Wax* 1953; *Miss Sadie Thompson, Crime Wave, Tennessee Champ, Riding Shotgun, Apache, Vera Cruz* 1954. As Charles Bronson—*Drum Beat* 1954; *Big House USA, Target Zero* 1955; *Jubal* 1956; *Run of the Arrow* 1957; *Gang War, Showdown at Boot Hill, Machine Gun Kelly, When Hell Broke Loose* 1958; *Never So Few* 1959; *The Magnificent Seven* 1960; *Master of the World, A Thunder of Drums* 1961; *X-15, Kid Galahad* 1962; *The Great Escape, 4 for Texas* 1963; *The Sandpiper, Battle of the Bulge* 1965; *This Property Is Condemned* 1966; *The Dirty Dozen* 1967; *La Bataille de San Sebastian/Guns for San Sebastian* (Fr./It./Mex./US), *Villa Rides, Adieu l'Ami* (Fr.), *C'era una Volta il West/Once Upon a Time in the West* (It./US) 1968; *Twinky/Lola* (UK/It.), *You Can't Win 'Em All/The Dubious Patriots* (UK), *Città Violenta/The Family* (It./Fr.), *De la part des Copains/Cold Sweat* (Fr./It.) 1970; *Quelqu'un derrière la Porte/Someone Behind the Door* (Fr.), *Soleil rouge* (Fr./It./Sp.) 1971; *Joe Valachi/I Segreti di Cosa Nostra/The Valachi Papers* (It./Fr.), *Chato's Land, The Mechanic* 1972; *Valdez il Mezzosangue/Chino/Valdez the Halfbreed/The Valdez Horses* (It./Sp./Fr.), *The Stone Killer* (US/UK) 1973; *Mr. Majestyk, Death Wish* 1974; *Breakout, Hard Times* 1975; *Breakheart Pass, St. Ives, From Noon Till Three* 1976; *The White Buffalo* (as Wild Bill Hickok), *Telefon* 1977; *Love and Bullets* (UK), *Caboblanco* (UK), *Borderline* 1980; *Death Hunt* 1981; *Death Wish 2* 1982; *10 to Midnight* 1983; *The Evil That Men Do* 1984; *Death Wish 3* 1985; *Murphy's Law* 1986; *Assassination, Death Wish 4: The Crackdown* 1987; *Messenger of Death* 1988; *Kinijite/Forbidden Subjects* 1989; *The Indian Runner* 1991; *Death Wish 5: The Face of Death* 1994.

Bronston, Samuel. Producer. *b.* 1909, Bessarabia, Rumania. *d.* 1994. *ed.* Sorbonne. Entered films as a salesman for MGM in France. In the early 40s he served as production executive for Columbia; left in 1943 to form his independent Samuel Bronston Productions. Made little impact until the late 50s, when he began producing spectacular epics in Spain. Early success encouraged him to invest in the building of enormous studios near Madrid; he was single-handedly responsible for putting Spain on the map as a center for international film production. But he borrowed heavily and overextended his investment and by 1964 was forced to suspend all business activities. The ensuing court litigations prevented him from further production. In 1971 he announced that he was resuming his film activity with a monumental production of *Isabella of Spain,* but the plan never materialized.

FILMS INCLUDE: *Jack London* 1943; *John Paul Jones* 1959; *King of Kings, El Cid* 1961; *55 Days at Peking* 1963; *The Fall of the Roman Empire, Circus World* 1964; *The Mysterious House of Dr. C.* 1976.

Brook, Clive. Actor. *b.* Clifford Brook, June 1, 1887, London. *d.* 1974. Suave leading man of British and American stage and screen. The son of a gold-mining magnate and an opera singer, he began his working life as an insurance clerk and newspaper reporter. After returning from WW I service with the rank of major, he made his stage debut in 1918. By 1920 he was appearing on the London stage and in British silent films. His screen career reached a high point in Hollywood (1924–34), where he became established as a reliable leading man, usually in roles epitomizing stiff-upper-lipped suavity and distinction. His clipped accent enhanced his screen presence after the advent of sound. Among his strongest portrayals were the lead roles in VON STERNBERG's *Underworld* and *Shanghai Express.* In 1935 he returned to Britain, where he also appeared in films, the last of which, *On Approval* (1945), he also produced and directed. He subsequently appeared occasionally on the stage and British TV, returning to the big screen only once in *The List of Adrian Messenger* (1963). His widow is a former co-star, Mildred Evelyn. Their children, Faith (*b.* 1922) and Lyndon (*b.* 1926) Brook, are also actors.

FILMS INCLUDE: In the UK—*Trent's Last Case* 1920; *Daniel Deronda* 1921; *Debt of Honor* 1922; *Woman to Woman* 1923. In the US—*The Recoil, The Mirage, Christine of the Hungry Heart* 1924; *When Love Grows Cold, Enticement, Déclassé, Playing with Souls, If Marriage Fails, The Home Maker, Compromise, The Woman Hater, Seven Sinners, The Pleasure Buyers* 1925; *Three Faces East, You Never Know Women, For Alimony Only, The Popular Sin* 1926; *Afraid to Love, Barbed Wire, Underworld, Hula, French Dressing, The Devil Dancer* 1927; *Midnight Madness, The Yellow Lily, Forgotten Faces, The Perfect Crime* 1928; *Interference, A Dangerous Woman, The Four Feathers, Charming Sinners, The Return of Sherlock Holmes* (as Holmes), *The Laughing Lady* 1929; *Slightly Scarlet, Sweethearts and Wives, Anybody's Woman* 1930; *Scandal Sheet, East Lynne, Tarnished Lady, The Lawyer's Secret, Silence, Twenty-Four Hours, Husband's Holiday* 1931; *Shanghai Express, The Man from Yesterday, The Night of June 13th, Sherlock Holmes* (again as Holmes) 1932; *Cavalcade, Midnight Club, If I Were Free* 1933; *Gallant Lady, Where Sinners Meet, Let's Try Again* 1934. In the UK—*The Love Affair of the Dictator/Loves of a Dictator* 1935; *Love in Exile* 1936; *The Lonely Road* 1937; *Action for Slander* 1938; *The Ware Case, Return to Yesterday* 1939; *Convoy* 1940; *Freedom Radio/The Voice in the Night* 1941; *Breach of Promise* 1942; *The Flemish Farm* 1943; *Shipbuilders* 1944; *On Approval* (also dir., prod., sc.) 1945; *The List of Adrian Messenger* (US; filmed in Ireland) 1963.

Brook, Sir Peter. Director. Born Mar. 21, 1925, in London. While still a student at Oxford in 1943, he made an amateur film, *Sentimental Journey.* That same year he went to London to direct his first play, 'Dr. Faustus.' While directing dozens of impressive stage productions in London, Paris, Moscow, and New York, he has also directed a handful of intellectually stimulating, but at times pretentious British films, which seem extensions of his stage experiments. In 1970 he founded in Paris the experimental International Center of Theater Research. In 1974 it became the Centre for International Creation, the site of experimental, improvisational workshops that provide the backbone for his theatrical productions. In 1951 he married actress Natasha Parry.

FEATURE FILMS: *The Beggar's Opera* 1953; *Moderato Cantabile* (also co-sc.; Fr./It.), *Lord of the Flies* (also sc.) 1963; *The Ride of the Valkyrie* (short), *The Persecution and Assassination of Jean-Paul Marat as Performed by the Inmates of the Asylum of Charenton Under the Direction of the Marquis de Sade/Marat-Sade* 1967; *Tell Me Lies* (also prod.) 1968; *King Lear* (release delayed from 1969) 1971; *Meetings With Remarkable Men* 1979; *La Tragédie de Carmen/The Tragedy of Carmen/Carmen* (Fr.) 1983; *Swann in Love* (sc. only) 1984; *The Mahabharata* 1990; *Looking for Richard* (act. only) 1996.

Brooke, Hillary. Actress. Born Beatrice Peterson, on Sept. 8, 1914, in Astoria, Long Island, N.Y. *ed.* Columbia. She came to films in 1937 via modeling and the stage. Throughout the 40s and most of the 50s, she played both comic and dramatic second leads in A pictures and later some leading roles in low-budget films. She was also a regular on the TV series 'My Little Margie.' In 1960 she married MGM's general manager, Ray Klune.

FILMS INCLUDE: *New Faces of 1937* 1937; *The Adventures of Sherlock Holmes* 1939; *New Moon, The Philadelphia Story* 1940; *Dr. Jekyll and Mr. Hyde, Mr. and Mrs. North* 1941; *To the Shores of Tripoli, Counter-Espionage, Wake Island* 1942; *Sherlock Holmes Faces Death* 1943; *Lady in the Dark, Jane Eyre, Standing Room Only, Ministry of Fear* 1944; *The Crime Doctor's Courage, The Woman in Green, The Enchanted Cottage* 1945; *Road to Utopia, Strange Impersonation, Monsieur Beaucaire* 1946; *Big Town, Big Town After Dark, The Strange Woman* 1947; *The Fuller Brush Man* 1948; *Africa Screams, Alimony, Bodyhold* 1949; *The Admiral Was a Lady, Beauty on Parade, Vendetta* 1950; *Insurance Investigator, The Lost Continent* 1951; *Abbott and Costello Meet Captain Kidd, Never Wave at a WAC, Confidence Girl* 1952; *The Lady Wants a Mink, Invaders From Mars, The Maze* 1953; *Heat Wave* 1954; *Bengazi* 1955; *The Man Who Knew Too Much* 1956; *Spoilers of the Forest* 1957.

Brooke, Van Dyke. American director, actor. A veteran of the stage, he entered films with Kalem in 1909 and for the next six years directed scores of one-, two-, and three-reelers, in most of which he also appeared as an actor. He was responsible for many of the early films of John Bunny and Maurice Costello, among other screen personalities of the day, but his career was most closely linked with that of Norma TALMADGE, opposite whom he starred in numerous productions under his own direction through 1915. His career as a director ended at that point, but he continued playing character roles in films through 1921.

FILMS INCLUDE: As director only—*The Artist's Revenge* 1909; *A Dixie Mother* 1910; *Her Hero* 1911; *The Adventure of the Italian Model, The Money Kings, Billy's Burglar* 1912; *Just Show People, A Soul in Bondage, Cupid Through a Keyhole, His Silver Bachelorhood, The Honorable Algernon* 1913; *John Rance Gentleman, The Hidden Letters, Sunshine and Shadows* 1914; *Rags and the Girl* (also sc.) 1915. As director-actor—*Conscience/The Baker Boy* 1910; *Counsel for the Defense, The Adventure of the Retired Army Colonel, O'Hara Squatter and Philosopher, Ida's Christmas* 1912; *O'Hara Helps Cupid, O'Hara as a Guardian Angel, Wanted a Stronghand, Under the Daisies, The Doctor's Secret, Father's Hatband, Fanny's Conspiracy* 1913; *Sawdust and Salome, The Salvation of Kathleen, His Little Page, Officer John Donovan* (also sc.), *Old Reliable, Cupid Versus Money, The Right of Way, Politics and the Press, The Peacemaker, Memories in Men's Souls, Under False Colors, Goodbye Summer, A Daughter of Israel* 1914; *The Barrier of Faith, A Daughter's Strange Inheritance, Janet of the Chorus, Elsa's Brother, A Pillar of Flame, The Criminal* 1915. As actor only—*The Leading Lady, My Old Dutch* (also sc.), *The Thumb Print* 1911; *The Fortune Hunter* 1920; *The Passionate Pilgrim, Straight Is the Way, The Crimson Cross, A Midnight Bell, The Son of Wallingford* 1921.

Brooks, Albert. Actor, director, screenwriter. Born Albert Einstein, on July 22, 1947, in Los Angeles. *ed.* Carnegie Tech. The son of comedian Harry Einstein (alias 'Parkyakarkus'), a sidekick of Eddie Cantor, he started out as a standup comic and TV performer, appearing regularly in 1969 in the variety show 'Dean Martin Presents the Golddiggers.' He gained popularity on 'Saturday Night Live,' to which he contributed in 1975–76 a series of highly entertaining filmed comedy shorts. Entering films as an actor in 1976, he subsequently also directed and wrote for the screen.

FILMS (as actor): *Taxi Driver* 1976; *Real Life* (also dir., co-sc.) 1979; *Private Benjamin* 1980; *Modern Romance* (also dir., co-sc.) 1981; *Twilight Zone—The Movie* 1983; *Unfaithfully Yours* 1984; *Lost in America* (also dir., co-sc.) 1985; *Broadcast News* 1987; *Defending Your Life* (also dir., sc.) 1991; *I'll Do Anything, The Scout* (also co-sc.) 1994; *Mother* (also dir.) 1996.

Brooks, Geraldine. Actress. *b.* Geraldine Stroock, Oct. 29, 1925, New York City. *d.* 1977. The daughter of a costume manufacturer and a designer, she made her first stage appearance in a musical at 17 and after appearing in summer stock and touring with the Theatre Guild in a repertory of Shakespeare plays enrolled at the American Academy of Dramatic Arts. A petite, pretty brunette, she was signed at Warner Bros. and brought to Hollywood in 1947. She played convincing ingenue roles in a number of films, but, disappointed with the quality of most of her pictures, she accepted an offer by director William Dieterle to play Anna Magnani's younger sister in his Italian production *Vulcano/Volcano* (1950), which was intended to compete at the box office with Roberto Rossellini's *Stromboli.* The film didn't do very well (neither did), but she stayed in Europe for a couple of additional movies, then returned to the US, where she devoted most of her energies to the stage and TV, appearing only rarely in films. She also became an accomplished nature photographer and in 1975 published a book of her bird photographs, *Swan Watch,* with accompanying essays by her second husband (from 1964), novelist-screenwriter Budd SCHULBERG. She died of cancer at 52.

FILMS: *Possessed, Cry Wolf* 1947; *Embraceable You, An Act of Murder/Live Today for Tomorrow* 1948; *The Younger Brothers, The Reckless Moment, Challenge to Lassie* 1949; *This Side of the Law, Vulcano/Volcano* (It.), *Ho Sognato il Paradiso/Streets of Sorrow* (It.) 1950; *J'était une Pêcheresse* (Fr.) 1951; *Le Gantelet vert/The Green Glove* (Fr./US) 1952; *Street of Sinners* 1957; *Johnny Tiger* 1966; *Mr. Ricco* 1975.

Brooks, James L. Director, producer, screenwriter. Born on May 9, 1940, in North Bergen, N.J. *ed.* NYU. He started out as a copyboy with CBS News in New York, eventually becoming a TV newswriter. In 1965 he moved to Los Angeles to work for David L. Wolper's documentary company. Showing a growing interest in the entertainment aspect of television, he conceived the idea for the series 'Room 222' (1969–74). Forming a partnership with fellow writer Allan Burns ('The Bullwinkle Show'), he embarked on the big time by creating the enormously successful 'Mary Tyler Moore Show' (1970–77). He later produced such series as 'Taxi,' 'The Associates,' and 'Cheers.' Having conquered television, Brooks then turned his attention to motion pictures. In 1983 he made an auspicious debut as a film director with *Terms of Endearment,* the winner of five Academy Awards: best picture, best director, best screenplay, best actress, and best supporting actor. He was again nominated for best picture and best screenplay Oscars for *Broadcast News* (1987), a film he based on his real-life experience in the CBS newsroom. It was named best film and Brooks was honored as best director by the New York Film Critics. Brooks subsequently produced several box-office hits.

FILMS: *Real Life* (act.), *Starting Over* (co-prod., sc.) 1979; *Modern Romance* (act.) 1981; *Terms of Endearment* (dir., co-prod., sc.) 1983; *Broadcast News* (dir., co-prod., sc.) 1987; *Big* (co-prod.) 1988; *Say Anything* (exec. prod.), *The War of the Roses* (co-prod.) 1989; *I'll Do Anything* (dir., co-prod., sc.) 1994.

Brooks, Louise. Actress. *b.* Nov. 14, 1906, Cherryvale, Kans. *d.* 1985. A lawyer's daughter. She began her professional career at age 15 as a dancer with the Ruth St. Denis company. Appearances in 'George White's Scandals' and the 'Ziegfeld Follies' led to a Hollywood contract and a 1925 film debut in a bit role. A pretty, shapely brunette with a boyish bob hair style, she was cast at first in routine flapper comedies but gradually emerged as a talented actress in such films as Hawks's *A Girl in Every Port* and Wellman's *Beggars of Life*. But her true worth as an artist was revealed in Germany, where she gave some remarkable performances for director G. W. PABST in *Pandora's Box* and *Diary of a Lost Girl*. She was particularly magnetic in the former as Lulu, a nymphomaniac devastated by her insatiable desires. She gave another sparkling performance in a French film, *Prix de Beauté*, then returned to Hollywood, where she was offered minor roles in minor films.

Unable or unwilling to re-acclimate herself to the film colony, she retired from the screen in 1931 and made her living as a nightclub dancer. In 1936 she made a futile attempt at a comeback and meekly accepted bit roles or leads in B Westerns. She finally retired in 1938. In the early 40s she made occasional radio appearances in New York but eventually gave up show business altogether and found employment as a sales clerk at New York's Saks Fifth Avenue. By the late 40s she had become a recluse, completely avoiding the public eye. But in the mid-50s she was rediscovered by film cultists when some of her old films were re-screened in Europe and the US. In 1956 she settled in Rochester, New York, at the urging of James Card, curator of the George Eastman House collection. There she studied film and devoted herself to writing for film periodicals. In 1982 she received accolades for the style and intelligence of her book *Lulu in Hollywood*, a collection of essays about her life and other screen personalities. She died of a heart attack poor, alone, but not forgotten. She was married briefly (1926–28) to director Edward SUTHERLAND.

FILMS: *The Street of Forgotten Men* (bit) 1925; *The American Venus, A Social Celebrity, It's the Old Army Game, The Show-Off, Love 'Em and Leave 'Em, Just Another Blonde/The Girl from Coney Island* 1926; *Evening Clothes, Rolled Stockings, The City Gone Wild, Now We're in the Air* 1927; *A Girl in Every Port, Beggars of Life* 1928; *The Canary Murder Case, Die Büchse der Pandora/Pandora's Box* (Ger.), *Das Tagebuch einer Verlorenen/Diary of a Lost Girl* (Ger.) 1929; *Prix de Beauté/The Beauty Prize/Miss Europe* (Fr.), *Windy Riley Goes to Hollywood* (2-reel short dir. by Fatty Arbuckle) 1930; *It Pays to Advertise, God's Gift to Women, The Public Enemy* (bit), *The Steel Highway* 1931; *Empty Saddles* 1936; *When You're in Love* (bit, as a chorus girl), *King of Gamblers* (bit), *Overland Stage Raiders* 1938.

Brooks, Mel. Director, screenwriter, actor. Born Melvin Kaminsky, on June 28, 1926, in Brooklyn, N.Y. A compulsive funnyman, he began doing impressions as a child, then took up amateur drumming and piano playing. After WW II service as a combat engineer, he played drums in Catskills resorts, eventually becoming a social director and resident comic at Grossinger's. To avoid confusion with trumpet player Max Kaminsky, he changed his name to Brooks, borrowing his mother's maiden name, Brookman. In 1949 he began a decade-long stint as a writer and occasional performer on Sid Caesar's TV programs 'The Admiral Broadway Revue,' 'Your Show of Shows,' and their follow-ups. In 1960 he gained popularity with a now-legendary recording (with Carl Reiner) of 'The 2,000-Year-Old Man.' In 1963 he made the Oscar-winning cartoon short *The Critic* and in 1965 created (with Buck Henry) the successful TV spy-spoof series 'Get Smart.' During the 60s he also appeared as a guest on TV talk shows, displaying a robust, irreverent, instinctive sensibility for manic offbeat comedy.

In 1968 Brooks made his debut as a feature director with *The Producers,* a film many consider a masterpiece of zany comedy. He followed it with other screen comedies, often inventive, sometimes tasteless, but almost always hilariously funny. In 1980 he established his own production company, Brooksfilms, but his later efforts have largely failed to capture public or critical fancy. He won an Academy Award for the original screenplay of *The Producers* and received Oscar nominations for the script of *Young Frankenstein* and the lyrics of the title song of *Blazing Saddles.* His second wife (from 1964), Anne BANCROFT, co-starred in *To Be or Not to Be* (1983), his remake of the Lubitsch classic.

FILMS: *The Critic* (anim. short; sc., act.) 1963; *The Producers* (dir., sc.) 1968; *Putney Swope* (act.) 1969; *The Twelve Chairs* (dir., sc., act.) 1970; *Shinbone Alley* (voice only) 1971; *The 2,000-Year-Old-Man* (anim.; sc., voice only), *Blazing Saddles* (dir., co-sc. lyr., act.), *Young Frankenstein* (dir., co-sc.) 1974; *Silent Movie* (dir., co-sc., act.) 1976; *High Anxiety* (dir., prod. co-sc. act.) 1977; *The Muppet Movie* (act.) 1979; *The Elephant Man* (exec. prod.) 1980; *History of the World Part One* (dir., prod., co-sc. act.) 1981; *To Be or Not to Be* (prod., co-sc., act.) 1983; *The Doctor and the Devils* (exec. prod.) 1985; *The Fly* (exec prod.), *Solarbabies* (exec. prod.) 1986; *84 Charing Cross Road* (exec. prod.), *Spaceballs* (dir., prod., co-sc., act.) 1987; *Look Who's Talking Too* (voice only) 1990; *Life Stinks* (dir., prod., act., co-sc.) 1991; *Robin Hood: Men in Tights* (dir., prod., act., co-sc.) 1993; *The Little Rascals, The Silence of the Hams* (unbilled cameo) 1994; *Dracula: Dead and Loving It* 1995.

Brooks, Phyllis. Actress. *b.* Phyllis Steiller, on July 18, 1914, in Boise, Idaho. *d.* 1995. A pretty blonde, she was an artist's model before entering films in 1934. She was briefly known as Mary Brooks. For the most part she played leading roles in low-budget films, but was also cast in some supporting roles in A pictures before retiring in 1945 to wed Harvard football star Robert MacDonald. She also played some ingenue leads on Broadway.

FILMS INCLUDE: *I've Been Around* 1934; *Lady Tubbs, To Beat the Band, Another Face* 1935; *You Can't Have Everything, Dangerously Yours 1937*; *City Girl, Rebecca of Sunnybrook Farm, In Old Chicago, Little Miss Broadway, Straight Place and Show, Up the River, Charlie Chan in Honolulu* 1938; *Charlie Chan in Reno* 1939; *Slightly Honorable* 1940; *The Shanghai Gesture* 1941; *No Place for a Lady* 1943; *Lady in the Dark* 1944; *The Unseen, High Powered, Dangerous Passage* 1945.

Brooks, Richard. Director, screenwriter. *b.* May 18, 1912, Philadelphia. *d.* 1992. *ed.* Temple U. He began his career as a sports reporter for the Philadelphia *Record* and later became a radio writer, announcer, and commentator for NBC in New York. Moving to Los Angeles as a radio writer in 1941, he began collaborating on screenplays for Hollywood films the following year and had several minor productions to his credit before going into WW II service with the Marines. After the war, he wrote a first novel, *The Brick Foxhole* (1945), which provided the basis for the film *Crossfire* (1947). In transition to screen, the novel turned from a thriller involving bias against homosexuals to a thriller indicting anti-Semitism. Brooks, who returned to screenwriting, later wrote two other novels, *Boiling Point* (1948) and *The Producer* (1951). He made his bow as a film director in 1950 with *Crisis,* an intriguing but somewhat sluggish political thriller. With the exception of *Deadline USA* (1952), a strong Bogart drama about a newspaper's struggle against the mob, Brooks's early films were unexciting.

He hit his stride in 1955 with *The Blackboard Jungle,* a rather sensational but powerful drama about violence in the American school system. After this he took his place among Hollywood's leading directors. Writing his own screenplays, he has specialized in the adaptation of literary material from the stage and from novels, at times with considerable success. He made most of his films in the 50s and early 60s for MGM but became his own independent producer in 1965. He won an Academy Award for the screenplay of *Elmer Gantry* and was nominated for Oscars as the writer of *The Blackboard Jungle,* the director and co-writer of *Cat on a Hot Tin Roof,* the director and writer of *The Professionals,* and the director and writer of *In Cold Blood.* He was married to Jean SIMMONS.

FILMS: As screenwriter—*Men of Texas* (addnl. dial.), *Sin Town* (addnl. dial.) 1942; *Don Winslow of the Coast Guard* (serial; addnl. dial.), *White Savage* 1943; *My Best Gal* (story), *Cobra Woman* (co-sc.) 1944; *Swell Guy, Brute Force, Crossfire* (novel basis only, *The Brick Foxhole*) 1947; *To the Victor* (story, sc.), *Key Largo* (co-sc.) 1948; *Any Number Can Play* 1949; *Mystery Street* (co-sc.), *Storm Warning* (co-story, co-sc.) 1950. As director-screenwriter—*Crisis* 1950; *The Light Touch* 1951; *Deadline USA* (also story) 1952; *Battle Circus, Take the High Ground* (dir. only) 1953; *The Flame and the Flesh* (dir. only), *The Last Time I Saw Paris* (dir., co-sc.) 1954; *The Blackboard Jungle* 1955; *The Last Hunt, The Catered Affair* (dir. only) 1956; *Something of Value* 1957; *The Brothers Karamazov, Cat on a Hot Tin Roof* (dir., co-sc.) 1958; *Elmer Gantry* 1960; *Sweet Bird of Youth* 1962; *Lord Jim* (also prod.) 1965; *The Professionals* (also prod.) 1966; *In Cold Blood* (also prod.) 1967; *The Happy Ending* (also prod., story) 1969; *$/Dollars* 1971; *Bite the Bullet* (also prod.) 1975; *Looking for Mr. Goodbar* 1977; *Wrong Is Right* (also prod.) 1982; *Fever Pitch* 1985; *Fifty Years of Action!* (doc., act. only) 1986; *Listen Up* (doc. about Quincy Jones) 1990.

Brophy, Edward. Actor. *b.* Feb. 27, 1895, in New York City. *d.* 1960. *ed.* U. of Virginia; Hamilton Inst. (N.Y.). He made his first film appearance in *Yes or No* (1920), with Norma Talmadge, and subsequently played character roles in scores of films, typically as a valet (in the "Falcon" series) or as a small-time gangster or dumb cop. Most memorable of his later roles was that of the corrupt little politician in *The Last Hurrah.*

FILMS INCLUDE: *Yes or No* 1920; *West Point* 1927; *The Cameraman* 1928; *Spite Marriage* 1929; *Free and Easy, Dough Boys, Our Blushing Brides* 1930; *Parlor Bedroom and Bath, The Champ, A Dangerous Affair* 1931; *Freaks, Speak Easily, Flesh* 1932; *What! No Beer?, Broadway to Hollywood* 1933; *The Thin Man* 1934; *Naughty Marietta, The Whole Town's Talking, China Seas, People Will Talk, Mad Love* 1935; *Strike Me Pink, Woman Trap, The Case Against Mrs. Ames, Career Woman* 1936; *Michael Strogoff* 1937; *A Slight Case of Murder* 1938; *You Can't Cheat an Honest Man* 1939; *Calling Philo Vance, Golden Gloves, The Great Profile* 1940; *The Bride Came C.O.D., The Gay Falcon* 1941; *All Through the Night, Broadway, Larceny Inc.* 1942; *Air Force* 1943; *Cover Girl, It Happened Tomorrow* 1944; *Wonder Man* 1945; *The Falcon's Adventure* 1946; *It Happened on Fifth Avenue* 1947; *Arson Inc.* 1949; *Roaring City, Danger Zone* 1951; *The Last Hurrah* 1958.

Brosnan, Pierce. Actor. Born on May 16, 1951, in County Meath, Ireland. Suave, handsome leading man of TV and films. At 11 he moved with his family to London, where he started his working career as a cab driver and commercial illustrator. He then joined an experimental theater workshop and trained at the Drama Centre before appearing professionally on the London stage in 1976 and making his screen debut in 1980. An intended brief visit to America in 1982 turned into a long stay when he was picked to star in the popular TV series 'Remington Steele.' Upon the series' cancellation in 1986, Brosnan was announced as the choice to become the screen's next James Bond. But the unexpected temporary revival of the TV series forced him to give up the plum movie role until it came back around to him in 1996 with *Goldeneye.* He portrayed Phileas Fogg in the lavish miniseries 'Around the World in 80 Days.'

FILMS: *The Long Good Friday, The Mirror Crack'd* 1980; *Nomads* 1986; *The Fourth Protocol* 1987; *Taffin, The Deceivers* 1988; *Mister Johnson* 1990; *The Lawnmower Man* 1992; *Mrs. Doubtfire* 1993; *Love Affair* 1994; *Goldeneye* 1995; *Dante's Peak, The Mirror Has Two Faces* 1996.

Broughton, James. Avant-garde filmmaker. Born in 1912, in San Francisco. *ed.* Stanford; New School for Social Research. A poet and playwright, he made a first experimental film in 1946, in collaboration with sculptor-writer Sidney Peterson. Later working mainly on his own, in Europe as well as in the US, he made lyrically inspired films, several of which are considered key works of the postwar avant-garde.

FILMS INCLUDE: *The Potted Psalm* (with Sidney Peterson) 1946; *Mother's Day* 1948; *Adventures of Jimmy* 1950; *4 in the Afternoon, Loony Tom, The Happy Lover* 1951; *The Pleasure Garden* 1953; *The Bed* 1968; *Nuptiae* 1969; *The Golden Positions* 1970; *This Is It* 1971; *Dreamwood* 1972; *High Kukus* 1973; *Testament* 1974; *The Water Circle* 1975; *Etrogeny, Together* (with Joel Singer) 1976; *Windmobile, Song of the Godbody* (both with Singer) 1977; *Hermes Bird* 1979; *The Gardener of Eden* (with Singer), *Shaman Psalm* (both with Singer) 1981.

Brown, Blair. Actress. Born in 1948, in Washington, D.C. Intelligent-looking leading lady of the American stage, TV, and films. Trained at the National Theatre School of Canada, she played Shakespeare and other classical roles on stage, starred in TV series 'Days and Nights of Molly Dodd,' and gave several convincing performances in films. Divorced from actor Richard JORDAN.

FILMS: *The Choirboys* 1977; *One-Trick Pony, Altered States* 1980; *Continental Divide* 1981; *A Flash of Green* 1984; *Stealing Home* 1988; *Strapless* 1990; *Passed Away* 1992.

Brown, Bryan. Actor. Born on June 23, 1947, near Sydney, Australia. Sinewy leading man of stage and screen. He began acting professionally in Sydney, then went to London, where he joined the National Theatre in 1974. Back home, he made his feature film debut in 1977 and soon attracted international attention for his performances in *Breaker Morant* and several other major Australian productions. Hollywood leading roles followed, memorably in *F/X* and *Gorillas in the Mist.* He also starred in the British TV series 'A Town Like Alice' and the American miniseries 'The Thorn Birds.' He married actress Rachel Ward in 1983.

FEATURE FILMS: *Love Letters from Teralba Road* 1977; *The Irishman, Newsfront, Third Person Plural, Money Movers, Weekend of Shadows, The Chant of Jimmie Blacksmith* 1978; *Palm Beach, Cathy's Child, The Odd Angry Shot, Breaker Morant* 1979; *Blood Money, Stir* 1980; *The Winter of Our*

Dreams 1981; *Far East* 1982; *Give My Regards to Broad Street* (UK), *Bones/Parker* 1984; *Rebel, The Shiralee, The Empty Beach* 1985; *The Umbrella Woman/The Good Wife, F/X* (US), *Tai-Pan* (US) 1986; *Cocktail* (US), *Gorillas in the Mist* (US) 1988; *Confidence* 1989; *Blood Oath* 1990; *Sweet Talker* (also co-wr. story), *Prisoners of the Sun/Blood Oath* 1991; *Blame It on the Bellboy* 1992.

Brown, Clarence. Director. *b.* May 10, 1890, Clinton, Mass. *d.* 1987. *ed.* U. of Tennessee. Trained as an engineer, then worked in the automobile industry and operated his own car sales agency before turning to films in 1915 as an assistant to director Maurice TOURNEUR. The five years he spent as a disciple (and film editor) of the great European master were reflected later in the aesthetic care, pictorial quality, and romantic flavor of Brown's own films, which he began to direct in 1920. Having established his reputation in 1925 with *The Eagle,* starring Rudolph Valentino and Vilma Banky, Brown joined MGM and soon became one of the company's top directors. Above all, he became known as the man who could handle the company's most difficult star, Greta GARBO, and bring out the best of her. He directed two of her silent films—*Flesh and the Devil* and *A Woman of Affairs*—and five of her most successful talkies—*Anna Christie, Romance, Inspiration, Anna Karenina,* and *Conquest.*

Brown directed many quality productions for MGM through the early 50s, achieving his best moments in excursions into rural Americana in films like *Ah Wilderness!, Of Human Hearts, The Human Comedy, The Yearling,* and *Intruder in the Dust.* The latter is his only film with a clear social message, a plea for racial tolerance. For the most part, he subjugated his themes to his pictorial vision and was unabashedly sentimental in his celebration of romanticism. From 1947 he also produced all his films. After retiring from filmmaking in 1953 he became a successful businessman. In 1971 he donated land valued at $300,000 to his alma mater and helped establish the Clarence Brown Theatre for the Performing Arts at the university, in Knoxville. The first two of his three marriages were to actresses: Mona MARIS and Alice JOYCE.

FILMS: *The Great Redeemer* (under Maurice Tourneur's supervision), *The Last of the Mohicans* (co-dir. with Tourneur) 1920; *The Foolish Matrons* (co-dir. with Tourneur) 1921; *The Light in the Dark* (also co-sc.) 1922; *Don't Marry for Money, The Acquittal* 1923; *The Signal Tower, Butterfly* 1924; *Smouldering Fires, The Eagle, The Goose Woman* 1925; *Kiki* 1926; *Flesh and the Devil* 1927; *The Trail of '98, A Woman of Affairs* 1928; *The Wonder of Women, Navy Blues* 1929; *Anna Christie, Romance* 1930; *Inspiration, A Free Soul, Possessed* 1931; *Emma, Letty Lynton, The Son-Daughter* 1932; *Looking Forward, Night Flight* 1933; *Sadie McKee, Chained* 1934; *Anna Karenina, Ah Wilderness!* 1935; *Wife Versus Secretary, The Gorgeous Hussy* 1936; *Conquest/Maria Walewska* 1937; *Of Human Hearts* 1938; *Idiot's Delight, The Rains Came* 1939; *Edison the Man* 1940; *Come Live with Me* (also prod.), *They Met in Bombay* 1941; *The Human Comedy* (also prod.) 1943; *The White Cliffs of Dover* 1944; *National Velvet* 1945; *The Yearling, Song of Love* (also prod.) 1947; *Intruder in the Dust* (also prod.), *To Please a Lady* (also prod.) 1950; *Angels in the Outfield* (also prod.) 1951; *It's a Big Country* (co-dir with 5 others), *When in Rome, Plymouth Adventure* 1952; *Never Let Me Go* (prod. only) 1953.

Brown, David. Producer, production executive. Born July 28, 1916, in New York City. *ed.* Stanford U.; Columbia School of Journalism. A former reporter, editor in chief of *Liberty Magazine,* managing editor of *Cosmopolitan,* and prolific short-story writer, he began his association with films in 1953 at 20th Century-Fox as story editor, then became head of the scenario department. It was there that he supervised and befriended the studio boss's son, Richard ZANUCK. Brown later served in various executive capacities at Fox. In 1969, when young Zanuck became the studio's president, Brown was appointed executive vice president of creative operations. He was ousted from the company along with Zanuck and followed him to Warner Bros., where he served in 1971–72 as executive vice president and member of the board of directors. In July of 1972 he formed with Zanuck Jr. the Zanuck-Brown company, releasing through Universal. The independent company was responsible for two of the biggest moneymaking films of all time, *The Sting* (a best picture Oscar winner, 1973) and *Jaws* (1975). Brown is the husband of Helen Gurly Brown, author of *Sex and the Single Girl* and editor of *Cosmopolitan.* After the Zanuck-Brown partnership was dissolved in 1988, Brown became president of Manhattan Project Ltd. For a list of production credits, see ZANUCK, Richard Darryl.

Brown, Georgia. Actress, singer. *b.* Georgia Klot, Oct. 21, 1933. *d.* 1992. She gained popularity as a cabaret singer, then starred in both the London and the New York productions of 'The Threepenny Opera' and 'Oliver!' Her film appearances were sporadic.

FILMS INCLUDE: *A Study in Terror* (UK/Ger.) 1965; *The Fixer* (US) 1968; *Lock Up Your Daughters* 1969; *The Raging Moon/Long Ago Tomorrow* 1971; *Tales That Witness Madness, Nothing but the Night* 1973; *Galileo* (US/UK) 1975; *The Seven Per Cent Solution* (US), *The Bawdy Adventures of Tom Jones* 1976; *Love at Stake* 1988.

Brown, Harry. Screenwriter, novelist, poet. *b.* Apr. 30, 1917, Portland, Me. *d.* 1986, of emphysema. *ed.* Harvard. He worked briefly for *Time* and *The New Yorker* magazines, then, toward the end of his WW II Army service, began writing war stories. His novel *A Walk in the Sun* (1944) was turned into an excellent motion picture by Lewis Milestone in 1946. Much of his writing for the screen deals with war, but he also has written, alone and in collaboration, screenplays for other types of dramas and Westerns. He won an Academy Award in 1951 for his part on the screenplay of *A Place in the Sun.* In the early 60s he moved to Mexico, where he wrote several novels, including the autobiographical *A Quiet Place to Work.*

FILMS (alone or in collaboration): *The True Glory* (doc.) 1945; *A Walk in the Sun, The Other Love* 1947; *Arch of Triumph, Wake of the Red Witch* 1948; *Sands of Iwo Jima, The Man on the Eiffel Tower* 1949; *Kiss Tomorrow Goodbye* 1950; *Apache Drums* (novel basis only), *A Place in the Sun, Only the Valiant* 1951; *Bugles in the Afternoon, The Sniper, Eight Iron Men* (from own play) 1952; *All the Brothers Were Valiant* 1953; *Many Rivers to Cross, The Virgin Queen* 1955; *D-Day the Sixth of June, Between Heaven and Hell* 1956; *The Deep Six, The Fiend Who Walked the West* 1958; *Ocean's 11* 1960; *El Dorado* (novel basis only, *The Stars in Their Courses*) 1967.

Brown, Harry Joe. Director, producer. *b.* Sept. 22, 1890, Pittsburgh. *d.* 1972. *ed.* U. of Michigan; U. of Syracuse (law). After several years of acting and directing for traveling companies, stock, vaudeville, and Broadway revues, he entered motion pictures in 1920. One of his early assignments was as chief engineer of illumination and lighting effects on Erich von Stroheim's *Foolish Wives* (1922). He also worked as a cameraman and production manager on several other films. Before long, he was producing low-budget Fred Thomson Westerns for Monogram and by 1925 he was heading his own production company, for which he directed and produced numerous oaters and action pictures, mostly starring Reed Howes, through 1927. He then directed or produced for another company many silent and early sound Ken MAYNARD Westerns. In 1933 he gave up directing and became a producer of some major productions for Warner Bros., Fox, and other studios. He returned to directing only once, in 1944, with the musical film *Knickerbocker Holiday,* which he also produced. In the late 40s and throughout the 50s he produced many Westerns in association with actor Randolph SCOTT. His first wife was actress Sally EILERS. Their son, Harry Joe Brown, Jr. (*b.* 1934), is also a film producer.

FILMS INCLUDE: As director-producer (complete)—*Bashful Buccaneer* 1925; *Danger Quest, Racing Romance, Broadway Billy, The Dangerous Dude, Fighting Thorobreds, The Self Starter, The Windjammer, One Punch O'Day, Moran of the Mounted, The High Flyer, Rapid Fire Romance, The Winner, Kentucky Handicap, The Night Owl, Stick to Your Story* 1926; *The Scorcher, Romantic Rogue, The Royal American, The Racing Fool* 1927; *Knickerbocker Holiday* 1944. As director only (complete)—*The Land Beyond the Law, Gun Gospel* 1927; *The Wagon Show, The Code of the Scarlet* 1928; *The Lawless Legion, The Royal Rider, The Wagon Master, Senor Americano* 1929; *Parade of the West, Lucky Larkin, The Fighting Legion, Mountain Justice, Song of the Caballero, Sons of the Saddle, The Squealer* 1930; *Millie, Woman of Experience/Registered Woman* 1931; *Madison Square Garden* 1932; *The Billion Dollar Scandal, I Love That Man, Sitting Pretty* 1933; As producer only—*The Mask of Lopez, The Silent Stranger, The Dangerous Coward* 1924; *Easy Money, Youth's Gamble* 1925; *The Red Raiders* 1927; *The Glorious Trail, The Phantom City* 1928; *Cheyenne, The California Mail* 1929; *Captain Blood, The Florentine Dagger, I Found Stella Parrish, The Case of the Curious Bride, Dangerous* 1935; *Ceiling Zero, Hearts Divided, The Great O'Malley* 1936; *Another Dawn* 1937; *Alexander's Ragtime Band* (assoc. prod.) 1938; *The Rains Came* (assoc. prod.), *Hollywood Cavalcade* (assoc. prod.) 1939; *Johnny Apollo* (assoc. prod.), *Down Argentine Way* (assoc. prod.), *Four Sons, Young People* 1940; *Western Union* (assoc. prod.), *Moon Over Miami, Wild Geese Calling* 1941; *The Desperadoes, Sahara* 1943; *Gunfighters* 1947; *Coroner Creek* 1948; *The Doolins of Oklahoma, The Walking Hills* 1949; *The Nevadan, Fortunes of Captain Blood* 1950; *Santa Fe, Man in the Saddle* 1951; *Hangman's Knot* 1952; *The Stranger Wore a Gun, The Last Posse* 1953; *Three Hours to Kill* 1954; *Ten Wanted Men, A Lawless Street* 1955; *Seventh Cavalry* 1956; *The Tall T, Decision at Sundown* 1957; *Screaming Mimi, Buchanan Rides Alone* 1958; *Ride Lonesome* 1959; *Comanche Station* 1960; *The Son of Captain Blood* 1964; *A Time for Killing* 1967.

Brown, Jim. Actor. Born James Nathaniel Brown, on Feb. 17, 1935, on St. Simon Island, off the Georgia coast. Raised in the black ghetto area of Manhasset, Long Island, he excelled in athletics in high school and was All-American in both football and lacrosse at Syracuse University. As a star fullback of the Cleveland Browns from 1957 to 1967, he shattered a number of National Football League records, including most yardage gained, and was one of the game's most exciting players. A handsome, virile man, he began appearing in films in 1964 and in 1967 retired from football to become a movie star, the first bona-fide black male "sex symbol" of the American screen. Not to be confused with James (Jim) Brown.

FILMS INCLUDE: *Rio Conchos* 1964; *The Dirty Dozen* 1967; *Dark of the Sun, The Split, Ice Station Zebra* 1968; *Tick Tick Tick, El Condor, The Grasshopper* 1970; *Slaughter, Black Gunn* 1972; *Slaughter's Big Rip-off, I Escaped from Devil's Island, The Slams* 1973; *Three the Hard Way* 1974; *Take a Hard Ride* 1975; *Kid Vengeance* (Isr.) 1977; *Fingers* 1978; *One Down, Two to Go* 1982; *The Running Man* 1987; *I'm Gonna Git You Sucka* 1988; *L.A. Heat* 1989; *Twisted Justice* 1990.

Brown, Joe E(vans). Actor. *b.* July 28, 1892, Holgate, Ohio. *d.* 1973. A circus acrobat at nine, he later played semipro baseball and performed in vaudeville and burlesque, finally reaching Broadway in 1918. He first brought his elastic face and broad slapstick style to the screen in 1928, and in the 30s and early 40s gained popularity as the wide-mouthed star of a long string of low-budget, lowbrow farces. Retired from films in 1943 but later returned to the screen in occasional prestige roles, memorably in a rare dramatic part in *The Tender Years* (1947), as an engaging Captain Andy in *Show Boat* (1951), and as an amorous millionaire in *Some Like It Hot* (1959). Autobiography: *Laughter Is a Wonderful Thing* (1959). Not to be confused with actor Joe Brown (*b.* Feb. 11, 1885, in N.Y.C.) who played character roles in films of the late 20s and early 30s.

FILMS INCLUDE: *Crooks Can't Win, Hit the Show, The Circus Kid* 1928; *Molly and Me, My Lady's Past, On With the Show, Painted Faces, Sally* 1929; *Song of the West, Hold Everything, Top Speed, Maybe It's Love, The Lottery Bride, Going Wild* 1930; *Sit Tight, Broad Minded, Local Boy Makes Good* 1931; *Fireman Save My Child, The Tenderfoot, You Said a Mouthful* 1932; *Elmer the Great, Son of a Sailor* 1933; *The Circus Clown* 1934; *Alibi Ike, Bright Lights, A Midsummer Night's Dream* (as Flute) 1935; *Sons o' Guns, Polo Joe* 1936; *Riding on Air, Fit for a King* 1937; *Wide Open Faces, The Gladiator, Flirting With Fate* 1938; *$1,000 a Touchdown, Beware Spooks!* 1939; *So You Won't Talk?* 1940; *Shut My Big Mouth* 1942; *Chatterbox* 1943; *Casanova in Burlesque, Pin Up Girl* 1944; *The Tender Years* 1947; *Show Boat* 1951; *Around the World in 80 Days* 1956; *Some Like It Hot* 1959; *It's a Mad Mad Mad Mad World, The Comedy of Terrors/The Graveside Story* 1963.

Brown, Johnny Mack. Actor. *b.* Sept. 1, 1904, Dothan, Ala. *d.* 1974. An All-American halfback at the University of Alabama and a Rose Bowl hero in 1926, he had his first taste of acting in school, and upon graduation he turned down professional football offers and headed for Hollywood. In 1927 he was signed to an MGM contract and for several years played lead roles in top-budget productions for them. Following his success in the title role of King Vidor's *Billy the Kid* (1930), he played in Westerns, mostly B grade, for various companies, including Paramount, Republic, Universal, and finally Monogram, usually riding his horse Reno. In all, he appeared in close to 200 films. He was on the list of the top moneymaking Western stars for every year between 1942 and 1950. In 1953 he retired from the screen, became manager-host of a restaurant, and subsequently made only occasional appearances in films.

FILMS INCLUDE: *The Bugle Call* (bit), *The Fair Co-Ed* 1927; *The Divine Woman, Soft Living, The Play Girl, Our Dancing Daughters, Annapolis, A Lady of Chance, A Woman of Affairs* 1928; *Coquette, The Valiant, The Single Standard, Jazz Heaven* 1929; *Undertow, Montana Moon, Hurricane, Billy the Kid* (title role) 1930; *The Great Meadow, The Secret Six, The Last Flight* 1931; *Flames, The Vanishing Frontier, 70,000 Witnesses* 1932; *Fighting with Kit Carson* (serial), *Saturday's Millions, Female* 1933; *Three on a Honeymoon, Belle of the Nineties* 1934; *Rustlers of Red Dog* (serial), *The Courageous Avenger* 1935; *The Desert Phantom, Lawless Land* 1936; *Wild West Days* (serial), *Wells Fargo, Born to the West* 1937; *Flaming Frontiers* (serial) 1938; *The Oregon Trail* (serial), *Oklahoma Frontier* 1939; *Chip of the Flying U, West of Carson City, Law and Order* 1940; *Bury Me Not on the Lone Prairie, The Man from Montana, The Masked Rider* 1941; *Ride 'Em Cowboy, The Silver Bullet, Stagecoach Buckaroo, The Old Chisholm Trail, Deep in the Heart of Texas* 1942; *The Ghost Rider, The Texas Kid* 1943; *Range Law, West of the Rio Grande* 1944; *Gun*

Smoke, The Navajo Trail 1945; *Under Arizona Skies, Trigger Fingers* 1946; *Raiders of the South, Valley of Fear* 1947; *Frontier Agent, Triggerman* 1948; *The Fighting Ranger, Stampede* 1949; *Over the Border* 1950; *The Man from Sonora, Oklahoma Outlaws* 1951; *Texas City, Dead Man's Trail* 1952; *Canyon Ambush* 1953; *The Bounty Killer, Requiem for a Gunfighter* 1965; *Apache Uprising* 1966.

Brown, Karl. Director, screenwriter, director of photography. *b.* 1897, McKeesport, Pennsylvania, the son of stage and screen performers. *d.* 1990. Entered films in 1912 as a lab assistant, later becoming a still photographer. After playing a bit in D. W. GRIFFITH's *Home Sweet Home* (1914), he became Billy BITZER's assistant cameraman and worked on many Griffith films through 1920, including *The Birth of a Nation* (1915) and *Intolerance* (1916). Adept at special effects, he is credited with the invention of a double-printing process that gave an unearthly radiance to the image of Jesus Christ in the 'Judean Story' of the latter film. As a director of photography in the early 20s, he worked mainly with director James CRUZE. Their association culminated in Cruze's monumental production *The Covered Wagon* (1923). In 1926, Brown ventured into screenwriting and directing. He was only modestly successful at both and his efforts were confined mostly to B pictures. He was married to actress-aviator Edna May Cooper. Memoirs: *Adventures With D. W. Griffith* (1976).

FILMS INCLUDE: As director of photography—*The Avenging Conscience* (asst. phot.) 1914; *Intolerance* (2nd phot.), *The Traveling Salesman* (co-phot.) 1916; *Stagestruck* 1917; *Hearts of the World* (2nd phot.), *Battling Jane* 1918; *A Romance of Happy Valley* (2nd phot.) 1919; *The City of Masks, The Life of the Party* 1920; *Brewster's Millions, Crazy to Marry* 1921; *One Glorious Day, The Dictator, The Old Homestead, Thirty Days* 1922; *The Covered Wagon, Hollywood, Ruggles of Red Gap* 1923; *The Fighting Coward, The Enemy Sex, The City That Never Sleeps, Merton of the Movies, The Garden of Weeds* 1924; *The Goose Hangs High,, Beggar on Horseback, The Pony Express* 1925; *Mannequin* 1926. As director—*Stark Love* (also prod., sc.), *His Dog* 1927; *Prince of Diamonds* (co-dir. with A. H. Van Buren) 1930; *Flames* 1932; *The White Legion* (also story), *In His Steps* (also sc.) 1936; *Michael O'Halloran, Federal Bullets* (also sc.) 1937; *The Port of Missing Girls* (also story, sc.), *Numbered Woman* (also sc.), *Barefoot Boy* (also sc.), *Under the Big Top* (also sc.) 1938. As screenwriter (alone or in collaboration)—*The Mississippi Gambler* (co-story only) 1930; *Fast Workers* 1933; *One in a Million* 1934; *Tarzan Escapes* (story only) 1936; *Gangster's Boy* (also co-story) 1938; *A Woman Is the Judge* 1939; *My Son Is Guilty* (story only), *The Man With Nine Lives, Gangs of Chicago, Military Academy, Before I Hang* (co-story only) 1940; *Mr. District Attorney, I Was a Prisoner on Devil's Island* 1941; *Hitler Dead or Alive* 1942; *The Ape Man* 1943; *The Chicago Kid* (story only) 1945.

Brown, Nacio Herb. American composer. *b.* Feb. 22, 1896. *d.* 1964. A former real estate man, he joined MGM at the very start of the sound era and subsequently composed some scores and numerous songs, often in collaboration with Arthur FREED. At one time married to actress Anita Page.

FILMS INCLUDE: *The Broadway Melody* ('You Were Meant for Me,' etc.), *The Hollywood Revue* ('Singin' in the Rain,' etc.), *The Pagan* ('Pagan Love Song,' etc.) 1929; *Whoopee!, Montana Moon* 1930; *The Barbarian, Going Hollywood* ('Temptation,' etc.) 1933; *Hollywood Party, Student Tour* 1934; *Broadway Melody of 1936, A Night at the Opera* ('Alone') 1935; *San Francisco* 1936; *Babes in Arms* ('Good Morning') 1939; *Ziegfeld Girl* ('You Stepped Out of a Dream') 1941; *Holiday in Mexico* 1946; *The Kissing Bandit, On an Island with You* 1948; *The Bribe* 1949; *Pagan Love Song* 1950; *Singin' in the Rain* 1952.

Brown, Rowland. Director, screenwriter. *b.* Nov. 6, 1900, Akron, Ohio. *d.* 1963. *ed.* U. of Detroit; Detroit School of Fine Arts. A former fashion illustrator and sports cartoonist, he arrived in Hollywood in 1928 and began his film career as a laborer on the Fox lot, later working up to property boy and gagman. By 1930 he was on the payroll as a screenwriter, and in 1931 he directed his first film, *Quick Millions,* which received excellent critical acclaim. Critics hailed Brown as an original new talent with a keen eye for detail, a sharp perception of character, and an exciting visual style. Brown fulfilled his promise with two other similarly intriguing films, *Hell's Highway* (1932) and *Blood Money* (1933) and then directed no more.

An uncompromising individualist, he found himself at odds with the studio system, and his film career became studded with unrealized projects and last-minute replacements by other directors. The final blow came when he punched a producer in a fit of rage. He then tried his luck in England, where he was assigned to direct the prestigious *The Scarlet Pimpernel* but was removed from the helm after less than a month. Upon returning to the US, he wrote a number of original stories and screenplays, made an abortive try as a playwright and Broadway producer in 1942, and all but disappeared from the Hollywood scene.

FILMS: As director—*Quick Millions* (also co-sc.) 1931; *Hell's Highway* (also co-sc.) 1932; *Blood Money* (also co-sc.) 1933. As screenwriter—*Points West* (sc.) 1929; *Doorway to Hell* (story) 1930; *Skyline* (co-sc., uncredited) 1931; *What Price Hollywood* (co-sc.), *State's Attorney* (co-sc.) 1932; *Leave It to Blanche* (co-sc.) 1934; *Widow's Might (co-sc.)* 1935; *Robin Hood of El Dorado* (co.sc., uncredited), *The Devil Is a Sissy* (story) 1936; *Boy of the Streets* (story) 1937; *Angels With Dirty Faces* (story) 1938; *The Lady's From Kentucky* (story) 1939; *Johnny Apollo* (co-sc.) 1940; *Nocturne* (co-story) 1946; *The Nevadan* (addnl. dial.) 1950; *Kansas City Confidential* (co-story) 1952.

Brown, Tom. Actor. *b.* Thomas Edward Brown, Jan. 6, 1913, New York City. *d.* 1990. The son of vaudevillian Harry Brown and musical comedy star Marie (Francis) Brown, he attended the Professional Children's School in New York and performed on radio and stage from infancy. He was nine when he reached Broadway and ten when he made his debut in silent films. He is best remembered as a clean-cut boy-next-door type in Hollywood talkies of the 30s. Appealingly baby-faced, he became typecast as a cadet, collegian, or the kid brother of the hero or heroine in numerous high- and low-budget films of Universal, MGM, and other studios. After returning from WW II combat service as a paratrooper, he vainly attempted to shake the clean-cut image by playing heavies and other character parts. He was recalled for action in the Korean War, out of which he emerged as a lieutenant colonel. He then appeared only rarely in films but could be seen regularly on TV in the 'Gunsmoke' and 'General Hospital' series.

FILMS INCLUDE: *The Hoosier Schoolmaster* 1924; *The Wrongdoers* 1925; *The Lady Lies* 1929; *Queen High* 1930; *Tom Brown of Culver, Fast Companions, Hell's Highway* 1932; *Destination Unknown, Three-Cornered Moon* 1933; *This Side of Heaven, The Witching Hour, Anne of Green Gables* 1934; *Black Sheep, Annapolis Farewell, Freckles* 1935; *And Sudden Death, Rose Bowl* 1936; *Maytime, Navy Blue and Gold, The Man Who Cried Wolf* 1937; *In Old Chicago, Merrily We Live, The Duke of West Point* 1938; *Big Town Czar, Ex-Champ, Sergeant Madden* 1939; *Margie* 1940; *Niagara Falls* 1941; *Hello Annapolis* 1942; *Adventures of Smiling Jack* (serial), *The Payoff* 1943; *The House on 92nd Street* 1945; *Buck Privates Come Home* 1947; *The*

Duke of Chicago 1949; *Operation Haylift* 1950; *Fireman Save My Child* 1954; *The Quiet Gun* 1957; *The Notorious Mr. Monks* 1958; *The Choppers* 1961.

Brown, Vanessa. Actress. Born Smylla Brind, on Mar. 24, 1928, in Vienna. At the age of 13 she appeared on Broadway in 'Watch on the Rhine' and at 16 made her screen debut in *Youth Runs Wild* (1944), billed as Tessa Brind. Changing her name to Vanessa Brown, she went on to play many fetching ingenue roles in films, as well as on the stage, radio, and TV, through the early 50s, when she retired to marry TV director Mark Sandrich, Jr. She later returned to acting occasionally, in character parts. Since her semiretirement, she has written numerous newspaper and magazine articles, freelanced for 'The Voice of America' broadcasts, and published a novel and a nonfiction book.

FILMS INCLUDE: As Tessa Brind—*Youth Runs Wild* 1944. As Vanessa Brown—*I've Always Loved You, Margie* 1946; *The Late George Apley, The Ghost and Mrs. Muir, Mother Wore Tights, The Foxes of Harrow* 1947; *Big Jack, The Secret of St. Ives, The Heiress* 1949; *Tarzan and the Slave Girl, Three Husbands* 1950; *The Basketball Fix* 1951; *The Fighter, The Bad and the Beautiful* 1952; *Rosie* 1967; *Bless the Beasts and the Children* 1971; *The Witch Who Came from the Sea* 1976.

Browne, Coral. Actress. *b.* July 23, 1913, in Melbourne, Australia. d. 1991. A veteran of the London stage, she made only sporadic film appearances, usually in sophisticated character roles. Married actor Vincent PRICE in 1974.

FILMS INCLUDE: *The Amateur Gentleman* 1936; *Black Limelight* 1938; *Let George Do It* 1940; *Piccadilly Incident* 1946; *Auntie Mame* (US) 1958; *The Roman Spring of Mrs. Stone* (US/UK) 1961; *Dr. Crippen* 1964; *The Night of the Generals* 1967; *The Legend of Lylah Clare* (US), *The Killing of Sister George* (US) 1968; *The Ruling Class* 1972; *Theatre of Blood* 1973; *The Drowning Pool* (US) 1975; *American Dreamer* (US) 1984; *Dreamchild* 1985.

Browne, Roscoe Lee. Actor. Born on May 2, 1925, in Woodbury, N.J. *ed.* Lincoln U. (Pa.); Middlebury; Columbia. An international track star and a champion middle-distance runner during his college days, he was a sales representative for a liquor company and taught French and literature at Lincoln University before making his professional acting debut in a New York Shakespeare Festival production of 'Julius Caesar' in 1956. He has since played character roles in several Broadway plays and in a number of films. On the screen, he has specialized in the portrayal of cynical Uncle Toms or calculating middle-class blacks. He is the published author of poems and short stories.

FILMS INCLUDE: *The Connection* 1962; *Black Like Me* 1964; *Terror in the City* 1966; *The Comedians* 1967; *Uptight* 1968; *Topaz* 1969; *The Liberation of L. B. Jones* 1970; *Cisco Pike* 1971; *The Cowboys* 1972; *The World's Greatest Athlete, Superfly T.N.T.* 1973; *Uptown Saturday Night* 1974; *Logan's Run* 1976; *Twilight's Last Gleaming* 1977; *Nothing Personal* (Can.) 1980; *Legal Eagles, Jumpin' Jack Flash* 1986; *Oliver & Company* (voice only), *Open Window* (short), *Moon 44* (W. Ger.) 1988; *The Mambo Kings* 1992; *Naked in New York* 1994; *Babe* (voice only), *Last Summer in the Hamptons* 1995; *Dear God, The Pompatus of Love* 1996.

Browning, Tod. Director. *b.* July 12, 1882, Louisville, Ky. *d.* 1962. At 16 he ran away from home to join a traveling circus as a contortionist and a clown. Later he was a vaudeville comedian and sometime around 1915 joined BIOGRAPH as an actor. He appeared in Griffith's *The Mother and the Law,* in 1916, and in the same year was one of the director's assistants on *Intolerance.* After writing several screenplays, he became a director in 1917. His early output consisted mostly of routine melodramas and adventure films. The turning point came in 1925 when MGM's production boss, Irving Thalberg, approved Browning's pet project, *The Unholy Three,* as a vehicle for Lon CHANEY. The film, a melodrama about the criminal feats of a trio of crooks—a transvestite ventriloquist (Chaney), a dwarf (Harry Earles), and a strongman (Victor McLaglen)—was the beginning of a remarkable collaboration between Browning, a director with a taste for the macabre, and Chaney, an actor who could make the most grotesque seem real. Under Browning's direction, Chaney brought to the silent screen a wonderful gallery of grotesque portrayals, often playing dual roles of extreme contrast.

Chaney's death in 1930 frustrated Browning's plans to make him the star of his forthcoming sound film, *Dracula.* Despite a rather static production and a stodgy performance by the substitute vampire, Bela LUGOSI, the 1931 expressionistic film has become a classic of the horror genre. But Browning's most controversial, most macabre and grotesque work came the following year. Abnormal humans of every shape and aberration were assembled from all over the world to appear in *Freaks.* Midgets, dwarfs, armless and legless living beings, sword swallowers, and bearded ladies provided some of the most ghastly and grotesque sights in film history. Compassionate as it was for the plight of its unfortunate characters, the film was tainted with melodramatic excess and was accused of being exploitative and sensational. After a San Diego preview in which one woman ran screaming up the aisle, the film was drastically cut and later completely shelved. For 30 years it was banned in England, and only in recent years has it been reappearing on American screens. In 1939 Browning went into prosperous retirement in his Santa Monica home, where he lived in relative seclusion until his death at 80.

FILMS: *Jim Bludso, A Love Sublime, Hands Up, Peggy the Will-o'-the-Wisp, The Jury of Fate* 1917; *The Eyes of Mystery, Which Woman, The Deciding Kiss, Revenge, The Legion of Death, The Brazen Beauty, Set Free (also sc.)* 1918; *The Unpainted Woman, The Wicked Darling, The Exquisite Thief, A Petal on the Current, Bonnie Bonnie Lassie* (also co-sc.) 1919; *The Virgin of Stamboul* (also co-sc.) 1920; *Outside the Law* (also story, co-sc.), *No Woman Knows* (also co-sc.) 1921; *The Wise Kid, Man Under Cover, Under Two Flags* (also co-adapt.) 1922; *Drifting* (also co-sc.), *White Tiger* (also story, co-sc.) *The Day of Faith* 1923; *The Dangerous Flirt, Silk Stocking Sal* 1924; *The Unholy Three, The Mystic* (also story), *Dollar Down* 1925; *The Black Bird* (also story), *The Road to Mandalay* (also co-story) 1926; *The Show, The Unknown* (also story), *London After Midnight* (also story) 1927; *The Big City* (also story), *West of Zanzibar* 1928; *Where East Is East* (also co-story), *The Thirteenth Chair* 1929; *Outside the Law* (remake; also co-sc.) 1930; *Dracula, The Iron Man* 1931; *Freaks* 1932; *Fast Workers* 1933; *Mark of the Vampire* 1935; *The Devil Doll* (also co-sc.) 1936; *Miracles for Sale* 1939.

Brownlow, Kevin. Director, film editor, film historian. Born on June 2, 1938, in Crowborough, England. *ed.* University Coll. The son of artists, he grew up in London devoting much of his youth to collecting films. His favorite, at age 11, was a two-reel clip of Abel Gance's masterpiece *Napoléon,* a film Brownlow would spend many of his adult years painstakingly restoring to its original glory. At 14 he began making his own first film, *The Capture,* a 9.5 mm adaptation of a Maupassant story. It took him three years to complete, with money he earned from articles for an amateur movie magazine. At 17, he entered the film industry as an editing apprentice at a documentary house. In 1956, when he was 18, the precocious Brownlow began directing his first feature, *It Happened Here,* a film based on the invented premise of a Nazi invasion of Britain during WW II. He endured many setbacks before completing the film in 1964 and finally exhibiting it commercially in 1966, to generally enthusiastic reviews. Meanwhile, he earned his living as an editor and occasional director of documentary shorts. In 1965 he joined Tony RICHARDSON's Woodfall Films, where he edited Lindsay Anderson's featurette *The White Bus* (1965) and Richardson's *Red and Blue* (1966) and *The Charge of the Light Brigade* (1967). In 1968 Brownlow published *How It Happened Here,* a witty account of the making of his film, and *The Parade's Gone By,* a beautifully illustrated, lovingly recreated eyewitness history of the silent screen. He followed the latter with two similar tomes, *The War, the West, and the Wilderness* (1978) and *Hollywood: The Pioneers* (1979). These books provided the model for 'Hollywood' (1980), a 13-part TV series Brownlow directed with David Gill for British TV. In 1983, he made another highly regarded three-part TV series, 'Unknown Chaplin,' which contained Chaplin material never before seen. In a similar manner, he later assembled 'Buster Keaton: A Hard Act to Follow.' But Brownlow's crowning achievement remains the skillful, tireless, obsessive frame-by-frame restoration of *Napoléon,* Abel Gance's 1927 five-hour "lost" masterpiece, which Brownlow started as a boy and first exhibited to the public in 1979. In recognition of his contribution to French culture, the French decorated him a chevalier of the Legion of Honor.

FEATURE FILMS: *It Happened Here* (co-dir., co-prod. co-sc. with Andrew Mollo) 1966; *The Charge of the Light Brigade* (superv. edit.) 1967; *Winstanley* (co-dir., co-sc. with Mollo) 1975; *Napoléon* (restored) 1952–1979.

Bruce, David. Actor. *b.* Andrew McBroom, Jan. 6, 1914, Kankakee, Ill. *d.* 1976. *ed.* Northwestern. Clean-cut leading man and second lead in Hollywood films of the 40s, following experience in stock.

FILMS INCLUDE: *The Man Who Talked Too Much, The Sea Hawk, Santa Fe Trail, A Dispatch From Reuters, The Letter* 1940; *Singapore Woman, The Sea Wolf, Sergeant York* 1941; *Corvette K–225, Calling Dr. Death, Gung Ho!, Honeymoon Lodge, The Mad Ghoul* 1943; *Ladies Courageous, Christmas Holiday, Moon Over Las Vegas, South of Dixie, Can't Help Singing* 1944; *Lady on a Train, Salome Where She Danced, That Night With You* 1945; *Susie Steps Out* 1946; *Prejudice* 1949; *Young Daniel Boone, Timber Fury* 1950; *Masterson of Kansas* 1955.

Bruce, Nigel. Actor. *b.* William Nigel Bruce, Sept. 4, 1895, Ensenada, Mexico, to British parents visiting as tourists. *d.* 1953. After WW I service with the British army, in which he was gravely wounded, he went on stage, appearing in many London and Broadway productions. A decade later he made his debut in British films and in 1934 began a solid Hollywood career as a supporting actor. The son of a baronet, he played convincing, often bumbling, upper-class characters or Colonel Blimp types but is best remembered for the role of Dr. Watson in Basil RATHBONE's 'Sherlock Holmes' series, a role he also played for eight years on radio. He was married to actress Violet Campbell (Shelton).

FILMS INCLUDE: *Red Aces* 1929; *The Squeaker, Escape* (UK) 1930; *Lord Chamber's Ladies* (UK) 1932; *Channel Crossing* (UK), *I Was a Spy* (UK) 1933; *Coming-Out Party, Springtime for Henry, Stand Up and Cheer, Treasure Island* 1934; *The Scarlet Pimpernel* (UK), *Becky Sharp, Jalna, She, The Man Who Broke the Bank at Monte Carlo* 1935; *The Trail of the Lonesome Pine, Under Two Flags, The Charge of the Light Brigade* 1936; *The Last of Mrs. Cheyney* 1937; *Kidnapped, Suez* 1938; *The Hound of the Baskervilles, The Adventures of Sherlock Holmes* 1939; *Rebecca, The Bluebird, Lillian Russell, A Dispatch From Reuters, Hudson's Bay* 1940; *The Chocolate Soldier, Suspicion* 1941; *Roxie Hart, This Above All, Sherlock Holmes and the Voice of Terror, Journey for Margaret* 1942; *Forever and a Day* 1943; *The Pearl of Death, Frenchman's Creek* 1944; *Son of Lassie, The Corn Is Green* 1945; *Terror by Night, Dressed to Kill* 1946; *The Two Mrs. Carrolls, The Exile* 1947; *Julia Misbehaves* 1948; *Vendetta* 1950; *Hong Kong* 1951; *Bwana Devil, Limelight* 1952; *World for Ransom* 1954.

Bruce, Virginia. Actress. *b.* Helen Virginia Briggs, Sept. 29, 1910, Minneapolis. *d.* 1982. Leading lady of Hollywood films of the 30s and early 40s. Raised in Fargo, N.D., she went to Los Angeles with the intent of attending UCLA but was lured away by the glamour of movies and began playing bit parts in early Paramount talkies. Her roles improved considerably in MGM productions of the 30s, but although she played numerous leads she never became a front-rank star and was assigned mostly to the company's low-budget fare. She briefly retired from the screen during her marriage (1932–34) to the former screen idol John GILBERT. In 1937 she married director J. Walter RUBEN, who died in 1942. Her third husband was a Turkish immigrant 12 years her junior. She continued appearing in films, in gradually diminishing roles through 1960, when she played Kim Novak's mother in *Strangers When We Meet.*

FILMS INCLUDE: *Fugitives* (bit), *Blue Skies* (bit), *Woman Trap, The Love Parade* 1929; *Lilies of the Field, Only the Brave, Slightly Scarlet, Young Eagles, Safety in Numbers, Whoopee!* 1930; *Hell Divers* 1931; *The Miracle Man, Sky Bride, Winner Take All, Downstairs, Kongo* 1932; *Jane Eyre* (title role in Monogram version), *The Mighty Barnum* 1934; *Society Doctor, Shadow of Doubt, Times Square Lady, Escapade, The Murder Man, Metropolitan* 1935; *The Garden Murder Case, The Great Ziegfeld, Born to Dance* 1936; *Women of Glamour, When Love Is Young, Between Two Women, Wife Doctor and Nurse* 1937; *The Bad Man of Brimstone, Arsene Lupin Returns, The First 100 Years, Yellow Jack, Woman Against Woman, There Goes My Heart* 1938; *Let Freedom Ring, Society Lawyer, Stronger Than Desire* 1939; *The Man Who Talked Too Much, Hired Wife* 1940; *The Invisible Woman, Adventure in Washington* 1941; *Pardon My Sarong, Careful Soft Shoulders* 1942; *Action in Arabia, Brazil* 1944; *Love Honor and Goodbye* 1945; *Night Has a Thousand Eyes* 1948; *State Department—File 649* 1949; *The Reluctant Bride* (UK) 1952; *Istanbul* (Turkey) 1953; *Two Grooms to a Bride* 1957; *Strangers When We Meet* 1960.

Bruckheimer, Jerry. Producer. Born in Detroit. *d.* 1996. *ed.* University of Arizona (psychology). Partner of the late Don SIMPSON, with whom he produced some of the highest grossing films of all time, big-budget adventures with such stars as Eddie Murphy and Tom Cruise. All their joint efforts were filmed in conjunction with Paramount until 1990, when the two parties split amicably. In 1991, they signed a multi-year development deal with Disney. Bruckheimer earned the nickname "Mr. Outside," for his hands-on filmmaking experience, to Simpson's "Mr. Inside" well-connected existence within the filmmaking community.

FILMS INCLUDE: *Farewell, My Lovely* 1975; *March or Die* 1977; *American Gigolo, Defiance* 1980; *Thief* 1981; *Cat People* (exec. prod.), *Young Doctors in Love* 1982; *Flashdance* 1983; *Beverly Hills Cop, Thief of Hearts* 1984; *Top Gun* 1986; *Beverly Hills Cop II* 1987; *Days of Thunder* 1990; *Bad Boys, Crimson Tide, Dangerous Minds* 1995; *The Rock* 1996; *Con Air* 1997.

Bruckman, Clyde. Director, screenwriter. *b.* 1894, San Bernadino, Calif. *d.* 1955. A former journalist, he began in films as a staff screenwriter at Warners. In the early 20s he started working for Buster KEATON as idea and gagman and became the comedian's regular collaborator as screenwriter and, later, co-director of the Civil War comedy classic *The General* (1926). He subsequently directed comedies of Monty Banks, Harold Lloyd, Laurel and Hardy, and W. C. Fields, but his directing career ended in 1935. Twenty years later, driven to drink by professional failure and marital problems and armed with a pistol he had borrowed from Buster Keaton, he shot himself to death in the rest room of a Hollywood restaurant after a meal for which he could not pay.

FILMS: As screenwriter, in collaboration—*Rouged Lips, The Three Ages, Our Hospitality* 1923; *Sherlock Jr., The Navigator* 1924; *Seven Chances, Keep Smiling* 1925; *For Heaven's Sake* 1926; *The Cameraman* (co-story only) 1928; *Professor Beware* (co-story only) 1938; *Swingtime Johnny* (sc. alone) 1943; *She Gets Her Man* 1945. A director—*The General* (co-dir., co-sc. with Buster Keaton), *Horse Shoes, Call of the Cuckoos* (short), *Putting Pants on Philip* (short), *Love 'Em and Feed 'Em* (short), *The Battle of the Century* (short) 1927; *A Perfect Gentleman, Leave 'Em Laughing* (short), *The Finishing Touch* (short) 1928; *Welcome Danger* (also co-story) 1929; *Feet First* 1930; *Everything's Rosie* 1931; *Movie Crazy* 1932; *Too Many Highballs* (short), *The Human Fish* (short), *The Fatal Glass of Beer* (short) 1933; *Spring Tonic, The Man on the Flying Trapeze* 1935.

Brunel, Adrian. Director. *b.* 1892, Brighton, England. *d.* 1958. A former actor and singer, he entered the motion picture industry as a film salesman in 1915. Two years later he began directing war propaganda shorts and commercial feature films. In 1920 he founded Minerva Films with Leslie HOWARD, through which he turned out satirical shorts such as *The Bump, £5 Reward,* and *Bookworms.* His reputation rests on his feature films of the silent era rather than his later talkies. Often wrote his own scripts.

FEATURE FILMS: *The Cost of a Kiss* 1917; *A Temporary Lady* 1921; *The Man Without Desire* 1923; *Lovers in Araby* 1924; *Land of Hope and Glory* (sc. only), *Blighty* 1927; *The Constant Nymph, The Vortex, A Light Woman* 1928; *The Crooked Billet* 1929; *Elstree Calling* (co-dir. with Alfred Hitchcock) 1930; *Taxi to Paradise, I'm an Explosive, Follow the Lady, Little Napoleon, Two Wives for Henry, The Laughter of Fools* 1933; *Important People, Badger's Green* 1934; *Cross Currents, Vanity, Variety, The City of Beautiful Nonsense, While Parents Sleep* 1935; *Prison Breaker, Love at Sea, The Invader* 1936; *The Return of the Scarlet Pimpernel* (sc. only) 1937; *The Lion Has Wings* (co-dir. with Michael Powell and Brian Desmond Hurst), *The Girl Who Forgot* 1939.

Brusati, Franco. Director, screenwriter. *b.* 1922, in Milan, of Austrian parents. *d.* 1993. Briefly a journalist, he turned to Italian films as a screenwriter in 1950, and began directing occasionally in 1955, but attracted little attention until the 70s, when he received international acclaim for *Bread and Chocolate* (1973) and *To Forget Venice* (1979). The former film depicted with engaging humor the bitter travails of an Italian expatriate restaurant worker in Switzerland. The latter film, somewhat pretentious, relied more on style than substance to win its Oscar nomination for best foreign picture of 1980.

FILMS INCLUDE: As co-screenwriter—*Atto di Accusa* 1950; *Honeymoon Deferred* (UK), *Anna* 1951; *Moglie per una Notte, Le Infedeli/The Unfaithfuls* 1952; *L'Etá dell'Amore* 1953; *I Tre Ladri, Ulisse/Ulysses* 1955; *Via Marqutta/Run with the Devil* 1960; *Smog, Una Vita violenta* 1962; *Seduto alla sua destra/Seated at His Right, Romeo e Giulietta/Romeo and Juliet* 1968. As director/co-screenwriter—*Il Padrone sono me* 1955; *Il Disordine/Disorder* 1962; *Tenderly/Il Suo Modo di Fare/The Girl Who Couldn't Say No* 1968; *I Tulipani di Haarlem/The Tulips of Harlem* 1970; *Pane e Cioccolata/Bread and Chocolate* 1973; *Dimemticare Venezia/To Forget Venice* 1979; *Lo Zio indegno* 1989.

brute. A high-intensity arc spotlight used as the largest standard studio lamp. With a current rating of 225 amps and equipped with a 48-inch-diameter lens, it is particularly advantageous in lighting sets for color filming.

Bryan, Jane. Actress. Born Jane O'Brien, on June 11, 1918, in Hollywood, Calif. Attractive girl-next-door type of ingenue of Warner Bros. films of the late 30s. Retired from the screen at the age of 21 to marry the president of the Rexall Drug Company.

FILMS INCLUDE: *The Case of the Black Cat* 1936; *Marked Woman, Kid Galahad, Confession* 1937; *A Slight Case of Murder, The Sisters, Girls on Probation, Brother Rat* 1938; *Each Dawn I Die, The Old Maid, These Glamour Girls, We Are Not Alone, Invisible Stripes* 1939; *Brother Rat and a Baby* 1940.

Bryan, John. Art director, producer. *b.* 1911, London. *d.* 1969. He began designing stage sets at the age of 16. At 20 he entered films, beginning as draftsman and assistant art director on such noted British productions as *The Ghost Goes West* and *Things to Come* (both 1936). After becoming an art director in the late 30s, he designed many important British films and was especially noted for his work on Shaw and Dickens adaptations. He won an Academy Award for designing the sets of David Lean's *Great Expectations.* More recently, he was the production designer on *Becket.* In 1951 he became a producer, working in that capacity for various British production organizations until his death.

FILMS INCLUDE: As art director—*Pygmalion* 1938; *Major Barbara* 1941; *The Adventures of Tartu, 2000 Women, Millions Like Us* 1943; *Fanny by Gaslight* 1944; *Great Expectations, Caesar and Cleopatra* 1946; *Blanche Fury* 1947; *Oliver Twist* 1948; *The Passionate Friends* 1949; *Madeleine, The Golden Salamander* 1950; *The Flying Dutchman, The Magic Box* 1951; *Becket* 1964. As producer—*The Card/The Promoter* 1952; *The Million Pound Note/Man with a Million* 1953; *The Purple Plain* 1954; *The Spanish Gardener* (also sc.) 1956; *The Secret Place* 1957; *Windom's Way* 1958; *The Horse's Mouth* 1959; *There Was a Crooked Man* 1960; *The Girl on the Boat* 1961; *Tamahine* 1963; *After the Fox* 1966; *The Touchables* 1968.

Brynner, Yul. Actor. *b.* July 12, 1915, Sakhalin, an island east of Siberia and north of Japan. *d.* 1985. His true origins have been calculatedly shrouded in mystery, Brynner himself helping to spread conflicting versions about his date and place of birth and the identity of his parents. At one time he claimed that as children he and his half sister Vera, later a concert singer, had been adopted by gypsies and brought to Paris, where at the age of 13 Yul joined a gypsy group and began singing and playing the balalaika in nightclubs. (But in the 70s Brynner finally acknowledged a part-gypsy ancestry and became active in the cause of gypsy rights.) According to a 1989 biography by his son, Rock, *Yul: The Man Who Would Be King,* Brynner was born on July 11, 1920, in Vladivostok, Russia.

The facts about Brynner's later life are less contradictory. In his late teens he was a high trapeze flyer with the Paris Cirque d'Hiver but was grounded after almost being crippled by a fall. After recovering from his injuries, he joined the Pitoeff Repertory Company as a stagehand and apprentice actor. At the same time, he attended the Sorbonne. He later became a protégé of actor Michael Chekhov, who brought him to the US in 1940 with his Shakespeare company. Fluent in several languages,

Brynner was recruited in 1942 by the US Office of War Information for the duration of the war as a radio commentator in French. Brynner made it to Broadway in 1946, appearing with Mary Martin in 'Lute Song,' and in 1949 made his film debut as a villain in a B picture, *Port of New York.* But he devoted most of his energies in the late 40s to the fledgling TV industry, both as an actor and a director. His big break came in 1951 when he was chosen to står as the king in the hit Broadway musical 'The King and I,' for which he won a slew of awards and critical praise. He stayed with the show through 1,246 performances, then went to Hollywood, where he repeated his success in the film version, winning the best actor Oscar in the process. Keeping the Siamese king's shaved head as a trademark, Brynner went on to star in numerous Hollywood and international films of varying quality, bringing to the screen a mysterious, magnetically forceful hero personality. In 1960 he wrote the book *Bring Forth the Children.* In the late 60s he moved to Switzerland and became a Swiss citizen, but in 1972 he returned to Hollywood. In 1975 he returned to Broadway in a flop musical, 'Home Sweet Homer,' but in 1977 he scored a hit with the Broadway revival of 'The King and I.' In September of 1983 Brynner was diagnosed as having lung cancer and was given only months to live. Defiantly, he carried on with a coast-to-coast "farewell engagement" of yet another revival of 'The King and I,' which started in 1981 and ended triumphantly on Broadway just four months before his October 1985 death. In all, he gave 4,625 performances as the King of Siam over the course of 30 years. Brynner, whose first (1944–60) of three wives had been actress Virginia GILMORE, married for the fourth time in 1983. His bride was Kathy Lee, the Malaysian principal dancer of his touring company. After he passed away, the American Lung Association released a haunting series of commercials in which the dying actor pleaded with smokers to kick the habit that had cost him his life.

FILMS: *Port of New York* 1949; *The King and I, The Ten Commandments* (as Rameses), *Anastasia* 1956; *The Brothers Karamazov* (as Dimitri Karamazov), *The Buccaneer* 1958; *The Journey, The Sound and the Fury, Solomon and Sheba* (as Solomon) 1959; *Le Testament d'Orphée/The Testament of Orpheus* (cameo; Fr.), *Once More with Feeling, Surprise Package, The Magnificent Seven* 1960; *Escape from Zahrain, Taras Bulba* (title role) 1962; *Kings of the Sun* 1963; *Flight From Ashiya, Invitation to a Gunfighter* 1964; *Morituri/Saboteur—Code Name Morituri* 1965; *The Poppy Is Also a Flower* (cameo), *Cast a Giant Shadow, Return of the Seven, Triple Cross* (Fr./UK) 1966; *The Double Man* (UK), *The Long Duel* (UK) 1967; *Villa Rides* 1968; *The File of the Golden Goose* (UK), *The Madwoman of Chaillot* (UK) 1969; *Battle of Neretva* (Yug./It./Fr.), *The Magic Christian* (cameo; UK) 1970; *Indio Black sai che to dico: sei un Gran Figlio di. . . /Adios Sabata* (It./Sp.), *Catlow* (Sp.), *The Light at the Edge of the World* (US/It./Sp.), *Romance of a Horsethief* (US/Yug.) 1971; *Fuzz* 1972; *Le Serpent/The Serpent* (Fr./Ger.), *Westworld* 1973; *The Last Warrior* 1975; *Futureworld, Con la Rabbia aqli Occhi/Anger in His Eyes/Death Rage* (It.) 1976.

Buchanan, Edgar. Actor. *b.* William Edgar Buchanan, Mar. 21, 1902, Humansville, Mo. *d.* 1979. *ed.* U. of Oregon. He went into dentistry but found little satisfaction in his work and in 1939 drifted into films. He soon became a fixture in Western films, playing convincing character roles, typically as a corrupt sheriff or judge, or a rugged old-timer. He often managed to stay likable even when playing villain roles. Buchanan played in close to 100 films, mostly Westerns. He co-starred in the TV series 'Hopalong Cassidy' (1949–51), 'Judge Roy Bean' (title role; 1956), 'Petticoat Junction' (1963–70), and 'Cade's County' (1971–72).

FILMS INCLUDE: *My Son Is Guilty* 1939; *When the Daltons Rode, Too Many Husbands, The Sea Hawk, Arizona* 1940; *Penny Serenade, Texas* 1941; *Tombstone, The Talk of the Town* 1942; *City Without Men, Destroyer* 1943; *Buffalo Bill, The Impatient Years* 1944; *The Guardsman* 1945; *Abilene Town, Renegades, The Walls Came Tumbling Down* 1946; *The Sea of Grass, Framed* 1947; *Coroner Creek, The Black Arrow, The Man from Colorado, The Untamed Breed* 1948; *Red Canyon, The Walking Hills, Any Number Can Play* 1949; *The Big Hangover, Cheaper by the Dozen, The Great Missouri Raid* 1950; *Rawhide, Silver City* 1951; *The Big Trees* 1952; *Shane* 1953; *Destry, Human Desire* 1954; *Wichita, Lonesome Trail* 1955; *Come Next Spring* 1956; *Spoilers of the Forest* 1957; *The Sheepman* 1958; *King of the Wild Stallions, Edge of Eternity, Four Fast Guns* 1959; *Cimarron* 1960; *The Comancheros* 1961; *Ride the High Country* 1962; *McLintock, A Ticklish Affair, Move Over Darling* 1963; *The Rounders* 1965; *Gunpoint* 1966; *Welcome to Hard Times* 1957; *Angel in My Pocket* 1969; *Benji* 1974.

Buchanan, Jack. Actor singer, dancer. *b.* Walter John Buchanan, Apr. 2, 1890, Helensburgh, Scotland. *d.* 1957. *ed.* Glasgow Academy. A former clerk and amateur performer, he made his professional debut in 1911 in variety shows, later appearing in London stage musicals. He sang and danced his way through many London productions before making his film debut in 1917. Tall, dashing, and debonair, he was a well-known British film star when he made his Broadway debut in 'Charlot's Revue' (1924), with Beatrice Lillie and Gertrude Lawrence. In 1929–30 he appeared in several Hollywood films, including the lead role opposite Jeannette MacDonald in Lubitsch's *Monte Carlo.* Back in England, he resumed brisk stage and screen activity. He directed or produced several films. His career sagged in the 40s, but was revived in 1953 by his memorable appearance in the Hollywood musical *The Band Wagon.*

FILMS INCLUDE: *Auld Lang Syne* 1917; *Her Heritage* 1919; *The Audacious Mr. Squire* 1923; *The Happy Ending* 1924; *Bulldog Drummond's Third Round* 1925; *Confetti* 1927; *Toni* 1928; *Paris* (US) 1929; *Monte Carlo* (US) 1930; *Man of Mayfair* 1931; *Goodnight Vienna/Magic Night* 1932; *Yes Mr. Brown* (also co-dir. with Herbert Wilcox), *That's a Good Girl* (also dir.) 1933; *Brewster's Millions* 1935; *Limelight/Backstage, When Knights Were Bold* 1936; *The Sky's the Limit* (also prod.) 1937; *Sweet Devil* (prod. only), *Break the News* (also prod., co-dir. with Lee Garmes) 1938; *The Gang's All Here/The Amazing Mr. Forrest* (also co-prod.), *The Middle Watch* 1939; *Bulldog Sees It Through* 1940; *Happidrome* (co-prod. only) 1943; *The Band Wagon* (US) 1953; *As Long As They Are Happy, Josephine and Men, Les Carnets du Major Thompson/The French They Are a Funny Race* (Fr.) 1955.

Buchholz, Horst. Actor. Born on Dec. 4, 1932, in Berlin. After early work as a very young radio and stage performer, he began his film career by lending his voice to the dubbing of foreign pictures. Julien DUVIVIER noted his acting performance in Berlin's Schiller Theater and gave him his first onscreen role, in *Marianne de ma Jeunesse* (1955). Later that year he received the Cannes Festival Award for his performance in Helmut Kautner's *Himmel ohne Sterne/Sky Without Stars.* After starring in the internationally successful *The Confessions of Felix Krull* (1957), he began gaining worldwide recognition with romantic leads in British and American films. Married French actress Myriam Bru, 1958.

FILMS INCLUDE: *Marianne de ma Jeunesse/Marianne* (Fr./Ger.), *Himmel ohne Sterne/Sky Without Stars* 1955; *Regine, Die Halbstarken* 1956; *Herrscher ohne Krone/King in Shadow, Robinson soll nicht sterben/The Girl and the Legend, Die*

Bekenntnisse des Hochstaplers Felix Krull/The Confessions of Felix Krull, Monpti 1957; *Nasser Asphalt* 1958; *Das Totenschiff* (Ger./Mex.), *Tiger Bay* (UK) 1959; *The Magnificent Seven* (US) 1960; *Fanny* (US), *One Two Three* (US) 1961; *Nine Hours to Rama* (US), *La Noia/The Empty Canvas* (It./Fr.) 1963; *La Fabuleuse Aventure de Marco Polo/Marco the Magnificent* (as Marco Polo; Fr./It./Afg./Eg.), *Colpo Grosso a Galata Bridge/That Man in Istanbul* (It./Fr./Sp.) 1965; *Johnny Banco—Geliebter Taugenichts/Johnny Banco* (Ger./Fr./It.) 1967; *Cervantes/The Young Rebel* (Sp./Fr./It.) 1968; *The Great Waltz* (as Johann Strauss, Jr.; US) 1972; *The Catamount Killing* (UK) 1975; *Da Dunkerque alla Vittoria/From Hell to Victory* (It./Fr./Sp.), *Avalanche Express* (US) 1979; *Aphrodite* 1982; *Sahara* (US/It.) 1984; *Code Name: Emerald* (US) 1985; *And the Violins Stopped Playing* (US/Pol.) 1989; *Fuga Dal Paradiso/Escape from Paradise* (It./Fr./Ger.) 1990; *Aces: Iron Eagle III* 1992; *Faraway So Close* 1993.

Buchman, Sidney. Screenwriter, producer. *b.* Mar. 27, 1902, Duluth, Minn. *d.* 1975. *ed.* U. of Minnesota; Columbia. Started his professional career as assistant stage director at London's Old Vic. After returning to the US, he wrote several plays, none of which was successful. Set out for Hollywood in 1930 as a contract screenwriter for Paramount, and in 1934 he moved over to Columbia. It was here that he contributed some of his best script work, alone or in collaboration, notably for such sophisticated comedies as *Theodora Goes Wild, Mr. Smith Goes to Washington, Here Comes Mr. Jordan,* and *The Talk of the Town.* A favorite writer of Columbia's boss Harry Cohn, Buchman also produced a number of the studio's films.

In 1942, Buchman began supervising Columbia's production and later moved up to the position of vice president and assistant production chief. But everything changed for him in 1951, when he admitted former membership in the Communist party to the House Un-American Activities Committee. When he refused to name names, he was found guilty of contempt of Congress, fined $150, and given a year's suspended sentence. Blacklisting followed, and he was unable to find work in films until the early 60s, when he was hired by 20th Century-Fox as writer and producer in Europe. He resided in Cannes, France, in the last decade of his life.

FILMS INCLUDE (as screenwriter): *Matinee Ladies* (co-story) 1927; *Beloved Bachelor* (dial.) 1931; *The Sign of the Cross* (adapt., dial.), *If I Had a Million* 1932; *From Hell to Heaven* 1933; *Whom the Gods Destroy, Broadway Bill* (uncredited) 1934; *Love Me Forever, She Married Her Boss* 1935; *The King Steps Out, Adventure in Manhattan, Theodora Goes Wild* 1936; *The Awful Truth, Lost Horizon* (both co-sc., uncredited) 1937; *Holiday* 1938; *Mr. Smith Goes to Washington* 1939; *The Howards of Virginia* 1940; *Here Comes Mr. Jordan* 1941; *The Talk of the Town* 1942; *Sahara* (co-sc., uncredited) 1943; *A Song to Remember, Over 21* (both also prod.) 1945; *The Jolson Story* (co-story, uncredited) 1947; *To the Ends of the Earth* (prod. and uncredited co-sc. only) 1948; *Jolson Sings Again* (also prod.) 1949; *Saturday's Hero* 1951; *The Mark* 1961; *Cleopatra* 1963; *The Group* (also prod.) 1966; *La Maison sous les Arbres/The Deadly Trap* 1972.

Buchowetzki (also **Buchowetski), Dimitri.** Director. *b.* 1885, Russia. *d.* 1932. After law studies, he began directing films in Czarist Russia, then emigrated to Germany in the wake of the October Revolution. Unlike many of his former colleagues, he made a successful transition to German films. In 1919 he directed a series of Max Linder shorts and the following year began directing ambitious costume dramas, often starring Emil Jannings and Pola NEGRI. When Negri went to Hollywood, she requested his importation as director of her films. He was brought in with much fanfare in 1924 but failed to impress the studio bosses and did not fare well in the American phase of his career. By the turn of the sound era, he had been reduced to directing only German versions of Hollywood productions.

FEATURE FILMS: In Germany—*Die Brüder Karamasoff/The Brothers Karamazov* (co-dir. with Carl Froelich), *Das Experiment des Professor Mithrany, Die letzte Stunde* 1920; *Danton/All for a Woman* (also sc.), *Der Galiläer, Sappho/Mad Love* (also sc.), *Der Stier von Olivera* (co-dir. with Erich Schonfelder) 1921; *Die Gräfin von Paris, Othello, Peter der Grosse/Peter the Great* 1922; *Das Karussell des Lebens* (also co-sc.; Ger./Sw.) 1923. In the US—*Men* (also story), *Lily of the Dust* 1924; *The Swan* (also sc.), *Graustark* 1925; *The Crown of Lies, The Midnight Sun, Valencia* (also co-story) 1926; *Weib im Dschungel* (German version of *The Letter*), *Le Requisitoire* (French version of *Manslaughter*) 1930; *Die Nacht der Entscheidung* (German version of *The Virtuous Sin*), *Stamboul* 1931.

Buckner, Robert. Screenwriter, producer. Born on May 28, 1906, in Crewe, Va. *ed.* U. of Virginia; U. of Edinburgh (Scotland). Started at 20 as London correspondent for the New York *World.* Later worked as an instructor at the Belgian Military Academy and as editor with several large New York publishers. A contributor of fiction to American and British magazines, he began writing original stories and screenplays for Hollywood films in 1937. From the early 40s through the late 50s he was also active as producer, for Warner Bros. and later other studios.

FILMS INCLUDE: As screenwriter, alone or in collaboration—*Gold Is Where You Find It, Jezebel, Comet Over Broadway* 1938; *The Oklahoma Kid, Dodge City, Espionage Agent* (story only), *Angels Wash Their Faces* 1939; *Primrose Path* (co-play basis only), *Virginia City, My Love Came Back, Knute Rockne—All American, Santa Fe Trail* 1940; *Dive Bomber* 1941; *Yankee Doodle Dandy* (also story) 1942; *Confidential Agent* (also prod.) 1945; *Rogues' Regiment* (also prod., co-story) 1948; *Sword in the Desert* (also prod.), *Free for All* (also prod.) 1949; *Deported* (also prod.) 1950; *Bright Victory* (also prod.) 1951; *The Man Behind the Gun* 1953; *To Paris With Love* (UK), *A Prize of Gold* (UK) 1955; *Safari* (UK), *Love Me Tender* 1956; *House of Secrets/Triple Deception* (UK) 1957; *From Hell to Texas* (also prod.) 1958; *Return of the Gunfighter* 1968. As producer only—*Gentleman Jim* 1942; *Mission to Moscow, The Desert Song* 1943; *Uncertain Glory, God Is My Co-Pilot, San Antonio* 1945; *Devotion, Nobody Lives Forever* 1946; *Cheyenne, Life with Father* 1947.

Bucquet, Harold S. Director. *b.* Apr. 10, 1891, London. *d.* 1946. In the US from the mid-30s, he began his film career as a director of short subjects. Later directed a string of "Dr. Kildare" films for MGM, as well as some other features, the most ambitious of which was *Dragon Seed,* with Katharine Hepburn, which he co-directed with Jack Conway from the book by Pearl S. Buck.

FEATURE FILMS: *Young Dr. Kildare* 1938; *Calling Dr. Kildare, On Borrowed Time, The Secret of Dr. Kildare* 1939; *Dr. Kildare's Strange Case, We Who Are Young, Dr. Kildare Goes Home, Dr. Kildare's Crisis* 1940; *The Penalty, The People vs. Dr. Kildare, Dr. Kildare's Wedding Day, Kathleen* 1941; *Calling Dr. Gillespie, The War Against Mrs. Hadley* 1942; *The Adventures of Tartu* (UK) 1943; *Dragon Seed* (co-dir., with Jack Conway) 1944; *Without Love* 1945.

Buena Vista. See DISNEY, Walt.

Buetel, Jack. Actor. *b.* Jack Beutel, Sept. 5, 1916, Dallas. *d.* 1989. He gained some stage experience with the Dallas Little

Theater while making his living as an insurance clerk. In 1940 he played Billy the Kid in Howard Hughes's controversial film *The Outlaw,* opposite Jane Russell. It would probably have made him a star, but the film ran into censorship trouble when released briefly in 1941 and again in 1943. It was not seen by the general public until 1950, when interest had cooled considerably. The long delay, plus the years he spent in WW II service with the Navy, combined to keep Buetel out of other films in the 40s. Howard Hawks wanted him to play a key role, opposite John Wayne, in his 1948 Western classic *Red River,* but Howard Hughes, who had Buetel under contract, refused to loan him out. The part eventually went to Montgomery Clift and made him a star. Buetel was convinced Hughes was undermining his career because the eccentric producer believed Buetel had had an affair with one of Hughes's girlfriends. He appeared in a handful of low-budget Westerns in the 50s, then disappeared from the Hollywood scene.

FILMS: *The Outlaw* 1941, 1943, 1950; *Best of the Badmen* 1951; *The Half-Breed, Rose of the Cimarron* 1952; *Jesse James' Women* (as Frank James) 1954; *Mustang* 1959.

Bugs Bunny. Popular Warner Bros. cartoon character, an indomitable, wisecracking rabbit, created collectively in 1936 by a group of artists led by Chuck JONES and Friz FRELENG. The original sketch for the character was submitted by a Warners story man named Bugs Hardaway. For the purpose of identification he marked the model sheets "Bugs' Bunny." The name stuck. Mel Blanc supplied Bugs's voice for the sound track, which was frequently accented by the immortal phrase, "What's up, Doc?" A feature-length anthology of old Bugs Bunny classic cartoons was released theatrically in 1975 under the title *Bugs Bunny Superstar.* Other anthologies followed, including *The Bugs Bunny/Road Runner Movie* (1979) and *Bugs Bunny's 3rd Movie: 1001 Rabbit Tales* (1982). He was one of the many cartoon luminaries with a cameo in *Who Framed Roger Rabbit*? (1988)

Bujold, Geneviève. Actress. Born July 1, 1942, in Montreal. Educated in a convent and at the Quebec Conservatory of Drama. The daughter of a French-Canadian bus driver, she worked her way through drama school as an usherette at a Montreal cinema. Made her stage debut in a Canadian production of 'The Barber of Seville,' and played her first film role in the Canadian co-production *The Adolescents* (1964). On a visit to Europe, she was picked by director Alain Resnais to appear opposite Yves Montand in the film *La Guerre est finie* (1966). She subsequently appeared in other French and Canadian productions and made her mark as an international star in 1969 as Anne Boleyn in the Anglo-American film *Anne of the Thousand Days,* for which she received an Oscar nomination. Her performances exude sensitivity, warmth, and youthful maturity. She has since been active in supporting roles. In 1967 she married Paul ALMOND, who directed several of her films. They divorced in 1973.

FILMS INCLUDE: *La Fleur de l'Age ou les Adolescentes/The Adolescents* (Can./Fr./It./Jap.) 1964; *La Guerre est finie/The War Is Over, Le Roi de Coeur/King of Hearts* (Fr./It.) 1966; *Le Voleur/The Thief of Paris* (Fr./It.) 1967; *Isabel* (Can.) 1968; *Anne of the Thousand Days* (as Anne Boleyn; UK) 1969; *Acte du Coeur/Act of the Heart* (Can.) 1970; *The Trojan Women* (as Cassandra; Gr./UK) 1971; *Journey* (Can.) 1972; *Kamouraska* (Can.), *Earthquake* (US) 1974; *L'Incorrigible/Incorrigible* (Fr.) 1975; *Swashbuckler* (US), *Obsession* (US), *Alex and the Gypsy/Love and Other Crimes* (US) 1976; *Un autre Homme une autre Chance/Another Man Another Chance* (Fr./US) 1977; *Coma* (US) 1978; *Sherlock Holmes: Murder by Decree* (UK/Can.) 1979; *The Last Flight of Noah's Ark* (US), *Final Assignment* (Can.) 1980; *Monsignor* (US) 1982; *Tightrope* (US), *Choose Me* (US) 1984; *Trouble in Mind* (US) 1985; *The Moderns* (US), *Dead Ringers* (Can.) 1988; *Les Noces de Papier/A Paper Wedding* (Can.), *Secret Places of the Heart, False Identity* 1990; *Rue du Bac* 1991; *What a Night* 1992; *Mon Amie Mar* 1994; *Pinocchio* 1996; *The House of Yes* 1997.

Bulajič, Veljko. Director. Born on Mar. 23, 1928, in Montenegro, Yugoslavia. He started out as a journalist, then directed several short Yugoslavian documentaries before going to Rome in 1950 to attend the Centro Sperimentale cinema school. He later worked as assistant to such Italian directors as Zampa, Fellini, and De Sica, then returned to Yugoslavia in 1958. He received international recognition for his first feature film, *Train Without a Timetable* (1958), and won several awards for his feature-length documentary *Skopje 1963.* He has since remained established as one of the major talents of the Yugoslavian cinema. In the late 60s he began undertaking ambitious, large-scale international productions.

FEATURE FILMS: *Train Without a Timetable* 1958; *War* 1960; *Boom Town* 1961; *Kozara/Hill of Death* 1963; *Skopje 1963* (doc.) 1964; *A Glance at the Pupil of the Sun* 1966; *Battle of Neretva* (Yug./It./Fr.) 1970; *Assassination in Sarajevo/The Day That Shook the World* (Yug./Czech.) 1976; *Donator* 1989.

Bulgaria. Wars, foreign domination, international strife, and general economic backwardness have combined to delay and decelerate the development of a film industry in this Balkan nation. Its first film, *Bulgarians Are Gallant,* was turned out in 1910, two years after the proclamation of Bulgaria's independence. It was directed by Vassil Gendov, a spirited pioneer who for several years worked entirely alone at building his country's film production. In the early 20s, Gendov was joined by Boris Greshov, who is considered to have been Bulgaria's top director in the years between the world wars. Gendov, Greshov, and several other pioneers worked under adverse conditions with primitive equipment and negligible funds.

It wasn't until 1933 that Gendov directed the country's first talkie. Some 50 films in all were produced by the outbreak of World War II, during which Bulgaria's film resources were harnessed to the propaganda machine of the Axis powers. Feature film production was resumed in 1944, and in 1948 the industry was nationalized by the Communist government. Early films under the new order tended to follow the example of Soviet films of the period both in style and in choice of themes. WW II and highlights in the nation's history were the usual subjects of films, which were intended more to inspire and instill pride than to entertain. Leading directors of the period include Zahari Zhdanov and Anton Marinovich. In the late 50s a trend began to appear with the development of a new generation of directors, led by Rangel Vulchanov and Vulo Radev. By the mid-60s contemporary themes were being seen on Bulgarian screens, with detective stories and suspense films as well as social dramas with modern-day backgrounds.

Vulchanov's *Sun and Shadow* (1962) and Radev's *The Peach Thief* (1964) were among the first internationally important Bulgarian productions. Since then, Bulgarian films have been shown regularly in film festivals, often winning prestigious awards. Some 20 features and 200 short subjects are being produced every year. Among the prominent current feature directors, in addition to Vulchanov and Radev, are Hristo Hristov, Lyudmil Staikov, Zako Heskiya, and Nikola Korabov.

Most Bulgarian films are produced at a modern production center near Sofia, which has large, fully equipped sound stages for features, documentaries, and educational and scientific shorts. A thriving animation studio turns out many quality animated shorts every year. The state offers a four-year course for directors, cinematographers, and film critics. However, there is no established film school, and young filmmakers are often trained in other countries.

Bullock, Sandra. American actress. Born 1966. After a brief stint in TV movies, this charming, lovely leading lady endeared herself to audiences everywhere with her star turn in the box office smash *Speed* 1994. She has gone on to become one of the most recognized and popular stars in Hollywood.

FILMS INCLUDE: *Love Potion No. 9* 1992; *Demolition Man, Wrestling Ernest Hemingway, The Thing Called Love* 1993; *Speed* 1994; *The Net, While You Were Sleeping* 1995; *A Time to Kill, In Love and War, Two If By Sea* 1996; *Speed 2: Cruise Control* 1997.

Bumstead, Henry. American art director. Beginning in the late 40s, he designed the sets for many major Hollywood productions, notably several Hitchcock classics. He was Oscar-nominated for *Vertigo* (1958) and won Academy Awards for *To Kill a Mockingbird* (1962) and *The Sting* (1973).

FILMS INCLUDE: *Saigon* 1948; *Song of Surrender Streets of Laredo* 1949; *The Furies* 1950; *Sailor Beware* 1951; *Come Back Little Sheba* 1952; *The Bridges at Toko-Ri* 1954; *The Man Who Knew Too Much, The Vagabond King* 1956; *I Married a Monster from Outer Space, Vertigo* 1958; *Cinderfella* 1960; *Come September* 1961; *To Kill a Mockingbird* 1962; *A Gathering of Eagles* 1963; *Father Goose* 1964; *The War Lord* 1965; *Topaz, Tell Them Willie Boy Is Here* 1969; *Slaughterhouse Five* 1972; *High Plains Drifter, The Sting* 1973; *The Front Page* 1974; *The Great Waldo Pepper* 1975; *Family Plot* 1966; *Slap Shot* 1977; *A Little Romance* 1979; *The World According to Garp* 1982; *The Little Drummer Girl* 1984; *Warning Sign* 1985; *Psycho III* 1986; *Funny Farm* 1988; *Her Alibi* 1989; *Ghost Dad* 1990; *Absolute Power* 1997.

Bunny, John. Actor. *b.* Sept. 21, 1863, New York City. *d.* 1915. The son of a British naval officer who had emigrated to the US, he grew up in Brooklyn, where he clerked in a neighborhood market before running away to join a roving minstrel show. He then worked his way up to the legitimate theater as an actor, stage manager, and director for various stock companies. In 1910 he joined Vitagraph and within months emerged as the first comic star of the American screen. Genial and rotund (he weighed about 300 pounds), he captivated audiences the world over with his roaring mirth and merry charm. During his five years in films, he made more than 160 short comedies and a number of dramatic appearances (*Vanity Fair, The Pickwick Papers,* etc.), relying on a refined pantomime style to bring alternating laughter and tears to silent film audiences. Much of his comedy material revolved around his immense size or concerned extramarital escapades, with homely Flora FINCH usually playing the perfect foil as his scrawny, ferocious wife. After John's death, George Bunny (1870–1952) tried to take his brother's place in films, capitalizing on their strong resemblance, but had little success with his few pictures for Goldwyn. He subsequently played character parts in features of the 20s.

FILMS INCLUDE: *Jack Fat and Slim Jim at Coney Island, In Neighboring Kingdoms* 1910; *The New Stenographer, Her Crowning Glory, Her Hero, Dr. Cupid, The Subduing of Mrs. Nag, The Leading Lady, My Old Dutch, A Tale of Two Cities, The Politician's Dream, Vanity Fair* 1911; *The First Violin, The Troublesome Step-Daughters, Stenographers Wanted, Cure for Pokeritis, Chumps, How He Papered the Room, Pandora's Box, A Bogus Napoleon, Leap Year Proposals, Diamond Cut Diamond, Bunny's Suicide, Bunny All at Sea, Bunny at the Derby, Freckles, Ida's Christmas* (as Santa Claus) 1912; *And His Wife Came Back, The Locket, Bunny Blarneyed/The Blarney Stone, Bunny as a Reporter, Bunny for the Cause, Bunny's Dilemma, Bunny's Honeymoon, The Autocrat of Flapjack Junction, John Tobin's Sweetheart, There's Music in the Hair, The Pickwick Papers* (filmed in England) 1913; *Father's Flirtation, Pigs Is Pigs, Polishing Up, The Honeymooners, Bunny Buys a Harem, Bunny in Disguise, Bunny's Birthday, Bunny's Mistake, Love's Old Dream, Love Luck and Gasoline* 1914; *How Cissy Made Good* 1915.

Buñuel, Luis. Director. *b.* Feb. 22, 1900, Calanda, Spain. *d.* 1983. The son of well-to-do landowners, he was educated by Jesuit priests, then went to the University of Madrid, where he befriended Salvador Dali, Garcia Lorca, and other future Spanish intellectuals. In 1920 he founded a cinema club at the university, one of the earliest in Europe. In 1925 he went to Paris, was accepted as a student at the Académie du Cinéma, and within a year was assigned as assistant director to Jean EPSTEIN on the film *Mauprat.* In 1927 he was Mario Nalpas's assistant on *La Sirène des Tropiques/Siren of the Tropics* and the following year was back with Epstein, working on *La Chute de la Maison Usher/The Fall of the House of Usher.*

During a three-day exchange of fantasies and dreams, Buñuel and DALI wrote a script for a surrealist film, which the former shot in two weeks with some assistance from Dali. The resulting 24-minute film, *Un Chien Andalou/An Andalusian Dog,* consisted of a series of unrelated and unexplainable images, the only unifying element of which was their power to shock. In one a hand seems to be devoured by ants; in another, a young woman's eyeball is slashed methodically with a razor. The film was enthusiastically received in a special screening before a gathering of Paris surrealists, who accepted Buñuel and Dali into their ranks. It is still widely shown in film societies and at universities.

In 1930, Buñuel directed his surrealist masterpiece, *L'Age d'Or/The Golden Age,* in which he laid the ideological foundations for much of his subsequent work. His savage assault on the Church, the establishment, and middle-class morality, first launched in this film, was to become for him an obsessive mission for many years to come. Dali was again to collaborate on the script, but the two young Spaniards parted ways after only a day or two of exchange of ideas. Dali's name remained in the screen credits, however. Buñuel's next film, *Las Hurdes/Land Without Bread* (1932), was a horrifying documentary account, surrealistically flavored, of the plight of village peasants, hopelessly enchained by their poverty and ignorance. As it turned out, this was his last film for many years.

Between 1933 and 1935, Buñuel was dubbing American films for Paramount and Warners, first in Paris, then in Spain. In 1935–36 he was executive producer on four routine Spanish films. The following year he contributed to a political documentary compiled from newsreels, *Madrid 36,* then went to Paris, where he supervised the production of Jean-Paul Le Chanois's *Spain 39.* In 1938, with the Spanish Civil War raging at home, Buñuel went on a special mission to Hollywood as a technical advisor on pro-Loyalist American films. He worked on one MGM project that was soon abandoned after it became clear that Franco was winning the war. Jobless and penniless, Buñuel arrived in New York and began to work for the Museum of Modern Art.

Here, from newsreel and documentary footage, he compiled a feature-length anti-Nazi film that has never been released, then worked on a series of propaganda films about the American Army. But he was dropped from the latter project because, in his words, "Dali called me an atheist." In 1944–46 he was again dubbing and supervising foreign versions for Warners in Hollywood. He was considered for the assignment as director of *The Beast with Five Fingers* and worked briefly on the preparatory stages of the project, but the job went to Robert Florey. After another abortive project, this time in France, Buñuel went to Mexico in 1947 and there renewed his long-suspended activity as film director.

Ostensibly, Buñuel seemed to be making an adjustment to the requirements of commercial cinema, accepting most projects suggested to him by producers and turning out films that proved entertaining enough for general audiences. But the iconoclastic fervor of the past began creeping back into his films, at first in disguise, as in *Los Olvidados/The Young and the Damned* (1950), then more and more audaciously until exploding with full force in *Nazarin* (1959) and *Viridiana* (1961). The latter, strangely enough, was produced in Spain with the blessings of the Spanish government and under the scrutiny of its censors. Only after the film's release did Franco's regime realize its meaning. The film was promptly banned.

Buñuel was unique among cinema's leading directors in his almost total disregard of technical virtuosity. His films were usually told in a straightforward manner with little stylistic adornment or tricky effects; yet his ideas come across not only on the intellectual level but as an aesthetic experience as well. Working economically and quickly (some suggest he actually disliked the shooting stage of a film), he was considered a good commercial risk by producers. His main concern remained what he put across and not how. His chief target was still the Church, which he attacked some times with vicious ferocity, at others with his own brand of irony and black humor ("Thank God I am still an atheist," he is quoted as saying).

Buñuel's preoccupation with sexual aberrations and far out fetishes and the iconoclastic nature of his work have made him the subject of public outcry since the beginning of his film career. As far back as 1932, in the wake of the *L'Age d'Or* controversy, Henry Miller wrote in a Paris journal: "They call Buñuel everything: traitor, anarchist, pervert, defamer, iconoclast. But lunatic they do not call him. It is true, it is lunacy he portrays, but it is not his lunacy. This stinking chaos which for a brief hour or so amalgamates under his wand, this is the lunacy of civilization, the record of man's achievement after ten thousand years of refinement."

Late in his career, Buñuel's biting criticism of various social institutions mellowed somewhat, but he still spoke with one of the boldest voices in the industry, and through such films as *Diary of a Chambermaid* (1964), *Simon of the Desert* (1965), *Belle de Jour* (1967), *The Milky Way* (1969), *Tristana* (1970), *The Discreet Charm of the Bourgeoisie* (1972), and *Le Fantôme de la Liberté* (1974) he maintained his long-standing reputation for integrity and courageous candor.

FILMS (as director): *Un Chien anadalou/An Andalusian Dog* (co-dir., co-prod., co-sc. with Salvador Dali; also edit., act.; Fr.) 1928; *L'Age d'Or/The Golden Age* (also co-sc. with Dali, edit.; Fr.) 1930; *Las Hurdes/Tierra sin Pan/Land Without Bread/Unpromised Land* (also edit.; Sp.) 1932; *Gran Casino/En el Viejo Tampico* (Mex.) 1947; *El Gran Calavera/The Great Madcap* (Mex.) 1949; *Los Olvidados/The Young and the Damned* (also co-sc.; winner of best direction prize at Cannes Festival; Mex.) 1950; *Susana/Demonio y Carne/The Devil and the Flesh* (Mex.), *La Hija del Engaño/Daughter of Deceit* (Mex.), *Una Mujer sin Amor* (Mex.), *Subida al Cielo/Mexican Bus Ride* (winner of best avant-garde film prize at Cannes; Mex.) 1951; *El Bruto/The Brute* (also co-sc.; Mex.), *Robinsón Crusoe/The Adventures of Robinson Crusoe* (also co-sc.; Mex.), *El/This Strange Passion* (also co-sc.; Mex.) 1952; *Abismos de Pasión/Cumbres Borrascosas/Wuthering Heights* (also sc.; Mex.), *La Ilusión Viaja en Tranvïa/The Illusion Travels by Streetcar* (Mex.) 1953; *El Río y la Muerte/The River and Death* (also co-sc.) 1954; *Ensayo de un Crimen/The Criminal Life of Archibaldo de la Cruz/Rehearsal for a Crime* (also co-sc.; Mex.) 1955; *Cela s'appelle l'Aurore* (also co-sc.; Fr./It.), *La Mort en ce Jardin/La Muerte en este Jardin/Gina/Evil Eden/Death in the Garden* (also co-sc.; Fr./Mex.) 1956; *Nazarin* (also co-sc.; winner of Special Jury Prize at Cannes Festival; Mex.) 1959; *La Fièvre monte à El Pao/Los Ambiciosos/Republic of Sin* (also co-sc.; Fr./Mex.) 1960; *La Joven/The Young One/Island of Shame* (also adapt., co-sc.; Mex.), *Viridiana* (also co-sc.; co-winner of Grand Prize at Cannes Festival; Sp./Mex.) 1961; *El Angel Exterminador/The Exterminating Angel* (also dial., co-sc.; Mex.) 1962; *Le Journal d'une Femme de Chambre/Diary of a Chambermaid* (also co-sc.; Fr./It.) 1964; *Simón del Desierto/Simon of the Desert* (also story, co-sc.; Mex.) 1965; *Belle de Jour* (also co-sc.; Fr./It.) 1967; *La Voie lactée/The Milky Way* (also co-sc.; Fr./It.) 1969; *Tristana* (also adapt., co-sc.; Fr./It./Sp.) 1970; *Le Charme discret de la Bourgeoisie/The Discreet Charm of the Bourgeoisie* (also co-story, co-sc.; winner of best foreign language film Academy Award; Fr.) 1972; *Le Fantôme de la Liberté* (also co-sc.; Fr.) 1974; *Cet Obscur Objet du Desir/That Obscure Object of Desire* (also co-sc.; Fr.) 1977; *Belle du Jour* (first American release) 1995.

Buono, Victor. Actor. *b.* 1938, San Diego. *d.* 1982. *ed.* Villanova. He acted in stock and on TV ('The Untouchables' series) before making an auspicious film debut in Robert Aldrich's *What Ever Happened to Baby Jane?* (1962), for which he received an Oscar nomination. Weighing 300 pounds, he was cast mostly as a heavy in a variety of Hollywood and Italian productions.

FILMS INCLUDE: *What Ever Happened to Baby Jane?* 1962; *Four for Texas* 1963; *The Strangler* (title role), *Robin and the Seven Hoods* 1964; *Hush Hush. . . Sweet Charlotte* (as Bette Davis's father); *The Greatest Story Ever Told, Young Dillinger* 1965; *The Silencers* 1966; *Who's Minding the Mint?* 1967; *Beneath the Planet of the Apes* 1970; *The Wrath of God* 1972; *Arnold* 1973; *Lo Strangolatore di Vienna/The Mad Butcher* (It.), *Moon Child* 1974; *The Evil* 1978; *The Man With Bogart's Face/Sam Marlow Private Eye* 1980.

Burel, Léonce-Henry. Director of photography, director. Born on Nov. 23, 1892, in Indret, France. *ed.* Inst. des Beaux-Arts (Paris); Nantes U. He came to films in 1915 and over the years distinguished himself as one of France's most durable and capable lensmen. He collaborated with some of France's greatest directors—Abel Gance, Jacques Feyder, Jean Renoir, and Robert Bresson—recording memorable images in many important French films. In 1951 he won the Venice Festival Award for the photography of Bresson's *The Diary of a Country Priest.* He also directed three films: *La Conquête des Gaules* (1922), *L'Evadée* (co-dir., 1922), and *La Fada* (1932).

FILMS INCLUDE (as director of photography): *Alsace* 1915; *Le Gaz mortels* 1916; *Mater Dolorosa* 1917; *La Dixième Symphonie* 1918; *J'accuse* 1919; *La Roue/The Wheel, Crainquebille* 1922; *Visage d'Enfants* 1923; *L'Image* 1924; *Napoléon* 1926; *L'Equipage* 1928; *Danton* 1931; *Abus de Confiance/Abused Confidence, La Mort du Cygne/Ballerina* 1937; *Retour àl'Aube/She Returned at Dawn* 1938; *La Vénus aveugle* 1941; *Les Mystères de Paris* 1943; *Les Casse-Pieds/The Spice of Life* 1949; *Le Journal d'un Curé de Campagne/Diary of a Country Priest* 1951; *La Véritésur Bébé Donge* 1952; *Marianne de ma Jeunesse/Marianne of My Youth* 1955; *Un Condamné à Mort s'est échappé/A Man Escaped* 1956; *Pickpocket* 1959; *Le Procès de Jeanne d'Arc/The Trial of Joan of Arc* 1962; *Un Drole de Paroissien/Thank Heaven for Small Favors, Chair de*

Poule/Highway Pickup 1963; *Les Compagnons de la Marguerite* 1966; *Bonaparte et la Revolution* 1971.

Burfield, Joan. See FONTAINE, Joan.

Burge, Stuart. Director. Born on Jan. 15, 1918, in Brentwood, England. Trained as a civil engineer, he entered the British theater as an actor and began directing in 1948. He has directed many distinguished stage and TV plays, mainly from the classic repertoire, and in the 60s turned out four film adaptations of theatrical productions.

FILMS: *There Was a Crooked Man* 1960; *Uncle Vanya* 1963; *Othello* (version starring Laurence Olivier) 1965; *The Mikado* 1967; *Julius Caesar* (version starring Charlton Heston and John Gielgud) 1970.

Burgess, Dorothy. Actress. *b.* Mar. 4, 1907, Los Angeles. *d.* 1961. The daughter of actress Grace Burgess and a niece of Fay Bainter, she started out as a specialty dancer and became a Broadway ingenue at 17. She starred in a number of Broadway plays and musicals before going to Hollywood with the advent of sound to play the female lead in *In Old Arizona.* Her film career wavered later between leads in independent B pictures and secondary roles for major studios. She returned to the stage in 1934 but was back in Hollywood in the early 40s for an occasional supporting role.

FILMS INCLUDE: *In Old Arizona, Pleasure Crazed, Protection, A Song of Kentucky* 1929; *Swing High, Recaptured Love* 1930; *Taxi, Play Girl, The Stoker* 1932; *Ladies They Talk About, What Price Decency?, Strictly Personal, Hold Your Man, From Headquarters, Easy Millions* 1933; *Fashions of 1934, Orient Express, A Modern Hero, The Circus Clown, Gambling* 1934; *A Village Tale* 1935; *I Want a Divorce* 1940; *Lady for a Night* 1942; *Girls in Chains* 1943.

Burke, Billie. Actress. *b.* Mary William Ethelbert Appleton Burke, Aug. 7, 1885, Washington, D.C. *d.* 1970. The only child of William (Billy) Burke, a singing clown in the Barnum and Bailey circus, she adopted her father's nickname before making her debut on the London stage in 1903. The family had moved to London when Billie was eight, and she received her education in England and in France. She appeared on the English stage for four years, then, after her father's death, she was brought to New York in 1907 to star opposite John Drew in 'My Wife.'

A delicate beauty of piquant personality, she soon was the toast of Broadway. Celebrities like Mark Twain, Enrico Caruso, James M. Barrie, and W. Somerset Maugham were among her backstage admirers. In 1913 the latter escorted her to a New Year's Eve party at the Astor Hotel, where she met Florenz ZIEGFELD. The following year the producer and the actress eloped and were married in a Hoboken, N.J., parsonage. Until Ziegfeld's death in 1932 they lived in a Hastings-on-Hudson estate, surrounded by a menagerie that included an elephant, two bears, two lion cubs, 15 dogs, and a herd of deer.

In 1915, Miss Burke accepted an offer of $300,000 from film pioneer Thomas H. INCE to appear in the film *Peggy.* She went on to star in about a dozen silent films, with Ziegfeld acting as her agent. In 1921 she returned to Broadway. In 1931, in an attempt to help her husband financially—he had been wiped out by the 1929 crash—she went back to Hollywood and into sound films. She played some leads and scores of delightful supporting roles in her new screen image as a feather-brained, twittery comedienne, memorably in *Topper* (1937) and its sequels, and as Glinda, the Good Fairy, in *The Wizard of Oz* (1939). In 1936 she acted as an advisor on the film *The Great Ziegfeld,* in which she was portrayed by Myrna Loy. She was nominated for an Academy Award for *Merrilly We Live* (1938). Autobiographies: *With a Feather on My Nose* (1949); *With Powder on My Nose* (1959).

FEATURE FILMS: *Peggy, Gloria's Romance* (serial) 1916; *The Mysterious Miss Terry, Arms and the Girl, The Land of Promise* 1917; *Eve's Daughter, Let's Get a Divorce, In Pursuit of Polly, The Make-Believe Wife* 1918; *Good Gracious Annabelle!, The Misleading Widow, Sadie Love, Wanted—A Husband* 1919; *Away Goes Prudence, The Frisky Mrs. Johnson* 1920; *The Education of Elizabeth* 1921; *Glorifying the American Girl* (unbilled cameo) 1929; *A Bill of Divorcement* 1932; *Christopher Strong, Dinner at Eight, Only Yesterday* 1933; *Finishing School, Where Sinners Meet, We're Rich Again, Forsaking All Others* 1934; *Only Eight Hours, Society Doctor, After Office Hours, Becky Sharp, Doubting Thomas, A Feather in Her Hat, She Couldn't Take It, Splendor* 1935; *My American Wife, Piccadilly Jim, Craig's Wife* 1936; *Parnell, Topper, The Bride Wore Red, Navy Blue and Gold* 1937; *Everybody Sing, Merrily We Live, The Young in Heart* 1938; *Topper Takes a Trip, Zenobia, Bridal Suite, The Wizard of Oz* (as Glinda, the Good Fairy), *Eternally Yours, Remember?* 1939; *The Ghost Comes Home, And One Was Beautiful, The Captain Is a Lady, Irene, Dulcy, Hullabaloo* 1940; *Topper Returns, One Night in Lisbon, The Wild Man of Borneo* 1941; *The Man Who Came to Dinner, What's Cookin', In This Our Life, They All Kissed the Bride, Girl Trouble* 1942; *Hi Diddle Diddle, Gildersleeve on Broadway, You're a Lucky Fellow Mr. Smith, So's Your Uncle* 1943; *The Laramie Trail* 1944; *Swing Out Sister, The Cheaters* 1945; *Breakfast in Hollywood, The Bachelor's Daughters* 1946; *The Barkleys of Broadway, And Baby Makes Three* 1949; *Father of the Bride, Boy From Indiana, Three Husbands* 1950; *Father's Little Dividend* 1951; *Small Town Girl* 1953; *The Young Philadelphians* 1959; *Sergeant Rutledge, Pepe* 1960.

Burke, Johnny. Lyricist. *b.* Oct. 3, 1908, Antioch, Calif. *d.* 1964. A former entertainer, he appeared in vaudeville, the 'Ziegfeld Follies,' and short musical films of the late 20s and early 30s. At one time he was also pianist for Irving Berlin. From the mid-30s he contributed numerous songs for Hollywood films and the recording industry, including such hits as 'Moonlight Becomes You,' 'Personality,' and 'Life Is So Peculiar.' From 1940 he collaborated with James VAN HEUSEN, and together they won an Academy Award for the song 'Swinging on a Star' in the film *Going My Way* (1944). They composed many other songs for Bing Crosby. For additional credits of their collaboration (1940–55), see VAN HEUSEN, James.

FILMS INCLUDE: *Murder at the Vanities* 1934; *Go West Young Man, Pennies from Heaven* 1936; *Double or Nothing* 1931; *Doctor Rhythm, Sing You Sinners* 1938; *East Side of Heaven, The Star Maker* 1939; *Road to Singapore, Rhythm on the River* 1940.

Burkina Faso. Formerly Upper Volta (until 1984), this tiny, impoverished, landlocked country in West Africa has been one of the pioneers and leading forces in AFRICAN cinema. The efforts of its determined and creative filmmakers have been helped by a tradition of cinematic innovation and government arts support inherited from France, the country's former colonizer. At the same time, the films are distinctively African, borrowing from indigenous folklore and focusing on contemporary social tensions. Burkina Faso's first film was *A Minuit l'Indépendance* (1961), a government-funded documentary on the ceremonies celebrating the newly won independence of many African nations. The first feature-length film was *Le Sang de parias/The Pariahs' Blood* (1972) by Mamadou Djim Kola. Gaston KABORÉ's *Wend Kuuni/The Gift of God* (1982), the tale of a mute orphan adopted by a weaver in pre-colonial times, gained international recognition for the director and his country, as did his later work *Zan Boko* (1988). Idrissa OUEDRAOGO, director of *Yaaba* (1989), a magical story of rural life, is another prominent figure in Burkinese film. Drissa Touré and Pierre Yaméogo are also promising Burkinese directors.

Burkina Faso's capital, Ouagadougou, is an acknowledged center of African film. FESPACO, the Pan-African Film Festival, has been held here since 1969; it occurs biannually, alternating with the Film Days in Carthage, Tunisia. Ouagadougou is also the base for FEPACI, the Pan-African Federation of Filmmakers, presided over by Gaston Kaboré, and for CINAFRIC, black Africa's first commercially-run studio complex. A bilateral production agreement has given Burkina Faso access to French funds for co-productions between the two nations.

Burks, Robert. Director of photography. *b.* 1910, Newport Beach, Calif. *d.* 1968. He started out as a special-effects expert for Warner Bros., working in that capacity on many prestige pictures from 1944 to 1949. He then became a top-ranking director of photography, for Warners and later for Paramount, providing the camera work for most of Alfred HITCHCOCK's films in the 50s and the 60s. He won an Academy Award for the color photography of Hitchcock's *To Catch a Thief* (1955).

FILMS INCLUDE: As special-effects man—*In This Our Life* 1942; *Arsenic and Old Lace* 1944; *Escape in the Desert, Pride of the Marines* 1945; *The Verdict, Night and Day, The Big Sleep* 1946; *The Unfaithful, My Wild Irish Rose, The Unsuspected, Cry Wolf, Possessed* 1947; *Key Largo* 1948; *The Younger Brothers* 1949. As director of photography—*A Kiss in the Dark, The Fountainhead, Task Force* (co-phot.), *Beyond the Forest* 1949; *The Glass Menagerie* 1950; *The Enforcer, Strangers on a Train, Come Fill the Cup* 1951; *Room for One More, Mara Maru* 1952; *The Desert Song, Hondo, I Confess* 1953; *Dial M for Murder, Rear Window* 1954; *To Catch a Thief, The Trouble with Harry* 1955; *The Man Who Knew Too Much, The Vagabond King* 1956; *The Wrong Man, The Spirit of St. Louis* (co-phot.) 1957; *Vertigo* 1958; *The Black Orchid, North by Northwest, But Not for Me* 1959; *The Rat Race* 1960; *The Great Impostor, The Pleasure of His Company* 1961; *The Music Man* 1962; *The Birds* 1963; *Marnie* 1964; *Once a Thief, A Patch of Blue* 1965; *A Covenant with Death, Waterhole #3* 1967; *Chubasco* (co-phot.) 1968.

Burness, Pete. Animator. Born on June 16, 1910, in Los Angeles. Worked for various animation units in the 40s, including MGM's Tom and Jerry cartoons. In 1949 he joined UPA, where he created the company's most popular cartoon character, Mister Magoo, a myopic, bulbous-nosed, short-tempered little man with more than an accidental resemblance to W. C. Fields. He won an Academy Award for best cartoon short for *When Magoo Flew* (1953), *Mister Magoo's Puddle Jumper* (1956). Burness's later work includes TV's long-running cartoon program of the 60s, 'Bullwinkle Show.'

ANIMATED SHORTS INCLUDE: *Bungled Bungalow* 1950; *Sloppy Jalopy, Captains Outrageous, The Dog Snatcher* 1952; *Magoo Goes West, Safety Spin, When Magoo Flew* (Academy Award) 1953; *Magoo Goes Skiing, Destination Magoo* 1954; *Magoo Express, Stagedoor Magoo* 1955; *Mister Magoo's Puddle Jumper* 1956.

Burnett, Carol. Actress, comedienne, singer. Born on Apr. 26, 1933, in San Antonio, Tex. *ed.* UCLA. The daughter of a movie theater owner, she appeared in New York revues before gaining popularity as a regular on the Garry Moore TV show in the late 50s. Her career blossomed further in the 60s with a couple of Broadway shows, several lavish TV specials, and finally her own highly successful weekly television revue program, 'The Carol Burnett Show.' Among numerous prizes, she won five Emmy Awards. A truly versatile actress, she received the best actress prize at the San Sebastian Festival for her role in *A Wedding* (1978). In 1980, she won a much-publicized $1.6 million libel suit against the *National Enquirer.* In 1985 she was elected to the Academy of Television Arts and Sciences Hall of Fame. One of her three children is actress-singer Carrie Hamilton.

FILMS: *Who's Been Sleeping in My Bed?* 1963; *Pete 'n' Tillie* 1972; *The Front Page* 1974; *A Wedding* 1978; *Health* 1979; *The Four Seasons, Chu Chu and the Philly Flash* 1981; *Annie* 1982; *Noises Off* 1992.

Burnett, Charles. Director/screenwriter, also cameraman. Born in 1944 in Vicksburg, Miss. *ed.* Los Angeles Community College (electronics); UCLA (theater, arts, film, writing, languages). Revered independent African-American director of disturbing works on the black family. Burnett enjoyed a renewed interest in his earlier, overlooked films upon the highly publicized release of his *To Sleep with Anger*, a brooding low-budget film that won awards from the Los Angeles Film Critics Association and the National Society of Film Critics, among others.

FILMS INCLUDE: *Killer of Sheep* (also prod., sc., ph., ed.) 1977; *My Brother's Wedding* (also prod., sc., ph.) 1983; *Bless Their Little Hearts* (sc., ph.) 1984; *Guests of Hotel Astoria* (ph.) 1989; *To Sleep With Anger* (also sc.) 1990.

Burnett, W(illiam) R(iley). Novelist, screenwriter. *b.* Nov. 25, 1899, Springfield, Ohio. *d.* 1982. *ed.* Ohio State. Worked for seven years as a statistician for the state of Ohio before turning to writing, in 1928. Specialized in crime and gangster stories. His first novel, *Little Caesar* (published 1929), provided the basis for the 1931 Mervyn LeRoy film (starring Edward G. Robinson), which was among the pace setters in the gangster film cycle of the 30s. Several others of his many novels were adapted for the screen, notably *Iron Man, The Dark Command, High Sierra, Nobody Lives Forever,* and *The Asphalt Jungle.* Burnett began writing screenplays, alone or in collaboration, early in the 30s. He contributed, along with his novels and stories, many original scripts and adaptations for motion pictures into the 60s.

FILMS INCLUDE: *Little Caesar* (novel basis), *The Finger Points* (co-story, co-sc.), *Iron Man* (novel) 1931; *The Beast of the City* (story), *Scarface* (co-sc.), *Law and Order* (novel, *Saint Johnson*) 1932; *Dark Hazard* (novel) 1934; *The Whole Town's Talking* (story), *Dr. Socrates* (novel) 1935; *36 Hours to Kill* (story) 1936; *King of the Underworld* (novel, *Dr. Socrates)* 1939; *Dark Command* (novel) 1940; *High Sierra* (co-sc., from own novel), *The Get-Away* (co-sc.) 1941; *This Gun for Hire* (co-sc.), *Wake Island* (co-story, co-sc.) 1942; *Background to Danger* (sc.), *Crash Dive* (story), *Action in the North Atlantic* (co-dial.) 1943; *San Antonio* (co-story, co-sc.) 1945; *Nobody Lives Forever* (sc., from own novel) 1946; *Belle Starr's Daughter* (story, sc.), *Yellow Sky* (story) 1948; *The Asphalt Jungle* (novel), *Vendetta* (sc.) 1950; *Iron Man* (novel), *The Racket* (sc.) 1951; *Arrowhead* (novel, *Adobe Walls*) 1953; *Dangerous Mission* (co-sc.) 1954; *Captain Lightfoot* (story, co-sc.), *Illegal* (co-sc.), *I Died a Thousand Times* (sc., from own novel, *High Sierra*) 1955; *Accused of Murder* (co-sc., from own novel *Vanity Row*) 1956; *The Badlanders* (novel, *The Asphalt Jungle*) 1958; *September Storm* (sc.) 1960; *Sergeants Three* (story, sc.) 1962; *Cairo* (novel), *The Great Escape* (co-sc.) 1963; *Cool Breeze* (novel, *The Asphalt Jungle*) 1972.

Burnette, Smiley. Actor. *b.* Lester Alvin Burnette, Mar. 18, 1911, in Summum, Ill. *d.* 1967, of leukemia. The son of a preacher, he began appearing in local radio and vaudeville shows after graduating from high school. He and his friend Gene

AUTRY, an aspiring cowboy singer, appeared together on stage and on the National Barn Dance radio show for several years. They entered films in 1934, and between 1935 and 1942 appeared together in 81 motion pictures, with Burnette playing Autry's comic sidekick, Frog Milhouse. From 1940 to 1952 Burnette appeared regularly on the list of the top ten money-making Western stars, the first supporting actor to achieve that distinction.

In all, Burnette appeared in some 200 Western films. Among his other screen partners were Allan "Rocky" Lane, Sunset Carson, and Charles Starrett. He also wrote more than 300 Western songs, many of which were used in his films. He retired from the movies in 1953 but appeared on TV from 1963 to 1967 as the railroad engineer in the series 'Petticoat Junction.'

FILMS INCLUDE: *Mystery Mountain* (serial), *In Old Santa Fe* 1934; *The Phantom Empire* (serial), *Tumblin' Tumbleweeds* 1935; *Border Patrolman, The Singing Cowboy* 1936; *Dick Tracy* (serial), *Manhattan Merry-Go-Round* 1937; *The Stadium Murders, Under Western Stars, Rhythm of the Saddle* 1938; *South of the Border* 1939; *Rancho Grande* 1940; *Down Mexico Way* 1941; *Cowboy Serenade* 1942; *The Desert Horseman* 1946; *Terror Trail* 1947; *Last Days of Boot Hill* 1948; *Quick on the Trigger, Laramie* 1949; *Across the Badlands* 1950; *Cyclone Fury, Bonanza Town* 1951; *Smoky Canyon* 1952; *Winning of the West* 1953.

Burns, Bob. Actor. *b.* Aug. 2, 1893, Van Buren, Ark. *d.* 1956. A vaudeville and nightclub comedian of hillbilly humor, he also enjoyed some popularity on radio and in films of the 30s. Typically played plain country folks who overcome their naïveté with innate common sense. Nicknamed "Bazooka" after the crude wind instrument he invented and played. Also known as "The Arkansas Philosopher."

FILMS INCLUDE: *Quick Millions* 1931; *The Singing Vagabond, The Courageous Avenger* 1935; *Rhythm on the Range, Guns and Guitars, The Big Broadcast of 1937* 1936; *Mountain Music, Wells Fargo, Waikiki Wedding* 1937; *The Arkansas Traveler, Radio City Revels, Tropic Holiday* 1938; *I'm From Missouri, Our Leading Citizen* 1939; *Alias the Deacon, Comin' Round the Mountain, Prairie Schooners* 1940; *Belle of the Yukon* 1944.

Burns, George. Actor. *b.* Nathan Birnbaum, on Jan. 20, 1896, in New York City. *d.* 1996. He started out in vaudeville as a singer in a children's quartet. Later he tried a roller-skating act and finally comedy. In 1925 he met Gracie ALLEN, with whom he formed the Burns and Allen comedy team. They married the following year and became popular in vaudeville, on radio, and in TV and films. In 1975, after an absence of 35 years, Burns, long-since widowed, made a triumphant comeback to the screen with an Oscar-winning performance in the comedy *The Sunshine Boys.* In 1977 he scored another success, playing the title role in *Oh God!* In the late 80s and early 90s, approaching 100, he was still going strong, starring in films and TV specials, chomping on his cigar, flirting with the ladies, writing popular books, and scoffing at the notion of retirement. Author: *I Love Her, That's Why; Living It Up, or They Still Love Me in Altoona!; The Third Time Around; How to Live to Be 100, or More!: The Ultimate Diet, Sex, and Exercise Book; Dr. Burns' Prescription for Happiness; Dear George: Advice and Answers From America's Leading Expert on Everything from A to Z; Gracie; Wisdom of the 90s.*

FEATURE FILMS: *The Big Broadcast* 1932; *College Humor, International House* 1933; *Six of a Kind, We're Not Dressing, Many Happy Returns* 1934; *Love in Bloom, The Big Broadcast of 1936, Here Comes Cookie* 1935; *College Holiday, The Big Broadcast of 1937* 1936; *A Damsel in Distress* 1937; *College Swing* 1938; *Honolulu* 1939; *The Solid Gold Cadillac* (narr. only) 1956; *The Sunshine Boys* 1975; *Oh God!* 1977; *Sergeant Pepper's Lonely Hearts Club Band, Movie Movie* 1978; *Just You and Me Kid, Going in Style* 1979; *Oh God! Book II* 1980; *Oh God! You Devil* 1984; *18 Again!* 1988; *Radioland Murders* 1994.

Burns, Ralph. Composer, music director. Born on June 29, 1922, in Newton, Mass. He won Academy Awards for the orchestrations of *Cabaret* and *All That Jazz.*

FILMS INCLUDE: *Cabaret* 1972; *Mame, Lenny* 1974; *Lucky Lady* 1975; *New York New York* 1977; *Movie Movie* 1978; *Urban Cowboy* 1980; *Annie, My Favorite Year, Jinxed!* 1982; *National Lampoon's Vacation, Star 80* 1983; *The Muppets Take Manhattan* 1984; *Perfect* 1985; *In the Mood* 1987; *All Dogs Go To Heaven, Bert Rigby You're a Fool* 1989.

burnt up. Description of a film that is overexposed.

Burr, Raymond. Actor. *b.* May 21, 1917, New Westminster, B.C., Canada. *d.* 1993. *ed.* Stanford; U. of California; Columbia. He came to films in 1946 after several years on stage and radio and was immediately put to work as a smooth heavy. For the next decade his stout frame was seen in many pictures, both major and minor, almost invariably as a villain. His magnetic voice and sad eyes often had a humanizing effect on the scores of ominous characters he played. In 1957 he made a sharp switch from villain to hero as the star of the popular TV series 'Perry Mason,' a role with which he was identified for the next eight years. This and the subsequent TV series 'Ironside,' in which he played a detective who is confined to a wheelchair, limited his feature film activity. He maintained homes in Los Angeles, where he grew orchids, and in the Fiji Islands, where he ran a copra plantation. In 1988 he formed Royal Blue, a TV production company. Until just before his death he remained active in TV, reprising in specials his Perry Mason and Ironside characters.

FILMS INCLUDE: *San Quentin* 1946; *Desperate* 1947; *Ruthless, Sleep My Love, Raw Deal, The Pitfall, Walk a Crooked Mile, Adventures of Don Juan* 1948; *Bride of Vengeance, Black Magic, Red Light, Abandoned* 1949; *Key to the City, Love Happy, Borderline* 1950; *M, His Kind of Woman, The Magic Carpet, New Mexico, A Place in the Sun* 1951; *Mara Maru, Horizons West, Meet Danny Wilson* 1952; *The Blue Gardenia, Tarzan and the She-Devil, Fort Algiers* 1953; *Gorilla at Large, Casanova's Big Night, Rear Window, Passion* 1954; *You're Never Too Young, A Man Alone* 1955; *Godzilla* (Jap.), *Please Murder Me, Ride the High Iron, Great Day in the Morning, A Cry in the Night* 1956; *Crime of Passion, Affair in Havana* 1957; *Desire in the Dust* 1960; *P.J.* 1968; *Tomorrow Never Comes* (UK/Can.) 1978; *The Return/The Alien's Return* 1980; *Out of the Blue, Airplane II: The Sequel* 1982; *Godzilla 1985* (Jap.) 1985; *Delirious* 1991.

burst wipe. See WIPE.

Burstall, Tim. Director, producer. Born on Apr. 20, 1929, in Stockton-on-Tees, England. He moved to Australia with his family when he was eight and after graduating from college worked for two years as a film librarian in Canberra. In 1952 he made several trips to Antarctica as a journalist. Settling in Melbourne, he formed a film company and in 1959 began directing and producing children's shorts. In 1965, he went to the US on a study grant and while attending UCLA film classes was assistant on Martin Ritt's *Hombre.* Returning to Melbourne, he directed his first feature, *2,000 Weeks* (1978), a forerunner in the revival of Australian cinema in the 70s. He provided the rebirth further momentum with *Alvin Purple* (1973), a voyeuristic comedy made on a shoestring budget, which became

Australia's highest grossing film to that date. Despite his penchant for lusty themes, and his sometimes crass treatment of them, Burstall's contribution to the new Australian cinema is widely acknowledged.

FILMS INCLUDE: *2,000 Weeks* 1968; *Stork* 1971; *Libido* ('The Child' episode), *Alvin Purple/The Sex Therapist* 1973; *Alvin Rides Again, Petersen/Jock Petersen* 1974; *End Play* 1975; *Eliza Frazer* 1976; *High Rolling* (prod. only) 1977; *The Last of the Knucklemen* 1979; *Attack Force Z* 1980; *Duet for Four* 1982; *Kangaroo* 1986.

Burstyn, Ellen. Actress. Born Edna Rae Gillooly, on Dec. 7, 1932, in Detroit, to a middle-class Irish family. At 18 she left home to seek fame and fortune as a model in Texas and New York, under the name Edna Rae. She became Keri Flynn when she danced in a Montreal nightclub chorus line and changed again to Erica Dean for a screen test in the mid-50s. In 1957 she broke the Broadway barrier, appearing in the play 'Fair Game,' under the name Ellen McRae. She retained the name through the mid-60s while acting in a couple of films and many TV programs, including 'The Doctors' series, and finally became Ellen Burstyn when she entered her third, since aborted, marriage.

Her big breaks came after she had spent an interlude studying acting seriously with Lee Strasberg at the Actors Studio. She scored on the screen in the early 70s, winning both the New York and the National Film Critics awards for her performance in *The Last Picture Show.* She was also nominated for Oscars for that film and for *The Exorcist.* Her career peaked in 1975, when, at the age of 43, she won both the best actress Academy Award for *Alice Doesn't Live Here Anymore* and the Broadway Tony Award for her performance in the play 'Same Time, Next Year.' She herself packaged *Alice*—found the script, provided additional dialogue, selected the director and players, and sold it to Warner Bros. for 10 percent of the profits. In the late 70s and early 80s she was nominated twice more for Oscars as best actress, for *Same Time, Next Year* and *Resurrection.* After Lee Strasberg's death in 1982, she was named co-artistic director (with Al Pacino) of the Actors Studio, a post she held until 1987. She served as president of Actors Equity from 1982 to 1985. In 1986 she starred in the TV comedy series 'The Ellen Burstyn Show.'

FILMS: *For Those Who Think Young, Goodbye Charlie* (both as Ellen McRae) 1964; *Pit Stop* (as Ellen McRae) 1969; *Tropic of Cancer, Alex in Wonderland* 1970; *The Last Picture Show* 1971; *The King of Marvin Gardens* 1972; *The Exorcist* 1973; *Harry and Tonto* 1974; *Alice Doesn't Live Here Anymore* 1975; *Providence* (Fr.) 1977; *A Dream of Passion* (Gr.), *Same Time Next Year* 1978; *Resurrection* 1980; *Silence of the North* (Can.) 1981; *The Ambassador, In Our Hands* (doc.) 1984; *Twice in a Lifetime* 1985; *Dear America: Letters Home from Vietnam* (doc.; voice only), *Hello Actors Studio* (doc.) 1987; *Hanna's War* 1988; *Dying Young* 1991; *The Cemetery Club* 1993; *Ed Wood, When a Man Loves a Woman* 1994; *The Baby-Sitters Club, How to Make an American Quilt, Roommates* 1995; *Mars Attacks!, Spitfire Grill* 1996.

Burton, Richard. Actor. *b.* Richard Walter Jenkins, Jr., in 1925, Pontrhydfen, South Wales. *d.* 1984. The 12th of 13 children of a coal miner, he won a scholarship to Oxford, thanks to the tutelage of his schoolmaster, Philip Burton, from whom he later acquired his professional name. Just before entering the university, he made his stage debut in Liverpool in 'Druid's Rest' in 1943. The following year he went with that play to London. From 1944 to 1947 he served with the Royal Air Force as a navigator. He returned to the stage in 1948 and the same year made his debut in British films in *The Last Days of Dolwyn.* It was on the set of this film that he met his first wife, Welsh actress Sybil Williams.

Burton's reputation as a fine actor began with his performance in the London production of Christopher Fry's 'The Lady's Not for Burning' (1949). In 1950 he played the same role on Broadway, to much critical acclaim. Alternating between stage and screen, and between England and the US, he played in his first American film, *My Cousin Rachel,* in 1952. The following year he played Hamlet with the Old Vic Company at the Edinburgh Festival. He stayed with that company through several other Shakespearean productions. In the meantime, he continued making his mark in such films as *The Robe, Prince of Players,* and *Alexander the Great.* Broadway audiences saw more of him in 'Time Remembered' (1957) and the musical 'Camelot' (1960). He was also seen on TV as Heathcliff in 'Wuthering Heights' (1958).

On the set of 20th Century-Fox's multimillion-dollar production of *Cleopatra,* Burton's status changed from that of a highly respected actor to that of a widely admired and publicized movie star. The new adulation followed his much publicized and often sensational off-screen romance with Elizabeth TAYLOR, who played Cleopatra to his Mark Antony. Their love story continued making headlines after the film's release in 1963, when he divorced Sybil to marry Miss Taylor, who had left her fourth husband, singer Eddie Fisher. When Burton came to New York City in 1964 to play Hamlet in the John Gielgud production, huge crowds gathered nightly on Broadway, besieging the stage door in a manner reminiscent of matinee-idol days. In that year he also published a novel, *A Christmas Story.*

Burton's new status as a superstar was reflected in the 60s in the huge salaries he and his wife and screen partner commanded—averaging a million dollars each per picture—but several of their films were panned by critics and failed to click at the box office. Burton, who was blessed with a commanding screen presence and one of the finest speaking voices around, was nominated for Academy Awards seven times—as best supporting player for *My Cousin Rachel* (1952) and as best actor for *The Robe* (1953), *Becket* (1964), *The Spy Who Came in From the Cold* (1965), *Who's Afraid of Virginia Woolf?* (1966), *Anne of the Thousand Days* (1969), and *Equus* (1977)—but never won the coveted Oscar. The Burtons divorced early in the 70s, reconciled and separated several times amid much publicity, remarried in 1975, and divorced again the following year, each later marrying another partner. Burton, whose turbulent life was frequently accented by heavy drinking and passionate explosions, seemed to be finally within reach of calm respectability when he died suddenly of a cerebral hemorrhage. Befitting his international status and his loyalty to his roots, he was buried in Switzerland wearing red, the national color of Wales. His fourth wife, Sally, a former BBC continuity girl, and actress daughter, Kate Burton (*b.* Feb. 16, 1957, Geneva), were at his side.

FILMS: In the UK—*The Last Days of Dolwyn/Dolwyn, Now Barabbas Was a Robber* 1949; *Waterfront, The Woman With No Name/Her Panelled Door* 1950; *Green Grow the Rushes* 1951. In the US—*My Cousin Rachel* 1952; *The Desert Rats, The Robe* 1953; *Prince of Players* (as Edwin Booth), *The Rains of Ranchipur* 1955; *Alexander the Great* (title role) 1956; *Sea Wife* (UK), *Amère Victoire/Bitter Victory* (Fr.) 1957; *Look Back in Anger* (UK) 1959; *The Bramble Bush, Ice Palace* 1960; *The Longest Day* 1962; *Cleopatra* (as Mark Antony; US/UK), *The V.I.P.s* (UK) 1963; *Becket* (as Thomas à Becket; UK/US), *The Night of the Iguana, Hamlet* (filmed Broadway play) 1964; *What's New Pussycat?* (cameo; US/Fr.), *The Sandpiper, The Spy Who Came in From the Cold* (UK) 1965; *Who's Afraid of Virginia Woolf?* 1966; *The Taming of the Shrew* (as Petruchio; US/It.), *Doctor Faustus* (as Faust; also co-dir. with Nevill Coghill, co-prod.; UK/It.), *The Comedians* (US/Fr.) 1967;

Boom! (US/UK), *Candy* (US/Fr./It.) 1968; *Where Eagles Dare* (UK), *Staircase, Anne of the Thousand Days* (as King Henry VIII; UK) 1969; *Raid on Rommel, Villain* (UK) 1971; *Hammersmith Is Out, Sutjeska* (as Marshal Tito; Yug.), *Bluebeard* (title role; Hung.), *The Assassination of Trotsky* (as Trotsky; Fr./It.) 1972; *Divorce His Divorce Hers* (3-hr., 2-pt. TV drama), *Rappresaglia/Massacre in Rome* (It.) 1973; *Il Viaggio/The Voyage* (It.), *The Klansmen* 1974; *Jackpot* 1975; *Exorcist II: The Heretic, Equus* 1977; *The Medusa Touch* (UK), *The Wild Geese* (UK), *California Suite* (cameo) 1978; *Sergeant Steiner 2/Breakthrough* 1979 (W. Ger.) 1979; *Circle of Two* (Can.) 1980; *Absolution* (UK; release delayed from 1978) 1981; *Wagner* (title role; UK/Hung./Aus.; orig. for TV) 1983; *1984* (UK) 1984.

Burton, Tim. Director. Born in 1960, in Burbank, Calif. The son of a Parks Department employee, he spent many reclusive childhood hours watching cartoons and horror films on TV and began drawing cartoons while still in grade school. He won a Disney fellowship to study animation at the California Institute of the Arts and at age 20 began working at DISNEY as an apprentice animator. He achieved success with his own first animated film, the six-minute, award-winning short *Vincent* (1982), modeled after and narrated by his childhood hero, Vincent Price. Turning to live-action shorts, he made a version of *Hansel and Gretel* featuring an all-Asian cast. He next directed for Disney *Frankenweenie,* a 30-minute live-action parody of *Frankenstein* in which the monster is a dog. Deemed too scary for children, the film was never released, but it led to Burton being hired by Warner Bros. as the director of *Pee-wee's Big Adventure,* which became a box-office hit. Meant for the kiddie market, the film struck certain critics with its originality, visual inventiveness, and eye for the absurd, qualities that became Burton's hallmarks and were strongly evident in his next three films, the box-office sleeper *Beetlejuice,* the blockbuster hit *Batman,* and the widely acclaimed adult fairy tale *Edward Scissorhands.* The sequel *Batman Returns* extended the original movie's weird symbolism of childhood images and adult obsessions. Following *Batman Returns* he signed a deal to produce films for Disney.

FEATURE FILMS: *Pee-wee's Big Adventure* 1985; *Beetlejuice* 1988; *Batman* 1989; *Edward Scissorhands* (also co-story, co-prod.) 1990; *Batman Returns* (also co-prod.) 1992; *Tim Burton's The Nightmare Before Christmas* (co-prod., story) 1993; *Cabin Boy* (co-prod.), *Ed Wood* 1994; *Mars Attacks!* 1996.

Burum, Stephen H. Director of photography. Born ca. 1940, in Visalia, Calif. Raised in the San Joaquin Valley, he attended Reedly College, then transferred to the UCLA Film School as a classmate of Francis Ford Coppola. He continued there as a student-teacher in the master's program, under the tutelage of cinematographers James Wong HOWE and Charles G. CLARKE. He gained field experience shooting a mini-budget feature in 1969 and Army films during his military service as a draftee, then worked in television, winning an Emmy Award for the special-effects cinematography of public TV's famous 'Cosmos' series. He was credited with additional footage on *The Black Stallion* and as second-unit cameraman (aerials and transitions) on Coppola's *Apocalypse Now* (both 1979) before graduating to full cinematographer in the early 80s. He soon became established as one of Hollywood's leading craftsmen in his field.

FILMS INCLUDE: *Wild Gypsies* 1969; *The Escape Artist* 1982; *The Outsiders, Rumble Fish, Uncommon Valor* 1983; *Body Double* 1984; *St. Elmo's Fire, The Bride* 1985; *Nutcracker* 1986; *The Untouchables* 1987; *Arthur 2 on the Rocks* 1988; *Casualties of War, The War of the Roses* 1989; *I Love You to Death* (addnl. phot.) 1990.

Buscemi, Steve. Actor, performance artist. Born in 1958 in Brooklyn, N.Y. A collaborator in theater with Mark Boone, Jr., and in marriage with performance artist and choreographer Jo Andres, he has consistently appeared in quirky films with a strong cult following. Often cited for his performance in *Parting Glances* as an offbeat video artist dying of AIDS.

FILMS INCLUDE: *The Way It Is or Eurydice in the Avenues* 1984; *No Picnic, Parting Glances, Sleepwalk* 1986; *Force of Circumstance, Heart, Kiss Daddy Goodnight* 1987; *Call Me, Coffee and Cigarettes Part Two* (short), *Heart of Midnight, Vibes* 1988; *Bloodhounds of Broadway, Borders, Mystery Train, New York Stories, Slaves of New York* 1989; *King of New York, Miller's Crossing, Tales From the Darkside: The Movie* 1990; *Zandalee*, 1991; *In the Soup* 1992; *Airheads, Floundering, The Hudsucker Proxy* 1994; *Desperado, Things to Do in Denver When You're Dead* 1995; *Escape From L.A., Fargo, Kansas City, The Search for One-Eyed Jimmy, Somebody to Love, Trees Lounge* (also dir.) 1996.

Busch, Mae. Actress. *b.* Jan. 20, 1897, Melbourne, Australia. *d.* 1946. In the US from childhood, she was educated in a New Jersey convent. While still in her teens she joined the Keystone company, appearing in such early films as *The Agitator/The Cowboy Socialist* (1912) and *A Favorite Fool* (1915), the latter with Eddie Foy, with whom she also appeared in several Broadway plays. She played lead roles in many other early silents, then rose to prominence with her starring role in Erich von Stroheim's *Foolish Wives* (1922). She remained active in films until the mid-30s. In 1930 she began appearing regularly in LAUREL AND HARDY two-reel comedies and feature films, sometimes as a vamp, at other times as Hardy's wife, and often as a foil of the duo's antics. At one time she was married to actor Francis MCDONALD.

FILMS INCLUDE: *The Agitator/The Cowboy Socialist* 1912; *A One Night Stand, Settled at the Seaside, A Rascal's Foolish Way/A Polished Villain, A Favorite Fool, The Best of Enemies* 1915; *The Worst of Friends, Because He Loved Her, Better Late Than Never, Wife and Auto Trouble, A Bath House Blunder* 1916; *The Fair Barbarian* 1917; *The Grim Game* 1919; *The Devil's Pass Key, Her Husband's Friend* 1920; *A Parisian Scandal, The Love Charm* 1921; *Foolish Wives, Pardon My Nerve!, Brothers Under the Skin, Only a Shop Girl* 1922; *The Christian, Souls for Sale* 1923; *Name the Man, The Shooting of Dan McGrew, A Woman Who Sinned, Bread, Broken Barriers, Married Flirts, The Triflers* 1924; *Frivolous Sal/Flaming Love, The Unholy Three, Camille of the Barbary Coast, Time the Comedian* 1925; *The Miracle of Life, The Nut-Cracker, Fools of Fashion, The Truthful Sex* 1926; *Tongues of Scandal, Husband Hunters, Perch of the Devil, Beauty Shoppers* 1927; *San Francisco Nights, Fazil, Black Butterflies, While the City Sleeps* 1928; *Alibi, Unaccustomed as We Are* (first Laurel and Hardy talking short; as Hardy's wife), *A Man's Man* 1929; *Young Desire* 1930; *Chickens Come Home* (L & H short), *Wicked* 1931; *Their First Mistake* (L & H short), *The Man Called Back, Scarlet Dawn* 1932; *Blondie Johnson, Sucker Money, Cheating Blondes, Lilly Turner, Dance Girl Dance, Sons of the Desert* (L & H feature; as Mrs. Hardy) 1933; *Oliver the Eighth* (L & H short), *Beloved, Going Bye-Bye* (L & H short), *Them Thar Hills* (L & H short), *I Like It That Way, The Live Ghost* (L & H short) 1934; *Tit for Tat* (L & H short), *Stranded* 1935; *The Bohemian Girl* (L & H feature; as Mrs. Hardy) 1936; *Daughter of Shanghai* 1937; *Prison Farm, Nancy Drew—Detective* 1938; *Women Without Names* 1940; *The Mad Monster* 1942; *The Blue Dahlia* (bit) 1946.

Busch, Niven. Novelist, screenwriter. *b.* Apr. 26, 1903, in New York City. *d.* 1991. *ed.* Princeton. An associate editor of *Time* magazine and a regular contributor to *The New Yorker,* he went to Hollywood in the early 30s and became a screenwriter for various studios. Although he wrote original stories and screenplays for films of varied genres, he gained a reputation mostly for his Westerns, into which he often introduced psychoneurotic elements. His novel *Duel in the Sun* (1944) provided the story basis for the large-scale Selznick-Vidor film of that name (1947). In the 70s, he was teaching and lecturing on film at various California universities and in the mid-80s became a teaching fellow at Princeton. He played a bit role in the film *The Unbearable Lightness of Being* (1988). Formerly (1942–52) married to actress Teresa WRIGHT.

FILMS INCLUDE (as screenwriter, alone or in collaboration): *The Crowd Roars, Miss Pinkerton, Scarlet Dawn* 1932; *College Coach* (also co-story) 1933; *The Man with Two Faces, He Was Her Man, The Big Shakedown, Babbitt* 1934; *Three Kids and a Queen, Lady Tubbs* 1935; *In Old Chicago* (novel basis only, *We the O'Learys*) 1938; *Off the Record, Angels Wash Their Faces* 1939; *The Westerner* 1940; *Belle Starr* (co-story only) 1941; *The Postman Always Rings Twice, Till the End of Time* (novel basis only, *They Dream of Home*) 1946; *Duel in the Sun* (novel basis only), *Pursued, Moss Rose* (adapt. only) 1947; *The Capture* (also prod.), *The Furies* (novel basis only) 1950; *Distant Drums* (also story) 1951; *The Man from the Alamo* (co-story only), *The Moonlighter* (also story) 1953; *The Treasure of Pancho Villa* 1955.

Busey, Gary. Actor. Born on June 29, 1944, in Goose Creek, Tex. *ed.* Coffeyville Jr. Coll.; Kansas State Coll.; Oklahoma State Coll. On graduating college in 1963, he joined the Rubber Band as a drummer and, as Teddy Jack Eddy, later played drums with Leon Russell, Kris Kristofferson, and Willie Nelson. He got into movies in 1971 and in the next two decades played a wide range of lead and supporting parts in a variety of films. He was nominated for an Academy Award for his title role in *The Buddy Holly Story* (1978). He co-starred in the TV series 'The Texas Wheelers' (1974–75). In 1988 he was badly hurt in a motorcycle accident, which soon focused attention on the need for stricter helmet laws.

FILMS: *Angels Hard as The Come* 1971; *Dirty Little Billy, The Magnificent Seven Ride* 1972; *The Last American Hero/ Hard Driver, Lolly Madonna XXX/The Lolly-Madonna War, Hex* 1973; *Thunderbolt and Lightfoot* 1974; *The Gumball Rally, A Star Is Born* 1976; *Straight Time, Big Wednesday, The Buddy Holly Story* (title role) 1978; *Foolin' Around, Carny* 1980; *Barbarosa* 1982; *D. C. Cab* 1983; *The Bear* 1984; *Silver Bullet, Insignificance* (UK) 1985; *Let's Get Harry, Eye of the Tiger* 1986; *Lethal Weapon* 1987; *Bulletproof* 1988; *Hider in the House* 1989; *Act of Piracy* (release delayed from 1987), *Predator 2* 1990; *My Heroes Have Always Been Cowboys, Point Break* 1991; *The Player, Under Siege* 1992; *The Firm, Rookie of the Year* 1993; *Chasers, Drop Zone, Surviving the Game* 1994; *Sticks and Stones* 1996; *Lost Highway* 1997.

Bushell, Anthony. Actor, director, producer. Born on May 19, 1904, in Westerham, England. *ed.* Oxford. In 1924 he began a distinguished acting career on the London stage and in 1927 came to New York to star in the Broadway production of 'Her Cardboard Lover,' with Jeanne Eagels. He made his start in films in 1929 in *Disraeli,* at the insistence of the picture's star, George Arliss. He then played in about a dozen other Hollywood films before returning to England in 1932. He played leading parts in many British films until the outbreak of WW II; then, upon his discharge from the British Army, he became Laurence OLIVIER's general manager and associate producer on *Hamlet* (1949). While continuing his acting career, he began directing and producing films of some merit but later centered most of his activity as producer, director, and actor on British TV.

FILMS INCLUDE: As actor—*Disraeli* (US) 1929; *Journey's End* (US), *The Flirting Widow* (US), *Three Faces East* (US) 1930; *The Royal Bed* (US), *Born to Love* (US), *Chances* (US), *Five Star Final* (US), *Expensive Women* (US) 1931; *A Woman Commands* (US), *Vanity Fair* (US), *Escapade* (US), *The Silver Greyhound, Sally Bishop* 1932; *The Ghoul, I Was a Spy, Channel Crossing, Soldiers of the King/The Woman in Command* 1933; *Red Wagon, Lilies of the Field* 1934; *The Scarlet Pimpernel* 1935; *Dark Journey, The Return of the Scarlet Pimpernel, Farewell Again/Troopship* 1937; *The Lion Has Wings* 1939; *The Small Back Room* 1938; *The Miniver Story* 1950; *High Treason* 1951; *Who Goes There/The Passionate Sentry* 1952; *The Black Knight, The Purple Plain* 1954; *The Battle of the River Plate/Pursuit of the Graf Spee* 1956; *Amère Victoire/Bitter Victory* (Fr.) 1957; *The Wind Cannot Read* 1958; *Desert Mice* 1959. As director (complete)—*Angel With the Trumpet* (also act.) 1949; *The Long Dark Hall* (co-dir.; also prod., act.) 1951; *The Red Beret/Paratrooper* (2nd-unit dir.; also act.) 1953; *Hell Below Zero* (2nd-unit dir.) 1954; *Richard III* (assoc. dir.) 1955; *Bhowani Junction* (2nd-unit. dir.; US/UK) 1956; *The Prince and the Showgirl* (assoc. dir.) 1957; *The Terror of the Tongs* (also act.) 1961; *A Woman's Privilege* (short) 1962.

Bushman, Francis X. Actor. *b.* Francis Xavier Bushman, Jan. 10, 1883, Norfolk, Va. (or Baltimore, Md.). *d.* 1966. He began acting in stock while still a boy but in 1911 abandoned the stage for the screen, starting his new career with the Essanay company in Chicago. A handsome man of sturdy physique (he had earlier worked as a sculptor's model), he was the object of unprecedented adulation among cinema audiences of the pre-20s. His popularity reached a peak when he joined Metro soon after its formation in 1915. He was rushed from one set to the other, playing hundreds of dashing romantic roles. His popularity dimmed considerably when his female admirers discovered that he had been secretly married to Beverly BAYNE, his co-star in the 1916 *Romeo and Juliet* and in many other films. (She was the second of his four wives.) But he continued appearing in many films and in 1926 played his most famous role as the Roman Messala, Ramon Novarro's rival in *Ben-Hur.* It is said that he refused to use a double for the chariot race sequence that provided the climax of this film.

Bushman's earnings were estimated at a million dollars a year, and he lived royally until his fortune was wiped out in the 1929 stock market crash. He later made a financial comeback in radio soap operas, but his film career came to a virtual halt by the early 30s. He played only occasional roles, some of them quite interesting, such as Bernard Baruch in *Wilson,* King Saul in *David and Bathsheba,* and Moses in *The Story of Mankind.* His son Ralph had a brief career as a film actor, sometimes using the name Francis X. Bushman, Jr.

FILMS INCLUDE: *His Friend's Wife, The Rosary, The New Manager, The Gordian Knot, Fate's Funny Frolic, Lost Years, Bill Bumper's Bargain* (as Mephisto), *The Madman* 1911; *The Mail Order Bride, The Melody of Love, Alias Billy Sargent, Out of the Depths, Napatia the Greek Singer, The Eye That Never Sleeps, A Good Catch, The Laurel Wreath of Fame, The Passing Shadow, White Roses, Twilight, The Magic Wand, The Fall of Montezuma* (as Cortez), *Neptune's Daughter, The Voice of Conscience, Chains, The House of Pride, The Penitent, The Virtue of Rags* 1912; *When Soul Meets Soul, The 13th Man, The Farmer's Daughter, Discovery, The Spy's Defeat, Let No Man Put Asunder, A Brother's Loyalty* (dual role), *The Power of*

Conscience, Tony the Fidler, The Toll of the Marshes, The Stigma 1913; *The Hour and the Man, Through the Storm, The Other Girl, Shadows, The Moon's Ray, Ashes of Hope, The Elder Brother, Fingerprints, The Countess, Trinkets of Tragedy, The Night Hawks, One Wonderful Night, The Masked Wrestler, Under Royal Patronage, The Plum Tree, Sparks of Fate, A Splendid Dishonor, The Other Man, In the Glare of the Lights, Blood Will Tell, Every Inch a King, The Battle of Love* 1914; *The Ambition of the Baron, The Accounting, Stars Their Courses Change, The Great Silence, The Return of Richard Neal, Graustark, The Slim Princess, The Second in Command, The Silent Voice, Pennington's Choice* 1915; *Man and His Soul, The Wall Between, A Million a Minute, Romeo and Juliet* (as Romeo), *In the Diplomatic Service* (also dir., sc.) 1916; *The Great Secret* (serial), *Their Compact, The Adopted Son, The Voice of Conscience, Red White and Blue Blood* 1917; *Under Suspicion, The Brass Check, With Neatness and Dispatch, Cyclone Higgins D.D., Social Quicksands, A Pair of Cupids, The Poor Rich Man* 1918; *God's Outlaw, Daring Hearts* 1919; *Smiling All the Way* 1920; *Modern Marriage* 1923; *The Masked Bride* 1925; *Ben-Hur* (as Messala), *The Marriage Clause* 1926; *The Lady in Ermine, The Thirteenth Juror* 1927; *The Grip of the Yukon, Say It with Sables, Midnight Life, The Charge of the Gauchos* 1928; *The Call of the Circus, The Dude Wrangler, Once a Gentleman* 1930; *Hollywood Boulevard* 1936; *Dick Tracy* (serial) 1937; *Wilson* (as financier Bernard Baruch) 1944; *David and Bathsheba* (as King Saul) 1951; *Apache Country, The Bad and the Beautiful* 1952; *Sabrina* 1954; *The Story of Mankind* (as Moses) 1957; *The Phantom Planet* 1962; *The Ghost in the Invisible Bikini* 1966.

business. Any minor movement (such as a step, a gesture, a facial expression) used by an actor as part of his interpretation of a role.

Butler, Bill (Wilmer). Director of photography. Born on Apr. 7, 1921, in Colorado. *ed.* Iowa Wesleyan; State Univ. of Iowa. A leading Hollywood cinematographer of the 70s and 80s. He was nominated for an Oscar for *One Flew Over the Cuckoo's Nest* (1975). He also worked in TV, winning an Emmy for the TV movie *Raid on Entebbe* (1977). Not to be confused with the British film editor of the same name whose credits include *A Clockwork Orange.*

FILMS INCLUDE: *Fearless Frank* 1967; *The Rain People* 1969; *Adam's Woman* (Austral.) 1970; *Drive He Said* 1971; *The Conversation* 1974; *Jaws, One Flew Over the Cuckoo's Nest* (co-phot.) 1975; *Bingo Long Traveling All-Stars and Motor Kings, Lipstick* 1976; *Demon Seed* 1977; *Capricorn One, Grease, Damien—Omen II* 1978; *Ice Castles, Rocky II* 1979; *It's My Turn* 1980; *Stripes* 1981; *Rocky III* 1982; *The Sting II* 1983; *Rocky IV* 1985; *Big Trouble* 1986; *Biloxi Blues, Child's Play* 1988.

Butler, David. Director. *b.* Dec. 17, 1894, San Francisco. *d.* 1979. *ed.* Stanford U. The son of a stage director, he began acting professionally at three, making his film debut in 1915. He later appeared in D. W. Griffith's *The Greatest Things in Life* (1918) and in such silent films as *Upstairs and Down* (1919), *The Sky Pilot* (1921), *The Village Blacksmith* (1922), *The Temple of Venus* (1923), *In Hollywood with Potash and Perlmutter* (1924), *Code of the West* (1925), *The Plastic Age, The Quarterback* (1926), *Seventh Heaven* (1927), and *Salute* (1929). At the same time, he continued appearing on stage and became stage manager of the Morosco Theater in Los Angeles in 1923. Four years later he began directing motion pictures for Fox. In a directing career spanning 40 years, he turned out scores of entertaining films for Fox, Paramount, and Warner Bros., typically light comedies and glossy musicals. He gained a reputation as a dependable and efficient, if impersonal, director, who could be relied upon to complete quality productions on time and within budget. He occasionally also produced, and often collaborated on the stories and screenplays of, his films.

FILMS: *High School Hero* (also co-story) 1927; *The News Parade* (also co-story), *Win That Girl, Prep and Pep* 1928; *Masked Emotions* (co-dir. with Kenneth Hawks), *Fox Movietone Follies of 1929* (also story), *Chasing Through Europe* (co-dir. with Alfred Werker), *Sunny Side Up* (also sc.) 1929; *High Society Blues, Just Imagine* (also sc.) 1930; *A Connecticut Yankee, Delicious* 1931; *Business and Pleasure, Down to Earth, Handle with Care* (also story) 1932; *Hold Me Tight, My Weakness* (also co-sc.) 1933; *Bottoms Up* (also co-story, co-sc.), *Handy Andy, Have a Heart* (also co-sc.) *Bright Eyes* (also co-story) 1934; *The Little Colonel, Doubting Thomas, The Littlest Rebel* 1935; *Captain January, White Fang, Pigskin Parade* 1936; *Ali Baba Goes to Town, You're a Sweetheart* 1937; *Kentucky Moonshine, Straight Place and Show, Kentucky* 1938; *East Side of Heaven* (also co-story), *That's Right You're Wrong* (also prod., co-story) 1939; *If I Had My Way* (also prod., co-story), *You'll Find Out* (also prod., co-story) 1940; *Caught in the Draft, Playmates* (also prod., co-story) 1941; *Road to Morocco* 1942; *They Got Me Covered, Thank Your Lucky Stars* 1943; *Shine On Harvest Moon, The Princess and the Pirate* 1944; *San Antonio* 1945; *Two Guys from Milwaukee, The Time the Place and the Girl* 1946; *My Wild Irish Rose* 1947; *Two Guys from Texas* 1948; *John Loves Mary, Look for the Silver Lining, It's a Great Feeling, The Story of Seabiscuit* 1949; *The Daughter of Rosy O'Grady, Tea for Two* 1950; *Lullaby of Broadway, Painting the Clouds with Sunshine* 1951; *Where's Charley?, April in Paris* 1952; *By the Light of the Silvery Moon, Calamity Jane* 1953; *The Command, King Richard and the Crusades* 1954; *Jump Into Hell* 1955; *Glory* (also prod.), *The Girl He Left Behind* 1956; *The Right Approach* 1961; *C'mon Let's Live a Little* 1967.

Butler, Frank. Actor, screenwriter. *b.* Dec. 28, 1890, Oxford, England. *d.* 1967. A graduate of Oxford, he started out as a stage actor and after coming to the US played character roles in many Hollywood films of the 20s, typically portraying distinguished gentlemen and aristocrats. He was briefly billed as F. R. Butler. He turned to screenwriting in 1927 and subsequently wrote numerous scripts, alone or in collaboration, for Hal Roach, Paramount, and other studios, specializing in comedy and light fare but occasionally collaborating on dramas and action films. His credits include a couple of LAUREL AND HARDY features and several HOPE and CROSBY "Road" pictures. He won an Academy Award for co-scripting *Going My Way* (1944).

FILMS INCLUDE: As actor—*Behold My Wife* 1920; *The Great Moment, The Sheik* 1921; *Beyond the Rocks* 1922; *My American Wife, The Tiger's Claw, Bluebeard's 8th Wife, The Call of the Wild* 1923; *The King of Wild Horses* 1924; *Satan in Sables* 1925; *Made for Love, The Fighting Buckaroo, The Passionate Quest* 1926. As screenwriter (alone or in collaboration)—*No Man's Law* 1927; *The Big Killing, Just Married* 1928; *China Bound* (co-story only), *Untamed* 1929; *Montana Moon* (also co-story), *Strictly Unconventional, Those Three French Girls, Remote Control* 1930; *This Modern Age* 1931; *Prosperity* 1932; *College Humor, The Way to Love* 1933; *Babes in Toyland* 1934; *Bonnie Scotland* 1935; *Strike Me Pink, The Milky Way, The Princess Comes Across* 1936; *Champagne Waltz, Waikiki Wedding* 1937; *Tropic Holiday, Give Me a Sailor* 1938; *Paris Honeymoon, Never Say Die, The Star Maker* 1939; *Road to Singapore, Untamed, Rangers of Fortune, I Want a Divorce* 1940; *Road to Zanzibar, Aloma of the South Seas* 1941; *My Favorite Blonde, Beyond the Blue Horizon, Wake Island,*

Road to Morocco 1942; *China, Hostages* 1943; *Going My Way* 1944; *A Medal for Benny, Incendiary Blonde* 1945; *The Kid from Brooklyn* 1946; *California, The Perils of Pauline, Golden Earrings* 1947; *Whispering Smith* 1949; *Road to Bali* 1953; *Strange Lady in Town* 1955; *The Miracle* 1959.

Butler, Hugo. Screenwriter. *b.* May 4, 1914, Calgary, Alberta, Canada. *d.* 1968. A journalist and playwright, he went to Hollywood in 1937 and wrote a number of noteworthy screenplays and adaptations through the early 50s. He shared an Academy Award nomination for the story of *Edison the Man* (1940).

FILMS INCLUDE: *Big City* 1937; *A Christmas Carol* 1938; *The Adventures of Huckleberry Finn, Society Lawyer* 1939; *Young Tom Edison, Wyoming, Edison the Man* (story only) 1940; *Barnacle Bill* 1941; *Lassie Come Home* 1943; *The Southerner* 1945; *From This Day Forward, Miss Susie Slagle's* 1946; *Roughshod* 1949; *A Woman of Distinction* (story only) 1950; *The Prowler, He Ran All the Way, The Big Night* 1951; *The First Time* 1952; *Sodoma e Gomorra/Sodom and Gomorrah* (It./Fr./US) 1961; *Eva* (Fr./It.) 1962; *A Face in the Rain* 1963; *The Legend of Lylah Clare* 1968.

Butler, Lawrence W. Special effects technician. *b.* 1908, Akron, Ohio. *d.* 1988. He dropped out of a Burbank, Calif., high school at 15 to become an assistant to his father, William Butler, a special and optical effects director for Warner Bros. He later worked for producer Alexander Korda in England, then in the US, winning an Academy Award for the marvelous special effects of *The Thief of Bagdad* (1940). He also gained Oscar nominations for *That Hamilton Woman* (1941), *Jungle Book* (1942), and *A Thousand and One Nights* (1945). After a brief stint at Warners during WW II, he joined Columbia, where he headed the special effects department for nearly three decades. At the 1976 Oscar ceremony, he shared with Roger Banks a scientific/technical Academy Award for "the concept of applying low inertia and stepping electric motors to film transport systems and optical printers for motion picture production."

FILMS INCLUDE: *Things to Come, The Man Who Could Work Miracles* 1936; *Fire Over England, Dark Journey* 1937; *South Riding* 1938; *The Thief of Bagdad* 1940; *That Hamilton Woman/Lady Hamilton, Lydia* 1941; *Jungle Book, To Be or Not to Be, Casablanca* 1942; *Destination Tokyo, The Adventures of Mark Twain* 1944; *Tonight and Every Night, A Thousand and One Nights* 1945; *Saratoga Trunk* 1946; *The Lady From Shanghai* 1948; *The Devil at Four O'Clock* 1961; *Panic in the Year Zero* 1962; *Robinson Crusoe on Mars* 1964; *In Harm's Way* 1965; *Marooned* 1969; *The Gospel Road* 1973.

butterfly. An aluminum reflector used in outdoor filming to diffuse harsh sunlight and soften shadows. Also, a small overhead silk or linen screen used for a similar purpose.

Butterworth, Charles. Actor. *b.* July 26, 1896, South Bend, Ind. *d.* 1946. *ed.* Notre Dame. Holder of a law degree, he turned to journalism but finally chose the stage, playing supporting roles in several Broadway musicals and light plays. In films from 1930, he did some comedy leads but mostly supporting parts, typically as a reticent, indecisive, balding bachelor of the leisure class. He was killed in a car crash.

FILMS INCLUDE: *The Life of the Party* 1930; *Illicit, Side Show, The Mad Genius* 1931; *Manhattan Parade, Love Me Tonight* 1932; *The Nuisance, My Weakness, Penthouse* 1933; *The Cat and the Fiddle, Student Tour, Hollywood Party, Bulldog Drummond Strikes Back* 1934; *Orchids to You, Baby Face Harrington, The Night Is Young* 1935; *Magnificent Obsession, The Moon's Our Home, Half Angel, Rainbow on the River* 1936; *Swing High Swing Low, Every Day's a Holiday* 1937; *Thanks for the Memory* 1938; *Let Freedom Ring* 1939; *The Boys from Syracuse, Second Chorus* 1940; *Sis Hopkins* 1941; *What's Cooking?* 1942; *This Is the Army* 1943; *The Sultan's Daughter, Bermuda Mystery* 1944.

Buttolph, David. Composer, music director. Born on Aug. 3, 1902, in New York City. In Hollywood since 1934, he composed the musical score of many major films, first for Fox, then for Warner Bros. and other production companies. But from the 50s mostly for routine Westerns and action pictures.

FILMS INCLUDE: *The World Moves On* 1934; *Show Them No Mercy* 1935; *Pigskin Parade* 1936; *Love Is News* 1937; *Stanley and Livingstone, The Three Musketeers* 1939; *Star Dust, Four Sons, The Man I Married, The Return of Frank James, Chad Hanna* 1940; *Tobacco Road, Western Union* 1941; *My Favorite Blonde, This Gun for Hire* 1942; *Crash Dive, Guadalcanal Diary* 1943; *The House on 92nd Street, Nob Hill* 1945; *My Darling Clementine, Somewhere in the Night, Shock* 1946; *The Brasher Doubloon, Boomerang, Kiss of Death, 13 Rue Madeleine, The Foxes of Harrow* 1947; *To the Victor, Rope, June Bride, One Sunday Afternoon* 1948; *Roseanna McCoy, Colorado Territory* 1949; *Pretty Baby* 1950; *The Enforcer, Along the Great Divide* 1951; *Lone Star* 1952; *The Man Behind the Gun, House of Wax* 1953; *Phantom of the Rue Morgue, Bounty Hunter* 1954; *Long John Silver* 1955; *The Lone Ranger, The Burning Hills* 1956; *The Big Land* 1957; *The Horse Soldiers* 1959; *Guns of the Timberland* 1960; *PT-109* 1963; *The Man From Galveston* 1964.

Buttons, Red. Actor, entertainer. Born Aaron Chwatt, on Feb. 5, 1919, in New York City. The son of an immigrant milliner, he was raised on the Lower East Side. At the age of 12 he won an amateur night contest, and at 16 he was a combination bellboy-singer in a Bronx tavern, where he became known as Red Buttons after his loud uniform. He later worked in Catskill Mountain resorts and also as a burlesque comedian. In 1942 he made his Broadway debut, playing a supporting role in 'Vickie.' During his Army service in World War II he appeared in the stage production of 'Winged Victory' and later in its film version. He became the star of his own TV show in 1953 but was out of work when he was selected to play the role of Sergeant Joe Kelly in the film *Sayonara* in 1957. He won an Academy Award as best supporting actor for this tragic portrayal and has since appeared in many other films.

FILMS: *Winged Victory* 1944; *13 Rue Madeleine* (bit) 1947; *Footlight Varieties* 1951; *Sayonara* 1957; *Imitation General* 1958; *The Big Circus* 1959; *One Two Three* 1961; *Five Weeks in a Balloon, Hatari!, The Longest Day, Gay Purr-ee* (voice only) 1962; *A Ticklish Affair* 1963; *Your Cheatin' Heart, Up From the Beach, Harlow* (Carroll Baker version) 1965; *Stagecoach* 1966; *They Shoot Horses Don't They?* (Acad. Award nom.) 1969; *Who Killed Mary Whats'ername?* 1971; *The Poseidon Adventure* 1972; *Gable and Lombard* 1976; *Viva Knievel!, Pete's Dragon* 1977; *Movie Movie* 1978; *C.H.O.M.P.S* 1979; *When Time Ran Out* 1980; *18 Again!* 1988; *The Ambulance, Into Thin Air* 1990; *It Could Happen To You* 1994.

buyer. A member of the props or wardrobe department whose job is to find, buy, or rent items needed for a film.

Buzzell, Edward (Eddie). Director. *b.* Nov. 13, 1895, Brooklyn, N.Y. *d.* 1985. A Broadway musical comedy star, he appeared in several feature films of the late 20s, including *Midnight Life* (1928) and *Little Johnny Jones* (1929), then wrote, directed, and starred in a series of 26 Columbia comedy shorts. He made his debut as a feature director in 1932 and subsequently turned out many run-of-the-mill productions, for Columbia, Universal, Paramount, MGM, and other studios, mainly comedies and light fare, including a couple of lesser Marx Brothers vehicles, *At the Circus* (1939) and *Go West* (1940).

FEATURE FILMS: *The Big Timer, Hollywood Speaks, Virtue* 1932; *Child of Manhattan, Ann Carver's Profession, Love Honor and Oh Baby!* 1933; *Cross Country Cruise, The Human Side* 1934; *Transient Lady, The Girl Friend* 1935; *Three Married Men, The Luckiest Girl in the World* 1936; *As Good as Married* 1937; *Paradise for Three, Fast Company* 1938; *Honolulu, At the Circus* 1939; *Go West* 1940; *The Get-Away, Married Bachelor* 1941; *Ship Ahoy, The Omaha Trail* 1942; *The Youngest Profession, Best Foot Forward* 1943; *Keep Your Powder Dry* 1945; *Easy to Wed, Three Wise Fools* 1946; *Song of the Thin Man* 1947; *Neptune's Daughter* 1949; *A Woman of Distinction, Emergency Wedding* 1950; *Confidentially Connie* 1953; *Ain't Misbehavin'* (also co-sc.) 1955; *Mary Had a Little...* (UK) 1961.

buzz track. A sound track carries a nondistinct background noise, or "room tone," rather than clear modulations or speech. It is usually recorded after a dialogue scene or a documentary interview while everyone on the set remains silent. It is used to help the editor bridge "mute" gaps between lines of dialogue which might otherwise sound eerily unnatural. See also ROOM TONE.

b/w. A common abbreviation for black-and-white film as distinguished from color.

Byington, Spring. Actress. *b.* Oct. 17, 1886, Colorado Springs, Colo. *d.* 1971. Orphaned at an early age, she made her stage debut at 14 with a Denver stock company; after numerous stage appearances with touring companies, she made her Broadway debut in 1924. She entered films in 1933, playing supporting roles in some 100 movies, typically as a pleasant young-in-spirit, often pixilated mother, most memorably in *You Can't Take It with You,* for which she was nominated for an Oscar as best supporting actress. She was a fixture in the "Jones Family" film series (1936–40). She also starred in the TV series 'December Bride' and was a regular on 'Laramie.'

FILMS INCLUDE: *Little Women* 1933; *The Werewolf of London, Mutiny on the Bounty, Way Down East, Ah! Wilderness* 1935; *Stage Struck, Dodsworth, The Charge of the Light Brigade, Theodora Goes Wild* 1936; *Green Light, A Family Affair, The Road Back, Penrod and Sam* 1937; *The Buccaneer, Jezebel, The Adventures of Tom Sawyer, You Can't Take It with You* 1938; *The Story of Alexander Graham Bell, Quick Millions* 1939; *The Blue Bird, Young As You Feel, A Child Is Born* 1940; *The Devil and Miss Jones, Meet John Doe* 1941; *Roxie Hart, Rings on Her Fingers, The Vanishing Virginian* 1942; *Presenting Lily Mars, Heaven Can Wait* 1943; *I'll Be Seeing You* 1944; *The Enchanted Cottage, Captain Eddie* 1945; *Dragonwyck* 1946; *Cynthia, Singapore* 1947; *B. F.'s Daughter* 1948; *In the Good Old Summertime* 1949; *Louisa, Devil's Doorway* 1950; *Angels in the Outfield* 1951; *No Room for the Groom, Because You're Mine* 1952; *The Rocket Man* 1954; *Please Don't Eat the Daisies* 1960.

Byrd, Ralph. Actor. *b.* Apr. 22, 1909, Dayton, Ohio. *d.* 1952. Rugged hero of many Hollywood serials and action pictures of the 30s and 40s. Also played supporting parts in better-grade films. He is most closely identified with the role of Dick Tracy.

FILMS INCLUDE: *Hell Ship Morgan, Swing Time* 1936; *S.O.S. Coast Guard* (serial), *Blake of Scotland Yard* (serial), *Dick Tracy* (serial), *San Quentin, Criminals of The Air* 1937; *Dick Tracy Returns* (serial), *Born to Be Wild* 1938; *Dick Tracy's G-Men* (serial), *Mickey the Kid* 1939; *The Howards of Virginia, Misbehaving Husbands, Drums of the Desert, Northwest Mounted Police* 1940; *Dick Tracy vs. Crime Inc.* (serial), *Son of Monte Cristo, Desperate Cargo, Dark Streets of Cairo, A Yank in the R.A.F.* 1941; *Duke of the Navy, Jungle Book, Moontide, Ten Gentlemen from West Point* 1942; *Guadalcanal Diary* 1943; *Tampico* 1944; *The Vigilante* (serial) 1947; *Jungle Goddess* 1948; *Union Station* 1950; *My Favorite Spy* 1951; *Dick Tracy vs. the Phantom Empire* (serial) 1952.

Byrne, David. Singer, actor, director. Born on May 14, 1952, in Dumbarton, Scotland. Having moved with his family to Baltimore at age seven, he studied photography, performance, and video production at the Rhode Island School of Design and the Maryland Inst. Coll. of Art. He gained great popularity in the 80s as the lead singer and songwriter of the rock band Talking Heads. He conceived and starred in the hit rock concert film *Stop Making Sense* (1984); directed, co-wrote, and narrated *True Stories* (1986); shared an Academy Award for the original score of *The Last Emperor* (1987); and composed the score for *Married to the Mob* (1988). His songs were heard in several other films, including *King of Comedy* (1983), *Something Wild* (1986), and *Down and Out in Beverly Hills* (1986).

Byrne, Gabriel. Actor. Born in 1950, in Dublin. *ed.* University Coll., Ireland. Dark, thoughtful leading man of stage and screen. An archaeologist and later a teacher of Spanish at a girls' school, he became involved in amateur dramatics, then joined the experimental Focus Theatre, and eventually Dublin's Abbey Theatre. He was 29 by the time he made his film debut and 36 when he broke through as an international star. Divorced from his *Siesta* co-star Ellen BARKIN.

FILMS: *The Outsider* 1979; *Excalibur* 1981; *The Keep, Wagner, Hanna K.* 1983; *Defence of the Realm/Defense of the Realm, Gothic* (as Lord Byron) 1986; *Lionheart, Siesta, Julia and Julia, Hello Again* 1987; *A Soldier's Tale, The Courier* 1988; *Diamond Skulls* 1989; *Miller's Crossing, Hakon Hakonsen/Shipwrecked* (Nor.) 1990; *Dark Obsession* (UK) 1989; *Cool World* 1992; *Point of No Return, Into the West* 1993; *Little Women, A Simple Twist of Fate, Trial By Jury* 1994; *Frankie Starlight, The Usual Suspects* 1995; *Dead Man, Mad Dog Time, The Last of the High Kings* (also co-sc.), *Somebody Is Waiting* (co-prod.) 1996; *The End of Violence, Smilla's Sense of Snow* 1997.

Byron, Kathleen. Actress. Born on Jan. 11, 1922, in London. Trained as a student with the Old Vic, then went directly into British films. She played leads and second leads in major British films of the 40s but has been seen infrequently, mostly in supporting roles, since the 50s.

FILMS INCLUDE: *The Young Mr. Pitt* 1942; *The Silver Fleet* 1943; *A Matter of Life and Death/Stairway to Heaven* 1946; *Black Narcissus* 1947; *The Small Back Room* 1948; *Madness of the Heart* 1949; *Prelude to Fame, The Reluctant Widow* 1951; *Tom Brown's Schooldays* 1951; *The Gambler and the Lady* 1952; *Young Bess* 1953; *Profile* 1954; *Hand in Hand* 1961; *Night of the Eagle/Burn Witch Burn* 1962; *Hammerhead* 1958; *Twins of Evil* 1971; *The Abdication* 1974; *The Elephant Man* 1980; *From a Far Country* 1981.

Byron, Walter. Actor. *b.* June 11, 1901, Leicester, England. *d.* 1972. Elegant leading man and supporting player of Hollywood films of the 20s and 30s. Starred opposite Gloria Swanson in Erich von Stroheim's ill-fated *Queen Kelly* (1928), which was exhibited in Europe but never commercially released in the US. Later teamed with such stars as Bette Davis and Jean Harlow but appeared mostly in routine films and never achieved prominence.

FILMS INCLUDE: *Queen Kelly, The Awakening* 1928; *The Sacred Flame* 1929; *Not Damaged, The Dancers* 1930; *The Lion and the Lamb, The Reckless Hour, The Last Flight, The Yellow Ticket, Leftover Ladies* 1931; *The Menace, Three Wise Girls, Sinners in the Sun, This Sporting Age, The Savage Girl* 1932; *Grand Slam, Kiss of Araby, East of Fifth Avenue, Charlie Chan's Greatest Case* 1933; *Man of Two Worlds, Once to Every*

Woman, British Agent 1934; *Folies-Bergère, Don't Bet on Blondes* 1935; *Mary of Scotland* 1936; *As Good as Married* 1937; *Trade Winds* 1939.

Byrum, John. Director, screenwriter. Born on Mar. 14, 1947, in Winnetka, Ill. A graduate of the NYU Film School, he started as an apprentice on industrial and underground films, then began writing scripts for low-budget films in England and the US. He broke through mainstream American cinema in the late 70s, as a screenwriter, then as a director, but had limited success in either capacity.

FILMS INCLUDE: As screenwriter—*Mahogany* 1975; *Harry and Walter Go to New York* 1976; *Sphinx* 1981; *Scandalous* 1984. As director-screenwriter—*Inserts* (UK) 1976; *Heart Beat* 1979; *The Razor's Edge* 1984; *The Whoopee Boys* 1986; *The War at Home 1990.*

C

Caan, James. Actor. Born on Mar. 26, 1939, in the Bronx, N.Y. *ed.* Michigan State; Hofstra Coll. The son of a kosher meat dealer, he grew up in Sunnyside, in the borough of Queens, N.Y., where he excelled in high school basketball and other sports. While attending college he supported himself as a bouncer, waiter, lifeguard, and summer camp counselor. He began acting at the Neighborhood Playhouse in New York in 1960 and made his stage debut off Broadway in 'La Ronde.' Following some TV work, he first appeared on the screen in 1963, playing an unbilled bit in *Irma La Douce.* His Hollywood career meandered through unmemorable roles until the early 70s, when he exploded on the scene with two intense performances, on TV as dying football player Brian Piccolo in 'Brian's Song' (1970) and on the screen as the brutish Sonny Corleone in *The Godfather* (1972). He was nominated for an Emmy for the former and for an Oscar for the latter. For a decade he remained one of the American screen's top box-office draws. He took a first stab at directing with *Hide in Plain Sight* (1980). But after giving one of his best performances in *Thief* (1981) he found few roles in the 1980s to boost his sagging career. In the 1990s, two broad performances as garrulous hucksters—in *For the Boys* and *Honeymoon in Vegas*—and one as a victimized romance writer in *Misery* re-established him in film, this time as a character actor. Casual and amiable, he is a sports enthusiast and participates professionally in rodeo competition, a devotion that has earned him the nickname "The Jewish Cowboy." He also owns a stable of racehorses.

FILMS: *Irma la Douce* (bit) 1963; *Lady in a Cage* 1964; *The Glory Guys, Red Line 7000* 1965; *El Dorado, Games* 1967; *Countdown, Journey to Shiloh, Submarine X-1* (UK) 1968; *The Rain People* 1969; *Rabbit Run* 1970; *T. R. Baskin* 1971; *The Godfather* 1972; *Slither, Cinderella Liberty* 1973; *The Gambler, Freebie and the Bean, The Godfather Part II* (cameo) 1974; *Funny Lady, Rollerball, Gone with the West, The Killer Elite* 1975; *Harry and Walter Go to New York, Silent Movie* (unbilled cameo) 1976; *Another Man Another Woman* (Fr.), *A Bridge Too Far* (UK), *Un autre Homme une autre Chance/Another Man Another Chance* (Fr./US) 1977; *Little Moon & Jud McGraw, Comes a Horseman* 1978; *Chapter Two* 1979; *Hide in Plain Sight* (also dir.) 1980; *Thief, Les Uns et les Autres/Bolero* (Fr.) 1981; *Kiss Me Goodbye* 1982; *Gardens of Stone* 1987; *Alien Nation* 1988; *Nowhere Man, Dad* 1989; *Dick Tracy* (bit), *Misery* 1990; *The Dark Backward, For the Boys* 1991; *Honeymoon in Vegas* 1992; *Things to Do in Denver When You're Dead* 1995; *Bulletproof, Eraser* 1996.

Cabanne, Christy. Director. *b.* William Christy Cabanne, April 16, 1888, St. Louis, Mo. *d.* 1950. *ed.* Annapolis. Had a brief Navy career before entering films in 1910 as an actor in D. W. GRIFFITH productions. He later became Griffith's assistant, then began a directing career in 1913 under his supervision. Immediately asserted himself as a top-ranking director, handling such stars as the Gish sisters, Wallace Reid, Mae Murray, Francis X. Bushman, and Douglas Fairbanks in his film debut in *The Lamb.* He worked as a casting director and second-unit director on the silent *Ben-Hur* (1926) and subsequently directed routine low-budget productions.

FILMS INCLUDE (complete from 1915): *The Vengeance of Galora, The Adopted Brother* (also sc.) 1913; *The Smugglers of Sligo, The Dishonored Medal, The Great Leap/Until Death Do Us Part, The Life of General Villa, Arms and the Gringo, The Rebellion of Kitty Belle, For Those Unborn, Her Awakening, The Odalisque, The Sisters* 1914; *The Lost House, Enoch Arden, The Outlaw's Revenge* (re-edited version of *The Life of General Villa*), *The Absentee* (also co-sc.), *The Failure* (also sc.), *The Lamb, The Martyrs of the Alamo* (also sc.), *Double Trouble* (also sc.) 1915; *Daphne and the Pirate, The Flying Torpedo* (battle scenes only), *Sold for Marriage, Reggie Mixes In, Flirting with Fate, Diane of the Follies* 1916; *One of Many, The Slacker* (also sc.), *Miss Robinson Crusoe* (also co-sc.), *National Red Cross Pageant* 1917; *Draft 258* (also co-sc.), *Cyclone Higgins D.D.* (also sc.) 1918; *Fighting Through* (also sc.), *The Pest, A Regular Fellow, The Mayor of Filbert, God's Outlaw* (also sc.), *The Beloved Cheater* 1919; *The Triflers, Burnt Wings* (also co-sc.), *The Notorious Mrs. Sands, Life's Twist, The Stealers* 1920; *What's a Wife Worth?* (also sc.), *Live and Let Live* (also sc.), *The Barricade, At the Stage Door* (also sc.) 1921; *Beyond the Rainbow, Till We Meet Again* (also story) 1922; *The Average Woman, The Spitfire, The Sixth Commandment* (also prod.), *Lend Me Your Husband, Youth for Sale, Is Love* (also story) 1924; *The Midshipman, The Masked Bride* (begun by Josef von Sternberg) 1925; *Monte Carlo* 1926; *Altars of Desire* 1927; *Nameless Men, Driftwood, Annapolis, Restless Youth* 1928; *Conspiracy, The Dawn Trail* 1930; *Carne de Cabaret* (Spanish version of *Ten Cents a Dance*), *The Sky Raiders, Convicted, Graft* 1931; *Hotel Continental, The Midnight Patrol, Hearts of Humanity, The Western Limited, Red-Haired Alibi, The Unwritten Law* 1932; *The Eleventh Commandment, Daring Daughters, The World Gone Mad, Midshipman Jack* 1933; *Money Means Nothing, Jane Eyre, A Girl of the Limberlost, When Strangers Meet* 1934; *Behind the Green Lights, Rendezvous at Midnight, One Frightened Night, The Keeper of the Bees, Storm Over the Andes* (and Spanish version, *Asalto sobre el Chaco*), *Another Face* 1935; *The Last Outlaw* 1936; *We*

Who Are About to Die, Criminal Lawyer, Don't Tell the Wife, The Outcasts of Poker Flat, You Can't Beat Love, Annapolis Salute (also sc.), *The Westland Case* 1937; *Everybody's Doing It, Night Spot, This Marriage Business, Smashing the Spy Ring* 1938; *Mutiny on the Blackhawk, Tropic Fury, Legion of Lost Flyers* 1939; *Man from Montreal, Danger on Wheels, Alias the Deacon, Hot Steel, Black Diamonds, The Mummy's Hand, The Devil's Pipeline* 1940; *Scattergood Baines, Scattergood Pulls the String, Scattergood Meets Broadway* 1941; *Scattergood Rides High, Drums of the Congo, Timber, Top Sergeant, Scattergood Survives a Murder* 1942; *Keep 'Em Slugging* 1943; *Dixie Jamboree* 1944; *The Man Who Walked Alone* (also assoc. prod., story) 1945; *Sensation Hunters* 1946; *Scared to Death, Robin Hood of Monterey* (also story), *King of the Bandits* 1947; *Black Trail, Silver Trails* 1948.

cableman. A crew member on a film set whose function is to handle cables and wires for sound hookups.

Cabot, Bruce. *b.* Jacques Etienne de Bujac, Apr. 20, 1904, Carlsbad, N.M. *d.* 1972. *ed.* U. of the South (Sewanee, Tenn.). Grandson of a French ambassador to the US. He tried a variety of odd occupations before talking David O. Selznick into giving him a screen test when they met at a Hollywood party. Made film debut in 1932 and subsequently played numerous rugged he-man roles, frequently in B pictures, occasionally as a heavy, most memorably as the hero who saved Fay Wray from the clutches of the ape in *King Kong.* After WW II service as an intelligence and operations officer in Europe and Africa, he returned to Hollywood but spent much of the 50s working and living in Europe. He again returned to Hollywood in the 60s, in character roles. He died of cancer. Two of his three wives were actresses Adrienne AMES and Francesca de Scaffa.

FILMS INCLUDE: *Roadhouse Murder* 1932; *Lucky Devils, King Kong, Disgraced, Flying Devils, Ann Vickers, Midshipman Jack* 1933; *Shadows of Sing Sing, Finishing School, Murder on the Blackboard, His Greatest Gamble, Redhead, Men of the Night* 1934; *Show Them No Mercy* 1935; *Don't Gamble with Love, The Robin Hood of El Dorado, The Three Wise Guys, Fury, The Last of the Mohicans, The Big Game, Legion of Terror* 1936; *Sinner Take All, Bad Guy* 1937; *Sinners in Paradise, The Bad Man of Brimstone, Smashing the Rackets, Tenth Avenue Kid* 1938; *Homicide Bureau, Dodge City, Traitor Spy, My Son Is Guilty* 1939; *Susan and God, Captain Caution* 1940; *The Flame of New Orleans, Sundown* 1941; *Wild Bill Hickok Rides* 1942; *The Desert Song* 1944; *Divorce, Salty O'Rourke, Fallen Angel* 1945; *Smoky, Avalanche* 1946; *Angel and the Badman, Gunfighters* 1947; *Sorrowful Jones* 1949; *Fancy Pants* 1950; *Best of the Badmen* 1951; *Lost in Alaska* 1952; *The Treasure of Rommel* (It.) 1955; *The Quiet American, The Sheriff of Fractured Jaw* (UK) 1958; *John Paul Jones* 1959; *The Comancheros* 1961; *Hatari!* 1962; *McLintock!* 1963; *Law of the Lawless* 1964; *In Harm's Way, Cat Ballou* 1965; *The Chase* 1966; *The War Wagon* 1967; *The Green Berets* 1968; *The Undefeated* 1969; *Chisum, WUSA* 1970; *Big Jake, Diamonds Are Forever* 1971.

Cabot, Sebastian. Actor. *b.* July 6, 1918, London. *d.* 1977. A school dropout at 14, he was a garage helper and a cook before turning actor on British radio, stage, and screen. Since the 50s mostly in Hollywood films. Burly (280 pounds), courtly, and usually bearded, he played heavies as well as amiable characters. Popular in the TV series 'Checkmate' (1960–62) and 'Family Affair' (1966–71). He died of a stroke at 59.

FILMS INCLUDE: *Foreign Affairs* 1935; *Secret Agent* 1936; *The Agitator* 1944; *Othello* (as Iago) 1946; *They Made Me a Fugitive* 1947; *Laughter in Paradise* 1951; *Ivanhoe, Babes in Bagdad* 1952; *Romeo and Juliet* 1954; *Kismet* 1955; *Omar Khayyam, Dragoon Wells Massacre* 1957; *In Love and War, Terror in a Texas Town* 1958; *The Angry Hills* 1959; *Seven Thieves, The Time Machine* 1960; *Twice Told Tales* 1963; *The Family Jewels* 1965; *The Jungle Book* (v/o) 1969.

Cabot, Susan. Actress. *b.* Harriet Shapiro, July 9, 1927, Boston. *d.* 1986. Pretty, brunette leading lady of Hollywood action films of the 50s, often in exotic roles. Breaking into features at 23, after brief experience on the stage and early TV, she initially seemed headed for a promising career. But a four-year hiatus to marry and raise a family halted her progress and led to her permanent retirement in 1959. In December of 1986, she was beaten to death in her Encino, Calif., home. Her 22-year-old college-student son, Timothy Scott Roman, was arrested and charged with her murder.

FILMS: *On the Isle of Samoa* 1950; *Flame of Araby, Tomahawk, The Enforcer* 1951; *The Battle at Apache Pass, Duel at Silver Creek, Son of Ali Baba* 1952; *Gunsmoke* 1953; *Ride Clear of Diablo* 1954; *Sorority Girl* 1957; *War of the Satellites, Fort Massacre, Machine Gun Kelly* 1958; *Surrender Hell!, The Wasp Woman* 1959.

Cacoyannis, Michael. Director. Born Mikhalis Kakogiannis on June 11, 1922, in Limassol, Cyprus, of Greek parentage. The son of a knighted Cypriot lawyer and political leader, he studied and practiced law in England. During WW II, he produced Greek programs for the BBC and attended acting and directing schools. He joined the Old Vic Company in 1946 and made his acting debut in 'Salome' the same year. After giving up acting in 1951, for two years he unsuccessfully sought directing assignments in Britain and the US. He returned to Greece and in 1953 began directing his first film, *Windfall in Athens.* His next, *Stella* (1955), starred Melina Mercouri and won several international awards. Cacoyannis's reputation as Greece's leading film director was established by *Electra* (1961), considered by some as the finest screen interpretation of a Greek tragedy. He later gained popular recognition with *Zorba the Greek* (1964). As a noted stage director of classical plays, he received critical praise for his off-Broadway production 'The Trojan Women' (1963). In 1986 he returned to films after a long absence with *Sweet Country,* a film many critics deemed "disappointing." In 1971 he directed a screen adaption of the play. In addition, Cacoyannis writes his own scripts.

FILMS: *Windfall in Athens/Sunday Awakening* 1954; *Stella* 1955; *A Girl in Black* 1956; *A Matter of Dignity/The Final Lie* 1958; *Our Last Spring/Eroica* 1960; *Il Relitto/The Wastrel* (It.), *Electra* 1961; *Zorba the Greek* 1964; *The Day the Fish Came Out* 1967; *The Trojan Women* 1971; *The Story of Jacob and Joseph* (for TV) 1974; *Attila '74* (doc.) 1975; *Iphigenia* 1977; *Sweet Country* 1986; *Zoe* 1989; *Up Down and Sideways* 1992; *Pano Kato ke Plagios* 1993.

Caesar, Sid. Comic actor. Born on Sept. 8, 1922, in Yonkers, N.Y. He started out as a musician, and after studying the saxophone and clarinet at Manhattan's Juilliard School of Music, he began playing with various bands. He switched to comedy during his WW II stint with the Coast Guard and was a featured comedian in the service show 'Tars and Spars' and then its subsequent film version. In the late 40s, after successful appearances in nightclubs and in the Broadway hit 'Make Mine Manhattan,' he began performing on TV and in the early 50s gained much popularity as the co-star of the TV comedy program 'Your Show of Shows.' He later brought his hilarious character studies to other television programs, but his big-screen appearances have been sporadic and have rarely taken full advantage of the broad range of his comic talent. In 1989 he returned to Broadway in 'Sid Caesar and Company.' Autobiography: *Where Have I Been?* (1982).

FILMS: *Tars and Spars* 1946; *The Guilt of Janet Ames* 1947; *It's a Mad Mad Mad Mad World* 1963; *A Guide for the Married Man, The Busy Body, The Spirit Is Willing* 1967; *Ten from Your Show of Shows* (feature-length compilation of TV sketches) 1973; *Airport 1975* 1974; *Silent Movie* 1976; *Fire Sale* 1977; *The Cheap Detective, Grease* (cameo) 1978; *The Fiendish Plot of Dr. Fu Manchu* 1980; *History of the World Part One* 1981; *Grease 2* 1982; *Over the Brooklyn Bridge, Cannonball Run II* 1984; *Stoogemania* 1985; *The Emperor's New Clothes* 1987.

Cage, Nicolas. Actor. Born Nicholas Coppola, on Jan. 7, 1964, in Long Beach, Calif. A nephew of director Francis Ford Coppola, he dropped out of high school to become an actor, making his debut on TV in 1981. He got into features the following year and rapidly became established as one of the American screen's most distinctive young talents. Intense in his approach to roles, he is said to have slashed his arm in preparation for his part in *Racing with the Moon,* had two teeth pulled for *Birdy,* and swallowed a live cockroach for *Vampire's Kiss.*

In 1995, Cage was placed on the "A" list of Hollywood actors with a gut-wrenching, critically acclaimed portrayal of an alchoholic screenwriter who eventually drinks himself to death in the Mike Figgis-directed *Leaving Las Vegas.* It was for this performance that he was named best actor by the New York and Los Angeles Film Critics Associations, the Golden Globes, as well as receiving the Oscar. Cage is married to actress Patricia ARQUETTE.

FILMS: As Nicholas Coppola—*Fast Times at Ridgemont High* 1982. As Nicolas Cage—*Valley Girl, Rumble Fish* 1983; *Racing with the Moon, The Cotton Club, Birdy* 1984; *The Boy in Blue* (Can.), *Peggy Sue Got Married* 1986; *Raising Arizona, Moonstruck* 1987; *Vampire's Kiss, Tempo di Uccidere/Killing Time/The Short Cut* (It./Fr.) 1989; *Fire Birds, Wild at Heart* 1990; *Zandalee* 1991; *Honeymoon in Vegas* 1992; *Red Rock West* 1993; *Guarding Tess, It Could Happen To You, Trapped in Paradise* 1994; *Kiss of Death, Leaving Las Vegas* 1995; *The Rock* 1996; *Con Air, Face/Off* 1997.

Cagney, James. Actor. *b.* James Francis Cagney Jr., July 17, 1899, New York City. *d.* 1986. *ed.* Columbia. The son of an Irish bartender and a Norwegian mother, he grew up on the Lower East Side and helped support his family as a waiter and poolroom racker, among other occupations. To supplement his income he joined a Yorkville area revue as a female impersonator. In 1920 he was in the chorus of the Broadway production 'Pitter-Patter,' and after touring in vaudeville with his wife Frances, he began playing leads on Broadway in 1925. Following the success of 'Penny Arcade,' he was brought to Hollywood in 1930 with co-star Joan Blondell to appear in the film version, renamed *Sinners' Holiday.*

Signed by Warner Bros., Cagney became a star within a year on the strength of his performance in *The Public Enemy* as a ruthless Prohibition gangster who, in a memorable scene, smashes a grapefruit into the face of gang moll Mae Clarke. This heralded the cocky, pugnacious characters he was to portray in subsequent films. An atypical Hollywood star, he was short and ordinary looking, but his eager energy and two-fisted vitality made him an ideal lead for the gangster films and the social dramas of the Depression era. Later he proved his acting versatility by effectively playing such diverse roles as Bottom in *A Midsummer Night's Dream* (1935), George M. Cohan in *Yankee Doodle Dandy* (in which he sang and danced and for which he won the 1942 best actor Oscar), Lon Chaney in *Man of a Thousand Faces* (1957), and a caricature of a dynamic American businessman in *One Two Three* (1961), after which he announced his retirement.

Will Rogers once remarked of Cagney, "Every time I see him work, it looks to me like a bunch of firecrackers going off all at once." The actor directed one film, *Short Cut to Hell* (1957), a so-so remake of *This Gun for Hire.* In 1942 he formed Cagney Productions with his brother, William (*b.* 1902, N.Y.C.; *d.* 1988), a former actor who produced several of Cagney's movies. His sister, Jean Cagney (*b.* Mar. 25, 1919, N.Y.C.; *d.* 1984), is a stage and TV actress who appeared in a number of films. The adulation of Cagney continued long after his announced retirement. In 1974 he became the first actor to receive the Life Achievement Award of the American Film Institute. In 1980 he was similarly honored by Washington's Kennedy Center and in 1984 he was decorated with the Medal of Freedom, the US government's highest civilian award. During 20 years of retirement he lived in quiet seclusion on a farm in upstate New York, repeatedly rejecting offers to return to the movies. But in 1981, responding to the advice of doctors that his deteriorating health would benefit from increased activity, he accepted an offer by director Milos Forman to play the small but crucial role of a police inspector in the film *Ragtime.* Cagney's comeback was applauded enthusiastically by the public and critics, encouraging him to defy diabetes, a circulatory ailment, and the effects of several strokes, and play the lead role as a crochety ex-boxer in a made-for-TV movie, *Terrible Joe Moran* in 1984. Two years later, on Easter Sunday, he died of cardiac arrest on his farm. "America lost one of her finest artists," Cagney's friend, President Ronald Reagan, eulogized. Autobiography: *Cagney by Cagney* (1975).

FILMS: *Sinners' Holiday, Doorway to Hell* 1930; *Other Men's Women, The Millionaire, The Public Enemy, Smart Money, Blonde Crazy* 1931; *Taxi, The Crowd Roars, Winner Take All* 1932; *Hard to Handle, Picture Snatcher, The Mayor of Hell, Footlight Parade, Lady Killer* 1933; *Jimmy the Gent, He Was Her Man, Here Comes the Navy, The St. Louis Kid* 1934; *Devil Dogs of the Air, G-Men, The Irish in Us, Frisco Kid, A Midsummer Night's Dream* (as Bottom) 1935; *Ceiling Zero, Great Guy* 1936; *Something to Sing About* 1937; *Boy Meets Girl, Angels with Dirty Faces* 1938; *The Oklahoma Kid, Each Dawn I Die, The Roaring Twenties* 1939; *The Fighting 69th, Torrid Zone, City for Conquest* 1940; *The Strawberry Blonde, The Bride Came C.O.D.* 1941; *Captains of the Clouds, Yankee Doodle Dandy* (as George M. Cohan) 1942; *Johnny Come Lately* 1943; *Blood on the Sun* 1945; *13 Rue Madeleine* 1947; *The Time of Your Life* 1948; *White Heat* 1949; *Kiss Tomorrow Goodbye, The West Point Story* 1950; *Starlift* (cameo), *Come Fill the Cup* 1951; *What Price Glory* 1952; *A Lion Is in the Streets* 1953; *Run for Cover, Love Me or Leave Me, The Seven Little Foys* (as George M. Cohan), *Mister Roberts* 1955; *Tribute to a Bad Man, These Wilder Years* 1956; *Short Cut to Hell* (dir. only; appears briefly in prologue), *Man of a Thousand Faces* (as Lon Chaney) 1957; *Never Steal Anything Small, Shake Hands with the Devil* 1959; *The Gallant Hours* (as Admiral "Bull" Halsey) 1960; *One Two Three* 1961.

Cahiers du Cinéma. Perhaps the single most influential magazine devoted to the serious study of film as an art form. In 1947 André BAZIN founded *La Revue du Cinéma,* which in 1951 became *Cahiers du Cinéma.* Jacques DONIOL-VALCROZE was co-editor with Bazin, who continued running *Cahiers* until his death in 1958. The guiding editorial principle of *Cahiers* has been the *politique des auteurs*—the AUTEUR THEORY—which it proclaimed and formulated under Bazin's guidance. *Cahiers* attracted a number of young film devotees to its staff as writers and critics. Eventually, many of them went on to make films of their own, providing the core of the French NOUVELLE VAGUE, or New Wave. Among them were Jean-Luc Godard, François

Truffaut, Claude Chabrol, Jacques Rivette, and Eric Rohmer. The Nouvelle Vague movement can therefore be considered a direct outgrowth of the ideas and theories promulgated by *Cahiers du Cinéma.* Briefly in the late 60s an American edition, *Cahiers du Cinéma in English,* was published in New York with Andrew SARRIS as editor. The French edition is still in publication, monthly.

Cahn, Edward L. Director, producer. *b.* Feb. 12, 1899, in Brooklyn, N.Y. *d.* 1963. Attended UCLA and worked nights as a film cutter at Universal. By 1926 he was chief film editor for the studio and in 1931 began his prolific directing career. With the exception of one of his earliest films, *Law and Order,* starring Walter Huston as Wyatt Earp, his output, in a variety of genres, consisted of routine, low-budget films. After 1950 he produced many of the films he directed.

FILMS: *Homicide Squad* (co-dir. with George Melford) 1931; *Law and Order, Radio Patrol, Afraid to Talk* 1932; *Laughter in Hell, Emergency Call* 1933; *Confidential* 1935; *Bad Guy* 1937; *Redhead* 1941; *Main Street After Dark, Dangerous Partners* 1945; *Born to Speed, Gas House Kids in Hollywood* 1947; *The Checkered Coat, Bungalow 13* 1948; *I Cheated the Law, Prejudice* 1949; *The Great Plane Robbery, Destination Murder, Experiment Alcatraz* 1950; *Two Dollar Bettor* 1951; *The Creature with the Atom Brain, Betrayed Women* 1955; *Girls in Prison, The She-Creature, Flesh and the Spur, Runaway Daughters, Shake Rattle and Rock* 1956; *Voodoo Woman, Zombies of Mora-Tau, Dragstrip Girl, Invasion of the Saucer Men, Motorcycle Gang* 1957; *Jet Attack, Suicide Battalion, It!—The Terror from Beyond Space, The Curse of the Faceless Man, Hong Kong Confidential, Guns Girls and Gangsters* 1958; *Riot in Juvenile Prison, Invisible Invaders, The Four Skulls of Jonathan Drake, Pier 5—Havana, Inside the Mafia, Vice Raid* 1959; *Gunfighters of Abilene, A Dog's Best Friend, Oklahoma Territory, Three Came to Kill, Twelve Hours to Kill, Noose for a Gunman, The Music Box Kid, Cage of Evil, The Walking Target* 1960; *The Police Dog Story, Frontier Uprising, Operation Bottleneck, Five Guns to Tombstone, The Gambler Wore a Gun, When the Clock Strikes, You Have to Run Fast, Secret of Deep Harbor, The Boy Who Caught a Crook, Gun Fight, Gun Street, The Clown and the Kid* 1961; *Incident in an Alley* 1962; *Beauty and the Beast* 1963.

Cahn, Sammy. Lyricist. *b.* Samuel Cohen, on June 18, 1913, in New York City. *d.* 1993. A classic Tin Pan Alley lyricist from 1935, he supplied lyrics for many films, often working in collaboration with composers Jule STYNE or Jimmy VAN HEUSEN. Of 30 Academy Award nominations, he won awards for the title song of *Three Coins in the Fountain* (1954), 'All the Way' from *The Joker Is Wild* (1957), 'High Hopes' from *A Hole in the Head* (1959), and 'Call Me Irresponsible' from *Papa's Delicate Condition* (1963). Known informally (with Jimmy Van Heusen) as Frank SINATRA'S personal composer, having written over 80 songs he has recorded. Autobiography: *I Should Care* (1974).

FILMS INCLUDE: *Argentine Nights* 1940; *Youth on Parade* ('I've Heard This Song Before,' etc.) 1942; *Crazy House, Lady of Burlesque* 1943; *Follow the Boys* ('I'll Walk Alone,' etc.), *Knickerbocker Holiday* 1944; *Anchors Aweigh* ('I Fall in Love Too Easily,' etc.), *The Stork Club* 1945; *The Sweetheart of Sigma Chi* ('Five Minutes More,' etc.), *The Kid from Brooklyn* 1946; *It Happened in Brooklyn* ('Time After Time,' etc.) 1947; *Romance on the High Seas* ('It's Magic,' etc.) 1948; *It's a Great Feeling* 1949; *Rich Young and Pretty* ('We Never Talk Much,' etc.) 1951; *Because You're Mine* 1952; *Peter Pan, Three Sailors and a Girl* (also prod.), *April in Paris* 1953; *Three Coins in the Fountain* 1954; *The Tender Trap, Love Me or Leave Me* 1955; *The Court Jester, Meet Me in Las Vegas, Anything Goes* 1956; *Pal Joey, The Joker Is Wild* 1957; *The Long Hot Summer, Indiscreet, Paris Holiday* 1958; *A Hole in the Head* 1959; *High Time* ('The Second Time Around,' etc.) 1960; *Pocketful of Miracles* 1961; *Boys' Night Out, How the West Was Won* 1962; *Papa's Delicate Condition, Come Blow Your Horn* 1963; *Robin and the Seven Hoods* ('My Kind of Town,' etc.) 1964; *The Oscar* 1966; *Thoroughly Modern Millie* 1967; *Star!* 1968; *A Touch of Class* 1973; *Journey Back to Oz* 1974; *Paper Tiger* 1975; *The Duchess and the Dirtwater Fox* (co-lyrics) 1976; *The Stud* (UK) 1978; *Boardwalk* (cameo appearance only) 1979; *Heidi's Song* 1982.

Caine, Michael. Actor. Born Maurice Joseph Micklewhite, Jr., on Mar. 14, 1933, in London. Coarsely debonair star of British and international films, highly popular after playing the title role as a self-centered lothario in *Alfie* (1966) and portraying atypical, bespectacled, vulnerable heroes in a succession of espionage thrillers of the late 60s. The son of a cockney fish-market porter and a cleaning-woman mother, he left school at 15 and worked at a variety of odd jobs. Got the acting bug a year later when he served tea in a London theater, and began appearing in amateur plays while working as a laborer. After serving with the British army in Korea and Germany, he began playing small parts in provincial theaters and on British TV and from the mid-50s appeared in bit roles in British films. Caine first attracted attention in the role of an effete young officer in the film *Zulu* (1964) and has since proved himself a versatile, as well as popular, screen personality. He was nominated for Academy Awards as best actor for his performances in *Alfie* (1966), *Sleuth* (1972), and *Educating Rita* (1983), and finally won the Oscar as best supporting actor for his role in Woody Allen's *Hannah and Her Sisters* (1986). Known for his omnipresence on-screen, he said of selecting roles, "First of all I choose the great ones, and if none of those come, I choose the mediocre ones, and if they don't come—I choose the ones that are going to pay the rent." Divorced from actress Patricia Haines, he married in 1973 Shakira Caine (*b.* Shakira Baksh, Feb. 23, 1947, Guyana), an exotic former Miss Guyana finalist who co-starred in *The Man Who Would Be King.*

FILMS: *A Hill in Korea* 1956; *How to Murder a Rich Uncle* 1957; *The Key, Blind Spot* 1958; *The Two-Headed Spy* 1959; *Foxhole in Cairo, The Bulldog Breed* 1960; *The Day the Earth Caught Fire* 1961; *Solo for Sparrow* 1962; *The Wrong Arm of the Law* 1963; *Zulu* 1964; *The Ipcress File* 1965; *Alfie, The Wrong Box, Gambit, Funeral in Berlin* 1966; *Hurry Sundown, Billion Dollar Brain, Woman Times Seven* 1967; *Tonight Let's All Make Love in London* (doc.), *Deadfall, The Magus* 1968; *Play Dirty, The Italian Job, The Battle of Britain* 1969; *Too Late the Hero* 1970; *The Last Valley, Get Carter, Kidnapped* 1971; *Zee and Company/X Y & Zee, Pulp, Sleuth* 1972; *The Black Windmill, The Marseille Contract/The Wilby Conspiracy, The Destructors* 1974; *The Romantic Englishwoman, The Man Who Would Be King* 1975; *Peeper, Harry and Walter Go to New York, The Eagle Has Landed* 1976; *A Bridge Too Far, Silver Bears* 1977; *The Swarm, California Suite* 1978; *Ashanti, Beyond the Poseidon Advenure* 1979; *The Island, Dressed to Kill* 1980; *The Hand, Escape to Victory/Victory* 1981; *Deathtrap* 1982; *Educating Rita, Beyond the Limit* 1983; *The Jigsaw Man, Blame It on Rio, Water* 1984; *The Holcroft Covenant* 1985; *Hannah and Her Sisters, Sweet Liberty, Mona Lisa, Half Moon Street* 1986; *The Fourth Protocol* (also exec. prod.), *The Whistle Blower, Jaws: The Revenge, Surrender* 1987; *Without a Clue* (as Sherlock Holmes), *Dirty Rotten Scoundrels* 1988; *Bullseye!* 1989; *A Shock to the System, Mr. Destiny* 1990; *Noises Off, The*

Muppets' Christmas Carol (v/o) 1992; *On Deadly Ground* 1994; *Blood and Wine* 1997.

Calamai, Clara. Actress. Born on Sept. 7, 1915, in Prato, Italy. Made her film debut in 1938 and soon developed into Italy's foremost star during the war years, notably in films directed by Blasetti. Her most memorable part was in Visconti's *Ossessione* (1942), a film that marked the beginnings of the neo-realist school in Italian cinema. After the war, her roles declined, with the exception of another strong performance in a Visconti film, *White Nights.*

FILMS INCLUDE: *Ettore Fieramosca* 1939; *Boccaccio* 1940; *Regina di Navarra* 1941; *Ossessione* 1942; *Adultera* 1944; *La Resa di Titi/The Merry Chase* 1945; *Ultimo Amore* 1946; *Le Notti Bianche/White Nights* 1957; *Aphrodite* 1958; *Le Streghe/The Witches* 1967.

Calhern, Louis. Actor. *b.* Carl Henry Vogt, Feb. 16, 1895, in New York City. *d.* 1956. Tall and imposing romantic leading man of Hollywood silents of the early 20s, he is best remembered for his powerful character roles in MGM films of the 50s, notably as the criminal mastermind in *The Asphalt Jungle,* as Justice Oliver Wendell Holmes in *The Magnificent Yankee,* and as Caesar in *Julius Caesar.* Also made numerous Broadway appearances. Was married to screen actresses Ilka Chase, Julia Hoyt, Natalie Schafer, and Marianne Stewart. He died of a heart attack in Tokyo during the filming of *The Teahouse of the August Moon.*

FILMS INCLUDE: *The Blot, What's Worth While?* 1921; *Woman Wake Up!* 1922; *The Last Moment* 1923; *Stolen Heaven, The Road to Singapore, Blonde Crazy* 1931; *Okay America!, Night After Night* 1932; *Frisco Jenny, 20,000 Years in Sing Sing, The Woman Accused, Diplomaniacs, Duck Soup* 1933; *The Man with Two Faces, The Affairs of Cellini, The Count of Monte Cristo* 1934; *The Arizonian, The Last Days of Pompeii* 1925; *The Gorgeous Hussy* 1936; *The Life of Emile Zola* 1937; *Juarez* 1939; *Dr. Ehrlich's Magic Bullet* 1940; *Heaven Can Wait* 1943; *Up in Arms, The Bridge of San Luis Rey* 1944; *Notorious* 1946; *Arch of Triumph* 1948; *The Red Pony, The Red Danube* 1949; *Nancy Goes to Rio, Annie Get Your Gun* (as Buffalo Bill), *The Asphalt Jungle, A Life of Her Own, Devil's Doorway, Two Weeks with Love* 1950; *The Magnificent Yankee* (as Justice Oliver Wendell Holmes) 1951; *Invitation, Washington Story, We're Not Married, The Prisoner of Zenda* 1952; *Julius Caesar* (title role), *Latin Lovers* 1953; *Rhapsody, Executive Suite, Men of the Fighting Lady, The Student Prince, Betrayed* 1954; *The Blackboard Jungle, The Prodigal* 1955; *High Society* 1956.

Calhoun, Rory. Actor. Born Francis Timothy Durgin, on Aug. 8, 1922 (or 1918), in Los Angeles. Ruggedly handsome leading man of Hollywood films. Raised in poverty by his mother and a stepfather named McCown, he was often in trouble with the law and spent several months of his juvenile years in reformatories and prisons. Reformed by a priest, he worked as a lumberjack, miner, cowboy, and forester before drifting into films as a result of a chance meeting with Alan Ladd. He went virtually unnoticed at 20th Century-Fox under his initial billing as Frank McCown. But after changing studios and converting his name to Rory Calhoun, he gradually advanced from supporting roles to leads, mostly in Westerns and action pictures. He also starred in the TV series 'The Texan' (1958–60) and in many other television programs. His 21-year marriage to actress Lita Baron was dissolved in 1970. He is an amateur artist and author of *The Man from Padera.*

FILMS INCLUDE: As Frank McCown—*Something for the Boys, Sunday Dinner for a Soldier* 1944; *The Bullfighters, Nob Hill, The Great John L.* 1945. As Rory Calhoun—*The Red House, Adventure Island* 1947; *Miraculous Journey* 1948; *Massacre River, Sand* 1949; *A Ticket to Tomahawk, Rogue River* 1950; *I'd Climb the Highest Mountain, Meet Me After the Show* 1951; *With a Song in My Heart, Way of a Gaucho* 1952; *Powder River, How to Marry a Millionaire* 1953; *River of No Return, Dawn at Socorro, Four Guns to the Border, A Bullet Is Waiting* 1954; *Ain't Misbehaving, The Treasure of Pancho Villa* 1955; *The Spoilers, Raw Edge, Red Sundown, Flight to Hong Kong* 1956; *The Big Caper, The Hired Gun* 1957; *Apache Territory* 1958; *Marco Polo* (It.) 1960; *The Colossus of Rhodes* (It.) 1961; *Requiem for a Heavyweight* 1962; *The Gun Hawk* 1963; *Young Fury, Black Spurs* 1965; *Apache Uprising* 1966; *Dayton's Devils* 1968; *Night of the Lepus* 1972; *Love and the Midnight Auto Supply* 1977; *The Main Event* 1979; *Motel Hell* 1980; *Angel* 1984; *Avenging Angel* 1985; *Hell Comes to Frogtown* 1988; *Bad Jim* 1990; *Pure Country* 1992.

calibration. 1. The process of measuring and marking focus settings and f-stop values on a camera's lens assembly in preparation for a shot that involves a gradual or sudden change of distance or light conditions. During filming, the assistant cameraman, or focus puller, will adjust the lens to the predetermined settings, leaving the camera operator free to concentrate on composition and camera movement and assuring that the shot remains in focus and properly exposed. 2. In animation terminology, a calibration is the marked position on the background that indicates the extent of camera movement for each frame.

caligarisme. A term coined by French critics and social analysts to describe the psychological phenomenon and the expressionist style of post–WW I German films associated with Robert Wiene's *The Cabinet of Dr. Caligari.*

call. The summons to performers and technical crews to report on a set or location at a specific time for a day's shooting. The call schedule is usually prepared by the assistant director and is referred to as the "call sheet."

Callan, Michael. Actor, dancer, singer. Born Martin Calinieff, on Nov. 22, 1935, in Philadelphia. A former nightclub entertainer, he has been playing light leads in films and on TV since the late 50s. Formerly married to actress Patricia Harty, his co-star in the TV series 'Occasional Wife' (1966–67).

FILMS INCLUDE: *They Came to Cordura* 1958; *The Flying Fontaines* 1959; *Mysterious Island* (UK), *Because They're Young* 1960; *Gidget Goes Hawaiian* 1961; *The Interns, 13 West Street, Bon Voyage* 1962; *The Victors* 1963; *The New Interns* 1964; *Cat Ballou, You Must Be Joking!* 1965; *The Magnificent Seven Ride* 1972; *Frasier the Sensuous Lion* 1973; *Lepke* 1975; *Record City* 1977; *The Cat and the Canary* (UK) 1978; *Double Exposure* (also prod.) 1982; *Chained Heat* 1983; *Freeway* 1988.

Calleia, Joseph. Actor. *b.* Joseph Spurin-Calleja, Aug. 14, 1897, Malta. *d.* 1975. Menacing character player of Hollywood films, often in darkly mysterious roles. He was memorable as Mae West's dashing masked lothario in *My Little Chickadee* and in such films as *Gilda* and *Touch of Evil.* On the screen from the early 30s, following a radio and stage singing career in England and the US. He collaborated on the screenplay of a B picture, *The Robin Hood of El Dorado* (1936).

FILMS INCLUDE: *His Woman* 1931; *Public Hero No. 1* 1935; *Riffraff, After the Thin Man* 1936; *Algiers, Marie Antoinette* 1938; *Juarez, Golden Boy* 1939; *My Little Chickadee* 1940; *The Monster and the Girl* 1941; *Jungle Book, The Glass Key* 1942; *For Whom the Bell Tolls, The Cross of Lorraine* 1943; *The Conspirators* 1944; *Gilda* 1946; *The Beginning or the End, Lured* 1947; *The Noose Hangs High, Four Faces West* 1948; *Captain Carey USA, Vendetta, Branded* 1950; *Valentino* 1951; *The Iron Mistress* 1952; *The Treasure of Pancho Villa* 1955; *Hot Blood, Serenade* 1956; *Wild Is the Wind, Touch of Evil* 1958; *Cry Tough* 1959; *The Alamo* 1960; *Johnny Cool* 1963.

Callow, Simon. Actor, director, author. Born June 15, 1949, in London, England. *ed.* Cambridge University, England; University of Belfast, Ireland; The London Drama Centre. Gained prominence as an actor for his early work in London theater, specifically for creating the role of Mozart in Peter Shaffer's 'Amadeus.' Appearing in the Milos FORMAN's film version as a minor character, he has since built an impressive resumé of both comic and dramatic performances, most notably in *A Room with a View* (1985) and *Four Weddings and a Funeral* (1994). His first effort as a film director, *The Ballad of the Sad Café* (1991), was met with mixed reviews. He is the author of several books on the subject of acting.

FILMS INCLUDE: *Amadeus* 1984; *A Room with a View* 1985; *The Good Father, Maurice* (also dir.) 1987; *Manifesto* 1988; *Postcards from the Edge* 1990; *The Ballad of the Sad Café* (dir. only), *The Crucifer of Blood* 1991; *Howards End* 1992; *Four Weddings and a Funeral, Street Fighter* 1994; *Ace Ventura: When Nature Calls, Jefferson in Paris* 1995; *James and the Giant Peach* (v/o) 1996.

Calmettes, André. Director, actor. *b.* Apr. 18, 1861, Paris. *d.* 1942. A stage actor for 20 years, and, beginning in 1908, the artistic director of the Film d'Art series of screen adaptations of distinguished plays. He co-directed the first important production of that group, *The Assassination of the Duke de Guise* (1908) and during the next three years directed several others. He retired from films in 1913, returning only briefly as an actor.

FILMS INCLUDE: As director—*L'Assassinat du Duc de Guise/The Assassination of the Duke de Guise* (co-dir. with Charles Le Bargy) 1908; *L'Arlésienne, La Tosca, La Tour de Nesle, Macbeth, Résurrection* 1909; *L'Avare, Don Carlos, Werther* 1910; *Camille Desmoulins, Madame Sans-Gêne* 1911; *Les Trois Mousquetaires* 1912; *Ferragus* 1913. As actor—*Le Petit Chose* 1922; *La Closerie des Genêts* 1925.

Calthrop, Donald. Actor. *b.* Apr. 11, 1888, London. *d.* 1940. A stage actor from 1906, he entered films in 1918. In the 20s and 30s he was among the most prominent character actors on the British screen. Typically cast as a villain, most memorably in early Hitchcock films. A drinking problem finally hurt his career and contributed to his early death, of a heart attack.

FILMS INCLUDE: *Wanted a Widow* 1916; *The Gay Lord Quex* 1918; *Nelson* 1919; *Shooting Stars* 1928; *Atlantic, Blackmail* 1929; *Juno and the Paycock, Elstree Calling, Two Worlds, Loose Ends, Murder* 1930; *The Ghost Train* 1931; *Number 17, Rome Express* 1932; *Sorrell and Son, I Was a Spy, Orders Is Orders* 1933; *The Clairvoyant, Scrooge* 1935; *Broken Blossoms* 1936; *Fire Over England, Dreaming Lips* 1937; *Let George Do It* 1940; *Major Barbara* 1941.

Calvert, Phyllis. Actress. Born Phyllis Bickle, on Feb. 18, 1915, in London. On the stage from childhood, she switched from dance to drama following an injury. She was a popular star in British films of the 40s and played leads in several Hollywood productions late in the decade. Her subsequent screen appearances were scattered, but she still appears occasionally on the stage, and early in the 70s she starred in the BBC TV series 'Kate.' She is the widow of actor-turned-publisher Peter Murray-Hill (1908–57).

FILMS INCLUDE: *The Arcadians* (bit) 1927; *Inspector Hornleigh* 1938; *Two Days to Live* 1939; *They Came by Night, Let George Do It* 1940; *Kipps/The Remarkable Mr. Kipps* 1941; *The Young Mr. Pitt* 1942; *The Man in Grey* 1943; *Fanny by Gaslight/Man of Evil* 1944; *Madonna of the Seven Moons, They Were Sisters* 1945; *The Magic Bow, Men of Two Worlds/Kisenga—Man of Africa* 1946; *Time Out of Mind* (US) 1947; *My Own True Love* (US), *The Golden Madonna* 1949; *The Woman with No Name/Her Paneled Door* 1950; *Appointment with Danger* (US), *Mr. Denning Drives North* 1951; *Mandy/The Story of Mandy/The Crash of Silence* 1952; *The Net/Project M-7* 1953; *It's Never Too Late* 1954; *Indiscreet* 1958; *Oscar Wilde* 1960; *The Battle of the Villa Fiorita* 1965; *Twisted Nerve* 1968; *Oh! What a Lovely War* 1969; *The Walking Stick* 1970.

Calvet, Corinne. Actress. Born Corinne Dibos, on Apr. 30, 1925, in Paris. Shapely leading lady of Hollywood films of the 50s, following French screen debut in 1945. Despite some good opportunities in both comedies and dramas, her career reached an impasse in the early 60s, and by the end of the decade she was seeking employment outside the industry. Five aborted marriages included (1948–53) that to actor John Bromfield. Autobiography: *Has Corinne Been a Good Little Girl?*

FILMS INCLUDE: In France—*La Part de l'Ombre* 1945; *Pétrus* 1947. In the US—*Rope of Sand* 1949; *When Willie Comes Marching Home, My Friend Irma Goes West* 1950; *Quebec, On the Riviera, Peking Express* 1951; *Sailor Beware, What Price Glory* 1952; *Thunder in the East, Powder River, Flight to Tangiers* 1953; *Le Avventure di Giacomo Casanova/Sins of Casanova* (It.) 1954; *Napoléon* (Fr.), *Bonnes a tuer/One Step to Eternity* (Fr.), *So This Is Paris, The Far Country* 1955; *Plunderers of Painted Flats* 1959; *Bluebeard's Ten Honeymoons* (UK) 1960; *Hemingway's Adventures of a Young Man* 1962; *Apache Uprising* 1966; *Too Hot to Handle* 1976; *Dr. Heckyl and Mr. Hype* 1980; *The Sword and the Sorcerer* 1982.

Cambridge, Godfrey. Actor. *b.* Feb. 26, 1933, New York City. *d.* 1976. The son of immigrants from British New Guinea, he grew up in Harlem and Nova Scotia. After briefly attending Hofstra College and CCNY, he worked in various capacities, including bouncer, judo instructor, and taxi driver. Began appearing in off-Broadway stage plays in the late 50s and made his screen debut as a young hoodlum in *The Last Angry Man* (1959). Following appearances in the early 60s in the off-Broadway production 'The Blacks' and the Broadway play 'Purlie Victorious,' he gained popularity as a funnyman on TV, leading to meatier parts and finally leads in films. He was stricken with a fatal heart attack on the set of the TV movie *Victory at Entebbe,* in which he was to portray the Ugandan president Idi Amin Dada.

FILMS INCLUDE: *The Last Angry Man* 1959; *Gone Are the Days!/Purlie Victorious* 1963; *The Troublemaker* 1964; *The Busy Body, The President's Analyst* 1967; *The Biggest Bundle of Them All, Bye Bye Braverman* 1968; *Watermelon Man, Cotton Comes to Harlem* 1970; *The Biscuit Eater, Come Back Charleston Blue* 1972; *Whiffs, Friday Foster* 1975; *Scott Joplin* 1977.

cameo. A brief, often unbilled film appearance by a well-known star. It is sometimes inserted for comic effect, such as Bing Crosby's showing up momentarily and unexpectedly in a film starring Bob Hope. But more frequently it is intended as a publicity gimmick to enhance the box-office potential of a film, as was the case with the many brief guest appearances by famous stars in *Around the World in 80 Days* and *Pepe.*

cameo shot. A shot photographed against a neutral or blacked-out background, using the barest of props in order not to detract from the principle subject of the shot. See also LIMBO.

camera, hand-held. A portable, lightweight motion-picture camera that is held in the hands of the cameraman and steadied against his body without the use of a tripod. Hand-held cameras, originally designed for newsreel photography, have been widely used by documentary and avant-garde filmmakers. Since the early 60s there has been an increase in the use of hand-held cameras in the production of feature films, both as a matter of convenience and for achieving a greater sense of realism for certain scenes.

camera, motion picture. The basic tool of the filmmaker, a motion picture camera operates on the same optical principles as a still camera but with a fundamental difference: it is designed to record not single images but a succession of images at regular intervals on a continuous band of film. When these still images are projected on a screen at a steady rate of speed, an illusion of motion is obtained. To achieve such results, the motion picture camera is equipped with special mechanisms that assure the precision and smoothness of its operation.

Early motion picture cameras were crude wooden boxes with unreliable mechanisms and had to be cranked by hand, but even before the turn of the century, Edison's KINETOGRAPH and the Lumière CINEMATOGRAPH incorporated the essential features of the modern motion picture camera: a light-tight interior in which film is drawn by a sprocket wheel and pulled down through a gate so that images can be exposed at regular intervals when a frame is stopped behind an aperture equipped with a light-gathering lens. The Edison and Lumière motion picture cameras were the culmination of research and experimentation dating back to the 1820s and the discovery of the principles of still photography by Frenchmen Joseph-Nicéphore NIÉPCE and Louis DAGUERRE.

The first important step toward cinematography was taken in 1877 by American Edward MUYBRIDGE, who recorded the phases of movement of a galloping horse by serially tripping the shutters of 24 stationary still cameras. Muybridge's experiments in the analysis of motion led to further explorations by the German Ottomar ANSCHUTZ and the French Etienne-Jules MAREY. The latter devised a photographic gun with which he was able, in 1882, to record serially the movements of a bird in flight at a rate of 12 photographs (or chronophotographs, as he called them) per second. By 1888 the first motion picture camera was completed by William Kennedy Laurie Dickson at Edison's New Jersey lab, and on December 28, 1895, the brothers LUMIÈRE, Louis and Auguste, gave the first public demonstration of projected films, at the Grand Café in Paris, with their combination camera-projector.

An essential development in making possible motion picture photography and projection was the invention of celluloid film by American George EASTMAN in 1889. Thomas Alva EDISON made an important contribution for fixing standard film dimensions and the distance between perforations. The brothers Lumière contributed the shuttle and claw mechanism, and British inventor Robert William PAUL originated the MALTESE CROSS, both essential for intermittent movement. The major problem plaguing camera designers in the formative years of cinema was the difficulty in obtaining precise registration of film in the camera. Since photographed images are enlarged hundreds of times during projection, the slightest inaccuracy in the positioning of successive frames behind the lens produces jerkiness and flickering on the screen.

These and other mechanical problems were ironed out by 1920 when the wooden camera with its unstable components was replaced by sturdy precision-built apparatus that (with improvements and modifications) have remained basically unchanged. Although motion picture cameras come in a variety of sizes, designs, styles, and capacities, essentially they all operate on similar principles. Their function is largely determined by film-gauge size: the standard gauge for professional cinematography is 35 mm, about the same as it has been since Edison's Kinetograph. The recent advent of wide-screen processes was accompanied by wider gauges, such as 65 and 70 mm. However, 16 mm cameras (known as substandard because of their narrower gauge, not their quality) were for many years used strictly for amateur cinematography. But a trend set by wartime newsreels, and augmented by documentary and avant-garde filmmakers as well as TV, has in recent years turned the 16 mm camera into a perfectly legitimate tool of the professional cinematographer. Its place as the camera of the amateur has been taken by the super-8 camera and the now rapidly obsolescing 8 mm camera.

Irrespective of gauge, film is driven through a motion picture camera by two mechanisms. One, which runs continuously, draws unexposed film from a storage chamber, known as a "magazine," or from a feed spool, and after exposure drives the film into another magazine or onto a take-up spool. The other mechanism, intermittent in its action, causes each frame of film to stop momentarily behind the camera aperture, just long enough for it to be exposed to light and to an image formed through the camera lens. A shutter mechanism is synchronized with the intermittent drive, so that each frame of film receives light during exposure but is protected from light entering the lens while it is pulled down to make room for the next frame. The continuous mechanism drives the film through the camera by means of sprocket wheels whose teeth engage film perforations.

In professional cameras, pressure rollers prevent disengagement of the perforations. The intermittent mechanism alternately holds the film stationary and rapidly pulls it down. To prevent the tearing of film from such sudden snatches, slack loops of film are formed above and below the intermittent mechanism of motion picture cameras as well as projectors. The intermittent mechanism of professional cameras is a highly complex assembly of precision parts. It works by means of a series of co-ordinated motions, and one of its important components is a shuttle whose one or more claws engage film perforations. The shuttle pulls each frame down into position behind the aperture. As the claws disengage from the perforations, the shuttle moves upward and one or two register pins, or pilot pins, engage the perforations and hold the frame steady for an exposure free of vibrations. As this is being accomplished, the shuttle starts the cycle all over again by pulling down another frame whose perforations are engaged by its claws. All this takes place within a fraction of a second.

Most professional motion picture cameras are driven by an electric motor, while many amateur cameras and some portable professional ones use a spring mechanism. Electric (and battery-operated) motors have the advantage not only of saving the time and effort involved in repeatedly winding a spring of limited length, but also of ensuring that the camera mechanism will be operating at a constant rate of speed. The various camera motors in use are usually grouped into three main types—synchronous, interlocked, or variable-speed. Since the advent of sound, professional motion picture cameras are equipped with BLIMPS, which are soundproof covers designed to render motors noiseless during the shooting of sound films. Cameras designed for synchronous sound recording are equipped with a device for recording the sound track on the film itself, magnetically, optically, or both ways.

In early professional cameras film magazines were housed inside the camera body. Magazines for most modern professional cameras are detachable and mounted on top of the camera body. Many have a capacity of 1,000 feet or more of film.

Lenses are mounted on a camera by either of two methods: the single-screw or bayonet mount, which requires the removal of one lens and its replacement by another; and the turret mount, which is a rotating disc on which three or more lenses are mounted. The latter can be rotated so that any one of the lenses can be placed in position in front of the camera aperture. Recently a single variable-focus zoom lens has replaced the turret on some cameras, but most professional motion picture cameras are still equipped with a turret mount.

The camera operator can view the image as it is recorded on film through any of a number of viewing systems. In early days, viewing was accomplished through the back of the film with the aid of an eyepiece. Later, a viewing device working independently of the lens optical system was attached to the side of the camera, making viewing of action possible even while the camera was moving and making correction for PARALLAX relatively simple. While this viewing system is still used on portable cameras, some motion picture cameras are equipped with a monitoring viewfinder in which the photographed image is reproduced for viewing on a relatively large screen. It is a useful guide for the operator during panning and traveling shots. An important innovation was the introduction of the REFLEX viewing system in Germany during the 30s. The system provides the operator with an accurate image devoid of parallax, as if he were viewing the action directly through the lens. Among the various controls at the disposal of a camera operator are: a starting switch, which activates the camera; a footage counter, which indicates the amount of film exposed; a frame counter, which records the passage of individual frames to facilitate the making of fades, dissolves, and special effects; an exposure speed indicator, or tachometer, for variable-speed motors; an automatic safety switch that stops the camera action when film isn't being properly driven; a focusing control; a built-in range finder, or telemeter; a variable-shutter control; and an automatic dissolve control. The more numerous the controls, the more flexible is the camera's action, but few if any cameras are equipped with all the available controls.

Motion picture cameras require a variety of accessories, the most essential of which are a tripod and tripod head and a changing bag for loading and unloading magazines even in direct sunlight. In recent years, camera design has moved in the direction of lightweight, compact cameras that are easily portable, can be held in the hand, and generally operate as an integral part of the cameraman.

camera angle. See ANGLE, CAMERA.

camera jam. A failure of a camera mechanism usually caused by the piling up of film the perforations of which are not properly engaged.

cameraman. General descriptive and familiar term for a person operating a motion picture camera. Professionally, a distinction is made between the DIRECTOR OF PHOTOGRAPHY, or the lighting cameraman (also called the "cinematographer"), and the CAMERA OPERATOR, who is the person actually operating the camera. The director of photography and camera operator are also known as the "first cameraman" and "second cameraman" respectively. The camera crew also includes an ASSISTANT CAMERAMAN and a second assistant cameraman, the latter sometimes also known as the "slate boy" or "clapper boy."

cameraman, assistant. See ASSISTANT CAMERAMAN.

camera movement. The panning, tilting, tracking, or zooming of a motion picture camera. There are certain conventions that are universally observed in camera movement. As a rule, a cameraman will run the camera in a static position for a brief moment before beginning the movement, and again after the movement is completed and the camera comes to rest. This not only makes for a smooth look on the screen but also provides the editor with a choice between a static or a moving situation when he cuts from one shot to another. Another widely observed rule is that movement begins and ends on specific points of interest that have been preselected, with the entire movement rehearsed before shooting. The direction of camera movement is as important as the direction of subject movement within the frame. Thus, a pan from left to right would normally not be followed with a pan from right to left, and so on, just as the movement of a performer from left to right would not be followed by the same subject's movement in the opposite direction.

camera operator. Also known as "second cameraman." The person who actually operates the camera during production, following instructions from the DIRECTOR and the DIRECTOR OF PHOTOGRAPHY. Unlike the director of photography, he is concerned not with the lighting of the sets or the composition of the shot but with accomplishing smooth camera movement and producing pictorial images that are deemed satisfactory by the director.

camera report. A sheet filled in daily, usually by the ASSISTANT CAMERAMAN, which contains information pertinent to the day's shooting. It lists such details as the number of takes shot, the amount of film footage exposed and recommendations concerning the selection of takes, and general and particular comments.

caméra-stylo. A term coined in 1948 by French director Alexandre ASTRUC, which literally means "camera-pen." It expresses the idea that cinema has become an autonomous art with a specific language of its own and is a legitimate mode of artistic expression. The artist who creates the film is the director who also writes his own scripts and thus has creative control over the production. Astruc's ideas, expressed in the magazine *L'Ecran Français,* provided the foundation for the AUTEUR THEORY of the French NOUVELLE VAGUE in the 50s. See also AUTEUR THEORY; BAZIN, ANDRÉ; CAHIERS DU CINÉMA; NOUVELLE VAGUE.

Camerini, Mario. Director. *b.* Feb. 6, 1895, Rome. *d.* 1981. After law studies and WW I service as a light infantry officer, he entered films in 1920 as assistant to his cousin, director Augusto GENINA. Began directing in 1923 and by the 30s, along with Alessandro BLASETTI, was considered one of Italy's most important directors. He is largely responsible for the successful acting career of Vittorio DE SICA, whom he cast as the star of a series of somewhat melancholy sentimental comedies between 1932 and 1939, and for the artistic development of many Italian directors who started as his assistants, among them Cesare Zavattini and Renato Castellani. After WW II he remained unaffected by the neorealist movement and continued to direct entertaining commercial productions. He collaborated on the screenplays of most of his own films as well as on several scripts for other directors, including King Vidor's *War and Peace* (1956).

FILMS (as director and generally also co-screenwriter): *Jolly—Clown da Circo* 1923; *La Casa dei Pulcini* 1924; *Maciste contro lo Sceicco, Voglio Tradire mio Marito* 1925; *Saetta—Principe per un Giorno* 1926; *Kiff Tebbi* 1927; *Rotaie* 1929; *La Riva dei Bruti* 1930; *Figaro e la sua Gran Giornata* 1931; *L'Ultima Avventura, Gli Uomini che Mascalzoni!* 1932; *T'Amerò sempre, Cento di questi Giorni, Giallo* 1933; *Il Cappello a tre Punte, Come le Foglie* 1934; *Darò un Milione, Il Grande Appello/The Last Roll-Call, Ma non è una Cosa seria/But It's Nothing Serious* (and German version, *Der Mann der nicht nein sagen kann,* released two years later) 1936; *Il Signor Max* 1937; *Batticuore* 1938; *Il Documento Fatale, I Grandi Magazzini* 1939; *Centomila Dollari, Una Romantica Avventura* 1940; *I Promessi Sposi/The Spirit and the Flesh* 1941; *Una Storia d'Amore* 1942; *T'amerò sempre* (remake) 1943; *Due Lettere Anonime* 1945; *L'Angelo e il Diavolo* 1946; *La Figlia del Capitano/The Captain's Daughter* 1947; *Molti Sogni per le Strade/Woman Trouble* 1948; *Due Mogli sono Troppe, Il Brigante Musolino* 1950; *Moglie per una Notte/Wife for a Night* 1951; *Gli Eroi della Domenica* 1952; *Ulisse/Ulysses* 1954; *La Bella Mugnaia!/The Miller's Beautiful Wife* 1955; *Suor Letizia/The Awakening* 1956; *Vacanze a Ischia/Holiday Island* 1957; *Primo Amore* 1958; *Via Margutta/Run with the Devil, Crimen/And Suddenly It's Murder* 1960; *I Briganti*

Italiani/Seduction of the South 1961; *Kali Yug—La Dea della Vendetta, Il Mistero del Tempio Indiano* 1963; *Delitto quasi Perfetto* 1966; *Io non vedo tu non parli lui non sente* 1971; *Don Camillo e i Giovani d'Oggi* 1972.

Cameron, James. Director, screenwriter. Born on Aug. 16, 1954, in Kapuskasing, Ont., Canada. The son of an engineer, he majored in physics at California State University, but after graduating drove a truck to support an addictive screenwriting habit. He landed his first professional film job as art director, miniature-set builder, and process projection supervisor on producer Roger Corman's *Battle Beyond the Stars* (1980). After a lame debut as a director the following year, Cameron earned a substantial living as an uncredited script doctor, then returned to directing, scoring a huge success with *The Terminator,* a sizzling futuristic action picture starring Arnold Schwarzenegger, which became the box-office sleeper of 1984. It was the first of several films Cameron was to make in collaboration with his first wife, producer Gale Anne HURD. *Aliens* (1986) confirmed his growing reputation as one of Hollywood's most skilled directors of science fiction action films. His next film, *The Abyss* (1989), was a commercial and critical disappointment, but it was followed by the big hit *Terminator 2: Judgment Day* (1991), a sequel to his earlier film. Having divorced Hurd, he married director Kathryn BIGELOW in 1989.

FILMS (as director): *Piranha II: The Spawning* (also co-sc.) 1981; *The Terminator* (also co-sc.) 1984; *Rambo: First Blood Part II* (co-sc. only) 1985; *Aliens* (also co-story, sc.) 1986; *The Abyss* (also sc.) 1989; *Terminator 2: Judgment Day* (also prod., co-sc.), *Point Break* (exec. prod. only) 1991; *True Lies* (also prod., co-sc.) 1994; *Strange Days* (co-prod., co-sc.) 1995; *Titanic* 1997.

Cameron, Rod. *b.* Nathan Roderick Cox, Dec. 7, 1910, Calgary, Alberta, Canada. *d.* 1983. A former laborer and construction worker, he began his film career as a stunt double for Buck Jones and a stand-in for Fred MacMurray, and then in 1939 started playing bit parts in a variety of Paramount productions, gradually moving into leads in Westerns. Tall (6' 4") and strongly built, he starred in numerous low- and medium-budget Westerns, serials, and action pictures, as well as in the TV series 'City Detective,' 'Coronado,' and 'State Trooper.' In 1960 he provided fodder to Hollywood's gossip machine when he divorced his second wife to marry her mother.

FILMS INCLUDE: *The Old Maid* (scene cut from final print) 1939; *The Quarterback, Christmas in July, North West Mounted Police* 1940; *The Monster and the Girl, Nothing but the Truth, The Night of January 16th, No Hands on the Clock* 1941; *The Remarkable Andrew* (as Jesse James), *True to the Army, The Fleet's In, Priorities on Parade, Wake Island, The Forest Rangers* 1942; *G-Men vs. the Black Dragon* (serial), *Secret Service in Darkest Africa* (serial), *The Commandos Strike at Dawn, No Time for Love, The Kansan, Riding High, Gung Ho!* 1943; *Mrs. Parkington, Riders of Santa Fe, The Old Texas Trail* 1944; *Beyond the Pecos, Salome—Where She Danced, Renegades of the Rio Grande, Swing Out Sister, Frontier Gal* 1945; *The Runaround* 1946; *Pirates of Monterey* 1947; *Panhandle, River Lady, Belle Starr's Daughter* 1948; *Strike It Rich, Stampede, Brimstone* 1949; *Dakota Lil, Short Grass* 1950; *Oh! Susanna, Stage to Tucson, Cavalry Scout, The Sea Hornet* 1951; *Ride the Man Down, Fort Osage, Wagons West, Woman of the North Country, The Jungle* 1952; *San Antone, The Steel Lady* 1953; *Southwest Passage, Hell's Outpost* 1954; *Double Jeopardy, Headline Hunters, The Fighting Chance* 1955; *Passport to Treason* (UK), *Yaqui Drums* 1956; *Spoilers of the Forest* 1957; *Escapement/The Electronic Monster* (UK), *The Man Who Died Twice* 1958; *The Gun Hawk* 1963; *Las Pistoles no Discuten/Bullets Don't Lie* (Sp.) 1964; *The Bounty Killer, Requiem for a Gunfighter* 1965; *Winnetou und sein Freund Old Firehand* (Ger.) 1966; *Evel Knievel, The Last Movie* 1971; *Psychic Killer* 1975; *Jessie's Girl* 1976; *Love and the Midnight Auto Supply* 1978.

Camp, Colleen. Actress. Born in 1953, in San Francisco. Capable, appealing young lead of American films and TV. A performer from age three, she was working as a bird trainer when she was discovered by an agent and placed on the 'Dean Martin Show.' In features from 1973, she has been seen mainly in low-budget productions.

FILMS INCLUDE: *Battle for the Planet of the Apes* 1973; *Smile, Funny Lady* 1975; *Death Game* 1977; *Game of Death, Apocalypse Now* 1979; *Cloud Dancer* 1980; *They All Laughed* 1981; *The Seduction* 1982; *Smokey and the Bandit III, Valley Girl* 1983; *Joy of Sex, The Rosebud Beach Hotel, City Girl* (also assoc. prod.) 1984; *Police Academy 2: Their First Assignment, Clue* 1985; *Walk Like a Man, Police Academy 4: Citizens on Patrol* 1987; *Illegally Yours, Track 29* 1988; *Wicked Stepmother* 1989; *My Blue Heaven* 1990; *The Vagrant* 1991; *Wayne's World* 1992; *Greedy* 1994; *The Baby-Sitters Club, Die Hard with a Vengeance, Three Wishes* 1995; *Speed 2: Cruise Control* 1997.

Camp, Joe. Director, producer, screenwriter. *b.* Apr. 20, 1939, in St. Louis, Mo. *d.* 1940, in Dallas, Tex. *ed.* U. of Mississippi. A former advertising and real-estate executive, he produced and directed industrial films and commercials before venturing into independent feature production in 1973. He set up his own production company in Dallas and with an initial investment of just over $500,000, mostly borrowed from friends, he turned out his first film, *Benji* (1974), a warmhearted if rather silly children's picture about the heroics of a little dog. Circumventing normal industry channels, he promoted and distributed the film himself, scoring a huge hit at the box office with an initial gross of more than $30 million. He continued exploiting his one-dog industry on TV, as well as in feature films, well into the late 80s.

FILMS: *Benji* 1974; *Hawmps* 1976; *For the Love of Benji* 1977; *The Double McGuffin* 1979; *Oh Heavenly Dog!* 1980; *Benji the Hunted* 1987.

Campanile, Pasquale Festa. See FESTA CAMPANILE, Pasquale.

Campbell, Colin. Director. *b.* 1880(?), Scotland. Deceased. Came to the US as a young man and, following stage experience as actor and director, became a prominent film director during the formative years of American cinema. One of his first films, the three-reel *Cinderella* (1911), employed a cast of 300, and the nine-reel *The Spoilers* (1914), starring William Farnum, was among the most ambitious and profitable films of the era. He turned out some 500 films of various lengths between 1911 and 1922, mostly for Selig and Mutual, including some of Tom Mix's early Westerns, but was all but forgotten by the mid-20s. He should not be confused with a stage and screen actor Colin Campbell (1883–1966), also Scottish born, who played light character parts in many films from 1914, or with actor Colin Campbell (*b.* 1937) who appeared in British films of the 60s.

FILMS INCLUDE: *Cinderella* 1911; *Monte Cristo/The Count of Monte Cristo* (also sc.), *The Coming of Columbus, The God of Gold* (also sc.), *Kings of the Forest* (also sc.), *Sammy Orpheus, Old Songs and Memories, The Little Organ Player of San Juan, Greater Wealth* 1912; *Alas! Poor Yorick!* (also sc.), *In the Long Ago, A Wise Old Elephant, An Old Actor* (also sc.), *A Wild Ride* (also sc.), *Thor Lord of the Jungles, Alone in the Jungle* 1913; *The Salvation of Nancy O'Shaughnessy* (also sc.), *The Tragedy of Ambition, Vengeance Is Mine, The Lily of the Valley, Hearts and Masks* (also sc.), *The Losing Fight* (also sc.),

Her Sacrifice (also sc.), *The Spoilers, Chip of the Flying U, The Story of the Blood Red Rose, In the Days of the Thundering Herd, The Wilderness Mail* (also sc.), *In Defiance of the Law* (also sc.) 1914; *The Carpet from Bagdad, The Rosary, The Runt* (also sc.), *The Vision of the Shepherd, Sweet Alyssum* 1915; *The Ne'er-Do-Well, Thou Shalt Not Covet, The Crisis* (also sc.), *The Garden of Allah* 1916; *Beware of Strangers, Who Shall Take My Life?* 1917; *The City of Purple Dreams, The Still Alarm* (also sc.), *A Hoosier Romance* (also sc.), *The Yellow Dog, The Sea Flower, Little Orphan Annie, Tongues of Flame* 1918; *The Beauty Market, The Railroader, The Thunderbolt* 1919; *The Corsican Brothers, Moon Madness, When Dawn Came* 1920; *The First Born, Black Roses, Where Lights Are Low, The Swamp, The Lure of Jade* 1921; *Two Kinds of Women, The World's a Stage* (also co-sc.) 1922; *Three Who Paid, The Buster, Bucking the Barrier, The Grail* 1923; *Pagan Passions, The Bowery Bishop* 1924.

Campbell, Eric. Actor. *b.* 1870(?), in Dunoon, Scotland. *d.* 1917. He was a member of the English Fred Karno troupe, which nurtured the talents of Charlie CHAPLIN. Chaplin invited him to perform in his films in 1916, and he played in all but one of Chaplin's comedies of the Mutual period, 1916–17. Huge-framed and mean-looking, he provided an ideal villainous adversary for the little Charlie. He is best remembered as the street thug Chaplin subdues with a lamppost in *Easy Street.* More typically, Campbell appeared as a bearded, heavily made-up, well-to-do tyrant. His career was cut short in 1917 when he was killed in a car accident.

FILMS: *The Floorwalker, the Fireman, The Vagabond, The Count, The Pawnshop, Behind the Screen, The Rink* 1916; *Easy Street, The Cure, The Immigrant, The Adventurer* 1917.

Campbell, Louise. Actress. Born Louise Weisbecker, in 1915, in Chicago. *ed.* Northwestern U.; DePaul U.; Chicago School of Expression. Redheaded leading lady of Hollywood films of the late 30s, following work experience as a dental assistant and as a drama instructor at DePaul. She was married to actor Horace MCMAHON.

FILMS: *Wild Money, Bulldog Drummond Comes Back, Bulldog Drummond's Revenge, Night Club Scandal* 1937; *Scandal Street, Bulldog Drummond's Peril, Men with Wings, The Buccaneer* 1938; *The Star Maker* 1939; *Emergency Squad, Anne of Windy Poplars, Bowery Boy* 1940; *Devil Ship* 1947.

Campbell, William. Actor. Born in 1926, in Newark, N.J. Went to Hollywood in 1950, after stock and Broadway and has since played sharp, calculating characters in many films, mostly in supporting roles, occasionally in leads. He played Caryl Chessman in *Cell 2455 Death Row* (1955).

FILMS INCLUDE: *The Breaking Point* 1950; *Inside the Walls of Folsom Prison, The People Against O'Hara* 1951; *Holiday for Sinners* 1952; *Battle Circus, Escape from Fort Bravo* 1953; *The High and the Mighty* 1954; *Cell 2455 Death Row, Battle Cry, Man Without a Star, Running Wild* 1955; *Backlash, Love Me Tender* 1956; *The Naked and the Dead, The Sheriff of Fractured Jaw* 1958; *The Young Racers* 1963; *The Secret Invasion* 1964; *Hush Hush... Sweet Charlotte* 1965; *Blood Bath* 1966; *Pretty Maids All in a Row* 1971; *Black Gunn* 1973; *Dirty Mary Crazy Larry* 1974.

Campion, Jane. Director, Born in 1955, in Wellington, New Zealand. A graduate of the Australian Film, Television, and Radio School, she first attracted notice when her nine-minute 1982 student project, *Peel,* won an award at Cannes. Her subsequent shorts, including the half-hour *A Girl's Story* and *Passionless Moments* (both 1984) led to her growing reputation and to her widely acclaimed first feature, *Sweetie* (1989), an off-beat horrific comedy centering on Campion's favorite subject, family relationships. Competing at Cannes, the film was the object of controversy, with reactions ranging from adulation to damnation. It was followed by *An Angel at My Table* (1990), a three-hour feature about the troubled youth of New Zealand writer Janet Frame. Originally made for TV, the film met with success during its screenings at the New York and Venice Film Festivals. Her next film, *The Piano*, shared the Palme d'Or at Cannes (with Chen Kaige's *Farewell My Concubine*) in 1993.

FEATURE FILMS: *Sweetie* (also co-sc.) 1989; *An Angel at My Table* 1990; *The Piano* (also sc.) 1993; *The Portrait of a Lady* 1996.

Campogalliani, Carlo. Actor, director. Born on Oct. 10, 1885, in Concordia, Italy. Following some stage experience, entered Italian films in 1910 and soon became popular as the dashing star of many early silent productions. Before long, he began directing his own films as well as those featuring other stars of the day, including his own wife, Letizia Quaranta. In the mid-20s he went to Argentina, where he directed a number of films and helped organize the film industry, but returned to Europe with the switch-over to sound and directed many more Italian films through the early 60s.

FILMS INCLUDE: As actor—*Re Lear/King Lear* 1910; *Promessi Sposi, Il Noturno di Chopin, La Crocetta d'Oro* 1913; *L'Epopea Napoleonica, Il Romanzo di un Re* 1914; *Romanticismo* 1915; *La Nave dei Morti* 1919. As director-actor—*Treno reale* 1915; *L'Isola tenebrosa, La Serata d'Honore di Buffalo* 1916; *L'Aeronave in Fiamme, L'Ombra che parla* 1918; *Maciste I, La Casa della Paura, Maciste contro la Morte, Scacco Matto, Un Simpatico Mascalzone* 1919; *Il Teschio d'Oro* 1921; *Bresaglio Umano, L'Antenato* 1922; *La Vuelta del Toro* (Arg.) 1924. As director—*Quando si ama* 1915; *L'Amazzone macabra* 1916; *Il Marchi Rosso* 1918; *Cortile* 1930; *Medico per Forza, La Laterna del Diavolo* 1931; *Stadio* 1934; *Montevergine/La Grande Luce/The Great Light* 1938; *La Notte delle Beffe* 1940; *Cuori nella Tormenta, Il Bravo di Venezia* 1941; *Perdizione* 1942; *Musica proibita* 1943; *L'Innocente Casimirio* 1945; *La Gondola del Diavolo* 1947; *La Mano della Morta* 1949; *Bellezze in Bicicletta* 1951; *L'Orfana del Ghetto, Foglio di Via* 1954; *La Canzone del Cuore* 1955; *L'Angelo della Alpi* 1957; *Capitan Fuoco* 1958; *Il Terrore dei Barbari/Goliath and the Barbarians* 1959; *Fontana di Trevi, Maciste nella Valle dei Re/Son of Samson* 1960; *Ursus/Mighty Ursus, Rosmunda e Alboino/Sword of the Conqueror* 1961.

Camus, Marcel. Director. *b.* Apr. 21, 1912, Chappes, France. *d.* 1982. Prepared for a career as an art teacher, but after spending most of WW II as a prisoner of war, entered French films as an assistant and technical advisor to Decoin, Feyder, Becker, Buñuel, and other directors. After directing a short in 1950, he made his debut as a feature director several years later and won international acclaim with his second film, *Orfeu Negro/Black Orpheus* (1958), a hauntingly beautiful film shot in Brazil. The film was honored with first prizes at both the Cannes and Venice film festivals and won the Hollywood Academy Award as best foreign film. Camus's subsequent films, also set mostly in exotic locations, failed to ignite a similar interest by the critics or the public. He collaborated on all his scripts.

FEATURE FILMS: *Morte en Fraude/Fugitive in Saigon* 1957; *Orfeu Negro/Black Orpheus* 1958; *Os Bandeirantes* 1960; *L'Oiseau de Paradis/Dragon Sky* 1962; *Le Chant du Monde* 1965; *L'Homme de New York* 1967; *Vivre la Nuit* 1968; *Le Mur de l'Atlantique, Un Eté sauvage* (also co-sc.) 1970; *Os Pastoris da Noite/Otalia de Bahia* (also co-sc.; Braz./Fr.) 1977.

can. 1. A round metal container for the storage of film. The term "in the can" means that a film has been completed. 2. A simple light source consisting of a 1,000-watt lamp in a rectangular housing. 3. A slang term for a set of headphones used by soundmen in monitoring a recording.

Canada. The world's second-largest country in land area, and one of the richest in per capita income, sparsely populated Canada is, paradoxically, one of the least significant centers of feature film production among the developed nations. One important reason is the close proximity of that nation to the United States, which historically has exerted considerable influence on Canadian culture and economy. Dependence on American capital and American products inhibited the development of the Canadian motion picture industry from the start. Surrendering control over the local feature film market to exporters, distributors, and exhibitors from its southern neighbor, and to a lesser extent from England, Canada concentrated instead on the production of documentaries. As early as 1900 the Canadian Pacific Railway company set up a film unit to produce shorts aimed at encouraging immigration. But commercial motion picture production was slow to emerge, and it wasn't until 1914 that Canada's first feature film, *Evangeline,* was brought to the screen. Feature film production continued sporadically through the 20s, but the vulnerable local industry suffered a severe setback during the switch to sound. Hope was restored in the early 30s by the success of *The Viking* (1931), a romantic drama set against the background of seal fishing in Newfoundland, but the film turned out to be an isolated triumph, and the dominance of Hollywood in the Canadian market continued unabated.

Although feature production remained relatively dormant, the arrival in 1939 of John GRIERSON as the government's film commissioner and head of the newly established National Film Board of Canada provided tremendous impetus to the establishment of Canada as one of the world's leading centers of documentary film production. The Board's reputation was established during WW II when it produced two notable documentary propaganda series— "Canada Carries On" and "The World in Action"—as well as numerous military training films, educational, industrial, and agricultural shorts, and cartoons. It was an immensely productive and enthusiastic period for the Canadian nonfiction film industry, a period that saw the development of such talented filmmakers as Stuart LEGG, Norman MCLAREN, George DUNNING, and Raymond SPOTTISWOODE.

The excellence of the Film Board's production continued after the war and Grierson's departure in 1945, but feature films were still being made only sporadically, and the few that were produced were rarely exhibited abroad and were poorly attended at home. Although some modest gains were made by young filmmakers, especially in the French-speaking province of Quebec during the 50s, feature film production was largely neglected by the country's money men, and little progress was made. Talented young directors like Norman JEWISON, Sidney J. FURIE, Arthur HILLER, Silvio NARRIZANO, and Ted KOTCHEFF, were driven away by apathy to pursue successful careers in Hollywood and London. One film that enjoyed a degree of success beyond Canada's own borders was Irvin KERSHNER's *The Luck of Ginger Coffey* (1964), a Canadian-American co-production.

In a belated but much welcomed effort to combat the predominance of foreign feature films on the Canadian screens, the Canadian Film Development Corporation was established by an Act of Parliament in 1967 to foster feature production and encourage filmmakers through investments, grants, and loans. By 1970 the annual feature film production had risen to 25 compared with only 3 in 1960. Still, despite displays of talent by such directors as Paul Almond, Claude JUTRA, Donals Shebib, William Fruet, and Eric Till, Canadian feature film production in the 70s was generally characterized by creative timidity and often by mediocrity. As the decade drew to a close, the only film that had won a measure of true international success was Kotcheff's *The Apprenticeship of Duddy Kravitz* (1974).

Canadian film in the 80s and 90s broke through its historic torpor. Productions such as David CRONENBERG's horror pictures and Denys ARCAND's art-house hits, *The Decline of the American Empire* and *Jesus of Montreal*, became increasingly marketable to international audiences. But much of interest occurred beyond the commercial mainstream. Women filmmakers (Lea Pool, Cynthia Scott, Patricia Rozema, Gail Singer) achieved considerable stature during this period. Immigrant filmmakers (Atom Egoyan from Egypt, Deepa Mehta from India) added their own cultural imprint to Canadian productions. Canada's vibrant avant-garde included such artists as Jean Pierre Lefebvre, Michael Snow, and Guy Maddin. Reinforcing the vitality of Canadian film was the generous support of the federal National Film Board and provincial governments.

In addition to its creative output, Canada has contributed in other ways to the North American film industry. Toronto, Ontario, hosts the annual Festival of Festivals, among the largest and best programmed film festivals in the world. One of the largest theater chains in North America, Cineplex Odeon, is also based in Toronto. Canada (in particular Vancouver, British Columbia) has increasingly played host to US-financed film and television production, which benefits from lower costs and local talent.

Canale, Gianna Maria. Actress. Born on Sept. 12, 1927, in Reggio di Calabria, Italy. Dark, mysterious beauty of Italian and international films, often seen in costume dramas, typically in the role of a temptress. A runner-up in the Miss Italy beauty contest, she entered films in 1946. Several of her early productions were directed by Riccardo FREDA, whom she later married. In the 50s and early 60s she appeared in American, British, and French, as well as Italian, productions.

FILMS INCLUDE: *Rigoletto* 1946; *Il Cavaliere misterioso* 1948; *Il Bacio di una Morta/A Dead Woman's Kiss, Totò le Makò, Il Figlio di d'Artagnan* 1949; *La Vendetta di Aquila Nera* 1950; *Go for Broke* (US), *Tradimento* 1951; *Vedi Napoli. . . e poi muori/See Naples and Die, La Leggenda del Piave, Spartaco* 1952; *Dramma nella Casbah/The Man from Cairo* (It./US), *Teodora Imperatrice di Bisanzio/Theodora Slave Empress* 1953; *Madame du Barry* (Fr./It.) 1954; *Napoléon* (Fr.) 1955; *Donne Sole, Le Schiave di Cartagine/The Sword and the Cross* 1956; *I Vampiri/The Vampires, Le Fatiche di Ercole/Hercules, La Gerusalemma liberata/The Mighty Crusaders* 1957; *The Silent Enemy* (UK), *The Whole Truth* (UK), *La Rivolta dei Gladiatori/The Warrior and the Slave Girl* 1958; *Il Cavaliere del Diavolo* 1959; *Les Nuits de Raspoutine/L'Ultimo Zar/The Night They Killed Rasputin* (Fr./It.), *La Venere dei Pirati/Queen of the Pirates* 1960; *The Secret of Monte Cristo* (UK), *Maciste contro il Vampiro/Goliath and the Vampires* 1961; *Il Conquistatore di Corinto/The Centurion, Il Figlio di Spartacus/The Slave* 1962; *La Tigre dei Sette Mari/Tiger of the Seven Seas* 1963; *Il Leone di San Marco/The Lion of St. Mark* 1964.

candela. Internationally accepted unit of measurement for determining the intensity of a light source. Commonly abbreviated as "cd," it was established as a standard in 1936, replacing the original unit of light measurement, the candle.

candid camera. A filming method involving the photographing of real people in real situations in which the subjects are unaware that they are being photographed. Of particular value in documentary filming, where a natural reflection of reality is desired. See also CINÉMA VÉRITÉ.

candlepower. The illuminating capacity of a light source, measured originally by candle units and since 1936 by CANDELA (cd) units. The candlepower rating of a fixture helps the lighting cameraman to determine the illumination intensity of the fixture at any given distance.

Candy, John. Actor. *b.* Oct. 31, 1950, Toronto. *d.* 1994. Chubby, likeable, light character star of Hollywood films. He began performing as an 11th grader and continued acting while studying journalism at Toronto's Centennial Community College. Following minor appearances in low-budget films of the early 70s, he joined Second City and became a regular on the satirical troupe's TV programs. He won Emmy Awards in 1982 and 1983 for writing on SCTV's comedy sketches. He became increasingly popular in the 80s as a movie funnyman, playing lead roles by the end of the decade.

FILMS INCLUDE: *Face-Off* 1971; *Class of '44* 1973; *It Seemed Like a Good Idea at the Time* 1975; *Tunnelvision, The Clown Murders* 1976; *The Silent Partner* 1978; *Lost and Found, 1941* 1979; *The Blues Brothers* 1980; *Heavy Metal, Stripes* 1981; *National Lampoon's Vacation, Going Berserk* 1983; *Splash* 1984; *Brewster's Millions, Summer Rental, Volunteers* 1985; *The Great Outdoors, Armed and Dangerous, Little Shop of Horrors* 1986; *Spaceballs, Planes, Trains, and Automobiles* 1987; *The Great Outdoors, Hot to Trot* 1988; *Who's Harry Crumb?* (also exec. prod.), *Speed Zone, Uncle Buck* 1989; *Delirious, Home Alone, The Rescuers Down Under* (v/o) 1990; *Nothing But Trouble, Only the Lonely, JFK* 1991; *Once Upon a Crime* 1992; *Wagons East* 1994; *Canadian Bacon* 1995.

Cannes Film Festival. See FILM FESTIVALS.

Cannon, Dyan. Actress. Born Samille Diane Friesen, on Jan. 4, 1937, in Tacoma, Wash. *ed.* U. of Washington. The daughter of a Baptist insurance broker and a Jewish housewife, she began singing at a Seattle Reform synagogue. After two years of college, she moved to Los Angeles, where she worked as a showroom model. In the early 60s she played a couple of minor roles in films and appeared in a number of Broadway flops and numerous TV programs. She retired from show business in 1965 after marrying Cary GRANT and bearing him his only child, a girl. She was granted a divorce in 1968, after which she returned to acting in the role of the uptight Alice in *Bob & Carol & Ted & Alice,* for which she was honored by the New York Film Critics as best supporting actress of 1969. She was nominated for an Academy Award for that film and later for *Heaven Can Wait* (1978). Typically seen in "sexy" roles. In 1976 she wrote, produced, directed, and co-edited a 42-minute film, *Number One,* under the sponsorship of the American Film Institute. It was nominated for an Academy Award.

FILMS: *The Rise and Fall of Legs Diamond, This Rebel Breed* 1960; *Bob & Carol & Ted & Alice* 1969; *Le Casse/The Burglars* (Fr.), *The Anderson Tapes, Doctors' Wives, The Love Machine, Such Good Friends* 1971; *Shamus, The Last of Sheila* 1973; *Child Under a Leaf* (Can.) 1974; *Heaven Can Wait, Revenge of the Pink Panther* 1978; *Coast to Coast, Honeysuckle Rose* 1980; *Deathtrap, Author! Author!* 1982; *Caddyshack II* 1988; *End of Innocence* (also dir., prod., sc.) 1990; *The Pickle* 1993; *Out To Sea, That Darn Cat* 1997.

Cannon Group. US-based motion picture production and distribution company. It was founded in 1967 as Cannon Films by Dennis Friedland and Chris Dewey. At first known mainly for sexploitation films, it earned greater respectability with the release of the low-budget drama *Joe* in 1970. In 1979, Cannon was acquired by two Israeli producers, Menahem GOLAN and Yoram GLOBUS, who began intensively producing modestly budgeted films for worldwide independent distribution. Some, like *Death Wish 3* (1985) were pure exploitation, while others, like *Runaway Train* (1985), had more substance. For a time, Cannon was producing more films than many major studios. In 1987, Italian executive Giancarlo Parretti purchased the Cannon Group and renamed it Pathé Communications Corp. Golan and Globus at first remained with the company, but resigned within the next few years.

Cannon, Robert. American animator. b. 1901. *d.* 1964. A former DISNEY employee and a leading figure in the formation and achievements of the independent UPA. A master of design and economy of movement. He created and directed such simple-lined pseudosurrealistic cartoon characters as Gerald McBoing Boing (Academy Award, 1950) and Christopher Crumpet.

FILM CARTOONS INCLUDE: *Fear* 1945; *Brotherhood of Man* 1947; *Gerald McBoing Boing* 1950; *Madeline, Willie the Kid, The Oompahs* 1952; *Gerald's Symphony, Christopher Crumpet's Playmate* 1953; *Fudget's Budget, Ballet Oop* 1954; *The Jaywalker* 1955; *Department of the Navy* 1958; *Moonbird* 1960.

Canonero, Milena. Costume designer. Working in British then also American films, she established a reputation as one of the best in her profession. She won Academy Awards for *Barry Lyndon* (1975) and *Chariots of Fire* (1981) and an Oscar nomination for *Out of Africa* (1984).

FILMS INCLUDE: *A Clockwork Orange* 1971; *Barry Lyndon* 1975; *Midnight Express* 1978; *The Shining* 1980; *Chariots of Fire* 1981; *The Hunger* 1983; *Give My Regards to Broad Street, The Cotton Club* 1984; *Out of Africa* 1985; *Tucker: The Man and His Dream* 1988; *Dick Tracy, The Godfather Part III, Naked Tango* (prod.), *Reversal of Fortune* 1990; *Single White Female* 1992.

Canova, Judy. Comedienne, singer. *b.* Juliet Canova, Nov. 20, 1916, Jacksonville, Fla. *d.* 1983. Clowned and sang in vaudeville, then on Broadway in Ziegfeld's 'Calling All Stars,' before making her screen debut as part of a family act in Busby Berkeley's *In Calinte* (1935). Her hillbilly humor and ear-bursting yodel were her trademark in many other films as well as in a ten-year stretch on radio. She returned to the screen in 1976 after an absence of nearly two decades. She was the mother of TV actress Diana Canova (*b.* June 1, 1953, West Palm Beach, Fla.).

FILMS: *In Caliente, Going Highbrow* 1935; *Artists and Models, Thrill of a Lifetime* 1937; *Scatterbrain* 1940; *Sis Hopkins, Puddin' Head* 1941; *Sleepytime Gal, True to the Army, Joan of Ozark* 1942; *Sleepy Lagoon, Chatterbox* 1943; *Louisiana Hayride* 1944; *Hit the Hay* 1945; *Singing in the Corn* 1946; *Honeychile* 1951; *Oklahoma Annie, The WAC from Walla Walla* 1952; *Untamed Heiress* 1954; *Carolina Cannonball, Lay That Rifle Down* 1955; *The Adventures of Huckleberry Finn* 1960; *Cannonball* 1976.

Cantinflas. Actor. *b.* Mario Moreno Reyes, Aug. 12, 1911, in Mexico City. *d.* 1993. Started out as a song-and-dance man in tent shows, then gained popularity as a circus clown, acrobat, and bullring buffoon. Appearing in Mexican films since 1936, he developed into one of the most beloved film comics of the Spanish-speaking world. He became internationally renowned after playing the role of Passepartout in Mike Todd's *Around the World in 80 Days* (1956). *Pepe* (US, 1960), another star-studded vehicle, was made to capitalize on his newly found popularity but failed both critically and commercially. Author: *Cantinflas: Apologia de un Humilde.*

FILMS INCLUDE: *No te engañes Corazón* 1936; *Ahi está el Detalle* 1940; *Ni Sangre ni Arena* (also prod.), *El Gandarme desconcido* 1941; *El Circo* 1942; *Los Tres Mosqueteros/The Three Musketeers, Romeo y Julieta/Romeo and Juliet* 1943;

Gran Hotel 1944; *El Mago* 1949; *El Bombero atómico* 1951; *Arriba el Telón* 1954; *Around the World in 80 Days* (US) 1956; *Pepe* (US) 1960; *El Extra* 1962; *El Padrecito* 1964; *Su Exelencia* 1966; *Don Quijote sin Mancha* 1968; *El Ministro y Yo* 1976; *El Patrullero 777* 1978.

Canton, Mark. Executive. Born on June 19, 1949, in New York City. *ed.* UCLA. After serving in the 70s as vice president for motion picture development at MGM, he became vice president of production at Warner Bros. in 1980. By 1989, he was Warner Bros.'s vice president for motion picture production. In 1991 he moved to Columbia Pictures, where he became chairman. In 1994, he gained the top position at TriStar Pictures as well, as chairman of the Columbia TriStar Motion Picture Companies under the umbrella of Sony Pictures Entertainment. But in 1996, he was released from his contract primarily because of the studio's poor showing at the box office. See COLUMBIA PICTURES.

Cantor, Eddie. Comic actor, singer. *b.* Edward Israel Iskowitz, Jan. 31, 1892, New York City, to Lower East Side immigrants from Russia. *d.* 1964. An orphan from early childhood, he began entertaining professionally at 14, and after working for a while as a singing waiter in Coney Island, he edged his way to great popularity in vaudeville and burlesque. He got his first big break in 'The Midnight Frolics' (1916), then starred in the Ziegfeld Follies and such Broadway hits as 'Kid Boots' (1926) and 'Whoopee' (1930), playing roles he later repeated in films. He made his film debut in 1926 and enjoyed considerable popularity after the advent of sound. However, most of his film vehicles were of mediocre quality and made little use of his stage presence and inimitable style. During the 30s he starred in his own highly popular radio show.

Cantor's rolling "banjo eyes" and unique speech pattern were imitated by Keefe Brasselle in the not-too-successful film biography *The Eddie Cantor Story* (1953). Cantor, whose activities were limited after a heart attack in 1952, was honored in 1956 with a special Academy Award "for distinguished service to the film industry." Ida Tobias, his wife for 48 years who was immortalized in the song lyrics "Ida, sweet as apple cider," died in 1962. Cantor wrote four autobiographical volumes, *My Life Is in Your Hands* (1928), *Take My Life* (1957), *The Way I See It* (1959), and *As I Remember Them* (1962).

FILMS: *Kid Boots* 1926; *Special Delivery* (also story) 1927; *Glorifying the American Girl* 1929; *Whoopee!* 1930; *Mr. Lemon of Orange* (co-sc. only), *Palmy Days* (also co-story, co-sc.) 1931; *The Kid from Spain* 1932; *Roman Scandals* 1933; *Kid Millions* 1934; *Strike Me Pink* 1936; *Ali Baba Goes to Town* 1937; *Forty Little Mothers* 1940; *Thank Your Lucky Stars* 1943; *Show Business* (also prod.), *Hollywood Canteen* (cameo) 1944; *If You Knew Susie* (also prod.) 1948; *The Story of Will Rogers* (cameo) 1952.

Canudo, Ricciotto. Film critic, theoretician. *b.* Jan. 2, 1879, Gioia delle Colle, Italy. *d.* 1923. After going to Paris in 1902, he soon became a leading figure in French cultural life, playing host to such artists as Picasso, Dufy, and Léger. He began writing film criticism in 1907, and his theoretical writings on film as a means of expression provided a foundation for subsequent European thinking on the aesthetics of the cinema. He coined the phrase "the seventh art" to describe the then-new art of film and in 1920 founded the Club of the Friends of the Seventh Art in Paris. In 1923 he planned a scenario for a film in collaboration with Marcel L'Herbier but died before the project got under way.

Canutt, Yakima. Actor, stuntman, second-unit director. *b.* Enos Edward Canutt, Nov. 29, 1895, Colfax, Wash. *d.* 1986. A ranch hand from boyhood, he joined a Wild West show at 17, later winning many prizes for his riding and roping stunts. The title of rodeo world champion led to his being cast for stunts and bit parts in Westerns in the early 20s, and he became a cowboy star in 1924. His films were typically fast-paced, action-filled adventures in which he performed all his own stunts, never using a double. They were released, however, for the most part by small independent companies and seldom reached wide markets, preventing Canutt from becoming a truly front-rank cowboy hero. Nor did his voice register well in talkies, and with the transition to sound he returned to stunt work and also started a new career as a screen villain.

His exploits as a stuntman became legendary, and his amazing leaps from and onto horses and wagons are the most spectacular the screen has ever seen. He also doubled for cowboy stars John Wayne, Roy Rogers, and Gene Autry, among others. At the same time, and often in the same film, he played supporting parts, usually as a heavy. His many portrayals of Indians led to the assumption that he was himself an Indian or a half-breed, but his parentage was Irish-Scots-Dutch. His exotic name Yakima was the result of a newsphoto caption identifying him as "The Cowboy From Yakima" during a rodeo contest early in his career.

In the late 30s, Canutt began setting up stunt sequences for other directors and soon became a second-unit director, one of the best in the business. In that capacity he directed breathtaking action sequences of some of Hollywood's most spectacular films. He also directed a number of low-budget Westerns in the 40s. He was awarded a special Oscar (1966) "for creating the profession of stuntman as it exists today and for the development of many safety devices used by stuntmen everywhere."

FILMS INCLUDE: As actor—*Romance and Rustlers, Ridin' Mad* 1924; *The Riding Comet, White Thunder, Scar Hanan, The Human Tornado* 1925; *The Outlaw Breaker, Hellhound of the Plains, The Fighting Stallion, Desert Greed* 1926; *The Iron Rider* 1927; *Bad Man's Money, Captain Cowboy* 1929; *Firebrand Jordan, Bar-L Ranch, Canyon Hawks* 1930; *Pueblo Terror* 1931; *Fighting Texans* 1933; *Lawless Frontier* 1934; *Circle of Death, Westward Ho!* 1935; *The Oregon Trail, King of the Pecos* 1936; *The Mysterious Pilot* (serial) 1937; *Stagecoach, Gone With the Wind* 1939; *The Dark Command, The Ranger and the Lady* 1940; *The Great Train Robbery* 1941; *In Old Oklahoma* 1943; *Hidden Valley Outlaws* 1944; *Rocky Mountain* 1950; *The Far Horizon* 1955. As director (complete)—*Sheriff of Cimarron* 1945; *Oklahoma Badlands, Carson City Raiders, Sons of Adventure* 1948. As 2nd-unit director—*Stagecoach* 1939; *The Dark Command* 1940; *In Old Oklahoma* 1943; *Wyoming* 1945; *Angel and the Badman* 1947; *The Doolins of Oklahoma* 1949; *Ivanhoe* 1950; *Knights of the Round Table* 1954; *Helen of Troy* 1955; *Zarak* 1956; *Ben-Hur* 1959; *Spartacus* 1960; *El Cid* 1961; *How the West Was Won* 1962; *The Fall of the Roman Empire* 1964; *Cat Ballou* 1965; *Khartoum* 1966; *The Flim-Flam Man* 1967; *Rio Lobo, Song of Norway* 1970; *Breakheart Pass* 1976.

Capellani, Albert. Director. *b.* 1870, Paris. *d.* 1931. Began directing films for Pathé in 1905, after gaining acting and administrative experience on the stage. From short comedies he moved to ambitious spectacles, often adaptations of literary classics (his *Les Misérables,* 1912, was five hours long), which were rather static and theatrical but highly regarded by those who sought to legitimize film as an art. His reputation brought him an invitation to direct in the US, and between 1915 and 1922 he piloted a good number of American films, often starring Alla NAZIMOVA or Clara Kimball YOUNG. In 1923 he returned to France afflicted with paralysis and retired from films. His brother, actor Paul Capellani (1884–1944), appeared occasionally in Albert's French and American films.

FILMS INCLUDE: In France—*La Peine du Talion, Aladin/Aladdin* 1906; *Don Juan, Cendrillon/Cinderella* 1907; *Le Chat botté/Puss 'n Boots, Peau d'Ane, Jeanne d'Arc/Joan of Arc* 1908; *L'Assommoir, La Mort du Duc d'Enghien* 1909; *Le Voile du Bonheur, Les Deux Orphelines* 1910; *Le Courrier de Lyon, Athalie, Notre Dame de Paris/The Hunchback of Notre Dame* 1911; *L'Arlésienne, Les Misérables, Les Mystères de Paris* 1912; *Peau de Chagrin, Germinal* 1913; *Le Tragique Amour de Mona Lisa, Quatre-Vingt-Treize* 1914. In the US—*The Face in the Moonlight, The Impostor, The Flash of an Emerald* (also sc.), *Camille* 1915; *The Common Law, The Dark Silence, The Feast of Life, La Vie de Bohème, The Foolish Virgin* (also sc.) 1916; *The Easiest Way, An American Maid* 1917; *Daybreak, The Richest Girl, Social Hypocrites, The House of Mirth, Eye for Eye* 1918; *Out of the Fog, The Red Lantern, Oh Boy!, The Virtuous Model* 1919; *The Fortune Teller* 1920; *The Inside of the Cup* (also co-sc.), *The Wild Goose* 1921; *Sisters, The Young Diana* 1922.

Capote, Truman. *b.* Sept. 30, 1924, New Orleans. *d.* 1984. Writer. Two of the works by this pint-sized (5' 3"), falsetto-voiced American author have been adapted to the screen by others: the novella *Breakfast at Tiffany's,* in 1961, and the nonfiction chiller *In Cold Blood,* in 1967. He has also collaborated on four scripts and played one of the leading roles in the film *Murder by Death* (1976).

FILMS (as screenwriter, in collaboration): *Stazione Termini/Indiscretion of an American Wife* (dial. only; It.) 1953; *Beat the Devil* (UK/It.) 1954; *The Innocents* (UK/US) 1961; *Trilogy* (from three of his own short stories; orig. shown on TV) 1969.

Capra, Frank. Director. *b.* 1897, in Palermo, Sicily. *d.* 1991. At the age of six he had moved with his family to California, where his father made a meager living as an orange picker. One of seven children, Capra sold newspapers and played a banjo in Los Angeles honky-tonks, among other occupations, to help the family budget and pay for his own education. Upon graduating as a chemical engineer from the California Institute of Technology in 1918, he enlisted in the Army as a private. After being demobilized, with the rank of second lieutenant, he could find no work in his profession, and began drifting about the West, selling books and mining stocks door to door and playing poker for a living. In 1922, down to his last nickel, he double-talked his way into directing a one-reel film adaptation of a Rudyard Kipling ballad, *Fultah Fisher's Boarding House,* for a small San Francisco–based company. He earned $75 for this first effort as director.

Capra realized he knew nothing about the film medium, so he took a job as an apprentice at a small film lab in return for food and lodging. For a year he printed, dried, and spliced amateur films, then began processing the daily rushes of a Hollywood comedy director, Bob Eddy. He next began to work for Eddy as a propman and film editor, then moved on to the Hal Roach studios as gagman for "Our Gang" comedies. He was fired after six months, but thanks to a recommendation from Will Rogers, he was hired in 1925 by Mack Sennett as gag writer for comedian Harry LANGDON.

When Langdon moved to First National the following year, he took Capra along as a director. Capra co-authored and co-directed (with Harry Edwards) Langdon's classic comedy *Tramp Tramp Tramp,* although he received screen credit as co-writer only. He then directed two other superior Langdon films, *The Strong Man* and *Long Pants.* However, Langdon, swell-headed with success, fired Capra and spread the rumor that he, not Capra, was responsible for the creative handling of these films.

Unable to find further employment in Hollywood, Capra went to New York in 1927, and got a job directing *For the Love of Mike,* a film featuring Claudette Colbert, a stage actress making her screen debut. The resulting flop sent Miss Colbert back to the stage and left Capra unemployed. (Seven years later, another Capra-Colbert collaboration, *It Happened One Night,* was to win Oscars for both.) A dejected Capra next returned to Hollywood and meekly accepted a $75-a-week salary (down from $600) for grinding out two-reel comedies for Sennett. Then came the turning point in his career, a contract to direct for Harry COHN and Columbia Pictures.

The decade-long association that resulted was to propel Columbia into the status of a major studio and Capra into the position of a leading Hollywood director.

Enjoying total creative freedom and absolute autonomy on the set, Capra made a succession of highly successful films from the mid-30s to the mid-40s. In these fable-like comedies, the recurrent theme was that of an idealistic individual, an improbable hero bucking all odds and thwarting the antisocial schemes of materialistic cynics. Films like *It Happened One Night, Mr. Deeds Goes to Town, You Can't Take It with You,* and *Mr. Smith Goes to Washington* all shared a basic faith in the essential goodness of the common man and the inevitable triumph of honesty and justice over (usually bureaucracy-driven) selfishness and deceit. Even the atypical *Lost Horizon* was a variation on the same theme. During this down-and-out Depression period, the formula clicked repeatedly with both the critics and the public; Capra reaped three Academy Awards within five years for the direction of *It Happened One Night* (1934), *Mr. Deeds Goes to Town* (1936), and *You Can't Take It with You* (1938). Only his darker view of the common man, *Meet John Doe* (1941), failed to generate wide critical or commercial appeal.

One way he was able to present such a unified view was his repertory of actors and crew. Leads like James Stewart, Gary Cooper, and Barbara Stanwyck projected the blend of earnest commonness and individuality that fueled his films; supporting cast members like Edward Arnold and Thomas Mitchell provided the corruption or skepticism needed to generate the drama. Also important was his screenwriter Robert RISKIN, who, beginning with *American Madness* (1932), and continuing through some of Capra's greatest successes (*It Happened One Night, Mr. Deeds Goes to Town*) helped to define the Capra film and the screwball comedy form.

During WW II, Capra, back in the service, directed a much-heralded Army documentary series, "Why We Fight." The first of the series, *Prelude to War,* won the best documentary Oscar in 1942. Capra's postwar activity slackened considerably after his discharge with the rank of colonel. After the war, he formed his own production company, Liberty Films, and hoped for a future as an independent. He felt his first Liberty film, the comedy-drama *It's a Wonderful Life* (1946), was his best film to date and would successfully reintroduce him to the postwar public. But the formula that suited a Depression audience looking for optimistic answers proved too simplistic for postwar audiences awakened to ambiguity. Capra was slow to adjust to the changing times. His total output after the mid-40s was limited to seven films. He also directed four hour-long television science programs for the Bell System: 'Our Mr. Sun,' (1956); 'Hemo the Magnificent,' 'The Strange Case of the Cosmic Rays' (1957); and 'The Unchained Goddess' (1958). In 1971 he published an autobiography, *Frank Capra: The Name Above the Title,* a lively, if boastful, reminder that Capra was the first of Hollywood's directors (excluding directors who financed their own films) whose name preceded the film title in the credits.

In the 1970s, when the copyright on *It's a Wonderful Life*

elapsed and was not renewed, the movie became a Christmastime staple on TV, and still serves to introduce new generations to the man who captured the archetypal conflict between the common man and the powers that be. His son, Frank Capra, Jr., is a film producer. His grandson, Frank Capra III, is an assistant director.

FILMS: *Fultah Fisher's Boarding House* (short) 1922; *Tramp Tramp Tramp* (co-dir., co-sc.), *The Strong Man* 1926; *Long Pants, His First Flame* (co-sc. only), *For the Love of Mike* 1927; *That Certain Thing, So This Is Love, The Matinee Idol, The Way of the Strong, Say It with Sables* (also co-story), *Submarine, The Power of the Press* 1928; *The Younger Generation, The Donovan Affair, Flight* (also dial.) 1929; *Ladies of Leisure, Rain or Shine* 1930; *Dirigible, The Miracle Woman, Platinum Blonde* 1931; *Forbidden* (also story), *American Madness* 1932; *The Bitter Tea of General Yen, Lady for a Day* 1933; *It Happened One Night, Broadway Bill* 1934; *Mr. Deeds Goes to Town* (also prod.) 1936; *Lost Horizon* (also prod.) 1937; *You Can't Take It with You* (also prod.) 1938; *Mr. Smith Goes to Washington* (also prod.) 1939; *Meet John Doe* (also prod.) 1941; *Prelude to War* (doc.), *The Nazis Strike* (doc.; co-dir. with Anatole Litvak) 1942; *Divide and Conquer* (doc.; co-dir with Litvak), *Battle of Britain* (doc.; co-dir.), *Battle of Russia* (doc.; prod. only), *Battle of China* (doc.; co-dir. with Litvak) 1943; *The Negro Soldier* (doc.), *War Comes to America* (doc.; prod. only), *Tunisian Victory* (doc.; co-dir. with Roy Boulting), *Arsenic and Old Lace* 1944; *Know Your Enemy: Japan* (doc.; co-dir. with Joris Ivens), *Two Down and One to Go* (doc.) 1945; *It's a Wonderful Life* (also prod., co-sc.) 1947; *State of the Union* (also co-prod.) 1948; *Riding High* (also prod.) 1950; *Here Comes the Groom* (also prod.) 1951; *A Hole in the Head* (also prod.) 1959; *Pocketful of Miracles* (also prod.) 1961.

Caprice, June. Actress. *b.* 1899, Arlington, Va. *d.* 1936. Bright-eyed star of Hollywood silents, mainly for Fox. Typically portrayed youthful innocence, in the style of Mary Pickford. She was married to screen actor-director Harry Millarde.

FILMS INCLUDE: *Caprice of the Mountains, Little Miss Happiness, The Ragged Princess, The Mischief Maker* 1916; *A Modern Cinderella, Miss USA, A Child of the Wild, Every Girl's Dream, A Small Town Girl* 1917; *The Heart of Romance, The Camouflage Kiss, Blue-Eyed Mary, Miss Innocence* 1918; *Oh Boy!, The Love Cheat, A Damsel in Distress, The Ragged Princess* 1919; *Pirate Gold* (serial), *In Walked Mary, Rogues and Romance* 1920; *Sky Ranger* (serial) 1921.

Capshaw, Kate. Actress. Born in 1953, in Fort Worth, Tex. *ed.* U of Mo. Pert, curly-haired leading lady of Hollywood films of the 80s and early 90s. Married to Steven SPIELBERG after his divorce from Amy IRVING.

FILMS: *A Little Sex* 1982; *Indiana Jones and the Temple of Doom, Best Defense, Dreamscape, Windy City* 1984; *Power, Space Camp* 1986; *Black Rain* 1989; *Love at Large* 1990; *My Heroes Have Always Been Cowboys* 1991; *Love Affair* 1994; *How To Make an American Quilt, Just Cause* 1995.

caption. A printed line shown on the screen to introduce a scene, describe a location, specify a date, etc. Sometimes also used interchangeably with SUBTITLE.

Capucine. Actress. *b.* Germaine Lefebvre, Jan. 6, 1933, Toulon, France. *d.* 1990, a suicide. A former haute-couture Paris model of classic features and slim figure, she came to the US in the late 50s and became a protegée of agent-producer Charles FELDMAN. She studied English intensively, and after drama training by Gregory Ratoff, made her screen debut in 1960. During her brief Hollywood starring career, she was intimately associated with producer Darryl F. Zanuck and actors William Holden and Peter Sellers. By the mid-60s she was back in Europe, where she appeared in international co-productions. She spent her final years in reclusive retirement in Lausanne, Switzerland. Suffering from profound depression, she jumped to her death from her eighth-floor penthouse apartment.

FILMS INCLUDE: *Song Without End, North to Alaska* 1960; *A Walk on the Wild Side, The Lion* (UK) 1962; *The Pink Panther, The Seventh Dawn* (US/UK) 1964; *What's New Pussycat?* 1965; *Le Fate/The Queens* (It./Fr.) 1966; *The Honey Pot* (US/UK/It.) 1967; *Fräulein Doktor* (It./Yug.), *Fellini Satyricon* (It./Fr.) 1969; *Soleil Rouge/Red Sun* (Fr./Sp.) 1971; *Exquisite Cadaver* (Sp.) 1972; *L'Incorrigible/Incorrigible* (Fr.) 1975; *Per Amore* (It.) 1976; *The Con Artists* (It.) 1977; *Ritratto di Borghese in Nero/Nest of Vipers* (It.) 1978; *Da Dunkerque alla Vittoria/From Hell to Victory* (It./Fr./Sp.), *Arabian Adventure* (UK), *Jaguar Lives* (US) 1979; *Trail of the Pink Panther* (UK) 1982; *Curse of the Pink Panther* (UK) 1983.

Cara, Irene. Actress, singer. Born on Mar. 18, 1958, in New York City. Leading lady of American stage, TV, and sporadic films, usually in ethnic roles.

FILMS INCLUDE: *Aaron Loves Angela* 1975; *Sparkle* 1976; *Fame* 1980; *D.C. Cab* 1983; *City Heat* 1984; *Certain Fury, Killing 'em Softly* (Can.) 1985; *Busted Up* (Can.) 1987; *Happily Ever After* (v/o) 1990; *Maximum Security* 1991.

Carax, Leos. Director, screenwriter, actor. Born Alexander Oscar Dupont in 1961 in Suresnes, France. After writing film criticism, he arrived in international film circles as a 22-year-old prodigy. His first feature as director-screenwriter, *Boy Meets Girl* (1984), was a notable debut at Cannes and the New York Film Festival. Filmed in high contrast black-and-white (by cinematographer Jean-Yves Escoffier), this episodic romance harkened back to France's Nouvelle Vague (new wave). Carax followed with a science-fiction-tinged production about a mysterious virus, *Mauvais Sang/Bad Blood* (1986), shot by Escoffier in color. A third film, the more commercially oriented, three-character melodrama, *Les Amants Du Pont Neuf* (1991), did not meet with the critical approval of the earlier pictures. Appearing in leading roles in all of these films is Carax collaborator Denis Lavant. The director's nom de cinema, "Leos Carax," is an anagram of his first two names, Alex Oscar.

FILMS (as director and screenwriter): *Boy Meets Girl* 1984; *Mauvais Sang/Bad Blood, King Lear* (act. only) 1987; *Les Ministères de l'art* (act. only) 1988; *Les Amants du Pont Neuf* 1991.

carbon-arc lamps. Studio lamps and projector bulbs whose light originates in an electric arc generated between two carbon electrodes. Carbon-arc lamps provide a steadier light when they operate on direct current rather than alternating current.

Cardiff, Jack. Director, director of photography. Born on Sept. 18, 1914, in Yarmouth, England. Entered British films at four as a child actor and continued as a camera assistant at 13. By 1936 he was a competent camera operator and worked in that capacity on such distinguished productions as *As You Like It, The Ghost Goes West* (both 1936), *Knight Without Armor,* and Britain's first three-color technicolor film, *Wings of the Morning* (both 1937). As a color expert he photographed many travelogue shorts and was a second-unit cameraman on *The Four Feathers* (1939). With the Crown Film Unit of the Ministry of Information during WW II, he photographed many documentaries, including the excellent *Western Approaches* (1944). He later became one of England's most accomplished directors of photography and provided the dazzling color camerawork for some of the country's most prestigious productions. He received an Academy Award for the cinematography of *Black Narcissus* (1947). Also worked on some American and international productions and in the late 50s turned to directing.

FILMS INCLUDE: As director of photography—*Western Approaches* (doc.) 1944; *Caesar and Cleopatra* (co-phot.), *A Matter of Life and Death/Stairway to Heaven* 1946; *Black Narcissus* 1947; *The Red Shoes* 1948; *Under Capricorn* (co-phot.) 1949; *The Black Rose* 1950; *Pandora and the Flying Dutchman, The Magic Box, The African Queen* 1951; *The Master of Ballantrae* 1953; *The Barefoot Contessa* 1954; *War and Peace* (co-phot.), *The Brave One* 1956; *Legend of the Lost, The Prince and the Showgirl* 1957; *The Vikings* 1958; *The Journey* 1959; *Fanny* 1961; *Scalawag* 1973; *The Prince and the Pauper/Crossed Swords, The Fifth Musketeer* 1977; *Death on the Nile* 1978; *Avalanche Express* 1979; *The Dogs of War* 1980; *Ghost Story* 1981; *The Wicked Lady* 1983; *Conan the Destroyer* 1984; *Cat's Eye, Rambo: First Blood Part II* 1985; *Tai-Pan* 1986; *Million Dollar Mystery* 1987. As director (complete)—*Intent to Kill* 1958; *Beyond This Place* 1959; *Sons and Lovers, Scent of Mystery* 1960; *Satan Never Sleeps* (addnl. seg. only), *The Lion, My Geisha* 1962; *The Long Ships* 1964; *Young Cassidy* (co-dir. with John Ford), *The Liquidator* 1965; *The Mercenaries/Dark of the Sun* 1967; *La Motocyclette/Girl on a Motorcycle/Naked Under Leather* (also adapt., phot.; Fr./UK) 1968; *The Mutations, Penny Gold* 1974; *Ride a Wild Pony/Wild Pony* 1976.

Cardinale, Claudia. Actress. Born on Apr. 15, 1939, in Tunis, to Italian parents. In 1957 she won a beauty contest and a trip to the Venice Film Festival. She later attended acting classes at the Centro Sperimentale film school in Rome and before long began playing secondary roles in pictures. Italy was then in dire need of a new international star to replace Gina Lollobrigida and Sophia Loren, both of whom had been lost to Hollywood. Producer Franco CRISTALDI chose Cardinale, took charge of her career, and later married her. A well-proportioned, husky-voiced dark beauty, she attained international stardom by the early 60s, but despite continuous employment in Italian, French, British, and American films has never reached the popularity of Lollobrigida or Loren. At Venice in 1984 she was named best actress in an Italian film for her role in *Claretta.*

FILMS INCLUDE: *Anneaux d'Or* (short; Fr.) 1956; *Goha* (Fr.) 1957; *Les Noces Vénetienne* (Fr./It.), *I Soliti Ignoti/Big Deal on Madonna Street* 1958; *Un Maledetto Imbroglio/The Facts of Murder, Upstairs and Downstairs* (UK) 1959; *Il Bell'Antonio, Rocco e i suoi Fratelli/Rocco and His Brothers* 1960; *La Ragazza con la Valigia/Girl with a Suitcase, La Viaccia/The Love Makers* 1961; *Cartouche* (Fr./It.) 1962; *Otto e Mezzo/8½, Il Gattopardo/The Leopard, La Ragazza di Bube/Bebo's Girl* 1963; *The Pink Panther* (US), *Circus World* (US), *Gli Indifferenti/Time of Indifference, Il Magnifico Cornuto/The Magnificent Cuckold* 1964; *Vaghe Stelle dell'Orsa/Sandra* 1965; *Blindfold* (US), *Lost Command* (US), *The Professionals* (US), *Le Fate/The Queens* 1966; *Una Rosa per Tutti/A Rose for Everyone, Don't Make Waves* (US) 1967; *C'era una Volta il West/Once Upon a Time in the West, The Hell with Heroes* (US), *Il Giorno della Civetta/Mafia* 1968; *Ruba al Prossimo Tuo/A Fine Pair* 1969; *Popsy Pop/The Butterfly Affair* 1970; *Krasnaya Palatka/La Tenda rossa/The Red Tent* (USSR/It.), *Les Petroleuses/The Legend of Frenchy King* (Fr./It./Sp.), *L'Udienza* 1971; *Il Giorno del Furore* 1973; *Libera Amore Mio* 1974; *A Mezzanotte va la Ronda del Piacere/Midnight Pleasures, Beato Loro, Gruppo di Famiglia in uno Interno/Conversation Piece* 1975; *Qui comincia l'avventura/The Immortal Bachelor* 1976; *Il Prefetto di Ferro, L'Arma, La Petite Fille en Velours bleu, Corleone* 1978; *I Briganti* (also prod.), *Escape to Athena* (UK), *L'Ingorgo/Traffic Jam* 1979; *La Pelle, The Salamander* (UK/US/It.) 1981; *Le Cadeau/The Gift* (Fr./It.), *Fitzcarraldo* (Ger.) 1982; *Enrico IV/Henry IV, Claretta* 1984; *L'Eté prochain/Next Summer* (Fr./It.), *La Storia/History* 1985; *Un Homme amoureux/A Man in Love* (Fr./It.) 1987; *La Revolution Française/The French Revolution* (Fr./W. Ger./It./Can.) 1989; *Atto di Dolore, La Batalla de los Tres Reyes* 1990; *588 Rue Paradis* 1992; *Son of the Pink Panther* 1993; *She Doesn't Think So* 1994.

Carère, Christine. Actress. Born Christine de Borde, on July 27, 1930, in Dijon, France. In French films from 1950, she was brought to the US with much fanfare to star in the Hollywood adaptation of Françoise Sagan's *A Certain Smile.* But after a couple of other roles, she returned to France. She is married to French actor Philippe Nicaud.

FILMS INCLUDE: *Folie douce, Olivia* 1951; *Un Caprice de Caroline Chérie* 1953; *Sang et Lumière, Cadet Rousselle* 1954; *Femmes libres, L'Affaire des Poisons* 1955; *Don Juan, Bonjour Jeunesse* 1956; *Les Collegiennes/The Twilight Girls* 1957; *A Certain Smile* (US), *Mardi Gras* (US) 1958; *A Private's Affair* (US) 1959; *I Deal in Danger* (US) 1966.

Carette, Julien. Actor. *b.* Dec. 23, 1897, Paris. *d.* 1966. Came to films in 1932 from the French music hall and the legitimate stage and played some 100 character roles, typically as a common man, most memorably in Jean Renoir's movies of the late 30s. He died as the result of burns he had suffered in an accident. Often billed under surname only, Carette.

FILMS INCLUDE: *L'Affaire est dans le Sac* 1932; *Gribouille/Heart of Paris, La Grande Illusion/Grand Illusion* 1937; *Entrée des Artistes/The Curtain Rises, La Marseillaise, La Bête humaine/The Human Beast* 1938; *La Règle du Jeu/The Rules of the Game* 1939; *Battements de Coeur* 1940; *Adieu Léonard* 1943; *Sylvie et le Fantôme/Sylvie and the Phantom, Les Portes de la Nuit/Gates of the Night* 1946; *Une si Jolie Petite Plage/Riptide* 1948; *Occupe-toi d'Amélie/Oh Amelia!* 1949; *Marie du Port* 1950; *Sans laisser d'Adresse, L'Auberge rouge/The Red Inn* 1951; *La Fête à Henriette/Holiday for Henrietta* 1952; *Crime et Châtiment/Crime and Punishment* 1956; *Le Joueur* 1958; *Archimède le Clochard/The Magnificent Tramp, La Jument verte/The Green Mare* 1959; *Les Pieds-Nickelés* 1964.

Carewe, Edwin. Director. *b.* Mar. 5, 1883, Gainesville, Tex. *d.* 1940. A stage actor from his teens, he spent a few months as a hobo before launching his screen career as an actor with Lubin in 1910. From 1914 he directed many films for Metro, First National, and other studios, including his own production company, among them a number of ambitious and successful silent productions, but his career faltered after the advent of sound. His daughter, Rita Carewe (1908–55), appeared in several of his films.

FILMS: *Across the Pacific* (also sc.) 1914; *The Cowboy and the Lady, Cora, Marse Covington, Destiny, or the Soul of a Woman, The Final Judgment* 1915; *The Upstart, Her Great Price, The Snowbird, God's Half Acre, The Dawn of Love, The Sunbeam* 1916; *The Barricade, Her Fighting Chance, The Greatest Power, The Trail of the Shadow, Their Compact, The Voice of Conscience* 1917; *The Splendid Sinner, The Trail to Yesterday, The House of Gold, Pals First* 1918; *The Great Romance, False Evidence, Way of the Strong, Shadows of Suspicion, Easy to Make Money, The Right to Lie* 1919; *Isobel or the Trail's End, The Web of Deceit, Rio Grande* 1920; *My Lady's Latchkey, Habit, Playthings of Destiny, The Invisible Fear, Her Mad Bargain* 1921; *A Question of Honor, I Am the Law* (also exec. prod.), *Silver Wings* (prologue directed by John Ford) 1922; *Mighty Lak' a Rose* (also prod.), *The Girl of the Golden West* (also exec. prod.), *The Bad Man* (also prod.) 1923; *A Son of the Sahara* (also prod.), *Madonna of the Streets* (also prod.) 1924; *My Son* (also prod.), *The Lady Who Lied* (also prod.), *Joanna* (also prod.), *Why Women Love* (also prod.) 1925; *High Steppers* (also prod.), *Pals First* (remake; also prod.) 1926; *Resurrection* (also prod., co-adapt.) 1927; *Ramona, Revenge* (also prod.) 1928; *Evangeline* (also prod.) 1929; *The Spoilers* 1930; *Resurrection* (remake) 1931; *Are We Civilized?* 1934.

Carey, Harry. Actor. *b.* Henry DeWitt Carey II, Jan. 16, 1878, the Bronx, N.Y. *d.* 1947. *ed.* NYU. Tried his hand at various occupations, including the writing of melodramas, before entering films with Biograph in 1909. Appeared in many early D. W. GRIFFITH productions and by 1917 had emerged as a star of Westerns and action pictures under John FORD and other directors. He worked closely with Ford on 26 productions, often as a character called Cheyenne Harry, occasionally collaborating with him on stories, scripts, producing, and directing. In the 30s, following an impressive performance in *Trader Horn* (1931), Carey began a second phase of his career as a reliable character actor, a phase that continued until his death in 1947 of a coronary thrombosis. The following year John Ford dedicated the film *The Three Godfathers* "to the memory of Harry Carey—bright star of the early Western sky." His second wife, Olive (1895–1988), also appeared in films using the professional names Olive Fuller Golden and Olive Carey. Their son is Harry CAREY, Jr.

FILMS INCLUDE: *Bill Sharkey's Last Game* 1909; *An Unseen Enemy, Friends, The Musketeers of Pig Alley, Heredity, The Informer, My Hero, A Cry for Help* 1912; *An Adventure in the Autumn Woods, Love in an Apartment Hotel, Brothers, Broken Ways, The Sheriff's Baby, The Hero of Little Italy, Olaf—An Atom, Two Men of the Desert* 1913; *Judith of Bethulia, The Master Cracksman* (also dir.), *McVeagh of the South Seas* (also dir., sc.) 1914; *Graft* (serial), *Just Jim* 1915; *A Knight of the Range* (also sc.), *The Three Godfathers, Love's Lariat* (also co-dir.), *Behind the Lines* 1916; *The Fighting Gringo, Straight Shooting, The Secret Man, A Marked Man, Bucking Broadway* 1917; *The Phantom Riders* (also prod.), *Wild Women, Hell Bent, Three Mounted Men* 1918; *Roped, A Fight for Love, Bare Fists, Riders of Vengeance* (also co-sc.), *The Outcasts of Poker Flat, The Ace of the Saddle, The Rider of the Law, A Gun Fightin' Gentleman* (also co-sc.), *Marked Men* 1919; *Bullet Proof, Human Stuff* (also co-sc.), *Sundown Slim* (also prod.), *West Is West, Hearts Up* (also story) 1920; *The Freeze Out, The Wallop, The Fox, Desperate Trails* 1921; *Man to Man* 1922; *Crashin' Thru, The Miracle Baby* 1923; *The Flaming Forties, The Night Hawk, Roaring Rails* 1924; *Soft Shoes, Silent Sanderson, The Texas Trail, The Bad Lands* 1925; *Satan Town* 1926; *A Little Journey, Slide Kelly Slide* 1927; *The Border Patrol* 1928; *The Vanishing Legion* (serial), *Trader Horn, Bad Company* 1931; *The Last of the Mohicans* (serial), *Law and Order* 1932; *Barbary Coast, The Last Outpost* 1935; *The Prisoner of Shark Island, Sutter's Gold* 1936; *Kid Galahad, Souls at Sea* 1937; *You and Me, King of Alcatraz* 1938; *Mr. Smith Goes to Washington* 1939; *They Knew What They Wanted* 1940; *The Shepherd of the Hills, Sundown, Among the Living* 1941; *The Spoilers* 1942; *Air Force* 1943; *The Great Moment* 1944; *Duel in the Sun* 1946; *The Sea of Grass, Angel and the Badman* 1947; *Red River, So Dear to My Heart* 1948.

Carey, Harry, Jr. Actor. Born on May 16, 1921, in Saugus, Calif. The son of actor Harry CAREY, he made his film debut in 1947, after a six-year stint in the Navy, as a protégé of John Ford. Began as shy and boyish and gradually matured into an all-purpose supporting player, mainly in Westerns.

FILMS INCLUDE: *Rolling Home* (bit) 1946; *Pursued* 1947; *Red River* 1948; *Three Godfathers, She Wore a Yellow Ribbon* 1949; *Wagonmaster, Rio Grande, Copper Canyon* 1950; *Warpath* 1951; *Monkey Business* 1952; *Niagara, Gentlemen Prefer Blondes, Beneath the 12-mile Reef* 1953; *The Silver Lode* 1954; *The Long Gray Line, Mister Roberts* 1955; *The Searchers* 1956; *Rio Bravo* 1959; *The Great Impostor* 1960; *The Comancheros* 1961; *Cheyenne Autumn* 1964; *Shenandoah* 1965; *The Rare Breed, Alvarez Kelly* 1966; *The Way West* 1967; *The Devil's Brigade, Bandolero!* 1968; *Death of a Gunfighter, The Undefeated* 1969; *The Moonshine War, Dirty Dingus Magee* 1970; *Big Jake, Something Big* 1971; *E Poi Lo Chiamorono il Magnifico* (It./Fr.) 1972; *Cahill U.S. Marshal* 1973; *Take a Hard Ride* 1975; *Nickelodeon* 1976; *The Long Riders* 1980; *Endangered Species* 1982; *Gremlins* 1984; *Mask* 1985; *The Whales of August* 1987; *Cherry 2000, Illegally Yours* 1988; *Breaking In* 1989; *Bad Jim, Back to the Future Part III, Exorcist III* 1990.

Carey, MacDonald. Actor. *b.* Mar. 15, 1913, Sioux City, Iowa. *d.* 1994. *ed.* U. of Wisconsin; U. of Iowa. Mild-mannered, often bland leading man of Hollywood films of the 40s and 50s. Began his screen career in 1942 after several years of singing and acting on radio and on the stage, capped by a successful stint in the 1941 Broadway production of 'Lady in the Dark.' He spent the 40s as a contract player with Paramount, playing leads and second leads, mainly in routine productions. Later free-lanced with various studios without improving the quality of his films. On TV from the early 50s, he starred in such series as 'Dr. Christian,' 'Lock Up,' and 'Mr. Blandings.' From 1965 he headed the cast of the TV daytime soap opera 'Days of Our Lives.' He wrote a book of poetry, *A Day in the Life.*

FILMS INCLUDE: *Dr. Broadway, Take a Letter Darling, Wake Island* 1942; *Shadow of a Doubt, Salute for Three* 1943; *Suddenly It's Spring* 1947; *Hazard, Dream Girl* 1948; *Bride of Vengeance* (as Cesare Borgia), *Streets of Laredo, The Great Gatsby, Song of Surrender* 1949; *South Sea Sinner, Comanche Territory, The Lawless, Copper Canyon, Mystery Submarine* 1950; *The Great Missouri Raid, Excuse My Dust, Meet Me After the Show, Let's Make it Legal* 1951; *My Wife's Best Friend* 1952; *Count the Hours, Outlaw Territory* 1953; *Fire Over Africa* 1954; *Stranger at My Door, Odongo* 1956; *John Paul Jones* (as Patrick Henry), *Blue Denim* 1959; *The Damned/These Are the Damned* (UK), *Stranglehold* (UK) 1962; *Tammy and the Doctor* 1963; *End of the World* 1977; *American Gigolo* 1980; *It's Alive III: Island of the Alive* 1987.

Carey, Phil(ip). Actor. Born July 15, 1925, in Hackensack, N.J. *ed.* U. of Miami. After stock experience and service with the US Marines, he entered films early in the 50s. Has played leading roles in B action pictures and second leads in some A pictures. Among other TV roles, he played the title role in the series 'Philip Marlowe' (1959–60).

FILMS INCLUDE: *Operation Pacific, I Was a Communist for the FBI, Inside the Walls of Folsom Prison* 1951; *Man Behind the Gun, Springfield Rifle* 1952; *Calamity Jane, Gun Fury, The Nebraskan* 1953; *Massacre Canyon, Pushover* 1954; *The Long Gray Line, Mister Roberts, Three Stripes in the Sun* 1955; *Wicked As They Come* 1957; *Screaming Mimi* 1958; *The Trunk* (UK) 1960; *Black Gold* 1963; *Dead Ringer, The Time Travelers* 1964; *The Great Sioux Massacre* 1965; *Three Guns for Texas* 1968; *Backtrack, Once You Kiss a Stranger* 1969; *The Seven Minutes* 1971; *Fighting Mad* 1976.

Carey, Timothy. American actor. Born in 1925. Character player of Hollywood films, typically as a repulsive villain. Memorable in Kubrick's *The Killing* and *Paths of Glory.*

FILMS INCLUDE: *Bloodhounds of Broadway* 1952; *White Witch Doctor* 1953; *Crime Wave* 1954; *East of Eden, Finger Man* 1955; *The Killing, The Last Wagon* 1956; *Paths of Glory* 1957; *Revolt in the Big House* 1958; *One-Eyed Jacks* 1961; *Convicts 4* 1962; *Bikini Beach* 1964; *Waterhole 3, A Time for Killing* 1967; *Head* 1968; *What's the Matter with Helen?, Minnie and Moskowitz* 1971; *The Outfit* 1972; *Peeper, The Killing of a Chinese Bookie* 1976.

Carfagno, Edward C. Art director, production designer. In a career spanning five decades, he collaborated on the set design of many major productions, mainly for MGM. He won Academy Awards for *The Bad and the Beautiful, Julius Caesar,* and *Ben-Hur,* and was nominated for Oscars several more times.

FILMS INCLUDE: *The Youngest Profession* 1943; *The Thin Man Goes Home* 1944; *Good News* 1947; *The Barkleys of Broadway, Neptune's Daughter* 1949; *Quo Vadis* 1951; *The Bad and the Beautiful* 1952; *Julius Caesar, The Story of Three Loves* 1953; *Executive Suite* 1954; *Tea and Sympathy* 1956; *Something of Value* 1957; *Ben-Hur* 1959; *Period of Adjustment, The Wonderful World of the Brothers Grimm* 1962; *Sunday in New York* 1963; *Viva Las Vegas* 1964; *The Cincinnati Kid* 1965; *The Shoes of the Fisherman* 1968; *The Hindenburg* 1975; *Looking for Mr. Goodbar* 1977; *Time After Time* 1979; *Little Miss Marker* 1980; *The Sting II, Sudden Impact* 1983; *All of Me, Tightrope* 1984; *Pale Rider* 1985; *Heartbreak Ridge* 1986; *Bird* 1988; *Pink Cadillac* 1989.

Carle, Gilles. Director. Born in 1929, in Maniwaki, Quebec, Canada. After studies at Montreal's Ecole des Beaux-Arts, he worked as a newspaper graphic artist and book illustrator. He turned out his first short, *Manger,* for the National Film Board of Canada in 1961 and his first feature, *La Vie heureuse de Lépold Z,* in 1965. He has since become established as one of the leading filmmakers of the French-Canadian cinema. A versatile artist, he has written novels, plays, short stories, and film criticism, and is a partner in a publishing company. He was among the founders of the film magazine *L'Ecran* and among the designers of the Quebec pavillion at Expo '67.

FEATURE FILMS: *La Vie heureuse de Léopold Z/The Merry World of Leopold Z* 1965; *Le Viol d'Une Jeune Fille douce/The Rape of a Sweet Young Girl* 1968; *Red* 1970; *La Vraie Nature de Bernadete* 1972; *La Mort d'un Bucheron/Death of a Lumberjack, Les Corps célestes/The Heavenly Bodies* 1973; *La Tête de Normand St.-Onge* 1975; *L'Ange et la Femme* 1976; *Fantastica* 1980; *Les Plouffe* 1981; *The Great Chess Movie* 1982; *Maria Chapdeleine* 1983.

Carlino, Lewis John. Screenwriter, director. Born on Jan. 1, 1932, in New York City. *ed.* USC. A playwright and novelist, he began writing screenplays in the mid-60s. He occasionally also directs.

FILMS (as screenwriter) *Seconds* 1966; *The Fox* 1967; *The Brotherhood* 1968; *The Mechanic/Killer of Killers* (also co-prod.) 1972; *A Reflection of Fear* 1973; *Crazy Joe* 1974; *The Sailor Who Fell from Grace with the Sea* (also dir.; UK) 1976; *I Never Promised You a Rose Garden* 1977; *The Great Santini/The Ace* (also dir.) 1979; *Resurrection* 1980; *Class* (dir. only) 1983; *Haunted Summer* 1988.

Carlisle, Kitty. Actress, singer. Born Catherine Holtzman on Sept. 3, 1914, New Orleans. *ed.* Lausanne, Paris; RADA. Following dramatic and operatic training, she starred in Broadway musicals and several Hollywood films early in the 30s. Returned briefly to films in the early 40s. Later seen as a regular panelist on TV's 'To Tell the Truth' quiz show. In 1976 she was appointed chairman of New York State's Council on the Arts. She is the widow of playwright Moss HART.

FILMS: *Murder at the Vanities, She Loves Me Not, Here Is My Heart* 1934; *A Night at the Opera* 1935; *Larceny with Music* 1943; *Hollywood Canteen* 1944; *Radio Days* 1987.

Carlisle, Mary. Actress. Born on Feb. 3, 1912, in Boston. Blue-eyed, blonde star of medium- and low-budget Hollywood films of the 30s. Typically played sweet coeds. The stepdaughter of industrialist Henry J. Kaiser, she retired from the screen early in the 40s after marrying actor-socialite James Blakeley, who later became a 20th Century-Fox executive. In 1951, Miss Carlisle took over the management of the Elizabeth Arden beauty salon in Hollywood.

FILMS INCLUDE: *Madame Satan* 1930; *This Reckless Age, Night Court, Grand Hotel* 1932; *College Humor, Ladies Must Love, The Sweetheart of Sigma Chi* 1933; *Palooka, This Side of Heaven, Murder in the Private Car, Girl of My Dreams* 1934; *Grand Old Girl, Great Hotel Murder, It's in the Air* 1935; *Lady Be Careful* 1936; *Hotel Haywire, Double or Nothing, Hold 'Em Navy* 1937; *Dr. Rhythm, Tip-Off Girls, Hunted Men, Touchdown Army, Illegal Traffic* 1938; *Fighting Thoroughbreds, Beware Spooks* 1939; *Dance Girl Dance* 1940; *Rags to Riches* 1941; *Baby Face Morgan* 1942; *Dead Men Walk* 1943.

Carlsen, Henning. Director. Born on June 4, 1927, in Aalborg, Denmark. Began writing and directing documentary shorts in 1949. His first feature-length film, *Dilemma* (1962), was a semidocumentary investigation of apartheid shot half-secretly in South Africa. In 1966 he gained wide recognition for his screen adaptation of Knut Hamsun's novel *Hunger.* He remained in the forefront of Danish cinema through the 70s and 80s. He also directed for the stage and TV, and taught at the Danish Film School.

FEATURE FILMS: *Dilemma/A World of Strangers* (also sc.; shot in English in South Africa) 1962; *How About Us?/Epilogue* 1963; *The Cats* (also co-sc.; Sw.) 1965; *Hunger* (also exec. prod.; co-sc.; Den./Nor./Sw.) 1966; *People Meet and Sweet Music Fills the Heart* (also co-prod., co-sc.; Den./Sw.) 1967; *Klabautermanden/We Are All Demons* (also prod., co-sc.) 1969; *Er i bange?/Are You Afraid?* (also prod., co-sc.) 1971; *Oh to Be on the Bandwagon* (also co-sc.) 1972; *Un Divorce heureux* (also co-sc.; Fr.) 1974; *When Svante Disappeared* 1976; *Did Somebody Laugh?, A Street Under the Snow* 1978; *Your Money or Your Life* 1981; *Oviri/Gaugin—Le Loup dans le Soleil/The Wolf at the Door* (Den./Fr.) 1986.

Carlson, Richard. Actor, director. *b.* Apr. 29, 1912, Albert Lea, Minn. *d.* 1977. A *summa cum laude* graduate of the University of Minnesota, he taught there briefly after receiving his M.A. degree but soon became involved with the theater as an actor, director, and writer. After several Broadway appearances, he made his screen debut in 1938 and for the next three decades appeared in numerous films, playing leads in B pictures and supporting roles in major productions. In the 50s he branched out into directing and demonstrated technical skill and good visual sense in the handling of five productions. He also wrote articles and stories for leading magazines and contributed scripts for various TV series. He starred in the TV series 'I Led Three Lives' and 'McKenzie's Raiders' and appeared in episodes of many others.

FILMS INCLUDE: As actor—*The Young in Heart, The Duke of West Point* 1938; *Winter Carnival, These Glamour Girls, Dancing Co-Ed* 1939; *The Ghost Breakers, The Howards of Virginia, Too Many Girls, No No Nanette* 1940; *Back Street, Hold That Ghost, The Little Foxes, West Point Widow* 1941; *Fly by Night, My Heart Belongs to Daddy, White Cargo* 1942; *Presenting Lily Mars, The Man from Down Under* 1943; *So Well Remembered* 1947; *Behind Locked Doors* 1948; *King Solomon's Mines* 1950; *Valentino, A Millionaire for Christy, The Blue Veil* 1951; *Retreat Hell!, Flat Top* 1952; *The Magnetic Monster, It Came from Outer Space, Seminole, The Maze, All I Desire* 1953; *Creature from the Black Lagoon* 1954; *The Last Command, Bengazi* 1955; *Three for Jamie Dawn* 1956; *The Helen Morgan Story* 1957; *Tormented* 1960; *The Power* 1968; *The Valley of Gwangi, Change of Habit* 1969. As director—*Riders to the Stars* (also act.), *Four Guns to the Border* 1954; *The Saga of Hemp Brown, Appointment with a Shadow* 1958; *Kid Rodelo* 1966; *The Power* 1968; *Valley of Gwangi, Change of Habit* 1969.

Carlsten, Rune. Director. Born on July 2, 1893, in Stockholm. A stage director with Sweden's Royal Dramatic Theater, he entered films in 1918 as an actor and the following year became a director. He is considered one of the better "lesser" directors of the Swedish cinema.

FILMS INCLUDE: *The Bomb* 1919; *Family Traditions* 1920; *A Modern Robinson* 1921; *The Young Nobleman* 1924; *Dangerous Paradise* 1931; *House of Silence* 1933; *Doktor Glas* 1942; *Anna Lans* 1943; *Black Roses* 1945; *The Eternal Bond* 1947.

Carlyle, David. See PAIGE, Robert.

Carmichael, Hoagy. Songwriter, actor. *b.* Hoagland Howard Carmichael, Nov. 22, 1899, Bloomington, Ind. *d.* 1981. *ed.* Indiana U. (law). He gave up a brief legal practice to become a bandleader and arranger and soon became a famous songwriter. His 'Stardust' (1931) is one of the most popular songs in the annals of Tin Pan Alley. Has also composed songs for many films, beginning in 1936. 'In the Cool Cool Cool of the Evening,' for the film *Here Comes the Groom,* won a 1951 Academy Award. He made occasional film appearances, often playing himself, usually remembered for his scenes sitting at the piano, a cigarette dangling from the side of his mouth. Memoirs: *The Stardust Road* (1946); *Sometimes I Wonder* (1965).

FILMS INCLUDE (as song composer): *Anything Goes* 1936; *Every Day's a Holiday, College Swing, Sing You Sinners, Thanks for the Memory* 1938; *Road Show* 1941; *True to Life* 1943; *To Have and Have Not* (also act.) 1944; *Johnny Angel* (also act), *The Stork Club* 1945; *Canyon Passage, The Best Years of Our Lives* (both also act.) 1946; *Night Song* (also act.) 1947; *Johnny Holiday* (also act.), *Young Man with a Horn* (act. only) 1950; *Here Comes the Groom* 1951; *Belles on Their Toes, The Las Vegas Story* (both also act.) 1952; *Gentlemen Prefer Blondes* 1953; *Timberjack* (also act.), *Three for the Show* 1955.

Carmichael, Ian. Actor. Born on June 18, 1920, in Hull, England. *ed.* Scarborough Coll. Made his stage debut in 1939 as a robot in *R.U.R.,* then achieved some success in British comedy revues before entering films in 1948. He has appeared mostly in comedy films, often as a naïve bumbler. Portrayed Lord Peter Wimsey, the hero of Dorothy L. Sayers's detective novels, in several series produced by British TV.

FILMS INCLUDE: *Bond Street* 1948; *Meet Mr. Lucifer* 1953; *Betrayed, The Colditz Story* 1954; *Storm Over the Nile, Simon and Laura* 1955; *Private's Progress* (lead) 1956; *Brothers in Law* 1957; *I'm All Right Jack, Left Right and Center* 1959; *School for Scoundrels* 1960; *Double Bunk* 1961; *Heavens Above* 1963; *Hide and Seek* 1964; *Smashing Time* 1967; *Seven Magnificent Deadly Sins* 1971; *From Beyond the Grave* 1975; *The Lady Vanishes* 1979; *Dark Obsession (Diamond Skulls)* 1989.

Carminati, Tullio. Actor. *b.* Count Tullio Carminati de Brambilla, Zara, Dalmatia, then Italy, now Yugoslavia. *d.* 1971. On the Italian stage from age 15, he made his screen debut in 1912 and was soon a leading star of Italian silent films. In 1920 he returned to the stage and often starred opposite Eleonora Duse. He came to the US in 1925 and for a number of years enjoyed popularity as a suave matinee idol on Broadway and in films. By 1935, however, he was back in Europe, as the star of British, Italian, and French productions. After a period of relative inactivity during WW II, he returned to the screen in character roles, including small parts in several large-scale US productions filmed in Europe.

FILMS INCLUDE: In Italy—*Il Bacio di Margherita da Cortona* 1912; *La mia Vita per la tua* 1914; *Romanticismo, La Maschera di Caino* 1915; *Il Presagio, La Menzogna, Amore tradito* 1916; *La Donna abbandonata, La Via delle Luce* 1917; *Madame Flirt* 1918; *Follia, Il Segreto* 1919; *Amore stanco* 1920; *La Principessa d'Azzurro* 1921. In Germany—*Mensch gegen Mensch* 1924. In the US—*The Bat, The Duchess of Buffalo* 1926; *Stage Madness, Honeymoon Hate* 1927; *Three Sinners* 1928; *Gallant Lady, Moulin Rouge, One Night of Love* 1934; *Let's Live Tonight, Paris in the Spring* 1935. In Europe—*La Marcia Nuziale* (It.) 1935; *The Three Maxims* (UK) 1936; *The Street Singer, The Show Goes On* (UK), *Sunset in Vienna/Suicide Legion* (UK), *London Melody/Girl in the Street* (UK) 1937; *Safari* (US) 1940; *La Vita torna* (It.) 1943; *L'Apocalisse, Sinfonia fatale* 1946; *La Chartreuse de Parme* (Fr./It.) 1948; *The Golden Madonna* (UK) 1949; *La Beauté di Diable/Beauty and the Devil* (Fr./It.) 1950; *Gli Uomini non guardano il Cielo/The Secret Conclave* (It.) 1952; *Roman Holiday* (US) 1953; *Giovanna d'Arco al Rogo/Joan at the Stake* (It.) 1954; *A Breath of Scandal* (US) 1960; *El Cid* (US/It.) 1961; *Hemingway's Adventures of a Young Man* (US) 1962; *The Cardinal* (US) 1963.

Carnahan, Suzanne. See PETERS, Susan.

Carné, Marcel. Director. *b.* Aug. 18, 1909, Paris. *d.* 1996. After serving as an apprentice to his father, a cabinetmaker, he worked briefly as an insurance clerk while studying film at night technical school. Entered films in 1928 as assistant cameraman to Georges PÉRINAL on Jacques FEYDER's *Les Nouveaux Messieurs* and the following year was René CLAIR's assistant director on *Sous Les Toits de Paris.* During his years of apprenticeship (1928–35) he co-directed a short amateur documentary with a friend, made several two-minute publicity commercials, and wrote about film for various French magazines. After assisting Feyder on three major films, *Le Grand Jeu* (1933), *Pension Mimosa* (1934), and *La Kermesse héroïque* (1935), he made his debut as feature director in 1936.

Working closely with poet-screenwriter Jacques PRÉVERT, Carné rose to great prominence in the French cinema of the late 30s and early 40s. Their collaboration produced such memorable films as *Drôle de Drame/Bizarre Bizarre, Quai des Brumes/Port of Shadows,* and *Le Jour se lève/Daybreak,* which were permeated with romantic fatalism and have become prime examples of the "poetic realism" school of the French cinema of the period. During the Nazi Occupation Prévert and Carné made the haunting 15th-century period piece *Les Visiteurs du Soir/The Devil's Envoys,* in which they attempted to symbolize Hitler's tyranny, and reached the peak of their artistic achievement with *Les Enfants du Paradis/Children of Paradise,* one of the most aesthetically satisfying films of all time.

Carné's stature with the critics and the public diminished considerably in the postwar years. The beginning of his decline coincided with his breakup with Prévert in 1948, following the mid-production cancellation of their unfinished film *La Fleur de l'Age,* but their split probably had to do more with the changing social scene and public taste. Carné, a film technician of the old school who never went out on location when he could build his exteriors in the studio, came to symbolize the "stagnancy" of the traditional French cinema in the eyes of the young critics of the New Wave and other tastemakers who deemed him out of vogue despite a respectable crop of postwar films.

FILMS: *Nogent—Eldorado du Dimanche* (amateur doc.; co-dir with Michel Sanvoisin; also co-sc.) 1929; *Jenny* 1936; *Drôle de Drame/Bizarre Bizarre* 1937; *Quai des Brumes/Port of Shadows, Hotel du Nord* 1938; *Le Jour se lève/Daybreak* 1939; *Les Visiteurs du Soir/The Devil's Envoys* 1942; *Les Enfants du Paradis/Children of Paradise* 1945; *Les Portes de la Nuit/Gates of the Night* 1946; *La Marie du Port* (also co-sc.) 1950; *Juliette ou la Clé des Songes* (also co-sc.) 1951; *Thérèse Raquin/The Adulteress* (also co-sc.) 1953; *L'Air de Paris* (also co-sc.) 1954; *Le Pays d'ou Je viens* (also co-sc.) 1956; *Les Tricheurs/The Cheaters* 1958; *Terrain vague* (also co-sc.) 1960; *Du Mouron pour les Petits Oiseaux* (also co-sc.) 1963; *Trois Chambres à Manhattan* (also co-sc.) 1965; *Les Jeunes Loups/The Young Wolves* 1968; *Les Assassins de l'Ordre* (also co-sc.) 1971; *La Merveilleuse Visite* (also co-sc.) 1974; *La Bible* (feature-length doc. made for TV and theatrical release) 1976.

Carney, Art. Actor. Born Arthur William Matthew Carney, on Nov. 4, 1918, in Mount Vernon, N.Y. He started as a funnyman with a dance band and developed his comic skills as second banana to such funnymen as Fred Allen, Edgar Bergen, and Bert Lahr. During WW II he was hit by shrapnel at Normandy's Omaha Beach landing, and the injury left him with a slight limp. He returned to acting and gradually built a reputation as a solid dramatic and comic actor on Broadway ('The Rope Dancers,' 'The Odd Couple,' 'The Prisoner of Second Avenue,' etc.) and on TV, gaining wide popularity as Ed Norton, the sewer worker, in Jackie Gleason's classic comedy series 'The Honeymooners.' A brooder and habitual worrier, as well as a former alcoholic, he had to leave the successful Broadway run of 'The Odd Couple' in 1960 to enter a psychiatric hospital but was soon back working on the stage and TV and in occasional films. He won the best actor Academy Award for his performance as a 72-year-old in Paul Mazursky's film *Harry and Tonto* (1974) as well as six Emmys for his TV work.

FILMS: *Pot o' Gold* (bit) 1941; *The Yellow Rolls-Royce* 1964; *A Guide for the Married Man* 1967; *Harry and Tonto* 1974; *W. W. and the Dixie Dance Kings* 1975; *Won Ton Ton—The Dog Who Saved Hollywood* 1976; *The Late Show, Scott Joplin* 1977; *House Calls, Movie Movie* 1978; *Ravagers, Sunburn, Going in Style* 1979; *Steel/Look Down and Die/Men of Steel, Defiance, Roadie* 1980; *St. Helen's, Take This Job and Shove It* 1981; *Better Late Than Never* 1983; *Firestarter, The Naked Face* (UK), *The Muppets Take Manhattan* 1984; *Last Action Hero* 1993.

Carney, Augustus. American actor. Deceased. One of the most popular comedy stars of the American screen in the pre-Chaplin era. A veteran of vaudeville, he entered films in 1909 and first gained notice in the 'Hank and Lank' one-reel comedies of 1910. His popularity reached a peak in 1911–12 as a character called Alkali Ike in a series of Essanay broad slapstick comedies with a rustic flavor. At the height of his success, Alkali Ike dolls were being sold throughout America in considerable numbers. Carney quit films in 1915 and was soon forgotten.

FILMS INCLUDE: *Alkali Ike's Auto* 1911; *Alkali Ike's Love Affair, Alkali Beats Broncho Billy, Alkali Ike Plays the Devil* 1912; *Alkali Ike's Mother-in-Law, Alkali Ike's Misfortunes, Alkali Ike and the Hypnotist* 1913; *The Absentee, The Failure, The Martyrs of the Alamo* 1915; *Blue Blood and Red* 1916.

Carnovsky, Morris. Actor. *b.* Sept. 5, 1898, St. Louis. *d.* 1992. A grocer's son, he began a stage career in 1919 that was studded with numerous distinguished Broadway appearances. He made his screen debut in 1937 and appeared regularly in films, playing character roles, from 1943 to 1951, when he became a victim of the Hollywood blacklist following an appearance before the House Un-American Activities Committee in which he refused to affirm past membership in the Communist party.

FILMS INCLUDE: *The Life of Emile Zola, Tovarich* 1937; *Edge of Darkness* 1943; *Address Unknown, The Master Race* 1944; *Rhapsody in Blue, Our Vines Have Tender Grapes* 1945; *Cornered* 1946; *Dead Reckoning, Dishonored Lady* 1947; *Saigon* 1948; *Thieves' Highway* 1949; *Cyrano de Bergerac* 1950; *The Second Woman* 1951; *Vu du Pont/A View from the Bridge* (Fr./It.) 1962; *The Gambler* 1974; *Joe's Bed-Stuy Barbershop: We Cut Heads* 1983.

Carol, Martine. Actress. *b.* Maryse Mourer, May 16, 1922, Biarritz, France. *d.* 1967. Started her acting career on the French stage using the name Maryse Arley. Following her screen debut in 1943, she played supporting parts in a number of films before her first starring role in 1948. During the early 50s she reigned supreme as the French screen's leading box-office attraction, preceding Brigitte Bardot as the country's number one sex symbol. A ripe-mouthed, voluptuous blonde, she is best remembered for her seminude scenes, but it was the combination of her attractive personality and a certain degree of acting ability, as well as her inviting sexuality, that made her an important star in her day. Memorable in Richard Pottier's *Caroline Chérie* (1951), René Clair's *Les Belles de Nuit* (1952), Max Ophüls's *Lola Montès* (1955), and such lavish costume productions as *Adorable Créatures* (1952), *Lucrèce Borgia* (1953), *Madame Du Barry* (1954), and *Nana* (1955), all directed by her husband, CHRISTIAN-JAQUE. The decline in her career in the late 50s coincided with the rise of Bardot. An attempt to revive her fading glory in Italian, British, and American films ended in failure. She died of a heart attack at 45.

FILMS INCLUDE: *La Ferme aux Loups* 1943; *Voyage-Surprise* 1947; *Les Amants de Vérone/The Lovers of Verona* 1949; *Nous irons à Paris, Méfiez-vous des Blondes* 1950; *Caroline Chérie, Le Désir et l'Amour* 1951; *Les Belles de Nuit/Beauties of the Night, Adorable Créatures/Adorable Creatures* 1952; *Un Caprice de Caroline Chérie, Lucrèce Borgia/Sins of the Borgias* (as Lucrezia Borgia), *La Spiaggia* (It.) 1953; *Destinées/Daughters of Destiny* (as Lysistrata), *Secrets d'Alcôve/Il Letto/The Bed, Madame Du Barry* (title role) 1954; *Nana* (title role), *Lola Montès/The Sins of Lola Montes* (title role), *Les Carnets de Major Thompson/The French They Are a Funny Race* 1955; *Around the World in 80 Days* (cameo; US), *Difendo il mio Amore/Defend My Love* (It.) 1956; *Action of the Tiger* (UK), *Nathalie Agent secret/The Foxiest Girl in Paris* 1957; *La Prima Notte* (It./Fr.) 1958; *Ten Seconds to Hell* (US) 1959; *Austerlitz* (as Josephine), *La Française et l'Amour/Love and the Frenchwoman* 1960; *Le Cave se rebiffe/Money Money Money/The Counterfeiters of Paris, Vanina Vanini* (It./Fr.) 1961; *Hell Is Empty* (It.) 1966.

Carol, Sue. Actress. *b.* Evelyn Lederer, Oct. 30, 1907, Chicago. *d.* 1982. A socialite, she enjoyed a special status in Hollywood, where she played leads in films of the late 20s and early 30s, typically as a bouncy flapper. Retired after marrying one of her leading men, Nick STUART. After their divorce she became a talent agent and discovered, among others, Alan LADD, who became her fourth husband, in 1942. In the 70s she operated the Alan Ladd Hardware and Gifts store in Palm Springs. Mother of actress Alana and actor David Ladd.

FILMS INCLUDE: *Slaves of Beauty, Soft Cushions* 1927; *Skyscraper, Beau Broadway, The Cohens and the Kellys in Paris, The Air Circus, Win That Girl, Captain Swagger* 1928; *The Exalted Flapper, Girls Gone Wild, Why Leave Home, Chasing Through Europe* 1929; *Lone Star Ranger, The Golden Calf, The Big Party, She's My Weakness, Dancing Sweeties* 1930; *Graft, In Line of Duty* 1931; *Secret Sinners, Straightaway* 1933; *A Doctor's Diary* 1937.

Carolco Pictures Inc. Motion picture production company. It was founded as Carolco Service Inc., a foreign sales organization, by Mario Kassar and Andrew Vajna in 1976. The company then became an independent movie producer, scoring a big success with its first feature, the Sylvester Stallone vehicle *First*

Blood (1982), which spawned two sequels (*Rambo* and *Rambo III*). Specializing in big-budget action films, Carolco was the model of the successful "indie" until it began to be rocked by financial troubles. Although making money from hits like *Basic Instinct*, the company suffered the burden of major flops like *Chaplin* (both 1992). In 1993, Carolco underwent financial restructuring. Vajna left in 1989 to form his own production company.

Caron, Leslie. Actress, dancer. Born on July 1, 1931, in Boulogne-Billancourt, near Paris, to a French father, a chemist, and an American-born mother, a former dancer. Miss Caron took up ballet at ten and at 16 was dancing with Roland Petit's Ballets des Champs Elysées when she was seen by Gene KELLY, who chose her as his co-star in *An American in Paris* (1951). The film launched her on a starring career in MGM musicals, in which she demonstrated natural charm, a fetching gamine personality, and graceful dancing. In between films she appeared on the stage, on Broadway, in London, and in Paris. Gradually she broadened her range to include serious drama as well as light films and scored a personal triumph as a dramatic actress in the British *The L-Shaped Room* (1962). She won her second British Film Academy Award for her performance in that film (the first had been for *Lili,* in 1953 she received Oscar nominations for both), but her subsequent roles, in Hollywood and elsewhere, have been mostly unrewarding. Her first husband (1951–54) was meat-packing heir George Hormel. Her second marriage, in 1956, to British producer-director Peter HALL, ended in divorce in 1966, with actor Warren BEATTY as a corespondent. In 1969 she married producer Michael Laughlin.

FILMS: *An American in Paris, The Man with a Cloak* 1951; *Glory Alley* 1952; *The Story of Three Loves, Lili* 1953; *The Glass Slipper, Daddy Long Legs* 1955; *Gaby* 1956; *Gigi, The Doctor's Dilemma* (UK) 1958; *The Man Who Understood Women* 1959; *Austerlitz* (Fr./It.), *The Subterraneans* 1960; *Fanny* 1961; *Guns of Darkness* (UK), *The L-Shaped Room* (UK), *Les Quatre Vérités/Three Fables of Love* (Fr./It./Sp.) 1962; *Father Goose* 1964; *A Very Special Favor* 1965; *Promise Her Anything, Paris brule-t-il?/Is Paris Burning?* (Fr./US) 1966; *Il Padre di Famiglia/The Head of the Family* (It./Fr.) 1968; *Madron* (US/Isr.) 1970; *Chandler* 1971; *Nicole* (Fr.), *Purple Night* 1972; *Serail* (Fr.) 1976; *L'Homme qui aimait les Femmes/The Man Who Loved Women* (Fr.), *Valentino* (as Nazimova; UK) 1977; *Goldengirl* 1979; *Tous Vedettes* (Fr.), *Contract* (Pol.) 1980; *Chanel Solitaire* 1981; *Imperativ/Imperatives* (Ger.) 1982; *La Diagonale du Fou/Dangerous Moves* (Fr.) 1984; *Unapproachable* 1987; *Warriors and Sinners* 1988; *Courage Mountain, Guerriers et captives* (Fr.) 1989; *Damage* 1992; *Funny Bones* 1995.

Carpenter, Carleton. Actor, singer, dancer. Born July 10, 1926, in Bennington, Vt. Gangling song-and-dance man of MGM musicals of the early 50s after an early career as a nightclub magician and Broadway performer. Best remembered for the comic-musical duet 'Aba Daba Honeymoon' with Debbie Reynolds in the film *Two Weeks with Love* (1950), a lively number they later turned into a hit recording. Carpenter subsequently appeared in a number of nonmusical films, then went back to the stage and nightclubs and began to write mystery novels, returning to the screen only occasionally.

FILMS INCLUDE: *Lost Boundaries* 1949; *Three Little Words, Summer Stock, Two Weeks with Love, Father of the Bride* 1950; *Vengeance Valley, The Whistle at Eaton Falls* 1951; *Fearless Fagan, Sky Full of Moon* 1952; *Take the High Ground* 1953; *Up Periscope* 1959; *Some of My Best Friends Are...* 1971; *Simon* 1980; *The Prowler* 1981.

Carpenter, John. Director. Born on Jan. 16, 1948, in Carthage, N.Y. He was raised in Bowling Green, Kentucky, where his violinist father taught music at Western Kentucky University. Fascinated with film, he began making amateur fantasy movies as a child. In 1968, he dropped out of Western Kentucky U. just short of graduation and transferred to the University of California's film school. During his four years at USC he made a dozen short films and collaborated as co-writer, co-cameraman, composer, and assistant director on the Oscar-winning live-action short *The Resurrection of Broncho Billy* (1970). With schoolmate Dan O'BANNON, the would-be special-effects magician, and $1,000 from the school, Carpenter began working on what would eventually become his first feature, *Dark Star* (1974). Finally completed at a total cost of $60,000, the science fiction film would become a cult classic. He used a bigger budget and achieved a stronger impact with his next film, *Assault on Precinct 13* (1976), a harrowing drama of a police station under siege by a youth gang, an idea borrowed from the Howard Hawks western *Rio Bravo.* It was with his third feature that Carpenter became established as one of Hollywood's most bankable directors. Produced on a shoestring budget of $300,000, his effectively executed horror movie *Halloween* (1978) grossed $60 million worldwide, thus becoming the most profitable independent production up to its day. As he often does, the director co-wrote the screenplay and composed the intense music score. Adept at generating suspense and narrative drive, Carpenter also uses horror and science fiction metaphorically to explore the dark side of modern American culture—personal isolation and distrust in *The Thing*, urban decay in *Escape from New York*, and mass communications in *They Live.* However, his films are often uneven in quality, sometimes overshadowed by their own expensive special effects and the conventional demands of the genres in which they are placed. In 1979 he married actress Adrienne BARBEAU. He co-wrote *Report from the Besieged City and Other Poems* (1985).

FEATURE FILMS: *Dark Star* (also prod., co-sc., mus.) 1974; *Assault on Precinct 13* (also sc., mus.) 1976; *The Eyes of Laura Mars* (sc. only), *Halloween* (also co-sc., mus.) 1978; *Elvis* (orig. for TV) 1979; *The Fog* (also co-sc., mus.) 1980; *Escape from New York* (also co-sc., co-mus.), *Halloween Two* (co-prod., co-sc., co-mus. only) 1981; *The Thing, Halloween Three: Season of the Witch* (co-prod., co-mus. only) 1982; *Christine* (also co-mus.) 1983; *The Philadelphia Experiment* (exec. prod. only), *Starman* 1984; *Black Moon Rising* (story, co-sc only), *Big Trouble in Little China* (also co-mus.) 1986; *Prince of Darkness* (also sc. [as Martin Quatermass], co-mus.) 1987; *Halloween Four: The Return of Michael Myers* (theme mus. only), *They Live* (also co-mus.) 1988; *Halloween Five: The Revenge of Michael Myers* (theme mus. only) 1989; *Memoirs of an Invisible Man* 1992; *The Silence of the Hams* (act. only) 1994; *In the Mouth of Madness, Village of the Damned* (also co-sc.) 1995; *Escape from L.A.* 1996.

Carr, Mary. Actress. *b.* Mary Kennevan, 1874, Philadelphia. *d.* 1973. A veteran of the stage, she entered films at middle age and became famous for her strong portrayals of devoted mothers and grandmothers in Hollywood silents and early talkies. Received top billing in many of her films. Early in her career she was variously billed as Mrs. Carr, Mary K. Carr, Mary Kennavan, Mary Kennevean, and Mrs. William Carr. Subsequent appearances sporadic.

FILMS INCLUDE: *The City of Failing Light, The Flames of Johannis, Light at Dusk* 1916; *The Barrier* 1917; *My Own United States, The Birth of a Race* 1918; *The Lion and the Mouse, Mrs. Wiggs of the Cabbage Patch* (title role) 1919; *Over the Hill to the Poorhouse* 1920; *Thunderclap* 1921; *Silver Wings* 1922; *The Custard Cup, Loyal Lives, The Daring Years,*

Broadway Broke, On the Banks of the Wabash 1923; *Painted People, Damaged Hearts, Roulette, Why Men Leave Home, For Sale, The Woman on the Jury, The Spirit of the USA, Three Women, East of Broadway* 1924; *Easy Money, The Night Ship, Capital Punishment, The Parasite, Go Straight, Drusilla with a Million, The Wizard of Oz, A Slave of Fashion, Pleasures of the Rich, The Night Patrol, The Night Watch, Somebody's Mother, The Red Kimono* 1926; *The Show Girl, Special Delivery, The Fourth Commandment, Jesse James, On Your Toes* 1927; *Lights of New York* 1928; *Some Mother's Boy* 1929; *Hot Curves, The Midnight Special* 1930; *Beyond Victory* 1931; *Pack Up Your Troubles* 1932; *Change of Heart* 1934; *The World Accuses* 1935; *East Side of Heaven* 1939; *The Oregon Trail* 1945; *Friendly Persuasion* 1956.

Carradine, David. Actor, singer, songwriter. Born on Dec. 8, 1936, in Hollywood, Calif. *ed.* San Francisco State. Tall, lanky, unpredictable, and free-spirited like his father, John CARRADINE, he spent several restless years working at manual occupations and experimenting with psychedelic drugs before entering films as a bit player in 1964. The following year he appeared in the Broadway production of 'The Royal Hunt of the Sun' and in the fall of 1966 played the title role in the short-lived TV series 'Shane.' He then returned to the big screen in secondary roles that were often ruthless or villainous. His big break came in 1972, when he was chosen to star in the internationally popular TV series 'Kung Fu.' Leading roles in films followed, culminating in his moving portrayal of folk singer Woody Guthrie in *Bound for Glory* (1976) and the lead male role opposite Liv Ullman in Ingmar Bergman's German-made film *The Serpent's Egg* (1977). But on the whole he has been undiscriminating about his choice of roles and appeared in numerous cheap films unworthy of his talent. An unorthodox, spontaneous actor, he is also a singer, songwriter, and an occasional folk concert performer. He is half brother of actors Keith and Robert CARRADINE. Thrice married, he had a stormy six-year relationship with actress Barbara HERSHEY, which produced a son, Free.

FILMS INCLUDE: *Taggart* 1964; *Bus Riley's Back in Town* 1965; *The Violent Ones* 1967; *Heaven with a Gun, Young Billy Young, The Good Guys and the Bad Guys* 1969; *The McMasters, Macho Callahan* 1970; *Boxcar Bertha* 1972; *Mean Streets* (bit) 1973; *You and Me* (also dir.; release delayed from 1972), *Death Race 2000* 1975; *Cannonball, Bound for Glory* (as folk singer Woody Guthrie) 1976; *Gray Lady Down, The Serpent's Egg* (Ger./US), *Thunder and Lightning* 1977; *Moonbeam Rider, Deathsport* 1978; *Circle of Iron, Fast Charlie... The Moonbeam Rider* 1979; *Cloud Dancer, The Long Riders* (as outlaw Cole Younger) 1980; *Safari 3000/Rally/Two in the Bush, Q/Winged Serpent, Trick or Treats* 1982; *Lone Wolf, Americana* (also dir., prod.) 1983; *The Warrior and the Sorceress, On the Line* (Sp.) 1984; *P.O.W.: The Escape, Armed Response* 1986; *Wheels of Terror/The Misfit Brigade* (UK), *Crime Zone* (also co-assoc. prod.) 1988; *Try This On for Size* (Fr.), *Nowhere to Run, Warlords, Future Force* (also assoc. prod.) 1989; *Sundown: The Vampire in Retreat, Think Big, Future Zone, Sonny Boy* (also song) 1990; *Dune Warriors, Roadshow Prophets* 1991; *Capital Punishment, First Force, Double Trouble, Distant Justice, Waxwork II* 1992; *Bird of Prey* 1996.

Carradine, John. Actor. *b.* Richmond Reed Carradine, Feb. 5, 1906, Greenwich Village, New York City. *d.* 1988. The son of a noted attorney-poet-painter father and surgeon mother, he was first a painter and a sculptor, working his way down South sketching portraits in office-building lobbies. In New Orleans he decided on an acting career and made his stage debut in a local production of 'Camille' in 1925. He later joined a Shakespearean stock company, beginning a lifelong love affair with the works of the Bard. In 1927 he hitchhiked West, again supporting himself with quick sketch portraits on his journey. Failing in Hollywood to get film work, he appeared in local stage productions until his screen debut in 1930. For several years he played small roles in films under the name John Peter Richmond, switching to John Carradine when he signed a Fox contract in 1935.

Carradine soon began an impressive career as a character actor which stretched over five decades and more than 220 films of all genres. His tall, reedy figure and gaunt, saturnine features made him at times a spectacular villain and at other times an eccentric, offbeat, philosophizing friend. He occasionally played leads in B pictures, typically in horror ones, as a sadist or demented scientist, and portrayed Count Dracula three times on the screen. But some of his finest portraits were in supporting roles, memorably in *The Grapes of Wrath* and many other John FORD classics. In between films he also appeared in numerous stage plays, often in Shakespearean and other classic roles, and in many TV productions. In Hollywood, Carradine had a reputation as an eccentric and a ham. He was known as the "Bard of the Boulevard" for his habit of reciting Shakespeare in his booming voice while walking the streets. His three dissolved marriages produced five sons, three of them actors, David, Keith, and Robert CARRADINE.

FILMS INCLUDE: As John Peter Richmond—*Tol'able David* 1930; *Bright Lights* 1931; *The Sign of the Cross* 1932; *The Invisible Man* 1933; *Cleopatra, The Black Cat* 1934; *Clive of India, Cardinal Richelieu, Les Misérables, Bride of Frankenstein, The Crusades* 1935. As John Carradine—*Anything Goes, The Prisoner of Shark Island, Under Two Flags, White Fang, Mary of Scotland, Romona, Dimples, The Garden of Allah, Winterset* 1936; *This Is My Affair, Captains Courageous, Ali Baba Goes to Town, The Hurricane, The Last Gangster, Thank You Mr. Moto* 1937; *Of Human Hearts* (as Abraham Lincoln), *Four Men and a Prayer, Kidnapped, Alexander's Ragtime Band, Submarine Patrol* 1938; *Jesse James, The Three Musketeers, Stagecoach, The Hound of the Baskervilles, Captain Fury, Frontier Marshal, Drums Along the Mohawk* 1939; *The Grapes of Wrath, The Return of Frank James, Brigham Young—Frontiersman, Chad Hanna* 1940; *Western Union, Blood and Sand, Man Hunt, Swamp Water* 1941; *Son of Fury, Whispering Ghosts, Reunion in France* 1942; *I Escaped from the Gestapo, Captive Wild Woman, Hitler's Madman* (as Nazi hangman Gen. Reinhard Heydrich), *Isle of Forgotten Sins* 1943; *Revenge of the Zombies, Voodoo Man, The Adventures of Mark Twain* (as Bret Harte), *The Invisible Man's Revenge, Return of the Ape Man, The Mummy's Ghost, Bluebeard* (title role) 1944; *House of Frankenstein* (as Dracula), *Captain Kidd, House of Dracula* (title role) 1945; *Face of Marble* 1946; *The Private Affairs of Bel-Ami* 1947; *C-Man* 1949; *Casanova's Big Night, Johnny Guitar, The Egyptian* 1954; *The Kentuckian* 1955; *The Court Jester, The Black Sleep, The Ten Commandments* (as Aaron), *Around the World in 80 Days* 1956; *The Unearthly, The Story of Mankind* 1957; *The Proud Rebel, The Last Hurrah* 1958; *The Cosmic Man* (title role), *Invisible Invaders* 1959; *The Adventures of Huckleberry Finn* 1960; *The Man Who Shot Liberty Valance* 1962; *The Patsy, Cheyenne Autumn* 1964; *Munster Go Home!, Billy the Kid vs. Dracula* (as Dracula) 1966; *Dr. Terror's Gallery of Horrors* 1967; *The Astro-Zombies, The Hostage* 1968; *Blood of Dracula's Castle, The Good Guys and the Bad Guys, Las Vampiras* 1969; *The McMasters, Myra Breckinridge* 1970; *Horror of the Blood Monsters, The Seven Minutes* 1971; *Boxcar Bertha, Richard, Everything You Always Wanted to Know About*

Sex but Were Afraid to Ask 1972; *Terror in the Wax Museum, Hex* 1973; *The House of the Seven Corpses* 1974; *Mary Mary Bloody Mary* 1975; *The Shootist, The Last Tycoon* 1976; *The Sentinel, The White Buffalo, Crash, Shock Waves/Death Corps* 1977; *Vampire Hookers, The Bees* 1978; *Monster, Nocturna* 1979; *Shock Waves, The Boogey Man* 1980; *The Howling, The Nesting* 1981; *Satan's Mistress* 1982; *Evils of the Night* 1983; *The Ice Pirates* 1984; *Prison Ship 2005/Star Slammer* 1985; *Monster in the Closet, Peggy Sue Got Married, The Tomb* 1986.

Carradine, Keith. Actor, singer, songwriter. Born Aug. 8, 1949, in San Mateo, Calif. Lanky actor of effortless sexuality. The son of John CARRADINE, half brother of David CARRADINE, and brother of Robert CARRADINE, he began acting in high school drama productions and briefly attended Colorado State University as a theater-arts major. Impatient with academic studies, he left college after less than one semester to seek acting jobs and in 1969 landed a role in the Los Angeles production of 'Hair.' This led to a small role in Robert ALTMAN's film *McCabe and Mrs. Miller* (1971) and eventually to leads in films of Altman and other directors. He played one of the leads, an unscrupulous rock singer, in Altman's *Nashville* (1975) and won an Academy Award for the song 'I'm Easy,' which he wrote and sang in the film. In recent years he was notable as the down-home suitor to Madonna in the video for 'Material Girl' and as the originator of the title role in the Broadway musical 'The Will Rogers Follies.' He is the father of actress Martha PLIMPTON.

FILMS: *McCabe and Mrs. Miller, A Gunfight* 1971; *Emperor of the North Pole, Hex* 1973; *Thieves Like Us, Antoine et Sebastian* (Fr.), *Run Run Joe!* 1974; *Idaho Transfer, You and Me* (release delayed from 1972), *Nashville* (also songs) 1975; *Lumière* (Fr.) 1976; *Welcome to L.A., The Duellists* (UK) 1977; *Pretty Baby, Sgt. Pepper's Lonely Hearts Club Band* 1978; *Old Boyfriends, An Almost Perfect Affair* 1979; *The Long Riders* (as outlaw Jim Younger) 1980; *Southern Comfort* 1981; *Choose Me* 1984; *Maria's Lovers* (also co-song), *Trouble in Mind* 1985; *L'Inchiesta/The Investigation* 1987; *The Moderns, Backfire* 1988; *Street of No Return* (Fr./Port.), *Cold Feet* 1989; *Dr. Grassler, Daddy's Dyin'... Who's Got the Will?* 1990; *The Ballad of the Sad Cafe* 1991; *Crisscross* 1992; *Andre, Mrs. Parker and the Vicious Circle* 1994; *The Ties That Bind, Wild Bill* 1995; *A Thousand Acres* 1997.

Carradine, Robert. Actor. Born in 1954, in Los Angeles. Youngest son of John CARRADINE, brother of Keith and half brother of David CARRADINE. Began appearing in films while still in his teens and rapidly advanced from juvenile supporting roles to leads.

FILMS: *The Cowboys* 1972; *Mean Streets* 1973; *Aloha Bobby and Rose* 1975; *Jackson County Jail, The Pom Pom Girls, Cannonball, Massacre at Central High* 1976; *Joyride, Orca* 1977; *Coming Home, Blackout* (Can./Fr.) 1978; *The Long Riders* (as outlaw Bob Younger), *The Big Red One* 1980; *Heartaches* (Can.) 1981; *T.A.G.: The Assassination Game* 1982; *Wavelength* 1983; *Revenge of the Nerds, Just the Way You Are* 1984; *Number One with a Bullet, Revenge of the Nerds II: Nerds in Paradise* 1987; *Buy and Cell, All's Fair, Rude Awakening* 1989; *The Player* 1992.

Carré, Ben. Art director. *b.* Benjamin J. Carré, Dec. 5, 1883, Paris. *d.* 1978. Pioneer designer of American movie sets. A scenic painter of stage productions at the Paris Opera, the Comédie Française, and Covent Garden, he began working at the Pathé Gaumont films studios in 1901. In 1912 he came to the US as a designer for the Eclair Studios at Fort Lee, New Jersey, where he began a long association with French-born director Maurice Tourneur. Working on many key productions of the silent era, he is credited with helping set the high visual standards of American cinema in its formative years. His career as an art director ended in 1937 but he went on painting backgrounds for such MGM films as *The Wizard of Oz* (1939), *Meet Me in St. Louis* (1944), and *An American in Paris* (1951). He painted murals for the General Motors Pavilion at New York's 1964 World's Fair.

FILMS INCLUDE: *La Course aux Poitrons* 1907; *The Dollar Mark* 1912; *Mother, The Pit* 1914; *Alias Jimmy Valentine, Trilby, Camille* 1915; *La Vie de Bohème* 1916; *The Poor Little Rich Girl, The Undying Flame, Barbary Sheep* 1917; *The Blue Bird, A Doll's House, Prunella* 1918; *Victory, In Old Kentucky* 1919; *The River's End* 1920; *Bob Hampton of Placer* 1921; *Cytherea, The Red Lily* 1924; *The Phantom of the Opera* (underground scenes only), *The Masked Bride* 1926; *Don Juan, Mare Nostrum* 1927; *The Red Dance* 1928; *The Iron Mask, The Cock-Eyed World* 1929; *River's End* 1930; *Riders of the Purple Sage* 1931; *Dante's Inferno* (inferno scenes only), *A Night at the Opera* 1935; *Great Guy* 1936.

Carrel, Dany. Actress. Born Suzanne Chazelles du Chaxel, on Sept. 20, 1935, in Tourane, Annam, Indochina, to French parents. Petite ingenue, then leading lady of French films and some international co-productions.

FILMS INCLUDE: *Dortoir des Grandes, Maternité clandestine* 1953; *La Cage aux Souris* 1954; *Les Indiscrètes, La Môme Pigalle/The Maiden* 1955; *Des Gens sans Importance, Les Possedées/Passionate Summer, Club de Femmes, Elisa* 1956; *Escapade, Que les Hommes sont Bêtes, Porte de Lilas/Gates of Paris, Pot-Bouille* 1957; *La Moucharde/Woman of Sin, Racconti d'Estate/Love on the Riviera* (It./Fr.) 1958; *Ce Corps tant desirée, Les Dragueurs/The Chasers, Die Gans von Sedan* (Ger./Fr.), *Les Naufrageurs* 1959; *The Enemy General* (US) 1960; *Les Mains d'Orlac/The Hands of Orlac* (Fr./UK) 1961; *Une Souris chez les Hommes* 1964; *La Prisonnière/The Woman Prisoner* 1968; *Les Portes de Feu* 1972.

Carrera, Barbara. Actress. Born in 1951 in Managua, Nicaragua, to an American father, an employee of the US Embassy, and a Nicaraguan mother. Convent-educated in Europe and the US, she became a high-fashion model at 17. Her chiseled facial structure and exotic appearance drew the attention of filmmakers during a fashion show at Cannes, leading to her screen debut. In 1985 she joined the cast of the TV series 'Dallas.'

FILMS: *Puzzle of a Downfall Child* 1970; *The Master Gunfighter* 1975; *Embryo* 1976; *The Island of Dr. Moreau* 1977; *When Time Ran Out* 1980; *Condorman* 1981; *I, the Jury* 1982; *Lone Wolf McQuade, Never Say Never Again* 1983; *Wild Geese II* 1985; *Love at Stake, The Underachievers* 1988; *Wicked Stepmother, Loverboy, The Favorite* 1989; *Love Is All There Is* 1996.

Carreras, Michael. Director, producer, screenwriter. Born in 1927, in London. In British films from age 16, as an apprentice and later a publicity director, he began directing shorts in 1955, features in 1957. But his activity as a director has been sparse and he is mainly known as a producer of horror and fantasy pictures for Hammer Films, the British company founded and headed by his father, Sir James Carreras (1900–1990).

FILMS INCLUDE: As director—*The Steel Bayonet* (also prod.) 1957; *Visa to Canton/Passport to China* (also prod.) 1960; *The Savage Guns* (US/Sp.) 1962; *Maniac* 1963; *The Curse of the Mummy's Tomb* (also prod.) 1964; *Slave Girls/Prehistoric Women* (also prod.) 1967; *The Lost Continent* (also prod.) 1968; *Call Him Mr. Shatter* (also co-prod.) 1975. As producer—*Murder by Proxy/Blackout, The Stranger Came Home/The Unholy Four* (also sc.) 1954; *The Snorkel* 1958; *Ten Seconds to Hell* (UK/US), *The Mummy* 1959; *Hell Is a City, The*

Two Faces of Dr. Jekyll/House of Fright 1960; *The Curse of the Werewolf* (exec. prod.) 1961; *The Pirates of Blood River* (exec. prod.) 1962; *The Damned/These Are the Damned* (exec. prod.) 1963; *Fanatic/Die! Die! My Darling* (exec. prod.), *She* 1965; *One Million Years B.C.* (also sc.) 1966; *Moon Zero Two* (also sc.) 1969; *Creatures the World Forgot* (also sc.) 1971; *Crescendo* 1972; *Demons of the Mind* 1973.

Carrey, Jim. Actor, comedian. Born James Eugene Carrey on January 17, 1962, in Toronto, Canada. Combining an outrageous, offbeat style of physical comedy with the ability to create presence on the silver screen has made this former stand-up comic a box office megastar as well as a household name virtually overnight. His meteoric rise to celebrity came with his first starring role in *Ace Ventura, Pet Detective* (1994) which earned over $100 million in its first month of release, as did almost all of his subsequent films with the exception of *The Cable Guy* (1996). Able to command millions in salary, he has joined the ranks of the highest paid stars in the history of film.

After playing small, supporting roles in films, Carrey was a series regular on Keenan Ivory WAYANS's television comedy 'In Living Color,' where he created memorable characters and established himself as a wickedly funny character comedian extraordinaire. An equally gifted dramatic actor, he turned the heads of many critics with his powerful performance as the alchoholic older brother in the TV movie 'Doing Time on Maple Drive.' Other than that role, he is known as America's funny man.

FILMS: *Finders Keepers* 1984; *Once Bitten* 1985; *Peggy Sue Got Married, The Dead Pool* 1988; *Earth Girls Are Easy, Pink Cadillac* 1989; *High Strung* 1991; *Ace Ventura Pet Detective* (also co-sc.), *Dumb & Dumber, The Mask* 1994; *Ace Ventura: When Nature Calls, Batman Forever* 1995; *The Cable Guy* 1996; *Liar, Liar* 1997.

Carrière, Jean-Claude. French screenwriter. Born in 1931. One of France's leading scriptwriters of the 60s and 70s, he has been a frequent collaborator of Luis BUÑUEL and has also worked with such directors as Pierre Etaix, Louis Malle, Jacques Deray, Jean-Luc Godard, and Volker Schlondorff.

FILMS INCLUDE (as screenwriter in collaboration): *Le Soupirant/The Suitor* 1963; *Le Journal d'une Femme de Chambre/Diary of a Chambermaid* 1964; *Yoyo/Yo Yo, Viva Maria* 1965; *Hotel Paradiso* (US/UK) 1966; *Le Voleur/The Thief of Paris, Belle de Jour* 1967; *La Piscine/The Swimming Pool, La Voie lactée/The Milky Way* (also act.) 1969; *Borsalino* 1970; *Taking Off* (US), *Un peu de Soleil dans l'Eau froid* 1971; *La Cagna/Liza* (It./Fr.), *Un Homme est mort/The Outside Man, Le Charme discret de la Bourgeoisie/The Discreet Charm of the Bourgeoisie* 1972; *France Société anonyme, Le Fantôme de la Liberté* 1974; *Léonor* 1975; *Les Oeufs brouilles* 1976; *Le Gang, Julie Pot de Colle, Le Diable dans la Boîte, Cet Obscur Objet du Désir/That Obscure Object of Desire* 1977; *Die Blechtrommel/The Tin Drum* (Ger./Fr./Yugoslavia./Pol.) 1979; *Sauve qui peu (la Vie)/Every Man for Himself* 1980; *Die Falschung/Circle of Deceit* (Ger./Fr.) 1981; *Le Retour de Martin Guerre/The Return of Martin Guerre* 1982; *Danton, La Tragédie de Carmen* 1983; *Un Amour de Swann/Swann in Love* 1984; *The Unbearable Lightness of Being* (US) 1988; *Milou en Mai/Milou in May, Valmont* 1989; *Cyrano de Bergerac, The Mahabharata* 1990; *The Ogre* 1996.

Carrière, Mathieu. Born on Aug. 2, 1950, in Hannover, Germany, a psychiatrist's son. On the stage as an amateur from childhood, he made his screen debut at 13, playing the adolescent hero of Rolf Thiele's adaptation of Thomas Mann's *Tonio Kröger* (the protagonist as an adult was portrayed by Jean-Claude Brialy). Two years later Carrière played the title role in Volker Schloendorff's *Der junge Törless/Young Torless*. He then began performing in films internationally. As a handsome romantic leading man in the 70s, he worked mainly in France.

FILMS INCLUDE: *Tonio Kröger* (title role as an adolescent; Ger./Fr.) 1964; *Der junge Törless/Young Torless* (Ger./Fr.) 1966; *Gates to Paradise* (Pol./Yug.) 1967; *L'Amore breve/Lo Stato d'Assedio* (It.) 1969; *Le Petit Matin* (Fr.), *Rendez-vous à Bray* (Fr.) 1971; *Malpertuis* (Belg./Fr.), *Bluebeard* (Hung.) 1972; *Don Juan 73/Ms. Don Juan* (Fr.), *Il n'y a pas de Fumée sans Feu/Where There's Smoke* (Fr.) 1973; *La Jeune Fille assassinée/Charlotte* (Fr.) 1974; *India Song* (Fr.), *Isabelle devant le Désir* (Fr.), *Né pour l'Enfer* (Fr.), *Blondy* (It.) 1975; *Police Python 357/The Case Against Ferro* (Fr.), *Der Fangschuss/Coup de Grace* (Ger./Fr.) 1976; *Les Indiens sont encore loin* (Fr.), *Bilitis* (Fr.) 1977; *L'Associé/The Associate* (Fr./Ger.) 1979; *Wege in der Nacht/Ways in the Night* (Ger.) 1980; *La Femme de l'Aviateur/The Aviator's Wife* (Fr.) 1981; *La Passante de Sans-Souci/La Passante* (Fr./Ger.) 1982; *Die Flambierte Frau/A Woman in Flames* (Ger.) 1983; *The Bay Boy* (Can./Fr.) 1984; *Le Neveu de Beethoven/Beethoven's Nephew* (also co-sc.; Fr./Ger.), *Bras de Fer, Marie Ward* (Fr.) 1985; *Terminus* (Fr./Ger./Hung.) (v/o), *Johann Strauss le roi sans couronne, El Placer de Matar/The Pleasure of Killing* (Fr.) 1987; *Ceremonie d'amour, L'Oeuvre au noir/The Abyss, Sanguines* (Fr.) 1988; *Zugzwang/Fool's Mate* (also dir., sc.) (Ger.) 1989; *Malina* (Fr.) 1991; *Dieu que les Femmes Sont Amoureuses* 1994.

Carrillo, Leo. Actor. *b.* Aug. 6, 1880, Los Angeles. *d.* 1961. A graduate of St. Vincent of Loyola, he was a newsman and cartoonist before becoming a dialect comedian in vaudeville and later on the legitimate stage. Entering films in the late 20s, he became one of Hollywood's busiest character actors of the 30s and 40s, at first playing leads—as in *Love Me Forever* (1935), opposite Grace Moore—but later typically providing comedy relief as an amiable Latin. In the early 50s, after retiring from the screen, he played Pancho, Duncan RENALDO's sidekick, in 'The Cisco Kid' TV series.

FILMS INCLUDE: *Mister Antonio* 1929; *Hell Bound, Homicide Squad, The Guilty Generation* 1931; *Girl of the Rio, The Broken Wing, Deception* 1932; *Parachute Jumper, Racetrack, Obey the Law, Moonlight and Pretzels* 1933; *Four Frightened People, Viva Villa!, Manhattan Melodrama, The Gay Bride* 1934; *The Winning Ticket, In Caliente, Love Me Forever* 1935; *The Gay Desperado* 1936; *History Is Made at Night, The Barrier, Manhattan Merry-Go-Round* 1937; *The Girl of the Golden West, Blockade, City Streets, Too Hot to Handle* 1938; *Society Lawyer, The Girl and the Gambler, Rio, The Chicken Wagon Family* 1939; *Twenty-Mule Team, Lillian Russell* (as nightclub operator Tony Pastor), *Wyoming, Captain Caution* 1940; *Horror Island, Barnacle Bill* 1941; *Sin Town, American Empire* 1942; *Crazy House* 1943; *Ghost Catchers, Gypsy Wildcat, Bowery to Broadway* 1944; *Crime Incorporated, Mexicana* 1945; *The Fugitive* 1947; *The Girl from San Lorenzo* 1950.

Carroll, Diahann. Actress, singer. Born on July 17, 1935, in the Bronx, N.Y. At age ten received a Metropolitan Opera scholarship for studies at New York's High School of Music and Art. While studying sociology at NYU, she modeled and began singing in nightclubs and performing on TV, making both her Broadway ('House of Flowers') and Hollywood (*Carmen Jones*) debuts in 1954. Subsequently starred in Broadway's 'No Strings' (Tony Award, 1962) and in TV's 'Julia' (1968–71), the first regular series to star a black personality. Nominated for an Oscar for her performance in *Claudine* (1974). Oddly, she's made only one more film since then, with several television credits. In 1984 she joined the cast of the TV series 'Dynasty.' Autobiography: *Diahann* (1986).

FILMS: *Carmen Jones* 1954; *Porgy and Bess* 1959; *Goodbye Again, Paris Blues* 1961; *Hurry Sundown* 1967; *The Split* 1968; *Claudine* 1974; *The Five Heartbeats* 1991.

Carroll, Gordon. Producer. Born on Feb. 2, 1928, in Baltimore. *ed.* Princeton. Came to films via advertising in 1958.

FILMS INCLUDE: *The World of Suzie Wong* 1961; *How to Murder Your Wife* 1965; *Luv, Cool Hand Luke* 1967; *The April Fools* 1969; *Pat Garrett and Billy the Kid* 1973; *Alien* 1979; *Blue Thunder* 1983; *The Best of Times, Aliens* 1986; *Red Heat* 1988; *Alien 3* 1992.

Carroll, John. Actor, singer. *b.* Julian LaFaye, July 17, 1905, New Orleans. *d.* 1979. At 12 he ran away from home and supported himself as a newsboy, steelworker, and seaman, among other things. Later, in Europe, he studied voice and raced cars for prize money. Broke into films in the late 20s as a stuntman and had worked his way up to leads with RKO by 1935. Combining a good singing voice with virile good looks, he reached his peak in the early 40s as a leading man in light MGM fare. Later appeared mostly in action pictures for Republic and other studios. Carroll had an off-screen reputation in Hollywood as a playboy, but he invested wisely and retired from films in the late 50s as a wealthy man. From 1936 to 1940 he was married to actress Steffi Duna.

FILMS INCLUDE: *Hearts in Exile* 1929; *Monte Carlo* 1930; *Hi Gaucho!* 1935; *Murder on a Bridle Path* 1936; *Zorro Rides Again* (serial), *We Who Are About to Die* 1937; *Rose of the Rio Grande* 1938; *Only Angels Have Wings* 1939; *Congo Maisie, Phantom Raiders, Susan and God, Hired Wife, Go West* 1940; *Sunny, Lady Be Good, This Woman Is Mine* 1941; *Rio Rita, Flying Tigers* 1942; *Hit Parade of 1943* 1943; *Bedside Manner* 1945; *A Letter for Evie* 1946; *Fiesta, Wyoming, The Flame* 1947; *I Jane Doe* 1948; *Surrender* 1950; *Belle le Grand* 1951; *The Farmer Takes a Wife* 1953; *Geraldine* 1954; *Decision at Sundown* 1957; *Plunderers of Painted Flats* 1959.

Carroll, Leo G. Actor. *b.* Oct. 25, 1892, Weedon, England, of Irish parents. *d.* 1972. Began in the theater in 1911 and made his London and New York debuts in 1912. Commuted for many years between London and Broadway and added Hollywood to his busy itinerary in 1934. His heavy brows and impeccable diction were his stock-in-trade in many distinguished character roles in American and some British films, notably six Hitchcock thrillers. Also seen frequently on TV, notably as Cosmo Topper in the 'Topper' series and as Mr. Waverly in 'The Man from U.N.C.L.E.'

FILMS INCLUDE: *Sadie McKee, The Barretts of Wimpole Street, Outcast Lady* 1934; *Clive of India* 1935; *London by Night* 1937; *A Christmas Carol* (as Marley's Ghost) 1938; *The Private Lives of Elizabeth and Essex, Wuthering Heights, Tower of London* 1939; *Rebecca, Waterloo Bridge* 1940; *Suspicion, Scotland Yard, Bahama Passage* 1941; *Spellbound, The House on 92nd Street* 1945; *Song of Love, Forever Amber, The Paradine Case* 1947; *So Evil My Love* 1948; *The Happy Years, Father of the Bride* 1950; *The First Legion, Strangers on a Train, The Desert Fox* 1951; *The Snows of Kilimanjaro* 1952; *The Bad and the Beautiful, Young Bess* 1953; *We're No Angels* 1955; *The Swan* 1956; *North by Northwest* 1959; *The Prize* 1963; *The Spy with My Face* 1966; *From Nashville with Music* 1969.

Carroll, Madeleine. Actress. *b.* Marie-Madeleine Bernadette O'Carroll, Feb. 26, 1906, West Bromwich, England. *d.* 1987. *ed.* Birmingham U. A French teacher and a hat model before her London stage debut in 1927. She began appearing in British films the following year. Before long she was a popular star locally and after playing leads in two Hitchcock thrillers, *The 39 Steps* and *Secret Agent,* she came to Hollywood in 1936 under contract to Walter Wanger and 20th Century-Fox. A beautiful and ladylike blonde, she decorated many Hollywood productions and in 1943 became an American citizen. After her sister's death in the London Blitz of WW II, she returned to England to work in war relief, then made only three postwar film appearances before retiring. She subsequently worked for UNESCO and made occasional appearances on the stage, or radio, and on TV. She was married and divorced four times. Her second husband (1942–46) was actor Sterling HAYDEN, her third French film producer Henri Lavorel, and her fourth (1950–65) *Life* magazine publisher Andrew Heiskell.

FILMS: In the UK—*The Guns of Loos, The First Born, What Money Can Buy* 1928; *The Crooked Billet, L'Instinct* (Fr.), *The American Prisoner, Atlantic* 1929; *Young Woodley, The W Plan, French Leave, Escape, School for Scandal, Madame Guillotine* 1930; *The Kissing Cup Race, Fascination, The Written Law* 1931; *Sleeping Car, I Was a Spy* 1933; *The World Moves On* 1934; *The Dictator/Loves of a Dictator, The 39 Steps* 1935; *Secret Agent* 1936. In the US—*The Case Against Mrs. Ames, The General Died at Dawn, Lloyds of London* 1936; *On the Avenue, The Prisoner of Zenda, It's All Yours* 1937; *Blockade* 1938; *Cafe Society, Honeymoon in Bali* 1939; *My Son My Son, Safari, North West Mounted Police* 1940; *Virginia, One Night in Lisbon* 1941; *Bahama Passage, My Favorite Blonde* 1942; *White Cradle Inn/High Fury* (UK) 1946; *An Innocent Affair/Don't Trust Your Husband* 1948; *The Fan* 1949.

Carroll, Nancy. Actress. *b.* Ann Veronica La Hiff, Nov. 19, 1904, New York City. *d.* 1965. On the musical stage from age 16, and a Broadway chorine at 18, she entered films in 1927 and became very popular with the advent of talkies, when her singing and dancing ability as well as her acting could be shown to advantage. A vivacious star with flaming red hair and a cupid-bow mouth, she enjoyed a great following through the mid-30s and was reported to have received more fan mail than any other Hollywood star of the period. She was nominated for an Oscar for *The Devil's Holiday* (1930). She was equally proficient as a bubbly comedienne and a sensitive dramatic actress, but by the end of the decade her popularity had waned and she retired from the screen. In 1950–51 she co-starred in the early TV series 'The Aldrich Family.' Her first of three husbands was playwright Jack Kirkland.

FILMS: *Ladies Must Dress* 1927; *Abie's Irish Rose, Easy Come Easy Go, Chicken a la King, The Water Hole, Manhattan Cocktail* 1928; *The Shopworn Angel, The Wolf of Wall Street, The Sin Sister, Close Harmony, The Dance of Life, Illusion, Sweetie* 1929; *Dangerous Paradise, Honey, Paramount on Parade, The Devil's Holiday, Follow Thru, Laughter* 1930; *Stolen Heaven, The Night Angel, Personal Maid* 1931; *The Man I Killed/Broken Lullaby, Wayward, Scarlet Dawn, Hot Saturday, Under-Cover Man* 1932; *Child of Manhattan, The Woman Accused, The Kiss Before the Mirror, I Love That Man* 1933; *Springtime for Henry, Transatlantic Merry-Go-Round, Jealousy* 1934; *I'll Love You Always, After the Dance, Atlantic Adventure* 1935; *There Goes My Heart, That Certain Age* 1938.

Carson, Jack. Actor. *b.* John Elmer Carson, Oct. 27, 1910, Carmen, Manitoba, Canada. *d.* 1963. *ed.* Carleton Coll. Came to films from vaudeville in 1937 and played scores of impressive supporting roles, ranging from numbskull buffoons and back-slapping pests in comedies and musicals to callous heels in Westerns and dramas. His facial expressions were among the most flexible in the business, and his beefy frame added a pathetic quality to his frequent characterizations of cowardly bullies. In the 40s he teamed with Dennis MORGAN in a series of

Doris DAY musicals. He died at 53 of stomach cancer. Among his four wives was actress Lola ALBRIGHT (1952–58).

FILMS INCLUDE: *Stage Door, You Only Live Once, Two Many Wives* 1937; *Vivacious Lady, Bringing Up Baby, Carefree* 1938; *Mr. Smith Goes to Washington, Destry Rides Again* 1939; *I Take This Woman, Enemy Agent, Lucky Partners, Typhoon* 1940; *Mr. and Mrs. Smith, The Strawberry Blonde, Love Crazy, The Bride Came C.O.D., Navy Blues* 1941; *The Male Animal, Larceny Inc., Wings for the Eagle, Gentleman Jim* 1942; *The Hard Way, Princess O'Rourke, Thank Your Lucky Stars* 1943; *The Doughgirls, Arsenic and Old Lace, Hollywood Canteen, Shine on Harvest Moon, Make Your Own Bed, Roughly Speaking* 1944; *Mildred Pierce* 1945; *One More Tomorrow, Two Guys from Milwaukee, The Time the Place and the Girl* 1946; *Love and Learn* 1947; *April Showers, Romance on the High Seas, Two Guys from Texas* 1948; *It's a Great Feeling, My Dream Is Yours, John Loves Mary* 1949; *Bright Leaf, The Good Humor Man* 1950; *Mr. Universe, The Groom Wore Spurs* 1951; *Red Garters, Dangerous When Wet, A Star Is Born, Phffft* 1954; *Ain't Misbehavin'* 1955; *The Bottom of the Bottle* 1956; *The Tattered Dress* 1957; *Cat on a Hot Tin Roof, Rally Round the Flag Boys!* 1958; *The Bramble Bush* 1960; *King of the Roaring 20s* 1961.

Carson, L.M. "Kit." Screenwriter, actor, director. Born in Dallas, Tex. *ed.* New York University (film). Best known for his screenplay for *David Holzman's Diary* (1967), he has been only sporadically active in scriptwriting, acting, and directing capacities since then. Formerly married to actress Karen BLACK, by whom he has a son, actor Hunter Carson.

FILMS INCLUDE: *David Holzman's Diary* (sc., act.) 1967; *The Lexington Experience* (sc.) 1970; *The American Dreamer* (dir., sc.) 1971; *The Last Word* (sc.) 1979; *Breathless* (sc.) 1983; *Chinese Boxes* (act., sc.), *Paris, Texas* (story adaptation) 1984; *The Texas Chainsaw Massacre Part 2* (assoc. prod., sc., song) 1986; *Running on Empty* (act.) 1988.

Carson, Robert. Screenwriter. Born on Oct. 6, 1909, in Clayton, Washington. Wrote screenplays for many Hollywood films, mostly in collaboration. He shared an Academy Award for the script of *A Star Is Born* (1937).

FILMS INCLUDE: *A Star Is Born, The Last Gangster* 1937; *Men with Wings* 1938; *Beau Geste, The Light That Failed* 1939; *Western Union* 1941; *The Tuttles of Tahiti* 1942; *The Desperadoes* 1943; *Perilous Holiday* 1946; *You Gotta Stay Happy* 1948; *Sailor Beware* 1951; *Pushover* 1954; *Ain't Misbehaving, You're Never Too Young* 1955; *Action of the Tiger* 1957; *Advance to the Rear* 1964.

Carson, Sunset. Actor. *b.* Michael Harrison, Nov. 12, 1922, in Plainview, Tex. *d.* 1990. A rodeo performer from his early teens, he played bits in several films before making his 1943 debut as feature player in the United Artists all-star film *Stage Door Canteen.* The following year he became a cowboy star for Republic and the company changed his name to Sunset Carson, to coincide with the fictional name of the Western hero he was to portray in the company's films of the 40s. He also rode for RKO and Warners and appeared in TV Westerns.

FILMS INCLUDE: *Stage Door Canteen* 1943; *Code of the Prairie, Firebrands of Arizona* 1944; *Bandits of the Badlands, Oregon Trail* 1945; *The El Paso Kid, Days of Buffalo Bill, Alias Billy the Kid* 1946; *Sunset Carson Rides Again* 1948; *Indian Territory* 1950; *Seabo* 1977.

Carstairs, John Paddy. Director. Screenwriter. *b.* John Keys, in 1910, London. *d.* 1970. Entered films in 1928 as an assistant cameraman, became a screenwriter in 1931 and director in 1934. Turned out numerous British films and TV episodes, mostly in a light vein. He was also the author of many humorous novels, and his paintings have been exhibited internationally. Memoirs: *Honest Injun* (1942), *Hadn't We the Gaiety* (1945), *Kaleidoscope and a Jaundiced Eye* (1946).

FILMS INCLUDE (as director): *Paris Plane* 1934; *Night Ride, Incident in Shanghai, Double Exposure* 1937; *The Saint in London* 1939; *He Found a Star* 1941; *Dancing with Crime* 1947; *Sleeping Car to Trieste* 1948; *The Chilton Hundreds/The Amazing Mr. Beecham* 1949; *Tony Draws a Horse* 1950; *Talk of a Million* 1951; *Treasure Hunt, Made in Heaven* 1952; *Trouble in Store* 1953; *Up to His Neck* 1954; *Man of the Moment* 1955; *Up in the World* 1956; *The Big Money, The Square Peg* 1958; *Tommy the Toreador* 1959; *Sands of the Desert* 1960; *A Weekend with Lulu* 1961; *Im Namen des Teufels/The Devil's Agent* (Ger./UK) 1962.

Carter, Helena. Actress. Born Helen Rickerts, on Aug. 24, 1923, in New York City. A former model, she made her film debut in 1947 and played some leading lady roles until her retirement early in the 50s.

FILMS INCLUDE: *Time Out of Mind, Something in the Wind* 1947; *Intrigue, River Lady* 1948; *The Fighting O'Flynn* 1949; *South Sea Sinner, Kiss Tomorrow Goodbye* 1950; *Double Crossbones, Fort Worth* 1951; *Bugles in the Afternoon, The Golden Hawk* 1952; *The Pathfinder, Invaders from Mars* 1953.

Carter, Helena Bonham. See BONHAM CARTER, Helena.

Carter, Janis. Actress. Born Janis Dremann, on Oct. 10, 1917, in Cleveland. Trained for opera in New York, she performed on the musical stage, and several Broadway appearances led to a screen contract. A pretty blonde, she played leading ladies in many B pictures of the 40s, occasionally portraying "the other woman" in higher-budget films. In the 50s she cohosted a TV quiz show.

FILMS INCLUDE: *Cadet Girl* 1941; *I Married an Angel* 1942; *Lady of Burlesque* 1943; *The Girl in the Case, The Mark of the Whistler, One Mysterious Night, The Missing Juror, Together Again* 1944; *The Fighting Guardsman, One Way to Love* 1945; *The Notorious Lone Wolf, Night Editor* 1946; *Framed* 1947; *Miss Grant Takes Richmond, Slightly French* 1949; *A Woman of Distinction, The Woman on Pier 13* 1950; *My Forbidden Past, Santa Fe, Flying Leathernecks* 1951; *The Half-Breed* 1952.

cartoon. See ANIMATION.

Cartwright, Veronica. Actress. Born in 1949, in Bristol, England. Child performer, then leading lady and second lead of Hollywood films. As a teenager she co-starred in the TV series 'Daniel Boone' (1964–66). The older sister of TV child star Angela Cartwright (*b.* Sept. 9, 1952), she married director Richard Compton.

FILMS INCLUDE: *In Love and War* 1958; *The Children's Hour* 1961; *The Birds, Spencer's Mountain* 1963; *One Man's Way* 1964; *Inserts* (UK) 1976; *Goin' South, Invasion of the Body Snatchers* 1978; *Alien* 1979; *Nightmares, The Right Stuff* 1983; *My Man Adam* 1985; *Flight of the Navigator, Wisdom* 1986; *The Witches of Eastwick* 1987; *Valentino Returns* 1988; *False Identity* 1989; *Man Trouble* 1992; *Candyman: Farewell To the Flesh* 1995.

Caruso, Anthony. American actor. Born in 1915(?). In Hollywood films since the early 40s, typically as a mobster or in other unpleasant character parts.

FILMS INCLUDE: *Johnny Apollo* 1940; *Tall Dark and Handsome* 1941; *Always in My Heart* 1942; *Watch on the Rhine* 1943; *And Now Tomorrow* 1944; *Objective Burma!, Crime Doctor's Courage* 1945; *Tarzan and the Leopard Woman* 1946; *Wild Harvest* 1947; *To the Victor* 1948; *Scene of the Crime, The Threat, The Undercover Man* 1949; *The Asphalt Jungle* 1950; *The Iron Mistress* 1952; *Fighter Attack* 1953; *Phantom of the*

Rue Morgue 1954; *Hell on Frisco Bay* 1955; *When Gangland Strikes* 1956; *Baby Face Nelson* 1957; *Legion of the Doomed* 1958; *Never Steal Anything Small* 1959; *Most Dangerous Man Alive* 1961; *Young Dillinger* 1965; *Flap* 1970; *The Legend of Earl Durand* 1975; *Mean Johnny Barrows* 1976.

Caruso, David. Actor. Born January 17, 1956, in Forest Hills, N.Y. Intense, talented red-headed character actor who played supporting roles in films from 1980 until he found stardom and critical success on television in the controversial cop series 'N.Y.P.D. Blue.' After a year on the series, a very public contract negotiation ensued resulting in Caruso's departure to pursue lucrative film offers. His first two films, *Kiss of Death* and *Jade* (both 1995), were met with mediocre response from audiences and critics alike.

FILMS: *Without Warning* 1980; *First Blood, An Officer and a Gentleman* 1982; *Thief of Hearts* 1984; *Blue City* 1986; *China Girl* 1988; *Twins, King of New York* 1990; *Hudson Hawk* 1991; *Mad Dog and Glory* 1993; *Jade, Kiss of Death* 1995.

Carver, Lynne. Actress. *b.* Virginia Reid Sampson, Sept. 13, 1916, Lexington, Ky. *d.* 1955. Ingenue, then leading lady, of Hollywood films from the mid-30s to the late 40s. A blue-eyed, blonde beauty-contest winner, she was billed as Virginia Reid during the early stage of her career.

FILMS INCLUDE: As Virginia Reid—*Down to Their Last Yacht, Kid Millions* 1934; *Roberta* 1935. As Lynne Carver—*Maytime, Madame X, The Bride Wore Red* 1937; *Everybody Sing, A Christmas Carol* (as Bess), *Young Dr. Kildare* 1938; *The Adventures of Huckleberry Finn* (as Mary Jane) 1939; *Bitter Sweet, Broadway Melody of 1940, Sporting Blood, Dulcy* 1940; *The Man from Cheyenne, Tennessee Johnson* 1942; *Law of the Valley* 1944; *Flame of the West* 1945; *Drifting Along* 1946; *Crossed Trails* 1948.

Carver, Steve. Director. Born on Apr. 5, 1945, in Brooklyn, N.Y. *ed.* U. of Buffalo; Washington U. (M.F.A.). A former news photographer for UPI and a college film instructor, he became a directing and writing fellow at the American Film Institute's Center for Advanced Studies in 1970. After serving as Dalton Trumbo's assistant on *Johnny Got His Gun* (1971) and a writing and editing apprenticeship at New World, he was given his first opportunity to direct under the tutelage of Roger CORMAN. He specializes in hard-hitting action fare.

FEATURE FILMS: *The Arena* 1973; *Big Bad Mama* 1974; *Capone* 1975; *Drum* 1976; *Fast Charlie the Moonbeam Rider/Fast Charlie and the Moonbeam* 1979; *Steel/Look Down and Die/Men of Steel* 1980; *An Eye for an Eye* 1981; *Lone Wolf McQuade* (also prod.) 1983; *Jocks* 1987; *Bulletproof* 1988; *River of Death* 1990.

Carvey, Dana. Actor, comedian. Born June 2, 1955, in Missoula, Mont. *ed.* San Francisco State University. He got his break on NBC's 'Saturday Night Live,' where he created many memorable characters, several of which he remains closely identified with. The talented and endearing former stand-up comic found box office success on the big screen with fellow SNL alum Mike Myers in *Wayne's World* (1992) and its sequel. His subsequent films, all comedies, have fared well but none have generated quite as much attention.

FILMS: *Halloween II* 1981; *Racing with the Moon, This Is Spinal Tap* 1984; *Tough Guys* 1986; *Opportunity Knocks* 1990; *Wayne's World* 1992; *Wayne's World 2* 1993; *Clean Slate, The Road to Wellville, Trapped in Paradise* 1994.

Casares, Maria. Actress. Born Maria Casares Quiroga, on Nov. 21, 1922, in Coruña, Spain. The daughter of a loyalist politician and diplomat, she volunteered as a nurse during the Spanish Civil War and after Franco's victory sought asylum in France. After studying acting at the Paris Conservatoire, she began appearing on the stage in the early 40s and made her screen debut in Carné's *Les Enfants du Paradis/Children of Paradise.* A superb stage tragedienne with the Comédie Française and later with the Théatre National Populaire, she dominated the screen with her dark beauty and powerful personality in sporadic film appearances. Memorable as Death in Cocteau's *Orphée/Orpheus* (1950).

FILMS: *Les Enfants du Paradis/Children of Paradise, Les Dames du Bois de Boulogne/Ladies of the Park* 1945; *Roger-la-Honte, La Septième Porte, La Revenche de Roger-la-Honte, L'Amour autour de la Maison* 1946; *La Chartreuse de Parme, Bagarres/The Wench* 1948; *L'Homme qui revient de Loin* 1949; *Orphée/Orpheus* 1950; *Ombre et Lumière* 1951; *Testament d'Orphée/Testament of Orpheus* 1960; *La Reine verte* 1964; *La Lectrice* 1989; *Les Chevaliers de la table ronde* 1990.

Caserini, Mario. Director. *b.* 1874, Rome. *d.* 1920. A former painter, he entered Italian films as an actor in 1905 and turned to directing in 1907. He was among the leading directors of the so-called "golden age" of the embryonic Italian film industry. His prolific output consisted mainly of ambitious literary adaptations, and romantic melodramas, historical pageants, many of which had worldwide distribution. His wife, Maria Caserini, starred in several of his films.

FILMS INCLUDE: *Otello/Othello, Garibaldi* 1907; *Marco Visconti, Romeo e Giulietta/Romeo and Juliet* 1908; *Beatrice Cenci, Giovanna d'Arco/Joan of Arc, Macbeth* 1909; *Amleto/Hamlet, Anna Garibaldi, Il Cid, Federico Barbarossa, Lucrezia Borgia* 1910; *L'Adultera, La Mala Pianta* 1911; *I Cavalieri di Rodi, Dante e Beatrice, Infamia Araba, Mater Dolorosa, Parsifal, Siegfried, La Ribalta* 1912; *Gli Ultimi Giorni di Pompei/The Last Days of Pompeii, Ma l'Amor mio non muore, Nerone e Agrippina, Romanticismo, Somnambulismo* 1913; *La Gorgona* 1914; *La Pantomima della Morte* 1915; *La Divetta del Regimento, Maschera di Misterio, Vita e Morte, La Vittima dell'Amore* 1916; *Resurrezione/Resurrection, La Via piu lunga, Il Dramma di una Notte* 1917; *La Signora Arlecchino, Il Filo della Vita, Una Notte a Calcutta, Primerose, Capitan Fracassa* 1918; *Anima tormentata, L'Imprevisto, Musica profana, Tragedia senza Lacrime, Il Romanzo di una Vespa, Il Miracolo* 1919; *Fior d'Amore, Sorella, La Voce del Cuore, La Modella* 1920.

Casey, Bernie. Actor. Born on June 8, 1939, in Wyco, W. Va. *ed.* Bowling Green U. (M.F.A.). A former football pro with the San Francisco Giants and Los Angeles Rams, he studied drama with Jeff Corey and began appearing in films and on TV in the late 60s. Memorable for his dual role in *Dr. Black and Mr. Hyde* (1976), a black version of the Stevenson classic.

FILMS INCLUDE: *Guns of the Magnificent Seven* 1969; *Black Chariot* 1971; *Black Gunn, Boxcar Bertha, Hit Man* 1972; *Cleopatra Jones, Maurie* 1973; *Cornbread Earl and Me* 1975; *The Man Who Fell to Earth* (UK), *Dr. Black and Mr. Hyde/The Watts Monster* 1976; *Brothers* 1977; *Sharkey's Machine* 1982; *Never Say Never Again* 1983; *Revenge of the Nerds* 1984; *Spies Like Us* 1985; *Steel Justice* 1987; *Rent-a-Cop, Backfire, I'm Gonna Git You Sucka* 1988; *Bill and Ted's Excellent Adventure* 1989; *Another 48 Hours, Chains of Gold* 1990.

Cash, Jim. Screenwriter. One of contemporary Hollywood's most dependable and highest paid writers and script doctors. Usually works in collaboration with Jack Epps, Jr., specializing in dialogue while the latter takes on plot structure and continuity.

FILMS INCLUDE: *The Postman Always Rings Twice* 1981; *Top Gun, Legal Eagles* 1986; *The Secret of My Success* 1987; *Turner & Hooch* 1989; *Dick Tracy* 1990.

Cash, Rosalind. Actress. *b.* Dec. 31, 1938, in Atlantic City,

N.J. *d.* 1995. Strong leading lady of and star of many African-American films of the 70s.

FILMS: *Klute, The Omega Man* 1971; *Melinda, The New Centurions, Hickey and Boggs* 1972; *The All-American Boy* 1973; *Uptown Saturday Night, Amazing Grace* 1974; *Cornbread Earl and Me* 1975; *Dr. Black and Mr. Hyde/The Watts Monster, The Monkey Hustle* 1976; *The Class of Miss MacMichael* 1978; *Keeping On* (orig. for TV) 1981; *Wrong Is Right* 1982; *Go Tell the Spartans, The Adventures of Buckaroo Banzai Across the Eighth Dimension* 1984; *The Offspring/From a Whisper to a Scream* 1987; *Forced March* 1989.

Caspary, Vera. Screenwriter, novelist. *b.* Nov. 13, 1904, Chicago. *d.* 1987. She started out as a freelance writer, contributing stories and articles to magazines. For a while she edited *The Dance* magazine. Several of her novels were turned into movies, including the best-seller *Laura.* In addition, she wrote a number of screenplays and adaptations directly for the screen.

FILMS INCLUDE: *Working Girls* (co-play basis only, 'Blind Mice') 1931; *The Night of June 13th* (story basis only) 1932; *Such Women Are Dangerous* (story), *Private Scandal* (co-story) 1934; *I'll Love You Always* (co-sc.) 1935; *Easy Living* (story) 1937; *Scandal Street* (story), *Service De Luxe* (co-story) 1938; *Lady from Louisiana* (co-sc.) 1941; *Laura* (novel basis only) 1944; *Claudia and David* (adapt. only), *Bedelia* (co-sc. from own novel; UK) 1946; *A Letter to Three Wives* (adapt.) 1949; *Three Husbands* (co-sc. from own story), *I Can Get It for You Wholesale* (adapt.) 1951; *The Blue Gardenia* (story), *Give a Girl a Break* (story) 1953; *Les Girls* (story) 1957; *Bachelor in Paradise* (story) 1961.

Cass, Henry. Director. Born on June 24, 1902, in London. A former stage actor, he directed numerous plays for various British theatrical companies as well as many feature films and several shorts. The sentimental but highly sensitive *The Glass Mountain* (1948) and *Last Holiday* (1950) are memorable among his many routine films. The latter provided Alec Guinness with one of his best screen roles.

FEATURE FILMS: *Lancashire Luck* 1937; *29 Acacia Avenue/The Facts of Love* 1945; *The Glass Mountain* 1948; *No Place for Jennifer* 1949; *Last Holiday* 1950; *Young Wives' Tale* 1951; *Father's Doing Fine, Castle in the Air* 1952; *The Reluctant Bride, No Smoking* 1955; *Bond of Fear, Break-away, The High Terrace* 1956; *Professor Tim, The Crooked Sky, Booby Trap* 1957; *Blood of the Vampire* 1958; *Boyd's Shop* 1959; *The Man Who Couldn't Walk, The Hand* 1960; *Mr. Brown Comes Down the Hill* 1966; *Give a Dog a Bone* 1968; *Happy Deathday* 1969.

Cass, Peggy. Actress. Born on May 21, 1924, in Boston. Made her professional stage debut in 1945 on an Australian tour with 'The Doughgirls.' Later appeared in many revues and Broadway stage productions, mainly in comedy parts, winning a Tony Award for her performance in the role of Agnes Gooch in 'Auntie Mame.' She was nominated for a best supporting actress Oscar for repeating that role in the 1958 screen version of the play. Her film appearances have been rare, but she is seen often on TV as a guest of talk shows and a panelist on game shows.

FILMS: *The Marrying Kind* 1952; *Auntie Mame* 1958; *Gidget Goes Hawaiian* 1961; *If It's Tuesday This Must Be Belgium, Age of Consent* (Austral.) 1969; *Paddy* (Ire.) 1970; *Cheaters* 1984.

Cassavetes, John. Actor, director, screenwriter. *b.* Dec. 9, 1929, New York City, the son of a Greek-born businessman. *d.* 1989. Cassavetes became interested in acting while majoring in English at Colgate, and after his graduation he enrolled at the American Academy of Dramatic Arts. He made his stage debut with a Providence, R.I., stock company and subsequently gained a reputation as a fine, intense actor in films and numerous live TV dramas. In 1960 he used his earnings as the star of the TV detective series 'Johnny Staccato' to finance his first film, *Shadows,* a semi-improvised production about a love affair between a white boy and a black girl, which he shot on 16 mm stock at the cost of a mere $40,000. The film won the Critics Award at the Venice Film Festival and as a result he was hired to direct two studio-mold productions, *Too Late Blues* (1962) and *A Child Is Waiting* (1963). Neither did well with the critics or at the box office.

Resentful of studio interference, Cassavetes returned to independent filmmaking and to his controversial style, which depends more on the personality and improvisational ability of the actors than on a prepared script and preplanned camera work. In films like *Faces* (1968) and *Husbands* (1970), he dealt with marital problems and women's lib by utilizing harsh techniques and hand-held camera effects. The result was self-indulgent, unpolished, and erratic but striking and audience-involving. *Minnie and Moskowitz* (1971) was an entertaining interlude preceding Cassavetes's next marital drama, *A Woman Under the Influence* (1974). Here Cassavetes departed from his style by writing a fully detailed script prior to production, and he extracted marvelous performances from his friend Peter FALK and wife Gena ROWLANDS, who had appeared in most of his films. Falk and Cassavetes used their own money to finance the film. All crews and actors, including members of the director's own family, worked on deferred salaries. Dismayed with the distribution of his previous films, Cassavetes, Falk, and Rowlands traveled from coast to coast promoting, distributing, and booking the film directly with motion picture theaters.

The director himself provided the essential key to his approach when he said, "I am more interested in the people who work with me than in the film itself, or in cinema." That's perhaps why his films are further than most from the conventions of art or entertainment, but at their very best moments are closer than most to truth, or at least to the subjective reality of its participants. Critics and audiences either love or hate Cassavetes's freewheeling work. His films are as disturbing as they are erratic, leaving no one indifferent. Cassavetes's life and career were the subject of the 1984 Michael Ventura documentary *I'm Almost Not Crazy.* All three of the director's children—Nicholas, Alexandra, and Xan—appeared in some of their father's films. Of the three, only Nick Cassavetes (b. 1959, New York City) forged a career of his own as an actor, in low-budget films of the late 80s and in the 90s turned to directing his father's as well as his own material for film.

FILMS: As actor—*14 Hours* (extra) 1951; *Taxi* 1953; *The Night Holds Terror* 1955; *Crime in the Streets* 1956; *Edge of the City, Affair in Havana* 1957; *Saddle the Wind, Virgin Island* (UK) 1958; *The Webster Boy* (UK) 1962; *The Killers* 1964; *The Dirty Dozen, Devil's Angels* 1967; *Rosemary's Baby, Gli Intoccabili/Machine Gun McCain* (It.) 1968; *Roma come Chicago/Bandits in Rome* (It.), *If It's Tuesday It Must Be Belgium* (cameo) 1969; *Two-Minute Warning, Mikey and Nicky* 1976, *The Fury, Brass Target* 1978; *Whose Life Is It Anyway?* 1981; *The Incubus* (Can.), *Tempest* 1982; *Marvin and Tige* 1983. As director—*Shadows* 1961; *Too Late Blues* (also prod., co-sc.) 1962; *A Child Is Waiting* 1963; *Faces* (also sc.) 1968; *Husbands* (also sc., act.) 1970; *Minnie and Moskowitz* (also sc.) 1971; *A Woman Under the Influence* (also sc.) 1974; *The Killing of a Chinese Bookie* (also sc.) 1976; *Gloria* (also prod., sc.) 1980; *Love Streams* (also co-sc., act.) 1984; *Big Trouble* 1986; *She's So Lovely* (sc.) 1997.

Cassel, Jean-Pierre. Actor. Born Jean-Pierre Crochon, Oct. 27, 1932, Paris. A small-time stage, film, and TV player when discovered in 1956 by Gene KELLY, then in Paris for the shooting of *The Happy Road.* Tall and whimsical, with a facile smile, Cassel established himself in several Philippe de BROCA comedies and found his niche in farcical romantic roles in both French and international productions.

FILMS INCLUDE: *Pigalle-Saint-Germain-des-Près* 1950; *The Happy Road, A Pied à Cheval et en Voiture* 1957; *Le Désordre et la Nuit, En Cas de Malheur/Love Is My Profession* 1958; *Les Jeux de l'Amour/The Love Game, Candide* (title role) 1960; *Le Farceur/The Joker, L'Amant de Cinq Jours/The Five Day Lover* 1961; *Les Sept Péchés capitaux/Seven Capital Sins, Le Caporal épinglé/The Elusive Corporal, Arséne Lupin contre Arsène Lupin, Cyrano et d'Artagnan* 1962; *Un Monsieur de Compagnie/Male Companion, Alta Infedeltà/High Infidelity* (It./Fr.), *La Ronde* 1964; *Those Magnificent Men in Their Flying Machines* (UK), *Les Fêtes Gallantes* 1965; *Paris brûle-t-il?/Is Paris Burning?* (Fr./US) 1966; *Jeu de Massacre/The Killing Game* 1967; *L'Armée des Ombres, L'Ours et la Poupée/The Bear and the Doll, Oh What a Lovely War!* (UK) 1969; *La Rupture* 1970; *Le Charme discret de la Bourgeoisie/The Discreet Charm of the Bourgeoisie, Baxter* (UK) 1972; *Le Mouton enragé/The French Way, The Three Musketeers* (as Louis XIII; UK), *Murder on the Orient Express* (UK/US) 1974; *The Four Musketeers* (UK), *Docteur Françoise Gailland/No Time for Breakfast* 1975; *Folies Bourgeoises* 1976; *Les Rendez-vous d'Anna, Who Is Killing the Great Chefs of Europe?* (US/Ger.) 1978; *Du Dunkerque alla Vittoria/From Hell to Victory* (It./Fr./Sp.) 1979; *Le Soleil en Face* 1980; *La Vie continue* 1981; *La Truite/The Trout* 1982; *Nudo di Donna/Portrait of a Woman Nude* (It./Fr.), *Vive la Sociale* 1983; *Tranches de Vie* 1985; *Chouans!, Mangeclous, Migrations* 1988; *Vado a riprendermi il gatto* (It.) 1989; *Mister Frost* (US) 1990; *In Heaven as on Earth* 1992; *Petain* 1993; *The Maid, Ready to Wear* 1994; *The Ceremony, Judgment in Stone* 1997.

Cassel, Seymour. Actor. Born on Jan. 22, 1935, in Detroit. As a boy, he traveled with his mother, a burlesque performer. After completing high school, he began performing in stock, then trained at the American Theatre Wing and the Actors Studio, where he took part in a workshop by John CASSAVETES, who became his mentor. A solid character player, he was nominated for an Academy Award as best supporting actor for Cassavetes's *Faces* (1968).

FILMS INCLUDE: *Juke Box Racket* 1960; *Too Late Blues* 1962; *The Killers* 1964; *The Sweet Ride, Coogan's Bluff, Faces* 1968; *The Revolutionary* 1970; *Minnie and Moskowitz* (as Moskowitz) 1971; *The Killing of a Chinese Bookie, The Last Tycoon* 1976; *Scott Joplin, Black Oak Conspiracy, Death Game, Valentino* (UK) 1977; *Convoy* 1978; *California Dreaming* 1979; *The Mountain Men* 1980; *Double Exposure* 1982; *Love Streams* 1984; *Eye of the Tiger* 1986; *Tin Men, Survival Game* 1987; *Johnny Be Good, Track 29* (UK) 1988; *Wicked Stepmother* 1989; *Dick Tracy, Cold Dog Soup* 1990; *White Fang, Mobsters* 1991; *In the Soup, Diary of a Hitman, Honeymoon in Vegas, Cold Heaven* 1992; *Chain of Desire, Indecent Proposal, Short Cuts* 1993; *Chasers, Imaginary Crimes, It Could Happen to You* 1994; *Dead Presidents, Four Rooms* 1995; *Trees Lounge, When Pigs Fly* 1996.

cassette. 1. A lightproof container into which a roll of film can be inserted for loading a camera in broad daylight. The insertion or removal of the roll into and from the cassette must, however, be performed in darkness. See also CHANGING BAG. 2. A container for the recording and replay of audio- or videotapes. Videocassette equipment has largely replaced motion picture apparatus as a more convenient means of recording and playing movies at home and in small gatherings. Its widespread use revolutionized the viewing habits of millions, contributing to a steep decline in motion-picture theater attendance and leading to a corresponding massive audience interest in older movies, which can be cheaply rented or purchased, or copied directly off TV screens.

Cassidy, Hopalong. See BOYD, William.

Cassidy, Jack. Actor, singer, dancer. *b.* Mar. 5, 1927, Richmond Hill, N.Y. *d.* 1976. Made his Broadway debut at 15 as a member of the chorus line in 'Something for the Boys' and in the 50s and 60s became established as a star of the musical stage. He also appeared in many revues and nightclub acts and on TV programs, both light and dramatic, often with his second wife, actress-singer Shirley JONES. However, his film appearances were sporadic. He portrayed John Barrymore in *W. C. Fields and Me* (1976), his final screen appearance. He died at 49, in a fire that destroyed his Los Angeles apartment. His son David Cassidy (*b.* Apr. 12, 1950, New York City) is a popular singer and co-star of the TV series 'The Partridge Family' and 'Man Undercover.' Another son, Shaun Cassidy (*b.* Sept. 27, 1958, Los Angeles), is a successful actor-singer and co-star of the TV series 'The Hardy Boys' and 'Breaking Away.'

FILMS: *Look in Any Window* 1961; *The Chapman Report* 1962; *FBI Code 98* 1964; *The Cockeyed Cowboys of Calico County* 1970; *Bunny O'Hare* 1971; *The Eiger Sanction* 1975; *W. C. Fields and Me* (as John Barrymore) 1976; *The Private Files of J. Edgar Hoover* (as Damon Runyon) 1978.

Cassidy, Joanna. Actress. Born on Aug. 2, 1944, in Camden (or Haddonfield), N.J. *ed.* Syracuse U. Dependable leading lady of Hollywood films of the 70s and 80s. Also very busy on TV.

FILMS INCLUDE: *Bullitt* (bit) 1968; *Fools* (bit) 1970; *The Laughing Policeman* 1973; *The Outfit, Bank Shot* 1974; *Night Child* 1975; *Stay Hungry* 1976; *The Late Show, Stunts* 1977; *The Glove* 1979; *Night Games* 1980; *Blade Runner* 1982; *Under Fire* 1983; *Club Paradise* 1986; *The Fourth Protocol* (UK) 1987; *Who Framed Roger Rabbit? 1969* 1988; *The Package* 1989; *Where the Heart Is, May Wine* 1990; *Don't Tell Mom the Babysitter's Dead, Lonely Hearts, All-American Murder* 1991; *Vampire in Brooklyn* 1995; *Chain Reaction* 1996.

cast. 1. The performers appearing in a film, including stars, featured players, bit players, and extras. 2. To select the performers for a film.

Castellani, Renato. Director. *b.* Sept. 4, 1913, Finale Ligure, Italy. *d.* 1985. Spent part of his childhood in Argentina, where his father worked for Eastman Kodak. Continued his education in Switzerland and studied architecture in Milan before entering Italian films in the late 30s as screenwriter for Soldati, Camerini, and Blasetti. Made his directorial debut in 1941. The elegant, decorative style of his WW II–period films gave way to an optimistic, fantasy-inspired neorealism in the postwar years best exemplified by *Sotto il Sole di Roma/Under the Sun of Rome,* Best Italian Film, Venice (1948), *É Primavera/It's Forever Springtime* (1949), and *Due Soldi di Speranza/Two Cents Worth of Hope,* shared Best Film, Cannes (1952). However, he returned to detached elegance in 1954 with the British production of *Romeo and Juliet* (Golden Lion, Venice 1954), but his subsequent films failed to re-ignite critical interest. From the late 60s he worked mainly for Italian TV. He co-scripted all the films he directed, as well as many films of other directors.

FILMS: *Un Colpo di Pistola* 1941; *Zaza* 1942; *La Donna della Montagna* 1943; *Mio Figlio Professore/Professor My Son* 1946; *Sotto il Sole di Roma/Under the Sun of Rome* 1948; *É Primavera/It's Forever Springtime* 1949; *Due Soldi di Speranza/Two Cents Worth of Hope* 1952; *Giulietta e Romeo/Romeo and Juliet* (UK) 1954; *I Sogni nel Cassetto* 1957; *Nella Città l'Inferno/And the Wild Wild Women* 1958; *Il Brigante* 1961; *Mare Matto* 1962; *Tre Notti d'Amore/Three Nights of Love* ("La Vedova" episode), *Controsesso* ("Una Donna d'Afari" episode) 1964; *Sotto il Cielo Stellato* 1966; *Questi Fantasmi/Ghosts Italian Style* 1967; *Una Breva Stagione* 1969; *Leonardo da Vinci* (condensed from 5-part TV special) 1972.

Castellano, Richard. Actor. *d.* Sept. 4, 1933, in the Bronx, N.Y. *d.* 1988. *ed.* Columbia. Character player of the American stage, TV, and occasional films; at his most convincing in the portrayal of Italian-Americans and other ethnic types. He was nominated for an Oscar as best supporting player for his performance in *Lovers and Other Strangers* (1970) in a role he had earlier played on Broadway. He ran a construction company before starting his acting career in 1963 with the New Yiddish Theatre.

FILMS: *A Fine Madness* (bit) 1966; *Lovers and Other Strangers* 1970; *The Godfather* 1972; *Night of the Juggler* 1979.

Castiglioni, Iphigenie. See KINSKEY, Leonid.

casting director. The person responsible for the selection and hiring of players for a film. In the heyday of the studio system, this task was usually carried out by an executive on the studio payroll, with the aid of a staff of casting clerks. He was often empowered to negotiate contracts with the chosen players. Nowadays, however, the typical casting director is an independent professional who maintains a specialized bureau, servicing the industry. In the 80s, casting directors began receiving prominent screen credit for their work.

Castle, Nick. Dance director. *b.* Mar. 21, 1910, Brooklyn, N.Y. *d.* 1968. A former vaudeville dancer, he entered films in the mid-30s as choreographer for Fox, then worked for Universal, MGM and other studios. He was among Hollywood's leading dance directors, working with such hoofers as Fred Astaire, Gene Kelly, Ann Miller, Judy Garland, Betty Grable, and Shirley Temple. He was the father of film director Nick CASTLE.

FILMS INCLUDE: *One in a Million* 1935; *Sally Irene and Mary, Rebecca of Sunnybrook Farm* 1938; *The Little Princess* 1939; *Swanee River, Down Argentine Way* 1940; *Hellzapoppin* 1941; *Orchestra Wives* 1942; *Stormy Weather, This Is the Army* 1943; *Something for the Boys* 1944; *Thrill of Brazil* 1946; *Summer Stock, Nancy Goes to Rio* 1950; *Rich Young and Pretty, Royal Wedding* 1951; *Everything I Have Is Yours* (with Gower Champion), *Skirts Ahoy* 1952; *Here Come the Girls* 1953; *Red Garters* 1954; *Seven Little Foys* 1955; *Anything Goes, That Certain Feeling* 1956; *Pocketful of Miracles* 1960; *State Fair* 1962.

Castle, Nick. Director. Born on Sept. 21, 1947, in Los Angeles. *ed.* Santa Monica Coll.; U. of Southern California. The son of the famed choreographer of the same name, he appeared as a child in such films as *Artists and Models* (1955) and *Anything Goes* (1956). At USC's film school, he worked with John Carpenter and others on the Oscar-winning live-action short *The Resurrection of Broncho Billy* (1970). He then wrote screenplays for Carpenter and others, making his debut as a director in 1982.

FILMS: As screenwriter—*Halloween* 1978; *Skatetown U.S.A.* 1979; *Escape from New York* 1981. As director—*T.A.G.: The Assassination Game* (also sc.) 1982; *The Last Starfighter* 1984; *The Boy Who Could Fly* (also sc., act.) 1986; *Tap* (also sc.) 1989; *Dennis the Menace* 1993; *Mr. Wrong* 1996.

Castle, Peggie. Actress. *b.* Dec. 22, 1926, Appalachia, Va. *d.* 1973. A former model, this sultry blonde played leads in numerous Hollywood B pictures of the 50s. Later she was a regular on the TV series 'The Lawman' and 'The Outlaws.' Becoming increasingly addicted to alcohol, she retired in 1962 and died 11 years later of liver cirrhosis. Also billed as Peggy Castle.

FILMS INCLUDE: *Buccaneer's Girl, Mr. Belvedere Goes to College* 1950; *Payment on Demand, Air Cadet* 1951; *Wagons West, Invasion U.S.A.* 1952; *I the Jury, 99 River Street, Son of Belle Starr* 1953; *The Long Wait, Jesse James' Women, The White Orchid* 1954; *Target Zero, Finger Man* 1955; *Two-Gun Lady, The Oklahoma Woman, Miracle in the Rain* 1956; *The Beginning of the End, The Counterfeit Plan, Back from the Dead* 1957; *Seven Hills of Rome* 1958.

Castle, William. Director, producer. *b.* Apr. 24, 1914, New York City. *d.* 1977. He broke into show business at the age of 15, getting a small part in a Broadway show by falsely representing himself as a nephew of Samuel Goldwyn. He went through a variety of acting, producing, and writing jobs before going to Hollywood as an actor in 1937. After a transitional period as a dialogue director, he began directing on his own in 1943. In the following three decades he turned out numerous low-budget films, showing some flair for crime and action situations. In the late 50s he took on the additional function of producer and subsequently specialized in chillers and horror films, most of which were panned by critics for "poor taste" but fared handsomely at the box office. A shrewd promoter, Castle would draw attention to his films by such gimmicks as insuring audiences with Lloyds of London should any of them die of fright during the exhibition of *Macabre* (1958). For *The Tingler* (1959) some theater seats were wired to produce mild electric shocks. "I've modeled my career on P. T. Barnum," he once said. His most ambitious and best-known film as producer was *Rosemary's Baby* (1968), which he did not direct. He also produced a number of TV shows, including the hour-long series 'Circle of Fear' (1972). He portrayed a producer in Hal Ashby's *Shampoo* and a director in John Schlesinger's *The Day of the Locust* (both 1975). At the time of his death of a heart attack he was producing the film *200 Lakeview Drive* for MGM. Autobiography: *Step Right Up! I'm Gonna Scare the Pants Off America* (1976).

FILMS: As director—*The Chance of a Lifetime, Klondike Kate* 1943; *The Whistler, She's a Soldier Too, The Mark of the Whistler, When Strangers Marry* 1944; *Voice of the Whistler* (also co-sc.), *The Crime Doctor's Warning* 1945; *Just Before Dawn, The Mysterious Intruder, The Return of Rusty, The Crime Doctor's Man Hunt* 1946; *The Crime Doctor's Gamble* 1947; *Texas Brooklyn and Heaven, The Gentleman from Nowhere* 1948; *Johnny Stool Pigeon, Undertow* 1949; *It's a Small World* (also co-sc.) 1950; *The Fat Man, Hollywood Story, The Cave of the Outlaws* 1951; *Serpent of the Nile, Fort Ti, Conquest of Cochise, Slaves of Babylon* 1953; *Drums of Tahiti, Charge of the Lancers, Battle of Rogue River, Jesse James vs. the Daltons, The Iron Glove, The Law vs. Billy the Kid* 1954; *Masterson of Kansas, The Americano, New Orleans Uncensored, The Gun That Won the West, Duel on the Mississippi* 1955; *The Houston Story, Uranium Boom* 1956. As director-producer—*Macabre* 1958; *House on Haunted Hill, The Tingler* 1959; *13 Ghosts* 1960; *Homicidal* (also narrator), *Mr. Sardonicus* 1961; *Zotz!* 1962; *13 Frightened Girls, The Old Dark House* 1963; *Strait-Jacket* 1964; *The Night Walker, I Saw What You Did* 1965; *Let's Kill Uncle* 1966; *The Busy Body, The Spirit Is Willing* 1967; *Project X, Rosemary's Baby* (prod. only) 1968; *Riot* (prod. only) 1969; *Shanks* (dir. only) 1974; *Bug* (prod., co-sc. only) 1975.

Cates, Gilbert. Director. Born Gilbert Katz, on June 6, 1934, in New York City. *ed.* Syracuse U. (B.S.; M.A.). He entered the entertainment industry as a guide at New York's NBC Studios, and by the late 50s had worked his way up to producer and director of game shows. In the late 60s he began producing Broadway plays. It was with the screen adaptation of one of these, *I Never Sang for My Father,* that he made an impressive bow as a feature film director in 1970. Concentrating on TV movies and specials, he returned to features only sporadically, with mixed results. In 1989 he was honored by the Directors Guild of America with the Robert B. Aldrich award. His brother, Joseph Cates (*b.* Joseph Katz, 1924), is a pioneer TV producer-director with three low-budget features to his credit. Joseph is the father of actress Phoebe CATES.

FEATURE FILMS: *I Never Sang for My Father* (also prod.) 1970; *Summer Wishes, Winter Dreams* 1973; *One Summer Love/Dragonfly* (also prod.) 1976; *The Promise* 1979; *The Last Married Couple in America, Oh God! Book II* (also prod.) 1980; *Backfire* 1988.

Cates, Phoebe. Actress. Born in 1964, in New York City. Lovely brunette leading lady. The daughter of TV producer-director Joseph Cates and niece of director Gilbert CATES, she was a dance prodigy and a fashion model before starting her acting career. Married actor Kevin KLINE.

FILMS: *Paradise, Fast Times at Ridgemont High* 1982; *Private School* 1983; *Gremlins* 1984; *Date with an Angel* 1987; *Bright Lights Big City, Shag* (UK) 1988; *I Love You to Death* (unbilled cameo), *Gremlins 2: The New Batch, Heart of Dixie* 1990; *Drop Dead Fred* 1991; *Bodies Rest and Motion* 1993; *Princess Caraboo* 1994.

Catlett, Walter. Actor. *b.* Feb. 4, 1889, San Francisco. *d.* 1960. *ed.* St. Ignatius Coll. Entered films in the mid-20s after extensive experience as a vaudeville and stage comedian. Played scores of supporting roles, mostly comic, typically as a fidgety, flustered, exasperated scatterbrain.

FILMS INCLUDE: *Second Youth* 1924; *Summer Bachelors* 1926; *The Music Master* 1927; *Why Leave Home?* 1929; *Happy Days, The Golden Calf, The Floradora Girl, The Big Party* 1930; *The Front Page, Platinum Blonde* 1931; *Cock of the Air, Back Street, Big City Blues, Okay America, Rain, Rockabye* 1932; *Mama Loves Papa, Only Yesterday* 1933; *The Captain Hates the Sea* 1934; *A Tale of Two Cities* 1935; *Mr. Deeds Goes to Town, Cain and Mabel, Banjo on My Knee* 1936; *On the Avenue, Love Is News, Wake Up and Live, Love Under Fire* 1937; *Every Day's a Holiday, Bringing Up Baby* 1938; *Zaza, Going Places* 1939; *Spring Parade* 1940; *Horror Island, Manpower, Unfinished Business, It Started with Eve* 1941; *My Gal Sal, Yankee Doodle Dandy* 1942; *They Got Me Covered, His Butler's Sister* 1943; *Up in Arms, Ghost Catchers* 1944; *I'll Be Yours* 1947; *The Boy with Green Hair* 1948; *Look for the Silver Lining, The Inspector General* 1949; *Dancing in the Dark* 1950; *Father Takes the Air, Here Comes the Groom* 1951; *Friendly Persuasion* 1956; *Beau James* 1957.

Caton-Jones, Michael. Director. Born in 1958, in Broxburn, Scotland. Gained notice with incisive, poignant view of Profumo affair in *Scandal*; has since applied same light but probing view to films about varieties of American life.

FILMS INCLUDE: *Scandal* 1989; *Memphis Belle* 1990; *Doc Hollywood* (also act.) 1991; *This Boy's Life* 1993; *Rob Roy* 1994; *The Jackal* 1997.

Cattrall, Kim. Actress. Born on Aug. 21, 1956, in Liverpool, England. Trained at New York's American Academy of Dramatic Arts, she appeared on the Canadian stage and in isolated films of the 70s before finding her niche as a sexy comedienne in Hollywood movies of the 80s. She was memorable in the Oliver Stone TV mini-series, 'Wild Palms.'

FILMS INCLUDE: *Rosebud* 1976; *Tribute* (Can.) 1980; *Ticket to Heaven* 1981; *Porky's* 1982; *Police Academy* 1984; *Turk 182!, City Limits* 1985; *Big Trouble in Little China* 1986; *Mannequin* 1987; *Masquerade, Midnight Crossing* 1988; *Brown Bread and Sandwiches* (Can.), *Goodnight, Michelangelo* 1989; *The Bonfire of the Vanities, Honeymoon Academy* 1990; *Star Trek VI: The Undiscovered Country, Smokescreen* 1991; *Split Second* 1992; *Live Nude Girls* 1995; *Unforgettable* 1996.

catwalk. A suspended overhead structure in a studio allowing crewmen access to lighting and sound equipment high above the studio floor. Also called "rigging" or "scaffolding."

Caulfield, Joan. Actress. *b.* Beatrice Joan Caulfield, June 1, 1922, in Orange, N.J. *d.* 1991. A former model, she played ingenues on Broadway before entering films in the mid-40s. For several years she was among Paramount's top stars, radiating delicate femininity and demure beauty but rarely much else. Retired from the screen in 1950 after marrying producer Frank Ross (they divorced in 1960) and subsequently made only occasional film appearances. However, she was seen in much TV, including the series 'My Favorite Husband' and 'Sally,' and was active in summer stock.

FILMS: *Duffy's Tavern* 1945; *Blue Skies, Miss Susie Slagle's, Monsieur Beaucaire* 1946; *Dear Ruth, Welcome Stranger, The Unsuspected, Variety Girl* 1947; *The Sainted Sisters, Larceny* 1948; *Dear Wife, The Petty Girl* 1950; *The Lady Says No* 1951; *The Rains of Ranchipur* 1955; *Cattle King* 1963; *Red Tomahawk* 1967; *Buckskin* 1968; *The Daring Dobermans* 1973; *Pony Express Rider* 1976.

Cavalcanti, Alberto. Director, producer, screenwriter, art director. *b.* Alberto de Almeida-Cavalcanti, Feb. 6, 1897, Rio de Janeiro. *d.* 1982. After studying law and architecture in Switzerland, he went to Paris, where he became close to the young avant-garde art movement. He began his film career in the early 20s as an innovative set decorator for Marcel L'HERBIER on such films as *L'Inhumaine* (1923, in collaboration with Fernand LEGER) and *Feu Mathias Pascal* (1925, in collaboration with Lazare MEERSON). But he seemed to reject the avant-garde when he began directing on his own in 1926. His films of the period typically dealt with ordinary daily lives, and in retrospect, their melancholy realism sprinkled with touches of poetic fantasy can be seen as precursors of the "poetic realism" that was to characterize the French cinema of the 30s. In 1934 he accepted John GRIERSON's invitation to join the G.P.O. Film Unit in England. As a producer-director and sound expert, Cavalcanti made an important contribution to the development of the British documentary movement at the G.P.O. and from 1939 the Crown Film Unit.

In 1942, Cavalcanti joined Michael Balcon's Ealing studios as a feature director, introducing the influence of documentary filmmaking into fiction films. In 1949 he returned to Brazil, where he joined the Vera Cruz production group and as head of production infused new life into a dormant industry. But three years later he was fired on suspicions of Communist activities, and shortly after, he returned to Europe. In Austria he directed, for East Germany, *Herr Puntila und sein Knecht Matti* from the play by BRECHT with the help of the author, who later called the film the only faithful screen adaptation of his work. Cavalcanti subsequently directed several other features and worked in British and French TV. In 1968 he taught at UCLA. For decades he was among the most important and influential figures on the international film scene. Author of the book *Film e Realidad (Film and Reality).*

FILMS (as director): In France—*Rien que les Heures* (doc.; also prod., co-sc.) 1926; *La P'tite Lilie, Yvette* (also sc.), *En Rade/Sea Fever* (also co-sc.) 1927; *Le Train sans Yeux* (filmed in 1926) 1928; *Le Capitaine Fracasse* (also co-sc.), *La Jalousie du Barbouillé* (also sc., asst. dir.), *Le Petit Chaperon rouge* (also co-dial.), *Vous verrez la Semaine prochaine* 1929; *Toute sa Vie* (and Portuguese version, *A Cançao do Berco*) 1930;

Dans une Ile perdue, A Mi-Chemin du Ciel, Les Vacances du Diable 1931; *Tour de Chant* (doc.; also sc.), *En lisant le Journal, Le Jour du Frotteur* (also sc.), *Revue Montmartroise, Nous ne ferons jamais le Cinéma* (doc.) 1932; *Le Mari Garçon, Plaisirs defendu* 1933; *SOS Radio Service* (doc.), *Coralie & Cie* (also sc.) 1934. In the UK—*Pett and Pott* (short; also sc.), *New Rates* 1934; *Coal Face* (doc.; also sc.) 1935; *Message from Geneva* (doc.; also sc.) 1936; *We Live in Two Worlds* (doc.), *The Line to Tcherva Hut* (doc.), *Who Writes to Switzerland* (doc.; also sc.) 1937; *Four Barriers* (doc.; also sc.) 1938; *Men of the Alps* (doc.), *Midsummer Day's Work* (doc.; also sc.) 1939; *The Yellow Caesar* (compilation doc.) 1941; *Film and Reality* (compilation anthology for the British Film Institute), *Went the Day Well?/48 Hours, Alice in Switzerland* (short), *Greek Testament* (doc.) 1942; *Watertight* 1943; *Champagne Charlie* 1944; *Dead of Night* ("The Ventriloquist's Dummy" episode) 1945; *Nicholas Nickleby, They Made Me a Fugitive/I Became a Criminal* 1947; *The First Gentleman* 1948; *For Them That Trespass* 1949. In Brazil—*Simão o Caolho* (also prod.) 1952; *O Canto do Mar* (also prod., co-story) 1953; *Mulher de Verdade* (also prod.) 1954. In Austria—*Herr Puntila und sein Knecht Matti* (also co-addnl. dial.) 1955. In Romania—*Castle in the Carpathians* 1957. In Italy—*La Prima Notte/Les Noces Venitiennes* 1958. In the UK—*The Monster of Highgate Pond* (short) 1960. In Israel—*Thus Spake Theodor Herzl/The Story of Israel* (doc.; also sc.) 1967.

Cavalier, Alain. Director. Born Alain Fraissé, on Sept. 14, 1931, in Vendôme, France. After graduating from the IDHEC film school in Paris, he worked as an assistant to Edouard MOLINARO and Louis MALLE. He made his directing debut in 1958 with a short, *Un Americain.* His first feature, in 1962, received only mild critical and commercial appreciation. Despite evident talent, he has had only rare subsequent assignments. He won the Prix Delluc for his 1981 film *Un Etrange Voyage.*

FEATURE FILMS: *Le Combat dans l'Ile* (also co-story) 1962; *L'Insoumis* (also sc.) 1964; *Mise à Sac* (also co-story, co-sc.) 1967; *La Chamade* (also co-sc.) 1968; *Le Plein de Super* (also sc.) 1976; *Martin et Lea* (also co-sc.) 1978; *Ce Répondeur ne prend pas de Message* (also c-sc.) 1979; *Une Etrange Voyage* (also co-sc.) 1981; *Thérèse* (also co-sc.) 1986; *Portraits d'Alain Cavalier* 1988.

Cavanagh, Paul. Actor. *b.* 1895, Chislehurst, England. *d.* 1959. *ed.* Cambridge. On the London stage and in several British films before coming to Hollywood in 1930, he acted in scores of films until the late 50s, initially in romantic leads and later typically as a dapper, mustachioed villain.

FILMS INCLUDE: *Tesha/A Woman in the Night* (UK), *The Runaway Princess* (UK) 1928; *Strictly Unconventional, Grumpy, The Storm, The Virtuous Sin* 1930; *Unfaithful, Born to Love, Always Goodbye, Transgression, The Squaw Man* 1931; *Devil's Lottery, The Crash, A Bill of Divorcement* 1932; *Tonight Is Ours, The Kennel Murder Case* 1933; *Tarzan and His Mate, The Notorious Sophie Lang, Menace* 1934; *Goin' to Town, Splendor* 1935; *Champagne Charlie* 1936; *Crime Over London* 1938; *The Under-Pup, Reno* 1939; *I Take This Woman* 1940; *Maisie Was a Lady* 1941; *Captains of the Clouds* 1942; *The Gorilla Man, The Hard Way* 1943; *The Scarlet Claw* 1944; *The Man in Half Moon Street, The House of Fear, The Woman in Green* 1945; *Night and Day, The Verdict* 1946; *Humoresque, Dishonored Lady, Ivy* 1947; *Secret Beyond the Door, The Black Arrow* 1948; *Madame Bovary* 1949; *Hollywood Story, The Desert Fox* 1951; *The Mississippi Gambler, House of Wax, The All-American* 1953; *Casanova's Big Night, The Raid, Magnificent Obsession* 1954; *The Purple Mask, The Prodigal* 1955; *Diane* 1956; *She Devil* 1957; *The Four Skulls of Jonathan Drake* 1959.

Cavanaugh, Hobart. Actor. *b.* Sept. 22, 1886, Virginia City, Nev. *d.* 1950. Stage veteran who played character roles in scores of Hollywood films, often as a henpecked husband, nervous clerk, or assortment of other meek, sometimes nasty, little men.

FILMS INCLUDE: *San Francisco Nights* 1928; *I Cover the Waterfront, Lilly Turner* 1933; *The Key, Madame Du Barry* 1934; *Bordertown, Dr. Socrates, A Midsummer Night's Dream, Captain Blood* 1935; *Wife vs. Secretary, Cain and Mabel* 1936; *Three Smart Girls* 1937; *Rose of Washington Square* 1939; *Santa Fe Trail* 1940; *I Wanted Wings, Horror Island, Skylark* 1941; *My Favorite Spy, The Magnificent Dope* 1942; *Sweet Rosie O'Grady* 1943; *Jack London, Kismet* 1944; *Lady on a Train* 1945; *Black Angel, Margie* 1946; *A Letter to Three Wives* 1949; *Stella* 1950.

Cavani, Liliana. Director. Born on Jan. 12, 1936, in Emilia, near Modena, Italy. *ed.* U. of Bologna (B.A. in classic literature; Ph.D. in linguistics). A graduate of Rome's Centro Sperimentale film school, she made documentaries and dramas for Italian television before venturing into feature films in the late 60s. Her films typically echo political and social concerns with some emphasis on violence and sex. Her best-known picture, *The Night Porter* (1974), which deals with the sado-masochistic relationship between an ex-Nazi officer and his former concentration camp rape victim, enjoyed commercial success in the US despite a negative reaction from most critics. She has also staged operas.

FILMS: *Francesco d'Assisi* (also co-sc.; orig. made for TV) 1966; *Galileo* (also co-sc.; It./Bulg.) 1968; *I Cannibali/The Cannibals* (also story, co-sc.) 1969; *L'Ospite/The Hospital* (also co-sc.) 1971; *Milarepa* 1973; *Il Portiere di Notte/The Night Porter* (also co-story, co-sc.) 1974; *Oltre il Bene e il Male/Beyond Good and Evil* (also co-sc.; It./Fr./Ger.) 1977; *La Pelle/The Skin* (also co-sc.) 1981; *Oltra la Porta/Beyond the Door* (also co-sc.) 1982; *Berlin Affair* (also co-sc.) 1985; *Francesco/St. Francis of Assisi* (also co-sc.) 1988; *Where Are You, I'm Here?* 1993.

Cavett, Frank. Screenwriter. *b.* Dec. 27, 1907, Jackson, Ohio. *d.* 1973. *ed.* Ohio U.; Yale. Entered films in 1929 as an assistant director. A screenwriter since 1939, mostly in collaboration. He won an Academy Award in 1944 for co-scripting *Going My Way* and in 1952 for collaborating on the original story of *The Greatest Show on Earth.*

FILMS INCLUDE: *Vanity Street* (co-story only) 1932; *Rulers of the Sea* 1939; *Tom Brown's Schooldays* 1940; *Second Chorus* 1941; *Syncopation* 1942; *Going My Way* 1944; *The Corn Is Green* 1945; *Smash-Up* (co-story) 1947; *Across the Wide Missouri* (co-story) 1951; *The Greatest Show on Earth* (co-story) 1952.

Cayatte, André. Director. *b.* Feb. 3, 1909, Carcassonne, France. *d.* 1989. Abandoned a law practice to become a journalist and novelist, then turned to films in 1938 as screenwriter and from 1942 as director. Emphasizing content over form, Cayatte often used film as a polemical tool to express his ideas on social and moral problems. The best known of his films—*Justice Is Done* (winner of the Grand Prize at the Venice Film Festival), *We Are All Murderers* (winner of special Jury Prize at Cannes), *Avant le Déluge* (winner of International Critics' Prize at Cannes), and *Le Dossier Noir*—denounced various aspects of the French judicial system, such as the jury and capital punishment. But he also directed a number of tender romantic films, notably an updated version of 'Romeo and Juliet,' *Les Amants de Vérone.* His *La Vie conjugale/Anatomy of a Marriage* was made as two separate films, *My Days with Jean Marc* and *My Nights with Françoise,* analyzing the same problem-filled marriage from two different points of view. Several of his films won prizes at film festivals, including the Cannes and Venice. He scripted or co-scripted all of his films.

FILMS: *La Fausse Maîtresse* 1942; *Au Bonheur des Dames/Shop-Girls of Paris, Pierre et Jean* 1943; *Le Dernier Sou, Sérénade aux Nuages, Roger-la-Honte* 1945; *La Revanche de Roger-la-Honte* 1946; *Le Chanteur inconnu* 1947; *Les Dessous des Cartes* 1948; *Les Amants de Vérone/The Lovers of Verona, Retour à la Vie* ("Tante Emma" episode) 1949; *Justice est faite/Justice Is Done* 1950; *Nous sommes tous des Assassins/We Are All Murderers* 1952; *Avant le Déluge* 1954; *Le Dossier Noir* 1955; *Oeil pour Oeil/An Eye for an Eye* 1957; *Le Miroir à Deux Faces/The Mirror Has Two Faces* 1958; *Le Passage du Rhin/Tomorrow Is My Turn* 1960; *Le Glaive et la Balance/Two Are Guilty* 1963; *La Vie conjugale/Anatomy of a Marriage* (as two separate films, *My Days with Jean Marc* and *My Nights with Françoise*) 1964; *Piège pour Cendrillon/A Trap for Cinderella* 1965; *Les Risques du Métier* 1967; *Les Chemins de Katmandou* 1969; *Mourir d'aimer/To Die of Love* 1971; *Il n'y a pas de Fumée sans Feu/Where There's Smoke* 1973; *Le Testament/The Verdict* 1975; *A Chacun son Enfer* 1977; *La Raison d'Etat, Justices, L'Amour en Question* 1978.

Cazale, John. Actor. *b.* 1936, Boston, Mass. *d.* March 12, 1978. *ed.* Oberlin College, Oh., Boston University (drama). Edgy, haunted character actor with stage experience (winning Obies in 1968 for 'The Indians Want the Bronx' and in 1971 for 'The Line') who came to prominence with his role as Fredo in *The Godfather* (1972). He died suddenly of cancer after appearing in five of the most acclaimed films of the 70s.

FILMS: *The Godfather* 1972; *The Conversation, The Godfather, Part II* 1974; *Dog Day Afternoon* 1975; *The Deer Hunter* 1978.

Cazenove, Christopher. Actor. Born on Dec. 17, 1945, in Winchester, England. *ed.* Eton, Oxford. Well-bred, British leading man. Trained at the Bristol Old Vic Theatre School, he began appearing almost simultaneously in the late 60s on the West End stage, on TV, and in films. He made his Broadway debut in 'Goodbye Fidel' (1980). Married actress Angharad Rees.

FILMS INCLUDE: *Julius Caesar, There's a Girl in My Soup* 1970; *Royal Flash* 1975; *East of Elephant Rock* 1976; *Zulu Dawn* 1979; *Eye of the Needle* (US) 1981; *Heat and Dust* 1983; *Until September* (US) 1984; *Mata Hari* (US) 1985; *The Fantasist* 1986; *Souvenir* 1989; *Three Men and a Little Lady* 1990; *Aces: Iron Eagle III* 1991.

Cecchi D'Amico, Suso. Screenwriter. Born Giovanna Cecchi, on July 21, 1914, in Rome. The daughter of author and screenwriter Emilio Cecchi, she started out as a journalist and as a translator of English-language plays. At the end of WW II she turned to screenwriting, collaborating with such directors as Luigi Zampa and Vittorio De Sica on key neorealist films. Later also worked with Antonioni and Visconti, among other directors.

FILMS INCLUDE (screenplays usually in collaboration): *Mio Figlio Professore/Professor My Son, Vivere in Pace/To Live in Peace* 1946; *L'Onorevole Angelina/Angelina, Fabiola, Il Delitto di Giovanni Episcopo/Flesh Will Surrender* 1947; *Ladri di Biciclette/The Bicycle Thief, Proibito Rubare/Guaglio, La Mura di Malapaga/Au-delà des Grilles/The Walls of Malapaga* (story only) 1948; *E Primavera/It's Forever Springtime* 1949; *Miracolo a Milano/Miracle in Milan, Bellissima* 1951; *Altri Tempi/Times Gone By, Processo alla Città/A Town on Trial, I Vinti* 1952; *Tempi Nostri/Anatomy of Love, Siamo Donne/We the Women, La Signora senza Camelie/Camille Without Camelias* 1953; *Senso* 1954; *Le Amiche/The Girl Friends* 1955; *Le Notti Bianche/White Nights* 1957; *I Soliti Ignoti/Big Deal on Madonna Street, Nella Città l'Inferno/And the Wild Wild Women* 1958; *Estate Violenta/Violent Summer* 1959; *Rocco e i suoi Fratelli/Rocco and His Brothers, Risate di Gioia/The Passionate Thief* 1960; *Il Relitto/The Wastrel, I Due Nemici/The Best of Enemies* (It./UK) 1961; *Boccaccio '70, Salvatore Giuliano* 1962; *Il Gattopardo/The Leopard* 1963; *Gli Indifferenti/Time of Indifference* 1964; *Casanova '70, Vaghe Stelle dell'Orsa/Sandra* 1965; *The Taming of the Shrew* (US/It.), *Lo Straniero/The Stranger* 1967; *Metello* 1970; *La Mortadella/Lady Liberty* 1972; *Ludwig, Fratello Sole Sorella Luna/Brother Sun Sister Moon* 1973; *Gruppo di Famiglia in uno Interno/Conversation Piece* 1975; *Caro Michele, L'Innocente/The Innocent* 1976; *Gesu di Nazareth/Jesus of Nazareth* 1977; *Un Scandalo per Bene, Cuore* 1984; *Speriamo che sia Femmina/Let's Hope It's a Girl, Le Due Vite di Mattia Pascal/The Two Lives of Mattia Pascal, La Storia/History* 1985; *Oci Ciornie/Dark Eyes, I Picari* 1987; *Ti Presento un'Amica* 1988; *Stradivari* 1989; *Il Male Oscuro* 1990.

cel. In animation, a transparent sheet of celluloid or plastic on which original pencil drawings representing phases of action are traced by hand or transferred by a xerography process. By placing one or more cels on top of a background drawing, and changing cels between exposures of individual frames, apparent motion is achieved. Both the background drawing, which remains unchanged, and the cels are punched with holes that mount on pins to assure perfect registration when they are placed on a table under the animation camera. See also ANIMATION; BRAY, John Randolph.

Celi, Adolfo. Actor. *b.* July 27, 1922, Sicily. *d.* 1986. *ed.* Rome Acad. Husky character player with stage background. On the Italian screen from the late 40s, he was extremely busy in international films from the mid-60s, often playing heavies.

FILMS INCLUDE: *Un Americano in Vacanza* 1946; *Proibito Rubare/Guaglio* (lead; It.), *Natale al Campo/Escape Into Dreams* (It.) 1948; *L'Homme de Rio/That Man from Rio* (Fr./It.), *Un Monsieur de Compagnie/Male Companion* (Fr./It.) 1964; *E Venne un Uomo/And There Came a Man* (It./Fr.), *Von Ryan's Express* (US), *The Agony and the Ecstasy* (as Giovanni de Medici; US), *Thunderball* (UK) 1965; *El Greco* (It./Fr.), *Le Roi de Coeur/King of Hearts* (Fr./It.), *Grand Prix* (US) 1966; *The Bobo* (UK), *The Honey Pot* (US/UK/It.), *Ad ogni Costo/Grand Slam* (It./Sp./Ger.) 1967; *Il Padre di Famiglia/The Head of the Family* (It./Fr.), *Dalle Ardenne all'Inferno/Dirty Heroes* (It./Fr./Ger.), *Diabolik/Danger: Diabolik* (It./Fr.) 1968; *Midas Run* (US), *Un Detective/Detective Belli* (It.), *L'Alibi* (also co-dir., co-sc.; It.) 1969; *In Search of Gregory* (UK/It.) 1970; *Fragment of Fear* (UK), *Murders in the Rue Morgue* (US/It./Sp./Ger.) 1971; *La Mala Ordina/The Italian Connection* (It./Ger.) 1972; *Fratello Sole Sorella Luna/Brother Sun Sister Moon* (It.), *Gli Ultimi 10 Giorni di Hitler/Hitler: The Last Ten Days* (It./UK) 1973; *Libera Amore mio* (It.), *Le Fantôme de la Liberté* (Fr./It.), *And Then There Were None/Ten Little Indians* (UK) 1974; *The Devil Is a Woman* (UK/It.), *Amici miei/My Friends* (It.) 1975; *The Next Man* (US), *Le Grand Escogriffe* (Fr.), *Signore e Signori Buonanotte* (It.), *Sandokan* (It.) 1976; *Les Passagers* (Fr.) 1977; *Caffe Express/Café Express* 1980; *Monsignor* (US) 1982.

Celluloid. Trademark for a clear, transparent cellulose derivative widely in use as a base or support of film stock. The "cell" side of film is glossy in appearance and is readily distinguishable from the dull emulsion side, which carries the photographic image. Raw stock of film is supplied with the "cell" side up and the emulsion facing the center of the roll.

cement. A liquid adhesive used in splicing two clips of film by pressure contact. To assure permanent adhesion, the emulsion on the surface of at least one film clip must be scraped off. The two clips are then joined by a device called a SPLICER. This process is known as a HOT SPLICE, as distinguished from the dry TAPE SPLICE, which involves the use of clear adhesive tape.

Central Casting Corporation. A bureau set up in 1926 and maintained by all major Hollywood studios through AMPTP as a pool for supplying extras for film productions. In 1976, Central Casting ceased to be maintained by the studios and was sold to Production Payments, Inc.

Centro Sperimentale di Cinematografia (C.S.C.). Western Europe's oldest film school, established in Rome in 1935 by the Mussolini regime and headed by Luigi CHIARINI during its first eight years. Still financed by the Italian government and now directed by Angelo Libertini, it is a center for serious film research, and important theoretical works have been written and translated there. It has also issued several film publications, notably *Bianco e Nero.*

Located at 1524 Via Tuscolana, Rome, next to the Cinecittà film studios, C.S.C. offers programs in direction, production, camera, editing, set and costume design, sound, and acting. The school facilities include sound stages, a television studio, laboratories, and fully equipped cutting rooms.

century stand. A small three-legged stand designed to support diffusers or other lighting-related devices.

Cervi, Gino. Actor. *b.* May 3, 1901, Bologna, Italy. *d.* 1974. The son of a theater critic, he made his stage debut in 1924 and entered films in 1932. Robust and commanding, he was for many years a pillar of the Italian film industry, playing a wide assortment of leads and character roles in a variety of film genres. Established his reputation in Blasetti's *The Iron Crown* (1940) and *Four Steps in the Clouds* (1942) and became internationally popular in the role of Peppone, the militant Communist mayor, in Duvivier's *The Little World of Don Camillo* and its several sequels. His son, Tonino Cervi, is a film director and producer.

FILMS INCLUDE: *L'Armata azzurra* 1932; *T'Amero Sempre* 1933; *Frontiere* 1934; *Aldebaran* 1935; *Amore, I Due Sergenti* 1936; *Ettore Fieramosca, Un'Avventura di Salvator Rosa* 1939; *Una Romantica Avventura, Melodie Eterne/Eternal Melodies, La Corona di Ferro/The Iron Crown* 1940; *I Promessi Sposi/The Spirit and the Flesh* 1941; *Quattro Passi fra le Nuvole/Four Steps in the Clouds, Don Cesare di Bazan* 1942; *Lo Sbaglio di essere Vivo/My Widow and I* 1945; *Le Miserie del Signor Travet/His Young Wife, Un Uomo Ritorno/Revenge, Aquila Nera, L'Angelo e il Diavolo* 1946; *Daniele Cortis, Furia, I Miserabili/Les Miserables* (as Jean Valjean) 1947; *Anna Karenina* (UK), *Fabiola* 1948; *Guglielmo Tell/William Tell* 1949; *Il Cristo proibito/Strange Deception/Forbidden Christ, Donne senza Nome/Women Without Names* 1950; *O.K. Nerone/O.K. Nero!* (as Emperor Nero) 1951; *La Regina di Saba/The Queen of Sheba* (as King Solomon), *Le Petit Monde de Don Camillo/The Little World of Don Camillo* (Fr./It.), *Moglie per una Notte/Wife for a Night* 1952; *La Signora senza Camelie/Camille Without Camelias, Stazione Termini/Indiscretion of an American Wife, Le Retour de Don Camillo/The Return of Don Camillo* (Fr./It.) 1953; *Frou-Frou* 1955; *Gli Innamorati/Wild Love, Beatrice Cenci* 1956; *Sans Famille* (Fr./It.), *La Maja Desnuda/The Naked Maja* (as King Carlos of Spain) 1958; *Le Grand Chef/The Big Chief* (Fr./It.) 1959; *Femmine di Lusso/Love the Italian Way, L'Assedio di Siracusa/Siege of Syracuse* 1960; *La Rivolta degli Schiavi/The Revolt of the Slaves* 1961; *Le Crime ne paie pas/Crime Does Not Pay* (Fr./It.) 1962; *La Smania Addossò/The Eye of the Needle* 1963; *Becket* (US/UK) 1964; *Don Camillo e i Giovani d'Oggi, Uccidere in Silenzio* 1972.

César. The French Oscar.

Chabrol, Claude. Director. Born on June 24, 1930, in Paris. The product of a typical Paris bourgeois environment, he studied pharmacy, intending to enter the family business. But after military service he veered toward cinema, at first in the publicity department of the Paris bureau of Fox, then as writer and film critic for *Arts* and *Cahiers du Cinéma.* In 1957 he co-authored (with Eric ROHMER) an analytical book on HITCHCOCK. The following year Chabrol made his debut as director with *Le Beau Serge,* a film he was able to finance himself with an inheritance from his first wife. Chabrol was the first of the young group of critics at *Cahiers* to break through the barrier of French commercial cinema with a feature film. Through the production company he set up (AJYM), he also helped the careers of such New Wave directors as Jacques RIVETTE, Eric Rohmer, and Philippe de BROCA.

Chabrol gained respectability and international recognition with his films of the late 50s, particularly with *Les Cousins* and *Les Bonnes Femmes,* proving himself the most technically skilled and least pretentious of the newly emerging NOUVELLE VAGUE. In the early 60s his stature diminished considerably with a succession of commercially inspired critical failures, but he returned to good form late in the decade with such films as *Les Biches* and *La Femme Infidèle.* He reached another peak in 1978 with *Violette Nozière* in 1978. In the 1980s, he worked with producer Marin Karmetz to produce four films, including *Story of Women*, a study of a French woman led to make her living performing illegal abortions during WW II. In the 1990s, he has done two remakes—one of *Dr. Mabuse* called *Club Extinction*, one of *Madame Bovary*.

Chabrol, whose admiration for the Hitchcock thriller style is evident in some of his own films (*The Champagne Murders, This Man Must Die, Poulet au vinaigre/Cop au Vin*), is more typically concerned with exploring, in a curiously detached way, personal relationships (*Les Cousins, Les Biches*). His favorite target remains the urban French petite bourgeoisie, the milieu of his youth. Stéphane AUDRAN, Chabrol's second wife (they married in 1964 and divorced in the late 80s) played increasingly important parts in most of his films. He himself appeared in two of his own films as well as in several made by his friends. He received credit as "technical consultant" on Godard's *Breathless.* He has written or collaborated on most of his films' scripts.

FILMS: *Le Beau Serge/Bitter Reunion* (also prod., sc.) 1958; *Les Cousins/The Cousins* (also prod., sc.), *A Double Tour/Leda/Web of Passion* 1959; *Les Bonnes Femmes* (also adapt.) 1960; *Les Godelureaux* (also co-sc.) 1961; *Les Sept Péchés capitaux/Seven Capital Sins* ("Greed" episode), *L'Oeil du Malin/The Third Lover* (also sc.), *Ophélia* (also co-sc.) 1962; *Landru/Bluebeard* 1963; *Les plus Belles Escroqueries du Monde/The Beautiful Swindlers* ("L'Homme qui vendit la Tour Eiffel" episode), *Le Tigre aime la Chair fraîche/The Tiger Likes Fresh Blood* 1964; *Paris vu par. . . /Six in Paris* ("La Muette" episode; also sc.; act.), *Marie-Chantal contre le Docteur Kha* (also co-sc.), *Le Tigre se parfume à la Dynamite/An Orchid for the Tiger* (also act.) 1965; *La Ligne de Démarcation* (also co-sc.) 1966; *Le Scandale/The Champagne Murders* (French and English versions), *La Route de Corinthe/Who's Got the Black Box?* (also act.) 1967; *Les Biches/The Does/The Girlfriends* (also sc., act.) 1968; *La Femme Infidèle/Unfaithful Wife* (also sc.), *Que la Bête meure/This Man Must Die* (also co-sc.) 1969; *Le Boucher* (also story, sc.), *La Rupture/The Breakup* (also sc.) 1970; *Juste avant la Nuit/Just Before Nightfall* (also sc.) 1971; *La Décade prodigieuse/Ten Days' Wonder, Docteur Popaul* 1972; *Les Noces rouges/Wedding in Blood* (also sc.), *De Grey—Le Banc de Désolation* (made for TV) 1973; *Nada/The Nada*

Gang (also co-sc.), *Histoires insolites* (series of four TV films) 1974; *Une Partie de Plaisir/A Piece of Pleasure/Pleasure Party, Les Innocents aux Mains sales/Dirty Hands* (also sc.), *Les Magiciens* 1975; *Folies Bourgeoises* (also co-sc.) 1976; *Alice ou la Dernière Fugue/Alice or the Last Escapade* (also sc.) 1977; *Les Liens de Sang* (also co-sc.), *Violette Nozière/Violette* 1978; *Le Cheval d'Orgueil/The Horse of Pride/The Proud Ones* (also co-sc.) 1980; *Les Fantomes du Chapelier/The Hatmaker* (also sc.) 1982; *Les Sang des Autres/The Blood of Others* (Fr./Can.) 1984; *Poulet au Vinaigre/Cop au Vin* (also co-sc.) 1985; *Inspector Lavardin* (also co-sc.) 1986; *The Cry of the Owl, Masques* (also co-sc.) 1987; *Sale destin!* (act. only) 1987; *Une Affaire de femmes/Story of Women* (also sc.), *Alouette, je te plumerai* 1988; *Docteur M* (also sc.) 1989; *Jours tranquilles à Clichy/Quiet Days in Clichy* (also sc.) 1990; *Club Extinction, Madame Bovary* 1991; *Betty, L'Oeil de Vichy/The Eye of Vichy* (doc.) 1993; *L'Enfer* 1994; *The Ceremony, Judgment in Stone* 1996.

Chadwick, Helene. Actress. *b.* Nov. 25, 1897, Chadwicks, N.Y. *d.* 1940. Blonde leading lady of Hollywood silents, typically starred in romantic and domestic melodramas. Played supporting roles in a number of talkies. The first wife of director William WELLMAN, she died at 42 as a result of injuries she had incurred in a fall.

FILMS INCLUDE: *The Challenge* 1916; *The Iron Heart, The Angel Factory* 1917; *Naulahka* 1918; *An Adventure in Hearts, Girls, Caleb Piper's Girl, Solitary Sin, Heartsease* 1919; *Scratch My Back, Cupid the Cowpuncher, The Cup of Fury* 1920; *Godless Men, Made in Heaven, The Old Nest, Dangerous Curve Ahead* 1921; *The Glorious Fool, Yellow Men and Gold, The Dust Flower, The Sin Flood, Brothers Under the Skin* 1922; *Gimme, Quicksands, Reno* 1923; *The Masked Dancer, Why Men Leave Home, Love of Women, Her Own Free Will, The Border Legion, Trouping with Helen, The Dark Swan/The Black Swan* 1924; *The Recreation of Brian Kent, The Woman Hater, The Golden Cocoon* 1925; *Pleasures of the Rich, The Still Alarm, Hard Boiled, Dancing Days* 1926; *Stolen Pleasures, The Bachelor's Baby, The Rose of Kildare, Stage Kisses* 1927; *Women Who Dare, Modern Mothers, Say It with Sables, Confessions of a Wife* 1928; *Father and Son* 1929; *Men Are Like That* 1930; *Hell Bound* 1931; *Mary Burns Fugitive* 1935.

Chaffey, Don. Director. *b.* Aug. 5, 1917, in Hastings, England. *d.* 1990. Began his film career in 1944 as an assistant in the art department of Gainsborough Pictures and within two years was promoted to art director. In 1950 he directed his first feature, the children's film *The Mysterious Poacher,* for which he won a medal at the Venice Festival. He subsequently directed several other children's shorts and features, including Walt Disney's *The Three Lives of Thomasina* (1963), as well as many adult comedies and dramas. He is best remembered for the cult classic *Jason and the Argonauts* (1963), a fantasy based on Greek mythology with special effects by Ray Harryhausen. In the 80s he worked mostly for TV.

FEATURE FILMS: *The Mysterious Poacher* 1950; *The Case of the Missing Scene* 1951; *Skid Kids* 1953; *Time Is My Enemy* 1954; *The Secret Tent* 1956; *The Girl in the Picture, The Flesh Is Weak* 1957; *A Question of Adultery, The Man Upstairs* 1958; *Danger Within/Breakout* 1959; *Dentist in the Chair* 1960; *Nearly a Nasty Accident, Greyfriars Bobby, A Matter of WHO* 1961; *The Prince and the Pauper, The Webster Boy* 1962; *The Horse Without a Head, Jason and the Argonauts, The Three Lives of Thomasina* (US/UK) 1963; *A Jolly Bad Fellow/They All Died Laughing* 1964; *The Crooked Road* (also co-sc.; UK/Yug.) 1965; *One Million Years B.C.* 1966; *The Viking Queen* 1967; *A Twist of Sand* 1968; *Creatures the World Forgot* 1971; *Charley One-Eye* 1973; *Persecution/The Terror of Sheba* 1974; *Ride a Wild Pony* 1976; *Pete's Dragon* 1977; *The Magic of Lassie* 1978; *C.H.O.M.P.S.* 1979.

Chahine, Youssef (pronounced and also spelled **Yussef Shahin**). Director. Born on Jan. 25, 1926, in Alexandria, Egypt. The best known and most highly regarded Egyptian filmmaker. The son of a well-to-do lawyer, he was raised as a Christian and educated at Victoria College, an exclusive high school where studies were conducted in English. After a year at Alexandria University, he went to the US, where for two years he trained as an actor at the Pasadena Playhouse. Returning to Egypt in 1948, he entered the film industry and began directing in 1950. From the start he asserted himself as a skilled technician. Although his early films only occasionally veered far from the thematic concerns of commercial cinema, they were frequently distinguished by the director's eclectic personality and bold visual style. He is credited with having discovered Omar Sharif (then Michael Shalhoub), who made his debut in Chahine's *Struggle in the Valley* (1953). Chahine's career was by necessity affected by political events at home. During the heyday of Gamal Abdel Nasser's push for Pan-Arabism, for example, he was assigned to direct the nationalistic epic *El Naser Sallah-e-din/Salladin* (1963). But he continued handling strictly commercial ventures like *Sand of Gold* (1966), an Arabic version of the bullring drama *Blood and Sand.* After Egypt's stunning defeat by Israel in 1967, his films became increasingly political and social. Clues to his personality and state of mind can be found in his autobiographical film *Alexandria. . . Why?* (1978), winner of the Special Jury Prize at the 1979 Berlin Festival, and its sequel, *An Egyptian Story* (1982).

FILMS: *Father Amin* 1950; *Son of the Nile, The Great Clown* 1951; *Lady on the Train, Women Without Men* 1952; *Struggle in the Valley* 1953; *Devil of the Sahara/Devil of the Desert* 1954; *Struggle on the Pier/Black Waters* 1955; *You Are My Love* 1956; *Farewell to Your Love* 1957; *The Iron Gate/Cairo Station* (also act.), *Jamila the Algerian* 1958; *Forever Yours* 1959; *In Your Hands* 1960; *A Lover's Call, A Man in My Life* 1961; *Salladin/Salladin the Victorious* 1963; *Dawn of a New Day* 1964; *The Ring Seller* 1965; *Sand of Gold* 1966; *People of the Nile* (released in 1972) 1967; *The Land/The Earth* 1969; *The Choice* 1970; *The Sparrow* 1973; *The Return of the Prodigal Son* 1975; *Alexandria. . . Why?* 1978; *An Egyptian Story* 1982; *Adieu Bonaparte* (Egypt/Fr.) 1984; *Le Sixiéme Jour* 1986; *Sarikat Sayfeya* 1988; *Iskindiriah Kaman Oue Kaman, Alexandria—Now and Forever* 1990.

Chakiris, George. Actor, singer, dancer. Born Sept. 16, 1933, in Norwood, Oh., to parents of Greek origin. A one-time choirboy, he made his film debut in 1947 singing in the chorus of *Song of Love,* under the pseudonym George Kerris. He later attended a dance school in Hollywood and appeared as a dancer in such musical films as *Gentlemen Prefer Blondes* (1953), *White Christmas, The Girl Rush, There's No Business Like Show Business, Brigadoon* (all 1954), and *Meet Me in Las Vegas* (1956). In 1957 he made his debut as a dramatic actor and in 1961 acted, danced, and sang as Bernardo in *West Side Story,* a performance that won him that year's best supporting actor Academy Award. His subsequent film roles, in the US and abroad, have been for the most part unrewarding. In 1985 he joined the cast of the TV series 'Dallas.'

FILMS INCLUDE (as actor): *Under Fire* 1957; *West Side Story* 1961; *Two and Two Make Six/A Change of Heart/The Girl Swappers* (UK) 1962; *Diamond Head, La Ragazza di Bube/Bebo's Girl* (It./Fr.), *Kings of the Sun* 1963; *Flight from Ashiya* (US/Jap.), *633 Squadron* (US/UK) 1964; *The High Bright*

Sun/McGuire Go Home! (UK) 1965; *Paris brûle-t-il?/Is Paris Burning?* (Fr./US) 1966; *Les Demoiselles de Rochefort/The Young Girls of Rochefort* (Fr.) 1967; *Le Rouble à Deux Faces/The Day the Hot Line Got Hot* (Fr./Sp.) 1968; *The Big Cube* (US/Mex.) 1969; *Why Not Stay for Breakfast* (UK) 1980; *Jekyll and Hyde. . . Together Again* 1982; *Pale Blood* 1991.

Challis, Christopher. Director of photography. Born on Mar. 18, 1919, in London. *ed.* Wimbledon Coll. Entered the British film industry in his late teens as camera assistant on newsreels. After WW II service as cameraman with the RAF, he became a camera operator, then was promoted to lighting cameraman in 1947. His work, and especially his lush color photography, has been noted for its technical excellence.

FILMS INCLUDE: *The End of the River* 1947; *The Small Back Room* 1948; *Gone to Earth/The Wild Heart, The Elusive Pimpernel* 1950; *The Tales of Hoffman* 1951; *24 Hours of a Woman's Life* 1952; *Genevieve, The Story of Gilbert and Sullivan* 1953; *Malaga, The Flame and the Flesh* 1954; *Quentin Durward, Footsteps in the Fog, Oh Rosalinda* 1955; *The Battle of the River Plate/The Pursuit of the Graf Spee, The Spanish Gardener* 1956; *Ill Met By Moonlight/Night Ambush, Windom's Way* 1958; *Blind Date/Chance Meeting* 1959; *Sink the Bismarck, The Grass Is Greener* 1960; *HMS Defiant/Damn the Defiant* 1962; *An Evening with the Royal Ballet* (co-phot.), *The Victors* 1963; *The Long Ships, A Shot in the Dark* 1964; *Those Magnificent Men in Their Flying Machines* 1965; *Arabesque, Kaleidoscope* 1966; *Two for the Road* 1967; *Chitty Chitty Bang Bang* 1968; *Staircase* 1969; *The Private Life of Sherlock Holmes* 1970; *Villain, Mary Queen of Scots, Catch Me a Spy* 1971; *The Little Prince* 1974; *Mr. Quilp* 1975; *The Incredible Sarah* 1976; *The Deep* 1977; *Force 10 from Navarone* 1978; *The Mirror Crack'd* 1980; *Evil Under the Sun* 1982; *Top Secret!* 1984; *Steaming* 1985.

Chamberlain, Richard. Actor. Born George Richard Chamberlain, Mar. 31, 1935, in Beverly Hills, Calif. *ed.* Pomona Coll. He trained and hoped to become a painter, but after returning from a 16-month stint as an infantry company clerk in Korea, he chose acting instead. He studied voice at the Los Angeles Conservatory of Music and drama with Jeff Corey. A tall, blond, clean-cut leading man, he entered films early in the 60s, but it was on TV that he established himself as a popular star in the title role of the long-running 'Dr Kildare' series (1961–66). For several years he successfully tried to shake off the image associated with that role by tackling ambitious parts on the British stage (including 'Hamlet') and in British films. His popularity stretched into the 80s, when he scored well in such TV miniseries as 'Shogun' (1980) and 'The Thorn Birds' (1983). Chamberlain, who has a fine singing voice, has made several vocal recordings.

FILMS: *The Secret of the Purple Reef* 1960; *A Thunder of Drums* 1961; *Twilight of Honor* 1963; *Joy in the Morning* 1965; *Petulia* (US/UK) 1968; *The Madwoman of Chaillot* (UK) 1969; *Julius Caesar* (as Octavius; UK) 1970; *The Music Lovers* (as Tchaikovsky; UK) 1971; *Lady Caroline Lamb* (as Lord Byron; UK) 1972; *The Three Musketeers* (as Aramis; UK/Fr.), *The Towering Inferno* 1974; *The Four Musketeers* (as Aramis; UK/Fr.) 1975; *The Slipper and the Rose* (as Cinderella's Prince; UK), *The Count of Monte Cristo* (UK) 1976; *The Last Wave* (Austral.) 1977; *The Swarm* 1978; *Bells/Murder by Phone* (Can.) 1981; *King Solomon's Mines* 1985; *Allan Quatermain and the Lost City of Gold* 1987; *The Return of the Musketeers* 1989; *Bird of Prey* 1996.

Champion, Gower. Dancer, choreographer, actor, director. *b.* June 21, 1919, Geneva, Ill. *d.* 1980. Began dancing professionally in Los Angeles night spots at 15 and made his first appearance in a Broadway musical three years later. After returning from WW II service in 1945 he joined Marjorie Belcher, whom he had known in high school, to form the Gower and Bell dance team. They were married in 1947 and as Marge and Gower Champion rose to fame in film musicals of the 50s. Beginning in 1948 Gower branched out into stage and TV choreography and directing and in the 60s and 70s directed and choreographed such Broadway musical hits as 'Bye Bye Birdie,' 'Carnival,' 'Hello Dolly!,' 'I Do I Do,' 'The Happy Time,' and a revival of 'Irene.' He directed his first film, *My Six Loves,* in 1963. Earlier he had choreographed some of the dance numbers in the films in which he and Marge Champion appeared. They divorced in 1973. He died of a rare blood cancer just hours before the premiere of '42nd Street,' the musical that was to mark his triumphant return as a Broadway director.

FILMS INCLUDE: As dancer-actor—*Till the Clouds Roll By* 1946; *Words and Music* 1948; *Mr. Music* 1950; *Show Boat* 1951; *Lovely to Look At, Everything I Have Is Yours* (also co-chor.) 1952; *Give a Girl a Break* (also co-chor.) 1954; *Jupiter's Darling, Three for the Show* 1955. As choreographer—*The Girl Most Likely* 1957. As director—*My Six Loves* 1963; *Bank Shot* 1974.

Champion, Marge. Dancer, actress. Born Marjorie Celeste Belcher, on Sept. 2, 1921, in Hollywood, Calif. The daughter of a ballet coach of many screen stars, Ernest Belcher, and half sister of actress Lina BASQUETTE, she began dancing as a child and later became a model for the heroine of Walt Disney's *Snow White* and for the Blue Fairy in *Pinocchio.* As Marjorie Bell she appeared in three films of 1939. In 1945 she teamed up with dancer-choreographer Gower CHAMPION, whom she married in 1947. A capable dramatic actress as well as a dancer, she appeared with Gower in all his films of the 50s. In addition, she played straight roles in three nonmusical films of the late 60s. The Champions divorced in 1973. In 1975 she won an Emmy Award for the choreography of the TV special 'Queen of the Stardust Ballroom.' That same year she choreographed the dance numbers in John Schlesinger's film *The Day of the Locust.*

FILMS (for credits of the 50s see CHAMPION, Gower): As actress—*Honor of the West, The Story of Vernon and Irene Castle, Sorority House* 1939; *The Party, The Swimmer* 1968; *The Cockeyed Cowboys of Calico County* 1970. As choreographer—*The Day of the Locust* 1973; *Whose Life Is It Anyway?* 1981.

Champlain, Yves. See ALLÉGRET, Yves.

Chan, Jackie. Actor, director, screenwriter, producer. Born Chan Kwong-Sang on Apr. 7, 1954, in Hong Kong. One of Asia's most popular and durable film stars, he became an internationally known director-screenwriter. Born into poverty by immigrant parents, he moved with his family to Australia in 1960, where he was enrolled into the Chinese Opera Research Institute at age seven. There he spent ten years in physically demanding (and abusive) training for the Peking Opera, which included mime, acrobatics, and martial arts. With his training, he secured work as a child actor in more than twenty films. In the 70s, due to the international popularity of Asian martial arts films, Chan was able to work his way up from stuntman to bit-player to star. In *New Fists of Fury*, he was tapped as a possible successor to the late Bruce Lee. But Chan proved resistant to stereotyping and soon found his niche in a field he virtually created: comedy kung fu (*Half a Loaf of Kung-Fu*).

Chan contracted in 1980 with his new studio, Golden Harvest, to direct and write his own projects, debuting with *The Young Master*. He spent a brief and unhappy period in the US in the early 80s, resulting in the ill-conceived *Big Brawl* and the *Cannonball Run* pictures. Returning to Hong Kong, he created a series of action comedies, starting with *Project A* in 1983, and made appearances in a number of other films. All of these films spotlight Chan's physical grace, honed from years of training, and his unforced, eager-to-please charm. Most famously, these films contain elaborate set-pieces capped by death-defying stunts that Chan planned and executed by himself: falling handcuffed off a five-story clock tower (*Project A*), sliding down a live electrical wire (*Police Story*), rollerskating under a moving diesel truck (*Winners and Sinners*). One such stunt—a swing from a tree limb for *Armor of God*—nearly killed him. In addition to his acting and directing duties, Chan also trains his stunt crew and supervises the postproduction on his projects.

FILMS INCLUDE (as actor): *Little Tiger from Canton* 1971; *New Fist of Fury*, *Shaolin Wooden Men* 1976; *Killer Meteor*, *Snake-Crane Art of Shaolin* 1977; *To Kill with Intrigue*, *Half A Loaf of Kung-Fu*, *Magnificent Bodyguard*, *Snake in the Eagle's Shadow*, *Spiritual Kung-Fu*, *Dragon Fist*, *Drunken Monkey in a Tiger's Eye (Drunken Master)* 1978; *Fearless Hyena* 1979; *The Young Master* (also dir., co-sc.), *The Big Brawl* 1980; *The Cannonball Run* 1981; *Dragon Lord* (also dir., co-sc.) 1982; *Winners and Sinners*, *The Cannonball Run II*, *Project A* (also co-dir., co-sc.) 1983; *Wheels on Meals* 1984; *My Lucky Stars*, *Twinkle Twinkle Lucky Stars*, *First Mission*, *The Protector*, *Police Story* (also dir., co-sc.) 1985; *Armor of God* (also dir., co-s.) 1986; *Project A, Pt. II* (also dir., co-s.) 1987; *Dragons Forever*, *Police Story, Pt. II* (also dir., co-s.) 1988; *Mr. Canton and Lady Rose* (also dir., co-s.) 1989; *Island on Fire* 1991; *Twin Dragons*, *Armor of God II: Operation Condor* (also dir., co-s.), *Police Story III: Supercop* (also dir., co-s.) 1992; *City Hunter* 1993; *Rumble in the Bronx*, *Supercop* 1996; *First Strike* 1997.

Chandler, Chick. Actor. *b.* Jan. 18, 1905, in Kingston, N.Y. *d.* 1988. The son of an Army surgeon, he attended a military school but eventually chose acting and appeared in vaudeville and on the legitimate stage. Played some leads and numerous supporting parts, mostly comic, in a variety of Hollywood films.

FILMS INCLUDE: *Red Love* 1925; *Melody Cruise, Blood Money* 1933; *The Party's Over* 1934; *Murder on a Honeymoon, Circumstantial Evidence* 1935; *Tango, Three of a Kind* 1936; *Time Out for Romance, Born Reckless* 1937; *Alexander's Ragtime Band, Mr. Moto Takes a Chance, While New York Sleeps, Time Out for Murder* 1938; *Hotel for Women, Hollywood Cavalcade* 1939; *Swanee River, Tom Brown's School Days* 1940; *The Bride Came C.O.D.* 1941; *The Magnificent Dope, The Big Shot* 1942; *Action in the North Atlantic* 1943; *Seven Doors to Death, Irish Eyes Are Smiling* 1944; *Captain Eddie* 1945; *Mother Wore Tights* 1947; *Family Honeymoon* 1949; *The Great Rupert* 1950; *The Lost Continent* 1951; *Battle Cry* 1955; *The Naked Gun* 1956; *It's a Mad Mad Mad Mad World* 1963; *Nightmare in the Sun* 1964; *The Girl Who Knew Too Much* 1969.

Chandler, George. Actor. *b.* June 30, 1902, in Waukegan, Ill. *d.* 1985. *ed.* U. of Illinois. A former vaudevillian billed as "The Musical Nut," he played a variety of character parts in some 150 Hollywood films.

FILMS INCLUDE: *The Cloud Dodger* 1928; *The Kid's Clever* 1929; *The Floradora Girl, The Last Dance* 1930; *Man of the World* 1931; *Me and My Gal* 1932; *Bureau of Missing Persons* 1933; *The Country Doctor, Fury, Libeled Lady* 1936; *Nothing Sacred* 1937; *Jesse James* 1939; *The Return of Frank James, Arizona* 1940; *Western Union, Tobacco Road* 1941; *Isle of Missing Men* 1942; *The Ox-Bow Incident* 1943; *It Happened Tomorrow, Since You Went Away* 1944; *Captain Eddie* 1945; *Behind the Mask* 1946; *Dead Reckoning* 1947; *The Paleface* 1948; *The Happy Years* 1950; *Across the Wide Missouri* 1951; *Hans Christian Andersen* 1952; *The High and the Mighty* 1954; *Spring Reunion* 1957; *Dead Ringer* 1964; *Apache Uprising* 1966; *Buckskin* 1968; *One More Train to Rob* 1971; *Pickup on 101* 1972; *Escape to Witch Mountain* 1975; *Griffin and Phoenix* (TV movie) 1976.

Chandler, Helen. Actress. *b.* Feb. 1, 1906, Charleston, S.C. *d.* 1965. *ed.* a Charleston convent; Professional Children's School (N.Y.C.). A stage actress from childhood, she played teenagers and ingenues on Broadway before going to Hollywood in the late 20s. Memorable as the feminine lead in *Outward Bound* and *Dracula.* She retired from the screen in the mid-30s, returning briefly to the stage. Little heard of afterward. Screenwriter Cyril Hume and actor Bramwell FLETCHER were among her several husbands.

FILMS INCLUDE: *The Music Master, The Joy Girl* 1927; *Mother's Boy, Salute* 1929; *The Sky Hawk, Rough Romance. Outward Bound* 1930; *Dracula, Daybreak, Salvation Nell, The Last Flight, A House Divided* 1931; *Vanity Street, Behind Jury Doors* 1932; *Christopher Strong, Alimony Madness, Dance Hall Hostess, Goodbye Again* 1933; *Long Lost Father, Midnight Alibi, Unfinished Symphony* 1934; *It's a Bet* (UK) 1935; *Mr. Boggs Steps Out* 1938.

Chandler, Jeff. Actor. *b.* Ira Grossel, Dec. 15, 1918, Brooklyn, N.Y. *d.* 1961. After WW II service, he performed briefly in radio dramas, then made his film debut in 1947. His curly, prematurely gray hair and ruggedly handsome features gave him a distinctive look that made him a favorite with female audiences, although most of his roles were in male-oriented Westerns and action pictures. Played both romantic leads and exotic roles, three times portraying Cochise on the screen. He was nominated for an Oscar for one of these portrayals in *Broken Arrow* (1950). He died at 42 of blood poisoning following surgery.

FILMS: *Johnny O'Clock, The Invisible Wall, Roses Are Red* 1947; *Mr. Belvedere Goes to College, Sword in the Desert, Abandoned/Abandoned Woman* 1949; *Broken Arrow* (as Cochise), *Two Flags West, Deported* 1950; *Bird of Paradise, Smuggler's Island, Iron Man, Flame of Araby* 1951; *The Battle at Apache Pass* (again as Cochise), *Red Ball Express, Yankee Buccaneer, Because of You* 1952; *The Great Sioux Uprising, East of Sumatra* 1953; *War Arrow, Taza, Son of Cochise* (cameo, as Cochise), *Yankee Pasha, Sign of the Pagan* 1954; *Foxfire, Female on the Beach, The Spoilers* 1955; *Toy Tiger, Away All Boats, Pillars of the Sky* 1956; *Drango, The Tattered Dress, Jeanne Eagels* 1957; *Man in the Shadow, The Lady Takes a Flyer, Raw Wind in Eden* 1958; *Stranger in My Arms, Thunder in the Sun, The Jayhawkers, Ten Seconds to Hell* 1959; *A Story of David* (as King David; orig. made for TV), *The Plunderers* 1960; *Return to Peyton Place* 1961; *Merrill's Marauders* 1962.

Chandler, Lane. Actor. *b.* Robert Lane Oakes, June 4, 1899, Culbertson, Mont. *d.* 1972. *ed.* Montana Wesleyan Coll. Tall and husky, he worked as a garage mechanic in Los Angeles while awaiting an opportunity to break into films. Began playing bits in 1924 and was starring in low-budget Paramount Westerns by 1927. With the coming of sound he was relegated to second leads in A features but went on playing occasional leads in Westerns. From the early 40s, only in character parts.

FILMS INCLUDE: *Open Range* 1927; *Legion of the Condemned, Love and Learn, The First Kiss, Red Hair, The Big Killing* 1928; *The Studio Murder Mystery, The Single Standard* 1929; *Rough Waters, Lightning Express* (serial) 1930; *The Reckless Rider, The Hurricane Horseman* 1931; *Cheyenne Cyclone, Wyoming Whirlwind* 1932; *Fra Diavolo, Sagebrush*

Trail 1933; *Texas Tornado* 1934; *Hearts in Bondage* 1936; *The Lone Ranger* (serial), *Heroes of the Alamo* 1938; *The Man in the Iron Mask* 1939; *North West Mounted Police* 1940; *Pride of the Yankees, Reap the Wild Wind* 1942; *Casanova Brown, Laura* 1944; *Along Came Jones* 1945; *Duel in the Sun* 1946; *Pursued* 1947; *Samson and Delilah* 1949; *Montana* 1950; *Thunder Over the Plains* 1953; *Prince of Players* 1955; *Quantrill's Raiders* 1958; *Requiem for a Gunfighter* 1965.

Chandler, Raymond. Novelist, screenwriter. *b.* July 22, 1888, Chicago. *d.* 1959. Spent his youth in England, where he attended Dulwich College and began a career as a journalist. Following WW I service, he returned to the US and went into business. In the early 30s he began selling short stories to magazines and before long became a highly successful writer of mystery novels. His favorite protagonist, private eye Philip Marlowe, has been portrayed in films by such stars as Humphrey Bogart, Dick Powell, Robert Montgomery, Elliot Gould, and Robert Mitchum. Films adapted by others from his novels are *The Falcon Takes Over* (from *Farewell My Lovely*) 1942; *Time to Kill* (from *The High Window*) 1943; *Murder My Sweet* (from *Farewell My Lovely*) 1945; *The Big Sleep* 1946 and 1978; *Lady in the Lake, The Brasher Doubloon* (from *The High Window*) 1947; *Marlowe* (from *The Little Sister*) 1969; *The Long Goodbye* 1973; and *Farewell My Lovely* 1975. In addition, Chandler wrote a number of solid screenplays for Hollywood films, mostly in collaboration.

FILMS (screenplays): *Double Indemnity, And Now Tomorrow* 1944; *The Unseen* 1945; *The Blue Dahlia* (from own story) 1946; *Strangers on a Train* 1951.

Chaney, Lon. Actor. *b.* Alonso Chaney, Apr. 1, 1883, Colorado Springs, Colo. *d.* 1930. The son of deaf-mute parents, he learned from childhood to communicate through pantomime and facial expression. As a boy, he worked at Colorado Springs's opera house as a stagehand, scene painter, and property boy, occasionally playing bit parts. At 17 he went on the road as an actor with a play he wrote with his brother. After several not-too-successful touring seasons in musical comedy, he went to Hollywood in 1912 and began one of the most legendary acting careers in film history. Between 1913 and 1930 he played more than 150 widely diverse film roles, frequently villainous, sometimes bizarre and macabre, almost always pathetic and moving. He was known as "The Man of a Thousand Faces" for his ability to play an endless variety of parts and for his mastery of the art of makeup (he wrote the entry on makeup for one edition of the *Encyclopedia Britannica*).

Chaney's disguises often involved physical hardship: for *The Penalty* (1920), in which he played a legless criminal, he had his legs bound tightly behind him, and walked and jumped on his knees; to feel Quasimodo's agony in *The Hunchback of Notre Dame* (1923), he wore a hump weighing 40 pounds plus a harness weighing 30. Among his many other memorable roles were those in *He Who Gets Slapped, The Unholy Three, The Phantom of the Opera* and *Tell It to the Marines.* Some of his best films of the late 20s were directed by Tod BROWNING.

In 1915 Chaney directed six films for Universal, also writing the screenplays for two of them. At the height of his prestige, in the 20s, he was often instrumental in decisions involving the production and direction of his films. Chaney shunned the transition to sound but in 1930 was finally persuaded to play in a sound remake of *The Unholy Three.* The film was a success, but just one month after its release Chaney died of bronchial cancer. His fascinating life story was told in the 1957 film *Man of a Thousand Faces,* starring James CAGNEY. His son, Lon CHANEY, Jr., has done many horror roles in films.

FILMS INCLUDE (complete from 1916; features complete from 1914): *Poor Jake's Demise* (first credited role), *The Sea Urchin, The Trap, Back to Life, Almost an Actress, Bloodhounds of the North* 1913; *The Lie, The Honor of the Mounted, Discord and Harmony, The Embezzler, The Lamb the Woman the Wolf, The Forbidden Room, The Oubliette, Richelieu, The Pipes of Pan, Lights and Shadows, A Night of Thrills* 1914; *The Star of the Sea, Threads of Fate, The Measure of a Man, Such Is Life, The Grind, The Stool Pigeon* (dir. only), *For Cash* (dir. only), *The Oyster Dredger* (dir., sc. only), *The Violin Maker* (also dir.), *The Trust* (also dir.), *Mountain Justice, The Chimney's Secret* (also dir., sc.), *The Fascination of the Fleur de Lis, A Mother's Atonement, The Millionaire Paupers, Father and the Boys, Stronger Than Death* 1915; *The Grip of Jealousy, Tangled Hearts, The Gilded Spider, Bobbie of the Ballet, The Grasp of Greed, The Mark of Cain, If My Country Should Call, The Place Beyond the Winds, The Price of Silence* 1916; *The Piper's Price, Hell Morgan's Girl, The Girl in the Checkered Coat, The Mask of Love, The Flashlight, A Doll's House* (as Nils Krogstad), *Fires of Rebellion, The Rescue, Pay Me/Vengeance of the West, Triumph, Anything Once, Bondage, The Scarlet Car* 1917; *The Grand Passion, Broadway Love, The Kaiser—Beast of Berlin* (as Admiral Alfred von Tirpitz), *Fast Company, A Broadway Scandal, Riddle Gawne, That Devil Bateese, The Talk of the Town, Danger—Go Slow* 1918; *The Wicked Darling, False Faces, A Man's Country, Paid in Advance, The Miracle Man, When Bearcat Went Dry, Victory* 1919; *Daredevil Jack* (serial), *Treasure Island* (as blind pirate Pew), *The Gift Supreme, Nomads of the North, The Penalty* 1920; *Outside the Law, For Those We Love, Bits of Life, The Ace of Hearts* 1921; *The Trap, Voices of the City/The Night Rose, Flesh and Blood, The Light in the Dark, Shadows, Oliver Twist* (as Fagin), *Quincy Adams Sawyer, A Blind Bargain* 1922; *All the Brothers Were Valiant, While Paris Sleeps, The Shock, The Hunchback of Notre Dame* (as Quasimodo) 1923; *The Next Corner, He Who Gets Slapped* 1924; *The Monster, The Unholy Three, The Phantom of the Opera* (title role), *The Tower of Lies* 1925; *The Black Bird, The Road to Mandalay* 1926; *Tell It to the Marines, Mr. Wu, The Unknown, Mockery, London After Midnight* 1927; *The Big City, Laugh Clown Laugh, While the City Sleeps, West of Zanzibar* 1928; *Where East Is East, Thunder* 1929; *The Unholy Three* (sound remake of 1925 silent) 1930.

Chaney, Lon, Jr. Actor. *b.* Creighton Chaney, Feb. 10, 1906, in Oklahoma City, *d.* 1973. The son of Lon CHANEY, he trained to become a plumber. He began his screen career in 1932, initially using his real name, which he changed to Lon Chaney, Jr., in 1935. His career was undistinguished until 1940, when he impressed critics as Lennie in *Of Mice and Men.* In the 40s he played a succession of monster roles in horror films, including Frankenstein's monster, Dracula, the Mummy, and several times as the Wolf Man. Big and hulking, with impassive, craggy features, he appeared in about 150 films, mostly horror pictures and Westerns, typically as a villain or some other heavy.

FILMS INCLUDE: *The Last Frontier* (serial), *Girl Crazy* 1932; *Scarlet River* 1933; *Sixteen Fathoms Deep* 1934; *Accent on Youth, Captain Hurricane* 1935; *Ace Drummond* (serial), *The Singing Cowboy* 1936; *Secret Agent X-9* (serial), *Second Honeymoon, Slave Ship* 1937; *Alexander's Ragtime Band, Submarine Patrol, Mr. Moto's Gamble* 1938; *Jesse James, Frontier Marshal, Union Pacific* 1939; *Of Mice and Men, One Million B.C., North West Mounted Police* 1940; *Man-Made Monster, Billy the Kid, The Wolf Man* (title role) 1941; *The Ghost of Frankenstein* (as the Monster), *The Mummy's Tomb* 1942; *Eyes of the Underworld, Frankenstein Meets the Wolf Man* (as the Wolf Man), *Son of Dracula* (title role), *Crazy House* (cameo), *Calling Dr. Death* 1943; *Weird Woman, Cobra Woman, Ghost Catchers, The Mummy's Ghost, Dead Man's Eyes* 1944; *House of Frankenstein* (as the Wolf Man), *The Mummy's Curse, The Frozen Ghost, Strange Confession, House of Dracula* (as the Wolf Man), *The Daltons Ride Again, Pillow of Death* 1945; *My Favorite Brunette* 1947; *Albuquerque, Abbott and Costello Meet Frankenstein* (as the Wolf Man), *Sixteen Fathoms Deep* 1948; *Captain China* 1949; *Only the Valiant, Behave Yourself* 1951; *High Noon, Springfield Rifle, The Black Castle* 1952; *A Lion Is in the Streets* 1953; *The Boy from Oklahoma, Casanova's Big Night* 1954; *Big House U.S.A., Not as a Stranger, I Died a Thousand Times* 1955; *The Indestructible Man, Pardners* 1956; *Cyclops* 1957; *The Defiant Ones* 1958; *La Casa del Terror/Face of the Screaming Werewolf* (Mex.), *The Devil's Messenger* (as the Devil, Sw./US), *The Alligator People* 1959; *The Phantom* 1961; *The Haunted Palace* 1963; *Law of the Lawless, Witchcraft* (UK) 1964; *Town Tamer* 1965; *Apache Uprising, Johnny Reno* 1966; *Welcome to Hard Times, Dr. Terror's Gallery of Horrors/The Blood Suckers* 1967; *The Frontiersman, Buckskin* 1968; *A Time to Run* 1970; *Dracula vs. Frankenstein* 1973.

change-over. The process of switching from one projector to another during the exhibition of a multireel film so that there is no pause in the projection. The standard 35 mm magazine contains 2,000 feet for a running time of 20 minutes, but change-overs may occur at intervals of up to 60 minutes, depending on the type of equipment. In order to achieve a smooth transition from one projector to the other, CUE MARKS appear at the upper right-hand corner of the screen to alert the projectionist that the end of the reel is approaching and that he must switch on the alternate machine. Automatic change-over systems are slowly replacing the traditional procedure.

changing bag. A lightproof, closely woven, satin-lined black bag with two close-fitting sleeves which permits the loading and unloading of film magazines even in direct sunlight. The magazine is inserted through a zippered opening. The cameraman, or more often his assistant, can then handle the loading or unloading through the sleeves, which come with elastic cuffs. The changing bag is an invaluable accessory on locations distant from a darkroom; not only does it prevent the fogging of film due to open-air loading, but it is also useful in investigating the causes of a camera jam without ruining exposed or yet-to-be-exposed film stock. See also CASSETTE.

Channing, Carol. A comic actress, entertainer. Born on Jan. 31, 1921, in Seattle, the daughter of a well-known Christian Science lecturer. Exuberant, saucer-eyed entertainer of the American stage, nightclubs, TV, and occasional movies. She dropped out of Bennington College in 1941 to start a professional career that culminated with her memorable Broadway portrayal of Lorelei Lee in Anita Loos's 'Gentlemen Prefer Blondes,' in which she sang in her inimitable raspish voice 'Diamonds Are a Girl's Best Friend.' The song remains her trademark. She later starred in several other Broadway productions, including 'Show Girl' and 'Hello Dolly!' and on numerous TV shows. She has appeared in only a handful of films but was nominated for a best supporting actress Oscar for her performance in *Thoroughly Modern Millie* (1967). In 1995, after an extensive national tour and to the delight of theater-goers everywhere, Channing returned to Broadway as Dolly Levi in 'Hello Dolly!' with a record-breaking number of performances, receiving a special Tony Award for her lifetime of achievements.

FILMS: *Paid in Full* 1950; *The First Traveling Saleslady* 1956; *Thoroughly Modern Millie* 1967; *Skidoo* 1968; *Shinbone Alley* (v/o) 1971; *Sgt. Pepper's Lonely Hearts Club Band* (cameo) 1978; *Thumbelina* (v/o) 1994.

Channing, Stockard. Actress. Born Susan Stockard, on Feb. 13, 1944, in New York City. The daughter of a wealthy shipping executive, she was educated at private schools and became interested in dramatics while attending Radcliffe College. After graduation, she appeared for a while with the Theater Company of Boston and with various repertory groups while trying unsuccessfully to crash Broadway. Things began turning around for her in the early 70s, when she went to Los Angeles to appear in a West Coast stage production of 'Two Gentlemen of Verona.' After playing bits in a couple of films and leads on TV, she landed the lead feminine role in Mike Nichols's *The Fortune* (1975) and won rave reviews for holding her own opposite male stars Jack Nicholson and Warren Beatty in this offbeat comedy. She was 33 when she played a high-school senior in *Grease* (1978). After starring in her own TV series in 1979–80, she returned to the stage, winning the admiration of critics and a Tony Award for 'Joe Egg' in 1985. Her film career in the 80s was less spectacular, being limited to intermittent appearances, mostly in lower-budget productions. She has been married four times.

FILMS: *The Hospital* (bit) 1971; *Up the Sandbox* (bit) 1972; *The Fortune* 1975; *Sweet Revenge/Dandy the All American Girl, The Big Bus* 1976; *The Cheap Detective, Grease* 1978; *Silent Victory, The Fish That Saved Pittsburgh* 1979; *Safari 3000* 1982; *Without a Trace* 1983; *Heartburn, The Men's Club* 1986; *A Time of Destiny* 1988; *Staying Together* 1989; *Meet the Applegates* 1991; *Married To It* 1992; *Six Degrees of Separation* 1993; *Smoke, To Wong Foo Thanks for Everything Julie Newmar* 1995; *First Wives Club* (unbilled cameo), *Moll Flanders, Up Close and Personal* 1996.

Chaplin, Charlie (Sir Charles Spencer Chaplin). Actor, director, producer, screenwriter, composer. *b.* Apr. 16, 1889, London. *d.* 1977. The son of music hall entertainers who separated when he was one year old, he accompanied his mother on her frequent travels, absorbing the stage atmosphere from a tender age. At five he took his first turn on the stage under unhappy circumstances, when his mother's voice cracked in the middle of a singing performance and he was rushed onstage to take over. This was the beginning of the end of his mother's career. Shortly afterward his father died, and Charlie and his older half brother Sydney CHAPLIN suddenly found themselves hungry little urchins roaming the streets of cockney London while their mother was suffering a complete breakdown. The boys, who resorted to dancing on the streets and passing a hat for pennies, were placed in an orphanage for destitute children.

Thanks to his mother's connections, however, Charlie was able to join a troupe of child dancers, the Eight Lancashire Lads. He was now eight and a professional performer. Later he played child parts in London stage plays, including the opening show at the Hippodrome in 1900 and the premiere performance of 'Peter Pan' in 1904. When he was 17 he took the first important step of his career when he joined the successful Fred Karno company, where Sydney had already become established as a popular comic. The Karno company consisted of several troupes that performed throughout Britain and abroad, and it was with Karno that Chaplin acquired his basic comic skills and the rudiments of the style that was to be immortalized in his films.

Chaplin went on a US tour with one of the troupes in 1910 and again in 1912, and it was during the latter tour that Mack SENNETT, the boss of Keystone, caught a glimpse of him playing a drunken reveler in the show 'A Night in a London Music Hall.' In December 1913, Chaplin joined Keystone, but his first film, *Making a Living,* in which he played a smooth villain, wearing a high hat, a frock coat, a drooping mustache, and a monocle, disappointed Sennett. Chaplin's performance was adequate although it hardly suggested the emergence of the greatest screen clown of all time. But it was then that the now-famous Chaplin screen character began to metamorphose.

Already in his second film, *Kid Auto Races at Venice,* he is seen wearing a bowler, baggy trousers, and a mashed mustache and using a cane as an indispensable prop. In early films for Keystone he played mainly in support of such established comedy stars as Ford STERLING, Chester CONKLIN, Fatty ARBUCKLE, and Mabel NORMAND. The films were directed by Henry LEHRMAN, Mabel Normand, Sennett himself, and others. A veteran of 11 one- and two-reel films after less than three months as a screen actor, Chaplin was seized with an urge to direct. He assisted Miss Normand with the direction of his 12th film and wrote and directed solo his 13th, *Caught in the Rain.* With the creative control he had now acquired, he began shaping and refining the lovable, naïve character of Charlie the Tramp.

Chaplin made 35 films during his year at Keystone, many of which he also wrote and directed. It was a formative year of experimentation and discovery during which he learned to adapt all he had learned on the music hall stage to the medium of film. By the end of the year he was a popular screen comedian, successful enough to demand and receive $1,250 a week when he signed with Essanay in 1915, up from the $175 he had been earning at Keystone, plus a $10,000 bonus. The Essanay period saw the full bloom of Charlie's screen character, the invincible vagabond, the resilient little fellow with an eye for beauty and a pretense of elegance who stood up heroically and pathetically against overwhelming odds and somehow triumphed.

The final touches were applied in *The Tramp,* released in April of 1915 and generally accepted as Chaplin's first masterpiece. Charlie was now making fewer films with an increasing attention to quality. At the end of his first year with Essanay his contract was renewed at $5,000 a week. In the middle of 1916 he moved on to Mutual, where he was offered an unprecedented salary of $10,000 a week plus a bonus of $150,000. The contract called for 12 films yearly and promised him complete creative control. The Mutual period was highly creative and inventive; it is memorable for such gems as *The Rink, Easy Street, The Cure, The Immigrant,* and *The Adventurer.* Chaplin proved himself an inmitable pantomimist capable of moving his audiences from laughter to tears with a subtle gesture or a bold sweep of movement, as graceful as a ballet dancer.

In 1918 he signed a contract with First National for more than a million dollars for just eight two-reel films. It was for First National that Chaplin made his famous parody of war in the trenches, *Shoulder Arms* (1918), and *The Kid* (1921), his even more famous first feature-length film. The latter was hailed as a masterpiece and was second only to *The Birth of a Nation* in box-office returns up to that time. *The Kid* revealed Chaplin's growing tendency to inject sentiment into his films, a tendency that would later result in bittersweet pathos, an echo of the haunting memories of his Dickensian childhood. Chaplin was by now an international celebrity, known and beloved the world over.

In 1919, Chaplin founded United Artists Corporation in partnership with Mary PICKFORD, Douglas FAIRBANKS, and D. W. GRIFFITH. Three years later he made a triumphant tour of Europe, during which he was amazed and delighted by the extent of his popularity abroad—he later described his impressions in the book *My Wonderful Visit* (1922). In 1923, after his return, he directed *A Woman of Paris,* his only silent film in which he did not star (he did play a walk-on). Although the film solidified Chaplin's reputation as a director, it was not a commercial success. His next film, *The Gold Rush* (1925), is considered by many to be his greatest masterpiece, a tender and poetic culmination of his film art, containing some of the most memorable moments of comedy and pathos in his entire body of work. The first Academy Award presentation (1927–28) awarded him a special Oscar "for versatility and genius in writing, acting, directing, and producing *The Circus,*" his next film. He never won a regular Academy Award.

The coming of sound presented a problem for Chaplin, the essence of whose art was pantomime. He decided to ignore the technical phenomenon by simply making his next project, *City Lights* (1931), a silent film. His only concession to the sound track were effects and a musical score, which he composed and conducted himself, a practice he was to follow in his subsequent films. Despite warnings from his friends in the industry, *City Lights* was an unqualified commercial success as well as an artistic triumph. Five years passed before he presented his next film, *Modern Times,* again a silent and another hit.

Despite his continued success and popularity, Chaplin was evidently uncomfortable with the requirements of the feature-length format and the inevitability of dialogue. His sound-era features were spaced years apart and became more and more appreciated for vignette highlights and less and less for their total impact as fully integrated productions. In *The Great Dictator* (1940) he poked fun at fascism, playing a dual role as both a Jewish barber and a grotesque caricature of Hitler. It was his last appearance as the little tramp and to many of his fans the end of an era in film comedy. Bitterness rather than fun characterized his next film, *Monsieur Verdoux* (1947), a serious pacifist appeal disguised as a comedy-of-errors variation on the Bluebeard theme. And pathos, not laughs, was at the essence of *Limelight* (1952).

Although almost from the start of his career Chaplin was a beloved international celebrity, with fame came notoriety, press scrutiny, and incredible outbursts from moral purists and political conservatives. The first outcry came during WW I, when Chaplin was attacked for not returning to Europe for service in the armed forces. As it turned out, he did volunteer but was turned down for medical reasons. He was also a tireless campaigner for the sale of US War Bonds. Then there was the moral indignation over his marital affairs and his penchant for lovely teenagers. His first wife was Mildred Harris, a 16-year-old film extra when he married her in 1918. They divorced two years later. His second bride was yet another 16-year-old beauty, Lolita MacMurray, who changed her name to Lita Grey, hoping for a career in films. Chaplin was 35 when he married her in 1924. The marriage lasted three years and produced two sons, actors Charles Chaplin Jr. (1925–1968), who appeared in several films, and Sydney CHAPLIN. Their parents' bitter and prolonged divorce case captured headlines and ended in a million-dollar settlement. Chaplin was 44 when in 1936 he married secretly, at sea, the 19-year-old Paulette GODDARD. Their marriage was not revealed until 1936, the year *Modern Times* was released, starring Miss Goddard, who also co-starred in Chaplin's next film, *The Great Dictator.* They were divorced in 1942.

Shortly before that liaison ended, the newspapers were filled with lurid details of a paternity suit brought against Chaplin by Joan Barry, an aspiring actress. He was found innocent of violating the Mann Act (transporting a minor across state lines for immoral purposes) but was ruled the father of the child. Amid the clamor of the court case, Chaplin finally settled on a permanent relationship with his fourth wife, Oona O'Neill, the daughter of playwright Eugene O'Neill. They were married in 1943 despite her father's strong disapproval. Miss O'Neill was 18, Chaplin 54.

Chaplin's political critics were even more vociferous than his moral detractors. The fact that in 42 years of US residence he never acquired American citizenship was broadly resented, and the themes of such films as the assembly-line satire *Modern Times* and the pacifist *Monsieur Verdoux* did not endear him to conservatives. Rumors of his Communist leanings, which began during WW II when he was among the first to advocate the opening of a second front in Russia, intensified into a smear campaign in 1947 with the release of *Monsieur Verdoux.* Spearheaded by the American Legion, pressure groups organized to boycott the film and were successful in limiting its circulation. It was the dawn of the McCarthy era, and Chaplin was subpoenaed by the House Un-American Activities Committee to testify on his alleged Communist affiliations. He wired back: "I am not a Communist; neither have I ever joined any political party or organization in my life. I am what you call a peacemonger." His protestations were in vain, and there were demands for his deportation. In 1952, when Chaplin and Oona were in mid-Atlantic on their way to the London premiere of *Limelight,* word came that the attorney general had instructed immigration authorities to deny Chaplin a re-entry visa unless he submitted to an inquiry of his moral worth.

Chaplin vowed never to return to America, the country that had made him rich, famous, and unhappy. He settled down in Vevey, Switzerland, in the splendor of a large estate with Oona and their eight children, including Geraldine CHAPLIN who later developed into a capable leading lady in films. His next film, *A King in New York* (1957), made in England, was again more a product of bitterness than of genius, a series of unfunny pokes at the American way of life. Chaplin's eagerly awaited comeback film after a long respite, *The Countess from Hong Kong,* made in England with American money in 1966, was even more disappointing. Critics panned it as uninspired and old-fashioned, and the public stayed away, despite such box-office draws as Marlon Brando and Sophia Loren in the lead roles.

In 1972, shortly after reaffirming his determination never to step on American soil, Chaplin returned to the US to accept a second special Academy Award, for "the incalculable effect he has had on making motion pictures the art form of this century." He was enthusiastically received at the Oscar ceremony and at a party thrown in his honor later on at New York's Philharmonic Hall. People cheered him everywhere. "This is my renaissance," he said. "I'm being born again." Early in 1975, Chaplin, the former London street urchin, was knighted by the Queen. He was now addressed as Sir Charles. Several months after Chaplin's death, his body mysteriously disappeared from the village cemetery in Vevey. It was later recovered.

There is hardly a superlative in the English language regarding greatness which wasn't bestowed on Charlie Chaplin during his lifetime by fellow artists and critics. George Bernard Shaw called him "the only genius developed in motion pictures." Mack Sennett thought of him as "the greatest artist who ever lived." And though his later work was flawed and his achievements as a director are contestable, the admiration for Chaplin the actor, the mimic, the eloquent comedian, is universal. His *My Autobiography* (1964) is a valuable account of the man's life but tells little of the artist's work or his inner world. The definitive book on Chaplin is still Theodore Huff's *Charles Chaplin* (1951).

FILMS: As actor—at Keystone: *Making a Living, Kid Auto Races at Venice, Mabel's Strange Predicament, Between Showers, A Film Johnnie, Tango Tangles, His Favorite Pastime, Cruel Cruel Love, The Star Boarder, Mabel at the Wheel, Twenty Minutes of Love, The Knockout, Tillie's Punctured Romance* 1914. As actor-director-writer—*Caught in a Cabaret* (act., sc., co-dir. with Mabel Normand), *Caught in the Rain, A Busy Day, The Fatal Mallet, Her Friend the Bandit, Mabel's Busy Day, Mabel's Married Life* (last three act., sc., co-dir. with Mabel Normand), *Laughing Gas, The Property Man, The Face on the Barroom Floor, Recreation, The Masquerader, His New Profession, The Rounders, The New Janitor, Those Love Pangs, Dough and Dynamite, Gentlemen of Nerve, His Musical Career, His Trysting Place, Getting Acquainted, His Prehistoric Past* 1914. At Essanay: *His New Job, A Night Out, The Champion, In the Park, A Jitney Elopement, The Tramp, By the Sea, Work, A Woman, The Bank, Shanghaied, A Night in the Show* 1915; *Carmen, Police* 1916; *Triple Trouble* (compiled from old, unused Chaplin material) 1918. At Mutual: *The Floorwalker, The Fireman, The Vagabond, One A.M., The Count, The Pawnshop, Behind the Screen, The Rink* 1916; *Easy Street, The Cure, The Immigrant, The Adventurer* 1917. At First National: *A Dog's Life, The Bond* (propaganda film made for the Liberty Loan Committee), *Shoulder Arms* 1918; *Sunnyside, A Day's Pleasure* 1919; *The Nut* (cameo in a Fairbanks film), *The Kid, The Idle Class* 1921; *Pay Day* 1922; *The Pilgrim* 1923. For United Artists: *A Woman of Paris* (also prod., cameo part only) 1923; *The Gold Rush* (also prod.) 1925; reissued 1942 with music and commentary by Chaplin; *The Circus* (also prod.) 1928; reissued 1969; *City Lights* (also prod., mus.) 1931; reissued 1950; *Modern Times* (also prod., mus.) 1936; *The Great Dictator* (also prod., mus.) 1940; *Monsieur Verdoux* (also prod., mus.) 1947; *Limelight* (also prod., mus., songs, chor.) 1952. In the UK: *A King in New York* (also prod., mus.) 1957; *The Countess from Hong Kong* (also mus.; cameo role) 1967.

Chaplin, Geraldine. Actress. Born on July 31, 1944, in Santa Monica, Calif. Charlie CHAPLIN's firstborn from his marriage to Oona O'Neill, she was educated in Swiss schools and began her professional career as a dancer with the Royal Ballet in England. Lean, pallid, and solemn, she has been playing leads in international films since the mid-60s, doing some of her best work for her longtime companion, director Carlos SAURA.

FILMS: *Limelight* (bit, as a child; US) 1952; *Par un Beau Matin d'Eté* (Fr.) 1964; *Doctor Zhivago* (US) 1965; *Andremo in Città* 1966; *Stranger in the House/Cop-Out* (UK), *The Countess from Hong Kong* (bit; UK), *J'ai tué Raspoutine/I Killed Rasputin* (Fr./It./Ger.), *Peppermint frappé* (Sp.) 1967; *Stress es tres tres* (Sp.) 1968; *La Madriguera/Honeycomb* (also co-sc.; Sp.) 1969; *El Jardin de las Delicias/The Garden of Delights, The Hawaiians* (US) 1970; *Sur un Arbre perché* (Fr.) 1971; *La Casa sin Fronteras* (Sp.), *Zero Population Growth/Z.P.G.* (UK), *Innocent Bystanders* (UK) 1972; *Aña y los Lobos/Ana and the Wolves, Y el projimo?* 1973; *Verflucht dies Amerika!/La Banda de Jaider* (Sp./Ger.), *The Three Musketeers* (as Anne of Austria; UK) 1974; *The Four Musketeers* (as Anne of Austria; UK), *Nashville* (US) 1975; *Buffalo Bill and the Indians* (as Annie Oakley; US); *Cria Cuervos/Cria!* (Sp.), *Scrim* 1976; *Welcome to L.A.* (US), *Elisa Vida mìa/Elisa My Love* (Sp.), *Noroit* (Fr.), *In Memoriam* (Sp.), *Une Page d'Amour* (Belg./Fr.), *Roseland* (US) 1977; *Los Ojos Vendados* (Sp.), *A Wedding* (US), *Remember My Name* (US), *L'Adoption* (Fr.), *The Masked Bride* 1978; *Mama cumple Cien Años/Mama Turns 100* (Sp.), *La Viuda de Montiel/Montiel's Widow* (Chile), *Mais ou et donc Ormecar* (Fr.) 1979; *Le Voyage en Douce* (Fr.), *The Mirror Crack'd* (UK) 1980; *Les Uns et les autres/Bolero* (Fr.) 1981; *La Vie est un Roman/Life Is a Bed of Roses* (Fr.) 1983; *L'Amour par Terre/Love on the Ground* (Fr.) 1984; *White Mischief* (UK) 1987; *The Moderns* (UK) 1988; *Je veux rentrer a la maison* (Fr.), *The Return of the Musketeers* 1989; *The Children* 1990; *Buster's Bedroom* 1991; *Chaplin* 1992; *Age of Innocence* 1993; *Words Upon the Windowpane* 1994; *Home for the Holidays* 1995; *Cousin Bette* 1997.

Chaplin, Saul. Composer, arranger, musical director, producer. Born Saul Kaplan, on Feb. 19, 1912, in Brooklyn, N.Y. *ed.* NYU. A songwriter from age 20, he composed for Tin Pan Alley, vaudeville, and the Broadway stage. In films since the late 30s. He won Academy Awards for his collaborations on the scoring and orchestration of *An American in Paris* (1951), *Seven Brides for Seven Brothers* (1954), and *West Side Story* (1961). Producing since the early 60s.

FILMS INCLUDE: *Manhattan Merry-Go-Round* 1937; *Argentine Nights* 1940; *Crazy House* 1943; *Meet Me on Broadway* 1946; *The Countess of Monte Cristo* 1948; *On the Town* (vocal arrangements only) 1949; *Jolson Sings Again* (musical advisor only), *Summer Stock* 1950; *An American in Paris* 1951; *Lovely to Look At* 1952; *Kiss Me Kate* 1953; *Give a Girl a Break, Seven Brides for Seven Brothers* 1954; *High Society* 1956; *Les Girls* (assoc. prod. only) 1957; *Merry Andrew* (also assoc. prod.) 1958; *Can-Can* (assoc. prod. only) 1960; *West Side Story* 1961; *The Sound of Music* (assoc. prod. only) 1965; *Star!* (prod. only) 1968; *Man of La Mancha* (assoc. prod. only) 1972; *That's Entertainment Part 2* (co-prod. only) 1976.

Chaplin, Syd(ney). Actor. *b.* Mar. 17, 1885, Cape Town, South Africa. *d.* 1965. The half brother of Charlie CHAPLIN, he too grew up in abject poverty on the sidewalks of London. They shared the misery of hunger and orphanage and the thrill of vagabond life. Syd was the first to go on the stage and the first to break into the big time as a member of the famous Fred Karno company. It was through his efforts that Charlie was accepted as a member of the troupe. Charlie eventually repaid Syd by getting him into Keystone films in Hollywood.

Syd, who had been considered the more talented of the brothers at Karno, remained a second-rank comic in films. Unlike Charlie, he blended into the slapstick mold of knockabout comedy without developing a distinctive style. Typically he appeared with his hair parted down the middle, an upward-twisting mustache, wearing rumpled shirts with high collars and oversized shoes. His humor was quite vulgar, and Mack SENNETT frequently had to cut Syd's off-color scenes. In 1915 he starred in a series of shorts as a character named Gussle.

Early in 1916, Syd quit acting to take charge of Charlie's booming business affairs. He was instrumental in securing for his half brother the lucrative contracts with Mutual and First National. At the same time, he played occasional roles in Charlie's films, and he later returned to the screen in both leads and supporting parts, memorably in the 1925 version of *Charley's Aunt.* Syd never acquired American citizenship, and after some trouble with the Internal Revenue, he returned to England in the late 20s.

FILMS INCLUDE: *Fatty's Wine Party* 1914; *A Submarine Pirate, Gussle's Day of Rest, Giddy Gay and Ticklish, That Springtime Feeling, Hushing the Scandal* 1915; *A Dog's Life, Shoulder Arms* 1918; *No One to Guide Him* 1919; *King Queen Joker* (also dir., story, sc.) 1921; *Pay Day* 1922; *The Pilgrim, Her Temporary Husband, The Rendezvous* 1923; *Galloping Fish, The Perfect Flapper* 1924; *Charley's Aunt, The Man on the Box* 1925; *Oh! What a Nurse!, The Better 'Ole* 1926; *The Missing Link, The Fortune Hunter* 1927; *A Little Bit of Fluff* (UK) 1928.

Chaplin, Sydney. Actor. Born on Mar. 21, 1926, in Los Angeles. *ed.* Lawrenceville Acad. The son of Charlie CHAPLIN and actress Lita Grey, he was named after Charlie's half brother Sydney CHAPLIN. His parents separated when he was nine months old, and Sydney was brought up by his mother. After completing his education and serving a two-and-a-half-year stint with the Army, he joined the Circle Theater in Los Angeles. In 1952 he made his film debut in his father's *Limelight,* but his career in films has been spotty and irregular. He has fared much better on the Broadway stage, starring in such musicals as 'Bells Are Ringing,' 'Subways Are for Sleeping,' and 'Funny Girl.'

FILMS INCLUDE: *Limelight* 1952; *Confession/The Deadliest Sin* (UK); *Land of the Pharaohs* 1955; *Pillars of the Sky* 1956; *Quantez* 1957; *The Countess from Hong Kong* (UK) 1967; *Le Clan des Siciliens/The Sicilian Clan* (Fr.), *The Adding Machine* (US/UK) 1969; *Song of the Balalaika* 1971; *The Contract* (Fr.) 1974; *Satan's Cheerleaders* 1977.

Chapman, Edward. Actor. *b.* Oct. 13, 1901, Harrogate, England. *d.* 1977. Solid character player of British stage and screen. Formerly a bank clerk, he made his stage debut in 1924 and entered films after the transition to sound. He figured prominently in scores of movies in a career spanning four decades, with a time out for WW II service in the RAF.

FILMS INCLUDE: *Juno and the Paycock, Murder* 1930; *Happy Ever After* 1932; *Things to Come, Rembrandt* 1936; *The Citadel* 1938; *The Four Just Men/The Secret Four, Inspector Hornleigh on Holiday* 1939; *The Happy Valley* 1940; *Jeannie, Ships with Wings, They Flew Alone/Wings and the Woman* 1941; *It Always Rains on Sunday, The October Man* 1947; *The History of Mr. Polly, Madeleine* 1949; *Night and the City* 1950; *The Card/The Promoter, Mandy/The Crash of Silence, Folly to Be Wise* 1952; *The Intruder* 1953; *Bhowani Junction, X the Unknown* 1956; *School for Scoundrels, Oscar Wilde* 1960; *A Stitch in Time* 1963; *The Man Who Haunted Himself* 1970.

Chapman, Graham. Actor, screenwriter. *b.* Jan. 8, 1941, Leicester, England. *d.* 1989, of spinal cancer. With Cambridge classmate John CLEESE, he began writing comedy material for British TV in the 60s. Together they conceived the idea for the hit comedy show 'Monty Python's Flying Circus,' which ran in Britain from 1969 to 1974, and later enjoyed cult success in the US and other markets. He appeared in and collaborated on the scripts of the TV programs and the series of movies that followed. He also worked in other films as actor and writer.

FILMS INCLUDE (as actor): *Doctor in Trouble, The Magic Christian* (also co-sc.), *The Rise and Rise of Michael Rimmer* (also co-sc.) 1970; *The Magnificent Seven Deadly Sins* (co-sc. only), *The Statue* 1971; *And Now For Something Completely Different* (also co-sc.), *Rentadick* (co-sc. only) 1972; *Monty Python and the Holy Grail* (as King Arthur; also co-sc.) 1974; *The Odd Job* (also co-prod., co-sc.) 1978; *Monty Python's Life of Brian* (title role; also co-sc.) 1979); *Monty Python Live at the Hollywood Bowl, The Secret Policeman's Other Ball* 1982; *Monty Python's The Meaning of Life* (also co-sc.), *Yellowbeard* (also co-sc.) 1983.

Chapman, Marguerite. Actress. Born on March 9, 1920, in Chatham, N.Y. Leading lady of Hollywood films of the 40s and 50s; mostly in Columbia low- to medium-budget features, often action dramas. Later appeared in numerous TV plays. Formerly married to British producer-director Anthony HAVELOCK-ALLAN, she is now semiretired, living in Hawaii.

FILMS INCLUDE: *On Their Own, Charlie Chan at the Wax Museum* 1940; *Navy Blues, The Body Disappears* 1941; *Spy Smasher* (serial), *Submarine Raider, Parachute Nurse, A Man's World* 1942; *Murder in Times Square, Appointment in Berlin, Destroyer* 1943; *Counter-Attack, Pardon My Past* 1945; *The Walls Came Tumbling Down* 1946; *Mr. District Attorney* 1947; *Relentless, Gallant Blade, Coroner Creek* 1948; *The Green Promise* 1949; *Kansas Raiders* 1950; *Flight to Mars* 1951; *Man Bait, Sea Tiger, Bloodhounds of Broadway* 1952; *The Seven Year Itch* 1955; *The Amazing Transparent Man* 1960.

Chapman, Michael. Director of photography, director. Born on Nov. 21 1935, in New York City. He worked on New York–area documentaries before going west as a camera operator for cinematographer Gordon WILLIS and others on such films as *The Godfather, Klute,* and *Jaws.* As a lighting cameraman from 1973, he contributed fine visuals to many major films of the 70s and 80s, notably for Martin SCORSESE. He took a first stab at directing in 1983. Married director-writer Amy JONES.

FILMS INCLUDE: As director of photography—*The Last Detail* (also act.) 1973; *The White Dawn* 1974; *Taxi Driver, The Front, The Next Man* 1976; *Fingers, The Last Waltz, Invasion of the Body Snatchers* 1978; *Hardcore, The Wanderers* 1979; *Raging Bull* 1980; *Dead Men Don't Wear Plaid, Personal Best* 1982; *The Man with Two Brains* 1983; *Shoot to Kill, Scrooged* 1988; *Ghostbusters II* 1989; *Kindergarten Cop, Quick Change* 1990. As director—*All the Right Moves* 1983; *The Clan of the Cave Bear* 1986; *The Fugitive, Rising Sun* 1993; *Primal Fear, Space Jam* 1996.

chapter play. Film industry colloquial term for SERIAL.

character role. A role in a motion picture requiring a mature performance on the part of an actor or actress in an attempt to represent a distinctive character type rather than a standard romantic lead, ingenue, or juvenile part. Character roles are sometimes performed by stars, especially as they grow older, but they are usually played by actors or actresses who specialize in the portrayal of particular types or who are capable of playing a wide range of roles. Some character actors have achieved remarkable screen careers without ever acquiring star status.

Charell, Erich (also **Erik).** Director. *b.* 1895, Breslau, Germany. *d.* 1974. A highly successful producer-director of stage operettas and light revues, he was invited by producer Erich Pommer to direct *Der Kongress tanzt/The Congress Dances* (1931), a musical extravaganza of early German sound cinema. The film was made in three versions (German, English, and French) and enjoyed great commercial success the world over. As a result, Charell was invited to Hollywood to direct *Caravan* (1934) starring Charles Boyer and Loretta Young. However, the film was a failure, and Charell disappeared from film, except for collaborations on the screenplay of *Casbah* (1948) and several unimportant German films.

FILMS (as director): *Der Kongress tanzt/The Congress Dances* (German, French, and English versions; Ger.) 1931; *Caravan* (English and French versions; US) 1934.

Charisse, Cyd. Actress, dancer. Born Tula Ellice Finklea, on Mar. 8, 1921, in Amarillo, Tex. A ballet student from childhood, she joined the Ballet Russe at 13 and during a European tour in 1939 she married her ballet instructor, Nico Charisse. She broke into films in 1943 as a bit player, under the name of Lily Norwood. But it was as Cyd Charisse, under contract to MGM from 1946, that she soon developed into a popular star of screen musicals, the alluringly beautiful, leggy, and statuesque dance partner of Gene KELLY and Fred ASTAIRE. She was among the finest and certainly the most scintillating female dancers that ever adorned the silver screen. But the decline of the Hollywood musical in the late 50s forced her into dramatic roles, in which she was just another pretty, competent actress. In the 60s she appeared in a number of European films as well as occasional Hollywood productions and rare TV offerings. She also teamed up in a nightclub revue with her second husband, crooner Tony MARTIN, whom she married in 1948, the year following her divorce from Nico Charisse. In 1972 she starred in an Australian stage production of 'No No Nanette'; in 1992 she appeared briefly in 'Grand Hotel.' With Tony Martin, she published a dual autobiography, *The Two of Us* (1976).

FILMS: *Mission to Moscow, Something to Shout About* 1943; *The Harvey Girls, Ziegfeld Follies, Three Wise Fools, Till the Clouds Roll By* 1946; *Fiesta, The Unfinished Dance* 1947; *On an Island with You, Words and Music* 1948; *The Kissing Bandit, East Side West Side, Tension* 1949; *Mark of the Renegade* 1951; *Singin' in the Rain, The Wild North* 1952; *Sombrero, The Band Wagon, Easy to Love* (unbilled cameo) 1953; *Brigadoon, Deep in My Heart* 1954; *It's Always Fair Weather* 1955; *Meet Me in Las Vegas* 1956; *Invitation to the Dance, Silk Stockings* 1957; *Twilight for the Gods, Party Girl* 1958; *Un Deux Trois Quatre/Les Collants noirs/Black Tights* (Fr.) 1960; *Cinque Ore in Contanti/Five Golden Hours* (It./UK) 1961; *Two Weeks in Another Town* 1962; *Assassinio Made in Italy/Assassination in Rome* (It.) 1963; *The Silencers* 1966; *Maroc 7* (UK) 1967; *Warlords of Atlantis* (UK) 1978; *Visioni privati/Private Screening* (It) 1990.

Charleson, Ian. Actor. *b.* Aug. 11, 1949, Edinburgh. *d.* 1990. *ed.* Edinburgh U. (architecture). Trained at the London Academy of Music and Dramatic Art, he played leads, including 'Hamlet,' on the London stage, and prominent roles in several films, most memorably in *Chariots of Fire,* as the Presbyterian Olympic runner who refused to compete on the Sabbath. He seemed headed for a brilliant career when he died of AIDS at 40.

FILMS: *Jubilee* 1978; *Chariots of Fire* 1981; *Gandhi* 1982; *Ascendency* 1983; *Louisiane* (Fr./Can.), *Greystoke: The Legend of Tarzan Lord of the Apes* 1984; *Car Trouble* 1986; *Opera* (It.) 1987.

Charrier, Jacques. Actor. Born on Nov. 6, 1936, in Metz, France. Defied family military tradition to work in the arts, first ceramics, then the stage, and finally in 1958, in films. Boyishly handsome, he has played charming but rather bland leading roles. He made the headlines when he married Brigitte BARDOT, his co-star in *Babette Goes to War* (1959). It was a rocky affair from the start, accompanied by his nervous breakdowns and attempted suicides, and ended in divorce the following year.

FILMS INCLUDE: *Les Tricheurs/The Cheaters* 1958; *Babette s'en va-t-en Guerre/Babette Goes to War, Les Dragueurs/The Chasers* 1959; *La Main chaude* 1960; *La Belle Américaine* 1961; *Les Sept Péchés capitaux/Seven Capital Sins, L'Oeil du Malin/The Third Lover, Carmen di Trastevere* (It./Fr.) 1962; *La Vie conjugale/Anatomy of a Marriage* 1964; *Les Créateurs* 1966; *Le plus Vieux Métier du Monde/The Oldest Profession* 1967; *Sirokko/Winter Wind* (Hung./Fr.) 1969; *Les Soleils de l'Ilede Paques, Les Volets clos* 1973; *L'Affaire Dreyfus* (prod. only) 1975.

Chartoff, Robert. Producer. Born on Aug. 26, 1933, in New York City. *ed.* Union Coll. (A.B.); Columbia (LL.B.). In partnership with Irwin WINKLER he has turned out a number of successful Hollywood films since the late 60s. Later established his own company, Chartoff Productions.

FILMS INCLUDE: (all in collaboration with Irwin Winkler): *Point Blank* 1967; *The Split* 1968; *They Shoot Horses Don't They?* 1969; *Leo the Last* (UK), *The Strawberry Statement* 1970; *The Gang That Couldn't Shoot Straight* 1971; *The New Centurions, The Mechanic, Up the Sandbox* 1972; *Busting, S*P*Y*S** (US/UK), *The Gambler* 1974; *Breakout* 1975; *Peeper, Rocky, Nickelodeon* 1976; *New York New York, Valentino* (UK) 1977; *Comes a Horseman* 1978; *Rocky II* 1979; *Raging Bull* 1980; *True Confessions* 1981; *Rocky III* 1982; *The Right Stuff* 1983; *Rocky IV* 1985; *The Return of the Musketeers, Rocky V* 1990.

Chase, Barrie. See CHASE, Borden.

Chase, Borden. Screenwriter. *b.* Frank Fowler, Jan. 11, 1900, New York City. *d.* 1971. Left school at 14 and earned a living at an assortment of odd jobs. In his late teens he was a boxer and a cab driver, then served a year in the Navy. During the Roaring 20s he was, by his own account, a chauffeur for a gang boss. After his employer's body was found riddled with bullets (by rival Al Capone?), he worked in the construction of

New York's Holland Tunnel. The death of a co-worker in an accident in the tunnel provided him with the material for his first screenplay, *Under Pressure* (1935). He subsequently wrote numerous short stories for leading magazines and several novels, some of which were adapted to the screen by others. He borrowed his pen name from the familiar milk company and bank. Beginning in 1943 he wrote many screenplays, alone or in collaboration, for quality Westerns and action pictures, often from his own stories. His daughter, Barrie Chase (born 1934, New York City), is an actress-dancer who played supporting roles in several films of the early 60s.

FILMS (screenplay unless otherwise indicated): *Under Pressure* 1935; *Midnight Taxi* (story only) 1937; *The Devil's Party* (novel only), *Trouble Wagon* 1938; *Blue White and Perfect* (story only) 1941; *The Navy Comes Through, Dr. Broadway* (both story only) 1942; *Harrigan's Kid* (story only), *Destroyer* 1943; *The Fighting Seabees* 1944; *This Man's Navy, Flame of the Barbary Coast* 1945; *I've Always Loved You* 1946; *Tycoon* 1947; *Man from Colorado* (story only), *Red River* 1948; *The Great Jewel Robber, Montana, Winchester '73* 1950; *Iron Man* 1951; *Lone Star, Bend of the River, The World in His Arms* 1952; *Sea Devils, His Majesty O'Keefe* 1953; *Vera Cruz* (story only) 1954; *The Far Country, Man Without a Star* 1955; *Backlash* 1956; *Night Passage* 1958; *Ride a Crooked Trail* 1958; *Gunfighters of Casa Grande* 1965; *A Man Called Gannon, Backtrack* 1969.

Chase, Charlie (also **Charley).** Actor, director, screenwriter. *b.* Charles Parrott, Oct. 20, 1893, Baltimore. *d.* 1940. Brother of director James Parrott. In vaudeville and musical comedy before joining Mack SENNETT's Keystone in 1914 as second-banana comedian. Appeared in several Chaplin vehicles, then moved on to Triangle and Fox. From 1915 on he also directed many of his own comedies as well as some starring Fatty ARBUCKLE and Ford STERLING. Chase was only modestly successful as a comedian or a director until 1921, when he joined the Hal Roach studios as a director-writer. Using his real name, Charles Parrott, he directed some of Roach's brightest and most inventive comedies of the early 20s, demonstrating a flair for wit and light charm, with films starring Harry "Snub" POLLARD and others. In 1924 he switched back to acting, again using the pseudonym Charlie Chase, and enjoyed a great deal of popularity in two-reel comedies for his characterizations of a dapper but bashful man about town who invariably runs into trouble or of a meek, hen-pecked husband. Chase directed some of these, again under the name Charles Parrott, while others were brilliantly directed by Leo MCCAREY.

The advent of sound found Chase not only with a good speaking voice but also with a talent for singing, which he employed from time to time in his films. He also began playing supporting parts in feature films. In 1937 he moved over to Columbia as a comedian and a director of shorts starring Andy CLYDE, The THREE STOOGES, and others. At about this time he began drinking heavily and died of a heart attack at age 46.

FILMS INCLUDE: As actor only—*The Knockout, The Masquerader, His New Profession, The Rounders, His Musical Career, Tillie's Punctured Romance* (all with Chaplin) 1914; *All Wet* 1924; *Bad Boy, His Wooden Wedding, Innocent Husbands, The Rat's Knuckles, What Price Goofy?* 1925; *Crazy Like a Fox, Dog Shy, Mighty Like a Moose, There Ain't No Santa Claus* 1926; *Movie Night, Modern Love, You Can't Buy Love, Crazy Feet* 1929; *The Real McCoy, Whispering Whoopee, Fifty Million Husbands* 1930; *The Pip from Pittsburgh, Rough Seas* 1931; *The Tabasco Kid, Young Ironsides* 1932; *Sons of the Desert* (with Laurel & Hardy), *Fallen Arches, Nature in the Wrong* 1933; *Kelly the Second* 1936; *From Bad to Worse* 1937; *Time Out for Trouble* 1938; *Pie a la Maid, Rattling Romeo* 1939; *South of the Boudoir, The Heckler, His Bridal Fright* 1940. As director only—*The Hunt* (co-dir. with Ford Sterling), *Dirty Work in a Laundry, Only a Messenger Boy* 1915; *All at Sea* 1919; *Why Go Home?, Live and Learn* 1920; *His Best Girl, Big Game, Blue Sunday, The Hustler* 1921; *Days of Old, In the Movies, The Dumb Bell, The Stone Age* 1922; *The Courtship of Miles Sandwich, Sold at Auction, Jack Frost* 1923; *The Bargain of the Century* 1933; *Oh What a Knight!* 1937; *The Old Raid Mule, Tassels in the Air, Ankles Away* (also sc.), *Halfway to Hollywood, Violent Is the Word for Curly, Mutts to You, A Nag in the Bag, Flat Foot Stooges* 1938; *Mutiny on the Body, Boom Goes the Groom, Saved by the Belle, Static in the Attic* 1939. As director-actor—*The Anglers* 1914; *Do-Re-Mi-Fa* 1915; *A Dash of Courage* 1916; *Chased Into Love* (also sc.) 1917; *Hello Trouble* 1918; *Ship Ahoy!* (also sc.) 1919; *Kids Is Kids* 1920; *Sherman Said It, Midsummer Mush, Luncheon at Twelve* 1933; *The Cracked Iceman* (co-dir. with Eddie Dunn), *Four Parts* (co-dir. with Dunn), *I'll Take Vanilla* (co-dir. with Dunn), *Another Wild Idea* (co-dir. with Dunn), *It Happened One Day* (co-dir. with Dunn), *Something Simple* (co-dir. with Walter Weems), *You Said a Hateful!, Fate's Fathead, The Chases of Pimple Street* 1934; *Okay Toots!* (co-dir. with William Terhune), *Poker at Eight, Southern Exposure, The Four-Star Boarder, Nurse to You* (co-dir. with Jefferson Moffitt), *Manhattan Monkey Business* (co-dir. with Harold Law), *Public Ghost No. 1* (co-dir. with Law), *Life Hesitates at 40* (co-dir. with Law), *The Count Takes the Count* (co-dir. with Law), *Vamp Till Ready* (co-dir. with Law), *On the Wrong Trek* (co-dir. with Law), *Neighborhood House* (co-dir. with Law) 1936.

Chase, Chevy. Actor. Born Cornelius Crane Chase, on Oct. 8, 1943, in New York City. *ed.* Bard Coll. (B.A.); CCC Institute of Audio Research; MIT (M.A.). The grandson of plumbing tycoon Cornelius Crane and son of book editor Ned Chase, he started out in the late 60s as a writer for *Mad* magazine. He also wrote comedy material and performed for various satirical groups and educational television's 1971 comedy show 'The Great American Dream Machine.' A chance meeting with TV producer Lorne Michaels led to a stint as a writer and performer on TV's popular 'Saturday Night Live' in 1976. After a season of deadpan wisecracks and well-timed pratfalls, and Emmy Awards for acting and writing, the preppy, affable comedian sought greener pastures in feature films. Following initial success, he had to overcome interim career setbacks and a drug problem stemming from work-related back injuries before becoming firmly established as a bankable star. He adopted his professional name from the Maryland town of Chevy Chase, a suburb of Washington.

FILMS: *The Groove Tube* 1974; *Tunnelvision* 1976; *Foul Play* 1978; *Oh Heavenly Dog, Caddyshack, Seems Like Old Times* 1980; *Under the Rainbow, Modern Problems* 1981; *National Lampoon's Vacation, Deal of the Century* 1983; *Fletch, National Lampoon's European Vacation, Sesame Street Presents: Follow That Bird, Spies Like Us* 1985; *Three Amigos* 1986; *The Couch Trip, Funny Farm, Caddyshack II* 1988; *Fletch Lives, National Lampoon's Christmas Vacation* 1989; *L.A. Story* (uncred. cameo), *Nothing But Trouble, Memoirs of an Invisible Man* 1991; *Cops and Robbersons* 1994; *Man of the House* 1995; *Vegas Vacation* 1997.

Chatterton, Ruth. Actress. *b.* Dec. 24, 1893, New York City. *d.* 1961. The daughter of a successful architect, she made her stage debut in stock at 12, reached Broadway at 18, and triumphed at 20 as the star of 'Daddy Long Legs.' But it wasn't until she was in her mid-30s that she made her screen debut in *Sins of the Fathers* (1928), opposite Emil Jannings.

She had a successful Hollywood career, playing an assortment of leads, often as tense and distraught, sometimes misguided, women. She was nominated for Oscars as best actress for *Madame X* (1929) and *Sarah and Son* (1930), and is best remembered for her role as the wife in Dodsworth (1936). She left Hollywood after completing that film, appeared in two British productions, then retired from films altogether, returning occasionally to Broadway, several times as actress and once as director. Miss Chatterton, who had authored a Broadway play, 'Monsieur Brotonneau,' in 1930, wrote several successful novels in the 50s. An active, liberated woman, she was also a licensed pilot and flew her own plane cross-country. Her three husbands were all actors: Ralph FORBES (1924–32), George BRENT (1932–34), and Barry Thomson (1942–*d.* 1960).

FILMS: *Sins of the Fathers* 1928; *The Doctor's Secret, The Dummy, Madame X, Charming Sinners, The Laughing Lady* 1929; *Sarah and Son, Paramount on Parade, The Lady of Scandal/The High Road, Anybody's Woman, The Right to Love* 1930; *Unfaithful, The Magnificent Lie, Once a Lady* 1931; *Tomorrow and Tomorrow, The Rich Are Always with Us, The Crash* 1932; *Frisco Jenny, Lilly Turner, Female* 1933; *Journal of a Crime* 1934; *Lady of Secrets, Girls' Dormitory, Dodsworth* 1936; *The Rat, A Royal Divorce* (both UK) 1938.

Chautard, Emile. Director, actor. *b.* 1881, Paris. *d.* 1934. He was first a stage actor in Paris and entered films there in 1909. Directed several French films before emigrating to the US in 1914. In Hollywood, he directed big-budget productions of little distinction through the mid-20s, then returned to acting in character roles, often portraying French types.

FILMS INCLUDE: As director—*La Légende de l'Aigle* (Fr.), *Le Poison de l'Humanité* (Fr.) 1911; *La Dame de Monsoreau* (Fr.), *L'Aiglon* (Fr.) 1912; *Le Mystère de Chambre jaune* (Fr.) 1913; *L'Appentie* (Fr.) 1914; *The Arrival of Perpetua, The Boss, The Little Dutch Girl* 1915; *Love's Crucible, Sudden Riches, Human Driftwood, Friday the 13th, The Heart of a Hero, All Man, The Rack* 1916; *The Hungry Heart, The Web of Desire, The Man Who Forgot, The Family Honor, The Fires of Youth, Forget-Me-Not, The Eternal Temptress, Under False Colors, Magda, The Heart of Ezra Greer* 1917; *The Marionettes, The House of Glass, Her Final Reckoning, The Ordeal of Rosetta, A Daughter of the Old South, Under the Greenwood Tree* 1918; *Out of the Shadow, The Marriage Price, Eyes of the Soul, His Parisian Wife, Paid in Full, The Mystery of the Yellow Room* 1919; *The Black Panther's Cub* 1921; *Living Lies, The Glory of Clementina, Youth to Youth* (also prod.), *Forsaking All Others* 1922; *Daytime Wives* 1923; *Untamed Youth* 1924. As actor—*Paris at Midnight* (as Balzac's Père Goriot), *Broken Hearts of Hollywood, Bardelys the Magnificent, My Official Wife, The Flaming Forest* 1926; *Upstream, Seventh Heaven, The Love Mart* 1927; *The Noose, His Tiger Lady, Out of the Ruins, Adoration, Lilac Time* 1928; *The House of Horror, Times Square, South Sea Rose* 1929; *L'Enigmatique Monsieur Parkes* (French-language version of *Slightly Scarlet), Le Petit Café* (French-language version of *Playboy of Paris), Morocco* 1930; *The Road to Reno* 1931; *Shanghai Express, The Man from Yesterday* 1932; *The Three Musketeers* (serial), *Design for Living* 1933; *Man of Two Worlds* 1934.

Chayefsky, Paddy. Playwright, screenwriter. *b.* Sidney Chayefsky, Jan. 29, 1923, Bronx, N.Y. *d.* 1981. *ed.* CCNY. As a young man, he tried breaking into show business as a stand-up comic. He wrote his first play, a musical, while recuperating in England from injuries incurred from a German land mine in WW II action. After discharge he worked briefly at his uncle's print shop, played a bit (as a photographer) in the film *A Double Life* (1947), then began writing short stories and radio and TV dramas, which typically dealt with the lives of ordinary people in sympathetic, realistic terms. In 1955 he won an Oscar as well as a Cannes Festival award for the script of *Marty,* a simple, touching love story about a Bronx butcher and a plain schoolteacher, which he adapted from one of his own TV plays. In 1971 he won another Academy Award for the story and screenplay of *The Hospital,* which he wrote directly for the screen. He won a third Oscar for the original screenplay of *Network* (1976). In between Hollywood awards he wrote the Broadway plays 'Middle of the Night' (1956), 'The Tenth Man' (1959), 'Gideon' (1961), and 'The Passion of Joseph D' (1964), as well as 'The Latent Homosexual' (1968), which never reached New York. He also continued writing screenplays, causing a controversy in 1980, when he asked that his name be removed from the credits as the screenwriter of *Altered States,* which he had adapted from his 1978 novel. The script was attributed to Sidney Aaron, his first and Hebrew names. He died of cancer the following year.

FILMS: *As Young As You Feel* (story basis only) 1951; *Marty* (sc., from own teleplay) 1955; *The Catered Affair* (teleplay basis only) 1956; *The Bachelor Party* (sc., from own teleplay) 1957; *The Goddess* (story, sc.) 1958; *Middle of the Night* (sc., from own play) 1959; *The Americanization of Emily* (sc.) 1964; *Paint Your Wagon* (adapt.) 1969; *The Hospital* (story, sc.) 1971; *Network* 1976; *Altered States* (sc., uncredited, from own novel) 1980.

cheat. The "dishonest" but expedient act of arbitrarily changing the position of performers or props in relation to the background when switching camera angles. For example, two actors are seen together in one shot. The director now cuts to a closer shot from a new angle, so only one of the actors is facing the camera. The director changes the position of the actors with no regard to the exact positions they occupied in the previous shot, so that he can achieve the desired effect of the new shot by emphasizing the actor facing the camera. The other actor is thus "cheated" out of the shot, partly or entirely, in a way the director hopes is not too noticeable to audiences.

Checchi, Andrea. Actor. *b.* Oct. 21, 1916, Florence, Italy. *d.* 1974. Leading man of Italian films for three decades. A graduate of Rome's Academia di Belle Arti, he made his screen debut in *1860* (1934), a film directed by his drama instructor, Alessandro BLASETTI. Checchi became a highly popular star during the WW II years and was among the few professional actors who were in demand by directors of the postwar neorealist movement. During his last year he was active on Italian TV and exhibited his paintings in art shows. He died at 57 of a rare virus infection.

FILMS INCLUDE: *1860* 1934; *Vecchia Guardia* 1935; *Amore* 1936; *Luciano serra Pilota* 1938; *Ettore Fieramosca, I Grandi Magazzini* 1939; *L'Assedio dell'Alazar, Senza Cielo* 1940; *Tragica Notte, Via delle Cinque Lune* 1941; *Giacomo l'Idealista* 1942; *Due Lettere Anonime* 1945; *Roma Città Libera* 1946; *Caccia Tragica/Tragic Hunt, Eleonora Duse* 1947; *Il Grido della Terra/The Earth Cries Out, Au-delà des Grilles/Le Mura di Malapaga/The Walls of Malapaga* 1948; *Paolo e Francesca/Paolo and Francesca* 1949; *Il Capitano nero* 1950; *Achtung Banditi!, Alti Tiempi/Times Gone By, L'Eroe sono Io* (also co-dir.) 1951; *Tempi Nostri, La Signora senza Camelie* 1953; *Casa Ricordi/House of Ricordi* 1954; *Il Tesoro di Rommel/Rommel's Treasure* 1955; *Terrore sulla Città* 1956; *Die Tausend Augen des Dr. Mabuse/The 1000 Eyes of Dr. Mabuse, La Ciociara/Two Women* 1960; *L'Assassino/The Lady Killer of Rome, L'Oro di Roma* 1961; *Italiano Brava Gente* 1964; *Made in Italy* 1965; *El Che Guevara* 1968; *Waterloo* 1970; *Un Apprezzato Professionista di Sicuro Avvenire* 1972.

Cheech and Chong. Comedy team that in the late 70s and early 80s specialized in low-grade, drug-related humor in a series of cheap, crude films that for a while raked in high profits at the box office. Of the duo, Richard MARIN (Cheech) was the small, excitable Latin, while Tommy CHONG played the tall, laid-back Anglo. The team debuted in 1978 and broke up in 1984.

Chen, Joan. Actress. Born Chen Chong in 1961 in China. Slender, delicate screen lead and supporting player adept in both dramatic and action-adventure roles. Debuted in Chinese films in late adolescence and in US films in young adulthood. Regular on the TV series 'Twin Peaks.'

FILMS INCLUDE: *Little Flower* (China), *Awakening* (China) 1980; *Dim Sum: A Little Bit of Heart* 1985; *Tai-Pan* 1986; *The Night Stalker, The Last Emperor* (UK/China) 1987; *The Blood of Heroes* 1990; *Turtle Beach* (Austral.) 1992; *The Joy Luck Club, Heaven and Earth* 1993; *Golden Gate, On Deadly Ground, Turtle Beach* 1994; *The Hunted, Judge Dredd, Wild Side* 1995.

Chen Kaige. Director. Born in 1952 in Beijing, China. One of the most prominent and accomplished of the post–Cultural Revolution Chinese directors. Son of Chen Huaikai, also a well-known film director, he was forced at 14 by the Cultural Revolution to interrupt school and work as a rubber plantation farmer, soldier, and factory hand. He entered the Beijing Film Academy in 1978. Following some shorts and television work, Chen created three colorful features, all set in China's recent past: *Yellow Earth*, *The Big Parade*, and *King of Children*. After leaving China for a stint in New York City (1987–90), Chen returned to his homeland to film *Life on a String*, a fable set in remote Mongolia about a blind man searching for a magic cure to recover sight. His 1993 feature, *Farewell My Concubine*, shared the Palme d'Or at Cannes (with Jane Campion's *The Piano*) and further widened his international reputation. Chen's films are renowned both for their emotional delicacy and their lavish spectacle, using an extensive palette of color and state-of-the-art film technology. His cinematographer for his first two films was Zhang Yimou, later a director in his own right. Chen writes his own scripts.

FILMS INCLUDE: *Yellow Earth* 1984; *The Big Parade* 1985; *King of Children* 1987; *Life on a String* 1991; *Farewell My Concubine/Farewell to My Concubine* 1993; *Temptress Moon* 1997.

Chenal, Pierre. Director. Born Pierre Cohen, on Dec. 5, 1903, in Paris. A former journalist, he began directing experimental shorts in 1927, starting with *Paris-Cinéma*. After turning to features in the early 30s, he occupied a prominent position in the French cinema of the decade and received high praise for such films as *Crime et Châtiment/Crime and Punishment* (1935), *The Late Mathias Pascal* (1937), and *L'Alibi* (1937). But later French critics re-evaluated his work of the period and termed it mediocre and overpraised. During the German Occupation of WW II, he escaped to South America, where he made a number of films. Returning to France, he directed a commercially successful comedy, *Clochemerle* (1947), but was unable to regain his prewar status and by the early 60s had all but disappeared from films.

FEATURE FILMS: *Le Martyre de l'Obèse, La Rue sans Nom* 1933; *Crime et Châtiment/Crime and Punishment* 1935; *Les Mutinés de l'Elseneur* 1936; *Il Fu Mattia Pascal/L'Homme de nulle Part/The Late Mathias Pascal* (Fr./It.), *L'Alibi* 1937; *L'Affaire Lafarge, La Maison du Maltais/Sirocco* 1938; *Le Dernier Tournant/The Postman Always Rings Twice* 1939; *Todo un Hombre* (Arg.) 1943; *El Mueroto falta a la Città* (Arg.) 1944; *Se abre el Abismo* (Arg.) 1945; *El Viaje sin Regreso* (Arg.), *La Foire aux Chimères/The Devil and the Angel* 1946; *Clochemerle/The Scandals of Clochemerle* 1948; *El Idolo* (Chile) 1949; *Confesiònal Amanecer* (Chile), *Sangre Negra/ Native Son* (Arg.; in English) 1951; *Section des Disparus, Le Fleuve d'Argent* 1956; *Rafles sur la Ville/Sinners of Paris, Jeux dangereux/Dangerous Games* 1958; *La Bête à l'Affût* 1959; *Les Nuits de Raspoutine/L'Ultimo Zar/The Night They Killed Rasputin* (Fr./It.) 1960; *L'Assassin connaît la Musique* 1963.

Cher. Singer, actress. Born Cherilyn LaPiere (Sarkisian), on May 20, 1946, in El Centro, Calif. Raised by her abandoned, ten-times married, ex-actress mother, she surmounted an unstable childhood and as a teenager started a modest career as a backup singer in a Manhattan recording studio. It was there, in 1964, that she met, married, and teamed up with singer Sonny Bono (*b.* Salvatore Bono, on Feb. 16, 1935, Detroit). Following a modest start as "Caesar and Cleo," they finally clicked as "Sonny and Cher," turning out the first of several hit records in 1965. Their growing popularity prompted their own TV variety show, 'The Sonny and Cher Comedy Hour,' which premiered in 1971 and ended when the couple divorced in 1974. Their daughter, Chastity Bono (*b.* Mar. 4, 1969), was a regular on the show. The feline, exotically attired Cher continued for a season with her own show, 'Cher' but when audiences dwindled she reteamed with her former husband in 'The Sonny and Cher Show' (1976–77). By that time she was carrying Elijah Blue, the product of her brief (1975–77), unhappy second marriage to drug-addicted rock star Gregg Allman. Continuing on her own, Cher starred in opulent TV specials, in which she flaunted her slick, skinny figure in outrageous costumes. But she soon tired of the Hollywood glitz, returned to New York, and auditioned for director Robert ALTMAN, who cast her in the play, then the film version of *Come Back to the Five and Dime, Jimmy Dean, Jimmy Dean*. In this and subsequent films, she proved herself a capable actress, with expressive, soulful eyes to augment her natural manner. She was nominated for an Academy Award as best supporting actress for *Silkwood* (1983). She shared the best actress prize at Cannes for *Mask* (1985) and won the Oscar as best actress for her performance in *Moonstruck* (1987).

FILMS: *Good Times* 1967; *Chastity* 1969; *Come Back to the Five and Dime, Jimmy Dean, Jimmy Dean* 1982; *Silkwood* 1983; *Mask* 1985; *The Witches of Eastwick, Suspect, Moonstruck* 1987; *Mermaids* 1990; *The Player* (cameo) 1992; *Ready to Wear* 1994; *Faithful* 1996.

Cherkassov (also **Cherkasov), Nikolai.** Actor. *b.* Nikolai Konstantinovich Cherkassovin, July 27, 1903, Leningrad. *d.* 1966. A graduate of the St. Petersburg (now Leningrad) Theater Institute, he first appeared on the stage in 1926 and made his film debut the following year. One of the USSR's most commanding actors, he was cast in leading roles of heroic proportions in many outstanding Soviet films, notably the title role in Eisenstein's two-part *Ivan the Terrible* (1944–46). In the late 30s he served as a deputy of the Supreme Soviet. Awarded Order of Lenin in 1939 and People's Artist of the USSR in 1947. Author: *Notes of a Soviet Actor* (1951). Not to be confused with Nikolai P. Cherkasov, or Cherkassov, also known as N. Cherkasov-Sergeiev, who played the title role in Pudovkin's *General Suvorov* (1941) and leads in other Soviet films.

FILMS INCLUDE: *Poet and Czar, His Excellency* 1927; *Happiness* 1932; *Hectic Days* 1935; *Girl Friends* 1936; *The Baltic Deputy, Peter the First* (Pt. I; as Alexei, Peter's son) 1937; *Treasure Island, Friends, Captain Grant's Children, The Man with the Gun, Alexander Nevsky* (title role) 1938; *The Conquests of Peter the Great* (*Peter the First,* Pt. II; again as Alexei), *Lenin in 1918* (as Maxim Gorky) 1939; *His Name Is Sukhe-Bator* 1942; *Ivan the Terrible* (Pts. I, II; title role)

1944/46; *In the Name of Life, Spring* 1947; *Academician Ivan Pavlov/Ivan Pavlov* (again as Maxim Gorky), *The Battle of Stalingrad/The First Front* (in two parts; as Franklin D. Roosevelt) 1949; *Alexander Popov* (title role), *Mussorgsky* 1950; *Rimsky-Korsakov* (title role) 1953; *They Knew Mayakovsky* (title role) 1955; *Don Quixote* (title role) 1957; *Legacy* 1963; *La Nuit des Adieux* (Fr.) 1965.

Cherrill, Virginia. Actress. *b.* Apr. 12, 1908, in Carthage, Ill. *d.* 1996. A society girl, she had no previous acting experience when seen by Charlie CHAPLIN at a boxing match and chosen for the memorable lead as the blind flower girl whom Chaplin loves in *City Lights* (1931). She went on to star in several other Hollywood films but retired in 1933 after marrying Cary GRANT (one of her five husbands). After their 1935 divorce, she went to England, where she appeared in two "quota quickies," both co-starring James Mason in his first film roles. She then re-retired from films to marry the ninth Earl of Jersey, a union that lasted from 1937 to 1946.

FILMS: *City Lights, Girls Demand Excitement, The Brat, Delicious* 1931; *Fast Workers, The Nuisance, Charlie Chan's Greatest Case, Ladies Must Love, He Couldn't Take It* 1933; *White Heat* 1934; *Late Extra/What Price Crime?* (UK) 1935; *Troubled Waters* (UK) 1936.

Chevalier, Maurice. Entertainer, singer, actor. *b.* Sept. 12, 1888, Paris. *d.* 1972. The youngest of the nine children of an alcoholic house painter, he quit school at 11 to earn a living as an apprentice engraver and factory worker. He broke into show business as an acrobat, but an accident forced him to switch to singing in Paris cafés and variety halls. He overcame the handicap of a limited voice by enriching his act with comedy and zestful charm and before long became established as a popular entertainer. His big break came in 1909, at 21, when he was hired by the Folies-Bergère as the revue partner of the legendary musical star Mistinguett, who became his lover off as well as on the stage.

A year earlier, in 1908, Chevalier had made the first of several appearances in silent French films, but the musical stage remained his principal medium. Wounded and captured during the first year of WW I, he spent more than two years in a German prisoner-of-war camp, where he learned English from a fellow inmate. He was decorated with a Croix de Guerre. Returning to the stage, he became a top-billed star of the music halls and soon became world famous, in his trademark boulevardier outfit of a straw hat and bow tie, for his *joie de vivre,* suggestive swagger, and twinkling, roguish blue eyes. In 1929 he went to Hollywood and enjoyed great popularity with American audiences as the gay, sophisticated star of such romantic screen classics as Ernst LUBITSCH's *The Love Parade* and *The Merry Widow.* He left Hollywood in anger in 1935 when Irving THALBERG insisted Chevalier get second billing to Grace MOORE in a film, but continued his screen appearances in France and England. In 1938 he was decorated a Chevalier of the Legion of Honor. Toward the end of WW II he was accused of collaborating with the Nazis but was later vindicated and, more popular than ever, returned to entertaining. In 1947 he brought his one-man show to New York but was refused reentry in 1951 for having signed the Communist-inspired "Stockholm Appeal" for banning nuclear weapons. He returned to the US and to Hollywood films, however, in the late 50s. In 1958 he won a special Oscar "for his contributions to the world of entertainment for more than half a century." Next to De Gaulle, Chevalier was probably the best-known Frenchman abroad, one of the great entertainers of the era, a legend in his own time.

FILMS: In France—*Trop Credule* (short) 1908; *Un Marié qui se fait attendre* (short), *La Mariée recalcitrante* (short), *Par Habitude* (short) 1911; *La Valse renversante* (short), *Une Soirée mondaine* (short) 1917; *Le Match Criqui-Ledoux* (short), *Le Mauvais Garçon* 1922; *Gonzague* (medium-length), *Jim Bougne Boxeur* (medium-length), *L'Affaire de la Rue de Lourcine* (medium-length) 1923; *Par Habitude* (medium-length remake of 1911 short) 1924. In the US—*Bonjour New York!* (three-reel travelog) 1928; *Innocents of Paris* (and French-language version, *La Chanson de Paris), The Love Parade* (and French-language version, *Parade d'Amour*) 1929; *Paramount on Parade* (and several foreign-language versions), *The Big Pond* (and French-language version, *La Grande Mer), Playboy of Paris* (and French-language version, *Le Petit Café*) 1930; *El Cliente Seductor* (2-reel Spanish-language film shot in France), *The Stolen Jools* (2-reel comedy produced by Hollywood's Masquers Club), *The Smiling Lieutenant* (and French-language version, *Le Lieutenant souriant*) 1931; *Toboggan* (short; Fr.), *One Hour with You* (and French-language version, *Une Heure près de toi), Make Me a Star* (cameo), *Love Me Tonight* 1932; *A Bedtime Story, The Way to Love* (and French-language version, *L'Amour guide*) 1933; *The Merry Widow* (and French-language version, *La Veuve joyeuse*) 1934; *Folies Bergère* (and French-language version, *L'Homme des Folies Bergère*) 1935; *The Beloved Vagabond* (UK) 1936. In France—*L'Homme du Jour/The Man of the Hour, Avec le Sourire/With a Smile* 1937; *Break the News* (UK) 1938; *Pièges/Personal Column* 1939; *Le Silence est d'Or/Man About Town* 1947; *Paris 1900* (compilation doc.) 1948; *La Roi/A Royal Affair, Ma Pomme/Just Me* 1950; *Schlager-parade* (cameo; Ger.) 1953; *Cento Anni d'Amore* (It.), *J'avais Sept Filles/My Seven Little Sins* 1954; *Rendez-vous avec Maurice Chevalier* (doc.) 1956; *Love in the Afternoon* (US) 1957; *Gigi* (US) 1958; *Count Your Blessings* (US) 1959; *Can-Can* (US), *Un Deux Trois Quatre!/Les Collants noirs/Black Tights* (narrator), *A Breath of Scandal* (US), *Pepe* (cameo; US) 1960; *Fanny* (US) 1961; *Jessica* (US/Fr./It.), *In Search of the Castaways* (US/UK) 1962; *A New Kind of Love* (cameo; US) 1963; *Panic Button* (US), *I'd Rather Be Rich* (US) 1964; *Monkeys Go Home!* (US) 1967; *The Aristocats* (off-screen title song only) 1970.

Chiari, Mario. Art director. *b.* July 14, 1909, Florence, Italy. *d.* 1989. Although trained as an architect, he entered Italian films in 1940 as assistant and script collaborator of Alessandro BLASETTI and helped the director on such notable films as *La Corona di Ferro* (1941) and *Fabiola* (1948). He also directed a number of shorts and an episode of a feature film, but it was as art director from the early 50s that he made an important contribution to Italian and international cinema.

FILMS INCLUDE (as art director): *Miracolo a Milano/Miracle in Milan* (costumes only), *Vulcano/Volcano* 1951; *La Carrozza d'Oro/The Golden Coach, La Nemica* 1952; *I Vitelloni* 1953; *Carosello Napoletano/Neapolitan Carousel, Le Rouge et le Noir* 1954; *War and Peace* (US) 1956; *Le Notti Bianche/White Nights* 1957; *Il Gobbo/The Hunchback of Rome* 1960; *Barabba/Barabbas* 1961; *La Città Prigioniera/Conquered City* 1962; *La Bibbia/The Bible* (It./US) 1966; *Doctor Dolittle* (US) 1967; *Un Tranquillo Posto di Campagna/A Quiet Place in the Country* 1968; *Fraülein Doktor* (It./Yug.) 1968; *Ludwig* 1973; *King Kong* (co-art dir.; US) 1976; *Clair de Femme* (Fr./It.) 1979.

Chiari, Walter. Actor. *b.* Walter Annichiarico, 1924, in Verona, Italy. *d.* 1991. Darkly handsome leading man of Italian and some international films, whose affable personality and flair for comedy roles also kept him active on the stage and in TV.

FILMS INCLUDE: *Vanità* 1947; *I Cadetti di Guascogna* 1950; *Bellissima, O.K. Nerone/O.K. Nero, Il Sogno di Zorro* 1951; *La Minute de Verité/The Moment of Truth* (Fr.), *Gran*

Varietà 1953; *Un Giorno di Pretura/A Day in Court, Questa è la Vita/Of Life and Love, Le Rouge et le Noir* (Fr.) 1954; *Nana* (Fr.), *Pepote, Donatella* 1955; *Amore a Prima Vista, The Little Hut* (US) 1957; *Bonjour Tristesse* (US), *Festa di Maggio/Premier Mai* 1958; *Femmine di Lusso/Love the Italian Way, A Breath of Scandal* (US) 1960; *Copacabana Palace/Girl Game* (Braz./It./Fr.) 1962; *Le Corniaud/The Sucker* (Fr./It.), *Made in Italy* 1965; *Falstaff/Chimes at Midnight* (Sp./Switz.) 1966; *Capricio all'Italiana* 1968; *Monte Carlo or Bust/Those Daring Young Men in Their Jaunty Jalopies* (UK/Fr./It.) 1969; *Joe Valachi—I Segreti di Cosa Nostra/The Valachi Papers* 1972; *Zig-Zag* (Fr./Hung.) 1974; *La Banca di Monate* 1976; *Italiano como me* 1977; *Ridiamo insieme* 1979.

Chiarini, Luigi. Film theoretician, critic, director, screenwriter. *b.* June 20, 1900, Rome. *d.* 1975. The holder of a law degree, he turned to journalism, contributing to various literary publications. In 1935 he published his first of several books on film, *Cinematografo,* and founded the famous Italian film school Centro Sperimentale di Cinematografia. He remained head of the school until 1943 and continued as one of its directors through 1950. In 1937 he founded *Bianco e Nero,* one of the world's most respected film publications, which he edited until 1951. For many years a leading figure in Italian culture, he devoted most of his energies to film and was considered by many as the dean of the Italian cinema. His books on film theory include *Problemi del Film* (1939), an anthology he co-edited with Umberto Barbaro; *Cinque Capitoli sul Film* (1941); *Il Film nei Problemi dell'Arte* (1949); *Il Film nella Battaglia delle Idee* (1954); and *Arte e Tecnica del Film* (1962). He also directed several films and collaborated on the screenplays of others. His work as a director is considered cold and stylistic. During much of the 60s he served as director of the Venice Film Festival. Chiarini's six-year term (1962–68) as head of the festival was marked by controversy and criticism of his flamboyance and dictatorial one-man policies. He was toppled from the post in 1968 after a bitter confrontation with radical leftists and retreated into academic life as professor of film history and criticism at the University of Urbino, a position he held until his death at 75. He recorded the events that brought about his resignation from the Venice Festival in the book *Of Lions and Other Beasts.*

FILMS: As director-screenwriter—*Via delle Cinque Lune, La Bella Addormentata/Sleeping Beauty* 1942; *La Locandiera* 1943; *Ultimo Amore* 1946; *Patto col Diavolo* 1949. As screenwriter alone—*La Peccatrice* 1940. As screenwriter in collaboration—*Stazione Termini/Indiscretion of an American Wife, Siamo Donne/We the Women, Tempi Nostri/The Anatomy of Love, Amore in Città/Love in the City* 1953; *Ioamo. . . tu ami/I Love You Love, Viva l'Italia* (co-story only) 1961.

Chiaureli, Mikhail. Director, actor. *b.* Jan. 25, 1894, in Tiflis, Georgia, Russia. *d.*(?) A former sculptor, he played an important part in the development of the Georgian branch of Soviet cinema, first as actor in the early 20s, then as director since 1928. His early films were impressive, almost neorealistic in style. They included *Khabarda* (1931), a sharp satire on personality cults. Ironically, Chiaureli himself eventually became a leader in the Stalin personality cult in postwar Soviet films. Although his idolization of the tyrant reached ridiculous levels in flag-waving productions like *The Vow* and *The Fall of Berlin,* Chiaureli, winner of the Order of Lenin in 1935, handled these and other films with considerable skill. After Stalin's death, he made only two films, then vanished from view.

FILMS (as director): *In the Last Hour* (short), *First Cornet Streshnev* (co-dir. with Efim Dzigan) 1928; *Saba* 1929; *Khabarda* (also co-sc.), *Out of the Way!* 1931; *The Last Masquerade* (also sc.) 1934; *Arsen* (also co-sc.) 1937; *The Great Dawn/The Great Glow/They Wanted Peace* (also co-sc.) 1938; *Georgi Saakadze* (2 parts) 1942–43; *The Vow* (also co-sc.) 1946; *The Fall of Berlin* (two parts; also co-sc.) 1949–50; *The Unforgettable Year 1919* 1952; *Otar's Widow* 1958; *The Story of a Girl* (also co-sc.) 1960.

China. The world's most populous nation was one of the slowest to develop its own film industry. Film clips were exhibited in Shanghai by American and French showmen as early as 1896, but it was not until 1908 that the first locally made fiction film was produced, an adaptation of scenes from a Chinese opera, *Tingchun Mountain.* Many of China's early films were similarly derived from staged opera productions or light comedies. The first company to produce films on a regular basis—the Asia Motion Picture Company—was set up in 1908 by an American, Benjamin Polaski, in partnership with two Chinese businessmen. Although their films attracted large audiences in China's big cities, they were rarely seen abroad. A more sophisticated network of production and distributorship was established in 1917 by the Commercial Press, a foreign-owned Shanghai-based publishing house. The company produced newsreels and documentary films as well as entertainment features. The first wholly owned Chinese film company, Ming Hsing, was formed in 1922. Many small companies became active in the film business in the early 20s, but few survived longer than a few years. Among the more successful films of the early period were *Sea Oath* (1921), *Beauties and Skeletons* (1922), and *Orphan Rescues Grandfather* (1923).

The coming of sound created not only an additional financial burden on the struggling industry but also a new technical challenge and the problem of producing synchronized talkies for a multidialect population. One result was the decentralization of production and the mushrooming of small film companies in various regional cities. Films in Cantonese manufactured in Canton and Hong Kong earned hard foreign currency for their producers because they were often exported to communities of Chinese emigrés in the US and elsewhere.

The early Chinese talkies were technically primitive, but the growing internal political strife and the increasing external threat from Japan soon resulted in a greater awareness of social and political issues on the Chinese screen and contributed to a rapid maturation of the Chinese cinema. Cheng Bu-kao's *Wild Torrent* (1933) dealt with the oppression of peasants by landlords. Tsai Chu-sheng's *The Song of the Fishermen* (1934) took up the cause of Yangtse boatmen. It won a prize at the Moscow Festival of 1935. Other important films of the period include *Dawn Over the Metropolis, The Angry Tide of China's Seas, The Existence of the Nation, The Outcry of Women, and Crossroads.*

After the Japanese invasion of Shanghai in 1937, the large film community in that city dispersed. Some directors, writers, technicians, and actors found exile in Hong Kong or on Taiwan, but others followed the fleeing leadership of the Government to Hankow, then to Chungking. The conquering Japanese took over the film studios in the captured territories and converted them for use in the production of propaganda films, often with the collaboration of technicians and actors who stayed behind.

The civil war that was touched off by Japan's surrender in 1945 extended into a struggle for control of the Chinese cinema. The Communist followers of Mao Tse-tung had the upper hand over Chiang Kai-shek's Nationalists in that cultural war as they eventually would in the political conflict. Among several impressive films made by leftists during that transitional period were *Spring River Flows East/Tears of the Yangtse* (1947), *Lights of Ten Thousand Homes* (1948), *Crows and Sparrows* (1949), *The Bridge* (1949), and *Daughters of China* (1949).

Soon after the establishment of the People's Republic of

China, in October of 1949, the film industry was nationalized. The Ministry of Culture set up a Film Administration Bureau with two main divisions, one concerned with film production and processing and the other with distribution and exhibition. Seven major studios and numerous smaller production units were activated. The first major film produced by the nationalized industry was a Sino-Soviet co-production, *Victory of the Chinese People* (1950). Other early films included *The White-Haired Girl, New Heroes and Heroines,* and *The Life of Wu Hsun.* The latter film was hurriedly removed from the screens despite great initial success after it met with the personal displeasure of Chairman Mao, who was not known as a film enthusiast.

Propaganda and indoctrination themes characterized most of the films produced in China in the ensuing years. Filmmakers generally tackled "safe" subjects, echoing the Government's political and economic line in films set against a modern background or adapting approved historic sagas and revolutionary stage operas to the screen. There was a brief spate of originality during Mao's Hundred Flowers campaign in the mid-50s which encouraged brief speech, but the industry soon reverted to mass mediocrity. In 1964, annual production reached 480 feature films, 3,000 newsreels, 1,400 scientific films, and more than 200 cartoons. However, production was drastically reduced in the wake of the Cultural Revolution, and the film industry entered a lengthy period of decline from which it began emerging only during the political thaw of the late 70s.

China enjoyed a flowering of creativity during the 80s, mirroring the cultural and economic reforms of the nation. The re-opened Beijing Film Academy—a national school for directors that closed during the Cultural Revolution—graduated its first class in 1982. Christened the "fifth generation," these directors (Chen Kaige, Huang Jianxin, Zhang Yimou, and others) had privileged exposure to Western film and sought to bring the same quality to their national cinema. While willing to operate within conventional genres and political limitations, the new directors' works brought great advances to Chinese cinema: elliptical narratives, fresh subject matter, and technical advances in color and camerawork. A number of enduring works emerged from this period, including Tian Zhuangzhuang's *The Horse Thief* (1987), Chen's *Yellow Earth* (1983), Huang's *The Black Cannon Incident* (1983), Zhang's *Red Sorghum* (1988), and Xie Fei's *Hibiscus Town* (1987).

To some degree, the Chinese government tolerated the reform movement and was content to collect the international royalties from these productions. Nevertheless, the government's Film Bureau continued to license and censor films, demanding adherence to the four basic principles: the leadership of the Communist Party, adherence to the socialist road, the preservation of national dignity, and attention to the sensibilities of ethnic minorities. Particularly in the latter half of the decade, the Bureau banned films outright or heavily reworked them; an example of the latter tendency was Chen's *The Big Parade* (1985), to which propagandistic voiceovers and a triumphant martial climax were ordered by the government.

With the political repression following the 1989 massacre in Tiananmen Square, official Chinese film production has returned to safe nationalistic epics and period pieces. Although Chen, Zhang, and others continue to work in China, their productions are often financed with foreign money—Germany and Britain for Chen's *Life on a String* (1991), Japan for Zhang's *Ju Dou* (1989) and *Raise the Red Lantern* (1991).

Film exhibition in China is plagued with chronic problems. There are relatively few fixed motion picture theaters in China, and many of these are now in disrepair. Traditionally, the largest audiences have been reached by mobile projection teams that travel from village to village in every administrative area of the country. Films are even shown on boats turned for the occasion into floating theaters. When the picture shown is not in the local dialect, a member of the projection team acts as a translator, providing a vocal running commentary as the film feeds through the projector.

china (graph) pencil. A grease pencil used by film editors to mark up the work print for dissolves, fades, etc. Indispensable in the cutting room.

chinese dolly. A complex traveling shot combining the pulling back of the camera with a sweeping PAN. So called because it is executed with the dolly tracks laid at a slant in relation to the subject being photographed.

Chodorov, Edward. Playwright, screenwriter, producer. *b.* Apr. 17, 1904, New York City. *d.* 1988. *ed.* Brown U. A former Broadway stage manager, entered films as publicity director for Columbia. From the early 30s he wrote many screenplays alone or in collaboration and occasionally produced. Also wrote a number of Broadway plays, including 'King Lady,' 'Those Endearing Young Charms,' and 'Oh Men! Oh Women!' In 1953 he was blacklisted by the Hollywood studios, after being identified as a Communist Party member by choreographer Jerome ROBBINS and refusing to cooperate with the House Un-American Activities Committee. Brother of Jerome CHODOROV.

FILMS INCLUDE (as screenwriter): *Mayor of Hell, The World Changes* 1933; *Madame Du Barry* 1934; *The Story of Louis Pasteur* (uncredited), *Craig's Wife, Snowed Under* 1936; *The League of Frightened Men* (assoc. prod. only) 1937; *Rich Man Poor Girl* (prod. only), *Yellow Jack, Woman Against Woman* (also prod.), *Spring Madness* (also prod.) 1938; *Tell No Tales* (prod. only) 1939; *The Man from Dakota* (prod. only) 1940; *Those Endearing Young Charms* (play basis only) 1945; *Undercurrent* 1946; *The Hucksters* (adapt. only) 1947; *Road House* (also prod.) 1948; *Kind Lady* 1951; *Oh Men! Oh Women!* (play basis only) 1957.

Chodorov, Jerome. Playwright, screenwriter. Born on Aug. 10, 1911, in New York City. *ed.* U. of Pennsylvania. Brother of Edward CHODOROV. A former New York *World* reporter, he began writing screenplays in the mid-30s, sometimes in collaboration with Joseph FIELDS. They later collaborated on Broadway plays, including 'My Sister Eileen' (1940) and its musical version, 'Wonderful Town' (1953), 'Junior Miss' (1952), 'Anniversary Waltz' (1954), and 'The Ponder Heart' (1956).

FILMS INCLUDE: *The Case of the Lucky Legs* 1935; *Dancing Feet* 1936; *Devil's Playground, Reported Missing* 1937; *Rich Man Poor Girl* 1938; *Conspiracy* 1939; *The Mad Empress, Two Girls on Broadway, Dulcy* 1940; *Louisiana Purchase* 1941; *My Sister Eileen* 1942; *Junior Miss* (play basis only), *Those Endearing Young Charms* 1945; *Man from Texas* 1948; *Happy Anniversary* 1959.

choker. A slang term for a tight close-up, usually limited to a performer's face.

Chomon, Segundo de (also known as **Sogon de Chomon** and **Segundo Chaumont**). Pioneer director, animator, and cameraman. *b.* Oct. 18, 1871, Teruel, Spain. *d.* 1929. Began in Spanish films in 1902, turning out newsreel clips and a great many trick films that rivaled the films of Méliès for originality and inventiveness. He is credited with advancing the single-frame technique, optical dissolves, and complex studio traveling shots. From 1906 to 1909 he worked mainly in France, then returned to Spain, where he established his own production company in 1910. In 1912 he went to Italy, where his inventiveness and technical expertise as a cameraman contributed greatly to the international success of Giovanni Pastrone's *Cabiria* (1914). In the 20s he was employed mainly as a special-effects expert.

FILMS INCLUDE: As director—In Spain: *Los Guapos del Parque, Hotel Electrico* 1905. In France: *La Maison hantée, Les Ombres chinoises, La Passion de Jesus, La Legende du Fantôme, Le Chevalier mystère, Voyage à la Planète Jupiter* 1907; *Mars, Cuisine magnetique, La Table magique, Transformation elastique, Les Jouets vivants, Fabrique d'Argent* 1908; *Liquefaction des Corps durs, Voyage au Centre de la Terre, Voyage dans la Lune, Sculpteur moderne* 1909. In Spain: *Amor Gitano, La Expiacion, El Puente de la Muerte, La Fatalidad, Adios se un Artista, Flores y Perlas* 1910; *Pulgacirto* 1911. As cameraman—In Italy: *Padre* 1912; *Tigris* 1913; *Cabiria* (co-phot.) 1914. As special-effects man—In Italy: *Maciste all'Inferno* 1925. In France: *Napoléon* 1927.

Chong, Rae Dawn. Born in 1962, in Vancouver, B.C., Canada. The daughter of actor-director Tommy CHONG, of Cheech and Chong fame, she began performing on TV at 12, then developed into an appealing young lead in films.

FILMS: *Stony Island* 1978; *La Guerre du Feu/Quest for Fire* (Fr./Can.) 1981; *Cheech and Chong's The Corsican Brothers, Beat Street, Fear City, Choose Me* 1984; *American Flyers, City Limits, Commando, The Color Purple* 1985; *Soul Man* 1986; *The Squeeze, The Principal* 1987; *Far Out Man, Tales from the Darkside: The Movie* 1990; *Amazon, Common Bonds* 1991; *When the Party's Over, Chaindance, In Exile* 1992; *Hideaway* 1995; *Small Time* 1996.

Chong, Tommy (Thomas). Actor, director, screenwriter. Born on May 24, 1938, in Edmonton, Alta., Canada. A rhythm-and-blues guitar player with various Canadian combos, he switched to comedy, teaming up with Richard MARIN to form an improvisation duo. As CHEECH AND CHONG, they broke into movies in the late 70s and for several years enjoyed some popularity with a series of lowbrow, low-budget, high-profit, drug-related comedies. Chong doubled as director of several of his films and collaborated on the screenplays of most. He is the father of Rae Dawn CHONG.

FILMS (as actor): *Up in Smoke* (also co-sc.) 1978; *Cheech and Chong's Next Movie* (also dir., co-sc.) 1980; *Cheech and Chong's Nice Dreams* (also dir., co-sc.) 1981; *Things Are Tough All Over* (also co-sc.), *It Came from Hollywood* 1982; *Still Smokin'* (also dir., co-sc.), *Yellowbeard* 1983; *Cheech and Chong's The Corsican Brothers* (also dir., co-sc.) 1984; *After Hours* 1985; *Far Out Man* (also dir., sc.) 1990; *Ferngully* (v/o), *Spirit of '76* 1991; *Ready to Wear* (cameo) 1994; *National Lampoon's Senior Trip* 1995; *Faithful* 1996.

Chopra, Joyce. Director, producer. Born in 1938. *ed.* Brandeis University, Waltham, Mass. (comparative literature); Neighborhood Playhouse, N.Y. After making several documentaries, she made her feature debut with the well-regarded *Smooth Talk* (1985), which introduced actress Laura Dern in the intense story of a teenage girl's sexual awakening.

FILMS INCLUDE: *Martha Clarke, Light and Dark* (dir., ed., prod.) 1981; *Smooth Talk* (dir.) 1985; *The Lemon Sisters* (dir.) 1989; *Murder in New Hampshire* 1991.

Chrétien, Henri. Inventor. *b.* Feb. 1, 1879, Paris. *d.* 1956. Invented the anamorphic lens, which he exhibited in 1927 as the Hypergonar. Director Claude Autant-Lara experimented with the lens in a short, *Construire un Feu* (1928), but the invention was neglected until 1952, when it was acquired by 20th Century-Fox and then adapted for the company's CinemaScope process, which was launched the following year. Anamorphic lenses are now used in a variety of wide-screen processes. See also: ANAMORPHIC LENS; CINEMASCOPE; PANAVISION.

Christensen (also **Christiansen** in the US), **Benjamin.** Director. *b.* Sept. 28, 1879, Viborg, Denmark. *d.* 1959. *ed.* U. of Copenhagen (medicine). Started out in show business as an opera singer in 1902. Later became a stage actor and director and from 1906 appeared as an actor in occasional Danish films. In 1913 he made an impressive debut as director of *The Mysterious X,* in which he also starred and which first revealed his preoccupation with the mysterious and the macabre, a preoccupation that was to be superlatively expressed in his best-known film, *Häxan/Witchcraft Through the Ages,* which he directed in Sweden and in which he appeared as Satan. The film remains a masterpiece of the horror genre, a horrifyingly vivid record in striking lights and shades of diabolism and satanic practices from the Middle Ages to the 20th century. The international reputation of the film (although it was banned in many countries for scenes of cruelty and nudism), resulted in an invitation to work for UFA in Berlin. He directed three German films and played the lead role in Carl Dreyer's *Mikaël/Chained* (1924). In 1925 he arrived in Hollywood, where he directed a number of films through the late 20s, mostly mysteries, some spiced with black humor. In the early 30s he returned to Denmark, where he turned out several routine films during WW II.

FILMS: In Denmark—*The Mysterious X* (also sc., act.) 1913; *Night of Vengeance* (also sc., act.) 1915. In Sweden—*Häxan/Witchcraft Through the Ages* (also sc., act.) 1922. In Germany—*Unter Juden/Among Jews, Seine Frau die Unbekannte/His Mysterious Adventure* (also sc.) 1923; *Die Frau mit dem schlechten Ruf/The Woman Who Did* 1925. In the US—*The Devil's Circus* (also story, sc.) 1926; *Mockery* (also story) 1927; *The Hawk's Nest, The Haunted House* 1928; *Seven Footprints to Satan, The House of Horror, The Mysterious Island* (some footage only; final direction credited to Lucien Hubbard) 1929. In Denmark—*Children of Divorce* (also sc.) 1939; *The Child* (also co-sc.) 1940; *Come Home with Me* 1941; *The Lady with the Light Gloves* 1943.

Christian, Linda. Actress. Born Blanca Rosa Welter, on Nov. 13, 1923, in Tampico, Mexico. The daughter of a Dutch oilman, she grew up in Venezuela, South Africa, Holland, Switzerland, and Palestine, in the last of which she worked at the office of the British censor and attended medical school. She broke into Hollywood films in the mid-40s as a starlet but despite considerable beauty never gained much popularity as a leading lady. She became better known for her off-screen romances widely reported in the fan magazines. Her husbands included actors Tyrone POWER and Edmund PURDOM.

FILMS INCLUDE: *Holiday in Mexico* 1946; *Green Dolphin Street* 1947; *Tarzan and the Mermaids* 1948; *The Happy Time, Battle Zone* 1952; *Slaves of Babylon* 1953; *Athena* 1954; *Thunderstorm* 1956; *The House of the Seven Hawks* 1959; *The V.I.P.s* (UK) 1963; *The Beauty Jungle/Contest Girl* (UK) 1964; *Il Momento della Verità/The Moment of Truth* (It./Sp.) 1965; *Bel Ami 2000/How to Seduce a Playboy* (Aus./Fr./It.) 1966.

Christian, Paul. See HUBSCHMID, Paul.

Christian-Jaque. Director. *b.* Christian Maudet, on Sept. 4, 1904, in Paris. *d.* 1994. *ed.* Ecole des Beaux-Arts, Ecole des Arts Decoratifs (Paris; architecture). Started out as a journalist and film critic and in 1926 entered the industry as a poster designer and later became a set decorator and assistant to Julien DUVIVIER and other directors. In 1932 he made his own debut as director. A prolific worker and a solid technician, he was among the most commercially successful French directors, equally adept at drama, comedy, and action films. From time to time he enjoyed critical approval as well, and he won the best director award at Cannes for his lively period adventure farce *Fanfan la*

Tulipe (1952). An elegant man of confident charm, Christian-Jaque has been married five times. Three of his wives were actresses, Simone Renant, René Faure, and the late Martine CAROL. The latter starred in many of his films of the 50s.

FEATURE FILMS: *Le Bidon d'Or* 1932; *Adhémar Lampiot, Le Tendron d'Achille, Ça Colle, La Boeuf sur la Langue* 1933; *L'Hôtel du Libre-Echange* 1934; *Compartiment des Dames seules, Le Père Lampion, Sous la Griffe, La Sonnette d'Alarme, La Famille Pont-Biquet, Sacré Léonce, Voyage d'Agrément* 1935; *Monsieur Personne, Un de la Légion, L'Ecole des Journalistes, Rigolboche, Josette, On ne roule pas Antoinette* 1936; *La Maison d'en face, A Venise une Nuit, Les Perles de la Couronne/The Pearls of the Crown* (co-dir. with Sacha Guitry), *François Ier/Francis the First, Les Dégourdis de la Onzième* 1937; *Les Pirates du Rail, Ernest le Rebelle, Les Disparus de Saint-Agil/Boys' School* 1938; *Raphaël le Tatoué, C'était moi, L'Enfer des Anges* 1939; *Le Grand Elan* 1940; *L'Assassinat du Père Noël/Who Killed Santa Claus?, Premier Bal* 1941; *La Symphonie Fantastique* 1942; *Voyage sans Espoir* 1943; *Carmen* (also co-sc.; release delayed from 1942; It./Fr.), *Sortilèges/The Bellman, Boule de Suif/Angel and Sinner* (also co-adapt.) 1945; *Un Revenant/A Lover's Return* (also co-adapt.) 1946; *La Chartreuse de Parme/La Certosa di Parma* (also co-sc.; Fr./It.), *D'Homme à Hommes/Man to Men* (also co-sc.; Fr./Switz.) 1948; *Singoalla/The Wind Is My Lover/The Mask and the Sword* (also co-sc.; Sw./Fr.), *Souvenirs perdus* (also co-adapt.) 1950; *Barbe-Bleue/Bluebeard* (also adapt.) 1951; *Fanfan la Tulipe/Fanfan the Tulip* (also prod., co-adapt.), *Adorables Créatures/Adorable Creatures* (also co-sc.) 1952; *Lucrèce Borgia/Lucrezia Borgia/Sins of the Borgias* (also co-sc.; Fr./It.) 1953; *Destinées/Daughters of Destiny* ("Lysistrata" episode; Fr./It.), *Madame du Barry* (also co-sc.) 1954; *Nana* (also co-sc.) 1955; *Si tous les Gars du Monde/If All the Guys in the World* (also co-sc.) 1956; *Nathalie/The Foxiest Girl in Paris* (also prod., co-adapt.) 1957; *La Loi c'est la Loi/The Law Is the Law* (also co-adapt.; Fr./It.) 1958; *Babette s'en va-t-en Guerre/Babette Goes to War* 1959; *La Française et l'Amour/Love and the Frenchwoman* ("Divorce" episode) 1960; *Madame Sans-Gêne/Madame* (also co-sc.; Fr./It./Sp.) 1961; *Les Bonnes Causes/Don't Tempt the Devil* (also co-sc.; Fr./It.) 1963; *La Tulipe noire/The Black Tulip, Le Repas des Fauves* 1964; *Le Gentleman de Cocody/Man from Cocody* (also co-sc.; Fr./It.), *Guerre secrète/The Dirty Game* (co-dir. with Terence Young, Carlo Lizzani, and Werner Klingler; also co-sc.; Fr./It./Ger.), *La Fabuleuse Aventure de Marco Polo/Marco the Magnificent* (co-dir. with Denys de la Patellière and Noel Howard; Fr./It./Afg./Eg./Yug.) 1965; *La Seconde Vérité, Le Saint prend l'Affût* 1966; *Deux Billets pour Mexico/Dead Run* (also co-sc.; Fr./It./Ger.) 1967; *Les Amours de Lady Hamilton/Lady Hamilton/The Making of a Lady* (Fr./It./Ger.) 1968; *Les Pétroleuses/The Legend of Frenchy King* 1971; *Dr. Justice* 1975; *La Vie Parisienne* 1978.

Christians, Mady. Actress. *b.* Margarethe Maria Christians, Jan. 19, 1900, Vienna. *d.* 1951. Distinguished personality of the European and American stage who had a secondary career in German and Hollywood films. She first came to the US in 1912, when she appeared with her parents in a German-speaking theater they established in New York. In 1912, having made one American film, billed as Margarete Christians, she returned to Europe to study under Max REINHARDT and in the 20s starred in many German stage productions and films as well as in occasional Broadway plays. In 1933, when the Nazis came to power, she returned to the US for good and began commuting between Hollywood and Broadway. In films, she played mostly supporting character parts, but her stage triumphs were many, notably as Gertrude to Maurice Evans's Hamlet (1938) and the title role in 'I Remember Mama' (1944). Shortly before her death, she was blacklisted by Hollywood after she was labeled a Communist sympathizer during the McCarthy era investigations.

FILMS INCLUDE: In the US—*Audrey* 1916. In Germany—*Der Mann ohne Namen* 1920; *Das Weib des Pharao/The Loves of Pharaoh* 1921; *Malmaison* 1922; *Die Budden-brooks, Das Spiel der Königin/Ein Glas Wasser, Der verlorene Schuh, Der Wetterwart, Die Finanzen des Grossherzogs/The Grand Duke's Finances* 1923; *Mensch gegen Mensch* 1924; *Der Abenteurer, Der Farmer aus Texas, Die Verrufenen/Slums of Berlin, Ein Walzertraum/The Waltz Dream* 1925; *Nanette macht alles, Die Königin vom Moulin Rouge* 1926; *Grand Hotel, Königin Luise/Queen Luise, Der Sohn der Hagar/Out of the Mist* 1927; *The Runaway Princess* (UK), *Duel* (Fr.) 1928; *Das brennende Herz/The Burning Heart, Dich hab'ich geliebt/Because I Loved You* 1929; *Die Frau von der man spricht* 1931; *Friederike, Der Schwarze Husar* 1932; *Ich und die Kaiserin* (and UK version, *The Only Girl/Heart Song;* in both as Empress Eugenie) 1933. In the US—*A Wicked Woman* 1934; *Escapade* 1935; *Come and Get It* 1936; *Seventh Heaven, The Woman I Love, Heidi* 1937; *Address Unknown, Tender Comrade* 1944; *All My Sons, Letter from an Unknown Woman* 1948.

Christiansen, Benjamin. See CHRISTENSEN, Benjamin.

Christie, Al(bert). Director, producer. *b.* Nov. 24, 1886, London, Ontario, Canada. *d.* 1951. Began his film career in 1909, working in various capacities for the Nestor company. In 1912 he was put in charge of the production of a series of short Westerns, "The Wild West Weekly," but it was in the comedy field that he would later make his name. He directed numerous comedy shorts for Nestor, then Universal, many of them starring Betty Compson and the comedy team of Eddie Lyons and Lee Moran. By mid-1916 he had set up his own production company, a virtual laugh factory that turned out a great many inexpensive and simple-minded but often popular two-reel comedies each year as well as occasional full-length comedy features. Next to Mack Sennett and Hal Roach he was the most prolific and best-known producer of comedy shorts during the silent era. He continued producing through the late 30s, mainly in the service of Columbia and Educational.

FILMS INCLUDE: As director—*When the Mummy Cried for Help, All Aboard, Almost a King* (also sc.), *Little Egypt Malone, Mrs. Plum's Pudding* (feature; also co-sc.), *Eddie's Little Love Affair* (also co-sc.), *Wanted: A Leading Lady* (also sc.), *Love and a Savage* (also sc.) 1915; *Wanted: A Husband* 1916. As director-producer—*Seminary Scandal, Never Lie to Your Wife* 1916; *Five Little Widows, Who's Looney Now?* 1917; *Out of the Night, Wedding Blues, The Reckless Sex, So Long Letty* (feature) 1920; *Kiss and Make Up, See My Lawyer* (feature) 1921; *One Stormy Knight, That Son of Sheik* 1922; *The Chased Bride* 1923; *Reckless Romance* (feature; prod. only), *Savage Love, Bright Lights* 1924; *Charley's Aunt* (feature; prod. only), *Stop Flirting* (feature; co-prod. only), *Madame Behave* (feature; prod. only), *Hot Doggie* 1925; *Up in Mabel's Room* (feature; prod. only), *Seven Days* (feature; prod. only), *The Nervous Wreck* (feature; prod. only) 1926; *Meet the Folks* 1927; *Tillie's Punctured Romance* (feature; prod. only) 1928; *The Carnation Kid* (feature; prod. only), *Divorce Made Easy* 1929; *Charley's Aunt* (feature; remake), *Sweethearts on Parade* (feature; prod. only) 1930. As producer—*Girls Will Be Boys* 1931; *He's a Honey, Hollywood Runaround* 1932; *Static* 1933; *Rural Romeos, Second-Hand Husbands* 1934; *College Capers, Dame Shy, Moon Over Manhattan* 1935; *Home on the Range, Spooks*

1936; *The Bashful Ballerina, Playboy Number One, Koo Koo Korrespondence Skool* 1937; *Pardon My Accident* 1938.

Christie, Julie. Actress. Born on Apr. 14, 1941, in Chukua, Assam, India, on her father's tea plantation. Educated in England and France, she trained for the stage at London's Central School of Music and Drama and made her debut with a repertory company in 1957. She began playing small roles in films in 1962 and got her first lead the following year in John SCHLESINGER's *Billy Liar* (1963). It was Schlesinger who provided her with a tailor-made role in *Darling* (1965), which made her an international star and the winner of the best actress Oscar and the New York Film Critics Award, among other prizes. A striking beauty with unusual facial features and a beguiling personality, she remained a leading star of British and American films through the late 60s and 70s, and sustained her appeal well into the 80s. She was nominated for a second Oscar for her performance in *McCabe and Mrs. Miller* (1971).

FILMS: *Crooks, Anonymous* 1962; *The Fast Lady, Billy Liar* 1963; *Young Cassidy* (UK/US), *Darling, Doctor Zhivago* (US) 1965; *Fahrenheit 451* 1966; *Far from the Madding Crowd* 1967; *Petulia* (UK/US) 1968; *In Search of Gregory* (UK/It.) 1970; *The Go-Between, McCabe and Mrs. Miller* (US) 1971; *Don't Look Now* (UK/Fr./It.) 1973; *Shampoo* (US), *Nashville* (cameo; US) 1975; *Demon Seed* (US) 1977; *Heaven Can Wait* (US) 1978; *Memoirs of a Survivor* 1981; *Les Quarantièmes Rugissants/The Roaring Forties* (Fr.) 1982; *The Return of the Soldier, Heat and Dust* 1983; *The Gold Diggers* 1984; *Power, Miss Mary* (Arg.) 1986; *Fools of Fortune* 1990; *Dragonheart, Hamlet* 1996.

Christopher, Dennis. Actor. Born Dennis Carelli, on Dec. 2, 1955, in Philadelphia. *ed.* Temple U. Open-faced, blond young lead of Hollywood films. On the screen from his mid-teens, he is best remembered as the determined biker in *Breaking Away.* He also appeared in TV and on the New York stage.

FILMS INCLUDE: *The Young Graduates, Blood and Lace* 1971; *Fellini's Roma* (bit; It.) 1972; *Three Women, September 30 1955* 1977; *A Wedding* 1978; *Breaking Away, California Dreaming* 1979; *Fade to Black* 1980; *Chariots of Fire* (UK) 1981; *Don't Cry It's Only Thunder* 1982; *Jake Speed, Flight of the Spruce Goose* 1986; *Alien Predator* 1987; *A Sinful Life, Circuitry Man* 1990; *Dead Women in Lingerie, Doppelganger* 1991; *Circuitry Man II* 1994.

chromatic aberration. A lens defect causing colored fringes at the edges of a photographed image. The defect prevents different color rays from converging on the same plane.

chronotography. The photographic recording of successive phases of movement for the purpose of scientific study, as exercised by MUYBRIDGE and MAREY in the 1870s and 1880s. Essentially just a succession of stills, it paved the way for the invention of cinematography. Sophisticated methods of stop-motion chronotography are still used for the scientific analysis of fast-moving objects, such as the study of ballistics.

Chukhrai, Grigori. Director. Born on May 23, 1921, in Melitopol, Ukraine (USSR). His studies at the Soviet State film school (VGIK) were interrupted by WW II, in which he served as a parachutist and infantry officer and was wounded five times and decorated for valor. Returning to school, he studied under directors ROMM and YUTKEVICH and started his professional career as the former's assistant. Began directing in the mid-50s and immediately established himself in the front rank of the Soviet cinema. His first solo film, *The Forty-First* (1956), was an important turning point, representing a marked departure from the hero cult theretofore prevalent in Soviet war films. It received the Jury Prize at the Cannes Festival. *Ballad of a Soldier* (1959), also an award winner at Cannes, treated war with compassion and sincerity, rare in an industry noted for reliance on propaganda. The first Soviet film ever entered in an American festival, it won the top prize at San Francisco in 1960. It also earned Chukhrai the highest Soviet cultural award, the Order of Lenin. His next, *Clear Skies* (1961), attacked the personality cult and decried the horrors of the Stalinist era. Chukhrai's romanticism introduced a refreshing new spirit into the drabness of conventional social realism. In 1966, he was appointed the head of the newly formed Moscow Experimental Film Unit. But his subsequent output was sparse and undistinguished.

FILMS: *Nazar Stodolya* (co-dir. with K. Ivchenko) 1955; *The Forty-First* 1956; *Ballad of a Soldier* 1959; *Clear Skies* 1961; *There Was an Old Couple* 1965; *People!* 1966; *Stalingrad/Battle of Stalingrad/Memory* (doc.) 1970; *Untypical Story* 1977.

Churchill, Marguerite. Actress. Born on Dec. 25, 1909, in Kansas City, Mo. Attended New York's Professional Children's School and Theatre Guild Drama School and made her Broadway debut at 13. An attractive brunette, she came to Hollywood shortly after the advent of sound and played feminine leads in many films of the early 30s, mostly B pictures, including several in the horror genre. She returned to Broadway in 1932, for the hit play 'Dinner at Eight' and again in 1937, after retiring from the screen. Subsequently appeared in only one picture in 1950. She was married to cowboy star George O'BRIEN from 1933 to 1948. When last heard from, she was living in Portugal.

FILMS: *The Valiant, Pleasure Crazed, They Had to See Paris, Seven Faces* 1929; *Harmony at Home, Born Reckless, Good Intentions, The Big Trail* 1930; *Girls Demand Excitement, Charlie Chan Carries On, Quick Millions, Riders of the Purple Sage, Ambassador Bill* 1931; *Forgotten Commandments* 1932; *Girl Without a Room* 1933; *Without Children, Penthouse Party* 1935; *Man Hunt, The Walking Dead, Murder by an Aristocrat, Dracula's Daughter, Alibi for Murder, The Final Hour, Legion of Terror* 1936; *Bunco Squad* 1950.

Churchill, Sarah. Actress. *b.* Oct. 7, 1914, London, the daughter of Sir Winston Churchill. *d.* 1982. Trained in ballet, she became a dancer at 17 and made her professional debut on the London stage in the chorus of 'Follow the Sun' in 1936. She made her first dramatic appearance on the stage in 1939 and on the screen the following year, then joined the WAAF, in which she served until 1945. Made her US stage debut in 1949, touring with 'The Philadelphia Story,' and her first New York appearance in 1951, in the Broadway production of 'Gramercy Ghost.' She appeared in only a handful of films, playing her best-known screen role opposite Fred Astaire in *Royal Wedding* (US, 1951). The first of her three husbands was actor Vic Oliver. She was also a painter and the author of two books of verse.

FEATURE FILMS: *Who's Your Lady Friend?* 1937; *Spring Meeting, He Found a Star* 1941; *Sinfonia fatale/When in Rome* (It.), *Daniele Cortis* (It.) 1947; *All Over Town* 1949; *Royal Wedding/Wedding Bells* (US) 1951; *Serious Charge/Immortal Charge/A Touch of Hell* 1959.

Chytilová, Véra. Director. Born on Feb. 2, 1929, in Ostrava, Czechoslovakia. Majored in philosophy and architecture at Charles University and worked briefly as a draughtsman, but her side career as a fashion model brought her in contact with film people and she soon entered the industry as a continuity clerk. In 1957, having worked her way up to assistant director, she enrolled at the FAMU film school in Prague. While there, she directed several shorts and in 1962 turned out her graduation film, the medium-length *Ceiling,* which immediately placed her among the emerging formalists of the Czech new wave. Her subsequent films as director have typically combined elements of *cinéma vérité* and formalism and revealed the influence of the French Nouvelle Vague. Her best-known film in the West, *Daisies* (1966), is a complex modern fable in which she used bold, inventive filming, cutting, and color-processing techniques to mock and disparage manifestations of consumerism, conformism, indifference, and vapidity in Czech society. The film was officially condemned and banned by the authorities, but finally released in 1967, when it won the top prize at the Bergamo festival. Increasingly at odds with the political tastemakers of the state-controlled Czech cinema, she was forced to seek financing in Belgium for her next project, which did not materialize until 1970. She was unable to make another film until 1976–77. But Chytilová steadfastly held her ground and consistently refused to compromise her ideas or style. She has collaborated on most of her own screenplays, usually with screenwriter and sometimes director Ester Krumbachova (*b.* 1923). Chytilová's second husband, Jaroslav Kuçera (*b.* 1929, Prague), has been her regular cameraman.

FILMS: *Villa in the Suburbs* (short) 1959; *Mr. K—Green Street* (short) 1960; *Academy Newsreel* (short) 1961; *Ceiling* (medium-length), *A Bagful of Fleas* 1962; *Something Different/Another Way of Life* 1963; *Pearls of the Deep* (one episode) 1965; *Daisies* (release delayed from 1966) 1967; *Fruit of Paradise/We May Eat of the Fruit of the Trees of the Garden* 1970; *The Apple Game* 1977; *Panelstory/Prefab Story/Apartment House Story* 1980; *Calamity* 1982; *Chytilova vs. Forman* (for TV) 1983; *The Very Late Afternoon of a Faun* 1984; *Wolf Chalet* 1986; *Sasek a Kralovna/The Jester and the Queen* 1988; *Kopytem sem, Kopytem tam/Tainted Horseplay* 1989.

Ciampi, Yves. Director. *b.* Feb. 9, 1921, Paris. *d.* 1982. Began making amateur films while a medical student in the late 30s and continued turning out documentary and avant-garde shorts throughout his internship. His studies and film work were interrupted by the Occupation during WW II, when much of his time was spent in activities as a member of the French Resistance. After the Liberation, he was decorated with the Legion d'Honneur and in 1946 he qualified as a physician. However, instead of pursuing a medical career, he intensified his involvement in film and after serving briefly as an assistant director began working on his first feature in 1948. It was released in 1950. Much of his work was routine, but several of his films stand out for their originality and quality. In 1956 he married Japanese actress Keiko Kishi, who appeared in two of his pictures.

FEATURE FILMS: *Suzanne et ses Brigands, Un Certain Monsieur* 1950; *Un Grand Patron/The Perfectionist* (also co-sc.) 1951; *Le plus Heureux des Hommes* 1952; *L'Esclave* 1953; *Le Guérisseur* 1954; *Les Héros sont fatigués/Heroes and Sinners* (also co-sc.) 1955; *Typhon sur Nagasaki/Typhoon Over Nagasaki* (also adapt.; Fr./Jap.) 1957; *Le Vent se lève/Time Bomb* (also co-sc.; Fr./It.) 1959; *Qui êtes-vous Monsieur Sorge?* (also co-story) 1960; *Liberté I* (also co-story) 1961; *Le Ciel sur la Tête/Sky Above Heaven* (also co-sc. Fr./It.) 1964; *A quelque Jours près/A Matter of Days* (also story, co-sc.; Fr./Czech.) 1969.

Ciannelli, Eduardo. Actor. *b.* Aug. 30, 1887, the Island of Ischia, off Italy. *d.* 1969. *ed.* U. of Naples (medicine). Started in opera, as a baritone, touring Italy and the Continent. After WW I service with the Italian army, he came to the US, where he began a long and successful career as character actor on the stage and in films. He made his Broadway debut in 1925, in 'Rose Marie,' and subsequently appeared in many plays, notably as the evil Trock Estrella in 'Winterset,' a role he later repeated on the screen. He also co-authored the play 'Foolscap,' which enjoyed a moderate success on Broadway in 1933. In films from 1933, he soon developed into one of the most menacing among Hollywood's character actors. Craggy-faced, suave-mannered, and evil-eyed, he typically played criminal masterminds and gang bosses, though he could occasionally be seen in benevolent roles. From the early 50s he worked mostly in Italy.

FILMS INCLUDE: *Reunion in Vienna* 1933; *The Scoundrel* 1935; *Winterset* 1936; *Criminal Lawyer, Marked Woman* 1937; *Gunga Din* 1939; *Strange Cargo, Foreign Correspondent, The Mummy's Hand, Kitty Foyle* 1940; *I Was a Prisoner on Devil's Island, Paris Calling* 1941; *Cairo* 1942; *For Whom the Bell Tolls, They Got Me Covered* 1943; *The Conspirators, The Mask of Dimitrios, Passage to Marseille* 1944; *A Bell for Adano, Dillinger* 1945; *Perilous Holiday* 1946; *California, Seven Keys to Baldpate, The Lost Moment* 1947; *The Creeper* 1948; *Vulcano/Volcano* (It.) 1950; *The People Against O'Hara* 1951; *The Stranger's Hand* (UK), *Mambo* (It.), *Attila* (It./Fr.) 1954; *Helen of Troy* (US/It.) 1956; *Houseboat* 1958; *Der Besuch/The Visit* (Ger./Fr./It./US) 1964; *The Chase* 1966; *The Brotherhood* 1968; *Mackenna's Gold, Stiletto, The Secret of Santa Vittoria* 1969; *Boot Hill* (It.) 1970.

Cicognini, Alessandro. Composer. Born on Jan. 25, 1906, in Pescara, Italy. *ed.* Milan's Conservatory of Music. Began composing scores for Italian films in 1936. They are traditional in style but often offbeat in orchestration and are frequently performed by chamber-size groups. Won recognition for scores for De Sica's films of the neorealist period.

FILMS INCLUDE: *Il Corsare nero* 1936; *La Corona di Ferro/The Iron Crown* 1940; *Quattro Passi fra le Nuvole/Four Steps in the Clouds* 1942; *Sciuscià/Shoeshine* 1946; *Ladri di Biciclette/The Bicycle Thief* 1948; *Miracolo a Milano/Miracle in Milan* 1951; *Umberto D* 1952; *Siamo Donne/We the Women, Stazione Termini/Indiscretion of an American Wife, Pane Amore e Fantasia/Bread Love and Dreams* 1953; *L'Oro di Napoli/Gold of Naples* 1954; *Ulisse/Ulysses, Summer Madness/Summertime* (UK/US) 1955; *Il Tetto/The Roof, Loser Takes All* (UK) 1956; *Padri e Figli/Fathers and Sons* 1957; *Anna di Brooklyn/Fast and Sexy, The Black Orchid* (US) 1958; *The Pigeon That Took Rome* (US) 1962.

Cilento, Diane. Actress. Born on Oct. 5, 1933, in Brisbane, Australia (some sources: Apr. 2, 1934, Rabaul, New Guinea). The daughter of Sir Ralph West Cilento, a world-renowned authority on tropical medicine as well as a distinguished attorney, and Lady Cilento, a gynecologist, she attended New York's American Academy of Dramatic Arts, then London's Royal Academy of Dramatic Art (RADA), before making her screen debut in 1952 and her stage debut the following year. An attractive blonde, she subsequently appeared in many London and some Broadway stage productions and played leads in British and occasional Hollywood films. She was nominated for an Oscar for her performance in *Tom Jones* (1963). Formerly (1962–73) married to actor Sean Connery, she is the mother of actor Jason Connery. She is the author of the novels *The Manipulator* and *The Hybrid.*

FILMS INCLUDE: *Wings of Danger/Dead on Course, Moulin Rouge* 1952; *Meet Mr. Lucifer* 1953; *The Passing Stranger* 1954; *The Angel Who Pawned Her Harp* 1955; *The Admirable Crichton, The Truth About Women* 1957; *Jet Storm* 1959; *The Full Treatment/Stop Me Before I Kill, The Naked Edge* 1961; *I Thank a Fool* 1962; *Tom Jones* 1963; *The Third Secret, Rattle of a Simple Man* 1964; *The Agony and the Ecstasy* (US) 1965; *Hombre* (US) 1967; *Negatives* 1968; *Zero Population Growth/Z.P.G.* 1972; *Hitler: The Last Ten Days, The Wicker Man* 1973; *Duet for Four* (Austral.) 1982; *The Boy Who Had Everything* (Austral.) 1984.

Cimino, Michael. Director, screenwriter, producer. Born in 1943 in New York City. The son of a music publisher, he grew up in Old Westbury, Long Island, and attended private schools. While studying graphic arts at Michigan State, he edited the university's satirical publication *The Spartan* and participated in weightlifting competition. He then studied painting, architecture, and art history at Yale, where he earned an M.F.A. degree and became involved in school dramatics. After a six-month stint with the Army Reserves, he went to New York, where he worked as an editing apprentice for a documentary production house and trained in acting and the ballet. By the end of the 60s he had emerged as a successful director of TV commercials. In 1971 he moved to Hollywood and began collaborating on screenplays, and in 1974 made a successful debut as a director with a Clint Eastwood vehicle, *Thunderbolt and Lightfoot.*

Cimino waited four years for the release of his next film, but *The Deer Hunter* was well worth the wait. The visually stunning, emotionally charged Vietnam saga was shot in American and Thai locations under the most difficult conditions, extending way beyond schedule and budget. But it was generally hailed as a masterpiece. One respected critic called it "the greatest anti-war movie since *The Grand Illusion*." It was nominated for nine Academy Awards, winning five Oscars, including best picture and best director.

Cimino next embarked on an even more ambitious project, *Heaven's Gate,* a monumental epic of the Johnson County (Wyoming) massacre in 1892 of more than 100 immigrant settlers by land barons. The director's passion for period detail and historical accuracy and unexpected hardships during filming combined to swell production costs from $12 million to $38 million. When it was finally released in 1980, at a running length of 219 minutes, it was widely criticized as a beautiful, at moments brilliant, but plotless, structureless, self-indulgent mess. The film was immediately withdrawn from distribution, then briefly re-released in an abbreviated 149-minute version. Although *Heaven's Gate* found a minority of admirers in the US and was much liked abroad, financially it was an unmitigated disaster, one of the costliest flops in movie history. Its very title became synonymous with failure. Cimino was viewed by the Hollywood community as a present-day Erich von Stroheim. Five years would pass before he could land another assignment. His later films have received mixed reviews at best.

FILMS: As screenwriter—*Silent Running* (co-sc.) 1972; *Magnum Force* (co-sc.) 1973. As director—*Thunderbolt and Lightfoot* (also sc.) 1974; *The Deer Hunter* (also co-sc.) 1978; *Heaven's Gate* (also sc.) 1980; *Year of the Dragon* (also co-sc.) 1985; *The Sicilian* (also co-prod.) 1987; *Desperate Hours* (also co-prod.) 1990; *Sunchaser* 1996.

cinch marks. Scratch marks on the surface of film caused by the presence of abrasive particles between coils or by careless winding of a film roll.

cinéaste. Term of French origin, coined by Louis DELLUC but now also widely used in English-speaking countries. In its broad, original sense it described anyone connected with the making of films—artists, technicians, even businessmen—as well as people engaged in the study and criticism of film and its aesthetics. With time, the term has acquired a much narrower application and is now used mostly in reference to a director or other creative filmmaker.

Cinecittà. Italy's largest film studio complex, founded in 1937 and situated some six miles from downtown Rome. The name literally means "cinema city," but the studios were popularly dubbed "Hollywood on the Tiber" because of the tremendous production activity there after WW II by American film companies for reasons of economy and tax shelter. The late 60s and early 70s saw a marked decline in the use of the studio's facilities by American and other foreign production companies, threatening the Italian film industry with a severe crisis, but the situation has since stabilized.

Cine-Eye. See VERTOV, Dziga.

cinema. 1. Derived from the Greek word for "movement," the term was originally used as a contraction of "Cinematograph." It gradually evolved into an all-encompassing term, referring to motion pictures as a whole, as an art or form of expression. 2. In British use, a motion picture theater.

Cinema Nôvo (literally: **new cinema**). A "new wave" movement that flourished in the 60s in Brazil. It aimed to create a national film culture free of foreign influence. Formed as a co-operative, the movement was led by Glauber Rocha and included, among other directors, Ruy Guerra and Nelson Pereira dos Santos. Its films reflected a concern with social themes but were also characterized by a search for a bold aesthetic style that sometimes bordered on the bizarre. Several of the Cinema Nôvo films—notably Rocha's *Deus e o Diablo na Terra do Sol* (1964) and *Antonio-das-Mortes* (1969), Dos Santos's *Vidas Secas* (1962), and Guerra's *Oz Fuzis* (1964)—enjoyed success abroad, at international festivals and in art houses. But the movement suffered from a failure to communicate with its intended audience, the Brazilian public, which has traditionally shown a marked preference for light entertainment films, mainly musical carnival comedies. This combined with severe censorship restriction by Brazilian authorities led to the movement's decline by the late 60s. See also BRAZIL.

CinemaScope. Trade name copyrighted by 20th Century-Fox for a wide-screen process based on an ANAMORPHIC system developed by Professor Henri CHRÉTIEN. The system involves special lenses that compress and distort images during filming and spread them out undistorted during projection, over an area wider than the normal motion picture screen. In theory, the anamorphic effect has been known since the 1860s. Several anamorphic processes have been patented since 1898. The most successful of these was developed and demonstrated by Chrétien late in the 20s. French director Claude AUTANT-LARA experimented with Chrétien's invention on several short documentaries, but it seemed to have no commercial value and was soon shelved. In the frantic search by Hollywood studios early in the 50s for wide-screen systems to counter the threat of television, 20th Century-Fox took an option on Chrétien's invention and named it CinemaScope. *The Robe,* the first film made under the new system, opened at New York's Roxy Theater in September of 1953. Its commercial success led to the adoption of the system by other major studios and to the rise of rival anamorphic systems, including WarnerScope, TechniScope, PanaScope, and the versatile SuperScope and PANAVISION. The CinemaScope image, photographed on normal 35 mm film, is about two-and-a-half times as wide as it is high when it is projected, an aspect ratio of 2.35:1, as compared with the conventional screen aspect ratio of 1.33:1. The aspect ratio for 70 mm CinemaScope is 2.2:1. See also WIDE-SCREEN PROCESSES.

cinémathèque. French term for film archives, sometimes used broadly in other languages to denote film clubs or theaters that specialize in the exhibition of art films.

Cinémathèque Française. The world's most famous film archives. Founded in 1936 in Paris by Henri LANGLOIS and Georges FRANJU, it played an important part in the early development of the young directors of the French New Wave, who spent many hours in its screening rooms viewing millions of feet of old and new films. The Cinémathèque has a vast collection of films, stills, film books, and original documents concerning the history of the cinema. After 1945, the Cinémathèque operated under the auspices of the government-supported Centre National du Cinéma, but following a dispute in 1968, involving Langlois' anarchical working methods, the subsidy was withdrawn. The then Minister of Culture, André Malraux, announced his intention to remove Langlois from his post but was forced to back down under pressure from demonstrators and threats by famous directors to refuse permission for the screenings of their works at the Cinémathèque. In 1969 the French government established its own film archives, the Service des Archives de Film du Centre National de la Cinématographie, outside Paris. The Cinémathèque continued to function under the direction of Langlois (until his death early in 1977) as an independent body, relying on private funds for support. In 1972, the Cinémathèque began operating the Musée du Cinéma, a film museum that attempts to capture the spirit of the art through the display of artifacts and reconstructed sets from various periods of film history. It also publishes a journal, *Archives*.

cinematic. Having qualities attributable to characteristic properties of motion pictures. The adjective is often used as the opposite of "stagy" or "theatrical."

cinematograph. A motion picture projector or camera; more specifically, the combination camera-projector used by the brothers LUMIÈRE of France at the turn of the century. Spelled *cinématographe* in France.

cinematographer. The person in charge of lighting a set and photographing a film. More formally known as a DIRECTOR OF PHOTOGRAPHY.

cinéma vérité (literally: **cinema truth**). A style of filmmaking. Practitioners of *cinéma vérité* attempt to capture truth on film by observing, recording, and presenting reality without exercising directorial control or otherwise utilizing conventional film techniques to affect the veracity of a situation. Historically, the concept of *cinéma vérité* may be traced back to Dziga VERTOV, who advocated and practiced objective filmmaking using real people and actual events in accordance with his *Kino-Glaz* (Cine-Eye) theory and *Kino-Pravda* (cinema truth) technique. Vertov called for the exclusion from cinema of anything not emanating from real life itself and, governed by this stricture, took his camera with him wherever he went in order to be able to record bits of reality, often catching people being themselves with a hidden candid-camera technique. He called this technique "Improvised Life." But Vertov also believed in manipulating his material through the MONTAGE method of editing in order to interpret reality in line with revolutionary dogma and arrive at "the purest possible essence of truth," in contrast with the stance of present-day practitioners of *cinéma vérité* who disdain any deviation from the principles of total objectivity.

Vertov was also hampered by the cumbersome camera equipment that was available in Russia during the late 1910s and early 20s, while the *cinéma vérité* movement of the 60s and 70s was able to flourish because of the advent of compact, lightweight cameras and sound recorders and fast film requiring minimal lighting. In the US, Robert FLAHERTY also foreshadowed today's *cinéma vérité* with his documentary of Eskimo life, *Nanook of the North* (1922). Like his contemporary Vertov, Flaherty sought to record on film actual people in real situations. Unlike Vertov, he did not seek to enhance the emotional impact of his films through editing; but Flaherty, too, manipulated reality by idealizing his material and by carefully setting up and sometimes even re-creating scenes.

The growing tendency toward realism on the screen after WW II, and especially Italian neo-realism with its emphasis on true-to-life on-location cinematography, provided further impetus to the growth of the *cinéma vérité* movement, as did the NOUVELLE VAGUE in France, which discarded conventional film techniques. A more important development was the sponsoring by the television industry of lighter, more compact and mobile 16 mm cameras with provisions for direct synchronized sound to facilitate and speed up coverage of news and sports events. Program-hungry TV also provided a stage for experimentation by documentary filmmakers attracted by the immediacy of the medium and by the opportunity to make sponsored films regularly.

The *cinéma vérité* movement as we know it today developed simultaneously in France and the US in the late 50s and early 60s along parallel but distinct lines. In France the term was coined as a translation of Vertov's *Kino-Pravda* to describe the method employed by Jean ROUCH and Edgar Morin on the feature-length documentary *Chronique d'un Eté/Chronicle of a Summer* (1961), which comprised a series of street interviews with the people of Paris. Other filmmakers of the French *cinéma vérité* movement include Jacques Rozier, Chris MARKER, François REICHENBACH, and Mario Ruspoli. The movement spread from France to Canada, where the leading exponent of the technique is Michel Brault, who worked as a cameraman on *Chronique d'un Eté* and another Rouch documentary, *La Punition* (1963).

The American school of *cinéma vérité* prefers to call its method "Direct Cinema." The movement grew out of the association in the late 50s between Richard LEACOCK and Robert Drew, who intially called their approach "Living Cinema." They were later joined by such filmmakers as D. A. PENNEBAKER and the MAYSLES brothers. The French school of *cinéma vérité* and the American Direct Cinema share in common the objective of recording truthful drama on film by capturing people in real situations. Both schools tend to minimize the role of the director, preferring the term "filmmaker," and glorify the function of the cameraman as the immediate link between the camera and the subject. The production method of either group is characterized by casual attention to technical quality and the use of lightweight, hand-held cameras and portable sound equipment to capture the spontaneity of a real situation. Scripts, actors, studios, or any other components that characterize the artificiality of fiction film are avoided, as are preplanned camera setups and technical refinements that may interfere with the immediacy and spontaneity of the action, and interpretive narration that may distort objective truth.

However, the two movements differ fundamentally in approach. The French school, as represented by Rouch and his followers, believes in using the camera as a catalyst, hoping to reach into a deeper truth by encouraging and stimulating subjects to open up and reveal their real thoughts and feelings through interviews and conversations. On the other hand, the American Direct Cinema school, as represented by Leacock and his colleagues, uses the camera functionally as a silent observer of the reality unfolding before it. Passivity is a key characteristic of the method that seeks to arrive at the truth by allowing people to reveal themselves in unguarded moments while forgetting about the presence of the camera or its crew. Intervention to provoke response is strictly eschewed. In the editing stage, the Americans tend to cut the filmed material into a coherent form, while the French prefer to preselect and predetermine the extent of their material, editing in the camera, so to speak, and then presenting the shot footage in its totality without the benefit of compressing the material in the cutting room.

Critics of both methods reject the claim that *cinéma vérité* can acheive an objective truth, arguing that the mere presence of the camera is bound to influence the reality before it and that subjective selection inevitably takes place whether through the arbitrary imposition of a theme as practiced by the French or through the sifting of material in the cutting room as practiced by the Americans.

cinemobile. A self-contained vehicular unit for filming on location. The buslike vehicle, designed and created in the US by Fouad Said, accommodates all necessary film equipment as well as a production crew of 50. It even has space for several dressing rooms and bathrooms. It is rapidly replacing the cumbersome caravan of trucks necessary for on-location production before the development of lightweight motion-picture equipment.

Cineorama. The world's first multiscreen system. Patented in 1897 by Raoul Gromoin-Sanson, it was presented publicly during the 1900 world's exposition in Paris. The system used ten synchronized projectors that threw ten images simultaneously on a circular panoramic screen measuring 100 meters in circumference. The spectacle drew huge crowds but was withdrawn after only three performances by order of the police for reasons of safety. See also MULTISCREEN.

Cinerama. A wide-screen process originally utilizing three cameras and three projectors to record and project a single image. The three 35 mm cameras were set up to record three aspects of a single image simultaneously: one camera facing directly ahead and the other two slightly to the right and left. When projected on a special huge screen, curved to an angle of about 165 degrees, at 26 frames per second, the images blended together to produce an illusion of vastness and plasticity. Three electronically synchronized projectors were used, the middle one projecting straight ahead and the other two projecting to the right and left in a crisscross arrangement.

Developed by Fred WALLER of Paramount's special-effects department, the system was first introduced at New York's 1939 World's Fair as Vitarama, and at that time the process involved 11 projectors. In 1952 the improved and simplified process described above made its sensational public bow in New York with *This Is Cinerama,* a thrill-filled travelogue type of film, which featured a roller-coaster ride, a plane flight over the Grand Canyon, and several other spectacular scenes. Other episodic Cinerama films followed until 1962, when the first story feature in the process, *How the West Was Won,* was released. Although commercially successful, Cinerama left much to be desired technically. The three images did not always match properly, causing an irritating jarring effect where the three images joined. As a result, the three-lens system was abandoned and a single-lens, 70 mm process, similar to other current wide-screen processes except for its curved screen, was adopted.

Multiple camera-projector systems date back to 1896, when the French inventor Raoul Grimoin-Sanson used ten projectors to show a panoramic picture on a huge circular screen. He called the process Cineorama. Director Abel GANCE used a triple-panel screen to project his 1927 *Napoléon.* He called his system POLYVISION. Following the exploitation of Cinerama, other processes were attempted, including Cinemiracle, Thrillerama, Wonderama, Disney's Circarama, Quadravision, and the technically inferior Soviet system KINOPANORAMA.

cinex strip. A short test strip of film printed by the laboratory and sent along with the DAILIES as an indication of the possible printing range from the negative. Each frame of the strip is printed at a different light level, gradually increasing in intensity from very light to very dense. With color film, the cinex strip provides a gradation of color filter selection.

circuit. A chain of motion picture theaters owned by the same organization. It has the advantage of booking films centrally for all its houses and enjoying special rates in dealing with film distributors.

Cissé, Souleymane. Director, screenwriter, producer. Born in 1940 in Bamako, Mali, Africa. He began his film career as a projectionist after Mali gained its independence in 1960. In 1963, he received the first of several scholarships to study cinema in the Soviet Union at the State Institute of Cinema (VGIK). After returning home in 1969, he made newsreels and documentaries for the Mali State Information Service. His first fiction film was *Cinq Jours d'une vie* (1972). He has since become one of Africa's most admired filmmakers, drawing on indigenous folklore and experience to explore conflicts in Mali society, particularly that between change and tradition. In 1987, he directed, wrote, and produced *Yeelen,* the mythic story of a power struggle between two magicians, called by *Film Comment* "the best African film ever made."

FILMS INCLUDE: *Cinq Jours d'une vie/Five Days in a Life* 1972; *Den Muso/The Young Girl* 1974; *Baara/Work* 1978; *Finyé/The Wind* 1982; *Yeelen/The Light* 1987.

city symphonies. Documentary films attempting to capture through images and sounds the physical and spiritual essence and the life pulse of a big city, often in a dawn-to-dusk chronology. These films are usually patterned after Walter RUTTMANN's *Berlin: Symphony of a Big City* (1927). City symphony films have been made about several major European metropolises (*Stockholm: Rhythm of a City,* 1947, etc.) and big cities on other continents. New York City has long been a favorite of documentary filmmakers, and its cacophonous harmony the subject of a number of city symphonies.

Clair, René. Director. *b.* René-Lucien Chomette, Nov. 11, 1898, Paris. *d.* 1981. The son of a soap merchant, he grew up above his father's store on Rue des Halles in the famous market quarter of the French capital. At the age of seven he began writing and directing his own plays with a toy puppet theater he was given for his birthday. During his high school days he wrote a great deal of poetry, which went unpublished. Though a better-than-average student, he failed his final exams. In 1917 he volunteered to drive an ambulance on the battle front and expressed his disenchantment with war in a group of unpublished poems he entitled "La Tête de l'Homme." Several months later he was invalided out with an injured spinal column. Under physical and mental stress, he retired briefly to a Dominican monastery.

After the armistice, Clair flirted with the ideology of the intellectual left and began writing for a Paris journal. In 1920, thanks to some friends in the industry, he began playing leads in films. His name changed to René Clair, he appeared in *Le Lys de la Vie* (1920), *Le Sens de la Mort,* and the Feuillades serials *L'Orpheline* and *Parisette* (all 1921). He loathed acting but was intrigued by the idea of filmmaking, so in 1922 he went to Brussels, where his brother Henri was working as assistant to director Jacques de BARONCELLI, and spent several months studying cinema technique.

The following year Clair was assigned his first film as director-writer. He wrote the initial draft for *Paris qui dort* in one night and completed the film within three weeks. It contained the core elements of Clair's cinema—the stylish charm, the exhilarating wit, the celebration of movement, and the intuitive sense of comic timing. But it wasn't until the satiric farce *The Italian Straw Hat* (1927), which many consider his silent masterpiece, that Clair drew international recognition. Although he was initially skeptical about the value of sound in the cinema, he not only adapted easily to talkies but became a pioneer in the creative use of the sound track, using music, sound effects, and dialogue in imaginative, unorthodox ways to expand the meaning and power of his visuals, directly or by counterpoint. Clair's early talkies, especially *Le Million* (1931), were among his finest films and influenced filmmakers everywhere. Although briefly associated with the French avant-garde (his second film, *Entr'acte,* remains a masterpiece of pure cinema), from the very start he considered film as a medium of entertainment. He developed into one of the most original stylists in world cinema, a complete filmmaker who always wrote or collaborated on the films he directed and constantly explored the possibilities of visual form, movement, and sound. He expressed many of his ideas about cinema in magazine articles, which were assembled in the book *Reflexion Faite* (1951) and a sequel, *Cinéma d'Hier, Cinéma d'Aujourd'hui* (1970). He also wrote prefaces to his published screenplays, three novels, and several short stories, and translated the play 'Born Yesterday' into French.

Rarely shooting on location and relying mostly on studio-built exteriors, Clair created his own distinctive world in which he proceeded to express his satirical view of life. His early films, ostensibly optimistic comedies, were often underlined with bitter irony that might well have suggested a profound pessimism. Indeed, in his later films, he veered toward tragicomedy, depicting the human condition more grimly but always with a fundamental love of humanity. Profoundly French, he made his least successful films during his sojourns in England and the US, where he overextended his preoccupation with fantasy *ad absurdum.* Still, even his Anglo-Saxon films are all highly entertaining and contain ample illustrations of his subtle irony and precision of style. Early in the 60s he was elected to the French Academy. His brother, Henri Chomette (1896–1941), dubbed by Siodmak "the obscure Clair," directed a number of avant-garde and commercial films in the 20s and 30s.

FILMS (as director-screenwriter): In France—*Paris qui dort/The Crazy Ray, Entr'acte* 1924; *Le Fantôme du Moulin Rouge* 1925; *Le Voyage imaginaire* 1926; *La Proie du Vent, Un Chapeau de Paille d'Italie/The Italian Straw Hat/The Horse Ate the Hat* 1927; *La Tour* (doc. short), *Les Deux Timides* 1928; *Sous les Toits de Paris/Under the Roofs of Paris* 1930; *Le Million, A Nous la Liberté* 1931; *Quatorze Juillet/July 14th* 1933; *Le Dernier Milliardaire* 1934. In the UK—*The Ghost Goes West* 1935; *Break the News* 1938. In France—*Un Village dans Paris* (doc. short; co-prod. only), *Air Pur* (unfinished) 1939. In the US—*The Flame of New Orleans* 1941; *I Married a Witch* 1942; *Forever and a Day* (one episode; took over for Hitchcock) 1943; *It Happened Tomorrow* 1944; *And Then There Were None* 1945. In France—*La Silence est d'Or/Man About Town* 1947; *La Beauté du Diable/Beauty and the Devil (Fr./It.)* 1950; *Les Belles de Nuit/Beauties of the Night* (Fr./It.) 1952; *Les Grandes Manoeuvres/The Grand Maneuver* (Fr./It.) 1955; *Porte de Lilas/Gates of Paris* (Fr./It.) 1957; *La Française et l'Amour/ Love and the Frenchwoman* ("Marriage" episode) 1960; *Tout l'Or du Monde* (Fr./It.) 1961; *Les Quatre Vérités/Three Fables of Love* ("Two Pigeons" episode, Fr./It./Sp.) 1962; *Les Fêtes galantes (Fr./Rum.)* 1965.

Claire, Ina. Actress. *b.* Ina Fagan, Oct. 15, 1892, Washington, D.C., of Irish ancestry. *d.* 1985. A vaudeville comedienne at 13, she made her screen debut in 1915, was featured on the stage in the 'Ziegfeld Follies' of 1915 and 1916, and starred in 'The Gold Diggers' (1919) for nearly two years. In the 20s she developed into a Broadway favorite, and in 1929, after a long absence, she returned to the screen as the star of the first film version of *The Awful Truth,* a role she had originated on the stage in 1922. She went on to display her bubbly comedy style in several other films but reserved most of her appearances for the stage, where until retirement in 1954 she excelled in sophisticated comedy. Her second of three husbands (1929–31) was screen idol John GILBERT.

FILMS INCLUDE: *Wild Goose Chase, The Puppet Crown* 1915; *Polly with a Past* 1920; *The Awful Truth* 1929; *The Royal Family of Broadway* (as Ethel Barrymore), *Rebound* 1931; *The Greeks Had a Name for Them* 1932; *Ninotchka* 1939; *Stage Door Canteen, Claudia* 1943.

Clampett, Bob. Animator. *b.* May 8, 1915, San Diego. *d.* 1984. A graduate of the Otis Art School, he worked briefly for Disney, for whom he designed the first Mickey Mouse doll. In 1931 he joined the staff of the Harman-Ising Studio. Working with such innovators as Chuck JONES and Tex AVERY, he helped create the Warner Bros. animated series 'Merrie Melodies' and 'Looney Tunes.' He played a crucial role in the development of the humorous style of the Warner cartoon and in the creation of such characters as Porky Pig, Bugs Bunny, Daffy Duck, and Tweety. As a director from 1937, he developed his own recognizable animation style, which was characterized by boldness, aggressiveness, and robust humor. His association with Warner Bros. lasted 16 years, after which he worked briefly as a producer for Columbia and Republic, before starting his own company. Working mainly for TV, he enjoyed some success with the animated program 'Beany and Cecil,' the winner of three Emmys.

CARTOONS INCLUDE: *Porky's Badtime Story* 1937; *What Price Porky, The Daffy Doc* 1938; *Porky's Movie Mystery, Kristopher Kolumbus Jr., Jeepers Creepers, The Film Fan* 1939; *Ali Baba Bound* 1940; *Meet John Doughboy* 1941; *The Wacky Rabbit, A Tale of Two Kitties, Coal Black and de Sebben Dwarfs* 1942; *Tin Pan Alley Cats, Corny Concerto* 1943; *What's Cookin' Doc?, Russian Rhapsody* 1944; *Draftee Daffy* 1945; *Book Revue, The Great Piggy Bank Robbery* 1946.

clapper boards. See CLAPSTICKS; SLATE.

clapsticks. A pair of hinged boards attached to the slate which are clapped together before or after each take in shooting dialogue once camera and sound equipment are running at synchronous speed. The loud crack resulting from the sudden clap later provides the film editor with a reference mark for the synchronization of picture and sound track. Clapsticks have gradually been replaced by electronic synchronization techniques. Also called "clapper boards" or "clappers." See also SLATE.

Clare, Mary. Actress. *b.* July 17, 1894, London. *d.* 1970. A prolific performer of the London stage from age 16, she also played character parts in many silent and sound British films, often in intense, overpowering roles.

FILMS INCLUDE: *The Black Spider* 1920; *A Prince of Lovers/The Life of Lord Byron* (as Lady Caroline Lamb), *Foolish Monte Carlo* (US) 1922; *Becket* (as Queen Eleanor) 1923; *The Constant Nymph* 1928; *Hindle Wakes* 1931; *Jew Suss/Power* 1934; *The Clairvoyant, Lorna Doone, Mr. Hobo* 1935; *The Mill on the Floss, Young and Innocent/The Girl Was Young, The Rat* 1937; *The Citadel, The Lady Vanishes, Climbing High, The Challenge* 1938; *Mrs. Pym of Scotland Yard* (title role), *On the Night of the Fire/The Fugitive, A Girl Must Live* 1939; *This Man Is Dangerous/The Patient Vanishes* 1941; *Next of Kin* 1942; *Oliver Twist* 1948; *The Black Rose* 1950; *Moulin Rouge, The Beggar's Opera* 1953; *Mambo* (It.) 1954; *The Price of Silence* 1960.

Clark, Bob. Director. Born Benjamin Clark on Aug. 5, 1941, in New Orleans. *ed.* Hillsdale Coll. (Mich.). Long a resident of Canada, he began and pursued much of his career there, usually working with limited budgets. His films occasionally rose above mediocrity (*Murder by Decree, A Christmas Story*). But he scored his biggest commercial success with the trashy *Porky's* and its sequels.

FEATURE FILMS: *Children Shouldn't Play with Dead Things* (also co-prod., co-sc.) 1970; *Dead of Night/Deathdream* (also prod., sc.) 1972; *Black Christmas* (also prod.) 1974; *Breaking Point* (also co-prod.) 1976; *Murder by Decree* (also co-prod., story) 1978; *Tribute* 1980; *Porky's* (also co-prod., sc.) 1982; *Porky's II: The Next Day* (also co-prod., co-sc.), *A Christmas Story* (also co-prod., co-sc.) 1983; *Rhinestone* (also lyrics) 1984; *Turk 182!* 1985; *From the Hip* (also co-prod. co-sc.) 1987; *Loose Cannons* (also co-sc.) 1990; *It Runs in the Family* 1994.

Clark, Candy. Actress. Born on June 20, 1947, in Norman, Okla. Vivacious leading lady of Hollywood films of the 70s; a former fashion model. Nominated for an Oscar for her performance in *American Graffiti* (1973).

FILMS INCLUDE: *Fat City* 1972; *American Graffiti* 1973; *I Will I Will. . . for Now, The Man Who Fell to Earth* (UK) 1976; *Handle with Care/Citizens Band* 1977; *The Big Sleep* (UK) 1978; *When You Comin' Back Red Ryder?, More American Graffiti* 1979; *National Lampoon Goes to the Movies* 1981; *Q* 1982; *Blue Thunder, Amityville 3-D* 1983; *Hambone and Hillie* 1984; *Cat's Eye* 1985; *At Close Range* 1986; *The Blob* 1988; *Blind Curve* 1989; *Original Intent* 1990; *Cool As Ice, Deuce Coupe* 1991; *Buffy the Vampire Slayer* 1992; *Radioland Murders* 1994.

Clark, Dane. Actor. Born Bernard Zanville, on Feb. 18, 1913, in Brooklyn, N.Y. *ed.* Cornell; St. John's U. (N.Y.). Unable to capitalize on his law degree in the midst of the Depression, he worked on a road gang, boxed, modeled, and played semipro baseball before making his Broadway debut in 1934. He broke into films in 1942 and, despite his small size, typically played many leads, as a brooding pugnacious tough guy in the John Garfield mold. But he never gained the latter's prominence on the Warners lot. Still active on TV but rarely on the big screen.

FILMS INCLUDE: As Bernard Zanville—*Sunday Punch, The Glass Key, Wake Island, The Pride of the Yankees* 1942; *Action in the North Atlantic* 1943. As Dane Clark—*Destination Tokyo, The Very Thought of You, Hollywood Canteen* 1944; *God Is My Co-Pilot, Pride of the Marines* 1945; *A Stolen Life, Her Kind of Man* 1946; *That Way with Women, Deep Valley* 1947; *Whiplash, Embraceable You, Moonrise* 1948; *Without Honor* 1949; *Backfire, Barricade* 1950; *Fort Defiance, Never Trust a Gambler* 1951; *Go Man Go!, Blackout/Murder by Proxy* 1954; *Toughest Man Alive* 1955; *Massacre* 1956; *Outlaw's Son* 1957; *The McMasters* 1970; *The Woman Inside* (Can.) 1981; *Last Rites* 1988.

Clark, Fred. Actor. *b.* Frederic Leonard Clark, Mar. 9, 1914, Lincoln, Calif. *d.* 1968. *ed.* Stanford U., AADA. A veteran of the Broadway stage (from 1938), he made his screen debut in 1947 as a detective in *The Unsuspected.* Bald and dour-looking, he played dozens of character roles, often comic, typically as a short-tempered businessman or bumbling villain. His first wife was actress Benay Venuta.

FILMS INCLUDE: *The Unsuspected* 1947; *Hazard* 1948; *Alias Nick Beal, Flamingo Road, White Heat* 1949; *Sunset Boulevard, The Jackpot* 1950; *The Lemon Drop Kid, Meet Me After the Show, A Place in the Sun* 1951; *Three for Bedroom C* (lead role), *Dreamboat* 1952; *The Caddy, How to Marry a Millionaire* 1953; *Abbott and Costello Meet the Keystone Kops, Daddy Long Legs, The Court-Martial of Billy Mitchell* 1955; *Miracle in the Rain, The Solid Gold Cadillac* 1956; *Don't Go Near the Water* 1957; *Auntie Mame* 1958; *The Mating Game* 1959; *Visit to a Small Planet, Bells Are Ringing* 1960; *Boys' Night Out* 1962; *Move Over Darling* 1963; *The Curse of the Mummy's Tomb* 1965; *The Horse in the Grey Flannel Suit, Skidoo* 1968; *I Sailed to Tahiti with an All Girl Crew* 1969.

Clark, James B. Film editor, director. Born on May 14, 1908, in Stillwater, Minn. *ed.* Ohio U. He worked in his family restaurant business before going to London, where he started his career as a film editor in 1936. He joined 20th Century-Fox, for whom he edited numerous films in the UK and the US through the late 50s. He was nominated for an Oscar for *How Green Was My Valley* (1941). Becoming a director, he specialized in adventure and nature dramas meant mainly for the children's market.

FILMS INCLUDE: As editor—*Wings of the Morning* (UK), *Under the Red Robe* (UK) 1937; *Keep Smiling/Smiling Along* (UK), *Inspector Hornleigh* (UK) 1938; *Busman's Honeymoon/Haunted Honeymoon* (UK) 1940; *How Green Was My Valley* 1941; *Roxie Hart* 1942; *Holy Matrimony* 1943; *Buffalo Bill, The Keys of the Kingdom* 1944; *Leave Her to Heaven* 1946; *The Foxes of Harrow, The Late George Apley* 1947; *Road House* 1948; *I Was a Male War Bride* 1949; *My Blue Heaven* 1950; *The Desert Fox* 1951; *Five Fingers* 1952; *23 Paces to Baker Street* 1956; *An Affair to Remember* 1957. As director (complete)—*Under Fire* 1957; *Sierra Baron, Villa* 1958; *The Sad Horse* 1959; *A Dog of Flanders, One Foot in Hell* 1960; *The Big Show* (also co-prod.), *Misty* 1961; *Drums of Africa, Flipper* 1963; *Island of the Blue Dolphins* 1964; *. . . And Now Miguel* 1966; *My Side of the Mountain* 1969; *The Little Ark* 1972.

Clark, Jim. Film editor, director. Born in 1931, in Boston, Lincolnshire, England. Entering films as an apprentice in 1952, he emerged in the 60s as one of Britian's premier film cutters. He was far less successful, however, when he ventured into directing in the late 60s and early 70s. Returning to the cutting table, he won an Oscar as well as the British Acadmy Award for editing *The Killing Fields* (1984).

FILMS INCLUDE: As editor—*One Wish Too Many* 1956; *The Grass Is Greener* 1960; *The Innocents* 1961; *Charade* (US) 1963; *The Pumpkin Eater* 1964; *Darling* 1965; *Midnight Cowboy* (consultant only) 1969; *The Day of the Locust* (US), *The Adventure of Sherlock Holmes' Smarter Brother* 1975; *Marathon Man* (US) 1976; *Yanks, Agatha* 1979; *Honky Tonk Freeway* (US) 1981; *Privates on Parade* 1982; *The Killing Fields* 1984; *The Mission* 1986. As director—*The Christmas Tree* (also co-sc.) 1966; *Every Home Should Have One/Think Dirty* 1970; *Rentadick* 1972; *Madhouse* 1974.

Clark, Marguerite. Actress. *b.* Feb. 22, 1883, Avondale, Ohio. *d.* 1940. Came to films from the stage in 1914, scoring an immediate success as the heroine of Allan Dwan's *Wildflower.* A tiny, dark-haired beauty, she continued playing sweet innocent maidens well into her 30s, rivaling Mary Pickford for popularity. She remained one of the best loved and highest paid Hollywood silent screen stars until her retirement in 1921. She had spent her entire career with Famous Players-Paramount.

FILMS: *Wildflower, The Crucible* 1914; *The Goose Girl, Gretna Green, The Pretty Sister of Jose, The Seven Sisters, Helene of the North, Still Waters, The Prince and the Pauper* (in dual title role) 1915; *Mice and Men, Molly Make Believe, Silks and Satins, Little Lady Eileen, Out of the Drifts, Miss George Washington, Snow White* (title role) 1916; *The Fortunes of Fifi, The Valentine Girl, The Amazons, Bab's Diary, Bab's Burglar, Bab's Matinee Idol, The Seven Swans* 1917; *Rich Man Poor Man, Prunella, Uncle Tom's Cabin* (in the dual role of Topsy and Eva), *Out of a Clear Sky, Little Miss Hoover* 1918; *Mrs. Wiggs of the Cabbage Patch, Three Men and a Girl, Come Out of the Kitchen, Let's Elope, Girls, Widow by Proxy, Luck in Pawn* 1919; *A Girl Named Mary, Easy to Get, All of a Sudden Peggy* 1920; *Scrambled Wives* 1921.

Clark, Petula. Actress, singer. Born on Nov. 15, 1932, in Epsom, England. During WW II she became popular as a child singer on the BBC and in London concert halls and at the age of 11 began playing child roles in British films. She remained on the screen through adolescence and early maturity, mostly in syrupy roles in films of little consequence, then left for Paris, where she achieved great popularity in the late 50s and early 60s as a concert and recording artist. Her popularity spread into the English-speaking world in the mid-60s after pop hits such as 'Downtown,' plus a number of specials on American TV. She was soon back in two musical films as a highly paid star.

FILMS INCLUDE: *A Medal for the General/The Gay Intruders* 1944; *Murder in Reverse, I Know Where I'm Going* 1945; *London Town* 1946; *Vice Versa, Holiday Camp* 1947; *Easy Money, Here Come the Huggetts* 1948; *The Romantic Age, Dance Hall* 1950; *White Corridors* 1951; *The Card/The Promoter* 1952; *The Runaway Bus* 1953; *Track the Man Down* 1955; *That Woman Opposite* 1957; *Finian's Rainbow* (US) 1968; *Goodbye Mr. Chips* (US/UK) 1969; *Never Never Land* 1981.

Clark, Susan. Actress. Born Nora Golding, on Mar. 8, 1940, in Sarnid, Ontario, Canada. Leading lady of Hollywood films of the late 60s and the 70s, following a stage career that she began as a child. A graduate of London's Royal Academy of Dramatic Art, she made her screen debut in *Banning* (1967). She won an Emmy for her portrayal of athlete Babe Didrickson Zaharias in the TV movie *Babe* (1983). She married her co-star in that production, ex-football pro Alex Karras. They later co-starred in the series 'Webster' and began producing TV movies.

FILMS INCLUDE: *Banning* 1967; *Madigan, Coogan's Bluff* 1968; *Tell Them Willie Boy Is Here* 1969; *Skullduggery, The Forbin Project* 1970; *Valdez Is Coming, Skin Game* 1971; *Showdown* 1973; *The Midnight Man, Airport 1975* 1974; *Night Moves, The Apple Dumpling Gang* 1975; *Murder By Decree* (UK/Can.) 1978; *The North Avenue Irregulars, Real Life, City on Fire* (Can.), *Promises in the Dark* 1979; *Double Negative* (Can.) 1980; *Nobody's Perfekt* 1981; *Porky's* (Can.) 1982.

Clarke, Charles G(alloway). Director of photography. *b.* Mar. 10, 1899, Potter Valley, Calif. *d.* 1983. After repeated attempts to break into the theater as an actor, he entered films in 1919 as laboratory assistant on D. W. Griffith productions. The following year he advanced to assistant cameraman, to become a full-fledged director of photography in the early 20s. Best work from 1937 under contract to 20th Century-Fox. He earned four Academy Award nominations in the 40s for his work at 20th Century-Fox. During the 1944 Oscar ceremony he received a special technical award for "the development and practical application of a device for composing artificial clouds into motion picture scenes during production photography." Clarke's technical innovations date back to the silent era when he designed a battery-run camera motor which later became standard equipment. He was also known for his gutsy ruggedness, and was much in demand for outdoor cinematography under difficult physical conditions.

FILMS INCLUDE: *The Half-Breed* (co-phot.) 1922; *The Light That Failed* 1923; *Tiger Love* 1924; *Top of the World, Friendly Enemies* 1925; *Whispering Smith* 1926; *Upstream* 1927; *Four Sons* (co-phot.) 1928; *Masquerade* (co-phot.), *The Exalted Flapper, Words and Music* 1929; *So This Is London* 1930; *Viva Villa!, Annabelle's Affairs* 1931; *The Cat and the Fiddle, Tarzan and His Mate* 1934; *Shadow of Doubt, Pursuit* 1935; *The Return of the Cisco Kid* 1939; *Yesterday's Heroes* 1940; *Moontide* 1942; *Guadalcanal Diary* 1943; *Tampico* 1944; *Margie* 1946; *Miracle on 34th Street, Captain from Castile* 1947; *The Iron Curtain, That Wonderful Urge* 1948; *Sand, Slattery's Hurricane* 1949; *I'll Get By, The Big Lift* 1950; *Destination Gobi* 1953; *Suddenly, Black Widow, Night People* 1954; *Prince of Players, Violent Saturday, The Virgin Queen, The Man in the Gray Flannel Suit* 1955; *Carousel* 1956; *The Wayward Bus* 1957; *The Barbarian and the Geisha* 1958; *These Thousand Hills, The Sound and the Fury* 1959; *Flaming Star* 1960; *Return to Peyton Place* 1961; *Madison Avenue* 1962.

Clarke, Mae. Actress. *b.* Aug. 16, 1907, in Philadelphia. *d.* 1992. The daughter of a motion-picture-theater organist, she started out as a cabaret dancer at 16 and two years later began playing supporting roles in stage musicals and dramas. She made her film debut in 1929 and for several years was a successful leading lady in such films as *Frankenstein, Waterloo Bridge,* and *The Front Page,* in which she gave a good performance as the pathetic Molly Malloy. But among nostalgic cinema buffs she is most closely identified with one of her smaller roles, that of a gang moll who gets a grapefruit pushed in her face by James CAGNEY in *The Public Enemy.* Despite some good opportunities in second features, Miss Clarke's career quickly declined and by the late 30s she was reduced to bit parts and unbilled cameo appearances, although she returned occasionally to leads in B action pictures. Her first of three dissolved marriages was to Lew Brice, Fanny Brice's brother.

FILMS INCLUDE: *Big Time, Nix on Dames* 1929; *The Fall Guy, The Dancers* 1930; *Men on Call, The Front Page, The Public Enemy, The Good Bad Girl, Waterloo Bridge, Frankenstein, Reckless Living* 1931; *Three Wise Girls, The Final Edition, The Impatient Maiden, Night World* 1932; *Fast Workers, Parole Girl, Turn Back the Clock, Penthouse, Made on Broadway, Lady Killer* 1933; *Nana, This Side of Heaven, Let's Talk It Over, The Man with Two Faces* 1934; *The Daring Young Man, Silk Hat Kid* 1935; *The House of a Thousand Candles, Hearts in Bondage, Great Guy* 1936; *Trouble in Morocco* 1937; *Women in War* 1940; *Flying Tigers* 1942; *Here Come the Waves, And Now Tomorrow* 1944; *Kitty* 1945; *Daredevils in the Clouds* 1948; *King of the Rocket Men* (serial) 1949; *Annie Get Your Gun* 1950; *The Great Caruso* 1951; *Because of You, Singin' in the Rain* 1952; *Magnificent Obsession* 1954; *Women's Prison, Not as a Stranger* 1955; *Ask Any Girl* 1959; *A Big Hand for the Little Lady* 1966; *Thoroughly Modern Millie* (bit) 1967; *The Watermelon Man* (bit) 1970.

Clarke, Shirley. Director. *b.* Shirley Brimberg, in 1925, in New York City. *d.* 1997. *ed.* Stephens College; Johns Hopkins U.; Bennington Coll.; U. of North Carolina. The product of a well-to-do Jewish family, she grew up on Park Avenue and at 14 took up dancing with Martha Graham and other teachers and companies. She presented her first work as a choreographer at 17 and at 21 became president of the National Dance Association. Her exploration of movement led in 1953 to her conversion to filmmaking. After several dance-related shorts, she began applying principles of choreography to the filming and editing of nondance subjects. In *Bridges-Go-Round* (1959), for example, she achieved dance-like movement by the superimposition and rhythmic cutting of shots of New York bridges. The 20-minute *Skyscraper* (also 1959), which she co-directed, was nominated for an Oscar in the live-action short category and won prizes at Venice and Edinburgh. She adapted *cinéma vérité* techniques for her first feature, *The Connection* (1961). Shot in black and white with a minuscule budget, the independently produced film (money was raised by the promise of profit-sharing) caused much controversy. Adopted from Jack Gelber's Living Theatre drama about heroin junkies, it was hailed as exhilaratingly spontaneous by many admirers, who saw it as a groundbreaker for an alternative American cinema. But most American critics deemed it crude and offensive. It became a test case of censorship regulations when New York State banned it for a year because of its liberal use of foul language.

In 1962 Ms. Clarke co-founded, with Jonas Mekas, the Film-Makers Cooperative, a nonprofit company for the distribution of independent films. The following year she shared an

Academy Award for the feature-length documentary, *Robert Frost: A Lover's Quarrel with the World.* She also released her second feature, *The Cool World,* a drama about a ghetto street gang which she shot on location in Harlem with a largely non-professional cast. This time the response of the critical establishment was mostly favorable, though some still found in her work deficiencies of structure and technique. Controversy erupted again over her next feature. *Portrait of Jason* (1967), a 105-minute single-camera interview with a black male prostitute, was found repulsive by most reviewers. But it was well liked in Europe, where it won festival prizes and was called by Ingmar Bergman "the most fascinating film I've ever seen."

Feeling she was ready to take on a commercial venture, she went to Hollywood to discuss with studio executives a project based on a Shelley Winters screenplay. She would later recreate her bitterness and near breakdown over the frustrating experience in a moving personal appearance in Agnès Varda's film *Lions Love* (1969). Her disappointment led her to shift her interest from film to the exploration of video as a medium of expression. In 1976 she moved to the West Coast and began teaching video and film at UCLA.

FILMS: *Dance in the Sun* (also prod., phot., edit.) 1953; *In Paris Parks* (also prod., phot., edit.) 1954; *Bullfight* (also prod., phot., edit.) 1955; *A Moment in Love* (also prod., phot., edit.) 1957; *The Skyscraper* (co-dir. with Willard Van Dyke), *Loops* (also prod., phot., edit.) 1958; *Bridges-Go-Round* (also prod., phot., edit.) 1959; *A Scary Time* (also co-sc., phot.) 1960; *The Connection* (also co-prod., edit.) 1962; *Robert Frost: A Lover's Quarrel with the World* (co-dir.), *The Cool World* (also co-sc., edit.) 1963; *Man in the Polar Regions* (11-screen presentation for Expo '67), *Portrait of Jason* (also prod. edit., off-camera voice), *24 Frames per Second* (also edit.) 1977; *Initiation* (also edit.) 1978; *Mysterum* (also edit.) 1979; *Four Journeys Into Mystic Time* (also edit.) 1980; *Savage/Love* (also edit.) 1981; *Tongues* (also edit.) 1983; *Ornette: Made in America* (also edit.) 1986.

Clarke, T. E. B. Screenwriter. *b.* Thomas Ernest Bennett, June 7, 1907, Watford, England. *d.* 1989. *ed.* Cambridge. A former police officer, advertising man, and journalist, he came to films in 1943 and subsequently wrote original stories and screenplays for many outstanding British motion pictures, notably some of Ealing's brightest comedies. He won an Academy Award and a Venice Festival Award for the script of *The Lavender Hill Mob* (1951). He also received Oscar nominations for the comedy *Passport to Pimlico* and the drama *Sons and Lovers.* He was the author of 15 novels and travel books, a play, and an autobiography, *This Is Where I Came In* (1974).

FILMS INCLUDE: *Champagne Charlie* 1944; *Johnny Frenchman, Dead of Night* 1945; *Hue and Cry* 1947; *Against the Wind* 1948; *Passport to Pimlico, The Magnet* 1949; *The Blue Lamp* 1950; *The Lavender Hill Mob* (also story), *Encore* ("The Ant and the Grasshopper" episode) 1951; *The Titfield Thunderbolt* 1953; *Law and Disorder* 1956; *Barnacle Bill/All at Sea* 1957; *A Tale of Two Cities, Gideon's Day/Gideon of Scotland Yard* 1958; *Sons and Lovers* 1960; *The Horse Without a Head* 1963; *A Man Could Get Killed* (US) 1966.

Clavell, James. Director, producer, screenwriter, novelist, playwright. *b.* Oct. 10, 1924, Sydney, Australia. *d.* 1994. *ed.* Birmingham U., England. A captain with the British Royal Artillery, he spent half of WW II in a Japanese prisoner-of-war camp. Was a salesman before venturing into a TV pilot deal, which brought him to the US in 1953. He began writing for the screen in 1958 and directing and producing the following year. His most successful film as director has been *To Sir with Love* (1967). A naturalized American since 1963, he is now better known as a best-selling novelist. Three of his novels, *King Rat* (1962), *Tai Pan* (1966), and *Shogun* (1975) have been adapted to the screen by others.

FILMS: As screenwriter—*The Fly* 1958; *Watusi* 1959; *The Great Escape* 1963; *633 Squadron* 1964; *The Satan Bug* 1965. As director-producer-screenwriter—*Five Gates to Hell* 1959; *Walk Like a Dragon* 1960; *The Sweet and the Bitter* (Can.) 1962; *To Sir with Love* (UK) 1967; *Where's Jack?* (dir. only; UK) 1968; *The Last Valley* (UK) 1971.

claw. A metal tooth in the intermittent-movement section of a camera and some projectors which engages a perforation in the film and pulls the film down frame by frame. Some machines are equipped with double claws, one above the other, so that if one perforation is broken the next one is engaged.

Clayburgh, Jill. Actress. Born on Apr. 30, 1944, in New York City. Tall, blue-eyed leading lady of the American stage and screen. The daughter of a wealthy, socially prominent family, she was educated at the exclusive Brearley School and Sarah Lawrence College. While at the latter, she began acting in summer stock at the Williamstown (Mass.) Theater Festival, then joined the Charles Street Repertory Theater in Boston. Moving to New York, she appeared in several off-Broadway productions, finally emerging as a star in the 70s in such Broadway musicals as 'The Rothschilds' and 'Pippin.' She had made her film debut in 1969 but did not rise to prominence as a screen personality until 1976, when she portrayed actress Carole Lombard in the biographical film *Gable and Lombard* and played the lead in *Silver Streak.* Both films failed with the critics but established her as a star. In 1978 she was named best actress at the Cannes Festival for her performance in *An Unmarried Woman,* a film for which she was also nominated for an Oscar. She was nominated again for an Oscar in the following year, for *Starting Over,* but her choice of roles in the 80s was less fortunate. Having ended a five-year, live-in relationship with actor Al PACINO, she married playwright David RABE in 1979.

FILMS: *The Wedding Party* 1969; *The Telephone Book* 1971; *Portnoy's Complaint* 1972; *The Thief Who Came to Dinner* 1973; *The Terminal Man* 1974; *Gable and Lombard* (as Carole Lombard), *Silver Streak, Griffin and Phoenix* (TV movie) 1976; *Semi-Tough* 1977; *An Unmarried Woman* 1978; *La Luna* (It.), *Starting Over* 1979; *It's My Turn* 1980; *First Monday in October* 1981; *I'm Dancing as Fast as I Can* 1982; *Hanna K* (Fr.) 1983; *Where Are the Children?* 1986; *Shy People* 1987; *Beyond the Ocean, Rich in Love* 1990; *Whisper in the Dark* 1992; *Naked in New York* 1994.

Clayton, Ethel. Actress. *b.* 1884, Champaign, Ill. *d.* 1966. Convent educated. She entered films in 1910, beginning her career in one-reel Essanay comedies. In 1912 she joined LUBIN and soon became the most popular star on the company's stable. Many of her films of the period were directed by her husband, Joseph Kaufman, who died in 1919. Her second husband was actor Ian KEITH. She later joined World, and still later Paramount, typically appearing in romantic and domestic melodramas, and remained a leading Hollywood star until the early 20s. She continued playing character parts through the late 30s.

FILMS INCLUDE: *Art and Honor, When the Earth Trembled* 1913; *The Lion and the Mouse, The Fortune Hunter* 1914; *The College Widow, The Sporting Duchess, The Great Divide* 1915; *Husband and Wife, A Woman's Way* 1916; *The Stolen Paradise* 1917; *Stolen Hours, The Witch Woman, Journey's End, The Soul Without Windows, The Woman Beneath, The Dormant Power, Easy Money, Whims of Society* 1918; *Maggie Pepper, Pettigrew's Girl, The Woman Next Door, Men Women and Money, A Sporting Chance, Mystery Girl* 1919;

The 13th Commandment, The Young Mrs. Winthrop, A Lady in Love, The Ladder of Lies, Crooked Streets, The City Sparrow, The Sins of Rosanne, More Deadly Than the Male 1920; *The Price of Possession, Sham, Wealth, Beyond, Exit the Vamp* 1921; *Her Own Money, The Cradle, For the Defense, If I Were Queen* 1922; *Can a Woman Love Twice?, The Remittance Woman* 1923; *The Mansion of Aching Hearts, Wings of Youth, Lightnin'* 1925; *Sunny Side Up, Risky Business, His New York Wife* 1926; *The Princess from Hoboken* 1927; *Mother Machree* 1928; *Hit the Deck, The Call of the Circus* 1930; *Hotel Continental, The Crooked Circle* 1932; *Secrets* 1933; *Artists and Models* 1937; *The Buccaneer* 1938; *Ambush* 1939.

Clayton, Jack. Director. *b.* 1921, in Brighton, England. *d.* 1995. Went to work for London Films at 14 and for several years performed various functions, eventually moving up to assistant director, then film editor. During WW II he served with the film unit of the RAF, as cameraman, editor, director, and finally the unit's commanding officer. After the war, he worked as a production manager on Alexander Korda's *An Ideal Husband* (1948) and functioned as associate producer on such films as *The Queen of Spades* (1949), *Flesh and Blood* (1950), *Moulin Rouge* (1953), *Beat the Devil* (1954), and *I Am a Camera* (1955). He then turned to directing with the medium-length *The Bespoke Overcoat* (1955), a prize winner at the Venice Film Festival. His first feature as a director, *Room at the Top* (1958), led a trend in British films toward raw sensuality and frank treatment of social issues. He subsequently directed a number of fine if less original productions through 1967. After a long absence, he returned to films in 1974 as the director of Hollywood's lavishly decorative but disappointing adaptation of F. Scott Fitzgerald's *The Great Gatsby.* Nearly a decade had gone by before he could land another film assignment. He married and divorced actresses Christine NORDEN and Katherine Kath.

FILMS (as director): *Naples Is a Battlefield* (doc.; also sc. co-phot., uncredited) 1944; *The Bespoke Overcoat* (medium length; also prod.) 1955; *Room at the Top* 1958; *The Innocents* (also prod.) 1961; *The Pumpkin Eater* 1964; *Our Mother's House* (also prod.; UK/US) 1967; *The Great Gatsby* (US) 1974; *Something Wicked This Way Comes* (US) 1983; *The Lonely Passion of Judith Hearne* 1987.

Cleese, John. Actor, screenwriter. Born on Oct. 27, 1939, in Weston-Super-Mare England. *ed.* Clifton Coll.; Cambridge. Tall (6' 4"), eccentric comic star of British TV and films. The son of an insurance salesman, he began his acting career with the Cambridge University Footlights revue, performing alongside David Frost and Peter COOK. With Cambridge classmate Graham CHAPMAN, he began writing comedy material for British TV in the 60s. Together they conceived the idea for the hit comedy show 'Monty Python's Flying Circus' which also featured Terry Gilliam, Eric Idle, Terry Jones, and Michael Palin. It ran in Britain from 1969 to 1974, and later attracted large audiences in the US and other markets. He appeared in and collaborated on the scripts of the TV programs and the series of movies that followed. His popularity soared after his portrayal of the bumbling, pompous, explosive Basil Fawlty in the TV series 'Fawlty Towers.' He won the British Academy Award as best actor for his performance in *A Fish Called Wanda* (1988) and was nominated for an Oscar for the screenplay of that film. Formerly married to actress Connie Booth. Co-author: *Families and How to Survive Them.*

FILMS: *Interlude, The Bliss of Mrs. Blossom* 1968; *The Best House in London* 1969; *The Rise and Rise of Michael Rimmer* (also co-sc.) *The Magic Christian* (also co-sc.) 1970; *The Statue* 1971; *And Now For Something Completely Different* (also co-sc.), *Rentadick* (co-sc. only), *The Love Ban* 1972; *Romance with a Double Bass* 1974; *Monty Python and the Holy Grail* (also co-sc.) 1975; *Pleasure at Her Majesty's/Monty Python Meets Beyond the Fringe* (also co-sc.) 1976; *Monty Python's Life of Brian* (also co-sc.), *Away from It All* (short; dir., narr. only), *The Secret Policeman's Ball* 1979; *Monty Python Live at the Hollywood Bowl, The Great Muppet Caper, Time Bandits* 1981; *The Secret Policeman's Other Ball, Privates on Parade* 1982; *Monty Python's The Meaning of Life* (also co-sc.), *Yellowbeard* 1983; *Silverado* (US) 1985; *Clockwise* 1986; *The Secret Policeman's Third Ball* 1987; *A Fish Called Wanda* (also co-exec. prod., co-story, sc.) 1988; *The Big Picture* (cameo), *Erik the Viking* 1989; *An American Tail: Fievel Goes West* (v/o), *Bullseye!* 1991; *Splitting Heirs* 1993; *The Jungle Book, Mary Shelley's Frankenstein, The Swan Princess* (v/o) 1994; *Fierce Creatures* (also co-prod., co-sc.) 1997.

Clemens, William B. Director. Born on Sept. 10, 1905, in Saginaw, Mich. Entered films in the early 30s as editor for Warners. Directed B pictures for this and other companies from the mid-30s to the mid-40s, specializing in mysteries.

FILMS: *Man Hunt, The Law in Her Hands, The Case of the Velvet Claws, Down the Stretch, Here Comes Carter* 1936; *Once a Doctor, The Case of the Stuttering Bishop, Talent Scout, Footloose Heiress, Missing Witness* 1937; *Torchy Blane in Panama, Accidents Will Happen, Mr. Chump, Nancy Drew—Detective* 1938; *Nancy Drew—Reporter, Nancy Drew—Trouble Shooter, Nancy Drew and the Hidden Staircase, The Dead End Kids on Dress Parade* 1939; *Calling Philo Vance, King of the Lumberjacks, Devil's Island* 1940; *She Couldn't Say No, Knockout, The Night of January 16th* 1941; *A Night in New Orleans, Sweater Girl* 1942; *Lady Bodyguard, The Falcon in Danger, The Falcon and the Co-Eds* 1943; *The Falcon Out West, Crime by Night* 1944; *The Thirteenth Hour* 1947.

Clément, Aurore. Actress. Born in France. Following her 1973 debut in Louis Malle's *Lacombe, Lucien*, she established herself as a versatile lead of the French screen. Married to production designer Dean TAVOULARIS.

FILMS INCLUDE: *Lacombe Lucien* 1973; *Caro Michele* 1975; *Le Crabe-Tambour, Le Juge Fayard dit le "sheriff"* 1977; *Les Rendez-Vous d'Anna, Travels with Anita* 1978; *Buone Notizie, Caro Papa* 1979; *5% de Risque* 1980; *L'Amour des Femmes* 1981; *Les Fantômes du Chapelier, Toute une nuit/All Night Long* 1982; *Les Années 80, El Sur* 1983; *Paris, Texas* 1984; *Festa di Laurea, Je vous salue, Marie/Hail Mary, El Suizo—Un Amour En Espagne* 1985; *Mosca Addio* 1987; *Der Einbruch* (uncred.), *Gemini: The Twin Stars* 1988; *Comédie d'amour* 1989; *Stan the Flasher* 1990.

Clement, Dick (Richard). Director, screenwriter. Born on Sept. 5, 1937, in West Cliff-on-Sea, England. Entered British films and TV as screenwriter in the mid-60s and has collaborated on the scripts of such films as *The Jokers* (1967), *Hannibal Brooks* (1968), *Villain* (1971), and *The Prisoner of Zenda* (1979). Turned director in 1969.

FILMS (as director): *Otley* (also co-sc.) 1969; *A Severed Head, Catch Me a Spy* (also-sc.), *Keep Your Fingers Crossed* 1971; *Porridge/Doing Time* (also co-sc.) 1979; *Bullshot* 1983; *Water* (also co-sc.) 1985; *The Commitments* 1991.

Clément, René. Director. *b.* Mar. 18, 1913, in Bordeaux, France. Deceased. He terminated his studies in architecture to enter French films as a cameraman and assistant director in 1934. In 1936 he began directing short documentaries, an activity that took him to such faraway places as Tunisia and Yemen. He contracted typhoid and was arrested three times before completing his color documentary *L'Arabie interdite* (1937). After the Liberation of France, he began his career as a feature director with a remarkable semidocumentary, *La Bataille du Rail,* a meticulous reconstruction of the exploits of the French Resistance. This was followed by an assignment as technical consultant to COCTEAU on *Beauty and the Beast* and as collaborator of NOËL-NOËL on *Le Père Tranquille.*

Clément's subsequent work, both in French and in international films, showed an increasing fascination with visual effect and technical stylistics. However, he remained faithful to his documentary origins, and his insistence on authenticity of detail in his films nearly approached an obsession. He was more successful with his French-made films (*Forbidden Games, Gervaise*) than with his frequent international co-productions, though his London-made comedy *Knave of Hearts* was impressive. Clément, whose preoccupation with WW II themes might have ended with the ambitious but not very successful *Is Paris Burning?,* showed a flair for the *film noir* with *Purple Noon* and *Rider on the Rain,* among others.

Clément was not prolific, completing only some 15 films in 25 years, but he occupies a solid position among French postwar directors as a member of the middle generation between the Old Guard and the New Wave. He won Academy Awards for best foreign-language film for *The Walls of Malapaga* and *Forbidden Games.* The latter film, his best known and most memorable, also won the grand prize at the 1952 Venice Festival.

FILMS: Shorts—*Soigne ton Gauche* 1936; *L'Arabie interdite* (also sc., phot.) 1937; *La Grande Chartreuse* 1938; *La Bièvre* 1939; *Le Triage* 1940; *Ceux du Rail* 1942; *La Grande Pastorale* 1943; *Chefs de Demain* 1944. Features—*La Bataille du Rail/Battle of the Rails* (also sc.), *Le Père Tranquille/Mr. Orchid* 1946; *Les Maudits/The Damned* (also co-adapt.) 1947; *Au-delà des Grilles/Le Mura di Malapaga/The Walls of Malapaga* (It./Fr.) 1949; *Le Château de Verre* (also co-sc; Fr./It.) 1950; *Jeux interdits/Forbidden Games* (also co-adapt., co-dial.) 1952; *Monsieur Ripois/Knave of Hearts/Lovers Happy Lovers* (also co-sc.; Fr./UK) 1954; *Gervaise* 1956; *Barrage contre le Pacifique/La Diga sul Pacifico/This Angry Age/The Sea Wall* (also co-sc.; It./Fr.) 1958; *Plein Soleil/Purple Noon/Lust for Evil* (also co-sc.; It./Fr.) 1959; *Quelle Joie de vivre/Che Gioia vivere* (also co-sc.; It./Fr.) 1961; *Le Jour et l'Heure/The Day and the Hour* (also co-sc.; Fr./It.) 1963; *Les Félins/Joy House/The Love Cage* (also co-sc.) 1964; *Paris brûle-t-il?/Is Paris Burning?* (Fr./US) 1966; *Le Passager de la Pluie/Rider on the Rain* (Fr./It.) 1970; *La Maison sous les Arbres/The Deadly Trap* (Fr./US) 1971; *La Course du Lièvre à travers les Champs/And Hope to Die* (Fr./US) 1972; *La Baby-Sitter* (It./Fr./Ger.) 1975.

Clementi, Pierre. Actor. Born in 1942, in Paris. Darkly handsome, fierce-eyed leading man of French films and European co-productions. Typically seen in temperamental and sometimes decadent, cruel roles. Also active on the Paris stage and closely associated as an experimental filmmaker with the French underground film movement. In 1976 he directed a first film, *Visa de Censure.*

FILMS INCLUDE: *Il Gattopardo/The Leopard* (It./Fr.) 1963; *Un Homme de trop/Shock Troops* (Fr./It.), *Belle de Jour* (Fr./It.) 1967; *Benjamin, Partner* (It.), *Scusi—facciamo l'Amore?/Listen—Let's Make Love* (It./Fr.) 1968; *La Voie lactée/The Milky Way* (Fr./It.), *Antenna* (Hol.), *Porcile/Pigsty/Pig Pen* (It./Fr.), *I Cannibali/The Cannibals* (It.), *Il Conformista/The Conformist* (It.) 1970; *La Pacifista/The Pacifist* (It./Fr./Ger.) 1971; *La Cicatrice interieure* 1972; *Steppenwolf* (UK/It./Ger.), *Sweet Movie* (Fr./Can./Ger.) 1974; *L'Affiche rouge* 1976; *Les Apprentis Sorciers* 1977; *La Chanson de Roland* 1978; *Cauchemar* 1980; *Quartet* (UK/Fr.) 1981; *Exposed* (US/Fr.) 1983; *Es ist nicht leicht ein Gott zu sein/It Isn't Easy Being God* (Ger./It./USSR/Fr./Switz.) 1990.

Clements, Sir John. Actor. *b.* Apr. 25 1910, London. *d.* 1988. *ed.* Cambridge. A distinguished stage actor and director since 1930, he appeared in British films since 1935, at first in leads and later in sporadic supporting roles. He has also directed and produced one film, *Call of the Blood* (1948). Knighted in 1968. Married actress Kay HAMMOND.

FILMS INCLUDE: *Once in a New Moon* 1935; *Things to Come, Rembrandt* 1936; *Knight Without Armor* 1937; *South Riding* 1938; *The Four Feathers* 1939; *Convoy* 1940; *This England, Ships with Wings* 1941; *Tomorrow We Live/At Dawn We Die* 1942; *Undercover* 1943; *They Came to a City* 1944; *Call of the Blood* (also dir.) 1948; *Train of Events* 1949; *The Silent Enemy* 1958; *The Mind Benders* 1962; *Oh! What a Lovely War* 1969; *Gandhi* 1982; *The Jigsaw Man* 1984.

Clements, Stanley. Actor. *b.* July 16, 1926, Long Island, N.Y. *d.* 1981. The winner of an amateur singing contest at age 11, he entered films early in the 40s and for a while played tough teenagers. After military service (1946–47), he returned to the screen in young adult leads and supporting roles, but still on the tough side, in very-low-budget films. In the late 50s he appeared in several Bowery Boys films. His first wife (1945–48) was actress Gloria GRAHAME.

FILMS INCLUDE: *Tall Dark and Handsome* 1941; *I Wake Up Screaming, Smart Alecks* 1942; *The More the Merrier, Sweet Rosie O'Grady* 1943; *Going My Way* 1944; *Salty O'Rourke* 1945; *Hazard, The Babe Ruth Story* 1948; *Bad Boy, Johnny Holiday* 1949; *Destination Murder* 1950; *Pride of Maryland* 1951; *Boots Malone, Army Bound, Jet Job* 1952; *Off Limits, Hot News* 1953; *Robber's Roost* 1955; *Hot Shots* 1956; *Spook Chasers, Looking for Danger* 1957; *In the Money* 1958; *Sniper's Ridge* 1961; *Tammy and the Doctor* 1963; *Panic in the City* 1968; *Hot Lead and Cold Feet* 1978.

Cleveland, George. Actor. *b.* 1886, Sydney, Nova Scotia, Canada. *d.* 1957. A veteran of the stage (from 1903), he played character parts in some 150 Hollywood films of the 30s, 40s, and early 50s, typically as a crusty but kindly old man. Played Gramps in the 'Lassie' TV series.

FILMS INCLUDE: *Monte Carlo Nights* 1934; *The Keeper of the Bees* 1935; *Revolt of the Zombies* 1936; *Streets of New York* 1939; *The Haunted House* 1940; *All That Money Can Buy* 1941; *The Spoilers, The Big Street* 1942; *Drums of Fu Manchu* 1943; *It Happened Tomorrow, Home in Indiana* 1944; *Dakota, Pillow of Death* 1945; *Little Giant, Courage of Lassie, Angel on My Shoulder* 1946; *Mother Wore Tights, My Wild Irish Rose* 1947; *Albuquerque, A Date with Judy* 1948; *Miss Grant Takes Richmond* 1949; *Frenchie* 1950; *Flaming Feather* 1951; *Carson City* 1952; *Walking My Baby Back Home* 1953; *Untamed Heiress, The Outlaw's Daughter* 1954.

cliff-hanger. 1. An adventure serial consisting of several episodes, each of which ends on a suspenseful note to hold the audience in expectation of the next. 2. The suspenseful moment at the end of a serial chapter in which the hero or heroine seems to be in a dire predicament; hence, any situation or event whose outcome is suspensefully uncertain.

Clifford, Graeme. Director. Formerly an editor of British films, he moved to Hollywood in the late 70s and after several editing assignments began directing in the early 80s.

FILMS INCLUDE: As editor—*Images* (Ire.) 1972; *Don't Look Now* 1973; *The Rocky Horror Picture Show* 1975; *The Man Who Fell to Earth* 1976; *Convoy* (US), *F.I.S.T.* (US) 1978; *The Postman Always Rings Twice* (US) 1981. As director—*Frances* (US) 1982; *Burke and Wills* (Austral.) 1986; *Gleaming the Cube* (US) 1989; *Ruby Cairo* 1993.

Clift, Montgomery. Actor. *b.* Edward Montgomery Clift, Oct. 17, 1920, Omaha, Nebr. *d.* 1966. Made his debut in summer stock at 14 and before long was appearing on Broadway in increasingly important roles. He was among the founding members of the Actors Studio in 1947. After turning down several Hollywood offers, he made his screen debut in 1948 and immediately established himself as a promising young star. He received an Academy Award nomination for his very first appearance, in Fred Zinnemann's *The Search.* Other Oscar nominations followed, for *A Place in the Sun, From Here to Eternity,* and *Judgment at Nuremberg.* An intelligent and sensitive actor, he appeared in few films but consistently drew acclaim for his portrayals of introspective, troubled heroes, roles he endowed with a rare psychological dimension.

Off screen he gained a reputation as a loner and nonconformist, and following an automobile accident in 1957 there were rumors of heavy drinking, abuse of drugs, and odd behavior on and off the set. The accident scarred his face and ruined his good looks but gave his screen presence added strength and pathos. During the production of *Freud* (1962), in which he played the title role, he was operated on for the removal of cataracts in both eyes. He died of a heart attack at the age of 45.

FILMS: *The Search, Red River* 1948; *The Heiress* 1949; *The Big Lift* 1950; *A Place in the Sun* 1951; *I Confess, From Here to Eternity, Stazione Termini/Indiscretion of an American Wife* (It.) 1953; *Raintree County* 1957; *The Young Lions* 1958; *Lonelyhearts, Suddenly Last Summer* 1959; *Wild River* 1960; *The Misfits, Judgment at Nuremberg* 1961; *Freud* (title role) 1962; *L'Espion/The Defector* (Fr./Ger.) 1966.

Clifton, Elmer. Director. *b.* 1892, Chicago. *d.* 1949. A former stage actor, he began his film career in 1914. Starred in *John Barleycorn* (1914) and played romantic leads in two major D. W. GRIFFITH productions, *The Birth of a Nation* (1915) as Phil Stoneman, and *Intolerance* (1916) as Rhapsode in the Babylonian episode. He stayed on briefly as Griffith's assistant and soon began directing on his own. Piloted a number of major productions during the silent era, including films starring Dorothy Gish and Clara Bow but was relegated to Buck Jones vehicles and other low-budget Westerns, serials, and action pictures after the coming of sound.

FILMS INCLUDE: *The Artist's Wife* (short; also act.) 1915; *Her Official Fathers* (co-dir.), *The Flame of Youth, The Midnight Man, Flirting with Death, The Man Trap* 1917; *The Flash of Fate, The Two-Soul Woman* (also sc.), *The Guilt of Silence, Smashing Through, The Eagle, Winner Takes All, Battling Jane, Kiss or Kill* (also sc.) 1918; *The Hope Chest, Boots, Peppy Polly, Nugget Nell, Nobody Home/Out of Luck* 1919; *Mary Ellen Comes to Town, Way Down East* (2nd-unit dir. only) 1920; *Down to the Sea in Ships* (also prod.) 1922; *Six Cylinder Love* 1923; *The Warrens of Virginia, Daughters of the Night* 1924; *Wives at Auction* (also story), *The Truth About Men* 1926; *The Wreck of the Hesperus* 1927; *Let 'Er Go Gallegher, Beautiful but Dumb, Virgin Lips, Tropical Nights* 1928; *The Devil's Apple Tree* 1929; *Maid to Order* 1931; *Skull and Crown, Pals of the Range, Captured in Chinatown* (also co-sc.) 1935; *Custer's Last Stand* (serial), *Gambling with Souls* 1936; *Death in the Air, Mile a Minute Love, Crusade Against Rackets* 1937; *Wolves of the Sea* (also sc.), *Crime Afloat, The Secret of Treasure Island* (serial) 1938; *Crashing Thru* 1939; *Isle of Destiny* 1940; *Hard Guy, Swamp Woman* 1941; *Deep in the Heart of Texas, The Old Chisholm Trail* (also sc.) 1942; *The Days of Old Cheyenne, Return of the Rangers* (also sc.) 1943; *Captain America* (serial; co-dir. with John English), *Seven Doors to Death* (also sc.), *Gangsters of the Frontier* (also sc.) 1944; *Three in the Saddle* 1945; *The Judge, Not Wanted* 1949; *The Silver Bandit* 1950.

Cline, Eddie (Edward F.). Director. *b.* Nov. 7, 1892, Kenosha, Wis. *d.* 1961. Following some stage experience, entered films in 1913 as one of Mack SENNETT's Keystone Cops, then became Sennett's assistant and directed many Keystone comedies, including "Bathing Beauties" shorts from 1916 to 1918. Probably the foremost comic talent to come out of the Sennett school, Cline later directed scores of comedy features for various studios in addition to hundreds of shorts. Between 1920 and 1923 he collaborated with Buster KEATON on the direction of many of the latter's comedies. In 1925 he rejoined Sennett at Pathé and directed many two-reelers starring Alice Day, Andy Clyde, Ben Turpin, Madeline Hurlock, Carole Lombard, etc. His work in the sound era culminated in the early 40s with some of W. C. FIELD's most hilarious comedy features, *My Little Chickadee, The Bank Dick,* and *Never Give a Sucker an Even Break,* and with the helter-skelter Olsen and Johnson slapstick vehicle *Crazy House.* But he ended the decade and his career with the starvation-budget Monogram studio.

FILMS INCLUDE (features complete): Shorts—*The Winning Punch, His Busted Trust, Sunshine* 1916; *The Dog Catcher's Love, The Pawnbroker's Heart, A Bedroom Blunder, That Night* 1917; *The Kitchen Lady, Those Athletic Girls, His Smothered Love, The Summer Girls, Whose Little Wife Are You?, Hide and Seek Detectives* 1918; *Cupid's Day Off, East Lynne with Variations, When Love Is Blind, Hearts and Flowers* 1919; *One Week, Convict 13, The Scarecrow, Neighbors* (all co-dir., co-sc. with Buster Keaton) 1920; *The Haunted House, Hard Luck, The High Sign, The Playhouse, The Boat* (all co-dir., co-sc. with Keaton) 1921; *The Paleface, Cops, My Wife's Relations, The Frozen North, The Electric House, Day Dreams* (all co-dir., co-sc. with Keaton) 1922; *The Balloonatic, The Love Nest, The Three Ages* (feature; all co-dir., co-sc. with Keaton), *Circus Days* (feature), *The Meanest Man in the World* (feature) 1923; *When a Man's a Man* (feature), *The Plumber, Little Robinson Crusoe* (feature), *Good Bad Boy* (feature), *Captain January* (feature), *Along Came Ruth* (feature) 1924; *Bashful Jim, Tee for Two, Cold Turkey, Love and Kisses, Dangerous Curves Behind, The Rag Man* (feature), *Old Clothes* (feature) 1925; *The Gosh-Darn Mortgage, Spanking Breezes, A Love Sundae, The Ghost of Folly, Puppy Lovetime, Smith's Baby, When a Man's a Prince, Flirty Four-Flushers, Gooseland, A Harem Knight, A Blonde's Revenge* 1926; *The Jolly Jilter, Let It Rain* (feature), *Soft Cushions* (feature), *The Girl from Everywhere, The Bullfighters* 1927; *Hold That Pose, Love at First Sight, Ladies' Night in a Turkish Bath* (feature), *Vamping Venus* (feature), *Man Crazy, The Head Man* (feature), *The Crash* (feature) 1928. Features—*Broadway Fever, His Lucky Day, The Forward Pass* 1929; *In the Next Room, Sweet Mama, Leathernecking, The Widow from Chicago, Hook Line and Sinker* 1930; *Cracked Nuts, The Naughty Flirt, The Girl Habit* 1931; *Million Dollar Legs* 1932; *So This Is Africa, Parole Girl* 1933; *The Dude Ranch, Peck's Bad Boy* 1934; *When a Man's a Man, The Cowboy Millionaire* 1935; *It's a Great Life, F-Man* 1936; *On Again Off Again, Forty Naughty Girls, High Flyers* 1937; *Hawaii Calls, Go Chase Yourself, Breaking the Ice, Peck's Bad Boy with the Circus* 1938; *My Little Chickadee, The Villain Still Pursued Her, The Bank Dick* 1940; *Meet the Chump, Hello Sucker, Never Give a Sucker an Even Break* 1941; *Snuffy Smith the Yard Bird, What's Cookin'?, Private Buckaroo, Give Out Sisters, Behind the Eight Ball* 1942; *He's My Guy, Crazy House* 1943; *Swingtime Johnny, Ghost Catchers, Moonlight and Cactus, Night Club Girl, Slightly Terrific* 1944; *See My Lawyer, Penthouse Rhythm* 1945; *Bringing Up Father* 1946; *Jiggs and Maggie in Society, Jiggs and Maggie in Court* (co-dir. with William Beaudine) 1948.

clip. A brief section of film removed in editing from the footage of a shot. Sometimes called a "cut" or a "trim." In a narrower sense, the term applies to a section of film taken from existing STOCK FOOTAGE, and inserted into a film in editing.

Clive, Colin. Actor. *b.* Clive Greig, Jan. 20, 1898, St. Malo, France (the date given in most sources, although his death certificate says 1900). *d.* 1937. Son of a British colonel, he abandoned a military career because of a knee injury and turned to the stage. In Hollywood and British films from 1930, he played leads and second leads, typically on the brooding side, and is best remembered for the title role in *Frankenstein* (1931), as Rochester in *Jane Eyre* (1934), and as the pianist Orlac in *Mad Love/The Hands of Orlac* 1935. He was married to character actress Jean de Casalis (1896–1966). His death in his late 30s was attributed to pulmonary and intestinal disorders.

FILMS: *Journey's End* 1930; *The Stronger Sex* (UK), *Frankenstein* 1931; *Lily Christine* (UK) 1932; *Christopher Strong, Looking Forward* 1933; *The Key, One More River, Jane Eyre* 1934; *Clive of India, The Right to Live, The Bride of Frankenstein, Mad Love/The Hands of Orlac, The Girl from 10th Avenue, The Man Who Broke the Bank at Monte Carlo* 1935; *The Widow from Monte Carlo* 1936; *History Is Made at Night, The Woman I Love* 1937.

Clive, E. E. Actor. *b.* Edward E. Clive, 1879, Monmouthshire, Wales. *d.* 1940. Left medical school at 22 to go on the London stage. In 1912 he came to the US, where he produced, directed, and acted in stage productions, and, in 1933, began his Hollywood career, playing numerous character roles, often a dour butler or a stern Englishman.

FILMS INCLUDE: *The Invisible Man* 1933; *Bulldog Drummond Strikes Back, Charlie Chan in London, Riptide* 1934; *The Bride of Frankenstein, The Mystery of Edwin Drood, A Tale of Two Cities, Captain Blood* 1935; *Little Lord Fauntleroy, Dracula's Daughter, Camille, Libeled Lady, Charge of the Light Brigade, Lloyds of London* 1936; *Maid of Salem, Bulldog Drummond Escapes* 1937; *Kidnapped, Submarine Patrol* 1938; *The Last Warning, The Little Princess, The Hound of the Baskervilles, The Adventures of Sherlock Holmes* 1939; *The Earl of Chicago, Pride and Prejudice, Foreign Correspondent* 1940.

Cloche, Maurice. Director. *b.* June 17, 1907, Commercy, France. *d.* 1990. A former artist, he made his entry into films with several short documentaries, one of which, *Le Mont-Saint-Michel—Merveille de l'Occident* (1934), won a gold medal at the Venice Biennale. Turned to feature films in 1937, achieving his best form ten years later with *Monsieur Vincent,* the winner of the French cinema's Grand Prix as the best film of 1947 as well as an Oscar as best foreign film. But the bulk of his prolific output was mediocre. In 1940, Cloche founded a film society for young talent that became the foundation for France's distinguished film school, the Institute of Advanced Film Studies. In his later years he was hampered by a long bout with Parkinson's Disease.

FILMS INCLUDE: *Ces Dames aux Chapeaux verts/The Ladies in the Green Hats* 1937; *Le Petit Chose, La Vie est magnifique* 1938; *Nord Atlantique* 1939; *Sixième Etage* 1941; *Feu sacré* 1942; *L'Invité de la Onzième Heure* 1945; *Jeux de Femmes* 1946; *Coeur de Coq, Monsieur Vincent* 1947; *Docteur Laënnec* 1948; *La Cage aux Filles* 1949; *La Porteuse de Pain* 1950; *Never Take No for an Answer* (co-dir. with Ralph Smart; UK) 1951; *Domenica* 1952; *Nuits andalouses* 1954; *Un Missionnaire* 1955; *Adorable Démons* 1956; *Marchands de Filles/The Girl Sellers/Girl Merchants* 1957; *Les Filles de la Nuit/Girls of the Night, Prisons de Femmes* 1958; *Le Fric, Bal de Nuit* 1959; *Touchez pas aux Blondes!* 1960; *Cocagne* 1961; *La Porteuse de Pain* (remake) 1963; *Requiem pour un Caïd* 1964; *Le Vicomte règle ses Comptes/The Viscount* (French-, Italian-, Spanish-, and English-language versions) 1967; *Un Killer per sua Maestà/Le Tueur aime les Bonbons* (co-dir. with Richard Owens; It./Fr.) 1968; *Mais toi tu es Pierre* 1971.

Clonblough, G. Butler. See SEYFFERTITZ, Gustav von.

Clooney, George. Actor. *b.* May 6, 1961, in Lexington, Ky. *ed.* Northern Kentucky University. Handsome, confident leading man of stage and screen. The son of broadcaster Nick Clooney and nephew of singer-actress Rosemary CLOONEY, he came to prominence as the hearthrob Dr. Doug Ross on the television series 'ER.' Prior to that success, he had appeared for years in numerous TV pilots and sitcoms. With the advent of his meteoric rise to celebrity came several high profile film roles including the romantic comedy *One Fine Day* (1996) and the much anticipated *Batman and Robin* (1997), the fourth installment of the Warner Bros. box office giant with Clooney assuming the lead role, replacing Val KILMER.

FILMS: *And They're Off* 1982; *Return of the Killer Tomatoes* 1988; *Red Surf* 1990; *Unbecoming Age* 1992; *From Dusk Till Dawn, One Fine Day* 1996; *Batman and Robin, The Peacemaker* 1997.

Clooney, Rosemary. Singer, actress. Born on May 23, 1928, in Maysville, Ky. Began career at age 13, singing with her sister Betty on Cincinnati radio. Later became a band vocalist and rose to instant fame with her recording of 'Come-on-a-My-House.' She subsequently starred in a number of films, but her screen career petered out. In 1977 she authored an autobiography, *This for Remembrance,* in which she told of her harrowing experiences during confinement to the psychotic ward of a California hospital and of her recovery. The following year NBC presented a TV dramatization of her plight, 'Escape from Madness.' In 1982 she was impersonated by Sondra LOCKE in yet another TV movie about her tragedy, *Rosie: The Rosemary Clooney Story.* In the 1980s and 90s, she has revitalized her career as a jazz stylist. Formerly married to José FERRER. She is the aunt of actor George CLOONEY.

FILMS: *The Stars Are Singing, Here Come the Girls* 1953; *Red Garters, White Christmas* 1954; *Deep in My Heart* 1955.

Cloquet, Ghislain. Director of photography. *b.* 1925, Belgium. *d.* 1982. In France from boyhood, he began his career in the early 50s as a cameraman on Alain Resnais's shorts. In the 60s and 70s he worked for Robert Bresson and other leading French directors, and was behind the camera on films by Americans Arthur Penn and Woody Allen. He shared the Academy Award for the cinematography of Roman Polanski's *Tess,* a project he took over after the sudden death of Geoffrey UNSWORTH.

FILMS INCLUDE: *Les Statues meurent aussi* 1953; *Nuit et Brouillard/Night and Fog* (co-phot.), *Toute la Mémoire du Monde* 1956; *Un Amour de Poche/Nude in His Pocket* 1957; *Le Trou/The Night Watch* 1960; *La Belle Américaine* 1961; *Le Feu Follet/The Fire Within* 1963; *Mickey One* (US) 1965; *Au Hasard Balthazar* 1966; *Mouchette, Les Demoiselles de Rochefort/The Young Girls of Rochefort* 1967; *Benjamin, Mazel Tov ou Le Mariage/Marry Me! Marry Me!* 1968; *Une Femme douce/A Gentle Creature* 1969; *Peau d'Ane/Donkey Skin* 1971; *Love and Death* (US) 1975; *Tess* (co-phot.) 1979; *Chère inconnue/I Sent a Letter to My Love* 1980; *Four Friends* (US) 1981.

Close, Glenn. Actress. Born on Mar. 19, 1947, in Greenwich, Conn. *ed.* Coll. of William and Mary. A 12th-generation New Englander, she was raised on the family's 500-acre estate, occasionally accompanying her Harvard-trained surgeon father on his trips to a clinic he opened in Belgian Congo (now Zaire). While still at high school, she organized and performed with a repertory troupe called Fingernails ("The Group With Polish"), and later toured with various folk-singing groups. After graduating from college with a degree in drama and speech, she began performing on the New York stage. Director George Roy Hill, who saw her in the Broadway musical 'Barnum,' cast her in the role of Robin Williams's liberated mother in *The World According to Garp* (1982), her film debut. She proved a natural for the movies, reaching peaks of success with vicious roles in *Fatal Attraction* and *Dangerous Liaisons,* for both of which she was nominated for Academy Awards as best actress. She was also nominated for Oscars as best supporting actress for *Garp, The Big Chill,* and *The Natural.* On her frequent returns to Broadway, she has won the Tony for 'The Real Thing,' 'Death and the Maiden,' and a triumphant turn as Norma Desmond in Andrew Lloyd Webber's production of 'Sunset Boulevard.' In recent years she has distinguished herself on the small screen, in well-received TV movies 'Sarah, Plain and Tall' and 'Stones for Ibarra.' Twice divorced, she lives in New York City as a single mother. An accomplished lyric soprano, she traditionally sings the National Anthem in the New York Mets home opening-day games.

FILMS: *The World According to Garp* 1982; *The Big Chill* 1983; *The Stone Boy, The Natural, Greystoke: The Legend of Tarzan, Lord of the Apes* (dubbed v/o) 1984; *Maxie, Jagged Edge* 1985; *Fatal Attraction, Light Years* (v/o, English version only of 1982 animated French-Swiss-German film *Les Maîtres du Temps), Do You Mean There Are Still Real Cowboys?* (doc.; prod. only) 1987; *Dangerous Liaisons* 1988; *Immediate Family* 1989; *Orders, Reversal of Fortune, Hamlet, The White Cow* 1990; *Meeting Venus, Hook* (uncred. cameo) 1991; *The House of the Spirits* 1993; *The Paper* 1994; *101 Dalmations, Mars Attacks!, Mary Reilly* 1996; *Paradise Road* 1997.

close shot (c.s.). A shot closer than a medium shot but not as tight as a CLOSE-UP. When the subject is a person, he or she is framed from the top of the head to the waist. When it is an object, the shot is relative to the size of that object.

close-up (abbreviated **c.u.)** A shot taken from a short distance or through a telephoto lens which brings to the screen a magnified, detailed part of a person or an object. A close-up of a person, for example, might show only his head, a shot of a car's interior might reveal just the steering wheel. A close-up is used to draw attention to a significant detail to clarify a point, designate a meaning, or heighten the dramatic impact of a film's plot.

Clothier, William. Director of photography. Born in 1903, in Decatur, Ill. Entered films as camera assistant in 1923 and later contributed some impressive aerial photography to the film *Wings.* Worked as director of photography in Mexico and Spain for several years but because of union restrictions returned to Hollywood as assistant cameraman after WW II service as an Army Air Corps captain. He did not become a full lighting cameraman until the 40s, and it was not until the 60s that he established a reputation for his superb handling of outdoor color cinematography, working for such directors as Ford, Walsh, Wellman, McLaglen, and Peckinpah, among others. He has also contributed excellent aerial photography for films shot by others.

FILMS INCLUDE: *For You I Die* 1947; *Sofia* 1948; *Once a Thief* 1950; *Phantom from Space* 1953; *The High and the Mighty* (aerial phot. only), *Track of the Cat* 1954; *The Sea Chase, Blood Alley* 1955; *Seven Men from Now* 1956; *Bombers B-52* 1957; *Darby's Rangers, Lafayette Escadrille* 1958; *The Horse Soldiers* 1959; *The Alamo* 1960; *Ring of Fire, The Deadly Companions, The Comancheros* 1961; *The Man Who Shot Liberty Valance, Merrill's Marauders* 1962; *Donovan's Reef, McLintock* 1963; *A Distant Trumpet, Cheyenne Autumn* 1964; *Shenandoah* 1965; *The Rare Breed, Stagecoach* 1966; *The Way West, The War Wagon* 1967; *Firecreek, The Devil's Brigade, Bandolero* 1968; *The Hellfighters, The Undefeated* 1969; *The Cheyenne Social Club, Chisum, Rio Lobo* 1970; *Big Jake* 1971; *The Train Robbers* 1973.

Clouse, Robert. American director. Specializes in featherbrained movies with heavy-duty action. His *Enter the Dragon* is widely admired by martial-arts aficionados.

FILMS INCLUDE: *Darker Than Amber, Dreams of Glass* (also prod., sc.) 1970; *Enter the Dragon* 1973; *Black Belt Jones, Golden Needles* 1974; *The Ultimate Warrior* (also sc.) 1975; *The Pack* (also sc.) 1977; *The Amsterdam Kill* (also sc.) 1978; *The Game of Death* 1979; *The Big Brawl* (also sc.) 1980; *Force: Five* (also sc.) 1981; *Deadly Eyes* 1982; *Gymkata* 1985.

Cloutier, Suzanne. Actress. Born in 1927, in Ottawa, Canada. A former New York model, she played leads in international films of the late 40s and 50s, notably as Desdemona in Orson Welles's *Othello.* Formerly married to Peter USTINOV.

FILMS INCLUDE: *Temptation* (US) 1946; *Au Royaume des Cieux* (Fr.) 1949; *Juliette ou la Clef des Songes* (Fr.) 1950; *Derby Day* (UK) 1951; *Othello* (US/It.) 1952; *Doctor in the House* (UK) 1954; *Romanoff and Juliet* (US) 1961.

Clouzot, Henri-Georges. Director. *b.* Nov. 20, 1907, Niort, France. *d.* 1977. Poor vision and ill health forced him to abandon plans for a naval career, so, hoping to be a diplomat, he studied political science. He served as secretary to a right-wing politician but soon was drawn to writing, first as a newspaper reporter and from the early 30s as screenwriter and occasional playwright. Between 1931 and 1933 he collaborated on many scripts, mostly for routine French films, and worked as assistant director to Anatole LITVAK and E. A. Dupont. Deteriorating health forced his retirement from any activity in 1933 and he spent the next few years convalescing in a sanatorium.

Clouzot returned to screenwriting in 1938, and in 1942 he made his debut as director with a minor but effective thriller, *L'Assassin habite au 21.* His next film, *Le Corbeau,* brought him at once fame and notoriety. An excellent suspense drama about a small French town terrorized by an epidemic of poison-pen letters, it commented sharply on the quality of French provincial life. However, a Nazi-run company produced the film, and false allegations followed that it was used in Germany for anti-French propaganda. After the liberation, the film was temporarily banned from exhibition and Clouzot was suspended from any motion-picture activity for six months. He did not make another film until 1947.

An excellent craftsman, Clouzot was an acknowledged master of suspense, a sort of French Hitchcock, but unlike the latter, totally lacking in humor. His films are typically morbid and violent, their suspense often unrelenting. Among the most thrilling and best known are *The Wages of Fear* and *Les Diaboliques,* both of which enjoyed great commercial success abroad. His nonthrillers also reflect his pessimistic view of society and its institutions. Even his lovers (in *Manon, La Vérité,* etc.) are typically amoral and destined to torment each other. Clouzot usually wrote his own scripts, often a free adaptation of a successful novel. He was a meticulous worker, planning every film shot long before production actually began. He had a reputation as a tyrant on the set, often working his actors and technicians to the point of exhaustion until he got what he considered perfect results.

Continuous ill health hampered Clouzot's activity in his final years and aborted several of his projects. His wife, Brazil-born Vera Clouzot (*b.* Vera Amado, 1921; *d.* 1960), appeared in three of his films. In 1984, the French government declared his *Le Mystère Picasso/The Mystery of Picasso* (1956) a national treasure.

FILMS (as director and co-screenwriter): *La Terreur des Batignolles* (short) 1931; *L'Assassin habite au 21/The Murderer*

Lives at Number 21 1942; *Le Corbeau/The Raven* 1943; *Quai des Orfèvres/Jenny Lamour* 1947; *Manon, Retour à la Vie* ("Le Retour de Jean" episode) 1949; *Miquette et sa Mère/Miquette* 1950; *Le Salaire de la Peur/The Wages of Fear* 1953; *Les Diaboliques/Diabolique* 1955; *Le Mystère Picasso/The Mystery of Picasso* (feature-length doc.) 1956; *Les Espions* 1957; *La Vérité/The Truth* 1960; *L'Enfer* (unfinished due to Clouzot's illness; later produced in 1994) 1964; *La Prisonnière/The Female Prisoner* 1968.

Cluzet, Francois. Actor. French lead known for consistent work in films by leading French directors (Chabrol, Tavernier, Blier), including role as adoptive fan in Bertrand Tavernier's *Round Midnight* (1986).

FILMS INCLUDE: *Le Cheval d'orgueil/The Horse of Pride, Cocktail Molotov* 1979; *L'Eté meurtrier/One Deadly Summer, Les Fantômes du Chapelier/The Hatter's Ghosts* 1982; *Coup de Foudre/Entre Nous, Vive la Sociale!* 1983; *Les Enragés* 1984; *Elsa, Elsa!* 1985; *Association de Malfaiteurs, Autour de Minuit/Round Midnight, Etat d'âme, Rue du départ* 1986; *Jaune revolver* 1987; *Une Affaire de femmes/Story of Women, Chocolat, Deux, Un Tour de manège* 1988; *Force majeure, La Révolution Française, Trop belle pour toi/Too Beautiful for You* 1989.

Clyde, Andy. Actor. *b.* Mar. 25, 1892, Blairgowrie, Scotland. *d.* 1967. Began his film career in the mid-20s, playing second banana to Billy BEVAN and other comic stars in scores of silent and sound Mack SENNETT two-reel comedies. From 1928 played grizzled character parts in feature films, often Westerns, and in the 40s was William BOYD's sidekick in numerous Hopalong Cassidy Westerns. He was also a regular on the TV series 'The Real McCoys' (1957–63), 'Lassie' (1958–64), and 'No Time for Sergeants' (1964–65). He was married to Elsie Tarron, a one-time Mack Sennett Bathing Beauty. Both his brother, David Clyde (1885–1945), and sister, Jean Clyde (1889–1962), were also in films.

FILMS INCLUDE: *His New Mama* (short) 1924; *Sea Dog's Tale* (short) 1926; *The Goodbye Kiss, Blindfold* 1928; *Midnight Daddies* 1930; *Million Dollar Legs* 1932; *The Little Minister* 1934; *Annie Oakley* 1935; *Two in a Crowd* 1936; *It's a Wonderful World* 1939; *Abe Lincoln in Illinois, Hopalong Cassidy* 1940; *Outlaws of the Desert* 1941; *This Above All* 1942; *Roughly Speaking* 1945; *The Green Years, The Plainsman and the Lady* 1946; *Gunslingers* 1950; *The Road to Denver* 1955.

Clyde, June. Actress. Born June Tetrazini, on Dec. 2, 1909, in St. Joseph, Mo. Appeared in vaudeville as Baby Tetrazini from age seven, and later in stage musicals before making her screen debut in 1929. The following year she married screen director Thornton FREELAND. Played leading ladies in Hollywood films of the early 30s, topping the bill in B pictures and supporting in bigger productions. During her husband's stint in England in the late 30s, she appeared in British films and on the London stage.

FILMS INCLUDE: *Tanned Legs* 1929; *Hit the Deck, The Cuckoos, Midnight Mystery* 1930; *Men Are Like That, The Mad Parade, Morals for Women, Arizona, The Secret Witness* 1931; *Steady Company, Radio Patrol, The Cohens and the Kellys in Hollywood, Thrill of Youth, Strange Adventure, Back Street, The All-American* 1932; *A Study in Scarlet, Her Resale Value, Forgotten, Only Yesterday* 1933; *I Hate Women, Hollywood Party* 1934; *Dance Band* (UK), *She Shall Have Music* (UK) 1935; *Land Without Music/Forbidden Music* (UK) 1936; *Intimate Relations, School for Husbands* (UK) 1937; *Poison Pen* (UK) 1939; *Country Fair, Sealed Lips* 1941; *Seven Doors to Death* 1944; *Hollywood and Vine* 1945; *Behind the Mask* 1946; *Night Without Stars* 1953; *The Story of Esther Costello* (UK) 1957.

Coates, Anne V. Editor. Born in 1925, Reigate, England. *ed.* Bartrum Coll. A former nurse at a plastic surgery hospital, she began editing British films in the early 50s and for three decades worked on numerous major productions, including several Hollywood films. She won an Academy Award for editing *Lawrence of Arabia* (1962) and was nominated for Oscars for *Becket* (1964) and *The Elephant Man* (1980). She was married to director Douglas HICKOX.

FILMS INCLUDE: *The Pickwick Papers* 1952; *Lost/Tears for Simon* 1955; *The Horse's Mouth* 1958; *Tunes of Glory* 1960; *Lawrence of Arabia* 1962; *Becket* 1964; *Those Magnificent Men in Their Flying Machines* 1965; *Hotel Paradiso* 1966; *The Bofors Gun* 1968; *The Italian Job* 1969; *The Adventurers* 1970; *Bequest to the Nation/The Nelson Affair* 1973; *Murder on the Orient Express* 1974; *The Eagle Has Landed* 1976; *The Medusa Touch* (also co-prod.) 1978; *The Elephant Man* 1980; *Ragtime* 1981; *The Pirates of Penzance* 1983; *Greystoke: The Legend of Tarzan, Lord of the Apes* 1984; *Lady Jane, Raw Deal* 1986; *Masters of the Universe* 1987; *Farewell to the King* (co-edit.), *Listen to Me* 1989; *I Love You to Death* 1990; *Chaplin* 1992; *In the Line of Fire* 1993; *Pontiac Moon* 1994.

Cobb, Irvin S. Playwright, novelist, actor. *b.* June 23, 1876, Paducah, Ky. *d.* 1944. *ed.* U. of Georgia; Dartmouth (law degree). A newspaper reporter from his teens, he was the editor of his hometown newpaper at 19. Later worked for various New York dailies and was a regular contributor to *The Saturday Evening Post,* for which he covered some phases of WW I in Europe. Wrote a number of plays, many novels, and numerous short stories, and several of his books and stories were adapted into films. His *Judge Priest* stories provided the material for John FORD's 1934 film by the same title, starring Will ROGERS. He also wrote titles for several silent films, including *Pardon My French* and *Peck's Bad Boy* (both 1921). Cobb played prominent roles in occasional films from early silent days.

FILMS INCLUDE (as actor): *The Arab* 1915; *Go and Get It* 1920; *The Great White Way* (cameo) 1924; *Steamboat 'Round the Bend* 1935; *Everybody's Old Man* (title role), *Pepper* 1936; *Hawaii Calls, The Young in Heart, The Arkansas Traveler* 1938.

Cobb, Lee J. Actor. *b.* Leo Jacob, Dec. 8, 1911, New York City. *d.* 1976. Outstanding character player of the American stage, TV, and films. The son of a compositor at *The Jewish Daily Forward,* he was raised on New York's Lower East Side and showed early promise as a virtuoso child violinist, but a broken wrist ended his plans for a musical career. At 17 he ran away from home, going to Hollywood in an unsuccessful bid for a career in films. Returning to New York, he began acting in radio dramas while studying accounting nights at CCNY. In 1931 he was back in California, where he made his stage debut at the Pasadena Playhouse, and in 1935, again in New York, he joined the famed Group Theatre and appeared in such plays as 'Waiting for Lefty' and 'Golden Boy.' His stage career culminated in 1949, when he created on Broadway the role of Willy Loman in Arthur Miller's 'Death of a Salesman' to rave reviews. He repeated the role in 1966 in a highly esteemed TV version. He is also remembered by TV audiences for his role of Judge Garth in the long-running 'The Virginian' series. In films from 1934, he played some leads and numerous character roles, often as a menacing heavy, sometimes as an imposing patriarch or a brooding community leader or business executive. Memorable as Johnny Friendly, the union racketeer in *On the Waterfront* (1954) and as Fyodor Karamazov in *The Brothers Karamazov* (1958), roles for which he was nominated for Academy Awards as best supporting actor.

FILMS: *The Vanishing Shadow* (serial) 1934; *North of the Rio Grande, Rustler's Valley, Ali Baba Goes to Town* 1937;

Danger on the Air 1938; *The Phantom Creeps* (serial), *Golden Boy* 1939; *This Thing Called Love, Men of Boys Town* 1941; *Paris Calling* 1942; *The Moon Is Down, Tonight We Raid Calais, Buckskin Frontier, The Song of Bernadette* 1943; *Winged Victory* 1944; *Anna and the King of Siam* 1946; *Boomerang, Johnny O'Clock, Captain from Castile* 1947; *Call Northside 777, The Miracle of the Bells, The Luck of the Irish, The Dark Past* 1948; *Thieves' Highway* 1949; *The Man Who Cheated Himself, Sirocco, The Family Secret* 1951; *The Fighter* 1952; *The Tall Texan* 1953; *Yankee Pasha, Gorilla at Large, On the Waterfront, Day of Triumph* (orig. made for TV) 1954; *The Racers, The Road to Denver, The Left Hand of God* 1955; *The Man in the Gray Flannel Suit, Miami Exposé* 1956; *12 Angry Men, The Garment Jungle, The Three Faces of Eve* 1957; *The Brothers Karamazov, Man of the West, Party Girl* 1958; *The Trap, Green Mansions, But Not for Me* 1959; *Exodus* 1960; *The Four Horsemen of the Apocalypse, How the West Was Won* 1962; *Come Blow Your Horn* 1963; *Our Man Flint* 1966; *In Like Flint* 1967; *Las Vegas 500 Millones/They Came to Rob Las Vegas* (Sp./It./Fr./Ger.), *Il Giorno della Civetta/Mafia* (It./Fr.), *Coogan's Bluff* 1968; *Mackenna's Gold* 1969; *The Liberation of L. B. Jones, Macho Callahan* 1970; *Lawman* 1971; *The Man Who Loved Cat Dancing, The Exorcist* 1973; *La Polizia sta a guardere* (It.) 1974; *Venditore di Palloncini/The Last Circus Show* (It.), *Ultimatum alla Città/Ultimatum, Mark il Poliziotta/Blood, Sweat, and Fear* (It.), *That Lucky Touch* (UK) 1975; *Nick the Sting, La Legge violenta della Squadra anticrimine/Cross Shot* (It.) 1976; *Arthur Miller on Home Ground* 1979.

Coburn, Charles. Actor. *b.* June 19, 1877, Savannah, Ga. *d.* 1961. At 17 he became manager of a Savannah theater where he had started three years earlier as a program boy. He later turned to acting, making his Broadway debut in 1901. In 1906 he organized the Coburn Shakespeare Players with his first wife, Ivah Wills. He resisted entering films until the mid-30s but then made numerous screen appearances in key character roles, typically as a hardened businessman or politician with a vulnerable heart. Won the Academy Award as best supporting actor in 1943 for his role in *The More the Merrier.* He was also nominated for Oscars for *The Devil and Miss Jones* (1941) and *The Green Years* (1946).

FILMS: *Boss Tweed* (title role) 1933; *The People's Enemy* 1935; *Of Human Hearts, Yellow Jack, Vivacious Lady, Lord Jeff* 1938; *Idiot's Delight, Made for Each Other, The Story of Alexander Graham Bell, Bachelor Mother, In Name Only, Stanley and Livingstone* 1939; *Road to Singapore, Florian, Edison the Man, Three Faces West, The Captain Is a Lady* 1940; *The Lady Eve, The Devil and Miss Jones, Our Wife, Unexpected Uncle, H. M. Pulham Esq.* 1941; *Kings Row, In This Our Life, George Washington Slept Here* 1942; *The More the Merrier, The Constant Nymph, Heaven Can Wait, My Kingdom for a Cook, Princess O'Rourke* 1943; *Knickerbocker Holiday, Wilson, The Impatient Years, Together Again* 1944; *A Royal Scandal, Rhapsody in Blue, Over 21, Shady Lady* 1945; *Colonel Effingham's Raid, The Green Years* 1946; *Lured* 1947; *The Paradine Case, B. F.'s Daughter, Green Grass of Wyoming* 1948; *Impact, Everybody Does It, The Doctor and the Girl, The Gal Who Took the West, Yes Sir That's My Baby* 1949; *Peggy, Louisa, Mr. Music* 1950; *The Highwayman* 1951; *Has Anybody Seen My Gal?, Monkey Business* 1952; *Trouble Along the Way, Gentlemen Prefer Blondes* 1953; *The Rocket Man, The Long Wait* 1954; *How to Be Very Very Popular* 1955; *The Power and the Prize, Around the World in 80 Days* 1956; *Town on Trial, How to Murder a Rich Uncle, The Story of Mankind* (as Hippocrates) 1957; *The Remarkable Mr. Pennypacker, Stranger in My Arms, John Paul Jones* (as Benjamin Franklin) 1959; *Pepe* 1960.

Coburn, James. Actor. Born on Aug. 31, 1928, in Laurel, Neb. The son of an auto mechanic, he studied acting at Los Angeles City College, the University of Southern California, and with Stella Adler in New York, then made his stage debut at the La Jolla Playhouse in 'Billy Budd.' Following some TV work in commercials and live plays, he made his film debut in 1959 and for a while was cast in supporting roles, often as a gunslinger. Tall, lithe, craggy-faced, and nonchalantly charming, he gradually worked up to better roles and by the late 60s became a popular star as the Bond-like hero of two light, action-filled espionage spoofs, *Our Man Flint* and *In Like Flint.* His own company, Panpiper, produced another successful vehicle, *The President's Analyst.* He later established Armageddon Productions and occasionally directed series episodes for TV. He was second-unit director on Sam Peckinpah's film *Convoy* (1978) and collaborated on the story of *Circle of Iron* (1979).

FILMS: *Ride Lonesome, Face of a Fugitive* 1959; *The Magnificent Seven* 1960; *Hell Is for Heroes* 1962; *The Great Escape, Charade* 1963; *The Man from Galveston, The Americanization of Emily* 1964; *Major Dundee, A High Wind in Jamaica, The Loved One* 1965; *Our Man Flint, What Did You Do in the War Daddy?, Dead Heat on a Merry-Go-Round* 1966; *In Like Flint, Waterhole No. 3, The President's Analyst* 1967; *Duffy* (US/UK), *Candy* (US/Fr./It.) 1968; *Hard Contract* 1969; *The Last of the Mobile Hot-Shots/Blood Kin* 1970; *Giù la Testa/Duck You Sucker!* (It./Sp.), *The Honkers, The Carey Treatment* 1972; *Pat Garrett and Billy the Kid, The Last of Sheila, Harry in Your Pocket* 1973; *Una Ragione per Vivere e una per Morire/A Reason to Live a Reason to Die* (It.), *The Internecine Project* (UK) 1974; *Jackpot* (It.), *Bite the Bullet, Hard Times* 1975; *Sky Riders* (US/Ger.), *The Last Hard Man, Midway* 1976; *White Rock* (doc.; on-screen narrator; UK), *Cross of Iron* (UK/Ger.) 1977; *Circle of Iron* (co-story only; UK), *Firepower* (UK), *The Muppet Movie* (cameo), *Goldengirl* 1979; *The Baltimore Bullet, Mr. Patman* (Can.), *Loving Couples* 1980; *High Risk, Looker* 1981; *Martin's Day* (Can.) 1984; *Death of a Soldier* (Austral.) 1986; *Walking After Midnight* 1988; *Call from Space, Tag till himlen* (Ger.) 1989; *Young Guns II* 1990; *Hudson Hawk* 1991; *Sister Act 2: Back in the Habit* 1993; *Deadfall, Maverick* 1994; *Eraser, The Nutty Professor* 1996; *Keys to Tulsa* 1997.

Cochran, Steve. Actor. *b.* Robert Alexander Cochran, May 25, 1917, Eureka, Calif. *d.* 1965. *ed.* U. of Wyoming. He was a railway hand, a cowpuncher, and a store detective at Macy's before beginning his stage career in Detroit. He later appeared in stock, reached Broadway in 1944, and made his film debut the following year. Tall and virile, he often portrayed heels and insensitive lovers, playing some of his best roles at Warners in the early 50s. In 1948 he costarred with Mae WEST in the Broadway revival of 'Diamond Lil' and in 1953 formed his own film company, Robert Alexander Productions. In 1957 he went to Italy to play the grim lead in Antonioni's *Il Grido/The Outcry.* Shortly before his sudden death aboard his yacht in 1965, he wrote, directed, produced, and starred in the film *Tell Me in the Sunlight,* which was released posthumously two years later.

FILMS INCLUDE: *Wonder Man* 1945; *The Kid from Brooklyn, The Chase, The Best Years of Our Lives* 1946; *Copacabana* 1947; *A Song Is Born* 1948; *White Heat* 1949; *The Damned Don't Cry, Highway 301, Dallas* 1950; *Storm Warning, Inside the Walls of Folsom Prison, Tomorrow Is Another Day, Jim Thorpe—All-American, The Tanks Are Coming* 1951; *The Lion and the Horse, Operation Secret* 1952; *She's Back on Broadway, The Desert Song, Back to God's Country* 1953; *Carnival Story, Private Hell 36* 1954; *Come Next Spring, Slander* 1956; *Il Grido/The Outcry* (It.) 1957; *I Mobster* 1958; *The Beat Generation* 1959; *The Deadly Companions/Trigger Happy*

1961; *Of Love and Desire* 1963; *Mozambique* (UK) 1965; *Tell Me in the Sunlight* (also dir., prod., co-title song; release delayed from 1964) 1967.

Coco, James. Actor. *b.* Mar. 21, 1929, New York City. *d.* 1987. Chubby, balding character player of the American stage, TV, and films. Made his stage debut as a child but worked as a toy salesman, night clerk, waiter, and dishwasher, among other occupations, before making his first New York appearance as an adult in 1957. Subsequently played supporting roles in many stage productions, on Broadway, off Broadway, and on the road, winning the first of two Obie Awards for 'The Moon in the Yellow River' in 1959. He achieved breakthrough success as the tragicomic lead in Neil Simon's 'Last of the Red Hot Lovers' (1969), a role especially tailored for him by the playwright. In films since 1964, mainly in comic support roles, he was playing character leads by the early 70s. Starred in the TV series 'Calucci's Department' and 'The Dumplings.' He was nominated for an Oscar as best supporting actor for *Only When I Laugh* (1981) and won an Emmy in 1983 for an appearance in the TV series 'St. Elsewhere.' Waging a life-long battle with obesity, Coco gained, lost, and regained hundreds of pounds during his career. In 1984, he wrote *The James Coco Diet Book.* He completed another book, *Cooking with Coco,* just before his death at 56 of a heart attack.

FILMS: *Ensign Pulver* 1964; *Generation* 1969; *End of the Road, The Strawberry Statement, Tell Me That You Love Me Junie Moon* 1970; *A New Leaf, Such Good Friends* 1971; *Man of La Mancha* (as Sancho Panza) 1972; *The Wild Party* 1975; *Murder by Death* 1976; *Bye Bye Monkey, The Cheap Detective, Charleston* 1978; *Scavenger Hunt* 1979; *Wholly Moses* 1980; *Only When I Laugh* 1981; *The Muppets Take Manhattan* 1984; *Hunk* 1987; *That's Adequate* (release delayed) 1989.

Cocteau, Jean. Poet, novelist, essayist, painter, playwright, director, screenwriter, set designer, actor. *b.* July 5, 1889, Maisons-Lafitte, near Paris, *d.* 1963. Began writing at ten and was a published poet, magazine editor, and the young darling of the international intellectual set by age 16 and a leading figure in French cultural life between the World Wars. Active in many art movements, he participated in practically every phase of the literary and plastic arts. But above all, he remained a poet, and his work in the cinema must be seen as an extension of his poetic vision. In the mid-20s, during a period of personal depression, he became addicted to opium but was eventually cured.

Cocteau made his first film, *The Blood of a Poet* (1930), with the financial backing of the Vicomte de Noailles (who also financed Buñuel's *L'Age d'Or*). This gave Cocteau complete freedom from the conventions of the medium about which, according to his own testimony, he knew little at the time. *Le Sang d'un Poète/The Blood of a Poet* is a wholly personal expression of the poet's inner life, his fears and obsessions, his relationship with the living world around him, and his preoccupation with the idea of death.

These themes were to be expanded and elaborated upon in Cocteau's two other personal films, *Orpheus* (1950) and *The Testament of Orpheus* (1960). All three films have been criticized by his detractors as pretentious and self-centered, which they partly are. But they are also among the most inventive and aesthetically satisfying in the history of cinema. Cocteau's other important films are *Beauty and the Beast* (1945), a haunting adaptation of a fairy tale, rich in visual imagery and lyrical expression, and *Les Parents terribles* (1948), an adaptation of his own stage play about family entanglements, and a *tour de force* of screen acting.

Cocteau's favorite actor was Jean MARAIS, his intimate friend, who appeared in practically every one of his films. In addition to directing and writing his own films, Cocteau contributed screenplays or dialogue to the works of other directors, for films ranging from routine to important. Some of these, such as Delannoy's *L'Eternel Retour,* seem to be more strongly imprinted with the personality of Cocteau than with that of their director.

Cocteau was a member of the French, German, and American academies and honorary president of the Cannes Film Festival. His manifesto on film, *Entretiens autour de Cinématographe (Cocteau on the Film)* was published in 1952.

FILMS: As director-writer—*Le Sang d'un Poète/The Blood of a Poet* (also edit., narr.) 1930 (first shown publicly in 1932); *La Belle et la Bête/Beauty and the Beast* (with technical assistance by René Clément) 1946; *L'Aigle à Deux Têtes/Eagle with Two Heads* (from own play), *Les Parents terribles/The Storm Within* (from own play) 1948; *Orphée/Orpheus, Coriolan* (16 mm short) 1950; *La Villa Santo-Sospir* (16 mm short) 1952; *Le Testament d'Orphée/The Testament of Orpheus* (also act.) 1960. As screenwriter—*La Comédie du Bonheur* (adapt., dial.; release delayed from 1939–40) 1942; *Le Baron fantôme* (dial.; off-screen voice) 1943; *Les Dames du Bois de Boulogne/Ladies of the Park* (dial.) 1945; *Ruy Blas* (sc., dial.), *L'Amore* ("Una Voce Umana" episode; play basis only, *La Voix humaine*; It.), *La Leggenda di Sant' Orsola* (short art film; commentary; It.) 1948; *Les Noces de Sable* (commentary written and narrated by Cocteau) 1949; *Les Enfants terribles/The Strange Ones* (co-sc., dial., from own novel) 1950; *Venise et ses Amants* (art film; commentary), *The Emperor's Nightingale* (commentary for French version of Jíri Trnka's 1948 Czech film) 1951; *La Corona Negra* (sc.; Sp./Fr.) 1952; *Gate of Hell* (French preface to Kinugasa's Japanese film) 1953; *Intimate Relations* (in English; play basis only, *Les Parents terribles*) 1954; *Le Bel Indifférent* (short; one-act play basis only), *A l'Aube du Monde* (short; commentary) 1957; *Le Musée Grevin* (doc.; personal appearance and improvised dialogue in one sequence), *Django Reinhardt* (short; preface) 1959; *La Princesse de Clèves* (adapt., dial.) 1961; *Thomas l'Imposteur/Thomas the Imposter* (co-sc., co-dial. from own novel) 1965.

code numbers. Matching numbers printed at one-foot intervals on the edges of both a positive print and its intended sound track to provide the editor with sync marks throughout the work print. (They are not to be confused with edge numbers, which serve to match up positive and negative film in lab processing.) The printing is made by a coding machine equipped with a revolving printing head and set to mark numbers sequentially at the one-foot intervals.

Cody, Bill. Actor *b.* William Joseph Cody, Jr., Jan. 5, 1891, Winnipeg, Canada. *d.* 1948. *ed.* St. John's U. (Minn.). Acted in vaudeville and stock before entering films as a stuntman early in the 20s. By 1925 he was starring in his own Western series and soon developed into a popular cowboy star. His films were typically filled with no-nonsense action, leaving little room for romance and none for comic relief. In 1927 he formed Bill Cody Productions and began directing and writing his own pictures. But his company soon folded when his distributor, Pathé, dropped out of the feature field. He went over to Universal, continuing his starring career through the early 30s. He later joined a traveling Wild West show but went on playing supporting parts in occasional films. His son, Bill Cody, Jr., was also in films.

FILMS INCLUDE: *Moccasins, Border Justice, Riders of Mystery, The Fighting Sheriff, Cold Nerve* 1925; *King of the Saddle, The Galloping Cowboy* 1926; *The Arizona Whirlwind, Born to Battle* 1927; *Laddie Be Good, The Price of Fear* 1928; *Slim Fingers, Wolves of the City, Eyes of the Underworld* 1929; *Under Texas Skies* 1930; *The Montana Kid, Oklahoma Jim,*

Land of Wanted Men, Ghost City 1931; *Texas Pioneers, Law of the North, Mason of the Mounted* 1932; *Frontier Days* 1934; *Cyclone Ranger* 1935; *The Fighting Gringo* 1939.

Cody, Iron Eyes. Actor. *b.* Oskie Cody, 1907, in Oklahoma Territory. *d.* 1991. Following in his father's footsteps, he began performing in circuses and Wild West shows at an early age, making his first film appearance as an extra at 12. Like his father, he became a consultant on Indian lore and equipment renter to Hollywood filmmakers while appearing in films and touring with Tim McCoy's and Buck Jones's shows and with the Ringling Brothers & Barnum and Bailey Circus. He also appeared extensively on TV. Famous as the Indian shedding a tear over the destruction of the environment in TV ecology spots and print advertising. Autobiography: *Iron Eyes: My Life as a Hollywood Indian* (1982).

FILMS INCLUDE: *Back to God's Country* (extra) 1919; *The Covered Wagon* 1923; *The Iron Horse, The Scarlet Letter* 1924; *The Road to Yesterday* 1925; *War Paint* 1926; *The Wolf Song* 1929; *Cimarron* 1931; *The Plainsman* 1937; *Union Pacific* 1939; *North West Mounted Police, Kit Carson* 1940; *Western Union* 1941; *Valley of the Sun* 1942; *The Senator Was Indiscreet, The Unconquered* 1947; *Blood on the Moon, The Paleface* 1948; *Massacre River, Sand* 1949; *Comanche Territory, Broken Arrow, Cherokee Uprising* 1950; *Ace in the Hole/The Big Carnival, The Last Outpost, Fort Defiance* 1951; *Red Mountain, Son of Paleface* 1952; *Sitting Bull* (as Chief Crazy Horse) 1954; *White Feather* 1955; *Comanche* 1956; *Alias Jesse James* 1959; *Heller in Pink Tights* 1960; *Black Gold* 1963; *The Great Sioux Massacre* (again as Crazy Horse) 1965; *Nevada Smith* 1966; *A Man Called Horse, El Condor* 1970; *Grayeagle* 1977; *Monsters in the Closet* 1987; *Spirit of '76* 1991.

Cody, Lew. Actor. *b.* Louis Joseph Coté, Feb. 22, 1884, Berlin, N.H. *d.* 1934. Suave, debonair star of Hollywood silents and early talkies. He quit medical studies to go on the stage in vaudeville and stock. Entered films in 1915, initially as Lewis J. Cody, and by the early 20s was much in demand as a leading man, often a seducer, sometimes a heel, always a charmer. He was married to screen star Mabel NORMAND.

FILMS INCLUDE: *The Mating, Comrade John* 1915; *The Cycle of Fate* 1916; *A Branded Soul* 1917; *Treasure of the Sea, The Demon, For Husbands Only, Borrowed Clothes, Mickey* 1918; *Don't Change Your Husband, The Life Line, The Beloved Cheater* 1919; *The Butterfly Man* 1920; *The Sign on the Door, Dangerous Pastime* 1921; *The Secrets of Paris, The Valley of Silent Men* 1922; *Souls for Sale, Within the Law, Rupert of Hentzau* (title role), *Lawful Larceny, Reno* 1923; *The Woman on the Jury, The Shooting of Dan McGrew, Revelation, Three Women, Husbands and Lovers, So This Is Marriage* 1924; *Man and Maid, The Sporting Venus, A Slave of Fashion, Exchange of Wives, Time the Comedian, The Tower of Lies, His Secretary* 1925; *The Gay Deceiver, Monte Carlo* 1926; *Adam and Evil, Tea for Three, The Demi-Bride, On Ze Boulevard* 1927; *Beau Broadway, Wickedness Preferred* 1928; *A Single Man* 1929; *What a Widow, Divorce Among Friends* 1930; *Dishonored, Three Rogues, Beyond Victory, Sweepstakes, A Woman of Experience, The Common Law, Sporting Blood, X Marks the Spot* 1931; *The Tenderfoot, 70,000 Witnesses, The Crusader, A Parisian Romance, Madison Square Garden, Undercover Man* 1932; *I Love That Man, Sitting Pretty, Wine Women and Song* 1933; *Private Scandal, Shoot the Works* 1934.

Coen, Joel & Ethan. Director, screenwriters. Born in 1958, in St. Louis Park, Minn. *ed.* Simon's Rock Coll. (Mass.). With brother Ethan Coen (*b.* 1958, St. Louis Park, Minn. *ed.* Princeton) as his producer and co-screenwriter, they broke into films in the mid-80s after training at NYU. Initially working with a minuscule budget, the duo became immediately recognized for their originality and flamboyance. In addition to their own films, they co-wrote the screenplay for Sam Raimi's *Crime Wave* (1986). They received an Academy Award for their original screenplay for the black comedy *Fargo* (1996).

FILMS (Joel as director-screenwriter, Ethan as producer-screenwriter): *Blood Simple* (also edit.) 1984; *Raising Arizona* 1987; *Miller's Crossing* 1990; *Barton Fink* 1991; *The Hudsucker Proxy* 1994; *Fargo* 1996.

co-feature. A film intended for release as one part of a double feature; usually a low- or medium-budget picture.

Coffee, Lenore J. Screenwriter. *b.* 1897, San Francisco. *d.* 1984. *ed.* Dominican Coll. (San Rafael, Calif.). She wrote screenplays, alone and in collaboration, for numerous Hollywood silents and talkies. Typical of her work are several Warner Bros. romantic melodramas of the 40s, but she was equally at home with suspense thrillers.

FILMS INCLUDE (alone or in collaboration): *The Better Wife* 1919; *The Forbidden Woman* 1920; *Ladyfingers* 1921; *The Right That Failed, Sherlock Brown* 1922; *Temptation* (story only), *Wandering Daughters* (titles only), *The Age of Desire* (titles only), *Daytime Wives* (co-story only), *Thundering Dawn* 1923; *Fools' Highway, Bread* (adapt. only), *The Rose of Paris* (co-adapt. only) 1924; *Hell's Highroad, East Lynne* 1925; *The Volga Boatman, For Alimony Only* 1926; *The Night of Love, Lonesome Ladies, The Angel of Broadway* 1927; *Chicago* 1928; *Desert Nights* 1929; *Street of Chance* (dial. only), *The Bishop Murder Case* 1930; *Arsene Lupin* 1932; *Evelyn Prentice, Four Frightened People* 1934; *Age of Indiscretion* (story only), *Vanessa: Her Love Story* 1935; *Suzy* 1936; *Four Daughters* 1938; *Good Girls Go to Paris* (co-story only) 1939; *My Son My Son!, The Way of All Flesh* 1940; *The Great Lie* 1941; *The Gay Sisters* 1942; *Old Acquaintance* 1943; *Till We Meet Again, Marriage Is a Private Affair* 1944; *Tomorrow Is Forever* 1946; *The Guilt of Janet Ames* (story only) 1947; *Beyond the Forest* 1949; *Lightning Strikes Twice* 1951; *Sudden Fear* 1952; *Young at Heart, The End of the Affair, Footsteps in the Fog* 1955; *Another Time Another Place* (novel basis only) 1958; *Cash McCall* 1960.

Cohan, George M. Actor, singer, dancer, songwriter, playwright, screenwriter. *b.* July 4, 1878, Providence, R.I. *d.* 1942. The celebrated Broadway producer-writer-entertainer appeared sporadically in films from 1916. Several of his plays provided the basis for film scripts. Among them his stage dramatization of Earl Derr Biggers's 'Seven Keys to Baldpate' (filmed 1917, 1925, 1929, 1935, 1947) and his plays 'Gambling' (1934), 'Song-and-Dance Man,' and 'Home Towners (both 1936), 'The Miracle Man' (1919, 1932), and 'Elmer the Great' (1933). In addition, he wrote several original screenplays and produced the film *Little Nellie Kelly* (1940), which was based on his play of the same name. Some of his songs have been heard frequently in films. Among them 'Yankee Doodle Dandy,' 'Give My Regards to Broadway,' and 'Over There.' James CAGNEY portrayed Cohan in an Oscar-winning performance in the film tribute *Yankee Doodle Dandy,* completed in 1942, while Cohan was still alive, but not officially released until 1943. (Cagney again played Cohan as a cameo in the film *Seven Little Foys,* 1955.) Cohan's daughter, Helen Cohan, played leads in a couple of films of the early 30s but retired because of failing health.

FILMS INCLUDE (as actor): *Broadway Jones, Seven Keys to Baldpate* 1917; *Hit-the-Trail Haliday* 1918; *The Phantom President* 1932; *Gambling* 1934.

Cohen, Larry. Director, screenwriter, producer. Born Lawrence G. Cohen, on July 15, 1938, in New York City. *ed.* U. CCNY; NYU. The son of a realtor, he started out as a page at

NBC's New York studios, but within months was writing scripts for entertainment programs and TV series. In films from the mid-60s, as a screenwriter, then also as a director and producer, he specializes in action, horror, the offbeat, and the bizarre. Not to be confused with several other screenwriters billed as Laurence or Lawrence Cohen.

FILMS: As screenwriter—*Return of the Seven, I Deal in Danger* 1966; *Daddy's Gone a-Hunting* 1969; *El Condor* 1970; *The American Success Company/American Success/Success* 1980; *I, the Jury* 1982; *Scandalous* (co-story only) 1984; *Maniac Cop* (also prod.) 1986; *Best Seller* 1987. As director-screenwriter—*Bone* 1972; *Black Caesar* (also prod.), *Hell Up in Harlem* (also prod.) 1973; *It's Alive!* (also prod.) 1974; *God Told Me To/Demon* (also prod.) 1976; *The Private Files of J. Edgar Hoover* (also prod.), *It Lives Again* (also prod.) 1978; *Full Moon High* (also prod.) 1981; *Q/The Winged Serpent* (also prod.) 1982; *Perfect Strangers/Blind Alley, Special Effects* 1984; *The Stuff* (also exec. prod.) 1985; *Return to Salem's Lot, It's Alive III: Island of the Alive* (also exec. prod.), *Deadly Illusion* (co-dir.) 1987; *Wicked Stepmother* (also exec. prod.) 1989; *Friend to Friend* (prod. only), *Into Thin Air, Ambulance* 1990; *The Heavy, The Man Who Loved Hitchcock* 1991; *The Apparatus* (also dir., sc.) 1992; *Guilty as Sin* 1993.

Cohen, Rob. Producer, director, screenwriter, executive. *b.* March 12, 1949, in Cornwall-on-Hudson, N.Y. *ed.* Amherst College, Mass.; Harvard University, Cambridge, Mass. Dynamic and driven everyman of Hollywood films who began his long successful career bringing to the screen films such as *Mahogany* (1975) and *The Wiz* (1978) for Motown Records film prouctions. He has also become a premier producer and director of TV commercials in addition to his occasional feature film directing projects.

FILMS INCLUDE: As producer or executive producer except where noted—*Mahogany* 1975; *The Bingo Long Traveling All-Stars & Motor Kings* 1976; *Scott Joplin—King of Ragtime* 1977; *Almost Summer, Thank God, It's Friday, The Wiz* 1978; *A Small Circle of Friends* (dir.), *The Razor's Edge, Scandalous* (also dir, sc.) 1984; *The Legend of Billy Jean* 1985; *Ironweed, Light of Day, The Monster Squad, The Running Man, The Witches of Eastwick* 1987; *The Serpent and the Rainbow* 1988; *Bird on a Wire, Disorganized Crime* 1990; *The Hard Way* 1991; *Dragon: The Bruce Lee Story* (dir., sc. only) 1993; *Dragonheart* (dir.), *Daylight* (dir.) 1996.

Cohl, Emile. Animation pioneer. *b.* Emile Courtet, Jan. 4, 1857, Paris. *d.* 1938. Apprenticed as a jeweler, he began drawing caricatures during his military service. After returning to civilian life, he became a political cartoonist for various French publications. One day in 1905 he stormed into the offices of the GAUMONT film company in Paris, enraged that one of his cartoon ideas had been borrowed for a film poster. To appease him, Louis FEUILLADE, then Gaumont's head, suggested Cohl come work for the company. He began as idea man and writer of Gaumont shorts. Late in 1907 he turned director, first of little trick films and soon after of animated cartoons and some puppet films.

Utilizing the American invention of stop-motion photography (one turn, one picture), he made some 100 brief animated films between 1908 and 1918, drawing every frame of his films himself. His drawing was simple and schematic, almost primitive, but he infused his characters with much life and humor. He is credited with being the first to develop a regular cartoon character, Fantoche, a little man who "appeared" in many of his films. Leaving Gaumont, Cohl worked for Pathé from 1910 and for Eclair from 1912. The latter company sent him to the US, where he worked in Fort Lee, N.J., on Baby Snookums ('The Newlyweds and Their Baby') cartoons until 1914.

When he returned to work in France on the eve of WW I, Cohl found the competition stiffening and was unable to adapt to the new trends in animation. He made no films after 1918. Living in abject poverty, completely forgotten, he fell victim at 81 to a freak accident. One night, while rooming in a slum neighborhood with no electricity, his long white beard caught fire from a candle. He was rushed to a hospital, where he died in agony several weeks later. An Emile Cohl prize is awarded annually in France for excellence in animation.

FILMS INCLUDE: *Fantasmagorie/Metamorphosis/Black and White, Le Journal animé, Le Cauchemar de Fantoche/The Puppet's Nightmare, L'Automat, Les Allumettes animé/Animated Matches* 1908; *Les Transfigurations, La Valise diplomatique, L'Omlette fantastique/Magic Eggs, L'Eventail animé/Historical Fan, Clair de la Lune espagnole/The Man in the Moon/The Moon-Struck Matador, La Bataille d'Austerlitz, Monsieur Clown chez les Lilliputiens, Don Quichotte/Don Quixote* 1909; *Le Songe d'un Garçon de Café/Cafe Waiter's Dream/The Hasher's Delirium, Le Tout Petit Faust/The Beautiful Margaret, Histoire des Chapeaux, Le Baron de Crac/The Wonderful Adventures of Herr Munchhausen* 1910; *Les Aventures d'un Bout de Papier, Le Musée des Grotesques, La Boite diabolique* 1911; *Les Exploits de Feu-Follet, Campbell Soups, La Marseillaise, The Newlyweds and Their Baby* series (US) 1912; *He Wants What He Wants When He Wants It* (US), *Clara's Mysterious Toys* (US), *A Vegetarian's Dream* (US), other films in "Newlyweds" and "Moving World" series 1913; *Le Ouistiti de Toto* 1914; *Le Voisin trop gourmand* 1915; *La Main mysterieuse* 1916; *Les Aventures des Pieds Nickelés* series 1918.

Cohn, Harry. Executive. *b.* July 23, 1891, New York City. *d.* 1958. The son of an immigrant tailor, he quit school at an early stage and began to work at a variety of jobs—as a chorus boy in a play, a shipping clerk for a music publishing house, a fur salesman, and a pool hustler. In 1912 he teamed up with Harry Ruby (later a famous Broadway composer) in a short-lived vaudeville act. Cohn then worked briefly as a trolley conductor and began a mildly successful career as a song plugger. In 1918 he became personal secretary to film pioneer and founder of Universal, Carl LAEMMLE, for ten years the employer of Harry's brother, Jack Cohn (*b.* Oct. 27, 1889, N.Y.C.; *d.* 1956). In 1920 the Cohn brothers and a fellow Laemmle employee, Joe Brandt, struck out on their own, forming the C.B.C. Films Sales Company.

Jack Cohn and Brandt remained in New York to run the company's administration and sales, while Harry was dispatched to Hollywood to begin production. After starting from scratch on the film capital's Poverty Row, Harry steadily advanced the fortunes of the company, which in 1924 became Columbia Pictures. Gambling on new ideas and luring talent from other studios, Cohn was able to elevate Columbia to the status of a major Hollywood studio in the 30s and into a virtual gold mine in the 40s.

Harry Cohn was notorious for his ruthlessness and vulgarity. He ruled his studio like a despot, spying on employees through informers and a hidden-microphone system, hiring and firing at will, courting the strong and humiliating the weak. He was known as "Harry the Horror" until Ben HECHT gave him the nickname that stuck, "White Fang." A vigorous, outspoken man who used profanity freely, Cohn seemed to savor his reputation as the toughest of Hollywood's moguls and made sure that his occasional acts of charity and benevolence were kept secret.

Cohn was personally responsible for the development of many stars, notably Rita HAYWORTH, but clashed frequently with his stars, directors, and writers, and the turnover at Columbia was the greatest of any Hollywood studio. Throughout his career as production head in Hollywood he was engaged in a power struggle with his brother Jack, who still ran the company's headquarters in New York. Their battles were so intense that for many months they spoke to each other only through intermediaries. In 1932, Harry successfully avoided Jack's attempt to oust him and from then on solidified his position as the real boss of Columbia.

Harry Cohn was probably the most feared and hated man in Hollywood, but even his enemies acknowledged his uncanny sense of what made a picture successful and also his ability to run a studio effectively and profitably. Cohn is the subject of an intriguing biography by Bob Thomas, *King Cohn* (1967).

Cohn, Jack. See COHN, Harry.

Colbert, Claudette. Actress. *b.* Claudette Lily Chauchoin, on Sept. 13, 1905, in Paris. *d.* 1996. She came to New York as a child of six and attended Washington Irving High School and the Art Students League, intending to become a fashion designer. A chance meeting at a party led to her stage debut in 1923 and to subsequent ingenue roles on Broadway, 1925–29. She made her screen debut in a 1927 silent shot in Paramount's Astoria, Queens, N.Y., studios. Her screen career started in earnest in 1929, after the advent of sound. At first she played a mixture of roles, from fluffy comedy to tearful soap opera and occasional *femme fatale* parts—in C. B. DE MILLE's *The Sign of the Cross* and *Cleopatra,* for example. But after playing a screwball heiress in CAPRA's *It Happened One Night,* a performance for which she won the 1934 best actress Academy Award, she found her niche in sophisticated comedy and became one of Hollywood's leading female interpreters of the genre. She was nominated for Oscars for *Private Worlds* (1934) and *Since You Went Away* (1944). She remained a popular Hollywood star through the mid-50s, after which she occasionally returned to the stage. Miss Colbert's first husband (1928–35) was actor-director Norman FOSTER. Late in 1935 she married Dr. Joel Pressman, who had treated her for sinus trouble. He left her a widow in 1968. In 1984 the Film Society of Lincoln Center honored her with a special tribute.

FILMS: *For the Love of Mike* 1927; *The Hole in the Wall, The Lady Lies* 1929; *L'Enigmatique M. Parkes* (French-language version of *Slightly Scarlet*), *The Big Pond* (and French-language version, *La Grande Mare*), *Young Man of Manhattan, Manslaughter* 1930, *Honor Among Lovers, The Smiling Lieutenant, Secrets of a Secretary, His Woman* 1931; *The Wiser Sex, The Misleading Lady, The Man from Yesterday, The Phantom President, The Sign of the Cross* 1932; *Tonight Is Ours, I Cover the Waterfront, Three-Cornered Moon, Torch Singer* 1933; *Four Frightened People, It Happened One Night, Cleopatra, Imitation of Life* 1934; *The Gilded Lily, Private Worlds, She Married Her Boss, The Bride Comes Home* 1935; *Under Two Flags* 1936; *Maid of Salem, I Met Him in Paris, Tovarich* 1937; *Bluebeard's Eighth Wife* 1938; *Zaza, Midnight, It's a Wonderful World, Drums Along the Mohawk* 1939; *Boom Town, Arise My Love* 1940; *Skylark* 1941; *Remember the Day, The Palm Beach Story* 1942; *So Proudly We Hail, No Time for Love* 1943; *Since You Went Away* 1944; *Practically Yours, Guest Wife* 1945; *Tomorrow Is Forever, Without Reservations, The Secret Heart* 1946; *The Egg and I* 1947; *Sleep My Love* 1948; *Family Honeymoon, Bride for Sale* 1949; *Three Came Home, The Secret Fury* 1950; *Thunder on the Hill, Let's Make It Legal* 1951; *The Planter's Wife/Outpost in Malaya* (UK) 1952; *Daughters of Destiny* (Fr.) 1953; *Royal Affairs in Versailles* (Fr.) 1954; *Texas Lady* 1955; *Parrish* 1961.

Cole, George. Actor. Born on Apr. 22, 1925, in London. The son of a cockney butcher and a cleaning woman, he got into acting by answering a help wanted ad, and became a protégé of actor Alastair SIM. Two years after his first stage appearance, he made his British film debut in 1941. During the peak years of his career in the 50s, he played many leading comedy roles, typically as a confused, silly young man. Married actresses Eileen Moore (1954–66) and Penny Morrell (from 1968).

FILMS INCLUDE: *Cottage to Let/Bombsight Stolen* 1941; *The Demi-Paradise/Adventure for Two* 1943; *Henry V* 1944; *Quartet* 1948; *Morning Departure/Operation Disaster* 1950; *Laughter in Paradise, Scrooge/A Christmas Carol* (as Scrooge as a young man) 1951; *Top Secret/Mr. Potts Goes to Moscow, Who Goes There?/The Passionate Sentry* 1952; *Will Any Gentleman. . . ?, Our Girl Friday/The Adventures of Sadie, The Intruder* 1953; *Happy Ever After/Tonight's the Night, The Belles of St. Trinian's* 1954; *A Prize of Gold, The Constant Husband, Quentin Durward* 1955; *The Green Man* 1956; *Blue Murder at St. Trinian's* 1957; *Too Many Crooks* 1958; *The Bridal Path* 1959; *The Pure Hell of St. Trinian's* 1960; *The Anatomist* 1961; *Cleopatra* (US/UK) 1963; *One Way Pendulum* 1965; *The Great St. Trinian's Train Robbery* 1966; *The Vampire Lovers* 1970; *Fright* 1971; *Gone in 60 Seconds* 1974; *The Blue Bird* (as the Dog; US/USSR) 1976.

Cole, Jack. Dance director. *b.* Apr. 27, 1914, New Brunswick, N.J. *d.* 1974. Choreographed many dance numbers for Hollywood films starting in the mid-40s, notably working with Rita HAYWORTH and Marilyn MONROE. Occasionally also danced and acted in films.

FILMS INCLUDE: *Moon Over Miami* 1941; *Kismet, Cover Girl* 1944; *Tonight and Every Night, Gilda* 1945; *The Jolson Story, Down to Earth* 1947; *On the Riviera, Meet Me After the Show* 1951; *The Merry Widow* 1952; *The I Don't Care Girl, Gentlemen Prefer Blondes* 1953; *River of No Return, There's No Business Like Show Business* 1954; *Three for the Show, Kismet, Gentlemen Marry Brunettes* 1955; *Designing Woman, Les Girls* 1957; *Some Like It Hot* 1959; *Let's Make Love* 1960.

Cole, Lester. Screenwriter. *b.* June 19, 1904, New York City. *d.* 1985. The son of immigrants from Poland, he dropped out of school at 16 to become a stage director and aspiring playwright. After appearing as an actor in several plays and films of the late 20s and early 30s, he began writing screenplays in Hollywood, where he became a union activist and one of the founders of the Screen Writers Guild in 1933. His career ended abruptly in 1947, when he was cited for contempt of Congress, after he had challenged the right of the House Un-American Activities Committee to ask questions about his political affiliation. As one of the "Hollywood Ten," he was imprisoned for a year and blacklisted by the industry. He left behind an unfinished script that would eventually be rewritten by John Steinbeck for Elia Kazan's *Viva Zapata.* After his release from prison, he worked as a short-order cook, waiter, and manual laborer, among other odd jobs. He moved to London in 1961 but later returned to the US and settled in San Francisco. He collaborated on several screenplays under assumed names and later taught screenwriting at the University of California at Berkeley.

FILMS INCLUDE: *If I Had a Million* 1932; *Charlie Chan's Greatest Case* 1933; *Sleepers East* 1934; *Under Pressure* 1935; *The President's Mystery* 1936; *The Jury's Secret, The Crime of Dr. Hallet* 1938; *Winter Carnival* 1939; *The Invisible Man Returns, The House of Seven Gables, When the Daltons Rode* 1940; *Footsteps in the Dark, Among the Living* 1941; *Night Plane from Chungking* 1942; *Hostages* 1943; *None Shall Escape* 1944; *Objective Burma!, Blood on the Sun* 1945; *Fiesta, The Romance of Rosy Ridge* 1947; *High Wall* 1948; *Operation Eichmann* (under pseudonym Lewis Copley) 1961; *Born Free* (under pseudonym Gerald L. C. Copley; UK) 1966.

Cole, Nat "King." Singer, pianist, *b.* Nathaniel Adams Coles, on Mar. 17, 1919, Montgomery, Ala. *d.* 1965. Highly popular jazz pianist and velvet-voiced crooner, he made occasional film appearances, including a starring role (as W. C. Handy) in *St. Louis Blues* (1958). Died of lung cancer at 45. His daughter, Natalie Cole, is a talented, award-winning singer-songwriter.

FILMS: *Here Comes Elmer* 1943; *Pin-Up Girl, Stars on Parade, Swing in the Saddle* 1944; *See My Lawyer* 1945; *Breakfast in Hollywood* 1946; *Make-Believe Ballroom* 1949; *The Blue Gardenia, Small Town Girl* 1953; *Kiss Me Deadly* 1955; *Istanbul, China Gate* 1957; *St. Louis Blues* 1958; *The Night of the Quarter Moon* 1959; *Cat Ballou* 1965.

Coleman, Dabney. Actor. Born on Jan. 3, 1932, in Austin, Tex. *ed.* Virginia Military Institute; U. of Texas. Tall, mustachioed character player of Hollywood TV and films. He prepared to become a lawyer, but was drawn to acting at school. After training at the Neighborhood Playhouse, he began appearing in films in the mid-60s, at first in dramatic roles. Gradually, he found his niche in comedy. His career took off following his amusing portrayal of the mean boss in *9 to 5* (1980). His TV credits include the series 'That Girl' (1966–67), 'Mary Hartman, Mary Hartman' (1976–78), and 'Buffalo Bill' (1983–84).

FILMS: *The Slender Thread* 1965; *This Property Is Condemned* 1966; *The Scalphunters* 1968; *Downhill Racer* 1969; *I Love My Wife* 1970; *Cinderella Liberty* 1973; *The Dove, The Towering Inferno* 1974; *The Other Side of the Mountain, Bite the Bullet* 1975; *Black Fist/The Black Streetfighter, Midway* 1976; *Rolling Thunder, Viva Knievel!* 1977; *North Dallas Forty* 1979; *Nothing Personal, How to Beat the High Cost of Living, Melvin and Howard, 9 to 5* 1980; *On Golden Pond, Modern Problems* 1981; *Young Doctors in Love, Tootsie* 1982; *War Games* 1983; *The Muppets Take Manhattan, Cloak and Dagger* 1984; *The Man with One Red Shoe* 1985; *Dragnet* 1987; *Hot to Trot* 1988; *Where the Heart Is, Short Time* 1990; *Meet the Applegates* 1991; *There Goes the Neighborhood* 1992; *Amos and Andrew* 1993; *Clifford* 1994.

Coleman, Nancy. Actress. Born in Dec. 30, 1917, in Everett, Wash. *ed.* U. of Washington. Leading lady and second lead of Warner Bros. films of the 40s, following radio and stage experience and a Broadway debut in 1941. Typically played a timid, neurotic character. Retired shortly after marrying the studio publicity chief, Whitney Bolton. Later returned to the stage and occasional films.

FILMS: *Kings Row, Dangerously They Live, The Gay Sisters, Desperate Journey* 1942; *Edge of Darkness* 1943; *In Our Time* 1944; *Devotion* (as Anne Brontë), *Her Sister's Secret* 1946; *Violence* 1947; *Mourning Becomes Electra* 1948; *Man from Tangier* 1953; *Slaves* 1968.

Colette. Novelist, screenwriter. *b.* Gabrielle-Sidonie Colette, Jan. 28, 1873, Saint-Sauveur-en-Puisaye, France. *d.* 1954. A film critic as early as 1916, this popular French novelist wrote screenplays and dialogue for French films beginning in 1917 and collaborated on screen adaptations of several of her own novels.

FILMS: *La Vagabonde* (sc. from own novel; Fr./It.) 1917; *La Flamme cachée* (orig. sc.) 1920; *La Vagabonde* (remake; addnl. scenes, from own novel), *Filles en Uniforme* (dial. for this French-language version of the German *Mädchen in Uniform*) 1932; *Lac aux Dames* (dial.) 1934; *Divine* (co-sc., dial.) 1935; *Claudine à l'Ecole* (novel basis only) 1937; *Gigi* (dial., from own story) 1949; *Julie de Carneilhan* (story basis only), *Minne l'Ingenue libertine/Minne* (novel basis only), *Chéri* (dial. from own novel) 1950; *Olivia/Pit of Loneliness* (sc.) 1951; *Les Sept Péchés capitaux/Seven Deadly Sins* (Rossellini's "Envy" episode based on her story *La Chatte*) 1952; *Le Ble en Herbe/The Game of Love* (novel basis only) 1954; *Mitsou* (story basis only) 1956; *Gigi* (story basis only; US) 1958.

Colleano, Bonar. Actor. *b.* Bonar Sullivan II, Mar. 14, 1924, New York City. *d.* 1958 in a car crash. At the age of five he joined the Colleano family acrobatic circus act and at 12 went to England, where he performed in music halls, on radio, and eventually on the legitimate stage. He made his film debut in 1944. A fine actor of distinctive lean looks, he appeared in many British films, typically as a crook or a wisecracking Yank. He was married to actress Susan SHAW.

FILMS INCLUDE: *Starlight Serenade* 1944; *The Way to the Stars/Johnny in the Clouds* 1945; *A Matter of Life and Death/Stairway to Heaven, Wanted for Murder* 1946; *One Night with You, Good Time Girl, Sleeping Car to Trieste* 1948; *Give Us This Day/Salt to the Devil* 1949; *Dance Hall, Pool of London* 1950; *A Tale of Five Cities/A Tale of Five Women* 1951; *Eight Iron Men* (US) 1952; *The Flame and the Flesh, The Sea Shall Not Have Them* 1954; *Joe Macbeth* 1955; *Zarak* 1956; *Interpol/Pickup Alley, Fire Down Below* 1957; *No Time to Die/Tank Force* 1958.

Collette, Toni. Actress. *b.* 1972, in Sydney, Australia. *ed.* National Institute of Dramatic Art, Sydney, Australia. This attractive, gifted comedic actress came to prominence in her native Australia for her leading performance in *Muriel's Wedding* (1994), a film which found success in the US as well. She began as stage actress and has since embarked on an international film career including several in America.

FILMS: *The Efficiency Expert* (Austral.) 1992; *Muriel's Wedding* (Austral.) 1994; *Arabian Knight* 1995; *The Pallbearer, Emma* 1996; *Cosi* 1997.

Colli, Tonino Delli. See DELLI COLLI, Tonino.

Collier, Constance. Actress. *b.* Laura Constance Hardie, Jan. 22, 1878, in Windsor Berks, England. *d.* 1955. A distinguished actress on the British and American stage, she began as a chorus girl in musical revues, then developed into a fine dramatic player. She made her film debut in 1916 in D. W. Griffith's *Intolerance,* and continued making infrequent but impressive appearances in Hollywood films of the 30s and 40s, typically playing stately ladies of the grand-manner school. She authored several plays.

FILMS INCLUDE: *Intolerance, Tongues of Men, The Code of Marcia Gray, Macbeth* (as Lady Macbeth) 1916; *Bleak House* (UK) 1920; *The Bohemian Girl* (UK) 1922; *Shadow of Doubt* 1935; *Professional Soldier, Girls' Dormitory, Little Lord Fauntleroy* 1936; *Wee Willie Winkie, Stage Door, A Damsel in Distress* 1937; *Zaza* 1939; *Susan and God* 1940; *Kitty, The Dark Corner, Monsieur Beaucaire* 1946; *The Perils of Pauline* 1947; *Rope, An Ideal Husband* (UK) 1948; *Whirlpool* 1950.

Collier, Lois. Actress. Born Madelyn Jones, Mar. 21, 1919, in Salley, S.C. Leading lady of Hollywood B pictures of the 40s; formerly on local stage and radio. Often in exotic, mysterious parts. She co-starred in the early TV series 'Boston Blackie' (1951–53).

FILMS INCLUDE: *A Desperate Adventure* 1938; *Gauchos of Eldorado* 1941; *The Phantom Plainsman* 1942; *Cobra Woman, Weird Woman, Jungle Woman, Ladies Courageous* 1944; *Jungle Queen* (serial), *The Naughty Nineties, Penthouse Rhythm, The Crimson Canary* 1945; *The Cat Creeps, Girl on the Spot, A Night in Casablanca, Wild Beauty* 1946; *Slave Girl* 1947; *Out of the Storm* 1948; *Miss Mink of 1949* 1949; *Humphrey Takes a Chance* 1950; *Flying Disc Man from Mars* (serial) 1951; *Missile Monsters* 1958.

Collier, William ("Buster"), Jr. Actor. *b.* Feb. 12, 1902, New York City. *d.* 1986. The son of Broadway star, playwright, and movie character actor William Collier, Sr. (*b.* Nov. 12, 1866, New York City; *d.* 1944), he began appearing with his celebrated father on the stage while still a child and made his screen debut at age 14. In the 20s he developed into a popular leading man of silent films. He made a successful transition to sound but retired in the mid-30s and became an agent with William Morris.

FILMS INCLUDE: *The Bugle Call* 1916; *Everybody's Sweetheart* 1920; *The Heart of Maryland, The Girl from Porcupine, At the Stage Door* 1921; *Cardigan, The Good Provider, The Secrets of Paris* 1922; *The Enemies of Women, The Age of Desire, Pleasure Mad* 1923; *Leave It to Gerry, Fools' Highway, The Sea Hawk, Wine of Youth, The Lighthouse by the Sea* 1924; *The Reckless Sex, The Devil's Cargo, The Verdict, Eve's Secret, Playing with Souls, The Wanderer* 1925; *The Lucky Lady, The Rainmaker, God Gave Me Twenty Cents, The Lady of the Harem, Just Another Blonde* 1926; *The Broken Gate, Backstage, Convoy, The Sunset Derby, Dearie, The Desired Woman, Stranded, The College Widow* 1927; *So This Is Love, The Tragedy of Youth, A Night of Mystery, The Lion and the Mouse, Women They Talk About, Beware of Bachelors* 1928; *The Red Sword, Hardboiled Rose, Tide of Empire, One Stolen Night, The Donovan Affair, The Bachelor Girl, New Orleans, Two Men and a Maid, The College Coquette* 1929; *The Melody Man, A Royal Romance, Fox Movietone Follies of 1930, Rain or Shine* 1930; *Little Caesar, Reducing, Cimarron, Street Scene, The Big Gamble, The Secret Witness* 1931; *Dancers in the Dark, The Phantom Express, The Fighting Gentleman, Behind Jury Doors, Speed Demon* 1932; *The Story of Temple Drake, Her Secret* 1933; *All of Me, Public Stenographer* 1934; *The People's Enemy* 1935.

Collinge, Patricia. Actress. *b.* Sept. 20, 1894, Dublin. *d.* 1974. On the London stage from age ten, she made her Broadway debut at 14 and later became a distinguished personality of the American theater. She went to Hollywood in 1941 to repeat her Broadway role in the screen version of *The Little Foxes* and was nominated for an Oscar for her portrayal of Aunt Birdie in that film. Subsequently played character roles in a handful of other films. She was the author of a play, several books, and many short stories.

FILMS: *The Little Foxes* 1941; *Shadow of a Doubt* 1943; *Tender Comrade, Casanova Brown* 1944; *Teresa* 1951; *Washington Story* 1952; *The Nun's Story* 1959.

Collins, Alf(red). British director of early silents, a former music hall comic who made early chase comedies and one-reel dramas for Gaumont. He is reputed to have used modern editing techniques, such as the close-up and the traveling shot, long before Griffith.

FILMS INCLUDE: *Rip Van Winkle, The Pickpocket, Marriage by Motor* 1903; *Behind the Scenes, The Haunted Houseboat* 1904; *Mutiny on a Russian Battleship/Potemkin, The Burglar* 1905; *Dolly Varden* 1906; *Catch the Kid* 1907; *Black Eyed Susan* 1908; *Quicksilver Pudding* 1909; *The Coster's Phantom Fortune* 1910; *A Maid of the Alps* 1912.

Collins, Cora Sue. Actress. Born on Apr. 19, 1927, in Beckley, W. Va. Child performer of Hollywood films of the 30s and early 40s, an expert tap dancer. Retired from the screen at 17. She later married a wealthy Virginian and settled on his 3,000-acre Nevada ranch. Their second home, in Mexico, is a society gathering place.

FILMS INCLUDE: *The Strange Case of Clara Deane* 1932; *Jennie Gerhardt, Queen Christina* 1933; *Treasure Island, Evelyn Prentice, The Scarlet Letter, Little Men* 1934; *Anna Karenina, Magnificent Obsession* 1935; *The Adventures of Tom Sawyer* 1938; *Blood and Sand* 1941; *Get Hep to Love* 1942; *Weekend at the Waldorf, Youth on Trial, Roughly Speaking* 1945.

Collins, Joan. Actress. Born on May 23, 1933, in London, the daughter of a theatrical booking agent. After two years of studies at the British Royal Academy of Dramatic Art, she made her London stage debut in 'A Doll's House' (1946) and her British film debut in 1952. During the next two years she played in nine films, typically as an erring juvenile, then went to Hollywood, where her sultry sex appeal helped establish her as a star. With her career declining in the 70s, she was back in England, reduced to roles in horror films and sexploitation movies like *The Stud* and *The Bitch,* which were based on novels by her younger sister (*b.* Oct. 4, 1941), best-selling author Jackie Collins. In 1980, she suffered a personal tragedy when her daughter Katy was struck by a car, sustaining severe brain injuries. But the advent of the TV series 'Dynasty' in the following year infused new life into Miss Collins's career and brought her sudden fame and fortune. As the scheming, devilish Alexis Carrington Colby, she gained millions of new admirers and soon achieved superstar status. Voluptuously sexy as ever at age 50, she posed seminude for *Playboy* magazine in 1983 and made millions from appearing in perfume commercials. In addition to several well-publicized affairs (including Nicky Hilton, Rafael Trujillo, Warren Beatty, and Ryan O'Neal), she has been married several times, including once to actor Anthony NEWLEY (1963–70). Autobiography: *Past Imperfect* (1978, updated 1984).

FILMS: In UK—*Lady Godiva Rides Again* 1951; *Judgment Deferred, The Womans's Angle, I Believe in You, Decameron Nights* 1952; *Cosh Boy/The Slasher, Turn the Key Softly, The Square Ring* 1953; *Our Girl Friday/The Adventures of Sadie, The Good Die Young* 1954. In US—*Land of the Pharaohs, The Virgin Queen, The Girl in the Red Velvet Swing* (as Evelyn Nesbit Thaw) 1955; *The Opposite Sex* 1956; *Sea Wife* (UK), *Island in the Sun* (UK), *Stopover Tokyo, The Wayward Bus* 1957; *The Bravados, Rally 'Round the Flag Boys!* 1958; *Seven Thieves, Esther and the King* (as Queen Esther) 1960; *The Road to Hong Kong* (UK/US) 1962; *La Congiuntura* (It.) 1965; *Warning Shot* 1967. In UK—*Subterfuge* (US/UK), *If It's Tuesday This Must Be Belgium* (cameo; US), *Can Heironymus Merkin Ever Forget Mercy Humppe and Find True Happiness?* 1969; *L'Amore breve/Lo Stato d'Assedio* (It.), *Up in the Cellar* (US), *The Executioner* 1970; *Quest for Love, Revenge/Terror from Under the House/Inn of the Frightened People* 1971; *The Aquarian, Tales from the Crypt, Fear in the Night* 1972; *Tales That Witness Madness, Dark Places* 1973; *Call of the Wolf, The Referee/Football Crazy* 1974; *Alfie Darling* 1975; *I Don't Want to Be Born/The Devil Within Her, The Bawdy Adventures of Tom Jones, The Great Adventure* 1976; *Empire of the Ants* (US) 1977; *The Stud, The Big Sleep, The Day of the Fox* 1978; *The Bitch, Zero to Sixty* (Can.), *Sunburn* (US), *A Game for Vultures* 1979; *Growing Pains, Homework* 1980; *The Nutcracker* 1982; *A Midwinter's Tale* 1995.

Collins, Ray. Actor. *b.* 1888, Sacramento, Calif., the son of a noted drama critic. *d.* 1965. On the stage from the age of six, he appeared in stock, developed on Broadway, and reached a career peak with Orson WELLES's Mercury Theater. He followed the director to Hollywood, where he appeared in Welles's first two productions, and stayed to play some 75 character roles in a broad range of films. He later (1957–65) played Lieutenant Tragg in the long-running TV series 'Perry Mason.'

FILMS INCLUDE: *Citizen Kane* 1941; *Crime Doctor, The Magnificent Ambersons, The Big Street* 1942; *The Human Comedy* 1943; *The Seventh Cross, The Hitler Gang* 1944; *Leave Her to Heaven* 1945; *The Best Years of Our Lives, Two Years Before the Mast* 1946; *The Bachelor and the Bobby-Soxer, A Double Life* 1947; *Good Sam, Command Decision* 1948; *The*

Fountainhead, The Heiress 1949; *Francis, Summer Stock* 1950; *Desert Song, The Kid from Left Field* 1953; *Rose Marie* 1954, *The Desperate Hours* 1955; *The Solid Gold Cadillac, Never Say Goodbye* 1956; *Touch of Evil* 1958; *I'll Give My Life* 1959.

Collins, Stephen. Actor. Born on Oct. 1, 1947, in Des Moines, Iowa. *ed.* Amherst. Leading man of Hollywood TV and films, following experience on the New York stage. Married actress Faye Grant.

FILMS: *All the President's Men* 1976; *Between the Lines* 1977; *Fedora* (Ger./Fr.) 1978; *The Promise, Star Trek—The Motion Picture* 1979; *Loving Couples* 1980; *Brewster's Millions* 1985; *Choke Canyon/On Dangerous Ground, Jumpin' Jack Flash* 1986; *The Big Picture* (cameo) 1989; *Stella* 1990; *First Wives Club* 1996.

Collinson, Peter. Director. *b.* 1936, Lincolnshire, England. *d.* 1980. Began directing British features in the late 60s, following experience on the stage and in TV commercials. Showed initial promise with original, if somewhat pretentious, films like *The Penthouse* (1967) and *Up the Junction* and *The Long Day's Dying* (both 1968), winning an award at the San Sebastian Film Festival for the latter. Later turned out a succession of stylish, if empty, action adventures, demonstrating his versatility but also a still ill-defined personal style.

FILMS: *The Penthouse* (also sc.) 1967; *Up the Junction, The Long Day's Dying* (also co-prod.) 1968; *The Italian Job* 1969; *You Can't Win 'Em All* 1970; *Fright* 1971; *Innocent Bystanders* 1972; *The Man Called Noon* 1973; *Straight on Till Morning* (also prod.), *Open Season* (US), *And Then There Were None/Ten Little Indians* 1974; *The Spiral Staircase* 1975; *The Sell Out* 1976; *Tigers Don't Cry* 1977; *Tomorrow Never Comes* 1978; *The Earthling* 1980.

Collyer, June. Actress. *b.* Dorothea Heermance, Aug. 19, 1907, New York City. *d.* 1968. The debutante daughter of a New York lawyer and a former actress, she played aristocratic leading ladies in Hollywood films of the late 20s and early 30s. Retired in 1934. Died of bronchial pneumonia three months after the death of her husband (since 1931), comedian Stuart ERWIN, with whom she had co-starred in films and in the TV series 'The Trouble with Father' and 'The Stu Erwin Show.' She was the sister of TV's game show host and MC Bud Collyer.

FILMS INCLUDE: *East Side West Side* 1927; *Woman Wise, Me Gangster, Four Sons, Hangman's House, Red Wine* 1928; *Not Quite Decent, Illusion, The River of Romance, The Love Doctor* 1929; *Three Sisters, A Man from Wyoming, Sweet Kitty Bellairs, Extravagance, Charley's Aunt* 1930; *Alexander Hamilton, Honeymoon Lane, Dude Ranch, Damaged Love, Drums of Jeopardy, The Brat* 1931; *Revenge at Monte Carlo, Before Midnight* 1933; *Cheaters* 1934; *The Ghost Walks* 1935.

Colman, Ronald. Actor. *b.* Feb. 9, 1891, Richmond, England. *d.* 1958. Orphaned at 16, he began work as an office boy with the British Steamship Company, a position he held for five years, during which he dabbled in amateur dramatics. Invalided out of WW I service on the French front, he turned to the stage in 1916. He played bits in some short British films and in 1918 began appearing in features. In 1920 he emigrated to the US and for a couple of years seemed to be getting nowhere, either on the stage or in films. The turning point came in 1923, after Lillian GISH saw him in a play and chose him as her leading man in *The White Sister.* From there on, Colman developed into one of Hollywood's most popular romantic stars and was one of the few screen personalities who managed to sustain a dominant position in both silent and sound films.

Suave, dignified, and gentle, he personified the aristocratic gentlemanly, romantic hero who did not go out of style after the switch to sound. His silent period was highlighted by a commanding performance in *Beau Geste* and a series of romantic dramas co-starring Vilma BANKY. His mellow, richly modulated voice became an additional asset with the advent of the talkies. Among his most striking performances in sound films were those in *Arrowsmith, A Tale of Two Cities, Lost Horizon,* and *If I Were King.* He was nominated for Oscars for *Bulldog Drummond* and *Condemned* (both 1929) and *Random Harvest* (1942); but won an Academy Award toward the end of his career for a less-impressive performance, a dual role in *A Double Life,* as an actor playing Othello both on and off the stage. He was married to actresses Thelma Victoria Maud (1918–35) and Benita HUME (from 1938). He is the subject of a biography, *Ronald Colman—A Very Private Person* (1975), written by his daughter, Juliet Benita Colman.

FILMS: In the UK—*The Toilers, A Daughter of Eve, Sheba, Snow in the Desert* 1919; *A Son of David, Anna the Adventuress, The Black Spider* 1920. In the US—*Handcuffs or Kisses* 1921; *The White Sister* 1923; *The Eternal City, $20 a Week, Tarnish, Romola* 1924; *Her Night of Romance, A Thief in Paradise, His Supreme Moment, The Sporting Venus, Her Sister from Paris, The Dark Angel, Stella Dallas, Lady Windermere's Fan* 1925; *Kiki, Beau Geste* (title role), *The Winning of Barbara Worth* 1926; *The Night of Love, The Magic Flame* 1927; *Two Lovers* 1928; *The Rescue, Bulldog Drummond* (title role), *Condemned* 1929; *Raffles* 1930; *The Devil to Pay, The Unholy Garden, Arrowsmith* (title role) 1931; *Cynara* 1932; *The Masquerader* 1933; *Bulldog Drummond Strikes Back* (again as Drummond) 1934; *Clive of India* (as Baron Robert Clive), *The Man Who Broke the Bank at Monte Carlo, A Tale of Two Cities* (as Sydney Carton) 1935; *Under Two Flags* 1936; *Lost Horizon, The Prisoner of Zenda* (dual role) 1937; *If I Were King* (as François Villon) 1938; *The Light That Failed, Lucky Partners* 1940; *My Life with Caroline* 1941; *The Talk of the Town, Random Harvest* 1942; *Kismet* 1944; *The Late George Apley* (title role) 1947; *A Double Life* 1948; *Champagne for Caesar* 1950; *Around the World in 80 Days* (cameo) 1956; *The Story of Mankind* (as the Spirit of Man) 1957.

Colonna, Jerry. Comic actor. *b.* Gerardo (Gerald) Luigi Colonna, 1904, Boston. *d.* 1986. Started out as a trombone player but soon discovered the comic value of his wild rolling eyes, walrus mustache, and bellowing voice, and began a successful stint as a comedian in nightclubs and musical revues. By the late 30s his popularity led to a radio contract on the Bob HOPE show and to comic appearances in light films, including a number of Hope vehicles.

FILMS INCLUDE: *52nd Street, Rosalie* 1937; *College Swing, Little Miss Broadway* 1938; *Naughty but Nice* 1939; *Road to Singapore, Comin' Round the Mountain* 1940; *Sis Hopkins, Ice Capades* 1941; *True to the Army, Priorities on Parade, Star Spangled Rhythm* 1942; *Atlantic City* 1944; *It's in the Bag* 1945; *Road to Rio* 1947; *Kentucky Jubilee* 1951; *Meet Me in Las Vegas* 1956; *Andy Hardy Comes Home* 1958; *Road to Hong Kong* (cameo) 1961; *The Bob Hope Vietnam Christmas Show* (made for TV but later released theatrically) 1966.

color chart and gray scale. A chart containing 32 color patches side by side with a ten-step gray scale. It is used for checking how various colors will reproduce as shades of gray if it becomes necessary to make black-and-white prints of color film.

color cinematography. The search for a color effect in films began in the earliest days of cinema. Experimentation proceeded along three basic courses: the development of (1) hand-painted films, tinted or toned; (2) additive color systems; and (3) subtractive color systems. The earliest and simplest method of applying color to film was by tinting or toning. Tinting consists in applying one or more colors to individual frames of a film, usually by hand after exposure; toning consists in bathing an entire film or sections of a film in a color solution. In tinting, different colors may appear on the same image; in toning the entire frame has the same color value.

Hand-painted films were made as early as 1894 and were in wide use by 1910. Many of Georges MÉLIÈS's trick films were tinted. In the original print of the 1903 *The Great Train Robbery* the gunshot blast at the conclusion of the film was tinted red. D. W. GRIFFITH tinted sequences of many of his famous films, including *The Birth of a Nation* and *Intolerance.* Sergei EISENSTEIN used tinting sparingly in *Potemkin* and other films of the mid-20s. Among the early tinting processes, the French-developed Pathé color was the most accurate and reliable. It was used widely in films of all nations until the advent of sound. Tinting and toning were dropped temporarily in the late 20s when they were found to interfere with sound-track reproduction. Their use was resumed after a special tinted stock was introduced late in 1929. Tinting and toning are still occasionally used in films.

Of the two true-color-reproduction systems, additive and subtractive, the additive color process was the first to be explored and developed, mainly because it made possible the recording and projection of color on black-and-white stock. The various additive systems entailed the use of color filters on both the photography and projection apparatus, while subtractive systems also depend on dyed emulsions on the film stock.

The theoretical principle of color photography was recognized as early as 1785, but the earliest patents for color film were not registered until late in the 19th century. Primitive additive color processes employed a variety of methods and devices, none of which was very successful. The first practicable and commercially successful color system was Kinemacolor, patented in England in 1906 by George Albert Smith and exploited by Smith and Charles Urban through their Natural Colour Kinematograph Company. After experimenting with several short films, they produced the first major color film, *The Durbar at Delhi,* in 1911.

Kinemacolor was a two-color additive process utilizing black-and-white film and red-orange and blue-green filters. The film was shot and projected at 32 frames per second, twice the normal speed, so that the red-orange and blue-green images alternated. A rotating color wheel in front of the projector and the phenomenon of persistence of vision combined to bring the colors together. The result was not altogether unpleasing, but the system had several drawbacks, not least of which were eye strain, rapid wear and tear of film, and the sudden drifting of colors from one part of the frame to another. Competing two-color additive systems, like the French Gaumont Color and the American Prizma Color, had similar drawbacks. Early attempts with three-color additive processes, although they rendered truer color reproduction, presented even graver technical problems and were soon abandoned.

In 1915 two Americans, Herbert T. Kalmus and Daniel F. Comstock, began experimenting with an additive two-color process they called Technicolor, utilizing a camera with two apertures, each equipped with its own color filter, one red and one green. The system was more advanced than most of the period but often produced unwanted color fringes and halos during projection. In the early 20s, Technicolor, now a corporation, came up with a two-color subtractive system. The print consisted of two thin layers of film welded together after being exposed and dyed, one with red-orange, the other blue-green. The first color film made by this method was *Toll of the Sea* (1922). Although research and experimentation with additive color systems continued through the mid-40s, the subtractive process was well in the lead with the film industry by the late 20s. In addition to Douglas FAIRBANKS's celebrated *The Pirate* (1926), some other features and many shorts were made in two-color Technicolor or similar processes.

During the switch to sound, Hollywood studios used Technicolor as an added attraction for many of their musical films, and many other films included color sequences. But the limited effect of the two-color system did not justify the extra expense, and by 1932, after the initial novelty had worn off, hardly any Hollywood films were made in color. At that critical point Technicolor announced a truly advanced color system, a three-color process that was to dominate the industry for many years to come, made possible by the invention of a special beam-splitter camera equipped with two 45-degree prisms in the form of a cube. In operation, light from a photographed object entering the camera through a single lens is deflected by the prisms and is absorbed by negatives sensitive to each of the primary photographic colors—green, blue, and red. The three negatives are each printed as a positive relief image called a "matrix," from which the final release print is made.

The first film to be made with the three-strip camera and the three-color printing technique was the famous short subject *La Cucaracha* (1933), and the first feature film produced in three-color Technicolor was Rouben Mamoulian's *Becky Sharp* (1935). The new process was universally hailed for its pleasing natural effect, and color returned to the American screen. Technicolor reached a peak of prestige with the release of *Gone With the Wind* (1939). In the early 40s, Technicolor simplified its process with the introduction of the monopack (one film) system, which made it possible to shoot Technicolor films with ordinary motion picture cameras.

The percentage of American and European films made in Technicolor or in any other of the other rapidly growing number of three-color processes increased every year. By the early 50s, at least in Hollywood, color was the rule rather than the exception in film production. The advent of various wide-screen processes in the 50s was accompanied by the development of color systems incorporating an anamorphic lens. The best known of these is Technicolor's Technirama. Among the major trade names for three-color systems are the American Eastman Color; the German, then Russian, Agfacolor (and its derivative Sovcolor); the Italian Ferraniacolor; and the Belgian-French Gevacolor.

Color cinematography entails problems of economical, technical, and aesthetic nature. Color film stock is almost twice as expensive as black and white, and so is the cost of developing and printing. In addition, color photography of exteriors is subject to variations in the intensity and tone of natural light during different hours of the day and during periods of sunshine and cloudiness. This limits the effective number of days or hours of the day during which more or less consistent color photography can be obtained. The slightest variation in color may present a problem of "matching" when two or more shots, taken at different times, are spliced in editing. However, color cinematography has come a long way since its crude early days.

For many years, color was used primarily as a gimmick and few attempts were made to explore its aesthetic capacities. Early colors were often loud and gaudy, emphasizing the novelty of the process over black and white rather than its uniqueness. But gradually, as the technical problems were ironed out, attention shifted to the artistic use of color. In the 40s, Powell and Pressburger splashed colors luxuriously on such British films as *Black Narcissus* and *The Red Shoes.* In the 50s, color was being used judiciously in such films as Huston's *Moulin Rouge* in the

West and Kinugasa's *Gate of Hell* in the East. The 60s saw Antonioni paint inanimate objects to obtain desired color effects in *The Red Desert.* In the 70s, Coppola used golden tones with chiaroscuro effects to create the sense of a tragic, vanished time in *The Godfather*. Cinematographer Nestor Almendros developed the use of natural light in period films such as *Days of Heaven* (1978). In the 80s and 90s, directors Spike Lee and Jonathan Demme have used drenched colors that evoke a technicolor past in decidedly contemporary settings. But for most filmmakers, color has remained a commercial commodity, a sugar coating now routinely applied to nearly all films.

color consultant. A person assigned to the production of a motion picture whose function is to advise the director and the lighting cameraman on matters pertaining to color. The function is today virtually obsolete.

color correction. The alteration of specific color values, usually by means of filters, either during filming or during printing in the laboratory.

color film. Film with one or more layers of color-sensitive emulsions.

color filter. A colored substance, in the form of gelatin or glass, placed in front of a camera lens. The filter permits the passage of light rays of its own color but absorbs light rays of complementary colors.

color sensitivity. The degree of response of a film's emulsion to colors in the visible range of the spectrum.

color temperature. A measure of the color value of a light source expressed in degrees Kelvin. The instrument for measuring color temperature is the color-temperature meter, also known as a "three-color meter."

colorization. A computer-aided process by which black-and-white films are converted to color for showing on TV screens. The conversion practice, which became widespread in the mid- to late 80s, and affected many Hollywood classics of the 30s and 40s, met with fierce objections by filmmakers, who termed it a vulgar assault on the creative rights of artists. Although colorization is still practiced, its progress was slowed by the organized protest, by technical imperfections, and by higher than expected costs.

Colpi, Henri. Film editor, director. Born on July 15, 1921, in Brigue, Switzerland. Studied film editing at IDHEC in Paris but after graduating turned to film journalism, as editor of the magazine *Ciné-Digest.* In 1947 he edited a critical anthology, *Le Cinéma et ses Hommes* and he is also the author of a book on film music, *Defense et Illustration de la Musique dans le Film* (1963). He began his direct involvement with films in 1950, editing or directing several short subjects. From 1955 to 1961 he edited several important Alain RESNAIS films, as well as Chaplin's controversial *A King in New York.* In 1961 he directed his first full-length feature film, *Une aussi longue Absence,* which won the grand prize at the Cannes Film Festival. He has since also directed for French TV.

FILMS INCLUDE: As editor—*La Pointe courte* 1954; *Nuit et Brouillard/Night and Fog* 1955; *Le Mystère Picasso/The Mystery of Picasso* 1956; *A King in New York* (UK) 1957; *Hiroshima mon Amour* 1959; *L'Année dernière à Marienbad/ Last Year at Marienbad* 1961; *Détruire dit-elle/Destroy She Said* 1969; *Chantons sous l'Occupation* 1976; *Dilitis* 1977; *Offret/ Sacrificatio/Le Sacrifice/The Sacrifice* (also technical consultant; Swed./Fr.) 1986. Features as director (complete)—*Une aussi longue Absence/The Long Absence* 1961; *Codine* (also co-story, edit., co-music) 1963; *Mona—l'Etoile sans Nom* 1967; *Heureux qui comme Ulysse* (also co-sc.) 1970; *L'Ile mystérieuse/The Mysterious Island of Captain Nemo* (co-dir. with Juan Antonio Bardem; Fr./Sp.) 1973.

Coltrane, Robbie. Born in 1950 in Rutherglen, Scotland. *ed.* Glasgow School of Art. Broad, hale supporting player. Trained in the Traverse Theater in Edinburgh, he has established himself in a wide range of British and American comedy and drama.

FILMS INCLUDE: *La Morte en Direct* 1979; *Flash Gordon* 1980; *Subway Riders* 1981; *Britannia Hospital, Scrubbers* 1982; *Ghost Dance, Krull, Loose Connections* 1983; *Chinese Boxes* 1984; *Defence of the Realm, Revolution, The Supergrass, National Lampoon's European Vacation* 1985; *Absolute Beginners, Caravaggio, Mona Lisa* 1986; *Eat the Rich, The Secret Policeman's Third Ball, The Strike* 1987; *The Fruit Machine, Midnight Breaks* 1988; *Bert Rigby, You're a Fool, Henry V, Lenny Live, Let It Ride* 1989; *Nuns on the Run, Perfectly Normal* 1990; *The Pope Must Die* 1991; *Triple Bogey on a Par 5 Hole* 1992; *The Adventures of Huck Finn* 1993.

Coluche. Actor. *b.* Michel Colucci, 1944, Paris. *d.* 1986. An abrasive stand-up comic in café-theaters and music halls, he acquired a lovable, teddy-bear personality when he began appearing in films. Although he specialized in comedy, he won a César as best actor for a straight role in *Tchao Pantin* (1983), a sordid psychological thriller. He was at the peak of his career, widely adored by French moviegoers, when he was killed in a motorcycle accident.

FILMS INCLUDE: *Le Pistonné/The Man with Connections* (bit) 1970; *L'Aile ou la Cuisse* 1976; *Vous n'aurez pas l'Alsace et la Lorraine* (also dir., sc.) 1977; *Le Maître d'Ecole* 1981; *Banzaï, La Femme de Mon Pote/My Best Friend's Girl, Tchao Pantin* 1983; *Le Vengéance du Serpent a Plumes* 1984; *Les Rois du Gag* 1985.

Columbia Pictures. American motion picture production and distribution company, incorporated in 1924. It was an outgrowth the of C.B.C./Film Sales Company, founded in 1920 by the brothers Harry and Jack Cohn, and Joe Brandt, all former employees of Carl LAEMMLE. From a fly-by-night little company on Hollywood's Poverty Row, Columbia developed into a major studio in the 30s thanks largely to the dynamic leadership of Harry COHN and the creative talent of Frank CAPRA. Still trailing such companies as MGM, Fox, Warners, and Paramount in both prestige and size, however, Columbia concentrated its efforts in the 40s on the production of many slick and profitable B pictures and occasional commercial blockbusters starring Rita Hayworth, notably *Gilda.* Also very successful at the box office were *The Jolson Story* and its sequel, *Jolson Sings Again.* Between 1940 and 1946 the company's gross income doubled and its net profit was up six and a half times.

The two-pronged crisis that rocked Hollywood in the late 40s had only a mild effect on Columbia. Since the company owned no motion picture theaters, it was spared the upheaval shared by other major studios that had to divest themselves of their theater chains because of new antitrust laws. And the threat from television which all but ruined some companies was met realistically early in the 50s when Columbia became the first major studio to learn to live with the new medium through its subsidiary Screen Gems. Profits from sales of old films to TV were channeled into new film production, and before long the company was solidly entrenched at the top.

Among the films that contributed to the growth of Columbia in both box-office returns and prestige since the late 40s were *All the King's Men, Born Yesterday, From Here to Eternity, The Caine Mutiny, On the Waterfront, The Bridge on the River Kwai, Dr. Strangelove, Lawrence of Arabia, Easy Rider,* and *Oliver!* In 1968 the company reorganized, changing its corporate title from Columbia Pictures Corporation to Columbia Pictures Industries, with Columbia Pictures and

Screen Gems as its major divisions. Financial setbacks in the 70s, which brought the company to the brink of bankruptcy, led to the ascent of a new management team headed by Alan Hirschfield and David Begelman. They turned out such box-office hits as *Shampoo* (1975) and *Close Encounters of the Third Kind* (1977); but Begelman was forced to leave in 1978, in the wake of an embezzlement scandal. His successor as production chief, Frank Price, was responsible for successes like *Kramer vs. Kramer* (1979), *Tootsie* (1982), and *Ghostbusters* (1984). Price was succeeded in 1986 by British producer David Puttnam, but Puttnam's multi-year contract was terminated in 1987, when he was replaced by Dawn Steel. The Coca-Cola company, which had purchased Columbia for $750 million in 1982, sold the studio to Japan's Sony Corporation for a whopping $3.4 billion in 1989. Coca-Cola had introduced a new production company, TRISTAR PICTURES, which continued with Columbia Pictures under the aegis of Sony Pictures Entertainment.

After Sony wrote off exorbitant losses, Peter Guber and Jon Peters were ousted from their expensive contracts. In an effort to get the studio back on its feet financially, John Calley, former head of MGM-US, was brought on board as COO and president, with Jeff Sagansky in as co-president. Amy Pascal and Robert Cooper were made heads of Columbia Pictures and TriStar, respectively, while Mark Canton and Marc Platt were excused from their former positions.

Columbus, Chris. Director, screenwriter. Born in 1959 in Spangler, Pa. *ed.* New York University (film). Youth-oriented screenwriter and, later, director. He sold his first screenplay before graduating from N.Y.U. (*Jocks*) and also worked on a children's cartoon series, "Galaxy High School." After writing scripts for several films executive-produced by Steven Spielberg (beginning with *Gremlins*), he went on to direct one of the top-grossing films of all time, *Home Alone* (1990).

FILMS INCLUDE: *Gremlins* (sc.), *Reckless* (sc.) 1984; *The Goonies* (sc.), *Young Sherlock Holmes* (sc.) 1985; *Little Nemo in Slumberland* (animated) (sc.) 1986; *Adventures in Babysitting* (dir.) 1987; *Heartbreak Hotel* (dir., sc.) 1988; *Home Alone* (dir.) 1990; *Only the Lonely* (dir., sc.) 1991; *Home Alone 2: Lost in New York* (dir.) 1992; *Nine Months* (also co-prod.) 1995; *Jingle All the Way* (prod. only)1996.

combined print. See COMPOSITE PRINT.

Comden, Betty. Playwright, lyricist, screenwriter. Born Elizabeth Cohen, on May 3, 1917, in Brooklyn, N.Y. *ed.* NYU. Collaborated with Adolph GREEN on many successful Broadway musicals and the screenplays and songs of some of Hollywood's brightest musical films. She played bits in *Greenwich Village* (1944), *Garbo Talks* (1984), *Slaves of New York* (1989), and *The Teddy Bear Habit* (1990).

FILMS INCLUDE: *Good News* 1947; *Take Me Out to The Ball Game* (songs only), *On the Town, The Barkleys of Broadway* 1949; *Singin' in the Rain* 1952; *The Band Wagon* 1953; *It's Always Fair Weather* 1955; *Auntie Mame* 1958; *Bells Are Ringing* 1960; *What a Way to Go!* 1964.

Comencini, Luigi. Director. Born on June 8, 1916, in Salo, Italy. After studying architecture in Milan he became interested in film and founded, together with director Alberto LATTUADA, the Cineteca Italiana film archives in Milan. A journalist and film critic, he made his debut as director with a short documentary, *Bambini in Città,* in 1946. His early feature films indicated a neorealistic trend, but the commercial success of *Bread Love and Dreams* (1954), starring Gina LOLLOBRIGIDA and Vittorio DE SICA, paved the way to other films of mass audience appeal. He has collaborated on scripts of many of his own films as well as those of other directors. His daughter, Francesca Comencini, is a budding director who won the Venezia De Sica Award for *Pianoforte* in 1984. Of his children, Cristina Comencini is a screenwriter and Paola Comencini a designer.

FEATURE FILMS: *Proibito rubare/Guaglio* (also co-sc.) 1948; *L'Imperatore di Capri* 1949; *Persiane chiuse/Behind Closed Shutters* 1950; *Heidi* (Switz.), *La Tratta delle Bianche/ Girls Marked Danger* 1952; *Pane Amore e Fantasia/Bread Love and Dreams* (also co-sc.), *La Valigia dei Sogni* 1953; *Pane Amore e Gelosia/Frisky* (also co-sc.) 1954; *La Bella di Roma* (also co-sc.) 1955; *La Finestra sul Luna Park* (also co-sc.) 1956; *Mariti in Città* (also co-sc.) 1957; *Mogli pericolose* (also story, co-sc.) 1958; *Und das am Montagmorgen* (Ger.), *Le Sorprese dell'Amore* 1959; *Tutti a Casa/Everybody Go Home!* (also co-sc.) 1960; *A Cavallo della Tigre* (also co-sc.) 1961; *Il Commissario* 1962; *La Ragazza di Bube/Bebo's Girl* (also co-sc.) 1963; *Tre Notte d'Amore/Three Nights of Love* ('Fatebenefratell' episode), *La Mia Signorina* ('Eritrea' episode; also co-sc.), *Le Bambole/The Dolls* ('Treatise in Eugenics' episode), *Il Compagno Don Camillo, La Bugiarda/Six Days a Week* (also co-sc.) 1965; *Incompreso/Vita col Figlio* 1966; *Italian Secret Service* (also co-story, co-sc.) 1968; *Infanzia Vocazione e Prime Esperienze di Giacomo Casanova—Veneziano* (also co-story), *Senza Sapere niente di Lei* (also co-sc.) 1969; *Le Avventure di Pinocchio* (also co-sc.) 1971; *Lo Scopone scientifico/The Scientific Cardplayer* 1972; *Delitto d'Amore* (also co-sc.), *Mio Dio come sono Caduta in Basso/Till Marriage Do Us Part* (also co-story, co-sc.) 1974; *La Donna della Demonica/The Sunday Woman, Signore e Signori Buonanotte/Goodnight Ladies and Gentlemen* (two episodes; also co-sc.), *Basta che non si sappia in Giro* ('L'Equivoco' episode), *Quelle Strane Occasioni* ('L'Ascensore' episode) 1976; *Il Gatto* 1977; *L'Ingorgo—Una Storia impossibile/ Bottleneck/Traffic Jam* (also co-sc.) 1979; *Voltati Eugenio* (also co-story, co-sc.) 1980; *Cercasi Gesu* (also co-story, co-sc.) 1982; *Cuore* (also co-sc.) 1984; *La Storia/History* (also co-sc.) 1985; *A Boy from Calabria* 1987; *La Bohème* 1988; *Buon Natale Buon Anno/Merry Christmas, Happy New Year* (also co-sc.) 1990; *Bread and Wine* 1992.

Comer, Anjanette. Actress. Born on Aug. 7, 1942, in Dawson, Tex. *ed.* Baylor U. Leading lady of Hollywood films from the mid-60s, following some exposure on TV.

FILMS INCLUDE: *Quick Before It Melts, The Loved One* 1965; *The Appaloosa* 1966; *Banning* 1967; *Guns for San Sebastian, In Enemy Country* 1968; *Rabbit Run* 1970; *The Baby* 1973; *The Night of the Thousand Cats* 1974; *The Manchu Eagle Murder Caper Mystery, Lepke* 1975; *Fire Sale* 1977.

Comfort, Lance. Director. *b.* 1908, Harrow, England. *d.* 1967. He entered the industry in 1926 as animator-cameraman, first on medical films, then on features. In 1941 he made his debut as director and subsequently piloted a good number of British films, typically routine thrillers.

FEATURE FILMS: *Hatter's Castle, Penn of Pennsylvania/ Courageous Mr. Penn* 1941; *Those Kids from Town, Squadron Leader X* 1942; *Escape to Danger, Old Mother Riley—Detective, When We Are Married* 1943; *Hotel Reserve* 1944; *Great Day* 1945; *Bedelia* 1946; *Temptation Harbor* 1947; *Daughter of Darkness* 1948; *Silent Dust* 1949; *Portrait of Clare* 1950; *The Girl on the Pier* 1953; *Bang You're Dead, Eight O'Clock Walk* 1954; *Man in the Road* 1956; *Face in the Night, At the Stroke of Nine, The Man from Tangier* 1957; *Make Mine a Million, The Ugly Duckling* 1959; *The Breaking Point/The Great Armored Car Swindle, Rag Doll/Young Willing and Eager, Pit of Darkness* 1961; *The Painted Smile/Murder Can Be Deadly* 1962; *The Break, Tomorrow at Ten, Touch of Death, Live It Up/Sing and Swing* 1963; *Blind Corner in the Dark* 1964; *Devils of Darkness, Be My Guest* 1965.

Comingore, Dorothy. Actress. *b.* Aug. 24, 1913, Los Angeles. *d.* 1971. *ed.* U. of California. Following some stage experience in stock, she broke into films as Linda Winters in Columbia comedy shorts of the mid-30s. She appeared with the THREE STOOGES, played leads in a couple of low-grade Westerns, and bits in a handful of other films before getting her big chance in Orson Welles's *Citizen Kane* (1941). She seemed destined for stardom after portraying Kane's pathetic protégée and second wife but subsequently appeared in supporting roles in only three scattered films. Her career was dealt a final blow in 1951, when she was blacklisted, in the wake of the House Un-American Activities Committee hearings.

FEATURE FILMS: As Linda Winters—*Prison Train, Comet Over Broadway* 1938; *Trade Winds, Blondie Meets the Boss, North of the Yukon, Five Little Peppers and How They Grew, Scandal Sheet, Mr. Smith Goes to Washington, Cafe Hostess/Street of Missing Women* 1939; *Pioneers of the Frontier* 1940. As Dorothy Comingore—*Citizen Kane* 1941; *The Hairy Ape* 1944; *Any Number Can Play* 1949; *The Big Night* 1951.

commissary. A studio's restaurant or cafeteria.

Como, Perry. Singer. Born Pierino Roland Como, on May 18, 1912, in Canonsburg, Pa. A barber at 15, he later began singing with bands (initially as Nick Perido) and, as a crooner with an amiable, relaxed style, became a recording star in the 40s. Featured in several musical films but reached a career peak as star of his own TV show in the 50s and 60s. He is a resident of Jupiter, Florida.

FILMS: *Something for the Boys* 1944; *Doll Face* 1945; *If I'm Lucky* 1946; *Words and Music* 1948.

Companeez, Jacques. Screenwriter. *b.* Mar. 5, 1906, St. Petersburg, Russia. *d.* 1956. An engineer by profession, he began his film career in Berlin in 1931. In 1936 he moved to France, where he wrote screenplays for many films, including a number of artistic and commercial successes. In hiding during the Nazi Occupation, he worked anonymously on a number of uncredited scripts. His daughter, Nina Companeez (*b.* 1938, Paris), was a highly regarded screenwriter in the 60s and began directing films in the 70s.

FILMS INCLUDE: *Nächte von St. Petersburg* (Ger.) 1934; *A Dog's Life* (Czech.), *Ave Maria* (Ger.) 1936. In France—*Les Bas-Fonds/The Lower Depths* 1936; *Feu, Nostalgie/The Postmaster's Daughter, L'Alibi* 1937; *La Maison du Maltais/Sirocco, Gibraltar/It Happened in Gibraltar, Coup de Feu, Katia, Pièges/Personal Column, La Mer en Flammes* 1939; *L'Inévitable M. Dubois* 1943; *Un Ami viendrâ ce Soir/A Friend Will Come Tonight* 1945; *Adieu Chérie, La Foire aux Chimères* 1946; *La Maison sous la Mer, Les Maudits/The Damned, Contre-Enquête/Counter Investigation* 1947; *Un Flic, Carrefour des Passions* (also co-prod.) 1948; *Souvenirs perdus* 1950; *Casque d'Or* 1951; *Adorable Créatures, Le Fruit défendu/Forbidden Fruit* 1952; *Les Compagnes de la Nuit/Companions of the Night, La Rage au Corps* 1953; *Les Amants du Tage, Escale à Orly* 1954; *La Sorcière* 1955; *Folies-Bergère* 1956.

compilation film. Film assembled in the cutting room from pre-existing library footage. Most compilation films are classified as documentaries since they derive their material from nonfiction sources and aim to influence or educate, but some are made purely as entertainment, combining clips from old movies to create a new production of mass appeal. The first compilation films were made in the late 1890s, as soon as producers discovered safe means of duplicating and splicing existing footage. The first famous example is Edwin S. Porter's *The Life of an American Fireman* (1903), which combined newly shot material with library stock of firemen in action.

The main source of material for the compilation film has been the newsreel, which by 1910 was being issued regularly in several countries. In France during that year, Gaumont produced a compilation report on the Portuguese revolution. Over the years, the newsreel mushroomed into a massive archive of historically significant visual documentation. The enormous outpour of newsreel footage during WW I provided a virtually infinite source of material for compilation films, which proliferated during and immediately after the war both for the purpose of political propaganda and as a means of quick commercial exploitation. The five-reel *America Answers* (1918) was the US Government's offical record of the war. Other political and military events were being assembled into compilation films during that period. In the US, the Mutual company had released a seven-reel feature in 1914, *The Life of Villa,* which depicted Pancho Villa's insurrection in Mexico by combining newsreel footage and reconstructed scenes under the supervision of D. W. Griffith.

In the Soviet Union, where the factual film had been recognized by Lenin as a useful tool of the Revolution, and where the scarcity of raw stock forced filmmakers to experiment with existing footage, the compilation film was elevated to an art form in the 20s. Dziga Vertov's 13-reel *History of the Civil War* (1921) was an early example of the use of montage techniques to increase the emotional impact of a compilation film. Even more ambitious in scope was the work of Esther Shub in the late 20s, which covered Russian history from 1896 through the Revolution in three compilation films, *The Fall of the Romanov Dynasty* and *The Great Road* (both 1927) and *The Russia of Nicholas II and Leo Tolstoy* (1928).

In the West, too, the compilation film became more sophisticated and better edited during the 20s. Significant examples include Cecil Hepworth's *Through Three Reigns* (1922), Wilfred Day's *Royal Remembrances* (1929), and Basil Wright's *Conquest* (1929) in England; Otto Nelson and Terry Ramsaye's *The March of the Movies* (1927) in the US; and Walter Ruttman's *Die Melodie der Welt* (1929) in Germany. The 30s saw the creation in America of "The March of Time" series, which often employed compilation methods in its presentations. Among several outstanding compilation films in the decade were two that dealt with the Spanish Civil War, Luis Buñuel's *Madrid 1936/Loyal Spain Take Arms!* (1936) and Shub's *Spain* (1939).

During WW II a propaganda battle raged between the Allies and the Axis nations via the compilation film. The US contribution to this audiovisual war included Frank Capra's "Why We Fight" series (1943–44) and Samuel Spewack's *The World at War* (1943). Britain produced Alberto Cavalcanti's *Yellow Caesar* (1940), a critique of Mussolini; Fred Watt's *Curse of the Swastika* (1940); and Paul Rotha's *Total War in Britain* (1945). A combined Anglo-American effort resulted in Carol Reed and Garson Kanin's *The True Glory* (1945). From Russia came a Dovzhenko-Solntseva-Avdeyenko collaboration, *The Fight for Our Soviet Ukraine* (1943). Canada packaged a wartime series, *The World in Action.* Postwar rehabilitation problems were eloquently depicted in Rotha's *World of Plenty* (1943), *Land of Promise* (1945), and *The World Is Rich* (1947).

In the years following WW II, compilation films have been made on a variety of subjects, from Nicole Védrès's nostalgic *Paris 1900* (France, 1947) to Stuart Legg's history of aviation, *Powered Flight* (UK, 1953). But the grim memories of the war continued to haunt compilation filmmakers, especially in Europe, for quite a number of years. Among the most striking examples of their product are Alain Resnais' *Nuit et Brouillard/Night and Fog* (France, 1955), Erwin Leiser's *Mein*

Kampf (Sweden, 1960), Rotha's *Das Leben von Adolf Hitler/The Life of Adolf Hitler* (Germany, 1961), Frédéric Rossif's *Le Temps du Ghetto* (France, 1961), Mikhail Romm's *Ordinary Fascism* (USSR, 1965), and Marcel Ophüls's *Le Chagrin et la Pitié/The Sorrow and the Pity* (France/Switzerland/Germany, 1971). Notable postwar compilation films on other subjects include Joris Ivens and Vladimir Pozner's *Lied der Strome/Song of the Rivers* (East Germany, 1954), about the international trade union movement; George Morrison's *Miss Eire* (Ireland, 1959), a portrait of life in the Irish Republic; Rossif's *Mourir à Madrid/To Die in Madrid* (France, 1963), a review of the Spanish Civil War from its origins in 1931 to Franco's consolidation of power in 1939; and Marcel Ophüls's *A Sense of Loss* (US/Switz., 1972), about the conflict in Northern Ireland, and *The Memory of Justice* (UK/Germany, 1976), an examination of the conflicts in Algeria and Vietnam, evoking the memory of the Nuremberg Trials.

Examples of compilation films made primarily for entertainment are Robert Youngson's amusing collections of old movie clips, *When Comedy Was King* (1960), *Days of Thrills and Laughter* (1961), and *30 Years of Fun* (1963); Jack Haley, Jr.'s, reprise of 100 MGM musicals, *That's Entertainment* (1974), and its sequel, Gene Kelly's *That's Entertainment Part 2* (1976), and the American Film Institute's *America at the Movies* (1976).

composite dupe negative. A duplicate negative that carries both image and sound in synchronization. See also DUPE NEGATIVE.

composite master. A fine-grain positive print from which a COMPOSITE DUPE NEGATIVE for release printing can be directly made.

composite print. The positive print of a film combining picture and sound track in synchronization. In order for picture and sound to be reproduced simultaneously during projection, the two must be properly staggered, allowing for the distance (ADVANCE) between the picture and sound gates of a projector (21 frames for 35 mm and 26 frames for 16 mm). Also called a "combined print."

compositing. In movie special effects, the process of combining two or more separate images to create an image that would otherwise be difficult or impossible to achieve. Compositing can be done optically, using the BLUE SCREEN PROCESS and an OPTICAL PRINTER to rephotograph separate images onto a single frame. It can also be done digitally, by translating images into digital form and combining them on a computer (see DIGITAL EFFECTS).

Compson, Betty. Actress. *b.* Eleanor Luicime Compson, Mar. 18, 1897, Beaver, Utah. *d.* 1974, the daughter of a mining engineer. She started out in vaudeville at 15, billed as "The Vagabond Violinist." A stunning blonde, she broke into films in 1915 as the heroine of Al CHRISTIE's comedy shorts. She appeared in dozens of these during the next three years, then emerged as a dramatic star in *The Miracle Man* (1919), opposite Lon CHANEY. She was one of Hollywood's top stars during the 20s, appearing in numerous silent films from Paramount and other studios. She closed out the silent phase of her career on an upbeat note, playing two of her most memorable roles in Tod Browning's *The Big City* and Josef von Sternberg's *The Docks of New York* (1928). She was nominated for a best actress Academy Award for *The Barker* (also 1928). She made a smooth transition to sound and for a while continued to play leads, but she gradually slipped into minor productions and supporting parts and finally retired from the screen in 1948. Her first of three husbands was director James CRUZE.

FILMS INCLUDE: *Wanted: A Leading Lady* 1915; *His at Six O'Clock* 1916; *A Bold Bad Night* 1917; *Betty Makes Up, The Border Raiders* 1918; *The Terror of the Range* (serial), *The Prodigal Liar, The Devil's Trail, The Miracle Man* 1919; *Prisoners of Love, At the End of the World, For Those We Love, Ladies Must Live, The Little Minister* 1921; *The Law and the Woman, The Green Temptation, Always the Woman, The Bonded Woman, To Have and to Hold, Kick In* 1922; *The Rustle of Silk, The Woman with Four Faces, Hollywood, Woman to Woman* (UK), *The White Flower* 1923; *The Stranger, Miami, The Enemy Sex, The Female, The Garden of Weeds, The Fast Set, White Shadow* 1924; *Locked Doors, New Lives for Old, Eve's Secret, Paths to Paradise, The Pony Express, Counsel for the Defense* 1925; *The Wise Guy, Palace of Pleasure, The Belle of Broadway* 1926; *The Ladybird, Say It with Diamonds, Temptations of a Shop Girl, Cheating Cheaters* 1927; *Love Me and the World Is Mine, The Big City, Masked Angel, Court-Martial, The Docks of New York, The Barker* 1928; *Scarlet Seas, Weary River, On with the Show, The Time the Place and the Girl, Street Girl, The Great Gabbo, Skin Deep, Woman to Woman* (remake; UK) 1929; *The Case of Sergeant Grischa, Isle of Escape, Midnight Mystery, The Czar of Broadway, Inside the Lines, Those Who Dance, The Spoilers, The Boudoir Diplomat, She Got What She Wanted* 1930; *The Lady Refuses, Virtuous Husband, Three Who Loved, The Gay Diplomat* 1931; *The Silver Lining* 1932; *West of Singapore, Destination Unknown* 1933; *False Pretenses* 1935; *Hollywood Boulevard* 1936; *The Port of Missing Girls, A Slight Case of Murder* 1938; *News Is Made at Night* 1939; *Strange Cargo* 1940; *Mr. and Mrs. Smith, The Invisible Ghost* 1941; *Second Chance* 1947; *Here Comes Trouble* 1948.

Compton, Fay. Actress. *b.* Virginia Lilian Emeline Compton Mackenzie, Sept. 18, 1894, London. *d.* 1978. Made her stage debut at 12 and went on to a long, distinguished stage career. She starred in silent British films and early talkies, then switched to character parts. Familiar to worldwide TV audiences for her role as the crusty old aunt in 'The Forsyte Saga' series. A sister of novelist Sir Compton Mackenzie, she was the mother of director Anthony PELISSIER from the first of her four marriages. Her last two husbands were actors, Leon Quartermaine and Ralph Michael (Ralph Champion Shotter).

FILMS INCLUDE: *She Stoops to Conquer* 1914; *One Summer's Day* 1917; *Judge Not* 1920; *A Woman of No Importance, The Old Wives' Tale* 1921; *A Bill of Divorcement* 1922; *This Freedom, The Loves of Mary Queen of Scots* 1923; *The Eleventh Commandment* 1924; *The Happy Ending* 1925; *London Love* 1926; *Robinson Crusoe* 1927; *Zero* 1928; *Fashions in Love* (US) 1929; *Cape Forlorn/Love Storm, Tell England/The Battle of Gallipoli* 1931; *Waltzes from Vienna/Strauss's Great Waltz* 1933; *Autumn Crocus* 1934; *The Mill on the Floss* 1937; *So This Is London* 1939; *The Prime Minister* (as Queen Victoria) 1941; *Odd Man Out* 1946; *Nicholas Nickleby* 1947; *London Belongs to Me/Dulcimer Street* 1948; *Britannia Mews/The Forbidden Street* 1949; *Blackmailed* 1950; *Laughter in Paradise* 1951; *Othello* (as Emilia), *Lady Possessed* (US) 1952; *Aunt Clara* 1954; *Town on Trial* 1956; *The Story of Esther Costello* 1957; *The Haunting, Uncle Vanya* 1963; *The Virgin and the Gypsy* 1970.

computer animation. A technique in which special effects artists use a computer to manipulate images that are digitally stored. The images can be live-action footage or artwork that have been scanned into the computer, or they can be COMPUTER-GENERATED IMAGERY. To produce the illusion of movement, the animator can specify the position of the moving objects in each frame, or he can specify their positions at key points, allowing the computer to trace their movements from point to point according to programmed procedures. The computer can also be used to embellish the image by distorting, coloring, or shading. Computer animation is increasingly being used to replace or enhance more laborious traditional techniques, such as stop-motion and cartoon animation, which rely on frame-by-frame filming of objects or drawings that have been slightly altered in the interval between frames. See also DIGITAL EFFECTS.

computer-generated imagery (CGI). In movie special effects, images created directly on a computer (without first being photographed or painted elsewhere). They are often combined digitally with live action, as when a computer-generated mountain range is added as a background or a computer-generated ghost chases after an actor. See DIGITAL EFFECTS and COMPUTER ANIMATION.

cone lights. A family of cone-shaped floodlight units designed to cover large areas with soft, diffused light. Its main members are the senior, junior, and baby cone.

Conklin, Chester. Actor. *b.* Jan. 11, 1888, Oskaloosa, Iowa. *d.* 1971. Began in stock and vaudeville, then worked as a circus clown before being hired by Mack SENNETT as a Keystone Cop in 1913. With a walrus mustache as a trademark, he played second banana in some of Charlie CHAPLIN's early comedies and teamed up with Mack SWAIN in the "Ambrose-Walrus" series of comedy shorts. He usually played Droppington, a fumbling little fellow, or Walrus, a mischievous little imp. In 1920 he went to Fox, where he appeared in many Sunshine Comedies, and he later freelanced, teaming up with various comedians, including W. C. FIELDS. From the early 20s until the late 40s he played occasional leads and numerous supporting roles in feature films. But his broad comedy style found little expression in talkies and by 1950 his career had ended. In 1954 he was reported to be working as Santa Claus in a Los Angeles department store. In 1961 he entered a nursing home, and four years later, at the age of 77, he married another convalescent. The bride, 65, was his fourth. All his marriages were childless.

FILMS INCLUDE: *Making a Living* (Chaplin's first film), *Mabel's Strange Predicament, Between Showers, Tango Tangles, Cruel Cruel Love, Twenty Minutes of Love, Caught in a Cabaret, The Face on the Barroom Floor, The Masquerader, Dough and Dynamite, Tillie's Punctured Romance* (all starring Chaplin), *The Anglers* 1914; *Love Speed and Thrills, Ambrose's Sour Grapes, A One Night Stand, The Best of Enemies, The Cannon Ball* 1915; *Dizzy Heights and Daring Hearts, Cinders of Love, A Tugboat Romeo* 1916; *The Pullman Bride, A Clever Dummy, An International Sneak* 1917; *It Pays to Exercise, Ladies First, The Village Chestnut* 1918; *Uncle Tom's Cabin* (a burlesque), *Yankee Doodle in Berlin* 1919; *Chicken a la Cabaret* 1920; *Skirts* 1921; *Desire, Anna Christie* 1923; *Greed* 1923–24; *Galloping Fish* 1924; *The Phantom of the Opera, The Great Love, The Pleasure Buyers, The Masked Bride, A Woman of the World* 1925; *Behind the Front, A Social Celebrity, Say It Again, We're in the Navy Now, The Duchess of Buffalo, The Nervous Wreck* 1926; *A Kiss in a Taxi, McFadden's Flats, Cabaret, Rubber Heels, Two Flaming Youths, Tell It to Sweeney* 1927; *Tillie's Punctured Romance, Gentlemen Prefer Blondes, The Big Noise, Fools for Luck, Varsity, Taxi 13, The Haunted House* 1928; *The House of Horror, The Studio Murder Mystery, Fast Company, The Virginian* 1929; *Swing High* 1930; *Her Majesty Love* 1931; *Hallelujah I'm a Bum* 1933; *Modern Times* 1936; *Every Day's a Holiday* 1938; *Hollywood Cavalcade* 1939; *The Great Dictator* 1940; *Knickerbocker Holiday, Hail the Conquering Hero* 1944; *The Perils of Pauline* 1947; *The Beautiful Blonde from Bashful Bend* 1949; *Paradise Alley* 1962; *A Big Hand for the Little Lady* 1966.

Connelly, Marc. Playwright, screenwriter, stage director. *b.* Marcus Cook, Dec. 13, 1890, McKeesport, Pa. *d.* 1980. Originally a reporter, he collaborated with George S. KAUFMAN in the 20s on a string of successful Broadway plays, then won the 1930 Pulitzer Prize for his most celebrated play 'The Green Pastures.' Among the many films adapted by others from his plays or original stories are *Dulcy, To the Ladies* (1923), *Merton of the Movies* (1924, 1947), *Beggar on Horseback* (1925), *Helen of Troy* (1927), *Not So Dumb* (from *Dulcy;* 1930), *Make Me a Star* (1932), *Elmer and Elsie* (1934), and *The Farmer Takes a Wife* (1953). In addition he wrote a number of screenplays directly for films, alone and in collaboration. He directed many stage plays and co-directed the film version of *The Green Pastures* (1936). He was a professor at Yale and wrote short stories, and a novel, *Survival from Quam* (1965), and *Voices of Stage: A Book of Memoirs* (1968). Once married to screen actress Madeline HURLOCK.

SCREENPLAYS INCLUDE: *Cradle Song* 1933; *The Green Pastures* (also co-dir., from own play) 1936; *Captains Courageous* 1937; *I Married a Witch* 1942; *Reunion in France* 1943; *Crowded Paradise* (addnl. scenes only) 1956.

Conner, Bruce. Filmmaker. Born in 1933, in McPherson, Kans. *ed.* U. of Wichita; U. of Nebraska; U. of Colorado; Brooklyn Museum Art School. A painter and a sculptor, he became involved in films after moving to San Francisco in the late 50s. Popular among underground film audiences for his rhythmic, sometimes humorous cutting, and occasional use of erotic material. His films, typically short, are often constructed from randomly assembled bits and pieces of borrowed footage.

FILMS INCLUDE: *A Movie* 1958; *Cosmic Ray* 1962; *Vivian* 1964; *Report* 1965; *Looking for Mushrooms* 1966; *Breakaway* 1967; *Liberty Crown* 1970; *Marilyn Times Five* 1973; *Crossroads, Take the 5:10 to Dreamland* 1976; *Valse triste* 1977; *Mongoloid* 1978; *America Is Waiting* 1981.

Connery, Sean. Actor. Born Thomas Connery, on Aug. 25, 1930, in Edinburgh, Scotland. The son of a truckdriver and a charlady, he left school at 15 to join the British Navy and later worked in such capacities as bricklayer, lifeguard, and coffin polisher. In his spare time he became involved in bodybuilding, a preoccupation that began paying off in swimming-trunk modeling assignments. In 1950 he represented Scotland in the Mr. Universe contest and in 1951 landed a part in the chorus of the London production of 'South Pacific.' After gaining some acting experience in repertory, he began, in 1954, playing small roles in films and bigger ones on British TV. His film career was going no place in particular when in 1962 he was chosen from among several contenders to portray the screen incarnation of James Bond, the popular secret-agent hero of Ian Fleming's adventure novels. Connery leaped to sudden fame in the first of the Bond films, *Dr. No,* and became closely identified with the role, which he repeated in several other successful productions. His charm, wit, and virility made him an ideal Bond and, before long, a superstar. In the ensuing years, he tried gallantly, and eventually successfully, to shake off the sexy spy image by offering a wide range of strong screen portrayals, often sans toupee and glamour. Although he returned twice more to impersonate Bond, in 1971 and 1983, he took advantage of the intervening years to become firmly established as one of the screen's most reliable, versatile, and popular leading men. He won the British Academy Award as best actor for *The Name of the Rose* (1986) and a Hollywood Oscar as best supporting actor for *The Untouchables* (1987). He is often now cast as a seasoned mentor teamed with a younger hero, a role he played to comic effect as Harrison Ford's father in *Indiana Jones and the Last Crusade* (1989). But he continues to be a convincing romantic lead, as in his performance opposite Michelle Pfeiffer in the espionage thriller *The Russia House* (1990).

Connery directed a documentary film, *The Bowler and the Bonnet,* in 1969, but it was never released. His brother, Neil Connery (*b.* 1938), played leads in a couple of films of the late 60s, then retired from acting to become a plasterer. A devoted family man, with "Scotland Forever" and "Mom and Dad" tattooed on his arm, Sean is the father of actor Jason Connery (*b.* Jan. 11, 1963, London) from his 12-year marriage (1962–73) to actress Diane CILENTO. He shares homes in Marbella (Spain) and the Bahamas with a second wife, the French-Moroccan painter Micheline Roquebrune.

FILMS: *Lilacs in the Spring/Let's Make Up* (bit) 1954; *No Road Back* 1956; *Hell Drivers, Time Lock, Action of the Tiger* 1957; *Another Time Another Place, A Night to Remember* 1958; *Darby O'Gill and the Little People* (US), *Tarzan's Greatest Adventure* 1959; *The Frightened City, On the Fiddle/Operation Snafu* 1961; *The Longest Day* (US), *Dr. No* (as James Bond) 1962; *From Russia with Love* (as James Bond) 1963; *Marnie* (US), *Woman of Straw, Goldfinger* (as James Bond) 1964; *The Hill, Thunderball* (as James Bond) 1965; *A Fine Madness* (US) 1966; *You Only Live Twice* (as James Bond) 1967; *Shalako* 1968; *The Molly Maguires* (US) 1970; *Krasnaya Palatka/The Red Tent* (USSR/It.), *The Anderson Tapes* (US), *Diamonds Are Forever* (as James Bond) 1971; *The Offence* 1973; *Zardoz, Murder on the Orient Express* (UK/US) 1974; *Ransom/The Terrorists, The Wind and the Lion* (US), *The Man Who Would Be King* 1975; *Robin and Marian* (as Robin Hood), *The Next Man* (US) 1976; *A Bridge Too Far* 1977; *The First Great Train Robbery/The Great Train Robbery, Meteor* (US), *Cuba* (US) 1979; *Time Bandits, Outland* (US) 1981; *Wrong Is Right/The Man with the Deadly Lens* (US), *Five Days One Summer* (US) 1982; *Never Say Never Again* 1983; *Sword of the Valiant* 1984; *Highlander, The Name of the Rose* (It./Fr./Ger.) 1986; *The Untouchables* (US) 1987; *The Presidio* (US), *Memories of Me* (as himself) 1988; *Indiana Jones and the Last Crusade, Family Business* 1989; *The Hunt for Red October, Russia House* 1990; *Highlander 2: The Quickening, Robin Hood: Prince of Thieves* 1991; *Medicine Man* 1992; *Rising Sun* 1993; *A Good Man in Africa* 1994; *First Knight, Just Cause* (exec.-prod.) 1995; *Dragonheart* (v/o), *The Rock* (also co-exec.-prod.) 1996.

Connick, Harry, Jr. Musician, actor. Born Sept. 11, 1967, in New Orleans, La. Lanky crooner best known for lush, jazzy renditions of Tin Pan Alley classics in *When Harry Met Sally. . .* (1989). A musical child prodigy, he began performing with New Orleans jazz groups when he was six. He first appeared in movies in 1990.

FILMS: *When Harry Met Sally. . .* (arranger, singer) 1989; *Memphis Belle* (act.), *The Godfather Part III* (singer) 1990; *Little Man Tate* (act.) 1991; *Copycat* 1995; *Independence Day* 1996; *Excess Baggage* 1997.

Connolly, Walter. Actor. *b.* Apr. 8, 1887, Cincinnati. *d.* 1940. *ed.* St. Xavier Coll. (Cincinnati); U. of Dublin. A distinguished Broadway actor, he made his film debut in 1932. During his seven years in Hollywood he played dozens of memorable character parts, often in leads, notably as Claudette Colbert's millionaire father in *It Happened One Night* (1934), an irate editor in *Nothing Sacred* (1937), and the title role of *The Great Victor Herbert* (1939).

Films: *Washington Merry-go-round, Man Against Woman, No More Orchids* 1932; *The Bitter Tea of General Yen, Paddy the Next Best Thing, Lady for a Day, Master of Men, Man's Castle* 1933; *Eight Girls in a Boat, It Happened One Night, Once to Every Woman, Twentieth Century, Whom the Gods Destroy, Servants' Entrance, Lady by Choice, The Captain Hates the Sea, Broadway Bill, White Lies* 1934; *Father Brown Detective, She Couldn't Take It, So Red the Rose, One Way Ticket* 1935; *Soak the Rich, The Music Goes 'Round, The King Steps Out, Libeled Lady* 1936; *The Good Earth, Nancy Steele Is Missing, Let's Get Married, The League of Frightened Men, Nothing Sacred, First Lady* 1937; *Penitentiary, Start Cheering, Four's a Crowd, Too Hot to Handle* 1938; *The Girl Downstairs, The Adventures of Huckleberry Finn, Bridal Suite, Good Girls Go to Paris, Coast Guard, Fifth Avenue Girl, Those High Grey Walls, The Great Victor Herbert* (title role) 1939.

Connor, Kevin. Director. Born in 1937, in London. He entered the film industry as an apprentice at 16. In the late 60s he became an editor and in that capacity worked on such films as *Oh! What a Lovely War* (1969), *The Magic Christian* (1970), and *Young Winston* (1972). He then turned to directing, specializing in low-budget horror and fantasy films.

FILMS: *From Beyond the Grave/Creatures/The Creatures from Beyond the Grave* 1973; *The Land That Time Forgot* 1975; *Trial by Combat/Choice of Weapons/Dirty Knights' Work, At the Earth's Core* 1976; *The People That Time Forgot* 1977; *Warlords of Atlantis* 1978; *Arabian Adventure* 1979; *Motel Hell* (US) 1980; *The House Where Evil Dwells* (US) 1982.

Connors, Chuck. Actor. *b.* Kevin Joseph Connors, Apr. 10, 1921, in Brooklyn, N.Y. *d.* 1992. *ed.* Seton Hall Coll. A professional baseball player for the Brooklyn Dodgers, Chicago Cubs, and other major league clubs, he began playing bit roles in films early in the 50s, then leads in B pictures. Rangy and tough, he became a film star in the 60s following his success on TV, notably in 'The Rifleman' series (1958–63). Seen mostly in Westerns and action pictures. From the mid-70s on, he appeared mainly in shoestring-budget productions, occasionally in villainous roles. His second wife (1963–72) was actress Kamala Devi.

FILMS INCLUDE: *Pat and Mike* 1952; *South Sea Woman* 1953; *The Human Jungle* 1954; *Target Zero, Three Stripes in the Sun, Good Morning Miss Dove* 1955; *Hold Back the Night, Hot Rod Girl, Walk the Dark Street* 1956; *Tomahawk Trail, Death in Small Doses, Designing Woman, The Hired Gun* 1957; *The Big Country* 1958; *Geronimo* (title role) 1962; *Flipper, Move Over Darling* 1963; *Synanon* 1965; *Ride Beyond Vengeance* 1966; *Captain Nemo and the Underwater City* 1970; *The Deserter, Support Your Local Gunfighter* 1971; *The Proud and the Damned, Embassy* 1972; *Soylent Green* 1973; *99 44/100% Dead* 1974; *Wolf Larsen/Legend of the Sea Wolf* (title role; It.), *Pancho Villa* 1975; *Tourist Trap* 1979; *Virus* (Jap.) 1980; *Airplane 2: The Sequel* 1982; *Target Eagle* (Sp.) 1983; *The Vals/Valley Girls* (release delayed from 1983) 1985 *Balboa* (filmed in 1982) 1986; *Summer Camp Nightmare/The Butterfly Nightmare* 1987; *Terror Squad, Skinheads, Salmonberries* 1989.

Connors, Michael (Mike). Actor. Born Kreker Ohanian, on Aug. 15, 1925, in Fresno, Calif. *ed.* UCLA. Earned his B.A. degree after WW II service with the Air Force. Began law studies but decided to switch to acting and played a lawyer in his stage debut. Tall and masculine, he entered films early in the 50s, at first using the name Touch Connors. Steadily progressed from supporting parts to lead roles but for the most part has appeared in undistinguished productions. He also starred in the TV series 'Tightrope' (1959–60), 'Mannix' (1967–75), and 'Today's F.B.I.' (1981–82).

FILMS INCLUDE: *Sudden Fear* 1952; *The 49th Man, Island in the Sky, Sky Commando* 1953; *Naked Alibi* 1954; *Five Guns West* 1955; *Jaguar, The Day the World Ended, Swamp Women/Swamp Diamonds/Cruel Swamp, Shake Rattle and Rock, The Ten Commandments* 1956; *Live Fast Die Young, Suicide Battalion* 1958; *Good Neighbor Sam, Panic Button, Where Love Has Gone* 1964; *Harlow* (Carroll Baker version), *Situation Hopeless but Not Serious* 1965; *Stagecoach* 1966; *Kiss the Girls and Make Them Die* 1967; *Cruise Missile* 1978; *Avalanche Express* 1979; *Too Scared to Scream* (filmed in 1982) 1985; *Fist Fighter, Friend to Friend* 1990.

Conrad, Con. Composer. *b.* Conrad K. Dober, June 18, 1891, New York City. *d.* 1938. A successful Broadway composer, he went to Hollywood with the advent of sound and wrote songs and scores for early talkies. Won the first Oscar ever awarded for a song, 'The Continental,' from the film *The Gay Divorcee* (1934).

FILMS INCLUDE: *Broadway, Words and Music, Fox Movietone Follies* 1929; *Happy Days, Let's Go Places* 1930; *Palmy Days* 1931; *Wine Women and Song* 1933; *Gift of Gab, The Gay Divorcee* 1934; *Reckless, Here's to Romance* 1935; *The Great Ziegfeld* 1936; *The Story of Vernon and Irene Castle* 1939.

Conrad, Robert. Actor. Born Conrad Robert Falk, on Mar. 1, 1935, in Chicago. *ed.* Northwestern U. Handsome, muscular leading man of American TV and occasional films. A former boxer and nightclub singer, he gained popularity as the star of such TV series as 'Hawaiian Eye,' 'The Wild Wild West,' 'The D.A.,' and 'The Duke,' but made only scattered appearances in feature films. He directed several of his own TV episodes and one feature film. His daughter, Nancy Conrad, is an actress.

FILMS: *Thundering Jets* (bit) 1958; *Palm Springs Weekend* 1963; *Young Dillinger* (as Pretty Boy Floyd) 1965; *Murph the Surf/Live a Little Steal a Lot/You Can't Steal Love* 1975; *The Bandits* (also dir.; Mex.) 1976; *Sudden Death* 1977; *The Lady in Red* 1979; *Wrong Is Right* 1982; *Jingle All the Way* 1996.

Conrad, William. Actor, director, producer. *b.* Sept. 27, 1920, in Louisville, Ky. *d.* 1994. A former trumpet player and radio-drama writer-performer, he came to films in the mid-40s, following WW II service as a fighter pilot, and played an assortment of character roles, often as mustached, cold-blooded heavies, or detectives. In the late 50s he turned director and producer, at first of TV series, then of motion pictures. In the early 60s, he was the off-screen narrator of the popular TV cartoon series 'The Bullwinkle Show.' In the early 70s he starred in TV series 'Cannon' (1971–76) as an overweight private eye. He played the title role in the 'Nero Wolf' series in 1981.

FILMS INCLUDE: As actor—*The Killers* 1946; *Body and Soul* 1947; *Arch of Triumph, Sorry Wrong Number, Joan of Arc* 1948; *Tension, Any Number Can Play, East Side West Side* 1949; *Dial 1119, One Way Street* 1950; *Cry Danger* 1951; *Lone Star* 1952; *Cry of the Hunted, The Desert Song* 1953; *The Naked Jungle* 1954; *Five Against the House* 1955; *Johnny Concho* 1956; *The Ride Back* (also prod.) 1957; *–30–* 1959; *Moonshine County Express* 1977. As director—*The Man from Galveston* 1964. As director-producer—*Two on a Guillotine, My Blood Runs Cold, Brainstorm* 1965. As executive producer—*An American Dream* 1966; *A Covenant with Death, First to Fight, The Cool Ones* 1967; *Countdown, Chubasco* 1968; *Assignment to Kill* 1969.

Conried, Hans. Actor. *b.* Apr. 15, 1917, Baltimore. *d.* 1982. *ed.* Columbia. Acted in radio dramas in Hollywood for three years before making his film debut in 1938. Appeared in numerous productions in roles ranging from bits to leads. During WW II, specialized in Nazi parts. Most often he played eccentric comedy roles, sometimes sinister, utilizing a clipped English diction or a variety of foreign accents for added comic effect. Best remembered for the lead role in the fantasy film *The 5,000 Fingers of Dr. T.* (1953). Among numerous TV roles, he is memorable as Uncle Tonoose on 'The Danny Thomas Show' (1958–64) and as the voice of Snidley Whiplash in the cartoon series 'The Bullwinkle Show' (1961–62).

FILMS INCLUDE: *Dramatic School* 1938; *It's a Wonderful World* 1939; *Dulcy* 1940; *Underground, The Gay Falcon* 1941; *Joan of Paris, Saboteur, The Big Street, Nightmare, Once Upon a Honeymoon, Journey Into Fear* 1942; *Hitler's Children, Hostages, A Lady Takes a Chance, Crazy House* 1943; *Passage to Marseille, Mrs. Parkington* 1944; *The Senator Was Indiscreet* 1947; *My Friend Irma, On the Town* 1949; *Nancy Goes to Rio, Summer Stock* 1950; *Three for Bedroom C, The World in His Arms, Big Jim McLain* 1952; *The Twonky, The 5,000 Fingers of Dr. T.* 1953; *Davy Crockett King of the Wild Frontier* 1955; *Bus Stop* 1956; *Jet Pilot* 1957; *Rock-a-Bye Baby* 1958; *My Six Loves* 1963; *The Patsy* 1964; *The Brothers O'Toole* 1973; *The Shaggy D.A.* 1976; *The Cat from Outer Space* 1978; *Oh God! Book II* 1980.

console. A control panel used in the sound studio for recording, re-recording, monitoring, and combining the various sound tracks during a mix. See also MIX.

Constantine, Eddie. Actor, singer. *b.* Oct. 29, 1917, in Los Angeles, to Russian immigrants. *d.* 1993. The son of an opera baritone, he was sent to Vienna to study voice but after returning to the US got no further than the chorus of New York's Radio City Music Hall and extra parts in a few films. When his wife, dancer Helene Mussel, joined the Ballets de Monte Carlo, he followed her to Paris, where he began singing in nightclubs. Became a protégé and intimate friend of Edith Piaf, soon achieving popularity as a recording artist. After appearing in a made-in-Egypt independent American film, in 1953, he soared to instant popularity in France in a role that would become pivotal in his career. As Lemmy Caution, the hard-boiled, womanizing, whiskey-drinking American private eye, inspired by Peter Cheyney's mysteries, he played the hero of an entire series of popular French films of the 50s and early 60s, culminating in Jean-Luc Godard's tribute-parody *Alphaville.* Constantine became so closely identified with the role that he named one of his children Lemmy. Constantine later starred in films of other genres, but rarely varied his basic tough-hero acting style. Author of a novel, *Le Proprietaire,* an English-language translation of which was published in the US in 1976 under the title *The Godplayer.*

FILMS INCLUDE: *Egypt by Three* (US), *La Môme Vert de Gris/Poison Ivy, Cet Homme est dangereux/This Man Is Dangerous* 1953; *Les Femmes s'en balancent, Avanzi di Galera* (It.) 1954; *Ça va barder, Je suis un Sentimental* 1955; *Les Truands* 1956; *Folies-Bergère, L'Homme et l'Enfant, Le Grand Bluff* 1957; *Incognito, Ces Dames préfèrent le Mambo/ Dishonorable Discharge* 1958; *Passport to Shame/Room 43* (UK), *Du Rififi chez les Femmes/Riff Raff Girls, SOS Pacific* (UK), *The Treasure of San Teresa/Hot Money Girl* (UK/Ger.) 1959; *Bomben auf Monte Carlo* (Ger.) 1960; *Le Chien de Pique, Mani in Alto* (It.), *Lemmy pour les Dames* 1961; *Les Sept Péchés capitaux/Seven Capital Sins, Cléo de 5 à 7/Cleo from 5 to 7, L'Empire de la Nuit* 1962; *A toi de faire Mignonne/Your Turn Darling* 1963; *Nick Carter va tout casser/Nick Carter casse tout/License to Kill* (title role), *Lucky Jo* 1964; *Alphaville: Une Etrange Aventure de Lemmy Caution/Alphaville, Je vous salue Maffia/Hail Mafia!, Nick Carter et le Trefle rouge* 1965; *Cartes sur Table/Attack of the Robots* 1966; *Lions Love* (US) 1969; *Malatesta* (Ger.) 1970; *Warnung vor einer heiligen Nutte/ Beware of a Holy Whole* (Ger.) 1971; *Souvenir de Gibraltar* (Bel.) 1975; *Le Couple témoin* 1977; *It Lives Again* (US) 1978; *Die dritte Generation/The Third Generation* (Ger.) 1979; *The Long Good Friday* (UK) 1980; *Boxoffice* (US) 1982; *Fluchtpunkt Berlin/Flight to Berlin* (Ger./UK) 1984; *Paul Chevrolet and the Ultimate Hallucination* (Holl.) 1985; *Frankenstein's Aunt* 1986.

contact printing. The method of printing in which the emulsion of the negative comes in direct contact with the emulsion of the positive it reproduces while moving together past an exposing aperture. It is the simplest, cheapest, and fastest method of film printing.

Conte, Richard. Actor. *b.* Nicolas Peter Conte, Mar. 24, 1914, in Jersey City, N.J. *d.* 1975. The son of a barber, he worked as a Wall Street messenger and truck driver before having his first brush with show business as a performing waiter at a Connecticut resort. Elia KAZAN saw him there in 1935 and offered him a scholarship at New York's Neighborhood Playhouse. He appeared, as Nicholas Conte, in an isolated film in 1939, then, following a number of critical successes on Broadway, he signed a contract with 20th Century-Fox in 1943 and soon developed into one of the studio's dependable leading men. He played a variety of roles but was most typically cast as a world-weary hero or cynical gangster. After directing a film in Yugoslavia in 1969, he worked mainly in Italy until his untimely death of a heart attack.

FILMS INCLUDE: *Heaven with a Barbed Wire Fence* 1939; *Guadalcanal Diary* 1943; *The Purple Heart* 1944; *A Bell for Adano, Captain Eddie, The Spider* 1945; *A Walk in the Sun, Somewhere in the Night* 1946; *13 Rue Madeleine, The Other Love* 1947; *Call Northside 777, Cry of the City* 1948; *House of Strangers, Thieves' Highway, Whirlpool* 1949; *The Sleeping City* 1950; *Under the Gun, Hollywood Story* 1951; *The Fighter, The Raiders* 1952; *The Blue Gardenia* 1953; *Highway Dragnet, New York Confidential, The Big Combo, Bengazi, Target Zero* 1955; *I'll Cry Tomorrow* 1956; *Full of Life, The Brothers Rico* 1957; *This Angry Age* 1958; *They Came to Cordura* 1959; *Ocean's 11* 1960; *Who's Been Sleeping in My Bed?* 1963; *Circus World* 1964; *The Greatest Story Ever Told* (as Barabbas), *Synanon* 1965; *Assault on a Queen* 1966; *Tony Rome, Hotel* 1967; *Lady in Cement* 1968; *Operation Cross Eagles* (also dir.) 1969; *Explosion* 1970; *The Godfather* 1972; *L'Onorata Famiglia/The Big Family* (It.), *Tony Arzenta/Big Guns/No Way Out* (It./Fr.), *La Polizia vuole Giustizia/The Violent Professionals* (It.) 1973; *Il Boss/The New Mafia* 1974; *Roma violenta/Street Killers, Un Urlo dalle Tenebre/Who Are You Satan?* 1975.

Conti, Bill. Composer. Born on Apr. 13, 1942, in Providence, R.I. *ed.* Louisiana State U.; Juilliard. A piano prodigy as a child, he formed his own band at 15. He scored his first film in Italy, while touring there with a jazz combo. Much of his Hollywood work is refreshingly original. But his theme for *Rocky,* one of his best-known movie scores, for which he was Oscar-nominated, was partly borrowed from an anonymous Baroque composition. He won an Academy Award for the score of *The Right Stuff* (1983).

FILMS INCLUDE: *Blume in Love* (mus. supvr. only) 1973; *Harry and Tonto* 1974; *Next Stop Greenwich Village, Rocky* 1976; *Citizen's Band/Handle with Care* 1977; *An Unmarried Woman, The Big Fix* 1978; *The Seduction of Joe Tynan* 1979; *Gloria, Private Benjamin* 1980; *For Your Eyes Only* 1981; *Split Image, That Championship Season* 1982; *Bad Boys, The Right Stuff* 1983; *Mass Appeal, The Karate Kid* 1984; *F/X, Big Trouble* 1986; *Happy New Year, Baby Boom, Broadcast News* 1987; *Betrayed* 1988; *Lean on Me* 1989; *Rookie of the Year, By the Sword* 1993; *8 Seconds* 1994; *Bushwacked* 1995; *Entertaining Angels* 1997.

Conti, Tom. Actor. Born on Nov. 22, 1941, in Paisley, Scotland. Dark, brooding, small-framed leading man of British and American stage, TV, and films. Trained as a classical pianist at the Glasgow's Royal Scottish Academy of Music, he later took up acting at the Glasgow College of Drama. Appeared in regional rep, making his London debut in 1973. He also performed on Broadway, winning a Tony for 'Whose Life Is It Anyway?.' In films from 1974, typically in soulful roles, he was nominated for an Academy Award for his performance in *Reuben, Reuben* (1983).

FILMS: *Flame* 1974; *Galileo* 1975; *Eclipse, Full Circle/The Haunting of Julia* 1976; *The Duellists* 1977; *Merry Christmas Mr. Lawrence, Reuben Reuben* (US) 1983; *American Dreamer* (US) 1984; *Miracles* (US), *Saving Grace* (US), *Heavenly Pursuits/The Gospel According to Vic* 1986; *Beyond Therapy* 1987; *The Summer of White Roses, Shirley Valentine* 1989; *Sombody Else's America* 1996.

continuity. The uninterrupted progression of related shots, scenes, and sequences necessary to maintain a logical development of theme or story in a film. Since motion pictures are frequently shot out of sequence, care must be taken to avoid breaks in the flow of action and dialogue as well as discrepancies in the minutest details. The appearance of performers, props, costumes, and backgrounds must match exactly from one shot to the next so that the illusion of sequential filming is maintained.

continuity clerk. Also, "continuity girl," "script girl," "script supervisor," or "script clerk." A member of a filming crew, often a woman, stationed by the camera, whose job it is to assure the film's CONTINUITY. She takes notes of the details of each take, records the dialogue actually spoken, describes the action of the players and their exact positions and attire, notes any departure from the written script, reminds the director of the direction of the action (from right to left or left to right), instructs the clappers what number to use on each shot, records the number of takes, their duration, etc. Her notes form a film's log and are typed daily on CONTINUITY SHEETS.

continuity sheets. Records maintained by the CONTINUITY CLERK indicating scenes and slate number of each shot, the number of takes and their quality, the type of lens used and its aperture, the actual dialogue spoken, details of the action, the props, and the players' attire, etc. The sheets are used as a reference for possible RETAKES and INSERTS and for guidance for the prop and wardrobe departments and eventually the film editor.

The term is also used to describe the list of key numbers of each scene in proper continuity, prepared by the film editor to match the negative print during negative cutting.

continuity title. A narrative title explaining a film's plot or furnishing a line of dialogue and usually occupying the full screen between scenes of photographed images. It was widely used in silent films but is rarely used in talkies.

contract player. An actor or actress under a term contract with a studio or a producer, as distinguished from one hired to perform in a particular production.

contrast. The ratio between the lightest and darkest tonal areas of a shot either in the scene itself or in its photographic reproduction. In a studio setup, the lighting contrast is established by the ratio of KEY LIGHT to FILL LIGHT.

contrast glass. An eyepiece used by a director of photography to determine contrast when lighting a set for a take.

Conway, Jack. Director. *b.* July 17, 1887, Graceville, Minn. *d.* 1952. A high school dropout, he worked on a railroad before becoming a stage actor with a West Coast Belasco stock company in 1907. Two years later he began playing lead roles at Nestor, one of California's first film studios, and starred in, among others, *Her Indian Hero* (1909), *Arizona Bill* (1911), and *The Valley of the Moon* (1914). Under the influence of D. W. GRIFFITH, whose assistant he was for a while, he turned to directing, completing his first feature in 1915. He subsequently directed numerous silent and sound films, which were noted for their level of technical excellence, if not for consistency of theme or style. A dependable, speedy craftsman, he adapted well to the MGM studio machine, for which he turned out many glossy, star-studded productions. Among his best-appreciated films were *Viva Villa!* (1934) and *A Tale of Two Cities* (1935). Several of his romantic comedies have also received critical attention. But his forte was dramatic action, with his protagonists mostly males.

FEATURE FILMS: *The Penitents* 1915; *The Silent Battle, The Beckoning Trail, The Social Buccaneer, The Mainspring, The Measure of a Man* 1916; *Her Soul's Inspiration, Polly Redhead, A Jewel in Pawn, Come Through, The Little Orphan* (also act.), *The Charmer, The Bond of Fear, Because of a Woman* 1917; *Little Red Decides, Her Decision, You Can't Believe Everything, Desert Law, A Diplomatic Mission* 1918; *A Royal Democrat/Democracy* (also act.), *Lombardi Ltd.* 1919; *Riders of the Dawn, The Servant in the House, The Dwelling Place of Light, The Money Changers, The U.P. Trail* 1920; *The Spenders, The Kiss, A Daughter of the Law, The Killer* (also act.), *The Lure of the Orient* (also act.), *The Rage of Paris, The Millionaire* 1921; *Step on It!, Across the Deadline, Another Man's Shoes, Don't Shoot, The Long Chance* 1922; *The Prisoner, Quicksands, Sawdust, What Wives Want, Trimmed in Scarlet, Lucretia Lombard* 1923; *The Trouble Shooter, The Heart Buster, The Roughneck* 1924; *The Hunted Woman, The Only Thing* 1925; *Soul Mates, Brown of Harvard* 1926; *The Understanding Heart, Twelve Miles Out* 1927; *The Smart Set, While the City Sleeps, Bringing Up Father, Alias Jimmy Valentine* 1928; *Our Modern Maidens, Untamed* 1929; *They Learned About Women* (co-dir. with Sam Wood), *The Unholy Three* 1930; *New Moon, The Easiest Way, Just a Gigolo* 1931; *Arsene Lupin, But the Flesh Is Weak, Red-Headed Woman* 1932; *Hell Below, The Nuisance, The Solitaire Man* 1933; *Viva Villa!, The Girl from Missouri, The Gay Bride* 1934; *One New York Night, A Tale of Two Cities* 1935; *Libeled Lady* 1936; *Saratoga* 1937; *A Yank at Oxford, Too Young To Handle* 1938; *Let Freedom Ring, Lady of the Tropics* 1939; *Boom Town* 1940; *Love Crazy, Honky-Tonk* 1941; *Crossroads* 1942; *Assignment in Brittany* 1943; *Dragon Seed* (co-dir. with Harold S. Bucquet) 1944; *High Barbaree, The Hucksters* 1947; *Julia Misbehaves* 1948.

Conway, Tim. Actor. Born on Dec. 15, 1933, in Willoughby, Ohio. *ed.* Bowling Green State U. Began as a writer-director with a Cleveland TV station and became established as a comic performer on 'The Steve Allen Show.' He later co-starred in the 'McHale's Navy' TV series and hosted his own TV show. He won three Emmys as actor and one as writer for his work on 'The Carol Burnett Show.' He played comic character roles in occasional films, mainly Disney features for the juvenile market. His son, Tim Conway, Jr., is also an actor.

FILMS INCLUDE: *McHale's Navy* 1964; *The World's Greatest Athlete* 1973; *The Apple Dumpling Gang* 1975; *Gus, The Shaggy D.A.* 1976; *The Billion Dollar Hobo* 1978; *The Apple Dumpling Gang Rides Again, The Prize Fighter* 1979; *The Private Eyes* (also co-sc.) 1981; *Cannonball Run II* 1984; *The Longshot* (also sc., co-songs) 1986; *Dear God* 1996; *Speed 2: Cruise Control* 1997.

Conway, Tom. Actor. *b.* Thomas Charles Sanders, Sept. 15, 1904, St. Petersburg, Russia, to British parents. *d.* 1967. *ed.* Brighton College (England). The brother of actor George SANDERS, he came to Hollywood in 1940 after stage experience in England. He appeared in many films and played suave leads in low-budget productions. In 1942 he inherited the title role in "The Falcon" series started by his brother the year before. A heavy drinker, he died at 63 of liver cirrhosis.

FILMS INCLUDE: *Sky Murder* 1940; *The Trial of Mary Dugan, The Bad Man, Lady Be Good, Tarzan's Secret Treasure* 1941; *Mr. and Mrs. North, Rio Rita, Grand Central Murder, The Falcon's Brother, Cat People* 1942; *The Falcon Strikes Back, I Walked with a Zombie, The Seventh Victim* 1943; *The Falcon Out West, A Night of Adventure, The Falcon in Hollywood* 1944; *Two O'Clock Courage, The Falcon in San Francisco* 1945; *Whistle Stop, The Falcon's Alibi, Criminal Court* 1946; *Lost Honeymoon* 1947; *One Touch of Venus* 1948; *I Cheated the Law* 1949; *The Great Plane Robbery* 1950; *Painting the Clouds with Sunshine* 1951; *Confidence Girl* 1952; *Tarzan and the She-Devil* 1953; *Prince Valiant* 1954; *Barbados Quest/Murder on Approval* (UK) 1955; *The Last Man to Hang* (UK), *Death of a Scoundrel* 1956; *Voodoo Woman* 1957; *The Atomic Submarine* 1959; *What a Way to Go!* 1964.

Coogan, Jackie. Actor. *b.* John Leslie Coogan, Jr. Oct. 24, 1914, Los Angeles, the son of vaudevillians. *d.* 1984. *ed.* Villanova; USC. His first screen appearance was in *Skinner's Baby* at 18 months old. He was a regular attraction at age four in an Annette Kellerman revue when an impressed Charlie CHAPLIN caught the act in Los Angeles. Chaplin used Jackie in the two-reel *A Day's Pleasure* and made him the co-star of his first feature length film, *The Kid.* The bright-eyed little ragamuffin in a tattered cap and oversized trousers won the hearts of movie audiences from the start. His career as an international child star was phenomenal and his every move was reported in the world press.

Coogan's salary was among Hollywood's highest; he received a half-million-dollar bonus just for switching from First National to Metro, with a contract calling for wages of $1 million plus a percentage of the profits in two years. The money was kept in trust by his parents, with the boy getting only $6.25 a week as allowance. But his popularity waned as he grew up. The turning point was probably symbolized in a newsmaking hair-cutting ceremony at 12, when his famous rumpled bob was shorn to the clicking of cameras, and MGM promptly seized the opportunity to produce *Johnny Get Your Hair Cut,* which showed Jackie before and after the big event. In 1927 he played his last role as a child star. The following year he headlined a show at London's Palladium; then, in 1930, he made a brief screen comeback in *Tom Sawyer* and in 1931, in *Huckleberry Finn,* but by the mid-30s he was all but forgotten.

In 1935, the same year he was supposed to receive the estimated $4 million he had earned as a child star, he was injured in an automobile crash that took the life of his father and child actor Junior Durkin. However, his mother and his new stepfather were in no hurry to part with the money, to the detriment of Jackie, who had married starlet Betty GRABLE in 1937 and now found himself unable to support his bride. He filed suit against his family in 1938 for the assets of Jackie Coogan Productions, Inc., but the case dragged on for months before finally being settled. By that time the assets of the company had dwindled to a mere $252,000, of which Coogan received half. However, the legal issue led to the passage of California's Child Actors Bill, popularly known as the Coogan Act, which was designed to prevent the repetition of such abuses, by creating court-administered trust funds for juvenile actors.

In the meantime, Coogan's marriage to Betty Grable was on the rocks. They were divorced in 1940, with "money matters" cited as the cause. He later married three more times, always to show girls. Two of the marriages—to actresses Flower Parry (1941–43) and Ann McCormick (1946–51)—ended in divorce. His widow is dancer Dorothea Lamphere. During WW II, Coogan served as a flight officer and was the first glider pilot to land Allied troops behind Japanese lines in Burma. In the ensuing years, he occasionally returned to the screen in character parts, often as a mean, slimy heavy. But he had a prolific career on television, where he is said to have appeared in some 1,400 shows. On the small screen he was best known as the bald, grotesque Uncle Fester in the ghoulish TV series 'The Addams

Family' (1964–66). Jackie's younger brother, Robert Coogan (*b.* Dec. 13, 1925, Glendale, Calif.; *d.* 1978), also appeared in films, initially as a juvenile and later in character roles. A grandson, Keith Mitchell, also known as Keith Coogan (*b.* Jan. 13, 1970, Palm Springs, Calif.), is a TV and movie actor.

FILMS INCLUDE (silents complete): *Skinner's Baby* 1917; *A Day's Pleasure* 1919; *The Kid, Peck's Bad Boy* 1921; *My Boy, Trouble, Oliver Twist* 1922; *Daddy, Circus Days, Long Live the King* 1923; *Little Robinson Crusoe, A Boy of Flanders* 1924; *The Rag Man, Old Clothes* 1925; *Johnny Get Your Hair Cut, The Bugle Call, Buttons* 1927; *Tom Sawyer* 1930; *Huckleberry Finn* 1931; *Home on the Range* 1935; *College Swing* 1938; *Million Dollar Legs, Sky Patrol* 1939; *Kilroy Was Here* 1947; *French Leave* 1948; *Skipalong Rosenbloom* 1951; *Outlaw Women* 1952; *The Proud Ones* 1956; *The Joker Is Wild, The Buster Keaton Story* 1957; *High School Confidential, Lonelyhearts* 1958; *The Beat Generation, Night of the Quarter Moon* 1959; *Sex Kittens Go to College* 1960; *John Goldfarb Please Come Home* 1964; *A Fine Madness* 1966; *The Shakiest Gun in the West* 1968; *Marlowe* 1969; *Cahill US Marshal* 1973; *The Manchu Eagle Murder Caper Mystery* 1975; *Dr. Heckyl and Mr. Hype* 1980; *The Escape Artist* 1982; *The Prey* 1984.

Cook, Clyde. Actor. *b.* Dec. 16, 1891, Australia. *d.* 1984. He began as a performer at 12, with an act of acrobatic dancing between rounds of boxing matches. At 16 he moved to England, where he entertained in music halls. Arriving in the US after WW I service with the British Navy, he began playing comic roles in Mack Sennett's Keystone comedies. Small and wiry, he was nicknamed "The Kangaroo Boy" for his acrobatic talents. In 1920 he switched to Fox, appearing in many of the company's Sunshine Comedies, often opposite Chester CONKLIN, then joined Hal Roach. In the early 20s he began playing dramatic as well as comic character roles in feature films. In 1927–28 he co-starred with Louise FAZENDA in several popular slapstick comedy features. He remained active on the screen through the early 50s. His credits are sometimes confused with those of a silent-film cinematographer of the same name.

FILMS INCLUDE: *Don't Tickle, The Huntsman* 1920; *Skirts* 1921; *The Eskimo* 1922; *He Who Gets Slapped, So This Is Marriage* 1924; *Miss Nobody, The Winning of Barbara Worth* 1926; *White Gold, The Brute, The Climbers, Simple Sis, The Bush Leaguer, Barbed Wire, A Sailor's Sweetheart, Good Time Charley* 1927; *Beware of Married Men, Domestic Troubles, Five and Ten Cents Annie, Pay as You Enter, The Docks of New York, Celebrity, Beware of Bachelors, The Spieler* 1928; *Captain Lash, Strong Boy, A Dangerous Woman, Masquerade, In the Headlines, Taming of the Shrew* (as Grumio), *Jazz Heaven* 1929; *The Dude Wrangler, The Dawn Patrol, Sunny* 1930; *Daybreak, Never the Twain Shall Meet* 1931; *Blondie of the Follies* 1932; *Oliver Twist* 1933; *Barbary Coast* 1935; *The White Angel* 1936; *Wee Willie Winkie, Love Under Fire* 1937; *Kidnapped* 1938; *The Little Princess* 1939; *The Sea Hawk* 1940; *White Cargo* 1942; *The Man from Down Under* 1943; *To Each His Own, The Verdict* 1946; *Pride of Maryland* 1951; *Loose in London* 1953; *Donovan's Reef* (bit) 1963.

Cook, Donald. Actor. *b.* Sept. 26, 1900, Portland, Ore. *d.* 1961. A former bank clerk and vaudevillian, he made his Broadway debut as Donn Cook in 1926 and entered films early in the 30s. Played leads and second leads, mostly in B pictures but also in some important A's. His best opportunity came in the male lead in *Jennie Gerhardt,* but he remained a gray, second-rank Hollywood personality throughout the rest of his career. Fared much better in frequent Broadway stage appearances from 1937, notably 'Claudia,' 'Private Lives,' and 'The Moon Is Blue.'

FILMS INCLUDE: *Unfaithful, The Public Enemy, The Mad Genius* 1931; *The Man Who Played God, The Trial of Vivienne Ware, The Conquerors* 1932; *Frisco Jenny, Private Jones, The Kiss Before the Mirror, Jennie Gerhardt, Baby Face, Brief Moment, The World Changes, Fury of the Jungle, Fog* 1933; *Long Lost Father, The Ninth Guest, Viva Villa!, The Most Precious Thing in Life, Jealousy* 1934; *Behind the Evidence, The Casino Murder Case, Gigolette* 1935; *Show Boat, Ring Around the Moon, Beware of Ladies* 1936; *Two Wise Maids* 1937; *Bowery to Broadway, Murder in the Blue Room* 1944; *Patrick the Great, Here Come the Co-eds, Blonde Ransom* 1945; *Our Very Own* 1950.

Cook, Elisha, Jr. Actor. *b.* Dec. 26, 1906, in San Francisco. *d.* 1995. On the stage from age 14, he performed in vaudeville, in stock, and on Broadway and made an isolated film appearance in 1929, repeating his stage role as the romantic juvenile lead in *Her Unborn Child.* Returning to Broadway, he appeared in several other stage productions before settling permanently in Hollywood in 1936. Slightly built and shifty-eyed, he soon became typecast in films as a small-time gangster, often a fall guy and a victim of his own violent milieu. Memorable as the hood Wilmer in *The Maltese Falcon* (1941) and as the mysterious drummer Cliff March in *Phantom Lady* (1944). Because of his jockey-size frame, he has been called the screen's lightest heavy. He also appeared in numerous TV episodes and in the 80s he played a recurring role of a crime czar nicknamed "Ice Pick" in the series 'Magnum P.I.'

FILMS INCLUDE: *Her Unborn Child* 1929; *Two in a Crowd* 1936; *Love Is News, They Won't Forget* 1937; *Submarine Patrol, Newsboys' Home* 1938; *Grand Jury Secrets* 1939; *The Stranger on the Third Floor, Tin Pan Alley* 1940; *Love Crazy, The Maltese Falcon, I Wake Up Screaming* 1941; *A-Haunting We Will Go* 1942; *Phantom Lady, Up in Arms, Dark Waters* 1944; *Dillinger* 1945; *Cinderella Jones, The Falcon's Alibi, The Big Sleep* 1946; *Fall Guy, Born to Kill, The Long Night, The Gangster* 1947; *Flaxy Martin, The Great Gatsby* 1949; *Behave Yourself* 1951; *Don't Bother to Knock* 1952; *Shane, I the Jury* 1953; *Drum Beat* 1954; *The Killing* 1956; *Chicago Confidential, Voodoo Island, Baby Face Nelson* 1957; *House on Haunted Hill* 1959; *Platinum High School, College Confidential* 1960; *One-Eyed Jacks* 1961; *Black Zoo, The Haunted Palace, Johnny Cool* 1963; *Blood on the Arrow* 1964; *Welcome to Hard Times* 1967; *Rosemary's Baby* 1968; *The Great Bank Robbery* 1969; *El Condor* 1970; *The Great Northfield Minnesota Raid, Blacula* 1972; *Emperor of the North Pole, Electra Glide in Blue* 1973; *The Outfit* 1974; *Messiah of Evil, Winter Hawk, The Black Bird* 1975; *St. Ives* 1976; *The Champ, 1941* 1979; *Carny, Tom Horn* 1980; *Harry's War* 1981; *Hammett* 1982.

Cook, Fielder. Director. Born on Mar. 9, 1923, in Atlanta. *ed.* Washington and Lee; U. of Birmingham (England). After WW II service with the Navy's amphibious forces, he began his career in advertising. A TV director from the early 50s, he made an auspicious debut as a motion picture director with *Patterns,* an incisive drama of the power struggle behind the scenes of a big corporation's executive suite. His subsequent, rather sporadic output has been variable in quality.

FILMS INCLUDE: *Patterns* 1956; *Home Is the Hero* (Ire.) 1959; *A Big Hand for the Little Lady* (also prod.) 1966; *How to Save a Marriage—and Ruin Your Life, Prudence and the Pill* (some scenes dir. by Ronald Neame) 1968; *Eagle in a Cage* (UK) 1971; *From the Mixed-Up Files of Mrs. Basil E. Frankweiler* 1973.

Cook, Peter. Actor, humorist. *b.* Nov. 17, 1937, in Torquay, England. *d.* 1995. *ed.* Cambridge. Irreverent comedian-writer of 'Beyond the Fringe' fame, for which he shared a Tony Award on

Broadway with collaborator Dudley MOORE. His second wife was actress Judy Huxtable.

FILMS: *The Wrong Box* 1966; *Bedazzled* (also co-sc.) 1967; *A Dandy in Aspic* 1968; *Monte Carlo or Bust/Those Daring Young Men in their Jaunty Jalopies, The Bed Sitting Room* 1969; *The Rise and Rise of Michael Rimmer* 1971; *The Adventures of Barry Mackenzie* (Austral.) 1972; *The Hound of the Baskervilles* (as Sherlock Holmes) 1978; *Yellowbeard* (also co-sc.; US) 1983; *Supergirl* 1984; *Whoops, Apocalypse, The Princess Bride* 1987; *Without a Clue* 1988; *Getting It Right, Great Balls of Fire, Kokoda Crescent* (sc.) 1989; *Black Beauty* 1994.

cookie. From the greek word *kukaloris,* the breaking up of light. It is a metal screen with variously shaped cutout areas. When placed in front of a light source it casts shadows in a variety of patterns for arty effects in a scene.

Coolidge, Martha. Director. Born in 1946, in New Haven, Conn. *ed.* Rhode Island School of Design; School of Visual Arts; Columbia; NYU graduate film school. Involved in filmmaking from age 18, she was behind the camera as director or crew member on many documentary shorts and commercials in the late 60s, when she also produced a children's show for Canadian TV. In the 70s, after directing such festival-bound documentaries as *David Off and On* (1972), *More Than a School* (1973), and *Old-Fashioned Woman* (1974), she gained wider recognition in 1976 with *Not a Pretty Picture,* a feature about a woman filmmaker directing a re-creation of a traumatic rape experience. In 1978 Francis Ford COPPOLA then invited her to develop a rock 'n' roll musical at his Zoetrope Studios but after two years he ran out of money for the project. With the financial help of Peter BOGDANOVICH, she was able to complete her first fiction feature, *The City Girl,* but before it could get released, she scored a box-office success with the low-budget teen movie *Valley Girl* (1983). She is one of a small but growing number of women directors working steadily in Hollywood today.

FEATURE FILMS: *Not a Pretty Picture* 1976; *Valley Girl* 1983; *The City Girl* (release delayed from 1982), *Joy of Sex* 1984; *Real Genius* 1985; *Plain Clothes* 1988; *That's Adequate* (act.) 1989; *The Friendly, Rope Dancing* 1990; *Rambling Rose* 1991; *Lost in Yonkers* 1993; *Angie, Beverly Hills Cop III* (act. only) 1994; *Three Wishes* 1995; *Out to Sea* 1997.

Coop, Denys. Director of photography. *b.* July 20, 1920, Reading, England. *d.* 1981. Entered British films at 16 as camera assistant and worked in that capacity on numerous productions, including *Goodbye Mr. Chips, The Fallen Idol, The Third Man,* and *Richard III.* He was camera operator on *The Guns of Navarone* and *Lolita.* As a lighting cameraman from 1962, he created fine black-and-white and color images for many British and some American productions of the 60s and 70s. He shared an Academy Award for the special visual effects of *Superman* (1978).

FILMS INCLUDE: *A Kind of Loving* 1962; *The Mind Benders, Billy Liar, This Sporting Life* 1963; *King and Country* 1964; *One-Way Pendulum, Bunny Lake Is Missing* 1965; *The Double Man* 1967; *The Birthday Party* 1968; *My Side of the Mountain* (US/Can.) 1969; *The Executioner, Ryan's Daughter* (2nd-unit phot. only) 1970; *10 Rillington Place* 1971; *The Little Ark* (US/Hol.), *Asylum* 1972; *The Vault of Horror* 1973; *Rosebud* (US), *Inserts* (US) 1975; *Superman* (process phot. only; US) 1978; *Venom* 1982.

Cooper, Ben. Actor. Born on Sept. 30, 1930, in Hartford, Conn. *ed.* Columbia. Baby-faced leading man and second lead of Hollywood films, mostly Westerns, after juvenile experience on stage and radio and in TV.

FILMS INCLUDE: *Side Street* 1950; *Thunderbirds* 1952; *The Woman They Almost Lynched, Sea of Lost Ships* 1953; *Johnny Guitar* 1954; *The Last Command, The Eternal Sea, The Rose Tattoo, Headline Hunters* 1955; *A Strange Adventure* 1956; *Duel at Apache Wells, Outlaw's Son* 1957; *The Chartroose Caboose* 1960; *Gunfight at Comanche Creek* 1963; *Arizona Raiders* 1965; *Waco* 1966; *Red Tomahawk* 1967; *One More Train to Rob, Support Your Local Gunfighter* 1971.

Cooper, Chris. Actor. *b.* Christopher W. Cooper, July 9, 1951, in Kansas City, Mo. *ed.* University of Missouri. Known primarily for his impressive, subdued acting style in many of acclaimed independent producer-director John SAYLE's films, this theatrically trained actor has developed a successful career far from the mainstream of celebrity and Hollywood. Respected and admired for his roles in *Matewan* (1987) and more recently in *Lone Star* (1996), Cooper stays close to the stage and chooses his film and television roles with care. He is married to actress-writer Marianne Leone.

FILMS: *Bad Timing* 1980; *Matewan* 1987; *City of Hope, Guilty By Suspicion* 1991; *This Boy's Life* 1993; *Money Train* 1995; *Lone Star, A Time to Kill* 1996; *Great Expectations* 1997.

Cooper, Gary. Actor. *b.* Frank James Cooper, May 7, 1901, Helena, Montana. *d.* 1961. The son of a Montana state supreme court justice, he received his elementary schooling in England, later attending Wesleyan College, an agricultural school, in Montana and Grinnell College in Iowa. After graduation, he worked briefly as a guide at Yellowstone National Park and began submitting political cartoons to his hometown newspaper, the Helena *Independent.* In 1924, Cooper set out for California, hoping to become a cartoonist for a Los Angeles newspaper. Instead he found himself a door-to-door salesman for a photographer and space salesman for theater curtain advertising. In 1925 he was introduced by friends to Hollywood casting directors and began playing cowboy extras in Westerns. During 1925 and early 1926 he appeared briefly in many films, including *The Thundering Herd, Wild Horse Mesa, The Vanishing American, The Eagle,* and *The Enchanted Hill.* He also played heavies in several two-reelers. His big break came in 1926, when he was cast as a last-minute replacement for the second lead in Goldwyn's *The Winning of Barbara Worth,* starring Ronald COLMAN and Vilma BANKY.

The film was a big box-office hit and it started Cooper on his way to becoming one of Hollywood's all-time great stars. Tall, handsome, and laconic, with a shy smile and a hesitant delivery, he had an immediate appeal to both male and female audiences and steadily moved to the top. In the eyes of millions the world over he came to personify the strong, silent American, a man of action and few words. At first taken lightly by the critics, he received more press coverage for his romantic escapades (Clara Bow, Lupe Velez, Evelyn Brent, etc.) than for his acting in films. But he soon settled down, married socialite Veronica Balfe, who had briefly appeared in films as Sandra Shaw, and gradually developed a natural aptitude for screen acting. By the mid-30s he was generally accepted as a capable performer.

His physique and nonchalant manner had been effective from the start in romantic and adventure films. Now his slightly awkward mannerisms and delayed reactions also proved to be perfect assets for screen comedy, under the guidance of such directors as LUBITSCH and CAPRA. But above all, he remained most closely identified with his roles as a man of the American West. The diversity of his roles was reflected in two of his Oscar nominations: *Mr. Deeds Goes to Town* (1936), and *The Pride of the Yankees* (1942). He won his first Academy Award, as well as the New York Film Critics Award, for *Sergeant York* (1941).

Cooper received another Oscar in 1952 for *High Noon,* perhaps his most memorable film, and received a Special

Academy Award in the 1960 ceremony, held in April of 1961, "for his many memorable screen performances and the international recognition he, as an individual, has gained for the motion picture industry." His close friend, James Stewart, accepted this last award in Cooper's behalf with tears in his eyes. He had just learned, along with a few other Cooper intimates, that the beloved star was suffering from incurable cancer. On May 13, 1961, about one month later, Gary Cooper died at 60.

FEATURE FILMS (excluding some 30 appearances as extra): *The Winning of Barbara Worth* 1926; *It, Children of Divorce, Arizona Bound, Wings, Nevada, The Last Outlaw* 1927; *Beau Sabreur, The Legion of the Condemned, Doomsday, Half a Bride, Lilac Time, The First Kiss, The Shopworn Angel* 1928; *Wolf Song, Betrayal, The Virginian* 1929; *Only the Brave, Paramount on Parade, The Texan, Seven Days Leave, A Man from Wyoming, The Spoilers, Morocco* 1930; *Fighting Caravans, City Streets, I Take This Woman, His Woman* 1931; *Make Me a Star* (cameo), *Devil and the Deep, If I Had a Million, A Farewell to Arms* 1932; *Today We Live, One Sunday Afternoon, Design for Living, Alice in Wonderland* (as the White Knight) 1933; *Operator 13, Now and Forever* 1934; *The Wedding Night, The Lives of a Bengal Lancer, Peter Ibbetson* (title role) 1935; *Desire, Mr. Deeds Goes to Town, Hollywood Boulevard* (cameo), *The General Died at Dawn* 1936; *The Plainsman* (as Wild Bill Hickok), *Souls at Sea* 1937; *The Adventures of Marco Polo* (title role), *Bluebeard's Eighth Wife, The Cowboy and the Lady* 1938; *Beau Geste* (title role), *The Real Glory* 1939; *The Westerner, North West Mounted Police* 1940; *Meet John Doe, Sergeant York* (title role) 1941; *Ball of Fire, The Pride of the Yankees* (as Lou Gehrig) 1942; *For Whom the Bell Tolls* 1943; *The Story of Dr. Wassell* (title role), *Casanova Brown* 1944; *Along Came Jones* (also prod.), *Saratoga Trunk* 1945; *Cloak and Dagger* 1946; *Unconquered, Variety Girl* (cameo) 1947; *Good Sam* 1948; *The Fountainhead, It's a Great Feeling* (cameo), *Task Force* 1949; *Bright Leaf, Dallas* 1950; *You're in the Navy Now/USS Teakettle, Starlift* (cameo), *Distant Drums, It's a Big Country* 1951; *High Noon, Springfield Rifle* 1952; *Return to Paradise, Blowing Wild* 1953; *Garden of Evil, Vera Cruz* 1954; *The Court-Martial of Billy Mitchell* (as Gen. Billy Mitchell) 1955; *Friendly Persuasion* 1956; *Love in the Afternoon* 1957; *Ten North Frederick, Man of the West* 1958; *The Hanging Tree, Alias Jesse James* (cameo), *They Came to Cordura, The Wreck of the Mary Deare* 1959; *The Naked Edge* (UK) 1961.

Cooper, Dame Gladys. Actress. *b.* Dec. 18, 1888, Lewisham, London, England. *d.* 1971. A chorine at 16, she became famous for her delicate beauty and was the foremost pinup girl during WW I. In the early 20s she achieved stardom on the legitimate British stage and managed London's Playhouse Theatre. She appeared occasionally in silent British films from 1913, but her major screen career began in 1940 in Hollywood, where for three decades she played distinguished character roles exemplifying British dignity. She was three times nominated for an Academy Award, for *Now Voyager* (1942), *The Song of Bernadette* (1943), and *My Fair Lady* (1964). She also appeared in the TV series 'The Rogues' (1964). Her third husband was actor Philip Merivale. Autobiography: *Gladys Cooper* (1931).

FILMS: In the UK—*The Eleventh Commandment* 1913; *Dandy Donovan, The Gentleman Cracksman* 1914; *The Real Thing at Last, The Sorrows of Satan* 1916; *Masks and Faces, My Lady's Dress* 1917; *Unmarried* 1920; *The Bohemian Girl* 1922; *Bonnie Prince Charlie* 1923; *The Iron Duke* 1934. In the US—*Rebecca, Kitty Foyle* 1940; *That Hamilton Woman* (as Lady Nelson), *The Black Cat* 1941; *This Above All, Eagle Squadron, Now Voyager* 1942; *Forever and a Day, Mr. Lucky, Princess O'Rourke, The Song of Bernadette* 1943; *The White Cliffs of Dover, Mrs. Parkington* 1944; *The Valley of Decision, Love Letters* 1945; *The Green Years, The Cockeyed Miracle, Beware of Pity* (UK) 1946; *Green Dolphin Street, The Bishop's Wife* 1947; *Homecoming, The Pirate* 1948; *The Secret Garden, Madame Bovary* 1949; *Thunder on the Hill* 1951; *At Sword's Point* 1952; *The Man Who Loved Redheads* (UK) 1955; *Separate Tables* 1958; *The List of Adrian Messenger* 1963; *My Fair Lady* 1964; *The Happiest Millionaire* 1967; *A Nice Girl Like Me* (UK) 1969.

Cooper, Jackie. Actor. Born John Cooper, Jr., on Sept. 15, 1921, in Los Angeles. A nephew of film director Norman TAUROG, he began appearing in Bobby Clark and Lloyd Hamilton comedies at three and later was in eight episodes of the "Our Gang" series. During the 30s he was one of Hollywood's most popular child stars, making audiences cry and laugh at his mishaps and antics in a long succession of tearjerkers. He was nominated for best actor Academy Award for his performance in *Skippy* (1930), which was directed by his uncle. He was teamed with Wallace BEERY in several successful films, notably *The Champ* (1931), *The Bowery* (1933), and *Treasure Island* (1934).

Cooper's career declined in the early 40s, and after WW II service he attempted a comeback in B films, then tried summer stock and Broadway, later touring with the national company of 'Mr. Roberts' as Ensign Pulver. He finally launched a highly successful career on TV, starring in the series 'The People's Choice' (1955–58) and 'Hennessey' (1959–62) and becoming an Emmy Award–winning director and executive producer. In 1972 he made his debut as film director with *Stand Up and Be Counted.*

FILMS INCLUDE: *Fox Movietone Follies, Sunny Side Up* 1929; *Skippy, Donovan's Kid, The Champ, Sooky* 1931; *When a Feller Needs a Friend, Divorce in the Family* 1932; *Broadway to Hollywood, The Bowery* 1933; *Lone Cowboy, Treasure Island, Peck's Bad Boy* 1934; *Dinky, O'Shaughnessy's Boy* 1935; *Tough Guy, The Devil Is a Sissy* 1936; *Boy of the Streets* 1937; *White Banners, Gangster's Boy, That Certain Age, Newsboys' Home* 1938; *Scouts to the Rescue* (serial), *Spirit of Culver, Streets of New York, Two Bright Boys, What a Life!, The Big Guy* 1939; *Seventeen, The Return of Frank James, Gallant Sons* 1940; *Life with Henry, Ziegfeld Girl, Her First Beau, Glamour Boy* 1941; *Syncopation, Men of Texas, The Navy Comes Through* 1942; *Where Are Your Children?* 1944; *Stork Bites Man, Kilroy Was Here* 1947; *French Leave* 1948; *Everything's Ducky* 1961; *The Love Machine* 1971; *Stand Up and Be Counted* (dir. only) 1972; *Chosen Survivors* 1974; *Superman* 1978; *Superman II* 1980; *Superman III* 1983; *Superman IV: The Quest for Peace, Surrender* 1987.

Cooper, Melville. Actor. *b.* Oct. 15, 1896, Birmingham, England. *d.* 1973. He made his stage debut in 1914 at Stratford-on-Avon, his British film debut in 1934. In Hollywood from 1936, he played numerous character parts of great versatility, often droll, from butlers and crooks to officers and gentlemen. Pudgy and thoroughly unromantic, he played his most memorable part in *Pride and Prejudice,* as the ridiculously pompous Mr. Collins who woos the heroine, Greer Garson.

FILMS INCLUDE: In the UK—*The Calendar/Bachelor's Folly* 1931; *The Private Life of Don Juan* 1934; *The Scarlet Pimpernel* 1935. In the US—*The Gorgeous Hussy* 1936; *The Last of Mrs. Cheyney, Thin Ice, Tovarich* 1937; *The Adventures of Robin Hood* (as the Sheriff of Nottingham), *Dawn Patrol* 1938; *The Sun Never Sets* 1939; *Rebecca, Pride and Prejudice, Too Many Husbands* 1940; *Scotland Yard, The Lady Eve, The Flame of New Orleans* 1941; *This Above All, Random Harvest,*

Life Begins at Eight-Thirty 1942; *The Immortal Sergeant, Holy Matrimony* 1943; *13 Rue Madeleine* 1947; *Enchantment* 1948; *The Red Danube* 1949; *Love Happy, Father of the Bride* 1950; *It Should Happen to You* 1954; *Moonfleet, The King's Thief* 1955; *Around the World in 80 Days* 1956; *The Story of Mankind* 1957; *From the Earth to the Moon* 1958.

Cooper, Merian C. Director, producer. *b.* Oct. 24, 1893, Jacksonville, Fla. *d.* 1973. The son of a lawyer who later became chairman of Florida's Federal Reserve Board, he was adventure-prone from childhood, spending a good deal of his time training to improve his skills in boxing, wrestling, and swimming, and dreaming of becoming a daring explorer. At 18, he entered Annapolis as a cadet but for some reason resigned during his graduating year and became a merchant marine. Following an interlude as a newspaperman in Minneapolis, Des Moines, and St. Louis, he joined the Georgia National Guard and participated in Mexican border expeditions against Pancho Villa. Transferring to the infantry, then the Aviation Corps, he trained as a pilot and caught the tail end of WW I as an aerial observer over German lines. Shot down twice, he was a badly burned prisoner of war in a German hospital when the armistice was declared. After his release and recovery, he stayed in Europe and became involved in the activities of the American Relief Association. Moved by the plight of the Poles, who were battling incursions by Red Army Bolsheviks, he joined the Kosciusko Squadron, a ten-man volunteer American aerial unit of the Polish Air Force. Again shot down, he was captured by Russian Cossacks and spent nearly a year in jails and forced-labor camps. He finally escaped in April of 1921 and made his way to Warsaw, where he was decorated for exceptional bravery by President Pilsudski.

Returning to New York, he became a reporter for the *Daily News,* then a feature writer for the *New York Times.* But his penchant for adventure soon caused him to quit and offer his services as a first officer on a schooner bound for an around-the-world expedition to record strange places and customs for articles, books, and films. When the expedition's cameraman quit, Cooper cabled Ernest B. SCHOEDSACK, a rangy newsreel daredevil he had met in postwar Europe. Together, they shot exotic rare footage in Ethiopia and the pilgrimage to Mecca, which they intended to incorporate into a feature-length film. But the negatives went up in flames when their ship caught fire. Undaunted, they returned to New York to raise money and with Marguerite Harrison, an adventurous sponsor, set off to Arabistan (later Khuzistan) in southwest Persia (now Iran), where they joined the annual summer migration of 50,000 feudal Bakhtiari tribesmen and their half million grazing livestock across the formidable Zardeh Kuh mountain range, sharing with the natives the hardships of the hegira. The result of their travails was *Grass* (1925), a remarkable, though flawed, feature-length documentary that caused a sensation when Paramount released it in movie theaters. Cooper wrote a diary of the expedition, also titled *Grass.* Encouraged by their success, and now financed by Paramount's Jesse Lasky, Cooper and Schoedsack next collaborated on *Chang* (1927), a fictionalized documentary they filmed for nearly two years in the jungles of northern Siam (now Thailand). Focusing on the hazardous lives of a tribal family and its survival battle against tigers, leopards, and rampaging elephants, the film was a spectacular box-office success. The elephant stampede sequence was projected in Magnascope, an image-magnifying system that was used to highlight climactic scenes of major films of the period. Clips from the stampede and other action footage would for many years show up in Hollywood jungle films. The influence of *Chang* on famous jungle pictures like *Trader Horn* and *Tarzan the Ape Man* was considerable.

Cooper and Schoedsack next tried their hand at a fiction feature, enjoying critical success with their version of the Empire-building adventure, *Four Feathers* (1929), which they shot partly on location in Sudan and Tanganyika. Cooper then took leave from the film business to return to his first love, the airplane. He invested his movie profits in the fledgling airline industry and became one of the first stockholders and directors of Western Airlines and Pan American Airways. In his leisure time he began developing the outline of the story that would provide the basis for *King Kong* (1933), perhaps the most famous adventure picture of all time. After failing to persuade MGM and Paramount to sponsor his project, Cooper found a responsive ear at RKO, a studio he joined early in 1931 as an executive assistant to production chief David O. SELZNICK. While producing the thriller classic *The Most Dangerous Game* (1932), Cooper met Willis O'BRIEN, a model animation and special effects wizard whose ideas and skills would become instrumental in creating and putting into believable motion the mechanical gorilla who would be climbing the Empire State Building in the memorable climax of *King Kong.* Combining innovative technical feats with exhilarating thrills, a memorable music score, and a simple-minded but captivating story which could best be described as a variation on the Beauty and the Beast fairy tale, *King Kong* proved an immediate hit at the box office, returning $5 million in North American rentals on a $650,000 investment. The film went on to become a classic of its genre and part of American culture and folklore. *King Kong* was Cooper's last film as a director. After its completion in 1933, he succeeded Selznick as vice president in charge of production at RKO. In 1936 he became vice president of Selznick International Pictures.

During WW II, Cooper served as a colonel with the US Army Air Corps and was chief of staff to General Claire Chennault in China. Cooper retired from the service as a US Air Force brigadier general. In 1947 he formed Argosy Pictures with John FORD and co-produced several of the director's films. He is the author of several books, including *The Sea Gypsy, Grass, Under the White Eagle, Things Men Die For,* and *King Kong.* In 1952 he co-produced the first Cinerama presentation, *This Is Cinerama.* The same year he received a special Academy Award "for his many innovations and contributions to the art of motion pictures." He was married to actress Dorothy JORDAN.

FILMS INCLUDE: Documentaries—*The Lost Empire/In Quest of the Golden Prince* (title writer, editor) 1924; *Grass/Grass: A Nation's Battle for Life/Grass: The Epic of a Lost Tribe* (co-prod., co-dir. with Ernest B. Schoedsack and Marguerite Harrison; co-phot. with Schoedsack; also personal appearance) 1925; *Chang* (doc. drama; co-prod., co-dir. with Schoedsack) 1927; *Gow the Head Hunter* (co-phot. with Schoedsack) 1928. Fiction feature films as producer-director—*The Four Feathers* (co-prod. with Schoedsack; co-dir. with Schoedsack and Lothar Mendes; also co-phot.), *King Kong* (co-prod., co-dir. with Schoedsack; also co-sc.) 1933. Features as producer or executive producer, alone or in collaboration—*The Most Dangerous Game, The Phantom of Crestwood* 1932; *Son of Kong, Lucky Devils, Morning Glory, Ann Vickers, Little Women, Flying Down to Rio* 1933; *The Lost Patrol, The Crime Doctor* 1934; *She, The Last Days of Pompeii* 1935; *The Toy Wife* 1938; *The Fugitive* 1947; *Fort Apache* 1948; *Three Godfathers, She Wore a Yellow Ribbon, Mighty Joe Young* 1949; *Wagonmaster, Rio Grande* 1950; *The Quiet Man, This Is Cinerama* 1952; *The Sun Shines Bright* 1953; *The Searchers* 1956; *The Best of Cinerama* 1963.

Cooper, Miriam. Actress. *b.* 1891, Baltimore. *d.* 1976. *ed.* Cooper Union. Expressive, dark-eyed star of early Hollywood silents. Played leading roles in D. W. GRIFFITH's *Home Sweet*

Home, The Birth of a Nation (as Margaret Cameron), and *Intolerance* (as the Friendless One in the modern story), and starred in many films directed by Raoul WALSH, her husband from 1916 to 1926. She retired from the screen in 1924 and for several decades lived on her alimony and the considerable income she had earned as a star. But she spent her final years in poverty and obscurity in Charlottesville, Va. In 1974, two years before her death, she published an autobiography, *Dark Lady of the Silents* (1973).

FILMS INCLUDE: *A Blot in the 'Scrutcheon, Battle of Pottsburg Bridge, The Drummer Girl of Vicksburg, The Girl in the Caboose, The Pony Express Girl* 1912; *The Turning Point, The Farm Bully* 1913; *The Stolen Radium, Home Sweet Home, The Dishonored Medal, The Gunman, The Odalisque* 1914; *The Birth of a Nation, The Burned Hand* 1915; *Intolerance* 1916; *The Honor System, The Silent Lie, The Innocent Sinner, Betrayed* 1917; *The Woman and the Law, The Prussian Cur* 1918; *Evangeline, Should a Husband Forgive?* 1919; *The Deep Purple* 1920; *The Oath, Serenade* 1921; *Kindred of the Dust* 1922; *Her Accidental Husband, The Girl Who Came Back, Daughters of the Rich, Is Money Everything?, The Broken Wing* 1923; *After the Ball* 1924.

Cooper, Wilkie. Director of photography. Born on Oct. 19, 1911, in London. Entered British films as a child actor and at age 15 switched to the camera department. Worked his way up through various stages to lighting cameraman by the mid-30s. He has since worked on many British and some Hollywood productions. Married to actress Peggy Bryan.

FILMS INCLUDE: *Conquest of the Air* (co-phot.; release delayed to 1940) 1936; *Trunk Crime/Design for Murder* 1939; *Ships with Wings* 1941; *The Big Blockade, The Foreman Went to France/Somewhere in France* 1942; *Went the Day Well?/48 Hours, My Learned Friend* 1943; *Champagne Charlie, Fiddlers Three* 1944; *The Rake's Progress/Notorious Gentleman* 1945; *I See a Dark Stranger/The Adventuress, Green for Danger* 1946; *Captain Boycott, Mine Own Executioner* 1947; *London Belongs to Me/Dulcimer Street* 1948; *The Hasty Heart* 1949; *Stage Fright* 1950; *The Long Dark Hall* 1951; *Sea Devils* 1953; *Svengali* 1954; *Geordie/Wee Geordie* 1955; *Seven Waves Away/Abandon Ship, The Admirable Crichton* 1957; *The 7th Voyage of Sinbad* 1958; *I Aim at the Stars, The Three Worlds of Gulliver* 1960; *Mysterious Island* 1961; *Mouse on the Moon, Jason and the Argonauts* 1963; *One Million Years B.C.* 1966; *Hammerhead* (co-phot.) 1968; *Cromwell* (2nd unit) 1970; *Please Sir!* 1972.

Coote, Robert. Actor. *b.* Feb. 4, 1909, London, *d.* 1982. *ed.* Hurstpierpoint Coll., Sussex, UK. On the stage from age 16, he appeared in England, South Africa, and Australia before arriving in Hollywood in the late 30s. Played pompous Englishmen in many films, with time out for WW II service as a squadron leader with the Canadian Air Force. Played Colonel Pickering in the original Broadway cast of 'My Fair Lady.' In the mid-60s he appeared in the TV series 'The Rogues.'

FILMS INCLUDE: *Sally in Our Alley* (UK) 1931; *Loyalties* (UK) 1933; *A Yank at Oxford* (US-UK) 1938; *Gunga Din* 1939; *You Can't Fool Your Wife* 1940; *The Commandoes Strike at Dawn* 1942; *A Matter of Life and Death/Stairway to Heaven* (UK) 1946; *The Ghost and Mrs. Muir, Forever Amber* 1947; *Bonnie Prince Charlie* (UK), *The Three Musketeers* (as Aramis), *Berlin Express* 1948; *The Red Danube* 1949; *The Elusive Pimpernel* (UK) 1950; *The Desert Fox* 1951; *The Prisoner of Zenda, Scaramouche, Othello* (as Roderigo) 1952; *The Swan* 1956; *The Horse's Mouth* (UK), *Merry Andrew* 1958; *The League of Gentlemen* (UK) 1960; *A Man Could Get Killed, The Swinger* 1966; *The Cool Ones* 1967; *Prudence and the Pill* 1968; *Kenner* 1969; *Theatre of Blood* (UK) 1973.

Copland, Aaron. Composer. *b.* Nov. 14, 1900, Brooklyn, N.Y. *d.* 1990. The distinguished composer of 'Appalachian Spring,' 'Billy the Kid,' 'Rodeo,' and countless other musical works. Widely extolled as the Dean of American Music, he also scored several films, notably *The Heiress,* for which he won a 1949 Academy Award.

FILMS INCLUDE: *The City, Of Mice and Men* 1939; *Our Town* 1940; *North Star* 1943; *Fiesta* (orig. suite) 1947; *The Red Pony, The Heiress* 1949; *Something Wild* 1961; *Love and Money* 1982.

Coppola, Francis Ford. Director, screenwriter. Born on Apr. 7, 1939, in Detroit. His parents were Carmine Coppola (*b.* June 11, 1910, New York City; *d.* 1991), the first flute of the NBC Symphony Orchestra under Toscanini, and the former Italia Pennino, who once acted in Italian films. He grew up in the New York borough of Queens, where he developed an early interest in amateur filmmaking. He made his first film with an 8 mm camera at age ten, after recovering from a year-long bout with polio. While studying drama at Hofstra College he wrote the book and lyrics for a couple of school-produced musicals, but returned to his first love, the movies, at the film department of UCLA. While there, he tried for an early entry into the commercial market in 1961 with *Tonight for Sure,* a soft-core, rather dull-witted "nudie" film he produced and directed. Nothing about this poorly made color feature could foretell the future of Coppola as one of the leading directors of American cinema. Also at UCLA, he wrote a screenplay, *Pilma Pilma,* which won a Samuel Goldwyn Award in 1962 but was never produced.

It was through his association with Roger CORMAN that Coppola made his breakthrough. After helping the producer-director in various capacities on a number of films (see credits listing below), he was awarded with the opportunity to direct a low-budget horror film, *Dementia 13* (1963), which he made in Ireland. He married the film's set decorator, Eleanor Neil, that same year. But four more years were to elapse before he directed his next film, *You're a Big Boy Now* (1967), which he presented as his M.F.A. thesis at UCLA. This zestful, lighthearted film looked much better than its low budget allowed, partly because many on the crew and actors volunteered their time. (Between these first two films, Coppola had collaborated on a number of scripts and performed other production work.) On the strength of his success with this latter film, Coppola was entrusted with the direction of an expensive Hollywood musical, *Finian's Rainbow* (1968). The film failed, as did Coppola's next production, *The Rain People* (1969).

In 1969, with the financial backing of Warner Bros., Coppola established American Zoetrope, a small production facility, in a San Francisco warehouse. He appointed as vice president a promising filmmaker named George LUCAS. They hoped to shape the studio into a springboard for other young directors. The plan never materialized. After only one film, Lucas's *THX–1138,* Coppola found himself on the verge of bankruptcy, $300,000 in debt. But he bounced back the following year, sharing the Academy Award for the script of *Patton,* and in 1972 he directed *The Godfather,* one of the biggest moneymakers of all time and winner of the best picture Academy Award. A masterful operatic-scale epic of the dark world of a Mafia family, *The Godfather* remains widely acclaimed as of one of the great American films of all time, a mythic portrayal of family ties and the ruthlessness of business.

The following year he produced, but did not direct, another success, *American Graffiti,* and in 1974 he reached a peak of achievement with two films, *The Conversation,* a taut and intelligent inner view of the surveillance business, which won him high critical praise, and *The Godfather, Part II,* a sequel that unexpectedly matched (and some say surpassed) its predecessor in style and dramatic impact. Interweaving the story of two generations of the Corleone family, it deepened the first film's thematic concerns, exploring immigrant ambition and the insidiousness of a powerful man's moral decay. The film won seven Academy Awards, two of which went to Coppola personally, for best picture, best director, and best screenplay, the latter in collaboration with author Mario Puzo. Later that decade, Coppola supervised the television repackaging of the two *Godfather* films as *The Godfather Saga*, a chronological reordering and expansion of the story that garnered praise in its own right.

In 1975, Coppola devoted much of his energies to the publishing of a San Francisco magazine, *City,* which folded the following year. He sunk more of his money into expanding American Zoetrope, then mortgaged everything else he owned to cover the mounting costs of his next ambitious project. The production of *Apocalypse Now,* a compelling odyssey of the war in Vietnam, patterned after Joseph Conrad's *Heart of Darkness,* was fraught with every imaginable disaster. Logistical mishaps, serious illnesses, and a destructive typhoon played havoc with the shooting schedule on location in the Philippines, stretching it to 16 arduous months and bloating the original budget of $12 million to more than $30 million. Eleanor Coppola described the madness of it all in her diary-style book *Notes* (1979), and the story was later the subject of the documentary *Hearts of Darkness: A Filmmaker's Apocalypse* (1991). With some reservations, *Apocalypse Now* met with a chorus of approval and had surprising box-office appeal. It tied for the Palme d'Or at the 1979 Cannes film festival and won two Oscars.

His reputation enhanced and his financial health partly restored, Francis Coppola (he had dropped his middle name back in 1977) now focused on forging American Zoetrope into a full-scale production factory on studio property he acquired in Los Angeles. But he soon ran into deep financial difficulties, resulting mostly from the folly of *One from the Heart* (1982), a visually lavish, but empty stylistic exercise that proved a fiasco with critics and audiences alike. Coppola's financial state was further weakened by *The Cotton Club* (1984), a musically rich gangster film set in Harlem in the 20s; this film was another production nightmare and box-office disappointment. Coppola was forced to assume huge personal debts; American Zoetrope (later Zoetrope Studios) filed for Chapter 11 bankruptcy in 1990.

Coppola continued to direct smaller films presenting different facets of American experience; many received critical praise, though not on the same scale as the *Godfather* films. *The Outsiders* and *Rumble Fish* (both 1983) were interesting, if overly stylized, adaptations of two youth novels by S. E. Hinton. Some critics considered *Peggy Sue Got Married* (1986) one of his best films, a deceptively light, elegiac story of a woman time-traveling to her teenage past. *Gardens of Stone* (1987) was a well-acted drama about the American homefront during the Vietnam War. *Tucker: The Man and His Dream* (1988) was a lush 40s period piece about real-life car manufacturer Preston Tucker, whom Coppola presents as an icon of American entrepeneurship challenging the establishment.

In 1990, Coppola reached back to the roots of his earlier triumphs, unveiling the third part of *The Godfather* saga. While neither as flawless in execution nor as commercially successful as its predecessors, *The Godfather Part III* was critically well received. Rounding out the story of crime boss Michael Corleone (played in all three films by Al Pacino), the film shows how his hunger for redemption is overwhelmed by the weight of his past. The film earned Academy Award nominations for best picture and for Coppola as director.

As a producer, Coppola helped develop many major young talents of the American screen, both behind and in front of the cameras. He also supported the production of works by veteran artists, like Kurosawa's *Kagemusha* (1980). In 1981 he produced the triumphant Radio City Music Hall screenings of Abel Gance's 1927 silent masterpiece *Napoleon.* Francis's father, Carmine Coppola, composed and conducted the grand score for the presentation, as well as for several of his son's films. In the 90s, Francis Coppola mounted an ambitious new cycle of classic horror films. He directed and produced the first of these, *Bram Stoker's Dracula* (1992), an imaginative reworking of the old vampire story that some found rich and stylish and others overstuffed.

Over the years Francis Coppola has teetered between success and disaster, often rising like a phoenix from the ashes every time his career seems doomed. He remains one of America's most creative, if erratic, filmmakers, his place in motion picture history secured by the *Godfather* films. He continues to work frequently with his family: in addition to Carmine's contributions, his sister, Talia SHIRE, his cousin, Nicolas CAGE, and his daughter, Sofia Coppola, have appeared in his films. His son, Gian Carlo, was killed in 1986 in a Maryland boating accident, which also involved Ryan O'Neal's son, while Coppola was filming *Gardens of Stone.*

FILMS: *Tonight for Sure!* (dir., sc., prod.) 1961; *The Playgirls and the Bellboy/The Bellboy and the Playgirls* (dir., sc. of addnl. sequences for US re-edited vers. of 1958 West German film *Mit Eva fing die Sünde an*), *Premature Burial* (asst. dir.), *The Magic Voyage of Sinbad* (adapt. English vers. of 1953 Soviet film *Sadko*), *Tower of London* (dial. dir.) 1962; *Battle Beyond the Sun* (adapt. English vers. of '59 Soviet film *Nebo Zovyot*), *The Young Racers* (sound; 2nd-unit dir.), *The Terror* (assoc. prod.; 2nd-unit dir.), *Dementia 13/The Haunted and the Hunted* (dir., sc.) 1963; *This Property Is Condemned* (co-sc.), *Paris brule-t-til?/Is Paris Burning?* (co-sc.) 1966; *You're a Big Boy Now* (dir., sc.) 1967; *The Wild Racers* (2nd-unit dir.), *Finian's Rainbow* (dir.) 1968; *The Rain People* (dir., sc. from own story, 'Echoes') 1969; *Patton* (co-sc.) 1970; *THX–1138* (exec. prod.) 1971; *The Godfather* (dir. co-sc.) 1972; *American Graffiti* (exec. prod.) 1973; *The Conversation* (dir. sc., co-prod.), *The Godfather Part II* (dir. co-sc. co-prod.), *The Great Gatsby* (sc.) 1974; *The Black Stallion* (exec. prod.), *Apocalypse Now* (dir., co-sc. co-prod., co-music) 1979; *Kagemusha* (co-exec. prod.) 1980; *The Escape Artist* (co-exec. prod.), *One from the Heart* (dir., co-sc.), *Hammett* (co-exec. prod.) 1982; *The Black Stallion Returns* (exec. prod.), *The Outsiders* (dir.), *Rumble Fish* (dir., co-sc.) 1983; *The Cotton Club* (dir., co-sc.) 1984; *Mishima* (co-exec. prod.) 1985; *Peggy Sue Got Married* (dir.) 1986; *Gardens of Stone* (dir., co-prod.), *Lionheart* (co-exec. prod.), *Tough Guys Don't Dance* (co-exec. prod.) 1987; *Tucker: The Man and His Dream* (dir.) 1988; *New York Stories* (dir co-sc. "Life Without Zoe" episode) 1989; *The Godfather Part III* (dir., prod., co-sc.) 1990; *Bram Stoker's Dracula* (dir., co-prod.) 1992; *Mary Shelly's Frankenstein* (co-prod. only); *Don Juan DeMarco* (exec. prod. only) 1995; *Jack* 1996.

Coppola, Talia. See SHIRE, Talia.

co-production. A collaboration between producers in two or more countries resulting in the production of a film or group of films, often in two or more language versions. The practice proliferated in Europe immediately after WW II, when neighboring countries began pooling their financial resources and artistic talent in an effort to widen the markets for their films. Co-productions are commonplace today. In addition to the advantages of increased capital and larger viewing audiences, the system enables producers in one country to enjoy various monetary incentives offered by governments of other countries for the encouragement of local production, such as financing and tax exemptions, as well as, in some countries, comparatively cheap labor.

copter mount. A camera platform that is attached to a helicopter for aerial shots. It protects the camera from excessive vibrations during flight. Also known by the trade name Tyler Mount.

copy. A positive print made from a positive original, such as a reproduction of a reversal color film.

Corbett, Stanley. See CORBUCCI, Sergio.

Corbucci, Sergio. Director. *b.* 1926, in Rome. *d.* 1990. A former film critic, he entered the industry as an assistant director, graduating to director in the early 50s. His early films were melodramas and occasional comedies, but he later specialized in pseudohistorical spectacles and stylish spaghetti Westerns, sometimes using the pseudonym Stanley Corbett. He collaborated on many of his own scripts as well as several for films of other directors.

FILMS INCLUDE: *Salvate mia Figlia* 1951; *La Peccatrice dell'Isola/The Island Sinner* (also co-sc.) 1953; *I Due Marescialli/Two Colonels* (also co-sc.), *Romolo e Remo/Duel of the Titans* (also story, co-sc.), *Maciste contro il Vampiro/Goliath and the Vampires* (co-dir. with Giacomo Gentilomo; also co-sc.) 1961; *Il Figlio di Spartacus/The Slave* 1962; *Il Girono più Corto* (also co-sc.) 1963; *Minnesota Clay* (also co-sc.) 1965; *Django, Un Dollaro a Testa/Navajo Joe, Johnny Oro* 1966; *I Crudeli/The Hellbenders, Bersaglio Mobile* (also co-sc.) 1967; *Il Grande Silenzio* (also story, co-sc.), *Il Mercenario/The Mercenary* (also co-sc.), *Gli Specialisti* 1969; *Vamos a Matar Compañeros/Companeros* (also prod., co-sc.; Sp./It.) 1971; *Viva la Muerte. . . tua!* 1972; *Che e'entriamo noi con la Rivoluzione?* (also co-story, co-sc.), *La Banda J & S—Cronaca criminale del Far-West* (also co-story, co-sc.) 1973; *Tre Tigri contro Tre Tigri/The Con Arists* (co-dir., co-sc.), *Ecco noi per esempio* 1977; *La Mazzetta* 1978; *Giallo napoletano, Atti Atrocissima de Amore e di Vendetta* 1979; *Supersnooper/Super Fuzz* (also co-sc.) 1980.

Corby, Ellen. Actress. Born Ellen Hansen, on June 3, 1913, in Racine, Wis. After 12 years as a script girl she turned to acting. She has played scores of character roles from the mid-40s, typically as a fussy spinster or a busybody. Memorable as the lovelorn aunt in *I Remember Mama* (1948), a role for which she was nominated for an Academy Award. In the early 70s she was a regular on the TV series 'The Waltons,' (1972–79) for which she won three Emmy Awards.

FILMS INCLUDE: *The Dark Corner* 1946; *I Remember Mama* 1948; *Little Women, The Dark Past, Madame Bovary* 1949; *Caged, Harriet Craig* 1950; *The Mating Season* 1951; *The Big Trees* 1952; *Shane* 1953; *About Mrs. Leslie, Sabrina* 1954; *Illegal* 1955; *Macabre, Vertigo* 1958; *Visit to a Small Planet* 1960; *A Pocketful of Miracles* 1961; *The Caretaker* 1963; *The Strangler* 1964; *Hush Hush. . . Sweet Charlotte* 1965; *The Night of the Grizzly* 1966; *The Gnome-Mobile* 1967; *The Legend of Lylah Clare* 1968; *A Fine Pair* 1969; *Support Your Local Gunfighter* 1971; *Napoleon and Samantha* 1972.

Corday, Mara. Actress. Born Marilyn Watts, on Jan. 3, 1932, in Santa Monica, Calif. A former chorus girl and photographer's model, she played leading ladies and assorted sultry, often tempestuous "broads" in Hollywood films of the 50s, mostly low budget. Widow of actor Richard LONG.

FILMS INCLUDE: *Two Tickets to Broadway* 1951; *Sea Tiger* 1952; *The Lady Wants Mink* 1953; *Dawn at Socorro, So This Is Paris* 1954; *Tarantula, Man Without a Star, The Man from Bitter Ridge, Foxfire* 1955; *A Day of Fury, Raw Edge, The Naked Gun* 1956; *The Black Scorpion, The Giant Claw* 1957; *Girls on the Loose* 1958; *The Gauntlet* 1977; *Sudden Impact* 1983.

Corday, Paula. See CORDAY, Rita.

Corday, Rita (Paula). Actress. *b.* 1924, in Switzerland. *d.* 1992. Began her Hollywood career in 1943 as Rita Corday, changed the name to Paule Croset in 1947 and to Paula Corday in the early 50s. Under any name, she was not a very successful leading lady and soon retired from the screen. Married to producer Harold Nebenzal.

FILMS INCLUDE: *Hitler's Children, Mr. Lucky, The Falcon Strikes Back* 1943; *The Body Snatcher, The Falcon in San Francisco* 1945; *The Truth About Murder, Dick Tracy vs. Cueball, The Falcon's Alibi* 1946; *The Exile* 1947; *The Sword of Monte Cristo, Too Young to Kiss* 1951; *The Black Castle, You for Me* 1952; *The French Line* 1956.

Corey, Jeff. Actor. Born Aug. 10, 1914, in New York City. Worked as a sewing machine salesman before embarking on a stage acting career in the mid-30s. Played a wide range of character roles in Hollywood films of the 40s. A victim of blacklisting, he was absent from the screen for most of the 50s, a decade he devoted to establishing and running an acting school. He returned to films in the 60s in supporting roles of increased importance. He also appeared frequently on TV and directed many episodes of various series.

FILMS INCLUDE: *Third Finger, Left Hand* 1940; *All That Money Can Buy/The Devil and Daniel Webster* 1941; *Paris Calling, Roxie Hart* 1942; *The Moon Is Down, My Friend Flicka* 1943; *The Killers* 1946; *Brute Force, The Gangster* 1947; *Joan of Arc* 1948; *Home of the Brave* 1949; *Bright Leaf* 1950; *14 Hours, Only the Valiant* 1951; *Red Mountain* 1952; *The Balcony* 1963; *Lady in a Cage* 1964; *Mickey One, The Cincinnati Kid* 1965; *Seconds* 1966; *In Cold Blood* 1967; *The Boston Strangler* 1968; *True Grit, Butch Cassidy and the Sundance Kid* 1969; *Beneath the Planet of the Apes, Getting Straight, They Call Me Mr. Tibbs, Little Big Man* (as Wild Bill Hickok) 1970; *Shoot-Out, Catlow* 1971; *Paper Tiger* (UK) 1975; *The Premonition, The Last Tycoon* 1976; *Moonshine County Express, Oh God!* 1977; *The Wild Geese* (UK), *Jennifer* 1978; *Butch and Sundance: The Early Days* 1979; *Battle Beyond the Stars* 1980; *The Sword and the Sorcerer* 1982; *Conan the Destroyer* 1984; *Creator* 1985; *Messenger of Death* 1988; *Bird on a Wire* 1990; *Deception* 1993; *Color of Night, Surviving the Game* 1994.

Corey, Wendell. Actor. *b.* Mar. 20, 1914, in Dracut, Mass., the son of a Congregational minister. *d.* 1968. Made his first stage appearance as an amateur in 1934 and his professional debut the following year. He reached Broadway in 1942, and after scoring a success in the 1945 production of 'Dream Girl' was signed by producer Hal Wallis to a film contract. A versatile, dependable actor, but lacking heroic looks or charisma, he played leading roles in many films in the next two decades, usually straight, square, and upright, occasionally unsympathetic, at his best as a skeptic or cynic. He served as president of the Academy of Motion Picture Arts and Sciences and as a director of the Screen Actors Guild. In 1965 he was elected to the Santa Monica city council, but he failed in his bid for the Republican nomination for a congressional seat the following year.

FILMS: *Desert Fury* 1947; *I Walk Alone, Man-Eater of Kumaon, The Search, Sorry Wrong Number* 1948; *The Accused, Any Number Can Play, Holiday Affair* 1949; *Thelma Jordon/The File on Thelma Jordon, No Sad Songs for Me, The Furies, Harriet Craig* 1950; *The Great Missouri Raid* (as Frank James), *Rich Young and Pretty, The Wild Blue Yonder* 1951; *Carbine Williams, The Wild North, My Man and I* 1952; *Hell's Half Acre, Laughing Anne, Rear Window* 1954; *The Big Knife* 1955; *The*

Killer Is Loose, The Bold and the Brave, The Rack, The Rainmaker 1956; *Loving You* 1957; *The Light in the Forest* 1958; *Alias Jesse James* (as Jesse James) 1959; *Blood on the Arrow* 1964; *Agent for H.A.R.M., Waco, Picture Mommy Dead, Women of the Prehistoric Planet, Cyborg 2087* 1966; *Red Tomahawk* 1967; *Buckskin, The Astro-Zombies* 1968.

Corman, Roger. Director, producer. Born on Apr. 5, 1926, in Detroit. *ed.* Stanford U. (engineering); Oxford. After three years' service with the Navy, he joined 20th Century-Fox as a messenger boy, hoping somehow to break into films. Soon after, he became a story analyst for the company. He then left for England, where he spent a term at Oxford doing graduate work in English literature. Returning to Hollywood, he worked briefly as a literary agent. In 1953 he re-entered films as producer and screenwriter and in 1955 made his debut as director. He has since been one of Hollywood's most prolific filmmakers and by 1970 had completed some 45 films as producer-director and 30 additional films as producer or executive producer. He worked mostly for American International Pictures, a small, independent company known for its low-budget exploitation films.

Beginning with extremely low budgets, Corman tackled a wide array of genres, from Westerns and gangster films to science fiction and teenage hot-rod and rock movies. In 1957 alone he turned out nine films, some of which were completed in two or three days. In the early 60s he moved into somewhat larger budgets and slicker productions with a cycle of horror pictures based on the tales of Edgar Allan Poe. Most of these films, which were highly successful at the box office, were written by novelist Richard Matheson, designed by Daniel HALLER, and photographed by Floyd CROSBY, Murnau's veteran cameraman. They regularly starred Vincent PRICE and helped establish Corman's reputation as Hollywood's master of the macabre in the 60s.

Corman's cult following among film buffs is especially strong in France and in England. *The Masque of the Red Death* and *The Tomb of Ligeia,* both made in England in 1964, are considered the best examples of his horror style. A rare departure from the genre was *The Intruder* (1961), a personal statement by Corman on race relations in the South. In his capacity as producer, he helped develop promising young talent, including Francis Ford COPPOLA, Peter BOGDANOVICH, Martin SCORSESE, Jonathan DEMME, and Haller, his former art director and now a director. Several of Corman's films were produced by his brother Gene Corman (*b.* Sept. 24, 1927, Detroit), his partner in the New World Pictures company they established in 1970. Roger's wife, Julie Corman, also produces. Corman's hectic schedule slackened in the late 60s; by the early 70s he was active more as a producer and executive than as a director. He branched out into distribution, importing to the US such European films as Bergman's *Cries and Whispers* and Fellini's *Amarcord.* Corman appeared in some of his own films as well as in several made by others. One of his more substantial roles was that of a lawyer in Wim Wender's *The State of Things* (1982). In 1983 Corman sold New World to a group of investors for $17 million. He immediately set up another production company, Millenium. In 1984 he founded the New Horizons company to produce his films and in 1985 established the Concorde company as its distribution wing. In 1990 he returned to directing for the first time in nearly 20 years with *Frankenstein Unbound.* He is the subject of a feature-length documentary by Christian Blackwood, *Roger Corman—Hollywood's Wild Angel* (1978). Corman's 1990 autobiography is titled *How I Made a Hundred Movies in Hollywood and Never Lost a Dime.*

FILMS: As director-producer—*Five Guns West, Apache Woman* 1955; *The Day the World Ended, Swamp Women* (dir. only), *The Oklahoma Woman, Gunslinger, It Conquered the World* 1956; *Not of This Earth, The Undead, Naked Paradise/Thunder Over Hawaii, Attack of the Crab Monsters, Rock All Night, Teenage Doll, Carnival Rock, Sorority Girl, The Viking Women and the Sea Serpent* 1957; *War of the Satellites, The She Gods of Shark Reef* (dir. only), *Machine Gun Kelly, Teenage Caveman* 1958; *I Mobster, A Bucket of Blood, The Wasp Woman* 1959; *Ski Troop Attack, The House of Usher, The Little Shop of Horrors, The Last Woman on Earth* 1960; *Creature from the Haunted Sea, Atlas, The Pit and the Pendulum* 1961; *The Intruder, Premature Burial, Tales of Terror/Poe's Tales of Terror, Tower of London* (dir. only) 1962; *The Raven, The Terror, "X" the Man with the X-Ray Eyes, The Haunted Palace, The Young Racers* 1963; *The Secret Invasion* (dir. only), *The Masque of the Red Death* (UK/US), *The Tomb of Ligeia* 1964; *The Wild Angels* 1966; *The St. Valentine's Day Massacre, The Trip* 1967; *How to Make It* (dir. only) 1969; *Bloody Mama, Gās-s-s-s. . . or It May Become Necessary to Destroy the World in Order to Save It!* 1970; *Von Richtofen and Brown* (dir. only) 1971; *Frankenstein Unbound* (also co-sc.) 1990. As producer (partial list)—*Highway Dragnet* (co-prod., co-sc.) 1953; *Monster from the Ocean Floor* 1954; *The Beast with a Million Eyes* (exec. prod.) 1955; *Stakeout on Dope Street* (exec. prod.) 1958; *Crime and Punishment USA* (exec. prod.) 1959; *The Wild Ride* (exec. prod.) 1960; *Dementia 13/The Haunted and the Hunted* (US/Ire.; exec. prod.) 1963; *Blood Bath* (exec. prod.) 1966; *A Time for Killing* (co-prod.; also dir. some scenes, uncredited) 1967; *The Wild Racers* (exec. prod.), *Targets* (exec. prod.) 1968; *The Dunwich Horror* (exec. prod.) 1970; *Boxcar Bertha* 1972; *I Escaped from Devil's Island* (co-prod.) 1973; *Big Bad Mama, Cockfighter* 1974; *Capone, Death Race 2000* 1975; *Jackson County Jail* (exec. prod.), *Eat My Dust!, Fighting Mad* 1976; *Grand Theft Auto* (exec. prod.), *I Never Promised You a Rose Garden* (co-exec. prod.), *Thunder and Lightning* 1977; *Deathsport, Piranha* (co-exec. prod.), *Outside Chance* (co-prod.), *Avalanche* 1978; *Monster, Saint Jack, Rock 'n' Roll High School* 1979; *Battle Beyond the Stars* 1980; *Smokey Bites the Dust* 1981; *Forbidden World* 1982; *Love Letters/My Love Letters, Space Raiders/Star Child* 1983; *Cocaine Wars* (co-prod.) 1985; *Stripped to Kill* (exec. prod.), *Munchies, Big Bad Mama II* 1987; *The Lawless Land* (co-exec. prod.), *The Drifter* (exec. prod.), *Daddy's Boys, Crime Zone* (exec. prod.) 1988;, *Two to Tango* (co-prod.), *Heroes Stand Alone* (exec. prod.), *Transylvania Twist* (exec. prod.) 1989; *Streets* (exec. prod.) 1990; *Dracula Rising* 1992; *Chayette Warrior, Reflections on a Crime* 1994.

Corneau, Alain. Director. Born in 1943, in Meung-sur-Loire, France. A jazz musician before turning to films, he spent some time in the US studying and playing with various bands. After several years as an assistant director, he wrote the script for Nadine Trintignant's *Défense de Savoir* (1972), then scored a critical success with his first film as director, *France Société anonyme* (1974).

FILMS: *France Société anonyme* (also so-sc.) 1974; *Police Python 357/The Case Against Ferro* (also co-sc.) 1976; *La Menace* (also co-sc.) 1977; *Série noire* (also co-sc.) 1979; *Le Chois des Armes/Choice of Arms* (also co-sc.) 1981; *Fort Saganne* (also co-sc.) 1984; *Nocturne indien* (also co-sc.) 1989.

Cornelius, Henry. Director. *b.* Aug. 18, 1913, South Africa. *d.* 1958. Studied under Max REINHARDT and was an actor and stage director in Berlin before leaving for France in 1933 after the Nazi takeover. While a student at the Sorbonne, he entered films as an assistant editor. In 1935 he went to England as assistant editor on René CLAIR's *The Ghost Goes West* and was soon elevated to full film editor. Among the notable films on which he worked in that capacity were *The Drum/Drums*

(1938) and *The Four Feathers* (1939). During WW II he produced, directed, and wrote many documentaries in South Africa. Returned to British films as associate producer and screenwriter on *It Always Rains on Sunday* (1947) and from 1949 was a director. Made two of the wittiest, funniest, and most charming British comedies of the postwar wave of humor, *Passport to Pimlico* and *Genevieve,* which reflected the deft style of his mentor, René Clair. Died during production of the film *Law and Disorder* (which was completed by Charles Crichton).

FILMS: *Passport to Pimlico* 1949; *The Galloping Major* (also co-sc.) 1951; *Genevieve* (also prod.) 1953; *I Am a Camera* 1955; *Next to No Time* (also sc.), *Law and Disorder* (co-dir.) 1958.

Cornell, Joseph. Filmmaker, artist. *b.* 1903, Nyack, N.Y. *d.* 1972. Avant-garde filmmaker who applied techniques from the fine arts to a visionary body of film. Known primarily for his collages and boxes created out of found images, he employed these methods in making films over a period of three decades. The most celebrated example of his work is *Rose Hobart* (1937), a surreal tribute to the eponymous Hollywood starlet, drawn from images clipped and re-assembled from a minor jungle spectacle, *East of Borneo* (1931). Directors such as Stan Brakhage, Jonas Mekas, and Ken Jacobs have cited his works as influences. Dates can be appended only conditionally to his work; some were as long as thirty years in the making.

FILMS INCLUDE: *Rose Hobart* 1937; *Gnir Rednow, Curtains of June* 1955 *Aviary* 1956; *Nymphlight, Angel* 1957; *Cotillions-The Children's Party-The Midnight Party* (a trilogy filmed in the 30s, cut in 1968); *A Legend for Fountains* (filmed 1957, released 1970).

Cornenweth, Jordan. Director of photography. One of Hollywood's most creative cinematographers of the 70s and 80s. He won the British Academy Award for *Blade Runner* (1982).

FILMS INCLUDE: *Trilogy* 1969; *Brewster McCloud* 1970; *Play It as It Lays* 1974; *Zandy's Bride, The Front Page* 1974; *Gable and Lombard* 1976; *Citizens Band/Handle with Care* 1977; *Altered States* 1980; *Cutter and Bone/Cutter's Way* 1981; *Blade Runner* 1982; *Peggy Sue Got Married* 1986; *Gardens of Stone* 1987; *U2: Rattle and Hum* (co-phot.) 1988.

Cornfield, Hubert. Director. Born on Feb. 9, 1929, in Istanbul. The son of an overseas sales executive for American film companies, he began his association with the film medium in various capacities at a young age. From the mid-50s through the mid-70s he directed infrequent features in a variety of styles and with varying success, then moved to Paris.

FILMS: *Sudden Danger* 1955; *Lure of the Swamp, Plunder Road* 1957; *The Third Voice* (also prod., co-sc.) 1959; *Angel Baby* (co-dir. with Paul Wendkos) 1961; *Pressure Point* (also co-sc.) 1962; *The Night of the Following Day* (also prod., sc.) 1969; *Les Grandes Moyens* (also co-sc.; Fr.) 1976.

Corri, Adrienne. Actress. Born Adrienne Riccoboni, on Nov. 13, 1930, in Glasgow, Scotland. London stage debut, 1948; film debut, 1951. A pretty redhead, she has made numerous screen, stage, and TV appearances in the UK and the US, in both leading and supporting roles. At one time married to actor Daniel MASSEY.

FILMS INCLUDE: *The Romantic Age/Naughty Arlette* 1949; *Quo Vadis?, The River* 1951; *The Kidnappers/The Little Kidnappers* 1953; *Lease of Life, Make Me an Offer* 1954; *The Feminine Touch, Three Men in a Boat* 1956; *The Rough and the Smooth/Portrait of a Sinner* 1959; *The Anatomist, The Hellfire Club* 1961; *Corridors of Blood* (release delayed from 1958), *The Tell-Tale Heart* 1962; *Lancelot and Guinevere/Sword of Lancelot* 1963; *Bunny Lake Is Missing, A Study in Terror, Doctor Zhivago* (US) 1965; *The Viking Queen, Africa Texas Style!* (UK/US), *Sept fois Femme/Woman Times Seven* (Fr./It./US) 1967; *The File of the Golden Goose, Moon Zero Two* 1969; *A Clockwork Orange* 1971; *Vampire Circus* 1972; *Madhouse* 1974; *Rosebud* (US) 1975; *Revenge of the Pink Panther* 1978; *The Human Factor* 1979.

Corrigan, Lloyd. Actor, director, screenwriter. *b.* Oct. 16, 1900, San Francisco. *d.* 1969. *ed.* U. of California. The son of screen actress Lillian Elliott, he entered films in the mid-20s as an actor but soon after gravitated toward screenwriting. Turned to directing in the early 30s with only modest success and returned full cycle to acting by the end of the decade. A pudgy little man, he played light character roles, from jovial to anxious.

FILMS INCLUDE: As screenwriter—*Hands Up!, Miss Brewster's Millions, Wet Paint, The Campus Flirt* 1926; *Señorita, She's a Sheik, Wedding Bill$, Swim Girl Swim* 1927; *Red Hair* (co-adapt.), *Hot News* (co-adapt.), *What a Night* (co-story only) 1928; *The Mysterious Dr. Fu Manchu, The Saturday Night Kid, Sweetie* 1929; *The Return of Dr. Fu Manchu, Anybody's War* 1930; *Hold 'Em Navy* 1937; *Touchdown Army* 1938. As director—*Follow Thru* (co-dir., co-sc. with Laurence Schwab), *Along Came Youth* (co-dir. with Norman McLeod) 1930; *Daughter of the Dragon, The Beloved Bachelor* 1931; *No One Man, The Broken Wing* 1932; *He Learned About Women* (also story) 1933; *La Cucaracha* (two-reeler) 1934; *Murder on a Honeymoon* 1935; *Dancing Pirate* 1936; *Night Key* 1937; *Lady Behave* 1938. As actor—*The Splendid Crime* 1925; *Young Tom Edison, The Ghost Breakers, The Return of Frank James, Captain Caution, The Lady in Question* 1940; *Men of Boys Town, Kathleen* 1941; *The Great Man's Lady, Eyes of the Underworld, Lucky Jordan, Tennessee Johnson* 1942; *The Mantrap* (lead role), *Hitler's Children* 1943; *Since You Went Away* 1944; *The Thin Man Goes Home* 1945; *She Wolf of London, The Chase* 1946; *The Big Clock, A Date with Judy* 1948; *Dancing in the Dark* 1949; *Cyrano de Bergerac* 1950; *The Last Outpost* 1951; *Son of Paleface* 1952; *Return from the Sea* 1954; *The Manchurian Candidate* 1962; *It's a Mad Mad Mad Mad World* 1963.

Corrigan, Ray ("Crash"). Actor. *b.* Raymond Bernard, Feb. 14, 1902, in Milwaukee. *d.* 1976. A former electrician and physical education instructor, he entered films in 1934 as stuntman and bit player. By 1936 he was starring in serials and action pictures, earning the nickname "Crash" for his daredevil stunts. For several years he co-starred in the popular Western series "The Three Mesquiteers," with Bob LIVINGSTON and Max Terhune. Later he co-starred in another cowboy trio series, "The Range Busters," with Terhune and John "Dusty" King. From the mid-40s, in supporting roles. In 1950 he hosted the children's show 'Crash Corrigan's Ranch' on TV. Retired in the late 50s to pursue business ventures, including Corriganville, a ranch he rented out to studios as a movie location.

FILMS INCLUDE: *Mystery Ranch* 1934; *The Singing Vagabond* 1935; *Undersea Kingdom, Darkest Africa* (both serials), *The Three Mesquiteers* 1936; *The Painted Stallion* (serial), *Come On Cowboys!, Trigger Trio* 1937; *The Purple Vigilantes, Pals of the Saddle* 1938; *Wyoming Outlaw* 1939; *The Range Busters* 1940; *Fugitive Valley* 1941; *Texas Trouble Shooters* 1942; *Cowboy Commandos* 1943; *Renegade Girl* 1947; *Zamba* 1949; *Killer Ape* 1953; *Domino Kid* 1957; *It! The Terror from Beyond Space* 1958.

Cort, Bud. Actor. Born Walter Edward Cox, on Mar. 29, 1950, in New Rochelle, N.Y. *ed.* NYU. Juvenile leading man and supporting player of Hollywood films. Memorable as the flight-obsessed youth in Robert Altman's *Brewster McCloud* and as the suicide-prone kid in Hal Ashby's cult favorite *Harold and Maude.*

FILMS INCLUDE: *M*A*S*H, The Strawberry Statement, Gass-s-s-s, The Traveling Executioner, Brewster McCloud* 1970; *Harold and Maude* (1971); *Why Shoot the Teacher?* (Can.) 1977; *Die Laughing, She Dances Alone* (Austral.) 1980; *Love Letters, Hysterical* 1983; *Electric Dreams, The Secret Diary of Sigmund Freud* (title role) 1984; *Maria's Lovers* 1985; *Invaders from Mars* 1986; *Love at Stake* 1988; *The Chocolate War* 1989; *Out of the Dark, Brain Dead* 1990; *Going Under* 1991; *Ted and Venus* (also dir., co-sc.) 1992; *Heat* 1995.

Cortese (in Hollywood: **Cortesa), Valentina.** Actress. Born on Jan. 1, 1924, in Milan. In Italian films from age 15, she advanced from bits to lead roles in wartime comedies and dramas. After starring in the British-Italian co-production *The Glass Mountain* (1948), she was invited to Hollywood, where she played lead roles in several films, spelling her name Cortesa, and married one of her co-stars, Richard BASEHART. (They divorced in 1970.) After a few years she returned to Europe and subsequently appeared in Italian and international productions. She won the New York Film Critics best supporting actress award and an Academy Award nomination for her portrayal of a grotesque fading film star in Truffaut's *Day for Night* (1973).

FILMS INCLUDE: *Orizzonte Dipinto* 1940; *Il Bravo de Venezia, La Cena delle Beffe, Primo Amore* 1941; *Soltano un Bacio, Quatra Pagina* 1942; *Chi l'ha visto?* 1943; *Un Americano in Vacanza/A Yank in Rome, Roma Città libera* 1946; *Il Passatore/A Bullet for Stefano, I Miserabili/Les Miserables* 1947; *L'Ebreo errante/The Wandering Jew, The Glass Mountain* (UK) 1948; *Black Magic* (US), *Thieves' Highway* (US) 1949; *Malaya* (US), *Donne senza Nome/Women Without Names* 1950; *The House on Telegraph Hill* (US) 1951; *The Secret People* (UK) 1952; *Donne proibite/Angels of Darkness* 1953; *The Barefoot Contessa* (US) 1954; *Le Amiche/The Girl Friends, Shadow of the Eagle* 1955; *Calabuch/Rocket from Calabuch, Magic Fire* (US) 1956; *Barabba/Barabbas* 1961; *Der Besuch/ The Visit* (Ger./Fr./It./US) 1964; *Giulietta degli Spiriti/Juliet of the Spirits* 1965; *Soleil noir/Black Sun* (Fr./It.), *The Legend of Lylah Clare* (US) 1968; *The Secret of Santa Vittoria* (US) 1969; *Erste Liebe/First Love* (Switz./Ger.), *Les Caprices de Marie/Give Her the Moon* (Fr./It.) 1970; *The Assassination of Trotsky* (as Mme. Trotsky (Fr./It.) 1972; *Fratello Sole Sorella Luna/Brother Sun Sister Moon, La Nuit Americaine/Day for Night* (Fr.) 1973; *Apassionata, Tendre Dracula* (Fr.) 1974; *Le Grand Escogriffe* (Fr.) 1976; *Nido de Viudas/Widow's Nest* 1977; *When Time Ran Out* 1980; *La Ferdinanda* 1982; *Giovane Toscanini/Young Toscanini* (It.) 1988; *The Adventures of Baron Munchausen* 1989.

Cortez, Ricardo. Actor, director. *b.* Jacob Krantz (also spelled Kranze), Sept. 19, 1899, Vienna. *d.* 1977. Brother of cinematographer Stanley CORTEZ. At the age of three he was brought to New York, where he later sold newspapers and worked as a runner on Wall Street to help support his immigrant parents. After some stage experience, he was signed by Paramount in the early 20s and groomed as a Latin-lover type and possible heir to Rudolph Valentino. Tall, dark, and handsome, and famous for his "bedroom eyes," he starred as an exotic romantic hero in numerous silent and early sound films and played Greta Garbo's lover in her first Hollywood film, *The Torrent* (1926). From the early 30s he appeared mostly in B pictures, continuing to play leads into the early 40s. He was the original Sam Spade in the 1931 version of *The Maltese Falcon.* Later switched to character roles, often playing suave villains. He also skillfully directed a number of low-budget productions in 1939–40. After retiring from films, he became a stockbroker. He was the husband of actress Alma Rubens, who died in 1931.

FILMS INCLUDE: As actor—*Sixty Cents an Hour, Children of Jazz, The Call of the Canyon* 1923; *A Society Scandal, The Bedroom Window, Feet of Clay, The City That Never Sleeps, This Woman, Argentine Love* 1924; *The Swan, Not So Long Ago, In the Name of Love, The Pony Express, The Spaniard* 1925; *The Torrent, Volcano, The Cat's Pajamas, The Sorrows of Satan, The Eagle of the Sea* 1926; *New York, Mockery, The Private Life of Helen of Troy* (as Paris) 1927; *The Grain of Dust, Prowlers of the Sea, Ladies of the Night Club, The Gun Runner, Excess Baggage* 1928; *The Younger Generation, New Orleans, The Phantom in the House, The Lost Zeppelin, Midstream* 1929; *Montana Moon, Her Man* 1930; *Illicit, Ten Cents a Dance, The Maltese Falcon, White Shoulders, Transgression, Bad Company, Reckless Living* 1931; *Men of Chance, No One Man, Symphony of Six Million, 13 Women, The Phantom of Crestwood, Flesh* 1932; *Broadway Bad, Midnight Mary, Torch Singer, Big Executive, The House on 56th Street* 1933; *The Big Shakedown, Mandalay, Wonder Bar, The Man with Two Faces, A Lost Lady, The Firebird* 1934; *I Am a Thief, The White Cockatoo, Shadow of Doubt, Special Agent* 1935; *Man Hunt, The Walking Dead, The Case of the Black Cat* 1936; *Her Husband Lies, Talk of the Devil, West of Shanghai, The Californian* 1937; *City Girl* 1938; *Mr. Moto's Last Warning, Charlie Chan in Reno* 1939; *Murder Over New York* 1940; *I Killed That Man, A Shot in the Dark, World Premiere* 1941; *Tomorrow We Live* 1942; *Make Your Own Bed* 1944; *The Locket* 1946; *Blackmail* 1947; *Bunco Squad* 1950; *The Last Hurrah* 1958. As director (complete)—*Inside Story* 1938; *Chasing Danger, The Escape, Heaven with a Barbed-Wire Fence* 1939; *City of Chance, Free Blonde and 21, Girl in 313* 1940.

Cortez, Stanley. Director of photography. Born Stanislaus Krantz (also spelled Kranze) on Nov. 4, 1908, in New York City. *ed.* NYU. Brother of Ricardo CORTEZ, he began as an assistant to Steichen and other noted portrait photographers. In 1926 he became a motion picture assistant cameraman and in 1937 made his first feature film as director of photography. He soon gained a reputation for the quality of his camera work, although he served more often in B pictures than in major productions. In 1942 he won the Film Critics of America award for the photography of Welles's *The Magnificent Ambersons.* In 1932 he directed one short film, *Scherzo.*

FILMS INCLUDE: *Four Days Wonder* 1937; *Lady in the Morgue* 1938; *For Love or Money, Risky Business* 1939; *Meet the Wildcat* 1940; *The Black Cat* 1941; *Bombay Clipper, Eagle Squadron, The Magnificent Ambersons* 1942; *Flesh and Fantasy* (co-phot.) 1943; *Since You Went Away* (co-phot.) 1944; *Smash-Up* 1947; *The Secret Beyond the Door* 1948; *The Man on the Eiffel Tower, The Underworld Story* 1950; *Fort Defiance* 1951; *The Diamond Queen* 1953; *Riders to the Stars* 1954; *Black Tuesday, Night of the Hunter* 1955; *Top Secret Affair, The Three Faces of Eve* 1957; *Thunder in the Sun* 1959; *The Angry Red Planet, Dinosaurus* 1960; *Back Street* 1961; *Shock Corridor* 1963; *The Naked Kiss* 1964; *Nightmare in the Sun, Young Dillinger* 1965; *The Ghost in the Invisible Bikini* 1966; *Blue* 1968; *The Bridge at Remagen* 1969; *Tell Me That You Love Me Junie Moon* (title sequence only) 1970; *The Date* 1971; *Un autre Homme une autre Chance/Another Man Another Chance* (Fr.) 1977; *Damien—Omen II* (special phot. only) 1978; *When Time Ran Out* (special phot. only) 1980.

Corti, Axel. Director. Born in 1933 in Paris. Active in French and Austrian TV and theater, he established himself in film through the "Where to and Back" trilogy about pre- and postwar Vienna. Based on the screenplays of Georg Stefan Troller, they offer a contained social history of the time and place.

FILMS INCLUDE: *Der Verweigerung/The Refusal* 1972;

Totstellen/The Condemned 1975; *Donauwalzer/Waltzes of the Danube* (act. only), *A Woman's Pale Blue Handwriting* (also sc.) 1984; *An uns glaubt Gott nicht mehr/God Does Not Believe In Us, Santa Fe* 1985; *Welcome to Vienna* (also sc.) 1986; *The King's Whore* (also sc.) 1990.

Cosby, Bill. Actor, comedian. Born on July 12, 1937, in Philadelphia. *ed.* Temple U. of Massachusetts. Popular star of American TV and occasional films. A high school dropout, he joined the Navy in 1956, but earned a diploma through correspondence and on his discharge in 1960 enrolled at Temple University on a football scholarship. He started his career as a stand-up comic in nightclubs and gained prominence on such TV shows as 'I Spy,' 'The Bill Cosby Show,' and 'Fat Albert and the Cosby Kids.' He has also appeared as a guest on numerous other TV programs, frequently on 'The Electric Company' kiddie show, and has won a number of Emmy Awards. He has also received several Grammy awards for his comedy recordings. In the 70s he began appearing in films. In 1984 he returned to television and, taking complete creative control, turned the family-oriented 'The Cosby Show' into the top-rated program of the late 80s and one of the most successful series in the history of the medium. In the process he amassed a fortune, becoming one of the wealthiest entertainers in America. Bucking the trend, he based his operations in New York and taped his shows in Queens. An effort to revive the old Groucho Marx TV show, 'You Bet Your Life,' failed. He holds a Ph.D. degree in education and is very active in the affairs of the African-American community. Author: *The Wit and Wisdom of Fat Albert; Bill Cosby's Personal Guide to Power Tennis; Fatherhood; Time Flies.*

FILMS: *Man and Boy, Hickey and Boggs* 1972; *Uptown Saturday Night* 1974; *Let's Do It Again* 1975; *Mother Juggs & Speed* 1976; *A Piece of the Action* 1977; *California Suite* 1978; *The Devil and Max Devlin* 1981; *Bill Cosby—Himself* (concert film) 1982; *Leonard Part 6* (also prod., story) 1987; *Ghost Dad* 1990; *Meteor Man* 1993; *Jack* 1996.

Coslow, Sam. Songwriter, occasional producer. *b.* Samson Coslow, Dec. 27, 1902, New York City. *d.* 1982. Wrote lyrics for numerous Hollywood films from the beginning of the sound era, often in collaboration with composer Arthur Johnston. Sometimes composed the music himself. During the 40s, produced several features and shorts for Paramount and other companies, sharing an Academy Award for the two-reel short *Heavenly Music* (1943). Autobiography: *Cocktails for Two* (1977).

FILMS INCLUDE: As songwriter—*Thunderbolt, River of Romance, The Time the Place and the Girl, The Dance of Life, Fast Company, Broadway Scandals* 1929; *Behind the Make-Up, The Vagabond King, Honey, Paramount on Parade, Reno* (under pseudonym Leslie Barton) 1930; *College Humor, Too Much Harmony* 1933; *Murder at the Vanities, You Belong to Me, Belle of the Nineties* 1934; *The Gilded Lily, Ruggles of Red Gap, Coronado* 1935; *Poppy, Klondike Annie, It's Love Again, 100 Men and a Girl, Rhythm on the Range* 1936; *Champagne Waltz, Turn Off the Moon, Mountain Music, Thrill of a Lifetime* 1937; *You and Me* 1938; *St. Louis Blues* 1939; *Song of the South* 1946; *His Kind of Woman* 1951; *An Alligator Named Daisy* (UK) 1955. As producer—*Dreaming Out Loud* (co-prod.; also songs) 1940; *Heavenly Music* (short; co-prod.) 1943; *Out of This World* (also co-story) 1945; *Copacabana* (also songs) 1947.

Cosmatos, George Pan. Director. Born Yorgo Pan Cosmatos on Jan. 4, 1941, in Greece. *ed.* London Film School. An assistant on such productions as *Exodus* and *Zorba the Greek,* he made commercials before becoming a much-traveled feature director in the early 70s. He broke through the low-budget barrier with *Rambo* (1985), a box-office smash that allowed him to flaunt his technical mastery of action scenes.

FILMS INCLUDE: *The Beloved/Restless* (also sc., co-prod.; Ger./UK) 1971; *Rappresaglia/Massacre in Rome* (also co-sc.; It.) 1973; *The Cassandra Crossing* (also co-sc.; UK/It./Ger.) 1977; *Escape to Athena* (also co-story; UK) 1979; *Of Unknown Origin* (Can.) 1983; *Rambo: First Blood Part II* (US) 1985; *Cobra* (US) 1986; *Leviathan* (US) 1989; *Tombstone* (US) 1993; *The Shadow Conspiracy* 1997.

Cosmopolitan Productions. See DAVIES, Marion; HEARST, William Randolph.

Costa-Gavras, Constantin. Director. Born Konstantinos Gavras, in 1933, in Kilvia, Greece. The son of a middle-level atheist bureaucrat of the Greek government, he received a strict Orthodox education, at the insistence of his mother. Since his father, a WW II resistance fighter, was repeatedly jailed after the war on suspicion of Communist activity, young Kostantinos was denied entry into a Greek university and was refused a visa to study in the US. At 18 he went to Paris, where he graduated from the Sorbonne three years later with a degree in literature. A cinema devotee since childhood, he then studied filmmaking at IDHEC (Institut des Hautes Etudes Cinématographiques) in Paris. After a period of apprenticeship as assistant director to Yves ALLÉGRET, René CLAIR, and Jacques DEMY, among others, he made his debut as director in 1965 with a commercially successful suspense thriller, *The Sleeping Car Murders.* He gained international prominence with his political thriller, *Z,* a virtuoso indictment of the repressive Greek junta regime, notable for its gripping suspense and realistic camera work. The film was nominated for Academy Awards for best picture and best director. It won Oscars for best foreign language film and best editing. The New York Film Critics named Costa-Gavras best director of 1969. Demonstrating that he was opposed to tyranny anywhere and under any flag, he followed *Z* with another political film, *The Confession,* again starring his favorite actor, Yves Montand, this time as the victim of a Communist witchhunt in Czechoslovakia. In *State of Siege,* Montand is a CIA agent meddling in the affairs of Uruguay. In 1975 he shared the best director prize at Cannes for *Special Section,* a recreation of Vichy government days in WW II France. He shared a Golden Palm (best film) in Cannes and a best screenplay adaptation Oscar for his first American film, *Missing* (1982), a piercing, factually based drama about American-sanctioned political atrocities in post-Allende Chile. As with most of Costa-Gavras's works, the film caused much controversy, as did his pro-Palestinian melodrama *Hanna K.* (1983). He appeared as an actor in *La Vie devant soi/Madame Rosa* (1977).

A naturalized Frenchman since 1956, Costa-Gavras is married to freelance journalist and former Chanel model Michele Ray, world famous for her daring journalistic adventures and her captivity at the hands of the Viet Cong. She was the producer of his *Family Business* (1986). Costa-Gavras became president of the Cinémathèque Française in 1982.

FILMS: *Compartment Tueurs/The Sleeping Car Murders* (also sc.) 1965; *Un Homme de Trop/Shock Troops* (also sc.) 1967; *Z* (also co-sc.) 1969; *L'Aveu/The Confession* 1970; *Etat de Siège/State of Siege* (also co-sc.) 1972; *Section speciale/Special Section* (also co-sc.) 1975; *Clair de Femme* (also sc.) 1979; *Missing* (also co-sc.; US) 1982; *Hanna K.* (also prod.) 1983; *Conseil de Famille/Family Business* (also sc.) 1986; *Betrayed* (US) 1988; *Music Box* 1990; *La Petite Apocalypse* 1993; *The Dreyfuss Affair* 1994; *Rasputin* 1995; *The Stupids* (act. only) 1996; *Mad City* 1997.

Costello, Dolores. Actress. *b.* Sept. 17, 1905, Pittsburgh. *d.* 1979. She and her sister Helene COSTELLO began appearing as children in Vitagraph films starring their celebrated father, Maurice COSTELLO. After attending school and modeling for such top New York illustrators as James Montgomery Flagg, she returned to the screen at 17, playing bit roles in East Coast productions. Following the success of the sisters' dance duet on the New York stage in the 'George White Scandals' of 1924, they were signed by Warner Bros. Dolores's renewed screen career started slowly, but she gained sudden stardom when John BARRYMORE chose her as his leading lady in *The Sea Beast* (1926), a romanticized screen adaptation of *Moby Dick.* They were married in 1928.

A delicate blonde beauty who projected patrician poise, Miss Costello went on to become one of the leading box-office stars of the late silent and early sound era, but she retired early in the 30s to give birth to a daughter, Dolores Ethel Mae, and a son, future actor John BARRYMORE, Jr. Following her 1935 divorce from the senior Barrymore, she returned to films, in mature roles that revealed a ripened acting ability, memorably as Freddie Bartholomew's mother in *Little Lord Fauntleroy* (1936) and as Isabel Amberson in Orson Welles's *The Magnificent Ambersons* (1942). Shortly after the release of the latter she retired to her California avocado farm.

FILMS INCLUDE (complete from 1923): *A Geranium, The Child Crusoes, His Sister's Children* 1911; *The Meeting of the Ways, The Money Kings, The Troublesome Step-Daughters, A Juvenile Love Affair, Vultures and Doves, Ida's Christmas* 1912; *The Hindoo Charm, Fellow Voyagers* 1913; *Etta of the Footlights* 1914; *The Evil Men Do, How Cissy Made Good* (cameo) 1915; *The Glimpses of the Moon, Lawful Larceny* 1923; *Greater Than a Crown* 1925; *The Sea Beast, Mannequin, Bride of the Storm, The Little Irish Girl, The Third Degree* 1926; *When a Man Loves, A Million Bid, Old San Francisco, The Heart of Maryland, The College Widow* 1927; *Tenderloin, Glorious Betsy* 1928; *The Redeeming Sin, Noah's Ark, The Glad Rag Doll, Madonna of Avenue A, Show of Shows, Hearts in Exile* 1929; *Second Choice* 1930; *Expensive Women* 1931; *Little Lord Fauntleroy, Yours for the Asking* 1936; *The Beloved Brat, Breaking the Ice* 1938; *King of the Turf, Whispering Enemies, Outside These Walls* 1939; *The Magnificent Ambersons* 1942; *This Is the Army* 1943.

Costello, Helene. Actress *b.* Helen Costello, June 21, 1903, in New York City. *d.* 1957. Along with her sister Dolores COSTELLO, she began appearing as a child in Vitagraph films starring their father, Maurice COSTELLO, and other personalities of the day. After attending private schools, modeling in New York, and dancing with her sister in the 'George White Scandals' of 1924, she returned to films and for a short while rivaled her sister's popularity. However, her career soon waned, and shortly after the advent of sound she disappeared from the screen, except for a bit part in a 1935 film. At one time (1930–32) she was married to director-actor Lowell SHERMAN.

FILMS INCLUDE: *A Geranium, The Child Crusoes* 1911; *The First Violin, The Money Kings, The Troblesome Step-Daughters, Rip Van Winkle, The Night Before Christmas* 1912; *The Doctor's Secret, The Hindoo Charm, Fellow Voyagers* 1913; *The Evil Men Do, How Cissy Made Good* (cameo) 1915; *The Man on the Box, The Ranger of Big Pines* 1925; *Wet Paint, Don Juan, The Honeymoon Express, The Love Toy, Millionaires, While London Sleeps* 1926; *The Heart of Maryland, Good Time Charley, The Broncho Twister, In Old Kentucky, Husbands for Rent, Finger Prints, The Fortune Hunter* 1927; *Lights of New York, The Midnight Taxi, Burning Up Broadway, Comrades, The Circus Kid, Broken Barriers* 1928; *The Fatal Warning* (serial), *When Dreams Come True* 1929; *Riff-Raff* 1935.

Costello, Lou. Actor. *b.* Louis Francis Cristillo, Mar. 6, 1906, Paterson, N.J. *d.* 1959. Worked as a newsboy, soda fountain clerk, hot shop salesman, and prizefighter before going to Hollywood in the late 20s in an attempt to break into films. But the only film work he could get was as a laborer on the MGM and Warner lots and eventually some stunt assignments. He went into vaudeville and burlesque instead and in 1931 teamed up with Bud ABBOTT to form one of the most successful comedy teams in show business. With tall, lean Abbott playing straightman to short, pudgy funnyman Costello, the team was a top box-office attraction in films of the 40s and early 50s. After the team split up in 1957, Costello appeared without his partner in one film, *The 30-Foot Bride of Candy Rock* (1959), just before his death of a heart attack at 53. For other film credits and career details see ABBOTT, Bud; ABBOTT AND COSTELLO.

Costello, Maurice. Actor. *b.* Feb. 22, 1877, in Pittsburgh. *d.* 1950. Father of Dolores and Helene COSTELLO. A matinee idol for 15 years, he was among the first important American stage actors to turn to the screen. After a few years with Edison, he moved to Vitagraph in 1908, where he had his biggest triumph in 1911 as Sydney Carton in the three-reel *A Tale of Two Cities.* At the height of his popularity he was billed as "The Dimpled Darling." He went on to play a variety of lead roles, switching to character roles in the mid-20s. He directed many of his own films. Impoverished and all but forgotten by the time he reached 60, he sued his daughters for support in 1939.

FILMS INCLUDE: *Salome, Richard III, Antony and Cleopatra, Julius Caesar, The Merchant of Venice* 1908; *Ruy Blas, Saul and David, King Lear, A Midsummer Night's Dream* (as Lysander) 1909; *Conscience of the Baker Boys, A Broken Spell, Uncle Tom's Cabin* 1910; *The New Stenographer, A Tale of Two Cities* (as Sydney Carton), *My Old Dutch* 1911; *The First Violin, Counsel for the Defense, The Money Kings, As You Like It* (as Orlando), *The Night Before Christmas* 1912; *The Ambassador's Disappearance* (also dir.), *The Weapon* (also dir.), *Extremities* (also dir.), *The Intruder* (also co-dir.), *The Spirit of the Orient* (also dir.), *A Faithful Servant* (also dir.), *The Hindoo Charm* (also dir.), *The Joys of a Jealous Wife* (also dir.), *The Lonely Princess* (also dir.), *Cupid versus Women's Rights* (also dir.), *Fellow Voyagers* (also co-dir.), *The Warmakers* (also co-dir.) 1913; *Iron and Steel* (also co-dir.), *Mr. Barnes of New York* (also co-dir.), *The Mysterious Lodger* (also co-dir.), *The Moonstone of Fez* (also co-dir.), *The Blood Rub* (also co-dir.), *The Peacemaker, The Plot* (also co-dir.) 1914; *The Evil Men Do* (also co-dir.), *The Criminal, The Man Who Couldn't Beat God* (also co-sc.), *Tried for His Own Murder* 1915; *The Crown Prince's Double, The Crimson Satin Mystery* (serial) 1916; *The Captain's Captain/Cap'n Abe's Niece* 1918; *The Cambrick Mask, The Man Who Won, The Girl Woman* 1919; *Tower of Jewels, Human Collateral, Deadline at Eleven* 1920; *Conceit* 1921; *Determination* 1922; *The Glimpses of the Moon, Fog Bound, Man and Wife, None So Blind* 1923; *Let No Man Put Asunder, Roulette, Week End Husbands, Virtuous Liars, Love of Women, The Story Without a Name, The Law and the Lady* 1924; *The Mad Marriage* 1925; *The Last Alarm, The Wives of the Prophet* 1926; *Johnny Get Your Hair Cut, Wolves of the Air, Camille, The Shamrock and the Rose, Spider Webs* 1927; *The Wagon Show, Eagle of the Night* (serial), *Black Feather* 1928; *Hollywood Boulevard* 1936; *A Little Bit of Heaven* 1940; *Lady from Louisiana* 1941.

Costner, Kevin. Actor, director, producer. Born on Jan. 18, 1955, in Compton, near Los Angeles, Calif. *ed.* California State, Fullerton. Leading star of Hollywood films of the late 80s and early 90s. He joined a community theater group while pursuing a marketing degree in college. After graduating and getting married, he worked in marketing for a month before deciding he preferred an acting career. Following small parts in tiny-budget exploitation films, he played bits in two major productions, but found his scenes on the cutting-room floor: In *Frances* (1982) he had one speaking line, as actor Luther Adler, and in *The Big Chill* (1983) he was the corpse in the opening credit sequence. Gradually, his roles improved, and he achieved star status with the role of the upright and humane Eliot Ness in *The Untouchables* (1987). By the end of the decade he had become established as one of Hollywood's best liked, most bankable, and highest paid leading men. In 1989 he formed his own production company, TIG, and in the following year directed his first film, the much admired *Dances with Wolves,* which won seven Academy Awards, including best director and best picture.

FILMS: *Shadows Run Black* (release delayed to 1986) 1981; *Chasing Dreams* (release delayed to 1989) 1982; *Night Shift* 1982; *Stacy's Knights, Table for Five, Testament* 1983; *The Gunrunner* (Can.; release delayed to 1989) 1984; *Fandango, American Flyers, Silverado* 1985; *Sizzle Beach U.S.A.* (release delayed from late 70s) 1986; *The Untouchables* (as crime buster Eliot Ness), *No Way Out* 1987; *Bull Durham* 1988; *Field of Dreams* 1989; *Revenge* (also exec. prod.), *Dances with Wolves* (also dir., co-prod.) 1990; *Robin Hood: Prince of Thieves, JFK* 1991; *The Bodyguard* (also co-prod.) 1992; *A Perfect World* 1993; *The War, Wyatt Earp* (also co-prod.) 1994; *Rapa Nui* (co-prod. only), *Waterworld* (also co-prod.) 1995; *Tin Cup* 1996.

costume designer. The person who conceives and draws designs for costumes to be worn by performers in films. The sketches are usually done in color after a careful study of the script, pending the approval of the producer, the director, and the art director. Probably the best-known costume designer in Hollywood history is Paramount's Edith HEAD, winner of many Academy Awards. Other well-known studio-era costume designers include Adrian and Orry-Kelly. In recent years, active costume designers have included Theadora Van Runkle, Patricia Norris, and Theoni V. Aldredge.

costumer. The man or woman responsible for the acquisition of clothes and their maintenance throughout a film's production. They are usually assigned to a major film several weeks before the start of production. After studying the script, they begin gathering items of apparel from available sources such as the studio wardrobe or rental establishments. They supervise the fittings of secondary players and extras. They also assist the stars in dressing before every shooting session. According to union rules, their responsibility covers "anything that is worn."

Cottafavi, Vittorio. Director. Born on Jan. 30, 1914, in Modena, Italy. After studying law, philosophy, and literature in Rome, he attended that city's Centro Sperimentale di Cinematografia and, following graduation in 1938, entered the industry as screenwriter for ALESSANDRINI and later was assistant to BLASETTI and DE SICA. Made his debut as director in 1942 with *I Nostri Sogni,* starring De Sica. After exploring several genres, from melodramas to documentaries, he found his niche in the late 50s with methodological and pseudohistorical spectaculars, which were hailed by young critics of the French *Cahiers du Cinéma* as the stylish works of a true *auteur,* an opinion few other critics endorse. In the late 60s he switched to Italian television, for which he has directed adaptations of literary classics.

FILMS: *I Nostri Sogni* 1942; *Lo Sconosciuto di San Marino* (co-dir. with Michael Waszynski) 1946; *La Grande Strada* (co-dir. with Waszynski) 1948; *La Fiamme che non si Spegne* 1949; *Una Donna ha Ucciso* 1951; *Il Boia di Lilla* 1952; *Il Cavaliere di Maison Rouge, Traviata '53, In Amore si Pecca in Due* 1953; *Unna Donna Libera, Avanzi di Galera, Nel Gorgo del Peccato* 1954; *Fiesta Brava* (doc.; Sp.) 1956; *La Rívolta dei Gladiatori/The Warrior and the Slave* 1958; *Le Legioni di Cleopatra/Legions of the Nile, Messalina* 1959; *La Vendetta di Ercole/Goliath and the Dragon/The Vengeance of Hercules* 1960; *Le Vergini di Roma/Amazons of Rome* (co-dir. with Carlo Bragaglia), *Ercole alla coquista di Atlantide/Hercules and the Captive Women* 1961; *I Cento Cavalieri/The Hundred Horsemen* 1964.

Cotten, Joseph. Actor. *b.* May 15, 1905, Petersburg, Va. *d.* 1995. *ed.* Hickman School of Expression (Washington, D.C.). Sold paint and advertising space and wrote occasional drama reviews for the *Miami Herald* while struggling to establish himself as an actor. In 1930 he was engaged by David Belasco as understudy and assistant stage manager and soon after began appearing on Broadway. In 1937 he joined Orson WELLES's Mercury Theater, leaving two years later to play the lead opposite Katharine HEPBURN in the Broadway hit 'The Philadelphia Story.' He made his first film appearance in *Too Much Johnson* (1938), a 40-minute farce made by Welles for insertion into an aborted stage production, and in 1941 was brought to Hollywood by Welles to play leading parts in the latter's first three feature productions, *Citizen Kane, The Magnificent Ambersons,* and *Journey Into Fear.*

Cotten's intelligent face, resonant voice, and low-keyed presence was later used effectively in such thrillers as Hitchcock's *Shadow of a Doubt* and Carol Reed's *The Third Man,* as well as in a string of romantic leads throughout the 40s and early 50s. He won the best actor award at the Venice Festival for his performance in *Portrait of Jennie* (1948). His career declined sharply in the late 50s, when he began appearing in a great number of inferior productions. He hosted several TV shows in the late 50s and early 60s. Widowed in 1960, he married actress Patricia MEDINA that same year. Autobiography: *Vanity Will Get You Somewhere* (1987).

FEATURE FILMS: *Citizen Kane, Lydia* 1941; *The Magnificent Ambersons, Journey Into Fear* (also co-sc.) 1942; *Shadow of a Doubt, Hers to Hold* 1943; *Gaslight, Since You Went Away* 1944; *I'll Be Seeing You, Love Letters* 1945; *Duel in the Sun* 1946; *The Farmer's Daughter* 1947; *Portrait of Jennie* 1948; *Under Capricorn* (UK), *Beyond the Forest, The Third Man* (UK) 1949; *Gone to Earth/The Wild Heart* (narr. only; UK), *Two Flags West, Walk Softly Stranger* 1950; *September Affair, Half Angel, Peking Express, The Man with a Cloak* 1951; *Othello* (It./Mor./US), *Untamed Frontier, The Steel Trap* 1952; *Niagara, A Blueprint for Murder, Egypt by Three* (narr. only) 1953; *Von Himmel gefallen/Special Delivery* (Ger./US) 1955; *The Bottom of the Bottle, The Killer Is Loose* 1956; *The Halliday Brand* 1957; *Touch of Evil* (cameo), *From the Earth to the Moon* 1958; *The Angel Wore Red/La Sposa Bella* (US-It.) 1960; *The Last Sunset* 1961; *Hush Hush. . . Sweet Charlotte, The Great Sioux Massacre* 1965; *The Oscar, The Money Trap, Gli Uomini del Passo Pesanti/The Tramplers* (It.) 1966; *I Crudeli/The Hell Benders* (It./Sp.), *Brighty of the Grand Canyon, Jack of Diamonds* (US/Ger.), *Some May Live* (UK) 1967; *Petulia* (US/UK), *Un Giorno di Fuoco/Days of Fire/Gangster '70* (It.), *Comanche Blanco/White Comanche* (Sp.) 1968; *Latitude Zero* (US/Jap.), *E Vene l'Ora della Vendetta/Hour of Vengeance* (It.) 1969; *The Grasshopper, Tora! Tora! Tora!* 1970; *The Abominable Dr. Phibes* (UK), *La Figlia di Frankenstein/Lady Frankenstein* (It.) 1971; *Lo Scopone Scientifico/The Scientific Card Player* (It.), *Gli Orrori del Castello di Norinberga/Baron Blood* (It/Fr.), *Doomsday Voyage* 1972; *Soylent Green, A Delicate Balance* 1973; *F for Fake* (Fr.) 1974; *Il Giustiziere sfida la Città/Syndicate Sadists* (It.), *Timber Tramps* 1975; *Sussuri Nel Buio* (It.), *Twilight's Last Gleaming, Airport '77* 1977; *The Wild Geese* (UK), *L'Ordre et la Sécurité du Monde*

(Fr.), *Caravans* 1978; *L'Isola degli Uomini Pesci/Island of the Fishmen/The Island of Mutations/Screamers* (It.), *S.O.S Concorde/The Concorde Affair* (It.), *Trauma* 1979; *Guyana, Cult of the Damned/Guyana, Crime of the Century* (Mex./Sp./Panam.), *The Survivor* (Austral.), *The Hearse* 1980; *Delusion, Heaven's Gate* 1981; *The House Where Evil Dwells* 1982.

Coulouris, George. Actor. *b.* Oct. 1, 1903, Manchester, England. *d.* 1989. Balding, wicked-looking character player of British and American stage and screen. Leaving home at 20, he was a waiter on an ocean liner before enrolling as a student at London's Central School of Dramatic Art. He made his London stage debut in 1925, appearing with Charles LAUGHTON in Shakespearean repertory at the Old Vic. He first appeared on Broadway in 1929 and in 1937 became one of the original members of Orson Welles's Mercury Theater, playing Marc Antony in a celebrated modern-dress production of 'Julius Caesar.' In Hollywood from 1933, he appeared in numerous films, typically playing shrewd or villainous characters. Memorable as Walter Parks Thatcher, young Kane's guardian, in Welles's *Citizen Kane.* He remained active until the mid-80s, when he became increasingly disabled by Parkinson's disease.

FILMS INCLUDE: *Christopher Bean* 1933; *All This and Heaven Too, The Lady in Question* 1940; *Citizen Kane* 1941; *Assignment in Brittany, This Land Is Mine, For Whom the Bell Tolls, Watch on the Rhine* 1943; *None but the Lonely Heart, Mr. Skeffington, The Master Race, The Conspirators* 1944; *Confidential Agent, Hotel Berlin, A Song to Remember, Lady on a Train* 1945; *The Verdict, Nobody Lives Forever* 1946; *Where There's Life, California* 1947; *Joan of Arc, Sleep My Love* 1948; *Kill or Be Killed* 1950; *An Outcast of the Islands* 1951; *Doctor in the House* 1954; *Tarzan and the Lost Safari* 1957; *I Accuse, Tank Force* 1958; *Beast of Marseille* 1959; *Surprise Package* 1960; *King of Kings* 1961; *The Crooked Road* 1964; *The Skull* 1965; *Arabesque* 1966; *Land Raiders* 1969; *Blood from the Mummy's Tomb* 1971; *Papillon* 1973; *Murder on the Orient Express* 1974; *Shout at the Devil, The Ritz* 1976; *L'Anti Cristo/The Tempter* (It.) 1978; *The Long Good Friday* 1980.

counter key. See MODELING LIGHT.

counterpoint. In film theory, the combining of image and sound in such a way that the visual image and the sound track accompanying it denote different meanings, though they both may represent the same object. The term is borrowed from music terminology. Opposite of PARALLELISM.

Courant, Curt(is) (Kurt). Director of photography. Born in 1895(?), in Germany, of Jewish parents. One of Europe's finest cameramen during the 20s and 30s, he began his career during WW I in Italian and German films. In 1933 he left Germany for fear of the Nazis and worked in France, England, and the US. Among the many directors he collaborated with are Fritz Lang, Hitchcock, Renoir, Carné, Gance, Ophuls, and Chaplin. His son, Willy Kurant, also a director of photography, has worked for directors of the French New Wave, including Godard.

FILMS INCLUDE: In Germany—*Hilde Warren und der Tod* (co-phot.) 1917; *Hamlet* (co-phot.) 1920; *Peter der Grosse/Peter the Great* (co-phot.) 1922; *Quo Vadis* (It.) 1924; *Ich Liebe Dich* 1926; *Die Frau in Mond/By Rocket to the Moon/Woman in the Moon* (co-phot.), *Das brennende Herz/Burning Heart* 1929; *Der Weisse Teufel* (co-phot.) 1930; *Rasputin* 1932. In France—*Ciboulette* 1933; *Amok* 1934; In the UK—*Perfect Understanding* 1933; *The Man Who Knew Too Much* 1934; *The Iron Duke* 1935; *Broken Blossoms* 1936. In France—*Le Puritain, La Bête Humaine/The Human Beast, Louise* 1938; *Le Jour se lève/Daybreak* 1939; *De Mayerling à Sarajevo/Mayerling to Sarajevo* (co-phot.) 1940. In the US—*Monsieur Verdoux* (co-phot.) 1947; *It Happened in Athens* 1962.

Courcel, Nicole. Actress. Born Nicole Marie-Anne Andrieux, on Oct. 21, 1930, in Saint-Cloud, France. The discovery of director Jacques BECKER, she made her debut in his *Antoine et Antoinette* (1947) and later appeared in his *Rendez-vous de Juillet* (1949). She developed in the 50s into one of the most capable young leads of the French screen.

FILMS INCLUDE: *Antoine et Antoinette/Antoine and Antoinette* (bit) 1947; *Rendez-vous de Juillet* 1949; *La Marie du Port* 1950; *Les Amants de Bras-Mort* 1951; *Les Amours finissent à l'Aube* 1953; *Marchandes d'Illusions/Nights of Shame, Les Clandestines/Vice Dolls, Huis clos/No Exit, Papa Maman la Bonne et moi/Mama Papa the Maid and I* 1954; *La Sorcière, Le Cas du Dr. Laurent/The Case of Dr. Laurent, Club de Femmes* 1956; *Ein Mann geht durch die Wand/The Man Who Walked Through the Wall* (Ger.) 1959; *Le Testament d'Orphée/The Testament of Orpheus, Le Passage du Rhin/Tomorrow Is My Turn* 1960; *Le Vergini di Roma/Amazons of Rome* (It./Fr.) 1961; *Les Dimanches de Ville d'Avray/Sundays and Cybele* 1962; *Verspätung in Marienborn/Stop Train 349* (Ger./Fr./It.) 1964; *The Night of the Generals* (UK/Fr.) 1967; *L'Etrangleur* 1970; *L'Aventure c'est l'Aventure/Money Money Money, Le Rempart des Beguines/Rampart of Desire* 1972; *Un Officier de Police sans Importance* 1973; *La Gifle/The Slap* 1974; *Thomas* 1974; *L'Esprit de Famille* 1979.

Court, Hazel. Actress. Born in 1926, in Sutton Coldfield, England. A good-looking redhead, she entered British films as a Gainsborough studios hopeful in the mid-40s but usually played unrewarding parts in undistinguished films. She saved her best for last, closing her career in the early 60s with effective leads in three Roger CORMAN horror classics. Divorced from actor Dermot Walsh (1949–63), she retired from the screen after marrying actor Don TAYLOR in 1964.

FILMS INCLUDE: *Champagne Charlie* 1944; *Dreaming* 1945; *Meet Me at Dawn, Carnival, Gaiety George/Showtime* 1946; *Dear Murderer, Bond Street, Holiday Camp* 1947; *Forbidden* 1949; *Ghost Ship* 1952; *Counterspy* 1953; *The Curse of Frankenstein* 1957; *Model for Murder* 1958; *The Man Who Could Cheat Death* 1959; *The Shakedown* 1960; *Dr. Blood's Coffin, Mary Had a Little...* 1961; *Premature Burial* (US) 1962; *The Raven* (US) 1963; *The Masque of the Red Death* (UK/US) 1964.

Courtenay, Tom. Actor. Born on Feb. 25, 1937, in Hull, England, the son of a ship painter. *ed.* University Coll., London. After training at the Royal Academy of Dramatic Art, he made his stage debut in 1960 in the Old Vic production of 'The Seagull.' The following year he took over Albert Finney's role in 'Billy Liar' and later played the part in the film version. He made an immediate impact on critics and audiences alike with his first British film, *The Loneliness of the Long Distance Runner,* and has since played other impressive leading roles in UK and US films, typically as a misunderstood, nonconforming youth. His promising screen career inexplicably stalled in 1971, but his stage work continues to thrive. In 1977 he made a belated Broadway debut in 'Otherwise Engaged.' Courtenay's return to the screen in 1983 was marked by an Academy Award nomination as best actor for his remarkable performance in *The Dresser* (1983). He had been previously nominated for an Oscar best supporting actor for *Doctor Zhivago* (1965). He is married to stage actress Cheryl Kennedy.

FILMS: *The Loneliness of the Long Distance Runner, Private Potter* 1962; *Billy Liar* 1963; *King and Country* 1964; *Operation Crossbow, King Rat* (US), *Doctor Zhivago* (US) 1965; *Night of the Generals* (UK/Fr.), *The Day the Fish Came*

Out 1967; *A Dandy in Aspic, Otley* 1968; *One Day in The Life of Ivan Denisovich* (UK/Nor.), *Keep Your Fingers Crossed, Catch Me a Spy* (UK/Fr.) 1971; *The Dresser* 1983; *Happy New Year, Leonard Part 6* 1987; *Let Him Have It* 1993.

Courtneidge, Dame Cicely. Actress. *b.* Apr. 1, 1893, Sydney, Australia. *d.* 1980. Ebullient comedienne of British music halls and the legitimate stage, she played eccentric characters and leads in British films of the 30s, sometimes partnering with husband, Jack HULBERT. Later in occasional character parts. Autobiography: *Cicely* (1953).

FILMS: *Elstree Calling* 1930; *The Ghost Train* 1931; *Jack's the Boy/Night and Day* 1932; *Soldiers of the King/The Woman in Command* 1933; *Aunt Sally/Along Came Sally* 1934; *Me and Marlborough, The Perfect Gentleman* (US), *Things Are Looking Up* 1935; *Everybody Dance* 1936; *Take My Tip* 1937; *Under Your Hat* 1940; *Miss Tulip Stays the Night* 1955; *Spider's Web* 1960; *The L-Shaped Room* 1962; *The Magnificent Men in Their Flying Machines* 1965; *The Wrong Box* 1966; *Not Now My Darling* 1973.

Cousteau, Jacques-Yves. Oceanographer, director. Born on June 11, 1910, in Saint-André, France. *d.* 1997. *ed.* Naval Academy (Brest). As a French naval officer in the mid-30s, he became interested in underwater exploration and was partly responsible for the invention of the aqualung, a portable breathing apparatus for divers. In 1942 he began recording his explorations on film, using an underwater camera of his own design. Developing his camera skills through a series of excellent shorts, he made a big splash in 1956 with his first feature length film, *The Silent World,* which he co-directed with Louis MALLE. The film won the Palme d'Or (the grand prize) at the Cannes Festival as well as Hollywood's best documentary Academy Award. Another Oscar went to his second feature, *World Without Sun* (1964). He also made many TV specials recounting the scientific adventures of his now-famous ship, *Calypso.*

FEATURE FILMS: *Le Monde du Silence/The Silent World* 1956; *Le Monde sans Soleil/World Without Sun* 1964; *Le Voyage au bout du Monde/Voyage to the Edge of the World* (co-dir with Philippe Cousteau) 1976.

Coutard, Raoul. Director of photography. Born on Sept. 16, 1924, in Paris. Following military service with the French forces in Indochina, he worked as a still photographer and combat reporter for *Life, Paris Match,* and other magazines. Entering films through newsreels and documentaries, he later introduced such journalistically inspired elements as camera mobility, hand-held techniques, and rapid pans into the feature films of such New Wave directors as GODARD, TRUFFAUT, and DEMY. He has been equally impressive when called upon to turn out glossy images within the confines of traditional camera techniques. His contribution to the aesthetics of Godard's films in particular has been enormous. His first film as director, *Hoa Binh* (1970), shot in Vietnam, was received favorably by US and European critics.

FILMS INCLUDE: *Pêcheur d'Islande* 1959; *Á Bout de Souffle/Breathless, Tirez sur le Pianiste/Shoot the Piano Player, Le Petit Soldat* 1960; *Lola, Jules et Jim, Une Femme est une Femme/A Woman Is a Woman, Chronique d'un Eté/Chronicle of a Summer* (co-phot.), *Tire au Flanc/The Army Game* 1961; *La Poupée, Vivre sa Vie/My Life to Live, L'Amour a Vignt Ans/Love at Twenty* (Truffaut episode) 1962; *Les Carabiniers, Les Mepris/Contempt* 1963; *Bande à part/Band of Outsiders, La Peau Douce/The Soft Skin, Un Monsieur de Compagne/Male Companion, Une Femme Mariée/The Married Woman* 1964; *Alphaville, Pierrot le Fou* 1965; *Made in USA* 1966; *The Sailor from Gibraltar* (UK), *La Chinoise* 1967; *Le Week-End/Weekend, La Mariée etait en Noir/The Bride Wore Black* 1968; *Z* 1969; *Hoa Binh* (dir., sc. only), *L'Aveu/The Confession* 1970; *Les Aveux les plus doux, L'Explosion* 1971; *The Jerusalem File* (co-phot.), *Embassy* 1972; *Allez-vous perdre ailleurs/A Pain in the A...* 1973; *Le Crabe-Tambour* 1977; *La Légion saute sur Kolwezi* (dir. only) 1980; *Passion, S.A.S. à San Salvador* (dir. only) 1982; *Prénom: Carmen/First Name Carmen* 1983; *La Diagonale du Fou/Dangerous Moves, La Garce* 1984; *Max Mon Amour/Max My Love* 1986; *Peau de Vaches* 1989.

coverage. The act of filming all the necessary footage, from all setups and angles, that may be required for editing a fluid sequence in the cutting room.

cover shot. Extra footage shot for a scene as protection against the possibility that the shots already filmed may not work. Also known as an "insurance take."

Cowan, Jerome. Actor. *b.* Oct. 6, 1897, in New York City. *d.* 1972. He came to films from vaudeville, stock, and Broadway in 1936 and subsequently played well over 100 diversified character roles, typically intelligent and urbane, often wearing a pencil-thin mustache. Occasionally in lead roles. Memorable as a doomed detective in *The Maltese Falcon* and as Charles Peabody, Dagwood's boss, in the later episodes of the "Blondie" movie series. Also seen in the TV series 'Tycoon' and 'Alias Smith and Jones.'

FILMS INCLUDE: *Beloved Enemy* 1936; *You Only Live Once, Shall We Dance, The Hurricane* 1937; *The Goldwyn Follies* 1938; *The Old Maid, The Great Victor Herbert* 1939; *Castle on the Hudson, Torrid Zone, City of Conquest, Victory* 1940; *High Sierra, The Great Lie, Kiss the Boys Goodbye, The Maltese Falcon* 1941; *Moontide, Street of Chance* 1942; *Mission to Moscow, Song of Bernadette, Find the Blackmailer* 1943; *Mr. Skeffington, Crime by Night* 1944; *Blonde Ransom, Getting Gertie's Garter* 1945; *My Reputation, The Kid from Brooklyn, Claudia and David* 1946; *The Miracle on 34th Street, Cry Wolf* 1947; *So This Is New York, The Night Has a Thousand Eyes, June Bride, Arthur Takes Over* 1948; *The Fountainhead, The Girl from Jones Beach* 1949; *Young Man with a Horn, Dallas* 1950; *The West Point Story, Criminal Lawyer* 1951; *The System* 1953; *Visit to a Small Planet* 1960; *Pocketful of Miracles* 1961; *Critic's Choice* 1963; *The Patsy* 1964; *Frankie and Johnny* 1965; *Penelope* 1966; *The Gnome-Mobile* 1967; *The Comic* 1969.

Coward, Sir Noel. Playwright, screenwriter, novelist, director, producer, actor, composer. *b.* Dec. 16, 1899, Teddington, England. *d.* 1973. On the stage from the age of 12, he went on to become one of the most creative and controversial figures of the British theater. He was the author of numerous plays, mostly sophisticated comedies, several of which have been adapted to the screen. He also wrote a number of novels, two autobiographical volumes, short stories, and many songs, including the famous 'Mad Dogs and Englishmen.' His association with films began in 1918, when he played two bit parts in D. W. GRIFFITH's *Hearts of the World.* Later screen activity consisted of acting, screenwriting, producing, and directing. In 1942 he received a special Academy Award "for his outstanding production achievement" on *In Which We Serve,* a magnificent WW II sea saga that he produced, co-directed (with David LEAN), scored, and starred in.

FILMS: *Hearts of the World* (act.) 1918; *The Queen Was in the Parlor* (sc.), *Easy Virtue, The Vortex* (both play basis) 1927; *Private Lives* (play basis) 1931; *Cavalcade, Tonight Is Ours, Bitter Sweet, Design for Living* (all play basis) 1933; *The Scoundrel* (act.) 1935; *Bitter Sweet* (remake; play basis) 1940; *In Which We Serve* (prod., co-dir., music, act.), *We Were Dancing* (play basis, 'Tonight at 8:30') 1942; *This Happy Breed* (prod., play basis) 1944; *Blithe Spirit* (co-prod., sc., from own play), *Brief Encounter* (co-prod., so-sc., from own play) 1945; *The*

Astonished Heart (sc., from own play, music, act.) 1950; *Meet Me Tonight/Tonight at 8:30* (remake; play basis) 1952; *Around the World in 80 Days* (cameo) 1956; *Our Man in Havana, Surprise Package* (both act.) 1960; *Paris When It Sizzles* (act.) 1964; *Bunny Lake Is Missing* (act.) 1965; *Pretty Polly/A Matter of Innocence* (story basis) 1967; *Boom!* (act.), *Star!* (contains material from his plays) 1968; *The Italian Job* (act.) 1969.

Cox, Alex. Director. Born on Dec. 15, 1954, in Liverpool, England. He studied law at Oxford but was drawn to the stage and began directing and acting in plays staged by the university's drama society. Following film production studies at the University of Bristol, he went to the US and in 1981 enrolled at the UCLA film school on a Fulbright scholarship. Unable to find work in the film industry after graduating, he took a job with a car repossession company. This experience, coupled with his interest in punk rock, provided the impetus for Cox's first film, *Repo Man* (1984), a critical success and an instant cult favorite. Punk rock remained the inspiration for his next movie, the made-in-Britain *Sid and Nancy,* a recreation of the bizarre love affair between singer Sid Vicious of the Sex Pistols and an American groupie.

FILMS: *Repo Man* (also sc.) 1984; *Sid and Nancy* (also co-sc.; UK) 1986; *Straight to Hell* (also co-sc.), *Walker* (also co-edit.) 1987; *Highway Patrolman* 1991; *Dead Beat, Floundering, Queen of the Night* 1994; *Death and the Compass* 1997.

Cox, Paul. Director. Born on Apr. 16, 1940 in Venlo, Holland. The son of a film producer, he spent his early childhood as a WW II evacuee. After art school training in still photography, he went to Australia in 1963 as part of a student exchange program by Melbourne University. He returned home after a year but was back in Australia as an immigrant in 1965. He opened a photography studio in Melbourne and immediately became established as one of the country's most widely exhibited and frequently published photographers. At the same time, starting with *Matuta* (1965), he began making highly personal short fiction and documentary films, typically dealing with his favorite subjects, loneliness and alienation, often in metaphysical terms. Graduating to features in the mid-70s, Cox quickly established a reputation as an honest, if eccentric, director who stamps his films with a true personal mark and humanistic passion. His *Lonely Hearts* was named best film at the 1982 Australian Film Awards and Outstanding Film of the Year at the London Film Festival. *Man of Flowers* won the Jury Prize at the 1983 Chicago Film Festival. Based on his own painful experience, *My First Wife* (1984), depicting the breakdown of a man deserted by his spouse, won the awards for best director and best screenplay at the Australian Film Awards. It starred his favorite actress, Wendy HUGHES.

FEATURE FILMS: *Illuminations* (also sc., co-edit.) 1976; *Inside Looking Out* (also prod., co-sc., co-phot. co-edit.) 1977; *Kostas* (also idea) 1979; *Lonely Hearts* (also co-sc.) 1982; *Man of Flowers* (also co-prod., co-sc.) 1983; *My First Wife* (also co-prod., co-sc.) 1984; *Cactus* (also co-prod., co-sc.) 1986; *Vincent: The Life and Death of Vincent Van Gogh* (doc.; also sc., phot. edit.) 1987; *Island* (also prod., sc.) 1989; *The Golden Braid* (also act., prod, sc.) 1990; *A Woman's Tale* 1991.

Cox, Ronny. Actor. Born on Aug. 23, 1938, in Cloudcroft, N.M. *ed.* Eastern New Mexico U. Character player of Hollywood films; occasionally in leads, typically in determined or tough portrayals. Memorable as the villainous executive in two Paul Verhoeven films, *Robocop* and *Total Recall.* Also much on TV.

FILMS INCLUDE: *The Happiness Cage, Deliverance* 1972; *Bound For Glory* 1976; *The Car* 1977; *Gray Lady Down, Harper Valley P.T.A.* 1978; *The Onion Field* 1979; *Taps* 1981; *The Beast Within, Some Kind of a Hero* 1982; *Beverly Hills Cop, Courage/Raw Courage* 1984; *Vision Quest* 1985; *Hollywood Vice Squad* 1986; *Beverly Hills Cop II, Steel Justice, Robocop* 1987; *One Man Force, Total Recall* 1990; *Scissors, Captain America* 1991; *Past Midnight* 1992; *Murder at 1600* 1997.

Cox, Wally. Actor. *b.* Wallace M. Cox, on Dec. 6, 1924, in Detroit. *d.* 1973. *ed.* CCNY; NYU. After WW II Army service, he operated a men's jewelry store, then began appearing in nightclubs in 1948 as a comedian. In the 50s he gained popularity as the shy, unworldly hero of the TV series 'Mr. Peepers' and 'Hiram Holliday.' Himself a bespectacled, shy little man with a high-pitched voice, he began making regular film appearances in the 60s.

FILMS INCLUDE: *State Fair* 1962; *Spencer's Mountain* 1963; *Fate Is the Hunter, The Yellow Rolls-Royce, The Bedford Incident* 1964; *A Guide for the Married Man* 1967; *The One and Only Genuine Original Family Band* 1968; *The Cockeyed Cowboys of Calico County* 1970; *The Barefoot Executive* 1971.

Coyote, Peter. Actor. Born Peter Cohon, in 1942. Versatile lead and character player of the American screen. A former San Francisco dock worker, he joined a local radical mime group. A restless young man, he quit acting at 23 and roamed the country in a mobile home, killing birds and selling their feathers to earn a living. He was nearly 40 by the time he drifted into movies in 1980. A memorable role as the scientist "Keys" in E.T. led to a busy career and many strong, offbeat characterizations, often in leads.

FILMS INCLUDE: *Die Laughing, Tell Me A Riddle* 1980; *Southern Comfort* 1981; *E.T. the Extra-Terrestrial, Endangered Species, Out* 1982; *Timerider, Cross Creek* 1983; *Slayground* (UK), *Strangers Kiss, Heartbreakers* 1984; *Kerouac, Jagged Edge* 1985; *Outrageous Fortune, Un Homme amoureux/A Man in Love* (Fr./It.), *Stacking* 1987; *Baja Oklahoma* 1988; *Heart of Midnight* 1989; *The Man Inside* 1990; *Crooked Hearts* 1991; *Exposure, Bitter Moon* 1992; *Kika* 1993; *Moonlight and Valentino* (unbilled) 1995; *Unforgettable* 1996.

Crabbe, Larry ("Buster"). Actor. *b.* Clarence Lindon Crabbe, Feb. 17, 1907, Oakland, Calif. *d.* 1983. *ed.* USC. Grew up in Hawaii, where he developed into an outstanding swimmer and all-around high school athlete. After placing fourth at the 1928 Amsterdam Olympics, he won the gold medal in the 400-meter free-style swimming event in the 1932 Los Angeles Olympics, breaking a record previously held by another would-be action star, Johnny WEISSMULLER. Like Weissmuller, Crabbe headed for Hollywood and early in his screen career was called upon to portray Tarzan, but unlike Weissmuller, he later diversified into other action-hero roles, mostly in Westerns and adventure serials, and became immensely popular with young audiences as the screen incarnation of science fiction heroes Flash Gordon and Buck Rogers. In the 40s he portrayed Billy the Kid in many PRC-studio low-budget Westerns, with Al "Fuzzy" ST. JOHN as his comic sidekick. When screen roles became scarce he toured with an aquacade and in the 50s starred in the TV series 'Captain Gallant of the French Foreign Legion' with his son, Cullen "Cuffy" Crabbe. He later became athletic director for a resort hotel in the Catskills and became involved in the swimming-pool business. Authored *Energetics* (1970), a physical fitness book for the over-50 set. He was an active member of the planning committee for the 1984 Los Angeles Olympics at the time of his sudden death of a heart attack.

FILMS INCLUDE: *Good News* (extra) 1930; *Maker of Men* (bit) 1931; *The Most Dangerous Game* 1932; *King of the Jungle, Tarzan the Fearless* (feature and serial versions), *The Sweetheart of Sigma Chi* 1933; *Search for Beauty, You're Telling Me, We're Rich Again* 1934; *Nevada, Hold 'Em Yale* 1935;

Flash Gordon (serial), *Arizona Raiders, Desert Gold, Lady Be Careful, Rose Bowl* 1936; *King of Gamblers, Sophie Lang Goes West, Thrill of a Lifetime, Daughter of Shanghai* 1937; *Red Barry* (serial), *Flash Gordon's Trip to Mars* (serial and feature version, *Mars Attacks the World*), *Tip-Off Girls, Hunted Men, Illegal Traffic* 1938; *Buck Rogers* (serial), *Million Dollar Legs* 1939; *Flash Gordon Conquers the Universe* (serial), *Sailor's Lady* 1940; *Billy the Kid Wanted, Jungle Man* 1941; *Jungle Siren, Mysterious Rider, Queen of Broadway, Wildcat* 1942; *Blazing Frontier* 1943; *Valley of Vengeance* 1944; *Shadows of Death* 1945; *Swamp Fire* 1946; *The Sea Hound* (serial), *Last of the Redmen* 1947; *Caged Fury* 1948; *Pirates of the High Seas* (serial), *Captive Girl* 1950; *King of the Congo* (serial) 1952; *Gun Brothers* 1956; *Badman's Country* 1958; *Gunfighters of Abilene* 1960; *The Bounty Killers, Arizona Raiders* 1965.

crab dolly. An elaborate wheeled platform on which a camera is mounted for complex shots. It is equipped with hydraulic steering controls that permit the operator a combination of camera movements in any direction. See also DOLLY.

Crabtree, Arthur. Director. *b.* 1900, Shipley, England. *d.* 1975. Entered British films as an assistant cameraman in 1929, becoming a director of photography in 1935. Directed some commercially successful British films from the mid-40s to the late 50s.

FILMS: *Madonna of the Seven Moons* 1944; *They Were Sisters* 1945; *Caravan* 1946; *Dear Murderer* 1947; *Quartet* (one episode), *The Calendar* 1948; *Don't Ever Leave Me* 1949; *Lilli Marlene* 1950; *Hindle Wakes* 1951; *The Wedding of Lilli Marlene* 1953; *Death Over My Shoulder, West of Suez* 1957; *Morning Call, Fiend Without a Face* 1958; *Horrors of the Black Museum* 1959.

Craig, James. Actor. *b.* James Henry Meador, Feb. 4, 1912, Nashville, Tenn. *d.* 1985. After graduating from the Rice Institute, where he excelled at football and tennis, he headed for Hollywood, where he studied acting while supporting himself with odd jobs and occasional extra appearances in films. Graduating to bits, supporting parts, and finally leads in second features, he was given his best acting opportunity when he portrayed a Faustian character torn between the Devil (Walter HUSTON) and orator Daniel Webster (Edward ARNOLD) in *All That Money Can Buy* (1941), a delightful adaptation of Stephen Vincent Benét's story 'The Devil and Daniel Webster.' Darkly handsome and bearing a strong resemblance to Clark Gable, he was then recruited by MGM as the superstar's replacement during WW II. But despite his natural charm and pleasant soft-tough screen personality, he appeared mostly in routine productions and never became a major star. His three marriages, to actresses Mary June Ray, Jill Jarman, and Sumie Jassi, all ended in divorce.

FILMS INCLUDE: *Thunder Trail* 1937; *The Big Broadcast of 1938, The Buccaneer* 1938; *Flying G-Men* (serial), *The Man They Could Not Hang* 1939; *Winners of the West* (serial), *Zanzibar, South to Karanga, Seven Sinners, Kitty Foyle* 1940; *Unexpected Uncle, All That Money Can Buy* 1941; *Valley of the Sun, Friendly Enemies, Seven Miles from Alcatraz, The Omaha Trail* 1942; *The Human Comedy, Swing Shift Maisie* 1943; *The Heavenly Body, Lost Angel, Kismet, Marriage Is a Private Affair* 1944; *Our Vines Have Tender Grapes, Dangerous Partners, She Went to the Races* 1945; *Boys Ranch* 1946; *Dark Delusion* 1947; *Northwest Stampede* 1948; *Side Street* 1950; *Drums in the Deep South* 1951; *Hurricane Smith* 1952; *Fort Vengeance* 1953; *Massacre, While the City Sleeps* 1956; *Cyclops* 1957; *Four Fast Guns* 1960; *Fort Utah* 1967; *Arizona Bushwhackers* 1968; *Bigfoot* 1970; *The Doomsday Machine* 1973.

Craig, Michael. Actor. Born Michael Gregson, on Jan. 27, 1928, in Poona, India. The son of a British serviceman, he went to England at three, to Canada at ten, then returned to England, where he made his stage debut in repertory in 1949. In the same year he began playing extra parts in films and landed his first speaking role in 1954. His roles gradually increased in importance. He played leads in many films of the late 50s and early 60s, then settled for character roles. Has also acted with the Royal Shakespeare Company in London and New York.

FILMS INCLUDE: *Passport to Pimlico* 1949; *Malta Story, Svengali* 1954; *Passage Home* 1955; *The Black Tent, Yield to the Night/Blonde Sinner, House of Secrets/Triple Deception* 1956; *Campbell's Kingdom* 1957; *The Silent Enemy, Nor the Moon by Night/Elephant Gun, Sea of Sand/Desert Patrol* 1958; *Sapphire, Upstairs and Downstairs* 1959; *The Angry Silence* (also co-story), *Cone of Silence/Trouble in the Sky, Doctor in Love* 1960; *Payroll, No My Darling Daughter!, Mysterious Island* (US/UK) 1961; *A Pair of Briefs, Life for Ruth/Walk in the Shadow, La Città Prigioniera/Conquered City* (It.) 1962; *The Iron Maiden/The Swingin' Maiden, Stolen Hours* (US) 1963; *Vaghe Stelle dell'Orsa/Sandra* (It.), *Life at the Top* 1965; *Modesty Blaise* 1966; *Star!* (US) 1968; *The Royal Hunt of the Sun* (UK/US) 1969; *Country Dance/Brotherly Love* 1970; *A Town Called Hell* (Sp.) 1971; *The Vault of Horror* 1973; *Ride a Wild Pony* 1976; *The Irishman* (Austral.) 1978; *Turkey Shoot/Escape 2000* (Austral.) 1981; *Stanley* 1983.

Craig, Stuart. Art director. One of the most creative production designers of British and American films of the 80s. He shared Academy Awards for the sets of *Gandhi* (1982), *Dangerous Liaisons* (1988), and *The English Patient* (1996).

FILMS INCLUDE: *The Elephant Man* 1980; *History of the World Part I* 1981; *Gandhi* 1982; *Cal* 1983; *Greystoke: The Legend of Tarzan Lord of the Apes* 1984; *The Mission* 1986; *Cry Freedom* 1987; *Dangerous Liaisons* 1988; *The English Patient* 1996.

Crain, Jeanne. Actress. Born on May 25, 1925, in Barstow, Calif. A beauty contest winner (Miss Long Beach) at age 16, she turned to modeling and the following year was named "Camera Girl of 1942." Hollywood was quick to beckon and she made her film debut in 1943. A trim figure and exquisite features were her main assets in a starring career that lasted through the 50s and gradually fizzled out in the 60s. Occasionally she was called upon to try serious acting, as in *Pinky* (Oscar nomination for portrayal of black girl passing for white) and *O. Henry's Full House*, but for the most part she was limited to lending a pretty face to the décor of light films. Married in 1945 to actor Paul Brook (né Brinkman), she is the mother of seven.

FILMS: *The Gang's All Here* 1943; *Home in Indiana, In the Meantime Darling, Winged Victory* 1944; *State Fair, Leave Her to Heaven* 1945; *Centennial Summer, Margie* 1946; *You Were Meant for Me, Apartment for Peggy* 1948; *A Letter to Three Wives, The Fan, Pinky* 1949; *Cheaper by the Dozen, I'll Get By* (cameo) 1950; *Take Care of My Little Girl, People Will Talk* 1951; *The Model and the Marriage Broker, Belles on Their Toes, O. Henry's Full House* ("The Gift of the Magi" episode) 1952; *Dangerous Crossing, City of Bad Men, Vicki* 1953; *Duel in the Jungle* 1954; *Man Without a Star, Gentlemen Marry Brunettes, The Second Greatest Sex* 1955; *The Fastest Gun Alive* 1956; *The Tattered Dress, The Joker Is Wild* 1957; *Guns of the Timberland* 1960; *Twenty Plus Two* 1961; *Madison Avenue, Ponzio Pilato/Pontius Pilate* (It./Fr.), *Neferite Regina del Nilo/Queen of the Nile* (as Nefertite; It.), *Col Ferro e col Fuoco/Invasion 1700/Daggers of Blood* (It./Fr./Yug.) 1962; *Hot Rods to Hell/52 Miles to Terror* 1967; *Skyjacked* 1972; *The Night God Screamed* 1975.

crane. A large, wheeled support that carries a camera on a pivoted arm. The base of the crane is a heavy trolley to which a long BOOM is attached. At the end of the boom a platform is mounted on which the camera is installed as well as three seats—for the director, the camera operator, and a camera assistant. The crane movements are regulated through a power-driven hydraulic system. Counterbalance weights at the other end of the boom allow it to be raised 20 or more feet above the ground, lowered, or swiveled, either hydraulically or mechanically, by the operator from his seat on the platform. The crane is one of the most complex pieces of equipment on a set and is invaluable in shooting large-scale sequences in studios or outdoor locations which require complicated camera movement. In industry slang, the crane is sometimes called a "whirly."

Cravat, Nick. Actor. *b.* 1911. *d.* 1994. Pint-sized acrobat who performed with Burt LANCASTER during the latter's circus days. He demonstrated some dazzling stunts as Lancaster's sidekick in two films of the early 50s and afterward appeared irregularly in motion pictures.

FILMS INCLUDE: *My Friend Irma* 1949; *The Flame and the Arrow* 1950; *Ten Tall Men* 1951; *The Crimson Pirate* 1952; *Veils of Bagdad* 1953; *King Richard and the Crusaders* 1954; *Three-Ring Circus, Davy Crockett King of the Wild Frontier* 1955; *The Story of Mankind* 1957; *Run Silent Run Deep* 1958; *The Way West* 1967; *The Scalphunters* 1968; *Valdez Is Coming* 1971; *Ulzana's Raid* 1972; *The Midnight Man* 1974; *The Island of Dr. Moreau* 1977.

Craven, Frank. Actor, playwright, screenwriter. *b.* 1875, Boston. *d.* 1945. A veteran Broadway character player and the author of many light stage plays, he went to Hollywood with the change to sound and became active in films as screenwriter and actor. He also directed one film, *That's Gratitude* (1934). He is best remembered as the narrator–stage manager in both the stage and screen versions of *Our Town.* Played a wide variety of character parts in many other films.

FILMS INCLUDE: As writer—*New Brooms* (play basis) 1925; *The First Year* (play basis) 1926; *Too Many Cooks* (play basis) 1931; *The First Year* (remake; play basis), *Handle with Care* (co-sc.) 1932; *Her First Mate* (co-play basis, 'Salt Water') 1933; *Sons of the Desert* (orig. story), *That's Gratitude* (sc. from own play; also dir.) 1934; *Annapolis Farewell* (co-sc.) 1935; *Our Town* (co-sc.; also act.) 1940. As actor—*The Very Idea* 1929; *State Fair* 1933; *He Was Her Man, Let's Talk It Over* 1934; *Car 99, Vagabond Lady, Barbary Coast* 1935; *Small Town Girl, The Harvester* 1936; *Penrod and Sam, Blossoms on Broadway* 1937; *You're Only Young Once* 1938; *Miracles for Sale, Our Neighbors—The Carters* (lead role) 1939; *Our Town* (top billed in narrator role; also co-sc.) *City for Conquest* 1940; *The Lady from Cheyenne, The Richest Man in Town* (lead) 1941; *In This Our Life, Pittsburgh, Through Different Eyes* (lead), *Girl Trouble, Keeper of the Flame* 1942; *Dangerous Blondes, Son of Dracula* 1943; *Jack London, Destiny* 1944; *Colonel Effingham's Raid* 1946.

Craven, Wes. Director. Born on Aug. 2, 1949, in Cleveland. *ed.* Wheaton Coll. (B.A.); Johns Hopkins (M.A. in philosophy). After teaching humanities, he entered films in 1970 as a production assistant, then worked as a film editor on several low-budget productions. Turning a director, he specialized in horror and the bizarre, finally scoring a major hit with *A Nightmare on Elm Street* (1984). He also directed TV movies and episodes of series, including 'The Twilight Zone.'

FILMS: *Last House on the Left* (also sc., edit.) 1972; *The Hills Have Eyes* (also sc., edit.), *Deadly Blessing* (also co-sc.) 1981; *Swamp Thing* (also sc.) 1982; *A Nightmare on Elm Street* (also sc.) 1984; *The Hills Have Eyes II* (also sc.) 1985; *Deadly Friend* 1986; *A Nightmare on Elm Street 3: Dream Warriors* (co-sc. co-exec prod. only) 1987; *The Serpent and the Rainbow* 1988; *Shocker* (also sc., exec. prod.) 1990; *The People Under the Stairs* (also sc., co-exec. prod.) 1991; *Wes Craven's New Nightmare* (also sc., act.) 1994; *Vampire in Brooklyn* 1995; *Scream* 1996.

Crawford, Anne. Actress. *b.* Imelda Crawford, 1920, Palestine. *d.* 1956. Blonde, oval-faced leading lady and second lead of British films of the 40s and early 50s. She died at 35 of leukemia.

FILMS INCLUDE: *Prison Without Bars* 1938; *They Flew Alone/Wings and the Woman, The Peterville Diamond* 1942; *The Dark Tower, Millions Like Us* 1943; *2,000 Women* 1944; *They Were Sisters* 1945; *Caravan, Bedelia* 1946; *Master of Bankdam, Daughter of Darkness* 1947; *Night Beat, The Blind Goddess* 1948; *Trio* 1950; *Thunder on the Hill* (US) 1951; *Street Corner/Both Sides of the Law* 1953; *Knights of the Round Table* (as Morgan le Fay), *Mad About Men* 1954.

Crawford, Broderick. Actor. *b.* William Broderick Crawford, Dec. 9, 1911, in Philadelphia. *d.* 1986. Hulking, coarse-featured, gruff-voiced character star of stage, screen, and television. The son of vaudevillian Lester (Robert) Crawford and famed comedienne Helen Broderick, he accompanied his parents on their tours and played bit parts in their comedy routines. After completing his high school education at Dean Academy in Franklin, Mass., he enrolled at Harvard at the insistence of his parents, but dropped out after three weeks and for a while worked as a New York waterfront longshoreman and a tanker seaman. Returning to acting, he performed on radio and in 1934 made his legitimate stage debut in London. Following his 1935 Broadway debut, he was signed by Goldwyn for films and played supporting roles in several minor Hollywood productions. He was back on Broadway in 1937, creating the role of Lennie in Steinbeck's 'Of Mice and Men,' but despite his great success he continued to play unimportant parts in routine films for many years, typically as a thug. In 1949, after 12 years of screen work, he became an overnight star, thanks to a dynamic portrayal of ruthless politican Willie Stark in Robert Rossen's adaptation of Robert Penn Warren's *All the King's Men,* a performance for which he won the 1949 best actor Oscar as well as the New York Film Critics Award. But after two other impressive leads, in the comedy *Born Yesterday* and the drama *The Mob,* Crawford was back in unrewarding roles in lesser films, with the notable exception of Fellini's *Il Bidone* (1955), in which he played a delightful swindler. On TV he starred in the series 'Highway Patrol' (1955–59), 'King of Diamonds' (1961–62), and 'The Interns' (1970). He spent much of the 60s and 70s in Italy and Spain, appearing indiscriminately in cheap Westerns and adventure epics. Increasingly bitter and disillusioned in his later years, Crawford had a reputation as a heavy drinker and barroom brawler.

FILMS INCLUDE: *Woman Chases Man, Submarine D-1* 1937; *Start Cheering* 1938; *Ambush, Sudden Money, Undercover Doctor, Island of Lost Men, Beau Geste, The Real Glory, Eternally Yours* 1939; *Slightly Honorable, I Can Give You Anything But Love, Baby, When the Daltons Rode, Seven Sinners, Trail of the Vigilantes, Texas Rangers Ride Again* 1940; *The Black Cat, Tight Shoes, Badlands of Dakota, South of Tahiti* 1941; *North to the Klondike, Larceny Inc., Butch Minds the Baby, Broadway, Men of Texas, Sin Town* 1942; *The Runaround, Black Angel* 1946; *Slave Girl* 1947; *The Time of Your Life, Sealed Verdict* 1948; *Bad Men of Tombstone, A Kiss in the Dark, Night Unto Night, Anna Lucasta, All the King's Men* 1949; *Cargo to Capetown, Convicted, Born Yesterday* 1950; *The Mob* 1951; *Lone Star, Scandal Sheet, Stop You're Killing Me* 1952; *Last of the Comanches, The Last Posse* 1953; *Night People,*

Human Desire, Down Three Dark Streets 1954; *Il Bidone/The Swindle* (It.), *New York Confidential, Big House USA, Not as a Stranger* 1955; *The Fastest Gun Alive, Between Heaven and Hell* 1956; *The Decks Ran Red* 1958; *La Vendetta di Ercole/Goliath and the Dragon* 1960; *Square of Violence* (Yug./US), *Convicts Four* 1962; *El Valle de las Espadas/The Castilian* (Sp./US) 1963; *A House Is Not a Home* 1964; *Up from the Beach* 1965; *Kid Rodello* (US/Sp.), *Texas Kid/El Tejano/The Texican* (Sp./US), *The Oscar* 1966; *Red Tomahawk, The Vulture* (US/UK/Can.), *Per un Dollaro di Gloria* (Sp./It.) 1967; *Hell's Bloody Devils* (release delayed from 1967) 1970; *Ransom Money* 1971; *Embassy* 1972; *Terror in the Wax Museum* 1973; *Proof of the Man* (Jap.) 1977; *The Private Files of J. Edgar Hoover* (as Hoover) 1978; *A Little Romance* 1979.

Crawford, Joan. Actress. *b.* Lucille Fay Le Sueur, Mar. 23, 1904, San Antonio, Tex. *d.* 1977. Worked as a laundress, waitress, and shopgirl before starting a modest dancing career as a result of winning a Charleston contest. As Billie Cassin (her stepfather's name) she appeared in night spots in Detroit and Chicago and was in a Broadway chorus line when she was spotted by MGM for a Hollywood contract. A nationwide publicity contest to find her a suitable screen name resulted in "Joan Crawford." A top film star over an amazing span of nearly five decades, she rode the Hollywood tide with driving ambition, hard work, and remarkable adaptability.

During the flapper era of the late 20s she rivaled Clara Bow as the personification of Charleston-dancing flaming youth. In the socially conscious 30s she was the incarnation of the Depression-wise working girl reaching out for the top. Later in the decade and in the early WW II years she represented Hollywood glamour at its shiniest. In the 40s, following the termination of her MGM contract after being written off as "box-office poison," she bounced back as a superstar at Warner Bros. in a new image, playing the suffering heroine of pulp melodramas and winning a 1945 Academy Award for her performance as the sacrificing mother in *Mildred Pierce*. She was Oscar-nominated twice more: for *Possessed* (1947) and *Sudden Fear* (1952). During the 50s she played mature femme fatales, and in the 60s, when again she was considered through in the business, she came back triumphantly in the horror genre as the co-star of her former rival, Bette Davis, in the surprise box-office hit *What Ever Happened to Baby Jane?*

Broad-shouldered and somber-faced, Miss Crawford never ranked among Hollywood's great sex symbols, nor has she been counted among the screen's most accomplished actresses; yet few in filmdom have rivaled her for star glamour and for durability as a top-ranking celluloid queen. Three of her four husbands were actors, Douglas Fairbanks, Jr. (1928–33), Franchot Tone (1935–39), and Philip Terry (1942–46). Her fourth husband was Alfred Steele, board chairman of Pepsi-Cola, whom she married in 1956. Widowed in 1959, she became active with the beverage company as a board member and publicity executive but returned to the screen every time she was offered a role. She wrote two volumes of memoirs, *A Portrait of Joan* (1962) and *My Way of Life* (1971). Her adopted daughter, Christina, portrayed her as a cruel, manipulative mother in a best-selling biography, *Mommie Dearest* (1978). Faye Dunaway impersonated Crawford in the book's 1981 screen adaptation.

FILMS: *Lady of the Night, Proud Flesh, Pretty Ladies, Old Clothes, The Only Thing, Sally Irene and Mary* 1925; *The Boob, Tramp Tramp Tramp, Paris* 1926; *The Taxi Dancer, Winners of the Wilderness, The Understanding Heart, The Unknown, Twelve Miles Out, Spring Fever* 1927; *West Point, Rose Marie, Across to Singapore, The Law of the Range, Four Walls, Our Dancing Daughters, Dream of Love* 1928; *The Duke Steps Out, The Hollywood Revue of 1929, Our Modern Maidens, Untamed* 1929; *Montana Moon, Our Blushing Brides, Paid* 1930; *Dance Fools Dance, Laughing Sinners, This Modern Age, Possessed* 1931; *Grand Hotel, Letty Lynton, Rain* 1932; *Today We Live, Dancing Lady* 1933; *Sadie McKee, Chained, Forsaking All Others* 1934; *No More Ladies, I Live My Life* 1935; *The Gorgeous Hussy, Love on the Run* 1936; *The Last of Mrs. Cheyney, The Bride Wore Red* 1937; *Mannequin, The Shining Hour* 1938; *Ice Follies of 1939, The Women* 1939; *Strange Cargo, Susan and God* 1940; *A Woman's Face, When Ladies Meet* 1941; *They All Kissed the Bride, Reunion in France* 1942; *Above Suspicion* 1943; *Hollywood Canteen* 1944; *Mildred Pierce* 1945; *Humoresque* 1946; *Possessed, Daisy Kenyon* 1947; *Flamingo Road, It's a Great Feeling* (cameo) 1949; *The Damned Don't Cry, Harriet Craig* 1950; *Goodbye My Fancy* 1951; *This Woman Is Dangerous, Sudden Fear* 1952; *Torch Song* 1953; *Johnny Guitar* 1954; *Female on the Beach, Queen Bee* 1955; *Autumn Leaves* 1956; *The Story of Esther Costello* 1957; *The Best of Everything* 1959; *What Ever Happened to Baby Jane?* 1962; *The Caretakers* 1963; *Straight-Jacket* 1964; *I Saw What You Did* 1965; *Berserk* (UK) 1967; *Trog* 1970.

Crawford, Michael. Actor. Born Michael Dumble-Smith, on Jan. 19, 1942, in Salisbury, England. Light, pleasant leading man of British stage, screen, and television. A former St. Paul's Cathedral choirboy, he dropped out of school at 15 to begin a busy professional career in BBC radio, early TV, and films. He achieved perhaps his greatest success on the stage in the 80s, starring in the musical 'Barnum' and scoring a huge hit in both the London and New York productions of 'The Phantom of the Opera'. He won Broadway's Tony Award for the latter in 1988.

FILMS INCLUDE: *Soap Box Derby, Blow Your Own Horn* 1958; *Two Living One Dead* 1962; *Two Left Feet, The War Lover* 1963; *The Knack* 1965; *A Funny Thing Happened on the Way to the Forum* (US) 1966; *The Jokers, How I Won the War* 1967; *Hello Dolly* (US) 1969; *The Games, Hello-Goodbye* (US) 1970; *Alice's Adventures in Wonderland* (as the White Rabbit) 1972; *Condorman* 1981.

Creative Artists Agency (CAA). Powerful Hollywood talent agency, once headed by Michael Ovitz, who co-founded it in 1975, leaving in 1995 for a post at Disney. Also leaving the agency, in 1996, was Ron Meyer who joined Universal studios. Since then, its client list has dwindled slightly but it still reads like a who's who of Hollywood's most sought-after actors, directors, and screenwriters.

credits. 1. A list of the names of the principals involved in the production of a motion picture with their functions—*e.g.*, the stars, the featured players, the director, the producer, the screenwriter, the director of photography. The list appears as titles, usually at the beginning or end of a film, or both. Since the early 50s there has been a tendency to substitute straight credit listings with more imaginative methods involving superimposition over action scenes, bold designs, animation, and special effects. 2. A list of titles of films in which an actor, a director, or some other individual has been involved.

Cregar, Laird. Actor. *b.* Samuel Laird Cregar, July 28, 1916, Philadelphia. *d.* 1944. *ed.* Winchester Acad. (England); Pasadena Community Playhouse. A big (6' 3"), burly man, he was a nightclub bouncer, among other odd occupations, before breaking into films in 1940. His screen career was to last only five years, but during that brief period he emerged as one of Hollywood's most memorable heavies, notably in his last two films, *The Lodger* (as Jack the Ripper) and *Hangover Square*. He died at age 28 as a result of a crash diet that weakened his heart.

FILMS: *Granny Get Your Gun, Oh Johnny How You Can*

Love, Hudson's Bay 1940; *Blood and Sand, Charley's Aunt, I Wake Up Screaming* 1941; *Joan of Paris, Rings on Her Fingers, This Gun for Hire, Ten Gentlemen from West Point, The Black Swan* 1942; *Hello Frisco Hello, Heaven Can Wait* (as the Devil), *Holy Matrimony* 1943; *The Lodger* (as Jack the Ripper) 1944; *Hangover Square* 1945.

Crenna, Richard. Actor. Born on Nov. 30, 1926, in Los Angeles. *ed.* USC. Leading man of Hollywood and international films. As a teenager performed in many radio serials and later was a regular on the TV series 'Our Miss Brooks' (1952–55), 'The Real McCoys' (1957–63), and 'Slattery's People' (1964–65). Made his screen debut in the early 50s but did not appear regularly in films until the late 60s.

FILMS: *Red Skies of Montana, The Pride of St. Louis, It Grows on Trees* 1952; *Our Miss Brooks, Over-Exposed* 1956; *John Goldfarb Please Come Home* 1965; *Made in Paris, The Sand Pebbles* 1966; *Wait Until Dark* 1967; *Star!* 1968; *Midas Run, Marooned* 1969; *La Spina dorsale del Diavolo/The Deserter* (It./Yug.), *Catlow, Red Sky at Morning, Doctors' Wives* 1971; *Un Flic/A Cop/Dirty Money* (Fr.) 1972; *Jonathan Livingston Seagull* (v/o), *The Man Called Noon* 1973; *Breakheart Pass* 1976; *The Evil* 1978; *Wild Horse Hank* (Can.) 1979; *Stone Cold Dead* (Can.), *Death Ship* 1980; *Body Heat* 1981; *First Blood* 1982; *Table for Five* 1983; *The Flamingo Kid* 1984; *Rambo: First Blood Part II, Summer Rental* 1985; *50 Years of Action* (narr.) 1986; *Rambo III* 1988; *Leviathan* 1989; *Hot Shots! Part Deux* 1993; *Jade, A Pyromaniac's Love Story, Sabrina* 1996.

Crews, Laura Hope. Actress. *b.* Dec. 12, 1879, San Francisco. *d.* 1942. The daughter of a carpenter and a stage actress, she made her debut in stock at age four, retiring three years later to attend school. She returned to the stage at 19 as an ingenue and soon after played leading ladies on Broadway, finally finding her niche as a character actress. She arrived in Hollywood during the transition to sound as a speech coach but soon began appearing in films. Typically played mothers and society matrons whose endearing manners sometimes masked poisonous thoughts. Best remembered as the silly Aunt Pittypat in *Gone With the Wind.*

FILMS INCLUDE: *Charming Sinners* 1929; *New Morals for Old, Rockabye* 1932; *The Silver Cord, Ever in My Heart* 1933; *The Age of Innocence* 1934; *Behold My Wife, Escapade* 1935; *Camille, The Road Back, Confession, Angel* 1937; *Doctor Rhythm, The Sisters, Thanks for the Memory* 1938; *Idiot's Delight, The Star Maker, The Rains Came, Remember?, Gone With the Wind* 1939; *The Blue Bird, The Lady with Red Hair* 1940; *The Flame of New Orleans, One Foot in Heaven* 1941; *The Man Who Came to Dinner* 1942.

Crichton, Charles. Director. Born on Aug. 6, 1910, in Wallasey, England. *ed.* Oxford. He entered British films early in the 30s as editor and worked in that capacity on such distinguished productions as *Sanders of the River* (1935), *Things to Come, Elephant Boy* (1936), and *The Thief of Bagdad* (1940). In 1941 he directed a short, *The Young Veterans,* and three years later began directing features for the Ealing studios. Some of his work has shown the influence of the British documentary movement. Reached his peak in the late 40s and early 50s with such films as *Hue and Cry* (1947), *The Lavender Hill Mob* (1951), and *The Titfield Thunderbolt* (1953), three of Ealing's brightest comedies. He proved equally adept at drama with *The Divided Heart* (1954), but his subsequent output was for the most part unexceptional. In 1962 his career suffered a setback when he quit in mid-production as director of *Birdman of Alcatraz* over a dispute with producer-star Burt LANCASTER. He subsequently worked mainly in TV, directing episodes for the popular 'The Avengers' series, among others. But in 1988 he returned to the big screen triumphantly with *A Fish Called Wanda,* for which he was nominated for an Academy Award as best director.

FEATURE FILMS: *For Those in Peril* 1944; *Painted Boats/The Girl on the Canal, Dead of Night* ("The Golfing Story" episode) 1945; *Hue and Cry* 1947; *Against the Wind, Another Shore* 1948; *Train of Events* ('The Orchestra Conductor' episode) 1949; *Dance Hall* 1950; *The Lavender Hill Mob* 1951; *Hunted/The Stranger in Between* 1952; *The Titfield Thunderbolt* 1953; *The Love Lottery, The Divided Heart* 1954; *The Man in the Sky/Decision Against Time* 1956; *Law and Disorder, Floods of Fear* (also sc.) 1958; *The Battle of the Sexes* 1959; *The Boy Who Stole a Million* (also co-sc.) 1960; *The Third Secret* 1964; *He Who Rides a Tiger* 1965; *Tomorrow's Island* (doc.; also sc.) 1968; *A Fish Called Wanda* (also co-story) 1988.

Crichton, Michael. Novelist, screenwriter, director. Born John Michael Crichton, on Oct. 23, 1942, in Chicago. The son of the executive editor of *Advertising Age,* he grew up in Roslyn, N.Y., and after graduating *summa cum laude* from Harvard, he taught anthropology at England's Cambridge. He then returned to Harvard for medical studies. By the time he received his M.D. degree he had published half a dozen paperback thrillers under the pen name John Lange. He later authored highly successful science-suspense novels under his own name (*The Andromeda Strain, The Terminal Man,* etc.) as well as under such pseudonyms as Michael Douglas (for a collaboration with his younger brother Douglas) and Jeffrey Hudson. After seeing several of his books turned into films by others, he directed a TV movie from his own novel, *Binary,* in 1972, and his first feature film, the stylish, inventive futurist thriller *Westworld,* the following year. His novel about genetically engineered dinosaurs was turned into the phenomenally successful 1993 movie *Jurassic Park*, for which he co-wrote the screenplay. He received the Mystery Writers' Edgar Award in 1968 and 1980.

FILMS: *The Andromeda Strain* (novel basis) 1971; *The Carey Treatment* (novel basis, *A Case of Need,* under pseudonym Jeffrey Hudson), *Dealing: or the Berkeley-to-Boston Forty-Brick Lost-Bag Blues* (co-novel basis), *Binary* (TV movie, from his own novel under pseudonym John Lange; also dir.) 1972; *Extreme Close-Up* (sc.), *Westworld* (dir., sc.) 1973; *The Terminal Man* (novel basis) 1974; *Coma* (dir., sc.) 1978; *The First Great Train Robbery/The Great Train Robbery* (dir., sc., novel basis; UK) 1979; *Looker* (also sc.) 1981; *Runaway* (dir., sc.) 1984; *Physical Evidence* (dir.) 1989; *Jurassic Park* (novel basis, co-sc.), *Rising Sun* (novel basis, co-sc.) 1993; *Congo* (co-sc), *Disclosure* (co-prod.) 1995; *Twister* (co-sc., co-prod.) 1996; *The Lost World* 1997.

Crisp, Donald. Actor, director. *b.* July 27, 1880, Aberfeldy, Scotland. *d.* 1974. *ed.* Eton; Oxford. Fought and wounded in the Boer War. In the US from 1906, he spent two years on the stage, acting and singing in musicals, then joined Biograph in 1908 as an actor. He was Griffith's assistant on *The Birth of a Nation* (1915) and *Broken Blossoms* (1919) and appeared in the former as General Grant and in the latter as Lillian Gish's brutal father, Battling Burrows. He was absent from the screen for a brief period during WW I, when he served as a British secret agent in Russia. In 1922 he supervised the operations of the Famous-Lasky studios in Bombay. Between 1914 and 1930 he directed many films with such stars as Douglas Fairbanks and John Barrymore and co-directed Buster Keaton's *The Navigator.* As an actor he appeared in hundreds of films over a period of 55 years, playing a variety of character roles, ranging from ruthless military men to genial grandfathers. Best remembered as the grand old man in *How Green Was My Valley,* for which he won the 1941 Academy Award for best supporting actor, and later in the *Lassie* movie series. With his film roles slackening in the 50s, he served as an adviser on film production loans for the Bank of Italy (later the Bank of America). His second wife (1932–44) was screenwriter Jane MURFIN.

FILMS INCLUDE: As director—*Her Father's Silent Partner, The Mysterious Shot* (also act.), *The Newer Woman* (also act.), *Their First Aquaintance, The Tavern of Tragedy* (also act.), *Another Chance* (also act.), *The Idiot, Sands of Fate, The Warning* (also act.), *The Niggard* (also act.), *The Little Country Mouse* 1914; *An Old-Fashioned Girl Ramona* (also act. billed as James Needham) 1916; *The Eyes of the World, His Sweetheart, The Bond Between, The Cook of Canyon Camp* (also story, co-sc.), *Lost in Transit, The Countess Charming, The Clever Mrs. Carfax* 1917; *Jules of the Strongheart, The House of Silence, Believe Me Xantippe, The Firefly of France, Less Than Kin, The Goat* 1918; *The Way of a Man with a Maid, Under the Top, Venus in the East, The Poor Boob, Johnny Get Your Gun, Love Insurance, Why Smith Left Home, It Pays to Advertise* 1919; *Too Much Johnson, The Six Best Cellars, Miss Hobbs, Held by the Enemy* 1920; *Appearances* (US/UK), *The Princess of New York, The Barbarian, The Bonnie Brier Bush* (also act.; US/UK) 1921; *Ponjola* 1923; *The Navigator* (co-dir. with Buster Keaton) 1924; *Don Q Son of Zorro* (also act.) 1925; *Sunnyside Up, Young April* 1926; *Nobody's Widow, Man Bait, Vanity, The Fighting Eagle, Dress Parade* 1927; *Stand and Deliver, The Cop* 1928; *Runaway Bride* 1930. As actor—*The French Maid* 1907; *Sunshine Sue* 1910; *The Primal Call, Out from the Shadow, The Battle, The Failure* 1911; *When Kings Were the Law* 1912; *Two Men of the Desert* 1913; *The Great Leap, The Battle of the Sexes, Home Sweet Home, The Escape, The Avenging Conscience* 1914; *The Birth of a Nation* (as Gen. U. S. Grant), *The Commanding Officer, May Blossom* 1915; *Joan the Woman* (also 2nd-unit dir.) 1916; *Broken Blossoms* 1919; *The Black Pirate* 1926; *The River Pirate, The Viking* (as Leif Ericsson) 1928; *The Pagan, Trent's Last Case, The Return of Sherlock Holmes* 1929; *Scotland Yard* 1930; *Svengali, Kick In* 1931; *Red Dust* 1932; *The Key, The Crime Doctor, What Every Woman Knows, The Little Minister* 1934; *Vanessa: Her Love Story, Laddie, Oil for the Lamps of China, Mutiny on the Bounty* 1935; *The White Angel, Mary of Scotland, The Charge of the Light Brigade, Beloved Enemy* 1936; *Parnell, The Life of Emile Zola* 1937; *Jezebel, Beloved Brat, Dawn Patrol, Valley of the Giants, The Amazing Dr. Clitterhouse, The Sisters* 1938; *Juarez, Daughters Courageous, Wuthering Heights, The Oklahoma Kid, The Old Maid, The Private Lives of Elizabeth and Essex* 1939; *Dr. Ehrlich's Magic Bullet, Brother Orchid, The Sea Hawk, City for Conquest* 1940; *Shining Victory, Dr. Jekyll and Mr. Hyde, How Green Was My Valley* 1941; *The Gay Sisters, Forever and a Day, Lassie Come Home* 1943; *The Uninvited, The Adventures of Mark Twain, National Velvet* 1944; *Son of Lassie, The Valley of Decision* 1945; *Hills of Home* 1948; *Whispering Smith* 1949; *Bright Leaf* 1950; *Prince Valiant* 1954; *The Long Gray Line, The Man from Laramie* 1955; *The Last Hurrah* 1958; *A Dog of Flanders, Pollyanna* 1960; *Greyfriars Bobby* (US/UK) 1961; *Spencer's Mountain* 1963.

Cristaldi, Franco. Producer. *b.* Oct. 3, 1924, Turin, Italy. *d.* 1992. Studied law but was attracted to films and started out as a producer of documentaries. Moved on to feature films in 1953 as Italy's youngest producer and was responsible for a number of important productions. In 1977 he was elected president of the International Federation of Film Producers Associations (IFFPA).

FILMS INCLUDE: *La Pattuglia Sperduta* 1953; *Il Seduttore, Camilla* 1954; *Mio Figlio Nerone/Nero's Mistress* 1956; *Kean, Le Notti bianche/White Nights* 1957; *I Soliti Ignoti/Big Deal on Madonna Street* 1958; *Kapò* 1960; *L'Assassino/The Lady Killer of Rome, Divorzio all'Italiana/Divorce Italian Style* 1961; *Salvatore Giuliano* 1962; *I Compagni/The Organizer, La Ragazza di Bube/Bebo's Girl* 1963; *Sedotta e Abbandonata/Seduced and Abandoned, Gli Indifferenti/Time of Indifference* 1964; *Vaghe Stelle dell'Orsa/Sandra* 1965; *Una Rosa per tutti/A Rose for Everyone, La Cina è Vicina/China Is Near* 1967; *Ruba al Prossimo Tuo/A Fine Pair* 1969; *Krasnaya Palatka/The Red Tent* (USSR/It.), *Nel Nome del Padre/In the Name of the Father* 1971; *Il Caso Mattei/The Mattei Affair, Lady Caroline Lamb* (exec. prod.; UK) 1972; *Re: Lucky Luciano, Amarcord* 1973; *Beato Loro* 1975; *Qui comincia l'avventura* 1976; *Mogliamante/Wifemistress* 1977; *Cristo si è fermato a Eboli/Christ Stopped at Eboli/Eboli* 1979; *Caffe Express/Café Express* 1980; *E la Nave va/And the Ship Sails On* 1983; *The Name of the Rose* 1986; *Nuovo Cinema Paradiso/Cinema Paradiso* 1989; *Vanille Fraise* 1989; *C'era un castello con 40 cani* 1990.

Cromwell, James. Actor, director. Born Jamie Cromwell, January 27, in Los Angeles. *ed.* Carnegie Institute of Technology, Pittsburgh, Pa. This stalwart, dependable, and talented character actor spent many years on the stage as an actor and director in regional theater, eventually moving to television with a recurring role on the sitcom classic 'All In the Family.' His feature film debut came in 1976 with the comedy-mystery *Murder by Death*, but it wasn't until his breakthrough performance as the farmer in the Australian film *Babe* (1995) that his talent was fully recognized with an Academy Award nomination as best supporting actor.

FILMS: *Murder by Death* 1976; *The Cheap Detective* 1978; *Nobody's Perfect* 1980; *The Man with Two Brains* 1983; *Revenge of the Nerds, Tank* 1984; *A Fine Mess* 1986; *Revenge of the Nerds II: Nerds in Paradise* 1987; *The Rescue* 1988; *Pink Cadillac* 1989; *The Babe* 1992; *Romeo Is Bleeding* 1994; *Babe* 1995; *Star Trek: First Contact, The People vs. Larry Flynt* 1996; *L.A. Confidential* 1997.

Cromwell, John. Director. *b.* Dec. 23, 1888, Toledo, Ohio. *d.* 1979. On the stage from 1907, arrived Hollywood 1928, following substantial success as a Broadway actor, director, and producer. Appeared as actor in *The Dummy* (1929), he turned to film directing and over the next three decades proved himself a competent technician and capable actors' director and at times a sensitive storyteller. He turned out many glossy productions in the standard studio mold, some of which were of exceptional quality, notably *Of Human Bondage* (1934), *The Prisoner of Zenda* (1937), *Abe Lincoln in Illinois* (1940), *So Ends Our Night* (1941), *The Enchanted Cottage* (1945), and *Anna and the King of Siam* (1946). He made only occasional films after the early 50s, when he returned to the stage as actor, director, and playwright. Married four times, all to actresses, Alice Indahl, Marie Goff, Kay JOHNSON, and Ruth Nelson.

FILMS: *Close Harmony* (co-dir. with Edward Sutherland), *The Dance of Life* (co-dir. with Sutherland), *The Mighty* (also act.) 1929; *Street of Chance, The Texan, For the Defense, Tom Sawyer* 1930; *Scandal Sheet, Unfaithful, The Vice Squad, Rich Man's Folly* 1931; *The World and the Flesh* 1932; *Sweepings, The Silver Cord, Double Harness, Ann Vickers* 1933; *Spitfire, This Man Is Mine, Of Human Bondage, The Fountain* 1934; *Village Tale, Jalna, I Dream Too Much* 1935; *Little Lord Fauntleroy, To Mary with Love, Banjo on My Knee* 1936; *The Prisoner of Zenda* 1937; *Algiers* 1938; *Made for Each Other, In Name Only* 1939; *Abe Lincoln in Illinois, Victory* 1940; *So Ends Our Night* 1941; *Son of Fury* 1942; *Since You Went Away* 1944; *The Enchanted Cottage* 1945; *Anna and the King of Siam* 1946; *Dead Reckoning, Night Song* 1947; *Caged* 1950;

The Company She Keeps, The Racket 1951; *The Goddess* 1958; *The Scavengers* 1959; *A Matter of Morals* (Sw./US) 1960; *Three Women* (as actor only) 1977; *A Wedding* (as actor only) 1978.

Cromwell, Richard. Actor. *b.* Roy M. Radabaugh, Jan. 8, 1910, Los Angeles. *d.* 1960. An artist-decorator, he became interested in acting while painting mask portraits of Hollywood stars. After two days of work as an extra on *The King of Jazz* (1930), he got the leading part in *Tol'able David* and went on to play youthful leads and supporting roles in many films. Boyish and mild-mannered, he was usually cast in shy, soft-spoken, or neurotic roles. His career was interrupted by WW II service with the Coast Guard, after which he returned to the screen only once. He was briefly (1945–46) married to Angela LANSBURY. He died at 50 of cancer.

FILMS INCLUDE: *Tol'able David* 1930; *Fifty Fathoms Deep, Shanghaied Love, Maker of Men* 1931; *Emma, The Strange Love of Molly Louvain, Tom Brown of Culver, The Age of Consent, That's My Boy* 1932; *This Day and Age, Above the Clouds, Hoopla* 1933; *Carolina, Among the Missing, When Strangers Meet* 1934; *The Lives of a Bengal Lancer, Life Begins at 40, Annapolis Farewell* 1935; *Poppy* 1936; *Our Fighting Navy/Torpedoed!* (UK), *The Road Back, The Wrong Road* 1937; *Jezebel, Come on Leathernecks!, Storm Over Bengal* 1938; *Young Mr. Lincoln* 1939; *Enemy Agent, The Villain Still Pursued Her* 1940; *Parachute Battalion, Riot Squad* 1941; *Baby Face Morgan* 1942; *Bungalow 13* 1948.

Cronenberg, David. Director, screenwriter. Born on May 15, 1943, in Toronto. *ed.* U. of Toronto (literature). Horror director whose work has transcended the genre, achieving mainstream recognition. The son of a newspaper stamp columnist and a professional pianist, he wrote a prize-winning story in his college freshman year. While still at school, he was drawn to film and in 1966 made the shorts *Transfer* and *From the Drain.* Working independently, he turned out his first feature in 1969. Horrific, gruesome, stylistically innovative, pervaded with anxiety about sexuality and modern life, his films slowly built a cult following. His 1981 film *Scanners* brought him wider exposure; *The Dead Zone* (1983), the only film he has directed but not written, showed he could create suspense through characters and atmosphere rather than gore. He scored a major hit with his remake of *The Fly* (1988), which succeeded as both a gruesome horror movie and as a tragedy of love, error, and mortality. He achieved broad critical acceptance with *Dead Ringers* (1988), a harrowing psychosexual drama of twin gynecologists locked in a bizarre symbiosis. The film won Genie Awards for best film and best screenplay and the Los Angeles Film Critics' nod as best director. Cronenberg went on to adapt William S. Burroughs's hallucinatory novel *Naked Lunch*.

Although he is much in demand in Hollywood, he still works mainly out of his home base in Toronto, where he lives with his wife and three children, usually writing his own scenarios. His sister, Denise, designed the costumes for *The Fly* and for *Naked Lunch*. It has been conjectured that the slow, agonizing deaths of his ever-ailing parents profoundly influenced David Cronenberg's psyche and his fascination with the morbid and the macabre.

FEATURE FILMS (as director): *Stereo* (also prod, sc., phot., ed.) 1969; *Crimes of the Future* (also prod., sc., phot.) 1970; *Shivers/The Parasite Murders/They Came from Within* (also sc.) 1975; *Rabid/Rage* (also sc.) 1977; *Fast Company* (also co-sc.) 1978; *The Brood* (also sc.) 1979; *Scanners* (also sc.) 1981; *Videodrome* (also sc.) 1982; *The Dead Zone* 1983; *Into the Night* (act. only) 1985; *The Fly* (also co-sc., act. as a gynecologist) 1986; *Dead Ringers* (also co-prod., co-sc.) 1988; *Nightbreed* (act. only) 1990; *Naked Lunch* (also sc.) 1991; *M. Butterfly* 1993; *Trial by Jury* (act. only) 1994; *To Die For* (act. only) 1995; *Crash* 1997.

Cronjager, Edward. Director of photography. *b.* 1904, US. *d.* 1960. In Hollywood as an assistant cameraman from the early 20s, he graduated to cinematographer in 1925. Was in charge of the photography of numerous films of Paramount, RKO, Fox, and other studios, achieving high standards in both outdoor and indoor scenes, initially in black and white and later in color cinematography. Married and divorced actress Kay Sutton, who appeared in several films of the late 30s.

FILMS INCLUDE: *Womanhandled* 1925; *Let's Get Married, Say It Again, The Quarterback* 1926; *Paradise for Two, Man Power, The Gay Defender* 1927; *Sporting Goods, Easy Come Easy Go, Just Married, Warming Up* 1928; *Nothing but the Truth, Fashions in Love, Fast Company, The Virginian* (co-phot.) 1929; *Seven Keys to Baldpate* 1930; *Cimarron* 1931; *The Conquerors* 1932; *Sweepings, Diplomaniacs* 1933; *Spitfire* 1934; *Roberta, Jalna* 1935; *The Texas Rangers* 1936; *Nancy Steele Is Missing, Wife Doctor and Nurse* 1937; *Escape, The Gay Caballero* 1940; *Sun Valley Serenade, Western Union, Rise and Shine* 1941; *To the Shores of Tripoli, The Pied Piper, Friendly Enemies, Life Begins at 8:30* 1942; *Heaven Can Wait, The Gang's All Here* 1943; *Home in Indiana, Irish Eyes Are Smiling* 1944; *Nob Hill* 1945; *Canyon Passage* 1946; *Desert Fury* (co-phot.), *Honeymoon* 1947; *Relentless* 1948; *The Capture, House by the River* 1950; *I'd Climb the Highest Mountain* 1951; *Lure of the Wilderness* 1952; *Beneath the 12-Mile Reef, Treasure of the Golden Condor* 1953; *The Siege at Red River* 1954.

Cronyn, Hume. Actor. Born on July 18, 1911, in London, Ontario, Canada, the son of a prominent Canadian politician, Hume Blake Cronyn. *ed.* Ridley Coll.; McGill (law); AADA. He made his stage debut with the Montreal Repertory Theatre in 1930 while still a student. By 1934 he had reached Broadway and soon gained a reputation for excellence and versatility as both actor and director. He became especially adept at portraying ordinary people—at times fanciful, at others pathetic, and on occasion quite despicable. In 1942 he married the late Jessica TANDY, who teamed with him in many plays, memorably in the two-character 'The Fourposter.' Cronyn's screen career, although secondary to his stage work, has been consistently impressive in memorable supporting parts of a tremendous range. He was nominated for an Academy Award for *The Seventh Cross* (1944). Cronyn, who appeared in two of Hitchcock's films in the 40s, later wrote the adaptations for that director's *Rope* (1948) and *Under Capricorn* (1949).

FILMS: *Shadow of a Doubt, Phantom of the Opera, The Cross Of Lorraine* 1943; *Lifeboat, The Seventh Cross* 1944; *Main Street After Dark* 1945; *The Sailor Takes a Wife, A Letter for Evie, The Green Years, The Postman Always Rings Twice, Ziegfeld Follies* 1946; *The Beginning of the End, Brute Force* 1947; *The Bride Goes Wild* 1948; *Top o' the Morning* 1949; *People Will Talk* 1951; *Crowded Paradise* 1956; *Sunrise at Campobello* 1960; *Cleopatra* 1963; *Hamlet* (as Polonius) 1964; *The Arrangement, Gaily Gaily* 1969; *There Was a Crooked Man* 1970; *Conrack, The Parallax View* 1974; *Honky Tonk Freeway, Rollover* 1981; *The World According to Garp* 1982; *Impulse* 1984; *Brewster's Millions, Cocoon* 1985; *Batteries Not Included* 1987; *Cocoon: The Return* 1988; *The Pelican Brief* 1993; *Camille* 1994; *Marvin's Room* 1996.

Crosby, Bing. Singer, actor. *b.* Harry Lillis Crosby, May 2, 1903, Tacoma, Wash. *d.* 1977. *ed.* Gonzaga U. (Spokane). Began as a vocalist-drummer with a small combo while still attending college. By 1926 was singing with the Paul Whiteman band and in 1930 made his film debut as a member of the band.

He adopted the professional name of "Bing Crosby," reportedly borrowing the "Bing" from his favorite comic strip, 'The Bingville Bugle.' Going solo the following year, he appeared in nightclubs and eight Mack SENNETT shorts and signed a recording contract. Soon he was the star of his own radio show (theme song 'Where the Blue of the Night'), and his records began selling by the millions. Through radio, records, and films he became America's most popular crooner of the 30s and one of the most successful and influential entertainers of all time.

Crosby's relaxed manner and casual delivery set a crooning style that was widely imitated for decades. As a screen personality he made up for a slight build, average looks, and protruding ears with engaging warmth and an affable manner. In the 30s he starred in light musical films that emphasized crooning and romancing. In the 40s he emerged a capable comedian in the profitable "Road" series with Bob HOPE and Dorothy LAMOUR and won an Academy Award for his dramatic portrayal of a Catholic priest in *Going My Way* (1944). He was nominated for Oscars for two subsequent dramatic roles—*The Bells of St. Mary's* (1945) and *The Country Girl* (1954)—but it was in light films that he made his lasting contribution to the American screen.

Crosby amassed a fortune from radio, records, films, and TV during his four decades as entertainer and invested wisely in a wide array of business ventures. Second in wealth only to Bob Hope among show people, his fortune was at one time estimated at anywhere between 200 and 400 million dollars, including holdings in real estate, banking, oil and gas wells, broadcasting, and the Coca-Cola company. He was executive producer of the film *Final Chapter—Walking Tall* (1977). His four sons from his first marriage (in 1930) to singer Dixie Lee—Gary (*b.* 1933; *d.* 1995), Dennis (*b.* 1935; *d.* 1991), Phillip (*b.* 1935), and Lindsay (*b.* 1938; *d.* 1989)—all attempted careers in films but none was successful. Widowed in 1952, Crosby married screen actress Kathryn GRANT (30 years his junior) in 1957. She bore him two more boys and a girl, Mary Crosby (*b.* Sept. 14, 1959, Los Angeles), a TV and film actress, famous as the girl who shot J.R. in the 'Dallas' series. He died of a heart attack at 73 while pursuing his favorite pastime, playing golf. Crosby collaborated on an autobiography, *Call Me Lucky,* in 1953. *Bing and Other Things,* a memoir by Kathryn Crosby (Grant) appeared in 1967, and *Bing,* an authorized biography by Charles Thomson in 1975. After his death, an unflattering portrait of the star as a selfish and callous manipulator emerged in a critical biography, *Bing Crosby—The Hollow Man* (1981) by Donald Shepherd and Robert F. Slatzer. An account of abuse and frequent child-beating was included in a confessional memoir, *Going My Own Way* (1983) by son Gary Crosby. When Bing's youngest son by Dixie Lee, Lindsay Crosby, shot himself to death in 1989 because he ran out of money to support his family, it was revealed the star had stipulated in his will that none of his sons could touch a trust fund he had left them before reaching age 65. Bing's brother, bandleader Bob Crosby (*b.* George Robert Crosby, Aug. 23, 1913, Spokane, Wash.; *d.* 1993), appeared in occasional films of the 40s and 50s.

FILMS (not including shorts and uncredited cameo appearances): *King of Jazz* 1930; *Reaching for the Moon* 1931; *The Big Broadcast* 1932; *College Humor, Too Much Harmony, Going Hollywood* 1933; *We're Not Dressing, She Loves Me Not, Here's My Heart* 1934; *Mississippi, The Big Broadcast of 1936, Two for Tonight* 1935; *Anything Goes, Rhythm on the Range, Pennies from Heaven* 1936; *Waikiki Wedding, Double or Nothing* 1937; *Dr. Rhythm, Sing You Sinners* 1938; *Paris Honeymoon, East Side of Heaven, The Star Maker* 1939; *Road to Singapore, If I Had My Way, Rhythm on the River* 1940; *Road to Zanzibar, Birth of the Blues* 1941; *Holiday Inn, Road to Morocco, Star Spangled Rhythm* 1942; *Dixie* 1943; *Going My Way, Here Come the Waves* 1944; *Duffy's Tavern, The Bells of St. Mary's* 1945; *Road to Utopia, Blue Skies* 1946; *Variety Girl, Welcome Stranger, Road to Rio* 1947; *The Emperor Waltz* 1948; *A Connecticut Yankee in King Arthur's Court, Top o' the Morning* 1949; *Riding High, Mr. Music* 1950; *Here Comes the Groom* 1951; *Just for You, Road to Bali* 1952; *Little Boy Lost* 1953; *White Christmas, The Country Girl* 1954; *Anything Goes, High Society* 1956; *Man on Fire* 1957; *Say One for Me* 1959; *Let's Make Love, High Time, Pepe* 1960; *Road to Hong Kong* 1962; *Robin and the 7 Hoods* 1964; *Stagecoach* 1966; *That's Entertainment* (on-screen narrator) 1974.

Crosby, Floyd. Director of photography. *b.* Dec. 12, 1899, New York City. *d.* 1985. Worked on Wall Street, in the stock exchange before turning to still photography and, in the early 30s, to cinematography. Made his name as the man behind the camera on important documentaries of Robert Flaherty, Pare Lorentz, and Joris Ivens, and in 1931 won an Academy Award for the cinematography of the celebrated Murnau-Flaherty semi-documentary *Tabu.* Not until the early 50s, however, did he begin working on Hollywood feature entertainment. He started out prominently with such major films as Robert Rossen's *The Brave Bulls* (1951) and Fred Zinnemann's *High Noon* (1952) but never allied himself with a major studio. He subsequently worked independently on numerous low-budget productions, including many of the stylish horror and action pictures of Roger CORMAN. He was the father of popular folk-rock singer David Crosby (*b.* Aug. 14, 1941, Los Angeles).

FILMS INCLUDE: *Tabu* 1931; *The River* (co-phot.) 1937; *Power and the Land* (co-phot.), *Fight for Life* 1940; *My Father's House* 1947; *Of Men and Music* (co-phot.) 1950; *The Brave Bulls* (co-phot.) 1951; *High Noon* 1952; *Man in the Dark* 1953; *Five Guns West, Oklahoma* (2nd-unit phot.), *The Naked Street* 1955; *Naked Paradise, Attack of the Crab Monsters* 1957; *The Old Man and the Sea* (2nd-unit phot.), *War of the Satellites, Machine Gun Kelly, I Mobster* 1958; *The Wonderful Country* (co-phot.), *Crime and Punishment USA* 1959; *The Fall of the House of Usher* 1960; *The Pit and the Pendulum, The Explosive Generation, A Cold Wind in August* 1961; *The Premature Burial, Tales of Terror* 1962; *The Raven, The Young Racers, The Yellow Canary, X—The Man with the X-Ray Eyes* 1963; *Sallah* (Isr.), *Comedy of Terrors, Bikini Beach, Pajama Party* 1964; *How to Stuff a Wild Bikini* 1965; *Fireball 500* 1966; *The Cool Ones* 1967; *The Arousers* (co-phot.) 1973.

Croset, Paule. See CORDAY, Rita.

Crosland, Alan. Director. *b.* Aug. 10, 1894, New York City. *d.* 1936 in a car crash. An actor and stage manager from age 15, he joined the Edison company in 1912, working in various capacities before turning director in 1914. Turned out numerous shorts before piloting his first feature in 1917. Subsequently worked for a number of studios, mostly on routine productions. His career got a great lift when he joined Warner Bros. in 1925 and directed *Don Juan* (1926), the first feature with synchronized music, and *The Jazz Singer* (1927), the first talkie. He was married to silent star Elaine Hammerstein. Their son, Alan Crosland Jr., was a film editor and occasional director in the 40s and 50s.

FEATURE FILMS: *Kidnapped, Chris and His Wonderful Lamp, Knights of the Square Table, Light in Darkness* (also sc.), *The Little Chevalier, The Apple-Tree Girl* 1917; *The Unbeliever, The Whirlpool* 1918; *The Country Cousin* 1919; *The Flapper, Youthful Folly, Broadway and Home, Greater Than Fame, Point of View* 1920; *Worlds Apart, Is Life Worth Living?, Room and Board* 1921; *Slim Shoulders, Why Announce Your Marriage?* (also co-story, co-sc.), *The Prophet's Paradise, Shadows of the Sea, The Snitching Hour, A Face in the Fog* 1922; *Enemies of Women, Under the Red Robe* 1923; *Three Weeks, Miami* (also prod.), *Unguarded Women, Sinners in Heaven* 1924; *Contraband, Compromise, Bobbed Hair* 1925; *Don Juan* 1926; *When a Man Loves, The Beloved Rogue, Old San Francisco, The Jazz Singer* 1927; *Glorious Betsy, The Scarlet Lady* 1928; *On with the Show, General Crack* 1929; *The Furies, Song of the Flame, Big Boy, Viennese Nights, Captain Thunder* 1930; *Children of Dreams* 1931; *The Silver Lining, Week Ends Only* 1932; *Hello Sister* 1933; *Massacre, Midnight Alibi, The Personality Kid, The Case of the Howling Dog* 1934; *The White Cockatoo, It Happened in New York, Mr. Dynamite, Lady Tubbs, King Solomon of Broadway, The Great Impersonation* 1935.

Cross, Ben. Actor. Born Bernard Cross, on Dec. 16, 1947, in London. Solemn, high-cheekboned leading man of British films. A high-school dropout at 15, he worked as a window washer, then as a stage hand, prop master, and master carpenter for the Welsh National Opera and as a set builder for the Wimbledon Theatre. Drawn to acting, he trained at the Royal Academy of Dramatic Arts and made his stage debut in 1972. He was an established stage and TV performer by the time he achieved international fame as the star of the film *Chariots of Fire* (1981), which won the best picture Oscar.

FILMS: *Great Expectations* (bit; TV movie in US; theatrically released in UK) 1974; *A Bridge Too Far* 1977; *Chariots of Fire* 1981; *Coming Out of the Ice* 1984; *The Assisi Underground, L'Attenzione/The Lie* (It.) 1985; *The Unholy* 1988; *Paperhouse* 1989; *The House of the Lord* 1990; *The Eye of the Widow* 1991; *First Knight* 1995.

cross cutting. The technique of intercutting two independent sequences to and fro in the course of editing so that a relationship is established between the parallel actions. Crosscutting is the key to tension building in chase scenes, with emphasis shifting back and forth from pursuer to pursued. The technique was elevated to an art by D. W. GRIFFITH in *The Birth of a Nation* (1915) and *Intolerance* (1916) but appeared as early as 1903 in Porter's *The Great Train Robbery.*

cross-plot. A one-page abridged breakdown sheet that shows at a glance the main requirements of a shooting schedule, such as actors, equipment, props. See BREAKDOWN.

cross-wheel. See MALTESE CROSS.

Crothers, Scatman. Actor. *b.* Benjamin Sherman Crothers, May 23, 1910, Terre Haute, Ind. *d.* 1986. A jazz singer-drummer-guitarist, he began performing at age 14. In the mid-30s he formed his own band and toured the Midwest, playing in communities where black men were seldom seen before. Drifting into Los Angeles in the late 40s, he performed on early TV and made his screen debut in the early 50s. A lanky man with a toothy smile, he played many character roles in films, memorably in *The Shining* and *Twilight Zone: The Movie.* His many TV appearances included the role of Louie, the garbage collector, in the series 'Chico and the Man' (1974–78). His nickname was derived from "scatting," the technique of improvising nonsense syllables to jazz melodies, at which he excelled.

FILMS INCLUDE: *Yes Sir Mr. Bones* 1951; *Meet Me at the Fair* 1952; *Walking My Baby Back Home* 1953; *Johnny Dark* 1954; *Between Heaven and Hell* 1956; *The Sins of Rachel Cade* 1960; *Lady in a Cage, The Patsy* 1964; *The Great White Hope, The Aristocats* (v/o) 1970; *The King of Marvin Gardens, Lady Sings the Blues* 1972; *The Fortune, Coonskin, One Flew Over the Cuckoo's Nest* 1975; *Stay Hungry, The Shootist, Silver Streak* 1976; *The Cheap Detective* 1978; *The Shining, Bronco Billy* 1980; *Deadly Eyes/The Rats* 1982; *Twilight Zone: The Movie, Two of a Kind* 1983; *The Journey of Natty Gann* 1985; *The Transformers* (v/o) 1986.

Crouse, Lindsay. Actress. Born Lindsay Ann Crouse, on May 12, 1948, in New York City. *ed.* Radcliffe. The daughter of playwright-librettist-screenwriter Russel Crouse (1893–1966), she began her performing career as a modern and jazz dancer, then moved to acting on the stage, in TV, and in films. She was nominated for an Academy Award as best supporting actress in *Places in the Heart* (1984) and gave a memorable role as the lead in *House of Games* (1987). She is also an accomplished flutist and pianist. Formerly married to playwright David MAMET.

FILMS: *All the President's Men* 1976; *Slap Shot, Between the Lines* 1977; *Prince of the City* 1981; *The Verdict* 1982; *Daniel* 1983; *Iceman, Places in the Heart* 1984; *House of Games* 1987; *Lemon Sky* 1988; *Communion* 1989; *Desperate Hours* 1990; *Being Human* 1994; *Bye, Bye Love, The Indian in the Cupboard* 1995; *The Juror* 1996.

crowd artist. See EXTRA.

Crowe, Cameron. Director, screenwriter. Born July 13, 1957, in Palm Springs, Calif. *ed.* California State University, San Diego. Former rock journalist who wrote for *Rolling Stone* as a teenager and adapted his own novel, *Fast Times At Ridgemont High*, for the screen. Since then, he has become a director-screenwriter whose films take a hip, wry, reflective approach to 80s and 90s youth culture. His talent for creating fascinating characters earned him an Academy Award nomination for his original screenplay *Jerry Maguire* (1996).

FILMS INCLUDE: *American Hot Wax* (act.) 1978; *Fast Times At Ridgemont High* (sc. from book) 1982; *The Wild Life* (prod., sc.) 1984; *Say Anything* (dir., sc.) 1989; *Singles* (dir., sc.) 1992; *Jerry Maguire* 1996.

Crowe, Russell. Actor. *b.* 1964, in New Zealand. Athletic, charismatic leading man of Australian and American films. A child actor in his native land, he had a television series at the age of six, after which he was absent from the screen for twelve years. His welcomed return to acting resulted in the Australian Film Institute award for supporting actor in *Proof* and the best actor award for his performance in *Romper Stomper*. His appealing presence and versatility on film gained the attention of Hollywood, most notably for his performance in *The Sum of Us* (1994), leading to substantial roles in American films.

FILMS: In Australia—*Blood Oath, The Crossing* 1990; *Prisoner of the Sun* 1991; *The Efficiency Expert, Proof, Romper Stomper, Spotswood* 1992; *Hammers Over the Anvil, Love in Limbo, The Silver Stallion, King of the World, Brumbies* 1993; *For the Moment, The Sum of Us* 1994. In the US—*The Quick and the Dead, Virtuosity* 1995; *L.A. Confidential, Rough Magic* 1997.

Crowley, Pat(ricia). Actress. Born on Sept. 17, 1933, in Olyphant, Pa. A former child model, she received her education at New York's High School of Performing Arts. Played leads and second leads in Hollywood films and TV in the 50s and 60s. Her many television appearances included the starring role in the series 'Please Don't Eat the Daisies' (1965–67).

FILMS INCLUDE: *Forever Female, Money from Home, Red Garters* 1954; *The Square Jungle* 1955; *Walk the Proud Land, Hollywood or Bust* 1956; *Key Witness* 1960; *The Scarface Mob* 1962; *The Wheeler Dealers* 1963; *To Trap a Spy* 1966; *The Biscuit Eater* 1972; *Off the Wall* 1977.

Crown Film Unit. See DOCUMENTARY.

Cruise, Tom. Actor. Born Thomas Cruise Mapother IV, on July 3, 1962, in Syracuse, N.Y.. Leading star of Hollywood films of the 80s and 90s. As a boy he suffered from dyslexia and from the breakup of his nomadic family, which kept him moving around the continent, living for brief spells in Louisville, Ottawa, and Cincinnati, where he attended a Franciscan seminary. Finally settling with his remarried mother in Glen Ridge, N.J., he got into acting in high school after a knee injury forced him to quit the wrestling team. Eager to get started, he moved to New York City in 1980 and eked out a living as a busboy and maintenance worker before his film debut in *Endless Love* (1981). At first he was considered just another of Hollywood's "Brat Pack," the new wave of juvenile leads that swept the American screen in the 80s. But in role after role, he proved to be more than just a handsome young man with a winning smile and by the end of the decade he had developed into a genuine superstar. After a strong, mature performance in *Rain Man* (1988), he was nominated for an Academy Award as best actor for his portrayal of Vietnam vet Ron Kovic in *Born on the Fourth of July* (1989). In 1996 he made the leap to producing and starring in the box-office blockbuster *Mission: Impossible*, as well as earning an Oscar nomination as best actor for his sincere, high-energy performance in *Jerry Maguire* (also 1996). Divorced from actress Mimi ROGERS, he is married to actress Nicole KIDMAN.

FILMS: *Endless Love, Taps* 1981; *Losin' It, The Outsiders, Risky Business, All the Right Moves* 1983; *Legend* 1985; *Top Gun, The Color of Money* 1986; *Cocktail, Rain Man* 1988; *Born on the Fourth of July* 1989; *Days of Thunder* (also co-story) 1990; *Far and Away, A Few Good Men* 1992; *The Firm* 1993; *Interview with a Vampire* 1994; *Mission: Impossible* (also co-prod.), *Jerry Maguire* 1996.

Cruze, James. Director, former actor. *b.* James Cruze Bosen, on Mar. 27, 1884, Ogden, Utah. *d.* 1942. The son of a Mormon family of Danish descent, he worked as a fisherman in the Bering Strait to pay his way through drama school. By age 16 he was an actor, appearing in medicine shows, road shows, and stock. In 1906 he became a member of the famed Belasco company and appeared frequently on Broadway. In 1908 he joined the Thanhouser film company and starred in many of its films, including several serials. In 1916 he moved on to Lasky, still as an actor, and in 1918 made his directorial debut.

A facile, energetic, prolific worker, Cruze directed numerous films in the 20s and 30s, many of which have been lost and are unavailable for evaluation. His range of subjects was wide—romantic comedies starring Wallace REID, broad slapstick with "Fatty" ARBUCKLE, suspense thrillers, and large-scale epics. Several of his Arbuckle films were withdrawn from release in 1921 as a result of the Arbuckle scandal. He is best known for *The Covered Wagon* (1923), a meticulously reconstructed Western that influenced not only future Westerns but also historic epics and documentary films. His *Hollywood* of the same year, an unusual fantasy film, contained bold references to the "Fatty" Arbuckle scandal that was rocking Hollywood at the time.

Contemporary critics were even more impressed with Cruze's surrealistic *Beggar on Horseback* (1925), an inventive expressionist film. He made another successful Western that year, *The Pony Express,* but another attempt at historic reconstruction, *Old Ironsides* (1926), was unappreciated by both the critics and the public.

Among Hollywood studio bosses, Cruze had a reputation as a rapid worker and reliable craftsman. He was seldom choosy about his subjects and as a result turned out many routine films, a fact that tends to obscure his important contributions to the art of film. He adjusted easily to the requirements of sound, and his talkies of the 30s include several films of interest and charm.

Cruze married and divorced actresses Marguerite SNOW and Betty COMPSON.

FILMS: As actor (partial list)—*A Boy of the Revolution, She* 1911; *Dr. Jekyll and Mr. Hyde, East Lynne, The Arab's Bride, Lucille, Undine, The Thunderbolt, The Star of Bethlehem* 1912; *Cymbeline, The Marble Heart, Tannhauser, The Legend of Provence* 1913; *Frou Frou, Joseph in the Land of Egypt, Cardinal Richelieu's Ward* (as Richelieu), *The Million Dollar Mystery* (serial) 1914; *Zudora* (serial) 1914–15; *The Patriot and the Spy, Armstrong's Wife* 1915; *The Call of the East, Nan of Music Mountain* 1917; *Belive Me Xantippe* 1918; *Johnny Get Your Gun* 1919. As director (complete)—*Too Many Millions* 1918; *The Dub, Alias Mike Moran, The Roaring Road, You're Fired, The Love Burglar, Valley of the Giants, An Adventure in Hearts, Hawthorne of the U.S.A., The Lottery Man* 1919; *Mrs. Temple's Telegram, Terror Island, A Full House, The Sins of St. Anthony, What Happened to Jones?, Always Audacious* 1920; *The Charm School, The Dollar-a-Year Man, Food For Scandal, Leap Year/Skirt Shy* (not released), *The Fast Freight* (not released), *Gasoline Gus, Crazy to Marry* 1921; *One Glorious Day, Is Matrimony a Failure?, The Dictator, The Old Homestead, Thirty Days* 1922; *The Covered Wagon, Hollywood, Ruggles of Red Gap* (also prod.), *To the Ladies* (also prod.) 1923; *Merton of the Movies* (also prod.), *The Fighting Coward* (also prod.), *The Garden of Weeds* (also prod.), *The City That Never Sleeps* (also prod.), *The Enemy Sex* (also prod.) 1924; *The Pony Express* (also prod.), *Beggar on Horseback* (also prod.), *The Goose Hangs High* (also prod.), *Marry Me* (also prod.), *Welcome Home* (also prod.), *Waking Up the Town* (also co-story) 1925; *Mannequin* (also prod.), *The Waiter from the Ritz* (also prod.), *Old Ironsides* (also prod.) 1926; *We're All Gamblers* (also prod.), *The City Gone Wild* (also prod.) 1927; *On to Reno, The Red Mark, Excess Baggage* (also prod.), *The Mating Call* 1928; *The Duke Steps Out* (also prod.), *A Man's Man* (also prod.), *The Great Gabbo* 1929; *Once a Gentleman* (also prod.), *She Got What She Wanted* (also exec. prod.) 1930; *Salvation Nell* (also exec. prod.) 1931; *If I Had a Million* (two episodes), *Washington Merry-Go-Round* (also exec. prod.) 1932; *Racetrack* (also exec. prod.), *Sailor Be Good, I Cover the Waterfront, Mr. Skitch* 1933; *David Harum, Their Big Moment* 1934; *Helldorado, Two-Fisted* 1935; *Sutter's Gold* 1936; *The Wrong Road* 1937; *Prison Nurse, Gangs of New York, Come On Leathernecks!* 1938.

Cryer, Jon. Actor. Born on Apr. 16, 1965, in New York City. Juvenile lead of stage and screen. The son of actor David Cryer and songwriter-actress Gretchen Cryer.

FILMS INCLUDE: *No Small Affair* 1984; *Pretty in Pink* 1986; *Morgan Stewart's Coming Home, Superman IV: The Quest for Peace, O.C. and Stiggs, Dudes, Hiding Out/Adult Education* 1987; *Penn and Teller Get Killed* 1990; *Hot Shots!* 1991; *The Pompatus of Love* 1996.

Crystal, Billy. Actor. Born on Mar. 14, 1947, in Long Beach, N.Y. *ed.* Marshall U.; NYU Film School. Popular comedian and leading man. The son of a jazz concert producer and a nephew of a record manufacturer, he grew up in a show business atmosphere and began touring coffee houses and college campuses as a stand-up comedian at a young age. He gained popularity on TV talk shows, then scored his first success portraying a gay youth in the hit comedy series 'Soap' (1977–81). His popularity increased after a season (1984–85) on 'Saturday Night Live.' He established himself as a romantic lead in *When Harry Met Sally. . .* (1989) and became known to audiences worldwide as the host of several Oscar telecasts. He made his directorial debut with *Mr. Saturday Night* (1992).

FILMS: *Rabbit Test* 1978; *This Is Spinal Tap* 1984; *Running Scared* 1986; *The Princess Bride, Throw Momma from the Train* 1987; *Memories of Me* (also co-prod. co-sc.) 1988; *When Harry Met Sally. . .* 1989; *City Slickers* (also exec. prod.) 1991; *Mr. Saturday Night* (also dir., prod., co-sc.) 1992; *City Slickers 2: The Legend of Curly's Gold* (also co-prod., co-sc.) 1994; *Forget Paris* (also dir., prod., co-sc.) 1995; *Hamlet* 1996; *Father's Day* 1997.

c.s. An abbreviation commonly used in scripts to designate a CLOSE SHOT.

c.u. An abbreviation commonly used in scripts to designate a CLOSE-UP shot.

Cuba. A newsreel account of the extinction of a fire inaugurated film production on this Caribbean island in 1897. Regular production of short fiction films began in 1908. Most of the films of the period were directed by Enrique Diaz Quesada, who completed his first feature length film, *Manuel Garcia,* in 1913. Cuban silent films often dealt with social and revolutionary themes. The sound era opened with the musical short *Maracas y Bongoes,* followed by the feature *La Serpiente Roja.* Characteristically, Cuban sound films of the 30s, 40s, and 50s were for the most part light musicals and comedies with little attention to quality. Many Americans associated the Cuban film industry with its thriving porno branch, which supplied many a stag party with smuggled clandestine entertainment.

Shortly after the Castro revolution, a central body, Instituto Cubano del Arte y Industria Cinematográficos (ICAIC), was set up by the government to handle the country's film production, distribution, and exhibition. Film was declared a tool of the revolution, and filmmakers were encouraged to make films relevant to the social and political aims of the regime. Since 1960 an average of four feature films have been produced annually, but the backbone of the Cuban film industry is educational shorts and propaganda documentaries. Characteristically, Cuban documentaries, and often also the feature films, are didactic and militant, with "Yankee imperialism" a frequent target.

Some of these films, like *Now* (1965) and *LBJ* (1968), extended their anti-American theme into a depiction of American "brutality" at home and in the Far East, respectively, and so went beyond merely depicting the US as the principal enemy of the Cuban revolution. The anti-American bias eased in the 70s, but Cuban films continue to be revolutionary in content and tone.

In 1992, the ICAIC was forcibly merged with the film department of the armed services, a move officials attributed to economics, but which was branded by independent filmmakers as a further move to restrict artistic freedom. Recent years have been marked by censorship of films critical of Cuban life, including such hugely popular features as *Alicia en el Pueblo de Maravillas*, *El Encanto del Regreso*, *Adorables mentiras*, and others, regardless of whether the films contain any overt political themes. Filmmakers have been imprisoned for making "counter-revolutionary" films, and many, such as director/screenwriter Jesus Diaz, have fled the country.

Among leading Cuban film directors of the last fifty years are Santiago ALVAREZ, Tomás GUTIÉRREZ ALEA, Sergio Giral, Mañuel Octavio Gomez, and Humberto SOLAS.

cue. A designated signal, in the form of an action, a marking, or a line of dialogue which alerts a performer to enter, speak, etc., or a technician to activate equipment.

cue cards. Large cardboard panels on which dialogue or narration are hand-printed. They are held by an assistant next to the camera for the benefit of a performer who cannot remember his lines and are popularly known as "idiot cards." In many cases, cue cards have been replaced by the Tele-Prompter, an electronic device mounted on or next to the camera which achieves the same purpose with more precision.

cue mark. 1. A mark made by the editor on a work print, either by scratching or by a chinagraph pencil, to indicate the point at which narration is to start, music is to fade in or out, sound effects are to be introduced, etc. 2. A small dot appearing on a corner of the frame of a release print to indicate the approach of the end of a reel, thus alerting the projectionist to switch on the motor of his second projector and to be ready for the moment of CHANGE-OVER from one machine to the other.

Cugat, Xavier. Bandleader. *b.* Jan. 1, 1900, Barcelona, Spain. *d.* 1990. Came to the US from Havana, where he was raised from age three. He was a cartoonist for the Los Angeles *Times* before introducing his first band at Hollywood's Cocoanut Grove in 1928. In the 30s and 40s he was known as America's "Rhumba King" and did much to introduce and popularize Latin rhythms in the US. He appeared in occasional films, playing genial characters, usually himself, and leading his orchestra memorably in MGM musicals of the 40s. Inactive after suffering a stroke in 1971. The third of his four wives was singer-actress Abbe Lane. The fourth was TV entertainer Charo. Autobiography: *Rhumba Is My Life* (1948).

FILMS INCLUDE: *Go West Young Man* 1936; *You Were Never Lovelier* 1942; *Stage Door Canteen* 1943; *Two Girls and a Sailor, Bathing Beauty* 1944; *Weekend at the Waldorf* 1945; *Holiday in Mexico, No Leave No Love* 1946; *This Time for Keeps* 1947; *Luxury Liner, On an Island with You, A Date with Judy* 1948; *Neptune's Daughter* 1949; *Chicago Syndicate* 1955; *The Monitors* (cameo) 1969; *The Phynx* (cameo) 1970.

Cukor, George. Director. *b.* July 7, 1899, New York City. *d.* 1983. Drawn to the stage in his teens, he entered the theater professionally in 1919 as stage manager for a Chicago company. The following year he became resident director of a stock company in Rochester, N.Y. By 1926 he was directing such stars as Ethel Barrymore, Jeanne Eagels, and Laurette Taylor on Broadway. In 1929 he joined the mass exodus of Broadway talent to a Hollywood undergoing the big switch to sound.

First engaged as a dialogue director, Cukor coached the actors of Milestone's *All Quiet on the Western Front,* among other films. In 1930 he co-directed three films for Paramount, handling the acting and the dialogue while leaving the action sequences to experienced veteran directors of the silent screen. The following year he made his debut as solo director with *Tarnished Lady,* starring Tallulah Bankhead. But his stay with Paramount was brief. He was sacked by Ernst Lubitsch from the set of *One Hour with You* (1932). Lubitsch, who started out as producer of the film, got the director's credit as well. Cukor then followed his friend David O. SELZNICK to RKO and later to MGM. Their professional association, which resulted in such memorable films as *A Bill of Divorcement, Dinner at Eight,* and *Little Women,* came to an end in 1938, when Selznick fired Cukor from the set of *Gone With the Wind* only ten days after the start of production.

In the meantime, Cukor had solidified his position in Hollywood with such films as *Camille* and *Holiday.* Disheartening as the *Gone With the Wind* affair must have been, he was able to bounce back with two successive triumphs, *The Women* and *The Philadelphia Story.* He experienced a certain creative drought in the 40s, particularly in the fiasco of *Two-Faced Woman,* memorable forever as the film that hastened Greta Garbo's retirement. (Ironically, it was Cukor who had guided Garbo to her best screen performance, in *Camille.*) But he came back strongly late in the decade and in the early 50s with two Tracy-Hepburn comedies, a couple of Judy Holliday vehicles, and *A Star Is Born,* which is believed by some to be one of his finest films.

Almost from the start of his career Cukor has been typed by film critics as an "actor's director" and, more specifically, as a "woman's director." This reputation has been substantiated over the years by some remarkable performances he was able to extract from such famous stars as Greta Garbo, Katharine Hepburn, Norma Shearer, and Joan Crawford. But the label does not do full justice to Cukor's contribution to the cinema. True, he was essentially a man of the theater and much of his film style is attributable to the influence of the stage. While his material was often adapted from the stage, and even his characters were frequently theater people, most of his films look nothing like photographed stage plays.

Cukor's handling of scenes was seldom flamboyant and he rarely exhibited technical virtuosity for its own sake. But his handling of action, when required, was often skillful and his camera work as fluid as anyone else's. He did not write his own scripts, but he selected his material with tasteful discretion. His most fruitful collaboration was with writer Garson KANIN. In 1964, Cukor received an Academy Award for the direction of *My Fair Lady,* decidedly not among his best films. He continued directing sporadically into his 80s.

FILMS: *Grumpy* (co-dir. with Cyril Gardner), *The Virtuous Sin* (co-dir. with Louis Gasnier), *The Royal Family of Broadway* (co-dir. with Gardner) 1930; *Tarnished Lady, Girls About Town* 1931; *One Hour with You* (co-dir. with Lubitsch; credited to Lubitsch), *What Price Hollywood, A Bill of Divorcement, Rockabye* 1932; *Our Betters, Dinner at Eight, Little Women* 1933; *David Copperfield* 1935; *Sylvia Scarlett, Romeo and Juliet* 1936; *Camille* 1937; *Holiday, Zaza* 1938; *Gone With the Wind* (replaced by Victor Fleming; uncredited), *The Women* 1939; *The Philadephia Story, Susan and God* 1940; *A Woman's Face, Two-Faced Woman* 1941; *Her Cardboard Lover* 1942; *Keeper of the Flame* 1943; *Resistance and Ohm's Law* (doc. for Army Signal Corps), *Gaslight, Winged Victory* 1944; *Desire Me* (co-dir. with Mervyn LeRoy, neither credited), *A Double Life* 1947; *Edward My Son* (US/UK), *Adam's Rib* 1949; *Born Yesterday, A Life of Her Own* 1950; *The Model and the Marriage Broker, The Marrying Kind, Pat and Mike* 1952; *The Actress* 1953; *It Should Happen to You, A Star Is Born* 1954; *Bhowani Junction* 1956; *Les Girls, Wild Is the Wind* 1957; *Heller in Pink Tights, Song Without End* (completed for the deceased Charles Vidor; declined screen credit), *Let's Make Love* 1960; *The Chapman Report* 1962; *My Fair Lady* 1964; *Justine* (replaced Joseph Strick) 1969; *Travels with My Aunt* (also co-prod.; UK) 1973; *The Blue Bird* (US/USSR) 1976; *The Corn Is Green* (TV movie) 1979; *Rich and Famous* 1981.

Culkin, Macaulay. Actor. Born on Aug. 26, 1980, in New York, N.Y. Blond exemplar of late-20th century childhood impishness. After making his stage debut in New York at age four, he spent the next years of his childhood in a mix of classical and commercial training, including study with the School of the American Ballet (with George Balanchine) and appearances in TV commercials and a Michael Jackson video. Following the success of *Home Alone* he became one of the highest paid stars in Hollywood.

FILMS: *Rocket Gibraltar* 1988; *See You in the Morning, Uncle Buck* 1989 *Jacob's Ladder, Home Alone* 1990; *Only the Lonely, My Girl* 1991; *Home Alone 2: Lost in New York* 1992; *The Good Son, The Nutcracker* 1993; *Getting Even with Dad, The Pagemaster, Ritchie Rich* 1994.

Culp, Robert. Actor. Born on Aug. 16, 1930, in Berkeley, Calif. *ed.* Stockton; Coll. of the Pacific; Washington U.; San Francisco State. Leading man of the American stage, TV, and films, typically in cynical roles. Made his stage debut on Broadway at age 21. Later appeared in several off-Broadway productions, but it was on TV that he became a star, in such series as 'Trackdown' and 'I Spy.' He also wrote scripts for some of the episodes of 'The Rifleman' and 'I Spy.' His film appearances have been sporadic. In the early 70s he ventured for the first time into directing. At one time married to actress France NUYEN.

FILMS: *PT-109* 1963; *The Raiders, Sunday in New York, Rhino!* 1964; *Bob & Carol & Ted & Alice* 1969; *Hannie Caulder* 1971; *Hickey and Boggs* (also dir.) 1972; *The Castaway Cowboy* 1974; *Inside Out* (UK) 1975; *Sky Riders* (US/Ger.), *Breaking Point* (Can.), *The Great Scout and Cathouse Thursday* 1976; *Goldengirl* 1979; *Turk 182!* 1985; *Big Bad Mama II* 1987; *Silent Night Deadly Night III: Better Watch Out!, Pucker Up and Bark Like a Dog* 1989; *Timebomb, Nameless* 1991; *The Pelican Brief* 1993; *Panther* 1995.

Culver, Roland. Actor. *b.* Aug. 31, 1900, London. *d.* 1984. *ed.* Highgate Coll.; RADA. An RAF pilot during World War I, he made his stage debut in 1925 and entered British films in 1931. Often played droll character parts typifying a British gentleman. Seen in some US films starting in the mid-40s.

FILMS INCLUDE: *Flat No. 9* 1931; *77 Park Lane, There Goes the Bride* 1932; *Nell Gwyn* 1934; *Accused* 1936; *Paradise for Two/The Gaiety Girls* 1937; *French Without Tears, Night Train to Munich/Night Train* 1939; *Quiet Wedding* 1940; *This England* 1941; *The Day Will Dawn/The Avengers, The First of the Few/Spitfire* 1942; *The Life and Death of Colonel Blimp, Dear Octopus/The Randolph Family* 1943; *On Approval, Dead of Night, Perfect Strangers/Vacation from Marriage* 1945; *To Each His Own* (US), *English Without Tears/Her Man Gilbey, Wanted for Murder* 1946; *Down to Earth* (US), *Singapore* (US) 1947; *The Emperor Waltz* (US), *Isn't It Romantic?* (US) 1948; *The Great Lover* (US) 1949; *Trio* 1950; *Hotel Sahara, The Late Edwina Blake/Obsessed, Encore* 1951; *The Hour of 13, Folly to Be Wise* 1952; *Betrayed* (US/UK) 1954; *The Man Who Loved Redheads, Touch and Go, The Ship That Died of Shame* 1955; *Safari* 1956; *The Vicious Circle/The Circle* 1957; *Bonjour Tristesse, Rockets Galore/Mad Little Island, Next to No Time* 1958; *A Pair of Briefs, Term of Trial* 1962; *The Iron Maiden/The Swingin' Maiden* 1963; *The Yellow Rolls-Royce* 1964; *Thunderball* 1965; *A Man Could Get Killed* (US) 1966; *In Search of Gregory* (UK/It.) 1970; *Fragment of Fear* 1971; *A Bequest to the Nation/The Nelson Affair, The Legend of Hell House, The Mackintosh Man* 1973; *The Greek Tycoon* (US) 1978; *Rough Cut* 1980; *Britannia Hospital, The Missionary* 1982.

Cummings, Constance. Actress. Born Constance Halverstadt, on May 15, 1910, in Seattle, Wash., the daughter of an attorney and Kate Cummings, a concert soprano. She made her stage debut at 16 in stock and in 1928 reached Broadway as a chorus girl in musicals. Early in the 30s she went to Hollywood, where she played leads in more than 20 films, both dramas and light fare, in the course of four years, but her roles rarely matched her sophistication and considerable acting talent, which she was better able to demonstrate on the Broadway stage. In the mid-30s she left the US for England, where she continued her acting career on the stage and in films. She was married to the late British playwright and stage producer Benn W. Levy.

FILMS INCLUDE: In the US—*The Criminal Code, The Last Parade, Traveling Husbands, Lover Come Back, The Guilty Generation* 1931; *Behind the Mask, Attorney for the Defense, The Big Timer, Movie Crazy* (opposite Harold Lloyd), *Night After Night, American Madness, The Last Man, Washington Merry-Go-Round* 1932; *The Billion Dollar Scandal, Broadway Thru a Keyhole, The Charming Deceiver, The Mind Reader* 1933; *Glamour, This Man Is Mine, Looking for Trouble* 1934; *Remember Last Night* 1935; In the UK—*Seven Sinners/Doomed Cargo, Strangers on a Honeymoon* 1936; *Busman's Honeymoon/Haunted Honeymoon* 1940; *This England* 1941; *The Foreman Went to France/Somewhere in France* 1942; *Blithe Spirit* 1945; *Into the Blue/Man in the Dinghy* 1951; *John and Julie* 1955; *The Intimate Stranger/Finger of Guilt* 1956; *Battle of the Sexes* 1959; *Sammy Going South/A Boy Ten Feet Tall, In the Cool of the Day* (US; filmed in Greece) 1963; *Dead Man's Folly* (TV movie in the US) 1986.

Cummings, Irving. Actor, director. *b.* Oct. 9, 1888, New York City. *d.* 1959. Appeared with Lillian Russell's stage company before entering films in 1909. He was a popular leading man in many silent pictures, then turned director in the early 20s. His initial films as director, both silents and talkies, were mostly in the action vein, often sprinkled with humor. From the mid-30s he specialized in 20th Century-Fox musicals and light films and directed some of the best-known vehicles of, among others, Shirley Temple, Alice Faye, and Betty Grable. Not a very original director but a consistent craftsman of solid entertainment. He was married to silent screen actress Ruth Sinclair.

FILMS: As actor (partial list)—*Camille, The Faith Healer* 1912; *The Bells, Ashes, The Fight for Right* 1913; *Jane Eyre, The Last Volunteer, Uncle Tom's Cabin, The Million Dollar Mystery* (serial) 1914; *The Diamond from the Sky* (serial) 1915; *The Saleslady, The Gilded Cage, The Lure of the Mask* 1916; *An American Widow, The Whip, A Royal Romance, Rasputin the Black Monk* 1917; *The Interloper, Toys of Fate, The Woman Who Gave* 1918; *Auction of Souls, The Bluffer, Mandarin's Gold, The Scar, Don't Change Your Husband, Men Women and Money, Secret Service, Everywoman* 1919; *Sex, The Round-Up* 1920; *The Saphead, Old Dad* 1921; *The Eternal Flame* 1922; *Rupert of Hentzau* 1923. As director (complete)—*The Man from Hell's River* (also prod., sc., act.), *Flesh and Blood* (also prod.), *Paid Back, Broad Daylight, The Jilt, Environment* (also prod.) 1922; *The Drug Traffic* (also exec. prod.), *East Side West Side* (also prod.), *Broken Hearts of Broadway* (also prod.) 1923; *Stolen Secrets, Fools' Highway, The Dancing Cheat, Riders Up, In Every Woman's Life, The Rose of Paris* 1924; *As Man Desires* (also act.), *One Year to Live, The Desert Flower, Just a Woman, Infatuation* 1925; *The Johnstown Flood, Rustling for Cupid, The Midnight Kiss, The Country Beyond* (also co-sc.), *Bertha the Sewing Machine Girl* 1926; *The Brute* 1927; *The Port of Missing Girls, Dressed to Kill* (also co-story), *Romance of the Underworld/Romance and Bright Lights* 1928; *In Old Arizona* (co-dir. with Raoul Walsh), *Not Quite Decent, Behind That Curtain* 1929; *Cameo Kirby, On the Level, A Devil with Women* 1930; *A Holy Terror, The Cisco Kid, Attorney for the Defense, The Night Club Lady, Man Against Woman* 1932; *Man Hunt, The Woman I Stole, The Mad Game* 1933; *I Believed in You, Grand Canary, The White Parade* 1934; *It's a Small World, Curly Top* 1935; *Nobody's Fool, The Poor Little Rich Girl, Girls' Dormitory, White Hunter* 1936; *Vogues of 1938, Merry-Go-Round of 1938* 1937; *Little Miss Broadway, Just Around the Corner* 1938; *The Story of Alexander Graham Bell, Hollywood Cavalcade, Everything Happens at Night* 1939; *Lillian Russell, Down Argentine Way* 1940; *That Night in Rio, Belle Starr, Louisiana Purchase* 1941; *My Gal Sal, Springtime in the Rockies* 1942; *Sweet Rosie O'Grady, What a Woman!* (also prod.) 1943; *The Impatient Years* (also prod.) 1944; *The Dolly Sisters* 1945; *Double Dynamite* 1951.

Cummings, Jack. Producer. *b.* 1905, New Brunswick, Canada. *d.* 1989. A nephew of MGM boss Louis B. MAYER, he joined the studio at 17. Worked his way up from MGM office boy through script clerk, assistant director, and short-subject director-producer before becoming a feature producer in 1934. In charge of many successful MGM musicals.

FILMS INCLUDE: *The Winning Ticket* 1935; *Born to Dance* 1936; *Broadway Melody of 1937, Yellow Jack* 1937; *Broadway Melody of 1940, Go West* 1940; *I Dood It* 1943; *Bathing Beauty* 1944; *Easy to Wed* 1946; *The Romance of Rosy Ridge, Fiesta* 1947; *Neptune's Daughter, The Stratton Story* 1949; *Three Little Words, Two Weeks with Love* 1950; *Texas Carnival* 1951; *Lovely to Look At* 1952; *Sombrero, Kiss Me Kate!* 1953; *Seven Brides for Seven Brothers, The Last Time I Saw Paris* 1954; *Interrupted Melody* 1955; *The Teahouse of the August Moon* 1956; *The Blue Angel* 1959; *Can Can* 1960; *The Second Time Around* 1961; *Bachelor Flat* 1962; *Viva Las Vegas* 1964.

Cummings, Robert (Bob). Actor. *b.* Clarence Robert Orville Cummings, June 10, 1908, Joplin, Mo. *d.* 1990. *ed.* Drury Coll.; Carnegie Tech.; AADA. An enterprising young man, he started out on Broadway in 1931 after faking a British accent and presenting himself as Blade Stanhope Conway, Englishman. He broke into films in a similar fashion in 1935 after faking a southern drawl and presenting himself as Brice Hutchens, Texan. He later reclaimed his real name and went on to become a popular screen star in many light romantic Hollywood comedies, typically playing affable, bumbling young men. But he was also effective in occasional dramatic roles, in films like *Kings Row, The Lost Moment,* and *Dial M for Murder.* In the 50s and early 60s, looking as youthful as ever, he starred successfully in the TV series 'The Bob Cummings Show' (1955–59; 1961–62) and 'My Living Doll' (1964–65). He won an Emmy for his dramatic performance in the Studio One TV version of 'Twelve Angry Men.' A health food devotee, he attributed his sustained boyish looks to balanced nutrition and vitamins. He wrote a book on the subject, *How to Stay Young and Vital.* Three times married, Cummings was the father of seven.

FILMS: *Sons of the Desert* (crowd extra) 1933; *The Virginia Judge, So Red the Rose, Millions in the Air* 1935; *Desert Gold, Arizona Mahoney, Border Flight, Forgotten Faces, Three Cheers for Love, Hollywood Boulevard, The Accusing Finger* 1936; *Hideaway Girl, The Last Train from Madrid, Souls at Sea, Sophie Lang Goes West, Wells Fargo* 1937; *College Swing, You and Me, The Texan, Touchdown Army, I Stand Accused* 1938; *Three Smart Girls Grow Up, The Under-Pup, Rio, Everything Happens at Night, Charlie McCarthy Detective* 1939; *And One Was Beautiful, Private Affairs, Spring Parade, One Night in the Tropics* 1940; *Free and Easy, The Devil and Miss Jones, Moon Over Miami, It Started with Eve* 1941; *Kings Row, Saboteur, Between Us Girls* 1942; *Forever and a Day, Princess O'Rourke, Flesh and Fantasy* 1943; *You Came Along* 1945; *The Bride Wore Boots, The Chase* 1946; *Heaven Only Knows, The Lost Moment* 1947; *Sleep My Love, Let's Live a Little* (also co-prod.) 1948; *The Accused, Free for All, Tell It to the Judge, The Black Book/Reign of Terror* 1949; *Paid in Full, The Petty Girl, For Heaven's Sake* 1950; *The Barefoot Mailman* 1951; *The First Time* 1952; *Marry Me Again* 1953; *Lucky Me, Dial M for Murder* 1954; *How to Be Very Very Popular* 1955; *My Geisha* 1962; *Beach Party* 1963; *What a Way to Go!, The Carpetbaggers* 1964; *Promise Her Anything, Stagecoach* 1966; *Five Golden Dragons* 1967.

Cummins, Peggy. Actress. Born on Dec. 18, 1925, in Prestatyn, North Wales. A stage actress at 12, she played teenagers, then pert leading ladies in British and some American films of the 40s and 50s.

FILMS INCLUDE: *Dr. O'Dowd* 1940; *English Without Tears/Her Man Gilbey* 1944; *The Late George Apley* (US), *Moss Rose* (US) 1947; *Green Grass of Wyoming* (US), *Escape* 1948; *That Dangerous Age/If This Be Sin* 1949; *My Daughter Joy/Operation X, Gun Crazy* (US) 1950; *Street Corner/Both Sides of the Law, Always a Bride* 1953; *The Love Lottery, To Dorothy a Son/Cash on Delivery* 1954; *Carry on Admiral, Hell Drivers, Night of the Demon* 1957; *The Captain's Table* 1958; *Dentist in the Chair* 1960; *In the Doghouse* 1961.

Cunard, Grace. Actress. *b.* Harriet Mildred Jeffries, 1894,

Columbus, Ohio. *d.* 1967. On the stage from her early teens, she entered films with Biograph in 1910. In 1913 she married director-actor Francis FORD. They moved to Universal, where she soon became celebrated as the studio's "serial queen." She often collaborated with Ford on the screenplays and direction of their films. By 1916 they were among Hollywood's most popular action stars. Their careers suffered after their divorce around 1918. She later married stuntman and bit player Jack Shannon (1892–1968) and appeared with decreasing frequency and diminishing importance in a variety of films through the early 40s.

FILMS INCLUDE: *Before Yorktown* 1911; *An Indian Legend* 1912; *The Favorite Son* 1913; *Lucille Love—The Girl of Mystery* (serial; also co-sc.), *The Mysterious Rose* 1914; *The Heart of Lincoln, Phantom of the Violin* (also sc.), *The Broken Coin* (serial; also sc.), *The Campbells Are Coming* (also sc.), *And They Called Him Hero* (also sc.), *The Hidden City* (also sc.), *Three Bad Men and a Girl* 1915; *The Bandit's Wager* (also sc.), *Peg o' the Ring* (serial; also sc.) 1916; *The Purple Mask* (serial), *Her Better Self, The Man Hater* 1917; *After the War* 1918; *Elmo the Mighty* (serial) 1919; *The Girl in the Taxi* 1921; *Emblems of Love, The Last Man on Earth* 1924; *Outwitted, The Kiss Barrier* 1925; *Exclusive Rights* 1926; *Blake of Scotland Yard* (serial), *The Denver Dude* 1927; *Masked Angel, The Price of Fear, The Chinatown Mystery* (serial) 1928; *Untamed* 1929; *A Lady Surrenders* 1930; *Resurrection* 1931; *Ladies They Talk About* 1933; *We're in the Legion Now/The Rest Cure* 1936.

Cundey, Dean. American director of photography. A lighting cameraman from the mid-70s, he worked frequently with director John CARPENTER, and during the 80s gradually developed into one of Hollywood's leading cinematographers. He was nominated for an Academy Award for *Who Framed Roger Rabbit?* (1989).

FILMS INCLUDE: *Where the Red Fern Grows* 1974; *Halloween* 1978; *Rock 'n' Roll High School* 1979; *The Fog* 1980; *Escape from New York* 1981; *The Thing* 1982; *Psycho II* 1983; *Romancing the Stone* 1984; *Back to the Future* 1985; *Big Trouble in Little China* 1986; *Project X* 1987; *Big Business, Who Framed Roger Rabbit?* 1988; *Road House, Back to the Future Part II* 1989; *Jurassic Park* 1993.

Cunningham, Sean S. Director, producer. Born on Dec. 31, 1941, New York City. *ed.* Franklin & Marshall (B.A.); Stanford (M.F.A.). After a brief stint as an actor, he became a stage manager and later the producer of the Mineola Theatre in Long Island. Several of his plays moved on to Broadway. In 1971 he formed a film production company and began producing and directing commercials, industrials, documentaries, and eventually features. Specializing in exploitation films, he scored a commercial hit with the gory *Friday the 13th* (1980).

FEATURE FILMS (as director-producer): *Here Come the Tigers* 1978; *Friday the 13th* 1980; *A Stranger Is Watching* 1982; *Spring Break* 1983; *The New Kids* 1985; *Deepstar Six, The Horror Show* 1989; *House III* (prod.) 1990; *House IV* (prod.) 1991; *Jason Goes to Hell: The Final Friday* (prod.) 1993.

Cuny, Alain. Actor. Born on July 12, 1908, in Saint-Malo, France. Quit medical school to attend the Ecole des Beaux-Arts in Paris and became a painter. First entered French films as costume and set designer for CAVALCANTI, FEYDER, and RENOIR. After drama studies with Charles Dullin, he turned to acting on the stage and in films in the late 30s. A highly cultivated man, he made few but imposing appearances in French and Italian films, beginning with romantic leads and later veering toward characterizations of intellectuals. Memorable as the agonized philosopher in *La Dolce Vita* (1960).

FILMS INCLUDE: *Remorques/Stormy Waters* 1941; *Les Visiteurs du Soir/The Devil's Envoy* 1942; *Baron Fantôme/The Phantom Baron* 1943; *Il Cristo Proibito/Strange Deception* 1950; *Camicie Rosse/Anita Garibaldi* 1951; *La Signora senza Camelie/Camille Without Camellias* 1952; *Notre Dame de Paris/The Hunchback of Notre Dame* 1956; *Les Amants/The Lovers* 1958; *La Dolce Vita* 1960; *Peau de Banane/Banana Peel* 1964; *La Voie lactée/The Milky Way, Fellini Satyricon* 1969; *Uomini Contro, Valparaiso Valparaiso* 1970; *L'Udienza* 1972; *Il Maestro i Margarita* 1973; *Emmanuelle, Touchez pas al Femme blanche* 1974; *Il Contesto* 1975; *I Prosseneti, Cadaveri Eccellenti* 1976; *El Recurso del Metedo* (Mex./Cuba/Fr.) 1978; *Cristo si è fermato a Eboli/Christ Stopped at Eboli* 1979; *Quartetto Basileus/Basileus Quartet* 1982; *Detective* 1985; *Camille Claudel* 1988.

Currie, Finlay. Actor. *b.* Jan. 20, 1878, Edinburgh, Scotland. *d.* 1968. An organist and choirmaster, he made his stage debut in 1898, his screen debut in 1932. Played impressive character roles in many notable UK and US films, often as patriarchs or other men of authority. Best remembered as the convict Magwitch in Lean's *Great Expectations* (1946).

FILMS INCLUDE: *The Frightened Lady/Criminal at Large, Rome Express* 1932; *The Good Companions, Orders Is Orders* 1933; *The Edge of the World* 1937; *The 49th Parallel/ The Invaders* 1941; *The Day Will Dawn/The Avengers, Thunder Rock* 1942; *I Know Where I'm Going* 1945; *Great Expectations* 1946; *The Brothers* 1947; *Bonnie Prince Charlie, Sleeping Car to Trieste* 1948; *Treasure Island* (as Capt. Billy Bones; US/UK), *The Black Rose* (US/UK), *Trio, The Mudlark* 1950; *People Will Talk* (US), *Quo Vadis* (as the apostle Peter; US) 1951; *Kangaroo* (US), *Walk East on Beacon* (US), *Ivanhoe* (US/UK) 1952; *Treasure of the Golden Condor* (US) 1953; *Rob Roy the Highland Rogue/Rob Roy* (UK/US), *The End of the Road* (lead) 1954; *Footsteps in the Fog* (US/UK), *Captain Lightfoot* (US) 1955; *Zarak* 1956; *The Little Hut* (US), *Saint Joan* 1957; *Naked Earth, La Tempesta/Tempest* (It.) 1958; *Ben-Hur* (US), *Solomon and Sheba* (as King David; US) 1959; *Kidnapped, The Adventures of Huckleberry Finn* (US) 1960; *Francis of Assisi* (as Pope Innocent III; US) 1961; *The Inspector/Lisa* (UK/US) 1962; *Murder at the Gallop, Cleopatra* (US/UK), *Billy Liar, The Three Lives of Thomasina* (US/UK) 1963; *The Fall of the Roman Empire* (US) 1964; *Bunny Lake Is Missing* 1965.

Curry, Tim. Actor. Born on Apr. 19, 1946, in Cheshire, England. *ed.* Birmingham U. Gaunt leading man of British stage, television, and films. He portrayed Mozart on Broadway in 'Amadeus' (1981) and William Shakespeare in a TV movie biography of the playwright. Best known for his role as Dr. Frank-N-Furter in both the stage and screen versions of the cult classic *The Rocky Horror Picture Show,* he has also appeared in American films.

FILMS INCLUDE: *The Rocky Horror Picture Show* (UK) 1975; *The Shout* (UK) 1978; *Times Square* 1980; *Annie* 1982; *The Ploughman's Lunch* (UK) 1983; *Legend* (UK), *Clue* 1985; *Pass the Ammo* 1988; *The Hunt for Red October* 1990; *Oscar, Ferngully* (v/o) 1991; *Passed Away, Home Alone 2: Lost in New York* 1992; *The Three Musketeers* 1993; *The Shadow* 1994; *Congo, The Pebble and the Penguin* (v/o) 1995; *Lover's Knot, Muppet's Treasure Island* 1996; *McHale's Navy* 1997.

Curtin, Valerie. Actress, screenwriter. Born on Mar. 31, 1945?, in Jackson Heights, New York City. The daughter of a popular radio actor, she moved into films after some stage experience, and was relegated mostly to supporting roles. In the late 70s she began writing screenplays, often in collaboration with her husband, director Barry LEVINSON. She is a cousin of TV (and occasionally movie) comedienne Jane Curtin (*b.* Sept. 6, 1947, Cambridge, Mass.) of 'Saturday Night Live' fame.

FILMS INCLUDE: As actress—*Alice Doesn't Live Here Anymore* 1975; *All the President's Men* 1976; *Silent Movie, Silver Streak* 1977; *A Different Story* 1978; *Why Would I Lie?* 1980; *Maxie* 1985; *Down and Out in Beverly Hills, Big Trouble* 1986. As co-screenwriter—*. . . And Justice for All* 1979; *Inside Moves* 1980; *Best Friends* 1982; *Unfaithfully Yours* 1984; *Toys* (sc.) 1992.

Curtis, Alan. Actor. *b.* Harold Neberroth, July 24, 1909, Chicago. *d.* 1953. Darkly handsome, he was a male model before coming to films in 1936. Played both romantic leads and villains, mostly in routine films with several notable exceptions, including the pivotal role of a framed murder suspect in *Phantom Lady* (1944). Married and divorced his *New Wine* co-star, Ilona MASSEY. Died at 43 following a kidney operation.

FILMS INCLUDE: *Winterset* (bit) 1936; *Mannequin, Yellow Jack, The Shopworn Angel, The Duke of West Point* 1938; *Good Girls Go to Paris, Hollywood Cavalcade* 1939; *Four Sons* 1940; *High Sierra, Buck Privates, We Go Fast, New Wine* 1941; *Two Tickets to London, Hitler's Madman, Gung Ho!* 1943; *Phantom Lady, The Invisible Man's Revenge, Destiny* 1944; *See My Lawyer, The Naughty Nineties, Shady Lady, The Daltons Ride Again* 1945; *Flight to Nowhere, Inside Job, Renegade Girl* 1946; *Philo Vance's Gamble* 1947; *The Enchanted Valley* 1948; *I Pirati di Capri/The Pirates of Capri* (It.), *Apache Chief* 1949.

Curtis, Jamie Lee. Actress. Born on Nov. 22, 1958, in Los Angeles. The daughter of movie stars Tony CURTIS and Janet LEIGH, she began performing on TV while still a teenager, then co-starred in the series 'Operation Petticoat' (1977–78). Making her film debut in 1978, she was relegated at first mainly to horror movies. But gradually she developed into a competent leading lady in a wide range of comic as well as dramatic roles, memorably in *A Fish Caled Wanda* (1988). She married actor Christopher GUEST in 1984.

FILMS: *Halloween* 1978; *The Fog, Prom Night, Terror Train* (Can.) 1980; *Road Games* (Austral.), *Halloween II* 1981; *Love Letters/My Love Letters, Trading Places* 1983; *Grandview U.S.A., Adventures of Buckaroo Banzai Across the Eighth Dimension* 1984; *Perfect* 1985; *Amazing Grace and Chuck/Silent Voice, Un Homme amoureux/A Man in Love* (Fr./It.) 1987; *Dominick and Eugene/Nicky and Gino, A Fish Called Wanda* (UK) 1988; *Blue Steel* 1990; *Queens Logic* 1991; *My Girl, Forever Young* 1992; *Mother's Boys, My Girl 2, True Lies* 1994; *House Arrest* 1995; *Fierce Creatures* 1997.

Curtis, Tony. Actor. Born Bernard Schwartz, on June 3, 1925, in the Bronx, N.Y. The son of an immigrant tailor, he grew up in poverty in a tough section of the Bronx and by age 11 was a member of a notorious street gang. It was in a neighborhood settlement house that he had his first taste of acting, playing a little girl in an adventure drama about King Arthur. After WW II service with the Navy, during which he was wounded on Guam, he attended CCNY and took acting classes at New York's Dramatic Workshop. He began his professional career with a stock company that toured the Catskill Mountain "Borscht Circuit," then appeared briefly off Broadway. In 1949 he was signed for movies by Universal and was initially billed as James Curtis, then Anthony Curtis. Within two years, thanks to his pretty-boy looks, the pressure of fan mail, and publicity buildup, he was a star. At first typecast as juvenile delinquents, then as swashbuckling heroes and Arabian Nights caliphs (with a Bronx accent!), he gradually broadened his range and in 1957 surprised critics with his nervously energetic performance in *The Sweet Smell of Success* as the unprincipled press agent Sidney Falco. He followed this in 1958 with another acceptable dramatic performance in *The Defiant Ones,* which earned him a best actor Oscar nomination. Another successful performance, in the Roaring Twenties comedy *Some Like It Hot* (1959), led to many light roles in films of the 60s. Curtis's three marriages include those to actresses Janet LEIGH (1951–62) and Christine KAUFMANN (1963–67). The former union produced actress Jamie Lee CURTIS. In the early 70s he starred in the TV series 'The Persuaders.' In 1977 he published a first novel, *Kid Andrew Cody & Julie Sparrow.* Reduced mainly to supporting roles in minor films in the 80s, he found time to develop his skills as an artist. His paintings, especially the Marilyn Monroe portraits, fetch considerable sums.

FILMS: *Criss Cross, City Across the River, The Lady Gambles, Johnny Stool Pigeon* 1949; *Francis, I Was a Shoplifter, Winchester '73, Sierra, Kansas Raiders* 1950; *The Prince Who Was a Thief* 1951; *Flesh and Fury, No Room for the Groom, Son of Ali Baba* 1952; *Houdini* (title role), *The All-American* 1953; *Forbidden, Beachhead, Johnny Dark, The Black Shield of Falworth* 1954; *Six Bridges to Cross, So This Is Paris, The Purple Mask* 1955; *The Square Jungle, Trapeze, The Rawhide Years* 1956; *Mister Cory, The Sweet Smell of Success, The Midnight Story* 1957; *The Vikings, Kings Go Forth, The Defiant Ones* 1958; *The Perfect Furlough, Some Like It Hot, Operation Petticoat* 1959; *Pepe* (cameo), *Who Was That Lady?, The Rat Race, Spartacus* 1960; *The Great Imposter* 1961; *The Outsider, Taras Bulba* 1962; *Forty Pounds of Trouble, The List of Adrian Messenger* 1963; *Captain Newman M.D., Wild and Wonderful, Goodbye Charlie, Paris When It Sizzles* 1964; *Sex and the Single Girl, The Great Race, Boeing Boeing* 1965; *Not with My Wife You Don't, Chamber of Horrors* (cameo), *Arrivederci Baby!* (UK) 1966; *Don't Make Waves* 1967; *La Cintura di Castita/On My Way to the Crusades I Met a Girl Who. . . /The Chastity Belt* (It./US), *The Boston Strangler* 1968; *Monte Carlo or Bust/Those Daring Young Men in Their Jaunty Jalopies* (UK/It/Fr.) 1969; *You Can't Win 'Em All/The Dubious Patriots* (UK), *Suppose They Gave a War and Nobody Came* 1970; *Capone* (as Al Capone), *Lepke* (title role) 1975; *The Count of Monte Cristo* (UK), *The Last Tycoon* 1976; *Casanova & Co./Some Like It Cool* (title role; Ger./Aus./It./Fr.) 1977; *The Manitou, Sextette, The Bad News Bears Go to Japan* 1978; *Little Miss Marker, The Mirror Crack'd* (UK) 1980; *Brainwaves, Othello: The Black Commando* (as Iago) 1982; *Where Is Parsifal?* 1984; *Insignificance* (UK), *Balboa* 1985; *Club Life* 1986; *The Last of Philip Banter* (Sp.) 1987; *Lobster Man from Mars, Midnight, Walter & Carlo in America* (Den.) 1989; *Prime Target, Center of the Web* 1991; *Naked in New York* 1994; *The Celluloid Closet* 1995.

Curtiz, Michael. Director. *b.* Miháli Kertész, Dec. 24, 1888, Budapest, of Jewish parentage. *d.* 1962. *ed.* Markoszy U.; Royal Academy of Theater and Art, Budapest. The son of an architect and opera singer, he is said to have made his first appearance on the stage at 11, in an opera starring his mother. At 17 he ran away from home to join a traveling circus and the following year made his professional stage debut in Budapest. He entered Hungarian films in 1912 as an actor and within months began directing. Shortly after, he spent several months in Copenhagen brushing up on film technique at the Nordisk studios and assisting August BLOM on the epic *Atlantis* (1913). He served briefly with a Hungarian army film unit in WW I and after his discharge, in 1915, he married a 17-year-old actress, Lucy Doraine, who would star frequently in his European films (they divorced in 1923). In 1917 Curtiz was appointed production director at Budapest's largest studio, Phönix Films. In 1919, when Béla Kun's Communist regime nationalized the Hungarian film industry, he sought political refuge in Austria and Germany, where he continued to direct, rapidly gaining an international reputation. Accounts of his early work are conflicting, and no reliable list of his complete European credits exists. However, his German-language films of the 20s were more carefully documented. Several of these, especially the sumptuous epics *Sodom and Gomorrah* (1922) and *Moon of Israel* (1924), made a strong impression on the Hollywood moguls.

In 1926 he was brought to Hollywood by Harry WARNER. For the next quarter of a century he completed well over 100 films for Warner Bros., many of them routine but some showing substantial talent and creative energy. In the eyes of many critics he became closely identified with the Hollywood studio system. He has often been dismissed as a superbly skilled technician who served his studio well, subordinating his personality to the requirements of the machine. But certain of his films of the 30s and 40s tend to contradict this simple assessment.

His Errol Flynn cycle gave the American screen some of its best-remembered romantic adventures. He also did some excellent work with Bogart, Garfield, and Cagney. His *Mildred Pierce* resurrected the career of Joan Crawford, and *Casablanca,* for which he won an Academy Award, is an enduring light masterpiece and can hardly be dismissed as "the happiest of happy accidents," in the words of critic Andrew Sarris. Curtiz worked in every film genre imaginable—social drama, musical comedy, Westerns, sea sagas, swashbuckling romances, gangster and prison melodramas, horror films, mystery thrillers, etc. His forceful personality frequently broke through the most routine material, and it was often difficult to tell who was subservient to whom, Curtiz to the studio system or the studio system to Curtiz. More often than not, they seemed to be one and the same. Curtiz had the reputation of being a virtual dictator on the set. He ruled his actors and technicians with an iron hand and is said to have been hated by both. His films of the 50s, after he left the Warners mold, were considerably inferior to his earlier work; they tended to diminish his stature and obscure his achievements of the 30s and 40s. Curtiz's second wife (1928–61) was screenwriter Bess MEREDYTH.

FILMS (complete from 1919): In Hungary—*Today and Tomorrow* (also act.), *The Last Bohemian* 1912; *My Husband Lies, Captive Soul* 1913; *Princess Pongyola, Slaves of the Night* (also act.), *The Golden Shovel, Borrowed Babies, The Vagrant, Bánk Bán* 1914; *Loved by Two* 1915; *The Doctor, Black Rainbow, The Firmness of the Hungarian Soil, The Silver Goat, The Wolf, The Carthusian, The Apothecary, The Seven of Clubs* 1916; *Man of the Soil, The Charlatan, The Road to Peace, Nobody's Son, The Secret of St. Job Forest, The Red Samson, John the Tenant, The Last Dawn, The Colonel, The Death Bell, Master Zoard, The Story of a Penny, Invasion, Spring in Wintertime* 1917; *Donkey Skin, Alraune* (co-dir.), *The Ugly Boy, The Lady with Sunflowers, The Scorpion, The Wellington Mystery, The Devil, Judas, Ninety-Nine, Lu the Cocotte, Lulu, The Magic Waltz, The Merry Widow* 1918; *John the Younger Brother, Liliom* (unfinished) 1919. In Austria/Germany—*Die Dame mit dem schwarzen Handschuh, Die Gottesgeissel* 1919; *Der Stern von Damaskus, Die Dame mit den Sonnenblumen, Herzogin Satanella, Boccaccio, Miss Tutti Frutti* (It.) 1920; *Cherchez la Femme, Frau Dorothy's Bekenntnis, Wege des Schreckens/Labyrinth des Grauens* 1921; *Sodom und Gomorrah/Legende von Sünde und Stafe/The Queen of Sin and the Spectacle of Sodom and Gomorrah* (in 2 parts) 1922–23; *Samson und Dalila* (production supervisor only on film directed by Alexander Korda), *Die Lawine/Avalanche, Der junge Medardus, Namenlos* 1923; *Ein Spiel ums Leben, Harun al Raschid, Die Sklavenkönigin/Moon of Israel* 1924; *Celimene—la Poupée de Montmartre/Das Spielzeug von Paris/Red Heels* (Fr./Aus./Ger.) 1925; *Der goldene Schmetterling/The Road to Happiness* (Aus./Ger./Den.), *Fiaker Nr. 13* 1926. In the US—*The Third Degree, A Million Bid, The Desired Woman, Good Time Charley* 1927; *Tenderloin* 1928; *Noah's Ark, The Glad Rag Doll, The Madonna of Avenue A, The Gamblers, Hearts in Exile* 1929; *Mammy, Under a Texas Moon, The Matrimonial Bed, Bright Lights, A Soldier's Plaything, River's End* 1930; *Dämon des Meeres* (German-language version of Lloyd Bacon's *Moby Dick*), *God's Gift to Women, The Mad Genius* 1931; *The Woman from Monte Carlo, Alias the Doctor* (co-dir. with Lloyd Bacon), *The Strange Love of Molly Louvain, Doctor X, Cabin in the Cotton* 1932; *20,000 Years in Sing Sing, The Mystery of the Wax Museum, The Keyhole, Private Detective 62, Goodbye Again, The Kennel Murder Case, Female* 1933; *Mandalay, Jimmy the Gent, The Key/High Peril, British Agent* 1934; *Black Fury, The Case of the Curious Bride, Front Page Woman, Little Big Shot, Captain Blood* 1935; *The Walking Dead, The Charge of the Light Brigade* 1936; *Stolen Holiday, Mountain Justice, Kid Galahad/The Battling Bellhop, The Perfect Specimen* 1937; *Gold Is Where You Find It, The Adventures of Robin Hood* (co-dir. with William Keighley), *Four's a Crowd, Four Daughters, Angels with Dirty Faces* 1938; *Sons of Liberty* (short), *Dodge City, Daughters Courageous, The Private Lives of Elizabeth and Essex/Elizabeth the Queen, Four Wives* 1939; *Virginia City, The Sea Hawk, Santa Fe Trail* 1940; *The Sea Wolf, Dive Bomber* 1941; *Captains of the Clouds, Yankee Doodle Dandy* 1942; *Casablanca, Mission to Moscow, This Is the Army* 1943; *Passage to Marseille, Janie* 1944; *Roughly Speaking, Mildred Pierce* 1945; *Night and Day* 1946; *Life with Father, The Unsuspected* 1947; *Romance on the High Seas* 1948; *My Dream Is Yours* (also prod.), *Flamingo Road, The Lady Takes a Sailor* 1949; *Bright Leaf, Young Man with a Horn, The Breaking Point* 1950; *Force of Arms, Jim Thorpe—All-American* 1951; *I'll See You in My Dreams, The Story of Will Rogers* 1952; *The Jazz Singer, Trouble Along the Way* 1953; *The Boy from Oklahoma, The Egyptian, White Christmas* 1954; *We're No Angels* 1955; *The Vagabond King, The Scarlet Hour* (also prod.), *The Best Things in Life Are Free* 1956; *The Helen Morgan Story* 1957; *King Creole, The Proud Rebel* 1958; *The Hangman, The Man in the Net* 1959; *The Adventures of Huckleberry Finn, A Breath of Scandal* 1960; *Francis of Assisi, The Comancheros* 1961.

Cusack, Cyril. Actor. *b.* Nov. 26, 1910, in Durban, South Africa. *d.* 1993. Raised in Ireland, he made his first stage and screen appearances at age seven, and after studies at the Dominican College in Newburgh (County Kildare) and University College in Dublin, joined the Abbey Players in 1932. He subsequently appeared in numerous plays in Ireland, England, and the US. In the mid-40s he began playing regularly in films. Because of his dimunitive size, he was confined mainly to supporting roles, although he sometimes played character leads. Of his six children, Sinead (*b.* 1948) and Sorcha Cusack became actresses.

FILMS INCLUDE: *Knocknagow* 1917; *Late Extra, The Man Without a Face* 1935; *Inspector Hornleigh Goes to It/Mail Train* 1941; *Odd Man Out* 1947; *Escape, The Small Back Room* 1948; *The Blue Lagoon* 1949; *Gone to Earth/The Wild Heart, The Elusive Pimpernel/The Fighting Pimpernel* 1950; *Soldiers Three* (US), *The Blue Veil* (US), *The Secret of Convict Lake* (US) 1951; *Saadia* (US) 1954; *The Man Who Never Was, The Spanish Gardener* 1956; *Ill Met by Moonlight/Night Ambush, The Rising of the Moon* (Ire.) 1957; *Gideon's Day/Gideon of Scotland Yard, Shake Hands with the Devil* (Ire.) 1959; *A Terrible Beauty/The Night Fighters* 1960; *Johnny Nobody* 1961; *Waltz of the Toreadors, I Thank a Fool* 1962; *80,000 Suspects* 1963; *The Spy Who Came in from the Cold* 1965; *Where the Spies Are, I Was Happy Here/Time Lost and Time Remembered, Fahrenheit 451*

1966; *The Taming of the Shrew* (as Gremio; US/It.) 1967; *Galileo* (title role; It.), *Oedipus the King* 1968; *David Copperfield, Country Dance/Brotherly Love* 1970; *Sacco e Vanzetti/Sacco and Vanzetti* (It./Fr.), *King Lear* (as the Duke of Albany; UK/Den.), *Harold and Maude* (US), *Tam Lin/The Devil's Widow* 1971; *Più Forte Ragazzi!/All the Way Boys!* (It.) 1972; *The Day of the Jackal* (UK/Fr.), *The Homecoming* (US/UK) 1973; *The Abdication* 1974; *Children of Rage* 1975; *Lo Mano spietata della Legge/The Bloody Hands of the Law/Execution Squad* 1976; *Pointin'* (Ire.) 1979; *True Confessions* (US) 1981; *Wagner* 1983; *1984* 1984; *The Outcasts* (Ire.) 1985; *Little Dorrit* (as Frederick Dorrit) 1987; *My Left Foot* 1989; *The Fool* 1990; *Far and Away* 1991.

Cusack, Joan. Actress. Born on Oct. 11, 1962, in Evanston, Ill. *ed.* Piven Theatre Workshop, Evanston; U. Of Wisconsin, Madison. Character comedienne of the 80s, often portraying young airheads. She was absent from the big screen during 1985–86 when she was a regular on TV's 'Saturday Night Live.' She was nominated for an Academy Award as best supporting actress for *Working Girl* (1988). Sister of actor John CUSACK.

FILMS: *My Bodyguard* 1980; *Class* 1983; *Sixteen Candles, Grandview U.S.A.* 1984; *The Allnighter, Broadcast News* 1987; *Stars and Bars, Married to the Mob, Working Girl* 1988; *Say Anything* 1989; *Heart of Midnight, Men Don't Leave, My Blue Heaven* 1990; *The Cabinet of Dr. Ramirez* 1991; *Hero, Toys* 1992; *Addams Family Values* 1993; *Corinna Corinna* 1994; *Nine Months* 1995; *Mr. Wrong, Two Much* 1996; *In and Out* 1997.

Cusack, John. Actor. Born on June 28, 1966, in Evanston, Ill. The younger brother of Joan CUSACK, he trained from the age of eight at his hometown's Piven Theatre Workshop. At 12 he was doing commercials for radio and TV. Entering films in 1983, he first appeared in productions also featuring his sister. Before long he developed into a popular juvenile lead, then young leading man, in characters ranging from sincere to sly. Offscreen, he achieved some notoriety for his anarchic lifestyle. In 1990 he was sentenced to three years probation for drunk driving.

FILMS: *Class* 1983; *Sixteen Candles, Grandview U.S.A.* 1984; *The Sure Thing, Better Off Dead, The Journey of Natty Gann* 1985; *Stand by Me, One Crazy Summer* 1986; *Hot Pursuit, Broadcast News* 1987; *Eight Men Out, Tapeheads* 1988; *Say Anything, Fat Man and Little Boy* 1989; *The Grifters* 1990; *True Colors, Shadows and Fog, Roadshow Prophets* 1991; *The Player, Map of the Human Heart, Bob Roberts* 1992; *Money for Nothing* 1993; *Bullets Over Broadway, Floundering, The Road to Wellville* 1994; *City Hall* 1996; *Grosse Pointe Blank* 1997.

Cushing, Peter. Actor. Born on May 26, 1913, in Kenley, England. Formerly a surveyor's clerk, he made his stage debut in 1935, after training at London's Guildhall School of Music and Drama, then came to the US, where he appeared on Broadway and played supporting roles in several Hollywood films. He made his British film debut in *Hamlet* (1948) and beginning in the mid-50s became closely identified with his roles as the gaunt, cold-blooded master of Hammer's horror films, particularly the role of Baron Frankenstein, which he played a number of times. The typecasting led the actor to complain, "If I played *Hamlet*, they'd call it a horror film." Autobiography: *Peter Cushing* (1986), supplemented by *Past Forgetting* (1988).

FILMS INCLUDE: In the US—*The Man in the Iron Mask* 1939; *A Chump at Oxford, Vigil in the Night* 1940; *They Dare Not Love* 1941. In the UK—*Hamlet* 1948; *Moulin Rouge* (UK/US) 1953; *The Black Knight* (UK/US) 1954; *The End of the Affair* 1955; *Alexander the Great* (US) 1956; *Time Without Pity, The Curse of Frankenstein* (as Baron Frankenstein), *The Abominable Snowman* 1957; *Dracula/Horror of Dracula* (as Dr. Van Helsing), *The Revenge of Frankenstein* (as Baron Frankenstein, disguised as Dr. Stein) 1958; *The Hound of the Baskervilles* (as Sherlock Holmes), *The Mummy, John Paul Jones* (US) 1959; *The Flesh and the Fiends/Mania/Psycho Killers/The Fiendish Ghouls, Cone of Silence/Trouble in the Sky, Suspect/The Risk, Sword of Sherwood Forest* (as Sheriff of Nottingham), *The Brides of Dracula* (as Dr. Van Helsing) 1960; *The Naked Edge* (US/UK), *Cash on Demand* 1961; *Captain Clegg/Night Creatures* 1962; *The Man Who Finally Died* 1963; *Dr. Terror's House of Horrors, The Evil of Frankenstein* (as Baron Frankenstein), *The Gorgon* 1964; *She, The Skull, Dr. Who and the Daleks* 1966; *Island of Terror* 1966; *Frankenstein Created Woman* (as Baron Frankenstein), *Torture Garden* 1967; *Blood Beast Terror/The Vampire Beast Craves Blood, Corruption* 1968; *Frankenstein Must Be Destroyed* (as Baron Frankenstein) 1969; *Scream and Scream Again, The Vampire Lovers* 1970; *I Monster, The House That Dripped Blood, Twins of Evil* 1971; *Asylum, Dr. Phibes Rises Again, Dracula A.D. 1972* (as Count Dracula) 1972; *The Satanic Rites of Dracula/Count Dracula and His Vampire Brides* (as Dr. Van Helsing), *Frankenstein and the Monster from Hell* (as Dr. Frankenstein), *The Creeping Flesh, And Now the Screaming Starts* 1973; *Legend of the Werewolf/The Legend of the Seven Golden Vampires/The Seven Brothers and One Sister Meet Dracula* (as Dr. Van Helsing), *Madhouse, The Beast Must Die, The Ghoul* 1974; *Call Him Mr. Shatter* (Hong Kong), *From Beyond the Grave* 1975; *Trial by Combat/Choice of Weapons/Dirty Knights' Work, At the Earth's Core* 1976; *The Uncanny, Die Standarte* (Ger.), *Shock Waves/Death Corps* (US), *Star Wars* (US) 1977; *Count Dracula and His Vampire Bride* 1978; *Arabian Adventure* 1979; *Misterio en la Isla de los Monstrous/Monster Island* (Sp.) 1980; *Black Jack* 1981; *House of the Long Shadows* 1983; *Sword of the Valiant, Top Secret!* (US) 1984; *Biggles/Biggles Adventure in Time* 1986.

cut. Abrupt transition from one scene to another without using an optical effect such as a dissolve, a wipe, or a fade. It is achieved by splicing the last frame of one scene with the first frame of the next.

"Cut!" Command by the director to camera and sound crew to switch off equipment upon completion of a shot.

cutaway. A shot of an action or object related to but not an immediate part of a principal scene. It is designed to draw attention from the main action temporarily or to comment on it as an aside. Technically, it is a useful device for the editor in bridging a time lapse or in avoiding a JUMP CUT. Directors make sure that their cameramen shoot cutaway footage whenever possible to provide the editor with additional material with which to work. A typical cutaway is a shot of the reaction of spectators at an athletic event, a close-up of a bystander's face, or a shot of a clock showing the passage of time. Cutaways can also be used as symbolic comments, such as a shot of ocean waves following a stormy love scene; or as a humorous device, such as a series of running-gag shots of someone continuously doing something funny "in the meantime," the main action continuing to unfold.

cut back. The return, in editing, to the main scene of action after an insert or a CUTAWAY.

cutter. A person who performs the mechanical duties of cutting and splicing film. Sometimes the term is used to describe a person who cuts and splices film creatively, more appropriately known as an EDITOR. But it can also be applied to an assistant editor.

cutting. The craft and art of assembling separate lengths of motion picture film into a unified whole. See EDITING; MONTAGE.

cutting negative. The process of cutting a negative to match the final work print as completed by the editor. The cut negative is used for the preparation of dupe negatives or other intermediate materials from which the composite prints are made.

cutting on action. Cutting from one shot to another while the subject of the shot is in motion. It has long been realized by film editors that the sudden change in the physical elements of an image as a result of a cut is made less noticeable when the attention of the viewer is distracted by the movement of a subject on the screen than when the cut is made on a static note. In shooting, the movement in both shots is filmed as a complete action and at the same speed. This enables the editor to splice both pieces of film as a matched action. For the technique to be effective, in the second shot the subject should occupy the same sector of the frame he had occupied in the first shot, but the second shot must be taken from a different angle.

cutting outline. In the production of documentary and compilation films, a sketchy description of scenes in continuity prepared by a writer as a guide for the editor when the latter is assembling the rough cut of a film for which there is as yet no written script.

cutting room. The editor's workshop. It is usually equipped with a workbench, a winding mechanism, a film synchronizer, a viewer, a bin fitted with pegs or pins, splicing materials, storage shelves, and a MOVIOLA or, more typically nowadays, a flat-bed editing table.

Cutts, Graham. Director. *b.* 1885, Brighton, England. *d.* 1958. *ed.* Pierpoint Coll. A marine engineer, he entered the film business as an exhibitor. In the 20s he directed some of Britain's most commercially successful silent film attractions. Far less important as a director of sound films. His daughter, Patricia Cutts (1926–74), was a child actress and a leading lady of British films, also known as Patricia Wayne. She committed suicide by an overdose of sleeping pills.

FILMS INCLUDE: *While London Sleeps, Flames of Passion* 1922; *Woman to Woman* 1923; *The Passionate Adventure* 1924; *The Blackguard, The Rat* 1925; *The Sea Urchin* 1926; *Confetti* 1927; *God's Clay* 1928; *Glorious Youth, The Return of the Rat* 1929; *The Sign of Four* 1932; *Three Men in a Boat* 1933; *Aren't Men Beasts?* 1937; *Just William* 1939; *Air Transport Support* (doc.) 1945; *Combined Operations* (doc.) 1946.

Cybulski, Zbigniew. Actor. *b.* Zbyszek Cybulski, Nov. 3, 1927, Kniaze, Ukraine. *d.* 1967. *ed.* Academy of Commerce and Journalism, Cracow (Poland). On the Polish stage from 1953, he made his film debut the following year and quickly became internationally known. Typically appearing in dark glasses, and often in angry-young-man roles, he personified Poland's perplexed postwar youth. Just before his death in a railway accident he was preparing his first film as a director. Andrzej WAJDA's *Everything for Sale* (1968) was inspired by and dedicated to the memory of Czybulski and the vacuum he left behind.

FILMS INCLUDE: *A Generation* 1954; *Three Stars* 1955; *Shipwrecks* 1957; *Ashes and Diamonds, The Eighth Day of the Week* (Pol./Ger.) 1958; *Baltic Express/Night Train* 1959; *Parting, See You Tomorrow* (also co-sc.), *Innocent Sorcerers* 1960; *L'Amour à Vingt Ans/Love at Twenty* (Fr./It./Jap./Pol./Ger.), *La Poupée/He She or It!* (Fr.) 1962; *How to Be Loved* 1963; *To Love* (Sw.) 1964; *Salto, The Saragossa Manuscript* 1965; *The Code, Christmas Eve* 1966; *Jovita, The Murderer Leaves a Clue* 1967.

cycle. In animation, a group of drawings representing the phases of a repetitious action, such as walking. A labor-saving shortcut, the cycle permits the use of the same motion over and over again, the length of the action being determined by the requirements of the story.

cyclorama. A curved cloth hung in a studio as a backdrop to represent sky. It was in vogue in the 20s but is infrequently used today because of its artificiality. Also known as "cyc" or "panorama cloth." The bank of lights used for illuminating the cyclorama is called a "cycstrip."

Czechoslovakia. This small, binational, European country—which, with the fall of the Iron Curtain, split into the Czech Republic and Slovakia in 1991—began its contribution to world cinema long before the actual invention of motion pictures. As early as 1818 Bohemian anatomist and physiologist Johannes Evangelista Purkinje (1787–1869) wrote on the phenomenon of PERSISTENCE OF VISION as part of his research in the physiology of the senses. In the 1840s and 1850s he developed a number of optical and mechanical devices in an attempt to project moving images on a screen and in 1861 used animation to depict the functions of the human heart.

Actual film production began in Prague in June of 1898, when Jan Krizenecky (1868–1921), an architect and amateur photographer, shot and projected three film strips with Lumiere equipment he had bought in Paris. The first permanent motion picture theater opened in Prague in 1907, and the first film production company, Kinofa, was formed the following year by Antonin Pech (1874–1928), a stage director. Pech produced and directed a variety of comic and dramatic shorts, including an adaptation of Gounod's *Faust* (1912), but specialized mainly in documentary films. His company folded in 1912. Another noted Czech film pioneer was Max Urban (*b.* 1882), who founded the Fotokinema (later ASUM) company and made numerous films, many of which starred his wife, actress Andula Sedlackova, among them a screen version of Smetana's *The Bartered Bride* (1913). Illusionfilm, headed by Alois Jalovec (1867–1932), was another busy production company that flourished during the early years of Czech cinema.

Film production was severely curtailed during WW I, but the emergence of Czechoslovakia as an independent nation in 1918, after centuries of political subjugation, brought about an aura of creative exuberance. Film production was greatly expanded, and hopes were high for the development of a national cinema matching the quality of imported films. By 1922 as many as 34 feature films had been produced annually, but most were mediocre productions, and competition from abroad forced local output down to only eight features in 1924. A gradual recovery began in the following year, and as the silent era drew to a close, several fine films were turned out by the Czech studios, including Karel LAMAC's *The Good Soldier Schweik* (1926), Gustav MACHATY's *The Kreutzer Sonata* (1926) and *Erotikon* (1929), Martin FRIÇ's *The Organist of St. Vitus* (1929), and Karl Junghans' *Such Is Life* (1929).

The advent of sound posed a new obstacle for the local industry, a language barrier to the exportation of films abroad. Still, despite that difficulty and the financial repercussions of the Depression, the film industry continued to show steady if modest progress, increasing its output from seven features in 1930 to 43 in 1937, partly owing to protective measures by the government, such as the imposition of a quota system and the levying of a special tax on imported films. Producers, on their part, helped their own cause by turning out many light entertainment films of universal appeal. Machaty's *Extase/Esctasy* (1933), with its sensational nude scenes of young Hedy Kiesler (later LAMARR), was a tremendous international hit. Other successful Czech productions of the 30s included Josef Rovensky's *The River/Young Love* (1933), Friç's *Janosik* (1936), and Otakar VÁVRA's *Humoresque* (1939). The studios at Barrandov, a suburb of Prague, in which this and many other films were made, were among the most modern and best equipped in Europe. In addition to features, some distinguished documentaries were produced in the 30s, notably Karel Plicka's *The Earth Sings* (1933), which garnered much praise at the 1934 Venice Festival. There was also some noteworthy experimental work by young Czech filmmakers.

Under the Nazi Occupation during WW II, film production fell to an average of about a dozen features a year. During the war years the Barrandov studios were utilized mainly by the Germans, and the few Czech films made there tended to be insignificant escapist fare. In 1943 a national film archive was established. In August of 1945, just months after the Liberation and the re-establishment of the republic, the film industry was nationalized. A national film school, FAMU, was opened in Prague, and a new generation of directors was being trained for the future. Meanwhile, some of the experienced old-timers, like Friç, Vávra, and Jiři WEISS, kept feature production alive, though the main emphasis in the early postwar years was on documentaries, cartoons, and puppet films.

The revived industry received an invigorating lift in 1947 when Karel Stekly's *The Strike* won the Grand Prize at the Venice Film Festival. Another film that enjoyed international success in 1947 was Jiří TRNKA's puppet-animation feature *The Czech Year.* The same year saw the establishment of a separate Slovak branch of the Czechoslovakian film industry with its own feature, documentary, and animation studios.

The first graduates of the FAMU school joined the cadre of filmmakers in 1951, but the early 50s proved to be lean years for the Czechoslovak cinema, both in quantity and quality, as they were for the film industries of the rest of Eastern Europe. Inhibition characterized the typical feature film as directors conformed to a style of social realism imposed from above, often working from committee-written scripts. Themes were culled from the nation's past. Historical sagas, national literature and folklore, and the painful and heroic memories of WW II provided the main source for plots while directors shied from contemporary themes and topical issues.

The situation gradually improved as the 50s drew to a close and the political atmosphere grew increasingly more relaxed. One film that heralded the coming change was Vojtech JASNY's *September Nights* (1957), which treated critically Stalinist-era abuses and personality cult manifestation in the armed forces. By the early 60s a "new wave" of talented and eager young directors had emerged that was soon to achieve international acclaim. They differed widely in approach and style but were united by a desire for personal expression and a spirit of experimentation and creative assertiveness. Broadly speaking, the "new wave" flowed along two streams, one concerned with the exploration of ideas and the other with social observation often underscored by a satirical view of human frailties and foibles.

Leading directors of the first group included Véra CHYTILOVÁ, Evald SCHORM, Jan NEMEC, and Jaromil Jires. The second group was led by Milos FORMAN, Ivan Passer, and Jirí MENZEL. Vávra, János KADÁR, and Elmar Klos were among the veteran directors who shared in the surge of the new wave. This brief but highly productive period in Czechoslovak cinema, which came to be known as the "Prague Spring," temporarily made the national industry a prominent member of the international film community. Such films as Forman's *Loves of a Blonde* (1965) and *The Firemen's Ball* (1967), Chytilová's *Daisies* (1966), Passer's *Intimate Lighting* (1966), Nêmec's *Diamonds of the Night* (1964) and *A Report on the Party and the Guests* (1966), Menzel's *Closely Watched Trains* enjoyed great success not only at prestigious film festivals but also on commercial screens in the West.

The Soviet invasion of August 1968 abruptly ended the Prague Spring. Renewed censorship and restrictions on free expression silenced the voices that for several years had given Czechoslovak cinema a sense of identity and pride. Several of the leading directors sought and found employment abroad, most notably Forman, who achieved success in Hollywood after initial difficulties. The 70s were barren years for the Czechoslovak film industry with most productions lacking originality or above-standard quality. Dim hopes for a revival were awakened late in the decade with the return to work of Menzel and Chytilovà.

By the early 90s, with the breakup of the country into the Czech Republic and Slovakia, film output had dwindled to a handful of features per year. However, with the establishment of several new production companies and with the international successes of such Czech films as *Elementary School* (1991) by young director Jan Sverák, the spirit of filmmaking in the region seems to have been reborn with the expulsion of the former totalitarian regime. With recent efforts concentrating on political documentaries, the situation for feature films is still murky, but the Czech and Slovakian cinemas will be important arenas to watch in coming years. One rising new director to appear in the 90s was Jan Sverak, whose *Kolya* (1996), which he directed and co-produced, won the Academy Award for best foreign film.

Czinner, Paul. Director. *b.* 1890, Budapest. *d.* 1972. A child violin prodigy, he went to Vienna at 14, eventually acquired a doctorate in philosophy and literature, and later worked as a journalist. He also wrote a play and produced several before directing his first film in Vienna in 1919. He rose to prominence in 1924 with the German film *Nju,* a triangle drama noted for its psychological depth. The film starred Elisabeth BERGNER, who became Czinner's wife and appeared in most of his subsequent pictures. He began directing in England in 1930, and in 1933, after the Nazis came to power, he emigrated with his wife to that country, where they continued their film activity. In 1940 they came to the US, where Miss Bergner starred in several films while Czinner produced and directed Broadway plays. After a tour of Australia, they returned to England. There Czinner developed special multiple-camera techniques to record distinguished opera and ballet performances for the screen.

FILMS: In Austria—*Homo immanis/Der Unmensch* 1919; *Inferno* 1920. In Germany—*Nju/Husbands or Lovers* (also sc.) 1924; *Der Geiger von Florenz/Impetuous Youth/The Violinist of Florence* (also sc.), *Liebe* (also sc.) 1926; *Dona Juana* (also co-sc.) 1927; *Fräulein Else* (also sc.) 1929; *Ariane* (and English-language version, *The Loves of Ariane;* also co-sc.) 1931; *Der Träumende Mund/Dreaming Lips* (also co-sc.) 1932. In England—*The Woman He Scorned/The Way of Lost Souls* 1930; *Catherine the Great* 1934; *Escape Me Never* 1935; *As You Like It* 1936; *Dreaming Lips* 1937; *Stolen Life* 1939; *Don Giovanni* 1955; *Kings and Queens, Salzburg Pilgrimage* (both shorts) 1956; *The Bolshoi Ballet* 1957; *The Royal Ballet* 1959; *Der Rosenkavalier* 1962; *Romeo and Juliet 1966.*

D

Da Costa, Morton. Director. *b.* Morton Tecosky, Mar. 7, 1914, Philadelphia. d. 1989. *ed.* Temple U. On Broadway as an actor from 1942 and a director from 1950, he ventured twice into films to direct the screen versions of plays he had turned into hits on the stage, then directed one more film before returning to Broadway. Author of *Morton Da Costa's Book of Needlepoint* (1975).

FILMS: *Auntie Mame* 1958; *The Music Man* (also prod.) 1962; *Island of Love* (also prod.) 1963.

Dafoe, Willem. Actor. Born July 22, 1955, in Appleton, Wis. Talented, versatile leading man of stage and films. One of eight children of a surgeon and a nurse, he dropped out of the University of Wisconsin (Milwaukee) and toured the US and Europe with Theatre X, an experimental troupe. He eventually settled in New York, where he joined another experimental ensemble, the Wooster Group, in the city's SoHo section. In films from the early 80s, he was initially typecast as a demented youth but gradually moved to better roles and soared to prominence after being nominated for an Academy Award as best supporting actor for his performance as Sgt. Elias in *Platoon* (1986). He is still a member of the Wooster Group and lives in New York with its director, Elizabeth Lecompte, and their son, Jack.

FILMS: *The Loveless, The Hunger* 1983; *New York Nights, Streets of Fire, Roadhouse 66* 1984; *To Live and Die in L.A.* 1985; *Platoon* 1986; *Dear America* (doc.; co-narr. only), *Off Limits* 1987; *The Last Temptation of Christ* (title role), *Mississippi Burning* 1988; *Triumph of the Spirit, Born on the Fourth of July* 1989; *Cry-Baby* (cameo), *Wild at Heart* 1990; *Flight of the Intruder* 1991; *White Sands, Light Sleeper* 1992; *Body of Evidence* 1993; *Clear and Present Danger, Tom and Viv* 1994; *The English Patient* 1996; *Night and the Moment, Speed 2: Cruise Control* 1997.

D'Agostino, Albert S. Art director. *b.* Dec. 27, 1893, New York City. *d.* 1970. He started out as a scenic designer for the stage, entering films as an assistant art director around 1918. He worked for MGM, Universal, and finally RKO, where he contributed memorable sets, often in collaboration with Walter E. Keller, for Val Lewton's horror classics of the early 40s. As RKO's supervising art director, he collaborated on the design of much of the studio's repertoire through the late 50s. He was nominated for Academy Awards for *The Magnificent Brute, The Magnificent Ambersons, Flight for Freedom, Step Lively*, and *Experiment Perilous*.

FILMS INCLUDE: *Salvation Nell, Ramona* 1928; *Today* 1930; *Blood Money, I Cover the Waterfront* 1933; *Great Expectations* 1934; *The Werewolf of London, The Mystery of Edwin Drood, The Raven* 1935; *Dracula's Daughter, The Invisible Ray, The Magnificent Brute* 1936; *Professor Beware* 1938; *The Stranger on the Third Floor* 1940; *Cat People, My Favorite Spy, Journey Into Fear, The Magnificent Ambersons* 1942; *Flight for Freedom, I Walked with a Zombie, The Leopard Man, The Seventh Victim, The Ghost Ship, This Land Is Mine, Forever and a Day, Mr. Lucky* 1943; *Curse of the Cat People, Step Lively, Mademoiselle Fifi, None but the Lonely Heart, The Master Race* 1944; *Experiment Perilous, Murder My Sweet, Isle of the Dead, The Body Snatcher, The Enchanted Cottage, The Bells of St. Mary's* 1945; *Cornered, Bedlam, Notorious, Sister Kenny, The Spiral Staircase, The Stranger* 1946; *Crossfire, Mourning Becomes Electra, The Long Night* 1947; *Berlin Express, Blood on the Moon, The Boy with Green Hair, I Remember Mama, Rachel and the Stranger* 1948; *The Set-Up, The Window, They Live by Night* 1949; *The Thing, On Dangerous Ground, The Racket* 1951; *Clash by Night, The Lusty Men, The Narrow Margin, The Big Sky* 1952; *The Hitch-Hiker, Androcles and the Lion* 1953; *Back from Eternity* 1956; *Run of the Arrow* 1957; *I Married a Woman* 1958.

Dagover, Lil. Actress. *b.* Marie Antonia Sieglinde Marta Liletts, Sept. 30, 1897, Madiven, Java. *d.* 1980. The daughter of a Dutch forest ranger, she was sent to Germany for her elementary education. She broke into German films thanks to her marriage at age 20 to veteran actor Fritz Daghofer (1872–1936), 25 years her senior. They divorced in 1919 but not before he had introduced her to director Robert Wiene and other notables of the German cinema. She made her screen debut in Fritz Lang's *Harakiri* (1919) and, immediately after, played the feminine lead in Wiene's classic of expressionism, *The Cabinet of Dr. Caligari*. A dark beauty with large, expressive eyes, she usually played frail, menaced heroines. She starred in scores of German films as well as in some Swedish (1926–27) and French (1928–29) and one American film (1931). She was an important international star in the 20s and early 30s and continued to play supporting parts into the late 70s. She was named State Actress of Germany in 1937 and was awarded the West German Cross of Merit in 1967.

FILMS INCLUDE: *Harakiri, Das Kabinett das Dr. Caligari/The Cabinet of Dr. Caligari, Die Spinnen/The Spiders* 1919; *Das Geheimnis von Bombay, Der Richter von Zalamea, Spiritismus, Die Toteninsel* 1920; *Das Medium, Der Müde Tod/Between Two Worlds/Beyond the Wall/Destiny* 1921; *Dr. Mabuse der Spieler/Dr. Mabuse the Gambler, Phantom, Tiefland* 1922; *Liebe macht blind/Love Makes Us Blind* 1923; *Komödie des Herzens* 1924; *Tartüff/Tartuffe, Zur Chronik von Grieshuus/At the Grey House* 1925; *Die Brüder Schellenberg/The Two Brothers, Giftas/Married Life* (Sw.) 1926; *Nur eine Tänzerin/Only a Dancing Girl* (Sw./Ger.), *His English Wife/Discord* (Sw.), *Orient-express* 1927; *Ungarische Rhapsodie/Hungarian Rhapsody, Le Tourbillon de Paris* (Fr.) 1928; *Le Grande Passion* (Fr.), *Monte Cristo* (Fr.), *Die Ehe, Es flüstert die Nacht/Hungarian Nights* 1929; *Das alte Lied, Der weisse Teufel/The White Devil, Boykott* 1930; *Elisabeth von Oesterreich, Der Kongress tanzt/The Congress Dances, The Woman from Monte Carlo* (US) 1931; *Barberina—die Tänzerin von Sans-Souci* 1932; *Johannisnacht* 1933; *Der Flüchtling aus Chicago, Eine Frau die weiss was sie will* 1934; *Lady Windermeres Fächer/Lady Windermere's Fan, Der höhere Befehl* 1935; *Schlussakkord, Fridericus, August der Starke, Das Mädchen Irene* 1936; *Die Kreutzersonate/The Kreutzer Sonata* 1937; *Dreiklang* 1938; *Friedrich Schiller, Bismarck* 1940; *Musik in Salzburg* 1944; *Es kommt ein Tag* 1950; *Bekenntnisse des Hochstaplers Felix Krull/The Confessions of Felix Krull* 1957; *Buddenbrooks* 1959; *Die seltsame Gräfin* 1961; *Der Fussgänger/The Pedestrian* 1974; *Der Richter und sein Henker/End of the Game* 1975; *Die Standarte* 1977; *Geschichten aus der Wienerwald/Tales from the Vienna Woods* 1979.

Daguerre, Louis. Inventor, physician, painter. *b.* Nov. 18, 1789, Cormeilles-en-Parisis, France. *d.* 1851. A noted stage set designer and co-inventor of photography with Joseph-Nicéphore NIÉPCE. After experimenting separately, they signed a contract for joint work in 1829. Four years later Niépce died, and Daguerre carried on the work with his son, Isidore. In 1839 he displayed to the Paris Academy of Science a successful photographic process that yielded a clear picture on a silvered copper plate. He called his photos "daguerreotypes."

Dahl, Arlene. Actress. Born on Aug. 11, 1924, in Minneapolis, of Norwegian extraction. *ed.* Minnesota Business Coll.; Minnesota Coll. of Music; Minnesota Institute of Art; U. of Minnesota (design). Stagestruck in high school, she joined a local drama group and supported herself with part-time jobs as a lingerie buyer, junior copywriter, and model for various department stores. She made it to Broadway in 1945, became the Rheingold beer girl of 1946, was signed to a contract by Warner Bros. in 1947, and moved on to MGM the following year. A ravishing redhead, she was one of the most beautiful and glamorous women that ever adorned the screen, and her Hollywood roles were more decorative than ambitious. Since 1959 she has appeared only occasionally in films but has been seen in stage and TV productions from time to time. In the early 80s she appeared regularly in the daytime soap opera 'One Life to Live.' She has written a syndicated column as well as several books on feminine beauty care. Her successful Arlene Dahl Enterprises also markets lingerie and cosmetics. The first two of her five husbands were Lex BARKER (1951–52) and Fernando LAMAS (1954–60).

FILMS: *Life with Father, My Wild Irish Rose* 1947; *The Bride Goes Wild, A Southern Yankee* 1948; *Scene of the Crime, The Black Book/Reign of Terror* 1949; *Ambush, The Outriders, Three Little Words, Watch the Birdie* 1950; *Inside Straight, No Questions Asked* 1951; *Caribbean* 1952; *Jamaica Run, Desert Legion, Sangaree, The Diamond Queen, Here Come the Girls* 1953; *Woman's World, Bengal Brigade* 1954; *Slightly Scarlet, Wicked As They Come* (UK) 1956; *Fortune Is a Woman/She Played with Fire* (UK) 1957; *Journey to the Center of the Earth* 1959; *Kisses for My President* 1964; *Les Ponyettes* (Fr.) 1968; *The Road to Katmandou* 1969; *Land Raiders* 1970; *Night of the Warrior* (with son Lorenzo Lamas) 1991.

Dahl, John. Director, screenwriter. *b.* 1956, in Billings, Mont. *ed.* U. of Montana; Montana State U.; American Film Institute, Los Angeles. Starting out as a storyboard artist for films, he then moved on to assistant directing while still a student at AFI. After training, he found success directing shorts and music videos, finally breaking into features with his striking and daring technique as a director. A favorite among critics, his career reached a peak with the modern noir classics *Red Rock West* (1993) and *The Last Seduction* (1994).

FILMS: As director—*The Dungeonmaster* (asst. dir. only) 1984; *Something Wild* 1986; *Married to the Mob* (storyboard only) 1988; *Kill Me Again* (sc. only) 1989; *Red Rock West* (also sc.) 1993; *The Last Seduction* 1994; *Unforgettable* 1996.

Dahlbeck, Eva. Actress. Born on Mar. 8, 1920, in Saltsjö-Duvnäs, Sweden. Died in Du Blé en Liasses 1971. Trained at Stockholm's Royal Dramatic Theater, she made her stage debut in 1941 and first appeared in films the following year. She is best known as the platinum-blonde heroine of several Ingmar BERGMAN films, particularly his comedies, and for her part in the American film *The Counterfeit Traitor*. She was named best actress at the 1958 Cannes Festival for her performance in Bergman's *Brink of Life*. She wrote the script for Arne Mattson's *Woman of Darkness* (1966), a play, a book of poetry, and more than ten novels.

FILMS INCLUDE: *Ride Tonight* 1942; *Black Roses* 1945; *Eva* 1948; *Only a Mother* 1949; *Unser Dorf/The Village* (Switz.), *Defiance, Secrets of Women* 1952; *Barabbas* 1953; *A Lesson in Love* 1954; *Dreams, Smiles of a Summer Night* 1955; *Brink of Life* 1957; *A Matter of Morals* (US/Sw.) 1960; *The Counterfeit Traitor* (US) 1962; *All These Women, Loving Couples* 1964; *Morianna/I the Body, The Cats* 1965; *Les Créatures* (Fr./Sw.) 1966; *The Red Mantle/Hagbard and Signe* (Den./Ice./Sw.), *People Meet and Sweet Music Fills the Heart* (Den./Sw.) 1967; *Tintomara* 1970.

Dailey, Dan. Actor. *b.* Dec. 14, 1914, New York City. *d.* 1978. The son of a hotel man, he began in show business as a child with a minstrel show. Later he was a song-and-dance man in vaudeville, appeared with Minsky's burlesque troupe, and also worked as a grocery clerk, golf caddy, and shoe salesman, among other things. He made his Broadway debut in 1937, playing a small part in 'Babes in Arms.' Following a lead role in 'Stars in Your Eyes' (1939), he was signed by MGM to a Hollywood contract. But it wasn't until he came back from WW II service, as a lieutenant, that he had starring roles, mostly with Fox, often in musicals about show-biz people. He was nominated for a best actor Oscar for *When My Baby Smiles at Me* (1948). From the late 50s he appeared mostly on the stage, in Las Vegas nightclubs, and on TV ('Four Just Men,' 'The Governor and J.J.,' and 'Faraday and Company.').

FILMS INCLUDE: *The Captain Is a Lady, The Mortal Storm, Dulcy, Susan and God* 1940; *Ziegfeld Girl, Lady Be Good* 1941; *Panama Hattie* 1942; *Mother Wore Tights* 1947; *You Were Meant for Me, Give My Regards to Broadway, When My Baby Smiles at Me* 1948; *Chicken Every Sunday, You're My Everything* 1949; *When Willie Comes Marching Home, I'll Get By, A Ticket to Tomahawk, My Blue Heaven* 1950; *Call Me Mister, I Can Get It for You Wholesale* 1951; *The Pride of St. Louis* (as baseball player Dizzy Dean), *What Price Glory, Meet Me at the Fair* 1952; *Taxi, The Girl Next Door, The Kid from Left Field* 1953; *There's No Business Like Show Business* 1954; *It's Always Fair Weather* 1955; *Meet Me in Las Vegas, The Best Things in Life Are Free* 1956; *The Wings of Eagles, Oh Men! Oh Women!, The Wayward Bus* 1957; *Pepe* 1960; *Hemingway's Adventures of a Young Man* 1962; *The Private Files of J. Edgar Hoover* 1978.

dailies. Roughly assembled prints of scenes shot the previous day. They are processed overnight and are frequently known as "rushes" because of their hasty assembly. These ungraded prints are projected daily, usually early in the morning, for critical viewing by the producer, director, cameraman, and crew to ascertain that all the required shots are completed, or "in the can," and that no retakes are necessary. Dailies are shown untrimmed and in order of shooting with no regard for continuity. The daily print is later used by the editor as part of his work print in assembling the film. Film dailies are now often supplemented by video assist devices, which allow a director on the set to review videotape of a shot immediately after filming.

Dale, Jim. Actor, singer, songwriter. Born James Smith, on Aug. 15, 1935, in Rothwell, England. Trained as a ballet dancer, he began his professional career in 1951 as a stage comedian and later enjoyed some success as a pop singer. He also worked as a radio disc jockey and has been appearing on British TV since 1957. In films since the early 60s, he appeared in several of the "Carry On" comedy series. He has composed music and written lyrics for several of his own stage and TV productions. He wrote the lyrics for the title song of the film *Georgy Girl* (1966) and for the theme song of *Shalako* (1968).

FILMS INCLUDE (as actor): *Raising the Wind/Roommates* 1961; *Nurse on Wheels, Carry on Cabby* 1963;

Carry on Spying, Carry on Cleo 1964; *The Big Job* 1965; *Carry on Cowboy, Carry on Screaming* 1966; *Follow That Camel* 1967; *Carry on Doctor* 1968; *Lock Up Your Daughters* 1969; *The National Health* 1973; *Digby/Digby—The Biggest Dog in the World* 1974; *Joseph Andrews, Pete's Dragon* (US) 1977; *Hot Lead and Cold Feet* (US) 1978; *The Spaceman and King Arthur/Unidentified Flying Oddball* 1979; *Scandalous* 1984; *The Adventures of Huckleberry Finn* 1985; *Carry on Columbus* 1992.

Dale, Virginia. Actress, dancer. Born in 1919(?). Light leading lady of Hollywood films of the 40s. Had her best opportunity as Fred Astaire's dancing partner in *Holiday Inn*, then slipped back into B films.

FILMS INCLUDE: *No Time to Marry, Start Cheering* 1938; *Idiot's Delight, Death of a Champion* 1939; *All Women Have Secrets, Buck Benny Rides Again, Parole Fixer, The Quarterback, Love Thy Neighbor* 1940; *World Premiere, Kiss the Boys Goodbye* 1941; *Holiday Inn* 1942; *Headin' for God's Country* 1943; *Dragnet, The Hucksters* 1947; *Docks of New Orleans* 1948; *Danger Zone* 1951.

Daley, Cass. Actress, singer. *b.* Katharine Daley, July 17, 1915, Philadelphia. *d.* 1975. Gawky, buck-toothed comedienne whose loud zany singing, dancing, and comedy style enlivened Paramount musicals of the 40s. The daughter of a streetcar conductor, she was first a straight band vocalist but soon displayed a talent for knockabout comedy and became highly popular in nightclubs and on radio. She starred in the "Ziegfeld Follies" of 1936. She retired from show business in the early 50s to raise a family and was attempting a comeback in the early 70s, when she died in a freak accident. Alone at home, she fell over a glass coffee table, and a shard of glass slashed her neck.

FILMS: *The Fleet's In, Star Spangled Rhythm* 1942; *Crazy House, Riding High* 1943; *Out of This World, Duffy's Tavern* 1945; *Ladies' Man, Variety Girl* 1947; *Here Comes the Groom* 1951; *Red Garters* 1954; *The Spirit Is Willing* 1967; *The Phynx, Norwood* 1970.

Dali, Salvador. Painter, writer. *b.* Mar. 11, 1904, Figueras, Spain. *d.* 1989. The flamboyant, eccentric, publicity-conscious surrealist artist, who claimed his waxed mustache acted as an antenna for the muses, made his most important contribution to cinema early in his career as Luis BUÑUEL's collaborator on *Un Chien Andalou* (1929) and *L'Age d'Or* (1930). Although Dali later came to denounce the merits of cinema as an art, in 1945 he designed the memorable surrealistic dream sequence for Hitchcock's *Spellbound* and in 1951 the sets and costumes for the Spanish film *Don Juan Tenorio*. He later directed a number of surrealist amateur shorts.

Dalio, Marcel. Actor. *b.* Israel Moshe Blauschild, July 17, 1900, Paris, to Rumanian immigrants. *d.* 1983. In French films since 1933, he rose to prominence in Duvivier's *Pépé le Moko* and Renoir's *La Grande Illusion* and *Rules of the Game*. At the outbreak of WW II, after his picture appeared on posters depicting "the typical Jew," he was forced to flee Europe. He found refuge in the US, where he played numerous secondary roles in a variety of films, typically as a comical foreigner. After the war, he resumed his activity in European films while retaining his Hollywood ties. Dalio, who played a supporting part in *Casablanca*, co-starred as Capt. Renaud in the TV series of the same title in 1955–56.

FILMS INCLUDE: In France—*Mon Chapeau* 1933; *Un Grand Amour de Beethoven/The Life and Loves of Beethoven* 1936; *Pépé le Moko, La Grande Illusion/Grand Illusion, Les Perles de la Couronne/The Pearls of the Crown, L'Alibi, Gribouille/Heart of Paris* 1937; *La Maison du Maltais/Sirocco, Entrée des Artistes/The Curtain Rises* 1938; *La Règle du Jeu/The Rules of the Game* 1939. In the US—*Unholy Partners* 1941; *Joan of Paris, The Shanghai Gesture, The Pied Piper* 1942; *Casablanca, Tonight We Raid Calais, The Constant Nymph, Paris After Dark, The Desert Song, The Song of Bernadette* 1943; *Pin Up Girl, Wilson* (as Clemenceau), *To Have and Have Not* 1944; *A Bell for Adano* 1945. In France—*Pétrus* 1946; *Les Maudits/The Damned, Temptation Harbor* (UK) 1947; *Snowbound* (UK), *Dédée d'Anvers/Dedee* 1948; *Les Amants de Vèrone/The Lovers of Verona* 1949; *Hans le Marin* 1950. In the US—*On the Riviera, Rich Young and Pretty* 1951; *The Merry Widow, The Snows of Kilimanjaro, The Happy Time* 1952; *Gentlemen Prefer Blondes* 1953; *Lucky Me, Sabrina* 1954; *Razzia sur la Chnouf/Razzia* (Fr.) 1955; *Anything Goes, Miracle in the Rain* 1956; *Tip on a Dead Jockey* 1957; *Lafayette Escadrille, The Perfect Furlough* 1958; *The Man Who Understood Women, Pillow Talk* 1959; *Can-Can, Classe tous Risques/The Big Risk* (Fr./It.) 1960; *The Devil at 4 O'Clock* 1961; *Jessica* (US/Fr./It.), *Cartouche* (Fr./It.) 1962; *The List of Adrian Messenger, Donovan's Reef* 1963; *Un Monsieur de Compagnie/Male Companion* (Fr./It.) 1964; *Lady L* (US/Fr./It.) 1965; *Made in Paris, How to Steal a Million, Tendre Voyou/Tender Scoundrel* (Fr./It.) 1966; *La 25e Heure/The 25th Hour* (Fr./It./Yug.) 1967; *How Sweet It Is!* 1968; *Justine* 1969; *Catch-22, The Great White Hope* 1970. In France—*Les Aventures de Rabbi Jacob/The Mad Adventures of Rabbi Jacob* 1973; *L'Aile et la Cuisse, L'Ombre de Château* 1976; *La Communion Solennelle, Une Page d'Amour* (Belg./Fr.) 1977; *Le Paradis des Riches* 1978; *Brigade mondaine* 1979; *Vaudoux aux Caraïbes* 1980.

Dall, John. Actor. *b.* John Jenner Thompson, 1918, New York City. *d.* 1971. *ed.* Columbia. After preparing for the stage at the Theodore Irvine School of the Theater and the Pasadena Playhouse, he made his Broadway debut in walk-on parts in 1941. He played his first lead in the 1944 production of 'Dear Ruth.' In 1946 he played his first and best screen role, opposite Bette Davis in *The Corn Is Green*, for which he was nominated for an Academy Award. His sporadic screen career included memorable leads in Hitchcock's *Rope* and Joseph H. Lewis's *Gun Crazy*. He died of a heart attack at 52.

FILMS: *The Corn Is Green* 1946; *Something in the Wind* 1947; *Rope, Another Part of the Forest* 1948; *Deadly Is the Female* 1949; *Gun Crazy* 1950; *The Man Who Cheated Himself* 1951; *Spartacus* 1960; *Atlantis the Lost Continent* 1961.

Dalle, Beatrice. Actress. Born on December 19, 1964, in Le Mans, France. Captivating French lead best known for performance in title role in *Betty Blue*.

FILMS INCLUDE: *37.2 Le Matin/Betty Blue, Ona Volé Charlie Spencer!* 1986; *La Visione del Sabba/The Witches' Sabbath* 1988; *Les Bois noirs, Chimère* 1989; *La Vengeance d'une femme/A Woman's Revenge* 1990; *Night on Earth* 1992.

Dallesandro, Joe. Actor. Born in 1948. Long-haired sexual icon who sulked through some of the most famous films of directors Andy WARHOL and Paul MORRISSEY.

FILMS INCLUDE: *The Loves of Ondine* 1967; *Flesh, Lonesome Cowboys* 1968; *Trash* 1970; *Heat* 1972; *Andy Warhol's Frankenstein* 1973; *Blood for Dracula, Donna e Bello* (Ital.), *The Gardener* 1974; *Black Moon, Je T'Aime Moi Non Plus* (Fr.) 1975; *La Marge* (Fr.) 1976; *Un Cuore Semplice* (Fr.) 1978; *Tapage Nocturne* (Fr.) 1979; *Seeds of Evil* 1980; *Merry Go Round* 1983; *The Cotton Club* 1984; *Critical Condition* 1987; *Sunset* 1988; *Private War* 1989; *Cry-Baby, Double Revenge* 1990; *Wild Orchid II: Two Shades of Blue* 1992; *Sugar Hill* 1994.

Dalrymple, Ian. Screenwriter, producer, director. *b.* Aug. 26, 1903, Johannesburg, South Africa. *d.* 1989. *ed.* Cambridge. A film editor from 1927 to 1935, he branched into screenwriting in 1933, turning out some of Britain's better scripts of the 30s.

In the 40s he also began producing and directing, with the Crown Film Unit during the war and with his own Wessex Films afterward. At one time he served as chairman of the British Film Academy.

FILMS INCLUDE: As screenwriter—*Taxi for Two* (co-dial., edit.) 1929; *The Good Companions* 1933; *Storm in a Teacup* 1937; *The Divorce of Lady X, Pygmalion, South Riding, The Citadel* 1938; *Q Planes/Clouds Over Europe, French Without Tears, The Lion Has Wings* (also prod.), *A Window in London/Lady in Distress* 1939; *Old Bill and Son* (also dir.) 1940; *Pimpernel Smith* 1941. As producer—*London Can Take It* 1940; *Listen to Britain* 1941; *Coastal Command* 1942; *Close Quarters* 1943; *Perfect Strangers* 1945; *The Woman in the Hall* (also co-sc.) 1947; *Esther Waters* (also dir.) 1948; *Dear Mr. Prohack* (also co-sc.) 1949; *The Wooden Horse* 1950; *The Heart of the* Matter (also sc.) 1952; *Three Cases of Murder* (co-prod., co-sc.) 1954; *Raising a Riot* (co-prod., co-sc.) 1955; *A Hill in Korea* (also sc.) 1956; *The Admirable Crichton* 1957; *A Cry from the Streets* 1958; *Calamity the Cow* 1967.

Dalton, Audrey. Actress. Born on Jan. 21, 1934, in Dublin. *ed.* Convent of the Sacred Heart (Dublin); RADA. Leading lady and second lead of Hollywood films of the 50s, following some stage experience. Later mainly on TV.

FILMS INCLUDE: *My Cousin Rachel, The Girls of Pleasure Island, Titanic* 1953; *Casanova's Big Night, Drum Beat* 1954; *The Prodigal* 1955; *Deadliest Sin* 1956; *The Monster That Challenged the World* 1957; *Separate Tables* 1958; *Mr. Sardonicus* 1961; *Kitten with a Whip* 1964; *The Bounty Killer* 1965.

Dalton, Dorothy. Actress. *b.* 1894, Chicago. *d.* 1972. A stage actress with a Midwest touring company, she was noticed by Thomas INCE during a Los Angeles engagement and he took personal charge of her screen career, directing some of her films and supervising many others. A dimpled beauty, she played many choice roles for Ince and later for Paramount and was a prominent star when she retired from the screen in 1924 to marry Broadway producer Arthur Hammerstein.

FILMS INCLUDE: *Pierre of the Plains, Across the Pacific* 1914; *The Disciple* 1915; *D'Atragnan* (as Queen Anne), *The Jungle Child, The Vagabond Prince, The Female of the Species/The Vampire* 1916; *The Weaker Sex, Chicken Casey, The Dark Road, The Flame of the Yukon, Love Letters* 1917; *Flare-Up Sal, Love Me, The Mating of Marcella, The Kaiser's Shadow, Green Eyes, Vive la France!, Quicksand* 1918; *Extravagance, The Lady of Red Butte, The Homebreaker, The Market of Souls, L'Apache* 1919; *Black Is White, The Dark Mirror, Guilty of Love, A Romantic Adventuress* 1920; *The Idol of the North, Fool's Paradise, Behind Masks* 1921; *Moran of the Lady Letty, The Crimson Challenge, The Woman Who Walked Alone, The Siren Call, On the High Seas* 1922; *Fog Bound, The Law of the Lawless, Dark Secrets* 1923; *The Moral Sinner, The Lone Wolf* 1924.

Dalton, Timothy. Actor. Born on Mar. 21, 1944, in Colwyn Bay, Wales. Tall (6' 2"), dark, handsome, green-eyed, cleft-chinned, sardonic leading man of British stage, screen, and television. He trained briefly at the National Youth Theatre, then for three years at the Royal Academy of Dramatic Art, before joining the Birmingham Repertory Theatre. Moving to the Royal Shakespeare Company, he rapidly established a reputation as a capable young performer of classical roles, much in the mold of Richard Burton. His early film roles were typically in period pieces. He emerged from relative obscurity in the late 80s, when he was cast twice as superspy James Bond. He is said to have performed most of his own stunts in both films.

FILMS: *The Lion in Winter* (as King Philip of France) 1968; *Cromwell* (as Prince Rupert), *Wuthering Heights* (as Heathcliff) 1970; *Mary Queen of Scots* (as Henry, Lord Darnley) 1971; *Vollmacht zum Mord/Permission to Kill* (UK/Aus.) 1975; *El Hombre que supo Amar* (Sp.) 1976; *Sextette* (US) 1978; *Agatha* 1979; *Flash Gordon* 1980; *Chanel Solitaire* 1981; *The Doctor and the Devils* 1985; *The Living Daylights* (as James Bond) 1987; *Hawks* 1988; *Brenda Starr, Licence to Kill* (as James Bond) 1989; *The King's Whore* 1990; *The Rocketeer* 1991; *Naked in New York* 1994; *The Beautician and the Beast* 1997.

Daltrey, Roger. Singer, actor. Born on Mar. 1, 1944, in London. The popular lead singer for The Who appeared in dramatic lead roles in occasional films, memorably in eccentric Ken RUSSELL productions.

FILMS: *Woodstock* (doc.) 1970; *Tommy* (title role; also co-mus.), Lisztomania (as Franz Liszt) 1975; *The Legacy* 1978; *The Kids Are Alright* 1979; *McVicar* (also co-prod.) 1980; *Mack the Knife, Cold Justice* 1989; *The Teddy Bear Habit, Father Jim, If Looks Could Kill, Teen Agent* 1991; *Buddy's Song* 1992; *Lightning Jack* 1994.

Daly, John. Producer, executive. Born in 1937, in London. The son of a cockney dockworker and ex-professional boxer, he dropped out of school at 15 and, after working as a teaboy in Covent Garden, was a waiter in the Merchant Navy. Returning to London, he became an insurance salesman. A chance meeting with actor David HEMMINGS led to a partnership in Hemdale, a company they founded in 1967, as a talent agency that eventually became involved in recording, TV, and movie management and production. In 1971 Daly bought Hemmings's share in the business and several years later he moved his operations to the US. Initially specializing in low-budget projects, Daly became known as a maverick independent producer who took chances on films turned down by the large studios. He also developed a reputation as a shrewd and tough businessman, as busy in the courts fighting off litigation as he was managing his thriving business. He moved into the big time in the mid-80s, scoring a box-office blockbuster with *The Terminator* and garnering an Academy Award for *Platoon*. He was among the sponsors of another Oscar winner, *The Last Emperor*.

FILMS INCLUDE (as producer or executive producer, alone or in collaboration): *Images* 1972; *Sunburn* (also co-sc.) 1979; *High Risk, Race to the Yankee Zephyr* (Austral./NZ) 1981; *Yellowbeard* 1983; *The Terminator* 1984; *Falcon and the Snowman* 1985; *Salvador, At Close Range, Hoosiers, Platoon* 1986; *River's Edge, Best Seller* 1987; *Love at Stake* 1988; *Shag, Vampire's Kiss, Miracle Mile, Criminal Law, The Boost* 1989; *Out Cold, Staying Together* 1990; *Persuasion* 1995.

Daly, Robert A. Executive. Born on Dec. 8, 1936, in New York City. *ed.* Brooklyn College, Hunter College. With Warner Bros. since the early 80s. He began his entertainment career at CBS-TV in 1955, eventually becoming president of CBS Entertainment (1977). In 1980, he was named co-chairman and co-chief executive officer of Warner Bros., Inc. Since 1982, he has been the company's chairman and CEO. With president Terry Semel, he presided over such blockbuster successes as *The Lethal Weapon* and *Batman* series, bringing Warner Bros. to a leading position in the industry.

Damiani, Damiano. Director. Born on July 23, 1922, in Pasiano, Italy. *ed.* Academia di Belle Arti (Milan). Began directing documentaries in 1946 while still a student and turned out some 30 shorts in ten years before becoming a screenwriter and assistant director on features in the mid-50s. He made his directorial debut in 1960 and won a prize at the San Sebastian Festival for his very first feature film, *Il Rossetto/Lipstick*. He has co-scripted most of his own films.

FILMS: *Il Rossetto/Lipstick* 1960; *Il Sicario* 1961; *L'Isola di Arturo/Arturo's Island* 1962; *La Rimpatriata/The Reunion, La Noia/The Empty Canvas* 1963; *Le Ho Amate Tutte* 1965; *La Strega in Amore/The Witch/Aura* 1966; *Quien Sabe?/A Bullet for the General* 1967; *Il Giorno della Civetta/Mafia* 1968; *Una Ragazza piuttosto Complicata* 1969; *La Moglie piú Bella* 1970; *Confessione di un Commissario di Polizia al Procuratore della Republica/Confessions of a Police Captain* 1971; *Girolimoni il Mostro di Roma/Assassins of Rome* 1973; *Perche si Uccide un Magistrato, The Devil Is a Woman* (UK/It.) 1975; *Un Genio Due Compari Un Pollo* 1976; *I Am Afraid* 1977; *Goodbye and Amen* 1978; *L'Ultimo nome* 1979; *Amityville II: The Possession* 1982; *Octopus* 1984; *Attacco alla Piovra/The Pizza Connection* 1985; *L'Inchiesta/The Investigation* 1987; *Giocodi Masacro, Il Sole Buio/The Dark Sun* 1990; *Angel of Death* 1992.

D'Amico, Suso Cecchi. See CECCHI D'AMICO, Suso.

Damita, Lili. Actress. *b.* Liliane-Marie-Madeleine Carré, on July 19, 1901, in Bordeaux, France. *d.* 1994. A music hall performer from the age of 16, she succeeded the famed Mistinguette as the star of the Casino de Paris revue. In French films from 1921, she first used the name Damita del Rojo, then Lily Seslys, before settling for Lili Damita in 1923. Between 1926 and 1928 she appeared in German, Austrian, and British films, then left for Hollywood at the invitation of Samuel Goldwyn. She played leads in a number of early talkies but was given more print space for her tempestuous marriage to Errol Flynn (1935–42) than for her career as an actress. She retired from the screen after marrying Flynn. Their son, former actor Sean Flynn, disappeared in Vietnam, where he served as a war correspondent in the early 70s.

FILMS INCLUDE: In France—*L'Empereur des Pauvres, Corsica* 1921; *Fille sauvage* 1922; *La Voyante* 1923; *Le Retour* 1924. In Austria/Germany—*Célimène—Poupée de Montmartre/Das Spielzeug von Paris/Red Heels* (Fr./Ger./Aus.) 1925; *Geheimnisse einer Seele/Secrets of a Soul, Der Goldene Schmetterling/The Golden Butterfly* (Den./Aus.), *Fiaker Nr. 13, Man spielt nicht mit der Liebe* 1926; *Die letzte Nacht/Forbidden Love* (and UK version, *The Queen Was in the Parlour*), *Die berühmte Frau/The Dancer of Barcelona* 1927; *Die grosse Abenteurerin, Die Frau auf der Folter/A Scandal in Paris* 1928. In the US—*The Rescue, The Bridge of San Luis Rey, The Cock-Eyed World* 1929; *Fighting Caravans, The Woman Between, Friends and Lovers* 1931; *This Is the Night, The Match King* 1932; *Goldie Gets Along* 1933; *Brewster's Millions* 1935; *The Devil on Horseback* 1936.

Damon, Mark. Actor, executive. Born on Apr. 22, 1933, in Chicago. *ed.* UCLA (B.A. in literature; M.A. in business administration). In films from the mid-50s, he was signed by 20th Century-Fox as a contract player in 1958 and for several years played handsome leads in inconsequential films. In 1962 he moved to Italy, where for the next 13 years he starred in dozens of spaghetti Westerns and action pictures. Returning to the US in 1976, he formed and presided over Producers Sales Organization, an international distribution company, and became involved in production. In 1987 he founded a production company, Vision International.

FILMS INCLUDE: As actor—*Inside Detroit, Between Heaven and Hell* 1956; *Young and Dangerous* 1957; *Life Begins at 17, The Party Crashers* 1958; *This Rebel Breed, House of Usher* 1960; *The Longest Day, Beauty and the Beast, Chronache di un Convento/The Reluctant Saint* (It./US) 1962; *The Young Racers, I Tre Volti della Paura/Black Sabbath* (It./Fr./US), *Sfida al Re di Castiglia/The Tyrant of Castile* (It./Sp.) 1963; *I Cento Cavalieri/100 Horsemen, Il Figlio di Cleopatra/Son of Cleopatra* (It./Egy.) 1964; *Agente Segreto 777 Operazione Mistero* (It.), *Johnny Oro/Ringo and His Golden Pistol* (It.), *Johnny Yuma* (It.) 1966; *Lo Sbarco di Anzio/Anzio* (It.), *Nude... si muore/The Young, the Evil, and the Savage* (It.) 1968; *Tutto per tutto* (It./Sp.) 1969; *Lo chiamavanoo Verità/They Called Him Truth* (It.) 1972; *Il Pleniluno delle Vergini/The Devil's Wedding Night* (It.), *Crypt of the Living Dead* 1973; *There Is No. 13* (It./Ger.) 1976. As producer or executive producer (alone or in collaboration)—*The Arena* 1973; *The Choirboys* 1977; *Das Boot/The Boat* (Ger.) 1981; *The Neverending Story* (Ger./UK) 1984; *9½ Weeks, Short Circuit* 1986; *The Lost Boys* 1987; *Mac and Me, Bat 21, High Spirits, Dark Angel, Wild Orchid* 1988; *Vietnam Texas, I Come in Peace* 1990; *Wild Orchid II: Two Shades of Blue* 1992.

Damone, Vic. Singer, actor. Born Vito Rocco Farinola, on June 12, 1928, in Brooklyn, N.Y. After tying for first place on the Arthur Godfrey 'Talent Scouts' show in 1945, he became a popular nightclub, TV, and recording star. He played romantic leads in a number of films beginning in the early 50s. His first wife was actress Pier ANGELI. Haunted by back taxes and his fading career, he was forced into bankruptcy in 1971 but later resumed his career as a Las Vegas entertainer. He married actress Diahann CARROLL in 1989.

FILMS: *Rich Young and Pretty, The Strip* 1951; *Deep in My Heart, Athena* 1954; *Hit the Deck, Kismet* 1955; *Meet Me in Las Vegas* (cameo) 1956; *An Affair to Remember* (voice only) 1957; *Hell to Eternity* 1960; *Spree* 1967.

Dana, Viola. Actress. *b.* Virginia Flugrath, June 28, 1897, Brooklyn N.Y. *d.* 1987. Along with her younger sister (future screen actress Shirley Mason), she began appearing on the stage as dancer and actress while still a child and played unbilled bits in Edison films from age 13. Following her success in the title role of the Broadway hit 'Poor Little Rich Girl' (1913), she began playing starring roles in films. She was a leading Metro star for most of the silent era, but her career ended with the advent of sound. Her first husband was director John H. Collins; her second, screen cowboy Maurice "Lefty" Flynn.

FILMS INCLUDE: *Cohen's Luck, Gladiola, Children of Eve* 1915; *The Flower of No Man's Land, The Light of Happiness, The Gates of Eden, The Cossack Whip* 1916; *Rosie O'Grady, Blue Jeans, The Mortal Sin, Lady Barnacle, Aladdin's Other Lamp, The Girl Without a Soul* 1917; *A Weaver of Dreams, Riders of the Night, The Only Road, Opportunity, Flower of the Dusk* 1918; *The Gold Cure, The Microbe, Satan Junior, The Parisian Tigress, False Evidence* 1919; *The Willow Tree, The Chorus Girl's Romance, Blackmail, Cinderella's Twin* 1920; *The Offshore Pirate, Puppets of Fate, The Match-Breaker, Life's Darn Funny, There Are No Villains* 1921; *Fourteenth Lover, Glass Houses, Seeing's Believing, June Madness, The Five Dollar Baby, Love in the Dark* 1922; *Her Fatal Millions, Crinoline and Romance, Rouged Lips, The Social Code, In Search of a Thrill* 1923; *The Heart Bandit, Revelation, Merton of the Movies, Don't Doubt Your Husband, Open All Night, Along Came Ruth, The Beauty Prize* 1924; *Forty Winks, As Man Desires, The Necessary Evil, Winds of Chance, The Great Love* 1925; *Bigger Than Barnum's, Kosher Kitty Kelly, The Ice Flood, Wild Oats Lane, The Silent Lover* 1926; *Naughty Nanette, The Lure of the Night Club, Salvation Jane* 1927; *That Certain Thing* 1928; *One Splendid Hour, Two Sisters, The Show of Shows* 1929.

Dance, Charles. Actor. Born on Oct. 10, 1946, in Worcestershire, England. Leading man of British stage, TV, and film. The son of an engineer and a waitress, he worked as a plumber's assistant and trained as a graphic designer at the Plymouth College of Art and the Leicester College of Art. He was drawn to acting while working as a stagehand in a West End theater. In 1970 he began performing with a touring company, and after acting in provincial repertory he joined the Royal Shakespeare Company in 1975, playing leads in many of its productions through 1980. He made his screen debut the following year. He impersonated D. W. Griffith in *Good Morning Babylon.*

FILMS INCLUDE: *For Your Eyes Only* 1981; *Plenty* (US) 1985; *The Golden Child* (US) 1986; *White Mischief, Good Morning Babilonia/Good Morning Babylon* (as D.W. Griffith; It./Fr./US) 1987; *Hidden City, Pascali's Island* 1988; *Secret Places of the Heart* 1989; *Alien 3* 1992; *Last Action Hero* 1993; *Century, China Moon* 1994; *Michael Collins* 1996.

Dandridge, Dorothy. Actress, singer, dancer. *b.* Nov. 9, 1923, Cleveland, Ohio. *d.* 1965. The daughter of a minister and stage and screen actress Ruby Dandridge (b. Mar. 3, 1902, Memphis Tenn.), she began performing professionally at four, teaming up with her sister Vivian in a song-and-dance act as "The Wonder Children." Later she became a regular on the radio and TV series 'Beulah' and gained fame and popularity as a sultry nightclub entertainer. She made her screen debut in a bit part in the Marx Brothers classic *A Day at the Races* (1937) and subsequently played small roles in Hollywood films of the 40s. In the late 50s she was among the first black performers to achieve star status in the American cinema, as the leading lady of two sumptuous productions, *Carmen Jones* (1954) and *Porgy and Bess* (1959). She was nominated for an Oscar as best actress for the former. But early in the 60s she lost all her money in a get-rich-quick oil-investment scheme and was forced into bankruptcy. Just before she was scheduled to open at New York's Basin Street East, she was found dead in her Hollywood apartment from an overdose of barbiturates. Her first husband was dancer Harold NICHOLAS. She had collaborated on an autobiography, which was published posthumously in 1970 as *Everything and Nothing: The Dorothy Dandridge Tragedy.*

FILMS: *A Day at the Races* 1937; *Going Places* 1938; *Four Shall Die* 1940; *Lady from Louisiana, Sundown, Sun Valley Serenade, Bahama Passage* 1941; *Drums of the Congo, Lucky Jordan* 1942; *Hit Parade of 1943* 1943; *Since You Went Away, Atlantic City* 1944; *Tarzan's Peril/Tarzan and the Jungle Queen, The Harlem Globetrotters* 1951; *Bright Road, Remains to Be Seen* 1953; *Carmen Jones* 1954; *Island in the Sun* 1957; *The Decks Ran Red* 1958; *Porgy and Bess, Tamango* 1959; *Moment of Danger/Malaga* (UK) 1960.

Dane, Karl. Actor. *b.* Karl Daen, Oct. 12, 1886, Copenhagen. *d.* 1934. He made his stage debut at 14 at his father's Copenhagen theater. Arriving in Hollywood during WW I, he impersonated Chancellor von Bethmann-Hollweg in three anti-German propaganda features of 1918–19. But his screen career failed to prosper until 1925, when he made a strong impression in the role of a gangly, tobacco-chewing doughboy in the WW I epic *The Big Parade*. He subsequently enjoyed considerable popularity as a character comedian in the waning years of the silent era and with George K. Arthur in a series of comedy shorts. However, his thick accent proved too much of a handicap with the advent of sound. He tried earning a living as a carpenter and a mechanic and finally wound up manning a hotdog stand. A has-been at 48, he shot himself to death.

FILMS INCLUDE: *The Triumph of Venus* (as Mars), *My Four Years in Germany, To Hell with the Kaiser* 1918; *The Great Victory/Wilson or the Kaiser?/The Fall of the Hohenzollerns, Daring Hearts* 1919; *The Everlasting Whisper, Lights of Old Broadway, The Big Parade* 1925; *The Son of the Sheik, The Scarlet Letter, Bardelys the Magnificient, La Boheme, Monte Carlo, War Paint* 1926; *The Red Mill, Slide Kelly Slide, Rookies, The Enemy* 1927; *Baby Mine, The Trail of '98, Circus Rookies, Alias Jimmy Valentine, Detectives, Brotherly Love* 1928; *The Duke Steps Out, Speedway, All at Sea, China Bound, Navy Blues* 1929; *Montana Moon, Free and Easy, The Big House, Billy the Kid* 1930; *Whispering Shadows* (serial) 1933.

Danes, Claire. Actress. Born April 12, 1979, in New York City. *ed.* Lee Strasberg Theatre Institute. A dancer by the age of six, this young leading lady of stage, television, and film got her start off Broadway and quickly made a name for herself on the short-lived but critically praised TV series 'My So-Called Life.' She has moved on to a promising career in feature film with her debut in *Little Women* (1994).

FILMS: *Little Women* 1994; *Home for the Holidays, How to Make an American Quilt* 1995; *Romeo & Juliet, To Gillian on Her 37th Birthday* 1996.

D'Angelo, Beverly. Actress. Born on Oct. 15, 1953, in Columbus, Ohio. Energetic, blonde leading lady of American films and TV. Following art studies in Italy, she worked as a cartoonist for the Hanna-Barbera studios, then switched careers and began touring as a coffeehouse singer and later as a vocalist with a rock band named Elephant. She appeared on Broadway in the rock musical 'Rockabye Hamlet.' Making her screen debut in 1977, she proved a capable actress in both dramatic (as Patsy Cline in *Coal Miner's Daughter*) and comic (*National Lampoon's Vacation*) roles.

FILMS: *The Sentinel, Annie Hall, First Love* 1977; *Every Which Way but Loose* 1978; *Hair, Highpoint* (Can.) 1979; *Coal Miner's Daughter* 1980; *Honky Tonk Freeway, Paternity* 1981; *National Lampoon's Vacation* 1983; *Finders Keepers* 1984; *National Lampoon's European Vacation, Big Trouble* 1985; *Maid to Order, In the Mood/The Woo Woo Kid, Aria* ('Rigoletto' segment; UK) 1987; *High Spirits, Trading Hearts* 1988; *National Lampoon's Christmas Vacation, Cold Front* 1989; *Daddy's Dyin'. . . Who's Got the Will?, Pacific Heights* (unbilled cameo) 1990; *The Pope Must Die/The Pope Must Diet* (UK), *Lonely Hearts, The Miracle* 1991; *Man Trouble* 1992; *Lightning Jack, Lonely Hearts* 1994; *Edie & Pen, Eye for an Eye* 1996; *Nowhere* 1997.

Dangerfield, Rodney. Actor, comedian. Born Jacob Cohen, on Nov. 22, 1921, in Babylon, L.I., N.Y. He started his career at 19 as Jack Roy, a stand-up comic in nightclubs of the 40s. Unable to sustain a living income, he went into business in 1951 but continued performing on weekends. Resuming his show business career full time in 1963, he gradually gained popularity in TV talk shows and variety programs as a self-effacing schlemiel who "gets no respect." In 1969 he opened his own Manhattan nightclub, Dangerfield's. In the 80s he enjoyed some success in movie comedies.

FILMS: *The Projectionist* 1970; *Caddyshack* 1980; *Easy Money* (also co-sc.) 1983; *Back to School* (also co-story) 1986; *Moving* 1989; *The Scout* 1990; *Ladybugs* 1992; *Natural Born Killers* 1994; *Meet Wally Sparks* (also co-sc.) 1997.

Daniell, Henry. Actor. *b.* Mar. 5, 1894, London. *d.* 1963. A veteran of the London stage and Broadway, he played versatile character roles in scores of Hollywood films of the 30s, 40s, and 50s, most memorably and convincingly as a suave villain or cold-blooded authoritarian. He died shortly after completing his part in the shooting of *My Fair Lady*, ending a long career as one of the cinema's top heavies.

FILMS INCLUDE: *Jealousy, The Awful Truth* 1929; *Last of the Lone Wolf* 1930; *The Unguarded Hour* 1936; *Camille* (as the Baron de Varville), *Madame X, The Thirteenth Chair, The Firefly* 1937; *Marie Antoinette, Holiday* 1938; *We Are Not Alone, The Private Lives of Elizabeth and Essex* 1939; *All This and Heaven Too, The Sea Hawk, The Great Dictator* 1940; *The Philadelphia Story, A Woman's Face* 1941; *Sherlock Holmes and the Voice of Terror, Nightmare* 1942; *Mission in Moscow* (as Von Ribbentrop), *Watch on the Rhine* 1943; *Jane Eyre* 1944; *The Suspect, Hotel Berlin, The Body Snatcher, The Woman in Green* (as Prof. Moriarty), *Captain Kidd* (as King William III) 1945; *Song of Love* (as Franz Liszt), *The Exile* 1947; *Wake of the Red Witch* 1948; *Siren of Atlantis* 1949; *Buccaneer's Girl* 1950; *The Egyptian* 1954; *The Prodigal* 1955; *The Man in the Gray Flannel Suit, Lust for Life* 1956; *The Sun Also Rises, Les Girls* 1957; *Witness for the Prosecution, From the Earth to the Moon* 1958; *The Four Skulls of Jonathan Drake* 1959; *The Comancheros* 1961; *Madison Avenue, The Notorious Landlady, Five Weeks in a Balloon, The Chapman Report* 1962; *My Fair Lady* 1964.

Daniels, Bebe. Actress. *b.* Phyllis Daniels, Jan. 14, 1901, in Dallas. *d.* 1971. The daughter of a Scottish-born father who managed a touring theatrical company starring her Spanish-born mother, she was appearing regularly in plays by the time she reached four. At nine she made her screen debut in the Selig company two-reeler *The Common Enemy*, then played other child parts in numerous other shorts, mostly Westerns and adventure pictures, while attending a Los Angeles convent. At 14 she began playing adult roles in two-reel Hal Roach comedies, starring Snub Pollard and Harold Lloyd. From 1914 to 1918 she was featured in some 200 of these shorts, including most of the "Lonesome Luke" and "The Winckle" series with Lloyd.

In 1919, Miss Daniels signed a long-term contract with Paramount. She subsequently starred in several DE MILLE films and many other Paramount features through the rest of the silent era. Typically, she played light leads, impish, warm, often comic. But occasionally she portrayed hardened, experienced playgirls and a variety of other roles. Next to Gloria Swanson and Pola Negri, Miss Daniels was the most popular Paramount star of the silent period. Among her leading men were Wallace Reid and Rudolph Valentino. With the advent of the talkies, she was dropped by Paramount and signed up with RKO where, in the popular 1929 production *Rio Rita*, she proved she could not only talk but also sing. In 1930 she married Ben LYON, her co-star in *Alias French Gertie* and several subsequent films.

By the mid-30s the Hollywood careers of both Lyon and Daniels were on a decline, and in 1936 the couple accepted an offer to appear at the London Palladium. They remained in London through WW II, appearing in music halls, on the stage, and in a long-running radio show on BBC, and entertaining US troops. In 1946 they returned to Hollywood, where Lyon took an executive position with Fox, then, in 1949, went back to England, where the couple headlined another popular 50s family radio show 'Life with the Lyons.'

FILMS INCLUDE: *The Common Enemy* 1910; *An Awful Romance, Luke's Society Mixup, Luke's Movie Muddle* 1916; *Lonesome Luke on Tin Can Alley, Lonesome Luke's Honeymoon, Stop! Luke! Listen!, Lonesome Luke's Wild Women, Over the Fence, Pinched, Bliss, Birds of a Feather, Rainbow Island, The Flirt, We Never Sleep* 1917; *The Lamb, Here Come the Girls, Fireman Save My Child, An Ozark Romance, Nothing but Trouble* 1918; *Young Mr. Jazz, The Marathon, Spring Fever, Just Neighbors, Be My Wife, The Rajah, Soft Money, Bumping Into Broadway, Captain Kidd's Kids, Male and Female, Everywoman* 1919; *Why Change Your Wife?, The Dancin' Fool, Oh Lady Lady, She Couldn't Help It, Sick Abed, The 14th Man, You Never Can Tell* 1920; *Ducks and Drakes, Two Weeks to Pay, The March Hare, One Wild Week, The Affairs of Anatol, The Speed Girl* 1921; *Nancy from Nowhere, North of the Rio Grande, Nice People, Pink Gods, Singed Wings* 1922; *The World's Applause, Glimpses of the Moon, His Children's Children, The Exciters* 1923; *The Heritage of the Desert, Daring Youth, Unguarded Women, Monsieur Beaucaire, Dangerous Money, Sinners in Heaven, Argentine Love* 1924; *Miss Bluebeard, The Crowded Hour, The Manicure Girl, Lovers in Quarantine, Wild Wild Susan, The Splendid Crime* 1925; *Miss Brewster's Millions, The Palm Beach Girl, Volcano, The Campus Flirt, Stranded in Paris* 1926; *A Kiss in a Taxi, Senorita, Swim Girl Swim, She's a Sheik* 1927; *Hot News, The Fifty-Fifty Girl, Take Me Home, Feel My Pulse, What a Night!* 1928; *Rio Rita* 1929; *Love Comes Along, Alias French Gertie, Dixiana, Lawful Larceny* 1930; *Reaching for the Moon, My Past, The Maltese Falcon* 1931; *Silver Dollar* 1932; *42nd Street, Cocktail Hour, Counsellor-at-Law* 1933; *Registered Nurse* 1934; *Music Is Magic* 1935; *The Return of Dean* (UK) 1939; *Hi Gang!* (based on radio series; UK) 1941; *Life with the Lyons* (UK) 1953; *The Lyons in Paris* 1955.

Daniels, Jeff. Actor. Born in 1955, in Georgia. *ed.* Central Michigan U. Placid leading man of Hollywood films, often playing young professionals in conflict. He began his career on the stage, first gaining notice in the off-Broadway production of 'Johnny Got His Gun,' for which he won an Obie Award. On the screen from the early 80s, notably as the feckless husband in *Terms of Endearment* (1983) and the Depression screen hero come to life in *The Purple Rose of Cairo* (1985). In recent years he founded his own theatrical company.

FILMS: *Ragtime* 1981; *Terms of Endearment* 1983; *The Purple Rose of Cairo, Marie* 1985; *Heartburn, Something Wild* 1986; *Radio Days* 1987; *The House on Carroll Street, Sweet Hearts Dance* 1988; *Checking Out* 1989; *Love Hurts, Welcome Home Roxy Carmichael* 1990; *The Butcher's Wife* 1991; *There Goes the Neighborhood* 1992; *Dumb and Dumber, Speed, Terminal Velocity* 1994; *101 Dalmations, 2 Days in the Valley, Fly Away Home* 1996; *Trial and Error* 1997.

Daniels, William. Actor. Born on Mar. 31, 1927, in Brooklyn, N.Y. *ed.* Northwestern. Character player of the American stage, TV, and films. An entertainer from age four, he toured the New York area with his parents as part of The Daniels Family song-and-dance troupe, later playing juvenile roles on the legitimate stage, including a boy's part in 1943 in Broadway's 'Life With Father.' As an adult, he drew attention in the original production of Edward Albee's 'The Zoo Story' (1960), then in the stage (1962) and screen (1963) versions of *A Thousand Clowns*. His film career was boosted when he played the role of Dustin Hoffman's father in *The Graduate* (1967). Daniels is married to actress Bonnie Bartlett, his co-star in the 1980s TV series 'St. Elsewhere,' for which they both won Emmy Awards.

FILMS: *Family Honeymoon* 1949; *Ladybug Ladybug* 1963; *A Thousand Clowns* 1965; *The President's Analyst, The Graduate, Two for the Road* 1967; *Marlowe* 1969; *1776* (lead, as John Adams) 1972; *The Parallax View* 1974; *Black Sunday, Oh God!* 1977; *The One and Only* 1978; *Sunburn* 1979; *The Blue Lagoon* 1980; *All Night Long, Reds* 1981; *Blind Date* 1987; *Her Alibi* 1989.

Daniels, William H. Director of photography. *b.* 1895, Cleveland. *d.* 1970. *ed.* USC. One of the most distinguished lighting cameramen in the history of American cinema, he was a brilliant innovator who varied his style from picture to picture, to match each film's theme as well as each director's vision. Daniels began as assistant camera operator with the Triangle company in 1917 and became first operator at Universal in 1918 and director of photography in 1921. He achieved outstanding mood effects on films of Erich von STROHEIM in the early 20s and reached a peak of personal prestige during his long employment (1924–43) with MGM. In the 30s he became known as "GARBO's cameraman." He worked on most of the star's pictures and was not only able to capture her unique features glowingly but also to win her confidence and trust. Out of consideration for her fears and temperament, he insisted that all Garbo scenes be shot on closed sets with no one but the essential crew present. In 1947, after a period of illness, Daniels joined Universal. The following year he won an Academy Award for the starkly realistic photography of Jules Dassin's *The Naked City*. In both the 50s and 60s, he demonstrated a skill with color photography no less impressive than his celebrated work in black and white. President of American Society of Cinematographers 1961–63.

FILMS INCLUDE: *Blind Husbands* (cam. op.) 1919; *The Devil's Passkey* (cam. op.) 1920; *Foolish Wives* (co-phot.) 1922; *Merry-Go-Round* (co-phot.) 1923; *Helen's Babies* 1924; *Greed* (co-phot.), *The Merry Widow* (co-phot.) 1925; *Dance Madness, The Torrent, Monte Carlo, The Boob, The Temptress* (co-phot.), *Bardelys the Magnificent* 1926; *Flesh and the Devil* 1927; *Love, Bringing Up Father, The Actress, The Mysterious Lady, Woman of Affairs* 1928; *The Trial of Mary Dugan, Wild Orchids, The Last of Mrs. Cheyney, The Kiss* 1929; *Anna Christie, Romance* 1930; *Inspiration, A Free Soul, Susan Lennox: Her Fall and Rise* 1931; *Mata Hari, Grand Hotel* 1932; *Rasputin and the Empress, The White Sister, Dinner at Eight* 1933; *Queen Christina, The Barretts of Wimpole Street, The Painted Veil* 1934; *Naughty Marietta, Anna Karenina* 1935; *Rose Marie, Romeo and Juliet* 1936; *Camille, Broadway Melody of 1938, The Last Gangster* 1937; *Marie Antoinette* 1938; *Idiot's Delight, Ninotchka* 1939; *The Shop Around the Corner, The Mortal Storm* 1940; *So Ends Our Night, Back Street* 1941; *Keeper of the Flame* 1942; *Girl Crazy* 1943; *Brute Force, Lured* 1947; *The Naked City* 1948; *Winchester '73, Harvey* 1950; *Bright Victory* 1951; *Pat and Mike, Plymouth Adventure* 1952; *Thunder Bay, The Glenn Miller Story* 1953; *The Far Country* 1954; *The Shrike, Strategic Air Command* 1955; *Night Passage, My Man Godfrey* 1957; *Cat on a Hot Tin Roof, Some Came Running* 1958; *A Hole in the Head, Never So Few* 1959; *Can-Can, Ocean's 11* 1960; *Come September* 1961; *How the West Was Won* (co-phot.) 1962; *Come Blow Your Horn, The Prize* 1963; *Von Ryan's Express, Marriage on the Rocks* (also prod.) 1965; *Assault on a Queen* (also assoc. prod.) 1966; *In Like Flint, Valley of the Dolls* 1967; *Marlowe* 1969; *Move* 1970.

Danner, Blythe. Actress. Born on Feb. 3, 1943, in Philadelphia. *ed.* Bard Coll. Leading lady of American stage, TV, and films of the 70s. She won a Tony Award for her performance in Broadway's 'Butterflies Are Free' and co-starred in the short-lived TV series 'Adam's Rib.' Married writer-producer Bruce Paltrow. Their daughter is actress Gwyneth PALTROW.

FILMS: *To Kill a Clown, 1776* (as Martha Jefferson) 1972; *Lovin' Molly* 1974; *Hearts of the West* 1975; *Futureworld* 1976; *The Great Santini* 1979; *Man, Woman, and Child* 1983; *Brighton Beach Memoirs* 1986; *Another Woman* 1988; *Mr. and Mrs. Bridge* 1989; *Alice* 1990; *The Prince of Tides* 1991; *To Wong Foo Thanks for Everything Julie Newmar* 1994; *Homage* 1996; *Mad City, Myth of Fingerprints* 1997.

Danning, Sybil. Actress. Born in 1950, in Vienna. Sexy, blonde bombshell of international films. Having spent part of her childhood in California, she was working as a dental assistant in Salzburg in 1970 when she agreed to appear in softcore German sexploitation films. Decorative roles in legitimate but mostly poor features followed.

FILMS INCLUDE: *Urlaubsreport/Swedish Love Games, Das Mädchen mit der heissen Masche/The Loves of a French Pussycat* 1971; *Bluebeard* 1972; *The Three Musketeers* 1974; *The Four Musketeers* 1975; *The Prince and the Pauper/Crossed Swords, Operation Thunderbolt* 1977; *The Concorde—Airport '79, Meteor* 1979; *Battle Beyond the Stars, How to Beat the High Cost of Living, The Man with Bogart's Face* 1981; *Julie Darling* 1982; *Chained Heat, The Salamander, Hercules* 1983; *They're Playing with Fire, The Seven Magnificent Gladiators, Jungle Warriors* 1984; *Howling II: Your Sister Is a Werewolf, Private Property/Young Lady Chatterley II, Reform School Girls, The Tomb* 1986; *Warrior Queen, Amazon Women on the Moon* 1987; *L.A. Bounty* 1989.

Dano, Royal. Actor. Born on Nov. 16, 1922, in New York City. *d.* 1994. *ed.* NYU. Tall, brawny supporting player of Hollywood films, mainly of the action variety, often in bad-guy roles. Seen in numerous productions from 1950.

FILMS INCLUDE: *Undercover Girl* 1950; *Under the Gun, The Red Badge of Courage* 1951; *Bend of the River* 1952; *Johnny Guitar* 1954; *The Far Country, The Trouble with Harry* 1955; *Tribute to a Bad Man, Moby Dick* 1956; *Crime of Passion* 1957; *Saddle the Wind, Man of the West* 1958; *Never Steal Anything Small* 1959; *The Adventures of Huckleberry Finn, Cimarron* 1960; *King of Kings* (as Peter) 1961; *Savage Sam* 1963; *7 Faces of Dr. Lao* 1964; *Gunpoint* 1966; *Welcome to Hard Times* 1967; *Day of the Evil Gun* 1968; *The Undefeated* 1969; *The Great Northfield Minnesota Raid* 1972; *Cahill US Marshall, Electra Glide in Blue* 1973; *Big Bad Mama* 1974; *The Wild Party, Messiah of Evil* 1975; *The Outlaw Josey Wales, The Killer Inside Me* 1976; *In Search of Historic Jesus* 1979; *Take This Job and Shove It* 1981; *Hammett* 1982; *Something Wicked This Way Comes, The Right Stuff* 1983; *Teachers* 1984; *Red Headed Stranger* 1986; *House II: The Second Story* 1987; *Killer Klowns from Outer Space* 1988; *Ghoulies II* 1989; *Spaced Invaders* 1990.

Danova, Cesare. Actor. *b.* 1926, Italy. *d.* 1992. Leading man of Italian cinema who later played leads and second leads in Hollywood films.

FILMS INCLUDE: *La Figlia del Capitano/The Captain's Daughter* (It.) 1947; *Processo contro Ignoti/Genoese Dragnet* (It.) 1952; *Don Giovanni/Don Juan* (title role; Aus.) 1955; *The Man Who Understood Women* 1959; *Valley of the Dragons* 1961; *Tender Is the Night* 1962; *Cleopatra, Gidget Goes to Rome* 1963; *Viva Las Vegas* 1964; *Boy Did I Get the Wrong Number!, Chamber of Horrors* 1966; *Che!* 1969; *Mean Streets* 1973; *Scorchy* 1976; *Tentacles* (It.) 1977; *National Lampoon's Animal House* 1978.

Danson, Ted. Actor. Born Edward Bridge Danson III, on Dec. 29, 1947, in San Diego. *ed.* Kent School; Stanford U.; Carnegie Mellon U. Tall (6' 2"), dark, pleasant leading man of American TV and films. Best known for his role as Sam Malone, the womanizing bartender, in the long-running TV series 'Cheers.' The son of a noted archeologist/anthropologist, he grew up in Arizona, where his father served as a university professor and museum president. He turned to acting at boarding school and began his career on the New York stage in the late 60s. Divorced from his wife of many years, he is now married to actress Mary STEENBURGEN.

FILMS: *The Onion Field* 1979; *Body Heat* 1981; *Creepshow* 1982; *Little Treasure* 1985; *Just Between Friends, A Fine Mess* 1986; *Three Men and a Baby* 1987; *Cousins, Dad* 1989; *Three Men and a Little Lady* 1990; *Made in America* 1993; *Getting Even with Dad, Pontiac Moon* (also co-exec. prod.) 1994.

Dante, Joe. Director. Born in Morristown, N.J. Entering the film world as a promotion specialist, he became a protégé of Roger CORMAN, and began editing in 1973, and directing in

1976. A proficient technician, he is most at home with action-fantasy material.

FILMS: *Hollywood Boulevard* (co-dir. edit.) 1976; *Piranha* (also edit.) 1978; *Rock 'n' Roll High School* (co-story only) 1979; *The Howling* (also edit.) 1982; *Twilight Zone—The Movie* (one segment) 1983; *Gremlins* 1984; *Explorers* 1985; *Innerspace, Amazon Women on the Moon* (co-dir.) 1987; *The 'Burbs* 1989; *Gremlins 2: The New Batch, Monoliths* 1990; *Sleepwalkers* (act.) 1991; *Matinee* 1993; *Beverly Hills Cop III* (act. only), *The Silence of the Hams* (act. only) 1994; *The Phantom* (co-exec. prod. only) 1996.

Dantine, Helmut. Actor. *b.* Helmut Guttman, Oct. 7, 1917, Vienna. *d.* 1982, of a massive coronary, Vienna. *ed.* U. of California. He came to the US in the late 30s as a fugitive from the German Anschluss of Austria and, after gaining acting experience as a member of the Pasadena Community Players, entered films in 1941. Darkly handsome, with chiseled features, he played leads and second leads in Warner Bros. pictures of the 40s, specializing in Nazi roles during the WW II years. He directed one undistinguished film, *Thundering Jets*, in 1958. That same year he married actress Nicola Schenck (professional name: Niki Dantine), the daughter of Nicholas M. Schenck, the former president of Loew's, Inc. In 1959, Dantine became vice president and in 1970 president of the Schenck Enterprises film production and distribution organization. He later appeared in films only sporadically, in small roles.

FILMS INCLUDE: *International Squadron* 1941; *To Be or Not to Be, Mrs. Miniver* 1942; *Casablanca, Edge of Darkness, Mission to Moscow, Northern Pursuit* 1943; *Passage to Marseille, The Mask of Dimitrios* 1944; *Hotel Berlin, Escape in the Desert* 1945; *Shadow of a Woman* 1946; *Whispering City* 1948; *Call Me Madam, Guerrilla Girl* 1953; *Alexander the Great, War and Peace* 1956; *The Story of Mankind, Hell on Devil's Island* 1957; *Thundering Jets* (dir. only), *Fraulein, La Tempesta/Tempest* (It./Fr./Yug.) 1958; *Operation Crossbow* 1965; *Bring Me the Head of Alfredo Garcia* (also exec. prod.) 1974; *The Wilby Conspiracy* (exec. prod. only), *The Killer Elite* (also exec. prod.) 1975; *The Fifth Musketeer* (Aus.) 1977.

Danton, Ray(mond). Actor, director. *b.* Sept. 19, 1931, New York City. *d.* 1992. *ed.* Carnegie Tech. Leading man of Hollywood and international films, at his most effective in smooth gangster roles. Entered films in the mid-50s, following radio and stage experience and military service. From the mid-60s he often worked in Europe. Also much TV. In the early 70s he directed low-budget horror films. Married to actress Julie ADAMS.

FILMS INCLUDE: As actor—*Chief Crazy Horse, The Spoilers, I'll Cry Tomorrow* 1955; *Outside the Law* 1956; *Too Much Too Soon, Tarawa Beachhead* 1958; *The Big Operator, The Beat Generation* 1959; *The Rise and Fall of Legs Diamond* (title role), *Ice Palace* 1960; *Portrait of a Mobster* (as "Legs" Diamond), *The George Raft Story* (title role) 1961; *A Majority of One, The Longest Day, The Chapman Report* 1962; *FBI Code 98* 1964; *The Spy Who Went Into Hell* (Ger.) 1965; *New York appelle Super Dragon/Secret Agent Super Dragon* (Fr./It./Ger.) 1966; *El Mercenario/The Last Mercenary* (Sp./It./Ger.) 1970; *The Centerfold Girls* 1974; *Pursuit, Six-Pack Annie* 1975. As director—*The Deathmaster* 1972; *Crypt of the Living Dead* 1973; *Psychic Killer* (also co-sc.) 1975.

Daquin, Louis. Director. *b.* May 30, 1908, Calais, France. *d.* 1980. After law studies and a brief career in advertising and journalism, he entered French films in 1932 as assistant to Chenal, Duvivier, Gance, and Grémillon. In 1941 he made an auspicious debut as a director with *Nous les Gosses/Portrait of Innocence*, an unpretentious, heartwarming film about school children which succeeded in sneaking through Nazi Occupation censors despite its "objectionable" poetic realism. He was a member of the Comité de Libération du Cinéma Français and helped with the production of the documentary *Le Journal de la Résistance* (1945). He received much critical acclaim for *Le Point du Jour* (1948), a starkly realistic film about miners. His radical ideas concerning human and social problems, and his uncompromising filmic approach, made him an outcast in the French industry, and in the late 50s he worked in Austria, Romania, and West Germany. His made-in-Austria *Bel-Ami* (1954) was held up by the French censors and not released until three years later. He is the author of the book *Le Cinéma—Notre Métier* (1960). Served as director of studies at IDHEC.

FILMS: *Le Joueur* (French version of Gerhard Lamprecht's Der Spieler) 1938; *Nous les Gosses/Portrait of Innocence* 1941; *Madame et le Mort, Le Voyageur de la Toussaint* 1943; *Premier de Cordée* 1944; *Patrie* 1946; *Les Frères Bouquinquant* 1947; *Le Point du Jour* 1948; *La Parfum de la Dame en Noir* 1949; *Matre après Dieu/Skipper Next to God* 1951; *Bel-Ami* (Aus.) 1954; *Ciulinii Baraganului/Les Chardons du Baragan* (Rum.) 1957; *Trube Wasser/Les Arrivistes* (E. Ger.) 1960; *Le Foire aux Cancres* 1963.

Darabont, Frank. Director, screenwriter. Born 1959, in France. Getting his start in films as a production assistant on the hokey horror flick *Hell Night* (1981), the fledgling filmmaker sold his first screenplay, which has never been produced, and then earned screen credit for rewriting the script for *A Nightmare on Elm Street 3: Dream Warriors* (1987), leading to other scripts or film and television. But it was his ambitious effort, the touching and effective *The Shawshank Redemption* (1994), based on the Stephen King novella, which brought critical acclaim and a Directors Guild Award nomination along with Writers Guild and Academy Award nominations for his adapted screenplay.

FILMS: *Hell Night* (prod. asst. only) 1981; *Crimes of Passion* (set dec. only) 1984; *A Nightmare on Elm Street 3: Dream Warriors* (sc. only) 1987; *The Blob* (sc. only), *The Fly II* (sc. only) 1988; *Mary Shelley's Frankenstein* (sc. only), *The Shawshank Redemption* (dir., sc.) 1994.

D'Arbanville, Patti. Actress. Born in 1951, in New York City. Raised in Greenwich Village, she landed her first job while a baby, in Ivory Soap commercials. In her early teens, she worked as a disc jockey and played a small role in Andy Warhol's *Flesh*. At 17, she moved to Paris, where she became a fashion model and appeared in a couple of films. She was a mature 21 by the time she returned to the US and settled in Los Angeles in 1973 to launch a Hollywood career in films and television.

FILMS: *Flesh* 1968; *La Maison* (Fr.) 1969; *La Saigne* (Fr.) 1971; *The Crazy American Girl* (Fr.) 1972; *L'Amour* 1973; *Rancho Deluxe* 1975; *Big Wednesday* 1978; *The Main Event, Time After Time* 1979; *The Fifth Floor, Hog Wild* (Can.) 1980; *Modern Problems* 1981; *Real Genius, The Boys Next Door* 1985; *Call Me, Fresh Horses* 1988; *Wired* 1989; *Frame Up 2* 1992; *The Fan* 1996.

Darby, Kim. Actress. Born Deborah Zerby, on July 8, 1947, in Hollywood, Calif. The daughter of performers billed as the "Dancing Zerbies," she danced and sang professionally from childhood (as Derby Zerby) and made her mark on TV in the 'Mr. Novak' and 'Run for Your Life' series. After making her screen debut as an extra in *Bye Bye Birdie* (1963), she played plain, spunky leads in films of the late 60s and early 70s. She was briefly married to actor John Stacy.

FILMS: *Bus Riley's Back in Town, The Restless Ones* 1965; *The Karate Killers* (TV movie; shown theatrically abroad) 1967;

True Grit, Generation 1969; *The Strawberry Statement, Norwood* 1970; *The Grissom Gang* 1971; *The One and Only* 1978; *Better Off Dead* 1985; *Teen Wolf Too* 1987.

Darc, Mireille. Actress. Born Mireille Aigroz, May 15, 1938, in Toulon, France. A former model, she broke into French films via TV in 1960 and has become a popular leading lady thanks to her tomboyish vitality and comic talent.

FILMS INCLUDE: *Les Distractions* 1960; *La Bride sur le Cou/Please Not Now, Les Nouveaux Aristocrates* 1961; *Virginie* 1962; *Monsieur, Chasse à l'Homme/Male Hunt, Les Barbouzes/The Great Spy Chase* 1964; *Galia, Du Rififi à Paname/The Upper Hand* 1966; *Le Week-End/Weekend* 1968; *Monte Carlo or Bust/Those Daring Young Men in Their Jaunty Jalopies* (UK/Fr./It.), *Jeff* 1969; *Madly* (also story basis), *Borsalino* (bit) 1970; *Laisse aller—c'est une Valse* 1971; *Le Grand Blond avec une Chaussure noire/The Tall Blond Man with One Black Shoe, Il n'y a pas de Fumée sans Feu/Where There's Smoke* 1973; *Les Seins de Glace/Icy Breasts* 1974; *L'Ordinateur des Pompes funèbres* 1976; *Les Passagers, L'Homme pressé, Mort d'un Pourri* 1977; *Les Ringards* 1978.

Darcel, Denise. Actress. Born Denise Billecard, on Sept. 8, 1925, in Paris. *ed.* U. of Dijon. A nightclub singer, she went to Hollywood in 1947, played sensual leads in a number of films, then returned to nightclubs and acted in dinner theaters and in TV commercials.

FILMS: *To the Victor* 1948; *Thunder in the Pines, Battleground* 1949; *Tarzan and the Slave Girl* 1950; *Westward the Women, Young Man with Ideas* 1952; *Dangerous When Wet, Flame of Calcutta* 1953; *Vera Cruz* 1954; *Seven Women from Hell* 1961.

D'Arcy, Roy. Actor. *b.* Roy Francis Giusti, Feb. 10, 1894, San Francisco. *d.* 1969. After university studies in Germany, he spent some time in the jungles of Brazil on a business venture and held various executive posts upon returning to the US. He made his screen debut in 1919, spent the early 20s in vaudeville and stock, and reappeared in films in 1925, playing a memorable role as the leering, lecherous crown prince in von Stroheim's *The Merry Widow*. He subsequently portrayed villainous characters in many films until his retirement in the late 30s.

FILMS INCLUDE: *Oh Boy!* 1919; *The Merry Widow, Graustark, The Masked Bride* 1925; *La Boheme, Monte Carlo, The Gay Deceiver, The Temptress, Bardelys the Magnificent, Valencia* 1926; *Frisco Sally Levy, Lovers?, Adam and Evil, On ze Boulevard, The Road to Romance* 1927; *The Actress, Forbidden Hours, Beware of Blondes* 1928; *The Last Warning, The Black Watch, The Woman from Hell* 1929; *Sherlock Holmes* 1932; *Flying Down to Rio* 1933; *Orient Express* 1934; *Revolt of the Zombies, Hollywood Boulevard* 1936; *Chasing Danger* 1939.

Darin, Bobby. Singer, songwriter, actor. *b.* Robert Walden Cassotto, May 14, 1936, New York City. *ed.* Hunter Coll. *d.* 1973. Having lost his father before birth, he was raised by his mother with the aid of welfare. In the late 50s he emerged as a highly successful nightclub and recording singing star and won two Grammy Awards in 1960 for his rendition of 'Mack the Knife,' which sold 2 million copies. He subsequently played both light and dramatic roles in films and was nominated for an Oscar for his portrayal of a shell-shocked GI in *Captain Newman, M.D.* (1964). Long plagued by heart trouble, he died at 37 following an operation. His first wife was actress Sandra DEE.

FILMS: *Pepe* 1960; *Come September* 1961; *Too Late Blues, State Fair, Hell Is for Heroes, Pressure Point, If a Man Answers* 1962; *Captain Newman M.D.* 1964; *That Funny Feeling* (also music and title song) 1965; *Gunfight in Abilene, Stranger in the House/Cop-Out* (UK) 1967; *The Happy Ending* 1969; *Happy Mother's Day—Love George* 1973.

Darling, William. Art director. *b.* Wilhelm Sandorhazi, Sept. 14, 1882, Sandor, Hungary. *d.* 1963. In US films since 1920 after university studies in Budapest. He did his most important work for 20th Century-Fox after 1933. He shared Academy Awards for the art direction of *Cavalcade* (1933), *The Song of Bernadette* (1943), and *Anna and the King of Siam* (1946). He worked frequently for director John FORD.

FILMS: *Her Mad Bargain* 1921; *What Price Glory* 1926; *Paid to Love, A Girl in Every Port* 1928; *The Black Watch* 1929; *City Girl, Men Without Women, Common Clay* 1930; *Bad Girl, The Yellow Ticket* 1931; *While Paris Sleeps* 1932; *Cavalcade, Pilgrimage, Zoo in Budapest, Berkeley Square* 1933; *The World Moves On, Judge Priest* 1934; *Dante's Inferno, Folies Bergere, In Old Kentucky, Way Down East, The Little Colonel, Steamboat Round the Bend* 1935; *Captain January, Poor Little Rich Girl, Under Two Flags, Message to Garcia, The Prisoner of Shark Island, Lloyds of London, Dimples* 1936; *Wee Willie Winkee, Wake Up and Live, Seventh Heaven, On the Avenue* 1937; *In Old Chicago* 1938; *Jesse James, Stanley and Livingstone, The Rains Came* 1939; *Brigham Young—Frontiersman* 1940; *Hangmen Also Die, The Song of Bernadette* 1943; *The Keys of the Kingdom* 1944; *Anna and the King of Siam* 1946.

Darnell, Linda. Actress. *b.* Monetta Eloyse Darnell, Oct. 16, 1921, Dallas. *d.* 1965. The daughter of a postal clerk, she was driven by an ambitious stage mother into tap-dance lessons at age five, modeling and talent competitions at 11, and beauty contests at 14. Well developed for her age, she won a regional "Gateway to Hollywood" contest at 16 and was screen-tested by RKO. Two years later she was signed by 20th Century-Fox to a seven-year contract and rapidly developed into one of the studio's top stars. An exotic brunette beauty with a perfect complexion, she started out playing doll-like virginal heroines (*The Mark of Zorro*) and faithful young wives (*Blood and Sand*), but gradually switched to sultry temptresses (*Forever Amber*). Whatever her role, she was a decorative type of actress and was rarely effective when given the opportunity to show her talent.

Just the same, Linda Darnell was among Hollywood's most popular stars in the 40s, but her career declined sharply in the early 50s following the termination of her Fox contract, after which she appeared mostly in minor productions. She was seen in only one film after 1957 but could be glimpsed occasionally on the stage and in TV dramas. Her first (1943–52) of three husbands was cameraman Peverell J. MARLEY.

FILMS: *Hotel for Women, Daytime Wife* 1939; *Star Dust, Brigham Young, The Mark of Zorro, Chad Hanna* 1940; *Blood and Sand, Rise and Shine* 1941; *The Loves of Edgar Allan Poe* 1942; *City Without Men, The Song of Bernadette* (unbilled, as the Virgin Mary) 1943; *It Happened Tomorrow, Buffalo Bill, Summer Storm, Sweet and Lowdown* 1944; *Hangover Square, The Great John L., Fallen Angel* 1945; *Centennial Summer, Anna and the King of Siam, My Darling Clementine* 1946; *Forever Amber* 1947; *The Walls of Jericho, Unfaithfully Yours* 1948; *A Letter to Three Wives, Slattery's Hurricane, Everybody Does It* 1949; *No Way Out, Two Flags West* 1950; *The Thirteenth Letter, The Guy Who Came Back, The Lady Pays Off* 1951; *Saturday Island, Island of Desire, Night Without Sleep, Blackbeard the Pirate* 1952; *Donne Proibite/Angels of Darkness* (It.), *Second Chance* 1953; *This Is My Love* 1954; *Gli Ultimi Cinque Minuti* (It.) 1955; *Dakota Incident* 1956; *Zero Hour* 1957; *El Valle de las Espadas/The Castilian* (Sp./US) 1963; *Black Spurs* 1965.

D'Arrast, Harry d'Abbadie. Director. *b.* 1897, Argentina, of French-Basque nobility. *d.* 1968. *ed.* Lycée de de Sailly (Paris); Bradford U. (England). While recuperating from severe WW I wounds in France, he met director George Fitzmaurice, who urged him to come to the US and try his hand in films. Arriving in Hollywood in 1922, he first worked as a researcher and technical adviser on Chaplin's *A Woman of Paris* (1923), then as Chaplin's assistant on *The Gold Rush* (1925). Between 1927 and 1933 he directed seven Hollywood films, five silents and two talkies, all noted for their wit and elegance, for their brilliant photography and perfect pace. In addition, he co-directed, but did not receive screen credit for, *Raffles* (1930). Despite high critical acclaim and some box-office success, he was often at odds with studio bosses and producers, and by 1934 he could no longer find work in Hollywood. He went to Spain, where he directed a film based on Alarcón's *The Three-Cornered Hat*, starring his wife, Eleanor Boardman, then returned to Hollywood, where he spent several idle years. In 1946 he returned to France and spent the rest of his life at the family castle in the Basses-Pyrenees and in Monte Carlo, managing to eke out a living at the Casino roulette table.

FILMS: *Service for Ladies, A Gentleman of Paris, Serenade* 1927; *The Magnificent Flirt* (also co-sc.), *Dry Martini* 1928; *Raffles* (uncredited; completed by George Fitzmaurice), *Laughter* (also co-story) 1930; *Topaze* 1933; *It Happened in Spain/The Three-Cornered Hat* (Sp.) 1934.

Darren, James. Actor. Born James Ercolani, on June 8, 1936, in Philadelphia. Coached in acting by Stella Adler, he entered films in the mid-50s and became popular with teeny-boppers for his leads in *Gidget* and other youth-oriented productions. For a while he was also successful as a recording artist. He has played both light and dramatic roles in films but never did quite shake off the teenage-idol image. Also seen in the TV series 'Time Tunnel' (1966).

FILMS INCLUDE: *Rumble on the Docks* 1956; *The Brothers Rico, Operation Madball* 1957; *Gidget, The Gene Krupa Story* 1959; *All the Young Men, Let No Man Write My Epitaph* 1960; *The Guns of Navarone* 1961; *Diamond Head, Gidget Goes to Rome* 1963; *For Those Who Think Young, The Lively Set* 1964; *Venus in Furs* 1970; *The Boss' Son* 1978.

Darrieux, Danielle. Actress. Born on May 1, 1917, in Bordeaux, France. The daughter of an army doctor who died when she was seven, she was raised in Paris and was a 14-year-old cello student at the Conservatoire when her mother entered her in an audition for an adolescent role in the film *Le Bal* (1931). It was the start of a glorious long career in French and international films which saw her progress from fragile romantic ingenues to chic, elegant, sophisticated women-of-the-world roles. Throughout that long period she remained one of the screen's major stars, known and admired the world over as the embodiment and the essence of French femininity. During the Nazi occupation in WW II, she was marked for execution by the French underground for entertaining German troops but was later exonerated and resumed her film career. In addition to French productions, she also made films in the US, the UK, Germany, Italy, Spain, Czechoslovakia, and Hungary. She has also appeared on the stage and in the 60s entertained as a singer in concert and on records. In 1970, still delicate and lovely, she replaced Katharine HEPBURN in the lead role in the Broadway musical 'Coco.' She has been married three times, to director Henri DECOIN (1934–40), to international playboy-diplomat Porfirio Rubirosa (1942–47), and (from 1948) to author Georges Mitsinkides.

FILMS INCLUDE: *Le Bal* 1931; *Château de Rêve* 1933; *Mauvaise Graine, Volga en Flammes, Le Crise est finie, Dédé, L'Or dans la Rue* 1934; *Quelle Drôle de Gosse, Le Domino Vert* 1935; *Mademoiselle Mozart/Meet Miss Mozart, Mayerling, Club de Femmes, Port-Arthur/I Give My Life, Tarass Boulba* 1936; *Abus de Confiance/Abused Confidence, Mademoiselle ma Mère* 1937; *The Rage of Paris* (US), *Katia, Retour à l'Aube/She Returned at Dawn* 1938; *Battements de Coeur* 1939; *Premier Rendez-Vous/Her First Affair, Caprices* 1941; *Adieu Chérie, Au Petit Bonheur* 1946; *Ruy Blas, Jean de la Lune* 1948; *Occupe-toi d'Amélie/Oh Amelia* 1949; *La Ronde* 1950; *Rich Young and Pretty* (US), *La Maison Bonnadieu* 1951; *Le Plaisir, La Vérité sur Bébé Donge, Five Fingers* (US), *Adorable Créatures* 1952; *Le Bon Dieu sans Confession, Madame de. . . /The Earrings of Madame De* 1953; *Le Rouge et le Noir* 1954; *Napoléon, Bonnes à tuer/One Step to Eternity, L'Amant de Lady Chatterley/Lady Chatterley's Lover* 1955; *Alexander the Great* (US), *Typhon sur Nagasaki* (Fr./Jap.) 1956; *Pot-Bouille* 1957; *Un Drôle de Dimanche, Le Désordre et la Nuit/Night Affair* 1958; *Marie-Octobre, Les Yeux de l'Amour* 1959; *The Greengage Summer/Loss of Innocence* (UK) 1961; *Landru/Bluebeard* 1963; *Patate/Friend of the Family* 1964; *Le Coup de Grâce, Le Dimanche de la Vie* 1965; *Les Demoiselles de Rochefort/The Young Girls of Rochefort* 1967; *24 Heures de la Vie d'une Femme/24 Hours in a Woman's Life, Les Oiseaux vont mourir au Pérou/Birds of Peru* 1968; *La Maison de Campagne/A House in the Country* 1969; *Roses rouges et Piments verts/The Lonely Woman* 1975; *L'Année sainte* 1976; *Le Cavaleur/Practice Makes Perfect* 1979; *Une Chambre en Ville* 1982; *En haut des Marches* 1983; *Le Lieu du Crime/Scene of the Crime* 1986; *Quelques Jours avec moi/A Few Days with Me* 1988; *Bille en Tête* 1989; *Le Jour de Rois* 1990.

Darro, Frankie. Actor. *b.* Frank Johnson, Dec. 22, 1917, Chicago. *d.* 1976. The son of circus aerialists, he made his film debut at six and continued playing child roles in films throughout the silent era. Maturing into adolescent roles in the 30s, he often played tough kids of the Depression era, then played leads in low-budget Monogram action programmers. Because of his small frame, he also portrayed many jockeys and pint-size punks. Gradually he drifted into bit roles and finally stunt work and all but disappeared from public view after the early 50s, except for an occasional movie role and a spot on TV's 'The Red Skelton Show.' Also billed as Frankie Darrow.

FILMS: *Judgment of the Storm, The Signal Tower* 1924; *So Big* 1925; *Mike, Memory Lane, Kiki* 1926; *Long Pants, Flesh and the Devil, Little Mickey Grogan* (title role) 1927; *The Circus Kid* (title role) 1928; *The Rainbow Man* 1929; *The Lightning Warrior* (serial), *The Mad Genius, The Public Enemy* 1931; *The Mayor of Hell, Tugboat Annie, Wild Boys of the Road* 1933; *No Greater Glory, Broadway Bill* 1934; *Phantom Empire* (serial), *Little Men* 1935; *Charlie Chan at the Race Track* 1936; *Racing Blood, Saratoga, Thoroughbreds Don't Cry* 1937; *Reformatory, Juvenile Court* 1938; *Chasing Trouble, Laughing at Danger* 1940; *High School Hero* 1946; *That's My Man* 1947; *Trouble Makers* 1948; *Fighting Fools* 1949; *Riding High* 1950; *Across the Wide Missouri* 1951; *Operation Petticoat* 1959; *The Carpetbaggers* (bit) 1964; *Hook Line and Sinker* (bit) 1969.

Darrow, John. Actor. Born Harry Simpson, on July 17, 1907, in New York City. Began acting in stock directly out of high school, entering films at 20. During the early 30s he enjoyed some popularity as a leading man, mainly in B productions, but he retired from the screen by mid-decade and later became one of Hollywood's most successful agents.

FILMS INCLUDE: *High School Hero* 1927; *The Racket, Avalanche, Prep and Pep* 1928; *Girls Gone Wild, The Argyle Case* 1929; *Cheer Up and Smile, Hell's Angels* 1930; *The Lady Refuses, Everything's Rosie, The Bargain, Fanny Foley Herself* 1931; *The Midnight Lady, Alias Mary Smith, The All American* 1932; *Strange People, Midshipman Jack* 1933; *I Give My Love, Flirtation Walk* 1934; *A Notorious Gentleman* 1935; *Crime Over London* (UK) 1936.

Darvi, Bella. Actress. *b.* Bayla Wegier, Oct. 28, 1928, Sosnowiec, Poland. *d.* 1971. In Paris from infancy, she was placed in a concentration camp at age 12 when the Germans occupied the city she lived in. It was in Paris in 1951 that she attracted the attention of movie mogul Darryl F. ZANUCK and his wife, Virginia. They paid her gambling debts at various Riviera casinos and took her back to their Hollywood home. As a Zanuck protégée she was given a screen test and launched on a brief and unremarkable film career. Her screen name was derived from the combined first names of Darryl and Virginia Zanuck. After only three disappointing Hollywood films, and amidst scandalous rumors, she was thrown out of the Zanuck house by Mrs. Zanuck and her Fox contract was terminated. She returned to Europe and appeared in a number of undistinguished French and Italian productions.

FILMS INCLUDE: *Hell and High Water* (US), *The Egyptian* (US) 1954; *The Racers* (US), *Je suis un Sentimental* (Fr.) 1955; *Le Gorille vous salve bien/Gorilla* (Fr.) 1957; *Le Pain des Jules* (Fr.), *Il Rossetto/Lipstick* (It./Fr.) 1960; *Les Petites Filles modèles* 1971.

Darwell, Jane. Actress. *b.* Patti Woodward, Oct. 15, 1879, Palmyra, Mo. *d.* 1967. The daughter of a railroad president who claimed to be a direct descendant of Andrew Jackson, she made her stage debut in 1906. She appeared in a handful of films in 1913–15, several under the direction of Cecil B. DE MILLE, then returned to the stage, resuming her screen career fully in 1930. She subsequently played character roles in scores of films, often in kind, sometimes dominating, motherly roles. Won an Academy Award for her portrayal of Ma Joad in *The Grapes of Wrath* (1940).

FILMS INCLUDE: *The Master Mind, The Only Son, Ready Money, Rose of the Rancho* 1914; *After Five, The Goose Girl, The Reform Candidate* 1915; *Tom Sawyer* 1930; *Huckleberry Finn* 1931; *Back Street, Hot Saturday* 1932; *Bondage, Only Yesterday, Design for Living, Roman Scandals* 1933; *Wonder Bar, David Harum, Bright Eyes, The Scarlet Empress, The White Parade* 1934; *One More Spring, Life Begins at Forty, Curly Top* 1935; *The Country Doctor, Captain January, Little Miss Nobody, Poor Little Rich Girl, White Fang, Ramona, Star for a Night, Craig's Wife* 1936; *Love Is News, Slave Ship, Wife Doctor and Nurse* 1937; *Three Blind Mice, Little Miss Broadway* 1938; *Jesse James, The Rains Came, Gone With the Wind* 1939; *The Grapes of Wrath, Chad Hanna, Brigham Young* 1940; *All That Money Can Buy* 1941; *All Through the Night* 1942; *The Ox-Bow Incident* 1943; *The Impatient Years, Sunday Dinner for a Soldier* 1944; *Three Wise Fools, My Darling Clementine* 1946; *Three Godfathers, Red Canyon* 1949; *Wagonmaster, Caged* 1950; *The Lemon Drop Kid* 1951; *We're Not Married* 1952; *The Bigamist* 1953; *There's Always Tomorrow* 1956; *The Last Hurrah* 1958; *Mary Poppins* 1964.

Da Silva, Howard. Actor. *b.* Howard Silverblatt, May 4, 1909, Cleveland. *d.* 1986. The son of a dress cutter and a women's rights activist, he was raised in the Bronx, then moved with his family to Pittsburgh, where he worked in the steel mills to pay his way through the Carnegie Institute of Technology. He made his New York stage debut in 1929 and subsequently played with distinction many character roles on Broadway, culminating in the part of Jud in the musical hit 'Oklahoma!' (1943). Concurrently, he pursued a successful career as a character actor in films, specializing in mean heavy roles. In 1951 he refused to affirm or deny membership in the Communist party in hearings before the House Un-American Activities Committee and as a result was blacklisted by the Hollywood studios. He remained active, though, on Broadway, as an actor, director, producer, and playwright, and returned to films in the 60s.

FILMS INCLUDE: *Once in a Blue Moon* 1936; *Golden Boy* 1939; *Abe Lincoln in Illinois* 1940; *The Sea Wolf, Sergeant York* 1941; *Native Land, The Big Shot, Reunion in France, Keeper of the Flame* 1942; *Tonight We Raid Calais* 1943; *The Lost Weekend* 1945; *The Blue Dahlia, Two Years Before the Mast* 1946; *Blaze of Noon, Unconquered* 1947; *The Great Gatsby, They Live by Night, Border Incident* 1949; *The Underworld Story, Tripoli* 1950; *Fourteen Hours, Three Husbands, M* 1951; *David and Lisa* 1963; *The Outrage* 1964; *Nevada Smith* 1966; *1776* (as Benjamin Franklin) 1972; *The Great Gatsby* 1974; *The Private Files of J. Edgar Hoover* 1978; *Mommie Dearest* 1981; *Garbo Talks* 1984.

Dassin, Jules. Director. Born Julius Dassin, on Dec. 18, 1911, in Middletown, Conn. One of eight children of a Russian Jewish immigrant barber, he moved with his family to the Harlem section of New York City and attended high school in the Bronx. After drama studies in Europe, he made his debut as an actor in 1936 with New York's Yiddish Theater. He later wrote radio scripts and in 1940 went to Hollywood, where, after a brief induction as assistant director at RKO, he began directing short subjects for MGM. The last of these, *The Tell-Tale Heart* (1941), resulted in his promotion to feature director. His early films were inconsequential, mildly entertaining suspense and comedy fare. In the late 40s he seemed to have at last found his stride with three dynamic on-location slice-of-life dramas, *Brute Force, The Naked City,* and *Thieves' Highway,* but just as he was gaining recognition as a director with something to say and an interesting way of saying it, he was forced into exile in Europe as a result of the House Un-American Activities Committee hearings, in which he was identified as a Communist by Edward Dmytryk.

Dassin's first stop was England, where he directed another intelligent film in his new-found semidocumentary style, *Night and the City*. He later turned up in France with a suspense gem, *Du Rififi chez les Hommes/Rififi. He Who Must Die* fetched prizes at Eastern-block festivals but was poorly received in the West, as was the French-Italian production *Where the Hot Wind Blows.* Then in the 60s came his Greek period and films starring his second wife, Melina MERCOURI. The best known of these, *Never on Sunday,* discovered the Mediterranean for Americans, but in Europe it was forgivingly dismissed as a naïve American's view of a world he understands only superficially. *Topkapi,* another commercially successful venture, was a colorful and highly entertaining jewel-robbery caper. But on the whole, Dassin's films of the European period have lacked the direction and conviction of his earlier American films. He has produced and co-scripted most of his own films since 1950.

FEATURE FILMS: In the US—*Nazi Agent, The Affairs of Martha, Reunion in France* 1942; *Young Ideas* 1943; *The Canterville Ghost* 1944; *A Letter for Evie, Two Smart People* 1946; *Brute Force* 1947; *The Naked City* 1948; *Thieves' Highway* 1949. In Europe—*Night and the City* (US/UK) 1950; *Du Rififi chez les Hommes/Rififi* (also co-sc., act.; Fr.) 1955; *Celui qui doit mourir/He Who Must Die* (also co-sc.; Fr./It.) 1957; *La Legge/La Loi/Where the Hot Wind Blows* (also co-sc.; It./Fr.) 1958; *Never on Sunday* (also prod., sc., act.; Gr.) 1960; *Phaedra* (also prod., co-sc., act.; Gr./US) 1962; *Topkapi* (also prod.; US) 1964; *10:30 P.M. Summer* (also co-prod., co-sc.; US/Sp.) 1966; *Survival* 1967 (doc.; also co-prod.; US/Isr.), *Uptight* (also prod., co-sc.; US) 1968; *La Promesse de l'Aube/Promise at Dawn* (also prod., sc., act., impersonating Russian screen actor Ivan Mozhukhin/Mosjoukine; Fr./US) 1970; *The Rehearsal* (semi-doc. about massacre of students by Greek junta) 1974; *A Dream of Passion* (also prod., sc.) 1978; *Circle of Two* (Can.) 1980.

Dasté, Jean. Actor. Born on Aug. 18, 1904, in Paris. Primarily a stage actor, he made few but distinguished film appearances. He played the leads in Jean VIGO's *Zéro de Conduite/Zero for Conduct* (1933) and *L'Atalante* (1934) and had important supporting roles in several Jean RENOIR productions. In 1947 he founded the Comédie de St.-Etienne stage company and became its director. His wife, Marie-Héléne Dasté (b. Dec. 2, 1902, Lyngly, Denmark), is also a stage and film actress.

FILMS INCLUDE: *Boudu sauvé des Eaux/Boudu Saved from Drowning* 1932; *Zéro de Conduite/Zero for Conduct* 1933; *L'Atalante* 1934; *Le Crime de Monsieur Lange/The Crime of Monsieur Lange* 1936; *La Grande Illusion/Grand Illusion* 1937; *Remorques/Stormy Waters* 1941; *Adieu Léonard* 1943; *Muriel* 1963; *La Guerre est finie/The War Is Over* 1966; *Z* 1969; *L'Enfant sauvage/The Wild Child* 1970; *Les Jours gris* 1974; *Le Petit Marcel* 1976; *L'Homme qui aimait les Femmes/The Man Who Loved Women* 1977; *La Chambre Verte/The Green Room, Molière* 1978; *Mon Oncle d'Amérique* 1980; *L'Amour á Mort* 1984; *La Moine et la Sorcière/Sorceress* 1987.

Dauphin, Claude. Actor. *b.* Claude Legrand, Aug. 19, 1903, Corbeil, France, into a family of music-hall performers. *d.* 1978. Starting as a set designer, he soon switched to stage acting and made his screen debut in 1930. Charming and elegant, he played leads and supporting roles in many French, British, American, and international films, typically in sophisticated, cosmopolitan roles.

FILMS INCLUDE: *Langrevin Père et Fils* 1930; *La Fortune* 1931; *Faubourg Montmartre* 1932; *L'Abbé Constantin, La Fille du Régiment* 1933; *Le Voyage impévu/The Slipper Episode, Dédé* 1934; *Paris-New York, Conflit/The Affair Lafont, Entrée des Artistes/The Curtain Rises* 1938; *Cavalcade d'Amour, Menaces* 1939; *Les Deux Timides* 1941; *La Belle Aventure/Twilight* 1945; *English Without Tears/Her Man Bilbey* (UK) 1946; *Jean de la Lune* 1948; *Deported* (US/It.) 1950; *Casque d'Or* 1951; *Le Plaisir, April in Paris* (US) 1952; *Little Boy Lost* (US) 1953; *Phantom of the Rue Morgue* (US), *Innocent in Paris* (UK) 1954; *Les Mauvaises Rencontres* 1955; *The Quiet American* (US) 1958; *The Full Treatment/Stop Me Before I Kill* (UK) 1961; *La Diable et les Dix Commandements/The Devil and the Ten Commandments, Tiara Tahiti* (UK) 1961; *Symphonie pour un Massacre/Symphony for a Massacre* 1963; *La Bonne Soupe, Der Besuch/The Visit* (Ger./US/It./Fr.) 1964; *Compartiment Tueurs/The Sleeping Car Murder, Lady L* (US/Fr./It.) 1965; *Paris brûle-t-il?/Is Paris Burning?* (Fr./US), *Grand Prix* (US) 1966; *Two for the Road* (US/UK) 1967; *Barbarella* 1968; *Hard Contract* (US), *The Madwoman of Chaillot* (UK) 1969; *L'Important c'est d'aimer/That Most Important Thing: Love* 1974; *La Course a l'Echalote/The Wild Goose Chase* 1975; *Le Locataire/The Tenant* 1976; *La Vie devant soi/Madame Rosa, Le Point de Mire* 1977; *Le Pion* 1978.

Davenport, Dorothy. Actress, producer, director, screenwriter. *b.* in 1895, Boston. *d.* 1977. The daughter of character actor Harry DAVENPORT and silent screen comedienne Alice Davenport (b. 1864, N.Y.C.; deceased) who appeared in several early Chaplin shorts, she starred in numerous silent films, often opposite her husband, Wallace REID. After Reid's tragic death, she appeared in the film *Human Wreckage,* which warned against the danger of narcotics. She then turned producer, director, and screenwriter, using the name Dorothy Reid.

FILMS INCLUDE: As actress—*Her Indian Hero* 1909; *The Best Man Wins* 1911; *Almost a Suicide, His Only Son* 1912; *Our Lady of the Pearls, The Lightning Bolt, The Cracksman's Reformation, A Hopi Legend, The Fires of Fate, Retribution* 1913; *The Intruder, The Countess Betty's Mine, The Accomplished Mrs. Thompson, The Way of a Woman, The Voice of the Viola, A Gypsy Romance, The Siren* 1914; *Fruit of Evil, The Unknown, The Adventurer, The Explorer* 1915; *The Way of the World, The Unattainable, Black Friday* 1916; *The Girl and the Crisis, Treason, The Squaw Man's Son* 1917; *The Fighting Chance* 1920; *Every Woman's Problem* 1921; *The Test, The Masked Avenger* 1922; *Human Wreckage* 1923; *The Satin Woman* 1927; *Hellship Bronson* 1928; *Man Hunt* 1933. As producer—*Broken Laws* (also act.) 1924; *The Red Kimono* (also act.), *The Earth Woman* 1926; *The Dude Wrangler* (co-prod.) 1930; *Honeymoon Limited, Women Must Dress* (also co-sc.) 1935; *Paradise Isle* 1937; *Rose of the Rio Grande* 1938; *Terror in the City* 1966. As director—*Linda* (also exec. prod.) 1929; *Sucker Money* 1933; *Road to Ruin* (also co-sc.), *Woman Condemned* (also co-sc.) 1934. As screenwriter—*Prison Break* 1938; *The Haunted House* 1940; *Redhead* 1941; *Curley* 1947; *Who Killed Doc Robbin?* 1948; *Impact* 1949; *Rhubarb* 1951; *Footsteps in the Fog* 1955.

Davenport, Harry. Actor. *b.* Jan. 19, 1866, New York City, *d.* 1949. Descended from a long line of actors, he began his stage career at five. Entering films as an actor in 1914, he turned to directing in the following year with a long series of comedy shorts featuring himself and Rose Tapley as the characters Mr. and Mrs. Jarr. While continuing to act in films of others, he also directed ten feature films from 1915 to 1917, but his main screen career came after the advent of sound, when he played scores of character roles in Hollywood films, usually as distinguished and kindly elderly gentlemen. His first wife was actress Alice Davenport; his second, actress Phyllis Rankin. He was the father of actresses Ann, Kate, and Dorothy DAVENPORT, and actor Arthur Rankin.

FILMS INCLUDE: As director—*The Jarr Family Discovers Harlem* (also act.), *Mr. Jarr and the Lay Reformer* (also act.), *Mr. Jarr and the Dachshund* (also act.), *Mrs. Jarr and the Beauty Treatment* (also act.), *The Island of Regeneration, The Making Over of Geoffrey Manning* 1915; *For a Woman's Fair Name, The Supreme Temptation* 1916; *A Woman Alone, Tillie Wakes Up, The Millionaire's Double, The False Friend, A Son of the Hills, A Man's Law* 1917. As actor—*Fogg's Millions* 1914; *C.O.D., Father and the Boys* 1915; *The Wheel of the Law* 1916; *Sowers and Reapers* 1917; *Dawn* 1919; *Her Unborn Child* 1929; *My Sin* 1931; *The Scoundrel* 1935; *Three Men on a Horse, The Case of the Black Cat* 1936; *They Won't Forget, The Life of Emile Zola, Wells Fargo* 1937; *You Can't Take It with You, The Sisters* 1938; *The Story of Alexander Graham Bell, Juarez, Gone With the Wind, The Hunchback of Notre Dame* 1939; *Dr. Ehrlich's Magic Bullet, All This and Heaven Too, Foreign Correspondent* 1940; *I Wanted Wings, That Uncertain Feeling* 1941; *Kings Row, Son of Fury, Larceny Inc., Tales of Manhattan* 1942; *The Ox-Bow Incident, Jack London* 1943; *Kismet, The Impatient Years, Meet Me in St. Louis, Music for Millions* 1944; *The Thin Man Goes Home, The Enchanted Forest* 1945; *Adventure, Courage of Lassie, Claudia and David* 1946; *The Farmer's Daughter, The Bachelor and the Bobby-Soxer* 1947; *Three Daring Daughters, That Lady in Ermine* 1948; *Down to the Sea in Ships, Little Women, That Forsyte Woman* 1949; *Riding High* 1950.

Davenport, Nigel. Actor. Born on May 23, 1928, in Shelford Cambridge, England. *ed.* Cheltenham Coll.; Trinity Coll., Oxford. Character lead and supporting player of the British stage, TV, and films. On the stage from the early 50s, he made his film debut in 1959 and has since played pivotal roles in numerous productions, typically in tough characterizations.

FILMS INCLUDE: *Look Back in Anger* 1959; *Peeping Tom* 1960; *In the Cool of the Day* (US) 1963; *The Third Secret* 1964; *A High Wind in Jamaica* (UK/US), *Sands of the Kalahari, Life at the Top* 1965; *Where the Spies Are, A Man for All Seasons* (as the Duke of Norfolk) 1966; *Sebastian, The Strange Affair, Play Dirty* 1968; *Sinful Davey, The Royal Hunt of the Sun* (as explorer Hernando De Soto; UK/US), *The Virgin Soldiers* 1969; *The Mind of Mr. Soames, No Blade of Grass* 1970; *The Last Valley, Villain, Mary Queen of Scots* (UK/US), *Living Free* 1971; *Charley-One-Eye* 1973; *Phase IV* (US) 1974; *Stand Up Virgin Soldiers, The Island of Dr. Moreau* (US) 1977; *An Eye for an Eye* 1978; *Zulu Dawn* 1979; *Nighthawks* (US), *Chariots of Fire* 1981; *Greystoke: The Legend of Tarzan Lord of the Apes* 1984; *Caravaggio* 1986; *Without a Clue, Upper Crust* 1988.

Daves, Delmer. Director, screenwriter, producer. *b.* July 24, 1904, San Francisco. *d.* 1977. *ed.* Stanford U. (law). He broke into films as a prop boy on James Cruze's *The Covered Wagon* (1923) while still in college, and later served as technical adviser on productions involving college backgrounds. Next he appeared in several films as an actor, including *The Duke Steps Out* (1929) and *The Bishop Murder Case* (1930) and began collaborating on original stories and screenplays, among them *Shipmates* (1931), *Dames* (1934), *Flirtation Walk* (1935), *The Petrified Forest* (1936), *Professor Beware* (1938), *Love Affair* (1939), and *You Were Never Lovelier* (1942). As a director since 1943, for Warner Brothers and later Fox and other studios, he continued to write many of his own screenplays and still later also doubled as producer on some of his films through his own company, Diamond-D Productions. Daves was a meticulous craftsman and a showy stylist with a penchant for complicated crane shots. Although variable in thematic quality, his films were always interesting to watch and were often imbued with humanity and sympathetic understanding for characters in conflict with their environment. Especially effective were his Westerns, some of which show the influence of the period of his youth spent living among Hopi and Navajo Indians. He was married (from 1938) to actress Mary Lou Lander.

FILMS (as director): *Destination Tokyo* (also co-sc.), *The Very Thought of You* (also co-sc.), *Hollywood Canteen* (also sc.) 1944; *Pride of the Marines* (also co-sc.) 1945; *The Red House* (also sc.), *Dark Passage* (also sc.) 1947; *To the Victor* 1948; *A Kiss in the Dark, Task Force* (also sc.) 1949; *Broken Arrow* 1950; *Bird of Paradise* (also prod., sc.) 1951; *Return of the Texan* 1952; *Treasure of the Golden Condor* (also sc.), *Never Let Me Go* 1953; *Demetrius and the Gladiators, Drum Beat* (also sc.) 1954; *Jubal* (also co-sc.), *The Last Wagon* (also co-sc.) 1956; *3:10 to Yuma* 1957; *Cowboy, Kings Go Forth, The Badlanders* 1958; *The Hanging Tree, A Summer Place* (also prod., sc.) 1959; *Parrish* (also prod., sc.), *Susan Slade* (also prod., sc.) 1961; *Rome Adventure* (also prod., sc.) 1962; *Spencer's Mountain* (also prod., sc.) 1963; *Youngblood Hawke* (also prod., sc.) 1964; *The Battle of the Villa Fiorita* (also prod., sc.) 1965.

Davi, Robert. Actor. Born 1953. *ed.* Hofstra University; Actors Studio. Dark-haired supporting player often with an intimidating screen presence. He spent his early years studying drama, moving into television, primarily in movies and miniseries since the early 80s. Over the years he has amassed a long line of feature film appearances, typically as the heavy, villainous tough guy with the occasional comedic turn.

FILMS: *Rage* 1980; *City Heart* 1984; *The Goonies* 1985; *Raw Deal* 1986; *Wild Thing* 1987; *Action Jackson, Die Hard, Traxx* 1988; *Licence to Kill* 1989; *Deceptions, Maniac Cop II, Peacemaker, Predator 2* 1990; *Legal Tender, The Taking of Beverly Hills* 1991; *Center of the Web, Christopher Columbus: The Discovery, Wild Orchid 2: Two Shades of Blue* 1992; *Son of the Pink Panther* 1993; *Cops and Robbersons* 1994; *Showgirls* 1995.

Davidovich, Lolita. Actress. Born Lolita David. Arresting lead best known for title role as Baltimore stripper and Huey Long paramour Blaze Starr in *Blaze* (1989).

FILMS INCLUDE: *The Big Town, Adventures in Babysitting* 1987; *Blaze* 1989; *The Object of Beauty, The Inner Circle* 1991; *Leap of Faith* 1992; *Cobb, Intersection* 1994; *Touch* 1996; *Jungle 2 Jungle* 1997.

Davies, John Howard. Actor, TV director. Born in 1939, in London. The son of screenwriter Jack Davies (b. 1913, London), he starred as a child in several distinguished British films. Later became a TV director for the BBC, helming many small-screen productions, including the popular 'Monty Python's Flying Circus' comedy series.

FILMS: *Oliver Twist* (title role) 1948; *The Rocking Horse Winner* 1949; *Tom Brown's School Days* (title role), *The Magic Box* 1951.

Davies, Marion. Actress. *b.* Marion Cecilia Douras, Jan. 3, 1897, Brooklyn, N.Y. *d.* 1961. Convent-educated, she made her stage debut in a Broadway chorus line at 16. She made several other stage appearances, modeled, was featured in the 'Ziegfeld Follies' of 1916 and made her screen debut the following year, in *Runaway Romany.* Around that time she met newspaper magnate William Randolph Hearst, who took an immediate personal interest in her career, vowing to make her Hollywood's greatest star. He formed a company, Cosmopolitan Pictures, for the sole purpose of producing her films, and mobilized the immense resources of the Hearst press to publicize her film appearances and praise them to the sky. From 1919 to 1923 the Cosmopolitan films were released by Paramount. Despite a good deal of publicity, they all lost money, largely because Hearst demanded the most expensive production values for his protégée. He is said to have lost as much as $7 million dollars on the Cosmopolitan film ventures over the years, yet he insisted that Davies keep playing fragile, innocent, virginal heroines. The Hearst patronage might have made her one of the most famous of the Hollywood stars, but it also made her one of the most unsuccessful at the box office.

In 1924, Cosmopolitan and Davies moved over to the Goldwyn Company, and when Goldwyn merged with Metro shortly after to form MGM, Cosmopolitan was part of the package. Louis B. Mayer, MGM's production chief, was quick to realize the potential value of associating with Hearst, both in terms of free publicity and social prestige. Davies lavishly entertained society and royalty in her studio bungalow and in the several homes she shared with Hearst, including a Beverly Hills mansion, a palatial 110-room, 55-bath Santa Monica beach house, and their famous San Simeon castle-by-the-sea. The Hearst-Davies affair, caricaturized by Orson Welles in the controversial *Citizen Kane* (1941), was sincere and lasting. They would have married had Mrs. Hearst consented to a divorce. When the Hearst empire suffered a financial setback in the mid-30s, it was Miss Davies (who had by now accumulated a personal fortune) who saved the day by chipping in a million-dollar personal loan. Only after Hearst's death, in 1951, did she finally marry for the first time (to one Horace G. Brown).

Miss Davies's career had begun slipping seriously with the advent of sound. Because she tended to stutter, she was seen mostly in brief scenes and her roles required fewer and fewer dialogue lines. In 1934 Hearst broke off with MGM after several choice roles he had intended for his protégée went instead to Irving Thalberg's wife, Norma Shearer. The 1937 financial troubles of the Hearst empire also marked the end of the film career of Marion Davies. She retired, renowned and wealthy, and spent the rest of her years as a successful business executive.

FILMS: *Runaway Romany* 1917; *Beatrice Fairfax* (serial), *Cecilia of the Pink Roses, The Burden of Proof* 1918; *The Belle of New York, Getting Mary Married, The Dark Star, The Cinema Murder* 1919; *April Folly, The Restless Sex* 1920; *Buried Treasure, Enchantment* 1921; *The Bride's Play, Beauty's Worth, The Young Diana, When Knighthood Was in Flower* (as Mary Tudor) 1922; *Adam and Eva, Little Old New York* 1923; *Yolanda, Janice Meredith* 1924; *Zander the Great, Lights of Old Broadway* 1925; *Beverley of Graustark* 1926; *The Red Mill, Tillie the Toiler, Quality Street, The Fair Co-Ed* 1927; *The Patsy, The Cardboard Lover, Show People* 1928; *Marianne, The Hollywood Revue of 1929* 1929; *Not So Dumb, The Florodora Girl* 1930; *The Bachelor Father, It's a Wise Child, Five and Ten* 1931; *Polly of the Circus, Blondie of the Follies* 1932; *Peg o' My Heart, Going Hollywood* 1933; *Operator 13* 1934; *Page Miss Glory* 1935; *Hearts Divided, Cain and Mabel* 1936; *Ever Since Eve* 1937.

Davies, Terence. British director, writer. Known for his unsparing, yet feeling portraits of postwar working class Britain, often drawn from his personal experiences. His 1988 *Distant Voices, Still Lives* was widely hailed at the Cannes and other film festivals.

FILMS INCLUDE: *Distant Voices Still Lives* (also sc.) 1988; *The Long Day Closes* (also sc.) 1993; *The Neon Bible* 1995.

Davies, Valentine. Screenwriter. Born on Aug. 25, 1905, in New York City. A playwright and novelist, he began writing for the screen in 1941. Won the 1947 Academy Award for his original story *Miracle on 34th Street.* Wrote and also directed the film *The Benny Goodman Story* (1955).

FILMS INCLUDE: *Syncopation* (story only) 1942; *Three Little Girls in Blue* 1946; *Miracle on 34th Street* (story only) 1947; *You Were Meant for Me, Chicken Every Sunday* 1948; *It Happens Every Spring* 1949; *On the Riviera* 1951; *The Glenn Miller Story* 1954; *The Benny Goodman Story* (also dir.), *The Bridges at Toko-Ri, Strategic Air Command* 1955; *Bachelor in Paradise* 1961.

Davis, Andrew. Director, producer, cinematographer, screenwriter. Born in Chicago. Son of stage actor Nate Davis, he studied journalism at the University of Illinois and worked for a time as a PBS reporter. In 1969, he served on *Medium Cool* as an assistant to cinematographer Haskell Wexler (who was also the film's director, writer, and co-producer). Until the 80s, Davis worked as a cinematographer, but he broke into directing in 1978 with the critically praised independent feature *Stony Island.* He then became known as a successful action director able to inject the genre with intelligence, humor, and believability. He is also known for his use of realistic urban settings, often in his native Chicago. With *Above the Law* (1988) and *Under Siege* (1992), he respectively launched and broadened the career of actor Steven Seagal. With *The Fugitive* (1993), Davis became one of Hollywood's most sought-after directors.

FILMS INCLUDE: *Cool Breeze* (phot.), *Private Parts* (phot.), *Hit Man* (phot.) 1972; *The Slams* (phot.) 1973; *Lepke* (phot.), *The Terror of Dr. Chancey* (phot.) 1975; *Stony Island* (dir., prod., sc.) 1978; *Over the Edge* (phot.) 1979; *The Final Terror* (dir.) 1981; *Angel* (phot.) 1983; *Code of Silence* (dir.) 1985; *Above the Law* (prod., dir., sc., story, co-phot.) 1988; *The Package* (prod., dir.) 1989; *Schweitzer* (act.) 1990; *Under Siege* (dir.) 1992; *The Fugitive* (dir.) 1993; *Steal Big Steal Little* 1995; *Chain Reaction* 1996.

Davis, Bette. Actress. *b.* Ruth Elizabeth Davis, Apr. 5, 1908, Lowell, Mass. *d.* 1989. The daughter of a patent attorney and a portrait photographer who divorced when she was seven, she decided on an acting career while still a freshman at high school. However, the ordeals of her early career offered little encouragement to the young woman who was to become recognized as the "first lady of the American screen." After some light experience in school productions and in semiprofessional stock, she was rejected as a student by Eva Le Gallienne and enrolled instead at John Murray Anderson's drama school. On her very first professional engagement with a stock company in Rochester, N.Y., she was fired by director George Cukor. In 1928 she appeared with the off-Broadway Provincetown Players and the following year made her Broadway debut in a domestic comedy, 'Broken Dishes.' Early in 1930 she failed a screen test at Goldwyn, but later in the year she was successfully tested and signed by Universal. When the studio's boss, Carl Laemmle, first saw her he commented that she had "as much sex appeal as Slim Summerville." But the determined Miss Davis clung to her new career.

After appearing in a number of indifferent roles in routine productions, she attracted favorable attention as George Arliss's leading lady in *The Man Who Played God* (1932). This was the first of Miss Davis's long succession of films under a long-term contract with Warner Brothers. Her efforts at Warners varied in quality, but gradually, through her hard work and perseverance, her forceful personality began glowing through her roles. She had to fight for her right to star as Mildred, the nasty, selfish waitress in John Cromwell's *Of Human Bondage* (1934) on a loan-out to RKO. She finally got the role and responded with a sterling performance, the first of many electrifying appearances that were to establish her over the years as the American screen's most accomplished actress.

Still Warners continued offering her mediocre vehicles but she capably survived the worst of them, and critics constantly praised her acting while panning her films. In 1935 she won her first Oscar for *Dangerous,* an inconsequential tearjerker. The following year she had a meaty role in *The Petrified Forest,* but her subsequent two vehicles were again of poor script quality. The strong-willed Miss Davis, who had practically clawed her way to the top, became rebellious. She refused another unsuitable role and was suspended without pay. She accepted an offer from England to appear in a couple of European productions, but Warners, to whom she was bound by contract until 1942, issued an injunction. She promptly sued the company but lost in the ensuing court battle. To her surprise, Warners not only paid her legal expenses but began treating her with greater respect and offered her roles to suit her temperament and talent.

During the following decade Miss Davis reached a new artistic maturity. She began to strive for limits beyond the mere effect of her fiery personality by gradually developing an arsenal of personal screen mannerisms and perfecting her acting techniques. Her appeal was strongest to feminine audiences. They loved her best when she played women at their worst—bitchy, ambitious characters who proudly pursued their selfish goals. They also identified with her when she was good, suffering the heartthrobs and disappointments of love. Male audiences were less responsive.

In 1938, Miss Davis won her second Academy Award, for *Jezebel*. Her stature grew with every film she made in the early 40s; but by the end of the decade her career seemed headed for oblivion. The indomitable Miss Davis then countered with one of her greatest performances, in *All About Eve* (1950), for which she was named best actress by the New York Film Critics. Late in the 50s her career again faltered. But she emerged triumphant in the early 60s, this time with a couple of made-to-measure horror films, *What Ever Happened to Baby Jane?* and *Hush*

Hush. . . Sweet Charlotte. She received another Academy Award nomination for the former film, the final of ten career Oscar nominations, more than any other actress.

Miss Davis told of her uphill struggle, conquests and disappointments, as well as her four marriages and divorces, in a frank, intelligent autobiography, *The Lonely Life* (1962). Her first husband (1932–38) was bandleader Harmon Oscar "Ham" Nelson. Her second (1941–43) was businessman Arthur Farnsworth, who left her a widow; her third (1945–45) artist William Grant Sherry; and fourth, actor Gary MERRILL (1950–60). Miss Davis's daughter by her third marriage, Barbara Davis (Sherry) Hyman, stunned many of the star's admirers when in 1985, in the book *My Mother's Keeper,* she portrayed her mother as a domineering, abusive, grotesque alcoholic. Miss Davis refuted the allegations in 1987, in an updated autobiography, *This 'N That.*

Miss Davis continued her reign as one of the screen's grandest, most durable stars. In 1977 she became the fifth recipient of the American Film Institute's Life Achievement Award, the first woman to be so honored. She was also awarded a special César by the French film industry and in 1987 was honored by the Film Society of Lincoln Center at its annual tribute for cinema's greats. Although she had undergone a mastectomy in 1983 and suffered several strokes during her hospitalization, she resumed performing and making public appearances with characteristic courage, knowing her cancer was terminal. She died at 81 in France, en route back from yet another life achievement tribute, at the San Sebastian Film Festival. Not long before her death she said, "You know what they'll write on my tombstone? 'She did it the hard way.'"

FILMS: *Bad Sister, Seed, Waterloo Bridge* 1931; *Way Back Home, The Menace, Hell's House, The Man Who Played God, So Big, The Rich Are Always with Us, The Dark Horse, The Cabin in the Cotton, Three on a Match* 1932; *20,000 Years in Sing Sing, Parachute Jumper, The Working Man, Ex-Lady, Bureau of Missing Persons* 1933; *Fashions of 1934, The Big Shakedown, Jimmy the Gent, Fog Over Frisco, Of Human Bondage, Housewife* 1934; *Bordertown, The Girl from Tenth Avenue, Front Page Woman, Special Agent, Dangerous* 1935; *The Petrified Forest, The Golden Arrow, Satan Met a Lady* 1936; *Marked Woman, Kid Galahad, That Certain Woman, It's Love I'm After* 1937; *Jezebel, The Sisters* 1938; *Dark Victory, Juarez* (as Empress Carlota von Habsburg), *The Old Maid, The Private Lives of Elizabeth and Essex* (as Queen Elizabeth I) 1939; *All This and Heaven Too, The Letter* 1940; *The Great Lie, The Bride Came C.O.D., The Little Foxes, The Man Who Came to Dinner* 1941; *In This Our Life, Now Voyager* 1942; *Watch on the Rhine, Thank Your Lucky Stars, Old Acquaintance* 1943; *Mr. Skeffington, Hollywood Canteen* 1944; *The Corn Is Green* 1945; *A Stolen Life, Deception* 1946; *Winter Meeting, June Bride* 1948; *Beyond the Forest* 1949; *All About Eve* 1950; *Another Man's Poison* (UK), *Payment on Demand* 1951; *Phone Call from a Stranger, The Star* 1952; *The Virgin Queen* (as Queen Elizabeth I) 1955; *Storm Center, The Catered Affair* 1956; *John Paul Jones* (cameo, as Catherine the Great), *The Scapegoat* (UK) 1959; *A Pocketful of Miracles* 1961; *What Ever Happened to Baby Jane?* 1962; *La Noia/The Empty Canvas* (It.), *Dead Ringer, Where Love Has Gone* 1964; *Hush Hush. . . Sweet Charlotte, The Nanny* (UK) 1965; *The Anniversary* (UK) 1967; *Connecting Rooms* (UK) 1970; *Bunny O'Hare* 1971; *Madame Sin* (TV film, shown in theaters abroad), *Lo Scopone scientifico/The Scientific Cardplayer* 1972; *Burnt Offerings* 1976; *Return from Witch Mountain, Death on the Nile* 1978; *The Watcher in the Woods* (UK) 1980; *The Whales of August* 1987; *Wicked Stepmother* 1989.

Davis, Brad. Actor. *b.* Nov. 6, 1949, Tallahassee, Fla. *d.* 1992. The winner of a music talent contest at 17, he moved to Atlanta, where he began performing on the stage. Off-Broadway and TV roles followed training at the American Academy of Dramatic Arts. He launched his screen career in 1978 with an impressive debut as the hero of *Midnight Express.* He died just 14 years later of AIDS.

FILMS: *Midnight Express* 1978; *A Small Circle of Friends* 1980; *Chariots of Fire* 1981; *Querelle* (Ger./Fr.) 1982; *Heart, Cold Steel* 1987; *Rosalie Goes Shopping* 1990; *Hangfire* 1991.

Davis, Carl. Composer. Born on Oct. 28, 1936, in Brooklyn, N.Y. *ed.* Queens Coll.; Bard Coll.; New England Coll. of Music. He was a pianist with the Robert Shaw Chorale and composer for stage revues before moving to London in 1961. He wrote scores for British stage productions and many films, winning the British Academy Award for the music of *The French Lieutenant's Woman.* Davis, who is also a conductor with the London Philharmonic, is renowned for his scores for revived silent classics like *Napoléon, The Crowd, Greed,* and *Intolerance.*

FILMS INCLUDE: *The Bofors Gun* 1968; *Up Pompeii* 1971; *Rentadick* 1972; *The National Health* 1973; *Man Friday* 1975; *The French Lieutenant's Woman* 1981; *Champions* 1983; *King David* 1985; *The Girl in a Swing* 1988; *Scandal, The Rainbow* 1989; *Frankenstein Unbound* 1990; *The Trial, Widow's Peak* 1994.

Davis, Desmond. Director. Born in 1928, in London. He broke into British films at 16 as a clapper boy and following WW II service with the Army Film Unit returned as a cameraman. He collaborated on occasional screenplays and worked as camera operator on such films as *A Taste of Honey* (1961), *The Loneliness of the Long Distance Runner* (1962), and *Tom Jones* (1963). He directed shorts from 1950, but it wasn't until 1963 that he made his debut as a feature director. He subsequently piloted a handful of stylish films that revealed an empathy for women's plight in modern society. In 1970 he formed a production company with the star of two of these, Rita Tushingham, but for the next decade occupied himself with TV work. He returned to the big screen in 1981 with a successful, though uncharacteristic mythological epic, *Clash of the Titans.*

FILMS: *Girl with Green Eyes, The Uncle* (also co-sc.) 1964; *I Was Happy Here/Time Lost and Time Remembered* (also co-sc.) 1965; *Smashing Time* 1967; *A Nice Girl Like Me* (also co-sc.) 1969; *Clash of the Titans* 1981; *The Sign of Four* (orig. for TV) 1983; *Ordeal by Innocence* 1984.

Davis, Geena. Actress. Born Virginia Davis, Jan. 21, 1957, in Wareham, Mass. *ed.* Boston U. Genial, unpretentious leading lady of the American screen. The daughter of an engineer and a teacher's aide, she attended Boston schools and began acting with a repertory company in New Hampshire. In 1979 she moved to New York, where she worked as a salesgirl in a dress shop and modeled briefly before landing a supporting role in the film *Tootsie* (1982). She went on to play leads in a number of scary movies and starred in two light TV series ('Buffalo Bill', 'Sara'), then responded to the challenge of a more difficult role, winning the Academy Award as best supporting actress for *The Accidental Tourist* (1988). She achieved household name recognition with her performance as a fugitive housewife who excels at small-time robbery in the dark fantasy *Thelma and Louise* (1991). Her 1987 marriage to actor Jeff GOLDBLUM, her co-star in *The Fly* and other films, ended in 1990. She was married to director Renny Harlin, with whom she combined forces in 1995 to star in the box-office bomb *Cutthroat Island,* a big-budget pirate film fraught with troubles from the beginning. The two re-teamed the next year for the unconventional action-thriller *The Long Kiss Goodnight*, this time to positive response from audiences as well as critics.

FILMS: *Tootsie* 1982; *Fletch, Transylvannia 6-5000* 1985; *The Fly* 1986; *Beetlejuice, The Accidental Tourist* 1988; *Earth Girls Are Easy* 1989; *Quick Change* 1990; *Thelma and Louise* 1991; *A League of Their Own, Hero* 1992; *Angie, Speechless* 1994; *Cutthroat Island* 1995; *The Long Kiss Goodnight* 1996.

Davis, George W. Art director. Born on Apr. 17, 1914, in Kokomo, Ind. *ed.* USC. He designed the sets for numerous 20th Century-Fox productions of the 40s and 50s. In 1959 he moved over to MGM, replacing the retired Cedric Gibbons as supervising art director. He was nominated for Academy Awards 13 times, winning the Oscar twice, for *The Robe* (1953) and *The Diary of Anne Frank* (1959).

FILMS INCLUDE: *The Ghost and Mrs. Muir* 1947; *House of Strangers* 1949; *All About Eve* 1950; *David and Bathsheba* 1951; *The Robe* 1953; *The Egyptian* 1954; *Love Is a Many-Splendored Thing, The Seven-Year Itch* 1955; *Funny Face* 1957; *The Diary of Anne Frank* 1959; *The Time Machine, Cimarron, Butterfield 8, Home from the Hill* 1960; *Two Weeks in Another Town, Period of Adjustment, Mutiny on the Bounty, Ride the High Country, Sweet Bird of Youth, The Wonderful World of the Brothers Grimm, How the West Was Won* 1962; *Twilight of Honor* 1963; *The Americanization of Emily, The Unsinkable Molly Brown* 1964; *A Patch of Blue* 1965; *Mr. Buddwing* 1965; *Point Blank* 1967; *The Shoes of the Fisherman* 1968; *The Gypsy Moths* 1969; *Brewster McCloud* 1970; *Wild Rovers* 1971.

Davis, Jim. Actor. *b.* Marlin Davis, Aug. 26, 1915, Edgerton, Mo. *d.* 1981. *ed.* William Jewell Coll. (Liberty, Mo.). Heavyset leading man and supporting player of Hollywood films. A former rigger with a traveling tent circus, he arrived in Los Angeles as an oil salesman and somehow managed to get into movies. Had his best opportunity as the co-star of Bette Davis in *Winter Meeting* (1948) but later appeared mostly in routine low-budget productions, often of the action variety. Making a comeback on TV, he enjoyed his greatest success in his final three years, playing Jock, the silver-haired patriarch of the Ewing clan, in the popular series 'Dallas.' Early in his career he was also billed as James Davis, which led to a confusion of his credits with those of a black actor of the same name.

FILMS INCLUDE: *White Cargo* 1942; *What Next Corporal Hargrove?* 1945; *Gallant Bess* 1946; *The Beginning or the End, The Romance of Rosy Ridge* 1947; *Winter Meeting* 1948; *Hellfire, Brimstone* 1949; *Hi-Jacked, California Passage* 1950; *Cavalry Scout* 1951; *The Big Sky* 1952; *Jubilee Trail* 1954; *Timberjack* 1955; *The Bottom of the Bottle, The Maverick Queen* 1956; *The Badge of Marshal Brennan, Apache Warrior, Raiders of Old California, The Last Stage-coach West* 1957; *Wolf Dog* 1958; *Alias Jesse James* 1959; *Noose for a Gunman* 1960; *Frontier Uprising, The Gambler Wore a Gun* 1961; *Iron Angel* 1964; *Zebra in the Kitchen* 1965; *Fort Utah, El Dorado* 1967; *The Road Hustlers* 1968; *Five Bloody Graves* 1969; *Monte Walsh, Rio Lobo* 1970; *Big Jake* 1971; *The Honkers, Bad Company* 1972; *Dracula vs. Frankenstein* 1973; *The Parallax View* 1974; *The Choirboys* 1977; *Comes a Horseman* 1978; *The Day Time Ended* 1980.

Davis, Judy. Actress. Born in 1956, in Perth, Australia. Australia's best known leading lady. She dropped out of convent school in her teens to become a rock band vocalist. Later she attended the West Australia Institute of Technology and trained for the stage at Sydney's National Institute of Dramatic Arts. Making her screen debut in 1977, she drew wide acclaim two years later for her mature portrayal of the defiant heroine of Gillian Armstrong's *My Brilliant Career.* That performance gained her a Sammy at the Australian Film Awards and the best actress award by the British Film Academy. Her subsequent awards included the 1983 Moscow Festival best actress prize for *Winter of Our Dreams* (1981) and an Oscar nomination for *A Passage to India* (1984). She impersonated Israel's Premier Golda Meir as a young woman (Ingrid Bergman played Meir in her later years) in the TV movie *A Woman Called Golda.* In 1992 she was nominated for an Academy Award for her performance as a separated wife in *Husbands and Wives.* She married actor Colin Friels, her co-star in *Kangaroo* (1986).

FILMS: *High Rolling* 1977; *My Brilliant Career* 1979; *Hoodwink, Winter of Our Dreams, Heatwave* 1981; *Who Dares Wins/The Final Option* (UK) 1982; *A Passage to India* (UK) 1984; *Kangaroo* 1986; *High Tide* 1987; *Georgia* 1989; *Impromptu* 1990; *Barton Fink, Naked Lunch* 1991; *Where Angels Fear to Tread, Husbands and Wives* 1992; *The New Age, The Ref* 1994; *Children of the Revolution* 1996; *Blood and Wine* 1997.

Davis, Joan. Actress. *b.* Madonna Josephine Davis, June 29, 1907, St. Paul, Minn., the daughter of a train dispatcher. *d.* 1961. She began performing on the stage as a child, and after marrying comedian Sy Wills in 1931, she teamed up with him in the vaudeville comedy act of Wills and Davis. Upon settling in Hollywood in 1934, she made her screen debut in comedy shorts and appeared in her first feature film the following year. A gangling, loose-jointed, raucous comedienne who would punch herself in the jaw to produce laughs, she used her knockabout slapstick style in comedy leads and supporting roles in many films through the early 50s. During the 40s she was also highly popular as a radio star, and in 1950 she formed her own production company to produce her own successful TV comedy series, 'I Married Joan.' Her daughter, Beverly Wills (1934–63), also appeared in occasional films.

FILMS INCLUDE: *Millions in the Air* 1935; *The Holy Terror, On the Avenue, Wake Up and Live, Angel's Holiday, Thin Ice, Life Begins in College, Love and Hisses* 1937; *Sally Irene and Mary, Josette, My Lucky Star, Hold That Co-Ed, Just Around the Corner* 1938; *Tail Spin, Daytime Wife* 1939; *Free Blonde and 21* 1940; *Hold That Ghost, Sun Valley Serenade, Two Latins from Manhattan* 1941; *Yokel Boy, Sweetheart of the Fleet* 1942; *Two Senoritas from Chicago, Around the World* 1943; *Beautiful but Broke, Show Business, Kansas City Kitty* 1944; *She Gets Her Man, George White's Scandals* 1945; *She Wrote the Book* 1946; *If You Knew Susie* 1948; *Make Mine Laughs* 1949; *Traveling Saleswoman, Love That Brute* 1950; *The Groom Wore Spurs* 1951; *Harem Girl* 1952.

Davis, Nancy. Actress. Born Anne Frances Robbins, on July 6, 1921, in New York City. *ed.* Girls Latin School, Chicago; Smith Coll. Following in the footsteps of her mother, Edith, a former actress, she began performing on the stage after graduating from college. In 1949, she became an MGM contract player and for the next decade played supporting roles, then leads in films of that studio and others, never attaining star status. In 1952 she became the second wife of fellow actor Ronald REAGAN and in 1958 retired from the screen. She then devoted herself to raising their two children and two stepchildren and to her husband's political career. Despite her frail appearance, she proved herself a bastion of strength during his campaigns and during his terms as Governor of California (1967–74) and President of the United States (1981–89). She was a staunch protector of the President against real and imagined foes and influenced certain policy and personnel decisions, sometimes, as it turned out, with the guidance of an astrologer. She was also the subject of a fierce Kitty Kelley biography and a couple of clearly autobiographical novels written by her daughter, Patti Davis. Autobiography: *Nancy* (1980).

FILMS: *The Doctor and the Girl* 1949; *East Side West Side, Shadow on the Wall* 1950; *Night Into Morning* 1951; *It's a Big Country, Shadow in the Sky, Talk About a Star* 1952; *Donovan's Brain* 1953; *Hellcats of the Navy* 1957; *Crash Landing* 1958.

Davis, Ossie. Actor, director, producer, playwright, screenwriter. Born on Dec. 18, 1917, in Cogdell, Ga. *ed.* Howard U. The son of a railroad engineer, he came to New York after college, hoping for a career as a writer, but worked as a janitor, stock clerk, and garment center handcart pusher before discovering the theater during his WW II military service. He made his Broadway debut in 1946 and during the 50s played impressive supporting roles in plays and occasional films. In 1961 he triumphed on Broadway as the author and star of 'Purlie Victorious' and two years later repeated his success on the screen with a film adaptation called *Gone Are the Days!* In 1970 he turned out his first film as director, *Cotton Comes to Harlem*, to good notices and excellent box-office returns. Mr. Davis, who with his wife, Ruby DEE, is active in civil rights and humanitarian causes, is head of Third World Cinema, a film production company formed in the early 70s to encourage black and Puerto Rican talent.

FILMS: As actor—*No Way Out* 1950; *Fourteen Hours* 1951; *The Joe Louis Story* 1953; *Gone Are the Days!* (also sc., from own play 'Purlie Victorious'), *The Cardinal* 1963; *Shock Treatment* 1964; *The Hill* 1965; *A Man Called Adam* 1966; *The Scalphunters* 1968; *Sam Whiskey, Slaves* 1969; *Let's Do It Again* 1975; *Hot Stuff, The House of God* 1979; *Harry and Son* 1984; *Avenging Angel* 1985; *School Daze, Do the Right Thing* 1988; *Joe Versus the Volcano* 1990; *Jungle Fever* 1991; *Gladiator* 1992; *Get On the Bus* 1996. As director—*Cotton Comes to Harlem* (also co-sc.) 1970; *Kongi's Harvest* (US/Nigeria) 1971; *Black Girl* 1972; *Gordon's War* 1973; *Countdown at Kusini* (also co-sc., act.; US/Nigeria) 1976.

Davis, Sammi. Actress. Born in 1965, in Kidderminster, Worcestershire, England. Exuberant, blonde young lead of British films. Convent-educated and with no formal training, she began performing with a local drama society, then toured for two years with Birmingham's Big Brum Theatre company, before moving on to London. Following her memorable screen debut in *Mona Lisa* (1986), in the role of a 15-year old junkie prostitute, she has been much in demand by film directors.

FILMS: *Mona Lisa* 1986; *Lionheart, Hope and Glory, A Prayer for the Dying* 1987; *Consuming Passions, The Lair of the White Worm* 1988; *The Rainbow* 1989; *Shadow of China, Horseplayer* 1991; *Four Rooms* 1995.

Davis, Sammy, Jr. Actor, singer, dancer. *b.* Dec. 8, 1925, New York City. *d.* 1990. The son of vaudeville hoofers, he was on the road before his third birthday and joined his uncle Will Mastin's all-black family act of seven males and seven females before he reached four. During the Depression the act was gradually reduced in size until it emerged as the Will Mastin Trio, consisting of Sammy Davis, Jr., his father, and his uncle. Little Sammy soon developed into a highly versatile entertainer who could not only sing and dance but also mimic, tell jokes, and play an assortment of musical instruments. The troupe went through many ups and downs while crisscrossing the country countless times.

Meanwhile, young Davis started making inroads on his own as a recording artist and TV personality. He was at the peak of his form in 1954 when a car accident cost him his left eye and caused other injuries that threatened to end his career. But within months he was back, demonstrating even more of the energy and determination that had characterized his entertainment style from the start. In 1956 he made both his Broadway ('Mr. Wonderful') and Hollywood (*The Benny Goodman Story*) debuts. Other films followed, including several that featured Frank Sinatra's "Rat Pack," of which Davis was a member.

A multitalented man of boundless energy, Davis sustained his reputation as one of America's top entertainers despite attacks from both blacks and whites on such occasions as his marriage (second of three) to Swedish actress May BRITT, his conversion to Judaism, and his sudden switch from Kennedy Democrat to Nixon Republican. In 1985 he underwent reconstructive hip surgery that enabled him to dance again. In 1989, after announcing he finally won a long battle with alcohol and cocaine dependency, Davis celebrated a successful comeback by co-starring in the movie *Tap* and embarking on a world tour with Frank Sinatra and Liza Minnelli. But soon after he was diagnosed as having throat cancer. Eight months later he died, at 64. Autobiographies: *Yes, I Can* (1965), *Why Me?* (1989).

FILMS: *Rufus Jones for President* 1933; *The Benny Goodman Story* 1956; *Anna Lucasta* 1958; *Porgy and Bess* 1959; *Ocean's 11, Pepe* 1960; *Sergeants 3, Convicts 4* 1962; *Die Dreigroschenoper/The Threepenny Opera* (Ger.), *Johnny Cool* 1963; *Robin and the 7 Hoods* 1964; *Nightmare in the Sun* 1965; *A Man Called Adam* 1966; *Salt and Pepper* (UK) 1968; *Sweet Charity* 1969; *One More Time* (also exec. prod.) 1970; *Diamonds Are Forever* (cameo) 1972; *Save the Children* (filmed concert) 1973; *Gone with the West* 1975; *Stop the World—I Want to Get Off* 1978; *The Cannonball Run* 1981; *Heidi's Song* (voice only) 1982; *Cannonball Run II* 1984; *The Perils of P.K.* 1986; *Moon Over Parador* 1988; *Tap* 1989.

Davison, Bruce. Actor. Born in 1946, in Philadelphia. Versatile character lead and supporting player of stage, screen, and television. An art major at Penn State, he got into acting when, on a dare, he auditioned for a school play. After training at NYU's theater program, he made his stage debut with the Lincoln Center Repertory, later playing leading roles in such plays as 'The Elephant Man' and 'The Glass Menagerie.' In films from the late 60s. In 1986 he married actress Lisa Pelikan.

FILMS INCLUDE: *Last Summer* 1969; *The Strawberry Statement* 1970; *Willard* 1971; *Ulzana's Raid* 1972; *Mame* 1974; *Mother Jugs & Speed* 1976; *Short Eyes* 1977; *Brass Target, French Quarter* 1978; *High Risk* 1981; *Crimes of Passion* 1984; *Spies Like Us* 1985; *The Ladies Club* 1986; *Wheels of Terror/The Misfit Brigade* (UK) 1987; *Longtime Companion, Steel and Lace* 1990; *Oscar* 1991; *The Baby Sitters Club* 1995; *The Crucible, Grace of My Heart, Homage, It's My Party* 1996; *Lovelife* 1997.

Daw, Marjorie. Actress. Born in 1902, in Colorado Springs, Colo. Leading lady of Hollywood silents. Trained as an opera singer, she broke into films at 13 as a protégée of Geraldine Farrar and played juveniles in a number of Cecil B. DE MILLE productions. She soon graduated to romantic leads and during 1918–19 was the frequent screen partner and love interest of Douglas Fairbanks, Sr. She went on to star in numerous silent films but retired from the screen with the advent of sound. At one time married to director A. Edward Sutherland.

FILMS INCLUDE: *The Warrens of Virginia, The Unafraid, The Puppet Crown, The Secret Orchard, The Chorus Lady, Out of the Darkness* 1915; *Joan the Woman* 1916; *The Jaguar's Claws, Rebecca of Sunnybrook Farm, Conscience, A Modern Musketeer* 1917; *Mr. Fix-It, He Comes Up Smiling, The Sunset Princess, Arizona* 1918; *The Knickerbocker Buckaroo, His Majesty the American, The Sunset Princess* 1919; *The River's End, Don't Ever Marry, The Great Redeemer, Dinty* 1920; *Bob Hampton of Placer, The Butterfly Girl, Experience, Fifty Candles, Cheated Hearts* 1921; *Penrod, Love Is an Awful Thing, A Fool There Was, The Long Chance, The Pride of*

Palomar 1922; *Wandering Daughters, Rupert of Hentzau, Going Up, The Barefoot Boy, The Dangerous Maid* 1923; *Gambling Wives, Revelation, Greater Than Marriage* 1924; *Fear-Bound, His Master's Voice, East Lynne* 1925; *In Borrowed Plumes, Redheads Preferred* 1926; *Outlaws of the River, Topsy and Eva, Home Made, Spoilers of the West* 1927.

Dawley, J. Searle. American director of early silent films. Died 1950. A former actor, stage producer, and sometime playwright, he joined the Edison company in 1907 as special consultant to Edwin S. PORTER on the handling of actors. He soon began collaborating with Porter on the direction of films, with Porter handling the action and Dawley the acting and dramatic development. One of their earliest collaborative efforts was *Rescued from an Eagle's Nest* (1907), which starred an unknown young actor, D. W. Griffith. Dawley directed some 300 one-reel films for Edison and for Porter's independent company, Rex. When Porter joined Famous Players in 1912, Dawley came along as his executive assistant, creative consultant, and director. He made many shorts and features, often adaptations of literary classics, which starred such players as Mary Pickford, Marguerite Clark, and John Barrymore. Dawley remained a successful director through the early 20s, after which he retired from the screen.

FILMS INCLUDE: *Rescued from an Eagle's Nest* (co-dir. with Edwin S. Porter) 1907; *The Prince and the Pauper* (also sc.), *Hansel and Gretel* (also sc.), *Faust* (also sc.), *Bluebeard* 1909; *Michael Strogoff* (also sc.), *Frankenstein* (also sc.), *A Christmas Carol* 1910; *Aida* (co-dir. with Oscar Apfel), *The Doctor, Van Bibber's Experiment, The Battle of Bunker Hill, Under the Tropical Sun, The Battle of Trafalgar* 1911; *Treasure Island, The Charge of the Light Brigade, Partners for Life, Aladdin Up-to-Date* 1912; *Mary Stuart* (also sc.), *In the Bishop's Carriage* (co-dir. with Porter), *Tess of the D'Urbervilles* (also sc.), *The Port of Doom* (also sc.), *Leah Kleschna* 1913; *An American Citizen, The Day of Days, A Woman's Triumph, The Lost Paradise, Marta of the Lowlands, One of Millions* (also sc.), *In the Name of the Prince of Peace* (also sc.) 1914; *The Daughter of the People* (also sc.), *Four Feathers, Helene of the North, Still Waters* 1915; *Mice and Men, Out of the Drifts, Molly Make-Believe, Silks and Satins, My Lady Eileen, The Rainbow Princess, Miss George Washington, Snow White* 1916; *The Valentine Girl, Bab's Diary, Bab's Burglar* 1917; *The Seven Swans* (also sc.), *The Lie, Rich Man Poor Man* (also sc.), *The Death Dance, Uncle Tom's Cabin* (also sc.) 1918; *Twilight, The Phantom Honeymoon* (also sc.), *Everybody's Business* (also sc.) 1919; *The Harvest Moon* (also sc.) 1920; *A Virgin Paradise, Beyond Price* 1921; *Who Are My Parents?/A Little Child Shall Lead Them* 1922; *As a Man Lives, Has the World Gone Mad?, Broadway Broke* 1923.

Dawn process. An early GLASS SHOT process attributed to director-cameraman Norman Dawn ca. 1905. It made possible simple and economical composite effects through the shooting of action while the performers were stationed either in front of or behind backgrounds painted on glass and mounted in a wooden frame in front of the camera.

Dawson, Ralph. Film editor. Born on Apr. 18, 1897, in Westboro, Mass. In films from 1919, he was the winner of three Academy Awards for editing *A Midsummer Night's Dream, Anthony Adverse,* and *The Adventures of Robin Hood.*

FILMS INCLUDE: *Lady of the Night* 1925; *If I Were Single* 1927; *Tenderloin, The Singing Fool* 1928; *The Desert Song* 1929; *Under a Texas Moon, Outward Bound* 1930; *Girl Missing* 1933; *The Story of Louis Pasteur, A Midsummer Night's Dream* 1935; *Anthony Adverse* 1936; *Another Dawn, The Prince and the Pauper* 1937; *The Dawn Patrol, Four Daughters, The Adventures of Robin Hood* 1938; *The Great Lie* 1941; *Kings Row* 1942; *Mr. Skeffington* 1944; *Saratoga Trunk* 1945; *Ivy* 1947; *All My Sons, An Act of Murder* 1948; *Undertow* 1949; *Harvey* 1951; *Island in the Sky* 1953; *Hondo, The High and the Mighty* 1954; *Flight to Hong Kong* 1956.

Day, Doris. Actress, singer. Born Doris von Kappelhoff, on Apr. 3, 1924, in Cincinnati. An auto accident forced her to abandon a budding dancing career at 15 and she turned instead to singing. In the early 40s she gained popularity as a vocalist with the Bob Crosby and Les Brown bands, and by the middle of the decade she was a highly successful recording star. She entered films in 1948 as a last-minute replacement for Betty Hutton in the Warner Bros. musical *Romance on the High Seas* and promptly became an audience favorite as the freckle-faced girl-next-door heroine of light musicals and occasional dramas. By the early 50s she was the most popular female star in the US and one of the highest paid. In the late 50s and early 60s she was the virginal heroine of a succession of pseudosophisticated bedroom farces, mostly at Universal, opposite such would-be seducers as Rock Hudson and Cary Grant. She was nominated for an Oscar for one of these films, *Pillow Talk* (1959).

In her book *Doris Day: Her Own Story* (1975) she revealed for the first time that behind the ever-cheerful facade there was a woman far from happy. She was hospitalized for a year at 13, went on the road at 16, married a "psychopath" musician at 17, and entered another unsuccessful union at 22. Her third marriage, to producer-manager Marty MELCHER, lasted 17 seemingly blissful years, but upon his death in 1968 she discovered that he had either mismanaged or embezzled her entire life's earnings of $20 million and had left her flat broke. After recovering from an ensuing nervous breakdown, she bounced back as a TV star with 'The Doris Day Show' (1968–73), which ran for several successful seasons (she had been committed to do the series by her late husband without her knowledge). In 1974 she was awarded more than $22 million in damages from her former lawyer, who had helped Melcher manage her business and wipe out her fortune. After more than a decade's absence, she returned to the spotlight in 1985–86 as the host of a cable TV show, 'Doris Day and Friends.'

FILMS: *Romance on the High Seas* 1948; *My Dream Is Yours, It's a Great Feeling* 1949; *Young Man with a Horn, Tea for Two, The West Point Story* 1950; *Storm Warning, Lullaby of Broadway, On Moonlight Bay, I'll See You in My Dreams, Starlift* (cameo) 1951; *The Winning Team, April in Paris* 1952; *By the Light of the Silvery Moon, Calamity Jane* 1953; *Lucky Me* 1954; *Young at Heart, Love Me or Leave Me* 1955; *The Man Who Knew Too Much, Julie* 1956; *The Pajama Game* 1957; *Teacher's Pet, Tunnel of Love* 1958; *It Happened to Jane, Pillow Talk* 1959; *Please Don't Eat the Daisies, Midnight Lace* 1960; *Lover Come Back, That Touch of Mink, Jumbo* 1962; *The Thrill of It All, Move Over Darling* 1963; *Send Me No Flowers* 1964; *Do Not Disturb* 1965; *The Glass-Bottom Boat* 1966; *Caprice* 1967; *The Ballad of Josie, Where Were You When the Lights Went Out?, With Six You Get Eggroll* 1968.

Day, Josette. Actress. *b.* Josette Dagory, July 31, 1914, Paris. *d.* 1978. She made her film debut at the age of five and later appeared on the stage and as a child dancer in the Paris Opera. Returned to the screen as an adult in the early 30s and played leads in many French films, memorably as Beauty in Cocteau's *Beauty and the Beast* (1945). Divorced from playwright-director Marcel PAGNOL, she retired from the screen in the late 40s to marry a Belgian industrialist, who left her a widow in 1960.

FILMS INCLUDE: *La Pocharde* 1919; *Allô Berlin. . . Ici Paris* 1932; *Le Barbier de Séville* 1934; *Aux Portes de Paris*

1935; *Ménilmontant, Club de Femmes* 1936; *L'Homme du Jour/The Man of the Hour, Education de Prince/The Bargekeeper's Daughter, Le Patriote/The Mad Emperor* 1938; *La Fille de Puisatier/The Well-Digger's Daughter* 1941; *Arlette et l'Amour* 1943; *La Belle et la Bête/Beauty and the Beast* 1946; *Les Parents terribles/The Storm Within* 1948; *Swiss Tour/Four Days' Leave* (Switz.), *La Révoltée/Stolen Affections* 1949.

Day, Laraine. Actress. Born Laraine Johnson, on Oct. 13, 1917, in Roosevelt, Utah. A descendant of a prominent Mormon pioneer leader and one of eight children of a well-to-do grain dealer, she began her stage career with the Long Beach Players after her family moved to California. She made her screen debut in 1937, playing a bit in *Stella Dallas,* and then had leads in several George O'Brien Westerns at RKO under her real name before signing an MGM contract in 1939. It was under the screen name Laraine Day that she gained popularity in the role of Nurse Mary Lamont, the fiancée of Lew Ayres in the "Dr. Kildare" series, and went on to play a variety of leads at MGM, RKO, and other studios in medium-budget films of the 40s and 50s. A devout Mormon, she never smokes or drinks, not even coffee. During her second marriage (1947–60), to baseball manager Leo Durocher, she took an active interest in the game and was known as "the first lady of baseball." She wrote a volume of memoirs: *Day with Giants* (1952). Her first husband (1942–47) had been singer Ray Hendricks, and the third (from 1960) is TV producer Michael Grilkhas. Author also of *The America We Love.*

FILMS INCLUDE: *Stella Dallas* 1937; *Border G-Men, Painted Desert* 1938; *Sergeant Madden, Calling Dr. Kildare, Tarzan Finds a Son* 1939; *I Take This Woman, And One Was Beautiful, Foreign Correspondent, My Son My Son!, Dr. Kildare's Crisis* 1940; *The Trial of Mary Dugan, The Bad Man, Dr. Kildare's Wedding Day, Kathleen, Unholy Partners* 1941; *Fingers at the Window, Journey for Margaret* 1942; *Mr. Lucky* 1943; *The Story of Dr. Wassell, Bride by Mistake* 1944; *Those Endearing Young Charms, Keep Your Powder Dry* 1945; *The Locket* 1946; *Tycoon* 1947; *My Dear Secretary* 1948; *I Married a Communist/The Woman on Pier 13, Without Honor* 1949; *The High and the Mighty* 1954; *Toy Tiger, Three for Jamie Dawn* 1956; *The Third Voice* 1960; *House of Dracula's Daughter* 1972.

Day, Marceline. Actress. Born on Apr. 24, 1907, in Colorado Springs, Colo. Leading lady of late Hollywood silents and early talkies, mostly at MGM. Best remembered for her starring roles in *The Beloved Rogue* (1927), opposite John Barrymore, and *The Cameraman* (1928), opposite Buster Keaton. She also teamed with comedians Harry Langdon, Stan Laurel, and Charlie Chase, among others, but slipped into low-budget action pictures in the early 30s and retired from the screen. Her sister, Alice Day (b. Nov. 7, 1905, Colorado Springs, Colo.), a former Mack Sennett bathing beauty, also played leads in films of the 20s and early 30s.

FILMS INCLUDE: *The Taming of the West, The Wall Street Whiz, The Splendid Road, The White Outlaw* 1925; *The Barrier, That Model from Paris, College Days, The Boy Friend, The Gay Deceiver, Fools for Fashion* 1926; *The Beloved Rogue, Rookies, Captain Salvation, The Road to Romance, London After Midnight* 1927; *The Big City, A Certain Young Man, The Cameraman, Driftwood, Detectives, Under the Black Eagle, Freedom of the Press, Restless Youth, Stolen Youth* 1928; *The Jazz Age, The Wild Party, The One Woman Idea, A Single Man, Trent's Last Case* 1929; *Paradise Island, Temple Tower, Sunny Skies* 1930; *The Mad Parade, Sky Raiders* 1931; *The Fighting Fool, Arm of the Law, The Crusader* 1932; *The Telegraph Tail, Via Pony Express, The Flaming Signal* 1933; *Damaged Lives* (release delayed from 1933) 1937.

Day, Richard. Art director. *b.* May 9, 1896, Victoria, B.C., Canada. *d.* 1972. In Hollywood from 1918, he began as a set decorator on Erich von STROHEIM's earliest films at Universal, *Blind Husbands* (1919) and *The Devil's Pass Key* (1920). He stayed on with von Stroheim through his moves to MGM, Paramount, and United Artists, and for the remainder of the silent era collaborated with the director on the art direction and the costume design of the latter's elaborate productions. On his own from the early 30s, Day proved himself one of the most capable and imaginative art directors in the business, designing many distinguished productions for United Artists, 20th Century-Fox, and RKO. His sets, whether period or modern, have been noted for their realism. He won Academy Awards for his work on *The Dark Angel* (1935), *Dodsworth* (1936), *How Green Was My Valley* (1941), *This Above All* and *My Gal Sal* (both 1942), *A Streetcar Named Desire* (1951), and *On the Waterfront* (1954).

FILMS INCLUDE (alone or in collaboration): *Foolish Wives* 1921; *Merry-Go-Round* 1922; *Greed* 1923–25; *The Merry Widow* 1925; *Bardelys the Magnificent, Beverly of Graustark* 1926; *The Enemy, The Student Prince* 1927; *The Wedding March, Queen Kelly* 1928; *Whoopee!* 1930; *Arrowsmith, Street Scene, The Front Page* 1931; *Rain, The Kid from Spain* 1932; *Hallelujah I'm a Bum, The Bowery, Roman Scandals* 1933; *Nana, The House of Rothschild, Bulldog Drummond Strikes Back* 1934; *The Wedding Night, Barbary Coast, The Mighty Barnum, Cardinal Richelieu, The Call of the Wild, The Dark Angel, Clive of India, Les Miserables* 1935; *These Three, The Gay Desperado, Come and Get It, Dodsworth* 1936; *Stella Dallas, Dead End, The Hurricane* 1937; *The Goldwyn Follies, The Cowboy and the Lady, The Adventures of Marco Polo* 1938; *Hollywood Cavalcade, Swanee River, Drums Along the Mohawk, The Hound of the Baskervilles, Young Mr. Lincoln* 1939; *The Return of Frank James, The Mark of Zorro, Lillian Russell* 1940; *How Green Was My Valley, Tobacco Road, Blood and Sand, Man Hunt* 1941; *This Above All, My Gal Sal, The Black Swan, Tales of Manhattan, Moontide* 1942; *The Ox-Bow Incident* 1943; *The Razor's Edge, Boomerang, Miracle on 34th Street, The Ghost and Mrs. Muir* 1947; *Captain from Castile, Force of Evil, Joan of Arc* 1948; *My Foolish Heart* 1949; *Cry Danger, A Streetcar Named Desire* 1951; *Hans Christian Andersen* 1952; *On the Waterfront* 1954; *Solomon and Sheba* 1959; *Exodus* 1960; *Something Wild* 1961; *Cheyenne Autumn* 1964; *The Greatest Story Ever Told* 1965; *The Chase* 1966; *Valley of the Dolls* 1967; *The Boston Strangler* 1968; *Tora! Tora! Tora!* 1970.

Day, Robert. Director. Born on Sept. 11, 1922, in Sheen, England. Entered British films at 16 as a camera assistant, graduating to director of photography in the 40s. A director since the mid-50s, he started out auspiciously with a suspenseful Alistair Sim black comedy, *The Green Man,* but with the exception of another comedy, *Two-Way Stretch,* with Peter Sellers, his output has consisted of smooth but inconsequential farces and adventures. Has also worked in Hollywood and has directed several made-for-TV movies. Married Dorothy PROVINE.

FILMS: *The Green Man* 1956; *Stranger's Meeting* 1957; *Grip of the Strangler/The Haunted Strangler* 1958; *First Man Into Space, Life in Emergency Ward 10, Bobbikins* 1959; *Two-Way Stretch, Tarzan the Magnificent* (also co-sc.) 1960; *The Rebel/Call Me Genius* 1961; *Corridors of Blood* (release delayed from 1958), *Operation Snatch* 1962; *Tarzan's Three Challenges* (also co-sc.; US) 1963; *She* 1965; *Tarzan and the Valley of Gold* (US/Switz.) 1966; *Tarzan and the Great River* (US) 1967; *Tarzan and the Jungle Boy* (prod. only; US/Switz.) 1968; *The Man with Bogart's Face/Sam Marlowe Private Eye* (US) 1980.

day-for-night cinematography. The process of simulating night scenes while shooting in broad daylight, usually with the aid of filters and through underexposure. In most cases this is done for reasons of economy (to save the payment of night overtime to performers and crew) and speed of production.

Day-Lewis, Daniel. Actor. Born on Apr. 29, 1957, in London. Princely stage and screen leading man of astonishing range. The son of noted author and England's Poet Laureate, Cecil Day-Lewis (C. Day Lewis), and stage/screen actress Jill Balcon, and grandson of British movie mogul Sir Michael BALCON, he ran away from boarding school at 13. The following year he made his first film appearance, playing a bit as a car vandal in John Schlesinger's *Sunday, Bloody Sunday.* At 15, he wrote and acted in his first play, 'Breakout.' After training with the Bristol Old Vic, he embarked on an increasingly prominent professional stage career that culminated in his 1982 West End debut in 'Another Country.' On the screen, he continued to amaze international audiences with the brilliance of his performances in a widely diverse range of roles: a gay cockney punk in *My Beautiful Laundrette,* an upper-class twit in *A Room with a View,* an irresistible lover in *The Unbearable Lightness of Being,* a wilds-trained frontiersman in *The Last of the Mohicans,* and a crippled writer-painter in *My Left Foot,* for which he won the Academy Award as best actor in 1989.

FILMS: *Sunday Bloody Sunday* 1971; *Gandhi* 1983; *The Bounty* 1984; *The Insurance Man, My Beautiful Laundrette* 1985; *A Room with a View* 1985; *Nanou* (UK/Fr.) 1987; *The Unbearable Lightness of Being, Stars and Bars* 1988; *My Left Foot, Eversmile, New Jersey* 1989; *The Last of the Mohicans* 1992; *The Age of Innocence, In the Name of the Father* 1993; *The Crucible* 1996.

daylight. In photographic terms, the total amount of measurable light, combining both sunlight and skylight. The color temperature of daylight is much greater than that of sunlight, which is the amount of light reaching a photographed subject directly from the sun.

daylight leading spool. A special reel with opaque flanges that hold film tightly in place so that only the outer layers may be affected when the film is loaded or unloaded in broad daylight. Such safety spools are more commonly used in 16 mm cinematography than in 35 mm work.

Dean, Basil. Director, producer, screenwriter. *b.* Sept. 27, 1888, Croydon, England. *d.* 1978. On the British stage as an actor from 1906, he later produced and directed many plays and films. In 1932 he founded and headed Associated Talking Pictures, Ltd., a forerunner of the Ealing studios. He discovered and advanced the careers of such performers as Gracie Fields, George Formby, and his former wife Victoria HOPPER. He was the guiding spirit behind the formation of ESNA (Entertainments National Service Association), Britain's equivalent of America's U.S.O., during WW II. Autobiography: *Mind's Eye* (1973).

FILMS INCLUDE (as producer-director): *The Constant Nymph* (prod., co-dir., from own co-play) 1928; *The Return of Sherlock Holmes* 1929; *Escape, Birds of Prey/The Perfect Alibi* 1930; *Sally in Our Alley* (prod. only) 1931; *The Impassive Footman/Woman in Chains* 1932; *Loyalties, Three Men in a Boat* (prod. only), *The Constant Nymph* (remake; dir., sc. only from own co-play) 1933; *Autumn Crocus, Java Head* (prod. only) 1934; *Lorna Doone* 1935; *Whom the Gods Love* 1936; *Penny Paradise* 1938; *21 Days/21 Days Together* (dir. only; release delayed from 1937), *Mozart* 1940.

Dean, Eddie. Actor, singer. Born Edgar Dean Glosup, in 1910(?) in Posey, Tex. Singing cowboy star of Hollywood films of the 40s. He made his name as a Western singer on radio from 1930 and started playing bit roles in films in 1936. He reached his peak in the mid-40s, when he was among the top ten most popular cowboy stars, but soon after retired from films.

FILMS INCLUDE: *Western Jamboree* 1938; *Renegade Trail* 1939; *Golden Trail* 1940; *Sierra Sue* 1941; *Fighting Bill Fargo* 1942; *King of the Cowboys* 1943; *Song of Old Wyoming* 1945; *Romance of the West* 1946; *Wild Country* 1947; *Stars Over Texas* 1948; *Varieties on Parade* 1951.

Dean, James. Actor. *b.* James Byron Dean, Feb. 8, 1931, Marion, Ind. *d.* 1955 in an auto crash. The son of a dental technician, he moved with his family to Los Angeles at age five, but after his mother's death, he returned to the Midwest at age nine and was raised by relatives on their Iowa farm. After graduating from high school, he returned to California, where he attended Santa Monica Junior College and UCLA. He began acting with James Whitmore's little theater group, appeared in occasional TV commercials, and played bit parts in several films. In 1951 he went to New York, where after hanging around the theater district earning his living as a busboy, he got a part in Broadway's 'See the Jaguar.' He later observed classes at the Actors Studio, played bits in TV dramas, and returned to Broadway in 'The Immoralist' (1954). This last appearance resulted in a screen test at Warners and one of the most spectacularly brief careers of any screen star. In just more than a year, and in only three films, Dean became a widely admired screen personality, a personification of the restless American youth of the mid-50s, an embodiment of the title of one of his films, *Rebel Without a Cause.* He was nominated for Academy Awards as best actor for *East of Eden* (1955) and *Giant* (1956). Dean was killed in a highway crash while driving his Porsche to Salinas, to compete in a racing event. His adulation by fans grew posthumously to legendary proportions. Many of them refused to accept his death, and a James Dean cult developed into a mass mystique of a kind that surrounded the personality of no other star since Valentino. Numerous posthumous biographies of James Dean have been published. Echoes of the Dean adulation fill Altman's fiction feature *Come Back to the Five and Dime, Jimmy Dean, Jimmy Dean* (1982) and James Bridges's *September 30, 1955* (1978), the date of the star's death.

FILMS: *Sailor Beware* (bit), *Fixed Bayonets* (bit) 1951; *Has Anybody Seen My Gal* (bit) 1952; *Trouble Along the Way* (bit) 1953; *East of Eden, Rebel Without a Cause* 1955; *Giant* 1956.

Dean, Priscilla. Actress. *b.* 1896, in New York City, into a theatrical family. *d.* 1988. As an infant she accompanied her parents on their tours and began performing in their stock company while still a child. She was an accomplished actress by ten and made her screen debut at 14. After appearing in a number of one-reelers at Biograph and other studios, she joined Universal in 1911 and soon became established as the principal soubrette in the Eddie Lyons-Lee Moran comedy series. She made her leap to stardom in features as a result of her popularity as the heroine of the 1917 serial *The Gray Ghost.* She subsequently starred in many Universal silent dramas, notably Tod Browning's *The Virgin of Stamboul* (1920) and *Under Two Flags* (1922). Her popularity diminished in the late 20s, and she slipped into minor films with poverty-row studios. She was married to actor Wheeler Oakman.

FILMS INCLUDE: *Mother* 1914; *Love Dynamite and Baseball* 1916; *The Gray Ghost* (serial), *Even As You and I, The Hand That Rocks the Cradle, Beloved Jim* 1917; *The Two-Soul Woman, The Brazen Beauty, Kiss or Kill, She Hired a Husband, Wildcat of Paris* 1918; *The Wicked Darling, Forbidden, The Exquisite Thief, Silk Lined Burglar, Paid in Advance* 1919; *The Virgin of Stamboul* 1920; *Outside the Law, Reputation, Conflict*

1921; *Wild Honey, Under Two Flags* 1922; *The Flame of Life, The White Tiger, Drifting* 1923; *Storm Daughter, The Siren of Seville, A Cafe in Cairo* 1924; *The Crimson Runner* 1925; *West of Broadway, The Speeding Venus, Forbidden Waters, The Danger Girl* 1926; *Birds of Prey, The Dice Woman, Jewels of Desire* 1927; *Behind Stone Walls* 1932.

De Antonio, Emile. Filmmaker. *b.* 1920, Scranton, Pa. *d.* 1989. *ed.* Harvard. The son of a well-to-do physician, he was at different times a longshoreman, a barge captain, a peddler, a war surplus broker, a book editor, and a college instructor at William and Mary. In the early 60s, De Antonio, called by his friends D, began making antiestablishment documentary and compilation films that reflected his Marxist leanings. Just before his death of a heart attack, he completed *Mr. Hoover and I,* depicting his life as seen through the files of the FBI, 10,000 pages of surveillance material which he retrieved through a suit based on the Freedom of Information Act. He was instrumental in influencing Andy Warhol toward experimentation in film.

FILMS INCLUDE (as director-producer): *Point of Order!* (from the TV footage of the 1954 Army-McCarthy hearings) 1964; *That's Where the Action Is* (about New York City's mayoral campaign) 1965; *Rush to Judgment* (based on Mark Lane's investigation of the JFK assassination) 1967; *America Is Hard to See* (about Senator Eugene McCarthy) 1968; *In the Year of the Pig* (a radical view of the Vietnam War) 1969; *Milhouse: A White Comedy* (a satire on President Nixon) 1971; *Painters Painting* (about New York's art world) 1973; *Underground* (interviews with five members of the Weather Underground; co-dir. with Haskell Wexler) 1976; *In the King of Prussia* (about the Pennsylvania trial of Roman Catholic radicals) 1982; *Mr. Hoover and I* 1990.

Dearden, Basil. Director, producer, screenwriter. *b.* Basil Dear, Jan. 1, 1911, Westcliffe, England. *d.* 1971. Worked in the theater before entering British films as an assistant to Basil DEAN and production manager, associate producer, and screenwriter at Ealing. He changed his name to avoid confusion with that of Dean. In 1941 he co-directed the first of several Will Hay comedies with the actor and in 1943 directed his first solo film. In the late 40s he began a long association with producer-writer Michael RELPH, which resulted in many intelligent and sometimes controversial films. Dearden dealt soberly and discreetly with such difficult social problems as race relations (*Sapphire*) and homosexuality (*Victim*), and also demonstrated a knack for lighthearted comedy in such films as *The Smallest Show on Earth* and *Man in the Moon* and a flair for dazzling action in films like *Khartoum* and *The Assassination Bureau.* Two of Dearden's films, *The Blue Lamp* and *Sapphire,* won British Film Academy Awards. He was killed in a car crash. His son, James DEARDEN, is also a director and screenwriter.

FILMS (as director): *The Black Sheep of Whitehall* (co-dir. with Will Hay) 1941; *The Goose Steps Out* (co-dir. with Hay) 1942; *My Learned Friend* (co-dir.), *The Bells Go Down* 1943; *Halfway House, They Came to a City* (also co-sc.) 1944; *Dead of Night* ("Hearse Driver" episode) 1945; *The Captive Heart* 1946; *Frieda* 1947; *Saraband for Dead Lovers/Saraband* 1948; *Train of Events* (co-dir. with Sidney Cole and Charles Crichton; co-sc.) 1949; *The Blue Lamp, Cage of Gold* 1950; *Pool of London* 1951; *I Believe in You* (co-dir., co-prod., co-sc.), *The Gentle Gunman* (also co-prod.) 1952; *The Square Ring* (co-dir., co-prod.) 1953; *The Rainbow Jacket* 1954; *Out of the Clouds* (co-dir., co-prod.), *The Ship That Died of Shame* (also co-prod., co-sc.) 1955; *Who Done It?* (co-dir., co-prod.) 1956; *The Smallest Show on Earth* 1957; *Violent Playground* 1958; *Sapphire* 1959; *The League of Gentlemen, Man in the Moon* (also co-sc.) 1960; *The Secret Partner, Victim* (also co-prod.) 1961; *All Night Long* (co-dir., co-prod.), *Life for Ruth/Walk in the Shadow* 1962; *The Mind Benders, A Place to Go* 1963; *Woman of Straw* 1964; *Masquerade* 1965; *Khartoum* 1966; *Only When I Larf* 1968; *The Assassination Bureau* 1969; *The Man Who Haunted Himself* (also co-sc.) 1970.

Dearden, James. Director, screenwriter. Born September 14, 1949, in London. *ed.* New College, Oxford, England. Son of the late director Basil DEARDEN, he began his film career as a production runner, then worked as an editor of commercials and documentaries and as an assistant director. In 1978, he won the Silver Bear Award at the Berlin Film Festival for *The Contraption*, a short he wrote, produced, and directed. Another short, *Diversion* (1979), became the basis for his screenplay for *Fatal Attraction* (1987), which earned him an Academy Award nomination. He branched into feature directing with *Pascali's Island* (1988).

FILMS INCLUDE: *Fatal Attraction* (sc.) 1987; *Pascali's Island* (dir., sc.) 1988; *A Kiss Before Dying* (dir., sc.) 1991.

d'Eaubonne, Jean. See EAUBONNE, Jean d'.

de Banzie, Brenda. Actress. *b.* 1915, Manchester, England. *d.* 1981. Leading lady and character actress of British stage (from 1935), films (from 1942), and television. Memorable in David Lean's *Hobson's Choice* (1954). Also seen in some Hollywood productions.

FILMS INCLUDE: *The Long Dark Hall* 1951; *I Believe in You* 1952; *Hobson's Choice, The Purple Plain* 1954; *A Kid for Two Farthings, Doctor at Sea* 1955; *The Man Who Knew Too Much* (US) 1956; *Too Many Crooks* 1958; *The 39 Steps* 1959; *The Entertainer* 1960; *The Mark, Flame in the Streets, Come September* (US) 1961; *A Pair of Briefs* 1962; *The Pink Panther* (US) 1964; *Pretty Polly/A Matter of Innocence* 1967.

de Baroncelli, Jacques. See BARONCELLI, Jacques de.

De Bont, Jan. Director, director of photography. Born on Oct. 22, 1943, in Holland. Trained at the Amsterdam Film Academy, he embarked on a Hollywood career on the strength of his vivid images for several Dutch films for Paul VERHOEVEN and Fons RADEMAKERS. As a director, he has helmed two top-grossing films in the 90s, one of which, *Twister* (1996), broke box-office records.

FILMS INCLUDE: In Holland—*Turkish Delight* 1973; *Keetje Tippel/Cathy Tippel* 1975; *Max Havelaar* 1976; *Soldier of Orange* 1979. In US—*Private Lessons* 1981; *I'm Dancing as Fast as I Can* 1982; *Cujo, All the Right Moves, The Fourth Man* (Holl.) 1983; *The Jewel of the Nile, Flesh and Blood* 1985; *Ruthless People* 1986; *Die Hard* 1988; *Black Rain* 1989; *The Hunt for Red October* 1990; As director—*Speed* 1994; *Twister* 1996; *Speed 2: Cruise Control* (also Prod. co-scr.) 1997.

de Broca, Philippe. See BROCA, Philippe de.

De Brulier, Nigel. Actor. *b.* 1878, England. *d.* 1948. Versatile character player of numerous Hollywood silents and talkies, often in dominating roles, such as Cardinal Richelieu in the 1921 and 1935 productions of *The Three Musketeers* and in the 1929 *The Iron Mask,* and as Simonides in the silent *Ben-Hur.* Remembered by serial followers as the mysterious Shazam in *The Adventures of Captain Marvel* (1941).

FILMS INCLUDE: *Ghosts* 1915; *The Pursuit of the Phantom* 1914; *Ghosts, The Spanish Jade* 1915; *Ramona, Intolerance* (bit), *Purity, The Dumb Girl of Portici* 1916; *The Bond Between* 1917; *The Kaiser, The Beast of Berlin, Kultur, The Romance of Tarzan* 1918; *The Boomerang, Sahara* 1919; *The Virgin of Stamboul* 1920; *The Four Horsemen of the Apocalypse, The Three Musketeers* (as Cardinal Richelieu), *The Devil Within* 1921; *A Doll's House* (as Dr. Rank), *Omar the Tentmaker* 1922; *Salome, The Hunchback of Notre Dame, Rupert of Hentzau* 1923; *A Boy of Flanders, Mademoiselle*

Midnight, Three Weeks, Wild Oranges 1924; *Ben-Hur* (as Simonides), *The Ancient Mariner* 1925; *Don Juan, The Greater Glory* 1926; *The Beloved Rogue, Wings, Surrender* 1927; *Divine Sinner, Loves of an Actress, Two Lovers* 1928; *Noah's Ark, The Iron Mask* (again as Cardinal Richelieu), *The Wheel of Life* 1929; *The Green Goddess, Moby Dick, Redemption* 1930; *Son of India* 1931; *I'm No Angel* 1933; *Viva Villa!* 1934; *A Tale of Two Cities, Charlie Chan in Egypt, The Three Musketeers* (again as Cardinal Richelieu) 1935; *The Garden of Allah, Mary of Scotland* 1936; *Zorro Rides Again* (serial) 1937; *The Man in the Iron Mask, Tower of London, The Hound of the Baskervilles* 1939; *The Mad Empress, One Million B.C.* 1940; *The Adventures of Captain Marvel* (serial) 1941; *Tonight We Raid Calais* 1943.

Decaë, Henri. Director of photography. *b.* July 31, 1915, in Saint-Denis, France. *d.* 1987. Began making amateur shorts while still a boy and entered the industry as a sound recordist and editor. After WW II service as a cameraman with the French Air Force, he produced, directed, and photographed documentary shorts as well as industrial and commercial films. As a director of photography since the late 40s, he introduced documentary freedom into French feature films and became a favorite of several New Wave directors, notably Melville, Chabrol, and Malle. He works best outdoors, and early in his career often employed hand-held cameras, but later showed considerable ability with disciplined, studio-made, flashier cinematography, and his services have been sought for big-budget international productions.

FILMS INCLUDE: *Le Silence de la Mer* 1947; *Les Enfants Terribles/The Strange Ones* 1949; *Ascenseur pour l'Echafaud/Frantic, Le Beau Serge, Les Amants/The Lovers, Les Cousins* 1958; *Les Quatre Cents Coups/The 400 Blows, A Double Tour/Leda/Web of Passion* 1959; *Plein Soleil/Purple Noon, Les Bonnes Femmes* 1960; *Léon Morin Prêtre* 1961; *Les Sept Péchés capitaux/Seven Deadly Sins* (Godard, Demy, Vadim episodes), *La vie Privée/A Very Private Affair, Cybèle ou les Dimanches de Ville-d'Avray/Sundays and Cybele, L'Aîné des Ferchaux/Magnet of Doom* 1962; *Le Jour et l'Heure/The Day and the Hour, Dragées au poivre/Sweet and Sour, La Tulipe noire/The Black Tulip* 1963; *Les Félins/Joy House/The Love Cafe, La Ronde/Circle of Love* 1964; *Le Corniaud/The Sucker, Viva Maria* 1965; *Hotel Paradiso* (US/UK) 1966; *The Night of the Generals* (UK/Fr.), *Le Voleur/The Thief of Paris, The Comedians* (US/Fr.) 1967; *Castle Keep* (US), *Le Clan des Siciliens/The Sicilian Clan* 1969; *Hello-Goodbye* (US), *The Only Game in Town* (US) 1970; *The Light at the Edge of the World* (US/It.) 1971; *Le Droit de l'Aimer* 1972; *Two People* (US) 1973; *La Course a l'Echalote/The Wild Goose Chase, Seven Men at Daybreak/Operation Daybreak* (UK) 1975; *Bobby Deerfield* (US) 1977; *The Boys from Brazil* (US) 1978; *An Almost Perfect Affair* (US) 1979; *The Island* (US), *Le Coup du Parapluie* 1980; *Le Professionnel* 1981; *Exposed* (US) 1983.

DeCamp, Rosemary. Actress. Born on Nov. 14, 1913, in Prescott, Ariz. A veteran of stage and radio, she played supporting roles in numerous films of the 40s and 50s, mostly for Warner Bros., often as the sympathetic sister, mother, or friend of the heroine. She also appeared frequently on TV and was a regular on the series 'The Bob Cummings Show' and 'That Girl.'

FILMS INCLUDE: *Cheers for Miss Bishop, Hold Back the Dawn* 1941; *Jungle Book, Yankee Doodle Dandy* 1942; *This Is the Army* 1943; *The Merry Monahans, Bowery to Broadway* 1944; *Practically Yours, Rhapsody in Blue, Blood on the Sun, Pride of the Marines, Weekend at the Waldorf, Danger Signal* 1945; *From This Day Forward, Two Guys from Milwaukee* 1946; *Nora Prentiss* 1947; *Night Unto Night, Look for the Silver Lining, The Story of Seabiscuit* 1949; *The Big Hangover* 1950; *Night Into Morning, On Moonlight Bay* 1951; *Scandal Sheet* 1952; *By the Light of the Silvery Moon, So This Is Love* 1953; *Many Rivers to Cross, Strategic Air Command* 1955; *13 Ghosts* 1960; *Saturday the 14th* 1981.

De Carlo, Yvonne. Actress. Born Peggy Yvonne Middleton, on Sept. 1, 1922, in Vancouver, B.C., Canada. A dancer from childhood, she appeared in nightclubs and on the stage before making her film debut in 1942. After a long succession of secondary roles, she was cast by Walter WANGER in the title role of *Salome—Where She Danced* (1945), followed by *The Song of Scheherazade* and *Slave Girl*, and became typecast as an exotic temptress, representing Hollywood's idea of an Arabian Nights beauty. When she wasn't busy wearing harem attire, she frequently was seen as a Western heroine or dance hall girl. On the rare occasions when she was required to act she showed a surprising aptitude, and demonstrated a special knack for comedy in the British-made *Hotel Sahara* (1951) and *The Captain's Paradise* (1953). On TV she starred in the comic horror series 'The Munsters' (1964–66). In 1971 she appeared on Broadway in the musical 'Follies.' She married (in 1955) and later divorced Hollywood stuntman and sometime actor Robert Morgan. Autobiography: *Yvonne* (1987).

FILMS: *Harvard Here I Come!, This Gun for Hire, Road to Morocco, Lucky Jordan, Youth on Parade* 1942; *Rhythm Parade, The Crystal Ball, Salute for Three, For Whom the Bell Tolls, So Proudly We Hail!, Let's Face It, True to Life, The Deerslayer* 1943; *Standing Room Only, The Story of Dr. Wassell, Rainbow Island, Kismet, Practically Yours, Here Come the Waves* 1944; *Bring on the Girls, Salome—Where She Danced* (first lead role), *Frontier Gal* 1945; *Song of Scheherazade, Brute Force, Slave Girl* 1947; *Black Bart* (as dancer-adventuress Lola Montez), *Casbah, River Lady* 1948; *Criss Cross, Calamity Jane and Sam Bass* (as Calamity Jane), *The Gal Who Took the West* 1949; *Buccaneer's Girl, The Desert Hawk* (as Scheherazade) 1950; *Tomahawk, Hotel Sahara* (UK), *Silver City* 1951; *The San Francisco Story, Scarlet Angel, Hurricane Smith* 1952; *Sombrero, She Devils, Fort Algiers, The Captain's Paradise* (UK) 1953; *La Castiglione* (Fr./It.), *Border River, Happy Ever After/Tonight's the Night* (UK/US), *Passion* 1954; *Shotgun* 1955; *Flame of the Islands, Magic Fire, Raw Edge, Death of a Scoundrel, The Ten Commandments* 1956; *Band of Angels* 1957; *La Spada e la Croce/Mary Magdalene* (as Mary Magdalene; It.) 1958; *Timbuktu* 1959; *McLintock!* 1963; *A Global Affair, Law of the Lawless* 1964; *Tentazioni proibite* (semidoc.; It.) 1965; *Munster Go Home!* 1966; *Hostile Guns* 1967; *The Power, Arizona Bushwhackers* 1968; *The Delta Factor* 1970; *The Seven Minutes* 1971; *The Girl on the Late Late Show* (TV movie), *The Mark of Zorro* (TV movie) 1974; *It Seemed Like a Good Idea at the Time* (UK/Can.), *Arizona Slim* 1975; *Won Ton Ton: the Dog Who Saved Hollywood* (cameo), *Blazing Stewardesses* 1976; *La Casa de la Sombras/House of Shadows* (Arg.), *Satan's Cheerleaders* 1977; *Nocturna, Silent Scream* 1979; *Guyana, Cult of the Damned* (Mex./Sp./Panam.), *The Man with Bogart's Face* 1980; *The Munster's Revenge* (TV movie), *Play Dead* 1981; *Liar's Moon* 1982; *Vultures in Paradise/Flesh and Bullets* 1983; *A Masterpiece of Murder* (TV movie), *American Gothic* 1988; *Mirror, Mirror* 1990; *Oscar* 1991.

Decoin, Henri. Director. *b.* Mar. 18, 1896, Paris. *d.* 1969. A former athlete, WW I aviator, and sportswriter, he entered French films in 1929 as an assistant director and screenwriter. A director from 1933, he turned out many solid commercial productions, some of which starred his second (1935–41) wife, Danielle DARRIEUX. Decoin was a prolific and technically competent director who made up for his lack of originality with skillful handling of story material. He often collaborated on his own scripts, mostly by providing additional dialogue. He was also the author of a sports novel and several stage plays.

FILMS: *Les Requins du Pétrole, Les Bleus du Ciel, Je vous aimerai toujours* 1933; *Toboggan* (also sc.) 1934; *Le Domino vert* 1935; *Mademoiselle ma Mère, Abus de Confiance/Abused Confidence* (also co-sc.) 1937; *Retour à l'Aube/She Returned at Dawn* 1938; *Battements de Coeur* 1940; *Premier Rendez-Vous/Her First Affair* (also sc.) 1941; *Les Inconnus dans la Maison/Strangers in the House, Mariage d'Amour* (also co-sc.), *Le Bienfaiteur* (also sc.) 1942; *L'Homme de Londres* (also sc.), *Je sui avec toi* 1943; *La Fille du Diable/Devil's Daughter* (also co-sc.) 1946; *Non Coupable/Not Guilty, Les Amants du Pont Saint-Jean* 1947; *Les Amoureux sont seuls au Monde Monelle* 1948; *Entre Onze Heures et Minuit/Between Eleven and Midnight* (also co-sc.), *Au Grand Balcon* 1949; *Trois Télégrammes/Paris Incident* (also co-sc.) 1950; *Clara de Montargis* (also sc.), *Le Désir et l'Amour* 1951; *La Vérité sur Bébé Dónge* 1952; *Les Amants de Tolède/The Lovers of Toledo, Dortoir des Grandes/Inside a Girls' Dormitory* (also co-sc.) 1953; *Secrets d'Alcôve/Il Letto/The Bed* ("The Billet" episode; also co-sc.), *Les Intrigantes* 1954; *Bonnes à tuer/One Step to Eternity* (also co-sc.), *Razziá sur la Chnouff/Razzia* (also co-sc.), *L'Affaire des Poison* (also co-sc.) 1955; *Folies-Bergère, Le Feu aux Poudres* (also sc.), *Tous peuvent me tuer* (also co-sc.) 1957; *Charmants Garçons, La Chatte/The Cat* (also co-sc.) 1958; *Pourquoi viens-tu si tard?* (also co-sc.), *Nathalie Agent secret* 1959; *La Chatte sort ses Griffes* (also co-sc.), *Tendre et Violente Elisabeth/Passionate Affair* (also co-sc.), *La Française et l'Amour/Love and the Frenchwoman* ("L'Enfance" episode) 1960; *Maléfices/Where the Truth Lies* (also co-sc.), *Le Pavé de Paris* (also co-sc.) 1961; *Le Masque de Fer* 1962; *Parias de la Gloire* 1963; *Nick Carter va tout casser* 1964.

De Cordoba, Pedro. Actor. *b.* Sept. 28, 1881, New York City, to Cuban-French parents. *d.* 1950. Tall, gaunt character player of numerous silent and sound films. A former opera basso and stage actor, on the screen he typically portrayed aristocratic Latins, often benevolent, sometimes sinister.

FILMS INCLUDE: *Carmen* (as Escamillo), *Temptation* 1915; *Maria Rosa* 1916; *Runaway Romany* 1917; *The New Moon* 1919; *The World and His Wife* 1920; *The Inner Chamber, When Knighthood Was in Flower* 1922; *The Purple Highway, Enemies of Women* 1923; *The Desert Sheik, The Bandolero* 1924; *The New Commandment* 1925; *The Crusades, Captain Blood* 1935; *Rose of the Rancho, The Devil Doll, Anthony Adverse, Ramona, The Garden of Allah* 1936; *Maid of Salem* 1937; *Juarez, The Light That Failed* 1939; *My Favorite Wife, Earthbound, The Ghost Breakers, The Sea Hawk, The Mark of Zorro* 1940; *Blood and Sand, Aloma of the South Seas* 1941; *The Corsican Brothers, Son of Fury, Saboteur* 1942; *For Whom the Bell Tolls, The Song of Bernadette* 1943; *Uncertain Glory* 1944; *The Keys of the Kingdom* 1945; *Swamp Fire* 1946; *The Beast with Five Fingers* 1947; *Samson and Delilah* 1949; *Comanche Territory, Crisis* 1950.

De Cordova, Frederick. Director. Born on Oct. 27, 1910, in New York City. *ed.* Northwestern. He came to films from the stage in 1944 as a dialogue director and graduated to full director the following year. Turned out many routine medium-budget entertainment features through the mid-60s but has been active mainly in TV since the mid-50s, producing and directing such programs as the 'Burns and Allen Show,' 'December Bride,' the 'George Gobel Show,' the 'Jack Benny Program,' the 'Smothers Brothers Show,' and 'My Three Sons.' In 1971 he became the producer of NBC's 'Tonight Show.' Memoirs: *Johnny Came Lately* (1988).

FILMS: *Too Young to Know* 1945; *Her Kind of Man* 1946; *That Way with Women, Love and Learn, Always Together* 1947; *Wallflower, For the Love of Mary, The Countess of Monte Cristo* 1948; *Illegal Entry, The Gal Who Took the West* 1949; *Buccaneer's Girl, Peggy, The Desert Hawk* 1950; *Bedtime for Bonzo, Katie Did It, Little Egypt, Finders Keepers* 1951; *Here Come the Nelsons, Bonzo Goes to College, Yankee Buccaneer* 1952; *Column South* 1953; *I'll Take Sweden* 1965; *Frankie and Johnny* 1966.

De Corsia, Ted. Actor *b.* Sept. 29, 1904, Brooklyn, N.Y. *d.* 1973. He toured in stock and performed on radio before his film debut in 1948. On the screen played numerous character roles, often as a mean, ugly villain.

FILMS INCLUDE: *The Naked City, The Lady from Shanghai* 1948; *Neptune's Daughter, It Happens Every Spring* 1949; *Cargo to Capetown* 1950; *The Enforcer, Inside the Walls of Folsom Prison, A Place in the Sun* 1951; *The Turning Point* 1952; *Man in the Dark* 1953; *Crime Wave, 20,000 Leagues Under the Sea* 1954; *The Big Combo, The Man with the Gun, Kismet* 1955; *Slightly Scarlet, The Killing, Mohawk* 1956; *Gunfight at the O.K. Corral, The Midnight Story, The Joker Is Wild, Baby Face Nelson* 1957; *Enchanted Island, The Buccaneer* 1958; *Inside the Mafia* 1959; *Oklahoma Territory, From the Terrace* 1960; *Blood on the Arrow* 1964; *Nevada Smith* 1966; *King's Pirate* 1967; *Five Card Stud* 1968; *The Delta Factor* 1970.

De Cuir, John. Art director, production designer. Born on June 4, 1918, in San Francisco. *ed.* Chouinard Art School. He joined Universal in 1938 and began designing sets in the mid-40s. In 1949 he moved over to 20th Century-Fox, where he later specialized in large-scale productions with elaborate, sometimes gaudy décors. He was nominated for Academy Awards 11 times, winning Oscars for *The King and I, Cleopatra,* and *Hello Dolly!*. His son, John De Cuir, Jr. (*b.* Aug. 4, 1941, Burbank, Calif.; *ed.* USC), is also a Hollywood production designer (*Top Gun,* etc.).

FILMS INCLUDE: *White Tie and Tails* 1946; *Brute Force* 1947; *The Naked City, Casbah* 1948; *Snows of Kilimanjaro, My Cousin Rachel, Call Me Madam* 1953; *Three Coins in the Fountain, There's No Business Like Show Business* 1954; *Daddy Long Legs* 1955; *The King and I* 1956; *Island in the Sun* 1957; *South Pacific, A Certain Smile* 1958; *The Big Fisherman* 1959; *Cleopatra* 1963; *Circus World* 1964; *The Agony and the Ecstasy* 1965; *A Man Could Get Killed* 1966; *The Taming of the Shrew* 1967; *Hello Dolly!* 1969; *On a Clear Day You Can See Forever* 1970; *Once Is Not Enough* 1975; *That's Entertainment Part 2* 1976; *The Other Side of Midnight* 1977; *Love and Bullets* (UK) 1979; *Raise the Titanic!* 1980; *Monsignor, Dead Men Don't Wear Plaid* 1982; *Ghostbusters* 1984; *Legal Eagles* 1986.

Dee, Frances. Actress. Born Jean Dee, on Nov. 26, 1907, in Los Angeles. *ed.* U. of Chicago. Starting in films as an extra in 1929, she rose to prominence the following year as Maurice Chevalier's co-star in *Playboy of Paris* and went on to play lovely leading ladies and second leads in many Hollywood productions through the early 50s. She married one of her screen partners, Joel McCrea, in 1933.

FILMS INCLUDE: *Words and Music* (extra) 1929; *Follow Thru* (bit), *Playboy of Paris, Along Came Youth* 1930; *June Moon, An American Tragedy, Rich Man's Folly* 1931; *This Reckless Age, Nice Women, Love Is a Racket, The Night of June 13th, If I Had a Million* 1932; *King of the Jungle, The Silver Cord, Blood Money, Little Women* 1933; *Coming Out Party, Finishing School, Of Human Bondage* 1934; *Becky Sharp, The Gay Deception* 1935; *Half Angel* 1936; *Souls at Sea, Wells Fargo* 1937; *If I Were King* 1938; *Coast Guard* 1939; *So Ends*

Our Night, A Man Betrayed 1941; *Meet the Stewarts* 1942; *I Walked with a Zombie, Happy Land* 1943; *Patrick the Great* 1945; *The Private Affairs of Bel-Ami* 1947; *Four Faces West* 1948; *Payment on Demand* 1951; *Because of You* 1952; *Mister Scoutmaster* 1953; *Gypsy Colt* 1954.

Dee, Ruby. Actress. Born Ruby Ann Wallace, on Oct. 27, 1923, in Cleveland. *ed.* Hunter Coll. The daughter of a railroad porter and a schoolteacher, she grew up in Harlem, where she began her acting career with the American Negro Theatre. Her 1946 Broadway debut, in 'Anna Lucasta,' was unanimously praised by the critics. She has since appeared in many other plays and on numerous TV programs. In films since the early 50s, she has played increasingly more important roles, particularly in films involving the race issue. She and her husband since 1948, Ossie DAVIS, have been active in various civil rights and humanitarian causes.

FILMS: *No Way Out, The Jackie Robinson Story* 1950; *The Tall Target* 1951; *Go Man Go!* 1954; *Edge of the City* 1957; *St. Louis Blues* 1958; *Take a Giant Step, Virgin Island* 1960; *A Raisin in the Sun* 1961; *Gone Are the Days!/Purlie Victorious, The Balcony* 1963; *The Incident* 1967; *Uptight* (also co-sc.) 1968; *Buck and the Preacher, Black Girl* (cameo) 1972; *Countdown at Kusini* (US/Nigeria) 1976; *Do the Right Thing* 1988; *Just Cause* 1995.

Dee, Sandra. Actress. Born Alexandra Zuck, on Apr. 23, 1942, in Bayonne, N.J. A model while still in grade school, she later broke into TV and made her film debut before her 15th birthday. Popular with young audiences, she starred in many teenage-oriented productions, typically playing cute, glamorous nymphets on the threshold of romantic maturity. She was married to teen idol Bobby DARIN.

FILMS INCLUDE: *Until They Sail* 1957; *The Reluctant Debutante, The Restless Years* 1958; *Imitation of Life, Gidget, A Summer Place* 1959; *A Portrait in Black* 1960; *Romanoff and Juliet, Tammy Tell Me True, Come September* 1961; *If a Man Answers* 1962; *Tammy and the Doctor, Take Her She's Mine* 1963; *I'd Rather Be Rich* 1964; *That Funny Feeling* 1965; *A Man Could Get Killed* 1966; *Rosie!* 1968; *The Dunwich Horror* 1970; *Ad est di Marsa Matruh* (It.) 1971.

Deed, André. Actor. *b.* André Chapuis, 1884, Le Havre, France. *d.* 1938. A former revue and music hall singer and acrobat, he entered French films in 1905 and before long became one of the screen's first popular comic stars. His popularity was international, and as was the case with other early screen comedians in the silent era, he was known in different countries by different names, often after the character he played in films. In France he was known as Boireau or Gribouille, in Italy as Cretinetti, in the Spanish-speaking world as Torribo or Sanchez, and in the English-speaking world as Foolshead or Jim. He remained popular through 1915 but continued appearing occasionally in films through 1928. He died poor and forgotten ten years later.

FILMS INCLUDE: *Boireau déménage* 1905; *Le Chevalier Mystère* 1907; *L'Homme Singe* 1908; *Cretinetti alla Guerra* (It.) 1909; *Boireau domestique* 1913; *Cretinetti e le Donne* (It.) 1915; *Graine au Vent* 1928.

deep focus. Sharp definition of all objects in front of a camera, both far and near, in the same shot. The effective range in which ordinary camera lenses can produce images in focus is limited by the laws of DEPTH OF FIELD. But the development of a deep-focus lens late in the 30s opened new possibilities for directors and cameramen. Director of photography Gregg TOLAND explored those new possibilities with great effectiveness in the 40s, most notably in Orson Welles's *Citizen Kane* (1941) and William Wyler's *The Best Years of Our Lives* (1946). By using a deep-focus shot, a director may comment visually on relationships between characters and events situated at different planes without resorting to an interruptive cut or unnecessarily moving his camera to cover the entire scene. See also BAZIN, André.

DEFA (Deutsche Film Aktien Gesellschaft). East Germany's state-owned film organization, an umbrella under which all the country's studios operated until the unification with West Germany in 1990. The enormous DEFA Film Studio Babelsberg, comprising 107 acres near Berlin, was sold in 1991 to Compagnie Générale des Eaux, a French real estate and media company. See also GERMANY.

De Filippo, Eduardo. Director, playwright, screenwriter, actor. *b.* Eduardo Passarelli, May 24, 1900, Naples. *d.* 1984. The son of a famous Neapolitan actor, he absorbed the atmosphere of the stage from early childhood and at 13 joined the Neapolitan dialect company of Eduardo Scarpetta. In 1932 he founded a highly successful stage company, along with brother Peppino De Filippo (1903–80) and sister Tina De Filippo (1898–1963) and enjoyed great popularity as a comic actor, director, producer, and dramatist. He was one of Italy's foremost playwrights. Several of his more than 50 plays, typically boisterous, lusty comedies inspired by *commedia dell'arte* and reflecting the lively spirit of the people of Naples, have been performed on the London and New York stages and in theaters throughout the Western world. While continuing their stage activity, the De Filippos brought the traditions of the Neapolitan theater to the Italian screen in 1933 when they began a series of appearances in films, but they separated after WW II.

Eduardo branched into film directing in 1940 and through the late 50s turned out a group of amiable films, in all of which he also acted and for most of which he also collaborated on the screenplay. Several of his films as director-actor-screenwriter were based on his own plays, notably *Napoli Milionaria, Filumena Marturano,* and *Questi Fantasmi.* He also collaborated on the scripts of De Sica's *Yesterday Today and Tomorrow* (1963) and *Marriage Italian Style* (1964). The latter was a refilming of his own play 'Filumena Marturano.'

FILMS INCLUDE: As actor only—*Tre Uomini in Frak* 1933; *Il Cappello a tre Punte* 1934; *Sono stato io!/It Was I!* 1937; *Ma l'Amor mio non Muore* 1938; *Il Sogno di tutti* 1940; *La Vita ricomincia/Life Begins Anew* 1945; *Assunta Spina/Scarred* (also sc.) 1947; *Altri Tempi/Times Gone By* 1951; *Le Ragazze di Piazza di Spagna/Three Girls from Rome* 1952; *Villa Borghese* 1953; *L'Oro di Napoli/Gold of Naples* 1954; *Raw Wind in Eden* (US) 1958; *Fantasmi a Roma/Ghosts of Rome, It Happened in the Park, Tutti a Casa/Everybody Go Home!* 1960. As director-actor-screenwriter (complete)—*In Campagna è caduta una Stella* 1940; *Ti conosco Mascherina!* 1943; *Napoli Milionaria/Side Street Story* 1950; *Filumena Marturano* 1951; *I Sette Peccati Capitali/Les Sept Péchés capitaux/Seven Capital Sins* ("Avarice" and "Anger" episodes), *Marito e Moglie/Husband and Wife, Ragazze da Marito* 1952; *Napoletani a Milano* 1953; *Questi Fantasmi* 1954; *Fortunella* (dir.-act. only) 1958; *Il Sogno di una Notte di Mezza Sbornia* (dir.-act. only) 1959; *Oggi Domani Dopodomani/Kiss the Other Sheik* ("L'Ora di Punta" episode; dir., sc. only) 1965; *Spara Forte. . . più Forte. . . non capisco/Shoot Loud. . . Louder. . . I Don't Understand* 1966.

definition. The sharpness and clarity of detail of a photographed image. The defining power of a lens is determined by its ability to form sharp and detailed images by concentrating or dispersing rays of light from an object.

Defore, Don. Actor. *b.* Aug. 25, 1917, Cedar Rapids, Iowa. *d.* 1993. *ed.* U. of Iowa; Pasadena Community School Theater.

After some experience in stock, he made his screen debut in 1937 and his Broadway bow the following year. During the 40s and the 50s he played some leads and many second leads in Hollywood films, typically as a smiling, gullible, urbanized yokel. He was a regular on the TV series 'Ozzie and Harriet' and 'Hazel.'

FILMS INCLUDE: *Kid Galahad* 1937; *Brother Rat* 1938; *We Go Fast* 1941; *The Male Animal* 1942; *The Human Comedy, A Guy Named Joe* 1943; *Thirty Seconds Over Tokyo* 1944; *The Affairs of Susan, You Came Along, The Stork Club* 1945; *Without Reservations* 1946; *It Happened on Fifth Avenue, Ramrod* 1947; *Romance on the High Seas, One Sunday Afternoon* 1948; *Too Late for Tears, My Friend Irma* 1949; *Dark City, Southside 1-1000* 1950; *A Girl in Every Port, No Room for the Groom, Jumping Jacks* 1952; *Battle Hymn* 1957; *A Time to Live and a Time to Die* 1958; *The Facts of Life* 1960; *A Rare Breed* 1981.

De Forest, Lee. Inventor. *b.* Aug. 26, 1873, in Council Bluffs, Iowa. *d.* 1961. Many of his 300 patented inventions contributed to the development of motion pictures, radio, and TV, including a method of synchronizing sound on film (Phonofilm), which he introduced in 1923, dubbing and blooping systems, and a camera blimp. The Motion Picture Academy awarded him a special Oscar, during the 1960 ceremony, "for his pioneering inventions which brought sound to the motion picture."

De Fuentes, Fernando. Director. *b.* Dec. 13, 1895, Vera Cruz, Mexico. *d.* 1958. A leading figure in the fertile years of the Mexican cinema of the 30s. A former movie-house manager and film editor, he began directing in the early 30s and before long became established as one of his country's foremost filmmakers. Several of his films dealt passionately with the experience of the Mexican revolution, focusing on such heroes as Pancho Villa and Emiliano Zapata. Many others were traditional popular entertainment fare, including Mexico's first color film, *Así se quiere en Jalisco* (1942), which enjoyed worldwide distribution.

FILMS INCLUDE: *El Anónimo* 1932; *El Prisionero 13, La Calandria, El Tigre de Yautepec, El Compadre Mendoza* 1933; *El Fantasma del Convento, Cruz Diablo* 1934; *Vamónos con Pancho Villa/Let's Go with Pancho Villa, La Familia Dressel* 1935; *Allá en el Rancho Grande/Rancho Grande* 1936; *Bajo el Cielo de México/Beneath the Sky of Mexico, La Zandunga* 1937; *La Casa del Ogro/The House of the Ogre* 1938; *Papacito lindo/Sugar Daddy* 1939; *Allá en el Tropico* 1940; *Creo en Dios* 1941; *Así se quiere en Jalisco* 1942; *Doña Barbara* 1943; *El Rey se divierte* 1944; *La Selva de Fuego* 1945; *La Devorada* 1946; *Allá en el Rancho Grande* (remake) 1948; *Crimen y Castigo/Crime and Punishment* 1950; *Canión de Cuña* 1952; *Tres Citas con el Destino* 1953.

de Funès, Louis. See FUNÈS, Louis de.

De Grasse, Joseph. Director. *b.* 1873, Bathurst, N.B., Canada. *d.* 1940. The elder brother of Sam DE GRASSE, he started out as a journalist and a stage actor and entered films in 1910 as an actor in early silents. Several years later he switched to directing and turned out melodramas and action pictures until the mid-20s, including many of Lon Chaney's early vehicles. He then returned briefly to acting and among other roles played the lead opposite Colleen Moore in *So Big* (1925).

FILMS INCLUDE: *All for Peggy, Father and the Boys* 1915; *The Grip of Jealousy, Tangled Hearts, The Gilded Spider, The Grasp of Greed, The Mark of Cain, The Place Beyond the Winds, The Price of Silence* 1916; *Hell Morgan's Girl, A Doll's House, Pay Me/The Vengeance of the West* (also story), *Triumph, Anything Once, The Winged Mystery* 1917; *The Rough Lover, A Broadway Scandal, After the War, The Wildcat of Paris* 1918; *The Market of Souls, L'Apache* 1919; *The Brand of Lopez, Forty-Five Minutes from Broadway* 1920; *Bonnie May* (co-dir.), *The Midlanders* (co-dir.), *The Old Swimmin' Hole* 1921; *A Tailor Made Man* 1922; *The Girl I Loved, Thundergate* 1923; *Flowing Gold* 1924; *The Hidden Way* 1926.

De Grasse, Robert. Director of photography. *b.* Feb. 9, 1900, Maplewood, N.J. *d.* 1971. *ed.* USC. A nephew of film director Joseph DE GRASSE and actor Sam DE GRASSE, he joined Universal as a camera assistant while still a student and was a full-fledged cinematographer by the time he reached 21. During the 20s he worked mostly on low-budget action silents, but when sound came in he was downgraded to camera operator, reputedly at his own request. He was back again as a director of photography in the mid-30s and subsequently photographed many of RKO's more prestigious productions.

FILMS INCLUDE: *Desperate Trails* (co-phot.) 1921; *Crashin' Thru* (co-phot.) 1923; *Three Pals* 1926; *Beyond London Lights* 1928; *Fury of the Wild* 1929; *Break of Hearts, Alice Adams, Freckles, Seven Keys to Baldpate* 1935; *A Woman Rebels, Quality Street* 1936; *The Outcasts of Poker Flat, Stage Door* 1937; *Vivacious Lady, Carefree, Having Wonderful Time* 1938; *The Story of Vernon and Irene Castle, Bachelor Mother, Fifth Avenue Girl* 1939; *Vigil in the Night, Kitty Foyle* 1940; *My Favorite Spy, Pittsburgh* 1942; *Forever and a Day* (co-phot.), *Lady of Burlesque, The Leopard Man* 1943; *Tall in the Saddle, Step Lively* 1944; *The Body Snatcher* 1945; *Badman's Territory, Crack-Up* 1946; *The Bachelor and the Bobby-Soxer* 1947; *Miracle of the Bells* 1948; *Home of the Brave, The Window* 1949; *The Men* 1950; *The First Legion* 1951; *Marry Me Again* 1953.

De Grasse, Sam. Actor. *b.* 1875, Bathurst, N.B., Canada. *d.* 1953. One of the meanest, slimiest, and most convincing villains of the silent screen. Entering films in 1912, he initially played some romantic leads, occasionally opposite Lillian Gish. But he was best suited for dastardly roles. He played the ruthless adversary to many a hero. He was particularly memorable in the adventure films of Douglas FAIRBANKS. Brother of Joseph DE GRASSE.

FILMS INCLUDE: *The Beat of the Year* 1914; *The Birth of a Nation* (as Senator Charles Sumner), *The Martyrs of the Alamo* 1915; *The Good Bad Man, An Innocent Magdalene, The Half-Breed, Intolerance, Diane of the Follies* 1916; *Jim Bludso, Wild and Woolly, The Winged Mystery* 1917; *The Narrow Path* 1918; *Sis Hopkins, Heart of the Hills, Blind Husbands* 1919; *The Devil's Passkey* 1920; *Courage* 1921; *Robin Hood* (as Prince John), *Forsaking All Others* 1922; *Circus Days, The Spoilers, In the Palace of the King* (as King Philip II of Spain), *Tiger Rose, The Courtship of Miles Standish* 1923; *Painted People, The Virgin* 1924; *One Year to Live, Sally Irene and Mary* 1925; *The Black Pirate, Broken Hearts of Hollywood, The Eagle of the Sea, Love's Blindness* 1926; *When a Man Loves, The Fighting Eagle* (as Talleyrand), *The Country Doctor, The King of Kings* (as the Pharisee), *The Wreck of the Hesperus* (lead) 1927; *The Man Who Laughs* (as King James II), *The Racket, Our Dancing Daughters* 1928; *The Last Performance* (release delayed from 1927), *Wall Street* 1929; *Captain of the Guard* 1930.

De Grunwald, Anatole. Producer, screenwriter, playwright. *b.* Dec. 25, 1910, St. Petersburg, Russia. *d.* 1967. *ed.* Cambridge; Sorbonne. The son of a Czarist diplomat, he escaped to England as a child during the Revolution. At first a journalist, he entered British films as a screenwriter in 1939 and from 1943 also doubled as a producer. He became the director of Two Cities, then formed his own production company in

1946, often collaborating with his younger brother, producer Dimitri de Grunwald.

FILMS INCLUDE: As screenwriter only—*French Without Tears* 1939; *Freedom Radio, Quiet Wedding* 1940; *Jeannie, Pimpernel Smith/Mister V* 1941; *A Day Will Dawn/The Avengers, Tomorrow We Live/At Dawn We Die, The First of the Few/Spitfire* 1942. As producer-writer—*The Demi-Paradise/ Adventure for Two* 1943; *The Way to the Stars/Johnny in the Clouds* 1945; *English Without Tears/Her Man Gilbey* (co-sc. only) 1946; *Bond Street* 1947; *The Winslow Boy* 1948; *The Queen of Spades* (prod. only), *The Last Days of Dolwyn/Dolwyn* (prod. only) 1949; *The Holly and the Ivy* 1952; *Innocents in Paris* (prod. only) 1953; *The Doctor's Dilemma* 1958; *Libel* 1959; *Come Fly with Me* (prod. only), *The V.I.P.s* (prod. only) 1963; *The Yellow Rolls-Royce* (prod. only) 1964; *Stranger in the House/Cop-Out* (exec. prod. only) 1967.

DeHaven, Carter. Actor, director. *b.* 1896, Chicago. *d.* 1977. Popular, versatile figure of vaudeville, the legitimate stage, and films. He entered films in his late teens and appeared in many silent productions, often opposite his wife, the former Flora Parker. He also directed and produced several films as well as many stage plays and was Chaplin's assistant on *Modern Times* (1936). Father of Gloria DEHAVEN and producer Carter DeHaven, Jr.

FILMS INCLUDE: As actor—*The College Orphan* 1915; *Get the Boy, From Broadway to a Throne* 1916; *Close to Nature, Why Divorce?* 1919; *Beating Cheaters, Twin Beds* 1920; *Marry the Poor Girl, My Lady Friends* 1922; *A Ring for Dad* 1923; *The Great Dictator* 1940; *The Notorious Landlady* 1962. As director—*The Wrong Door, A Gentleman of Nerve* 1916; *The Losing Winner* 1917; *What Could Be Sweeter?* 1920; *The Panic's On* 1922; *Say It with Diamonds* 1923.

DeHaven, Gloria. Actress. Born July 23, 1924, Los Angeles. The daughter of popular entertainers Carter DEHAVEN and Flora Parker, she accompanied her parents on the vaudeville circuit as a child. At 11 she appeared as an extra in Chaplin's *Modern Times* (1936), on which her father worked as assistant director. She played bits in other films during her teens and later made her name as a vocalist with the Bob Crosby and Jan Savitt bands. In the early 40s she joined MGM as a starlet and was soon being featured regularly in the studio's musicals, typically as a vivacious, glamorous lead or second lead. Her career slipped in the 50s with the decline of the screen musical, but she continued appearing on the stage and in TV. Her first (1944–50) of several husbands was actor John PAYNE. She was the sister of the late producer Carter DeHaven, Jr.

FILMS INCLUDE: *Modern Times* (extra) 1936; *The Great Dictator* (extra), *Susan and God* 1940; *The Penalty, Two-Faced Woman* (bit) 1941; *Best Foot Forward, Thousands Cheer* 1943; *Broadway Rhythm, Two Girls and a Sailor, Step Lively, The Thin Man Goes Home* 1944; *Between Two Women* 1945; *Summer Holiday* 1948; *Scene of the Crime, The Doctor and the Girl, Yes Sir That's My Baby* 1949; *The Yellow Cab Man, Three Little Words* (as her mother, Flora Parker DeHaven), *Summer Stock, I'll Get By* 1950; *Two Tickets to Broadway* 1951; *Down Among the Sheltering Palms* 1953; *So This Is Paris, The Girl Rush* 1955; *Won Ton Ton—The Dog Who Saved Hollywood* (cameo) 1976; *Bog* 1978; *Evening in Byzantium* 1979; *Out to Sea* 1997.

de Havilland, Olivia. Actress. Born on July 1, 1916, in Tokyo. *ed.* Notre Dame Convent (Belmont, Calif.), Mills Coll. The daughter of a British patent attorney and a former actress, she was brought to California at age three by her mother, after her parents' divorce, along with her younger sister, Joan FONTAINE. While a freshman in college (in 1933) Miss de Havilland appeared in a local production of 'A Midsummer Night's Dream' and was chosen by Max Reinhardt to play Hermia in both his stage (Hollywood Bowl, 1934) and screen (Warner Bros., 1935) versions of the play. She was then signed by Warners to a seven-year contract and went on to play delicate, sweetly appealing heroines in films dominated by the personality of some of the studio's top male stars, particularly Errol Flynn, whose romantic partner she was in many an adventure yarn. In a marked departure from her customary passive roles, she was cast as Melanie in *Gone With the Wind* (1939), on loan-out to Selznick, and showed considerable dramatic ability in a demanding part. Back at Warners, she rebelled for better roles there and was put on a six-month suspension. When Warners wouldn't release her from her contract at the end of the seven-year term, claiming her obligation should be extended for the duration of the suspension, she sued the studio and won a landmark decision that set the outside limit of a studio-player contract at seven years, including periods of suspension.

Miss de Havilland, absent from the screen for the three-year duration of the court battle, celebrated her comeback in 1946 with an Academy Award–winning performance in *To Each His Own.* She won another best actress Oscar in 1949 for *The Heiress.* She was also chosen best actress two years in succession (1948 and 1949) by the New York Film Critics for her performances in *The Snake Pit* and *The Heiress,* and was nominated for Oscars for *Gone With the Wind* (1939), *Hold Back the Dawn* (1941), and *The Snake Pit* (1948). She also won the Venice Festival prize for the latter. Just when she was becoming established as one of Hollywood's leading dramatic actresses, she left the screen temporarily for Broadway, returning only sporadically to films, and never regained her hard-earned stature. Having divorced novelist Marcus Goodrich, her husband since 1946, she married Pierre Galante, the editor of *Paris Match,* in 1955, and moved to France. She recollected her life in Paris in the book *Every Frenchman Has One* (a liver, not a mistress). She has since appeared in a handful of films, mostly shot in Europe but some in Hollywood, and has made occasional appearances on Broadway and American TV.

FILMS: *A Midsummer Night's Dream, Alibi Ike, The Irish in Us, Captain Blood* 1935; *Anthony Adverse, The Charge of the Light Brigade* 1936; *Call It a Day, The Great Garrick, It's Love I'm After* 1937; *Gold Is Where You Find It, The Adventures of Robin Hood, Four's a Crowd, Hard to Get* 1938; *Wings of the Navy, Dodge City, The Private Lives of Elizabeth and Essex, Gone With the Wind* 1939; *Raffles, My Love Came Back, Santa Fe Trail* 1940; *Strawberry Blonde, Hold Back the Dawn, They Died with Their Boots On* 1941; *The Male Animal, In This Our Life* 1942; *Thank Your Lucky Stars* (cameo), *Princess O'Rourke, Government Girl* 1943; *Devotion, The Well-Groomed Bride, To Each His Own, The Dark Mirror* 1946; *The Snake Pit* 1948; *The Heiress* 1949; *My Cousin Rachel* 1953; *That Lady, Not as a Stranger* 1955; *The Ambassador's Daughter* 1956; *The Proud Rebel* 1958; *Libel* (UK) 1959; *The Light in the Piazza* 1962; *Lady in a Cage* 1964; *Hush Hush. . . Sweet Charlotte* 1965; *The Adventures* 1970; *Pope Joan* (UK) 1972; *The Fifth Musketeer/ Behind the Iron Mask, Airport '77* 1977; *The Swarm* 1978.

Dehn, Paul. Screenwriter, playwright, lyricist, film critic. *b.* Nov. 5, 1912, in Manchester, England. *d.* 1976. *ed.* Oxford. A prolific and versatile writer, he began reviewing films for London daily newspapers in 1936 and subsequently authored plays, opera librettos, poetry, and books and lyrics for stage musicals. He shared an Oscar for his very first work in film, as co-author (with James Bernard) of the original story of *Seven Days to Noon* (1951). Later wrote many screenplays, alone and in collaboration, as well as lyrics to screen songs, and in 1958 won the British Film Academy Award for the script of *Orders to Kill*.

FILMS INCLUDE (as screenwriter): *Seven Days to Noon* (co-story only) 1951; *Moulin Rouge* (lyrics only) 1952; *I Am a Camera* (lyrics only) 1955; *Orders to Kill* 1958; *The Innocents* (lyrics only) 1961; *Goldfinger* (co-sc.) 1964; *The Spy Who Came in from the Cold* (co-sc.) 1965; *The Deadly Affair* 1966; *The Night of the Generals* (co-sc.), *The Taming of the Shrew* (co-sc.) 1967; *Beneath the Planet of the Apes* (also co-story), *Fragment of Fear* (also assoc. prod.) 1970; *Escape from the Planet of the Apes* 1971; *Conquest of the Planet of the Apes* 1972; *Battle for the Planet of the Apes* (story only) 1973; *Murder on the Orient Express* 1974.

Dekker, Albert. Actor. *b.* Albert van Dekker, Dec. 20, 1904, Brooklyn, N.Y. *d.* 1968. *ed.* Bowdoin Coll. On the stage from 1927, he was an established Broadway actor by the time he made his screen debut in 1937. Tall and husky, he played strong character roles, often as a menacing villain. Memorable in the title role of *Dr. Cyclops* (1940). In 1945–46 he served a term in the California legislature as a Democratic assemblyman from the Hollywood district. In the 60s he was busier on the stage than in films, both as actor and director, and lectured in colleges on poetry and drama. His death from suffocation was believed to be a suicide but was ruled an accident.

FILMS INCLUDE: *The Great Garrick* 1937; *Marie Antoinette* 1938; *The Man in the Iron Mask* (as King Louis XIII), *Beau Geste* 1939; *Dr. Cyclops* (title role), *Strange Cargo, Seven Sinners* 1940; *Honky Tonk, Among the Living* (dual-role lead) 1941; *Wake Island, Once Upon a Honeymoon* 1942; *In Old Oklahoma, The Woman of the Town* 1943; *Experiment Perilous* 1944; *Salome—Where She Danced, Incendiary Blonde, Hold That Blonde* 1945; *Suspense, The Killers, Two Years Before the Mast* 1946; *California, Slave Girl, The Pretender* (title role), *Cass Timberlane, Gentleman's Agreement* 1947; *Fury at Furnace Creek* 1948; *Tarzan's Magic Fountain* 1949; *The Furies* 1950; *As Young As You Feel* 1951; *Wait Till the Sun Shines Nellie* 1952; *The Silver Chalice* 1954; *East of Eden, Kiss Me Deadly, Illegal* 1955; *She Devil* 1957; *These Thousand Hills, Middle of the Night, The Wonderful Country, Suddenly Last Summer* 1959; *Come Spy with Me* 1967; *The Wild Bunch* 1969.

De La Motte, Marguerite. Actress. *b.* June 22, 1902, Duluth, Minn. *d.* 1950. Petite brunette star of Hollywood silents. Trained as a dancer, supposedly under Pavlova, she entered films in 1918 and rose to fame as the love interest in several Douglas FAIRBANKS productions. She starred in many silents of the 20s but played only minor roles in occasional talkies. She was married to actor John BOWERS.

FILMS INCLUDE: *Arizona* 1918; *The Pagan God, For a Woman's Honor, A Sage Brush Hamlet* 1919; *The Hope, The Mark of Zorro* 1920; *The Nut, The Three Musketeers* (as Constance) 1921; *Shattered Idols, The Jilt, Shadows* 1922; *What a Wife Learned, The Famous Mrs. Fair, Scars of Jealousy, Just Like a Woman, Wandering Daughters, Desire, Richard the Lion-Hearted* 1923; *Behold This Woman, The Beloved Brute, East of Broadway, Those Who Dare, In Love with Love* 1924; *Cheaper to Marry, Flattery, Daughters Who Pay, Children of the Whirlwind, The People vs. Nancy Preston* 1925; *Fifth Avenue, Red Dice, The Unknown Soldier, Meet the Prince, The Last Frontier, Pals in Paradise* 1926; *The Final Extra, The Kid Sister, Ragtime, Broadway Madness* 1927; *The Iron Mask* (as Constance), *Montmartre Rose* 1929; *Shadow Ranch* 1930; *A Woman's Man* 1934; *Reg'lar Fellers* 1942.

Delannoy, Jean. Director. Born on Jan. 12, 1908, in Noisy-le-Sec, France. *ed.* Lille U. The son of a bureaucrat and brother of silent screen actress Henriette Delannoy, he entered French films in the late 20s as an actor and in the early 30s became a feature editor and a director of shorts. A feature director since 1935, he asserted himself in the 40s with such fine, sensitive productions as *L'Eternel Retour* and *La Symphonie Pastorale* and won the Grand Prix for the latter at the 1946 Cannes Festival. He shared the International Prize at the Venice Festival for *God Needs Men*. He gained a reputation for technical excellence and meticulous craftsmanship, but his films of the 50s and 60s were for the most part routine thrillers, historical epics, and melodramas with little to say. In the late 50s his work was the subject of ferocious attacks by the young critics of the French New Wave, who accused him of emotional frigidity. From the early 70s he engaged mainly in TV work, but he returned to the big screen after a long absence in 1988.

FEATURE FILMS: *Paris-Deauville* 1935; *La Vénus de l'Or* (also co-sc.) 1938; *Le Diamant noir, Macao L'Enfer de Jeu* 1940; *Fièvres* 1941; *L'Assassin a peur la Nuit, Pontacarral Colonel d'Empire* 1942; *L'Eternel Retour/The Eternal Return* 1943; *Le Bossu* 1944; *La Part de l'Ombre/Blind Desire* (also co-sc.) 1945; *La Symphonie Pastorale* (also co-sc.) 1946; *Les Jeux sont faits/The Chips Are Down* (also co-sc.) 1947; *Aux Yeux du Souvenir/Souvenir* (also co-sc.), *Le Secret de Mayerling* (also co-sc.) 1949; *Dieux a besoin des Hommes/God Needs Men* 1950; *Le Garçon sauvage/Savage Triangle* 1951; *La Minute de Vérité/The Moment of Truth* 1952; *Destinées/Daughters of Destiny* ("Joan of Arc" episode), *Secrets d'Alcôve, Il Letto/The Bed* ("Pompadour Bed" episode; also co-sc.), *La Route Napoléon* 1953; *Obsession* (also co-sc.) 1954; *Chiens perdus sans Collier* (also co-sc.) 1955; *Marie Antoinette, Notre Dame de Paris/The Hunchback of Notre Dame* 1956; *Maigret tend un Piège/Inspector Maigret* (also co-sc.) 1958; *Guinguette* (also co-sc.), *Maigret et l'Affaire Saint-Fiacre* (also co-sc.) 1959; *Le Baron de l'Ecluse* (also co-sc.), *La Française et l'Amour/Love and the Frenchwoman* ("Adolescence" episode) 1960; *La Princesse de Clèves, Le Rendez-Vous* (also co-sc.) 1961; *Vénus impériale* 1962; *Les Amitiés particulières/This Special Friendship* 1964; *Le lit à deux Places/The Double Bed* (co-dir.), *Le Majordôme* 1965; *Les Sultans* (also co-sc.) 1966; *Le Soleil des Voyous/Action Man* (also co-sc.) 1967; *La Peau de Torpédo* (also co-sc.) 1970; *Pas Folle la Guêpe* (also co-sc.) 1972; *Bernadette* (also co-sc.) 1988; *The Hunchback of Notre Dame, God Needs Men* 1990; *Special Friendship* 1992.

De Laurentiis, Dino. Producer. Born on Aug. 8, 1919, in Torre Annuziata, Italy. The son of a Naples pasta manufacturer, he left home at 17 to enroll at Rome's Centro Sperimentale di Cinematografia. He supported himself as an extra, actor, prop-man, unit manager, and assistant director and by the time he was 20 produced his first film. Temporarily sidetracked by WW II military service, he returned to production in 1946 and scored an international box-office hit by combining eroticism with neorealism in *Bitter Rice* (1948). The film launched the screen career of its sensuous star, Silvana MANGANO, who became his wife in 1949. In the early 50s he joined forces with Carlo PONTI to form the Ponti-De Laurentiis production company, which produced a number of major films, including Fellini's *La Strada* (1954) and *The Nights of Cabiria* (1956), both winners of best foreign film Oscars. But the partnership was dissolved in 1957. De Laurentiis then turned to the production of expensive international spectacles and in the early 60s built Dinocittà, an enormous studio complex near Rome, as a production base for his epics. However, the crisis in the Italian film industry and the failure of his epics to make money forced him to close down the studios, and in the early 70s he sold them to the Italian government and moved his base of operations to the United States.

Working out of New York and Hollywood, he enjoyed initial success at the box office. But his company, De Laurentiis Entertainment Group (DEG), and its Wilmington, North Carolina, studios, were crippled badly by a string of big-budget flops (*Tai-Pan, Dune,* etc.) in the mid-80s. In 1988 De Laurentiis was forced to resign as chairman of the board and soon after DEG filed for bankruptcy. His daughter, Raffaella De Laurentiis, is an independent producer serving as DEG's head of production.

FILMS INCLUDE (as producer or executive producer): *L'Amore canta* 1941; *Il Bandito* 1946; *La Figlia del Capitano* 1947; *Riso Amaro/Bitter Rice* 1948; *Il Lupo della Sila/Lure of the Sila* 1949; *Il Brigante Musolino* 1950; *Anna, Guardie Ladri* 1951; *Europa '51* in 1952; *Ulisse/Ulysses, Mambo, La Strada* 1954; *L'Oro di Napoli/Gold of Naples, Guendalina, La Bella Mugnaia/The Miller's Beautiful Wife* 1955; *War and Peace, Le Notti di Cabiria/Cabiria/Nights of Cabiria* 1956; *La Diga sul Pacifico/This Angry Age, The Sea Wall* 1957; *La Tempesta/Tempest* 1958; *La Grande Guerra/Great War, Giovanna e le altre/Five Branded Women* 1959; *Tutti a Casa/Everybody Go Home* 1960; *I due Nemici/The Best of Enemies, Barabba/Barabbas* 1961; *Il Mafioso* 1963; *La Bibbia/The Bible* 1966; *Lo Straniero/The Stranger* 1967; *Lo Sbarco di Anzio/Anzio, Barbarella* 1968; *Waterloo* 1970; *Joe Valachi—i segreti di Cosa Nostra/The Valachi Papers* 1972; *The Stone Killer, Serpico* 1973; *Death Wish, Casanova* 1974; *Three Days of the Condor, Mandingo* 1975; *Drum, King Kong* 1976; *Orca, The White Buffalo, The Serpent's Egg* (Ger./US) 1977; *Hurricane, The Brink's Job, King of the Gypsies* 1978; *Hurricane* 1979; *Flash Gordon* 1980; *Ragtime* 1981; *Conan the Barbarian* 1982; *The Dead Zone* 1983; *The Bounty, Dune, Silver Bullet, Year of the Dragon* 1985; *Tai-Pan, Blue Velvet, Crimes of the Heart* 1986; *The Bedroom Window, Million Dollar Mystery* 1987; *Desperate Hours* 1990; *Kuffs, Once Upon a Crime* 1992; *Body of Evidence* 1993; *Assassins* 1995; *Daylight, Unforgettable* 1996; *Breakdown* 1997.

Del Carril, Hugo. Actor, director, producer. *b.* Piero Bruno Ugo Fontana, Nov. 30, 1912, Buenos Aires. *d.* 1989. A major figure in Argentine cinema, he first gained popularity on radio as an announcer and tango singer. He made his film debut in 1936 as an actor-singer in *Los Muchachos de Antes no usban Gomina* and quickly developed into one of the most beloved entertainers of the Argentine screen with such films as *Life Is a Tango* and *La Cumparsita.* After costarring with Eva Perón in *La Cabalgata del Circo* ("The Circus Cavalcade," 1945), he became an admirer and protégé of Argentine President Juan Perón, and his career became closely linked to the rise and fall of the Peronist regime. Making his debut as a director in 1949, Del Carril three years later turned out one of the most important of all Argentine films, *La Aguas bajan turbias,* a technically superior production that candidly exposed exploitative conditions of rural workers. Amazingly, Perón approved the project, which was based on a novel by a Communist writer he himself had put in jail. The film received a Special Mention by international critics at the 1952 Venice Festival. Del Carril went on to make a dozen more films but he found opportunities limited after the fall of Perón in 1955. When the dictator returned to power in 1973, he appointed Del Carril as head of the National Film Institute, but Perón's death in 1976 spelled the end of the director's career. Del Carril's second wife was actress Ana Maria Lynch, who appeared in a couple of Hollywood films of the early 60s under the name Ana St. Clair.

FILMS INCLUDE (as director-actor): *Historia del 900* 1949; *Sucros de Sangre* 1950; *Las Aguas bajan turbias/Dark River/The River of Blood* 1952; *La Quintrala* 1955; *Una Cita con la Vida* (dir. only) 1958; *Las Tierras blancas, Culpable* 1959; *Esta Tierra es mia* 1960; *Amorina* 1961; *Yo maté a Facundo* 1975.

Delerue, Georges. Composer. *b.* Mar. 12, 1925, Roubaix, France. *d.* 1992. Studied under Darius MILHAUD. One of the leading scorers of the modern French cinema, he wrote the music for numerous French and international shorts and feature films as well as for the concert hall, ballet, the stage, and TV. He was known for his prolific output, lyrical style, and knack for capturing mood and character through music.

FILMS INCLUDE: *Un Amour de Poche/Nude in His Pocket* 1957; *Hiroshima mon Amour* 1959; *Tirez sur le Pianiste/Shoot the Piano Player* 1960; *Le Farceur/The Joker, L'Amant de Cinq Jours/The Five Day Lover, Une aussi longue Absence/The Long Absence* 1961; *Jules et Jim/Jules and Jim, Cartouche* 1962; *Le Mèpris/Contempt* 1963; *La Peau douce/The Soft Skin, The Pumpkin Eater* (UK), *Un Monsieur de Compagnie/Male Companion, L'Homme de Rio/That Man from Rio* 1964; *Le Corniaud/The Sucker, Viva Maria* 1965; *Le Roi de Coeur/King of Hearts, A Man for All Seasons* (UK) 1966; *Le Vieil Homme et l'Enfant/The Two of Us* 1967; *Women in Love* (UK), *A Walk with Love and Death* (US) 1969; *Anne of the Thousand Days* (UK), *Il Conformista/The Conformist* (It./Fr.), *La Promesse de l'Aube/Promise at Dawn* (Fr./US) 1970; *Les Deux Anglaises et le Continent/Two English Girls* 1971; *The Day of The Jackal* (UK/Fr.) *La Nuit américaine/Day for Night, The Day of the Dolphin* (US) 1973; *Le Gifle/The Slap* 1974; *L'Important c'est d'aimer/That Most Important Thing: Love* 1975; *Femmes Fatales/Calmos* 1976; *Julie Pot de Colle, Julia* (US), *Le Point de Mire, Tendre Poulet* 1977; *Va voir Maman. . . Papa travaille, La Petite Fille en Velours bleu, Préparez vos Mouchoirs/Get Out Your Handkerchiefs* 1978; *Le Cavaleur/Practice Makes Perfect, L'Amour en fuite/Love on the Run, A Little Romance* (US) 1979; *Le Dernier Métro/The Last Metro* 1980; *La Femme d'a Coté/The Woman Next Door, Garde à Vue, True Confessions* (US), *Rich and Famous* (US) 1981; *A Little Sex* (US) 1982; *Man, Woman, and Child* (US), *Vivement Dimanche!/Confidentially Yours, Silkwood* (US) 1983; *Agnes of God* (US) 1985; *Salvador* (US), *Platoon* (US) *Crimes of the Heart* (US) 1986; *Un Homme amoureux/A Man in Love, The Lonely Passion of Judith Hearne* (UK) 1987; *Biloxi Blues* (US), *A Summer Story* (UK), *Memories of Me* (US) 1988; *Beaches* (US), *Heartbreak Hotel* (US), *Steel Magnolias* (US), *La Revolution Francaise/The French Revolution* 1989; *Georg Elser/Seven Minutes* (W. Ger./US), *Joe Versus the Volcano* (US) 1990.

Del Guidice, Filippo. Producer. *b.* Mar. 26, 1892, Trani, Italy. *d.* 1961. A lawyer, he settled in England in 1933 and subsequently joined Two Cities Films as a legal advisor and later as producer, production supervisor, and managing director. Produced, co-produced, or supervised a number of distinguished British films before retiring to a monastery in 1958.

FILMS INCLUDE: *French Without Tears* 1939; *In Which We Serve* 1942; *The Demi-Paradise/Adventure for Two* 1943; *The Way Ahead* 1944; *Henry V, The Way to the Stars/Johnny in the Clouds, Blithe Spirit* 1945; *Beware of Pity, Mr. Emmanuel, School for Secrets, Men of Two Worlds* 1946; *Odd Man Out, Vice Versa, The October Man, Fame Is the Spur* 1947; *Hamlet* 1948.

Dell, Gabriel. Actor. *b.* Gabriel Del Vecchio, Oct. 7, 1919, Brooklyn, N.Y. *d.* 1988. One of the original Dead End Kids, whose screen careers were launched by Sidney Kingsley's 1935 Broadway play 'Dead End.' He worked with the group through its various mutations: the Little Tough Guys, the East Side Kids, and the Bowery Boys. He also played supporting roles in other films and in many Broadway and off-Broadway plays.

FILMS INCLUDE: *Dead End* 1937; *Crime School, Little Tough Guy, Angels with Dirty Faces* 1938; *They Made Me a Criminal, Hell's Kitchen, Angels Wash Their Faces, Dress Parade* 1939; *You're Not So Tough, Give Us Wings* 1940; *Mob Town* 1941; *Mr. Wise Guy* 1942; *Mug Town* 1943; *Bowery Champs* 1944; *Come Out Fighting* 1945; *Bowery Buckaroos* 1947; *Angels in Disuise* 1949; *Blonde Dynamite* 1950; *Escape from Terror* 1960; *Who Is Harry Kellerman...* 1971; *Earthquake* 1974; *The Manchu Eagle Murder Caper Mystery* 1975; *The Escape Artist* 1982.

Delli Colli, Tonino (Antonio). Director of photography. Born on Nov. 20, 1923, in Rome. He entered Italian films in his teens as a camera assistant and by 21 was a full-fledged cinematographer. A masterful technician, he was entrusted in 1952 with the photography of Italy's first color film, *Totò a Colori.* His art reached full maturity in the 60s, when he displayed a great versatility behind the camera with subjects ranging from the urban realism of Pasolini to the dazzling outdoor cinematography of Sergio Leone's "spaghetti Westerns."

FILMS INCLUDE: *Il Paese senza Pace* 1942; *Fugitive Lady* (US) 1951; *Totò a Colori* 1952; *Amori di Mezzo Secolo, Le Rouge et le Noir* 1954; *Poveri ma Belli/Poor but Beautiful* 1956; *Primo Amore* 1958; *Morgan il Pirata/Morgan the Pirate* 1960; *Il Ladro di Bagdad/The Thief of Bagdad, Accatone* 1961; *Mamma Roma* 1962; *El Verdugo/Not on Your Life* (Sp.) 1963; *Il Vangelo Secondo Matteo/The Gospel According to St. Matthew* 1964; *Uccellacci e Uccellini/The Hawks and the Sparrows, Il Buono il Brutto il Cattivo/The Good the Bad and the Ugly* 1966; *La Cina è Vicina/China Is Near* 1967; *Il Giorno della Civetta/Mafia, C'era una Volta il West/Once upon a Time in the West* 1968; *Porcile/Pig Pen/Pigsty* 1969; *Pussycat Pussycat I Love You* (US) 1970; *Il Decamerone/The Decameron, Homo Eroticus/Man of the Year* 1971; *Pilgrimage* (US), *I Racconti di Canterbury/The Canterbury Tales* 1972; *Lacombe Lucien* 1973; *Salo o le Centiventi: Giornate di Sodoma/Salo 120 Days of Sodom* 1975; *Pasqualino Settebellezze/Seven Beauties, Caro Michele* 1976; *Anima Persa, Un Taxi mauve* (Fr./It./Ire.), *I Nuovi Mostri/Viva Italia* 1977; *Caro Papa* (It./Fr./Can.), *Primo Amore* 1978; *Fatto di Sangue fra Due Uomini per causa di una Vedova/Blood Feud/Revenge* 1979; *Sunday Lovers* 1980; *Fantasma d'Amore, Storie di Ordinaria Follia/Tales of Ordinary Madness* 1981; *Trenchcoat* (US) 1983; *Once Upon a Time in America* (US) 1984; *Ginger e Fred/Ginger and Fred* (co-phot.) 1985; *The Name of the Rose* 1986; *La Voce della Luna/The Voice of the Moon* 1990.

Delluc, Louis. Director, screenwriter, novelist, film critic, theorist. *b.* Oct. 14, 1890, Cadouin, France. *d.* 1924. In Paris as a student from age 15, he left school before graduation to begin a career in journalism. He took an interest in theater and later also in films, about which he wrote extensively for various periodicals and for a number of books. He also played an important role in founding cinema clubs in France and generally in advancing the status of cinema as an art. In the early 20s he directed several films, most of which starred his wife, Eve Francis. The few films he made were noted for their preoccupation with memory, manipulation of time, and the psychological insight of their scripts, which he wrote himself. But his death from tuberculosis at the age of 33 did not allow the full development of his skills as a filmmaker. It is as a writer and theorist that he made his greatest contribution to the cinema. In addition to his own production, he wrote scripts for several other films, including Germaine Dulac's *La Fête espagnole* (1919). Le Prix Delluc, the highest award bestowed annually by French cinema for achievements in filmmaking, is named after him.

FILMS (as director-writer): *Fumée noir* (co-dir. with Rene Coiffard), *Le Silence* 1920; *Fièvre, Le Chemin d'Enroa/L'Américain, Le Tonnerre/Evangéline et le Tonnerre* 1921; *La Femme de nulle part* 1922; *L'Inondation* 1924.

Delon, Alain. Actor. Born on Nov. 8, 1935, in Sceaux, France. The product of a broken home, he was expelled from several Catholic schools and became a butcher's apprentice. At 17 he enlisted in the French marines and served as a parachutist in Indochina during the Dienbienphu siege. Upon returning to civilian life, his pretty-boy good looks soon paved the way for his film debut in 1957. Before long, he was much in demand for lead roles in French and international productions, but despite unique opportunities in films of such directors as Clément, Visconti, and Antonioni, for a while he had difficulties in shaking off the pretty-boy image that had launched his screen career. Dynamic and aggressive both on- and offscreen, he branched into film production.

Late in 1968, Delon and his then-wife (1964–69), actress Natalie Delon (*b.* Francine Canovas, 1938), were the central figures in a major murder, drug, and sex scandal that rocked the French capital, following the discovery of the body of Delon's bodyguard in a garbage dump. Although he was cleared of criminal suspicion, Delon admitted to intimate association with underworld characters which dated back to his premovie years. The affair did not hurt his career; rather it promoted his public image as a "toughie" offscreen as well as on. In 1981 he took a first shot at directing with *Pour la Peau d'un Flic/For a Cop's Hide.* He won a César Award for his performance in *Notre Histoire* (1984).

FILMS INCLUDE: *Quand la Femme s'en mêle* 1957; *Christine* 1958; *Faibles Femmes/Women Are Weak* 1959; *Plein Soleil/Purple Noon/Lust for Evil, Rocco e i suoi Fratelli/Rocco and His Brothers* (It./Fr.) 1960; *Quelle Joie de Vivre* 1961; *L'Eclisse/Eclipse* (It./Fr.), *Le Diable et les Dix Commandments/The Devil and the Ten Commandments* 1962; *Il Gattopardo/The Leopard* (It./Fr.), *Mélodie en Sous-Sol/Any Number Can Win, La Tulipe noire/The Black Tulip* 1963; *Les Félins/Joy House/The Love Cage, L'Insoumis, The Yellow Rolls-Royce* (UK) 1964; *Once a Thief* (US/Fr.) 1965; *Lost Command* (US), *Texas Across the River* (US), *Paris brûle-t-il?/Is Paris Burning?* (Fr./US) 1966; *Les Aventuriers/The Last Adventure, Le Samourai/The Godson, Diaboliquement vôtre/Diabolically Yours* 1967; *Histoires extraordinaires/Spirits of the Dead, La Motorcyclette/The Girl on a Motorcycle* (Fr./UK), *Adieu l'Ami* 1968; *La Piscine/The Swimming Pool, Jeff* (also prod.), *Le Clan des Siciliens/The Sicilian Clan* 1969; *Borsalino* (also prod.), *Le Cercle rouge* 1970; *Madly/The Love Mates* (also prod.), *Doucement les Basses, La Veuve Couderc/The Widow Couderc, Soleil rouge/Red Sun* 1971; *The Assassination of Trotsky* (Fr./It.), *Un Flic/Dirty Money* 1972; *Traitement de Choc/Shock, Scorpio* 1973; *Les Seins de Glaces/Icy Breasts, Creezy, Le Gifle/The Slap* 1974; *Zorro, Flic Story, Le Gitan* 1975; *Mr. Klein* (also co-prod.), *Comme un Boomerang* (also co-prod., co-sc.) 1976; *Le Gang, Armaguedon, L'Homme pressé, Mort d'un Pourri* 1977; *The Concorde—Airport '79* (US) 1979; *Trois Hommes á abbatre/Three Men to Destroy* 1980; *Tehran–43/Teheran Incident* (USSR/Switz./Fr.), *Pour la Peau d'un Flic/For a Cop's Hide* (also dir., co-sc.), 1981; *Le Choc, Le Battant* (also dir., co-sc.) 1982; *Un Amour de Swann/Swann in Love, Notre Histoire/Our Story* 1984; *Parole de Flic/Cop's Honor* 1985; *Le Passage/The Passage* (also co-prod., co-adapt.) 1986; *Nouvelle Vague* 1990; *Let Sleeping Cops Lie, Dancing Machine* 1991; *The Return of Casanova* 1992.

Delorme, Danièle. Actress. Born Gabrielle Girard, on Oct. 9, 1926, in Levallois-Perret, France. In French films since 1942, she initially played frail, sad, sometimes malicious young heroines. Her best role came in Jacqueline Audry's version of *Gigi*. Divorced from actor Daniel GÉLIN, she is married to director-actor Yves ROBERT and has produced several of the films he has directed.

FILMS INCLUDE: *Felicie Nanteuil* 1942; *Gigi, La Cage aux Filles* 1949; *Miquette et sa Mère/Miquette, Minne—l'Ingenue libertine/Minne, Agnès de rien, Souvenirs perdus* 1950; *Sans laisser d'Adresse, Olivia/Pit of Loneliness* 1951; *La Jeune Folle/Desperate Decision* 1952; *Les Dents longues* 1953; *Le Guérisseur, Si Versailles m'était conté/Royal Affairs in Versailles, Huis Clos/No Exit* 1954; *Casa Ricordi/House of Ricordi* (It./Fr.), *Le Dossier noir* 1955; *Voici le Temps des Assassins/Deadlier Than the Male* 1956; *Les Misérables, Prison de Femmes* 1958; *La Guerre des Boutons/War of the Buttons* (co-prod. only), *Le Septième Juré/The Seventh Juror* 1962; *Marie Soleil* (also prod.) 1964; *Alexandre le bienheureux/Very Happy Alexander* (prod. only) 1968; *Le Voyou/The Crook* 1970; *Absences répétées* 1972; *Belle* 1973; *Un Elephant ça trompe énormément/Pardon mon Affaire* 1976; *Nous irons tous au Paradis* 1977; *La Barricade du Point du Jour* 1978; *La Drolesse/The Hussy* (co-prod. only) 1979.

Delpy, Julie. Actress. Born 1969, in Paris, France. Born into a theatrical family, this alluring beauty made her stage debut at an early age. Discovered by French filmmaker Jean-Luc GODARD when he cast her in *Detective* (1985), she has gone on to become an international star. Known primarily to American audiences through art-house releases, she has begun to work more in American films such as *Before Sunrise* (1995).

FILMS: *Detective* (Fr.) 1985; *Bad Blood* (Fr.), *King Lear* (Switz./US) 1987; *Europa, Europa* (Fr./Ger.), *Voyager* (Fr./Ger./Gr.)1991; *Blue* (Fr./Pol./Switz.), *The Three Musketeers* (US), *Younger and Younger* 1993; *Killing Zoe* (US), *Red* (Fr./Pol./Switz.), *White* (Fr.) 1994; *Before Sunrise* (US) 1995; *Live Nude Girls* (US) 1996; *Tykho Moon* 1997.

Del Rio, Dolores. Actress. *b.* Lolita Dolores Martinez Asunsolo Lopez Negrette, Aug. 3, 1905, Durango, Mex. *d.* 1983. The daughter of a banker and second cousin of Ramon NOVARRO, she was educated in a convent. By age 16 she was married to writer Jaime Del Rio. Director Edwin CAREWE was struck by her dark beauty and invited her to Hollywood to appear in his film *Joanna* (1925). She went on to star in many silent films of Carewe and other directors. One of the most beautiful women ever to grace the American screen, her career suffered from frequent typecasting in ethnic and exotic roles, even more so after the coming of sound, when her Latin accent made typecasting almost unavoidable. She was popular enough to remain active in Hollywood films through the early 40s. In 1930 she married art director Cedric GIBBONS. Shortly after their 1941 divorce, she was seen in *Journey Into Fear* (1942).

Unsatisfied with her Hollywood career, Miss Del Rio returned to Mexico in 1943, where she signed a lucrative contract that gave her a percentage of the profits of her films. Her Mexican career was much more rewarding. Among her many films of the 40s were several directed by Emilio Fernandez, including the famed *Maria Candelaria,* and John Ford's *The Fugitive*. In the 60s she returned occasionally to Hollywood films in character parts.

FILMS INCLUDE: In the US—*Joanna* 1925; *High Steppers, The Whole Town's Talking, Pals First, What Price Glory* 1926; *Resurrection, The Loves of Carmen* 1927; *The Gateway of the Moon, No Other Woman, The Red Dance, Ramona, Revenge* 1928; *The Trail of '98, Evangeline* 1929; *The Bad One* 1930; *The Girl of the Rio, Bird of Paradise* 1932; *Flying Down to Rio* 1933; *Wonder Bar, Madame Du Barry* 1934; *In Caliente, I Live for Love, The Widow from Monte Carlo* 1935; *Accused* (UK) 1936; *Devil's Playground, Lancer Spy* 1937; *International Settlement* 1938; *The Man from Dakota* 1940; *Journey Into Fear* 1942. In Mexico—*Flor Silvestre, Maria Candelaria* 1943; *Bugambilia, Los Abandonadas* 1944; *La Otra* 1946; *The Fugitive* 1947; *Historia de una Mala Mujer* (Argen.) 1948; *Dona Perfecta* 1950; *La Cucaracha* 1958; *Flaming Star* (US) 1960; *Cheyenne Autumn* (US) 1964; *C'era una Volta/More Than a Miracle* (It.), *Rio Blanco* 1967; *The Children of Sanchez* (US/Mex.) 1978.

Del Ruth, Roy. Director. *b.* Oct. 18, 1895, Philadelphia. *d.* 1961. A young journalist, he entered films in 1915 as a screenwriter and gagman for Mack SENNETT. Two years later he began directing two-reel comedies, which starred Bill Turpin, Billy Bevan, and Harry Langdon, among others. Del Ruth turned to feature films in the mid-20s. A solid craftsman in the best Hollywood tradition, he turned out a number of atmospheric dramas for Warners in the early 30s, then switched to lavish MGM musicals. Despite their technical excellence, few of his films rose above routine entertainment. He was the brother of gagman, writer, and sometime director Hampton Del Ruth.

FEATURE FILMS: *Eve's Lover, Hogan's Alley* 1925; *Three Weeks in Paris, The Man Upstairs, The Little Irish Girl, Footloose Widows, Across the Pacific* 1926; *Wolf's Clothing, The First Auto, Ham and Eggs at the Front* 1927; *If I Were Single, Five and Ten Cent Annie, Powder My Back, The Terror, Beware of Bachelors* 1928; *Conquest, The Desert Song, The Hottentot, The Gold Diggers of Broadway* 1929; *The Aviator, Hold Everything, The Second Floor Mystery/The Second Story Murder, Three Faces East, The Life of the Party, Divorce Among Friends* 1930; *My Past, The Maltese Falcon, Side Show, Blonde Crazy/Larceny Lane* 1931; *Taxi, Beauty and the Boss, Winner Take All, Blessed Event* 1932; *Employees' Entrance, The Mind Reader, The Little Giant, Bureau of Missing Persons, Captured, Lady Killer* 1933; *Bulldog Drummond Strikes Back, Upper World, Kid Millions* 1934; *Broadway Melody of 1936, Folies-Bergère* (also French version, *L'Homme des Folies-Bergère*), *Thanks a Million* 1935; *It Had to Happen, Private Number, Born to Dance* 1936; *On the Avenue, Broadway Melody of 1938* 1937; *Happy Landing, My Lucky Star* 1938; *Tail Spin, The Star Maker, Here I Am a Stranger* 1939; *He Married His Wife* 1940; *Topper Returns, The Chocolate Soldier* 1941; *Maisie Gets Her Man* 1942; *Du Barry Was a Lady* 1943; *Broadway Rhythm, Barbary Coast Gent* 1944; *It Happened on Fifth Avenue* (also prod.) 1947; *The Babe Ruth Story* (also prod.) 1948; *Red Light* (also prod.), *Always Leave Them Laughing* 1949; *The West Point Story* 1950; *On Moonlight Bay, Starlift* 1951; *About Face* 1952; *Stop You're Killing Me, Three Sailors and a Girl* 1953; *Phantom of the Rue Morgue* 1954; *The Alligator People* 1959; *Why Must I Die?* 1960.

De Luise, Dom. Actor. Born on Aug. 1, 1933, in Brooklyn, N.Y. *ed.* Tufts U. Bald, chubby comic character player of the American stage, TV, and films. Began his career in Cleveland repertory and first gained popularity on TV as Dominick the Great, a bumbling magician, on 'The Garry Moore Show.' He later starred in his own TV variety program and made several Broadway appearances, memorably in 'The Last of the Red Hot Lovers.' On the screen from the mid-60s. He directed himself in *Hot Stuff* (1980). He married actress Carol Arthur, who appeared in occasional movies and TV shows.

FILMS INCLUDE: *Fail Safe* 1964; *The Glass Bottom Boat* 1966; *The Busy Body* 1967; *What's So Bad About Feeling Good?* 1968; *Norwood, The Twelve Chairs* 1970; *Every Little Crook and Nanny* 1972; *Blazing Saddles* 1974; *The Adventure of Sherlock Holmes' Smarter Brother* 1975; *Silent Movie* 1976; *The World's Greatest Lover* 1977; *Sextette, The End, The Cheap*

Detective 1978; *Hot Stuff* (also dir.), *The Muppet Movie* 1979; *Fatso, The Last Married Couple in America, Smokey and the Bandit II, Wholly Moses!* 1980; *The Cannonball Run, History of the World: Part I* (as Nero) 1981; *The Best Little Whorehouse in Texas* 1982; *Cannonball Run II, Johnny Dangerously* 1984; *Haunted Honeymoon, An American Tail* (voice only) 1986; *Spaceballs* (voice only) 1987; *Going Bananas, Oliver & Company* (voice of Fagin) 1988; *Loose Cannons* 1990; *An American Tail: Fievel Goes West* (voice only) 1991; *Almost Pregnant* 1992; *Happily Ever After* (voice only) 1993; *All Dogs Go to Heaven* (voice only) 1996.

Delvaux, André. Director. Born on Mar. 21, 1926, in Héverlé, near Louvain, Belgium. He studied German philosophy at the Free University of Brussels and at the same time attended piano classes at Belgium's Royal Conservatory. He later taught at the university and in 1950 began accompanying on the piano silent films at the Belgian Cinémathèque and fell in love with the cinema. He was appointed head of a program of film education for Belgian teachers and organized a seminar on the language of film at the Free University's department of sociology. In 1960 he made a four-part series about Federico Fellini for Belgian TV, the first of several series about film directors he would turn out for television during the 60s. Graduating to features in the middle of the decade, he won several international prizes for his first full-length film, the Belgian-made *Die Man die zijn Haar kort liet knippen/L'Homme au Crâne rasé/The Man Who Had His Hair Cut Short* (1966), including a British Academy Award. He won the Prix Louis Delluc for his third feature, the French-Belgian co-production *Rendez-vous à Bray* (1971).

FEATURE FILMS: *Die Man die zijn Haar kort liet knippen/L'Homme au Crâne rasé/The Man Who Had His Hair Cut Short* (also co-sc.) 1966; *Un Soir un Train* (also sc.) 1968; *Rendez-vous à Bray* (also sc.) 1971; *Belle* (also sc.) 1973; *Een Vrouw tussen Hond en Wolf/Femme entre Chien et Loup/Woman in a Twilight Garden/Women of Twilight* (also sc.) 1979; *To Woody Allen: From Europe with Love* 1980; *Benvenuta* (also sc.) 1983; *Babel-Opera* (also sc.) 1985.

Demarest, William. Actor. *b.* Feb. 27, 1892, St. Paul, Minn. *d.* 1983. A former vaudeville, carnival, and stock performer and a professional boxer, he made his screen debut in 1926 and later played well over 100 character parts, often cunning but kind, in a wide variety of films, including several by director Preston STURGES. He was nominated for an Oscar for his role in *The Jolson Story* (1946). Familiar to TV viewers as Uncle Charley in the long-running series 'My Three Sons' (1965–72).

FILMS INCLUDE: *When the Wife's Away* 1926; *Fingerprints, The Jazz Singer* 1927; *A Girl in Every Port, The Escape* 1928; *Broadway Melody* 1929; *The Crash* 1932; *Fog Over Frisco* 1934; *Diamond Jim* 1935; *Easy Living, Big City* 1937; *Rebecca of Sunnybrook Farm* 1938; *Mr. Smith Goes to Washington* 1939; *The Farmer's Daughter, Tin Pan Alley, The Great McGinty* 1940; *The Lady Eve, Sullivan's Travels, The Devil and Miss Jones* 1941; *My Favorite Spy, Pardon My Sarong* 1942; *Hail the Conquering Hero, The Miracle of Morgan's Creek* 1944; *Along Came Jones* 1945; *The Jolson Story* 1946; *The Perils of Pauline, Variety Girl* 1947; *Night Has a Thousand Eyes* 1948; *Sorrowful Jones* 1949; *Jolson Sings Again* 1949; *Riding High* 1950; *The First Legion* 1951; *What Price Glory* 1952; *Escape from Fort Bravo* 1953; *The Far Horizons* 1955; *Hell on Frisco Bay* 1956; *King of the Roaring Twenties* 1961; *It's a Mad Mad Mad Mad World* 1963; *Viva Las Vegas* 1964; *That Darn Cat* 1965; *The Wild McCullochs* 1975.

De Marney, Derrick. Actor. *b.* Sept. 21, 1906, London. *d.* 1978. Handsome, British leading man and supporting player. On the stage from age 17, he made his screen debut at 22 and for two decades remained quite popular. His brother, Terence De Marney (1909–71), was also a stage and screen actor.

FILMS INCLUDE: *Adventurous Youth* 1928; *Shadows* 1931; *The Private Life of Henry VIII* 1933; *The Scarlet Pimpernel, Music Hall* 1934; *Things to Come, Land Without Music/Forbidden Music* 1936; *Victoria the Great* (as D'Israeli), *Young and Innocent/The Girl Was Young* 1937; *Sixty Glorious Years/Queen of Destiny* (as D'Israeli), *Blonde Cheat* (US) 1938; *The Spider, The Lion Has Wings* 1939; *Dangerous Moonlight/Suicide Squadron* 1941; *The First of the Few/Spitfire* 1942; *Latin Quarter/Frenzy* 1945; *Uncle Silas/The Inheritance* 1947; *Sleeping Car to Trieste* 1948; *She Shall Have Murder* 1950; *Meet Mr. Callaghan* 1954; *Private's Progress* 1956; *Doomsday at Eleven* 1962; *The Projected Man* 1966.

Demeny, Georges. Inventor, cinema pioneer. *b.* June 12, 1850, Douai, France. *d.* 1917. A physiologist, he was the assistant and later the collaborator of Professor Etienne-Jules MAREY on his photographic research of movement. In 1891, Demeny developed the Phonoscope, which permitted the viewing of a series of photographs of lip movement which had been recorded by Marey. In 1892, Demeny patented an apparatus that created an illusion of motion by recording a quick succession of individual images and in 1893 he introduced a camera derived from Marey's chronophotographe but equipped with a beater intermittent movement, a vital step toward the development of movie cameras and projectors.

De Mille, Cecil B. Director, producer, screenwriter. *b.* Cecil Blount de Mille, Aug. 12, 1881, Ashfield, Mass. *d.* 1959. The son of an Episcopalian lay preacher who also taught at Columbia and wrote plays, he was orphaned at age 12. His mother, the former Beatrice Samuel, an Englishwoman of Jewish descent, who also wrote occasional plays, supported the family by opening a school for girls, and later a successful theatrical company. Following in the footsteps of his older brother, William DE MILLE, he then became interested in the theater and enrolled at New York's Academy of Dramatic Arts. He made his acting debut on Broadway in 1900. Two years later he married a stage colleague, Constance Adams.

During his next dozen years as actor and general manager of his mother's company, he collaborated with brother William on a number of moderately successful plays and often worked closely with David Belasco. In 1913 he went into partnership with vaudeville musician Jesse L. LASKY and glove salesman Samuel Goldfish (later GOLDWYN). They formed a motion picture firm, the Jesse L. Lasky Feature Play Company, and traveled to Hollywood to produce their first venture, *The Squaw Man* (1914). De Mille, who was named director-general of the company, co-produced and co-directed the film with Oscar APFEL. Six reels long, *The Squaw Man* was a colossal film by the standards of the day and enjoyed commercial and critical success. It helped solidify the position of the infant company and immediately established De Mille as a director to be reckoned with in the not-yet-thriving Hollywood community.

Before long, the Lasky company grew into Paramount, a giant of the industry, with De Mille as its acknowledged creative force. Not only did he personally produce and direct many of the company's films during these formative years, but he also supervised the company's entire output, often lending a hand at the writing of scripts and directing of sequences in films assigned to other directors. He brought to the screen longer and more elaborate productions and was largely responsible for Hollywood's switch from two- and three-reelers to feature films. He is generally acknowledged as the man who more than anyone else helped Hollywood become the world's greatest film center.

De Mille was a born showman. He had a knack for anticipating public taste and gauging the nation's changing moods. He made do without big-name stars and instead developed his own roster of regular players. He put the money he thus saved where he thought it might do the most good—into better production values and luxurious settings. Among the stars he developed were Gloria Swanson, Bebe Daniels, soprano Geraldine Farrar, Julia Faye, Wallace Reid, Monte Blue, and Elliott Dexter. Over the years, De Mille handled every existing film genre and formulated some that never existed before.

These films were highly successful, reflecting as well as influencing American lifestyles in the 20s. The same formula—explicit visual description of sin redeemed by verbal Christian ethic—was used by De Mille with even greater commercial success in his mammoth spectacles, *The Ten Commandments, The King of Kings, The Sign of the Cross, Cleopatra, The Crusades,* etc. Above all, De Mille was a master storyteller who shunned camera trickery and audience manipulation and developed his plots traditionally and skillfully. His films were often described as simple-minded and vulgar, but in sheer narrative skill and judicial pacing of action, De Mille had few competitors in Hollywood or elsewhere. His films moved and were always entertaining.

De Mille spent most of his career with Paramount, apart from a period in the mid-20s when he struck out on his own, and in the early sound era, which he spent briefly and unhappily at MGM. In all, he produced and directed 70 films and participated in some form in the production of many more. From 1936 to 1945, De Mille hosted and directed a popular weekly radio show, 'Lux Radio Theatre,' which consisted of radiophonic adaptations of famous films and stage plays with the participation of many of Hollywood's and Broadway's best known performers. He was forced to abandon the series after a dispute with the union of radio artists, AFRA (now AFTRA, including television). He also made occasional appearances in films, notably in the 1950 *Sunset Boulevard.* His *Autobiography* was published posthumously in 1959.

FILMS (as director-producer): *The Squaw Man* (co-dir., co-prod., co-sc. with Oscar C. Apfel), *Brewster's Millions* (co-dir., uncredited with Apfel), *The Master Mind* (co-dir., uncredited, with Apfel), *The Only Son* (co-dir., uncredited, with Apfel and others), *The Man on the Box* (co-dir., uncredited, with Apfel), *The Call of the North* (co-dir. with Apfel; also sc.), *The Virginian* (also sc., co-edit.), *What's His Name* (also sc., edit.), *Rose of the Rancho* (also sc., edit.), *The Ghost Breaker* (co-dir., uncredited, with Apfel) 1914; *The Girl of the Golden West* (also sc., edit.), *After Five* (co-dir., uncredited, with Apfel), *The Warrens of Virginia* (also edit.), *The Unafraid* (also sc., edit.), *The Captive* (also co-sc., edit), *The Wild Goose Chase* (also edit.), *The Arab* (also co-sc., edit.), *Chimmie Fadden* (also sc., edit.), *Kindling* (also sc., edit.), *Carmen* (also edit.), *Chimmie Fadden Out West* (also co-sc., edit.), *The Cheat* (also edit.) 1915; *The Golden Chance* (also sc., edit.), *Temptation* (also edit.), *The Trail of the Lonesome Pine* (also sc., edit.), *The Heart of Nora Flynn* (also edit.), *Maria Rosa* (also edit.), *The Dream Girl* (also edit.) 1916; *Joan the Woman* (also edit.), *Romance of the Redwoods* (also co-sc., edit.), *The Little American* (also co-sc., edit.), *The Woman God Forgot* (also edit.), *The Devil Stone* (also edit.) 1917; *The Whispering Chorus* (also edit.), *Old Wives for New* (also edit.), *You Can't Have Everything* (also co-edit.), *Till I Come Back to You, The Squaw Man* (remake) 1918; *Don't Change Your Husband, For Better for Worse, Male and Female* 1919; *Why Change Your Wife?, Something to Think About* 1920; *Forbidden Fruit, The Affairs of Anatol, Fool's Paradise* 1921; *Saturday Night, Manslaughter* 1922; *Adam's Rib, The Ten Commandments* 1923; *Triumph, Feet of Clay* 1924; *The Golden Bed, The Road to Yesterday* 1925; *The Volga Boatman* 1926; *The King of Kings* 1927; *The Godless Girl, Dynamite* 1929; *Madame Satan* 1930; *The Squaw Man* (second remake) 1931; *The Sign of the Cross* 1932; *This Day and Age* 1933; *Four Frightened People, Cleopatra* 1934; *The Crusades* 1935; *The Plainsman* 1937; *The Buccaneer* 1938; *Union Pacific* 1939; *North West Mounted Police* 1940; *Reap the Wild Wind* 1942; *The Story of Dr. Wassell* 1944; *Unconquered* 1947; *Samson and Delilah* 1949; *The Greatest Show on Earth* 1952; *The Ten Commandments* 1956.

De Mille, Katherine. Actress. Born Katherine Lester, on June 29, 1911, in Vancouver, B.C., Canada. *d.* 1995. Orphaned as a child, she was adopted by director Cecil B. DE MILLE at nine. She appeared in many films of the 30s and 40s, usually as a jilted, jealous, or just plain unhappy woman in second leads or supporting roles, but also in darkly exotic leads. Formerly married to Anthony QUINN.

FILMS INCLUDE: *Madam Satan* 1930; *Viva Villa!, The Trumpet Blows, Belle of the Nineties* 1934; *All The King's Horses, Call of the Wild, The Crusades* 1935; *Drift Fence, The Sky Parade, Ramona, Banjo on My Knee* 1936; *Charlie Chan at the Olympics, Love Under Fire, Under Suspicion* 1937; *Blockade* 1938; *In Old Caliente* 1939; *Isle of Destiny, Dark Streets of Cairo, Ellery Queen Master Detective* 1940; *Aloma of the South Seas* 1941; *Black Gold, Unconquered* 1947; *The Man from Del Rio* (bit) 1956.

De Mille, William C(hurchill). Director, playwright, screenwriter. *b.* July 25, 1878, Washington, D.C. *d.* 1955. *ed.* Columbia. The elder brother of Cecil B. DE MILLE, he was an established playwright when Cecil was still groping for artistic direction. Essentially a man of the theater, he saw little substance in his brother's plans of becoming a filmmaker and turned down an offer to become a co-founder of the Lasky company. But following Cecil's initial success William, too, went to Hollywood, where he directed and produced with some success. He also wrote many original screenplays and adaptations of his own plays for other directors, including his brother Cecil.

FILMS (as director): *The Only Son* (co-dir., uncredited, with Oscar Apfel and others) 1914; *The Ragamuffin* (also sc.), *The Blacklist* (also co-sc.), *The Sowers, Maria Rosa* (also sc.), *The Clown, Common Ground, Anton the Terrible, The Heir to the Hoorah* (also co-sc.) 1916; *Hashimura Togo, The Ghost House, The Secret Game* 1917; *One More American, The Honor of His House, The Widow's Might, The Mystery Girl, Mirnady Smiles* 1918; *The Tree of Knowledge, Prince Chap, Conrad in Quest of His Youth, Midsummer Madness* 1920; *What Every Woman Knows, The Last Romance, After the Show, Miss Lulu Bett* 1921; *Bought and Paid For, Clarence, Nice People* 1922; *The World's Applause, Grumpy, Only 38, Don't Call It Love, The Marriage Maker* 1923; *Icebound, The Bedroom Window, The Fast Set* 1924; *Locked Doors, Men and Women, Lost: A Wife, New Brooms, The Splendid Crime* (also story) 1925; *The Runaway, For Alimony Only* 1926; *The Little Adventuress* 1927; *Craig's Wife, Tenth Avenue* 1928; *The Doctor's Secret* (also sc.), *The Idle Rich* 1929; *This Mad World, Passion Flower* 1930; *Two Kind of Women* 1932; *His Double Life* (co-dir. with Arthur Hopkins) 1934.

Demme, Jonathan. Director, screenwriter, producer. Born on Feb. 22, 1944, in Baldwin, N.Y. One of the most supple-minded and inventive American directors of the postwar era. As a youngster he moved with his family to Miami, where he attended high school. At the University of Florida, he began writing film reviews. After a stint in the Air Force, he was introduced by his father, the public-relations director for the Fontainbleau Hotel, to producer Joseph E. LEVINE, who hired young Demme to write releases for Avco-Embassy in New York. After several years of publicity work for various movie companies and writing for the trade journal *Film Daily,* he left in 1969 for London, where he became involved in the production of TV commercials. He functioned as a music coordinator for producer Irwin ALLEN on John Hough's *Eyewitness/Sudden Terror* (1970), then did publicity for low-budget mogul Roger CORMAN, who gave him his first opportunity to produce and write. Making his directing debut in 1974, Demme soon attracted critics' attention for his ingenuity and style. He won wide praise for *Citizens Band/Handle with Care* (1977) and *Last Embrace* (1979), and international acclaim for *Melvin and Howard* (1980). In *Something Wild* and *Married to the Mob*, he brought to full fruition his ability to portray the idiosyncratic varieties of American life. His greatest success thus far has been the Academy Award–winning thriller, *The Silence of the Lambs* (1991). Working within the genre of psychological suspense, he fashioned a rich, intelligent movie driven by the symbiotic relationship between FBI trainee Jodie FOSTER and cultured serial killer Anthony HOPKINS. His next film *Philadelphia* (1993), received critical praise and is widely considered the first "commercially successful" mainstream film to deal with the serious reality of AIDS. Since 1984, he has also directed a variety of accomplished documentaries, on topics ranging from Haiti to his clergyman cousin, and has produced several films. He frequently works with the same crew, including cinematographer Tak Fujimoto and Craig McKay. Divorced from producer Evelyn Purcell, he married painter Joanne Howard.

FILMS: As producer/co-screenwriter—*Angels Hard as They Come* 1971; *The Hot Box* 1972; *Black Mama White Mama* (co-story only) 1973. As director—*Caged Heat/Renegade Girls* (also sc.) 1974; *Crazy Mama* 1975; *Fighting Mad* (also sc.) 1976; *Citizens Band/Handle with Care* 1977; *Roger Corman: Hollywood's Wild Angel* (act. only), *The Incredible Melting Man* (act. only) 1978; *Last Embrace* 1979; *Melvin and Howard* 1980; *Ladies and Gentlemen, the Fabulous Stains* (sc. only) 1982; *Swing Shift, Stop Making Sense* (also co-sound) 1984; *Something Wild* (also co-prod.) 1986; *Swimming to Cambodia* 1987; *Haiti Dreams of Democracy* (doc., also prod.); *Married to the Mob* 1988; *Miami Blues* (prod. only) 1990; *The Silence of the Lambs* 1991; *Cousin Bobby* (doc.); *Amos & Andrew* (exec. prod. only) 1992; *Philadelphia* 1993; *Devil in a Blue Dress* (exec.-prod. only) 1995; *That Thing You Do* (co-prod., cameo) 1996; *Ulee's Gold* (exec.-prod.) 1997.

Demongeot, Mylène. Actress. Born Marie Hélène Demongeot, on Sept. 28, 1936, in Nice, France. A pretty, sexy blonde, she made her film debut in 1953 and asserted herself with *The Witches of Salem/The Crucible* in 1957. She has since starred in numerous French and several international films. She heads a production company, Kangourou Films, in partnership with her husband, director Marc Simenon, the son of novelist Georges Simenon.

FILMS INCLUDE: *Les Enfants de l'Amour* 1953; *Frou-Frou* 1955; *It's a Wonderful World* (UK) 1956; *Les Sorciéres de Salem/Witches of Salem/The Crucible, Une Manche et la Belle/What Price Murder* 1957; *Bonjour Tristesse* (UK/US), *Soi Belle et tais-toi/Be Beautiful and Shut Up* 1958; *Faibles Femmes/Women Are Weak, Le Vent se lève/Time Bomb, La Notte Brava/On Any Street/Bad Girls Don't Cry* (It./Fr.), *La Battaglia di Maratona/The Giant of Marathon* (It.), *Upstairs and Downstairs* (UK) 1959; *The Singer Not the Song* (UK), *Les Trois Mousquetaires/The Three Musketeers* (as Milady) 1961; *Doctor in Distress* (UK) 1963; *Fantômas* 1964; *Onkel Toms Hütte/Uncle Tom's Cabin* (Ger./Fr./It./Yug.), *Furia à Bahia pour OSS 117/OSS 117—Mission for a Killer* 1965; *Tendre Voyou/Tender Scoundrel* 1966; *The Private Navy of Sgt. O'Farrell* (US) 1968; *Le Champignon* 1970; *L'Explosion* 1971; *Les Pavillion de Verre* 1972; *Par le Sang des autres/By the Blood of Others* 1973; *Les Noces de Porcelaine* 1974; *L'Echappatoire* 1977; *Le Batard* 1983; *Paulette, Tenue du Soirée/Ménage* 1986.

De Mornay, Rebecca. Actress. Born in 1961, in Los Angeles. Striking blonde leading lady of the American screen. Raised in Europe, she received her high school education in Austria. On returning to the US, she enrolled at Lee Strasberg's Los Angeles Institute, then apprenticed at Francis Ford COPPOLA's Zoetrope Studios, where she made her debut playing a bit in *One from the Heart.* Best known for her performance as the enterprising escort to Tom Cruise in *Risky Business* (1983).

FILMS: *One from the Heart* 1982; *Risky Business, Testament* 1983; *The Slugger's Wife, The Trip to Bountiful, Runaway Train* 1985; *Beauty and the Beast* (as Beauty) 1987; *And God Created Woman, Feds* 1988; *Dealers* 1989; *Backdraft* 1991; *The Hand That Rocks the Cradle* 1992; *Guilty as Sin, The Three Musketeers* 1993; *Never Talk to Strangers* (also co-exec. prod.) 1995; *Winner* 1996.

Dempsey, Patrick. Actor. Born in 1966, in Lewiston, Maine. Juvenile lead, then young leading man of Hollywood films. A state downhill-skiing champion during his high school days, he began his performing career as an amateur magician-juggler-puppeteer and later appeared professionally on the stage. On the screen from 1985, he was ideally cast in *In the Mood* (1987) as the "Woo Woo Kid," a hapless California teenager who in the 40s made headlines because of his publicized affairs with older women.

FILMS: *Heaven Help Us* 1985; *Meatballs III* 1986; *Can't Buy Me Love, In the Mood/The Woo Woo Kid* 1987; *In a Shallow Grave, Some Girls* 1988; *Loverboy* 1989; *Coup De Ville, Happy Together* 1990; *Run, Mobsters* 1991; *Outbreak* 1995.

Dempster, Carol. Actress. *b.* 1902. *d.* 1991. A peppy, athletic brunette dancer, she was brought to the attention of D. W. GRIFFITH by still photographer Hendrik Sartov, who was to replace Billy Bitzer as Griffith's favorite cinematographer. The famous director not only made her the star of most of his films of the 20s but reputedly fell in love with her and sought to marry her. However, in 1926 she walked out on her contract with Griffith to marry an investment broker and retired from the screen. In addition to playing in the Griffith films, she had occasionally starred in films made by other directors, notably opposite John Barrymore in Albert Parker's *Sherlock Holmes* (1922).

FILMS INCLUDE: *The Greatest Thing in Life* (dancing bit) 1918; *The Hope Chest, A Romance of Happy Valley, The Girl Who Stayed at Home, True Heart Susie, Scarlet Days* 1919; *The Love Flower* 1920; *Dream Street* 1921; *Sherlock Holmes, One Exciting Night* 1922; *The White Rose* 1923; *America, Isn't Life Wonderful?* 1924; *Sally of the Sawdust, That Royle Girl* (both with W. C. Fields) 1925; *The Sorrows of Satan* 1926.

Demy, Jacques. Director. *b.* June 5, 1931, in Pont-Château, France. *d.* 1990. After art studies in Nantes and film studies in Paris, he became assistant to animator Paul Grimault in 1952 and to documentarist Georges Rouquier in 1954. In 1956 he directed the first of several shorts and in 1960 made a substantial debut as feature director with *Lola,* a film he dedicated to Max Ophüls, the director of *Lola Montès.* In *Lola* as well as in his subsequent films, Demy reveals tender romanticism, a penchant for decorative elegance, a strong sense of nostalgia, and a preoccupation with the themes of chance, absence, and relative time. His third film, *The Umbrellas of Cherbourg,* is revolutionary in its concept as a musical in which every word of dialogue is sung (to a score by Michel Legrand). It is also rich in color (photography by Jean Rabier) and imaginative in design (Bernard Evein). It did win the Palme d'Or (grand prize) at the Cannes Festival. In *The Young Girls of Rochefort,* he repeated the formula with lesser success. His made-in-America film, *The Model Shop,* did not create much of a stir. In 1982, however, he won the Grand Prix du Cinéma for *Une Chambre en Ville.* Demy always wrote or collaborated on his own scripts. In 1962 he married director Agnès VARDA. He died at 59 of a brain hemorrhage brought on by leukemia.

FILMS (as director-writer): Shorts—*Le Sabotier du Val de Loire* 1956; *Le Bel Indifférent* 1957; *Musée Grévin* (co-dir. with J. Masson) 1958; *La Mère et l'Enfant* (co-dir. with Masson), *Ars* 1959. Features—*Lola* 1961; *Les Sept Péchés capitaux/Seven Capital Sins* ("Lust" episode) 1962; *La Baie des Anges/Bay of the Angels* 1963; *Les Parapluies de Cherbourg/The Umbrellas of Cherbourg* 1964; *Les Demoiselles de Rochefort/The Young Girls of Rochefort* 1967; *The Model Shop* (also prod.; US) 1969; *Peau d'Ane/Donkey Skin* 1971; *The Pied Piper of Hamelin/The Pied Piper* (UK/Ger.) 1972; *L'Evenement le plus Important depuis que l'Homme a marché sur la Lune/A Slightly Pregnant Man* 1973; *Lady Oscar* (in English; Jap./Fr.) 1978; *Une Chambre en Ville/A Room in Town* 1982; *Parking* 1985; *Trois Places pour le 26* 1988.

Dench, Dame Judi. Actress. Born on Dec. 9, 1934, in York, England. *ed.* The Mount School, York; Central School of Speech Training and Dramatic Art. Lusty leading lady and supporting player of British stage, screen, and television. She made her stage debut as Ophelia in an Old Vic Liverpool production of 'Hamlet' and has since been highly regarded for her performances in Shakespeare and the classic repertoire. Her screen appearances have been relatively few, but usually memorable. She won British Film Academy Awards for *Four in the Morning* (1965) and *A Handful of Dust* (1988).

FILMS: *The Third Secret* 1964; *Four in the Morning, A Study in Terror/Fog* 1965; *He Who Rides a Tiger* 1966; *A Midsummer Night's Dream* 1968; *Luther* 1973; *Dead Cert* 1974; *Wetherby* 1985; *A Room with a View* 1986; *84 Charing Cross Road* 1987; *A Handful of Dust* 1988; *Henry V* 1989; *Jack and Sarah* 1995; *Goldeneye, Hamlet* 1996.

Deneuve, Catherine. Actress. Born Catherine Dorléac, on Oct. 22, 1943, in Paris. The daughter of veteran stage and screen actor Maurice Dorléac and the younger sister of the late Françoise DORLÉAC, she made her screen debut while still a schoolgirl of 13, assuming the maiden name of her mother, who was also an actress. Despite the patronage of star-maker Roger VADIM, she did not achieve any prominence until her appearance seven years later in Demy's *The Umbrellas of Cherbourg* (1963). An exquisite, fragile beauty, aloof and detached in manner, she developed into France's leading female screen personality and one of the top stars on the international film scene in the late 60s. She was particularly effective as the frigid, mentally disoriented character in Polanski's macabre *Repulsion* (1965), the innocent-conniving 18th-century virgin in Deville's *Benjamin* (1968), and the erotic, enigmatic protagonist of Buñuel's *Belle de Jour* (1967) and *Tristana* (1970). In 1971 she formed her own production company, Les Films de la Citrouille. She was named best foreign actress at the David Donatello Awards for her performance in *The Last Metro* (1980) and was nominated for an Academy Award for her performance in *Indochine* (1992). In the 80s, as beautiful and elegant as ever, she advertised Chanel perfumes so successfully on American TV that in 1986 she launched a fragrance bearing her own name. Liberated and independent in her private life, she had a child by Vadim in 1963 and another by Marcello MASTROIANNI in 1972 but did not marry either. Her marriage to British photographer David Bailey ended in divorce.

FILMS INCLUDE: *Les Collégiennes* 1956; *Les Petits Chats/Wild Roots of Love* 1959; *Les Portes claquent* 1960; *Les Parisiennes/Tales of Paris* ("Sophie" episode) 1962; *Le Vice et la Vertu/Vice and Virtue, Vacances Portugaises* 1963; *Les Parapluies de Cherbourg/The Umbrellas of Cherbourg, La Chasse à l'Homme/Male Hunt, Un Monsieur de Compagnie/Male Companion* 1964; *Repulsion* (UK), *Le Chant du Monde* 1965; *La Vie de Château, Les Créatures* 1966; *Les Demoiselles de Rochefort/The Young Girls of Rochefort, Belle de Jour* 1967; *Benjamin, Manon 70, Mayerling* (Fr./UK), *La Chamade* 1968; *The April Fools* (US), *La Sirène de Mississippi/Mississippi Mermaid* 1969; *Tristana* 1970; *Peau d'âne/Donkey Skin, Ça n'arrive qu'aux autres/It Only Happens to Others* 1971; *La Cagna/Liza* (It./Fr.), *Un Flic/Dirty Money* 1972; *L'Evenement le plus important depuis que l'Homme a marché sur la Lune/A Slightly Pregnant Man* 1973; *Touchez pas la Femme blanche, La Femme aux Bottes rouges/The Woman with Red Boots, Fatti di Gente Perbene/La Grande Bourgeoise* (It./Fr.) 1974; *L'Aggression/Act of Aggression, Le Sauvage/The Savage/Lovers Like Us, Zig Zig/Zig-Zag, Hustle* (US) 1975; *Si c'était a refaire/Second Chance* 1976; *Anima Persa, March or Die* (UK) 1977; *L'Argent des Autres, Ecoute Voir...* 1978; *A nous deux/An Adventure for Two* (Fr./Can.), *Ils sont grand ces Petits* 1979; *Le Dernier Métro/The Last Metro, Je vous aime* 1980; *Le Choix des Armes/Choice of Arms, Hotel des Amériques* 1981; *Le Choc* 1982; *L'African/The African, The Hunger* (US) 1983; *Le Bon Plaisir, Fort Saganne, Paroles et Musique/Love Songs* (Can./Fr.) 1984; *Speriamo che sia Femmina/Let's Hope It's a Girl* (It./Fr.) 1985; *Le Lieu du Crime/Scene of the Crime* 1986; *Frequence meurtre/Frequency Murder, Drole d'endroit Pour Une Recontre/A Strange Place to Meet* (also prod.) 1988; *Helmut Newton: Frames from the Edge* (documentary) 1989; *Indochine* 1992; *La Reine Blanche* 1992; *Belle de Jour* (first American release), *The Convent* 1995; *Ma Saison Préférée, Voleurs* 1996.

Denham, Maurice. Actor. Born on Dec. 23, 1909, in Beckenham, England. A former engineer, he made his stage debut in 1934. He has played numerous character roles in British films since the mid-40s.

FILMS INCLUDE: *Daybreak, Jassy, The Man Within/The Smugglers, Blanche Fury, The End of the River* 1947; *Escape, London Belongs to Me/Dulcimer Street* 1948; *The Blue Lagoon, Madness of the Heart, The Spider and the Fly, Landfall* 1949; *The Net/Project M-7* 1953; *The Million Pound Note/Man with a Million, The Purple Plain, Carrington V.C./Court Martial* 1954; *Doctor at Sea, Simon and Laura* 1955; *23 Paces to Baker Street* (US), *Checkpoint* 1956; *Barnacle Bill/All at Sea, Night of the Demon* 1957; *The Captain's Table* 1958; *Our Man in Havana* 1959; *Sink the Bismarck!, Two-Way Stretch* 1960; *The Mark* 1961; *The Nanny, Operation Crossbow* 1965; *Caccia alla Volpe/After the Fox* (It./UK/US) 1966; *The Long Duel, Torture Garden* 1967; *Negatives* 1968; *Midas Run* (US), *The Best House in London* 1969; *The Virgin and the Gypsy* 1970; *Sunday Bloody Sunday, Nicholas and Alexandra* 1971; *The Day of the Jackal* 1973; *Luther* 1974; *Shout at the Devil* 1976; *Julia* (US) 1977; *From a Far Country* 1981; *Mr. Love* 1986; *84 Charing Cross Road* 1987.

De Niro, Robert. Actor. Born on Aug. 17, 1943, in New York City. *ed.* Rhodes School (N.Y.C.); High School of Music and Art (N.Y.C.). Trained for the stage by Stella Adler and Lee Strasberg, he appeared in off-Broadway productions and with touring companies before entering films in the late 60s. He gave interesting characterizations in several low-budget Brian De Palma films but attracted little attention until 1973, when he etched a sensitive portrayal of a dying baseball player in John Hancock's *Bang the Drum Slowly* and gave an incisive performance as a simple-minded smalltime hood in Martin SCORSESE's *Mean Streets.* His performance in the latter began an ongoing working relationship between the actor and director, each highlighting the other's portrayal of Italian-American life on the edge. The following year he won an Academy Award as best supporting actor for his portrait of the young Vito Corleone in *The Godfather Part II.* He topped these achievements in 1976 with a memorable performance in the role of a psychotic cabbie alienated by the moral and physical squalor of New York in Scorsese's *Taxi Driver,* affirming his position as one of the finest American screen actors of the 70s. He was again nominated for an Oscar for *The Deer Hunter* (1978) and won a second Academy Award, this time as best actor, for his portrait of boxer Jake La Motta in Scorsese's *Raging Bull* (1980). He shared the best actor prize at the Venice Film Festival for *True Confessions* (1981). An intense, perceptive performer, he remained a forceful figure on the American screen in the 80s and 90s, in a variety of roles ranging from a blank, violent Mafia kingpin in Scorsese's *GoodFellas* (1990) to a softhearted bounty hunter in *Midnight Run* (1988). His company, Tribeca Films, and New York production facility, Tribeca Film Center, have stimulated filmmaking in the city. He made his directorial debut with *A Bronx Tale* (1993). He was married (1975–78) to actress Diahnne ABBOTT.

FILMS: *Trois Chambres à Manhattan* (bit; Fr.) 1965; *Greetings* 1968; *The Wedding Party* (release delayed from 1967), *Sam's Song/The Swap* 1969; *Hi Mom!, Bloody Mama* 1970; *Born to Win, Jennifer on My Mind, The Gang That Couldn't Shoot Straight* 1971; *Bang the Drum Slowly, Mean Streets* 1973; *The Godfather Part II* 1974; *Taxi Driver, The Last Tycoon* (as Monroe Stahr), *Novecento/1900* (It.) 1976; *New York New York* 1977; *The Deer Hunter* 1978; *Raging Bull* 1980; *True Confessions* 1981; *The King of Comedy* 1983; *Once Upon a Time in America, Falling in Love* 1984; *Brazil* 1985; *The Mission* (UK) 1986; *Angel Heart, The Untouchables* (as Al Capone), *Dear America* (doc.; voice only) 1987; *Midnight Run* 1988; *Jacknife, We're No Angels* (also exec. prod.) 1989; *GoodFellas, Awakenings* 1990; *Guilty by Suspicion, Backdraft, Cape Fear* 1991; *Thunderheart* (co-prod. only), *Mad Dog and Glory, Night and the City* 1992; *This Boy's Life, A Bronx Tale* (also dir., co-prod.) 1993; *Mary Shelley's Frankenstein* 1994; *Casino, Heat* 1995; *Faithful* (co-prod. only), *The Fan, Marvin's Room, Sleepers* 1996; *Cop Land* 1997.

Denison, Michael. Actor. Born on Nov. 1, 1915, in Doncaster, England. *ed.* Harrow; Oxford. Smooth, mild-mannered leading man of the British stage (from 1938) and films (from 1940). Married to Dulcie GRAY. Autobiography: *Overture and Beginners* (1973).

FILMS INCLUDE: *Tilly of Bloomsbury* 1940; *Hungry Hill* 1946; *My Brother Jonathan* 1947; *The Blind Goddess, The Glass Mountain* 1948; *Landfall* 1949; *The Franchise Affair* 1950; *The Magic Box* 1951; *The Importance of Being Earnest, Angels One Five* 1952; *There Was a Young Lady/The Frightened Bride* 1953; *The Truth About Women* 1957; *Faces in the Dark* 1960; *Dark River* 1990; *Shadowlands* 1993.

Denmark. Despite the small size of its native market and its relatively limited resources, this country reigned supreme for several years (1909–14) as Europe's most prosperous film center. Its films rivaled those of Hollywood for popularity on the screens of Paris, London, Berlin, and New York.

Film production in Denmark began as early as 1898, but it was in 1906 that the founding of NORDISK Films Kompagni by Ole Oleson provided the impetus for the remarkable rise of the Danish cinema. In the very first year, Nordisk turned out no less than 32 films, and by 1910 more than 100 annually. From the start the company was an entertainment factory, turning out with great regularity and little pretension well-made melodramas, risqué romances, farcical comedies, adaptations of literary classics, and sensational thrillers of mystery and intrigue.

Among the leading directors of the period were Viggo Larsen, August Blom, Urban Gad, Holger Madsen, Robert Dinesen, and Benjamin Christensen. Their stars, Valdemar Psilander, Olaf Fonss, and in particular superstar Asta Nielsen, enjoyed great international popularity. It was from Denmark that Hollywood imported the idea and image of the vamp and the taste for shocking subjects. Such films as Holger Madsen's *The Morphine Takers* (1911) and *Opium Dreams* (1914), banned in several countries in Europe, were sensations in American movie theaters.

The outbreak of WW I dealt a severe blow to the Danish film industry and marked the beginning of the end of its "golden age." For a while, production intensified to satisfy the needs of German theaters cut off completely from any other source of film supply. But the rest of the European market and the lucrative American market were disappearing. In 1916 production at Nordisk reached a record 124 films, but in 1917 production dropped to 81, by 1921 to 17, by 1925 to four, and by 1928 to a single feature film. Other Danish production companies fared no better. The crisis resulted in a mass exodus of talent to other lands. Directors like Christensen and Carl DREYER and stars like Nielsen were forced to seek employment elsewhere. The only films of the Danish cinema internationally successful in the 20s were the comedies of Harold Madsen and Carl Schenstrom, the Laurel and Hardy of Europe.

The coming of sound hurt the Danish film industry further, for the language barrier only compounded its difficulties in regaining world markets. But film production in the 30s gradually increased in response to the demands of local theaters and, paradoxically, WW II provided Danish cinema with a healthy shot in the arm. The spirit of resistance to German Occupation stimulated film production, mostly of government-sponsored documentaries but also feature films. Christensen and Dreyer were by now repatriated. Dreyer directed a number of documentaries and in 1943 created his masterpiece, *Day of Wrath.* A new crop of directors developed during the war and flourished immediately after. Lau Lauritzen, Jr., made a splash in 1945 with *The Red Earth.* The following year the husband-wife team of Bjarne and Astrid Henning-Jensen made several documentaries and an engrossing feature film, *Ditte Daughter of Man,* the first Danish film to enjoy international success in a long time.

The recovery of the Danish picture industry since the war has been slow but steady. Nordisk is still active today and the oldest film production company in the world in continuous existence. For the most part, the country's output still consisted of light comedy films of interest to the local market and, more recently, of pornographic films aimed at world markets. But in the late 60s a new generation of serious filmmakers began to manifest itself, largely as a result of the establishment in 1965 of the Danish Government Film Foundation, which sponsored local production through guaranteed loans and encouraged creativity through a system of awards and inducements.

In recent years, financing of Danish feature films has become more difficult as production costs rise and private and government funds become more scarce. Attendance at Danish cinemas has also decreased, from 59 million visits annually in

1953 to 9 million in 1991. An increasing number of Danish films are international co-productions, often with Sweden or other Scandinavian countries, but also with France and Italy.

Among Denmark's most prominent filmmakers in recent decades have been Jorgen Roos, its top documentarian; Henning Carlsen, the director of *Hunger* (1966); Palle Kjaerulff-Schmidt, director of *Once There Was a War* (also 1966); Bille August, director of Cannes Palme d'Or winners *Pelle the Conqueror* (1988) and *The Best Intentions* (1992); Elizabeth Rygard and Hans-Henrik Jorgensen, veteran documentary directors; and gifted newcomers Susanne Bier and Birger Larsen.

Dennehy, Brian. Actor. Born on July 9, 1938, in Bridgeport, Conn. *ed.* Columbia U. Heavyset character lead and supporting player of the American stage, screen, and TV. Following a five-year stretch with the Marines, which included a stint in Vietnam, he took up acting with New York coaches while earning a living as a salesman, bartender, and truck driver. On the screen from 1977, he soon became established as a solid performer, in roles that range from the ruthlessly tough to the reliably congenial.

FILMS: *Looking for Mr. Goodbar, Semi-Tough* 1977; *F.I.S.T., Foul Play* 1978; *Butch and Sundance: The Early Days, 10* 1979; *Little Miss Marker* 1980; *Split Image, First Blood* 1982; *Never Cry Wolf, Gorky Park* 1983; *Finders Keepers, The River Rat* 1984; *Cocoon, Silverado, Twice in a Lifetime* 1985; *F/X, The Check Is in the Mail, Legal Eagles* 1986; *Dear America* (doc.; voice only), *Best Seller, The Belly of an Architect* (UK) 1987; *Return to Snowy River* (Austral.), *Miles from Home, Cocoon: The Return* 1988; *Georg Elser/Seven Minutes* (W. Ger./US), *Presumed Innocent* 1990; *FX 2: The Deadly Art of Illusion, Gladiator* 1991; *Seven Minutes* 1992; *The Stars Fell on Henrietta, Tommy Boy* 1995; *Romeo and Juliet* 1996.

Denner, Charles. Actor. *b.* May 29, 1926, in Tarnów, Poland. *d.* 1995. In France from age four, he made his stage debut in 1946 and was an established dramatic performer by the time he made his first screen appearance in 1956. He has since appeared in many French films, giving a wide variety of strong characterizations, memorably in the title role of Claude Chabrol's *Landru/Bluebeard* (1963) and in the lead in Alain Jessua's *La Vie à l'envers/Life Upside Down/Inside Out* (1964).

FILMS INCLUDE: *La Meilleure Part* 1956; *Ascenseur pour l'Echafaud/Frantic* 1958; *Landru/Bluebeard* 1963; *La Vie à l'envers/Life Upside Down/Inside Out* 1964; *Compartiment Tueurs/The Sleeping Car Murder, Marie-Chantal contre Docteur Kha* 1965; *Le Voleur/The Thief of Paris, Le Vieil Homme et l'Enfant/The Two of Us* 1967; *La Mariée était en Noir/The Bride Wore Black* 1968; *Z* 1969; *Le Voyou/The Crook* 1970; *Les Assassins de l'Ordre* 1971; *L'Aventure c'est l'Aventure/Money Money Money, Une Belle Fille comme moi/Such a Gorgeous Kid Like Me* 1972; *L'Héritier/The Inheritor, Les Gaspards/The Holes/The Down-in-the-Hole Gang* 1973; *Toute une Vie/And Now My Love* 1974; *Peur sur la Ville/Night Caller* 1975; *Mado, Si c'était à refaire* 1976; *La Première Fois, L'Homme qui aimait les Femmes/The Man Who Loved Women* 1977; *Robert et Robert* 1978; *Le Coeeur à l'enver* 1980.

Denning, Richard. Actor. Born Ludwig [later Louis] A. Denninger, in 1914, in Poughkeepsie, N.Y. *ed.* Woodbury Coll. Blond, handsome, athletic leading man and supporting player of numerous Hollywood films since 1937, seen mostly in grade-B action adventures. Familiar to TV viewers as the star of such series as 'Mr. and Mrs. North,' 'The Flying Doctor,' and 'Michael Shayne,' and as the governor in the series 'Hawaii Five-O.' He was married to actress Evelyn ANKERS.

FILMS INCLUDE: *Hold 'Em Navy* 1937; *Her Jungle Love, The Buccaneer* 1938; *King of Chinatown, Some Like It Hot, Million Dollar Legs, Union Pacific* 1939; *Geronimo, Seventeen, Parole Fixer, Golden Gloves, North West Mounted Police* 1940; *Adam Had Four Sons* 1941; *Beyond the Blue Horizon, The Glass Key, Quiet Please—Murder* 1942; *Black Beauty* 1946; *Unknown Island* 1948; *No Man of Her Own, Double Deal* 1950; *Insurance Investigator* 1951; *Okinawa, Scarlet Angel, Hangman's Knot* 1952; *The 49th Man, Target Hong Kong, The Glass Web* 1953; *Creature from the Black Lagoon, Target Earth, Battle of Rogue River* 1954; *Creature with the Atom Brain, The Magnificent Matador* 1955; *Assignment Redhead/Million Dollar Manhunt* (UK) 1956; *The Day the World Ended* 1956; *An Affair to Remember, The Black Scorpion* 1957; *The Lady Takes a Flyer* 1958; *Twice Told Tales* 1963; *I Sailed to Tahiti with an All Girl Crew* 1969.

Dennis, Sandy. Actress. *b.* Sandra Dale Dennis, Apr. 27, 1937, Hastings, Nebr. *d.* 1992. After some experience in local stock, she headed for New York and the Actors Studio and soon began appearing in off-Broadway plays. In 1961 she made her screen debut, playing a supporting role in Elia Kazan's *Splendor in the Grass* (1961), but it was on Broadway that she emerged as a star, winning two Tony Awards in succession, for 'A Thousand Clowns' and 'Any Wednesday.' She followed these triumphs with an Academy Award for best supporting actress in her first substantial screen role, in *Who's Afraid of Virginia Woolf?* (1966). A honey-blonde, distinctive actress with intense, almost nervous, mannerisms and a muttering speech pattern, she went on to play leads in other films, memorably as a young teacher in a tough New York school in *Up the Down Staircase* (1967). In 1976 she separated from jazz musician Gerry Mulligan, with whom she had lived for many years.

FILMS: *Splendor in the Grass* 1961; *Who's Afraid of Virginia Woolf?* 1966; *Up the Down Staircase* 1967; *The Fox, Sweet November* 1968; *That Cold Day in the Park* (Can./US), *A Touch of Love/Thank You All Very Much* (UK) 1969; *The Out-of-Towners* 1970; *The Only Way Out Is Dead* (Can.) 1971; *Mr. Sycamore* 1975; *Nasty Habits* (UK), *God Told Me To* 1976; *Demon, The Three Sisters* 1977; *The Four Seasons* 1981; *Come Back to the Five and Dime, Jimmy Dean, Jimmy Dean* 1982; *Another Woman, 976-EVIL* 1988; *Parents* 1989.

Denny, Reginald. Actor. *b.* Reginald Leigh Daymore, Nov. 20, 1891, Richmond, Surrey, England. *d.* 1967. On the London stage from the age of eight, he made his film debut in Hollywood in 1919 and for the next 15 years starred in numerous silent and early sound comedy-adventure films, usually portraying a vigorous man of action à la Fairbanks. In the mid-30s he switched to dapper character roles, and because of his marked British accent he was typically cast as an amiable though sometimes asinine Englishman, memorably as Algy in the Bulldog Drummond series of the late 30s. In all he appeared in some 200 films, including 24 shorts in the "Leather Pushers" series (1922–24), in which he starred, as well as in stage plays, such as 'My Fair Lady,' and on TV. Denny was also active in the aviation industry, pioneering and developing the first pilotless radio-controlled aircraft successfully flown in the US.

FILMS INCLUDE: *Bringing Up Betty, The Oakdale Affair* 1919; *A Dark Lantern, 39 East* 1920; *The Iron Trail, Footlights, Disraeli, Tropical Love* (also sc.) 1921; *The Kentucky Derby, Sherlock Holmes* 1922; *The Abysmal Brute, The Thrill Chaser* 1923; *Sporting Youth, The Reckless Age, The Fast Worker* 1924; *Oh Doctor!, I'll Show You the Town, Where Was I?, California Straight Ahead* 1925; *Skinner's Dress Suit, Rolling Home, Take It from Me, What Happened to Jones, The Cheerful Fraud* 1926; *Fast and Furious* (also story), *Out All Night, On Your Toes* 1927; *That's My Daddy* (also story), *Good Morning Judge, The Night*

Bird 1928; *Red Hot Speed, Clear the Decks, His Lucky Day, One Hysterical Night* (also story, dial., edit.) 1929; *What a Man!, Madam Satan, Embarrassing Moments, A Lady's Morals, Those Three French Girls, Oh for a Man!* 1930; *Kiki, Parlor Bedroom and Bath, Private Lives, Stepping Out* 1931; *Strange Justice, The Iron Master* 1932; *The Barbarian, Only Yesterday, Fog* 1933; *The Lost Patrol, Of Human Bondage, The World Moves On, Dancing Man, We're Rich Again, The Little Minister* 1934; *No More Ladies, Anna Karenina* 1935; *The Preview Murder Mystery, Romeo and Juliet* 1936; *Bulldog Drummond Comes Back, Beg Borrow and Steal* 1937; *Bulldog Drummond's Peril, Four Men and a Prayer, Blockade* 1938; *Arrest Bulldog Drummond* 1939; *Rebecca, Spring Parade, Seven Sinners* 1940; *Appointment for Love, International Squadron* 1941; *Captains of the Clouds, Sherlock Holmes and the Voice of Terror, Eyes in the Night* 1942; *Song of the Open Road* 1944; *Love Letters* 1945; *My Favorite Brunette, The Macomber Affair, The Secret Life of Walter Mitty* 1947; *Mr. Blandings Builds His Dream House* 1948; *Abbott and Costello Meet Dr. Jekyll and Mr. Hyde* 1953; *Cat Ballou* 1965; *Assault on a Queen, Batman* 1966.

density. The relative opacity of a filmed image; the degree to which it limits the amount of light passing through it. Density is measured with the aid of a densitometer in terms of logarithmic units.

De Palma, Brian. Director. Born on Sept. 11, 1940, in Newark, N.J. He grew up in Philadelphia, where, he confesses, he became fascinated by blood, gore, and terror, watching his father, an orthopedic surgeon, operate on his patients. As a physics major at Columbia University, he was drawn to drama. He joined the Columbia Players and with a second-hand 16 mm Bolex began making film shorts, starting with *Icarus* (1960) and *660124: The Story of an IBM Card* (1961). On the strength of a prize-winning third short, *Wotan's Wake* (1962), he won an MCA writing fellowship to Sarah Lawrence College, where he spent two years working on his first feature, *The Wedding Party* (released briefly in 1969). Money earned by making documentaries helped him start *Murder à la Mode* (1967), his first released feature. *Greetings* (1968), an anarchic satire, brought him the first wide recognition and some critical praise. De Palma followed it with a funnier sequel, *Hi Mom!* (1970), and another offbeat comedy before he ventured into what has become known as his "Hitchcock phase" with *Sisters* (1973). Paying a tribute to the great master of the thriller film, De Palma first openly imitated or borrowed from Hitchcock, but eventually expanded and elaborated on Hitchcockian themes and images, developing a style all his own. His early lower-budget thrillers, although superbly manufactured, were too bloody and garish for the average taste and infuriated many critics. But De Palma began gaining respectability with *Dressed to Kill* (1980) and following several critical setbacks, reached his apex in the late 80s with such high-powered productions as *The Untouchables* (1987) and *Casualties of War* (1989). A superb technician, he was finally crafting material worthy of his bold, often dazzling, visual flair. A major critical and financial disappointment, *The Bonfire of the Vanities*, led to much Hollywood self-analysis and placed De Palma in a position for a comeback, which he began working toward with the psychological thriller *Raising Cain* and the more fully realized gangster film *Carlito's Way*. In 1996, De Palma found box-office success with *Mission: Impossible* starring Tom Cruise.

FEATURE FILMS: *Murder à la Mode* (also sc., edit.), *Greetings* (also co-sc., edit.) 1967; *The Wedding Party* (co-dir., co-prod., co-sc., co-edit. with Cynthia Munroe and Wilford Leach; his first feature; release delayed from 1964) 1969; *Dionysus in '69* (co-dir. with Robert Fiore and Bruce Rubin; also co-phot., co-edit.; 8 and 16 mm recording of stage performance; release delayed from 1968), *Hi Mom!* (also co-story, sc.) 1970; *Get to Know Your Rabbit* 1972; *Sisters* (also story, co-sc.) 1973; *Phantom of the Paradise* (also sc.) 1974; *Obsession* (also co-story), *Carrie* 1976; *The Fury* 1978; *Home Movies* 1979; *Dressed to Kill* 1980; *Blow Out* 1981; *Scarface* 1983; *Body Double* 1984; *Wise Guys* 1986; *The Untouchables* 1987; *Casualties of War* 1989; *The Bonfire of the Vanities* 1990 (also pr., uncred. act.); *Raising Cain* (also sc.) 1992; *Carlito's Way* 1993; *Mission: Impossible* 1996.

Depardieu, Gérard. Actor. Born on Dec. 27, 1948, in Chateauroux, France. One of the principal leading men of the French cinema of the 70s and its top male star of the 80s. A juvenile delinquent in his teens, he took up acting as therapy, on the recommendation of a prison psychologist. While training at dramatic school, he made his film debut at 16 in Roger Leenhardt's short, *Le Beatnik et le Minet* (1965). He later performed on TV and on the stage, before returning to the screen for the long stretch in 1970. A strong, brawny man of powerful presence, with crude yet expressive facial features, he gradually evolved into a screen personality reminiscent of the late Jean Gabin: commanding, versatile, and amazingly prolific. His persuasive portrayals range from gruff to sensitive, from common men to prominent figures like Danton and Rodin. His *Cyrano de Bergerac* (1990), was praised by critics as the definitive portrait of the Rostand character. He won Césars for *The Last Metro* (1980) and *Cyrano,* and the best actor prize at Venice for *Police* (1985), among many other awards. He directed himself in *La Tartuffe* (1984) and co-produced Satyajit Ray's Indian-French film *Branches of the Tree* (1990).

FILMS INCLUDE: *Le Cri du Cormoran le Soir au-dessus des Jonques* 1970; *Le Tueur* 1971; *Nathalie Granger, L'Affaire Dominici* 1972; *Deux Hommes dans la Ville, Rude Journée pour la Ville, Les Gaspards/The Holes* 1973; *Les Valseuses/Going Places, Stavisky* 1974; *Vincent François Paul et les autres/Vincent Francois Paul and the Others, Pas si méchant que ça/The Wonderful Crook, 7 Morts sur Ordonnance, Maîtresse* 1975; *1900* (It.), *La Dernière Femme/The Last Woman, Barocco* 1976; *Baxter—Vera Baxter, Le Camion, René la Canne, Violanta* (Switz.), *La Nuit tous les Chats sont gris* 1977; *Préparez vos Mouchoirs/Get Out Your Handkerchiefs, Bye Bye Monkey* (It./Fr.), *Le Sucre* 1978; *Les Chiens, L'Ingorgo/Traffic Jam* (It./Fr./Sp.), *Buffet froid* 1979; *Le Dernier Métro/The Last Metro, Mon Oncle d'Amérique, Loulou, Inspecteur la Bavure, Je vous aime* 1980; *Le Choix des Armes/Choice of Arms, La Femme d'a Coté/The Woman Next Door, La Chèvre* 1981; *Le Retour de Martin Guerre/The Return of Martin Guerre, Le Grand Frère* 1982; *Danton* (title role), *La Lune dans le Caniveau/The Moon in the Gutter, Les Compères* 1983; *Fort Saganne, Le Tartuffe* (also dir., sc.), *Rive Droite Rive Gauche* 1984; *Une Femme ou Deux/One Woman or Two, Police* 1985; *Tenue du Soirée/Ménage, Jean de Florette, Les Fugitifs* 1986; *Sous le Soleil de Satan/Under Satan's Sun* 1987; *Camille Claudel* (as Auguste Rodin), *Deux* 1988; *Trop Belle pour toi/Too Beautiful for You, Je vous rentre à la Maison* 1989; *Cyrano de Bergerac* (title role), *Green Card* (US) 1990; *Thanks for Life, Uranus* 1991; *Tous les Matins du Monde/Every Morning of the World, 1492: The Conquest of Paradise* (US/Sp./Fr./UK) 1992; *Germinal* 1993; *Le Colonel Chabert, My Father the Hero* (US), *Pure Formality* 1994; *Rasputin* 1995; *Bogus* (US), *Hamlet* (US/UK), *The Horseman on the Roof, LeGarcu, The Secret Agent, Unhook the Stars* (US) 1996; *She's So Lovely* (co-exec. prod. only) 1997.

Depp, Johnny. Actor, musician. Born in 1964, in Kentucky. Raised in Miramar, Florida, he started his own rock group at 13 and later played lead guitar with The Kids band. He turned to acting in the mid-80s and gained popularity in the role of police officer Tom Hanson, who masquerades as a high school student in the TV series '21 Jump Street.' His career in films was boosted tremendously by the title role in the 1990 hit *Edward Scissorhands.*

FILMS: *A Nightmare on Elm Street* 1984; *Private Resort* 1985; *Platoon* 1986; *Cry-Baby, Edward Scissorhands* 1990; *Freddy's Dead: The Final Nightmare* (cameo) 1991; *American Dreamers* 1992; *Benny & Joon, What's Eating Gilbert Grape* 1993; *Ed Wood* 1994; *Don Juan DeMarco, Nick of Time* 1995; *Dead Man* 1996; *Donnie Brasco* 1997.

depth of field. The range of distance from the camera, at a particular lens setting, at which all images will remain in reasonably sharp focus. The permissible depth of field for a shot depends on the focal length of the lens, its aperture, and the distance at which it is focused.

depth of focus. The infinitely small range at which the distance between a lens and the film in the camera will produce a reasonably sharp image. The slightest change in the position of film inside the camera during exposure may result in out-of-focus images.

De Putti, Lya. Actress. *b.* 1901, Vesce, Hungary. *d.* 1931. Reputedly the daughter of a baron and wife of a count, she began as a dancer in Budapest vaudeville, then turned to classical ballet in Berlin. She later starred in vamp type of roles in films of the German UFA company, including E. A. Dupont's famous *Variety* (1925). In 1926 she went to Hollywood, where she starred in several films. She died in New York of pneumonia following an operation.

FILMS INCLUDE: In Germany—*Das indische Grabmal/The Indian Tomb* 1921; *Ilona, Der brennende Acker/Burning Soil, Phantom, Othello* 1922; *Die Fledermaus, Thamar—das Kind der Berge* 1923; *Komödianten* 1924; *Eifersucht/Jealousy, Im Namen des Kaisers, Variété/Variety* 1925; *Manon Lescaut* 1926. In the US—*The Prince of Tempters, The Sorrows of Satan, God Gave Me Twenty Cents* 1926; *The Heart Thief* 1927; *Buck Privates, Midnight Rose, The Scarlet Lady* 1928. In the UK—*The Informer* 1929.

Deray, Jacques. Director. Born Jacques Deray-Desrayaud, on Feb. 19, 1929, in Lyons. In Paris from age 12, he studied drama with René Simon and played small roles on the stage and in films before moving behind the camera as an assistant director in 1952. He worked in that capacity on many productions until 1960, when he turned out his first feature as a director. He soon established a reputation as a competent craftsman with an assertive visual style.

FILMS (as director and co-screenwriter): *Le Gigolo* 1960; *Rififi à Tokyo/Rififi in Tokyo* 1961; *Symphonie pour un Massacre/Symphony for a Massacre* 1963; *Par un Beau Matin d'Eté* 1964; *L'Homme de Marrakesh/That Man George/Our Man in Marrakesh* 1966; *Avec la Peau des autres* 1967; *La Piscine/The Swimming Pool* 1969; *Borsalino* 1970; *Doucement les Basses, Un peu de Soleil dans l'Eau froide* 1971; *Un Homme est mort/The Outside Man* 1972; *Borsalino and Co.* 1974; *Flic Story* 1975; *Le Gang* 1977; *Un Papillon sur l'Epaule/Butterfly on the Shoulder* 1978; *Trois Hommes à abbatre/Three Men to Destroy* 1980; *Le Marginal* 1983; *On ne meurt que deux fois/He Died with His Eyes Open* 1985; *Les Bois noirs* 1989.

Derek, Bo. Actress. Born Mary Cathleen Collins, on Nov. 20, 1956, in Torrance, Calif. Exquisite beauty of the American screen. The daughter of a motorcycle salesman and a hairdresser to the stars, she was introduced, at age 16, through her mother's connections, to actor-director-photographer John DEREK. He took charge of her life and career. To avoid legal problems, he whisked her off to Germany and in 1974, after she turned 18, he divorced his wife to marry her. After a slow start, she soared to fame in 1979 as the object of Dudley Moore's sexual fantasies in Blake Edwards's film *10.* However, her submission to her husband's guidance proved harmful to the rest of her career. He featured her in a succession of awfully scripted movies he directed and photographed himself, the only redeeming feature of which was the loveliness of her chiseled face and naked body.

FILMS: *Orca* 1977; *10* 1979; *A Change of Seasons* 1980; *Fantasies/And Once Upon a Love* (release delayed from 1976), *Tarzan the Ape Man* (also prod.) 1981; *Bolero* (also prod.) 1984; *Ghosts Can't Do It* (also prod.) 1990; *Tommy Boy* 1995.

Derek, John. Actor, director. Born Derek Harris, on Aug. 12, 1926, in Hollywood, Calif. The son of a writer-director, Lawson Harris, and a minor screen actress, Dolores Johnson, he was put under contract to David O. Selznick while still a teenager but did not make his screen debut until he returned from WW II service. A darkly handsome young man with pretty-boy good looks, he immediately was popular with the bobby-sox crowd and was accordingly cast mainly in costume adventure yarns appealing to young people. Disappointed in his acting career, he developed an interest in still photography and became a proficient still photographer. In the late 60s he turned to directing low-budget motion pictures, on some of which he was also the cameraman. Formerly married to French starlet Patti Behrs, Swiss sexpot Ursula ANDRESS, and American TV star Linda Evans, he married Bo DEREK in 1974 and, in Svengali fashion, assumed control of her life and career. He directed and photographed her latest films, which many say belong more in the softcore porno genre than in the mainstream feature category.

FILMS: As actor—*Since You Went Away* (extra) 1944; *I'll Be Seeing You* (bit) 1945; *A Double Life* (bit) 1947; *Knock on Any Door, All the King's Men* 1949; *Rogues of Sherwood Forest* 1950; *Mask of the Avenger, Saturday's Hero, The Family Secret* 1951; *Scandal Sheet, Thunderbirds* 1952; *Prince of Pirates, Ambush at Tomahawk Gap, The Last Posse. Mission Over Korea, Sea of Lost Ships, The Outcast, The Adventures of Hajji Baba* 1954; *Prince of Players, An Annapolis Story, Run for Cover* 1955; *The Leather Saint, The Ten Commandments* (as Joshua) 1956; *Fury at Showdown, Omar Khayyam, The Flesh Is Weak* (UK) 1957; *High Hell, Il Corsaro della Mezza Luna* (It.) 1958; *I Battellieri del Volga/Prisoner of the Volga* (It.) 1959; *Exodus* 1960; *Nightmare in the Sun* (also co-prod.) 1965. As director—*Once Before I Die* (also prod., act.) 1966; *A Boy. . . a Girl* (also sc., phot.), *Childish Things* (also phot.) 1969; *Fantasies/And Once Upon a Love* (also phot.; release delayed from 1976), *Tarzan the Ape Man* (also phot.) 1981; *Bolero* (also sc., phot.) 1984; *Ghosts Can't Do It* (also phot.) 1990.

Deren, Maya. Avant-garde filmmaker. *b.* 1917, Kiev, Russia. *d.* 1961. As a child, she immigrated with her Jewish family to the US, where her father, a psychiatrist, joined the staff (and later became the director) of the State Institute for the Feeble-Minded, in Syracuse, New York. After receiving her high school education at the League of Nations School in Geneva, Switzerland, she studied journalism at the University of Syracuse. On an impulse, she got married and moved with her husband to New York City, where she completed her B.A. degree at NYU. Following a divorce, she went for her master's degree in literature at Smith College. Intending to write a book about dance, she accompanied black dancer-choreographer Katherine Dunham on a national tour, during which she met and in 1942 married Czech filmmaker Alexander Hammid (*b.* Alexander Hackenschmied, Dec. 17, 1907, Linz, Austria). Together they started working on her first film, *Meshes in the Afternoon* (1943), an 18-minute short in which time and space were manipulated to achieve a twilight zone between dream and reality. A dark beauty, she played the principal role in the film, which is widely considered a milestone in the annals of experimental cinema. Although less well known, her subsequent films, were similarly striking lyrical explorations of the dream-versus-reality theme. She died at 44, after a series of brain hemorrhages, leaving behind a legacy of inspired cine-poetry.

Dern, Bruce. Actor. Born on June 4, 1936, in Winnetka, near Chicago. The grandson of a former governor of Utah and the nephew of the Secretary of War in FDR's cabinet and of poet-playwright Archibald MacLeish, he attended prep school (Choate) but dropped out of college (U. of Pennsylvania) to pursue an acting career. Following several supporting roles on and off Broadway, he made his film debut in 1960 playing a bit in Kazan's *Wild River.* In the next few years he played small roles, often bellhops and police clerks in numerous TV shows. Critics and film directors slowly began taking notice of his ability, and he was eventually able to demonstrate his versatility in a wide range of interesting roles, including leads. He was nominated for an Oscar for best supporting actor for *Coming Home* (1978) and the best actor prize at the Berlin Film Festival for *That Championship Season* (1982). He is the father of actress Laura DERN by his marriage to actress Diane LADD.

FILMS: *Wild River* 1960; *Bedtime Story* 1963; *Marnie* 1964; *Hush Hush. . . Sweet Charlotte* 1965; *The Wild Angels* 1966; *The St. Valentine's Day Massacre, Waterhole #3, The Trip, The War Wagon* 1967; *Psych-Out, Will Penny, Hang 'em High* 1968; *Support Your Local Sheriff!, Castle Keep, Number One, They Shoot Horses Don't They?* 1969; *Rebel Rousers* (release delayed from 1967), *The Cycle Savages* (release delayed from 1969), *Bloody Mama* 1970; *Drive He Said, The Incredible Two-Headed Transplant* 1971; *The Cowboys, Silent Running, Thumb Tripping, The King of Marvin Gardens* 1972; *The Laughing Policeman* 1973; *The Great Gatsby* 1974; *Smile, Posse* 1975; *Family Plot, Won Ton Ton—The Dog Who Saved Hollywood, Folies Bourgeoises/The Twist* (Fr.) 1976; *Black Sunday* 1977; *Coming Home, The Driver* 1978; *Middle Age Crazy* 1980; *Tattoo* 1981; *Harry Tracy—Desperado* (Can.), *That Championship Season* 1982; *On the Edge* 1986; *The Big Town* 1987; *World Gone Wild 1969* 1988; *The 'Burbs* 1989; *After Dark My Sweet* 1990; *Diggstown* 1992; *Wild Bill* 1995; *Down Periscope, Last Man Standing, Mulholland Falls* (unbilled) 1996.

Dern, Laura. Actress. Born in 1966, in Los Angeles. Tall (5' 10") languid blonde lead of the American screen. The daughter of actors Bruce DERN and Diane LADD, she appeared as a child extra in several of her father's films and had a walk-on in her mother's *Alice Doesn't Live Here Anymore* (1974). After training at the Lee Strasberg Theatre Institute, she made her screen acting debut in 1980, and was highly praised for her roles in *Smooth Talk* (1985) and *Rambling Rose* (1991), two varieties of women confronting their sexuality. Nominated for an Academy Award as best actress for the latter, Dern and Ladd (nominated as supporting actress for the same film) made Oscar history as the first mother/daughter to receive nominations in the same year.

FILMS: *Alice Doesn't Live Here Anymore* 1974; *Foxes* 1980; *Ladies and Gentlemen—The Fabulous Stains* 1981; *Teachers* 1984; *Mask, Smooth Talk* 1985; *Blue Velvet* 1986; *Haunted Summer* 1988; *Fat Man and Little Boy* 1989; *Wild at Heart* 1990; *Rambling Rose* 1991; *Jurassic Park, A Perfect World* 1993; *Citizen Ruth* 1996.

de Rochemont, Louis. Producer. *b.* Jan. 13, 1899, Chelsea, Mass. *d.* 1978. *ed.* MIT; Harvard. After a six-year stint as an officer in the US Navy (1917–23), he worked for various newsreel companies in capacities ranging from cameraman to executive. In 1934, dissatisfied with the shallow content of American newsreels, he created (with Roy E. Larsen of Time, Inc.) "The March of Time," a novel concept in screen journalism which offered cinema audiences a dynamic, in-depth view of the news. The series won an Academy Award in 1936. In 1940, de Rochemont produced and directed the first feature of "The March of Time," *The Ramparts We Watch,* a dramatization of the impact of WW II on a small American town. In 1943 he joined 20th Century-Fox, for which, the following year, he produced the Oscar-winning documentary *The Fighting Lady,* made in association with the US Navy. After WW II, still as producer for Fox, he pioneered in the trend toward realism and on-location shooting of Hollywood features with such semi-documentary fictionalized true-life dramas as *The House on 92nd Street* and *Boomerang.* He later became an independent producer, forming Louis de Rochemont Associates with former colleagues at March of Time. Among his subsequent films were some in Cinerama and other widescreen processes. His brother, Richard de Rochemont (*b.* Dec. 13, 1903, Chelsea, Mass.; *d.* 1982), and his son, Louis de Rochemont III (*b.* Dec. 14, 1930, N.Y.C.), were also filmmakers.

FILMS INCLUDE: *Metropolitan Opera, The First World War* (compilation film; co-dir.) 1934; *The Ramparts We Watch* (also dir.) 1940; *We Are the Marines* (doc.; also dir.) 1942; *The Fighting Lady* (also edit.) 1944; *The House on 92nd Street* 1945; *13 Rue Madeleine, Boomerang* 1947; *Lost Boundaries* 1949; *The Whistle at Eaton Falls* 1951; *Walk East on Beacon* 1952; *Martin Luther* 1953; *Animal Farm* (UK) 1954; *Cinerama Holiday* (also sc.) 1955; *Windjammer* (in Cinemiracle) 1958; *Man on a String* 1960; *The Roman Spring of Mrs. Stone* 1961.

De Santis, Giuseppe. Director. Born on Feb. 11, 1917, in Fondi, Italy. After philosophy studies at the University of Rome and literature and film training at Rome's Centro Sperimentale di Cinematografia he began writing for the magazine *Cinema.* He frequently criticized contemporary (late 30s and early 40s) trends in Italian films, advocating instead the approach that was later to become known as NEOREALISM. In 1942, while still working for the magazine, he collaborated on the script of Visconti's first feature film, *Ossessione.* Following other contributions as screenwriter and assistant director, he directed his first film, *Caccia tragica/Tragic Hunt* in 1947. In this and three subsequent films he pleaded for improved social conditions in postwar Italy. But his sincerity as a social reformer was marred by ideological incoherence and a tendency toward sensationalism. His second film, *Bitter Rice,* was the sexiest of the neorealist productions and had audiences the world over queuing up to see Silvana Mangano in the briefest of hot pants loving and suffering in the rice fields of the Po Valley. His fourth, *Rome 11 O'Clock,* was a powerful but also gruesome and sensational story about a group of unemployed girls who are killed when a stairway collapses under the weight of too many applicants for a secretarial job. De Santis's importance as a filmmaker diminished after he switched from social themes to intimate dramas, in conformity with the trend in Italian cinema since the early 50s.

FILMS (as director-co-screenwriter): *Giorni di Gloria* (one episode) 1945; *Caccia tragica/Tragic Hunt* 1947; *Riso amaro/Bitter Rice* 1949; *Non c'e Pace tra gli Ulivi/Under the Olive Tree* Italiani 1950; *Roma Ore 11/Rome 11 O'Clock* 1952; *Un Marito per Anna Zaccheo/A Husband for Anna* 1953; *Giorni d'Amore/Days of Love* 1954; *Uomini e Lupi/Men and Wolves* 1956; *La Strada lunga un Anno* 1958; *La Garçonnière* (It./Fr.) 1960; *Italiani brava Gente* (It./USSR) 1964; *Un Apprezzato Professionista di Sicuro Avvenire* 1972.

De Santis, Pasqalino (Pasquale). Italian director of photography. Superb craftsman who after several years as camera operator for Gianni Di Venanzo (*Salvatore Giuliano, 8½, Juliet of the Spirits, The 10th Victim,* etc.) became a noted cinematographer himself. He won an Oscar for the cinematography of Franco Zeffirelli's *Romeo and Juliet* (1969), becoming the first foreigner to win an Academy Award in that category. He also won the Italian David Di Donatello Award a number of times.

FILMS INCLUDE: *C'era una Volta/More Than a Miracle* 1967; *Romeo and Juliet* (UK/It.), *Gli Amanti/A Place for Lovers* 1968; *La Caduta degli Dei/Götterdämmerung/The Damned* (co-phot.) 1969; *Morte a Venezia/Death in Venice* 1971; *L'Assassinat de Trotsky/The Assassination of Trotsky* (Fr./It.) 1972; *A Proposito Lucky Luciano/Re: Lucky Luciano* 1973; *Lancelot du Lac/Lancelot of the Lake* (Fr.) 1974; *Gruppo di Famiglia in uno Interno/Conversation Piece* 1975; *Cadaveri Eccelenti/Illustrious Corpses, L'Innocente/The Innocent* 1976; *Una Giornata speciale/A Special Day* (It./Can.), *Le Diable probablement/The Devil Probably* (Fr.) 1977; *Cristo si è fermato a Eboli/Christ Stopped at Eboli/Eboli* 1979; *La Terrazza/The Terace* 1980; *Tre Fratelli/Three Brothers* 1981; *Misunderstood* (US), *L'Argent* (Fr.) 1983; *Carmen* 1985; *Dimenticare Palermo/ To Forget Palermo* (It./Fr.) 1990.

Deschanel, Caleb. Director of photography, director. Born on Sept. 21, 1941, in Philadelphia to a French father and a Quaker mother. *ed.* Johns Hopkins U.; USC Film School. After training at the American Film Institute, he apprenticed under cinematographer Gordon Willis and began making commercials, shorts, and documentaries. A lighting cameraman of features from 1979, he impressed from the start with his vivid imagery. He was nominated for Oscars for *The Right Stuff* (1983) and *The Natural* (1984). His achievements as an occasional director were less spectacular. His wife Mary Jo Deschanel is an actress.

FILMS: As cinematographer—*Apocalypse Now* (2nd-unit phot.), *More American Graffiti, The Black Stallion, Being There* 1979; *Let's Spend the Night Together, The Black Stallion Returns* (addnl. phot. only), *The Right Stuff* 1983; *The Natural* 1984; *The Slugger's Wife* 1985; *50 Years of Action!* 1986. As director—*The Escape Artist* 1982; *Crusoe* 1989; *It Could Happen to You* 1994; *Fly Away Home* 1996.

De Sica, Vittorio. Director, actor. *b.* July 7, 1902, Sora, Italy. *d.* 1974. He grew up in Naples in a middle-class, low-income environment. While in his teens he contributed to the family resources by working as an office clerk but soon found acting a more satisfying escape from the drudgery of his youth. He made his screen debut in 1918 in *The Clemenceau Affair,* but his acting career did not begin in earnest until 1923 when he joined Tatiana Pavlova's stage company. A handsome man, he was a successful matinee idol by the late 20s and before long formed his own company to produce stage plays, in many of which he co-starred with his first wife, Giuditta Rissone. He made a name as a suave leading man in Italian films, mostly light comedies, and became immensely popular with female audiences.

During WW II he became attracted to directing. His first four films as director were routine light productions in the tradition of the Italian cinema of the day. But his fifth, *The Children Are Watching Us,* marked the beginning of De Sica's collaboration with author and screenwriter Cesare Zavattini, a creative relationship that was to give the world two of the most significant films of postwar Italian neorealism, *Shoeshine* (1946) and *The Bicycle Thief* (1948). In both films De Sica and Zavattini examined the chaotic urban conditions in the aftermath of the war with incisive simplicity and disarming sincerity. In both films social and economic conditions on the streets of Rome were drawn in stark detail as background to a personal emotional drama revolving around a tender human relationship, of two shoeshine boys in *Shoeshine,* of father and son in *The Bicycle Thief.* In both films De Sica achieved marvelous results with nonprofessional actors, infusing his characters with his deep humanity and tenderness. The winner of a best foreign film Oscar and other international awards, *The Bicycle Thief* not only remains a supreme example of neorealism but is also widely accepted as one of the great films of all time.

De Sica's next film in collaboration with Zavattini was the satirical fantasy *Miracle in Milan* (1950), which wavered between optimism and despair in its allegorical treatment of the plight of the poor in an industrial society. *Umberto D* (1952), a sad, disturbing film-poem about old age and loneliness, which he dedicated to the memory of his father, was De Sica's last neorealist film and temporarily his last masterpiece. With the notable exception of *Two Women* (1960), a solid work enhanced by the excellent performance of Sophia Loren, his subsequent output as director was for a long while markedly less inspired and significant.

Throughout his career as director, De Sica continued to act in films so that he could finance the kinds of film he wanted to make. He turned almost exclusively to acting in the late 50s and enjoyed great popularity in the role of the affable *maresciallo* (rural police officer) in Comencini's *Bread Love and Dreams* (1954) and several sequels in a comedy series co-starring Gina Lollobrigida. He was at his best playing light roles requiring deft irony and flashy charm but proved himself capable of a solid dramatic performance in Rossellini's *General della Rovere* (1959). In the 60s he was back in the director's chair, turning out such successful box-office ventures as *Yesterday Today and Tomorrow* and *Marriage Italian Style* (both 1964), and also quite a few commercial and critical failures, all the while continuing to appear as an actor in films of other directors. And then, when he seemed to have settled on ending his career in mediocrity, De Sica made a dramatic comeback as a director to be reckoned with in 1971 with *The Garden of the Finzi-Continis,* an exquisite, hauntingly beautiful, and deeply disturbing film about the gradual disintegration of Jewish freedom and dignity in Fascist Italy, a work permeated with the humanity and tenderness of De Sica's films of old.

In all, De Sica directed some 25 films, four of which won Oscars as best foreign films: *Shoeshine, The Bicycle Thief, Yesterday Today and Tomorrow,* and *The Garden of the Finzi-Continis.* He appeared as an actor in more than 150 films. He died at 72 following surgery for the removal of a cyst from his lungs. He was survived by his second wife, former Spanish actress Maria Mercader, with whom he had lived since 1942 but whom he could legally marry only in 1968 after adopting French citizenship, which enabled him to divorce his first wife. The eldest son of De Sica and Mercader, Manuel, composed the music for *The Garden of the Finzi-Continis*; the younger, Christian, is a pop singer and an actor.

FILMS: As director (complete)—*Rose Scarlatte* (also act.) 1940; *Maddalena Zero in Condotta* (also co-sc., act.), *Teresa Venerdi/Doctor Beware* (also co-sc., act.) 1941; *Un Garibaldino al Convento* (also co-sc., act.) 1942; *I Bambini ci Guardano/The Children Are Watching Us* (also co-sc.) 1943; *La Porta Del Cielo* (also co-sc.), *Sciuscia/Shoeshine* 1946; *Ladri di Biciclette/ The Bicycle Thief/Bicycle Thieves* (also prod.) 1948; *Miracolo a Milano/Miracle in Milan* (also prod., co-sc.) 1950; *Umberto D* (also co-prod., co-sc.) 1952; *Stazione Termini/Indiscretion of an American Wife* (also prod.) 1953; *L'Oro di Napoli/Gold of Naples* (also co-sc., act.) 1954; *Il Tetto/The Roof* (also prod.)

1956; *La Ciociara/Two Women* (It./Fr.; also co-sc.) 1960; *Il Giudizio Universale* (also act.) 1961; *Boccaccio '70* ("The Raffle" episode; It./Fr.), *I Sequestrati di Altona/The Condemned of Altona* (It./Fr.) 1962; *Il Boom, Ieri Oggi Domani/Yesterday Today and Tomorrow* (It./Fr.) 1963; *Matrimonio all'Italiana/Marriage Italian Style* (It./Fr.) 1964; *Un Monde nouveau/Un Mondo nuovo/A Young World* (Fr./It.), *Caccia alla Volpe/After the Fox* (It./US/UK) 1966; *Le Streghe/The Witches* ("A Night Like Any Other" episode; It./Fr.), *Sept fois Femme/Woman Times Seven* (Fr./US) 1967; *Amanti/A Place for Lovers* (also co-sc.; It./Fr.) 1968; *I Girasoli/Sunflower* (It./Fr.) 1969; *Il Giardino dei Finzi-Contini/The Garden of the Finzi-Continis* (It./Ger.) 1971; *Lo Chiameremo Andrea* 1972; *Una Breve Vacanza/A Brief Vacation* 1973; *Il Viaggio/The Voyage* 1974.

As actor (partial list)—*The Clemenceau Affair* 1918; *La Compagnia dei Matti* 1928; *La Vecchia Signora* 1931; *Gli Uomini che Mascalzoni* 1932; *Passa l'Amore* 1933; *La Canzone del Sole* 1934; *Darò un Milione, Amo te Sola, Tempo massimo* 1935; *Lohengrin* 1936; *Napoli d'Altri Tempi, Il Signor Max* 1937; *La Mazurka di Papà, Le Due Madri/The Two Mothers* 1938; *Castelli in Aria, I Grandi Magazzini* 1939; *Manon Lescaut, La Peccatrice* 1940; *I nostri Sogni* (also co-sc.) 1942; *Dieci Minuti di Vita* 1943; *Roma Città libera* 1946; *Domani è troppo tardi/Tomorrow Is Too Late* 1950; *Altri Tempi/Times Gone By* 1952; *Madame De. . . /The Earrings of Madame De* 1953; *Pane Amore e Fantasia/Bread Love and Dreams, Il Letto/The Bed* 1954; *Pane Amore e Gelosia/Frisky, Peccato che si una Canaglia/Too Bad She's Bad, Il Segno di Venere, La Bella Mugnala/The Miller's Beautiful Wife, Il Bigamo/The Bigamist* 1955; *Mio Figlio Nerone/Nero's Mistress* (as Seneca), *Monte Carlo, Padri e Figli/Fathers and Sons/The Tailor's Maid, Souvenir d'Italie* 1956; *Amore e Chiacchiere, Vacanze a Ischia/Holiday Island, A Farewell to Arms* (US) 1957; *Anna di Brooklyn* 1958; *Il Moralista/The Moralist, Il Generale della Rovere/General della Rovere* 1959; *It Started in Naples* (US), *The Millionairess* (UK), *The Angel Wore Red* (US), *Austerlitz* (as Pope Pius XII) 1960; *Le Meraviglie di Aladino/The Wonders of Aladdin* (as Genie), *Lafayette* (as secret agent Edward Bancroft; Fr./It.) 1962; *The Amorous Adventures of Moll Flanders* (UK) 1965; *The Biggest Bundle of Them All* (US/It.), *The Shoes of the Fisherman* (US) 1968; *Snow Job* 1971; *Delitto Mattei* 1973; *Andy Warhol's Dracula* 1974; *C'eravamo tanto Amati/We All Loved Each Other So Much* 1975.

Desmond, William. Actor. *b.* William Mannion, in 1878, Dublin. *d.* 1949. Stocky, muscular, square-jawed star of Hollywood silents. In the US from infancy, he was raised in New York. A veteran of vaudeville and the legitimate stage, he directed his own theatrical company before entering films in 1915. Initially, he played leads in society melodramas, but in the early 20s he moved into serials and action pictures at Universal, enjoying great popularity for several years. Nearly 50 at the advent of sound, he began playing secondary roles, mainly in serials and Westerns. He was married to actress Mary McIvor, a leading lady of William S. Hart.

FILMS INCLUDE: *Kilmeny, Peer Gynt* 1915; *Peggy, The Waifs, The Sorrows of Love, Lieutenant Danny U.S.A., The Dawn Maker, The Criminal* 1916; *Blood Will Tell, Paws of the Bear, Master of His Home, Flying Colors, The Sudden Gentleman* 1917; *The Sea Panther, Society for Sale, An Honest Man, Hell's End, Beyond the Shadows, The Pretender* 1918; *The Prodigal Liar, The Mints of Hell, A Sage Brush Hamlet, Dangerous Waters* 1919; *The Prince and Betty, Twin Beds, Women Men Love* 1920; *The Parish Priest, The Child Thou Gavest Me, Dangerous Toys, Fightin' Mad* 1921; *Perils of the Yukon* (serial), *Night Life in Hollywood* (cameo, as himself) 1922; *Around the World in 18 Days* (serial), *Beasts of Paradise* (serial), *The Phantom Fortune* (serial), *McGuire of the Mounted, Shadows of the North, The Extra Girl* (cameo) 1923; *The Riddle Rider* (serial), *The Breathless Moment, Big Timber, The Measure of a Man, The Sunset Trail* 1924; *Ace of Spades* (serial), *Perils of the Wild* (serial), *Outwitted, Duped, Blood and Steel, The Burning Trail, The Meddler* 1925; *Strings of Steel* (serial), *The Winking Idol* (serial) 1926; *Return of the Riddle Rider* (serial), *Tongues of Scandal, Red Clay* 1927; *The Mystery Rider* (serial), *The Vanishing Rider* (serial), *The Devil's Trademark* 1928; *No Defense* 1929; *Battling with Buffalo Bill* (serial), *Hell Bent for Frisco* 1931; *Heroes of the West* (serial), *The Jungle Mystery* (serial) 1932; *Clancy of the Mounted* (serial), *Gordon of Ghost City* (serial), *The Phantom of the Air* (serial), *The Three Musketeers* (serial), *Mr. Broadway* 1933; *The Perils of Pauline* (serial), *The Red Rider* (serial), *Tailspin Tommy* (serial), *The Vanishing Shadow* (serial) 1934; *The Roaring West* (serial), *Powdersmoke Range* 1935; *The Black Coin* (serial), *Hollywood Boulevard* 1936; *Winners of the West* (serial), *A Little Bit of Heaven* 1940.

Desny, Ivan. Actor. Born Ivan Desnitzky, in 1922, in Peking, to Russian emigrés fleeing the Revolution. He was educated in France and during the Nazi occupation was interned in a German labor camp. He entered films as an extra after the liberation. Since the early 50s he has played suave leads, often romantic, and supporting roles, often mysterious or smoothly sinister, in many French, British, German, Italian, and some American films.

FILMS INCLUDE: *Bonheur en Location* (Fr.) 1949; *Madeleine* (UK) 1950; *La P. . . respectueuse/The Respectful Prostitute* (Fr.), *La Signora senza Camelie/Camille Without Camelias/The Lady Without Camelias* (It.), *Weg ohne Umkehr/No Way Back* (Ger.) 1953; *Un Acte d'Amour/Act of Love* (US/Fr.), *Die Goldene Pest/The Golden Plague* (Ger.) 1954; *Frou-Frou* (It./Fr.), *Lola Montès/The Sins of Lola Montes* (Fr./Ger.) 1955; *Anastasia* (US), *Rosen für Bettina/Ballerina* 1956; *Une Vie/End of Desire/A Life* (Fr.), *Der Satan lockt mit Liebe* (Ger.), *Le Miroir à deux Faces/The Mirror Has Two Faces* (Fr.) 1958; *Song Without End* (US) 1960; *Bon Voyage* (US) 1962; *Tendre Voyou/Tender Scoundrel* (Fr./It.) 1966; *J'ai tué Raspoutine* (Fr.) 1967; *Les Cañones de San Sebastian/Guns for San Sebastian* (Mex./Fr./It./US) 1968; *Mayerling* (UK/Fr.) 1968; *Kleine Mutter/Little Mother* (Ger.), *Nocturno* (Ger.) 1972; *Faustrecht der Freiheit/Fox and His Friends/Fist-Right of Freedom* (Ger.), *Falsche Bewegung/Wrong Move* (Ger.), *Paper Tiger* (UK) 1975; *Die Eroberung der Zitadelle* (Ger.) 1977; *Halbe-Halbe* (Ger.) 1978; *Die Ehe der Maria Braun/The Marriage of Maria Braun* (Ger.) 1979; *Berlin Alexanderplatz* (Ger.), *Malou* (Ger.) 1980; *Lola* (Ger.) 1981; *Flügel und Fesseln/L'Avenir d'Emilie/The Future of Emily* (Ger./Fr.) 1984; *Le Caviar rouge* (Fr./Switz.) 1985; *Offret/Sacrificatio/Le Sacrifice/The Sacrifice* (Swed./Fr.) 1986; *Quicker Than the Eye* (Switz.) 1989.

De Toth, André. Director. Born Sásvrái Farkasfawi Tóthfalusi Tóth Endre Antai Mihaly, on May 15, 1913, in Mako, Hungary, the son of a former Hussar officer. While preparing for a law degree at the University of Budapest, he entered Hungarian films in 1931 as screenwriter, editor, second-unit director, and sometime actor. As Endre Tóth, he directed several Hungarian films just before the outbreak of WW II, then went to England, where he worked for Alexander Korda as second-unit director on *The Thief of Bagdad* (1940). He next went to Hollywood and worked briefly as a truck driver before returning to film work as Korda's second-unit director on *Jungle Boy*

(1942). The following year he made his Hollywood debut as director. His films were typically gutsy Westerns and action dramas, noted for their curious detachment and casual attitude toward violence and treachery. He shared an Academy Award nomination for the original story of *The Gunfighter* (1950), which was directed by Henry KING. The fact that he had only one eye hampered little the visual excellence of his films. In 1953 he directed what is probably the best of the 3-D features, *House of Wax.* After the late 50s he worked mostly in Europe, but he kept returning to the US to explore potential projects. His first (1944–52) wife was Veronica LAKE.

FILMS: In Hungary—*Wedding in Toprin, At 5:40, Two Girls of the Street, Six Weeks of Happiness, Semmelweiss* 1938–39. In the US—*Passport to Suez* 1943; *None Shall Escape, Dark Waters* 1944; *Ramrod, The Other Love* 1947; *Pitfall* 1948; *Slattery's Hurricane* 1949; *The Gunfighter* (co-story only) 1950; *Man in the Saddle* 1951; *Carson City, Springfield Rifle, Last of the Comanches* 1952; *House of Wax, The Stranger Wore a Gun, Thunder Over the Plains* 1953; *Crime Wave/The City Is Dark, Riding Shotgun, Tanganyika, The Bounty Hunter* 1954; *The Indian Fighter* 1955; *Monkey on My Back, Hidden Fear* (also co-sc.) 1957; *The Two-Headed Spy* (UK), *Day of the Outlaw* 1959; *Man on a String, Morgan il Pirata/Morgan the Pirate* (supervising dir., co-sc.; It./Fr.) 1960; *I Mongoli/The Mongols* (supervising dir.; It./Fr.) 1961; *Oro per i Cesari/Gold for the Caesars* (supervising dir.; It./Fr.) 1963; *Billion Dollar Brain* (exec. prod. only; UK) 1967; *Play Dirty* (also exec. prod. UK) 1968; *El Condor* (prod. only) 1970.

deuce. Slang term for a 2,000-watt lamp used in lighting a set.

Deutch, Howard. Director. Born in New York City. *ed.* Ohio State U. The son of a noted music publisher, he engaged in the making of music videos and film trailers before moving into features in 1986, under he aegis of producer-director-writer John HUGHES.

FILMS: *Pretty in Pink* 1986; *Some Kind of Wonderful* 1987; *The Great Outdoors* 1988; *Article 99* 1992; *Getting Even with Dad* 1994.

Deutsch, Adolph. Composer, conductor, musical director. *b.* Oct. 20, 1897, London. *d.* 1980. In Hollywood from the late 30s following a long spell on Broadway, he scored numerous films for Warner Bros., MGM, and other studios, winning Academy Awards for the orchestrations of *Annie Get Your Gun, Seven Brides for Seven Brothers,* and *Oklahoma!*

FILMS INCLUDE: *Fools for Scandal* 1938; *Across the Pacific* 1942; *Action in the North Atlantic, Northern Pursuit* 1943; *Uncertain Glory* 1944; *The Mask of Dimitrios* 1945; *Nobody Lives Forever, Three Strangers* 1946; *Blaze of Noon* 1947; *Intruder in the Dust, Little Women, Take Me Out to the Ball Game* 1949; *Annie Get Your Gun* 1950; *Torch Song, The Band Wagon* 1953; *Seven Brides for Seven Brothers* 1954; *Oklahoma!* 1955; *Tea and Sympathy* 1956; *Funny Face, Les Girls* 1957; *The Matchmaker* 1958; *Some Like It Hot* 1959; *The Apartment* 1960; *Go Naked in the World* 1961.

Deutsch, Helen. Screenwriter. *b.* Mar. 21, 1912, New York City. *d.* 1992. *ed.* Barnard Coll. She collaborated on a number of major Hollywood productions from the mid-40s through the mid-60s. Her stage work includes the book for the Broadway musical 'Carnival.'

FILMS INCLUDE: *The Seventh Cross, National Velvet* 1944; *Golden Earrings* 1947; *The Loves of Carmen* 1948; *King Solomon's Mines, Kim* 1950; *It's a Big Country, Plymouth Adventure* 1952; *Lili* 1953; *The Flame and the Flesh* 1954; *The Glass Slipper, I'll Cry Tomorrow* 1955; *Forever Darling* 1956; *The Unsinkable Molly Brown* 1964; *Valley of the Dolls* 1967.

Devane, William. Actor. Born on Sept. 5, 1939, in Albany, N.Y. Leading man of the American stage, TV, and films. A graduate of the American Academy of Dramatic Arts, he began with the New York Shakespeare Festival and appeared in a number of off-Broadway productions before gaining wider recognition during the 70s as a result of several impressive performances on TV, including the role of John F. Kennedy in 'The Missiles of October,' and of John Henry Falk in 'Fear on Trial.' At the same time, he gradually progressed from supporting parts to leads in feature films. In 1979 he signed one of TV's most lucrative contracts to play the lead in the miniseries 'From Here to Eternity.' He later co-starred in the long-running series 'Knots Landing,' which limited his big-screen activity in the 80s.

FILMS: *In the Country* (16 mm feature) 1967; *The Pursuit of Happiness, Three Hundred Year Weekend* (also co-addnl. dial.), *My Old Man's Place, McCabe and Mrs. Miller, La Mortadella/Lady Liberty* (It.) 1971; *Irish Whiskey Rebellion* 1973; *Report to the Commissioner* 1975; *Family Plot, Marathon Man* 1976; *The Bad News Bears in Breaking Training, Rolling Thunder* 1977; *The Dark, Yanks* 1979; *Honky Tonk Freeway* 1981; *Testament* 1983; *Hadley's Rebellion* 1984; *Vital Signs* 1990.

developer. The chemical agent used at a laboratory to make visible the latent image on exposed film. Also, the person at the lab responsible for running developing machines.

Deville, Michel. Director. Born on Apr. 13, 1931, in Boulogne-sur-Seine, France. Entered French films in 1951 as an assistant to Henri DECOIN. A director since 1958, he was among the few French filmmakers of his generation who rejected the influence of the New Wave, focusing instead on old-fashioned, lighthearted entertainment, which he executed with facility and technical proficiency. He usually collaborated on his own scripts, often with Nina Companeez (see Jacques COMPANEEZ).

FILMS: *Une Balle dans le Canon* (co-dir. with Charles Gérard) 1958; *Ce Soir ou Jamais* (also prod.; co-sc.) 1960; *Adorable Menteuse* (also prod.; co-sc.) 1961; *A cause à cause d'une Femme* (also prod.; co-sc.) 1962; *L'Appartement des Filles* (also co-sc.) 1963; *Lucky Jo* (also co-story) 1964; *On a volé la Joconde* (also co-story) 1965; *Martin Soldat* (also co-story) 1966; *Tendres Requins* 1967; *Benjamin ou les Mémoires d'un Puceau/Benjamin/Benjamin—The Diary of an Innocent Young Boy* (also co-story) 1968; *Bye Bye Barbara* (also co-sc.) 1969; *L'Ours et la Poupée/The Bear and the Doll* (also co-sc.) 1970; *Raphaël ou le débauché* 1971; *La Femme en Bleu* (also sc.) 1973; *Le Mouton enragé/Love at the Top/The French Way* 1974; *L'Apprenti salaud* (also sc.) 1977; *Le Dossier 51* (also co-sc.) 1978; *Le Voyage en douce/Sentimental Journey* 1980; *Eaux profondes* 1981; *La Petite Bande* 1983; *Péril en la Demure/Death in a French Garden/Peril* 1985; *Le Paltoquet* 1986; *La Lectrice* 1988; *Nuit d'Eté en Ville* 1990; *Toutes Peines Confondues* 1992; *Aux Petits Bonheurs* 1993.

Devine, Andy. Actor. *b.* Jeremiah Schwartz, Oct. 7, 1905, Flagstaff, Ariz. *d.* 1977. *ed.* St. Mary and St. Benedict Coll.; Arizona State Teacher's Coll.; Santa Clara U. A football star in his college days, the big, husky (and later fat) Devine arrived in Hollywood in 1926 hoping to become a movie actor. After a number of BITS he began playing supporting parts in a variety of light silent films. His raspy voice, the result of a childhood accident, was deemed at first unsuitable for sound but later turned into an asset as Devine became typecast as a country bumpkin and later as comic sidekick for Roy Rogers and other screen cowboys in numerous Westerns. In the early 50s he played Jingles, Guy Madison's sidekick in the TV series 'Wild Bill Hickok,' and later starred in his own series, 'Andy's Gang.' He served for several years as honorary mayor of Van Nuys, California.

FILMS INCLUDE: *We Americans, Red Lips* 1928; *Hot Stuff* 1929; *The Spirit of Notre Dame* 1931; *Destry Rides Again, Tom Brown of Culver, The Man from Yesterday* 1932; *Doctor Bull, Saturday's Millions* 1933; *Wake Up and Dream, The President Vanishes* 1934; *The Farmer Takes a Wife, Way Down East* 1935; *Romeo and Juliet* 1936; *A Star Is Born, The Road Back* 1937; *In Old Chicago, Dr. Rhythm, Yellow Jack, Men with Wings* 1938; *Stagecoach, Never Say Die* 1939; *Little Old New York, Danger on Wheels, The Devil's Pipeline, When the Daltons Rode* 1940; *The Flame of New Orleans, South of Tahiti, Raiders of the Desert* 1941; *Corvette K–225, Crazy House* 1943; *Ali Baba and the Forty Thieves, Follow the Boys, Babes on Swing Street* 1944; *Sudan* 1945; *Canyon Passage* 1946; *Slave Girl* 1947; *Eyes of Texas* 1948; *Never a Dull Moment* 1950; *New Mexico, The Red Badge of Courage* 1951; *Montana Belle* 1952; *Island in the Sky* 1953; *Pete Kelly's Blues* 1955; *Around the World in 80 Days* 1956; *The Adventures of Huckleberry Finn* 1960; *Two Rode Together* 1961; *The Man Who Shot Liberty Valance, How the West Was Won* 1962; *It's a Mad Mad Mad Mad World* 1963; *Zebra in the Kitchen* 1965; *The Ballad of Josie* 1968; *Myra Breckinridge* 1970; *Won Ton Ton—The Dog Who Saved Hollywood* (bit) 1976; *A Whale of a Tale, The Mouse and His Child* (animated film; voice only) 1977.

De Vinna, Clyde. Director of photography. *b.* 1892, Sedalia, Mo. *d.* 1953. *ed.* U. of Arkansas. A cinematographer from 1915, he was behind the camera on many silent and sound films for Ince, MGM, and other studios. At his best with outdoor photography.

FILMS INCLUDE: *D'Artagnan, The Raiders, Civilization* (co-plot.), *The Captive God* 1916; *Blood Will Tell, The Flame of the Yukon* 1917; *Blindfolded, Patriotism* 1918; *Playthings of Passion* 1919; *The Man Who Dared* 1920; *Face of the World* 1921; *Yellow Men and Gold* 1922; *Lost and Found on a South Sea Island* (co-phot.), *The Victor, The Wild Party* 1923; *Sporting Youth* 1924; *Ben-Hur* (co-phot.), *War Paint* 1926; *Winners of the Wilderness, California, The Frontiersman, Spoilers of the West*) 1927; *The Law of the Range, The Adventurer, White Shadows in the South Seas* (co-phot.) 1928; *The Pagan* 1929; *Trader Horn* 1931; *Tarzan the Ape Man* 1932; *Eskimo* 1933; *Tarzan and His Mate, Treasure Island* 1934; *West Point of the Air, Ah Wilderness!* 1935; *Bad Man of Brimstone* 1937; *Of Human Hearts* 1938; *Blackmail* 1939; *20-Mule Team, Phantom Raiders* 1940; *Barnacle Bill* 1941; *The Immortal Sergeant* 1943; *Sword of the Avenger* 1948; *The Jungle* 1952.

De Vito, Danny. Actor, director, producer. Born on Nov. 17, 1944, in Neptune, N.J. *ed.* Oratory Prep School. Diminutive (5') character star of the American stage, TV, and films. After training at the Wilfred Academy of Hair and Beauty Culture, he began his working life at 18 as a hairdresser at his sister's salon. Determined to act, he attended the American Academy of Dramatic Arts, then made his New York stage debut in 1969 and his first film appearance the following year. Starting in bits and walk-ons, his career picked up momentum after he repeated his stage role in the screen version of *One Flew Over the Cuckoo's Nest* (1975). He gradually evolved into a popular comic screen personality, especially in the wake of his success in the role of Louie De Palma in the hit TV series 'Taxi' (1978–83), for which he won an Emmy as best supporting actor in 1981. At his best in hypertense, frenzied, sly characterizations. In the late 80s he turned to directing. His black comedy *The War of the Roses* (1989) was a commercial and critical success, and made him a sought-after director in Hollywood. He is married to actress Rhea Perlman, best known for her Emmy-winning role Carla in the TV sitcom 'Cheers.'

FILMS (as actor): *Dreams of Glass* 1970; *La Mortadella/Lady Liberty* (It.) 1971; *Scalawag, Hurry Up or I'll Be 30* 1973; *One Flew Over the Cuckoo's Nest* 1975; *Deadly Hero, Car Wash* 1976; *The Van, The World's Greatest Lover* 1977; *Goin' South* 1978; *Going Ape* 1981; *Terms of Endearment* 1983; *Romancing the Stone, Johnny Dangerously* 1984; *Head Office, The Jewel of the Nile* 1985; *Wise Guys, My Little Pony* (voice only), *Ruthless People* 1986; *Tin Men, Throw Momma from the Train* (also dir.) 1987; *Twins* 1988; *The War of the Roses* (also dir.) 1989; *Other People's Money* 1991; *Batman Returns, Hoffa* (also dir.) 1992; *Jack the Bear* (also dir.) 1993; *Junior, Renaissance Man, Reality Bites* (co-prod. only) 1994; *Get Shorty* (also co-prod.) 1995; *Feeling Minnesota* (co-prod. only), *Mars Attacks, Matilda* (also dir., prod.), *Sunset Park* (co-prod. only) 1996; *Hercules* (voice only), *L.A. Confidential* 1997.

Dewaere, Patrick. Actor. *b.* Patrick Maurin, Jan. 26, 1947, Saint-Brieuc (Brittany), France. *d.* 1982, a suicide. A second-generation actor, he borrowed a grandmother's last name when he began performing with an improvisation group in 1968. In films from the early 70s, he rapidly developed into a popular leading man, rivaling Gérard Depardieu, with whom he co-starred in Bertrand Blier's *Les Valseuses/Going Places* (1974). He began working on *Edith and Marcel,* in which he was to portray Piaf's lover, boxing champion Marcel Cerdan, when he was found dead of a self-inflicted gun shot. The role went to Marcel Cerdan, Jr.

FILMS INCLUDE: *Les Mariés de l'An II, La Maison sous les Arbres/The Deadly Trap* 1971; *Au long de la Rivière* 1973; *Les Valseuses/Going Places* 1974; *Catherine et Cie/Catherine & Co., Adieu Poulet/The French Detective* 1975; *Marcia Trionfale/Victory March* (It.), *F comme Fairbanks* 1976; *La Stanza del Vescovo* (It.), *Le Juge Fayard dit le Sheriff* 1977; *Préparez vos Mouchoirs/Get Out Your Handkerchiefs* 1978; *Coup de Tête/Hothead, L'Ingorgo/Traffic Jam* (It./Fr./Sp./Ger.), *Série noire* 1979; *Un Mauvais Fils* 1980; *Plein Sud/Heat and Desire, Beau-Père* 1981; *Paco l'Infallible* (release delayed from 1979), *Paradis pour tous* 1982.

Dewhurst, Colleen. Actress. *b.* June 3, 1926, Montreal. *d.* 1991. The daughter of a hockey player, she dropped out of Downer College for Young Ladies (now Lawrence University) in Milwaukee. She worked as an elevator operator and gym instructor before enrolling at New York's American Academy of Dramatic Arts. She made her Broadway debut in 1955 and before long developed into one of the leading personalities of the New York stage, winning Tony Awards for 'All the Way Home' and 'A Moon for the Misbegotten' on Broadway and several Obies for her off-Broadway performances. Her film appearances were sporadic. She twice married and twice divorced actor George C. SCOTT. Their son is actor Campbell Scott. She had a recurring part on TV sitcom 'Murphy Brown.' At one time president of Actors' Equity Association.

FILMS: *The Nun's Story* 1959; *Man on a String* 1960; *A Fine Madness* 1966; *The Last Run* 1971; *The Cowboys* 1972; *MCQ* 1974; *Annie Hall* 1977; *The Third Walker* (Can.), *Ice Castles* 1978; *When a Stranger Calls* 1979; *Final Assignment* (Can.) 1980, *Tribute* (Can.) 1980; *The Dead Zone* 1983; *The Boy Who Could Fly* 1986; *Obsessed* (Can.) 1988; *Bed and Breakfast* 1989; *Termini Station* 1990.

De Wilde, Brandon. Actor. *b.* Andre Brandon De Wilde, Apr. 9, 1942, Brooklyn, N.Y. *d.* 1972. The son of a stage manager and an actress, he made his Broadway debut at seven in 'The Member Of The Wedding' to great critical acclaim and was the first child ever to win the Donaldson Award for an outstanding stage performance. He played the role for 492 performances before repeating it in 1952 for the Hollywood screen version. He became internationally famous the following year as the child star of the classic western *Shane,* a performance for which he was nominated for an Oscar. In 1953–54 he starred in his own TV series, 'Jamie,' and later played youthful roles in a variety of films, memorably in *Blue Denim, All Fall Down,* and *Hud.* He died at 30 as a result of injuries suffered in a traffic accident near Denver, where he was to appear in a stage production of 'Butterflies Are Free.'

FILMS: *The Member of the Wedding* 1952; *Shane* 1953; *Goodbye My Lady* 1956; *Night Passage* 1957; *The Missouri Traveler* 1958; *Blue Denim* 1959; *All Fall Down* 1962; *Hud* 1963; *Those Calloways, In Harm's Way* 1965; *The Deserter* (US/Sp.) 1971; *Wild in the Sky/Black Jack* 1972.

De Wolfe, Billy. Actor. *b.* William Andrew Jones, Feb. 18, 1907, Wollaston, Mass. *d.* 1974. Stagestruck from childhood, he began his show business career at 18 as a dancer-comic in vaudeville and nightclub revues. From the early 40s he played occasional but memorable light supporting roles in which he used his lisping diction and toothy smile for comic effect.

FILMS: *Dixie* 1943; *Duffy's Tavern* 1945; *Miss Susie Slagle's, Our Hearts Were Growing Up, Blue Skies* 1946; *Dear Ruth, Variety Girl, The Perils of Pauline* 1947; *Isn't It Romantic?* 1948; *Dear Wife, Tea for Two* 1950; *Lullaby of Broadway, Dear Brat* 1951; *Call Me Madam* 1953; *Billie* 1965; *The World's Greatest Athlete* 1973.

Dexter, Anthony. Actor. Born Walter Reinhold Alfred Fleischmann, on Jan. 19, 1919, in Talmage, Nebr. *ed.* U. Of Iowa (M.A.). A stage actor before and after his WW II army service. Made his film debut with a fanfare of publicity in the title role of *Valentino* (1951) but has since appeared mainly in low-budget, low-quality action pictures.

FILMS INCLUDE: *Valentino* 1951; *The Brigand* 1952; *Captain John Smith and Pocahontas* 1953; *Captain Kidd and the Slave Girl, Black Pirates* 1954; *He Laughed Last* 1956; *The Story of Mankind, The Parson and the Outlaw* 1957; *12 to the Moon* 1960; *Thoroughly Modern Millie* 1967.

Dexter, Elliott. Actor. *b.* 1870, Galveston, Tex. *d.* 1941. Handsome leading man of Hollywood silents. A veteran of vaudeville and the legitimate stage, he starred in numerous screen productions for Cecil B. DE MILLE and other directors, listing among his leading ladies such stars as Mary Pickford and Gloria Swanson. He married and later divorced actress Marie Doro, his co-star in De Mille's *The Heart of Nora Flynn* (1916) and other films. Retired from the screen in 1925.

FILMS INCLUDE: *The Masqueraders* 1915; *The Heart of Nora Flynn, The Lash, Diplomacy, Daphne and the Pirate, Public Opinion* 1916; *A Romance of the Redwoods, A Castle for Two, The Rise of Jennie Cushing, Lost and Won* 1917; *Woman and Wife, The Whispering Chorus, Old Wives for New, We Can't Have Everything, The Squaw Man* 1918; *Don't Change Your Husband, For Better for Worse, Maggie Pepper* 1919; *Behold My Wife, Something to Think About* 1920; *The Witching Hour, The Affairs of Anatol, Forever/Peter Ibbetson, Don't Tell Everything* 1921; *Grand Larceny, The Hands of Nara, Enter Madame* 1922; *Adam's Rib, Only 38, Broadway Gold, The Common Law, Flaming Youth* 1923; *By Divine Right, The Spitfire, For Woman's Favor, The Fast Set, The Age of Innocence, The Triflers* 1924; *Capital Punishment, The Verdict, Wasted Lives, Stella Maris* 1925.

De Young, Cliff. Actor. Born on Feb. 12, 1945, in Inglewood, Calif. *ed.* California State Coll., Illinois State U. Leading man and supporting player of the American stage, TV, and films. On the screen sporadically from the early 70s, most actively in the late 80s.

FILMS INCLUDE: *Pilgrimage* 1972; *Harry and Tonto* 1974; *Blue Collar* 1978; *Shock Treatment* 1981; *Independence Day/Follow Your Dream, The Hunger* 1983; *Reckless, Protocol* 1984; *Secret Admirer* 1985; *F/X, Flight of the Navigator* 1986; *Pulse, In Dangerous Company, Fear* 1988; *Rude Awakening, Glory, Bulldance/Forbidden Sun* (UK) 1989; *Flashback* 1990; *Crackdown* 1991; *To Die Standing* 1994; *Tales from the Crypt Presents Demon Knight* 1995; *The Craft, The Substitute* 1996.

DGA. Directors Guild of America, Inc., encompassing directors and assistant directors in both films and television. It has offices in Los Angeles, New York, and Chicago. It publishes a magazine and bestows annual achievement awards in addition to its regular functions as a union.

Dhéry, Robert. Actor, director, screenwriter, playwright. Born Robert Foullcy, on Apr. 27, 1921, in Héry, France. A circus performer from age 14, he turned to the legitimate stage after studies at the Paris Conservatory. Also in films since the early 40s, he specialized in burlesque comedy roles, at first as actor and later also as director and screenwriter. He scored a personal triumph with his stage revue 'La Plume de ma Tante,' which enjoyed long runs in London and New York. His best-known film outside France is *La Belle Américaine* (the Beautiful American of the title is a Cadillac). His wife, Colette Brosset, appears regularly in his plays and films.

FILMS INCLUDE: As actor—*Monsieur des Lourdines* 1942; *Les Enfants du Paradis/Children of Paradise* 1944; *Sylvie et le Fantôme* 1945; *Les Aventures des Pieds-Nickelés* (also sc.) 1947; *Ah! les Belles Bacchantes/Peek-a-Boo* (as himself; also sc.) 1954; *La Communale* 1965; *Three Men on a Horse* 1969; *On est toujours trop bon avec les Femmes* 1971; *Malevil* 1981; *La Passion Béatrice/Beatrice* 1987. As director-screenwriter-actor—*La Patronne* (dir. only), *Branquignol* 1949; *Bertrand Coeur de Lion* 1950; *La Belle Américaine* 1961; *Allez France!/The Counterfeit Constable* 1964; *Le Petit Baigneur* 1968.

diagonal action. Action taking place diagonally across the screen, as from the lower left-hand corner to the upper right-hand corner. Diagonal flow of action is considered to be dynamic in its effect on the senses of the viewer.

diagonal splicing. A method of splicing sound film diagonally, rather than in a straight line, so that the gradual slope of the joint may minimize the clicking sound that a splice characteristically produces as it passes through the sound head of a projector.

dialing. Slang term for the act of controlling sound during filming. To dial out a sound is to eliminate an unwanted noise in a recording.

dialogue. In a film, all spoken lines. Since the cinema is essentially a visual medium, dialogue is, or should be, used more sparingly than in the theater, supplementing action rather than substituting for it.

dialogue director. The person assigned to coach players in the delivery of lines and frequently also in the execution of movement during rehearsals and during filming. Dialogue directors were in great demand in Hollywood during the early sound period, when veteran directors of silent films lacked the experience necessary for handling spoken words. A Broadway-to-Hollywood exodus was begun by directors experienced in coaching actors but ignorant of film techniques. Many present-day Hollywood directors began their film career this way, notably George Cukor, who was dialogue director on Lewis Milestone's *All Quiet on the Western Front* (1930). Dialogue directors are infrequently used in today's film industry.

dialogue track. Sound track carrying the dialogue portion of a film, as distinguished from music or sound effects. The separate tracks are eventually combined in the MIX. Keeping separate tracks allows the mixer more flexibility and is essential for films that are designed to be dubbed into foreign languages. In foreign versions the dialogue track is simply substituted while the music and sound effects remain unchanged.

dialogue writer. A person specializing in the writing of dialogue lines for a film rather than complete screenplays. The distinction between a dialogue writer and a screenwriter is rarely made in American or British films, but in France dialogue writing has long been a highly regarded specialty. The best known and busiest French *dialoguiste* was Henri JEANSON.

Diamant-Berger, Henri. Director, producer, screenwriter, critic. *b.* June 9, 1895, Paris. *d.* 1972. While studying law he became involved in amateur dramatics and at 20 began directing and producing French silent films. From 1916 to 1919, while continuing his activity as producer-director, he published and edited the magazine *Film,* and in 1918 he wrote the first of several books on film, *Le Cinéma.* That same year he came to the US to attempt French-American co-productions and establish and organize the PATHÉ laboratories in Fort Lee, N.J., and after returning to France established the Pathé labs in Vincennes and the film studios at Billancourt. In 1925 he was back in the US as a director of several Hollywood productions. He returned to the US once more in 1940 as a film representative in California for the Free French government in exile. A versatile and highly prolific man, he has directed, produced, or written more than 100 films while holding active posts with various film organizations.

FILMS INCLUDE: As director—*Le Lord Ouverier* 1915; *Paris pendant la Guerre* (doc.) 1916; *Les Quatre Cavaliers de l'Apocalypse, Ils y viennent tous au Cinéma* (also prod., sc.) 1917; *Le Feu sacré* 1920; *Le Trois Mousquetaires* (serial) 1921–22; *Le Mauvais Garcon* (also prod.) 1922; *Vingt Ans après* (serial also prod.) 1922–23; *Gonzague* (also prod.), *L'Affaire de la Rue de Loureine, Jim Bougne Boxeur* (also prod.) 1923; *Le Roi de la Vitesse* (also prod.), *La Marche du Destin, L'Emprise* 1924; *Fifty-Fifty* (also prod.; US) 1925; *Lover's Island* (also prod.; US), *The Unfair Sex* (also prod.; US) 1926; *Rue de la Paix, Education de Prince* 1927; *Paris la Nuit* (also story), *Sola* 1930; *Clair de Lune, La Bonne Aventure, Les Trois Mousquetaires* (remake), *Milady* 1932; *Miquette et sa Mère* 1933; *La Grande Vie* (also sc.) 1934; *Arsène Lupin Détective* (also prod.) 1937; *La Vierge Folle* 1938; *La Maternelle* (also prod.) 1948; *Monsieur Fabre/The Amazing Monsieur Fabre* (also prod.) 1951; *Le Chasseur de Chez Maxim's* (also prod.) 1953; *Messieurs les Ronds-de-Cuir* (also prod.) 1959; *Song of the Balalaika* 1971. As producer—*La Belle Américaine* (co-prod.) 1961; *Un Drôle de Paroissien/Thank Heaven for Small Favors* 1963; *Allez France!/The Counterfeit Constable* 1964; *La Sentinelle endormie* 1965.

Diamond, I. A. L. Screenwriter. *b.* Itek Dommnici, 1920, Ungeny, Rumania (now Moldova). *d.* 1988. In the US since 1929, he grew up in the Crown Heights section of Brooklyn where he became known as Isadore or Izzy Diamond. After winning a scholarship in a New York Metropolitan Area mathematics championship, he went to Columbia University, where he wrote much of the material for the university variety show. When a colleague suggested his byline was "too Jewish," Diamond impulsively chose the initials I.A.L., which stood for the Interscholastic Algebra League, of which he had been champion in 1936 and 1937. The puzzling initials stuck for the duration of his career. He went to Hollywood directly out of college and for several years wrote screenplays for routine light films. His career took an important turn in the mid-50s when he began collaborating with director Billy WILDER on the trenchant screenplays of the latter's films (their first joint venture: *Love in the Afternoon*). They shared an Academy Award for the screenplay of *The Apartment.* Diamond doubled as associate producer on their later collaborations.

FILMS (mostly in collaboration): *Murder in the Blue Room* 1944; *Never Say Goodbye, Two Guys from Milwaukee* 1946; *Always Together, Love and Learn* 1947; *Romance on the High Seas* (dial. only), *Two Guys from Texas* 1948; *It's a Great Feeling* (story only), *The Girl from Jones Beach* 1949; *Love Nest, Let's Make It Legal* 1951; *Monkey Business, Something for the Birds* 1952; *That Certain Feeling* 1956; *Love in the Afternoon* 1957; *Merry Andrew* 1958; *Some Like It Hot* 1959; *The Apartment* 1960; *One Two Three* 1961; *Irma La Douce* 1963; *Kiss Me Stupid* 1964; *The Fortune Cookie* 1966; *Cactus Flower* 1969; *The Private Life of Sherlock Holmes* 1970; *Avanti!* 1972; *The Front Page* 1974; *Fedora* (Ger./Fr.) 1978.

diaphragm. A regulating device in the form of adjustable metal blades which controls the amount of light entering a camera lens and striking the film. It is also known as an "iris," because of the similarity of its function to that of the iris of the human eye.

Diaz, Cameron. Actress. Born August 30, 1972, in San Diego, Calif. A former model, this striking blond of Cuban and Native American extraction quickly became an overnight sensation with her starring role opposite Jim CARREY in the box office topper *The Mask* (1994). Subsequently, she has earned several top roles, in each offering impressive performances.

FILMS: *The Mask* 1994; *Feeling Minnesota, The Last Supper, She's the One* 1996; *Head Above Water, A Life Less Ordinary, My Best Friend's Wedding* 1997.

DiCaprio, Leonardo. Actor. Born Leonardo Wihelm DiCaprio, November 11, 1974, in Los Angeles. *ed.* Center for Enriched Studies, Los Angeles. Slim and youthful, this handsome young actor got his start on television sitcoms but quickly made the leap to feature films where he consistently takes on challenging roles with great aplomb. Reaching stardom at an early age, he has impressed critics and audiences with his versatility, specifically with his Academy Award–nominated turn as the mentally challenged boy in *What's Eating Gilbert Grape* (1993).

FILMS: *Critters 3, Poison Ivy* 1992; *This Boy's Life, What's Eating Gilbert Grape* 1993; *The Basketball Diaries, A Hundred and One Nights, The Quick and the Dead, Total Eclipse* (Fr./US) 1995; *Marvin's Room, Romeo & Juliet* 1996.

Dickerson, Ernest. Cinematographer and director. Born in 1952 in Newark, N.J. *ed.* Howard Univ. (architecture), NYU (film). Following his first cinematography job photographing surgery for the medical school at Howard Univ., he established himself at NYU through his work as a cinematographer on films by fellow student Spike LEE (*Sarah, Joe's Bed-Stuy Barbershop: We Cut Heads*). Since then he has acted as cinematographer for many of Lee's feature films, infusing images (particularly those in *Do the Right Thing* and *Malcolm X*) with lyricism, rage, and epic scale. He has photographed music videos for Miles Davis and Bruce Springsteen, among others. He directed his first movie, *Juice*, in 1992.

FILMS INCLUDE: *The Brother from Another Planet* 1984; *Krush Groove* 1985; *She's Gotta Have It* (also act.) 1986; *Eddie Murphy Raw* 1987; *School Daze, The Laser Man* 1988; *Do the Right Thing* 1989; *Def by Temptation, Fright House, Mo' Better Blues* 1990; *Jungle Fever, Sex, Drugs, Rock & Roll* 1991; *Cousin Bobby, Malcolm X, Juice* (dir., co-sc., story only) 1992; *Surviving the Game* 1994; *Bulletproof* 1996.

Dickinson, Angie. Actress. Born Angeline Brown, on Sept. 30, 1931, in Kulm, N.D. *ed.* Immaculate Heart Coll.; Glendale Coll. The winner of a beauty contest, she broke into films as a starlet in 1954 and for several years played bits and small roles. Her big break came in 1959 when she played the female lead in Howard Hawks's *Rio Bravo.* She subsequently played engaging leads in many Hollywood productions, but her film vehicles have been mostly routine. Also much on TV, including many TV movies and starring role in the 'Police Woman' series (1974–78). Divorced from college football star Gene Dickinson, she married and separated from composer Burt BACHARACH in 1965. They divorced in 1980.

FILMS INCLUDE: *Lucky Me* 1954; *Man with the Gun* 1955; *Gun That Man Down* 1956; *China Gate* 1957; *Cry Terror* 1958; *Rio Bravo* 1959; *The Bramble Bush, Ocean's 11* 1960; *The Sins of Rachel Cade, Fever in the Blood* 1961; *Rome Adventure, Jessica* 1962; *Captain Newman M.D., The Killers* 1964; *The Art of Love* 1965; *The Chase, Cast a Giant Shadow* 1966; *Point Blank, The Last Challenge* 1967; *Sam Whiskey, Young Billy Young, Some Kind of a Nut* 1969; *Pretty Maids All in a Row, The Resurrection of Zachary Wheeler* 1971; *The Outside Man* (Fr.) 1973; *Big Bad Mama* 1974; *Klondike Fever, Dressed to Kill* 1980; *Charlie Chan and the Curse of the Dragon Queen, Death Hunt* 1981; *Big Bad Mama II* 1987; *Even Cowgirls Get the Blues* 1994; *Sabrina* 1995.

Dickinson, Desmond. Director of photography. Born on May 25, 1902, in London. Entered British films in 1919 as lab assistant and during the 20s worked his way up from camera assistant and operator to lighting cameraman. Was associated mainly with minor productions until WW II, during which he directed a number of propaganda documentaries for the British government. Returning to the industry, he was assigned as cinematographer to major films and in 1958 won the Venice Festival award and the British Film Academy award for the photography of Laurence Olivier's *Hamlet.* During the 50s, Dickinson worked frequently on the films of Anthony ASQUITH.

FILMS INCLUDE: *A Woman Redeemed* (co-phot.) 1927; *The Guns of Loos* (co-phot.) 1928; *Jealousy* 1931; *Dick Turpin* 1933; *Chips* 1938; *Men of Two Worlds, Hungry Hill* 1946; *Fame Is the Spur* 1947; *Hamlet* 1948; *The Rocking Horse Winner* 1949; *The Woman in Question* 1950; *Encore, The Browning Version* 1951; *Meet Me Tonight/Tonight at 8:30, The Importance of Being Earnest* 1952; *The Man Between* 1953; *Gentlemen Marry Brunettes (US), The Adventures of Quentin Durward* 1955; *Fire Down Below* 1957; *Orders to Kill* 1958; *Sparrows Can't Sing* 1963; *Murder Most Foul* 1964; *A Study in Terror* 1965; *Berserk* 1967; *Baby Love* 1968; *Trog* 1970; *Who Slew Auntie Roo?* 1971; *Tower of Evil/Horror of Snape Island/ Beyond the Fog* 1972.

Dickinson, Thorold. Director. *b.* Nov. 16, 1903, Bristol, England. *d.* 1984. He produced college plays while attending Oxford and after graduating worked in the British film industry in various capacities, including assistant director, screenwriter, sound editor, film editor, and production manager. He turned out his first film as director in 1937 and after two conventional thrillers and a Spanish Civil War documentary established his reputation with *Gaslight* (1940), a stylish suspense thriller, noted for its period atmosphere and fluid camera work. The negative of the film was acquired by MGM and destroyed, to assure an exclusive market for the studio's own version of *Gaslight,* which was directed by George Cukor in 1944. But several prints turned up later on and the film was exhibited in the US in 1952 as *Angel Street.* Dickinson reaffirmed his reputation with a WW II training-propaganda documentary *Next of Kin* (1942) and received high critical acclaim for a visually striking adaptation of Pushkin's *The Queen of Spades* (1949). The filming of his *Secret People* (1952) was minutely documented in a book by director Lindsay Anderson, *The Making of a Film: The Story of "Secret People."* Dickinson's last picture was *Hill 24 Doesn't Answer* (1955), an episodic drama about Israel's War of Independence which, although it was the first important feature produced in Israel, was among the lesser achievements of Dickinson as director. In 1952–53 he served as chairman of the British Film Academy. From 1956 till 1960 Dickinson headed the UN Office of Public Information and during that period supervised, but did not direct, several documentaries for the international body. In 1958–66 he was president of the International Federation of Film Societies. In 1967 he began teaching film theory at the University of London, becoming the first film professor at any British university. Upon retiring in 1971 he published a book, *A Discovery of Cinema.* He was also the author of *Soviet Cinema* (1948).

FILMS: *The High Command* 1937; *Spanish ABC* (doc.) 1938; *The Arsenal Stadium Mystery* 1939; *Yesterday Is Over Your Shoulder* (doc. short), *Gaslight/Angel Street* 1940; *Next of Kin* (semidoc.; also co-sc.), *The Prime Minister* 1942; *Men of Two Worlds/Kisenga—Man of Africa* (semidoc.; also co-sc.) 1946; *The Queen of Spades* 1949; *Secret People* (also co-sc.) 1952; *Hill 24 Doesn't Answer* (also co-prod.; Isr.) 1955.

Dickson, Gloria. Actress. *b.* Thais Dickerson, Aug. 13, 1916, Pocatello, Idaho. *d.* 1945. The daughter of a banker who died when she was 12, she gained acting experience with stock and touring companies before her screen debut with Warner Bros. in 1937. Her first role, in Mervyn LeRoy's *They Won't Forget,* was also her most memorable. She subsequently played leads in minor films and second leads in more important productions. She died at 29 in a fire that destroyed her rented Hollywood home.

FILMS INCLUDE: *They Won't Forget* 1937; *Gold Diggers in Paris, Racket Busters, Secrets of an Actress, Heart of the North* 1938; *They Made Me a Criminal, Waterfront, On Your Toes, No Place to Go, Private Detective* 1939; *Tear Gas Squad, I Want a Divorce, King of the Lumberjacks* 1940; *This Thing Called Love, The Big Boss, Mercy Island* 1941; *The Affairs of Jimmy Valentine* 1942; *Power of the Press, Lady of Burlesque, The Crime Doctor's Strangest Case* 1943; *Rationing* 1944.

Dickson, William Kennedy Laurie. Inventor. *b.* 1860, Château St. Buc, Minihic-sur-Ranse, France, of English-Scotch parents. *d.* 1935. In the US from 1879, he was employed in New York City's Edison Electric Works. In 1885 he was transferred to EDISON's private research laboratory in Menlo Park, N.J., and in 1887 was assigned by Edison to develop a motion picture apparatus at the new Orange, N.J., labs. His efforts, under Edison's supervision, were crowned with success in 1889 when he demonstrated before Edison the Kinetophonograph, an apparatus capable of projecting pictures in synchronization with a phonograph record. His work provided the technical basis for Edison's Kinetograph camera and Kinetoscope viewer.

It was also Dickson who designed BLACK MARIA, the world's first film studio for Edison, and "directed" Edison's very first films. He also devised equipment for developing and printing motion-picture film. Dickson left Edison's employ in 1895 and worked briefly with Latham on the development of the Panopticon. The following year he joined the American Mutoscope and Biograph Company and collaborated with Eugene LAUSTE on constructing the American Biograph projection apparatus. In 1897 he returned to Europe as Biograph's supplier of film footage of European events. He wrote two books of interest on the study of the early technical development of American cinema: *The Life and Inventions of Thomas Edison* (1894) and *History of the Kinematograph, Kinetoscope, and Kinetophonograph* (1895). See also EDISON, Thomas Alva.

Diegues, Carlos. Director. Born on May 19, 1940, in Maceio, Brazil. *ed.* Catholic University of Rio de Janeiro (law).

During his school days, he was active in the political affairs of the academic community and became film critic of *O Metropolitano,* a publication of the Metropolitan Union of Students. While becoming established as a critic and a poet, he began directing film shorts in 1960. With his first feature, *Ganga Zumba* (1964), the saga of a 17th-century slave rebellion, he asserted himself as a new vital force in Brazil's Cinema Novo movement. After the compelling *Xica da Silva,* he returned to the historical scene of his first film with *Quilombo* (1984), one of Brazil's most expensive and elaborate productions to that date. His reputation was later enhanced by such films as *Subway to the Stars* (1988) and *Better Days Ahead* (1989). He writes his own screenplays, alone or in collaboration.

FEATURE FILMS: *Ganga Zumba* 1964; *A Grande Cidade/The Big City* 1966; *Os Heredeiros/The Inheritors* 1969; *Qunado o Carnaval chegar/When Carnival Comes* 1972; *Joana a Francesca* 1973; *Xica da Silva/Xica* 1976; *Chuvas de Verao/Summer Showers/A Summer Rain* 1977; *Bye Bye Brasil/Bye Bye Brazil* 1980; *Quilombo* (Braz.) 1984; *Um Trem para as Estrelas/Train to the Stars/Subway to the Stars* (Baz./Fr.) 1988; *Dias Melhores Virao/Better Days Ahead* (Braz.) 1989.

Dieterle, William. Director, former actor. *b.* Wilhelm Dieterle, July 15, 1893, in Ludwigshafen, Germany. *d.* 1972. The youngest of nine children of a poverty-stricken family, he hustled for money early, wheeling and dealing in scrap, among other juvenile enterprises. Beginning an acting career in his teens, he appeared with various theatrical groups in Germany and Switzerland before joining Max REINHARDT in Berlin in 1918. At the same time, he appeared in scores of German silent films, including *Fiesco* (1913), *The Pied Piper of Hamelin* (1916), *Lukrezia Borgia* (1922), *Waxworks* (1924), and *Faust* (1926). From 1923 he directed German films in which he invariably appeared. The co-star of his first film as a director, *Der Mensch am Wege,* was 21-year-old Marlene DIETRICH. In 1930 he emigrated to Hollywood, where he developed into a dependable craftsman in the Warner Bros. mold. His best work at the beginning of his contract, with such films as the exciting *The Last Flight* and the delicious *Her Majesty Love,* and toward its end, when he handled the company's prestigious biopics of Pasteur, Zola, Juarez, and others.

In 1939 he moved to RKO, for which he directed a competent version of *The Hunchback of Notre Dame* and one of his best films, *All That Money Can Buy,* a classic of Americana adapted from Stephen Vincent Benét's *The Devil and Daniel Webster.* If during the 30s Dieterle was mostly respected for his pedantic technical proficiency and meticulous craftsmanship, in the 40s he occasionally demonstrated a capacity for romantic expression in such films as Paramount's *Love Letters* and Selznick's *Portrait of Jennie.* Dieterle, who in 1941, with Fritz LANG, had financed the immigration of Bertolt Brecht and Kurt Weill to the US, came under attack by McCarthyists in 1947 for his sympathy for liberal causes, reflected in films like *Blockade* (1938), which dealt with the Spanish Civil War. Although he was never directly charged with anything, his passport was confiscated in 1951, and again in 1953. Though his name never appeared on the infamous black list, he found worthy directing assignments elusive. His progressively poorer films of the 50s reflected and in turn accelerated his fall from grace. He went to Europe, where he made one Italian and two German films. Dieterle then returned to the US for a disastrous last production, which failed miserably under three different titles, in three release opportunities, before finally retiring in 1965.

FILMS (as director): In Germany—*Der Mensch am Wege* (also sc., act.) 1923; *Der Mann der nicht lieben darf/Das Geheimnis des Abbe X/Behind the Altar* (also sc., act.) 1927; *Geschlecht in Fesseln/Sex in Chains* (also act.), *Der Heilige und ihr Narr/The Saint and Her Fool* (also act.) 1928; *Frühlingsrauschen* (also act.), *Ich lebe fur Dich* (also act.), *Ludwig der Zweite—König von Bayern* (also act.), *Das Schweigen im Walde* (also act.), *Eine Stunde Glück* (also act.) 1929. In the US—*Der Tanz geht weiter* (German-language version of William Beaudine's *Those Who Dance*; also act.), *Die Maske fällt* (German-language version of Frank Lloyd's *The Way of All Men*) 1930; *Kismet* (German-language version of John Francis Dillon's 1930 film of same title), *The Last Flight, Her Majesty Love* 1931; *Man Wanted, Jewel Robbery, The Crash, Six Hours to Live, Scarlet Dawn, Lawyer Man* 1932; *Grand Slam, Adorable, The Devil's in Love, Female, From Headquarters* 1933; *Fashions of 1934, Fog Over Frisco, Madame Du Barry, The Firebird* 1934; *The Secret Bride, A Midsummer Night's Dream* (co-dir. with Max Reinhardt), *Dr. Socrates* 1935; *The Story of Louis Pasteur, The White Angel, Satan Met a Lady/Men on Her Mind* 1936; *The Great O'Malley, Another Dawn, The Life of Emile Zola* 1937; *Blockade* 1938; *Juarez, The Hunchback of Notre Dame* 1939; *Dr. Ehrlich's Magic Bullet, A Dispatch from Reuters* 1940; *All That Money Can Buy* (also prod.) 1941; *Syncopation* (also prod.), *Tennessee Johnson* 1942; *Kismet* 1944; *I'll Be Seeing You, Love Letters, This Love of Ours* 1945; *The Searching Wind* 1946; *The Accused, Portrait of Jennie, Rope of Sand* 1949; *Vulcano/Volcano* (also prod.; It.), *Paid in Full, Dark City* 1950; *September Affair, Peking Express* 1951; *Red Mountain, The Turning Point, Boots Malone* 1952; *Salome* 1953; *Elephant Walk* 1954; *Magic Fire* (also prod.) 1956; *Omar Khayyam* 1957; *Il Vendicatore/Dubrowsky* (also act.; It./Yug.) 1959; *Die Fastnachtsbeichte* (Ger.), *Herrin der Welt* (Ger.) 1960; *The Confession/Quick Let's Get Married/7 Different Ways* 1964.

Dietrich, Marlene. Actress. *b.* Maria Magdalene Dietrich, Dec. 27, 1901, Berlin. *d.* 1992. Her early life was shrouded in mystery, mainly as a result of her own conflicting statements and the intended fabrications by press agents upon her arrival in America in 1930. Until an enterprising reporter dug up her birth certificate in East Berlin, in 1964, she was believed to have been born Maria Magdalena von Losch in 1904. As it turned out, Edouard von Losch, a cavalry lieutenant, was her stepfather. Her own father, Louis Erich Otto Dietrich, an officer in the Royal Prussian Police, died when she was still a child. Von Losch was killed on the Russian front toward the end of WW I. One way or another, she was brought up strictly in an upper-middle-class conservative home. In her teens she took violin lessons, hoping for a career in the concert halls. But a wrist injury ended that dream and she began thinking of becoming an actress. After failing an audition with Max Reinhardt in 1921, she joined the chorus line of a touring musical revue. The following year she was auditioned again and accepted as a student in Reinhardt's drama school.

Soon after, she began playing small roles on the stage and in German films. Her most substantial part during that period was a supporting role in the film *Tragedy of Love* (1923), for which she was selected by a young Czech production assistant named Rudolf Sieber. They married in 1924 and in 1925 had a daughter, Maria (later known as actress Maria Riva). They never divorced but lived apart for most of the next four decades. He died in 1975.

Gradually, Miss Dietrich's stage and screen roles grew in importance and by the late 20s she was quite popular as a leading lady and was compared in some German magazines with Greta Garbo and Elisabeth Bergner. But before Dietrich's discovery by American film director Josef von STERNBERG, her success was only moderate and confined to the German-speaking world.

In Germany to direct *The Blue Angel* with Emil Jannings, von Sternberg had long been in search of an actress who could exude the sexuality of the film's seductive vamp, Lola Lola. He saw Dietrich performing on the stage and immediately decided that his search was over. According to his autobiography, *Fun in a Chinese Laundry,* von Sternberg molded Dietrich's personality radically to conform to his conception of the part. Their Svengali-Trilby relationship resulted in a film classic of great raw power and an unqualified international success. Even before *The Blue Angel* was released, Dietrich was signed to a Paramount contract, and in 1930 she went to Hollywood, leaving her husband and daughter behind. In Hollywood, von Sternberg continued his transformation of Marlene from a plump fraulein into a glamorous, sensuous star and woman of mystery. Paramount billed her as their answer to MGM's Greta Garbo, with a magnificent pair of legs as an extra edge. Six of Dietrich's first seven Hollywood films were made by von Sternberg; six highly personal, self-indulgent, lyrical-exotic films that made von Sternberg an enigma to the public and Marlene Dietrich a legend and a myth.

In 1935, after the completion of *The Devil Is a Woman,* the Sternberg-Dietrich collaboration was ended, probably by Paramount in response to disappointing box-office returns on their investment in the star. Dietrich began to work for other directors and eventually for other studios, in a wider variety of roles. But essentially she continued playing variations of Lola Lola, and most of her vehicles remained echoes of *The Blue Angel.*

In 1937, while in England to film *Knight Without Armor,* Dietrich was approached by Nazi agents with tempting offers to return to German films; it is said that she was visited by Joachim von Ribbentrop, then ambassador to England, with a personal and very generous offer from Hitler himself. She turned the offer down and as a result her films were banned in Germany. She became an American citizen in 1939, and during WW II she entertained US troops, participated in war bond drives, and made anti-Nazi propaganda broadcasts in German. She was awarded the Medal of Freedom and named Chevalier of the French Legion of Honor.

In 1948, Dietrich became "the world's most glamorous grandmother" when her daughter, Maria, gave birth to a son. Her preoccupation with Maria was deep and she spent much time with her. In the 50s, when her film career began to wane, the legendary Marlene began a new phase of her career as a recording star and cabaret performer. She sang to packed houses in London, Paris, Moscow, Las Vegas, and New York. In the early 70s she was still glamorous and very popular. And the vogue among American women for wearing slacks, which she started at the height of her fame, is still much in evidence everywhere. Rarely seen in public in her last years, she agreed to participate in a screen biography of herself by Maximilian SCHELL, in which she is heard on tape but never seen. The result, *Marlene* (1984), is a fascinating montage of old film clips enhanced by a lively, revealing interview with the star. Her death in 1992 was internationally mourned. An unflattering biography, *Marlene: An Intimate Memoir,* was published in 1993 by Maria Riva, her daughter. Author: *Marlene Dietrich's ABC* 1961; *My Life Story* 1979; *Marlene* 1987.

FILMS: In Germany—*Der kleine Napoleon/So sind die Männer/Napoleons kleiner Bruder, Tragödie der Liebe/Tragedy of Love, Der Mensch am Wege* 1923; *Der Sprung ins Leben* 1924; *Die freudlose Gasse/The Street of Sorrow/Streets of Sorrow/The Joyless Street* (unbilled extra) 1925; *Manon Lescaut, Eine Dubarry von heute/A Modern Du Barry, Kopf hoch Charly!, Madame wünscht keine Kinder/Madame Wants No Children* 1926; *Der Juxbaron, Sein grösster Bluff, Café Electric/Wenn ein Weib den Weg verliert/Die Liebesbörse* (Aus./Ger.) 1927; *Prinzessin Olala/The Art of Love* 1928; *Ich küsse ihre Hand Madame/I Kiss Your Hand Madame, Die Frau nach der man sich sehnt/Three Loves, Das Schiff der verlorenen Menschen/The Ship of Lost Men* (Ger./Fr.), *Gefahren der Brautzeit* 1929; *Der blaue Engel/The Blue Angel* 1930. In the US—*Morocco* 1930; *Dishonored* 1931; *Shanghai Express, Blonde Venus* 1932; *Song of Songs* 1933; *The Scarlet Empress* (as Catherine the Great) 1934; *The Devil Is a Woman* 1935; *Desire, The Garden of Allah* 1936; *Knight Without Armor* (UK), *Angel* 1937; *Destry Rides Again* 1939; *Seven Sinners* 1940; *The Flame of New Orleans, Manpower* 1941; *The Lady Is Willing, The Spoilers, Pittsburgh* 1942; *Follow the Boys* (cameo in magic act, being sawed in half by Orson Welles), *Kismet* 1944; *Martin Roumagnac/The Room Upstairs* (Fr.) 1946; *Golden Earrings* 1947; *A Foreign Affair* 1948; *Jigsaw* (cameo) 1949; *Stage Fright* (US/UK) 1950; *No Highway/No Highway in the Sky* (UK/US) 1951; *Rancho Notorious* 1952; *Around the World in 80 Days* (cameo) 1956; *Montecarlo/The Monte Carlo Story* (It.) 1957; *Witness for the Prosecution, Touch of Evil* (cameo) 1958; *Judgment at Nuremberg* 1961; *Black Fox* (doc.; narrated) 1962; *Paris When It Sizzles* (cameo) 1964; *Schöner Gigolo—Armer Gigolo/Just a Gigolo* 1979; *Marlene* (voice only) 1984.

Dietz, Howard. Lyricist, librettist, publicity executive. *B.* Sept. 8, 1896, New York City. *d.* 1983. *Ed.* Columbia. After WW I service with the Navy, he worked briefly as a newspaperman, then went into advertising. He joined Goldwyn Pictures as publicity director and, when the company merged with Metro in 1924, retained that position with MGM. He is credited with creating the company's trademark, Leo the Lion, and its Latin motto, *Ars Gratia Artis.* In 1940 he was appointed MGM's vice president in charge of publicity (he retired from the studio in 1957). At the same time, Dietz pursued another successful career as lyricist and opera and musical comedy librettist. Among his collaborations with composer Arthur SCHWARTZ were such songs as 'Dancing in the Dark' and 'Alone Together.' Among his musical shows were 'Dear Sir' (1924), 'Merry-Go-Round' (1927), 'The Little Show' (1929), 'Three's a Crowd' (1930), 'The Band Wagon' (with George S. Kaufman; 1931), 'Inside USA' (1948), and 'Jennie' (1963). He also wrote English adaptations of 'La Bohème' and 'Die Fledermaus' for the Metropolitan Opera. He was married to designer and costumer Lucinda Ballard. Autobiography: *Dancing in the Dark* (1975).

FILMS INCLUDE: *Love* 1928; *Battle of Paris* 1929; *The Lottery Bride* 1930; *Hollywood Party* (also prod.) 1934; *Under Your Spell* 1936; *Her Kind of Man* 1946; *Three Daring Daughters* 1947; *Dancing in the Dark* 1950; *The Band Wagon, Torch Song* 1953.

differential focusing. The utilization of the depth-of-field factor for placing the main action of a scene in sharp focus while keeping the background blurred.

Diffring, Anton. Actor. *b.* Oct. 20, 1918, Coblenz, Germany. *d.* 1989. A graduate of Berlin's Academy of Drama, he performed on the stage in Canada and the US before starting his screen career in the UK in 1950. He played character roles in numerous British and international productions, often portraying Nazis or other villains.

FILMS INCLUDE: *State Secret/The Great Manhunt* 1950; *Hotel Sahara* 1951; *Red Beret/Paratrooper, Albert R.N.* 1953; *Betrayed* 1954; *The Colditz Story, I Am a Camera* 1955; *House of Secrets/Triple Deception* 1957; *The Man Who Could Cheat*

Death 1959; *Circus of Horrors* 1960; *Incident at Midnight* 1963; *The Heroes of Telemark* 1965; *The Blue Max, Fahrenheit 451* 1966; *The Double Man* 1967; *Counterpoint* (US) 1968; *Where Eagles Dare* 1969; *Zeppelin* 1971; *Dead Pigeon on Beethoven Street* (Ger.) 1972; *The Beast Must Die* 1974; *Call Him Mr. Shatter* (Hong Kong), *Seven Men at Daybreak/Operation Daybreak* 1975; *Potato Fritz* (Ger.) 1976; *Vanessa* (Ger.), *L'Imprécateur* (Fr.), *Les Indiens sont encore loin* (Switz./Fr.), *Valentino* 1977; *Tusk* 1979; *Escape to Victory/Victory* 1981; *Der Sommer der Samurai* 1986; *Richard und Cosima* (as Franz Liszt) 1987.

diffuser. Transluscent material attached to a lighting unit for the purpose of softening the light falling on a subject. Diffusion filters are sometimes used in conjunction with the lens to soften hard lines of subjects being photographed.

digital effects. Special visual effects produced by manipulating images that are stored in a computer in binary digital form (as a string of 1s and 0s). The images can be movie frames or artwork scanned into a computer or pictures generated by the computer. The effects artist uses the computer to composite the images (put different elements together in one frame) and manipulate them in various ways. A computer-generated image of a charging dinosaur, for example, can be placed behind a filmed image of a man running away. In MORPHING, one image (such as a woman) is transformed into another (such as a panther). Digital effects can also be used to enhance filmed scenes (for example, adding computer-generated snow to make a blizzard out of a flurry) and to remove elements the audience is not supposed to see (such as the wires holding up a flying superhero).

The digital images composited on the computer are transferred to film either by filming them off the computer's cathode ray tube or by using a laser to scan the images directly onto the film.

Digital effects are increasingly taking the place of more traditional techniques of optical compositing, in which two or more filmed, drawn, or painted images are combined on an OPTICAL PRINTER. However, because of the expense of digital work, many images are still created optically and probably will be for some time. See also COMPUTER ANIMATION.

digital sound track. A movie sound track created by converting sound into binary digital information. In the theater, the digital information is converted back into audible sound. First used with films in the 90s, the technology is regarded by many as an improvement on traditional optical sound tracks, which are recorded photographically on film and are converted from light impulses to sound during projection. Digital sound differs from optical sound in its greater dynamic range (allowing greater loudness for gunshots and car crashes), its greater range of frequencies (allowing more faithful reproduction of low-end sounds, like explosions, and high-end sounds, like violins), and the greater discreteness of its stereo effects.

Digital sound systems can be single or double, depending on whether the sound track is contained on the film itself or on a separate compact disk (CD). Dolby SR-D, a single system, prints its digital data directly between the film perforations. Universal's DTS, a double system, uses compact disks played in electronic synchronization with the film projector.

Diller, Barry. Executive. Born on Feb. 2, 1942, in San Francisco. He was only 24 when he joined ABC-TV as assistant to the vice president in charge of programming. Within three years he rose to vice president of East Coast Features and Program Development. In 1974, Diller moved over to Paramount Pictures as chairman and chief executive officer, becoming one of Hollywood's most powerful decision makers. In 1984 he resigned to take over the reins at 20th Century-Fox. He was largely responsible for the rapid development of Fox Television as a viable alternative network. In a major shake-up, he resigned from Fox in February, 1992. He went on to become chairman and CEO of QVC Network, the home shopping cable service; in that capacity, he launched an unsuccessful bidding war in 1993–94 between QVC and Viacom for control of his former employer Paramount. He purchased and has combined three separate companies: Silver King Communications, Inc.; The Home Shopping Network, and Savoy Pictures Entertainment, into one entity.

Diller, Phyllis. Comedienne. Born Phyllis Driver, on July 17, 1917, in Lima, Ohio. *ed.* Sherwood Music School; Bluffton Coll. (Ohio). She was nearly 40, a mother of five working as an advertising copywriter for a California radio station, when she made a sensational comedy debut at San Francisco's Purple Onion. Other nightclub and TV engagements followed and before long she was nationally popular as a frowzy, mop-headed, grotesque, self-mocking comedienne with a spine-chilling laugh and a robust delivery of crude one-liners, many at the expense of her first husband, "Fang." In the 60s she appeared in a handful of films, several times as the screen partner of Bob Hope. In 1970 she appeared on Broadway for several months in the title role of 'Hello Dolly.' Author: *Phyllis Diller's Housekeeping Hints, Phyllis Diller's Marriage Manual, Phyllis Diller's The Complete Mother, The Joys of Aging and How to Avoid Them.*

FILMS: *Splendor in the Grass* 1961; *Boy Did I Get a Wrong Number, The Fat Spy* 1966; *Eight on the Lam, Mad Monster Party* (animated puppet film; voice only) 1967; *The Private Navy of Sgt. O'Farrell, Did You Hear the One About the Traveling Saleslady?* 1968; *The Adding Machine* (UK/US) 1969; *Pink Motel* 1983; *The Bone Yard* 1991; *The Nutcracker Prince* (voice only) 1991; *Wisecracks* 1992; *Happily Ever After* (voice only) 1993.

Dillman, Bradford. Actor. Born on Apr. 14, 1930, in San Francisco. *ed.* Yale. Sensitive, thoughtful, intelligent leading man and character player of stage, TV, and films. He made his Broadway debut in 1953 and scored a success three years later in 'Long Day's Journey Into Night.' In films since 1958, he was seen at first in youthful roles, but he gradually moved into more varied characterizations, ranging from hero to villain. He won the Cannes Festival acting award for *Compulsion* (1959). In addition to features, he appeared in scores of TV movies and series episodes. He married model-actress Suzy PARKER.

FILMS INCLUDE: *A Certain Smile, In Love and War* 1958; *Compulsion* 1959; *Crack in the Mirror* 1960; *Circle of Deception* (UK), *Sanctuary, Francis of Assisi* (title role) 1961; *A Rage to Live* 1965; *The Plainsman* 1966; *Sergeant Ryker, Jigsaw* 1968; *The Bridge at Remagen* 1969; *Suppose They Gave a War and Nobody Came* 1970; *Brother John, The Mephisto Waltz, Escape from the Planet of the Apes, The Resurrection of Zachary Wheeler* 1971; *The Iceman Cometh, The Way We Were* 1973; *99 44/100% Dead, Chosen Survivors, Gold* (UK) 1974; *Bug* 1975; *The Enforcer* 1976; *The Lincoln Conspiracy* (as John Wilkes Booth), *The Amsterdam Kill, Mastermind* 1977; *The Swarm, Piranha* 1978; *Love and Bullets* (UK) 1979; *Guyana: Cult of the Damned* 1980; *Sudden Impact* 1983; *Treasure of the Amazon* (Mex.) 1985; *Man Outside* 1988; *Heroes Stand Alone* 1989.

Dillon, John Francis (Jack). Director, actor. *b.* July 13, 1884, New York City. *d.* 1934. He entered films as an actor in 1913 and began directing comedy shorts and features the following year. During the 20s he established a reputation as a proficient director of commercially successful romantic dramas and comedies, including several popular "flapper age" romps featuring some of Hollywood's glamour stars of the day. Along with his prolific output as a director, he continued playing supporting roles in sporadic films through 1927 and was billed interchangeably as John Francis Dillon or Jack Dillon. His acting credits are often confused with those of John T. Dillon (1866–1937), also billed as Jack Dillon, and John Webb Dillion (1877–1949), also billed as Jack Dillion or Jack Dillon. Toward the end of his career he was reduced mainly to B pictures. Married to actress Edith Haller.

FEATURE FILMS (as director): *The Key to Yesterday* (also act.) 1914; *Indiscreet Corinne* 1917; *Betty Takes a Hand, Limousine Life, Heiress for a Day, Nancy Comes Home, The Love Swindle, Beans* 1918; *She Hired a Husband, A Taste of Life, The Silk-Lined Burglar, The Follies Girl, Love's Prisoner, Burglar by Proxy* (also sc.) 1919; *The Right of Way, Suds, Blackbirds* 1920; *The Plaything of Broadway, Children of the Night, The Roof Tree* 1921; *Gleam O'Dawn, The Yellow Stain, The Cub Reporter, Calvert's Valley, Man Wanted* 1922; *The Broken Violin, The Self-Made Wife, Flaming Youth* 1923; *Lilies of the Field, The Perfect Flapper, Flirting with Love* 1924; *If I Marry Again, One Way Street, Chickie, The Half-Way Girl, We Moderns* 1925; *Too Much Money, Don Juan's Three Nights, Midnight Lovers, Love's Blindness* 1926; *The Sea Tiger, The Prince of Headwaiters, Smile Brother Smile* (also act.), *The Crystal Cup, Man Crazy* 1927; *The Noose, The Heart of a Follies Girl, Out of the Ruins* 1928; *Scarlet Seas, Children of the Ritz, Careers, Fast Life* 1929; *Sally, Spring Is Here, Bride of the Regiment, The Girl of the Golden West, Kismet, One Night at Susie's* 1930; *Millie, The Finger Points, The Reckless Hour, Pagan Lady* 1931; *The Cohens and Kellys in Hollywood, Behind the Mask, Man about Town, Call Her Savage* 1932; *Humanity* 1933; *The Big Shakedown* 1934.

Dillon, Kevin. Actor. Born August 19, 1965, in Mamaroneck, New York. The younger brother of Matt DILLON, he has distinguished himself as a sturdy actor in meditative lead roles as well as a competent hero in lighter fare.

FILMS INCLUDE: *No Big Deal, Heaven Help Us* 1985; *Platoon* 1986; *Dear America: Letters Home from Vietnam* 1987; *The Blob, The Remote Control, The Rescue, War Party* 1988; *Immediate Family* 1989; *The Doors, A Midnight Clear* 1991; *No Escape* 1994.

Dillon, Matt. Actor. Born on Feb. 18, 1964, in New Rochelle, N.Y. Natural, spontaneous juvenile lead, then leading man of the American screen. A grand nephew of cartoonist Alex Raymond, the creator of the 'Flash Gordon' and 'Jungle Jim' comic strips, he was a 14-year-old junior high school student when he was discovered by a casting director and auditioned successfully for his first film role. During the 80s he emerged as one of the more gifted and charismatic of the new crop of Hollywood's young stars, distinguishing himself particularly with his gritty performance in *Drugstore Cowboy* (1989). His younger brother, Kevin DILLON, is also an film actor.

FILMS: *Over the Edge* 1979; *Little Darlings, My Bodyguard* 1980; *Liar's Moon, Tex* 1982; *Rumble Fish, The Outsiders* 1983; *The Flamingo Kid* 1984; *Target, Rebel* (Austral.) 1985; *Native Son* 1986; *Dear America* (doc.; voice only), *The Big Town* 1987; *Kansas* 1988; *The Bloodhounds of Broadway, Drugstore Cowboy* 1989; *A Kiss Before Dying* 1991; *Singles* 1992; *Mr. Wonderful, The Saint of Fort Washington* 1993; *Golden Gate* 1994; *Frankie Starlight, To Die For* 1995; *The Albino Alligator, Beautiful Girls, Grace of My Heart* 1996; *In and Out* 1997.

Dillon, Melinda. Actress. Born on Oct. 13, 1939, in Hope, Ark. Talented lady of the American stage and screen. She burst on the Broadway scene in 1962 with an emotionally charged performance as Honey in the original production of 'Who's Afraid of Virginia Woolf?' She subsequently appeared in many other plays and TV programs and was first seen on the screen in 1969, but began appearing regularly in films in the late 70s. She was nominated for Academy Awards as best supporting actress for *Close Encounters of the Third Kind* (1977) and *Absence of Malice* (1981).

FILMS: *The April Fools* (bit) 1969; *Bound for Glory* 1976; *Slap Shot, Close Encounters of the Third Kind* 1977; *F.I.S.T.* 1978; *Absence of Malice* 1981; *A Christmas Story* 1983; *Songwriter* 1984; *Harry and the Hendersons* 1987; *Staying Together* 1989; *The Game, Spontaneous Combustion* 1990; *The Prince of Tides* 1991; *Demolition Man* 1993; *Sioux City, To Wong Foo Thanks for Everything Julie Newmar* 1994; *How to Make an American Quilt* 1995; *Entertaining Angels* 1996.

dimension–150. A WIDE-SCREEN PROCESS in which 70 mm prints are projected on a deeply curved screen.

DIN. A system for rating the speed of film EMULSION. It is widely used in parts of Europe but rarely in the US, where the ASA rating system prevails. DIN stands for Deutsche Industrie Norm, the German standards body that devised the system.

dinky inky. A small, low-wattage spotlight.

diopter lens. A supplementary lens placed in front of a regular camera lens for extreme close-up photography.

diorama. A miniature scale model of a motion picture set.

Di Palma, Carlo. Director of photography. Born on Apr. 17, 1925, in Rome. Entered Italian films as an assistant camera operator in 1942 and graduated to lighting cameraman in 1954. But it was not until the mid-60s that he gained an international reputation for the outstanding color cinematography of ANTONIONI's *Red Desert* and *Blow-Up.* He sometimes uses the pseudonym Charles Brown. In 1973 he made his debut as director with *Teresa la Ladra,* starring Monica Vitti, but later returned to cinematography. In the 80s he began collaborating regularly with director Woody ALLEN.

FILMS INCLUDE: *Ivan* 1954; *La Lunga Notte del '43* 1960; *L'Assassino/The Lady Killer of Rome* 1961; *Omicron* 1963; *Deserto Rosso/Red Desert* 1964; *I Tre Volti* (one episode) 1965; *Blow-Up* 1966; *The Appointment* (US) 1969; *Drama della Gelosia/The Pizza Triangle* 1970; *La Pacifista/The Pacifist* 1971; *Teresa la Ladra/Teresa the Thief* (dir. only) 1973; *Qui comincia l'Avventura* 1976; *Amo non amo* 1979; *La Tragedia di un Uomo ridicolo/Tragedy of a Ridiculous Man* 1981; *Identificazione di una Donna/Identification of a Woman* 1982; *Gabriela* (Braz.), *The Black Stallion Returns* (US) 1983; *Hannah and Her Sisters, Off Beat* (US) 1986; *Radio Days, The Secret of My Success, September* (US) 1987; *Alice* (US) 1990; *Shadows and Fog, Husbands and Wives* (US) 1992; *Manhattan Murder Mystery* (US) 1993; *Mighty Aphrodite* 1995; *Everyone Says I Love You, Mission: Impossible* 1996.

direct cinema. See CINÉMA VÉRITÉ.

direct cut. The same as CUT, but often used in scripts to convey more emphatically a preference for that and no other form of transition, such as a DISSOLVE.

directional. Pertaining to a direction in space; a term used to describe a variety of optical, electronic, and acoustic devices that characteristically have a limited angle of projection or acceptance, such as spotlights, antennas, screens, and particularly microphones. A directional microphone, for instance, is one that is selective with reference to the directions from which it best picks up sound waves.

director. In films, the person responsible for the creative aspects, both interpretive and technical, of a motion picture production. In addition to orchestrating the action in front of the camera and guiding the acting and the dialogue, the film director controls camera position and movement, sound, lighting, and all other ingredients that contribute to the final look of a motion picture. In carrying out the task of transforming a screenplay into a film, he supervises a versatile crew of artists and technicians, each responsible for his own area of specialty but all answerable to the director, who has the final word on all aspects of production during filming.

Directors enjoyed a considerable degree of creative freedom during the early days of the cinema, though only a few took advantage of that freedom to create anything worthwhile. However, as the film business grew into an industry, the efficient but restrictive studio system wrested from most American directors such an essential component of artistic filmic expression as choice of script, cast, cameraman, and editor. While his European colleague continued working with a certain measure of autonomy, the average American director became a studio employee with a producer or production supervisor looking over his shoulder during filming and making the all-important decisions of the final cut. Certain directors with strong personalities and impressive box-office track records—like John Ford, Alfred Hitchcock, Ernst Lubitsch, Otto Preminger, George Stevens, Billy Wilder, and William Wyler—managed to maintain their creative independence within the studio system. But the typical Hollywood director was for many years a hireling appointed to execute the wishes of producers and movie moguls. Obstinate geniuses like Erich von Stroheim and Orson Welles found out the hard way how expendable talent was in a system dominated by money tycoons.

Under the studio system, most directors were interchangeable, and little of their personal mark could be detected in the final product. In most cases, it was easier to identify a film by its "look" as the product of a certain studio than as the work of a particular director. It is not, therefore, surprising that only a relatively few directors were known to the general public by name and that for so many years the film's stars, not the director, were the main attraction at the box office.

The late 50s saw a gradual elevation in the status of the American director as a result of the decline of the studio system and the reassessment by French critics of the body of work of many previously neglected filmmakers and their ranking in a pantheon of *auteurs* (see AUTEUR THEORY). The growing sophistication of film audiences and the increasing interest among students of film as an academic subject also contributed to the emergence of the American director in the 60s and 70s as the real star of many films, whose name above the title often now carries more weight than the name of the actors in the principal roles.

Ideally, the complete filmmaker should be a director-producer-writer all in one. But it does not often work out this way (see HYPHENATES). When a director does not develop his or her own projects, the director is hired by a producer at some early stage in the project to execute the production of a film. He may or may not be a party to the selection of the story or subject of the film, but it is important that he be involved in the preparation of the shooting script, preferably that he write the screenplay himself, alone or in collaboration. Other preproduction stages the director may or may not (but should) be involved in are casting, selection of technical crews and locations, and determination of the pictorial design of the film with the art director. In fact, one way some movies achieve the signature look of a director is through the repeated grouping of a technical staff—cinematographer Tak Fujimoto and editor Craig Mckay in Jonathan Demme movies, cinematographer Ernest Dickerson and production designer Wynn Thomas in Spike Lee movies.

Some directors, Hitchcock for one, plan their films carefully and rarely deviate from their scripts, notes, and storyboards once filming has begun. Others, like Fellini, like to improvise and make on-the-spot changes in the script or the visual aspects of the film. But advance preparation by all directors is thorough and meticulous, for film is a highly expensive medium and mistakes and last-minute changes or adjustments can prove costly and embarrassing. Again, the director may or may not be involved in the postproduction stage of a project, the all-important phase of editing, in which final determinations are made about the shape, meaning, and pace of a film. Since the development of VCRs in the 1980s, directors who are displeased with studio editing of their movie sometimes release to video a "director's cut," which usually includes additional or re-edited footage. The greater the involvement of the director in all phases of production, the more acceptable is his claim for authorship of the film.

director, assistant. See ASSISTANT DIRECTOR.

director of photography. The person in charge of lighting a set and photographing a film. Also known as "first cameraman," "lighting cameraman," or "cinematographer," he is responsible for transforming the screenwriter's and director's concepts into real visual images.

In the early days of cinema, camera work was handled by one man who not only operated the camera, but often also developed the film and printed it in the laboratory. But as the art of film progressed and grew in complexity, the duties of the cameraman became more specific and his contributions to the quality of a film more vital. Many of the technical innovations credited to director D. W. Griffith originated with his cameraman, Billy Bitzer, or came about as a result of the close creative partnership between the two men. Other leading creative cameramen who have contributed greatly to the advancement of cinema art over the years include Nestor Almendros, Joseph August, William Daniels, Ernest Dickerson, Karl Freund, Lee Garmes, James Wong Howe, Charles B. Lang, Henry Miller, Sven Nykvist, Charles Rosher, Leon Shamroy, Karl Struss, Gregg Toland, Geoffrey Unsworth, and Haskell Wexler.

The modern director of photography does not physically operate the camera. This is done by a CAMERA OPERATOR. Others in the crew under the charge of the director of photography are the first ASSISTANT CAMERAMAN, also known as the "focus-puller," and the second assistant cameraman, also known as the "clapper boy" or the "loader." This leaves the director of photography free to deal with his main responsibility—creating the appropriate mood, atmosphere, and visual style of each and every shot and sustaining these qualities throughout the entire film.

The director of photography's involvement in a film begins some time before the actual start of production. He is usually consulted by the producer and director about a variety of technical details, including the choice of film stock and laboratory. He normally scouts the proposed locations to ascertain their suitability and to determine the type and number of cameras and lighting equipment that may be needed for shooting. The art director and set decorator consult him on the placement of lighting units and camera riggings in every set. Once shooting begins, the director of photography is second in importance on the set only to the director.

Working closely together, the director and the director of photography determine the camera angles, setup, and movement for every shot. The latter then selects the proper lens and filter that will best achieve the former's concept of the shot, determines the exposure, and sets up the lights to achieve the particular effect desired. The camera operator takes over from there. Later, the director of photography joins the director in viewing the dailies, or rushes, to evaluate his earlier work and make necessary adjustments for future shooting. At the conclusion of production, the director of photography supervises the grading of the first print in the lab to assure that the desired degree of brightness and the right color tone are achieved for the images the public will eventually see on the screen.

Directors Guild of America. See DGA.

disc synchronization. See SOUND.

Disney, Walt. Animator, producer, executive. *b.* Dec. 5, 1901, Chicago. *d.* 1966. The man who would one day become the most famous name in film animation and children's entertainment began his working life as a schoolboy, delivering newspapers. At 14 he enrolled at the Kansas City Art Institute and at 16 volunteered as a Red Cross ambulance driver in France during the waning months of WW I. Returning to the US in 1919, he went to work for a commercial art studio in Kansas City, where he met Ub IWERKS, another young and promising artist, who was to become his lifelong collaborator. They joined the Kansas City Film Ad Company, where they made animated commercials and a series of satirical animated cartoons on their own and selling them to a local theater under the title of Laugh-O-Grams. Encouraged by the results, Disney formed his own cartoon production company, Laugh-O-Gram, but soon went bankrupt and headed for Hollywood, where in 1923, in partnership with his older brother, Roy, and with the creative help of Iwerks, he began producing a series of animation-live action cartoons called "Alice in Cartoonland."

In 1927, Disney and Iwerks initiated a new cartoon series, "Oswald the Rabbit," and the following year created Mickey Mouse. The first two Mickey cartoons, *Plane Crazy* and *Gallopin' Gaucho,* were silent; but Disney, a stickler for perfection and technical quality, quickly switched to sound with the third, *Steamboat Willie,* utilizing an improvised early sound system. Disney himself provided Mickey's characteristic high-pitched voice on the sound track. Encouraged by the success of their sound experiments, the Disney team started the "Silly Symphony" cartoon series, in which the action on the screen was created to match the beat of a prerecorded music track rather than the other way around, as had been the custom. The first of these were *The Skeleton Dance* (1929) and the best known and most successful, *The Three Little Pigs* (1933).

In the meantime, the success of Mickey Mouse spawned a whole menagerie of animal cartoon characters, some of whom became popular "stars" in their own right, notably Minnie Mouse, Mickey's mate, Donald Duck, Goofy (originally named Dippy Dawg), and Pluto. Disney continued to strive for technical improvement of his product. As early as 1931 some of the cartoons were made in two-strip color and by the mid-30s the entire studio output was in three-strip Technicolor. The Disney team also developed the multiplane camera, a breakthrough in animation technique that made it possible to create animated films with more intricate action and with a greater sense of perspective and depth.

The Disney organization had meanwhile grown into a virtual animation factory, employing hundreds of men and women and realizing profits from the merchandising of a whole array of products associated with the studio's cartoon characters. By 1934, Disney began the production of a feature-length animated cartoon, at a great risk of company resources, money, and prestige. *Snow White and the Seven Dwarfs* premiered in December 1937, and was released in February of 1938, proving an enormous success at the box office. Other Disney feature cartoons followed, the most controversial of which was *Fantasia* (1940), an ambitious attempt to marry animation with classical music. It won Disney many new admirers among serious filmgoers and eventually became a big moneymaker through repeated re-releases over the years.

During WW II, the Disney company turned out a great many training and morale-boosting films, culminating in the live-action animation feature documentary *Victory Through Air Power* (1943). It was a trying period for the company, in the wake of a 1941 strike by animators against Disney's authoritative rule and naturalistic drawing style, which resulted in a mass resignation from the studio and the formation of UPA (United Productions of America). But the company survived both that crisis and wartime production restrictions, and went on to new heights.

After some success with features combining live action with animation, production expanded to include pure action films, the first of which was *Treasure Island* (1950). At the same time, production began on a fascinating series of nature documentaries, known as the "True-Life Adventure" series, that followed the success of the half-hour short *Seal Island* (1948). The first of these features was *The Living Desert* (1953) and the last, *Jungle Cat* (1960). Several films in the series won Academy Awards. Altogether Disney collected 29 Oscars for his films.

By now, Disney was America's undisputed king of family entertainment in America. He formed a subsidiary, the Buena Vista company, as a distributing arm for the Disney films, thus freeing himself of any dependence on other powers in the industry. In October of 1954 he launched a weekly anthology TV series, 'Disneyland,' which ran for decades under different names and on different networks. The following year he opened Disneyland, a 160-acre fantasy-amusement park in Anaheim, Calif., one of the world's major tourist attractions.

By the mid-60s, Disney's avuncular presence had become known to millions through his weekly introductions to the Disney TV series. It came as a shock, then, when the great showman died on December 15, 1966, of acute circulatory collapse following surgery for the removal of a lung tumor. For the company's history following his death, see the Walt DISNEY COMPANY.

FEATURE FILMS (as producer or executive producer): *Snow White and the Seven Dwarfs* 1937; *Pinocchio, Fantasia* 1940; *The Reluctant Dragon, Dumbo* 1941; *Bambi* 1942; *Saludos Amigos, Victory Through Air Power* 1943; *The Three Caballeros* 1945; *Make Mine Music, Song of the South* 1946; *Fun and Fancy Free* 1947; *Melody Time, So Dear to My Heart* 1948; *Ichabod and Mr. Toad* 1949; *Cinderella, Treasure Island* 1950; *Alice in Wonderland* 1951; *The Story of Robin Hood* 1952; *Peter Pan, The Sword and the Rose, The Living Desert* 1953; *Rob Roy—The Highland Rogue, The Vanishing Prairie, 20,000 Leagues Under the Sea* 1954; *Davy Crockett—King of the Wild Frontier, Lady and the Tramp, The African Lion, The Littlest Outlaw* 1955; *The Great Locomotive Chase, Davy Crockett and the River Pirates, Secrets of Life, Westward Ho the Wagons* 1956; *Johnny Tremain, Perri, Old Yeller* 1957; *The Light in the Forest, White Wilderness, Tonka* 1958; *Sleeping Beauty, The Shaggy Dog, Darby O'Gill and the Little People, Third Man on the Mountain* 1959; *Toby Tyler, Kidnapped, Pollyanna, Jungle Cat, Ten Who Dared, The Swiss Family Robinson, The Sign of Zorro* 1960; *101 Dalmatians, The Absent-Minded Professor, The Parent Trap, Nikki—Wild Dog of the North, Greyfriars Bobby, Babes in Toyland* 1961; *Moon Pilot, Bon Voyage, Big Red, Almost Angels, The Legend of Lobo, In Search of the Castaways* 1962; *Son of Flubber, Miracle of the Wild Stallions, Savage Sam, Summer Magic, The Incredible Journey, The Sword in the Stone* 1963; *The Misadventures of Merlin Jones, A Tiger Walks, The Three Lives of Thomasina, The Moon-Spinners, Mary Poppins, Emil and the Detectives* 1964; *Those Calloways, The Monkey's Uncle, That Darn Cat* 1965; *The Ugly Dachshund, Lt. Robin Crusoe—USN, The Fighting*

Prince of Donegal, Follow Me Boys 1966; *Monkeys Go Home!, Adventures of Bullwhip Griffin, The Gnome-Mobile, The Jungle Book, The Happiest Millionaire* 1967.

Disney Company, The Walt. American motion picture production and distribution company. For many years, the studio was virtually synonymous with its namesake and head, animator Walt DISNEY, who, with his brother Roy, founded the company in 1923. The studio's rise to fame and prosperity began with the first sound Mickey Mouse cartoon, *Steamboat Willie* (1928), and continued with their numerous animated features, beginning with *Snow White* in 1937. Publicly traded since 1940, the company not only led the field in animation, but came to dominate and define the family entertainment industry. In the 50s, the studio branched into live-action features (such as *20,000 Leagues Under the Sea*), nature features, and television production. In 1955, the company entered a new arena when the successful theme park Disneyland opened in Anaheim, California.

When Walt Disney died in 1966, his death was a blow, which sent the company into a downward spiral. Its movies gained a reputation for mediocrity at a time when "family" movies were increasingly considered box-office poison. The Disney TV anthology series continued, but steadily declined in quality and audience. A group of Disney animators, led by Don BLUTH, left in 1979, citing a deterioration in the studio's artistic standards. The company's major strong point was its theme park business, which expanded to include Walt Disney World, near Orlando, Fla., in 1971 and a park in Tokyo in 1983.

The turnaround in the studio's fortunes began in 1983, when Ron MILLER, Walt Disney's son-in-law, became chief executive. Miller founded Touchstone Pictures, designed to make films targeted to adults while Walt Disney Pictures continued to make family-oriented films. The first Touchstone release, *Splash* (1984), was a big commercial success, but it came too late for Miller, who was in a power struggle with Roy E. Disney, a major shareholder and the son of Walt's brother Roy. Late in 1984, Miller was ousted; the former president of Paramount, Michael EISNER, became chairman and CEO of the Walt Disney Company, while Frank Wells, formerly a Warner Bros. Executive, became president and Roy E. Disney vice chairman.

Building on what Miller had begun, Eisner brought the Walt Disney Company back to prosperity. With Jeffrey KATZENBERG, chairman of the company's movie-making division (the Walt Disney Studios), he resuscitated the careers of stars such as Bette MIDLER and Richard DREYFUSS and developed a strategy of producing tightly budgeted films with wide appeal such as *Stakeout*, *Honey I Shrunk the Kids*, *Pretty Woman*, and *Sister Act*. Disney's stature as the leading animation studio was also revived with a successful series of new musical animated features, including *Beauty and the Beast, The Lion King* and *Pocahontas*.

However, the untimely death of executive Frank Wells put into motion the exit of Katzenberg, who assumed he would be offered the now vacant position. Chief Michael Eisner filled the position himself and shortly thereafter engineered a multibillion dollar merger with Cap Cities/ABC. The shock came with the announcement that co-founder and head of CAA Michael Ovitz would be coming on board as second in command. In a little over a year, Ovitz made his exit with a reported $90 million payoff. The company, meanwhile, continues to register strong profits and is the industry leader in box office grosses.

In its television endeavors, Disney made up for the loss of its weekly network series with the pay-cable Disney Channel (established by Miller in 1983). Disney's home-video, recording, publishing, and merchandising enterprises have also flourished. The Euro Disney theme park, established near Paris in 1992, has so far proved successful, but the movie studio has not been without box-office disappointments. But for now, Disney has restored its reputation as the first word in family entertainment while building a new reputation as a general-interest motion picture studio.

dissolve. A screen effect of gradually fusing one shot into another. It is achieved by the overlapping of two lengths of film so that, as the last frames of the first shot gradually darken or fade out, they are blended with the opening frames of the next scene, which gradually brighten or fade in. The effect on the screen is that of one scene seeming to melt into another. Some cameras are equipped with dissolve controls, but normally the effect is produced by OPTICAL PRINTING in the lab.

Also known as a "lap dissolve," the effect is used as a transitional device, usually to indicate a time lapse or a change in location, as distinct from a direct cut, which tends to suggest concurrent action. The length of any particular dissolve depends on the desired effect—a slow dissolve indicating a long time lapse, a relatively quick dissolve indicating a brief passage of time. Technically, the length of the dissolve is measured by the total number of frames required to complete the effect. Since a dissolve demands the superimposition of the end of one scene onto the beginning of the next, at least six extra feet of film must be shot for each scene for the lab to have the necessary footage to achieve the effect. Using a CHINAGRAPH (grease) pencil, the editor indicates a dissolve by marking the desired length of film on his work print with a diagonal line.

distortion. An optical malformation of an image, usually as a result of an inconsistency in the magnification of the image between the edges and the center of the frame. Distortions may result accidentally from the use of a defective lens or a miscalculated placement of the camera, or they may be achieved intentionally for an artistic effect. German director F. W. Murnau often resorted to the use of unusual camera angles. These resulted in startling distortions, adding to the significance of some key sequences in *The Last Laugh* (1924), for example. Weird effects have been achieved in TV commercials by shooting close-ups of subjects with a fish-eye lens.

distributor. The person or company acting as a "middleman" between film producers and exhibitors, usually for a percentage of the profits but sometimes for a flat fee. Or the distributor may buy the rights to a film from the producer and rent out prints of it to exhibitors.

Di Venanzo, Gianni. Director of photography. *b.* Dec. 18, 1920, Teramo, Italy. *d.* 1966. Entered Italian films during WW II as camera assistant to Tonti, Martelli, and others, and worked in that capacity or as camera operator on some key neorealist productions, including Visconti's *Ossessione* and *La Terra Trema,* Rossellini's *Open City* and *Paisan,* and De Sica's *Miracle in Milan.* As a lighting cameraman from the early 50s, he soon proved himself a master at creating mood through the lens. He worked for Fellini and Rosi, among others, but his stark, melancholy visual style was most beneficial to several important films of ANTONIONI. His premature death at 45 during the production of *The Honey Pot* robbed the Italian cinema of one of its outstanding cinematographers.

FILMS INCLUDE: *Achtung Banditi!* 1951; *Amore in Città/Love in the City* 1953; *Cronache di Poveri Amanti* 1954; *Le Amiche/The Girl Friends* 1955; *Lo Scapolo* 1956; *Kean, Il Grido/The Outcry, La Sfida* 1957; *I Soliti Ignoti/Big Deal on Madonna Street* 1958; *I Delfini/The Dauphins* 1960; *La Notte/The Night* 1961; *L'Eclisse/The Eclipse, Salvatore Giuliano, Eva* 1962; *Otto e Mezzo/8½, La Ragazza di Bube/*

Bebo's Girl, Le Mani sulla Città 1963; *Gli Indifferenti/ Time of Indifference* 1964; *Il Momento della Verità/The Moment of Truth, Giulietta degli Spiriti/Juliet of the Spirits, La decima Vittima/The Tenth Victim* 1965; *The Honey Pot* (US/UK/It.) 1967.

Divine. Transvestite performer. *b.* Harris Glenn Milstead, Oct. 19, 1945, Baltimore. *d.* 1989. A high school chum of John WATERS, he later starred in many of the cult director's films, usually impersonating obese, garishly dressed, often depraved female characters. Dominating the screen with his 300-pound frame, he gained fame and cult-star status after appearing in the midnight classic *Pink Flamingos* (1972), but found his greatest recognition (and even affection) as the game Baltimore housewife and mother in *Hairspray* (1988). He died shortly after the premiere of that movie. Also appeared on the stage and in cabaret and became a European disco star.

FILMS INCLUDE: *Roman Candles* 1966; *Eat Your Makeup* 1968; *Mondo Trasho, Multiple Maniacs* 1970; *Pink Flamingos* 1972; *Female Trouble* 1974; *Polyester* 1981; *Lust in the Dust* 1985; *Trouble in Mind* 1986; *Hairspray* 1988; *Out of the Dark* 1989.

Dix, Richard. Actor. *b.* Ernest Carlton Brimmer, July 18, 1894, St. Paul, Minn. *d.* 1949. *ed.* Northwestern; U. of Minnesota. While a medical student, he began acting in campus plays and eventually gave up the idea of medical practice for a career on the stage. After some experience in stock and WW I service, he made his Broadway debut in 1919 ('The Hawk'). Two years later he made his screen debut and immediately clicked as a star. Tall, rugged, and square-jawed, he often played the strong, silent type, and enjoyed considerable popularity in the 20s as a hero capable of dealing calmly with every situation. Among his notable silent film roles was that of the hero in the modern part of De Mille's *The Ten Commandments* and as an Indian in *The Vanishing American.* He spent most of the silent period with Paramount, but early in the 30s he moved to RKO and other companies. His best known early sound vehicle was *Cimarron.* Despite the film's huge financial and critical success and a personal Oscar nomination, Dix found himself subsequently drifting into second features. For the rest of his career he appeared mostly in B pictures, typically in the action vein. In the mid-40s he played "The Whistler" in a series of adventure films. He died at 55 of a heart attack. His son, Robert Dix, has also appeared in films, in both leads and supporting parts.

FILMS INCLUDE: *Not Guilty, The Sin Flood, Dangerous Curve Ahead, Poverty of Riches* 1921; *Yellow Men and Gold, The Glorious Fool, The Wall Flower, Fools First* 1922; *The Christian, Quicksands, The Ten Commandments, Souls for Sale, Racing Hearts, To the Last Man, The Call of the Canyon* 1923; *The Stranger, Icebound, Unguarded Women, Sinners in Heaven, Manhattan* 1924; *A Man Must Live, Too Many Kisses, Men and Women, The Lucky Devil, The Vanishing American, Womanhandled* 1925; *The Quarterback, Let's Get Married, Say It Again* 1926; *Paradise for Two, Knockout Reilly, Man Power, Shanghai Bound, The Gay Defender* 1927; *Sporting Goods, Warming Up, Easy Come Easy Go, Moran of the Marines* 1928; *Redskin, Nothing but the Truth, The Wheel of Life, The Love Doctor, Seven Keys to Baldpate* 1929; *Lovin' the Ladies, Shooting Straight* 1930; *Cimarron, Donovan's Kid, The Public Defender, Secret Service* 1931; *The Lost Squadron, Hell's Highway, The Conquerors* 1932; *The Great Jasper, Day of Reckoning, Ace of Aces* 1933; *Stingaree, West of the Pecos* 1934; *The Tunnel/Transatlantic Tunnel* (UK), *The Arizonian* 1935; *Yellow Dust, Special Investigator* 1936; *The Devil's Playground, It Happened in Hollywood* 1937; *Blind Alibi, Sky Giant* 1938; *Twelve Crowded Hours, Man of Conquest, Reno* 1939; *The Marines Fly High, Cherokee Strip, Men Against the Sky* 1940; *The Roundup* 1941; *Tombstone, American Empire* 1942; *Eyes of the Underworld, The Kansan, The Ghost Ship* 1943; *The Whistler* 1944; *The Power of the Whistler* 1945; *The Mysterious Intruder* 1946; *The Thirteenth Hour* 1947.

Dixon, Donna. Actress. Born on July 20, 1957, in Alexandria, Va. A beautiful blonde, she quit anthropology and premedical studies at Mary Washington University to become a popular model and cover girl. After co-starring in the TV series 'Bosom Buddies' (1980–82), she began appearing in films. She married actor and *Doctor Detroit* co-star Dan AYKROYD.

FILMS: *Doctor Detroit, Twilight Zone—The Movie* 1983; *Spies Like Us* 1985; *The Couch Trip, Lucky Stiff* 1988; *Speed Zone, It Had to Be You* 1989; *Wayne's World* 1992; *Exit to Eden* 1994.

Dixon, Jean. Actress. *b.* July 14, 1896, Waterbury, Conn. *D.* 1981. Partly educated in France, she made her debut on the Paris stage in a play starring Sarah Bernhardt, and her first Broadway appearance in 1921. She appeared in many stage productions, on the road and on Broadway, before and after her screen debut in 1929. She played character parts in many films of the 30s, typically as a wisecracking friend of the heroine.

FILMS INCLUDE: *The Lady Lies* 1929; *The Kiss Before the Mirror* 1933; *Sadie McKee* 1934; *I'll Love You Always, She Married Her Boss* 1935; *My Man Godfrey, The Magnificent Brute* 1936; *You Only Live Once* 1937; *Joy of Living, Holiday* 1938.

Dmytryk, Edward. Director. Born on Sept. 4, 1908, in Grand Forks, British Columbia, to Ukrainian immigrants. After his mother died, and his father moved to San Francisco and remarried, he found himself a neglected and abused child of six who had to contribute to the family budget by peddling newspapers even while attending grammar school. At age 15 he began working for Paramount in Hollywood as a messenger boy and later was employed as assistant in various phases of production. From 1930 to 1939 he was film editor, counting among his credits the noted *Ruggles of Red Gap* (1935). During this period he directed *The Hawk* (also 1935), but his career as director officially begins in 1939. His early films were mostly routine action and light fare. His first interesting work was *Hitler's Children* (1943), an engrossing anti-fascist drama. Next he directed two exciting suspense thrillers, *Murder My Sweet* (from Raymond Chandler's *Farewell My Lovely*) and *Cornered,* both starring Dick Powell. Dmytryk won respect among film critics with his 1947 *Crossfire,* Hollywood's first serious attempt to deal with the subject of racial discrimination (anti-Semitism in this case, although the subject of the original novel was homosexuality).

The year 1947 was a fateful one in Dmytryk's life. He was investigated and found guilty of Communist affiliations (he had joined the Communist Party in 1945) by the House Un-American Activities Committee, and as one of the HOLLYWOOD TEN he was sentenced to one year in jail. After his release, he went into self-imposed exile in England, where he directed three films, including the socially aware *Give Us This Day.* In 1951 he returned to the US and gave testimony in the second round of the committee hearings, which helped incriminate several of his former colleagues. As a result of his "purging" testimony, he was immediately removed from the industry's blacklist. After his reinstatement, he seemed to be on the right creative track with such creditable films as *The Sniper, The Caine Mutiny,* and *Broken Lance,* but his subsequent work has not been as even in quality as it was and is much less original in approach and treatment, especially when he has had big budgets at his disposal. In the late 70s Dmytryk taught film at the University of Texas at Austin and in 1981 was appointed a filmmaking professor at the

University of Southern California. Married actress Jean Porter, his second. Autobiography: *It's a Hell of a Life but Not a Bad Living* (1979).

FILMS: *The Hawk* 1935; *Television Spy* 1939; *Emergency Squad, Golden Gloves, Mystery Sea Raider, Her First Romance* 1940; *The Devil Commands, Under Age, Sweetheart of the Campus, The Blonde from Singapore, Secrets of the Lone Wolf, Confessions of Boston Blackie* 1941; *Counter-Espionage, Seven Miles from Alcatraz* 1942; *Hitler's Children, The Falcon Strikes Back, Captive Wild Woman, Behind the Rising Sun* 1943; *Tender Comrade, Murder My Sweet/Farewell My Lovely* 1944; *Back to Bataan, Cornered* 1945; *Till the End of Time* 1946; *Crossfire, So Well Remembered* (UK) 1947; *Obsession/The Hidden Room* (UK), *Give Us This Day/Salt to the Devil* (UK) 1949; *Mutiny, The Sniper, Eight Iron Men* 1952; *The Juggler* 1953; *The Caine Mutiny, Broken Lance, The End of the Affair* (UK) 1954; *Soldier of Fortune, The Left Hand of God* 1955; *The Mountain* (also prod.) 1956; *Raintree County* 1957; *The Young Lions* 1958; *Warlock* (also prod.), *The Blue Angel* 1959; *Cronache di un Convento/The Reluctant Saint* (also prod.; It./US), *Walk on the Wild Side* 1962; *The Carpetbaggers, Where Love Has Gone* 1964; *Mirage* 1965; *Alvarez Kelly* 1966; *Lo Sbarco di Anzio/Anzio* (English version; It.), *Shalako* (UK) 1968; *Bluebeard* (also co-story, co-sc.; Hung.) 1972; *The Human Factor* (UK/US) 1975; *He Is My Brother* 1976.

documentary. In the broadest sense, a factual film depicting actual events and real people. The term was first used by John GRIERSON in a review of Robert FLAHERTY's *Moana* in the New York *Sun,* in February of 1926. It was derived from *documentaire,* a term used by the French to describe travel films. Grierson later defined documentary as "the creative treatment of actuality," but other definitions abound for this significant form of filmic expression, most of them more restrictive, none fully satisfactory. Many theoreticians feel that a true documentary must communicate social ideas and values and aim to bring about a change for the better in social and economic conditions. But others see it as a form of artistic journalism that may cover a broad range of factual subjects, social, scientific, educational, and instructional, as well as recreational.

The roots of the documentary go back to the NEWSREEL, which in turn goes back to the very beginning of film history. Many, in fact, most, of the short subjects made in the 1890s in the US, France, and elsewhere were factual, at first depictions of everyday happenings and soon real or fake coverage of newsworthy events. By the end of the first decade of the 20th century, filmmakers in several countries were turning out a variety of small, factual, general- and special-interest films that went beyond simple fragmentary newsreels. Although some of these were several reels long, most were primitively structured and merely descriptive, lacking a viewpoint. Early examples of ambitious factual films in Britain include *The Durbar at Delhi/The Delhi Durbar* (1911), more than two hours long and filmed in India in Kinemacolor, and the 90-minute-long *Scott's Antarctic Expedition/The Undying Story of Captain Scott* and *Animal Life in the Antarctic,* which was released in several segments between 1911 and 1913. In the US, D. W. GRIFFITH supervised *The Life of Villa* (1914), a seven-reel production that combined authentic newsreel footage and studio reconstruction to tell the story of Villa's resurrection in Mexico. In the same year, Americans John Ernest and George M. Williamson made a five-reel underwater science feature, *Thirty Leagues Under the Sea.* Microphotography was used experimentally in *How Life Begins* (1916).

The outbreak of WW I brought about a spate of compilation films heavily flavored with propaganda and nationalistic bias. Authentic wartime footage was also incorporated into some fiction features, like Griffith's *Hearts of the World* (1918). In the years immediately following the war, the scope of the fact film broadened and filmmakers in various countries began groping for an expressive style for the nonfiction motion picture.

But it was in the United States that the creative documentary was born in 1922 with the release of Robert Flaherty's remarkable record of Eskimo life, *Nanook of the North.* It wasn't simply a fascinating anthropological account of an exotic lifestyle but a dramatically powerful interpretation of reality. The commercial success of *Nanook* led to similar explorations of life in distant lands, like Flaherty's *Moana* (1926) and Merian COOPER and Ernest B. SCHOEDSACK's *Grass* (1925) and *Chang* (1927). In Europe, too, significant advances were made during the 20s. In Russia, Dziga VERTOV used montage and other manipulative techniques to achieve "the purest possible essence of truth" in his *Kino-Pravda* newsreel series and feature-length real-life films like *Cinema Eye* (1924), *Stride Soviet!* (1926), and *Man with a Movie Camera* (1929). Esther SHUB made a series of impressive compilation films summarizing Russian history; Sergei EISENSTEIN's *October/Ten Days That Shook the World* (1928) reconstructed events of the Russian Revolution with documentary authenticity; and Victor Turin's *Turksib* (1929) was a skillful documentary of the construction of the trans-Siberian railroad.

In France, Léon Poirier (*La Croisière noire,* 1926), Marc ALLÉGRET (*Voyage au Congo,* 1927), and Jean EPSTEIN (*Finis Terrae,* 1929) followed the Flaherty example by going to exotic lands for their material. Alberto CAVALCANTI initiated the CITY SYMPHONIES style of documentary with *Rien que les Heures* (1926), a highly original study of Paris and its people, which was followed in Germany by Walter RUTTMANN's *Berlin—Symphony of a Big City* (1927), a classic of rhythmic montage, and later in other countries by various filmmakers. Also in the vein of the personal, expressive documentary was Jean VIGO's *A propos de Nice* (1930), inspired by the candid camera techniques of Vertov's *Man with a Movie Camera,* and Joris IVENS's exercises in patterns of movement, *The Bridge* (1928) and *Rain* (1929).

During the 20s, significant strides were also made in the concept and technique of the scientific and educational documentary. In the US, Max FLEISCHER tried to explain complex ideas in simple visual terms in the partly animated *Einstein's Theory of Relativity* (1923). In the USSR, PUDOVKIN demonstrated Pavlov's experiments with conditioned reflexes in the feature-length documentary *Mechanics of the Brain* (1925). Educational and scientific films of quality were similarly being made during the 20s in England, France, and particularly Germany, where the UFA company set up a special unit for the production of nonfiction motion pictures.

It was in England during the 30s that the documentary acquired that added dimension of social purpose. The guiding hand behind the movement to give the nonfiction film a responsible public voice was Grierson, a Scotsman who had studied the effect of the communication media on public opinion on a fellowship in the US. In 1928 he joined the newly established Empire Marketing Board, a British government agency set up to co-ordinate food supplies within the British Empire. The Board's Film Unit was created to publicize its work, but under Grierson's guidance it soon developed into a vital creative force.

Successfully persuading his superiors that film could be turned into a powerful instrument of public education, Grierson gathered around him a group of bright young men that included Edgar Anstey, Arthur Elton, Stuart Legg, Paul Rotha, Harry Watt, and Basil Wright, who made up in enthusiasm and talent for their lack of experience as filmmakers. The basic premise underlining the work of Grierson and his associates was that the documentary must be created in response to a social need and must fulfill a public service. Although they were motivated by a passion for social action, their films were characteristically reserved and underplayed. In style, they were often poetic and aesthetically pleasing even though form was always subordinated to content.

In 1933, when the EMB was disbanded, Grierson's film unit was absorbed by Britain's General Post Office. The GPO FILM UNIT was taken over by the Ministry of Information at the outbreak of WW II in September of 1939 and was renamed the Crown Film Unit in April of the following year. Among the many notable films created by the unit during one of the most glorious decades in the history of the documentary were Grierson's own *Drifters* (1929), Flaherty's *Industrial Britain* (1932), Rotha's *Contact* (1933), Elton's *Aero-Engine* (1934), Legg's *BBC—The Voice of Britain* (1935), Rotha's *The Face of Britain* and *Shipyard* (both 1935), Anstey and Elton's *Housing Problems* (1935), Wright's *Song of Ceylon* (1935), Cavalcanti's *Coal Face* (1935), Wright and Watt's *Night Mail* (1936), Watt's *Enough to Eat* (1936), Wright's *Children at School* (1937), and Watt's *North Sea* (1939).

In 1939, the Canadian government appointed Grierson film commissioner and chief executive of the newly formed National Film Board, an organization that would soon develop into one of the world's most important centers of documentary production. In the United States, meanwhile, the documentary movement in the 30s lacked the centralized organization of its British counterpart and the institutional sponsorship that would have assured it of a continual flow of production. But its social concern was equally keen, and the style it chose for expressing it often more pointed and blunt. Some of the films were politically motivated, usually by leftist ideology. Typical of these were Seymour Stern's *Imperial Valley* (1931), which decried the exploitation of labor in the California fruit fields, and Ivens's *The Spanish Earth* (1937), a fervent call for support for the Republicans in the Spanish Civil War with commentary written and narrated by Ernest Hemingway.

A more moderate but still penetrating social message was contained in the documentaries sponsored by US Government agencies during the New Deal era, notably Pare LORENTZ's *The Plow That Broke the Plains* (1936), which dramatized the problems of soil conservation in the Great Plains, and *The River* (1937), a study of erosion in the Mississippi River basin. The music for both films was composed by Virgil Thomson. Aaron Copland wrote the musical score for another milestone documentary of the 30s, *The City* (1939), a plea for the planning of urban communities. *The City* was directed by Willard VAN DYKE and Ralph Steiner, both former cameramen for Lorentz.

An influential voice in the American documentary from 1935 through 1951 was THE MARCH OF TIME series, which combined newly shot newsreel material with stock footage and staged scenes to cover a variety of factual subjects, typically with a conservative political slant. In 1938 the Roosevelt Administration inaugurated the US FILM SERVICE, Pare Lorentz as production chief. Among the films the UFS produced were Ivens's *Power and the Land* (1940), about the impact of electricity on rural areas; Lorentz's *The Fight for Life* (1941), which explored the problems of maternity in the slums; and Flaherty's *The Land* (1942), about agriculture during the Depression. But the emphasis on social action in these films alienated certain congressmen, and the Film Service was voted out of existence in 1942. The unit was then absorbed into the Office of War Information. American documentary films made independently just before America's entry into WW II included Willard Van Dyke's *Valley Town* (1940), a study of the human consequences of automation, and Herbert KLINE's exposition of the conflict between modernity and tradition in a remote Mexican town, *The Forgotten Village* (1941), from a script by John Steinbeck.

Germany's efforts in this area were particularly striking, notably Leni RIEFENSTAHL's remarkable filmic record of the 1934 Nazi party rally in Nuremberg, *Triumph des Willens/Triumph of the Will* (1935), and her equally stunning spectacle of the 1936 Berlin Olympics, *Olympia* (1938), a hymn to physical superiority. Other prewar documentaries turned out by Josef Goebbels's propaganda machine included *Blutendes Deutschland* (1933), *Bilddokumente* (1935), and *Für Uns* (1937). On the other extreme of the political spectrum were the many official propaganda documentary films made by the Soviet regime, mostly for local consumption, and isolated individual efforts supporting Socialist causes by such filmmakers as Luis BUÑUEL (*Las Hurdes/Land Without Bread,* Spain, 1932); Ivens (*Song of Heroes/Komsomol,* USSR, 1932; *Borinage,* with Henri STORCK, Belgium, 1933; *New Earth,* Holland, 1934; and *The 400 Million,* US, 1939); and Jean RENOIR (*La Vie est à nous,* France, 1936). Notable nonpolitical European documentaries of the 30s included Storck's *Images d'Ostende* (Belgium, 1930), Jan Kucera's *Construction* (Czechoslovakia, 1933), John Ferno's (Fernhout) *Easter Island* (Holland, 1934), and Jean Painlevé's *L'Hippocampe* (France, 1934).

The value of the documentary film as a tool of propaganda, morale boosting, and military training was recognized early in the conflict by all combatant nations. As a result, the documentary flourished during the war years as never before or since, both in terms of quantity of output and technical quality of production. Germany, with its well-oiled propaganda machinery and a head start of several years in official brainwashing tactics under the guidance of Josef Goebbels, had the initial advantage in the propaganda war. Some of Germany's most impressive early war films focused on glorifying the might of the Nazi armed forces. These included Hans Bertram's *Feuertaufe/Baptism of Fire* (1940), which recorded the role of the air force in the conquest of Poland; Dr. Fritz Hippler's *Feldzug in Polen* (1940), which documented the contribution of the ground forces to the same campaign; and *Sieg im Westen/Victory in the West* (1941), about the conquest of France. Dr. Hippler was also responsible for *Der ewige Jude/The Eternal Jew* (1940), a vicious anti-Semitic propaganda "documentary."

In Great Britain, government and private industry joined forces to harness the country's filmmaking talent to the war effort. The Ministry of Information assumed control over the Crown Film Unit. Its large output was supplemented by that of the various service units. Many of Britain's early war films were intended as morale boosters for the local population in the wake of the London Blitz. But the scope broadened to include films of war record, information, and instruction, and several effective fictionalized semidocumentary features. The long list of quality war documentaries included Cavalcanti's *The First Days* (1939); Humphrey Jennings and Harry Watt's *Britain Can Take It* (1940); Watt's *Target for Tonight* (1941); Jennings's brilliant impressionistic study of the sight and sounds of wartime England, *Listen to Britain* (1941); J. B. Holmes's *Coastal Command* (1942); Jennings's *Fires Were Started* (1943); Roy Boulting's *Desert Victory* (1943); Pat Jackson's *Western Approaches* (1944); and *The True Glory* (1945), an Anglo-American collaborative effort directed by Carol Reed and Garson Kanin. Dramatized semidocumentaries included *The Lion Has Wings* (directed by Michael Powell, Brian Desmond

Hurst, and Adrian Brunel, 1939); *In Which We Serve* (directed by Noel Coward and David Lean, 1942); *Next of Kin* (directed by Thorold Dickinson, 1942); and *The Way Ahead* (directed by Carol Reed, 1944).

In the United States, anti-Nazi propaganda documentaries were being made even before America's entry into the war. "The March of Time" led the way with *Inside Nazi Germany* (1938), *Canada at War* (1939), *The Ramparts We Watch* (1940), and *America Speaks Her Mind* (1941). Shortly after Pearl Harbor, production was undertaken on a massive scale, mainly under the aegis of the War Department and the civilian Office of War Information. Hundreds of documentary and compilation films were turned out, ranging from simple orientation and training shorts for GIs to elaborate and technically superior information and propaganda features.

The creative resources of the commercial American cinema were tapped for the war effort. Among leading Hollywood directors who lent their talents to the undertaking were Frank CAPRA, John FORD, John HUSTON, and William WYLER. One of the most celebrated products of this effort was the "Why We Fight" indoctrination series produced by Col. Frank Capra for the War Department's Army Pictorial Service. Several of the feature-length films in this highly successful series were also widely exhibited to civilians on the home front. Among the best in the series were *Prelude to War* (1943), directed by Capra; *The Nazis Strike* (1943), directed by Capra and Maj. Anatole LITVAK; *The Battle of Russia* (1943), directed by Lt. Col. Litvak; and the seventh and last film in the series, *War Comes to America* (1945), also directed by Litvak. Another notable series of the period was the "ARMY-NAVY SCREEN MAGAZINE."

Other exceptional American war documentaries included Comdr. John Ford's *The Battle of Midway* (1942), Capt. John Huston's *Report from the Aleutians* (1943), Maj. Huston's *The Battle of San Pietro* (1945), Lt. Col. William Wyler's *The Memphis Belle* (1944), and Louis DE ROCHEMONT's *The Fighting Lady* (1944). A major contributor to the cinematic war effort was Walt DISNEY, whose animation studios turned out hundreds of thousands of feet of information and training films for Uncle Sam, capped by the impressive feature-length animation and live-action color production *Victory Through Air Power* (1943).

Several of Russia's leading directors were also recruited for the production of wartime documentaries, among them Pudovkin and DOVZHENKO. Soon after the Nazi invasion, the Soviets started their "Fighting Film Album," multi-episode reports from the front which were released in monthly installments from November 1941 through the end of 1942. Directors of individual episodes included Sergei Gerasimov, Gregori Kozintsev, Sergei Yutkevitch, Boris Barnet, and Ilya Trauberg. Most Russian feature-length wartime documentaries were compilation films, among them *Defeat of the German Armies Near Moscow* (directed by Leonid Varlamov and Ilya Kopalin, 1942), *Leningrad in Combat* (directed by Roman KARMEN and several others, 1942), *Day of War* (edited by Mikhail Slutsky from footage supplied by 240 cameramen, 1942), *Stalingrad* (directed by Leonid Varlamov, 1943), *The Fight for the Soviet Ukraine* (directed by Yulia Solntseva and Y. Avdeyenko under the supervision of Alexander Dovzhenko, 1943), *Victory in the Ukraine* (directed by Dovzhenko and Solntseva, 1945), and *Berlin* (directed by Yuli Raizman and Yelizaveta Svilova, 1945).

The end of WW II signaled a sudden drop in the level of activity in the documentary field. One Western nation—Canada—has continually turned out high-quality documentaries and scientific, instructional, and experimental films for worldwide distribution. Notable Canadian productions include *The Feeling of Rejection* (1947), *Corral* (1954), *City of Gold* (1956), *Universe* (1960), *Lonely Boy* (1962), and *Warrendale* (1967). Elsewhere, postwar documentary production has been mixed. In Italy, documentary elements were prevalent in the feature films of the neorealist movement of the 40s and early 50s, but few notable full-length nonfiction films have since been produced. A certain commercial success on an international scale was enjoyed by Gualtiero JACOPETTI's sensational bizarre documentary *Mondo Cane* (1962), which was followed by several sequels.

In France, the memories of WW II lingered in documentary films for years after the Liberation. Outstanding films in this context include Henri Cartier-Bresson's *Le Retour* (1946), René Clément's *La Bataille du Rail/Battle of the Rails* (1946), Alain RESNAIS' *Nuit et Brouillard/Night and Fog* (1955), and Marcel OPHÜLS's *Le Chagrin et la Pitié/The Sorrow and the Pity* (1971). War in general was protested in RESNAIS'S *Guernica* (1950) and Georges FRANJU's *Hôtel des Invalides* (1952). Notable documentaries on other subjects include Georges ROUQUIER's ode to nature, *Farrebique* (1946); Franju's shockingly poetic *Le Sang des Bêtes/The Blood of Beasts* (1949); Jean GRÉMILLON's *Les Charmes de l'Existence* (1949); Henri-Georges CLOUZOT's *Le Mystère Picasso/The Picasso Mystery* (1956); Painlevé's science films; the politically committed documentaries of Chris MARKER; and the productions of the *cinéma vérité* movement of the 60s and 70s led by Jean ROUCH.

In Belgium, Storck emerged as the leading figure after the departure of Joris Ivens, and in Holland top postwar names have included Bert HAANSTRA, Nicolai van der Heyde, Herman van der Horst, and John Ferno. In Germany, Heinz Sielmann acquired an international reputation with his wildlife films.

While documentary production in Western Europe had to depend mainly on private sponsorship for continuing output, government sponsorship in the East assured the nonstop flow of factual films, usually tailored to current information and propaganda needs of the existing regime. Many of the film studios in the Soviet Union specialize in documentary production. In addition to 30 to 40 feature-length documentary films, more than 1,000 factual shorts are being produced each year. Leading directors since WW II include Roman Karmen, Ilya Kopalin, and Yuli RAIZMAN. The nationalized film industries in the Soviet satellite countries have equally emphasized documentary production. Among leading directors of the movement in Bulgaria are Roumen Grigorov, Hristo Kovachev, Yuli Stroyanov, and Nevena Toshava. Several outstanding documentary features were made during the 50s in Czechoslovakia by Ján KADÁR and Elmar KLOS. In East Germany, leading documentarians include Jürgen Böttcher, Karl Gass, Walter Heynowski, Gerhard Scheumann, and Andrew and Annelie Thorndike. Women have figured prominently as directors of Hungarian documentaries, notably Livia Gyaramathy and Marianne Szemes. Male directors include Jozsef Csoke, Agoston Kollanyi, and Istvan Timar. Leading figures in the highly reputed Polish documentary movement include Jerzy Bossak (*Requiem for 500,000,* etc.), Jerzy HOFFMAN (*Patria o Muerte, Market of Miracles,* etc.), Tadeusz Jaworski, Kazimierz Karabasz, Jan Lomnicki (*The End of the Road, Meetings with Warsaw,* etc.), Janus Majewski, and Wladislaw Slesicki. Among the top documentarians in Rumania are Ion Bostan, Eric Nussbaum, Savel Stiopul, and Gheorghe Vitandis. Hundreds of documentaries, mostly shorts, are turned out annually in Yugoslavia by such directors as Ante Babaja, Purisa Djordjevic, and Krsto Skanata.

Cut off from government sponsorship, the British documentary movement never regained its former glory in the postwar years, although it enjoyed a period of creative rebirth during the 50s with the advent of the FREE CINEMA group under the leadership of Lindsay ANDERSON, Karel REISZ, and Tony RICHARDSON.

In the United States, too, television became the leading sponsor and programmer of documentary films in the postwar years. Partly out of a sincere desire to serve the community better and partly in response to pressure from the Federal Communications Commission (FCC) for a continual flow of public affairs programming, the TV networks and many of the affiliated and independent stations initiated a regular schedule of documentary fare.

Outstanding series have included CBS's 'See It Now,' produced by Edward R. Murrow and Fred Friendly and famous for its courageous confrontations with Senator Joe McCarthy; 'CBS Reports' (*Harvest of Shame,* among other memorable documentaries); NBC's 'Victory at Sea' compilation series; NBC's 'White Paper' and 'Project XX' series, and such outstanding specials as *Vincent Van Gogh: A Self Portrait, Shakespeare: Soul of an Age, The Louvre,* and *The Tunnel*; CBS's 'The Twentieth Century' and the commercially successful '60 minutes'; ABC's 'Close-Up!,' and several important contributions from such producers outside the networks as Drew Associates (*Yanki No!, The Children Are Watching,* etc.) and David Wolper (*The Making of the President,* etc.). America's public television network encouraged experimentation in documentary production and played host to several important *cinéma vérité* projects by such filmmakers as the MAYSLES brothers, Arthur Barron, and Frederick Wiseman, and to Craig Gilbert's controversial 12-hour series 'An American Family' (1973). In the 1990s, brothers Ken and Ric Burns created a massive, affecting mix of personal stories, vivid images, and strong historical background in their multipart PBS series, 'The Civil War.'

The development of lightweight 16 mm hand-held equipment for TV also benefited documentary filmmakers operating outside that industry, permitting not only greater mobility but also more intimacy between camera and subject and an increased sense of reality and immediacy. Feature-length documentary production for theatrical release has been sparse in America as elsewhere in the West in the postwar years, but a good number of remarkable nonfiction films reached the big screen. These include Robert Flaherty's *Louisiana Story* (1948); Sidney Meyers's *The Quiet One* (1949); James Algar's nature documentaries for Walt Disney, *The Living Desert* (1953), *The Vanishing Prairie* (1954), and *Secrets of Life* (1956); Lionel Rogosin's *On the Bowery* (1956), *Come Back Africa* (1960), and *Black Fantasy* (1972); Ben Maddow, Sidney Meyers, and Joseph Strick's *The Savage Eye* (1959); Bruce Brown's *The Endless Summer* (1966); Shirley Clarke's *Portrait of Jason* (1967); Frederick Wiseman's *The Titicut Follies* (1967) and *High School* (1969); D. A. Pennebaker's *Don't Look Back* (1967), *Monterey Pop* (1969), and *Sweet Toronto* (1971); Robert Snyder's *The Henry Miller Odyssey* (1969) and *The World of Buckminster Fuller* (1974); David Maysles, Albert Maysles, and Charlotte Zwerin's *Salesman* (1969) and *Gimme Shelter* (1970); Budd Boetticher's *Arruzza* (1971); Walon Green's *The Hellstrom Chronicle* (1971); Bruce Brown's *On Any Sunday* (1971); Emile de Antonio's satirical *Millhouse* (1971), and *Painters Painting* (1973); Richard T. Heffron's *Fillmore* (1972); Howard Smith-Sarah Kernochan's *Marjoe* (1972); Keith Merrill's *The Great American Cowboy* (1973); William Richert's *First Position* (1973); Jerry Bruck, Jr.'s, *I.F. Stone's Weekly* (1973); Jerome Hill's *Film Portrait* (1973); Arthur R. Dubs and Heinz Seilman's *Vanishing Wilderness* (1974); Cinda Firestone's *Attica* (1974); Peter Davis' *Hearts and Minds* (1974); David Helpern, Jr.'s, documentary about director Nicholas Ray, *I'm a Stranger Here Myself* (1975); Dick Robinson's semidocumentary *Brother of the Wind* (1975); Philippe Mora's compilation film *Brother Can You Spare a Dime?* (1975); Richard Cohen's *Hurry Tomorrow* (1975); Emile de Antonio, Mary Lampson, and Haskell Wexler's *Underground* (1976); Barbara Kopple's *Harlan County USA* (1976); and Herbert Kline's *The Challenge* (1977).

The 1980s and 90s saw a loosening of the documentary form, in films that were more subjective or followed a nonlinear structure, like Michael Moore's excoriation of General Motors, *Roger and Me* (1989). Other notable documentaries focused on current issues, like the new face of strike-busting in Barbara Kopple's *American Dream* (1989), gender switching, as seen through the practice of highly ritualized cross-dressing in Jennie Livingston's *Paris Is Burning* (1990), or the search for justice in a murder case, in Errol Morris's *The Thin Blue Line* (1988).

Internationally, documentary film production by far outnumbers the output of fiction films, in developed, developing, and underdeveloped nations alike. Many of these films compete annually in international festivals that specialize in documentaries and nonfiction shorts. Among the best known are the festivals held in Bologna, Budapest, Chicago, Edinburgh, Nyon, Oberhausen, and the American Film and Video Festival.

Dodd, Claire. Actress. *b.* Dec. 29, 1908, New York City. *d.* 1973. A former Ziegfeld showgirl, she appeared in numerous films of the 30s, typically portraying the seductive, socially prominent "other woman" who threatens to steal the film's hero away from the heroine. But she also played occasional leads in lower-budget productions and was Della Street in several Perry Mason mysteries.

FILMS INCLUDE: *Our Blushing Brides* 1930; *The Secret Call, An American Tragedy, Up Pops the Devil, The Road to Reno, Girls About Town* 1931; *Two Kinds of Women, The Broken Wing, Man Wanted, This Is the Night, The Match King, Dancers in the Dark* 1932; *Hard to Handle, Ex-Lady, Elmer the Great, Footlight Parade* 1933; *Massacre, Gambling Lady, Journal of a Crime, Babbitt* 1934; *Roberta, The Case of the Curious Bride, The Glass Key, The Pay-Off* 1935; *The Singing Kid, The Case of the Velvet Claws, Navy Born* 1936; *Fast Company, Three Loves Has Nancy* 1938; *Charlie Chan in Honolulu* 1939; *If I Had My Way, Slightly Honorable* 1940; *The Black Cat, In the Navy* 1941; *Don Winslow of the Navy* (serial), *The Mad Doctor of Market Street* 1942.

Doillon, Jacques. Director, screenwriter. Born on Mar. 15, 1944, in Paris. He entered French cinema as an assistant film editor in 1966, later graduating to editor. A director of shorts from 1969 and features from 1972, he became known for his idiosyncratic, emotionally distant handling of oblique themes, making his highly regarded films often inaccessible to wide audiences. He usually writes his own scripts, sometimes in collaboration with Jean-François Goyet.

FILMS INCLUDE: *L'An 01* 1972; *Les Doigts dans la Tête* 1974; *Un Sac de Billes* 1975; *La Femme qui pleure* 1978; *La Drolesse* 1979; *La Fille prodigue* 1981; *La Pirate* 1984; *La Vie de Famille, La Tentation d'Isabelle* 1985; *La Fille de Quinze Ans* 1989; *La Vengeance d'une Femme* 1990; *Le Jeune Werther/Young Werther* 1993; *Germaine and Benjamin* 1994; *Ponette* (also sc.) 1996.

Dolan, Robert Emmett. Composer, music director, arranger, conductor, producer. *b.* Aug. 3, 1908, Hartford, Conn. *d.* 1972. A veteran Broadway conductor, composer, and arranger, he went to Hollywood in the early 40s as musical director for Paramount. Scored, arranged, and conducted many musical and dramatic films and in the 50s produced three musicals, *White Christmas* (1954), *The Girl Rush* (1955), and *Anything Goes* (1956). He later returned to the stage.

FILMS INCLUDE (as composer or musical director): *Birth of the Blues* 1941; *Holiday Inn, Star Spangled Rhythm* 1942; *Dixie* 1943; *Lady in the Dark* 1944; *The Bells of St. Mary's, Incendiary Blonde, Murder He Says, Salty O'Rourke, The Stork Club* 1945; *Blue Skies, Monsieur Beaucaire, Road to Utopia* 1946; *Dear Ruth, My Favorite Brunette, The Perils of Pauline, Welcome Stranger* 1947; *Saigon, Good Sam* 1948; *The Great Gatsby, Sorrowful Jones* 1949; *My Son John* 1952; *The Three Faces of Eve* 1957; *The Man Who Understood Women* 1959.

Dolby Laboratories Inc. San Francisco-based company whose innovative sound systems are widely used in motion picture production and exhibition. The patented Dolby noise-reduction system was first developed by Ray Dolby for the recording industry in 1965. In the 70s, it was adapted for use in motion pictures, beginning with *Quiet Revolution* (1972). In addition to its noise-reduction system, Dolby developed a stereo system that could produce realistic four-channel sound using an optical sound track on standard 35 mm prints (see also STEREOPHONIC SOUND). Dolby Stereo first gained national attention when it was used on release prints of the blockbuster hit *Star Wars* in 1977; since then, many theaters in the US and other countries have been equipped with the decoding box needed to use the system. In the 90s, the company introduced Dolby SR-D, a DIGITAL SOUND TRACK system featuring even greater crispness and range in intensity and frequency.

dolly. A wheeled platform on which a camera (with its operator) is mounted for traveling shots. Dollies differ in size, capabilities, and complexity. Typically, they are hydraulically powered and their operation is completely silent. Sometimes they move on tracks. Their sturdiness assures smooth and accurate camera movement. The dolly is operated by a person other than the camera operator, allowing the latter to concentrate on other aspects of his work, such as panning, tilting, and generally obtaining the desired shot without having to concern himself with the mechanics of smooth tracking. The dolly can be equipped with a BOOM, at the end of which the camera is installed. This allows raising, lowering, and pivoting the camera at various angles. The most elaborate version of the dolly is the CRAB DOLLY, whose wheels can move not only forward and back but also sideways and in any direction between.

dolly shot. Also called "traveling," "trucking," or "tracking shot." A moving shot of a moving or stationary subject exercised by mounting the camera on a dolly or camera truck. To dolly-in (or track-in) is to move the camera toward the subject; to dolly-out (or track-out) is to move the camera away from the subject.

Domergue, Faith. Actress. Born on June 16, 1925, in New Orleans. A sultry brunette, she entered films in the late 40s as a protégée of Howard HUGHES, who promoted her career at great expense during his tenure as boss of RKO. Despite the publicity fanfare, the public remained indifferent to her charms, and after marrying director Hugo FREGONESE (they've since divorced), she stayed on in films as the leading lady of low-budget action and science-fiction films. Retired in the mid-50s and after a long absence returned to the screen in the 60s, playing mainly supporting roles, mostly in Europe. Author: *My Life with Howard Hughes* (1972).

FILMS INCLUDE: *Young Widow* 1946; *Vendetta, Where Danger Lives* 1950; *Duel at Silver Creek* 1952; *Timeslip/The Atomic Man* (UK), *The Great Sioux Uprising* 1953; *This Is My Love* 1954; *Cult of the Cobra, It Came from Beneath the Sea, This Island Earth* 1955; *California* 1963; *Track of Thunder* 1967; *L'Amore Breve* (It.) 1969; *The Gamblers* 1970; *Man with Icy Eyes, Legacy of Blood, Una sull'altra/One on Top of the Other* (It./Fr./Sp.) 1971; *The House of Seven Corpses* 1974.

Donahue, Troy. Actor. Born Merle Johnson, Jr., on Jan. 27, 1936, in New York City. Blond, blue-eyed leading man of Hollywood films of the 60s. While studying journalism at Columbia University, he began appearing in stock productions, making his screen debut in 1957. In 1959 he was signed by Warner Bros. as a contract player and soon emerged as the heart-throb of female teenagers. His popularity was enhanced by co-starring parts in the TV series 'Surfside Six' (1960–62) and 'Hawaiian Eye' (in 1962–63). After several years of high visibility, he gradually drifted into lesser roles. He disappeared from the screen in the mid-70s but returned in the mid-80s with indiscriminate abandon, appearing in numerous basement-budget productions aimed directly at the home video market. Having married and divorced actress Suzanne PLESHETTE in 1964, he married actress Valerie Allen in 1966.

FILMS INCLUDE: *Man Afraid* 1957; *This Happy Feeling, Voice in the Mirror* 1958; *The Perfect Furlough, Imitation of Life, A Summer Place* 1959; *The Crowded Sky* 1960; *Parrish, Susan Slade* 1961; *Rome Adventure* 1962; *Palm Springs Weekend* 1963; *A Distant Trumpet* 1964; *My Blood Runs Cold* 1965; *Come Spy with Me, Rocket to the Moon/Those Fantastic Flying Fools* (UK) 1967; *Sweet Saviour* 1971; *Cockfighter/Born to Kill, Seizure, The Godfather Part II* 1974; *The Legend of Frank Woods* 1977; *Tin Man* 1983; *Grandview U.S.A.* 1984; *Low Blow* 1986; *Cyclone* (cameo) 1987; *Assault of the Party Nerds, Bad Blood* 1989; *Cry-Baby* (cameo), *Nudity Required, Shock 'Em Dead, Omega Cop* 1990; *Double Trouble, Deadly Diamonds, Sounds of Silence* 1991.

Donald, James. Actor. *b.* May 18, 1917, in Aberdeen, Scotland. *d.* 1993. *ed.* Edinburgh U.; McGill. Introspective leading man and supporting player of the British stage (from 1935), films (from 1941), and television (from 1946). He has also been seen in a number of American productions.

FILMS INCLUDE: *The Missing Million* 1941; *In Which We Serve* 1942; *The Way Ahead* 1944; *Broken Journey, The Small Voice/Hideout* 1948; *Edward My Son* (US/UK), *Trottie True/The Gay Lady* 1949; *Cage of Gold* 1950; *White Corridors* 1951; *Brandy for the Parson, The Gift Horse/Glory at Sea* 1952; *The Pickwick Papers* (as Mr. Winkle), *The Net/Project M-7* 1953; *Beau Brummel* (US/UK) 1943; *Lust for Life* (as Theo Van Gogh; US) 1956; *The Bridge on the River Kwai* 1957; *The Vikings* (US) 1958; *Third Man on the Mountain* 1959; *The Great Escape* (US) 1963; *King Rat* (US) 1965; *Cast a Giant Shadow* (US) 1966; *The Jokers, Quatermass and the Pit/Five Million Years to Earth* 1967; *Hannibal Brooks, The Royal Hunt of the Sun* (as King Carlos V; US/UK) 1969; *David Copperfield* (as Mr. Murdstone; orig. made for US TV; US/UK) 1970; *Conduct Unbecoming* 1975; *The Big Sleep* 1978.

Donald Duck. Popular cartoon character introduced by Walt DISNEY in 1936 in the short *Orphans' Benefit.* Like all Disney characters, the little duck, usually clad in sailor's blue and white, has distinctive human characteristics. Unlike the calm MICKEY MOUSE, he is an excitable little fellow, hotheaded and always eager to challenge adversaries.

Donaldson, Roger. Director. Born on Nov. 15, 1945, in Ballarat, Australia. At 19 he emigrated to New Zealand, where he opened a still photography studio. Turning to motion pictures, he made several documentaries and dramatic shorts before directing his first feature in 1977. The film, *Sleeping Dogs,* showed his inexperience, but had the distinction of being the first New Zealand film ever released in the US. He fared far better with his next, *Smash Palace* (1981), an insightful drama of family upheaval, paving his way to the spectacular British/American production, *The Bounty* (1984), then to Hollywood.

FEATURE FILMS: In New Zealand—*Sleeping Dogs* (also prod.) 1977; *Smash Palace* (also prod., co-sc.) 1981. In UK—*The Bounty* 1984. In US—*Marie* 1985; *No Way Out* 1987; *Cocktail* 1988; *Cadillac Man* 1990; *White Sands* 1992; *The Getaway* 1994; *Species* 1995; *Dante's Peak* 1997.

Donat, Robert. Actor. *b.* Mar. 18, 1905, Withington, Manchester, England. *d.* 1958. The son of a Polish immigrant and a British mother, he began taking elocution lessons at 11 to overcome a stutter and developed an exceptionally fine and versatile voice that was to make him a leading actor of British stage and films. He made his stage debut at 16 and played a variety of Shakespearean and classical roles in repertory and with touring companies before appearing in his London debut in 1930. Tall, handsome, and romantically dashing, he was soon noticed by film producers. After turning down a Hollywood offer by Irving Thalberg, he accepted a contract with Alexander Korda and became internationally famous as the romantic lead in *The Private Life of Henry VIII* (1933). He was rushed to Hollywood to star in *The Count of Monte Cristo* (1934) but didn't like the town or the prospect of becoming a conventional movie star. Returning to England, he established himself as a highly respected and popular actor of both stage and screen.

He played the leads in some of Britain's finest films of the 30s and early 40s, ranging from Hitchcock's adventurous *The 39 Steps* to René Clair's comedy-fantasy *The Ghost Goes West,* in which he played the title role. He won an Academy Award for his performance in *Goodbye Mr. Chips* (1939), in which he aged on the screen from 25 to 83. But Donat's career was severely hampered by a lifelong bout with chronic asthma, as well as by nagging insecurities and self-doubts. He was seriously ill during the production of his last film, *The Inn of the Sixth Happiness* (1958), and was barely able to complete his role with the aid of oxygen tanks. His last spoken words on the screen were prophetically: "We shall not see each other again, I think. Farewell." He died at 53 before the picture was released. In addition to his film performances, Donat left the imprint of his great voice in a memorable series of poetry recordings. His second wife (from 1953) was actress Renée ASHERSON.

FILMS: *Men of Tomorrow* 1932; *That Night in London, Cash/For Love or Money, The Private Life of Henry VIII* 1933; *The Count of Monte Cristo* (as Edmond Dantes; US) 1934; *The 39 Steps, The Ghost Goes West* 1935; *Knight Without Armor* 1937; *The Citadel* 1938; *Goodbye Mr. Chips* (title role) 1939; *The Young Mr. Pitt* (as William Pitt) 1942; *The Adventures of Tartu* 1943; *Perfect Strangers/Vacation from Marriage* 1945; *Captain Boycott* (cameo as Charles Parnell) 1947; *The Winslow Boy* 1948; *The Cure for Love* (also dir., prod.) 1949; *The Magic Box* (as film pioneer William Friese-Greene) 1951; *Lease of Life* 1954; *The Inn of the Sixth Happiness* 1958.

Donath, Ludwig. Actor. *b.* Mar. 5, 1900, Vienna. *d.* 1967. A graduate of Vienna's Royal Academy of Music and Dramatic Arts, he made his stage debut in 1924 and gained prominence in Berlin from 1928 to 1933. He left Germany after the Nazi takeover and arrived in Hollywood in the early 40s. Because of his foreign accent he was cast in a succession of WW II anti-Nazi films and later played a variety of character roles, memorably as Papa in both *The Jolson Story* (1946) and *Jolson Sings Again* (1949). In the early 50s he was blacklisted by the Hollywood studios in the wake of the House Un-American Activities Committee hearings and did not return to the screen until just before his death from leukemia at 67.

FILMS INCLUDE: *Lady from Chungking* 1942; *The Strange Death of Adolf Hitler* (in dual role as Hitler and his double), *Hostages, Hangmen Also Die* 1943; *The Hitler Gang, The Story of Dr. Wassell* 1944; *Counter-Attack* 1945; *Gilda, The Jolson Story, The Devil's Mask, The Return of Monte Cristo* 1946; *To the Ends of the Earth, Sealed Verdict* 1948; *The Fighting O'Flynn, The Great Sinner, Jolson Sings Again* 1949; *Mystery Submarine* 1950; *The Great Caruso, Sirocco, Journey Into Light* 1951; *Sins of Jezebel, The Veils of Bagdad* 1953; *Torn Curtain* 1966.

Donen, Stanley. Director. Born on Apr. 13, 1924, in Columbia, S.C. *ed.* U. of South Carolina. A dancer from age ten, he made his Broadway debut in 1940 as a chorus boy in 'Pal Joey,' starring Gene Kelly. The following year he assisted Kelly on the choreography of 'Best Foot Forward,' again also appearing in the chorus, and in 1943 repeated as both assistant choreographer and chorus boy in the film version of the musical. He subsequently choreographed or co-choreographed many other films, including *Cover Girl* (1944), *Holiday in Mexico, No Leave No Love* (both 1946), *This Time for Keeps* (1947), *Big City, A Date with Judy* (both 1948), and *Take Me Out to the Ball Game* (also co-sc.; 1949). He made his directorial bow as Kelly's co-director in the sparkling musical *On the Town.* He later co-directed with Kelly several other superior MGM musicals and on his own directed other lively musicals and light films. In the 60s, working mostly abroad, he also ventured into the suspense genre, successfully with *Charade* and less so with *Arabesque* but demonstrated he was still at his best at light romance with *Two for the Road.* He married actress Yvette MIMIEUX in 1972.

FILMS: *On the Town* (co-dir. with Gene Kelly) 1949; *Royal Wedding* 1951; *Singin' in the Rain* (co-dir., co-chor. with Kelly), *Love Is Better Than Ever, Fearless Fagan* 1952; *Give a Girl a Break* (also co-chor.) 1953; *Seven Brides for Seven Brothers, Deep in My Heart* 1954; *It's Always Fair Weather* (co-dir., co-chor. with Kelly) 1955; *Funny Face, The Pajama Game* (co-dir., co-prod. with George Abbott), *Kiss Them for Me* 1957; *Indiscreet* (also prod.), *Damn Yankees* (co-dir., co-prod. with Abbott) 1958; *Once More with Feeling, Surprise Package, The Grass Is Greener* (all also prod.) 1960; *Charade* (also prod.) 1963; *Arabesque* (also prod.) 1966; *Two for the Road, Bedazzled* (both also prod.) 1967; *Staircase* (also prod.) 1969; *The Little Prince* (also prod.) 1974; *Lucky Lady* 1975; *Movie Movie* (also prod.) 1978; *Saturn 3* (prod. only) 1980; *Blame It on Rio* 1984.

Doniol-Valcroze, Jacques. Director, journalist. *b.* Mar. 15, 1920, Paris. *d.* 1989. An assistant editor of the prestigious *La Revue du Cinéma,* he was influential in the development of the French New Wave in the 50s as co-founder and co-editor (with André BAZIN) of the magazine *Cahiers du Cinéma.* In 1955 he began directing short films and since 1959 directed a number of features, but his own work as a filmmaker, while always intelligent, was neither substantial nor memorable. He also appeared as an actor in several films, collaborated on scripts of other directors, and wrote a novel, *Les Portes du Baptistère.* He died of a heart attack during the opening night ceremony of an international TV festival in Cannes.

FEATURE FILMS (as director-writer): *L'Eau à la Bouche/A Game for Six Lovers* 1960; *Le Coeur battant/The French Game* 1961; *La Dènonciation/The Immoral Moment* 1962; *Le Viol/The Rape* (Fr./Swed.) 1967; *La Maison des Bories* 1970; *L'Homme au Cerveau greffé* 1972; *Anne ou la Mort d'un Pilote* 1974.

Donlan, Yolande. Actress. Born June 2, 1920, in Jersey City, N.J. The daughter of character actor James Donlan (1889–1938), she was convent-educated in Los Angeles and at 16 began playing bits and secondary parts in Hollywood films, under her real name, and as Yolande Mollot. She also performed on the stage, making her Broadway debut in 1944. In 1946 she played Billie Dawn in the Boston production of 'Born Yesterday' and the following year scored a big success repeating the same role on the London stage. She stayed in England, where she appeared in many other theatrical productions and several films. Her second husband is director Val GUEST. Autobiography: *Shake the Stars Down* (1976; in US *Third Time Lucky,* 1977).

FILMS INCLUDE: In US—*Pennies from Heaven, After the Thin Man* 1936; *The Champagne Waltz, Rosalie* 1937; *Love Finds Andy Hardy, Sweethearts* 1938; *The Great Man Votes, Idiot's Delight, The Oklahoma Kid, Man About Town* 1939; *I Take This Woman, Turnabout, Devil Bat* 1940; *Dark Streets of Cairo, Roadshow, Unfinished Business* 1941; *Du Barry Was a Lady, Girl Crazy* 1944. In UK—*Miss Pilgrim's Progress* 1950; *Mr. Drake's Duck* 1951; *Penny Princess* 1952; *They Can't Hang Me* 1955; *Tarzan and the Lost Safari* 1957; *Expresso Bongo* 1959; *Jigsaw* 1962; *80,000 Suspects* 1963; *The Adventures* (US) 1970; *Seven Nights in Japan* 1976.

Donlevy, Brian. Actor. *b.* Feb. 9, 1899, Portadown, Ireland, the son of a whiskey distiller. *d.* 1972. He was raised in the US from early childhood. When still in his teens he joined General John Pershing's Mexican border expedition against Pancho Villa as a bugler, then again lied about his age to become a pilot with the famous Lafayette Escadrille in WW I. Husky and barrel-chested, he became a model for shirts back in civilian life and made his acting debut in 1924 with a walk-on in a Broadway play and a small part in a New York–made film. Larger stage and screen parts soon followed. He made his niche in Hollywood in tough villain roles, memorably as the sadistic sergeant in *Beau Geste,* for which he was nominated for an Oscar as best supporting actor. But he also played many arrogant, two-fisted heroes, and even assayed comedy roles, in a screen career that spanned four decades. His second wife was actress Marjorie Lane.

FILMS INCLUDE: *Jamestown* (bit) 1923; *Damaged Hearts, Monsieur Beaucaire* (bit) 1924; *School for Wives* 1925; *A Man of Quality* 1926; *Mother's Boy* 1929; *Barbary Coast* 1935; *Strike Me Pink, Human Cargo, High Tension* 1936; *Crack-Up, This Is My Affair, Born Reckless* 1937; *In Old Chicago, Sharpshooters* 1938; *Jesse James, Union Pacific, Beau Geste, Behind Prison Gates, Destry Rides Again* 1939; *The Great McGinty* (title role), *When the Daltons Rode, Brigham Young* 1940; *I Wanted Wings, Billy the Kid, Hold Back the Dawn, South of Tahiti, Birth of the Blues* 1941; *The Remarkable Andrew* (as the ghost of Andrew Jackson), *Two Yanks in Trinidad, A Gentleman After Dark, Wake Island, The Glass Key, Nightmare, Stand By for Action* 1942; *Hangmen Also Die* 1943; *The Miracle of Morgan's Creek, An American Romance* 1944; *The Virginian, Canyon Passage, Our Hearts Were Growing Up, Two Years Before the Mast* 1946; *The Beginning or the End, The Song of Scheherazade, The Kiss of Death, Heaven Only Knows, Killer McCoy* 1947; *A Southern Yankee* 1948; *Command Decision, The Lucky Stiff, Impact* 1949; *Shakedown* 1950; *Fighting Coast Guard* 1951; *Hoodlum Empire* 1952; *The Big Combo* 1955; *The Creeping Unknown, Cry in the Night* 1956; *Cowboy* 1958; *Never So Few* 1959; *The Errand Boy* 1961; *The Curse of the Fly* 1965; *Waco* 1966; *Hostile Guns, Arizona Bushwhackers* 1968; *Pit Stop* 1969.

Donnell, Jeff. Actress. *b.* July 10, 1921, South Windham, Me. *d.* 1988. *ed.* Yale Drama School. Although 21 when she broke into films in the early 40s, she was cast in teenage roles for several years before graduating to second leads and occasional light leads and finally into matronly roles. She played George Gobel's wife in TV's 'George Gobel Show' (1954–58), appeared in the series 'Matt Helm' (1975–76), and in 1979 joined the cast of the soap opera 'General Hospital.' She was briefly (1954–56) married to Aldo RAY, her second of four husbands.

FILMS INCLUDE: *My Sister Eileen* 1942; *A Night to Remember* 1943; *Once Upon a Time, Three Is a Family* 1944; *Over 21* 1945; *The Unknown* 1946; *Mr. District Attorney* 1947; *Roughshod* 1949; *In a Lonely Place, The Fuller Brush Girl* 1950; *Thief of Damascus, Because You're Mine* 1952; *The Blue Gardenia, So This Is Love* 1953; *The Guns of Fort Petticoat, Sweet Smell of Success, My Man Godfrey* 1957; *Gidget Goes Hawaiian, Force of Impulse* 1961; *The Iron Maiden/The Swingin' Maiden* (UK) 1963; *The Comic* 1969; *Tora! Tora! Tora!* 1970; *Stand Up and Be Counted* 1972.

Donnelly, Ruth. Actress. *b.* May 17, 1896, Trenton, N.J., the daughter of a newspaperman. *d.* 1982. She started her career at 17 as a chorine in a touring musical and shortly after reached Broadway. She appeared in many stage plays, including several George M. Cohan productions, before making her screen debut in 1927. For the next 30 years she appeared in scores of films, typically in fast-talking, sharp-tongued supporting roles, often as a snoopy spinster, shrewish wife, or flippant friend of the heroine.

FILMS INCLUDE: *Rubber Heels* 1927; *Transatlantic* 1931; *Blessed Event* 1932; *Employees' Entrance, Hard to Handle, Bureau of Missing Persons, Footlight Parade, Female* 1933; *Mandalay, Wonder Bar, Housewife* 1934; *Metropolitan, Hands Across the Table* 1935; *Mr. Deeds Goes to Town, Cain and Mabel* 1936; *A Slight Case of Murder, The Affairs of Annabel* 1938; *Mr. Smith Goes to Washington* 1939; *My Little Chickadee* 1940; *Model Wife, You Belong to Me, Rise and Shine* 1941; *The Bells of St. Mary's* 1945; *Cinderella Jones* 1946; *The Snake Pit* 1948; *Where the Sidewalk Ends* 1950; *The Secret of Convict Lake* 1951; *The Spoilers* 1955; *Autumn Leaves* 1956; *The Way to the Gold* 1957.

Donner, Clive. Director. Born on Jan. 21, 1926, in London, the son of a violinist and a boutique operator. He entered British films at 15 as assistant editor and in the early 50s edited such notable productions as *Scrooge/A Christmas Carol, The Card/The Promoter,* and *Genevieve.* As a director since the mid-50s, he demonstrated a flair for visual stylishness and sensitivity, but he tended to accept assignments indiscriminately and his output over the years was uneven. He has also directed documentaries and many TV movies and episodes of TV series in addition to his feature films, as well as a number of stage productions. He married costume designer Jocelyn Rickards.

FEATURE FILMS: *The Secret Place* 1957; *Heart of a Child* 1958; *Marriage of Convenience, The Sinister Man* 1961; *Some People* 1962; *The Caretaker/The Guest* 1963; *Nothing but the Best* 1964; *What's New Pussycat?* (US) 1965; *Luv* (US) 1967; *Here We Go Round the Mulberry Bush* (also prod.) 1968; *Alfred the Great* 1969; *Vampira/Old Dracula* 1974; *The Nude Bomb/The Return of Maxwell Smart* (US) 1980; *Charlie Chan and the Curse of the Dragon Queen* (US) 1981; *Stealing Heaven* 1988.

Donner, Jörn. Director, writer. Born on Feb. 5, 1933, in Helsinki, to wealthy Swedish-speaking parents of German descent. He began writing seriously in his early teens and by the time he was 18 published a collection of short stories. That same year, 1951, he enrolled at the Helsinki University, majoring in political science and Swedish literature, and began writing film criticism for Finnish newspapers. During the 50s he directed a number of short films but remained known primarily as a writer of film essays, poetry, fiction, and reportage. Later in 1959,

Donner began an 18-month tour of duty as a civilian hospital orderly in lieu of military service, which he was spared as a conscientious objector. He then traveled through central Europe, a journey that resulted in the book *Report from the Danube,* and in 1961 he published a scathing critical study of the work of Ingmar Bergman in which he labeled the director's films as irrelevant to the problems of contemporary society. Donner made his own bow as a feature film director in Sweden in 1963 with *A Sunday in September,* a study of the breakdown of a marriage which won a special prize at the Venice Film Festival for the best first work by a director. This and several of his subsequent films starred Harriet ANDERSSON, a veteran of Bergman's stock company who became not only Donner's favorite actress but also his live-in lover.

Donner directed several more films in Sweden through 1967, steadily gaining a reputation as a sincere observer of the contemporary social scene. But his maverick personality and unorthodox filming style made him unpopular with the Swedish critical establishment and he returned to Finland in 1967. His Finnish films have been for the most part lighter and more personal and he appeared in several of them as an actor. He has also taken charge of the dormant Finnish film industry and revitalized it as a producer and mentor of its young generation of film directors. In 1978 he was named managing director of the Swedish Film Institute, a post he held for three years. He subsequently devoted his energies to producing and to writing novels.

FILMS (as director-screenwriter): Shorts—*Morning in the City* 1954; *In These Days* 1955; *Porkala* 1956; *Water* 1957; *Testimonies of Her* 1963. Features—*A Sunday in September* 1963; *To Love* 1964; *Adventure Starts Here* 1965; *Mondo Teeno/Teenage Rebellion* (doc.; Sw. sequence only; US/UK), *Stimulantia* ("He-She" episode), *Rooftree* (also edit.) 1967; *Black on White* (also exec. prod., edit., act.) 1968; *69* (also co-exec. prod., act.) 1969; *Portraits of Women* (also exec. prod., edit., act.), *Anna* (also co-exec. prod.) 1970; *Perkele!/Fuck Off!—Images of Finland* (also exec. prod.) 1971; *Tenderness* (also exec. prod.) 1972; *Hangover* (revised version of *Tenderness,* intended for international distribution; also exec. prod.) 1973; *The World of Ingmar Bergman* (doc.) 1975; *The American Dream* (exec. prod. only) 1976; *Home and Refuge* (prod. only) 1977; *Bluff Stop* (exec. prod. only), *Manrape/Man Cannot Be Raped* (also co-prod.) 1978; *Fanny and Alexander* (exec. prod. only) 1983; *After the Rehearsal* (prod. only) 1984; *Paradise America* (prod. only) 1990.

Donner, Richard. Director, producer. Born in 1939, in New York City. A former off-Broadway actor, he moved to California in 1958 and began directing documentaries, industrial films, and commercials. After directing episodes for 'Wanted Dead or Alive' and other TV series, he turned to feature films, sporadically from the early 60s, regularly from the mid-70s. A superior technician, he has done well with crowd-pleasing movies, especially action spectacles.

FEATURE FILMS: *X-15* 1961; *Salt and Pepper* (UK) 1968; *Twinky/Lola* (UK/It.) 1969; *The Omen* 1976; *Superman* 1978; *Inside Moves* 1980; *The Toy* 1982; *Ladyhawke* (also co-prod.), *The Goonies* (also co-prod.) 1985; *Lethal Weapon* (also co-prod.), *The Lost Boys* (exec. prod. only) 1987; *Scrooged* (also co-prod.) 1988; *Lethal Weapon 2* (also co-prod.) 1989; *Lethal Weapon 3* (also co-prod.) 1992; *Maverick* (also co-prod.) 1994; *Assassins* (also pro.) 1995.

D'Onofrio, Vincent Phillip. Actor. Born 1960 in Brooklyn, New York. Tall, brooding supporting actor who drew attention as the disturbed cadet in Stanley Kubrick's *Full Metal Jacket* (1987) after establishing himself on the legitimate stage at the American Stanislavsky Theatre.

FILMS INCLUDE: *The First Turn-On!!* 1984; *Adventures in Babysitting, Full Metal Jacket* 1987; *Mystic Pizza* 1988; *The Blood of Heroes, Signs of Life* 1989; *Naked Tango* 1990; *Crooked Hearts, Dying Young, Fires Within, JFK* 1991; *The Player, Malcolm X* 1992; *Household Saints, Mr. Wonderful* 1993; *Being Human, Ed Wood, Imaginary Crimes, Nunzio's Second Cousin* 1994; *Strange Days, Stuart Saves His Family* 1995; *Feeling Minnesota, The Whole Wide World, Winner* 1996; *Boy's Life 2* 1997.

Donohoe, Amanda. Actress. Sensuous, intriguing, uninhibited leading lady of British films. A graduate of the London School of Speech and Drama, she entered films in the late 80s and became a favorite of director Ken RUSSELL. She has done much work on TV from the early 90s, including regular appearances on 'L.A. Law'.

FILMS INCLUDE: *Foreign Body* 1986; *Castaway* 1987; *The Lair of the White Worm* 1988; *The Rainbow, Diamond Skulls (Dark Obsession)* 1989; *Tank Malling, Paper Mask* 1990; *The Madness of King George* 1994; *Liar, Liar* 1997.

Donohue, Jack. Director. *b.* John Francis Donohue, Nov. 3, 1908, New York City. *d.* 1984. After being an apprentice bank clerk and iron worker, he began his show business career in 1927 as a chorus boy in the 'Ziegfeld Follies.' He was later featured as a dancer in vaudeville and choreographed musical numbers for Broadway shows. In Hollywood as a dance director from 1934, he created dance numbers for Shirley TEMPLE and Esther WILLIAMS, among others. He made his debut as a film director in 1948. His output, mostly light fare, was sporadic and variable in quality. He also directed numerous TV variety programs, including scores of Frank Sinatra and Red Skelton shows.

FILMS: *Close-Up* 1948; *The Yellow Cab Man* 1950; *Watch the Birdie* 1951; *Calamity Jane* (dance numbers only) 1953; *Lucky Me* 1954; *Babes in Toyland* 1961; *Marriage on the Rocks* 1965; *Assault on a Queen* 1966.

Donskoy, Mark. Director. *b.* Mar. 12, 1897, Odessa, Russia. *d.* 1981. Having served with the Red Army from the October Revolution until 1920, part of the time as a prisoner of the Whites, he enrolled at a Crimean medical school and specialized in the study of psychiatry and the physiology of the human brain. For some reason, he transferred to law school and after graduation worked as prosecutor for the Ukrainian police and published many articles on jurisprudence. In 1925, he turned his interest to the arts and began writing novels, plays, and finally a screenplay. The following year he went to Moscow to present his scenario at the film studios, decided to remain, and enrolled in Sergei EISENSTEIN's class at the State Film Institute. At the same time, he began his apprenticeship in the Soviet film industry as assistant editor.

A feature director since 1928, he gained international fame in the late 30s for his "Gorky Trilogy," a three-part biography of the noted Russian author who had befriended Donskoy in the mid-30s. The trilogy comprises *The Childhood of Maxim Gorky* (1938), *My Apprenticeship* (also known as *On His Own, Out in the World,* or *Among People,* 1939), and *My Universities* (also known as *University of Life,* 1940). Subsequently, Donskoy acquired a reputation as Gorky's best screen interpreter and took his place in the pantheon of Soviet directors alongside Eisenstein, PUDOVKIN, and DOVZHENKO. Donskoy was among the most decorated artists of the Soviet Union. Among his many awards were the Stalin Prize (1941, 1946, 1948), the Order of Lenin (1944, 1971), People's Artist of the Soviet Union (1966), and Hero of Socialist Labor (1971). His work is characterized by warmth and human compassion.

FILMS: *Life* (short; also co-dir. with Mikhail Auerbach,)

1927; *In the Big City* (also co-dir. with Auerbach,) 1928; *The Value of a Man* (co-dir. with Auerbach), *The Pigeon/The Fop* 1929; *Alien Shore* 1930; *Fire* 1931; *Song About Happiness* (co-dir. with Vladimir Legoshin) 1934; *The Childhood of Maxim Gorky* (first film in "Gorky Trilogy"; also co-sc.) 1938; *My Apprenticeship/On His Own/Out in the World/Among People* (second in "Gorky Trilogy"; also co-sc.) 1939; *My Universities/ University of Life* (third in "Gorky Trilogy"; also co-sc.), *Brother of a Hero* 1940; *Romantics/Children of the Soviet Arctic* 1941; *The Signal/Beacon/The Lighthouse* (episode in "Fighting Film Album" #9), *How the Steel Was Tempered/Heroes Are Made* (also sc.) 1942; *The Rainbow* 1944; *Unconquered/The Taras Family* (also co-sc.) 1945; *Village Teacher* 1947; *Alitet Leaves for the Hills* 1949; *Our Champions/Sporting Fame* (doc.) 1950; *Mother/1905* (also co-sc.) 1956; *At Great Cost/The Horse That Cried* 1957; *The Gordeyev Family* (also co-sc.) 1959; *Hello Children!* 1962; *A Mother's Heart/Sons and Mothers* 1966; *A Mother's Devotion* 1967; *Nadyezhda* 1973.

Dooley, Paul. Actor. Born on Feb. 22, 1928, in Parkersburg, W. Va. Versatile character player of the American stage, films, and TV. A frustrated cartoonist, he turned to acting, performing with the Second City and on Broadway. On the screen from the late 60s, he gained good exposure in several Robert ALTMAN films.

FILMS INCLUDE: *What's So Bad About Feeling Good?* 1968; *The-Out-of-Towners* 1970; *Up the Sandbox* 1972; *Death Wish* 1974; *Slap Shot* 1977; *A Wedding* 1978; *A Perfect Couple* (lead), *Rich Kids, Breaking Away, Health* 1979; *Popeye* 1980; *Paternity* 1981; *Endangered Species, Kiss Me Goodbye* 1982; *Strange Brew, Going Berserk* 1983; *Sixteen Candles* 1984; *Monster in the Closet* 1986, *Big Trouble* 1986; *O.C. and Stiggs* 1987; *Last Rites* 1988; *Flashback* 1989; *Shakes the Clown, The Player* 1992.

dope sheet. 1. A list of shots taken, prepared by the cameraman or his assistant; a camera report. 2. A descriptive list of the contents of a reel of film maintained by a film library for classification and identification.

Doran, Ann. Actress. Born on July 28, 1911, in Amarillo, Tex. One of the busiest and least-heralded character actresses in Hollywood, she has played a wide variety of supporting roles in some 200 films since the mid-30s. Also much on TV.

FILMS INCLUDE: *Charlie Chan in London* 1934; *Way Down East* 1935; *Palm Springs* 1936; *Devil's Playground* 1937; *You Can't Take It with You, Blondie* 1938; *The Green Hornet* (serial), *Mr. Smith Goes to Washington* 1939; *Untamed* 1940; *Meet John Doe, Penny Serenade* 1941; *My Sister Eileen, Yankee Doodle Dandy* 1942; *Air Force, Old Acquaintance* 1943; *The Story of Dr. Wassell, Mr. Skeffington* 1944; *Pride of the Marines* 1945; *The Strange Love of Martha Ivers* 1946; *My Favorite Brunette, Magic Town* 1947; *Pitfall, The Snake Pit, Sealed Verdict* 1948; *The Fountainhead, Beyond the Forest* 1949; *Never a Dull Moment, Riding High* 1950; *The People Against O'Hara* 1951; *Love Is Better Than Ever* 1952; *The Eddie Cantor Story* 1953; *The High and the Mighty, Them* 1954; *The Desperate Hours, Rebel Without a Cause* 1955; *The Deep Six* 1958; *A Summer Place, Cast a Long Shadow, Warlock* 1959; *Captain Newman M.D.* 1963; *The Carpetbaggers* 1964; *Mirage* 1965; *The Hostage* 1966; *Rosie* 1967; *Once You Kiss a Stranger* 1969; *The Hired Hand* 1971; *The First Monday in October* 1981; *Wildcats* 1986.

Dorff, Stephen. Actor. Born July 29, 1974, in California. Darkly handsome young lead of American films whose career was launched in television movies. He then made a splash in the independent film *S.F.W.* (1995) but, prior to that, had impressive turns in *The Power of One* (1992) and *Backbeat* (1993).

FILMS: *The Gate* 1987; *The Power of One* 1992; *Backbeat* 1993; *Judgment Night* 1993; *A Hundred and One Nights, Reckless, S.F.W.* 1995; *I Shot Andy Warhol* (as Candy Darling) 1996; *Blood and Wine, City of Industry* 1997.

Dorléac, Françoise. Actress. *b.* Mar. 21, 1942, Paris. *d.* 1967. The daughter of screen actor Maurice Dorléac and the sister of star Catherine DENEUVE, she made her screen debut in 1959 following some stage experience. A charming, elegant, radiant, and talented actress, she was at the height of an international starring career when she was killed in a car accident at the age of 25.

FILMS INCLUDE: *Mensonges* 1959; *La Fille aux Yeux d'Or/The Girl with the Golden Eyes, Ce Soir ou Jamais, Le Jeu de la Vérité, Tout l'Or du Monde* 1961; *Arsène Lupin contre Arsène Lupin* 1962; *L'Homme de Rio/That Man from Rio, La Chasse a l'Homme/Male Hunt, La Peau douce/The Soft Skin* 1964; *Genghis Khan* (US/UK/Ger./Yug.) 1965; *Where the Spies Are* (UK), *Cul-de-Sac* (UK) 1966; *Les Demoiselles de Rochefort/The Young Girls of Rochefort, Billion Dollar Brain* (UK) 1967.

Dorn, Philip. Actor. *b.* Hein Van Der Niet, Sept. 30, 1901, Scheveningen, the Netherlands. *d.* 1975. *ed.* Academy of Fine Arts and Architecture (The Hague). The youngest of nine children, he was drawn early to the stage, made his debut at 14, and before long was playing leads in Dutch and other European theaters under the name Fritz Van Dongen. He was a popular matinee idol and film actor by the time WW II broke out and he made his way to America. In Hollywood from 1939, he played leads in many films, often portraying anti-Nazi patriots and Continental lovers. In the late 40s he switched to more mature character roles, memorably as Papa to Irene Dunne's Mama in *I Remember Mama* (1948). Dorn was hampered by ill health from the start. Long plagued by phlebitis, he suffered the first of a series of strokes in 1945. In the early 50s he returned to Europe, where he appeared in a number of films and plays, but retired in 1955 following an injury in a stage accident. He spent his remaining years confined to his California home, living in retirement with his wife, Dutch actress Marianne Van Dam.

FILMS INCLUDE: *De Kribbebyter/The Cross-Patch* (Hol.) 1936; *Der Tiger von Eschnapur* (Ger.) 1937; *Der Indische Gambal* (Ger.) 1938; *Die Reise nach Tilsit* (Ger.) 1939; *Enemy Agent, Ski Patrol, Escape* 1940; *Ziegfeld Girl, Underground, Tarzan's Secret Treasure* 1941; *Calling Dr. Gillespie, Random Harvest* 1942; *Reunion in France, Chetniks, Paris After Dark* 1943; *Passage to Marseille* 1944; *Escape in the Desert, Blonde Fever* 1945; *I've Always Loved You* 1946; *I Remember Mama* 1948; *The Fighting Kentuckian* 1949; *Spy Hunt* 1950; *Sealed Cargo* 1951; *Der träumende Mund* (Ger.), *Salto Mortale* (Ger.) 1953.

Dörrie, Doris. Director, screenwriter. Born in 1955 in Hanover, West Germany. *ed.* Hochschule fur Film und Fernsehen, Munich. German director-screenwriter known for her dark comic approach to sexual identity and male-female relations. She was known for her documentaries and for her critically acclaimed short film *The First Waltz* (1978) before making her feature film directorial debut with *Straight Through the Heart* (1983). She scored an international hit with the feature *Men* (1985).

FILMS INCLUDE: *Der Hauptdarsteller* (act. only) 1977; *Mitten Ins Herz/Straight Through the Heart* (dir.) 1983; *Im Innern des Wals* (dir., sc.) 1985; *King Kongs Faust* (act. only), *Manner/Men* (dir., sc.); *Paradies* (dir., sc.) 1986; *Wann—Wenn Nicht Jetzt?* (sc.) 1987; *Me and Him* (dir., sc.) 1988; *Geld* (dir., sc.) 1989; *Happy Birthday Türkel* (also sc.) 1991; *Nobody Loves Me* 1994.

Dors, Diana. Actress. *b.* Diana Fluck, Oct. 23, 1931, Swindon, England. *d.* 1984. *ed.* Royal Academy of Dramatic Art. Buxom, platinum-blonde leading lady of British and some American films. The daughter of a railway clerk, she launched her career as an entertainer at 13 and made her screen debut at 14. Almost from the start, she was groomed as a sex symbol and England's answer to Marilyn Monroe, but the public remained largely apathetic toward her frank, exaggerated sexuality. Her playgirl image, on and off the screen, disguised her occasional sincere efforts at real acting. A survivor of meningitis and two operations for the removal of tumors, she died of cancer at 52.

FILMS INCLUDE: *The Shop at Sly Corner* 1946; *Holiday Camp* 1947; *Good Time Girl, Oliver Twist, Here Come the Huggets* 1948; *Diamond City* 1949; *Dance Hall* 1950; *Lady Godiva Rides Again* 1951; *The Weak and the Wicked* 1954; *A Kid for Two Farthings, Value for Money, An Alligator Named Daisy* 1955; *Yield to the Night/Blonde Sinner* 1956; *The Long Haul, The Unholy Wife* 1957; *I Married a Woman* 1958; *Passport to Shame/Room 43* 1959; *Scent of Mystery* (US) 1960; *On the Double* (US), *King of the Roaring Twenties* (US) 1961; *Allez France!/The Counterfeit Constable* (Fr.) 1964; *The Sandwich Man* 1966; *Berserk, Danger Route* 1967; *Hammerhead* 1968; *Baby Love* 1969; *There's a Girl in My Soup, Deep End* 1970; *Hannie Caulder* 1971; *The Pied Piper/The Pied Piper of Hamelin, The Amazing Mr. Blunden, Nothing but the Night* 1972; *Theatre of Blood, From Beyond the Grave, Craze/The Infernal Doll* 1973; *Swedish Wildcats/The Groove Room* 1974; *Adventures of a Taxi Driver* 1975; *Adventures of a Private Eye* 1977; *Confessions from the David Galaxy Affair* 1979; *Steaming* 1984.

D'Orsay, Fifi. Actress. *b.* Yvonne Lussier, Apr. 16, 1904, Montreal. *d.* 1983. One of 12 children of a postal clerk, she was convent-educated and worked as a typist before making her show-biz bid in 1923 as a chorus girl in 'Greenwich Village Follies.' She subsequently entertained in vaudeville, at first with the famous Gallagher and Shean, then in her own act, and in 1929 she made her film debut, opposite Will Rogers, in *They Had to See Paris.* Although she had never set foot in France, she was billed and typecast in early Hollywood talkies as a Parisian sex symbol, playing both leads and supporting roles as an empty-headed floozy. After 1935 she returned sporadically to films and played TV in character parts and devoted much of her time to lecturing on religion. In 1971 she made a nostalgic comeback in the Broadway musical 'Follies.'

FILMS INCLUDE: *They Had to See Paris, Hot for Paris* 1929; *Women Everywhere, On the Level, Those Three French Girls* 1930; *Mr. Lemon of Orange, Women of All Nations, Young As You Feel* 1931; *Girl from Calgary* 1932; *Going Hollywood* 1933; *Wonder Bar* 1934; *Accent on Youth* 1935; *Three Legionnaires* 1937; *The Gangster* 1947; *What a Way to Go!* 1964; *The Art of Love* 1965; *Assignment to Kill* 1968.

Dorziat, Gabrielle. Actress. *b.* Gabrielle Sigrist Moppert, Jan. 15, 1886, Epernay, France. *d.* 1979. A veteran of the Paris stage since 1900, she played aristocratic, authoritarian, often severe character roles in some 70 French films since 1922.

FILMS INCLUDE: *L'Infante a la Rose* 1922; *Mayerling* (as Empress Elizabeth of Austria), *Samson* 1936; *Le Mensonge de Nina Petrovna/The Lie of Nina Petrovna, La Dame de Pique* 1937; *La Vierge Folle, Mollenard/Hatred, Le Drame de Shanghai/The Shanghai Drama* 1938; *La Fin du Jour/The End of a Day* 1939; *De Mayerling a Sarajevo/Mayerling to Sarajevo* (as Archduchess Maria Therese) 1940; *Premier Rendez-Vous/Her First Affair* 1941; *Falabalas/Paris Frills, Adieu Cherie* 1945; *Monsieur Vincent* 1947; *Ruy-Blas, Les Parents terribles/The Storm Within* 1948; *Manon* 1949; *So Little Time* (UK) 1952; *Little Boy Lost* (US) 1953; *Un Acte d'Amour/Act of Love* (Fr./US), *Madame Du Barry* 1954; *Mitsou* 1956; *Les Espions* 1957; *Katia/Magnificent Sinner* 1960; *Gigot* (US), *Un Singe en Hiver/Monkey in Winter* 1962; *Germinal* 1963.

Dos Santos, Nelson Pereira. See PEREIRA DOS SANTOS, Nelson.

dot. A small, flat, round disk placed in front of a light source as a diffuser.

double. A person who takes the place of an actor in a shot, either because the particular scene involves exposure to danger or requires special athletic ability or skills (riding, juggling, etc.) that the actor may not have. Since the double is usually similar in build and coloring to the actor, and his actions are recorded from a safe distance and cut to match the close-ups of the actor, the viewing public is seldom aware of the impersonation. See also STAND-IN; STUNT PLAYER.

double bill. See B PICTURE; DOUBLE FEATURE.

double broad. See BROAD.

double exposure. The recording of two different images on the same length of film as a result of exposing the same negative twice through the camera or a printer. Double exposure may occur accidentally, by unknowingly running previously exposed film through the camera, or by design if some special effect is desired.

double feature. A program at a motion picture theater consisting of the showing of two full-length features. It is seldom presented at first-run theaters but still occurs in second-run houses and revival theaters.

double framing. See SKIP FRAMING.

double system. The recording of sound in synchronization with the visuals but on a separate track. The camera and the sound recorder are driven simultaneously by a synchronous motor. The sound is not recorded directly onto the picture film, as it is in SINGLE-SYSTEM RECORDING, but on separate magnetic film or tape. The double system not only offers better quality of sound but also provides the editor with greater flexibility in cutting the film and matching the sound. The double system is the normal procedure of filming with synchronous sound, while the single system is used in situations where speedy production is of the essence and sound quality is of secondary importance, such as in newsreels or low-budget documentary films.

double take. An initial mild reaction by a player followed by a second, much more emphatic delayed reaction, usually for comic effect, often to suggest that an idea or situation had not been completely understood by the player at first.

Douglas, Bill. Scottish-born British director. Sponsored by the British Film Institute, he set out in 1970 to explore his roots on film. The result was a remarkable three-part document known as 'The Bill Douglas Trilogy,' in which the director recreated his childhood and adolescence in a wretched mining town, with the help of local actors and a great deal of imagination and skill. The trilogy, which took eight years to complete, was hailed in Britain, US, and elsewhere as a unique achievement.

FILMS INCLUDE: *My Childhood* 1972; *My Kin Folk* 1973; *My Way Home* 1978; *Comrades* 1987.

Douglas, Gordon. Director. *b.* Dec. 5, 1909, New York City. *d.* 1993. On the stage while still a toddler, he went to Hollywood in the late 20s and after working briefly for MGM and Paramount joined the Hal Roach studios as actor, casting director, and occasional gagman. He appeared in "The Boy Friends" comedy series and in 1936 began directing "Our Gang" comedy shorts, among them *Bored of Education, Spooky Hooky* (1936), *Rushin' Ballet, Roamin' Holiday, Mail and Female, Our Gang Follies of 1938* (1937), *Bear Facts, Hide and Shriek,* and

The Little Ranger (1938). He also co-directed the Our Gang feature *General Spanky* in 1936. From 1939 through the early 70s he directed a great number of motion pictures for various studios, mostly for RKO, Columbia, Warner Bros., and 20th Century-Fox. Specializing at first in comedy and later in action and adventure films, he was known more for his technical efficiency and visual polish than for a singular personal style or message.

FEATURE FILMS: *General Spanky* (co-dir. with Fred Newmeyer) 1936; *Zenobia* 1939; *Saps at Sea* 1940; *Road Show* (co-dir. with Hal Roach and Hal Roach, Jr.), *Broadway Limited, Niagara Falls* 1941; *The Devil with Hitler, The Great Gildersleeve* 1942; *Gildersleeve's Bad Day, Gildersleeve on Broadway* 1943; *A Night of Adventure, Gildersleeve's Ghost, Girl Rush, The Falcon in Hollywood* 1944; *Zombies on Broadway, First Yank Into Tokyo* 1945; *Dick Tracy vs. Cueball, San Quentin* 1946; *If You Knew Susie, The Black Arrow, Walk a Crooked Mile* 1948; *Mr. Soft Touch* (co-dir. with Henry Levin), *The Doolins of Oklahoma* 1949; *The Nevadan, The Fortunes of Captain Blood, Rogues of Sherwood Forest, Kiss Tomorrow Goodbye, Between Midnight and Dawn* 1950; *The Great Missouri Raid, Only the Valiant, I Was a Communist for the FBI, Come Fill the Cup* 1951; *Mara Maru, The Iron Mistress* 1952; *She's Back on Broadway, The Charge at Feather River, So This Is Love* 1953; *Them!, Young at Heart* 1954; *The McConnell Story, Sincerely Yours* 1955; *Santiago* 1956; *The Big Land, Bombers B-52* 1957; *Fort Dobbs, The Fiend Who Walked the West* 1958; *Up Periscope, Yellowstone Kelly* 1959; *Gold of the Seven Saints, The Sins of Rachel Cade, Claudelle Inglish* 1961; *Follow That Dream* 1962; *Call Me Bwana* 1963; *Robin and the 7 Hoods, Rio Conchos* 1964; *Sylvia, Harlow* (Carroll Baker version) 1965; *Stagecoach, Way. . . Way Out* 1966; *In Like Flint, Chuka, Tony Rome* 1967; *The Detective, Lady in Cement* 1968; *Skullduggery, Barquero, They Call Me Mr. Tibbs* 1970; *Skin Game* (co-dir., uncredited) 1971; *Slaughter's Big Rip-Off* 1973; *Viva Knievel!* 1977.

Douglas, Illeana. Actress, screenwriter. Charming, unassuming leading and character actress of American stage and film, most notably for director Martin SCORSESE. She began her career in New York working on the off-Broadway stage and landing bit parts in films until Scorsese cast her in a supporting role in *New York Stories* (1989). From then on her working relationship with the scion of filmmaking led to more important roles in *GoodFellas* (1990) and the remake of *Cape Fear* (1991). Her star turn came with her role as the wronged sister in Gus VAN SANT's *To Die For* (1995) followed by the well-received independent film *Grace of My Heart* (1996). Douglas is the granddaughter of actor Melvyn DOUGLAS.

FILMS: *The Last Temptation of Christ* (bit) 1988; *New York Stories* 1989; *GoodFellas* 1990; *Cape Fear, Guilty by Suspicion* 1991; *Alive, Household Saints* 1993; *Quiz Show* 1994; *Search and Destroy, To Die For* 1995; *Grace of My Heart* 1996.

Douglas, Kirk. Actor. Born Issur Danielovitch (later changed to Isidore Demsky), on Dec. 9, 1916, in Amsterdam, N.Y., to illiterate Russian Jewish peasant immigrants. He worked as a waiter to put himself through St. Lawrence University, where he excelled in wrestling and dabbled in school dramatics, then wrestled professionally and worked as an usher and bellhop, among other things, to put himself through the American Academy of Dramatic Arts. He made his Broadway debut in 1941 but after only two small roles left for WW II service in the Navy. In 1945 he returned to Broadway in chunkier parts and did some radio work before embarking on a screen career the following year. In 1949 he emerged as a front-rank star with a convincing performance as an unscrupulous boxer punching his way to the top in *Champion.* It was the type of role he was to portray best and most often in ensuing films—cocky, selfish, intense, forceful, and egocentric. He was nominated for Academy Awards for *Champion, The Bad and the Beautiful,* and *Lust for Life* and won the N.Y. Critics Award as best actor for his powerful portrayal of Vincent Van Gogh in the latter film.

Ambitious and dynamic off as well as on the screen, Douglas formed his own company, Bryna Productions, in 1955, through which he turned out his own films as well as those of other stars. He later formed another company, Joel Productions. Approaching 60 and still playing leading men, he began directing some of his films in the early 70s. While continuing to star in films during the 80s, Douglas allotted more and more of his time for a variety of voluntary civic duties and testified before Congress on discrimination and on the abuse of the elderly. A Goodwill Ambassador for the State Department and the USIA since 1963, he was the recipient in 1981 of the Presidential Medal of Freedom. In 1983, he received the Jefferson Award for public service as a private citizen. In recognition of his contribution to the arts, the French government named him Chevalier of the Legion of Honor in 1985. He won the American Cinema Award in 1987, the German Golden Kamera Award in 1988, and the National Board of Review's career achievement award in 1989. He is the father of actor-producer Michael DOUGLAS. He has published two novels: *Dance with the Devil* (1990) and *The Secret* (1992). Autobiography: *The Ragman's Son* (1988).

FILMS: *The Strange Love of Martha Ivers* 1946; *Mourning Becomes Electra, Out of the Past* 1947; *I Walk Alone, The Walls of Jericho, My Dear Secretary* 1948; *A Letter to Three Wives, Champion* 1949; *Young Man with a Horn, The Glass Menagerie* 1950; *Along the Great Divide, The Big Carnival* (originally titled *Ace in the Hole), Detective Story* 1951; *The Big Trees, The Big Sky* 1952; *The Bad and the Beautiful, The Story of Three Loves, The Juggler* 1953; *Act of Love* (US/Fr.), *20,000 Leagues Under the Sea* 1954; *The Racers, Ulisse/Ulysses* (title role; It.), *Man Without a Star, The Indian Fighter* 1955; *Lust for Life* (as Vincent Van Gogh) 1956; *Top Secret Affair, Gunfight at the O.K. Corral* (as Doc Holliday) 1957; *Paths of Glory, The Vikings* 1958; *Last Train from Gun Hill, The Devil's Disciple* 1959; *Strangers When We Meet, Spartacus* (title role; also exec. prod.) 1960; *The Last Sunset, Town Without Pity* (US/Ger./Switz.) 1961; *Lonely Are the Brave, Two Weeks in Another Town* 1962; *The Hook, The List of Adrian Messenger, For Love or Money* 1963; *Seven Days in May* 1964; *In Harm's Way, The Heroes of Telemark* (UK) 1965; *Cast a Giant Shadow, Paris Brûle-t-il?/Is Paris Burning?* (as General Patton; Fr./US) 1966; *The Way West, The War Wagon* 1967; *A Lovely Way to Die, The Brotherhood* 1968; *The Arrangement* 1969; *There Was a Crooked Man* 1970; *Summertree* (prod. only), *The Light at the Edge of the World* (also prod.), *A Gunfight, Catch Me a Spy* (UK) 1971; *Un Uomo da Rispettare/The Master Touch* (It.) 1972; *Scalawag* (also dir.) 1973; *Once Is Not Enough, Posse* (also dir., prod.) 1975; *Holocaust 2000/The Chosen* (It./UK) 1977; *The Fury* 1978; *The Villain, Home Movies* 1979; *Saturn 3* (UK), *The Final Countdown* 1980; *The Man from Snowy River* (Austral.) 1982; *Eddie Macon's Run* 1983; *Tough Guys* (also credited as Issur Danielovitch, creative consultant) 1986; *Oscar* 1991; *Welcome to Veraz* 1992; *Greedy* 1994.

Douglas, Melvyn. Actor. *b.* Melvyn Edouard Hesselberg, Apr. 5, 1901, Macon, Ga. *d.* 1981. The son of a Russian-born concert pianist and a housewife of Scottish descent, he was drawn to acting at high school and made his stage debut in Chicago in 1919, after returning from WW I military service as a medical orderly. For several years he appeared in stock and toured with various companies, finally making his Broadway debut in 1928, playing a gangster in 'A Free Soul.' Other Broadway roles followed, highlighted by the hit 'Tonight or Never,' and he was brought to Hollywood to repeat the part in the film version. Other Hollywood roles followed in rapid succession, including that of Greta Garbo's leading man in *As You Desire Me* (1932), but he was unhappy with the way his Hollywood career was shaping up and in 1934 returned to Broadway as an actor and a director. He was soon back in Hollywood, however, under contract to Columbia (and later also MGM), and into a series of characterizations that was to make him one of the most popular stars of the 30s and early 40s.

A tall, dapper man with intelligent good looks and a debonair manner, Douglas found his niche in romantic and marital comedies as the suave, sophisticated leading man of such stars as Garbo, Colbert, Crawford, Dietrich, Loy, and Dunne. He was the man who liberated Irene Dunne's body and spirit in *Theodora Goes Wild* (1936) and who made Garbo laugh in *Ninotchka* (1939). In 1942 he went to Washington as the director of the Arts Council of the Office of Civilian Defense, then enlisted as a private in the Army the following year. Demobilized a major, he returned to Hollywood but found his renewed screen career unrewarding and by the early 50s was back on Broadway. On the stage, he soon acquired a reputation as a fine, serious actor and won a Tony Award for his portrayal of a Presidential aspirant in 'The Best Man.'

It wasn't until the early 60s that Douglas returned to films, this time as a character actor, and he promptly won an Academy Award as best supporting actor in *Hud* (1963). He was nominated for a best actor Oscar for *I Never Sang for My Father* (1970), and won a second Academy Award in the supporting actor category for *Being There* (1979). He also began appearing in TV plays and won an Emmy Award for 'Do Not Go Gentle into That Good Night.' Douglas's second wife (since 1931) was former stage actress and Congresswoman Helen GAHAGAN, the beautiful star of *She* (1935). Their granddaughter is actress, writer, director Illeana DOUGLAS.

FILMS: *Tonight or Never* 1931; *Prestige, The Wiser Sex, Broken Wing, As You Desire Me, The Old Dark House* 1932; *The Vampire Bat, Nagana, Counsellor-at-Law* 1933; *Woman in the Dark, Dangerous Corner* 1934; *The People's Enemy, She Married Her Boss, Mary Burns Fugitive, Annie Oakley* 1935; *The Lone Wolf Returns* (title role), *And So They Were Married, The Gorgeous Hussy, Theodora Goes Wild* 1936; *Women of Glamour, Captains Courageous, I Met Him in Paris, Angel, I'll Take Romance* 1937; *Arsene Lupin Returns* (title role), *There's Always a Woman, The Toy Wife, Fast Company, That Certain Age, The Shining Hour, There's That Woman Again* 1938; *Tell No Tales, Good Girls Go to Paris, Ninotchka, The Amazing Mr. Williams* 1939; *Too Many Husbands, He Stayed for Breakfast, Third Finger Left Hand* 1940; *This Thing Called Love, That Uncertain Feeling, A Woman's Face, Our Wife, Two-Faced Woman* 1941; *We Were Dancing, They All Kissed the Bride* 1942; *Three Hearts for Julia* 1943; *The Sea of Grass, The Guilt of Janet Ames* 1947; *Mr. Blandings Builds His Dream House* 1948; *My Own True Love, A Woman's Secret, The Great Sinner* 1949; *My Forbidden Past, On the Loose* 1951; *Billy Budd* 1962; *Hud* 1963; *Advance to the Rear, The Americanization of Emily* 1964; *Rapture* 1965; *Hotel* 1967; *I Never Sang for My Father* 1970; *One Is a Lonely Number, The Candidate* 1972; *Le Locataire/The Tenant* (Fr.) 1976; *Twilight's Last Gleaming* (US/Ger.) 1977; *The Seduction of Joe Tynan, Being There* 1979; *The Changeling* (Can.), *Tell Me a Riddle* 1980; *Ghost Story* 1981.

Douglas, Michael. Actor, producer. Born on Sept. 25, 1944, in New Brunswick, N.J. *ed.* Black Fox Military Academy; Choate; U. of California. The son of Kirk DOUGLAS, he entered the industry in the mid-60s as an assistant director but later in the decade turned to acting on TV, on the stage, and in films. He made an auspicious start as a producer (in collaboration) with *One Flew Over the Cuckoo's Nest,* a film that captured all five top Oscars, including best picture, for 1975. In the early 80s, playing a succession of heroes, he developed into a popular movie star. Later in the decade, he demonstrated a capacity for greater depth and wider range (particularly in playing characters of problematic morality) in such films as *Fatal Attraction* (1986), *Wall Street* (1987), and *Falling Down* (1993). He won an Academy Award as best actor for his portrayal of a greedy, ruthless inside trader in *Wall Street*.

FILMS (as actor): *Hail Hero!* 1969; *Adam at 6 A.M.* 1970; *Summertree* 1971; *Napoleon and Samantha* 1972; *One Flew Over the Cuckoo's Nest* (co-prod. only) 1975; *Coma* 1978; *The China Syndrome* (also prod., co-sc.), *Running* (Can.) 1979; *It's My Turn* 1980; *The Star Chamber* 1983; *Romancing the Stone, Starman* (exec. prod. only) 1984; *A Chorus Line, Jewel of the Nile* 1985; *Fatal Attraction, Wall Street* 1987; *Black Rain, The War of the Roses* 1989; *Shining Through, Basic Instinct* 1992; *Falling Down* 1993; *Disclosure* 1994; *The American President* 1995; *The Ghost and the Darkness* 1996; *Face/Off* (ex-prod. only), *The Game* 1997.

Douglas, Paul. Actor. *b.* Nov. 4, 1907, Philadelphia, a doctor's son. *d.* 1959. *ed.* Yale. He was drawn to drama at high school but after leaving college became a professional football player, with Philadelphia's Frankford Yellow Jackets, then a radio sportscaster and news commentator. He made his Broadway debut in 1935, in the comedy 'Double Dummy,' but returned to radio and was nearly 40 when Garson Kanin chose him to play the gruff, loud-mouthed scrap tycoon in one of Broadway's longest-running hits, 'Born Yesterday.' By the time he made his screen debut in 1948 he was a mature, burly, middle-aged man, but he proved to be an appealing film personality and an effective actor, especially in comedy leads. He died of a heart attack at 52. The last two of his five marriages were to screen actresses, Virginia Field and his widow, Jan STERLING.

FILMS: *A Letter to Three Wives* 1948; *It Happens Every Spring, Everybody Does It* 1949; *The Big Lift, Love That Brute, Panic in the Streets* 1950; *Fourteen Hours, The Guy Who Came Back, Angels in the Outfield* 1951; *When in Rome, Clash by Night, We're Not Married* 1952; *Never Wave at a WAC* 1953; *Forever Female, Executive Suite, The Maggie/High and Dry* (UK), *Green Fire* 1954; *Joe Macbeth* (UK) 1955; *The Leather Saint, The Solid Gold Cadillac, The Gamma People* (UK) 1956; *This Could Be the Night, Beau James* 1957; *Fortunella* (It.) 1958; *The Mating Game* 1959.

Douglas, Robert. Actor. Born Robert Douglas Finlayson, on Nov. 9, 1909, in Bletchley, England. On the London stage from 1927, he made several appearances in British films, in both leads and supporting parts. After serving in WW II, he came to Hollywood, where he played suave villains in many adventure films, crossing swords with Errol Flynn and Robert Taylor, among others. In the late 50s he became a TV director and in 1964 piloted a British feature, *Night Train to Paris.*

FILMS INCLUDE: In the UK—*P.C. Josser* 1931; *The Blarney Stone/The Blarney Kiss* 1933; *London Melody/Girl in the Street* 1937; *The Challenge, Over the Moon* 1938; *The Lion Has Wings* 1939. In the US—*The Decision of Christopher Blake* (lead), *Adventures of Don Juan* 1948; *The Fountainhead, Homicide* 1949; *Barricade, The Flame and the Arrow, Spy Hunt, Kim, Mystery Submarine* 1950; *Target Unknown, Thunder on the Hill* 1951; *At Sword's Point, Ivanhoe, The Prisoner of Zenda*

1952; *The Desert Rats, Fair Wind to Java, Flight to Tangier* 1953; *Saskatchewan, King Richard and the Crusades* 1954; *The Scarlet Coat* (as Benedict Arnold), *The Virgin Queen, Good Morning Miss Dove* 1955; *Helen of Troy* (as Agamemnon) 1956; *The Young Philadelphians* 1959; *Night Train to Paris* (dir. only; UK) 1964.

Douglass, Kent. See MONTGOMERY, Douglass.

Dourif, Brad. Actor. Born on Mar. 18, 1950, in Huntington, W. Va. Blond, baby-faced leading man and character player; effective in sensitive or deranged roles. He performed for three years with New York's Circle Repertory Company before getting into films and TV. He was nominated for an Oscar and won the British Academy Award at the very start of his screen career, for *One Flew Over the Cuckoo's Nest* (1975) and played memorable roles in *Wise Blood, Ragtime,* and *Mississippi Burning.*

FILMS INCLUDE: *W.W. and the Dixie Dancekings* (bit), *One Flew Over the Cuckoo's Nest* 1975; *The Eyes of Laura Mars* 1978; *Wise Blood* 1979; *Heaven's Gate* 1980; *Ragtime* 1981; *Dune* 1984; *Blue Velvet, Impure Thoughts* 1986; *Fatal Beauty* 1987; *Child's Play, Mississippi Burning* 1988; *Medium Rare* 1989; *The Exorcist: 1990, Spontaneous Combustion, Sonny Boy, Stephen King's Graveyard Shift, Child's Play 2* (voice only), *Hidden Agenda* 1990; *Child's Play 3* (voice only) 1991; *Critters 4, Common Bonds/Chaindance* (Can.), *Dead Certain* (Can./UK/US), *London Kills Me* (UK) 1992; *Color of Night* 1994; *Murder in the First* 1995.

Douy, Max. Art Director, set designer. Born on June 20, 1914, in Issy-Les Moulineaux, France. Beginning as an assistant to Meerson, Trauner, and others, he came into his own in 1942 and has become one of France's most stylish and inventive set designers. He has worked mainly with AUTANT-LARA but also for Becker, Bresson, Grémullen, Astruc, and Buñuel. His brother, Jacques Douy (*b.* 1924), is also a successful art director.

FILMS INCLUDE: *Dernier Atout* 1942; *Lumière d'Eté, Adieu Léonard* 1943; *Le Ciel est à vous* 1944; *Les Dames du Bois de Boulogne/Ladies of the Park, Falbalas/Paris Frills* 1945; *Le Diable au Corps/Devil in the Flesh, Quai des Orfèvres/Jenny Lamour* 1947; *Manon, Occupe-toi d'Amélie/Oh Amelia!* 1949; *L'Auberge rouge/The Red Inn* 1951; *Le Bon Dieu sans Confession* 1953; *Le Blé en Herbe/The Game of Love, L'Affaire Maurizius, Le Rouge et le Noir* 1954; *French Cancan/Only the French Can, Les Mauvaises Recontres* 1955; *Cela s'appelle l'Aurore, Margerite de la Nuit, La Traversée de Paris/Four Bags Full* 1956; *Celui qui doit mourir/He Who Must Die* 1957; *En Case de Malheur/Love Is My Profession, Le Joueur* 1958; *La Jument verte/The Green Mare* 1959; *Phaedra* 1962; *Le Meurtier/Enough Rope* 1963; *Topkapi* (US) 1964; *Le plus vieux Métier du Monde/The Oldest Profession* 1967; *Castle Keep* (US) 1969; *Boulevard du Rhum/Rum Runner, La Cavale* 1971; *Black and White in Color* (Ivory Coast/Fr.) 1976; *Vous n'aurez pas l'Alsace et la Lorraine* 1977.

Dove, Billie. Actress. Born Lillian Bohney, on May 14, 1900, in New York City. A former artist's model and Ziegfeld showgirl, she was among the loveliest leading ladies of Hollywood's silent era, energetically publicized as "The American Beauty," and was chosen to co-star with Douglas Fairbanks in the sumptuous early color production *The Black Pirate* (1926). She starred in many silent and early sound films before retiring in 1932 to marry a wealthy rancher. Earlier (1923–29) she had been married to director Irvin WILLAT. In 1962 she returned briefly to the screen playing a bit in the film *Diamond Head.*

FILMS: *Get-Rich-Quick Wallingford, At the Stage Door* 1921; *Polly of the Follies, Beyond the Rainbow, Youth to Youth* 1922; *Madness of Youth, All the Brothers Were Valiant, Soft Boiled, The Thrill Chaser, Lone Star Ranger* 1923; *Yankee Madness, On Time, Try and Get It, The Wanderer of the Wasteland, The Roughneck* 1924; *The Folly of Vanity, The Air Mail, The Light of the Western Stars, Wild Horse Mesa, The Lucky Horseshoe, The Fighting Heart, The Ancient Highway* 1925; *The Black Pirate, The Marriage Clause, Kid Boots, The Lone Wolf Returns* 1926; *An Affair of the Follies, Sensation Seekers, The Tender Hour, The Stolen Bride, American Beauty, The Love Mart* 1927; *The Heart of a Follies Girl, The Yellow Lily, The Night Watch, Adoration* 1928; *Careers, The Man and the Moment, Her Private Life, Painted Angel* 1929; *The Other Tomorrow, A Notorious Affair, Sweethearts and Wives, One Night at Susie's* 1930; *The Lady Who Dared, The Age of Love* 1931; *Cock of the Air, Blondie of the Follies* 1932; *Diamond Head* (bit) 1962.

Dovzhenko, Alexander Petrovich. Director. *b.* Sept. 12, 1894, Sosnitsa, Ukraine. *d.* 1956. The son of an illiterate Cossack peasant, he was encouraged to complete his education by his semiliterate grandfather and at age 19 became a primary-school teacher. A heart condition kept him out of military service during WW I and he spent the war and revolution years teaching as well as studying economics. In the early 20s he became active in the Communist Party and was awarded with diplomatic posts abroad, at first as secretary to the Soviet embassy in Warsaw, then as secretary of the consulate in Berlin. Returning to Kiev in 1923, he chose a new career as magazine cartoonist and book illustrator.

In 1926 he was seized with a passion to make films and set out to Odessa, where the nearest film studios were located. According to his own memoirs, published in 1939, he had little or no idea of how films were made and had seen only a handful, but at 32 he became convinced that his future as an artist should be tied to this "entirely new and original" art for the masses. He wrote one script, which remained unproduced, then another, for the film *Vasya the Reformer,* which he also co-directed. In 1928 he made his first important film, *Zvenigora,* a lyrical epic of the Ukraine in which elements of history and folklore, stark realism and tender poetry, obvious propaganda and subtle satire blend into an exciting whole. The film was enthusiastically received in Moscow. Legend has it that after the premiere, EISENSTEIN and PUDOVKIN displayed their recognition of Dovzhenko as their equal by joining him in an all-night drinking romp.

Dovzhenko's next film, *Arsenal,* a classic of the silent Soviet cinema, offers a dazzling display of visual virtuosity whose vivid images linger long in memory and is both a deeply committed political manifesto and a passionately lyrical film-poem. Dovzhenko's next film, *Earth* (sometimes known as *Soil*), is considered by many his masterpiece. One of the last great films of the Soviet silent period, it is a work of great aesthetic beauty, a philosophical-lyrical poem of the glory of nature and the inevitabilities of life and death. It was denounced by official Soviet critics as "counter-revolutionary" and "defeatist." Other high points in his career were the film *Aerogard* (also known as *Air City* or *Frontier*) and *Shchors* (sometimes spelled *Shors*), both fiercely patriotic and both among the most exciting Soviet films of the 30s.

Dovzhenko died of a heart attack at 62. A diary he kept from 1941 reveals his deep resentment against working conditions in the Soviet film industry, which he blamed for having prevented him from completing many projects.

During WW II, Dovzhenko began to shift the emphasis of his creative work from filmmaking to the writing of screenplays as well as novels and short stories. After his death, his widow, Yulia SOLNTSEVA, who had frequently assisted him on his films, directed several films from his writings, notably the memorable *Poem of the Sea.* After his death also, the Kiev studio was renamed the Dovzhenko studio.

FILMS (as director-screenwriter): *Vasya the Reformer* (co-dir. with F. Lokatinsi and Yosif Rona), *Love's Berry* (short) 1926; *The Diplomatic Pouch* 1927; *Zvenigora* 1928; *Arsenal* 1929; *Earth/Soil* 1930; *Ivan* 1932; *Aerogard/Frontier/Air City* 1935. Assisted by Yulia Solntseva—*Shchors/Shors* 1939; *Liberation* 1940; *The Battle for Our Soviet Ukraine* (doc.; sc. and supervision only) 1943; *Ukraine in Flames* (full title: *Victory in the Ukraine and the Expulsion of the Germans from the Boundaries of the Ukrainian Soviet Earth* (doc.; co-dir.) 1945; *Native Land* (narr. and edit. only) 1946; *Michurin/Life in Bloom* (release delayed from 1947) 1949. Films directed by Yulia Solntseva from Dovzhenko's scripts or writings: *Poem of the Sea* 1958; *Story of the Flaming Years* 1961; *Alexander Dovzhenko* (dir. by Yavheniya Hryhorovych) 1964; *The Enchanted Desna* 1965; *The Unforgettable* 1968.

Dow, Peggy. Actress. Born Peggy Josephine Varnadow, on Mar. 18, 1928, in Louisiana. Attractive leading lady of Hollywood films who retired from the screen after only a few productions to marry an Oklahoma oil millionaire.

FILMS: *Undertow* 1949; *Woman in Hiding, Shakedown, The Sleeping City, Harvey* 1950; *Bright Victory, You Never Can Tell, Reunion in Reno, I Want You* 1951.

Down, Lesley-Anne. Actress. Born Lesley Down, on Mar. 17, 1954, in London. Leading lady of British and American films. The daughter of a caretaker and an amateur singer-dancer, she started out as a teen model and at 16 won a contest for "The Prettiest Teenager in England." On the screen from the late 60s, she gained prominence following her success in the role of Lady Georgina Worsley in the TV series 'Upstairs Downstairs' (1976–77). In the 80s she got as much newsprint for her off-screen romances as she did for her movie roles. After breaking up with her boyfriend of ten years, Hollywood screenwriter Bruce Robinson, she married a penniless Argentine assistant director she had met on the Cairo location of *Sphinx* (1981). She divorced him to marry director William FRIEDKIN, but soon after the birth of their son divorced him amidst a nasty custody battle, then married cameraman Don Fauntleroy.

FILMS INCLUDE: *The Smashing Bird I Used to Know/House of Unclaimed Women, All the Right Noises* 1969; *Countess Dracula* 1970; *Assault/In the Devil's Garden* 1971; *Pope Joan* 1972; *Scalawag, From Beyond the Grave* 1973; *Brannigan* 1975; *The Pink Panther Strikes Again* 1976; *A Little Night Music* 1977; *The Betsy, The First Great Train Robbery/The Great Train Robbery* 1978; *Hanover Street* 1979; *Rough Cut* 1980; *Sphinx* 1981; *Nomads* 1986; *Scenes from the Goldmine* 1987; *Death Wish V: The Face of Death* 1994; *Birds of Prey* 1996.

Downey, Robert. American director. Born in June 1936. A high-school dropout, he joined the Army at age 16 and was discharged three years later. He later was a pitcher in semipro baseball, worked as a waiter, and began a modest acting career. His initial work in films was in 16 mm. He first drew critical recognition with his 1965 *Chafed Elbows,* which he turned out at the cost of only $25,000. The irreverent, absurd, almost insane humor characteristic of that film has also flavored his subsequent efforts. He is the father of actor Robert DOWNEY JR.

FILMS: *Babo 73* (also sc.) 1963; *Chafed Elbows* (also prod., sc.) 1965; *No More Excuses* (also sc., act.) 1968; *Putney Swope* (also sc.) 1969; *Pound* (also sc.) 1970; *You've Got to Walk It Like You Talk It or You Lose Your Beat* (act. only), *Is There Sex After Death?* (act. only) 1971; *Greaser's Palace* (also sc.) 1972; *Two Tons of Turquoise to Taos Tonight* (also sc.) 1976; *The Gong Show Movie* (co-sc. only), *Up the Academy* 1980; *America/This Is America—The Movie Not the Country* (also sc.) 1986; *Rented Lips* 1988; *Too Much Sun* (dir., sc.) 1991.

Downey, Robert, Jr. Actor. Born on Apr. 5, 1965, in New York City. The son of director Robert DOWNEY, he made his screen debut at age five in the dog-theme film, *Pound,* and later appeared in several other of his father's films. He spent much of his youth hopping from coast to coast. At 15, he moved to Los Angeles and attended Santa Monica High School. But he dropped out of the 11th grade and returned to New York, where he worked as a shoe salesman and as a busboy at a SoHo restaurant while auditioning for roles. In 1985–86 he was a regular on TV's 'Saturday Night Live,' a prelude to a hectic movie career that saw him appear in an amazing number of films of the late 80s, at first in juvenile support, then as an exuberant, uninhibited leading man, particularly adept at physical humor. He was nominated for an Academy Award for his performance in the title role in *Chaplin* (1992).

FILMS INCLUDE: *Pound* 1970; *Greaser's Palace* 1972; *Up the Academy* 1980; *Baby It's You* 1983; *Firstborn* 1984; *Tuff Turf, Weird Science, To Live and Die in L.A.* 1985; *Back to School, America* 1986; *The Pick-Up Artist, Less Than Zero* 1987; *Johnny Be Good, Rented Lips, 1969* 1988; *True Believer, That's Adequate, Chances Are* 1989; *Three of Hearts, Air America* 1990; *Too Much Sun, Soapdish* 1991; *Chaplin* 1992; *Heart and Souls* 1993; *Natural Born Killers, Only You* 1994; *Danger Zone, Home for the Holidays, Restoration, Richard III* 1995; *One Night Stand* 1997.

Downs, Cathy. Actress. *b.* 1924. *d.* 1976. Pleasant, outdoors-type leading lady of Hollywood films. A former model, she became a Fox contract player in 1944. She seemed destined for success when she played the title role in John Ford's *My Darling Clementine* (1946), but most of her subsequent roles were in lower-budget action pictures. She was married to actor Joe Kirkwood, the screen's Joe Palooka.

FILMS INCLUDE: *Diamond Horseshoe, State Fair, The Dolly Sisters* 1945; *The Dark Corner, Do You Love Me?, My Darling Clementine* 1946; *For You I Die, The Noose Hangs High, Panhandle* 1948; *Massacre River* 1949; *The Sundowners, Short Grass* 1950; *Triple Cross* 1951; *Gobs and Gals* 1952; *Bandits of the West* 1953; *The Phantom from 10,000 Leagues, She-Creature* 1956; *The Amazing Colossal Man* 1957; *Missile to the Moon* 1958.

Downs, Johnny. Actor, song-and-dance man. *b.* Oct. 10, 1913, in Brooklyn. N.Y. *d.* 1994. He entered films as a child and appeared in the "Our Gang" series and other comedy shorts as well as several silent features. After touring in vaudeville and appearing on Broadway in the early 30s, he returned to the screen as a juvenile lead in B musicals and light romantic films, often with a college setting. His film career slowing down in the mid-40s, he returned to Broadway, then performed in nightclubs and on TV.

FILMS INCLUDE: *Outlaws of Red River, Valley of the Giants* 1927; *The Trail of '98, The Crowd* 1928; *Babes in Toyland* (as Little Boy Blue) 1934; *College Scandal, The Virginia Judge, So Red the Rose, Coronado* 1935; *Everybody's Old Man, The First Baby, Pigskin Parade, College Holiday* 1936; *Turn Off the Moon, Blonde Trouble, Thrill of a Lifetime* 1937; *Hunted Men, Algiers, Hold That Co-Ed, Swing Sister Swing* 1938; *Parents on Trial, Hawaiian Nights, Laugh It Off* 1939; *A Child Is Born, I Can't Give You Anything but Love Baby, Sing Dance Plenty Hot, Melody and Moonlight, Slightly Tempted* 1940; *Honeymoon for Three, Adam Had Four Sons, Redhead, Sing Another Chorus, All American Co-Ed, Moonlight in Hawaii* 1941; *The Mad Monster, Behind the Eight Ball* 1942;

Adventures of the Flying Cadets (serial), *Campus Rhythm, Harvest Melody* 1943; *What a Man!, Trocadero* 1944; *Forever Yours, Rhapsody in Blue* 1945; *The Kid from Brooklyn* 1946; *Square Dance Jubilee* 1949; *Hills of Oklahoma* 1950; *Cruisin' Down the River* 1953.

downstage. The foreground, that portion of the set closest to the camera.

Drach, Michel. Director. *b.* Oct. 19, 1930, Paris. *d.* 1990, of lung cancer. He was a painter before entering French films in his late teens as an assistant to his cousin, director Jean-Pierre MELVILLE. At the age of 21 he established his own production company, Port Royal Films, through which he released three shorts he directed during the 50s. After several years as a TV director, he turned out his first feature film, *On n'enterre pas le Dimanche,* in 1959. The film was made on a tight budget and was technically flawed but was imbued with the sincere humanism that would characterize the director's later product. It won the Prix Delluc for that year. Drach went on to develop into one of the most respected directors of the new French cinema. In 1961 he married Marie-José NAT, leading lady of several of his films.

FILMS (as director and co-screenwriter): Shorts—*Les Soliloques du Pauvre/Le Revenant* 1951; *La Mer sera haute à 16 heures* 1954; *Auditorium* 1957. Features—*On n'enterre pas le Dimanche* 1959; *Amélie ou le Temps d'aimer* 1961; *Les Belles Conduites/La Bonne Occase* 1964; *Safari Diamants* 1965; *Elise ou la Vraie Vie* 1970; *Les Violons du Bal* 1974; *Parlez moi d'Amour* 1975; *Le Passé simple/Replay* 1977; *Le Pull-Over rouge* 1979; *Guy de Maupassant* 1982; *Il est Génial Papy* 1987.

Dragotti, Stan. Director. Born on Oct. 4, 1932, in New York City. *ed.* Cooper Union; School of Visual Arts. Starting out as a sketch artist, he was eventually promoted to art director at a large advertising agency. After some training as an actor, he began directing TV commercials, among them the award-winning "I Love New York" campaign. He directed his first feature in 1972, but his subsequent output has been sparse.

FEATURE FILMS: *Dirty Little Billy* (also co-prod., co-sc.) 1972; *Love at First Bite* 1979; *Mr. Mom* 1983; *The Man with One Red Shoe* 1985; *She's Out of Control* 1989; *Necessary Roughness* 1991.

Drake, Betsy. Actress. Born on Sept. 11, 1923, in Paris, to American parents. A former model, she played leads in a number of films beginning in 1948 and the following year married one of her co-stars, Cary GRANT. They later divorced. She has since directed a psychodrama therapy project at UCLA and authored a novel, *Children, You're Very Young* (1971), which derived from that experience.

FILMS: *Every Girl Should Be Married* 1948; *Dancing in the Dark* 1949; *Pretty Baby* 1950; *The Second Woman* 1951; *Room for One More* 1952; *Will Success Spoil Rock Hunter?* 1957; *Intent to Kill* (UK), *Next to No Time* (UK) 1958; *Clarence the Cross-Eyed Lion* 1965.

Drake, Dona. Actress. *b.* Rita Novella, 1920, in Mexico City. *d.* 1989. A small-framed, temperamental dynamo, she started out as a band vocalist under the name Rita Rio. In the 40s and early 50s she played fiery second leads, and occasional leads, in films of Paramount and other studios.

FILMS INCLUDE: *Aloma of the South Seas, Louisiana Purchase* 1941; *Road to Morocco, Star Spangled Rhythm* 1942; *Let's Face It* 1943; *Without Reservations, Dangerous Millions* 1946; *Another Part of the Forest* 1948; *The Girl from Jones Beach, The Doolins of Oklahoma* 1949; *Fortunes of Captain Blood* 1950; *Valentino* 1951; *Kansas City Confidential* 1953; *Princess of the Nile* 1954.

Drake, Frances. Actress. Born Frances Dean, on Oct. 22, 1908, in New York City. Educated in Canada and England, she began her career as a nightclub dancer in London, where she made both her stage and screen debuts under her real name in 1933. Returning to the US in 1934, she played leads in many Hollywood productions of the 30s, often as the terrified heroine of horror and mystery tales. She retired in 1939 after marrying a son of the 19th Earl of Suffolk.

FILMS INCLUDE: *The Jewel* (UK) 1933; *Two Hearts in Waltz Time* (UK), *Bolero, The Trumpet Blows, Ladies Should Listen, Forsaking All Others* 1934; *Transient Lady, Les Misérables, Mad Love* 1935; *The Invisible Ray, The Preview Murder Mystery, Florida Special, And Sudden Death, I'd Give My Life* 1936; *Midnight Taxi, Love Under Fire* 1937; *There's Always a Woman, The Lone Wolf in Paris* 1938; *It's a Wonderful World* 1939; *I Take This Woman* 1940; *The Affairs of Martha* 1942.

Drake, Tom. Actor. *b.* Alfred Alderdice, Aug. 5, 1918, Brooklyn, N.Y. *d.* 1982. Having made his stage debut in stock at 18 and the first of several Broadway appearances at 20, he made a tentative screen debut, billed as Richard Alden, in *The Howards of Virginia* (1940). Unable to secure more film roles, he returned to the stage, and it wasn't until 1944 that he reappeared on the screen as the clean-cut, mild-mannered young lead of MGM films. It was he who was on Judy Garland's mind when she sang 'The Boy Next Door' in *Meet Me in St. Louis,* and it was as a boy-next-door that he was typecast for much of his early career. But his bland style failed to sustain interest in the postwar years, and by the early 50s he was out of his MGM contract and into diminishing roles in mostly minor films. From the early 60s he was seen infrequently on the stage and in films and TV and to supplement his income worked as an automobile salesman. In 1976 he produced and directed a low-budget Canadian film, *The Keeper.*

FILMS INCLUDE: *The Howards of Virginia* 1940; *Two Girls and a Sailor, Maisie Goes to Reno, The White Cliffs of Dover, Mrs. Parkington, Meet Me in St. Louis* 1944; *This Man's Navy* 1945; *The Green Years, Courage of Lassie, Faithful in My Fashion* 1946; *I'll Be Yours, Cass Timberlane, The Beginning or the End* 1947; *Hills of Home, Words and Music* (as Richard Rodgers) 1948; *Mr. Belvedere Goes to College, Scene of the Crime* 1949; *FBI Girl* 1951; *Sangaree* 1953; *Sudden Danger* 1955; *Cyclops, Raintree County* 1957; *Warlock* 1959; *The Bramble Bush* 1960; *The Sandpiper* 1965; *The Singing Nun* 1966; *Red Tomahawk* 1967; *Warkill* 1968; *The Spectre of Edgar Allan Poe* 1973; *Savage Abduction* 1975; *The Keeper* (prod., dir. only; Can.) 1976.

drapes. Curtains or any pieces of cloth used for decorating a set or changing its acoustic quality.

DreamWorks SKG. For the first time in decades, this new motion picture studio was created by a triumvirate of arguably the most powerful and successful of Hollywood players of the latter part of this century: filmmaker Steven SPIELBERG; former Disney executive Jeffrey KATZENBERG; and music mogul David GEFFEN. With an announcement in the fall of 1995, DreamWorks SKG was formed with the intention of becoming a full-fledged studio/company representing all areas of entertainment, including animation. To date, the television offerings have been less than anticipated but much more is expected from the Hollywood "dream team" in the future.

Dreier, Hans. Art director. *b.* Aug. 21, 1885, Bremen, Germany. *d.* 1966. An architect, he worked in South Africa before entering German films in 1919. In 1923 he came to the US at the invitation of Paramount, later becoming the head of that studio's art department. Through the early 50s he designed hundreds of elegant sets, alone or in collaboration, for many of

Hollywood's most distinguished productions, notably on films of von Sternberg, Lubitsch, Mamoulian, King Vidor, and De Mille. He received Academy Awards for *Frenchman's Creek* (1944), *Samson and Delilah* (1949), and *Sunset Boulevard* (1950).

FILMS INCLUDE: *Danton/All for a Woman* (Ger.) 1921; *Forbidden Paradise* 1924; *Underworld* 1927; *The Last Command, The Dragnet, The Street of Sin, The Patriot, The Docks of New York* 1928; *The Case of Lena Smith, Betrayal, Thunderbolt* 1929; *The Love Parade, The Vagabond King, Morocco* 1930; *Dishonored, The Smiling Lieutenant, An American Tragedy* 1931; *Dr. Jekyll and Mr. Hyde, Shanghai Express, The Man I Killed/Broken Lullaby, One Hour with You, Love Me Tonight, Trouble in Paradise* 1932; *I'm No Angel, Song of Songs, Design for Living* 1933; *The Scarlet Empress, Death Takes a Holiday, Cleopatra* 1934; *The Devil Is a Woman, Ruggles of Red Gap, The Crusades, Lives of a Bengal Lancer* 1935; *Desire, The General Died at Dawn, The Texas Rangers* 1936; *The Plainsman, Make Way for Tomorrow, Wells Fargo, Maid of Salem, High Wide and Handsome, Angel* 1937; *Bluebeard's Eighth Wife, You and Me* 1938; *Dr. Cyclops, Union Pacific* 1939; *Typhoon, North West Mounted Police, Road to Singapore* 1940; *Hold Back the Dawn, I Wanted Wings* 1941; *The Major and the Minor, The Glass Key, Reap the Wild Wind, The Palm Beach Story* 1942; *For Whom the Bell Tolls* 1943; *The Story of Dr. Wassell, Lady in the Dark, Frenchman's Creek, Going My Way, Double Indemnity* 1944; *Hold That Blonde, The Unseen* 1945; *Blue Skies, The Virginian* 1946; *Unconquered, Road to Rio* 1947; *The Big Clock, Sorry Wrong Number, The Emperor Waltz, So Evil My Love* 1948; *The Great Gatsby, Samson and Delilah* 1949; *Sunset Boulevard* 1950; *A Place in the Sun* 1951.

Dreifuss, Arthur. Director. Born on Mar. 25, 1908, in Frankfurt am Main, Germany. A child prodigy conductor-pianist, he later became a choreographer and producer of stage musicals. In Hollywood from 1935 as a dance director, he began directing films early in the 40s. He has since turned out many low-budget pictures, some of which he also co-wrote and produced.

FILMS: *Mystery in Swing* 1940; *Reg'lar Fellers* 1941; *Baby Face Morgan, The Boss of Big Town, The Pay-Off* 1942; *Sarong Girl, Melody Parade, Campus Rhythm, Nearly Eighteen* 1943; *The Sultan's Daughter, Ever Since Venus* (also co-sc.) 1944; *Eadie Was a Lady, Boston Blackie Booked on Suspicion, Boston Blackie's Rendezvous, The Gay Senorita, Prison Ship* 1945; *Junior Prom, Freddie Steps Out, High School Hero* (also co-sc.) 1946; *Vacation Days, Betty Co-Ed* (also co-sc.), *Little Miss Broadway* (also co-sc.), *Two Blondes and a Redhead, Sweet Genevieve* (also co-sc.) 1947; *Glamour Girl, Mary Lou, I Surrender Dear* 1948; *An Old-Fashioned Girl* (also prod., co-sc.), *Manhattan Angel, Shamrock Hill* (also prod.) 1949; *There's a Girl in My Heart* (also prod., songs) 1950; *Life Begins at 17* 1958; *The Last Blitzkrieg, Juke Box Rhythm* 1959; *The Quare Fellow* (also story, co-sc.; UK/Ire.) 1962; *Riot on Sunset Strip, The Love-Ins* (also co-sc.) 1967; *For Singles Only* (also co-sc.), *A Time to Sing, The Young Runaways* 1968.

dress. To add props to a set to enhance its décor.

Dresser, Louise. Actress. *b.* Louise Kerlin, Oct. 5, 1878, Evansville, Ind. *d.* 1965. A veteran of vaudeville and Broadway musicals, she played strong character leads and supporting parts, typically stern and dramatic, in both silent and sound Hollywood films, memorably as Catherine the Great (opposite Rudolph Valentino) in *The Eagle* (1925), as Al Jolson's loving mother in *Mammy* (1930), and as Will Rogers's co-star in a number of films. After her retirement in 1937, she devoted her time to Hollywood's Motion Picture Country House and Hospital, where she died at 86.

FILMS INCLUDE: *The Glory of Clementine, Enter Madame* 1922; *Prodigal Daughters, The Fog, Ruggles of Red Gap, To the Ladies* 1923; *The Next Corner, The City That Never Sleeps* 1924; *Enticement, Percy, The Eagle* (as Catherine the Great), *The Goose Woman* (title role) 1925; *Fifth Avenue, The Blind Goddess, Broken Hearts of Hollywood, Padlocked, Gigolo* 1926; *The Third Degree, Mr. Wu, White Flannels* 1927; *The Garden of Eden, A Ship Comes In, The Air Circus, Mother Knows Best* (title role) 1928; *Not Quite Decent, The Madonna of Avenue A* 1929; *Mammy* (title role), *The 3 Sisters, Lightnin'* 1930; *Caught* 1931; *Stepping Sisters* 1932; *State Fair, Doctor Bull, Cradle Song* 1933; *David Harum, The World Moves On, The Scarlet Empress* (as Empress Elizabeth), *Servants' Entrance, A Girl of the Limberlost* 1934; *The County Chairman* 1935; *Maid of Salem* 1937.

Dressler, Marie. Actress. *b.* Leila Marie Koerber, Nov. 9, 1869, Coburg, Canada. *d.* 1934. The daughter of a music teacher, she joined a stock company at 14 and by the time she was 20 had become a seasoned veteran in light opera and on the legitimate stage. She made it to Broadway in 1892 and became a vaudeville headliner shortly after the turn of the century. One of the nations' leading comediennes, she made her screen debut as Charlie Chaplin's costar in *Tillie's Punctured Romance* (1914), an adaptation of one of her stage vehicles. She also appeared in several other film comedies of the period but remained essentially a vaudeville and musical comedy star. Her stage career suffered a severe setback in the 20s, largely because of her activity in a labor dispute, but in 1927 MGM screenwriter Frances MARION got her back into films.

She quickly developed into a popular star, especially in comedies co-starring Polly MORAN. Her popularity increased after the advent of sound, and her screen career received an enormous boost from her surprise casting in a serious character part, as Marthy, the waterfront hag, in *Anna Christie* (1930). She won the best actress Academy Award for her tragicomic performance that same year in *Min and Bill,* opposite Wallace Beery. A homely woman of enormous girth, she was unlikely star material, but in the early 30s she was among Hollywood's most popular personalities and for four years was the number one box-office attraction in the country. Her autobiography was candidly titled *The Life Story of an Ugly Duckling.*

FILMS: *Tillie's Punctured Romance* 1914; *Tillie's Tomato Surprise* 1915; *Tillie Wakes Up, The Scrublady* 1917; *The Cross Red Nurse, The Agonies of Agnes* 1918; *The Callahans and the Murphys, The Joy Girl, Breakfast at Sunrise* 1927; *Bringing Up Father, The Patsy* 1928; *The Divine Lady, The Hollywood Revue, The Vagabond Lover* 1929; *Chasing Rainbows, Anna Christie, The Girl Said No, One Romantic Night, Caught Short, Let Us Be Gay, Min and Bill* 1930; *Reducing, Politics* 1931; *Emma, Prosperity* 1932; *Tugboat Annie, Dinner at Eight, Christopher Bean* 1933.

Drew, Ellen. Actress. Born Terry Ray, on Nov. 23, 1915, in Kansas City, Mo. A barber's daughter, she worked as a salesgirl and elevator operator before winning a local beauty contest and deciding to try her luck in Hollywood. Making her bid in 1936, she played bit roles, under her real name, in some two dozen films. As Ellen Drew since 1938, she played vivacious leads in many films through the 50s. Her second (1941–50) of four husbands was screenwriter Sy BARTLETT.

FILMS INCLUDE: *College Holiday, Hollywood Boulevard, Rhythm on the Range* 1936; *Make Way for Tomorrow* 1937; *The Buccaneer, Bluebeard's Eighth Wife, Sing You Sinners, If I Were King* 1938; *The Lady's from Kentucky, The Gracie Allen Murder*

Case 1939; *Geronimo, Buck Benny Rides Again, French Without Tears, Women Without Names, Christmas in July* 1940; *The Mad Doctor, The Monster and the Girl, Reaching for the Sun, The Parson of Panamint, Our Wife, The Night of January 16th* 1941; *The Remarkable Andrew, My Favorite Spy* 1942; *Night Plane from Chungking* 1943; *The Imposter* 1944; *China Sky, Isle of the Dead, Man Alive* 1945; *Johnny O'Clock, The Swordsman* 1947; *Man from Colorado* 1948; *The Crooked Way* 1949; *Davy Crockett Indian Scout, The Baron of Arizona, Cargo to Capetown, Stars in My Crown* 1950; *The Great Missouri Raid, Man in the Saddle* 1951; *Outlaw's Son* 1957.

Dreyer, Carl Theodor. Director. *b.* Feb. 3, 1889, Copenhagen. *d.* 1968. The illegitimate son of a Swedish farmer and his housekeeper, he spent his early months in Danish foster homes and after his mother's death, in 1891, was adopted by a newspaper typographer's strict Lutheran family, in an emotionally arid environment. In 1912 he began writing his own column and at the same time entered films as a title writer for the Nordisk company. Gradually he moved on to the writing of scripts and to occasional editing assignments, and by 1918 he felt secure enough in his knowledge of picture making to begin directing his first film, *The President,* completed in 1919. Dreyer's directorial debut hardly held much promise for the film career of a man later to be recognized as the greatest creative talent in the history of Danish cinema.

Dreyer's second film, *Leaves from Satan's Book,* was much more ambitious and even more pretentious in its attempt to emulate the multi-episode construction of Griffith's *Intolerance.* But some of the carefully constructed scenes, especially in the Spanish Inquisition episode, already contained the pictorial vision that was to make *The Passion of Joan of Arc* and *Day of Wrath* such highly acclaimed masterpieces. The shaky economic state of the Danish film industry forced Dreyer to seek assignments abroad and, with few exceptions, he was to make his subsequent films in Norway, Sweden, France, and Germany. But no matter where he directed, he found himself in constant conflict with producers and backers. They regarded him as an obstinate artist, and a costly one, because of his fanatic attention to detail and atmosphere.

Dreyer's fascination with human psychology and the complexities of the conscious and subconscious mind became evident in his third film, *The Parson's Widow* (also known as *The Witch Woman* or *The Fourth Marriage of Dame Margaret*), a lusty, ribald tale filmed in Norway with Swedish funds. It was even more apparent in *Mikael* (also variously known as *Chained, Heart's Desire,* or *The Story of the Third Sex*), the study of a man (played by director Benjamin Christensen) tormented by his homosexual tendencies. It was in France that Dreyer directed his first masterpiece, *The Passion of Joan of Arc,* a powerful if sometimes flawed drama of the last day of Joan's life, noted for its tapestry-like visual textures, the force of its frequent close-ups, and the superior performance of Renée Falconetti in her only film role. The film, which took a year and a half to complete and whose elaborate sets were constructed at great cost, was a huge critical success but a commercial disaster.

Dreyer next became involved in a dispute with his French producers over another project and sued them for breach of contract. He eventually won the case, but not before he had to endure several years of inactivity. Five years passed before he made his next film, *Vampyr (Vampire,* subtitled *The Strange Adventures of Allan Gray* and also known as *Castle of Doom*). The film, which he produced independently in partnership with a rich Dutch baron, is an eerie excursion into a twilight zone between reality and dream, a world of the mind in which nothing is definite and little is clear. The sparse dialogue in this, his first sound film, was postsynchronized in three language versions, German, English, and French. *Vampire,* as was to be expected, was another financial flop. The double-edged commercial failure and critical snub resulted in a decade of cinematic inactivity for Dreyer. It wasn't until 1942 that he made a tentative comeback in films, with a documentary short about mothers for the Danish government. The following year, at the height of the Nazi occupation of Denmark, he directed the film for which he is probably known best, the slow, ponderous, monumental drama of witchhunt, faith, and human passion, *Day of Wrath.*

Fearing persecution by the Nazi authorities because of the allusions of *Day of Wrath* to the tyranny of the Occupation, Dreyer fled to Sweden, where he remained for the rest of the war years and where he directed the rather banal two-character drama *Two People.* He returned to Denmark after the war but was unable to find a sponsor for a feature film for another ten years and instead devoted his energies to documentary shorts, mostly for the Danish government. In 1952, in recognition of his achievements, that government leased to Dreyer the Dagmar Bio, Copenhagen's most luxurious motion picture theater, thus assuring him a comfortable living as a theater manager and freedom from financial worries. But the director wasn't ready to retire on his laurels. He still had two masterpieces in him, made over a ten-year span, *Ordet/The Word* and *Gertrud.* Several important projects remained unrealized at the time of his death.

It is perhaps unfortunate that the impression most film goers have of Dreyer's work is derived from familiarity with only one of his films, *Day of Wrath.* It is undoubtedly one of Dreyer's most important films, but its deliberate, ponderous pace creates a somewhat misleading image of him as a gloomy, heavy-handed director whose work might test the patience of even the most dedicated film-society audience, a view not substantiated by some of his lesser-known films.

The credits below do not include features or shorts for which Dreyer wrote screenplays but which he did not himself direct.

FILMS (as director-writer): *The President* 1919; *Leaves from Satan's Book, The Parson's Widow/The Witch Woman/The Fourth Marriage of Dame Margaret* 1920; *Love One Another, Once Upon a Time* 1922; *Mikael/Chained* (Ger.) 1924; *Master of the House, The Bride of Glomdal* 1925; *La Passion de Jeanne d'Arc/The Passion of Joan of Arc* (Fr.) 1928; *Vampyr/Vampire/ The Strange Adventure of Allan Gray/Castle of Doom* 1932; *Help for Mothers/Good Mothers* (short) 1942; *Vredens Dag/Day of Wrath* 1943; *Two People* 1945; *Water from the Land* (short) 1946; *The Danish Village Church* (short), *The Struggle Against Cancer* (short) 1947; *They Caught the Ferry* (short) 1948; *Thorvalden* (short) 1949; *The Storstrom Bridge* (short) 1950; *The Castle Within a Castle* (short), *Ordet/The Word* 1955; *Gertrud* 1964.

Dreyfuss, Richard. Actor. Born on Oct. 29, 1947, in Brooklyn, N.Y. Leading character star of Hollywood films of the 70s. An attorney's son, he spent his early childhood in Brooklyn and in Bayside, Queens, moving at nine with his family to Los Angeles, where he began his acting career at the Beverly Hills Jewish Center. He studied for a year at the San Fernando Valley State College, then, as a conscientious objector, spent the next two years in alternate service, as a clerk at a Los Angeles hospital. In the late 60s and early 70s he commuted from coast to coast, doing Broadway, off Broadway, repertory, and improvisational comedy, as well as guest appearances on television. He made his film debut as a supporting player in

1968, but it was not until 1973 that he rose to prominence with a solid portrayal of Baby Face Nelson in a B picture, *Dillinger,* and with a sensitively etched lead role as an ambivalent college-bound boy in *American Graffiti.* He drew further attention and praise the following year for his intense and intelligent portrait of an aggressive youth in Montreal's Jewish ghetto in the Canadian film *The Apprenticeship of Duddy Kravitz,* and attained box-office viability with two commercial blockbusters, *Jaws* (1975) and *Close Encounters of the Third Kind* (1977). He played his first romantic lead in *The Goodbye Girl* (1977), for which he won an Academy Award as best actor. Compact and typically projecting an air of egocentric cockiness, Dreyfuss has relied on intelligence, energy, and personal integrity, rather than looks and charisma, to gain his place among the leading personalities of the American screen in the 70s. Personal problems, including a serious accident and temporary involvement with drugs, set back Dreyfuss's career in the early 80s. But later in the decade he made a terrific comeback in *Down and Out in Beverly Hills* and *Tin Men,* and in 1995 earned another Oscar nomination as best actor for the title role in *Mr. Holland's Opus.*

FILMS: *Valley of the Dolls* (bit), *The Graduate* (bit) 1967; *The Young Runaways* 1968; *Hello Down There* 1969; *Dillinger* (as Baby Face Nelson), *American Graffiti* 1973; *The Apprenticeship of Duddy Kravitz* (Can.), *The Second Coming of Suzanne* 1974; *Jaws* 1975; *Inserts, Victory at Entebbe* (TV movie) 1976; *Close Encounters of the Third Kind, The Goodbye Girl* 1977; *The Big Fix* (also co-prod.) 1978; *The Competition* 1980; *Whose Life Is It Anyway?* 1981; *The Buddy System* 1984; *Down and Out in Beverly Hills, Stand by Me* 1986; *Tin Men, Stakeout, Nuts* 1987; *Moon Over Parador* 1988; *Let It Ride, Always* 1989; *Postcards from the Edge* 1990; *Once Around, Rosencrantz and Guildenstern Are Dead, What About Bob?* 1991; *Lost in Yonkers, Another Stakeout* 1993; *Silent Fall* 1994; *The American President, Mr. Holland's Opus* 1995; *James and the Giant Peach* (voice only), *Mad Dog Time* 1996; *Night Falls on Manhattan* 1997.

Driscoll, Bobby. Actor. *b.* May 3, 1937, Cedar Rapids, Iowa. *d.* 1968. Child star of Hollywood films of the 40s and early 50s, memorable in several Disney productions and as the boy who witnesses a murder in Ted Tezlaff's thriller *The Window* (1949), following which he won a special Academy Award as "the outstanding juvenile actor of 1949." He was the first "live" actor to sign a long-term contract with Disney's animation studios, where he starred in such popular productions as *Song of the South* (1946), *So Dear to My Heart* (1948), and *Treasure Island* (1950). His career faltered, however, when he reached his teens, and he was unable to obtain work in films or on TV except on scattered occasions. Unable to adjust to the new conditions, he became a drug addict and was arrested several times for various offenses. In 1965 he moved to New York City, where three years later his body was found in the rubble of an abandoned tenement, the victim of a heart attack. He was buried in a pauper's grave. It was not until 1969, a full year after the burial, that, through fingerprints, the body was identified as that of Driscoll.

FILMS: *Lost Angel* 1943; *The Sullivans, Sunday Dinner for a Soldier* 1944; *The Big Bonanza, Identity Unknown* 1945; *From This Day Forward, Miss Susie Slagle's, So Goes My Love, OSS, Song of the South* 1946; *If You Knew Susie, Melody Time* 1948; *So Dear to My Heart, The Window* 1949; *Treasure Island* (as Jim Hawkins) 1950; *When I Grow Up* 1951; *The Happy Time* 1952; *Peter Pan* (voice only) 1953; *The Scarlet Coat* 1955; *The Party Crashers* 1958.

Driver, Minnie. Actress. Born in 1970. Charming, spirited ingenue of the silver screen. This talented young actress endeared herself to audiences on both sides of the Atlantic as the plump, awkward teen in *Circle of Friends* (1995), and gained the attention of critics and Hollywood.

FILMS: *Circle of Friends* (Ire./US), *Golden Eye* 1995; *Big Night, Sleepers* 1996; *The Flood, Grosse-Point Blank* 1997.

drive-in. An open-air motion picture theater into which audiences drive in their cars. The film is projected onto a large screen and viewed from the vehicle. Small individual speakers are attached to each car, as well as heaters in cold weather. From their introduction in 1933 through the 1950s, drive-ins were extremely popular in the United States, especially in rural areas; in 1958, there were 4000 drive-ins across the country. Their typical audience was composed of families with children, who were spared the problem of baby-sitting by taking the whole family out at a reduced cost (charges are per car plus a nominal fee per person), and teenage couples, who could see a film while enjoying privacy. Many drive-in theaters switched in the late 60s from the traditional family picture to sexploitation films. This brought about an indignant reaction in some communities, not so much to the program itself but to the showing of erotic material that might be seen by unwilling passersby from the highway. The change in programming, combined with the advent of the VCR, contributed to the demise of the drive-in. As of 1992, there were fewer than 1000 drive-ins in operation in the US.

Dru, Joanne. Actress. *b.* Joanne LaCock, on Jan. 31, 1923, in Logan, W. Va. *d.* 1996. A former model and showgirl, she made her film debut in 1946. She played leads in a variety of films of the 40s and 50s but is best remembered as the feminine touch in such male-centered Western classics as Howard Hawks's *Red River* (1948) and John Ford's *She Wore a Yellow Ribbon* (1949) and *Wagonmaster* (1950). Her first two husbands were screen actors Dick HAYMES (1941–49) and John IRELAND (1949–56). She is the sister of TV host Peter Marshall (LaCock), who appeared in several films.

FILMS INCLUDE: *Abie's Irish Rose* 1946; *Red River* 1948; *All the King's Men, She Wore a Yellow Ribbon* 1949; *Wagonmaster, 711 Ocean Drive* 1950; *Vengeance Valley, Mr. Belvedere Rings the Bell* 1951; *Return of the Texan, The Pride of St. Louis, My Pal Gus* 1952; *Thunder Bay, Outlaw Territory* 1953; *Forbidden, The Siege at Red River, Three Ring Circus* 1954; *The Warriors, Sincerely Yours* 1955; *Hell on Frisco Bay* 1956; *Durango* 1957; *The Light in the Forest* 1958; *The Wild and the Innocent* 1959; *September Storm* 1960; *Sylvia* 1965; *Super Snooper/Super Fuzz* (It./US) 1980.

dry run. A full rehearsal during which actors go through their moves and speak their lines with the cameras not running. Often the cameras and their crews are also present and go through their motions as if they were filming.

duarc. A double-arc unfocused lamp used for filler light in color photography.

Duarte, Eva. See PERÓN, Eva.

dubbing. 1. Sound mixing; the combining of several sound tracks (dialogue, music, sound effects, etc.) into one master recording that eventually becomes the sound track of a motion picture film. 2. A process of sound recording in which a voice, which may or may not be that of the actor appearing on the screen, is synchronized with the lip movement of the film actor. Dubbing is most often used in the making of foreign-language versions of a film, but sometimes dialogue in the original language is dubbed. The Italian film industry is notorious for dubbing most dialoguc lines in the sound studio after the film production is completed.

Dubois, Marie. Actress. Born on Jan. 12, 1937, in Paris. Leading lady and second lead of the French stage, TV, and films. A charming blonde, she has been a favorite interpreter of directors of the French New Wave as well as of those of the traditional old school.

FILMS INCLUDE: *Le Signe du Lion/The Sign of Leo* 1959; *Tirez sur le Pianiste/Shoot the Piano Player* 1960; *Une Femme est une Femme/A Woman Is a Woman, Jules et Jim/Jules and Jim* 1961; *La Croix des Vivants/Cross of the Living* 1962; *La Chasse à l'Homme/Male Hunt, La Ronde/Circle of Love, Week-end à Zuydcoote/Weekend at Dunkirk* 1964; *Les Grandes Gueules/Wise Guys, Les Fêtes galantes* 1965; *La Grande Vadrouille/Don't Look Now* 1966; *Le Voleur/The Thief of Paris* 1967; *Ce Sacré Grand-Père/The Marriage Came Tumbling Down, Le Rouble à Deux Faces/The Day the Hot Line Got Hot, Stuntman* (It./Fr.) 1968; *Monte Carlo or Bust/Those Daring Young Men in Their Jaunty Jalopies* (UK/Fr./It.) 1969; *La Maison des Bories* 1970; *L'Oeuf* 1971; *Les Arpenteurs* (Switz.) 1972; *Le Serpent/The Serpent, L'Escapade* (Switz.) 1973; *Vincent François Paul et les autres/Vincent Francois Paul and the Others* 1975; *Les Mal Partis, Du bout du Lèvres, Nuit d'Or, L'Innocente/The Innocent* 1976; *La Menace* 1977; *Mon Oncle d'Amérique, La Petite Sirène* 1980.

Duchamp, Marcel. Painter, sculptor, avant-garde filmmaker. *b.* 1887, Blainville, France. *d.* 1968. This unorthodox artist whose work influenced cubism, Dadaism, and futurism early in the century dabbled in abstract cinema as an extension of his experimentation in art. He directed *Anemic Cinema* (1925) and *Abstract* (1927) and collaborated on the scripts of several avant-garde films. He also appeared in René Clair's *Entr'acte* (1924), in which he was seen pursuing his greatest passion, playing chess.

Dudley Ward, Penelope. Actress. *b.* Aug. 4, 1914, London. *d.* 1982. Refined, charming brunette leading lady of some major British films of the late 30s and early 40s. Also on the stage. She retired from acting following her 1948 marriage to director Carol REED.

FEATURE FILMS: *Escape Me Never, Moscow Nights/I Stand Condemned* 1935; *The Citadel* 1938; *Hell's Cargo/Dangerous Cargo* 1939; *Convoy, The Case of the Frightened Lady/The Frightened Lady* 1940; *Major Barbara* 1941; *In Which We Serve* 1942; *The Demi-Paradise/Adventure for Two* 1943; *The Way Ahead/Immortal Battalion, English Without Tears/Her Man Gilbey* 1944.

Dudow, Slatan. Director. *b.* Jan. 30, 1903, Zaribrod, Bulgaria. *d.* 1963. The son of a railway worker, he joined a revolutionary group at 17 and participated in street fighting with Bulgarian police, which was precipitated by a Moscow-inspired strike in Sofia, went to Berlin in 1922 to study architecture and became involved instead in the theater and politics. He studied directing at the Berlin University and organized a workers' theater. In 1929 he went to Moscow to research a thesis on the Soviet theater and in the following year directed his first film, the documentary *Wie der Berliner Arbeiter wohnt* ("How the Berlin Worker Lives"). He is best known for his second film, *Kühle Wampe* (1932), a radical, Communist-inspired depiction of social and economic conditions in Germany, based on a screenplay by Bertolt BRECHT and Ernest Ottwald. The film caused much controversy and was banned in Germany for "insulting Hindenburg and religion." A member of the German Communist party, Dudow was forced to flee to France, then settled in Switzerland, where he spent the WW II years writing in obscurity. After the war he returned to East Germany and resumed his directorial career, winning the state award three times. He was killed in a car accident, leaving a film unfinished. He had collaborated on the scripts of most of his films.

FILMS: *Wie der Berliner Arbeiter wohnt* (doc.) 1930; *Kühle Wampe/Whither Germany?/To Whom Does the World Belong?* 1932; *Bulles de Savon/Seifenblasen/Soap Bubbles* (experimental short; Fr.) 1934; *Unser Tägliche Brot/Our Daily Bread* 1949; *Familie Benthin* (co-dir. with Kurt Matzig 1950); *Frauenschicksale* 1952; *Stärker als die Nacht* 1954; *Der Hauptmann von Köln* 1956; *Verwirrung der Liebe* 1958; *Christine* (unfinished) 1963.

Duff, Howard. Actor. *b.* Nov. 24, 1913, Bremerton, Wash. *d.* 1990. Gritty leading man and character player of the American screen. After drama studies and an apprenticeship with the Seattle Repertory Playhouse, he made his name on radio as the original Sam Spade. Following WW II service with the Army, he made his film debut in 1947. After supporting roles in several major films, he began playing leads in B pictures, mostly of the action genre. Typically cast as a tough hero, often a cop. In 1951, he married one of his co-stars, Ida LUPINO, who in the late 50s also appeared with him in the TV series 'Mr. Adams and Eve' (1957–58). They divorced in 1973. He later starred in the TV series 'Dante' (1960–61) and 'Felony Squad' (1966–69). Gradually reduced to supporting roles, he appeared in numerous TV movies and series episodes of the 70s and 80s, and was a regular on the series 'Flamingo Road' (1981–82) and 'Knots Landing' (1984–85). After a decade-long absence, he returned sporadically to feature films in the late 70s, in solid character parts.

FILMS INCLUDE: *Brute Force* 1947; *The Naked City, All My Sons* 1948; *Red Canyon, Calamity Jane and Sam Bass, Illegal Entry, Johnny Stool Pigeon* 1949; *Woman in Hiding, Shakedown, Spy Hunt* 1950; *The Lady from Texas/Steel Town* 1951; *Models Inc.* 1952; *Roar of the Crowd* 1953; *Private Hell 36, Tanganyika* 1954; *Women's Prison* 1955; *Broken Star, Flame of the Islands, While the City Sleeps* 1956; *Boys' Night Out* 1962; *Panic in the City* 1968; *The Late Show* 1977; *A Wedding* 1978; *Kramer vs. Kramer* 1979; *Double Negative* (Can.), *Oh God!: Book II* 1980; *Monster in the Closet* 1986; *No Way Out* 1987.

Duigan, John. Director born in Australia. Known for his thoughtful explorations of young people coming of age (*The Year My Voice Broke, Flirting*) as well as his unsentimental film biography of martyred activist clergyman Archbishop Oscar Romero (*Romero*).

FILMS INCLUDE: *The Trespassers* (also prod. and sc.) 1976; *Mouth to Mouth* (also prod. and sc.) 1978; *Dimboola* 1979; *The Year My Voice Broke* (also sc.) 1988; *Romero* 1989; *Flirting* (also sc.) 1992; *Wide Sargasso Sea* (also co-sc.) 1993; *Sirens* 1994.

Dukakis, Olympia. Actress. Born on June 20, 1931, in Lowell, Mass., the daughter of Greek immigrants. A fencing champion and a theater fanatic during her studies at Boston University (B.A., M.F.A.), she was among the founders of the Charles Playhouse in Boston. In the early 60s, she began performing on the New York stage, off and on Broadway, and later taught drama at NYU and Yale. On the screen in character roles sporadically, and at times reluctantly, from 1964, she kept a relatively low profile before winning an Academy Award for her performance in *Moonstruck* (1987). With her husband, actor Louis Zorich, she founded the Whole Theatre company in Montclair, New Jersey, where she acted and directed when not engaged for outside assignments. The company closed for financial reasons in 1990. She is a first cousin of Michael Dukakis, the former Governor of Massachusetts and the Democratic candidate for the US Presidency in the 1988 elections.

FILMS: *Twice a Man* (experimental) 1963; *Lilith* 1964; *John and Mary* 1969; *Made for Each Other* 1971; *The Rehearsal, Death Wish* 1974; *The Wanderers, Rich Kids* 1979; *The Idolmaker* 1980; *National Lampoon Goes to the Movies/National Lampoon's Movie Madness* 1981; *Flanagan* 1985;

Moonstruck 1987; *Working Girl* 1988; *Look Who's Talking, Dad, Steel Magnolias* 1989; *In the Spirit, Look Who's Talking Too* 1990; *Ruby Cairo* 1991; *The Cemetery Club, Over the Hill* 1992; *Look Who's Talking Now* 1993; *Digger, I Love Trouble* 1994; *Jeffrey, Mighty Aphrodite, Jerusalem, Mr. Holland's Opus* 1995.

Duke, Bill. Actor, director. Born on Feb. 26, 1943, in Poughkeepsie, N.Y. *ed.* Boston Univ., NYU Sch. of the Arts. Multitalented character actor known for his work in action movies. The movies he has directed have been praised for their performances and the ways the films break with conventional cinematic structures. He is also a writer of children's literature and a member of the board of directors for the American Film Institute.

FILMS INCLUDE (as actor): *Car Wash* 1976; *American Gigolo* 1980; *Commando* 1985; *Predator, No Man's Land* 1987; *Action Jackson* 1988; *Bird on a Wire* 1990; *Street of No Return* (US/Fr./Port.), *A Rage in Harlem* (dir. only) 1991; *The Cemetery Club* (dir. only), *Deep Cover* (dir. only) 1992; *Sister Act II: Back in the Habit* (act., dir.) 1993; *Hoodlum* 1997.

Duke, Patty. Actress. Born Anna Marie Duke, on Dec. 14, 1946, in Elmhurst, N.Y. *ed.* Quintano School for Young Professionals, N.Y.C. A professional actress at seven, she had two films, some 50 TV shows, and many stage appearances behind her by the time she zoomed to stardom on Broadway before her 13th birthday as the young Helen Keller in 'The Miracle Worker' (1959). She repeated the role for the 1962 film version, winning an Academy Award for best supporting actress, the youngest person ever to receive this award at the time. Later in the 60s she gained popularity with 'The Patty Duke Show' comedy series (1963–66) on TV and subsequently appeared in numerous TV movies and segments of series, winning three Emmy Awards in the process. But her feature film career as an adult has been far less fulfilling. A product of a broken home, she has had a turbulent personal life. Having divorced director Harry Falk, Jr., and rock promoter Michael Tell, she married actor John Astin in 1972 and for a decade was billed as Patty Duke Astin. After their divorce in the early 80s, she remarried and reclaimed her original billing. In 1985–88 she served as president of the Screen Actors Guild. Author: *Surviving Sexual Assault* (1983); *Call Me Anna* (1987).

FILMS: *I'll Cry Tomorrow* (extra) 1955; *Somebody Up There Likes Me* (extra) 1956; *Country Music Holiday, The Goddess* 1958; *4-D Man, Happy Anniversary* 1959; *The Miracle Worker* 1962; *Billie* 1965; *The Daydreamer* 1966; *Valley of the Dolls* 1967; *Me Natalie* 1969; *You'll Like My Mother* 1972; *The Swarm* 1978; *By Design* (Can.) 1981; *Willy Milly/Something Special/I Was a Teenage Boy* 1986; *Prelude to a Kiss* 1992.

Dulac, Germaine. Director. *b.* Charlotte-Elisabeth-Germaine Saisset-Schneider. Nov. 17, 1882, Amiens, France. *d.* 1942. The daughter of a cavalry captain, she was raised by a grandmother in Paris, where she studied various forms of art with an emphasis on music and the opera. In 1905 she married engineer-novelist Marie-Louis Albert-Dulac (they divorced in 1920) and under his influence veered toward journalism. As one of the leading radical feminists of her day, she was editor of *La Française,* the organ of the French suffragette movement. She also doubled as theater and cinema critic of the publication and became increasingly enamored with film as an art form. In 1915 she formed, with her husband, a small production company, Delia Film, and began directing highly inventive, small-budget pictures. Chronologically, she was the second woman director in French films, after Alice Guy-Blaché, a contemporary of Méliès.

Dulac, who had been strongly influenced by American films, visited the US in 1921, met with D.W. GRIFFITH, and was duly impressed by the filming techniques and organizational methods of the emerging studio system. With *La Fête Espagnole* and her masterpiece, *La Souriante Madame Beudet,* Dulac emerged as a leading figure in the impressionist movement in French films.

In the late 20s, she was an important part of the "second avant-garde" of the French cinema with the surrealistic *La Coquille et le Clergyman* and a number of other experimental films. In these as well as in her theoretical writing, her goal was "pure" cinema, free from any influence from literature, the stage, or even the other visual arts. She talked of "musically constructed" films, or "films made according to the rules of visual music." The latter film, insightfully depicting the plight and state of mind of an unhappy housewife, has been called by some the first truly feminist film ever made and one of the finest examples of psychological drama in silent cinema.

Dulac was also instrumental in the development of cinema clubs throughout France in the mid-20s. Sound put an end to her experimentations and her career as a director. From 1930 until her death she was in charge of newsreel production at Pathé, then at Gaumont.

FILMS: *Les Soeurs Ennemies* 1916; *Géo le Mystérieux Vénus Victrix ou dans l'Ouragan de la Vie* 1917; *Ames de Fous* (serial; also sc.), *Le Bonheur des Autres* 1918; *La Fête espagnole, La Cigarette* (also co-sc.) 1919; *Malencontre* 1920; *La Belle Dame sans Merci* 1921; *La Mort du Soleil, Werther* (unfinished) 1922; *La Souriante Madame Beudet, Gossette* (serial) 1923; *Le Diable dans la Ville* 1924; *Ame d'Artiste* (also co-sc.), *La Folie des Vaillants* 1925; *Antoinette Sabrier* 1926; *La Coquille et le Clergyman, L'Invitation au Voyage, Le Cinéma au Service de l'Histoire* (compilation film) 1927; *La Princesse Mandane, Disque 927* (abstract film), *Thèmes et Variations* (abstract film), *Germination d'un Haricot* (doc.) 1928; *Etude Cinégraphique sur une Arabesque* 1929.

Dullea, Keir. Actor. Born on May 30, 1936, in Cleveland. He was raised in New York's Greenwich Village, where his parents ran a bookstore, and after attending Rutgers University and San Francisco State College began acting in stock and with various repertory companies. He made his New York debut in 1956, in the revue 'Sticks and Stones,' and after appearing off Broadway in 1959 in 'Season of Choice' made an impressive film debut as a disturbed juvenile delinquent in *The Hoodlum Priest* (1961). He played another disturbed youth in *David and Lisa* (1963), a role for which he won the best actor award at the San Francisco Film Festival. He went on to portray a number of intense, sensitive young men in other films and was memorable in the lead in *2001: A Space Odyssey* (1968). In 1970 he made his Broadway debut in 'Butterflies Are Free.' But on the screen his misses outnumbered his hits in the 70s and 80s.

FILMS: *The Hoodlum Priest* 1961; *David and Lisa* 1963; *Le Ore nude/The Naked Hours* (It.), *Mail Order Bride, The Thin Red Line* 1964; *Bunny Lake Is Missing* 1965; *Madame X* 1966; *The Fox, 2001: A Space Odyssey* 1968; *De Sade* (title role) 1969; *Pope Joan* 1972; *Il Diavolo nel Cervello* (It./Fr.), *Paperback Hero* (UK/Can.) 1973; *Paul and Michelle* (UK/Fr.), *Black Christmas/Silent Night Holy Night* (UK) 1974; *Full Circle/The Haunting of Julia* (UK/Can.) 1976; *Welcome to Blood City* (UK/Can.) 1977; *Leopard in the Snow* (UK/Can.), *Because He's My Friend* (Austral.) 1978; *Brainwaves* 1982; *The Next One, Blind Date, 2010* 1984; *Oh What a Night* 1994.

Dumbrille, Douglas. Actor. *b.* Oct. 13, 1889, Hamilton, Ontario, Canada. *d.* 1974. As a young man, he quit a bank clerk's job to join a stock company and, following his Broadway debut as Banquo in the 1924 production of 'Macbeth,' sold the Ontario onion farm he owned to devote himself to a stage career. He had many Broadway plays behind him by the time he started his Hollywood career in the early 30s. He played character roles in more than 200 films, often as a suave villain or corrupt tycoon or politician. On TV he was seen regularly on the series 'You'll Never Get Rich' and 'China Smith.' In 1960, at the age of 70, he married Patricia Mowbray, the 28-year-old daughter of his friend, actor Alan Mowbray.

FILMS INCLUDE: *His Woman* 1931; *The Wiser Sex* 1932; *King of the Jungle, Voltaire, The World Changes* (as Buffalo Bill) 1933; *Journal of a Crime, Broadway Bill, Treasure Island* 1934; *The Lives of a Bengal Lancer, Naughty Marietta, Cardinal Richelieu, Crime and Punishment, Peter Ibbetson* 1935; *The Lone Wolf Returns, Mr. Deeds Goes to Town, The Princess Comes Across* 1936; *A Day at the Races, The Emperor's Candlesticks, The Firefly, Ali Baba Goes to Town* 1937; *The Buccaneer, Mr. Moto in Danger Island, Crime Takes a Holiday, Kentucky* 1938; *The Three Musketeers* (as Athos), *Captain Fury, Charlie Chan at Treasure Island* 1939; *Slightly Honorable, Virginia City* 1940; *The Big Store* 1941; *King of the Mounties* (serial) 1942; *Du Barry Was a Lady* 1943; *Uncertain Glory, Lost in a Harem* 1944; *Jungle Queen* (serial), *A Medal for Benny, The Frozen Ghost* 1945; *Road to Utopia, The Cat Creeps, Monsieur Beaucaire* 1946; *Riding High* 1950; *Son of Paleface* 1952; *Julius Caesar* 1953; *The Ten Commandments* 1956; *The Buccaneer* 1958; *Johnny Cool* 1962; *Shock Treatment* 1964.

Dumont, Margaret. Actress. *b.* Margaret Baker, Oct. 20, 1889, Brooklyn, N.Y. *d.* 1965. Starting out as a singer, she made her Broadway debut in a George M. Cohan play at 18 and during the 20s became a fixture in the zany stage comedies of the MARX BROTHERS. She later appeared in seven of their films, triggering many laughs as the stately, statuesque, perfect foil for their antics. She appeared with equally stuffy serenity and absurd aplomb in films of W. C. Fields, Laurel and Hardy, Jack Benny, and other comedians, as well as in an assortment of general character roles.

FILMS INCLUDE: *A Tale of Two Cities* (bit) 1917; *The Cocoanuts* 1929; *Animal Crackers* 1930; *The Girl Habit* 1931; *Duck Soup* 1933; *A Night at the Opera* 1935; *Anything Goes* 1936; *A Day at the Races, High Flyers, Wise Girl* 1937; *Dramatic School* 1938; *At The Circus* 1939; *The Big Store, Never Give a Sucker an Even Break* 1941; *Born to Sing, Sing Your Worries Away* 1942; *The Dancing Masters* 1943; *Up in Arms, Bathing Beauty* 1944; *The Horn Blows at Midnight, Diamond Horseshoe* 1945; *Little Giant* 1946; *Three for Bedroom C, Stop You're Killing Me* 1952; *Auntie Mame* 1958; *Zotz!* 1962; *What a Way to Go!* 1964.

Dunaway, Faye. Actress. Born Jan. 14, 1941, in Bascom, Fla. The daughter of a career Army officer, she was raised and educated in various American and European towns. After attending the University of Florida and the School of Fine and Applied Arts at Boston University, she headed for New York in search of an acting career. She joined the Lincoln Center Repertory Company in 1962 and appeared in such plays as 'A Man for All Seasons' and 'After the Fall.' Her performance in the off-Broadway production 'Hogan's Goat' led to her 1967 screen debut in *The Happening.* A few months later she made a considerable impact in the role of gun moll Bonnie Parker in *Bonnie and Clyde,* for which she was nominated for an Oscar. A cool green-eyed, blonde beauty, she became one of the most sought-after female stars in Hollywood and international films during the 1960s and 1970s. She was again nominated for an Academy Award for *Chinatown* (1974) and finally won the Oscar for *Network* (1976). In 1981, she gave a brilliant portrayal of Joan Crawford in the film *Mommie Dearest.* After a relatively dormant period in the early 80s, she made a strong comeback in *Barfly* (1987). As have several top female stars past their ingenue years, she found a high-quality outlet in TV movies, producing and appearing in the 1990 entry *'Cold Sassy Tree.'*

FILMS: *The Happening, Hurry Sundown, Bonnie and Clyde* (as Bonnie Parker) 1967; *The Thomas Crown Affair* 1968; *The Extraordinary Seaman, Gli Amanti/A Place for Lovers* (It.), *The Arrangement* 1969; *Puzzle of a Downfall Child, Little Big Man* 1970; *Doc* 1971; *La Maison sous les Arbres/The Deadly Trap* 1972; *Oklahoma Crude* 1973; *The Three Musketeers* (as Milady), *Chinatown, The Towering Inferno* 1974; *The Four Musketeers* (as Milady), *Three Days of the Condor* 1975; *Voyage of the Damned* (UK), *Network* 1976; *Eyes of Laura Mars* 1978; *The Champ* 1979; *The First Deadly Sin* 1980; *Mommie Dearest* 1981; *The Wicked Lady* 1983; *Ordeal by Innocence* (UK), *Supergirl* 1984; *Barfly* 1987; *Midnight Crossing, Burning Secret* 1988; *The Handmaid's Tale, Wait Until Spring Bandini* (Bel./Fr./It./US), *On a Moonlit Night* 1990; *Arizona Dream, The Temp* 1993; *Even Cowgirls Get the Blues* 1994; *Don Juan DeMarco* 1995; *The Albino Alligator, The Chamber, Drunks, Dunstan Checks In* 1996; *In Praise of Older Women* 1997.

Duncan, Bud (Albert). See HAMILTON, Lloyd.

Duncan, William. Actor, director, screenwriter. *b.* 1880, Scotland, *d.* 1961. In the US from age ten, he ran a physical culture school and acted on the stage before entering films with the Selig Polyscope Company in 1912 as an actor-director, mainly of outdoor action fare. His rugged athletic physique and virile good looks helped him become one of the most popular Western stars of his day. He directed most of his own films, often writing his own scripts. Early in his career, Tom Mix played the second lead in several films starring and directed by Duncan. In 1916, Duncan joined Vitagraph and soon became the studio's leading serial star and director. He married one of his leading ladies, Edith Johnson (1895–1969), in 1921. Soon after, they both moved to Universal, where they ended their screen careers in 1924. They later toured in vaudeville. Another William Duncan (*b.* Feb. 6, 1874; *d.* 1945) played supporting roles in B westerns of the 30s, including several in the "Hopalong Cassidy" series.

FILMS INCLUDE (as actor-director): *The Dynamiters* (also sc.), *A Rough Ride with Nitroglycerine* 1912; *A Matrimonial Deluge* (also sc.), *The Suffragette, Billy's Birthday Present* (also sc.), *Juggling with Fate* (dir. only), *Made a Coward, An Embarrassed Bridegroom, His Father's Bridegroom* (also sc.), *Religion and Gun Practice, The Law and the Outlaw* (dir. only), *The Jealousy of Miguel and Isabella, The Senorita's Repentance, The Taming Of Texas Pete, An Apache's Gratitude* (also sc.), *The Good Indian, Galloping Romeo, Rejected Lover's Luck, Howlin' Jones, The Silver Grindstone, The Escape of Jim Dolan* (dir. only), *Buck's Romance* (also sc.) 1913; *Romance of the Forest Reserve* (dir. only), *Marrying Gretchen, Marian the Holy Terror, The Servant Question Out West, Anne of the Mines* (act. only) 1914; *The Chalice of Courage* (act. only) 1915; *The Last Man* (act. only), *God's Country and the Woman* (act. only) 1916; *Aladdin from Broadway* (act. only), *Dead Shot Baker, The Tenderfoot, The Fighting Trail* (serial) 1917; *Vengeance and the Woman* (serial) 1917–18; *A Fight for Millions* (serial) 1918; *Smashing Barriers* (serial), *Man of Might* 1919; *The Silent Avenger* (serial) 1920; *Fighting Fate* (serial), *Where Men Are Men, Steelheart, No Defense* 1921; *The Silent Vow, When Danger Smiles* 1922; *Smashing Barriers* (feature version of 1919 serial), *The Steel Trail* (serial), *Playing It Wild* 1923; *The Fast Express* (serial), *Wolves of the North* (serial) 1924.

Duning, George. Composer. Born on Feb. 25, 1908, in

Richmond, Ind. *ed.* Cincinnati Conservatory of Music; U. of Cincinnati. In films since 1939 as arranger, then orchestrator from 1944. In 1947 he began scoring films, mostly for Columbia. Since the early 60s he has scored numerous TV series and TV movies.

FILMS INCLUDE: *Down to Earth, The Guilt of Janet Ames, Johnny O'Clock* 1947; *To the Ends of the Earth, The Man from Colorado, Dark Past* 1948; *Jolson Sings Again, Johnny Allegro* 1949; *From Here to Eternity* 1953; *The Man from Laramie* 1955; *The Eddie Duchin Story, Picnic* 1956; *Pal Joey, 3:10 to Yuma* 1957; *The Last Angry Man, Cowboy* 1958; *The World of Suzie Wong, The Devil at 4 O'Clock* 1961; *The Notorious Landlady* 1962; *Toys in the Attic* 1963; *Ensign Pulver* 1964; *Dear Brigitte* 1965; *Any Wednesday* 1966; *Terror in the Wax Museum* 1973; *The Man with Bogart's Face* 1980.

Dunn, James. Actor. *b.* Nov. 2, 1905, New York City. *d.* 1967. Following some stage experience and a 1930 Broadway debut, he went to Hollywood, where he became a nice-guy type of leading man of many B pictures of the 30s and early 40s. When given the opportunity, he proved himself a capable actor, as in the role of Jimmy Nolan in *A Tree Grows in Brooklyn* (1945), for which he won the Academy Award for best supporting actor. But his hopes for a more substantial screen career failed to materialize. By 1950 he was out of films and returned to the screen only occasionally in the 60s. One of his three wives was actress Frances GIFFORD.

FILMS INCLUDE: *Bad Girl, Over the Hill* 1931; *Dance Team, Handle with Care* 1932; *Sailor's Luck, Arizona to Broadway* 1933; *Stand Up and Cheer, Change of Heart, Baby Take a Bow, 365 Nights in Hollywood, Bright Eyes* 1934; *The Daring Young Man, Bad Boy, The Pay-Off* 1935; *Two-Fisted Gentleman* 1936; *We Have Our Moments, Living on Love* 1937; *Shadows Over Shanghai* 1938; *Pride of the Navy* 1939; *Hold That Woman* 1940; *The Living Ghost* 1942; *Government Girl* 1943; *Leave It to the Irish* 1944; *A Tree Grows in Brooklyn* 1945; *Killer McCoy* 1947; *The Golden Gloves Story* 1950; *The Bramble Bush* 1960; *Hemingway's Adventures of a Young Man* 1962; *The Oscar* 1966.

Dunn, Michael. Actor. *b.* Gary Neil Miller, Oct. 20, 1934, Shattuck, Okla. *d.* 1973. A dwarf, he courageously pursued an acting career beyond the obvious freak roles and in the early 60s made a strong bid for recognition in the Broadway play 'The Ballad of the Sad Cafe.' He received an Oscar nomination for his first major film, *Ship of Fools* (1965), in which he played a compassionate observer of the human scene. He subsequently appeared in other films, plays, and TV episodes. He was found dead, a possible suicide, in his London hotel room during the filming of *The Abdication.*

FILMS INCLUDE: *Pity Me Not* 1960; *Without Each Other* 1962; *Ship of Fools* 1965; *You're a Big Boy Now* 1967; *No Way to Treat a Lady, Madigan, Boom!* 1968; *Justine* 1969; *Murders in the Rue Morgue* 1971; *House of Freaks/Frankenstein's Castle of Freaks/The Mutations, Werewolf of Washington* 1973; *The Abdication* 1974.

Dunne, Griffin. Actor, producer. Born June 8, 1955, in New York City. Dark-haired, bright-eyed leading man of American films of the 80s. The son of TV and film producer Dominick Dunne, he trained for the stage at the Neighborhood Playhouse and with Uta HAGEN, making his screen debut in 1975. His career was helped by the lead role in Martin Scorsese's *After Hours* (1985). He also co-produced that film, as well as several others, through Double Play Productions, a company he had formed in partnership with Amy Robinson. He married actress Carey LOWELL in 1989.

FILMS: *The Other Side of the Mountain* (bit) 1974; *Head Over Hills/Chilly Scenes of Winter* (also co-prod.) 1979; *The Fan* (bit), *An American Werewolf in London* 1981; *Baby It's You* (co-prod. only) 1983; *Cold Feet, Almost You, Johnny Dangerously* 1984; *After Hours* (also co-prod.) 1985; *Who's That Girl, Amazon Women on the Moon* 1987; *Le Grand Bleu/The Big Blue* (Fr.), *Running on Empty* (co-prod. only) 1988; *Me and Him, Perugia, White Palace* (co-prod. only) 1990; *Once Around* (also co-prod.), *My Girl, Stepkids* 1991; *Straight Talk, Big Girls Don't Cry. . . They Get Even, The Pickle* 1992; *I Like It Like That, Naked in New York, Quiz Show* 1994; *Search and Destroy* 1995; *Addicted To Love* (dir. only) 1997.

Dunne, Irene. Actress. *b.* Irene Marie Dunn, Dec. 20, 1898, Louisville, Ky., the daughter of a Federal steamship inspector and a pianist. *d.* 1990. A graduate of the Chicago Musical College, she failed a singing audition at New York's Metropolitan Opera in 1920 and turned instead to musical comedy, starring in her debut in the road company of 'Irene.' She made her first Broadway appearance in 1922, in 'The Clinging Vine,' and was an established leading lady of the musical stage when she starred as Magnolia in Ziegfeld's highly successful road-company production of 'Show Boat' in 1929. She was signed to a Hollywood contract by RKO and made her screen debut the following year. For the next 22 years she starred in a wide assortment of motion pictures, ranging from sweet romances and melodramatic tearjerkers to musicals and madcap comedies. Regardless of genre, she always appeared regal and dignified and remained among Hollywood's top-ranking stars until her retirement in the early 50s. A staunch Republican, she devoted herself to political activity and in 1957 was appointed by President Eisenhower as an alternate delegate to the UN's 12th General Assembly. She never returned to acting, except for sporadic TV appearances. In 1965 she was elected to the board of directors of Technicolor. In 1985 she was among six distinguished Americans honored at Washington's Kennedy Center for their achievements in the performing arts. She was nominated for best actress Oscars for *Cimarron* (1931), *Theodora Goes Wild* (1936), *The Awful Truth* (1937), *Love Affair* (1939), and *I Remember Mama* (1948).

FILMS: *Leathernecking* 1930; *Cimarron, Bachelor Apartment, The Great Lover, Consolation Marriage* 1931; *Symphony of Six Million, Back Street, Thirteen Women* 1932; *No Other Woman, The Secret of Madame Blanche, The Silver Cord, Ann Vickers, If I Were Free* 1933; *This Man Is Mine, Stingaree, The Age of Innocence* 1934; *Sweet Adeline, Roberta, Magnificent Obsession* 1935; *Show Boat, Theodora Goes Wild* 1936; *High Wide and Handsome, The Awful Truth* 1937; *Joy of Living* 1938; *Love Affair, Invitation to Happiness, When Tomorrow Comes* 1939; *My Favorite Wife* 1940; *Penny Serenade, Unfinished Business* 1941; *Lady in a Jam* 1942; *A Guy Named Joe* 1943; *The White Cliffs of Dover, Together Again* 1944; *Over 21* 1945; *Anna and the King of Siam* 1946; *Life with Father* 1947; *I Remember Mama* 1948; *Never a Dull Moment, The Mudlark* (as Queen Victoria) 1950; *It Grows on Trees* 1952.

Dunne, Philip. Director, screenwriter, producer. *b.* Feb. 11, 1908, New York City. *d.* 1992. *ed.* Harvard. In Hollywood from the mid-30s, after a brief business and banking career, he wrote many distinguished screenplays before turning director in 1955. His work as a director was intelligent but often heavy-handed. He wrote the screenplays for most of the films he directed. He was a speech writer for John F. Kennedy during the 1960 election campaign. He married actress Amanda Duff.

FILMS INCLUDE: As screenwriter (alone or in collaboration)—*The Count of Monte Cristo* 1934; *Helldorado* 1935; *The Last of the Mohicans* 1936; *Lancer Spy* 1937; *Suez* 1938; *Stanley and Livingstone, Swanee River, The Rains Came* 1939;

Johnny Apollo 1940; *How Green Was My Valley* 1941; *Son of Fury* 1942; *The Late George Apley, Forever Amber, The Ghost and Mrs. Muir* 1947; *Escape* 1948; *Pinky* 1949; *David and Bathsheba, Way of a Gaucho* (also prod.) 1952; *The Robe* 1953; *Demetrius and the Gladiators, The Egyptian* 1954; *The Agony and the Ecstasy* 1965. As director (complete)—*Prince of Players* (also prod.), *The View from Pompey's Head* (also prod., sc.) 1955; *Hilda Crane* (also sc.) 1956; *Three Brave Men* (also sc.) 1957; *Ten North Frederick* (also sc.), *In Love and War* 1958; *Blue Denim* (also co-sc.) 1959; *Wild in the Country* 1961; *The Inspector/Lisa* (UK/US) 1962; *Blindfold* (also co-sc.) 1966.

Dunning, George. Animator, director. *b.* 1920, Toronto, Ont., Canada. *d.* 1979. He joined the National Film Board of Canada in 1943, set up his own company in 1949, and left for England in 1956. He established a reputation for originality, deriving his themes from an irrational, surrealist world. Several of his films won international awards, and his feature-length *The Yellow Submarine* was a great commercial success. He did TV commercials, TV cartoon series ('The Beatles,' etc.), industrial films, and theatrical cartoons.

FILMS INCLUDE: *Auprès de ma Blonde* 1943; *Grim Pastures* 1944; *Three Blind Mice* 1945; *Cadet Rousselle* 1946; *The Wardrobe* 1959; *The Flying Man, The Apple* 1962; *Canada Is My Piano* 1966; *Yellow Submarine* 1968; *Moon Rock* 1970.

Dunnock, Mildred. Actress. *b.* Jan. 25, 1904, Baltimore. *d.* 1991. *ed.* Johns Hopkins; Columbia. She dabbled in amateur dramatics while still in high school but at the insistence of her parents went on to college and a teaching career at New York's Brearly School. However, she finally succumbed to the acting bug and, after appearing with various groups, made her Broadway debut in 1931. She scored a personal triumph in 1940 in the role of a Welsh schoolteacher in 'The Corn Is Green,' a character part she was to repeat in her screen debut in the 1945 film version of the play, in support of Bette Davis. She subsequently played memorable character roles in many other plays, films, and TV dramas, notably as the wife in 'Death of a Salesman,' which she portrayed on Broadway (1949) and in the film (1951) and TV (1966) versions. She was nominated for an Oscar for her performances in *Death of a Salesman* (1951) and *Baby Doll* (1956).

FILMS: *The Corn Is Green* 1945; *Kiss of Death* 1947; *Death of a Salesman, I Want You* 1951; *Viva Zapata!, The Girl in White* 1952; *The Jazz Singer, Bad for Each Other* 1953; *The Trouble with Harry* 1955; *Love Me Tender, Baby Doll* 1956; *Peyton Place* 1957; *The Nun's Story* 1959; *The Story on Page One, Butterfield 8* 1960; *Something Wild* 1961; *Sweet Bird of Youth* 1962; *Behold a Pale Horse, Youngblood Hawke* 1964; *Seven Women* 1965; *What Ever Happened to Aunt Alice?* 1969; *The Spiral Staircase* (UK) 1975; *One Summer Love/Dragonfly* 1976; *The Pick-Up Artist* 1987.

dupe negative. A negative made from a fine-grain positive print; short for "duplicate negative." The purpose of making duplicate negatives is most often to preserve the original negative from deterioration when multiple reproduction of prints becomes necessary, or to make reproduction possible at several labs at the same time. The process of making dupe negatives is known as "duping," and the print used for duplication is a "duping print."

Duprez, June. Actress. *b.* May 14, 1918, London. *d.* 1984. Leading lady of British and later Hollywood films. Typically cast in exotic roles, memorably in *The Four Feathers* (1939) and *The Thief of Bagdad* (1940). She was the daughter of American vaudevillian and character actor Fred Duprez (1884–1938), who appeared in many British films of the 30s.

FILMS: In UK—*The Amateur Gentleman* (bit), *The Crimson Circle, The Cardinal* 1936; *The Spy in Black/U-Boat 29* 1938; *The Lion Has Wings, The Four Feathers* 1939; *The Thief of Bagdad* 1940. In the US—*Little Tokyo USA, They Raid by Night* 1942; *Forever and a Day, Tiger Fangs* 1943; *None but the Lonely Heart* 1944; *The Brighton Strangler, And Then There Were None* 1945; *That Brennan Girl* 1946; *Calcutta* 1947; *1 + 1/Exploring the Kinsey Reports* (US/Can.) 1961.

Durand, Jean. Director. *b.* Dec. 15, 1882, Paris. *d.* 1946. An important figure in the early years of French cinema, he was instrumental in the development of slapstick comedy and action genres in French films. Between 1907 and 1929, he turned out scores of silent shorts and feature films, often without the benefit of script or rehearsals, including the "Calino" (1907–11) and "Onésime" (1912–13) series, and a series of takeoffs on the American Western starring Joe Hamman and Durand's wife, Berthe Dagmar.

FILMS INCLUDE: *La Prairie en Feu* 1907; *Arizona Bill, L'Attaque d'un Train* 1909; *Pendaison à Jefferson City* 1911; *Cent Dollars, Mort ou Vif* 1912; *Le Collier Vivant* 1915?, *Serpentin au Harem* 1919; *Impéria* (serial) 1920; *Marie la Gaieté* 1921; *Marie la Bohémienne* 1922; *Face aux Loups* 1926; *Palaces* 1927; *L'Ile d'Amour* 1928; *La Femme rêvée* 1929.

Durante, Jimmy. Comedian, songwriter, entertainer. *b.* James Francis Durante, Feb. 10, 1893, New York City. *d.* 1980. Son of a sideshow barker, he was nicknamed "Schnozzola" for his long, bulbous nose. He began his long show-business career at 16, playing ragtime piano in Bowery nightclubs. Teaming up with Lou Clayton and Eddie Jackson, he became a big success on the vaudeville and nightclub circuits. In 1928 they made it to New York's Palace and in 1929 were featured on Broadway in Ziegfeld's 'Show Girl.' He made his film debut the following year and signed a five-year contract with MGM. Throughout the 30s he commuted between Hollywood and Broadway, gaining popularity both in stage musicals and in films. Later he brought his appealing buffoonery, delightful malapropisms, and hoarse singing voice to radio and TV. His durable career extended into the 70s, when he could still be seen in Las Vegas nightclubs or on TV specials frantically waving his hat and cane and signing off his appearances with his trademark line "Goodnight Mrs. Calabash, wherever you are."

FILMS: *Roadhouse Nights* 1930; *New Adventures of Get-Rich-Quick Wallingford, The Cuban Love Song* 1931; *The Passionate Plumber, The Wet Parade, Speak Easily, Blondie of the Follies, The Phantom President* 1932; *What! No Beer?, Hell Below, Broadway to Hollywood, Meet the Baron* 1933; *Palooka, George White's Scandals, Hollywood Party, Strictly Dynamite, She Learned About Sailors, Student Tour* 1934; *Carnival* 1935; *Sally Irene and Mary, Start Cheering, Little Miss Broadway, Forbidden Music* 1938; *Melody Ranch* 1940; *You're in the Army Now* 1941; *The Man Who Came to Dinner* 1942; *Two Girls and a Sailor* 1944; *Music for Millions* 1945; *Two Sisters from Boston* 1946; *It Happened in Brooklyn, This Time for Keeps* 1947; *On an Island with You* 1948; *The Great Rupert, The Milkman* 1950; *Beau James* (unbilled cameo) 1957; *Pepe* 1960; *Jumbo* 1962; *It's a Mad Mad Mad Mad World* 1963.

Duras, Marguerite. Novelist, playwright, screenwriter, director. Born Marguerite Donnadieu, in Apr. 2, 1914, in Giadinh, Indochina (now Vietnam), to French parents, both teachers. She went to live in Paris at 18 and studied mathematics, law, and political science at the Sorbonne. In 1935 she became a civil servant in the Ministry for Colonial Affairs. During WW II she was active in the Resistance and in 1945 she joined the Communist Party. She published her first novel in 1943 and had her first play produced in 1955. She often issued her works in several forms successively, first as a novel, then as an adaptation into a play, a teleplay, or a screenplay, or all three. The search for the essence of time and the exploration of human relationships are at the core of her writings, which are characteristically concerned more with how characters relate to each other, especially women to men, rather than with expounding a situation or developing a plot. Romance and passion accent many of her works, which are rich in stylized, often poetic dialogue. Several of her novels have been adapted to the screen by others, including René Clement's *Barrage contre le Pacifique/La Diga sul Pacifico/This Angry Age/The Sea Wall* (1958) and Tony Richardson's *The Sailor from Gibraltar* (1967). She made her first direct contribution to films with the original screenplay for Alain Resnais' *Hiroshima mon Amour* (1959) and later wrote several other scripts, alone or in collaboration. She began directing films in 1966, typically emphasizing script and atmosphere over camera technique. Her novel *The Lover* was made into a movie in 1992.

FILMS: As screenwriter—*Hiroshima mon Amour* 1959; *Moderato Cantabile* (co-sc. from own novel) 1960; *Une aussi longue Absence/The Long Absence* (co-sc., from own novel) 1961; *10:30 P.M. Summer* (co-sc. from own novel; US/Sp.), *Les Rideaux blancs, La Voleuse* (dial.) 1966; *Ce que savait Morgan* (co-sc.) 1974. As director-writer—*La Musica* (co-dir. with Paul Seban) 1966; *Détruire dit-elle/Destroy She Said* 1969; *Jaune le Soleil* (also co-edit.) 1971; *Nathalie Granger* (also music), *La Ragazza di Passaggio/La Femme du Ganges* (It./Fr.) 1973; *India Song* (also voice) 1975; *Des Journées entières dans les Arbres/Days in the Trees, Son Nom de Venises dans Calcutta Desert* 1976; *Le Camion* (also act.), *Baxter—Vera Baxter* 1977; *Le Navire Night, Aurelia Steiner* (a four-shorts omnibus) 1979; *Agatha et les Lectures limitées, L'Homme Atlantique* (experimental; medium-length; also voice) 1981; *Il Dialogo di Roma/Dialogue de Rome* (doc.; also voice; It.) 1983; *Les Enfants* 1985.

Durbin, Deanna. Actress, singer. Born Edna Mae Durbin, on Dec. 4, 1921, in Winnipeg, Man., Canada. Raised in California from infancy, she demonstrated a talent for singing at an early age and at 14 was recommended to MGM by a talent agent. The studio put her in a musical short, *Every Sunday* (1936), together with another promising youngster, Judy Garland, and when it came to choosing between the two, they picked Garland and dropped Durbin. She was signed instead by Universal and within months proved to be a wise investment, saving the studio from bankruptcy with the hefty box-office receipts of her first feature film, *Three Smart Girls.* Shortly before that she had captured nationwide attention singing on the Eddie Cantor radio show, and the success of the film made her an instant star. Appearing in a succession of tailor-made vehicles that exploited her wholesome sweetness and bubbling personality as well as her excellent singing voice, she quickly became an internationally popular star, one of the top box-office attractions of the late 30s and early 40s.

In 1938 she shared a special Academy Award with Mickey Rooney for "bringing to the screen the spirit and personification of youth." Durbin matured on the screen from a peppy adolescent into a starry-eyed romantic beauty and was Hollywood's highest-paid woman star when she suddenly retired from films in 1948. She has been living in wealthy retirement in France with her third husband, director Charles David.

FILMS: *Every Sunday* (short), *Three Smart Girls* 1936; *100 Men and a Girl* 1937; *Mad About Music, That Certain Age* 1938; *Three Smart Girls Grow Up, First Love* 1939; *It's a Date, Spring Parade* 1940; *Nice Girl?, It Started with Eve* 1941; *The Amazing Mrs. Holliday, Hers to Hold, Her Butler's Sister* 1943; *Christmas Holiday, Can't Help Singing* 1944; *Lady on a Train* 1945; *Because of Him* 1946; *I'll Be Yours, Something in the Wind* 1947; *Up in Central Park, For the Love of Mary* 1948.

Durfee, Minta. Actress. *b.* 1897, Los Angeles. *d.* 1975. Comic lead of the silent screen. She entered show business as a chorus girl at 17. In 1908 she married Roscoe ("Fatty") ARBUCKLE and with him joined the Keystone film company in 1913. She appeared as a comic leading lady in a dozen of Charlie CHAPLIN's earliest films, as well as in many of her husband's comedies. She left Arbuckle in 1918 and retired from the screen. They separated legally in 1921 and divorced in 1925. She later returned to films in occasional cameo roles and made some appearances on TV.

FILMS INCLUDE: *Fatty's Day Off, Fatty at San Diego, Fatty's Flirtation* 1913; *Making a Living* (Chaplin's first film), *A Film Johnnie, Twenty Minutes of Love, Cruel Cruel Love, Caught in a Cabaret, The Knockout, The Masquerader, His New Profession, The Rounders, The New Janitor, Tillie's Punctured Romance* (all with Chaplin), *Fatty's Finish, The Alarm, Fatty and the Heiress, Fatty's Debut, Leading Lizzie Astray, Fatty's Wine Party, Fatty and Minnie He-Haw, Ambrose's First Falsehood* 1914; *Ambrose's Fury, Ambrose's Little Hatchet, Hearts and Planets, Love Speed and Thrills, The Home Breakers, Fatty's Reckless Fling, Fatty's Faithful Fido, When Love Took Wings, Our Dare Devil Chief, Fido's Tin Type Tangle, Dirty Work in a Laundry, Fickle Fatty's Fall, A Village Scandal* 1915; *The Great Pearl Tangle, Bright Lights, His Wife's Mistake, The Other Man* 1916; *Mickey* 1918; *Naughty Marietta* (bit) 1935; *How Green Was My Valley* (bit) 1941; *It's a Mad Mad Mad Mad World* (bit) 1963; *The Unsinkable Molly Brown* (bit) 1964.

Durkin, Junior. Actor. *b.* James Durkin, 1915, New York City. *d.* 1935. The son of actress Florence Edwards, he made his professional stage debut at the age of 2½, playing Cupid in the musical comedy 'Some Night.' He later appeared in many plays and musicals, notably in 'Poppy' with W. C. Fields. In the early 30s he played juveniles in Hollywood films, memorably as Huck Finn in *Tom Sawyer* (1930) and *Huckleberry Finn* (1931). He was 20 when he died in a car crash during an outing with fellow juvenile actor Jackie Coogan. Coogan was the only survivor in the crash that also killed the driver, Coogan's father, and another passenger. Not to be confused with character actor James Durkin (1879–1934), who was also active in Hollywood films of the early 30s.

FILMS INCLUDE: *Recaptured Love, The Santa Fe Trail, Tom Sawyer* 1930; *The Conquering Horde, Huckleberry Finn* 1931; *Hell's House* 1932; *Man Hunt* 1933; *Little Men* 1934.

Durning, Charles. Actor. Born on Feb. 28, 1923, in Highland Falls, N.Y. *ed.* NYU. Beefy character player of the American stage and screen, often in tough, dominant roles. The son of an Army officer, he left home at 15 and supported himself with an odd assortment of menial jobs, including boxing, iron work and construction. After serving with distinction (Silver Star) in the Korean War, he attended Columbia and NYU, and studied acting on the GI Bill. Frustrated in his bid for roles, he supported himself as a cab driver, elevator operator, bartender, and Fred Astaire School dance instructor. Finally making his professional stage debut in 1960, he gained experience and exposure in several productions of the New York Shakespeare Festival. His first big break came in 1972, when he won the Drama Desk Award for his performance in 'That Championship Season.' On the screen from 1965, he gradually developed into a dependable supporting player and by the early 80s reached the stature of a character star. He was nominated for Oscars as best supporting actor for *The Best Little Whorehouse in Texas* and *To Be or Not to Be.* He won a Tony in 1990 for the

Broadway revival of 'Cat on a Hot Tin Roof.' He has also figured prominently on TV, particularly in a regular role on the sitcom 'Evening Shade.'

FILMS: *Harvey Middleman—Fireman* 1965; *Hi Mom!, I Walk the Line* 1970; *The Pursuit of Happiness* 1971; *Dealing, Deadhead Miles* 1972; *Sisters, The Sting* 1973; *The Front Page* 1974; *Dog Day Afternoon, The Hindenburg* 1975; *Breakheart Pass, Harry and Walter Go to New York* 1976; *Twilight's Last Gleaming, An Enemy of the People, The Choirboys* 1977; *The Fury, The Greek Tycoon, Tilt* 1978; *The Muppet Movie, North Dallas Forty, Starting Over, When a Stranger Calls* 1979; *Die Laughing, The Final Countdown* 1980; *True Confessions, Sharkey's Machine* 1981; *The Best Little Whorehouse in Texas, Tootsie* 1982; *To Be or Not to Be, Two of a Kind* 1983; *Hadley's Rebellion, Mass Appeal* 1984; *Stick, The Man with One Red Shoe, Stand Alone, Private Conversations* (doc.), *Death of a Salesman* (TV movie in US; theatrically released abroad) 1985; *Big Trouble, Where the River Runs Black, Tough Guys, Solarbabies* 1986; *Happy New Year, The Rosary Murders* 1987; *Cop/Blood on the Moon, A Tiger's Tale, Far North* 1988; *Dick Tracy, Fatal Sky, Project Alien* 1990; *V.I. Warshawski* 1991; *Brenda Starr* 1992; *The Music of Chance* 1993; *The Hudsucker Proxy, I.Q.* 1994; *Home for the Holidays* 1995; *The Last Supper, Spy Hard* 1996.

Duryea, Dan. Actor. *b.* Jan. 23, 1907, White Plains, N.Y. *d.* 1968. After graduating from Cornell, he worked for six years in advertising before making his Broadway debut in 1935. Rave reviews for his portrayal of the weakling son Leo in the Broadway hit 'The Little Foxes' led to his screen debut in the screen version of the play. From the start of his film career he was typecast as a cynical, sneering villain whom women found strangely fascinating. Among his most memorable roles were those as the antagonist of Edward G. Robinson in two Fritz Lang dramas of the 40s, *The Woman in the Window* and *Scarlet Street.* In addition to making some 60 films, he also appeared in many TV dramas, including the series 'China Smith' (1952–55) and 'Peyton Place' (1967–68). He died of cancer.

FILMS: *The Little Foxes, Ball of Fire* 1941; *The Pride of the Yankees, That Other Woman* 1942; *Sahara* 1943; *Man from Frisco, The Woman in the Window, Ministry of Fear, Mrs. Parkington, None but the Lonely Heart* 1944; *Main Street After Dark, The Great Flamarion, The Valley of Decision, Along Came Jones, Lady on a Train, Scarlet Street* 1945; *Black Angel, White Tie and Tails* 1946; *Black Bart, Another Part of the Forest, River Lady, Larceny* 1948; *Criss Cross, Manhandled, Too Late for Tears, Johnny Stool Pigeon* 1949; *One Way Street, Winchester '73, The Underworld Story* 1950; *Al Jennings of Oklahoma, Chicago Calling* 1951; *Thunder Bay, Sky Commando, Thirty-Six Hours/Terror Street* (UK) 1953; *Ride Clear of Diablo, Rails Into Laramie, World for Ransom, Silver Lode, This Is My Love* 1954; *The Marauders, Foxfire* 1955; *Storm Fear* 1956; *Battle Hymn, The Burglar, Night Passage, Slaughter on Tenth Avenue* 1957; *Kathy O'* 1958; *Platinum High School* 1960; *Six Black Horses* 1962; *He Rides Tall, Do You Know This Voice?, Walk a Tightrope, Taggart* 1964; *The Bounty Killer, The Flight of the Phoenix* 1965; *Incident at Phantom Hill, Un Fiume di Dollari/The Hills Run Red* (It.) 1966; *Five Golden Dragons* (UK) 1967; *The Bamboo Saucer* 1968.

Duryea, George. Actor. *b.* Dec. 20, 1898, Rochester, N.Y. *d.* 1963. *ed.* Columbia; Carnegie Tech. A veteran of the stage, he made his screen debut in 1928, playing lead roles in major productions under his real name. In 1931, after changing his name to Tom Keene, he began the second phase of his career as the star of numerous Westerns. His most important film during that period was King Vidor's classic of the Depression years, *Our Daily Bread* (1934). In 1944 he again changed his name, this time to Richard Powers, under which he played mostly character roles.

FILMS INCLUDE: As George Duryea—*Marked Money* 1928; *Honky Tonk, Thunder, Tide of Empire, In Old California, The Godless Girl* 1929; *Bean Bandit, Tol'able David, Pardon My Gun, Night Work, The Dude Wrangler* 1930. As Tom Keene—*Sundown Trail* 1931; *Partners, Ghost Valley, Beyond the Rockies* 1932; *Cheyenne Kid, Cross Fire, Scarlet River* 1933; *Our Daily Bread* 1934; *Hong Kong Nights* 1935; *Timothy's Quest, Desert Gold* 1936; *The Law Commands, Old Louisiana* 1937; *The Painted Trail* 1938; *Wanderers of the West* 1941; *Where Trails End* 1942. As Richard Powers—*Up in Arms* 1944; *Sergeant Mike* 1945; *San Quentin* 1946; *Crossfire* 1947; *Berlin Express, Blood on the Moon* 1948; *Desperadoes of the West* (serial) 1950; *Red Planet Mars* 1952; *Wetbacks* 1956; *Plan 9 from Outer Space* 1959.

Duse, Eleonora. Actress. *b.* Oct. 3, 1858, Vigevano, Italy. *d.* 1924. The internationally celebrated stage actress appeared in only one film, *Cenere* (1916), which she also helped script and direct. Disappointed with the quality of this sole permanent record of her thespian ability, she had the film withdrawn from circulation, but it was later re-released as *Madre.* Several prints have survived to this day. She died in Pittsburgh during a highly successful American tour.

Dutton, Charles S. Actor. Born on Jan. 30, 1951, in Baltimore, Md. *ed.* Towson State, Yale School of Drama. Rich-voiced character actor of screen, stage, and television. Turning his life around following a stint in jail, he studied acting at Yale, eventually distinguishing himself on Broadway. In the 1990s he starred in the TV series 'Roc,' while continuing to deliver an impressive array of complex, multidimensional characters.

FILMS INCLUDE: *No Mercy* 1987; *Crocodile Dundee II* 1988; *Jacknife, An Unremarkable Life* 1989; *Q&A* 1990, *Mississippi Masala, Alien* 3, *The Distinguished Gentleman* 1992; *Menace II Society* 1993; *A Low Down Dirty Shame, Nick of Time, Surviving the Game* 1994; *Cry the Beloved Country* 1995; *Last Dance* (unbilled), *Get on the Bus, A Time to Kill* 1996.

Duvall, Robert. Actor. Born on Jan. 5, 1931, in San Diego, Calif. *ed.* Principia Coll. (Ill.). An admiral's son, he came to New York following two years of military service in Korea, and after a period of training at the Neighborhood Playhouse began acting in stock and off Broadway. He made a memorable film debut as Gregory Peck's feeble-minded next-door neighbor in *To Kill a Mockingbird* (1962) and has subsequently played an impressive range of distinctive character roles that demonstrate not only his versatility as an actor but a valuable knack for blending anonymously into his roles without drawing attention to himself. As a result he has become one of the most sought-after character leads and supporting players in Hollywood today. He won the best actor Academy Award for *Tender Mercies* (1983), following Oscar nominations as best supporting actor for *The Godfather* (1972) and *Apocalypse Now* (1979), and as best actor for *The Great Santini* (1980). He also shared the best actor prize at Venice for *True Confessions* (1981), in addition to many other international awards. He impersonated Dwight D. Eisenhower in the TV movie *Ike* (1979). Having made a documentary in 1977, Duvall skillfully directed a first feature, *Angelo, My Love,* in 1983. Won accolades for his portrayal of a flinty cowboy in the 1989 TV miniseries 'Lonesome Dove.'

FILMS: *To Kill a Mockingbird* 1962; *Nightmare in the Sun, Captain Newman, M.D.* 1964; *The Chase* 1966; *Countdown, The Detective, Bullitt* 1968; *True Grit, The Rain People* 1969;

*M*A*S*H, The Revolutionary* 1970; *THX-1138, Lawman* 1971; *The Godfather, The Great Northfield Minnesota Raid* (as Jesse James), *Joe Kidd, Tomorrow* 1972; *Badge 373, Lady Ice, The Outfit* 1973; *The Conversation, The Godfather Part II* 1974; *Breakout, The Killer Elite* 1975; *The Seven-Per-Cent Solution* (as Sherlock Holmes's Dr. Watson), *Network, The Eagle Has Landed* (UK) 1976; *We're Not the Jet Set* (doc.; dir.; co-prod. only), *The Greatest* 1977; *The Betsy, Invasion of the Body Snatchers* (cameo) 1978; *Apocalypse Now, The Great Santini/The Ace* 1979; *True Confessions, The Pursuit of D. B. Cooper* 1981; *Tender Mercies* (also co-prod., co-songs), *Angelo, My Love* (dir., prod. sc. only) 1983; *The Stone Boy, The Natural* 1984; *Sanford Meisner* (doc. interview) 1985; *Belizaire the Cajun* (also creative consultant), *The Lightship, Let's Get Harry* 1986; *Hotel Colonial* (It./US) 1987; *Colors* 1988; *The Handmaid's Tale, Days of Thunder, A Show of Force* 1990; *Convicts, Hearts of Darkness: A Filmmaker's Apocalypse, The Plague, Rambling Rose* 1991; *Newsies* 1992; *Falling Down, Wrestling Ernest Hemingway, Geronimo: An American Legend* 1993; *The Paper* 1994; *The Scarlet Letter, Something to Talk About, The Stars Fell on Henrietta* 1995; *A Family Thing* (also co-prod.), *Phenomenon, Sling Blade* 1996.

Duvall, Shelley. Actress. Born July 7, 1949, in Houston, Tex., a lawyer's daughter. Tall, gangly, and toothy, she was discovered at a Houston party by director Robert ALTMAN, who cast her in a featured role in the film *Brewster McCloud* (1970) although she had had no acting experience. She has since become a leading lady of Hollywood films, starring regularly in Altman productions, displaying sensitivity and versatility in a variety of roles. She was named best actress at Cannes for her performance in Altman's *Three Women* (1977). She was ideally cast as Olive Oyl in the director's *Popeye* (1980). But in the 80s her screen career was put on a back burner to accommodate her increasing activity as the producer of the 'Faerie Tale Theater' series and other children's and adult programs for TV through her own company, Think Entertainment.

FILMS: *Brewster McCloud* 1970; *McCabe and Mrs. Miller* 1971; *Thieves Like Us, Un Homme qui dort* (voice only) 1974; *Nashville* 1975; *Buffalo Bill and the Indians* 1976; *Annie Hall* (cameo), *Three Women* 1977; *The Shining, Popeye* (as Olive Oyl) 1980; *Time Bandits* (UK) 1981; *Roxanne* 1987; *Suburban Commando* 1991; *Underneath* 1994; *Portrait of a Lady* 1996; *Changing Habits* 1997.

Duvivier, Julien. Director. *b.* Oct. 8, 1896, Lille, France. *d.* 1967. Educated at a Jesuit school, he attended Lille University, but dropped out to pursue an acting career. After local experience, he performed in Paris, where he became an assistant to experimental director André Antoine who encouraged him to turn to cinema. In 1918 he entered French films as assistant director (to Feuillade, L'Herbier, etc.) and occasional screenwriter. In 1919 he directed his first film. His films of the 20s gained little notice, but in the 30s he gradually emerged as one of the "Big Five" of French cinema, alongside René Clair, Jacques Feyder, Jean Renoir, and Marcel Carné. He established an international reputation for his "poetic realism" in such films as *David Golder, Poil de Carotte, Maria Chapdelaine, La Bandera, The Golem, Pépé le Moko, They Were Five, Un Carnet de Bal, La Fin du Jour,* and *La Charrette Fantôme.* In 1938 he was invited to Hollywood to direct *The Great Waltz,* a lavish if somewhat kitschy biography of Johann Strauss.

After the invasion of France, Duvivier returned to America, where he spent the war years directing a number of expensive films, memorably two multistar pictures made up of several episodes, *Tales of Manhattan* and the more successful *Flesh and Fantasy.* In 1945 he returned to Europe, where he continued as a director of French films and films of other nations, including the British *Anna Karenina* starring Vivien Leigh. Most notable among his postwar pictures was *The Little World of Don Camillo,* for which he won a prize at Venice. His career as director spanned almost 50 years, paralleling the development of French cinema, from Feuillade to Godard. He scripted or co-scripted most of his own films.

FILMS: *Haceldama/Le Prix du Sang* 1919; *La Réincarnation de Serge Renaudier* 1920; *Les Roquevillard, L'Ouragan sur la Montagne, Der Unheimliche Gast* (Ger.) 1922; *Le Reflet de Claude Mercoeur* 1923; *Credo ou la Tragédie de Lourdes, Coeurs farouches, La Machine à refaire la Vie* (doc.; co-dir.), *L'Oeuvre immortelle* (Belg.) 1924; *L'Abbé Constantin, Poil de Carotte* 1925; *L'Agonie de Jérusalem, L'Homme à l'Hispano* 1926; *Le Mariage de Mademoiselle Beulemans, Le Mystère de la Tour Eiffel* 1927; *Le Tourbillon de Paris* 1928; *La Vie miraculeuse de Thérèse Martin, La Divine Croisière, Maman Colibri* 1929; *Au Bonheur des Dames, David Golder* 1930; *Les Cinq Gentlemen maudits/Sous la Lune du Maroc* (and German-language version, *Die fünf verfluchten Gentlemen*), *Allo Berlin? Ici Paris!, Poil de Carotte* (a sound version), *La Vénus du Collège* 1932; *La Tête d'un Homme, La Machine à refaire la Vie* (sound version), *Le Petit Roi* 1933; *La Paquebot "Tenacity," Maria Chapdelaine/The Naked Heart* 1934; *Golgotha, La Bandera/Escape from Yesterday* 1935; *Le Golem/The Golem* (Fr./Czech.), *L'Homme du Jour/Man of the Hour, La Belle Equipe/They Were Five* 1936; *Pépé le Moko, Un Carnet de Bal* 1937; *The Great Waltz* (US) 1938; *La Fin du Jour/The End of a Day, La Charrette fantôme* 1939; *Untel Père et Fils/The Heart of a Nation* 1940; *Lydia* (US) 1941; *Tales of Manhattan* (US) 1942; *Flesh and Fantasy* (also prod.; US) 1943; *The Impostor* (also prod.; US) 1944; *Panique/Panic* 1946; *Anna Karenina* (UK) 1948; *Au Royaume des Cieux/The Sinners* 1949; *Black Jack/Captain Black Jack* (also prod.; Fr./UK/Sp.) 1950; *Sous le Ciel de Paris/Under the Paris Sky, Le Petit Monde de Don Camillo/The Little World of Don Camillo* (Fr./It.) 1951; *La Fête à Henriette/Holiday for Henrietta* 1952; *Le Retour de Don Camillo/The Return of Don Camillo* (Fr./It) 1953; *L'Affaire Maurizius/On Trial* 1954; *Marianne de ma Jeunesse/Marianne of My Youth* (Fr./Ger.) 1955; *Voici le Temps des Assassins/Deadlier Than the Male* 1956; *L'Homme à l'Imperméable/The Man in the Raincoat* (Fr./It.), *Pot-Bouille* (Fr./It.) 1957; *La Femme et la Pantin/The Female* (Fr./It.), *Marie Octobre* 1959; *La Grande Vie/Das kunstseidene Mädchen* (Fr./Ger.), *Boulevard* 1960; *La Chambre ardente/The Burning Court* (Fr./It./Ger.), *Le Diable et les Dix Commandements/The Devil and the Ten Commandments* (Fr./It.) 1962; *Chair de Poule/Highway Pickup* (Fr./It.) 1963; *Diaboliquement Vôtre/Diabolically Yours* (Fr./It./Ger.) 1967.

Dvorak, Ann. Actress. *b.* Ann McKim, Aug. 2, 1912, New York City. *d.* 1979. The daughter of a Biograph studio manager and silent screen leading lady Anna Lehr, she appeared as Baby Anna Lehr in a few silent films. She re-entered films at the advent of sound as a dance instructor and leggy chorine in MGM musicals. But it was as a dramatic actress under the aegis of Howard Hughes that she made her mark in 1932 as the heroine of *Sky Devils,* opposite Spencer Tracy, and as Paul Muni's sister in *Scarface.* That same year her contract was bought out by Warner Bros. She played leads in some good dramas, like *G-Men,* and lively musicals, like *Thanks a Million,* but on the whole was dissatisfied with her roles and often clashed with the studio management. In 1940 she accompanied her first (1932–46) of three husbands, director Leslie FENTON, on his return trip to England to serve in WW II and she drove an ambulance as her part in the war effort. She also appeared in three

British films before returning to Hollywood as a freelance actress. She retired from the screen in 1951.

FILMS INCLUDE: *Ramona* (title role, as child) 1916; *The Hollywood Revue of 1929* 1929; *Free and Easy* 1930; *The Guardsman* 1931; *Sky Devils, The Crowd Roars, The Strange Love of Molly Louvain, Scarface, Love Is a Racket, Stranger in Town, Three on a Match* 1932; *The Way to Love, College Coach* 1933; *Massacre, Midnight Alibi, Housewife, Murder in the Clouds* 1934; *Sweet Music, G-Men, Bright Lights, Dr. Socrates, Thanks a Million* 1935; *We Who Are About to Die* 1936; *Racing Lady, Midnight Court, Manhattan Merry-Go-Round* 1937; *Merrily We Live, Gangs of New York* 1938; *Blind Alley* 1939; *Cafe Hostess, Girls of the Road* 1940; *Squadron Leader X* (UK) 1942; *Escape to Danger* (UK) 1943; *Flame of Barbary Coast, Masquerade in Mexico* 1945; *Abilene Town* 1946; *The Private Affairs of Bel-Ami, The Long Night* 1947; *The Walls of Jericho* 1948; *Our Very Own, A Life of Her Own, The Return of Jesse James* 1950; *I Was an American Spy, The Secret of Convict Lake* 1951.

Dwan, Allan. Director. *b.* Joseph Aloysius Dwan, Apr. 3, 1885, Toronto, the son of a clothing merchant. *d.* 1981. Educated at Notre Dame, where he studied electrical engineering, played football, and acted in campus plays. He went to work for a Chicago illumination company that was introducing the mercury vapor arc, a predecessor of neon light, into the market. In 1909 he was assigned to supervise the use of this new light source to one of his company's first customers, the Essanay studios in Chicago. Learning that the company was short on good material, he began selling the studio stories he had written in college and was soon asked to join Essanay as a scenario editor.

Dwan remained a director, learning his craft while shooting films. In the course of two years, from mid-1911 to mid-1913, he turned out more than 250 films for the American Film Company, mostly one-reel Westerns but also dramas, comedies, and documentaries. He also supervised the production of many more pictures of a second filming unit headed by Wallace REID. Dwan not only produced and wrote all the scripts for these products of his early career but also edited and himself physically cut the films. He attributed much of the development of his visual style to D. W. GRIFFITH, whose films he avidly watched and into whose camp he dispatched spies to investigate his methods. But the development of Dwan's own techniques is clearly partly attributable to his training as an engineer.

From the start, Dwan demonstrated an uncommon knack for solving technical problems with practical innovations. As early as 1915 he employed the dolly shot (using a Ford car) so that he could more effectively follow the walk of actor William H. Crane in *David Harum.* The same year, he helped Griffith solve the problem of photographing the huge set of *Intolerance* by suggesting the construction of an elevator on a railroad track so that the camera could go up or down and forward or backward at the same time. Later he helped develop several lighting and electronic devices and with the coming of sound was the first to demonstrate the practicability of dollying with a microphone. In mid-1913, Dwan joined Universal, for which he directed many films in little over a year and produced and supervised the production of a second company, whose films were alternately directed by Wallace Reid and Marshall Neilan.

The leading lady of many Dwan films at Universal was Pauline Bush. They married in 1915 and divorced several years later. His second wife was a former Ziegfeld Girl. Late in 1914, Dwan joined Famous Players, for which he helmed several successful Mary Pickford vehicles. In 1916 he began a happy association with Douglas FAIRBANKS which resulted in some of the best films (eleven in all) in the careers of both the director and the star. Dwan reached a peak of prestige in the 20s when, in addition to piloting several highly successful Fairbanks vehicles, he also directed several expensive productions of Gloria SWANSON and other famous Paramount and Fox stars.

Dwan made a smooth transition to talkies, although he wasn't overjoyed with the coming of sound. His most successful early talkie was *While Paris Sleeps* (1932). He directed his next three films in England. After returning to Hollywood in 1934 he found himself relegated to B pictures at Fox. For the next couple of years he turned out routine melodramas and comedies. After directing two commercially successful Shirley TEMPLE vehicles (*Heidi* and *Rebecca of Sunnybrook Farm*), he temporarily regained big-time status with *Suez* (1938) but soon was back on the B grind, directing mostly routine films with the notable exception of *Frontier Marshal* (1939), an exciting Western.

It wasn't until the mid-40s that Dwan returned to good form with a series of four fast-paced comedies he directed for Edward Small. Late in 1945 he went to work for Republic, where until 1945 he ground out many routine films and one excellent war film, *Sands of Iwo Jima.* Dwan wound up his career with a group of low-budget but highly acclaimed Westerns. He directed his last film, in a career spanning 50 years, at age 76. At 82 he was preparing yet another production for Warner Bros., a Korean War picture titled *Marine!,* but the project was abandoned when Jack Warner sold the studio.

Dwan was among Hollywood's most prolific directors, with more than 400 films to his credit as director, in addition to hundreds more that he produced, supervised, or wrote.

FILMS (as director, complete as of 1915) employed; features complete: *Brandishing a Bad Man, Rattlesnakes and Gunpowder, The Angel of Paradise Ranch, The Yiddisher Cowboy, The Poisoned Flume, Three Million Dollars, The Gunman, The Gold Lust* 1911; *The Locket, The Mormon, Fidelity, The Coward, The Haters, The Green Eyed Monster, The Marauders, The Animal Within, The Battleground, The Fear, Calamity Anne's Ward, The Power of Love* 1912; *The Fugitive, Calamity Ann Detective, Angel of the Canyons, The Animal* (also sc.), *Another Man's Life, Ashes of Three, When Luck Changes, Cupid Throws a Brick, The Spirit of the Flag, The Call to Arms* (also sc.), *Criminals, Back to Life, The Menace* (also sc.) 1913; *The Lie, Discord and Harmony, The Embezzler* (also sc.), *Tragedy of Whispering Creek, The Forbidden Room, Richelieu* (also sc.), *Wildflower* (also co-sc.), *The County Chairman* (also sc.), *The Straight Road, The Unwelcome Mrs. Hatch, Honor of the Mounted, The Hopes of Blind Alley* (also co-sc.), *The Conspiracy* 1914; *The Dancing Girl, David Harum, The Love Route, The Commanding Officer, May Blossom, The Pretty Sister of Jose, A Girl of Yesterday, The Foundling, Jordan Is a Hard Road* (also sc.) 1915; *Betty of Greystone, The Habit of Happiness* (also story, co-sc.), *The Good Bad Man, An Innocent Magdalene, The Half-Breed, Manhattan Madness, Fifty-Fifty* (also story) 1916; *Panthea* (also sc.), *The Fighting Odds, A Modern Musketeer* (also sc.) 1917; *Mr. Fix-It* (also sc.), *Bound in Morocco* (also sc.), *He Comes Up Smiling* 1918; *Cheating Cheaters, Getting Mary Married, The Dark Star, Soldiers of Fortune* 1919; *The Luck of the Irish, The Forbidden Thing* (also prod., co-sc.) 1920; *A Perfect Crime* (also prod., sc.), *A Broken Doll* (also prod., sc.), *The Scoffer* (also prod.), *The Sin of Martha Queed* (also prod., sc.), *In the Heart of a Fool* (also prod.) 1921; *The Hidden Woman* (also prod.), *Superstition* (also prod.), *Robin Hood* 1922; *The Glimpses of the Moon* (also prod.), *Lawful Larceny* (also prod.), *Zaza* (also prod.), *Big Brother* (also prod.) 1923; *A Society Scandal* (also sc.), *Manhandled* (also prod.), *Her Love Story* (also prod.), *Wages of*

Virtue (also prod.), *Argentine Love* (also prod.) 1924; *Night Life of New York* (also prod.), *Coast of Folly* (also prod.), *Stage Struck* (also prod.) 1925; *Sea Horses* (also prod.), *Padlocked* (also prod.), *Tin Gods* (also prod.), *Summer Bachelors* (also prod.) 1926; *The Music Master* (also prod.), *West Point* (one-reel doc. in sound), *The Joy Girl* (also prod.), *East Side West Side* (also sc.), *French Dressing* (also prod.) 1927; *The Big Noise* (also prod.) 1928; *The Iron Mask, Tide of Empire, The Far Call, Frozen Justice, South Sea Rose* 1929; *What a Widow!* (also prod.), *Man to Man* 1930; *Chances, Wicked* 1931; *While Paris Sleeps* 1932; *Her First Affair* (UK), *Counsel's Opinion* (UK) 1933; *I Spy/The Morning After* (UK), *Hollywood Party* (co-dir. with Richard Boleslawski and Roy Ronland, uncredited) 1934; *Black Sheep* (also story), *Navy Wife* 1935; *Song and Dance Man, Human Cargo, High Tension, 15 Maiden Lane* 1936; *Woman-Wise, That I May Live, One Mile from Heaven, Heidi* 1937; *Rebecca of Sunnybrook Farm, Josette, Suez* 1938; *The Three Musketeers, The Gorilla, Frontier Marshal* 1939; *Sailor's Lady, Young People, Trail of the Vigilantes* 1940; *Look Who's Laughing* (also prod.), *Rise and Shine* 1941; *Friendly Enemies, Here We Go Again* (also prod.) 1942; *Around the World* (also prod.) 1943; *Up in Mabel's Room, Abroad with Two Yanks* 1944; *Brewster's Millions, Getting Gertie's Garter* (also co-sc.) 1945; *Rendezvous with Annie* (also assoc. prod.) 1946; *Calendar Girl* (also assoc. prod.), *Northwest Outpost* (also assoc. prod.), *Driftwood* 1947; *The Inside Story* (also prod.), *Angel in Exile* (co-dir. with Philip Ford) 1948; *Sands of Iwo Jima* 1949; *Surrender* (also assoc. prod.) 1950; *Belle Le Grande, The Wild Blue Yonder* 1951; *I Dream of Jeanie, Montana Belle* 1952; *Woman They Almost Lynched, Sweethearts on Parade* (also assoc. prod.) 1953; *Flight Nurse, Silver Lode, Passion, Cattle Queen of Montana* 1954; *Escape to Burma, Pearl of the South Pacific, Tennessee's Partner* (also co-sc.) 1955; *Slightly Scarlet, Hold Back the Night* 1956; *The River's Edge, The Restless Breed* 1957; *Enchanted Island* 1958; *Most Dangerous Man Alive* (release delayed from 1958) 1961.

Dykstra, John. Special effects artist. Born on June 3, 1947, in Long Beach, Calif. A still photographer while attending design school, he got his start in films by collaborating on the special effects of John Trumbull's *Silent Running* (1972). The following year, however, he went to work for Berkeley's Institute of Urban Development, where he participated in a sophisticated project applying cinematography and visual effects to the construction of miniature cityscape models. He re-entered films triumphantly as the innovative special effects supervisor on George LUCAS's *Star Wars* (1977), winning two Academy Awards for his effort. He shared the regular Oscar in the visual effects category and won a scientifical/technical special award for the invention and development of the DYKSTRAFLEX motion control camera system. For *Star Wars*, Dykstra served as head of a company Lucas called INDUSTRIAL LIGHT & MAGIC (ILM), which was to become Hollywood's best-known supplier of visual effects. Dykstra left ILM to form his own company, Apogee, through which he produced the first five episodes and the motion picture version of *Battlestar Galactica* (1979).

FILMS INCLUDE: *Silent Running* 1972; *Star Wars* 1977; *Battlestar Galactica* (also prod.), *Avalanche Express, Star Trek: The Motion Picture* 1979; *Firefox* 1982; *Invaders from Mars* 1986; *The Unholy, My Stepmother Is an Alien* 1988; *Batman and Robin* 1997.

Dykstraflex. A computerized motion control camera system that allows a camera and a model (such as a spaceship) to move together in prearranged patterns. Because the motions are computer-controlled, they can be repeated exactly many times, making it easier to create traveling MATTES and to add embellishments in separate passes of the camera (such as engine glows for spaceships). The Dykstraflex is named for its principal inventor, special effects artist John DYKSTRA, who used it in the making of *Star Wars* (1977).

dynamic cutting. A film-editing style, characteristic of polemic documentaries and propaganda films, in which separate shots are joined or contrasted in such a manner as to give significant expression to basically nonpartisan material. In dynamic cutting, the film's impact is achieved in the cutting room rather than during the original shooting, typically through clever juxtaposition and rapid pacing.

Dzigan, Yefim (also **Efim**). Director. *b.* 1898, Byelorussia. *d.* 1982. Among the lesser figures of the Soviet cinema, he is best known for the film *We Are from Kronstadt* (1936), for which he gained international recognition, winning the Grand Prize at the 1937 Paris World's Fair.

FILMS INCLUDE: *Trumpeter Treshney* 1928; *The War God* 1929; *Woman's World* 1932; *We Are from Kronstadt* 1936; *If War Comes Tomorrow* (doc.) 1938; *Moscow Music Hall* (filmed revue; co-dir. with Sergei Gerasimov and Mikhail Kalatozov) 1946; *Jambul* 1953; *Prologue 1956.*

E

Eagels, Jeanne. Actress. *b.* June 26, 1894, Kansas City, Mo. *d.* 1929. A celebrated beauty, she appeared on the stage from the age of seven. Became famous in the role of Sadie Thompson in 'Rain.' She made only a handful of Hollywood films before her death from an overdose of heroin. Her life story was told in *Jeanne Eagels,* a 1957 movie starring Kim Novak.

FILMS: *The House of Fear* 1915; *The World and The Woman* 1916; *The Fires of Youth, Under False Colors* 1917; *The Cross Bearer* 1918; *Man Woman and Sin* 1927; *The Letter, Jealousy* 1929.

Eagle, S. P. See SPIEGEL, Sam.

Eagle-Lion Films. British film distribution company and American film production company. The name was first used for a distribution company founded in 1944 by British film mogul Arthur Rank, but was then adopted for an American production company founded in 1946. The latter company was short-lived, producing a number of B films (including comedies and crime melodramas) until 1950, beginning with *It's a Joke, Son* (1947). However, its output, which included early films by director Anthony Mann, has received a good critical reputation. Eagle-Lion merged with Film Classics in 1950, becoming Eagle-Lion Classics, and was taken over by United Artists the following year.

Ealing comedies. A cluster of sophisticated satirical films produced in the late 40s and early 50s at England's Ealing Studios under the leadership of Sir Michael Balcon. Typically British in their irreverent, self-deprecating, understated humor, these comedies enjoyed universal success. Screenwriters William Rose and T. E. B. Clarke were largely responsible for the success of the Ealing comedies, which were directed by Henry Cornelius, Robert Hamer, Alexander Mackendrick, and Charles Crichton, among others. Alec Guinness was a frequent star. Among the most successful of the genre were *Passport to Pimlico, Kind Hearts and Coronets, Whiskey Galore/Tight Little Island* (all 1949), *The Lavender Hill Mob* (1951), and *The Ladykillers* (1955).

Earle, Edward. Actor. *b.* 1884, Toronto, Ont., Canada. *d.* 1972. Blue-eyed, blond romantic leading man of numerous Hollywood silents. He entered films with the Edison company in 1915, following extensive experience in vaudeville and musicals and on the legitimate stage. Starred in many productions, opposite Mary Pickford and other popular leading ladies. Played supporting roles in talkies through the early 50s.

FILMS INCLUDE: *The Innocence of Ruth, The Gates of Eden* 1916; *For France* 1917; *Blind Adventure* 1918; *His Bridal Night, The Miracle of Love* 1919; *The Law of the Yukon* 1920; *East Lynne, Passion Fruit* 1921; *False Fronts, The Man Who Played God, The Streets of New York* 1922; *Broadway Broke* 1923; *The Dangerous Flirt, The Family Secret, Gambling Wives, The Lure of Love* 1924; *The Lady Who Lied, The Splendid Road* 1925; *Irene, The Greater Glory, A Woman's Heart* 1926; *Spring Fever* 1927; *The Wind* 1928; *Kid Gloves, Spite Marriage, Smiling Irish Eyes, The Hottentot* 1929; *In the Next Room, Second Honeymoon* 1930; *A Woman of Experience* 1931; *Alimony Madness* 1933; *Little Miss Marker* 1934; *Magnificent Obsession* 1935; *Her Jungle Love* 1938; *East Side of Heaven* 1939; *Seventeen* 1940; *The Dancing Masters* 1943; *The Harvey Girls* 1946; *The Beginning or the End* 1947; *Command Decision, That Midnight Kiss* 1949; *The Stranger Wore a Gun* 1953.

Eason, B. Reeves ("Breezy"). Director. *b.* 1886, Friar Point, Miss. *d.* 1956. He left the produce business to go into acting in stock and vaudeville. In 1913 he joined the American Film Company as director and then piloted numerous shorts and action features for various motion picture companies, specializing in serials and low-budget action films. His talent for directing action (but not actors) was exemplified by the exciting mass-movement sequences he handled in his capacity as second-unit director on grand-scale pictures directed by others. Among many action-filled scenes he handled was the famous chariot race in the silent version of *Ben-Hur* (1925), employing more than 40 cameramen; the exciting charge sequence in *The Charge of the Light Brigade* (1936); and the burning of Atlanta sequence in *Gone With the Wind* (1939). Low budgets and speedy schedules prevented him from generating much excitement in his own films as director.

FILMS INCLUDE: *The Day of Reckoning, The Assayer of Lone Gap, The Spirit of Adventure* 1915; *Nine-Tenths of the Law* (also sc., act.) 1918; *The Moon Riders* (serial), *Human Stuff* (also co-sc.), *Blue Streak McCoy* (also sc.), *Pink Tights, Two Kinds of Love* (also co-sc. act.) 1920; *The Big Adventure, Colorado, Red Courage, The Fire Eater* 1921; *Pardon My Nerve!, When East Comes West, Rough Shod, The Lone Hand* 1922; *Around The World* (serial), *His Last Race* 1923; *Trigger Finger, Women First, Flashing Spurs* 1924; *Fighting the Flames, Border Justice, Fighting Youth, Ben-Hur* (2nd-unit dir.), *The Shadow on the Wall* 1925; *The Sign of the Claw, The Test of Donald Norton* 1926; *The Denver Dude, The Prairie King, Painted Pony* 1927; *A Trick of Hearts, The Flyin' Cowboy* (also sc.), *Riding for Fame* (also sc.) 1928; *The Lariat Kid, The Winged Horseman* (co-dir. with Arthur Rosson) 1929; *Troopers Three* (co-dir. with Norman Taurog), *The Roaring Ranch* (also sc.), *Trigger Tricks* (also sc.), *Spurs* (also sc.) 1930; *The Galloping Ghost* (serial), *The Vanishing Legion* (serial) 1931; *The Last of the Mohicans* (serial; co-dir. with Ford Beebe), *The Sunset Trail, Honor of the Press, The Heart Punch* 1932; *Cornered, Behind Jury Doors, Alimony Madness, Revenge at Monte Carlo, Her Resale Value, Dance Hall Hostess* 1933; *Law of the Wild* (serial; co-dir. with Armond L. Schaefer) 1934; *The Phantom Empire* (serial; co-dir. with Ottol Brower), *The Adventures of Rax and Rinty* (serial; co-dir. with Ford Beebe), *The Fighting Marines* (serial; co-dir, with Joseph Kane) 1935; *The Charge of the Light Brigade* (2nd-unit dir.), *Darkest Africa* (serial; co-dir. with Kane), *The Undersea Kingdom* (co-dir. with Kane), *Red River Valley* 1936; *Empty Holsters, Prairie Thunder* 1937; *Sergeant Murphy, The Kid Comes Back* 1938; *Gone With the Wind* (2nd-unit dir.), *Blue Montana Skies, Mountain Rhythm* 1939; *Men with Steel Faces* (co-dir. with Bower) 1940; *Murder in the Big House, Spy Ship* 1942; *The Phantom* (serial), *Truck Busters* 1943; *Black Arrow* (serial), *The Desert Hawk* (serial) 1944; *Duel in the Sun* (2nd-unit dir.) 1947; *Rimfire* 1949; *Dallas* (2nd-unit dir.) 1950.

Eastman, George. Inventor, manufacturer. *b.* July 12, 1854, Waterville, N.Y. *d.* 1932, a suicide after a long illness. At age six he moved with his family to Rochester, N.Y., where his father founded the Eastman Commercial College. Two years later his father died, and by age 14 George was forced to leave school to help support his family as a messenger boy and office clerk. An amateur photographer, he began inventing photographic processes while in his early 20s. In 1880 he started manufacturing gelatin dry plates to replace the messy wet collodion process then prevalent in still photography. In 1884 he introduced paper roll film and, soon after, began marketing an inexpensive box camera, the Number 1 Kodak, which immediately became popular. His invention of perforated celluloid film in 1889 enabled W. K. L. Dickson and Thomas Alva Edison to perfect their motion picture apparatus and begin producing their films in a size (35 mm) that remains standard to this day. Eastman, whose invention made him very wealthy, was a noted philanthropist and contributed millions to institutions of learning, culture, and public health. The Eastman House in Rochester, N.Y., is a center of cinema research and contains valuable collections related to the early history of film.

Eastman Color. Three-color process that has gained wide acceptance by film studios the world over since its introduction in the early 50s. Its main advantages over Technicolor and other color systems at the time were easier processing at a lower cost and less light needed during photography. Eastman Color was used in the production of many 3-D and CinemaScope films of the 50s. The Japanese film *Gate of Hell,* one of the most striking color productions ever made, was shot in Eastman Color.

Eastwood, Clint. Actor, director, producer. Born Clinton Eastwood, Jr., on May 31, 1930, in San Francisco. *ed.* Los Angeles City Coll. A child of the Depression, he spent his early boyhood trailing a father who pumped gas along dusty roads all over the West Coast. Young Clint rarely spent more than a semester in one school, and after graduating from high school, he worked as a logger, steel-furnace stoker, and gas pumper. After a four-year stint (1950–54) with the Army Special Services, he settled in Hollywood in 1955 as a small-time actor. He enjoyed a modest success as a character named Rowdy Yates in the TV Western series 'Rawhide,' which ran for eight seasons from the late 50s through the mid-60s.

But it was in Italy that he found his fame and fortune, as the laconic, supercool "Man With No Name" hero of three violence-filled "spaghetti Westerns" by Sergio LEONE, *A Fistful of Dollars, For a Few Dollars More,* and *The Good the Bad and the Ugly* (1964–66). Enormously popular worldwide, the trilogy catapulted Eastwood into top-ranking box-office stardom and established his screen image as a lanky, tight-lipped, beleaguered hero, a role he continued to play back in the States in a succession of Don SIEGEL films in the late 60s and in his own films as director from the early 70s. He heads his own production company, Malpaso Productions.

The film that firmly established Eastwood as a superstar and with which he remained most closely identified throughout his career was Siegel's *Dirty Harry* (1971). An exciting but controversial action picture, called excessively brutal by some, and blatantly fascist by others, it was followed by four sequels in a span of 17 years.

As a director, Eastwood gradually won the respect of many critics for his no-nonsense approach to filmmaking and his intuitive ability to handle action fluidly. In 1980 the New York Museum of Modern Art held a retrospective of Eastwood films. In 1985, following a retrospective at the Cinématheque Française, he was decorated Chevalier des Arts et Lettres by the French government. In 1986–88 he served as the elected mayor of Carmel, California.

Eastwood's 1988 biographical film *Bird*, based on the life of jazz legend Charlie Parker, gained international acclaim and heightened his critical standing. The dark revisionist Western *Unforgiven* (1992) won an Oscar for best picture and extended the critical view, setting him in iconic relief as both actor and director. After decades of competency and artlessness, he is seen as a spare, epic directorial master and an actor who makes aging seem not only acceptable but glamorous.

Eastwood's marriage (from 1953) to Maggie Johnson ended in 1980, amidst publicity over his open affair with one of his co-stars, Sondra LOCKE. That relationship, too, fell apart in the late 80s. His next romantic interest was actress Frances Fisher, with whom he has a daughter. Eastwood was married again in 1996 to Tina Ruiz. A longtime jazz aficionado, he has featured jazz music in many of his movies and played jazz piano in *In the Line of Fire*.

FILMS (as actor): *Revenge of the Creature, Francis in the Navy, Lady Godiva, Tarantula* 1955; *Never Say Goodbye, The First Traveling Saleslady, Star in the Dust* 1956; *Escapade in Japan* 1957; *Ambush at Cimarron Pass, Lafayette Escadrille* 1958; *Per un Pugno di Dollari/A Fistful of Dollars* 1964; *Per Qualche Dollari in piu/For a Few Dollars More* 1965; *Il Buono il Brutto il Cattivo/The Good, the Bad and the Ugly* 1966; *Le Streghe/The Witches* (De Sica episode) 1967; *Hang 'Em High, Coogan's Bluff* 1968; *Where Eagles Dare, Paint Your Wagon* 1969; *Two Mules for Sister Sara, Kelly's Heroes* 1970; *The Beguiled, Play Misty for Me* (also dir.), *Dirty Harry* 1971; *Joe Kidd* 1972; *High Plains Drifter* (also dir.), *Breezy* (dir. only), *Magnum Force* 1973; *Thunderbolt and Lightfoot* 1974; *The Eiger Sanction* (also dir.) 1975; *The Outlaw—Josey Wales* (also dir.), *The Enforcer* 1976; *The Gauntlet* 1977; *Every Which Way but Loose* 1978; *Escape from Alcatraz* 1979; *Bronco Billy* (also dir.), *Any Which Way You Can* 1980; *Firefox* (also dir., prod.), *Honkytonk Man* (also dir., prod.) 1982; *Sudden Impact* (also dir., prod.) 1983; *Tightrope* (also co-prod.), *City Heat* 1984; *Pale Rider* (also dir., prod.) 1985; *Heartbreak Ridge* (also dir., prod) 1986; *The Dead Pool, Bird* (dir., prod. only) 1988; *Thelonius Monk: Straight, No Chaser* (doc.; exec. prod. only), *Pink Cadillac* 1989; *White Hunter Black Heart* (also dir., prod.), *The Rookie* (also dir.) 1990; *Unforgiven* (also dir, prod.) 1992; *In the Line of Fire, A Perfect World* (also dir.) 1993; *Casper* (v/o) 1994; *The Bridges of Madison County* (also dir.), *The Stars Fell on Henrietta* (co-prod. only) 1995; *Absolute Power* (also dir.) 1997.

Eaton, Shirley. Actress. Born in 1936, in London. Shapely, blonde leading lady, employed to decorative advantage in many British films of the late 50s and 60s. Memorable as the girl painted gold in the James Bond adventure, *Goldfinger.*

FILMS INCLUDE: *You Know What Sailors Are, The Belles of St. Trinian's, Doctor in the House* 1954; *Sailor Beware/Panic in the Parlor* 1956; *Doctor at Large, Three Men in a Boat, The Naked Truth/Your Past Is Showing* 1957; *Carry on Sergeant* 1958; *Carry on Nurse* 1959; *Life Is a Circus, Carry on Constable* 1960; *A Weekend with Lulu* 1961; *The Girl Hunters* 1963; *Rhino!* (US), *Goldfinger* 1964; *The Naked Brigade* (US/Gr.) 1965; *Ten Little Indians, Around the World Under the Sea* (US) 1966; *Eight on the Lam* (US), *Sumuru/The Million Eyes of Su-Muru* 1967; *Kiss & Kill/The Blood of Fu Manchu* (US/UK/Ger./Sp.) 1968.

Eaubonne, Jean d'. Art Director. *b.* 1903, Talence, France. *d.* 1971. Trained as a sculptor and a painter, he was an assistant to designer Lazare Meerson before being given his first opportunity to design for films on Jean Cocteau's *Le Sang d'un Poéte/The Blood of a Poet,* in 1930. He subsequently worked on many distinguished French productions for Cocteau, Max Ophüls, Feyder, Becker, and others. In the last decade of his career he worked often in Hollywood. Noted for his baroque, refined style.

FILMS INCLUDE: *Le Sang d'un Poéte/The Blood of a Poet* 1930; *Pour un Sou d'Amour* 1932; *De Mayerling é Sarajevo/Mayerling to Sarajevo* 1940; *La Loi du Nord* (release delayed from 1939) 1942; *Macadam/Back Streets of Paris* 1946; *La Chartreuse de Parme* 1948; *Black Magic* (US) 1949; *Orphée/Orpheus, La Ronde* 1950; *Le Plaisir, Casque d'Or* 1952; *Madame de. . . /The Earrings of Madame De, Rue de l'Estrapade* 1953; *Touchez pas au Grisbi/Grisbi* 1954; *Lola Montés* 1955; *Amére Victoire/Bitter Victory* 1957; *Montparnasse 19/Modigliani of Montparnasse, The Reluctant Debutante* (US) 1958; *Crack in the Mirror* (US) 1960; *The Big Gamble* (US), *Madame Sans-Gêne/Madame* 1961; *Love Is a Ball* (US), *Charade* (US) 1963; *Paris When It Sizzles* 1964; *Lady L* (US/Fr./It.) 1965; *Custer of the West* (US) 1968; *Le Drapeau noir flotte sur la Marmite* 1971.

Ebsen, Buddy. Actor, dancer. Born Christian Rudolph Ebsen, on Apr. 2, 1908, in Belleville, Ill. Trained in his father's dance school, he appeared as a dancer in vaudeville and on Broadway, often with sister Vilma, before going into films. He played supporting roles in screen musicals of the 30s and early 40s. He was the original Tin Man in *The Wizard of Oz* (1939), but after nine days of shooting he was poisoned by his makeup and was replaced by Jack HALEY. After an eight-year absence, he returned to films as a dramatic actor in 1950. He struck it rich as the head of 'The Beverly Hillbillies' clan in the long-running (1962–71) TV series and later starred in 'Barnaby Jones' (1973–80) and 'Matt Houston' (1984–85).

FILMS INCLUDE: *Broadway Melody of 1936* 1935; *Captain January, Born to Dance, Banjo on My Knee* 1936; *Broadway Melody of 1938* 1937; *The Girl of the Golden West, Yellow Jack, My Lucky Star* 1938; *Four Girls in White* 1939; *Parachute Battalion* 1941; *Sing Your Worries Away* 1942; *Under Mexicali Stars* 1950; *Thunder in God's Country* 1951; *Night People, Red Garters* 1954; *Davy Crockett* 1955; *Attack* 1956; *Breakfast at Tiffany's* 1961; *The Interns* 1962; *Mail Order Bride* 1964; *The One and Only Genuine Original Family Band* 1968.

echo chamber. An enclosure in which a microphone and a loudspeaker are set up so that amplified sound can travel back and forth, creating a reverberation that results in a recorded echo effect. Also, an electronic device designed to produce that effect during recording or mixing. For example, the echo chamber is used when it is desired to have dialogue sound as if it were recorded in a cave or a cathedral or any other place that would be expected to produce an echo.

Eddie Awards. See A.C.E.

Eddy, Helen Jerome. Actress. *b.* 1897, New York City. *d.* 1990. Tall, genteel star and supporting player of American silents, then character player of Hollywood talkies of the 30s. Raised in Los Angeles, she attended the University of California at Berkeley and entered films in 1915. She specialized in well-bred heroines and characters until her retirement in 1940. Early in her career she was billed as Helen Eddy.

FILMS INCLUDE: *The Red Virgin, The Gentleman from Indiana* 1915; *Madame la Presidente, Pasquale* 1916; *His Sweetheart, Rebecca of Sunnybrook Farm* 1917; *Jules of the Strong Heart, Old Wives for New* 1918; *The Turn in the Road, The Boomerang, The Man Beneath, The Trembling Hour, The Tong Man* 1919; *Pollyanna, The County Fair, A Light Woman, The Forbidden Thing* 1920; *The First Born, The Other Woman* 1921; *The Flirt, When Love Comes* 1922; *To the Ladies* 1923; *Marry Me, The Dark Angel* 1925; *Padlocked* 1926; *Camille, Quality Street* 1927; *Chicago After Midnight, Two Lovers* 1928; *The Divine Lady* 1929; *War Nurse* 1930; *Reaching for the Moon, Girls Demand Excitement, Skippy, Sooky, Mata Hari* 1931; *Madame Butterfly* 1932; *The Bitter Tea of General Yen, The Masquerader, Torch Singer* 1933; *Riptide* 1934; *The Keeper of the Bees* 1935; *Klondike Annie, The Country Doctor, Winterset, Stowaway* 1936; *City Streets* 1938; *Strike Up the Band* 1940.

Eddy, Nelson. Singer, actor. *b.* June 29, 1901, Providence, R.I. *d.* 1967. As a boy he sang soprano in church choirs. After moving to Philadelphia in his teens, he worked as a switchboard operator, shipping clerk, and finally newspaper reporter before winning a competition in 1922 to join the Philadelphia Civic Opera. He sang in many of the group's productions and in 1924 played Tonio in *Pagliacci* at the New York Metropolitan Opera (but not with the Met company). A successful concert tour and radio appearances in the early 30s led to a movie contract with MGM. He enjoyed phenomenal popularity after teaming with Jeanette MACDONALD in a series of saccharine operettas, beginning with *Naughty Marietta* in 1935. Billed as "America's Sweethearts" or the "Singing Sweethearts," Eddy and Macdonald became the most popular screen duo of their day. Their bittersweet films, which have since become high camp, were blockbusters at the box office in the innocent days preceding America's entry into WW II. When the partnership finally came to an end (with *I Married an Angel,* in 1942), Eddy's film career went downhill. He continued to appear, however, in concerts and nightclubs and made occasional recordings. In 1967, during an Australian tour, he collapsed onstage and died of a stroke.

FILMS: *Broadway to Hollywood, Dancing Lady* 1933; *Student Tour* 1934; *Naughty Marietta* 1935; *Rose Marie* 1936; *Maytime, Rosalie* 1937; *The Girl of the Golden West, Sweethearts* 1938; *Let Freedom Ring!, Balalaika* 1939; *New Moon, Bitter Sweet* 1940; *The Chocolate Soldier* 1941; *I Married an Angel* 1942; *The Phantom of the Opera* 1943; *Knickerbocker Holiday* 1944; *Make Mine Music* (v/o) 1946; *Northwest Outpost* 1947.

Eden, Barbara. Actress. Born Barbara Jean Huffman, on Aug. 23, 1934, in Tucson, Ariz. A former all-American cheerleader and a teenage pop singer, she has had a modest career as a leading lady in films but has fared much better as a TV star in the series 'How to Marry a Millionaire' (1957–59), 'I Dream of Jeannie' (1965–70), and 'Harper Valley P.T.A.' (1981–82). She was married to actor Michael Ansara from 1958 to 1973. She is president of Mi-Bar Productions and is a director of Security First National Bank of Chicago.

FILMS: *Back from Eternity* 1956; *The Wayward Girl* 1957; *A Private's Affair* 1959; *Twelve Hours to Kill, Flaming Star, From the Terrace* 1960; *All Hands on Deck, Voyage to the Bottom of the Sea* 1961; *The Wonderful World of the Brothers Grimm, Swingin' Along, Five Weeks in a Balloon* 1962; *The Yellow Canary* 1963; *The Brass Bottle, The 7 Faces of Dr. Lao, The New Interns, Ride the Wild Surf* 1964; *Quick Let's Get Married* 1971; *The Amazing Dobermans* 1977; *Harper Valley P.T.A.* 1978; *Jaws 3-D* 1983; *Chattanooga Choo Choo* 1984.

Edens, Roger. Composer, arranger, music supervisor, producer. *b.* Nov. 9, 1905, Hillsboro, Tex. *d.* 1970. A former piano accompanist for ballroom dancers, he went to Hollywood in 1933 to write special material for Ethel Merman films at Paramount. In 1935 he joined MGM as a musical supervisor and occasional composer and arranger, notably of Judy Garland songs ('Dear Mr. Gable,' etc.). In the early 40s he became associate producer to Arthur FREED while continuing to compose, score, and arrange MGM musicals. He won Academy Awards for collaborating on the scoring of *Easter Parade, On the Town,* and *Annie Get Your Gun.* He also produced a number of films after the mid-50s.

FILMS INCLUDE: *Kid Millions* 1934; *Born to Dance* 1936; *Broadway Melody of 1938* 1937; *Everybody Sing* 1938; *The Wizard of Oz* (arrangements only), *Babes in Arms* 1939; *Strike Up the Band, Go West, Little Nelly Kelly* 1940; *Ziegfeld Girl, Lady Be Good, Babes on Broadway* 1941; *Presenting Lily Mars* 1943; *Thousands Cheer, Meet Me in St. Louis* (mus. super., assoc. prod. only) 1944; *Yolanda and the Thief* (mus. super., assoc. prod. only) 1945; *The Harvey Girls* (mus. super., assoc. prod. only), *Ziegfeld Follies* 1946; *Good News* (also assoc. prod.) 1947; *Easter Parade* 1948; *Take Me Out to the Ball Game, On the Town* 1949; *Annie Get Your Gun* 1950; *Show Boat, An American in Paris* (both assoc. prod. only) 1951; *The Band Wagon* (assoc. prod. only) 1953; *Deep in My Heart* (prod. only), *A Star Is Born* 1954; *Funny Face* (also prod.) 1957; *The Unsinkable Molly Brown* (assoc. prod. only) 1964; *Hello Dolly* (assoc. prod. only) 1969.

Edeson, Arthur. Director of photography. *b.* Oct. 24, 1891, New York City. *d.* 1970. *ed.* CCNY. A portrait photographer, he entered the film industry with the Eclair company in 1911. Toward the end of the decade, he began a long association with Douglas FAIRBANKS, Sr., first as a camera operator and later as a director of photography. In 1918 he was among the founders of A.S.C. In 1929, at the dawn of the sound era, Edeson pioneered in location sound photography as the cameraman of the successful Western *In Old Arizona.* A superb black-and-white artist and a master at creating atmosphere, he reached the peak of his long career with Warner Bros. in the 30s and early 40s. He retired in 1949.

FILMS INCLUDE: *The Dollar Mark* 1914; *Hearts in Exile* 1915; *In Again Out Again, Wild and Woolly, Reaching for the Moon* (all camera operator only), *Souls Adrift* 1917; *Mr. Fix-It* (cam. oper. only) 1918; *Cheating Cheaters, Eyes of Youth* 1919; *The Forbidden Woman* 1920; *The Three Musketeers* 1921; *Robin Hood* 1922; *The Thief of Bagdad* 1924; *One-Way Street, Lost World, Stella Dallas* 1925; *The Bat* 1926; *McFadden's Flats, The Patent Leather Kid, The Gorilla* 1927; *Me Gangster* 1928; *In Old Arizona* 1929; *All Quiet on the Western Front, The*

Big Trail (co-phot.) 1930; *Waterloo Bridge, Frankenstein* 1931; *The Old Dark House* 1932; *A Study in Scarlet, The Invisible Man* (co-phot.) 1933; *Mutiny on the Bounty, Ceiling Zero* 1935; *Gold Diggers of 1937* 1936; *They Won't Forget* (co-phot.) 1937; *Each Dawn I Die* 1939; *Castle on the Hudson, They Drive by Night* 1940; *Sergeant York* (battle sequences only), *The Maltese Falcon* 1941; *The Male Animal, Across the Pacific, Casablanca* 1942; *Thank Your Lucky Stars* 1943; *The Mask of Dimitrios, The Conspirator* 1944; *Three Strangers, Nobody Lives Forever* 1946; *My Wild Irish Rose* 1947; *The Fighting O'Flynn* 1949.

Edeson, Robert. Actor. *b.* 1868, New Orleans. *d.* 1931. Virile hero, then solid character player of numerous Hollywood silents and early talkies. The son of a theatrical producer and manager, he had an early start as a stage actor and was a seasoned veteran by the time he made his screen debut in 1914. Starred in many films, often in tough man-of-action roles. In the 20s appeared regularly in sumptuous C. B. DE MILLE productions, usually in commanding character parts.

FILMS INCLUDE: *The Call of the North, Where the Trail Divides* 1914; *Man's Prerogative, The Absentee, Mortmain, The Cave Man, How Molly Made Good* 1915; *The Light That Failed* 1916; *The Public Defender* 1917; *Sealed Hearts* 1919; *Extravagance* 1921; *The Prisoner of Zenda* 1922; *Has the World Gone Mad!, Luck, The Silent Partner, To the Last Man, The Ten Commandments* 1923; *Thy Name Is Woman, Mademoiselle Midnight, Triumph, Men, Feet of Clay* 1924; *The Golden Bed, The Rag Man, Men and Women, Blood and Steel, The Danger Signal, Keep Smiling, Hell's Highroad, The Scarlet West, Braveheart* 1925; *Whispering Smith, The Volga Boatman, Eve's Leaves, The Blue Eagle* 1926; *Altars of Desire, The King of Kings* (as Matthew), *The Heart Thief* 1927; *Chicago, Tenth Avenue, The Power of the Press, George Washington Cohen* 1928; *The Doctor's Secret, Marianne, Dynamite* 1929; *Cameo Kirby, The Way of All Men, Big Money, The Lash/Adios* 1930.

edge numbers. Serial numbers (and key letters) printed during the manufacturing stage on the edge of raw negative film at one-foot intervals. Duplicated on positive prints during processing, these numbers help editors and negative cutters to match the negative with the work print once editing is completed.

Edison, Thomas Alva. Inventor. *b.* Feb. 11, 1847, Milan, Ohio. *d.* 1931. The son of a timber dealer of Dutch descent, he had little formal education and was tutored for the most part by his mother, a teacher of Scottish descent. He began experimenting with telegraphic devices at age ten. At 12 he began working as a newspaper and candy vendor on the Port Huron–Detroit train. At 15 he became a telegraph operator. Continued experimentation led to his first patented invention, the stock ticker, in 1868, and later to several improved telegraphic systems. In 1871 he set up a plant in Newark, N.J., which manufactured devices for Western Union. In 1876 he gave up his factory and founded a research laboratory in Menlo Park, N.J., from which there emanated a great number of important inventions, including the carbon microphone essential to the practicability of Bell's telephone, the phonograph, and the incandescent lamp that made modern electricity possible.

Edison, or "The Wizard of Menlo Park" as he now came to be called, moved his lab to larger quarters at Orange, N.J., in 1887. Here he set a staff to work on developing his mechanical visions, among them a motion picture apparatus. Edison envisioned the motion picture machine as an instrument "that should do for the eye what the phonograph did for the ear." He entrusted his assistant, W. K. L. DICKSON, with the construction of the apparatus. In 1889 the Edison Kinetophonograph (also known as the Kinetophone), capable of showing film (just invented by EASTMAN) in synchronization with a phonograph record, became a reality. In 1891 the offspring of the Kinetophonograph, the Kinetograph camera and the Kinetoscope viewer, were successfully demonstrated. In accordance with Edison's specifications, George Eastman supplied his newly invented celluloid film roll for the newly invented apparatus on 35 mm stock with four perforations on each side of the frame, standards that remain unchanged to this day. Edison manufactured his early films at his BLACK MARIA, the world's first studio, constructed in 1893 by Dickson.

For reasons of his own, Edison at first neglected to develop a practicable projector for public viewing of his films on a screen. Instead, his Kinetoscope was exploited as a peep-show novelty that could be viewed only privately by one person at a time. Finally realizing the commercial potential of public showings of film, he contracted to acquire the rights to the Jenkins-Armat Vitascope projector, an improvement of his own invention. On April 23, 1896, the Edison Vitascope was publicly unveiled in a program of projected films accompanying a vaudeville show at New York's Koster & Bial Music Hall, on 34th Street and Broadway. The program consisted of 12 short subjects, one of them hand-colored, and marked the birth in America of a new form of art and a great new industry.

In 1909 the Edison organization and several other major embryonic motion picture companies joined forces to form the Motion Picture Patents Company, a trust designed to block the encroachment of the many independent producers seeking a piece of the new business. Antitrust action resulted in the dissolution of the monopoly in 1917, and that same year the Edison Company went out of the film business. Edison, called by Einstein "the greatest inventor of all time," having laid the mechanical foundations of cinema, went on to numerous other inventions until shortly before his death at 84. Edison's career was romanticized in two MGM films, *Young Tom Edison,* starring Mickey Rooney, and *Edison the Man,* starring Spencer Tracy, both released in 1940.

editing. The process of selecting, assembling, and arranging motion picture shots and corresponding sound tracks in coherent sequence and flowing continuity. A significant phase of film production editing begins as soon as the first day's shooting is completed and the exposed footage has been processed and printed by the lab. As filming proceeds, the footage arrives in the CUTTING ROOM in installments known as DAILIES or rushes, which eventually add up to the editor's WORK PRINT. The footage is received in a crude state, containing printable shots and copies of SOUND TRACKS in the order and length in which they have been filmed and recorded.

Editing is a laborious, exacting, multistage process that is both a craft and an art. The editor and his assistants must perform many routine, time-consuming chores before they can even begin their involvement in the creative aspect of their work. Each foot of film must be matched and synchronized with the corresponding sound track (see CODE NUMBERS; SYNCHRONIZATION) and each roll examined and catalogued. As it continues to arrive in the cutting room, the footage is viewed repeatedly. The best takes and camera angles are selected, and sequences are joined in the order specified by the script. The process continues until all filming is completed and all footage is "IN THE CAN." With all the needed visuals and sound tracks in the cutting room, and all material aligned, synchronized, and arranged more or less according to the intended continuity, the editor can proceed with the creative task of continually trimming down, refining, and reshaping the material to achieve the desired content, construction, and rhythm within each sequence and through the production as a whole. This is done in three main stages, compressing the footage first to a ROUGH CUT, second to a FINE CUT, and third—and last—to an approved WORK PRINT that is acceptable to the director and producer. At each stage, the footage is repeatedly passed through the VIEWER and the MOVIOLA. Scenes are spliced and re-spliced with tape (dry splice) or liquid cement (wet splice), and transitional effects like fades, dissolves, and wipes are tentatively worked and reworked into the print by CHINA (GRAPH) PENCIL. Toward the end of the process, the editor's work print is a smudged mess of wound celluloid seemingly held together by a thread.

The approved work print is the result of weeks or months of painstaking work during which the editor, under the supervision of the director or producer, has, ideally, turned tens of thousands of feet of orderless film into a motion picture of content and sensibility. Each shot has been carefully selected and trimmed and every superfluous frame eliminated. Shots have been arranged and juxtaposed within scenes to create meaning, mood, or effect. Each scene has been sharpened and compressed into its essential length and added to other scenes, composing a sequence, and sequences have been made to flow into one another in flawless continuity. SOUND EFFECTS and music tracks have been added to the dialogue and narration tracks, and transitional effects (dissolves, fades, etc.) and titles have been designated and prepared for optical printing.

Two important final procedures remain before the edited work print can be turned into a RELEASE PRINT for showing to an audience. One involves the sound portion of the film, the other the visuals. The first procedure is the MIX, in which several separate sound tracks (dialogue, narration, sound effects, music; sometimes multiples of each) are combined into a single sound track in an especially equipped sound studio. Working from detailed cue sheets prepared earlier, the supervising sound editor and the film editor, usually in the presence of the director or producer, collaborate closely to bring about a delicate balance among the different sounds, stressing some and de-emphasizing others, fading sounds in and out, overlapping sounds, and, when necessary, altering sounds to achieve acoustic effects. Occasionally, the number of tracks involved and the complexity of an assignment call for a premix before the final mix can be accomplished. In recent years, the work of sound effects editing has been recognized as a separate craft from film editing. (See SOUND CREW.)

The other procedure is called MATCHING, or "matching negative." The work print is turned over to a negative cutter, who matches it frame by frame with the original negative. Using white gloves and extreme care, the negative cutter cuts and splices the precious negative exactly the way the work print has been cut and edited. He is guided by the edge numbers and by detailed instructions from the editor. Finally, the cut negative and the mixed sound track are sent to the laboratory for printing, with specific instructions about the desired tonal quality and density of each sequence. The trial print that comes back from the lab is called an ANSWER PRINT (also known as an "approval print"). It is screened and carefully examined for light grading, color balance, and other optical details. If the result is unsatisfactory, corrections are requested; the lab may have to turn out several answer prints before one is finally approved. The approved answer print serves as a standard by which subsequent release prints are prepared.

Many editors now use VIDEO EDITING SYSTEMS to streamline their work. In these systems, film frames are transferred to videotape, allowing the editor to view them on a monitor and rearrange them electronically without having to resort to physical cutting of a work print. The editor can also try out a number of alternative sequences before settling on a final version. The frames are coded by computer, simplifying the matching process.

editing room. See CUTTING ROOM.

Editola. Trade name for a compact editing machine. Similar in function to the Moviola, it differs from the latter in that it provides viewing through a continuous run of the film rather than through intermittent motion.

editor. In motion picture production, the person responsible for EDITING a film. Working behind the scenes, away from the glare of publicity and the glamorous surroundings of the film set, the film editor is an unsung member of a motion picture's creative team. Yet the success or failure of a production may hinge on the quality of his work. Sharp film editing can make a mediocre production look good and a good production look even better. Conversely, sloppy editing can undo a solid script and even negate fine efforts by the director, the actors, and technical crews.

In the early days of cinema, editing amounted to little more than simple cutting—trimming edges and splicing loose ends to arrange shots in elementary continuity. The term CUTTER, still used today for an editor, is a vestige of those primitive days. Gradually, through such landmark productions as Edwin S. Porter's *The Great Train Robbery* (1903), D. W. Griffith's *The Birth of a Nation* (1915), and Sergei Eisenstein's *Potemkin* (1925), an expressive language of editing evolved that enhanced the film's narrative and emotional power. The film cutter became a film editor, exercising a complex art as well as a demanding craft, and editing conventions developed that were passed on from one editor to another and continually refined in cutting rooms around the world.

The individual contribution of an editor to a film varies from situation to situation. Some editors with proven skills are given a great deal of autonomy and creative freedom, while others execute their craft mechanically under precise instructions by the director or producer. Sometimes, when working on a high-budget film, an editor may become involved in the preproduction stages of a project and may be invited to attend the actual shooting of some complicated scenes, but normally his role is confined to the cutting room. That role may be great or small, depending on the stage of the footage shot.

Certain directors prepare their scripts and shoot their films with such meticulous care that there is little left for the editor to do but exercise technical expertise, manual dexterity, and a sense of precise timing, in following the director's plan. Frequently, however, the editor is called upon to bring to the production not just his professional skill but also objective judgment, personal taste, and a capacity to articulate vaguely defined directorial intentions by selecting, arranging, and pacing miles of filmed footage into a unified narrative whole. It is not uncommon for an editor to correct or cover up in the cutting room errors or omissions committed during filming on the set. But in the final analysis, film remains a director's medium, and the editor can react only to the material before him, which has been conceived and shot by the director. More often than not, the finished film reflects the personality and temperament of the director rather than the editor. The editor's role is somewhat more pivotal in documentary films, for which no shooting script exists, than in planned fiction productions.

Some directors like to work regularly with the same editors. Notable examples are the collaborations between director Cecil B. De Mille and editor Anne Bauchens, between director Claude Chabrol and editor Jacques Gaillard, between director Joseph Losey and editor Reginald Beck, between director Arthur Penn and editor Dede Allen, between director Jonathan Demme and editor Craig McKay, and between director Woody Allen and editors Ralph Rosenblum (in earlier films) and Susan E. Morse (in more recent films). Such close collaboration facilitates communication between director and editor and probably results in some saving of time and the avoidance of cutting by trial and error, as the editor learns to anticipate the director's intentions. But many directors have worked with a variety of editors with equally successful results. A few directors have maintained complete control by editing their own films, most notably David Lean. Several directors, including Lean, started their careers as editors, among them Dorothy Arzner, Hal Ashby, Charles Frend, Anthony Harvey, Seth Holt, Peter Hunt, Robert Parrish, Mark Robson, John Sturges, and Robert Wise. Wise claims that his previous experience in the cutting room has helped him "visualize the scenes as they will look on the screen before they are shot." Another way his editing experience has helped him, he says, is in the ability to shoot a sequence completely out of continuity, a skill that can result in great savings in money and time.

Prominent editors past and present include, in addition to those named above, Albert Akst, who worked on several big MGM musicals; George Amy, who edited some of the best Warner Bros. films of the 30s and 40s; Britain's Robert Bates; MGM's Margaret Booth; France's Claudine Bouché, who worked on Truffaut's films of the 60s; David Bretherton (*Cabaret,* etc.); Britain's Anne Coates (*Lawrence of Arabia, Becket,* etc.); France's Henri Colpi, who directed several films on his own; France's Anne-Marie Cortet, a frequent collaborator of Jacques Demy; France's Cecile Decugis, who works with Eric Rohmer; Adrienne Fazan, who edited several of Vincente Minnelli's best musicals for MGM; Verna Fields (*American Graffiti, Jaws,* etc.); Rudi Fehr, who did his best work for Warners in the 40s; Britain's Anthony Gibbs (*Tom Jones,* etc.); Gerald Greenberg (*The French Connection,* etc.); France's Agnes Guillemot, who worked on most of Jean-Luc Godard's and several of Trauffaut's films; Britain's Jack Harris (*Great Expectations,* etc.); Doane Harrison, a frequent collaborator of Billy Wilder; Columbia's Gene Havlick; William Hornbeck, an outstanding Paramount editor (*The Heiress, A Place in the Sun, Shane,* etc.), who did some of his best work in Britain in the late 30s (*Rembrandt, Things to Come, The Four Feathers,* etc.); Michael Kahn (*Raiders of the Lost Ark, Fatal Attraction,* etc.); Britain's Ralph Kemplen (*Moulin Rouge, Oliver!,* etc.); Harold Kress (*Mrs. Miniver, The Yearling, The Poseidon Adventure, The Towering Inferno,* etc.); Viola Lawrence (*Here Comes Mr. Jordan, The Lady from Shanghai,* etc.); France's Raymond Lamy, the regular collaborator of Robert Bresson; Britain's Russell Lloyd, a frequent collaborator of John Huston; Warren Low, for many years with Warners, then Paramount; Daniel Mandell, one of the highest rated in the business, who did some of his best work for William Wyler (*Wuthering Heights, The Little Foxes, The Best Years of Our Lives,* etc.) and Billy Wilder (*The Apartment,* etc.); Owen Marks (*Casablanca,* etc.); Barbara McLean, who often worked with Henry King and Joseph L. Mankiewicz at Fox; Britain's Reginald Mills (*The Red Shoes, The Servant,* etc.); Conrad Nervig, who won the first Oscar ever for editing, for *Eskimo,* in 1934; Sam O'Steen (*Chinatown,* etc.); Britain's Tom Priestly; William Reynolds (*The Godfather, The Sting, The Turning Point,* etc.); Dorothy Spencer (*Stagecoach, My Darling Clementine, Cleopatra, Earthquake*); Fredric and William Steinkamp (*Tootsie, Out of Africa,* etc.); George Tomasini, who edited several of Alfred Hitchcock's best American films, including *Rear Window, Vertigo, North by Northwest,* and *Psycho;* Britain's Ernest Walter; Ferris Webster (*The Manchurian Candidate, The Great Escape,* etc.); Ralph Winters (*King Solomon's Mines, Quo Vadis, Seven Brides for Seven Brothers, Ben-Hur,* the 1976 version of *King Kong,* etc.); William Ziegler (*My Fair Lady,* etc.); and Peter Zinner (*The Godfather, The Deer Hunter, An Officer and a Gentleman,* etc.).

Traditionally, editing has been one of the few movie crafts wide open to women, most likely because the position involves little contact with the male-dominated technical crews, but also because it requires manual dexterity rather than brawn and an observant aesthetic eye. The quality of an editor's work can be discerned by such details as the smooth matching of action, the creative use of dissolves and fades, and the general flow of the continuity. Often, an editing job is considered successful when it goes unnoticed on the screen. Ironically, an editor invests weeks or months of intensive work to achieve the impression that he has done nothing at all.

Edlund, Richard. Special effects artist. Born on Dec. 6, 1940, in Fargo, N.D. A photo enthusiast from childhood, he joined the Navy after graduating from high school and received intensive photography and camera repair training at the US Naval Photographic School. He became interested in motion pictures when he was stationed in Japan and after returning home he enrolled in University of Southern California film program. After several years with a small optical effects firm and an attempt at experimental filmmaking, he was recruited by John DYKSTRA as first cameraman on the special effects unit of *Star Wars* (1977). He shared an Academy Award for his work on the film and stayed on with George Lucas's Industrial Light & Magic as a key employee. Known as a virtual wizard of special effects, he went on to share additional Oscars for *The Empire Strikes Back, Raiders of the Lost Ark,* and *Return of the Jedi,* as well as receiving several other nominations. He also won two special Awards in the Scientific/Engineering category for "the concept and engineering of a beam-splitter optical composite motion picture printer" and for "the engineering of the Empire Motion Picture Camera System." In 1983, he formed his own effects company, Boss Film Studios, and has since created astonishing visuals for such movies as *Ghostbusters* and *Ghost.*

FILMS INCLUDE: *Star Wars* 1977; *The Empire Strikes Back* 1980; *Raiders of the Lost Ark* 1981; *Poltergeist* 1982; *Return of the Jedi* 1983; *Ghostbusters, 2010* 1984; *Fright Night* 1985; *Poltergeist II: The Other Side, Big Trouble in Little China, The Boy Who Could Fly* 1986; *Masters of the Universe, The Monster Squad* 1987; *Die Hard, Big Top Pee-wee* 1988; *Ghost* 1990; *Alien* 3 1992, *Air Force One* 1997.

Edouart, Farciot. Special effects artist. *b.* 1897 (?), Calif. *d.* 1980. Perfecter of the BACK PROJECTION or rear projection technique for simulating moving backgrounds, also referred to as process photography (see PROCESS SHOT). In the 1920s he headed the special effects department at Paramount, where he developed several TRAVELING MATTE techniques before focusing on rear projection. By the early 30s he was the premier expert in Hollywood on process photography and helped to make it an essential part of the special effects of the studio era. Among his achievements was the development of the triple-head process projector, which used three projectors to increase the intensity of the background image. He remained with Paramount for many years. He shared two Oscars, for *I Wanted Wings* (1941) and *Reap the Wild Wind* (1942).

FILMS INCLUDE: *Alice in Wonderland* 1933; *Lives of a Bengal Lancer* 1935; *The Plainsman* 1937; *Spawn of the North* 1938; *Union Pacific* 1939; *Dr. Cyclops, The Ghost Breakers, Road to Singapore* 1940; *Sullivan's Travels* 1941; *Reap the Wild Wind* 1942; *Double Indemnity, The Uninvited* 1944; *Road to Utopia* 1945; *Monsieur Beaucaire, The Strange Love of Martha Ivers* 1946; *Unconquered* 1947; *The Paleface* 1948; *A Connecticut Yankee in King Arthur's Court* 1949; *Sunset*

Boulevard 1950; *Detective Story* 1951; *The Turning Point* 1952; *The Naked Jungle* 1953; *Sabrina* 1954; *The Desperate Hours, To Catch a Thief* 1955; *Teacher's Pet, Vertigo* 1958; *Visit to a Small Planet* 1960; *One-Eyed Jacks, Pocketful of Miracles* 1961; *It's a Mad Mad Mad Mad World* 1963; *Roustabout* 1964; *The Spirit Is Willing* 1967; *Rosemary's Baby* 1968.

educational films. A broad category encompassing all films intended primarily to inform and instruct rather than to entertain. Educational films are produced most often in 16 mm, for exhibition at schools and before groups and organizations as well as for transmission over television. Some educational films are made in 35 mm, for showing in big auditoriums and motion picture theaters, and some in 8 mm and Super 8, for broader and cheaper circulation.

Educational Pictures. A motion picture production company, established in 1919, initially for the purpose of making educational films for schools. Instead, the company became a virtual factory for comedy shorts, in the 20s featuring such stars as Lloyd Hamilton and Lupino Lane. Educational continued to prosper in the early 30s despite the generally poor quality of its tight-budget shorts but went out of business at the end of the decade. Operating from studios in Astoria, Queens, N.Y., it managed to employ top East Coast talent during and in between Broadway and vaudeville engagements. Among the stars who worked for Educational at one time or another were Buster Keaton, Harry Langdon, Edward Everett Horton, Charlotte Greenwood, Bert Lahr, Irene Ryan, Milton Berle, the Ritz Brothers, and Danny Kaye.

Edwards, Anthony. Actor. Born on July 19, 1962, in Santa Barbara, Calif. Blond, gentle lead and supporting player, often in comic roles. The grandson of an architect who helped design the Walt Disney studios in the 30s and worked for Cecil B. DE MILLE as a conceptual artist, he began acting at 12 and appeared in numerous plays and commercials during his teens. After training at London's Royal Academy of Arts and at USC, he made his screen debut in 1982. His television work includes the series 'Northern Exposure' and the critically hailed 'ER.'

FILMS: *Fast Times at Ridgemont High* 1982; *Heart Like a Wheel* 1983; *Revenge of the Nerds* 1984; *The Sure Thing, Gotcha!* 1985; *Top Gun* 1986; *Summer Heat, Revenge of the Nerds II* 1987; *Mr. North* 1988; *How I Got Into College, Hawks, Miracle Mile* 1989; *Downtown* 1990; *Delta Heat, Landslide, Pet Sematary II* 1992; *Charlie's Ghost Story* (also dir.), *The Client* 1994.

Edwards, Blake. Director, producer, screenwriter, former actor. Born William Blake McEdwards, on July 26, 1922, in Tulsa, Okla. The grandson of silent screen director J. Gordon Edwards, and the son of stage director and movie production manager Jack McEdwards, he broke into films in the early 40s as an actor, appearing in such productions as *Ten Gentlemen from West Point* (1942). *A Guy Named Joe* (1943), *In the Meantime Darling* (1944), *The Best Years of Our Lives* (1947), *Leather Gloves* and *Panhandle* (both 1948). He also co-produced and co-scripted the latter film and later gained a reputation as a bright screenwriter for Richard QUINE and other directors. He made his debut as a film director in 1955 and almost immediately won recognition as a promising new talent in the field, thanks to the flamboyant style and the effervescent scripts of many of his early films.

Edwards reached a peak of success in the late 50s and early 60s with parallel triumphs in both television and films. For TV he created the popular series 'Peter Gunn' (1958–60), 'Mr. Lucky' (1959–60), and 'Dante' (1960–61). For the big screen he directed a diverse number of superior productions: the service farce *Operation Petticoat,* the romantic comedy *Breakfast at Tiffany's,* the suspenseful thriller *Experiment in Terror,* the bleak social drama *Days of Wine and Roses,* and the hilarious Inspector Clouseau spoofs, *The Pink Panther* and *A Shot in the Dark.* But in 1965, following the expensive debacle of the slapstick extravaganza *The Great Race,* Edwards's career began a decade-long slide at the box office and in the review columns. Constant feuds with the studios reached their shrillest level over *Darling Lili* (1970), a costly Paramount musical starring Julie ANDREWS, whom Edwards married (his second) in 1969. After further disappointments at MGM, accompanied by rifts over cutting rights, Edwards exiled himself to England, where he was able to regain viability in 1975 with the first of several *Pink Panther* sequels. He returned to Hollywood with a vengeance in 1979, scoring a huge box-office hit with *10.* The following year he vented his fury at Tinseltown's establishment with *S.O.B.,* a vicious autobiographical satire of the movie industry. But following another success with *Victor/Victoria* (1982), for which he won a French César and an Italian David Di Donatello Award as best foreign film, Edwards's career seemed once more headed toward a long eclipse. Edwards is an exhibited painter and sculptor. His daughter, Jennifer Edwards, is a screen actress; his son Geoffrey, a screenwriter.

FILMS: As screenwriter (alone or in collaboration)—*Panhandle* (also coprod., act.), *Leather Gloves* (also act.) 1948; *Stampede* (also coprod.) 1949; *Sound Off, Rainbow 'Round My Shoulder* 1952; *All Ashore, Cruisin' Down the River* 1953; *Drive a Crooked Road, The Atomic Kid* (story only) 1954; *My Sister Eileen* 1955; *Operation Mad Ball* 1957; *The Couch* (story only), *Walk on the Wild Side* (addnl. scenes only, uncredited), *The Notorious Landlady* 1962; *Soldier in the Rain* 1963; *Inspector Clouseau* 1968. As director—*Bring Your Smile Along* (also co-story, sc.) 1955; *He Laughed Last* (also co-story, sc.) 1956; *Mister Cory* (also sc.) 1957; *This Happy Feeling* (also sc.) 1958; *The Perfect Furlough, Operation Petticoat* 1959; *High Time* 1960; *Breakfast at Tiffany's* 1961; *Experiment in Terror* (also prod.) 1962; *Days of Wine and Roses* 1963; *The Pink Panther* (also co-sc.), *A Shot in the Dark* (also prod., co-sc.) 1964; *The Great Race* (also co-story) 1965; *What Did You Do in the War Daddy?* (also prod., co-story) 1966; *Gunn* (also story, co-sc.) 1967; *The Party* (also prod., story, co-sc.) 1968; *Darling Lili* (also prod., co-sc.) 1970; *Wild Rovers* (also co-prod., sc.) 1971; *The Carey Treatment* 1972; *The Tamarind Seed* (also sc.) 1974; *The Return of the Pink Panther* (also prod., co-sc.) 1975; *The Pink Panther Strikes Again* (also prod., co-sc.) 1976; *Revenge of the Pink Panther* (also prod., story, co-sc.) 1978; *10* (also prod., sc.) 1979; *S.O.B.* (also co-prod., sc.) 1981; *Victor/Victoria* (also co-prod., sc.), *Trail of the Pink Panther* (also co-prod., co-sc.) 1982; *Curse of the Pink Panther* (also co-prod., co-sc.), *The Man Who Loved Women* (also co-prod. co-sc.) 1983; *Micki and Maude* 1984; *A Fine Mess, That's Life!* (also co-sc.) 1986; *Blind Date* 1987; *Sunset* (also sc.) 1988; *Skin Deep* (also sc.) 1989; *Switch* (also sc.) 1991; *Son of the Pink Panther* (also sc.) 1993.

Edwards, Cliff. Singer, actor. *b.* June 14, 1895, Hannibal, Mo. *d.* 1971. He began his career in St. Louis saloons, where his singing to the accompaniment of a ukulele earned him the nickname "Ukulele Ike." After making a national hit of a song called 'Ja Da,' he became a vaudeville headliner. In 1936 he replaced Rudy Vallee as the star of 'George White's Scandals' and for several years was highly popular on Broadway in such shows as 'Lady Be Good,' 'Sunny,' and 'Ziegfeld Follies.' An invitation to Hollywood followed. In one of his first films, *The Hollywood Revue,* he introduced the song 'Singin' in the Rain.' He subsequently played supporting roles in scores of other films. Edwards supplied the off-screen voice of Jiminy Cricket for Disney's *Pinocchio* (1940) and sang the Oscar-winning song 'When You Wish upon a Star.'

FILMS INCLUDE: *The Hollywood Revue of 1929, Marianne, So This Is College* 1929; *Lord Byron of Broadway, Montana Moon, Way Out West, Good News, Dough Boys, Those Three French Girls* 1930; *Dance Fools Dance, Parlor Bedroom and Bath, The Prodigal, Laughing Sinners, The Sin of Madelon Claudet, Sidewalks of New York, Hell Divers* 1931; *Fast Life* 1932; *Flying Devils, Take a Chance* 1933; *George White's Scandals* 1934; *Red Salute* 1935; *They Gave Him a Gun, Saratoga, Between Two Women* 1937; *The Bad Man of Brimstone, The Girl of the Golden West* 1938; *Maisie, Gone With the Wind* 1939; *His Girl Friday, Pinocchio* (voice of Jiminy Cricket), *Flowing Gold* 1940; *The Monster and the Girl, International Squadron* 1941; *American Empire* 1942; *The Falcon Strikes Back* 1943; *Fun and Fancy Free* (v/o) 1947; *The Man from Button Willow* (v/o) 1965.

Edwards, Harry. Director. *b.* 1888, London, Ontario. Deceased. Entered films in 1912 as a prop boy and gradually worked his way up to director of comedy shorts. Under the tutelage of Mack SENNETT he developed into one of the brightest comedy directors of the silent period, but with few exceptions his output consisted of short subjects, starring Harry Langdon, Billy Bevan, Ben Turpin, and Carole Lombard. He is best known as the director of the feature *Tramp, Tramp, Tramp* (1926), one of Langdon's finest comedies.

FILMS INCLUDE: Features—*Tramp Tramp Tramp* 1926; *His First Flame* 1927. Shorts—*Boobs in the Woods, Plain Clothes, Remember When?, Lucky Stars* 1925; *Saturday Afternoon* 1926; *A Hollywood Hero, The Best of Friends, The Golf Nut, Daddy Boy, Fiddlesticks* 1927; *The Beach Club, The Best Man, The Girl from Nowhere, A Dumb Waiter, The Campus Vamp* 1928; *Clunked on the Corner, Matchmaking Mamas* 1929.

Edwards, Henry. Director, actor. *b.* Ethelbert Edwards, Sept. 18, 1882, Weston-super-Mare, England, *d.* 1952. He directed and starred in numerous films starting in 1915, often appearing with his wife, Chrissie WHITE. In the 30s he turned almost exclusively to directing and in the 40s switched to acting in character parts.

FILMS INCLUDE: As actor-director—*A Welsh Singer* 1915; *East Is East* 1916; *Broken Threads* 1917; *The Hanging Judge* 1918; *The Kinsman* 1919; *The Amazing Quest of Mr. Ernest Bliss* 1920; *A Lunatic at Large, The Bargain* 1921; *Tit for Tat* 1922; *The Naked Man* 1923. As director only—*A Girl of London* 1925; *The Island of Despair* 1926; *The Barton Mystery* 1932; *Lord of the Manor* 1933; *The Man Who Changed His Name, Are You a Mason?, The Lash* 1934; *Squibs, Scrooge* 1935; *Juggernaut* 1936; *The Song of the Forge* 1937. As actor only—*Grim Justice* 1916; *The Cobweb* 1917; *The Flag Lieutenant* 1926; *The Fake* 1927; *The Call of the Sea* 1930; *Captain's Orders* 1937; *The Magic Bow, Green for Danger* 1946; *Take My Life* 1947; *London Belongs to Me, Oliver Twist, Quartet* 1948; *Madeleine, Trio* 1950; *The Lady with the Lamp, The Magic Box* 1951; *Trent's Last Case* 1952.

Edwards, J. Gordon. Director. *b.* 1885(?), Montreal. *d.* 1925. A stage actor and director, he began directing films for Fox in 1914 and was soon assigned to pilot the studio's expensive spectacles. From 1916 to 1919 he directed nearly all of Theda BARA's lavish productions and many of William FARNUM's heroic adventures. Later he was appointed Fox's production supervisor, while continuing to direct prestigious but superficial literary adaptations until his death in 1925. He was the grandfather of director Blake EDWARDS.

FILMS INCLUDE: *St. Elmo, Life's Shop Window* 1914; *Anna Karenina, A Woman's Resurrection, The Song of Hate, The Blindness of Devotion* (also sc.), *The Galley Slave* 1915; *Under Two Flags, Her Double Life, Romeo and Juliet, A Daughter of the Gods* (prod. only), *The Vixen* 1916; *The Darling of Paris, The Tiger Woman, Her Greatest Love, Heart and Soul, Camille, Cleopatra, The Rose of Blood* 1917; *The Forbidden Path, Madame Du Barry, The Soul of Buddha, Under the Yoke, When a Woman Sins, Salome* 1918; *The She-Devil, The Light, When Men Desire, The Siren's Song, A Woman There Was, The Lone Star Ranger, The Last of the Duanes, Wings of the Morning* 1919; *If I Were King, The Adventurer, Heart Strings, The Orphan, The Scuttlers* 1920; *The Queen of Sheba, His Greatest Sacrifice* 1921; *Nero* 1922; *The Silent Command, The Shepherd King, The Net* 1923; *It Is the Law* 1924.

Edwards, Penny. Actress. Born Millicent Edwards, on Aug. 24, 1928, in Jackson Heights, N.Y. With the Ziegfeld Follies at age 12, and later in several plays, she was groomed to stardom by Warner Bros., making her screen debut in 1947. But she soon wound up at Republic, relegated to leads in low-budget Westerns opposite Roy ROGERS and other saddle aces. Married to Universal casting director Ralph Winters, she is the mother of actress Deborah Winters.

FILMS INCLUDE: *My Wild Irish Rose, That Hagen Girl* 1947; *Two Guys from Texas* 1948; *Tucson* 1949; *Sunset in the West, North of the Great Divide, Trail of Robin Hood* 1950; *Spoilers of the Plains, Missing Women, Million Dollar Pursuit, Heart of the Rockies, In Old Amarillo, The Wild Blue Yonder* 1951; *Woman in the Dark, Captive of Billy the Kid, Pony Soldier* 1952; *Powder River* 1953; *The Dalton Girls, Ride a Violent Mile* 1957.

Edwards, Vince. Actor. Born Vincent Edward Zoimo, on July 9, 1928, in New York City. *ed.* Ohio State; U. of Hawaii; AADA. Intense, brooding leading man of American films and television. After a Broadway debut in the musical 'High Button Shoes' (1947), he appeared in many TV plays and began a gradual rise to leading roles in films. His screen career was briefly boosted by the popularity he gained as the star of the TV medical series 'Ben Casey' (1961–66). He later also starred in the short-lived series, 'Dr. Matt Lincoln' (1970–71). During the 60s he attempted a second career as a nightclub and recording singer.

FILMS INCLUDE: *Mr. Universe* 1951; *Sailor Beware, Hiawatha* 1952; *Rogue Cop* 1954; *The Night Holds Terror, Cell 2455 Death Row* 1955; *Serenade, The Killing* 1956; *The Three Faces of Eve, The Hired Gun* 1957; *Murder by Contract* 1958; *City of Fear* 1959; *Too Late Blues* 1962; *The Victors* 1964; *The Devil's Brigade, Hammerhead* 1968; *The Desperadoes* 1969; *The Mad Bomber* 1973; *The Seduction* 1982; *Space Raiders, Deal of the Century* 1983; *Sno-Line* 1986; *Return to Horror High* 1987; *Cellar Dweller* 1988; *The Gumshoe Kid* 1989.

Edzard, Christine. Director, screenwriter. Born in 1945 in Paris. Maker of meticulous films based on Victorian English sources. She began her career as theatrical assistant and designer. She and her husband and producer, Richard Goodwin, entered film with a screenplay of the tales of Beatrix Potter, produced in 1970. They later collaborated on a similar project based on Hans Christian Andersen (*Stories from A Flying Trunk*), with Edzard writing and directing and Goodwin co-producing. In 1975, Edzard and Goodwin set up Sands Films Studios in 1975 in the wharf area in London. There she directed *Little Dorrit*, a six-hour, two-part feature adaptation of the Dickens novel, renowned for its fidelity to the source and its narrative inventiveness (telling the tale twice, from the perspective of two different characters). This was followed by *The Fool*, a farce set in the world of finance in Victorian England. Both films starred stage and film actor Derek Jacobi.

FILMS INCLUDE (as director and screenwriter): *Stories from a Flying Trunk* 1979; *Biddy* 1983; *Little Dorrit, Pts. 1 & 2* 1987; *The Fool* 1990; *As You Like It* 1992.

effects. General term for all transitional devices and illusory optical tricks used in making motion pictures, as well as for some aspects of sound recording. Abbreviated in scripts as FX. See also: SPECIAL EFFECTS; SOUND EFFECTS.

effects box. See MATTE BOX.

effects track. Sound track containing sounds other than dialogue, music, or narration. Often these sounds—such as a door slamming, a gun popping—are not recorded during shooting but are either recorded separately or borrowed from a library of stock sound effects and synchronized with the appropriate shots. The effects track is combined with the dialogue and music tracks during the MIX.

Egan, Richard. Actor. *b.* July 29, 1921, San Francisco. *d.* 1977, of prostate cancer. *ed.* U. of San Francisco (B.A.); Stanford U. (M.A.). After serving in the Army in WW II, as a captain, instructing troops in judo and later seeing action in the Philippines, he taught public speaking at Northwestern University before arriving in Hollywood in 1949. Tall and rugged, he gradually worked his way up from supporting roles to virile leads in 20th Century-Fox melodramas and action pictures. After the late 60s seen mainly on TV or on tour in plays. He starred in the short-lived TV series 'Empire' (1962–63) and 'Redigo' (1963) and was a regular on the daytime soap opera 'Capitol.' He was married to actress Patricia Hardy.

FILMS INCLUDE: *The Damned Don't Cry, Undercover Girl* 1950; *Up Front, Hollywood Story, Bright Victory* 1951; *The Devil Makes Three, One Minute to Zero* 1952; *Split Second, The Glory Brigade* 1953; *Wicked Woman, Demetrius and the Gladiators, Gog, Khyber Patrol* 1954; *Underwater!, Untamed, Violent Saturday, Seven Cities of Gold, The View from Pompey's Head* 1955; *The Revolt of Mamie Stover, Love Me Tender* 1956; *Slaughter on Tenth Avenue* 1957; *Voice in the Mirror, The Hunters* 1958; *These Thousand Hills, A Summer Place* 1959; *Pollyanna, Esther and the King* (as King Ahasuerus of Persia) 1960; *The 300 Spartans* 1962; *Valley of Mystery* 1967; *The Destructors, Chubasco* 1968; *The Big Cube* 1969; *The Sweet Creek County War* 1979.

Eggar, Samantha. Actress. Born Victoria Samantha Eggar, on Mar. 5, 1938, in London. The daughter of a British army brigadier and a Dutch-Portuguese mother, she received a convent education. In her late teens she began stage acting. Producer Betty Box noticed her in a Shakespearean role and started her on a career in British and American films. She attracted international attention with *The Collector,* for which she was nominated for an Oscar and named best actress at the Cannes Film Festival. Since the mid-70s she has been most often seen in television films.

FILMS: *The Wild and the Willing* 1961; *Doctor Crippen, Doctor in Distress* 1963; *Psyche 59* 1964; *The Collector* (US/UK), *Return from the Ashes* (US/UK) 1965; *Walk Don't Run* (US) 1966; *Doctor Dolittle* (US) 1967; *The Molly Maguires* (US), *The Walking Stick, La Dame dans l'Auto avec des Lunettes et un Fusil/The Lady in a Car with Glasses and a Gun* (Fr./US) 1970; *The Light at the Edge of the World* (US/It./Sp.) 1971; *L'Etrusco Uccide Ancora/The Dead Are Alive* (It./Yug./Ger.) 1972; *The Seven-Per-Cent Solution* 1976; *Why Shoot the Teacher* (Can.), *The Uncanny, Welcome to Blood City* (Can./UK) 1977; *Il Grande Attaca/The Biggest Battle* (It.) 1978; *The Brood* 1979; *The Exterminator* (US) 1980; *Demonoid/Macabra* (US) 1981; *Curtains* 1983; *Ragin' Cajun* 1990; *Dark Horse* 1992; *Inevitable Grace, Round Numbers* 1994; *Hercules* (v/o) 1997.

Eggeling, Viking. Painter, avant-garde filmmaker. *b.* Oct. 21, 1880, Lund, Sweden. *d.* 1925. At 17 he went to Paris and ten years later moved to Switzerland, where he joined the Dada movement. In 1918 he began a lifelong association with the German painter Hans RICHTER. They experimented with abstract picture strips, through which they hoped to discover all the possible permutations of certain linear and spatial relationships, thus ascertaining the principles of "rhythm in painting." This led to their collaboration in Germany on an elaborate array of scroll paintings and eventually to their decision to utilize the scrolls as the basic material of animated films. For more than three years (1921 to 1924) Eggeling labored at completing thousands of drawings that were necessary to animate his scroll work. The result was a landmark in abstract cinema, the *Diagonalsymphonien/Diagonal Symphony,* which influenced experimental filmmakers of the period. Just before his death at 45 of septic angina, Eggeling completed two other animated films in the same vein, *Parallel* and *Horizontal.*

Eggerth, Marta. Actress, singer. Born on Apr. 17, 1912, in Budapest. On the stage from age 11, she became the reigning star of numerous filmed operettas in Germany and Austria during the golden age of that genre in Europe in the 30s. After the Anschluss, she and husband Jan KIEPURA, the Polish tenor who co-starred in most of her films, found refuge in the US. She appeared in two Judy Garland musicals of the early 40s but failed to impress Hollywood and resumed her activity in Europe after WW II. Now retired, she lives in New York.

FILMS INCLUDE: *Der Draufgänger, Eine Nacht im Grand-hotel, Die Bräutigamswitwe* (and UK version, *Bridegroom for Two*) 1931; *Where Is the Lady?* (UK), *Der Frauendiplomat, Kaiserwalzer, Das Blaue von Himmel, Es war einmal ein Walzer, Ein Lied ein Kuss ein Mädel, Traum von Schönbrunn* 1932; *Leise flehen meine Lieder* (and 1934 UK version, *Unfinished Symphony*), *Der Zarewitsch, Die Blume von Hawaii* 1933; *Mein Herz ruft nach Dir* (and UK version, *My Heart Is Calling*), *Die Czardasfürstin* 1934; *Casta Diva* (It.), *Die ganze Welt dreht sich um Liebe/The World's in Love, Die Blonde Carmen* 1935; *Das Hofkonzert, Das Schloss in Flandern* 1936; *Zauber der Bohème/The Charm of La Bohème* 1937; *For Me and My Gal* (US) 1942; *Presenting Lily Mars* (US) 1943; *Addio Mimi/Her Wonderful Lie* (It.) 1947; *La Valse brillante* (Fr.) 1950; *Das Land des Lächelns* 1952; *Frühling in Berlin* 1957.

Egypt. Regular film production materialized slowly in this ancient land at the crossroads of Africa and Asia, but from the late 20s to the early 90s, the Egyptian motion picture industry has dominated the market in the Arab world. Foreigners controlled the business at the start. Lumière shorts were shown in Alexandria as early as 1896, and all films exhibited in Egypt's dozen theaters had been imported until 1912, when an Italian named De Lagarne began producing shorts depicting local scenes. The first fiction films were produced in 1918 by the Italo-Egyptian Cinematographic Company, which was partly sponsored by the Bank of Rome. A step toward autonomous local production was taken in 1923 with the release of *The Civil Servant,* which was directed by Mohamed Baoumi, who had studied filmmaking in Germany. A more important landmark was *Laila* (1927), a tearful romantic melodrama that is considered Egypt's first major screen production. It was produced by its star, stage actress Aziza Amir, who also produced and starred in another successful silent production, *Daughter of the Nile* (1929).

The coming of sound represented a difficult transitional period for the industry. The first Egyptian talkie, *The Song of the Heart* (1932), was shot largely at a Paris studio. But once the technical problems had been overcome, sound presented the Egyptian cinema with the ingredients for a formula that remained its trademark for many years: the romantic comedy or melodrama sprinkled with song and dance numbers at regular intervals. This formula proved popular not only in Egypt but also in other parts of the Arab world and assured the Egyptian film industry of a sizable market for its productions.

Among the leading directors of the first decade of Egyptian talkies were Ahmed Galal, Nagib el-Rihani, and Mohamed Karim. But performing stars, not directors, dominated the fortunes of the industry for many years. These included actor Youssef Wahby, singer Mohamed Abdel-Wahab, singer-actor Farid el-Atrash, and singing idol Omm Kulthum, all of whom enjoyed great popularity throughout the Middle East. An important factor in the expansion of the Egyptian cinema in the 30s was the establishment of the large Misr studios in Cairo in 1935. Other production companies active during the formative period included Togo Mizrahi and Lama Brothers.

An important step forward took place in 1940 with the release of Kamal Selim's *Determination,* the first major Egyptian film dealing realistically with social problems and reflecting true conditions in Cairo's slum districts. The success of the film encouraged the growth of a school of realism in the Egyptian cinema, although light musicals continued as the main genre for at least another decade. The trend toward social realism picked up momentum under the aegis of the Ministry of National Culture and Guidance after the 1952 revolution. The Ministry encouraged the production of quality films of social concern but at the same time imposed strict censorship regulations that inhibited free expression of ideas unpalatable to President Nasser's regime. The regime also encouraged the production of foreign films on Egyptian soil but at the same time banned many imported films made by or starring persons known for their pro-Zionist sympathies, among them Otto Preminger, Elizabeth Taylor, Paul Newman, and Danny Kaye. In all, hundreds of films had been banned on various grounds by the time of the Six-Day War in 1967.

Among the leading directors that emerged in the Egyptian cinema in the 50s and 60s were Salah Abu Saif, Youssef Shahin, and Hussein Kamal. But the only Egyptian film personality who went on to enjoy international success was an actor, Omar SHARIF. A gradual break from themes of social concern and a return to light entertainment productions occurred during the 70s in keeping with the liberalized, Western-oriented atmosphere of the late President Sadat's regime.

The government withdrew much of its financial support for the film industry in the early 90s, leading to a spate of films oriented to a popular audience. However, the tradition of serious filmmaking continues; several Egyptian films of recent years have enjoyed both commercial success and critical praise. Among the 60 or so features produced in Egypt each year, many have attracted attention at international film festivals, including the auspicious first films of Daoud Abdel Sayed, director of *The Vagabonds* (1985), *The Search for Sayed Marzouk* (1991), and *Kit Kat* (1991).

In recent years, the Egyptian Film Institute has trained such promising filmmakers as the female director Asma El Bakri, whose first film was *Proud and Beggars* (1991–92). Egypt is also home to the Cairo International Film Festival.

Eichhorn, Lisa. Actress. Born on Feb. 4, 1952, in Reading, Pa. *ed.* Queens College (Kingston, Ontario, Canada). In England to pursue graduate literature studies at Oxford, she stayed for training at the Royal Academy of Dramatic Art and for her screen debut in *Yanks* (1979). She has since played intelligent leads in films and TV programs on both sides of the Atlantic.

FILMS: *Yanks, The Europeans* 1979; *Why Would I Lie* 1980; *Cutter's Way/Cutter and Bone* 1981; *The Weather in the Streets* 1983; *Wildrose* 1985; *Opposing Force* 1986; *Moon 44* 1989; *Grim Prairie Tales* 1990; *A Modern Affair, Sticks and Stones* 1996.

8 mm film. The narrowest-gauge film available for motion picture photography. Introduced in 1932 for use by amateurs, it was used primarily for home movies but also, because of the low price of the stock and its processing, in the experimental work of filmmakers of the avant-garde and the underground. More recently it has been used for the making of educational film. Since the mid-60s, 8 mm film has been gradually superseded by Super 8 film, which offers greater brightness and a much larger picture in projection. There has been an increased use of sound in both 8 mm and Super 8 systems.

Eikenberry, Jill. Actress. Born on Jan. 21, 1947, in New Haven, Conn. *ed.* Yale Drama School. Leading lady of American stage, screen, and television. In films from the late 70s (notably as Dudley Moore's heiress-fiancée in *Arthur*), she gained further wide exposure in the late 80s in the popular TV series 'L.A. Law.' She married actor Michael Tucker.

FILMS: *Between the Lines* 1977; *The End of the World in Our Usual Bed in a Night Full of Rain, An Unmarried Woman* 1978; *Butch and Sundance: The Early Days, Rich Kids* 1979; *Hide in Plain Sight* 1980; *Arthur* 1981; *Grace Quigley* 1984; *The Manhattan Project* 1986.

Eilbacher, Lisa. Actress. Born on May 5, 1952[?], in Dharan, Saudi Arabia. A commercials and TV performer from age seven, she made her feature film debut in 1972. Infrequent but good movie roles followed. Her younger sister, Cindy Eilbacher, is also a TV and movie actress.

FILMS: *The War Between Men and Women* 1972; *Run for the Roses/Thoroughbred* 1978; *On the Right Track* 1981; *An Officer and a Gentleman* 1982; *Ten to Midnight* 1983; *Beverly Hills Cop* 1984; *Thunder Alley* 1986; *Never Say Die* (New Zealand) 1988; *Leviathan* 1989; *A Modern Affair, Sticks and Stones* 1996.

Eilers, Sally. Actress. *b.* Dorothea Sally Eilers, Dec. 11, 1908, in New York City. *d.* 1978. A dancing student of Ernest Belcher, she began her film career in the mid-20s in Pathé shorts and, following bits and supporting roles in several features, graduated to leading lady in Mack Sennett's romantic feature *The Goodbye Kiss* in 1928. She played her best role in Frank Borzage's *Bad Girl* (1931), opposite James DUNN, who was her co-star in several other early talkies. At the peak of her career she was considered one of Hollywood's prettiest women, but she never developed into a major star and was seen mostly in low-budget productions. By the early 40s she had been reduced to occasional appearances in supporting roles. Retired in 1951. Her first two of four marriages were to cowboy star Hoot GIBSON (1930–33) and producer Harry Joe BROWN (1933–43).

FILMS INCLUDE: *Slightly Used, Sunrise* 1927; *Dry Martini, The Goodbye Kiss* 1928; *Sailor's Holiday, The Long Long Trial, Trial Marriage, Broadway Babies* 1929; *She Couldn't Say No, Roaring Ranch, Let Us Be Gay, Dough Boys* 1930; *Reducing, Parlor Bedroom and Bath, Quick Millions, The Black Camel, A Holy Terror, Bad Girl, Over the Hill* 1931; *Dance Team, Disorderly Conduct, Hat Check Girl* 1932; *Second-Hand Wife, State Fair, Sailor's Luck, Central Airport, Hold Me Tight, Made on Broadway, Walls of Gold* 1933; *She Made Her Bed, Three on a Honeymoon* 1934; *Carnival, Alias Mary Dow, Remember Last Night?* 1935; *Strike Me Pink, Florida Special, Without Orders* 1936; *We Have Our Moments, Talk of the Devil, Danger Patrol* 1937; *Lady Behave, Condemned Women, Tarnished Angel* 1938; *They Made Her a Spy, Full Confession* 1939; *I Was a Prisoner on Devil's Island* 1941; *Strange Illusion* 1945; *Coroner Creek* 1948; *Stage to Tucson* 1951.

Eisenstein, Sergei Mikhailovich. Director, film theoretician. *b.* Jan. 23, 1898, Riga, Latvia, *d.* 1948. The son of a Russian mother and an engineer-architect father of German-Jewish origin, he grew up in a cultured, materially comfortable bourgeois home and by the age of ten was fluent in Russian, English, French, and German. He was a voracious reader and displayed an early talent for drawing. His childhood was marred by frequent quarrels between his parents, who finally separated when he was eight. He stayed mostly with his father. In 1915 he enrolled at the Petrograd (Saint Petersburg) Institute of Civil Engineering. But his true passion during these student days became the theater, which he attended frequently, eventually resolving to give up engineering for a career in the arts.

Eisenstein's opportunity to break away from the vocation intended for him by his father came in the wake of the Revolution. In February of 1917 the Engineering Institute was converted into a militia center, and Eisenstein, like other students, began wearing a militia's armband. He began sketching the exciting scenes around him and was successful in selling several of his caricatures to the newspaper Petersburgkaya *Gazetta.* He signed them with the pseudonym "Sir Gay." Shortly after the October Revolution the Engineering Institute was closed; and at the outbreak of the Civil War early in 1918, Eisenstein, along with the other students, enlisted in the Red Army, while his father joined the opposing White Army.

Eisenstein spent two years in uniform, serving in a variety of capacities in various posts. Toward the end of his military service, late in 1919, the military construction unit to which he was attached was stationed near a town that had its own small theatrical company. The young soldier befriended members of the troupe and attended many of their rehearsals, then formed his own amateur group from among fellow servicemen and early in 1920 began directing a series of little productions. In the spring of 1918, Eisenstein transferred from his engineering unit to a theatrical troupe that was soon incorporated into the Political Directorate for the Western Front. After a long period of inactivity he was assigned to a unit in Minsk that decorated *agitprop* (propaganda) trains leaving for the front.

While still in uniform, Eisenstein took an interest in oriental culture and began teaching himself Japanese, the ideographic structure of which would later help him articulate his principles of MONTAGE. As soon as he was demobilized, he went to Moscow to enroll in the Oriental Language Department of the General Staff Academy, but a chance encounter with a childhood friend, actor Maxim Strauch, resulted in a change of plans and set in motion events that would soon lead to one of the most illustrious careers in the history of cinema. Strauch provided him not only with shelter and food but also with guidance and encouragement as the two went searching for work at one of the newly established workers' theaters. It was a difficult search because membership in these troupes was restricted almost exclusively to the working classes, but the two persevered and were finally accepted by the Proletkult Theater—Strauch as an actor, Eisenstein as a scenic designer.

This was an enthusiastic and adventurous if chaotic period in the Russian theater as in other arts. There were calls for completely abandoning all form of the traditional theater and public debates on the course that the new revolutionary theater should take. Each of the stage groups that proliferated during this period had its own ideas about the face of the new theater, and some of these were extremely bizarre. A leading voice in the debate was director Vsevolod Meyerhold, who would soon become Eisenstein's mentor and friend. One of Eisenstein's first assignments at the Proletkult Theater was designing the sets and costumes for a stage adaptation of Jack London's 'The Mexican.' He not only designed highly original stylized sets for the play but also contributed ideas for a key scene in the production—a boxing match—that employed dynamics more akin to the cinema than to the stage. Elevated to co-director of the play, his original ideas became the talk of Moscow's theatrical circles. After several less spectacular decorating jobs, Eisenstein tired of the Proletkult and responded to an advertisement that announced the recruiting of students to the new School for State Direction under Meyerhold.

Meyerhold's teaching methods, combining precise discipline and daring improvisation, suited Eisenstein's own temperament and technical-artistic background. Eisenstein was also influenced by the unconventional ideas promulgated in Leningrad by the FEX group. In the fall of 1922, Eisenstein was appointed administrative head and artistic director of the Peredvizhaniya Trupa, a splinter group of the Proletkult Theater, and immediately set about to put into practice the ideas he had been forming about new stage dynamics. It was during this time that he began expounding a theory he called the "montage of attractions," which would later provide the foundation for his ideas of montage in films. His first stage production, 'The Wise Man,' boasted action on several planes and exploding firecrackers under customers' seats, and included *Glumov's Diary,* a short film parody of contemporary newsreels. Subsequent productions brought him closer and closer to the realm of the cinema, especially 'Gas Masks' (1924), which he staged "on location" at a real Moscow gas factory, inviting the audience to occupy benches amid the greasy machinery and foul smells. The failure of the show to bridge artificiality with reality, as he had hoped to accomplish, convinced him of the limitations of the theater and gave final impetus to his determination to turn to films.

An avid filmgoer ever since his student days, Eisenstein was particularly impressed by the work of D. W. GRIFFITH, especially the American director's cutting techniques. In 1923 he briefly attended a film workshop that was held by Lev KULESHOV in the attic of Meyerhold's theater. Early in the following year, he helped his friend Esther SHUB re-cut a Soviet-government-approved version of Fritz LANG's *Dr. Mabuse der Spieler* (1922). He also experimented with Miss Shub in the re-editing of leftover fragments of films in various combinations in the manner of the Kuleshov school. It was with this meager experience that Eisenstein approached his first assignment as a film director, *Strike.*

Strike had been originally intended as the fifth episode of an eight-part epic, entitled *Towards Dictatorship*, which aimed at depicting various aspects of the revolutionary struggle before 1917. The series as a whole never materialized, but *Strike*, on its own, proved an impressive first feature by an inexperienced director. As would become his career-long habit, Eisenstein approached the filming with a great deal of preparatory work. He spent months researching the subject with scientific thoroughness and several more weeks writing the initial script. He planned the shooting in detail, although at that point he was just beginning to grasp the intricacies of film technique, aiming above all to achieve a "montage of shocks" as an outgrowth of his stage experiments with a "montage of attractions." When it came to the actual filming, Eisenstein was fortunate to have as a cameraman the experienced and talented Edward TISSÉ, who not only captured on film the imagery envisaged by Eisenstein but also taught the young director a great deal about the technique and artistry of filmmaking. Their association lasted through most of Eisenstein's career.

Deviating from the didactic scheme that had been planned for *Strike* by the party ideologues, Eisenstein turned the film into a dynamic experimental production that had its roots in his theatrical work and contained the seeds of a style that he would further develop in his future films.

The reaction of Soviet critics to the film's premiere in February of 1925 was mixed. *Pravda* called it "the first revolutionary creation of our cinema," but reviewers for other publications cried deviationism. The reaction of the public was on the whole unfavorable. However, *Strike* did enjoy some success abroad, and as a result Eisenstein was commissioned by the Central Committee to direct a film commemorating the revolution of 1905. Originally conceived as an eight-part epic covering the events of an entire crucial year, shooting was interrupted by bad weather, jeopardizing the deadline Eisenstein had been committed to meet, in time for the October Revolution anniversary celebrations. While filming in Odessa, he made up his mind to limit the film to only one of its intended episodes, the mutiny of the crew of a battleship, to symbolize the entire insurrection. The result was *The Battleship Potemkin* (1925), more familiar in the US as simply *Potemkin,* one of the most remarkable films in the history of the cinema.

Potemkin materialized from just a half-page portion of hundreds of pages of script that had been prepared for *The Year 1905.* It was an inspired production that flowed from Eisenstein's genius as the shooting progressed. The story was simple and fragmented, but the director's spontaneous treatment of it was astonishingly inventive, greatly enriching the grammar of the cinema. The bold imagery, the stylized compositions, and, above all, the powerful rhythmic editing all combined to create a film that international panels on several occasions voted the best of all time. The famous Odessa Steps sequence remains one of the most visually electrifying ever brought to the screen.

Eisenstein worked days and nights to complete the film in time for its scheduled December premiere, continually experimenting with various combinations and juxtapositions until the very last possible moment. The gala premiere at Moscow's Bolshoi Theater was an immense success, and the film's reception abroad was equally enthusiastic. It helped put the Soviet cinema on the international map and made Eisenstein an overnight celebrity. But at home the director soon found himself the object of envy and criticism. *Potemkin* was released by the authorities without adequate publicity and was relegated to second-rate theaters, where it played to half-empty houses. The film was criticized for, among other things, being too "formalistic" and far above the heads of the average audience, accusations that would be directed more vehemently at Eisenstein's subsequent films.

Eisenstein was well ahead in preparing the groundwork for *Zhunguo,* a film about China, when he was ordered to start production on *The General Line,* intended to propagandize the collectivization of agriculture. But after a month of shooting, he was told to make another quick adjustment and start work on a more urgent project, *October/Ten Days That Shook the World,* designated as an official entry in the festivities to commemorate the tenth anniversary of the 1917 Revolution.

Eisenstein was given the full cooperation of the authorities, and virtually the entire city of Leningrad was put at his disposal. He had carte blanche to use government property and personnel for the production; he was given access to the Czar's palace and permission to screen the city's population and the armed forces for the thousands of extras needed for the crowd scenes in the film. Taking his inspiration from John Reed's book *Ten Days That Shook the World* and several other sources, the director began exhaustive research, intending to make his film an epic history of the whole history of the proletarian revolution. But once again he finally chose to concentrate on only one episode to symbolize the period: the events at Petrograd (Leningrad) from February to October of 1917.

The filming of *October,* which Eisenstein co-directed with his close collaborator Grigori ALEXANDROV, proceeded at an intense clip, with two units often shooting simultaneously. Some 150,000 feet of film were accumulated in six months of shooting, and Eisenstein labored feverishly to edit the seemingly endless footage down to size in time for the anniversary celebrations. A first cut was ready by November 7, 1927. But just then, changes in the official political ideology, most importantly the expulsion of Leon Trotsky from the party, forced Eisenstein to make extensive last-minute changes in the film's content, resulting in the total elimination of about 1,000 feet—much of it under the personal scrutiny of Joseph Stalin—and drastic re-editing of the rest.

October represented a step beyond *Potemkin* in Eisenstein's continuing exploration into the essence of the cinema. It contained passages that were purely experimental, elevating his former ideas of "montage of attractions"—affecting emotion through the juxtaposition of visual images—to a higher plane of "intellectual montage," which attempted to convey abstract concepts through similar but more sophisticated means. Eisenstein even attempted to convey sound effects visually, suggesting gunfire by such means as the flickering of the lens diaphragm or the quivering of crystal chandeliers. *October* never achieved the success of *Potemkin,* at home or abroad.

Resuming production on *The General Line,* Eisenstein decided to simplify his experimentations and chose such obvious objects as a bull, a tractor, and a cream separator to symbolize the transition from primitive farming to mechanized modern agriculture. He also showed flexibility in allowing an illiterate peasant named Marfa Lapkina to occupy a focal position in the story, contrary to strict application of his principle of "typage." Still, he experimented extensively, utilizing, among other effects, what he called "overtonal montage," a method of cutting in which the arrangement of shots is determined by their dominant feature, such as length, tempo, or gradations of the black-and-white tonal scale. He also experimented in this production with what he termed *mise-en-cadre,* montage *within* a shot.

Completed in April of 1929, its release was postponed for seven months to allow Eisenstein to make drastic changes in the closing scenes on orders from Stalin. The new ending was more palatable to the authorities but not to the degree that would bring them to bestow on the film their official sanction. As a result, the film's title was changed from *The General Line,* which would imply authorized policy, to *Old and New.* After its November release, the film was widely criticized in the Soviet Union for "formalism," but by this time Eisenstein was touring Western Europe and about to embark on a voyage to America.

Like other Soviet artists, Eisenstein was increasingly experiencing difficulties with cultural officials at home during this politically sensitive period. But abroad he was still being revered by film enthusiasts as a high priest of the new cinema. This, coupled with his great interest in the new developments in filmic sound techniques, led him to look forward to his long-planned foreign sojourn.

The idea for a Hollywood trip had first arisen during the 1926 visit to Moscow of Douglas FAIRBANKS and Mary PICKFORD, who promised they would try to secure Eisenstein a contract with United Artists. Contacts with other Americans followed, and late in 1928 a tentative offer for a job with MGM came from Joseph SCHENCK (the position never materialized). In mid-August of 1929, Eisenstein, accompanied by colleagues Edward Tissé and Grigori Alexandrov, began the European leg of the long-awaited journey.

Harassment by police and other government agencies became a familiar experience to Eisenstein and his colleagues throughout their European visit, reflecting the growing suspicion in the West of Soviets. But the enthusiasm of film lovers who welcomed them everywhere more than compensated the travelers for the chilly official reception. After their expulsion from Zurich they returned to Berlin, then went to Hamburg and on to Paris, where Eisenstein helped Alexandrov make a short sound film, *Romance Sentimentale.* Next they stopped in England, where Eisenstein's lectures to London's Film Society had a lasting influence on the course of the British avant-garde. Back in Paris, after stopovers in Belgium and Holland, Eisenstein became the center of a raging controversy when a screening of *The General Line/Old and New* at the Sorbonne was canceled by orders of the police for reasons of "security."

He had just about given up on the prospect of an American trip, when Jesse LASKY arrived in Paris with an offer from Paramount. Eisenstein's arrival in America in mid-1930 was welcomed by a fanfare of studio publicity which totally confounded the director. He felt uncomfortable in the social milieu and, to worsen matters, had to spend much of his stay in the shadow of a smear campaign to have him deported. Professionally, he experienced difficulties in getting the approval of Paramount's production chiefs to a succession of contemplated projects. Among the first casualties were *The Glass House* and *Sutter's Gold.* The bitterest disappointment was the turning down by the studio of his screen adaptation of Theodore Dreiser's *An American Tragedy,* after the finished script had been enthusiastically endorsed by the novelist. With both parties at an apparent communication impasse, Eisenstein's contract with Paramount was terminated in October of 1930. The studio assured the director's early departure by buying him a return ticket to Moscow and announcing the date to the press.

However, just as he was preparing to leave, Eisenstein met Robert FLAHERTY, who inspired the frustrated director with his accounts of the virtues of independent film production. Flaherty also rekindled an old Eisenstein dream of visiting and working in Mexico. Further impetus came at the same time from correspondence from painter Diego Rivera, who urged Eisenstein to make a film about life in Mexico. The director turned for advice to one of his closest friends in Hollywood, Charles CHAPLIN, who suggested leftist novelist Upton Sinclair as a likely sponsor for such a venture. The project was eventually funded by Sinclair's wealthy wife with help from a silent partner or two; and in December of 1930, Eisenstein, accompanied by Tissé and Alexandrov, left Hollywood for Mexico, beginning a tragic episode that would haunt him all his life.

Eisenstein's troubles in Mexico started soon after his arrival, when he and his two companions were arrested by the authorities for no apparent good reason. Only after the intervention of 12 US senators and such public figures as Chaplin and Albert Einstein were they released. Free to pursue his project, by now titled *Que Viva Mexico!,* Eisenstein began exploring the Mexican countryside, filming certain scenes and events along the way. The original plan called for a panoramic travelogue of Mexico, the budget allowing three to four months of shooting. But the longer Eisenstein explored his subject and the more fascinated he became with the fierce beauty of the Mexican landscape and the sensuous, cruel poetry of the country's past and present life, the more grandiose his ideas for the film became, and as a result the production schedule and cost soon greatly exceeded the original plan and budget. He approached *Que Viva Mexico!* as a four-episode production with a prologue and an epilogue. The four stories—entitled "Sandunga," "Maguey," "Fiesta," and "Soldadera"—were to embody the spirit of Mexico and to express the clashing forces that have dominated the nation's experience through the ages: life and death, beauty and corruption, freedom and oppression, paganism and Christianity.

The preparation and production dragged on for months, Eisenstein's ideas expanding and changing as the shooting progressed. In Hollywood, Sinclair was growing increasingly impatient, although he was highly pleased with the partial rushes Eisenstein had sent him about 11 months after the start of production. Soon relations between sponsor and director became intolerably tense. Finally, in January of 1932, caving in to pressures by his family, Sinclair ordered the shooting stopped just as Eisenstein was preparing to film the last episode. The director pleaded for just a little bit more time and money to complete the project, but the novelist was adamant. Eisenstein was stranded in Mexico without money and cut off from access to the film footage that he had sent to Hollywood for processing.

Denied permission to re-enter the US, Eisenstein and his two colleagues spent several weeks in a border town before finally receiving transit visas for only one month. The director was shunned by Sinclair, who avoided seeing him, making instead indirect promises to ship the footage to Eisenstein in Moscow for editing. The promise was never kept. After Eisenstein's departure, Sinclair made the footage available to producer Sol LESSER, who used material from the "Maguey" episode to make a feature-length film, *Thunder Over Mexico* (1933), and other footage to prepare two shorts, *Death Day* and *Eisenstein in Mexico* (both 1934). In 1939, the original footage was eventually returned to Russia by the Sinclair estate. It was re-edited by Alexandrov as the USSR's "official" version and was ready for release in 1979.

Back in Moscow, meanwhile, Eisenstein was inconsolable over the abortion of the project, in which he had invested not only months of hard work but also a great deal of intellectual and emotional artistic energy. His repeated attempts to reclaim the original material for editing in Moscow were unsuccessful, and he now found himself the target of suspicion and criticism at home, as well. He was attacked in the Soviet press and in film circles for his long absence and for deviating in his work and theory from the officially endorsed tenets of Socialist Realism.

In January of 1935, he was singled out for attack by his colleagues at the All Union Conference of Cinematographic Workers and dismissed with a minor award during ceremonies to commemorate the 15th anniversary of the Soviet film industry. Proudly defying his detractors, Eisenstein set out to make his first sound feature, *Bezhin Meadow,* inspired by a Turgenev story. After weeks of scripting, casting, and location scouting, production began in the spring of 1935. But a series of illnesses that afflicted Eisenstein caused considerable delays in the shooting. No sooner had the filming resumed than it was again interrupted, this time for revisions in the script which were demanded by Boris Shumyatsky, the state's production boss and Eisenstein's chief nemesis. Despite several drastic revisions to satisfy Socialist Realism and the party line, work on *Bezhin Meadow* was stopped in March of 1937 on orders from Shumyatsky, who also published a vicious attack on the film in *Pravda.* A special conference was staged to condemn the work, and Eisenstein was forced to make a public confession of his "transgressions," repudiating his own film. "It was one of the most bitterly painful experiences in my creative life," Eisenstein later confided.

Eisenstein's apparent submission to the will of the Party earned him an early political reprieve that soon resulted in another important film assignment, *Alexander Nevsky* (1938). As insurance against stylistic experimentation or deviationist tendencies on the part of the appointed director, Eisenstein was assigned a team of trusted collaborators. Ironically, even the man chosen to portray Nevsky in the film, actor Nikolai CHERKASSOV, was a member of the Supreme Soviet.

Rich in imagery and dramatic power, *Alexander Nevsky* represented an extreme departure from Eisenstein's former cataclysmic work and theoretical writing. The breadth and splendor of its pageantry was operatic in scale, its impact enhanced by a magnificent original score by Sergei PROKOFIEV. The film enjoyed great success at home and abroad. *Alexander Nevsky* restored Eisenstein to his former prestigious position in the Soviet cinema, although the film was quietly withdrawn from circulation in the USSR after the signing of the German-Soviet Pact of 1939.

In February of 1939, Eisenstein was awarded the Order of Lenin, and in the following month he received the title Doctor of the Science of Art Studies. The director had been teaching filmmaking at the State Institute of Cinematography ever since 1928. Appointed head of the Institute's directing department in 1932. Eisenstein loved teaching, and his classes provided him with an island of tranquility during the many disappointments he suffered throughout his career. He also found solace in his theoretical writing, which both influenced and was influenced by his work as a director. The central theme of Eisenstein's theory is that "art is conflict." A basic ingredient in that theme is the montage, which to Eisenstein represented a clash between two images which creates a third, unseen, entity. In this equation, one plus one added up to three, rather than two.

The film for Eisenstein was a means of strengthening the social consciousness of the audience through the heightening of emotional response to the conflicts on the screen. He saw the cinema as concerned primarily with the senses, and he became increasingly concerned with the co-ordination of sense stimuli in the film, leading him to the exploration of the meaning of color and sound. The unity binding together the different aspects of sense stimuli was rhythm, and the resulting totality was termed by him a "synchronization of the senses." He identified five levels of montage which could be brought about to elicit the desired emotional response from an audience: metric, rhythmic, tonal, overtonal, and intellectual.

After the triumph of *Alexander Nevsky,* Eisenstein began another film project during the summer of 1939. *The Fergana Canal* was intended as an epic tribute to the fertilization of the deserts of Uzbekistan, spanning a period from Tamburlaine's era (the 16th century) to modern USSR. The project was abandoned after many months of preparation for unspecified reasons. Eisenstein's disappointment was alleviated in 1940, when he was appointed the artistic head of Mosfilm, USSR's largest film studio complex, in Moscow. Also during that year he directed a highly successful production of Wagner's 'Die Walkure' at the Bolshoi Theater.

Shortly after the premiere, Eisenstein began work on a monumental film production, *Ivan the Terrible,* conceived as a three-part epic about the life and times of Ivan IV, the Czar who first unified Russia in the 16th century. Eisenstein devoted a great deal of attention and time to developing the massive project. More than two years elapsed from the time he began researching and outlining the subject and the actual start of filming in April of 1943. He made hundreds of sketches for every scene and detail in the film, and by the time the cameras began to roll he had a clear vision of the film's powerful imagery. Part I of *Ivan* was filmed at the Alma Ata studios in Central Asia, to which the film workers of Moscow were evacuated when the capital came under heavy Nazi bombardment. It was completed late in December of 1944 and premiered in January of 1945 and was an instant success, winning for Eisenstein and several of his collaborators a Stalin Prize.

Encouraged by his triumph, Eisenstein rushed to complete Part II. Shooting was done mainly in Moscow from February to December of 1945. Editing was completed early in February of 1946, but during a celebration of that event and the Stalin Prize he had just received for Part I, the director suddenly collapsed of a heart attack in the middle of a dance. He was hospitalized, and during his long convalescence Part II of *Ivan* was shown privately to Stalin, who is said to have disliked it intensely. In September 1946 the Central Committee of the Communist Party in a sharply worded proclamation denounced Eisenstein for having "betrayed his ignorance of historical fact by showing the progressive bodyguard of Ivan the Terrible as a degenerate band rather like the Ku Klux Klan, and Ivan the Terrible himself, who was a strong man of will and character, as weak and indecisive, somewhat like Hamlet." The film was not publicly released until 1958. Part II of *Ivan* contained two color sequences, used to signify psychological meaning rather than to serve an aesthetic function.

Ignoring the warnings of his physician, Eisenstein resumed active work in September of 1946. He planned a panoramic history of the Soviet capital, entitled *Moscow 800.* The project never materialized. Instead, Eisenstein hoped to complete production on Part III of *Ivan the Terrible,* which, surprisingly, had been cleared by Stalin after a secret meeting with the director. But Eisenstein's health deteriorated rapidly, and he postponed the resumption of filming month after month. He continued teaching on a curtailed schedule and added several essays to his theoretical writings, which have been assembled into several volumes, including *Film Sense* (1942), *Film Form* (1949), *Notes of a Film Director* (1959), and *Film Essays with a Lecture* (1968). Eisenstein died of a heart attack on the morning of February 11, 1948, just 19 days after his 50th birthday, depriving cinema of one of its greatest creative giants.

FILMS: *Glumov's Diary* (five-minute short; also story) 1923; *Strike* (also co-sc.), *The Battleship Potemkin/Potemkin* (also co-sc.) 1925; *October/Ten Days That Shook the World* (co-dir., co-sc. with Grigori Alexandrov) 1928; *The General Line/Old and New* (co-dir., co-sc. with Alexandrov), *Sturm über la Sarraz/Kampf des unabhängigen gegen des kommerziellen Film* (two-reel short; co-dir. with Hans Richter and Ivor Montagu; also act.) 1929; *Romance sentimentale* (two-reel short; co-dir. with Alexandrov) 1930; *Que Viva Mexico!* (with assoc. dir. Alexandrov; unfinished) 1931–32; *Bezhin Meadow* (unfinished) 1935–37; *Alexander Nevsky* (with assoc. dir. Dmitri Vasiliev) 1938; *The Fergana Canal* (also co-sc.; unfinished) 1939; *Ivan the Terrible Part I* (also sc.) 1945; *Ivan the Terrible Part II/The Boyars' Plot* (also sc.; release delayed until 1958) 1946; *Ivan the Terrible Part III/The Battles of Ivan* (also sc.; unfinished) 1947.

Eisler, Hanns. Composer. *b.* July 6, 1898, Leipzig, Germany. *d.* 1962. A student of Arnold Schoenberg, he began composing for films and the stage in the late 20s, working with such luminaries of pre-Hitler German culture as Walter Ruttmann, Bertolt Brecht, and Slatan DUDOW. He got himself into trouble with the authorities over his association with Dudow on the latter's radical leftist film *Kühle Wampe* (1932), which Eisler scored to the lyrics of Brecht, and was forced to leave Germany after the official ban of the film in 1933. He then wandered through Europe, working in Holland, Russia, France, and England, on documentaries of Joris IVENS and occasional features (FEYDER's *Le Grand Jeu,* etc.). He arrived in the US at the outbreak of WW II and here composed for Broadway plays and Hollywood films (for Fritz Lang, Frank Borzage, and Jean Renoir, among others), revealing in his modernistic style great originality and a keen understanding of the function of film music. Long a Marxist, he was among the first Hollywood personalities to be called to testify in the 1947 hearings of the House Un-American Activities Committee. He was declared an unfriendly witness and was deported, to the protestations of his close friend Charlie CHAPLIN. He settled in East Germany and in addition to scoring occasional European films composed music for revolutionary workers' choruses, concert pieces, and East Germany's national anthem. He was the author of *Composing for the Films* (1947).

FILMS INCLUDE: *Opus III* (experimental short; Ger.) 1924; *Niemandsland/No Man's Land* (Ger.) 1930; *Kühle Wampe* (Ger.), *Komsomol* (USSR) 1932; *Nieuwe Gronden/New Earth* (Hol.), *Le Grand Jeu* (Fr.) 1934; *Abdul the Damned* (UK) 1935; *The 400,000,000* (US) 1939; *The Forgotten Village* (US) 1941; *Hangmen Also Die* (US) 1943; *None but the Lonely Heart* (US) 1944; *Jealousy* (US), *The Spanish Main* (US) 1945; *A Scandal in Paris* (US), *Deadline at Dawn* (US) 1946; *The Woman on the Beach* (US) 1947; *Unser täglich Brot/Our Daily Bread* (E. Ger.) 1949; *Herr Puntila und sein Knecht Matti* (Aus./E. Ger.), *Bel Ami* (Aus.), *Nuit et Brouillard/Night and Fog* (Fr.) 1955; *Fidelio* (sc., musical adapt. only; Aus.) 1956; *Les Sorcières de Salem/The Witches of Salem* (Fr./E. Ger.) 1957; *Les Arrivistes* (Fr.) 1960.

Eisner, Lotte. Film historian. *b.* 1896, Berlin. *d.* 1983. Author of influential studies of Lang and Murnau, and seminal exploration of early German cinema, *The Haunted Screen* (1952).

Eisner, Michael D. Executive. Born in Mt. Kisco, New York, on March 7, 1942. *ed.* Denison U., Granville, Ohio. Head of the Walt Disney Company, widely credited with revitalizing it in the 80s as a major movie studio. He began his career as a television executive, getting his start with CBS before spending eleven years with ABC (1966–76). He left ABC to become president and chief operating officer of Paramount Pictures. In 1984, he became chairman and chief executive officer of the Walt DISNEY COMPANY. With Jeffrey Katzenberg, chairman of the Walt Disney Studios, he helped to make Disney a box-office leader (with such films as *Pretty Woman*, 1990) and to restore its reputation as a maker of animated films (such as *Beauty and the Beast*, 1991). Eisner has also overseen the company's flourishing theme parks and its continuing profitability in television production, home video, publishing, and other fields, including the company's merger with ABC/Cap Cities in 1996.

Ekberg, Anita. Actress. Born on Sept. 29, 1931, in Malmö, Sweden. A statuesque, voluptuous blonde, she came to the US in 1951 to participate in the Miss Universe contest as Miss Sweden. After working briefly in modeling and nightclubs, she made a modest Hollywood debut in 1953. But it was in Italy that she got her best parts, first in King Vidor's *War and Peace,* then in Fellini's *La Dolce Vita* and his "Temptation of Dr. Antonio" episode in *Boccaccio '70,* in which her ample physical endowments were turned from sexual symbol to erotic caricature. Formerly married to actors Anthony STEEL (1956–62) and Rik Van Nutter (1963–75).

FILMS INCLUDE: *The Golden Blade* 1953; *Blood Alley, Artists and Models* 1955; *War and Peace, Back from Eternity, Zarak* (UK), *Hollywood or Bust* 1956; *Paris Holiday, Screaming Mimi, The Man Inside* (UK) 1958; *Nel Segno di Roma/Sign of the Gladiator* (It./Fr./Ger.) 1959; *La Dolce Vita* (It./Fr.) 1960; *I Mongoli/The Mongols* (It./Fr.) 1961; *Boccaccio '70* (It./Fr.) 1962; *Call Me Bwana, 4 for Texas* 1963; *The Alphabet Murders* (UK), *Way. . . Way Out* 1966; *Sept fois Femme* (Fr./It./US), *Il Cobra/The Cobra* (It./Sp.), *La Sfinge d'Oro/The Glass Sphinx* (It./Sp./Eg.) 1967; *If It's Tuesday This Must Be Belgium* 1969; *I Clowns/The Clowns* (It./Fr.) 1970; *Fangs of the Living Dead* 1973; *Das Tal der Witwen/The Valley of the Widows* (Ger.) 1974; *Suor omicidi/The Killer Nun* 1979; *The Daisy Chain* 1981; *Intervista* (cameo; It.) 1986; *Bambola* 1996.

Ekland, Britt. Actress. Born Britt-Marie Eklund, on Sept. 29, 1942, in Stockholm. Pretty leading lady of international films of the 60s and 70s; a former model. At one time the wife of Peter SELLERS, she married drummer Slim Jim Phantom McDonnell of the rock group Stray Cats in 1984.

FILMS INCLUDE: *Short Is the Summer* (Swed./Nor.) 1962; *Il Commandante* (It.) 1963; *Caccia alla Volpe/After the Fox* (It./US/UK) 1966; *The Bobo* (UK), *The Double Man* (UK) 1967; *The Night They Raided Minsky's* (US), *Gli Intoccabili/Machine Gun McCain* (It.) 1968; *I Cannibali/The Cannibals* (It.), *Stiletto* (US) 1969; *Get Carter* (UK), *Percy* (UK) 1971; *Asylum* (UK), *Baxter* (UK) 1972; *The Ultimate Thrill, The Man with the Golden Gun* (UK) 1974; *The Wicker Man* (UK), *Royal Flash* (UK) 1975; *High Velocity* (US), *Casanova & Co./Some Like It Cool* (Aus./Ger./It.), *Slavers* (Ger.) 1977; *King Solomon's Treasure* (Can./UK) 1978; *The Monster Club* (UK) 1980; *Satan's Mistress/Dark Eyes/Demon Rage* (US) 1982; *Fraternity Vacation* (US) 1985; *Moon in Scorpio* 1988; *Scandal* (UK), *Beverly Hills Vamp* (US) 1989; *The Children* 1990.

Elam, Jack. Actor. Born on Nov. 13, 1916, in Miami, Ariz. *ed.* Santa Monica Junior College, Calif. Formerly an accountant and hotel manager, since 1950 he has become one of Hollywood's major heavies. Tall and lean, with an evil leer (his left eye is sightless as a result of a childhood fight), he specializes in moronic thug roles in gangster dramas or as a malevolent gunslinger in Westerns.

FILMS INCLUDE: *Wild Weed* 1949; *An American Guerrilla in the Philippines, High Lonesome, The Sundowners, One Way Street* 1950; *Rawhide* 1951; *Kansas City Confidential, Rancho Notorious* 1952; *Ride Vaquero, Appointment in Honduras* 1953; *Vera Cruz, Cattle Queen of Montana* 1954; *The Far Country, Moonfleet, Kiss Me Deadly, Artists and Models, The Man from Laramie, Kismet* 1955; *Jubal* 1956; *Gunfight at the O.K. Corral, Night Passage, Baby Face Nelson* 1957; *The Gun Runners* 1958; *Edge of Eternity* 1959; *The Last Sunset, The Comancheros, Pocketful of Miracles* 1961; *4 for Texas* 1963; *The Rare Breed* 1966; *The Way West, The Last Challenge* 1967; *Firecreek, Never a Dull Moment, C'era una Volta il West/Once Upon a Time in the West* (It./US) 1968; *Support Your Local Sheriff* 1969; *Dirty Dingus Magee, Rio Lobo* 1970; *Support Your Local Gunfighter, The Wild Country, The Last Rebel* 1971; *Pat Garrett and Billy the Kid* 1973; *A Knife for the Ladies* 1974; *The Creature from Black Lake, The Winds of Autumn, Pony Express Rider* 1976; *Grayeagle* 1977; *The Norseman, Hot Head and Cold Feet* 1978; *The Apple Dumpling Gang Rides Again, The Villain* 1979; *The Cannonball Run* 1981; *Jinxed!* 1982; *Sacred Ground* 1983; *Cannonball Run II* 1984; *The Aurora Encounter* 1986; *Hawken's Breed* 1989; *Big Bad John* 1990; *Giant of Thunder Mountain, Suburban Commando* 1991; *Dead Presidents* 1996.

Eldridge, Florence. Actress. *b.* Florence McKechnie, Sept. 5, 1901, in Brooklyn, N.Y. *d.* 1988. On the New York stage from the age of 17, she became one of Broadway's most celebrated performers. She received the N.Y. Drama Critics Award (1956–57) as best actress for her performance in O'Neill's 'Long Day's Journey Into Night.' Her screen appearances were sporadic but memorable. Often in films starring her husband from 1927, Fredric MARCH.

FILMS: *Six Cylinder Love* 1923; *The Studio Murder Mystery, Charming Sinners, The Greene Murder Case* 1929; *The Divorcee, The Matrimonial Bed* 1930; *Thirteen Women*

1932; *Dangerously Yours, The Great Jasper, The Story of Temple Drake* 1933; *A Modern Hero* 1934; *Les Miserables* 1935; *Mary of Scotland* 1936; *Another Part of the Forest, An Act of Murder* 1948; *Christopher Columbus* 1949; *Inherit the Wind* 1960.

electrician. A member of a motion picture production crew who, under the supervision of the GAFFER, places and adjusts lights on the set, in the studio or on location.

Elfman, Danny. Composer. Born in 1954 in Los Angeles, Calif. Leading composer of witty, romantic, modernist scores. Began writing for movies as member of group Oingo Boingo. In 1985, with his first complete score (for *Pee-Wee's Big Adventure*), he developed an informal partnership with director Tim BURTON, for whom he would write several scores as baroque and elemental as the director's style. Composer of the theme for the TV comedy *The Simpsons*.

FILMS INCLUDE (as sole composer): *Pee-Wee's Big Adventure* 1985, *Back to School, Wisdom* 1986; *Summer School* 1987; *Beetlejuice, Midnight Run, Big-Top Pee-Wee, Hot to Trot, Scrooged* 1988; *Batman* 1989; *Nightbreed, Dick Tracy, Darkman, Edward Scissorhands* 1990; *Pure Luck* 1991; *Article 99, Batman Returns, Buffy the Vampire Slayer* 1992; *Army of Darkness, Sommersby, Tim Burton's Nightmare Before Christmas* (also assoc. prod.) 1993; *Black Beauty, Shrunken Heads* 1994; *Dolores Claiborne, To Die For* 1995; *Extreme Measures, The Frighteners, Mars Attacks, Mission: Impossible* 1996; *Men in Black* 1997.

Elg, Taina. Actress. Born on Mar. 9, 1930, in Helsinki. Leading lady of a handful of American and European films of the late 50s. A former dancer with the Sadler's Wells and Marquis de Cuevas ballet troupes.

FILMS INCLUDE: *The Prodigal* 1955; *Diane, Gaby* 1956; *Les Girls* 1957; *Imitation General* 1958; *Watusi, The 39 Steps* (UK) 1959; *Le Baccanti/The Bacchantes* (as Dirce; It./Fr.) 1961; *Hercules in New York* (as Nemesis) 1970; *Liebestraum* 1991.

Elizondo, Hector. Actor. Born on Dec. 22, 1936, in New York City, of Hispanic descent. Brooding character player of numerous plays, TV shows, and films. Trained at the Ballet Arts Company of Carnegie Hall and at Actors Studio. Married actress Carolee Campbell.

FILMS INCLUDE: *The Vixens* 1969; *The Landlord* 1970; *Valdez Is Coming, Born to Win* 1971; *Pocket Money, Deadhead Miles* 1972; *The Taking of Pelham One Two Three* 1974; *Report to the Commissioner* 1975; *Thieves* 1977; *Cuba* 1979; *American Gigolo* 1980; *The Fan* 1981; *Young Doctor in Love* 1982; *The Flamingo Kid* 1984; *Nothing in Common* 1986; *Leviathan* 1989; *Pretty Woman, Taking Care of Business* 1990; *Necessary Roughness, Frankie & Johnny, Pay Dirt, Final Approach* 1991; *Samantha, There Goes the Neighborhood* 1992; *Being Human, Beverly Hills Cop III, Exit to Eden, Getting Even with Dad* 1994; *Perfect Alibi* 1995; *Dear God 1996; Turbulence* 1997.

Ellenshaw, Peter. Special effects artist, production designer. Born on May 24, 1913, in London. Trained as an assistant to pioneer matte artist W. Percy Day, who would later become his stepfather, he entered the industry in 1934 as a matte painter for Alexander KORDA. After WW II service with the RAF, he free-lanced as a matte artist for Michael POWELL and other directors. In 1948 he joined Walt Disney's newly formed British production branch as a matte artist, effects specialist, and occasionally also as a production designer. He later worked in similar capacities for Disney in Hollywood, finally retiring in 1979. He shared an Academy Award for the special effects of *Mary Poppins* (1964) and Oscar nominations for the art direction of *Bedknobs and Broomsticks* (1971) and *The Island at the Top of the World* (1974).

FILMS INCLUDE: *Things to Come* 1936; *Rembrandt, Victoria the Great* 1937; *The Drum/Drums* 1938; *The Thief of Bagdad* 1940; *A Matter of Life and Death/Stairway to Heaven* 1946; *Black Narcissus* 1947; *The Red Shoes* 1948; *Treasure Island* 1950; *The Story of Robin Hood* 1952; *The Sword and the Rose* 1953; *20,000 Leagues Under the Sea* 1954; *Davy Crockett, King of the Wild Frontier* 1955; *The Great Locomotive Chase* 1955; *Johnny Tremain, Old Yeller* 1957; *Darby O'Gill and the Little People* 1959; *Kidnapped, Pollyanna* 1960; *The Absent-Minded Professor* 1961; *In Search of the Castaways* 1962; *Mary Poppins* 1964; *The Adventures of Bullwhip Griffin, The Gnome-Mobile, The Happiest Millionaire* 1967; *Blackbeard's Ghost, The Love Bug* 1968; *Bedknobs and Broomsticks* 1971; *Island at the Top of the World* 1974; *The Black Hole* 1979.

Elliott, Denholm. Actor. *b.* May 31, 1922, in London. *d.* 1992. *ed.* Malvern College. Dependable supporting player and occasional lead of the British stage and screen. Made his stage debut in 1945, shortly after being freed from a prisoner-of-war camp in Germany, where he had spent the last three years of WW II. From 1949 was seen in numerous British and some American films, often in pivotal roles. His first wife was actress Virginia MCKENNA.

FILMS INCLUDE: *Dear Mr. Prohack* 1949; *The Sound Barrier/Breaking Through the Sound Barrier, The Holly and the Ivy* 1952; *The Heart of the Matter, The Cruel Sea* 1953; *Lease of Life* 1954; *The Man Who Loved Redheads, The Night My Number Came Up* 1955; *Scent of Mystery* (US) 1960; *Station Six—Sahara* (UK/Ger.) 1963; *Nothing but the Best, The High Bright Sun/McGuire Go Home!* 1964; *King Rat* 1965; *Alfie, The Spy with a Cold Nose, Maroc 7* 1966; *Here We Go 'Round the Mulberry Bush, The Night They Raided Minsky's* (US), *The Sea Gull* (US/UK) 1968; *Too Late the Hero* (US) 1970; *The House That Dripped Blood, Percy, Quest for Love* 1971; *The Vault of Horror, A Doll's House* 1973; *The Apprenticeship of Duddy Kravitz* (Can.) 1974; *Russian Roulette* (US) 1975; *To the Devil a Daughter, Robin and Marian, Partners* (Can.), *Voyage of the Damned* 1976; *Sweeney 2, The Boys from Brazil* (US), *La Petite Fille en Velours bleu* (Fr.), *The Hound of the Baskervilles* 1978; *Zulu Dawn, Saint Jack* (US), *Cuba* (US) 1979; *Bad Timing/A Sensual Obsession* 1980; *Raiders of the Lost Ark* 1981; *Brimstone and Treacle, The Missionary* 1982; *The Wicked Lady, Trading Places* (US) 1983; *The Razor's Edge* (US), *A Private Function* 1984; *Defence of the Realm/Defense of the Realm, A Room with a View* 1986; *Maurice, September* 1987; *Return from the River Kwai, Stealing Heaven, Indiana Jones and the Last Crusade* (US) 1989; *Scorchers, Toy Soldiers* 1991; *Noises Off* 1992.

Elliott, Sam. Actor. Born on Aug. 9, 1944, in Sacramento, Calif. *ed.* U. of Oregon. Tough but kindly looking leading man of American films and much TV. In 1984 he married actress Katharine Ross.

FILMS: *Butch Cassidy and the Sundance Kid* (bit) 1969; *The Games* 1970; *Frogs, Molly and Lawless John* 1972; *Lifeguard* 1976; *The Legacy* 1979; *Mask* 1985; *Fatal Beauty* 1987; *Shakedown* 1988; *Road House, Prancer* 1989; *Sibling Rivalry* 1990, *Rush* 1991; *Gettysburg, Tombstone* 1993; *Beverly Hills Cop III, The Desperate Trail* 1994.

Elliott, William ("Wild Bill"). Actor. *b.* Gordon Nance, 1903, Pattonsburg, Mo. *d.* 1965. A former rodeo competitor, he made his screen debut in 1925 playing mostly supporting roles in non-Western films under his real name. After appearing in a Columbia serial, *The Great Adventures of Wild Bill Hickok* (1938), he adopted the character's sobriquet as part of his new professional name and went on to star in numerous Westerns of the 40s and early 50s, including many of the "Red Ryder" series.

FILMS INCLUDE: As Gordon Elliott—*The Plastic Age* (bit) 1925; *The Arizona Wildcat, The Private Life of Helen of Troy* (as Telemachus) 1927; *Beyond London Lights, The Passion Song, Restless Youth* 1928; *Broadway Scandals* 1929; *The Great Divide* 1930; *Wonder Bar* 1934; *Devil Dogs of the Air, The Girl from 10th Avenue, The Goose and the Gander* 1935; *Murder by an Aristocrat, The Case of the Velvet Claws* 1936; *Midnight Court, Wife Doctor and Nurse* 1937; *The Lady in the Morgue, The Devil's Party, The Great Adventures of Wild Bill Hickok* (serial) 1938. As Bill, "Wild Bill," or William Elliott—*Overland with Kit Carson* (serial), *Taming of the West* 1939; *The Return of Wild Bill* 1940; *King of Dodge City* 1941; *The Valley of Vanishing Men* (serial), *Vengeance of the West* 1942; *Calling Wild Bill Elliott, Wagon Tracks West* 1943; *Cheyenne Wildcat, Hidden Valley Outlaws* 1944; *Phantom of the Plains* 1945; *In Old Sacramento, Sheriff of Redwood Valley, The Plainsman and the Lady* 1946; *Wyoming, The Fabulous Texan* 1947; *Old Los Angeles* 1948; *The Last Bandit, Hellfire* 1949; *The Showdown* 1950; *Waco* 1952; *Rebel City* 1953; *Bitter Creek* 1954; *Sudden Danger* 1955; *Footsteps in the Night* 1957.

Ellis, Patricia. Actress. *b.* Patricia Gene O'Brien, May 20, 1916, Birmingham, Mich. *d.* 1970. Tall, blonde leading lady of numerous Warner Bros. B pictures of the 30s. The stepdaughter of a theatrical producer, she spent three years on the stage before making her film debut in 1932. She appeared in some 40 productions before retiring in 1940 to marry an industrialist. Died of cancer at 54.

FILMS INCLUDE: *Three on a March, Central Park* 1932; *The King's Vacation, Picture Snatcher, Elmer the Great, The Narrow Corner, The World Changes, 42nd Street* 1933; *Easy to Love, Here Comes the Groom, The Circus Clown, Let's Be Ritzy* 1934; *Hold 'Em Yale, A Night at the Ritz, Stranded, Bright Lights, The Case of the Lucky Legs, The Pay-Off* 1935; *Freshman Love, Love Begins at 20, Boulder Dam* 1936; *Step Lively Jeeves, Melody for Two* 1937; *The Lady in the Morgue, Block-Heads* 1938; *Back Door to Heaven, Fugitive at Large* 1939.

Ellis, Robert. Actor. *b.* June 27, 1892, Brooklyn, N.Y. *d.* 1935. Tall, blue-eyed, popular leading man in talkies. A veteran of the Chicago and New York stage, he entered films with Kalem in 1915 and for the next seven years shuffled between acting and directing duties, sometimes doubling in both. His marriages included actresses May ALLISON and Vera REYNOLDS. Another Robert Ellis (1933–73), also known as Bobby, played juvenile and young adult roles in films of the late 40s and 50s. His credits are also sometimes confused with those of an art director and a screenwriter of the same name.

FILMS INCLUDE (as actor): *The Apaches of Paris* (also dir.), *The Glory of Youth* (also dir.) 1915; *The Lifted Veil, The Fringe of Society* (dir. only) 1917; *Brown of Harvard* 1918; *The Imp* (dir. only), *Louisiana, The Spite Bride* 1919; *A Fool and His Money* (dir. only), *The Figurehead* (dir. only), *The Daughter Pays* (also dir.) 1920; *A Divorce of Convenience* (dir. only), *Handcuffs and Kisses, Ladies Must Live, Chivalrous Charley* (dir. only) 1921; *The Infidel, Love's Masquerade, The Woman Who Fooled Herself* (also co-dir. with Charles Logue), *Anna Ascends* 1922; *Dark Secrets, The Flame of Life, Mark of the Beast, The Wild Party, The Wanters* 1923; *The Law Forbids, For Sale, Lovers' Lane, Silk Stocking Sal, A Cafe in Cairo* 1924; *Capital Punishment, Forbidden Cargo, Lady Robin Hood, The Part-Time Wife, Northern Code* 1925; *The Girl from Montmartre, Ladies of Leisure, Whispering Canyon, Devil's Dice* 1926; *The Lure of the Night Club, Ragtime* 1927; *Marry the Girl, Freedom of the Press, Varsity, Restless Youth* 1928; *Broadway, The Love Trap, Tonight at Twelve, Night Parade* 1929; *The Undertow, What Men Want, The Squealer* 1930; *The Last Parade, The Good Bad Girl, Caught Cheating* 1931; *American Madness, The Last Man, White Eagle* 1932; *Soldiers of the Storm, The Sphinx, Police Call* 1933; *Madame Spy, A Girl of the Limberlost* 1934.

Ellison, James. Actor. *b.* James Ellison Smith, 1910, Guthrie Center, Iowa. *d.* 1994. After appearing in stock, he broke into films in 1932 as a romantic and second lead. From 1935 to 1937 he supported William BOYD in a string of "Hopalong Cassidy" Westerns in which he was featured in the role of Johnny Nelson. He appeared in other Westerns, memorably as Buffalo Bill in De Mille's *The Plainsman* (1937), as well as in many low-budget films of other genres, mostly romantic comedies and light mysteries. Retired from films in the early 50s, he entered the real estate business.

FILMS INCLUDE: *Play Girl* 1932; *Carolina* 1934; *Hopalong Cassidy, Reckless* 1935; *The Leathernecks Have Landed* 1936; *Borderland, The Plainsman, Annapolis Salute, The Barrier* 1937; *Vivacious Lady, Next Time I Marry* 1938; *Zenobia, Fifth Avenue Girl, Hotel for Women* 1939; *You Can't Fool Your Wife, Anne of Windy Poplars* 1940; *Play Girl, Charley's Aunt, Ice-Capades* 1941; *Careful Soft Shoulder, The Undying Monster, Army Surgeon* 1942; *Dixie Dugan, I Walked with a Zombie, The Gang's All Here* 1943; *Lady Let's Dance* 1944; *Hollywood and Vine* 1945; *G.I. War Brides* 1946; *The Ghost Goes Wild* 1947; *I Killed Geronimo, The Texan Meets Calamity Jane, Colorado Ranger, Fast on the Draw* 1950; *Dead Man's Trail* 1952; *Ghost Town* 1956; *When the Girls Take Over* 1963.

Elsom, Isobel. Actress. *b.* Isobel Reed, Mar. 16, 1893, Chesterton, Cambridge, England. *d.* 1981. On the British stage from 1911, she starred in numerous silent and some sound British pictures, then went to Hollywood, where she played many character parts, typically in the grande dame tradition. At one time married to director Maurice ELVEY.

FILMS INCLUDE: In the UK—*A Prehistoric Love Story* 1915; *Milestones* 1916; *Onward Christian Soldiers* 1918; *Aunt Rachel* 1920; *Debt of Honor* 1922; *The Wandering Jew* 1923; *The Last Witness* 1925; *Human Law* 1926; *The Other Woman* 1931; *Illegal* 1932; *The Primrose Path* 1934. In the US—*Ladies in Retirement* 1941; *Seven Sweethearts, You Were Never Lovelier* 1942; *Forever and a Day* 1943; *Between Two Worlds, Casanova Brown* 1944; *The Unseen* 1945; *Two Sisters from Boston, Of Human Bondage* 1946; *The Two Mrs. Carrolls, Monsieur Verdoux, The Ghost and Mrs. Muir* 1947; *The Paradine Case* 1948; *The Secret Garden* 1949; *Désirée* 1954; *Love Is a Many Splendored Thing* 1955; *Lust for Life* 1956; *The Young Philadelphians* 1959; *The Errand Boy* 1961; *My Fair Lady* 1964; *The Pleasure Seekers* 1965.

Elvey, Maurice. Director. *b.* William Seward Folkard, Nov. 11, 1887, Darlington, England. *d.* 1967. The most prolific director in British film history, he was raised in poverty, received no education, and began working for a living as a boy of nine. While still in his teens he became a stage actor and before long a director. His career as a film director began in 1913 and lasted 44 years, during which he turned out an astonishing number of films, some 300 features and innumerable shorts. Some of these were films of quality and many enjoyed success at the box office. They covered the range of film genres from melodrama to comedy. In addition to turning out his numerous British films, he also worked briefly in Hollywood in the mid-20s and occasionally on the Continent. Retired after losing an eye. He was married at one time to actress Isobel ELSOM.

FILMS INCLUDE: *The Great Gold Robbery, Maria Marten* 1913; *The Suicide Club, The Cup Final Mystery* 1914; *Florence Nightingale* 1915; *Vice Versa, When Knights Were Bold, The King's Daughter* 1916; *The Grit of a Jew, Flames, Justice, The Gay Lord Quex* 1917; *Hindle Wakes, Adam Bede, Nelson* 1918; *Bleak House, Comradeship/Comrades in Arms, Mr. Wu* 1919; *The Elusive Pimpernel, The Amateur Gentleman, At the Villa Rosa* 1920; *The Hound of the Baskervilles, The Adventures of Sherlock Holmes* (serial) 1921; *The Passionate Friends* 1922; *The Sign of Four, The Wandering Jew, Don Quixote, Sally Bishop* 1923; *My Husband's Wives* (US) 1924; *Curly Top* (US), *The Folly of Vanity* (US), *She Wolves* (US), *Every Man's Wife* (US) 1925; *The Flag Lieutenant, The Woman Tempted, Mademoiselle from Armentieres* 1926; *Hindle Wakes/ Fanny Hawthorn, Roses of Picardy, The Flight Commander* 1927; *Palais de Danse, You Know What Sailors Are* 1928; *High Treason* 1929; *Balaclava/Jews of Hell* (co-dir. with Milton Rosmer), *School for Scandal* 1930; *Sally in Our Alley* 1931; *In a Monastery Garden, The Lodger/Phantom Fiend, Diamond Cut Diamond/Blame the Woman* 1932; *Soldiers of the King/The Woman in Command, The Wandering Jew* 1933; *Princess Charming, Lily of Killarney/The Bride of the Lake, My Song for You* 1934; *The Tunnel/Transatlantic Tunnel, The Clairvoyant* 1935; *Spy of Napoleon, The Man in the Mirror* 1936; *A Romance in Flanders* 1937; *The Spider, Sons of the Sea* 1939; *Under Your Hat* 1940; *The Gentle Sex* (co-dir. with Leslie Howard), *The Lamp Still Burns* 1943; *Medal for the General/The Gay Intruders* 1944; *Beware of Pity* 1946; *The Late Edwina Black/Obsessed* 1951; *House of Blackmail* 1953; *What Every Woman Wants* 1954; *You Lucky People* 1955; *Stars in Your Eyes* 1956; *Second Fiddle* 1957.

Elwes, Cary. Actor. Born on Oct. 26, 1962, in London. *ed.* Sarah Lawrence; Actors Studio. Handsome, blond lead of British and American films from the mid-80s. Son of painter Dominic Elwes.

FILMS: *Another Country, Oxford Blues* 1984; *The Bride* 1985; *Lady Jane* 1986; *The Princess Bride* 1987; *Glory, Never on Tuesday* 1989; *Days of Thunder* 1990; *Hot Shots!, Leather Jackets* 1991; *Bram Stoker's* Dracula 1992; *The Crush, Robin Hood: Men in Tights* 1993; *The Chase, The Jungle Book* 1994; *Twister* 1996; *Kiss the Girls, Liar, Liar* 1997.

Ely, Ron. Actor. Born Ronald Pierce, on June 21, 1938, in Hereford, Tex. Tall (6' 4"), athletic leading man of Hollywood films who became the screen's 15th Tarzan. He portrayed the ape man in the 1966–68 TV series and in two offshoot feature films released in 1970. In 1979–81 he replaced Bert Parks as host of the "Miss America" pageant.

FILMS INCLUDE: *South Pacific* (bit), *The Fiend Who Walked the West* 1958; *The Remarkable Mr. Pennypacker* 1959; *The Night of the Grizzly, Once Before I Die* 1966; *Tarzan's Deadly Silence, Tarzan's Jungle Rebellion* 1970; *Doc Savage the Man of Bronze* 1975; *Mitgift/Killing Me Softly* (Ger.) 1976; *Slavers* (Ger.) 1977.

Emerson, Faye. Actress. *b.* July 8, 1917, Elizabeth, La. *d.* 1983. Raised in California; educated in a San Diego convent. She was spotted by a Warner Bros. talent scout while appearing in an amateur stage production. A cool, elegant beauty, she played the heroine in the studio's lesser films of the early 40s and second leads, typically as a corrupt or fallen woman, in major productions. Her second marriage, in 1944, to President Franklin D. Roosevelt's son Elliott, brought her great publicity and social prominence. It was dissolved in 1950. The following year she married bandleader Skitch Henderson, with whom she appeared frequently during her successful career as a TV personality in the 50s. They divorced in 1958. Miss Emerson also enjoyed some success on Broadway and as a newspaper columnist. Later in her life she made her home in Palma de Majorca. She died there of cancer at 65.

FILMS INCLUDE: *Bad Men of Missouri, Manpower, Blues in the Night* 1941; *Murder in the Big House, Lady Gangster, Secret Enemies* 1942; *Air Force, The Hard Way, The Desert Song* 1943; *Destination Tokyo, Uncertain Glory, Between Two Worlds, The Mask of Dimitrios, The Very Thought of You* 1944; *Hotel Berlin, Danger Signal* 1945; *Her Kind of Man, Nobody Lives Forever* 1946; *Guilty Bystander* 1950; *Main Street to Broadway* (cameo) 1953.

Emerson, Hope. Actress. *b.* Oct. 27, 1897, Hawarden, Iowa. *d.* 1960. A six-foot-two-inch 230-pound giant of a woman, she specialized in comedy during her vaudeville and Broadway years in the 20s and 30s but was exploited on the screen in such roles as a murderous masseuse in *Cry of the City* (1948) and a sadistic prison matron in *Caged* (1950). In a lighter vein, she was memorable as the circus strongwoman in *Adam's Rib* (1949).

FILMS INCLUDE: *Smiling Faces* 1932; *Cry of the City, That Wonderful Urge* 1948; *House of Strangers, Thieves' Highway, Roseanna McCoy, Dancing in the Dark, Adam's Rib* 1949; *Caged, Copper Canyon* 1950; *Double Crossbones, Belle le Grand* 1951; *Westward the Women* 1952; *The Lady Wants Mink* 1953; *Casanova's Big Night* 1954; *Untamed* 1955; *Guns of Fort Petticoat* 1957; *All Mine to Give* 1958; *Rock-a-Bye Baby* 1959.

Emerson, John. Director, screenwriter, producer, actor. *b.* May 29, 1874, Sandusky, Ohio. *d.* 1956. *ed.* Oberlin Coll.; U. of Chicago; Heidelberg. The son of an Episcopalian minister, he planned to follow in his father's footsteps but was sidetracked by the stage and became a Broadway actor and later a stage manager and a director. In 1912 he began writing screenplays, and appearing in occasional screen productions. In 1915 he joined the Triangle company, where, under the supervision of D. W. GRIFFITH, he directed some of Douglas Fairbanks's early pictures. He also wrote the screenplays for several of these in collaboration with his wife, Anita Loos. Their frothy scripts helped guide Fairbanks's style in the direction of social satire and shape the star's screen image for the remainder of his career. Emerson also directed such female stars as Norma and Constance Talmadge and gave Erich von Stroheim his first important opportunity as actor and assistant director. In the mid-20s he gave up directing for screenwriting and collaborated with Loos on, among other pictures, the adaptation of her play *Gentlemen Prefer Blondes.* He also produced several films and, in collaboration with his wife, wrote two books, *How to Write Photoplays* (1920) and *Breaking Into Movies* (1922). He also wrote many magazine articles on film.

FILMS INCLUDE: As director (complete)—*In Old Heidelberg* (also sc.) 1915; *His Picture in the Papers* (also co-sc.), *The Mystery of the Leaping Fish, The Social Secretary* (also co-sc.), *Macbeth* (also sc.), *Less Than Dust, The Americano* (also co-sc.) 1916; *In Again Out Again, Wild and Woolly, Down to Earth* (also co-sc.), *Reaching for the Moon* (also co-sc.) 1917; *Come On In* (also co-prod., co-sc.), *Goodbye Bill* (also co-prod., co-sc.) 1918; *Oh You Women!* (also so-sc.) 1919; *Polly of the Follies* (also co-sc.) 1922. As screenwriter (alone or in collaboration)—*The Agitator, Geronimo's Last Raid* 1912; *The Flying Torpedo* 1916; *Let's Get a Divorce, Hit-the-Trail Holliday* 1918; *Getting Mary Married, The Isle of Conquest* 1919; *The Perfect Woman* 1920; *Mama's Affair, Woman's Place* 1921; *Red Hot Romance* (also co-prod.) 1922; *Dulcy* 1923; *Three Miles Out* 1924; *Learning to Love* 1925; *Gentlemen Prefer Blondes* 1926; *The Fall of Eve* (co-story only) 1929; *The Struggle* (also co-story) 1931; *The Girl from Missouri* 1934. As producer (alone or in collaboration)—*A Temperamental Wife* (also co-story), *A Virtuous Vamp* 1919; *In Search of a Sinner* (also co-sc.), *The Love Expert* (also co-sc.), *Dangerous Business* (also co-sc.) 1920; *San Francisco* 1936; *Mama Steps Out* 1937.

Emery, John. Actor. *b.* 1905, New York City. *d.* 1964. Suave second lead and supporting player of the American stage and screen, often in smooth, sometimes treacherous roles. Occasionally in leads. At one time married to Tallulah BANKHEAD.

FILMS INCLUDE: *The Road Back* 1937; *Here Comes Mr. Jordan, The Corsican Brothers* 1941; *Eyes in the Night* 1942; *Assignment in Brittany* 1943; *Blood on the Sun, Spellbound, The Spanish Main* 1945; *The Voice of the Turtle* 1947; *The Woman in White, Let's Live Again* (lead), *Joan of Arc* 1948; *The Gay Intruders* (lead) 1949; *Rocketship X-M* 1950; *Double Crossbones* 1951; *The Mad Magician* 1954; *The Girl Can't Help It* 1957; *Ten North Frederick* 1958; *Youngblood Hawke* 1964.

EMI (Electrical and Musical Industries). British conglomerate that became active in film production and distribution in 1969 when it acquired ASSOCIATED BRITISH and with it Elstree Studios. In 1979, EMI was purchased by British conglomerate Thorn, which became Thorn-EMI. The company soon fell into financial difficulties and was forced to sell its film and television interests, which were acquired by the CANNON GROUP in 1986.

Emmer, Luciano. Director. Born on Jan. 19, 1918, in Milan. Abandoned law studies for filmmaking in 1940 and in collaboration with Enrico Gras wrote and directed an innovative series of short documentaries on art and artists, notable for their mood and pace, often achieved as a result of the dynamic editing of stills. Among them are *Racconto da un Fresco,* on Giotto (1941), *Il Paradiso Terrestre,* on Bosch (1946), and *Leonardo da Vinci* (1952), and *Picasso* (1954). His documentaries also include *Bianchi Pascoli* (1947), a visual essay on Allied cemeteries in Italy, and two lyrical films about Venice, *Romantici a Venezia* (1948) and *Isole nella Laguna* (1949). In 1950, Emmer turned out his first feature film, *Domenica d'Agosto,* a humorous, affectionate look at Italian middle-class mores in the neorealist vein. His subsequent features have been only modestly successful and from 1960 he has been concentrating mainly on TV production.

FEATURE FILMS: *Domenica d'Agosto/Sunday in August* (also co-sc.) 1950; *Parigi è sempre Parigi* (also co-sc.) 1951; *Le Ragazze di Piazza di Spagna/Three Girls from Rome* (also co-sc.) 1952; *Terza Liceo/High School* (also co-sc.) 1953; *Camilla* (also co-sc.) 1954; *Il Bigamo/The Bigamist* 1956; *Il Momento più Bello/The Most Wonderful Moment* 1957; *Paradiso terrestre/Ritual of Love* (compilation film; co-dir. with Robert Enrico; also co-sc.) 1959; *La Ragazza in Vetrina/The Girl in the Window* (also co-sc.) 1960.

Emmerich, Roland. Director, screenwriter, producer. Born November 10, 1955, in Stuttgart, West Germany. *ed.* Munich Film and Television School, W. Germany. An affinity for science fiction and high-gloss special effects have followed this filmmaker from his school days to a successful Hollywood career as director of one of the highest grossing films of all time, *Independence Day* (1996). His previous efforts abroad, mainly in the adventure-thriller genre, led to his first American success, the sci-fi thriller *Stargate* (1994).

FILMS: As director and screenwriter—*Joey, The Noah's Ark Principle* 1985; *Ghost Chase* 1988; *Moon 44* (W. Ger.; also prod.) 1990; *Eye of the Storm* (exec.-prod. only), *Universal Soldier* (dir. only) 1992; *Stargate* (Fr./US) 1994; *Independence Day* 1996.

Empire Film Board (EMB) Film Unit. See DOCUMENTARY.

Emshwiller, Ed. Filmmaker. *b.* 1925, East Lansing, Mich. *d.* 1990. *ed.* U. of Michigan; Ecole des Beaux Arts, Paris; Art Students League, New York. He gained his early reputation as a painter and an illustrator of science fiction books and magazines, under the signature EMSH. In the mid-50s he became involved in experimental filmmaking and during the 60s he handled the cinematography of the feature-length films of Adolfas Mekas (see Jonas MEKAS) and other avant-garde directors. From 1963–73 he collaborated on a series of dance films with choreographer Alwin Nikolais. At the same time he continued with his own experimental filmmaking, winning awards for his works at Oberhausen, Mannheim, and other international festivals. During the 70s, Emshwiller extended his visual probe to video. From 1972–79 he was artist in residence at the WNET (Channel 13) TV Lab in New York. His 1974 program 'Pilobolus and Joan' was named the year's best drama and most innovative program by the Corporation for Public Broadcasting. His experiments with multimedia presentations culminated in *Hunger* (1987), an electronic video opera for the Los Angeles Arts Festival, which employed live performance and interactive computer devices. Emshwiller became dean of film and video at the California Institute of the Arts in 1979 and served as provost from 1981 to 1986.

FILMS INCLUDE: *Paintings by Ed Emshwiller* 1955–58; *Dance Chromatic* 1959; *Lifelines* 1960; *Time of the Heathen* (co-dir.) 1961; *Thanatopsis* 1962; *Totem* (co-dir.) 1963; *Faces of America* 1965; *Relativity* 1966; *Fusion* (co-dir.) 1967; *Project Apollo* 1968; *Flesh and Voice* 1969; *Branches* 1970; *Choice Chance Woman Dance* 1970; *The Chalk Line* 1971; *Identities* 1973; *Pilobolus and Joan* (video), *Interrupted Solitude* 1974; *Inside Edges* 1975; *Collisions* 1976; *Slivers* 1977; *Dubs* 1978; *Sunstone* 1979; *Passes* (video) 1979–82; *Hunger* (video) 1987.

emulsion. The light-sensitive substance, consisting primarily of gelatin and silver salts, with which one side of a film base is coated and on which the photographic image is formed. The emulsion side, or dull side, of raw film stock (as opposed to the shiny base side) should face the lens in the camera gate. But exposed film is normally wound with the "emulsion in," that is, with the coated surface, or dull side, facing the core of the reel. "Emulsion speed" is the degree of light sensitivity of the film stock and is expressed as an exposure index number, such as the ASA speed rating.

Endfield, Cy. Director. *b.* Cyril Raker Endfield, Nov. 1914, South Africa. *d.* 1995. *ed.* Yale; New Theater School (N.Y.C.). Taught drama and produced for the stage before arriving in Hollywood as a writer in 1941. His early film career was interrupted by WW II service with the Army Signal Corps. He made his debut as a director in 1945 with several "Passing Parade" shorts at MGM and directed his first feature the following year at Monogram. He began attracting attention in 1950–51 with two taut, atmospheric suspense yarns, *The Underworld Story* and *The Sound of Fury/Try and Get Me,* but was identified as a Communist before the House Un-American Activities Committee in 1951 and was forced by Hollywood's blacklisting to work in England under pseudonyms (sometimes as C. Raker or C. Raker Endfield) or with no screen credit. In the early 60s he formed a production company with British actor Stanley BAKER, under which banner he directed two successful adventure pictures, *Zulu* and *Sands of the Kalahari.* He often writes his own scripts. In 1978, Endfield invented a computerized pocket-sized typewriter.

FILMS: In the US—*Gentleman Joe Palooka* (also sc.) 1946; *Stork Bites Man* 1947; *The Argyle Secrets* 1948; *Joe* pocket-sized typewriter.

FILMS: In the US—*Gentleman Joe Palooka* (also sc.) 1946; *Stork Bites Man* 1947; *The Argyle Secrets* 1948; *Joe Palooka in the Big Fight* 1949; *The Underworld Story* 1950; *The Sound of Fury/Try and Get Me* 1951; *Tarzan's Savage Fury* 1952. In the UK—*Limping Man* (uncredited; co-dir. with Charles De Lautour) 1953; *The Master Plan* (under pseudonym Hugh Baker) 1954; *Impulse* (uncredited; co-dir. with De Lautour), *The Secret* (also sc.) 1955; *Child in the House* (uncredited; co-dir. with De Lautour; also sc.) 1956; *Hell Drivers* (also sc.) 1957; *Sea Fury* (also co-sc.) 1958; *Jet Storm/Killing Urge* (also co-sc.) 1959; *Mysterious Island* (UK/US) 1961; *Hide and Seek, Zulu* (also co-prod., co-sc.) 1964; *Sands of the Kalahari* (also co-prod., sc.) 1965; *De Sade* (co-dir. with uncredited Roger Corman and Gordon Hessler; US/Ger.) 1969; *Universal Soldier* 1971; *Zulu Dawn* (sc. only) 1979.

Engel, Morris. Director. *b.* Apr. 8, 1918, New York City. He received international acclaim for *Little Fugitive* (1953), a highly imaginative film about the Coney Island adventure of a boy who is convinced he has killed his brother, which Engel filmed in collaboration with his wife, Ruth Orkin (1921–85). He followed this with two other low-budget films, *Lovers and Lollipops* (1955), which he also co-directed with his wife, and *Weddings and Babies* (1958), the winner of the Critics Award at the Venice Film Festival. All three films were notable for their on-location photography, shot in New York City with an innovative portable 35mm camera of his design. In 1968, he completed his film *I Need a Ride to California.* Ruth Orkin grew up in Hollywood, was the daughter of silent screen actress Mary Ruby, and worked at MGM Studios as a messenger. She was a successful photojournalist, and her photograph *American Girl in Italy* has achieved international recognition. Her photo-autobiography, *A Photo Journal,* was published in 1981. She gained praise before her death of cancer for *A World Through My Window* and *More Pictures From My Window,* photographs of Central Park through the seasons, taken from the window of the Engel's high-rise Manhattan apartment.

FILMS: *Little Fugitive* (co-dir., co-prod., co-sc., phot.) 1953; *Lovers and Lollipops* (co-dir., prod., sc., phot.) 1955; *Weddings and Babies* (dir., prod., sc.) 1958; *I Need a Ride to California* (dir.) 1968

VIDEOS: *A Little Bit Pregnant* (dir., phot.) 1994; *Camellia (dir., phot.) 1998*

Engel, Samuel G. Producer, screenwriter. *b.* Dec. 2, 1904, Woodridge, N.Y. *d.* 1984. *ed.* Union U. (Tenn.) (chemistry, pharmacology). He entered films in the early 30s as assistant director at Warner Bros., joined the script department in 1933, and began producing at 20th Century-Fox in 1936. During WW II he served as a Commander in the US Navy and with the Office of Strategic Services. His most important film as a producer and co-screenwriter is John Ford's *My Darling Clementine* (1946). He had a number of other commercially successful films to his credit. Engel was president of the Producers Guild of America from 1955–58, and as member of the Board of Governors of the Motion Picture Academy was credited with initiating the televising of the Oscar ceremonies. He retired in 1966. His son, Charles F. Engel, is a TV production executive.

FILMS INCLUDE: As screenwriter—*The Big Shakedown* (co-story only) 1934; *Sins of Man, Stowaway* 1936; *Johnny Apollo* (co-story only), *Earthbound* 1940; *Scotland Yard, Private Nurse* 1941. As producer—*Crack-Up, Lancer Spy* 1937; *We're Going to Be Rich, Gateway* 1938; *My Darling Clementine* (also co-sc.) 1946; *Sitting Pretty, The Street with No Name, Deep Waters* 1948; *Mr. Belvedere Goes to College, Come to the Stable* 1949; *Night and the City, The Jackpot* 1950; *Rawhide, Follow the Sun, The Frogmen* 1951; *Belles on Their Toes, Pony Soldier* 1952; *Taxi* 1953; *A Man Called Peter, Daddy Long Legs, Good Morning Miss Dove* 1955; *Boy on a Dolphin* 1957; *The Story of Ruth* 1960; *The Lion* 1962.

English, John. Director. *b.* 1903, Cumberland, England. *d.* 1969. Raised and educated in Canada, he settled in Hollywood in the mid-30s. Through the early 50s he directed numerous serials and low-budget action pictures for Republic, as well as many Westerns starring such cowboy heroes as Roy Rogers and Gene Autry.

FILMS INCLUDE (serials indicated by "S"): *His Fighting Blood* 1935; *Arizona Days, Zorro Rides Again* (S; co-dir. with William Witney) 1937; *Dick Tracy Returns* (S), *Hawk of the Wilderness* (S), *The Lone Ranger* (S; all co-dir. with Witney), *Call the Mesquiteers* 1938; *Dick Tracy's G-Men* (S), *Zorro's Fighting Legion* (S; both co-dir. with Witney) 1939; *Adventures of Red Ryder* (S), *Drums of Fu Manchu* (S), *King of the Royal Mounted* (S), *Mysterious Dr. Satan* (S; all co-dir. with Witney) 1940; *Adventures of Captain Marvel* (S), *Dick Tracy vs. Crime Inc.* (S), *Jungle Girl* (S), *King of the Texas Rangers* (S; all co-dir. with Witney) 1941; *Westward Ho!, The Phantom Plainsmen, Daredevils of the West* (S), *Overland Mail Robbery* 1943; *Captain America* (S; co-dir. with Elmer Clifton), *San Fernando Valley, Faces in the Fog* 1944; *Utah, Don't Fence Me In, The Phantom Speaks* 1945; *Murder in the Music Hall* 1946; *The Last Round-Up* 1947; *Loaded Pistols* 1948; *Riders in the Sky* 1949; *Mule Train, Blazing Sun* 1950; *Silver Canyon, Valley of Fire* 1951.

Englund, George H. Director, producer. Born on June 22, 1926, in Washington, D.C. In Hollywood since the late 50s, he has tackled some ambitious themes with modest results. He married actress Cloris LEACHMAN in 1955.

FILMS (as director-producer): *The World the Flesh and the Devil* (prod. only) 1959; *The Ugly American* 1963; *Signpost to Murder* (dir. only) 1965; *Dark of the Sun* (prod. only), *The Shoes of the Fisherman* (prod. only) 1968; *Zachariah* 1971; *Snow Job/The Great Ski Caper* 1972.

Englund, Ken. Screenwriter. Born on May 6, 1914, in Chicago. *ed.* Lane Tech. (Chicago). He started out as a magazine writer and later wrote material for vaudeville routines, radio shows, and stage musicals. Since 1938 he has collaborated on the screenplays of many films, mostly in the light vein, as well as many TV shows. A former president of the Writers Guild of America, West.

FILMS INCLUDE: *The Big Broadcast of 1938, Artists and Models Abroad* 1938; *Good Girls Go to Paris* 1939; *Slightly Honorable, The Doctor Takes a Wife, No No Nanette* 1940; *This Thing Called Love, Nothing but the Truth* 1941; *Rings on Her Fingers* 1942; *Sweet Rosie O'Grady* 1943; *Here Come the Waves* 1944; *The Unseen* 1945; *The Secret Life of Walter Mitty* 1947; *Good Sam* 1948; *A Millionaire for Christy* 1951; *Never Wave at a WAC* 1952; *Androcles and the Lion, The Caddy* 1953; *The Vagabond King* 1956; *The Wicked Dreams of Paula Schultz* 1968.

Englund, Robert. Actor. Born on June 6, 1948, in Glendale, Calif. Character player of Hollywood films. On the screen in relative obscurity from the mid-70s, he became a popular cult figure in the late 80s as a result of his portrayal of the horrific Freddy Krueger in *A Nightmare on Elm Street* (1984) and its sequels. He made his debut as a director in 1988.

FILMS: *Buster and Billie* 1974; *Hustle* 1975; *Stay Hungry, St. Ives, The Last of the Cowboys/The Great Smokey Roadblock, A Star Is Born, Eaten Alive* 1976; *Big Wednesday, Blood Brothers* 1978; *The Fifth Floor* 1980; *Dead and Buried, Galaxy of Terror* 1981; *Don't Cry, It's Only Thunder* 1982; *A*

Nightmare on Elm Street 1984; *A Nightmare on Elm Street, Part 2: Freddy's Revenge* 1985; *Never Too Young to Die* 1986; *A Nightmare on Elm Street, Part 3: Dream Warriors* 1987; *A Nightmare on Elm Street, Part 4: The Dream Master, 976-EVIL* (dir. only) 1988; *A Nightmare on Elm Street, Part 5: The Dream Child, The Phantom of the Opera* (title role) 1989; *The Adventures of Ford Fairlane* 1990; *Freddy's Dead: The Final Nightmare* 1991; *Dance Macabre* 1992; *Tobe Hooper's Night Terrors, Wes Craven's New Nightmare* 1994; *The Mangler* 1995.

Enrico, Robert. Director. Born on Apr. 13, 1931, in Liévin, France, of Italian descent, the son of a champion cyclist. Became involved in dramatics at the Sorbonne and, after studying film technique at IDHEC, began his professional career as a film editor and assistant director. In 1952 he began directing short subjects for French TV and during his tour of service in the late 50s he directed documentaries and training films for the French armed forces. He drew international attention in 1961 with the short fiction film *La Rivière du Hibou/Incident at Owl Creek,* which won a prize at the Cannes Festival and a Hollywood Academy Award. This and adaptations of two other short stories by Ambrose Bierce comprised his first full-length feature, *Au Coeur de la Vie,* which was released in 1962. He was entrusted with the first of two parts of the mammoth historical epic *The French Revolution,* released in 1989 to commemorate the bicentennial of Bastille Day.

FEATURE FILMS: *Au Coeur de la Vie* (3 episodes: "La Rivière du Hibou"/"Incident at Owl Creek," "Chikamauga," "L'Oiseau Moquerr") 1962; *La Belle Vie* (also sc.) 1963; *Les Grandes Gueules/The Wise Guys* (also co-sc.) 1965; *Les Aventuriers/The Last Adventure* (also co-sc.) 1967; *Tante Zita/Zita* (also co-sc.), *Ho!* (also co-sc.) 1968; *Un peu... beaucoup... passionnément* (also co-sc.), *Boulevard du Rhum/Rum Runner* (also co-sc.) 1971; *Les Caids* (also co-sc.) 1972; *Le Compagnon indesirable* 1973; *Le Secret* (also co-adapt.) 1974; *Le Vieux Fusil* (also co-sc.) 1975; *Coup de Foudre, Un Neveu silencieux* (also prod., co-sc) 1979; *L'Empreinte des Géants* (also co-sc.), *Pile ou Face* (also co-sc.) 1980; *Au Nom de tous les miens* (also co-sc.; Fr./Can.) 1983; *Zone rouge* (also co-sc.) 1986; *La Revolution Française: Les Années Lumière/The French Revolution: The Light Years* (also co-sc., Fr./W. Ger./It./Can.) 1989.

Enright, Ray. Director. *b.* Raymond E. Enright, Mar. 25, 1896, Anderson, Ind. *d.* 1965. He began his film career in 1914 as a cutter on early Chaplin comedies, then worked as a gagman and chief editor for Mack Sennett. After WW I service in France, he worked for Ince, then for Warner Bros., where he made his debut as a director in 1927 with a Rin Tin Tin adventure. During the 30s he specialized in light fare, directing breezy musicals and romances, with no particular flair, for Warners and First National. In the 40s, working for Universal, Columbia, RKO, and other studios, he switched to medium- and low-budget action pictures, including several gutsy Westerns that starred Randolph Scott.

FILMS: *Tracked by the Police, Jaws of Steel, The Girl from Chicago* 1927; *Domestic Troubles, Land of the Silver Fox* 1928; *The Little Wildcat, Stolen Kisses, Kid Gloves, Skin Deep* 1929; *Song of the West, Golden Dawn, Dancing Sweeties, Scarlet Pages* 1930; *Play Girl, The Tenderfoot* 1932; *Blondie Johnson, The Silk Express, Tomorrow at Seven, Havana Widows* 1933; *I've Got Your Number, 20 Million Sweethearts, The Circus Clown, Dames, The St. Louis Kid* 1934; *While the Patient Slept, Traveling Saleslady, Alibi Ike, We're in the Money, Miss Pacific Fleet* 1935; *Snowed Under, Earthworm Tractors, China Clipper* 1936; *Sing Me a Love Song, Ready Willing and Able, Slim, The Singing Marine, Back in Circulation* 1937; *Swing Your Lady, Gold Diggers in Paris, Hard to Get, Going Places* 1938; *Naughty but Nice, Angels Wash Their Faces, On Your Toes* 1939; *Brother Rat and a Baby, An Angel from Texas, River's End* 1940; *The Wagons Roll at Night, Thieves Fall Out, Bad Men of Missouri, Law of the Tropics* 1941; *Wild Bill Hickok Rides, The Spoilers, Men of Texas, Sin Town* 1942; *Good Luck Mr. Yates, The Iron Major, Gung Ho!* 1943; *China Sky, Man Alive, One Way to Love* 1945; *Trail Street* 1947; *Albuquerque, Return of the Badmen, Coroner Creek* 1948; *South of St. Louis* 1949; *Montana, Kansas Raiders* 1950; *Flaming Feather* 1952; *The Man from Cairo* 1953.

Ephron, Henry and Phoebe. Playwrights, screenwriters. Henry (*b.* May 26, 1912, N.Y.C.; *d.* 1992. *ed.* Cornell) and Phoebe (*b.* Phoebe Wolkind, Jan. 26, 1914, N.Y.C.; *d.* 1971. *ed.* Hunter Coll.) began their collaboration soon after their marriage in 1934. Their first stage hit, 'Three's a Family,' was produced on Broadway in 1943. 'Take Her She's Mine,' another Broadway success, in 1961, was later adapted for the screen. The Ephrons collaborated on many light screenplays from the mid-40s. Henry also produced several films, including *Carousel* (1956), *Desk Set* (1957), and *A Certain Smile* (1958). Henry authored a memoir of his collaboration with Phoebe, *We Thought We Could Do Anything* (1977). Their daughter is writer Nora EPHRON; another is production executive Amy Ephron. In 1978 he married actress June Gale, widow of Oscar LEVANT.

FILMS INCLUDE: *Bride By Mistake* 1944; *Always Together* 1947; *Wallflower* 1948; *John Loves Mary, Look for the Silver Lining* 1949; *The Jackpot* 1950; *On the Riviera* 1951; *Belles on Their Toes, What Price Glory* 1952; *There's No Business Like Show Business* 1954; *Daddy Long Legs* 1955; *Carousel* (also prod. by Henry) 1956; *Desk Set* (also prod. by Henry) 1957; *Take Her She's Mine* (play basis only) 1963; *Captain Newman M.D.* 1964.

Ephron, Nora. Screenwriter, journalist, novelist, director. Born on May 19, 1941, in New York City, the daughter of writers Henry and Phoebe EPHRON. *ed.* Wellesley. After gaining acclaim in the 1970s as a wit and essayist (*Crazy Salad*), she was nominated for an Academy Award for her debut screenplay collaboration, *Silkwood* (1983), for the romantic comedy *When Harry Met Sally...* (1989), and again in 1993 for *Sleepless in Seattle.* She adapted to the screen her own autobiographical novel, *Heartburn,* which was based on her failed marriage to reporter Carl Bernstein of Watergate fame. In 1992, she directed her first film. Formerly also married to writer Dan Greenberg, she is now wed to writer Nicholas Pileggi (*Wiseguy*).

FILMS: *Silkwood* 1983; *Heartburn* (from her own novel) 1985; *Crimes and Misdemeanors* (act. only), *When Harry Met Sally..., Cookie* 1989; *My Blue Heaven* (also co-exec. prod.) 1990; *Husbands and Wives* (act. only), *This Is My Life* (also dir.) 1992; *Sleepless in Seattle* (co-sc., also dir.) 1993; *Mixed Nuts* (also dir.) 1994; *Michael* (dir., co-scr.) 1996.

episode. 1. One of a number of self-contained, loosely connected parts comprising a motion picture. Episodes may be linked to one another by a common theme, as in Griffith's *Intolerance* (1916) and Allen-Coppola-Scorsese's *New York Stories* (1989); by narrative continuity, as in Duvivier's *Tales of Manhattan* (1942); or by both, as in Ophüls's (1950) and Vadim's (1963) *La Ronde.* 2. The weekly segment of an action serial, typically ending in a cliff-hanger situation to hold the audience in suspense until the showing of the next episode the following week.

Epstein, Jean. Director, film theoretician. *b.* Mar. 25, 1897, Warsaw to a French-Jewish father and Polish mother. *d.* 1953. In France from his teens after elementary schooling in

Switzerland, he studied biophysics and medicine at the University of Lyons. Worked briefly as a lab assistant and hospital intern before taking an interest in literature and the cinema. Under the influence of Louis DELLUC, he wrote his first film theory work, *Bonjour Cinéma,* in 1921. The following year he directed his first film, the biography *Pasteur.* His most successful film, *Coeur fidèle* (1923), a work of pictorial and editorial virtuosity, was a visual demonstration of some of the ideas about filmic style that he expressed in his theoretical writings. Following another remarkable film, *La Belle Nivernaise,* and several routine films in the commercial vein, he was drawn toward independent experimental work, turning out avant-garde films and later documentaries. Among his most satisfying late-silent-period works is an adaptation of Poe's *The Fall of the House of Usher* (1928), which was described by Henri Langlois as "the cinematic equivalent of a Debussy creation."

Epstein's films of the sound period were of lesser interest, but he continued making notable contributions with his theoretical works, including *Le Cinéma vu de l'Etna* (1936), *Le Cinéma du Diable* (1947), and *L'Esprit du Cinéma* (published posthumously, 1955). During the Nazi Occupation, Epstein was barred from the studios by the Vichy regime. He and his sister Marie (*b.* 1899), who collaborated on many of his scripts, were arrested by the Gestapo but were saved from deportation through the efforts of friends and the intervention of the Red Cross. In addition to her script work for her brother, Jean, Marie Epstein was Jean BENOIT-LÉVY's co-director on *Ames d'Enfants* (1928), *Peau de Péche* (1929), *Maternité* (1930), and *La Maternelle* (1933), and his screenwriter on *La Mort du Cygne/Ballerina* (1937), among other films.

FILMS: *Pasteur, Les Vendanges* (doc. short) 1922; *L'Auberge rouge/The Red Inn* (also sc.), *Coeur fidèle* (also sc.), *La Montagne infidèle* (doc. short) 1923; *La Belle Nivernaise* (also sc.), *Photogénies* (short), *Le Lion des Mogols* (also adapt.) 1924; *L'Affiche, Le Double Amour* 1925; *Les Aventures de Robert Macaire* (five-episode serial) 1925–26; *Au Pays de George Sand* (doc. short; also prod.), *Mauprat* (also prod.) 1926; *Six et Demi-Onze/6½ × 11* (also prod.), *La Glace á Trois Faces* (also prod.) 1927; *La Chute de la Maison Usher/The Fall of the House of Usher* (also prod.) 1928; *Finis Terrae* (also sc.) 1929; *Sa Tête* (also sc.), *Le Pas de la Mule* (doc. short) 1930; *Mor'Vran/La Mer des Corbeaux/The Sea of Ravens* (medium length), *Notre Dame de Paris* (doc. short), *Le Chanson des Peupliers* (illustrated song), *Le Cor* (illustrated song) 1931; *L'Or des Mers* (also sc.), *Les Berceaux* (illustrated song), *La Villanelle des Rubans* (illustrated song), *Le Vieux Challand* (illustrated song) 1932; *L'Homme á l'Hispano/The Man in the Hispano-Suiza* (also sc.) 1933; *Le Châtelaine du Liban* (also sc.), *La Vie d'un Grand Journal* (doc.) 1934; *Chanson d'Amour* (also adapt.) 1935; *Cuor di Vagabondo/Coeur de Gueux* (also adapt.; It./Fr.), *La Bretagne* (doc.), *La Bourgogne* (doc.) 1936; *Vive la Vie* (doc.; also co-sc.) 1937; *La Femme du Bout du Monde* (also sc.), *Les Bâtisseurs* (doc.), *Eau Vive* (doc. short; also sc.) 1938; *Artères de France* (doc. short; co-dir. with René Lucot) 1939; *Le Tempestaire* (also sc.) 1947; *Les Feux de la Mer* (doc. short) 1948.

Epstein, Julius J. Screenwriter. Born on Aug. 22, 1909, in New York City. *ed.* Penn State. The son of a livery stable proprietor. Epstein started out as a radio publicist but soon turned to writing one-act plays and, from 1935, screenplays. In 1939 he began a long and fruitful collaboration with his brother Philip G. Epstein (*b.* 1912, N.Y.C.; deceased) which lasted until 1958. They shared Academy Award honors for the screenplay of *Casablanca* (1943) and contributed to the success of many other films of Warner Bros. and other studios. They also collaborated on a number of stage plays. Julius occasionally ventured into producing. He was nominated for Oscars for his screenplays for *Four Daughters* (1938), *Pete 'n' Tillie* (1972), and *Reuben, Reuben* (1983). His first wife (1936–49) was actress Frances Sage.

FILMS INCLUDE (alone and in collaboration): *The Big Broadcast of 1936* (uncredited), *Living on Velvet, In Caliente, Broadway Gondolier* 1935; *Sons o' Guns* 1936; *Confession* 1937; *Four Daughters, Secrets of an Actress* 1938; *Daughters Courageous, Four Wives* 1939; *Saturday's Children, No Time for Comedy* 1940; *Strawberry Blonde, The Bride Came C.O.D.* 1941; *The Man Who Came to Dinner, The Male Animal* 1942; *Casablanca* 1943; *Mr. Skeffington* (also co-prod.), *Arsenic and Old Lace* 1944; *Romance on the High Seas* 1948; *Chicken Every Sunday* (co-play basis only) 1949; *Born Yesterday* (uncredited), *My Foolish Heart* 1950; *Forever Female* 1953; *The Last Time I Saw Paris* 1954; *Young at Heart, The Tender Trap* 1955; *Kiss Them for Me* 1957; *The Brothers Karamazov* (co-adapt. only) 1958; *Take a Giant Step* (also prod.), *Tall Story* 1960; *Fanny* 1961; *Light in the Piazza* 1962; *Send Me No Flowers* 1964; *Return from the Ashes* 1965; *Any Wednesday* (also prod.) 1966; *Pete 'n' Tillie* (also prod.) 1972; *Jacqueline Susann's Once Is Not Enough* 1975; *Cross of Iron* (UK/Ger.) 1977; *House Calls* (co-sc., co-story) 1978; *Reuben, Reuben* (also co-prod.) 1983.

Equity. Commonly used contraction for ACTORS' EQUITY ASSOCIATION.

Erice, Victor. Director, screenwriter. Born in 1940 in Carranza, Spain. Erice's career as a director bears a resemblance to that of the late Danish director Carl Theodor Dreyer: he directs features about once a decade, each graced with a sublime and meditative quality. After studies in economics and political science at the University of Madrid, he attended the Escuela Oficial de Cinematografia in Madrid, where he directed shorts (including a segment of *Los Desafios*, his first commercial release). He served as a film critic at two Spanish journals, *Nuestro Cine* and *Cuadernos de Arte y Pensamieto*. In 1973, he released his first full-length feature, *The Spirit of the Beehive*, to international acclaim. Set in the 30s, it tells the story of two village girls whose lives are transformed by the movies they see, especially *Frankenstein*. Erice's second release, *El Sur*—a drama between father and daughter that pays homage to Hitchcock's *Shadow of a Doubt*—came ten years later. His third feature, *El Sol del Membrillo/Dream of Light* (1992), is a study of the work of painter Antonio Lopez.

FILMS (as director-screenwriter): *Los Desafios* (segment) 1968; *The Spirit of the Beehive* 1973; *El Sur* 1983; *El Sol del Membrillo/Dream of Light, The Quince Tree Sun* 1992.

Erickson, Leif. Actor. *b.* William Wycliff Anderson, Oct. 27, 1911, Alameda, Calif., the son of a sea captain and a writer. *d.* 1986. *ed.* UCLA. A former band vocalist and trombone player, he first appeared in a film in 1933 as a soloist with the Ted Fio Rito Orchestra. His "acting" debut came two years later (as a corpse) in *Wanderer of the Wasteland* (1935). A big, brawny man, he subsequently played intelligent but rather bland second leads in numerous Hollywood films both before and after WW II, during which he was twice wounded in action. He was also often seen on Broadway and in television plays, as well as on the TV series 'High Chaparral' (1967–71). He was at one time married to actress Frances FARMER. His second of three wives was actress Margaret ("Maggie") Hayes.

FILMS INCLUDE: *The Sweetheart of Sigma Chi* 1933; *Wanderer of the Wasteland, Nevada* 1935; *College Holiday* 1936; *Waikiki Wedding, Conquest* 1937; *The Big Broadcast of* 1938, *Ride a Crooked Mile* 1938; *One Third of a Nation* 1939; *Nothing but the Truth, H. M. Pulham Esq.* 1941; *The Fleet's In, Eagle Squadron, Pardon My Sarong, Night Monster, Arabian Nights*

1942; *Blonde Savage, The Gangster* 1947; *Sorry Wrong Number, The Snake Pit, Joan of Arc* 1948; *The Lady Gambles* 1949; *Stella, Three Secrets, Dallas* 1950; *Show Boat* 1951; *Sailor Beware, With a Song in My Heart, Carbine Williams, My Wife's Best Friend* 1952; *Trouble Along the Way, Invaders from Mars* 1953; *On the Waterfront* 1954; *Tea and Sympathy* 1956; *The Vintage, Kiss Them for Me* 1957; *The Young Lions, Twilight of the Gods* 1958; *A Gathering of Eagles* 1963; *Straight-Jacket, The Carpetbaggers* 1964; *Mirage, I Saw What You Did* 1965; *Man and Boy* 1972; *Winter Hawk* 1975; *Twilight's Last Gleaming* 1977.

Ericson, John. Actor. Born Joseph Meibes, on Sept. 25, 1926, in Düsseldorf, Germany. A graduate of the American Academy of Dramatic Arts, he made both his Broadway ('Stalag 17') and Hollywood (*Teresa*) debuts in 1951. Despite good looks and fair opportunities, he never quite made it as a screen leading man.

FILMS INCLUDE: *Teresa* 1951; *Rhapsody, The Student Prince* 1954; *Green Fire, Bad Day at Black Rock, The Return of Jack Slade* 1955; *Forty Guns* 1957; *Day of the Badman* 1958; *Sotto Dieci Bandiere/Under Ten Flags* (It./US), *Pretty Boy Floyd* (title role) 1960; *Semiramis* (It.) 1963; *The 7 Faces of Dr. Lao* 1964; *The Destructors, The Bamboo Saucer/Collision Course, The Money Jungle* 1968; *Bedknobs and Broomsticks* 1971; *Hustler Squad* 1976; *Crash* 1977.

Ermler, Friedrich. Director. *b.* May 13, 1898, Rechitsa, Latvia (now USSR). *d.* 1967. Trained as a pharmacist, he served with the Russian army during WW I, then joined the Bolsheviks in the Revolutionary struggle. After the armistice he enrolled at Leningrad's Fine Arts Institute. In 1924 he joined an experimental film group as an actor and soon after turned to directing. His first important film, *Fragment of an Empire* (1929), was described by historian Paul Rotha as "the epitome of the Soviet sociological propaganda film, realized with extraordinary skill of technical achievement." His three subsequent masterpieces were *Counterplan* (1932), *The Great Citizen* (in two parts, 1938–39), and *The Turning Point* (1946). Ermler ranks among the leading directors of the Soviet cinema of the sound period. His films are noted for their strong sense of realism, often bordering on naturalism, and the psychological detail of their characters. In his best films he has demonstrated a measure of creative independence within the framework of the accepted line of party ideology.

FILMS: *Scarlet Fever* (doc.) 1924; *Children of the Storm* (co-dir., co-sc. with Eduard Johanson), *Katka's Reinette Apples* (co-dir. with Johanson) 1926; *The House in the Snow-Drifts, Parisian Cobbler* 1928; *Fragment of an Empire* (also co-sc.) 1929; *Counterplan/Pozor/Shame* (co-dir. with Sergei Yutkevich; also co-sc.) 1932; *Peasants* (also co-sc.) 1935; *The Great Citizen* (in 2 parts; also co-sc.) 1938–39; *Autumn* (experimental color short; co-dir. with several others) 1940; *She Defends Her Country/No Greater Love* 1943; *The Turning Point* 1946; *The Great Force* 1949; *Unfinished Story* 1955; *The First Day* 1958; *Dinner Time* 1962; *From New York to Issanaia Poliana* 1963.

Errol, Leon. Actor *b.* July 3, 1881, Sydney, Australia. *d.* 1951. In the US from his youth, he starred in vaudeville, burlesque, the 'Ziegfeld Follies' (1911–15), and on the legitimate stage before making his film debut in 1924. A highly versatile and talented comedian, he played leads and supporting roles in many silent and sound features but found the ideal outlet for his comic talent in some 100 two-reel comedy shorts (1933–51), in which he typically portrayed a bald, nervous, henpecked husband in trouble over drinking and extramarital affairs. The rubber-legged comedian reached the height of his popularity in the 40s and was still going strong, negotiating a TV series deal, at the time of his death at 70.

FEATURE FILMS INCLUDE: *Yolanda* 1924; *Sally, Clothes Make the Pirate* 1925; *The Lunatic at Large* 1927; *Only Saps Work* 1930; *One Heavenly Night, Finn and Hattie, Her Majesty Love* 1931; *Alice in Wonderland* 1933; *We're Not Dressing, The Notorious Sophie Lang, The Captain Hates the Sea* 1934; *Princess O'Hara, Coronado* 1935; *Make a Wish* 1937; *The Girl from Mexico, Career* 1939; *Mexican Spitfire, Pop Always Pays* 1940; *Six Lessons from Madame La Zonga, Moonlight in Hawaii, Never Give a Sucker an Even Break, Hurry Charlie Hurry* 1941; *Mexican Spitfire at Sea* 1942; *Follow the Band, Gals Inc., Higher and Higher* 1943; *Babes on Swing Street, The Invisible Man's Revenge* 1944; *She Gets Her Man, What a Blonde!, Mama Loves Papa* 1945; *Joe Palooka Champ* 1946; *The Noose Hangs High* 1948; *Footlight Varieties* 1951.

Erskine, Chester. Director, producer, screenwriter. *b.* Nov. 29, 1905, Vienna. *d.* 1986. *ed.* Union U. (Tenn.). He began an acting career at age 20, touring the US with a Shakespearean company. He later came to New York, where he started writing and directing vaudeville sketches. He scored his first Broadway success with 'Harlem' (1929), an all-black revue that he wrote, produced, and directed. After producing and directing several Broadway plays, he arrived in Hollywood in 1932 as assistant to director Lewis Milestone on *Rain.* Directed several routine films alone before returning to the stage. He resumed his screen activity with greater success than earlier in the mid-40s and ended it in the late 60s.

FILMS INLCUDE: *Master of Men* (co-story) 1933; *Midnight* (dir.) 1934; *Frankie and Johnnie* (dir.) 1935; *The Sailor Takes a Wife* (co-sc. from own play) 1946; *The Egg and I* (co-prod., dir., co-sc.) 1947; *All My Sons* (prod., sc.) 1948; *Take One False Step* (prod., dir., co-sc.) 1949; *The Belle of New York* (adapt.), *A Girl in Every Port* (dir., sc.) 1952; *Androcles and the Lion* (dir., co-adapt.), *Split Second* (co-story only) 1953; *Witness to Murder* (prod., sc.) 1954; *The Wonderful Country* (prod.) 1959; *The Invincible Six* (co-sc.) 1970.

Erwin, Stuart. Actor. *b.* Feb. 14, 1902, Squaw Valley, Calif. *d.* 1967. *ed.* U. of California. On the stage from 1924, he appeared in some 100 light films from 1928, often typecast as a sad-eyed, shy, bumbling but amiable, folksy guy. He was nominated for a best supporting actor Oscar for *Pigskin Parade* (1936). In the 50s he co-starred with wife June COLLYER in the TV series 'The Trouble With Father,' which eventually became 'The Stu Erwin Show' (1950–55).

FILMS INCLUDE: *Mother Knows Best* 1928; *The Exalted Flapper, Dangerous Curves, The Cock-Eyed World, Sweetie, This Thing Called Love* 1929; *Happy Days, Young Eagles, Love Among the Millionaires, Playboy of Paris, Only Saps Work, Along Came Youth* 1930; *No Limit, Dude Ranch, Up Pops the Devil, The Magnificent Lie* 1931; *Two Kinds of Women, Strangers in Love, The Misleading Lady, Make Me a Star, The Big Broadcast* 1932; *The Crime of the Century, International House, Hold Your Man, The Stranger's Return, Before Dawn, Going Hollywood* 1933; *Palooka* (as cartoon character Joe Palooka), *Viva Villa!, Chained, The Band Plays On* 1934; *After Office Hours* 1935; *Ceiling Zero, All American Chump, Women Are Trouble, Pigskin Parade* 1936; *Small Town Boy, Slim, Dance Charlie Dance, Second Honeymoon, I'll Take Romance* 1937; *Three Blind Mice, Passport Husband* 1938; *It Could Happen to You, Hollywood Cavalcade* 1939; *Our Town, When the Daltons Rode, Little Bit of Heaven* 1940; *The Bride Came C.O.D.* 1941; *Adventures of Martin Eden, Drums of the Congo* 1942; *He Hired the Boss* 1943; *The Great Mike* 1944; *Heaven Only Knows* 1947; *Father Is a Bachelor* 1950; *Main Street* 1953; *For the Love of Mike* 1960; *Son of Flubber* 1963; *The*

FILMS INCLUDE: *Carmen* (release delayed from 1943) 1945; *La Belle et la Bête/Beauty and the Beast, L'Idiot/The Idiot* 1946; *L'Aigle a deux Têtes/The Eagle Has Two Heads, Ruy Blas* 1948; *Orphée/Orpheus* 1950; *Fanfan la Tulipe* 1952; *Senso* (co-costumes) 1954; *Nana, Lola Montès* 1955; *Pot-Bouille* 1957; *Les Misérables* 1958; *Et Mourir de Plaisir/Blood and Roses* 1960; *Madame Sans-Gêne/Madame* 1961; *Gli Indifferenti/Time of Indifference* (It./Fr.) 1964; *Lady L* (co-costumes; US/Fr./It.) 1965; *Sept fois Femme/Woman Times Seven* 1967; *Mayerling* 1968.

Esmond, Carl. Actor. Born Willy Eichberger, on June 14, 1905, in Vienna. *ed.* U. of Vienna. A stage actor in Vienna and Berlin, he found refuge from Nazi persecution in London in 1933. He appeared in British films until 1938, when he settled in Hollywood. Smooth and elegant, he has played suave, often sinister, character roles in many films.

FILMS INCLUDE: In the UK—*Evensong* 1933; *Blossom Time/April Romance* 1934. In the US—*The Dawn Patrol* 1938; *Sergeant York, Sundown* 1941; *Pacific Rendezvous, Seven Sweethearts* 1942; *Margin for Error, First Comes Courage* 1943; *Address Unknown, The Story of Dr. Wassell, The Master Race, Experiment Perilous, Ministry of Fear* 1944; *Without Love, This Love of Ours* 1945; *The Catman of Paris* 1946; *Smash-Up, Slave Girl* 1947; *Walk a Crooked Mile* 1948; *The Desert Hawk, Mystery Submarine* 1950; *The World in His Arms* 1952; *The Racers* 1955; *From the Earth to the Moon* 1958; *Thunder in the Sun* 1959; *Hitler* (as Field-Marshal Wilhelm Keitel) 1962; *Morituri* 1965; *Agent for H.A.R.M.* 1966.

Esmond, Jill. Actress. *b.* Jill Esmond-Moore, Jan. 26, 1908, London. *d.* 1990. *ed.* RADA. She made her London stage debut at 14 and, after appearing in three British films, left for the US in 1931 with her husband, Laurence OLIVIER (they married in 1930 and divorced in 1940). She played leads in a number of Hollywood films of the early 30s, then returned to England with Olivier. She was back in Hollywood for the duration of WW II, this time as a character actress.

FILMS INCLUDE: In the UK—*The Chinese Bungalow* 1930; *The Skin Game, The Eternal Feminine* 1931. In the US—*Once a Lady* 1931; *Ladies of the Jury, State's Attorney, Is My Face Red?, Thirteen Women* 1932. In the UK—*F.P. 1* (UK/Ger.), *No Funny Business* 1933. In the US—*This Above All, The Pied Piper, Random Harvest, Journey for Margaret* 1942; *The White Cliffs of Dover, Casanova Brown, My Pal Wolf* 1944; *The Bandit of Sherwood Forest* 1946. In the UK—*Bedelia* 1946; *Escape* 1948. In the US—*Night People* 1954; *A Man Called Peter* 1955.

Essanay. A film production and distribution company founded in 1907 in Chicago by George K. Spoor and G. M. ("Broncho Billy") ANDERSON. The company's name was derived from the first letters of the partner's surnames, *S* and *A*. Its trademark, an Indian's head, was borrowed from the one-cent coin then in circulation. Essanay pioneered in the production of two genres of film, the Western and slapstick comedy. Anderson was in charge of the Western crew, which traveled extensively throughout the West shooting hundreds of "Broncho Billy" one- and two-reelers starring himself. The train in which the company traveled was equipped with a film lab so that film could be developed as soon as it was exposed. The series enjoyed considerable popularity until 1915.

In comedy, Essanay was one of the most active companies in the field. Calling itself "The House of Comedy Hits," it turned out numerous fast-paced farces at an unprecedented rate. Among its most successful series were the Snakesville comedies, taking place in a mythical village, and the "Alkali Ike" comedies, starring Augustus Carney. Ben Turpin, Francis X. Bushman, Beverly Bayne, Henry B. Walthal, and Max Linder were among the company's stars. Wallace Beery made his screen debut dressed as a woman in the 1914 Essanay series "Sweedie." Essanay reached the peak of its success in 1915 when it outbid Keystone for the services of Charlie Chaplin. During his Essanay period, lasting one year, Chaplin refined and further defined the character of his Tramp, adding subtlety and pathos to his comic antics.

Essanay's fortunes declined sharply after Chaplin's defection to Mutual early in 1916. Anderson sold his share in the business to Spoor and went into semiretirement. Spoor tried valiantly to keep the company going. But in 1917, Essanay, one of the last surviving members of the MOTION PICTURE PATENTS COMPANY, ceased operations and soon after disbanded.

Essex, Harry. Screenwriter, playwright, novelist, director. Born on Nov. 29, 1910, in New York City. *ed.* St. John's U. A former welfare worker and member of the Army Signal Corps in WW II, he has written prolifically for the stage, films, and TV since the late 30s. His screenplays, alone or in collaboration, have been mostly simple, unpretentious stories for low-budget science fiction and action films, four of which he also directed.

FILMS INCLUDE (as screenwriter): *Man-Made Monster* (co-story only) 1941; *Boston Blackie and the Law* 1943; *Dragnet* 1947; *He Walked by Night* (addnl. dial. only) 1948; *Undercover Girl, The Killer That Stalked New York* 1950; *The Fat Man* 1951; *The Las Vegas Story, Models Inc., Kansas City Confidential* 1952; *It Came from Outer Space, I the Jury* (also dir.) 1953; *Creature from the Black Lagoon* 1954; *Mad at the World* (also dir.) 1955; *Raw Edge* 1956; *The Lonely Man* 1957; *The Sons of Katie Elder* 1965; *Octaman* (also dir.) 1971; *The Cremators* (dir., prod. only), *Man and Boy* 1972; *Deaf Smith and Johnny Ears* 1973.

established. On record. Persons or objects are said to be established once they have been spotted by the camera in a sequence. Once they have been established, the positions they originally held must be accounted for in the continuity of the rest of the sequence. The usual way to circumvent this is to CHEAT.

establishing shot. A shot, usually a long shot or a full shot at the beginning of a sequence, which establishes the location, setting, and mood of the action. It provides the audience with an initial visual orientation, enabling it to see the interrelationship between the general setting and the detailed action in subsequent scenes.

Estabrook, Howard. Screenwriter. *b.* 1884, Detroit. *d.* 1978. A former stage actor-director-producer, he wrote screenplays for many commercially successful Hollywood productions, alone or in collaboration, from the late 20s to the late 50s. He won an Academy Award for the script of *Cimarron* (1931). Directed one routine film, *Heavenly Days* (1944).

FILMS INCLUDE: *The Port of Missing Girls, Dressed to Kill, Forgotten Faces, Varsity* 1928; *The Shopworn Angel, The Four Feathers, The Virginian* 1929; *Street of Chance, Slightly Scarlet, The Bad Man, Hell's Angels* 1930; *Kismet* 1931; *A Bill of Divorcement* 1932; *The Masquerader, The Bowery* 1933; *David Copperfield, Orchids to You, Way Down East* 1935; *Maid of Salem* (assoc. prod. only) 1936; *Wells Fargo* (assoc. prod. only) 1936; *International Lady, The Corsican Brothers* 1941; *New Wine* 1942; *The Human Comedy* 1943; *The Bridge of San Luis Rey, Heavenly Days* (also dir.) 1944; *The Virginian* (remake) 1946; *Lone Star* 1952; *Cattle Queen of Montana* 1955, *The Big Fisherman* 1959.

Estevez, Emilio. Actor. Born on May 12, 1962, in New York City. Capable, appealing lead of American films. The son of Martin SHEEN and elder brother of Charlie SHEEN, who took the original family surname, he began appearing on TV directly out of high school. He was 20 when he made his big-screen debut and established himself in the 80s through a variety of roles, mainly disaffected young men. He has also proved himself as an accomplished director and screenwriter. Divorced from singer/dancer Paula Abdul.

FILMS: *Tex* 1982; *The Outsiders, Nightmares* 1983; *Repo Man* 1984; *The Breakfast Club, St. Elmo's Fire, That Was Then. . . This Is Now* (also sc.) 1985; *Maximum Overdrive, Wisdom* (also dir., sc.) 1986; *Stakeout* 1987; *Young Guns* (as Billy the Kid) 1988; *Men at Work* (also dir., sc.) 1989; *Young Guns II* 1990; *Freejack, The Mighty Ducks* 1992; *Another Stakeout, Judgment Night, National Lampoon's Loaded Weapon* 1993; *D2: The Mighty Ducks* 1994; *The Jerky Boys* (exec.-prod. only) 1995; *D3: The Mighty Ducks, The War at Home* (dir., sc., prod.) 1996.

Eszterhas, Joe. Screenwriter, novelist. The author of the award-winning novel *Charlie Simpson's Apocalypse* (1974), he began writing for the screen in the late 70s and co-producing in the 80s. He drew attention to the growing involvement of superagents in shaping careers when he dropped Michael Ovitz and the Creative Artists Agency in 1989 following ongoing battles over career choices. His ability to write commercially successful, if sometimes controversial, scripts brought him into high demand in Hollywood. The sale of his original screenplay for *Basic Instinct* for $3 million set a record for screenwriters in the industry. His next two screenplays, *Sliver* (1993) and *Showgirls* (1995) met with tragedy at the box office, with the latter receiving an NC-17 rating, believed by many to be a curse for the commercial success of a film.

FILMS INCLUDE: *F.I.S.T.* 1978; *Flashdance* 1983; *Jagged Edge* 1985; *Big Shots, Hearts of Fire* 1987; *Betrayed* (also co-exec. prod.) 1988; *Checking Out* 1989; *The Music Box* (also co-exec. prod.) 1990; *Basic Instinct* 1992; *Nowhere to Run, Sliver* (also exec.-prod.) 1993; *Jade, Showgirls* 1995; *An Allen Smithee Film* 1997.

Etaix, Pierre. Director, actor. Born on Dec. 23, 1928, in Roanne, France. Trained as a painter, he began his film career in 1949 as a production assistant. He was engaged as a gagman and assistant to Jacques Tati on *Mon Oncle* (1958), then as an actor in Robert Bresson's *Pickpocket* (1959) and Claude de Givray's *Une Grosse Tête* 1962. At about the same period, he teamed up with the clown Nino in music hall, cabaret, and TV shows. In 1961–62 he co-directed, with Jean-Claude Carrière, two comedy shorts, the second of which, *Heureux Anniversaire,* was the winner of an Oscar. In 1962 he made the first of several piquant feature-length films, the comic style of which derives from the American silent shorts of the 20s and is particularly inspired by the comedies of Buster Keaton. Etaix has starred in all his films as director and has collaborated on their scripts with Carrière. His wife, actress Annie Fratellini, appeared with him in his *Le Grand Amour* (1969) and in Federico Fellini's *The Clowns* (1970). Etaix quit directing in the early 70s, but could be seen in films occasionally as an actor. After a long absence he reappeared on the screen in *Max Mon Amour* (1986), in the role of a detective.

FILMS (as director-actor and co-screenwriter): *Rupture* (short; co-dir. with Jean-Claude Carrière) 1961; *Heureux Anniversaire* (short; co-dir. with Carrière) 1962; *Le Soupirant/The Suitor* 1963; *Nous n'irons plus au Bois* (short) 1964; *Insomnie* (short), *Yoyo/Yo Yo* 1965; *Tant qu'on a la Santé/As Long As You're Healthy* 1966; *Le Grand Amour* 1969; *Pays de Cocagne, La Polonaise* (short) 1971; *Henry and June* (act. only) 1990.

Etting, Ruth. Singer actress. *b.* Nov. 23, 1896, David City, Nebr. *d.* 1978. Pioneer radio and recording star who popularized such sentimental songs as 'You Made Me Love You,' 'Shaking the Blues Away,' 'Everybody Loves My Baby,' and 'Ten Cents a Dance.' She also starred in several Ziegfeld Follies revues and Broadway musicals of the late 20s and early 30s, as well as in a number of early sound film shorts and three features. Her stormy life and career were pictured in the film biography *Love Me or Leave Me* (1955), in which she was portrayed by Doris Day. In that film, James Cagney played Etting's first husband, mobster Martin ("Moe the Gimp") Snyder, who, in a rage of jealousy, shot the singer's pianist Myrl Alderman (played by Cameron Mitchell), who became her second husband during Snyder's trial for attempted murder in 1938.

FEATURE FILMS: *Roman Scandals* 1933; *Hips Hips Hooray, Gift of Gab* 1934.

Eustache, Jean. Director. *b.* Nov. 30, 1938, Pessac, France. *d.* 1981. A film enthusiast from childhood, he began in the early 60s hanging around the Paris offices of the New Wave magazine *Cahiers du Cinéma,* where his wife worked as a secretary. After assisting on a short, he turned out his own, very personal, medium-length film, *Du Coté de Robinson,* which he would later combine with another medium-length autobiographical film, *La Père Noël a les Yeux bleus,* to form his first feature, *Les Mauvaises Fréquentations.* A self-effacing, ascetic man, he barely made a living at his chosen art, occasionally directing documentaries or editing films for other directors. But his early work was highly regarded by his colleagues and by many serious critics. He gained wide recognition in 1973 with *La Maman et la Putaine/The Mother and the Whore,* a nearly four-hour-long, black-and-white film about sex and emotion in which he achieved an improvisatory look through disciplined means. It won the Special Jury Prize and shared the International Critics Prize at the Cannes Film Festival. Eustache went on to direct only two more features and several shorts. He appeared as an actor in Jean-Luc Godard's *Weekend* (1967) and in Wim Wenders's *The American Friend* (1977). In 1980 he was hurt in an accident and for the next 15 months barely left his home. He took his own life by a gunshot just three weeks before his 43rd birthday.

FEATURE FILMS (as director-screenwriter): *Les Mauvaises Fréquentations/Bad Company* (comprising two medium-length episodes, "Du Côté de Robinson"/"Robinson's Place" and "Le Père Noël a les Yeux bleus"/"Santa Claus Has Blue Eyes") 1967; *La Maman et la Putain/The Mother and The Whore* 1973; *Mes Petites Amoureuses/My Little Loves* 1975; *Une Sale Histoire/A Dirty Story* 1977.

Evans, Clifford. Actor. *b.* Feb. 17, 1912, Senghenydd, South Wales. *d.* 1985. Sincere, virile leading man, then character player, of the British stage and screen. He was reaching a peak of popularity in the early 40s, when a long absence for WW II service irreversibly hurt his career.

FILMS INCLUDE: *The River House Mystery* 1935; *Ourselves Alone/River of Unrest* 1936; *The Mutiny of the Elsinore, Mademoiselle Docteur* 1937; *Luck of the Navy, His Brother's Keeper* 1939; *The Proud Valley* 1940; *Love on the Dole, Penn of Pennsylvania/The Courageous Mr. Penn* 1941; *The Foreman Went to France/Somewhere in France* 1942; *The Silver Darlings* 1947; *A Run for Your Money* 1950; *Valley of Song* 1953; *The Gilded Cage* 1955; *Passport to Treason* 1956; *Violent Playground* 1958; *S.O.S. Pacific* 1960; *The Curse of the Werewolf* 1962; *Kiss of the Vampire/Kiss of Evil* 1963; *The Long Ships* 1964; *A Twist of Sand* 1968; *One Brief Summer* 1970.

Evans, Dale. Actress, singer. Born Frances Octavia Smith, on Oct. 31, 1912, in Uvalde, Tex. Widowed at 17, she worked as a stenographer before breaking into show business as a radio and nightclub vocalist and reaching Hollywood in the early 40s.

In 1947 she married one of her leading men, cowboy star Roy ROGERS, with whom she continued to team in films and in his TV series, 'The Roy Rogers Show' (1951–57), riding her horse Buttermilk and singing their theme song 'Happy Trails to You.' Her personal life was often touched by tragedy. She had lost three of six children before they reached 21. She described her bringing up of a retarded child in the book *Angel Unaware.*

FILMS INCLUDE: *Orchestra Wives, Girl Trouble* 1942; *Swing Your Partner, The West Side Kid, In Old Oklahoma* 1943; *The Cowboy and the Senorita, Song of Nevada, The Yellow Rose of Texas* 1944; *Don't Fence Me In, Hitchhike to Happiness, Utah* 1945; *Helldorado, My Pal Trigger* 1946; *Apache Rose* 1947; *Down Dakota Way* 1949; *Twilight in the Sierras* 1950; *Pals of the Golden West* 1951.

Evans, Dame Edith. Actress. *b.* Feb. 8, 1888, London. *d.* 1976. She studied acting at night while working as a milliner and made her professional stage debut in 1912. Became famous for her brilliant performances of the classics on the London stage and later also on Broadway. Early in her career she appeared in two silent films, but it wasn't until 1948 that she returned to the screen. Her film appearances were infrequent but memorable, particularly her characterizations of Lady Bracknell in *The Importance of Being Earnest* (1952) and of the intrepid aunt in *Tom Jones* (1963). She received the New York Critics Award as best actress for her performance in *The Whisperers* (1967).

FILMS: *A Welsh Singer* 1915; *East Is East* 1916; *The Queen of Spades, The Last Days of Dolwyn/Dolwyn* 1949; *The Importance of Being Earnest* 1952; *The Nun's Story, Look Back in Anger* 1959; *Tom Jones* 1963; *The Chalk Garden* 1964; *Young Cassidy* 1965; *The Whisperers, Fitzwilly* 1967; *Prudence and the Pill* 1968; *The Madwoman of Chaillot, Crooks and Coronets/Sophie's Place* 1969; *Scrooge, David Copperfield, Upon This Rock* 1970; *A Doll's House* 1973; *Craze* 1974; *The Slipper and the Rose, Nasty Habits* 1976.

Evans, Gene. Actor. Born on July 11, 1922, in Holbrook, Ariz. In stock directly out of high school, he made his film debut in 1947 and subsequently played character roles, often on the heavy side, and occasional leads, in numerous Hollywood productions, most frequently in action films. He was also seen in numerous TV productions, including co-starring roles in 'My Friend Flicka' (1956–57) and 'Matt Helm' (1975–76).

FILMS INCLUDE: *Under Colorado Skies* 1947; *Larceny, Berlin Express* 1948; *It Happens Every Spring, Criss Cross* 1949; *Armored Car Robbery* 1950; *The Steel Helmet, Ace in the Hole/The Big Carnival, Force of Arms, I Was an American Spy, Fixed Bayonets* 1951; *Mutiny, Park Row* 1952; *Thunderbirds, Donovan's Brain* 1953; *The Long Wait* 1954; *The Sad Sack* 1957; *The Bravados* 1958; *The Giant Behemoth, Operation Petticoat* 1959; *Shock Corridor* 1963; *Nevada Smith, Apache Uprising* 1966; *The War Wagon* 1967; *Support Your Local Sheriff* 1969; *The Ballad of Cable Hogue, There Was a Crooked Man* 1970; *Support Your Local Gunfighter* 1971; *Walking Tall, Pat Garrett and Billy the Kid* 1973; *People Toys* 1974; *Devil Times Five* 1977; *The Magic of Lassie* 1978; *Blame It on the Night* (bit) 1984.

Evans, Joan. Actress. Born Joan Eunson, in 1934, in New York City. The daughter of a playwright father (Dale Eunson), and a novelist-screenwriter mother (Katherine Eunson), she made her stage debut at age eight, then starred briefly in films in youthful romantic roles.

FILMS: *Roseanna McCoy* 1949; *Our Very Own, Edge of Doom* 1950; *On the Loose* 1951; *Skirts Ahoy!, It Grows on Trees* 1952; *Column South* 1953; *The Outcast* 1954; *A Strange Adventure* 1956; *No Name on the Bullet, The Flying Fontaines* 1959; *The Walking Target* 1960.

Evans, Madge. Actress. *b.* July 1, 1909, New York City. *d.* 1981. A popular child star in silent films from age five, she made a successful transition to ingenue and leading lady roles on Broadway and in motion pictures. Typically played "nice," genial romantic heroine. Retired from the screen in 1938 and from the stage in 1943, after marrying playwright Sidney Kingsley. In 1952 she appeared as a panelist on the TV quiz show 'Masquerade Party.'

FILMS INCLUDE: *Shore Acres, The Sign of the Cross* 1914; *Alias Jimmy Valentine, The Seven Sisters, Zaza* 1915; *Sudden Riches, Seventeen, Husband and Wife, The Revolt, The Hidden Scar, Broken Chains* 1916; *Web of Desire, Maternity, Beloved Adventuress, Little Duchess, The Volunteer, The Corner Grocer, The Little Patriot, The Burglar, The Adventures of Carol* 1917; *Woman and Wife, Wanted: A Mother, Heredity, The Love Nest, The Golden Wall, Neighbours, The Gates of Gladness, The Power and the Glory* 1918; *The Love Defender, Home Wanted* 1919; *On the Bank of the Wabash* 1923; *Classmates* 1924; *Son of India, Sporting Blood, Guilty Hands, Heartbreak* 1931; *The Greeks Had a Word for Them, Lovers Courageous, Huddle, Fast Life* 1932; *Hallelujah I'm a Bum, Hell Below, The Nuisance, The Mayor of Hell, Made on Broadway, Dinner at Eight, Broadway to Hollywood, Beauty for Sale, Day of Reckoning* 1933; *Fugitive Lovers, The Show-Off, Stand Up and Cheer, Grand Canary, Paris Interlude, Death on the Diamond, What Every Woman Knows* 1934; *Helldorado, David Copperfield, Age of Indiscretion, Men Without Names, The Tunnel/Transatlantic Tunnel* (UK) 1935; *Exclusive Story, Moonlight Murder, Piccadilly Jim, Pennies from Heaven* 1936; *Espionage, The Thirteenth Chair* 1937; *Sinners in Paradise, Army Girl* 1938.

Evans, Maurice. Actor. *b.* June 3, 1901, in Dorchester, England. *d.* 1989. The son of a justice of the peace, an amateur playwright, he began his career as a boy singer and later appeared in his father's adaptations of Thomas Hardy's novels. He made his professional stage debut in 1926 and his first London appearance the following year. While striving for recognition, he operated a cleaning and dyeing establishment, but by 1929, when he scored a personal triumph in 'Journey's End,' he was successful enough to devote all his energies to the stage. In 1934 he joined the Old Vic company and the following year he left for the US to begin a long and illustrious career on Broadway, highlighted by eloquent interpretations of Shakespeare and Shaw. He became a US citizen in 1941, and during WW II he was put in charge of the Army Entertainment Section, Central Pacific Theater, with the rank of major. Evans's screen appearances were sporadic and his film roles not always consistent with his stature on the stage. His TV career was more prolific and prominent, however, consisting of many specials and a regular role in the 'Bewitched' series (1964–72). He won an Emmy for his performance in the 1961 TV production of 'Macbeth.'

FILMS: *White Cargo, Raise the Roof, Should a Doctor Tell?* 1930; *Wedding Rehearsal* 1932; *The Only Girl/Heart Song* 1933; *Scrooge* 1935; *Kind Lady* 1951; *Androcles and the Lion* (as Caesar), *Gilbert and Sullivan* (as Sullivan) 1953; *Macbeth* (made for TV; title role) 1959; *The War Lord* 1965; *Jack of Diamonds* 1967; *Planet of the Apes, Rosemary's Baby* 1968; *The Body Stealers, Beneath the Planet of the Apes* 1970; *Terror in the Wax Museum* 1973; *The Jerk* 1979.

Evans, Ray. Lyricist. Born on Feb. 4, 1915, in Salamanca, N.Y. He was a musician aboard cruise ships before beginning a successful collaboration with composer Jay LIVINGSTON, his former classmate at the University at Pennsylvania. They wrote numerous songs for radio, then for films. Broadway, and TV, including Academy Award winners 'Buttons and Bows' (from

The Paleface, 1948), 'Mona Lisa' (from *Captain Carey USA,* 1950), and 'Que Sera Sera' (from *The Man Who Knew Too Much,* 1956). Among their other popular tunes are 'To Each His Own,' 'Golden Earrings,' 'Tammy,' 'Silver Bells,' and 'Dear Heart,' and the TV themes for 'Bonanza' and 'Mr. Ed.' For film credits, see Jay LIVINGSTON.

Evans, Robert (Bob). Producer, production executive, former actor. Born Robert Shapera, on June 29, 1930, in New York City. As a child performer he appeared on more than 300 radio shows and in some films and stage plays. But he was forced to give up acting temporarily because of a collapsed lung, and at 21 he formed, with his brother, what became a thriving women's sportswear establishment. In 1957 he stumbled back into acting when Norma Shearer selected him to portray her late husband, film mogul Irving Thalberg, in the Lon Chaney biography *Man of a Thousand Faces.* He then played supporting roles in such films as *The Sun Also Rises* (1957) and *The Best of Everything* (1959) and the title role in *The Fiend Who Walked the West* (1958). Deciding to move into film production, he sold his share of the garment-industry enterprise Evan-Picone to Revlon at a huge profit and went to work for 20th Century-Fox as an independent producer. In 1966 he joined Paramount as vice president in charge of production and in 1969 rose to executive vice president. During his tenure he was responsible for such box-office blockbusters as *Barefoot in the Park* (1967), *The Odd Couple, Rosemary's Baby* (both 1968), *Goodbye Columbus* (1969), *Love Story* (1970), and *The Godfather* (1972). In 1974 he began producing independently under a contract to Paramount. Evans was one of Hollywood's most powerful men when his gilded world began collapsing into a hellish nightmare in the early 80s. First came his conviction on cocaine possession, for which he was made to pay penance by producing an hour-long TV special against drug abuse. Then there was the fiasco of *The Cotton Club* (1984), a box-office flop on which he had risked and lost money, prestige, and six years of productive life. In his effort to raise money to finish the project, he became briefly associated with Roy Radin, a man of a shady reputation. When Radin was murdered in 1983, Evans's name was dragged into the case as a material witness amidst rumors of suspicion. To add insult to injury, he was fired in 1985 from a co-starring role in Paramount's aborted *The Two Jakes,* the sequel to *Chinatown.* But in the late 80s Evans seemed to be on the road to a gradual recovery. He was back in business as an independent producer. However, his revival of the *Two Jakes* project, when released, received unfavorable reviews. In the 1990s, he again attempted a comeback with the much-ballyhooed but disappointing voyeuristic thriller *Sliver*. Evans's four wives include actress Ali MACGRAW and former Miss America Phyllis George.

FILMS: As actor—*Hey Rookie!* 1944; *Lydia Bailey* 1952; *Man of a Thousand Faces* (as Irving M. Thalberg), *The Sun Also Rises* 1957; *The Fiend Who Walked the West* (title role) 1958; *The Best of Everything* 1959; *Too Soon to Love* 1960. As producer—*Chinatown* 1974; *Marathon Man* 1976; *Black Sunday* 1977; *Players* 1979; *Popeye, Urban Cowboy* 1980; *The Cotton Club* 1984; *Desperate Hours* (act. only), *The Two Jakes* 1990; *Sliver* 1993; *Jade* 1995; *The Phantom* (co-prod.) 1996.

Evein, Bernard. Art director. Born on Jan. 5, 1929, in Saint-Nazaire, France. A graduate of IDHEC, he entered French films as assistant decorator at 20, but it was not until 1958 that he began designing sets on his own. At first (1958–60) in collaboration with Jacques Saulnier, then alone, he played a prominent part in defining the visual style of the French New Wave, working with such directors as Chabrol, Malle, Truffaut, Demy, and Godard.

FILMS INCLUDE: *Les Amants/The Lovers* 1958; *Les Cousins/The Cousins, Les 400 Coups/The 400 Blows, A Double Tour/Leda/Web of Passion* 1959; *Le Farceur/The Joker, Zazie dans le Métro/Zazie* 1960; *L'Amant de Cinq Jour/The Five-Day Lover, Lola, L'Année Dernière a Marienbad/Last Year at Marienbad* (costumes only), *Une Femme est une Femme/A Woman Is a Woman* 1961; *La Vie Privée/A Very Private Affair, Cléo de 5 à 7/Cleo from 5 to 7, Cybèle ou les Dimanches de Ville d'Avray/Sundays and Cybèle* 1962; *La Baie des Anges/Bay of the Angels, Le Jour et l'Heure/The Day and the Hour, Le Feu Follet/The Fire Within* 1963; *Les Parapluies de Cherbourg/The Umbrellas of Cherbourg* 1964; *Viva Maria* 1965; *Paris au Mois d'Aôut/Paris in the Month of August* 1966; *Les Demoiselles de Rochefort/The Young Girls of Rochefort, Sept fois Femme/Woman Times Seven* 1967; *L'Aveu/The Confession* 1970; *Le Bateau sur l'herbe* 1971; *L'Evènement le plus important depuis que l'homme a marché sur la lune, The Grand Bazar, Le Hasard et La Violence* 1973; *La Merveilleuse visite* 1974; *L'Alpagueur, Le Jouet, Néa* 1976; *La Vie devant soi/Madame Rosa* 1977; *Lady Oscar* 1979; *Chère Inconnue, Tous Vedettes* 1980; *Notre Histoire* 1984; *La Rumba, Thérèse* 1986; *Trois places pour le 26* 1988.

Everett, Chad. Actor. Born Raymond Cramton, on June 11, 1936, in South Bend, Ind. *ed.* Wayne State U. Leading man of Hollywood films and such TV series as 'The Dakotas' (1963), 'Medical Center' (1969–76), 'Hagen' (1980), and 'The Rousters' (1983–84).

FILMS INCLUDE: *Claudelle Inglish* 1961; *The Chapman Report* 1962; *Get Yourself a College Girl* 1964; *The Singing Nun* 1965; *Made in Paris, Johnny Tiger* 1966; *First to Fight, The Last Challenge* 1967; *The Impossible Years* 1968; *The Firechasers* 1970; *Airplane II: The Sequel* 1982; *Fever Pitch* 1985; *Heroes Stand Alone* 1989.

Everett, Rupert. Actor. Born on May 29, 1959, in Norfolk, England. Angular star of British films. An army major's son, he dropped out of Catholic school at 15 to pursue acting at the Central School of Speech and Drama, from which he was soon expelled for insubordination. He received his training, instead, as an apprentice with Glasgow's Citizen's Theatre. After originating the role of Guy Bennett in the 1982 London production of 'Another Country,' he repeated it in a triumphant screen debut in 1984. He was also seen to advantage in the TV movie *Princess Daisy* (1983) and other small-screen productions.

FILMS INCLUDE: *Another Country, Real Life* 1984; *Dance with a Stranger* 1985; *Duet for One, The Right Hand Man* (Austral.) 1986; *Chronicle of a Death Foretold, Gli Occhiali d'Oro, Hearts of Fire* 1987; *Tolérance* (Fr.) 1989; *The Comfort of Strangers* (US/It.) 1991; *Inside Monkey Zetterland* (US) 1993; *Cemetery Man, Dellamorte Dellamore, The Madness of King George, Ready to Wear* 1994; *Dunston Checks In* 1996; *My Best Friend's Wedding* 1997.

Everson, William K. Archivist, film historian. Born April 8, 1929, in Yeovil, Eng. Independent owner of one of the largest film collections in the US. A devotee of movies since his upbringing near the movie studios in London, Everson came to the US in the early 1950s (following a 1947–49 stint in the armed forces) and began purchasing (or "liberating") unwanted early films from studios about to destroy them. Since 1966, he has taught film history at the New School for Social Research and NYU, as well as at other colleges and universities. He has also written TV specials about the movies, as well as several books of film history, including *The Western* and *The Bad Guys*. Yet his greatest contribution remains his vast private collection, which now numbers several thousand entries, many of films that might otherwise have been forgotten.

Ewell, Tom. Actor. *b.* Yewell Tompkins, on Apr. 29, 1909, in Owensboro, Ky. *d.* 1994. He became involved in college dramatics at the University of Wisconsin and made his professional stage debut in 1928. He worked as a salesman at Macy's before getting his first Broadway role in 1934. He played bits in two 1940–41 films but remained rooted to the stage and was an established Broadway character comedian by the time he made a memorable leading screen debut, opposite Judy Holliday, in *Adam's Rib* (1949). His skill at caricaturing the foibles of the ordinary man was best exemplified in *The Seven Year Itch* (1955, opposite Marilyn Monroe), in which he repeated his 1952 Broadway triumph. In 1960–61 he starred briefly on TV in the 'Tom Ewell Show.' He later appeared regularly in the series 'Baretta' (1975–78) and 'Best of the West' (1981–82).

FILMS: *They Knew What They Wanted* 1940; *Desert Bandit* 1941; *Adam's Rib* 1949; *A Life of Her Own, An American Guerrilla in the Philippines, Mr. Music* 1950; *Up Front* 1951; *Finders Keepers, Lost in Alaska* 1952; *The Seven Year Itch* 1955; *The Lieutenant Wore Skirts, The Girl Can't Help It* 1956; *Tender Is the Night, State Fair* 1962; *Suppose They Gave a War and Nobody Came?* 1970; *To Find a Man/Sex and the Teenager, They Only Kill Their Masters* 1972; *The Great Gatsby* 1974; *Easy Money* 1983.

exchange. A regional bureau for the distribution of films to motion picture theaters. Film exchanges were started in the early days of American cinema by enterprising businessmen who acted as middlemen between film production and distribution companies, based mainly on the East and West coasts, and exhibitors in cities, towns, and villages throughout the United States. The exchange phenomenon remains uniquely American.

exciter lamp. A small, intense incandescent bulb capable of converting light waves into sound waves when its beam is focused on the sound track area of film. It is used both in the recording of optical sound tracks and in the projection of sound films.

executive producer. A person who is ultimately responsible for a film's production but who seldom takes part in any phase of the filmmaking. He is often in charge of several productions simultaneously and usually oversees general business aspects while leaving each venture to the actual charge of a PRODUCER.

exhibitor. The owner or operator of a theater, or chain of theaters, in which motion pictures are shown.

exploitation. The combined use of advertising, public relations, and other forms of promotion and sales techniques for the purpose of realizing the profit potential of a film.

exploitation films. Films made with little or no attention to quality or artistic merit but with an eye to a quick profit, usually via high-pressure sales and promotion techniques emphasizing some sensational aspect of the product. Films whose erotic or pornographic subject matter is thus exploited have been known as "sexploitation" films.

explosion wipe. See WIPE.

exposure. The process of subjecting film to light so that a latent image is produced on the emulsion. The degree of exposure is determined by the amount of light allowed to reach each frame during shooting. The determining factors in the degree of exposure are length of time and intensity of illumination.

exposure meter. An instrument for measuring the intensity of light falling on or being reflected from a subject or an area being photographed. The meter is activated when light strikes its photoelectric cell, providing the user with mathematically accurate exposure recommendations. There are two basic types of exposure meters: 1. the reflected-light meter, measuring light reflected *from* the subject, and 2. the incident-light meter, measuring the light falling *on* the subject. To get a reading of reflected light, the meter is held near the camera position and aimed toward the subject; to get a reading of incident light, the meter is held close to the subject and is aimed at the position of the camera. Either type of meter can be used to determine correct exposure, but generally speaking, reflected-light readings are preferred for determining the overall brightness of a scene, while incident-light reading is often found more suitable for close-ups and portraits. Some exposure meters are designed to be used for both reflected-light and incident-light measurements.

exposure sheets. In animation, special forms filled out by the animator as a guide for the animation cameraman. The sheets contain instructions regarding the proper order in which each CEL should be photographed in combination with the background, as well as information regarding the timing and speed of all movements, special optical effects desired, etc.

expressionism. A style of art which developed early in the 20th century into an influential movement in German painting, sculpture, literature, drama, and, finally, cinema. Expressionism, as defined by one of its exponents, seeks to "present the inner life of humanity rather than its outward appearance." Another has defined it as a "heightened reality, often via the nonobjective use of symbols, stereotyped characters, and stylization, in order to give objective expression to inner experience." In German cinema, in the years immediately following WW I, expressionism was characterized by extreme stylization of sets and décor as well as in the acting, lighting, and camera angles. The grossly distorted, largely abstract sets were as expressive as the actors, if not more. To assure complete control and free manipulation of the décor, lighting, and camera work, expressionist films were always shot in the studio, never outdoors, even when scenes called for exterior shooting. Lighting was deliberately artificial, emphasizing deep shadows and sharp contrasts; camera angles were chosen to emphasize the fantastic and the grotesque; and the actors externalized their emotions to the extreme.

Some of the finest and most intriguing films in all of silent cinema came out of the German expressionist movement. The prime example of German expressionism is *The Cabinet of Dr. Caligari* (1919). Other key films in the same strange, fantastic vein include *The Golem* (1920), *Der müde Tod/Between Worlds/Destiny* (1921), *Nosferatu, Dr. Mabuse the Gambler* (both 1922), and *Waxworks* (1924). Among the leading directors of the movement were Robert Wiene, Fritz Lang, Paul Leni, and F. W. Murnau. Among the writers, Carl Mayer was the most influential, with Thea von Harbou as a capable disciple. Cameramen included Karl Freund and Fritz Wagner, and the set designers, Hermann Warm, Walter Röhrig, Robert Herlth, and Otto Hunte. The influence of German expressionism was global and long-lasting. Traces of it are recognizable in the films of Alfred Hitchcock and Orson Welles, among many others.

EXT. The common abbreviation used in film scripts and camera reports to indicate an exterior scene, shot either out of doors, on location, or on a studio set simulating the outdoors. Opposite of INT.

extension tube. A cylindrical device used as an extension to hold the camera lens at an increased distance from the film in the camera. It is particularly useful for extremely close-up work.

extra. A member of the cast who speaks no lines and makes no gestures but is used primarily as part of the background or as part of a crowd. Extras are organized in the Screen Extras Guild. They are generally supplied in specified numbers and types by CENTRAL CASTING.

extreme close-up (abbreviated ECU or XCU). A very tight close-up shot that greatly magnifies a tiny object or shows a magnified view of part of an object or a person, such as a shot of a face featuring only the eyes, nose, and mouth. Sometimes called "big close-up." Extreme close-ups are useful for showing small objects in detail, but beyond this obvious utility they may be used effectively for dramatic impact or meaningful emphasis. See also CLOSE-UP.

extreme long shot (abbreviated ELS or XLS). A wide-angle shot providing a bird's-eye view of a vast area. Usually a static shot filmed from a high vantage point, it is most often used to establish the geography of an area or to suggest wide open spaces.

extremes. In animation, the key drawings at the beginning and end of an action usually drawn by the animator himself. Assistant animators, or in-betweeners, using the extremes as guides, then draw the intermediate phases of the action.

eye light. See KICKER.

eyepiece. An attachment at the end of a camera's viewing system which allows the cameraman to appraise his composition before shooting and to view the action during shooting. It is usually furnished with a rubber eyecup, to protect the viewer's eye, and with some cameras with an adjusting ring for individual eyesight. In some late models the pressure of an eye on the eyecup automatically activates a closing shutter to protect the film from light seeping through the viewing system.

Eythe, William. Actor. *b.* Apr. 7, 1918, Mars, Pa. *d.* 1957. Husky, pleasant, but rather colorless leading man of Hollywood films of the 40s. Also active on the stage as actor, director, and producer. Died at 38 of acute hepatitis, following a long bout with alcoholism.

FILMS: *The Ox-Bow Incident, The Song of Bernadette* 1943; *The Eve of St. Mark, Wilson, Wing and a Prayer* 1944; *A Royal Scandal, The House on 92nd Street* 1945; *Colonel Effingham's Raid, Centennial Summer* 1946; *Meet Me at Dawn, Mr. Reckless* 1948; *Special Agent* 1949; *Customs Agent 1950.*

Fabares, Shelley. Actress. Born on Jan. 19, 1942, in Santa Monica, Calif. A niece of Nanette FABRAY, she began performing on TV and in movies as a child, rising to popularity in the wake of 'The Donna Reed Show' (1958–63). At the peak of her film success in the late 60s she co-starred with Elvis PRESLEY in three films. A lead role on TV's 'Coach' revived her television career in the early 90s.

FILMS INCLUDE: *The Girl Rush* 1955; *Never Say Goodbye, Rock Pretty Baby* 1958; *Marjorie Morningstar, Summer Love* 1958; *Ride the Wild Surf* 1964; *Girl Happy* 1965; *Hold On!, Spinout* 1966; *Clambake* 1967; *A Time to Sing* 1968; *Hot Pursuit* 1987; *Love or Money?* 1988.

Fabian. Actor, singer. Born Fabian Forte, on Feb. 6, 1940, in Philadelphia. A teeny-bopper idol and successful pop singer from the age of 14, he played both light and dramatic roles in films from 1959, often in productions appealing to youngsters. Starred on TV in the 'Bus Stop' series and other shows. Since 1970 billed as Fabian Forte, his full name.

FILMS INCLUDE: *Hound-Dog Man* 1959; *High Time, North to Alaska* 1960; *Love in a Goldfish Bowl, Mr. Hobbs Takes a Vacation, Five Weeks in a Balloon, The Longest Day* 1962; *Ride the Wild Surf* 1964; *Dear Brigitte, Ten Little Indians* 1965; *Fireball 500, Dr. Goldfoot and the Girl Bombs* 1966; *Thunder Alley* 1967; *Maryjane, The Wild Racers* 1968; *The Devil's 8* 1969; *A Bullet for Pretty Boy* (as Charles "Pretty Boy" Floyd) 1970; *Little Laura and Big John* 1973; *The Day the Lord Got Busted (Soul Hustler)* 1976; *Disco Fever* 1978; *Kiss Daddy Goodbye/Revenge of the Zombie/The Vengeful Dead* 1981.

Fabian, Françoise. Actress. Born Michèle Cortès de Leone y Fabianera, on May 10, 1932, in Touggourt, Algeria, to a Spanish father and Polish-Jewish mother. She studied piano and attended the Algerian Conservatory of Dramatic Arts before going to Paris, where she attended the Conservatory and made her stage debut in the early 50s. She began appearing in films in 1955 but came into international prominence only in the late 60s with composed, intelligent performances in such films as Luis Buñuel's *Belle de Jour* and Eric Rohmer's *Ma Nuit chez Maud/My Night at Maud's.* She is the widow of film director Jacques BECKER and later married Marcel BOZZUFFI.

FILMS INCLUDE: *Mémoires d'un Flic* 1955; *Cette Sacrée Gamine/Mam'zelle Pigalle, Le Couturier de ces Dames/Fernandel the Dressmaker* 1956; *Le Feux aux Poudres, Michel Strogoff, Les Fanatiques/Bomb for a Dictator* 1957; *Les Violents* 1958; *La Brune que voilà* 1961; *Maigret voit Rouge* 1963; *La Jeune Morte* 1965; *Le Voleur/The Thief of Paris, Belle de Jour* 1967; *Ma Nuit chez Maud/My Night at Maud's, L'Américain* 1969; *Un Condé/The Cop* 1970; *Raphaël ou le débauché* 1971; *La Bonne Année/Happy New Year, Projection privée/Private Projection* 1973; *Per le Antiche Scale/Down the Ancient Stairs* (It./Fr.), *Perche si Uccide un Magistrato* (It.) 1975; *Salut l'Artiste, E la Donna crea l'Amore* (It.) 1976; *Madame Claude, Les Fougères bleues* 1977; *Noel dans une Maison de Rendez-vous* 1978; *Le Cercle des Passions, Benvenuta, L'Ami de Vincent* 1983; *Partir revenir* 1985; *Réunion* 1989; *Reflections in a Dark Sky* 1991.

Fabray, Nanette. Actress, singer. Born Ruby Bernadette Nanette Fabares, on Oct. 27, 1920, in San Diego. She began performing professionally at age five and at six was working in vaudeville with Ben Turpin. In 1927, at seven, she was featured as Baby Nan in several "Our Gang" comedy shorts. She returned to the screen briefly in 1939–40 as a supporting player, but it was on the Broadway stage that she made her name as a musical comedy star. Her only important film appearance was in the musical *The Band Wagon* (1953), in which she performed memorably with Fred Astaire and Jack Buchanan in the famous "Triplets" number. She won two Donaldson Awards for Broadway performances and three Emmys for her co-starring role in the Sid Caesar's TV series 'Caesar's Hour' (1954–56). She was also honored with the President's Distinguished Service Award and several humanitarian prizes. She is the widow of screenwriter Ranald MACDOUGALL.

FILMS INCLUDE: "Our Gang" Comedies 1927; *The Private Lives of Elizabeth and Essex* 1939; *A Child Is Born* 1940; *The Band Wagon* 1953; *The Happy Ending* 1969; *The Cockeyed Cowboys of Calico County* 1970; *Harper Valley P.T.A.* 1978; *Amy* 1981; *Personal Exemptions* 1988.

Fábri, Zoltàn. Director. Born in 1917, in Budapest. Trained as a painter and set designer at Budapest's Academy of Fine Arts, he later transferred to the Academy of Dramatic and Film Art and began his career as a stage director. He spent much of WW II as a prisoner of war and after the liberation gravitated toward film. He began directing in the early 50s and soon distinguished himself as one of the leading talents of the Hungarian "New Cinema." He has also written the scripts and designed the sets for several of his films as director. His Hungarian-American co-production *The Boys Of Paul Street* (1968) was nominated for an Oscar as best foreign film. He won the Jury Prize at the 1975 Moscow Festival for *141 Minutes from the Unfinished Sentence* and the Grand Prize in 1977 for *The Fifth Seal.* In the Berlin Festival of 1982 he won the Silver Bear for single outstanding achievement for his script of *Requiem.* In the 80s he served as president of the Union of Hungarian Cinema and Television Artists and taught at Budapest's Academy of Theater and Film Art.

FILMS: *Underground Colony* 1951; *The Storm* 1952; *Fourteen Lives* 1954; *Merry-go-round* (also co-sc., art dir.) 1955; *Professor Hannibal* (also co-sc.) 1956; *Summer Clouds* (also art dir.) 1957; *Anna* (also co-sc., art dir.) 1958; *The Brute* (also sc., art dir.) 1959; *The Last Goal* (also Art Dir.) 1961; *Darkness in Daytime* (also Sc., Art Dir.) 1963; *Twenty Hours* 1964; *A Hard Summer* (made for TV) 1965; *Late Season* 1967; *The Boys of Paul Street* (also co-sc.) 1968; *The Toth Family* 1970; *Ants' Nest* 1971; *One Day More One Day Less* 1973; *148 Minutes from the Unfinished Sentence* (also sc.) 1975; *The Fifth Seal* (also co-sc.) 1976; *The Hungarians* (also sc.) 1978; *Balint Fabian Meets God* (also sc.) 1980; *Requiem* (also sc.) 1981; *The Housewarming* (also sc.) 1983.

Fabrizi, Aldo. Actor. *b.* Nov. 1, 1905, Rome. *d.* 1990. Started out as a music hall comedian and began playing character roles in Italian films in the early 40s. Became internationally known for his dramatic portrayal of a courageous priest defying the Fascists in Rossellini's *Open City* (1945) and subsequently gained stature as a versatile character actor in both comedy and drama. He occasionally directed and wrote the screenplays for his films as an actor, but his efforts as a director were rarely seen outside Italy. After the mid-70s he was seen rarely on the screen, devoting his time instead to the writing of cookbooks.

FILMS INCLUDE: *Avanti C'è Posto* 1942; *Campo De'fiori/The Peddler and the Lady* 1943; *Roma Città Aperta/Open City* 1945; *Mio Figlio Professore/Professor My Son, Vivere in Pace/To Live in Peace* (also co-sc.) 1946; *Il Delitto Di Giovanni Episcopo/Flesh Will Surrender* (also co-sc.), *Tombolo* 1947; *Natale Al Campo 119/Escape Into Dreams* (also co-story) 1948; *Emigrantes* (also dir., sc.) 1949; *Prima Comunione/Father's Dilemma, Francesco Giullare Di Dio/Flowers of St. Francis, Tre Passi A Nord/Three Steps North* 1950; *Parigi è Sempre Parigi, Guardie E Ladri/Cops and Robbers, Altri Tempi/Times Gone By, La Famiglia Passaguai* (also dir., sc.) 1951; *Papà Diventa Mamma* (also dir., sc.) 1952; *Questa è La Vita/Of Life and Love* (one episode; also dir., sc.), *Cento Anni D'amore* 1954; *Donatella* 1955; *Festa Di Maggio/Premier May* 1957; *Il Maestro/The Teacher and The Miracle* (also dir., prod., co-sc.) 1958; *La Sposa Bella* 1959; *Le Meraviglie Di Aladino/The Wonders of Aladdin* 1962; *Made in Italy* 1965; *Three Bites of the Apple* (US) 1967; *Cose Di Cosa Nostra/The Godson* 1971; *Permettete Che Ami Vostre Figlia?, Touchez-pas La Femme Blanche* (Fr./It.) 1974; *C'ervamo Tanto Amati/We All Loved Each Other So Much/Those Were the Years* 1975; *Il Ginecologo Della Mutua* 1977; *Carefree Giovanni* 1985.

Fabrizi, Franco. Actor. *b.* Feb. 15, 1926, in Cortemaggiore, Italy. *d.* 1995. A stage actor from 1947, he made his film debut in 1952 and attracted attention the following year in the role of the leader of a group of aimless small-town youths in Fellini's *I Vitelloni.* Tall, blond, and handsome, he subsequently played leads and supporting roles in many European productions.

FILMS INCLUDE: *Carica Heroica* 1952; *I Vitelloni, Il Sacco Di Roma/The Pagans/The Barbarians* 1953; *La Romana/Woman of Rome, Camilla* 1954; *Le Amiche/The Girl Friends, Il Bidone/The Swindle, Calabuch/The Rocket from Calabuch* (Sp./It.) 1955; *Mariti In Città, Sait-on Jamais?/No Sun in Venice* (Fr./It.), *La Donna Del Giorno/The Doll That Took the Town* 1957; *Racconti D'estate/Love on the Riviera* 1958; *Le Notti Di Lucrezia/The Nights of Lucretia Borgia* (as Cesare Borgia), *Il Moralista/The Moralist, Un Maledetto Imbroglio/The Facts of Murder* 1959; *Via Margutta/Run with the Devil* 1960; *Orazi E Curiazi/Duel of Champions, Il Relitto/The Wastrel* 1961; *Il Criminale* 1962; *Signore E Signori/The Birds the Bees and the Italians* 1966; *Le Dolci Signore/Anyone Can Play* 1967; *El Millón De Madigan/Madigan's Millions* (Sp./It.) 1968; *Morte A Venezia/Death in Venice* 1971; *La Polizia Ringrazia* 1972; *Conoscenza Matrimoniale* 1973; *L'Aggression* (Fr./It.) 1975; *L'Affaire Suisse* (Switz./Fr./It.) 1978; *Ginger e Fred/Ginger and Fred* 1985; *Besame* 1987; *Il Piccolo Diavolo/The Little Devil* 1988.

fade. An optical effect that causes a scene to emerge gradually on the screen from complete blackness (fade-in), or a bright image to dim gradually into blackness (fade-out). The fade is a transitional device that usually signifies a distinct break in a film's continuity, indicating a change in time, location, or subject matter. Most films begin with a fade-in and end with a fade-out. The use of a fade-in/fade-out between sequences within a film is similar to the function of the beginning or end of a chapter in a book or of an act in a play. The length of the fade should be in keeping with the film's tempo and mood. Technically, a fade-in is achieved by a gradual increase of exposure for each frame until the image reaches full brightness; a fade-out is obtained by a gradual decrease of exposure for each frame with the last frame completely black. Normally, fades are made by the optical printer, but they can also be satisfactorily achieved by some cameras. Amateurs often use a fading solution to obtain fades chemically. The gradual increase or decrease in the level of sound in a film is similarly known as a fade-in or fade-out. Thus, typically, a motion picture script would start with the instruction "Fade in" on the picture side and "Fade in music" (or sound effects) on the sound side.

Fahey, Jeff. Actor. Born in 1956 in Buffalo, N.Y. Handsome leading and supporting actor of the American stage and screen. With experience as a ballet dancer and having worked at the Studio Arena Theatre in his hometown of Buffalo, Fahey began his film career in Lawrence Kasdan's *Silverado* (1985). He has worked extensively in TV movies while continuing to create believable characters in films, ranging from "the guy next door" to the "offbeat, psycho next door."

FILMS INCLUDE: *Silverado* 1985; *Psycho III* 1986; *Backfire* (US/Can.) 1987; *Split Decision* 1988; *True Blood* 1989; *The Last of the Finest, Impulse, White Hunter, Black Heart* 1990; *Body Parts, Iron Maze* 1991; *The Lawnmower Man, Sketch Artist* 1992; *Woman of Desire* 1993; *Wyatt Earp,* 1994.

Fain, Sammy. Composer, songwriter. *b.* Samuel Feinberg, June 17, 1902, New York City. *d.* 1989. A former club and radio pianist, he has written scores and songs for many films since the beginning of the sound era. Won Academy Awards for the song 'Secret Love' in the film *Calamity Jane* (1953) and for the title song of *Love Is a Many Splendored Thing* (1955).

FILMS INCLUDE: *It's A Great Life* 1929; *Footlight Parade, Moonlight and Pretzels* 1933; *Dames* 1934; *Sweet Music, Goin' to Town* 1935; *New Faces of 1937, Vogues of 1938* 1937; *Hellzapoppin* 1941; *I Dood It* 1943; *Two Girls and a Sailor, I'll Be Seeing You* (title Song) 1944; *Weekend At the Waldorf, Anchors Aweigh* 1945; *Two Sisters from Boston, No Leave No Love* 1946; *The Unfinished Dance, This Time for Keeps* 1947; *Three Daring Daughters* 1948; *Alice in Wonderland, Call Me Mister* 1951; *The Jazz Singer, Calamity Jane, Peter Pan* 1953; *Lucky Me* 1954; *Young at Heart, Love Is a Many Splendored Thing* 1955; *April Love* 1957; *Marjorie Morningstar, A Certain Smile, Mardi Gras* 1958; *Tender Is the Night* 1962; *Made in Paris* 1965; *Myra Breckinridge* 1970; *The Stepmother* 1973; *The Teacher* 1974; *The Specialist* 1975; *The Rescuers* 1977.

Fair, Elinor. Actress. *b.* 1902, Richmond, Va. *d.* 1957. Leading lady of Hollywood silents, following stage experience in vaudeville, musical comedy, and stock. At one time was married to screen cowboy William BOYD, who co-starred in several of her films. Retired shortly after the advent of sound.

FILMS INCLUDE: *The Road Through the Dark* 1918; *The Miracle Man, Words and Music, Love Is Love, Be a Little Sport, Vagabond Luck, The Lost Princess, Tin Pan Alley* 1919; *Occasionally Yours, Kismet, The Girl in No. 29, Broadway and Home* 1920; *It Can Be Done, A Dangerous Pastime, Through the Back Door* 1921; *White Hands, Big Stakes* 1922; *Driven, The Eagle's Feather, Has the World Gone Mad?, The Mysterious Witness* 1923; *The Law Forbids* 1924; *Gold and the Girl, The Wife Who Wasn't Wanted, Trapped, Timber Wolf* 1925; *The Volga Boatman, Bachelor Brides* 1926; *Jim the Conqueror, The Yankee Clipper* 1927; *Let 'Er Go Gallagher, My Friend from India* 1928; *Sin Town* 1929; *The Night Rider* 1932.

Fairbanks, Douglas. Actor. *b.* Douglas Elton Ulman, May 23, 1883, Denver, Colo. *d.* 1939. The son of a prominent Jewish lawyer and a Southern belle who were separated when he was five, he was raised by his mother, who reassumed the surname of her first husband, Fairbanks. Douglas made his stage debut at age 12, playing a newsboy with an Italian accent in a locally produced play. He continued appearing in occasional plays while attending the Colorado School of Mines. In 1900 the family moved to New York, where he joined an unsuccessful touring company. In 1902 he made his Broadway debut in 'Her Lord and Master.' In 1907, just as he was beginning to make it as a leading man, he left the stage to marry the daughter of an industrialist, Anna Beth Sully, and to work for her family's soap company. But he returned to the theater the following year when his father-in-law lost his fortune. In 1909, Doug's son, Douglas FAIRBANKS, Jr., was born.

By 1910, Douglas Sr. was an established Broadway star, widely admired for the same qualities that were to make him the silent screen's most beloved hero—cheerful exuberance, moral courage, a devil-may-care attitude, and physical agility, a prototype of the idealized image of the American male. In 1915, Fairbanks was lured to Hollywood by a generous contract with Triangle. The public took to him immediately and by 1916 he was popular and secure enough to establish his own production company, the Douglas Fairbanks Film Corporation, with an Artcraft-Paramount release. He had complete control of all phases of production and named members of his family to key positions in the company.

During a WW I Liberty Bond tour with Charlie CHAPLIN and Mary PICKFORD, Fairbanks fell in love with "America's Sweetheart." Having divorced his first wife, Fairbanks married Pickford in 1920 and after a whirlwind European honeymoon they settled in their Hollywood mansion, Pickfair, which soon became a social Mecca for the titled and the famous. Earlier, in 1919, Doug and Mary had gone into partnership with Chaplin and D. W. GRIFFITH, forming United Artists to distribute all their future productions. Both Fairbanks and Pickford reached the peak of their success in the 20s.

Fairbanks was as popular in his early tongue-in-cheek social comedies as he later became in a succession of swashbuckling adventures. And he was still fit and trim in 1929, when his stage-trained voice allowed him to make a smooth transition to sound. But as he clearly advanced in age, receding hair framing his still handsome but tired face, his popularity began to slip. The failure of *The Taming of the Shrew* (1929), the only film in which he co-starred with his wife, did not help the shaky marriage. The two separated in 1933 and in January 1936 they were divorced. In March he married ex-chorus girl Lady Sylvia Ashley (1904–77) and announced his retirement from acting. In December of 1939 he died in his sleep of a heart attack. Author: *Laugh and Live* (1917); *Making Life Worth While* (1918); *My Secret Success* (1922); *Youth Points the Way* (1924).

FILMS: *The Martyrs of the Alamo, The Lamb, Double Trouble* 1915; *His Picture in the Papers, The Habit of Happiness, The Good Bad Man, Reggie Mixes In, Flirting with Fate, The Mystery of the Leaping Fish* (two-reel short), *The Half Breed, Intolerance* (cameo), *Manhattan Madness, American Aristocracy, The Matrimaniac, The Americano* 1916; *In Again Out Again* (also prod.), *Wild and Woolly* (also prod.), *Down to Earth* (also prod., story), *The Man from Painted Post* (also prod., sc.), *Reaching for the Moon* (also prod.) 1917; *A Modern Musketeer* (also prod.), *Headin' South* (also prod.), *Mr. Fix-It* (also prod.), *Say! Young Fellow* (also prod.), *Bound in Morocco* (also prod.), *He Comes Up Smiling* (also prod.), *Arizona* (also dir., prod., sc.) 1918; *The Knickerbocker Buckaroo* (also prod., story, co-sc.), *His Majesty the American* (also prod., co-sc. under pseudonym Elton Banks), *Till The Clouds Roll By* (also prod., co-story, co-sc.) 1919; *The Mollycoddle* (also prod., co-sc.), *The Mark of Zorro* (as Zorro; also prod., co-sc. under pseudonym Elton Thomas) 1920; *The Nut* (also prod.), *The Three Musketeers* (as D'Artagnan; also prod.) 1921; *Robin Hood* (title role; also prod., sc. under pseudonym Elton Thomas) 1922; *The Thief of Bagdad* (title role; also prod., story under pseudonym Elton Thomas) 1924; *Don Q Son of Zorro* (again as Zorro; also prod.) 1925; *The Black Pirate* (also prod., story under pseudonym Elton Thomas) 1926; *Potselui Mary Pickford/The Kiss of Mary Pickford* (cameo; USSR), *The Gaucho* (also prod., story under pseudonym Elton Thomas) 1927; *The Iron Mask* (again as D'Artagnan; also prod., sc. under pseudonym Elton Thomas), *Show People* (cameo) 1928; *The Taming of the Shrew* (as Petruchio; also prod.) 1929; *Reaching for the Moon* (remake; also prod.), *Around the World in 80 Minutes* (also prod., co-dir. with Victor Fleming, co-sc. with Robert E. Sherwood) 1931; *Mr. Robinson Crusoe* (also prod.) 1932; *The Private Life of Don Juan* (as Don Juan; UK) 1934.

Fairbanks, Douglas, Jr. Actor. Born on Dec. 9, 1909, in New York City. The son of Douglas FAIRBANKS from the silent star's first marriage, to Anna Beth Sully, he was raised by his mother from age nine, when his parents divorced. He made his screen debut at age 13 as the boy star of *Stephen Steps Out*, an unsuccessful attempt by Jesse L. Lasky to exploit the magic of the Fairbanks name. Fairbanks Sr. took little interest in his son's career, confessing he had "no more paternal feelings than a tiger in the jungle for his cub." Only in the early 30s did father and son become close friends. Meanwhile, Douglas Jr. had to carve his own way through the Hollywood jungle, accepting any role that came his way, including bits and extra parts. To supplement his meager income, he wrote titles for silent films, and appeared occasionally on the Los Angeles stage. But his heart never was in acting and it wasn't until 1928, when he married Joan CRAWFORD, that he became more ambitious and began to emerge as a star.

Still, despite his dashing good looks and agreeable screen personality, he never became a superstar of the magnitude of his father, nor even of such contemporary film heroes as Ronald Colman and Errol Flynn. Instead, he seemed to thrive on his eminent social and political connections, in England as well as in the US, which included an intimately close relationship with the British royal family. During WW II, as a lieutenant commander in the US Navy, he participated in several combined Anglo-American operations. The British awarded him with an assortment of medals and decorations, and in 1949 he was knighted for "furthering Anglo-American amity." An avowed Anglophile, Fairbanks lived for many years in London after his retirement from the screen in the early 50s (in 1953–57 he hosted a London-based anthology series for American TV). Sharing his home was Mary Lee Hartford, the former wife of the A & P heir, whom he married in 1938, five years after his divorce from Miss Crawford. During the 60s he hosted and sometimes acted in a British-made TV drama series, 'Douglas Fairbanks Presents.' Later he and his wife sold their London home and settled in Palm Beach, Fla, where she died in 1988. Co-author: *The Fairbanks Album* (1975). Autobiographies: *The Salad Days* (1988), *A Hell of a War* (1993).

FILMS: *Stephen Steps Out* 1923; *The Air Mail, Wild Horse Mesa, Stella Dallas* 1925; *The American Venus, Padlocked, Broken Hearts of Hollywood* 1926; *Man Bait, Women Love Diamonds, Is Zat So?, A Texas Steer* 1927; *Dead Man's Curve, Modern Mothers, The Toilers, The Power of the Press, The Barker, A Woman of Affairs* 1928; *The Jazz Age, Fast Life, Our Modern Maidens, The Careless Age, The Show of Shows, The Forward Pass* 1929; *Party Girl, Loose Ankles, The Dawn Patrol, Little Accident, One Night at Susie's, Outward Bound, The Way of All Men* 1930; *Little Caesar, Chances, I Like Your Nerve* 1931; *Union Depot, It's Tough to Be Famous, Love Is a Racket, Scarlet Dawn* 1932; *Parachute Jumper, The Life of Jimmy Dolan, The Narrow Corner, Morning Glory, Captured* 1933; *Catherine the Great* (as Grand Duke Peter; UK), *Success at Any Price* 1934; *Mimi* (UK) 1935; *The Amateur Gentleman* (UK), *Accused* (UK) 1936; *Jump for Glory/When Thief Meets Thief* (UK), *The Prisoner of Zenda* (as Rupert of Hentzau) 1937; *Joy of Living, The Rage of Paris, Having Wonderful Time, The Young in Heart* 1938; *Gunga Din, The Sun Never Sets, Rulers of the Sea* 1939; *Green Hell, Safari, Angels Over Broadway* (also assoc. prod.) 1940; *The Corsican Brothers* (dual role) 1941; *Sinbad the Sailor* (title role), *The Exile* (also prod., sc.) 1947; *That Lady in Ermine* 1948; *The Fighting O'Flynn* (also prod., co-sc.) 1949; *State Secret* (UK) 1950; *Mister Drake's Duck* (UK) 1951; *Chase a Crooked Shadow* (prod. only; UK) 1958; *Moment of Danger/Malaga* (co-exec. prod. only; UK) 1960; *Ghost Story* 1981.

Falconetti, Renée (Maria). Actress. *b.* 1892, Sermano, Corsica. *d.* 1946. A celebrated actress and producer of the Paris stage, she made only one film appearance, but her performance, in Carl Dreyer's *La Passion de Jeanne d'Arc/The Passion of Joan of Arc* (1927) was so memorable that it assured her a place in film history. She died in Buenos Aires, where she had emigrated shortly before the outbreak of WW II.

Falk, Peter. Actor. Born on Sept. 16, 1927, in New York City. He began his adult life as a cook with the merchant marine and, after acquiring a B.A. from the New School for Social Research and an M.B.A. from Syracuse University in public administration, became an efficiency expert for the Budget Bureau of the state of Connecticut. Bored with adding figures, he became interested in amateur dramatics and in 1955 turned professional with the encouragement of Eva Le Gallienne. He first gained attention in the off-Broadway production of 'The Iceman Cometh,' which led to a busy career on Broadway and TV and in films. Adept at portraying Runyonesque hoodlums and big-city blue-collar characters, he won an Emmy Award for his portrayal of a truck driver in the TV play 'Price of Tomatoes' and three others for his title role as an eccentric detective in the popular 'Columbo' series (1971–77; late 80s revival plus several television movies based on the series in the late 80s and early 90s). He received Oscar nominations as best supporting actor for his work in the films *Murder Inc.* (1960) and *Pocketful of Miracles* (1961). In 1972 he won a Tony for his performance in Broadway's 'The Prisoner of Second Avenue.' His characters derive added authenticity from his squinty gaze, the result of the loss of an eye at the age of three.

FILMS: *Wind Across the Everglades* 1958; *The Bloody Brood* (Can.) 1959; *Pretty Boy Floyd, Murder Inc., The Secret of the Purple Reef* 1960; *Pocketful of Miracles* 1961; *Pressure Point* 1962; *The Balcony, It's a Mad Mad Mad Mad World* 1963; *Robin and the 7 Hoods, Italiani Brava Gente* (It./USSR) 1964; *The Great Race* 1965; *Penelope* 1966; *Luv* 1967; *Gli Intoccabili/Machine Gun McCain* (It.), *Lo Sbarco di Anzio/ Anzio* 1968; *Castle Keep* 1969 *Rosolino Paterno' Soldato/ Operation Snafu* (It.), *Husbands* 1970; *A Woman Under the Influence* 1974; *Murder by Death, Mikey and Nickey, Griffin and Phoenix* (TV movie released theatrically abroad) 1976; *Opening Night* (cameo), *The Cheap Detective, The Brink's Job* 1978; *The In-Laws* 1979; *The Great Muppet Caper* (cameo), *. . . All the Marbles* 1981; *Big Trouble* 1986; *Happy New Year, Der Himmel über Berlin/Les Ailes du Désir/Wings of Desire* (Ger./Fr.), *The Princess Bride* 1987; *Vibes* 1988; *Cookie* 1989; *In the Spirit, Tune in Tomorrow* 1990; *The Player* 1992; *Far Away, So Close!* 1993; *Roommates* 1995.

Falkenburg, Jinx. Actress. Born Eugenia Falkenburg, on Jan. 21, 1919, in Barcelona. Vivacious leading lady of Hollywood second features, mostly inexpensive comedies and musicals. Raised in Chile, where she attended Santiago College and was a tennis and swimming champion, she started her career in the US as a fashion model and cover girl. In her early films she was billed as Eugenia or Jinx Falkenberg, or Jinx Falken.

FILMS INCLUDE: *Strike Me Pink, Big Brown Eyes* 1936; *Nothing Sacred* 1937; *Song of the Buckaroo* 1938; *The Lone Ranger Rides Again* (serial) 1939; *Two Latins from Manhattan, Sing for Your Supper* 1941; *Sweetheart of the Fleet, Lucky Legs, Laugh Your Blues Away* 1942; *She Had What It Takes, Two Senoritas from Chicago* 1943; *Nine Girls, Cover Girl, Tahiti Nights* 1944; *The Gay Senorita* 1945; *Meet Me on Broadway, Talk About a Lady* 1946.

Famous Players. Film production company formed in 1912 by Adolph ZUKOR, following his great success in the American distribution of the French-made *Queen Elizabeth,* starring Sarah Bernhardt. Zukor modeled his Famous Players Film Company after the French Film d'Art company, which had produced *Queen Elizabeth,* turning out screen adaptations of classic novels and plays under the slogan "Famous Players in Famous Plays." In 1916 Zukor's company merged with Jesse L. LASKY's Feature Play company to form the Famous Players—Lasky Corporation. Soon after, the new corporation was merged with its distributing company, W. W. Hodkinson's PARAMOUNT Pictures Corporation.

Fanck, Dr. Arnold. Director. *b.* Mar. 6, 1889, Frankenthal, Germany. *d.* 1974. A geologist, he manifested his passion for mountain climbing in a series of post–WW I documentary and fiction films which initiated the trend to MOUNTAIN FILMS as a popular genre in the German cinema. Among his collaborators were Sepp Allgeier, Leni RIEFENSTAHL, G. W. PABST, and Tay GARNETT.

FILMS: *Das Wunder des Schneeschuhs/Marvels of Ski* (also co-sc.) 1921; *Pomperly's Kampf mit dem Schneeschuh, Im Kampf mit dem Berge;* (both co-dir., co-sc.) 1922; *Der Berg des Schicksals/Peak of Fate* (also sc., co-phot.) 1924; *Der heilige Berg/Peaks of Destiny* (also sc.) 1926; *Der grosse Sprung/The Big Jump* (also sc.) 1927; *Die weisse Hölle vom Piz Palü/The White Hell of Pitz Palu* (co-dir. with G. W. Pabst, co-sc.) 1929; *Stürme über dem Montblanc/Avalanche* (also sc.) 1930; *Der weisse Rausch/The White Frenzy/The White Ecstasy/The Ski Chase* 1931; *SOS Eisberg/SOS Iceberg* (co-dir. with Tay Garnett; also co-sc.) 1933; *Der ewige Traum* (also sc.) 1934; *Die Tochter des Samurai* (also sc.; Ger./Jap.) 1937; *Ein Robinson* (also co-sc.; in Chile) 1940.

Fantômas. Master criminal villain-hero of a series of pulp novels published in France between 1911 and 1914. Louis FEUILLADE brought the character to the screen in a series of five action serials with René Navarre in the title role. The international popularity of these multi-episode films influenced the serial trend in American films. In 1921, Fantômas was the hero of a Hollywood serial by that title, directed by Edward Sedgwick. The character reappeared on the French screen in 1932 under the direction of Paul Fejos; in 1947 with Jean Sacha directing; and in 1965, André Hunebelle. The latter version starred Jean Marais, with Louis de Funès and Mylène Demongeot supporting.

Fapp, Daniel L. Director of photography. Born on Apr. 4, 1901, in Kansas City, Kans. Entered films as a lab assistant and in the 20s joined Paramount's camera department. As a lighting cameraman since the early 40s, he was responsible for many quality productions at Paramount and other studios. His work is noted for its bold black-and-white and lavish color photography. He won an Academy Award for the cinematography of *West Side Story* (1961). Retired in 1969.

FILMS INCLUDE: *World Premiere* 1941; *Priorities on Parade* 1942; *And Now Tomorrow* 1944; *Hold That Blonde* 1945; *Kitty, To Each His Own* 1946; *Golden Earrings* 1947; *Dream Girl* 1948; *Sorrowful Jones* 1949; *No Man of Her Own, Union Station* 1950; *The Lemon Drop Kid, Sailor Beware* 1951; *The Stooge, Jumping Jacks* 1952; *Money from Home* 1953; *Living It Up, Knock on Wood* 1954; *The Far Horizons* 1955; *Artists and Models* 1956; *The Joker Is Wild* 1957; *Kings Go Forth, Desire Under the Elms* 1958; *Li'l Abner, The Five Pennies, On the Beach* 1959; *All the Young Men, Let's Make Love* 1960; *One Two Three, West Side Story* 1961; *Bachelor Flat* 1962; *A New Kind of Love, Fun in Acapulco, Move Over Darling, The Great Escape* 1963; *Send Me No Flowers, The Unsinkable Molly Brown* 1964; *I'll Take Sweden* 1965; *Our Man Flint, Lord Love a Duck* 1966; *Sweet November, Ice Station Zebra* 1968; *Marooned* 1969.

Faragoh, Francis Edward. Screenwriter. *b.* Oct. 16, 1898, in Budapest. *d.* 1966. *ed.* CCNY; Columbia. A playwright and short-story writer, he contributed several successful Hollywood screenplays, alone or in collaboration.

FILMS INCLUDE: *Her Private Affair* 1929; *Back Pay* 1930; *Little Caesar, Frankenstein* 1931; *The Last Man* 1932; *Becky Sharp, The Return of Peter Grimm* 1935; *Dancing Pirate* 1936; *My Friend Flicka* 1943; *Renegades* 1946; *Easy Come Easy Go* 1947.

Farentino, James. Actor. Born on Feb. 24, 1938, in Brooklyn, N.Y. *ed.* AADA. Assertive leading man of the American stage, TV, and occasional films. His career took off after a strong Broadway debut in the 1961 production of 'Night of the Iguana.' On TV he was seen in the series 'The Lawyers' (1969–72), 'Cool Million' (1972–73), 'Dynasty' (1981–82), 'Blue Thunder' (1984), and 'Mary' (1985–86), among numerous other productions.

FILMS INCLUDE: *Violent Midnight/Psychomania* 1963; *Ensign Pulver* 1964; *The War Lord* 1965; *The Pad* 1966; *Banning, Rosie* 1967; *Me Natalie* 1969; *Story of a Woman* 1970; *The Final Countdown* 1980; *Dead and Buried* 1981; *Her Alibi* 1989; *Bulletproof* 1996.

Farmer, Frances. Actress. *b.* Sept. 19, 1913, Seattle, Wash. *d.* 1970. A lawyer's daughter, she excelled as a high school student and during her studies at the University of Washington won a trip to the Soviet Union as first prize for an essay she submitted in competition to a radical magazine. She made her screen debut in 1936 and the following year began a concurrent stage career with the Group Theatre in New York, playing the female lead in 'Golden Boy' and other Broadway productions of the late 30s. Talented as well as beautiful, she seemed to be headed for a promising career on the stage and in films, but the problem of alcoholism brought her into frequent conflict with the law and forced her retirement in 1942. She spent a good part of the 40s in various mental institutions and by the late 50s was well enough to appear in a single film and to host a local TV program in Indianapolis. She died of cancer at 57. An autobiography, *Will There Really Be a Morning?,* was published posthumously in 1972. Miss Farmer's tragic life story was harrowingly recreated in the film *Frances* (1981), in which she was impersonated by Jessica LANGE. The first of her three husbands was actor Leif ERICKSON.

FILMS: *Too Many Parents, Border Flight, Rhythm on the Range, Come and Get It* 1936; *Exclusive, The Toast of New York, Ebb Tide* 1937; *Ride a Crooked Mile* 1938; *South of Pago-Pago, Flowing Gold* 1940; *World Premiere, Badlands of Dakota, Among the Living* 1941; *Son of Fury* 1942; *The Party Crashers* 1958.

Fargo, James. Director. Born on Feb. 24, 1938, in Republic, Wash. *ed.* U. of Washington. Action-oriented filmmaker with TV and cable experience.

FILMS: *The Enforcer* 1972; *Caravans* (Iran/US), *Every Which Way but Loose* 1978; *Game for Vultures* (UK) 1979; *Forced Vengeance* 1981; *Voyage of the Rock Aliens* 1987; *Born to Race* 1988.

Farley, Chris. Actor, comedian. *b.* February 15, 1964, in Wisconsin. Hyper-intense, pudgy comic actor who got his start doing improvisational comedy at Chicago's Second City, followed by several years as a regular on the NBC late-night series 'Saturday Night Live.' There he was able to showcase his talent for outrageous physical comedy leading to feature film work in his post-SNL days.

FILMS: *L.A. Story* 1991; *Wayne's World* 1992; *Coneheads, Wayne's World 2* 1993; *Airheads* 1994; *Tommy Boy* 1995; *Black Sheep* 1996; *Beverly Hills Ninja* 1997.

Farnsworth, Richard. Actor. Born on Sept. 1, 1920, in Los Angeles. He entered films at 16 as a stuntman and for four decades earned his keep by doubling for Roy ROGERS and other stars of Westerns and action pictures. Over the years, he played bits and tiny parts in occasional films. By the late 60s he had graduated to character roles and in the 70s he ventured into acting on a regular basis. He was nominated for an Oscar as best supporting actor for his performance in *Comes a Horseman* (1978) and Canada's best actor award for his lead role in *The Grey Fox* (1982).

FILMS INCLUDE: *A Day at the Races* 1937; *This Is the Army* 1943; *Red River* 1948; *The Wild One* 1953; *The Tin Star* 1957; *Spartacus* 1960; *Duel at Diablo, Texas Across the River* 1966; *Monte Walsh* 1970; *Pocket Money, Ulzana's Raid, The Life and Times of Judge Roy Bean* 1972; *The Soul of Nigger Charley* 1973; *The Duchess and the Dirtwater Fox* 1976; *Un Autre Homme une Autre Chance/Another Man Another Chance* (Fr.) 1977; *Comes a Horseman* 1978; *Tom Horn, Resurrection* 1980; *Ruckus, The Legend of the Lone Ranger* 1981; *Independence Day, The Grey Fox* (Can.) 1982; *The Natural, Rhinestone* 1984; *Into the Night, Sylvester* 1985; *Space Rage* 1986; *Witchery* 1988; *The Two Jakes, Misery* 1990; *Highway to Hell* 1992; *The Getaway, Lassie* 1994.

Farnum, Dustin. Actor. *b.* May 27, 1874, Hampton Beach, N.H. *d.* 1929. Brother of William FARNUM. On the stage from age 15, he made his screen debut in 1913. The following year brought him instant success as the star of C. B. DE MILLE's first film, *The Squaw Man.* He went on to play a variety of leading parts in many pictures but was most closely identified in the public mind with his cowboy roles. His career waned in the beginning of the 20s, but he continued starring in films until 1926.

FILMS INCLUDE: *Soldiers of Fortune, The Squaw Man* (title role), *The Virginian* (title role) 1914; *Cameo Kirby, Captain Courtesy, The Gentleman from Indiana, The Call of the Cumberlands, The Iron Strain* 1915; *David Garrick* (title role), *The Parson of Panamint, Ben Blair, Davy Crockett* (title role) 1916; *The Scarlet Pimpernel, The Spy, Durand of the Bad Lands* 1917; *The Light of the Western Stars* 1918; *A Man's Fight* 1919; *The Corsican Brothers* (dual lead role), *Big Happiness* 1920; *The Primal Law, The Devil Within* 1921; *Strange Idols, Oath-Bound, The Yosemite Trail* 1922; *Three Who Paid, The Buster, The Man Who Won, The Grail, Kentucky Days* 1923; *My Man* 1924; *The Flaming Frontier* (as General Custer) 1926.

Farnum, Franklyn. Actor. *b.* June 5, 1876, Boston. *d.* 1961. In vaudeville from age 12, he played in numerous stage plays and musicals before his film debut in 1914. Starred in scores of silent movies, mostly Westerns, and a number of serials. Played character parts after the coming of sound. No relation to Dustin or William Farnum.

FILMS INCLUDE: *Love Never Dies* 1916; *A Stormy Knight, The Clock* 1917; *Fast Company* 1918; *Vanishing Trails* (serial), *The Galloping Devil, The Land of Jazz* 1920; *The Fighting Stranger, The Hunger of the Blood, The Last Chance, The White Masks, The Struggle, The Raiders* 1921; *Gold Grabbers, Texas Angel Citizens, Gun Shy, So This Is Arizona, Smiling Jim, Trail's End, Cross Roads, The Firebrand* 1922; *It Happened Out West* 1923; *Battling Brewster* (serial), *A Two-Fisted Tenderfoot, Courage, A Desperate Adventure* 1924; *The Gambling Fool, Drug Store Cowboy, Border Intrigue* 1925; *Beyond the Rio Grande* 1930; *Three Rogues* 1931; *Human Targets* 1932; *Frontier Days* 1934; *Hopalong Cassidy, The Crusades* 1935; *The Preview Murder Mystery* 1936; *Saddle Leather Law* 1944; *Sunset Boulevard* 1950.

Farnum, William. Actor. *b.* July 4, 1876, Boston. *d.* 1953. On the stage from age 12, he later toured vaudeville in an athletic act with his brother Dustin FARNUM. He rose quickly to screen stardom with his very first film, *The Spoilers,* one of the most spectacular productions of the early silent era. He subsequently starred in scores of films, commanding one of the highest salaries in Hollywood. In 1925, during the filming of *A Man Who Fights Alone,* he was seriously injured and could play only minor parts till the end of the silent era. He later played character roles in sound films, often bits in remakes of films in which he had starred.

FILMS INCLUDE: *The Spoilers, The Sign of the Cross* 1914; *Samson* (title role), *The Plunderer, The Nigger, The Wonderful Adventure, The Broken Law, A Soldier's Oath* 1915; *Fighting Blood, The Bondman, A Man of Sorrow, The End of the Trail* 1916; *A Tale of Two Cities* (as Charles Darnay/Sydney Carton), *The Conqueror, American Methods, The Heart of a Lion, Les Miserables* (as Jean Valjean) 1917; *The Rainbow Trail, True Blue, Riders of the Purple Sage* 1918; *The Male Hunter, The Lone Star Ranger, The Last of the Duanes, Wolves of the Night, Jungle Trail* 1919; *If I Were King* (as François Villon), *The Adventurer, Drag Harlan* 1920; *His Greatest Sacrifice, Perjury* 1921; *A Stage Romance* (as Shakespearean actor Edmund Kean), *Shackles of Gold, Moonshine Valley, Without Compromise* 1922; *Brass Commandments, The Gunfighter* 1923; *The Man Who Fights Alone* 1924; *Du Barry Woman of Passion* (as King Louis XV) 1930; *Ten Nights in a Barroom, The Painted Desert, A Connecticut Yankee* (as King Arthur) 1931; *Mr. Robinson Crusoe* 1932; *Supernatural* 1933; *Are We Civilized?, The Count of Monte Cristo* 1934; *The Silver Streak, The Crusades* 1935; *Maid of Salem* 1937; *If I Were King* 1938; *Kit Carson* 1940; *A Woman's Face, The Corsican Brothers* 1941; *The Spoilers, Men of Texas* (as General Sam Houston), *Tennessee Johnson* 1942; *Hangmen Also Die* 1943; *The Mummy's Curse* 1944; *Captain Kidd* 1945; *The Perils of Pauline* 1947; *Bride of Vengeance, Samson and Delilah* 1949; *Lone Star, Jack and the Beanstalk* 1952.

Farr, Derek. Actor. *b.* Feb. 7, 1912, Chiswick, England. *d.* 1986. Leading man of British films, stage, and TV. A former schoolmaster, he made his stage debut in 1937 and his first film in 1939, but his early career was interrupted by WW II, during which he served as a lieutenant in the Royal Artillery. Often played men under challenge. His second wife (from 1947) was actress Muriel PAVLOW.

FILMS INCLUDE: *The Outsider* 1939; *Spellbound* 1940; *Freedom Radio/The Voice of the Night, Quiet Wedding* 1941; *Quiet Weekend* 1945; *Wanted for Murder* 1946; *Conspiracy in Teheran* 1947; *Bond Street* 1948; *Man on the Run* 1949; *Double Confession, Murder Without Crime* 1950; *Reluctant Heroes* 1951; *Young Wives' Tale* 1952; *Front Page Story* 1953; *Bang You're Dead, Eight O'Clock Walk* 1954; *The Dam Busters, Value for Money* 1955; *Vicious Circle/The Circle, Doctor at Large* 1957; *The Truth About Women* 1958; *Attempt to Kill* 1961; *The Projected Man* 1966; *Thirty Is a Dangerous Age Cynthia* 1968; *Pope Joan* 1972.

Farr, Felicia. Actress. Born on Oct. 4, 1932, in Westchester County, N.Y. *ed.* Penn State. Leading lady of a handful of Hollywood films, often Westerns, following some stage experience. Married Jack LEMMON in 1960.

FILMS INCLUDE: *Big House U.S.A.* 1955; *Timetable, Jubal, Reprisal!, The First Texan, The Last Wagon* 1956; *3:10 to Yuma* 1957; *Onionhead* 1958; *Hell Bent for Leather* 1960; *Kiss Me Stupid* 1964; *The Venetian Affair* 1967; *Kotch* 1971; *Charley Varrick* 1973; *That's Life!* 1986; *The Player* 1992.

Farrar, David. Actor. *b.* 1908, in Forest Gate, England. *d.*

1995. A former journalist, he went on the stage in 1932 and entered British films five years later. He reached his peak as a handsome, virile star in the late 40s. Later, also in Hollywood, he sometimes appeared in villainous roles. He retired in the early 60s, then settled in South Africa. Autobiography: *No Royal Road* (1948).

FILMS INCLUDE: *Return of the Stranger* 1937; *A Royal Divorce* 1938; *Penn of Pennsylvania* 1941; *Went the Day Well/48 Hours* 1942; *The Dark Tower, The Night Invader* 1943; *Meet Sexton Blake* 1944; *The Lisbon Story* 1946; *Black Narcissus, Frieda* 1947; *Mr. Perrin and Mr. Traill, The Small Back Room* 1948; *Cage of Gold, Gone to Earth/The Wild Heart* 1950; *Night Without Stars, The Late Edwina Blake/Obsessed* 1951; *Duel in the Jungle* (UK/US), *The Black Shield of Falworth* (US) 1954; *Escape to Burma* (US), *The Sea Chase* (US), *Pearl of the South Pacific* (US) 1955; *Lost/Tears for Simon* 1956; *I Accuse!* 1958; *Watusi, John Paul Jones* (US), *Solomon and Sheba* (as the Pharaoh; US) 1959; *Beat Girl/Wild for Kicks* 1960; *The 300 Spartans* (as Emperor Xerxes of Persia; US) 1962.

Farrar, Geraldine. Singer, actress. *b.* Feb. 28, 1882, Melrose, Mass. *d.* 1967. At 19 she took Europe by storm after her debut at Berlin's Royal Opera. From 1906 to 1922 she was one of the leading stars of New York's Metropolitan Opera, often singing opposite Caruso. Beautiful as well as talented, she was courted by Puccini and Toscanini. She starred in a string of early DE MILLE silent films, often opposite Wallace Reid, and later in the films of other directors. Her husband, Lou TELLEGEN (*d.* 1934), was Sarah Bernhardt's leading man.

FILMS: *Carmen, Temptation* 1915; *Maria Rosa, Joan the Woman* 1916; *The Woman God Forgot, The Devil Stone* 1917; *Turn of the Wheel, The Hell Cat* 1918; *Shadows, The Flame of the Desert, The Stronger Vow, The World and Its Women* 1919; *The Woman and the Puppet, The Riddle Woman* 1920.

Farrell, Charles. Actor. *b.* Aug. 9, 1901, Onset Bay, Mass. *d.* 1990. *ed.* Boston U. After some stage experience, he made his film debut in 1923 as an extra in *The Cheat.* He played supporting parts in other films until he hit his stride as Janet GAYNOR's co-star in a series of romantic vehicles, beginning in 1927 with *Seventh Heaven.* The pair enjoyed enormous popularity for seven years as the leading screen lovers of the period. Farrell's popularity declined in the mid-30s and he retired early in the 40s, subsequently making a fortune as the founder and manager of the Palm Springs Racquet Club. During the 50s he served for seven years as the mayor of Palm Springs, while starring on TV in 'My Little Margie' (1952–55) and the 'Charlie Farrell Show' (1956). He was married to actress Virginia Valli (*b.* 1895) from 1932 until her death in 1968. Not to be confused with a character player by the same name (*b.* Aug. 6, 1901, Dublin) who appeared in British films from 1912 to the late 50s.

FILMS: *The Cheat, The Hunchback of Notre Dame, Rosita, The Ten Commandments* (bits) 1923; *The Freshman, Wings of Youth, The Love Hour, Clash of the Wolves* 1925; *Sandy, A Trip to Chinatown, Old Ironsides* 1926; *The Rough Riders, Seventh Heaven* 1927; *Street Angel, Fazil, The Red Dance, The River* 1928; *Lucky Star, Sunny Side Up* 1929; *Happy Days, High Society Blues, City Girl, Liliom, The Princess and the Plumber* 1930; *The Man Who Came Back, Body and Soul, Merely Mary Ann, Heartbreak, Delicious* 1931; *After Tomorrow, The First Year, Tess of the Storm Country, Wild Girl* 1932; *Aggie Appleby Maker of Man, Girl Without a Room* 1933; *The Big Shakedown, Falling in Love/Trouble Ahead* (UK), *Change of Heart* 1934; *Fighting Youth, Forbidden Heaven* 1935; *The Flying Doctor* (UK) 1936; *Moonlight Sonata* (UK), *Midnight Menace/Bombs Over London* (UK) 1937; *Just Around the Corner, Flight to Fame* 1938; *Tail Spin* 1939; *The Deadly Game* 1941.

Farrell, Glenda. Actress. *b.* June 30, 1904, Enid, Okla. *d.* 1971. In stock from her early teens, she reached Broadway in 1928 and Hollywood the following year. She began her screen career as a tough gangster's moll in *Little Caesar* and other crime dramas but is best remembered for the numerous light films of the 30s in which she was typecast as a cynical, wisecracking, man-chasing blonde, often as the best friend of Joan BLONDELL and later as a determined reporter in the "Torchy Blane" series. From the 50s she played a variety of character roles on television and on Broadway, as well as in films. She won an Emmy Award in 1963 as best supporting actress for her performance in a 'Ben Casey' TV segment. Terminal lung cancer forced her to leave the Broadway cast of '40 Carats' in 1969.

FILMS INCLUDE: *Lucky Boy* (bit) 1929; *Little Caesar* 1931; *Life Begins, Three on a Match, I Am a Fugitive from a Chain Gang, The Match King* 1932; *The Mystery of the Wax Museum, Grand Slam, The Keyhole, Girl Missing, Gambling Ship, Lady for a Day, Bureau of Missing Persons, Man's Castle* 1933; *Hi Nellie!, The Big Shakedown, Dark Hazard, The Personality Kid* 1934; *Gold Diggers of 1935, Traveling Saleslady, Go Into Your Dance, In Caliente, Little Big Shot* 1935; *Nobody's Fool, High Tension, Gold Diggers of 1937* 1936; *Smart Blonde, Fly Away Baby, Torchy Blane the Adventurous Blonde* 1937; *Hollywood Hotel, Stolen Heaven, Prison Break, Exposed* 1938; *Torchy Blane in Chinatown* 1939; *Johnny Eager, The Talk of the Town* 1942; *City Without Men* 1943; *I Love Trouble* 1947; *Lulu Belle* 1948; *Apache War Smoke* 1952; *Girls in the Night* 1953; *Secret of the Incas, Susan Slept Here* 1954; *The Girl in the Red Velvet Swing* 1955; *Middle of the Night* 1959; *Kissin' Cousins, The Disorderly Orderly* 1964; *Tiger by the Tail* 1970.

Farrow, John V(illiers). Director. *b.* Feb. 10, 1904, Sydney, Australia. *d.* 1963. *ed.* Newington Coll. (Australia); Winchester Coll. (UK); Royal Naval Academy. A marine research specialist, he began writing short stories and plays during a four-year naval career. He arrived in Hollywood in the late 20s as a technical advisor on the filming of sea sequences and stayed as a screenwriter, working on the scripts of such films as *Sailor's Sweetheart, The Wreck of the Hesperus* (both 1927), *Ladies of the Mob, The First Kiss, Woman from Moscow* (all 1928), *Wolf Song, A Dangerous Woman, Wheel of Life* (all 1929), *Shadow of the Law, Seven Days' Leave* (both 1930), *Woman of Experience* (1931), *Last of the Pagans* (1935), and *Tarzan Escapes* (1936). He made his debut as a director in 1937 and gradually worked his way up from B features to full-budget productions. On occasion he proved himself a capable director of solid entertainment fare with such varied films as the realistic war-action *Wake Island* (1942), the thriller melodrama *The Big Clock* (1948), the dark political allegory *Alias Nick Beal* (1949), and the psychological Western *Hondo* (1953). He was also skilled in eliciting good performances from actors.

Farrow, who was injured during his early WW II stint as a lieutenant commander with the Royal Navy and invalided out of the service, became a convert to Catholicism and wrote a biography of Thomas More and a study of the Papacy, in addition to several novels. He collaborated on the scripts of a couple of his own films and shared in the Academy Award for the screenplay of *Around the World in 80 Days* (1956). He was the husband of Maureen O'SULLIVAN and father of Mia FARROW.

FILMS: *Men in Exile, West of Shanghai/War Lord* 1937; *She Loved a Fireman, The Invisible Menace, Little Miss*

Thoroughbred, My Bill, Broadway Musketeers 1938; *Women in the Wind, The Saint Strikes Back, Sorority House, Five Came Back, Full Confession, Reno* 1939; *Married and in Love, A Bill of Divorcement* 1940; *Wake Island* 1942; *The Commandos Strike at Dawn, China* 1943; *The Hitler Gang* 1944; *You Came Along* 1945; *Two Years Before the Mast* 1946; *California, Easy Come Easy Go, Blaze of Noon, Calcutta* 1947; *The Big Clock, Beyond Glory, The Night Has a Thousand Eyes* 1948; *Alias Nick Beal, Red Hot and Blue* (also co-sc.) 1949; *Where Danger Lives* (also prod.), *Copper Canyon* 1950; *His Kind of Woman, Submarine Command* 1951; *Ride Vaquero, Plunder of the Sun, Botany Bay, Hondo* 1953; *A Bullet Is Waiting* 1954; *The Sea Chase* (also prod.) 1955; *Back from Eternity* (also prod.) 1956; *The Unholy Wife* (also prod.) 1957; *John Paul Jones* (also co-sc.) 1959.

Farrow, Mia. Actress. Born Maria de Lourdes Villiers Farrow, on Feb. 9, 1945, in Los Angeles. The third of seven children of director John FARROW and actress Maureen O'SULLIVAN, she received a parochial-school education but grew up in a Hollywood atmosphere and frequently accompanied her parents on their travels. A small-framed, fragile child, she was the victim of polio at age nine and was felled frequently by childhood diseases, and still seems undernourished and frail. She made her stage debut in 1963, shortly after the death of her father, in an off-Broadway production of 'The Importance of Being Earnest,' and her first screen appearance the following year. Her career was spurred by a featured part in the TV soap opera series 'Peyton Place,' in which she appeared for two years, but was constantly interrupted by personal affairs. In 1966 she made headlines by marrying Frank SINATRA, 30 years her senior. The mismatch ended in a divorce in 1968.

After the breakup, Mia went on a flower-child binge and flew to India for a month of transcendental meditation with guru Maharishi Mahesh Yogi. She returned to Hollywood in time to bask in the glowing reviews of her performance in Roman Polanski's film *Rosemary's Baby.* Diminutive and fey, she subsequently played other fragile heroines. In February of 1970 she gave birth to twin boys. In September of that year she married their father, former Hollywood composer-conductor André PREVIN, now the principal conductor of the London Symphony Orchestra. They divorced in 1979, but not before they had one more natural son and adopted three orphan girls: two Vietnamese and one, Soon-Yi, Korean.

In the early 80s, after a brief entanglement with cinematographer Sven NYKVIST, Farrow became intimately associated with Woody ALLEN, replacing Diane KEATON as the director's emotional link and favorite screen heroine. Under Allen's direction, Farrow matured as an actress, expanding her range to include the tough gun moll in *Broadway Danny Rose* and the maternal perfect sister in *Hannah and Her Sisters*. As an unmarried couple, Farrow and Allen adopted a boy, Moses, and a girl, Dylan, and had a natural son, Satchel. Despite their closeness, Farrow and Allen continued to live in separate apartments, with Farrow caring for a household of nine children, four natural and five adopted.

After more than a decade, Farrow's partnership with Allen was shattered when she discovered that he was carrying on an affair with her teenaged daughter Soon-Yi Previn. Allen accused Farrow of being an unfit mother, while Farrow charged that Allen had molested the 7-year-old Dylan. Though that charge was not substantiated, Farrow was awarded custody of the three children. Farrow's final collaboration with Allen, 1992's *Husbands and Wives*, drew some interest for its mirroring of their personal trauma, but performed poorly at the box office. Her sister, Tisa Farrow, is also in films.

FILMS: *John Paul Jones* (bit) 1959; *Guns at Batasi* (UK) 1964; *A Dandy in Aspic* (UK), *Rosemary's Baby, Secret Ceremony* (UK) 1968; *John and Mary* 1969; *Blind Terror/See No Evil* (UK) 1971; *Follow Me/The Public Eye* (UK), *Docteur Popaul/Scoundrel in White* (Fr.) 1972; *The Great Gatsby* 1974; *Trikimia/The Tempest* (Gr./UK) 1975; *Full Circle* (UK/Can.) 1977; *Avalanche, A Wedding, Death on the Nile* 1978; *Hurricane/Forbidden Paradise* 1979; *The Haunting of Julia* (UK/Can.) 1981; *A Midsummer Night's Sex Comedy, The Last Unicorn* (v/o) 1982; *Zelig* 1983; *Broadway Danny Rose, Supergirl* (UK) 1984; *The Purple Rose of Cairo* 1985; *Hannah and Her Sisters* 1986; *Radio Days, September* 1987; *Another Woman, New York Stories* ("Oedipus Wrecks" episode), *Crimes and Misdemeanors* 1989; *Alice* 1990; *Shadows and Fog, Husbands and Wives* 1992; *Widow's Peak* 1994; *Reckless, Miami Rhapsody* 1995.

Fassbinder, Rainer Werner. Director. *b.* May 31, 1946, Bad Wörishofen, Bavaria, Germany. *d.* 1982. Immensely prolific director-writer of the German stage, TV, and films; a prominent voice of the new German cinema. A doctor's son, he was raised by his mother in Munich after his parents divorced when he was five. A film addict, he attended movies at a frenzied frequency. He dropped out of school and, after working at a variety of odd jobs, applied for enrollment at the Berlin Film School but was turned down. At age 20, he began making amateur shorts, the second of which featured his mother, who would later appear in many of his films under the name of Lilo Pempeit. Trained as an actor, he joined the Munich Action Theater in 1967 and the following year formed his own company, the Anti-Theater. Both were experimental, iconoclastic troupes. Fassbinder made his first feature film in 1969 after some experimentation with shorts in 1965–66, and subsequently turned out films at an amazing average rate of three or four a year, in addition to a large number of stage and TV productions.

Working at an indefatigable pace and taking advantage of subsidies and cash prizes made available by the German government, Fassbinder created his films not only rapidly but also uncompromisingly as true expressions of his enigmatic, rebelliously independent self. He surrounded himself with a closely knit nucleus of technicians and performers who operated as a virtual stock company under his loving but tyrannical control. He appeared as an actor in several of his own films as well as in those of others, sometimes using the pseudonym Fitz. His early films characteristically lacked flashy dramatic effect and stylistic flair, often denying the essential syntax of cinema language. The camera is usually static as it eavesdrops on lengthy conversations. The dialogue is typically mannered and monotone, the action and motivation ambiguous, and the décor sparse; and yet many of Fassbinder's scenes have had a spellbinding impact on audiences. His films, like his theater, are politically committed and uncompromising in their irreverence for social institutions. A recurrent theme is the misuse of power and the consequences of oppression. Some critics have compared his work with that of France's Jean-Luc GODARD while others have also detected the influence of the American cinema of the 50s and particularly the films of Douglas SIRK. He scored international triumphs with such films as *The Merchant of Four Seasons, The Bitter Tears of Petra von Kant, The Marriage of Maria Braun,* and *Veronika Voss* (he won the Golden Bear at the 1982 Berlin Festival for the latter). Tragically, the furious energy that fueled Fassbinder's creative drive also hastened his early end. Openly homosexual (although married for a while to one of his leading ladies, Ingrid Caven), and defiantly nonconformist, the director led a hectic lifestyle energized by cocaine and other drugs. He died of an overdose at the age of 36.

FILMS (as director-writer): *Der Stadtsreicher* (short; also act.) 1965; *Das kleine Chaos* (short; also act.) 1966; *Liebe ist kälter als der Tod* (also co-art dir., act.), *Katzelmacher* (also art dir., act.) 1969; *Götter der Pest/Gods of the Plague* (also act.), *Warum läuft Herr R. Amok?/Why Does Herr R. Run Amok?* (co-dir. with Michael Fengler), *Der amerikanische Soldat/The American Soldier* (also co-art dir., co-song, act.), *Die Niklashauser Fahrt* (co-dir., co-sc. with Fengler; also act.) 1970; *Rio Das Mortes* (also act.), *Pioniere in Ingolstadt/Recruits in Ingolstadt* (also act.), *Das Kaffeehaus* (for TV), *Whity* (also act.), *Warnung vor einer heiligen Nutte/Beware the Holy Whore* (also act.) 1971; *Händler der vier Jahreszeiten/The Merchant of Four Seasons* (also act.), *Die bitteren Tränen der Petra von Kant/The Bitter Tears of Petra von Kant, Acht Stunden sind kein Tag* (in five episodes) 1972; *Wildwechsel/Jail Bait, Welt am Draht* (in two episodes) 1973; *Angst essen Seele auf/Ali: Fear Eats the Soul/Ali* (also art dir.), *Martha, Nora Helmer* (for TV), *Fontane Effi Briest/Effi Briest* (also narr.), *Wie ein Vogel auf dem Draht* (medium length for TV) 1974; *Faustrecht der Freiheit/Fox/Fox and His Friends* (also act.), *Mütter Kusters Fahrtn zum Himmel/Mothe Kuster's Trip to Heaven/Mother Kuster Goes to Heaven* 1975; *Angst vor de Angst/Fear of Fear, Ich will doch nur dass Ihr mich liebt/I Only Want You to Love Me, Satansbraten/Satan's Brew, Schatten der Engel/Shadow of Angels* (co-sc. from own play, act. only), *Chineisisches Roulette/Chinese Roulette* 1976; *Bolweiser/The Stationmaster's Wife, Frauen in New York* (for TV) 1977; *Eine Reise ins Licht/Despair, Deutschland im Herbst/Germany in Autumn* (one episode; also act.), *In einem Jahr mit 13 Monden/In a Year of 13 Moons* (also phot., edit.) 1978; *Die Ehe der Maria Braun/The Marriage of Maria Braun* (dir. idea only), *Die dritte Generation/The Third Generation* (also phot.) 1979; *Berlin Alexanderplatz* (orig. 15-hour, 13-part TV presentation; also cameo) 1980; *Lili Marleen* (also act.), *Lola* (also exec. prod.), *Theater in Trance* (video doc.) 1981; *Die Sehnsucht der Veronika Voss/Veronika Voss* (dir. only), *Querelle* 1982.

fast motion. See ACCELERATED MOTION; SLOW MOTION.

Faulkner, William. Novelist, screenwriter. *b.* Sept. 9, 1897, New Albany, Miss. *d.* 1962. Several novels by this celebrated Nobel and Pulitzer Prize–winning author were adapted to the screen by others. He refused to tamper with his own work, although he did collaborate on a number of screenplays based on material originally written by others, working mainly for director Howard HAWKS. From 1932 to 1955, Faulkner commuted frequently between his hometown of Oxford, Mississippi, and Hollywood. In addition to his credited screenplay collaborations, he was involved without official acknowledgement in various stages of script preparation for many other films, mainly at 20th Century-Fox and Warner Bros., as well as numerous aborted projects. Films adapted from Faulkner's novels include *The Story of Temple Drake* (from *Sanctuary*, 1933), *Intruder in the Dust* (1949), *The Tarnished Angels* (from *Pylon*), *The Long Hot Summer* (from *The Hamlet;* both 1958), *The Sound and the Fury* (1959), *Sanctuary* (from *Sanctuary* and *Requiem for a Nun,* 1961), and *The Reivers* (1969). *Tomorrow* (1972) was adapted from his short story.

FILMS: *Today We Live* (dial. from own story, 'Turn About') 1933; *Lazy River* (addnl. dial., uncredited) 1934; *Sutter's Gold* (unused treatment), *The Road to Glory* (co-sc.), *Banjo on My Knee* (co-treatment; uncredited) 1936; *Slave Ship* (preliminary co-sc.; unused) 1937; *Four Men and a Prayer* (minor treatment revisions), *Submarine Patrol* (preliminary sc.; unused) 1938; *Gunga Din* (early treatment & dial. revision; uncredited), *Drums Along the Mohawk* (treatment; uncredited) 1939; *Air Force* (sc. for two scenes; uncredited), *Background to Danger* (minor revisions), *Northern Pursuit* (co-sc; uncredited) 1943; *To Have and Have Not* (co-sc.) 1944–45; *God Is My Co-Pilot* (treatment; uncredited), *The Southerner* (co-sc.; uncredited), *Mildred Pierce* (preliminary revision; uncredited) 1945; *The Big Sleep* (co-sc.) 1946; *Stallion Road* (preliminary sc.; uncredited), *Deep Valley* (early treatment; uncredited) 1947; *The Adventures of Don Juan* (preliminary revision; uncredited) 1948; *The Damned Don't Cry* (uncredited treatment, partly based on his story 'The Brooch') 1950; *Land of the Pharaohs* (co-story, co-sc.), *The Left Hand of God* (preliminary sc.; unused) 1955.

favoring. Having one of the players in a group face the camera or the microphone more directly than the others. The player thus emphasized in a shot is said to be favored.

Fawcett, Farrah. Actress. Born on Feb. 2, 1946, in Corpus Christi, Tex., the daughter of an oil contractor. *ed.* U. of Texas. Toothsome, radiant blonde beauty who became a popular pinup in the 70s through numerous TV commercials and magazine covers. She reached a peak of adulation during her one-season (1976–77) stint as co-star of the TV series 'Charlie's Angels,' which precipitated vast merchandising of Farrah dolls, T-shirts, wigs, and posters. She demonstrated limited acting ability in her subsequent few leads in feature films. But in the 80s she surprised critics with capable performances in the off-Broadway play 'Extremities' (1983) and the TV movie *The Burning Bed* (1984). During her marriage to actor Lee Majors in the late 70s she was billed as Farrah Fawcett-Majors. For many years she was the companion of actor Ryan O'NEAL, with whom she has a son.

FEATURE FILMS: *Um homme qui me plaît/Love Is a Funny Thing* (Fr./It.) 1969; *Myra Breckinridge* 1970; *Logan's Run* 1976; *Somebody Killed Her Husband* 1978; *Sunburn* 1979; *Saturn 3* (UK) 1980; *The Cannonball Run* 1981; *Extremities* 1986; *See You in the Morning* 1989; *Man of the House* 1995.

Fawcett, George. Actor. *b.* Aug. 25, 1860, Alexandria, Va. *d.* 1939. Stalwart character star of the American silent screen. A graduate of the University of Virginia, he was trained at Sargent's School of Acting, the forerunner of the American Academy of Dramatic Arts, and after many years on the stage, entered films around 1914. He played pivotal roles in several D. W. GRIFFITH productions and became one of Hollywood's busiest and most respected character actors, specializing in authoritative roles, often as a father, community leader, or a judge. His wife, Percy Haswell (1871–1945), also appeared in films, sometimes billed as Mrs. George Fawcett.

FILMS INCLUDE: *The Majesty of the Law* 1915; *Intolerance* (as Babylonian judge), *Crisis, The Country That God Forgot* 1916; *Panthea, The Cinderella Man* 1917; *Hearts of the World, The Great Love, The Hun Within* 1918; *The Hope Chest, A Romance of Happy Valley, The Girl Who Stayed at Home, I'll Get Him Yet, True Heart Susie, Nobody Home, Turning the Tables, Scarlet Days, The Greatest Question* 1919; *Two Weeks, Little Miss Rebellion* (dir. only), *The Branded Woman* 1920; *Lessons in Love, Such a Little Queen* (dir. only), *Little Italy, Nobody, Forever/Peter Ibbetson* 1921; *Polly of the Follies, Destiny's Isle, Manslaughter, The Old Homestead, Ebb Tide* 1922; *Drums of Fate, Java Head, Just Like a Woman, The Woman with Four Faces, Salomy Jane, His Children's Children* 1923; *Pied Piper Malone, The Breaking Point, Tess of the D'Urbervilles, Triumph, Broken Barriers, Her Love Story*

1924; *The Price of Pleasure, The Sporting Venus, The Verdict, The Merry Widow* (as King Nikita), *The Circle* 1925; *The Son of the Sheik* 1926; *Flesh and the Devil, Captain Salvation, Spring Fever, Love, The Valley of the Giants, The Private Life of Helen of Troy* 1927; *The Enemy, Tempest, Prowlers of the Sea, The Wedding March* (lead role, as Prince von Wildeliebe-Rauffenburg) 1928; *Lady of the Pavements, Tide of Empire, Innocents of Paris, The Four Feathers, The Gamblers, Hearts in Exile, Hot for Paris* 1929; *Ladies of Leisure, The Bad One, Swing High, Once a Gentleman* 1930; *A Woman of Experience, Personal Maid* 1931.

Fay, Gaby. See HOLDEN, Fay.

Faye, Alice. Actress. Born Alice Jeanne Leppert, on May 5, 1912, in New York City, the daughter of a policeman. She began dancing and singing professionally at age 14. In 1931 she was spotted in the chorus line of Broadway's 'George White's Scandals' by Rudy VALLEE, who signed her to tour with his band as a singer. Vallee insisted that Fox cast her in the film version of *George White's Scandals* (1934), and when his intended leading lady, Lilian Harvey, walked off the set, Alice was given the lead, over the objections of George White himself. (That same year, she was named by Vallee's wife in a stormy divorce case in court.) Signed to a Fox contract, she was first cast as a Harlow-type bleached blonde. But her husky speaking voice and mellow singing contralto were soon put to advantage in a string of lively musical films, and within two or three years she developed into a leading star of the genre.

She frequently feuded with studio boss Darryl F. Zanuck, who banned her radio appearances and in 1940 brought Betty Grable into Fox as a threat to Alice's position. Eventually, Grable did replace her as Fox's top musical star and surpassed her in popularity. In 1945, after a disastrous appearance in a drama, *Fallen Angel,* Miss Faye walked out on her contract and retired from the screen. She returned for an isolated appearance, miscast as Pat Boone's mother, in *State Fair* (1962). In 1973–74 she was reunited with former screen partner John PAYNE in a stage revival of the musical 'Good News.' She reappeared on the screen in 1978 in *Every Girl Should Have One.* Formerly married to singer Tony MARTIN, she has been married since 1941 to bandleader-actor Phil HARRIS. A grandmother of four, she still has active fan clubs around the world.

FILMS: *George White's Scandals, Now I'll Tell, She Learned About Sailors, 365 Nights in Hollywood* 1934; *George White's 1935 Scandals, Every Night at Eight, Music Is Magic* 1935; *King of Burlesque, Poor Little Rich Girl, Sing Baby Sing, Stowaway* 1936; *On the Avenue, Wake Up and Live, You Can't Have Everything, You're a Sweetheart* 1937; *In Old Chicago, Sally Irene and Mary, Alexander's Ragtime Band* 1938; *Tail Spin, Rose of Washington Square, Hollywood Cavalcade, Barricade* 1939; *Little Old New York, Lillian Russell* (title role), *Tin Pan Alley* 1940; *That Night in Rio, The Great American Broadcast, Weekend in Havana* 1941; *Hello Frisco Hello, The Gang's All Here* 1943; *Four Jills in a Jeep* (cameo) 1944; *Fallen Angel* 1945; *State Fair* 1962; *Won Ton Ton—The Dog Who Saved Hollywood* (cameo) 1976; *Every Girl Should Have One, The Magic of Lassie* 1978.

Faylen, Frank. Actor. *b.* Frank Ruf, Dec. 8, 1905, St. Louis, Mo. *d.* 1985. Versatile character player of numerous Hollywood films. The son of vaudevillians, he started out as a pantomimist and clown and had some success as an acrobatic song-and-dance man before entering films in the mid-30s. He played a wide range of character roles, memorably as the sadistic male nurse in *The Lost Weekend* (1945). He was a regular on the TV series 'The Many Loves of Dobie Gillis' (as Dobie's father) and 'That Girl.' He was married to the former Carol Hughes, who played the female lead in the 1940 serial *Flash Gordon Conquers the Universe* and in several B films.

FILMS INCLUDE: *Border Flight* (bit) 1935; *Bullets or Ballots* 1936; *Kid Galahad, They Won't Forget* 1937; *The Invisible Menace* 1938; *Nick Carter—Master Detective* 1939; *The Grapes of Wrath, No Time for Comedy* 1940; *Come Live with Me* 1941; *Address Unknown, And the Angels Sing, The Canterville Ghost* 1944; *The Lost Weekend* 1945; *The Blue Dahlia, To Each His Own, Blue Skies, It's a Wonderful Life* 1946; *California, The Perils of Pauline, Welcome Stranger, Variety Girl, Road to Rio* 1947; *Blood on the Moon* 1948; *Whispering Smith* 1949; *Francis* 1950; *14 Hours, Detective Story* 1951; *The Sniper* 1952; *Riot in Cell Block 11* 1954; *The McConnell Story* 1955; *Gunfight at the O.K. Corral* 1957; *The Monkey's Uncle* 1965; *Funny Girl* 1968.

Fazenda, Louise. Actress. *b.* June 17, 1895, Lafayette, Ind. *d.* 1962. She entered films in 1913 with Universal, where she developed into an eccentric comedienne in the studio's Joker shorts. She joined Mack SENNETT's Keystone in 1915 and after several months of playing standard comic supporting roles became one of the studio's principal female comic talents. A plain-looking woman but a highly gifted character actress, she was soon popular with audiences as the absurdly funny star of numerous two-reel comedies. She was particularly adept at portraying rural types. In the 20s and 30s she also appeared in a great many feature films. She was married to producer Hal B. WALLIS.

FILMS INCLUDE: *Almost an Actress, Mike and Jake at the Beach, The Cheese Special* 1913; *Traffic in Soles, Love and Graft* 1914; *The Great Vacuum Robbery, Ambrose's Fury, Ambrose's Little Hatchet, Stark Mad, A Versatile Villain* 1915; *Summer Girl, Bombs and Brides, The Judge* 1916; *Her Fame and Shame, Her Torpedoed Love* 1917; *Her Screen Idol, The Kitchen Lady* 1918; *Hearts and Flowers, A House Divided* 1919; *Down on the Farm, Married Life, It's a Boy* 1920; *The Beautiful and Damned, Quincy Adams Sawyer* 1922; *Main Street, The Spoilers, The Gold Diggers* 1923; *Abraham Lincoln/The Dramatic Life of Abraham Lincoln, Being Respectable, This Woman* 1924; *Déclassée, The Night Club, Grounds for Divorce, Bobbed Hair, Hogan's Alley* 1925; *The Bat, Ladies at Play/Loose Ankles, Footloose Widows, The Lady of the Harem, Millionaires* 1926; *The Cradle Snatchers, A Sailor's Sweetheart* 1927; *The Terror, Outcast, Tillie's Punctured Romance* (as Tillie, opposite W. C. Fields) 1928; *Noah's Ark, The Desert Song, The House of Horror* 1929; *No No Nanette, High Society Blues, Bride of the Regiment, Rain or Shine, Leathernecking* 1930; *Gun Smoke, Cuban Love Song* 1931; *Alice in Wonderland* 1933; *Wonder Bar, Caravan* 1934; *The Casino Murder Case, Broadway Gondolier* 1935; *Colleen* 1936; *Swing Your Lady* 1938; *The Old Maid* 1939.

FBO. Film Booking Offices of America. A film distribution and production company that evolved in the late 1910s through various corporate transmutations from the MUTUAL FILM CORPORATION. In 1926, FBO was acquired by Joseph P. KENNEDY, who eventually merged it with Radio-Keith-Orpheum, later known as RKO.

feature film. A motion picture, usually fictional and intended for theatrical release, which runs 3,000 feet (about 34 minutes) or longer. All films of lesser length and duration are classified as "shorts" or, sometimes, "featurettes."

feature player. Also, "featured player." Actor or actress playing a major supporting part but not a starring role, in a film. He or she is ranked below the stars in the billing (screen credits), usually after the main title.

feed reel. The reel around which film is originally wound.

It "feeds" through the camera (or projector) mechanism onto the TAKE-UP REEL. See also REEL.

Fegté, Ernst. Art director. *b.* Sept. 28, 1900, Hamburg, Germany. *d.* 1976. Entered the German film industry in 1919. In American films from the mid-20s, he created distinguished sets for many productions at Paramount and other studios and shared an Academy Award with Hans Dreier for his work on *Frenchman's Creek* (1945).

FILMS INCLUDE: *The Shock Punch, Womanhandled* 1925; *In Old Kentucky* 1927; *Big Executive* 1933; *Death Takes a Holiday, Kiss and Make Up* 1934; *Accent on Youth* 1935; *The General Died at Dawn* 1936; *Easy Living* 1937; *You and Me* 1938; *The Lady Eve* 1941; *The Palm Beach Story, I Married a Witch* 1942; *Five Graves to Cairo* 1943; *The Miracle of Morgan's Creek, The Uninvited* 1944; *Wonder Man, Frenchman's Creek, And Then There Were None* 1945; *I've Always Loved You, Specter of the Rose* 1946; *Christmas Eve, Angel and the Badman* 1947; *On Our Merry Way* 1948; *Canadian Pacific* 1949; *Destination Moon* 1950; *The Restless Breed* 1957; *Desire in the Dust* 1960; *B.S. I Love You* 1971.

Fehr, Rudi. Film editor. Born in 1911, in Berlin. He worked in the German film industry before fleeing the Nazis to Hollywood via Britain. During the 50s he served as director of postproduction operations at Warner Bros. He shared an Oscar nomination for editing *Prizzi's Honor* (1985). Married movie actress Maris Wrixon.

FILMS INCLUDE: *Invisible Enemies* (UK) 1935; *My Love Came Back* 1940; *All Through the Night, Desperate Journey* 1942; *Watch on the Rhine* 1943; *The Conspirators* 1944; *Humoresque* 1946; *Possessed* 1947; *Key Large* 1948; *The Inspector General* 1949; *The Desert Song* (prod. only), *House of Wax* 1953; *Dial M for Murder* 1954; *Land of the Pharaohs* 1955; *One from the Heart* 1981; *Prizzi's Honor* 1985.

Feist, Felix E. Director. *b.* Feb. 28, 1906, New York City. *d.* 1965. *ed.* Elmhurst Coll.; Columbia. The son of MGM's general sales manager, he started out as a film salesman but got interested in production and became a newsreel cameraman. In 1930 he returned to MGM as a producer of travelogues and director of screen tests. He left the studio briefly to direct his first feature, *The Deluge* (1933), at RKO, but returned in 1933 as a director and writer of shorts, including the 'Pete Smith Specialties,' 'The Passing Parade,' and the 'Crime Does Not Pay' series. He resumed directing features, under contract to Universal, in 1943, and later worked for RKO and other studios. He was a reliable, "nuts and bolts" director of routine low-budget productions.

FEATURE FILMS: *The Deluge* 1933; *All by Myself, You're a Lucky Fellow Mr. Smith* 1943; *This Is the Life, Pardon My Rhythm, The Reckless Age* (also prod.) 1944; *George White's Scandals* 1945; *The Devil Thumbs a Ride* (also sc.) 1947; *The Winner's Circle* 1948; *The Threat* 1949; *Guilty of Treason, The Golden Gloves Story* 1950; *The Man Who Cheated Himself, Tomorrow Is Another Day, The Basketball Fix* 1951; *The Big Trees, This Woman Is Dangerous* 1952; *The Man Behind the Gun, Donovan's Brain* (also sc.) 1953; *Pirates of Tripoli* 1955.

Fejos, Paul. Director. *b.* Pál Fejös, Jan. 24, 1897, Budapest. *d.* 1963. Following the sudden death of his pharmacist father, he was raised by his mother, who entered him in medical school. His studies were interrupted by WW I service as a battlefront medical orderly. Returning home, he worked as a set painter for operas, then films. After directing several Hungarian features, he emigrated to the US in 1923, first stopping at Vienna and Berlin, where he worked briefly for Max REINHARDT and Fritz LANG, then in Paris, here he staged a play. In 1926 he spent the last of his savings on a used car and headed for Hollywood. After being repeatedly rebuffed in attempts to infiltrate the industry, he secured a minuscule budget of $5,000 to produce a film. Using donated film stock, novice technicians, and volunteer actors, he turned out *The Last Moment* (1928), a visually fascinating silent feature depicting in flashback the recollections of a suicide victim. The film won high praise from Charlie CHAPLIN and others, leading to a contract for Fejos with Universal. His first film for the studio, the part-talkie *Lonesome* (1928) was also his most admired. A sensitively told story of big-city loneliness, it was also noted for its freewheeling camera techniques and was hailed by some as a forerunner of NEOREALISM. Fejos's next effort, *The Last Performance,* was far less successful, and after a couple of trouble-ridden projects, he moved over to MGM, where he directed the French and German language versions of George Hill's prison drama *The Big House.* He became an American citizen in 1930. Disillusioned and bitter, he left in 1931 for France, where he worked on two inconsequential films. The following year he returned to Budapest, where he directed the little-seen but highly reputed film, *Marie, A Hungarian Legend* (1932), starring Annabella. Fejos resumed his wandering a year later in Vienna and from there went to Denmark. In 1941 he returned to New York and became the research director of the Viking Fund.

FILMS: In Hungary—*Pan* (also sc.), *Hallucination* (also co-sc.), *The Resurrected* 1920; *The Black Captain, Arsene Lupin's Last Adventure* 1921; *Sensation/Pique Dame/The Queen of Spades* 1922; *The Stars of Eger* (also sc.; unfinished) 1923. In the US—*Land of the Lawless* (sc. only), *The Last Moment* (also sc.) 1927; *Lonesome* 1928; *Broadway, The Last Performance/Erik the Great* 1929; *Captain of the Guard* (film begun by Fejos as *La Marseillaise* but completed by John S. Robertson, who received sole director's credit), *Revolte dans la Prison* (French-language version of George Hill's *The Big House*), *Menschen hinter Gittern* (German-language version of *The Big House)* 1930. In France—*L'Amour à l'Américaine* (supvr. only) 1931; *Fantômas* (also sc.) 1932. In Hungary—*Tavaszi Zapor/Marie Légende hongroise/Marie/Spring Shower* (released in four versions—Hungarian, French, German, and English; also co-sc.), *Itel a Balaton* 1932. In Austria—*Sonnenstrahl* (also co-prod., co-story; Aus./Fr.), *Frühlingstimmen* 1933. In Denmark—*Millions in Flight* (also sc.) 1934; *Prisoner No. 1* (also story), *The Golden Smile* (also sc.) 1935. In Madagascar—*Black Horizons* (doc. in six parts; Den./Swed.) 1936. In the East Indies—A documentary in seven parts (Swed.) 1938; in Thailand—*A Handful of Rice* (doc.; Swed.) 1939. In Peru—*Yagua* (doc.) 1941.

Feld, Fritz. Actor. *b.* Oct. 15, 1900, Berlin. *d.* 1993. Appeared on the German stage and screen and was an assistant to Max REINHARDT before coming to the US in the mid-20s. Here he founded, with Joseph SCHILDKRAUT, the Hollywood Playhouse theater, wrote several screenplays, and played hundreds of amusing character roles and cameos in films and on TV, typically as a mad foreigner, eccentric director, or ritualistic headwaiter. His trademark was the popping sound of a champagne cork, which he made by bouncing the flat of his hand off his mouth. Married character actress Virginia Christine.

FILMS INCLUDE: *Der Golem und die Tänzerin* (Ger.) 1917; *The Last Command, A Ship Comes In* 1928; *Broadway, Black Magic, One Hysterical Night* 1929; *I Met Him in Paris, Lancer Spy, True Confession, Tovarich* 1937; *Hollywood Hotel, Bringing Up Baby, Gold Diggers in Paris, Go Chase*

Yourself, Campus Confessions, The Affairs of Annabel, Artists and Models Abroad 1938; *Idiot's Delight, When Tomorrow Comes, At the Circus* 1939; *Little Old New York, It's a Date, Victory* 1940; *World Premiere* 1941; *Maisie Gets Her Man, Iceland* 1942; *The Phantom of the Opera* 1943; *Knickerbocker Holiday* 1944; *George White's Scandals* 1945; *I've Always Loved You* 1946; *Carnival in Costa Rica, The Secret Life of Walter Mitty* 1947; *If You Knew Susie, Julia Misbehaves, Mexican Hayride* 1948; *Riding High, The Jackpot* 1950; *O. Henry's Full House* 1952; *Call Me Madam* 1953; *The Errand Boy, Pocketful of Miracles* 1961; *Promises! Promises!, Who's Minding the Store?* 1963; *The Patsy* 1964; *Three on a Couch* 1966; *Barefoot in the Park, Caprice* 1967; *The Wicked Dreams of Paula Schultz* 1968; *The Comic, Hello Dolly!* 1969; *The Computer Wore Tennis Shoes* 1970; *The Sunshine Boys* 1975; *Silent Movie* 1976; *Freaky Friday, The World's Greatest Lover* 1977; *Fun on a Weekend* 1979; *Herbie Goes Bananas* 1980; *History of the World Part I, All the Marbles* 1981; *Heidi's Song* (v/o) 1982; *A Fine Mess* 1986; *Homer and Eddie* 1989.

Feldman, Charles K. Producer. *b.* Charles Gould, Apr. 26, 1904, New York City. *d.* 1968, *ed.* U. of Mich.; USC. Orphaned in childhood, he was raised by adoptive parents and set up a law practice in Los Angeles in 1928. He abandoned it four years later to become president of Famous Artists, a leading talent agency, with clients among Hollywood's top producers, directors, and actors. In the early 40s he turned producer and was subsequently responsible for a good number of high-quality productions.

FILMS INCLUDE: *Pittsburgh* 1942; *Follow the Boys* 1944; *Uncle Harry* (exec. prod.) 1945; *Red River* (exec. prod.) 1948; *The Glass Menagerie* (co-prod.) 1950; *A Streetcar Named Desire* 1951; *The Seven Year Itch* (co-prod.) 1955; *North to Alaska* 1960; *Walk on the Wild Side* 1962; *The 7th Dawn* 1964; *What's New Pussycat?* (co-prod.) 1965; *The Group* (exec. prod.) 1966; *Casino Royale* (co-prod.), *The Honey Pot* 1967.

Feldman, Corey. Actor. Born on July 16, 1971, in Reseda, Calif. Bratty juvenile lead and supporting player of American TV and films, often paired with actor Corey HAIM in coming-of-age teen films. His career began at the age of three with extensive commercial work and then on to roles in the critically hailed *Stand By Me* (1986) and *The Lost Boys* (1987). But as he grew older his offscreen bouts with drug addiction halted an otherwise promising career.

FILMS INCLUDE: *Time After Time* 1979; *The Fox and the Hound* (v/o) 1981; *Friday the 13th—The Final Chapter, Gremlins* 1984; *Friday the 13th Part V: A New Beginning, The Goonies* 1985; *Stand by Me* 1986; *The Lost Boys* 1987; *License to Drive* 1988; *The 'Burbs* 1989; *Dream a Little Dream; Teenage Mutant Ninja Turtles: The Movie* (v/o) 1990; *Rock 'n' Roll High School Forever, Edge of Honor* 1991; *Meatballs 4, Round Trip to Heaven* 1992; *National Lampoon's Loaded Weapon, Stepmonster, Teenage Mutant Ninja Turtles III* 1993; *Maverick, National Lampoon's Last Resort* 1994; *A Dangerous Place, Dream A Little Dream 2* 1995; *Tales from the Crypt: Bordello of Blood* 1996.

Feldman, Marty. Actor. *b.* July 8, 1933, London. *d.* 1982. Pint-sized comedian with expressive facial features accentuated by huge bulging eyes. He began his career on the London variety stage as a musician but later turned to comedy. In the late 50s he entered British TV as a screenwriter on comedy shows and in 1967 made his debut as a comic performer on the small screen. In 1970 he starred in his own British TV comedy series, 'Marty.' In films from 1969, he gained popularity in the 70s thanks to delightful comic portrayals in Mel Brooks's *Young Frankenstein* and *Silent Movie*, and Gene Wilder's *The Adventure of Sherlock Holmes' Smarter Brother.* In 1977 he directed the first of two films. He died of a heart attack at 49.

FILMS: *The Bed Sitting Room* 1969; *Every Home Should Have One* 1970; *Young Frankenstein* (US) 1974; *The Adventure of Sherlock Holmes' Smarter Brother* (UK/US) 1975; *40 Gradi all'Ombra del Lenzuolo/Sex with a Smile* (It.), *Silent Movie* (US) 1976; *The Last Remake of Beau Geste* (also dir., co-story, co-sc.; US) 1977; *In God We Trust* (also dir., co-sc.) 1980; *Yellowbeard* 1983; *Slapstick (of Another Kind)* (release delayed from 1982) 1984.

Felix, Maria. Actress. Born Maria de Los Angeles Felix Guereña, in 1915, in Alamo, Mexico. Beautiful, passionate, and forceful star of many Mexican and some European films; a major box-office attraction in the Spanish-speaking world from the early 40s. Widowed by her fifth husband, she went into semiretirement in the early 70s.

FILMS INCLUDE: *El Peñon de las Animas* 1942; *Doña Barbara* 1943; *Amok* 1944; *Le Mujer de todos* 1946; *Rio Escondido/Hidden River, Vertigo* 1947; *Enamorada, Mare Nostrum* (Sp.) 1948; *Doña Diabla* 1949; *La Corona negra* (Sp.), *Messalina* (It.) 1951; *La Pasión desnuda* (Arg.) 1952; *Camelia* 1953; *La Belle Otéro* (Fr.) 1954; *French Cancan, Les Héros sont fatigués/Heroes and Sinners* (both Fr.) 1955; *La Escondida, Faustina* 1956; *Flor de Mayo/Beyond All Limits* 1957; *La Cucaracha* 1958; *La Fièvre monte à El Pao/Los Ambiciosos/Republic of Sin* (Fr./Mex.), *Sonatas* 1959; *La Estrella vacia/The Empty Star* 1960; *Juana Gallo* 1961; *La Bandida* 1962; *Amor y Sexo* 1963; *La Valentina* 1965; *Le Generala* 1970.

Felix, Seymour. Choreographer, director. *b.* Oct. 23, 1892, New York City. *d.* 1961. An amateur dancer from age nine, he began appearing in vaudeville at 15 and later became one of Broadway's leading dance directors, working on major musicals, including several Al Jolson productions. He went to Hollywood during the switch to sound and choreographed a number of lively musicals through the early 50s, winning an Academy Award for his work on *The Great Ziegfeld* (1936). He also directed two low-budget films.

FILMS INCLUDE: As director (complete)—*Girls Demand Excitement* 1931; *Stepping Sisters* 1932. As choreographer—*Sunnyside Up* 1929; *Just Imagine* 1930; *Delicious* 1931; *Hollywood Party* (co-chor.) 1934; *The Great Ziegfeld* 1936; *On the Avenue* 1937; *Alexander's Ragtime Band* 1938; *Rose of Washington Square* 1939; *Tin Pan Alley* 1940; *Yankee Doodle Dandy* (co-chor.) 1942; *Let's Face It* 1943; *Cover Girl* 1944; *Three Little Girls in Blue* 1946; *The I Don't Care Girl* 1953.

Felix the Cat. The most popular cartoon character on the American screen before the reign of Mickey Mouse. First introduced in 1914 by animator Pat Sullivan, Felix reached the height of his fame in the 20s. He bowed out to the competition in 1930 but returned in refined form on TV.

Fell, Norman. Actor. Born on Mar. 24, 1924, in Philadelphia. *ed.* Temple U. Busy character player of American TV and films. He took up drama training with Stella ADLER on returning from WW II action as a tail gunner over the Pacific and later enrolled at the Actors Studio. In the 50s he began playing small roles on the stage and on TV, making his screen debut in 1959. Over the next three decades he appeared in numerous productions, demonstrating dependable ability in both drama and comedy. His popularity in the role of Mr. Roper in the TV series 'Three's Company' (1977–79) spawned a spin-off series, 'The Ropers' (1979–80).

FILMS INCLUDE: *Pork Chop Hill* 1959; *Ocean's*

Eleven, Inherit the Wind 1960; *PT 109, It's a Mad Mad Mad Mad World* 1963; *The Killers* 1964; *The Graduate* 1967; *Bullitt* 1968; *If It's Tuesday This Must Be Belgium* 1969; *Catch–22* 1970; *Charley Varrick, The Stone Killer* 1973; *Airport 1975* 1974; *The End* 1978; *Paternity* 1981; *Stripped to Kill* 1987; *C.H.U.D. 2: Bud the Chud* 1989; *The Bone Yard* 1990; *For the Boys* 1991.

Fellini, Federico. Director. *b.* Jan. 20, 1920, Rimini, Italy. *d.* 1994. Born into a family of the provincial middle class. His father was a traveling salesman of confections, preserves, and coffee who expected Federico to one day become a lawyer; but the only aptitude the boy showed in school was for drawing. Details of Fellini's early life are muddled in confusion and contradiction since the chronology of events underwent several transformations in the director's own fertile imagination. This obscurity is all the more tantalizing in the case of a director like Fellini, whose films are often autobiographical and contain many flashes of memory, probably distorted and embellished by poetic license and Fellini's self-admitted penchant for lying.

This much is known with a degree of certainty about Fellini's early life: As a young boy, probably at the age of seven, he ran away from a boarding school to follow a traveling circus but was returned to his parents within several days. The incident left an indelible impression on Fellini's mind, and the circus became for him an enduring passion and a source of inspiration for his work as a film director. Fellini attended a succession of religious schools, none of which was much to his liking. He remembers himself as a poor student who disliked mathematics nearly as much as he did the humiliating punishment meted out by his teachers for minor infractions of school rules. During his last year in high school, in 1937, Fellini and several of his mates began leading the idle, empty street life the director would later depict so vividly in the film *I Vitelloni.* It was a purposeless life, devoid of a constructive focus or plans for the future and deriving its main gratification from the successful execution of mischievous pranks.

In the fall of 1938, Fellini left his hometown and headed for Florence, ostensibly for university studies. He stayed there six months, working as a proofreader and cartoonist for a comic-strip story magazine, an experience that would provide the background for his film *Lo Sceicco bianco/The White Sheik.* He then continued to Rome, where he enrolled at the University of Rome's law school but never attended classes, using his student status to avoid the draft. Instead, he worked briefly as a police and court reporter for the newspaper *Il Popolo di Roma,* then drew cartoons and wrote short stories for the satirical publication *Marc'Aurelio.* Fellini would later use his skill as a cartoonist to draw characters and scenes in preparation for all his films.

It was during this formative period in Rome that Fellini met and befriended veteran actor Aldo FABRIZI, who played a decisive role in attracting Fellini to the performing arts. Fellini drew sketches for Fabrizi's acts, then accompanied the actor's troupe as a designated "poet," actually carrying out a variety of utility duties such as those of wardrobe master, scenery painter, traveling secretary, and bit actor. This experience would later provide the background for Fellini's first film as a director (in collaboration with Alberto Lattuada), *Luci del Varietà/Variety Lights.* In 1940, Fellini began writing for radio and collaborating on scripts for films. He avoided the draft when his records were destroyed during the bombing of a military hospital. He later met and married a woman who would exert considerable influence on his life and art, actress Giulietta MASINA.

Shortly after the liberation of Rome, Fellini and several of his colleagues opened The Funny Face Shop, an arcade that provided American GIs with such services as quick portraits, caricatures, candid photos, and voice recordings for delivery to families back home. An unexpected visitor at the shop one day was director Roberto ROSSELLINI, who asked for Fellini's collaboration on the script of a documentary. The project eventually developed into a feature-length classic of Italian neorealism, *Open City* (1945). Fellini then went on to collaborate with Rossellini as a screenwriter and assistant director on *Paisan* (1946) and later contributed the story for one of the two episodes in Rossellini's *L'Amore* (1948), "Il Miracolo," in which a bleached-haired Fellini also co-starred with Anna Magnani.

Following several assignments in the late 40s as a co-screenwriter or assistant director for Pietro GERMI and Alberto LATTUADA, Fellini took a first stab at directing with *Luci del Varietà/Variety Lights* (1951), a collaborative effort with Lattuada from Fellini's own original story about a troupe of traveling actors. The film was not a success, and Fellini briefly returned to work as an assistant director to Germi. But he was now determined to direct again.

Fellini inherited almost by default his first assignment as a solo director. The film, *The White Sheik* (1952), had first been intended by the producers for Antonioni, then for Lattuada, but Fellini persisted and, after peddling the story among a number of prospective investors, finally found a producer who would let him direct this satirical farce about the world of the photo-strip comic book, a form of "literature" immensely popular among the Italian lower classes. The film failed at the box office.

Undaunted by the critical rejection and financial failure, Fellini immediately set out to make his next film, *I Vitelloni/The Young and the Passionate/The Loafers* (1953), an overwhelming success that established Fellini as a director of international standing. The film is a fond recollection of Fellini's own experience as an adolescent, telling with a balanced blend of drama and humor the story of an aimless quintet of good-for-nothing young loafers whose boredom is periodically relieved by practical jokes and other mischief. For a while Fellini considered a sequel to *I Vitelloni* called *Moraldo in Città,* which would have picked up Moraldo's story in Rome, but he soon abandoned the project. Moraldo, however, would later reappear in another Fellini film, *La Dolce Vita,* disguised as another character, Marcello.

Fellini scored an even greater international success with *La Strada* (1954), a profoundly moving and thoroughly humanistic story, replete with symbolism, of a half-witted waif and a brutal strongman who buys her for a plate of pasta and dominates her in body but never truly in spirit. The film was interpreted by some as an early manifesto of women's liberation, but it encompasses broader ideas, and its spirit of human liberation was hailed by the Catholic press as genuinely Christian. Leftist critics, however, attacked Fellini for betraying the concepts of neorealism. Giulietta Masina's unforgettable performance in that role established her reputation as an international star. *La Strada* was awarded an Oscar as best foreign film.

Fellini responded to the criticism from the Left with *Il Bidone/The Swindle* (1955), a starkly realistic and savagely bitter drama about a band of small-time swindlers who pitilessly cheat the poor. Despite thematic and technical flaws, it was a sincere social document and a worthy intermezzo between *La Strada* and *Le Notti di Cabiria* in what some critics have defined as Fellini's "trilogy of loneliness."

Le notti di Cabiria/The Nights of Cabiria/Cabiria (1957)

was another milestone in Fellini's development as an artist and provided Giulietta Masina with another opportunity to display her unique acting talent in a sensitively etched, touching role of a kindhearted, simple-minded prostitute whose dreams of modest happiness are mired by the reality of her situation. The film enjoyed great popularity internationally and fetched for Fellini another Academy Award as best foreign film.

La Dolce Vita (1960) was a triumphant successor to Fellini's international successes of the 50s. The film provided a sensational view of the decadent "sweet life" of Rome's society as seen through the eyes of Marcello, a journalist (played by Marcello Mastroianni), who loathes the degradation around him but seems incapable of extricating himself from the glitter of the Via Veneto and the allure of uninhibited orgies. *La Dolce Vita* was clearly autobiographical, with Marcello representing Moraldo (that is, Fellini), the member of the *I Vitelloni* quintet who left his hometown to seek a future in Rome. It won the grand prize at the 1961 Cannes Festival.

After turning out a memorable segment, "The Temptation of Dr. Antonio," for the episode film *Boccaccio '70* (1962), in which he sarcastically ridiculed sexual hypocrisy, Fellini brought to the screen one of his most personal and stylistically unorthodox films, *Otto e Mezzo/8½* (1963), supposedly so titled because it represented Fellini's eighth-and-a-half production (his seventh solo effort plus three collaborations, each counting as a half). As an autobiography, this film goes a step beyond Fellini's other celluloid self-portraits and is more in the nature of a confession or unabashed self-analysis. A mixture of fact and fantasy, it is a complex film, both in structure and content, and an inspired testimony to Fellini's originality and inventiveness. It won a first prize at the Moscow Film Festival and a third best foreign film Oscar for Fellini.

Giulietta degli Spiriti/Juliet of the Spirits (1965), Fellini's first color feature, is also an exercise in psychoanalysis, this time of the neuroses and fantasies of a woman (played by Giulietta Masina) who suspects her husband is betraying her. It is a visually dazzling, nearly gaudy production with no coherent plot but many absorbing psychological and social observations. *Fellini Satyricon* (1969) was rich in décor and bold in its imagery, but many critics considered it pretentious, excessive, and self-indulgent. *I Clowns/The Clowns* (1970), originally made for Italian television, was a personal tribute to the circus people Fellini had admired from childhood.

Fellini made a tentative but, to many of his admirers, an encouraging return to the kind of film that had made him successful in the 50s and early 60s with *Roma/Fellini's Roma* (1972), an affectionate satirical look at the Eternal City offering a kaleidoscopic synthesis of the director's own reminiscence and fantasy. With his next film, *Amarcord* (1973), his fourth best foreign language Oscar winner, Fellini returned to the top of his old form and to Rimini, the cradle of his boyhood memories and fantasies, but with *Casanova/Fellini's Casanova* (1976) he seemed to be again drifting from inspired free flights of personal fancy and toward a labyrinthine search of elusive new expressive forms. Fellini continued to tantalize and delight his admirers in the late 70s and throughout the 80s, experimenting with chamber filmmaking in *Orchestra Rehearsal* (1979), gliding into fantasy in *City of Women* (1981), cruising back to a bygone era in *And the Ship Sails On* (1983), reaching for melancholic nostalgia in *Ginger and Fred* (1985), and paying homage to himself in *Intervista* (1987). While none of these films ranked with the director's greatest, they were all unmistakably Fellini creations, all feasts for minds, hearts, and senses to savor and celebrate. As the decade came to a close, the director offered his many fans *Voices of the Moon* (1990), an evocation and summary of themes and obsessions that had occupied Fellini, the man and the filmmaker, since 8½. He received a lifetime achievement award at the 1992 Academy Awards.

FILMS: As co-screenwriter—*Il Pirata sono io* (gags only), *Non me lo dire* (gags only), *Lo vedi come sei?* (gags only) 1940; *Avanti c'è Posto* (story only), *Documento Z–3, Quarta Pagina* 1942; *Campo dè Fiori* (story only), *Apparizione, L'Ultima Carrozzella* (story only), *Chi l'ha visto?* 1943; *Roma Città aperta/Open City* (also asst. dir.) 1945; *Paisà/Paisan* (also asst. dir.) 1946; *Il Delitto di Giovanni Episcopo/Flesh Will Surrender, L'Ebreo errante/The Wandering Jew* (uncredited), *Il Passatore/A Bullet for Stefano* 1947; *Senza Pietà/Without Pity, L'Amore* (story of "Il Miracolo"/"The Miracle" episode; also act.) 1948; *In Nome della Legge/Mafia* (also asst. dir.), *Il Mulino del Po/The Mill on the Po* (also asst. dir.), *La Città dolente* 1949; *Francesco Giullare di Dio/Flowers of St. Francis* (also asst. dir.), *Il Camino della Speranza/The Path of Hope* (also asst. dir.) 1950; *Persiane chiuse, La Città si difende* (also asst. dir.) 1951; *Europa '51/The Greatest Love* (uncredited), *Il Brigante di Tacca del Lupo* (co-story, asst. dir. only), *Cameriera Bella Presenza Offresi* 1952; *Fortunella* 1958. As director and co-screenwriter—*Luci del Varietà/Variety Lights* (co-dir. with Alberto Lattuada) 1951; *Lo Sceicco bianco/The White Sheik* 1952; *I Vitelloni/The Young and the Passionate/The Loafers, Amore in Città/Love in the City* ("Un'Agenzia matrimoniale" episode) 1953; *La Strada* 1954; *Il Bidone/The Swindle* 1955; *Le Notti di Cabiria/The Nights of Cabiria/Cabiria* 1957; *La Dolce Vita* 1960; *Boccaccio '70* ("Le Tentazioni di Dottor Antonio"/"The Temptation of Dr. Antonio" episode) 1962; *Otto e Mezzo/8½* 1963; *Giulietta degli Spiriti/Juliet of the Spirits* 1965; *Histoires extraordinares/Tre Passi nel Delirio/Spirits of the Dead* ("Toby Dammit"/"Never Bet the Devil Your Head" episode; Fr./It.) 1968; *Fellini Satyricon* 1969; *I Clowns/The Clowns* 1970; *Roma/Fellini's Roma* 1972; *Amarcord* 1973; *Casanova/Fellini's Casanova* 1976; *Prova d'Orchestra/Orchestra Rehearsal* 1979; *La Città delle Donne/City of Women* 1981; *E la Nave va/And the Ship Sails On* 1983; *Ginger e Fred/Ginger and Fred* 1985; *Intervista* 1987; *La Voce della Luna/Voices of the Moon* 1990.

Fellows, Edith. Actress. Born on May 20, 1923, in Boston. Spirited child and teenage performer of Hollywood films of the 30s and early 40s, often in "rotten but nice" roles. She retired from the screen in her early 20s but later appeared on the stage and in TV.

FILMS INCLUDE: *Madame X* 1929; *Daddy Long Legs, Cimarron, Huckleberry Finn* 1931; *Emma* 1932; *Jane Eyre, Kid Millions, His Greatest Gamble, Mrs. Wiggs of the Cabbage Patch* 1934; *Dinky, Black Fury, The Keeper of the Bees, She Married Her Boss, One-Way Ticket* 1935; *Pennies from Heaven, Tugboat Princess* 1936; *Little Miss Roughneck, City Streets, The Little Adventures* 1938; *Pride of the Blue Grass, Give Little Peppers* 1939; *Music in My Heart, Nobody's Children, Her First Romance* 1940; *Her First Beau* 1941; *Girls' Town* 1942; *Lilith* 1964.

Fenton, Leslie. Director, former actor. *b.* Mar. 12, 1902, Liverpool, England. *d.* 1978. In the US from boyhood, he entered Hollywood films as an actor in the early 20s and played leads and character roles in numerous productions through the late 30s. Turning director, he made a number of solid masculine action films before retiring early in the 1950s. He was married at one time to actress Ann DVORAK.

FILMS INCLUDE: As actor—*Gentle Julia* 1924; *The Ancient Mariner, Thunder Mountain, East Lynne, Lazybones*

1925; *The Road to Glory, Black Paradise, Sandy, The Shamrock Handicap, What Price Glory* 1926; *The Showdown, The Dragnet, The First Kiss* 1928; *Broadway, The Man I Love, The Office Scandal, Paris Bound, The Last Performance, Dynamite* 1929; *The Public Enemy, Kick-In, The Guilty Generation* 1931; *The Hatchet Man, The Famous Ferguson Case, Air Mail* 1932; *Night Flight, Lady Killer* 1933; *Marie Galante* 1934; *Star of Midnight, The Casino Murder Case* 1935; *Murder on the Bridle Path* 1936; *House of Secrets* 1937; *Boys Town* 1938. As director (complete)—*Tell No Tales, Stronger Than Desire* 1939; *The Man from Dakota, The Golden Fleecing* 1940; *The Saint's Vacation* (UK) 1941; *There's a Future in It* (UK) 1943; *Tomorrow the World* 1944; *Pardon My Past* (also prod.) 1946; *On Our Merry Way/A Miracle Can Happen* (co-dir. with King Vidor), *Saigon, Lulu Belle* 1948; *Whispering Smith, Streets of Laredo* 1949; *The Redhead and the Cowboy* 1951.

Ferguson, Elsie. Actress. *b.* 1883, New York City. *d.* 1961. Hollywood silent star of the WW I era, following stage experience. For a while she specialized in society melodramas.

FILMS INCLUDE: *Barbary Sheep, The Rise of Jennie Cushing* 1917; *The Song of Songs, The Lie, The Danger Mark, Heart of the Wilds, A Doll's House, Under the Greenwood Tree* 1918; *His Parisian Wife, The Marriage Price, Eyes of the Soul, The Avalanche, A Society Exile, The Witness for the Defense* 1919; *His House in Order, Lady Rose's Daughter* 1920; *Footlights, Forever/Peter Ibbetson, Sacred and Profane Love* 1921; *Outcast* 1922; *Broadway After Dark* 1924; *The Unknown Lover* 1925; *Scarlet Pages* 1930.

Fernandel. Actor. *b.* Fernand Joseph Désiré Contandin, May 8, 1903, Marseille, France. *d.* 1971. The son of a semi-professional music hall entertainer, he began performing while still a child and later gained experience as an amateur comedian and light singer while earning a living as a bank teller, a docker, and a clerk at his father's wholesale grocery business. He turned professional in 1922 and before long became popular in vaudeville, operettas, and music hall revues. He made his film debut in 1930 and appeared in many minor productions before gaining national popularity playing a serious role in the screen adaptation of Maupassant's *Le Rosier de Madame Husson* (1932). His reputation was further enhanced by Marcel Pagnol's *Angèle* (1934), another serious-pathetic role.

Occasionally, Fernandel played other serious parts, but his fame and popularity were to rest on the more than 100 comic portrayals that made him France's top funnyman for four decades. His popularity quickly spread overseas and he became an audience favorite in the US, England, and other countries. His long, lugubrious face, horselike grin, and shy-mischievous manner represented for many filmgoers a virtual symbol of France. Among his most popular films were the "Don Camillo" series, in which he portrayed an eccentric Roman Catholic priest at war with his town's Communist mayor. Fernandel died of lung cancer during the production of what had been intended as the last episode in the series.

FILMS INCLUDE: *Le Blanc et le Noir, Paris-Beguin* 1931; *Le Rosier de Madame Husson/He, Les Gaietés de l'Escadron, La Porteuse de Pain* 1932; *L'Ordonnance/The Orderly* 1933; *Adéma ï Aviateur, Angèle* 1934; *Ferdinand le Noceur* 1935; *Un de la Legion, Josette* 1936; *François I/Francis the First, Le Dégourdis de lo Onzième, Un Carnet de Bal, Regain/Harvest, Hercule, Igance, Le Roi du Sport* 1937; *Le Schpountz/Heartbeat* 1939; *Fric-Frac* 1939; *La Fille du Puisatier/The Well-Digger's Daughter, Un Chapeau de Paille d'Italie/The Italian Straw Hat* 1940; *La Fille de Puisatier* 1941; *Simplet* (also dir.) 1942; *Adrien* (also dir. 1943); *Naïs* 1945; *Pétrus, Les Gueux au Paradis/Hoboes in Paradise* 1946; *Emile l'Africain, L'Armoire volante/The Cupboard Was Bare, Botta e Riposta* (It.) 1949; *Meurtres/Three Sinners* 1950; *Topaze, L'Auberge Rouge/The Red Inn, Adhémar* (also dir.) 1951; *La Table aux Crevés, Le Petit Monde de Don Camillo/The Little World of Don Camillo* (Fr./It.), *Le Fruit défendu/Forbidden Fruit, Coiffeur pour Dames/The French Touch* 1952; *Le Retour de Don Camillo/The Return of Don Camillo* (Fr./It.), *L'Ennemi Public No. 1/The Most Wanted Man* 1953; *Mam'zelle Nitouche* 1954; *Le Mouton à Cinque Pattes/The Sheep Has Five Legs* (in five roles), *Ali Baba* 1954; *Don Juan/Pantaloons, Around the World in 80 Days* (US), *Le Couturier de ces Dames/Fernandel the Dressmaker* 1956; *L'Homme à l'Imperméable/The Man in the Raincoat, Sénéchal le Magnifique/Senechal the Magnificent, Sous le Ciel de Provence/The Virtuous Bigamist* 1957; *Le Chômeur de Clochemerle/The Easiest Profession, La Loi c'est la Loi/The Law Is the Law, Paris Holiday* (US/Fr.) 1958; *Le Grand Chef/The Big Chief, La Vache et le Prisonnier/The Cow and I* 1959; *Crésus, Le Caïd* 1960; *Cocagne, Dynamite Jack* (dual role), *Don Camillo Monseigneur* 1961; *le Diable et les Dix Commandements/The Devil and the 10 Commandments* (as God) 1962; *La Cuisine au Beurre/My Wife's Husband* 1963; *L'Age Ingrat* (also co-prod.) 1964; *Don Camillo à Moscou* 1965; *Le Voyage du Père* 1966; *L'Homme à la Buick* 1967; *Heureux qui comme Ulysse* 1970.

Fernandez, Emilio. Director, actor. *b.* Mar. 26, 1904, El Seco, near Hondo, Coahuila, Mexico *d.* 1986. The most important single figure in Mexican cinema, he was born to a Spanish-Mexican father and Indian mother, hence his nickname "El Indio." At 19 he took part in Mexican revolutions and counter-revolutions, rising to the rank of lieutenant colonel. In 1923 he was sentenced to 20 years' imprisonment but escaped to California, where, until the amnesty in 1933, he earned a living playing bits and supporting roles in Hollywood films. He later achieved some prominence as an actor in Mexican films, then turned to directing in the early 40s. He soon achieved a worldwide reputation with a series of award-winning films that helped the Mexican industry gain an important place in international cinema. These films, most notably *Maria Candelaria* (1943), a grand prize winner at Cannes, and *La Perla/The Pearl* (1946), winner of the international prize at San Sebastian, were marked by dramatic pictorial compositions, stark contrasts, and striking overall visual style. Thematically, they reflected Fernandez's own background and the socioeconomic conditions that prevailed in Mexico during his youth. Most of them were photographed by Gabriel FIGUEROA and starred Pedro ARMENDARIZ. Fernandez's wife, Columba Dominguez, also appeared in several of his films.

Fernandez's prestige declined in the 50s, along with the quality of his films. He then returned to acting, re-emerging as a director only once every several years. Among the US films in which he appeared were *The Reward* (1965), *The Appaloosa, Return of the Seven* (both 1966), *A Covenant with Death, The War Wagon* (both 1967), *The Wild Bunch* (1969), *Pat Garrett and Billy the Kid* (1973), *Bring Me the Head of Alfredo Garcia* (1974), and *Lucky Lady* (1975). Fernandez, who once shot a film critic in the heat of a dispute, was found guilty of manslaughter in 1976 for killing a farm laborer during location scouting in northern Mexico, allegedly in self-defense. He served six months of a four-and-a-half-year term in jail.

FILMS (as director and co-screenwriter): *La Isla de la Pasión/Passion Island* 1941; *Soy puro Mexicano* 1942; *Flor Sylvestre* (also act.), *Maria Candelaria* 1943; *Las Abandonadas,*

Bugambilla 1944; *Pepita Jimenez* 1945; *La Perla/The Pearl, Enamorada* 1946; *Río Escondido/Hidden River* 1947; *Malcovia, Salón México* 1948; *Pueblerina, La Malquerida, Duelo en las Montañas* 1949; *The Torch* (US remake of *Enamorada), Un Dia de Vida, Victimas del Pecado* 1950; *La Bienamada, Acapulco, Islas Marias, Soave Patria, Siempre tuya* 1951; *Tu y el Mar, Cuando levanta la Niebla* 1952; *La Red/The Net, El Reportaje, El Rapto* 1953; *La Rosa Blanca, La Rebellion de los Colgados, Nostros Dos* (Sp.) 1954; *La Tierra del Fuego se Apaga* (Arg.) 1955; *Una Cita de Amor* 1956; *El Impostor/El Gesticulador* 1957; *Pueblito* 1962; *The Night of the Iguana* (assoc. dir. only; US) 1964; *Un Dorado de Pancho Villa/A Loyal Soldier of Pancho Villa* 1966; *El Crepúscolo de un Dios* 1968; *La Choca* 1973; *Zona Roja* 1976.

Ferrara, Abel. Director. Born in 1952, in the Bronx, N.Y. A film addict from childhood, he made 8 mm shorts before having his first feature released in 1979. Working with minuscule budgets, he received good critical notices and a cult following for *Ms. 45/Angel of Vengeance* (1981), a harrowing tale of revenge by a raped woman. He began to get mainstream attention with the provocative *Bad Lieutenant* (1992), built around an outstanding performance by Harvey Keitel as a corrupt policeman seeking redemption. Ferrara's work often features gory violence, but is also carefully stylized and moody. His TV credits include the pilot for the 1990 cop series 'Crime Story.'

FEATURE FILMS: *Driller Killer* 1979; *Ms. 45/Angel of Vengeance* 1981; *Fear City* 1984; *China Girl* 1987; *King of New York* (It.) 1989; *Cat Chaser* 1990; *Bad Lieutenant* (also co-sc.) 1992; *Dangerous Game* 1993; *Body Snatchers, Snake Eyes* 1994; *The Addiction* 1995; *The Funeral* 1996; *Black Out* 1997.

Ferrer, José. Actor, director. *b.* José Vicente Ferrer de Otero y Cintron, Jan. 8, 1909, in Santurce, Puerto Rico. *d.* 1992. In the US from childhood, he abandoned plans to become an architect when he discovered dramatics at Princeton and made his Broadway debut in 1935. Within several years he had established a solid reputation as a versatile actor who was capable of admirable performances in a wide range of roles, from the comic title role in 'Charley's Aunt' (1940) to Iago opposite Paul Robeson's Othello (1942). He began directing for Broadway in 1942 and was a widely respected actor-director by the time he made his screen debut as the Dauphin in *Joan of Arc* (1948), a performance for which he received an Academy Award nomination as best supporting actor. He achieved a similar distinction in films, although his bravura style has at times been too strong for the screen, and won an Academy Award for the title role of *Cyrano de Bergerac* (1950), a part he had previously played on Broadway. He received another Oscar nomination as best actor for his portrayal of crippled painter Toulouse-Lautrec in *Moulin Rouge* (1952). Ferrer directed a number of films in the late 50s and 60s. His work as a director has been labeled "interesting" rather than exciting and as a consequence he returned to acting in both plays and films. His first (1938–48) wife was stage actress Uta Hagen, and his third (1953–67) singer Rosemary CLOONEY. His son Miguel Ferrer (*b.* 1954) is also a screen actor.

FILMS (as actor): *Joan of Arc* (as the Dauphin) 1948; *Whirlpool, Crisis, Cyrano de Bergerac* (title role) 1950; *Anything Can Happen, Moulin Rouge* (as Toulouse-Lautrec) 1952; *Miss Sadie Thompson* 1953; *The Caine Mutiny* 1952–53; *Deep in My Heart* (as Sigmund Romberg) 1954; *The Shrike* (also dir.) 1955; *The Cockleshell Heroes* (also dir.; UK) 1956; *The Great Man* (also dir, co-sc.) 1957; *I Accuse!* (as Dreyfus; also dir.), *The High Cost of Loving* (also dir.) 1958; *Return to Peyton Place* (dir. only) 1961; *State Fair* (dir. only), *Lawrence of Arabia* (UK) 1962; *Nine Hours to Rama* (US/UK), *Verspätung in Marienborn/Stop Train 349* (Ger./Fr./It.) 1963; *Cyrano et D'Artagnan* (Fr.) 1964; *The Greatest Story Ever Told* (as Herod), *Ship of Fools* 1965; *Enter Laughing* 1967; *Cervantes/The Young Rebel* (Sp./It./Fr.) 1968; *El Clan de los Immorales/Order to Kill* (Sp.) 1974; *e' Lollipop/Lollipop/Forever Young Forever Free* (S. Africa) 1975; *Paco* (Sp.), *The Big Bus, Voyage of the Damned* (UK) 1976; *Crash!, The Sentinel, Who Has Seen the Wind* (Can.), *Behind the Iron Mask/The Fifth Musketeer* (as Athos; Aus.) 1977; *The Private Files of J. Edgar Hoover, Dracula's Dog/Zoltan Hound of Dracula, The Swarm, Fedora* (Ger.) 1978; *Natural Enemies* 1979; *The Big Brawl* 1980; *A Midsummer Night's Sex Comedy, Blood Tide* 1982; *The Being, To Be or Not to Be* 1983; *The Evil That Men Do, Dune* 1984; *Bloody Birthday* 1986; *Old Explorers* 1990; *Hired to Kill, The Horror of It All* (narr.) 1991; *Primary Motive* 1992.

Ferrer, Mel. Actor, director producer. *b.* Melchior Gaston Ferrer, Aug. 25, 1917, Elberon, N.J. The son of a Cuban-born surgeon and a Manhattan socialite, he went to prep school and attended Princeton University but dropped out in his sophomore year to become an actor in summer stock. To support himself he worked as an editor on a small Vermont newspaper and wrote a children's book, *Tito's Hat.* He broke into Broadway in 1938 as a chorus dancer in two musicals and made his New York debut as an actor two years later. His career was interrupted for one year by a bout with polio and was resumed in radio, on which he started as a disc jockey for small local stations and rose to producer-director of top-rated shows for NBC. In 1945 he made a modest debut as a film director at Columbia with the low-budget *The Girl of the Limberlost* (1945) and in the same year returned to acting on Broadway. In 1947 he was John Ford's assistant on the film *The Fugitive.*

Ferrer made his screen acting debut in 1949 and subsequently appeared in many films, typically as a sensitive, quietly reserved, at times woodenly cold leading man. He is best remembered for the role of the lame puppeteer in *Lili* (1953). His several efforts as a film director, with the notable exception of the suspenseful thriller *The Secret Fury* (1950), have been unsuccessful. He turned to producing in the late 60s. His third (1954–68) of four wives was actress Audrey HEPBURN, whom he directed in *Green Mansions* (1959). He produced another of her vehicles, *Wait Until Dark* (1967). In the 60s and 70s he worked mainly in Europe, appearing in countless, virtually untraceable cheap horror movies. Returning to the US, he was a regular on the TV series 'Behind the Screen' (1981–82) and 'Falcon Crest' (1981–84).

FILMS INCLUDE: As actor—*Lost Boundaries* 1949; *Born to Be Bad* 1950; *The Brave Bulls* 1951; *Rancho Notorious, Scaramouche* 1952; *Lili* 1953; *Knights of the Round Table* (as King Arthur), *Saadia* 1954; *Oh Rosalinda!* (UK), *Proibito/Forbidden* (It.) 1955; *War and Peace* (as Prince Andrei; US/It.), *Elena et les Hommes/Paris Does Strange Things* (Fr./It.) 1956; *The Vintage, The Sun Also Rises, Mayerling* 1957; *Fraulein* 1958; *The World the Flesh and the Devil* 1959; *L'Homme a Femmes* (Fr.), *Et Mourir de Plaisir/Blood and Roses* (Fr./It.) 1960; *Les Mains d'Orlac/The Hands of Orlac* (Fr./UK), *Legge di Guerra* (It.), *I Lancieri neri* (It.) 1961; *Le Diable et les Dix Commandements/The Devil and the Ten Commandments* (Fr.), *The Longest Day* (US/Fr.) 1962; *The Fall of the Roman Empire, Paris When It Sizzles* (cameo), *Sex and the Single Girl, El Señor de la Salle* (Sp.) 1964; *La Chica del Molino rojo/The Girl from the Red Cabaret* (Sp.) 1973; *L'Anticristo/The Temper* (It.) 1974; *Brannigan, Morte sospetta di una Minorenne* (It.) 1975; *Das Netz* (Ger.), *Il Corsaro nero* (It.), *Eaten Alive/Death Trap/Starlight Slaughter/ Legend of the Bayou/Horror Hotel* 1976; *La Ragazza dal Pigiami giallo* (It.), *L'Avvocato della Mala* (It.) 1977; *L'Isola di Uoimini Pesce/Island of the Fishmen/Fish Men/Screamers* (It.), *Hi-Riders, The Norseman* 1978; *Il Visitore/The Visitor* (It.) 1979; *The Fifth Floor, Il Fiume de Grande Caimano/Great Alligator* (It.), *Incubo sulla Citta' contaminata/City of the Walking Dead/Nightmare City* (It./Sp.) 1980; *Lili Marleen* (Ger.) 1981; *Mille Milliarde de Dollars* (Fr.) 1982. As director (complete)—*The Girl of the Limberlost* 1945; *The Secret Fury, Vendetta* (co-dir. with several uncredited directors) 1950; *Green Mansions* 1959; *Cabriola/Every Day Is a Holiday* (also exec. prod., story, co-sc.; Sp.) 1965. As producer—*El Greco* (co-prod.; also music, act. in title role; It./Fr.; filmed in Spain) 1964; *Wait Until Dark* 1967; *The Night Visitor* (Sw./Den.) 1971; *A Time for Loving* (also act.) 1972; *W* 1974.

Ferreri, Marco. Director. Born on May 11, 1928, in Milan. *d.* 1997. A university dropout, he worked as a liquor salesman and briefly as a journalist before beginning in films as a producer of commercials. In 1950 he launched a film magazine called "Documento Mensile." It was supposed to be screened regularly in Italian theaters as a mélange of newsreel, documentary, *cinéma vérité,* and fiction bits, but the idea was shelved after two issues. Ferreri then worked in various secondary capacities on a number of Italian neorealist features and in the late 50s went to Spain, where he made his debut as a feature director with three films noted for their abrasive humor. He returned to Italy in the wake of the success of one of these, *El Cochecito/The Wheelchair* (1960), at the Venice Festival. There Ferreri quickly established a reputation as an eclectic director with a biting humanistic theme and an anarchic poetic style. In his early films, he treated matrimonial relations, or the absence thereof, with a sense of pessimistic cynicism which reached a high mark of alienation and despair in his ambiguous masterpiece, *Dillinger è Morto/Dillinger Is Dead* (1969). Ferreri's Buñuel-like anarchic, antibourgeois theme exploded with its greatest ferocity in *La Grande Bouffe* (1973), in which people literally self-destruct in a mass eating orgy. Ferreri mocked the disintegration of sex roles and the nuclear family in *La Dernière Femme/The Last Woman* (1976), in which the hero slices off his sex organ with an electric carving knife; he then turned out his first English-speaking film, *Bye Bye Monkey* (1978), a continuation of his theme of the breakup of urban life, in which his hero is gang-raped by several women. Ferreri, a collaborator on all of his own scripts, won the International Critics Prize at Cannes for *The Wheelchair* (1960) and *La Grande Bouffe* (1973) and at San Sebastian for *Tales of Ordinary Madness* (1981).

FILMS (as director and co-screenwriter): *El Pisito* (Sp.) 1958; *Los Chicos* (Sp.) 1959; *El Cochecito/The Wheelchair/ The Little Coach* (Sp.) 1960; *Le Italiane e l'Amore* ("L'Infidelità Coniugale" episode) 1961; *Una Storia Moderna: L'Ape Regina/The Conjugal Bed* 1963; *La Donna Scimmia/The Ape Woman, Controsesso* ("Il Professore" episode) 1964; *Oggi Domani e Dopodomani* ("L'Uomo dei Cinque Palloni"/"The Man with the Balloons" episode) 1965; *Marcia Nuziale* 1966; *L'Harem* 1967; *L'Uomo dei Cinque Palloni/The Man with the Balloons* (expanded version) 1968; *Dillinger è Morto/ Dillinger Is Dead, Il Seme dell'Uomo/The Seed of Man* 1969; *L'Udienza* 1971; *Liza/La Cagna* (Fr./It.) 1972; *La Grande Bouffe* (Fr./It.) 1973; *Touchez pas la Femme Blanche* (also act.; Fr./It.) 1974; *L'Ultima Donna/La Dernière Femme/The Last Woman* (It./Fr.) 1976; *Bye Bye Monkey* (It./Fr.), *Ciao Male* 1978; *Chiedo Asilo/Pipi Caca Dodo/My Asylum/No Child's Land* 1979; *Storie di Ordinara Follia/Tales of Ordinary Madness* 1981; *Storia di Piera* 1983; *Il Futuro e Donna* 1984; *I Love You* 1986; *O come sono buoni i bianchi* 1987; *Nitrate Base* 1996.

Ferrero, Anna Maria. Actress. Born Anna Maria Guerra, in 1931, in Rome. Leading lady of Italian films of the 50s, usually in delicate roles. Married to actor Jean Sorel.

FILMS INCLUDE: *Il Cielo è Rosso/The Sky Is Red* 1949; *Domani è un altro Giorno, Il Cristo proibito/Strange Deception, Il Conte di S. Elmo/The Count of St. Elmo* 1950; *Le Due Verità* 1951; *Lo sai che i Papaveri, I Vinti, Le Infedeli* 1952; *Cronache di Poveri Amanti, Villa Borghese/It Happened in the Park, Giuseppe Verdi/The Life and Music of Giuseppe Verdi* 1953; *La Vedova* 1954; *War and Peace* (US) 1956; *Los Amantes del Desierto/Desert Warrior* (Sp./It.) 1958; *La Notte Brava/On Any Street/Bad Girls Don't Cry* 1959; *Il Mattatore/ Love and Larceny, Il Gobbo/The Hunchback of Rome* 1960; *L'Oro di Roma* 1961; *Una Domenica d'Estate* 1962; *Controsesso* 1964.

Ferretti, Dante. Art director. Born in 1943, in Italy. One of Europe's leading production designers in the 70s and 80s, he has received four Academy Award nominations for his rich, elaborate art direction. A favorite of PASOLINI and FELLINI, he maintains a reputation of exquisite artistry as a designer in American as well as foreign films.

FILMS INCLUDE: *Medea* 1970; *Il Decamerone/The Decameron, La Classe operaia va in Paradiso/Lulu the Tool* 1971; *I Racconti di Canterbury/The Canterbury Tales* 1972; *Il Fiore delle Mille e una Notte/The Arabian Nights, Mio Dio come sono Cadutta in Basso/Till Marriage Do Us Part* 1974; *Prova d'Orchestra/Orchestra Rehearsal* 1979; *La Città delle Donne/City of Women* 1981; *Storie di Ordinara Follia/Tales of Ordinary Madness* 1981; *La Nuit de Varennes* 1982; *E la Nave va/And the Ship Sails On* 1983; *Pianoforte* 1984; *Ginger e Fred/Ginger and Fred* 1985; *The Name of the Rose* 1986; *Adventures of Baron Munchausen* (UK) 1989; *Docteur M, La Voce della Luna/The Voice of the Moon, Hamlet* (US) 1990; *Lo Zio Indegno* (It.) 1991; *Bram Stoker's Dracula* (US) 1992; *The Age of Innocence* (US) 1993; *Interview with a Vampire* (US) 1994.

Ferzetti, Gabriele. Actor. Born Pasquale Ferzetti, on Mar. 17, 1925, in Rome. Handsome leading man and supporting player with patrician manner of numerous Italian films and some international productions. Also active on the Italian stage.

FILMS INCLUDE: *Via delle Cinque Lune* 1942; *Fabiola, I Miserabili* 1947; *Guglielmo Tell/William Tell* 1949; *Il Cristo proibito/Forbidden Christ* 1950; *Tre Storie proibite/Three Forbidden Stories* 1951; *Puccini* (title role) 1952; *La Provinciale/The Wayward Wife* 1953; *Le Avventure di Giacomo Casanova/Sins of Casanova* (as Casanova), *Casa Ricordi/ House of Ricordi* (as Puccini), *Camilla* 1954; *Le Amiche/The Girl Friends, Donatella* 1955; *Racconti d'Estate/Love on the Riviera, Tutti innamorati* 1958; *Annibale/Hannibal, Labbra Rosse/Red Lips, L'Avventura* 1960; *Jessica* 1962; *La Calda Vita* 1963; *La Bibbia/The Bible,* (as Lot; It./US) 1966; *A Ciascuno il suo/We Still Kill the Old Way* 1967; *Meglio Vedova/Better a Widow, Un Bellissimo Novembre/That Splendid November, Grazie Zia/Come Play with Me, C'era una Volta il West/Once Upon a Time in the West* 1968; *On Her Majesty's Secret Service* (UK) 1969; *L'Aveu/The Confession* (Fr./It.) 1970; *Mendiants et Orgeuilleux* (Fr.) 1972; *Gli Ultimi 10 Giorni di Hitler/Hitler: The Last Ten Days* (as Field Marshal Wilhelm Keitel; It./UK) 1973; *Il Portiere di Notte/The Night Porter, Corruzione al Palazzo di Giustizia* 1974; *Der Richter und sein Henker/End of the Game* (Ger./It.) 1975; *Le*

Guepier (Fr.), *A Matter of Time* (US/It.), *Potresti Essere mia Figlia* 1976; *Oedipus Orca* 1977; *L'Ordre et la Sécurité du Monde* (Fr.) 1978; *Sette Notte in Nero/The Psychic* 1979; *Inchon* (Korea/US) 1981; *Quartetto Basileus/The Basileus Quartet* (re-edited from '81 TV presentation) 1984; *Julia e Julia/Julia and Julia* 1987.

Fescourt, Henri. Director. *b.* Nov. 23, 1880, Bèziers, France. *d.* 1966. A former lawyer, music critic, and journalist, he began directing films in 1912. During the 20s he ranked among France's leading directors. His realistic films of the period are noted for their intelligence and discretion. He is the author of a number of books on cinema and other subjects.

FILMS INCLUDE: *Le Bonheur perdu* 1912; *Jeux d'Enfants* 1913; *Peine d'Amour* 1914, *La Menace* 1915; *Mathias Sandorf* (serial) 1921; *Rouletabille* 1922; *Mandrin* (serial), *Les Grands* 1924; *Le Fils d'Amérique, Les Misérables* 1925; *L'Occident* 1927; *La Maison du Maltais* 1928; *Monte Cristo* 1929; *Serments* (Sw.) 1931; *L'Occident* (remake) 1937; *Bar du Sud* 1938; *Retour de Flamme* 1942.

Festa Campanile, Pasquale. Director, screenwriter. Born on July 28, 1927, in Melfi, Italy. After law studies, he worked as a journalist and wrote short stories, novels, and plays. In the early 50s he began writing screenplays for Italian films, mostly in collaboration with Massimo Franciosa (*b.* July 23, 1924, Rome) or others. He began directing in the early 60s. His films as director have often dealt with aspects of sexuality. He writes his own scripts, alone or in collaboration. He shared an Oscar nomination for the original script of Nanni Loy's *The Four Days of Naples.*

FILMS INCLUDE: As screenwriter—*Faddija* 1950; *Gli Innamorati/Wild Love, Poveri ma Belli/Poor but Beautiful* 1956; *Giovani Mariti/Young Husbands* 1958; *Rocco e i suoi Fratelli/Rocco and His Brothers* 1960; *La Viaccia/The Love Makers, L'Assassino/The Lady Killer of Rome* 1961; *Le Quattro Giornate di Napoli/The Four Days of Naples* 1962; *Il Gattopardo/The Leopard* 1963. As director-screenwriter—*Un Tentativo Sentimentale* (co-dir. with Massimo Franciosa) 1963; *Le Voci bianche/White Voices* (co-dir. with Franciosa), *La Costanza della Regione* 1964; *Una Vergine per il Principe/A Maiden for a Prince* 1965; *Adulterio all' Italiana/Adultery Italian Style* 1966; *La Ragazza e il Generale/The Girl and the General, La Cintura di Castità/On My Way to the Crusades I Met a Girl Who. . .* (It./US) 1967; *Il Marito è mio e l'Amazzo quando mi Pare/Drop Dead!* 1968; *La Matriarca/The Libertine, Dove vai tutta Nuda?* 1969; *Scacco alla Regina, Con Quale Amore con Quanto Amore, Quando le Donne avevano la Coda/When Women Had Tails* 1970; *Il Merlo Maschio* 1971; *Jus Prima Noctis, La Calandria, Quando le Donne Persero la Coda* 1972; *L'Emigrante, Rugantino* 1973; *Soldier of Fortune* 1975; *Humunqus Hector* 1976; *Cara Sposa, Autostop, Parlami d'Amore Maria* 1977; *Il Ritorno di Casanova* (orig. for TV), *Corne Perdere una Moglie e Trovare un'Amante* 1978; *Bello ma Dannato, Gege Bellavita* 1979; *Il Ladrone* 1980; *Nessuno é peerfetto* 1981; *La Ragazza di Trieste* (from his own novel) 1982; *Bingo Bongo* 1983.

Fetchit, Stepin. Actor. *b.* Lincoln Theodore Monroe Andrew Perry, May 30, 1892, Key West, Fla. *d.* 1985. A medicine show and vaudeville performer, he arrived in Hollywood in the late 20s and over the next decade made a small fortune playing lazy, easily frightened comic characters that have since been identified as insulting stereotypes of African-Americans. He was the first black actor to receive featured billing in American movies. He is reputed to have made $2 million during the 30s, but he squandered his money, leading the lavish life of a star (at one time he owned 16 cars, including a pink Rolls-Royce, and employed 16 Chinese servants) and in 1947 he declared bankruptcy. In the late 60s he converted to the Black Muslim faith. In 1969 he endured a personal tragedy when his son Donald killed three people, then committed suicide, on the Pennsylvania Turnpike. In 1970 he sued CBS unsuccessfully for $3 million, charging defamation of character for the use of "out of context" clips of his movies as examples of black caricature in American films. He returned to the screen in the mid-70s after an absence of two decades. In 1976 he received a special Image Award from the Hollywood chapter of the NAACP and in 1978 he was elected to the Black Filmmakers Hall of Fame. He borrowed his screen name from a racehorse that had won him some money in his pre-Hollywood days.

FILMS INCLUDE: *In Old Kentucky* 1927; *The Tragedy of Youth* 1928; *The Ghost Talks, Hearts in Dixie, Show Boat, Fox Movietone Follies of 1929, Salute* 1929; *The Big Fight, Cameo Kirby, Swing High* 1930; *The Prodigal* 1931; *Carolina, David Harum, Stand Up and Cheer, Judge Priest* 1934; *Heldorado, The County Chairman, One More Spring, Charlie Chan in Egypt, Steamboat 'Round the Bend* 1935; *Dimples* 1936; *On the Avenue, Love Is News* 1937; *Zenobia* 1939; *Miracle in Harlem* (lead) 1947; *Bend of the River* 1952; *The Sun Shines Bright* 1953; *Amazing Grace* 1974; *Won Ton Ton—The Dog Who Saved Hollywood* 1976.

Feuillade, Louis. Director. *b.* Feb. 19, 1873, Lunel, France. *d.* 1925. The son of a wine broker, he attended a Catholic seminary. After completing compulsory military service in the cavalry, he married and began a modest career as an amateur actor, local reporter, and bullfight critic. In 1898 he settled in Paris, where he began writing for the right-wing, royalist press in 1902. In 1906 he began his association with French cinema as screenwriter and soon after also was working as director. In the following year he was appointed production chief of all Gaumont films but continued directing his own films while supervising the production of others. His personal output was phenomenally prolific. In less than 20 years he directed more than 800 films of varying lengths, also writing the scripts for virtually all of them. In addition, he wrote some 100 screenplays for other directors and supervised the production of countless other films. He created in a variety of genres—drama, comedy, adventure, historical epics—but became best known for his fantasy serials, most notably *Fantômas, Les Vampires,* and *Judex,* the dreamlike, hallucinatory quality of which resulted in compelling visual suspense. Neglected by film historians for many years, Feuillade was rediscovered by French *cinéastes* in the mid-40s as a result of a retrospective of his films in the CINÉMATHÈQUE FRANÇAISE. He has since been hailed as a great film pioneer and his contribution to the art of cinema has been compared by some chauvinistic French critics with that of the American D. W. Griffith. Many consider Feuillade a forerunner of German expressionism and the prime mover in the thriller and suspense film genres.

FILMS INCLUDE: *Le Billet de Banque, La Course au Potiron, Les Deux Gosses, La Porteuse de Pain* 1906; *L'Homme aimanté, La Course des Belles-Máres, La Sirène, Vive le Sabotage* 1907; *Une Dame vraiment bien, La Grève des Apaches, Prométhée, Un Tic* 1908; *Les Heures, L'Aveugle de Jérusalem, La Chatte métamorphosée en Femme, Le Huguenot, Judith et Holopherne, La Mort de Mozart, Le Printemps* 1909; *Mater Dolorosa, Benvenuto Cellini, Le Festin de Balthazar, Esther, L'Exode, Molière, Les Sept Péchés capitaux* 1910; the "Bébé" series (74 episodes, of variable lengths, the heroine of which is a child) 1910–13; "La Vietelle qu'elle est"/"Life as It Is" series (a realistic social drama series, 15 episodes) 1911–13; *Charles VI, Le Fils de la Sunamite, Aux Lions les Chrétiens* 1911; *Le Mort vivant, L'Anneau fatal, Le Proscrit* 1912; "Bout-de-Zan" series (53 adventure episodes) 1912–16; *L'Angonie de Byzance, Bonne Année, Le Revenant, La Gardienne du Feu, La Mort de Lucrèce* 1913; *Fantômas* (five multi-episode serials) 1913–14; *La Rencontre, Manon de Montmartre, L'Epreuve* 1914; *Les Vampires* (ten-episode serial) 1915–16; *Judex* (12-episode serial) 1916; *La Nouvelle Mission de Judex* (12-episode serial) 1917; *Tih Minh* (12-episode serial), *Vendémiaire* 1918; *Barrabas* (12-episode serial), *L'Homme sans Visage* 1919; *Les Deux Gamines* (12-episode serial), *L'Orpheline* (12-episode serial) 1921; *Parisette* (12-episode serial), *Le Fils du Flisbustier* (12-episode serial) 1922; *Vindicta* (5-episode serial) 1923; *L'Orphelin de Paris* (six-episode serial), *Lucette* 1924; *Le Stigmate* (six-episode serial) 1925.

Feuillère, Edwige. Actress. Born Caroline Vivette Edwige Cunati, on Oct. 29, 1907, in Vésoul, France. The daughter of an Italian architect and an Alsatian mother, she studied drama at the conservatories of Dijon and Paris and in 1930 began playing minor roles on the stage under the name Cora Lynn. The following year she married the stage actor Pierre Feuillère and joined the Comédie-Française. Both bonds lasted only two years. Meanwhile, she had started a career in films that saw her gradually developing into the "first lady" of the French cinema. She typically played elegant, desirable, but often heartless femmes fatales, in both dramas and comedies, and her reputation gained additional glitter from her sterling performances on the Paris stage. Jean Cocteau wrote 'L'Aigle à Deux Têtes' especially for her and she played the role of the Queen in both the stage (1946) and screen (1948) versions. She has also appeared on the London stage and on French TV and has produced and directed plays for her own stage company. She is a Chevalier of the Légion d'Honneur. In 1984 she was honored by the French Film Academy with a special César Award. Autobiography: *Les Feux de la Mémoire* (1977).

FILMS INCLUDE: *Le Cordon Bleu, La Perle* 1931; *Monsieur Albert* 1932; *Topaze* 1933; *Barcarole* (Ger.), *Golgotha, Stradivarius, Lucrèce Borgia/Lucrezia Borgia* (title role) 1935; *Mister Flow/Compliments of Mr. Flow, La Route heureuse* 1936; *Marthe Richard* (title role), *Feu!* 1937; *J'étais une Aventurière* 1938; *L'Emigrante* 1939; *Sans Lendemain, De Mayerling à Sarajevo/Mayerling to Sarajevo* 1940; *La Duchesse de Langeais/The Wicked Duchess* 1942; *L'Honorable Catherine/The Honorable Catherine* 1943; *La Part de l'Ombre/Blind Desire* 1945; *L'Idiot/The Idiot* 1946; *L'Aigle à Deux Têtes/Eagle with Two Heads, Woman Hater* (UK) 1948; *Souvenirs perdus* 1950; *Olivia/Pit of Loneliness* 1951; *Adorable Créatures/Adorable Creatures* 1952; *Le Blé en Herbe/The Game of Love* 1954; *Les Fruits de l'Eté/Fruits of Summer* 1955; *Quand la Femme s'en mêle* 1957; *En Cas de Malheur/Love Is My Profession* 1958; *Les Amours célèbres* 1961; *Aimez-Vous les Femmes?/A Taste for Women* 1964; *Scusi—facciamo l'Amore?/Listen—Let's Make Love* (It./Fr.) 1968; *Clair de Terre* 1970; *La Chair de l'Orchidée* 1974.

FEX (also **FEKS**). Fabrika Eccentricheskovo Aktyora, or Factory of the Eccentric Actor. An avant-garde movement formed early in the 20s by young Soviet stage directors who proposed to reshape the entire socialist theater according to the traditions of the circus and vaudeville, especially in the style of acting. Cinema-oriented from the start, the group, led by Grigori KOZINTSEV, Leonid TRAUBERG, and Sergei YUTKEVICH, made its first film, *The Adventures of Oktyabrina,* in 1924. This short farcical fantasy was followed by other films of an experimental nature which exerted some influence on future Soviet Cinema. The leaders of the movement went on to become important film directors. As a movement, FEX was pitted in a battle of theories against Dziga VERTOV and his Kino-Eye school on the one hand, and against Lev KULESHOV and his "experimental laboratory" on the other.

Feyder, Jacques. Director. *b.* Jacques Frédérix, July 21, 1885, Ixelles, Belgium. *d.* 1948. Frustrating his bourgeois parents' hope that he would pursue a military career by flunking the entrance exams to officers school, he worked instead for two years in a cannon foundry. He arrived in Paris in 1911 and began playing minor roles on the stage and in films but soon decided that his real interest was in making films. Shortly after he was assigned as assistant to director Gaston Ravel, WW I broke out. Most French directors were mobilized, and Feyder was given the opportunity to direct much sooner than he expected. His early films, short comedies for the most part, were competent but drew little attention. In 1917, shortly after marrying celebrated actress Françoise ROSAY, he was mobilized by the Belgian army and spent the rest of the war years as an actor with a military troupe directed by Victor FRANCEN.

Upon returning to France in 1919, Feyder began the phase of his career that was to establish his reputation during the 20s and 30s as a pioneer and leading exponent of the school of poetic realism in French cinema. His first major film, *L'Atlantide* (1921), was shot partly in the Sahara Desert and was the most expensive French production up to that date. His other important films of the 20s were *Crainquebille* (1922), from the story by Anatole France, which echoed German expressionism and at the same time heralded the poetic realism that was to take firm hold of the French cinema of the 30s; *Visage d'Enfants* (1925), which he shot in Switzerland; and *Thérèse Raquin* (1928), from Zola, which he shot in Berlin. The latter boasted a powerful performance by Gina Manès and is considered one of the finest films of the late silent era. Following the official ban of his irony-filled satire *Les Nouveaux Messieurs* (1928) for undermining "the dignity of Parliament and its ministers," Feyder accepted an invitation from MGM to work in Hollywood.

Feyder directed Greta Garbo's last silent film, *The Kiss* (1929), and two minor Ramon Novarro talkies, as well as several foreign-language versions of US films, but he found the Hollywood atmosphere incompatible with his temperament and returned to France in 1931. Here he solidified his reputation with three successful films starring his wife, *Le Grand Jeu* (1934), *Pension Mimosas,* and *La Kermesse héroïque/Carnival in Flanders* (1935). The latter, an elaborate period farce with contemporary political implications, was his most famous film, the winner of many international awards, including the New York Film Critics best foreign film award and the best direction prize at the Venice Festival. It was banned by Goebbels after the Nazi invasion, and Feyder was forced into refuge in Switzerland for the duration of WW II. He wrote the scripts for many of his own films, alone or in collaboration, as well as for Jean Grémillon's *Gardiens de Phare* (1929).

FILMS: *M. Pinson—Policier* (co-dir. with Gaston Ravel), *Têtes de Femmes—Femmes de Tête, Le Pied qui étreint* (in four episodes; also sc.), *Le Bluff* (also sc.), *Un Conseil d'Ami* (also sc.), *L'Homme de Compagnie, Tiens vous êtes à Poitiers?, Le Frère de Lait* (also sc.) 1916; *L'Instinct est Maître, Le Billard cassé* (also sc.), *Abrégeons les Formalités!* (also sc.), *La Trouvaille de Buchu* (also sc.), *Le Pardessus de Demi-Saison, Les Vieilles Femmes de l'Hospice, Le Ravin sans Fond* (co-dir. with Raymond Bernard) 1917; *La Faute d'Orthographe* (also sc.) 1919; *L'Atlantide* (also sc.) 1921; *Crainquebille* (also sc., art dir.) 1922; *Visages d'Enfants/Faces of Children* (also sc., art dir.; Switz.), *L'Image* (also sc.; Aus.), *Gribiche* (also sc.) 1925; *Carmen* (also sc.) 1926; *Au Pays du Roi lépreux* (also sc.; exteriors shot in Indochina) 1927; *Gardiens de Phare* (sc., art dir. only), *Thérèse Raquin/Du sollst nicht ehebrechen/Shadows of Fear* (also adapt.; Ger.), *Les Nouveaux Messieurs/The New Gentlemen* 1928; *The Kiss* (also co-sc.; US) 1929; *Anna Christie* (German and Swedish versions of Clarence Brown's film), *Le Spectre vert* (French version of Lionel Barrymore's *The Unholy Night*), *Si l'Empereur savait ça* and *Olympia* (French and German versions of Lionel Barrymore's *His Glorious Night;* all US) 1930; *Daybreak* (US), *Son of India* (US) 1931; *Le Grand Jeu* 1934; *Pension Mimosas, La Kermesse héroïque/Carnival in Flanders* (plus German version, *Klugen Frauen;* also co-sc.) 1935; *Knight Without Armor* (UK) 1937; *Fahrendes Volk* (and French version, *Les Gens du Voyage;* also co-sc.; Ger.) 1938; *La Loi du Nord* (also co-sc.; in France and Norway) 1942; *Une Femme disparaît/Portrait of a Woman* (also sc.; Switz.) 1942; *Maturareise* (production supervisor only; Switz.) 1943; *Macadam/Back Streets of Paris* (artistic supervisor only) 1946.

Field, Betty. Actress. *b.* Feb. 8, 1918, Boston. *d.* 1973. Raised in New York City's borough of Queens, she attended the American Academy of Dramatic Arts and made her professional acting debut in summer stock in 1933. The following year she reached Broadway and developed into a popular ingenue in George Abbott's comedy presentations of the late 30s. She made her screen debut in 1939, repeating her Broadway role in the film version of *What a Life!* Her provocative performance in *Of Mice and Men* (1940) established her reputation as a screen personality with more than just looks, and during the 40s she commuted between Broadway and Hollywood. Her film roles were typically neurotic and hard-bitten. After an absence of several years, she returned to the screen in the mid-50s in character parts, often portraying slovenly, understanding mothers. Her first of three husbands (1942–56) was playwright Elmer Rice, who wrote several plays especially for her. She died of a cerebral hemorrhage.

FILMS: *What a Life!* 1939; *Of Mice and Men, Seventeen* 1940; *Victory, The Shepherd of the Hills, Blues in the Night* 1941; *Kings Row, Are Husbands Necessary?* 1942; *Flesh and Fantasy* 1943; *The Great Moment, Tomorrow the World* 1944; *The Southerner* 1945; *The Great Gatsby* 1949; *Picnic, Bus Stop* 1956; *Peyton Place* 1957; *Hound-Dog Man* 1959; *Butterfield 8* 1960; *Birdman of Alcatraz* 1962; *Seven Women* 1966; *How to Save a Marriage—and Ruin Your Life, Coogan's Bluff* 1968.

Field, Sally. Actress. Born on Nov. 6, 1946, in Pasadena, Calif. Dramatic and comic lead who matured from a bubbly TV teenager to a determined everywoman in American films. The daughter of screen actress Margaret Field (later known as Maggie Mahoney), who played leads in B pictures of the late 40s, and the stepdaughter of actor Jock MAHONEY, she attended the Columbia Pictures acting workshop and was selected over 150 other candidates to play the title role in the TV series 'Gidget' (1965–66). Her success led to a starring role in the even more popular series 'The Flying Nun' (1967–70). Dissatisfied with being typecast in cute, undemanding parts, she enrolled at the Actors Studio and after three years of training emerged as a competent dramatic actress. In 1977 she won an Emmy Award for her performance in the four-hour TV movie *Sybil,* in which she portrayed a mentally disturbed woman fragmented into 16 personalities. Her motion picture breakthrough came in 1979, when she won the Academy Award and the best actress prize at Cannes for her strong portrayal of a union activist in *Norma Rae.* She garnered a second Oscar for *Places in the Heart* (1984), gaining notoriety for one exuberant phrase in her acceptance speech: "You like me, you *really* like me!" With her production company, Fogwood Films, she has branched into producing as well as acting. Divorced (1968–73) from screenwriter Steven Craig, she was also married to producer Alan Greisman.

FILMS: *The Way West* 1967; *Stay Hungry* 1976; *Smokey and the Bandit, Heroes* 1977; *The End* 1978; *Beyond the Poseidon Adventure, Norma Rae* 1979; *Smokey and the Bandit II* 1980; *Back Roads, Absence of Malice* 1981; *Kiss Me Goodbye* 1982; *Places in the Heart* 1984; *Murphy's Romance* (also exec. prod.) 1985; *Surrender* 1987; *Punchline* (also prod.) 1988; *Steel Magnolias* 1989; *Not Without My Daughter, Soapdish, Dying Young* (co-prod. only) 1991; *Mrs. Doubtfire, Homeward Bound: The Incredible Journey* (v/o) 1993; *Forrest Gump* 1994; *Eye for an Eye* 1995; *Homeward Bound 2: Lost in San Francisco* (v/o) 1996.

Field, Shirley Ann(e). Actress. Born on June 27, 1936, in London. A former model, she entered British films in 1956, following some experience in repertory. She gradually developed from bit player and pretty ingenue into a capable leading lady, but her screen career faded in the mid-60s.

FILMS INCLUDE: *Simon and Laura* 1955; *It's Never Too Late* 1956; *The Good Companions, The Silken Affair* 1957; *Horrors of the Black Museum, Upstairs and Downstairs* 1959; *Once More with Feeling* (US), *Peeping Tom, The Entertainer, Beat Girl/Wild for Kicks, Saturday Night and Sunday Morning, Man in the Moon* 1960; *The Damned/These Are the Damned, The War Lover* 1962; *Kings of the Sun* (US) 1963; *Doctor in Clover/Carnaby M.D., Alfie* 1966; *With Love in Mind* 1969; *House of the Living Dead* 1977; *My Beautiful Laundrette* 1985; *Getting It Right, The Rachel Papers, Shag: The Movie* (US) 1989; *Hear My Song* (US) 1991; *Carrington* 1995.

Field, Ted. Producer. *ed.* U. of Chicago, Pomona College. Originally co-owner of Field Enterprises of Chicago; later founder of Interscope Communications, production company for theater and TV films. Best known for producing star vehicle comedies and dramas.

FILMS INCLUDE: *Revenge of the Nerds* 1984; *Turk 182* 1985; *Critical Condition, Outrageous Fortune, Three Men and a Baby* 1987; *The Seventh Sign, Cocktail* 1988; *Bill and Ted's Excellent Adventure* (exec. prod.), *An Innocent Man* 1989; *The First Power* (exec. prod.), *Bird on a Wire, Three Men and a Little Lady* 1990; *Paradise* 1991; *The Hand That Rocks the Cradle, The Cutting Edge, FernGully. . . The Last Rainforest, Out on a Limb* 1992; *The Air Up There* 1994; *Operation Dumbo Drop, The Tie That Binds* 1995; *The Associate* 1996.

Fielding, Jerry. Composer. *b.* June 17, 1922, Pittsburgh, Pa. *d.* 1980. *ed.* Carnegie Tech. He scored many films and TV series, beginning in the early 60s.

FILMS INCLUDE: *Advise and Consent* 1962; *McHale's Navy* 1964; *The Wild Bunch* 1969; *Johnny Got His Gun, Lawman, Straw Dogs* (UK) 1971; *Junior Bonner, The Mechanic* 1972; *Scorpio* 1973; *The Outfit, The Super Cops, The Gambler* 1974; *The Killer Elite, The Black Bird* 1975; *The Bad News Bears, The Enforcer* 1976; *Demon Seed, Semi-Tough, The Gauntlet* 1977; *Gray Lady Down, The Big Sleep* (UK) 1978; *Beyond the Poseidon Adventure* 1979; *Funeral Home* (Can.) 1982.

field of view. Area covered by the camera lens at a particular instant. See also ANGLE, CAMERA.

Fields, Dorothy. Songwriter, librettist. *b.* July 15, 1905, Allenhurst, N.J. *d.* 1974. The daughter of comedian Lew FIELDS of Weber and Fields fame, and younger sister of playwrights-screenwriters Herbert and Joseph FIELDS, she began a highly successful career as a Broadway lyricist in 1928 and in the subsequent four decades wrote hundreds of songs for stage and screen musicals, often in collaboration with composer Jimmy McHugh. She won an Academy Award for the song 'The Way You Look Tonight' in the Astaire-Rogers film *Swing Time* (1936). She also wrote the books, usually in collaboration with brother Herbert, for several Broadway musical hits that were later brought to the screen, including 'Let's Face It,' 'Something for the Boys' 'Mexican Hayride,' 'Annie Get Your Gun,' and 'Up in Central Park.' She appeared as herself in the film *Stage Door Canteen* (1943).

FILMS INCLUDE: *The Time the Place and the Girl* 1929; *Love in the Rough* 1930; *Dance Fools Dance, Cuban Love Song* 1931; *Meet the Baron, Dancing Lady* 1933; *Roberta* ('Lovely to Look At,' etc.), *Hooray for Love, Every Night at Eight* ('I'm in the Mood for Love,' etc.), *I Dream Too Much, In Person* 1935; *The King Steps Out, Swing Time* ('The Way You Look Tonight,' etc.) 1936; *When You're in Love* 1937; *The Joy of Living* ('You Couldn't Be Cuter,' etc.; also co-story) 1938; *One Night in the Tropics* ('Remind Me,' etc.) 1940; *Father Takes a Wife* (co-sc.) 1941; *Let's Face It* (co-play basis) 1943; *Something for the Boys* (co-play basis) 1944; *Up in Central Park* (co-play basis and songs), *Mexican Hayride* (co-play basis) 1948; *Annie Get Your Gun* (co-play basis) 1950; *Excuse My Dust, Mr. Imperium, Texas Carnival* 1951; *Lovely to Look At, The Farmer Takes a Wife* 1952; *Sweet Charity* 1969.

Fields, Freddie. Producer, agent. Born on July 23, 1923 in Ferndale, N.Y. Founded multinational talent agency, Creative Management Associates, Ltd., in 1961; sold interest in 1975, with agency eventually becoming known as International Creative Management. From 1977 to 1983, he produced films for Paramount; from 1983 to 1985, he was president of MGM Film Co., and since then has been an independent producer for MGM/UA. As a producer, he is best known for successful commercial enterprises, including *Looking for Mr. Goodbar* and *Glory*. As agent, he has represented many of Hollywood's major stars, including Paul Newman and Barbra Streisand.

FILMS INCLUDE: *Lipstick* 1976; *Citizens Band/Handle with Care, Looking for Mr. Goodbar* 1977; *American Gigolo, Wholly Moses* 1980; *Victory* 1981; *Fever Pitch* 1985; *Poltergeist II, Crimes of the Heart* 1986; *Millenium, Glory* 1989.

Fields, Dame Gracie. Actress, singer. *b.* Grace Stansfield, Jan. 9, 1898, Rochdale, England. *d.* 1979. A music hall entertainer from the age of 13, she soared to unprecedented popularity in the early 30s on the stage and in films, both as a comedienne and as a singer. The spirited, undaunted personality she portrayed in her broad screen comedies helped spark optimism into the lives of British audiences during the Depression years. She was the top box-office draw and the highest paid actress in Britain for most of the decade. Her popularity was so great that Parliament was once adjourned early so that members could go home to listen to one of her radio broadcasts. Her Lancashire accent and style of humor were typically British, however (she was once described as England's counterpart of America's Will Rogers), and failed to ignite enthusiasm in American audiences, even when she appeared in three especially made-for-Hollywood films in the late 30s.

In 1940 she joined her second husband, actor-director Monty Banks, in his exile in America (having been born in Italy, he was declared an alien by British authorities when Italy joined WW II on the Axis side). In Hollywood she fared better with American audiences in two successful films in which she co-starred with Monty Woolley, *Holy Matrimony* and *Molly and Me*. She played a character part in *Paris Underground* before retiring from the screen. From the early 50s she lived in semi-retirement on Capri with her third husband. She was created Dame Commander of the Order of the British Empire in 1979.

FILMS: In the UK—*Sally in Our Alley* 1931; *Looking on the Bright Side* 1932; *This Week of Grace* 1933; *Love Life and Laughter, Sing As We Go* 1934; *Look Up and Laugh* 1935; *Queen of Hearts* 1936; *The Show Goes On* 1937; *We're Going to Be Rich* (UK/US), *Keep Smiling/Smiling Along* (UK/US) 1938; *Shipyard Sally* (UK/US) 1939. In the US—*Stage Door Canteen* (cameo), *Holy Matrimony* 1943; *Molly and Me, Paris Underground* 1945.

Fields, Herbert. Playwright, screenwriter. *b.* July 26, 1897, New York City. *d.* 1958. Son of comedian Lew Fields. Brother of Dorothy and Joseph Fields. A graduate of Columbia, he began as an actor, appearing in several plays and in the film *The Porcelain Lamp* (1921). He later directed and choreographed a number of Broadway productions, turning playwright in 1925. He authored many plays and librettos for stage musicals, sometimes in collaboration with his sister Dorothy. His stage works include 'Dearest Enemy' (1925), 'Hit the Deck!' (1927), 'A Connecticut Yankee' (1927), 'Fifty Million Frenchmen' (1929), 'The New Yorkers' (1930), 'Pardon My English' (1932), 'Panama Hattie' (1940), 'Let's Face It' (1941), 'Something for the Boys' (1943), 'Mexican Hayride' (1944), 'Annie Get Your Gun' (1946), 'Up in Central Park' (1947), and 'Redhead' (1959). He spent much of the 30s in Hollywood writing scripts for films, alone or in collaboration.

FILMS INCLUDE: *The Melody Man* (co-play basis only), *Leathernecking* (co-play basis only, 'Present Arms') 1930; *The Hot Heiress* 1931; *Let's Fall in Love* (also story), *Down to Their Last Yacht* (also co-story) 1934; *Mississippi, People Will Talk, Hands Across the Table* 1935; *Love Before Breakfast, The Luckiest Girl in the World* 1936; *Fools for Scandal, The Joy of Living* (co-story only) 1938; *Honolulu* (also co-story) 1939; *Father Takes a Wife* 1941; *Panama Hattie* (co-play basis only) 1942; *Let's Face It* (co-play basis only), *Du Barry Was a Lady* (co-play basis only) 1944; *Up in Central Park* (co-play basis only) 1948; *Slightly French* (story only) 1949; *Annie Get Your Gun* (co-play basis only) 1950; *Hit the Deck!* (play basis only) 1955.

Fields, Joseph. Playwright, screenwriter. *b.* Feb. 21, 1895, New York City. *d.* 1966. Son of comedian Lew Fields; brother of Dorothy and Herbert Fields. A graduate of NYU, he served with the American Expeditionary Forces in Europe during WW I and remained in Paris for four years after the Armistice. Returning to the US, he began writing articles and stories for magazines. Later wrote material for Ziegfeld shows and in the early 30s settled in Hollywood, where he collaborated on the stories and screenplays of many films, mainly light fare. One of his regular script collaborators was Jerome Chodorov, with whom he later wrote a number of successful Broadway comedies and musicals, including 'My Sister Eileen' (1940) and its musical version, 'Wonderful Town' (1953); 'Junior Miss' (1951); 'Anniversary Waltz' (1954); and 'The Ponder Heart' (1956). He also collaborated with Anita Loos on the hit musical 'Gentlemen Prefer Blondes' (1949), with Peter de Vries on 'The Tunnel of Love' (1957), and with Joshua Logan on 'Flower Drum Song' (1958), and directed a number of Broadway plays.

FILMS INCLUDE: *The Big Shot* 1931; *Pick Up* 1933; *Lightning Strikes Twice* 1934; *Annie Oakley* (co-story only), *$1,000 a Minute* 1935; *The Walking Dead* (co-story only), *Grand Jury* 1936; *When Love Is Young, Reported Missing* 1937; *Fools for Scandal, Rich Man Poor Girl* 1938; *The Girl from Mexico, The Spellbinder* 1939; *Mexican Spitfire* (also story), *Two Girls on Broadway, Dulcy* 1940; *Louisiana Purchase, My Sister Eileen* (from own co-play) 1942; *The Doughgirls* (play basis only) 1944; *Junior Miss* (co-play basis only) 1945; *A Night in Casablanca* 1946; *Lost Honeymoon* 1947; *Man from Texas* (also prod.) 1948; *The Farmer Takes a Wife, Gentlemen Prefer Blondes* (co-play basis only) 1953; *The Tunnel of Love* (from own co-play; also co-prod.) 1958; *Happy Anniversary* (from own co-play) 1959; *Flower Drum Song* (from own co-play; also co-exec. prod.) 1961.

Fields, Lew. Comic actor. *b.* Lewis Maurice Fields, 1867, New York City. *d.* 1941. Vaudeville, burlesque, stage, and screen comedian. Achieved popularity as partner with Joe WEBER in the Weber and Fields comedy team. The duo appeared in a scattered assortment of short and feature silent and sound films. Lew Fields was the father of lyricist Dorothy FIELDS and dramatists-screenwriters Herbert and Joseph FIELDS.

FILMS INCLUDE (with partner Joe Weber unless otherwise indicated): *Old Dutch* (Fields alone), *Two of the Bravest, The Best of Enemies, Fatty and the Broadway Stars* 1915; *The Worst of Friends* 1916; *The Corner Grocer* 1918; *Friendly Enemies* 1925; *Mike and Meyer* 1927; *23 Skidoo* (Fields alone), *The Duel* (Fields alone) 1930; *Blossoms on Broadway* 1937; *The Story of Vernon and Irene Castle* (Fields alone) 1939; *Lillian Russell* 1940.

Fields, W. C. Actor, screenwriter. *b.* William Claude Dukenfield, Feb. 10, 1879, Philadelphia. *d.* 1946. The son of a cockney immigrant who barely made ends meet by selling fruit and vegetables from a pushcart, he ran away from home at age 11 after a violent fight with his father. The homeless boy was frequently beaten in street brawls—one of which, according to Fields himself, resulted in his grotesquely bulbous nose—and spent many a night in jail. Years later, these bitter childhood experiences manifested themselves in the skepticism and misanthropy that characterized Fields's personality on- and off-screen.

From the age of nine Fields practiced juggling, believing he would one day become the world's greatest juggler. Strangely enough, it was this unlikely skill that started him on the road to success. At 14 he was hired as a juggler at an amusement park, the first step in a comedian-stuntman's career that saw him become a vaudeville headliner before he reached 20. In 1901 he went on a European tour, received top billing at the London Palace and the Paris Folies-Bergère, and gave a command performance at Buckingham Palace. In 1905 he appeared in his first Broadway play 'The Ham Tree,' and in 1915 made his film debut, an isolated screen appearance in a short called *Pool Sharks,* in which he gave a comical demonstration of his skill in billiards. He wasn't to make another film for a decade.

Meanwhile, Fields consolidated his position as a stage star, appearing in every version of the 'Ziegfeld Follies' from 1915 to 1921, as well as in 'George White's Scandals.' In 1923 he scored a personal triumph as the star of the hit Broadway musical comedy 'Poppy.' Two years later he appeared in the film adaptation of the play, now retitled *Sally of the Sawdust,* which was directed by D. W. Griffith. Subsequently, Fields appeared with varying success in a number of other silent films but really came into his own as a screen comedy star with the advent of sound, when his inimitable raspy voice could provide the final touch to his comic characterizations. Although he is best remembered for his many comedy roles, Fields gave one of his best characterizations in his only serious role, as Micawber in *David Copperfield* (1935). Fields's screen personality was now unlike any other film comedian's. His style was verbal rather than visual, and his philosophy represented a refreshing antithesis to prevailing moral attitudes.

On screen as off, Fields mistrusted all authority. He demonstrated flagrant contempt for the institution of the family and a deep suspicion of his fellow men. The attitudes he expressed in films were part of his off-screen personality as well, a bitter heritage of his lean years. His distrust of banks and bankers led him to deposit his savings in small amounts in almost every city and town in which he played or visited. At one point, he reportedly had as many as 700 savings accounts, under a variety of fictitious names, spread out all over the world.

Fields wrote the screenplays for many of his films, using such offbeat pseudonyms as Otis J. Criblecoblis and Mahatma Kane Jeeves. Thus his personal gripes and prejudices could be incorporated into his films to the point that it has become difficult to draw the line between his private and screen personalities. A braggart, a con man, a henpecked misogynist, a habitual drunk, and a confirmed misanthrope, Fields was not exactly a lovable figure. But audiences, particularly males, soon discovered that they shared many of his troubles and gripes, and his popularity grew to the proportions of a personality cult 20 years after his death. Fields was portrayed by Rod Steiger in the film biography *W. C. Fields and Me* (1976).

FILMS: *Pool Sharks* (short) 1915; *Janice Meredith* 1924; *Sally of the Sawdust* 1925; *That Royle Girl, It's the Old Army Game, So's Your Old Man* 1926; *The Potters, Running Wild, Two Flaming Youths* 1927; *Tillie's Punctured Romance, Fools for Luck* 1928; *The Golf Specialist* (short) 1930; *Her Majesty Love* 1931; *The Dentist* (short; also sc.), *Million Dollar Legs, If I Had a Million* 1932; *The Fatal Glass of Beer* (also sc.), *The Pharmacist* (short; also sc.), *The Barber Shop* (short; also sc.), *International House, Tillie and Gus, Alice in Wonderland* (as Humpty Dumpty) 1933; *Six of a Kind, You're Telling Me, The Old-Fashioned Way* (also story under pseudonym Charles Bogle), *Mrs. Wiggs of the Cabbage Patch, It's a Gift* (also story under pseudonym Charles Bogle) 1934; *David Copperfield* (as Micawber), *Mississippi, The Man on the Flying Trapeze* (also story under pseudonym Charles Bogle) 1935; *Poppy* 1936; *The Big Broadcast of 1938* 1938; *You Can't Cheat an Honest Man* (also story under pseudonym Charles Bogle) 1939; *My Little Chickadee* (also co-sc. with Mae West), *The Bank Dick* (also sc. under pseudonym Mahatma Kane Jeeves) 1940; *Never Give a Sucker an Even Break* (also story under pseudonym Otis Criblecoblis) 1941; *Tales of Manhattan* (a 20-minute episode that was eliminated from the final release print of the film but can be found in some private collections) 1942; *Follow the Boys* (cameo, in billiard routine), *Song of the Open Road* (as himself), *Sensations of 1945* (cameo) 1944.

Fiennes, Ralph. Actor. *b.* Raph Nathaniel Fiennes, December 22, 1962, in Suffolk, England. *ed.* Chelsea College of Art and Design, London; Royal Academy of Dramatic Art, London. Immensely talented, this tall, powerful actor received his early training at RADA and performed on the stage for England's National Theatre as well as the Royal Shakespeare Company, also working in television. He gained international attention and acclaim for his riveting portrayal of a demented Nazi war commandant in Steven Spielberg's modern masterpiece *Schindler's List* (1993), for which he was nominated for an Academy Award. He wowed Broadway in 1995 with his Tony Award winning performance as 'Hamlet,' and went on to astound critics and audiences with another stunning performance in *The English Patient* (1996), again nominated for the Oscar, this time as best actor.

FILMS: *The Baby of Macon, Schindler's List* 1993; *Quiz Show* 1994; *Strange Days* 1995; *The English Patient* 1996; *Oscar and Lucinda* 1997.

Fierstein, Harvey. Actor, playwright. *b.* June 6, 1954, in

Brooklyn, NY. *ed.* Pratt Institute, NY. Talented, endearingly funny, raspy-voiced character actor of the American stage, television, and screen. One of only a few openly gay performers in the industry, he was once labeled a "gay playwright" because of his Broadway play 'Torch Song Trilogy' (he later adapted it for the screen in 1988), detailing the life and loves of a New York drag queen, for which he earned the Tony Award for best play as well as best actor. He has gone on to further his career as a film actor where his dour but rubber-faced comic talents have lit up a number of major films including the blockbuster hit *Independence Day* (1996).

FILMS: *Garbo Talks, The Times of Harvey Milk* (doc.) 1984; *Torch Song Trilogy* (also co-prod., sc.) 1988; *Mrs. Doubtfire* 1993; *Bullets Over Broadway* 1994; *Dr. Jekyll and Ms. Hyde* 1995; *The Celluloid Closet, Everything's Relative, Independence Day* 1996; *Kull the Conqueror* 1997.

Figgis, Mike. Director. Born in 1949, in Kenya, to British parents who relocated to Newcastle, England, when he was eight. A former jazz musician, he became involved in drama after joining the People Show, an experimental group with which he toured Europe, South America, and the US. After his application to enroll at Britain's National Film School was turned down in 1976, he made a shoestring-budget 16 mm 15-minute short which he used to persuade Channel 4 to bankroll an hour-long film, *The House.* Its success paved the way to feature films and a promising Hollywood career. That career reached new heights with the critical and popular success of *Leaving Las Vegas* (1995), the tragic love story of an alcoholic intent on drinking himself to death and a prostitute dependent upon a life she hates. Figgis received Academy Award nominations for the script, which he adapted from the John O'Brien novel, as well as for directing. An accomplished musician, Figgis composed the music for this and several other of his films.

FEATURE FILMS: *Stormy Monday* (also sc., mus.) 1988; *Internal Affairs* (also co-mus.; US) 1990; *Liebestraum* (also sc.; UK), *Mr. Jones* 1991; *The Browning Version* 1994; *Leaving Las Vegas* 1995; *Foxfire* (co-exec. prod. only) 1996; *One Night Stand* (also co-prod., cameo) 1997.

"Fighting Film Album." See DOCUMENTARY; SOVIET UNION.

Figueroa, Gabriel. Director of photography. Born on Apr. 24, 1907, in Mexico. *d.* 1997. Orphaned in early childhood, he was forced to seek work as a boy, yet was able to pursue painting and still photography on his own. He became associated with a film studio in 1932, and in 1935 he went to Hollywood on its behalf to study motion picture photography as assistant to Gregg TOLAND. Returning to Mexico the following year, he began a prolific career as the cameraman of well over a hundred films, many of which won him international awards. He worked for BUÑUEL and FORD, among others, but his major contribution was on the films of Emilio FERNANDEZ, the dense atmosphere of which owes much to Figueroa's handling of the camera. He ranks among the leading directors of photography in world cinema.

FILMS: *Allá en el Rancho Grande* 1936; *Flor Sylvestre, Maria Candelaria* 1943; *Los Abandonadas, Bugambilla* 1944; *La Perla/The Pearl, Enamorada* 1946; *Rio Escondido/Hidden River* (co-phot.), *The Fugitive* (US/Mex.) 1947; *Tarzan and the Mermaids* (assoc. phot. only; US), *Malcovia, Salón México* 1948; *La Malquerida, Duelo en las Moñtanas* 1949; *The Torch* (US), *Un Dia de Vida, Victimas del Pecado, Los Olvidados/The Young and the Damned* 1950; *Tu y el Mar, Cuando levanta la Niebla, El* 1952; *Flor de Mayo/Beyond All Limits* 1957; *La Cucaracha* 1958; *Nazarin, La Fièvre monte à El Pao/Los Ambiciosos/Republic of Sin* 1959; *Macario, La Estrella Vacia/The Empty Star* 1960; *La Joven/The Young One, Animas Trujano/The Important Man* 1961; *El Angel Exterminador/The Exterminating Angel* 1962; *The Night of the Iguana* (US) 1964; *Simón del Desierto/Simon of the Desert* 1965; *The Big Cube* (US/Mex.) 1969; *Two Mules for Sister Sara* (US/Mex.), *Kelly's Heroes* (US/Yug.) 1970; *La Rosa Blanca* 1972; *Interval* 1973; *La Vida Cambia, Maten al Leon* 1976; *Under the Volcano* (US) 1984.

fill light. A secondary light used in filming to illuminate areas cast in shadow by the key light, thus preventing excessive contrast. Also known as "filler light" or "fill-in light." See also KEY LIGHT.

film, motion picture. A thin, flexible strip of transparent base material, coated with a light-sensitive emulsion on which photographic images are registered in taking motion pictures. The standard format of motion picture film for professional use—35 mm in width and 16 frames per foot, each frame nearly ¾ of an inch in height and each bordered by four perforations per side—was established as early as 1899, the first year of the commercial introduction of cellulose-base film by the Eastman Kodak company, to the specifications of W. K. L. DICKSON of Edison's laboratory. In 1917, these dimensions were officially adopted as industry standards by the Society of Motion Picture Engineers of America. Thirty-five mm film traveled through silent cameras at the rate of 16 frames per second. The standard speed of 35 mm film in sound equipment is 24 frames per second.

The high cost of 35 mm film stock and equipment led to the introduction of so-called "substandard" film sizes for the use of the amateur filmmaker. Of the variety of narrower-gauge films introduced over the years, only 16 mm and 8 mm survived into the 60s. In recent years there has been a noticeable increase in the use of 16 mm film by professional filmmakers, and Super 8 film is rapidly making the 8 mm gauge obsolete. Film gauges of up to 70 mm are used in wide-screen processes.

Prior to 1950 the base material of motion picture film was the highly flammable and perishable cellulose nitrate, which presented a constant hazard of fire in labs, cutting rooms, and theaters. It has since been superseded by a cellulose acetate base, commonly known as safety film.

The raw film stock used in shooting motion pictures produces a negative image in developing. Positive prints are then made of the negative. Reversal film, more common in amateur cinematography, is used in processing to produce a direct positive from the raw stock in the camera. Black-and-white film stock is coated with one layer of emulsion plus antihalation backing to prevent unwanted light reflection. Color film stock requires several layers of emulsion. Film stock must be handled and stored with care because it tends to expand in hot weather and contract in cold, to swell when wet and shrink when dry.

The sound track on 35 mm film appears as a strip along one edge, inside the perforations. It appears on both sides of 70 mm film, producing STEREOPHONIC sound reproduction. With the DOLBY system, stereophonic effects are also possible using standard 35 mm film. In the Dolby SR-D system, an additional DIGITAL SOUND TRACK appears between the film perforations.

Film stocks developed in recent years have allowed greater latitude of exposure within a variety of light conditions. Computer-controlled laboratory processing of film allows for increased creative precision in film development.

film club. Also, "film society." A film-appreciation group dedicated to activities concerning the art and history of the cinema, including discussions and the presentation of old and new films of artistic, historic, or sentimental value. Hundreds of film clubs operate around the world.

Film d'Art. A production company founded in 1908 in Paris for the purpose of bringing high-quality stage presentations to the mass-oriented screen. Sarah BERNHARDT and other notables of the Comédie-Française were engaged to star in a film repertory of classic plays under the direction of the most important stage directors of the day. The unfortunate filmic result was photographed theater, static and uninspired, which virtually halted the development of cinema for several years. But the trend proved beneficial in at least three ways: it brought better-educated audiences to movie theaters and enhanced the medium's prestige. It also had an important impact on the American film industry. In 1912 Adolph ZUKOR acquired the American exhibition rights to the three-to-four-reel Bernhardt film *Queen Elizabeth.* Its success encouraged him to establish his Famous Players in Famous Plays, the American equivalent of the Film d'Art. But most important, it convinced American production companies, which had been turning out single-reel films only, of the commercial viability of feature-length films.

film exchange. See EXCHANGE.

film festival. A program of film exhibitions to showcase new works, often an event that regularly recurs and lasts several days or weeks. Some but not all film festivals are competitive, with awards given. Film festivals can give valuable exposure to new works of high artistic quality, sometimes leading to international distribution for films that could otherwise expect only a limited release. Nearly every major film-producing country has at least one regular film festival to promote its domestic product; in addition, many festivals are international in scope. Annual awards given at prestigious international festivals such as Cannes (established in France in 1939) and Berlin can greatly increase a film's chances on the world market. The top prize at Cannes is the Palme d'Or (Golden Palm); the top prize at Berlin is the Golden Bear.

Some festivals showcase a particular form or genre, such as the Oberhausen (Germany) Short Film Festival and the International Tournée of Animation. Some concentrate on independent films, such as the Sundance Film Festival (US). Other important festivals include the New York Film Festival (sponsored by the Film Society of Lincoln Center), the Los Angeles International Film Festival, the Venice Film Festival, and the London Film Festival.

film library. 1. A collection of films or film clips stored and catalogued for possible future use as STOCK FOOTAGE in production. 2. A rental center for films of interest to schools, institutions, cinema clubs, and individuals. Films may be loaned out free of charge.

filmmaker. One who makes motion pictures, usually a director. The term is characteristically used to describe a person whose involvement in the making of films is creative rather than technical or business-oriented.

film noir. A term coined by French critics to describe a type of film that is characterized by its dark, somber tone and cynical, pessimistic mood. Literally meaning "dark (or "black") film," the term is derived from *roman noir,* "black novel," which was used by French critics of the 18th and 19th centuries to describe the British gothic novel. Specifically, *film noir* was coined to describe those Hollywood films of the 40s and early 50s which portrayed the dark and gloomy underworld of crime and corruption, films whose heroes as well as villains are cynical, disillusioned, and often insecure loners, inextricably bound to the past and unsure or apathetic about the future. In terms of style and technique, the *film noir* characteristically abounds with night scenes, both interior and exterior, with sets that suggest dingy realism, and with lighting that emphasizes deep shadows and accents the mood of fatalism. The dark tones and the tense nervousness are further enhanced by the oblique choreography of the action and the doom-laden compositions and camera angles.

Hollywood productions of the *film noir* style include John Huston's *The Maltese Falcon* (1941), *Key Largo* (1948), and *The Asphalt Jungle* (1950); Howard Hawks's *To Have and Have Not* (1944) and *The Big Sleep* (1946); Michael Curtiz's *Casablanca* (1942) and *Mildred Pierce* (1945); Tay Garnett's *The Postman Always Rings Twice* (1946); Billy Wilder's *Double Indemnity* (1944), *The Lost Weekend* (1945), *Sunset Boulevard* (1950), and *Ace in the Hole/The Big Carnival* (1951); Orson Welles's *The Lady from Shanghai* (1948); Otto Preminger's *Laura* (1944), *Fallen Angel* (1946), and *Where the Sidewalk Ends* (1950); Robert Siodmak's *Phantom Lady* (1944), *The Suspect* (1945), *Uncle Harry* (1945), *The Killers* (1946), *The Dark Mirror* (1946), and *Cry of the City* (1948); Jacques Tourneur's *Out of the Past* (1947); Charles Vidor's *Gilda* (1946); George Cukor's *Gaslight* (1944); Frank Tuttle's *This Gun for Hire* (1942); Fritz Lang's *The Woman in the Window* (1944), *Scarlet Street* (1945), and *The Big Heat* (1953); John Brahm's *The Lodger* (1944) and *Hangover Square* (1945); Alfred Hitchcock's *Spellbound* (1945); Lewis Milestone's *The Strange Love of Martha Ivers* (1946); Edward Dmytryk's *Murder My Sweet* (1944) and *Cornered* (1945); André De Toth's *Dark Waters* (1944) and *Pitfall* (1948); Stuart Heisler's *The Glass Key* (1942); Jean Negulesco's *The Mask of Dimitrios* (1944), *Three Strangers* (1946), *Nobody Lives Forever* (1946), and *Road House* (1948); Anthony Mann's *T-Men* (1948), *Raw Deal* (1948), and *Side Street* (1950); Fred Zinnemann's *Act of Violence* (1949); Rudolph Maté's *The Dark Past* (1948), *D.O.A.* (1950), and *Union Station* (1950); Henry Hathaway's *Kiss of Death* (1947) and *Call Northside 777* (1948); Robert Rossen's *Johnny O'Clock* (1947) and *Body and Soul* (1947); Abraham Polonsky's *Force of Evil* (1948); John Cromwell's *Dead Reckoning* (1947) and *The Racket* (1951); Robert Montgomery's *Lady in the Lake* (1947) and *Ride the Pink Horse* (1947); Delmer Daves's *Dark Passage* (1947); Robert Wise's *The Set-Up* (1949) and *The Captive City* (1952); Jules Dassin's *Brute Force* (1947), *The Naked City* (1948), *Thieves' Highway* (1949), and *Night and the City* (1950); John Farrow's *The Big Clock* (1948) and *Alias Nick Beal* (1949); Elia Kazan's *Boomerang* (1947) and *Panic in the Streets* (1950); Edgar G. Ulmer's *Ruthless* (1948); Joseph H. Lewis's *The Undercover Man* (1949) and *Gun Crazy* (1950); Nicholas Ray's *They Live by Night* (1949), *In a Lonely Place* (1950), and *On Dangerous Ground* (1952); Phil Karlson's *Scandal Sheet* (1952), *99 River Street* (1953), and *Tight Spot* (1955); Samuel Fuller's *Pickup on South Street* (1953); and Robert Aldrich's *Kiss Me Deadly* (1955).

The *film noir* trend, which had been influenced by a combination of factors, including an influx of immigrant directors from central Europe and the sobering effects of WW II and its aftermath, had all but run itself out by the mid-50s. But isolated films in the style have continued to be made in Hollywood, among them Welles's *Touch of Evil* (1958); Don Siegel's *Crime in the Streets* (1956), *Baby Face Nelson* (1957), *Madigan* (1968), and *Dirty Harry* (1971); Roger Corman's *The St. Valentine's Day Massacre* (1967); Peter Yates's *Bullitt* (1968); Robert Altman's *The Long Goodbye* (1973); Roman Polanski's *Chinatown* (1974); Robert Benton's *The Late Show* (1977); Lawrence Kasdan's *Body Heat* (1981); Ridley Scott's *Blade Runner* (1982); Richard Tuggle's *Tightrope* (1984); Alan

Rudolph's *Trouble in Mind* (1985); and Stephen Frears's *The Grifters* (1990).

The term *film noir* was also applied to certain French films of WW II and the postwar years and later to films of the New Wave which were influenced by the Hollywood crime movies. In its broader sense, the term has been used retroactively to describe expressionist German films of the 20s and Hollywood's gangster picture cycle of the 30s.

filmography. A list of the film work, usually in chronological order, of a particular director, writer, cameraman, actor, or anyone else connected with films. The term is borrowed from "bibliography," a list of works by an author.

filmology. The study and analysis of the psychological foundations of film aesthetics and their social, moral, and emotional consequences.

film strip. A strip of motion picture carrying a still photograph, or other graphic material, on each of its frames. The effect of projecting a film strip, unlike a motion picture, is not movement but a related series of static shots, usually accompanied by synchronized sound. Film strips have achieved a high degree of sophistication and are widely used as an audiovisual instruction tool and for business and sales presentations.

film theory. See THEORY, FILM.

filter. 1. A colored or neutral plate of gelatin or glass mounted in front of a camera or a film printer lens to modify the tone or the color balance of an image by absorbing part of the light spectrum. 2. In sound recording and reproduction, a device designed to select certain frequencies and reject others.

filter factor. A numerical factor indicating the increase in exposure necessary to compensate for loss of light through absorption when using a FILTER.

Finch, Flora. Actress. *b.* 1869, London. *d.* 1940. In the US from 1909, following a British stage career, she soon became famous as the scrawny, homely screen partner of chubby, ugly John BUNNY, in numerous Vitagraph comedies. They were among the earliest film comedians to be billed by name, and their series were popularly known as "Bunnyfinches" or "Bunnygraphs." After Bunny's death in 1915, Finch's career declined and she then formed the Flora Finch Film Company, through which she turned out crude slapstick comedies. She later played bit parts in feature films until the mid-30s.

FILMS INCLUDE: *Mrs. Jones Entertains, Jones and the Lady Book Agent* 1909; *All on Account of the Milk* 1910; *The New Stenographer, Subduing Mrs. Nag, The Politician's Dream* 1911; *The First Violin, Bunny and the Twins, A Cure for Pokeritis, Bunny's Suicide, Leap Year Proposals, Diamond Cut Diamond, Pandora's Box* 1912; *And His Wife Came Back, There's Music in the Hair, The Autocrat of Flapjack Junction, John Tobin's Sweetheart, Father's Hatband, Bunny's Mistake* 1913; *Love's Old Dream, Father's Flirtation, Bunny Buys a Harem, Polishing Up* 1914; *The Lady of Shallot, How Cissy Made Good, The Starring of Flora Finchurch* 1915; *A Night Out, Prudence the Pirate* 1916; *War Prides* 1917; *The Great Adventure* 1918; *Dawn, Oh Boy! His Better Half, Unwelcome Guest* 1919; *Birthright* 1920; *Lessons in Love* 1921; *Orphans of the Storm, When Knighthood Was in Flower, Man Wanted, Orphan Sally* 1922; *Luck* 1923; *Roulette, Monsieur Beaucaire* 1924; *The Adventurous Sex, Men and Women, The Wrongdoers* 1925; *Lover's Island, Fifth Avenue, The Brown Derby, Oh Baby!, A Kiss for Cinderella* 1926; *Captain Salvation, The Cat and the Canary, Rose of the Golden West, Quality Street* 1927; *The Wife's Relations, Five and Ten Cent Annie, The Haunted House* 1928; *The Faker, Come Across* 1929; *Sweet Kitty Bellairs* 1930; *The Scarlet Letter* 1934; *Show Boat* 1936; *The Women* 1939.

Finch, Jon. Actor. Born on Mar. 2, 1941, in Caterham, England. Leading man of British films, following seven years of experience in rep. He played the title role in Roman Polanski's controversial screen adaptation of *Macbeth* (1971).

FILMS INCLUDE: *The Vampire Lovers* 1970; *Sunday Bloody Sunday, Macbeth* (title role; UK/US) 1971; *Frenzy, Lady Caroline Lamb* (as William Lamb) 1972; *The Final Programme/Last Days of Man on Earth* 1973; *El Segundo Poder* (Sp.) 1977; *Death on the Nile* 1978; *The Sabina* (Sw./Sp.) 1979; *Giro City/And Nothing but the Truth* 1982; *Pop Pirates, Witching Time* 1984; *Game of Seduction* (Fr.) 1986.

Finch, Peter. Actor. *b.* William Mitchell, Sept. 28, 1916, London. *d.* 1977. The son of an Australian physicist and an English housewife who were divorced when he was two, he was raised by relatives in France, India, and from the age of ten in Australia. After drifting through a variety of jobs during the Depression, he finally found employment in vaudeville as a comedian's stooge. In 1935 he began acting in the legitimate theater and the following year made his screen debut in the first of several Australian films. He continued acting on the stage as well, forming his own company, and thanks to his good voice, became Australia's leading radio actor. He came to London in 1949 as a protégé of Laurence OLIVIER and immediately showed much promise both on the British stage and in films. Following a period of supporting roles on the screen, he hit his stride in the mid-50s, emerging as one of Britain's leading male stars. A ruggedly handsome man with weather-beaten features projecting intelligence and warmth, he proved himself capable of roles suggesting both strength and subtlety. He won the British Film Academy (BFA) best actor award several times, for his performances in *A Town Like Alice* (1956), *The Trials of Oscar Wilde* (1960), *No Love for Johnnie* (1961), and *Sunday Bloody Sunday* (1971). He was nominated for an Oscar for his sensitive portrayal of a homosexual doctor in the latter film and won Hollywood's Academy Award posthumously, and yet another BFA Award, for his rousing performance in the role of a demented newscaster in *Network* (1976). He died of a massive heart attack during a promotional campaign for *Network.* Finch also wrote, produced, and directed a short, *The Day* (1960).

FEATURE FILMS: In Australia—*The Magic Shoes* (unreleased) 1935; *Dad and Dave Come to Town/The Rudd Family Goes to Town* 1938; *Mr. Chedworth Steps Out, Ants in His Pants* 1939; *The Power and the Glory* 1941; *Rats of Tobruk* 1944; *Red Sky at Morning/Escape at Dawn* 1945; *A Son Is Born* 1946. In UK—*Eureka Stockade/Massacre Hill* (shot partly in Australia), *Train of Events* 1949; *The Wooden Horse, The Miniver Story* 1950; *The Story of Robin Hood* (as the Sheriff of Nottingham) 1952; *The Story of Gilbert and Sullivan/The Great Gilbert and Sullivan, The Heart of the Matter* 1953; *Elephant Walk* (US), *Father Brown/The Detective* 1954; *Make Me an Offer, The Dark Avenger/The Warriors, Passage Home, Josephine and Men, Simon and Laura* 1955; *A Town Like Alice, The Battle of the River Plate/Pursuit of the Graf Spee* 1956; *The Shiralee, Robbery Under Arms* 1957; *Windom's Way* 1958; *Operation Amsterdam, The Nun's Story* (US) 1959; *Kidnapped, The Trials of Oscar Wilde* (as Wilde) 1960; *The Sins of Rachel Cade* (US), *No Love for Johnnie* 1961; *I Thank a Fool* 1962; *In the Cool of the Day* (US) 1963; *Girl with Green Eyes, First Men in the Moon, The Pumpkin Eater* 1964; *Judith* (US/UK/Isr.) 1965; *The Flight of the Phoenix* (US), *10:30 P.M. Summer* (US/Sp.) 1966; *Far from the Madding Crowd* 1967; *The Legend of Lylah Clare* (US) 1968; *Krasnaya Palatka/The Red Tent* (It./USSR), *Sunday Bloody Sunday*

1971; *Something to Hide* 1972; *Lost Horizon* (US), *England Made Me, A Bequest to the Nation/The Nelson Affair* (as Lord Nelson) 1973; *The Abdication* 1974; *Network* 1976; *Raid on Entebbe* (TV movie, shown theatrically abroad; as Israel's Prime Minister Yitzhak Rabin) 1977.

finder. See VIEWFINDER.

Fine, Larry. See STOOGES, THE THREE.

fine cut. A refined version of the editor's WORK PRINT which marks a substantial improvement over the ROUGH CUT and approximates the final version of the film in continuity and length.

fine grain. Film stock in which the active chemicals in the emulsion consist of grains smaller than normal and which therefore produces a finer granular texture when developed. Fine-grain film is used mainly for duplicating work, in the preparation of a DUPE NEGATIVE, where sharp detail rather than emulsion speed is of the essence.

Finkel, Abem. Screenwriter. *b.* Dec. 6, 1889, New York City. *d.* 1948. *ed.* CCNY. A former stage manager, he collaborated on the screenplays of Warner Bros. films of the 30s and early 40s.

FILMS INCLUDE: *The Deceiver* 1931; *Hi Nellie* 1934; *Black Fury, Special Agent* 1935; *Black Legion, Marked Woman* 1937; *Jezebel, White Banners* 1938; *Sergeant York* 1941; *Tonight and Every Night* 1945; *Time Out of Mind* 1947.

Finklehoffe, Fred F. Screenwriter, playwright. *b.* Feb. 16, 1910, Springfield, Mass. *d.* 1977. *ed.* VMI; Yale (law). The co-author of 'Brother Rat' and producer of several other Broadway plays, he collaborated on the screenplays of Hollywood films of the 40s and early 50s, occasionally also producing. His first wife (1942–54) was the late singer-actress Ella Logan.

FILMS (alone or in collaboration) INCLUDE: *Brother Rat* (co-play basis only) 1938; *Brother Rat and a Baby, Strike Up the Band* 1940; *Babes on Broadway* (also story), *For Me and My Gal* 1942; *Best Foot Forward, Girl Crazy* 1943; *Meet Me in St. Louis* 1944; *Mr. Ace* (also story, co-songs) 1946; *The Egg and I* (also prod.) 1947; *Words and Music* 1948; *At War with the Army* (also prod.) 1951; *The Stooge* (also co-story) 1953.

Finland. Existing for generations under the political dominance of Russia and in the cultural shadow of Sweden, this Scandinavian country has been slow in developing its film industry, as it has been with other areas of culture and economy. Film production until the end of WW I consisted mostly of routine documentaries and occasional short fiction films. Lacking the opportunity to develop their craft in their native country, such Finnish-born directors as Mauritz STILLER and Gustaf MOLANDER rose to prominence in neighboring Sweden. The foundation for regular feature production in Finland was laid in 1919 when stage actors Erkki Karu and Teuvo Puro formed Suomi Film, through which they directed and produced a number of films of acceptable quality. Their frequent star was Ruth Svellmann, daughter of composer Jan Sibelius. The advent of sound was detrimental to the native film industry because of the unique position of Finnish in the language family (Finnish is unrelated to the Indo-European languages prevailing in Europe and the Americas).

The situation improved somewhat in the mid-30s when several companies pooled their resources, and production reached an average of a dozen feature films a year. Some of these, such as Nyrki Tapiovaara's *Juha* (1935), met high international standards. Other leading directors of the period included Risto Orko and Valentin Vaala. Finnish cinema reached a pinnacle both quantitatively and qualitatively in the early 50s with such internationally successful films as Erik Blomberg's *The White Reindeer* (1952) and Edvin Laine's *The Unknown Soldier* (1955). The end of the decade saw an artistic and economic decline, but the situation improved in the 60s, particularly after the return of director Jörn DONNER from Sweden in 1967. Donner established his own production company, which soon produced several successful films, including his own *Black on White* (1968) and *Portraits of Women* (1970), and *Fuck Off!—Images from Finland* (1971). In an effort to promote the production of films, the government helped establish the Finnish Film Foundation in 1969, but in the early 70s the Finnish film industry produced only a handful of films annually. Production has since increased, but in recent years theater admissions have been in decline. A planned merger between Finnkino (the largest Finnish motion picture company) and Danish Nordisk, which would have put Finnkino on a stronger financial footing, fell through in 1992.

Major Finnish directors in recent years have included Pertti Pasanen, Aki and Mika Kaurismaki, Matti Kassila, and Rauni Mollberg. Finnish-born Renny HARLIN emigrated to Hollywood to become a major director of American action films.

Finlay, Frank. Actor. Born on Aug. 6, 1926, in Farnworth, England. *ed.* RADA. Primarily a stage player, he has been impressive in his many film appearances since the early 60s. He was nominated for an Oscar for his performance as Iago in the film version of the National Theatre of Great Britain production of *Othello* (1965), co-starring Laurence Olivier in the title role.

FILMS INCLUDE: *The Loneliness of the Long Distance Runner, Life for Ruth/Walk in the Shadow* 1962; *Doctor in Distress, The Informers/Underworld Informers* 1963; *Hot Enough for June/Agent 8¾* 1964; *A Study in Terror* (as Inspector Lestrade), *Othello* (as Iago) 1965; *The Deadly Bees, The Jokers, Robbery* 1967; *Inspector Clouseau, The Shoes of the Fisherman* (US), *Twisted Nerve* 1968; *The Molly Maguires* (US), *Cromwell* 1970; *Assault/The Devil's Garden* 1971; *Gumshoe, Sitting Target* 1972; *Shaft in Africa* (US) 1973; *The Three Musketeers* (as Porthos) 1974; *The Four Musketeers* (as Porthos) 1975; *Murder by Decree* 1979; *The Return of the Soldier* 1981; *Enigma* 1982; *The Ploughman's Lunch* 1983; *1919* 1984; *Restless Natives* (voice of Freud), *Lifeforce* 1985; *Cthulhu Mansion* 1991; *Sparrow* 1993.

Finlayson, James (Jimmy). Actor. *b.* Aug. 27, 1887, Falkirk, Scotland. *d.* 1953. He was sent to Edinburgh by his well-to-do parents to study at the university but instead was drawn to the stage. He appeared in several plays in Scotland, then won a part in a play touring the US. When the troupe stopped in Los Angeles in 1916, Finlayson decided to stay and try his luck in films. After appearing briefly in Ince and L-KO comedies, he became a regular player with Mack SENNETT in feature-length comedies of the early 20s. In 1923 he joined Hal Roach, for whom he played leads and supporting parts in numerous comedies. Bald and mustached, with a noticeable squint and a special knack for effective double takes, he is best remembered as an explosive catalyst in Laurel and Hardy films from the late 20s. Continued appearing in films through the early 50s.

FILMS INCLUDE: *Married Life* 1920; *A Small Town Idol, Home Talent* 1921; *The Crossroads of New York, Homemade Movies* 1922; *Welcome Home* 1925; *Do Detectives Think?, Flying Elephants, Sugar Daddies, No Man's Law, The Second Hundred Years* 1927; *Ladies' Night in a Turkish Bath, Bachelor's Paradise, Lady Be Good, Show Girl* 1928; *Liberty, Two Weeks Off, Big Business, Men o' War, Hoosegow, Hard to*

Get, Wall Street 1929; *Chickens Come Home, Young Eagles, For The Defense, The Dawn Patrol* 1930; *Our Wife, Pardon Us* 1931; *The Chimp, Pack Up Your Troubles* 1932; *Fra Diavolo/The Devil's Brother* 1933; *Bonnie Scotland* 1935; *The Bohemian Girl, Our Relations* 1936; *Way Out West, Pick a Star* 1937; *Block-Heads* 1938; *Hollywood Cavalcade, The Flying Deuces, The Great Victor Herbert* 1939; *A Chump at Oxford, Saps at Sea* 1940; *To Be or Not to Be* 1942; *The Perils of Pauline* 1947; *Royal Wedding* 1951.

Finney, Albert. Actor Born on May 9, 1936, in Salford, England, the son of a bookie. He trained for the stage at the Royal Academy of Dramatic Art and made his debut in 1956 with the Birmingham Repertory Theatre. During the late 50s he appeared almost exclusively in Shakespearean roles. But in 1960 he burst forth as a dynamic personification of rebellious youth in 'Billy Liar' on the London stage and in Karel Reisz's film *Saturday Night and Sunday Morning.* He rapidly rose in prominence in plays and films written by John OSBORNE and directed by Tony RICHARDSON. In 1961 he received the best actor award at the Théatre des Nations international festival in Paris for his performance in 'Luther,' a play he subsequently brought to Broadway, and in 1963 he soared to international popularity with his boisterous performance in the film *Tom Jones.* He has since been hailed as a "second Olivier" (Sir Laurence himself dubbed him "the best actor of his generation"). In 1965 he formed his own production company, Memorial Enterprises, and in 1967 he directed himself in *Charlie Bubbles.* He was married to actresses Jane Wenham (1957–61) and Anouk AIMÉE (1970–78). He was nominated for Academy Awards for *Tom Jones, Murder on the Orient Express, The Dresser,* and *Under the Volcano.*

FILMS: *The Entertainer, Saturday Night and Sunday Morning* 1960; *Tom Jones* (title role), *The Victors* 1963; *Night Must Fall* (also co-prod.) 1964; *Two for the Road, Charlie Bubbles* (also dir.) 1967; *The Picasso Summer* 1969; *Scrooge* (title role) 1970; *Gumshoe* 1971; *Alpha Beta* 1973; *Murder on the Orient Express* (as detective Hercule Poirot) 1974; *The Duellists* 1977; *Loophole* 1980; *Wolfen* (US), *Looker* (US) 1981; *Shoot the Moon* (US), *Annie* (US) 1982; *The Dresser* 1983; *Under the Volcano* (US) 1984; *Orphans* (US) 1987; *The Endless Game* 1989; *Miller's Crossing* (US) 1990; *The Green Man* 1991; *The Playboys, Rich in Love* 1992; *The Browning Version, A Man of No Importance* 1994; *Run of the Country* 1995; *Washington Square* 1997.

Fiorentino, Linda. Actress. *b.* Clorina Fiorentino, March 9, 1960, in Philadelphia, Pa. *ed.* Rosemont College; Circle in the Square, New York City. Stunning, provocative leading lady who got her start primarily in television until she attracted attention with her performance in the teen film *Vision Quest* (1985). In a succession of films, she has proven her talent for playing the sultry seductress, particularly her wickedly funny turn in John DAHL's *The Last Seduction* (1994).

FILMS: *After Hours, Gotcha!, Vision Quest* 1985; *The Moderns* 1988; *Queens Logic, Shout* 1991; *Beyond the Law, Chain of Desire* 1992; *Acting On Impulse* 1993; *Charlie's Ghost Story, The Desperate Trail, The Last Seduction* 1994; *Jade* 1995; *Larger Than Life, Unforgettable* 1996; *Kicked in the Head,* 1997.

First National. A motion picture production and distribution company formed in 1917 by a group of exhibitors infuriated by the BLOCK-BOOKING practices of Famous Players-Lasky. Rather than be forced to buy a package of routine films in order to get one important production with a name star, like Mary Pickford, the exhibitors, led by J. D. Williams, decided to make their own films and set out to lure stars to the newly formed company. In short order, First National, or First National Exhibitors' Circuit, as it was formally known, signed up stars of the magnitude of Charlie Chaplin and Pickford and became an important factor in the industry. In the late 20s, First National was absorbed by Warner Bros.

first run. The initial showing of a motion picture at select theaters, usually at premium prices, before its release to neighborhood theaters. Auditoriums habitually selected for such showings are known as first-run theaters.

Firth, Colin. Actor. Born on Sept. 10, 1960, in Grayshott, England. Angel-faced leading man of British stage, TV, and films.

FILMS INCLUDE: *Another Country, 1919* 1984; *Restless Natives* 1985; *A Month in the Country* 1987; *Apartment Zero* 1988; *Valmont* (title role; Fr./UK) 1989; *Wings of Fame, The Pleasure Principle, Femme Fatale* 1990; *The Hour of the Pig* 1993; *Circle of Friends* 1995; *The English Patient* 1996; *A Thousand Acres* 1997.

Firth, Peter. Actor. Born on Oct. 27, 1953, in Bradford, England. Boyish, innocent-looking leading man of British stage, TV, and films. On television children's programs from age 15, he rose to prominence in 1953 on the strength of his performance in the National Theatre production of 'Equus.' He earned an Academy Award nomination as supporting actor for the same role in the 1977 screen version.

FILMS INCLUDE: *Brother Sun Sister Moon* (It./UK) 1972; *Diamonds on Wheels* 1973; *Aces High* 1976; *Joseph Andrews* (title role), *Equus* 1977; *When You Comin' Back Red Ryder?* (US), *Tess* (Fr./UK) 1979; *White Elephant* 1984; *Lifeforce, A Letter to Brezhnev* 1985; *A State of Emergency* 1986; *Born of Fire* 1987; *Prisoner of Rio* 1988; *Tree of Hands* 1989; *The Hunt for Red October* 1990; *The Rescuers Down Under* (v/o), *Shadowlands* 1993; *The Advocate* 1994; *An Awfully Big Adventure* 1995; *The English Patient* 1996.

Fischer, Gunnar. Director of photography. Born on Nov. 18, 1910, in Ljungby, Sweden. Entered Swedish films as an assistant cameraman in 1935 and graduated to cinematographer in 1942. Best known for his work for Ingmar BERGMAN on a dozen films through 1960, when they parted ways following a disagreement. His photography is noted for the tonal balance of its black-and-white imagery, and especially the texture of outdoor scenery. He is also a successful illustrator of children's books. His son, Peter Fischer, is also a director of photography.

FILMS INCLUDE: *Night in the Harbor* 1943; *Port of Call* 1948; *Three Strange Loves, To Joy* 1949; *High Tension, Illicit Interlude* 1950; *Secrets of Women, Monika* 1952; *Smiles of a Summer Night* 1955; *The Seventh Seal* 1956; *Wild Strawberries* 1957; *The Magician* 1958; *The Devil's Eye* 1960; *Two Living One Dead, Pleasure Garden* 1961; *Short Is the Summer* 1962; *My Love Is a Rose* 1963; *491* 1964; *Stimulantia* (co-phot.) 1967; *Made in Sweden* 1969; *Miss and Mrs. Sweden* 1970; *The Touch* (credit sequence only) 1971; *Don Juan* 1979.

Fischinger, Oskar. Animator. *b.* June 22, 1900, Gelnhausen, Germany. *d.* 1967. An avant-garde painter, he had begun toying with the idea of creating abstract visual interpretations of poetry and music at the age of 19 and became involved in film animation in the course of diagramming the emotional movements in a Shakespearean play. He made his first animated shorts in 1920 with the help of a wax-cutting machine of his own design. In 1926 he presented the first of a series of "absolute film" shorts, which he named *Study 1, Study 2,* etc. These "studies" gained in impact after the advent of sound, when they could be shown to the accompaniment of classical music and jazz. In 1928 he collaborated with Fritz Lang on the special effects of the German silent feature *Frau* *im Mond/The Woman in the Moon.* In 1933 he began exploring color with a special process he had helped to develop and in 1933 won a prize at the Venice Festival for his *Komposition in Blau/Composition in Blue.* The following year he went to Hollywood, where he made the animated short *Allegretto* to the tune of a jazz theme and worked on the special effects of *The Big Broadcast of 1937* (1936). He later worked with Walt Disney on the Bach "Toccata and Fugue" segment of *Fantasia* (1940), but his designs were considered too abstract and were included in the film in a modified form that he rejected. But he remained in Hollywood, where he continued making experimental shorts and advertising commercials. He won the Grand Prix at the Brussels Exhibition of 1949 for his *Motion Painting No. 1,* in which he used intricate designs and geometric forms to the accompaniment of Bach's Brandenburg Concerto No. 3.

FILMS INCLUDE: *Wax Experiments* 1926; *Orgelstäbe, Seelische Konstruktionen* 1927; *Dein Schicksal* 1928; *Das Hohenlied der Kraft* 1930; *Liebesspiel* 1931; *Kooloraturen* 1932; *Kreise* 1933; *Ein Spiel in Fraben* 1934; *Komposition in Blau/Composition in Blue* 1935; *Allegretto* 1936; *An Optical Poem* 1937; *American March* 1941; *Radio Dynamics* 1942; *Organic Fragment* 1945; *Motion Painting No. 1* 1947.

Fishburne, Laurence. Actor. Born Laurence Fishburne III on July 30, 1961, in Augusta, Ga. Stage-trained leading man and supporting player of American films. Raised in Brooklyn, N.Y, he worked on the daytime television serial "One Life to Live," before making his screen debut at age 12. Later he won a supporting role as a wigged-out soldier in *Apocalypse Now* by lying about his age. Following a series of supporting roles, often cast as heavies, he established himself as a more sympathetic film lead through his role as the principled father in *Boyz N the Hood.* He gained further attention with his riveting, balanced performance as Ike Turner in the Tina Turner biopic *What's Love Got to Do with It.* Awarded Tony for "Two Trains Running."

FILMS INCLUDE: *Cornbread Earl and Me* 1975; *Fast Break, Apocalypse Now* 1979; *Willie and Phil* 1980; *Death Wish II* 1982; *Rumble Fish* 1983; *The Cotton Club* 1984; *The Color Purple* 1985; *Quicksilver* 1986; *A Nightmare on Elm Street 3: Dream Warriors, Gardens of Stone* 1987; *School Daze, Red Heat* 1988; *King of New York* (It.), *Cadence* 1989; *Class Action* 1990; *Boyz N the Hood, Hearts of Darkness: A Filmmaker's Apocalypse* 1991; *Deep Cover* 1992; *What's Love Got to Do with It, Searching for Bobby Fischer* 1993; *Bad Company, The Tool Shed* 1994; *Higher Learning, Just Cause, Othello* 1995; *Fled* 1996; *Hoodlum* 1997.

Fisher, Carrie. Actress. Born on Oct. 21, 1956, in Los Angeles. The daughter of singer Eddie FISHER and actress Debbie REYNOLDS, she began her professional career at 12, performing in her mother's Las Vegas nightclub act. She dropped out of high school at 15 to devote all her time to show business and in 1973 made her Broadway debut in the chorus line of 'Irene,' the nostalgic revival starring her mother. She played her first film role in *Shampoo* (1975), portraying a sexy nymphet who seduces Warren Beatty, and after a year and a half of acting and speech training in London was selected to play the feminine lead, as planet princess Leia Organa, in George Lucas's hit space fantasy film *Star Wars* (1977) and its sequels. Her career nearly derailed in the mid-80s, when she entered a drug rehabilitation center to combat her addiction to cocaine, LSD, and other substances. She emerged from the experience with new insights and a basis for her first novel, *Postcards from the Edge* (1987), a national best-seller. She wrote the screenplay for the film adaptation of the book, in which Shirley MACLAINE and Meryl STREEP portrayed mother-daughter characters patterned after Debbie Reynolds and Carrie Fisher. Her 1990 follow-up best-seller *Surrender the Pink* chronicled her aborted marriage (1982–84) to singer Paul Simon. Her success as a novelist continued with *Delusions of Grandma* in 1993.

FILMS: *Shampoo* 1975; *Star Wars* 1977; *Mr. Mike's Mondo Video* 1979; *The Empire Strikes Back, The Blues Brothers* 1980; *Under the Rainbow* 1981; *Return of the Jedi* 1983; *Garbo Talks* 1984; *The Man with One Red Shoe* 1985; *Hannah and Her Sisters, Hollywood Vice Squad* 1986; *Amazon Women on the Moon* 1987; *Appointment with Death* (UK) 1988; *The 'Burbs, Loverboy, When Harry Met Sally...* 1989; *Postcards from the Edge* (sc. only), *Sibling Rivalry, Sweet Revenge* 1990; *Drop Dead Fred, Soapdish, This is My Life* 1991; *Sister Act* (co-sc., uncredited) 1992; *Star Wars, The Empire Strikes Back, Return of the Jedi* (all re-released special editions) 1997.

Fisher, Eddie. Singer, actor. Born Edwin Jack Fisher, Aug. 10, 1928, in Philadelphia. Teen idol crooner of the 50s who at his peak made the Hit Parade with regularity, starred on his own radio and TV shows, and appeared in three films. Paradoxically, he made bigger headlines at the ebb of his career as the center of a heavily publicized romantic storm when he divorced the popular Debbie REYNOLDS to marry one of the screen's great beauties, Elizabeth TAYLOR, in 1959. He made romantic-triangle news again in 1964 when Miss Taylor dumped him to marry her *Cleopatra* co-star, Richard Burton. Fisher later married and divorced actress-singer Connie STEVENS. He launched a semisuccessful comeback in the late 80s, returning to the nightclub circuit and releasing a critically acclaimed album after an absence of many years. In an unusual publicity stunt, when having a facelift in 1990 he allowed a film crew to interview him before and after, with extensive coverage of the procedure. He is the father of actress Carrie FISHER by Miss Reynolds.

FILMS: *All About Eve* (bit) 1950; *Bundle of Joy* 1956; *Butterfield 8* 1960; *The Bob Hope Vietnam Christmas Show* (made for TV but later shown theatrically) 1966; *Nothing Lasts Forever* 1984.

Fisher, Gerry. Director of photography. Born in 1926, in London. Entered British films in 1946 as a technician and camera assistant. After sharpening his skills as a camera operator on films of the early 60s, he made his debut as a lighting cameraman on Joseph Losey's *Accident* (1967). He was later responsible for the cinematography of many major British and international productions.

FILMS INCLUDE: *Accident, The Mikado* 1967; *Sebastian, Interlude, Secret Ceremony* 1968; *The Seagull, Hamlet, Ned Kelly, Macho Callahan* (US) 1970; *The Go-Between, Blind Terror/See No Evil, All the Right Noises* 1971; *Malpertius* (Belg./Fr.) 1972; *A Bequest to the Nation/The Nelson Affair, The Offence/The Offense, A Doll's House* 1973; *Butley* (UK/US), *S*P*Y*S* (UK/US), *Juggernaut* 1974; *Mr. Klein* (Fr.), *Aces High, The Romantic Englishwoman, The Adventure of Sherlock Holmes' Smarter Brother* (UK/US) 1975; *The Last Remake of Beau Geste* (US), *The Island of Dr. Moreau* (US) 1977; *Les Routes du Sud* (Fr.), *Fedora* (Ger./Fr.) 1978; *Wise Blood* (US/Ger.), *Don Giovanni* (Fr./It./Ger.) 1979; *The Ninth Configuration/Twinkle Twinkle Killer Kane* (US) 1980; *Wolfen* (US) 1981; *Yellowbeard, Lovesick* (US) 1983; *The Holcroft Covenant* 1985; *Highlander* 1986; *Man on Fire* (It./Fr.) 1987; *Running on Empty* 1988; *Dead Bang* 1989.

Fisher, Terence. Director. *b.* Feb. 23, 1904, London. *d.* 1980. Former merchant seaman and department-store window dresser, he entered British films as assistant editor in 1933, rising to film editor three years later. He was 44 by the time he was given his first opportunity to direct at the Rank Organisation in 1948. His early films were typically tender romantic dramas. In 1952, however, he joined the Hammer company and soon began to be identified with that studio's output of low-budget, rapid-schedule horror pictures. His films are noted for their gloss and rich color texture, but most lack the eerie gothic mood and the haunting impact of the American classics of the horror genre of the 30s. Fisher also directed for TV.

FILMS: *Colonel Bogey, To the Public Danger, Portrait from Life/The Girl in the Painting, Song of Tomorrow* 1948; *Marry Me* 1949; *The Astonished Heart, So Long at the Fair* (both co-dir. with Anthony Darnborough) 1950; *Home to Danger* 1951; *A Distant Trumpet, The Last Page, Stolen Face, Wings of Danger* 1952; *Four-Sided Triangle, Mantrap, Spaceways, Blood Orange* 1953; *Final Appointment, Mask of Dust, Face the Music, Children Galore, The Stranger Came Home/The Unholy Four, Murder by Proxy/Blackout* 1954; *Stolen Assignment, The Flaw* 1955; *The Last Man to Hang* 1956; *The Curse of Frankenstein, Kill Me Tomorrow* 1957; *Dracula/Horror of Dracula, The Revenge of Frankenstein* 1958; *The Hound of the Baskervilles, The Mummy, The Man Who Could Cheat Death, The Stranglers of Bombay* 1959; *The Brides of Dracula, The Sword of Sherwood Forest, The Two Faces of Dr. Jekyll/House of Fright/Jekyll's Inferno* 1960; *The Curse of the Werewolf* 1961; *The Phantom of the Opera; Sherlock Holmes und das Halsband des Tudes* (Ger./It./Fr.) 1962; *Sherlock Holmes* 1963; *The Horror of It All, The Earth Dies Screaming, The Gorgon* 1964; *Dracula—Prince of Darkness* 1965; *Island of Terror* 1966; *Frankenstein Created Woman, Night of the Big Heat/Island of the Burning Damned/Island of the Burning Doomed* 1967; *The Devil Rides Out/The Devil's Bride* 1968; *Frankenstein Must Be Destroyed!* 1969; *Frankenstein and the Monster from Hell* 1974.

fisheye lens. An extremely wide-angled lens that creates considerable linear distortion and is particularly effective in fantasy or nightmare sequences.

fishpole. A pole, resembling a fishing rod, at one end of which a microphone is suspended so that it can be positioned over a scene for recording dialogue. A fishpole is often used as a substitute for a MICROPHONE BOOM when the latter may prove too cumbersome to handle—in confined areas, for example.

Fisk, Jack. Director, production designer. Born on Dec. 19, 1934, in Ipava, Ill. *ed.* Cooper Union. He entered films as an art director, designing the sets of many Hollywood films of the 70s. In 1974 he married actress Sissy SPACEK, who would later star in his auspicious debut as a director, *Raggedy Man* (1981).

FILMS INCLUDE: As art director—*Angels Hard as They Come* 1971; *Badlands* 1973; *Phantom of the Paradise* 1974; *Carrie* 1976; *Days of Heaven, Eraserhead, Movie Movie* 1978; *Heart Beat* 1979. As director (complete)—*Raggedy Man* 1981; *Violets Are Blue* 1986; *Daddy's Dyin'. . . Who's Got the Will?* 1990.

Fitzgerald, Barry. Actor. *b.* William Joseph Shields, Mar. 10, 1888, Dublin. *d.* 1961. A veteran of Dublin's famed Abbey Theatre, he made his film debut in Hitchcock's British production of *Juno and the Paycock* (1930). He first came to the US with the Abbey Players in the late 20s and thereafter appeared frequently on Broadway. He was lured to Hollywood in 1936 by John FORD, to repeat his stage role in Sean O'Casey's *The Plough and the Stars,* and remained there as the movie colony's Irishman-in-residence, playing fanciful, heavily accented, ethnic near-caricatures with skill and whimsical charm. A notorious scene stealer, he was among Hollywood's prime character actors and won an Academy Award as best supporting actor for his role as Father Fitzgibbon in Leo McCarey's *Going My Way* (1944). Peculiarly, he was also nominated for the award in the best actor category. He was the brother of actor Arthur Shields (*b.* 1896. *d.* 1970).

FILMS: *Juno and the Paycock* (UK) 1930; *When Knights Were Bold* (UK) 1936; *The Plough and the Stars, Ebb Tide* 1937; *Bringing Up Baby, Marie Antoinette, Four Men and a Prayer, The Dawn Patrol* 1938; *The Saint Strikes Back, Pacific Liner, Full Confession* 1939; *The Long Voyage Home* 1940; *San Francisco Docks, The Sea Wolf, How Green Was My Valley, Tarzan's Secret Treasure* 1941; *The Amazing Mrs. Holliday, Two Tickets to London, Corvette K-225* 1943; *Going My Way, I Love a Soldier, None but the Lonely Heart* 1944; *Incendiary Blonde, Duffy's Tavern, And Then There Were None, The Stork Club* 1945; *Two Years Before the Mast* 1946; *California, Easy Come Easy Go, Welcome Stranger, Variety Girl* 1947; *The Naked City, The Sainted Sisters, Miss Tatlock's Millions* 1948; *Top o' the Morning, The Story of Seabiscuit* 1949; *Union Station* 1950; *Silver City* 1951; *The Quiet Man* 1952; *Happy Ever After/Tonight's the Night* (UK) 1954; *The Catered Affair* 1956; *Rooney* (UK) 1958; *Cradle of Genius* (doc.), *Broth of a Boy* (UK) 1959.

Fitzgerald, Geraldine. Actress. *b.* Nov. 24, 1912, Dublin. The daughter of a prominent attorney (his firm, E & T Fitzgerald, is mentioned in James Joyce's *Ulysses*), she began her acting career at Dublin's Gate Theatre, where she met another aspiring beginner, Orson WELLES. In 1934 she began appearing in low-budget British films. In 1936 she married a horse breeder and in 1938 moved to New York, where Welles gave her her American start in the Mercury Theater production of 'Heartbreak House.' The following year she went to Hollywood, where she played intense, often stern leads in Warner Bros. melodramas of the early 40s. She was nominated for a best supporting actress Oscar in *Wuthering Heights* (1939). Like her close friend Bette Davis, she constantly fought with the studio bosses over more suitable roles. Unlike Davis, she lost the fight, and her promising film career had faded by the end of the decade. She later returned to the screen in occasional character roles. In 1971 she made a triumphant comeback to ecstatic reviews in the Broadway revival of O'Neill's 'Long Day's Journey Into Night.' In 1946 she married wealthy businessman Stuart Scheftel, grandson of the founder of Macy's, who, as a dollar-a-year man, was chairman of New York Mayor John Lindsay's Youth Board. She helped him by forming street-corner theater groups. Her son from her first marriage, Michael Lindsay-Hogg, directed the Beatles film *Let It Be* (1970).

FILMS: In the UK—*Blind Justice, Open All Night* 1934; *The Lad, Ace of Spades, Three Witnesses, Department Store, Lieut. Daring R.N., Turn of the Tide* 1935; *Debt of Honor, Cafe Mascot* 1936; *The Mill on the Floss* 1937. In the US—*Wuthering Heights, Dark Victory* 1939; *A Child Is Born, 'Til We Meet Again* 1940; *Flight from Destiny, Shining Victory* 1941; *The Gay Sisters* 1942; *Watch on the Rhine* 1943; *Ladies Courageous, Wilson* 1944; *Uncle Harry* 1945; *Three Strangers, OSS, Nobody Lives Forever* 1946; *So Evil My Love* (US/UK) 1948; *The Late Edwina Blake/Obsessed* (UK) 1951; *Ten North Frederick* 1958; *The Fiercest Heart* 1961; *The Pawnbroker* 1965; *Rachel Rachel* 1968; *The Last American Hero* 1973; *Harry and Tonto* 1974; *Echoes of a Summer/The Last Castle* 1976; *The Mango Tree* (Austral.) 1977; *Ciao Male/Bye Bye Monkey* 1978; *Tristan and Isolt* (unreleased; Ire.) 1979; *Arthur* 1981; *Blood Link* (It.) 1982; *Easy Money*

1983; *Poltergeist II: The Other Side* 1986; *Arthur 2 on the Rocks* 1988.

Fitzmaurice, George. Director. *b.* Feb. 13, 1895, Paris. *d.* 1941. Emigrated in his early 20s to the US, where, having trained as a painter, he began as a set designer in the theater, then entered films as a screenwriter in 1908. A director from 1914, he demonstrated a certain visual flair in his films of the 20s and early 30s, many of which were commercially successful. Among the stars he directed were Pola Negri in *The Cheat,* Rudolph Valentino in *The Son of the Sheik,* Ronald Colman and Vilma Banky in *Night of Love,* and Greta Garbo in *Mata Hari* and *As You Desire Me.* His forte was the romantic drama. He was married to silent screen actress Diana Kane.

FEATURE FILMS: *When Rome Ruled, The Quest of the Scared Jewel* 1914; *Stop Thief, Who's Who in Society, The Commuters, The Money Master, Via Wireless, At Bay* 1915; *New York, Big Jim Garrity, Arms and the Woman, The Test, The Romantic Journey* 1916; *Kick-In, The On-the-Square Girl, The Hunting of the Hawk, Blind Man's Luck, The Recoil, The Iron Heart, The Mark of Cain, Sylvia of the Secret Service* 1917; *Innocent, The Naulahka, The Hillcrest Mystery, The Narrow Path, The Japanese Nightingale* 1918; *Common Clay, The Witness for the Defense, The Cry of the Weak, Our Better Selves, The Profiteers, The Avalanche, A Society Exile, Counterfeit* 1919; *On with the Dance, The Right to Love, Idols of Clay* 1920; *Paying the Piper* (also prod.), *Experience, Forever/Peter Ibbetson* 1921; *Three Live Ghosts, The Man from Home, To Have and to Hold, Kick In* 1922; *Bella Donna, The Cheat* (also prod.), *The Eternal City* 1923; *Cytherea, Tarnish* 1924; *A Thief in Paradise* (also exec. prod.), *His Supreme Moment, The Dark Angel* 1925; *The Son of the Sheik* 1926; *The Night of Love, The Tender Hour, Rose of the Golden West, The Love Mart* 1927; *Lilac Time, The Barker* 1928; *His Captive Woman, The Man and the Moment, The Locked Door, Tiger Rose* 1929; *The Bad One, Raffles* (co-dir. with Harry D'Abbadie D'Arrast) 1930; *The Devil to Pay, One Heavenly Night, Strangers May Kiss, The Unholy Garden* 1931; *Mata Hari, As You Desire Me* 1932; *All Men Are Enemies* 1934; *Petticoat Fever, Suzy* 1936; *The Last of Mrs. Cheyney* (completed for the deceased Richard Boleslawski; uncredited), *The Emperor's Candlesticks, Live Love and Learn* 1937; *Arsene Lupin Returns, Vacation from Love* 1938; *Adventure in Love* 1940.

Fix, Paul. Actor. *b.* Mar. 13, 1901, Dobbs Ferry, N.Y., the son of a brewer. *d.* 1983. He began his acting career with little theaters and stock companies and arrived in Hollywood in the early 20s. A versatile character actor, he appeared in some 300 films, often in Westerns and crime pictures, playing both villains and good guys. He was also a regular—the sheriff—on the 'Rifleman' TV series (1958–63).

FILMS INCLUDE: *Hoodoo Ranch* 1926; *The First Kiss* 1928; *Lucky Star* 1929; *Ladies Love Brutes* 1930; *The Last Mile, Back Street* 1932; *Zoo in Budapest* 1933; *The World Accuses* 1935; *The Prisoner of Shark Island, The Road to Glory, Winterset, After the Thin Man* 1936; *Souls at Sea* 1937; *Penitentiary* 1938; *Behind Prison Gates* 1939; *Black Friday, The Ghost Breakers, Dr. Cyclops* 1940; *Sherlock Holmes and the Secret Weapon, Pittsburgh* 1942; *Hitler—Dead or Alive* 1943; *The Fighting Seabees, Tall in the Saddle* 1944; *Flame of the Barbary Coast, Back to Bataan* 1945; *Tycoon* 1947; *Red River, Force of Evil* 1948; *Surrender* 1950; *What Price Glory* 1952; *Hondo* 1953; *Johnny Guitar, The High and the Mighty* 1954; *Blood Alley* 1955; *The Bad Seed, Towards the Unknown, Giant* 1956; *Night Passage* 1957; *To Kill a Mockingbird* 1963; *The Outrage* 1964; *Shenandoah, The Sons of Katie Elder* 1965; *Nevada Smith* 1966; *Welcome to Hard Times, El Dorado* 1967; *Day of the Evil Gun* 1968; *Young Billie Young, The Undefeated* 1969; *Zabriskie Point, Dirty Dingus Magee* 1970; *Shoot Out, Something Big* 1971; *Night of the Lepus* 1972; *Pat Garrett and Billy the Kid* 1973; *Grayeagle* 1977; *Wanda Nevada* 1979.

fixed camera. Filming setup in which the camera remains stationary throughout a shot. Opposite of "mobile camera."

fixed-focus lens. A lens that has no provision for focusing and thus remains at a fixed distance from the film plane. Although not very useful for close-up work, in which focusing is critical, a fixed-focus lens can render satisfactory results in filming objects at distances from six feet to infinity thanks to its great depth of field.

flag. A small GOBO, usually a rectangular sheet of black material, mounted on a stand in a studio to direct light away from the camera or to shade a part of the set.

Flaherty, Robert J. Director; "father" of the documentary. *b.* Feb. 16, 1884, Iron Mountain, Mich. *d.* 1951 *ed.* Michigan Coll. of Mines. The son of an iron-miner turned gold-prospector, he spent much of his childhood in remote prospecting camps. From his wanderings and encounters with Indians and other ethnic groups, he developed a passion for exploration. From 1910 to 1916 he carried out a series of expeditions in northern Canada on behalf of Sir William Mackenzie. Much of his exploration was done among the Eskimos around Hudson Bay. On one of these expeditions, in 1913, he took along a motion picture camera, hoping to defray some of the costs by selling a film about Eskimo life. While editing the footage in Toronto, he accidentally dropped a cigarette on the negative, and some 35,000 feet of film went up in flames. He salvaged the work print, however, and showed it to a number of friends, none of whom expressed much enthusiasm for the material.

Realizing that there was more to filmmaking than simply recording unrelated events, Flaherty returned to the Eskimo country in 1920 for the sole purpose of making a film. This time he was well prepared. He had obtained $50,000 in financial backing from Revillon Frères, fur merchants, and was able to take along sophisticated equipment, two cameras, a gasoline generator, lab materials for processing the film on the spot, and a projector, which enabled him to see the daily rushes as he went along. The result was *Nanook of the North,* a remarkable documentary record of the life and struggles of a courageous Eskimo man and his family, and a landmark in film history. What made *Nanook* so remarkable was its success in capturing the essence of primitive man's struggle for survival against the hostile forces of nature. The drama was provided by pitting Nanook as a protagonist against the North, the villain.

US distributors doubted the commercial potential of the film. It was eventually distributed by Pathé in 1922 and was a resounding success, both critically and commercially, all over the world. (A sad, ironic footnote was provided shortly after the film's completion by Nanook's death of starvation.) The film exerted considerable influence on the development of the motion picture documentary in many countries.

Producer Jesse L. LASKY commissioned Flaherty to go to the South Seas to make "another *Nanook.*" Working with an unlimited budget and backed by the facilities of a big commercial studio (Paramount), Flaherty came back after 20 months with a poetic record of Polynesian tribal life. The film was superior to *Nanook* in technique but, despite its great aesthetic beauty, far less truthful and consequently less powerful. It did poorly at the box office. By now, however, Flaherty was considered an expert on the exotic, and was assigned by MGM to co-direct (with Willard S. Van Dyke) a dramatic feature film, *White Shadows of the South Seas.* But Flaherty didn't care much for working with stars and had frequent disagreements with his collaborator over content and approach. He left production before the film's completion.

In 1928, Flaherty began a picture about the Pueblo Indians for Fox but did not get along with the studio brass and quit. The following year he formed a partnership with the celebrated German director F. W. MURNAU and they announced a whole array of joint projects. However, the only film to come out of the collaboration was *Tabu,* an exotic melodrama set against a South Sea island background. During production, a serious dispute developed between the two strong-minded directors, who differed greatly in personality and background. Murnau bought out Flaherty's interest in the picture and completed it himself. It turned out to be a very profitable film. Flaherty subsequently went to the British Isles, where he shot his celebrated documentary *Man of Aran,* an account of the life of a fisherman on a barren island off Ireland's west coast. He took three years to make it. Still in Britain, he then collaborated with Zoltán KORDA on *Elephant Boy,* a feature film adapted from a Kipling story. Flaherty directed the exteriors and Korda the interiors of the film, which starred Sabu in the title role.

After returning to the US, Flaherty made the documentary *The Land* for the Department of Agriculture, and finally *Louisiana Story,* for the Standard Oil Company of N.J. The latter told the story of a poor family in the bayous of Louisiana whose life and environment are changed by the arrival of an oil-drilling crew and equipment. Except for a few unconvincing sequences of re-enactment, *Louisiana Story* is another remarkable documentary in which Flaherty captures the flavor of a place and the nature of its people. Flaherty died before he was able to start production on two projects planned in the early 50s, *The Green Border,* about the division of Germany, and *East Is West,* about the Hawaiian Islands, both for the State Department.

Flaherty's wife, Frances, who collaborated on several of his films in various capacities, lectured on his work at universities and film clubs.

FILMS: Untitled documentary about Eskimo life (negative destroyed, work print lost; also prod., sc., phot., edit.) 1916; *Nanook of the North* (also prod., sc., phot., edit.) 1922; *The Pottery-Maker* (also sc., phot., edit.; short) 1925; *Moana* (also sc., phot., edit. with wife's assistance) 1926; *The Twenty-Four Dollar Island* (also prod., sc., phot., edit.; short) 1927; *White Shadows of the South Seas* (co-dir., co-sc.) 1928; *Tabu* (co-dir., co-sc.), *Industrial Britain* (also phot.; short; UK) 1933; *Man of Aran* (also sc., phot., assisted by wife; UK) 1934; *Elephant Boy* (co-dir.; UK) 1937; *The Land* (also sc., phot., narrated) 1942; *Louisiana Story* (also co-sc., with wife, 1948).

Flaiano (also **Flajano), Ennio.** Screenwriter. *b.* Mar. 5, 1910, Pescara, Italy. *d.* 1972. A former architect, journalist, drama critic, essayist, and novelist, he began writing for films in the early 40s and is best known for his collaborations (with FELLINI and PINELLI) on the screenplays of Fellini's films. Fellini himself describes Flaiano as "an unusually subtle writer, a sharp humorist, an impassioned reporter of Italian customs."

FILMS INCLUDE: *La Freccia nel Flanco* (co-sc. with Alberto Moravia) 1943; *Roma Città Libera* 1946; *Fuga in Francia/Flight Into France* 1948; *Luci del Varietà/Variety Lights* 1951; *Lo Sceicco Bianco/The White Sheik* 1952; *I Vitelloni, Villa Borghese* 1953; *Peccato che sia una Canaglia/Too Bad She's Bad, La Strada, La Romana/Woman of Rome* 1954; *Il Bidone, La Donna del Fiume, Il Segno di Venere* 1955; *Le Notti di Cabiria/The Nights of Cabiria* 1956; *Racconti d'Estate/Love on the Riviera, Fortunella* 1958; *La Dolce Vita* 1960; *La Notte/The Night* 1961; *Boccaccio '70* 1962; *Otto e Mezzo/8½* 1963; *El Verdugo/Not on Your Life* 1964; *Giulietta degli Spiriti/Juliet of the Spirits, La Decima Vittima/The Tenth Victim* 1965; *Le plus Vieux Metier du Monde/The Oldest Profession* (Fr./It./Ger.) 1967.

Flanagan, Bud. See O'KEEFE, Dennis.

flange. A metal or plastic disc attached to a rewinder to facilitate the uniform winding of film in the cutting room. Usually used in conjunction with a core. See also CORE, REWINDER.

flare. A bright spot or flash of light appearing on exposed film, usually caused by reflections from shiny objects or from internal camera reflections. Flare can usually be avoided by dulling shiny surfaces or by changing the camera angle.

flash. A shot of very brief duration, usually creating a sharp dramatic impact or shock effect.

flashback. A scene in a motion picture representing an earlier event than the one currently being depicted. The flashback is a useful narrative device that allows a screenwriter a degree of flexibility in the temporal structure of his plot. It may relate an event that occurred before the main story began or retrogress in time to depict a portion of the main story not previously shown. Flashbacks may be used to clarify an element of the plot (for example, to reconstruct the scene of a crime in a mystery film), to provide background information essential to the understanding of the current plot, or to supply keys to the understanding of characters or clues to their motivations (as in *Death of a Salesman*). Flashback inserts may be of any duration, from several frames representing a memory fragment being flashed briefly on the screen (as in *Hiroshima mon Amour*) to the length of nearly an entire film (as in *Citizen Kane* and *Rashomon*).

A flashback may be employed to relate the past story of a character or characters (as in *Dead Reckoning,* in which the entire plot unfolds as a Humphrey Bogart confession to a priest) or to enable several characters to tell their own versions of the same events (as in *Citizen Kane* and *Rashomon*), straining the objectivity of the camera with their subjective viewpoints. The ultimate in flashbacks is the flashback within a flashback. In *The Barefoot Contessa,* for example, Bogart, while attending Ava Gardner's funeral (the present), reminisces about the rainy night during which she visited his hotel room (flashback) to tell him about her wedding night (flashback within a flashback). Although generally a useful device in advancing a complicated plot, the multiple flashback can be absurdly confusing, as demonstrated by John Brahm's *The Locket* (1946), in which a flashback four layers deep (flashback within a flashback within a flashback within a flashback) makes Sheridan Gibney's muddled script hopelessly difficult to follow. See also FLASHFORWARD.

flashforward. The opposite of FLASHBACK. A scene in a motion picture representing an event that is expected, projected, or imagined to occur later than the one currently depicted. This narrative device has been employed less frequently than the flashback but can be quite useful in the futuristic structure of science-fiction stories or in depicting the hopes and dreams of a character.

flash frame. A fogged or overexposed film frame resulting from the camera's running below full speed. It is common for the first few frames of a shot to be overexposed because of the time required by the camera to reach the correct speed. Sometimes a frame is deliberately so exposed, to provide a film editor with a cue mark.

flashing. The brief exposure of film to light as a means of increasing the speed of its emulsion. This is sometimes done in the lab with film of low emulsion speed to make possible photography of acceptable exposure under relatively dark conditions.

flash pan. An extremely fast PAN shot that produces the effect of a near blur. It is used in shooting to make sudden transitions, often with the intent of creating a shock impact.

flat. 1. Lacking contrast; said of a photographic image of a restricted density range. 2. A large, flat, easily removable section of a studio set.

flat lighting. The even distribution of illumination on a set for the purpose of avoiding highlights and thus limiting the tonal range of a shot.

flat print. A standard motion picture print that may be projected through a normal lens, as opposed to a squeezed print, which requires projection through an ANAMORPHIC LENS system, such as CINEMASCOPE.

Flavin, James. Actor *b.* May 14, 1906, Portland, Me. *d.* 1976. A West Point graduate, he chose acting over a military career and after appearing with several stock companies entered films in the early 30s. He then played character parts in numerous Hollywood productions, typically portraying tough cops and crack Marine sergeants. He was also seen on hundreds of TV shows. In 1969 he appeared on Broadway in 'The Front Page' and just before his death completed the TV special 'The Francis Gary Powers Story,' in which he portrayed President Eisenhower. His wife, actress Lucille Browne, a heroine of several serials of the 30s, also died in 1976, two weeks after he did.

FILMS INCLUDE: *The Airmail Mystery* (serial; lead) 1932; *King Kong* 1933; *My Man Godfrey* 1936; *The League of Frightened Men* 1937; *The Duke of West Point* 1938; *The Gracie Allen Murder Case, Calling All Marines* 1939; *The Grapes of Wrath, The Great Profile* 1940; *Belle Starr* 1941; *Fingers at the Window, Ten Gentlemen from West Point, Gentleman Jim, Life Begins at Eight-Thirty* 1942; *Air Force, Corvette K-225* 1943; *Uncertain Glory, Laura* 1944; *Conflict, Anchors Aweigh* 1945; *Cloak and Dagger, Nobody Lives Forever* 1946; *Desert Fury, Nightmare Alley* 1947; *Mighty Joe Young* 1949; *South Sea Sinner* 1950; *Mister Roberts* 1955; *Wild Is the Wind* 1957; *The Last Hurrah* 1958; *In Cold Blood* 1967.

Fleischer, Dave and Max. Animators. Walt DISNEY's chief rivals in the 30s. Max (b. July 17, 1889, Vienna), in the US from childhood, began as cartoonist for Brooklyn *Daily Eagle,* later working for *Popular Science Monthly.* During WW I made instructional cartoons for the Army, then joined with brother Dave (*b.* July 14, 1894, N.Y.C.; *d.* 1979) in 1920 to create popular series of animated cartoons, such as *Out of the Inkwell, Betty Boop,* and *Popeye the Sailor.* Max acted mainly as producer and Dave as creative director of their films. A third brother, Louis Fleischer (1881–1985), was the team's music editor. In 1936 they made a medium-length animated film, *Popeye the Sailor Meets Sinbad the Sailor,* and in 1939 ventured on their first full-length cartoon *Gulliver's Travels.* Their next feature, *Mr. Bug Goes to Town* (1941), was a failure and soon after they parted ways, Dave becoming head of Columbia's cartoon department and Max going into industrial film production and TV. Max was the father of director Richard FLEISCHER.

Fleischer, Richard O. Director. Born on Dec. 8, 1916, in Brooklyn, N.Y. The son of animator Max FLEISCHER, he abandoned medical studies at Brown University to take up drama at Yale and in 1937 he organized a stage troupe, The Arena Players. He entered films in 1942, joining RKO as an editor on Pathé newsreels. The following year he began directing RKO shorts, among them many segments of the "This Is America" series, two-reel wartime documentaries in the style of "The March of Time." He was the originator and producer-director of another series, "Flicker Flashbacks," shorts compiled from silent films. Graduating to features in 1946, he soon proved himself a capable director of such crime and suspense dramas as *The Narrow Margin, Violent Saturday,* and *Compulsion,* and flamboyant adventures like *20,000 Leagues Under the Sea* and *The Vikings.* In the 60s he had his share of lavish flops with such high-budget productions as *Barabbas, Dr. Dolittle,* and *Che!,* but demonstrated a sure-handed technical flair even in his failures. In the 70s he returned to his specialty—crime and suspense—with mixed results. Eventually, he settled on no genre at all, indiscriminately accepting assignments of any type and any level of intelligence.

FEATURE FILMS: *Child of Divorce* 1946; *Banjo* 1947; *Design for Death* (full-length documentary), *So This Is New York, Bodyguard* 1948; *Make Mine Laughs, The Clay Pigeon, Follow Me Quietly, Trapped* 1949; *Armored Car Robbery* 1950; *The Narrow Margin, The Happy Time* 1952; *Arena* 1953; *20,000 Leagues Under the Sea* 1954; *Violent Saturday, The Girl in the Red Velvet Swing* 1955; *Bandido, Between Heaven and Hell* 1956; *The Vikings* 1958; *These Thousand Hills, Compulsion* 1959; *Crack in the Mirror* 1960; *The Big Gamble* 1961; *Barabba/Barabbas* (It.) 1962; *Fantastic Voyage* 1966; *Dr. Dolittle* 1967; *The Boston Strangler* 1968; *Che!* 1969; *Tora! Tora! Tora!* (co-dir. with Toshio Masuda and Kinji Fukasaku; US/Jap.) 1970; *10 Rillington Place* (UK), *Blind Terror/See No Evil* (UK), *The Last Run* 1971; *The New Centurions* 1972; *Soylent Green, The Don Is Dead* 1973; *The Spikes Gang, Mr. Majestyk* 1974; *Mandingo* 1975; *The Incredible Sarah* (UK) 1976; *The Prince and the Pauper/Crossed Swords* 1977; *Ashanti* 1979; *The Jazz Singer* 1980; *Tough Enough, Amityville 3-D* 1983; *Conan the Destroyer* 1984; *Red Sonja* 1985; *Million Dollar Mystery* 1987; *Call from Space (Showscan)* 1990.

Fleming, Bryant. See YOUNG, Gig.

Fleming, Rhonda. Actress. Born Marilyn Louis, on Aug. 10, 1922, in Los Angeles. The daughter of show people, she grew up in Hollywood and went almost straight out of Beverly Hills High School into films, at first as an extra. A ravishing redhead, she photographed exquisitely, especially in color, in a variety of leading lady roles, most typically as a hard-to-subdue good-bad girl. In 1971 she divorced her fourth husband (since 1966), producer-director Hall BARTLETT.

FILMS INCLUDE: *In Old Oklahoma* (bit) 1943; *Since You Went Away* (bit) 1944; *Spellbound, The Spiral Staircase* 1945; *Abilene Town* 1946; *Out of the Past, Adventure Island* 1947; *A Connecticut Yankee in King Arthur's Court, The Great Lover* 1949; *The Eagle and the Hawk* 1950; *The Redhead and the Cowboy, Cry Danger, The Last Outpost, Little Egypt, Crosswinds* 1951; *Hong Kong, The Golden Hawk* 1952; *Pony Express, Inferno, Those Redheads from Seattle* 1953; *Jivaro, Yankee Pasha* 1954; *Tennessee's Partner* 1955; *The Killer Is Loose, Slightly Scarlet, While the City Sleeps* 1956; *The Buster Keaton Story, Gunfight at the O.K. Corral, Gun Glory* 1957; *Home Before Dark* 1958; *Alias Jesse James, The Big Circus* 1959; *The Crowded Sky* 1960; *Le Rivolta degli Schiavi/The Revolt of the Slaves* (It./Sp./Ger.) 1961; *The Patsy* (cameo) 1964; *Una Moglie Americana/Run for Your Wife* (It./Fr.) 1965; *Backtrack* 1969; *Won Ton Ton—The Dog Who Saved Hollywood* (cameo) 1976; *The Nude Bomb* 1980.

Fleming, Victor. Director. *b.* Feb. 23, 1883, Pasadena, Calif. *d.* 1949. A former automobile mechanic and still photographer, he entered films in 1910 as assistant cameraman and worked on many of Allan DWAN's films from 1911. A director of photography at Triangle from 1915, he frequently worked under the supervision of D. W. GRIFFITH. He was the cameraman on several Douglas Fairbanks vehicles under Dwan's direction. Upon America's entry into WW I, he joined the intelligence bureau's photography section and later accompanied President Wilson to Europe as chief cameraman. Returning to Hollywood in 1919, making his debut with two Fairbanks films, he became a director. Fleming did not achieve a reputation among critics as one of Hollywood's great directors, but he was unquestionably a superior craftsman. He proved himself frequently capable of obtaining solid performances from actors and of turning out an elegant and entertaining product, and was especially adept at handling masculine action adventures. Some of his MGM films of the 30s are particularly engaging, notably *Bombshell, Treasure Island, Captains Courageous,* and the perennially popular *The Wizard of Oz.* He is also the accredited director of *Gone With the Wind,* for which he won the Academy Award, but so many people collaborated on this monumental production that it is difficult to determine responsibility for either its virtues or its faults. His last two films, *Adventure* and *Joan of Arc,* were notable failures.

FILMS: *When the Clouds Roll By* (co-dir. with Ted Reed) 1919; *The Mollycoddle* 1920; *Woman's Place, Mamma's Affair* 1921; *The Lane That Had No Turning, Red Hot Romance, Anna Ascends* 1922; *Dark Secrets, Law of the Lawless, To the Last Man, The Call of the Canyon* 1923; *Empty Hands, Code of the Sea* 1924; *The Devil's Cargo, Adventure, A Son of His Father, Lord Jim* 1925; *Blind Goddess, Mantrap* 1926; *The Rough Riders, The Way of All Flesh, Hula* 1927; *Abie's Irish Rose, The Awakening* 1928; *Wolf Song, The Virginian* 1929; *Common Clay, Renegades* 1930; *Around the World in 80 Minutes* (co-dir. with Douglas Fairbanks) 1931; *The Wet Parade, Red Dust* 1932; *The White Sister, Bombshell* 1933; *Treasure Island* 1934; *Reckless, The Farmer Takes a Wife* 1935; *The Good Earth* (dir. some scenes; uncredited), *Captains Courageous* 1937; *Test Pilot* 1938; *The Wizard of Oz, Gone With the Wind* 1939; *Dr. Jekyll and Mr. Hyde* (also prod.) 1941; *Tortilla Flat* 1942; *A Guy Named Joe* 1943; *Adventure* 1946; *Joan of Arc* 1948.

Flemyng, Robert. Actor. *b.* Jan. 3, 1912, in Liverpool. *d.* 1995. Character player of the British stage, films, and TV, typically in dignified roles. He made his stage debut in 1931 and later appeared in many theatrical productions in London and New York. He made his first film appearance in 1936, but his career was then interrupted by WW II service, for which he was awarded the Military Cross and the Order of the British Empire.

FILMS INCLUDE: *Head Over Heels/Head Over Heels in Love* 1936; *Bond Street* 1947; *The Guinea Pig* 1948; *Conspirator* (UK/US), *The Blue Lamp* 1950; *The Holly and the Ivy* 1952; *Cast a Dark Shadow* 1955; *The Man Who Never Was* 1956; *Funny Face* (US), *Let's Be Happy* 1957; *Windom's Way* 1958; *Blind Date/Chance Meeting* 1959; *A Touch of Larceny* 1960; *L'Orribile Segreto de Dr. Hitchcock/The Horrible Dr. Hitchcock* (title role; It.) 1962; *Mystery Submarine* 1963; *The Quiller Memorandum* (UK/US), *The Spy with a Cold Nose* 1966; *The Deadly Affair* 1967; *The Blood Beast Terror/The Vampire Beast Craves Blood* 1968; *Battle of Britain* 1969; *The Darwin Adventure, Young Winston, Travels with My Aunt* (UK/US) 1972; *The Medusa Touch, The 39 Steps* 1978; *Kafka* 1992; *Shadowlands* 1993.

Fletcher, Bramwell. Actor. *b.* Feb. 20, 1904, Bradford, England. *d.* 1988. Blond leading man and second lead of British and American stage, TV, and films. A former insurance clerk, he made his stage debut with the Shakespeare Memorial Company at Stratford-on-Avon, in 1927, and his first film appearance the following year. He first appeared on Broadway in 1929 and subsequently settled in the US, where he appeared in a number of Hollywood films and numerous stage plays. He made his last film appearance in 1943 but was later seen in some 200 TV productions and remained active on Broadway and on tour with various stage companies. A specialist in Shavian roles, he authored and starred in 'The Bernard Shaw Story' on Broadway in 1965. His first two of four marriages were to actresses Helen CHANDLER and Diana BARRYMORE.

FILMS INCLUDE: *Chick* (UK) 1928; *So This Is London, Raffles* 1930; *The Millionaire, Svengali, Daughter of the Dragon, Once a Lady* 1931; *The Silent Witness, A Bill of Divorcement, The Mummy* 1932; *Only Yesterday* 1933; *The Scarlet Pimpernel* (UK) 1935; *White Cargo, Random Harvest* 1942; *Immortal Sergeant* 1943.

Fletcher, Louise. Actress. Born in July, 1934, in Birmingham, Ala., the daughter of an Episcopal minister. She had an isolated and sometimes traumatic childhood, since both her parents were totally deaf. After graduating from the North Carolina State University, she did some acting in summer stock, then went to Los Angeles, where she worked as a physician's receptionist while studying acting at nights with Jeff Corey. In the late 50s and early 60s she appeared in episodes of such TV series as 'Wagon Train,' 'Lawman,' and 'The Untouchables,' but her television career was hampered by her height—five feet ten inches—which restricted her choice of male partners. In 1962 she married film producer Jerry Bick and two years later retired from acting when she was expecting her second child. More than a decade elapsed before she was back in front of a camera, playing a secondary role in Robert Altman's feature, *Thieves Like Us* (1974). Her performance impressed director Milos Forman, who assigned her the pivotal role of the coldblooded Nurse Ratched in his film *One Flew Over the Cuckoo's Nest* (1975). She won the best actress Academy Award for her superb, totally believable performance in that role. She is active in the cause of civil rights for the deaf. Her film roles have mostly dwindled, in recent years, to one-dimensional echoes of Nurse Ratched.

FILMS: *Thieves Like Us* 1974; *Russian Roulette, One Flew Over the Cuckoo's Nest* 1975; *Exorcist II: The Heretic* 1977; *The Cheap Detective* 1978; *The Magician of Lublin* (Isr./Ger.), *The Lady in Red, Natural Enemies* 1979; *The Lucky Star* (Can.), *Mama Dracula* (title role; Bel./Fr.) 1980; *Dead Kids* (Austral./N.Z.) 1981; *Brainstorm, Strange Invaders* 1983; *Firestarter* 1984; *Invaders from Mars, The Boy Who Could Fly* (cameo), *Nobody's Fool* 1986; *Flowers in the Attic* 1987; *Two Moon Junction* 1988; *Best of the Best* 1989; *Shadowzone, Blue Steel* 1990; *Twilight Blue, Blind Vision* 1991; *The Player* 1992; *Toll Booth* 1994; *Virtuosity* 1995.

flicker. An annoying flickering sensation during the projection of film which results from the inability of the human eye to perceive a continuous image under certain conditions. The illusion of continuous brightness and a steady image on the screen is produced by a phenomenon known as "persistence of vision," which allows the eye to interpret a rapid succession of alternating beats of light and dark as even illumination. When the frequency of light and dark is too slow to meet the minimum that is required for persistence of vision, a flickering sensation results. The problem was common during the early silent days, when films were projected at the slow rate of 16 frames per second. It was because of this that early motion pictures were called "flickers," or just "flicks," slang terms that are still in use today. To overcome the flicker effect, a three-bladed shutter was introduced that effectively increased the frequency of light and dark periods to 48 per second. Today's sound projectors operate at the speed of 24 frames per second and require a two-bladed shutter to produce a satisfactory, evenly illuminated picture.

flipover. Also "flip," "flipover wipe," "flip frame," or "flipwipe." A transitional optical effect in which an image appears to rotate on its horizontal or vertical axis and is then replaced by another image seemingly printed on the back of the original one. The effect is not unlike that produced by the flipping of book pages.

Flippen, Jay C. Actor. *b.* Mar. 6, 1898, Little Rock, Ark. *d.* 1971. On the stage from age 16, he made his Broadway debut in 1920 and was getting star billing by 1926. Except for a couple of isolated film appearances in the mid-30s, he made the switch from Broadway to Hollywood after WW II. Ruggedly built and craggy-featured, he played character parts, typically on the tough but nice side, in a variety of film genres but looked most comfortable in Westerns. In 1964, during the filming of *Cat Ballou,* he suffered an infection that led to the amputation of his right leg. But he resumed his work in films and TV from a wheelchair.

FILMS INCLUDE: *Marie Galante* 1934; *Brute Force* 1947; *Intrigue* 1948; *Down to the Sea in Ships, They Live by Night* 1949; *The Yellow Cab Man, Two Flags West, Winchester 73* 1950; *The Lemon Drop Kid, The People Against O'Hara, Flying Leathernecks* 1951; *Bend of the River* 1952; *The Wild One* 1954; *The Far Country, Strategic Air Command, Oklahoma!, Kismet* 1955; *The Killing* 1956; *Run of the Arrow* 1957; *Wild River* 1960; *How the West Was Won* 1962; *Cat Ballou* 1965; *Firecreek* 1968; *The Hellfighters* 1969; *The Seven Minutes* 1971.

Flon, Suzanne. Actress. Born in 1923, in Kremlin-Bicetre, France. Leading lady and supporting player of French films. Formerly Edith Piaf's secretary. She was named best actress at the 1961 Venice Festival for her performance in Claude Autant-Lara's *Tu ne tueras point/Non Uccidere/Thou Shalt Not Kill.*

FILMS INCLUDE: *Capitaine Blomet* 1947; *Dernier Amour, Suzanne et ses Brigands, La Cage aux Filles* 1949; *La Belle Image* 1951; *Procès au Vatican/Miracle of Saint Therese* 1952; *Moulin Rouge* (UK/US) 1953; *Mr. Arkadin/Confidential Report* (Sp./Switz.) 1955; *Tu ne tuera point/Non Uccidere/Thou Shalt Not Kill* 1961; *Un Singe en Hiver/A Monkey in Winter, Le Procès/The Trial* 1962; *Chateau en Suède/Nutty Naughty Chateau* 1963; *Le Train/The Train* (Fr./US/It.) 1964; *Le Soleil des Voyous/Action Man* 1967; *Tante Zita/Zita* 1968; *Les Silencieux/Escape to Nowhere* 1973; *Monsieur Albert, Mr. Klein* 1976; *Blackout* 1977; *Quartet* (UK/Fr.) 1981; *L'Eté meurtrier/One Deadly Summer* 1983; *La Vouivre* 1989.

Flood, James. Director. *b.* July 31, 1895, New York City. *d.* 1953. He entered films in 1912 as an assistant director at Biograph and in the early 20s began directing for Fox, then Warner Bros. and Tiffany. He continued working for various studios after the advent of sound, turning out many productions with routine efficiency.

FILMS: *Times Have Changed, When Odds Are Even* 1923; *The Tenth Woman* 1924; *The Man Without a Conscience, The Woman Hater, The Wife Who Wasn't Wanted, Satan in Sables* 1925; *Why Girls Leave Home, The Honeymoon Express* 1926; *The Lady in Ermine, Three Hours* 1927; *The Count of Ten, Domestic Meddlers, Marriage by Contract* 1928; *Midstream, Whispering Winds, Mister Antonio* 1929; *The Swellhead, Sisters* 1930; *Mother's Millions/She-Wolf/The She-Wolf of Wall Street* 1931; *The Mouthpiece, Life Begins, Under-Cover Man* 1932; *All of Me, Such Women Are Dangerous* 1934; *Wings in the Dark, Shanghai, We're Only Human* 1935; *Everybody's Old Man, The Lonely Road/Scotland Yard Commands* (UK) 1936; *Midnight Madonna* 1937; *Off the Record* 1939; *The Big Fix, Stepchild* 1947.

floodlight. A high-powered nondirectional lighting unit consisting of one or more lamps, used to illuminate a broad area of a set. The standard floodlight cannot be focused and its main function is to provide overall frontal lighting, but focusing floods, directional as well as focusable, are now widely in use as a compromise between the functions of floods and SPOTLIGHTS.

floor. That part of a studio on which shooting is in progress at a given time.

Florey, Robert. Director. *b.* Sept. 14, 1900, Paris. *d.* 1979. As a child, he became deeply interested in films while watching Georges Méliès work on his trick films at a nearby theater. After working briefly at 17 as a newspaper sportswriter, he switched to film reviews and interviews for *Cinémagazine,* France's earliest movie fan publication. At 19, while studying in Geneva, he entered the film industry, working in several capacities, including actor, screenwriter, and assistant director on a string of Swiss one-reelers, one of which, *Isidore à la Deveine,* he also directed. Upon returning to France, he became an assistant to Louis FEUILLADE and, among other duties, played a heavy in the latter's 1921 serial *L'Orpheline.* That same year Florey sailed for the US, hoping to recover his expenses by sending back articles about Hollywood. But he was immediately hired as a technical director on *Monte Cristo* (released in 1922), became a gag writer for Sunshine Comedies shorts starring Al St. John, and received several acting assignments.

Within months Florey was a popular member of the Hollywood social scene, an intimate friend of such screen luminaries as Charlie Chaplin, Douglas Fairbanks, and Rudolph Valentino. He became the director of foreign publicity for Fairbanks and Mary Pickford and in 1923 handled the publicity for Valentino's grand tour of the United States and Europe. That same year Florey directed his first American film, the two-reel comedy *Fifty-Fifty,* and began a long stint as an assistant director to such filmmakers as Louis J. Gasnier, Alfred Santell, Josef von Sternberg, John M. Stahl, Edmund Goulding, Christy Cabanne, Robert Z. Leonard, and King Vidor. In 1926 he was hired to write the script for *That Model from Paris* and ended up completing the direction of the film for the ailing Gasnier. He was then assigned his first feature as a director, *One Hour of Love,* and for the next two years alternated between directing minor films for "poverty row" studios and working as assistant director on major productions, such as Frank Borzage's *Seventh Heaven.* During that period (1927–28), Florey directed four experimental shorts, the best known of which is *The Life and Death of 9413—A Hollywood Extra,* a semiexpressionist fantasy shot to the beat of Gershwin's 'Rhapsody in Blue.' The others were *The Loves of Zero, Johann the Coffin Maker,* and *Skyscraper Symphony.* In addition, he turned out numerous screen tests and short subjects at Paramount's Long Island City studios, including the three-reelers *The Pusher-in-the-Face,* from a script by F. Scott Fitzgerald, and *Bonjour, New York,* featuring Maurice Chevalier.

From 1929 till 1950, Florey directed more than 60 feature films for Paramount, Warner Bros., and other studios. Most were routine B crime melodramas, but some were of more than passing interest, ranging from the Marx Brothers' first film comedy, *The Cocoanuts* (1929), through such stylish exercises in Gothic horror as *Murders in the Rue Morgue* (1932), starring Bela Lugosi, and *The Beast with Five Fingers* (1946), starring Peter Lorre. Florey also collaborated on the script of the original *Frankenstein* (1931) and was Charlie Chaplin's associate director on *Monsieur Verdoux* (1947).

In 1950, with the opportunities to work becoming scarce, Florey was among the first Hollywood directors to cross over to the competing medium of TV. He subsequently directed hundreds of television dramas, series episodes, and specials. A versatile man of unfulfilled potential, Florey was intimately involved with the development of American cinema without actually influencing its course. He wrote eight books and numerous articles on Hollywood history, ways, and personalities. In 1950 the French government made him a knight of the Légion d'Honneur for his contribution to film.

FEATURE FILMS: *One Hour of Love, The Romantic Age, Face Value* 1927; *Night Club* 1928; *The Hole in the Wall, The Cocoanuts* (co-dir. with Joseph Santley), *The Battle of Paris/The Gay Lady* 1929; *La Route est Belle* (French film made in the UK), *L'Amour Chante* (and German version, *Komm' zu mir zum Rendezvous,* and Spanish version, *El Professor de mi Señora;* all three versions filmed in Berlin for a French company), *Le Blanc et le Noir* (co-dir. with Marc Allégret; Fr.) 1930; *Murders in the Rue Morgue, The Man Called Back, Those We Love* 1932; *Girl Missing, Ex-Lady, The House on 56th Street* 1933; *Bedside, Smarty, Registered Nurse, I Sell Anything* 1934; *I Am a Thief, The Woman in Red, The Florentine Dagger, Don't Bet on Blondes, Going Highbrow, The Pay-Off, Ship Cafe* 1935; *The Preview Murder Mystery, Till We Meet Again, Hollywood Boulevard* 1936; *Outcast, King of Gamblers, Mountain Music, This Way Please, Daughter of Shanghai* 1937; *Dangerous to Know, King of Alcatraz* 1938; *Disbarred, Hotel Imperial, The Magnificent Fraud, Death of a Champion* 1939; *Parole Fixer, Women Without Names* 1940; *The Face Behind the Mask, Meet Boston Blackie, Two in a Taxi* 1941; *Dangerously They Live, Lady Gangster* (under pseudonym Florian Roberts) 1942; *The Desert Song* 1943; *Man from Frisco, Roger Touhy—Gangster* 1944; *God Is My Co-Pilot, Danger Signal* 1945; *The Beast with Five Fingers* 1946; *Tarzan and the Mermaids, Rogues' Regiment* 1948; *Outpost in Morocco, The Crooked Way* 1949; *The Vicious Years, Johnny One-Eye* 1950.

Flowers, Bess. Actress. *b.* 1900, in Sherman, Tex. *d.* 1984. *ed.* Oklahoma Coll. for Women; Carnegie Tech. Tall, statuesque, dignified player of numerous Hollywood silents and talkies. She entered films in the early 20s, after some experience in amateur dramatics, and initially played leading lady roles in low-budget Westerns and action silents. After the advent of sound she settled on a long and prolific career in featured roles in a number of productions and bit and extra appearances in hundreds of others. She is known among movie buffs as the "Queen of the Hollywood Extras." Her first husband was small-time film director Cullen Tate.

FILMS INCLUDE: *Hollywood, The Silent Partner, A Woman of Paris* 1923; *Irene, Hands Across the Border, The Greater Glory, Glenister of the Mounted, Laddie, Lone Hand Saunders* 1926; *Blondes by Choice* 1927; *We Faw Down* (Laurel and Hardy short; as Mrs. Laurel) 1928; *The Ghost Talks, Linda* 1929; *Lightnin'* 1930; *Bachelor Apartment* 1931; *Sinister Hands* 1932; *It Happened One Night* 1934; *Private Worlds* 1935; *The Golden Arrow, Anthony Adverse, My Man Godfrey, Forgotten Faces* 1936; *The Awful Truth, Paid to Dance, The Shadow* 1937; *Women in Prison, Holiday, The Lone Wolf in Paris* 1938; *Love Affair, Ninotchka* 1939; *Meet John Doe, Flame of New Orleans* 1941; *Double Indemnity* 1944; *Gilda* 1946; *Song of the Thin Man* 1947; *Sky Liner* 1949; *Born to Be Bad, All About Eve* 1950; *The Bad and the Beautiful* 1952; *The Greatest Show on Earth* 1953; *Rear Window* 1954; *The View from Pompey's Head* 1955; *Move Over Darling* 1963; *Good Neighbor Sam* 1964.

Flynn, Emmett J. Director. *b.* 1892, Denver, Colo. *d.* 1937. Entered films as an actor at 15 and later worked as an assistant director on a number of Mary Pickford films. A director from 1918, mostly for Fox, he had several prestigious silent productions to his credit, including Rudolph Valentino and John Gilbert vehicles. Retired at the switch to sound and died several years later, at 45.

FILMS: *The Alimony* 1917; *The Racing Strain* 1918; *A Bachelor's Wife, Bondage of Barbara, Virtuous Sinners, Yvonne from Paris, Eastward Ho!* 1919; *Leave It to Me, The Lincoln Highwayman* (also sc.), *Shod with Fire, The Valley of Tomorrow, Untamed, The Man Who Dared* 1920; *A Connecticut Yankee at King Arthur's Court, Shame* (also sc.) 1921; *The Last Trail* 1921; *Without Compromise, Monte Cristo, A Fool There Was* 1922; *Hell's Hole, In the Palace of the King* 1923; *Nellie the Beautiful Cloak Model, The Man Who Came Back, Gerald Cranston's Lady* 1924; *The Dancers, Wings of Youth, East Lynne* (also co-sc.) 1925; *The Yankee Señor, The Palace of Pleasure, Yellow Fingers* 1926; *Married Alive* 1927; *The Veiled Woman, Hold Your Man, The Shannons of Broadway* 1929.

Flynn, Errol. Actor. *b.* June 20, 1909, Hobart, Tasmania. *d.* 1959. The son of a distinguished Australian marine biologist and zoologist, he attended a number of fine schools in Australia and England and was expelled from most. At 15 he began clerking for a Sydney shipping company. At 16 he sailed to New Guinea to enter government service, but his adventurous spirit soon drove him to private enterprise, a search for gold. In 1930 he returned briefly to Sydney, purchased a boat, which he named *Sirocco,* and sailed back to New Guinea with three friends. He later described the seven-month sea voyage in his first of three books, *Beam Ends* (1937). In New Guinea he became manager of a tobacco plantation and dispatched a regular column for the Sydney *Bulletin.* Back in Australia, he was offered the role of Fletcher Christian in a semidocumentary feature-length film, *In the Wake of the Bounty.* In 1933 he set out for England, where he gained some acting experience with the Northampton Repertory Company. This led to a lead role in a low-budget mystery film produced by Warner's London branch, and this in turn to a Hollywood contract.

Flynn arrived in Hollywood in 1935. Before the year ended he was married (to actress Lili DAMITA) and an established star, following the success of *Captain Blood.* Tall, athletic, and exceptionally good-looking, he had no peer in costume adventure films. In movies like *The Charge of the Light Brigade, The Adventures of Robin Hood,* and *The Sea Hawk,* he made a splendid figure as a fearless fighter for justice and a noble leader of men. In addition to his sword-wielding roles, he was a gunfighter in epic Westerns beginning with *Dodge City* and a soldier in a number of World War II films, most notably *Objective Burma!* Ironically, Flynn was classified 4F and turned down by every branch of the armed services during WW II because of a combination of a heart defect, a recurrent malaria, and a measure of tuberculosis, a fact that hurt his ego considerably.

The consistency of Flynn's persona at the height of his career was due in part to his working mainly with two directors: Michael CURTIZ (*Captain Blood*, etc.) from 1935 to 1941, and Raoul WALSH (*Desperate Journey*, etc.) from 1942 to

1945. Alan Hale was often Flynn's burly sidekick, and in many films Olivia de Havilland was his leading lady.

Flynn, who enjoyed enormous popularity through the early 40s, soon began tiring of the dashing hero image and yearned for roles that would allow him to prove his worth as an actor, but rarely rose to the occasion when the opportunity presented itself. Off screen he was gaining a reputation as a rogue and a Casanova, and gossip columnists delighted in telling of his hedonistic exploits, amorous escapades, and barroom brawls. The semiserious intimations that made him a sort of living phallic symbol in the eyes of the public took a serious turn in 1942 when he was tried (and subsequently acquitted) on charges of statutory rape of two teenage girls aboard his yacht. The publicity resulted in a catch phrase, "In like Flynn," that gained national currency over the years. The same year he divorced Miss Damita. (The marriage had produced a look-alike son, Sean Flynn [*b.* 1941], who in the 60s starred in a number of European adventure pictures and in 1970, while covering the Southeast Asian war as a photographer-correspondent, disappeared and was presumed captured or dead.)

Flynn's popularity began to wane in the late 40s. Always known as a heavy drinker and smoker, he was now beginning to experiment with drugs, to which he became increasingly addicted. The effect of his hard-driving style of life soon became noticeable in his appearance and screen performances. In 1949 he divorced his second wife (since 1943), Nora Eddington, and in 1950 married actress Patrice WYMORE. In 1952 an embittered and debt-ridden Errol Flynn left Hollywood and set out for Europe to resurrect the pieces of his career. The several films he made in England and on the Continent were failures, and to make things worse, he lost every penny he had on an ill-fated production of *William Tell,* which was never completed. He returned to Hollywood in 1956 and the following year received good press notices for his performance as a drunken wastrel in *The Sun Also Rises.* He played drunks in his next two films as well, *Too Much Too Soon* (as John Barrymore) and *The Roots of Heaven.* His last picture, *Cuban Rebel Girls,* was a disastrous semidocumentary tribute to Fidel Castro, which Flynn also wrote, narrated, and co-produced. Flynn began writing his memoirs in 1958 with the help of a ghostwriter. His autobiography, *My Wicked, Wicked Ways,* was published posthumously in 1959. Flynn died of a heart attack on October 14, 1959, in Vancouver, Canada, at the age of 50. In a sensational 1980 biography, *Errol Flynn, the Untold Story,* Charles Higham painted an unflattering portrait of the star, suggesting Flynn was a Nazi agent in the service of the Gestapo and a bisexual who had affairs with several male celebrities.

FILMS: *In the Wake of the Bounty* (as Fletcher Christian; Austral.) 1933; *Murder at Monte Carlo* (UK), *The Case of the Curious Bride, Don't Bet on Blondes, Captain Blood* (title role) 1935; *The Charge of the Light Brigade* 1936; *Green Light, The Prince and the Pauper* (as Miles Hendon), *Another Dawn, The Perfect Specimen* 1937; *The Adventures of Robin Hood* (as Robin Hood), *Four's a Crowd, The Sisters, The Dawn Patrol* 1938; *Dodge City, The Private Lives of Elizabeth and Essex* (as the Earl of Essex) 1939; *Virginia City, The Sea Hawk, Santa Fe Trail* 1940; *Footsteps in the Dark, Dive Bomber* 1941; *They Died with Their Boots On* (as General Custer), *Desperate Journey, Gentleman Jim* (as boxer James J. Corbett) 1942; *Edge of Darkness, Thank Your Lucky Stars* (cameo), *Northern Pursuit* 1943; *Uncertain Glory* 1944; *Objective Burma!, San Antonio, Never Say Goodbye* 1946; *Cry Wolf, Escape Me Never* 1947; *Silver River* 1948; *Adventures of Don Juan* (as Don Juan), *It's a Great Feeling* (cameo), *That Forsyte Woman* (as Soames Forsyte) 1949; *Montana, Rocky Mountain* 1950; *Kim* (as Mahbub Ali), *Hello God* (semidocumentary feature), *Adventures of Captain Fabian* (also sc.) 1951; *Mara Maru, Against All Flags, Cruise of the Zaca* (color two-reeler record of Flynn's 1946 cruise to the South Seas; also dir, and narrated), *Deep-Sea Fishing* (one reel) 1952; *The Master of Ballantrae* (UK) 1953; *Il Maestro di Don Giovanni/Crossed Swords* (It.), *William Tell* (title role; unfinished), *Lilacs in the Spring/Let's Make Up* (UK) 1954; *The Dark Avenger/The Warriors* (as Prince Edward; UK), *King's Rhapsody* (UK) 1955; *Istanbul* 1956; *The Big Boodle, The Sun Also Rises* (as Mike Campbell) 1957; *Too Much Too Soon* (as John Barrymore), *The Roots of Heaven* 1958; *Cuban Rebel Girls* (also sc., co-prod., and narrated) 1959.

Flynn, Joe. Actor. *b.* Nov. 8, 1924, Youngstown, Ohio. *d.* 1974. *ed.* Notre Dame. Bespectacled character comedian of Hollywood films and TV. He co-starred in many Disney productions and in the TV series 'McHale's Navy' (1962–66). He died of a heart attack.

FILMS INCLUDE: *The Seven Little Foys* 1955; *The Boss* 1956; *Portland Expose* 1957; *This Happy Feeling* 1958; *Cry for Happy* 1961; *Lover Come Back* 1962; *McHale's Navy* 1964; *Divorce American Style* 1967; *The Love Bug* 1969; *The Computer Wore Tennis Shoes* 1970; *How to Frame a Figg, The Barefoot Executive, $1,000,000 Duck* 1971; *Now You See Him Now You Don't* 1972; *Camper John* 1973; *Superdad* 1974; *The Strongest Man in the World* 1975 (released posthumously); *The Rescuers* (v/o; released posthumously) 1977.

Flynn, John. Director. Born in Chicago. *ed.* George Washington U.; Stanford; UCLA. He started his working career in the mail room of MCA. Following a job with a public relations firm, he entered films in 1960 as a trainee script supervisor on *West Side Story.* After nearly a decade as an assistant director in TV and films, he turned out his own first film in 1968. His TV credits include the 1980 potboiler 'Marilyn—The Untold Story.'

FILMS: *The Sergeant* 1968; *The Jerusalem File* (Isr./US) 1972; *The Outfit* (also sc.) 1974; *Rolling Thunder* 1977; *Defiance* 1980; *Touched* 1983; *Best Seller* 1987; *Lock Up* 1989.

f-number. See F-STOP.

focal length. The distance between the center of a lens and the point on the film surface where a photographed image placed at infinity is brought to sharp FOCUS. It is given in inches or centimeters and normally engraved on the lens mount with the prefix f (i.e., f = 90 mm) and shouldn't be confused with the f = stop. A short-focal-length lens has a wide angle of view and a long-focal-length, or telephoto, lens has a narrow angle of view.

Foch, Nina. Actress. Born Nina Consuelo Maud Fock, on Apr. 20, 1924, in Leyden, Holland. The daughter of Dutch conductor-composer Dirk Fock and American showgirl and actress Consuelo Flowerton, a famous WW I poster girl, Nina was raised in Manhattan and after a brief early career as a concert pianist and amateur painter took up acting at the American Academy of Dramatic Arts. She appeared with little theater groups and with stock and touring companies before signing up with Columbia Pictures in 1943. Despite poor film vehicles during her early film career, she demonstrated from the start the screen presence and acting ability that soon helped her secure increasingly better roles. She made her Broadway debut in 1947 and eventually appeared on the stage in several Shakespearean productions. She also directed the play 'Ways and Means' (1967) and was John Houseman's assistant on the TV special 'A Night at Ford's Theater.' A chic, cool blonde, in films she typically portrayed aloof, sophisticated ladies, often fragile, sometimes neurotic. She has appeared in numerous TV productions in addition to many films and plays, including the series 'Shadow Chasers' (1985–86).

FILMS INCLUDE: *The Return of the Vampire* 1943; *Cry of the Werewolf, Shadows in the Night* 1944; *A Song to Remember, My Name Is Julia Ross, I Love a Mystery, Escape in the Fog* 1945; *Johnny O'Clock, The Guilt of Janet Ames* 1947; *The Dark Past, The Undercover Man, Johnny Allegro* 1949; *An American in Paris, St. Benny the Dip* 1951; *Scaramouche* (as Marie Antoinette), *Young Man with Ideas* 1952; *Sombrero* 1953; *Executive Suite* 1954; *You're Never Too Young, Illegal* 1955; *The Ten Commandments* 1956; *Three Brave Men* 1957; *Cash McCall, Spartacus* 1960; *Such Good Friends* 1971; *Salty, Mahogany* 1975; *Jennifer* 1978; *Rich and Famous* 1981; *Nomads* 1986; *Dixie Lanes* 1988; *Skin Deep* 1989; *Sliver* 1993; *It's My Party* 1996, *Til There Was You* 1997.

focus. The point at which an image obtains maximum definition in relation to the camera lens. Optically, it is the point of convergence or divergence of light rays on the lens. An image that is sharp and well defined is said to be "in focus," as opposed to a fuzzy, ill-defined, "out-of-focus" image. To secure an in-focus image, the distance from camera to object must be measured and the lens adjusted accordingly. See also FOCAL LENGTH, FOCUS PULLER, FOLLOW FOCUS.

focus puller. A member of the camera crew, usually the first assistant cameraman, whose job it is to adjust the lens in FOLLOW FOCUS situations. Prior to actual shooting, he measures and marks the distance between the lens and significant points in a TRAVELING SHOT, so that a smooth follow focus can be achieved during the TAKE.

fog. Unwanted density appearing on exposed film as a result of exposure to extraneous light, glare from the camera lens, the aging of raw stock, unsuitable storage or processing conditions, etc.

fog filter. A diffusing filter that is placed in front of a camera lens to produce a misty effect resembling fog. Simulated fog on a set can also be obtained with a fog gun, a portable device that heats and vaporizes air.

Foley artist. A member of the sound crew who, during a film's postproduction, creates certain sound effects heard on the EFFECTS TRACK, particularly those made by people rather than machines or natural objects. These may include kisses, punches, footsteps on different terrain with the appropriate shoes, and movement of fabrics.

Foley, James. Director, screenwriter. Born in New York City. *ed.* New York University; University of Southern California. A hip, spirited director who is very often involved with writing his own scripts, often giving himself a bit role. His major successes have been primarily thrillers or comedies with the exception of his polished direction of the ensemble piece *Glengarry Glen Ross* (1992), displaying his versatility with drama.

FILMS: *Reckless* 1984; *At Close Range* (also act.) 1985; *Who's That Girl?* 1987; *After Dark, My Sweet* (also sc.) 1990; *Glengarry Glen Ross* 1992; *Two Bits* 1995; *Fear, The Chamber* (also sc.) 1996.

follow focus. The continuous adjustment of the camera lens while shooting is in progress to accommodate the relative movement between camera and subject without loss of sharp focus. This becomes necessary whenever camera movement or subject movement causes a subject to move out of the DEPTH OF FIELD. See also FOCUS, FOCUS PULLER.

follow shot. A SHOT in which the camera moves about, following the action of a scene or the movement of a subject from one point to another. This can be done with any camera movement technique, such as a PAN, a TILT, a DOLLY SHOT, a TRACKING SHOT, or with a stationary camera by using a ZOOM LENS.

Folsey, George. Director of photography. *b.* 1898, New York City. *d.* 1990. Entered films at 14 as an office boy at the Lasky Players New York headquarters and at 15 became an assistant cameraman. Made his first film, as a lighting cameraman, at 19, taking over the duties of an absent director of photography, and went on to become one of Hollywood's leading cinematographers. He was among the trend setters in the gradual switch from harsh contrast to subtler, more softly lighted black-and-white cinematography. He was responsible for the remarkable photography of Mamoulian's *Applause* (1929) and was behind the camera on many glossy MGM productions in the 30s, 40s, and 50s. His son, George Folsey, Jr. (*b.* Jan. 17, 1939, Los Angeles), is a film editor and producer.

FILMS INCLUDE: *His Bridal Night* 1919; *The Fear Market, Sinners* 1920; *The Price of Possession* 1921; *The Bright Shawl* 1923; *The Enchanted Cottage* 1924; *Scarlet Saint* 1925; *The Savage* 1926; *American Beauty* 1927; *Lady Be Good* 1928; *Glorifying the American Girl, The Letter, Applause, The Cocoanuts* 1929; *Laughter, The Big Pond, Animal Crackers* 1930; *My Sin, The Cheat, The Smiling Lieutenant, The Royal Family of Broadway* 1931; *The Big Broadcast* 1932; *Reunion in Vienna, Going Hollywood* 1933; *Men in White, Operator* 13 1934; *Reckless* 1935; *The Great Ziegfeld* (co-phot.), *The Gorgeous Hussy* 1936; *The Last of Mrs. Cheyney* 1937; *Mannequin, The Shining Hour* 1938; *Million Dollar Legs, Remember?* 1939; *Come Live with Me* 1941; *A Guy Named Joe* (co-phot.), *Meet Me in St. Louis* 1944; *The Clock* 1945; *The Green Years, The Harvey Girls, Till the Clouds Roll By, The Ziegfeld Follies* 1946; *Green Dolphin Street* 1947; *State of the Union* 1948; *Take Me Out to the Ball Game, Adam's Rib* 1949; *Malaya, A Life of Her Own* 1950; *Night Into Morning, The Man with a Cloak* 1951; *Million Dollar Mermaid* 1952; *All the Brothers Were Valiant* 1953; *Executive Suite, Seven Brides for Seven Brothers* 1954; *The Cobweb* 1955; *Forbidden Planet, The Fastest Gun Alive* 1956; *Tip on a Dead Jockey* 1957; *Saddle the Wind, Imitation General* 1958; *Cash McCall* 1960; *The Balcony* 1963; *Glass Houses* 1972; *That's Entertainment Part II* (new sequences) 1976.

Fonda, Bridget. Actress. Born in 1964 in Los Angeles. *ed.* NYU (theater), Lee Strasberg Institute, New York. Slender, dynamic film lead of the late 1980s and 1990s. Scion of FONDA acting family (daughter of Peter, granddaughter of Henry), she has established herself as a multifaceted player in thrillers, dramas, and comedies. She projects modern-day confidence and sexuality, often with an undercurrent of soul-searching, similar to the persona of Barbara Stanwyck in an earlier era. She gained national prominence through her performance as cocky escort Mandy Rice-Davies in *Scandal*.

FILMS INCLUDE: *Aria, You Can't Hurry Love, Shag* 1988; *Scandal, Strapless* 1989; *The Godfather Part III, Roger Corman's Frankenstein Unbound* 1990; *Drop Dead Fred, Leather Jackets, Iron Maze, Out of the Rain, Doc Hollywood* 1991; *Single White Female, Singles* 1992; *Bodies Rest and Motion, Point of No Return, Army of Darkness* 1993; *Camilla, It Could Happen to You, Little Buddha, The Road to Wellville* 1994; *Balto* (v/o) 1995; *City Hall, Grace of My Heart* 1996; *Rough Magic, Touch* 1997.

Fonda, Henry. Actor. *b.* May 16, 1905, Grand Island, Nebr., a descendant of early Dutch settlers who founded the town of Fonda in upstate New York. *d.* 1982. When he was six months old, the family moved to Omaha, where his father set up a printing shop. Intending to become a newspaperman, young Fonda enrolled at the University of Minnesota as a journalism major but dropped out after two years and became an office boy at an Omaha credit company. In 1925 he was asked by a friend of the family, the mother of the then one-year-old Marlon Brando, to play the leading role in an amateur production at the Omaha Community Playhouse. He quit his office-boy job and stayed with the company for three years, receiving a small salary for doubling as the manager's assistant. In 1928, while he was playing a lead in New England summer stock, his path crossed that of a group of young theater aspirants who formed their own company to while away their summer vacation. Fonda joined the group, which included Joshua Logan, Myron McCormick, and later also Margaret Sullavan, Mildred Natwick, and James Stewart.

Fonda played a walk-on part in a Broadway play in 1929 and bit roles, but it was with the University Players that he developed his style. His leading lady was usually Margaret SULLAVAN, whom he married in 1931. They divorced in 1933. In 1934, Fonda played his first important Broadway part in the first edition of 'New Faces.' The same year he reaped enthusiastic notices for the title role in 'The Farmer Takes a Wife,' then went to Hollywood to repeat the role on the screen. Fonda's rise in films was meteoric. Within a year or two the shy young man, who shared a bachelor apartment with James Stewart, now another newcomer to Hollywood, was an established star and by the end of the decade internationally famous and admired.

Fonda's engaging sincerity, natural style of delivery, and characteristically "American" personality proved ideal for the screen. Through such personal landmarks as *The Trail of the Lonesome Pine, You Only Live Once,* and *Spawn of the North,* he reached the peak of his early Hollywood career with *Young Mr. Lincoln* and *The Grapes of Wrath.* He then demonstrated his versatility by playing comedy roles in *The Lady Eve, The Male Animal,* and *The Magnificent Dope.*

On the personal side, Fonda married the socially prominent Frances Seymour Brokaw in 1936. The marriage produced two children, Jane and Peter FONDA, both of whom were to become film stars in the 60s. (Peter's daughter Bridget FONDA became a film star in the 80s and 90s.) The marriage ended in tragedy in 1950, when Mrs. Fonda committed suicide in a rest home after suffering a mental collapse. Fonda subsequently married and divorced twice and in 1966 he married the vivacious Shirlee Adams, a former airline stewardess and model, his fifth wife. In 1942, Fonda enlisted for service with the Navy. He was later commissioned and served in the Pacific as an assistant operation and air combat intelligence officer. Lieutenant Fonda was awarded a Bronze Star and a Presidential Citation.

Fonda returned to Hollywood experienced and matured and the change was evident in his first postwar roles, in John Ford's *My Darling Clementine, The Fugitive,* and *Fort Apache,* and in Anatole Litvak's *The Long Night.* In 1948 he scored his greatest stage triumph, playing the title role in Broadway's 'Mister Roberts.' He stayed with the play for three years in New York and on the road. He repeated his stage role in the film version of *Mister Roberts.* His several Broadway appearances during the intervening period included 'The Caine Mutiny Court-Martial.' From the mid-50s on, Fonda alternated between screen and stage, to the appreciation of both film and theater audiences. He also starred in the TV series 'The Deputy' (1959–61) and 'The Smith Family' (1971–72) as well as in TV specials and such TV films as 'The Red Pony' and 'Clarence Darrow.' In 1978, Fonda received the Life Achievement Award by the American Film Institute. Gravely ill during the production of his last film, *On Golden Pond* (1981), Fonda was paid homage during the Oscar ceremonies that year (for 1980) with an honorary Academy Award for "the consummate actor, in recognition of his brilliant accomplishments and enduring contribution to the art of motion pictures." Just months before his death the following year, he won the Oscar as best actor for his glowing performance in that film.

FILMS: *The Farmer Takes a Wife, Way Down East, I Dream Too Much* 1935; *The Trail of the Lonesome Pine, The Moon's Our Home, Spendthrift* 1936; *You Only Live Once, Wings of the Morning, Slim, That Certain Woman* 1937; *I Met My Love Again, Jezebel, Blockade, Spawn of the North, The Mad Miss Manton* 1938; *Jesse James* (as Frank James), *Let Us Live, The Story of Alexander Graham Bell* (as Bell's associate, Thomas Augustus Watson), *Young Mr. Lincoln* (as Abraham Lincoln), *Drums Along the Mohawk* 1939; *The Grapes of Wrath* (as Tom Joad), *Lillian Russell, The Return of Frank James* (again as Frank James), *Chad Hanna* 1940; *The Lady Eve, Wild Geese Calling, You Belong to Me* 1941; *The Male Animal, Rings on Her Fingers, The Magnificent Dope, Tales of Manhattan, The Big Street* 1942; *The Immortal Sergeant, The Ox-Bow Incident* 1943; *My Darling Clementine* (as Wyatt Earp) 1946; *The Long Night, The Fugitive, Daisy Kenyon* 1947; *A Miracle Can Happen/On Our Merry Way, Fort Apache* 1948; *Jigsaw* (cameo) 1949; *Mister Roberts* (title role) 1955; *War and Peace* (as Pierre) 1956; *The Wrong Man, 12 Angry Men* (also co-prod.), *The Tin Star* 1957; *Stage Struck* 1958; *Warlock, The Man Who Understood Women* 1959; *Advise and Consent, The Longest Day* (as Brig. Gen. Theodore Roosevelt, Jr.) *How the West Was Won* 1962; *Spencer's Mountain* 1963; *The Best Man, Fail Safe* (as "The President"), *Sex and the Single Girl* 1964; *The Rounders, In Harm's Way, Battle of the Bulge, Guerre secrète/The Dirty Game* (Fr.) 1965; *A Big Hand for the Little Lady* 1966; *Welcome to Hard Times, Stranger on the Run* (originally made for TV) 1967; *Firecreek, Madigan, Yours Mine and Ours, The Boston Strangler, C'era una volta il West/Once Upon a Time in the West* (It./US) 1969; *The Cheyenne Social Club, There Was a Crooked Man. . . , Too Late the Hero* 1970; *Sometimes a Great Notion/Never Give an Inch* 1971; *Le Serpent/The Serpent* (Fr./Ger.), *Il Mio Nome e Nessuno/My Name Is Nobody* (It./Ger.), *Ash Wednesday* 1973; *Mussolini: Ultimo Atto/Mussolini: The Last Act/Mussolini: The Last Four Days* 1974; *Midway* (as Admiral Chester W. Nimitz), *The Last of the Cowboys/The Great Smokey Roadblock* 1976; *Tentacoli/Tentacles* (It.), *Il Grande Attaco/La Battaglia di Mareth/The Biggest Battle* (It.), *Rollercoaster* 1977; *The Swarm, Fedora* (cameo; Ger./It.) 1978; *Meteor, City on Fire* (Can.), *Wanda Nevada* 1979; *On Golden Pond* 1981.

Fonda, Jane. Actress. Born on Dec. 21, 1937, in New York City. *ed.* Vassar. The daughter of Henry FONDA, she was brought up on the West Coast until she was ten. When their father came to New York to appear in 'Mister Roberts,' she and brother Peter FONDA moved to a grandmother's home in Greenwich, Conn. Although Jane had occasional parts in school plays, she showed little interest in acting but agreed to appear with her father in the 1954 Omaha Community Theatre production of *The Country Girl.* Growing restless during her college days at Vassar, she went to Paris to study art. When she returned to New York, she took up modeling and twice made the cover of *Vogue*. A meeting with Lee Strasberg in 1958 led to studies at the Actors Studio and to a sudden passion for acting. In 1960 she made both her Broadway and Hollywood debuts and was immediately recognized as a potential star.

In 1965 she married French director Roger VADIM, the Svengali of sex goddesses, who tried to mold her into another Bardot, his effort culminating in the bizarre futuristic comic-book erotica *Barbarella* (1968).

In the late 60s, Fonda returned to the US and immediately plunged into fervent social activism, championing a variety of anti-Establishment causes and getting into trouble with the authorities over her actions on behalf of Black Panthers, Native Americans, and reluctant GIs. As part of her campaign to end the war in Southeast Asia, she formed with actor Donald Sutherland the Anti-War Troupe, which toured military camps in defiance of the Pentagon. She co-produced and co-wrote *F.T.A.* (*Free the Army,* 1972), a filmed record of the tour. With her second husband (1973–1990), antiwar militant Tom Hayden, and Haskell Wexler, she co-directed a documentary, *Introduction to the Enemy* (1974), an account of her controversial visit to North Vietnam. Her activities earned her the pejorative moniker "Hanoi Jane."

In 1969 she was nominated for an Oscar and won the New York Film Critics best actress award for her performance as a 1930s marathon dancer in *They Shoot Horses, Don't They?* She won the Academy Award as best actress, as well as another New York Critics award, for her performance as a brittle New York call girl in *Klute* (1971). In the late 70s, she returned to participation in the commercial cinema. She was nominated for a best actress Academy Award for *Julia* (1977) and captured her second Oscar as best actress for *Coming Home* (1978), a film dealing with the aftermath of the Vietnam War. Additional Academy Award nominations, for *The China Syndrome* (1979), *On Golden Pond* (1981) and *The Morning After* (1986) followed. *On Golden Pond* was her first pairing with her father, with whom she had had strained relations, and marked at least a symbolic reconciliation between the two.

In 1981, she ushered in an era of self-betterment through exercise (as well as an era of celebrity exercise books) with the publication of *Jane Fonda's Workout Book*, and accompanying record and videotape. Several exercise videotape sequels followed, amassing a fortune for her and making her the fitness guru of the 1980s.

In 1982, she helped finance her then-husband's election to the California State Assembly. In a 1988 TV interview, she apologized to Vietnam veterans and their families for posing at the controls of a North Vietnamese anti-aircraft gun during her 1972 visit to Hanoi. In 1991, she married broadcasting mogul Ted TURNER. She continued to appear in and produce films until she announced her retirement from acting in the early 90s.

FILMS: *Tall Story* 1960; *Walk on the Wild Side, The Chapman Report, Period of Adjustment* 1962; *In the Cool of the Day* 1963; *Sunday in New York, Les Félins/Joy House/The Love Cage* (Fr.), *La Ronde/Circle of Love* (Fr./It.) 1964; *Cat Ballou* 1965; *The Chase, La Curée/The Game Is Over* (Fr./It.), *Any Wednesday* 1966; *Hurry Sundown, Barefoot in the Park* 1967; *Histories extraordinaires/Spirits of the Dead* (Fr./It.), *Barbarella* (Fr./It.) 1968; *They Shoot Horses Don't They?* 1969; *Klute* 1971; *Tout va bien* (Fr.), *F.T.A./Free the Army* (also co-prod., co-sc.) 1972; *Steelyard Blues, A Doll's House* (as Nora) 1973; *Introduction to the Enemy* (doc.; co-dir. with Tom Hayden and Haskell Wexler) 1974; *The Blue Bird* (US/USSR) 1976; *Fun with Dick and Jane, Julia* (as writer Lillian Hellman) 1977; *Coming Home, Comes a Horseman, California Suite* 1978; *The Electric Horseman, The China Syndrome* 1979; *No Nukes, 9 to 5* 1980; *Rollover, On Golden Pond* 1981; *Agnes of God* 1985; *The Morning After* 1986; *Old Gringo* (also prod.), *Stanley and Iris* 1989.

Fonda, Peter. Actor, producer, director. Born on Feb. 23, 1939, in New York City. The son of Henry FONDA and brother of Jane FONDA, he was drawn to acting while still a boy. He scored his first success playing the lead in a school production of 'Harvey' as a student at the University of Omaha and made his Broadway debut in 1961 in 'Blood Sweat and Stanley Poole.' In films since 1963, he at first played nondescript "squares." The motorbike-riding "hippie" rebel image that he began cultivating in *The Wild Angels* (1966) culminated in the phenomenally successful *Easy Rider* (1969), which he also produced and co-scripted. In 1971 he directed his first film, *The Hired Hand,* a lyrical Western in which he also starred. In the 1980s he appeared mainly in low-grade, cheaply made productions. His daughter, Bridget FONDA (*b.* 1964), is a leading lady of Hollywood films.

FILMS (as actor): *Tammy and the Doctor, The Victors* 1963; *Lilith, The Young Lovers* 1964; *The Wild Angels* 1966; *The Trip* 1967; *Histories extraordinaries/Spirits of the Dead* (Fr./It.) 1968; *Easy Rider* (also prod., sc.) 1969; *The Hired Hand* (also dir.), *The Last Movie* 1971; *Two People* 1972; *Dirty Mary Crazy Larry, Open Season* 1974; *Idaho Transfer* (dir. only), *Race with the Devil, 92 in the Shade, Killer Force/The Diamond Mercenaries* 1975; *Futureworld, Fighting Mad* 1976; *Outlaw Blues* 1977; *High-ballin'* 1978; *Wanda Nevada* (also dir.) 1979; *The Cannonball Run* 1981; *Split Image* 1982; *Diajobu My Friend/All Right My Friend* (Jap.), *Dance of the Dwarfs/Jungle Heat, Spasms/Death Bite* (Can.) 1983; *Peppermint Frieden/Peppermint Freedom* (Ger.) 1984; *Certain Fury* 1985; *Mercenary Fighters* 1988; *Fatal Mission, The Rose Garden* (Ger./US) 1989; *Family Spirit, Reckless* 1991; *Bodies Rest and Motion, Deadfall, South Beach* 1993; *Love and a .45, Molly & Gina, Nadja* 1994; *Escape from L.A., Grace of My Heart* 1996; *Ulee's Gold* 1997.

Fong, Allen (Fong Yu-ping, Fong Yuk-ping). Director. Born on July 10, 1947 in Hong Kong. *ed.* Hong Kong Baptist College, USC (film). Inventive Hong Kong director best known for autobiographical family story, *Father and Son.* Member of the Feng Huang Motion Picture Company.

FILMS INCLUDE: *Father and Son* 1981; *Meiguo xin/Just Like the Weather* (also act.), *Aiqing Qianfeng Xunhao/Working Title* 1986; *Life Is Cheap. . . But Toilet Paper Is Expensive* (act. only) 1989; *Dancing Bull* (also pr.) 1990.

Fontaine, Joan. Actress. Born Joan de Beauvoir de Havilland, on Oct. 22, 1917, Tokyo, to British parents. In the US from childhood, she trailed far behind sister Olivia DE HAVILLAND in her early career. As Joan Burfield, she appeared with various West Coast stage companies and in 1935 made her screen debut under that name in a minor role, supporting Joan Crawford in MGM's *No More Ladies.* She then returned to the stage and it wasn't until 1937 that she began appearing regularly in films, mostly RKO B pictures, with the exception of *A Damsel in Distress,* in which she partnered with Fred Astaire, and *Gunga Din,* in which she was Douglas Fairbanks, Jr.'s, love interest. It was not until the early 40s that her career took off, thanks to leads in two Hitchcock films. She was nominated for an Oscar for *Rebecca* (1940), and *The Constant Nymph* (1943), and won the Academy Award, as well as the New York Film Critics Award, for her performance in *Suspicion* (1941).

Fontaine subsequently starred in numerous films, at first as innocent, refined heroines and later as sophisticated, sometimes bitchy and scheming, worldly women. In the 40s and 50s she had many real or imagined well-publicized feuds with sister Olivia. The first three of her four husbands were actor Brian AHERNE (1939–45), producer William Dozier (1946–51), and producer-screenwriter Collier Young (1952–61). A highly accomplished woman, she is a licensed pilot, champion balloonist, prize-winning tuna fisherman, and an expert golfer, as well as a licensed interior decorator and a Cordon Bleu cook. Autobiography: *No Bed of Roses* (1978).

FILMS: As Joan Burfield—*No More Ladies* 1935. As Joan Fontaine—*Quality Street, The Man Who Found Himself, You Can't Beat Love, Music for Madame, A Damsel in Distress, A Million to One* 1937; *Maid's Night Out, Blonde Cheat, Sky Giant, The Duke of West Point* 1938; *Gunga Din, Man of Conquest, The Women* 1939; *Rebecca* 1940; *Suspicion* 1941; *This Above All* 1942; *The Constant Nymph* 1943; *Jane Eyre* (title role), *Frenchman's Creek* 1944; *The Affairs of Susan* 1945; *From This Day Forward* 1946; *Ivy* 1947; *The Emperor Waltz, Kiss the Blood Off My Hands, Letter from an Unknown Woman, You Gotta Stay Happy* 1948; *Born to Be Bad* 1950; *September Affair, Darling How Could You!* 1951; *Something to Live For, Ivanhoe* (as Lady Rowena; UK/US) 1952; *Decameron Nights* (UK), *Flight to Tangier, The Bigamist* 1953; *Casanova's Big Night* 1954; *Othello* (extra) 1955; *Serenade, Beyond a Reasonable Doubt* 1956; *Island in the Sun, Until They Sail* 1957; *South Pacific* (extra), *A Certain Smile* 1958; *Voyage to the Bottom of the Sea* 1961; *Tender Is the Night* 1962; *The Witches/The Devil's Own* (UK) 1966.

Fontanne, Lynn. See LUNT, Alfred.

footage. In the broadest sense, any length of film—a shot, a scene, a sequence. More precisely, the length of film in terms of feet. Film length is commonly measured in feet in the US, the UK, and many other members of the Commonwealth. But in most other countries it is measured in meters; hence the French equivalent of footage is *métrage.* Sixteen frames make up a foot of 35 mm. At 24-frames-per second normal sound speed, one-and-a-half feet of film (or one foot and eight frames) take up one second of screen time. In one minute, 90 feet are shown; in 60 minutes 5,400 feet, etc. In 16 mm, where one foot equals 40 frames, the calculation is less simple. At 24-feet-per-second normal sound speed, 24 frames are shown in a one-second screen duration, 36 feet in a minute, and 2,160 feet in an hour. Of course, when film footage is obtained at camera speeds other than 24 frames per second, the above calculation guides do not apply.

FOOTAGE TABLE

	35 mm (24 f.p.s.) 1 Foot = 16 Frames		16 mm (24 f.p.s.) 1 Foot = 40 Frames	
SECONDS	FEET	FRAMES	FEET	FRAMES
1	1	8	—	24
2	3	—	1	8
3	4	8	1	32
4	6	—	2	16
5	7	8	3	—
10	15	—	6	10
30	45	—	18	—
MINUTES				
1	90	—	36	—
5	450	—	180	—
10	900	—	360	—
30	2,700	—	1,080	—
60	5,400	—	2,160	—

footage counter. A gauge device attached to a camera or a variety of other pieces of film equipment. It measures the amount of film exposed, printed, viewed, etc., in terms of feet. Fractions are expressed in frames rather than in parts of feet.

Foote, Horton. Screenwriter, playwright, producer. Born on Mar. 14, 1916, in Wharton, Tex. He began as a stage actor before turning his attention to play-writing. Considered one of the great American writers, Foote is effortless in his ability to write for both stage and screen. Drawing upon his childhood in southeast Texas, he wrote 'The Orphan's Home,' a series of nine plays chronicling the lives of four generations, yielding several film adaptations and critical praise. He received Academy Awards for his adaptation of Harper Lee's classic novel *To Kill a Mockingbird* (1962) and for *Tender Mercies* (1983), and was again nominated for *The Trip to Bountiful* (1985). He is the father of actors Hallie Foote and Horton Foote, Jr.

FILMS: *Storm Fear* 1956; *To Kill a Mockingbird* 1962; *Baby the Rain Must Fall* 1965; *The Chase* 1966; *Hurry Sundown* 1967; *Tomorrow* 1972; *Tender Mercies* (also co-prod.) 1983; *1918* (also co-prod.), *The Trip to Bountiful* (from his own play; also co-prod.) 1985; *On Valentine's Day* (from his own play, 'Valentine's Day') 1986; *Convicts* (co-prod., from his own play) 1991; *Of Mice and Men* (scr.) 1992.

Foran, Dick. Actor. *b.* John Nicholas Foran, June 18, 1910, Flemington, N.J. *d.* 1979. *ed.* Princeton. The son of a prominent New Jersey businessman who later became a US senator, he had intended to become a geologist but was attracted to singing and started his show business career as a radio and band vocalist. He made his screen debut in 1934 and appeared in several Fox B features as Nick Foran before changing his first name to Dick. Moving over to Warner Bros., he soon became established as the singing hero of a string of low-budget Westerns. He also played leads in many of the studio's minor dramatic features and second leads and supporting roles in major productions. In all, he appeared in nearly 100 films at various studios in a career that spanned four decades, as well as in many TV programs.

FILMS INCLUDE: *Stand Up and Cheer, Gentlemen Are Born* 1934; *Accent on Youth, Dangerous, Moonlight on the Prairie* 1935; *The Petrified Forest, Song of the Saddle, Treachery Rides the Range* 1936; *Black Legion, Guns of the Pecos, Cherokee Strip, She Loved a Fireman* 1937; *Over the Wall, Cowboy from Brooklyn, Four Daughters, Boy Meets Girl, The Sisters, Heart of the North* 1938; *Daughters Courageous, Four Wives* 1939; *Winners of the West* (serial), *My Little Chickadee, The Mummy's Hand, The House of Seven Gables* 1940; *Riders of Death Valley* (serial), *Four Mothers, Horror Island, In the Navy, Mob Town* 1941; *Ride 'Em Cowboy, Private Buckaroo, The Mummy's Tomb* 1942; *He's My Guy* 1943; *Guest Wife* 1945; *Fort Apache* 1948; *El Paso* 1949; *Al Jennings of Oklahoma* 1951; *Chicago Confidential* 1957; *Atomic Submarine* 1959; *Studs Lonigan* 1960; *Donovan's Reef* 1963; *Taggart* 1964; *Brighty of Grand Canyon* 1967.

Forbes, Bryan. Director, producer, screenwriter, former actor. Born John Theobald Clarke, on July 22, 1926, in Stratford-at-Bow, London, England. *ed.* Royal Academy of Dramatic Arts. On the stage from age 17, he made his screen acting debut in 1948, following service with British Army Intelligence. Became a screenwriter in the mid-50s and a director in the early 60s. At his best, his work is intelligent, mature, and subtly understated, but it has often bordered on pretentiousness. In 1969 he was appointed chief of production and managing director of Associated British (EMI) but resigned in 1971. Forbes is the author of several novels, a collection of short stories, and an autobiography, *Notes for a Life* (1974). He married actresses Constance Smith (1951–54) and Nanette NEWMAN (from 1954).

FILMS INCLUDE: As Actor—*The Small Back Room* 1948; *The Wooden Horse* 1950; *The World in His Arms* (US) 1952; *The Million Pound Note/Man with a Million* 1953; *An Inspector Calls, The Colditz Story* 1954; *The Baby and the Battleship* (also sc.), *Satellite in the Sky* 1956; *The Key, I Was Monty's Double* (also sc.) 1958; *The League of Gentlemen* (also sc.) 1960; *The Guns of Navarone* 1961; *A Shot in the Dark* 1964; *Restless Natives* (cameo) 1985. As screenwriter—*Cockleshell Heroes* 1955; *House of Secrets* 1956; *The Captain's Table* 1959; *The Angry Silence* (also co-prod.), *Man in the Moon* 1960; *Only Two Can Play* 1962; *Of Human Bondage* (also dir. addnl. scenes) 1964; *Hopscotch* (US) 1980. As director (complete)—*Whistle Down the Wind* (also co-exec. prod.) 1961; *The L-Shaped Room* (also sc.) 1962; *Seance on a Wet Afternoon* (also co-prod., sc.) 1964; *King Rat* (also sc.; US) 1965; *The Wrong Box* (also prod.) 1966; *The Whisperers* (also sc.) 1967; *Deadfall* (also sc.) 1968; *The Madwoman of Chaillot* 1969; *The Raging Moon/Long Ago Tomorrow* (also sc.) 1971; *The Stepford Wives* (US) 1975; *The Slipper and the Rose* (also co-sc.) 1976; *International Velvet* (also sc., prod.) 1978; *Les Séducteurs/Sunday Lovers* (British episode; Fr./It.) 1980; *Ménage à Trois/Better Late Than Never* (also sc.) 1982; *The Naked Face* (also sc.) 1984.

Forbes, Mary. Actress. *b.* Jan. 1, 1883, London. *d.* 1974. A veteran of the British stage, she played character parts in scores of Hollywood films and some Broadway plays, typically as a stately society matron. She was the mother of actress Brenda Forbes and actor Ralph FORBES. Retired in the late 40s and lived to the ripe age of 91. Not to be confused with actress Mary Elizabeth Forbes (1880–1964), who appeared in a few Hollywood silents.

FILMS INCLUDE: *Women Who Win* (UK) 1919; *The Child Thou Gavest Me* 1921; *Her Private Life, The Thirteenth Chair, Sunny Side Up, The Trespasser* 1929; *So This Is London, Holiday, East Is West* 1930; *Chances* 1931; *The Silent Witness, A Farewell to Arms* 1932; *Cavalcade, Bombshell* 1933; *Happiness Ahead* 1934; *Les Miserables, Anna Karenina, Captain Blood* 1935; *Another Dawn, Wee Willie Winkie, The Awful Truth* 1937; *You Can't Take It with You* 1938; *You Can't Cheat an Honest Man, The Adventures of Sherlock Holmes* 1939; *Nothing but the Truth* 1941; *Tender Comrade, Jane Eyre* 1944; *The Picture of Dorian Gray* 1945; *Terror by Night* 1946; *Ivy, The Exile* 1947; *You Gotta Stay Happy* 1948.

Forbes, Ralph. Actor. *b.* Ralph Taylor, Sept. 30, 1902, London. *d.* 1951. The son of Mary FORBES, he appeared on the British stage from childhood and in films from 1921. Arriving in Hollywood in 1926, after completing his university studies, he starred in many silents and early talkies, then played supporting roles. At one time he was married to Ruth CHATTERTON and later to Heather ANGEL.

FILMS INCLUDE: In the UK—*The Fifth Form at St. Dominic's* 1921; *Comin' Through the Rye* 1922. In the US—*Beau Geste* (as John Geste) 1926; *Mr. Wu, The Enemy* 1927; *The Latest from Paris, The Trail of '98, The Actress, Under the Black Eagle, The Whip, The Masks of the Devil, Restless Youth* 1928; *Lilies of the Field, The Green Goddess, Mamba, The Lady of Scandal, Inside the Lines, Her Wedding Night* 1930; *Beau Ideal* (title role), *The Bachelor Father* 1931; *Thunder Below, Smilin' Through* 1932; *Christopher Strong, Pleasure Cruise, The Phantom Broadcast, The Solitaire Man, The Avenger* 1933; *The Mystery of Mr. X, Riptide, Twentieth Century, The Barretts of Wimpole Street* 1934; *The Goose and the Gander, The Three Musketeers* (as the Duke of Buckingham) 1935; *Mary of Scotland, Romeo and Juliet* (as Paris), *Piccadilly Jim* 1936; *The Last of Mrs. Cheyney, Make a Wish* 1937; *Women Are Like That, Kidnapped, If I Were King* 1938; *The Hound of the Baskervilles, The Magnificent Fraud, The Private Lives of Elizabeth and Essex, Tower of London* (as Henry Tudor) 1939; *Curtain Call* 1940; *Frenchman's Creek* 1944.

forced perspective. A set design technique to create the illusion of increased depth. Foreground elements are constructed full-size, while background elements (mountains, buildings, etc.) are made small on such a scale as to give the appearance of great distance.

Ford, Aleksander (also **Alexander).** Director. *b.* Nov. 24, 1908, Lodz, Poland. *d.* 1980. *ed.* Warsaw U. A leading figure in the development of Polish cinema, he directed Polish films both before and after WW II. He began directing shorts in 1929 and full-length documentaries and feature films in 1930. In 1934 he went to Palestine to direct the film *Sabra.* He spent the WW II years in the Soviet Union, where he organized, with Jerzy Bossak, the Polish army's film unit, of which he was appointed chief. In 1945, after the nationalization of the Polish film industry, he was appointed the director of Film Polski, the government-run film organization. He was among the founders of the Lodz film school and for several years served as that revered institution's head. He later resumed directing, while also devoting time to the instruction and guidance of young filmmakers. He won a medal at the 1948 Venice Festival for *Border Street,* a story of the Warsaw Ghetto, and an award at Cannes in 1954 for *Five from Barska Street.* His *Knights of the Teutonic Order* (1960), a historic epic, was Poland's most expensive production to that date. During the 60s Ford experienced increasing difficulties in realizing his projects. His rift with Polish authorities culminated in 1969, when he emigrated to Israel. He later worked in Denmark and Germany, and died in Los Angeles.

FILMS: *At Dawn, Lodz—the Polish Manchester* (both shorts) 1929; *The Mascot* 1930; *Legion of the Streets* 1932; *Sabra/Chalutzim* (in Palestine), *Awakening* 1934; *Forward Cooperation* (doc.) 1935; *Road of Youth/Street of the Young/Children Must Laugh* 1936; *People of the Vistula* (co-dir.) 1937; *Maidanek* (short; co-dir.) 1944; *The Battle of Kolberg* (short; co-dir.) 1945; *Border Street* (also co-sc.) 1948; *Young Chopin* (also sc.) 1952; *Five from Barska Street* (also co-sc.) 1953; *The Eighth Day of the Week* (also sc.) 1958; *Kryzacy/The Knights of the Teutonic Order/Knights of the Black Cross* (also co-sc.) 1960; *The First Day of Freedom* 1964; *Der Arzt stellt fest/Angeklagt nach Paragraph 218/The Doctor Says/The Doctor Speaks Out* (sex ed. film; Switz./Ger.) 1966; *Good Morning Poland* (doc.) 1970; *The First Circle* (also sc.; Den./Ger.) 1972; *Der Martyrer/Sie sind frei Doktor Korczak/The Martyr* (Ger./Isr.) 1975.

Ford, Francis. Director, actor, screenwriter. *b.* Francis O'Feeney (O'Fearna). Aug. 15, 1882, Portland, Me. *d.* 1953. *ed.* Maine U. The older brother and mentor of John FORD, he began his career as an actor with various stock companies and occasionally appeared on Broadway. He entered films as an actor with Edison in 1907, later moving to Vitagraph and finally to Universal, where he became a director of shorts and action serials in 1913, in many of which he also starred. His regular co-star and co-writer was actress Grace CUNARD, whom he married in 1913. Ford, who had changed his surname while a stage actor, gave his brother John his adopted surname and first opportunity in films. It was as Francis's assistant that John Ford learned the rudiments of film technique. Years later, when Francis's career as director waned, the roles were reversed, Francis becoming a frequent character player in John's pictures as well as those of other directors, typically as a grizzly old-timer. His son, Philip Ford (*b.* Oct. 16, 1902, Portland, Me., *d.* 1976), directed a number of low-budget films in the late 40s and early 50s, as well as many TV programs.

FILMS INCLUDE: As director—*The Invaders* (co-dir. with Thomas H. Ince; also act.), *The Army Surgeon* (also act.) 1912; *When Lincoln Paid* (also act.), *The Favorite Son* (also act.), *Wynona's Vengeance* (also act.) 1913; *Washington at Valley Forge* (also co-sc., act.), *The Phantom Violin* (also act.), *Lucille Love—the Girl of Mystery* (serial; also co-sc., act.), *The Mysterious Rose* (also act.) 1914; *Three Bad Men and a Girl* (also act.), *The Hidden City* (also act.), *And They Called Him Hers, The Doorway of Destruction* (also act.), *The Broken Coin* (serial; also act.), *The Campbells Are Coming* (also prod., act.) 1915; *The Lumber Yard Gang* (also act.), *Chicken-Hearted Jim* (also sc., act.), *And They Called Him Hero, The Adventures of Peg o' the Ring* (serial; co-dir. with Jacques Jaccard; also act.), *The Bandit's Wager* (also act.) 1916; *The Purple Mask* (serial; also act.) 1916–17; *The Trail of Hate* (also sc.), *John Ermine of Yellowstone* (also act.), *Who Was the Other Man?* (also act.) 1917; *The Avenging Trail, Berlin Via America* (also prod., act.), *The Craving* 1918; *The Silent Mystery* (serial; also act.) 1918–19; *The Mystery of 13* (serial; also act.), *The Crimson Shoals* (also co-story) 1919; *The Man from Nowhere* (also act.) 1920; *Cyclone Bliss, The Stampede* (also act.), *I Am the Woman* 1921; *So This Is Arizona* (also act.), *Angel Citizens, Trail's End, Thundering Hoofs* (also act.), *They're Off* (also sc., act.), *Storm Girl* (also act.), *The Heart of Lincoln* (also prod., act.), *Gold Grabbers* 1922; *Cupid's Rustler* (also sc.), *A Rodeo Mixup* (also sc., act.), *Western Yesterdays* (also sc., act.), *Range Blood* (also sc.), *Lash of the Whip* (also sc.), *Midnight Shadows* (also sc.), *The Cowboy Prince, The Diamond Bandit* (also sc.), *The Lash of Pinto Pete, Western Feuds* (also act.) 1925; *The Winking Idol* (serial), *Her Own Story, The Ghetto Shamrock, False Friends* 1926; *Wolves of the Air* (also sc. as J. Francis O'Fearna), *Wolf's Trail* 1927; *Call of the Heart* 1928. As actor—*Custer's Last Raid* (as Custer) 1912; *Action* 1921; *The Village Blacksmith* 1922; *Haunted Valley* (serial) 1923; *In the Days of the Covered Wagon, Hearts of Oak, The Measure of a Man* 1924; *Soft Shoes, The Taming of the West, The Fighting Heart* 1925; *Speed Cop* 1926; *Upstream, Men of Daring, The Heart of Maryland, Uncle Tom's Cabin, The Wreck of the Hesperus* 1927; *Sisters of Eve* 1928; *The Black Watch* 1929; *The Jade Box* (serial), *Kathleen Mavourneen* 1930; *Seas Beneath* 1931; *Air Mail* 1932; *Pilgrimage, Charlie Chan's Greatest Case* 1933; *Murder in Trinidad, Judge Priest* 1934; *The Informer, Goin' to Town, The Arizonian, Steamboat Round the Bend* 1935; *The Prisoner of Shark Island, Charlie Chan at the Circus, Gentle Julia, Sins of Man* 1936; *Slave Ship* 1937; *In Old Chicago, The Texans* 1938; *Stagecoach, Young Mr. Lincoln, Drums Along the Mohawk* 1939; *Geronimo, Viva Cisco Kid!, South of Pago-Pago* 1940; *Tobacco Road* 1941; *King of the Mounties* (serial), *The Loves of Edgar Allan Poe* 1942; *The Ox-Bow Incident* 1943; *The Big Noise* 1944; *Hangover Square* 1945; *My Darling Clementine* 1946; *The Plunderers* 1948; *Wagonmaster* 1950; *The Quiet Man* 1952; *The Sun Shines Bright* 1954.

Ford, Glenn. Actor. Born Gwyllyn Samuel Newton Ford, on May 1, 1916, in Quebec. The son of a railroad executive, he was raised in California from age eight. He gained acting experience in plays staged by Santa Monica High School and after graduation began playing juvenile supporting parts and eventually leads with various West Coast stage companies. In 1939 he was tested and signed by Columbia Pictures. He was gaining momentum in the early 40s as a young leading man in films and on Broadway when his budding career was interrupted by WW II service with the Marines. During the war (in 1943) he married actress-dancer Eleanor POWELL. They divorced in 1959. Returning to the screen after his discharge, Ford soared to popularity in the late 40s as Rita Hayworth's leading man in *Gilda* and opposite Bette Davis in *A Stolen Life.* He subsequently starred in many films, demonstrating equal skill at playing drama (*The Blackboard Jungle, Trial,* etc.), comedy (*The Teahouse of the August Moon,* etc.), and action films, both of the thriller and Western variety. Typically portrayed amiable, easygoing, but tough and introspective heroes. In 1971–72 he starred in the TV series 'Cade's County.' He later appeared in a number of miniseries and occasional films. His second and third marriages were also to actresses, Kathryn Hays (1966–68) and Cynthia Hayward (from 1977). Autobiography: *Glenn Ford, RFD* (1970).

FILMS: *Heaven with a Barbed Wire Fence, My Son Is Guilty* 1939; *Convicted Woman, Men Without Souls, Babies for Sale, Blondie Plays Cupid, The Lady in Question* 1940; *So Ends Our Night, Texas, Go West Young Lady* 1941; *The Adventures of Martin Eden, Flight Lieutenant* 1942; *The Desperadoes, Destroyer* 1942; *Gilda, A Stolen Life, Gallant Journey* 1946; *Framed* 1947; *The Mating of Millie, The Loves of Carmen, The Return of October, The Man from Colorado* 1948; *The Undercover Man, Lust for Gold, Mr. Soft Touch, The Doctor and the Girl* 1949; *The White Tower, Convicted, The Flying Missile* 1950; *Follow the Sun, The Redhead and the Cowboy, The Secret of Convict Lake* 1951; *The Green Glove, Young Man with Ideas, Affair in Trinidad* 1952; *Terror on a Train/Time Bomb* (UK), *Plunder of the Sun, The Man from the Alamo, The Big Heat, Appointment in Honduras* 1953; *Human Desire* 1954; *The Americano, The Violent Men, The Blackboard Jungle, Interrupted Melody, Trial* 1955; *Ransom, Jubal, The Fastest Gun Alive, The Teahouse of the August Moon* 1956; *3:10 to Yuma, Don't Go Near the Water* 1957; *Cowboy, The Sheepman, Imitation General, Torpedo Run* 1958; *It Started with a Kiss* 1959; *The Gazebo* 1960; *Cimarron, Cry for Happy, Pocketful of Miracles* 1961; *The Four Horsemen of the Apocalypse, Experiment in Terror* 1962; *The Courtship of Eddie's Father, Love Is a Ball* 1963; *Advance to the Rear, Fate Is the Hunter* 1964; *Dear Heart, The Rounders* 1965; *El Mal/Rage* (Mex./US), *The Money Trap, Is Paris Burning?* 1966; *A Time for Killing, The Last Challenge* 1967; *Day of the Evil Gun* 1968; *Smith!, Heaven with a Gun* 1969; *Santee* 1973; *Midway* 1976; *Goodbye and Amen* (It.), *Superman* 1978; *The Visitor* (It./US) 1979; *Virus* (Jap.) 1980; *Happy Birthday to Me* 1981; *Raw Nerve* 1991.

Ford, Harrison. Actor. *b.* Mar. 16, 1892, Kansas City, Mo. *d.* 1957. Handsome, dashing leading man of Hollywood silents. Appeared in numerous productions from 1916, opposite some of the screen's most glamorous female stars, including Constance and Norma Talmadge, Gloria Swanson, Marion Davies, Clara Bow, and Marie Prevost. He retired from the screen in 1932.

FILMS INCLUDE: *Excuse Me* 1915; *Anton the Terrible* 1916; *The Crystal Gazer, The Sunset Trail, The Mysterious Mrs. M.* 1917; *The Cruise of the Make-Believe, A Pair of Silk Stockings, Such a Little Pirate* 1918; *The Third Kiss, The Veiled Adventure, The Lottery Man, Hawthorne of the USA* 1919; *A Lady in Love, Food for Scandal* 1920; *The Passion Flower, Wedding Bells, The Wonderful Thing, Love's Redemption* 1921; *Smilin' Through, Foolish Wives, Her Gilded Cage, The Primitive Lover, The Old Homestead, Shadows* 1922; *Vanity Fair* (as George Osborne), *Little Old New York, Maytime* 1923; *Three Miles Out, Janice Meredith* 1924; *Proud Flesh, Zander the Great, The Wheel, Lovers in Quarantine, The Marriage Whirl, That Royle Girl* 1925; *The Song and Dance Man, Hell's 400, Up in Mabel's Room, The Nervous Wreck* 1926; *The Night Bride, The Girl in the Pullman, The Rush Hour* 1927; *A Blonde for a Night, Just Married, Three Week-Ends* 1928; *Love in High Gear* 1932.

Ford, Harrison. Actor. Born on July 13, 1942, in Chicago. Handsome, rugged star of Hollywood films. The son of an Irish father and Russian-Jewish mother, he began acting while attending Ripon College in Wisconsin and, after briefly performing in summer stock, headed for Hollywood, where he signed as a contract player with Columbia, then Universal. He played secondary parts, typically as a cowboy, in a number of films of the late 60s and in such TV series as 'Gunsmoke,' 'The Virginian,' and 'Ironside.' Discouraged by the progress of his career, he dropped out of acting for a while and became a professional carpenter. But he returned to the screen in 1973, portraying Bob Falfa, a wise-guy racer in George Lucas's *American Graffiti.* Four years later he achieved "instant" popularity as co-star of Lucas's space fantasy *Star Wars,* in which he played Han Solo, the daring captain of a pirate starship. His popularity soared to superstar heights when he portrayed archeologist-adventurer Indiana Jones in the action-packed serial-inspired Steven Spielberg thriller *Raiders of the Lost Ark* and its two sequels. Gaining experience and maturity with every role, he proved himself a capable actor in drama and comedy as well, and was nominated for an Academy Award for his portrait of a big-city cop out of his element in Amish country in *Witness* (1985). Since the mid-80s, he has become one of Hollywood's favorite (and most bankable) leading men. He maintains homes in Los Angeles and rural Wyoming, with his second wife (from 1983), screenwriter (*E.T.,* etc.) Melissa Mathison.

FILMS: *Dead Heat on a Merry-Go-Round* 1966; *A Time for Killing* 1967; *Journey to Shiloh* 1968; *Getting Straight* 1970; *American Graffiti* 1973; *The Conversation* 1974; *Star Wars, Heroes* 1977; *Force 10 from Navarone* (UK) 1978; *Hanover Street* (UK), *The Frisco Kid, Apocalypse Now* (cameo), *More American Graffiti* 1979; *The Empire Strikes Back* 1980; *Raiders of the Lost Ark* 1981; *Blade Runner* 1982; *Return of the Jedi* 1983; *Indiana Jones and the Temple of Doom* 1984; *Witness* 1985; *The Mosquito Coast* 1986; *Frantic, Working Girl* 1988; *Indiana Jones and the Last Crusade* 1989; *Presumed Innocent* 1990; *Regarding Henry* 1991; *Patriot Games* 1992; *The Fugitive* 1993; *Clear and Present Danger, Jimmy Hollywood* (unbilled) 1994; *Sabrina* 1995; *Air Force One, The Devil's Own, Star Wars, The Empire Strikes Back, Return of the Jedi* (all re-released special editions) 1997.

Ford, John. Director. *b.* Sean Aloysius O'Feeney (O'Fearna), Feb. 1, 1895, Cape Elizabeth, Me. *d.* 1973. The 13th and youngest child of Irish immigrants, he was raised in Portland, Me., where his father owned a saloon. In 1913, after graduating from high school, he went to Hollywood to join his brother, Francis FORD. Sean O'Feeney, alias Jack Ford (he would not be known as John until 1923), began his Hollywood career as a set laborer and assistant prop man. Occasionally he was also employed as a stuntman and frequently doubled for his older brother, whom he closely resembled. Ford appeared as an extra, one of the hooded Ku Klux Klan riders, in Griffith's *The Birth of a Nation,* in 1915.

A director since 1917 (he might have directed a four-part film, *Lucille the Waitress,* as early as 1914), Ford made more than 30 films, mostly Westerns starring Harry CAREY, before moving from Universal to Fox in 1920. Many of these early films, as well as much of Ford's later silent product, were believed to be lost but have since emerged from such unlikely sources as the Czech Film Archive.

Ford directed two important silent films, *The Iron Horse* (1924) and *Four Sons* (1928). But his reputation as one of the great directors of the American cinema rests on his 40-year sound-film period, when he directed such screen classics as *The Informer, Stagecoach, Young Mr. Lincoln, The Grapes of Wrath, How Green Was My Valley, My Darling Clementine, She Wore a Yellow Ribbon, The Quiet Man, The Searchers,* and *The Man Who Shot Liberty Valance.* He worked in a variety of genres, including Westerns, comedies, stage adaptations, historical dramas, and war movies. To accept Ford's own assessment of his work—"I make Westerns"—leaves much unacknowledged.

Of all American directors, Ford had probably the clearest personal vision and the most consistent visual style. His ideas and his characters, are, like many things branded "American," deceptively simple. His heroes, such as Ethan Edwards (John Wayne) in *The Searchers* and Wyatt Earp (Henry Fonda) in *My Darling Clementine*, may appear simply to be loners, outsiders to established society who generally speak through action rather than words. But their conflict with society embodies larger themes in the American experience. With repeated viewings, the typical Ford film deepens into a meditation on frontier individualism versus encroaching, and apparently necessary, civilization.

Ford's films, particularly the Westerns, express a deep aesthetic sensibility for the American past and the spirit of the frontier. Ford was a folk artist, a master storyteller, and a poet of the moving image. His compositions have a classic strength in which masses of people and their natural surroundings are beautifully juxtaposed, often in breathtaking long shots, many in Monument Valley, the setting for several of his films. The movement of men and horses in his Westerns has rarely been surpassed for regal serenity and evocative power. The musical score, often variations on folk themes, plays a part more important than dialogue in many Ford films.

While focusing on the conflicts between individuals and society, Ford also championed the value and force of the group, as evidenced in his many military dramas (the Cavalry trilogy, *She Wore a Yellow Ribbon, The Long Gray Line*). In the making of his films, Ford expressed a similar sentiment for camaraderie through his repeated use of certain actors in the lead and supporting roles of his films. He was particularly close to Ward BOND and John WAYNE. Ford also frequently employed James STEWART, Henry FONDA, Victor MCLAGLEN, Harry CAREY, Sr., and Jr., and many others who over the years formed a sort of Ford stock company. He also felt an allegiance to places, shooting nine of his films in the panoramic Monument Valley, on the Arizona-Utah line, which is fondly known in Hollywood as "Ford Country" and by silent agreement is considered out of bounds to other directors.

During WW II, Ford was appointed chief of the Field Photographic Branch of the OSS. Initially, Ford's postwar films, like *Fort Apache, Wagonmaster, The Searchers*, and *The Man Who Shot Liberty Valance* did not enjoy the same reputation with tastemaker critics as did his earlier work. But by the 1960s, French and American auteurist critics (including the staff of *Cahiers du Cinéma* and Andrew Sarris) had brought about a critical re-evaluation in which Ford was viewed as a great artist of the screen, whose films reflected his changing outlook toward American individualism, society, and the powers of civilization.

The industry honored Ford with Academy Awards for the direction of *The Informer, The Grapes of Wrath, How Green Was My Valley,* and *The Quiet Man.* Two of his wartime documentaries also won Oscars: *The Battle of Midway* and *December 7th.* He also received the New York Film Critics Award four times. Long plagued with an eye ailment, Ford usually appeared in public with an eye patch or dark glasses. Failing health and a broken hip hampered his activity in his final years. He died of cancer at 78. His daughter, Barbara Ford (1923–85) was a film editor.

Ford was among the most durable creative directors of the American cinema, with some 50 years of continual high-quality work to his credit, all of it stamped with his unmistakable signature. When Orson WELLES was asked by a *Playboy* interviewer which American directors appealed to him most, he replied: "The old masters. . . By which I mean John Ford, John Ford, and John Ford."

FILMS: As Jack Ford—*The Tornado* (also sc., act.), *The Scrapper* (also sc., act.), *The Soul Herder, Cheyenne's Pal* (also story; all preceding are shorts), *Straight Shooting, The Secret Man, A Marked Man* (also story), *Bucking Broadway* 1917; *The Phantom Riders, Wild Women, Thieves' Gold, The Scarlet Drop* (also story), *Hell Bent* (also co-sc.), *A Woman's Fool, Three Mounted Men* 1918; *Roped, The Fighting Brothers* (short), *A Fight for Love, By Indian Post* (short), *The Rustlers* (short), *Bare Fists* (short), *Gun Law* (short), *The Gun Packer* (short), *Riders of Vengeance, The Last Outlaw* (short), *The Outcasts of Poker Flat, The Ace of the Saddle, The Rider of the Law, A Gun Fightin' Gentleman* (also co-story), *Marked Men* 1919; *The Prince of Avenue A, The Girl in No. 29, Hitchin' Posts, Just Pals* 1920; *The Big Punch* (also co-sc.), *The Freeze Out* (also co-sc.), *The Wallop, Desperate Trails, Action, Sure Fire, Jackie* 1921; *Little Miss Smiles, Silver Wings* (dir. the Prologue sequences), *The Village Blacksmith* 1922; *The Face on the Barroom Floor, Three Jumps Ahead* (also sc.) 1923. As John Ford—*Cameo Kirby, North of Hudson Bay, Hoodman Blind* 1923; *The Iron Horse, Hearts of Oak* 1924; *Lightnin', Kentucky Pride, The Fighting Heart, Thank You* 1925; *The Shamrock Handicap, Three Bad Men* (also co-sc.), *The Blue Eagle* 1926; *Upstream* 1927; *Mother Machree, Four Sons, Hangman's House, Napoleon's Barber* (short), *Riley the Cop* 1928; *Strong Boy, The Black Watch* (dial. dir. Lumsden Hare), *Salute* 1929; *Men Without Women* (also co-story; dial. dir. Andrew Bennison), *Born Reckless* (dial. dir. Andrew Bennison), *Up the River* (dial. dir. William Collier) 1930; *Seas Beneath, The Brat, Arrowsmith* 1931; *Air Mail, Flesh* 1932; *Pilgrimage* (dial. dir. William Collier), *Dr. Bull* 1933; *The Lost Patrol, The World Moves On, Judge Priest* 1934; *The Whole Town's Talking, The Informer, Steamboat 'Round the Bend* 1935; *The Prisoner of Shark Island, Mary of Scotland* 1936; *The Plough and the Stars* 1936; *Wee Willie Winkie, The Hurricane, The Adventures of Marco Polo* (dir. of some action sequences only), *Four Men and a Prayer, Submarine Patrol* 1938; *Stagecoach* (also prod.), *Young Mr. Lincoln, Drums Along the Mohawk* 1939; *The Grapes of Wrath, The Long Voyage Home* 1940; *Tobacco Road, Sex Hygiene* (Army doc.), *How Green Was My Valley* 1941; *The Battle of Midway* (Navy doc.; also co-phot., co-edit., co-narration), *Torpedo Squadron* (Navy doc.) 1942; *December 7th* (Navy doc.; co-dir. with Gregg Toland), *We Sail at Midnight* (Navy doc.) 1943; *They Were Expendable* (also prod.) 1945; *My Darling Clementine* 1946; *The Fugitive* (also co-prod.; in Mexico) 1947; *Fort Apache* (also co-prod.) 1948; *Three Godfathers* (also co-prod.), *She Wore a Yellow Ribbon* (also co-prod.), *Mighty Joe Young* (co-prod. only) 1949; *When Willie Comes Marching Home, Wagonmaster* (also co-prod.), *Rio Grande* (also co-prod.) 1950; *This Is Korea!* (Navy doc.) 1951; *What Price Glory, The Quiet Man* (also co-prod.) 1952; *The Sun Shines Bright* (also co-prod.), *Mogambo* 1953; *The Long Gray Line, Mister Roberts* (completed by Mervyn LeRoy when Ford became ill); *The Bamboo Cross* (TV drama), *Rookie of the Year* (TV drama) 1955; *The Searchers* 1956; *The Wings of Eagles, The Rising of the Moon* (in Ireland) 1957; *So Alone* (UK; short), *The Last Hurrah* (also prod.) 1958; *Gideon's Day/Gideon of Scotland Yard* (UK), *Korea* (Dept. of Defense doc.; also co-prod.), *The Horse Soldiers* 1959; *The Colter Craven Story* (TV film), *Sergeant Rutledge* 1960; *Two Rode Together, Flashing Spikes* (TV film), *The Man Who Shot Liberty Valance, How the West Was Won* ("Civil War" episode) 1962; *Donovan's Reef* (also prod.) 1963; *Cheyenne Autumn* 1964; *Young Cassidy* (co-dir. with Jack Cardiff, who received sole screen credit) 1965; *Seven Women* 1966; *Chesty* (doc.; orig. made for TV; release delayed from 1970) 1976.

Ford, Paul. Actor. *b.* Paul Ford Weaver, Nov. 2, 1901, Baltimore. *d.* 1976. Popular character player of the American stage, TV, and films. He was nearly 40, a father of five and an unemployed victim of the Depression, when he began his show business career with a puppet show sponsored by the WPA. He moved on to radio in the early 40s, made his Broadway debut in 1944, and his first film appearance the following year. He enjoyed great personal success in the role of an agitated colonel in both the Broadway production (1953) and the film version (1956) of *The Teahouse of the August Moon* and was popular as the harassed colonel in Phil Silvers's 'Sargeant Bilko' (1955–59) TV series and later in 'The Baileys of Balboa' (1964–65) series. He also triumphed on Broadway in 'Never Too Late' (1962) and repeated the role of a middle-aged expectant father in the 1965 film version of the play. His droopy jowls and mournful face were his trademarks in his often pompously comic roles.

FILMS INCLUDE: *The House on 92nd Street* 1945; *The Naked City* 1948; *Lust for Gold, All the King's Men* 1949; *Perfect Strangers* 1950; *The Teahouse of the August Moon* 1956; *The Matchmaker* 1958; *Advise and Consent, The Music Man* 1962; *It's a Mad Mad Mad Mad World* 1963; *Never Too Late* 1965; *The Russians Are Coming the Russians Are Coming, A Big Hand for the Little Lady* 1966; *The Comedians* 1967; *Lola* 1973; *Journey Back to Oz* (v/o) 1974.

Ford, Wallace. Actor. *b.* Samuel Jones Grundy, Feb. 12, 1898, Batton, England. *d.* 1966. He was raised in a London orphanage and spent his boyhood in various foster homes. Ran away at 11 to join a vaudeville troupe and eventually reached the legitimate stage. He appeared in many Broadway productions, often in leads, before going to Hollywood in 1930, where he played strong character leads and supporting roles in scores of films in a screen career that spanned three and a half decades.

FILMS INCLUDE: *Swellhead* 1930; *Possessed* 1931; *The Beast of the City, Freaks, Central Park* (lead) 1932; *Employees' Entrance, Night of Terror, Three-Cornered Moon, My Woman* 1933; *I Hate Women* (lead), *The Lost Patrol, Men in White* 1934; *The Whole Town's Talking, The Mysterious Mr. Wong, The Nut Farm* (lead), *The Informer, Mary Burns—Fugitive* 1935; *A Son Comes Home* 1936; *O.H.M.S./You're in the Army Now* (lead; UK), *Jericho/Dark Sands* (UK) 1937; *Back Door to Heaven* (lead) 1939; *Isle of Destiny, The Mummy's Hand* 1940; *Murder by Invitation* (lead), *Blues in the Night* 1941; *All Through the Night, The Mummy's Tomb* 1942; *Shadow of a Doubt, The Ape Man, The Cross of Lorraine* 1943; *Blood on the Sun, Spellbound* 1945; *The Green Years, Black Angel* 1946; *Dead Reckoning, Magic Town* 1947; *T-Men* 1948; *The Set-Up* 1949; *The Furies, The Breaking Point, Harvey* 1950; *He Ran All the Way* 1951; *Flesh and Fury* 1952; *Three Ring Circus* 1954; *The Man from Laramie, The Spoilers* 1955; *The First Texan, Johnny Concho, The Rainmaker* 1956; *The Matchmaker, The Last Hurrah* 1958; *Walrock* 1959; *A Patch of Blue* 1965.

Forde, Eugene. Director. *b.* Nov. 8, 1898, Providence, R.I. *d.* 1986. A stage actor at age five, he appeared in plays that starred Mary Pickford, Blanche Sweet, and William S. Hart early in the century, but "retired" at nine to enroll at a New York military school and later returned to acting as a juvenile lead in silent films. When he reached maturity, he once again retired from the screen and for several years worked as a bank teller in Hollywood. He returned to films as a script clerk and began directing comedy shorts in 1926 and feature films in 1928. Among his early features were several Tom Mix Westerns. During the 30s and early 40s he piloted many low- and medium-budget Hollywood productions, often detective mysteries and adventure yarns, mostly for Fox.

FILMS: *Daredevil's Reward, Painted Post, Son of the Golden West, Hello Cheyenne* 1928; *Outlawed, The Big Diamond Robbery* (also story) 1929; *Smoky* 1933; *Charlie Chan in London* 1934; *Mystery Woman, The Great Hotel Murder, Your Uncle Dudley* 1935; *The Country Beyond, 36 Hours to Kill* 1936; *Midnight Taxi, Step Lively Jeeves!, The Lady Escapes, Charlie Chan on Broadway, Charlie Chan at Monte Carlo* 1937; *International Settlement, One Wild Night, Meet the Girls* 1938; *Inspector Hornleigh* (UK), *The Honeymoon's Over* 1939; *Charlie Chan's Murder Cruise, Pier 13, Michael Shayne—Private Detective, Charter Pilot* 1940; *Sleepers West, Dressed to Kill, Buy Me That Town, Man at Large* 1941; *Right to the Heart, Berlin Correspondent* 1942; *The Crime Doctor's Strangest Case* 1943; *Shadows in the Night* 1944; *Backlash, Jewels of Brandenburg, The Crimson Key, The Invisible Wall* 1947.

Forde, Walter. Director. *b.* Thomas Seymour, in 1897, in Bradford, England. *d.* 1984. He started out as a pianist and comedian in vaudeville and in the early 20s began directing as well as starring in British slapstick shorts. He was England's only major comedy talent during the silent period and enjoyed great popularity. In 1923 he went to Hollywood, where he worked for Universal for two years. From the late 20s to the late 40s he directed many feature films in England, turning out comedies as well as enjoyable thrillers.

FEATURE FILMS: *Wait and See, What Next?* 1928; *The Silent House, Would You Believe It?* 1929; *Red Pearls, You'd Be Surprised, The Last Hour, Lord Richard in the Pantry* 1930; *Bed and Breakfast, Third Time Lucky, The Ringer, The Ghost Train, Splinters in the Navy* 1931; *Condemned to Death, Lord Babs, Jack's the Boy, Rome Express* 1932; *Orders Is Orders* 1933; *Jack Ahoy!, Chu-Chin-Chow* 1934; *Bulldog Jack/Alias Bulldog Drummond, Forever England/Born for Glory/Torpedo Raider, King of the Damned* 1935; *Land Without Music/ Forbidden Music* 1936; *Kicking the Moon Around/The Playboy/ Millionaire Merry-Go-Round, The Gaunt Stranger/The Phantom Strikes* 1938; *Let's Be Famous, The Four Just Men/The Secret Four, Cheer Boys Cheer, Happy Families, Inspector Hornleigh on Holiday* 1939; *Charley's (Big-Hearted) Aunt, Saloon Bar, Sailors Three/Three Cockeyed Sailors* 1940; *Inspector Hornleigh Goes to It/Mail Train, The Ghost Train* (remake), *Atlantic Ferry/Sons of the Sea* 1941; *Flying Fortess, The Peterville Diamond* 1942; *It's That Man Again* 1943; *Time Flies, One Exciting Night/You Can't Do Without Love* 1944; *The Master of Bankdam* 1947; *Cardboard Cavalier* 1949.

foreground. The part of a scene nearest to the camera, usually the area between the camera and the main subject. Commonly abbreviated "fg".

foreign version. A print for release in a language other than that of the original. Subtitles are superimposed or a new dialogue track is added to the original music and sound-effects tracks. In the early days of sound, original and foreign versions were made in tandem in the US and elsewhere, often with the same physical properties but different casts and directors (*e.g.*, the 1930 *Anna Christie* in English and German with Garbo in both, Marie Dressler/Salka Viertel, Charles Bickford/Hans Junkermann, and directors Clarence Brown/Jacques Feyder).

Foreman, Carl. Screenwriter, producer, director. *b.* July 23, 1914, Chicago. *d.* 1984. *ed.* U. of Illinois; Northwestern U.; John Marshall Law School. The son of Jewish immigrants from Russia, he began as a circus and carnival promoter, then turned freelance journalist and publicity writer. Made his debut as a screenwriter early in the 40s, collaborating on low-budget Bowery Boys films. This unpromising beginning was interrupted by WW II service with the US Army Signal Corps. In the late 40s he became an important part of Stanley Kramer's team, writing the screenplays for that producer's early excursions into serious, socially conscious filmmaking. But in 1951, just as he was nearing a peak of personal prestige with the completion of his script for *High Noon*—one of his best known films—he was blacklisted by the industry following testimony before the House Un-American Activities Committee in which he refused to confirm or deny Communist Party membership. He went into self-imposed exile in England, where for several years he worked in films "underground," hiding behind pseudonyms or turning out scripts anonymously. He was billed as Derek Frey, for example, as the screenwriter on Joseph Losey's *The Sleeping Tiger* (Losey himself used the pseudonym Victor Hanbury on that film) and was given no credit at all for his work on the celebrated *The Bridge on the River Kwai* and could not claim his share of the Academy Award as that film's co-writer. In 1958, however, he surfaced from his anonymity, setting up his own production company, Open Road Films, in London, distributing through Columbia. He subsequently became active in British films as both producer and screenwriter and in 1963 competently directed one film, *The Victors.* In 1968 he became president of Britain's Writers Guild and from 1965 to 1971 served as governor of the British Film Institute. He was awarded the title of Commander of the British Empire in 1970, but in 1975 he returned to the US after 23 years in exile and two years later signed a three-year contract with Universal as producer-writer, working independently under the umbrella of a small New York-based production company, appropriately named High Noon. In 1985, he was awarded his Oscar for *The Bridge on the River Kwai* posthumously.

FILMS INCLUDE (as screenwriter alone or in collaboration unless otherwise noted): In the US—*Bowery Blitzkrieg, Spooks Run Wild* 1941; *Rhythm Parade* 1942; *Dakota* (story only) 1945; *So This Is New York* 1948; *Champion, Home of the Brave* 1949; *Young Man with a Horn, The Men, Cyrano de Bergerac* 1950; *High Noon* 1952. In the UK—*The Sleeping Tiger* (under pseudonym Derek Frey) 1954; *The Bridge on the River Kwai* (uncredited) 1957; *The Key* (also exec. prod.) 1958; *The Guns of Navarone* (also exec. prod.; UK/US) 1961; *The Victors* (also prod., dir.; UK/US) 1963; *Born Free* (exec. prod. only) 1966; *Otley* (exec. prod. only), *Mackenna's Gold* (also co-prod.; US) 1969; *The Virgin Soldiers* (exec. prod. only), *Living Free* (exec. prod. only) 1971; *Young Winston* (also prod.) 1972; *Force 10 from Navarone* (prod., wrote outline only) 1978; *When Time Ran Out* 1980.

Forman, Milos. Director. Born on Feb. 18, 1932, in Cáslav, Czechoslovakia. The son of a Jewish professor of education and his Protestant wife, he lost both parents in Nazi concentration camps and was raised by relatives. A graduate of Prague's Academy of Music and Dramatic Art, he began writing screenplays in the mid-50s and participated in the preparation of the early Laterna Magika mixed-media presentations. He made his directorial debut in 1963 with two medium-length films, *Audition/Talent Competition* and *If There Were No Music.* He won the first prize at the Locarno Film Festival for his first feature, *Black Peter,* and scored critical and commercial triumphs with his next films, *Loves of a Blonde* and *The Firemen's Ball.* In these films Forman revealed his interest in the funny side of human foibles. He stressed improvisation in the development of his characters, and cast his actors with an eye for unveiling their own as well as the characters' inner secrets. His forte is ironic comedy and his milieu that of ordinary people in their daily lives, with the generation gap as a recurrent theme. His burst of free creativity was made possible by the brief "liberal spring" in Czech politics of the mid-60s.

Forman was in Paris in August of 1968, scouting a possible film project, when the Russians invaded his homeland. He remained in France as an expatriate and in 1969 came to New York with fellow director Ivan Passer. Following an abortive deal with Paramount, Forman was backed by Universal for his first American film, the successful *Taking Off* (1971), in which he returned to the generation gap theme. He was one of the international team of directors who covered the 1972 Munich Olympics in *Visions of Eight,* handling the decathlon episode. In 1975 he scored a tremendous personal triumph with the US film *One Flew Over the Cuckoo's Nest,* a big box-office hit and the winner in a sweep of all top five Academy Awards—best picture, best director, best screenplay, best actor, and best actress—a feat accomplished only once before, by Frank Capra's *It Happened One Night* (1934). Forman followed this success with a spirited and imaginative screen version of the musical *Hair* (1979) and a colorfully evocative adaptation of E.L. Doctorow's novel *Ragtime* (1981). He then scored another huge triumph with a sumptuous production of *Amadeus* (1984), the winner of several Oscars, including best picture and best director. An American citizen since 1975, Forman was appointed in that same year as a full professor and co-director of the film division of Columbia University. His first wife (1951–56) was Czech actress Jana BREJCHOVÁ.

FILMS: In Czechoslovakia—*Konkurs/Audition/Competition/Talent Competition* (medium-length; also co-sc.), *If It Weren't for Music* (medium-length; also co-sc.; last two films later shown together as a feature presentation) 1963; *Black Peter/Peter and Pavla* (also co-sc.) 1964; *Loves of a Blonde/A Blonde in Love* (also co-sc.) 1965; *The Firemen's Ball/Like a House on Fire* (also co-sc.) 1967. In the US—*Taking Off* (also co-sc.) 1971; *Visions of Eight* (doc.; "Decathlon" segment) 1973; *One Flew Over the Cuckoo's Nest* 1975; *Hair* 1979; *Ragtime* 1981; *Amadeus* 1984; *Heartburn* (act. only) 1986; *Valmont* (Fr./UK), *New Year's Day* (act. only) 1989; *The People vs. Larry Flynt* 1996.

format. The shape and proportions of a picture projected on a motion picture screen. A picture projected at the standard aspect ratio of 1.33:1 is said to be of a "flat format," the opposite of a "wide-screen format."

Formby, George. Actor. *b.* May 26, 1904, Wigan, England. *d.* 1961. Toothy, ukelele-toting music-hall entertainer who was England's most popular screen comedian in the late 30s and early 40s. Starting out regionally, in England's north, while still a boy, he became nationally famous through radio. His films, typically simpleminded, broad slapstick comedies, were hugely popular, mainly among British working-class audiences, but were rarely exported to the United States. In the British Isles and the countries of the Commonwealth he was a top box-office draw for a decade (1936–45). The postwar change in audiences' taste abruptly sealed his film career. He returned to the music halls and was regaining some of his popularity when he died of a heart attack at 57.

FILMS INCLUDE: *By the Shortest of Heads* 1915; *Boots Boots* 1934; *Keep Your Seats Please* 1936; *Keep Fit* 1937; *It's in the Air* 1938; *Trouble Brewing* 1939; *Let George Do It* 1940; *South American George* 1941; *Much Too Shy* 1942; *Get Cracking* 1943; *He Snoops to Conquer* 1944; *I Didn't Do It* 1945; *George in Civvy Street* 1946.

Forrest, Frederic. Actor. Born Dec. 23, 1936, in Waxahachie, Tex. *ed.* Texas Christian U.; U. of Oklahoma. Solid leading man and character player of the American stage, TV, and films. He began performing locally in Texas eventually moving on to New York. After training at the Actors Studio, he appeared in Greenwich Village cafés, then in off-Broadway productions. Making his screen debut in the late 60s, he achieved critical success with *The Rose* (1979), earning an Oscar nomination as supporting actor.

FILMS: *Futz* 1969; *When the Legends Die* 1972; *The Don Is Dead* 1973; *The Gravy Train/The Dion Brothers, The Conversation* 1974; *Permission to Kill* (UK) 1975; *The Missouri Breaks* 1976; *It Lives Again* 1978; *Apocalypse Now, The Rose* 1979; *One from the Heart, Hammett* (as author Dashiell Hammett) 1982; *Valley Girl* 1983; *The Stone Boy* 1984; *Where Are the Children?* 1986; *Stacking/Season of Dreams* 1987; *Tucker: The Man and His Dream, Valentino Returns* 1988; *The Dead Can't Lie, Music Box* 1989; *Cat Chaser, The Two Jakes* 1990; *Falling Down* 1992; *Trauma* 1993; *Chasers, Hidden Fears, Lassie* 1994; *The End of Violence* 1997.

Forrest, Sally. Actress. Born Katherine Sally Feeney, on May 28, 1928, in San Diego. A high school dance teacher, she entered films as a dancer in 1946 and played leads in a string of routine features of the early 50s.

FILMS INCLUDE: *Till the Clouds Roll By* 1947; *Not Wanted, Mr. Belvedere Goes to College* 1949; *Mystery Street* 1950; *Valentino, Hard Fast and Beautiful, Vengeance Valley, Excuse My Dust, The Strange Door, Bannerline* 1951; *Code 2* 1953; *Son of Sinbad* 1955; *While the City Sleeps* 1956.

Forrest, Steve. Actor. Born William Forrest Andrews, on Sept. 29, 1924, in Huntsville, Tex. The younger brother of Dana ANDREWS, he made a tentative film debut, in bit parts, as William Andrews, in 1943. Following military service in WW II, he attended UCLA, gained some stage and radio experience, then re-entered films in 1951, initially still using his real name. Manly and square-jawed, he played virile leads and supporting roles in motion pictures of all types. He starred in the TV series 'The Baron' (1966) and 'S.W.A.T.' (1975–76), and joined the cast of 'Dallas' in 1986.

FILMS INCLUDE: As William Andrews—*Crash Dive, The Ghost Ship* 1943; *Sealed Cargo* 1951; *Geisha Girl, Last of the Comanches* 1952. As Steve Forrest—*The Bad and the Beautiful* 1952; *The Clown, Battle Circus, Dream Wife, So Big, Take the High Ground* 1953; *Phantom of the Rue Morgue, Prisoner of War, Rogue Cop* 1954; *Bedevilled* 1955; *The Living Idol* 1957; *It Happened to Jane* 1959; *Jovanka e le Altre/Five Branded Women* (It./Yug.), *Heller in Pink Tights, Flaming Star* 1960; *The Second Time Around* 1961; *The Longest Day* 1962; *The Yellow Canary* 1963; *Rascal* 1969; *The Wild Country, The Late Liz* 1971; *North Dallas Forty* 1979; *Mommie Dearest* 1981; *Sahara* 1984; *Spies Like Us* 1985; *Amazon Women on the Moon* 1987.

Forst, Willi. Actor, director. *b.* Wilhelm Frohs, Apr. 7, 1903, Vienna. *d.* 1980. A leading star of Viennese-style operettas and fluffy musicals on the Austrian and German stage and screen. Highly popular in the early 30s, many of his prewar films were shown on US screens. He began directing his own films and those of other stars in 1933. Often wrote his own scripts.

FILMS INCLUDE: As actor—*Der Wegweiser* 1920; *Oh du lieber Augustin* 1922; *Cafe Electric* 1927; *Amor auf Ski* 1928; *Atlantik* 1929; *Zwei Herzen im 3/4-Takt/Two Hearts in Waltz Time* 1930; *Die lustigen Weiber von Wien, Der Raub der Mona Lisa/The Theft of the Mona Lisa* 1931; *Ein blonder Traum/A Blonde Dream* 1932; *Königswalzer/The Royal Waltz* 1936. As director—*Leise flehen meine Lieder/Unfinished Symphony* (also co-sc., Ger./Aus.) 1933; *Maskerade/Masquerade in Vienna* (also co-sc.; Aus.) 1934; *Mazurka* 1935; *Burgtheater/Vienna Burgtheater* (also co-sc.; Aus.) 1936; *Serenade* (also co-sc.) 1937; *Bel Ami* (also co-sc., act.) 1939; *Operette/Operetta* (also co-sc., act.) 1940; *Wiener Blut* (also act.) 1942; *Die Sünderin* (also co-sc.) 1950; *Im weissen Rössl/The White Horse Inn* 1952; *Dieses Lied bleibt bei Dir/Cabaret* 1954; *Kaiserjäger* 1956; *Wien—du Stadt meiner Traäume* (also co-sc.) 1957.

Forster, Robert. Actor. Born Robert Foster, Jr., on July 13, 1941, in Rochester, N.Y. *ed.* Heidelberg Coll. (Ohio); Alfred U.; Rochester U. Virile leading man of Hollywood films, following some stage experience. He got into films on the strength of his portrayal of Stanley Kowalski in a 1967 production of 'A Streetcar Named Desire.' Typically seen in offbeat, rebellious roles, he took a first jab at directing in 1986. He starred in the TV series 'Banyon' (1972–73) and 'Nakia' (1974).

FILMS: *Reflections in a Golden Eye* 1967; *The Stalking Moon* 1968; *Justine, Medium Cool* 1969; *Pieces of Dreams, Cover Me Babe* 1970; *Journey Through Rosebud* 1972; *The Don Is Dead* 1973; *Stunts* 1977; *Avalanche* 1978; *The Black Hole* 1979; *Alligator* 1981; *Vigilante* 1983; *Walking the Edge* 1985; *The Delta Force, Harry's Machine/Hollywood Harry* (also dir., prod.) 1986; *Committed, Esmeralda Bay* 1987; *Heat from Another Sun* 1988; *The Banker* 1989; *Peacemaker, Satan's Princess* 1990; *Diplomatic Immunity, 29th Street, Badge of Silence* 1991; *South Beach* 1992; *Scanners: The Showdown* 1994.

Forsyth, Bill. Director. Born William David Forsyth, on July 29, 1946, in Glasgow. A grocer's son, he dropped out of school at 17 to take a trainee job with a small local company producing documentaries and industrial films. While learning the various aspects of filmmaking, he began making experimental shorts of his own, using trims of unused stock and eventually formed a small film company with friends. After attending the National Film School, near London, for a term, he returned to making industrials and documentaries, and one dramatic production for the BBC, all the while dreaming of an opportunity to direct a feature film. Finally taking matters into his own hands, he used a mere $10,000 and the volunteer services of friends and of members of the Glasgow Youth Theater to turn out *That Sinking Feeling* (1979). Shot in 16 mm, in barely three weeks, the film—a witty, disarmingly insightful story of a bungled teen heist—was received with surprising enthusiasm at the Edinburgh and London Film Festivals. Its success enabled Forsyth to find commercial backing and a $400,000 budget for his next feature, *Gregory's Girl* (1981), a charming, spirited comic exploration of clumsy juvenile exuberance. It won the British Academy Award for best original screenplay and became a sleeper box-office hit in the US. Its success was overshadowed by *Local Hero* (1983), an inventive, gag-filled, delightful comedy about the effects of the North Sea oil boom on a sleepy Scottish coastal village. The emergence of Forsyth as a filmmaker gave a much-needed shot in the arm to a semidormant British film industry. In 1987 he made his first American film, a poetic, bittersweet adaptation of Marilynne Robinson's novel *Housekeeping*.

FEATURE FILMS (as director-screenwriter): *That Sinking Feeling* (also prod.) 1979; *Gregory's Girl* 1981; *Local Hero* 1983; *Comfort and Joy* 1984; *Housekeeping* (US) 1987; *Breaking In* (US) 1989; *Rebecca's Daughters* (US) 1992; *Being Human* (US) 1994.

Forsyth, Rosemary. Actress. Born in 1944, in Montreal. Tall (5' 9") leading lady of Hollywood films since the mid-60s, following a career in modeling and on TV.

FILMS INCLUDE: *Shenandoah, The War Lord* 1965; *Texas Across the River* 1966; *Where It's At, Whatever Happened to Aunt Alice?, Some Kind of a Nut* 1969; *How Do I Love Thee?* 1970; *Black Eye* 1974; *Gray Lady Down* 1978; *Disclosure, Exit to Eden* 1994.

Forsythe, John. Actor. Born on Jan. 29, 1918, in Penns Grove, N.J. *ed.* U. of North Carolina; Actors Studio. A college baseball player, he began his working career with a brief stint as radio broadcaster for the Brooklyn Dodgers. He then gravitated to acting, played minor roles on Broadway, and landed a supporting part in the film *Destination Tokyo* (1944). In 1947 he entered TV, the medium that was to make him famous and wealthy as the star of the long-running 'Bachelor Father' (1957–62) and other successful series. Early in the 50s he toured with the road company of 'Mister Roberts,' then took over Henry Fonda's part on Broadway (in 1956 he directed the City Center revival of the play). In 1953 he was again on Broadway, in 'The Teahouse of the August Moon.' A tall, handsome, Madison Avenue type, adept at both comedy and drama, he also began making his mark in movies in the 50s, memorably in Hitchcock's *The Trouble with Harry.* His busy TV schedule has limited the number of his film appearances. It included numerous dramas and TV movies, and starring roles in the series 'The John Forsythe Show' (1965–66), 'To Rome With Love' (1969–71), 'Charlie's Angels' (Charlie's voice, 1976–81), and 'Dynasty' (from 1981 through most of the 80s), his greatest success.

FILMS: *Destination Tokyo* 1944; *The Captive City* 1952; *The Glass Web, It Happens Every Thursday, Escape from Fort Bravo* 1953; *The Trouble with Harry* 1955; *The Ambassador's Daughter, Everything but the Truth* 1956; *Kitten with a Whip* 1964; *Madame X* 1966; *In Cold Blood* 1967; *Topaz, The Happy Ending* 1969; *Goodbye and Amen* (It.) 1978; *And Justice for All* 1979; *Scrooged* 1988.

Forte, Fabian. See FABIAN.

Fosco, Piero. See PASTRONE, Giovanni.

Fosse, Bob. Director, choreographer, dancer. *b.* Robert Louis Fosse, June 23, 1927, Chicago. *d.* 1987. The son of a vaudeville entertainer, he began performing on the vaudeville circuit as a child and was a seasoned veteran of many a burlesque show by the time he was 13. Later he teamed up with his first wife, Mary-Ann Niles, as a dancing duo in nightclubs and stage musicals. In the early 50s he appeared as a dancer and actor in several films, including *Kiss Me Kate* (1953) and *My Sister Eileen* (1955). During that period he married his second wife, his dancing partner Joan McCracken. In 1954 he began a successful stint as a Broadway choreographer, winning a Tony Award for his very first venture, 'The Pajama Game.' In 1957 he choreographed the film version of the hit musical, and he did the same for the stage (1955) and screen (1958) productions of 'Damn Yankees.' Other Broadway shows he choreographed were 'Bells Are Ringing' and 'New Girl in Town.' In 1959 he directed his first Broadway musical, 'Redhead,' which starred his third wife, dancer Gwen VERDON, and subsequently directed such hits as 'How to Succeed in Business Without Really Trying,' 'Sweet Charity,' 'Pippin,' 'Chicago,' all of which he also choreographed in his characteristic jazzy style.

Directing for the screen from 1969, Fosse won the best director Academy Award for his second effort, the dazzling 1972 film version of the Broadway musical 'Cabaret.' He next directed the somber Lenny Bruce biography, *Lenny.* In 1974 he co-choreographed and appeared as an actor in the film *The Little Prince,* and in 1977 he appeared in *Thieves.* In 1978, Fosse capped his Broadway career with yet another Tony Award–winning musical, 'Dancin',' a vibrant celebration of stage movement. After undergoing open-heart surgery, Fosse made *All That Jazz* (1979), a largely autobiographical film about a chain-smoking director who dies of a heart attack. The celluloid obituary seemed premature, as Fosse soon resumed full activity, turning out another film, *Star 80* (1983) and the Broadway musical 'Big Deal' (1986), which he based on Mario Monicelli's film *Big Deal on Madonna Street.* The following year he collapsed and died of a heart attack in his hotel room in Washington, D.C., just as the curtain was rising a few blocks away on his revival of his musical 'Sweet Charity.'

FILMS (as director): *Sweet Charity* (also chor.) 1969; *Cabaret* (also chor.) 1972; *Lenny* 1974; *All That Jazz* (also co-sc.) 1979; *Star 80* (also sc.) 1983.

Fossey, Brigitte. Actress. Born on Mar. 11, 1946, in Tourcoing, France, the daughter of a schoolteacher. She was only five years old when she gave a remarkable performance in René Clement's *Jeux interdits/Forbidden Games* (1952). At ten she appeared in Gene Kelly's made-in-France production *The Happy Road* (1957), then returned to her hometown to attend grade school and take up dancing and piano. After philosophy studies in Paris and training as translator-interpreter in Geneva, she returned to the screen as a young adult in the late 60s and has since played leads in many productions.

FILMS INCLUDE: *Jeux interdits/Forbidden Games* 1952; *The Happy Road* (US) 1957; *Le Grand Maulnes/The Wanderer* 1967; *Adieu l'Ami* 1968; *M comme Mathieu, Raphaël ou le débauché* 1971; *Les Valseuses/Going Places, L'Ironie du sort, La Brigade* 1974; *Le Chant de Départ, Le Bon et les Méchants/The Good and the Bad, Calmos/Femmes fatales, Les Fleurs du Miel* 1976; *Le Pays bleu, L'Homme qui aimait les Femmes/The Man Who Loved Women, Les Enfants du Placard* 1977; *Die gläserne Zelle* (Ger.), *L'Affaire suisse* 1978; *Quintet* (US), *Mais ou et donc Ornicar* 1979; *Un Mauvais Fils, La Boum* 1980; *Chanel Solitaire* (US/Fr.) 1981; *Imperativ* (Ger.), *La Boum 2, Enigma* (UK/Fr.) 1982; *Au Nom de tous les miens, La Scarlatine/Scarlet Fever* 1983; *Offret/Sacrificatio/Le Sacrifice/The Sacrifice* (Swed./Fr.) 1986; *Nuovo Cinema Paradiso/Cinema Paradiso* (It./Fr.) 1989; *The Last Butterfly* 1990 (Fr.); *Les Enfants du Naufrageur* (Fr.) 1992.

Foster, Dianne. Actress. Born Dianne Laruska, on Oct. 31, 1928, in Edmonton, Alberta, Canada. An actress and a model from age 13, she arrived in Hollywood via London and played leads in films of the 50s and early 60s.

FILMS INCLUDE: *The Quiet Woman* (UK) 1951; *Bad for Each Other* 1953; *Drive a Crooked Road, Three Hours to Kill* 1954; *The Violent Men, The Kentuckian* 1955; *Monkey on My Back, Night Passage, The Brothers Rico* 1957; *The Deep Six, Gideon's Day/Gideon of Scotland Yard* (UK), *The Last Hurrah* 1958; *King of the Roaring Twenties* 1961; *Who's Been Sleeping in My Bed?* 1963.

Foster, Jodie. Actress, director. Born Alicia Christian Foster, on Nov. 19, 1962, in Los Angeles, Calif. Versatile, amazingly mature child star of American and international films of the 70s, who blossomed into a solid leading lady in the 80s. Performing professionally from age three, she appeared in many Disney TV productions before graduating into feature films in 1972. While continuing to play child roles in family pictures for Disney and other studios, she electrified the film community and shocked many filmgoers with her astute characterizations of screen personae far exceeding her chronological age in maturity and sophistication. She was not quite 13 when she portrayed Iris, the drug-addicted teenage whore in *Taxi Driver,* and Miss Tallulah, a bawdy, provocative speakeasy queen in *Bugsy Malone* (both 1976), and not quite 14 when she played the title role of a young murderess in *The Little Girl Who Lived Down the Lane* (1977). Because of her tender age, she was replaced on the screen by an older sister in the nude scenes in the latter film. Jodie also starred in the short-lived TV series 'Paper Moon.' While accomplishing all that, Foster, who could read from age three, excelled scholastically at the Los Angeles Lycée Français, graduating in 1980 as the class valedictorian. She spoke her own lines in the French film *Moi, Fleur bleue* (1977). She continued performing in films and TV productions while earning 'A's toward her degree in literature at Yale. In 1981, she made front-page headlines when John W. Hinckley, Jr., who tried to assassinate President Ronald Reagan, attributed his deed to a desire to impress Foster, the object of his deluded obsessions. Having been nominated for an Academy Award for *Taxi Driver,* she won the best actress Oscar ten years later for her striking performance as a gang-rape victim in *The Accused* (1988). She won a second best actress Oscar for her performance as the astute, tenacious FBI agent Clarice Starling in *The Silence of the Lambs* (1991). Later in 1991, she made a respectable debut as a director with *Little Man Tate,* in which she also starred. She was again nominated as best actress for the title role in *Nell* (1994) and was met with less enthusiasm with her second directorial effort *Home for the Holidays* (1995).

FILMS: *Napoleon and Samantha, Kansas City Bomber* 1972; *Tom Sawyer* (as Becky Thatcher), *One Little Indian* 1973; *Alice Doesn't Live Here Anymore, Echoes of a Summer/The Last Castle* (US/Can.) 1975; *Taxi Driver, Bugsy Malone* (UK/US) 1976; *Freaky Friday, The Little Girl Who Lived Down the Lane* (Can.), *Il Casotto* (It.), *Moi Fleur bleue/Stop Calling Me Baby!* 1977; *Candleshoe* 1978; *Foxes, Carny* 1980; *O'Hara's Wife* 1982; *The Hotel New Hampshire, Le Sang des Autres/The Blood of Others* (Fr./Can.) 1984; *Mesmerized* (also co-prod.; UK/Austral./N.Z.) 1986; *Siesta* 1987; *Five Corners, Stealing Home, The Accused* 1988; *The Silence of the Lambs, Little Man Tate* (also dir.) 1991; *Backtrack, Shadows and Fog* 1992; *Sommersby* 1993; *Maverick, Nell* (also co-prod.) 1994; *Home for the Holidays* (dir., co-prod. only) 1995; *Contact* 1997.

Foster, Lewis R. Director, screenwriter. *b.* Aug. 5, 1900, Brookfield, Mo. *d.* 1974. A former reporter, he entered films in 1922 as a gag writer and script supervisor for Hal ROACH. Later, he directed a number of comedy shorts, including six Laurel and Hardy vehicles (*Double Whoopee, Bacon Grabbers, Angora Love, Unaccustomed As We Are, Men of War,* and *Berth Marks*). He made his debut as a feature director in 1936 but worked primarily as a screenwriter until the late 40s, when he turned mainly to directing, while continuing to collaborate on the screenplays of his own films. Among his many light screenplays are *Two in a Crowd, The Magnificent Brute* (both 1936), *Sons of the Legion, Some Like It Hot* (1939), *The Farmer's Daughter* (1940), *The Mayor of 44th Street* (1942), *The More the Merrier* (1943), *Can't Help Singing* (1944), *Never Say Goodbye* (1946), and *I Wonder Who's Kissing Her Now* (1947). He won an Academy Award for the original story of Frank Capra's *Mr. Smith Goes to Washington* (1939) and contributed ideas to René Clair's *It Happened Tomorrow* (1944). As a director, Foster was a capable craftsman who often managed to infuse more than routine interest into films that had started out as low-budget, run-of-the-mill adventure fare.

FEATURE FILMS (as director): *Love Letters of a Star* (co-dir. with Milton Carruth; also co-sc.) 1936; *She's Dangerous* (co-dir. with Carruth; also co-sc.), *Armored Car* (also co-sc.), *The Man Who Cried Wolf* 1937; *The Lucky Stiff* (also co-sc.), *El Paso* (also sc.), *Manhandled* (also co-sc.) 1949; *Captain China* (also co-sc.), *The Eagle and the Hawk* (also co-sc.) 1950; *The Last Outpost, Passage West* (also sc.), *Crosswinds* (also sc.) 1951; *Hong Kong* (also story) 1952; *Tropic Zone* (also sc.), *Jamaica Run* (also sc.), *Those Redheads from Seattle* (also sc.) 1953; *Crashout* (also co-sc.), *Top of the World* (also co-prod.) 1955; *The Bold and the Brave, Dakota Incident* 1956; *Tonka* (also co-sc.) 1958; *The Sign of Zorro* (co-dir. with Norman Foster) 1960.

Foster, Meg. American actress. Born on May 10, 1948. Intense leading lady of American TV and films, following training at New York's Neighborhood Playhouse. Typically in assertive roles. She played Detective Chris Cagney in TV's popular series 'Cagney & Lacey' before being replaced by Sharon Gless.

FILMS INCLUDE: *Adam at 6 A.M.* 1970; *Thumb Tripping* 1972; *Tender Flesh* 1976; *A Different Story* 1978; *Carny* 1980; *A Ticket to Heaven* 1981; *The Osterman Weekend* 1983; *The Emerald Forest* 1985; *Masters of the Universe* 1987; *They Live* 1988; *Leviathan, Relentless, Stepfather II: Make Room for Daddy, Tripwire* 1989; *Jezebel's Kiss, Blind Fury, Backstab* 1990; *Diplomatic Immunity, Relentless II: Dead On* 1991; *Project: Shadowchaser* 1992; *Best of the Best 2, Hidden Fears, Oblivion* 1993; *Immortal Combat, Shrunken Heads* 1994; *Undercover* 1995.

Foster, Norman. Director, actor. *b.* Norman Hoeffer, Dec. 13, 1900, Richmond, Ind. *d.* 1976. He dabbled briefly in journalism and after gaining experience in stock made his Broadway debut in 1926. On the stage and in many Hollywood films of the 30s, he played light leads opposite some of the top female stars of the day but mainly in minor productions. He turned to directing in 1936 and for several years turned out routine programmers for Fox, including many Mr. Moto and Charlie Chan detective yarns. He gained respectability in 1942 as the credited director of *Journey into Fear,* which had begun as an Orson Welles project. He subsequently directed an interesting, offbeat, folksy Western romance, *Rachel and the Stranger* (1948); a taut gangland drama, *Woman on the Run* (1950); an authentic semidocumentary saga of the West, *Navajo* (1952), featuring an all-Indian cast; as well as many mediocre films ranging from empty comedies to slick adventures of the Disney factory. He has also directed numerous episodes for TV series as well as TV plays. His former wives include actresses Claudette COLBERT and Sally Blane.

FILMS INCLUDE: As actor—*Gentlemen of the Press* 1929; *Young Man of Manhattan, Love at First Sight* 1930; *No Limit, It Pays to Advertise, Up Pops the Devil, Men Call It Love, Reckless Living* 1931; *Girl of the Rio/The Dove, Play Girl, Week-End Marriage, Smilin' Through, Prosperity* 1932; *State Fair, Pilgrimage, Professional Sweetheart, Walls of Gold* 1933; *Orient Express, Strictly Dynamite* 1934; *Behind the Evidence, Escape from Devil's Island* 1935; *High Tension, Fatal Lady* 1936. As director (complete)—*I Cover Chinatown* (also act.) 1936; *Fair Warning* (also sc.), *Think Fast Mr. Moto* (also co-sc.), *Thank You Mr. Moto* (also co-sc.) 1937; *Walking Down Broadway, Mr. Moto Takes a Chance* (also co-story), *Mysterious Mr. Moto* (also co-sc.) 1938; *Mr. Moto's Last Warning* (also co-sc.), *Charlie Chan in Reno, Mr. Moto Takes a Vacation* (also co-story, co-sc.), *Charlie Chan at Treasure Island* 1939; *Charlie Chan in Panama, Viva Cisco Kid* 1940; *Ride Kelly Ride, Scotland Yard* 1941; *Journey Into Fear* (co-dir. with uncredited Orson Welles) 1942; *Santa* (Mex.) 1943; *Hora de la Verdad* (Mex.) 1945; *Rachel and the Stranger, Kiss the Blood Off My Hands* 1948; *Tell It to the Judge* 1949; *Father Is a Bachelor* (co-dir. with Abby Berlin), *Woman on the Run* (also co-sc.) 1950; *Navajo* (doc.; also sc.), *Sky Full of Moon* (also sc.) 1952; *Sombrero* (also sc.) 1953; *Davy Crockett King of the Wild Frontier* (also co-sc.) 1955; *Davy Crockett and the River Pirates* (also co-sc.) 1956; *The Nine Lives of Elfego Baca* (orig. made for TV; also sc., songs) 1959; *The Sign of Zorro* (co-dir. with Lewis R. Foster; also co-sc.) 1960; *Die lustigen Weiber von Windsor/The Merry Wives of Windsor* (prod., sc., act. as Falstaff only; Aus.) 1965; *Indian Paint* (also sc.) 1966; *Brighty of the Grand Canyon* (also sc.) 1967.

Foster, Preston. Actor. *b.* Oct. 24, 1900, Ocean City, N.J. *d.* 1970. Drifted from job to job and dabbled in professional wrestling before breaking into show business as a singer with the Pennsylvania Grand Opera Company in Philadelphia. In the late 20s he made it to Broadway and in the early 30s began a prolific career as a two-fisted leading man of Hollywood films. A burly, dashing, six-foot-two 200-pounder, he played rugged heroes as well as occasional villains in some 100 films.

FILMS INCLUDE: *Nothing but the Truth, Follow the Leader* 1930; *Two Seconds, Doctor X, The Last Mile, I Am a Fugitive from a Chain Gang* 1932; *Ladies They Talk About, Corruption, The Man Who Dared, Devil's Mate, Hoopla* 1933; *Heat Lightning, Wharf Angel* 1934; *The People's Enemy, The Informer, The Arizonian, The Last Days of Pompeii, Annie Oakley, We're Only Human* 1935; *Muss 'Em Up, Love Before Breakfast* 1936; *We Who Are About to Die, The Plough and the Stars, The Outcasts of Poker Flat, You Can't Beat Love, The Westland Case, First Lady* 1937; *Double Danger, The Lady in the Morgue, Up the River, Submarine Patrol, The Last Warning* 1938; *News Is Made at Night, Missing Evidence* 1939; *Geronimo, North West Mounted Police, Moon Over Burma* 1940; *Unfinished Business* 1941; *Secret Agent of Japan, Night in New Orleans, Little Tokyo USA, Thunder Birds* 1942; *My Friend Flicka, Guadalcanal Diary* 1943; *Bermuda Mystery, Roger Touhy—Gangster* (title role) 1944; *Thunderhead, The Valley of Decision, Twice Blessed* 1945; *The Harvey Girls, Tangier, Inside Job* 1946; *King of the Wild Horses* 1947; *I Shot Jesse James, The Big Cat* 1949; *Tomahawk, The Big Night* 1951; *Kansas City Confidential* 1952; *I the Jury* 1953; *Destination 60,000* 1957; *The Man from Galveston, The Time Travelers* 1964; *Chubasco* 1968.

Foster, Susanna. Actress, singer. Born Suzanne DeLee Flanders Larson, on Dec. 6, 1924, in Chicago. An operatic singer from childhood, she was signed at 12 by MGM and was nearly 15 by the time she made her actual screen debut, with Paramount, in 1939. Graduating from singing teenager to leading-lady roles with Universal, she starred in one major production, playing the frightened prima donna in *The Phantom of the Opera* (1943). She was subsequently seen in low-budget films and by 1945 had disappeared from the screen. She appeared in operettas with her husband (from 1948), Wilbur Evans, but after their divorce in 1956 she went to work as a clerk with a Wall Street brokerage firm. In the 70s she was reported to be working as a check-in attendant in a Manhattan Turkish bath.

FILMS: *The Great Victor Herbert* 1939; *The Hard-Boiled Canary/There's Magic in Music, Glamour Boy* 1941; *Star Spangled Rhythm* 1942; *The Phantom of the Opera, Top Man* 1943; *This Is the Life, Bowery to Broadway, Follow the Boys, The Climax* 1944; *Frisco Sal, That Night with You* 1945.

Fowley, Douglas. Actor. Born Daniel Vincent Fowley, on May 30, 1911, in New York City. A veteran of the stage, he has played character parts in some 200 films since the early 30s, typically as a villain or gangster. Memorable as "the director" in *Singin' in the Rain* (1952). Produced and directed one low-budget film, *Macumba Love* (1960). He portrayed Doc Holliday in the TV series 'The Life and Legend of Wyatt Earp' (1955–61).

FILMS INCLUDE: *The Mad Game* 1933; *I Hate Women* 1934; *Two for Tonight* 1935; *Big Brown Eyes, 36 Hours to Live* 1936; *On the Avenue, Wake Up and Live, Charlie Chan on Broadway* 1937; *Mr. Moto's Gamble, Alexander's Ragtime Band, Submarine Patrol* 1938; *Dodge City, Lucky Night* 1939; *Street of Missing Women, Ellery Queen—Master Detective* 1940; *The Devil with Hitler* 1942; *Stand by for Action, Jitterbugs* 1943; *See Here Private Hargrove* 1944; *Don't Fence Me In* 1945; *Backlash, The Hucksters, Merton of the Movies* 1947; *Coroner Creek* 1948; *Mighty Joe Young, Battleground* 1949; *Edge of Doom* 1950; *Across the Wide Missouri* 1951; *Singin' in the Rain* 1952; *The Naked Jungle, The High and the Mighty* 1954; *These Thousand Hills* 1959; *Desire in the Dust* 1960; *Barabba/Barabbas* (It.) 1961; *Miracle of the Wild Stallions* 1963; *The 7 Faces of Dr. Lao* 1964; *Nightmare in the Sun* 1965; *The Good Guys and the Bad Guys* 1969; *Walking Tall* 1973; *Homebodies* 1974; *From Noon Till Three* 1976; *Black Oak Conspiracy, The White Buffalo* 1977; *The North Avenue Irregulars* 1979.

Fox, Edward. Actor. Born on Apr. 13, 1937, in London. Brother of James FOX. Blond leading man and supporting player of British films and TV. His aloof, patrician manner is well suited for the cynical or cruel roles he has often portrayed. Formerly married to actress Tracy Reed.

FILMS INCLUDE: *The Mind Benders* 1963; *The Jokers, The Long Duel, The Naked Runner, The Frozen Dead, I'll Never Forget What's 'Is Name* 1967; *Oh! What a Lovely War, Battle of Britain* 1969; *Skullduggery* (US) 1970; *The Go-Between* 1971; *The Day of the Jackal* (as "The Jackal"), *A Doll's House* (as Krogstad) 1973; *Galileo* (as the Cardinal Inquisitor) 1975; *The Squeeze, The Duellists, A Bridge Too Far* 1977; *The Big Sleep, Force 10 from Navarone, The Cat and the Canary* 1978; *Soldier of Orange* (Hol.) 1979; *The Mirror Crack'd* 1980; *Gandhi* 1982; *The Dresser, Never Say Never Again* 1983; *The Bounty, The Shooting Party* 1984; *Wild Geese II* 1985; *Return from the River Kwai* 1989; *Robin Hood* (originally intended as a feature, later scaled down for cable) 1991; *A Month by the Lake* 1995.

Fox, James. Actor. Born William Fox, on May 19, 1939, in London. Brother of Edward Fox. The product of a theatrical family, he entered British films for the first time in 1950 as a child of ten and, once again, in the early 60s as a mature leading man, in the process altering his first name from William to James. He has typically portrayed polished, refined, sometimes decadent or weakling characters. In 1973 he abandoned acting to become an active evangelist; but he returned to the screen in the early 80s. Autobiography: *Comeback: An Actor's Direction* (1983).

FILMS INCLUDE: *The Miniver Story, The Magnet* 1950; *The Lavender Hill Mob* 1951; *Timbuktu* (US) 1958; *The Secret Partner* 1961; *The Loneliness of the Long Distance Runner* 1962; *The Servant, Tamahine* 1963; *Those Magnificent Men in Their Flying Machines, King Rat* (US) 1965; *The Chase* (US) 1966; *Thoroughly Modern Millie* (US), *Arabella* (It.) 1967; *Isadora/The Loves of Isadora, Duffy* (US/UK) 1968; *Performance* 1970; *No Longer Alone* (religious film) 1978; *Runners* 1983; *Greystoke: The Legend of Tarzan Lord of the Apes, A Passage to India* 1984; *Absolute Beginners* 1986; *High Season, The Whistle Blower, Comrades, Hostage* 1987; *Farewell to the King, She's Been Away* 1989; *The Boys in the Island, The Russia House* 1990; *Patriot Games, Afraid of the Dark* 1991; *A Question of Attribution* 1992; *The Remains of the Day* 1993; *Hearts of Darkness: A Filmmaker's Apocalypse, Mrs. Parker and the Vicious Circle* (art dir. only) 1994; *Blue in the Face, Clockwork Fox, Cold Blooded* (cameo, co-prod.) 1995.

Fox, Michael J. Actor. Born on June 9, 1961, in Edmonton, Alberta, Canada. Diminutive (5' 4"), dynamic, likable star of American TV and films. One of five children of a Canadian Army career officer and a payroll clerk, he grew up in a succession of military bases. The family eventually settled in Vancouver, where Michael began performing on Canadian TV at age 15. At 18, he arrived in Los Angeles, hoping for a lucrative acting career, but found himself jobless and near starvation before landing small roles in a couple of movies and in the short-lived series 'Palmerstown, U.S.A.' (1980–81). His big break came in 1982, when he was cast as teenager Alex P. Keaton in the series 'Family Ties.' His charm and exuberance appealed to audiences and helped make the program one of the most successful of the 80s. His popularity soared even higher when in 1985 he starred as skateboarding Marty McFly in the hit comedy-fantasy film *Back to the Future.* Having established solid credentials in light roles, he began exploring occasional dramatic parts later in the 80s. In 1988 he married his 'Family Ties' co-star Tracy Pollan.

FILMS: *Midnight Madness* 1980; *Class of 1984* 1982; *Back to the Future, Teen Wolf* 1985; *Light of Day, Dear America* (doc.; v/o), *The Secret of My Success* 1987; *Bright Lights Big City* 1988; *Casualties of War* 1989; *Back to the Future II, Back to the Future III* 1990; *The Hard Way, Doc Hollywood* 1991; *Life with Mikey, For Love or Money* 1993; *Greedy, Where the River Flows North* 1994; *The American President, Blue in the Face* 1995; *The Frighteners, Homeward Bound 2: Lost in San Francisco* (v/o), *Mars Attacks!* 1996.

Fox, Wallace. Director. *b.* Mar. 9, 1895, Purcell, Okla. *d.* 1958. *ed.* West Texas Military Academy in San Antonio. Started as a black-face entertainer in minstrel shows. After performing briefly in vaudeville, he broke into films as a prop man in 1919 and later worked as assistant to director Edwin CAREWE. Debuting as a director in 1927, he turned out low-budget Westerns and action pictures, mostly for Monogram but also for such studios as RKO and Universal. In the 40s he directed many East Side Kids (Bowery Boys) comedies. In the early 50s he moved over to TV.

FILMS INCLUDE: *The Bandit's Son* 1927; *The Avenging Rider* 1928; *Come and Get It, The Amazing Vagabond, Laughing at Death* 1929; *Partners of the Trail* 1931; *The Cannonball Express, Devil on Deck* 1932; *Red Morning* 1935; *Yellow Dust* 1936; *Racing Lady* 1937; *The Mexicali Kid* 1938; *Pride of the Plains* 1940; *Bowery Blitzkrieg, Spooks Run Wild* 1941; *Bullets for Bandits, The Corpse Vanishes, Smart Alecks, Bowery at Midnight* 1942; *The Ghost Rider, The Girl from Monterey* 1943; *Men on Her Mind, The Great Mike* 1944; *Brenda Starr—Reporter* (serial), *Bad Men of the Border, Pillow of Death* 1945; *Gun Town* (also prod.), *Wild Beauty* (also prod.), *The Lawless Breed* (also prod.) 1946; *Jack Armstrong* (serial), *The Vigilante,* (serial) 1947; *Docks of New York, The Valiant Hombre* 1948; *The Daring Caballero, Western Renegades* 1949; *Over the Border* (also prod.), *Gunslingers* (also prod.), *Outlaw Gold* 1950; *Montana Desperado* 1951.

Fox, William. Executive. *b.* Wilhelm Fried, Jan. 1, 1879, Tulchva, Hungary, to German-Jewish parents. *d.* 1952. In the

US from the age of nine months, he grew up in a tenement on New York's Lower East Side. As the eldest of 13 children, six of whom survived their infancy, he helped support the family from an early age. At 11 he left school to work at a garment center sweatshop for 12 hours a day. Eventually he started his own garment business and was modestly successful. In 1904 he bought a failing Brooklyn penny arcade from J. Stuart BLACKTON and turned it into a booming operation. He soon developed his enterprise into a chain of 15 motion picture theaters in Brooklyn and Manhattan. Realizing there were more profits to be made in distribution, he started his own film exchange, The Greater New York Rental Company.

After successfully foiling an attempt by the monopolistic Patent Company to acquire his business, he decided to make his own films and formed the Box Office Attraction Company, which began production in 1912. Meanwhile, his theater chain as well as his rental firm continued to grow, and in 1915 he combined all three wings of his little empire—production, leasing, and exhibition—under one roof, the Fox Film Corporation. This soon developed from a modest family business (Fox's wife, Eve, selected scripts and sometimes supervised production) into a prosperous Hollywood studio employing such popular stars as Theda Bara, William Farnum, Betty Blythe, Annette Kellerman, and Tom Mix. Its big prestige picture in the 20s was Murnau's *Sunrise.* By the end of the decade the company was turning out some 50 films a year and its value was estimated at $200 million.

The ambitious Fox set out to expand his sizable empire further by acquiring hundreds of movie theaters and by purchasing a controlling interest in Loew's, Inc., the parent company of MGM, as well as a 45 percent interest in Gaumont-British, England's most important producing, distributing, and exhibiting company. Fox was only steps away from becoming Hollywood's most powerful magnate when the stock market collapse, government antitrust action, and a personal injury in an automobile crash which immobilized him for two months late in 1929, combined to shake the foundations of the Fox Corporation. In 1930, Fox was forced to sell his shares in the company to a group of bankers. Continual court litigations rapidly dwindled his assets and in 1936 he declared bankruptcy. In 1941 he was sentenced to a year's imprisonment for allegedly bribing a judge in his bankruptcy hearing. He served six months in a Pennsylvania penitentiary before being released on parole in 1943. He eventually paid off his debts and managed to live comfortably on the proceeds of some patents he still held. William Fox's eventful life story was dramatically told by author Upton Sinclair in the 1933 book *Upton Sinclair Presents William Fox.*

Fox Film Corporation. See 20TH CENTURY-FOX.

Foy, Bryan. Producer, director. *b.* Dec. 8, 1896, Chicago. *d.* 1977. A son of famous vaudeville entertainer Eddie Foy, brother of Eddie FOY, Jr., and himself popular on the vaudeville circuit as one of the Seven Little Foys, he left the stage in 1918 to become a director of comedy shorts at Fox. He later freelanced as a screenwriter and gag writer for Buster Keaton and others. In the mid-20s he joined Warner Bros., where his experience with sound on VitaPhone shorts led to his assignment to direct the feature *Lights of New York* (1928), a sort of landmark film, promoted by the studio as "the first 100 percent all-talking picture." Except for the novelty, it was a rather awkward motion picture, and after directing a number of low-budget films, Foy moved over to the producer's end of the business. For a while he headed the B unit at Warners. In the 40s he was associated with Fox and in the 50s was back with Warners, where he produced another technical landmark film, the 3-D *House of Wax* (1953). During his vaudeville days Foy wrote the hit song 'Mr. Gallagher and Mr. Shean.' Because of his long association with B pictures he was known jokingly in the industry as "Keeper of the B's."

FILMS INCLUDE: As director—*Lights of New York, The Home Towners* 1928; *Queen of the Night Clubs, The Royal Box* 1929; *The Gorilla* 1931. As producer—*Tomorrow's Children* 1934; *Crime School* 1938; *Berlin Correspondent, The Loves of Edgar Allan Poe* 1942; *Guadalcanal Diary* 1943; *Doll Face* 1946; *Trapped* 1949; *Breakthrough, I Was a Communist for the FBI, Inside the Walls of Folsom Prison* 1951; *The Lion and the Horse, The Miracle of Our Lady of Fatima* 1952; *House of Wax* 1953; *Crime Wave, The Mad Magician* 1954; *Blueprint for Robbery* 1961; *House of Women* 1962; *PT 109* 1963.

Foy, Eddie, Jr. Actor. *b.* Feb. 4, 1905, New Rochelle, N.Y. *d.* 1983. A son of the celebrated Eddie Foy, and brother of Bryan FOY, he began his career as one of the Seven Little Foys. On his own since the late 20s, Eddie Jr. made his Broadway debut in Ziegfeld's 'Show Girl' in 1929 and in the same year began appearing in supporting roles in feature films as well. He portrayed his famous father in several productions.

FILMS INCLUDE: *Queen of the Night Clubs* 1929; *Leathernecking* 1930; *Broadway Through a Keyhole* 1933; *Turn Off the Moon* 1937; *Secret Service of the Air, Frontier Marshal* (as his father) 1939; *Lillian Russell* (as his father) 1940; *Yankee Doodle Dandy* (as his father), *Moonlight Masquerade* 1942; *Dixie* 1943; *Wilson* (as his father), *And the Angels Sing* 1944; *The Farmer Takes a Wife* 1953; *Lucky Me* 1954; *The Pajama Game* 1957; *Bells Are Ringing* 1960; *Gidget Goes Hawaiian* 1961; *30 Is a Dangerous Age Cynthia* (UK) 1968.

f.p.s. Frames per second. The number of individual images produced every second as the film passes through the camera gate, or the number of individual images passing through the projector during exhibition. The standard silent 35 mm camera and projection speed was 16 f.p.s. The sound film standard is 24 f.p.s. Some wide-screen processes have experimented with 30 f.p.s.

Fraker, William A. Director of photography, director. Born in 1923, in Los Angeles. A graduate of the film school of USC, he entered the industry as a still photographer and after a period of transition in the cutting room became an assistant cameraman, camera operator, and finally, in 1967, a director of photography. He was immediately recognized as a rising new talent and within a year was entrusted with such top projects as *Rosemary's Baby* and *Bullitt.* His association with Lee Marvin on the set of *Paint Your Wagon* led to Fraker's first assignment as a director, *Monte Walsh* (1970), a fine, melancholy Western starring Marvin. Fraker was less successful with two other excursions into directing, but continued to impress as a cinematographer.

FILMS INCLUDE: As director of photography—*Forbid Them Not* (doc.; also co-prod.) 1962; *Games, The Fox* 1967; *The President's Analyst, Fade In, Rosemary's Baby, Bullitt* 1968; *Paint Your Wagon* 1969; *Dusty and Sweets McGee* 1971; *The Day of the Dolphin* 1973; *Rancho Deluxe, Coonskin, One Flew Over the Cuckoo's Nest* (co-phot.) 1975; *Lipstick* (co-phot.), *Gator* 1976; *Exorcist II: The Heretic, Looking for Mr. Goodbar, Close Encounters of the Third Kind* (co-phot.) 1977; *American Hot Wax, Heaven Can Wait* 1978; *Old Boyfriends, 1941* 1979; *The Best Little Whorehouse in Texas* 1982; *WarGames* 1983; *Irreconcilable Differences* (also act.) 1984; *Murphy's Romance* 1985; *Spacecamp* 1986; *Burglar, Baby Boom* 1987; *Chances Are, An Innocent Man* 1989; *The Freshman* 1990, *Memoirs of an Invisible Man* 1992;

Tombstone (assoc. prod. only) 1993; *There Goes My Baby, Street Fighter* 1994; *Father of the Bride II* 1995; *Vegas Vacation* 1997. As director (complete)—*Monte Walsh* 1970; *A Reflection of Fear* 1973; *The Legend of the Lone Ranger* 1981.

frame. One of the successive individual images that comprise a motion picture, or the space such an image occupies. Each frame is separated from the others by a horizontal border called a "frame line." The frame is the smallest coherent unit of a film. Like a still photograph, it may contain all the elements of a shot as far as composition is concerned, but it cannot convey motion unless it is shown in conjunction with preceding and following frames at a determined rate of frames per second (24 f.p.s. for 35 mm sound film). An average-length 90-minute feature film is made up of 129,600 separate frames.

frame counter. A gauging device attached to a camera which indicates the number of frames that have been exposed during filming.

framing. 1. Composing a shot. 2. Lining up a frame of the film in a projector or editing machine so that the picture is in register with the lens aperture. A correctly framed picture is said to be "in frame"; when frame lines are visible above or below the image, the picture is "out of frame."

Frampton, Hollis. Avant-garde filmmaker. *b.* Mar. 11, 1936, Wooster, Ohio. *d.* 1984. In the late 50s, in New York, he took an interest in still photography and during the 60s worked as a technician in a film laboratory. While there, he began exploring the physical properties and expressive potential of film. He soon began making experimental films, ranging widely in form but sharing the quality of structured precision. Among other areas, he experimented with interactive cinema, inviting audience participation. He wrote extensively on film theory. Although he never graduated high school (he did briefly attend Western Reserve University), he taught film at New York's Free University and Hunter College, and at the State University Media Center at Buffalo.

FILMS INCLUDE: *Manual of Arms* 1966; *Heterodyne* 1967; *Maxwell's Demon* 1968; *Palindrome, Artificial Light* 1969; *Zorn's Lemma* 1970; *Hapax Legomena* 1971; *Magellan* (unfinished) 1972.

France. No country other than the United States has contributed more to the technical and artistic development of the cinema than this culture-rich nation. Important ingredients of this contribution were the experiments in still photography early in the 19th century by Joseph-Nicéphore NIÉPCE and Louis DAGUERRE, who were the first to make pictures in a camera through the exposure of sensitive chemicals to light. In October of 1888, physiologist Etienne-Jules MAREY presented to the French Academy of Science a band of serial photographs of human and animal movement taken by his photographic gun, the *chronophotographe,* at 12 images per second, a great stride toward the invention of actual cinematography. Three months later Emile REYNAUD, a science teacher who had been experimenting with projection machines for several years, was granted a patent for his "Théâtre optique," a presentation system utilizing perforated celluloid strips of film. The show premiered at the 1889 World's Fair and was a fixture at the Musée Grévin between 1892 and 1900, during which time half a million spectators viewed the 12,800 performances. The program consisted of a number of highly inventive drawn animated shorts, including *Un Bon Bock* (15 min., 1889), *Clown et ses Chiens* (10 min., 1890), *Pauvre Pierrot* (15 min., 1891), *Un Rêve au Coin du Feu* (12 min., 1893), and *Autour d'une Cabine* (12 min., 1894).

The birth of the cinema as we know it today is acknowledged by many to have taken place on December 28, 1895, when Louis and Auguste LUMIÈRE presented the first program of projected films to a paying audience in the basement of the Grand Café on the Boulevard des Capucines in Paris. Early programs included the brothers' first film, *La Sortie des Usines Lumière,* which simply recorded workers as they were leaving the Lumière factory; *L'Arrivée d'un Train en Gare,* which jolted the audience with a shot of an oncoming train; and *L'Arroseur Arrosé,* a brief comic film that may be considered the screen's first farce as well as cinema's first bit of fiction. The Lumière catalog later contained other short-story films, but on the whole the brothers concentrated on recording scenes of real life, thus taking their place in cinema history as the precursors of the NEWSREEL and the DOCUMENTARY traditions.

The man who pioneered the creative fiction film was Georges MÉLIÈS, a conjurer and illusionist who, beginning with *Une Partie de Cartes* (1896), made hundreds of inventive and imaginative short films of various genres—drama, comedy, vaudeville, fairy tale, historic spectacle, etc.—but became best known and remembered for his clever and often humorous fantasy and trick movies, especially his futuristic parodies in the Jules Verne vein, several of which, including *Le Voyage dans la Lune/A Trip to the Moon* (1902), fascinate and amuse audiences even today.

In France a vast-scale commercial exploitation of the "new toy" came quickly on the heels of the early experiments. Not long after the historic Lumière presentation, Léon GAUMONT and Charles PATHÉ, laid the foundations to production organizations that would soon rise into movie empires. Gaumont, a manufacturer and merchant of photographic equipment, entered the film business in 1896, initially by developing motion picture apparatus but later that year branching into production and exhibition. Many of his early films were directed by his former secretary, Alice Guy (later GUY-BLACHÉ), probably the world's first woman director, who in 1900 was appointed head of production of the entire output of the Gaumont studios. She later came to the US, where she formed her own production company in 1910. The Gaumont company experimented with a sound system as early as 1902 and by 1907 had extended its film activities into foreign markets, including England, Germany, Russia, and the United States.

Gaumont's great rival, Pathé, would one day become known as the Napoleon of the cinema. A clever entrepreneur who had made a fortune in 1894 by charging fair crowds for the right to listen to early phonograph recordings, he was quick to realize the profit potential of the new medium of cinema and in 1896 began adding short films to his catalog of attractions. In the same year he formed the Pathé Frères company with his three brothers, and in 1901 he began devoting his energies solely to films. Pathé built a large studio at Vincennes and entrusted its creative management to Ferdinand ZECCA, a former café singer. Zecca acquired a reputation as a plagiarist, borrowing ideas and techniques from Méliès and the British film pioneers, but in his quest of exploitation material, he did introduce to the screen the genre of low-life and crime melodrama with films as realistic as *Histoire d'un Crime.* The Pathé company expanded rapidly, soon opening branches in various parts of the world. By 1908 it was an international empire, selling twice as many films in the United States as all American companies combined. It was by far the world's largest movie producer before the outbreak of WW I.

Pathé had a part interest in FILM D'ART. The company's first production was *L'Assassinat du Duc de Guise/The Assassination of the Duke de Guise* (1908). Unlike most earlier productions, which were typically made up of a succession of tableaux, or scenes, this film boasted a flowing continuity that permitted of character development and dramatic intensity. The dramatic format and grandeur of *L'Assassinat,* directed by Charles le Bargy and André CALMETTES, greatly influenced producers and filmmakers abroad, among them D. W. GRIFFITH. The international success of the film led to other grand Film d'Art spectacles, including adaptations of *Notre Dame de Paris/The Hunchback of Notre Dame* (1911) and *Les Misérables* (1912), both directed by Albert CAPELLANI; *Madame Sans-Gêne* (1911), directed by Calmettes; *La Dame aux Camelias* (1911), directed by Calmettes and Henri Pouctal; and *La Reine Elisabeth/Queen Elizabeth* (1912), directed by Louis Mercanton and Henri Desfontaines, the last two films starring Sarah BERNHARDT. Although these films were generally rather static photographed stage plays, they gave respectability to the cinema and drew to movie theaters a better-educated class of spectators. *Queen Elizabeth* played an important part in American film history. The proceeds of its distribution provided Adolph ZUKOR with the funds and impetus for his program of "Famous Players in Famous Plays," the cornerstone of PARAMOUNT.

In general, however, mediocrity prevailed in the French cinema of the period, with commercial rather than artistic considerations motivating most producers. Two of the most popular staples were slapstick comedy and adventure series. Among the leading comedians were André DEED, who created for the screen a Pierrot-like character called Gribouille in many comedy shorts in the *commedia dell'arte* style, and the dapper Max LINDER, who brought to film a more subtle, restrained, and sophisticated style of slapstick that influenced Charlie CHAPLIN and other great comedians of the silent screen. The series vogue began with Victorin JASSET's "Nick Carter" and reached its peak with Louis FEUILLADE's "Bout-de-zan" series (1912–16) and such serials as *Fantômas* (1913–14), *Les vampires* (1915–16), and *Judex* (1916), which successfully blended realism with fantasy and often also humor.

The outbreak of WW I dealt a severe blow to the French film industry. The commercial crisis in the French cinema continued after the Armistice, but a parallel development in the postwar years was the blossoming of a lively movement to elevate film to the status of a true form of art. The theoretical impetus was provided by Ricciotto CANUDO, who coined the name "the seventh art" to describe cinema and in 1920 founded the Club des Amis du 7e Art (The Club of the Friends of the Seventh Art) in Paris; and by Louis DELLUC, who played an important role in founding cinema clubs in France and himself directed a number of films noted for their psychological atmosphere, preoccupation with memory, and manipulation of time. Another important director in the movement, influenced by the contemporary avant-garde, was Germaine DULAC, who sought in several of her films to explore the unconscious and discover a mode of "pure cinema." Her best-known film was the surrealistic *La Coquille et le Clergyman* (1927), from a script by Antonin ARTAUD.

Jean EPSTEIN added to the theoretical writings of the period and, preaching what he taught, directed a number of films remarkable for their visual beauty and technical inventiveness, among them *L'Auberge rouge* (1923), *Coeur fidèle* (1923), and *La Chute de la Maison Usher* (1928), an adaptation of Edgar Allan Poe's *The Fall of the House of Usher.* Marcel L'HERBIER, a poet and playwright, participated in the screen experimentations of the early 20s, most notably with *Eldorado* (1921), *L'Inhumaine* (1923), and *Feu Mathias Pascal* (1925). Films of the avant-garde made during the 20s outside the confines of the commercial cinema included Man RAY's *Le Retour à la Raison* (1923), Fernand LÉGER's *Le Ballet mécanique* (1924), René CLAIR's *Entr'acte* (1924), Luis BUÑUEL's *Un Chien andalou* (1928) and *L'Age d'Or* (1930), and Jean COCTEAU's *Le Sang d'un Poète/The Blood of a Poet* (1930). These films drew large audiences of intellectuals at the ciné-clubs.

A dominant figure in 20s was Abel GANCE, a great technical innovator who constantly sought to extend the physical capacity of the medium. He used split-screen effects in *J'accuse* (1919), astounding visuals and rhythmic editing in *La Roue* (1923), and a whole array of inventions in his stupendous production of *Napoléon* (1927), including a triple-screen effect called Polyvision which was a precursor of CINERAMA. Another notable director was Belgian-born Jacques FEYDER, whose main films of the period were *L'Atlantide* (1921), *Crainquebille* (1922), and *Thérèse Raquin* (1928). Two directors whose work was impressive in the 20s but had greater impact in the 30s were René CLAIR and Jean RENOIR.

The early sound period in France as elsewhere was generally marked by stagnation, as many directors succumbed to the lure of dialogue at the expense of movement and action. Theatrical people like Marcel PAGNOL brought the stage tradition to the screen. A remarkable exception was the work of René Clair, who inventively exploited sound in such films as *Sous les Toits de Paris/Under the Roofs of Paris* (1930), *Le Million* (1931), *A nous la Liberté* (1931), and *Quatorze Juillet* (1933). Another outstanding contribution was made by Jean VIGO, whose career was cut short by his tragic early death. His *Zéro de Conduite/Zero for Conduct* (1933) and *L'Atalante* (1934) were unique blends of reality and fantasy which prefigured the poetic realism style that was to dominate the French cinema later in the 30s. Jean Renoir, who had established his credentials in the 20s with such films as *Nana* (1926) and *Tire-au-Flanc* (1928), now asserted his original talent with two films starring Michel Simon, *La Chienne* (1931) and *Boudu sauvé des Eaux/Boudu Saved from Drowning* (1932). Renoir anticipated neorealism with *Toni* (1935), which was filmed on actual locations with nonprofessional players, flirted with left-wing politics in *Le Crime de Monsieur Lange* (1936), *La Vie est à nous* (1936), and *La Marseillaise* (1938), and reached new peaks of cinematic expression with his masterpieces *La Grande Illusion/Grand Illusion* (1937), *La Bête humaine/The Human Beast* (1938), and *La Règle du Jeu/The Rules of the Game* (1939).

The French cinema entered one of its richest eras in the middle of the decade. In 1936, the CINÉMATHÈQUE FRANÇAISE was founded by Henri LANGLOIS, Jean MITRY, and Georges FRANJU. The style that most characterized the French cinema of the late 30s is known as poetic realism, a profoundly pessimistic, often fatalistic, but at the same time intrinsically romantic style that was best embodied on the screen in the personality of actor Jean GABIN. A key role in this school of cinematography was played by writers, particularly Charles SPAAK, Jacques PRÉVERT, and Henri JEANSON. Among the films that exemplified the style were Jacques FEYDER's *Pension Mimosas* (1935), Julien DUVIVIER's *La Bandera/Escape from Yesterday* (1935) and *Pépé le Moko* (1937), Renoir's *La Bête humaine/The Human Beast* (1938), Marcel CARNÉ's *Quai des Brumes/Port of Shadows* (1938) and *Le Jour se lève/Daybreak* (1939), and Jean GRÉMILLON's *Remorques/Stormy Waters* (made in 1939 but released in 1941). The theatrical tradition in the French cinema was preserved in the elegant but talkative productions of Sacha GUITRY.

The achievements of the late 30s placed France in the forefront of the world's creative cinema, but the outbreak of WW II rudely disrupted production and sent many of the leading directors scattering into hiding or exile. Duvivier, Clair, Renoir, and emigré Max OPHÜLS all went to Hollywood, and Feyder to Switzerland. Carné and Grémillon were the only established filmmakers who continued working during the Occupation. To avoid the scrutiny of German censorship, they typically resorted to themes of the distant past or obliquely stated allegory. Carné reached into medieval legend with the haunting, visually striking *Les Visiteurs du Soir/The Devil's Envoys* (1942) and achieved his artistic peak with his splendid evocation of the romantic theater of the 19th century with *Les Enfants du Paradis/Children of Paradise* (1945). Grémillon contributed the lyrical allegory of good versus evil *Lumière d'Eté* (1943) and the disguised tribute to French patriotism *Le Ciel est à vous/The Woman Who Dared* (1944). A director with lesser credentials during the 30s who reached maturity during the Occupation was Claude AUTANT-LARA, who was responsible for two charming if outdated romantic films, *Le Mariage du Chiffon* and *Lettres d'Amour* (both 1942), and a satire of the bourgeoisie, *Douce/Love Story* (1943).

Several new directors emerged during the war period, among them Robert BRESSON, who made an auspicious start with *Les Anges du Péché/Angels of the Street* (1943) and *Les Dames du Bois de Boulogne/Ladies of the Park* (1945). Another striking debut was made by Henri-Georges CLOUZOT, whose second film, *Le Corbeau/The Raven* (1943), established his reputation as a master of the suspense-thriller genre. After the Liberation this film was denounced as German-inspired anti-French propaganda. It was banned for two years and its director suspended for six months. Jean DELANNOY also made an impressive start during the occupation with *L'Eternel Retour/The Eternal Return* (1943), a modernized version of the Tristan and Isolde legend, as did Jacques BECKER with *Dernier Atout* (1942) and *Goupi Mains rouges/It Happened at the Inn* (1943). And 1943 marked the birth of IDHEC, the French cinema school.

The Centre National du Cinéma Française (CNC) was established in 1946 to regulate industry affairs. A quota system was initiated to protect national production from foreign competition, especially from Hollywood, and co-production with neighboring European countries was encouraged. The characteristic trend of the early postwar films was back to realism, with a penchant for the FILM NOIR style. Typical of these were Carné's *Les Portes de la Nuit/Gates of the Night* (1946), Duvivier's *Panique/Panic* (1946), Clouzot's *Quai des Orfèvres/Jenny Lamour* (1947), and Yves ALLÉGRET's *Dedée d'Anvers/Dedee* (1948) and *Une si Jolie Petite Plage/Riptide* (1949).

But suspenseful realism was by no means the exclusive style in the French cinema of the late 40s. René Clair returned from the US to direct the quaint, nostalgic *Le Silence est d'Or/Man About Town* (1947) and a rather lavish adaptation of the Faust legend, *La Beauté du Diable/Beauty and the Devil* (1950). Jacques Becker created two tenderly told, minutely detailed films of social observation, *Antoine et Antoinette/Antoine and Antoinette* (1947) and *Rendezvous de Juillet* (1949). Newcomer René CLÉMENT re-created episodes of the anti-Nazi resistance in *La Bataille du Rail/Battle of the Rails* (1946), then turned out a brisk psychological melodrama *Les Maudits/The Damned* (1947). Other impressive debuts were Roger LEENHARDT's *Les Dernières Vacances* (1948) and Jean-Pierre MELVILLE's *Le Silence de la Mer* (1949). Georges ROUQUIER composed a unique ode to nature in *Farrebique* (1946). Autant-Lara scandalized many with his masterpiece of adultery, *Le Diable au Corps/Devil in the Flesh* (1947), from a script by Jean AURENCHE and Pierre BOST, who became his regular collaborators. A major voice in French cinema of the late 40s was that of poet-playwright-artist Jean Cocteau, who contributed scripts for several films and himself directed the visually striking *La Belle et la Bête/Beauty and the Beast* (1946), the intimately claustrophobic *Les Parents terribles/The Storm Within* (1948), and the poetic fantasy *Orphée/Orpheus* (1950). In an entirely different vein, Jacques TATI first revealed his enormous comic talent in *Jour de Fête* (1949). Leading screen personalities of the 40s included Jean GABIN, RAIMU, Michel SIMON, Louis JOUVET, Viviane ROMANCE, Michèle MORGAN, and FERNANDEL, all of whom had been popular stars also in the 30s.

The early 50s were characterized by the dominance of the French film scene by the veteran directors, some of whom went on to new heights of achievement while others saw their reputations gradually decline. Among the outstanding films of the period: Becker's *Casque d'Or* (1952) and *Touchez pas au Grisbi/Grisbi* (1954); Autant-Lara's *L'Auberge rouge/The Red Inn* (1951); Bresson's *Le Journal d'un Curé de Campagne/Diary of a Country Priest* (1951) and *Un Condamné à Mort s'est échappé/A Man Escaped* (1956); Carné's *Thérèse Raquin/The Adulteress* (1953); André CAYATTE's indictments of the judicial and social system, *Justice est faite/Justice Is Done* (1950), *Nous sommes tous des Assassins/We Are All Murderers* (1952), and *Avant le Deluge* (1954); Clair's *Les Belles de Nuit/Beauties of the Night* (1952), and *Les Grandes Manoeuvres/The Grand Maneuver* (1955); Clément's *Jeux interdits/Forbidden Games* (1952) and *Gervaise* (1956); Clouzot's masterpiece of suspense, *Le Salaire de la Peur/Wages of Fear* (1953); American expatriate Jules DASSIN's *Du Rififi chez les Hommes/Rififi* (1955); Max Ophüls's last and most memorable films, *La Ronde* (1950), *Le Plaisir* (1952), *Madame de.../The Earrings of Madame De* (1953), and *Lola Montès* (1955); Renoir's *French Cancan/Only the French Can* (1955); and Tati's *Les Vacances de Monsieur Hulot/Mr. Hulot's Holiday* (1953) and *Mon Oncle/My Uncle* (1958).

Many leading directors turned out lavish but uninspired color movies. Typical of these were Autant-Lara's *Le Rouge et le Noir/The Red and the Black* (1954); Becker's *Ali Baba et les Quarantes Voleurs/Ali Baba and the 40 Thieves* (1954); and CHRISTIAN-JAQUE's *Fanfan la Tulipe/Fanfan the Tulip* (1952), starring Gérard PHILIPE, and *Nana* (1955), starring Martine CAROL. With the notable exceptions of Bresson and Tati, the work of none of the veteran directors showed consistent creative originality.

At this crossroad between peak achievement and stagnation, a group of young critics made its presence felt in the affairs of the French cinema. These men, among them Claude CHABROL, François TRUFFAUT, Jean-Luc GODARD, Eric ROHMER, and Jacques RIVETTE, gathered around André BAZIN, the co-founder with Jacques DONIOL-VALCROZE of the magazine CAHIERS DU CINÉMA. The group developed the AUTEUR THEORY, through which they exalted the works of certain neglected Hollywood directors and blamed the decadence of the French film industry on the inertia of the "old guard" of directors.

The *Cahiers* critics, as well as several other young filmmakers, began putting some of these new ideas into practice during the 50s, initially in shorts and by the end of the decade in feature-length films. Although the individual new directors varied widely in approach and style, they were conveniently lumped together by film journalists into a movement that became known as the NOUVELLE VAGUE, or New Wave. Ironically, the young director who helped pave the way for the movement into the mainstream of the French cinema, Roger VADIM, would become very much part of the commercial establishment against which the New Wave was rebelling. But at that juncture his *Et Dieu créa la Femme/And God Created*

Woman (1956) not only made Brigitte BARDOT a popular star but also proved to producers that the right combination of nonconformist, youthful exuberance and candid sexuality could crack open the coffers of the international box office for the dormant French cinema. Louis MALLE soon followed with two successes of his own, *Ascenseur pour l'Echafaud/Frantic* and *Les Amants/The Lovers* (both 1958). Claude Chabrol was the first of the *Cahiers* inner group to break through the barrier of the commercial cinema with *Le Beau Serge* (1958), partly thanks to money inherited from his wife. With the release of Truffaut's *Les 400 Coups/The 400 Blows* (1959) and Godard's *Á Bout de Souffle/Breathless* (1960), the *Nouvelle Vague* fully burst upon the scene. In 1962 *Cahiers du Cinéma* devoted an entire issue to the New Wave and listed 162 new directors working in France.

Among the leading directors of the new French cinema, in addition to those listed above, were Alexandre ASTRUC, whose feature career, dating back to 1955, influenced many young filmmakers; Jacques DEMY, who established an international reputation with *Lola* (1961) and showed great inventiveness with the musical *Les Parapluies de Cherbourg/The Umbrellas of Cherbourg* (1964); Georges FRANJU, who after many years of remarkable shorts proved himself in the 60s an excellent stylist of atmospheric features; Chris MARKER, an outstanding documentarian; Alain RESNAIS, a major talent whose cinematic exercises on the theme of time, like *Hiroshima mon Amour* (1959) and *L'Année dernière à Marienbad/Last Year at Marienbad* (1961), were among the most original and intellectually stimulating contributions of the New Wave; and Agnès VARDA, a former still-photographer whose visual flair and highly personal style became evident in such films as *La Pointe courte* (1956) and *Cléo de 5 à 7/Cleo from 5 to 7* (1962).

These and other new directors helped restore the international prestige of the French cinema during the 60s and at least temporarily revive the sagging economics of the national industry. Chabrol, Truffaut, Godard, and several of their colleagues became established in the forefront of world cinema. A newcomer, Claude LELOUCH, enjoyed great commercial international success with his romantic *Un Homme et une Femme/A Man and a Woman* (1966). Other names that emerged during the 60s included René ALLIO, Jacques Baratier, Jose Benazeraf, Claude BERRI, Bertrand BLIER, Yves BOISSET, Walerian BOROWCZYK, Serge BOURGUIGNON, Philippe de BROCA, Alain CAVALIER, Henri COLPI, Constantin COSTA-GAVRAS (who started a vogue with his political thriller Z, 1969), Jacques DERAY, Michel DEVILLE, Michel DRACH, Marguerite DURAS (who along with Alain ROBBE-GRILLET led a small movement of literary cinema), Robert ENRICO, Jean EUSTACHE, Philippe Garrel, Guy Gilles, José Giovanni, Claude de Givray, Marcel Hanoun, Alain JESSUA, Nelly KAPLAN, American William KLEIN, Serge Korber, Georges LAUTNER, Edouard Luntz, Jean-Pierre MOCKY, Gérard OURY, Gérard Pirès, documentarists François REICHENBACH and Frédéric ROSSIF, Yves ROBERT, Eric ROHMER, Jacques Rozier, Claude SAUTET, Pierre Schoendoerffer, Jean-Daniel Simon, Nadine TRINTIGNANT, and Jean Velère. An old-timer who made two of France's best films of the 60s was Luis Buñuel with *Le Journal d'une Femme de Chambre/The Diary of a Chambermaid* (1964) and *Belle de Jour* (1967). The former starred Jeanne MOREAU and the latter Catherine DENEUVE, the two leading female stars of the French cinema in the decade.

During the political upheaval of May 1968, the dissident directors, borrowing a term from the French Revolution, formed a self-styled Etats Généreaux du Cinéma and demanded that the industry be re-organized along Communist lines and financial aid dispensed to experimental and avant-garde films rather than commercially attractive projects. They also called for the replacement of IDHEC with a more "relevant" school. But little changed as a result of the rebellion, and after a brief period of turmoil the situation returned pretty much to its former state. Godard turned increasingly political, and a marginal group of militant filmmakers created a bit of a stir on the art-house circuit, but the main bulk of production continued to consist of commercially proven entertainment subjects. Production figures steadily rose in the early 70s, reaching a record feature output of 234 in 1974.

In an effort to elevate the sagging quality of production, the government instituted in the mid-70s a system that rewards exhibitors with tax cuts for showing quality films and conversely imposes heavy taxes on X-rated productions.

French films capture only about 30 percent of the market of French moviegoers, while American films capture 60 percent. Even so, domestic box-office share in France is ahead of that in other European countries. In Germany, for example, native films capture only about 13 percent of the market.

To combat the domination of big-budget American films, the French often rely on co-productions with other countries for financing and personnel, a strategy that reached its peak in the 60s, when about 75 percent of French movies were officially co-productions, most often with Italy. Today, French production companies such as CiBy 2000 and Studio Canal Plus regularly take advantage of Hollywood's bankability by investing in American films—a strategy that is little comfort to French filmmakers.

Adding to the pressure on the French film industry has been the increasing influence of television. As a result of competition from television, theatrical attendances have dropped, and exhibition has become more concentrated in the hands of large chains (particularly Pathé, Gaumont, and UGC).

Despite the problems of its film industry, France has continued to produce films of high artistic value and international commercial appeal. In addition to new works by such veteran directors as Chabrol, Rohmer, Godard, and Sautet, the 80s and 90s have seen the emergence of a number of talented directors, including Diane KURYS (*Entre Nous*, 1983), Bertrand TAVERNIER (*Un Dimanche à la Campagne*, 1984), Jean-Jacques ANNAUD (*Coup de Tête*, 1980), Léos CARAX (*Mauvais sang*, 1986), Luc BESSON (*La Femme Nikita,* 1990), Alain Corneau (*Tous les matins du monde,* 1991), Jean-Claude Brisseau (*Céline*, 1991), and Christine Pascal (*Le petit prince a dit*, 1991). French film stars of recent decades have included Philippe NOIRET, Patrick DEWAERE, Gérard DEPARDIEU, Anne GIRARDOT, Isabelle HUPPERT, Isabelle ADJANI, Michel Blanc, Daniel AUTEUIL, Emmanuelle BÉART, Juliette BINOCHE, and Julie DELPY.

Francen, Victor. Actor. *b.* Victor Franssen, Aug. 5, 1888, Tirlemont, Belgium, the son of a police commissioner. *d.* 1977. He began appearing in amateur plays at 15 and later abandoned a budding business career to become a professional actor. After gaining experience on the Brussels stage and on a tour of Russia, Canada, and South America, he began attracting attention on the Paris stage toward the end of WW I and later joined the Comédie-Française. He made his screen debut in the early 20s, and in the 30s became established as a popular star of the French cinema, typically playing suave, man-of-the-world lead roles. At the outbreak of WW II he went to Hollywood, where he was utilized throughout the 40s in the portrayal of Continental types, occasionally as a leading man but more often in strong character roles, typically as a top Nazi or a villainous mastermind. He continued appearing in both American and European productions through the late 60s.

FILMS INCLUDE: In France—*Le Logis de l'Horreur, Crepuscule d'Epouvante* 1922; *La Doute* 1924; *La Fin du Monde/The End of the World, L'Aiglon, Aprés l'Amour* 1931; *Mélo* 1932; *Les Ailes brisées* 1933; *L'Aventurier, Le Voleur* 1934; *Le Chemineau/The Open Road, Veille d'Armes/Sacrifice d'Honneur* 1935; *Le Roi/The King, La Porte du Large/The Great Temptation* 1936; *Nuits de Feu/The Living Corpse, Tamara la Complaisante, Feu!, Forfaiture* 1937; *J'accuse/That They May Live, La Vierge Folle* 1938; *Double Crime sur la Ligne Maginot/Crime in the Maginot Line, Entente Cordiale, La Fin du Jour/The End of a Day* 1939; *L'Homme du Niger/Forbidden Love* 1940. In the US—*Hold Back the Dawn* 1941; *The Tuttles of Tahiti, Ten Gentlemen from West Point, Tales of Manhattan* 1942; *Madame Curie, Mission to Moscow* (as Soviet diplomat Andrei Vyshinsky) 1943; *In Our Time, Passage to Marseilles, The Mask of Dimitrios, The Conspirators* 1944; *Confidential Agent, San Antonio* 1945; *Devotion, Night and Day* 1946; *The Beast with Five Fingers, The Beginning or the End* 1947; *To the Victor* 1948; *La Revoltée/Stolen Affections* (Fr.) 1949; *The Adventures of Captain Fabian* 1951; *Hell and High Water* 1954; *Bedevilled* 1955; *A Farewell to Arms* 1957; *Fanny* 1961; *La Grande Frousse/Top Crack* (Fr.) 1964.

Franciosa, Anthony (Tony). Actor. Born Anthony Papaleo, on Oct. 28, 1928, in New York City. An intense performer, he worked his way up in five years from bit parts off Broadway to a Broadway debut in 1953. His success in Broadway's 'A Hatful of Rain' (1955) led to an invitation from Hollywood to repeat the role on the screen, an effort that resulted in an Oscar nomination. He has since appeared in numerous films in a variety of lead roles. On TV, he starred in 'Valentine's Day' (1964–65), 'The Name of the Game' (1968–71), and 'Matt Helm' (1975–76), and was featured in the 1986 made-for-TV remake of 'Stagecoach,' among other series and programs. His second wife (1957–60) was Shelley WINTERS.

FILMS: *This Could Be the Night, A Face in the Crowd, A Hatful of Rain, Wild Is the Wind* 1957; *The Long Hot Summer* 1958; *La Maja Desnuda/The Naked Maja* (as Francisco Goya; It./US); *Career* 1959; *The Story on Page One* 1960; *Senilità* (It.), *Go Naked in the World* 1961; *Period of Adjustment* 1962; *Rio Conchos* 1964; *The Pleasure Seekers* 1965; *A Man Could Get Killed, Assault on a Queen, The Swinger* 1966; *Fathom* 1967; *The Sweet Ride, In Enemy Country* 1968; *A Man Called Gannon* 1969; *Across 110th Street* 1972; *Ghost in the Noonday Sun* 1974; *The Drowning Pool* 1975; *The World Is Full of Married Men* (UK), *Fire Power* (UK) 1979. *La Cicala* (It.) 1980; *Aiutami a Songare* 1981; *Julie Darling* (Can./Ger.), *Death Wish II, Tenebrae/Unsane* (It.) 1982; *Backstreet Dreams* 1990; *Double Threat, La Morte e di Moda* (It.) 1992; *City Hall* 1996.

Francis, Alec B. Actor *b.* 1869, London. *d.* 1934. A former barrister, he gained a certain popularity as a stage actor in England, then came to the US, where he joined Vitagraph in 1910. He played leads and later major supporting roles in numerous Hollywood silents and early talkies.

FILMS INCLUDE: *Vanity Fair* 1911; *Robin Hood* 1912; *The Spectre Bridegroom, The Crimson Cross* (as Christ) 1913; *The Man of the Hour, Adventures in Diplomacy, Lola/Without a Soul* 1914; *The Arrival of Perpetua, After Dark, Alias Jimmy Valentine* 1915; *The Ballet Girl, The Gilded Cage* 1916; *The Hungry Heart, The Cinderella Man* 1917; *Marionettes, The Face in the Dark, The Venus Model, The Glorious Adventure* 1918; *Day Dreams, Probation Wife, When Doctors Disagree, The Crimson Gardenia, City of Comrades, Heartease, The World and Its Women, Lord and Lady Algy, Flame of the Desert* 1919; *The Palliser Case, Earthbound, The Man Who Had Everything* 1920; *Godless Men, A Voice in the Dark, What's a Wife Worth?, Courage, The Great Moment, A Virginia Courtship* 1921; *Smilin' Through, Beyond the Rocks, The Man Who Saw Tomorrow, The Forgotten Law* 1922; *Children of Jazz, Three Wise Fools, The Gold Diggers, The Eternal Three, The Drivin' Fool, Lucretia Lombard* 1923; *The Human Terror, Beau Brummel* 1924; *The Bridge of Sighs, A Thief in Paradise, Capital Punishment, Charley's Aunt, Waking Up the Town, Man and Maid, The Coast of Folly, The Circle, Thunder Mountain, Wandering Footsteps, Thank You* 1925; *The Yankee Señor, Tramp Tramp Tramp, Three Bad Men, Forever After, The Return of Peter Grimm* 1926; *The Music Master, Camille, The Tender Hour* 1927; *The Shepherd of the Hills, Broadway Daddies, Life's Mockery, The Terror, The Companionate Marriage* 1928; *Evangeline, Evidence, The Mississippi Gambler, The Sacred Flame* 1929; *The Bishop Murder Case, The Case of Sergeant Grischa, Outward Bound, Feet First* 1930; *Arrowsmith, Mata Hari* 1931; *No Greater Love, The Last Mile, The Last Man* 1932; *Oliver Twist* (as Mr. Brownlow), *Looking Forward, Alice in Wonderland* (as the King of Hearts) 1933; *The Mystery of Mr. X, I'll Tell the World, Outcast Lady* 1934.

Francis, Anne. Actress. Born on Sept. 16, 1930, in Ossining, N.Y. A successful model and cover girl from age five, she played child roles on radio shows and became known as "The Little Queen of Soap Opera." She appeared on some early TV programs and made her screen debut with MGM in 1947. She played mostly bits and minor roles until the early 50s when she signed to Fox, where she developed into a leading lady of the second rank. She later returned to MGM and played for other studios as well, but, despite her blonde good looks and trim figure, she never became a popular star. However, she did prove herself capable of a wide range of roles, from fragile young things to hardened broads. She has also appeared frequently on TV, and in a brief but memorable role in 1965–66, starred in her own series, 'Honey West.'

FILMS INCLUDE: *This Time for Keeps* 1947; *Summer Holiday, Portrait of Jennie* 1948; *So Young So Bad* 1950; *The Whistle at Eaton Falls, Elopement* 1951; *Lydia Bailey, Dreamboat* 1952; *A Lion Is in the Streets* 1953; *Susan Slept Here, Rogue Cop* 1954; *Bad Day at Black Rock, Battle Cry, The Blackboard Jungle, The Scarlet Coat* 1955; *Forbidden Planet, The Rack* 1956; *Don't Go Near the Water* 1957; *Girl of the Night* 1960; *The Satan Bug, Brainstorm* 1965; *Funny Girl* 1968; *More Dead Than Alive, Impasse, Hook Line and Sinker* 1969; *Lost Flight* 1970; *Pancho Villa* (Sp.) 1972; *Born Again* (as Patti Colson) 1974; *The Return* 1980; *Little Vegas* 1990.

Francis, Connie. Singer, actress. Born Constance Franconero, on Dec. 12, 1938, in Newark, N.J. A first-prize winner on Arthur Godfrey's 'Talent Scouts' show at age 12 and later one of the most successful female pop singers of all time, she played youthful leads in several teen-oriented films of the early 60s. In her autobiography, *Who's Sorry Now* (1984), she dealt frankly with the rise and fall of her career and with such tragic low points in her life as the gangland murder of her brother, her brutal rape in 1974 in a Long Island motel, and her subsequent battle with emotional depression. She lost her voice after her rape, then spent years rebuilding it to performance caliber, taking her show on the road in sporadic concert tours through the early 90s.

FILMS: *Where the Boys Are* 1960; *Follow the Boys* 1963; *Looking for Love* 1964; *When the Boys Meet the Girls* 1965.

Francis, Eve. Actress. *b.* Aug. 24, 1896, Brussels. *d.* 1980. Radiantly beautiful star of the Paris stage who figured prominently in major silent productions of the French screen. She made her film debut in 1914 but became seriously involved with cinema after marrying legendary director and theorist Louis DELLUC in 1918. He left her a widow in 1924. She also worked for Germaine DULAC and Marcel L'HERBIER, often doubling as the latter's assistant director. She was decorated Chevalier of the Legion of Honor. Memoirs: *Temps héroïques* (1949).

FILMS INCLUDE: *La Dame blonde* 1914; *Ames de Fous* (serial) 1918; *La Fête espagnole, Fumée noire, Le Silence* 1920; *Fièvre, El Dorado, Le Chemin d'Erona* 1921; *La Femme de Nulle Part* 1922; *L'Indonaion* 1924; *Antoinette Sabrier* 1927; *Club de Femmes* 1936; *Forfaiture* (also asst. dir.) 1937; *La Brigade sauvage* (also asst. dir.) 1939; *La Comédie du Bonheur* (release delayed from 1939) 1942.

Francis, Freddie (Frederick). Director, director of photography. Born in 1917, in London. Started out as an apprentice to a still-photographer and at 17 entered British films as a clapper boy. He later advanced to camera assistant and, after WW II service as a director of photography with the Army Kinematographic Unit, returned to the industry as a camera operator. In that capacity he worked on such films as *Mine Own Executioner* (1947), *Outcast of the Islands* (1951), *Moulin Rouge* (1953), *Knave of Hearts, Beat the Devil,* and *Beau Brummell* (all 1954). After handling the second-unit photography of *Moby Dick* (1956), he graduated to director of photography and was responsible for the cinematography of such distinguished British productions as *Time Without Pity* (1957), *Room at the Top* (1959), *Saturday Night and Sunday Morning* (1960), *The Innocents* (1961), and *Night Must Fall* (1964). He won an Oscar for the cinematography of *Sons and Lovers* (1960). In the early 60s, while still winding up his career as a cinematographer, he turned to directing, specializing in horror pictures of varying quality, often for Hammer Films. While continuing to direct an occasional film, he returned to his roots in the 80s, once more excelling as a cinematographer.

FILMS: As director—*2 and 2 Make 6/A Change of Heart/The Girl Swappers, Vengeance/The Brain* (UK/Ger.) 1962; *Paranoiac* 1963; *Nightmare, The Evil of Frankenstein, Das Verrätertor/Traitor's Gate* (Ger./UK) 1964; *Dr. Terror's House of Horrors* (UK/US), *Hysteria, The Skull* 1965; *The Psychopath* 1966; *The Deadly Bees, They Came from Beyond Space, Torture Garden* 1967; *Dracula Has Risen from the Grave* 1968; *Mumsy Nanny Sonny and Girly/Girly* 1969; *Trog* 1970; *The Intrepid Mr. Twig* (short), *Tales from the Crypt* 1971; *Asylum, Tales That Witness Madness, The Creeping Flesh* 1973; *Son of Dracula, Craze, The Ghoul, Legend of the Werewolf* 1974; *The Doctor and the Devils* 1985; *Dark Tower* 1987. As director of photography—*A Hill in Korea/Hell in Korea* 1956; *Time Without Pity* 1957; *Room at the Top* 1959; *The Battle of the Sexes, Sons and Lovers, Saturday Night and Sunday Morning* 1960; *The Innocents* 1961; *Night Must Fall* 1964; *The Elephant Man* 1980; *The French Lieutenant's Woman* 1981; *Memed My Hawk, Dune* 1984; *Clara's Heart* 1988; *Her Alibi, Brenda Starr, Glory* 1989; *Man in the Moon* 1990; *Cape Fear, The Man in the Moon* 1991; *School Ties* 1992; *Princess Caraboo* 1994.

Francis, Kay. Actress. *b.* Katherine Edwina Gibbs, Jan. 13, 1903 (possibly 1899), Oklahoma City, Okla. *d.* 1968. The daughter of a businessman and an actress (Katherine Clinton), she went on the stage in 1925 following a convent education and employment as a stenographer and real estate agent. Summer stock and Broadway work led to a Hollywood contract in 1929. Despite a slight lisp, she was one of Hollywood's most glamorous and highly paid stars during the 30s, at first with Paramount, then with Warners, typically portraying stylish, worldly brunettes in romantic melodramas and occasional comedies. Toward the end of the decade, she gradually gave ground to Bette Davis in the Warners star hierarchy. By the early 40s she had been relegated mostly to B pictures. In 1945–46 she co-produced three low-budget Monogram films in which she starred, then went on tour with stock companies for four years before retiring from show business. Four marriages, all ending in divorce, included that to actor Kenneth MacKenna (1931–33), her third. She died of cancer at 65 and had willed most of her million-dollar estate to charity.

FILMS: *Gentlemen of the Press, The Cocoanuts, Dangerous Curves, Illusion, The Marriage Playground* 1929; *Behind the Makeup, Street of Chance, Paramount on Parade, A Notorious Affair, For the Defense, Raffles, Let's Go Native, The Virtuous Sin, Passion Flower* 1930; *Scandal Sheet, Ladies' Man, The Vice Squad, Transgression, Guilty Hands, Twenty-Four Hours, Girls About Town, The False Madonna* 1931; *Strangers in Love, Man Wanted, Street of Women, Jewel Robbery, One Way Passage, Trouble in Paradise, Cynara* 1932; *The Keyhole, Storm at Daybreak, Mary Stevens MD, I Loved a Woman, The House on 56th Street* 1933; *Mandalay, Wonder Bar, Doctor Monica, British Agent* 1934; *Living on Velvet, Stranded, The Goose and the Gander, I Found Stella Parish* 1935; *The White Angel* (as Florence Nightingale), *Give Me Your Heart* 1936; *Stolen Holiday, Another Dawn, Confession, First Lady* 1937; *Women Are Like That, My Bill, Secrets of an Actress, Comet Over Broadway* 1938; *King of the Underworld, Women in the Wind, In Name Only* 1939; *It's a Date, When the Daltons Rode, Little Men* 1940; *Play Girl, The Man Who Lost Himself, Charley's Aunt, The Feminine Touch* 1941; *Always in My Heart, Between Us Girls* 1942; *Four Jills in a Jeep* 1944; *Divorce, Allotment Wives* (both also co-prod.) 1945; *Wife Wanted* (also co-prod.) 1946.

Franciscus, James. Actor. *b.* Jan. 31, 1934, Clayton, Mo. *d.* 1991. *ed.* Yale. The handsome hero of such TV series as 'Naked City' (1958–59), 'Mr. Novak' (1963–65), 'Longstreet' (1971–72), 'Doc Elliot' (1974), and 'Hunter' (1977), he played leads in Hollywood and European films between television engagements.

FILMS: *Four Boys and a Gun* 1957; *The Mugger* 1958; *I Passed for White* 1960; *The Outsider* 1962; *Miracle of the White Stallions* 1963; *Youngblood Hawke* 1964; *Snow Treasure* 1968; *The Valley of Gwangi, Marooned* 1969; *Hell Boats* (UK), *Beneath the Planet of the Apes* 1970; *Il Gatto a Nove Code/The Cat O'Nine Tails* (It.) 1971; *Jonathan Livingston Seagull* (Jonathan's voice) 1973; *The Amazing Dobermans* 1977; *The Greek Tycoon, Good Guys Wear Black* 1978; *City on Fire* (Can.) 1979; *When Time Ran Out* 1980; *L'Ulimo Squalo/The Great White* (It.) 1981; *Butterfly* 1982.

Franju, Georges. Director. *b.* Apr. 12, 1912, Fougères, France. *d.* 1987. After completing his primary studies, he worked briefly for an insurance company and later as a packer in a noodle factory. After returning from military service in Algeria, in 1932, he studied theater décor and worked on the sets of the Folies-Bergère and the Casino de Paris music halls. In 1934 he befriended Henri LANGLOIS. With money they borrowed from the Langlois family, the two young men directed a 16 mm short, *Le Métro,* started a film magazine, which folded after two issues, and founded Le Cercle du Cinéma, a film club, in 1935. In 1937 they co-founded the CINÉMATHÈQUE FRANÇAISE, the famous film archives, and the following year Franju was elected the executive secretary of FIAF, the international federation of film archives. In 1949 he made the first of a dozen documentaries that were to establish him as a leading figure of the French cinema of the 50s. *Le Sang des Bêtes,* a graphic, uncompromisingly brutal and savage look at a Parisian slaughterhouse, revealed a paradoxical blend of compassion and cruelty, of lyrical gracefulness and blunt imagery, which was to characterize many of his future films, including the horror classic *Les Yeux Sans Visage (Eyes Without a Face).*

Influenced by German expressionism and at the same time deriving a taste for realism and atmosphere from the French cinema of the 30s, Franju's work provided an important link between the traditional French cinema and the New Wave of the 50s and 60s. But Franju never became part of the Nouvelle Vague or any other movement and throughout his career he occupied a unique position in the French cinema, maintaining an individuality that has not lent itself to simple classification. His feature films, which he began directing in the late 50s, were less disciplined and as a whole less successful than his shorts, yet they can be viewed as an extension of his documentary exploration and a broader mirror to his anarchic, at times downright nihilistic, world. His last feature was released in 1974, after which he made two more films for television. He spent his final years bitter over what he perceived to be neglect by film critics and historians.

FILMS: Shorts—*Le Métro* (co-dir. with Henri Langlois) 1934; *Le Sang des Bêtes* (also sc.) 1949; *En passant par la Lorraine* (also sc.) 1950; *Hôtel des Invalides* (also sc.) 1951; *Le Grand Méliès* (also sc.) 1952; *Monsieur et Madame Curie* (also sc.) 1953; *Les Poussières* (also sc.), *Navigation marchande* (also commentary) 1954; *A propos d'une Rivière/Le Saumon atlantique/Au Fil de la Rivière* (also sc.), *Mon Chien* (also sc.) 1955; *La Théâtre National Populaire* (also sc.), *Sur le Pont d'Avignon* (also sc.) 1956; *Notre Dame—Cathédrale de Paris* (also sc.) 1957; *La Première Nuit* (also adapt.) 1958; *Les Rideaux blancs* (for TV), *Marcel Allain* (for TV) 1966. Features—*La Tête contre les Murs/The Keepers* 1959; *Les Yeux sans Visage/Eyes Without a Face/Horror Chamber of Dr. Faustus* (also co-adapt.) 1960; *Pleins Feux sur l'Assassin/Spotlight on Murder* 1961; *Thérèse Desqueyroux/Therese* (also co-sc.) 1962; *Judex* 1964; *Thomas l'Imposteur/Thomas the Imposter* (also co-sc.) 1965; *La Faute de l'Abbé Mouret/The Demise of Father Mouret* (also co-sc.) 1970; *L'Homme sans Visage/Shadowman* (also co-music) 1974.

Frank, Harriet, Jr. See RAVETCH, Irving.

Frank, Melvin. Director, screenwriter, producer. *b.* Aug. 13, 1913, Chicago. *d.* 1988. While a student at the University of Chicago, he began a collaboration with classmate Norman PANAMA which resulted in a play. In 1938 they moved to Hollywood, where they collaborated on the scripts of light radio shows. Their work for Bob Hope led to their first contribution to films, the original story for Hope's comedy *My Favorite Blonde* (1942). In the 40s they wrote a series of engaging light scripts, mainly for Paramount, and in the 50s directed and produced entertaining films from their own scripts. They parted company in the early 60s, when Frank formed his own corporation in England and continued writing, directing, and producing on his own.

FILMS: As screenwriter (in collaboration with Norman Panama)—*My Favorite Blonde* (story only) 1942; *Happy Go Lucky, Thank Your Lucky Stars* 1943; *And the Angels Sing* 1944; *Duffy's Tavern* 1945; *Road to Utopia, Our Hearts Were Growing Up, Monsieur Beaucaire* 1946; *It Had to Be You* 1947; *Mr. Blandings Builds His Dream House* (also prod.), *A Southern Yankee* (story only), *The Return of October* 1948; *White Christmas* 1954. As director-producer-screenwriter (in collaboration with Norman Panama)—*The Reformer and the Redhead* 1950; *Strictly Dishonorable, Callaway Went Thataway* 1951; *Above and Beyond* 1953; *Knock on Wood* 1954; *The Court Jester, That Certain Feeling* 1956; *The Trap* (co-prod. only on film dir. by Panama), *The Jay-hawkers* (dir. alone with Panama as co-prod., co-sc.), *L'il Abner* (from their own Broadway musical) 1959; *The Facts of Life* (dir. alone; co-prod. with Panama) 1960. As director-producer-screenwriter (without Panama)—*The Road to Hong Kong* (prod., co-sc. only) 1962; *Strange Bedfellows* 1965; *Not with My Wife You Don't!* (co-story only on film dir., prod., sc. by Panama), *A Funny Thing Happened on the Way to the Forum* (prod. co-sc. only) 1966; *Buona Sera Mrs. Campbell* 1968; *A Touch of Class* 1973; *The Prisoner of Second Avenue* (dir., prod. only) 1975; *The Duchess and the Dirtwater Fox* (also co-lyrics) 1976; *Lost and Found* 1979; *Walk Like a Man* (dir. only) 1987.

Frank, Robert. Filmmaker and photographer. Born in 1924 in Zurich, Switzerland. Seminal photographer of the alienation of the 1950s (*The Americans*) who became one of the more distinctive film experimenters of his era. His first film, *Pull My Daisy* (1959) is an adaptation of 'The Beat Generation,' a play by Jack Kerouac.

FILMS INCLUDE (as director): *Pull My Daisy* (short, also pr., ed., phot.) 1959; *Sin of Jesus* (also ed.) 1961; *O.K. End Here* 1963; *Chappaqua* (phot. only) 1966; *Life-Raft Earth, Me and My Brother* (also ed., phot., sc.) 1969; *About Me: A Musical, Conversations in Vermont* (short, also phot.) 1971; *CS Blues* 1972; *Sunseed* (phot. only) 1973; *No Second Chances* (short, phot. only) 1974; *Diaries, Notes & Sketches—Volume 1, Reels 1–6: Lost Lost Lost* (act. only), *Keep Busy* 1975; *Energy and How to Get It, Life Dances On. . .* 1980; *This Song for Jack* 1983; *Candy Mountain* 1987; *I Will Not Make Any More Boring Art* (act. only) 1988; *Herzliche Wilkommen* (act. only), *UHF* (act. only) 1989.

Frankel, Benjamin. Composer. *b.* Jan. 31, 1906, London. *d.* 1973. An apprentice watchmaker in his youth, he studied music in Germany and earned his living as a nightclub jazz violinist while continuing his studies in London. He later gained note as the composer of eight symphonies and many other orchestral pieces, as well as numerous scores for stage and screen. A longtime member of the Communist Party, he incorporated principles of socialist realism in many of his works.

FILMS INCLUDE: *The Years Between* 1946; *Dancing with Crime, Mine Own Executioner* 1947; *Sleeping Car to Trieste* 1948; *Give Us This Day/Salt to the Devil* 1949; *Hotel Sahara, Appointment with Venus/Island Rescue, The Man in the White Suit* 1951; *The Importance of Being Earnest* 1952; *Footsteps in the Fog, A Kid for Two Farthings, Simon and Laura* 1955; *Brothers in Law* 1957; *Libel* 1959; *Guns of Darkness* 1962; *Night of the Iguana* 1964; *Battle of the Bulge* 1965.

Frankel, Cyril. Director. Born in 1921, in London. A documentary director with the Crown Film Unit, he moved on to middle-budget features in the mid-50s. He also directed numerous TV episodes for 'The Avengers' and other series.

FILMS INCLUDE: *Man of Africa* (doc.) 1953; *Devil on Horseback, Make Me an Offer* 1954; *It's Great to Be Young* 1956; *No Time for Tears* 1957; *She Didn't Say No, Alive and Kicking* 1958; *Never Take Sweets from a Stranger* 1960; *Don't Bother to Knock/Why Bother to Knock, On the Fiddle/Operation Snafu* 1961; *The Very Edge* 1963; *The Witches/The Devil's Own* 1966; *The Trygon Factor* 1967; *Permission to Kill* 1975.

Frankenheimer, John. Director. Born on Feb. 19, 1930, in Malba, N.Y., to a German-Jewish stockbroker father and an Irish Catholic mother. *ed.* LaSalle Military Acad.; Williams

Coll., where he excelled in tennis and participated in school dramatics. He first took an interest in films while serving in the Air Force (1951–53). At his request he was assigned to a newly formed film squadron, where he learned the fundamentals of film technique and made several documentary shorts. While still in uniform he made an unglamorous debut as a TV director on a local Los Angeles area show, sponsored by a cattle ranch, in which live cows were the stars. After his demobilization he joined CBS-TV in New York as assistant director. In November of 1954 he was promoted to director of the 'You Are There' program when Sidney Lumet resigned from the series to pursue a career in films. Frankenheimer went on to direct more than 125 TV plays, including many in the celebrated 'Playhouse 90' series. In 1956 he directed his first motion picture, *The Young Stranger,* a remake of a TV play he had directed on the 'Climax' series. It was an eclectic, promising first film and was well accepted by critics, but Frankenheimer found his initial film experience unnerving and confining and he returned to television. It wasn't until 1961 that he directed his second film, *The Young Savages.* This time he was in films to stay.

Frankenheimer scored a critical success with *All Fall Down,* a commercial one with *Birdman of Alcatraz,* and a combination of both with *The Manchurian Candidate,* all released in 1962. The latter film, a tingling masterpiece of political intrigue and suspense, won the admiration of millions of new viewers when it was made available for wide re-release in the late 80s. After *Seven Days in May* (1964), he seemed firmly entrenched at the top echelon of Hollywood's directors, a concerned observer of the American social and political scene who seemed capable of drawing a rewarding balance between form and content in his films. But then came a period of European residence and a long dry spell during which Frankenheimer seemed to be losing his edge by brandishing style for its own sake. After a string of critical and commercial disappointments over nearly a decade, he returned to the US and was back in his stride with the American Film Theatre's production of *The Iceman Cometh* (1973), the kind of intimate drama that he had done so well for live TV in the early days. He returned to the commercial mainstream in 1975 with *The French Connection II,* then scored another box-office hit with *Black Sunday* (1977). His output since then has been less successful.

FILMS: *The Young Stranger* 1957; *The Young Savages* 1961; *All Fall Down, Birdman of Alcatraz, The Manchurian Candidate* (also co-prod.) 1962; *Seven Days in May, Le Train/The Train* (Fr./It./US) 1964; *Seconds, Grand Prix* 1966; *The Fixer* 1968; *The Extraordinary Seaman* (release delayed from 1967), *The Gypsy Moths* 1969; *I Walk the Line* 1970; *The Horsemen* 1971; *L'Impossible Objet/Impossible Object* (Fr.), *The Iceman Cometh* 1973; *99 and 44/100% Dead* 1974; *The French Connection II* 1975; *Black Sunday* 1977; *Prophecy* 1979; *The Challenge* 1982; *52 Pick-Up* 1986; *Dead-Bang* 1989; *The Fourth War* 1990; *Year of the Gun* 1991; *The Island of Dr. Moreau* 1996.

Franklin, Carl. Director, screenwriter, actor. Born in 1949. *ed.* University of California, Berkeley; American Film Institute. He began as an actor on the off-Broadway stage and television. He left New York to train as a director at AFI, where he caught the eye of famed director Roger CORMAN who guided him into expanding his talents. Gifted in the art of FILM NOIR, Franklin found success with his acclaimed action-mystery *One False Move* (1992).

FILMS: *Five on the Black Hand Side* (act. only) 1979; *The Legend of the Golden Gun* (act. only) 1979; *One Cooks, The Other Doesn't* (act. only) 1983; *Nowhere to Run* (dir. only) 1989; *Full Fathom Five* (dir, sc., act.) 1990; *In the Heat of Passion* (act.), *One False Move* (dir. only) 1993; *Devil in a Blue Dress* (dir., sc.) 1995.

Franklin, Pamela. Actress. Born on Feb. 4, 1950, in Tokyo, to British parents. Trained as a ballet dancer, she entered British films at 11. She gradually matured on the screen from juvenile roles to ingenue leads.

FILMS INCLUDE: *The Innocents* 1961; *The Lion* 1962; *A Tiger Walks* (US), *Flipper's New Adventure* (US), *The Third Secret* 1964; *The Nanny* 1965; *Our Mother's House* (UK/US) 1967; *The Night of the Following Day* (US), *The Prime of Miss Jean Brodie, Sinful Davey* 1969; *David Copperfield* (as Dora; orig. for US TV), *And Soon the Darkness* 1970; *Necromancy* (US) 1972; *Ace Eli and Rodger of the Skies* (US), *The Legend of Hell House* (US) 1973; *The Food of the Gods* (US) 1976.

Franklin, Richard. Director. Born on July 15, 1948, in Melbourne. After attending Monash University, he went to the US for film studies at USC and was invited by his mentor, Alfred HITCHCOCK, as a guest observer on the set of *Topaz* (1969). Returning to Australia, he began directing episodes for TV series and documentary shorts. He graduated to features in 1975, and after some local experience was assigned to direct *Psycho II* (1983) in the US, a sequel to the Hitchcock classic.

FEATURE FILMS: In Australia—*The True Story of Eskimo Nell* 1975; *Fantasm* 1976; *Patrick* (also co-prod.) 1978; *The Blue Lagoon* (co-prod. only; US) 1980; *Road Games* (also prod.) 1981. In the US—*Psycho II* 1983; *Cloak and Dagger* 1984; *Into the Night* (act. only) 1985; *Link* (also prod.; UK) 1986; *FX2: The Deadly Art of Illusion* 1991; *Hotel Sorrento* 1995; *Brilliant Lies* 1997.

Franklin, Sidney. Director, producer. *b.* Mar. 21, 1893, San Francisco. *d.* 1972. He took an interest in films as a schoolboy and after working as a factory hand, stock boy, traveling salesman, and oil-field laborer, entered the film industry in 1913 as an actor and assistant cameraman. Within a year he was directing comedy shorts for the kiddie market in collaboration with his brother Chester M. Franklin (*b.* Sept. 1, 1890, San Francisco. *d.* 1948[?]) who was a former Sennett cartoonist. They graduated to features in 1915 but split up toward the end of WW I, when Chester was drafted. On his own, Sidney quickly established a reputation as an exacting craftsman who planned and executed his productions with great care. He also became known as a superb "woman's director," a man capable of eliciting sensitive performances from even mediocre actresses. Chester, meanwhile, remained a competent but unremarkable director of mainly routine productions. He remained active in films through 1936.

During his 20-year career as a director for First National, Warner Bros., and, from 1926, MGM, Sidney Franklin created many glossy productions that matched the glamour of such stars as Norma and Constance Talmadge, Mary Pickford, Marion Davies, Greta Garbo, Norma Shearer, Luise Rainer, and Jennifer Jones. At MGM he became a favorite of producer Irving THALBERG and was entrusted with some of the studio's most prestigious productions. After handling Shearer in *The Actress* (1928) and Garbo in *Wild Orchids* (1929), two stylish late silent films, he brought Alfred Lunt and Lynn Fontanne to the screen in *The Guardsman* (1931) and made another successful stage-to-screen adaptation with *Private Lives* (1931). His last film as a director (with the exception of a one-shot return to the helm in 1957) was *The Good Earth* (1937), a stupendous adaptation of Pearl Buck's novel, on which directors Sam Wood, George Hill, Fred Niblo, and Andrew Marton collaborated, receiving screen credits as associate directors.

Franklin's films as director were meticulously executed and technically faultless. The acting was invariably fine and the continuity smooth. But he was a stylish director rather than one with a singular style, and at MGM his personal signature was often buried deep beneath the exterior luster of the studio movie machine. After Thalberg's death, Franklin abandoned directing in favor of producing and in that capacity was responsible for some of MGM's most successful films of the 40s. His production of *Mrs. Miniver* won the 1942 best picture Academy Award. In that same year he received a special Oscar (the Irving G. Thalberg Award) for "consistent high quality of production achievement." In the early 50s he found himself at odds with the MGM management and working only on occasional projects. In 1957 he returned to directing with a new version of *The Barretts of Wimpole Street,* which he had directed for the studio in 1934. As soon as he had completed the project he walked out of MGM and into retirement. Franklin should not be confused with actor Sidney Franklin (1870–1931), who played character roles in numerous Hollywood silents of the 20s. Another Sidney Franklin, who was known as "The Bullfighter from Brooklyn," appeared in a number of films before his death in 1976.

FEATURE FILMS: As co-director with Chester M. Franklin—*Let Katie Do It* 1915; *Martha's Vindication, The Children in the House, Going Straight, The Little School Ma'am, Gretchen the Greenhorn, A Sister of Six* 1916; *Jack and the Beanstalk* (also co-sc.), *Aladdin and the Wonderful Lamp, The Babes in the Woods* 1917; *Treasure Island, Six Shooter Andy, The Bride of Fear, Fan Fan, Ali Baba and the Forty Thieves* 1918. As director—*Confession* (also sc.), *The Safety Curtain* (also co-sc.), *Her Only Way, The Forbidden City* 1918; *The Heart of Wetona, The Probation Wife, The Hoodlum, Heart o' the Hills* 1919; *Two Weeks, Unseen Forces* (also prod.) 1920; *Not Guilty, Courage* (also exec. prod.) 1921; *Smilin' Through* (also co-sc.), *The Primitive Lover, East Is West* 1922; *Brass, Dulcy, Tiger Rose* 1923; *Her Night of Romance* 1924; *Learning to Love, Her Sister from Paris* 1925; *Beverly of Graustark, The Duchess of Buffalo* 1926; *Quality Street* 1927; *The Actress* 1928; *Wild Orchids, The Last of Mrs. Cheyney* 1929; *Devil May Care, The Lady of Scandal, A Lady's Morals* 1930; *The Guardsman, Private Lives* 1931; *Smilin' Through* 1932; *Reunion in Vienna* 1933; *The Barretts of Wimpole Street* 1934; *The Dark Angel* 1935; *The Good Earth* (with the uncredited participation of several other directors) 1937; *The Barretts of Wimpole Street* (remake) 1957. As producer—*On Borrowed Time* 1939; *Waterloo Bridge* 1940; *Mrs. Miniver, Random Harvest* 1942; *Madame Curie* 1943; *The White Cliffs of Dover* 1944; *The Yearling* 1947; *Homecoming* 1948; *Command Decision* 1949; *The Miniver Story* 1950; *The Story of Three Loves, Young Bess, Torch Song* 1953.

Frankovich, M. J. ("Mike"). Producer. *b.* Sept. 29, 1910, in Bisbee, Ariz. *d.* 1992. *ed.* UCLA. The adopted son of comedian Joe E. BROWN, he was first brought into films at age 12 by Douglas FAIRBANKS, SR. as a child actor in *Rosita* (1923). Following a four-year stint as a radio producer and commentator, he re-entered films in 1938 as a screenwriter and adult actor. He appeared in *Yesterday's Heroes* (1940), *Buck Privates, The Great American Broadcast,* and *Meet John Doe* (all 1941), among other productions. After WW II service with the Army, he became an independent producer, making a number of films in Europe in the early 50s. He held a variety of executive positions with Columbia Pictures in England, beginning in 1955, and became chairman of the British branch of the organization in 1959. In 1962 he was put in charge of Columbia's international productions and in 1963 returned to Hollywood as vice president in charge of production of all the studio's pictures. In the late 60s he resigned his post to become an independent producer, releasing his films through Columbia. He was married to actress Binnie BARNES. He was the recipient of the Jean Hersholt Humanitarian Award in the 1984 Oscar ceremonies.

FILMS INCLUDE: *Fugitive Lady* 1951; *Decameron Nights* 1953; *Footsteps in the Fog* (co-prod.) 1955; *Joe Macbeth* 1956; *Bob & Carol & Ted & Alice* (exec. prod.), *Marooned, Cactus Flower* 1969; *The Looking Glass War* (exec. prod.), *There's a Girl in My Soup* (co-prod.) 1970; *Doctor's Wives, The Love Machine. $* 1971; *Butterflies Are Free* 1972; *40 Carats* 1973; *A Report to the Commissioner* 1975; *The Shootist, From Noon Till Three* (co-prod.) 1976.

Franz, Arthur. Actor. Born on Feb. 29, 1920, in Perth Amboy, N.J. *ed.* Blue Ridge Coll. Leading man, second lead, and later character player of Hollywood films, mainly B pictures of the action variety. Has also made frequent appearances on the stage and TV.

FILMS INCLUDE: *Jungle Patrol* 1948; *Red Stallion in the Rockies, Roseanna McCoy* 1949; *Sands of Iwo Jima, Three Secrets* 1950; *Abbott and Costello Meet the Invisible Man* (as the latter), *Flight to Mars, Submarine Command* 1951; *The Sniper, The Member of the Wedding, Eight Iron Men* 1952; *Invaders from Mars, The Eddie Cantor Story* 1953; *Flight Nurse, The Caine Mutiny* 1954; *Battle Taxi, New Orleans Uncensored* 1955; *Beyond a Reasonable Doubt* 1956; *Back from the Dead, The Unholy Wife* 1957; *The Young Lions, Monster on the Campus* 1958; *The Atomic Submarine* 1960; *The Carpetbaggers* 1964; *Alvarez Kelly* 1966; *Lo Sbarco di Anzio/Anzio* (It.), *The Sweet Ride* 1968; *So Long Blue Boy* 1973; *The Human Factor* (UK/US) 1975; *Sisters of Death* 1977; *That Championship Season* 1982.

Franz, Eduard. Actor. *b.* Oct. 31, 1902, Milwaukee. *d.* 1983. Character player of Hollywood films and TV with a long list of Broadway credits starting in the late 20s. Typically seen as a distinguished foreigner or prominent intellectual.

FILMS INCLUDE: *Killer at Large* 1947; *The Iron Curtain, Hollow Triumph/The Scar* 1948; *Wake of the Red Witch, Madame Bovary* 1949; *Francis, Whirlpool* 1950; *The Magnificent Yankee* (as Justice Louis Brandeis), *Molly, The Thing, The Great Caruso, The Desert Fox* 1951; *Because You're Mine* 1952; *The Jazz Singer, Dream Wife, Sins of Jezebel* (as Ahab) 1953; *Broken Lance* 1954; *Sign of the Pagan, Lady Godiva* (as King Edward) 1955; *The Ten Commandments* 1956; *A Certain Smile* 1958; *The Story of Ruth* 1960; *Francis of Assisi* 1961; *Hatari!* 1962; *Cyborg 2087* 1966; *The President's Analyst* 1967; *Johnny Got His Gun* 1971; *Twilight Zone—The Movie* 1983.

Fraser, Brendan. Actor. Born 1967, in Indianapolis. *ed.* Actor's Conservatory, Cornish College of the Arts, Seattle, Wash. Handsome, appealing young leading man of the American stage and screen. He began acting in television movies and after his feature debut with a small role in *Dogfight* (1991), he met with critical acclaim for his portrayal of a Neanderthal youth in modern society in the unlikely vehicle *Encino Man* (1992). Fraser often returns to the stage between films.

FILMS: *Dogfight* 1991; *Encino Man, School Ties* 1992; *Twenty Bucks, Younger and Younger* 1993; *Airheads, The Scout, With Honors* 1994; *Mrs. Winterbourne* 1996; *George of the Jungle* 1997.

Fraser, John. Actor. Born on Mar. 18, 1931, in Glasgow. Leading man and second lead of British films, the stage, and TV. He began his stage career a 16, while still a pupil at

Glasgow High School. Gradually matured from juvenile to adult roles.

FILMS INCLUDE: *The Dam Busters* 1953; *Touch and Go* 1955; *The Good Companions* 1957; *The Wind Cannot Read* 1958; *The Trials of Oscar Wilde, Tunes of Glory* 1960; *El Cid* (US/It.), *Fury at Smuggler's Bay* 1961; *Waltz of the Toreadors* 1962; *Tamahine* 1963; *Repulsion, Operation Crossbow* 1965; *A Study in Terror, Doctor in Clover/Carnaby M.D.* 1966; *Isadora/The Loves of Isadora* 1968; *Schizo* 1976.

Fraser, Richard. Actor. *b.* Mar. 15, 1913, Edinburgh, Scotland. *d.* 1971. *ed.* Cambridge; RADA. Leading man, second lead, and supporting player of Hollywood films of the 40s, following a brief career on the London stage. He later retired from acting and returned to England, where he became a business executive. At one time married to actress Ann GILLIS.

FILMS INCLUDE: *Man Hunt, A Yank in the RAF, How Green Was My Valley* 1941; *Joan of Paris, Desperate Journey* 1942; *Truck Busters, The Gorilla Man, Edge of Darkness, Holy Matrimony* 1943; *Ladies Courageous* 1944; *The Fatal Witness, Shadow of Terror, The Picture of Dorian Gray* (as James Vane) 1945; *Bedlam* 1946; *The Private Affairs of Bel Ami* 1947; *The Cobra Strikes, Rogues' Regiment* 1948; *The Red Danube* 1949.

Fraser, Ronald. Actor. Born on Apr. 11, 1930, in Ashton-under-Lyne, England. Chunky, crude-featured character player of British films and TV, usually in tough roles, often in uniform.

FILMS INCLUDE: *The Black Ice* (bit) 1957; *Bobbikins* (bit) 1959; *There Was a Crooked Man, The Sun-downers* (UK/Austral.) 1960; *The Long and the Short and the Tall/Jungle Fighters, I Due Nemici/The Best of Enemies* (It./UK) 1961; *In Search of the Castaways* (US/UK) 1962; *The V.I.P.s, Girl in the Headlines/The Model Murder Case* 1963; *The Beauty Jungle/Contest Girl, Allez France!/The Counterfeit Constable* (Fr.) 1964; *Victim Five/Code 7 Victim 5* 1965; *The Flight of the Phoenix* (US) 1966; *The Whisperers, Fathom* 1967; *Sebastian, The Killing of Sister George* (US) 1968; *Sinful Davey, The Bed Sitting Room* 1969; *Too Late the Hero* (US), *The Rise and Rise of Michael Rimmer* 1970; *The Magnificent Seven Deadly Sins* 1971; *Ooh You Are Awful!* 1972; *Get Charlie Tully* 1976; *The Wild Geese* 1978; *Trail of the Pink Panther* 1982; *Absolute Beginners* 1986; *Scandal* 1989; *Let Him Have It* 1991; *The Mystery of Edwin Drood* 1993.

Frawley, James. Director. Born in 1937, in Houston. *ed.* Carnegie Tech. Trained at the Actors Studio, he later taught there and ran the directors unit. As an actor, he performed with the comedy group The Premise and in New York plays, and appeared in such films as *Ladybug, Ladybug* (1963), *The Troublemaker* (1964), and *Wild, Wild Winter* (1966). He staged musical numbers for 'The Monkees' TV series, winning an Emmy Award, before directing his first feature film in 1971.

FILMS: *The Christian Licorice Store* 1971; *Kid Blue* 1973; *The Big Bus* 1976; *The Muppet Movie* 1979; *Fraternity Vacation* 1985; *Spies, Lies, and Naked Thighs* 1991.

Frawley, William. Actor. *b.* Feb. 26, 1887, Burlington, Iowa. *d.* 1966. A former vaudevillian, he appeared in some 150 Hollywood films of all genres, often playing gruff but amiable character roles. From the early 50s worked mainly on TV, portraying next-door-neighbor Fred Mertz in the popular series 'I Love Lucy' (1951–57) and 'The Lucy-Desi Comedy Hour' specials (1957–60). He later played Uncle Bub in 'My Three Sons' (1960–64).

FILMS INCLUDE: *Lord Loveland Discovers America* 1916; *Surrender* 1931; *Moonlight and Pretzels* 1933; *Miss Fane's Baby Is Stolen, Bolero, The Lemon Drop Kid* 1934; *Hold 'Em Yale!* 1935; *Strike Me Pink, Desire, The Princess Comes Across, The General Died at Dawn* 1936; *High Wide and Handsome, Something to Sing About* 1937; *Mad About Music, Professor Beware, Sons of the Legion* 1938; *Huckleberry Finn* (as "The Duke"), *Rose of Washington Square, Stop Look and Love* (lead) 1939; *Untamed, Rhythm on the River* 1940; *Footsteps in the Dark, The Bride Came C.O.D.* 1941; *Roxie Hart, Gentleman Jim* 1942; *The Fighting Seabees, Going My Way* 1944; *Lady on a Train* 1945; *Ziegfeld Follies, The Virginian* 1946; *Miracle on 34th Street, Monsieur Verdoux, Mother Wore Tights, My Wild Irish Rose* 1947; *The Babe Ruth Story, Good Sam, East Side West Side* 1949; *Pretty Baby, Kiss Tomorrow Goodbye* 1950; *The Lemon Drop Kid* (remake), *Rhubarb* 1951; *Rancho Notorious* 1952; *Safe at Home!* 1962.

Frazee, Jane. Actress, singer. *b.* Mary Jane Frehse, July 18, 1918, St. Paul, Minn. *d.* 1985. Raised in Duluth, she began singing and dancing professionally at age six with her sister, Ruth. They appeared together in nightclubs and vaudeville and sang on radio but split after arriving in Hollywood when Ruth failed her screen tests and abandoned acting to marry writer-producer Norman KRASNA. Jane went on to play leads in many B musicals and light Westerns of the 40s. From 1941–47 she was married to actor-director-screenwriter Glenn TRYON, the first of her four husbands. Bowing out of films in 1951, she appeared in the TV comedy series 'Beulah' (1952–53), then retired. In 1970 she moved to Newport Beach, California, where she sold real estate. She died at 67 of pneumonia, following a series of strokes.

FILMS INCLUDE: *Melody and Moonlight* 1940; *Buck Privates, Moonlight in Hawaii, Hellzapoppin* 1941; *What's Cookin', Almost Married, Get Hep to Love, Moonlight in Havana* 1942; *Hi 'Ya Chum, When Johnny Comes Marching Home* 1943; *Kansas City Kitty, Swing and Sway* 1944; *The Big Bonanza, Practically Yours, Ten Cents a Dance, Swingin' on a Rainbow* 1945; *Calendar Girl, Springtime in the Sierras* 1947; *Grand Canyon Trail, The Gay Ranchero* 1948; *Rhythm Inn* 1951.

Frazer, Robert. Actor. *b.* June 29, 1891, Worcester, Mass. *d.* 1944. Dashing romantic star of many Hollywood silents who later played character roles, often as a heavy, in numerous B action talkies and serials.

FILMS INCLUDE: *Robin Hood* (title role), *All on Account of a Ring* 1912; *Rob Roy* (title role), *The Holy City* (as Christ) 1913; *The Ballet Girl, The Feast of Life* 1916; *Her Code of Honor, Bolshevism on Trial* 1919; *Without Limit, Love Hate and a Woman* 1921; *Partners of the Sunset, Fascination, The Faithless Sex, How Women Love, When the Desert Calls* 1922; *As a Man Lives, Jazzmania, The Love Piker* 1923; *Women Who Give, Men, Traffic in Hearts, Bread, Broken Barriers, The Foolish Virgin* 1924; *Miss Bluebeard, The Charmer, The White Desert, The Scarlet West, The Keeper of the Bees, The Love Gamble, Why Women Love, The Splendid Road* 1925; *Desert Gold, The Isle of Retribution, The Speeding Venus, The City, Sin Cargo* 1926; *One Hour of Love, Wanted—A Coward, The Silent Hero, Out of the Past, Back to God's Country* 1927; *Burning Up Broadway, The Scarlet Dove, Black Butterflies, Out of the Ruins, City of Purple Dreams* 1928; *Sioux Blood, The Woman I Love, Careers, Frozen Justice* 1929; *Beyond the Law* 1930; *Ten Nights in a Barroom* 1931; *The Rainbow Trail, White Zombie* 1932; *The Three Musketeers* (serial), *The Vampire Bat* 1933; *Found Alive, Monte Carlo Nights* 1934; *The Miracle Rider* (serial), *The World Accuses* 1935; *The Black Coin* (serial), *The Clutching Hand* (serial), *The Garden of Allah* 1936; *Black Aces* 1937; *Religious Racketeer* 1938; *Navy Secrets, Juarez* 1939; *Dick Tracy vs. Crime Inc.* (serial), *Roar of the Press* 1941; *A Night for Crime*

1942; *Daredevils of the West* (serial) 1943; *Captain America* (serial), *The Tiger Woman* (serial), *Forty Thieves* 1944.

Frears, Stephen. Director. Born on June 20, 1941, in Leicester, England. A graduate of the Cambridge law school, he gravitated to drama and became Lindsay ANDERSON's assistant at the Royal Court Theatre and later on the films *If. . .* (1968) and *O Lucky Man!* (1973). He was also an assistant director on Karel Reisz's *Morgan* (1966) and Albert Finney's *Charlie Bubbles* (1968). At the same time, he was carving his own path as a director for British TV and in 1972 made his feature debut with the whimsical crime spoof *Gumshoe.* After intensive television activity in the 70s, he emerged in the 80s as one of Britain's freshest and most original talents, attracting international acclaim with *My Beautiful Laundrette* (1985) and other unconventional, socially perceptive feature films that were disturbing yet entertaining. He scored a critical and commercial triumph with his first Hollywood film, the sumptuous, sinister period piece *Dangerous Liaisons* (1988), a winner of several Academy Awards. He was nominated two years later as director for *The Grifters* (1990).

FEATURE FILMS: *Gumshoe* 1972; *Bloody Kids* 1980; *The Hit* 1984; *My Beautiful Laundrette* 1985; *Loving Walter/Walter and June* 1986; *Prick Up Your Ears, Sammy and Rosie Get Laid* 1987; *Dangerous Liaisons* (US) 1988; *The Grifters* (US) 1990; *Hero* (US) 1992; *The Snapper* 1993; *Mary Reilly* 1996; *The Van* 1997.

Freda, Riccardo. Director. Born Feb. 24, 1909, in Alexandria, Egypt, to Neapolitan parents. After university studies in Milan, he took up sculpture and later became an art critic for a daily newspaper. In Italian films since 1937 as screenwriter and production supervisor, following studies at the Centro Sperimentale, he made his debut as director in 1942. Resisting the trend toward neorealism in post–WW II Italian cinema, he specialized in grand-scale historic epics. More recently he turned to stylish adventure and horror pictures, which he sometimes signed with the pseudonym Robert Hampton or George Lincoln. His flamboyant visual style has made him a sort of cult figure among many film enthusiasts who admire his technique while ignoring the frequently thin content of his films. Freda collaborated on many of his own scripts. He has been largely inactive in films since the early 70s.

FILMS: *Don Cesare di Bazan* 1942; *Non Canto più* 1943; *Tutta la Città Canta* 1945; *Aquila Nera/The Black Eagle* 1946; *I Miserabili/Les Miserables* 1947; *Il Cavaliere Misterioso, Guarany* 1948; *Il Conte Ugolino, O Cacoulha do Barulho, Il Figlio di d'Artagnan* 1949; *Il Tradimento, La Vendetta di Aquila Nero, Vedi Napoli e poi Muori/See Naples and Die* 1951; *La Leggenda del Piave, Spartaco/Sins of Rome* 1952; *Teodora Imperatrice di Bisanzio/Theodora Slave Empress* 1953; *Da qui all'Eredite* 1955; *Beatrice Cenci, I Vampiri* 1956; *Agguato a Tangeri/Trapped in Tangiers* 1957; *Agi Murad—Il Diavolo Bianco/The White Warrior, Nel Segno di Roma* (2nd-unit dir. only), *Caltiki—Il Mostro Immortale/Caltiki—The Immortal Monster* 1959; *I Giganti della Tessaglia/The Giants of Thessaly* 1960; *I Mongoli/The Mongols* (action sequences only), *Caccia all'Uomo, Maciste alla Corte del Gran Khan/Samson and the Seven Miracles of the World* 1961; *Solo contro Roma/Alone Against Rome* (dir. arena sequences only), *Le Sette Spade del Vendicatore/The Seventh Sword, Maciste all'Inferno/The Witch's Curse, L'Orrible Segreto del Dottor Hitchcock/The Horrible Dr. Hitchcock, Lo Spectro/The Ghost, Oro per i Cesari/Gold for the Caesars* (action sequences only) 1962; *Il Magnifico Avventuriero* 1963; *Giulietta e Romeo/Romeo and Juliet* (also sc.) 1964; *Agente Coplan: Missione Spionaggio/The Exterminators* 1965; *A Doppia Faccia* 1969; *L'Iguana dalla Lingua di Fuoco* (also co-sc.) 1971; *Superhuman* 1979.

Frederick, Pauline. Actress. *b.* Beatrice Pauline Libbey, Aug. 12, 1883, Boston. *d.* 1938. The daughter of a railroad yardmaster. She made her show business debut at 19 as a chorus girl and within several years became established as one of Broadway's most popular leading ladies. She starred in many silent Hollywood films from 1915, spanning the gamut from heavy melodrama to sophisticated comedy. She switched to character roles in the early silent period, typically portraying domineering mothers. Her second (1917–20) of five husbands was actor-playwright-screenwriter Willard Mack. She died of an asthma attack.

FILMS INCLUDE: *The Eternal City, Sold, Zaza, Bella Donna* 1915; *Lydia Gilmore, Audrey, The Spider, The Woman in the Case, Ashes of Embers, The Moment Before* 1916; *Slave Island, Sleeping Fires, The Love That Lives, Hungry Heart* 1917; *Resurrection, Madame Jealousy, Her Final Reckoning, Fedora, La Tosca* 1918; *Out of the Shadow, One Week of Life, The Peace of Roaring River, Bonds of Love* 1919; *The Paliser Case, Madame X, A Slave of Vanity* 1920; *Roads of Destiny, Mistress of Shenstone, Salvage, The Sting of the Lash, Lure of Jade* 1921; *Two Kinds of Women, The Glory of Clementina* 1922; *Let No Man Put Asunder, Three Women, Married Flirts* 1924; *Smouldering Fires* 1925; *Her Honor the Governor, Devil's Island, Josselyn's Wife* 1926; *The Nest* 1927; *On Trial* 1928; *Evidence, The Sacred Flame* 1929; *This Modern Age* 1931; *Wayward, The Phantom of Crestwood* 1932; *Social Register* 1934; *My Marriage, Ramona* 1936; *Thank You Mr. Moto* 1937.

Free Cinema. A British documentary movement launched in 1956 by Lindsay ANDERSON, Karel REISZ, Tony RICHARDSON, and others to implement ideas advanced by Anderson and Reisz when they were editors (1946–52) of the magazine *Sequence.* The movement, which sprang out of the same political atmosphere that inspired the beginning of the New Left, attacked commercial British cinema for misjudging public demand by not showing people themes and plots relevant to their own lives. Free Cinema advocated "an expressive and personal use of the medium." In a published manifesto, the aims of the movement were summed up thus: "Implicit in our attitude is a belief in freedom, in the importance of people and in the significance of the everyday." Among the films created by the movement were *Oh Dreamland, Mama Don't Allow, Together, Every Day Except Christmas,* and *We Are the Lambeth Boys.* The Free Cinema's product did not always live up to the movement's declared standards, but it helped steer British commercial cinema in the direction of socially controversial subjects, dealing with contemporary problems against working-class settings. Reisz and Anderson themselves contributed two of the best films in this genre, Reisz with *Saturday Night and Sunday Morning* (1960) and Anderson with *This Sporting Life* (1963), on which Reisz participated as producer.

Freed, Arthur. Producer, lyricist. *b.* Arthur Grossman, Sept. 9, 1894, Charleston, S.C. *d.* 1973. He started out as a song plugger for a music publisher and later appeared with the Marx Brothers in vaudeville. After returning from WW I service, he went back to vaudeville and began writing songs and special material for nightclub revues, finally making it in 1923 with his first hit song, 'I Cried for You.' He was directing a stage musical in Hollywood when Irving Thalberg hired him as a lyricist for MGM in 1929, during the big outpouring of screen musicals at the dawn of the sound era. He wrote lyrics for numerous films, including *The Broadway Melody, The Hollywood Revue* ('Singin' in the Rain,' etc.), *The Pagan* (1929); *Lord Byron of Broadway, Montana Moon* (1930); *Blondie of the Follies* (1932); *The Barbarian, Hold Your Man, Stage Mother, Going Hollywood* ('Temptation,' etc., 1933); *Sadie McKee, Hollywood Party, Student Tour* (1934); *Broadway Melody of 1936* ('You Are My Lucky Star,' etc.), *A Night at the Opera* (1935); *San Francisco* ('Would You?') 1936, and *Broadway Melody of 1938* (1937). In 1939, after a successful tryout as the associate producer of *The Wizard of Oz,* Freed was elevated to producer and for the next two decades his name was synonymous with the glitter and high quality of the MGM musical.

Freed's credits read like a list of landmarks in the history of the genre. No one else was as instrumental in the development of Hollywood's unique gift to the world of entertainment, the screen musical of the 40s and 50s. A great judge of talent, he surrounded himself with directors like Vincente Minnelli, Busby Berkeley, Stanley Donen, and Charles Walters, as well as dynamic choreographers (Michael Kidd for one) and skilled musical directors (André Previn and others), and helped shape the careers of such stars as Judy Garland, Gene Kelly, Cyd Charisse, and June Allyson, among many, many others. Two of his films won best picture Oscars, *An American in Paris* (1951) and *Gigi* (1958), but his career waned in the early 60s with the demise of the screen musical. He was president of the Academy of Motion Picture Arts and Sciences (1963–66) and was decorated Chevalier of the French Légion d'Honneur in recognition of his cinema achievements.

FILMS (as producer): *Babes in Arms* (also song 'Good Morning') 1939; *Strike Up the Band* (also song 'Our Love Affair'), *Little Nellie Kelly* 1940; *Lady Be Good* (also songs), *Babes on Broadway* 1941; *Panama Hattie, For Me and My Gal* 1942; *Cabin in the Sky, Best Foot Forward, Du Barry Was a Lady, Girl Crazy* 1943; *Meet Me in St. Louis* (also sang as voice of Leon Ames) 1944; *The Clock, Yolanda and the Thief* (also songs) 1945; *The Harvey Girls, Ziegfeld Follies* (also song 'This Heart of Mine'), *Till the Clouds Roll By* 1946; *Good News* 1947; *Summer Holiday, The Pirate, Easter Parade, Words and Music* 1948; *Take Me Out to the Ball Game, The Barkleys of Broadway, Any Number Can Play, On the Town* 1949; *Annie Get Your Gun, Crisis, Pagan Love Song* (also songs) 1950; *Royal Wedding, Show Boat, An American in Paris* 1951; *The Belle of New York, Singin' in the Rain* (also songs, including title song) 1952; *The Band Wagon* 1953; *Brigadoon* 1954; *It's Always Fair Weather, Kismet* 1955; *Invitation to the Dance* 1956; *Silk Stockings* 1957; *Gigi* 1958; *Bells Are Ringing, The Subterraneans* 1960; *The Light in the Piazza* 1962.

Freeland, Thornton. Director. Born on Feb. 10, 1898, in Hope, N.D. A stage actor from boyhood, he joined Vitagraph at 18 and worked his way up to the position of director via such posts as assistant cameraman, cutter, assistant director (to GRIFFITH and LUBITSCH, among others), and production manager. Specialized in light, lively comedies and musicals. From the mid-30s he worked mainly in Britain. Retired from film activity in the late 40s. Married actress June CLYDE.

FILMS: In the US—*Three Live Ghosts* 1929; *Be Yourself!* (also co-sc.), *Whoopee!* 1930; *Six Cylinder Love, Terror by Night, The Secret Witness* 1931; *The Unexpected Father, Love Affair, Week-End Marriage, They Call It Sin* 1932; *Flying Down to Rio* 1933; *George White's Scandals* 1934. In the UK—*Brewster's Millions* 1935; *Skylarks, The Amateur Gentleman, Accused* 1936; *Paradise for Two/The Gaiety Girls, Jericho/Dark Sands* 1937; *Hold My Hand* 1938; *Over the Moon, So This Is London, The Gang's All Here* 1939. In the US—*Too Many Blondes, Marry the Boss's Daughter* 1941. In the UK—*Meet Me at Dawn* 1946; *Lucky Mascot/The Brass Monkey* 1947; *Dear Mr. Prohack* 1949.

Freeman, Everett. Screenwriter, producer. *d.* Feb. 2, 1911, in New York City. *d.* 1991. A former short-story writer and radio producer-writer, he began writing light screenplays in the late 30s, later also becoming active as producer. He also produced the 'Bachelor Father' series for TV. His brother, Devery Freeman (*b.* Feb. 18, 1913, N.Y.C.), is also a screenwriter.

FILMS INCLUDE (as screenwriter): *$1,000 a Minute* 1935; *Married Before Breakfast* 1937; *The Chaser* 1938; *Larceny Inc., George Washington Slept Here* 1942; *The Princess and the Pirate* 1944; *It Happened on Fifth Avenue, The Secret Life of Walter Mitty* 1947; *Lulu Belle* 1948; *Pretty Baby* 1950; *Jim Thorpe—All American* (also prod.) 1951; *Million Dollar Mermaid* 1952; *Destination Gobi* 1953; *My Man Godfrey* 1957; *Marjorie Morningstar* 1958; *Sunday in New York* (prod. only) 1964; *The Glass Bottom Boat* (also co-prod.) 1966; *Where Were You When the Lights Went Out?* (also co-prod.) 1968; *The Maltese Bippy* (also co-prod.) 1969; *Zigzag* (co-prod. only), *How Do I Love Thee* (also co-prod.) 1970.

Freeman, Kathleen. Actress. Born on Feb. 17, 1919, in Chicago. Spunky supporting player of scores of Hollywood films, typically in light character roles. She has also appeared in numerous TV shows, memorably in 'Topper' (1953–54) and 'The Beverly Hillbillies' (1969–71) series.

FILMS INCLUDE: *Casbah, The Naked City* 1948; *Mr. Belvedere Goes to College* 1949; *Lonely Hearts Bandits* 1950; *A Place in the Sun* 1951; *The Bad and the Beautiful, The Greatest Show on Earth, Monkey Business, O. Henry's Full House, The Prisoner of Zenda, Singin' in the Rain* 1952; *The Affairs of Dobie Gillis* 1953; *Artists and Models, The Far Country* 1955; *Houseboat, The Fly* 1958; *North to Alaska* 1960; *The Ladies Man* 1961; *The Nutty Professor* 1963; *The Disorderly Orderly* 1964; *The Rounders* 1965; *Three on a Couch* 1966; *Point Blank* 1967; *Support Our Local Sheriff* 1969; *The Ballad of Cable Hogue* 1970; *Stand Up and Be Counted* 1972; *The Norseman* 1978; *The Blues Brothers* 1980; *Heartbeeps* 1981; *The Best of Times, Malibu Bikini Shop* 1986; *Dragnet, Innerspace, In the Mood/The Woo Woo Kid* 1987; *Hollywood Chaos* 1989; *The Willies, Gremlins 2: The New Batch* 1990.

Freeman, Mona. Actress. Born Monica Freeman, on June 9, 1926, in Baltimore. A professional model while still attending high school, she was signed for the movies by Howard Hughes, who in turn sold her contract to Paramount. She gradually, and ever so slowly, matured on the screen from bright-eyed teenagers and innocent ingenues to leading lady roles. She was less successful in adult roles, appearing mostly in B productions, and her screen career ended in the late 50s. She later appeared on many TV programs. Her daughter, Monie Ellis, is an actress.

FILMS INCLUDE: *National Velvet, Our Hearts Were Young and Gay, Till We Meet Again, Together Again, Here Come the Waves* 1944; *Roughly Speaking, Junior Miss, Danger Signal* 1945; *Black Beauty, That Brennan Girl* 1946; *Dear Ruth, Mother Wore Tights* 1947; *Isn't It Romantic?* 1948; *Streets of Laredo, The Heiress* 1949; *Dear Wife, I Was a Shoplifter, Copper Canyon* 1950; *Branded, Dear Brat, Darling How Could You!, The Lady from Texas* 1951; *Flesh and Fury, Jumping Jacks, Thunderbirds* 1952; *Angel Face* 1953; *Battle Cry, The Road to Denver* 1955; *Hold Back the Night, Huk!*

1956; *Dragoon Wells Massacre* 1957; *The World Was His Jury* 1958.

Freeman, Morgan. Actor. Born on June 1, 1937, in Memphis, Tenn. Leading character player of the American stage, TV, and films. He joined the Air Force at 18 and after a five year stint took up acting at Los Angeles City College. He made his Broadway debut in the 1968 all-black revival of 'Hello Dolly,' starring Pearl Bailey, then gained wide exposure in 1971–76 as Easy Reader on Educational TV's 'The Electric Company.' On screen from the early 70s, he reached a peak of success in the late 80s, when he was nominated for a supporting actor Oscar and received the New York and Los Angeles Critics and the National Society of Film Critics best supporting actor awards for *Street Smart* (1987). He went on to be nominated for Academy Awards as best actor for his inspired performances in *Driving Miss Daisy* (1989) and *The Shawshank Redemption* (1994).

FILMS: *Who Says I Can't Ride a Rainbow?* 1971; *Brubaker* 1980; *Eyewitness* 1981; *Harry and Son, Teachers* 1984; *Marie, That Was Then. . . This Is Now* 1985; *Street Smart* 1987; *Clean and Sober* 1988; *Lean on Me, Phantom of the Mall, Driving Miss Daisy, Glory* 1989; *Johnny Handsome, The Bonfire of the Vanities* 1990; *Robin Hood: Prince of Thieves* 1991; *The Power of One, Unforgiven* 1992; *Bopha!* (dir. only) 1993; *The Shawshank Redemption* 1994; *Outbreak, Seven* 1995; *Chain Reaction, Moll Flanders* 1996; *Amistad, Kiss the Girls* 1997.

freeze frame. The effect of repeatedly printing a single frame so that the action seems to freeze on the screen into still-like motionlessness. The process can be used to lengthen a scene, to highlight a point, or for sheer dramatic effect. It was used very effectively in the final scene of *The 400 Blows,* which ends in a "frozen" close-up of the young hero.

Fregonese, Hugo. Director. *b.* Apr. 18, 1908, Buenos Aires. *d.* 1987. A former medical student, journalist, and cattleman, he came to New York in 1935 to study at Columbia and spent part of his American sojourn in Hollywood as a technical advisor in films with Latin-American backgrounds. He returned to Argentina in 1938 and entered the film industry as editor, assistant director, and a director of shorts, and made his debut as a feature director in 1943. He was back in Hollywood in 1949 and for the next couple of years directed B pictures for Universal. Despite low budgets and simple scripts, he managed to turn out a number of pictorially stimulating Westerns and gangster dramas. He deftly handled an offbeat prison comedy, *My Six Convicts* (1952), for producer Stanley Kramer, under the Columbia aegis, and then returned to his specialty of hard-hitting Westerns and crime melodramas, which at their best were as visually beautiful as they were inherently violent. But despite two solid productions in succession, *The Raid* (1954) for Fox and *Black Tuesday* (1955) for United Artists, which many consider his best, he found few offers to direct in Hollywood and was forced to work in Europe. Married actress Faith DOMERGUE.

FILMS: In Argentina—*Pampa Barbara* (co-dir. with Lucas Demare) 1943; *Donde Mueren las Palabras/Where Words Fail* 1946; *Apenas un Delincuente/Hardly a Criminal* 1947; *De Hombre a Hombre* 1949. In the US—*One Way Street, Saddle Tramp* 1950; *Apache Drums, Mark of the Renegade* 1951; *My Six Convicts, Untamed Frontier* 1952; *Blowing Wild, Decameron Nights* (US/UK), *Man in the Attic* 1953; *The Raid* 1954; *Black Tuesday* 1955; *I Girovaghi* (It.) 1956; *Seven Thunders/The Beast of Marseilles* (UK) 1957; *Live in Fear* (also prod., co-sc.), *Harry Black and the Tiger* (UK) 1958; *Marco Polo* (co-dir. with Piero Pierotti; It.) 1962; *Old Shatterhand/Shatterhand* (Ger./Fr./It./Yug.), *Die Todesstrahlen des Dr. Mabuse* (Ger./It./Fr.) 1964; *Pampa Salvaje/Savage Pampas* (also co-sc.; Sp./Arg./US) 1966; *La Mala Vida* (Arg.) 1973; *Más allá del Sol* (Arg.) 1975.

Freleng, Friz. Animator. *b.* Aug. 21, 1906, in Kansas City, Mo. *d.* 1995. In films from 1924, he joined Walt Disney in 1927 but after several months went to work on the "Krazy Kat" cartoon series at the Winkler Picture Corporation in New York. In 1930 he joined Warner Bros., where he stayed for three decades, creating numerous popular cartoons, typically emphasizing furious, sometimes violent, action. In 1963, with David H. DePatie, he established the DePatie-Freleng Enterprises, Inc., an independent animation production company, initially producing under the Warners umbrella. DePatie-Freleng created several successful cartoon series for TV, including the popular 'The Pink Panther,' as well as many commercials. In the 80s he produced or directed several compilation features of his cartoon shorts. He won five Academy Awards and three Emmys for his work for film and television.

FILMS INCLUDE: *Bugs Bunny and the Three Bears* 1944; *Sam the Pirate* 1946; *Tweety Pie and Sylvester* 1947; *Bugs Bunny Rides Again* 1948; *Canary Row* 1951; *Dog Pounded* 1953; *By Word of Mouse, Captain Hareblower, Bugs and Thugs* 1954; *Sandy Claws, Speedy Gonzalez, Pizzicato Pussycat, Tweety's Circus, Red Riding Hoodwinked* 1955; *Rabbitson Crusoe, Tugboat Granny, Tweet and Sour* 1956; *Birds Anonymous, Show Biz Bugs* 1957; *A Pizza Tweety-Pie, Knightly Knight Bugs* 1958; *The Loony Loony Loony Bugs Bunny Movie* (compilation) 1981; *Bugs Bunny Third Movie—1001 Rabbit Tales* (comp.) 1982; *Daffy Duck's Movie; Fantastic Island* (comp.) 1983.

Fremault, Anita. See LOUISE, Anita.

French, Harold. Director. Born on Apr. 23, 1897, in London. A former stage and screen actor, he began directing British films in 1937 and for decades turned out workmanlike if unspectacular productions. Better at directing actors in dialogue than at handling action and movement.

FILMS: *Cavalier of the Streets* 1937; *Dead Men Are Dangerous* 1939; *The House of the Arrow* 1940; *Major Barbara* (co-sc./part dir./uncredited), *Jeannie* 1941; *Secret Mission, Unpublished Story, The Day Will Dawn/The Avengers* 1942; *Dear Octopus/Randolph Family* 1943; *English Without Tears/Her Man Gilbey, Mr. Emmanuel* 1944; *Quiet Weekend* 1946; *White Cradle Inn* 1947; *The Blind Goddess, Quartet* ("The Alien Corn" episode), *My Brother Jonathan* 1948; *Adam and Evelyne/Adam and Evelyn* 1949; *Trio* (one episode), *The Dancing Years* 1950; *Encore* ("The Ant and the Grasshopper" and "Gigolo and Gigolette" episodes) 1951; *The Man Who Watched the Trains Go By/The Paris Express, The Hour of 13* 1952; *Isn't Life Wonderful, Rob Roy* 1953; *Forbidden Cargo* 1954; *The Man Who Loved Redheads* 1955.

Frend, Charles. Director. *b.* Nov. 21, 1909, Pulborough, England. *d.* 1977. *ed.* Oxford. Entered British films in 1931 as a film editor and worked in that capacity on four Hitchcock movies, *Waltzes from Vienna* (1933), *Secret Agent, Sabotage* (both 1936), and *Young and Innocent* (1937). Also edited, among other equally prestigious productions, *A Yank at Oxford, The Citadel* (both 1938), *Goodbye Mr. Chips* (1939), and *Major Barbara* (1941). He began directing in the early 40s and achieved his best work with semidocumentary war and adventure features. Also directed for British TV and was among the second-unit directors on David Lean's *Ryan's Daughter* (1970).

FILMS (as director): *The Big Blockade* (also act.) 1941; *The Foreman Went to France* 1942; *San Demetrio—London* 1943; *Johnny Frenchman, Return of the Vikings* (doc.) 1945;

The Loves of Joanna Godden 1947; *Scott of the Antarctic* 1948; *A Run for Your Money* (also co-sc.), *The Magnet* 1949; *The Cruel Sea* 1953; *Lease of Life* 1954; *The Long Arm/The Third Key* 1956; *Barnacle Bill/All at Sea* 1957; *Cone of Silence/Trouble in the Sky* 1960; *Girl on Approval* 1962; *Finché dura la Tempesta/Beta Som/Torpedo Bay* (It./Fr.) 1963; *The Sky Bike* (also sc.) 1967; *Ryan's Daughter* (2nd-unit dir. only) 1970.

Fresnay, Pierre. Actor. *b.* Pierre-Jules-Louis Laudenbach, Apr. 4, 1897, Paris. *d.* 1975. On the stage from age 15, he made his first of many appearances with the Comédie Française in 1915, the year in which he also made his screen debut. He became established as a leading stage actor in the 20s, but it wasn't until the early 30s that he became an important film personality, after portraying the title role in *Marius* (1931). He later played the leads in two other Pagnol screen adaptations, *Fanny* and *César,* and in many other distinguished French films, memorably in Jean Renoir's *La Grande Illusion/Grand Illusion* and Henri-Georges Clouzot's *Le Corbeau/The Raven.* In all he appeared in some 60 films, in addition to numerous plays. He was married to Yvonne Printemps, his frequent co-star on the stage and on the screen.

FILMS INCLUDE: *France d'abord* 1915; *L'Essor* 1921; *Les Mystères de Paris* 1922; *Rocambole* 1924; *La Vierge Folle* 1928; *Marius* (title role) 1931; *Fanny* (as Marius) 1932; *La Dame aux Camélias/Camille* (as Armand Duval, opposite his wife, Yvonne Printemps) 1934; *The Man Who Knew Too Much* (UK), *Koenigsmark* 1935; *Sous les Yeux d'Occident/Razumov, César* (as Marius) 1936; *Mademoiselle Docteur/Street of Shadows, La Grande Illusion/Grand Illusion* 1937; *Le Puritain, Adrienne Lecouvreur, Alerte en Méditerranée/SOS Mediterranean, Trois Valses/Three Waltzes* 1938; *La Charrette Fantôme* 1939; *Le Duel* (also dir.) 1940; *L'Assassin habite au 21/The Murderer Lives at Number 21, Les Inconnus dans la Maison* 1942; *La Main du Diable/Carnival of Sinners, Le Corbeau/The Raven* 1943; *Le Voyageur sans Bagages* 1944; *La Fille du Diable/The Devil's Daughter, Le Visiteur/Tainted* 1946; *Monsieur Vincent* (as church reformer Vincent de Paul) 1947; *Au Grand Balcon* 1949; *La Valse de Paris/The Paris Waltz* (as composer Jacques Offenbach), *Dieu à besoin des Hommes/God Needs Men* 1950; *Un Grand Patron/The Perfectionist, Monsieur Fabre/The Amazing Monsieur Fabre, Voyage en Amérique/Voyage to America* 1951; *Il est minuit Docteur Schweitzer* 1952; *Le Defroqué* 1954; *Les Avadés, Les Aristocrates* 1955; *Les Oeufs de l'Autruche/The Ostrich Has Two Eggs, Les Fanatiques/A Bomb for a Dictator* 1957; *La Millième Fenêtre, Les Vieux de la Vieille* 1960.

Freund, Karl. Director of photography, director. *b.* Jan. 16, 1890, Königinhof, Bohemia (now Czech Republic). *d.* 1969. Entered the film industry at 16 as an apprentice projectionist in Berlin. At 17 he became assistant cameraman and at 18 a newsreel cameraman for Pathé. A gifted innovator, he was experimenting with sound as early as 1908 and built his own camera to meet his high standards of quality. During the 20s he gained an international reputation as a master of daring angles, lighting effects, and camera movement in such German film classics as Murnau's *The Last Laugh,* Dupont's *Variety,* and Lang's *Metropolis.* He was once described by a film historian as "the Giotto of the screen." In 1926 he co-produced and co-scripted Walter Ruttmann's landmark documentary *Berlin—Die Symphonie einer Grossstadt/Berlin—Symphony of a Great City/Berlin—A Symphony of a Big City.* In 1929 he emigrated to the US, where he continued creating his beautiful images in Hollywood films. In 1937 he won an Academy Award for the photography of *The Good Earth.* In the early 30s he also demonstrated undeniable talent as a director, particularly with the fantasy films *The Mummy* and *Mad Love.* In 1944 he founded the Photo Research Corporation of Burbank, a manufacturer of light-measuring equipment, of which he was president until shortly before his death. In the 50s he left motion picture photography for TV work, becoming chief cinematographer for Desilu Productions.

FILMS INCLUDE: As director of photography: In Germany—*Der Liebling der Frauen* 1910; *Venetianische Nacht* 1914; *Satanas* 1919; *Der Bucklige und die Tänzerin, Der Golem wie er in die Welt kam/The Golem, Der Januskopf* (co-phot.), *Die Spinnen/The Spiders* (co-phot.) 1920; *Der verlorene Schatten/The Lost Shadow* 1921; *Der brennende Acker/Burning Soil* (co-phot.), *Lukrezia Borgia* (co-phot.), *Tiefland* 1922; *Die Austreibung* 1923; *Die Finanzen des Grossherzogs* (co-phot.), *Der letzte Mann/The Last Laugh, Mikäel/Chained* (co-phot.) 1924; *Varieté/Variety* 1925; *Tartüff/Tartuffe* 1926; *Metropolis* (co-phot.) 1927; *Fräulein Else* (co-phot.) 1929. In the US—*The Boudoir Diplomat* 1930; *Dracula, Bad Sister* 1931; *Murders in the Rue Morgue, Back Street, Air Mail* 1932; *The Kiss Before the Mirror* 1933; *Camille* (co-phot.), *The Good Earth, Parnell, Conquest* 1937; *Man-Proof, Letter of Introduction* 1938; *Rose of Washington Square, Golden Boy* (co-phot.), *Barricade, Balalaika* 1939; *Green Hell, Pride and Prejudice* 1940; *Blossoms in the Dust* (co-phot.), *The Chocolate Soldier* 1941; *Tortilla Flat* 1942; *Dubarry Was a Lady* 1943; *Cry Havoc, A Guy Named Joe, The Seventh Cross* 1944; *Without Love* 1945; *Undercurrent* 1946; *This Time for Keeps* 1947; *Key Largo* 1948; *South of St. Louis* 1949; *Montana, Bright Leaf* 1950. As director (complete)—*The Mummy* 1932; *Moonlight and Pretzels* 1933; *Madame Spy, The Countess of Monte Cristo, Uncertain Lady, I Give My Love, Gift of Gab* 1934; *Mad Love* 1935.

Frey, Sami. Actor. Born on Oct. 13, 1937, in Paris. Intriguing character player and occasionally leading man of the French stage and films, often in offbeat roles.

FILMS INCLUDE: *Pardonnez nos Offenses* 1956; *Jeux dangereux* 1958; *La Nuit des Traqués* 1959; *La Vérité/The Truth* 1960; *Gioventù di Notte* (It./Fr.) 1961; *Il Disordine/Disorder* (It./Fr.), *Les Sept Péchés capitaux/Seven Capital Sins* (Vadim episode), *Cleo de 5 à 7/Cleo from 5 to 7, Thérèse Desqueyrous/Therese* 1962; *L'Appartement des Filles* 1963; *Bande à part/Band of Outsiders* 1964; *Une Balle au Coeur* 1965; *Qui êtes-vous Polly Magoo?* 1966; *Manon 70* 1968; *Mister Freedom* 1969; *M comme Mathieu, Les Mariés de l'An deux, Jaune le Soleil* 1971; *Le Journal d'un Suicidé, Paulina 1880, César et Rosalie/Cesar and Rosalie* 1972; *Sweet Movie* (Can./Fr./Ger.) 1974; *Moi Pierre Rivière. . .* 1975; *Le Jeux du Solitaire, Néa* 1976; *Pourquoi pas?, Une Page d'Amour* (Belg./Fr.) 1977; *The Little Drummer Girl* (US) 1984; *Black Widow, Blood and Sand* (US) 1987; *La Fille de D'Artagnan* 1994.

Friç, Martin (Mac). Director, screenwriter, actor. *b.* Mar. 29, 1902, Prague. *d.* 1968. Injured seriously while flying a biplane in his teens, he took up painting during his recuperation period. Became a stage actor at 16, a set designer and laboratory assistant for Czech films at 17, and a screenwriter and film actor at 20. He directed his first film in 1928 and subsequently many Czech and several German films, some of which gained wide international circulation. Friç (pronounced Fritch) was billed in his German films as Mac Fric (pronounced Frick). After WW II he devoted much of his energy to teaching and guiding promising new filmmakers. He was the first film director to be honored as "National Artist" by the Communist Czech regime. He died of a heart attack the day Soviet tanks entered Prague to quell the liberal riots.

FILMS INCLUDE (as director): *Father Vojtech* (also sc., act.) 1928; *The Organist of St. Vitus* (also co-sc.), *Poor Girl* (also sc.) 1929; *All for Love* 1930; *Der Zinker* (co-dir. with Karel Lamac; Ger.), *He and His Sister* (co-dir. with Lamac), *Good Soldier Schweik* 1931; *Kantor Ideal, Sister Angelica* 1932; *Der Adjutant seiner Hoheit* (Ger./Czech.), *Revisor/The Inspector General, A Dog's Life* (also co-story, co-sc.), *The 12 Chairs* (also sc.), *The Ruined Shopkeeper, Closed Doors* 1933; *Der Doppelbräutigam* (Ger./Czech.), *Hej Rup!* (also co-story, co-sc.), *The Last Man* 1934; *Hero for a Night, The Eleventh Commandment* 1935; *Janosik* (also co-sc.), *Father Vojtech* (remake), *The Seamstress, Paradise Road* (Czech./Ger.) 1936; *The World Is Ours* (also co-story, co-sc.), *The Hordubals* 1937; *Madman in the Dark, School—Where Life Begins* 1938; *Christian* (also co-story), *The Reluctant Millionaire* 1939; *Baron Prášil/Baron Munchhausen, Catacombs, Second Tour* 1940; *The Hard Life of an Adventurer* 1941; *Experiment* 1943; *The Wedding Ring* 1945; *Beat 13* 1946; *Warning!* (also co-sc.), *Tales from Capek* (also co-sc.) 1947; *Homecoming, A Kiss at the Stadium* (also co-story, co-sc.) 1948; *Motorcycles* 1949; *Steel Town/Tempered Steel, The Trap* 1950; *The Emperor's Baker/The Emperor and the Golem* (also co-sc.) 1951; *The Mystery of the Blood* (also co-sc.) 1953; *Dog Heads* (also co-sc.) 1954; *Leave It to Me* (also co-sc.) 1955; *The Flood* (also co-sc.) 1958; *The Princess with the Golden Star* (also co-sc.) 1959; *King of Kings* 1963; *A Star Called Wormwood* 1964; *People on Wheels* 1966; *The Best Woman in My Life* 1968.

Fricker, Brenda. Actress. Born on Feb. 17, 1944 in Dublin, Ireland. Subtle stage-trained actress who sprang into the cinema mainstream with her Academy Award–winning performance as the tenacious mother of Daniel Day-Lewis in *My Left Foot.* Frequently cast in maternal roles.

FILMS: *The Quatermass Conclusion* (UK) 1980; *Bloody Kids* 1983; *Our Exploits at West Poley* 1986; *My Left Foot* 1989; *The Field* 1990; *Home Alone 2: Lost in New York, Utz* 1992; *So I Married an Axe Murderer* 1993; *Angels in the Outfield, A Man of No Importance* 1994; *Moll Flanders, A Time to Kill, Swann* 1996.

friction head. A panning and tilting TRIPOD head equipped with a sliding friction device to provide smooth camera movement.

Friedhofer, Hugo. Composer. *b.* May 3, 1902, San Francisco. *d.* 1981. A cellist's son, he intended at first to become a painter and did not start his musical training until the age of 18. Three years later he began performing with various symphony orchestras and in 1929 went to Hollywood as an arranger for Fox. He joined Warner Bros. as an orchestrator in 1934 and began composing for the screen in 1937. He subsequently scored or orchestrated many Hollywood films for various studios, winning an Academy Award for the score of *The Best Years of Our Lives* (1946).

FILM SCORES INCLUDE: *The Adventures of Marco Polo, Valley of the Giants* 1938; *Lifeboat, The Lodger, Home in Indiana, Wing and a Prayer* 1944; *The Best Years of Our Lives* 1946; *Body and Soul* 1947; *Joan of Arc* 1948; *Broken Arrow* 1950; *Ace in the Hole/The Big Carnival* 1951; *The Marrying Kind, The Outcasts of Poker Flat* 1952; *Hondo* (co-music), *Above and Beyond* 1953; *Vera Cruz* 1954; *Violent Saturday* 1955; *The Harder They Fall, The Revolt of Mamie Stover* 1956; *An Affair to Remember, The Sun Also Rises* 1957; *The Young Lions* 1958; *Woman Obsessed* 1959; *One-Eyed Jacks* 1961; *Geronimo* 1962; *The Secret Invasion* 1964; *Von Richthofen and Brown* 1971; *Private Parts* 1972.

Friedkin, William. Director. Born on Aug. 29, 1939, in Chicago. At 16 he began working in the mail room of a local TV station and within months had pulled his way up to studio floor manager. In less than a year he was directing local live broadcasts and not long after was handling network dramas and musical shows. In ten years he directed hundreds of local, network, and educational TV programs, including a number of well-received documentary specials. He made his big-screen directing debut with a minor film, *Good Times* (1967), a Sonny and Cher vehicle, but followed this with more ambitious projects, the old-burlesque-days nostalgia piece *The Night They Raided Minsky's,* the screen adaptation of Pinter's *The Birthday Party,* which he made in Britain, and the screen version of the off-Broadway play about gay men, *The Boys in the Band.* Friedkin next scored a tremendous commercial triumph with the action-filled box-office hit *The French Connection,* for which he won the best director Academy Award for 1971 and which received the best picture Oscar, as well as the awards for actor, screenplay, and editing. The film, which contained one of the most exciting chase sequences ever filmed, remains a landmark of screen suspense. Friedkin had another big commercial blockbuster with *The Exorcist* (1973), a sensational and exploitative, but nonetheless harrowingly gripping film, the success of which invited a number of sequels and imitations. But just when he seemed to be ensuring his place among Hollywood's elite, Friedkin experienced a string of commercial and critical failures. His career has yet to recover, though he remains highly regarded for his technical skills. In 1977 he married French actress Jeanne MOREAU, 11 years his senior. They divorced in 1980. His subsequent (1982–1985) marriage to British actress Lesley-Anne DOWN ended in a bitter custody battle over their son Josh. He is currently married to producer Sherry LANSING.

FILMS: *Good Times* 1967; *The Birthday Party* (UK), *The Night They Raided Minsky's* 1968; *The Boys in the Band* 1970; *The French Connection* 1971; *The Exorcist* 1973; *Sorcerer* (also prod.) 1977; *The Brink's Job* 1979; *Cruising* (also sc.) 1980; *Deal of the Century* 1983; *To Live and Die in L.A.* (also co-sc.) 1985; *The Guardian* (also co-sc.) 1990; *Rampage* (also sc.) 1992; *Blue Chips* (also sc.) 1994; *Jade* 1995.

Friedlander, Louis. See LANDERS, Lew.

Friedman, Seymour. Director. Born on Aug. 17, 1917, in Detroit. *ed.* Cambridge; St. Mary's Hospital Medical School (London). Entered films in 1937 as assistant editor, then became assistant director. After WW II service, he returned to Hollywood as director of routine, low-budget adventure films. Since the late 50s, a TV production executive.

FILMS INCLUDE: *Trapped by Boston Blackie* 1948; *Chinatown at Midnight, Bodyhold, Prison Warden, The Crime Doctor's Diary, The Devil's Henchman* 1949; *Bodyhold, Customs Agent* 1950; *Son of Dr. Jekyll, Criminal Lawyer* 1951; *Lone Shark* 1952; *Flame of Calcutta* 1953; *Khyber Patrol* 1954; *African Manhunt* 1955; *Secret of Treasure Mountain* 1956; *Belle Sommers* (production supervisor only) 1962.

Friend, Philip. Actor. Born on Feb. 20, 1915, in Horsham, England. *ed.* Bradfield Coll. Leading man and second lead of British, then also American films, following stage experience from 1935. He spent the late 40s and early 50s in Hollywood, where he was tried out, with no great success, as a swashbuckling hero of low-budget adventures. Also seen on Broadway and on TV. Married to actress Eileen Erskine.

FILMS INCLUDE: In the UK—*Midas Touch* 1939; *Pimpernel Smith/Mister V* 1941; *Next of Kin, In Which We Serve, The Day Will Dawn/The Avengers* 1942. In the US—*Enchantment* 1948; *My Own True Love, Sword in the Desert* 1949; *Buccaneer's Girl, Spy Hunt* 1950; *The Highwayman, Smuggler's Island, Thunder on the Hill* 1951. In the UK—

Desperate Moment, Background/Edge of Divorce 1953; *The Diamond Wizard* 1954; *Son of Robin Hood* 1958; *Web of Suspicion* 1959; *Stranglehold* 1962; *The Vulture* (US/Can./UK) 1967.

Friese-Greene, William. Inventor. *b.* William Green, Sept. 7, 1855, Bristol, England, *d.* 1921. A still photographer, he became interested in recording and projecting motion. Between 1885 and 1889 he developed and exhibited several projection apparatus based on the inventions of others. In 1889, he demonstrated a camera he had invented in collaboration with Mortimer Evans, a London civil engineer. However, the camera shot film at only four or five frames per second, which made it more suitable for sequential projection of still slides than for the showing of motion pictures. In 1891, Friese-Greene was jailed as a result of the bankruptcy of a company in which he was a partner. Undaunted, he continued patenting various motion picture devices after his release, including an improved camera, and stereoscopic and color systems, but most of his ideas proved impractical or premature. He died penniless, in the midst of a speech he was delivering to an indifferent audience at a film industry convention. His life and work were the subject of the film *The Magic Box* (1951), starring Robert DONAT and featuring many other distinguished players of the British screen.

Frings, Ketti. Screenwriter, playwright, novelist. *b.* Katherine Hartley, Feb. 28, 1915, Columbus, Ohio. *d.* 1981. Married former lightweight boxer Kurt Frings. She was an advertising copywriter, columnist, and ghost writer for film stars in fan magazines (under the pseudonym Anita Kilore) before becoming established as a novelist, screenwriter, and playwright. In 1958 she won the Pulitzer Prize for the play 'Look Homeward, Angel.'

FILMS INCLUDE: *Hold Back the Dawn* (novel basis only) 1941; *Guest in the House* 1945; *The Accused* 1949; *Thelma Jordan, Dark City* 1950; *The Company She Keeps* 1951; *Because of You, Come Back Little Sheba* 1953; *About Mrs. Leslie* 1954; *The Shrike, Foxfire* 1955; *By Love Possessed* 1961; *Mr. Sycamore* 1975.

Fritsch, Willy. Actor. *b.* Jan. 27, 1901, Kattowitz (Katowice), Germany (now Poland). *d.* 1973. After training as a mining engineer, he studied drama under Max REINHARDT and entered German films in the early 20s. He became a highly popular star of light operettas and romances, often opposite Lilian HARVEY or Käthe von NAGY.

FILMS INCLUDE: *Razzia* 1921; *Guillotine, Mutter und Kind* 1924; *Der Farmer aus Texas, Ein Walzertraum/Waltz Dream* 1925; *Schuldig/Guilty, Der letzte Walzer/The Last Waltz, Die selige Exzellenz/His Late Excellency* 1927; *Die Carmen von St. Pauli/Docks of Hamburg, Spione/Spies, Ungarische Rhapsodie/Hungarian Rhapsody* 1928; *Die Frau im Mond/Woman in the Moon/By Rocket to the Moon, Melodie des Herzens/Melody of the Heart* 1929; *Die Drei von der Tankstelle/Three from the Filling Station, Liebeswalzer, Hokuspokus/Hocuspocus* 1930; *Im Geheimdienst/In the Employ of the Secret Service, Der Kongress tanzt/The Congress Dances* 1931; *Ein blonder Traum/A Blond Dream, Ein toller Einfall/A Mad Idea* 1932; *Saison in Kairo, Walzerkrieg/War of the Waltzes/Waltz Time in Vienna* 1933; *Prinzessin Turandot* 1934; *Amphitryon* 1935; *Boccaccio* 1936; *Sieben Ohrfeigen/Seven Slaps* 1937; *Zwischen den Eltern/ Between the Parents* 1938; *Die Geliebte* 1939; *Wiener Blut/Vienna Blood* 1942; *Die Fledermaus/The Bat* 1945; *Film ohne Titel/Film Without a Name* 1947; *Die Du Barry* 1951; *Ungarische Rhapsodie/ Hungarian Rhapsody* 1953; *Schwarzwaldmelodie* 1956; *Verliebt in Heidelberg* 1964.

Fröbe, Gert. Actor. *b.* Karl-Gerhard Fröbe, Dec. 25, 1912, Planitz, Zwickau, Germany. *d.* 1988. A former violinist and stage decorator, he turned stage actor in the late 30s and cabaret performer in the mid-40s, following service in the German Army during WW II. Entering films in 1948, he played impressive character roles in many German and international productions, often as a dominant heavy. Best remembered in the title role of *Goldfinger* (1964). In 1965 Fröbe created an uproar by freely admitting past membership in the Nazi Party, but he later regained public affection when a Jewish survivor came forward to identify the actor as the man who saved his life by hiding his family from the Nazis. Fröbe was married five times.

FILMS INCLUDE: *Berliner Ballade/The Berliner* 1948; *Der Tag vor der Hochzeit, Salto Mortale* 1952; *Les Héros sont fatigués/Heroes and Sinners* (Fr./It.) 1955; *Celui qui doit mourir/He Who Must Die* (Fr./It.), *Robinson soll nicht sterben/The Girl and the Legend* 1957; *Das Mädchen Rosemarie/ Rosemary, Es geschah am hellichten Tag/It Happened in Broad Daylight* 1958; *Die 1000 Augen des Dr. Mabuse/The 1000 Eyes of Dr. Mabuse* 1960; *The Longest Day* (US) 1962; *Le Meutrier/Enough Rope* (Fr./It./Ger.), *Die Dreigroschenoper/ Threepenny Opera* 1963; *Peau de Banane/Banana Peel* (Fr./It.), *Tonio Kröger, Cent Mille Dollars au Soleil/Greed in the Sun* (Fr./It.), *Echappement libre/Backfire* (Fr./It./Sp.), *Goldfinger* (title role; UK) 1964; *A High Wind in Jamaica* (US/UK), *Those Magnificent Men in Their Flying Machines* (UK) 1965; *Du Rififi à Paname/The Upper Hand* (Fr./It./Ger.), *Paris brûle-t-il?/Is Paris Burning?* (Fr./US), *Triple Cross* (UK/Fr.) 1966; *Jules Verne's Rocket to the Moon/Those Fantastic Flying Fools* (UK) 1967; *Chitty Chitty Bang Bang* (UK) 1968; *Monte Carlo or Bust/Those Daring Young Men in Their Jaunty Jalopies* (UK/Fr./It.) 1969; *$/Dollars* (UK) 1971; *Ludwig* (It./Ger.) 1973; *And Then There Were None/Ten Little Indians* (UK/Fr./Ger./It.) 1975; *The Serpent's Egg* (Ger./US) 1977; *Tod oder Freiheit* 1978; *Bloodline* 1979; *Le Coup du Parapluie* 1980; *The Daisy Chain* 1981.

Froelich, Carl. Director. *b.* Sept. 5, 1875, Berlin. *d.* 1953. A pioneer of German cinema, he entered the fledgling industry in 1902 and was instrumental in the development of the German newsreel. In 1920 he established his own company and subsequently produced many of the films he directed. He was decorated by Goebbels for his contribution to German cinema during the Nazi period. Many of his films were commercially successful and enjoyed worldwide distribution.

FILMS INCLUDE: *Zu Spät* 1911; *Richard Wagner* 1913; *Die Brüder Karamasoff/The Brothers Karamazov* (co-dir.), *Die Toteninsel* (also co-sc.), *Irrende seelen* (also co-sc.), *Josef und seine Brüder/Joseph and His Brethren* (also sc.), *Der Taugenichts* (also co-sc.) 1922; *Mutter und Kind* 1924; *Kammermusik, Tragödie* 1925; *Rosen aus dem Süden* 1926; *Die grosse Pause, Violantha* 1927; *Lotte* 1928; *Die Nacht gehört uns* 1929; *Brand in der Oper* 1930; *Mitternachtsliebe* (co-dir. with Augusto Genina), *Luise—Königin von Preussen* 1931; *Die oder Keine* 1932; *Reifende Jugend, Der Choral von Leuten* 1933; *Frühlingsmärchen, Krach um Iolanthe* 1934; *Lisolette von der Pfalz/The Private Life of Louis XIV* (also co-sc.), *Ich war Jack Mortimer* 1935; *Wenn wir alle Engel wären/If We All Were Angels, Traumulus* 1936; *Heimat/Magda* 1938; *Es war eine rauschende Ballnacht* 1939; *Das Herz einer Königin* 1940; *Familie Buchholz* 1944; *Stips* 1951.

Froeschel, George. Screenwriter. *b.* Mar. 9, 1891, Vienna. *d.* 1979. A former lawyer, journalist, and novelist, he collaborated on screenplays for MGM from the early 40s. He shared in the Academy Award for the script of *Mrs. Miniver* (1942).

FILMS INCLUDE: *Waterloo Bridge, The Mortal Storm* 1940; *We Were Dancing, Mrs. Miniver, Random Harvest* 1942; *The White Cliffs of Dover* 1944; *Command Decision* 1949; *The Miniver Story* 1950; *The Unknown Man* 1951; *Scaramouche* 1952; *The Story of Three Loves, Never Let Me Go* 1953; *Rose Marie, Betrayed* 1954; *Quentin Durward* 1955; *Gaby* 1956; *Me and the Colonel* 1958; *I Aim at the Stars* (co-story only) 1960.

Fröhlich, Gustav. Actor, director. *b.* Mar. 21, 1902, in Hanover, Germany. *d.* 1987. A former journalist and editor, he turned to stage and screen acting in the mid-20s. Played leads in scores of German films, notably in Fritz Lang's *Metropolis.* Occasionally also directed.

FILMS INCLUDE: As actor—*Friesenblut* 1925; *Metropolis, Die elf Teufel, Jugendrausch/Eva and the Grasshopper, Der Meister von Nürnberg/The Meistersinger* 1927; *Angst, Heimkehr/Homecoming, Hurrah! Ich lebe!/ Hurrah I'm Alive!* 1928; *Asphalt, Das brennende Herz/The Burning Heart* 1929; *Brand in der Oper, Der unsterbliche Lump/The Immortal Vagabond, Zwei Menschen* 1930; *Voruntersuchung, Kismet* (German version of US film), *Gloria* (Ger./Fr.), *Liebeslied, Mein Leopold, Ein Walzer vom Strauss* (as Johann Strauss, Jr.), *Liebeskommando* 1931; *Kaiserwalzer* 1932; *Was Frauen traumen, Die Nacht der grossen Liebe/The Night of the Great Love* 1933; *Der Flüchtling aus Chikago* 1934; *Stradivari, Barcarole, Liebesleute* 1935; *Inkognito* 1936; *Die kleine und die grosse Liebe/Minor Love and the Real Thing* 1938; *Der grosse König* 1942; *Familie Buchholz* 1944; *Der grosse Fall* 1945; *Das verlorene Gesicht/Secrets of a Soul* 1948; *Die Sünderin/The Sinner* 1951; *Haus des Lebens* 1952; *Ball der Nationen* 1954. As director (complete)—*Rakoczy-Marsch* (co-dir. with Stefan Szekely; also act.) 1933; *Liebe und Trompetenklang/Abenteuer eines jungen Herrn in Polen* (also act.) 1934; *Leb' wohl Christina* (also co-sc.) 1945; *Wege im Zwielicht* (also act.) 1948; *Der Bagnosträfling* (also sc.) 1949; *Die Lüge* (also sc.) 1950; *Torreani* (also act.) 1951; *Seine Tochter ist der Peter* 1955.

front projection. A special effects technique in which a photographed background is projected from the front of the set to a screen behind the actors. Because the screen is highly reflective (typically made of Scotchlite, the same material used to reflect auto headlights from protective clothing), the projection light can be very dim, so that the actors and foreground objects do not reflect the projected image. The result is a bright and detailed background image, generally more convincing than that produced by the older method of BACK PROJECTION.

Front projection can also be used to place filmed action within the larger setting depicted by a MATTE PAINTING. For example, a painting of a cliffside might be prepared with a small hole; a patch of Scotchlite screen is placed behind the hole. A prefilmed scene of actors exploring a cave is then projected onto that screen. The camera photographs the composite of painting and filmed action; the result is a long shot of actors exploring a cave in the cliffside.

In front projection, a beam-splitter—a partially reflecting mirror—is used to place the beam of projected light in the same line of sight as the camera lens. The partial mirror is placed in front of the camera at a 45-degree angle, in such a way that the camera can photograph through it. The projector, placed next to the camera at a 90-degree angle, projects its light through the partial mirror, in such a way that some of the light bounces off the mirror and onto the screen. The camera then photographs the screen, along with the projected image.

Fruet, William (Bill). Director. Born in 1933, in Lethbridge, Alberta, Canada. Trained at the Canadian Theatre School in Toronto, he started his career as an actor. Later he began writing for television and occasionally directing industrial shorts. Following a brief enrollment at the UCLA film school, he returned to Canada as a film editor and screenwriter. His feature debut as a director, the prize-winning *Wedding in White* (1972) showed much promise, but many of his subsequent films were in the action-exploitation category.

FILMS INCLUDE: *Wedding in White* (also sc.) 1972; *Death Weekend/The House by the Lake* (also sc.) 1976; *Striking Back/Search and Destroy* 1979; *Funeral Home/Cries in the Night* (also prod.) 1981; *Death Bite/Spasms* 1983; *Bedroom Eyes* 1984; *Killer Party* 1986; *Blue Monkey* 1987.

Frye, Dwight. Actor. *b.* 1899, Denver, Colo. *d.* 1943. Small-framed character player of the New York stage, then Hollywood films, often in demented or pathetic roles. Memorable as the insect-devouring Renfield in the original *Dracula* and as Fritz, the mad, brain-switching hunchbacked dwarf, in the original *Frankenstein* (both 1931). He died suddenly of a heart attack in the midst of a prolific, if bizarre, career.

FILMS INCLUDE: *The Night Bird* (bit) 1928; *Man to Man/Barber John's Boy* 1930; *Dracula, The Maltese Falcon, The Black Camel, Frankenstein* 1931; *Attorney for the Defense* 1932; *The Vampire Bat, The Invisible Man* 1933; *The Bride of Frankenstein* 1935; *The Crime of Dr. Crespi* 1936; *The Man Who Found Himself, The Shadow* 1937; *Invisible Enemy* 1938; *Son of Frankenstein, The Man in the Iron Mask* 1939; *Gangs of Chicago, Phantom Raiders* 1940; *Mystery Ship* 1941; *Ghost of Frankenstein* 1942; *Frankenstein Meets the Wolf Man, Drums of Fu Manchu, The Wolf Man* 1943.

fs. Abbreviation used in scripts to denote "FULL SHOT."

f-stop. A setting indicating the relative aperture of a lens at its various diaphragm openings; hence, the capacity of the lens to admit light rays. It is expressed by a number that is obtained by dividing the FOCAL LENGTH of the lens by the effective diameter of its diaphragm. Among the most common *f*-stops—or standard *f* numbers calibrated on a camera lens—are 1.4, 2, 2.8, 4, 5.6, 8, 11, 16, and 22. Increasing the aperture by one *f*-stop doubles the amount of light transmitted through a lens. Decreasing the aperture by one *f*-stop halves the amount of transmitted light.

Fuentes, Fernando de. See DE FUENTES, Fernando.

Fuest, Robert. Director. Born in 1927, in London. A former painter and graphic designer, he entered British TV in 1957 as an art director and later directed numerous television programs and commercials. Several of his films of the 70s were noted for their stylishness, including the cult favorite *The Abominable Dr. Phibes*. Later worked mostly for TV.

FILMS INCLUDE: *Just Like a Woman* (also sc.) 1967; *And Soon the Darkness, Wuthering Heights* 1970; *The Abominable Dr. Phibes* 1971; *Dr. Phibes Rises Again* (also co-sc.) 1972; *The Final Programme/Last Days of Man on Earth* (also sc., art dir.) 1973; *The Devil's Rain* (US) 1975; *Aphrodite* (US) 1983.

Fujimoto, Tak. Director of photography. *ed.* London Film School. Distinctive Japanese-American cinematographer who got start in commercials as assistant to cinematographer Haskell Wexler. Has been Jonathan Demme's principal director of photography since *Caged Heat*, effecting through both drenched color and lighting the director's idiosyncratic views of America over the decades.

FILMS INCLUDE: *Badlands* 1973; *Caged Heat, Bootleggers* 1974; *Death Race 2000, Dr. Black, Mr. Hyde, Crazy Mama* (2nd unit); *Cannonball* 1976; *Chatter Box, Star Wars* (cam. op.) 1977; *Stony Island, Remember My Name* 1978; *The*

Watts Monster, Last Embrace 1979; *Borderline, Melvin and Howard, Where the Buffalo Roam* 1980; *National Lampoon Goes to the Movies* (part) 1982; *Heart Like a Wheel* 1983; *Swing Shift* 1984; *Ferris Bueller's Day Off, Pretty in Pink, Something Wild* 1986; *Backfire* 1987; *Cocoon: The Return, Married to the Mob, Sweet Hearts Dance* 1988; *84 Charlie Mopic* (assist.) 1989; *Miami Blues* 1990; *The Silence of the Lambs* 1991; *Philadelphia* 1993.

Fuller, Samuel. Director, producer, screenwriter. Born on Aug. 12, 1911, in Worcester, Mass. At age 12 he became a copyboy on the New York *Journal* and at 17 a crime reporter for the San Diego *Sun.* During the Depression years he wandered about the country on freight trains. He began writing short stories at the same time and in 1935 his first of several pulp novels, *Burn Baby Burn,* was published. In 1936 he became a screenwriter, collaborating on the script of James Cruze's *Gangs of New York* (1938), among other films. During WW II, he fought in North Africa and Europe with the First Infantry Division and was awarded the Bronze Star, the Silver Star, and a Purple Heart. Returning to Hollywood, he made his first film as a director in 1949.

Fuller, who writes most of his screenplays and often produces his own films, has been a controversial figure in American cinema. His output, mostly action pictures of the B category, reflects in its directness and brutal violence his experiences as a crime reporter, a tramp, and a soldier, and his protagonists are often corrupt and amoral. His coarse political views alienated critics of both the extreme Left and the extreme Right. Political views aside, most critics agree that Fuller has been a vital force in American cinema, a director with an exciting visual style who uses film as a dynamic means of expression. He is admired especially in France, where he now lives and where cultists consider him one of the most influential postwar directors. Retrospectives of his films are often shown in Europe.

In the 60s Fuller directed several episodes for various US TV series. After a long hiatus, he returned to features with *The Big Red One* (1980). The film, inspired by the director's own WW II combat experience with the First Infantry Division, was hailed by many as his masterpiece and one of the great American war dramas ever filmed. He appeared in the French films *Pierrot le Fou* (1965) and *Brigitte et Brigitte* (1966) and in the US films *The Last Movie* (1971) and *1941* (1979). Fuller appeared in several European and American films as an actor or as himself. In 1967 he married actress Christa Lang, his second.

FILMS: As screenwriter—*Hats Off* 1936; *It Happened in Hollywood* 1937; *Gangs of New York, Adventure in Sahara, Federal Man Hunt* 1938; *Bowery Boy* 1940; *Confirm or Deny* 1941; *Power of the Press* 1943; *Gangs of the Waterfront* (remake of *Gangs of New York*) 1945; *Shockproof* 1948; *The Tanks Are Coming* 1951; *Scandal Sheet* 1952; *The Command* 1954; *The Cape Town Affair* (remake of *Pickup of South Street;* see below) 1967; *Deadly Trackers* 1973; *The Klansman* 1974; *Let's Get Harry* (co-story only) 1986. As director-screenwriter—*I Shot Jesse James* 1949; *The Baron of Arizona, The Steel Helmet* (also prod.) 1950; *Fixed Bayonets* 1951; *Park Row* (also prod.) 1952; *Pickup on South Street* 1953; *Hell and High Water* 1954; *House of Bamboo* (also act.) 1955; *Run of the Arrow* (also prod.), *China Gate* (also prod.), *Forty Guns* (also prod.)1957; *Verboten!* (also prod.), *The Crimson Kimono* (also prod.) 1959; *Underworld U.S.A.* (also prod.) 1961; *Merrill's Marauders* 1962; *Shock Corridor* (also prod.) 1963; *The Naked Kiss* (also prod.) 1965; *Shark!* (release delayed from 1967; US/Mex.) 1969; *Dead Pigeon on Beethoven Street* (also act.) 1972; *The Big Red One* 1980; *White Dog* (also act.) 1982; *Les Voleurs de la Nuit/Thieves After Dark* (also act.; Fr.) 1984; *Street of No Return* (also act., co-ed.; US/Fr./Port.) 1989. As actor—*Pierrot le Fou* (Fr.) 1965; *Brigitte* (Fr.) 1966; *The Last Movie* 1971; *The Young Nurses* 1973; *Der Amerikanische Freund/The American Friend* (Ger.), *Scott Joplin* 1977; *Hammett, Die Stand der Dinge/The State of Things* (Ger.) 1982; *Slapstick of Another Kind* 1984; *Return to Salem's Lot* 1987; *Words* (act. only) 1996; *The End of Violence* (act. only) 1997.

full shot. A shot whose subject completely fills the screen. When the subject is a person his or her full body is included in the shot. The term is sometimes used interchangeably with LONG SHOT. In scripts and camera reports it is abbreviated "fs."

Fulton, John P. Special effects artist. *b.* 1902, Nebraska; moved to California in 1914. *d.* 1966. He was the son of Fitch Fulton, an artist who painted backdrops for vaudeville and later for movies, including *Gone With the Wind*. After studying electrical engineering and working as a surveyor, John Fulton entered the movies as an assistant cameraman. He was briefly a cinematographer before becoming head of Universal's special effects department, where he achieved fame for inventing the techniques that made Claude Rains invisible in *The Invisible Man*. He went on to do the special effects for many of Universal's classic horror films, including *The Mummy* and *Son of Frankenstein*, as well as numerous other productions. In the 40s he left Universal to work with Samuel Goldwyn, producing the ghostly twin effects in *Wonder Man*. In 1953, he became head of the effects department at Paramount (replacing the late Gordon Jennings), where he parted the Red Sea for Cecil B. De Mille's remake of *The Ten Commandments*. He continued working freelance after Paramount disbanded its effects department in the early 60s. Though a master of his craft, he never fulfilled his long-standing ambition to direct or produce. Winner of three Academy Awards ("AA" below).

FILMS INCLUDE: *Hell's Harbour* (phot. only) 1929; *Eyes of the World* (phot. only) 1930; *Waterloo Bridge, Frankenstein* 1931; *Air Mail, The Mummy, The Old Dark House* 1932; *The Invisible Man* 1933; *The Great Impersonation* (phot. only) 1935; *The Mystery of Edwin Drood, The Werewolf of London* 1935; *Dracula's Daughter, Show Boat, The Invisible Ray, The Sea Spoilers* (phot. only) 1936; *The Road Back* 1937; *Son of Frankenstein* 1939; *The Invisible Man Returns* 1940; *In the Navy, The Invisible Woman, Man Made Monster* 1941; *The Ghost of Frankenstein, Invisible Agent* 1942; *Calling Dr. Death, Frankenstein Meets the Wolf Man* 1943; *Ali Baba and the Forty Thieves, Follow the Boys, House of Frankenstein, Invisible Man's Revenge, The Scarlet Claw* 1944; *Here Come the Co-Eds, House of Dracula, Sudan, The Woman in Green, Wonder Man* (AA) 1945; *A Song Is Born* 1948; *Mad Wednesday* 1950; *The Naked Jungle* 1953; *Casanova's Big Night, Elephant Walk, Rear Window, Red Garters, Sabrina* 1954; *The Bridges at Toko-Ri* (AA), *Conquest of Space, The Desperate Hours, Strategic Air Command, To Catch a Thief, The Trouble with Harry, We're No Angels* 1955; *The Man Who Knew Too Much, The Rainmaker, The Ten Commandments* (AA) 1956; *Funny Face, Gunfight at the O.K. Corral, The Joker Is Wild, Omar Khayyam* 1957; *The Colossus of New York, Houseboat, I Married a Monster from Outer Space, King Creole, The Space Children* 1958; *Don't Give Up the Ship, Li'l Abner* 1959; *Visit to a Small Planet* 1960; *One-Eyed Jacks, The Pleasure of His Company* 1961; *Escape from Zahrain, Hatari!* 1962; *The Disorderly Orderly* 1964; *The Heroes of Telemark* (UK) 1965; *The Sea Pirate* (Fr./Sp./It.) 1967.

Funès, Louis de. Actor. *b.* July 31, 1914, Courbevoie, France, of Portuguese descent. *d.* 1983. Worked at a variety of odd jobs before beginning a career as a comic in Paris nightclubs and on radio. Has appeared in well over 100 French films, mostly routine, since 1945. At first played comic cameos, then soon developed into a star, and next to Fernandel was the French screen's most popular comedian in the 50s and 60s. His activity was curtailed in the mid-70s following a heart attack.

FILMS INCLUDE: *La Tentation de Barbizon* 1946; *Antoine et Antoinette/Antoine and Antoinette* 1947; *Le Roi du Bla-bla-bla, Boniface Somnambule* 1950; *Les Sept Péchés capitaux/The Seven Deadly Sins, Monsieur Taxi* 1952; *La Vie d'un Honnête Homme/The Virtuous Scoundrel, Capitaine Pantoufle* 1953; *Le Blé en Herbe/The Game of Love, La Mouton à Cinq Pattes/The Sheep Has Five Legs, Les Corsaires du Bois de Boulogne, La Reine Margot, Ah! les Belles Bacchantes/Peek-a-boo, Papa Maman la Bonne et Moi/Mama Papa the Maid and I* 1954; *Frou-frou, L'Impossible Monsieur Pipelet* 1955; *Courte Tête, La Traversée de Paris/Four Bags Full* 1956; *Comme un Cheveu sur la Soupe/Crazy in the Noodle* 1957; *Ni vu ni connu* 1958; *Candide* 1960; *La Belle Américaine* 1961; *Le Crime ne paie pas/Crime Does Not Pay, Le Diable et le Dix Commandements/The Devil and the Ten Commandments* 1962; *Le Gendarme de Saint-Tropez/The Gendarme of St. Tropez, Fantômas* 1964; *Le Corniaud/The Sucker; La Grande Vadrouille/Don't Look Now* (Fr./UK) 1966; *Oscar* 1967; *Le Tatoué* 1968; *Hibernatus* 1969; *Jo/The Gazebo, Sur un Arbre perché, La Folie des Grandeurs/Delusions of Grandeur* 1971; *Les Adventures de Rabbi Jacob/The Mad Adventures of Rabbi Jacob* 1973; *L'Aile et la Cuisse* 1976; *La Zizanie* 1978; *Le Gendarme et les Extraterrestres* 1979; *L'Avare/The Miser* (also co-dir.) 1980.

Funicello, Annette. Born on Oct.22, 1942, in Utica, N.Y. Perky, busty leading lady of lightweight Hollywood films of the 60s. Cheerleader of the Mouseketeers on Disney's 'Mickey Mouse Club' TV show, she graduated into Disney features, often billed simply as Annette. But she is best remembered clad in a swimsuit in a string of beach-party teenage romps produced by American-International, often co-starring Frankie AVALON. The popular team reunited to co-finance and star in the sleeper hit *Back to the Beach* (1987), to the delight of nostalgic fans. In 1992, Funicello made headlines by announcing that for several years she has been battling multiple sclerosis (MS).

FILMS: *Johnny Tremain* 1957; *The Shaggy Dog* 1959; *The Horsemasters, Babes in Toyland* 1961; *Beach Party* 1983; *The Misadventures of Merlin Jones, Muscle Beach Party, Bikini Beach, Pajama Party* 1964; *The Monkey's Uncle, How to Stuff a Wild Bikini, Ski Party* (cameo), *Dr. Goldfoot and the Bikini Machine* 1965; *Fireball 500* 1966; *Thunder Alley* 1967; *Head* 1968; *Back to the Beach* 1987.

Furie, Sidney J. Director. Born on Feb. 28, 1933, in Toronto. A producer-director for Canadian TV at 21, he began directing feature films in Canada in 1957, in England from 1960, and in Hollywood from 1966. His American films have been notable mainly for their surface visual style, rarely for substance.

FILMS: In Canada—*A Dangerous Age* (also prod., sc.) 1957; *A Cool Sound from Hell* (also prod., sc.) 1958. In the UK—*Dr. Blood's Coffin, The Snake Woman* 1960; *During One Night/Night of Passion* (also prod., sc.), *Three on a Spree, The Young Ones/Wonderful to Be Young!* 1961; *The Boys* (also prod.) 1962; *The Leather Boys, Wonderful Life/Swingers' Paradise* 1964; *The Ipcress File* 1965. In the US—*The Appaloosa* 1966; *The Naked Runner* (UK) 1967; *The Lawyer* (also co-sc.), *Little Fauss and Big Halsy* 1970; *Lady Sings the Blues* 1972; *Hit!* 1973; *Sheila Levine Is Dead and Living in New York* 1975; *Gable and Lombard* 1976; *The Boys in Company C* (also co-sc.) 1978; *The Entity* 1982; *Purple Hearts* (also prod., sc.) 1984; *Iron Eagle* (also co-sc.) 1986; *Superman IV: The Quest for Peace* 1987; *Iron Eagle II* (also co-sc.) 1988; *The Taking of Beverly Hills* (also co-story) 1991; *Ladybugs* 1992.

Furlong, Edward. Actor. *b.* August 2, 1977, Glendale, Calif. Youthful, intense young actor who debuted in the action-thriller *Terminator 2: Judgment Day* (1991), opposite Arnold SCHWARZENEGGER. His amazing versatility and commitment to develop his craft has enabled him to shine in a variety of roles.

FILMS: *Terminator 2: Judgment Day* 1991; *Pet Sematary II* 1992; *American Heart, Last Action Hero* 1993; *Brainscan, Little Odessa* 1994; *Before and After, The Grass Harp* 1996.

Furneaux, Yvonne. Actress. Born in 1928, in Lille, France. Brunette leading lady of British and continental films, often in exotic roles.

FILMS INCLUDE: *24 Hours in a Woman's Life/Affair in Monte Carlo, Meet Me Tonight/Tonight at 8:30* 1952; *The Master of Ballantrae, The Beggar's Opera* 1953; *Le Amiche/The Girl Friends* 1955; *The Dark Avenger/The Warriors, Lisbon* 1956; *The Mummy* 1969; *La Dolce Vita, Via Margutta, Le Comte De Monte-Cirsto/The Count of Monte Cristo* 1960; *I Lancieri Neri/Charge of the Black Lancers* 1961; *Io Semiramis/I Semiramis/Slave Queen of Babylon* 1962; *Le Meurtier/Enough Rope, Ii Criminals* 1963; *Repulsion* 1965; *Le Scandale/The Champagne Murders* 1966; *In Nome Del Popolo Italiano* 1972; *Frankenstein's Great Aunt Tillie* 1983.

Furness, Betty. Actress, consumer advocate. *b.* Elizabeth Mary Furness, on Jan. 3, 1916, in New York City. *d.* 1994. The daughter of radio pioneer and corporate executive George Furness, she was raised on Manhattan's Park Avenue and began modeling at 14 and appearing in films at 16. During the 30s she appeared in more than 30 Hollywood productions, playing leads in B pictures and second leads in some as well. In the early 40s she appeared in several Broadway shows. In 1949 she became TV's highest paid saleslady and for a decade pitched the merits of Westinghouse refrigerators on the air. In 1967 she was appointed President Johnson's Special Assistant for Consumer Affairs and later functioned as Chairman of New York State's Consumer Protection Board and Commissioner of New York City's Department of Consumer Affairs. She also wrote a consumer advocacy column for a leading magazine and in 1974 became Consumer Affairs Director for NBC's flagship TV station in New York, WNBC. She was a weekly contributor to NBC's 'The Today Show' and in 1988 hosted an informational chat spot called 'Betty's Attic.' She parted ways with NBC in 1992. Her first husband was song-writer Johnny GREEN and her third is CBS News executive Leslie Midgley.

FILMS INCLUDE: *Renegades of the West* 1932; *The Great Jasper, Cross Fire, Emergency Call, Professional Sweetheart, Midshipman Jack* 1933; *Beggars in Ermine, Gridiron Flash, The Band Plays On, A Wicked Woman* 1934; *Shadow of Doubt, McFadden's Flats, The Keeper of the Bees* 1935; *Magnificent Obsession, The Three Wise Guys, Swing Time, Mr. Cinderella, All-American Chump, The President's Mystery* 1936; *They Wanted to Marry, Fair Warning, Good Old Soak, It Can't Last Forever* 1937; *North of Shanghai* 1939.

Furse, Roger K. Art director. *b.* Sept. 11, 1903, Ightham, England. *d.* 1972. The son of Lieutenant General Sir William Furse, he was educated at Eton and at the Slade School for Fine Arts. After working as a portrait painter and a commercial artist in Paris, New York, and Philadelphia, he began designing sets for the London theater in the early 30s. He later rose to prominence through his long association with Sir Laurence OLIVIER as set designer of the latter's Shakespearean productions at the Old Vic and as art director of several of Olivier's films. He won an Academy Award for the sets of *Hamlet* (1948). His wife, Margaret Furse (1911–74), was a noted costume designer whose credits included such films as *Oliver Twist* (1948), *The Mudlark* (1951), *Becket* (1964), *The Lion in Winter* (1965), *Anne of the Thousand Days* (1969), and *Mary Queen of Scots* (1972). She was nominated for Oscars for the last five.

FILMS INCLUDE: *Henry V* (costumes only), *The True Glory* 1945; *Odd Man Out* 1947; *Hamlet* 1948; *Under Capricorn* (costumes only) 1949; *Ivanhoe* 1952; *Knights of the Round Table* (costumes only) 1953; *Richard III* 1956; *The Prince and the Show Girl, Saint Joan* 1957; *Bonjour Tristesse* 1958; *The Roman Spring of Mrs. Stone* 1961; *The Road to Hong Kong* 1962.

Furst, Anton. Production designer. *b.* Anthony Francis Furst in 1944 in Britain. *d.* 1991. *ed.* Royal College of Art. Highly imaginative designer best known for his dark and foreboding view of Gotham City in *Batman*. Originally an architect, he left the profession to design laser-light programs for rock concerts, and began film design work in Hollywood in the 1980s. At the height of his fame, he committed suicide.

FILMS INCLUDE: *Lady Chatterley's Lover, An Unsuitable Job for a Woman* 1981; *The Company of Wolves, The Frog Prince* 1985; *Full Metal Jacket* 1987; *High Spirits* 1988; *Batman* (Academy Award) 1989; *Awakenings* 1990.

Furthman, Jules. Screenwriter. *b.* Julius Grinnell Furthmann, Mar. 5, 1888, Chicago. *d.* 1960. *ed.* Northwestern. A former magazine and newspaper writer, he began submitting stories for films in 1915. A screenwriter from 1918, he used the pseudonym Stephen Fox, and occasionally Jules or Julius Grinnell, until 1920 because of the German sound of his real name. For the next 40 years Furthman wrote numerous screenplays, alone or in collaboration, working for directors with such divergent styles and temperaments as Josef von Sternberg and Howard Hawks. His brother, Charles Furthman (*b.* Oct. 3, 1884, Chicago. *d.* 1936), was also a screenwriter of some note.

FILMS INCLUDE: *Steady Company* (story only) 1915; *Souls in Pawn* 1917; *Up Romance Road, Japanese Nightingale* 1918; *Where the West Begins, Brass Buttons, A Sporting Chance, Victory* 1919; *Treasure Island, White Circle, The Great Redeemer, Land of Jazz* (also dir.), *The Texan* 1920; *The Big Punch, The Blushing Bride* (also dir.), *Colorado Pluck* (also dir.) 1921; *Arabian Love, The Love Gambler* 1922; *North of Hudson Bay, St. Elmo, The Acquittal* 1923; *Try and Get It* 1924; *Any Woman* 1925; *Hotel Imperial, Casey at the Bat, Fashions for Women* (co-adapt. only), *Barbed Wire, The Way of All Flesh, Underworld* (adapt. only), *The City Gone Wild* 1927; *The Dragnet, The Docks of New York* 1928; *Abie's Irish Rose, The Case of Lena Smith, Thunderbolt, New York Nights* 1929; *Common Clay, Renegades, Morocco* 1930; *Body and Soul, Yellow Ticket* 1931; *Shanghai Express, Blonde Venus* 1932; *Bombshell* 1933; *China Seas, Mutiny on the Bounty* 1935; *Come and Get It* 1936; *Spawn of the North* 1938; *Only Angels Have Wings* 1939; *The Shanghai Gesture* (co-adapt. only) 1941; *The Outlaw* 1943; *To Have and Have Not* 1944; *The Big Sleep, Moss Rose* 1946; *Nightmare Alley* 1947; *Peking Express* (adapt. only), *Jet Pilot* (also prod.) 1957; *Rio Bravo* 1959.

Fusco, Giovanni. Composer. *b.* Oct. 10, 1906, Sant' Agata dei Goti, Italy. *d.* 1968. A graduate of Rome's Santa Cecilia Academy. He began composing for the Italian screen in 1936. His scores for ANTONIONI from the early 50s to the mid-60s, at once discreet and evocative, are noted for their judicious instrumentation and compatibility with each film's theme and mood.

FILMS INCLUDE: *Il Cammino degli Eroi* (doc.) 1936; *Cronaca di un Amore/Story of a Love Affair* 1950; *La Signora senza Camelie/Camille Without Camellias, I Vinti* 1953; *Le Amiche/The Girl Friends* 1955; *Il Grido/The Outcry* 1957; *Hiroshima mon Amour* (co-music; Fr./Jap.) 1959; *L'Avventura, Il Rossetto/Lipstick* 1960; *L'Eclisse/Eclipse* 1962; *Deserto Rosso/Red Desert, Gli Indifferenti/Time of Indifference* 1964; *La Guerre est finie/The War Is Over* (Fr./Swed.) 1966; *Il Giorno della Civetta/Mafia* 1968.

f.x. Abbreviation used in scripts to denote effects (SOUND EFFECTS, SPECIAL EFFECTS, ETC.).

G

G. See RATING.

Gaal, Franciska (also **Franceska, Franziska**). Actress. *b.* Fanny Zilveritch, Feb. 1, 1904, Budapest. *d.* 1972. One of the most popular cabaret and stage performers in Central Europe between the World Wars, she also played lighthearted heroines in Hungarian, Austrian, and German romantic films of the early 30s. In 1938 she was brought to Hollywood with great fanfare by Cecil B. De Mille as the star of *The Buccaneer* and subsequently appeared in two other American films. In 1940 she returned to Budapest to visit her ailing mother and found herself trapped there for the duration of WW II. Miss Gaal, who had appeared sporadically on Broadway beginning in 1927, returned briefly to the New York stage in 1951, replacing Eva Gabor in 'The Happy Time.'

FILMS INCLUDE: *Fräulein Paprika* (Ger.) 1932; *Gruss und Kuss Veronika* (Ger.), *Skandal in Budapest* (Ger./Hung.) 1933; *Früchten/Csibi* (Aus./Hung.) 1934; *Spring Parade* (Hung.) 1935; *Katharina* (Aus.) 1936; *The Buccaneer* (US) 1938; *Paris Honeymoon* (US), *The Girl Downstairs* (US) 1939; *Fräulein Lilly* (Aus.) 1950.

Gaál, István. Director. Born on Aug. 25, 1933, in Salgotarjan, Hungary. An electrician's son, he trained to become an electrotechnician but opted for films instead and enrolled at Budapest's Academy of Dramatic and Cinematographic Arts. Graduating from the directing class in 1959, he was awarded an Italian State scholarship to the Centro Sperimentale in Rome, in recognition of his diploma work, *Surfacemen* (1957), a short about railroad workers. While in Rome, Gaál was employed as assistant to Italian directors and directed another short, *Etude* (1959). Back in Budapest, he directed three additional shorts before turning out his first feature film in 1964. Despite his meager output quantitatively, he has proved himself one of the outstanding talents of the new Hungarian cinema, a sensitive and versatile filmmaker and a keen observer of his country's social scene. He always writes his own scripts and edits his own films.

FEATURE FILMS: *Current* 1964; *The Green Years* 1965; *Baptism* 1967; *The Falcons* 1970; *Dead Landscape* 1971; *Legato/Ties* 1978; *Buffer Zone* 1981; *Orpheus and Eurydice* 1985.

Gabel, Martin. Actor. *b.* June 19, 1912, Philadelphia. *d.* 1986. *ed.* Lehigh U.; AADA. On Broadway from 1933, he appeared in several productions of Orson Welles's Mercury Theater company. In occasional films from the early 50s, he played character roles of a wide range, from comic to sinister. He also directed a solid dramatic film, *The Lost Moment* (1947), starring Robert Cummings and Susan Hayward, as well as a good number of Broadway plays. He co-produced several successful stage productions, including Broadway's hit play 'Life with Father.' He hosted the early TV quiz show 'With This Ring' (1951) and was a frequent panelist on 'What's My Line?' on which actress Arlene Francis (*b.* Oct. 20, 1908, Boston), his wife from 1946, was featured regularly.

FILMS: *The Lost Moment* (dir. only) 1947; *14 Hours, M* 1951; *Deadline USA, The Thief* 1952; *Tip on a Dead Jockey* 1957; *Marnie* 1964; *Lord Love a Duck* 1966; *Divorce American Style* 1967; *Lady in Cement* 1968; *There Was a Crooked Man* 1970; *The Front Page* 1974; *The First Deadly Sin* 1980.

Gabin, Jean. Actor. *b.* Jean-Alexis Moncorgé, May 17, 1904, Mériel, France. *d.* 1976. The son of café entertainers, he started out at age 14 as a laborer, but at 19 gave in to his father's urging and entered show business as a dancer with the Folies-Bergère. Played supporting parts in music halls and operettas before returning to the Folies as Mistinguette's leading man. He made his film debut in 1930, first rose to prominence in Duvivier's *Maria Chapdelaine* (1934), and subsequently established himself as a forceful screen personality, "the tragic hero of contemporary cinema," in the words of André Bazin. In the late 30s Gabin gained an international reputation as the strong, silent, and often deeply human hero, and more often, anti-hero, of such milestones of the French cinema as Duvivier's *Pépé le Moko,* Renoir's *La Grande Illusion,* and Carné's *Port of Shadows.* The quintessential Gabin role was that of an earthy loner, an outsider, usually a courageous, independent-minded member of the bourgeois or working class. But he also played a variety of other roles, ranging from hobo to tycoon.

During the Occupation, Gabin found refuge in Hollywood, but his two American films were flat and disappointing. After a period of adjustment in the mid-40s, Gabin had regained his stature as a leading figure of the French cinema by 1950. Instead of the young man of common origins he had typically played in prewar films, he now portrayed experienced, successful middle-aged men of confidence and authority. In 1963 he and FERNANDEL formed their own production company, Gafer Films. Gabin's 40-year career as a leading star has made him a national institution in France and one of the best known screen personalities the world over.

FILMS INCLUDE: *Chacun sa Chance* 1930; *Méphisto* 1931; *Paris-Beguin* 1932; *Adieux les Beaux Jours* 1933; *Maria Chapdelaine, Zouzou* 1934; *Golgotha, La Bandera/Escape from Yesterday* 1935; *La Belle Equipe/They Were Five, Les Bas-Fonds/The Lower Depths* 1936; *Pépé le Moko* (title role), *La Grande Illusion/Grand Illusion, Gueule d'Amour* 1937; *Quai des Brumes/Port of Shadows, La Bête humaine/The Human Beast* 1938; *Le Jour se lève/Daybreak* 1939; *Remorques/Stormy Waters* (release delayed from 1939) 1941; *Moontide* (US) 1942; *The Impostor* (US) 1944; *Martin Roumagnac/The Room Upstairs* 1946; *Au-delà des Grilles/La Mura di Malapaga/The Walls of Malapaga* 1949; *La Marie du Port* 1950; *La Nuit est mon Royaume/The Night Is My Kingdom* 1951; *Le Plaisir, La Minute de Vérité/The Moment of Truth* 1952; *Touchez pas au Grisbi/Grisbi, L'Air de Paris* 1954; *Le Port du Désir/The House on the Waterfront, Napoléon, French Cancan/Only the French Can, Razzia sur la Chnouf/Razzia, Gas-Oil* 1955; *Voici le Temps des Assassins/Deadlier Than the Male, La Traversée de Paris/Four Bags Full, Crime et Châtiment/Crime and Punishment* 1956; *Le Cas du Docteur Laurent/The Case of Dr. Laurent, Le Rouge est mis/Speaking of Murder* 1957; *Les Misérables* (as Jean Valjean), *Maigret tend un Piège/Inspector Maigret* (title role), *Le Désordre de la Nuit/Night Affair, En Cas de Malheur/Love Is My Profession, Les Grandes Familles/The Possessors* 1958; *Archimède le Clochard/The Magnificent Tramp* (also original idea), *Rue de Prairies/Rue de Paris* 1959; *Le Baron de l'Ecluse* 1960; *Le Président, Le Cave se rebiffe/The Counterfeiters of Paris/Money Money Money* 1961; *Un Singe en Hiver/A Monkey in Winter* 1962; *Mélodie en Sous-Sol/Any Number Can Win* 1963; *Monsieur* 1964; *L'Age ingrat* 1965; *Du Rififi à Paname/The Upper Hand* 1966; *Le Soleil des Voyous/Action Man/Leather and Nylon* 1967; *Le Clan des Siciliens/The Sicilian Clan* 1969; *Le Chat/The Cat, Le Drapeau noir flotte sur la Marmite* 1971; *Le Tueur* 1972; *L'Affaire Dominici, Deux Hommes dans la Ville/Two Against the Law* 1973; *Le Testament/The Verdict/Jury of One* 1975; *L'Année Sainte* 1976.

Gable, Clark. Actor. *b.* William Clark Gable, Feb. 1, 1901, Cadiz, Ohio. *d.* 1960. The son of a farmer-turned-oil-driller, he left school and home at 14 to work in a tire factory in nearby Akron. There he saw his first play and began working evenings backstage as a call boy for no pay. He was just beginning to play bit parts with the stock company when his father took him along to the Oklahoma oil fields. Reluctantly, he drilled for oil while dreaming of the theater. When he reached 21 he left his father and joined a traveling troupe. Stranded penniless in Oregon, he worked at lumberjacking and selling ties, among other odd jobs, before joining another traveling company. The troupe was headed by a veteran actress, Josephine Dillon, who took a personal interest in coaching the young Gable, 14 years her junior. Late in 1924 they were married and settled in Hollywood, where Gable was able to get occasional extra jobs in films, in Lubitsch's *Forbidden Paradise* (1924) and Von Stroheim's *The Merry Widow* (1925), for example.

Unable to get any further in movies, Gable separated from his wife (they divorced in 1930) and went on the road with touring stage companies. In 1928 he made it to Broadway, playing a romantic lead in *Machinal.* Another Broadway play, *Love Honor and Obey* (1930), in which he co-starred with Alice Brady, led to an engagement as the lead in the Los Angeles production of *The Last Mile.* Lionel Barrymore, with whom he had played on the road, arranged for a screen test at MGM. But Gable was turned down by the studio. Finally an agent persuaded Pathé to cast him in the role of the villain in a William Boyd Western, *The Painted Desert* (1931). Before the year was out, he was signed by MGM, and following a succession of supporting parts, often as a brute or a gangster, he was a promising new star. The film that clinched it for Gable was *A Free Soul,* in which he played a secondary role to Leslie Howard but stole the show and delighted audiences by pushing Norma Shearer around. Immediately after, he won the lead opposite Greta Garbo in *Susan Lennox: Her Fall and Rise* and opposite Joan Crawford in *Possessed.* That year, 1931, was a long and eventful one in Gable's life. Not only did he appear in a dozen films and entrench himself as a top MGM leading man, but he also married his second wife, Rhea Langham, a wealthy Texas socialite, 17 years his senior.

Over the next three years, Gable developed into a steady moneymaking star in the MGM stable, with such films as *Red Dust* and *Strange Interlude* to his credit, along with several routine vehicles. But it was at Columbia in 1934 that he scored his greatest triumph to date. Louis B. Mayer decided to loan him out for what was considered a minor project at Columbia—Frank Capra's *It Happened One Night.* Gable resisted the "demotion" but finally accepted the role, reluctantly, as did his co-star, Claudette Colbert. They both won Academy Awards.

Gable's popularity continued to rise throughout the 30s. A man's man and a woman's dreamboat, his name became synonymous with virility and sex appeal. By the end of the decade he was known in Hollywood and by film audiences as "The King."

About the only bad year Gable had in the decade was 1937; he was disastrously miscast in *Parnell* and was sued by an Englishwoman who charged he had fathered her 13-year-old daughter while he was visiting England in 1923. But he was able to prove that he was in Oregon at the time and made up for his failure in *Parnell* with a string of subsequent successes.

Separated since 1935 from his second wife, Gable was seeing much of actress Carole LOMBARD, who had divorced William Powell. She and Gable were married in 1939, shortly after his divorce, when he was in the midst of playing the most important role of his career—Rhett Butler in *Gone With the Wind.* To get Gable, producer David O. Selznick had had to take MGM as partner on the project, at an estimated cost of $25 million of the profits. But the gamble paid off handsomely. The film went on to become the greatest box-office attraction of all time and Gable as Butler was among its principal draws.

Gable's marriage to Lombard was soon considered one of the happiest in Hollywood. But tragedy struck in January of 1942: the plane on which Carole was returning from a War Bond drive crashed into a mountain, killing everyone aboard. Shortly after, the bereaved Gable joined the Air Force. He rose in rank from lieutenant to major and received the Distinguished Flying Cross and Air Medal for flying several bombing missions over Germany. He returned to the screen in 1945, in *Adventure.*

He gained weight, his age was beginning to tell, his nerves seemed to be shattered, and his popularity was slowly fading away. He took to drinking and was frequently shaking in front of the cameras. He remarried twice, first Lady Sylvia Ashley (1904–77) in 1949, and then Kay Spreckels in 1955. His MGM contract, which had expired in 1954, wasn't renewed. To film fans he was still the King, but as his kingdom, Hollywood, was dying, so was its monarch. He did his best postwar acting, and perhaps the best of his career in John Huston's *The Misfits* but did not live to see the good reviews. The strain of the production, in which he insisted on doing his own stunts, took its toll. He suffered a heart attack, and on November 16, 1960, he died. He also did not live to see his first and only child, John Clark, born to Kay Gable shortly after the King's death. John Clark Gable, a dead ringer for Kevin COSTNER, made his screen debut in *Bad Jim* (1990).

FILMS: As extra—*Forbidden Paradise, White Man* 1924; *Declasée/The Social Exile, The Peacemakers* (serial), *The Merry Widow, The Plastic Age* 1925; *North Star, The Johnstown Flood* 1926. As actor—*The Painted Desert, The Easiest Way, Dance Fools Dance, The Secret Six, The Finger Points, Laughing Sinners, A Free Soul, Night Nurse, Sporting Blood, Susan Lenox: Her Fall and Rise, Possessed, Hell Divers* 1931; *Polly of the Circus, Red Dust, Strange Interlude, No Man of Her Own* 1932; *The White Sister, Hold Your Man, Night Flight, Dancing Lady* 1933; *It Happened One Night, Men in White, Manhattan Melodrama, Chained, Forsaking All Others* 1934; *After Office Hours, The Call of the Wild* (as Jack Thornton), *China Seas, Mutiny on the Bounty* (as Fletcher Christian) 1935; *Wife vs. Secretary, San Francisco, Cain and Mabel, Love on the Run* 1936; *Parnell* (title role), *Saratoga* 1937; *Test Pilot, Too Hot to Handle* 1938; *Idiot's Delight, Gone With the Wind* (as Rhett Butler) 1939; *Strange Cargo, Boom Town, Comrade X* 1940; *They Met in Bombay, Honky Tonk* 1941; *Somewhere I'll Find You* 1942; *Adventure* 1945; *The Hucksters* 1947; *Homecoming, Command Decision* 1948; *Any Number Can Play* 1949; *Key to the City, To Please a Lady* 1950; *Across the Wide Missouri, Callaway Went That-away* (cameo) 1951; *Lone Star* 1952; *Never Let Me Go, Mogambo* (remake of *Red Dust*) 1953; *Betrayed* 1954; *Soldier of Fortune, The Tall Men* 1955; *The King and Four Queens* 1956; *Band of Angels* 1957; *Run Silent Run Deep, Teacher's Pet* 1958; *But Not for Me* 1959; *It Started in Naples* 1960; *The Misfits* 1961.

Gabor, Eva. Actress. *b.* Feb. 11, 1921, in Budapest. *d.* 1995. A former café singer and ice skater, she is the youngest of the glamorous GABOR sisters and the first to arrive in the US, in the late 30s. She had been appearing in Hollywood films since the early 40s, but it was on Broadway, in 'The Happy Time' (1950), that she achieved stardom. In the late 60s she became nationally popular in the TV comedy series 'Green Acres' (1965–71). Autobiography: *Orchids and Salamis* (1951).

FILMS INCLUDE: *Forced Landing* 1941; *A Royal Scandal* 1945; *The Wife of Monte Cristo* 1946; *Song of Surrender* 1949; *Paris Model* 1953; *The Mad Magician, The Last Time I Saw Paris* 1954; *Artists and Models* 1955; *My Man Godfrey, Don't Go Near the Water* 1957; *Gigi, The Truth About Women* 1958; *It Started with a Kiss,* 1959; *Love Island* 1960; *A New Kind of Love* 1963; *Youngblood Hawke* 1964; *The Aristocats* (v/o) 1970; *The Rescuers* (v/o) 1977; *The Princess Academy* 1987.

Gabór, Pál. Director. *b.* 1932, Budapest. *d.* 1987. Following studies at the University of Budapest and an art school, he became a teacher. Around 1960 he joined the newly formed Béla Balázs Studio, the experimental breeding ground for Hungary's new generation of filmmakers. He soon distingushed himself as one of the most talented of the group with several features centering on moral topics. However, he was little known internationally before the release of his *Angi Vera* (1979), a subdued yet searing indictment of the moral corruption and oppressive intellectual climate of totalitarian society. The film shared the International Critics Prize at Cannes, in the noncompeting category. He usually wrote his own scripts, alone or in collaboration.

FILMS INCLUDE: *Forbidden Ground* 1968; *Horizon* 1971; *Journey with Jacob* 1972; *Angi Vera* 1979; *Brady's Escape* (Hun./US) 1984; *The Bride Was Radiant* (Hun./It.) 1986.

Gabor, Zsa Zsa. Actress. Born Sari Gabor, on Feb. 6, 1918, in Budapest. Sister of Eva GABOR. Made her stage debut in Vienna at 15 and was Miss Hungary in 1936. In the US since 1941, she is famous more for many jewels and husbands (including George SANDERS and hotelier Conrad Hilton) than for acting achievements. The recipient of expensive gifts from General Rafael Trujillo, she was called by a congressman "the most expensive courtesan since Madame de Pompadour." She is one of the most glamorous women in America, and her film roles have been mostly decorative. A frequent sharp-tongued guest on TV talk shows, she has also appeared on the stage in stock and in 1970 starred in Broadway's 'Forty Carats.' In 1990 she recaptured headlines when she spent three days in jail for slapping a traffic cop in a highly publicized incident. She collaborated on an autobiography, *Zsa Zsa Gabor: My Story* (1960) and wrote *Zsa Zsa's Complete Guide to Men* (1969) and *How to Get a Man, How to Keep a Man, and How to Get Rid of a Man* (1971) before her 1991 autobiography, *One Lifetime Is Not Enough.*

FILMS INCLUDE: *Lovely to Look At, Moulin Rouge* 1952; *The Story of Three Loves, Lili* 1953; *Three Ring Circus* 1954; *Death of a Scoundrel* 1956; *The Girl in the Kremlin* 1957; *Touch of Evil, Queen of Outer Space* 1958; *Pepe* 1960; *Boys' Night Out* 1962; *Picture Mommy Dead, Arrivederci Baby* 1966; *Jack of Diamonds* 1967; *Up the Front* (UK) 1972; *Johann Strauss—Der König ohne Krone* (Aus./Ger./Fr.) 1986; *A Nightmare on Elm Street 3: Dream Warriors* 1987; *Happily Ever After* (v/o) 1990.

Gad, Urban. Director. *b.* Feb. 12, 1879, Korsor, Denmark. *d.* 1947. A pioneer of Danish cinema and one of the leading figures in that country's "golden age" prior to WW I, he enjoyed great success with films starring Asta NIELSEN, whom he discovered in 1910, married in 1912, and divorced in 1918. Gad also worked frequently in Germany (1912–22), where his films provided the model for some of the early productions of the expressionist movement of the 20s. He often wrote his own scripts. Author: *Filmen: Dens Midler op Maal* (1919).

FILMS INCLUDE: *Afgrunden/The Abyss* 1910; *Gypsy Blood, Hulda Rasmussen, The Woman Always Pays, Sins of the Children, The Power of Gold, Till Death* 1911; *Der Totentanz, Nina, Wenn die Maske fällt, Das Mädchen ohne Vaterland, Die arme Jenny, Komedianten* 1912; *Der Tod in Sevilla, Die Suffragette, Die Filmprimadonna, Engelein* 1913; *Das Kind ruft, Das Feuer, Zapatas Bande, Cinderella* 1914; *Weissen Rosen* 1915; *Die ewige Nacht* 1916; *Die Kleptomanin, Die neue Dalila, Der Schmuck des Rajah* 1918; *Der Breite Weg, Das Spiel von Liebe und Tod* 1919; *Christian Wahnschaffe, Weltbrand* 1921; *Henneles Himmelfahrt* 1922; *The Gay Huskies* 1926.

gaffer. The chief electrician on a film unit, responsible for the lighting of a set under instructions from the DIRECTOR OF PHOTOGRAPHY. Under his supervision the electrical crew positions the appropriate lamps before and during a shooting session.

gagman. A writer who specializes in the creation of jokes, visual as well as verbal. Gag writers were an essential part of the production team in the silent comedy era in Hollywood.

Gahagan, Helen. Actress, singer, politician. *b.* Nov. 25, 1900, Boonton, N.J. *d.* 1980. *ed.* Barnard Coll. Broadway leading lady and opera singer of the 20s and 30s who starred (memorably) in only one film, *She* (1935), in which she aged on the screen from a beautiful young woman to a 500-year-old wretch. She later went into politics and was twice elected to the US House of Representatives, serving as a Democratic congresswoman from the 14th District in California from 1945 to 1949. In 1950, however, she was defeated by Richard Nixon in her bid for a Senate seat. She was the author of *The Eleanor Roosevelt We Remember* (1963). Married from 1931 to actor Melvyn DOUGLAS, she was formally known as Helen Gahagan Douglas.

Gainsborough Pictures. See Léon GAUMONT and Sir Michael BALCON.

Gale, Bob. Screenwriter. Born in 1951, in St. Louis, Mo. A product of the film school of USC, he began a productive and highly profitable collaboration with fellow graduate Robert ZEMECKIS, at first for TV, then on feature films, with the latter usually directing and Gale writing and sometimes also producing.

FILMS: *I Wanna Hold Your Hand* (also assoc.-prod.) 1978; *1941* 1979; *Used Cars* (also prod.) 1980; *Back to the Future* (also co-prod.) 1985; *Back to the Future II* (also co-prod.) 1989; *Back to the Future III* (also co-prod.) 1990; *Looters* 1992; *Mr. Panback, The Underneath* 1995; *Tales from the Crypt: Bordello of Blood* 1996.

Galeen, Henrik. German screenwriter, director, and actor of Dutch or Czech origin. 1882. *d.* 1949. A former journalist and stage actor, he entered German films as actor in 1910. As screenwriter and director from 1914, he played an important part in steering German cinema in the direction of fantasy and horror and toward expressionism. Emigrated to the US in 1933 after the Nazi rise to power but made no American films and disappeared from public view.

FILMS INCLUDE: *Der Golem/The Golem* (co-dir. with Paul Wegener, sc., act.) 1914; *Peter Schlemihl* (co-sc., act.) 1915; *Der verbotene Weg* (dir., sc.), *Judith Trachtenberg* (dir., sc.), *Der Golem—wie er in die Welt Kam/The Golem* (co-sc.) 1920; *Nosferatu—eine Symphonie des Grauens/Nosferatu the Vampire* (sc.) 1922; *Stadt in Sicht* (dir., sc.) 1923; *Die Liebesbriefe der Baronin von S.* (dir., co-sc.), *Das Wachsfigurenkabinett/Waxworks/The Three Way Works* (sc.) 1924; *Zigano—der Brigant vom Monte Diavolo* (sc., act.) 1925; *Der Student von Prag/The Student of Prague/The Man Who Cheated Life* (dir., co-sc.) 1926; *Alraune* (dir., sc.), *Sein grösster Bluff* (co-dir. with Harry Piel) 1927; *After the Verdict* (dir.; UK) 1929; *Schatten der Unterwelt* (sc.) 1931; *Salon Dora Green* (dir.) 1933.

Gallagher, Peter. Actor. Born Aug. 19, 1955, Armonk, N.Y. Intense, brooding leading man of the American stage and screen. He began acting with Boston-area theater troupes while studying at Tufts University. After graduating in 1977 he appeared in the Broadway rivivals of 'Hair' and 'Grease,' later receiving a Tony nomination for 'Long Day's Journey Into Night.' He made his film debut in the role of a pop star in *The Idolmaker* (1980) and attracted wide notice as the yuppie husband in *sex, lies, and videotape* (1989) before his breakthrough role as a sleazy Hollywood studio executive in Robert ALTMAN's *The Player* (1992). A prolific actor in the late 80s and early 90s, he has been featured in TV miniseries ('An Inconvenient Woman') and telefilms as well as starring in the 1992 revival of 'Guys and Dolls' on Broadway, receiving a Tony nomination for the latter.

FILMS: *The Idolmaker* 1980; *Summer Lovers* 1982; *Dream Child* 1985; *My Little Girl* 1986; *High Spirits* 1988; *sex, lies, and videotape* 1989; *Tune in Tomorrow* 1990; *Late for Dinner* 1991; *Short Cuts, Malice, Watch It* 1993; *The Hudsucker Proxy, Mother's Boys, Mrs. Parker and the Vicious Circle* 1994; *While You Were Sleeping* 1995; *Last Dance, To Gillian on Her 37th Birthday* 1996; *Café Society* 1997.

Gallagher, Richard ("Skeets"). Actor. *b.* July 28, 1891, Terre Haute, Ind. *d.* 1955. Abandoned law studies for a long career as a song-and-dance man in vaudeville. He appeared in some 50 feature films and many shorts from the mid-20s, typically in lightweight second leads and supporting roles, sometimes in leads.

FILMS INCLUDE: *The Daring Years* 1923; *The Potters, New York, For the Love of Mike* 1927; *Alex the Great, The Racket, Stocks and Blondes* 1928; *Close Harmony, Fast Company, Pointed Heels* 1929; *Honey, The Social Lion, Love Among the Millionaires, Let's Go Native, Her Wedding Night* 1930; *It Pays to Advertise, Up Pops the Devil, Possessed* 1931; *The Trial of Vivienne Ware, Merrily We Go to Hell, The Night Club Lady, Bird of Paradise, The Conquerors, The Unwritten Law* 1932; *Easy Millions, Too Much Harmony, Alice in Wonderland* (as the White Rabbit) 1933; *Riptide, The Meanest Gal in Town* 1934; *The Perfect Clue* 1935; *Yours for the Asking, Polo Joe* 1936; *Espionage* 1937; *Idiot's Delight* 1939; *Brother Orchid* 1942; *The Duke of Chicago* 1949; *Three for Bedroom C* 1952.

Gallo, Mario. Director. *b.* July 31, 1878, Barletta, Italy. *d.* 1945, Buenos Aires. The father of Argentine cinema, he directed the first Argentine story-film, *El Fusillamiento de Dorrego* (1908), and other early silents.

FILMS INCLUDE: *El Fusillamiento de Dorrego* 1908; *Juan Moreira* 1909; *Revoluciòn de Mayo, Muerte Civil* 1910; *Balata de Maipó, Tierra baja* 1911.

Gallone, Carmine. Director. *b.* Sept. 18, 1886, Taggia, Italy, to a Neapolitan father and French mother. *d.* 1973. He began writing poems and plays as a teenager and won a national prize for a poetry collection in 1911. He entered films as a screenwriter the following year and in 1913 began a prodigiously prolific career as director. Many of his early films were "society" melodramas, some of which starred "diva" Lyda Borelli or his own wife, Soava Gallone (b. 1880, Warsaw. *d.* 1957), as well as ambitious costume pageants. In the late 20s and early 30s, Gallone worked in France, Germany, Britain, and Poland, but was recalled to Italy by the Fascist regime to direct *Scipione l'Africano* (1937), an ambitious but not too successful history-propaganda film, rumored to have been written by Mussolini himself. Gallone did an about-face in 1946, however, exalting the anti-Fascist resistance in *Before Him All Rome Trembled/Tosca.* His postwar product consisted mainly of opera films and pseudohistoric spectacles.

FILMS INCLUDE: *Il Bacio di Cirano* 1913; *La Donna Nuda* 1914; *Avatar, Fior di Male, Marcia Nuziale, Redenzione* 1915; *Malombra, La Falena* 1916; *Storia dei Tredici* 1917; *La Figlie del Mare* 1919; *Amleto e il suo Clown* 1920; *Nemesis* 1921; *Marcella, La Figlia della Tempesta, Il Colonnello Chabert* 1922; *Il Corsaro, Amore, La Cavalcata Ardente, Tormenta* 1923; *La Fiammata* 1924; *Gli Ultimi Gironi di Pompei/The Last Days of Pompeii* 1926; *Celle qui domine* (Fr.) 1927; *Liebeshölle/L'Inferno dell'Amore/Pawns of Passion* (Ger./Pol.) 1928; *Das Land ohne Frauen/Terra senza Donne/Bride 68* (Ger.) 1929; *Die Singende Stadt* (Ger.) 1930; *Le Chant du Marin,* (Fr.) *The City of Song/Farewell to Love* (UK), *Un Soir de Rafle* (Fr.) 1931; *Un Fils d'Amérique, Le Roi des Palaces, Ma Cousine de Varsovie* (all Fr.) 1932; *Mein Herz ruft nach Dir/Mon Coeur t'appelle/My Heart Is Calling* (Ger./Fr./Eng. versions) 1934; *Casta Diva* 1935; *Im Sonnenschein/Opernring/Thank You Madame* (Aus.) 1936; *scipione l'Africano/Scipio Africanus* 1937; *Marionette, Giuseppe Verdi* 1938; *Il Sogno di Butterfly/The Dream of Butterfly, Manon Lescaut* 1939; *Oltre l'Amore, Melodie eterne/Eternal Melodies* 1940; *La Regina di Navarra, Primo Amore* 1941; *La Due Orfanelle/The Two Orphans, Odessa in Fiamme* 1942; *Tristi Amori* 1943; *Il Canto della Vita* 1945; *Davanti a lui Tremava tutta Roma/Before Him All Rome Trembled/Tosca* 1946; *Rigoletto, Addio Mimi/Her Wonderful Lie, La Signora delle Camelie/La Traviata/The Lost One* 1947; *La Leggenda di Faust/Faust and the Devil* 1948; *Il Trovatore* 1949; *La Forza del Destino, Taxi di Notte/Singing Taxi Driver* 1950; *Messalina/ The Affairs of Messalina* 1951; *Puccini* 1952; *Cavalleria Rusticana/Fatal Desire* 1953; *Casa Ricordi/House of Ricordi, Casta Diva, La Figlia di Mata Hari* 1954; *Madama Butterfly, Don Camillo e l'Onorevole Peppone* 1955; *Tosca, Michel Strogoff/Michael Strogoff* 1956; *Polijuschka* 1958; *Cartagine in Fiamme/Carthage in Flames* 1960; *Don Camillo Monsignore ma non troppo* 1961; *La Monaca di Monza, Carmen di Trastevere* 1962.

Gam, Rita. Actress. Born on Apr. 2, 1928, in Pittsburgh, of French-Rumanian descent. The daughter of a clothing manufacturer, she grew up in Manhattan and after semisuccessful stabs at Broadway (from 1948) and TV (1950), she broke into films in 1952, playing the female lead opposite Ray Milland in the nontalking sound film *The Thief.* A striking beauty, she was typecast by Hollywood in decorative roles and from the late 50s worked mostly in Europe. She won a Berlin Festival award for her performance in a 1962 version of Sartre's *No Exit.* She was back in Hollywood films in the early 70s, in supporting roles. In the early 80s she ventured into the making of documentary films. Formely married to director Sidney LUMET and publisher Thomas H. Guinzburg.

FILMS INCLUDE: *The Thief* 1952; *Night People, Saadia, Sign of the Pagan* 1954; *Mohawk, Magic Fire* 1956; *Sierra Baron* 1958; *Annibale/Hannibal* (It.) 1960; *King of Kings* 1961; *Huis clos/No Exit* (Arg./US) 1962; *Klute, Such Good Friends, Shoot-Out* 1971; *Law and Disorder* (cameo) 1974; *The Gardener/Seeds of Evil* 1975; *Midnight* 1989.

Gambon, Michael. Actor. Born Oct. 19, 1940, in Dublin, Ireland. Respected actor who gained experience on the British stage before playing the lead in the hallucinatory British television serial 'The Singing Detective' (1986–87). He then made a powerful impression as the crude, violent thief in Peter Greenaway's *The Cook, the Thief, His Wife and Her Lover.*

FILMS INCLUDE: *The Beast Must Die* 1974; *Turtle Diary* 1985; *Paris by Night* 1988; *The Cook the Thief His Wife and Her Lover, A Dry White Season, The Rachel Papers* 1989; *Mobsters* 1991; *Toys* 1992; *The Browning Version, Clean Slate, A Man of No Importance, A Warrior* 1994; *Last Dance, Mary Reilly, Two Deaths* 1996; *Innocent Sleep, Nothing Personal,* 1997.

Gance, Abel. Director. *b.* Eugène Alexandre Péréthon, Oct. 25, 1889, Paris. *d.* 1981. The illegitimate son of a prosperous physician, Abel Flamant, he was raised by his working-class mother, Françoise Péréthon, and her live-in boyfriend (and later husband), a mechanic named Adolphe Gance. Under pressure to pursue a legal career, he began his working life as a lawyer's clerk but was irresistibly drawn to the theater and at 19 made his stage debut in Brussels. Returning to Paris, he played his first screen role in *Molière* (1909). He followed this with minor roles in other French films, then began writing occasional screenplays. He was on the verge of starvation throughout this period and fell seriously ill with tuberculosis. In 1911 he recovered sufficiently to form a film production company with a group of friends and directed his first picture, *La Digue.* His early films were not very successful and he returned briefly to the stage. He wrote a five-hour-long play, 'Victoire de Samothrace,' in which the great Sarah Bernhardt agreed to appear. But WW I broke out and the premiere never took place.

Gance's ill health kept him out of the service and he began directing films, with growing success. Despite the box-office appeal of many of his films, he was constantly at odds with management over his propensity to experiment with film technique, especially the use of close-ups and tracking shots, which were deemed confusing techniques at the time. But by 1917 he was considered important enough as a director for his picture to appear ahead of the stars' in a film's title sequence. This was to become a personal trademark in all Gance's silent films. After achieving two enormous commercial and critical successes, *Mater Dolorosa* (1917) and *La Dixième Symphonie* (1918), he was mobilized into the dwindling ranks of the armed forces in the final months of WW I.

During these months Gance became obsessed with the idea of making an ambitious cinematic pacifist statement on the futility of war, entitled *J'accuse/I Accuse.* He was discharged from the service following a near-encounter with death at a poison gas factory, but at his own request he was redrafted so that he could shoot the battle scenes of *J'accuse* with real soldiers and under real fire. The three-hour film, setting a triangle melodrama against the background of the war, enjoyed enormous success all over Europe. Its newsreel-like battle scenes were nothing short of sensational and its pacifist message, the first reaction to the horrors of WW I in a major film, had a strong impact on audiences everywhere. Certain sequences in the film achieved great power from a technique of rapid cutting, which Gance was later to perfect in such films as *La Roue* and *Napoléon* and which were to have a profound effect on the work of such masters of the Soviet cinema as EISENSTEIN, PUDOVKIN, and DOVZHENKO.

The filming of *La Roue,* Gance's next picture after *J'accuse,* was beset with problems from the start. He had fallen in love with a Film d'Art secretary, Ida Danis, and following a divorce from his wife, he was living in Paris with Ida, when both were felled by a flu epidemic. Gance recovered and was able to continue his work in stages, but Ida died the day the film was completed, in April of 1929. Shortly after, his closest friend and the star of several of his films, Séverin Mars, also died. The bereaved Gance left the editing of *La Roue* unfinished and sailed to America "to escape from myself."

He did not like Hollywood and its film-factory atmosphere and turned down a Metro offer to direct at several thousand dollars a week. His only fond memory of the trip was D. W. Griffith's excited reaction to *J'accuse* during a special screening in New York. Returning to France, Gance finally cut the footage of *La Roue*. The film, a melodrama set against a rail-yard background and enriched by authentic atmosphere and a display of montage technique, was hailed as a masterpiece by European intellectuals.

Gance's greatest triumph and the summary of his genius was his superspectacular production of *Napoléon,* a film that incorporated everything that had been known before about cinema technique, and much more. Parts of the film were shot by a combination of three synchronized cameras and shown on a wide triple screen, achieving an effect not unlike that of Cinerama some 30 years later. The triptych effect, called Polyvision, added breadth and sweep to the film's action highlights, in which thousands of extras participated. Gance also shot some scenes in 3-D and in color but decided against their incorporation into the final print, fearing they might distract audiences from the film's content.

Napoléon is virtually a lexicon of the entire technical grammar of the silent screen. Its camera mobility was nothing short of phenomenal in the late 20s. For some scenes, Gance had his cameramen hand-hold their then heavy and bulky apparatus; for others, he suspended a camera from wires and strapped another to a galloping horse. The film was presented in its entirety (17 reels) in the triple-screen format in only eight European cities. MGM, which acquired the American distribution rights, would not release *Napoléon* in its intended format, believing that the introduction of the new triple-screen effect would only further complicate the confusion created during this period with the switch to sound. The picture was shown in the US in a drastically cut, jumbled version and its reception by the public was disastrous.

Napoléon was Gance's last great creative work. His films of the sound era were, for the most part, commercial ventures controlled by the studios. In 1934 he made another technical innovation, adding stereophonic sound effects to *Napoléon* with a system he called Pictographe.

Over the years, *Napoleon* was presented in various lengths and forms as a patchup homage to a mythological relic. In 1979, however, the film re-emerged in its original glory at the Telluride Festival in Colorado, thanks to a painstaking 25-year reconstructive effort by British director-scholar Kevin BROWNLOW. Audiences, paying opera-level prices, interrupted scenes with wild cheers as the film unreeled for about five hours, accompanied by live symphonic orchestras—in London (1980; with music by Carl DAVIS), later in New York's Radio City Music Hall (1981; with music by Carmine Coppola), and in other major cities. Gance lived just long enough to witness his monumental final triumph. Gance died two weeks after his 92nd birthday, 18 days after the New York gala premiere of *Napoléon.*

FILMS: As screenwriter (alone or in collaboration)—*Le Portrait de Mireille, Le Glas du Père Césaire, La Légende de l'Arc-en-Ciel* 1909; *Paganini, La Fin de Paganini, Le Crime de Grand-Pére, Le Roi des Parfums, L'Aluminte, L'Auberge rouge, La Tragigue Amour de Mona Lisa* 1910; *Cyrano et d'Assoucy, Un Clair de Lune sous Richelieu, L'Electrocouté* 1911; *Une Vengénce d'Edgar Poe, La Mort du Duc d'Enghien, La Conspiration des Drapeaux, La Pierre philosophe* 1912; *L'Infirmière* 1914; *Napoleon auf St. Helena* (Ger.) 1929; *Leître de Forges* (also supvr.) 1933; *La Dame aux Camélias* (also supvr.) 1934; *Lumière et l'Invention du Cinématographe* (doc.; also narr.) 1953; *La Reine Margot* 1954. As director-screenwriter —*La Digue ou Pour sauveur la Hollande* 1911; *Le Nègre blanc* (also act.), *Il y a des Pieds au Plafond, Le Masque d'Horreur* 1912; *Un Drame au Château d'Acre, La Folie du Docteur Tube, L'Enigme de Dix Heures, La Fleur des Ruines, L'Héroisme de Paddy, Strass et Compagnie* 1915; *Fioritures/La Source de Beauté, Le Fou de la Falaise, Ce que les Flots racontent, Le Périscope, Les Gaz mortels, Le Droit à la Vie* 1916; *Barberousse, La Zone de la Mort, Mater Dolorosa* 1917; *La Dixième Symphonie* 1928; *J'accuse/I Accuse* 1919; *En tournant La Roue* (doc.) 1922; *La Roue, Au Secours!* 1923; *Napoléon/ Napoléon vu par Abel Gance* (also act.) 1927; *Autour de Napoléon* (doc.), *Danses, Galops, Marines* (triptych demonstrations) 1928; *La Fin du Monde/The End of the World* (also act.) 1931; *Mater Dolorosa* (remake) 1932; *Poliche, Napoléon Bonaparte* (abridged sound version of *Napoléon* 1934; *Le Roman d'un Jeune Homme pauvre, Lucrèce Borgia/Lucrezia Borgia, Jérôme Perreau/The Queen and the Cardinal* 1935; *Un Grand Amour de Beethoven/The Life and Loves of Beethoven, Le Voleur de Femmes* 1936; *J'accuse/That They May Live* (remake) 1938; *Louise* 1939; *Le Paradis perdu/Four Flights to Love* 1940; *La Vénus aveugle* 1941; *Le Capitaine Fracasse* 1943; *Quatorze Juillet* (short) 1953; *La Tour de Nesles* 1955; *Magirama* 1956; *Austerlitz/Battle of Austerlitz* 1960; *Cyrano et d'Artagnan* 1963; *Bonaparte et la Revolution* (sound remake of silent *Napoléon)* 1971.

Ganz, Bruno. Actor. Born on Mar. 22, 1941, in Zurich. Leading man of German and international films. Following military service in Switzerland, he began performing on the Berlin stage and by the late 60s was well established as a matinée idol. On the screen from the early 60s, he rose to prominence after appearing in Eric Rohmer's German-French production *The Marquise of O.* (1976). He subsequently figured prominently in some major films of the New German Cinema and European coproductions.

FILMS INCLUDE: *Chikita* 1961; *Der sanfte Lauf* 1967; *Sommergäste, Die Marquise von O./The Marquise of O.* 1975; *Lumière, Die Wildente/The Wild Duck* 1976; *Der Amerikanische Freun/The American Friend, Die linkshändike Frau/The Left-Handed Woman* 1977; *Schwarz und Weiss wie Tage und Nächte/Black and White Like Day and Night, Messer im Kopf/ Knife in the Head, The Boys from Brazil* (US) 1978; *Nosferatu—Phantom der Nachts/Nosferatu—the Vampire* (as Jonathan Harker), *Oggetti Smarriti* 1979; *La Provinciale/The Girl from Lorraine, La Vera Storia della Signora delle Camelie/La Dame aux Camélias* 1981; *Die Fälschung/Circle of Deceit, Dans la Ville blanche/In the White City* 1982; *Der Himmel über Berlin/Les Ailes du Déir/Wings of Desire* 1987; *Strapless* 1990; *Far Away, So Close!* 1993; *Children of Nature* 1994; *Saint Ex* 1996.

Ganz, Lowell. American screenwriter known for soft-edged comedy-dramas often built on odd premises, and frequently co-written with Babaloo MANDEL. He has worked several times with director Ron HOWARD.

FILMS: *Nightshift* 1982; *Splash* 1984; *Spies Like Us* 1985; *Gung Ho* 1986; *Vibes* 1988; *Parenthood* 1989; *City Slickers*

1991; *Mr. Saturday Night, A League of Their Own* 1992; *City Slickers II: Legend of Curly's Gold, Greedy* 1994; *Forget Paris* 1995; *Multiplicity* 1996; *Father's Day* 1997.

garbage matte. In special effects, a MATTE used to block out areas of a shot containing unwanted objects, such as stage lights, wires, and equipment. The garbage matte is usually roughly constructed out of black paper, since it does not need the detail of a matte used to block out a specific object.

Garbo, Greta. Actress. *b.* Greta Louisa Gustafsson, Sept. 18, 1905, Stockholm. *d.* 1990. The daughter of an unskilled laborer of peasant stock who was often out of work, she grew up in poverty in one of the Swedish capital's shabbiest districts. When she was 13 her father died and the following year she began work as a lather girl in a barbershop. She next found employment as a salesgirl in a large department store. As one of the better looking employees, she was chosen to appear in a short publicity film sponsored by the store, *How Not to Dress* (1921). This led to another publicity short, for a bakery, *Our Daily Bread* (1922), and later that year to the feminine lead in a slapstick comedy film, *Peter the Tramp.* Encouraged by her modest success, she applied for and won a scholarship to the Royal Dramatic Theater training school and soon began playing small roles on the stage as part of her training.

It was at the school that she was discovered by Mauritz STILLER, a Russian-Jewish immigrant who, with Victor Sjöström (Seastrom), dominated the Swedish cinema during its "golden age." Stiller was looking for a young actress to play the second lead in his forthcoming film, *The Story of Gösta Berling.* Garbo was recommended, tested, and selected for the part. In the following few years, the aspiring young actress and her famous mentor were inseparable. He coached her tirelessly, introduced her to his social circle, and took charge of her personal affairs.

The four-hour-long *Gösta Berling's Saga,* known alternately in English as *The Legend of Gösta Berling, The Atonement of Gösta Berling,* and *The Story of Gösta Berling,* scored well with European critics and launched Garbo as a promising new screen personality. She was given the second feminine lead in G. W. Pabst's *The Street of Sorrow/The Joyless Street,* in which her rival-to-be, Marlene Dietrich, appeared as an extra.

In Europe on a talent hunt in 1924, MGM production chief Louis B. MAYER offered Stiller a contract to work in Hollywood. Reluctantly, Mayer was forced to accept the director's condition that his discovery, Greta Garbo, would also be put on the MGM payroll. Stiller and Garbo arrived in New York in the summer of 1925. Studio publicity was at a loss on the image they were supposed to give Garbo.

Not until they saw the daily rushes of Garbo's first MGM film, *The Torrent,* did studio brass realize what a prize possession they had signed. As soon as the camera began to grind, the big, awkward, phlegmatic girl with the stooped shoulders and droopy eyes would suddenly come to life, electrifying the entire production crew with her magnetic personality. Even before the film was concluded, Mayer offered her a revised contract at a higher salary. When the film was released, in February of 1926, the critical and popular acclamation was unanimous: a new superstar was born and the Garbo myth began.

Garbo's only regret was that her mentor was not part of her triumph. Stiller was assigned to direct her next American picture, *The Temptress,* but after constant clashes with MGM executives he was replaced in mid-production by Fred Niblo. Stiller went over to Paramount, where he directed several films, but soon was also at odds with his new employers and in 1927 sailed home to Sweden, where he died the following year.

Garbo successfully protected her private life from the scrutiny of the press and the public. But neither she nor John Gilbert, her co-star in *Flesh and the Devil,* could hide from the probing camera eye that there was more to their passionate embraces than just good acting. When they were teamed again, in the film *Love* (1927), an adaptation of Tolstoy's *Anna Karenina,* the advertisements slyly read: "Garbo and Gilbert in *Love.*" But the ever elusive Garbo, tiring of the overbearing romantic bravado of the impulsive Gilbert, put an end to the affair in 1929. Over the years, she was reported nearly marrying director Rouben Mamoulian, conductor Leopold Stokowski, and nutrition expert Gaylord Hauser.

Of all the stars who have ever fired the imagination of film audiences, none has quite projected a magnetism and a mystique equal to Garbo's. Mysterious, unattainable, and ever-changing, she appealed to both male and female audiences. On the screen, as off, she represented a remote figure of loveliness—aloof, enigmatic, craving to be alone.

The publicity department put her on a high pedestal. When she appeared in her first talkie, *Anna Christie* (1930), the slogan "Garbo Talks!" filled much advertising space. When she appeared in her first comedy, *Ninotchka* (1939), the ads screamed: "Garbo Laughs!" The less communicative she became, the more the public clamored to hear about her and the more publicity obliged.

Garbo was twice named best actress by the New York film critics, for *Anna Karenina* in 1935 and for *Camille* in 1937. Amazingly, she never won an Academy Award, a situation belatedly remedied in 1954 when she received a special Oscar "for her unforgettable screen performances." In 1941, following the release of *Two-Faced Woman,* Garbo announced her retirement from films. True to character, she never explained why, though many feel it was not unrelated to the reception accorded *Two-Faced Woman,* which was greeted by the public and press alike as an unqualified disaster. She subsequently led the life of a semirecluse, dividing her time between Switzerland, the Riviera, and an Upper East Side New York apartment.

There was occasional talk of a projected comeback, but it never materialized. When she died at 84, the world mourned the passing of a legend. She left behind not only an estate valued at more than $200 million but a legacy of priceless nostalgia for a very special time in the history of American cinema. Half a century after she appeared in her last film, the Greta Garbo mystique remains intact. New audiences have discovered her on television and in special film festivals, and her older admirers have kept their memories alive.

FILMS: *Luffar Peter/Peter the Tramp* (Sw.) 1922; *Gösta Berling's Saga/The Legend of Gösta Berling/The Story of Gösta Berling/The Atonement of Gösta Berling* (Sw.) 1924; *Die freudlose Gasse/The Street of Sorrow/The Joyless Street* (Ger.) 1925; *The Torrent/Ibanez' Torrent, The Temptress* 1926; *Flesh and the Devil, Love* (as Anna Karenina) 1927; *The Divine Woman, The Mysterious Lady, A Woman of Affairs* 1928; *Wild Orchids, A Man's Man* (cameo), *The Single Standard, The Kiss* 1929; *Anna Christie* (title role; also German version), *Romance* 1930; *Inspiration, Susan Lenox: Her Fall and Rise, Mata Hari* (title role) 1931; *Grand Hotel, As You Desire Me* 1932; *Queen Christina* (title role) 1933; *The Painted Veil* 1934; *Anna Karenina* (title role) 1935; *Camille* (title role), *Conquest* (as Napoleon's mistress Maria Walewska) 1937; *Ninotchka* 1939; *Two-Faced Woman* 1941.

Garcia, Andy. Actor. Born on Apr. 12, 1956, in Havana. When he was five, his family fled the Castro regime to Miami Beach, where his father, a former lawyer, set up a prosperous cosmetic business. While attending the Florida International

University in Miami, young Garcia began performing in regional theater. In 1978 he moved to Los Angeles, where he appeared with an improvisational group and played bits on television, supplementing his income as a waiter and furniture hauler. In films from 1983, he gradually moved up from supporting to starring roles, typically playing intense, unrestrained, action-bound characters, like the young G-man in *The Untouchables* and the heir to the Corleone family business in *The Godfather: Part III.*

FILMS: *Blue Skies Again, A Night in Heaven* 1983; *The Lonely Guy* 1984; *The Mean Season* 1985; *Eight Million Ways to Die* 1986; *The Untouchables, Stand and Deliver* 1987; *American Roulette* 1978; *Black Rain* 1989; *Internal Affairs, A Show of Force, The Godfather: Part III* 1990; *Dead Again* 1991; *Jennifer 8, Hero* 1992; *When a Man Loves a Woman* 1994; *Steal Big, Steal Little, Things to Do in Denver When You're Dead* 1995; *The Disappearance of Garcia Lorca, Hoodlum, Night Falls on Manhattan* 1997.

Garcia Berlanga, Luis. See BERLANGA, Luis Garcia.

Gardenia, Vincent. Actor. *b.* Vincente Scognamiglio, Jan. 7, 1922, in Naples, Italy. *d.* 1992. Character player of the American stage, screen, and TV. In the US from early childhood, he was educated at New York City schools. He gave his first amateur performance in Brooklyn at age five, but did not start his professional career until he was in his mid-30s. He received a Tony Award for his performance in the Broadway production of 'The Prisoner of Second Avenue' (1971–72) and was nominated for an Oscar for his role in the film *Bang the Drum Slowly* (1973).

FILMS INCLUDE: *The House on 92nd Street* 1945; *Cop Hater* 1958; *Murder Inc.* 1960; *Mad Dog Coll* (as mobster Dutch Schultz), *The Hustler* 1961; *Vu du Pont/A View from the Bridge* (Fr./It.) 1962; *The Third Day* 1965; *Jenny, Where's Poppa?* 1970; *Little Murders* 1971; *Hickey and Boggs* 1972; *Bang the Drum Slowly* 1973; *Re: Lucky Luciano, Death Wish, The Front Page* 1974; *The Manchu Eagle Murder Caper Mystery* 1975; *Il Grande Rocket* (It.) 1976; *Fire Sale, Greased Lightning* 1977; *Heaven Can Wait* 1978; *Firepower* (UK), *Home Movies* 1979; *The Last Flight of Noah's Ark* 1980; *Death Wish II* 1982; *Movers and Shakers* 1985; *Little Shop of Horrors* 1986; *Moonstruck* 1987; *Skin Deep* 1989; *The Super* 1991.

Gardin, Vladimir. Director, actor. *b.* 1877, Moscow. *d.* 1965. A stage actor from 1898, he rose to prominence with Meyerhold's Moscow troupe after 1904. A film director after 1913, he specialized at first in adaptations from literary classics, soon gaining stature as one of Czarist Russia's most fashionable filmmakers. But after the Revolution his films were politically inspired, at first resorting to allegorical symbolism and later, toeing the party line, to social realism, in search of a mode of ideological expression. He was an early proponent of MONTAGE as a cinematic idiom. In 1919 he founded, in Moscow, Russia's first state cinema school and became its first director. In the early 20s he was instrumental in the development of the Ukrainian cinema and helped start the careers of PUDOVKIN and TISSÉ, both of whom worked on his film *Sickle and Hammer.* In the late 20s, Gardin abandoned directing for acting and played character parts in many Soviet films of the 30s and 40s. In 1935 he was named People's Artist for his achievements as an actor. He published three volumes of memoirs, in 1949, 1952, and 1960.

FILMS INCLUDE: As director—*Keys to Happiness* (co-dir., act.) 1913; *The Kreutzer Sonata, Anna Karenina* (both also sc.), *Days of Our Life* 1914; *Ghosts* (also sc.), *Petersburg Slums* (co-dir., co-sc.), *War and Peace* (co-dir., co-sc., act. as Napoleon) 1915; *Thought* (co-dir., sc.) 1916; *Our Heart* 1917; *The Iron Heel* (also sc.) 1919; *Sickle and Hammer* (assisted by Pudovkin), *Hunger—Hunger—Hunger* (co-dir. with Pudovkin) 1921; *The Duel* 1922; *A Specter Haunts Europe, Locksmith and Chancellor* (also co-sc. with Pudovkin) 1923; *The Landowner* 1924; *Cross and Mauser* 1925; *Czar and Poet* 1927; *Spring Song, 400 Million* 1929. As actor—*Dead Souls* 1929; *Counterplan* 1932; *Song About Happiness* 1934; *Peasants* 1935; *Dubrovsky* 1936; *Beethoven Concerto, Young Pushkin* 1937; *Pugachev* 1938; *Russian Ballerina* 1947.

Gardiner, Reginald. Actor. *b.* Feb. 27, 1903, Wimbledon, England. *d.* 1980. A graduate of London's Royal Academy of Dramatic Art, he appeared in British revues, plays, and films before delighting Broadway audiences in 1935 with a wallpaper imitation act in 'At Home Abroad.' He made his Hollywood debut the following year and subsequently played polished and urbane supporting roles, often in a pompous comic vein, in numerous films. Clipped speech and mustache were among his trademarks. An injury resulting from a fall forced his retirement in the mid-60s.

FILMS INCLUDE: *The Lovelorn Lady* (UK) 1932; *Just Smith* (UK) 1933; *Born to Dance* 1936; *A Damsel in Distress* 1937; *Marie Antoinette, Sweethearts* 1938; *The Flying Deuces* 1939; *The Doctor Takes a Wife, The Great Dictator, Dulcy* 1940; *A Yank in the R.A.F., Sundown, My Life with Caroline* 1941; *The Man Who Came to Dinner, Captains of the Clouds* 1942; *Immortal Sergeant, Sweet Rosie O'Grady, Claudia* 1943; *The Horn Blows at Midnight, Molly and Me, The Dolly Sisters* 1945; *Do You Love Me?, Cluny Brown* 1946; *I Wonder Who's Kissing Her Now* 1947; *That Lady in Ermine, That Wonderful Urge* 1948; *Wabash Avenue* 1950; *The Halls of Montezuma* 1951; *Androcles and the Lion* 1953; *Black Widow* 1954; *The Birds and the Bees* 1956; *The Story of Mankind* (as Shakespeare) 1957; *Back Street* 1961; *Mr. Hobbs Takes a Vacation* 1962; *What a Way to Go!* 1964; *Sergeant Deadhead, Do Not Disturb* 1965.

Gardner, Ava. Actress. *b.* Dec. 24, 1922, Grabton, near Smithfield, N.C. *d.* 1990. Seductive, husky-voiced star of Hollywood films of the 40s and 50s. One of six children of a poor tenant farmer, she had an unhappy, loveless childhood. She was preparing to become a secretary when a trip to New York changed the course of her life. A picture of her, taken by her photographer brother-in-law, found its way to MGM's casting department. A screen test was arranged in New York, the result of which took her to Hollywood in 1940. Here she was put on the standard training program for pretty starlets with good potential but no acting experience—drama and diction courses, calisthenics, makeup and grooming classes, and above all a great deal of publicity, before ever making a screen appearance. Months went by before she began playing minor roles in minor films. In 1942 she received much free publicity when she married Mickey ROONEY. They divorced the following year.

It wasn't until 1946 that Miss Gardner was discovered by the public, along with another newcomer, Burt Lancaster, in the screen adaptation of Hemingway's *The Killers.* A sensuous, sloe-eyed beauty, with a magnetic, tigress-like quality of sexuality, she replaced Rita Hayworth in the late 40s as Hollywood's love goddess and occupied that position until the ascent of Marilyn Monroe in the mid-50s. Having married and divorced (1945–47) the oft-married musician Artie Shaw, she married Frank SINATRA in 1951, following a stormy and much publicized courtship. They were separated in 1954 and divorced in 1957, whereupon Miss Gardner left Hollywood for the gay life of the international set in Madrid and surrounded herself with admiring rich playboys and famous matadors. She returned to the screen three years later, noticeably more mature but still very beautiful and still very much a star. Although her contribution to cinema was often merely decorative, Miss Gardner proved herself capable of potent, sometimes touching performances in the right roles. She was nominated for an Academy Award for *Mogambo* (1953). She extended her career in films through 1982. In 1985 she made her TV bow, appearing in the series 'Knots Landing' and portraying Agrippina, Nero's scheming mother, in the miniseries 'A.D.' She also appeared in the TV movies *The Long Hot Summer* (1985) and *Harem* (1986), her last role. She had just completed feeding material to a collaborator for an autobiography when she died of pneumonia in London at 67.

FILMS: *H.M. Pulham Esq.* 1941; *We Were Dancing, Joe Smith American, Sunday Punch, This Time for Keeps, Calling Dr. Gillespie, Kid Glove Killer* 1942; *Pilot No. 5, Hitler's Madman, Ghosts on the Loose, Reunion in France, Du Barry Was a Lady, Young Ideas, Lost Angel* 1943; *Swing Fever, Music for Millions, Three Men in White, Blonde Fever, Maisie Goes to Reno, Two Girls and a Sailor* 1944; *She Went to the Races* 1945; *Whistle Stop, The Killers* 1946; *The Hucksters, Singapore* 1947; *One Touch of Venus* (as the goddess Venus) 1948; *The Bribe, The Great Sinner, East Side West Side* 1949; *My Forbidden Past, Show Boat* (as Julie Laverne), *Pandora and the Flying Dutchman* (as Pandora) 1951; *Lone Star, The Snows of Kilimanjaro* 1952; *Ride Vaquero!, The Band Wagon* (cameo), *Mogambo* 1953; *Knights of the Round Table* (as Guinevere), *The Barefoot Contessa* 1954; *Bhowani Junction* 1956; *The Little Hut, The Sun Also Rises* 1957; *La Maja Desnuda/The Naked Maja* (as the Duchess of Alba; It./US), *On the Beach* 1959; *La Sposa Bella/The Angel Wore Red* (It./US) 1960; *55 Days at Peking* 1963; *Seven Days in May, The Night of the Iguana* 1964; *La Bibbia/The Bible* (as Sarah; It./US) 1966; *Mayerling* (as Empress Elizabeth; UK/Fr.) 1968; *The Devil's Widow/Tam Lin* (UK) 1971; *The Life and Times of Judge Roy Bean* (as famed actress Lily Langtry) 1972; *Earthquake* 1974; *Vollmacht zum Mord/Permission to Kill* (Aus./UK) 1975; *The Blue Bird* (as Luxury; US/USSR) 1976; *The Cassandra Crossing, The Sentinel* 1977; *City on Fire* (Can.) 1980; *The Kidnapping of the President* (Can.) 1980; *Priest of Love* (UK) 1981; *Regina* (Ger./It.) 1982.

Gardner, Helen. American actress. *b.* 1885(?). *d.* 1968. Star of the early American silent screen, often in exotic or "vamp" roles. In 1912 she formed her own production company, the Helen Gardner Picture Corporation, possibly the first star to undertake such an enterprise. She operated her own studio, in Tappan-on-the-Hudson, N.Y., until 1914. Her husband, Charles L. Gaskill, was often her director.

FILMS INCLUDE: *Arbutus, Vanity Fair* (as Becky Sharp) 1911; *Cleopatra* (title role; also prod.) 1912; *Alixe or the Test of Friendship, The Wife of Cain* (also prod.), *Sister to Carmen* (also prod.), *A Princess of Bagdad* (also prod.) 1913; *Pieces of Silver* (also prod.), *The Strange Story of Sylvia Gray, And There Was Light* 1914; *The Still Small Voice* 1915; *The Sleep of Cyma Roget/The Devil's Angel* 1920; *Sandra* 1924.

Garfein, Jack. Director. Born on July 2, 1930, in Mukacevo, Czechoslovakia. A survivor of the Auschwitz concentration camp, he came to the US in 1945 and after studies at the New School for Social Research began a career as a stage actor and director. He directed his first Broadway production 'End as a Man,' in 1953, and the following year joined the Actors Studio. He married a fellow member, actress Carroll BAKER, in 1955. They were divorced in 1969. Garfein, who has also directed a number of TV shows, worked as an assistant to Elia Kazan (on *Baby Doll*) and George Stevens (on *Giant*) before making an auspicious debut as a film director with *The Strange One* (1957), a screen adaptation of 'End as a Man.' He subsequently directed a couple of other Broadway productions but only one more film, *Something Wild* (1961), an offbeat, mildly interesting drama of a rapist-victim relationship which starred Miss Baker. He is the artistic director of the Harold Clurman Theater in New York and father of actress Blanche Baker.

FILMS: *The Strange One* 1957; *Something Wild* (also co-sc.) 1961.

Garfield, Allen. Actor. Born Allen Goorwitz, on Nov. 22, 1939, in Newark, N.J. Chubby character player of Hollywood films of the late 60s and 70s. Trained at the Actors Studio, he played a wide range of roles on the stage before making his screen debut in 1968. He has since contributed memorable characterizations to many films, proving especially adept at impersonating aggressive, indecent, often lecherous, obnoxiously corrupt types. From 1978 through 1983 he was billed as Allen Goorwitz, his real name, but later he switched back to Garfield.

FILMS INCLUDE: *Orgy Girls '69, Greetings* 1968; *Putney Swope, March of the Spring Hare/Roommates* 1969; *Hi Mom!, The Owl and the Pussycat* 1970; *Taking Off, Bananas, Cry Uncle* (lead), *Believe in Me, You've Got to Walk It Like You Talk It or You'll Lose Your Beat* 1971; *Get to Know Your Rabbit, The Candidate, The Organization* 1972; *Slither* 1973; *Busting, The Conversation, The Front Page* 1974; *Nashville* 1975; *Gable and Lombard* (as Louis B. Mayer), *Mother Jugs and Speed, Paco* 1976; *Skateboard, The Brink's Job* 1978; *The Stunt Man* (release delayed from 1978), *One Trick Pony* 1980; *Continental Divide* 1981; *One From the Heart, The State of Things* 1982; *The Black Stallion Returns, Get Crazy* 1983; *Irreconcilable Differences, Teachers, The Cotton Club* 1984; *Desert Bloom* 1986; *Beverly Hills Cop II* 1987; *Dick Tracy* 1990; *Club Fed* 1991; *Until the End of the World* 1992; *The Patriots* 1994; *Destiny Turns on the Radio* 1995.

Garfield, John. Actor. *b.* Julius Garfinkle, Mar. 4, 1913, New York City. *d.* 1952. The son of a poor immigrant Jewish tailor, he grew up on New York's tough Lower East Side, peddled newspapers on street corners, and got into frequent brawls with neighborhood gangs. He broke out of this apparent dead end by winning a state debating contest sponsored by *The New York Times*. As a result, he obtained a scholarship, which he used for studies at the Ouspenskaya Drama School, and served his apprenticeship with Eva Le Gallienne's Civic Repertory Theatre. After a period of vagrancy during which he traveled cross-country on freight trains, occasionally worked as a farmhand, and supposedly played a bit (as a sailor) in the film *Footlight Parade* (1933), he returned to New York and joined the Group Theatre, initially supporting himself as a Macy's sales clerk. In 1932 he married his high school sweetheart, Roberta Seidman. By 1936 he was playing leads in Broadway plays and in 1938 he was signed by Warner Bros. to star in the film *Four Daughters*.

Garfield's screen character was established from the very start and was not much at variance with his own personality—that of a cynical, defiant young man from the other side of the tracks, a resilient rebel with a chip on his shoulder who desperately tries to charm and muscle his way onward and upward. Despite the mediocrity of many of his films, Garfield's boyish virility and his ability to project a soulful interior underneath a pugnacious façade made him an attractive star to many filmgoers. When given a proper vehicle, he proved himself a sensitive and solid interpreter. He was nominated for Academy Awards as best supporting actor for *Four Daughters* (1938) and best actor for *Body and Soul* (1947).

In the mid-40s, Garfield left Warners, started his own production company, and also freelanced for various studios, but early in the 50s his career ended abruptly as a result of the

House Un-American Activities Committee investigation. He wasn't accused of anything in particular but was suspected of left-wing sympathies and was blacklisted for refusing to name friends as Communists. When he died of a heart attack in 1952, those close to him said it was the blacklisting that really killed him. Unfounded rumors persisted for years that the actor actually had taken his own life. Garfield's eldest daughter, Katherine, died in childhood of a strep throat infection. His son, David Patton Garfield (*b.* 1942), appeared in several films of the 60s as John Garfield, Jr. His daughter, Julie [Patton] Garfield (*b.* Jan. 10, 1946) has been performing in films since 1969.

FILMS: *Four Daughters* 1938; *They Made Me a Criminal, Blackwell's Island, Juarez* (as Porfirio Diaz), *Daughters Courageous, Four Wives, Dust Be My Destiny* 1939; *Castle on the Hudson, Saturday's Children, Flowing Gold, East of the River* 1940; *The Sea Wolf* (as George Leach), *Out of the Fog* 1941; *Dangerously They Live, Tortilla Flat* 1942; *Air Force, The Fallen Sparrow, Thank Your Lucky Stars* 1943; *Destination Tokyo, Between Two Worlds, Hollywood Canteen* 1944; *Pride of the Marines* 1945; *The Postman Always Rings Twice, Nobody Lives Forever, Humoresque* 1946; *Body and Soul, Gentleman's Agreement* 1947; *Force of Evil* 1948; *We Were Strangers* 1949; *Under My Skin, The Breaking Point* 1950; *He Ran All the Way* 1951.

Gargan, William. Actor. *b.* July 17, 1905, Brooklyn, N.Y. *d.* 1979. The son of a bill collector, he worked briefly at a number of white-collar jobs after leaving high school but quickly became bored with the routine and turned to acting in 1924. He made it to Broadway the following year and began playing bits in films in 1929. After scoring a personal triumph on the stage, he began a long and prolific career in Hollywood films. He played energetic, often gregarious leads in many B productions of the 30s and second leads in a number of major films, then gradually moved into character roles. He was nominated for an Oscar for his performance in *They Knew What They Wanted* (1940). He starred in the TV series 'Martin Kane, Private Eye' (1949–51) and its sequel, 'The New Adventures of Martin Kane' (1957). In 1960 he was forced into retirement by an operation for cancer of the larynx, during which his voice box was removed. He recounted the experience in a 1969 book, *Why Me?,* and returned to public view campaigning against smoking for the American Cancer Society, speaking through an artificial voice box. His brother, Edward Gargan (1902–64), played minor character roles in scores of films of the 30s and 40s.

FILMS INCLUDE: *Lucky Boy* (bit) 1929; *Follow the Leader* (bit) 1930; *His Woman* (bit) 1931; *The Misleading Lady, Rain, The Animal Kingdom* 1932; *Lucky Devils, The Story of Temple Drake, Night Flight, Headline, Shooters* 1933; *Four Frightened People, British Agent* 1934; *Black Fury, A Night at the Ritz, Broadway Gondolier* 1935; *Man Hunt, The Milky Way, Alibi for Murder, Flying Hostess* 1936; *You Only Live Once, Breezing Home, Wings Over Honolulu, Fury and The Woman, Reported Missing, Some Blondes Are Dangerous, Behind the Mike* 1937; *The Devil's Party, The Crowd Roars, Personal Secretary* 1938; *Broadway Serenade, Women in the Wind, House of Fear* 1939; *Double Alibi, Isle of Destiny, Star Dust, They Knew What They Wanted* 1940; *Cheers for Miss Bishop, Flying Cadets, I Wake Up Screaming* 1941; *Bombay Clipper, Miss Annie Rooney, Enemy Agents Meet Ellery Queen* (as Ellery Queen), *Destination Unknown, Who Done It?* 1942; *Swing Fever, The Canterville Ghost* 1944; *She Gets Her Man, Midnight Manhunt, The Bells of St. Mary's* 1945; *Behind Green Lights, Night Editor, Till the End of Time* 1946; *Daredevils of the Clouds* 1948; *Miracle in the Rain, The Rawhide Years* 1956.

Garland, Beverly. Actress. Born Beverly Fessenden, on Oct. 17, 1926, in Santa Cruz, Calif. *ed.* Glendale Coll. Leading lady of Hollywood films of the 50s, mainly in B pictures, typically in hardened "dame" roles. She was billed as Beverly Campbell in her film debut, *D.O.A.* Her career was hampered by frequent confrontations with producers and the press. She subsequently appeared on many TV shows and co-starred with Fred MacMurray in the popular series 'My Three Sons' (1969–72). In the late 60s she returned to the big screen in character roles. In 1983–86 she appeared in the TV series 'Scarecrow and Mrs. King,' and continued to make appearances in small roles on television.

FILMS INCLUDE: *D.O.A.* 1949; *The Glass Web* 1953; *Bitter Creek, The Miami Story* 1954; *New Orleans Uncensored, The Desperate Hours* 1955; *The Steel Jungle* 1956; *Chicago Confidential, The Joker Is Wild* 1957; *The Alligator People* 1959; *Stark Fear, Twice Told Tales* 1963; *Pretty Poison* 1968; *The Mad Room* 1969; *Airport 1975* 1974; *Where the Red Fern Grows* 1975; *Sixth and Main* 1977; *Roller Boogie* 1979; *It's My Turn* 1980.

Garland, Judy. Actress, singer. *b.* Frances Gumm, June 10, 1922, Grand Rapids, Minn. *d.* 1969. The child of vaudeville performers, she made her stage debut at three and was a seasoned trouper by the time she was five. Appearing with her two older sisters in the "Gumm Sisters Kiddie Act," on the stage and in several short films, she was billed as "the little girl with the great big voice." When she was nine the girls changed their stage name to Garland, at the suggestion of George Jessel. A year later Frances changed her name to Judy. The trio wasn't very successful under any name and it finally broke up when one of the sisters married. On her own, and prompted by an ambitious mother she was to bitterly describe in later years as "the real-life Wicked Witch of the West," Judy fared somewhat better. At 13 she was auditioned personally by MGM's production boss, Louis B. Mayer, who, impressed by her voice, signed her on a contract without a screen test.

Judy's first screen appearance was in a two-reel short, *Every Sunday,* also featuring Deanna Durbin. For her first feature, *Pigskin Parade,* Judy was loaned out to Fox, then, returning to MGM, she stole the show from a star-studded cast in *Broadway Melody of 1938,* when she sang 'Dear Mr. Gable' to a photograph of the star. In *Thoroughbreds Don't Cry* (1937) she was cast for the first time opposite Mickey Rooney, who was to become her frequent screen partner (nine times in all) in the juvenile phase of her career. Then came the film that made her a world-famous star, *The Wizard of Oz* (1939), in which, as wide-eyed little Dorothy, she played and sang her way to the hearts of millions. When she sang 'Over the Rainbow' in her distinctive trembling, emotion-choked voice with a built-in throb, an instant legend was born. She won a special Oscar as "the best juvenile performer of the year" for the role that had originally been intended for Shirley Temple.

Judy was still in her teens when she began being plagued by a weight problem. In an effort to contain her tendency to gain pounds, the studio put her on a strict diet and a doctor recommended pills. At the same time, the strain of work began taking its toll on her nervous system, and before long she was living on pills: pills to put her to sleep, pills to keep her awake, and pills to suppress her appetite. By the time she was 21 she was seeing a psychiatrist regularly. In 1941 she married the first of her five husbands, orchestra leader David Rose. In 1943, Judy and Rose separated and in 1945 she had her first divorce. Meanwhile, her career continued to prosper, not only in the movies but also on radio and in numerous personal appearances. One of her most successful films of the period was *Meet Me in St. Louis* (1944). A year after its release, she married the film's director, Vincente Minnelli. In 1946 their daughter, Liza Minnelli, was born. In 1951, Judy had her second divorce.

The dual pressure of stardom and personal unhappiness affected her career. She began showing up late for work or not at all, was suspended a couple of times, and finally, in 1950, was fired from the MGM lot. Depressed and bewildered, she made her first suicide attempt. Others were to follow. A temporary relief from her agony came in the person of Sid Luft, her third husband, who appointed himself her manager and arranged a triumphant engagement for Judy at the London Palladium. Her comeback road was subsequently paved with an even greater *tour de force,* a record-breaking 19-week engagement at New York's Palace Theater. In 1954, she returned to the screen, giving perhaps her finest performance, in *A Star Is Born* (1954), for which she was nominated for an Oscar. But the comeback was short-lived. The news Judy made in the late 50s involved lawsuits, counterlawsuits, nervous breakdowns, suicide attempts, and recurrent breakups with Luft.

In spite of all her troubles, in 1961 she gave a memorable concert at Carnegie Hall, played a magnificent dramatic vignette in Stanley Kramer's *Judgment at Nuremberg,* gaining another Oscar nomination (this time as supporting actress), and followed with another good dramatic performance in *A Child Is Waiting* (1963). But her long-awaited show on CBS television in 1963 had poor ratings and was canceled before the end of its scheduled run. Disappointed by this failure and exhausted from a custody battle with Sid Luft over their two children, one of whom is singer Lorna Luft, she flew to London for a concert with daughter Liza at the Palladium. Then, after divorcing Luft, in 1965, Judy married Mark Herron, a marginal actor seven years her junior. Six months later they separated and in 1967 Judy had her fourth divorce. Next, Judy was announced for a role in the film *Valley of the Dolls,* but Susan Hayward got the part.

Early in 1968, Judy went to London and there married her fifth husband, a 35-year-old discothéque manager named Mickey Deans. On June 22, 1969, she stumbled in the bathroom of her London apartment. She was found dead in the morning by Deans. The official coroner's verdict attributed her death to an accidental overdose of sleeping pills. Thousands of bereaved fans jammed the vicinity of the Manhattan funeral home where her body lay in state. The legend that had been Judy Garland was now a cult.

FILMS: Shorts—*The Meglin Kiddie Revue* 1929; *Holiday in Storyland, The Wedding of Jack and Jill* 1930; *The Old Lady and the Shoe* 1931; *La Fiesta de Santa Barbara* 1935; *Every Sunday* 1936. Features—*Pigskin Parade* 1936; *Broadway Melody of 1938, Thoroughbreds Don't Cry* 1937; *Everybody Sing, Love Finds Andy Hardy, Listen Darling* 1938; *The Wizard of Oz, Babes in Arms* 1939; *Andy Hardy Meets Debutante, Strike Up the Band, Little Nellie Kelly* 1940; *Meet the Stars No. 4* (short), *Cavalcade of the Academy Awards* (short), *Ziegfeld Girl, Life Begins for Andy Hardy* 1941; *Babes on Broadway, We Must Have Music* (short), *For Me and My Gal* 1942; *Presenting Lily Mars, Thousands Cheer, Girl Crazy* 1943; *Meet Me in St. Louis* 1944; *The Clock* 1945; *The Harvey Girls, Ziegfeld Follies, Till the Clouds Roll By* 1946; *The Pirate, Easter Parade, Words and Music* 1948; *In the Good Old Summertime* 1949; *Summer Stock* 1950; *A Star Is Born* 1954; *Pepe* (cameo) 1960; *Judgment at Nuremberg* 1961; *Gay Purr-ee* (v/o) 1962; *A Child Is Waiting, I Could Go On Singing* (UK) 1963.

Garmes, Lee. Director of photography. *b.* May 27, 1898, Peoria, Ill. *d.* 1978. After his parents' divorce, he was raised by a grandmother in Denver, Colo. He started his film career in 1916, directly after high school, as a painter's assistant and property boy at the Thomas H. Ince Studios. Later that year Garmes became assistant camerman, and through 1923 he worked on numerous comedy shorts and occasional features. In 1924 he became a lighting cameraman and soon distinguished himself as a creative cinematographer. In the late 20s he pioneered in the use of atmospheric photography, experimenting with the "Rembrandtian" north light, which called for highlighting significant detail while keeping the rest of a scene in low key. He was also among the first to use bare Mazda bulbs to light a whole set and helped devise the first CRAB DOLLY. From the mid-30s he occasionally ventured into producing and directing. He also did much of the physical directing on the films of Ben Hecht and Charles MacArthur, receiving screen credit as associate director. He did not receive screen credit for *Gone With the Wind,* although he photographed the first third of the film. Garmes was at his best with black and white but also did creditable color work. He won an Academy Award for Von Sternberg's *Shanghai Express.* He was at one time married to actress Ruth Hall.

FILMS INCLUDE: *The Hope Chest* (co-phot.) 1918; *Nugget Nell* (co-phot.) 1919; *Find Your Man* 1924; *Keep Smiling* (co-phot.) 1925; *The Show-Off, The Popular Sin* 1926; *The Garden of Allah, The Private Life of Helen of Troy* (co-phot.) 1927; *The Little Shepherd of Kingdom Come, The Yellow Lily* 1928; *Disraeli* 1929; *Lilies of the Field, Whoopee!* (co-phot.), *Morocco, Bright Lights* 1930; *Dishonored, City Streets, An American Tragedy* 1931; *Shanghai Express, Scarface, Strange Interlude, Smilin' Through* 1932; *Zoo in Budapest, Shanghai Madness* 1933; *Crime Without Passion* (also assoc. dir.) 1934; *Once in a Blue Moon, The Scoundrel* (both also assoc. dir.) 1935; *Dreaming Lips* (also co-prod., technical supervisor; UK), *The Lilac Domino* (prod. only; UK), *The Sky's the Limit* (co-dir. with Jack Buchanan only; UK) 1937; *Gone With the Wind* (co-phot.; uncredited) 1939; *Beyond Tomorrow* (prod. only), *Angels Over Broadway* (also co-dir. with Ben Hecht) 1940; *Lydia* (also co-prod.) 1941; *The Jungle Book, Footlight Serenade* 1942; *Forever and a Day* (co-phot.) 1943; *Since You Went Away* (co-phot.), *Guest in the House* 1944; *Love Letters* 1945; *The Searching Wind, Specter of the Rose* (also assoc. prod.), *Duel in the Sun* (co-phot.) 1946; *The Secret Life of Walter Mitty, Nightmare Alley, The Paradine Case* 1947; *Caught, My Foolish Heart* 1949; *Detective Story* 1951; *Actors and Sin* (also assoc. dir.), *The Captive City, The Lusty Men* 1952; *Land of the Pharaohs, The Desperate Hours* 1955; *D Day the Sixth of June* 1956; *The Big Fisherman* 1959; *Hemingway's Adventures of a Young Man* 1962; *A Big Hand for the Little Lady* 1966; *How to Save a Marriage and Ruin Your Life* 1968.

Garner, James. Actor. Born James Scott Bumgarner, on Apr. 7, 1928, in Norman, Okla. A high school dropout, he joined the merchant marine at 16. Later with the Army, he was wounded in the Korean War and awarded the Purple Heart. After his discharge, he briefly attended the University of Oklahoma and worked at a variety of odd jobs, as a gas station attendant, traveling salesman, carpet layer, and model of swim trunks. He chanced upon acting when a boyhood-friend-turned-producer offered him a nonspeaking role in the 1954 Broadway production of 'The Caine Mutiny Court-Martial.' Thanks to his tall, rugged frame, extreme good looks, and genial personality, he soon began landing small parts on TV and in films and in 1957 became the star of the popular TV series 'Maverick.' Starring roles in films followed and by the mid-60s he was among Hollywood's top-salaried leading men. He started his own production company, Maverick (later Cherokee), and parlayed his earnings into profitable investments in oil and real estate. His film roles declined in the early 70s, but he maintained his popularity with the TV series 'Nichols' (1971–72), 'The Rockford Files' (1974–80 [Emmy Award in 1977]), and the sequel series

'Bret Maverick' (1981–82). Hampered by a bad back, he continued appearing sporadically in films, and was nominated for an Academy Award as best actor for his performance in *Murphy's Romance* (1985). He has distinguished himself since in a variety of high-quality TV-movie performances.

FILMS: *Toward the Unknown, The Girl He Left Behind* 1956; *Shoot-Out at Medicine Bend, Sayonara* 1957; *Darby's Rangers* 1958; *Up Periscope* 1959; *Cash McCall* 1960; *The Children's Hour, Boys' Night Out* 1962; *The Great Escape, The Thrill of It All, The Wheeler Dealers, Move Over Darling* 1963; *The Americanization of Emily* 1964; *36 Hours, The Art of Love* 1965; *A Man Could Get Killed, Duel at Diablo, Mister Buddwing, Grand Prix* 1966; *Hour of the Gun* 1967; *How Sweet It Is, The Pink Jungle* 1968; *Marlowe, Support Your Local Sheriff* 1969; *A Man Called Sledge* 1970; *Support Your Local Gunfighter, Skin Game* 1971; *They Only Kill Their Masters* 1972; *One Little Indian* 1973; *The Castaway Cowboy* 1974; 1980; *The Fan* 1981; *Victor/Victoria* 1982; *Tank* 1984; *Murphy's Romance* 1985; *Sunset* (as Wyatt Earp) 1988; *The Distinguished Gentleman* 1992; *Fire in the Sky* 1993; *Maverick* 1994; *My Fellow Americans* 1996.

Garner, Peggy Ann. Actress, *b.* Feb. 3, 1931, Canton, Ohio. *d.* 1984. Child star of Hollywood films of the 40s. The daughter of an English-born attorney, she was driven by an ambitious stage mother into summer stock appearances and modeling assignments before she was six. After arriving in Hollywood as a child of seven, she appeared briefly in several productions of the late 30s, and in the early 40s demonstrated a mature capacity for acting, in such films as *The Pied Piper* (1942) and *Jane Eyre* (as the young Jane, 1944). She won a special Academy Award as the "outstanding child performer of 1945" for her sensitive performance in *A Tree Grows in Brooklyn.* But few of her subsequent roles were rewarding and her film career was all but finished by the early 50s. She made her Broadway debut in 1950 and subsequently appeared in many plays in New York and on the road. She also appeared in numerous TV dramas and series episodes but by the late 60s was making her living as a real estate broker. In the early 70s she became sales manager for a California automobile dealership. The first two of her three husbands were actors, Richard Hayes (1951–53) and Albert SALMI (1956–63).

FILMS INCLUDE: *Little Miss Thoroughbred* 1938; *In Name Only* 1939; *Abe Lincoln in Illinois* 1940; *The Pied Piper* 1942; *Jane Eyre* (Jane as a child), *The Keys of the Kingdom* 1944; *A Tree Grows in Brooklyn* (as Francie Nolan), *Nob Hill, Junior Miss* 1945; *Home Sweet Homicide* 1946; *Thunder in the Valley, Daisy Kenyon* 1947; *The Sign of the Ram* 1948; *Bomba the Jungle Boy, The Big Cat* 1949; *Teresa* 1951; *Black Widow* 1954; *The Cat* 1966; *A Wedding* 1978.

Garnett, Tay. Director, screenwriter. *b.* June 13, 1894, Santa Ana, near Los Angeles. *d.* 1977. *ed.* MIT. Serving as a flight instructor with the Naval Air Service in San Diego in WW I, he suffered an injury in a training crash that left him with a permanent limp and a lifelong reliance on a walking stick. During the latter phase of his service, which stretched until 1922, he was assigned to write and stage vaudeville-style shows for servicemen. Following his discharge, he went to Hollywood, where he found temporary employment as a gagman for Hal Roach, Mack Sennett, and other comedy producers. He contributed, uncredited, to the scripts of such Capra/Langdon features as *The Strong Man* (1926) and *Long Pants* (1927), but did receive screen credit for his contributions to many other films of the late silent period. In 1927 he joined the De Mille unit at Pathé and the following year began directing for that company. He first drew attention in the early 30s with such films as *Her Man* and *One Way Passage.* His subsequent career with Fox, MGM, and other studios was marked by inconsistency, occasionally reaching satisfying levels in such films as *China Seas, Slave Ship, Seven Sinners, The Valley of Decision,* and *The Postman Always Rings Twice.* The latter, regarded as his best film, is still widely admired as a prime example of American *film noir* of the 40s. But even his less accomplished productions were often noted for their flowing narrative and effective integration of background and plot. Garnett, who published a novel, *A Man Laughs Back,* in 1935, wrote the screenplays for many of his own films. From the late 50s he directed mostly for TV. Early in his career he married and divorced silent star Patsy Ruth Miller. In the 50s he married his third wife, actress Mari Aldon. Author: *A Man Laughs Back* (1935); *Light Up Your Torches and Pull Up Your Tights* (1973).

FILMS (as director): *Celebrity* (also co-sc.), *The Spieler* (also co-sc.) 1928; *The Flying Fool* (also co-sc.), *Oh Yeah!* (dial. dir. James Gleason; also sc., co-songs) 1929; *Officer O'Brien, Her Man* (also co-story) 1930; *Bad Company* (also co-sc.) 1931; *Prestige* (also co-adapt.), *Okay America, One Way Passage* 1932; *Destination Unknown, SOS Iceberg* (co-dir. with Arnold Fanck) 1933; *China Seas, She Couldn't Take It* 1935; *Professional Soldier* 1936; *Love Is News, Slave Ship, Stand-In* 1937; *Joy of Living* 1938; *Trade Winds* (also story), *Eternally Yours* (also prod., act.) 1939; *Slightly Honorable, Seven Sinners* 1940; *Unexpected Uncle* (prod. only), *Week End for Three* (prod. only), *Cheers for Miss Bishop* 1941; *My Favorite Spy* 1942; *Bataan, The Cross of Lorraine* 1943; *Mrs. Parkington* 1944; *The Valley of Decision* 1945; *The Postman Always Rings Twice* 1946; *Wild Harvest* 1947; *A Connecticut Yankee in King Arthur's Court* 1949; *The Fireball* (also co-sc.) 1950; *Cause for Alarm, Soldiers Three* 1951; *One Minute to Zero* 1952; *Main Street to Broadway* 1953; *The Black Knight* (UK/US) 1954; *Seven Wonders of the World* (Cinerama; co-dir. with four others) 1956; *A Terrible Beauty/The Night Fighters* (UK) 1960; *Cattle King* 1963; *The Delta Factor* (also prod., sc.) 1970; *Challenge to Be Free* (completed in 1972 as *The Mad Trapper;* also co-sc.) 1976; *Timber Tramp* (completed in 1972) 1977.

Garofalo, Janeane. Actress, comedian. Born September 28, 1964, in Newton, N.J. *ed.* Providence College, Rhode Island. A biting and quick wit helped launch her career early on as a comedian, particularly on television's MTV and as a series regular on HBO's sitcom 'The Larry Sanders Show,' before turning to feature films. She charmed audiences and critics alike with her performance as a lovestruck radio talk show host in *The Truth About Cats and Dogs* (1996).

FILMS: *Late for Dinner* 1991; *Reality Bites* 1994; *Bye Bye Love, Coldblooded, Now and Then* 1995; *The Truth About Cats and Dogs, Larger Than Life* 1996; *Copland, Romy and Michele's High School Reunion, Touch* 1997.

Garr, Teri. Actress. Born on Dec. 11, 1949, in Lakewood, Ohio. Blonde leading lady of the American screen. The daughter of actor Edward ("Eddie") Garr (1900–56), she began her career as a dancer, performing with the San Francisco Ballet at 13 and later appeared in the original road show of 'West Side Story.' Following some exposure in commercials, she began appearing in films in 1966 as Terry Garr, then Terri Garr, finally settling on Teri Garr. Her early career was helped by frequent appearances on 'The Sonny and Cher Comedy Hour' (1973–74). She made her first real impression on movie audiences as the wide-eyed girlfriend of Dr. Frankenstein in Mel Brooks's *Young Frankenstein* (1974) and has since played leads and supporting roles in numerous films, most successfully as a spirited comedienne in the Joan Blondell mold.

FILMS: *For Pete's Sake* 1966; *Maryjane, Head* 1968;

Changes 1969; *The Moonshine War* 1970; *The Conversation, Young Frankenstein* 1974; *Won Ton Ton—The Dog Who Saved Hollywood* 1976; *Oh God!, Close Encounters of the Third Kind* 1977; *Mr. Mike's Mondo Video, The Black Stallion* 1979; *Witches' Brew* 1980; *Honky Tonk Freeway* 1981; *One from the Heart, The Escape Artist, Tootsie* 1982; *The Sting II, The Black Stallion Returns, Mr. Mom* 1983; *Firstborn* 1984; *After Hours* 1985; *Miracles* 1986; *Full Moon in Blue Water* 1988; *Out Cold* 1989; *Waiting for the Light, Short Time* 1990; *The Player, Mom and Dad Save the World* 1992; *Dumb and Dumber, Ready to Wear* 1994; *Michael* 1996; *Changing Habits, A Simple Wish* 1997.

Garrett, Betty. Actress, singer, dancer. Born on May 23, 1919, in St. Joseph, Mo. The daughter of a traveling salesman who died when she was a teenager, she won a scholarship to New York's Neighborhood Playhouse and made her stage debut in 1938 in the Mercury Theater production of 'Danton's Death.' She later danced with the Martha Graham company and sang in nightclubs and at resort hotels and, while waiting for the big break, worked between engagements as a shopgirl and elevator operator. Her opportunity came in 1942 in the Broadway revue 'Let Freedom Ring.' Other Broadway appearances followed and after winning the Donaldson Award for her performance in 'Call Me Mister' (1946), she was signed by MGM on a movie contract. Her film career was short but memorable. In the late 40s she enlivened five MGM musicals with her singing, dancing, and bright comic acting, a bouncy and bubbly second lead, typically playing the best friend of the heroine. She took a sabbatical in 1950–51 to give birth to two sons but when she was ready to return for work found the MGM gates closed to her because of the confession of her husband (from 1944), Larry PARKS, before the House Un-American Activities Committee of past membership in the Communist party.

Garrett later appeared with her husband in a nightclub act and they toured the US with a play, but it wasn't until 1955 that she again appeared in a film, *My Sister Eileen,* at Columbia. Faithful to Parks, who was still blacklisted, she resisted a renewed screen career that would separate their careers and after appearing in one more film she retired from the screen. She and Parks appeared in stock and occasionally on TV (including her regular role as Archie Bunker's neighbor in 'All in the Family' [1973–75]). After Parks's death in 1975, she continued performing on the stage and played a regular role on television, as Mrs. De Fazio in the TV series 'Laverne and Shirley' (1976–81). In 1989 she appeared at the Pasadena Playhouse in a one-woman autobiographical show, 'No Dogs or Actors Allowed.' She brought it to New York in 1990. She resides in Seattle.

FILMS: *Big City, Words and Music* 1948; *Take Me Out to the Ball Game, Neptune's Daughter, On the Town* 1949; *My Sister Eileen* 1955; *The Shadow on the Window* 1957.

Garson, Greer. Actress. *B*orn on Sept. 29, 1908, in County Down, Ireland. *d.* 1996. *ed.* U. of London. She intended to become a teacher but instead joined an advertising agency, dabbling in amateur dramatics in her spare time. In 1932 she made her professional debut with the Birmingham Repertory Theatre and stayed with the company for two years. On the London stage from 1934, she was seen by visiting Hollywood mogul Louis B. Mayer, who signed her on an MGM contract. Her arrival in Hollywood was perfectly timed. MGM was in dire need of a high-caliber leading lady to fill the vacuum soon to be created by the retirement of Greta Garbo and Norma Shearer. Miss Garson became popular enough with her very first film, *Goodbye Mr. Chips,* for which she received her first nomination for an Academy Award (later nominations: *Blossoms in the Dust, Madame Curie, Mrs. Parkington, The Valley of Decision,* and *Sunrise at Campobello*). But the film that propelled her to the top was *Mrs. Miniver,* in which she symbolized the courage and gallantry of the British housewife during the Blitz. She won the best actress Academy Award for the role, which had been turned down by Shearer. Shortly after the film's release, in 1943, she married Richard NEY, the actor who played her son in the film (her first marriage had ended in divorce in 1937). She and Ney were divorced in 1947.

Through the mid-40s, Miss Garson was typecast in roles similar to that of Mrs. Miniver, combining moral courage and dedication as a wife and a mother. Her frequent co-star was Walter PIDGEON. Later in the decade, she was given an opportunity to demonstrate her versatility as an actress in a wider range of drama and in comedy, but the quality of her vehicles and her popularity began to slip after the end of WW II. In 1949 she married an oil magnate and several years later she retired from the screen. In 1958 she took over Rosalind Russell's role in Broadway's 'Auntie Mame' and in 1960 she made a one-shot screen comeback in the role of Eleanor Roosvelt in *Sunrise at Campobello.* She has subsequently appeared in occasional character parts and once in a while in specials on TV. She lives on a ranch near Santa Fe, New Mexico. She has received numerous awards for environmental and other civic and benevolent activities.

FILMS: *Goodbye Mr. Chips, Remember?* 1939; *Pride and Prejudice* (as Elizabeth Bennet) 1940; *Blossoms in the Dust, When Ladies Meet* 1941; *Mrs. Miniver* (title role), *Random Harvest* 1942; *The Youngest Profession, Madame Curie* (as Marie Curie) 1943; *Mrs. Parkington* (title role) 1944; *The Valley of Decision* 1945; *Adventure* 1946; *Desire Me* 1947; *Julia Misbehaves* 1948; *That Forsyte Woman/The Forsyte Saga* (as Irene Forsyte) 1949; *The Miniver Story* 1950; *The Law and the Lady* 1951; *Julius Caesar* (as Calpurnia), *Scandal at Scourie* 1953; *Her Twelve Men* 1954; *Strange Lady in Town* 1955; *Sunrise at Campobello* (as Eleanor Roosevelt), *Pepe* 1960; *The Singing Nun* 1966; *The Happiest Millionaire* 1967.

Garwood, Norman. Production designer. Visionary British designer able to infuse domestic worlds with varieties of surrealism, horror, and bizarre sensibility. Nominated for Academy Award for foreboding world of *Brazil.*

FILMS INCLUDE: *The Missionary, Time Bandits* 1981; *Brimstone and Treacle* 1982; *Bullshot, Red Monarch* 1983; *Water* 1984; *Brazil, Shadey* 1985; *Link* 1986; *The Princess Bride* 1987; *Glory* 1989; *Misery* 1990; *Hook* 1991; *Being Human* 1994.

Gasnier, Louis J. Director. *b.* Sept. 15, 1878, Paris. *d.* 1963. A former stage actor, director, and producer, he began directing comedy shorts for the French Pathé company in 1905. He discovered and directed the early films of Max LINDER, helping to mold his comedy style. Later also discovered and directed dramatic actor Jules BERRY. In 1912 he went to the US to run Pathé's American branch and helped the company's fortunes by directing such landmark serials as *The Perils of Pauline* (1914) and *The Exploits of Elaine* (1915), which were international box-office hits. He stayed in Hollywood as a director of features, mostly routine melodramas, returning to work in France only briefly in the early 30s. His Hollywood talkies were for the most part B pictures and he often needed the collaboration of dialogue directors in the handling of actors' lines.

FILMS INCLUDE: In France—*La Première Sortie d'un Colegien* 1905; *Le Pendu* 1906; *La Mort d'un Torèador* 1907; *Tirez s'il vous plaît* 1908; *Max fait du Ski* 1910. In the US—*The Perils of Pauline* (serial; co-dir. with Donald Mackenzie), *Detective Swift* (co-dir. with Mackenzie), *The Stolen Birthright* 1914; *The Exploits of Elaine* (serial; co-dir. with George B. Seitz) 1915; *The Shielding Shadow* (serial; co-dir. with Mackenzie), *Annabel's Romance, Hazel Kirke* 1916; *The*

Mystery of the Double Cross (serial) 1917; *The Seven Pearls* (serial), *Hands Up!* (serial) 1918; *The Tiger's Trail* (serial), *The Beloved Cheater* 1919; *The Corsican Brothers, The Butterfly Man, Kismet* 1920; *Good Women, A Wife's Awakening, Silent Years* 1921; *The Call of Home, Rich Men's Wives, Thorns and Orange Blossoms* 1922; *The Hero, Poor Men's Wives, Daughters of the Rich, Mothers-in-Law, Maytime* 1923; *Poisoned Paradise: The Forbidden Story of Monte Carlo, The Breath of Scandal, Wine, White Man, The Triflers* 1924; *The Parasite, The Boomerang, Parisian Love, Faint Perfume* 1925; *Pleasures of the Rich, Out of the Storm, Sin Cargo, That Model from Paris, Lost at Sea* 1926; *The Beauty Shoppers* 1927; *Streets of Shanghai, Fashion Madness* 1928; *Darkened Rooms* 1929; *Slightly Scarlet* (co-dir. with Edwin H. Knopf), *The Shadow of the Law, The Virtuous Sin* (co-dir. with George Cukor) 1930; *The Lawyer's Secret* (co-dir. with Max Marcin), *Silence* (co-dir. with Marcin) 1931; *The Strange Case of Clara Deane* (co-dir. with Marcin), *Forgotten Commandments* (co-dir. with William Schorr) 1932; *Gambling Ship* (co-dir. with Marcin), *Esperame* (Sp.), *Melodia de Arrabal* (Sp.), *Iris perdue et retrouvée* (Fr.), *Topaze* (Fr.) 1933; *Fedora* (Fr.), *Cuesta Abajo* (Sp.), *El Tango en Broadway* (Sp.) 1934; *The Last Outpost* (co-dir. with Charles Barton) 1935; *The Gold Racket, Bank Alarm* 1937; *La Immaculada* (Sp.) 1939; *Murder on the Yukon, The Burning Question/Tell Your Children/Reefer Madness* 1940; *Stolen Paradise* 1941; *Fight on Marines!* 1942.

Gassman, Vittorio. Actor. Born on Sept. 1, 1922, in Genoa. The son of an Austrian father and Florentine mother, a basketball star at high school, he later abandoned law studies to enroll at Rome's Accademia Nazionale di Arte Dramatica. He was a seasoned veteran of some 40 plays by the time he made his film debut in 1946. He started out as a dramatic player and because of his arrogant good looks was often typecast as an egocentric hero or a callous heel in adventure sagas and socio-romantic melodramas. By the early 50s he was one of the Italian screen's top leading men, but his reputation abroad remained limited and rested mainly on occasional box-office hits like *Bitter Rice* (1948) and *Anna* (1951). Meanwhile, he was gaining prestige as a stage actor, appearing with distinction in such productions as 'Tobacco Road' (for Visconti), 'Peer Gynt,' and 'Hamlet.' In 1952 he married American actress Shelley WINTERS and the following year came to the US and was signed by MGM. His Hollywood venture as well as the marriage came to an early, unhappy end and he was soon back in Italy, where he started his own stage company, Teatro Popolare Italiano, and resumed his activity in local films. In 1957 he directed himself in the film *Kean,* which enhanced his reputation for overacting under less than strict directorial control. In the late 50s Gassman began a new phase of his film career, proving himself a capable comedy actor and gained renewed popularity in the Italian and international markets with a succession of deftly handled lightweight roles. He won the best actor prize at Cannes for *Scent of a Woman* (1975).

FILMS INCLUDE: *Preludio d'Amore/Shamed* 1946; *L'Ebreo errante/The Wandering Jew, La Figlia del Capitano* 1947; *Riso Amaro/Bitter Rice, Il Cavaliere misterioso* (as Casanova) 1948; *Il Lupo della Sila/Lure of the Sila* 1949; *Il Tradimento, Anna* 1951; *La Corona Nera, Il Sogno di Zorro* 1952; *The Glass Wall* (US), *Sombrero* (US), *Cry of the Hunted* (US) 1953; *Rhapsody* (US), *Mambo* 1954; *La Donna piu Bella del Mondo/Beautiful but Dangerous* 1955; *War and Peace* (US/It.) 1956; *Kean* (also co-dir. with Francesco Rosi, co-sc.) 1957; *La Tempesta/Tempest, I Soliti Ignoti/Big Deal on Madonna Street* 1958; *The Miracle* (US), *La Grande Guerra/T he Great War* 1959; *Il Mattatore/Love and Larceny, Crimen/And Suddenly It's Murder* 1960; *Il Giudizio Universale* 1961; *Barabba/Barabbas* 1961; *Il Sorpasso/The Easy Life, La Marcia su Roma, I Mostri/Opiate '67, Il Successo* 1963; *Se Permettete. . . Parliamo di Donne/Let's Talk About Women, Il Gaucho* 1964; *La Guerra Secreta/The Dirty Game* 1965; *L'Armata Brancaleone, Il Diavolo Innamorato/The Devil in Love* 1966; *Il Profeta, Sept fois Femme/Woman Times Seven* (Fr./It./US), *Il Tigre/The Tiger and the Pussycat, Questi Fantasmi/Ghosts Italian Style* 1967; *L'Alibi* (also with Luciano Lucignani and Adolfo Celi; co-sc.) 1969; *Contestazione Generale, Il Divorzio* 1970; *L'Udienza* 1971; *In Nome del Popolo Italiano* 1972; *Senza Famiglie* (also dir.), *Tosca* 1973; *A Mezzanotte va la Ronda del Piacere/Midnight Pleasures, Profumo di Donna/Scent of a Woman, C'eravamo tanto Amati/We All Loved Each Other So Much* 1975; *Signore e Signori Buonanotte, Le Desert des Tartares* (Fr./It./Iran), *I Telefoni bianchi* 1976; *Anima Persa, I Nuovi Mostri/Viva Italia* 1977; *A Wedding* (US) 1978; *Due Pezzi di Pane/Happy Hobos, Caro Papa* (It./Fr./Can.), *Quintet* (US) 1979; *The Nude Bomb/The Return of Maxwell Smart* (US), *Camera d'Albergo, La Terrazza, Sono fotogenico* 1980; *Il Turno/Night Shift, Sharkey's Machine* (US) 1981; *Tempest* (US) 1982; *La Vie est un Roman/Life Is a Bed of Roses, Benvenuta* 1983; *Paradigme/Le Pouvoir du Mal* 1985; *I Soliti ignoti 20 Anni doppo/Big Deal on Madonna Street 20 Years Later* 1986; *La Famiglia/The Family, I Picari* 1987; *Lo Zio indegno/The Sleazy Uncle* 1989; *Dimenticare Palermo/To Forget Palermo, Sherherazade/The 1001 Nights* 1990; *I Divertimenti della Privata, Vita Tolgo il Disturbo/I Won't Disturb You* 1991; *El Largo Invierno/The Long Winter, Quando eravamo Repressi/When We Were Repressed* 1992; *Sleepers* (US) 1996.

gate. The part of the camera or projector mechanism in which the film is momentarily held while a frame is being exposed or projected. So called because it can be swung out on its hinges for threading or cleaning.

Gates, Nancy. Actress. Born on Feb. 1, 1926, in Dallas. An RKO starlet and juvenile player of the 40s, following radio and stage experience as a child, she graduated to leads in the 50s. Mainly in run-of-the-mill productions. She retired from the screen in 1960 after giving birth to twin daughters.

FILMS INCLUDE: *Come on Danger, The Tuttles of Tahiti, The Great Gildersleeve* 1942; *Hitler's Children, This Land Is Mine* 1943; *The Master Race, Nevada* 1944; *The Spanish Main* 1945; *Cheyenne Takes Over* 1947; *The Atomic City, The Member of the Wedding* 1952; *Hell's Half Acre, Suddenly* 1954; *No Man's Woman* 1955; *The Bottom of the Bottle, Wetbacks, World Without End, The Search for Bridey Murphy* 1956; *Some Came Running* 1959; *Comanche Station* 1960.

Gaudio, Tony. Director of photography. *b.* Gaetano Antonio Gaudio, 1885, Rome. *d.* 1951. A member of a family of photographic experts, he came to New York in his early 20s to head Vitagraph's film labs. On the West Coast from 1910, he was the lighting cameraman on hundreds of Hollywood films, including many distinguished productions, for Universal, Metro, Warners, and other studios. Particularly notable was his work for Warners in the 30s. He was among the founders of the American Society of Cinematographers and a highly regarded innovator in black-and-white cinematography. He won an Academy Award for his work on *Anthony Adverse* (1936). Sometimes billed as Gaetano Gaudio or Antonio Gaudio. In 1925 he directed two films, *Sealed Lips* and *The Price of Success.*

FILMS INCLUDE: *Their First Misunderstanding* 1911; *Classmates* 1914; *Big Termaine* 1916; *The Avenging Trail* 1917; *Pals First, Broadway Bill* 1918; *The Unpardonable Sin* (co-phot.) 1919; *In Old Kentucky, Kismet* 1920; *The Sin of Martha Queed* 1921; *East Is West, The Eternal Flame* 1922; *Ashes of Vengeance, Within the Law* 1923; *Secrets, Husbands and Lovers* 1924; *Déclassé, The Lady, Graustark* 1925; *The Temptress* (co-phot.), *The Gay Deceiver* 1926; *The Gaucho, An Affair of the Follies, Two Arabian Knights* (co-phot.), *The Notorious Lady* 1927; *The Racket* 1928; *On with the Show, Tiger Rose* 1929; *General Crack, Hell's Angels* (co-phot.) 1930; *Little Caesar* 1931; *Sky Devils, The Mask of Fu Manchu, Tiger Shark* 1932; *Voltaire, Ex-Lady, The Devil's Playground* 1933; *Mandalay* 1934; *Bordertown, Oil for the Lamps of China* 1935; *The Story of Louis Pasteur, The White Angel, Anthony Adverse* 1936; *Another Dawn, The King and the Chorus Girl, Kid Galahad, The Life of Emile Zola* 1937; *The Adventures of Robin Hood* (co-phot.), *The Dawn Patrol, The Amazing Dr. Clitterhouse, The Sisters* 1938; *Juarez, The Old Maid, We Are Not Alone* 1939; *The Fighting 69th, The Letter, Till We Meet Again, Brother Orchid* 1940; *The Great Lie, High Sierra, The Man Who Came to Dinner* 1941; *Larceny Inc.* 1942; *The Constant Nymph* 1943; *Days of Glory* 1944; *A Song to Remember* 1945; *I've Always Loved You, The Bandit of Sherwood Forest* 1946; *That's My Man* 1947; *The Red Pony* 1949.

gauge. Designation of the width of a film. Thirty-five mm film, commonly used in professional cinematography, is said to be of "standard gauge." Sixteen mm film, used by both professionals and amateurs, is said to be of "narrow gauge," or "substandard."

Gaumont, Léon. Pioneer film executive, inventor. *b.* May 10, 1864, Paris. *d.* 1946. A merchant of photographic equipment, in 1895 he established the Gaumont Company and in the following year began manufacturing motion picture apparatus. The commercial success of his chronophotographe, a camera-projector developed by Georges DEMENY, encouraged him to expand his activity into the production of films. The regular director of his films through 1907 was Alice GUY-BLACHÉ. Later directors included Louis Feuillade, Jacques Feyder, and Marcel L'Herbier. At the same time, Gaumont began experimenting with various film devices. One of his early inventions, in 1902, was the Chronophone, a sound system synchronizing motion pictures with a record player. His company expanded rapidly and soon comprised studios, labs, and a growing chain of movie theaters in Paris and other cities. After 1907 it extended its business activities into England, Germany, Russia, and even the United States. Gaumont continued with his technical research throughout the company's expansion.

In 1912 he introduced a program of "talking movies" into one of his Paris theaters, using an improved version of his Chronophone. In the same year he patented a three-color additive process, the Chronochrome, and in 1918 produced a short color film with that system. In 1928 he developed a sound system, which was used in the production of the first French talkie, *Eau de Nil.* However, the system was imperfect and was soon dropped. With competition from Hollywood cutting into his company's business, Gaumont retired in 1929. His retirement ended an era marked by the complete dominance of the French film industry by two pioneer giants—Léon Gaumont and Charles PATHÉ.

Gaumont's company was in part absorbed by Metro-Goldwyn-Mayer. Meanwhile, Gaumont British, originally founded as the London branch of Gaumont's, continued as an independent distributor and producer into the 1930s. After 1932, it was linked with Gainsborough Pictures, with Michael BALCON as head of production for both companies. Gaumont British produced several of Alfred HITCHCOCK's British films before the company collapsed following Balcon's departure in 1936.

Gavin, John. Actor. Born on Apr. 8, 1932, in Los Angeles. *ed.* Stanford U. Handsome, somewhat rigid leading man of Hollywood films, following a four-year stint as an air-intelligence officer in the Navy during and after the Korean War. He worked briefly as a press agent before making his screen debut in 1956. He also starred in the TV series 'Destry' (1964) and 'Convoy' (1965) and made his Broadway debut in 'Seesaw' in 1973. In 1971–73 he served as president of Screen Actors Guild. Gavin, whose mother was of Hispanic origin, majored in college in the economic history of Latin America, and became an expert in the field. Even while pursuing his acting career, he became involved in diplomatic affairs, serving for many years (1961–73) as an advisor to the Secretary General of the Organization of American States (OAS) and later as a consultant on Latin affairs to the State Department. In 1981–86 he served as the US Ambassador to Mexico. He is married to actress Constance Towers.

FILMS INCLUDE: *Behind the High Wall* 1956; *Four Girls in Town, Quantez* 1957; *A Time to Love and a Time to Die* 1958; *Imitation of Life* 1959; *Psycho, Spartacus, Midnight Lace, A Breath of Scandal* 1960; *Romanoff and Juliet, Tammy Tell Me True, Back Street* 1961; *Thoroughly Modern Millie* 1967; *The Madwoman of Chaillot* 1969; *Pussycat Pussycat I Love You* 1970; *One in the Morning* (It.) 1972; *Jennifer* 1978; *History of the World: Part I* 1981.

gay and lesbian cinema (queer cinema). In its narrowest sense, gay and lesbian cinema consists of films about homosexuality made by gay and lesbian people and directed primarily to a gay and lesbian audience. More broadly, it includes films on homosexuality made by straight people and directed to a mass (and therefore largely heterosexual) audience. However, there are several other aspects to consider in discussing gay and lesbian cinema. There is the phenomenon of "gay icons": directors, actors, and actresses (some homosexual or bisexual, some heterosexual) to whom the gay community is especially drawn, including Judy GARLAND, Bette DAVIS, Joan CRAWFORD, Marilyn MONROE, Louise BROOKS, Vincente MINNELLI, Marlene DIETRICH, Greta GARBO, Rudolph VALENTINO, George CUKOR, James DEAN, and Montgomery CLIFT. There is a "gay sensibility" through which gays and lesbians glean parallels to homosexual feelings and problems in films whose themes are not overtly gay. Though *Mildred Pierce* is not a product of a conscious gay cinema, it has nonetheless become adopted as a particular favorite of the gay community and would not seem out of place at a Gay and Lesbian Film Festival. There is also the checkered history of the portrayal of gays (explicit and implicit) in commercial films, largely for comic relief. Such representations include the "sissy" types that have proliferated in movie comedies, with Franklin PANGBORN, Grady SUTTON, and Antonio Fargas among the best-remembered clown mincers.

Gay and lesbian cinema proper—films made by, for, and about gays and lesbians—has had a fascinating and complex history. Gay and lesbian filmmakers have had to cope with public disapproval and indifference, villification of homosexuality in mainstream movies, the perception of gay films as unprofitable and marginal, and division among gay audiences due to the diversity of the gay experience.

According to Vito Russo's landmark study, *The Celluloid Closet*, the first gay film, presented in Berlin in 1919, was Richard Oswald's *Anders als die Anderen/Different from the Others*, which was plainly political in its encouragement of tolerance for what was called "the Third Sex." Another early classic is *Maadchen in Uniform* (Ger., 1932), the story of a schoolgirl with a romantic crush on her female professor. Such representations were possible in Weimar Germany, where, in some places, sexual exploration was practiced openly in the days before Hitler's policy of exterminating homosexuals alongside Jews and other "undesirables."

In Hollywood before the 1930s, representations of homosexuality were frequently used for comic relief or for condemnation, as in Cecil B. DE MILLE'S *The Sign of the Cross* (1932). A startling exception is *Salome* (1923), starring Alla NAZIMOVA and an all-gay cast, written and directed by her lover Natasha Rambova (both of whom were at different times wives of Valentino). But conservative opinion-makers deemed any representation of homosexuality shocking, and in 1930 the Production Code banned the depiction of homosexuality in any form.

Over the next thirty years, homosexuality was rarely more than alluded to on-screen. The late 40s and 50s were especially repressive times for gay filmmakers, who were dealing with a resistance to depictions of any kind of sexuality. Still, it was in this period that two of the most influential gay films were produced. Kenneth ANGER, a bored teenager working surreptitiously in his parents' garage, used found and stolen film stock to create *Fireworks* (1947). The avant-garde short juxtaposed images to capture the essence of male homosexuality. The film provoked legal action that eventually resulted in a Supreme Court decision that explicit handling of homosexual themes was not inherently obscene. That same year, playwright Jean Genet created his only film, *Un Chant d'Amour* (Fr.) which explored gay desire using the situational homosexuality of prisoners, the voyeuristic longing of their guard, and the violence that erupts with sexual repression.

By the late 50s, films had tentatively begun to explore previously taboo topics. In Hollywood, homosexuality was approached through insinuation, with tragic endings that were ultimately condemning, as in *Suddenly Last Summer, The Third Sex* (1959), *The Children's Hour, Advise and Consent* (1962), *Reflections in a Golden Eye* (1967), and *The Fox* (1968). But these negative portrayals paved the way for and played alongside more open-minded depictions. *Victim* (1961) was a landmark for its empathetic treatment of a closeted gay man who scores a personal triumph over his blackmailers. Films like *Darling* (1965) introduced the concept of bisexuality as a fact of life.

The floodgates of gay cinema opened at the end of the 60s, when the Production Code was dropped in favor of the MPAA ratings system. William FRIEDKIN'S *The Boys in the Band* (1970) offered a sustained and largely realistic look at gay life in the 60s in New York City. Gay and bisexual characters became more commonplace on the screen throughout the 70s in such hugely successful films as *Cabaret* (1972), *Dog Day Afternoon* (1975), and *La Cage aux Folles* (1978), the most commercially successful gay-themed film ever made.

Despite increasing exposure in commercial films, the true gay cinema had had its origins in the underground, and in the 70s that was where it stayed. Filmmakers like Andy WARHOL (*My Hustler,* 1965; *Lonesome Cowboys,* 1968) and John WATERS (*Pink Flamingos,* 1973) offered unapologetic if sensational glimpses of a growing gay subculture. The underground gay cinema was part of a growing avant-garde that eschewed the polished filmmaking Hollywood required. Its influences—the glamor of melodramas of the 40s and 50s and the spectacle of pornography—were readily visible, as was an edge absent from films that sought to please mass audiences. These influences came to a head with the ultimate "midnight movie," the paean to pansexuality, *The Rocky Horror Picture Show* (1976).

Friedkin's *Cruising* (1980) was a turning point. Gay activists protested and rioted over the film's negative portrayal of male homosexuality as a murderous impulse that can be "caught" like a disease. A critical and commercial failure, the film generated such opposition that it paradoxically helped to foster a more open era in gay and lesbian cinema. Such films as *Making Love* (1982), which presented a married man's "coming out," and *Kiss of the Spider Woman* (1985), which earned William HURT an Oscar for his portrayal of a gay political prisoner, were mainstream reflections of a growing gay and lesbian screen presence. Gay filmmakers flooded art houses with masterful and diverse examinations of the gay experience: *Taxi zum Klo* (Ger., 1981) with its hard sexual core; the touching lesbian love story *Entre-Nous/Between Us* (Fr., 1983); *Querelle* (Ger., 1982), Rainer Werner FASSBINDER'S disturbing portrait of a sailor's sexuality; *The Times of Harvey Milk* (1985), an Oscar-winning documentary on the assassination of the member of the San Francisco Board of Supervisors; *Mala Noche* (1986); *Dona Herlinda and Her Son* (Mex., 1986); *Desert Hearts* (1986); and representations of the effects of the early years of AIDS on the gay community, like *Parting Glances* (1986) and *Longtime Companion* (1990).

As gay filmmakers grew in numbers, straight filmmakers increasingly tended to portray gay characters honestly and without fanfare. In 1983, CHER was nominated for an Oscar for her performance in *Silkwood*, one of the first films with a character whose lesbianism was incidental to the plot. Stephen FREARS presented two men who happened to be gay in his exploration of racism in contemporary London in *My Beautiful Laundrette* (UK, 1986) and followed it with *Prick Up Your Ears* (UK, 1987), the life story of gay playwright Joe Orton. The Ismail MERCHANT and James IVORY (Merchant-Ivory) film *Maurice* (UK, 1987) depicted a gay man in turn-of-the-century England. Gus VAN SANT provided a crucial link as a gay auteur exploring gay subject matter in a film intended for general audiences, *My Own Private Idaho* (1991). The ambitious film enjoyed wide release due to its teen heartthrob leads, River PHOENIX and Keanu REEVES.

The late 80s and early 90s also saw a new facet of gay activism, in which self-proclaimed "queers" took a more confrontational approach to presenting their lives and concerns. This movement has been effectively embodied on the screen in the films of the late Derek JARMAN (*Edward II*, UK, 1991), Todd HAYNES'S *Poison* (1991), and the avant-garde video work of Sadie Benning. "Queer cinema" is a new term for films that are made by gays for gays, and that are usually radically imaginative in presentation, taking for granted their belief that being gay gives one a completely separate, distinct worldview.

In addition to those already named, current filmmakers involved in queer and gay/lesbian cinema include Neil JORDAN (*The Crying Game, Interview with the Vampire*), Pedro ALMODÓVAR (*Matador, Law of Desire),* Tom Kalin (*Swoon*), Jeff Arakki (*The Living End*), Jennie Livingston (*Paris Is Burning*), Edgar Michael Bravo (*I'll Love You Forever. . . Tonight*), Monika Treut (*My Father Is Coming*), Tilda Swinton (*Orlando*), Cheryl Dunye, Temistocles Lopez, Elle Spiro, Dawn Suggs, G. B. Jones, and Jerry Tartaglia.

Gaynor, Janet. Actress. *b.* Laura Gainor, Oct. 6, 1906, Philadelphia. *d.* 1984. After graduating from a San Francisco high school, she went to Los Angeles, hoping to get into films. She worked briefly as a bookkeeper in a shoe store and an usherette in a local theater, then began appearing as an extra in movies. She gradually worked her way up to bit parts in Hal Roach comedy shorts and a lead in a two-reel Western. Her first substantial part, under contract to Fox, came in *The Johnstown Flood* (1926). Within a year, she was the most important star on the Fox lot on the strength of her appeal in Murnau's masterpiece *Sunrise* and Borzage's box-office hit *Seventh Heaven.* She won the first Academy Award ever given in the best actress category, for her performances (early Oscars were often awarded for cumulative work) in *Sunrise, Seventh Heaven* (both 1927), and *Street Angel* (1928). Diminutive, dimpled, and sweetly wholesome, her appeal lay in her ability to project vulnerability and naïveté, even when playing prostitutes or misguided women. She often co-starred with equally wholesome Charles FARRELL. At the height of their popularity as a team, in the early 30s, they were known as "America's favorite lovebirds." In 1934, she was Hollywood's top box-office attraction.

After getting out of her Fox contract, Miss Gaynor scored handsomely in two successful Selznick films, *A Star Is Born* (Oscar nomination, 1937) and *The Young in Heart* (1938), then announced her retirement from the screen. Having married and divorced (1932–34) Lydell Peck, an attorney, in 1939 she married Gilbert ADRIAN, Hollywood's most famous costume designer. She emerged from retirement (much of it spent on a Brazilian ranch) occasionally in the 50s for radio and TV work and a mother part in the film *Bernadine.* She was widowed in 1959, and in 1964 she married Paul Gregory, a producer. In 1976 her still-life paintings were exhibited in a New York gallery. In 1978 she was honored with a special plaque from the Motion Picture Academy for "her truly immeasurable contribution to the art of motion pictures and for the pleasure and entertainment her unique artistry has brought to millions of film fans around the globe." Her final appearances came in 1980, in the short-lived Broadway stage adaptation of the film *Harold and Maude* and in an episode of the TV series 'Love Boat.' In 1983 she was critically injured in a traffic accident, in which her husband and actress-singer Mary MARTIN were also hurt. She sustained 11 broken ribs, a broken pelvis and collarbone, and various internal injuries from which she never fully recovered. Her death of pneumonia two years later was directly attributed by the coroner to these injuries.

FEATURE FILMS: *The Johnstown Flood, The Shamrock Handicap, The Midnight Kiss, The Blue Eagle, The Return of Peter Grimm* 1926; *Seventh Heaven, Sunrise, Two Girls Wanted* 1927; *Street Angel* 1928; *Four Devils* 1928–29; *Christina, Lucky Star, Sunny Side Up* 1929; *Happy Days, High Society Blues* 1930; *The Man Who Came Back, Daddy Long Legs, Merely Mary Ann, Delicious* 1931; *The First Year, Tess of the Storm Country* 1932; *State Fair, Adorable, Paddy the Next Best Thing* 1933; *Carolina, Change of Heart, Servants' Entrance* 1934; *One More Spring, The Farmer Takes a Wife* 1935; *Small Town Girl, Ladies in Love* 1936; *A Star Is Born* 1937; *Three Loves Has Nancy, The Young in Heart* 1938; *Bernadine* 1957.

Gaynor, Mitzi. Actress, dancer. Born Franceska Mitzi Gerber, on Sept. 4, 1930, in Chicago. Reputedly a descendant of Hungarian aristocracy (some sources give her name as Franceska Mitzi Marlene de Charney von Gerber), she followed in the footsteps of her ballerina mother and took up dancing at four. At 12 she became a member of the corps de ballet of the Los Angeles Civic Light Opera. She made her screen debut in 1950 and brightened a string of Fox musicals with her vivacity and chirpy charm. But her films did poorly at the box office and the studio dropped her option in 1954. That same year she married a talent agent, Jack Bean, who soon rejuvenated her career at Paramount and other studios. She scored nicely in *Anything Goes* (1956), opposite Bing Crosby, *The Joker Is Wild,* opposite Frank Sinatra, and *Les Girls,* opposite Gene Kelly (both 1957), and was selected by Joshua Logan among many competitors to star in his grandiose screen version of *South Pacific* (1958). But the film turned out to be a failure and hurt her career. She made her last film in 1963 and subsequently appeared successfully in stock and nightclubs and on TV.

FILMS: *My Blue Heaven* 1950; *Take Care of My Little Girl, Golden Girl* 1951; *We're Not Married, Bloodhounds of Broadway* 1952; *Down Among the Sheltering Palms, The I Don't Care Girl* 1953; *Three Young Texans, There's No Business Like Show Business* 1954; *Anything Goes, The Birds and the Bees* 1956; *The Joker Is Wild, Les Girls* 1957; *South Pacific* 1958; *Happy Anniversary* 1959; *Surprise Package* 1960; *For Love or Money* 1963.

Gazzara, Ben. Actor. Born Biago Gazzara on Aug. 28, 1930, in New York City. The son of an immigrant Sicilian laborer, he grew up on New York's tough Lower East Side and while reluctantly studying engineering at CCNY was dreaming of an acting career. He quit college after receiving a scholarship to study under Erwin Piscator, then joined the Actors Studio and was soon on his way to a Broadway success in such plays as 'Cat on a Hot Tin Roof' and 'A Hatful of Rain.' An intense, introverted actor, he showed great promise with his two first film roles, as a sadistic cadet in *The Strange One* (1957) and as an enigmatic rape suspect in the courtroom drama *Anatomy of a Murder* (1959). But with the notable exception of John Cassavetes's *Husbands* (1970), his subsequent films were of lesser consequence. He has been successful, though, as the star of the TV series 'Arrest and Trial' (1963–64) and 'Run for Your Life' (1965–68). His second wife (1961–79) was actress Janice RULE.

FILMS: *The Strange One* 1957; *Anatomy of a Murder* 1959; *Risate di Gioia/The Passionate Thief* (It.) 1960; *The Young Doctors* 1961; *Convicts 4, La Citta Prigioniera/Conquered City* (It.) 1962; *A Rage to Live* 1965; *The Bridge at Remagen* 1969; *Husbands* 1970; *The Neptune Factor* 1973; *Capone* 1975; *The Killing of a Chinese Bookie, Voyage of the Damned* (UK) 1976; *The Sicilian Connection, High Velocity* 1977; *Opening Night* 1978; *Saint Jack, Sidney Sheldon's Bloodline* 1979; *They All Laughed, Inchon, Storie di Ordinaria Follia/Tales of Ordinary Madness* (It./Fr.) 1981; *La Ragazza di Trieste/The Girl from Trieste* (It.) 1982; *Boogie Woogie, Uno Scandalo perbene* (It.) 1983; *Il Camorrista/The Professor* (It.) 1985; *Road House, Quicker Than the Eye* (Switz.) 1989; *Don Bosco, Silent Memory* 1990; *Parallel Lives* 1994; *Farmer and Chase, The Shadow Conspiracy* 1997.

geared head. A camera-support mount that makes it possible to PAN and TILT a camera by means of a mechanism composed of gear wheels and toothed rings.

Gedrick, Jason. Actor. Born in 1965, in Chicago. *ed.* Drake U. Brash young lead of American films. Soared to popularity among juvenile audiences as the star of the action picture *Iron Eagle* (1986).

FILMS: *Bad Boys, Risky Business* 1983; *Massive Retaliation* 1984; *The Zoo Gang, The Heavenly Kid* 1985; *Iron Eagle* 1986; *Stacking* 1987; *Promised Land* 1988; *Rooftops* 1989; *Crossing the Bridge* 1992.

Geer, Will. Actor. *b.* Mar. 9, 1902, Frankfort, Ind. *d.* 1978. The son of a postal worker and a teacher, he participated in high school dramatics and pursued the same interest while studying at the University of Chicago and at Columbia. He joined Eva Le Gallienne's National Repertory Company and made his Broadway debut in 'The Merry Wives of Windsor' (1928). He appeared in numerous stage productions and an occasional film in the 30s and 40s before settling on a Hollywood career as a character actor in 1948. Three years later, however, he was blacklisted for refusing to co-operate with the House Un-American Activities Committee and returned to the stage, appearing both on and off Broadway. It wasn't until 1962 that he returned to the screen, thanks to Otto PREMINGER, the first Hollywood director to defy the blacklist. From then Geer played character roles, often abrasive, sometimes sinister, in many

Hollywood productions, as well as on TV, notably in the long-running 'The Waltons.' His daughter, Ellen Geer, has played leads and supporting roles in several films of the 60s and 70s, as well as on TV.

FILMS INCLUDE: *The Misleading Lady* 1932; *Deep Waters* 1948; *Johnny Allegro, Lust for Gold, Anna Lucasta, Intruder in the Dust* 1949; *Commanche Territory, Winchester '73, Broken Arrow* 1950; *Double Crossbones, Bright Victory, The Tall Target* 1951; *Salt of the Earth* 1954; *Advise and Consent* 1962; *Black Like Me* 1964; *Seconds* 1966; *In Cold Blood, The President's Analyst* 1967; *Bandolero* 1968; *The Moonshine War, Pieces of Dreams* 1970; *Brother John* 1971; *Napoleon and Samantha, Jeremiah Johnson* 1972; *Executive Action* 1973; *Silence, Memory of Us* 1974; *The Manchu Eagle Murder Caper Mystery* 1975; *The Blue Bird* (US/USSR), *Moving Violation* 1976; *The Mafu Cage, The Billion Dollar Hobo* 1978.

Geeson, Judy. Actress. Born on Sept. 10, 1948, in Arundel, England. She attended London's Corona dramatic school and made her stage debut at nine. She began appearing on British TV at 12 and made her screen debut in the role of a fresh schoolgirl in *To Sir with Love* (1967). She has since played provocative leads in many British films. She married actor Kristoffer Tabori in 1985. Her sister, Sally Geeson (*b.* 1950), also appeared in films.

FILMS INCLUDE: *To Sir with Love, Berserk!* 1967; *Here We Go Round the Mulberry Bush, Prudence and the Pill, Hammerhead* 1968; *Three Into Two Won't Go, Two Gentlemen Sharing* 1969; *The Executioner, Good-bye Gemini* 1970; *10 Rillington Place, One of Those Things* 1971; *Fear in the Night* 1972; *Percy's Progress/It's Not the Size That Counts* 1974; *Brannigan* (UK/US), *Doomwatch* 1975; *Carry on England, The Eagle Has Landed* 1976; *Dominique* 1978; *Inseminoid/Horror Planet* 1980; *The Plague Dogs* (v/o) 1982.

Geffen, David. Producer. Born on February 21, 1943 in Brooklyn, N.Y. Largely self-made, highly respected executive of music industry, and later Broadway with, among others, the wildly successful Tony Award winning musical 'Rent,' and film production. After forming Geffen Records in 1980, he followed with development of Geffen Film Co., through which he has produced a number of idiosyncratic films, some of them substantial commercial hits. In 1994 he announced that he would join friends Steven SPIELBERG and Jeffrey KATZENBERG in the creation of a new motion picture studio, DreamWorks SKG.

FILMS INCLUDE: *Personal Best* 1982; *Risky Business* 1983; *Lost in America, After Hours* 1985; *Little Shop of Horrors* 1986; *Beetlejuice* (exec. pr.) 1988; *Men Don't Leave* 1990; *Defending Your Life* 1991; *Interview with a Vampire* 1994.

Gegauff, Paul. Screenwriter. *b.* 1922, Blotzheim, France. *d.* 1983. Claude Chabrol's favorite script collaborator. He also directed a film, *Reflux* (1961), and appeared as an actor in Godard's *Week-End/Weekend* (1968), in Vadim's *Le Vice et la Vertu/Vice and Virtue* (1963), and in Chabrol's *Une Partie de Plaisir/A Piece of Pleasure* (1975), co-starring in the latter with his wife, Danielle Gegauff. He also published several novels.

FILMS INCLUDE: *Les Cousins/The Cousins, A Double Tour/Leda/Web of Passion* 1959; *Plein Soleil/Purple Noon/Lust for Evil, Les Bonnes Femmes* 1960; *Les Godelureaux* 1961; *Ophélia* (under pseudonym Martial Matthieu) 1962; *Les Grands Chemins/Of Flesh and Blood* 1963; *Le Scandale/The Champagne Murders* (dial. only) 1967; *Les Biches* 1968; *More, Que la Bête meure/This Man Must Die* 1969; *Les Novices* 1970; *Docteur Popoul, La Décade prodigieuse/Ten Days' Wonder, La Vallée/The Valley* 1972; *Une Partie de Plaisir/A Piece of Pleasure* (also act.) 1975; *La Secte de Marrakech* 1979; *Ave Maria* 1984.

Gehr, Ernie. Avant-garde filmmaker. Born on July 20, 1943, in Milwaukee. He became involved in films shortly after arriving in New York in 1966. His work has often been described as minimalist and object-oriented, typically emphasizing technique and shunning emotional appeal. He has taught cinema at several colleges.

FILMS INCLUDE: *Morning Wait* 1968; *Transparency* 1969; *Serene Velocity* 1970; *Still* 1971; *Shift, Eureka* 1974; *Table* 1976; *Mirage* 1981.

Gelbart, Larry. Screenwriter. Born on Feb. 25, 1925, in Chicago. He was only 16 when he began writing radio material for Danny Thomas and other radio comedians. His contributions later extended to films, television, and plays. He won an Emmy Award in 1974 for episodes of TV's 'M*A*S*H', and Tony Awards for Broadway's 'A Funny Thing Happened on the Way to the Forum' (1962) and 'City of Angels' (1989), the latter a riotous musical spoof of 1940s Hollywood. He was nominated for Academy Awards for *Oh God!* (Writers Guild Award, 1977) and *Tootsie* (1982), the latter in collaboration. One of Hollywood's leading comedy writers, he is said to command a million-dollar fee per film, whether or not it is eventually produced. In addition to his signed work, he went uncredited for numerous script rewrites. In 1990 he was honored with a retrospective of his films at UCLA.

FILMS INCLUDE: *The Notorious Landlady* 1960; *The Thrill of It All* 1963; *A Funny Thing Happened on the Way to the Forum* (co-play basis only), *The Wrong Box* (UK), *Not with My Wife You Don't* 1966; *La Cintura di Castita/The Chastity Belt/On My Way to the Crusades I Met a Girl Who. . .* (It./US) 1968; *Ruba al Prossimo Tuo/A Fine Pair* (It.) 1969; *Oh God!* 1977; *Movie Movie* 1978; *Neighbors* 1981; *Tootsie* 1982; *Blame It on Rio* (also co-exec. prod.) 1984.

Gélin, Daniel. Actor. Born on May 19, 1921, in Angers, France. Entered French films in 1939, following drama studies at the Paris Conservatoire, and gradually developed from bits and light youth roles into one of the principal leads of the French cinema, typically appearing in sensitive, literate, man-of-the-world roles. He also directed one film, *Les Dents Longues* (1953), and is a published poet of some critical esteem. Formerly (1945–54) married to actress Danièle DELORME, he is the father of actress Maria SCHNEIDER of *Last Tango in Paris* fame. His son, Xavier Gelin, is also an actor.

FILMS INCLUDE: *Miquette et sa Mère/Miquette* 1940; *Premier Rendez-Vous/Her First Affair* 1941; *Un Ami viendra ce Soir/A Friend Will Come Tonight, Martin Roumagnac/The Room Upstairs* 1946; *Rendez-Vous de Juillet* 1949; *La Ronde, Dieu a besoin des Hommes/God Needs Men* 1950; *Edouard et Caroline/Edward and Caroline, Les Mains sales/Dirty Hands* 1951; *Le Plaisir, Adorables Créatures, La Minute de Vérité/The Moment of Truth* 1952; *Les Dents Longues* (also dir.), *Rue de l'Estrapade, L'Esclave* 1953; *La Neige était sale/The Snow Was Black, La Romana/Woman of Rome* (It.), *Sang et Lumière, Si Versailles m'était conté/Royal Affairs in Versailles, L'Affaire Maurizius* 1954; *Les Amants de Tage/Lovers' Net, Napoléon* (as Bonaparte) 1955; *Paris Coquin/Maid in Paris, The Man Who Knew Too Much* (US), *En effeuillant la Marguerite/Please Mr. Balzac* 1956; *Mort en Fraude, Retour de Manivelle/There's Always a Price Tag* 1957; *Charmants Garçons, La Fille de Hambourg/Port of Desire* 1958; *Julie la Rousse/Julie the Redhead* 1959; *Cartagine in Fiamme/Carthage in Flames* (It./Fr.), *Le Testament d'Orphee/Testament of Orpheus, La Proie pour Ombre, Austerlitz* 1960; *La Morte-Saison des Amours/The Season for Love* 1961; *The Longest Day* (US) 1962; *Les Vacances portugaises* 1963; *La Bonne Soupe/Careless Love* 1964; *Compartiment tueurs/The Sleeping Car Murder* 1965;

Paris brûle-t-il?/Is Paris Burning? (Fr./US), *La Ligne de Démarcation, Soleil noir/Black Sun* 1966; *Slogan, Détruire dit-elle/Destroy She Said* 1969; *Le Souffle au Coeur/Murmur of the Heart* 1971; *La Guele de L'Emploi* 1973; *Un Linceul n'a pas de Poches* 1974; *Trop c'est trop* 1975; *Nous irons tous au Paradis* 1977; *L'Honorable Société* 1978; *L'Oeil du Maître* 1979; *La Nuit de Varennes* 1982; *Les Enfants* 1985; *Itinéraire d'un Enfant gaté/Itinerary of a Spoiled Child* 1988; *Mr. Frost* (UK) 1990; *Un Type Bien* 1991; *Les Mormottes* 1993.

Gemini. A system combining a motion picture camera with a videotape camera. When the optical mechanisms of both cameras are interlocked, the system makes possible the simultaneous recording on film of the same image that is being recorded on videotape by the TV camera.

General Film Company. See MOTION PICTURE PATENTS COMPANY.

general release. The widespread distribution of a film for exhibition in motion picture theaters rather than a limited distribution for special showings.

Genina, Augusto. Director. *b.* Jan. 28, 1892, Rome. *d.* 1957. Entered Italian films in 1913 as a screenwriter and began directing within several months. An able craftsman, he directed some 150 films during 40 years, his subjects ranging from early Italian melodrama to Fascist propaganda, and won a number of awards at Venice. From the late 20s he also worked frequently in France, Germany, and Austria. He often wrote his own scripts. He was a cousin of director Mario CAMERINI, and the husband of Carmen Boni, who appeared in some of his films.

FILMS INCLUDE: *La Moglie di sua Eccelenza* 1913; *Il Segreto del Castello di Monroe, La Fuga degli Amanti* 1914; *Gelosia, Lulù* 1915; *La Drama della Corona, Conquista dei Diamanti, Il Sogno di un Giorno, La Menzogna, Il Presagio* 1916; *Maschiaccio, Femmina* 1917; *Addio Giovinezza!* 1918; *La Maschera e il Volto, Lucrezia Borgia, Bel Ami, La Donna e il Cadavere* 1919; *I Tre Sentimentali, I Diabolici, L'Avventura di Dio* 1920; *L'Innamorata* 1921; *Cyrano de Bergerac, Germaine* 1923; *Il Corsaro* (co-dir. with Carmine Gallone), *La Moglie bella* 1924; *Il Focolare Spento* 1925; *L'Ultimo Lord* 1926; *Die weisse Sklavin* (Ger.) 1927; *Liebeskarnaval* (Ger.), *Scampolo* (Ger.) 1928; *Quartier Latin* (Fr.) 1929; *Prix de Beauté* (Fr.) 1930; *Les Amants de Minuit* (co-dir. with Marc Allégret; Fr.), *Paris-Béguin* (Fr.), *La Femme en Homme* (Fr.) 1931; *Ne sois pas jalouse* (Fr.) 1932; *Nous ne sommes plus des Enfants* (Fr.) 1934; *Vergiss mein nicht* (Ger.) 1935; *La Gondole aux Chimères* (Fr.), *Blumen aus Nizza/Flowers from Nice* (Aus.), *Lo Squadrone Bianco/The White Squadron* 1936; *Naples au Baiser de Feu/The Kiss of Fire* (Fr.) 1937; *Castelli in Aria* (It./Ger.) 1939; *L'Assedio dell'Alcazar* 1940; *Bengasi* 1942; *Cielo sulla Palude* 1949; *L'Edera/Devotion* 1950; *Tre Storie Proibite/Three Forbidden Stories* 1952; *Maddalena* 1953; *Frou-Frou* (It./Fr.) 1955.

Genn, Leo. Actor. *b.* Aug. 9, 1905, London. *d.* 1978. The son of a prosperous merchant, he studied law at Cambridge and was a practicing barrister when he made his stage debut in 1930. For several years he continued offering legal services while gaining experience as a stage and screen player and had abandoned his law career entirely by the time he made his Broadway debut early in 1939. During WW II he served with the Royal Artillery, being promoted to lieutenant colonel in 1943 and awarded the Croix de Guerre in 1945. He was allowed several brief leaves of absence for film appearances. At the end of the war he joined the British unit investigating war crimes at the Belsen concentration camp, later serving as an assistant prosecutor for the Belsen trial. Genn's career received a boost from his subtle, sarcastic portrayal of the Constable of France in Laurence Olivier's film *Henry V* (1944), a small but memorable role. It resulted in an invitation to the US and one of his great stage successes in the 1946 Broadway production of Lillian Hellman's 'Another Part of the Forest.' Many stage and screen appearances followed on both sides of the Atlantic. In films, he played intelligent, personable, and typically understated character leads and supporting roles. He was nominated for an Oscar as best supporting actor for his portrayal of Gaius Petronius, Nero's counselor, in *Quo Vadis* (1951).

FILMS INCLUDE: *Immortal Gentleman* 1935; *Jump for Glory/When Thief Meets Thief, The Rat* 1937; *The Drum/Drums* 1938; *Ten Days in Paris/Missing Ten Days* 1939; *Contraband* 1940; *The Way Ahead, Tunisian Victory* (doc.; narrator), *Henry V* (as the Constable of France) 1944; *Green for Danger, Mourning Becomes Electra* (as Captain Adam Brant; US) 1947; *The Velvet Touch* (US), *The Snake Pit* (US) 1948; *No Place for Jennifer* 1949; *The Miniver Story, The Wooden Horse* 1950; *The Magic Box, Quo Vadis* (US) 1951; *Plymouth Adventure* (US), *24 Hours of a Woman's Life* 1952; *The Red Beret/Paratrooper, Personal Affair* 1953; *The Green Scarf* 1954; *L'Amant de Lady Chatterley/Lady Chatterley's Lover* (as Sir Clifford; Fr.) 1955; *Beyond Mombasa, Moby Dick* (as Starbuck) 1956; *The Steel Bayonet* 1957; *No Time to Die/Tank Force, I Accuse!* (as Major Picquart of Dreyfus case fame) 1958; *Too Hot to Handle/Playgirl After Dark* 1960; *The Longest Day* (US) 1962; *55 Days at Peking* (US) 1963; *Ten Little Indians* 1966; *Circus of Fear/Psycho-Circus* 1967; *Una Lucertola con la Pelle di Donna/A Lizard in a Woman's Skin* (It./Fr.) 1971; *Night of the Blood Monster* 1972; *Le Silencieux/Escape to Nowhere* (Fr.) 1973; *Sie sind frei Dr. Korczak/The Martyr* (Ger./Isr.) 1975.

George, Christopher. Actor. *b.* Feb. 25, 1929, Royal Oak, Minn. *d.* 1983. Tall, rugged leading man of American films and TV, usually in action dramas. He starred in the TV series 'The Rat Patrol' (1966–68) and 'The Immortal' (1970–71). Married actress Linda Day [George] (*b.* Dec. 11, 1944, San Marcos, Tex.), co-star of the TV series 'Mission Impossible.'

FILMS INCLUDE: *The Gentle Rains, El Dorado* 1966; *Ballad of Gavilan, Project X* 1968; *The Devil's 8, The 1,000 Plane Raid* 1969; *Tiger by the Tail, The Delta Factor, Chisum* 1970; *The Train Robbers, I Escaped from Devil's Island* 1973; *Dixie Dynamite, Midway, Grizzly* 1976; *Day of the Animals, Whiskey Mountain* 1977; *Questo si che l'Amore* (It.) 1978; *The Exterminator* 1980; *Graduation Day* 1981; *Enter the Ninja* 1982; *Mortuary* 1983.

George, Chief Dan. Actor. *b.* 1899, British Columbia, Canada. *d.* 1981. He was employed as a logger, stevedore, and construction worker before being forced out of manual labor by an injury in 1947. In the subsequent 12 years he served as chief of his tribe, the Tse-lal-watt Sioux. Retiring in 1959, he began his acting career in the Canadian TV series 'Caribou Country' (1960–61). In films from 1969, he is best remembered for his portrayal of the sage Old Lodge Skins in *Little Big Man* (1970), for which he was nominated for the best supporting actor Academy Award and won a New York Critics Award. He was a tireless campaigner for the hiring of Native Americans to portray Native Americans on the screen. He co-authored an autobiography: *You Call Me Chief* (1981).

FILMS: *Smith!* 1969; *Little Big Man* 1970; *Cancel My Reservation, Cold Journey* 1972; *Alien Thunder/Dan Candy's Law* 1973; *Harry and Tonto, The Beard and I* 1974; *The Outlaw—Josey Wales, Shadow of the Hawk* 1976; *Spirit of the Wind, Americathon* 1979.

George, Gladys. Actress. *b.* Gladys Anna Clare, Sept. 13, 1900, Patton, Me. *d.* 1954. The daughter of an actor and actress, she began her stage career as a child of three and later starred in vaudeville, in stock, and on Broadway. She appeared occasionally in silent films, but her main career as a Hollywood leading lady and second lead was in the 30s and 40s. Her forte on the stage was comedy, but in films she was more often cast in melodramas, memorably in *Valiant Is the Word for Carrie* (Oscar nomination, 1936), *The Roaring Twenties* (1939), and *The Way of All Flesh* (1940). She played character roles toward the end of her career and continued appearing in films until shortly before her death of cancer of the throat.

FILMS INCLUDE: *Red Hot Dollars* 1919; *The Woman in the Suitcase, Home Spun Folks* 1920; *The Easy Road, The House That Jazz Built* 1921; *Straight Is the Way* 1934; *Valiant Is the Word for Carrie* 1936; *They Gave Him a Gun, Madame X* 1937; *Love Is a Headache, Marie Antoinette* (as Madame Du Barry) 1938; *I'm from Missouri, The Roaring Twenties* 1939; *A Child Is Born, The House Across the Bay, The Way of All Flesh* 1940; *Hit the Road, The Maltese Falcon* 1941; *The Crystal Ball, The Hard Way* 1943; *Christmas Holiday, Minstrel Man* 1944; *Steppin' in Society* 1945; *The Best Years of Our Lives* 1946; *Millie's Daughter* 1947; *Flamingo Road* 1949; *Bright Leaf* 1950; *Lullaby of Broadway, He Ran All the Way, Detective Story* 1951; *It Happens Every Thursday* 1953.

George, Heinrich. Actor. *b.* Heinz Georg Schulz, Oct. 9, 1893, Stettin, Germany (now Poland). *d.* 1946. A stage and film actor from his teens, he rose to prominence as a character actor in the mid-20s. Although he had been an active member of the German Communist Party, he became an avid Nazi in 1933 and starred in several propaganda films, including the first Nazi film, *Hitlerjunge Quex* (1933), and the anti-Semitic *Jud Süss/Jew Suess* (1940). As a reward, he was appointed director of the Schiller Theater in Berlin. He died in a Soviet POW camp near Berlin.

FILMS INCLUDE: *Der Andere* 1913; *Kean* 1921; *Lukrezia Borgia* 1922; *Erdgeist/Earth Spirit, Der Mensch am Wege* 1923; *Der versunkene Flotte/The Wrath of the Seas* 1926; *Metropolis, Bigamie, Orientexpress* 1927; *Rutschbahn/Bondage, Song/Wasted Love, Das letzte Fort* 1928; *Manolescu* 1929; *Der Andere, Dreyfus/The Dreyfus Case* (as Emile Zola), *Der Mann der den Mord beging/The Man Who Committed the Murder* 1930; *1914—Die letzten Tage vom der Weltbrand/1914—The Last Days Before the War, Berlin-Alexanderplatz* 1931; *Reifende Jugend, Schleppzug M–17* (also dir.), *Hitlerjunge Quex* 1933; *Das Mädchen Johanna/Joan of Arc* 1935; *Ball in Metropol, Unternehmen Michael/The Private's Job, Der Biberpelz/The Beaver Coat* 1937; *Heimat/Magda* 1938; *Das unsterbliche Herz/The Immortal Heart* 1939; *Jud Süss/Jew Suess, Friedrich Schiller* 1940; *Kolberg* 1944.

George, Susan. Actress. Born on July 26, 1950, in London. The daughter of a saxophone player and a former showgirl, she began her own show business career as a tot, making her film debut at age four. At 12 she appeared in the London production of 'The Sound of Music,' and later played many roles on British TV. She returned to the screen in the early 60s and late in the decade began playing leads in both British and American films, typically in roles emphasizing her kittenish sexuality.

FILMS INCLUDE: *Come Fly with Me* (US) 1963; *Billion Dollar Brain* (bit), *The Sorcerers* 1967; *Up the Junction, The Strange Affair* 1968; *All Neat in Black Stockings* 1969; *The Looking Glass War, Twinky/Lola* (UK/It.) 1970; *Eyewitness/Sudden Terror, Straw Dogs, Fright* 1971; *La Banda J & S—Cronaca Criminale del West/Sonny and Jed* (It./Sp.) 1972; *Dirty Mary Crazy Larry* (US) 1974; *Mandingo* (US), *Out of Season* 1975; *A Small Town in Texas* (US) 1976; *Tomorrow Never Comes* (UK/Can.) 1978; *Enter the Ninja* (US) 1981; *Venom, The House Where Evil Dwells* (US) 1982; *The Jigsaw Man* 1984; *Lightning—The White Stallion* (US) 1986; *The Summer of White Roses* (also co-exec. prod.; UK/Yug.) 1989.

Gerasimov, Sergei. Director. *b.* May 21, 1906, Zlatoust, the Urals, Russia. *d.* 1985. Initially trained as a painter, he entered Soviet films as an actor in 1925, following studies at the Leningrad Institute of Stage Art, and became closely involved with the activities of FEX. He began directing in 1930 but for several years continued acting in others' films, including Pudovkin's *Deserter* (1933), typically in villainous roles. His first film of note, *Komsomolsk/City of Youth* (1938), glorified the volunteer spirit of Soviet youth in the socialist-realist style encouraged by the regime. His next film, *The New Teacher* (1939), attacked the shortcomings of the educational system, again with the approval and encouragement of the regime. In 1944 he joined the Communist party and in the same year he was appointed head of the documentary film studios. The following year he was appointed head of the acting and directing workshop at the Moscow Film School (VGIK), a post he held for 30 years. Throughout his career, Gerasimov remained faithful to the party line. In 1948 he was named People's Artist of the USSR. In 1949 he attended the Cultural and Scientific Conference for World Peace in New York City and in a speech denounced Hollywood films as violent and devoid of proper moral standards. In 1958 he directed his most ambitious production, a two-part screen adaptation of Mikhail Sholokov's novel *And Quiet Flows the Don,* regarded by many as one of the finest Soviet films of the period. For decades a major figure in Soviet cinema, Gerasimov won state prizes for his films *The New Teacher* (1939), *The Young Guard* (1948), and *The New China* (1950). In 1984, the year before his death of a heart attack, at 79, he was awarded the Lenin Prize, his country's highest honor, for his cumulative work and his final film, *Leo Tolstoy,* in which he also portrayed the Russian author.

FILMS: *22 Misfortunes* (co-dir. with D. Bartenev; also sc.) 1930; *The Forest* 1931; *The Heart of Solomon* (co-dir. with M. Kressin) 1932; *Do I Love You?* (also sc.) 1934; *The Bold Seven/Seven Brave Men* (also co-sc.) 1936; *Komsomolsk/City of Youth* (also co-sc.) 1938; *The Teacher/The New Teacher* (also sc.) 1939; *Fighting Film Album #1* ('Meeting With Maxim' episode), *Masquerade* (also sc., act.), *The Old Guard* (medium-length) 1941; *Moscow Music Hall/Film Concert for the Red Army's 25th Anniversary* (co-dir. with Efim Dzigan and Mikhail Kalatozov), *Invincible/The Unconquerable* (co-dir. with Kalatozov) 1943; *The Big Land/The Great Earth/The Ural Front* (also sc.) 1944; *Young Guard* (in two parts; also sc.) 1947–48; *Liberated China/The New China* (doc.; co-dir. with several others) 1950; *The Country Doctor* 1952; *Nadezhda* (also sc.) 1955; *Tikhi Don/And Quiet Flows the Don* (also sc.; in three parts) 1957–58; *Sputnik Speaking* (co-dir., co-sc.) 1959; *Men and Beasts* (also sc.; USSR/E. Ger.) 1962; *The Journalist* (also sc.) 1967; *By the Lake* (also sc.) 1970; *For the Love of Man* (also sc.) 1972; *Mothers and Daughters* 1974; *Le Rouge et le Noir/The Red and the Black* (in five parts; orig. for TV; also sc.) 1976; *Peter the Great* (in two parts: *The Youth of Peter; At the Beginning of Glorious Deeds*) 1981; *Leo Tolstoy* (also sc., act.) 1984.

Geray, Steven. Actor. *b.* Stefan Gyergyay Nov. 10, 1899, Uzhord, Czechoslovakia (now Uzhgorod, USSR). *d.* 1974. A member of the Hungarian National Theater, he also appeared in some 40 European films before coming to Hollywood in the early 40s. Played well over 100 character roles, often as a quietly menacing foreigner.

FILMS INCLUDE: *Dance Band* (UK) 1935; *A Star Fell from Heaven* (UK) 1936; *Inspector Hornleigh* (UK) 1939; *Man at Large* 1941; *Eyes in the Night, The Moon and Sixpence* 1942; *Appointment in Berlin, The Phantom of the Opera* 1943; *The Mask of Dimitrios, In Society, The Seventh Cross, The Conspirators* 1944; *Hotel Berlin, Spellbound, Cornered* 1945; *Gilda, So Dark the Night* 1946; *The Unfaithful, Blind Spot* 1947; *The Dark Past* 1948; *El Paso, Under My Skin, In a Lonely Place, All About Eve* 1950; *Affair in Trinidad, The Big Sky, O. Henry's Full House* 1952; *Call Me Madam, Gentlemen Prefer Blondes* 1953; *Knock on Wood* 1954; *Daddy Long Legs* 1955; *Attack!* 1956; *A Certain Smile* 1958; *Verboten!* 1959; *Ship of Fools* 1965; *The Swinger* 1966.

Gere, Richard. Actor. Born on Aug. 31, 1949, in Philadelphia. Intense, dreamy star of Hollywood films. The oldest of five children of an upstate New York farm family, he was a trumpet player and a gymnast at his high school in Syracuse. He won a scholarship to the University of Massachusetts but dropped out after two years to become a musician. He played various instruments with country, blues, bluegrass, and rock bands, then began acting in and composing for summer stock productions throughout New England. He performed with the Provincetown Players on Cape Cod and with the Seattle Repertory Theatre before making Broadway as an understudy for the lead in the musical 'Grease' in 1972. The following year he starred in the London production of the play, and later performed in several straight dramatic roles on both sides of the Atlantic. On the screen from the mid-70s, he first attracted wide attention in *Looking for Mr. Goodbar* (1977) and achieved top stardom and sex-symbol status with *Days of Heaven* (1978) and *American Gigolo* (1980). Gere proved himself a fine, sensitive, as well as attractive actor in *An Officer and a Gentleman* (1982) and other films, but later in the 80s his career took second place to his political and spiritual beliefs. Raised as a Methodist, he embraced Buddhism in the mid-70s. Following a 1978 visit to Tibetan refugee camps in Nepal, he became a disciple of the exiled Dalai Lama and subsequently devoted much of his energy and resources to the cause of Tibetan Buddhism. With composer Philip GLASS, he helped found Tibet House in Greenwich Village in 1988. He also took up the cause of Central American refugees, lobbying Congress on their behalf, after a personal fact-finding tour in 1986 of Nicaragua, Honduras, and El Salvador. He regained his box-office momentum in 1990 with the blockbuster hit *Pretty Woman*, and returned as an in-demand romantic lead in the early 90s. By signing on to play a gay man dying of AIDS, he resuscitated HBO's troubled production of Randy Shilts's controversial book about the AIDS crisis, *And the Band Played On*. Divorced from supermodel Cindy Crawford.

FILMS: *Report to the Commissioner* 1975; *Baby Blue Marine* 1976; *Looking for Mr. Goodbar* 1977; *Days Of Heaven, Bloodbrothers* 1978; *Yanks* (UK) 1979; *American Gigolo* 1980; *An Officer and a Gentleman* 1982; *Breathless, The Honorary Consul/Beyond the Limit* (UK/US) 1983; *The Cotton Club* 1984; *King David* (title role) 1985; *Power, No Mercy* 1986; *Miles from Home* 1988; *Internal Affairs, Pretty Woman* 1990; *Rhapsody in August* (Jap.; dir. Akira Kurosawa); *Final Analysis* (also co-exec. prod.), *Sommersby* (also co-exec. prod.) 1992; *Mr. Jones* (also co-exec. prod.) 1993; *Intersection* 1994; *First Knight* 1995; *Primal Fear* 1996; *The Jackal, Red Corner* 1997.

Gering, Marion. Director. *b.* June 9, 1901, Rostov-on-Don, Russia. *d.* 1977. A stage producer, director, and writer, he came to the US in 1924 with a trade commission for Siberian furs, then presented the play 'Gas' in Chicago and stayed on to found the Chicago Play Producing Company. He then directed Broadway plays and Hollywood films in the 30s, many of the latter medium-budget Paramount productions, often staring Sylvia SIDNEY. Later attempted to revive his declining career abroad without much success.

FILMS: *I Take This Woman, Twenty-Four Hours, Ladies of the Big House* 1931; *Devil and the Deep, Madame Butterfly* 1932; *Pick Up, Jennie Gerhardt* 1933; *Good Dame, Thirty-Day Princess, Ready for Love* 1934; *Rumba* 1935; *Rose of the Rancho, Lady of Secrets* 1936; *Thunder in the City* (UK) 1937; *She Married an Artist* 1938; *Sarumba* (also co-prod.; Cuba) 1950; *Violated Paradise* (also prod.; Jap./It.) 1963.

Germany. Although the German cinema achieved an important historic "first," it played an insignificant role in the development of the art of film until after WW I. On November 1, 1895, almost two months before the celebrated LUMIÈRE screening in Paris, the SKLADANOWSKY brothers, Max and Emil, presented the first moving pictures to a paying audience at the Berlin Wintergarten. The following year Oskar MESSTER began producing films for his own "movement theater." But on the whole, the early days of German cinema were characterized by scant and unimaginative production. A change for the better took place around 1910, when notable stage artists first began associating their names with film, until then considered an inferior, low-class-oriented medium. The leading figure in this movement was Max REINHARDT, the famed theatrical producer and director, whose services were recruited for films by Paul Davidson, the head of Projektion-A.G. Union.

In the years immediately preceding WW I hundreds of movie theaters were erected and two large film studios, Germany's first, were built near Berlin. Several film stars emerged, among them Henny PORTEN, Asta NIELSEN, and Paul WEGENER. The latter played the lead in the first version of *Der Student von Prag/The Student of Prague* (1913), a drama of the macabre in a style that would become a trademark of the German cinema in the 20s. Another quality production of the period was Max Mack's *Der Andere* (1913). But the typical German film of the prewar period was a farcical comedy or a static adaptation from literature or the stage. A vogue of mystery and detective films began in 1913.

The outbreak of WW I set Germany on a tragic course for several decades, but in the short run it had one beneficial effect. It enabled the national film industry to rid itself of foreign influence and establish its own firm independent foundation in the process. Production increased dramatically during the war years to keep the 2,000 cinema theaters supplied with diverting entertainment. Several large production concerns were established, with massive government aid, most importantly UFA (Universum Film Aktien Gesellschaft), which was founded in 1917 and remained a dominant force in the industry through the end of WW II. Among the directors who began emerging during the WW I period were Ernst LUBITSCH and Fritz LANG and among the actors Emil JANNINGS and Pola NEGRI.

The end of WW I signaled the beginning of a decade that would become known as the golden age of the German cinema. The most important films were characterized by two influences: EXPRESSIONISM on the one hand and the theater of the Max Reinhardt school on the other. The expressionist style in film was manifested on the screen in extremely stylized, grossly distorted studio sets, deliberately artificial lighting, emphasizing deep shadows and sharp contrasts, camera angles that emphasized the fantastic and grotesque, and an acting style that was exaggerated and externalized.

The nightmarish quality of the expressionist drama held a mysterious appeal to the tortured German soul during this period. The film that launched screen expressionism and came to symbolize it was Robert WIENE's *The Cabinet of Dr. Caligari* (1919), an eerie excursion into an insane universe of distorted shapes and twisted minds that remains one of the great classics of world cinema. Other key expressionist films included Paul Wegener and Carl Boese's *The Golem* (1920), Fritz Lang's *Der müde Tod/Between Worlds/Destiny* (1921) and *Dr. Mabuse the Gambler* (1922), F. W. MURNAU's *Nosferatu* (1922), Robert Wiene's *The Hands of Orlac* (1924), and Paul LENI's *Waxworks* (1924). In addition to the directors mentioned above, leading creative artists associated with screen expressionism included writer Carl MAYER, cameramen Karl FREUND and Fritz WAGNER, and set designers Hermann WARM, Walter RÖHRIG, Robert HERLTH, and Otto HUNTE.

Expressionism had run its course by 1925, but for several years it continued to influence filmmakers in Germany and elsewhere. The other major influence on the German cinema of the 20s, the one stemming from the tradition of the Reinhardt theater, manifested itself in several genres. Many of the leading film actors and directors of the period were products of the Reinhardt school, and naturally they incorporated ingredients of his stage style into their screen work. Among the characteristics of that style were light and shadow effects.

One of Reinhardt's most talented disciples was director Ernst Lubitsch, who brought to the screen the influence of his master's technique in handling large crowd scenes in a number of impressive costume films, notably *Madame Dubarry/Passion* (1919), *Anna Boleyn/Deception* (1920), *Sumurun/One Arabian Night* (1920), and *Das Weib des Pharao/The Loves of Pharaoh* (1922). Other elaborate costume films of the period which drew their inspiration from history included Dimitri BUCHOWETZKI's *Danton/All for a Woman* (1921) and *Othello* (1922) and Richard OSWALD's *Lukrezia Borgia* (1922). Spectacles deriving from folklore and legend included Ludwig BERGER's *Der verlorene Schuh/Cinderella* (1923) and Lang's *Die Nibelungen* (1924).

Another style that infiltrated the German cinema through the influence of the Reinhardt theater was the *Kammerspiel* (literally, "chamber play," that is, intimate drama). This style, characterized by sparse décor and intimate psychological content, was exemplified on the screen by such films as Leopold Jessner and Paul Leni's *Hintertreppe/Backstairs* (1921), Lupu PICK's *Schreben/Shattered* (1921) and *Sylvester* (1923), and Murnau's *Der letzte Mann/The Last Laugh* (1924). The influence of another notable stage director of the period, Erwin Piscator, could be discerned in Lang's masterpiece *Metropolis* (1927).

Two popular genres in the German cinema of the 20s were "street films" and "MOUNTAIN FILMS." The former vogue, launched by Karl GRUNE's *Die Strasse/The Street* (1923), were typically psychological melodramas in which the downtown street represented a dangerous lure and a force of tragic destiny for the imprudent male. Notable films in this group included G. W. PABST's *Die freudlose Gasse/The Street of Sorrow/The Joyless Street* (1925) and Bruno Rahn's *Dirnentragödie/Tragedy of the Streets* (1927). The mountain films exalted the beauty of nature and celebrated the triumph of the human body and spirit over the environment. Their chief exponents were Arnold FANCK, Leni RIEFENSTAHL, and Luis TRENKER. There were also significant achievements by the avant-garde movement during the 20s, notably Walter RUTTMANN's documentary *Berlin—Symphony of a Big City* (1927) and the experimental work by Hans RICHTER, Viking EGGELING, Oskar FISCHINGER, and Lotte REINIGER.

Films of high technical quality and artistic merit were but a small percentage of the large output by the nation's film industry during that period—averaging more than 200 features annually—most of which consisted of standard escapist fare of little or no lasting value.

The decline in the quality of production deepened after the coming of sound. Technically, the transition presented no problem to the German industry, which had been experimenting with optical sound for a decade and had developed its own system, independently of the American patents. Many of the early talkies were light musicals in the Viennese tradition, often made as co-productions with Austria. Among the most successful of these were Geza von Bolvary's *Zwei Herzen im dreiviertel Takt/Two Hearts in Waltz Time* (1930) and Erich CHARELL's *Der Kongress tanzt/The Congress Dances* (1931). Another popular genre of the early sound period was the romantic drama, often in a melancholy mood, a good example of which was Paul CZINNER's *Der träumende Mund/Dreaming Lips* (1932). One of the most effective early German talkies, *The Blue Angel* (1930), was directed by an American, Josef von STERNBERG. Other artistically significant films of the period include Pabst's *Die Dreigroschenoper/The Threepenny Opera* (1930) and Lang's *M* (1931) and *Das Testament des Dr. Mabuse/The Testament of Dr. Mabuse* (1933).

The political turmoil of the early 30s was reflected on the screen in a number of politically motivated films. On the liberal side were such films as Pabst's *Westfront 1918/Comrades of 1918* (1930) and *Kameradschaft* (1931), Victor TRIVAS's *Niemandsland/Hell on Earth* (1931), Leontine SAGAN's *Mädchen in Uniform* (1931), and Richard OSWALD's *Der Hauptmann von Köpenick* (1931). The committed Left was represented by Slatan DÜDOW's *Kühle Wampe* (1932) and the nationalist Right by such period pieces as Gustav Ucicky's *Das Flötenkonzert von Sanssouci* (1930) and *Yorck* (1931) and Trenker's *Der Rebell/The Rebel* (1932). Even before they came to power, the Nazis gained control over the nation's newsreel and propaganda shorts through their association with Alfred Hugenberg, UFA's board chairman, who was devoted to Hitler.

When the Nazis seized power in 1933, Joseph Goebbels, Hitler's minister of propaganda and public enlightenment, took charge of all forms of public expression. The Reichsfilmkammer exercised control not only over what films could or could not be made but also over who could or could not work in the industry. Jews were promptly purged. Liberals and independent-minded filmmakers were more subtly discouraged, and many left the industry on their own volition. Censorship was imposed, many old films were banned, and the stage was gradually set for the total nationalization of the film industry in 1942.

Goebbels was a skillful propagandist. He realized the powerful impact of film on the mind and emotions but was careful not to dilute that potential by overuse. Only a few of the major films produced by the state-controlled industry were overtly propagandistic, the bulk being devoted to escapist entertainment, mostly comedies. Large budgets and other means of support were lavished on productions chosen to express the Nazi ideology. A crew of 120, including some 40 cameramen, was put at the disposal of Leni Riefenstahl for her impressive cinematic record of the Nuremberg Nazi Party rally of 1934, *Triumph des Willens/Triumph of the Will* (1935), one of the most compelling examples of effective propaganda ever captured on film. Another Riefenstahl documentary, *Olympia* (1938), was a more subtle exposition of Nazi ideology. Other propaganda pieces of the prewar and WW II years included Hans Steinhoff's *Hitlerjunge Quex* (1933), Franz Seitz's *SA-Mann Brand* (1933), Franz Wenzler's *Hans Westmar/Horst Wessel* (1933), Veidt HARLAN's *Der Herrscher/The Ruler* (1937), the anti-British *Ohm Krüger* (Steinhoff, 1941), and the anti-Semitic *Jud Süss* (Harlan, 1940), *Die Rothschilds* (Erich Waschneck, 1940), and *Der ewige Jude* (Franz Hippler, 1940). A number of impressive examples of the COMPILATION FILM were also produced. There were also prestigious and expensive historical spectacles designed to promote national pride, among them tributes to

Frederick the Great and Bismarck. The most spectacular of the more than 1,000 productions made during the Nazi regime was Josef von BAKY's lavishly designed *Münchhausen* (1943), which was produced to celebrate the 25th anniversary of UFA.

The rehabilitation of the film industry in the early postwar years was relatively rapid, considering the physical devastation and the difficulties that arose from the division of parts of the country into zones controlled by the different Allied administrative policies. As part of the de-Nazification process, filmmakers in the Western zones were subjected to a complicated licensing policy that granted permits for the production of individual films only after careful scrutiny of the project's theme and the political past of the intended filmmaker. Key directors of the Nazi period like Harlan and Riefenstahl were blacklisted. Producer Erich Pommer was brought back to reorganize the industry. The movie theaters were inundated with imports, mainly from Hollywood. Most of the production facilities fell into the hands of the Soviets, under whose control the industry in the Eastern zone was nationalized in 1946. Some of the most significant films of the immediate postwar period were made in East Berlin by the state-run company DEFA, among them Wolfgang STAUDTE's *Die Mörder sind unter uns/The Murderers Are Among Us* (1946), Gerhard LAMPRECHT's *Irgendwo in Berlin/Somewhere in Berlin* (1946), Kurt Maetzig's *Ehe im Schatten/Marriage in the Shadows* (1947), and Erich Engel's *Affäre Blum* (1948). In the West, too, several of the better films of the early postwar period reflected the social concerns of the reconstruction years. These included Eugen York's *Morituri* (1948), Rudolph Jugert's *Film ohne Titel/Film Without a Name* (1948), Robert Stemmle's *Berliner Ballade/The Berliner* (1948), Pabst's *Der Prozess/The Trial* (1948), Wolfgang Liebeneiner's *Liebe '47* (1949), and Von Baky's *Der Ruf/The Last Illusion* (1949).

Following the official division of Germany into two national entities in 1949 (a division that lasted until reunification in 1990), the film industries of the Federal Republic of Germany (West Germany) and the German Democratic Republic (East Germany) developed along separate, diametrically opposed lines. In the East, themes of social concern were emphasized, many of the films dealing either with soul-searching memories of the country's Nazi past or with the struggles of the working class. Films in the latter category included Dudow's *Unser täglich Brot/Our Daily Bread* (1949) and *Stärker als die Nacht/Stronger Than the Night* (1954), Kurt Maetzig's two-part *Ernst Thälmann* (1954–55), Maetzig and Günter Reisch's *Das Lied der Matrosen/Sailor's Song* (1958), and Heiner Carow's *Sie nannten ihn Amigo/They Called Him Amigo* (1958). From the early 50s many East German films also dealt with contemporary personal problems, among them Dudow's *Frauenschicksale/ Women's Fate* (1952), Konrad Wolf's *Der geteilte Himmel/The Divided Sky* (1964) and *Ich war neunzehn/I Was 19* (1968), and Günther Rücker's *Die besten Jahre/The Best Years* (1965). Because of their dogmatic political slant, few of these feature films had wide distribution in the Western world. The industry gained more international attention with its many documentaries, and especially the fine compilation films by Andrew and Annelie Thorndike. Animation production was also stressed.

In West Germany, meanwhile, prosperity bred a public demand for escapist entertainment. Production figures rose rapidly as small film companies quickly proliferated. There were some attempts at serious drama, but on the whole the artistic level of the postwar German film remained remarkably low. A number of German stars gained an international reputation, mainly through appearances in co-productions with other countries. Among the most successful have been Curt JURGENS, Horst BUCHHOLZ, Hildegard(e) KNEF (Neff), Romy SCHNEIDER, Maria SCHELL, and Maximilian SCHELL. But for years the German director remained less known than his European colleagues.

Germany had to wait for its film renaissance until the late 60s and the 70s. But when it finally came, it was unleashed with a ferocity that has both shocked and perplexed audiences at home and abroad. The impetus for the Junger Deutscher Film, the name by which the new German cinema became known, was initiated in 1962 by the Oberhausen Manifesto, a document signed at the Oberhausen Film Festival by a group of 26 young writers and filmmakers who demanded freedom from industry conventions and commercial strictures in order to create a new German film.

In a belated response, the federal government responded in the late 60s with a program of grants for promising young filmmakers. A film institute was established in Berlin in 1968. Important support also came from German television, which over the years has maintained much higher standards than the film industry. The results began showing in the late 60s with a virtual avalanche of debut films by new directors.

The first productions to draw considerable international attention were Volker SCHLÖNDORFF's *Der junge Törless/Young Torless* (1966) and Alexander KLUGE's *Abschied von gestern/Yesterday's Girl* (1966). Other young filmmakers soon established themselves, among them Peter and Ulrich Schamoni, Edgar Reitz, Jean-Marie STRAUB, Roger Fritz, Hansjürgen Pohland, and Will Tremper.

The movement peaked in the 70s with directors Rainer Werner FASSBINDER, Werner HERZOG, and Wim WENDERS leading the way. Unlike the French New Wave, which developed mainly as a reaction to the conventional methods of the traditional cinema, the common denominator of the Young German Cinema was a spontaneous outrage at the quality of bourgeois life in affluent West Germany. Although the philosophies and styles of the individual directors vary widely, their work has been bound by a similar leftist revolutionary zeal and a humanistic, if often fatalistic, view of life. Their films are frequently too harsh and rigorous for common consumption and all too often incomprehensible to the average moviegoer. As a result, many of these films have been resounding flops at the box office at home, while enjoying great success at international film festivals and the art-house circuits abroad.

Two decades later, German films still lag far behind Hollywood films in attracting German audiences, despite the fact that Germany's annual movie attendances (119.9 million in 1991) are the highest in Europe. Even so, German filmmakers, supported by federal film subsidies, continue to produce original and interesting features that attract international attention. Talented new German directors of the 80s and 90s have included Agnieszka HOLLAND and Doris DÖRRIE (both women), Percy ADLON, Vadim Glowna, Eberhard Junkersdorf, Michael Klier, and Hans W. Geissendörfer.

Unification of East and West Germany in 1990 led to an artistically fertile crossover of talent and ideas, as well as providing subject matter for topical films on the social complexities of unification, such as Glowna's comedy *Der Brocken* (1991). Since unification, the DEFA Film Studio Babelsberg in the former East Germany, has been sold to Compagnie Générale des Eaux, a French company, with German filmmaker Volker Schlöndorff placed in charge of organizing production.

Germi, Pietro. Director. *b.* Sept. 14, 1914, Colombo, Liguria, Italy. *d.* 1974. Of lower-middle-class origin, he worked as a messenger and briefly attended a nautical school before deciding on an acting career. He enrolled at Rome's Centro Sperimentale di Cinematografia, where he studied acting and directing, supporting himself as an extra, bit actor, assistant director, and sometime writer. Making his debut as a film director in 1945, he started out as a disciple of the neorealist school. His early films were typically social dramas, dealing in contemporary issues against Sicilian backgrounds. Gradually he shifted from social drama to satirical comedy with socio-moral overtones but retained as his favorite milieu Sicily and its ignorant, poverty-stricken people. In the 60s he enjoyed worldwide commercial success with such films as *Divorce Italian Style* (Academy Award for script), *Seduced and Abandoned,* and *The Birds, the Bees, and the Italians* (grand prize at Cannes Festival). He collaborated on the scripts of all his own films and appeared in some of them as an actor. He died of hepatitis.

FILMS (as director and co-screenwriter): *Il Testimone* 1945; *Gioventù perduta/Lost Youth* 1947; *In Nome della Legge/Mafia* 1949; *Il Camino della Speranza/The Path of Hope* 1950; *La Cittá si difende/Four Ways Out* 1951; *La Presidentessa/ Mademoiselle Gobette, Il Brigante di Tacca del Lupo* 1952; *Gelosia* 1953; *Amori di Mezzo Secolo* (one episode) 1954; *Il Ferroviere/The Railroad Man/Man of Iron* (also act.) 1956; *L'Uomo di Paglia* (also act.) 1957; *Un Maledetto Imbroglio/The Facts of Murder* (also act.) 1959; *Divorzio all'Italiana/Divorce Italian Style* 1961; *Sedotta e Abbandonata/ Seduced and Abandoned* 1963; *Signori e Signore/The Birds the Bees and the Italians* 1966; *L'Immorale/The Climax/Too Much for One Man* 1967; *Serafino* 1968; *Le Castagne sono Buone/Till Divorce Do You Part* 1971; *Alfredo Alfredo* 1973; *Amici miei* (co-sc. only; replaced by Mario Monicelli as director before production began) 1975.

Gershwin, George. Composer. *b.* Sept. 26, 1898, Brooklyn, N.Y. *d.* 1937. The noted composer of concert and pop music, one of the leading creative forces on the American musical scene, spent some time in Hollywood, composing directly for the screen. In addition to his original film material, Gershwin music and songs initially written for the concert hall and the musical stage have been posthumously utilized in many Hollywood films. A romanticized story of Gershwin's life and career was told in the film biography *Rhapsody in Blue* (1945), with Robert ALDA portraying the composer. Brother of lyricist Ira GERSHWIN.

FILMS INCLUDE: *King of Jazz* 1930; *Delicious* 1931; *Girl Crazy* 1932; *Shall We Dance?, A Damsel in Distress* 1937; *The Goldwyn Follies* 1938; *Lady Be Good* 1941; *Girl Crazy* 1943; *Broadway Rhythm* 1944; *Rhapsody in Blue* 1945; *Ziegfeld Follies* 1946; *The Shocking Miss Pilgrim* 1947; *The Barkleys of Broadway* 1949; *Lullaby of Broadway, An American in Paris* 1951; *Three for the Show* 1955; *Funny Face* 1957; *Porgy and Bess* 1959; *Kiss Me Stupid* 1964; *When the Boys Meet the Girls* 1965; *Star!* 1968; *A Matter of Time* 1976.

Gershwin, Ira. Lyricist. *b.* Dec. 6, 1896, New York City. *d.* 1983. *ed.* CCNY. The elder brother of George GERSHWIN, he began writing lyrics for Tin Pan Alley and the stage in the early 20s, using the name Arthur Francis. Under his own name he later wrote books and lyrics for numerous plays and films, often in collaboration with his brother George. He won a Pulitzer Prize for the stage musical 'Of Thee I Sing' (1932). In the movie *Rhapsody in Blue* Ira was played by Herbert Rudley. For credits shared with his brother, see GERSHWIN, George.

FILMS INCLUDE: *Lady in the Dark, Cover Girl* 1944; *Where Do We Go from Here?* 1945; *A Star Is Born* 1954; *The Country Girl* 1955.

Gertz, Jami. Actress. Born on Oct. 28, 1965, in Chicago. Brunette young lead of Hollywood films of the 80s. The winner of a nationwide talent search for a role as the class shrew in the TV series 'Square Pegs' (1982–83), she later studied drama at NYU and appeared on the stage as well as on TV and in many films.

FILMS: *Endless Love, On the Right Track* 1981; *Alphabet City, Sixteen Candles* 1984; *Mischief/Heart and Soul* 1985; *Quicksilver, Crossroads, Solarbabies* 1986; *The Lost Boys, Less Than Zero* 1987; *Listen to Me, Renegades* 1989; *Don't Tell Her It's Me, Sibling Rivalry, Silence Like Glass* 1990; *Jersey Girls* 1992, *Twister* 1996.

Gherardi, Piero. Art director, costume designer. *b.* Nov. 20, 1909, Florence, Italy. *d.* 1971. A former architect, he entered Italian films after WW II. Made a great impression with the imaginative and highly original sets he created for Fellini in the late 50s and early 60s. He received Academy Awards for costume design for *La Dolce Vita* and *8½*.

FILMS INCLUDE: *Senza Pietà* 1947; *Camicie Rosse* 1952; *Anni facili* 1953; *Proibito* 1954; *Padri e Figli* 1956; *Le Notti di Cabiria/The Nights of Cabiria* 1957; *I Soliti Ignoti/Big Deal on Madonna Street* 1958; *La Dolce Vita, Kapò, Il Gobbo/The Hunchback of Rome* 1960; *8½, La Ragazza di Bube/Bebo's Girl* 1963; *Giulietta degli Spiriti/Juliet of the Spirits* 1965; *The Appointment* (US), *Quemada!/Burn!* 1969.

Ghione, Emilio. Director, actor, screenwriter. *b.* 1879, Turin, Italy. *d.* 1930. Pioneer of Italian cinema. The son of a painter and himself a miniaturist, he entered films as an extra in 1909 and soon became a leading actor, often starring opposite the famous Francesca BERTINI. In 1913 he became a director but continued acting in most of his films as well as writing his own scripts. He gained great popularity beginning in 1914 as the creator, director, and star of fantasy serials featuring a mysterious character, Za la Mort. He later published a novel, *L'Ombra di Za la Mort,* based on the screen adventures of the character. In the early 20s he worked briefly in Germany and late in the decade he tried to revive a fading career in France but became gravely ill and returned to Rome, where he died at 51.

FILMS INCLUDE: (as director-actor-screenwriter) *La Gerusalemme Liberata* (act. only) 1910; *San Francesco—il Poverello d'Assisi* (act. only) 1911; *Idillio Tragico* (act. only) 1912; *La Gloria, L'Arrivista* (both act. only), *La Cricca Dorata* 1913; *L'Amazone Mascherata, Ultimo Dovere, Za la Mort* (serial) 1914; *La Banda delle Cifre* (serial), *Anime Buie, Guglielmo Oberdan* 1915; *La Sposa della Morte* (dir. only), *La Grande Vergogna, Tormento Gentile, Un Drama Ignorato* 1916; *Il Triangolo giallo* (serial), *Don Pietro Caruso, L'Ultima Impressa* 1917; *I Topi Grigi* (serial), *Il Gorgo* 1918; *Dollari e Fraks* (serial) 1919; *Il Quadrante d'Oro* 1920; *Za la Mort contro Za la Mort* 1921; *Ultissime di Notte* 1922; *Il Sogno di Za la Vie* 1923; *La Nostra Patria* 1925.

Giannini, Giancarlo. Actor. Born on Aug. 1, 1942, in Spezia, Italy. Sad-eyed, tragicomic protagonist of Lina WERTMULLER's films. Trained at the Rome Academy of Drama, following studies in electronic engineering, he began his association with Miss Wertmuller while appearing in her play 'Two and Two Are No Longer Four' in the early 60s and later starred in most of her films, typically portraying flawed little guys bucking a system they cannot fully understand or accept. In 1973 he won the best actor award at Cannes for *Love and Anarchy.* He received much critical praise and an Oscar nomination for his performance in *Pasqualino Settebellezze/Seven Beauties* (1976), in the complex role of Pasqualino, a concentration camp inmate who chooses to suffer humiliation and degradation in a desperate effort to survive. He later appeared in Miss Wertmuller's first American-sponsored film, *A Nightful of Rain* (1977). Giannini, who is a partner in Wertmuller's production company, Liberty Films, has also appeared in many films of other directors.

FILMS INCLUDE: *Fango sulla Metropoli* 1965; *Rita la Zanzara/Rita the Mosquito* 1966; *Non Stuzzicate la Zanzara/Don't Sting the Mosquito, Arabella* 1967; *Lo Sbarco di Anzio/Anzio* 1968; *Fräulein Doktor, The Secret of Santa Vittoria* (US), *Le Sorelle* 1969; *Dramma della Gelosia/The Pizza Triangle/A Drama of Jealousy, Una Prostituta al Servizio del Pubblico* 1970; *Mio Padre Monsignore* 1971; *La Tarantola dal Ventre Nero/The Black Belly of the Tarantula, Mimi Metallurgio Ferito nell'Onore/The Seduction of Mimi, Ettore lo Fusto* 1972; *Film d'Amore e d'Anarchia/Love and Anarchy, Paolo il Caldo/The Sensuous Sicilian/The Sensual Man* 1973; *Tutto a Posto e Niente in Ordine/All Screwed Up, Travolti da un Insolito Destino nell'Azzurro Mare d'Agosto/Swept Away. . . By an Unusual Destiny in the Blue Sea of August, Fatti di Gente Perbene/La Grande Bourgeoise* 1974; *A Mezzanotte va la Ronda del Piacere* 1975; *Pasqualino Settebellezze/Seven Beauties, L'Innocente/The Innocent* 1976; *The End of the World in Our Usual Bed in a Night Full of Rain, I Nuovi Mostri* 1977; *Shimmy Lugano Tarantelle e Vino* 1978; *Fatto di Sangue/Revenge/Blood Feud, Viaggio con Anita/Travels with Anita/Lovers and Liars* 1979; *Lili Marleen* 1981; *I Capitoni* (also dir.), *American Dreamer* (US) 1984; *Fever Pitch* (US) 1985; *Saving Grace* (US) 1986; *I Picari* 1987; *New York Stories* ("Life Without Zoe" episode; US), *Lo Zio indegno, Brown Bread and Sandwiches* (Can.), *Tempo di Uccidere/The Killing Time/The Short Cut* (It./Fr.) 1989; *Il male oscuro/The Obscure Illness, Nel Giardino delle Rose/In the Rose Garden/Age of Discretion* 1990; *Once Upon a Crime* 1992; *Colpa di Coda* 1992; *Giovanni Falcone* 1993; *Come Due Croccodrilli* 1994; *A Walk in the Clouds* (US) 1995; *The Disappearance of Garcia Lorca* 1997.

Gibb, Cynthia. Actress. Born on Dec. 14, 1963, in Bennington, Vt. Brunette young lead of teen-oriented films of the late 80s and early 90s, following a co-starring role in the TV series 'Fame' (1983–86).

FILMS INCLUDE: *Youngblood, Modern Girls* 1986; *Malone* 1987; *Jack's Back, Short Circuit 2* 1988; *Death Warrant* 1990.

Gibbons, Cedric. Art director. *b.* Mar. 23, 1893, Dublin. *d.* 1960. The most celebrated and possibly the most important and influential production designer in the history of American films. The son of an architect, he worked briefly for his father, after graduating from New York's Art Students League, and entered films in 1915 as Hugo Ballin's assistant at the Edison Studios. Within two years he was assigned the responsibilities of an art director, moving over to Goldwyn in 1918. In 1924, he joined the staff of newly formed MGM, remaining with the company for 32 years as supervising art director. He designed most of his films in collaboration with other artists. His MGM contract assured him credit on all major studio productions. His name appeared on some 1,500 films, on many of which he worked only in a limited supervisory capacity. But many of his own designs were quite original and some influenced interior decoration in affluent American homes. The designer of the Oscar, the Academy Award statuette, he won that prize 11 times (designated "AA" below), out of 37 nominations, and in addition a special award for "consistent excellence" (1950). He also co-directed one film, *Tarzan and His Mate* (1934). At one time (1930–41) married to actress Dolores DEL RIO.

FILMS INCLUDE: *Thais* 1917; *The Unwritten Code* 1919; *The Woman and the Puppet, The Return of Tarzan, Earthbound, Madame X* 1920; *The Christian, The Green Goddess* 1923; *He Who Gets Slapped* 1924; *The Big Parade* 1925; *Ben-Hur* 1926; *The Student Prince* 1927; *The Big City, Our Dancing Mothers* 1928; *Hallelujah, The Bridge of San Luis Rey* (AA) 1929; *Anna Christie, The Big House* 1930; *Private Lives* 1931; *Grand Hotel* 1932; *Dinner at Eight* 1933; *The Merry Widow* (AA), *The Painted Veil, The Thin Man, The Barretts of Wimpole Street* 1934; *A Night at the Opera, Mark of the Vampire, Anna Karenina, China Seas, Mutiny on the Bounty, A Tale of Two Cities, David Copperfield* 1935; *Camille, San Francisco, Romeo and Juliet* 1936; *Captains Courageous, The Good Earth* 1937; *The Great Waltz, Marie Antoinette, Three Comrades* 1938; *Ninotchka* 1939; *Pride and Prejudice* (AA) 1940; *Blossoms in the Dust* (AA), *Honky Tonk* 1941; *Bataan, Cabin in the Sky, The Human Comedy, Lassie Come Home* 1943; *Gaslight* (AA) 1944; *The Picture of Dorian Gray, Yolanda and the Thief* 1945; *The Postman Always Rings Twice, The Yearling* (AA), *Ziegfeld Follies, The Green Years* 1946; *Lady in the Lake* 1947; *The Pirate, The Three Musketeers, Command Decision* 1948; *Little Women* (AA), *On the Town, Madame Bovary, Battleground* 1949; *An American in Paris* (AA) 1951; *The Bad and the Beautiful* (AA) 1952; *Julius Caesar* (AA) 1953; *Kismet* 1955; *Somebody Up There Likes Me* (AA), *Lust for Life* 1956.

Gibney, Sheridan. Screenwriter. *b.* June 11, 1903, New York City. *d.* 1988. *ed.* Phillips Exeter Acad.; Amherst. He has written plays, TV scripts, and opera librettos as well as screenplays. He shared in two separate Academy Awards, for the story and for the screenplay of *The Story of Louis Pasteur* (1936). He served as president of the Screen Writers Guild for a number of terms.

FILMS INCLUDE: *I Am a Fugitive from a Chain Gang* 1932; *The World Changes, The House on 56th Street* 1933; *The Story of Louis Pasteur, Green Pastures, Anthony Adverse* 1936; *Letter of Introduction* 1938; *Disputed Passage* 1939; *Cheers for Miss Bishop* 1941; *Once Upon a Honeymoon* 1942; *Our Hearts Were Young and Gay* (also prod.) 1944; *The Locket* 1947.

Gibson, Helen. See GIBSON, Hoot.

Gibson, Henry. Actor. Born on Sept. 21, 1935, in Germantown, Pa. *ed.* Catholic U of America. Squat comedian of American TV and films. On the stage from age seven, he gained popularity as a regular on the 'Rowan & Martin's Laugh-In' TV variety series (1968–71). His many, mainly small parts in films included a memorable role as a country music star in *Nashville* (1975), for which he was named best supporting actor by the National Society of Film Critics.

FILMS INCLUDE: *The Nutty Professor* 1963; *Kiss Me Stupid* 1964; *The Long Goodbye* 1973; *Nashville* 1975; *The Kentucky Fried Movie, The Last Remake of Beau Geste* 1977; *A Perfect Couple* 1979; *Health, The Blues Brothers* 1980; *The Incredible Shrinking Woman, Tulips* (Can.) 1981; *Monster in the Closet* 1986; *Innerspace* 1987; *Switching Channels* 1988; *Brenda Starr* 1989; *Gremlins 2: The New Batch, Tune in Tomorrow* 1990; *Tom and Jerry: The Movie* (voice) 1993.

Gibson, Hoot. Actor. *b.* Edmund Richard Gibson, Aug. 6, 1892, Takamah, Nebr. *d.* 1962. At 13 he joined a circus and, when he became stranded in Colorado, began to work as a cowpuncher. At 16 he was an accomplished rodeo performer in Wild West shows and in 1912 he won the title of "World's All-Around Champion Cowboy." That same year he entered films as an extra and stuntman, often doubling for Harry Carey and other Western stars of the period. In 1913 he married Helen Wegner, who, as Helen Gibson (née Rose Wegner, 1892–1977), soon became a popular star of serials and action pictures. But Hoot himself found the going much slower. He was beginning to play supporting roles in John FORD Westerns at Universal when he was called for WW I service, which he spent with the Army Tank Corps. Discharged in 1919, he returned to supporting roles in Ford Westerns but later that year was given his own two-reel series. In 1921, Gibson starred in his first feature films, John Ford's five-reelers *Action* and *Sure Fire*.

In his subsequent shorts and features, Gibson developed a novel type of Western hero, one who rarely carried a gun, and emphasized comedy over action. His Westerns boasted good production values and were quite popular in the 20s but lost much of their zing late in the decade when their plots thinned and their humor became stale. He continued to star in Westerns through 1936, when he retired from the screen, but returned to action in the early 40s and finally retired in 1944, except for an occasional role. Gibson, whose first marriage ended in 1920, later married and divorced actress Sally EILERS.

FILMS INCLUDE: *His Only Son* 1912; *Shotgun Jones* 1914; *Knight of the Range* 1916; *Straight Shooting, The Secret Man* 1917; *Headin' South* 1918; *The Rustlers, Gun Law, Roaring Dan* 1919; *Red Courage, Action, Sure Fire* 1921; *Ridin' Wild, The Galloping Kid, The Lone Hand, Trimmed* 1922; *Blinky, The Gentleman from America, The Thrill Chaser* 1923; *Hit and Run, The Sawdust Trail, Broadway or Bust* 1924; *The Calgary Stampede, The Taming of the West* 1925; *The Flaming Frontier, The Buckaroo Kid, The Phantom Bullet, Chip of the Flying U* 1926; *The Prairie King, The Silent Rider* 1927; *The Wild West Show, The Flyin' Cowboy, A Trick of Hearts* 1928; *King of the Rodeo, Smilin' Guns, The Winged Horseman, The Long Long Trail* 1929; *Roaring Ranch, The Mounted Stranger, Trigger Tricks* 1930; *Hard Hombre* 1931; *Spirit of the West, A Man's Land* 1932; *Dude Bandit* 1933; *Rainbow's End* 1935; *Powdersmoke Range, The Last Outlaw* 1936; *Blazing Guns* 1943; *Arizona Whirlwind* 1944; *Flight to Nowhere* 1947; *The Marshal's Daughter* 1953; *The Horse Soldiers* 1959; *Ocean's Eleven* 1960.

Gibson, Mel. Actor. Born on Jan. 3, 1956, in Peekskill, N.Y. Handsome, magnetic, spontaneous, animated, dark-haired, blue-eyed superstar of Australian and American films. The sixth of 11 children of an Irish-Catholic railroad brakeman and a former Australian opera singer, he moved with his family to Australia when he was 12, a move allegedly caused by economic distress and the father's desire to protect his older boys from the Vietnam draft. After graduating from high school, he enrolled at Sydney's National Institute of Dramatic Art, part of the University of New South Wales. While still a student, he made his screen debut in 1977 in an insignificant film. His performance caught the eye of director George Miller, who assigned him the title role in the futuristic action picture *Mad Max* (1979). The global success of the WW I drama *Gallipoli* (1981), for which he won the Australian Film Institute Award as best actor, launched Gibson as an international star. His popularity soared later that year, with the sequel box-office hit *Mad Max 2* (released in the US in 1982 as *The Road Warrior*) and peaked once more in the late 80s with his eccentric portrayal of a tough undercover cop in Hollywood's *Lethal Weapon* (1987) and its sequels (1989, 1991). In 1990 he proved himself capable of more complex roles with a strong performance in Franco Zeffirelli's *Hamlet.* In 1993, he made a respectable directorial debut, directing himself in *The Man Without a Face* and followed that effort with *Braveheart* (1995), a sweeping drama set in 13th century Scotland centered on the story of William Wallace (Gibson). With ten Academy Award nominations, Gibson took home the best director statue along with best picture.

Off-camera, Gibson is known to be a well-read quick wit who delights friends and associates with clever quips and puns. He maintains a rural lifestyle on an Australian ranch, far away from the limelight. He has his own production company, Icon Productions.

FILMS: *Summer City* 1977; *Mad Max, Tim* 1979; *Attack Force Z* 1980; *Gallipoli, Mad Max 2/The Road Warrior* 1981; *The Year of Living Dangerously* 1983; *The Bounty* (as Fletcher Christian; UK/US), *The River* (US), *Mrs. Soffel* (US) 1984; *Mad Max III/Mad Max Beyond Thunderdome* 1985; *Lethal Weapon* 1987; *Tequila Sunrise* 1988; *Lethal Weapon 2* 1989; *Bird on a Wire, Air America, Hamlet* (title role) 1990; *Lethal Weapon 3* 1991; *Forever Young* 1992; *The Man Without a Face* (also dir.) 1993; *Maverick* 1994; *Braveheart* (also dir., prod.), *Casper* (unbilled cameo), *Pocahontas* (v/o) 1995; *Ransom* 1996, *Father's Day* (unbilled cameo) 1997.

Gibson, Wynne. Actress. *b.* Winifred Gibson, July 3, 1905 (possibly 1899), New York City. *d.* 1987. She broke into show business as a chorus girl at 15 and appeared in vaudeville and in stock before reaching Broadway in 1928. Making her film debut the following year, she played leads and second leads in many Hollywood productions, typically portraying a hardened dame, often as a gangster moll or a tramp with a heart of gold. After her screen career ended, in 1943, she was an actors' agent in New York.

FILMS INCLUDE: *Nothing but the Truth* 1929; *The Fall Guy* 1930; *The Gang Buster, June Moon, Man of the World, City Streets, Kick In, Ladies of the Big House* 1931; *Two Kinds of Women, The Strange Case of Clara Deane, Lady and Gent, Night After Night, If I Had a Million, The Devil Is Driving* 1932; *The Crime of the Century, Her Bodyguard, Aggie Appleby—Maker of Men* 1933; *I Give My Love, The Captain Hates the Sea, The Crosby Case, Gambling* 1934; *Racketeers in Exile, Trapped by G-Men* 1937; *Gangs of New York* 1938; *Street of Missing Women, Cafe Hostess, Forgotten Girls* 1940; *Double Cross* 1941; *The Falcon Strikes Back, Mystery Broadcast* 1943.

Gielgud, Sir John. Actor. Born Arthur John Gielgud on Apr. 14, 1904, in London, of Lithuanian descent on his father's side and a grandnephew of legendary English actress Ellen Terry on his mother's. A graduate of RADA, he made his debut at the Old Vic in 1921 and subsequently became regarded as a leading exponent of the English theater and one of the most eminent Shakespearean interpreters of his generation. Although always impressive, his many screen appearances have been as a whole less distinguished than his work on the stage, perhaps because he has been less discriminating in his choice of film roles. He was nominated for an Oscar for his portrayal of King Louis VII of France in *Becket* (1964) and won an Academy Award as best supporting actor for his role as Dudley Moore's impeccable butler in *Arthur* (1981). In the 70s and 80s he also appeared in numerous television programs, miniseries, and TV movies. He is the author of *Early Stages* (1939), *Stage Directions* (1963), *Distinguished Company* (1972), and *An Actor and His Times* (1979).

FEATURE FILMS: *Who Is the Man?* 1924; *The Clue of the New Pin* 1929; *Insult* 1932; *The Good Companions* 1933; *Secret Agent* 1936; *Hamlet* (title role; medium-length doc.) 1939; *The Prime Minister* (as Disraeli) 1941; *Julius Caesar* (as Cassius; US) 1953; *Romeo and Juliet* (v/o, as the Chorus) 1954; *Richard III* (as Clarence) 1955; *The Barretts of Wimpole Street* (as father of Elizabeth Barrett), *Around the World in 80 Days* (cameo) 1956; *Saint Joan* (as Warwick) 1957; *Becket* (as King Louis VII of France), *Hamlet* (voice of Ghost; US) 1964; *The Loved One* (US) 1965; *Falstaff/Chimes at Midnight* (as Bolingbroke/King Henry IV; Sp./Switz.) 1966; *Sebastian, The Charge of the Light Brigade, The Shoes of the Fisherman* (as the elder Pope) 1968; *Assignment to Kill* (US) *Oh! What a Lovely War* 1969; *Julius Caesar* (title role) 1970; *Eagle in a Cage* 1971; *Lost Horizon* 1973; *Galileo, 11 Harrowhouse, Gold, Murder on the Orient Express* 1974; *Aces High* 1976; *Providence* (Fr.), *Joseph Andrews* 1977; *Murder by Decree* 1978; *A Portrait of the Artist as a Young Man, Caligula* (It./US), *The Human Factor* 1979; *Dyrygent/The Orchestra Conductor* (Pol.), *The Elephant Man, The Formula* (US) 1980; *Sphinx* (US), *Lion of the*

Desert/Omar Mukhtar—Lion of the Desert (Lybia/US), *Arthur* (US), *Chariots of Fire, Priest of Love* 1981; *Gandhi* 1982; *The Wicked Lady, Invitation to a Wedding, Wagner* 1983; *Scandalous* 1984; *The Shooting Party, Plenty* (US) 1985; *The Whistle Blower* 1987; *Appointment with Death, Arthur 2 on the Rocks* (US) 1988; *Getting It Right* 1989; *Prospero's Books* 1991; *Shining Through, The Power of One* 1992; *Dragonheart* (v/o), *First Knight* 1995; *Hamlet, The Leopard Sun* (narr.), *Looking for Richard, Portrait of a Lady, Shine* 1996.

Gifford, Frances. Actress. *b.* Mary Frances Gifford, on Dec. 7, 1920, Long Beach, Calif. *d.* 1994, of emphysema. She entered films directly out of high school but played mostly minor roles before gaining some popularity among juveniles as Nyoka, the fearless heroine of the serial *Jungle Girl* (1941). She went on to play secondary roles and some leads in Paramount features and in 1943 signed with MGM, where she stayed for the remainder of the 40s as a minor leading lady. In 1948 she was seriously injured in an automobile accident. After a slow recovery she appeared in only two films before retiring from the screen in 1953. Early in her career she was briefly married (1938–41) to actor James DUNN. In 1958, she entered a mental ward in a California hospital and was treated in mental hospitals periodically for the rest of her life.

FILMS INCLUDE: *Woman Chases Man, Stage Door* 1937; *Mr. Smith Goes to Washington, Mercy Plane* 1939: *Hold That Woman* 1940; *The Reluctant Dragon, Jungle Girl* (serial), *Louisiana Purchase, Border Vigilantes* 1941; *The Remarkable Andrew, Tombstone—The Town Too Tough to Die, Beyond the Blue Horizon, The Glass Key, American Empire* 1942; *Tarzan Triumphs, Cry Havoc* 1943; *Marriage Is a Private Affair* 1944; *Thrill of a Romance, Our Vines Have Tender Grapes, She Went to the Races* 1945; *Little Mr. Jim, The Arnelo Affair* 1947; *Luxury Liner* 1948; *Riding High* 1950; *Sky Commando* 1953.

Gilbert, Billy. Actor. *b.* Sept 12, 1893, Louisville, Ky. *d.* 1971. The son of Metropolitan Opera singers, he began performing at 12. In vaudeville and burlesque, he developed a suspense-filled sneezing routine that became his trademark in many comic screen portrayals and was also hilariously utilized for the cartoon character Sneezy on the sound track of Disney's *Snow White and the Seven Dwarfs* (1938). Tall and heavy (280 lbs.), he appeared in some 200 feature films and shorts and in light character roles in comic relief of straight players and support of leading comedians, notably LAUREL AND HARDY. Memorable as Herring (Field Marshal Hermann Goering) in Chaplin's *The Great Dictator* (1940). Gilbert directed two Broadway shows in the late 40s and authored a play, 'Buttrio Square,' which was produced in New York in 1952.

FILMS INCLUDE: *Bubbles of Trouble* 1916; *Dynamite Allen* 1921; *Noisy Neighbors* 1929; *The Music Box* (three-reel short), *Million Dollar Legs, Pack Up Your Troubles, Their First Mistake* (short) 1932; *Them Thar Hills* (two-reel short) 1934; *Sutter's Gold* 1936; *On the Avenue, The Outcasts of Poker Flat, The Toast of New York, The Firefly, Broadway Melody of 1938, 100 Men and a Girl, Music for Madame, Rosalie* 1937; *Snow White and the Seven Dwarfs* (voice/sneeze only), *Happy Landing, Joy of Living, Block-Heads, My Lucky Star* 1938; *The Under-Pup, Rio, Destry Rides Again* 1939; *His Girl Friday, Safari, The Great Dictator, A Little Bit of Heaven, Seven Sinners, Tin Pan Alley, No No Nanette* 1940; *Model Wife, Reaching for the Sun, One Night in Lisbon, Week-End in Havana* 1941; *New Wine, Song of the Islands, Valley of the Sun, Arabian Nights* 1942; *Crazy House, Anchors Aweigh* 1945; *The Kissing Bandit* 1948; *Bride of Vengeance* 1949; *Down Among the Sheltering Palms* 1953; *Five Weeks in a Balloon* 1962.

Gilbert, John. Actor. *b.* John Pringle, July 10, 1895, Logan, Utah. *d.* 1936. The son of the leading comic of the Pringle Stock Company, he broke into films through family connections in 1916 as an extra and bit player for the Thomas H. Ince company. Within a year he began playing featured parts and occasional leads, usually in unsympathetic roles or as the "other man." Occasionally he would collaborate on the scripts. One of his first good parts as a leading man was in First National's *Heart o' the Hills* (1919), opposite Mary Pickford. In this as well as in all his other films up to mid-1921 he was billed as Jack Gilbert. By the time he went to work for Fox in the early 20s he was quite popular and gaining momentum as a dashing leading man in such films as *Monte Cristo, Arabian Love,* and John Ford's *Cameo Kirby.* However, it was with MGM, from the mid- to the late-20s, that he became one of the great screen idols of his time. Appearing in one smash hit after another—*He Who Gets Slapped, The Merry Widow, The Big Parade, Bardelys the Magnificent*—he was, next to Valentino, the most widely admired celluloid lover of the era. And when Valentino died in 1926, Gilbert had no competitors in the romantic fervor and passion department.

Fans' adulation of Gilbert reached its highest peak in the late 20s, when he was teamed with Greta GARBO in three scorching screen romances in succession—*Flesh and the Devil, Love* (an adaptation of *Anna Karenina*), and *A Woman of Affairs.* (In 1933 he was to co-star with Garbo again in *Queen Christina.*) MGM was only too pleased to publicize an alleged offscreen romance, although Garbo later denied there had been any affair between them. The last three of Gilbert's four marriages were to actresses, Leatrice JOY (1923–24), Ina CLAIRE (1929–31), and Virginia BRUCE (1932–34).

The advent of sound marked a critical reversal in Gilbert's screen career. It was not so much that his voice was markedly high-pitched, as some popular film histories have suggested. True, the voice was far from ideal and did not carry the authority that his screen presence implied, but it was serviceable enough to carry him through ten talkies. Possibly the most important factor contributing to his downfall was that the type of passionate romantic drama that made him so popular went out of style at the close of the silent era and he wasn't a good enough actor to make an easy adjustment to a new type of role. Gilbert's frustrations led him to heavy drinking in his final years, which no doubt hastened his death, of a heart attack at 41.

FILMS: *Hell's Hinges, Bullets and Brown Eyes, The Aryan, The Apostle of Vengeance, The Phantom, Shell 43, The Eye of the Night, The Sin Ye Do* 1916; *Princess of the Dark, Happiness, The Millionaire Vagrant, Hater of Men, The Mother Instinct, The Devil Dodger, Golden Rule Kate, The Bride of Hate, The Dark Road, Love or Justice, Up or Down?* 1917; *Nancy Comes Home, Three X Gordon, Shackled, More Trouble, Wedlock, The Mask, The Dawn of Understanding* 1918; *The White Heather, The Busher, Widow by Proxy, The Red Viper, Heart o' the Hills, For a Woman's Honor, A Little Brother of the Rich, Should a Woman Tell?* 1919; *The Great Redeemer* (also co-adapt.), *The White Circle* (also co-sc.), *Deep Water* (also sc.), *The Servant in the House* 1920; *The Bait* (co-sc. only), *Love's Penalty* (dir., co-sc. only), *Shame, Ladies Must Live* 1921; *Gleam o' Dawn, Arabian Love, The Yellow Stain, Honor First, Monte Cristo, Calvert's Valley, A California Romance, The Love Gambler* 1922; *Truxton King, While Paris Sleeps/The Glory of Love* (release delayed from 1920), *The Madness of Youth, Saint Elmo, The Exiles, Cameo Kirby* 1923; *Just Off Broadway, The Wolf Man, A Man's Mate, Romance Ranch, The Lone Chance, His Hour, He Who Gets Slapped, Married Flirts* (cameo), *The Snob, The Wife of the Centaur* 1924; *The Merry Widow, The Big Parade* 1925; *La Boheme, Bardelys the Magnificent* 1926; *Flesh and the Devil, The Show, Twelve Miles Out, Love, Man Woman and Sin* 1927; *The Cossacks, Four Walls, The Masks of the Devil, Show People* (cameo), *A Woman of Affairs* 1928; *Desert Nights, A Man's Man* (cameo), *The Hollywood Revue, His Glorious Night* 1929; *Redemption, Way for a Sailor* 1930; *Gentleman's Fate, The Phantom of Paris* 1931; *West of Broadway, Downstairs* (also sc.) 1932; *Fast Workers, Queen Christina* 1933; *The Captain Hates the Sea* 1934.

Gilbert, Lewis. Director. Born on Mar. 6, 1920, in London. A former child actor on the London stage and British films, he worked as an assistant director in the late 30s, and during WW II was attached to the US Air Corps film unit. From 1944 to 1946 he directed documentaries, including *Sailors Do Care* (1944), *The Ten Year Plan* (1945), and *Arctic Harvest* (1946). He began his career as a feature director in 1947 with a children's film, *The Little Ballerina,* and after handling several minor productions, established his reputation during the 50s with a number of solid war dramas and taut thrillers. In 1961, in *The Greengage Summer* (US title: *Loss of Innocence*), he handled the subject of young love with remarkable sensitivity, but after his great commercial success with *Alfie* (1966), he undertook big-budget assignments like the James Bond thriller *You Only Live Twice* and the Harold Robbins expensive sex-saga fiasco *The Adventurers.* Smarting from the failure of the latter, Gilbert returned to sensitive explorations of young love in his films of the early 70s, but later in the decade he made a successful comeback as a box-office director with a second Bond thriller, *The Spy Who Loved Me* (1977). Later he recorded critical successes with the delightful feminist comedies *Educating Rita* (1983) and *Shirley Valentine* (1989), but backslid with the disastrous Liza MINNELLI vehicle *Stepping Out* (1991).

FEATURE FILMS: *The Little Ballerina* (also sc.) 1947; *Once a Summer, There Is Another Sun/Wall of Death* 1950; *The Scarlet Thread* 1951; *Emergency Call/Hundred Hour Hunt* (also co-sc.); *Time Gentlemen Please, Cosh Boy/The Slasher* (also co-sc.) 1952; *Johnny on the Run* (also prod.), *Albert R.N./Break to Freedom* 1953; *The Good Die Young, The Sea Shall Not Have Them* (both also co-sc.) 1954; *Cast a Dark Shadow* 1955; *Reach for the Sky* (also sc.) 1956; *The Admirable Crichton/Paradise Lagoon* 1957; *Carve Her Name with Pride* (also co-sc.), *A Cry from the Streets* (also exec. prod.) 1958; *Ferry to Hong Kong* (also exec. prod., co-sc.) 1959; *Sink the Bismarck!, Light Up the Sky* (also prod.) 1960; *The Greengage Summer/Loss of Innocence* 1961; *H.M.S. Defiant/Damn the Defiant!* 1962; *The Seventh Dawn* 1964; *Alfie* (also prod.) 1966; *You Only Live Twice* 1967; *The Adventurers* (also prod., co-sc.) 1970; *Friends* (also prod., story) 1971; *Paul and Michele* (also prod., story) 1974; *Seven Men at Daybreak/Operation Daybreak* 1975; *Seven Nights in Japan* (also prod.; UK/Fr.) 1976; *The Spy Who Loved Me* 1977; *Moonraker* 1979; *Educating Rita* (also prod.) 1983; *Not Quite Jerusalem/Not Quite Paradise* (also prod.) 1985; *Shirley Valentine* (also prod.) 1989; *The Haunted, Stepping Out* (also co-prod.) 1991.

Gilchrist, Connie. Actress. *b.* Rose Constance Gilchrist, Feb. 2, 1901, Brooklyn, N.Y. *d.* 1985. The daughter of an actress (Martha Daniels), she made her stage debut in London at 16 and, after touring France in repertory, performed for various US stage companies, finally reaching Broadway in 1935. In 1940 she was signed by MGM and subsequently played character roles in numerous films of that studio and others, typically portraying a mother or a spunky, outspoken governess or domestic.

FILMS INCLUDE: *Hullabaloo* 1940; *A Woman's Face, Billy the Kid, Barnacle Bill, Two-Faced Woman* 1941; *Johnny Eager, We Were Dancing, Tortilla Flat* 1942; *Thousands Cheer, Presenting Lily Mars, Cry Havoc* 1943; *Music for Millions* 1944; *Valley of Decision, Junior Miss* 1945; *The Hucksters, Song of the Thin Man, Good News* 1947; *Big City* 1948; *Act of Violence, A Letter to Three Wives, Little Women, The Story of Molly X* 1949; *Peggy, Louisa* 1950; *Here Comes the Groom, Thunder on the Hill* 1951; *Flesh and Fury* 1952; *Houdini* 1953; *It Should Happen to You* 1954; *The Far Country* 1955; *The Man in the Gray Flannel Suit* 1956; *Auntie Mame* 1958; *Some Came Running* 1959; *The Interns* 1962; *A House Is Not a Home* 1964; *Sylvia, The Monkey's Uncle, Tickle Me* 1965; *Some Kind of a Nut* 1969.

Gilford, Jack. Actor. *b.* Jacob Gellman, July 25, 1907, New York City. *d.* 1990. He grew up in Brooklyn's Williamsburg section, where his divorced, Rumanian-born mother supported her children as a bootlegger. A veteran vaudeville and revue comedian, he played comic character roles in many stage and TV productions as well as in a number of films, memorably as Hysetrium in *A Funny Thing Happened on the Way to the Forum* (1966), a role he had also played in the original Broadway musical. Blacklisted following a 1956 confrontation with the House Un-American Activities Committee, he appeared in no films or TV shows in the next decade. For a good number of years he was constantly in the public eye with his prize-winning Cracker Jack TV commercials. He was nominated for a best supporting actor Oscar for his performance in *Save the Tiger* (1972). He was married to actress Madeline Lee. Author (with wife, and Zero and Kate MOSTEL): *170 Years of Show Business.*

FILMS INCLUDE: *Hey Rookie, The Reckless Age* 1944; *Main Street to Broadway* 1953; *The Daydreamer, Mr. Buddwing, A Funny Thing Happened on the Way to the Forum* 1966; *Enter Laughing, The Incident, Who's Minding the Mint?* 1969; *Catch-22* 1970; *They Might Be Giants* 1971; *Harry and Walter Go to New York* 1976; *Cheaper to Keep Her, Wholly Moses* 1980; *Caveman* 1981; *Cocoon* 1985; *Arthur 2 on the Rocks, Cocoon: The Return* 1988.

Gillespie, A. Arnold ("Buddy"). Special-effects man, former art director. *b.* Oct. 14, 1899, El Paso, Tex. *d.* 1978. *ed.* Columbia; Art Students League. In films since 1922, he was art director for MGM from 1924 to 1936, then head of the company's special effects department. In all, he had hundreds of films to his credit and was the winner of four Academy Awards (designated "AA" below).

FILMS INCLUDE (alone or in collaboration): As art director—*Manslaughter* 1922; *Adam's Rib* 1923; *Ben-Hur* 1925; *La Bohème, The Road to Mandalay* 1926; *London After Midnight* 1927; *The Divine Woman, The Crowd* 1928; *Eskimo* 1934; *Mutiny on the Bounty* 1935. Special effects—*San Francisco* 1936; *The Good Earth* 1937; *The Wizard of Oz* 1939; *Mrs. Miniver* 1942; *A Guy Named Joe, Bataan* 1943; *Thirty Seconds Over Tokyo* (AA), *The White Cliffs of Dover* 1944; *They Were Expendable, The Clock, Yolanda and the Thief, Valley of Decision* 1945; *The Green Years* 1946; *Green Dolphin Street* (AA), *The Beginning or the End* 1947; *Command Decision* 1948; *The Secret Garden* 1949; *Scaramouche, The Bad and the Beautiful, Plymouth Adventure* (AA) 1952; *Above and Beyond, All the Brothers Were Valiant* 1953; *Rose Marie* 1954; *Forbidden Planet, High Society* 1956; *North by Northwest, Ben-Hur* (AA) 1959; *Atlantis the Lost Continent, The Four Horsemen of the Apocalypse* 1961; *Mutiny on the Bounty, Jumbo, How the West Was Won* 1962; *The Prize* 1953; *The Unsinkable Molly Brown* 1964; *The Greatest Story Ever Told* 1965.

Gilliam, Terry. Director, screenwriter, animator, actor. Born on Nov. 22, 1940, in Minneapolis. After graduating from Occidental College with a degree in political science, he worked in New York and Los Angeles as a writer-illustrator for magazines and advertising agencies. Dissatisfied with his lot, he moved to London where he began working for the BBC, and before long joined John Cleese, Terry Jones, Graham Chapman, Michael Palin, and Eric Idle in their zany television series 'Monty Python's Flying Circus' (1969–76). He participated in various capacities in the feature offsprings of the popular series, then asserted himself as a director of free imagination and a devilish sense of black humor. His *Brazil* (1985), a Kafkaesque excursion into near-future absurdities, highly praised when it opened in Europe, was the subject of a bitter battle with Universal, when the studio insisted on trimming the film by 17 minutes for its American release. Gilliam disappointed many admirers of that film with his ambitious but overblown Quixotic epic *The Adventures of Baron Munchausen* (1989). He continued to explore the intersection of fantasy and reality in *The Fisher King*, a tale of urban madness and redemption that received mixed reviews. He works out of London, where he lives with his wife, Maggie, and their three children.

FILMS: *And Now for Something Completely Different* (co-sc., anim., act.) 1972; *Monty Python and the Holy Grail* (co-dir. co-sc., anim., act.) 1975; *Jabberwocky* (dir., co-sc.) 1977; *Life of Brian* (co-sc., anim., act.) 1979; *Time Bandits* (dir., prod., co-sc.) 1981; *Monty Python Live at the Hollywood Bowl* (co-sc., act.) 1982; *Monty Python's the Meaning of Life* (co-sc., anim., act.) 1983; *Brazil* (dir., co-sc.), *Spies Like Us* (act.) 1985; *The Adventures of Baron Munchausen* (dir., co-sc., act.) 1989; *The Fisher King* (dir.) 1991; *Twelve Monkeys* (dir.)1995.

Gilliat, Sidney. Director, screenwriter, producer. *b.* Feb. 15, 1908, in Edgeley, England. *d.* 1994. *ed.* London U. (English & history). The son of a journalist who later became editor of the London *Evening Standard,* he entered British films in 1928 as assistant to screenwriter (later producer and director) Walter C. Mycroft, a former film critic at his father's newspaper. In the late 30s he began a long collaboration with Frank LAUNDER, first as writers and later also as co-producers through their partnership in Individual Pictures, which they formed in 1945. They both had made their debut as directors in 1942 and subsequently divided directing, producing, and writing duties between them. They were at their best with suspense and comedy films. Gilliat became chairman of the Shepperton studios in 1961. His younger brother, Leslie Gilliat (*b.* May 29, 1917, New Malden, England) was a producer and occasionally Sidney's collaborator.

FILMS INCLUDE: *Champagne* (co-titles) 1928; *The Ringer* (addnl. dial.), *A Gentleman of Paris* 1931; As screenwriter (alone or in collaboration)—*Rome Express* 1932; *Orders Is Orders, Friday the 13th* 1933; *Chu Chin Chow, Jack Ahoy, My Heart Is Calling* 1934; *Bulldog Jack/Alias Bulldog Drummond* 1935; *King of the Damned, Seven Sinners, The Man Who Changed His Mind/The Man Who Lived Again* 1936; *A Yank at Oxford, The Lady Vanishes* 1938; *Jamaica Inn* 1939; *Night Train to Munich/Night Train, The Girl in the News* 1940; *Kipps* 1941; *The Young Mr. Pitt* 1942; *2,000 Women* 1944; *I See a Dark Stranger* (also prod.) 1946; *Captain Boycott* (co-prod. only) 1947; *The Blue Lagoon* (also prod.) 1948; *The Belles of St. Trinian's* 1954; *Geordie/Wee Geordie* (also co-prod.) 1955; *The Green Man* (also co-prod.) 1956; *The Pure Hell of St. Trinian's* (also co-prod.) 1960. As director (complete)—*Partners in Crime* (short; co-dir. with Frank Launder) 1942; *Millions Like Us* (co-dir., co-sc. with Launder) 1943; *Waterloo Road* (also sc.) 1944; *The Rake's Progress/Notorious Gentleman* (also co-prod., co-sc.) 1945; *Green for Danger* (also co-sc.) 1946; *London Belongs to Me/Dulcimer Street* (also co-sc.) 1948; *State Secret* (also co-prod., sc.) 1950; *The Story of Gilbert and Sullivan/Gilbert and Sullivan* (also co-prod., co-sc.) 1953; *The Constant Husband* (also co-prod., co-sc.) 1955; *Fortune Is a Woman/She Played with Fire* (also co-prod., co-sc.) 1957; *Left Right and Centre* (also co-prod., co-sc.) 1959; *Only Two Can Play* (also co-prod.) 1962; *The Great St. Trinian's Train Robbery* (co-dir. with Launder) 1966; *Endless Night* (also sc.), *Ooh. . . You Are Awful/Get Charlie Tully* (co-exec. prod. only) 1972.

Gilling, John. Director, screenwriter. *b.* May 29, 1910, England. *d.* 1984. Entered British films in 1933 as assistant director and after WW II service with the Royal Navy began writing scripts. He made his debut as director in 1948 and subsequently turned out many low-to-medium-budget thrillers and adventure pictures. He continued to write screenplays for his own films as well as for those of others. Several of his horror pictures of the 60s struck a responsive chord among aficionados of the genre. In 1970 he emigrated to Spain, where he made his last film in 1974, became a painter, and died at 74. Married actress Lorraine Clewes.

FILMS (as director): *Escape from Broadmoor* (also sc.) 1948; *A Matter of Murder* (also sc.) 1949; *No Trace, Blackout* (both also sc.) 1950; *The Quiet Woman* (also sc.) 1951; *The Frightened Man* (also sc.), *Mother Riley Meets the Vampire* (also prod.), *The Voice of Merrill/Murder Will Out* (also sc.) 1952; *Recoil, Three Steps to the Gallows, Escape by Night* (all also sc.), *The Deadly Nightshade* 1953; *White Fire* (also co-sc.; US), *Double Exposure, The Embezzler* (all also sc.) 1954; *Tiger by the Tail* (also sc.), *The Gilded Cage* 1955; *The Gamma People, Odongo* (both also sc.) 1956; *High Flight, Interpol* 1957; *The Man Inside* 1958; *Bandit of Zhobe* (also sc.), *Idle on Parade* 1959; *The Flesh and the Fiends/Mania/Psycho Killers/ The Fiendish Ghouls* (also story, co-sc.), *The Challenge/It Takes a Thief* (also sc.) 1960; *Fury at Smuggler's Bay* (also prod., story, sc.), *The Shadow of the Cat* 1961; *The Pirates of Blood River* (also story, co-sc.) 1962; *The Scarlet Blade/The Crimson Blade* (also story, sc.) 1963; *Panic* (also co-story, sc.), *The Brigand of Kandahar* (also sc.) 1965; *The Plague of the Zombies, The Reptile, Where the Bullets Fly, The Night Caller/Blood Beast from Outer Space/Night Caller from Outer Space* 1966; *The Mummy's Shroud* (also sc.) 1967; *La Cruz del Diablo* (Sp.) 1974.

Gillis, Ann. Actress. Born Alma Mabel O'Connor, on Feb. 12, 1927, in Little Rock, Ark. She started as a child performer of Hollywood films of the late 30s and early 40s, often in brat roles. Although not quite of star caliber, she was popular among youngsters, but she was unsuccessful in her bid for a screen career as an adult. Formerly married to actor Richard FRASER, she now lives in England.

FILMS INCLUDE: *Garden of Allah* 1936; *Off to the Races* 1937; *The Adventures of Tom Sawyer* (as Becky Thatcher), *Little Orphan Annie* (title role), *Peck's Bad Boy* 1938; *The Under-Pup, Beau Geste* 1939; *Edison the Man, All This and Heaven Too* 1940; *Little Men, Nice Girl?* 1941; *In Society, Since You Went Away* 1944; *The Cheaters* 1945; *The Time of Their Lives* 1946; *Big Town After Dark* 1947; *2001: A Space Odyssey* (bit) 1968.

Gilmore, Stuart. Film editor, director. *b.* 1913, Tombstone, Ariz. *d.* 1971. He joined Paramount as an apprentice cutter at age 15 and began editing on his own in the late 30s, soon becoming Preston Sturges's favorite editor. After several middling outings as a director in the late 40s and early 50s he returned to the cutting room.

FILMS INCLUDE: As director (complete)—*The Virginian* 1946; *Hot Lead* 1951; *Captive Women, The Half-Breed, Target* 1952. As editor—*Wild Money* 1937; *Million Dollar Legs* 1939; *The Way of All Flesh* 1940; *The Lady Eve, Sullivan's Travels* 1941; *The Palm Beach Story* 1942; *The Miracle of Morgan's Creek, Hail the Conquering Hero, The Great Moment* 1944; *Road to Utopia* 1946; *The Conqueror, War and Peace* 1956; *The*

Enemy Below 1957; *Journey to the Center of the Earth* 1959; *The Alamo* 1960; *Hatari!* 1962; *Hawaii* 1966; *Thoroughly Modern Millie* 1967; *Sweet Charity* 1969; *Airport* 1970; *The Andromeda Strain* 1971.

Gilmore, Virginia. Actress. *b.* Sherman Virginia Poole, July 26, 1919, Del Monte, Calif. *d.* 1986. The daughter of a retired British army officer. She was educated at a Hollywood convent and made her stage debut at 15 with a San Francisco company. She was an experienced and proven actress by the time she broke into films in 1939. But her screen career as a leading lady for Goldwyn and Fox was less than spectacular. Her best opportunities came in Fritz Lang's *Western Union* and Jean Renoir's *Swamp Water* (both 1941), but most of her other roles were in minor productions. Before long she gave up on films for an on-again, off-again career on the stage (including Broadway) and television, and later as a drama coach. She taught drama at Yale from 1966 to 1968, then devoted much of her time to her role as a leader in Alcoholics Anonymous. She died at 66 of complications from emphysema, leaving a son from her one-time marriage (1944–60) to Yul BRYNNER.

FILMS: *Winter Carnival* 1939; *Manhattan Heartbeat, Ladie, Jennie* 1940; *Western Union, Tall Dark and Handsome, Swamp Water, Mr. District Attorney in the Carter Case* 1941; *Berlin Correspondent, The Loves of Edgar Allan Poe, The Pride of the Yankees, Orchestra Wives, That Other Woman, Sundown Jim* 1942; *Chetniks* 1943; *Wonder Man* 1945; *Close-Up* 1948; *Walk East on Beacon* 1952.

Gilroy, Frank D. Playwright, screenwriter, director, producer. Born on Oct. 13, 1925, in New York City. *ed.* Dartmouth Coll. (B.A., magna cum laude); Yale School of Drama. A TV writer from 1952, he contributed to 'Playhouse 90' and other anthology drama programs. He won an Obie Award for his first off-Broadway play, 'Who'll Save the Plowboy?' (1964, adapted from his 1957 teleplay) and both the Pulitzer Prize and Tony Award for his first Broadway play, 'The Subject Was Roses' (1964). He is also the author of several novels. Writing screenplays intermittently from the mid-50s, he made his debut as a film director in 1971.

FILMS: As screenwriter—*Fastest Gun Alive* 1956; *The Gallant Hours* 1960; *The Subject Was Roses* (from his own play) 1968; *The Only Game in Town* 1970. As director—*Desperate Characters* (also prod. sc.) 1971; *From Noon to Three* (also sc.) 1976; *Once in Paris* (also prod., sc.) 1978; *The Gig* (also sc.) 1985; *The Luckiest Man in the World* (also sc.) 1989.

Gingold, Hermione. Actress. *b.* Dec. 9, 1897, London, to an English mother and Austrian father. *d.* 1987. Rambunctious, irrepressible, tart-tongued character player of British and American stage and screen. A stage actress from the age of 11, she later became a leading revue comedienne and a favorite of audiences in both London and New York. She also made delightful, if less frequent, appearances in films and on TV, often in grotesque characterizations, memorably in *Gigi* and *Bell, Book and Candle* (both 1958). Autobiography: *The World Is Square* (1958).

FILMS INCLUDE: *Someone at the Door* 1936; *The Butler's Dilemma* 1943; *The Pickwick Papers* 1952; *Around the World in 80 Days* 1956; *Gigi, Bell Book and Candle* 1958; *The Naked Edge* 1961; *The Music Man* 1962; *I'd Rather Be Rich* 1964; *Harvey Middleman—Fireman, Rocket to the Moon/Those Fantastic Flying Fools* 1967; *A Little Night Music* 1977; *Garbo Talks* 1984.

Ginty, Robert. Actor, director. Born on Nov. 14, 1948, in New York City. *ed.* Yale. Taciturn leading man of mostly low-budget American films. He made an underwhelming debut as a director in 1989.

FILMS INCLUDE (as actor): *Bound for Glory, The Two-Minute Warning* 1976; *Coming Home* 1978; *The Exterminator* 1980; *Scarab* 1982; *Exterminator 2, The Act* 1984; *The Alchemist* (release delayed from 1981), *Warrior of the Lost World* (It.) 1985; *Programmed to Kill, Three Kinds of Heat* 1987; *Out on Bail, The Bounty Hunter* (also dir.) 1989; *Vietnam Texas* (also dir., co-prod.), *Madhouse* 1990; *Harley Davidson and the Marlboro Man* 1991.

Girard, Bernard. American director. Born in 1930(?). He entered the industry as a screenwriter in 1950 and, after directing for TV, made his debut as a motion picture director in 1957. Working mostly in television and only sporadically in feature films, he has turned out a number of routine melodramas but impressed with one solid caper thriller, *Dead Heat on a Merry-Go-Round* (1966). He often writes his own scripts.

FILMS: *Ride Out for Revenge, The Green-Eyed Blonde* 1957; *The Party Crashers* (also sc.), *As Young As You Are* 1958; *A Public Affair* (also co-prod., sc.) 1962; *Dead Heat on a Merry-Go-Round* (also sc.) 1966; *The Mad Room* (also co-sc.) 1969; *The Happiness Cage* 1972; *Gone with the West* 1975.

Girardot, Annie. Actress. Born on Oct. 25, 1931, in Paris. Sensual, talented leading lady of Paris stage and French and Italian films. An honor graduate of the Conservatoire de Paris, she was a member of the Comédie-Française from 1954 to 1957 and also performed on radio and TV and in Paris cabarets. In films since the mid-50s, she has often come up with solid performances and won several acting awards, including a Venice Festival prize for *Trois Chambres à Manhattan* (1965). She won a César, the French Oscar, for her performance in *Dorteur Françoise Gailland/No Time for Breakfast* (1975). She married Italian actor Renato Salvatori in 1962.

FILMS INCLUDE: *Treize à Table, L'Homme aux Clefs d'Or* 1956; *Le Rouge est mis/Speaking of Murder* 1957; *Maigret tend un Piège/Inspector Maigret* 1958; *Recours en Grâce, La Française et l'Amour/Love and the Frenchwoman, Rocco e i suoi Fratelli/Rocco and His Brothers* (It./Fr.), *Le Proie pour l'Ombre* 1960; *Smog* (It.), *Le Rendez-vous* 1961; *Le Crime ne paie pas/Crime Does Not Pay* 1962; *Le Vice et la Vertue/Vice and Virtue, I Compagni/The Organizer* (It./Fr./Yug.) 1963; *La Donna Scimmia/The Ape Woman* (It./Fr.), *La Bonne Soupe/Careless Love, Un Monsieur de Compagnie/Male Companion* 1964; *Guerre secréte/The Dirty Game, Trois Chambres à Manhattan* 1965; *Le Streghe/The Witches* (It./Fr.) 1966; *Vivre pour vivre/Live for Life* 1967; *Les Gauloises Bleues, Erotissimo* 1968; *It Rains in My Village* (Yug.), *Dillinger è morto/Dillinger Is Dead* (It.), *Il Seme dell'Uomo/The Seed of Man* (It.), *Un Homme qui me plaît/Love Is a Funny Thing* 1969; *Les Novices/The Novices* 1970; *Mourir d'Aimer/To Die of Love* 1971; *La Mandarine* 1972; *Traitement de Shoc/Shock, Il n'ya pas de Fumée sans Feu/Where There's Smoke* 1973; *La Giffle/The Slap* 1974; *Le Gitan, Docteur Françoise Gailland/No Time for Breakfast, Il pleut sur Santiago/It Is Raining on Santiago* 1975; *D'Amour et d'Eau Fraîche, Cours Après mois que je t'attrape/Run After Me Until I Catch You, Autopsie d'un Monstre* 1976; *A Chacun son Enfer, Jambon d'Ardenne, Le Dernier Baiser, Le Point de Mire, Tendre Poulet/Dear Detective/Dear Inspector* 1977; *La Zizanie, Vas y Maman, La Clé sur la Porte* 1978; *Le Cavaleur/Practice Makes Perfect, L'Ingorgo—una Storia impossibile/Traffic Jam* (It./Fr./Sp./Ger.) 1979; *On a volé la Cuisse de Jupiter/Jupiter's Thigh, Le Coeur à l'envers* 1980; *All Night Long* (US), *La Vie continue* 1981; *Adieu Blaireau, Partir revenir* 1985; *Cinq Jours en Juin* 1989; *Il y a des Jours. . . et des Lunes* 1990; *Merci la Vie, Toujours Seuls* 1991; *Prisonniers, Comedie d'Amour* 1992; *Les Braqueuses* 1994; *Les Miserables* 1995.

Girotti, Mario. See HILL, Terence.

Girotti, Massimo. Actor. Born on May 18, 1918, in Mogliano, Italy. Handsome, athletic, capable leading man of many Italian films since the late 30s. A graduate of an engineering school, he was a polo and swimming champion before making his film debut in Blasetti's *Dora Nelson* (1939). He has been equally successful in swashbuckling roles and in parts requiring sensitive acting. More recently in character roles.

FILMS INCLUDE: *Dora Nelson* 1939; *La Corona di Ferro/The Iron Crown, La Tosca* 1940; *Ossessione* 1942; *La Porta del Cielo, Il Dieci Comandamenti/The Ten Commandments* 1945; *Desiderio/Woman, Una Giorno nella Vita* 1946; *Caccia Tragica/Tragic Hunt, Giovnetù perduta/Lost Youth, Anni difficili/Difficult Years, Fabiola* 1947; *Molti Sogni Per le Strade/Woman Trouble, Natale al Campo 119/Escape Into Dreams, In Nome della Legge/Mafia* 1948; *Cronaca di un Amore/Story of a Love Affair* 1950; *Roma Ore undici/Rome 11 O'Clock, Spartaco* 1952; *L'Amour d'Une Femme* (Fr.) 1953; *Senso* 1954; *Marguerite de la Nuit* (Fr.) 1955; *Aphrodite* 1957; *Giuditta e Oloferne/Head of a Tyrant* (as Holophernes) 1958; *Erode il Grande, I Cosacchi/The Cossacks* (as Czar Alexander II) 1959; *Lettere di una Novizia/Rita* 1960; *I Giganti della Tessaglia/Duel of the Titans* 1961; *Oro di Cesari/Gold for the Caesars, Venus Imperiale* 1963; *La Fabuleuse Aventure de Marco Polo/Marco the Magnificent* 1965; *Le Streghe/The Witches* 1967; *Teorema, Medea* 1969; *Krasnaya Palatka/The Red Tent* (USSR/It.) 1971; *Gli Orrori del Castello di Norimberga/Baron Blood, Ultimo Tango a Parigi/Last Tango in Paris* 1972; *L'Innocente/The Innocent, Cagliostro, Mr. Klein* (Fr.) 1976; *Un Reitto delle Isole/An Outcast of the Islands* 1979; *Passione d'Amore* 1981; *Berlin Affair* 1985.

Gish, Annabeth. Actress. Born 1972 in Albuquerque, N.M. Lovely, expressive film actress who, as a youngster, made her film debut with *Desert Bloom* (1986). She stood out opposite Julia ROBERTS in *Mystic Pizza* (1988) and has came into her own in the 90s with more substantial, adult roles in major Hollywood films.

FILMS: *Desert Bloom, Hero in the Family* 1986; *Hiding Out* 1987; *Mystic Pizza* 1988; *Shag, When He's Not a Stranger* 1989; *Coupe de Ville* 1990; *The Last to Go* 1991; *Wyatt Earp* 1994; *Nixon* 1995; *Beautiful Girls, The Last Supper, Extreme Measures* 1996.

Gish, Dorothy. Actress. *b.* Mar. 11, 1898, Dayton, Ohio. *d.* 1968. A stage actress from age four, she shared with sister Lillian GISH the experience of constant travel, frequent unemployment, and occasional hunger. She was 14 when the sisters made their screen debut in Griffith's *An Uneasy Enemy,* in 1912. Early in their career they appeared side by side frequently, but later their paths crossed only periodically. However, they remained very close, and in her 1969 autobiography Lillian speaks fondly of her sister. Although Dorothy's importance as a silent screen star has been overshadowed by her sister's fame, she was an excellent actress and a star in her own right, appearing in many more films than Lillian. While Lillian was the silent screen's greatest dramatic actress, Dorothy excelled in pantomime and light comedy. A more down-to-earth heroine than her ethereal sister, she too enjoyed great popular success in films through the late 20s. She made her last silents in London, then returned to the stage, appearing only occasionally in films, in character parts. In 1920 she married James Rennie, her co-star in the film *Remodeling Her Husband,* which her sister directed. They divorced in 1935.

FILMS INCLUDE (complete from 1916): *An Unseen Enemy, The Musketeers of Pig Alley* (bit), *The New York Hat* (extra), *My Hero* 1912; *The Perfidy of Mary, The Lady and the Mouse, Almost a Wild Man, Her Mother's Oath, The Vengeance of Galora, The Adopted Brother, The Lady in Black, The House of Discord* 1913; *Judith of Bethulia* (bit), *The Mysterious Shot, The Floor Above, Liberty Belles, The Mountain Rat, Silent Sandy, The Newer Woman, Almost a Wild Man, Arms and the Gringo, The City Beautiful, The Painted Lady, Home Sweet Home, The Tavern of Tragedy, A Fair Rebel, The Wife, Sands of Fate, The Warning, The Availing Prayer, The Saving Grace, The Sisters, The Better Way* 1914; *An Old-Fashioned Girl, How Hazel Got Even, Minerva's Mission, Out of Bondage, Her Mother's Daughter, The Mountain Girl, Victorine, Bred in the Bone, Old Heidelberg, Jordan Is a Hard Road* 1915; *Betty of Greystone, Little Meena's Romance, Susan Rocks the Boat, The Little School Ma'am, Gretchen the Greenhorn, Atta Boy's Last Race, Children of the Feud* 1916; *The Little Yank, Stage Struck, Her Official Fathers* 1917; *Hearts of the World, The Hun Within, Battling Jane* 1918; *The Hope Chest, Boots, Peppy Polly, I'll Get Him Yet, Nugget Nell, Out of Luck, Turning the Tables* 1919; *Mary Ellen Comes to Town, Remodeling Her Husband, Little Miss Rebellion, Flying Pat* 1920; *The Ghost in the Garret* 1921; *Orphans of the Storm, The Country Flapper* 1922; *Fury, The Bright Shawl* 1923; *Romola* 1924; *Night Life of New York, The Beautiful City, Clothes Make the Pirate* 1925; *Nell Gwyn* (title role; UK) 1926; *London* (UK), *Tip Toes* (UK), *Madame Pompadour* (title role; UK) 1927; *Wolves/Wanted Men* (UK) 1930; *Our Hearts Were Young and Gay* 1944; *Centennial Summer* 1946; *The Whistle at Eaton Falls* 1951; *The Cardinal* 1963.

Gish, Lillian. Actress. *b.* Oct. 14, 1896, in Springfield, Ohio. *d.* 1993. The actress who is widely recognized as "The First Lady of the Silent Screen" took her first steps on the stage when she was five in a melodrama, 'In Convict Stripes.' Lillian's mother had taken to acting shortly before, during one of the frequent absences of her drifter husband, and was persuaded by friends to supplement the family income by letting her daughters, Lillian and Dorothy GISH, become child actresses. Lillian's most memorable experience during these lean years was a dancing part in a Sarah Bernhardt New York production. Their big chance came in 1912, when they ran into an old friend, a child actress they had known as Gladys Smith, whose name was now Mary Pickford, and she introduced them to director D. W. GRIFFITH. That same day both sisters acted in their first film, Griffith's *An Unseen Enemy.* Their mother was also in the cast.

Lillian was a made-to-order Griffith heroine. Her deceptive fragility, masking a great spiritual vibrance that could surge forth unexpectedly as physical strength, was perfectly suited to the Victorian sentiment of his dramas. She was deeply devoted to Griffith and admired him greatly, as she later revealed in her autobiography, *The Movies, Mr. Griffith and Me* (1969). Under Griffith's guidance, she developed into the most capable actress of the silent screen, an extraordinarily creative and dedicated performer whose work could uplift the most commonplace vehicle. She remained with Griffith until the early 20s, when they amicably parted ways over a salary dispute. Until then he had directed nearly all her films, most notably *Broken Blossoms, True Heart Susie, Way Down East,* and *Orphans of the Storm.*

Miss Gish directed her sister Dorothy in the film *Remodeling Her Husband* (1920), then starred in several major films of minor companies that gave her control over scripts and choice of directors. She received the same privileges when she joined MGM in 1925 and chose King Vidor and Victor Sjöström to direct her in *La Bohème* and *The Scarlet Letter*, respectively. Both films were highly successful. But her subsequent films for MGM did not fare very well commercially, and with Garbo emerging as a star, the company could afford to let Lillian Gish go in 1928. She appeared in one film for United Artists, after which she turned her back on Hollywood, which by now regarded her a "sexless antique."

Lillian then returned to her first love, the stage, and appeared in several Broadway plays in the 30s, including 'Uncle Vanya,' 'Camille,' and 'Hamlet' (as Ophelia opposite John Gielgud). In between plays, she acted in her last screen lead, in a Paramount film released early in 1934. From the early 40s she kept returning occasionally to the screen, in character parts, but devoted more of her energies to the stage and, later, also to television and lecture tours.

Miss Gish never married and, except for a persistent courtship by George Jean Nathan, managed to keep her private life shielded from publicity. In 1970 she was awarded a special Oscar for her cumulative work. In 1978 she returned to the screen after a long absence in Robert Altman's *A Wedding,* her 100th film. In 1984 she was the recipient of the American Film Institute's Life Achievement Award. Still amazingly resilient and energetic in her 90s, she continued appearing in films through the late 80s, her eighth decade on the screen. Her performance in her last film, *The Whales of August* (1987), opposite Bette DAVIS, was widely praised. Memoirs: *Life and Lillian Gish* (1932); *The Movies, Mr. Griffith and Me* (1969); *Dorothy and Lillian Gish* (1973); *An Actor's Life for Me* (1987).

FILMS: *An Unseen Enemy, Two Daughters of Eve* (bit), *In the Aisles of the Wild, The Musketeers of Pig Alley, My Baby* (bit), *Gold and Glitter, The New York Hat* (extra), *The Burglar's Dilemma, A Cry for Help, Oil and Water* (extra), *The Unwelcome Guest* (bit) 1912; *A Misunderstood Boy, The Left-Handed Man, The Lady and the Mouse, The House of Darkness, Just Gold, A Timely Interception, The Mothering Heart, During the Round-Up, An Indian's Loyalty, A Woman in the Ultimate, A Modest Hero, The Madonna of the Storm* 1913; *Judith of Bethulia, The Battle at Elderbush Gulch, The Green-Eyed Devil, The Battle of the Sexes, Lord Chumley, The Hunchback, The Quicksands, Man's Enemy, Home Sweet Home, The Rebellion of Kitty Belle, The Angel of Contention, The Tear That Burned, The Folly of Anne, The Sisters* 1914; *The Birth of a Nation* (as Elsie Stoneman), *The Lost House, Captain Macklin, Enoch Arden* (as Annie Lee, Enoch's wife), *The Lily and the Rose* 1915; *Daphne and the Pirate, Sold for Marriage, An Innocent Magdalene, Intolerance* (as the cradle rocker in the interludes), *Diane of the Follies, Pathways of Life, The Children Pay* 1916; *The House Built Upon Sand, Souls Triumphant* 1917; *Hearts of the World, The Great Love* (a Liberty Bond short), *The Greatest Thing in Life* 1918; *A Romance of Happy Valley, Broken Blossoms, True Heart Susie, The Greatest Question* 1919; *Remodeling Her Husband* (dir. only), *Way Down East* 1920; *Orphans of the Storm* 1922; *The White Sister* 1923; *Romola* (title role) 1924; *La Bohème* (as Mimi), *The Scarlet Letter* (as Hester Prynne) 1926; *Annie Laurie* 1927; *The Enemy, The Wind* 1928; *One Romantic Night* 1930; *His Double Life* 1933; *The Commandos Strike at Dawn, Top Man* 1943; *Miss Susie Slagle's* 1946; *Duel in the Sun* 1947; *Portrait of Jennie* 1949; *The Cobweb, The Night of the Hunter* 1955; *Orders to Kill* (UK) 1958; *The Unforgiven* 1960; *Follow Me Boys!* 1966; *Warning Shot, The Comedians* 1967; *A Wedding* 1978; *Hambone and Hillie* 1984; *Sweet Liberty* 1986; *The Whales of August* 1987.

Glaser, Paul Michael. Actor, director. Born on Mar. 25, 1943, in Cambridge, Mass. *ed.* Tulane (B.A.); Boston U. (M.A.). Intense young lead of American stage, TV, and films. Following five years in summer stock, he made his New York stage debut in 1968 in Joseph Papp's rock musical 'Rockabye Hamlet.' He later appeared in many off-Broadway plays and in such daytime soap operas as 'Love Is a Many Splendored Thing' (1969–70) and 'Love of Life' (1970–71). Although he has appeared in occasional films since 1971, it was on TV, as Detective Dave Starsky in the series 'Starsky and Hutch' (1975–79), that he became a popular star. He directed episodes of the series as well as a number of TV movies and feature films. Glaser lost his wife Elizabeth to AIDS, which she contracted from an infected blood transfusion in the early years of the epidemic. He continues their active role in promoting government allocations for pediatric treatment of the disease.

FEATURE FILMS: As actor—*Fiddler on the Roof* 1971; *Butterflies Are Free* 1972; *Phobia* (Can.) 1980. As director—*Band of the Hand* 1986; *The Running Man* 1987; *Blue Lightning* 1990; *The Cutting Edge* 1992; *The Air Up There* 1994; *Kazaam* 1996.

Glasmon, Kubec. See BRIGHT, John.

Glass, Philip. Composer. Born on Jan. 31, 1937, in Baltimore. The grandson of Orthodox Jewish immigrants from Russia,, he worked in his father's record store from age 12 while studying at Baltimore's Peabody Conservatory. At 15 he enrolled at the University of Chicago, where he excelled in piano and wrestling, then studied composition at Juilliard and became a pupil of Nadine Boulanger in Paris, on a Fulbright scholarship. He was most influenced, however, by sitar virtuoso Ravi Shankar, who introduced him to the music and spiritual world of the East. Having established an international reputation and a cult following as an innovative and bold minimalist composer of scintillating orchestral music, much of it inspired by rock and mysticism, he turned his attention to film scores in the 80s.

FILMS INCLUDE: *North Star, Mark Disuvero* (doc.) 1978; *Koyaanisqatsi* 1983; *Mishima* 1985; *Hamburger Hill* 1987; *Powaqqatsi, The Thin Blue Line* (doc.) 1988; *Mindwalk* 1990; *Candyman 2: Farewell to the Flesh* 1994; *The Secret Agent* 1996.

glass shot. A shot obtained through a glass plate on which part of the scene has been painted. The painting on the glass is photographed along with the action seen through the clear portion of the glass, providing the illusion of a complete setting. This SPECIAL EFFECT can be used to simulate elaborate locations without the need to construct expensive sets.

Glazer, Benjamin. Screenwriter. *b.* May 7, 1887, Belfast. *d.* 1958. A practicing attorney, he later became a journalist with the Philadelphia *Press.* He wrote several plays and stage adaptations before entering films in the early 20s. He wrote screenplays for many notable silent and sound Hollywood productions, alone or in collaboration, occasionally also producing or directing. In the late 20s he served for a period as head of production at Pathé. In the 30s he worked mainly for Paramount, functioning mostly as a producer.

FILMS INCLUDE (as screenwriter, alone or in collaboration): *A Trip to Paradise* (adapt. only) 1921; *Sinners in Silk* (story only) 1924; *The Merry Widow, Fine Clothes* 1925; *Memory Lane, The Skyrocket, The Gay Deceiver, Diplomacy, You Never Know Women, Everybody's Acting* 1926; *Flesh and the Devil, The Lady in Ermine, Seventh Heaven, A Gentleman of Paris* (adapt. only), *The Love Mart* 1927; *The Street of Sin* (co-assoc. prod., co-story only), *Happiness Ahead, Beggars of Life* (also prod.), *The Barker* 1928; *Strange Cargo* (prod., co-dir. with Arthur Gregor, story, dial. only), *The Dance of Life* 1929; *Tol'able David, The Boudoir Diplomat* 1930; *No Man of Her Own* (co-story only), *Mata Hari* 1932; *A Farewell to Arms, A Bedtime Story* (adapt. only), *The Way to Love* (also prod., co-story) 1933; *We're Not Dressing* (assoc. prod., adapt. only) 1934; *Enter Madame* (prod. only), *Paris in Spring* (prod. only), *The Big Broadcast of 1936* (prod. only) 1935; *Anything Goes* (prod. only), *Rhythm on the Range* (prod. only) 1936; *Mountain*

Music (prod. only), *Exclusive* (prod. only), *Double or Nothing* (prod. only) 1937; *Arise My Love* (co-story only) 1940; *Paris Calling* (also prod.), *Tortilla Flat* 1942; *Song of My Heart* (also dir.) 1948; *Carousel* (adapt. only) 1956.

Gleason, Jackie. Actor. *b.* Herbert John Gleason, Feb. 26, 1916, Brooklyn, N.Y. *d.* 1987, of cancer. The son of a poorly paid insurance clerk who disappeared when he was eight, he was raised by a struggling mother who worked as a subway change-booth attendant until she died when he was 16. A high school dropout, he received the bulk of his education in local pool halls and broke into show business at 15 after winning an amateur-night contest. He performed in vaudeville, carnivals, nightclubs, and roadhouses and in 1940 was signed to a film contract by Warner Bros. He played character roles in a number of films without much benefit to his career, and after several Broadway outings found his niche on TV as one of the medium's most popular stars. Starting with the 'The Life of Riley' (1949–50), 'Cavalcade of Stars' (1950–52), then 'The Jackie Gleason Show' (1952–55, 1956–59, 1961–70), he created and developed such memorable characters as Reggie Van Gleason, Joe the Bartender, Charlie the Loudmouth, and Ralph Kramden, the bus driver. The latter character became the central blustering figure in 'The Honeymooners' (1955–56), a comedy series that over the years achieved and maintained the status of a classic. In 1959, Gleason returned triumphantly to Broadway, winning a Tony Award for 'Take Me Along.' He then reappeared on the screen in starring roles, both comic and dramatic, and was nominated for an Academy Award for his portrait of legendary pool shark Minnesota Fats in *The Hustler* (1961). But he never achieved in films the appeal that made him a leading personality of American TV. Earlier in his career Gleason had had some success as the composer, arranger, and conductor of recorded mood music.

FILMS: *Navy Blues* 1941; *All Through the Night, Tramp Tramp Tramp, Larceny Inc., Lady Gangster, Escape from Crime, Orchestra Wives, Springtime in the Rockies* 1942; *The Desert Hawk* 1950; *The Hustler* 1961; *Gigot* (also story), *Requiem for a Heavyweight* 1962; *Papa's Delicate Condition, Soldier in the Rain* 1963; *Skidoo* 1968; *How to Commit Marriage, Don't Drink the Water* 1969; *How Do I Love Thee?* 1970; *Mr. Billion/The Windfall, Smokey and the Bandit* 1977; *Smokey and the Bandit II* 1980; *The Toy* 1982; *The Sting II, Smokey and the Bandit—Part 3* 1983; *Nothing in Common* 1986.

Gleason, James. Actor, screenwriter, playwright. *b.* May 23, 1886, New York City. *d.* 1959. The son of an actor and actress, he joined his parents' stock company in Oakland after returning from military service in the Spanish-American War. His career was again interrupted by WW I service, after which he began performing on Broadway. During the mid- to late-20s he wrote a number of plays and musicals, alone or in collaboration, several of which were later made into films, including *Is Zat So?* (1927), *The Shannons of Broadway* (1929, and again in 1938 as *Goodbye Broadway*), *Mammy, The Fall Guy,* and *Rain or Shine* (all 1930). He made his first screen appearance in 1922, but it wasn't until 1928 that he began appearing regularly in films. Early in his career as a screen actor he also collaborated on a number of scripts as a screenwriter or dialogue specialist, including *The Broadway Melody, High Voltage, His First Command* (all 1929), and *What a Widow!* (1930). He was dialogue director on *Oh Yeah!* (1929) and directed *Hot Tip* (1935). As an actor, Gleason soon established himself as one of the best liked character players of the American screen, portraying a rich gallery of big-city types—cops, robbers, reporters, gamblers, and fight managers, among many others—typically concealing a heart of gold beneath an ill-tempered façade. He played a recurring lead role as the slow-witted police inspector Oscar Piper in a series of mystery films of the 30s. In all he appeared in some 150 films. His wife, Lucille Gleason (*née* Webster, 1886–1947) also played character roles in films. Their son, Russell Gleason (1908–45), played leads, second leads, and supporting roles in a variety of films from 1929 until his fatal fall from a hotel window in 1945.

FILMS INCLUDE (as actor): *Polly of the Follies* 1922; *The Count of Ten* 1928; *The Flying Fool* (also dial.), *Oh Yeah!* (also dial. dir.), *The Shannons of Broadway* (lead; also dial., from own play) 1929; *The Swellhead* (lead; also co-dial.), *Puttin' On the Ritz, Dumbbells in Ermine* (also dial.), *The Matrimonial Bed, Her Man, Big Money* 1930; *Beyond Victory, It's a Wise Child, A Free Soul, Sweepstakes* 1931; *Blondie of the Follies, The Devil Is Driving* 1932; *Clear All Wires, Orders Is Orders* (lead; UK), *Hoopla* 1933; *Murder on the Blackboard* (lead) 1934; *Helldorado, Murder on a Honeymoon* (lead) 1935; *Murder on a Bridle Path* (lead), *The Ex-Mrs. Bradford, The Plot Thickens* (lead) 1936; *Forty Naughty Girls* (lead) 1937; *On Your Toes* 1939; *Meet John Doe, Here Comes Mr. Jordan, A Date with the Falcon* 1941; *Babes on Broadway, My Gal Sal, Footlight Serenade, Tales of Manhattan* 1942; *Crash Dive, A Guy Named Joe* 1943; *Once Upon a Time, Arsenic and Old Lace* 1944; *The Keys of the Kingdom, A Tree Grows in Brooklyn, The Clock, Captain Eddie* 1945; *The Hoodlum Saint, Home Sweet Homicide* 1946; *Down to Earth, The Bishop's Wife* 1947; *When My Baby Smiles at Me* 1948; *The Life of Riley, Take One False Step* 1949; *Key to the City, The Yellow Cab Man, Riding High, The Jackpot* 1950; *Come Fill the Cup, I'll See You in My Dreams* 1951; *We're Not Married, What Price Glory* 1952; *Suddenly* 1954; *The Night of the Hunter* 1955; *Spring Reunion* 1957; *The Last Hurrah* 1958.

Glen, John. Director. Born on May 15, 1932, in Sunbury-on-Thames, England. He entered British films as an apprentice at age 15, becoming a film editor in the late 60s. Among the many films he edited were *On Her Majesty's Secret Service* (1969), *Murphy's War* (1971), *A Doll's House* (1973), *Conduct Unbecoming* (1975), *The Spy Who Loved Me* (1977), *The Wild Geese,* and *Moonraker* (1979), and *The Sea Wolves* (1980). He doubled as a second-unit director on several of the latter films, then assumed directorial control over a string of glossy James Bond adventures.

FILMS: *For Your Eyes Only* 1981; *Octopussy* 1983; *A View to a Kill* 1985; *The Living Daylights* 1987; *Licence to Kill* 1989; *Aces: Iron Eagle III, Christopher Columbus: The Discovery* 1992.

Glenn, Scott. Actor. Born on Jan. 26, 1942, in Pittsburgh. *ed.* William & Mary Coll. Wiry, rugged leading man and second lead of the American screen. A former Marine and newspaper reporter, he attended the Actors Studio and appeared in several off-Broadway productions before his screen debut in 1970. Often seen in action roles, he usually performs his own stunts.

FILMS: *The Baby Maker* 1970; *Angels Hard As They Come* 1971; *Hex* 1973; *Nashville* 1975; *Fighting Mad* 1976; *She Came to the Valley, More American Graffiti, Apocalypse Now* 1979; *Urban Cowboy* 1980; *Cattle Annie and Little Britches* 1981; *Personal Best, The Challenge* 1982; *The Right Stuff, The Keep* 1983; *The River* 1984; *Wild Geese II* (UK), *Silverado* 1985; *Man on Fire* (It./Fr.) 1987; *Off Limits/Saigon* 1988; *Miss Firecracker* 1989; *The Hunt for Red October* 1990; *The Silence of the Lambs* 1991; *My Heroes Have Always Been Cowboys, Backdraft* 1991; *The Player* 1992; *Slaughter of the Innocents* 1993; *Reckless* 1995; *Carla's Song, Courage Under Fire, Edie and Pen* 1996.

Glennon, Bert. Director of photography, director. *b.* Nov. 19, 1895, Anaconda, Mont. *d.* 1967. Entered films in 1912 and worked as an assistant cameraman while attending Stanford University. A director of photography from 1916, he developed in the 20s into one of the leading craftsmen in his trade, a creative lighting cameraman whose career spanned a half-century of Hollywood history, and proved capable of satisfying the exacting requirements of such diverse directors as De Mille, Von Sternberg, Lubitsch, and Ford. He was far less successful in his stint as a director, from 1928 to 1932, and after turning out a number of mediocre low-budget productions, he resumed his distinguished career as a director of photography.

FILMS INCLUDE: As director of photography—*Ramona* 1916; *Eyes of the World* 1918; *The Kentucky Colonel* (co-phot.) 1920; *The Torrent, Cheated Love, The Kiss, A Daughter of the Law* 1921; *Ebb Tide, Burning Sands* 1922; *Salomy Jane, The Ten Commandments* (co-phot.), *Java Head* 1923; *Triumph, Changing Husbands* 1924; *The Dressmaker from Paris, Are Parents People?, Wild Horse Mesa, A Woman of the World* 1925; *Crown of Lies, Good and Naughty* 1926; *Barbed Wire, The City Gone Wild, Hotel Imperial, Underworld, Woman on Trial, We're All Gamblers* 1927; *The Last Command, The Patriot, The Street of Sin* (co-phot.) 1928. As director (complete)—*The Perfect Crime, Stepping High, The Air Legion, Gang War* 1928; *Syncopation* 1929; *Around the Corner, Second Wife* (co-sc. only), *Girl of the Port, Paradise Island* 1930; *In Line of Duty* 1931; *South of Santa Fe* 1932. As director of photography—*Blonde Venus* (co-phot.), *The Half-Naked Truth* 1932; *Christopher Strong, Gabriel Over the White House, Morning Glory, Alice in Wonderland* 1933; *The Scarlet Empress* 1934; *Lloyds of London, The Prisoner of Shark Island, Dimples* 1936; *The Hurricane* 1937; *Stagecoach, Young Mr. Lincoln, Drums Along the Mohawk* (co-phot.) 1939; *Our Town, The Howards of Virginia* 1940; *They Died with Their Boots On, Dive Bomber* (co-phot.), *Virginia* 1941; *Desperate Journey* 1942; *Mission to Moscow* 1943; *Destination Tokyo* 1944; *Hollywood Canteen, San Antonio* 1945; *The Red House* 1947; *Ruthless* 1948; *Wagonmaster, Rio Grande* 1950; *The Big Trees* 1952; *House of Wax* 1953; *The Mad Magician* 1954; *Davy Crockett and the River Pirates* 1956; *Sergeant Rutledge* 1960; *The Man from Galveston* 1964.

Glenville, Peter. Director. Born on Oct. 28, 1913, in London. The son of actors, he abandoned law studies at Oxford to begin an acting career on the stage in the early 30s. He was engaged to direct at the Old Vic in 1944 and subsequently produced and directed many distinguished productions in London and on Broadway. He appeared as an actor in several British films of the 40s and, beginning in 1955, has directed sporadically for the screen, usually handling the film versions of his stage hits.

FILMS: *The Prisoner* 1955; *Me and the Colonel* 1958; *Summer and Smoke* 1961; *Term of Trial* (also sc.) 1962; *Becket* 1964; *Hotel Paradiso* (also prod., co-sc., act.) 1966; *The Comedians* (also prod.) 1967.

Globus, Yoram. See GOLAN, Menahem.

Glover, Crispin. Actor. Born in 1964, in New York City. Oddball character player of Hollywood films, specializing in eccentric roles. The son of veteran character actor Bruce Glover and a dancer, he grew up in Los Angeles and at 14 made his stage debut as the eldest von Trapp kid in a local production of 'The Sound of Music.' He made his screen debut at 18 and was barely 20 when he portrayed George McFly, the bumbling father/suitor, in *Back to the Future* (1985). On and off the set, Glover's penchant for the bizarre is legendary. In 1987, he republished *Rat Catching*, a century-old text about killing vermin, illustrated with new pictures of mutilated rats. He followed this in 1988 with another weird publication, *Concrete Inspection*.

FILMS: *My Tutor* 1983; *Racing with the Moon, Friday the 13th—The Final Chapter, Teachers* 1984; *Back to the Future* 1985; *At Close Range* 1986; *River's Edge* 1987; *Where the Heart Is, Twister, Wild at Heart* 1990; *The Doors, Little Noises* 1991; *Rubin and Ed, Third Door Key* 1992; *Chasers, Even Cowgirls Get the Blues* 1994; *Dead Man* 1996.

Glover, Danny. Actor. Born on July 22, 1947, in San Francisco. *ed.* San Francisco State. Likeable, reliable, muscular character lead and supporting player of American films. Trained at the Black Actors Workshop of the American Conservatory Theatre, he appeared in many stage productions before making his screen debut in the late 70s. He received much praise for his portrayal of a brutal pivotal character in Steven Spielberg's *The Color Purple* (1985), then veered toward engaging roles in *Lethal Weapon* (1987), its sequels, and other films, gaining star-level popularity through his strong presence and appealing personality.

FILMS: *Escape from Alcatraz* 1979; *Chu Chu and the Philly Flash* 1981; *Out* 1982; *Iceman, Places in the Heart* 1984; *Witness, Silverado, The Color Purple* 1985; *Lethal Weapon* 1987; *Bat 21* 1988; *Lethal Weapon 2, Dead Man Out* 1989; *Predator 2, Flight of the Intruder* 1990; *To Sleep with Anger* (also exec. prod.), *A Rage in Harlem, Pure Luck* 1991; *Grand Canyon* 1991; *Lethal Weapon 3* 1992; *The Saint of Fort Washington, Bopha!* 1993; *Angels in the Outfield, Maverick* (unbilled cameo) 1994; *Operation Dumbo Drop* 1995; *Going West in America* 1996; *Gone Fishing* 1997.

Glover, John. Actor. Born on Aug. 7, 1944, in Salisbury, Md. Wiry, intense character player of the American stage and screen, typically in slimy, villainous roles. Intending to become a drama instructor, he attended Baltimore's Towson State Teachers College, but following graduation found ample opportunities to act in regional theater, then on the New York stage. On the screen fleetingly in the 70s, he's become a familiar face in films since the 80s.

FILMS INCLUDE: *Shamus* 1973; *Julia, Annie Hall* 1977; *Somebody Killed Her Husband* 1978; *Last Embrace* 1979; *Melvin and Howard* 1980; *The Incredible Shrinking Woman* 1981; *A Little Sex* 1982; *The Evil That Men Do* 1984; *White Nights* 1985; *52 Pick-Up* 1986; *Something Special* 1987; *Masquerade, A Killing Affair, Rocket Gibraltar, Scrooged* 1988; *Meet the Hollowheads, The Chocolate War* 1989; *Gremlins 2: The New Batch, Robocop 2* 1990; *Dora Was Dysfunctional, Ed and His Dead Mother* 1993; *In the Mouth of Madness* 1995; *Love! Valour! Compassion!* 1997.

Glover, Julian. Actor. Born on March 27, 1935 in London. *ed.* Royal Academy of the Dramatic Arts, London. Character actor, often cast as English or Germanic villainous types.

FILMS INCLUDE: *Tom Jones* 1963; *Girl with the Green Eyes* 1964; *I Was Happy Here, The Alphabet Murders* 1966; *Blood Fiend* 1967; *The Magus* 1968; *The Adding Machine, Alfred the Great* 1969; *Antony and Cleopatra, The Last Grenade, The Rise and Rise of Michael Rimmer, Wuthering Heights* 1970; *Nicholas and Alexandra* 1971; *Hitler: The Last Ten Days, The Internecine Project, Juggernaut, Luther* 1974; *Gulliver's Travels* 1977; *The Empire Strikes Back* 1980; *For Your Eyes Only* 1981; *Heat and Dust* 1983; *Cry Freedom, The Fourth Protocol, Hearts of Fire* 1987; *Indiana Jones and the Last Crusade* 1989; *Tusks* 1990; *King Ralph* 1991.

gobo. 1. An adjustable screen or mask mounted on a stand and used to shield the camera from direct light during shooting or to produce special lighting effects. 2. A movable sound-absorbent wall used in motion picture studios.

Godard, Jean-Luc. Director. Born on Dec. 3, 1930, in Paris, into an upper-middle-class family. The son of a doctor and a banker's daughter, he had his elementary and high school education in Nyon, Switzerland, and in Paris, then enrolled at the Sorbonne, ostensibly to study ethnology. During his university days he developed a passionate devotion to the cinema, spending endless hours at Left Bank cinema clubs and at the Cinémathèque, where in 1950 he met André BAZIN, François TRUFFAUT, Jacques RIVETTE, Eric ROHMER, and Claude CHABROL, with whom he would later form the nucleus of the French New Wave. Godard began contributing articles and film criticism for *La Gazette du Cinéma,* then CAHIERS DU CINÉMA, initially using the pseudonym Hans Lucas. Also in 1950, Godard helped finance, and appeared in, an experimental film by Rivette, *Quadrille,* in which four people around a table stare at each other for 40 minutes without saying a word.

In 1951, Godard toured North and South America. Godard began supporting himself with a variety of odd jobs. Meanwhile, he continued watching films at a fanatical rate, and his articles for *Cahiers* began reflecting an enthusiastic admiration of the work of little-known American directors of action films and at the same time a deep contempt for the traditional cinema, especially the commercial French film.

In 1954, Godard went back to Switzerland to attend services for his mother, who had been killed there in a car accident. He remained in that country to work as a laborer on a dam project. With his earnings he bought himself a 35 mm camera and made his first film, *Opération Béton,* a 20-minute short about the construction of the dam. In 1955, following a spurt of renewed activity in Paris as a contributor to *Cahiers du Cinéma,* he was back in Switzerland shooting a second short, *Une Femme coquette,* an adaptation of a de Maupassant story. Working as a one-man band, he produced, directed, and acted in the film as Jean-Luc Godard and wrote the screenplay and photographed and edited the film under the pseudonym Hans Lucas. Returning to Paris in 1956, Godard collaborated on films by Rohmer and Rivette, performing various functions, including acting. At the same time, he began contributing more regularly to *Cahiers* as well as to the magazine *Arts.*

Following three more shorts, Godard stunned the world with his first feature film, *Á Bout de Souffle/Breathless,* which was made in 1959 on a shoestring budget and released early in 1960. The film marked a significant break from orthodox cinema techniques, reshaping the traditional film syntax with its astonishing jump cuts and unsteady hand-held moving shots. It was a spontaneous, impulsive, vibrant, and totally original film that reflected the director's enchantment with the immediacy of the American gangster movie and his impatience with the laboriousness of the traditional techniques of "quality" cinema. It immediately established Godard as a leading spokesman of the NOUVELLE VAGUE movement.

Godard's next film, *Le Petit Soldat,* was a savage exposition of the Algerian conflict, a film as disturbing in the explicitness of the horrors it depicted as in the ambiguity of its characters and the political ideals they died for. The feminine lead in *Le Petit Soldat* and in several of Godard's subsequent films was played by Anna KARINA, who became the director's wife in 1961. They divorced in 1964.

Karina is a stripper who wants to have a baby and settle down, in one of Godard's most buoyant and charming films, *Une Femme est une Femme/A Woman Is a Woman* (1961), and a lonely, pathetic Paris prostitute in *Vivre sa Vie/My Life to Live* (1962), a curiously detached film in its Brechtian episodical structure and near-documentary style. Brechtian detachment and technical experimentation were also characteristic of *Les Carabiniers* (1963), an antiwar allegory that provoked such violently hostile reaction from audiences over its seemingly emotionless view of the horrors of war that Godard took the unusual step of responding to his critics from the pages of *Cahiers du Cinéma.*

The wide-screen polished color cinematography of *Le Mépris/Contempt* (1963) stood in sharp contrast to the grainy dreariness of *Les Carabiniers.* Adapted from an Alberto Moravio novel, this drama about the collapse of a marriage was turned by Godard into a tragedy that works on several levels, one of the most interesting of which is the examination of the relationship between cinema and reality.

With *Bande à Part/Band of Outsiders* (1964) Godard returned to the world of the gangster for the first time since *Breathless.* As in most of his films, the protagonists here are uprooted people, outsiders who defy the boundary between the real and the imagined. *Une Femme mariée/The Married Woman* (1964) was a conventionally structured sociological study of the alienation of a modern Parisian woman who can relate only on the physical level to both her husband and her lover. *Alphaville* (1965), Godard's excursion into science-fiction fantasy, showed much skill and technical inventiveness but failed to sustain its initial tension when it evolved into a lecture about the emotional wasteland of the electronic society of the present day. Man's conflict with an alienating world was also the theme of *Pierrot le Fou* (1965). This time the action takes place in the seemingly real world, but the distinction between what is real and imagined is kept intriguingly vague.

Gradually, Godard's films were becoming stripped of structure and conventional dramatic form, with an increasing emphasis on film as an essay, and cinema as a political and social instrument. *Masculin-Féminin/Masculine Feminine* (1966) was a free-form study of mores of Parisian youth. *Made in USA* (1966) had a crime story for an apparent plot but actually lacked a coherent structure and was fragmented into a bewildering kaleidoscope of comments on life, art, and reality. *Deux ou Trois Choses que je sais d'elle/Two or Three Things I Know About Her* (1967) told the story of a Paris housewife who indulges in prostitution for extra income with a generous sprinkling of opinions and ideas on a myriad of subjects. *La Chinoise* (1967), despite its fragmentation and political haranguing, was among Godard's most striking films since *Breathless.* The film featured in the leading role actress Anne Wiazemsky, who became Godard's second wife in June of 1967 and later appeared regularly in the director's films. This marriage, too, ended in divorce.

Godard's impact on the cinema of the 60s was cataclysmal and sweeping and his contribution to the art, thought, and language of the cinema significant. He used the camera not only creatively and inventively, rewriting the syntax of film grammar along the way, but also as a means of personal expression to tell "the truth 24 times a second." *Week-End/Weekend* (1968) represented the culmination of Godard's productive period, an anguished outcry against life's violence and man's cruelty to man.

After *Weekend* the director and critic suddenly disappeared. Instead, a new Godard surfaced, a revolutionary, didactic filmmaker who became obsessed with the spoken word and increasingly apathetic to cinema as a visual medium. He turned his back not only on the American films that had inspired the dreams of his youth but also on his own films, of which he began speaking with embarrassment and apologetic guilt. He dedicated himself to making "revolutionary films for revolutionary audiences," to expounding radical political ideas "as a secondary task in the struggle to liberate the oppressed from Capitalism." He began making films as a collective effort, working in groups named after such Soviet film figures as Dziga Vertov and Alexander Medvedkin. In the late 60s and early 70s he collaborated regularly with Jean-Pierre Gorin, a young Parisian rebel who became the revolutionary guru of the politically naïve Godard. In removing himself from the mainstream and subjugating his role as an artist to a mission as a political activist, Godard knowingly relinquished his following, along with it his once-considerable influence on the shaping of cinema as a thinking man's art.

In the late 70s and early 80s Godard underwent yet another metamorphosis. Abandoning his political wars and video experimentations, as well as his revolutionary base of operations in Grenoble, he moved to the Swiss town of Rolle in 1978, rediscovering himself and his love of film in the process. More restrained and philosophical in middle age, he refocused his sights on themes of universal humanistic concern in *Every Man for Himself* (1980), *Passion* (1982), and *First Name: Carmen* (1983). He even paid a renewed homage to American cinema in *Detective* (1985) but caused massive controversy with his updated story of Christ's birth *Hail Mary!,* inciting the condemnation of the Catholic Church. Although he seemed to be inching back to the fringes of the mainstream, Godard remained inaccessible to general audiences and even seasoned cinema sophisticates seemed puzzled by and less than wholly comfortable with his films of the late 80s, *King Lear* (1987) and *Nouvelle Vague* (1990). Godard won the best director award at the Berlin Festival for *Breathless* (1960) and the Golden Lion (best film) at Venice for *First Name: Carmen* (1983). In 1986, he was honored with a Special César Award for the body of his work.

FILMS (as director-screenwriter): Shorts—*Opération Béton* 1954; *Une Femme coquette* (also phot.) 1955; *Tous les Garçons s'appellent Patrick/Charlotte et Véronique* (dir. only) 1957; *Charlotte et son Jules* (also voice, dubbing for Belmondo), *Une Histoire d'Eau* (begun by Truffaut; footage reassembled by Godard; also narrator) 1958. Features—*Á Bout de Souffle/Breathless* (also act.) 1960; *Une Femme est une Femme/A Woman Is a Woman* 1961; *Les Sept Péchés capitaux/Seven Capital Sins* ("La Paresse"/"Laziness" episode), *Vivre sa Vie/My Life to Live, Rogopag* ("Le Nouveau Monde" episode) 1962; *Le Petit Soldat* (also act.; release delayed from 1960), *Les Carabiniers, Les Plus Belles Escroqueries du Monde* ("Le Grand Escroc" episode), *Le Mépris/Contempt* (also act.) 1963; *Bande à part/Band of Outsiders* (also narrator), *Une Femme mariée/The Married Woman* 1964; *Paris vu par. . . /Six in Paris* ("Montparnasse-Levallois" episode), *Alphaville/Une Etrange Aventure de Lemmy Caution, Pierrot le Fou* 1965; *Masculin-Féminin/Masculine Feminine, Made in USA* (also voice) 1966; *Deux ou Trois Choses que je sais d'elle/Two or Three Things I Know About Her* (also narrator), *Le Plus Vieux Métier du Monde* ("Anticipation" episode), *Loin du Viêtnam/Far from Vietnam* (co-dir. with five others), *La Chinoise* 1967; *Week-End/Weekend, Un Film comme les autres* 1968; *Amore e Rabbia/Vangelo '70/La Contestation/Love and Anger* ("L'Amore" episode; It./Fr.), *Le Gai Savoir, One A.M./One American Movie* (uncompleted), *Communications* (uncompleted), *One Plus One/Sympathy for the Devil* (UK), *British Sounds/See You at Mao* (medium-length; orig. made for British TV; co-dir. with Jean-Pierre Gorin; UK), *Le Vent d'Est/Wind from the East, Pravda* (co-dir. with Gorin and others; filmed in Czechoslovakia), *Lotte in Italia/Struggle in Italy* (co-dir. with Gorin) 1969; *Jusqu'à la Victoire/Till Victory* (PLO doc.; co-dir. with Gorin) 1970; *Vladimir et Rosa/Vladimir and Rosa* (co-dir. with Gorin and others) 1971; *Tous va bien* (co-dir. with Gorin), *Letter to Jane: Investigation of a Still* (co-dir. with Gorin) 1972; *Numéro Deux* (also co-prod.) 1975; *6 × 2: Sur et soux la Communication* (for TV), *Comment ça va* 1976; *Ici et ailleurs* 1977; *France Tour detour Deux Enfants* (for TV) 1978; *Sauve qui peut (la Vie)/Every Man for Himself* (also co-edit.) 1980; *Passion* (also edit.) 1982; *Prénom: Carmen/First Name Carmen* 1983; *Je vous salue Marie/Hail Mary!* (also edit.), *Détective* 1985; *Grandeur et Décadence d'un Petit Commerce du Cinéma* (16 mm) 1986; *Aria* ('Armide' segment; UK), *King Lear* (also act.; US/Switz.) 1987; *Soigne la Droite/Keep Up Your Right* (also edit., act.) 1988; *Nouvelle Vague/New Wave* (Switz./Fr.) 1990; *Allemagne Neuf Zéro/Germany Nine Zero* 1991; *Hélas Pour Moi/Woe Is Me* 1993; *JLG/JLG—Self-Portrait in December* 1994; *Forever Mozart* 1996.

Goddard, Paulette. Actress. *b.* Pauline Marion Levee (or Levy), June 3, 1905, Whitestone Landing, N.Y. *d.* 1990. A former fashion model, she was billed as "Peaches" when she made her stage debut as a Ziegfeld Girl in 'No Fooling' (1926). While on the road in 'Rio Rita' she met and married Edgar James, a wealthy lumber industrialist. In 1931 she drove out to Reno to obtain a quickie divorce and continued to Hollywood, hoping to get into pictures. Taking on her divorced mother's maiden name, Goddard, she got bit parts in a couple of films, was a Goldwyn Girl in *The Kid from Spain,* then was signed by Hal Roach as a member of his stock company. In 1932 she met Charlie CHAPLIN, who was taken by her striking beauty and cynical wit. They married secretly at sea in 1936 (some say as early as 1933), the year of the release of their joint venture, *Modern Times.* She was to appear in only one other Chaplin film, *The Great Dictator* (1940). Meanwhile, she was making it on her own as a rising star and was the leading contender for the role of Scarlett O'Hara in *Gone With the Wind* until the job was given to Vivien Leigh. In 1942 Miss Goddard divorced Chaplin and two years later married Burgess MEREDITH.

She was a top star at Paramount through the mid-40s, typically playing vivacious sirens, often exotic, at her best in comedy. She was nominated for an Academy Award as best supporting actress for her role in *So Proudly We Hail* (1943). But her career declined sharply late in the decade and came to a screeching halt in the mid-50s. Having divorced Meredith in 1949, she married novelist Erich Maria Remarque in 1958 and until his death in 1970 lived in luxurious retirement in Europe. In 1964 she made a one-shot comeback, in the Italian film *Time of Indifference.* At her death of heart failure, Swiss officials reported her year of birth was 1905, not 1911 as her professional biography claimed.

FILMS: As extra and bit player—*Berth Marks* (short), *The Locked Door* 1929; *City Streets, The Girl Habit* 1931; *The Mouthpiece, Show Business* (short), *Young Ironsides* (short), *Pack Up Your Troubles, Girl Grief* (short), *The Kid from Spain* 1932; *Roman Scandals* 1933; *Kid Millions* 1934. As roled actress—*Modern Times* 1936; *The Young in Heart, Dramatic School* 1938; *The Women, The Cat and the Canary* 1939; *The Ghost Breakers, The Great Dictator, North West Mounted Police* 1940; *Second Chorus, Pot o' Gold, Hold Back the Dawn, Nothing but the Truth* 1941; *The Lady Has Plans, Reap the Wild Wind, The Forest Rangers, Star Spangled Rhythm* (cameo) 1942; *The Crystal Ball, So Proudly We Hail* 1943; *Standing Room Only, I Love a Soldier* 1944; *Duffy's Tavern* (cameo) 1945; *Kitty, The Diary of a Chambermaid* 1946; *Suddenly It's Spring, Variety Girl* (cameo), *Unconquered* 1947; *An Ideal Husband* (UK), *On Our Merry Way/A Miracle Can Happen, Hazard* 1948; *Bride of Vengeance, Anna Lucasta* 1949; *The Torch* 1950; *Babes in Bagdad* 1952; *Vice Squad, Paris Model, Sins of Jezebel* (as Jezebel) 1953; *The Charge of the Lancers, The Stranger Came Home/The Unholy Four* (UK) 1954; *Gli Indifferenti/Time of Indifference* (It./Fr.) 1964.

Godfrey, Peter. Director. *b.* Oct. 16, 1899, London. *d.* 1970. A stage actor, producer, and director in England and

Ireland before turning to films, he arrived in Hollywood in the late 30s and after appearing in several films spent the bulk of his career with Warner Bros. as a director of medium-budget melodramas. In the 50s he switched to television. He also collaborated on the original story of one of the episodes of *Forever and a Day* (1943). During WW II, he entertained US troops as an amateur magician, aided by his wife, former actress Renee Haal.

FILMS: *The Lone Wolf Spy Hunt* 1939; *Unexpected Uncle* 1941; *Highway by Night* 1942; *Make Your Own Bed* 1944; *Hotel Berlin, Christmas in Connecticut* 1945; *One More Tomorrow* 1946; *The Two Mrs. Carrolls* (also act.); *Cry Wolf, That Hagen Girl, Escape Me Never* 1947; *The Woman in White, The Decision of Christopher Blake* 1948; *The Girl from Jones Beach, One Last Fling* 1949; *Barricade, The Great Jewel Robber, He's a Cockeyed Wonder* 1950; *One Big Affair* 1952; *Please Murder Me* 1956.

Goetz, William. Producer, studio executive. *b.* Mar. 24, 1903, New York City. *d.* 1969. After he dropped out of Pennsylvania College in the early 20s, he entered films as a production assistant and began making headway in the industry after becoming the son-in-law of MGM boss Louis B. Mayer. He joined Fox in 1930 as associate producer and became a vice president of 20th Century-Fox when the two companies merged in 1933. In 1942 he was elected to the company's board of directors and for two years substituted for Darryl Zanuck as production chief. He later formed International Pictures, and when the company merged with Universal in 1946, he became head of production for Universal International. In 1954 he formed William Goetz Productions and became an independent producer, releasing through Columbia, and later held executive positions with Columbia and Seven Arts. He was among the first Hollywood producers to take up the now common practice of paying leading stars a percentage of the profits of their pictures in lieu of a salary.

FILMS INCLUDE: As associate producer—*The Bowery* 1933; *Moulin Rouge, The House of Rothschild, The Affairs of Cellini, The Mighty Barnum* 1934; *Clive of India, Cardinal Richelieu, Les Miserables, Call of the Wild* 1935. As producer—*Jane Eyre* 1944; *The Man from Laramie* 1955; *Autumn Leaves* 1956; *Sayonara* 1957; *Me and the Colonel* 1958; *They Came to Cordura* 1959; *The Mountain Road, Song Without End* 1960; *Cry for Happy* 1961; *Assault on a Queen* 1966.

Golan, Menahem. Director, producer. Born on May 31, 1929, in Tiberias, Israel (then Palestine). A leading figure in the Israeli film industry, he began his career after the War Of Independence, in which he served as one of the first pilots of the Israeli Air Force. Following a long apprenticeship at the Habimah Theater in Tel Aviv as an assistant director, he went to London, where he studied directing at the Old Vic School and at the London Academy of Music and Drama. Returning to Israel, he directed a number of successful plays, then took an interest in Israel's budding film industry and went to New York to study filmmaking at NYU. After completing his studies, he worked for a while as an assistant to Roger Corman, then returned to Israel, where he produced and directed his first film, *El Dorado,* in 1963. He formed his own company, Noah Films, and subsequently turned out many films as a producer, a director, or both. In partnership with his cousin, Yoram Globus, he formed Golan-Globus Productions, a company that specialized in low-budget local films and through a subsidiary, Ameri-Euro Pictures, international co-productions. In 1979 they bought a controlling share of the New York-based CANNON Films, installing Golan as chairman of the board. Through ambitious expansion, frugal budgeting, and aggressive promotion the company soon became a leading force in American and international independent production, although much of its product was exploitative. However, overexpansion through acquisitions of production, distribution, and exhibition assets brought the company to the verge of collapse in the late 80s. Cannon Entertainment came under the control of Giancarlo Parretti's Pathé Communications. In 1989 Golan resigned, then formed a new company, 21st Century, through which he resumed production activities. Globus remained with Pathé and in 1990 was appointed president of MGM/UA when that studio was acquired by Parretti.

FILMS INCLUDE: *El Dorado* (prod., dir.) 1963; *Sallah* (prod.) 1964; *Trunk to Cairo* (prod., dir.; Isr./Ger.) 1966; *Tevye and His Seven Daughters* (prod., dir., co-sc.) 1968; *What's Good for the Goose* (dir., story, sc.; UK) 1969; *Margo* (dir., sc.), *Lupo* (dir., sc.) 1970; *Queen of the Road* (dir., sc.) 1971; *Escape to the Sun* (prod., dir., co-sc.; Isr./Fr./Ger.), *I Love You Rosa* (prod.) 1972; *Kazablan* (prod., dir., co-sc.) 1973; *The House on Chelouche Street* (prod.), *Topele* (prod.) 1974; *Lepke* (prod., dir.; US), *Diamonds* (prod., dir., co-sc.; Isr./Switz./US) 1975; *The Passover Plot* (exec. prod.; US/Isr.), *Vendetta* (co-prod.; Isr./It./US), *Lupo in New York* (prod.), *The Ambassador* (prod., dir.) 1976; *Operation Thunderbolt* (prod., dir., co-sc.) 1977; *Lemon Popsicle* (co-prod.), *It's a Funny Funny World* (co-prod.), *The Uranium Conspiracy* (dir., co-prod.; Isr./It.) 1978; *The Magician of Lublin* (dir., co-prod., co-sc.; Isr./Ger.) 1979; *The Happy Hooker* (co-prod.), *Dr. Heckyl and Mr. Hyde* (co-prod.), *The Apple* (dir., sc., co-prod.) 1980; *Enter the Ninja* (dir., co-sc.), *Body and Soul* (co-prod.) 1981; *Death Wish II* (co-prod.), *That Championship Season* (co-prod.) 1982; *10 to Midnight* (co-exec. prod.), *Nana* (co-prod.), *The Wicked Lady* (co-prod.), *Hercules* (co-prod.) 1983; *Sahara* (co-prod.), *The Naked Face* (co-prod.), *Love Stream* (co-prod.), *Over the Brooklyn Bridge* (dir., co-prod.), *Missing in Action, Grace Quigley* (co-prod.) 1984; *The Ambassador* (co-prod.), *Maria's Lovers* (co-exec. prod.), *Invasion U.S.A.* (co-prod.), *Berlin Affair* (It.), *Un Complicato Intrigo di Donne/Camorra* (co-prod.; It.), *King Solomon's Mines* (co-prod.), *Fool for Love* (co-prod.), *Runaway Train* (co-prod.) 1985; *The Delta Force* (dir., co-sc., co-prod.), *America 3000* (co-prod.), *Cobra* (co-prod.), *Invaders from Mars* (co-prod.), *The Texas Chainsaw Massacre Part 2* (co-prod.), *Otello/Othello* (It./US) (co-prod.), *52 Pick-Up* (co-prod.) 1986; *Over the Top* (dir., co-prod.), *Street Smart* (co-prod.), *Beauty and the Beast* (co-prod.), *Superman IV: The Quest for Peace* (co-prod.), *Dancers* (co-prod.), *Barfly* (co-exec. prod.), *Shy People* (co-exec. prod.), *King Lear* (co-prod.) 1987; *Going Bananas* (sc., co-prod.), *Powaggatsi* (co-exec. prod), *Puss in Boots* (co-prod.), *Hanna's War* (dir., sc., co-prod.), *A Cry in the Dark* (co-exec. prod.), *Haunted Summer* (co-exec. prod.) 1988; *Kinjite/Forbidden Subjects* (co-exec. prod.), *Cyborg* (co-exec. prod.), *Mack the Knife* (dir., sc., co-exec. prod.), *The Phantom of the Opera* (exec. prod.) 1989; *The Forbidden Dance* (co-exec. prod.), *Night of the Living Dead* (co-exec. prod.) 1990.

Gold, Ernest. Composer. Born on July 13, 1921, in Vienna. A descendant of a long line of concert hall musicians, he was a child prodigy and began composing at five. In 1938, after the German takeover of Austria, he emigrated to the US and began composing both pop and concert hall music. In Hollywood since the mid-40s, he began scoring major films in the late 50s and won an Academy Award for the music from *Exodus* (1960).

FILMS INCLUDE: *Smooth As Silk* 1946; *Wyoming* 1947; *Witness for the Prosecution, The Pride and the Passion* 1957; *Too Much Too Soon, The Defiant Ones* 1958; *On the Beach* 1959; *Inherit the Wind, Exodus* 1960; *The Last Sunset, Judgment at Nuremberg* 1961; *Pressure Point* 1962; *A Child Is*

Waiting, It's a Mad Mad Mad Mad World 1963; *Ship of Fools* 1965; *The Secret of Santa Vittoria* 1969; *The Wild McCullochs* 1975; *Fun with Dick and Jane, Cross of Iron* (UK/Ger.) 1977; *The Runner Stumbles* 1979; *Tom Horn* 1980; *Safari 3000* 1982; *Lost in America* 1985.

Gold, Jack. Director. Born on June 28, 1930, in London. Working in British films in various capacities since 1955, he directed for TV before turning out his first feature in 1968. He won praise for his sensitive directing of the TV-dramatized biography of flamboyant gay icon Quentin Crisp in 'The Naked Civil Servant.' Later, mainly the director of made-for-cable and television movies.

FILMS: *The Bofors Gun* 1968; *The Reckoning* 1969; *The National Health/Nurse Norton's Affair* 1973; *Who?, Man Friday* 1975; *Aces High* 1976; *The Medusa Touch* (also co-sc.), *The Sailor's Return* 1978; *Praying Mantis* 1982; *Red Monarch* 1983; *The Chain* 1985; *Ball-Trap on the Côte Sauvage* 1989.

Goldbeck, Willis. Director, screenwriter, producer. *b.* 1900, New York City. *d.* 1979. A former journalist, he began writing screenplays and film adaptations in the early 20s. In the 40s he directed many run-of-the-mill B pictures for MGM, including several of the "Dr. Kildare" series. He also wrote most of the "Dr. Kildare" scripts. In the mid-50s he turned producer.

FILMS INCLUDE: As screenwriter—*Scaramouche* 1923; *The Alaskan, Bluff, The Side Show of Life, Open All Night 1924*; *Peter Pan, Flower of Night* 1925; *Mare Nostrum, A Kiss for Cinderella* 1926; *Convoy, The Garden of Allah* 1927; *The Enemy, Lilac Time* (adapt. only) 1928; *Wild Orchids* (adapt. only), *Desert Nights* 1929; *Freaks* 1932; *Wednesday's Child* 1934; *Young Dr. Kildare* 1938; *Dr. Kildare's Crisis* 1940; *Calling Dr. Gillespie* 1942. As director (complete)—*Dr. Gillespie's New Assistant* 1942; *Dr. Gillespie's Criminal Case* 1943; *Rationing, Three Men in White* 1944; *Between Two Women, She Went to the Races* 1945; *Love Laughs at Andy Hardy, Dark Delusion* 1947; *Johnny Holiday* (also co-sc.) 1950; *Ten Tall Men* (also co-story) 1951. As producer—*I Died a Thousand Times* 1955; *The Lone Ranger* 1956; *Sergeant Rutledge* (co-prod.; also co-sc.) 1960; *The Man Who Shot Liberty Valance* (also co-sc.) 1962.

Goldberg, Whoopi. Actress. Born Caryn Johnson, on Nov. 13, 1949, in New York. *ed.* High School for the Performing Arts. Exuberant, animated black serio-comic star of the American stage, TV, and films. On the stage from age eight, she appeared in New York area productions and played small roles in Broadway musicals before moving to the West Coast in 1974. She performed with various drama and improvisation troupes in San Diego and San Francisco, then scored a personal hit in the one-woman 'Spook Show' with which she toured the US and Europe. Following a triumphant appearance on Broadway in 1984, she made a sensational screen debut in Steven Spielberg's *The Color Purple* (1985) in a moving performance that earned her an Academy Award nomination. Most of her subsequent film roles have been in the broad comedy vein. She won an Oscar as best supporting actress for *Ghost* (1990). In 1990 she co-starred in the TV comedy series 'Bagdad Cafe.' Her presence in *Sister Act*, one of the sleeper hits of 1991, guaranteed her a reported salary of $8 million for a return stint in its sequel, making her one of the highest paid actresses of all time. In 1992, she hosted her own syndicated talk show. She assumed her Jewish-sounding name through her first marriage. Her second, also ended, was to cinematographer David Claessen.

FILMS: *The Color Purple* 1985; *Jumpin' Jack Flash* 1986; *Burglar, Fatal Beauty* 1987; *The Telephone, Clara's Heart* 1988; *Homer and Eddie* 1989; *The Long Walk Home, Kiss Shot, Ghost* 1990; *Soapdish, House Party 2* (cameo) 1991; *The Player, Sister Act, Wisecracks, Sarafina!* 1992; *Made in America, Sister Act 2: Back in the Habit* 1993; *Corrina, Corrina, The Lion King* (v/o), *Naked in New York, The Pagemaster* (v/o), *Star Trek Generations* 1994; *Boys on the Side, The Celluloid Closet, Moonlight and Valentino* 1995; *The Associate, Bogus, Eddie, Ghosts of Mississippi, Theodore Rex* 1996.

Goldblum, Jeff. Actor. Born on Oct. 22, 1952, in Pittsburgh. Tall, gawky, expressive leading man of the American screen. A physician's son, he participated in the Carnegie-Mellon theater program while still attending high school, but his application to enroll at the university full time was turned down. Instead, he headed for New York, where he trained at Sanford Meisner's Neighborhood Playhouse. Within a year, he made his professional debut playing a bit in a Joe Papp production of Shakespeare in the Park. Small roles, on and off Broadway and in films, quickly followed, before he emerged in the 80s as an appealing screen lead, typically in cynically intelligent, often neurotic, offbeat roles. Having divorced actress Patricia Gaul, he was married to actress Geena DAVIS, from whom he was also later divorced.

FILMS: *Death Wish* (bit, as a mugger), *California Split* 1974; *Nashville* 1975; *Next Stop Greenwich Village, Special Delivery, St. Ives* 1976; *The Sentinel, Annie Hall, Between the Lines* 1977; *Remember My Name, Thank God It's Friday, Invasion of the Body Snatchers* 1978; *Threshold* (Can.) 1981; *The Big Chill, The Right Stuff* 1983; *The Adventures of Buckaroo Banzai Across the Eighth Dimension* 1984; *Into the Night, Silverado, Transylvannia 6-5000* 1985; *The Fly* 1986; *Beyond Therapy* 1987; *Vibes* 1988; *The Tall Guy* (UK), *Earth Girls Are Easy* 1989; *Mister Frost* (Fr./UK) 1990; *The Player, The Favor the Watch and the Very Big Fish, Deep Cover, Fathers and Sons* 1992; *Jurassic Park* 1993; *Lush Life* 1994; *Hideaway, Nine Months, Powder* 1995; *The Great White Hype, Independence Day, Mad Dog Time* 1996; *The Lost World* 1997.

Golden Globe Awards. See HOLLYWOOD FOREIGN PRESS ASSOCIATION.

Goldin, Sidney. Director, actor. *b.* 1880 in Odessa, Ukraine. *d.* 1937. Leading figure in the development of Yiddish filmmaking in the first decades of the 20th century. After emigrating with his family to the US when he was a child, he apprenticed with stage dramatist Lincoln Carter and worked for two years at film studio ESSANAY in Chicago before coming to New York in 1912 and directing films independently and for Carl LAEMMLE. A prolific filmmaker, he interested Yiddish audiences in films by employing in his works well-known personages from the Yiddish stage, like Molly Picon and Jacob Kalich. At the cusp of the 1920s he moved to Vienna to form his own production company, Goldin-Film. There, he produced several Yiddish films, until the end of the decade when he returned to the US to act and direct sound films. Following a success with the 1930 *Uncle Moses*, he worked little during the 1930s, affected at least in part by growing international anti-Semitism. He died of a heart attack in 1937, while directing his first film in over five years, *Dem Khazns Zundl/The Cantor's Son*.

FILMS INCLUDE: *Adventures of Lieutenant Petrosino, New York Society Life in the Underworld* 1912; *The Sorrows of Israel, Nihilist Vengeance, The Heart of a Jewess, Bleeding Hearts, The Black 107* 1913; *Uriel Acosta, Escaped from Siberia, Traffickers on Soles* 1914; *Last of the Mafia* 1915; *Ihre Vergangenheit/Her Past* (Aus.) 1921; *Führe Uns nicht in Versuchung/Lead Us Not into Temptation* (Aus.), *Hütet eure Töchter/Protect Your Daughters* (Aus.) 1922; *Ost und West/East and West* 1923; *Yisker* (Aus.) 1924; *Better Days* (act. only), *The Fightin' Comeback* (act. only) 1927; *East Side Sadie, Ad Mosay/The Eternal Prayer* 1929; *Mayn Yidishe Mame/My*

Jewish Mother, Sailor's Sweetheart, Eybike Naronim/Eternal Fools, Uncle Moses 1930; *Dem Khazns Zundl/The Cantor's Son* (replaced after death by Ilya Motyleff) 1937.

Goldman, Bo. Screenwriter. Born on Sept. 10, 1932, in New York City. *ed.* Princeton. Following a three-year stint with the Army, he began his career in 1958 as an associate producer on CBS-TV's 'Playhouse 90' and later produced and wrote for public television. He wrote the lyrics for the Broadway musical 'First Impressions' (1959). As a screenwriter, he shared the Academy Award for his first film, *One Flew Over the Cuckoo's Nest* (1975), then won another Oscar for *Melvin and Howard* (1980). One of Hollywood's highest paid writers (about $1 million per picture), he is often engaged as a script doctor, or rewrite master.

FILMS: *One Flew Over the Cuckoo's Nest, Der Richter und sein Henker/End of the Game* (Ger./It.) 1975; *The Rose* 1979; *Melvin and Howard* 1980; *Shoot the Moon* 1982; *Swing Shift* (uncredited) 1984; *Little Nikita* 1988; *Dick Tracy* (uncredited) 1990; *Scent of a Woman* 1992; *First Knight* (co-sc.) 1995; *City Hall* (co-sc.) 1996.

Goldman, James. Playwright, screenwriter, novelist. Born on June 30, 1927, in Chicago. *ed.* U. of Chicago; Columbia. He launched his career in 1961 with the play 'Blood, Sweat and Stanley Poole,' which he wrote in collaboration with his younger brother, William GOLDMAN. On his own, he established his reputation with the play 'The Lion in Winter' (1967) and won an Academy Award the following year for his screen adaptation of the historic drama. In addition to several other screenplays, he wrote the Broadway musical 'Follies' (1972), in collaboration with Stephen Sondheim.

FILMS: *The Lion in Winter* (from his own play) 1968; *They Might Be Giants, Nicholas and Alexandra* 1971; *Robin and Marian* 1976; *White Nights* 1985.

Goldman, William. Novelist, playwright, screenwriter. Born on Aug. 12, 1931, in Chicago, the younger brother of writer James GOLDMAN. *ed.* Oberlin Coll.; Columbia. Versatile, prolific, and highly successful, he has written short stories and children's fiction, as well as novels, plays, and screenplays, sometimes using the pseudonym Harry Longbaugh (the real name of one of Goldman's favorite historical personalities, the Sundance Kid). He won Academy Awards for *Butch Cassidy and the Sundance Kid* (1969) and *All the President's Men* (1976). In *Marathon Man* (1976), he created the Nazi dentist played by Laurence Olivier, inflicting torture on Dustin Hoffman while asking the unanswerable question, "Is it safe?" Goldman's nonfiction book *Adventures in the Screen Trade* (1983), offers behind-the-scenes insights into screenwriting and the movie business, while *Hype and Glory* (1990) scrutinizes the Cannes Film Festival. One of Hollywood's favorite script doctors, he is often called in to do uncredited revisions on ailing screenplays, such as the 1993 Arnold Schwarzenegger blockbuster *Last Action Hero*—a commercial failure despite Goldman's efforts.

FILMS: *Soldier in the Rain* (novel basis only) 1963; *Masquerade* 1965; *Harper* 1966; *No Way to Treat a Lady* (novel basis only) 1968; *Butch Cassidy and the Sundance Kid* 1969; *The Hot Rock* 1972; *The Stepford Wives, The Great Waldo Pepper* 1975; *All the President's Men, Marathon Man* (from his own novel) 1976; *A Bridge Too Far* 1977; *Magic* (from his own novel) 1978; *Butch and Sundance: The Early Days* 1979; *Heat* (from his own novel), *The Princess Bride* (from his own novel) 1987; *Misery* 1990; *Memoirs of an Invisible Man* (co-sc.) 1991; *Year of the Comet* 1992; *The Last Action Hero* (uncred.) 1993; *Maverick* 1994; *The Chamber* (co-sc.), *Extreme Measures* (co-sc.), *The Ghost and the Darkness* 1996; *Absolute Power* 1997.

Goldsmith, Jerry. Composer. Born on Feb. 10, 1929, in Los Angeles. *ed.* L.A. City Coll. Studied piano with Jacob Gimpel, composition and theory with Mario Castelnuovo-Tedesco, and film scoring under Miklos ROZSA at USC. Began his professional career in radio and later composed scores for leading TV shows ('Climax,' 'Playhouse 90,' 'Studio One,' 'Gunsmoke,' 'The Man from UNCLE,' etc.). A prolific composer, he has scored numerous Hollywood films since the late 50s, winning an Academy Award for the score of *The Omen* (1976) and picking up 13 Oscar nominations. He also composed chamber music and vocal works.

FILMS INCLUDE: *Black Patch* 1957; *Face of a Fugitive* 1959; *Studs Lonigan* 1960; *Freud* 1962; *Lilies of the Field, A Gathering of Eagles, The Prize, The Stripper* 1963; *Seven Days in May, Shock Treatment* 1964; *In Harm's Way, Von Ryan's Express* 1965; *Our Man Flint, A Patch of Blue, The Sand Pebbles, The Blue Max, Seconds* 1966; *In Like Flint, Warning Shot* 1967; *Bandolero! Planet of the Apes, The Detective* 1968; *The Illustrated Man, Justine, The Chairman* 1969; *Patton, The Ballad of Cable Hogue, Tora! Tora! Tora!, Rio Lobo* 1970; *The Mephisto Waltz, Escape from the Planet of the Apes, Wild Rovers, The Last Run* 1971; *The Other, The Man* 1972; *Shamus, The Don Is Dead, Papillon* 1973; *Chinatown, S*P*Y*S* 1974; *The Reincarnation of Peter Proud, The Wind and the Lion* 1975; *The Last Hard Men, Breakheart Pass, Logan's Run, The Omen* 1976; *Twilight's Last Gleaming, The Cassandra Crossing, Islands in the Stream, MacArthur, High Velocity, Damnation Alley* 1977; *Coma, Damien—Omen II, Capricorn One, The Swarm, The Boys from Brazil, Magic* 1978; *The First Great Train Robbery/The Great Train Robbery* (UK), *Alien, Star Trek—The Motion Picture* 1979; *Outland, Raggedy Man* 1981; *The Challenge, The Secret of Nimh, First Blood, Poltergeist* 1982; *Psycho II, Twilight Zone—The Movie, Under Fire* 1983; *The Lonely Guy, Gremlins* 1984; *Rambo: First Blood Part II* 1985; *Hoosiers* 1986; *Innerspace, Lionheart* 1987; *The 'Burbs, Leviathan, Criminal Law* 1989; *Total Recall, The Russia House, Not Without My Daughter* 1990; *Sleeping with the Enemy, Medicine Man* 1991; *Basic Instinct, Love Field, Mom and Dad Save the World, The Public Eye, Mr. Baseball* 1992; *Dennis the Menace* 1993; *I.Q.* 1994; *Congo, First Knight, Powder* 1995; *Chain Reaction, The Ghost and the Darkness* 1996; *Air Force One* 1997.

Goldstone, James. Director. Born on June 8, 1931, in Los Angeles. *ed.* Dartmouth Coll. (B.A.); Bennington Coll. (M.A.). A film story editor at age 19, he began directing for TV in 1958, graduating to feature films in the late 60s, and settling into made-for-television films in the 80s.

FILMS: *Jigsaw* 1968; *A Man Called Gannon, Winning* 1969; *Brother John, Red Sky at Morning, The Gang That Couldn't Shoot Straight* 1971; *They Only Kill Their Masters* 1972; *Swashbuckler* 1976; *Rollercoaster* 1977; *When Time Ran Out* 1980.

Goldwyn, Samuel. Producer. *b.* Shmuel Gelbfisz (later Samuel Goldfish), Aug. 27, 1882 (it is speculated his birth may have been in July of 1879), Warsaw. *d.* 1974. At age 11 he made his way, alone, to England, where he stayed with relatives and worked as a blacksmith's helper. At 13 he arrived in the US, alone and penniless. He found work as an apprentice glovemaker, in Gloversville, N.Y., at $3 a week, and took his education at night school. By the age of 15 he was an expert glove cutter and at 18 he went on the road as a glove salesman. Soon he was known as the best in the business. In 1910 he married Blanche Lasky, the sister of vaudeville performer and producer Jesse L. LASKY. In 1912, after the American glove industry suffered reversals from government policies of lower tariffs, Goldfish decided to look for a new means of livelihood. He persuaded his brother-in-law to enter the film business. In 1913 they formed the Jesse L. Lasky Feature Play Company with Lasky as president, Goldfish as treasurer and sales manager, and Cecil B. DE MILLE as director.

The trio's first picture, *The Squaw Man,* was a resounding financial success and provided the fledgling company with enough funds and confidence to produce a total of 21 films in its first year. In 1916 the company merged with Adolph ZUKOR'S FAMOUS PLAYERS. Goldfish was named chairman of the board of the new company, with Zukor president and Lasky vice president. But the partners soon began fighting over who was boss, and Zukor and Lasky agreed to buy Goldfish out for $900,000. Late that year, Goldfish formed a new partnership with Edgar SELWYN and others. They called the new company Goldwyn, combining the first syllable of Goldfish and the last of Selwyn. Goldfish grew fond of the name and in 1918 he legally changed his to Goldwyn.

The Goldwyn company recruited famous stars and top writers and announced a policy of quality productions. The company barely broke even. In 1922 Goldwyn was edged out of the corporation. When the failing Goldwyn company merged with Metro Pictures and Louis B. MAYER Productions to form METRO-GOLDWYN-MAYER, Samuel Goldwyn was not part of the deal. He thereafter vowed never to associate himself with partners again. In 1923 he formed Samuel Goldwyn Productions, with no partners, and himself in complete charge. Totally independent, with no studio bosses or board of directors to account to for his decisions, Goldwyn at last was free to prove himself the great showman he was. Sparing no expense and recruiting the best talent in the business, particularly the best screenwriters, he began producing films of high quality and meticulous production values.

Soon the words "Samuel Goldwyn Presents" came to mean the best in entertainment to millions of filmgoers. Although not himself creative, Goldwyn had the rare knack of consistently being able to put the right team together and inspire it with his intuitive artistry. His only close associate and confidante was his second wife, former Broadway actress Frances Howard (1903–76), whom he married in 1925 (he divorced his first wife in 1919). After bringing up their son, independent-producer-to-be Samuel GOLDWYN, Jr., she became quite active in all production phases of Goldwyn's films. A grandson, Tony Goldwyn (*b.* 1960), is an actor in television, stage, and films.

Many stars began their screen careers under the Goldwyn aegis, including Ronald Colman, Vilma Banky, Gary Cooper, Anna Sten, Teresa Wright, Danny Kaye, David Niven, Vera-Ellen, Farley Granger, Will Rogers, Lucille Ball, Susan Hayward, and Merle Oberon. Among the writers he employed were Robert Sherwood, Sinclair Lewis, Ben Hecht, MacKinlay Kantor, Lillian Hellman, and Sidney Kingsley. His most productive association was with William WYLER, who directed some of Goldwyn's most important productions, notably *The Best Years of Our Lives.* Goldwyn received the Irving Thalberg Memorial Award during the 1946 Oscar ceremonies for "consistently high quality of production." Besides earning fame as a filmmaker, Goldwyn was known for his great philanthropy and for some of the funniest malapropisms ever to grace the English language, or as they are called in Hollywood, Goldwynisms ("Include me out," "A verbal agreement isn't worth the paper it's written on," "Anyone seeing a psychiatrist should have his head examined," etc.).

FILMS INCLUDE: *Jubilo* 1919; *The Highest Bidder* 1921; *Potash and Perlmutter* 1923; *The Eternal City, Cytherea, Tarnish* 1924; *Ben-Hur* (co-prod.), *The Dark Angel, Stella Dallas* 1925; *The Winning of Barbara Worth* 1926; *The Night of Love, The Magic Flame, The Devil Dancer* 1927; *Two Lovers, The Awakening* 1928; *The Rescue, Bulldog Drummond Condemned* 1929; *Raffles, Whoopee!* 1930; *Street Scene, The Unholy Garden, Palmy Days, Arrowsmith* 1931; *The Greeks Had a Word for Them, Cynara, The Kid from Spain* 1932; *Roman Scandals* 1933; *Nana, We Live Again, Kid Millions* 1934; *The Wedding Night, The Dark Angel, Barbary Coast* 1935; *Strike Me Pink, Dodsworth, Come and Get It, These Three* 1936; *Dead End, Stella Dallas, The Hurricane* 1937; *The Goldwyn Follies, The Adventures of Marco Polo* 1938; *The Real Glory, Wuthering Heights* 1939; *The Westerner* 1940; *The Little Foxes* 1941; *Ball of Fire, The Pride of the Yankees* 1942; *North Star, Armored Attack* 1943; *Up in Arms, The Princess and the Pirate* 1944; *Wonder Man* 1945; *The Kid from Brooklyn, The Best Years of Our Lives* 1946; *The Secret Life of Walter Mitty, The Bishop's Wife* 1947; *A Song Is Born, Enchantment* 1948; *Roseanna McCoy, My Foolish Heart* 1949; *Edge of Doom* 1950; *Hans Christian Andersen* 1952; *Guys and Dolls* 1955; *Porgy and Bess* 1959.

Goldwyn, Samuel, Jr. Producer. Born on Sept. 7, 1926, in Los Angeles. *ed.* U. of Virginia. The son of legendary producer Samuel GOLDWYN, he served in the Army in WW II and was recalled to service in 1951. After WW II, he worked as a writer and associate producer for the J. Arthur Rank Organization in Britain, then returned to the US to serve as an associate producer for Universal. He worked in television before striking out on his own in 1955, establishing his own independent production company. After his father's death in 1974, he developed the Samuel Goldwyn Company into an independent film production and distribution company. Now a public company with Goldwyn as CEO and chairman, the company specializes in bringing foreign and American films of high artistic quality to a broad US market. Among the directors whose work it produced and/or distributed are Jim Jarmusch (*Stranger Than Paradise*, 1984), Alex Cox (*Sid and Nancy*, 1986), Robert Townsend (*Hollywood Shuffle*, 1987), Stephen Frears (*Prick Up Your Ears*, 1987), Kenneth Branagh (*Henry V*, 1989), David Lynch (*Wild at Heart*, 1990), Charles Burnett (*To Sleep with Anger*, 1990), John Sayles (*City of Hope*, 1991), and documentary filmmaker Roger Weisberg (*Road Scholar*, 1993). Goldwyn's company was also involved in theatrical exhibition and television and home video production. He has since sold his company to Metromedia. Among Goldwyn's TV production credits were the 59th and 60th Academy Awards shows (1987, 1988), the latter of which won an Emmy. Father of production executive John Goldwyn and actor Tony GOLDWYN.

FILMS INCLUDE (as producer): *The Man with the Gun* 1955; *Sharkfighters* 1956; *The Proud Rebel* 1958; *Huckleberry Finn* 1960; *The Young Lovers* (also dir.) 1965; *Cotton Comes to Harlem* 1970; *Come Back Charleston Blue* 1972; *The Golden Seal* 1983; *A Prayer for the Dying* 1987; *Mystic Pizza* (exec. prod.) 1988; *Stella* 1990.

Goldwyn, Tony. Actor. *b.* Anthony Goldwyn in 1960. *ed.* Brandeis University, M.A.; London Academy of Music and Art. His heritage undeniable, the grandson of legendary Hollywood mogul Samuel GOLDWYN and the son of successful film producer Samuel GOLDWYN, Jr., this talented, sensitive actor has already lived up to the family name. His stage background with the Williamstown Theatre coupled with an Obie Award–winning performance in the off-Broadway hit 'The Sum of Us' helped establish him as an intriguing actor with strong roles in important films. His brother John, is a Hollywood production executive.

FILMS: *Friday the 13th, Part VI: Jason Lives* 1986; *Gaby—A True Story* 1987; *Ghost* 1990; *Kuffs, Traces of Red* 1992; *The Pelican Brief* 1993; *Nixon, Reckless* 1995; *The Substance of Fire* 1996; *Kiss the Girls* 1997.

Golino, Valeria. Actress. Born on October 22, 1966 in Naples, Italy. *ed.* Spirited, exotic-looking actress with comedic flair. Born of Greco-Italian-Egyptian-French ancestry, she worked as a model before appearing at 17 in *Joke of Destiny* by Lina Wertmuller. Acted widely in European films, to much acclaim. Became known to mainstream audiences her for role as the olive-popping paramour in *Hot Shots!* (1991).

FILMS INCLUDE: *Scherzo del Destino in Agguato Dietro L'Angolo Come un Brigante di Strada/Joke of Destiny* 1983; *Blind Date* 1984; *Figlio Mio Infinamente Caro/My Dearest Son* 1985; *Piccoli Fuochi/Little Fires* 1985; *Asilo di Polizia/Dumb Dicks* 1986; *L'été dernier à Tanger/Last Summer in Tangiers, Storia d'Amore/Love Story, Gli Occhali d'Oro/The Gold-Rimmed Glasses* 1987; *Big Top Pee-Wee, Paura e Amore/Three Sisters, Rain Man* 1988; *Torrents of Spring* 1989; *The King's Whore, Il y a des jours. . . et des lunes, Tracce di Vita Amorosa/Traces of an Amorous Life* 1990; *Hot Shots!, The Indian Runner, Year of the Gun* 1991; *Hot Shots! Part Deux* 1993; *Clean Slate, Immortal Beloved* 1994; *Four Rooms, Leaving Las Vegas* 1995.

Golitzen, Alexander. Art director. Born on Feb. 28, 1907, in Moscow. Immigrating to the US at 16, he studied architecture at the University of Wisconsin and entered films in 1933 as an illustrator on MGM's *Queen Christina.* As an art director from 1935, he designed sets for major productions of various studios, finally settling at Universal, where he would become supervising art director in 1954, accumulating hundreds of screen credits. He shared Academy Awards for *Phantom of the Opera* (1943), *Spartacus* (1960), and *To Kill a Mockingbird* (1962), among 13 Oscar nominations.

FILMS INCLUDE: *The Call of the Wild* 1935; *The Hurricane* 1937; *Trade Winds* 1938; *Foreign Correspondent* 1940; *Sundown, That Uncertain Feeling* 1941; *Arabian Nights* 1940; *Phantom of the Opera* 1943; *The Climax* 1944; *Salome Where She Danced, Scarlet Street* 1945; *Magnificent Doll* 1946; *Smash-Up* 1947; *Letter to an Unknown Woman* 1948; *Sword in the Desert* 1949; *The World in His Arms* 1952; *All I Desire* 1953; *Sign of the Pagan* 1954; *All That Heaven Allows, The Far Country, Man Without a Star, This Island Earth, To Hell and Back* 1955; *Written on the Wind* 1956; *The Incredible Shrinking Man, Man of a Thousand Faces* 1957; *The Tarnished Angels, Touch of Evil* 1958; *Imitation of Life, Operation Petticoat, Pillow Talk* 1959; *The Great Imposter, Midnight Lace, Spartacus* 1960; *Back Street, Flower Drum Song, Lover Come Back* 1961; *Cape Fear, Lonely Are the Brave, That Touch of Mink, To Kill a Mockingbird* 1962; *The Thrill of It All, The Ugly American* 1963; *Father Goose, Send Me No Flowers* 1964; *Mirage, The War Lord* 1965; *The Appaloosa, Madame X, Gambit* 1966; *Thoroughly Modern Millie* 1967; *Coogan's Bluff* 1968; *Sweet Charity, Tell Them Willie Boy Is Here* 1969; *Airport, Colossus: The Forbin Project* 1970; *Play Misty for Me* 1971; *The Great Northfield Minnesota Raid, Slaughterhouse Five* 1972; *Earthquake* 1974.

Gomez, Thomas. Actor. *b.* July 10, 1905, New York City. *d.* 1971. Heavyset character player of Hollywood films, following stage experience from 1924. Entering films in the early 40s, he played many imposing character parts, typically as a crafty villain. Nominated for a best supporting actor Academy Award for his role in *Ride a Pink Horse* (1947).

FILMS INCLUDE: *Sherlock Holmes and the Voice of Terror, Arabian Nights, Pittsburgh* 1942; *White Savage, Corvette K-225, Crazy House* 1943; *Phantom Lady, Dead Man's Eyes, The Climax* 1944; *Frisco Sal* 1945; *Night in Paradise* (as Croesus) 1946; *Johnny O'Clock, Singapore, Ride a Pink Horse, Captain from Castile* 1947; *Casbah, Key Largo, Force of Evil* 1948; *Sorrowful Jones, That Midnight Kiss* 1949; *The Woman on Pier 13, The Eagle and the Hawk, The Furies, Kim* 1950; *Anne of the Indies* (as Blackbeard the pirate) 1951; *Macao, The Merry Widow, Pony Soldier* 1952; *Sombrero* 1953; *The Adventures of Haji Baba* 1954; *The Magnificent Matador* 1955; *The Conqueror, Trapeze* 1956; *John Paul Jones, But Not for Me* 1959; *Summer and Smoke* 1961; *Stay Away Joe* 1968; *Beneath the Planet of the Apes* 1970.

Go-Motion. A refinement of STOP MOTION animation in which motion is produced by computer-controlled rods attached to the body parts of a puppet. Prior to filming, the animator moves the rods manually to produce the desired action, while a programmer records the positions of the rods. The computer then plays back those positions, animating the puppet while the camera rolls. The rods are later blocked out by MATTES. The technique is more life-like than stop motion because the camera records the blur of the moving body parts. In stop motion, where individual static positions are photographed one frame at a time, the result can seem jerky and stroboscopic.

Gooding, Cuba, Jr. Actor. Born 1968, in the South Bronx, N.Y. The son of a musician, this charismatic and gifted actor grew up surrounded by the arts, enhancing his ability to create fascinating, believable characters first on the stage and eventually in television and film. His star turn in *Jerry Maguire* (1996) was greeted with critical acclaim and box office success, not to mention various awards including the Oscar for best supporting actor.

FILMS: *Coming to America* 1988; *Sing* 1989; *Boyz N the Hood* 1991; *A Few Good Men, Gladiator* 1992; *Daybreak, Judgment Night* 1993; *Lightning Jack* 1994; *Losing Isaiah, Outbreak* 1995; *Jerry Maguire* 1996.

Goodman, John. Actor. Born on June 20, 1952, in St. Louis. *ed.* Southwest Missouri State U. Beefy, likeable character lead of American films and television. After switching from football to drama in college, he headed in 1975 for New York, where for several years he eked out a living off-off Broadway and in out-of-town dinner theaters. His first break came in 1979, as a Christmas replacement for a featured role in the Broadway play 'Loose Ends.' It led to commercials and small character roles on TV and in films. He came into his own in the late 80s, following a successful 1985 Broadway appearance as Huck Finn's drunken father in 'Big River.' He began playing increasingly more important roles, even leads, in films and achieved great popularity in the late 80s as Roseanne Barr's wisecracking husband in the TV series 'Roseanne.'

FILMS: *Eddie Macon's Run, The Survivors* 1983; *Revenge of the Nerds, C.H.U.D.* 1984; *Maria's Lovers, Sweet Dreams* 1985; *True Stories* 1986; *Raising Arizona, Burglar, The Big Easy* 1987; *The Wrong Guys, Punchline, Everybody's All-American* 1988; *Sea of Love, Always* 1989; *Stella, Arachnophobia* 1990; *King Ralph* 1991; *The Babe, Barton Fink* 1992; *Born Yesterday, Matinee* 1993; *The Flintstones* 1994; *Mother Night* 1996.

Goodrich, Frances. Screenwriter, playwright. *b.* 1891, Belleville, N.J. *d.* 1984. *ed.* Vassar. A former actress, she wrote a number of plays (including the Pulitzer Prize–winning 'The Diary of Anne Frank') and many screenplays in collaboration with her third husband, Albert HACKETT (her second was writer-historian Hendrik Willem Van Loon).

FILMS INCLUDE: *Up Pops the Devil* (co-play basis only) 1930; *Penthouse* 1933; *The Thin Man* 1934; *Naughty Marietta, Ah! Wilderness* 1935; *Rose Marie, After the Thin Man* 1936; *The Firefly* 1937; *Thanks for the Memory* (co-play basis only) 1938;

Another Thin Man 1939; *The Hitler Gang, Lady in the Dark* 1944; *It's a Wonderful Life, The Virginian* 1946; *The Pirate, Summer Holiday, Easter Parade* 1948; *In the Good Old Summertime* 1949; *Father of the Bride* 1950; *Father's Little Dividend* 1951; *The Long Long Trailer, Give a Girl a Break, Seven Brides for Seven Brothers* 1954; *Gaby* 1956; *A Certain Smile* 1958; *The Diary of Anne Frank* (from own co-play) 1959; *Five Finger Exercise* 1962.

Goodwin, Ron(ald). Composer, arranger, conductor. Born in Plymouth, England. Began his career as an arranger for the BBC Dance Orchestra and later was a music director of a recording company and a conductor for British radio and TV. He has also appeared as a guest conductor with a number of leading symphony orchestras. Has composed scores for many British and some international productions since the late 50s.

FILMS INCLUDE: *Whirlpool* 1958; *I'm All Right Jack* 1959; *The Trials of Oscar Wilde* 1960; *Murder She Said* 1961; *Operation Crossbow, Those Magnificent Men in Their Flying Machines* 1965; *Where Eagles Dare* 1968; *Battle of Britain* 1969; *The Executioner* 1970; *Frenzy* 1972; *One of Our Dinosaurs Is Missing* 1975; *Escape from the Dark/The Littlest Horse Thieves* 1976; *Candleshoe, Force 10 from Navarone* 1978.

Goodwins, Leslie. Director. *b.* Sept. 17, 1899, London. *d.* 1969. In Hollywood from the early 30s, he directed several shorts before turning to feature films in 1936. He turned out many lowbrow, low-budget productions through the mid-50s, mainly for RKO, including the "Mexican Spitfire" series of the early 40s, starring Lupe Velez.

FEATURE FILMS: *With Love and Kisses* 1936; *Headline Crasher, Anything for a Thrill, Young Dynamite* 1937; *Almost a Gentleman, Crime Ring, Fugitives for a Night, Mr. Doodle Kicks Off, Tarnished Angel* 1938; *The Girl from Mexico, The Day the Bookies Wept, Sued for Libel* 1939; *Mexican Spitfire, Millionaire Playboy, Pop Always Pays, Men Against the Sky, Mexican Spitfire Out West* 1940; *Let's Make Music, They Met in Argentina, Parachute Battalion, Mexican Spitfire's Baby* 1941; *Mexican Spitfire at Sea, Mexican Spitfire Sees a Ghost, Mexican Spitfire's Elephant* 1942; *Silver Skates, Ladies' Day, Mexican Spitfire's Blessed Event, Gals Inc., The Adventures of a Rookie, Rookies in Burma* 1943; *Casanova in Burlesque, Goin' to Town, The Singing Sheriff, Murder in the Blue Room, Hi Beautiful!* 1944; *The Mummy's Curse, What a Blonde!, I'll Tell the World, Radio Stars on Parade, An Angel Comes to Brooklyn* 1945; *Riverboat Rhythm, Genius at Work, Vacation in Reno* 1946; *The Dragnet, The Lone Wolf in London* 1947; *Gold Fever* 1953; *Fireman Save My Child* 1954; *Paris Follies of 1956* 1955; *Tammy and the Millionaire* (co-dir. with Sidney Miller and Ezra Stone) 1967.

Goorwitz, Allen. See GARFIELD, Allen.

goose. A truck used for carrying camera and sound equipment.

Goosson, Stephen. Art director. *b.* Mar. 24, 1893, Grand Rapids, Mich. *d.* 1973. *ed.* Syracuse U. He was a practicing architect in Detroit before entering films with David SELZNICK in 1919. During the silent period he worked on major productions at various studios, finally finding permanent employment in 1930 at Columbia, where he soon assumed the responsibilities of supervising art director. His name was associated with some of that studio's finest films of the 30s and 40s.

FILMS INCLUDE: *The Love Light, Little Lord Fauntleroy* 1921; *The Eternal Flame, Oliver Twist* 1922; *The Hunchback of Notre Dame* 1923; *The Sea Hawk* 1924; *The Wreck of the Hesperus* 1927; *Skyscraper* 1928; *Just Imagine* 1930; *Lady for a Day* 1933; *One Night of Love, It Happened One Night* 1934; *Crime and Punishment, The Black Room* 1935; *The King Steps Out, Pennies from Heaven, Mr. Deeds Goes to Town, Theodora Goes Wild* 1936; *The Awful Truth, Lost Horizon* 1937; *Holiday, You Can't Take It with You* 1938; *The Little Foxes, Meet John Doe* 1941; *Cry Havoc* 1943; *Tonight and Every Night* 1945; *Gilda, The Jolson Story* 1946; *Dead Reckoning, Down to Earth* 1947; *The Lady from Shanghai, The Loves of Carmen, The Man from Colorado* 1948.

Gorcey, Leo. Actor. *b.* June 3, 1915, New York City. *d.* 1969. The son of Swiss-born veteran stage and screen actor Bernard Gorcey (1880–1955), he was working as an apprentice at his uncle's plumbing shop when he was persuaded by his father to try out for a role as one of a gang of juvenile delinquents in the original 1935 Broadway production of 'Dead End.' Despite no previous acting experience, he looked convincing in impersonating the hard-boiled, tough-talking slum boy Spit. The show was a hit and Gorcey went to Hollywood with others of the cast to appear in the 1937 film version, starring Humphrey Bogart. The "Dead End Kids" clicked with movie fans and were signed by Warner Bros. to appear in several crime melodramas. Gorcey, Huntz Hall, and some of the others later provided the core of the long-running low-budget "East Side Kids" series at Monogram and the eventual derivative series "The Bowery Boys." Gorcey's father, Bernard, and his brother David (1921–84) were also regulars in the latter series. Gorcey carried the tough little punk image into his offscreen life and had several close brushes with the law. He was married five times. He wrote an autobiography, *Dead End Yells, Wedding Bells, Cockle Shells, and Dizzy Spells.*

FILMS INCLUDE: *Dead End* 1937; *Mannequin, Crime School, Angels with Dirty Faces* 1938; *They Made Me a Criminal, Hell's Kitchen, Angels Wash Their Faces, Invisible Stripes* 1939; *The Ghost Creeps, Pride of the Bowery* 1940; *Road to Zanzibar, Flying Wild, Out of the Fog, Spooks Run Wild* 1941; *Mr. Wise Guy* 1942; *Destroyer* 1943; *Docks of New York* 1945; *So This Is New York* 1948; *Ghost Chasers* 1951; *Paris Playboys* 1954; *Crashing Las Vegas* 1956; *It's a Mad Mad Mad Mad World* (cameo) 1963; *The Phynx* (cameo) 1970.

Gordon, Bert I. Director-producer. Born on Sept. 24, 1922, in Kenosha, Wis. *ed.* U. of Wisconsin. A former producer of commercials and a production supervisor on the TV series 'Racket Squad,' he made his debut as a motion picture director in 1954. Has specialized in low-budget fantasy films involving special effects. He usually produces and sometimes writes the films he directs.

FILMS (as director-producer): *Serpent Island* 1954; *King Dinosaur* 1955; *Beginning of the End, Cyclops* (also sc.), *The Amazing Colossal Man* (also co-sc.) 1957; *Attack of the Puppet People* (also story), *War of the Colossal Beast* (also story), *The Spider/Earth vs. the Spider* (also story) 1958; *The Boy and the Pirates, Tormented* (also story) 1960; *The Magic Sword* (also story) 1962; *Village of the Giants* (also story) 1965; *Picture Mommy Dead* 1966; *How to Succeed with Sex* (dir. sc. only) 1970; *Necromancy* (also sc.) 1972; *The Mad Bomber* (also sc., phot.), *The Police Connection/Detective Geronimo* (also sc.) 1973; *The Food of the Gods* (also sc.) 1976; *Empire of the Ants* (also adapt.) 1977; *The Coming* 1983.

Gordon, C. Henry. Actor. *b.* Henry Racke, June 17, 1883, New York City, *d.* 1940. A cunning villain of scores of films from late 20s. Memorable as the evil khan speared by Errol Flynn at the climax of *The Charge of the Light Brigade* (1936). He died at 57 as a result of a leg amputation.

FILMS INCLUDE: *Renegades* 1930; *Berge in Flammen/The Doomed Battalion* (Ger.), *Once a Sinner, Charlie Chan Carries On, The Black Camel, Young as You Feel* 1931; *Mata*

Hari, Scarface, Jewel Robbery, Hell's Highway, Kongo 1932; *Rasputin and the Empress, Gabriel Over the White House, Penthouse, Night Flight* 1933; *Lazy River, Men in White, Stamboul Quest* 1934; *The Crusades* (as Philip of France) 1935; *Under Two Flags, The Charge of the Light Brigade* 1936; *Charlie Chan at the Olympics, Trapped by G-Men, Conquest* 1937; *Tarzan's Revenge, Invisible Enemy* 1938; *Man of Conquest* (as Santa Ana), *The Return of the Cisco Kid* 1939; *Passport to Alcatraz, Kit Carson* 1940.

Gordon, Keith. Actor, director. Born on Feb. 3, 1961, in New York City. A movie buff since childhood, always dreaming of becoming a filmmaker, he spent many hours of his spare time in his early teens helping the staff of the film department of the Museum of Modern Art. At the same time, he began playing juvenile roles in plays, films, and TV movies. Typically seen in sincere, nerdy characterizations, he gradually moved into young leads, and in 1988 made an auspicious debut as a director with *The Chocolate War*, following it up in 1992 with the critically acclaimed Vietnam drama *A Midnight Clear*.

FILMS: As actor—*Jaws II* 1978; *Home Movies, All That Jazz* 1979; *Dressed to Kill* 1980; *Christine* 1983; *The Legend of Billie Jean* 1985; *Back to School, Static* (also co-sc.; UK) 1986. As director—*The Chocolate War* (also sc.) 1988; *A Midnight Clear* 1992; *Mother Night* 1996.

Gordon, Lawrence. Producer. Born on March 25, 1936 in Belzoni, Miss. *ed.* Tulane U. Successful producer of both independent and studio releases, particularly action blockbusters. Originally an assistant to producer Aaron Spelling, he began producing films in the early 1970s. President of 20th Century-Fox from 1984–86. Brother and frequent partner of producer Charles Gordon.

FILMS INCLUDE: *Dillinger* (exec. pr.) 1973; *It's Not the Size That Counts* (exec. pr.) 1974; *Hard Times* 1975; *Rolling Thunder* (exec. pr.) 1977; *The End, The Driver, Hooper* (exec. pr.) 1978; *The Warriors* 1979; *Xanadu* 1980; *Paternity* 1981; *Jekyll and Hyde. . . Together Again, 48 Hours* 1982; *Streets of Fire* 1984; *Brewster's Millions* 1985; *Lucas, Jumpin' Jack Flash* 1986; *Predator* 1987; *Die Hard, The Couch Trip, The Wrong Guys* (exec. pr.) 1988; *Family Business, K-9, Field of Dreams, Leviathan, Lock Up* 1989; *Predator 2, Die Hard 2: Die Harder, Another 48 Hours* 1990; *Used People* 1992; *Boogie Nights* 1997.

Gordon, Leo. Actor, screenwriter. Born on Dec. 2, 1922, in New York City. *ed.* AADA. Heavyset supporting actor, usually in mean, brutal character parts, often in films of director Roger Corman. He has also written a number of screenplays, alone or in collaboration, including *Black Patch* (1957), *Hot Car Girl* (1958), *The Cat Burglar* (1961), *Tower of London* (1962), *The Bounty Killer* (1965), *Tobruk* (1966), and *You Can't Win 'Em All* (1970). Sometimes billed as Leo V. Gordon.

FILMS INCLUDE (as actor): *China Venture, Hondo* 1953; *Riot in Cell Block II* 1954; *Seven Angry Men, Soldier of Fortune, Tennessee's Partner, Man with the Gun* 1955; *The Conqueror, The Man Who Knew Too Much, Johnny Concho* 1956; *The Restless Breed, Black Patch* (also sc.), *Baby Face Nelson* (as Dillinger) 1957; *Apache Territory* 1958; *Noose for a Gunman* 1960; *The Intruder/I Hate Your Guts/Shame, Tarzan Goes to India* 1962; *The Haunted Palace, Kings of the Sun* 1963; *Kitten with a Whip* 1964; *The Night of the Grizzly, Beau Geste* 1966; *Tobruk* (also sc.), *The St. Valentine's Day Massacre, Hostile Guns* 1967; *Buckskin* 1968; *You Can't Win 'Em All* (also sc.) 1970; *My Name Is Nobody* (It./Fr./Ger.) 1973; *Nashville Girl* 1976; *Bog* 1978.

Gordon, Mary. Actress. *b.* Mary Gilmour, 1882, Scotland. *d.* 1963. She arrived in the US with a touring stage company and from the mid-20s played character roles in numerous Hollywood films, most memorably in the role of Mrs. Hudson, housekeeper for Sherlock Holmes, on the screen as well as in the radio series.

FILMS INCLUDE: *The Home Maker* 1925; *Black Paradise* 1926; *Naughty Nanette* 1927; *Dynamite* 1929; *The Black Camel* 1931; *The Little Minister* 1934; *The Bride of Frankenstein, Mutiny on the Bounty* 1935; *Mary of Scotland* 1936; *The Plough and the Stars* 1937; *Kidnapped, City Streets* 1938; *The Hound of the Baskervilles, The Adventures of Sherlock Holmes, Rulers of the Sea* 1939; *No No Nanette* 1940; *Appointment for Love* 1941; *The Mummy's Tomb* 1942; *Sherlock Holmes and the Secret Weapon* 1943; *Spider Woman* 1944; *The Woman in Green* 1945; *Little Giant* 1946; *West of Wyoming* 1950.

Gordon, Michael. Director. *b.* Sept. 6, 1909, Baltimore. *d.* 1993. *ed.* Johns Hopkins; Yale Drama School. A stage actor and director, he broke into films in 1940 as a dialogue director and film editor and made his debut as a director in 1942. He started out with low-budget crime films but in the late 40s and early 50s turned out a number of fine dramas, notably *Another Part of the Forest* (1948) and *Cyrano de Bergerac* (1950), which, despite their "staginess," have been among the American screen's more valiant attempts at serious drama. At that high point of his career, Gordon was blacklisted in the wake of the House Un-American Activities Committee Hollywood hearings and during the years that followed was able to direct only one film, in Australia. He returned to Hollywood in 1959 and in an extreme switch of style turned his attention to glossy entertainment films.

FILMS: *Boston Blackie Goes Hollywood, Underground Agent* 1942; *One Dangerous Night, Crime Doctor* 1943; *The Web* 1947; *Another Part of the Forest, An Act of Murder/Live Today for Tomorrow* 1948; *The Lady Gambles* 1949; *Woman in Hiding, Cyrano de Bergerac* 1950; *I Can Get It for You Wholesale, The Secret of Convict Lake* 1951; *Wherever She Goes* (also sc.; Austral.) 1953; *Pillow Talk* 1959; *Portrait in Black* 1960; *Boys' Night Out* 1962; *For Love or Money, Move Over Darling* 1963; *A Very Special Favor* 1965; *Texas Across the River* 1966; *The Impossible Years* 1968; *How Do I Love Thee?* 1970.

Gordon, Ruth. Actress, playwright, screenwriter. *b.* Ruth Gordon Jones, Oct. 30, 1896, Wollaston (Quincy), Mass., the daughter of a sea captain. *d.* 1985. As a youngster she went to New York and while struggling to crack Broadway appeared as an extra and bit player in silent films produced across the Hudson River at Fort Lee, N.J. Her initial reception was discouraging. Told she had no talent, she was dropped by the American Academy of Dramatic Arts after one term. Undaunted, she made her Broadway debut in 'Peter Pan' in 1915. But her first starring effort, in Booth Tarkington's 'Seventeen' (1918), invited a scathing review from Heywood Broun in the *New York Herald Tribune.* However, after personal triumphs in 'Ethan Frome' (1936) and 'A Doll's House,' she went on to become a widely admired stage performer. She returned to the screen in 1940, portraying Mary Todd Lincoln in John Cromwell's *Abe Lincoln in Illinois,* and appearing in a handful of other films of the early 40s. A long lull followed, during which she appeared in no films and only intermittently on the stage, notably as the original Dolly Levi in Broadway's 'The Matchmaker' (1954), on which the musical 'Hello Dolly!' would later be based. She focused instead on writing plays and screenplays, alone or in collaboration with her second husband (from 1942), Garson KANIN. They shared Academy Award nominations for *A Double Life* (1947), *Adam's Rib* (1949), and *Pat and Mike* (1952). Resuming her screen career in the mid-60s, she won over young, as well as older, audiences with a series of feisty, eccentric characterizations. She was nominated for an Academy Award as best supporting actress for *Inside Daisy Clover* (1965) and won the Oscar for her delicious portrait of a Manhattan witch in *Rosemary's Baby* (1968). Memoirs: *Myself Among Others* (1971), *My Side* (1976), *An Open Book* (1980). Novel: *Shady Lady* (1982).

FILMS: As actress—*Camille, The Whirl of Life* 1915; *Abe Lincoln in Illinois* (as Mary Todd Lincoln), *Dr. Ehrlich's Magic Bullet* 1940; *Two-Faced Woman* 1941; *Edge of Darkness, Action in the North Atlantic* 1943; *Inside Daisy Clover, Lord Love a Duck* 1966; *Rosemary's Baby* 1968; *What Ever Happened to Aunt Alice?* 1969; *Where's Poppa?* 1970; *Harold and Maude* 1971; *The Big Bus* 1976; *Every Which Way but Loose* 1978; *Boardwalk, Scavenger Hunt* 1979; *My Bodyguard, Any Which Way You Can* 1980; *Jimmy the Kid* 1983; *Delta Pi/Mugsy's Girls, Maxie* 1985; *The Trouble with Spies* (release delayed from 1984) 1987. As screenwriter—*Over 21* (play basis only) 1945; *A Double Life* 1948; *Adam's Rib* 1949; *The Marrying Kind, Pat and Mike* 1952; *The Actress* (from own play 'Years Ago,') 1953; *Rosie!* (adapt.) 1967.

Gordon, Stuart. Director, screenwriter. Born in 1946. He achieved fame as a horror film director with the witty, gruesome, and imaginative *Re-Animator* (1985), based on the work of H. P. Lovecraft. *From Beyond* (1986), also based on Lovecraft, was even more laden with special effects, though not as smoothly engaging as the first film. His subsequent directing efforts have received mixed reviews, though they continue to bear the stamp of his dark-humored intelligence. He wrote the co-story for *Honey, I Shrunk the Kids* and was to have directed before it was assigned to Joe Johnston.

FILMS INCLUDE (as director): *Re-Animator* (also co-sc.) 1985; *From Beyond* (also co-sc.) 1986; *Dolls* 1987; *Robojox/Robot Jox, Honey I Shrunk the Kids* (co-story only) 1989; *The Pit and the Pendulum* 1991; *Fortress* 1993; *Body Snatchers* (co-sc. only) 1994.

Goretta, Claude. Director. Born on June 23, 1929, in Geneva, the son of Italian immigrants. The holder of a law degree from the University of Geneva, he studied film at the British Film Institute under the auspices of which he made a short, *Nice Time* (1957), in collaboration with his countryman Alain TANNER. He later worked for Swiss TV and did not turn out his first feature until 1970. His films, made mainly in France, show a compassionate concern for the inner life of people and a keen observation of human behavior, down to minute, banal detail. The best known of these, *The Lacemaker* (1977), is a characteristically gentle yet incisive portrait of a naive girl rendered "voiceless" by her puzzling passivity. It won the Ecumenical Prize at the Cannes Festival. Although none of his subsequent productions have attained the quiet power of that film, Goretta remains, along with Tanner, a shining beacon safeguarding Swiss cinema from obscurity.

FEATURE FILMS: *Le Fou/The Madman* (also sc.) 1970; *Le Jour des Noces/The Wedding Day* (orig. made for TV) 1971; *L'Invitation/The Invitation* (also co-sc.) 1973; *Pas si méchant que ça/The Wonderful Crook* (also co-sc.) 1975; *La Dentellière/The Lacemaker* (also co-sc.) 1977; *Les Chemins de l'Exil ou Les Dernières Années de Jean-Jacques Rousseau/The Roads of Exile* (also co-sc.; orig. for TV) 1978; *La Provinciale/The Girl from Lorraine* (also co-sc.) 1981; *La Mort de Mario Ricci/The Death of Mario Ricci* (also sc.) 1983; *Orfeo/Orpheus* (also co-sc.; Fr./It./Can.) 1985; *Si le Soleil ne revenait pas* (also sc.) 1987; *Guillaume T—la Fouine* 1992.

Goring, Marius. Actor. Born on May 23, 1912, in Newport, Isle of Wight. Versatile performer of British stage and screen. The son of a noted physician, he was educated at Cambridge and at the universities of Frankfurt, Munich, Vienna, and Paris, and trained for the stage at the Old Vic dramatic school. On the stage from age 13, he played with the Old Vic and Sadler's Wells companies before making his screen debut in 1936. Although he remained primarily a stage actor, performing in French and German as well as in English, he has appeared in many films, in both leads and character roles, often cast as a decadent aristocrat.

FILMS INCLUDE: *Rembrandt* 1936; *The Spy in Black/U-Boat 29* 1939; *The Case of the Frightened Lady/Frightened Lady, Pastor Hall* 1940; *The Big Blockade* 1942; *Lilli Marlene* 1944; *Stairway to Heaven/A Matter of Life and Death* 1946; *Take My Life* 1947; *The Red Shoes, Mr. Perrin and Mr. Traill* 1948; *Odette* 1950; *Circle of Danger, Pandora and the Flying Dutchman* 1951; *The Man Who Watched the Trains Go By/The Paris Express, So Little Time* 1952; *The Barefoot Contessa* (US) 1954; *The Adventures of Quentin Durward/Quentin Durward* 1955; *Ill Met by Moonlight/Night Ambush* 1957; *I Was Monty's Double* 1958; *The Angry Hills* 1959; *Exodus* (US) 1960; *The Inspector/Lisa* (UK/US) 1962; *The Crooked Road, Up from the Beach* (US) 1965; *Le 25e Heure/The 25th Hour* (Fr./It./Yug.) 1967; *La Motocyclette/The Girl on a Motorcycle* (Fr./UK) 1968; *Erste Liebe/First Love* (Switz./Ger.) 1970; *Zeppelin* 1971; *La Petite Fille en Velours bleu* (Fr.) 1978.

Gorman, Cliff. Actor. Born on Oct. 13, 1936, in Jamaica, N.Y. *ed.* UCLA; U. of New Mexico; NYU. He drove a truck, then an ambulance, served as a probationary officer for delinquent youths, and worked for a collection company before scoring his first success on the stage in 'The Boys in the Band,' in 1968. In 1971 he won a Tony Award as best actor for portraying Lenny Bruce in the Broadway play 'Lenny.' He has been appearing in films since 1969.

FILMS: *Justine* 1969; *The Boys in the Band* 1970; *Cops and Robbers* 1973; *Rosebud* 1975; *An Unmarried Woman* 1978; *All That Jazz* 1979; *Night of the Juggler* 1980; *Angel* 1984.

Gosho, Heinosuke. Actor. *b.* Heiuemon Gosho, Feb. 1, 1902, Tokyo. *d.* 1981. The son of a geisha and a wealthy tobacco heir, he graduated from a business school before entering Japanese films as assistant director (to Shimazu) in 1923. A director since 1925, he made the first Japanese talkie, *The Neighbor's Wife and Mine,* in 1931. Despite recurrent bouts with tuberculosis from the late 30s, he was immensely prolific, turning out scores of films through the late 60s. Gosho, who was best known in the West for the film *Four Chimneys* (1953), paid great attention to detail, characterization, and atmosphere. The plots of his films usually dealt with common people, typically blending humor with pathos. He often wrote his own scripts. In 1949 he established his own production company.

FILMS INCLUDE: *Youth* (also sc.) 1925; *First Love* (also sc.), *Daughter* (also sc.), *The Girl Friend* (also sc.) 1926; *Tricky Girl* (also sc.), *The Village Bride* 1927; *The Road to God* 1928; *One Night of Passion* (also sc.) 1929; *Bachelors Beware* (also sc.) 1930; *The Neighbor's Wife and Mine* 1931; *Love in Tokyo* 1932; *Dancing Girls of Izu, The 19th Spring* 1933; *Everything That Lives* 1934; *Burden of Life* 1935; *The New Road* (also sc.) 1936; *Song of a Flower Basket* (also sc.) 1937; *Wooden Head* 1940; *New Snow* 1942; *The Girls of Izu* 1945; *Once More* 1947; *Image* (also sc.) 1948; *Dispersing Clouds* (also sc.) 1951; *Four Chimneys* 1953; *An Inn at Osaka* (also sc.), *The Valley Between Love and Death* 1954; *Growing Up/Adolescence* 1955; *Behold Thy Son, Elegy of the North* 1957; *Avarice* 1958; *White Fangs, When a Woman Loves* 1960; *As the Clouds Scatter* 1961; *A Million Girls* (also sc.) 1963; *An Innocent Witch* (also sc.) 1965; *Our Wonderful Years* 1966; *Rebellion of Japan* 1967; *A Girl of the Meiji Period* 1968.

Gossett, Louis, Jr. Actor. Born on May 27, 1936, in Brooklyn, N.Y. *ed.* NYU. Tall (6' 4") sinewy, commanding black character lead and supporting player of the American stage, TV, and films. The son of a porter and a maid, he turned to acting in high school, after a leg injury temporarily suspended his hopes for a basketball career. Following his Broadway debut at 17, he attended NYU on an athletic scholarship, while continuing to perform on TV and on the stage. He finally chose acting over basketball, turning down a contract offer from the New York Knicks. In the following years he appeared in numerous shows, plays, and films, attracting only modest attention, until 1977, when he won an Emmy Award for his performance in the TV miniseries 'Roots.' He was also impressive playing the title role of Egypt's president in the 1983 miniseries 'Sadat.' But the role for which he will be best remembered is that of the tough drill sergeant in the film *An Officer and a Gentleman* (1982), for which he won a best supporting actor Academy Award. He has participated in anti-drug campaigns and appeared in *Straight Up*, a 1990 video that preached abstinence from drugs, alcohol, and cigarettes to teenagers.

FILMS: *A Raisin in the Sun* 1961; *Leo the Last* (UK), *The Landlord, The Bushbaby* 1970; *The Skin Game* 1971; *Travels with My Aunt* 1972; *The Laughing Policeman* 1973; *The White Dawn* 1974; *J. D.'s Revenge, The River Niger* 1976; *The Deep, The Choirboys* 1977; *An Officer and a Gentleman* 1982; *Jaws 3-D* 1983; *Finders Keepers* 1984; *Enemy Mine* 1985; *Iron Eagle, Firewalker* 1986; *The Principal* 1987; *Iron Eagle II* 1988; *The Punisher* 1990; *Cover-Up, Toy Soldiers* 1991; *Keeper of the City, Aces: Iron Eagle III, Diggstown* 1992; *Blue Chips* (uncred.), *A Good Man in Africa* 1994; *Inside* 1997.

Gottlieb, Carl. American actor, screenwriter, director. Born on Mar. 18, 1938. He pursued parallel careers as a comic actor and comedy writer for such TV programs as 'The Odd Couple' series and the Flip Wilson and Bob Newhart Shows and won an Emmy Award for his writing contributions in 1969 to the 'Smothers Brothers Comedy Hour.' On the screen as an actor from the late 60s, he began collaborating on screenplays and sporadically directing in the early 80s.

FILMS: (as actor): *Maryjane* 1968; *The Committee/A Session with the Committee* 1969; *M*A*S*H* 1970; *Up the Sandbox* 1972; *Jaws* (also co-sc.) 1975; *Cannonball* 1976; *Which Way Is Up?* (co-sc. only) 1977; *Jaws* (co-sc. only) 1978; *The Jerk* (also co-sc.) 1979; *Caveman* (also dir., co-sc.) 1981; *The Sting II, Doctor Detroit* (co-sc., only), *Jaws 3-D* (co-sc. only) 1983; *Into the Night* (cameo) 1985; *Amazon Women on the Moon* (co-dir. only) 1987.

go-to-black. Colloquialism for "fade out." See FADE.

Goudal, Jetta. Actress. *b.* July 18, 1898, Versailles, France. *d.* 1985. She came to the US after WW I, following a modest stage career in Europe, and made several appearances on Broadway before making her screen debut in 1923. A tall, imposing brunette, she played exotic leads in many Hollywood silents but retired from the screen shortly after the arrival of sound. She was married to art director Harold Grieve.

FILMS INCLUDE: *The Bright Shawl, The Green Goddess* 1923; *Open All Night* 1924; *Salome of the Tenements, The Spaniard, The Coming of Amos, The Road to Yesterday* 1925; *Three Faces East, Paris at Midnight, Her Man o' War* 1926; *White Gold, Fighting Love, The Forbidden Woman* 1927; *The Cardboard Lover* 1928; *Lady of the Pavements* 1929; *Le Spectre Vert* (French-language version of *The Unholy Night*) 1930; *Business and Pleasure* 1932; *Tarnished Youth* 1933.

Gough, Michael. Actor. Born on Nov. 23, 1917, in Malaya, to British parents. *ed.* Wye Agricultural Coll. Tall, gaunt character player of the British stage and screen. Trained at the Old Vic School, he made his first stage appearance in 1936 and has since appeared in numerous plays in both leads and supporting parts. In films since the late 40s, he has frequently played sinister roles, sometimes in the lead.

FILMS INCLUDE: *Blanche Fury* 1947; *Anna Karenina, Saraband for Dead Lovers/Saraband* 1948; *The Small Back Room* 1949; *The Man in the White Suit, No Resting Place* 1951; *The Sword and the Rose* (as the Duke of Buckingham), *Rob Roy* (as the Duke of Montrose) 1953; *Richard III* 1955; *Dracula/Horror of Dracula, Horrors of the Black Museum* 1958; *The Horse's Mouth* 1959; *Konga* 1961; *Candidate for Murder, The Phantom of the Opera* 1962; *Black Zoo* (US) 1963; *Dr. Terror's House of Horrors, The Skull* 1965; *They Came from Beyond Space, Berserk* 1967; *A Walk with Love and Death* (US), *Women in Love* 1969; *Julius Caesar* (as Metellus Cimber), *Trog, The Corpse/Cauldron of Blood* 1970; *The Go-Between* 1971; *Savage Messiah, Henry VIII and His Six Wives* (as Norfolk) 1972; *Horror Hospital/Computer Killers* 1974; *Galileo* 1975; *The Boys from Brazil* (US) *L'Amour en Question* (Fr.) 1978; *Venom* 1982; *The Dresser* 1983; *Memed My Hawk, Top Secret!* (US), *Oxford Blues* (US) 1984; *Out of Africa* (US) 1985; *Caravaggio* 1986; *The Fourth Protocol* 1987; *The Serpent and the Rainbow* (US) 1988; *Batman* (US) 1989; *Strapless, Let Him Have It* 1990; *Blackeyes* 1991; *Batman Returns* 1992; *Wittgenstein* 1993; *The Advocate, Uncovered* 1994; *Batman Forever* 1995; *Batman and Robin* 1997.

Gould, Elliott. Actor. Born Elliott Goldstein, on Aug. 29, 1938, in Brooklyn, N.Y. The son of a Garment Center employee and a driving "stage mother," he began taking drama, diction, singing, and dancing instruction at the age of eight. He then appeared in song-and-dance routines in temples and hospitals, modeled, and popped up occasionally on the TV screen. On his summer vacations from Manhattan's Professional Children's School, he performed in the Catskills "borscht belt." He also studied ballet, which helped him break into a Broadway chorus line at age 18. But stage jobs were few and far between and to eat he sold vacuum cleaners and ran a hotel elevator, among other odd jobs. The turning point was provided by a chorus job in David Merrick's 'Irma La Douce,' which led to an audition for, and the lead in, 'I Can Get It for You Wholesale' (1962). The musical was only a mild success, but it became famous as the show that propelled Barbra Streisand to her phenomenal success. It did nothing for the career of Gould, despite excellent notices, but it led to a love affair with Miss Streisand and to their marriage in 1963.

As Barbra's fortunes soared, so did his sink. He found stage jobs scarce and instead became involved in managing his wife's TV enterprises. He got his first real break in years when he was cast in a supporting role in the film *The Night They Raided Minsky's*, in 1968. Within a year he was a movie star, an Oscar nominee (for *Bob & Carol & Ted & Alice*). The turnabout coincided with his 1967 divorce from Streisand and culminated in his memorable role as Trapper John in Robert Altman's irreverent blood-and-gore black comedy *M*A*S*H* (1970). In 1971 he became the first non-Swede to star in an Ingmar Bergman film, *The Touch.* Suddenly, Elliott Gould was the hot property in Hollywood and coming dangerously close to overexposure in just two or three years.

Gould's sudden success was a phenomenon of its times. Tall but not handsome, with puffy features and a mournful expression, these anti-heroic qualities attracted the admiration of young Americans. By the mid-70s, however, the Gould phenomenon had played itself out. Most of his many latter-day films have been minor. He married his second wife, Jennifer Bogart, twice—first in 1971, and after their 1975 divorce, again in 1977. His son by his first marriage, to Barbra Streisand, Jason Gould (*b.* 1967) began appearing in films in the late 80s.

FILMS: *The Night They Raided Minsky's* 1968; *Bob & Carol & Ted & Alice* 1969; *M*A*S*H, Getting Straight, Move, I Love My Wife* 1970; *The Touch* (Sw./US), *Little Murders* 1971; *The Long Goodbye* (as private eye Philip Marlowe) 1973; *Busting, S*P*Y*S, California Split* 1974; *Who?, Nashville* (cameo), *Whiffs* 1975; *Mean Johnny Barrows, I Will I Will. . . for Now, Harry and Walter Go to New York* 1976; *A Bridge Too Far* (UK) 1977; *The Silent Partner* (Can.), *Capricorn One, Matilda* 1978; *The Lady Vanishes* (UK), *Escape to Athena* (UK), *The Muppet Movie* (cameo) 1979; *The Last Flight of Noah's Ark, Falling in Love Again, Dirty Tricks* (Can.) 1980; *The Devil and Max Devlin* 1981; *The Naked Face, The Muppets Take Manhattan* (cameo), *Over the Brooklyn Bridge* 1984; *Inside Out* 1986; *The Telephone, Dangerous Love* 1988; *The Big Picture* (cameo), *The Night Visitor* 1989; *Scandalo Segreto/Secret Scandal* (It.) 1990; *Bugsy, Judgment, Dead Men Don't Die* 1991; *The Player* (cameo), *Exchange, Lifeguards* 1992; *The Glass Shield, Kicking and Screaming* 1995; *Camp Stories, Johns* 1997.

Gould, Harold. Actor. Born on December 10, 1923 in Schenectady, N.Y. *ed.* SUNY, Albany. Cornell U. (M.A., Ph.D.). Dapper silver-haired character actor of film and television, often featured in comedic roles. Originally an instructor of theater at Randolph Macon Women's College and assistant professor of drama at the University of California, he began his professional career in the late 1950s and won an Obie in 1969 for his performance in *Difficulty of Concentration*.

FILMS INCLUDE: *Two for the Seesaw, The Couch* 1962; *Marnie* 1964; *Inside Daisy Clover* 1965; *Harper, An American Dream* 1966; *The Arrangement, He and She* 1969; *The Lawyer* 1970; *Mrs. Pollifax: Spy, Where Does It Hurt?* 1971; *The Sting* 1973; *The Front Page* 1974; *Love and Death* 1975; *The Big Bus, Silent Movie* 1976; *The One and Only* 1978; *Seems Like Old Times* 1980; *The Dream Chasers* 1984; *The Fourth Wise Man* 1985, *Romero* 1989.

Goulding, Edmund. Director, screenwriter, composer. *b.* Mar. 20, 1891, London. *d.* 1959. On the London stage from age 12, he was a mildly successful actor-director-playwright by the time he left for military service in 1914. Upon his early discharge, as a wounded combatant, he emigrated to the US, where he began writing for the screen in 1916. In addition to original stories and scripts, alone or in collaboration, he wrote a novel, *Fury,* in 1922 (he directed it for the screen in 1923) and a hit play, 'Dancing Mothers,' in 1924. In 1925 he joined MGM as director-screenwriter. A man of culture and good taste, he brought to the screen a number of fine dramas (and on rarer occasions comedies), the most famous of which is the multistar MGM vehicle *Grand Hotel.* Among his other well known films was a silent adaptation of *Anna Karenina* starring Greta Garbo and entitled *Love,* and several highly melodramatic Bette Davis pictures, including *Dark Victory, The Old Maid,* and *The Great Lie.* He also directed Joan Fontaine to advantage in *The Constant Nymph,* Dorothy McGuire in *Claudia,* and Tyrone Power in his two most effective acting efforts, *The Razor's Edge* and *Nightmare Alley.* Goulding was among Hollywood's best handlers of actors, but he seems to have lacked a distinctive personal style. His films of the MGM period are very much in the studio's mold. When he moved to Warners, and later to Fox, he easily adapted to the styles typical of each of the studios. A versatile artist who often wrote his own scripts, he composed the score for one of his films, and wrote songs for two others.

FILMS: As screenwriter—*Little Lady Eileen* (co-story only; uncredited), *The Quest of Life* (co-play basis only, 'Ellen Young') 1916; *The Silent Partner* (story only) 1917; *The Ordeal of Rosetta* (story only) 1918; *The Imp, The Perfect Lover, The Glorious Lady* (story only), *A Regular Girl, Sealed Hearts* (co-story only) 1919; *A Daughter of Two Worlds, Madonnas and Men* (co-story only), *The Dangerous Paradise* (story only), *The Sin That Was His* 1920; *The Devil, Dangerous Toys, The Man of Stone* (co-story only), *Tol'able David* 1921; *Peacock Alley, The Seventh Day, Fascination, Broadway Rose, Till We Meet Again, Heroes of the Street* 1922; *Fury, Dark Secrets, Jazzmania, The Bright Shawl, Bright Lights of Broadway, Tiger Rose* 1923; *The Man Who Came Back, Dante's Inferno, Gerald Cranston's Lady* 1924; *The Dancers, The Scarlet Honeymoon* (story only), *Havoc, The Beautiful City* (story only), *The Fool* 1925; *Dancing Mothers* (co-play basis only) 1926; *Happiness Ahead* (story only) 1928; *The Broadway Melody* (story only) 1929; *The Grand Parade* (also prod.) 1930; *Flesh* (story only), *No Man of Her Own* (co-story only) 1932; *Two Girls on Broadway* (story only) 1940. As director—*Sun-Up* (also adapt.), *Sally Irene and Mary* (also sc.) 1925; *Paris* (also sc.) 1926; *Women Love Diamonds* (also story), *Love* (also prod.) 1927; *The Trespasser* (also sc., co-song) 1929; *Paramount on Parade* (co-dir. with ten others), *The Devil's Holiday* (also sc., music) 1930; *Reaching for the Moon* (also sc.), *The Night Angel* (also sc.) 1931; *Grand Hotel, Blondie of the Follies* 1932; *Riptide* (also sc.) 1934; *The Flame Within* (also prod., sc.) 1935; *That Certain Woman* (also sc.) 1937; *White Banners, The Dawn Patrol* 1938; *Dark Victory, The Old Maid, We Are Not Alone* 1939; *'Til We Meet Again* 1940; *The Great Lie* 1941; *Forever and a Day* (co-dir. with six others; also co-prod.), *The Constant Nymph, Claudia* 1943; *Of Human Bondage, The Razor's Edge* 1946; *Nightmare Alley* 1947; *Everybody Does It* 1949; *Mister 880* 1950; *We're Not Married* 1952; *Down Among the Sheltering Palms* 1953; *Teenage Rebel* (also song) 1956; *Mardi Gras* 1958.

Gowland, Gibson. Actor. *b.* Jan. 4, 1872, Spennymoor, Durham, England. *d.* 1951. Character star of Hollywood silents following stage experience in England and the US. Initially billed as T. H. Gowland. Best remembered for his strong lead roles in Erich von Stroheim's *Blind Husbands* (1919) and *Greed* (1923). He returned to England in the early 30s and ended his career in British films.

FILMS INCLUDE: *The Birth of a Nation* (bit), *Jewel* 1915; *Macbeth* (bit) 1916; *The Promise, Under Handicap, The Climber* 1917; *Breakers Ahead* 1918; *The Fighting Shepherdess, The Right of Way, Behind the Door* 1920; *Ladies Must Live* 1921; *Shifting Sands, Harbor Lights, Greed* 1923; *The Border Legion, Love and Glory, The Red Lily* 1924; *The Phantom of the Opera, The Prairie Wife* 1925; *The Outsider, Don Juan* (bit) 1926; *The First Auto, The Broken Gate, The Night of Love, Topsy and Eva, The Isle of Forgotten Women, The Land Beyond the Law* 1927; *Rose Marie* 1928; *The Mysterious Island* 1929; *The Sea Bat, Hell Harbor* 1930; *The Doomed Battalion* 1932; *S.O.S. Iceberg* 1933; *The Private Life of Don Juan* (UK) 1934; *The Mystery of Marie Celeste* (UK) 1936; *Cotton Queen* (UK) 1937.

GPO Film Unit. British government-sponsored documentary group that, under the supervision of John GRIERSON, produced films notable for their experimental quality and social significance in the 30s. The initials stand for General Post Office, under the auspices of which the unit operated. In 1940 it became the Crown Film Unit of the Ministry of Information.

Grable, Betty. Actress. *b.* Elizabeth Ruth Grable, Dec. 18, 1916, St. Louis, Mo. *d.* 1973. Trained from age 12 at the Hollywood Professional School, she began singing and dancing in the chorus line of Hollywood musical films before she reached 14. In 1931 she was signed by Sam GOLDWYN, who changed her name to Frances Dean and cast her in bits in several of his films, hoping to develop her into a star. Late in the following year, her contract was picked up by RKO and her name changed back to Grable. She was now playing leads in B musicals and comedies and bits in higher-grade pictures. She was still no more than an aspiring starlet in 1937 when she switched over to Paramount. That year she married former child star, Jackie COOGAN. Financial difficulties led to their divorce in 1940. The tide turned for Betty Grable that same year, when she was brought into Fox by Darryl F. Zanuck to use as a possible threat to his reluctant musical star Alice Faye.

With her peachy complexion glowing in Technicolor and her shapely legs displayed abundantly in lush musical films, Miss Grable suddenly bloomed into a top box-office star. Her popularity was at its peak during the WW II years, when GIs chose her as their number one "pinup girl." Fox publicity insured her famous legs with Lloyds of London for a million dollars, and she became the industry's highest paid star. In 1943 she married trumpeter-bandleader Harry James. (They divorced in 1965.) Her popularity began to wane in the early 50s and by the middle of the decade—coincidental with the decline of the film musical—her screen career was over. She subsequently appeared in nightclubs and occasional musical plays and was one of the rotation of stars heading the cast in Broadway's 'Hello, Dolly!' She died at 56 of lung cancer.

FILMS: *Happy Days, Let's Go Places, New Movietone Follies of 1930, Whoopee!* 1930; *Kiki, Palmy Days* 1931; *The Greeks Had a Word for Them, The Kid from Spain, Probation, Hold 'Em Jail* 1932; *Child of Manhattan, The Sweetheart of Sigma Chi, Cavalcade, Melody Cruise, What Price Innocence?* 1933; *By Your Leave, Student Tour, The Gay Divorcee* 1934; *The Nitwits, Old Man Rhythm, Collegiate* 1935; *Follow the Fleet, Pigskin Parade, Don't Turn 'Em Loose* 1936; *This Way Please, Thrill of a Lifetime* 1937; *College Swing, Give Me a Sailor, Campus Confessions* 1938; *Man About Town, Million Dollar Legs, The Day the Bookies Wept* 1939; *Down Argentine Way, Tin Pan Alley* 1940; *Moon Over Miami, A Yank in the R.A.F., I Wake Up Screaming* 1941; *Footlight Serenade, Song of the Islands, Springtime in the Rockies* 1942; *Coney Island, Sweet Rosie O'Grady* 1943; *Four Jills in a Jeep, Pin-Up Girl* 1944; *Diamond Horseshoe, The Dolly Sisters* 1945; *Do You Love Me?* (cameo) 1946; *The Shocking Miss Pilgrim, Mother Wore Tights* 1947; *That Lady in Ermine, When My Baby Smiles at Me* 1948; *The Beautiful Blonde from Bashful Bend* 1949; *Wabash Avenue, My Blue Heaven* 1950; *Call Me Mister, Meet Me After the Show* 1951; *The Farmer Takes a Wife, How to Marry a Millionaire* 1953; *Three for the Show, How to Be Very Very Popular* 1955.

grader. A lab technician responsible for determining and balancing the density and color of a negative film before it is printed. This is done for the most part by eye and its quality depends largely on the individual grader.

grading. The process of determining and balancing the density of each negative film frame before printing so that an overall unity of brightness and atmosphere is achieved in the projected print. Photographic exposure, however carefully calculated by the cameraman, tends to vary in tone and density. Should all frames by printed with the same printer-light intensity, some would be overexposed and others underexposed. Grading is designed to overcome this problem by adjusting the printer light to achieve the correct setting for every shot.

graduated filter. A variable-density filter designed to give non-uniform effects to different parts of the same scene. A common example is the sky filter, the top half of which is denser than the bottom, allowing skies to register vividly without affecting the rest of a scene.

Graetz, Paul. Producer. *b.* Apr. 4, 1899, Leipzig, Germany. *d.* 1966. The head of a small German production company, Terra Films, he was forced to flee to France during the Nazi takeover in 1933. In Paris he set up a new production company, Transcontinental Film, with a branch in Hollywood, and from the late 30s produced movies of both distinction and commercial appeal. Although working mostly in France, he acquired American citizenship. He was decorated a Chevalier of the Légion d'Honneur for his contribution to French cinema. He died during the production of his French-American film *Is Paris Burning?* (Not to be confused with a veteran character actor by the same name who died in 1937.)

FILMS INCLUDE: *Altitude 3,200* 1938; *La Charette Fantôme* 1939; *Untel Père et Fils/The Heart of a Nation* 1940; *Le Diable au Corps/Devil in the Flesh* 1947; *Dieu a besoin des Hommes/God Needs Men* 1950; *Roma Ore Undici/Rome 11 O'Clock* (It.) 1952; *Monsieur Ripois/Knave of Hearts/Lovers Happy Lovers* (Fr./UK) 1954; *Les Hommes en Blanc/The Doctors* 1955; *Amère Victoire/Bitter Victory* 1957; *Faibles Femmes/Women Are Weak* 1959; *La Giornata Balorda/From a Roman Balcony* (It./Fr.) 1960; *Vu du Pont/A View from the Bridge* 1962; *Paris brûle-t-il?/Is Paris Burning?* (Fr./US) 1966.

Graham, Sheilah. Columnist. *b.* Lily Sheil, September 1904, London. *d.* 1988. She had a cockney background, was brought up in an orphanage, matured into a London showgirl and model, and came to the US in 1933. Two years later she began a Hollywood column, which made her, along with Hedda Hopper and Louella Parsons, part of an influential triumvirate wielding considerable gossip power in the film capital. Her four-year love affair with F. Scott Fitzgerald in the closing years of his life is recounted in her book *Beloved Infidel* (1958), which was turned into a film in 1959, with Gregory Peck and Deborah Kerr playing the leads. She followed this with other volumes of Fitgerald memoirs, *The Real Scott Fitzgerald, The Rest of the Story, College for One,* and an autobiography, *A State of Heat* (1972). She also wrote *The Garden of Allah, How to Marry Super Rich, Confessions of a Gossip Columnist,* and *Hollywood Revisited* (1985), her last book. Fitzgerald modeled the heroine of his unfinished *The Last Tycoon* after her.

Grahame, Gloria. Actress. *b.* Gloria Grahame Hallward, Nov. 28, 1924, Los Angeles. *d.* 1981. The daughter of an industrial designer and a former minor actress, she began performing on the stage at age nine with the Pasadena Community Playhouse and later participated in Hollywood High School dramatics. After some experience in stock she made her Broadway debut as Gloria Hallward in 1943 and was signed to a film contract by MGM the following year. But it was not until the early 50s that she made her mark on Hollywood as a sensuous, sultry leading lady whose seductive voice, pouting lips, and inviting looks were perfectly suited to her typical role as a fallen woman or erring wife. She won an Academy Award as best supporting actress for her portrayal of a tramp in *The Bad and the Beautiful* (1952) and played a number of other meaty parts in the next four years. After that her roles diminished and her Hollywood career gradually declined; by the end of the decade she had retired from the screen. She later returned to films, mainly in low-budget productions. Her four marriages included actor Stanley CLEMENTS (1945–48) and directors Nicholas RAY (1948–52) and Cy HOWARD (1954–57). She died of cancer.

FILMS: *Blonde Fever* 1944; *Without Love* 1945; *It's a Wonderful Life* 1946; *It Happened in Brooklyn, Crossfire, Song of the Thin Man, Merton of the Movies* 1947; *A Woman's Secret, Roughshod* 1949; *In a Lonely Place* 1950; *The Greatest Show on Earth, Macao, Sudden Fear, The Bad and the Beautiful* 1952; *The Glass Wall, Man on a Tightrope, The Big Heat, Prisoners of the Casbah* 1953; *Human Desire, Naked Alibi* 1954; *The Good*

Die Young, Not as a Stranger, The Cobweb, Oklahoma! 1955; *The Man Who Never Was* (UK) 1956; *Ride Out for Revenge* 1957; *Odds Against Tomorrow* 1959; *Ride Beyond Vengeance* 1966; *Blood and Lace, The Todd Killings, Chandler* 1971; *The Loners* 1972; *Tarot* 1973; *Mama's Dirty Girls* 1974; *Mansion of the Doomed* 1976; *Head Over Heels/Chilly Scenes of Winter, A Nightingale Sang in Berkeley Square* (UK) 1979; *Melvin and Howard* 1980; *The Nesting* 1981.

Grahame, Margot. Actress. *b.* Feb. 20, 1911, Canterbury, Eng. *d.* 1982. Raised and educated in South Africa, she made her stage debut in Durban in 1926 and returned to England the following year with a touring company. A voluptuous blonde, she played leads in several British films of the 30s, then went to Hollywood, where she appeared in a number of films, notably in the role of Katie, Gypo's prostitute girl friend in John Ford's *The Informer* (1935). But she never reached stardom and eventually returned to England.

FILMS INCLUDE: *Rookery Nook/One Embarrassing Night* 1930; *The Love Habit, Uneasy Virtue, Glamour, Creeping Shadows/The Limping Man, Stamboul* 1931; *Innocents of Chicago/Why Saps Leave Home, Illegal* 1932; *I Adore You, Sorrell and Son* 1933; *The Broken Melody* 1934; *The Informer* (US), *The Arizonian* (US), *The Three Musketeers* (as Milady de Winter; US) 1935; *Crime Over London* (US/UK), *Two in the Dark* (US), *Counterfeit* (US), *Trouble Ahead* (US), *Night Waitress* (US) 1936; *Criminal Lawyer* (US), *The Soldier and the Lady* (US) 1937; *The Buccaneer* (US) 1938; *Broken Journey* 1948; *Black Magic* (US) 1949; *The Crimson Pirate* (US/UK), *The Venetian Bird/The Assassin* 1952; *The Beggar's Opera* 1953; *Orders Are Orders* 1954; *Saint Joan* 1957.

grain. A small particle of metallic silver formed on the photographic image during exposure and processing. Individual grains are invisible to the naked eye. Clumped together, they form the dark areas of a picture. But when greatly magnified on a theater screen the irregularity of their structure may produce the imperfect visual effect of "graininess."

Granger, Farley. Actor. Born on July 1, 1925, in San Jose, Calif. Spotted in a Los Angeles little theater production while still a pupil at North Hollywood High School, he was signed by Sam Goldwyn and made his film debut playing a Russian youth in *The North Star* (1943). He appeared in one other WW II propaganda film, *The Purple Heart* (1944), then went to war himself, returning to the screen in 1948 as one of two elitist student murderers in Hitchcock's *Rope.* He then returned to the Goldwyn fold and became typecast in pretty-boy-with-an-ugly-problem roles. He had vulnerable good looks that enabled him to project sensitive soulful young heroes, and many predicted for him a successful future as a Hollywood star, but his mismanaged career failed to live up to expectations, despite occasional good opportunities, like the role of the socialite tennis pro in Hitchcock's *Strangers on a Train* (1951). Following a series of minor vehicles in Hollywood, he went to Italy, where he gave his best performance as Alida Valli's betraying lover in Visconti's *Senso* (1954). He returned to Hollywood for two more films, then abandoned the screen for work on the stage and in TV. He returned to films in the late 60s, appearing mostly in obscure Italian productions.

FILMS INCLUDE: (complete through 1955), *The North Star/Armored Attack* 1943; *The Purple Heart* 1944; *Rope, Enchantment* 1948; *Roseanna McCoy, They Live by Night* 1949; *Side Street, Our Very Own, Edge of Doom* 1950; *Strangers on a Train, Behave Yourself, I Want You* 1951; *O. Henry's Full House* ("The Gift of the Magi" episode), *Hans Christian Andersen* 1952; *The Story of Three Loves* ("Mademoiselle" episode), *Small Town Girl* 1953; *Senso/The Wanton Contessa* (It.) 1954; *The Naked Street, The Girl in the Red Velvet Swing* 1955; *Rogue's Gallery* 1967; *Lo Chiamarano Trinità/They Call Me Trinity* (It.) 1971; *The Man Called Noon* (UK/It.), *Le Serpent/The Serpent* (Fr./Ger.), *White Fang* (It.), *Arnold* 1973; *La Polizia Chiede Aiuto* (It.) 1975; *The Prowler* 1981; *The Imagemaker* 1986.

Granger, Stewart. Actor. *b.* James Stewart, May 6, 1913, in London. *d.* 1993. *ed.* Epsom Coll.; Webber-Douglas School of Dramatic Art. He started his career in British films as an extra in 1933 and assumed his professional name in the late 30s to avoid confusion with Hollywood star James Stewart. After gaining some acting experience with various stage companies he returned to the screen as a leading man in 1939 and in the 40s, along with James Mason, developed into one of the British screen's two top romantic leading men and a consistent box-office draw. His tall, athletic physique and masculine profile attracted Hollywood's attention. In 1950 he signed with MGM and for the next seven years he played romantic swashbucklers, white hunters, and an assortment of other virile he-man types in the studio's high-budget adventure films. He later freelanced with various other studios in Hollywood and on the Continent. In the early 70s, with his film career in decline, he accepted starring roles on American TV. Granger became a US citizen in 1956. In 1971–72 he starred in the TV series 'The Man of Shiloh.' His first two of three aborted marriages were to actresses Elspeth March (1939–49) and Jean SIMMONS (1950–60). Autobiography: *Sparks Fly Upward* (1981).

FILMS: In the UK—*A Southern Maid* (extra) 1933; *Give Her a Ring* (bit); *Mademoiselle Docteur* (1937; *So This Is London* 1939; *Convoy* 1940; *Secret Mission* 1942; *Thursday's Child, The Lamp Still Burns, The Man in Grey* 1943; *Fanny by Gaslight/Man of Evil, Love Story/A Lady Surrenders, Madonna of the Seven Moons* 1944; *Waterloo Road, Caesar and Cleopatra* (as Appolodorus) 1945; *Caravan, The Magic Bow* (as Paganini) 1946; *Captain Boycott* 1947; *Blanche Fury, Saraband for Dead Lovers/Saraband, Woman Hater* 1948; *Adam and Evelyne/Adam and Evelyn* 1949. In the US—*King Solomon's Mines* (as Allan Quartermain) 1950; *Soldiers Three, The Light Touch* 1951; *The Wild North, Scaramouche, The Prisoner of Zenda* (as Rudolf Rassendyll/King Rudolf V) 1952; *Salome, Young Bess, All the Brothers Were Valiant* 1953; *Beau Brummel* (title role), *Green Fire* 1954; *Moonfleet, Footsteps in the Fog* (UK) 1955; *The Last Hunt, Bhowani Junction* (US/UK) 1956; *The Little Hut, Gun Glory* 1957; *The Whole Truth* (UK), *Harry Black/Harry Black and the Tiger* (UK) 1958; *North to Alaska* 1960; *The Secret Partner* (UK), *Sodoma e Gomorra/Sodom and Gomorrah* (as Lot; It./Fr./US) 1961; *Lo Spadaccino di Siena/Le Mercenaire/Swordsman of Siena* (It./Fr.), *La Congiura dei Dieci* (It.), *Marcia o Crepa/Hèros sans Retour/Commando* (It./Bel./Sp./Ger.) 1962; *Il Giorno più Corto* 1963; *The Secret Invasion, Unter Geiern/Frontier Hellcat* (Ger./It./Fr./Yug.) 1964; *The Crooked Road* (UK/Yug.), *Der Ölprinz/Rampage at Apache Wells* (Ger./Yug.), *Old Surehand I. Teil/Flaming Frontier* (Ger./Yug.), *Das Geheimnis der drei Dschunken/Red Dragon* (Ger./It.) 1965; *Das Geheimnis der gelben Mönche/Target for Killing/How to Kill a Lady* (Ger./Aus.), *Gern hab'ich die Frauen gekillt/Requiem for a Secret Agent* (Aus./It./Fr.) 1966; *The Last Safari* (UK), *The Trygon Factor* (UK) 1967; *Any Second Now* (TV movie) 1969; *Sherlock Holmes: The Hound of the Baskervilles* (as Holmes; TV movie) 1972; *The Wild Geese* (UK) 1978; *Hell Hunters* 1978.

Grant, Cary. Actor. *b.* Archibald Alexander Leach, Jan. 18, 1904, Bristol, England. *d.* 1986. The product of a poverty-stricken environment, he ran away from home at 13 to join a traveling acrobatic troupe as song-and-dance man and occasional juggler. Arriving in New York in 1920 on the troupe's US tour, he later found employment as a Coney Island lifeguard. During winter seasons, he carried advertising signs about on stilts when he wasn't engaged as a song-and-dance man in one-night stands. In 1923 he returned to England and began appearing in musical comedies. Arthur Hammerstein noticed him and brought him back to New York to appear in the musical 'Golden Dawn.' This was followed by other Broadway musicals and a summer 1931 engagement in St. Louis, where he played and sang in 12 operettas. He continued to Hollywood and signed a Paramount contract. After a rapid succession of good supporting roles, he was prominently cast as the man in the life of married Marlene Dietrich in Von Sternberg's *Blonde Venus.* Mae West then gave his career a lift when she chose him as her co-star in *She Done Him Wrong.*

In a few years Grant became established as an appealing straight romantic leading man. But it wasn't until 1937–38, now under joint contract with RKO and Columbia, that he hit his stride by unveiling his flair for screwball comedy in such films as *Topper, The Awful Truth, Bringing Up Baby,* and *Holiday.* It was this new screen personality, of a supersophisticated, witty, casual, debonair man-about-town at odds with an upside-down world that made Grant a perennial favorite of cinema audiences for more than three decades. Grant's youthful charm and mastery of his particular style kept the handsome man with the cleft in his chin top man on the Hollywood totem pole of romantic leads when most of his contemporaries either had passed away or were switching to character parts.

Grant's first four marriages ended in divorce: to actress Virginia CHERRILL (1933–35), heiress Barbara Hutton (1942–45), actress Betsy DRAKE (1949–59), and actress Dyan CANNON (1965–68). The latter gave him his only child, a girl, when he was past 60. Grant, never honored with an Oscar, received a special Academy Award in the 1970 ceremonies (for 1969) for his cumulative contribution to films. He had previously been nominated for Oscars twice, for *Penny Serenade* (1941) and *None but the Lonely Heart* (1944). Dashing and dapper to the last, he died of a stroke at 82, survived by his fifth wife (from 1981), nonactress Barbara Harris.

FILMS: *This Is the Night, Sinners in the Sun, Merrily We Go to Hell, The Devil and the Deep, Blonde Venus, Hot Saturday, Madame Butterfly* (as Lt. Pinkerton) 1932; *She Done Him Wrong, The Woman Accused, The Eagle and the Hawk, Gambling Ship, I'm No Angel, Alice in Wonderland* (as the Mock Turtle) 1933; *Thirty-Day Princess, Born to Be Bad, Kiss and Make-Up, Ladies Should Listen* 1934; *Enter Madame, Wings in the Dark, The Last Outpost* 1935; *Sylvia Scarlett, Big Brown Eyes, Suzy, Wedding Present, The Amazing Quest of Ernest Bliss/Romance and Riches/Amazing Adventure* (UK) 1936; *When You're in Love, Topper, The Toast of New York, The Awful Truth* 1937; *Bringing Up Baby, Holiday* 1938; *Gunga Din, Only Angels Have Wings, In Name Only* 1939; *His Girl Friday, My Favorite Wife, The Howards of Virginia* 1940; *The Philadelphia Story, Penny Serenade, Suspicion* 1941; *The Talk of the Town, Once Upon a Honeymoon* 1942; *Mr. Lucky* 1943; *Destination Tokyo, Once Upon a Time, None but the Lonely Heart, Arsenic and Old Lace* 1944; *Without Reservations* (cameo), *Night and Day* (as Cole Porter), *Notorious* 1946; *The Bachelor and the Bobby-Soxer, The Bishop's Wife* 1947; *Mr. Blandings Builds His Dream House, Every Girl Should Be Married* 1948; *I Was a Male War Bride* 1949; *Crisis* 1950; *People Will Talk* 1951; *Room for One More, Monkey Business* 1952; *Dream Wife* 1953; *To Catch a Thief* 1955; *The Pride and the Passion, An Affair to Remember, Kiss Them for Me* 1957; *Indiscreet, Houseboat* 1958; *North by Northwest, Operation Petticoat* 1959; *The Grass Is Greener* 1961; *That Touch of Mink* 1962; *Charade* 1963; *Father Goose* 1964; *Walk Don't Run* 1966.

Grant, Hugh. Actor. Born in 1962, in London. Boyish, sensitive, intelligent leading man of British stage, screen, and TV. Oxford-educated, he made his debut in the university-sponsored comedy film *Privileged* (1982). He later performed at the Nottingham Playhouse and formed his own revue group, the Jockeys of Norfolk. He shared the best actor prize at Venice for his professional debut in the film *Maurice* (1987). His mannered delivery and sophisticated, handsome looks make him a natural for film adaptations of classic novels.

FILMS: *Maurice* (UK) 1987; *White Mischief, The Lair of the White Worm* 1988; *Remando al Viento/Rowing with the Wind* (as Lord Byron) 1989; *Impromptu* (as Frederic Chopin), *Crossing the Line* 1990; *Bitter Moon, Four Weddings and a Funeral, Night Train to Venice, Sirens* 1994; *An Awfully Big Adventure, Nine Months, Restoration, Sense and Sensibility* 1995; *Extreme Measures* (also co-prod.) 1996.

Grant, James Edward. Screenwriter. *b.* 1902, USA. *d.* 1966. A popular pulp novelist, he settled in Hollywood in the mid-30s and contributed original stories and screenplays to many action films, including several John Wayne vehicles. He also produced one of his scripts *The Great John L.* (1945), and directed two of them, *Angel and the Badman* (1947) and *Ring of Fear* (1954).

FILMS INCLUDE (both original stories and screenplays, alone or in collaboration): *Whipsaw* 1935; *Big Brown Eyes, Grand Jury* 1936; *Danger—Love at Work* 1937; *Josette* 1938; *Miracles for Sale* 1939; *Music in My Heart, Boom Town* 1940; *Johnny Eager, The Lady Is Willing* 1942; *Belle of the Yukon* 1944; *The Great John L.* (also prod.) 1945; *Angel and the Badman* (also dir.) 1947; *The Plunderers* 1948; *Johnny Allegro, Sands of Iwo Jima* 1949; *Father Is a Bachelor, Surrender, California Passage* 1950; *Two of a Kind, The Bullfighter and the Lady, Flying Leathernecks* 1951; *Big Jim McLain* 1952; *Hondo* 1953; *Ring of Fear* (also dir.) 1954; *The Last Wagon* 1956; *Three Violent People* 1957; *The Sheepman, The Proud Rebel* 1958; *The Alamo* 1960; *The Comancheros* 1961; *Donovan's Reef, McLintock!* 1963; *Circus World* 1964; *Hostile Guns* 1967.

Grant, Kathryn (Kathy). Actress. Born Olive Kathryn Grandstaff, on Nov. 25, 1933, in Houston. *ed.* U. of Texas; UCLA. The winner of a string of beauty contests from the age of 14, she played leading roles in films of the 50s. Retired shortly after her 1957 marriage to Bing CROSBY. In the mid-70s she hosted a TV talk show in San Francisco.

FILMS INCLUDE: *Arrowhead* 1953; *Forever Female, Rear Window* 1954; *Cell 2455 Death Row, The Phenix City Story* 1955; *Five Against the House, Storm Center, The Wild Party* 1956; *Mister Cory, Guns of Fort Petticoat, The Brothers Rico, Operation Mad Ball* 1957; *The Seventh Voyage of Sinbad* 1958; *Anatomy of a Murder, The Big Circus* 1959.

Grant, Kirby. Actor. *b.* Kirby Grant Hoon, Jr., Nov. 24, 1911, Butte, Mont. *d.* 1985. *ed.* U. of Washington; American Conservatory of Music. A violin prodigy as a child, he later organized and led a dance band and sang on radio. In films from the mid-30s, he played leads in low-budget Westerns and other action pictures, often as a Canadian Mountie. He also starred in the TV series 'Sky King' (1953–54). He was billed as Robert Stanton in a couple of his early films. After retiring from acting, he became a public-relations executive and real-estate developer. He was killed in a car crash, on his way to view a space shuttle launch in Florida.

FILMS INCLUDE: *I Dream Too Much* 1935; *Lawless Valley* 1938; *Three Sons* 1939; *Bullet Code* 1940; *Blondie Goes Latin* 1941; *Hello Frisco Hello* 1943; *Destination Tokyo, The*

Ghost Catchers, Law Men 1944; *Bad Men of the Border, Easy to Look At* 1945; *The Spider Woman Strikes Back, The Lawless Breed* 1946; *Song of Idaho* 1948; *Trail of the Yukon* 1949; *Call of the Klondike* 1950; *Northwest Territory* 1951; *Yukon Gold* 1952; *Northern Patrol* 1953; *The Court-Martial of Billy Mitchell* 1955.

Grant, Lee. Actress, director. Born Lyova Haskell Rosenthal, on Oct. 31, 1927, in New York City. *ed.* Juilliard. The daughter of an actress-model, she made her stage debut at age four in a Metropolitan Opera production. At 11 she became a member of the American Ballet and at 14, after graduating from high school, won a scholarship to the Neighborhood Playhouse. Sidney Kingsley spotted her in a showcase production and cast her in the ingenue role of a shoplifter in 'Detective Story' (1949) on Broadway. She won the Critics Circle Award for her performance. In 1951 she repeated the role in the film version, was nominated for an Oscar, and won the best actress award at the Cannes Festival. Immediately after this spectacular screen debut she became a victim of the McCarthy-era Red Scare machine. She was blacklisted simply because her then-husband, the late playwright Arnold Manoff, had been on the blacklist and she refused to testify against him before the House Un-American Activities Committee. Except for occasional parts, she couldn't find work in films or on TV for the next 12 years. However, she continued to appear on the stage and in the 60s returned to the screen in a variety of memorable leads and character parts. She won the best supporting actress Academy Award for her role in *Shampoo* (1975), sandwiched between two additional Oscar nominations, for *The Landlord* (1970) and *Voyage of the Damned* (1976). Also much on TV, she won Emmy Awards in 1966 (for 'Peyton Place') and 1971 (for the drama 'Neon Ceiling'). She also played the title role in the short-lived series 'Fay' (1975–76). Since 1962 she has been married to producer Joe Feury. Having directed sporadically for the stage and TV, she turned to filmmaking in the late 70s. She tied for the best feature-length documentary Academy Award for her *Down and Out in America* (1986), an exposé of mass poverty, which she directed and narrated. She is the mother of actress Dinah MANOFF.

FILMS: As actress—*Detective Story* 1951; *Storm Fear* 1956; *Middle of the Night* 1959; *The Balcony, An Affair of the Skin* 1963; *Terror in the City* 1966; *Divorce American Style, In the Heat of the Night, Valley of the Dolls* 1967; *Buona Sera Mrs. Campbell, The Big Bounce, Marooned* 1969; *The Landlord, There Was a Crooked Man* 1970; *Plaza Suite* 1971; *Portnoy's Complaint* 1972; *The Internecine Project* 1974; *Shampoo* 1975; *Voyage of the Damned* 1976; *Airport '77* 1977; *Damien—Omen II, The Mafu Cage, The Swarm* 1978; *When You Comin' Back Red Ryder?* 1979; *Little Miss Marker* 1980; *Charlie Chan and the Curse of the Dragon Queen* 1981; *Visiting Hours* (Can.) 1982; *Teachers* 1984; *Sanford Meisner* (doc.; interviewee) 1985; *The Big Town* 1987; *A Billion for Boris* 1990; *Defending Your Life* 1991; *It's My Party, The Substance of Fire* 1996. As director—*The Stronger* (short) 1976; *The Wilmar 8* (doc.), *Tell Me a Riddle* 1980; *What Sex Am I?* (doc.; also narr.) 1985; *Down and Out in America* 1986; *Staying Together* 1992.

Grant, Richard E. Actor. Born on May 5, 1957, in Mbabane, Swaziland, the son of the country's minister of education. In 1976 he quit the University of Cape Town to form a biracial touring theater group comprising former students and members of Athol Fugard and Yvonne Bryceland's Space Theatre. Fed up with the sociopolitical climate of South Africa, he moved in 1982 to London, where he began performing in plays and films, with growing success. At his brightest in eccentric roles.

FILMS: *Withnail and I* 1987; *Hidden City* 1988; *How to Get Ahead in Advertising, Warlock* 1989; *Mountains of the Moon, Killing Dad, Henry and June* 1990; *L.A. Story, Hudson Hawk* 1991; *The Player, Bram Stoker's Dracula* 1992; *Ready to Wear* 1994; *Dangerous Minds, Jack and Sarah* 1995; *Portrait of a Lady, Twelfth Night* 1996.

Granville, Bonita. Actress. *b.* Feb. 2, 1923, New York City. *d.* 1988. The daughter of show people, she went on the stage at three and in the 30s became popular as a child performer in films, specializing in naughty little girl roles. Memorable as the little mischief maker of *These Three* (Oscar nomination, 1936) and as the leader of the hysteria-crazed pack of "bewitched" village girls in *Maid of Salem* (1937). In addition to her many vicious and mischievous roles she also played some engaging young leads and portrayed fictional girl detective Nancy Drew in the film series of the late 30s. She settled into routine leading lady roles in the 40s. She retired from the screen shortly after her 1947 marriage to Texas oilman and entrepreneur Jack Wrather and became an executive in his vast business empire, the Wrather Corporation, with holdings in oil wells, real estate, hotels, and entertainment enterprises, including the Muzak company and television programs. As Bonita Granville Wrather, she became the associate producer, then producer of her husband's 'Lassie' TV series. She held a series of executive positions in the company and succeeded her husband as board chairman after his death in 1984. She was also deeply involved in civic and cultural affairs, serving as chairman of the American Film Institute, trustee of the John F. Kennedy Center, and board member of various organizations and charities.

FILMS INCLUDE: *Westward Passage, Silver Dollar* 1932; *Cavalcade* 1933; *Ah Wilderness!* 1935; *These Three, The Garden of Allah* 1936; *The Plough and the Stars, Maid of Salem, Quality Street, Call It a Day, It's Love I'm After* 1937; *Merrily We Live, Beloved Brat, White Banners, Nancy Drew—Detective* 1938; *Nancy Drew—Reporter, Angels Wash Their Faces* 1939; *Forty Little Mothers, The Mortal Storm, Those Were the Days, Escape, Gallant Sons* 1940; *The People vs. Dr. Kildare, H. M. Pulham Esq.* 1941; *Syncopation, The Glass Key, Now Voyager* 1942; *Hitler's Children* 1943; *Andy Hardy's Blonde Trouble, Song of the Open Road, Youth Runs Wild* 1944; *The Beautiful Cheat* 1945; *Suspense, Breakfast in Hollywood, The Truth About Murder* 1946; *The Guilty* 1947; *Strike It Rich* 1948; *Guilty of Treason* 1950; *The Lone Ranger* 1956; *The Magic of Lassie* (co-prod. only) 1978.

Grapewin, Charley (Charles). Actor. *b.* Dec. 20, 1869, Xenia, Ohio. *d.* 1956. A veteran of vaudeville and the legitimate stage, he played character roles in more than 100 films, typically as a crusty old codger, most memorably as Grampa Joad in *The Grapes of Wrath* (1940) and Jeeter Lester in *Tobacco Road* (1941). In a departure from his typical role, he portrayed old Inspector Queen in several films of the "Ellery Queen" series of the early 40s starring Ralph Bellamy and later William Gargan.

FILMS INCLUDE: *The Shannons of Broadway* 1929; *Only Saps Work* 1930; *Hell's House, The Woman in Room 13* 1932; *The Kiss Before the Mirror, Pilgrimage, Don't Bet on Love* 1933; *The Quitter* (lead), *Caravan, Judge Priest, The President Vanishes* 1934; *Shanghai, Alice Adams* (as Mr. Lamb), *Rendezvous, Ah Wilderness!* 1935; *The Petrified Forest, The Voice of Bugle Ann, Libeled Lady* 1936; *The Good Earth, A Family Affair, Captains Courageous* (as Uncle Salters), *Big City* 1937; *Of Human Hearts, Three Comrades, Artists and Models Abroad* 1938; *The Wizard of Oz* (as Uncle Henry), *Sabotage* 1939; *The Grapes of Wrath* (as Grampa Joad), *Johnny Apollo, Earthbound, Rhythm on the River, Ellery Queen—Master Detective* (as Inspector Queen) 1940; *Tobacco Road* (lead, as

Jeeter Lester), *Ellery Queen and the Murder Ring* (as Inspector Queen) 1941; *They Died with Their Boots On* 1942; *Crash Dive* 1943; *Follow the Boys, The Impatient Years* 1944; *Gunfighters* 1947; *Sand* 1949; *When I Grow Old* 1951.

Grauman, Sidney Patrick. Theater owner. *b.* 1879. *d.* 1950. Hollywood's most famous movie exhibitor opened his first theater in the Yukon in the late 1890s, and went on to operate theaters in San Francisco both before and after the earthquake of 1904. By 1915, he had several theaters in northern California and one in New York. The first film at his first Los Angeles theater, the Million Dollar, was *The Silent Man* (1918), starring William S. Hart. He founded two more theaters in Los Angeles, the Rialto and the Metropolitan, before they were acquired by Paramount in 1924. His first theater on Hollywood Boulevard, the Egyptian, opened on Oct. 18, 1922, with the premiere of *Robin Hood*, starring Douglas Fairbanks. His second and more famous Hollywood theater, the Chinese, opened on May 19, 1927, with the premiere of Cecil B. DeMille's *King of Kings*. It became *de rigueur* for movie stars to leave their handprints and footprints in cement in the forecourt of Grauman's Chinese Theatre. In the 70s, the Mann Theatres Corporation (founded by Ted Mann) took over the Chinese and renamed it Mann's Chinese Theatre.

Graves, Peter. Actor. Born Peter Aurness, on Mar. 18, 1925, in Minneapolis. *ed.* U. of Minnesota. The brother of actor James ARNESS, he was a band musician and radio announcer before breaking into films in 1950. Tall and blond, he played occasional leads but mostly featured roles in films, memorably in *Stalag 17* (1953). But he is more familiar to audiences as the star of the popular TV series 'Mission Impossible.' (He is not to be confused with an actor by the same name [*b.* Oct. 21, 1911, London] who has played light leads and supporting roles in British and occasional Hollywood films since the early 40s.)

FILMS INCLUDE: *Rogue River* 1950; *Fort Defiance* 1951; *Red Planet Mars* 1952; *Stalag 17, Beneath the 12-Mile Reef* 1953; *The Raid, Black Tuesday* 1954; *The Long Gray Line, The Night of the Hunter, The Court-Martial of Billy Mitchell* 1955; *The Beginning of the End* 1957; *Wolf Larsen* 1958; *A Rage to Live* 1965; *Texas Across the River* 1966; *Valley of Mystery* 1967; *The Ballad of Josie, Sergeant Ryker* 1968; *The Five Man Army* 1970; *Sidecar Racers* 1975. *The Mysterious Monsters/Bigfoot the Mysterious Monster* 1976; *Cruise Missile* 1977; *Spree* 1978; *The Clonus Horror* 1979; *Airplane!* 1980; *Airplane II: The Sequel, Savannah Smiles* 1982; *Number One with a Bullet* 1987.

Graves, Ralph. Actor. *b.* Jan. 23, 1900, Cleveland. *d.* 1977. Tall, athletic, handsome leading man of Hollywood silents and early talkies. A discovery of D. W. Griffith, he entered films in 1918 following stage experience in stock. After four years with Griffith, he worked for Mack Sennett and later for other producers. He occasionally collaborated on the scripts and directed several of his own films.

FILMS INCLUDE: *Tinsel, Sporting Life* 1918; *Nobody Home, Scarlet Days, The Greatest Question, The White Heather* 1919; *Mary Ellen Comes to Town, Little Miss Rebellion, Polly with a Past* 1920; *Dream Street* 1921; *Come On Over, The Long Chance, Kindred of the Dust, The Jilt* 1922; *Prodigal Daughters, The Ghost Patrol, Out of Luck, The Extra Girl* 1923; *Yolanda, Daughters of Today* 1924; *Womanpower, The Country Beyond, Blarney* 1926; *Rich Men's Sons* (also dir.), *A Reno Divorce* (also dir., story), *The Swell-Head* (also dir.), *Alias the Deacon* 1927; *The Cheer Leader, That Certain Thing, Submarine, Bachelor's Paradise, The Sideshow, Bitter Sweets* 1928; *Fatal Warning* (serial), *The Eternal Woman, The Flying Fleet, The Glad Rag Doll, Flight* (also story), *The Song of Love* 1929; *Ladies of Leisure, Hell's Island* 1930; *Dirigible, Salvation Nell, A Dangerous Affair* 1931; *Huddle, War Correspondent* 1932; *Born to Be Bad* (story only) 1934; *The Black Coin* (serial) 1936; *Outlaws of the Orient* (story only) 1937; *Street of Missing Men* 1939; *Batman and Robin* (serial), *Alimony* 1949.

Graves, Rupert. Actor. Born June 30, 1963, in Weston-Super-Mare, England. Striking, attractive actor with an engaging onscreen presence. He achieved early success on the London stage with his ability to portray sensitive roles and has since distinguished himself on both sides of the Atlantic in the films *Maurice* (1987) and *The Madness of King George* (1994).

FILMS: *A Room with a View* 1985; *Maurice* 1987; *A Handful of Dust* 1988; *The Children* 1990; *Where Angels Fear to Tread* 1991; *Damage* 1992; *The Madness of King George* 1994; *Intimate Relations* 1996; *Innocent Sleep* 1997.

Gravey (known in the US as **Gravet**), **Fernand.** Actor. *b.* Fernand Mertens, Dec. 25, 1904, Brussels. *d.* 1970. The son of a theatrical couple, he began his stage career at five in a Brussels theater that was directed by his father. He was sent to school in England and later served with the British merchant marine. As a result he became bilingual, a fact that helpéd him to appear with success on both the Paris stage and Broadway and in French, British, and American films. He made his screen debut in 1930 and subsequently appeared in numerous French films. He enjoyed moderate popularity as the charming, elegant star of a number of Hollywood productions of the late 30s, memorably as Johann Strauss in *The Great Waltz* (1938). During WW II he served with distinction in the French Secret Army during the German Occupation, then became an officer of the Foreign Legion. He was wounded and received several decorations.

FILMS INCLUDE: *L'Amour chante* 1930; *Tu seras Duchesse* 1931; *Coiffeur pour Dames* 1932; *La Guerre des Valses* (Fr./Ger.), *Bitter Sweet* (UK) 1933; *The Queen's Affair* (UK) 1934; *Romance hongroise* 1935; *Mister Flow/Compliments of Mr. Flow, Le Grand Refrain/Symphonie d'Amour* 1936; *Le Mensonge de Nina Petrovna/The Lie of Nina Petrovna, The King and the Chorus Girl* (US) 1937; *Fools for Scandal* (US), *The Great Waltz* (as Johann Strauss; US) 1938; *Le Paradis perdu/Four Flights to Love* 1940; *Histoire de Rire/Foolish Husbands* 1941; *La Nuit fantastique, Le Capitaine Fracasse* 1942; *Domino* 1943; *La Ronde* 1950; *Si Versailles m'etait conté/Royal Affairs in Versailles* (as Molière) 1954; *Treize a Table, Mitsou* 1956; *Les Petits Matins* 1961; *How to Steal a Million* (US) 1966; *La Bataille de San Sebastian/Guns for San Sebastian* (Fr./It./US/Mex.) 1968; *The Madwoman of Chaillot* (UK) 1969; *Les Caprices de Marie/Give Her the Moon, La Promesse de l'Aube/Promise at Dawn* 1970.

Gray, Coleen. Actress. Born Doris Jensen, on Oct. 23, 1922, in Staplehurst, Nebr., of Danish descent. She became active in college dramatics at Hamline University (graduated summa cum laude) and appeared with various little theaters before breaking into films in the mid-40s. She has played competent leads in many Hollywood productions, mostly in crime dramas, Westerns, and action pictures. She co-starred in the TV series 'Window on Main Street' (1961–62).

FILMS INCLUDE: *State Fair* 1945; *Kiss of Death, Nightmare Alley* 1947; *Fury at Furnace Creek, Red River* 1948; *Sand* 1949; *Riding High, Father Is a Bachelor, The Sleeping City* 1950; *Lucky Nick Cain/I'll Get You for This, Apache Drums* 1951; *Models Inc., Kansas City Confidential* 1952; *Sabre Jet, The Vanquished* 1953; *Arrow in the Dust* 1954; *Las Vegas Shakedown, Tennessee's Partner* 1955; *The Killing* 1956; *The Vampire* 1957; *Hell's Five Hours, Johnny Rocco* 1958; *The Leech Woman* 1960; *Phantom Planet* 1961; *Town Tamer* 1965; *P.J.* 1968; *The Late Liz* 1971; *Cry from the Mountain* 1986.

Gray, Dolores. Actress, singer. Born on June 7, 1924, in Chicago. Statuesque, high-cheekboned blonde vocalist of Broadway and London stage musicals, she exported her striking presence to a handful of Hollywood films.

FILMS: *Lady for a Night* 1941; *Mr. Skeffingon* 1944; *It's Always Fair Weather, Kismet* 1955; *The Opposite Sex* 1956; *Designing Woman* 1957.

Gray, Dulcie. Actress. Born Dulcie Bailey, on Nov. 20, 1919 in Kuala Lumpur, West Malaysia. Soft-spoken, gentle-mannered leading lady of British films of the 40s. She married actor Michael DENISON in 1939.

FEATURE FILMS: *2,000 Women, Madonna of the Seven Moons* 1944; *A Place of One's Own, They Were Sisters* 1945; *Wanted for Murder, The Years Between, A Man About the House* 1946; *Mine Own Executioner* 1947; *My Brother Jonathan, The Glass Mountain* 1948; *The Franchise Affair* 1950; *Angels One Five* 1952; *There Was a Young Lady* 1953; *A Man Could Get Killed* (US) 1966.

Gray, Gilda. Actress. *b.* Marianna Michalska, Oct. 24, 1901, Krakow, Poland. *d.* 1959. In the US from age seven, she starred in a number of Hollywood silents and is credited with introducing the dance called "the shimmy."

FILMS INCLUDE: *Lawful Larceny* 1923; *Aloma of the South Seas* 1926; *Cabaret, The Devil Dancer* 1928; *Piccadilly* (UK) 1929; *Rose Marie, The Great Ziegfeld* 1936.

Gray, Lawrence. Actor, singer. *b.* July 28, 1898, San Francisco. *d.* 1970. Robust leading man of Hollywood late silents and early talkies. Starred opposite such leading ladies as Gloria Swanson, Marion Davies, Colleen Moore, and Betty Bronson. A production executive from the mid-30s, he spent the last 33 years of his life in Mexico as a co-ordinator between the American and Mexican film industries.

FILMS INCLUDE: *The Dressmaker from Paris, Are Parents People?, The Coast of Folly, Stage Struck* 1925; *The American Venus, The Untamed Lady, The Palm Beach Girl, Everybody's Acting, Kid Boots, Love 'Em and Leave 'Em* 1926; *Ankles Preferred, Convoy, The Telephone Girl, The Callahans and the Murphys, After Midnight, Pajamas, Ladies Must Dress* 1927; *Love Hungry, Shadows of the Night, The Patsy, Oh Kay!, Marriage by Contract* 1928; *Trent's Last Case, The Rainbow, Marianne, The Gay Nineties* 1929; *The Florodora Girl, Children of Pleasure, Spring Is Here, Sunny, Temptation* 1930; *Going Wild, Man of the World, She-Wolf* 1931; *Here Comes the Groom* 1934; *Timber War* 1936.

Gray, Nadia. Actress. Born Nadia Kujnir-Herescu, on Nov. 23, 1923, in Bucharest (or Berlin), to a Russian father and a Bessarabian mother. Cosmopolitan leading lady and second lead of numerous Continental, British, and American films. She arrived in Paris as a political refugee in the late 40s, after the Communist takeover of Rumania, with her first husband, a pilot and purportedly a former prince, and made her screen debut in 1948. She subsequently appeared in many international productions, perhaps most memorably in Fellini's *La Dolce Vita* (1960), in which she performed an intriguing stripping act in the orgy sequence. In the late 60s she married a Manhattan lawyer and moved to New York, where she headlined a nightclub show in 1976.

FILMS INCLUDE: *L'Inconnue d'un Soir* (Fr.) 1948; *Monseigneur* (Fr.), *The Spider and the Fly* (UK) 1949; *Night Without Stars* (UK), *Valley of the Eagles* (UK) 1951; *Top Secret/Mr. Potts Goes to Moscow* (UK), *Moglie per una Notte/Wife for a Night* (It.) 1952; *Puccini* (It.), *Gran Varietà* (It.), *La Vierge du Rhin* (Fr.) 1953; *Le Avventure di Giacomo Casanova/Sins of Casanova* (It./Fr.), *Casa Ricordi/House of Ricordi* (It./Fr.), *Carosello Napoletano/Neapolitan Carousel* (It.) 1954; *Musik im Blut* (Ger.) 1955; *Folies-Bergère* (Fr.), *Une Parisienne* (Fr./It.), *Sénéchal le Magnifique/Senechal the Magnificent (Fr./It.)* 1957; *Vacanze a Ischia/Holiday Island* (It./Fr./Ger.), *The Captain's Table* (UK) 1958; *La Dolce Vita* (It./Fr.), *Mr. Topaze/I Like Money* (UK), *Candide* (Fr.) 1960; *Maniac* (UK) 1963; *The Crooked Road* (UK/Yug.) 1965; *The Naked Runner* (UK), *Two for the Road* (US/UK), *Le plus Vieux Métier du Monde/The Oldest Profession* (Fr./It./Ger.) 1967; *Rue Haute* (Bel./Fr.) 1976.

Gray, Sally. Actress. Born Constance Vera Stevens, on Feb. 14, 1916, in Holloway, England. Beautiful blonde leading lady of British films of the 30s and 40s, following experience on the London stage from the age of ten. A nervous breakdown temporarily interrupted her career in the early 40s.

FILMS INCLUDE: *School for Scandal* 1930; *Checkmate* 1935; *Cheer Up* 1936; *Cafe Colette* 1937; *The Saint in London, A Window in London/Lady in Distress* 1939; *Dangerous Moonlight/Suicide Squadron* 1941; *Carnival, Green for Danger* 1946; *They Made Me a Fugitive* 1947; *Silent Dust* 1948; *Obsession/The Hidden Room* 1949; *Escape Route* 1952.

gray scale. A graduated range of tones extending from white through gray to black, used in the film laboratory as a standard for controlling the processing of black-and-white film.

Gray, Spalding. Actor. Born in 1941, in Barrington, R.I. On the stage from the mid-60s, he appeared in experimental productions in Houston and off Broadway, then toured the US, Europe, and Australia with a one-man show of autobiographical monologues. One of these, the fascinating *Swimming to Cambodia,* was filmed successfully by director Jonathan DEMME in 1987. He made his Broadway debut in 'Our Town' in 1988.

FILMS: *Cowards* 1970; *The Killing Fields* 1984; *Almost You* 1985; *Hard Choices, True Stories* 1986; *Swimming to Cambodia* (also sc.) 1987; *Stars and Bars, Clara's Heart, Beaches* 1988; *Heavy Petting* 1989; *King of the Hill, The Pickle* 1993; *The Paper* 1994, *Bad Company, Beyond Rangoon* 1995; *Diabolique, Gray's Anatomy* 1996; *Drunks* 1997.

Grayson, Kathryn. Actress, singer. Born Zelma Kathryn Hedrick, on Feb. 9, 1922, in Winston-Salem, N.C. Discovered by MGM talent scouts while she was singing on Eddie Cantor's radio show. She brought a florid coloratura soprano, a busty figure, a pretty heart-shaped face, and a perky turned-up nose to starring roles in many lavish musical films of the 40s and early 50s, mainly at MGM. Later appeared on the stage and in nightclubs. Formerly married to actor John Shelton (1940–46) and singer-actor Johnny Johnston (1947–51).

FILMS: *Andy Hardy's Private Secretary* 1941; *The Vanishing Virginian, Rio Rita, Seven Sweethearts* 1942; *Thousands Cheer* 1943; *Anchors Aweigh* 1945; *Ziegfeld Follies, Two Sisters from Boston, Till the Clouds Roll By* 1946; *It Happened in Brooklyn* 1947; *The Kissing Bandit* 1948; *That Midnight Kiss* 1949; *The Toast of New Orleans* 1950; *Grounds for Marriage, Show Boat* 1951; *Lovely to Look At* 1952; *The Desert Song, So This Is Love, Kiss Me Kate* 1953; *The Vagabond King* 1956.

Grazer, Brian. Producer. Born on July 12, 1951, in Los Angeles, Calif. Former script reader and talent agent who teamed with director Ron HOWARD to form production company Imagine Films Entertainment and has since produced a variety of commercially successful domestic dramas and comedies.

FILMS INCLUDE: *Night Shift* 1982; *Splash* 1983; *Real Genius* 1984; *Spies Like Us* 1985; *Armed and Dangerous* (also story) 1986; *Like Father Like Son* 1987; *Vibes* 1988; *The 'burbs, Parenthood, The Dream Team* 1989; *Cry-Baby* (co-exec. pr.), *Problem Child, Kindergarten Cop* 1990; *The Doors* (co-exec. pr.), *Closet Land* (co-exec. pr.), *Backdraft* (exec. pr.), *My Girl*

1991; *Far and Away, House Sitter, Boomerang* 1992; *Cop and a Half* 1993; *The Cowboy Way, Greedy, My Girl 2, The Paper* 1994; *Apollo 13* 1995; *No Fear, The Nutty Professor, Sgt. Bilko* 1996; *Liar, Liar* 1997.

Great Britain. See UNITED KINGDOM.

Greco, Juliette. Actress. Born in 1926, in Montpelier, France. A popular singer of Paris cafés frequented by existentialists in the mid-40s, she appeared in French and international films of the 50s and 60s. Her second husband (1966–77) was actor Michel PICCOLI.

FILMS INCLUDE: *Au Royaume des Cieux* 1949; *Orphée/Orpheus* 1950; *Sans laisser d'Adresse* 1951; *Le Gantelet vert/The Green Glove* (Fr./US) 1952; *Quand tu liras cette Lettre* 1953; *Eléna et les Hommes/Paris Does Strange Things* 1956; *The Sun Also Rises* (US) 1957; *Bonjour Tristesse* (UK), *Naked Earth* (UK), *The Roots of Heaven* (US) 1958; *Crack in the Mirror* (US) 1960; *The Big Gamble* (US) 1961; *Maléfices/Where the Truth Lies* 1962; *Onkel Toms Hütte/Uncle Tom's Cabin* (Ger./Fr./It./Yug.) 1965; *La Nuit des Généraux/The Night of the Generals* (Fr./UK) 1967.

Grede, Kjell. Director. Born in 1936, in Stockholm. *ed.* Stockholm U. One of Sweden's leading contemporary directors, a former assistant to Ingmar BERGMAN. He won the Special Jury Award at Venice for *Hip Hip Hurrah!* (1987). He usually writes his own scripts. Formerly (1960–72) married to actress Bibi ANDERSSON.

FEATURE FILMS: *Hugo and Josephine* 1967; *Harry Munter* 1969; *Claire Lust* 1972; *A Simple Melody* 1974; *My Beloved* 1979; *Hip Hip Hurrah!* 1987; *Good Evening, Mr. Wallenberg* 1990.

Greece. Regular film production in "the cradle of Democracy" did not start until the early 20s. The first important documentary, *Greek Wonder,* was made in 1921, and the first feature film, *A Child Abandoned,* in 1925. The latter set the tone and the style for a dominant genre in subsequent Greek films—highly emotional melodramas, staged rather theatrically and played by theater actors. Another genre that developed at the same time was light comedy, typically Mediterranean in humor and temperament. Films of both genres were usually augmented by folkloristic color and an abundance of song and dance. The first important Greek production was, inevitably, an adaptation of a classical tragedy, *Prometheus Bound,* produced and directed in 1927 by Dimitris Gaziadis. Other films of certain quality in that period were *Maria Pendaiosita* (1930) and the *Sorcerer of Athens* (1931), both directed by Achilles Madras, *Daphnis and Chloe* (1931), directed by Orestes Laskos, and Gaziadis's *Astero the Shepherd* (1932).

Film production in Greece declined sharply in quantity and quality during the Metaxas dictatorship (1936–41) and the German Occupation (1941–44), but in the midst of the civil war between royalists and Communists (1944–50) a revival began to take place which was due partly to the injection of American aid into the Greek economy in 1947. Studios were reconstructed and production picked up considerably. Greek directors of the early 50s were strongly influenced by Italian neorealism. Films such as Grigori Grigorious's *Bitter Bread* (1950) and Stelios Tatasopoulos's *Black Earth* (1952) were shot on location with nonprofessionals as actors.

In the mid-50s, Greece began moving into the forefront of international cinema. The film that provided the impetus was Michael CACOYANNIS's *Stella,* which was highly acclaimed at the 1956 Cannes Film Festival. Subsequently, Greek films began appearing with increasing frequency in international competition. In 1960, Melina MERCOURI, the star of *Stella,* won the Cannes best actress award for her performance in *Never on Sunday,* directed by expatriate American director Jules Dassin, her husband. (In the 1980s, Mercouri, as Greece's minister of culture and science, would promote government support of Greek filmmaking.) Another Greek star established during that period was Georges Foundas, who gained international recognition in *Stella, Never on Sunday,* and *Zorba the Greek,* and Irene PAPAS, the tragedienne of *Antigone* and *Electra.* On the lighter side, Aliki (Alice) Voyuklakis, "the Greek Brigitte Bardot," was winning fans in Europe.

Two Greek composers who became internationally famous for their melodic scores of Greek films are Manos HADJIDAKIS, who scored *Stella* and won an Academy Award for *Never on Sunday,* and Mikis THEODORAKIS, the composer of *Zorba the Greek.* Leading directors, in addition to Cacoyannis, included Nikos Koundouros (*The Magic City, The Ogre of Athens*), George Tzavellas (*Counterfeit Pound Sterling, Antigone*), Vassilis Georgiadis (*Good Morning Athens*), Theo Angelopoulos (*Megalexandros*), and Pantelis Voulgaris (*Engagement of Anna*). Creative filmmaking in Greece declined after the takeover of the government by a military junta in 1967, with many of the Greek artists in political prisons or in exile, but was on a revival course soon after the return to democracy in 1974. However, filmmakers had to face growing market pressures: lower cinema attendances (due in part to the spread of television, introduced to Greece in the late 60s) and the increasing domination of the market by American films.

By the 80s, several large studios, such as Finos Films, had closed and independent producers had dwindled to a few. Through the Greek Film Center (founded in 1970), the government increased its financial support for Greek filmmaking, spurring a renewal of the industry. Hellas Film was established to help promote Greek films internationally and oversee co-productions with foreign partners. Notable German directors of recent years have included Apostolis Doxiadis, George Stamboulopoulos, Costas Ferris, Tonia Marketaki, Nikos Vergitsis, and George Katakouzinos.

Green, Adolph. Librettist, lyricist, screenwriter, performer. Born on Dec. 2, 1915, in the Bronx, N.Y. A lifelong collaborator with Betty COMDEN, with whom he began performing in nightclubs in 1944, then wrote book and lyrics for many hit Broadway musicals and screenplays for a number of highly successful motion pictures. He also appeared as an actor in several films. He married actress Phyllis Newman in 1960.

FILMS: As screenwriter—*Good News* 1947; *Take Me Out to the Ball Game* (co-lyr. only), *The Barkleys of Broadway, On the Town* 1950; *Singin' in the Rain* 1952; *The Band Wagon* 1953; *It's Always Fair Weather* 1955; *Auntie Mame* 1958; *Bells Are Ringing* 1960; *What a Way to Go* 1964. As actor—*Greenwich Village* 1944; *Simon* 1980; *My Favorite Year* 1982; *Garbo Talks* 1984.

Green, Alfred E. Director. *b.* 1889, Ferris, Calif. *d.* 1960. He entered films in 1912 as an actor in the Selig Polyscope company's jungle dramas. He later became an assistant to Colin CAMPBELL and directed two-reel comedies before making his debut as a feature director in 1917. He gained success in the early 20s with a couple of Mary Pickford vehicles and later in the silent era enhanced his reputation with a number of box-office hits starring Wallace Reid, Thomas Meighan, and Colleen Moore. His career as a director extended into the mid-50s, but his silent films were mostly low-budget productions, which he turned out at an enormously prolific rate. Nonetheless, he had the reputation of being a solid craftsman who, although not too choosy about his material, was capable of delivering a smooth, entertaining product. He directed Bette Davis in her Oscar-winning performance in *Dangerous* (1935) and at various times handled such fine actors as John Barrymore, George Arliss, and Edward G. Robinson. His biggest commercial success in the talkie era, *The Jolson Story* (1946), came late in his career. But it was followed by a string of low-grade films, and by 1954 the aging Green, slowed by arthritis, was out of films and into routine TV fare.

FEATURE FILMS: *The Princess of Patches, Little Lost Sister, The Lad and the Lion* 1917; *The Web of Chance* 1919; *The Double-Dyed Deceiver, Silk Husbands and Calico Wives* 1920; *Just Out of College, The Man Who Had Everything, Through the Back Door* (co-dir. with Jack Pickford), *Little Lord Fauntleroy* (co-dir. with Pickford) 1921; *Come on Over, Our Leading Citizen, The Bachelor Daddy, The Ghost Breaker, The Man Who Saw Tomorrow, Back Home and Broke* 1922; *The Ne'er-Do-Well, Woman Proof* 1923; *Pied Piper Malone, In Hollywood with Potash and Perlmutter, Inez from Hollywood* 1924; *Sally, The Talker, The Man Who Found Himself* 1925; *Irene, Ella Cinders, It Must Be Love, Ladies at Play, The Girl from Montmartre* 1926; *Is Zat So?, The Auctioneer, Two Girls Wanted, Come to My House* 1927; *Honor Bound* 1928; *Making the Grade, Disraeli* 1929; *The Green Goddess, The Man from Blankley's, Old English, Sweet Kitty Bellairs* 1930; *Smart Money, Men of the Sky, The Road to Singapore* 1931; *Union Depot, It's Tough to Be Famous, The Rich Are Always with Us, The Dark Horse, Silver Dollar* 1932; *Parachute Jumper, Baby Face, The Narrow Corner, I Loved a Woman* 1933; *Dark Hazard, As the Earth Turns, The Merry Frinks, Housewife, Side Streets, A Lost Lady, Gentlemen Are Born* 1934; *Sweet Music, The Girl from 10th Avenue, The Goose and the Gander, Here's to Romance, Dangerous* 1935; *Colleen, The Golden Arrow, They Met in a Taxi, Two in a Crowd, More Than a Secretary* 1936; *Let's Get Married, The League of Frightened Men, Mr. Dodd Takes the Air, Thoroughbreds Don't Cry* 1937; *The Duke of West Point, Ride a Crooked Mile* 1938; *King of the Turf, The Gracie Allen Murder Case, 20,000 Men a Year* 1939; *Shooting High, South of Pago-Pago, Flowing Gold, East of the River* 1940; *Adventure in Washington, Badlands of Dakota* 1941; *The Mayor of 44th Street, Meet the Stewarts* 1942; *Appointment in Berlin, There's Something About a Soldier* 1943; *Mr. Winkle Goes to War, Strange Affair* 1944; *A Thousand and One Nights* 1945; *Tars and Spars, The Jolson Story* 1946; *The Fabulous Dorseys, Copacabana* 1947; *Four Faces West, The Girl from Manhattan* 1948; *Cover-Up* 1949; *The Jackie Robinson Story, Sierra* 1950; *Two Gals and a Guy* 1951; *Invasion USA* 1952; *Paris Model, The Eddie Cantor Story* 1953; *Top Banana* 1954.

Green, Guy. Director, former director of photography. Born in 1913, in Somerset, England. Entered British films in 1929 as an assistant cameraman and during WW II was the camera operator on such distinguished wartime productions as *One of Our Aircraft Is Missing* and *In Which We Serve* (both 1942). As a director of photography from 1944, he won an Academy Award for his work on David Lean's *Great Expectations* (1946) and was behind the camera on such films as *The Way Ahead* (1944), *Blanche Fury* (1947), *Oliver Twist* (1948), *The Passionate Friends/One Woman's Story* (1949), *Madeleine* (1951), *Captain Horatio Hornblower* (1951), *The Beggar's Opera* (1953), and *I Am a Camera* (1955). He then turned to directing and showed early promise with a number of well-executed modest-scale films, a promise that was fulfilled in 1960 and 1961 with two sensitive films many consider his best, *The Angry Silence* and *The Mark*. The success of these films led to directing assignments in Hollywood, to higher budgets, and to a string of disappointing films marred by exaggerated sentimentality and/or overblown pretense.

FILMS (as director): *River Boat* 1954; *Portrait of Alison* 1955; *Lost/Tears for Simon, House of Secrets/Triple Deception* 1956; *The Snorkel, Sea of Sand/Desert Patrol* 1958; *S.O.S. Pacific* 1959; *The Angry Silence* 1960; *The Mark* 1961; *Light in the Piazza* (US) 1962; *Diamond Head* (US) 1963; *A Patch of Blue* (also co-exec. prod., sc.; US) 1965; *Pretty Polly/A Matter of Innocence* 1967; *The Magus* 1968; *A Walk in the Spring Rain* (also co-exec. prod.; US) 1970; *Luther* 1973; *Once Is Not Enough/Jacqueline Susann's Once Is Not Enough* (US) 1975; *L'Avvocato del Diavolo* (It.) 1977.

Green, Janet. Screenwriter, playwright. Born on July 4, 1914, in Hitchin, England. A former actress, she began writing plays in the mid-40s and screenplays in the 50s, sometimes in collaboration with her husband, producer-writer John McCormick.

FILMS INCLUDE: *The Clouded Yellow* (also story) 1950; *Cast a Dark Shadow* (novel and play basis only) 1955; *Lost/Tears for Simon, The Long Arm/The Third Key* 1956; *Sapphire* 1959; *Midnight Lace* (play basis only; US) 1960; *Victim* 1961; *Life for Ruth/Walk in the Shadow* (from own play) 1962; *Seven Women* (US) 1966.

Green, Johnny. Composer, conductor, music director. *b.* Oct. 10, 1908, New York City. *d.* 1989. After graduating from Harvard (economics) at age 20, he first entered films as rehearsal pianist for Paramount in 1929. The following year he began arranging and composing for films while also pursuing a successful musical career as a bandleader in nightclubs, radio, and concert halls and a composer of hit songs, among them 'I Cover the Waterfront' and 'Body and Soul.' From 1949 till 1958 he served as MGM's general music director. Won Academy Awards for collaborations on the scoring of *Easter Parade, An American in Paris, West Side Story,* and *Oliver!*, among 14 Oscar nominations. In addition, he won an Academy Award in the one-reel live-action category for producing *The Merry Wives of Windsor Overture* (1953) in the MGM 'Concert Hall' series of shorts, of which he was the supervisor and regular conductor. Has was also active as a TV composer and concert hall conductor. He produced the first two Oscar telecasts (1953–54) and conducted ten more. As a liberal activist and a vocal civil rights campaigner for the Hollywood Independent Citizens Committee of the Arts, Sciences and Professions (HICCASP), Green came under the threat of the infamous blacklist in 1952. But a reluctant statement in which he asserted his patriotic beliefs saved his career. His second of three marriages was to actress Betty FURNESS. In 1943 he married the six-foot-tall former MGM starlet Bonnie Waters.

FILMS INCLUDE: *The Sap from Syracuse* 1930; *Start Cheering* 1938; *Stage Door Canteen* 1943; *Bathing Beauty* 1944; *Weekend at the Waldorf* 1945; *Easy to Wed* 1946; *Fiesta, Something in the Wind, It Happened in Brooklyn* 1947; *Easter Parade* 1948. *The Inspector General* 1949; *The Toast of New Orleans, Summer Stock* 1950; *The Great Caruso, An American in Paris* 1951; *It's a Big Country, Because You're Mine* 1952; *Rhapsody, Brigadoon* 1954; *Invitation to the Dance, High Society* 1956; *Raintree County* 1957; *Pepe* 1960; *West Side Story* 1961; *Bye Bye Birdie, Twilight of Honor* 1963; *Alvarez Kelly* 1966; *Oliver!* 1968; *They Shoot Horses Don't They?* (also assoc. prod.) 1969.

Green, Mitzi. Actress. *b.* Elizabeth Keno, Oct. 22, 1920, Bronx, N.Y. *d.* 1969. Child star of Paramount early talkies. She began performing on the stage at three in her parents' vaudeville act and entered films at nine. Publicized as Little Mitzi, she remained popular on the screen for several years through such parts as Becky Thatcher in *Tom Sawyer* (1930) and the title role in *Little Orphan Annie* (1932). She retired from the screen at 14, later returning in supporting adult roles in two films of the early

50s. She died of cancer at 48, leaving her husband of 27 years, director Joseph PEVNEY.

FILMS: *The Marriage Playground* 1929; *Honey, Paramount on Parade, Love Among the Millionaires, The Sante Fe Trail, Tom Sawyer* (as Becky Thatcher) 1930; *Finn and Hattie, Skippy, The Stolen Jools* (short), *Dude Ranch, Newly Rich, Huckleberry Finn* (again as Becky Thatcher) 1931; *Girl Crazy, Little Orphan Annie* (title role) 1932; *Transatlantic Merry-Go-Round* 1934; *Walk with Music* 1940; *Lost in Alaska, Bloodhounds of Broadway* 1952.

Green, Nigel. Actor. *b.* 1924, Pretoria, South Africa. *d.* 1972. Forceful character actor of many British and some Hollywood films, following stage and TV experience. Died of an accidental overdose of sleeping pills.

FILMS INCLUDE: *Meet Mr. Malcolm* 1953; *The Sea Shall Not Have Them* 1955; *Reach for the Sky* 1956; *Amère Victoire/Bitter Victory* (Fr.) 1957; *The Criminal/The Concrete Jungle, Sword of Sherwood Forest* (as Little John) 1960; *Mysterious Island* 1961; *Jason and the Argonauts* (as Hercules) 1963; *Zulu, The Masque of the Red Death* 1964; *The Ipcress File, The Skull, The Face of Fu Manchu* 1965; *Khartoum, Let's Kill Uncle; Deadlier Than the Male* 1966; *Tobruk* (US), *Africa—Texas Style!* (US/UK) 1967; *The Pink Jungle* (US), *Play Dirty* 1968; *Fräulein Doktor* (It./Yug.), *The Wrecking Crew* (US) 1969; *The Kremlin Letter* (US) 1970; *The Ruling Class* 1972.

Greenaway, Peter. Director, screenwriter. Born in 1942, in Wales. Ingenious, idiosyncratic British filmmaker. Trained as a painter at the Walthamstow Art College, he first exhibited his work in 1964. The following year he entered films as an editor and for the next 11 years worked in that capacity on numerous documentaries for Britain's Central Office of Information and other employers. Meanwhile, starting in 1966, he also directed experimental shorts and medium-length documentary films, several of which fetched top awards at international film festivals. He turned out his first feature, *The Falls,* in 1980 under the auspices of the British Film Institute. The highly acclaimed *The Draughtsman's Contract* (1983) established him internationally as a creative, original talent. Typically, his films offer stunning, distinctive visuals and sparse, enigmatic narratives. "Cinema is too rich and capable a medium to be merely left to story tellers," he stated. He was awarded a best artistic contribution prize at Cannes for *Drowning by Numbers* (1988). The controversy over the original X rating of his 1989 film *The Cook the Thief His Wife and Her Lover* forced the Motion Picture Association of America to reevaluate its rating system and assign a new category, NC-17, for films containing erotic but not blatantly pornographic material.

FILMS: Short (partial list)—*Train* 1966; *Five Postcards from Capital Cities* 1967; *Intervals* 1969; *Erosion* 1971; *Windows* 1975; *A Walk Through H, Vertical Features Remake* 1978; *Act of God, Zandra Rhodes* 1981; *Four American Composers* (TV series) 1983; *Making a Splash* 1984; *A TV Dante: Canto 5* 1984; *Inside Rooms: The Bathroom* 1985. Features (complete)—*The Falls* 1980; *The Draughtsman's Contract* 1983; *A Zed and Two Noughts* (UK/Holl.) 1985; *The Belly of an Architect* 1987; *Drowning by Numbers* 1988; *The Cook the Thief His Wife and Her Lover* (UK/Fr./Holl.) 1989; *Prospero's Books* 1991; *The Baby of Macon, Darwin* 1993; *Pillow Book* 1997.

Greenberg, Jerry. Film editor. American editor who distinguished himself in the 1970s with his work on furiously paced urban dramas, including *The French Connection*, and has since applied the same vigorous pacing to a variety of genres, including war dramas (*Apocalypse Now*) and epics (*Reds*).

FILMS INCLUDE: *The Subject Was Roses, Bye Bye Braverman* 1968; *Alice's Restaurant* (assoc. ed.) 1969; *The Boys in the Band* 1970; *The French Connection, They Might Be Giants* 1971; *Come Back Charleston Blue, The Stoolie* 1972; *Electra Glide in Blue, The Seven Ups* 1973; *The Taking of Pelham 1, 2, 3* 1974; *The Happy Hooker* 1975; *The Missouri Breaks* 1976; *Apocalypse Now, Kramer vs. Kramer* 1979; *Dressed to Kill, Heaven's Gate* 1980; *Reds* (addnl. ed.) 1981; *Still of the Night* 1982; *Scarface* 1983; *Body Double* 1984; *Savage Dawn* 1985; *No Mercy, Wise Guys* 1986; *The Untouchables* 1987; *The Accused* 1988; *National Lampoon's Christmas Vacation* 1989; *Awakenings, Collision Course* 1990.

Greene, Clarence. Producer, screenwriter. Born in 1918, in New York City. *ed.* St. John's U. (law). Formed a partnership with director Russell Rouse which resulted in a number of unconventional films. They shared Academy Awards for the story and screenplay of *The Well* (1951) and won the Oscar for the story of *Pillow Talk* (1959). Greene also co-produced and wrote for the TV series 'Tightrope.'

FILMS INCLUDE (as producer-screenwriter): *The Town Went Wild* 1945; *D.O.A.* (co-sc. only) 1950; *The Well* 1951; *The Thief* 1952; *Wicked Woman* 1954; *New York Confidential* 1955; *UFO* (prod. only), *The Fastest Gun Alive* (prod. only) 1956; *Thunder in the Sun* (prod. only) *Pillow Talk* (co-story only) 1959; *A House Is Not a Home* 1964; *The Oscar* 1966; *The Caper of the Golden Bulls* (prod. only) 1967; *Color Me Dead* (co-story basis only; Austral.) 1969; *D.O.A.* (co-story basis only) 1988.

Greene, David. Director. Born on Feb. 22, 1921, in Manchester, England. A former actor, he appeared in repertory with the Old Vic and other stage companies as well as in several British films of the late 40s, including *The Golden Madonna* (1949) and *The Wooden Horse* (1950). In 1951 he went on a US tour with Laurence Olivier's 'Antony and Cleopatra' and the following year moved to Canada, where for four years he was among the leading directors of Canadian TV. In 1956 he was back in the US as a director of TV dramas and in the early 60s commuted between London and New York, directing for both television and the stage. As a feature film director on both sides of the Atlantic since 1966, he has demonstrated both originality and stylistic flair.

FILMS: *The Shuttered Room* 1967; *Sebastian, The Strange Affair* 1968; *I Start Counting* (also prod.) 1969; *The People Next Door* (US) 1970; *Madame Sin* (made for TV; US) 1972; *Godspell* (also co-sc.; US) 1973; *The Count of Monte Cristo* 1976; *Gray Lady Down* (US) 1978; *Hard Country* (also prod.) 1981; *The Act* (co-prod. only) 1984.

Greene, Graham. Novelist, screenwriter, playwright. *b.* Oct. 2, 1904, Berkhamsted, England. *d.* 1991. *ed.* Oxford. The noted writer of adventure novels with psychological and religious overtones has written a number of important screenplays, and many of his books have been adapted to the screen by others. In the late 30s he was film critic for the *Spectator.* His reviews were collected in the book *Graham Greene on Film* (1972). His mother was a first cousin of author Robert Louis Stevenson. Another Graham GREENE is a Native American who was nominated for an Academy Award as best supporting actor for *Dances with Wolves* (1990).

FILMS: Novel or story basis—*Orient Express* (from *Stamboul Train/Orient Express*) 1934; *This Gun for Hire, Went the Day Well/48 Hours* 1942; *Ministry of Fear* 1944; *Confidential Agent* 1945; *The Man Within/The Smugglers, The Fugitive* (from *The Labyrinthine Ways*) 1947; *The Heart of the Matter* 1953; *The End of the Affair* 1955; *Across the Bridge, Short Cut to Hell* (from *This Gun for Hire*) 1957; *The Quiet American* 1958; *Travels with My Aunt* 1972; *England Made Me* 1973; *The Human Factor* 1980; *The Honorary Consul/Beyond the Limit* 1983. Screenplays—*21 Days/21 Days Together* (co-sc., release delayed from 1937) 1940; *Brighton Rock/Young Scarface* (co-sc. from own novel) 1947; *The Fallen Idol* (from own story, "The Basement Room") 1948; *The Third Man* 1949; *La Mano dello Straniero/The Stranger's Hand* (story, co-sc., co-prod.; It./UK) 1953; *Saint Joan* 1957; *Our Man in Havana* (from own novel) 1959; *The Comedians* (from own novel) 1967.

Greene, Lorne. Actor. *b.* Feb. 12 1915, Ottawa, Ont., Canada. *d.* 1987. *ed.* Queen's U. (Kingston, Ont.). He began acting in college productions, while studying chemical engineering and, after graduating, went into radio, soon becoming Canada's top newscaster. Moving to the US in the early 50s, he began appearing in TV shows, Broadway plays, and Hollywood movies. He enjoyed his greatest success in the starring role of Ben Cartwright in the long-running (1959–73) TV series 'Bonanza.' He later brought his solid frame, commanding personality, and authoritative voice to the series 'Griff' (1973–74), 'Battlestar Galactica' (1978–80), and 'Code Red' (1981–82). He was also the host/narrator of the nature documentary series 'Lorne Greene's Last of the Wild' (1974–79).

FILMS INCLUDE: *The Silver Chalice* 1954; *Tight Spot* 1955; *Autumn Leaves* 1956; *Peyton Place, The Hard Man* 1957; *The Gift of Love, Last of the Fast Guns, The Buccaneer* 1958; *The Trap* 1959; *The Errand Boy* (cameo) 1961; *Earthquake* 1974; *Tidal Wave* (Jap.) 1975; *Klondike Fever, Battlestar Galactica* (orig. for TV) 1979; *Conquest of the Earth* 1980.

Greene, Richard. Actor. *b.* Aug. 25, 1918, Plymouth, England. *d.* 1985. The son of an actor and actress and a descendant of British film pioneer William Friese-Greene, he joined a repertory company in his teens and at 20 was imported to Hollywood by 20th Century-Fox as a hopeful rival to MGM's Robert Taylor. Tall, handsome, and dimpled, he played leads in many of the studio's films of the late 30s and 40s. But although quite popular in his pretty-boy romantic and swashbuckling leads, he never reached top stardom. He continued playing leads in American, British, and Continental productions into the 60s and also starred in the British TV series 'Robin Hood' (1955–59; in US 'The Adventures of Robin Hood'). He died at 66 from a brain tumor, the result of injuries he had suffered in a fall three years earlier. At one time (1941–52) he was married to Patricia MEDINA.

FILMS INCLUDE: *Four Men and a Prayer, My Lucky Star, Submarine Patrol, Kentucky* 1938; *The Little Princess, The Hound of the Baskervilles, Stanley and Livingstone, Here I Am a Stranger* 1939; *Little Old New York, I Was an Adventuress* 1940; *Unpublished Story* 1941; *Flying Fortress* 1942; *The Yellow Canary* 1943; *Gaiety George/Showtime* (UK) 1946; *Forever Amber* 1947; *The Fan, The Fighting O'Flynn, That Dangerous Age/If This Be Sin* (UK), *Now Barabbas* (UK) 1949; *The Desert Hawk, My Daughter Joy/Operation X* (UK) 1950; *Lorna Doone* (as John Ridd) 1951; *The Black Castle, Rogue's March* 1952; *Captain Scarlett* 1953; *Contraband Spain* (UK) 1955; *Beyond the Curtain* (UK), *Sword of Sherwood Forest* (as Robin Hood; UK) 1960; *The Blood of Fu Manchu/Kiss and Kill* (UK/US/Ger./Sp.) 1968; *The Castle of Fu Manchu* (UK/Sp.) 1972; *Tales from the Crypt* 1971; *Special Effects* 1984.

Greene, William Howard. American director of photography. *b.* 1895(?). *d.* 1956. A color specialist since the early 20s, he photographed two-color sequences for *Ben-Hur* as early as 1925. Won special Academy Awards for the color photography of *The Garden of Allah* (1936), *A Star Is Born* (1937), and *Phantom of the Opera* (1943).

FILMS INCLUDE: *Trail of the Lonesome Pine, The Garden of Allah* 1936; *A Star Is Born, Nothing Sacred* 1937; *Jesse James* (co-phot.) 1939; *North West Mounted Police* (co-phot.) 1940; *Shepherd of the Hills* 1941; *Phantom of the Opera* (co-phot.) 1943; *Ali Baba and the Forty Thieves, Can't Help Singing, The Climax, Cobra Woman* 1944; *Salome Where She Danced* 1945; *A Night in Paradise* 1946; *Slave Girl* 1947; *The Big Cat* 1949; *When Worlds Collide* 1951; *The Brigand* 1952; *Raiders of the Seven Seas* 1953; *The Violent Men* 1955.

green print. A newly made positive print not dry enough for projection, or more generally, any print that has not been through a projector before and may require waxing or lubrication to prevent jamming in the projection gate.

Greenhut, Robert. Producer. Born in New York City. He entered films as a production assistant in 1967 and for a decade worked in various production capacities for New York–based directors like Woody ALLEN, Arthur HILLER, Milos FORMAN, Bob FOSSE, Sidney LUMET, Alan J. PAKULA, and Mike NICHOLS. After working as assistant director on such films as *The Panic in Needle Park* (1971) and *Last of the Red Hot Lovers* (1972), he gradually assumed production responsibilities as associate producer, then producer and executive producer. He was involved in the making of all of Woody Allen's films of the 80s, as well as many other critical and commercial successes of the decade.

FILMS INCLUDE: As associate producer—*Lenny* 1974; *Dog Day Afternoon* 1975; *The Front* 1976; *Hair* 1979. As producer or executive producer (alone or in collaboration)—*Annie Hall* 1977; *Interiors* 1978; *Manhattan* 1979; *Stardust Memories* 1980; *Arthur* 1980; *A Midsummer Night's Sex Comedy* 1982; *The King of Comedy, Zelig* 1983; *Broadway Danny Rose* 1984; *The Purple Rose of Cairo* 1985; *Hannah and Her Sisters, Heartburn* 1986; *Radio Days, September* 1987; *Big, Another Woman, Working Girl* 1988; *New York Stories, Crimes and Misdemeanors* 1989; *Postcards from the Edge, Alice* 1990; *Regarding Henry* 1991; *Shadows and Fog, A League of Their Own* 1992; *Bullets Over Broadway, Renaissance Man, Wolf* 1994; *Mighty Aphrodite* 1995; *Everyone Says I Love You, The Preacher's Wife* 1996.

greensman. Employee of a studio's construction department whose duties involve dressing sets with greenery, such as trees, plants, and shrubbery, and the maintenance of live greenery on the set or in storage.

Greenstreet, Sydney. Actor. *b.* Dec. 27, 1879, Sandwich, England. *d.* 1954. One of eight children of a leather merchant, he went to Ceylon at 18 in search of a fortune as a tea planter but was forced out of business by a drought and returned to England. He managed a brewery and tried several other jobs and to relieve the routine began attending an acting school. He made his London stage debut in 1902, playing a murderer in a production of 'Sherlock Holmes.' Two years later he went on tour in the US, made his Broadway debut in 'Everyman,' and subsequently appeared in numerous productions in New York and on the road, playing a wide range of roles, from Shakespeare to musical comedy. He spent most of the 30s with the Lunts at the Theatre Guild and in 1941 made an auspicious screen debut in the role of the mysterious and ruthless Kasper Guttman in John Huston's thriller *The Maltese Falcon.* He was nominated for an Academy Award for that performance. A bulky man, weighing nearly 300 pounds, he remained in Hollywood to play other mystery men and master villains, mostly in Warner Bros. melodramas. He was particularly effective when matched with fellow schemer Peter Lorre. Greenstreet's urbane ambiguous brand of villainy made him a favorite of film audiences of the 40s and one of the classic film villains of all time. Long plagued by diabetes and Bright's disease, he died at 75, four years after retiring from the screen.

FILMS: *The Maltese Falcon, They Died with Their Boots On* 1941; *In This Our Life* (cameo), *Across the Pacific* 1942;

Casablanca, Background to Danger 1943; *Passage to Marseille, Between Two Worlds, The Mask of Dimitrios, The Conspirators, Hollywood Canteen* (cameo) 1944; *Pillow to Post, Conflict, Christmas in Connecticut* 1945; *Three Strangers, Devotion, The Verdict* 1946; *That Way with Women, The Hucksters* 1947; *The Woman in White, The Velvet Touch, Ruthless* 1948; *It's a Great Feeling* (cameo), *Flamingo Road* 1949; *Malaya* 1950.

Greenwood, Charlotte. Actress. *b.* Frances Charlotte Greenwood, June 25, 1890, Philadelphia. *d.* 1978. An eccentric acrobatic dancer and comedienne in nightclubs, noted for her high kick, she made occasional appearances in early silent films. She returned to the screen in the late 20s, following a string of successes on the stage, and played leads in low-budget comedies, as well as supporting parts in musicals. Tall, energetic, and quite kooky, she added gaiety and spice to some Fox musical comedies of the 40s. Autobiography: *Never Too Tall* (1947).

FILMS INCLUDE: *Jane* 1915; *Baby Mine* 1928; *So Long Letty* 1930; *Parlor Bedroom and Bath, Palmy Days, The Man in Possession, Stepping Out, Flying High* 1931; *Cheaters at Play* 1932; *Orders Is Orders* (UK) 1933; *Star Dust, Young People, Down Argentine Way* 1940; *Tall Dark and Handsome, Moon Over Miami* 1941; *Springtime in the Rockies* 1942; *Dixie Dugan, The Gang's All Here* 1943; *Up in Mabel's Room, Home in Indiana* 1944; *Wake Up and Dream* 1946; *The Great Dan Patch, Oh You Beautiful Doll* 1949; *Peggy* 1950; *Dangerous When Wet* 1953; *Oklahoma!* 1955; *Glory, The Opposite Sex* 1956.

Greenwood, Joan. Actress. *b.* Mar. 4, 1921, Chelsea, London. *d.* 1987. Leading lady of British stage and films with husky, velvety voice and distinctive personality. The daughter of artist Sydney Earnshaw Greenwood, she was trained for the stage at the Royal Academy of Dramatic Art and made her London debut in 1938 and her first film appearance in 1940. She has also appeared on Broadway. She was married to actor André MORELL from 1960 until his death in 1978.

FILMS INCLUDE: *John Smith Wakes Up* 1940; *The Gentle Sex* 1942; *Latin Quarter/Frenzy* 1945; *A Girl in a Million* 1946; *The Man Within/The Smugglers, The October Man, The White Unicorn/Bad Sister* 1947; *Saraband for Dead Lovers/Saraband, The Bad Lord Byron* (as Caroline Lamb) 1948; *Whisky Galore/Tight Little Island, Kind Hearts and Coronets* 1949; *Flesh and Blood* 1950; *The Man in the White Suit, Le Passe-Muraille/Mr. Peek-A-Boo* (Fr.), *Young Wives' Tale* 1951; *The Importance of Being Earnest* (as Gwendolen) 1952; *Monsieur Ripois/Knave of Hearts/Lovers Happy Lovers* (Fr./UK), *Father Brown/The Detective* 1954; *Moonfleet* (US) 1955; *Stage Struck* (US) 1958; *Mysterious Island* (US/UK) 1961; *The Amorous Prawn/The Playgirl and the War Minister* 1962; *Tom Jones* 1963; *The Moon-Spinners* (US/UK) 1964; *Girl Stroke Boy* 1971; *The Hound of the Baskervilles* 1978; *The Water Babies* 1979; *Wagner* 1983; *Little Dorrit* 1987.

Greer, Jane. Actress. Born Bettejane Greer, on Sept. 9, 1924, in Washington, D.C. Driven by an ambitious stage mother, she took part in many beauty and talent contests as a child and modeled professionally at 12. She participated in high school dramatics and dropped out of school in her senior year to work as a vocalist with a nightclub band. Posing in a WAC uniform for a WW II recruiting poster led her to a Hollywood contract with Howard Hughes and a marriage to crooner Rudy VALLEE in 1943. Both associations ended in failure the following year. It wasn't until 1945 that Miss Greer made her screen debut with RKO. A deep-voiced, low-keyed performer, she played a number of interesting leads for that studio through the early 50s, then briefly joined MGM. She retired from the screen in 1953 to raise a family and has since returned intermittently to films, freelancing with various studios. One of her most memorable roles was that of Robert Mitchum's treacherous girlfriend in the 1947 *film noir* classic *Out of the Past.* In 1984 she re-emerged on the screen after a decade-long absence to play that character's mother in the film's remake, *Against All Odds.*

FILMS: As Bettejane Greer—*Two O'Clock Courage, Pan-Americana, George White's Scandals* 1945. As Jane Greer—*Dick Tracy* 1945; *The Falcon's Alibi, The Bamboo Blonde, Sunset Pass* 1946; *Sinbad the Sailor, They Won't Believe Me, Out of the Past* 1947; *Station West* 1948; *The Big Steal* 1949; *The Company She Keeps, You're in the Navy Now/USS Teakettle* 1951; *You for Me, The Prisoner of Zenda, Desperate Search* 1952; *The Clown, Down Among the Sheltering Palms* 1953; *Run for the Sun* 1956; *Man of a Thousand Faces* 1957; *Where Love Has Gone* 1964; *Billie* 1965; *The Outfit* 1973; *Against All Odds* 1984; *Just Between Friends* 1986; *Immediate Family* 1989.

Gregory, James. Actor. Born on Dec. 23, 1911, in the Bronx, N.Y. He gave up a budding Wall Street career for acting and appeared frequently on Broadway before making his film debut in the late 40s. He has since played character roles in many Hollywood films, often as a heavy or a tough cop. Also seen much on TV, including the series 'The Lawless Years' (1959–61) and 'Barney Miller' (1975–82).

FILMS INCLUDE: *The Naked City* 1948; *The Frogmen* 1951; *The Scarlet Hour* 1956; *The Young Stranger, The Big Caper* 1957; *Onionhead* 1958; *Al Capone* 1959; *X-15* 1961; *Two Weeks in Another Town, The Manchurian Candidate* 1962; *Captain Newman M.D., PT 109* 1963; *A Distant Trumpet* 1964; *The Sons of Katie Elder, A Rage to Live* 1965; *The Silencers, Murderers' Row* 1966; *The Ambushers* 1967; *The Secret War of Harry Frigg* 1968; *The Hawaiians, Beneath the Planet of the Apes* 1970; *Shoot Out, The Late Liz* 1971; *The Strongest Man in the World* 1975; *The Main Event* 1979.

Gregson, John. Actor. *b.* Mar. 15, 1919, Liverpool, England. *d.* 1975. Mild-mannered leading man of British films of the 50s, best remembered for his role in the comedy *Genevieve* (1953). He turned to acting in the late 40s after service with the Royal Navy in WW II. In the 60s and early 70s he played character roles in international productions. He also appeared frequently on British TV and starred in the long-running Scotland Yard series 'Gideon's Way.' He was married to actress Thea Gregory.

FILMS INCLUDE: *Saraband for Dead Lovers/Saraband, Scott of the Antarctic* 1948; *Whisky Galore/Tight Little Island* 1949; *Treasure Island* 1950; *The Lavender Hill Mob* 1951; *Angels One Five, The Brave Don't Cry, The Venetian Bird/The Assassin* 1952; *The Titfield Thunderbolt, The Weak and the Wicked, Genevieve* 1953; *A Conflict of Wings/Fuss Over Feathers, To Dorothy a Son/Cash on Delivery* 1954; *Above Us the Waves, Three Cases of Murder, Value for Money* 1955; *The Battle of the River Platte/Pursuit of the Graf Spee, Jacqueline* 1956; *Rooney* 1957; *Sea of Sand/Desert Patrol, The Captain's Table* 1958; *S.O.S. Pacific* 1959; *Faces in the Dark* 1960; *Hand in Hand, The Treasure of Monte Cristo/The Secret of Monte Cristo, The Frightened City* 1961; *Live Now Pay Later, The Longest Day* (US) 1962; *Tomorrow at Ten* 1963; *The Night of the Generals* 1967; *Fright* 1971; *The Tiger Lily* 1975.

Greist, Kim. Actress. Born on May 12, 1958, in Stamford, Conn. *ed.* New School for Social Research. A former model, she made her screen debut in 1984 and drew wide attention the following year in Terry Gilliam's *Brazil.* She also performed on the stage, off Broadway, and with the New York Shakespeare Festival, as well as in 'Miami Vice' and other TV programs.

FILMS: *C.H.U.D.* 1984; *Brazil* 1985; *Manhunter* 1986;

Throw Momma from the Train 1987; *Punchline* 1988; *Why Me?* 1989; *The Incredible Journey* 1992.

Grémillon, Jean. Director. *b.* Oct. 3, 1901, Bayeux, France. *d.* 1959. After music studies at the Paris Schola Cantorum, he was employed as a musician in an orchestra accompanying silent films. A meeting with cameraman Georges PÉRINAL led to an interest in filmmaking. He entered the industry as a title writer but soon took an interest in editing and directing. From 1923 he directed numerous short documentaries and experimental films. In 1927 he turned to features, winning acclaim among French intellectuals for such films as *Maldone* and *Gardiens de Phare.* But he found himself time and again unable to live with the demands of commercial French cinema and for a while in the 30s he sought work in Spain and Germany. Grémillon enjoyed his most successful period during WW II, with such films as *Remorques, Lumière d'Eté,* and *Le Ciel est à vous.* Again frustrated by his inability to realize ambitious artistic projects within the framework of the industry, he returned to documentary shorts in the 50s. He also began devoting much of his time to the Cinémathèque Française, of which he was president from 1943 to 1958. Grémillon, who frequently wrote his own scripts and also composed the music for many of his films, is considered by the French among their most gifted and personal directors, but his work is little known abroad.

FILMS: Shorts—*Chartres, Le Revêtement des Routes* 1923; *La Fabrication du Fil, Du Fil a l'Aiguille, La Fabrication du Ciment artificiel, La Bière, Le Roulement à Bille, Les Parfums, L'Etirage des Ampoules electriques, La Photogénie mécanique* 1924; *L'Education professionnelle des Conducteurs de Tramway, L'Electrification de la Ligne Paris-Vierzon, L'Auvergne, La Naissance des Cigognes, Les Acieries de la Marine et d'Homecourt* 1925; *La Croisière de l'Atalante* 1926; *Gratuites* 1927; *Bobs* 1928; *Le Petit Babouin* 1932; *Les Charmes de l'Existence* 1949; *Les Désastres de la Guerre* 1951; *Astrologie ou le Miroir de la Vie, Alchimie* 1952; *Au Coeur de l'Ile-de-France* 1954; *La Maison aux Images* 1955; *Haute Lisse* 1956; *André Masson et les Quatre Eléments* 1958. Features—*La Vie des Travailleurs Italiens en France* (full-length doc.; also edit.), *Un Tour au Large* (full-length doc.; also sc., edit., music) 1926; *Maldone* (also co-music) 1928; *Gardiens de Phare* (also edit.) 1929; *La Petite Lise* 1930; *Dinah la Métisse* 1931; *Pour un Sou d'Amour* (also edit.) 1932; *Gonzague/L'Accordeur* (also sc.) 1933; *La Dolorosa* (Sp.) 1934; *Centinella Alerta* (Sp.) 1935; *La Valse royale* (French-language version of Herbert Marisch's 1935 German film *Königswalzer), Pattes des Mouches* (also co-sc.; Fr./Ger.) 1936; *Gueule d'Amour* (Fr./Ger.) 1937; *L'Etrange Monsieur Victor* (Fr./Ger.) 1938; *Remorques/Stormy Waters* 1941; *Lumière d'Eté* 1943; *La Ciel est à vous/The Woman Who Dared* 1944; *Le 6 Juin à l'Aube* (full-length doc.; also sc., commentary, music) 1945; *Le Printemps de la Liberté* (also sc., music) 1948; *Pattes blanches* 1949; *L'Etrange Madame X* 1951; *L'Amour d'une Femme* (also co-sc.) 1954.

Grenfell, Joyce. Actress. *b.* Joyce Phipps, Feb. 10, 1910, London. *d.* 1979. Toothy comedienne of British stage and films. A former journalist and radio critic of *The Observer,* she made her stage debut in 1939, presenting her own monologues in a London revue, and her first film appearance in 1943. In the late 50s and early 60s she toured the United States, Canada, Australia, New Zealand, and other countries in a one-woman show that enjoyed great popularity. She also performed frequently on British radio and TV and in 1957 was elected president of England's Society of Women Writers and Journalists.

FILMS INCLUDE: *The Demi-Paradise/Adventure for Two, The Lamp Still Burns* 1943; *While the Sun Shines* 1947; *The Happiest Days of Your Life, A Run for Your Money* 1949; *Stage Fright* 1950; *Laughter in Paradise, The Galloping Major* 1951; *The Pickwick Papers* 1952; *Genevieve* 1953; *The Million Pound Note/Man with a Million, The Belles of St. Trinian's* 1954; *Happy Is the Bride, Blue Murder at St. Trinian's* 1957; *The Pure Hell of St. Trinian's* 1960; *The Old Dark House* (US/UK) 1963; *The Americanization of Emily* (US), *The Yellow Rolls-Royce* 1964.

Gréville, Edmond T. Director. *b.* June 20, 1906, Nice, France. *d.* 1966, a suicide. The son of a Protestant minister of English descent, he began as a journalist while still in his teens. His first effort as a filmmaker was a 1927 advertising short for the magazine *Vu,* for which he worked. He continued making advertising as well as experimental shorts while working as assistant director to Dupont, Gance, and Genina in 1929–30. He also appeared as an actor in Clair's *Under the Roofs of Paris.* At the same time, he was beginning to make himself a name as a novelist and playwright. A feature director from 1931, he made most of his films in France, with frequent outings to England and occasionally to other European countries. Certain of his films were acclaimed for their original style. His Dutch documentary *Forty Years,* commemorating Queen Wilhelmina's anniversary, won a gold medal at Venice.

FEATURE FILMS: *Le Train des Suicidès* (also sc., edit.) 1931; *Plaisirs de Paris* (uncredited; filmed partially in Berlin), *Le Triangle de Feu* (filmed in Berlin) 1932; *Remous/Whirlpool* (also co-sc., co-edit.) 1933; *Marchand d'Amour* (also sc.), *Princess Tam-Tam* 1935; *Gypsy Melody* (UK) 1936; *Brief Ecstasy* (UK), *Mademoiselle Docteur* (UK) 1937; *Secret Lives* (also sc.; UK), *What a Man!* (UK), *Veetig Jaren/Forty Years* (doc.; Hol.) 1938; *Menaces/Cinq Jours d'Angoisse* (also co-sc.) 1939; *Une Femme dans la Nuit* 1941; *Dorothée cherche l'Amour* (also co-adapt., co-dial.) 1946; *Pour une Nuit d'Amour/Passionnelle* (also co-sc.), *Le Diable souffle* (also co-sc.) 1947; *Noose* (UK), *Neit Tevergeefs/But Not in Vain* (Dutch- and English-language versions shot simultaneously; Hol.) 1948; *The Romantic Age* (also co-adapt.; UK) 1949; *Im Banne der Madonna* (never released; Ger./Fr.) 1950; *L'Enver du Paradis* (also sc.) 1953; *Le Port du Désir/Sauveur d'Epaves/The House on the Waterfront* (also co-adapt., co-dial., song lyrics), *Tant qu'il y aura des Femmes* 1955; *Je plaide non coupable/Guilty* (also sc.) 1956; *Quand sonnera Midi* 1958; *L'Ile du bout du Monde/Temptation* (also prod., co-sc.) 1959; *Beat Girl/Wild for Kicks* (also co-story; UK) 1960; *Les Mains d'Orlac/The Hands of Orlac* (French- and English-language versions; also co-sc.; Fr./UK), *Les Menteurs/The Liars/Twisted Lives* (also co-sc. under pseudonym Max Montagut) 1961; *L'Accident* (also co-sc.) 1963; *Peril au Paradis* (TV movie also co-prod., dial.; release delayed from 1964) 1967.

Grey, Jennifer. Actress. Born on March 26, 1960 in New York, N.Y. Spirited lead who made her screen debut in 1984 and became known for performance as a longing teenager in the coming-of-age movie *Dirty Dancing*. Daughter of actors Joel GREY and Jo Wilder.

FILMS INCLUDE: *Reckless, Red Dawn, The Cotton Club* 1984; *American Flyers* 1985; *Ferris Bueller's Day Off* 1986; *Dirty Dancing* 1987; *Light Years* (v/o) 1988; *Bloodhounds of Broadway* 1989; *The Sixth Family* 1990; *Stroke of Midnight* 1991; *Wind* 1992; *Lover's Knot* 1996.

Grey, Joel. Actor. Born Joel Katz, on Apr. 11, 1932, in Cleveland. Diminutive (5' 4") character star of the American stage and films. The son of comedian Mickey Katz, he made his professional stage debut at nine and by the time he reached his teens had developed into a versatile entertainer—singing and dancing as well as acting—in cabarets and nightclubs and on the legitimate stage. It wasn't until 1966, however, that he achieved stardom, winning the Tony Award for his performance as the Master of Ceremonies in the Broadway musical 'Cabaret.' He later won an Academy Award as best supporting actor for repeating the role in the 1972 screen version. He scored another Broadway hit in 1969 impersonating George M. Cohan in the musical 'George M,' and again in 1996 with the revival of 'Chicago.' His film appearances have been few but memorable. In 1982 he divorced his wife of 24 years, actress Jo Wilder. Their daughter is actress Jennifer GREY.

FILMS: *About Face* 1952; *Calypso Heat Wave* 1957; *Come September* 1961; *Cabaret* 1972; *Man on a Swing* 1974; *Buffalo Bill and the Indians, The Seven-Per-Cent Solution* 1976; *Remo Williams: The Adventure Begins. . .* 1985; *Kafka, The Player* (cameo) 1992; *The Music of Chance* 1993.

Grey, Nan. Actress. *b.* Eschal Miller, July 25, 1918, in Houston, Tex. *d.* 1993. Blonde leading lady and second lead of Hollywood films of the 30s, mostly in routine B productions. Married singer Frankie Laine in 1950.

FILMS INCLUDE: *The Firebird, Babbitt* 1934; *Sutter's Gold, Dracula's Daughter, Crash Donovan, The Sea Spoilers, Three Smart Girls* 1936; *Let Them Live, The Man in Blue, Love in a Bungalow* 1937; *The Jury's Secret, The Black Doll, The Storm, Girls' School, Reckless Living* 1938; *Three Smart Girls Grow Up, The Under-Pup, Tower of London* 1939; *The Invisible Man Returns, The House of the Seven Gables, Sandy Is a Lady, A Little Bit of Heaven, Margie* 1940; *Under Age* 1941.

Grey, Virginia. Actress. Born on Mar. 22, 1917, in Los Angeles. The daughter of silent comedy film director Ray Grey, who died when she was eight, she was raised by her mother, a cutter at Universal, who helped her get her first film role, at age ten, as Little Eva in *Uncle Tom's Cabin* (1927). She appeared in several other silent films as a child, left the screen to complete her schooling, then returned in the 30s as an adult, at first in small roles, then as a leading lady of numerous second features at MGM. A lissome blonde, she also played second leads in several of the studio's major productions. In 1942 she left MGM and began freelancing with various studios. Her career was both prolific and long-lasting. She played leads and supporting roles in numerous films through 1970. Although at one time romantically linked to Clark Gable, she never married.

FILMS INCLUDE: *Uncle Tom's Cabin* (as Eva) 1927; *The Michigan Kid, Heart to Heart* 1928; *Misbehaving Ladies* 1931; *Secrets* 1933; *Dames* 1934; *Gold Diggers of 1935* 1935; *The Great Ziegfeld* 1936; *Secret Valley, Bad Guy, Rosalie* 1937; *Test Pilot, Dramatic School, Shopworn Angel* 1938; *Idiot's Delight, Broadway Serenade, The Hardys Ride High, Thunder Afloat, The Women, Another Thin Man* 1939; *Three Cheers for the Irish, Hullabaloo* 1940; *Blonde Inspiration, The Big Store, Whistling in the Dark* 1941; *Mr. and Mrs. North, Tarzan's New York Adventure, Grand Central Murder* 1942; *Sweet Rosie O'Grady, Idaho* 1943; *Flame of Barbary Coast* 1945; *House of Horrors, Swamp Fire* 1946; *Wyoming, Unconquered* 1947; *So This Is New York, Unknown Island, Mexican Hayride, Jungle Jim* 1948; *The Threat* 1949; *Highway 301* 1950; *The Bullfighter and the Lady, Slaughter Trail* 1951; *Desert Pursuit* 1952; *A Perilous Journey* 1953; *Target Earth* 1954; *The Eternal Sea, The Last Command* 1955; *All That Heaven Allows, The Rose Tattoo, Accused of Murder* 1956; *Jeanne Eagels* 1957; *The Restless Years* 1958; *No Name on the Bullet* 1959; *Portrait in Black* 1960; *Flower Drum Song, Tammy Tell Me True, Back Street, Bachelor in Paradise* 1961; *Black Zoo* 1963; *The Naked Kiss* 1964; *Love Has Many Faces* 1965; *Madame X* 1966; *Rosie* 1967; *Airport* 1970.

Griem, Helmut. Actor. Born in 1940, in Hamburg. *ed.* Hamburg U. Blond leading man and supporting player of German and international films.

FILMS INCLUDE: *Bis zum Ende aller Tage/The Girl from Hong Kong* 1961; *La Caduta degli Dei/Götterdämmerung/The Damned* (It./Ger.) 1969; *The Mackenzie Break* (US) 1970; *Cabaret* (US) 1972; *Ludwig* (It./Fr./Ger.) 1973; *Children of Rage* (UK) 1975; *Il Deserto dei Tartari/Desert of the Tartars* (It./Fr./Iran), *Voyage of the Damned* (UK) 1976; *Deutchland im Herbst/Germany in Autumn, Die Glässerne Zelle/The Glass Cell, Sergeant Steiner/Breakthrough* 1978; *Berlin Alexanderplatz, Malou* 1980; *La Passante* (Fr./Ger.) 1982; *The Second Victory* (UK) 1986.

Grier, David Alan. Actor, comedian. Born June 30, 1955, in Detroit, Mich. *ed.* University of Michigan, Ann Arbor; Yale School of Drama. Heading straight to New York upon graduation from Yale, this gifted comedic actor found early success on the Broadway and off-Broadway stage, receiving a Tony nomination for his performance in 'The First' (1981). His tenure on television's 'In Living Color' opposite Jim CARREY and Keenan Ivory and Damon WAYANS, only confirmed his talents, leading to more substantial film roles.

FILMS: *Streamers* 1983; *A Soldier's Story* 1984; *Beer* 1985; *Amazon Women on the Moon, From the Hip* 1987; *I'm Gonna Git You Sucka, Off Limits* 1988; *Me and Him* 1989; *Almost an Angel, Loose Cannons* 1990; *Boomerang, The Player* 1992; *Blankman, In the Army Now* 1994.

Grier, Pam(ela). Actress. Born in 1949, in Winston-Salem N.C. Voluptuous heroine of black exploitation films of the 70s. She continued playing leads and second leads, mostly in low-budget productions, into the early 90s.

FILMS INCLUDE: *Beyond the Valley of the Dolls* 1970; *The Big Doll House* 1971; *The Big Bird Cage, Hit Man* 1972; *Black Mama White Mama, Twilight People, Coffy, Scream Blacula Scream* 1973; *The Arena, Foxy Brown* 1974; *Sheba Baby, Bucktown, Friday Foster* 1975; *Drum* 1976; *Greased Lightning* 1977; *Fort Apache: The Bronx* 1981; *Tough Enough, Something Wicked This Way Comes* 1983; *Stand Alone, Frankenstein 2000—The Vindicator* (Can./US) 1985; *The Allnighter* 1987; *Above the Law* 1988; *The Package* 1989; *Class of 1999* 1990; *Bill & Ted's Bogus Journey* 1991; *Posse* 1993; *Escape from L.A., Mars Attacks!* 1996.

Grierson, John. Producer, director, theoretician; founder of the British documentary movement. *b.* Apr. 25, 1898, Deanston, Scotland. *d.* 1972. After completing philosophy studies at Glasgow University, which were interrupted by WW I service on a British navy minesweeper, he lectured at Durham University. In 1924 he came to the US on a Rockefeller Research Fellowship to study the effects of communication media on public opinion. In February 1926 he was the first to use the term "documentary," in describing Robert Flaherty's *Moana,* in a film review in the New York *Sun.* He coined it from *documentaire,* a term used by the French for describing travelogues. Grierson's interest in the cinema, at that point, was that of a sociologist studying the impact of a medium on the public.

Returning to England in 1927, Grierson began exploring the possibilities for establishing a government-sponsored organization for making education and propaganda films. In 1928 he founded a film unit at the Empire Marketing Board (EMB) and set out to sea to direct his first film, *Drifters* (1929), a documentary about North Sea herring fishermen. It was received quite enthusiastically in Britain, long subjected to a tradition of studio-bound films. Grierson began expanding his film unit and soon had gathered around him a core of young trainees noted for their talent and enthusiasm.

Grierson directed only one more film, *The Fishing Banks of Skye,* in 1934. He was devoting his energy instead to organizing his unit and supervising the work of his young directors, among them Paul Rotha, Basil Wright, Stuart Legg, Harry Watt, and Edgar Anstey. Under his leadership the unit produced some 100 documentary films between 1930 and 1933. The emphasis in most was on social reform, a course that became a characteristic of the British documentary movement. In 1933, when the EMB was dissolved, Grierson's unit moved over to the GPO (General Post Office). Improved working conditions and increased budgets allowed Grierson and his directors to experiment with form and technique as well as with content. Some of the finest documentaries in memory were produced by the GPO Film Unit during this period, notably *Song of Ceylon* and *Night Mail*.

In 1937, Grierson left the unit and established Film Centre, an advisory organization that provided research know-how and production supervision for documentary filmmakers. In 1939 he was appointed Film Commissioner by the Canadian Government, and in that capacity he established the National Film Board of Canada, still noted today for the high quality of its documentary films. He resigned that post in 1945 and came to the USA, where he formed a company for producing films to promote international understanding, The World Today, Inc. In 1947 he was appointed director of Mass Media at UNESCO. From 1957 he hosted a weekly British TV show, from Scotland, 'This Wonderful World,' which featured a selection of documentary films from around the world.

Grierson was one of the leading figures in the history of the documentary, as a producer, organizer, and a driving creative force behind the development of a documentary movement in Britain and elsewhere. He is also considered the foremost theoretician of the documentary. Some of his extensive writing on the subject has been compiled by Forsyth Hardy in the book *Grierson on Documentary* (first published 1946; American edition 1947). In 1951–54 Grierson served as the executive producer of Group 3, an experimental unit that turned out a number of feature films.

FILMS INCLUDE: As producer—*Drifters* (also dir., sc.) 1929; *Conquest* (also edit.) 1930; *Upstream* 1931; *Industrial Britain* (also co-edit), *Aero-Engine* 1933; *The Fishing Banks of Skye* (also dir.), *So This Is London, Granton Trawler, Song of Ceylon* (also co-sc.) 1934; *BBC: The Voice of Britain* (co-prod.), *Coal Face* 1935; *Night Mail* 1936; *Trade Tattoo, Children at School, The Smoke Menace* (co-prod.), *We Live in Two Worlds* 1937; *The Face of Scotland* 1938; *The Londoners* (co-prod.) 1939; *Battle Is Their Birthright* (Can.) 1943; *When Asia Speaks* (Can.), *A Yank Comes Back* 1944. As executive producer—*Judgment Deferred, Brandy for the Parson* 1951; *The Brave Don't Cry, Laxdale Hall/Scotch on the Rocks, The Oracle, Time Gentleman Please, You're Only Young Twice* 1952; *Man of Africa* 1953; *Orders Are Orders* 1954.

Gries, Tom. Director. *b.* Thomas S. Gries, Dec. 20, 1922, Chicago. *d.* 1977. *ed.* Loyola Acad. (Chicago); Georgetown U. Following WW II service with the Marines, he started out as a reporter for the Chicago *Herald American* and later for *Variety*. In 1947 he went to Hollywood as a talent agent and two years later joined Stanley Kramer as a publicist and story aide. He moved into production in the early 50s as associate producer of *The Lusty Men* (1952), producer of *Donovan's Brain* (1953), and producer and co-writer on the feature-length nature documentary *Hunters of the Deep* (1954). He then switched to television, writing and directing episodes for many series. He won an Emmy Award in 1963 for his direction of the TV series 'East Side West Side' and again in 1973 for the TV movie 'Glass House.' Among his many other TV dramas was the adaptation of Leon Uris's 'QB VII.' In the late 60s, Gries began directing motion pictures, achieving unanimous critical acclaim for his uncommon Western *Will Penny* (1968). His subsequent films—typically odes to machismo—were less successful. He died of a heart attack while playing tennis during the editing stage of his final film, *The Greatest* (1977), the story of boxer Muhammad Ali.

FILMS: *Will Penny* (also co-exec. prod., sc.) 1968; *100 Rifles* (also co-sc.), *Number One* 1969; *The Hawaiians, Fools* (also co-exec. prod.) 1970; *Journey Through Rosebud* 1972; *Lady Ice* 1973; *Breakout* 1975; *Breakheart Pass* 1976; *The Greatest* 1977.

Griffies, Ethel. Actress. *b.* Ethel Woods, Apr. 26 1878, Sheffield England. *d.* 1975. Versatile character player of American and British films. Appearing professionally on the stage before her fourth birthday, she toured the British provinces as a child, finally making her London debut at 21. She was 46 by the time she made her first Broadway appearance in 1924. Apart from an isolated screen appearance in 1917, she began her screen career in the early 30s, in Hollywood, and subsequently played scores of supporting movie roles, some quite memorable.

FILMS INCLUDE: *The Cost of a Kiss* (UK) 1917; *Old English* 1930; *Waterloo Bridge* 1931; *Westward Passage, Love Me Tonight* 1932; *Alice in Wonderland* 1933; *We Live Again* 1934; *The Mystery of Edwin Drood, The Werewolf of London, Anna Karenina, The Return of Peter Grimm* 1935; *Kathleen* (Ire.) 1937; *We Are Not Alone* 1939; *Irene, Anne of Windy Poplars, The Stranger on the Third Floor* 1940; *A Yank in the R.A.F., Great Guns, How Green Was My Valley* 1941; *Time to Kill* 1942; *Holy Matrimony* 1943; *Jane Eyre, Music for Millions* 1944; *The Horn Blows at Midnight, Uncle Harry, Saratoga Trunk* 1945; *Devotion* 1946; *The Homestretch* 1947; *The Birds, Billy Liar* (UK) 1963; *Bus Riley's Back in Town* 1965.

Griffith, Andy. Actor. Born Andrew Samuel Griffith, on June 1, 1926, in Mount Airy, N.C. *ed.* U. of North Carolina. He studied to become a preacher, then switched to music and drama and after a brief stint as a teacher broke into show business with a preacher act on the Rotary circuit. In the late 40s and early 50s he played a British-accented Sir Walter Raleigh in the pageant 'Lost Colony,' but it was his natural drawling Blue Ridge accent that later established him as a popular favorite on the stage, in the movies, and on TV. He had a triumphant Broadway debut in 1955 as the star of 'No Time for Sergeants' and two years later made a strong impact with his first film role in *A Face in the Crowd*. He subsequently appeared in only a handful of films. It was on TV, however, that he registered his greatest success, as the folksy star of the long-running (1960–68, 1971) comedy series 'The Andy Griffith Show' and later of the drama series 'The Headmaster' and 'Matlock,' as well as many TV movies.

FILMS: *A Face in the Crowd* 1957; *No Time for Sergeants, Onionhead* 1958; *The Second Time Around* 1961; *Angel in My Pocket* 1969; *Hearts of the West* 1975; *Rustlers' Rhapsody* 1985.

Griffith, Corinne. Actress. *b.* Nov. 24, 1896, Texarkana, Tex. *d.* 1979. Educated at a New Orleans convent. She was signed in 1916 on a movie contract by the New York–based Vitagraph. In the early 20s, she moved to First National in Hollywood, where she became known as the "Orchid Lady" for her delicate beauty. Miss Griffith, whose stature as "the world's most beautiful woman" in the silent era equaled that of Hedy Lamarr in the talkie era, was rarely called upon to act, but remained highly popular through the end of the silent period. She appeared in a handful of talkies before retiring from the screen a wealthy woman. She then turned to business and writing. One of her dozen books, *Papa's Delicate Condition,* was adapted to the screen in 1963. Her several husbands included (1) actor-director Webster Campbell (1920–23), (2) screen producer Walter Morosco (1933–34), and (3) Washington Redskins owner Preston Marshall (1936–58). Campbell (1893–1972), a handsome leading man of the 1910s, directed several of her films of the early 20s.

FILMS INCLUDE; *The Last Man* 1916; *The Love Doctor* 1917; *The Menace, Miss Ambition, The Girl of Today* 1918; *Adventure Shop, Thin Ice, The Bramble Bush* 1919; *Human Collateral, The Garter Girl, The Tower of Jewels, The Whisper Market* 1920; *What's Your Reputation Worth?, Moral Fibre, The Single Track* 1921; *Island Wives, A Virgin's Sacrifice/A Woman's Sacrifice, Divorce Coupons* 1922; *The Common Law, Six Days* 1923; *Black Oxen, Lilies of the Field* (also exec. prod.), *Single Wives* (also exec. prod.), *Love's Wilderness* (also exec. prod.) 1924; *Déclassé/The Social Exile* (also exec. prod.), *The Marriage Whirl* (also exec. prod.), *Classified* (also exec. prod.), *Infatuation* (also exec. prod.) 1925; *Mademoiselle Modiste* (also exec. prod.), *Into Her Kingdom* (also exec. prod.), *Syncopating Sue* (also exec. prod.) 1926; *The Lady in Ermine* (also exec. prod.), *Three Hours* (also exec. prod.) 1927; *The Garden of Eden, Outcast* 1928; *The Divine Lady* (as Lady Hamilton), *Saturday's Children, Prisoners* 1929; *Lilies of the Field* (remake), *Back Pay* 1930; *Lily Christine* (UK) 1932.

Griffith, D. W. Director. *b.* David (Lewelyn) Wark Griffith, Jan. 22, 1875, La Grange, Ky. *d.* 1948. The single most important figure in the history of American film and one of the most influential in the development of world cinema as an art. His father, at one time a practicing physician, fought in the Mexican War. The Reconstruction took its toll on the Griffith family, and by the time David Wark was born it had been reduced to poverty. Raised in Louisville, young Griffith helped out by taking on various odd jobs at local establishments, but an accidental exposure to amateur dramatics caused him to decide to become an actor.

Assuming the stage name of Lawrence Griffith, David Wark joined Louisville's Meffert Stock Company in 1897 and for two seasons played supporting roles in a number of the troupe's productions. He then performed with little success for various touring companies, frequently penniless and usually spent his nights in flophouses with little hope of improving his lot. In 1906 he took his first wife, the young actress Linda ARVIDSON.

All during his lean years as an actor, Griffith made repeated attempts to establish himself as a writer. He wrote short stories, poems, and plays but saw little success in his literary endeavors until 1906–7, when a free-verse poem of his was published in *Leslie's Weekly* and he sold a play, 'A Fool and a Girl,' as a vehicle for actress Fanny Ward. But the play proved a commercial failure, and a disappointed Griffith turned his back on the theater to try his luck in the then little respected but, he hoped, less rigid and more lucrative world of the movies. He began making the rounds of various film studios in the New York area, trying to sell story ideas to producers and directors. He approached Edwin S. PORTER, who had gained fame as the director of *The Great Train Robbery* (1903). Porter turned down Griffith's idea for a film based on 'La Tosca' but offered him a leading role in an upcoming film, *Rescued from an Eagle's Nest* (1907). Reluctantly, Griffith accepted. As a writer, he met with more success at the BIOGRAPH studio, to which he sold a number of stories, later appearing as an actor in the films based on several of them, including *'Ostler Joe* and *At the Crossroads of Life* (both 1908).

Before long, Griffith was becoming a fixture at Biograph, getting involved in more and more areas of production and soon earning a chance to direct his first film, *The Adventures of Dollie* (1908). This film, like many of Griffith's other early productions, starred Miss Arvidson.

During the following 18 months, Griffith personally directed all the Biograph products. Thereafter, as Biograph's general director through the fall of 1913, he supervised the company's entire output and directed all or most of the major productions, an astonishing feat because of the sheer volume. He had personally directed an amazing total of some 450 films. Although most of these were one-reel long (some of the earliest films were shorter, a dozen of the later ones were two-reelers, and one film, *Judith of Bethulia,* released early in 1914, ran four reels), it was a pace of personal output rarely if ever paralleled by a film director.

Quantity alone did not make Griffith's early film career so extraordinary. From the very start, he showed a remarkable instinctive understanding of the creative potential of the medium, using inherently cinematic techniques—changing camera angles, intercutting, crosscutting, parallel action, camera movement, dramatic lighting, the close-up, the full shot, rhythmic editing, etc. He wasn't the first to employ these techniques, but he was the first to use them consciously and creatively, taking the linguistic components of film and molding them into a syntax, thus giving cinema and articulate language all its own. His innovative achievements in liberating the cinema from the restrictive traditions of the stage are all the more remarkable considering the theatrical roots of his background.

Griffith was fortunate to have had the cinematographic services and technical advice of a gifted, inventive cameraman, Billy (G. W.) BITZER. Their collaboration was among the most fertile partnerships in the history of the cinema. They worked together so closely on so many productions that it has become difficult to determine which one contributed what to many of their innovations.

Early on he recognized the need for a new style of performing for the screen, a style more subtle and restrained than the bombastic, exaggerated delivery then current on the stage. As early as 1909 he gathered a group of young actors and rehearsed them continually until he was able to extract from them performances that could withstand the magnifying eye of the motion picture camera. Before long he had developed a stock company of players that at one time or another included such future stars as Mary PICKFORD, Dorothy and Lillian GISH, Blanche SWEET, Mabel NORMAND, Mae MARSH, Florence LABADIE, Claire MCDOWELL, Henry B. WALTHALL, Robert (Bobby) HARRON, Alfred PAGET, Donald CRISP, Arthur JOHNSON, Jack PICKFORD, James KIRKWOOD, Owen MOORE, Wallace REID, and Harry CAREY. In 1910, Griffith began taking his troupe to California during the winter seasons to take advantage of the sunny climate and attain a greater variety of background scenery.

The sudden improvement in the quality of the Biograph product that resulted from Griffith's innovations did not go unnoticed by the public. Attendance rose dramatically as audiences came to expect superior entertainment from every Griffith production. Even the routine films were distinguished by their high production values and lively pace. Griffith's early films varied widely in genre and theme. Most dealt with the contemporary scene, but many were adaptations of period literature.

In mid-1911, Griffith took another important first step by directing *Enoch Arden* in two reels, a length then considered beyond the attention span of American film audiences. Gradually, his films were becoming more ambitious, not just in length but also in the treatment of serious subjects. Having demonstrated his skill at using the technical tools of the cinema expressively with such films as *The Lonely Villa* (1909), *Pippa Passes/The Song of Conscience* (1909), and *The Lonedale Operator* (1911), by 1912, Griffith had gained the self-confidence and the trust of his employers to enable him to explore themes of personal concern with greater scope and depth. In July of that year he turned out *A Man's Genesis,* a dramatized psychological study of Darwin's theory of evolution. *The Musketeers of Pig Alley,* released in October, was a realistic gangster drama that reflected the director's growing social concern. *The New York Hat,* released in December, was an atmospheric piece of Americana that mocked small-town puritanism and hypocrisy.

Seeking more freedom to express his expanding ideas and to satisfy his growing ambition, Griffith decided in the summer of 1913 to part company with Biograph and its restrictive policies. He left the studio, taking along most of his regular actors and the best of the technical crews, most importantly cameraman Billy Bitzer. In October joined Reliance-Majestic with the added title of head of production. Before he left Biograph, however, he had completed three key films, *The Massacre* and *The Battle of Elderbush Gulch,* and the third, the American cinema's first four-reeler, *Judith of Bethulia.* The two-reelers were remarkably complex films for their length and were noted for both their elaborate construction and vivid action scenes. *Judith,* a biblical epic, was considered a stupendous production at the time. Biograph released an expanded six-reel version of *Judith* in 1917, retitled *Her Condoned Sin.*

At Reliance-Majestic, Griffith spent little time on his duties as production chief. He was much too busy all through 1914 personally directing several feature-length films and secretly preparing his monumental *The Birth of a Nation* for production, to be released the following year. His first feature for his new employers, *The Battle of the Sexes/The Single Standard,* was a quickie production made cheaply to provide the new company with a much-needed cash flow. *The Escape* was a trashy melodrama undermined by a terrible script. *Home Sweet Home,* on the other hand, was an ambitious production with an all-star cast that foreshadowed the structure of *Intolerance* (1916). But it too was unsuccessful, as was the case with *The Avenging Conscience,* a psychological thriller.

The mediocrity of these productions could be blamed partly on Griffith's preoccupation with *The Birth of a Nation* (1915), a superlative epic of the Civil War which many historians consider the single most important film in the development of cinema as an art. It was certainly the most influential. Originally running about three hours in length, it was a stunning summary of all that had been known about filmmaking at the time and, much more, an elaborately constructed, complex production that remains effective to this day. Unanimously hailed as a great work of art, it was also an outstanding financial success, with long lines queueing up to see it at the unheard of price of two dollars a ticket. But *The Birth of a Nation* also generated criticism and stirred up a rage of controversy over its positive portrayal of the Ku Klux Klan and negative portrayal of African-Americans. Some black groups and white liberal groups condemned it as "a flagrant incitement to racial antagonism" and urged authorities in various states to ban its exhibition.

Griffith is said to have been bewildered and hurt by the charges of prejudice, and it is quite possible that he made his next film, *Intolerance,* partly in reaction to the controversy. *Intolerance,* released in the summer of 1916 after two years in the making, was a film of grandiose scale and design, dwarfing *The Birth of a Nation* in its mammoth ambition, cost, complexity, and length. Griffith invested much of his own money in this $2,500,000 production.

Intolerance proved to be a much lesser box-office attraction than *The Birth of a Nation* had been, largely because audiences found the labyrinthine structure and multiple plots too difficult to follow. The production ruined Griffith financially, hampering the progress of his career for several years. But it stands today as a monument to his creative talent, a film that despite its many flaws of conception and continuity proved as influential as *The Birth of a Nation* on future filmmakers, if not more. It was particularly influential in Russia, where Lenin ordered its importation in 1919 and where it was closely studied by film pupils and by such directors as EISENSTEIN and PUDOVKIN. In the US, episodes of *Intolerance* were released in 1919 as separate features, respectively titled *The Fall of Babylon* and *The Mother and the Law.*

In May of 1915, still basking in the triumph of *The Birth of a Nation* and already deeply involved in the production of *Intolerance,* Griffith had joined the newly formed TRIANGLE Corporation, along with Thomas H. INCE and Mack SENNETT. Together they formed a powerful triumvirate of director-producers as part of an ambitious scheme by the company to corner the market on prestigious quality productions. But the plan failed, placing Triangle in a precarious financial position. Griffith, now himself deeply in debt as a result of *Intolerance,* severed his connection with Triangle in March of 1917 and signed a contract with Artcraft, Adolph ZUKOR's company, releasing through Famous Players-Lasky (later Paramount). Soon after, he left for Europe, at the invitation of the British government, and while there made a WW I propaganda film, *Hearts of the World* (1918), in partnership with Zukor. Shot on location in England and France, and combining documentary footage with reconstructed scenes, this film proved more successful as a vehicle for the acting talents of Lillian and Dorothy Gish than as a topical drama, but it netted a quick profit at the box office and helped ease Griffith's financial burdens.

Returning to the US, Griffith made another war drama, *The Great Love* (1918), into which he incorporated some of the remaining on-location footage he had shot in England. The next few years were marked by a close association between Griffith and actress Lillian Gish, who starred in most of the films. He also produced for Artcraft a series of comedies starring her sister Dorothy.

In contrast with the ambitious scale of his previous feature productions, Griffith's postwar films of the late 1910s were intimate dramas of modest scope. No known print exists of *The Greatest Thing in Life* (1918). *A Romance of Happy Valley* (1919) was a charming rural drama that had also been thought lost until the recent discovery of a print at a Russian archive. *The Girl Who Stayed at Home* (1919) was a minor production. The best known and appreciated of Griffith's cycle of intimate dramas for Artcraft is *True Heart Susie* (1919), noted for its simple charm and unpretentious style and for superlative performances by its stars, Lillian Gish and Robert Harron. Griffith's last film for Artcraft was *Scarlet Days* (1919), his only feature-length Western.

In January of 1919, while still heavily engaged in fulfilling his contractual commitments to Artcraft, Griffith joined Douglas FAIRBANKS, Mary PICKFORD, and Charles CHAPLIN in forming the United Artists Corporation. The first film Griffith released through the new organization was *Broken Blossoms* (1919), the finest of his intimate films, a wonderfully atmospheric melodrama in which tenderness and violence are effectively balanced to achieve a poignant tragedy. Also in the hectic year of 1919, Griffith signed a three-picture deal with First National and set up his own studio complex at Mamaroneck, N.Y. In 1920 he incorporated his diverse enterprises under the umbrella of the D. W. Griffith Corporation (he had incorporated himself twice before, in 1913 and 1916).

Griffith's films for First National—*The Greatest Question* (1919), *The Idol Dancer* (1920), and *The Love Flower* (1920)—

were routine melodramas, evidently hurriedly made with a quick profit in mind. However, his independently made *Way Down East* (1920) turned out to be both an artistic triumph and an unexpected commercial hit, second only to *The Birth of a Nation* in box-office receipts.

Following an unsuccessful attempt to recapture the intimate poetic flavor of *Broken Blossoms in Dream Street* (1921), a film based on material by the same author and set against a similar background, Griffith successfully tackled a large-scale historical epic, *Orphans of the Storm* (1922). *Orphans* contained spectacular crowd scenes of the French Revolution which were shot skillfully on a 14-acre set in Mamaroneck re-creating 18th-century Paris. The film fared rather well at the box office but ended up losing money as a result of unexpected copyright and accounting problems. *One Exciting Night* (1922) was a misfired Griffith venture into the mystery thriller genre, and *The White Rose* (1923), a sentimental melodrama. With *America* (1924) Griffith regained his touch, turning out an impressive, pictorially exciting panorama of the Revolutionary War, the last of his great silent epics.

Isn't Life Wonderful (1924), Griffith's last independent production, was a compassionate romantic drama of postwar deprivation that decried the evils of WW I and exalted the power of love in the face of hardship. Like all Griffith's films for United Artists with the exception of *Way Down East,* it lost money, putting Griffith not only deeper in personal debt but also in conflict with his partners at the company.

In 1924, as his relations at United Artists soured beyond repair, the director signed a contract with Adolph Zukor to make films for Paramount. While gaining financial security and the logistic backing of a major studio, Griffith sacrificed his cherished freedom to create. Although he first enjoyed a special status at Paramount in recognition of his past achievements, before long Griffith began losing both his unique position and his own self-confidence as his productions failed at the box office.

Griffith's three films of the Paramount period, all made at the company's East Coast studios, were mediocre and uninspired. The first two, *Sally of the Sawdust* (1925) and *That Royle Girl* (1926), starred comedian W. C. FIELDS and lovely Carol DEMPSTER, with whom the director became infatuated. The third, *The Sorrows of Satan* (1926), was a visually lavish but dated, tiresome melodrama initially intended for C. B. DE MILLE. It proved a financial disaster and led to the premature dissolution of Griffith's contract with Zukor.

In April of 1927, Griffith returned to United Artists, but did not regain his creative independence. He signed a personal contract with Joseph SCHENCK, the company's controlling executive, according to which he gained the financial backing of Schenck's Art Cinema Corporation and in return forfeited to Schenck voting rights in the director's remaining United Artists stock as well as final script approval.

To carry out his first assignment under the new agreement, Griffith returned to Hollywood for the first time since 1919, discovering a thoroughly changed movie industry and a regimented studio system that tended to stifle personal creativity and initiative. Griffith's next three films—*Drums of Love* (1928), *The Battle of the Sexes* (1928), and *Lady of the Pavements* (1929)—reflected in their impersonal mediocrity the director's initial loss of orientation and self-confidence. But he regained the approval of critics and a brief resurgence of personal prestige with his first talkie, *Abraham Lincoln* (1930), an epic screen biography.

Griffith's last film, *The Struggle* (1931), was made independently and cheaply with proceeds from a large tax refund he had received unexpectedly. He was hoping to make a comeback as an independent producer with this somber drama of alcoholism and the futility of Prohibition. But audiences laughed at the clumsy sincerity of the production, and many critics ridiculed it mercilessly, although seen in retrospect the film has much in it to recommend. Gradually, he picked up the pieces, sold his shares in United Artists, and made some successful investments in ventures outside the movie industry. From time to time he became involved in negotiations for film projects that never materialized. In 1933 he wrote and narrated a fictionalized radio series based on his life.

In 1935, Griffith was invited to England to direct a remake of *Broken Blossoms.* But disagreements over details of production, especially casting, soon led to his departure, and the film, starring Emlyn Williams, was directed instead by Hans Brahm and released in 1936. Although Griffith was no longer making films, his legacy to the industry was not entirely forgotten. In the Academy Award ceremony for 1935, Griffith was awarded an honorary Oscar "for his distinguished creative achievements as director and producer and his invaluable initiative and lasting contributions to the progress of the motion picture arts."

Long divorced from Linda Arvidson, Griffith married Evelyn Baldwin, a young actress, in 1936, but the marriage did not last. In 1939 he was hired by Hal ROACH as a nominal producer on *One Million B.C.* and reputedly directed several scenes in this programme about the prehistoric. Later Griffith tried unsuccessfully to begin a new career as a Broadway producer. Although he owned a ranch in California, Griffith never really settled down but spent his remaining years in a succession of apartment-hotels.

FILMS (as director): Shorts—*The Adventures of Dollie, The Fight for Freedom, The Black Viper* (credit unconfirmed), *The Tavern Keeper's Daughter* (credit unconfirmed), *The Redman and the Child* (also sc.), *Deceived Slumming Party* (credit unconfirmed), *The Bandit's Waterloo* (also sc.), *A Calamitous Elopement* (also sc.), *The Greaser's Gauntlet* (also co-sc.), *The Man and the Woman* (credit unconfirmed; also sc.), *The Fatal Hour* (also sc.), *For Love of Gold* (also sc.), *Balked at the Altar* (also sc., act.), *For a Wife's Honor* (also sc.), *Betrayed by a Handprint* (also sc.), *Monday Morning in a Coney Island Police Court* (credit unconfirmed), *The Girl and the Outlaw* (also sc.), *Behind the Scenes: Where All Is Not Gold That Glitters* (also sc.), *The Red Girl* (also sc.), *The Heart of O Yama* (also sc., act.), *Where the Breakers Roar* (also co-sc.), *A Smoked Husband* (also sc.), *The Stolen Jewels* (also sc.), *The Devil* (also sc.), *The Zulu's Heart* (also sc.), *Father Gets in the Game* (also sc.), *The Barbarian Ingomar* (also sc.), *The Vaquero's Vow* (also sc.), *The Planter's Wife* (also sc.), *The Romance of a Jewess* (also sc.), *The Call of the Wild* (also sc.), *Concealing a Burglar* (also sc.), *After Many Years, The Pirate's Gold* (also co-sc.), *The Taming of the Shrew* (also co-sc.), *The Guerrilla* (also sc.), *The Song of the Shirt* (also co-sc.), *The Ingrate* (also sc.), *A Woman's Way* (also sc.), *The Clubman and the Tramp* (also sc.), *The Valet's Wife* (also sc.), *Money Mad* (also sc.), *The Feud and the Turkey* (also sc.), *The Reckoning* (also co-sc.), *The Test of Friendship* (also sc.), *An Awful Moment* (also sc.), *The Christmas Burglars* (also sc.), *Mr. Jones at the Ball* (also sc.), *The Helping Hand* (also sc.) 1908; *One Touch of Nature, The Maniac Cook* (also sc.), *Mrs. Jones Entertains* (also sc.), *The Honor of Thieves* (also sc.), *Love Finds a Way* (also sc.), *A Rural Elopement* (also sc.), *The Sacrifice* (also sc.), *The Criminal Hypnotist* (also sc.), *Those Boys!* (also sc.), *Mr. Jones Has a Card Party* (also sc.), *The Fascinating Mrs. Francis* (also sc.), *The Welcome Burglar* (also sc.), *Those Awful Hats* (also sc.), *The Cord of Life* (also sc.), *The Girls and Daddy* (also sc., act.), *The Brahma Diamond* (also sc.), *A Wreath in Time* (also sc.),

Edgar Allan Poe (also co-sc.), *Tragic Love* (also sc.), *The Curtain Pole* (also sc.), *His Ward's Love* (also sc.), *The Hindoo Dagger* (also sc.), *The Joneses Have Amateur Theatricals* (also sc.), *The Politician's Love Story* (also sc.), *The Golden Louis* (also sc.), *At the Altar* (also sc., act.), *His Wife's Mother* (also sc.), *The Prussian Spy* (also sc.), *A Fool's Revenge* (also sc.), *The Roué's Heart* (also sc.), *The Wooden Leg* (also sc.), *The Salvation Army Lass* (also sc.), *The Lure of the Gown* (also sc.), *I Did It Mama* (also sc.), *The Voice of the Violin* (also sc.), *The Deception, And a Little Child Shall Lead Them* (also sc.), *A Burglar's Mistake* (also sc.), *The Medicine Bottle* (also sc.), *Jones and His New Neighbors* (also sc.), *A Drunkard's Reformation* (also sc.), *The Road to the Heart* (also sc.), *Trying to Get Arrested* (also co-sc.), *A Rude Hostess* (also sc.), *Schneider's Anti-Noise Crusade* (also sc.), *The Winning Coat* (also sc.), *A Sound Sleeper* (also sc.), *Confidence* (also sc.), *Lady Helen's Escapade, A Troublesome Satchel, The Drive for a Life* (also sc.), *Lucky Jim, Twin Brothers, 'Tis an Ill Wind That Blows No Good* (also sc.), *The Eavesdropper* (also sc.), *The Suicide Club, The Note in the Shoe* (also sc.), *One Busy Hour* (also sc.), *Jones and the Lady Book Agent* (also sc.), *The French Duel* (also sc.), *A Baby's Shoe* (also sc.), *The Jilt* (also sc.), *Resurrection, Eloping with Aunty* (also sc.), *Two Memories* (also sc.), *The Cricket on the Hearth, Eradicating Aunty* (also sc.), *His Duty* (co-dir. with Frank Powell), *What Drink Did* (also sc.), *The Violin Maker of Cremona, The Lonely Villa, A New Trick* (also sc.), *The Son's Return* (also sc.), *Her First Biscuits* (also sc.), *The Faded Lilies* (also sc.), *Was Justice Served?* (also sc.), *The Peachbasket Hat* (also sc.), *The Mexican Sweethearts* (also sc.), *The Way of Man* (also sc.), *The Necklace, The Message, The Country Doctor* (also sc.), *The Cardinal's Conspiracy* (co-dir. with Powell), *The Friend of the Family* (also sc.), *Tender Hearts* (also sc.), *The Renunciation* (also sc.), *Sweet and Twenty, Jealousy and the Man* (also sc.), *A Convict's Sacrifice* (also sc.), *The Slave* (also sc.), *A Strange Meeting* (also co-sc.), *The Mended Lute, They Would Elope, Jones' Burglar* (also sc.), *The Better Way, With Her Card* (also sc.), *His Wife's Visitor* (also sc.), *Mrs. Jones's Lover/I Want My Hat* (also sc.), *The Indian Runner's Romance, Oh Uncle!* (also sc.), *The Seventh Day* (also sc.), *The Mills of the Gods* (also sc.), *Pranks* (credit unconfirmed), *The Little Darling* (also sc.), *The Sealed Room, 1776/The Hessian Renegades* (also co-sc.), *Comata the Sioux, The Children's Friend* (also sc.), *Getting Even* (also sc.), *The Broken Locket* (also sc.), *In Old Kentucky, A Fair Exchange, Leather Stocking, The Awakening, Wanted—A Child* (also sc.), *Pippa Passes/The Song of Conscience* (also co-sc.), *Fools of Fate, The Little Teacher, A Change of Heart, His Lost Love* (also sc.), *The Expiation* (also sc.), *In the Watches of the Night* (also sc.), *Lines of White on a Sullen Sea* (also co-sc.), *The Gibson Goddess* (also sc.), *What's Your Hurry?* (also sc.), *Nursing a Viper* (also co-sc.), *The Restoration* (also sc.), *The Light That Came* (also sc.), *Two Women and a Man* (also sc.), *A Midnight Adventure* (also sc.), *Sweet Revenge* (also sc.), *The Open Gate* (also co-sc.), *The Mountaineer's Honor* (also co-sc.), *The Trick That Failed, In the Window Recess, The Death Disc, Through the Breakers, The Redman's View, A Corner in Wheat* (also co-sc.), *In a Hempen Bag* (also sc.), *The Test, A Trap for Santa Claus* (also sc.), *In Little Italy, To Save Her Soul* (also sc.), *The Day After* (credit unconfirmed), *Choosing Her Husband* (also sc.) 1909; *The Rocky Road* (also sc.), *The Dancing Girl of Butte* (also sc.), *Her Terrible Ordeal* (also sc.), *On the Reef* (also sc.), *The Call* (also sc.), *The Honor of His Family, The Last Deal* (also sc.), *The Cloister's Touch, The Woman from Mellon's* (also sc.), *The Course of True Love, The Duke's Plan* (also sc.), *One Night and Then—* (also sc.), *The Englishman and the Girl* (also sc.), *His Last Burglary, Taming a Husband, The Final Settlement, The Newlyweds* (also sc.), *The Thread of Destiny, In Old California, The Converts, The Man, The Love of Lady Irma* (credit unconfirmed), *Faithful, The Twisted Trail, Gold Is Not All, His Last Dollar* (credit unconfirmed), *The Smoker* (credit unconfirmed), *As It Is in Life, A Rich Revenge, A Romance of the Western Hills, Thou Shalt Not, The Tenderfoot's Triumph* (credit unconfirmed), *The Way of the World, Up a Tree* (credit unconfirmed), *The Gold-Seekers, The Unchanging Sea* (also sc.), *Love Among the Roses, The Two Brothers* (credit unconfirmed), *Over Silent Paths, An Affair of Hearts, Ramona* (also co-sc.), *A Knot in the Plot* (credit unconfirmed), *The Impalement, In the Season of Buds, A Child of the Ghetto, A Victim of Jealousy, In the Border States, The Face at the Window, May and December* (credit unconfirmed), *Never Again* (credit unconfirmed), *The Marked Time-Table, A Child's Impulse, Muggsy's First Sweetheart, The Purgation, A Midnight Cupid, What the Daisy Said, A Child's Faith, A Flash of Light, As the Bells Rang Out, Serious Sixteen, The Call to Arms, Unexpected Help, An Arcadian Maid, Her Father's Pride, The House with Closed Shutters, A Salutary Lesson, When We Were in Our Teens* (credit unconfirmed), *An Old Story with a New Ending* (credit unconfirmed), *The Usurer, The Sorrows of the Unfaithful, Wilful Peggy, The Modern Prodigal, Muggsy Becomes a Hero* (credit unconfirmed), *The Affair of an Egg* (credit unconfirmed), *A Summer Idyll, Little Angels of Luck, A Mohawk's Way, In Life's Cycle, Summer Tragedy* (credit unconfirmed), *The Oath and the Man, Rose O'Salem-Town, Examination Day at School, The Iconoclast, A Gold Necklace* (credit unconfirmed), *That Chink at Golden Gulch, The Broken Doll, The Message of the Violin* (also sc.), *Two Little Waifs: A Modern Fairy Tale, Waiter No. 5, The Fugitive, Simple Charity, Sunshine Sue* (credit unconfirmed; also co-sc.), *The Song of the Wildwood Flute, His New Lid* (credit unconfirmed), *Not So Bad As He Seemed* (credit unconfirmed), *A Plain Song, Effecting a Cure, A Child's Stratagem, The Golden Supper, His Sister-in-Law* (credit unconfirmed; co-dir. with Powell), *The Lesson, White Roses* (credit unconfirmed), *Winning Back His Love* 1910; *The Two Paths, When a Man Loves, The Italian Barber* (also sc.), *His Trust, His Trust Fulfilled, Fate's Turning, Poor Sick Men* (credit unconfirmed), *A Wreath of Orange Blossoms* (credit unconfirmed), *Three Sisters, Heart Beats of Long Ago, What Shall We Do with Our Old, Fisher Folks, The Diamond Star, His Daughter, The Lily of the Tenements, The Heart of a Savage, A Decree of Destiny, Conscience, Was He a Coward?, Teaching Dad to Like Her* (credit unconfirmed), *The Lonedale Operator, The Spanish Gypsy, The Broken Cross, The Chief's Daughter, Paradise Lost* (credit unconfirmed), *Madame Rex, A Knight of the Road, His Mother's Scarf, How She Triumphed, The Two Sides, In the Days of '49, The New Dress, The Crooked Road* (credit unconfirmed), *The White Rose of the Wilds, A Romany Tragedy, A Smile of a Child, Enoch Arden Part I, Enoch Arden Part II, The Primal Call, Her Sacrifice* (credit unconfirmed), *Fighting Blood, The Thief and the Girl, The Jealous Husband* (credit unconfirmed), *Bobby the Coward, The Indian Brothers, A Country Cupid* (credit unconfirmed), *The Last Drop of Water, Out from the Shadow, The Ruling Passion, The Sorrowful Example, The Blind Princess and the Poet, The Rose of Kentucky, Swords and Hearts, The Stuff Heroes Are Made Of* (credit unconfirmed), *The Old Confectioner's Mistake* (credit unconfirmed), *The Squaw's Love, Dan the Dandy, The Revenue Man and the Girl, Her Awakening, The Making of a Man, Italian Blood, The Unveiling, The Adventures of Billy, The Long Road, Love in the Hills, The Battle, The Trail of Books, Through Darkened Vales, The Miser's Heart, Sunshine Through the Dark, A Woman Scorned,*

The Failure, Saved from Himself, As in a Looking Glass, A Terrible Discovery, The Voice of a Child 1911; *The Baby and the Stork* (credit unconfirmed), *A Tale of the Wilderness, The Eternal Mother* (also sc.), *The Old Bookkeeper, For His Son, A Blot in the 'Scutcheon, The Transformation of Mike, A Sister's Love* (credit unconfirmed), *Billy's Stratagem, The Mender of Nets, Under Burning Skies, The Sunbeam, A Siren of Impulse, A String of Pearls, Iola's Promise, The Root of Evil, The Goddess of Sagebrush Gulch, The Girl and Her Trust, The Punishment, Fate's Interception, The Female of the Species, Just Like a Woman, One Is Business the Other Crime, The Lesser Evil, The Old Actor, A Lodging for the Night, His Lesson, When Kings Were the Law, A Beast at Bay, An Outcast Among the Outcasts, Home Folks, A Temporary Truce, Lena and the Geese, The Spirit Awakened* (also sc.), *The School Teacher and the Waif, Man's Lust for Gold, An Indian Summer* (credit unconfirmed), *A Man's Genesis* (also co-sc.), *Heaven Avenges* (credit unconfirmed), *The Sands of Dee, The Black Sheep, The Narrow Road, A Child's Remorse, The Inner Circle, A Change of Spirit* (also co-sc.), *A Pueblo Legend* (also sc.), *An Unseen Enemy, Blind Love* (credit unconfirmed), *Two Daughters of Eve, Friends* (also sc.), *So Near Yet So Far, A Feud in the Kentucky Hills* (also sc.), *The Chief's Blanket* (credit unconfirmed), *In the Aisles of the Wild, The One She Loved, The Painted Lady* (also sc.), *The Musketeers of Pig Alley* (also sc.), *Heredity, The Massacre* (credit unconfirmed; also sc.), *Gold and Glitter* (credit unconfirmed), *My Baby* (credit unconfirmed), *The Informer, Brutality* (also sc.), *The New York Hat, My Hero* (credit unconfirmed; also sc.), *The Burglar's Dilemma, A Cry for Help, The God Within* 1912; *Three Friends, The Telephone Girl and the Lady, Pirate Gold* (credit unconfirmed), *An Adventure in the Autumn woods, The Tender-Hearted Boy* (credit unconfirmed), *A Misappropriated Turkey* (credit unconfirmed), *Brothers* (credit unconfirmed), *Oil and Water, Drink's Lure* (credit unconfirmed), *A Chance Deception* (credit unconfirmed), *Love in an Apartment Hotel* (credit unconfirmed), *Broken Ways, A Girl's Stratagem* (credit unconfirmed), *The Unwelcome Guest, Near to Earth* (credit unconfirmed), *Fate* (co-dir. with Powell), *A Welcome Intruder* (credit unconfirmed), *The Sheriff's Baby, The Hero of Little Italy* (credit unconfirmed), *The Perfidy of Mary* (credit unconfirmed), *The Little Tease* (also sc.), *A Misunderstood Boy, The Left-Handed Man* (credit unconfirmed), *The Lady and the Mouse, If We Only Knew* (credit unconfirmed), *The Wanderer* (credit unconfirmed; also sc.), *The House of Darkness, The Stolen Loaf* (credit unconfirmed), *The Yaqui Cur, Olaf an Atom* (credit unconfirmed), *Just Gold, His Mother's Son, The Ranchero's Revenge* (credit unconfirmed), *A Timely Interception* (credit unconfirmed), *Death's Marathon, The Switch Tower* (credit unconfirmed), *The Mothering Heart, In Diplomatic Circles* (credit unconfirmed), *Her Mother's Oath* (credit unconfirmed; also sc.), *The Sorrowful Shore* (credit unconfirmed), *The Mistake, Doing the Round-Up* (credit unconfirmed), *The Coming of Angelo* (credit unconfirmed; also sc.), *The Reformers or the Lost Art of Minding One's Business, An Indian's Loyalty* (credit unconfirmed), *Two Men of the Desert* 1913; *The Massacre* (also sc.), *The Battle at Elderbush Gulch* (also sc.), *Brute Force* 1914.

Features—*Judith of Bethulia* (also sc.), *The Battle of the Sexes/The Single Standard, The Escape, Home Sweet Home* (also co-sc.), *The Avenging Conscience* (also sc.) 1914; *The Birth of a Nation* (also co-sc.) 1915; *A Day with Governor Whitman* (doc. short), *Intolerance* (also prod., sc., mus.) 1916; *Her Condoned Sin* (expanded, retitled six-reel version of *Judith of Bethulia*) 1917; *Hearts of the World* (also prod., story under pseudonym of M. Gaston de Tolignac, sc. under pseudonym Capt. Victor Marier, co-mus.), *The Great Love* (also co-sc. under Marier pseudonym), *The Greatest Thing in Life* (also co-sc. under Marier pseudonym) 1918; *The World of Columbus* (charity-drive short), *A Romance of Happy Valley* (also sc. under Marier pseudonym), *The Girl Who Stayed at Home* (also co-sc.), *Broken Blossoms* (also prod., sc., co-mus.), *True Heart Susie, The Fall of Babylon* (the Babylonian episode of *Intolerance* presented as a feature), *The Mother and the Law* (the Modern episode of *Intolerance* presented as a feature), *Scarlet Days, The Greatest Question* 1919; *The Idol Dancer, The Love Flower* (also prod., sc.), *Way Down East* (also prod., co-sc.) 1920; *Dream Street* (also prod., sc. under pseudonym Roy Sinclair) 1921; *Orphans of the Storm* (also prod., sc. under pseudonym Gaston de Tolignac), *One Exciting Night* (also prod., story under pseudonym Irene Sinclair, sc.) 1922; *The White Rose* (also prod., story, sc. under pseudonym Irene Sinclair) 1923; *America* (also prod.), *Isn't Life Wonderful* (also prod., sc.) 1924; *Sally of the Sawdust* (also prod.) 1925; *That Royle Girl, The Sorrows of Satan* 1926; *Topsy and Eva* (dir. some scenes only, uncredited) 1927; *Drums of Love* (also prod.), *The Battle of the Sexes* 1928; *Lady of the Pavements* 1929; *Abraham Lincoln* 1930; *The Struggle* (also prod., co-sc., co-mus.) 1931.

Griffith, Edward H. Director. *b.* Aug. 23, 1894, Lynchburg, Va. Deceased. Educated in England and Germany. He started out as a newspaper reporter and magazine feature writer. Entered films as actor-screenwriter for the Edison company in 1915, following some stage experience. Soon after, he began directing two-reelers and, from 1917, feature films. His films are competently directed but mostly routine. Sometimes billed as E. H. Griffith.

FILMS: *Billy and the Big Stick, One Touch of Nature, The Awakening of Ruth* 1917; *Fit to Win, The End of the Road* 1919; *The Garter Girl, Bab's Candidate, The Vice of Fools* 1920; *Scrambled Wives, The Land of Hope, If Women Only Knew, Dawn of the East* 1921; *Free Air* 1922; *The Go-Getter, Sea Raiders, Unseeing Eyes* 1923; *Week-End Husbands, Another Scandal* 1924; *Bad Company, Headlines* 1925; *White Mice, Atta Boy* 1926; *The Price of Honor, Afraid to Love, Alias the Lone Wolf, The Opening Night* 1927; *Hold 'Em Yale!, Captain Swagger, Love Over Night* 1928; *The Shady Lady, Paris Bound, Rich People* 1929; *Holiday* 1930; *Rebound* 1931; *Lady with a Past, The Animal Kingdom* 1932; *Another Language* 1933; *Biography of a Bachelor Girl, No More Ladies* 1935; *Next Time We Love, Ladies in Love* 1936; *Cafe Metropole, I'll Take Romance* 1937; *Cafe Society, Honeymoon in Bali* 1939; *Safari* 1940; *Virginia* (also prod., co-story), *One Night in Lisbon* (also prod.), *Bahama Passage* (also prod.) 1941; *Young and Willing* (also prod.), *The Sky's the Limit* 1943; *Perilous Holiday* 1946.

Griffith, Hugh. Actor. *b.* May 30, 1912, Marian Glas, Anglesey, North Wales. *d.* 1980. A former bank clerk, he made his stage debut in 1939 and his first film appearance the following year. He played forceful, exuberant character roles in numerous plays and films, in the US as well as in Britain, and won an Academy Award as best supporting actor for his portrayal of Sheik Ilderim in *Ben-Hur* (1959). He was nominated for another Oscar for *Tom Jones* (1963).

FILMS INCLUDE: *Neutral Port* 1940; *London Belongs to Me/Dulcimer Street, So Evil My Love, The Last Days of Dolwyn/Dolwyn* 1948; *A Run for Your Money, Kind Hearts and Coronets* 1949; *Laughter in Paradise, The Galloping Major* 1951; *The Titfield Thunderbolt, The Beggar's Opera* 1953; *The Sleeping Tiger* 1954; *Ben-Hur* (US) 1959; *Exodus* (US) 1960; *The Counterfeit Traitor* (US), *The Inspector/Lisa* (UK/US), *Term of Trial, Mutiny on the Bounty* (US) 1962; *Tom Jones* (as Squire Western) 1963; *Hide and Seek* 1964; *The Amorous Adventures of Moll Flanders* 1965; *How to Steal a Million* (US)

1966; *Oh Dad Poor Dad...* (US), *The Sailor from Gibraltar* 1967; *Oliver!, The Fixer* (US) 1968; *Start the Revolution Without Me* (as Louis XVI; US), *Cry of the Banshee, Wuthering Heights* 1970; *The Abominable Dr. Phibes, Who Slew Auntie Roo?* 1971; *I Racconti di Canterbury/The Canterbury Tales* (It.) 1972; *Che?/What?* (It./Fr.), *Luther* (UK/US) 1973; *Craze, Legend of the Werewolf* 1974; *Loving Cousins* (It.), *The Passover Plot* (as Caiphas; Isr./US) 1976; *Casanova & Co.* (Aus./Ger./It./Fr.), *The Last Remake of Beau Geste* (US) 1977; *The Hound of the Baskervilles* (as Sir Henry Baskerville) 1978.

Griffith, Melanie. Actress. Born on Aug. 9, 1957, in New York City. Strapping (5' 9"), voluptuous star of Hollywood films of the late 80s and early 90s. The daughter of Hitchcock heroine Tippi HEDREN and real-estate developer Peter Griffith, she was raised on a ranch near Los Angeles. After some modeling, she made her screen debut in Arthur Penn's *Night Moves* (1975) playing a sexy nymphet, a role in which she would be typecast in several of her subsequent films. Following acting classes in New York with Stella Adler and a tantalizing performance in Brian De Palma's *Body Double* (1984), she was assigned meatier roles, then got her big break as the feisty, smarter-than-she-looks heroine of *Working Girl* (1988), for which she was nominated for a best actress Academy Award. Her career has faltered with a string of unambitious projects after her Oscar nomination, including an ill-advised remake of *Born Yesterday*, in which she starred with Don Johnson. Griffith's private life has been as much a subject of newsprint as has her movie career. A precocious juvenile, she was 14 when she fell in love with the then little-known actor Don JOHNSON, her mother's 22-year-old co-star in *The Harrad Experiment* (1973). After a period of cohabitation, they married in 1976; but their marriage ended in less than two years. In the 80s, Griffith became known for her drug and alcohol use. After completing *Working Girl* she checked into a Minnesota rehabilitation clinic and recovered from her dependency with the long-distance support of Johnson, whom she then remarried in June of 1989, only to divorce again several years later. The mother of three, she maintains homes in Aspen, Miami, and Beverly Hills and is now married to actor Antonio BANDERAS. Her younger half sister, Tracy Griffith, is a budding movie actress.

FILMS: *Night Moves, Smile, The Drowning Pool* 1975; *One on One, Joyride* 1977; *Underground Aces, Roar* 1981; *Body Double, Fear City* 1984; *Something Wild* 1986; *Cherry 2000, The Milagro Beanfield War, Stormy Monday* (UK), *Working Girl* 1988; *In the Spirit, Pacific Heights, The Bonfire of the Vanities* 1990; *Paradise, Shining Through* 1991; *A Stranger Among Us* 1992; *Born Yesterday* 1993; *Milk Money, Nobody's Fool* 1994; *Now and Then* 1995; *Mulholland Falls, Two Much* 1996.

Griffith, Raymond. Actor, producer, screenwriter. *b.* Jan. 23, 1890, Boston. *d.* 1957. The son of show people, he entered films with no stage experience in 1914 and subsequently appeared in numerous comedies and some dramas, in both leads and supporting roles. He also collaborated on several scripts. He retired from acting after playing his briefest and most memorable part, that of the dying French soldier in a trench with Lew Ayres in *All Quiet on the Western Front* (1930). He then turned producer, mainly for Fox.

FILMS INCLUDE: As actor—*A Scoundrel's Toll* 1916; *The Follies Girl* 1918; *The Crossroads of New York, Fools First* 1922; *Red Lights, The Day of Faith, White Tiger, The Eternal Three* 1923; *Changing Husbands, Poisoned Paradise, Lily of the Dust, Open All Night* 1924; *Forty Winks, The Night Club, Paths to Paradise, A Regular Fellow, When Winter Went, Fine Clothes* 1925; *Hands Up, Wet Paint, You'd Be Surprised* 1926; *Wedding Bills, Time to Love* 1927; *Trent's Last Case* 1929; *All Quiet on the Western Front* 1930. As production supervisor—*Gold Diggers of 1933, Voltaire* 1933. As producer or associate producer—*The Bowery* 1933; *Moulin Rouge, The House of Rothschild, The Affairs of Cellini, The Mighty Barnum* 1934; *Cardinal Richelieu, Les Miserables* 1935; *A Message to Garcia, Under Two Flags* 1936; *Seventh Heaven Thin Ice, Heidi, Second Honeymoon* 1937; *Rebecca of Sunnybrook Farm* 1938; *The Three Musketeers, Drums Along the Mohawk* 1939; *The Great Profile, The Mark of Zorro* 1940.

Griffith, Richard. Film historian and critic. *b.* Oct. 6, 1912, Winchester, Va. *d.* 1969, in a car crash. A graduate of Haverford College, he received a Rockefeller Foundation fellowship for research in film history. From 1935 he was motion picture critic and correspondent for various newspapers. In 1939 he joined the Museum of Modern Art film department as assistant curator. During WW II he was film editor for the Army Signal Corps and worked on, among other films, Frank Capra's *Why We Fight* documentary series. Between 1946 and 1949 he was executive director of New York's National Board of Review of Motion Pictures and from 1951 to 1965 curator of the Museum of Modern Art's Film Library. He edited the American edition of *Grierson on Documentary* (1947) and was co-author with Paul Rotha of the revised editions (since 1949) of *The Film Till Now* and the third edition of *Documentary Film.* He also wrote *The Movies* (with Arthur Mayer), *The World of Robert Flaherty,* and *Anatomy of a Motion Picture.*

Griggs, Loyal. American director of photography. *b.* 1906. *d.* 1978. Entered films directly out of high school in the mid-20s as an assistant in the special-effects branch of Paramount's camera department. He took nearly 30 years to graduate to director of photography but made the most of the opportunity, winning an Academy Award for the cinematography of the classic Western *Shane* (1953) just two years after making the grade as a lighting cameraman.

FILMS INCLUDE: *The Last Outpost* 1951; *Shane* 1953; *Elephant Walk, White Christmas* 1954; *The Bridges at Toko-Ri, Three-Ring Circus, We're No Angels* 1955; *Three Violent People, The Ten Commandments* 1956; *The Tin Star, The Sad Sack* 1957; *Hot Spell, The Buccaneer* 1958; *The Hangman* 1959; *Visit to a Small Planet, G.I. Blues* 1960; *Man-Trap* 1961; *Girls! Girls! Girls!* 1962; *Papa's Delicate Condition* 1963; *The Greatest Story Ever Told* (co-phot.), *In Harm's Way* 1965; *The Slender Thread* 1966; *Hurry Sundown* (co-phot.), *Banning* 1967; *P.J.* 1968; *Paint Your Wagon* (2nd-unit phot. only) 1969; *Tick... Tick... Tick* 1970; *Bunny O'Hare* (co-phot.) 1971.

Grimaldi, Alberto. Producer. Born in 1926, in Naples. An attorney, he entered the Italian motion picture industry as a legal counsel and was soon attracted by the business potential of film production. In 1962 he established his own production company, E.P.A., and the following year released his first production, a Zorro adventure. During the late 60s he made a quick fortune with several popular spaghetti Westerns, then turned to serious production with films by such directors as Fellini, Pasolini, and Bertolucci.

FILMS INCLUDE: *L'Ombra di Zorro* 1963; *Per qualche Dollaro in più/For a Few Dollars More* 1965; *Il Buono il Brutto il Cattivo/The Good the Bad and the Ugly* 1966; *Il Mercenario/ The Mercenary, Un Tranquillo Posto di Campagna/A Quiet Place in the Country* 1968; *Ehi Amico... c'è Sabata/Sabata, Fellini Satyricon, Quemada!/ Burn!* 1969; *Il Decamerone/The Decameron* 1971; *I Racconti di Canterbury/The Canterbury Tales, Man of La Mancha* (exec. prod.), *Ultimo Tango a Parigi/Last Tango in Paris* 1972; *Il Fiore delle Mille e una Notte/A Thousand and One Nights/The Arabian Nights* 1974; *Salo o le Centiventi Giornate di Sodoma/ Salo—The 120 Days of Sodom* 1975; *Cadaveri Eccellenti/ Illustrious Corpses, 1990, Casanova/Fellini's Casanova* 1976; *Viaggio con Anita/Travels with Anita/Lovers and Liars* 1979; *Ginger e Fred/Ginger and Fred* 1985.

Grimault, Paul. Animator. Born on Mar. 23, 1905, in Neuilly-sur-Seine, France. The son of an archeologist, he studied commercial art and began his career in advertising. With his earnings from cartoon commercials, he began making entertainment cartoons for the screen, at first short and later also feature length. His work is traditional in style but stands out for its intelligence and delicate lyricism. His *Le Petit Soldat* won first prize at Venice in 1948. His influence on the development of French animation has been considerable.

FILMS INCLUDE: *Go chez les Oiseaux, Les Passagers de la Grande Ourse* 1939; *Le Marchand de Notes* 1942; *L'Epouvantail* 1943; *Le Voleur de Paratonnerres, La Flûte magique* 1946; *Le Petit Soldat* 1947; *La Bergère et le Ramoneur* (feature) 1952; *Enrico* 1956; *La Faim du Monde* 1958; *Le Roi et l'Oiseau* (feature) 1967; *Le Diamant* 1970.

Grimes, Gary. Actor. Born on June 2, 1955, in San Francisco. Curly-haired, innocent-faced young lead of Hollywood films of the 70s.

FILMS: *Summer of '42* 1971; *The Culpepper Cattle Company* 1972; *Class of '44, Cahill—US Marshal* 1973; *The Spikes Gang* 1974; *Gus* 1976.

Grimes, Tammy. Actress. Born on Jan. 30, 1934, in Lynn, Mass., into a socially prominent family. *ed.* Stephens Coll.; Neighborhood Playhouse School of the Theatre. She made her New York stage debut in 1955 and, after appearing in a number of plays and revues, soared to Broadway stardom in 1960 as a result of her flamboyant performance in the title role of 'The Unsinkable Molly Brown,' for which she won both the Tony Award and the New York Drama Critics Award. She received both prizes again in 1970 for her part in the revival of 'Private Lives.' She starred on TV in 'The Tammy Grimes Show' in 1966. Her film appearances have been sporadic. She is the mother of actress Amanda PLUMMER.

FILMS: *Three Bites of the Apple* 1967; *Play It as It Lays* 1972; *Somebody Killed Her Husband* 1978; *The Runner Stumbles* 1979; *Can't Stop the Music* 1980; *The Last Unicorn* 1982; *America* 1986; *Mr. North* 1988; *Slaves of New York* 1989; *A Modern Affair* 1996.

Grinde, Nick. Director. *b.* Harry A. Grinde, Jan. 12, 1891, Madison, Wis. *d.* 1979. *ed.* U. of Wisconsin. Directed numerous low-budget Hollywood films—often lively crime and action dramas—for various studios over a period spanning the late 20s to the mid-40s. He then switched to TV and to producing commercials.

FILMS: *Riders of the Dark, Beyond the Sierras* 1928; *Morgan's Last Raid, The Desert Rider* 1929; *The Bishop Murder Case* (co-dir. with David Burton), *Good News* (co-dir. with Edgar J. McGregor), *Remote Control* (co-dir. with Mal St. Clair), *Wu Li Chang* (Spanish-language version of *Mr. Wu*) 1930; *This Modern Age* 1931; *Shopworn, Vanity Street* 1932; *Babes in Toyland* (co-sc. only) 1934; *Stone of Silver Creek, Border Brigands, Ladies Crave Excitement* 1935; *Public Enemy's Wife, Jailbreak* 1936; *Fugitive in the Sky, The Captain's Kid, White Bondage, Public Wedding, Love Is on the Air, Exiled to Shanghai* 1937; *Down in Arkansas* 1938; *Federal Man-Hunt, King of Chinatown, Sudden Money, The Man They Could Not Hang, A Woman Is the Judge* 1939; *Scandal Sheet, Convicted Woman, The Man with Nine Lives, Men Without Souls, Girls of the Road, Before I Hang, Friendly Neighbors* 1940; *Mountain Moonlight* 1941; *The Girl from Alaska* 1942; *We've Never Been Licked* (co-sc. only), *Hitler—Dead or Alive* 1943; *Road to Alcatraz* 1945.

grip. A general-purpose handyman, the movie set's counterpart of the theater's stagehand. His duties include laying DOLLY tracks, moving FLATS, setting up PARALLELS, building platforms, placing REFLECTORS and GOBOS, doing light carpentry, and generally performing tasks that require brawn. Grips are usually paid hourly wages. The head grip, officially known as "first company grip," is salaried weekly and is in charge of a crew of grips often numbering as many as 15.

Grodin, Charles. Actor. Born on Apr. 21, 1935, in Pittsburgh, the son of a dressmaking supply shop owner. *ed.* U. of Miami. Open-faced, shyly cynical, often quirky leading man of the American stage and screen, typically seen in comically flawed characterizations. Following a stint at the Pittsburgh Playhouse, he moved to New York, where he studied drama under Uta Hagen and Lee STRASBERG. He made his Broadway debut in 'Tchin Tchin' (1962) and (discounting a shelved film) his first screen appearance as Mia Farrow's obstetrician in *Rosemary's Baby* (1968). A protegé of Elaine MAY, he played his most memorable role as a bewildered newlywed heel on the prowl for another woman on his honeymoon, in her comedy gem *The Heartbreak Kid* (1972). Grodin, who has written, directed, and produced for the stage and TV, is also credited with a couple of movie screenplays. Twice married, he lives in Connecticut. Memoirs: *It Would Be So Nice If You Weren't Here* (1991).

FILMS: *Rosemary's Baby* 1968; *Sex and the College Girl/The Fun Lovers* (release delayed from 1964), *Catch-22* (as Aarfy Aardvark) 1970; *The Heartbreak Kid* 1972; *11 Harrowhouse* (also co-sc.) 1974; *King Kong* 1976; *Thieves* 1977; *Heaven Can Wait* 1978; *Sunburn, Real Life* 1979; *It's My Turn, Seems Like Old Times* 1980; *The Great Muppet Caper, The Incredible Shrinking Woman* 1981; *The Woman in Red, The Lonely Guy* 1984; *Movers and Shakers* (also sc., co-prod.) 1985; *Last Resort/Club Sandwich* 1986; *Ishtar* 1987; *The Couch Trip, You Can't Hurry Love, Midnight Run* 1988; *Taking Care of Business* 1990; *Beethoven* 1992; *Dave, Heart and Souls, So I Married an Axe Murderer, Beethoven's 2nd* 1993; *Clifford* 1994.

Grosbard, Ulu. Director. Born on Jan. 9, 1929, Antwerp, Belgium. *ed.* U. of Chicago; Yale Drama School. A former diamond cutter, he turned to directing plays in 1957 and has since staged a number of successful Broadway productions. Between plays, during the 60s, he apprenticed as an assistant director on several Hollywood productions (*Splendor in the Grass, West Side Story, The Hustler, The Pawnbroker,* etc.) and in 1968 turned out his own first film, *The Subject Was Roses.* He has since worked only sporadically in the film industry.

FILMS: *The Subject Was Roses* 1968; *Who Is Harry Kellerman and Why Is He Saying Those Terrible Things About Me?* (also co-prod.) 1971; *Straight Time* 1978; *True Confessions* 1981; *Falling in Love* 1984; *Georgia* (also co-prod.) 1995.

gross receipts. 1. The total amount of monies paid by theaters and theater chains to film distributors for the right to show a film. Also known as film RENTAL receipts or distributor's share of gross receipts. 2. The total amount paid to theaters by moviegoers in the form of ticket prices. Also known as BOX OFFICE receipts. 3. The total amount of money made by a film, including not only rental receipts, but also income from home video, pay-television, broadcast television, merchandising, soundtracks, book publishing, and music publishing.

Grot, Anton. Art director. *b.* Antocz Franziszek Groszewski, Jan. 18, 1884, Kelbasin, Poland. *d.* 1974. Following studies of design and illustration at the Kraków (Cracow) Art School and a technical college in Koenigsberg, Germany, he emigrated to the US in 1909. He entered the film industry in 1913 as an art director for the Lubin company and subsequently designed the sets of major silent productions of

Pathé, Fairbanks-Pickford, De Mille, and other producers. In 1927 he joined Warner Bros., where he remained until his retirement in the late 40s, influencing the characteristic look of the studio's productions during its pinnacle years of the 30s and 40s. He was nominated for five Academy Awards and during the 1941 presentations received a special scientific/technical Oscar for his invention of a water ripple and wave-illusion machine to help create light effects and bad-weather simulations in ocean sequences, first utilized in *The Sea Hawk* (1940). After retiring he devoted himself to painting.

FILMS INCLUDE: *The Mouse and the Lion* 1913; *Light at Dusk* 1916; *Arms and the Woman* 1917; *The Naulahka* 1918; *Rogues and Romance* 1920; *Dorothy Vernon of Haddon Hall, The Thief of Bagdad* (assoc. des.) 1924; *Don Q Son of Zorro* (assoc. des.), *The Road to Yesterday* 1925; *The Volga Boatman* 1926; *The King of Kings, White Gold* 1927; *The Barker* 1928; *Noah's Ark, Smiling Irish Eyes* 1929; *Lilies of the Field, No No Nanette* 1930; *Little Caesar, Body and Soul, Svengali, The Mad Genius* 1931; *The Hatchet Man, Doctor X* 1932; *20,000 Years in Sing Sing, Mystery of the Wax Museum, Footlight Parade, Gold Diggers of 1933* 1933; *British Agent* 1934; *Captain Blood, Dr. Socrates, A Midsummer Night's Dream* 1935; *Anthony Adverse, The White Angel* 1936; *The Life of Emile Zola, The Great Garrick, Tovarich* 1937; *They Made Me a Criminal, Juarez, The Private Lives of Elizabeth and Essex* 1939; *The Sea Hawk, A Dispatch from Reuter's* 1940; *The Sea Wolf* 1941; *The Conspirators* 1944; *Rhapsody in Blue, Mildred Pierce* 1945; *Nora Prentiss, The Two Mrs. Carrolls, Possessed, The Unsuspected* 1947; *Romance on the High Seas, June Bride* 1948; *Backfire* 1950.

Gruault, Jean. Screenwriter. Born in 1924 in Fontenay-sous-Bois, France. Originally a writer for left-wing theater, he became known for his screenplays for several landmark New Wave films.

FILMS INCLUDE: *Paris Nous Appartient/Paris Belongs to Us* 1960; *Jules et Jim/Jules and Jim, Vanina* (also act.) 1961; *Les Carabiniers* (also act.) 1963; *Suzanne Simonin, La Religieuse de Denis Diderot/The Nun* 1965; *La Prise de pouvoir par Louis XIV/The Rise of Louis XIV* 1966; *L'Enfant sauvage/The Wild Child* 1970; *Les Deux Anglaises et le Continent/Two English Girls, L'Histoire d/Adèle H./The Story of Adèle H.* 1971; *La Chambre Verte/The Green Room* 1975; *Il Messsia/The Messiah, Les Soeurs Brontë/The Brontë Sisters* 1978; *Mon oncle d'Amérique* 1979; *Via degli Specchi* 1982; *Les Années 80, La Vie est un roman/Life Is a Bed of Roses* 1983; *L'Amour à mort* 1984; *Mystère Alexina* 1985; *Golden Eighties* 1986; *Australia* 1989.

Gruber, Frank. American novelist, screenwriter. *b.* Feb. 2, 1904. *d.* 1969. Prolific author of many adventure novels and screenplays, mostly Westerns and mystery yarns.

FILMS INCLUDE: *Death of a Champion* (story basis only) 1939; *The Kansan* (novel basis only) 1943; *The Mask of Dimitrios* 1944; *Oregon Trail* (novel basis) 1945; *The French Key, Terror by Night, Dressed to Kill* (adapt.) 1946; *Bulldog Drummond at Bay* 1947; *Fighting Man of the Plains* (also story) 1949; *Dakota Lil* (story only), *The Cariboo Trail* 1950; *The Texas Rangers* (story only), *The Great Missouri Raid* (also story), *Warpath* (also story) 1951; *The Denver and the Rio Grande* (also story), *Hurricane Smith* 1952; *Pony Express* (story basis only) 1953; *Backlash* (novel basis only) 1956; *The Big Land* (novel basis only) 1957; *Twenty Plus Two* (from own novel; also prod.) 1961; *Town Tamer* (from own novel) 1965; *Arizona Raiders* (story basis only; remake of *The Texas Rangers*) 1967.

Gründgens, Gustaf (also **Gruendgens, Gustav**). Actor. *b.* Dec. 22, 1899, Düsseldorf, Germany. *d.* 1963, a suicide. He was a celebrated stage actor, director, and producer, and also played some key roles in German films of the 20s and 30s. Memorable as the gang chief in Lang's *M* (1931) and as the jealous husband in Ophüls's *Liebelei* (1933). He headed several German theaters from 1937, notably the Hamburg Schauspielhaus. He also directed a number of films. In the post–WW II years, Gründgens was never able to shake off accusations that he had collaborated with the Nazis. Famous for his interpretations of Faust's Mephisto, he was the prototype for the agonizing protagonist (played by Klaus Maria BRANDAUER) in Istvan Szabo's *Mephisto* (1981). The Oscar-winning film was based on a novel by Klaus Mann, the son of author Thomas Mann and the brother of Gründgens's first wife, Erika Mann. His second (1936–45) was actress Marianne Hoppe. He killed himself at age 63, during a visit to Manila.

FILMS INCLUDE: *Hokuspokus/Hocuspocus, Brand in der Oper/Fire in the Opera House* 1930; *Danton* (as Robespierre), *M, Der Raub der Mona Lisa/The Theft of the Mona Lisa, Yorck, Luise Königin von Preussen* 1931; *Eine Stadt steht Kopf* (dir. only), *Teilnehmer antwortet nichts, Die Gräfin von Monte Christo* 1932; *Liebelei, Der Tunnel* 1933; *Das Erbe von Pretoria, Die Finanzen des Grossherzogs/The Grand Duke's Finances* (dir. only), *Schwarzer Jäger Johanna* 1934; *Pygmalion* (as Robespierre), *Das Mädchen Johanna* 1935; *Capriolen* (also dir.) 1937; *Liebe im Gleitflug/Love in Stunt Flying* (also dir.) 1938; *Der Schritt vom Wege/The False Step* (dir. only) 1939; *Zwei Welten* (dir. only) 1940; *Friedemann Bach, Ohm Krüger* 1941; *Faust* (as Mephisto; also supervising dir.), *Ein Glas Wasser/A Glass of Water, Faust* (as Mephisto; also co-dir.) 1960.

Grune, Karl. Director. *b.* Jan. 22, 1890, Vienna. *d.* 1962. A former disciple of Max REINHARDT, he was an actor on the Berlin stage and the director of the city's Residenttheater before entering German films in 1918. His one important contribution to German cinema was the film *Die Strasse/The Street* (1923), a postexpressionist picture about a man who seeks liberation from marital doldrums in the alluring life of a city street, only to find danger and chaos and be forced to retreat to the safety of his home. The theme of the film provided the outline for a whole genre of German pictures known as "street films." In 1931 he left Germany, made one film in France, then settled in England, where he directed a number of sound films.

FILMS INCLUDE: *Der Mädchenhirt, Menschen in Ketten* (co-dir. with Friedrich Zelnik) 1919; *Die Jagd nach der Wahrheit, Nachtbesuch, Nacht ohne Morgen* 1920; *Mann über Bord* 1921; *Frauenopfer, Der Graf von Charolais, Der stärkste Trieb* 1922; *Schlagende Wetter, Die Strasse/The Street* (also co-sc.) 1923; *Arabella, Komödianten* 1924; *Eifersucht/Jealousy* 1925; *Die Brüder Schellenberg* (also co-sc.) 1926; *Am Rande der Welt/At the Edge of the World* (also co-sc.), *Königin Luise* 1927; *Marquis d'Eon—der Spion der Pompadour, Waterloo* 1928; *Katherine Knie* 1929; *Das gelbe Haus des King-Fu* 1931; *La Maison jaune* (French version of latter film; Fr.) 1932; *Abdul the Damned* (UK) 1935; *The Marriage of Corbal* (UK) 1936; *Pagliacci/A Clown Must Laugh* (UK) 1937.

Grünenwald, Jean-Jacques. Composer, organist. *b.* Feb. 2, 1911, Cran-Gevrier, near Annecy, France, of Swiss parentage. *d.* 1982. A protegé of Marcel Dupré, he was one of Europe's leading concert organists. He was also a well-known composer of concert-hall music. His scores for French films included several major productions of Robert BRESSON and Jacques BECKER.

FILMS INCLUDE: *Les Anges du Péché/Angels of the Streets* 1943; *Les Dames du Bois de Boulogne/Ladies of the Park* 1945; *Antoine et Antoinette/Antoine and Antoinette, Monsieur Vincent* 1947; *Le Journal d'un Curé de Campagne/*

Diary of a Country Priest, Edouard et Caroline/Edward and Caroline 1951; *La Verité sur Bébé Donge* 1952; *Les Amants de Tolède/The Lovers of Toledo* 1953; *Le Rage au Corps/Devil in the Flesh* 1954.

Grusin, Dave (David). Composer. Born in 1934, in Littleton, Col. A music director on the Andy Williams TV show for seven years in the 60s, he moved into features late in the decade and has since scored numerous major Hollywood productions. He won an Academy Award for *The Milagro Beanfield War* (1988).

FILMS INCLUDE: *Divorce American Style, The Graduate* 1967; *The Heart Is a Lonely Hunter* 1968; *Tell Them Willie Boy Is Here* 1969; *The Pursuit of Happiness* 1971; *The Great Northfield Minnesota Raid* 1972; *The Friends of Eddie Coyle* 1973; *The Yakooza, Three Days of the Condor* 1975; *The Front, Murder by Death* 1976; *The Goodbye Girl* 1977; *Heaven Can Wait* 1978; *. . . And Justice for All, The Champ, The Electric Horseman* 1978; *My Bodyguard* 1980; *Absence of Malice, On Golden Pond, Reds* 1981; *Author! Author!, Tootsie* 1982; *Racing with the Moon, The Pope of Greenwich Village* 1984; *The Goonies* 1985; *Lucas* 1986; *The Milagro Beanfield War, Clara's Heart, Tequila Sunrise* 1988; *The Fabulous Baker Boys* 1989; *Havana, The Bonfire of the Vanities* 1990; *The Firm* 1993; *The Cure* 1995; *Mulholland Falls* 1996.

Guardino, Harry. Actor. *b.* Dec. 23, 1925, in Brooklyn, N.Y. *d.* 1995. Tough-talking, tough-acting leading man and character player of American stage, TV, and films. Adept at comedy as well as drama.

FILMS INCLUDE: *Flesh and Fury* 1952; *Hold Back Tomorrow* 1955; *Houseboat* 1958; *Pork Chop Hill, The Five Pennies* 1959; *Jovanka e le Altre/Five Branded Women* (It./Yug.) 1960; *King of Kings* (as Barabbas) 1961; *Hell Is for Heroes, The Pigeon That Took Rome* 1962; *Rhino!* 1964; *Operazione San Gennaro/Treasure of San Gennaro* (It./Fr./Ger.) 1966; *The Adventures of Bullwhip Griffin, Valley of Mystery* 1967; *Madigan, Jigsaw, The Hell with Heroes* 1968; *Lovers and Other Strangers* 1970; *Dirty Harry, Red Sky at Morning* 1971; *They Only Kill Their Masters* 1972; *Capone, Whiffs* 1975; *St. Ives, The Enforcer* 1976; *Rollercoaster* 1977; *Matilda* 1978; *Goldengirl* 1979; *Any Which Way You Can* 1980.

Guarnieri, Ennio. Italian director of photography. One of Europe's leading cinematographers since the early 60s. He was behind the camera of films of Bolognini, Comencini, De Sica, Fellini, Ferreri, Pasolini, Wertmüller, and Zeffirelli, among other directors.

FILMS INCLUDE: *La Dolce Vita* (camera operator only), *I Giorni contati* 1960; *Una Storia moderna: L'Ape Regina/The Conjugal Bed* 1963; *Alta Infedeltá/High Infidelity* (co-sc.), *Le Voci bianche/White Voices* 1964; *Questa Volta parliamo di Uomini/Let's Talk About Men, Made in Italy* 1965; *Le Dolci Signore/Anyone Can Play, Arabella* 1967; *Meglio Veedova/Better a Widow* 1968; *Medea* 1970; *Fratello Sole Sorella Luna/Brother Sun Sister Moon, Ash Wednesday* (US), *Gli Ultimi 10 Giorni di Hitler/Hitler: The Last Ten Days* 1973; *Fatti di Gente perbene/La Grande Bourgeoisie, Il Viaggio/The Voyage* 1974; *Per le Antiche Scale/Down the Ancient Stairs, Der Richter und sein Henker/End of the Game* (Ger./It.) 1975; *Eredità Ferramonti/The Inheritance* 1976; *The Cassandra Crossing* (UK/It./Ger.), *Mogliamante/Wifemistress* 1977; *L'Ingorgo/Traffic Jam* 1979; *La Vera Storia della Signora dalle Camelie/La Dame aux Camélias* 1981; *Storia di Piera* 1982; *La Traviata* 1983; *Ginger e Fred/Ginger and Fred* (co-phot.) 1985; *Otello/Othello* (US/It.) 1986; *Mosca Addio, Dancers* (US) 1987.

Guazzoni, Enrico. Director. *b.* Sept. 18, 1876, Rome. *d.* 1949. A former painter and decorator, he directed many early Italian silents, typically historical spectaculars and ambitious literary adaptations. He designed the sets and costumes and wrote the scripts for most of his own films. His *Quo Vadis?* (1912) was a worldwide box-office hit. He continued directing into the early 40s but was less successful with sound films.

FILMS INCLUDE: *Un Invito a Pranzo* 1908; *Brutus, Agrippina, I Maccabei* 1910; *La Gerusalemme Liberata, Pinocchio* 1911; *Quo Vadis?* 1912; *Marcantonio e Cleopatra* 1913; *Caius Julius Caesar* 1914; *Ivan il Terribile, Alma Mater* 1915; *Madame Tallien* 1916; *Fabiola* 1917; *Lady Macbeth* 1918; *Il Sacco di Roma e Clemento VII* 1920; *Messalina* 1923; *La Sperdutta di Allah* 1928; *Myriam* 1929; *Il Domo del Mattino* 1932; *Signora Paradiso* 1934; *Il Re Burlone* 1935; *Ho Perduto mio Marito, I Due Sergenti, Re di Denari* 1936; *Il Dottore Antonio* 1938; *Il suo Destino* 1939; *La Figlia del Corsaro Verde* 1940; *Il Pirati della Malesia, Oro Nero* 1941; *La Fornarina* 1943.

Guber, Peter. Producer, executive. Born in 1939, in Newton, Mass., into an upper-middle-class Jewish family. After graduating from the University of Syracuse and attending the University of Florence, he went on to garner both a Master's in business administration and a law degree at New York University. Recruited by Columbia Pictures at entry level in 1968, he quickly advanced on the executive ladder and after four years became the company's head of worldwide production. He maintained that position for three years, during which he helped the studio achieve financial health through the judicious approval of projects (*The Way We Were, The Last Detail, Close Encounters of the Third Kind,* etc.) and astute financial management. He departed in 1976 to form his own company, Peter Guber's Filmworks, which he then merged with another company to form Casablanca Record and Filmworks. He scored a huge box-office hit with his first production, *The Deep* (1977). It was his first and last experience as a hands-on, on-location producer. But working behind the scenes, he soon became one of Hollywood's most successful producers and most powerful men. In 1980, Guber and his partners sold Casablanca to the Dutch conglomerate Philips/Siemens Polygram and under the auspices of the company set up Polygram Pictures, taking in as a partner producer Jon PETERS, a former hairdresser. They established the Guber-Peters company in 1983, which evolved through a 1988 merger into Guber-Peters-Barris Entertainment. Peters and Guber became known in the business as a shrewd and flamboyant duo who regularly took big chances and often scored huge hits. They had a seven-year contract with Warner Bros. when the giant Japanese Sony Corporation acquired Columbia Pictures from Coca-Cola for $3.5 billion late in 1989. In a bid to secure their services as chief executives for its American studio, Sony paid Guber and Peters nearly a billion dollars in fees and compensation, plus hundreds of millions in operating costs—exorbitant sums that catapulted the dynamic duo to the top of Tinseltown's heap. Then in one fell swoop Sony cleaned house, with Guber and Peters unceremoniously given the gate. They both are now independent producers.

FILMS INCLUDE (as producer or executive producer, usually in collaboration): *The Deep* 1977; *Midnight Express* 1978; *An American Werewolf in London* 1981; *Missing, Six Weeks* 1982; *Flashdance, D.C. Cab* 1983; *The Color Purple* 1985; *Youngblood* 1986; *The Witches of Eastwick, Innerspace* 1987; *Gorillas in the Mist, Rain Man* 1988; *Johnny Handsome, Tango and Cash, Batman* 1989; *The Bonfire of the Vanities* 1990; *Batman Returns* 1992; *This Boy's Life* 1993; *With Honors* 1994.

Guerra, Ruy. Director. Born on Aug. 22, 1931, in Lourenço Marques, Mozambique. The son of Portuguese settlers, he completed his education in Lisbon before enrolling at the IDHEC film school in Paris, in 1952. After working briefly as an assistant director to Jean Delannoy and Georges Rouquier, he went in 1958 to Brazil, where he stayed and soon became a leading figure in that country's Cinema Novo (New Cinema) movement. Following Mozambique's 1975 independence, he returned home to help organize the country's fledgling film industry but later resumed his work abroad. Guerra is a traditionalist in style whose films are typically driven by preset tempos and rhythms. The honesty of his themes and the authenticity of his locales give his films their originality. Guerra, who wrote or collaborated on his own scripts, also wrote the lyrics for Latin American pop songs. He also appeared as an actor in a number of films, including a leading role in Werner Herzog's *Aguirre, the Wrath of God* (1972).

FEATURE FILMS: *Os Cafajestes/Unscrupulous* (also co-sc.; Braz.) 1962; *Os Fuzis/The Guns* (also story co-sc., edit.; Braz.) 1964; *Sweet Hunters* (also story, co-sc., lyr.; Pan./Fr.) 1969; *Os Deuses e os Mortos/The Gods and the Dead* (also co-sc. co-edit.; Braz.) 1970; *A Queda/The Fall* (co-dir., co-sc., co-edit., lyr.; Braz.) 1978; *Mueda—Memoria e Massacre/Mueda—Memory and Massacre* (also co-phot. edit.; Mozam.) 1979; *Erendira* (Mex./Fr./Ger.) 1983; *Opera do Malandro* (also co-sc.; Braz.) 1986; *Kuarup* 1989.

Guerra, Tonino. Screenwriter. One of the Italian cinema's busiest and most highly regarded scripters since the early 60s. A favorite collaborator of Antonioni and Rosi, he also worked closely with De Sica, Fellini, Lattuada, Monicelli, Petri, Taviani, and other leading directors.

FILMS INCLUDE: *L'Avventura* 1960; *La Notte* 1961; *L'Assassino/The Lady Killer of Rome, L'Eclisse/Eclipse* 1962; *Deserto rosso/Red Desert, Matrimonio all'Italiana/Marriage Italian Style* 1964; *Casanova '70, La Decima Vittima/The Tenth Victim* 1965; *Blow-Up* (UK) 1966; *C'era una Volta/More Than a Miracle* 1967; *Gli Amanti/A Place for Lovers, Un Tranquillo Posto di Campagna/A Quiet Place in the Country* 1968; *I Girasoli/Sunflower* 1969; *Zabriskie Point* (US), *In Search of Gregory* (UK) 1970; *Il Caso Mattei/The Mattei Affair* 1972; *Bianco Rosso e. . . /White Sister, A proposito Lucky Luciano/Re: Lucky Luciano, Amarcord* 1973; *Cadaveri eccelenti/Illustrious Corpses, Caro Michele* 1976; *Cristo si è fermato a Eboli/Eboli* 1979; *Tre Fratelli* 1980; *Identificazione di una Donna/Identification of a Woman, La Notte di San Lorenzo/The Night of the Shooting Stars* 1982; *Nostalphia, E la Nave va/And the Ship Sails On* 1983; *Carmen/Bizet's Carmen, Kaos* 1984; *Ginger e Fred/Ginger and Fred* 1985; *O Melisskosmos* (Gr.) 1986; *Cronica de una Muerte anunciada, Good Morning Babylon/Good Morning Babilonia* 1987; *Il Frullo del Passero* 1988; *Landscape in the Mist* (Gr.) 1989; *Dimenticare Palermo/To Forget Palermo, Il male oscuro/The Obscure Illness, Il sole anche di notte/The Sun Also Shines at Night, Tutti stanno benne/Everybody's Fine* 1990.

Guest, Christopher. Actor, composer, screenwriter, director. Born on Feb. 5, 1948, in New York City. A veteran of TV comedy, he performed and wrote material for a variety of light entertainment programs, winning an Emmy Award for scripting a Lily Tomlin special in 1976. In 1984–85 he joined the cast of 'Saturday Night Live.' He also acted and wrote the music score for 'National Lampoon's Lemmings' off Broadway and appeared in Broadway stage productions. On the screen intermittently from the early 70s, he contributed to the script of *This Is Spinal Tap* (1984), a parody of rock documentaries in which he also starred as a member of the faux heavy metal band, Spinal Tap. The "band" proved so popular that they toured as a real band, further blurring the lines between satire and reportage. He made his debut as a director with *The Big Picture* (1989), a genial satire on contemporary Hollywood mores. He married actress Jamie Lee CURTIS in 1984.

FILMS (as actor): *The Hospital* 1971; *The Hot Rock* 1972; *Death Wish* 1974; *The Fortune* 1975; *Girlfriends* 1978; *The Last Word* 1979; *The Long Riders* 1980; *Heartbeeps* 1981; *This Is Spinal Tap* (also co-sc.) 1984; *Little Shop of Horrors* 1986; *Beyond Therapy, The Princess Bride* 1987; *Sticky Fingers* 1988; *The Big Picture* (also dir., co-sc.) 1989; *Shame of the Jungle* (voice) 1990; *Waiting for Guffman* (also dir.) 1997.

Guest, Lance. Actor. Born on July 21, 1960, in Saratoga, Calif. *ed.* UCLA. Clean-cut, curly-haired young lead of Hollywood films. His early career was helped by a regular role (1981–82) in the TV series 'Lou Grant.' He later appeared in the 'St. Elsewhere' series and in a number of TV movies.

FILMS: *Halloween II* 1981; *I Ought to Be in Pictures* 1982; *The Last Starfighter, Just the Way You Are* 1984; *Jaws: The Revenge* 1987; *The Wizard of Loneliness* 1988.

Guest, Val. Director, screenwriter, producer. Born in 1911, in London. A frustrated actor, he turned to film journalism, at first in England, then in Hollywood, where he worked for the Hollywood *Reporter* and the Los Angeles *Examiner* and supplied tips for Walter Winchell's column. Back in London, he began writing screenplays for British films in the mid-30s, specializing in comedy and thrillers. His contributions as a screenwriter included such Gainsborough comedy gems as *Oh, Mr. Porter!* (1937), *Alfs Button Afloat* (1938), *Ask a Policeman* (1939), and the remake of *The Ghost Train* (1941). He turned to directing in the early 40s and after a start in comedy shifted mainly to taut thrillers. A competent as well as prolific director, he created two science fiction films now recognized as classics of the genre, *The Quatermass Experiment* (1955) and *The Day the Earth Caught Fire* (1961). He is married to actress Yolande DONLAN, who starred in several of his films.

FILMS (as director-writer): *The Nose Has It* (short) 1942; *Miss London Ltd.* 1943; *Bees in Paradise, Give Us the Moon* 1944; *I'll Be Your Sweetheart* 1945; *Just William's Luck* 1947; *William Comes to Town* 1948; *Murder at the Windmill* 1949; *Miss Pilgrim's Progress, The Body Said No* 1950; *Mister Drake's Duck* 1951; *Penny Princess* (also prod.) 1952; *Life with the Lyons* 1953; *The Runaway Bus* (also prod.), *Men of Sherwood Forest, Dance Little Lady* 1954; *They Can't Hang Me, The Lyons in Paris, Break in the Circle, The Quartermass Experiment* 1955; *It's a Wonderful World, The Weapon* 1956; *Carry On Admiral/The Ship Was Loaded, Quatermass II, The Abominable Snowman* 1957; *The Camp on Blood Island, Up the Creek, Further up the Creek* 1958; *Expresso Bongo* (also prod.), *Yesterday's Enemy* 1959; *Life Is a Circus, Hell Is a City* 1960; *The Full Treatment/Stop Me Before I Kill* (also prod.), *The Day the Earth Caught Fire* (also prod.) 1961; *Jigsaw* (also prod.) 1962; *80,000 Suspects* (also prod.) 1963; *The Beauty Jungle/Contest Girl* (also prod.) 1964; *Where the Spies Are* (also co-prod.) 1965; *Casino Royale* (co-dir. with several others) 1967; *Assignment K* 1968; *When Dinosaurs Ruled the Earth* 1969; *Tomorrow* 1970; *The Persuaders* 1971; *Au Pair Girls* 1972; *Confessions of a Window Cleaner* 1973; *Killer Force/The Diamond Mercenaries* (dir. only) 1975; *The Boys in Blue* 1983.

Guffey, Burnett. Director of photography. *b.* May 26, 1905, Del Rio, Tenn. *d.* 1983. Entered films in 1923 as an assistant cameraman. The following year he handled the second-unit cinematography on John Ford's *The Iron Horse* but later returned to an assistant's position until 1928, when he became a camera operator. In the latter capacity he worked on several major productions, notably Ford's *The Informer* (1935), Alfred Hitchcock's *Foreign Correspondent* (1940), and Charles Vidor's *Cover Girl* (1944). Graduating to director of photography at

Columbia, he soon became one of the most respected lighting cameramen in the business, winning Academy Awards for the black-and-white cinematography of *From Here to Eternity* (1953) and the color cinematography of *Bonnie and Clyde* (1967).

FILMS INCLUDE: *The Soul of a Monster* 1944; *The Fighting Guardsman, My Name Is Julia Ross* 1945; *Gallant Journey* 1946; *Johnny O' Clock, Framed* 1947; *To the Ends of the Earth* 1948; *All the King's Men, Knock on Any Door, The Reckless Moment* 1949; *In a Lonely Place* 1950; *Sirocco* 1951; *The Sniper* 1952; *From Here to Eternity* 1953; *Human Desire* 1954; *The Violent Men* 1955; *The Harder They Fall* 1956; *The Brothers Rico, The Strange One* 1957; *Me and the Colonel, The Screaming Mimi* 1958; *Edge of Eternity, Gidget* 1959; *Let No Man Write My Epitaph* 1960; *Birdman of Alcatraz, Kid Galahad* 1962; *King Rat* 1965; *Bonnie and Clyde* 1967; *The Learning Tree* 1969; *The Great White Hope* 1970; *How to Succeed in Business Without Really Trying* 1976.

Guffroy, Pierre. Art director. Born in France. One of Europe's leading production designers since the early 60s, he has also provided lavish sets for a number of major international co-productions.

FILMS INCLUDE: *Le Testament d'Orphée/Testament of Orpheus* 1960; *La Dénociation/The Immoral Moment* 1962; *Pierrot le Fou* 1965; *L'Espion/The Defector* 1966; *Mouchette* 1967; *La Mariée était en Noir/The Bride Wore Black* 1968; *La Voie lactée/The Milky Way* 1969; *Le Passager de la Pluie/Rider on the Rain* 1970; *César et Rosalie/Cesar and Rosalie* 1972; *Le Fantome e la Libert Le Locataire/The Tenant* 1976; *Cet Obscure Objet du Désir/That Obscure Object of Desire* 1977; *Tess* 1979; *Hanna K.* 1983; *Pirates, Max Mon Amour* 1986; *The Unbearable Lightness of Being* (US), *Frantic* (US) 1988; *Valmont* 1989.

guide track. A sound track recorded in SYNC with a picture on location but not intended for use in the final film. Rather, it serves as a guide for the re-recording of the same sound under more ideal conditions by POSTSYNCHRONIZATION.

Guild, Nancy. Actress. Born on Oct. 11, 1925, in Los Angeles. Blonde leading lady of Hollywood films of the late 40s and early 50s. Divorced from actor Charles Russell, she married Broadway producer Ernest Martin and retired from the screen, devoting much of her time to charitable work.

FILMS: *Somewhere in the Night* 1946; *The Brasher Doubloon* 1947; *Give My Regards to Broadway* 1948; *Black Magic* 1949; *Abbott and Costello Meet the Invisible Man, Little Egypt* 1951; *Francis Covers the Big Town* 1953; *Such Good Friends* (cameo) 1971.

Guillemot, Agnès. Film editor. Born Agnès Perché in 1931 in Roubaix, France. *ed.* IDHEC, Paris. Accomplished editor of several landmark French New Wave films. Married to director Claude Guillemot.

FILMS INCLUDE: *Le Petit Soldat* 1960; *Une Femme est une femme/A Woman Is a Woman* 1961; *RoGoPag* (ed. part), *Vivre sa Vie/My Life to Live* 1962; *Les Carabiniers, Le Mépris/Contempt* 1963; *Bande à Part/Band of Outsiders, Une Femme mariée/A Married Woman, Les Plus belles escroqueries du monde* (ed. part) 1964; *Alphaville* 1965; *Made in U.S.A., Masculin-Féminin/Masculine Feminine* 1966; *Weekend* 1967; *Baisers volés/Stolen Kisses, La Sirène du Mississipi/Mississippi Mermaid, La Tréve* 1968; *Domicile conjugal/Bed and Board, L'Enfant sauvage/The Wild Child* 1970; *Cousin, Cousine* 1975; *Un Type comme moi ne devrait jamais mourir* 1976; *Le Pays Bleu* 1977; *Il y a longtemps que je t'aime* 1979; *Croque la Vie* 1981; *La Diagonale du Fou* 1984; *Escalier C* 1985; *La Brute, Fuegos* 1987; *La Lumière du lac* 1988; *Every Other Weekend* 1991.

Guillermin, John. Director. Born on Nov. 11, 1925, in London, to French-born parents. *ed.* Cambridge. He began his career in France in 1947 as a documentary filmmaker following WW II service with the RAF. Spent several months in Hollywood observing feature production. Returning to Britain in 1949, he wrote a couple of scripts and made his debut as a feature film director with *Torment*. Although small in scale, his early films revealed a sure-handed talent and eventually led to top budget productions of variable quality and eventually to large-scale Hollywood assignments. In the 80s he regressed into second-rate works.

FILMS: In the UK—*Torment* (also co-prod., sc.) 1949; *Smart Alec, Two on the Tiles, Four Days* 1951; *Song of Paris, Miss Robin Hood* 1952; *Operation Diplomat* (also co-sc.) 1953; *Adventure in the Hopfields, The Crowded Day* 1954; *Dust and Gold, Thunderstorm* 1955; *Town on Trial* 1957; *The Whole Truth, I Was Monty's Double* 1958; *Tarzan's Greatest Adventure* (also co-sc.) 1959; *The Day They Robbed the Bank of England, Never Let Go* (also co-story) 1960; *Waltz of the Toreadors, Tarzan Goes to India* (also co-sc.; UK/US/Ind.) 1962; *Guns at Batasi* 1964; *Rapture* (US/Fr.) 1965; *The Blue Max* 1966. In the US—*P.J.* 1968; *House of Cards, The Bridge at Remagen* 1969; *El Condor* 1970; *Skyjacked* 1972; *Shaft in Africa* 1973; *The Towering Inferno* 1974; *King Kong* 1976; *Death on the Nile* 1978; *Mr. Patman* (Can.) 1980; *Sheena* 1984; *King Kong Lives* 1986.

Guinness, Sir Alec. Actor. Born Alec Guinness de Cuffe, on Apr. 2, 1914, in London. A former advertising copywriter, he studied acting at the Fay Compton Studio of Dramatic Art and made his stage debut in a walk-on part in 1934. He gained experience and reputation with the Old Vic, where he played much Shakespeare, Shaw, and Chekhov from 1936. In 1938 he married Merula Salaman, an actress. Their son, Matthew Guinness, would later also become an actor. In 1941 he joined the Royal Navy as an ordinary seaman and obtained a commission the following year. In 1942 he was given special leave to make his New York stage debut in a propaganda play. In films since 1946 (he had made an isolated screen appearance in 1934), he soon became noted for his versatility and penchant for subtle disguises (he played eight parts, including a woman, in *Kind Hearts and Coronets*). He gained wide popularity in a string of bright British comedies and managed to look astonishingly different from film to film. Younger audiences know him better as the wise old spiritual warrior Obi-wan Kenobi in the *Star Wars* trilogy. He has also excelled in dramatic portrayals and won the best actor Academy Award for his excellent character study in *The Bridge on the River Kwai* (1957). In the 1980 Oscar ceremony (for 1979) he received an honorary Academy Award "for advancing the art of screen acting through a host of memorable and distinguished performances." In addition, Guinness secured Oscar nominations for *The Lavender Hill Mob* (for best actor; US release 1952), *The Horse's Mouth* (for best screenplay, 1958), *Star Wars* (for best supporting actor, 1977), and for *Little Dorrit* (for best supporting actor, US release 1988). In 1959 he was knighted by Queen Elizabeth for his achievements on the stage and screen. Autobiography: *Blessings in Disguise* (1985).

FILMS: *Evensong* (extra) 1934; *Great Expectations* (as Herbert Pocket) 1946; *Oliver Twist* (as Fagin) 1948; *Kind Hearts and Coronets, A Run for Your Money* 1949; *Last Holiday, The Mudlark* (as Disraeli) 1950; *The Lavender Hill Mob, The Man in the White Suit* 1951; *The Card/The Promoter* 1952; *The Captain's Paradise, The Malta Story* 1953; *Father Brown/The Detective, To Paris with Love* 1954; *The Prisoner, The Ladykillers* 1955; *The Swan* (US) 1956; *Barnacle Bill/All at Sea, The Bridge on the River Kwai* 1957; *The Horse's Mouth* (also sc.) 1958; *The Scapegoat, Our Man in Havana* 1959;

Tunes of Glory 1960; *A Majority of One* (US), *H.M.S. Defiant/Damn the Defiant!, Lawrence of Arabia* (as Prince Faisal) 1962; *The Fall of the Roman Empire* (as Marcus Aurelius; US) 1964; *Situation Hopeless but Not Serious* (US), *Doctor Zhivago* (as Yevgraf Zhivago; US) 1965; *Hotel Paradiso* (UK/US), *The Quiller Memorandum* (UK/US) 1966; *The Comedians* (US/Fr./Bermuda) 1967; *Cromwell* (as Charles I), *Scrooge* (as Marley's Ghost) 1970; *Fratello Sole Sorella Luna/Brother Sun Sister Moon* (as Pope Innocent III; It.), *Gli Ultimi 10 Giorni di Hitler/Hitler: The Last Ten Days* (as Adolf Hitler; It./UK) 1973; *Murder by Death* (US) 1976; *Star Wars* (US) 1977; *The Empire Strikes Back* (US), *Raise the Titanic* 1980; *Lovesick* (as Freud; US), *Return of the Jedi* (US) 1983; *A Passage to India* 1984; *Little Dorrit* (as William Dorrit) 1987; *A Handful of Dust* 1988; *Kafka* 1992; *Mute Witness* (unbilled cameo) 1995.

Guitry, Sacha. Playwright, director, screenwriter, actor. *b.* Alexandre-Pierre Georges Guitry, Feb. 21, 1885, St. Petersburg, Russia. *d.* 1957. The son of a celebrated French stage star, Lucien Guitry, he began an acting career in his early teens and wrote his first play at 17. Subsequently he wrote more than 120 plays, many of which enjoyed great success. Essentially a man of the theater, he engaged in film activity as director, screenwriter, and actor, mainly in order to bring his own plays to the screen. His films were typically static affairs, with little camera movement, but nonetheless fluid, charming, and rarely dull. In August of 1944, after the Liberation of Paris, he was arrested and charged with collaboration with the Nazis, but he was later vindicated. He was married four times, all to actresses: Charlotte Lysès, Yvonne Printemps, Geneviève de Séreville, and Lana Marconi.

FILMS (as director-screenwriter-actor): *Ceux de chez nous* (doc.; dir. only) 1915; *Roman d'Amour et d'Aventure* (act. only) 1917; *Le Blanc et le Noir* (sc. only) 1931; *Les Deux Couverts* (sc. only), *Pasteur* (in title role), *Bonne Chance* 1935; *Le Nouveau Testament* (co-dir. with Alexandre Ryder), *Le Roman d'un Tricheur/The Story of a Cheat, Faisons un Rêve, Le Mot de Cambronne, Mon Père avait raison* 1936; *Les Perles de la Couronne/The Pearls of the Crown* (co-dir. with Christian-Jaque; act. in 4 roles including Francis I and Napoleon III) 1937; *L'Accroche-coeur* (sc. only), *Quadrille, Désiré, Remontons les Champs-Elysées* (in several roles, including Louis XV and Napoleon III) 1938; *Ils étaient Neuf Célibataires/Nine Bachelors* 1939; *Le Destin Fabuleux du Désirée Clary/Mlle. Désirée* (as Napoleon) 1942; *Donne-moi tes Yeux* 1943; *La Malibran* 1944; *Le Comédien/The Private Life of an Actor* (as his father, Lucien Guitry), *Le Diable boiteux* (as Talleyrand) 1948; *Aux Deux Colombes, Toa* 1949; *Le Trésor de Cantenac* 1949; *Tu m'as sauvé la Vie* 1950; *Deburau, Adhémar ou le Jouet de Fatalité* (sc. only), *Le Poison* (dir., sc. only) 1951; *Je l'ai été trois fois, La Vie d'un Honnête Homme/The Virtuous Scoundrel* (dir., sc. only) 1953; *Si Versailles m'était conté/Royal Affairs in Versailles* (as Louis XIV) 1955; *Napoléon* (as Talleyrand), *Si Paris nous était conté* (as Louis XI) 1955; *Assassins et Voleurs/Lovers and Thieves* (dir., sc. only), *Le Trois font la Paire* (co-dir. with Clement Duhour, sc. only) 1957; *La Vie à Deux* (sc. only) 1958.

Gulager, Clu. Actor. Born on Nov. 16, 1928 in Holdenville, Okla. *ed.* Baylor U. Craggy-faced, virile supporting lead of television and screen. Son of cowboy celebrity John Gulager, he first appeared professionally on television in the 1950s. Best known as diffident lover of Ellen Burstyn in *The Last Picture Show*.

FILMS INCLUDE: *The Killers* 1964; *Winning* 1969; *The Last Picture Show* 1971; *McQ* 1974; *The Other Side of Midnight* 1977; *A Force of One* 1979; *Touched by Love* 1980; *Into the Night, The Return of the Living Dead* 1985; *Hunter's Blood, The Offspring, A Nightmare on Elm Street: Freddy's Revenge* 1986; *The Hidden* 1987; *Tapeheads* 1988; *I'm Gonna Git You Sucka* 1989; *My Heroes Have Always Been Cowboys* 1991.

Güney, Yilmaz. Director. *b.* Yilmaz Pütün, Sept. 9, 1937, in village near Adana, southern Turkey. *d.* 1984. One of seven children of a Kurdish peasant, he moved with his mother to Adana when his parents separated. He worked his way through high school and the university. He also began writing articles and short stories, and repeatedly got in trouble with the law over material that was considered subversive by the authorities. At 20 he was arrested for the first time. Long infatuated with the cinema, Güney entered films in 1958 as an actor-screenwriter, but his budding career was soon interrupted by a jail sentence on political charges. During his year-and-a-half (1960–62) imprisonment he completed a novel about poor peasants in southern Turkey, *They Died with Their Heads Bowed.* Trim and darkly handsome, he returned to acting after his release and quickly became one of Turkey's most popular screen personalities, typically portraying a tough underdog antihero of low-budget action films. Eventually he began producing his own films and in 1966 made his debut as a director. Most of his early films were undistinguished. Around 1970, however, he began asserting himself with a number of poignant films decrying social injustice that drew on his personal experience as a child of abject poverty and desperate hope. But in 1971 he was jailed again for two years for allegedly harboring left-wing terrorists. After his release, he resumed his film activities, but in 1975 he was arrested again, this time on the serious charge of killing a magistrate in a café brawl. The following year, he was sentenced to a jail term of 19 years, although his nephew had admitted to having been the real culprit. Amazingly—perhaps because of his popularity among his jailers—he was able to continue running his company, Güney Films, from prison. In addition to a novel, a book for his young son, memoirs, and political essays, he began writing detailed shooting scripts that enabled his associates to create two films—*The Herd* (1978) and *The Enemy* (1979)—exactly as he had envisioned them. In 1979, transferred to a harsher jail, he began working on his best known film, *Yol.* Drawing on his own harrowing experience as a prisoner and on stories by other political detainees, the film offered a scorching indictment of the Turkish sociopolitical system. It was shot under Güney's instructions by Serif Gören and smuggled abroad in sections. A year after the 1980 military takeover of the Turkish government, Güney managed to escape to Switzerland, where he completed the film's editing. *Yol* went on to share the Palme d'Or (best film) award at the 1982 Cannes Festival. With the financial support of the French Ministry of Culture, Güney then directed *The Wall* (1983), a film about a children's revolt in a Turkish prison, that disappointed many of his admirers. Repeated demands by Turkish authorities for his extradition from France and Greece went unheeded. In 1983 he was stripped of his Turkish citizenship. The following year, at the age of 47, he died in Paris of stomach cancer.

FILMS: As director-screenwriter-actor: *The Horse, the Woman, and the Gun* 1966; *Bullets Cannot Pierce Me, My Name Is Kerim* 1967; *Nuri the Flea* (co-dir.), *Seyyit Han/Bride of the Earth* 1968; *The Hungry Wolves, An Ugly Man* 1969; *Hope, Osman the Wanderer* (co-dir. with Serif Gören), *The Seven Bastards* (co-dir. with Irfan Atasoy) 1970; *The Fugitives, The Wrongdoers, The Example* (co-dir. with Gören), *Tomorrow Is the Last Day, The Hopeless Ones, Pain, Elegy, Baba/The Father* 1971; *The Friend, Anxiety* (co-dir. with Gören, sc. only) 1974; *The Poor Ones* (co-dir. with Yilmaz Atif; co-sc.) 1975. As screenwriter/director by proxy—*Sürü/The Herd* (field dir. Zeki Okten) 1978; *Düsman/The Enemy* (field dir. Okten) 1979;

Yol/The Way (field dir. Gören) 1982. As director-screenwriter—*Le Mur/The Wall* (Fr.) 1983.

Gunn, Bill. Screenwriter, director. *b.* c. 1930 in Philadelphia. *d.* 1989. Stage- and television-trained actor who became a writer and director, distinguishing himself as an insightful interpreter of contemporary African-American life in America. His *Ganja and Hess*, once seen as a standard vampire movie, has been reinterpreted as a multilayered study of conflicts within African-American culture. His play, *Black Picture Show*, was produced by the New York Shakespeare Festival in 1975. Author of *Rhinestone Sharecropping*, a novel.

FILMS INCLUDE (as screenwriter): *The Interns* (act. only) 1962; *Penelope* (act. only), *The Spy with My Face* (act. only) 1966; *The Angel Levine* (co-sc.), *The Landlord, STOP* (dir. only) 1970; *Ganja and Hess* (also dir.) 1973.

Gunn, Moses. Actor. *b.* Oct. 2, 1929, St. Louis. *d.* 1993. *ed.* Tennessee State U.; U. of Kansas. *d.* 1993. Leading black character player of the American stage (from 1962) and films (from 1964). His screen characterizations were strong and somewhat stylized.

FILMS INCLUDE: *Nothing but a Man* 1964; *What's So Bad About Feeling Good?* 1968; *The Great White Hope, WUSA* 1970; *Wild Rovers, Shaft, Eagle in a Cage* (UK) 1971; *The Hot Rock, Shaft's Big Score* 1972; *The Iceman Cometh* 1973; *Amazing Grace* 1974; *Cornbread Earl and Me, Rollerball, Aaron Loves Angela* 1975; *Remember My Name* 1978; *The Ninth Configuration* 1980; *Ragtime* 1981; *Amityville II: The Possession* 1982; *The NeverEnding Story* (Ger./UK), *Firestarter* 1984; *Certain Fury* 1985; *Heartbreak Ridge* 1986; *Leonard: Part 6* 1987; *Dixie Lanes* 1988; *The Luckiest Man in the World* (v/o) 1989.

Gurie, Sigrid. Actress. *b.* Sigrid Gurie Haukelid, May 18, 1911, Brooklyn, N.Y. *d.* 1969. Reared in Norway and Belgium, she returned to the US as an adult and became a protégée of Sam GOLDWYN, who publicized her as "The Siren of the Fjords." She played exotic or mysterious leading ladies in a number of films of the late 30s and 40s but never became an important or popular star, and retired from the screen in 1948. She died in Mexico City of an embolism.

FILMS: *The Adventures of Marco Polo, Algiers* 1938; *The Forgotten Woman, Rio* 1939; *Three Faces West* 1940; *Dark Streets of Cairo* 1941; *Voice in the Wind, Enemy of Women* 1944; *Sword of the Avenger, Sofia* 1948.

Gutiérrez Alea, Tomás. Director. Born on Dec. 11, 1928, in Havana. The son of a patent attorney, he was raised in upper-middle-class comfort but in his teens discovered Marxism and became active in Communist youth groups. While studying law at the University of Havana, Gutiérrez Alea, nicknamed Titón, began shooting amateur shorts with an 8 mm camera. One of these was made in collaboration with fellow-student Nestor ALMENDROS. After graduating, rather than start a law practice, he went to Rome and studied for two years at the Centro Sperimentale di Cinematografia film school. On returning to Cuba, he became involved in Fidel Castro's revolutionary movement and helped set up its clandestine film unit. In the period leading to and immediately following the 1959 Castro revolution, his documentary shorts became increasingly militant. In 1960 he was entrusted with directing the new regime's first official feature film, *Stories of the Revolution,* a semidocumentary reconstruction of incidents leading to the historic event. After turning out a Cuban version of the oft-filmed comedy *The Twelve Chairs* (1962) and a propagandist drama on a Haitian theme, Guttiérez Alea ridiculed the Kafkaesque side of Cuban officialdom in *Death of a Bureaucrat* (1966), his first film to capture international attention. The film received a special jury prize at the Karlovy Vary Festival, among other awards. The director's reputation reached its zenith with *Memories of Underdevelopment* (1968), a fiction film, integrating newsreel footage, exploring one man's alienation and soul-searching in postrevolutionary Havana. It was shown extensively abroad and won a number of international awards.

FEATURE FILMS: *Historias de la Revolución/Stories of the Revolution* (doc.) 1960; *Las Doce Sillas/The Twelve Chairs* 1962; *Cumbite* 1964; *La Muerte de un Búrocrata/Death of a Bureaucrat* 1966; *Memorias del Subdesarrollo/Memories of Underdevelopment* 1968; *Una Pelea Cubana contra los Demonios/A Cuban Fight Against the Demons* 1971; *La Ultima Cena/The Last Supper* 1976; *Los Sobrevivientes/The Survivors* 1978; *Hasta un Cierto Punto/Up to a Certain Point* 1984; *Letters from the Park* 1984; *Strawberry and Chocolate* 1994.

Gutowski, Gene (Eugene). Producer. Born on May 7, 1925, in Poland. Engaged in US TV and feature film production 1954–60, then formed his own company in London. Producer of Roman POLANSKI's British-made films of the late 60s.

FILMS INCLUDE: *Station Six Sahara* (UK/Ger.) 1963; *Repulsion* 1965; *Cul-de-Sac* 1966; *The Fearless Vampire Killers/Dance of the Vampires* 1967; *The Adventures of Gerard* (co-prod.) 1969; *A Day at the Beach* (co-prod.) 1970; *Romance of a Horsethief* 1971.

Guttenberg, Steve. Actor. Born on Aug. 24, 1958, in Brooklyn, N.Y. Amiable, exuberant, light leading man of Hollywood films. After graduating from New York's School of Performing Arts, he studied drama at Juilliard under John HOUSEMAN and attended classes by Lee Strasberg and Uta Hagen. On the New York stage from his teens, he moved to the West Coast in 1976, and after appearing in a TV movie made his feature film debut the following year. His career was boosted by a co-starring role in the popular *Police Academy* film series.

FILMS: *Rollercoaster, The Chicken Chronicles* 1977; *The Boys from Brazil* 1978; *Players* 1979; *Can't Stop the Music* 1980; *Diner* 1982; *The Man Who Wasn't There* 1983; *Police Academy* 1984; *Police Academy 2: Their First Assignment, Cocoon, Bad Medicine* 1985; *Police Academy 3: Back in Training, Short Circuit* 1986; *The Bedroom Window, Police Academy 4: Citizens on Patrol, Amazon Women on the Moon, Surrender, Three Men and a Baby* 1987; *High Spirits, Cocoon: The Return* 1988; *Don't Tell Her It's Me, Three Men and A Little Lady* 1990; *The Big Green, Home for the Holidays* 1995; *It Takes Two* 1996.

Guy-Blaché, Alice (also known as **Alice Guy** or **Alice Blaché).** Director, producer. *b.* Alice Guy, July 1, 1873, Saint-Monde, a suburb of Paris. *d.* 1968. The world's first woman director and possibly the first director of either sex to bring a story-film to the screen. The youngest of four daughters of a book publisher, she became a stenographer-typist at 16, after her father's death. It was as a secretary that she joined the Gaumont film company in 1896, but when the firm switched from the manufacture of cameras to the production of films later that year, Miss Guy became one of its pioneer directors. Her first film, *La Fée aux Choux* (1896)—a re-enactment of a fairy tale about children born in cabbages—preceded Meliès' story-films by a few months, according to several authoritative French historians, although others claim that her film wasn't made until 1900 or even later.

Miss Guy went on to make numerous one-reelers for Gaumont, sometimes at the pace of one or two a week, and by 1905 she was supervising a number of young directors as the company's producer-artistic director. In several of her films she experimented with sound. In 1907 she married Herbert Blaché, an Englishman of French descent who was at one time

Gaumont's chief cameraman and ran the company's branches in London, then Berlin. That same year the Blachés came to the US and set up a branch for Gaumont's products in Cleveland. Soon after, they moved to New York and in 1910 Alice, now known as Alice Guy-Blaché (and later as Alice Blaché), formed her own production company, Solax, through which she produced and directed numerous films, quickly establishing a reputation from the quality of her product. Before long she had moved her small studio in Flushing, N.Y., to larger quarters in Fort Lee, N.J. Her company prospered for several years but later declined and was reorganized as the US Amusement Company and, a short time later, as Popular Plays and Players.

By 1917 Alice Guy-Blaché gave in to the pressures of competition and pulled out of independent production. She continued directing for a while for larger studios, like Pathé and Metro, but after her divorce from Herbert Blaché in 1922 she returned to France with their two American-born children. However, despite repeated attempts, she was unable to obtain any directing assignments in her native land and she never made pictures again. She was a forgotten woman of 80 when the French government very belatedly recognized her contribution to the art of film, bestowing on her the Legion of Honor in 1953. In 1964 she returned to the US, where she spent the remaining four years of her life at the home of one of her daughters, in Mahwah, N.J., and where she died at 95.

FILMS INCLUDE: In France—*La Fée aux Choux* 1896; *Les Dangers de l'Alcoolisme* 1899; *La Danse des Saisons, Au Bal de Flore* 1900; *Hussards et Grisettes* 1901; *Le Pommier* 1902; *Le Voleur Sacrilège* 1903; *Paris la Nuit, Le Courrier de Lyon, Le Crime de la Rue du Temple* 1904; *La Esmeralda, Réhabilitation* 1905; *La Vie du Christ* (assisted by Victorin Jasset), *La Fée Printemps* 1906; *Fanfan la Tulipe* 1907. In the US—*Rose of the Circus, The Doll, The Violin Maker of Nuremberg* 1911; *The Face at the Window, Mignon, The Sewer* (prod. only), *Falling Leaves, In the Year 2000, Fra Diavolo, The Blood Stain, Playing Trumps, Phantom Paradise* 1912; *Beasts of the Jungle* (prod., sc. only), *Dick Whittington and His Cat* (also sc.), *The Pit and the Pendulum, A Terrible Night, The Little Hunchback, Rogues of Paris, The Star of India* 1913; *Beneath the Czar* (also sc.), *Shadows of the Moulin Rouge* (also sc.), *The Monster and the Girl, The Dream Woman* (also sc.), *The Woman of Mystery* (also sc.), *The Lure* (also sc.) 1914; *The Heart of a Painted Woman, My Madonna* (also sc.), *The Vampire* 1915; *What Will People Say?, The Waif* 1916; *The Adventurer, The Empress, A Man and the Woman* (also sc.), *House of Cards* (also sc.), *When You and I Were Young, Behind the Mask* 1917; *The Great Adventure* 1918; *Tarnished Reputations/A Soul Adrift* 1920.

Gwenn, Edmund. Actor. *b.* Sept. 26, 1875, Glamorgan, Wales. *d.* 1959. A veteran of the stage, he appeared in numerous West End productions from the early 1900s and was a personal favorite of Shaw. He later also appeared many times on Broadway. He made his screen debut in England back in 1916, but his film career really took shape in Hollywood in the 40s, when he developed into one of the American screen's most popular character actors. He typically played benevolent elders, often with a mischievous twinkle in the eye. He won an Academy Award as best supporting actor for *Miracle on 34th Street* (1947), in which he played a Macy's Santa Claus. Also memorable as a well-meaning forger in *Mister 880* (1950) and as the Captain in Hitchcock's *The Trouble with Harry* (1955).

FILMS: In the UK—*The Real Thing at Last* 1916; *Unmarried, The Skin Game* 1920; *How He Lied to Her Husband, The Skin Game* (sound version), *Hindle Wakes* 1931; *Money for Nothing, Frail Women, Condemned to Death, Love on Wheels, Tell Me Tonight/Be Mine Tonight* 1932; *The Good Companions, Cash/For Love or Money, Early to Bed, I Was a Spy, Channel Crossing, Smithy, Marooned, Friday the 13th* 1933; *Waltzes from Vienna/Strauss's Great Waltz* (as Johann Strauss), *The Admiral's Secret, Java Head, Passing Shadows, Warn London, Father and Son, Spring in the Air* 1934; *The Bishop Misbehaves* (US) 1935; *Sylvia Scarlett* (US), *The Walking Dead* (US), *Anthony Adverse* (as John Bonnyfeather; US), *Mad Holiday, Laburnum Grove* 1936; *Parnell* (US) 1937; *A Yank at Oxford, Penny Paradise* 1938; *Cheer Boys Cheer, An Englishman's Home* 1939. In the US—*The Earl of Chicago, The Doctor Takes a Wife, Mad Men of Europe, Pride and Prejudice* (as Mr. Bennet), *Foreign Correspondent* 1940; *Cheers for Miss Bishop, Scotland Yard, The Devil and Miss Jones, One Night in Lisbon, Charley's Aunt* 1941; *A Yank at Eton* 1942; *The Meanest Man in the World, Lassie Come Home, Forever and a Day* 1943; *Between Two Worlds* 1944; *The Keys of the Kingdom, Bewitched, Dangerous Partners, She Went to the Races* 1945; *Of Human Bondage* (as Thorpe Athelney), *Undercurrent* 1946; *Miracle on 34th Street, Life with Father, Green Dolphin Street, Thunder in the Valley* 1947; *Apartment for Peggy, Hills of Home* 1948; *Challenge to Lassie* 1949; *A Woman of Distinction, Pretty Baby, Mister 880, Louisa, For Heaven's Sake* 1950; *Peking Express, Sally and Saint Anne, Bonzo Goes to College, Les Misérables, Something for the Birds* 1952; *Mister Scoutmaster, The Bigamist* 1953; *Them, The Student Prince* 1954; *The Trouble with Harry, It's a Dog's Life* 1955; *Calabuch/The Rocket from Calabuch* (Sp.) 1956.

Gwynne, Anne. Actress. Born Marguerite Gwynne Trice, on Dec. 10, 1918, in Waco, Tex. *ed.* Stephens Coll. Leading lady and second lead of Hollywood films of the 40s, following some experience on the stage. Seen mostly in action and B horror pictures.

FILMS INCLUDE: *Unexpected Father* 1939; *Flash Gordon Conquers the Universe/Purple Death from Outer Space* (serial), *Black Friday, Spring Parade, Give Us Wings* 1940; *Nice Girl?, The Black Cat, Mob Town* 1941; *Jail House Blues, Ride 'Em Cowboy, The Strange Case of Dr. Rx, Broadway, Men of Texas, Sin Town, You're Telling Me* 1942; *Frontier Badmen* 1943; *Ladies Courageous, Weird Woman, South of Dixie, Moon Over Las Vegas, Murder in the Blue Room* 1944; *House of Frankenstein* 1945; *The Glass Alibi* 1946; *The Ghost Goes Wild, Killer Dill, Dick Tracy Meets Gruesome* 1947; *The Enchanted Valley* 1948; *Blazing Sun* 1950; *Breakdown* 1952; *Phantom of the Jungle* 1955; *Teenage Monster* 1958; *Adam at 6 A.M.* 1970.

Gwynne, Fred. Actor. *b.* July 10, 1926, New York City. *d.* 1993. Gigantic (6' 5"), mournful character player of American TV and films. After graduating from Harvard, he worked as a copywriter for a Manhattan advertising agency while at the same time pursuing an acting career off and on Broadway and in New York–based TV programs. His big break came in 1961–63 as co-star of the TV comedy-police series 'Car 54, Where Are You?' His success led to the role for which he remains best known, that of Herman Munster in the hit comedy-horror series 'The Munsters' (1964–66). He appeared intermittently in feature films, mainly in supporting roles, receiving warm notices for his final role as a skeptical judge in *My Cousin Vinny*. Gwynne was also the author/illustrator of several children's books.

FILMS: *On the Waterfront* 1954; *Munster Go Home* 1977; *La Luna* (It.) 1979; *Simon* 1980; *So Fine* 1981; *The Cotton Club* 1984; *Water* (UK) 1985; *Off Beat, The Boy Who Could Fly* 1986; *The Secret of My Success, Fatal Attraction, Ironweed* 1987; *Disorganized Crime, Pet Sematary* 1989; *Shadows and Fog, My Cousin Vinny* 1992.

Gynt, Greta. Actress. Born Margrethe Woxholt, in 1916, in Oslo. Blonde glamour girl of British films of the 40s, following some experience on the London stage. Often seen in crime melodramas.

FILMS INCLUDE: *Sangen till Henne/Song to Her* (Swed.) 1934; *It Happened in Paris* 1935; *The Road Back* (US), *The Last Curtain* 1937; *The Last Barricade* 1938; *The Dark Eyes of London/The Human Monster, The Arsenal Stadium Mystery* 1939; *Two For Danger, Bulldog Sees It Through* 1940; *The Common Touch* 1941; *Tomorrow We Live/At Dawn We Die* 1942; *Mr. Emmanuel* 1944; *London Town, Take My Life* 1946; *Dear Murderer* 1947; *Easy Money, The Calendar, Mr. Perrin and Mr. Traill* 1948; *Shadow of the Eagle* 1950; *Lucky Nick Cain* (US), *Soldiers Three* (US) 1951; *The Ringer* 1952; *Three Steps in the Dark* 1953; *Forbidden Cargo* 1954; *See How They Run* 1955; *Fortune Is a Woman* 1956; *Bluebeard's Ten Honeymoons* 1959; *The Runaway* 1966.

gyro head. A type of camera mount, incorporating a fast-revolving heavy flywheel, designed to assure camera stability during a PAN and a TILT.

H

Haanstra, Bert. Documentary producer-director, writer. Born on May 31, 1916, in Holten, Holland. The most original and best known of the postwar Dutch filmmakers, he began making amateur films as a young boy but earned his living as a painter and press photographer before directing his first professional short at the age of 33. However, once he broke through, he rose quickly to prominence. His second short, *Mirror of Holland* (1950), which he filmed himself, won the Grand Prix for documentaries at the Cannes Festival, and his subsequent efforts reaped awards of merit at an amazing rate. He received no fewer than 20 prizes for his short *Glass* and by 1970 had collected more than 50 international awards for his films. He made several documentaries on art and many shorts for the Royal Dutch-Shell film unit. His few stabs at feature films have been less successful than his celebrated documentary shorts.

FILMS INCLUDE (shorts are denoted "S"): *The Muider Group Revived* (S) 1949; *Mirror of Holland* (S) 1950; *Medieval Dutch Sculpture* (S), *Panta Rhei* (S) 1951; *The Dike Builders* (S) 1952; *The Changing Earth* (S), *The Wildcat* (S) 1953; *The Rival World* (S), *God Shiva* (S) 1955; *Rembrandt Painter of Man* (S) 1956; *Glass* (S), *Fanfare* 1958; *The M.P. Case* 1960; *Zoo* (S) 1962; *The Human Dutch* 1964; *Voice of the Water* 1967; *Bridges of Holland* (S) 1968; *Ape and Superape* 1973; *Doctor Pulder Sows Poppies/When the Poppies Bloom Again* 1976; *Mr. Slotter's Jubilee* 1979; *The Netherlands, In the Past People Could Laugh/The World of Simon Carmiggelt* 1982; *The Family of Chimps* 1984.

Haas, Charles F. Director. Born in 1913, in Chicago, *ed.* Harvard. He entered films in 1935 as an extra and assistant director at Universal. He later wrote, produced, and directed documentaries and industrial films and during WW II made training films for the Signal Corps. In 1946 he rejoined Universal as a producer and produced and wrote the screenplay for Frank Borzage's *Moonrise* (1949). He then returned to the industrial film field and began turning out promotional films for the Bell telephone system and directing TV programs. He made his first feature film as director in 1956 and for the next four years turned out a handful of adroit low-budget, lowbrow films. He then went back to TV.

FILMS: *Star in the Dust, Screaming Eagles, Showdown at Abilene* 1956; *Summer Love, Wild Heritage* 1958; *The Beat Generation, The Big Operator, Girls Town* 1959; *Platinum High School* 1960.

Haas, Dolly. Actress. Born in 1911, in Hamburg. A ballet dancer from age six, she became a popular star of German films of the early 30s. She later appeared in a couple of British films and one American period film. In 1987 she was the subject of a West German documentary by Rosa von Praunheim, *Dolly, Lotte, and Maria,* about her, Lotte Goslar, and Maria Piscator.

FILMS INCLUDE: *Eine Stunde Glück, Dolly macht Karriere/Dolly's Way to Stardom* 1930; *Liebeskommando/Love's Command, Der brave Sünder* 1931; *Es wird schon wieder besser* 1932; *Die kleine Schwinlerin, Der Page vom Dalmasse-Hotel* 1933; *Warum lügt Eräulein Käthe?* 1935; *Broken Blossoms* (UK) 1936; *Spy of Napoleon* (UK) 1937; *I Confess* (US) 1953.

Haas, Hugo. Actor, director, producer. *b.* Feb. 19, 1901, Brno, Czechoslovakia. *d.* 1968. A leading comic star in Czech films of the early 30s, and later as a director, he came to the US after the Nazi invasion and played character parts in many Hollywood films. During WW II he was an announcer on US broadcasts to Eastern Europe and a narrator of propaganda films. In the early 50s he began directing and producing, as well as starring in, a series of dreary, low-budget melodramas usually focusing on an inevitably doomed encounter between a crude middle-aged man and a young temptress.

FILMS INCLUDE: As actor: in Czechoslovakia—*The 11th Commandment* 1925; *Men Offside, The Good Soldier Schweik* 1930; *Necardee King of Kibitzers, Sister Angelica* 1932; *A Dog's Life* (also co-sc.), *The House in the Suburbs* (also co-sc.) 1933; *Mother's Boy* (also co-sc.), *The Last Man* 1934; *Hurrah for the Good Life* (also co-sc.) 1935; *The Road to Paradise* (also co-sc.) 1936; *Morality Above All* (also co-sc.) 1937; *A Begging World* (also co-sc.) 1938. In the US—*Days of Glory, Summer Storm, The Princess and the Pirate* 1944; *A Bell for Adano, Dakota* 1945; *Holiday in Mexico* 1946; *The Private Affairs of Bel-Ami, Fiesta, Northwest Outpost, The Foxes of Harrow* 1947; *My Girl Tisa, Casbah* 1948; *The Fighting Kentuckian* 1949; *King's Solomon's Mines, Vendetta* 1950. As director (complete): in Czechoslovakia—*A Camel Through a Needle's Eye* (co-dir.; also co-sc., act.) 1936; *Girl Defend Yourself!* (co-dir.; also co-sc., act.), *The Clucking Hen* (as sc.), *The White Plague/Skeleton on Horseback* (also sc., act.) 1937; *What Is Whispered* (also sc., act.) 1938. In the US—*Pickup* (also prod., co-sc., act.), *The Girl on the Bridge* (also prod., sc., act.) 1951; *Strange Fascination* (also prod., act.) 1952; *One Girl's Confession* (also prod., story, sc., act.), *Thy Neighbor's Wife* (also prod., sc., act.) 1953; *Bait* (also prod., act.), *The Other Woman* (also prod., act.) 1954; *Hold Back Tomorrow* (also prod., sc., act.) 1955; *Edge of Hell* (also prod., act.) 1956; *Hit and Run* (also prod., sc., act.), *Lizzie* (also act.) 1957; *Night of the Quarter Moon, Born to Be Loved* (also prod., sc., co-music., act.) 1959; *Paradise Alley* (also prod., sc., act.) 1962.

Haas, Lukas. Actor. Born on Apr. 16, 1976, in West Hollywood, Calif. Precocious juvenile lead of the American screen. Also seen on stage and TV. Discovered and encouraged by a kindergarten principal, he made his acting debut at age four.

FILMS: *Testament* 1983; *Witness* 1985; *Solarbabies* 1986; *Lady in White, The Wizard of Loneliness* 1988; *See You in the Morning* 1989; *The Music Box* 1990; *Rambling Rose* 1991; *Alan & Naomi, Leap of Faith* 1992; *Boys, Everyone Says I Love You, Mars Attacks!, Palookaville* 1996; *Johns* 1997.

Haas, Robert M. Art director. *b.* 1887, Newark, N.J. *d.* 1962. *ed.* U. of Pennsylvania. A former architect, he became associated with films in 1920 as art manager for Lasky. His work for Warner Bros. helped shape the distinct look of the studio's films of the 30s and 40s.

FILMS INCLUDE: *The Gilded Lily, Footlights, Forever/Peter Ibbetson* 1921; *Fury, The White Sister* 1923; *Romola* 1924; *Sackcloth and Scarlet* 1925; *The Reckless Lady, The Dancer of Paris* 1926; *She Goes to War* 1929; *Hell Harbor* 1930; *Bureau of Missing Persons, Lady Killer* 1933; *Dames* 1934; *Oil for the Lamps of China, The Story of Louis Pasteur* 1935; *Three Men on a Horse* 1936; *The King and the Chorus Girl, The Prince and the Pauper* 1937; *Jezebel* 1938; *Dark Victory, The Old Maid* 1939; *City of Conquest* 1940; *The Maltese Falcon, Four Mothers, The Man Who Came to Dinner, Strawberry Blonde* 1941; *Edge of Darkness* 1943; *Mr. Skeffington, Uncertain Glory* 1944; *Devotion, A Stolen Life* 1946; *Life with Father* 1947; *Johnny Belinda* 1948; *Beyond the Forest, The Inspector General* 1949; *The Glass Menagerie* 1950.

Hackett, Albert. Screenwriter. *b.* Feb. 16, 1900, in New York City. *d.* 1995. The son of stage and screen actress Florence Hackett (1882–1954) and brother of actor Raymond HACKETT, he appeared as a child actor on the stage and in films from the age of six. He later wrote plays and screenplays in collaboration with his wife, Frances Goodrich. For list of credits see GOODRICH, Frances.

Hackett, Buddy. Comedian, actor. Born Leonard Hacker, on Aug. 31, 1924, in Brooklyn, N.Y. He began his working life as an apprentice to his upholsterer father but was drawn irresistibly to comedy and broke into show business as a combination waiter-entertainer in the "borscht circuit" of the Catskill Mountains. Rotund, amiable, and quick-witted, he developed into one of the funniest and most inventive American stand-up comics, enjoying great success in nightclubs and TV guest spots. He has also made occasional incursions into the legitimate stage and films in light character roles. In 1956–57 he starred in the TV series 'Stanley.' In 1978 he portrayed Lou Costello in the TV movie *Bud and Lou.*

FILMS: *Walking My Baby Back Home* 1953; *Fireman Save My Child* 1954; *God's Little Acre* 1958; *All Hands on Deck, Everything's Ducky* 1961; *The Wonderful World of the Brothers Grimm, The Music Man* 1962; *It's a Mad Mad Mad Mad World* 1963; *Muscle Beach Party* 1964; *The Golden Head* (Hung./US) 1965; *The Love Bug, The Good Guys and the Bad Guys* (cameo) 1969; *Loose Shoes* 1980; *Hey Babe!* (Can.) 1984; *Scrooged* (as Scrooge) 1988; *The Little Mermaid* (anim.; v/o) 1989.

Hackett, Joan. Actress. *b.* May 1, 1942, New York City. *d.* 1983. *ed.* NYU. A former fashion model, she studied acting under Lee Strasberg and established her acting credentials on Broadway with a fine portrayal in 'Call Me by My Rightful Name' (1961). A polished and intelligent actress with a flair for both comedy and drama, she subsequently appeared in other Broadway productions and many TV presentations. On screen intermittently from 1966, she was nominated for an Academy Award for her performance in *Only When I Laugh* (1981). She died of cancer at 41.

FILMS: *The Group* 1966; *Will Penny, Assignment to Kill* 1968; *Support Your Local Sheriff* 1969; *Rivals* 1972; *The Last of Sheila* 1973; *The Terminal Man* 1974; *Mackintosh and T.J.* 1975; *Treasure of Matecumbe* 1976; *Mr. Mike's Mondo Video* 1978; *One Trick Pony* 1980; *Only When I Laugh* 1981; *The Escape Artist* 1982; *Flicks* (release delayed from 1981) 1987.

Hackett, Raymond. Actor. *b.* July 15, 1902, New York City. *d.* 1958. The son of stage and screen actress Florence Hackett (1882–1954) and brother of actor-turned-screenwriter Albert HACKETT, he made his stage debut at age four and played lead roles in silent and early sound Hollywood films. He was married to Blanche SWEET.

FILMS INCLUDE: *The Cruise of the Make-Believe* 1918; *The Country Flapper* 1922; *The Loves of Sunya* 1927; *Faithless Lover* 1928; *The Trial of Mary Dugan, Madame X, The Girl in the Show, Footlights and Fools* 1929; *Not So Dumb, The Bishop Murder Case, Numbered Men, Let Us Be Gay, Our Blushing Brides, On Your Back, The Sea Wolf, The Cat Creeps* 1930; *Seed* 1931.

Hackford, Taylor. Director. Born on Dec. 3, 1944, in Santa Barbara, Calif. After graduating from USC with a degree in international relations, he served two years as a Peace Corps volunteer in Bolivia. Returning home, he began his career with a TV station in Los Angeles. Later he started his own production company, New Visions. After winning an Academy Award for the live-action short *Teenage Father* (1978), he proved himself a capable feature director with *The Idolmaker* (1980). His prestige was greatly enhanced by the success of his next film, *An Officer and a Gentleman* (1982). Veering increasingly toward a producer's role later in the 80s, he merged his company with New Century Entertainment to form New Century/New Visions in 1988. But after a flurry of production activity, he announced late in 1990 that he was dissolving the business and devoting himself entirely to directing.

FEATURE FILMS: *The Idolmaker* 1980; *An Officer and a Gentleman* 1982; *Against All Odds* (also co-prod.) 1984; *White Nights* (also co-prod.) 1985; *La Bamba* (co-prod. only), *Chuck Berry: Hail! Hail! Rock 'n' Roll* (concert doc.) 1987; *Everybody's All-American* (also co-prod.) 1988; *The Long Walk Home* (exec. prod. only), *Sweet Talker* (co-exec. prod. only) 1990; *Queens Logic* (co-exec. prod. only) 1991; *Bound by Honor* 1993; *Dolores Claiborne* 1995; *When We Were Kings* (co-prod. only) 1996; *The Devil's Advocate* 1997.

Hackman, Gene. Actor. Born on Jan. 30, 1931, in San Bernardino, Calif. Character star of Hollywood films. The son of a journeyman pressman, he was raised in Danville, Ill., and at 16 dropped out of school to join the Marines. Discharged after three years of service, he moved to New York and for two years drifted from job to job. He later used the GI Bill to study commercial drawing, then journalism and TV production, and for a period moved across the country from one small town to another. Finally, in his early 30s, he attended the Pasadena Playhouse school in California and, after returning to New York, began getting small roles in summer stock, off Broadway, and TV.

Hackman's big break came in 1964 when he landed the lead part opposite Sandy Dennis in the Broadway comedy 'Any Wednesday.' This led to a brief but memorable scene in the film *Lilith* (1964). That film's star, Warren BEATTY, remembered Hackman when he was casting *Bonnie and Clyde* three years later and hired him to portray Clyde's brother Buck. Hackman's performance brought him his first Academy Award nomination. He picked up another nomination for *I Never Sang for My Father* (1970) and finally won the coveted Oscar for his performance in the role with which he has remained most closely identified, Popeye Doyle in *The French Connection* (1971). A superb, intuitive actor with an uncanny capacity to capture average characters down to their most minute emotional detail, Hackman followed this triumph with several other superlative true-to-life performances, most memorably in *The Conversation* (1974). Later, demonstrating remarkable versatility, he flaunted comic skills in *Superman* (1978) and its sequels. But his mainstay remained drama, and after hammering out one strong performance after another, he won the best actor prize at the Berlin Film Festival and a fourth Oscar nomination for *Mississippi Burning* (1988). In 1992, he captured a second Oscar for his best supporting actor performance in *Unforgiven*, Clint EASTWOOD's heralded Western. By consistently evoking varieties of everyman in his roles, he is one of the busiest, most sought-after screen personalities in Hollywood—and one of the highest paid.

FILMS: *Mad Dog Coll* (bit) 1961; *Lilith* 1964; *Hawaii* 1966; *A Covenant with Death, First to Fight, Banning, Bonnie and Clyde* 1967; *The Split* 1968; *Riot, The Gypsy Moths, Downhill Racer, Marooned* 1969; *I Never Sang for My Father* 1970; *Doctors' Wives, The Hunting Party* (UK), *The French Connection* 1971; *Cisco Pike, Prime Cut, The Poseidon Adventure* 1972; *Scarecrow* 1973; *The Conversation, Zandy's Bride, Young Frankenstein* (cameo) 1974; *French Connection II, Bite the Bullet, Night Moves, Lucky Lady* 1975; *The Domino Principle, A Bridge Too Far* (UK), *March or Die* (UK) 1977; *Superman* 1978; *Superman II* 1980; *All Night Long, Reds* 1981; *Eureka* (UK), *Under Fire, Uncommon Valor* 1983; *Misunderstood* 1984; *Target, Twice in a Lifetime* 1985; *Power, Hoosiers* 1986; *Superman IV: The Quest for Peace, No Way Out* 1987; *Another Woman, Bat 21, Split Decisions, Full Moon in Blue Water, Mississippi Burning* 1988; *The Package* 1989; *Loose Cannons, Narrow Margin, Postcards from the Edge* 1990; *Class Action* 1991; *Unforgiven* 1992; *The Firm, Geronimo: An American Legend* 1993; *Wyatt Earp* 1994; *Crimson Tide, Get Shorty, The Quick and the Dead* 1995; *The Birdcage, The Chamber, Extreme Measures* 1996; *Absolute Power* 1997.

Haden, Sara. Actress. *b.* 1897, Galveston, Tex. *d.* 1981. The daughter of a physician and a stage actress, she began acting professionally as a child and appeared in a number of Broadway productions during the 20s. In the 30s and 40s she played character roles in numerous films, most frequently for MGM, typically portraying plain secretaries and drab spinsters. Best remembered as Mickey Rooney's Aunt Milly in the "Andy Hardy" screen series.

FILMS INCLUDE: *Spitfire, The White Parade, Anne of Green Gables, Music in the Air* 1934; *Mad Love, Way Down East, Black Fury, Magnificent Obsession* 1935; *Captain January, Half Angel, Little Miss Nobody, Reunion* 1936; *The Last of Mrs. Cheyney, A Family Affair* 1937; *Out West with the Hardys* 1938; *The Hardys Ride High, The Secret of Dr. Kildare, Remember?* 1939; *The Shop Around the Corner, Boom Town* 1940; *The Trial of Mary Dugan, Love Crazy, Life Begins for Andy Hardy, H. M. Pulham Esq.* 1941; *Woman of the Year* 1942; *The Youngest Profession, Above Suspicion, Thousands Cheer* 1943; *Our Vines Have Tender Grapes* 1945; *She-Wolf of London, Mr. Ace* 1946; *The Bishop's Wife* 1947; *Rachel and the Stranger* 1948; *The Big Cat* 1949; *A Lion Is in the Streets* 1953; *Andy Hardy Comes Home* 1958.

Hadjidakis, Manos. Composer. Born in 1925, in Athens. One of the leading Greek composers of popular music, he has written the scores for dozens of Greek and international films. He won an Academy Award for the music and lyrics of the title song for the film *Never on Sunday* (1960).

FILMS INCLUDE: *Stella* 1954; *Drakos* 1956; *I Panorami* 1957; *We Have Only One Life* 1958; *Never on Sunday* 1960; *Madalena* 1961; *The 300 Spartans* (US), *It Happened in Athens* (US) 1962; *Nine Miles to Noon* (US), *In the Cool of the Day* (title song only; US), *Aliki/Aliki—My Love* 1963; *America America* (US), *Topkapi* (US) 1964; *Blue* (US) 1968; *The Invincible Six* (US/Iran) 1970; *Der Fussgänger/The Pedestrian* (Ger.), *Sweet Movie* (Can./Fr./Ger.) 1974; *Memed My Hawk* (UK) 1984.

Hadley, Reed. Actor. *b.* Reed Herring, 1911, Petrolia, Tex. *d.* 1974. He started out in little theaters, supplementing his income as a floorwalker. Later he appeared in stock and made his name as the voice of Red Ryder in the radio series. Tall and darkly handsome, he played leads, second leads, and character roles in many films, portraying both villains and "good guys," mostly in B pictures. He appeared as a regular on several TV series, including 'Racket Squad,' and 'Public Defender.'

FILMS INCLUDE: *Female Fugitive* 1938; *Zorro's Fighting Legion* (serial, as Zorro), *Calling Dr. Kildare* 1939; *I Take This Woman, The Bank Dick* 1940; *Adventures of Captain Marvel* (serial), *Whistling in the Dark* 1941; *Guadalcanal Diary* 1943; *In the Meantime Darling, Wing and a Prayer* 1944; *A Bell for Adano, Leave Her to Heaven* 1945; *Shock, The Dark Corner* 1946; *Captain from Castile* 1947; *A Southern Yankee, The Iron Curtain* 1948; *I Shot Jesse James* 1949; *The Baron of Arizona, Dallas, A Modern Marriage* 1950; *Kansas Pacific* 1953; *Highway Dragnet* 1954; *Big House USA* 1955; *Young Dillinger* 1965; *The St. Valentine's Day Massacre* 1967.

Haffenden, Elizabeth. Costume designer. *b.* 1906, Croydon, England. *d.* 1976. She entered British films in 1933 and was eventually put in charge of the costume department at Gainsborough Studios. She created the fashions for many major British and American films, alone or in collaboration, winning Academy Awards for *Ben-Hur* (1959) and *A Man for All Seasons* (1966).

FILMS INCLUDE: *Wedding Group/Wrath of Jealousy* 1936; *The Young Mr. Pitt* 1942; *Fanny by Gaslight* 1944; *The Wicked Lady* 1945; *The Magic Bow* 1946; *The Man Within/The Smugglers* 1947; *The Bad Lord Byron, Christopher Columbus* 1949; *Beau Brummel* 1954; *Invitation to the Dance, Bhowani Junction, Moby Dick, The Barretts of Wimpole Street* 1956; *Ben-Hur* 1959; *The Amorous Adventures of Moll Flanders* 1965; *A Man for All Seasons* 1966; *Half a Sixpence* 1967; *Chitty Chitty Bang Bang* 1968; *The Prime of Miss Jean Brodie* 1969; *Fiddler on the Roof* 1971; *Pope Joan* 1972; *The Day of the Jackal* 1973; *Luther* 1974.

Hageman, Richard. Composer, conductor. *b.* July 9, 1882, Leeuwarden, Holland. *d.* 1966. A concert pianist at six, he performed as an accompanist and later a conductor at Amsterdam's Royal Opera Company. He went to the US in 1906, becoming an American citizen in 1915. From 1914 to 1932 he conducted the orchestra of the New York Metropolitan Opera and later various other symphonic ensembles. In Hollywood from the late 30s, he composed scores for a number of films, winning acclaim for his adaptations of folk themes for several major John Ford productions. He shared the Academy Award for the score of *Stagecoach* (1939).

FILMS INCLUDE: *If I Were King* 1938; *Stagecoach* (co-composer) 1939; *The Long Voyage Home* 1940; *The Shanghai Gesture* 1941; *Angel and the Badman, The Fugitive, Mourning Becomes Electra* 1947; *Fort Apache* 1948; *Three Godfathers, She Wore a Yellow Ribbon* 1949; *Wagonmaster* 1950.

Hagen, Jean. Actress. *b.* Jean Shirley Verhagen, Aug. 3, 1923, Chicago. *d.* 1977. She went to New York in 1945, following graduation as a drama major from Northwestern University, and after several months as a radio performer and theater usherette launched her stage career on Broadway. She was signed by MGM on a movie contract in 1949 and showed much promise in her screen debut as Judy Holliday's home-wrecker in *Adam's Rib,* but with the notable exception of *The Asphalt Jungle* (1950) and *Singin' in the Rain* (1952), the film industry failed to take advantage of her versatile talent as a dramatic actress and comedienne. From 1953 to 1957 she played Danny Thomas's wife in the popular TV series 'Make Room for Daddy.' She died of throat cancer at 54.

FILMS: *Adam's Rib* 1949; *Side Street, Ambush, The Asphalt Jungle, A Life of Her Own* 1950; *Night Into Morning, No Questions Asked* 1951; *Singin' in the Rain, Carbine Williams, Shadow in the Sky* 1952; *Arena, Latin Lovers, Half a Hero* 1953; *The Big Knife* 1955; *Spring Reunion* 1957; *The Shaggy Dog* 1959; *Sunrise at Campobello* 1960; *Panic in the Year Zero* 1962; *Dead Ringer* 1964.

Hagerty, Julie. Actress. Born on June 15, 1955, in Cincinnati. Slender brunette leading lady of the American screen. The daughter of a musician and a former singer-model, she arrived in New York in the early 70s armed with six years of drama training and a modest modeling career of her own. While scaling the heights of the fashion business, she kept on attending drama classes with William HICKEY and at Juilliard, and made her acting debut in an off-off-Broadway Greenwich Village theater managed by her older brother, Michael. It led to her first movie role in *Airplane!* in 1980. Her scatterbrained, jittery persona in that film has characterized her performances in successive comedies.

FILMS: *Airplane!* 1980; *A Midsummer's Night's Sex Comedy, Airplane II: The Sequel* 1982; *Goodbye New York* (Isr./US), *Lost in America, Bad Medicine* 1985; *Beyond Therapy, Aria* (UK) 1987; *Bloodhounds of Broadway, Rude Awakening* 1989; *Reversal of Fortune* 1990; *What About Bob?* 1991; *Noises Off* 1992; *The Wife* 1996.

Haggard, Piers. Director. Born in 1939, in Scotland. *ed.* U. of Edinburgh. The son of actor Stephen Haggard and great grandnephew of novelist H. Rider Haggard of *She* and *King Solomon's Mines* fame, he began his career in the theater, in 1960, as an assistant to the artistic director of London's Royal Court. After several years as a director of plays and TV dramas, he made his debut as a screen director in 1969.

FILMS: *Wedding Night* (also co-sc.; Ire.) 1969; *The Blood on Satan's Claw/Satan's Skin/Satan's Claw* 1970; *The Fiendish Plot of Dr. Fu Manchu* (US), *Quatermass Conclusion* (orig. for TV) 1980; *Venom* 1982; *A Summer Story* 1988.

Hagman, Larry. Actor. Born on Sept. 21, 1931, in Fort Worth, Tex. The son of a small-town lawyer and a 17-year-old aspiring singer (she went on to become famous on Broadway as Mary MARTIN), he was raised by his divorced father in Weatherford, Texas, and later by a grandmother in California, occasionally shuttling to and from his mother's residence in New York. He was shunted around among numerous private schools, then dropped out of Bard College after a single year. Capping years in analysis, he began finding therapy in acting. When his career meandered, he enlisted in the Air Force, serving from 1952 to 1956, partly in London. On returning home, he began landing meatier roles, off and on Broadway and on TV, including a regular stint in 1961–63 in the daytime soap opera 'The Edge of Night.' His big break came in the popular comedy series 'I Dream of Jeannie' (1965–70), co-starring Barbara EDEN. It turned out to be only an interlude to his greatest success, the juicy role of the slimy J. R. Ewing in the long-running (1978–90), internationally popular hit series 'Dallas.' Hagman's hectic TV schedule limited his appearances in feature films.

FILMS: *Ensign Pulver, Fail Safe* 1964; *Sette contro la Morte/The Cavern* (It./Ger.), *In Harm's Way* 1965; *The Group* 1966; *Up in the Cellar* 1970; *Beware! The Blob* (also dir.) 1972; *Stardust* (UK), *Harry and Tonto* 1974; *Mother Jugs and Speed, The Big Bus, The Eagle Has Landed* (UK) 1976; *Checkered Flag or Crash* 1977; *Superman* 1978; *S.O.B.* 1981.

Haim, Corey. Actor. Born on Dec. 23, 1972, in Toronto. Bushy-haired juvenile lead typically featured in low-budget teen screwball comedies, often paired with Corey FELDMAN. He performed in commercials from age ten and appeared regularly on a children's show before making his feature debut in 1984.

FILMS: *Firstborn* 1984; *Secret Admirer, Silver Bullet, Murphy's Romance* 1985; *Lucas* 1986; *The Lost Boys* 1987; *License to Drive, Watchers* (Can.) 1988; *Dream a Little Dream* 1989; *Prayer of the Rollerboys, Dream Machine, Fast Getaway* 1991; *Fast Getaway 2, National Lampoon's Last Resort* 1994.

Haines, Randa. Director. Born on Feb. 20, 1945, in Los Angeles, Calif. Before turning to directing, she studied acting with Lee Strasberg and at the School of Visual Arts in New York. Her directorial debut, *Children of a Lesser God,* was widely praised for its evenhanded view of the life of a deaf woman.

FILMS: *Children of a Lesser God* 1986; *The Doctor* 1991; *Wrestling Ernest Hemingway* 1993; *A Family Thing* (co-prod. only) 1996.

Haines, William. Actor. *b.* Jan. 1, 1900, Staunton, Va. *d.* 1973. Popular, breezy star of light Hollywood silents and early talkies, he broke into films in 1922 via a new-faces contest that he had entered while working as an office boy on Wall Street. He became quite popular with movie audiences in smart-aleck type roles and was still cast as a college boy long after reaching maturity. He retired from the screen in the mid-30s and subsequently achieved some prominence as an interior decorator.

FILMS INCLUDE: *Brothers Under the Skin* 1922; *Three Wise Fools, Souls for Sale* 1923; *Three Weeks, True as Steel, Wine of Youth, The Midnight Express, Circe the Enchantress, The Wife of the Centaur* 1924; *A Fool and His Money, The Denial, A Slave of Fashion, The Tower of Lies, Little Annie Rooney, Sally Irene and Mary* 1925; *The Thrill Hunter, Mike, Memory Lane, Lovely Mary, Brown of Harvard, Tell It to the Marines* 1926; *A Little Journey, Slide Kelly Slide, Spring Fever* 1927; *West Point, The Smart Set, Excess Baggage, Show People, Alias Jimmy Valentine* 1928; *The Duke Steps Out, A Man's Man, Speedway, The Hollywood Revue, Navy Blues* 1929; *Free and Easy, Way Out West, Remote Control* 1930; *A Tailor-Made Man, Just a Gigolo* 1931; *Fast Life* 1932; *Young and Beautiful, The Marines Are Coming* 1934.

Hakim, Robert (born on Dec. 19, 1907), **Raymond** (*b.* Aug. 23, 1909; *d.* 1980), and **André** (born on Dec. 5, 1915). Producers. Born in Alexandria, Egypt, three brothers (a fourth, Raphael, is a film exporter) involved in film production from their teens. Robert and Raymond first worked for Paramount in Paris, then established their own company in 1934 and produced some major French films. In the 40s they shifted their activity to the US, then returned to France. André married a daughter of Darryl F. ZANUCK in the early 50s and became a producer for 20th Century-Fox.

FILMS INCLUDE: Produced by Robert and Raymond—*Samson* 1936; *Pépé le Moko, Marthe Richard* 1937; *La Bête humaine/The Human Beast* 1938; *The Southerner* (Robert co-prod. with David Loew; US) 1945; *Heartbeat* (US) 1946; *The Long Night* (US) 1947; *Without Honor* (US) 1949; *Casque d'Or* 1952; *Thérèse Raquin/The Adulteress* 1953; *Mam'zelle Nitouche* 1954; *Notre-Dame de Paris/The Hunchback of Notre Dame* 1956; *Pot-Bouille* 1957; *A Double Tour/Leda/Web of Passion* 1959; *Plein Soleil/Purple Noon, L'Avventura* (exec. prod.; It./Fr.), *Les Bonnes Femmes* 1960; *Une aussi Longue*

Absence/The Long Absence, L'Eclisse/Eclipse (It./Fr.), *Eva/The Devil's Woman* 1962; *Chair de Poule/Highway Pickup* 1963; *La Ronde/Circle of Love* 1964; *Belle de Jour* 1967; *Isadora/The Loves of Isadora* (UK) 1969; *Le Rempart des Béguines/Rampart of Desire* 1972; *La Marge* 1976. Produced by André—*L'Evential/Naughty Martine* 1947; *Mr. Belvedere Rings the Bell* (US) 1951; *O. Henry's Full House* (US) 1952; *Powder River* (US) 1953; *The Man Who Never Was* (US/UK), *Sea Wife* (UK) 1957; *La Bonne Soupe/Careless Love, Patate/Friend of the Family* 1964; *Hello-Goodbye* (US) 1970; *La Marge* 1976.

Halas, John. Animator, producer. Born on Apr. 16, 1912, in Budapest. A former apprentice of George PAL (1928–31), he began producing his own cartoons in 1934. In England from 1936, he formed Halas-Batchelor Cartoon Films in 1940 with his wife, Joy Batchelor. For list of credits see BATCHELOR, Joy.

halation. Unwanted flare or halo surrounding a photographed image on a film print. It is caused by light passing through the film's layer of emulsion and being reflected back into the emulsion from the film's base. The problem is virtually eliminated by coating the film during manufacture with a dark dye known as "antihalation backing." This dye prevents halation by absorbing much of the light passing through the emulsion and is then completely removed during processing.

Hale, Alan. Actor, director. *b.* Rufus Alan McKahan, Feb. 10, 1892, Washington D.C. *d.* 1950. He entered films in 1911, following an abortive try at a career as an opera singer, and throughout the silent era played starring and supporting roles in numerous screen productions. In the mid-20s he directed seven films for Cecil B. DE MILLE—*The Scarlet Honeymoon, The Wedding Song, Braveheart* (all 1925), *Forbidden Waters, The Sporting Lover, Risky Business* (all 1926), and *Rubber Tires* (1927). After playing leads in several early talkies, he became one of Hollywood's busiest character players, appearing in numerous films of Warner Bros. and other studios, often as a sidekick of Errol FLYNN, typically as a jovial, back-slapping muscleman. In all, he appeared in hundreds of films. Despite his busy schedule, he achieved some success as an inventor. His son and look-alike, Alan Hale, Jr. (1918–90), played character roles in numerous features from his teens and appeared in such TV series as 'Casey Jones' and 'Gilligan's Island.'

FILMS INCLUDE (as actor): *The Cowboy and the Lady* 1911; *The Prisoner of Zenda, By Man's Law* 1913; *Strongheart, Men and Women, The Cricket on the Hearth, Martin Chuzzlewit* (title role), *Masks and Faces, The Woman in Black* 1914; *After the Storm, The Americano, Adam Bede, Jane Eyre, Dora Thorne* 1915; *Pudd'n Head Wilson, The Woman in the Case, The Love Thief, The Scarlet Oath* 1916; *The Price She Paid, One Hour, Life's Whirlpool, The Eternal Temptress* 1917; *Moral Suicide* 1918; *The Four Horsemen of the Apocalypse, The Barbarian, The Great Impersonation* 1921; *A Doll's House* (as Trevald Helmer), *One Glorious Day, The Trap, The Dictator, Robin Hood* (as Little John) 1922; *Quicksands, The Covered Wagon, Main Street* (as Miles Bjornstam), *Cameo Kirby, Long Live the King* 1923; *Black Oxen, One Night in Rome* 1924; *Dick Turpin, Flattery* 1925; *Hearts and Fists* 1926; *Vanity, The Wreck of the Hesperus* 1927; *The Leopard Lady, Skyscraper, The Cop, Oh Kay!, Power, The Spieler* 1928; *Sal of Singapore, The Leatherneck, Sailor's Holiday, Red Hot Rhythm, The Sap* 1929; *She Got What She Wanted* 1930; *The Night Angel, Susan Lenox: Her Fall and Rise, The Sin of Madelon Claudet* 1931; *Union Depot, So Big* 1932; *What Price Decency?* 1933; *It Happened One Night, The Lost Patrol, Little Man What Now?, Of Human Bondage, Imitation of Life, Broadway Bill, Babbitt* (as Charlie McKelvey), *The Little Minister* 1934; *The Good Fairy, The Crusades, The Last Days of Pompeii* 1935; *A Message to Garcia, Our Relations* 1936; *The Prince and the Pauper, Jump for Glory/When Thief Meets Thief* (UK), *High Wide and Handsome, Stella Dallas, Thin Ice* 1937; *The Adventures of Marco Polo, Four Men and a Prayer, The Adventures of Robin Hood* (again as Little John), *Algiers, Valley of the Giants, The Sisters* 1938; *Dodge City, The Man in the Iron Mask* (as Porthos of the Three Musketeers), *Dust Be My Destiny, On Your Toes, The Private Lives of Elizabeth and Essex* 1939; *The Fighting 69th, Green Hell, Virginia City, They Drive by Night, The Sea Hawk, Tugboat Annie Sails Again, Santa Fe Trail* 1940; *The Strawberry Blonde, Footsteps in the Dark, Manpower* 1941; *Captains of the Clouds, Desperate Journey, Gentleman Jim* 1942; *Action in the North Atlantic, This Is the Army* 1943; *Destination Tokyo, The Adventures of Mark Twain* 1944; *Roughly Speaking, Hotel Berlin* 1945; *Night and Day, The Time the Place and the Girl* 1946; *The Man I Love, Pursued, Cheyenne, My Wild Irish Rose* 1947; *Adventures of Don Juan, Whiplash* 1948; *South of St. Louis, The Inspector General* 1949; *Stars in My Crown, Rogues of Sherwood Forest* 1950.

Hale, Barbara. Actress. Born on Apr. 18, 1921, in DeKalb, Ill. A former model, she played leads in many routine Hollywood productions of the 30s and 40s but is most closely identified with the role of Della Street in the long-running (1957–66) 'Perry Mason' TV series, for which she received an Emmy in 1959. Married to a former costar, Bill WILLIAMS. Their son is actor William KATT. Mother and son have appeared in Perry Mason TV movies in the late 80s and early 90s, directed by Katt.

FILMS INCLUDE: *Gildersleeve's Bad Day, The Seventh Victim, The Iron Major* 1943; *Higher and Higher, The Falcon Out West, The Falcon in Hollywood* 1944; *West of the Pecos, First Yank Into Tokyo* 1945; *Lady Luck* 1946; *A Likely Story* 1947; *The Boy with Green Hair* 1948; *The Clay Pigeon, The Window, Jolson Sings Again* 1949; *And Baby Makes Three, Emergency Wedding, The Jackpot* 1950; *Lorna Doone* 1951; *The First Time* 1952; *Seminole, Lone Hand, A Lion Is in the Streets* 1953; *Unchained, The Far Horizons* 1955; *The Houston Story, Seventh Cavalry* 1956; *The Oklahoman* 1957; *Desert Hell* 1958; *Buckskin* 1968; *Airport* 1970; *The Giant Spider Invasion* 1975; *Big Wednesday* 1978.

Hale, Creighton. Actor. *b.* Patrick Fitzgerald, May 14, 1882, Cork, Ireland. *d.* 1965. He made his stage debut as an infant with his father's touring company and came to the US on a tour with another Irish troupe in 1913. A dashing, elegant man, he entered films the following year and after playing secondary roles in a number of serials played dapper leads and second leads in many silent features of the late 1910s and 20s, then supporting and character roles in talkies of the 30s and 40s.

FILMS INCLUDE: *The Million Dollar Mystery* (serial), *The Three of Us* 1914; *The Exploits of Elaine* (serial), *A Fool There Was, The Old Homestead* 1915; *The Iron Claw* (serial), *Charity, Snow White* (as the prince) 1916; *The Seven Pearls* (serial) 1917; *Waifs, The Woman the Germans Shot* 1918; *The Great Victory/Wilson or the Kaiser/The Fall of the Hohenszollerens/Germany Must Pay, Oh Boy!, The Love Cheat, A Damsel in Distress, The Back Circle, The Thirteenth Chair* 1919; *The Idol Dancer, Way Down East, Child for Sale* 1920; *Forbidden Love* 1921; *Orphans of the Storm, Fascination, Her Majesty* 1922; *Trilby, Mary of the Movies, Broken Hearts of Broadway, Three Wise Fools* 1923; *Name the Man, The Marriage Circle, Wine of Youth, This Woman* 1924; *The Bridge of Sighs, Seven Days, Exchange Wives, Time the Comedian, The Shadow on the Wall, The Circle* 1925; *Beverly of Graustark, A Poor Girl's Romance, Oh Baby!, The Midnight Message* 1926; *Annie Laurie, The Cat and the Canary, Thumbs Down* 1927; *Rose-Marie, The House of*

Shame, Sisters of Eve 1928; *Seven Footprints to Satan, The Great Divide* 1929; *Holiday* 1930; *Prestige* 1932; *The Masquerader* 1933; *Hollywood Boulevard* 1936; *The Return of Dr. X* 1939; *Calling Philo Vance* 1940; *Larceny Inc.* 1942; *The Gorilla Man, Watch on the Rhine, Action in the North Atlantic* 1943; *Crime by Night* 1944; *The Two Mrs. Carrolls, The Perils of Pauline* 1947; *Beyond the Forest* 1949.

Hale, Georgia. Actress. *b.* 1906, St. Joseph, Mo. *d.* 1985. Working as an extra on the set of Roy William Neill's *By Divine Right/The Way Men Love* (1924), she was discovered by then-screenwriter Josef von Sternberg, who made her the star of his first film as a director, *Salvation Hunters,* in 1925. Later that year, she played her most memorable screen role as the subject of Charlie Chaplin's love and hallucinations in *The Gold Rush.* But the remainder of her career was largely undistinguished and she retired from the screen when sound came in.

FILMS: *By Divine Right/The Way Men Love* (extra) 1924; *The Salvation Hunters, The Gold Rush* 1925; *The Rainmaker, The Great Gatsby* (as Myrtle Wilson), *Man of the Forest* 1926; *Hills of Peril, The Wheel of Destiny* 1927; *A Woman Against the World, The Rawhide Kid, The Last Moment, A Trick of Hearts, Gypsy of the North, The Floating College* 1928.

Hale, Jonathan. Actor. *b.* Jonathan Hatley, 1891, Ontario, Canada, *d.* 1966, a suicide. He was a busy character player of more than 200 Hollywood films, often typecast as an exasperated businessman. Memorable as Mr. Dithers in the "Blondie" series. Also a fixture in "The Saint" and "Charlie Chan" adventures. He was a low-echelon diplomat prior to his film career.

FILMS INCLUDE: *Lightning Strikes Twice* 1934; *Alice Adams* 1935; *Fury, Charlie Chan at the Race Track* 1936; *You Only Live Once, Saratoga, Madame X* 1937; *Arsene Lupin Returns, Judge Hardy's Children, Her Jungle Love, The Saint in New York, Boys Town, Blondie* 1938; *The Story of Alexander Graham Bell, In Name Only, Barricade* 1939; *Johnny Apollo, The Saint Takes Over* 1940; *Blondie Goes Latin* 1941; *Calling Dr. Gillespie* 1942; *Hangmen Also Die, Sweet Rosie O'Grady* 1943; *Jack London, Since You Went Away, Dead Man's Eyes* 1944; *The Cat Creeps* 1946; *The Beginning or the End* 1947; *Johnny Belinda, Call Northside 777* 1948; *Strangers on a Train* 1951; *Riot in Cell Block 11* 1954; *The Night Holds Terror* 1955; *Jaguar* 1956; *Kiss Them for Me* 1957; *Four for Texas* 1963.

Hale, Louise Closser. Actress. *b.* Oct. 13, 1872, Chicago. *d.* 1933. Character player of the Broadway stage and Hollywood early talkies. On the screen she typically played tyrannical matrons.

FILMS INCLUDE: *The Hole in the Wall, Paris* 1929; *Big Boy, The Princess and the Plumber* 1930; *Born to Love, Daddy Long Legs, Devotion, Platinum Blonde* 1931; *The Man Who Played God, Shanghai Express, Letty Lynton, Rebecca of Sunnybrook Farm, Movie Crazy, Faithless, No More Orchids, The Son-Daughter* 1932; *The White Sister, Today We Live, The Barbarian, Another Language, Dinner at Eight* 1933.

Hale, Monte. Actor. Born on June 8, 1921, in San Angelo, Tex. Singing cowboy star of Republic Westerns of the late 40s and early 50s.

FILMS INCLUDE: *Steppin' in Society, The Big Bonanza* 1944; *The Purple Monster Strikes* (serial) 1945; *Home on the Range, The Man from Rainbow Valley* 1946; *Along the Oregon Trail, Under Colorado Skies* 1947; *California Firebrand, Son of God's Country* 1948; *Prince of the Plains, South of Rio* 1949; *The Vanishing Westerner, The Old Frontier* 1950; *Yukon Vengeance* 1954; *Giant* 1956.

Hale, Sonnie. Actor, singer, director. *b.* John Robert Hale Monro, May 1, 1902, London. *d.* 1959. *ed.* Beaumont College, Old Windsor. Short, oft-bespectacled, highly popular leading man of British stage and films. The son of actor Robert Hale and brother of revue star Binnie Hale, he made his stage debut in 1921 and rapidly found his niche in musical comedy. His popularity extended to films, in which he reached a peak of success in the early 30s. Later in the decade he also directed three films, all starring his second wife (1931–44) and frequent co-star, Jessie MATTHEWS. His first (1926–31) wife was actress Evelyn Laye.

FEATURE FILMS: As actor—*On with the Dance* 1927; *Happy Ever After, Tell Me Tonight/Be Mine Tonight* 1932; *Friday the Thirteenth, Early to Bed* 1933; *Evergreen, Wild Boy, My Song for You, My Heart Is Calling, Are You a Mason?* 1934; *Marry the Girl, First a Girl* 1935; *It's Love Again* 1936; *The Gaunt Stranger/The Phantom Strikes* 1938; *Let's Be Famous* 1939; *Fiddlers Three* 1944; *London Town/My Heart Goes Crazy* 1946. As director—*Head Over Heels/Head Over Heels in Love, Gangway* 1937; *Sailing Along* 1938.

Haley, Jack. Actor. *b.* Aug. 10, 1899, Boston. *d.* 1979. Lithe comedian of vaudeville, stage, and screen, forever remembered as the Tin Man in *The Wizard of Oz* (1939). After a long absence, he returned to the screen in 1970 in a cameo appearance in *Norwood,* directed by his son, Jack Haley, Jr. (*b.* Oct. 25, 1933), who also directed, produced, and scripted the MGM compilation film *That's Entertainment* (1974) and produced numerous TV specials on the history of motion pictures.

FILMS INCLUDE: *Broadway Madness* 1927; *Follow Thru* 1930; *Sitting Pretty* 1933; *Here Comes the Groom* 1934; *The Girl Friend, Coronado* 1935; *F-Man, The Poor Little Rich Girl, Pigskin Parade* 1936; *Wake Up and Live, Pick a Star, She Had to Eat, Danger—Love at Work* 1937; *Rebecca of Sunnybrook Farm, Alexander's Ragtime Band, Hold That Co-Ed, Thanks for Everything* 1938; *The Wizard of Oz* (as the Tin Man) 1939; *Moon Over Miami, Navy Blues* 1941; *Beyond the Blue Horizon* 1942; *Higher and Higher* 1943; *One Body Too Many* 1944; *George White's Scandals* 1945; *People Are Funny, Vacation in Reno* 1946; *Make Mine Laughs* 1949; *Norwood* (cameo) 1970.

Hall, Alexander. Director. *b.* 1894, Boston. *d.* 1968. On stage from age four, he began his film career as an actor, appearing in an early serial, *The Million Dollar Mystery* (1914). After WW I service, he returned to films as an editor and assistant director, becoming a full-fledged director in the early 30s. He turned out a number of skilled, sophisticated comedies and comedy-fantasy films, notably *This Thing Called Love, Here Comes Mr. Jordan, Bedtime Story,* and *Down to Earth,* but most of his output was routine. He was married to Lola LANE.

FILMS: *Sinners in the Sun, Madame Racketeer* (co-dir. with Harry Wagstaff Gribble) 1932; *The Girl in 419, Midnight Club, Torch Singer* (all co-dir. with George Somnes) 1933; *Miss Fane's Baby Is Stolen, Little Miss Marker, The Pursuit of Happiness, Limehouse Blues* 1934; *Goin' to Town, Annapolis Farewell* 1935; *Give Us This Night, Yours for the Asking* 1936; *Exclusive* 1937; *There's Always a Woman, I Am the Law, There's That Woman Again* 1938; *The Lady's from Kentucky, Good Girls Go to Paris, The Amazing Mr. Williams* 1939; *The Doctor Takes a Wife, He Stayed for Breakfast* 1940; *This Thing Called Love, Here Comes Mr. Jordan, Bedtime Story* 1941; *They All Kissed the Bride, My Sister Eileen* 1942; *The Heavenly Body, Once Upon a Time* 1944; *She Wouldn't Say Yes* 1945; *Down to Earth* 1947; *The Great Lover* 1949; *Love That Brute, Louisa* 1950; *Up Front* 1951; *Because You're Mine* 1952; *Let's Do It Again* 1953; *Forever Darling* 1956.

Hall, Anthony Michael. Actor. Born on Apr. 14, 1968, in Boston. Appealing blond juvenile lead to Hollywood films, originally in semi-nerdy roles, then later as a beefy jock. He was a regular on TV's 'Saturday Night Live' in 1985–86.

FILMS INCLUDE: *Six Pack* 1982; *National Lampoon's*

Vacation 1983; *Sixteen Candles* 1984; *The Breakfast Club, Weird Science* 1985; *Out of Bounds* 1986; *Johnny Be Good* 1988; *Edward Scissorhands* 1990; *Into the Sun, Me and the Mob* 1992; *Six Degrees of Separation* 1993; *A Gnome Named Gnorm* 1994; *Sunset Park* 1996.

Hall, Charles D. Art director. *b.* Aug. 19, 1899, England. *d.* 1968, England. Came to Hollywood after British stage experience. He is highly regarded for his work for Charlie CHAPLIN and for the imaginative sets of several key horror films of James Whale at Universal.

FILMS INCLUDE: *The Lying Truth* 1922; *The Gold Rush, The Phantom of the Opera* 1925; *The Cohens and Kellys* 1926; *The Cat and the Canary* 1927; *The Man Who Laughs, The Circus* 1928; *The Last Warning, Broadway* 1929; *All Quiet on the Western Front* 1930; *Dracula, City Lights, Frankenstein* 1931; *The Old Dark House* 1932; *The Invisible Man, By Candlelight* 1933; *The Black Cat, Little Man, What Now?* 1934; *The Good Fairy, The Bride of Frankenstein, Diamond Jim, Remember Last Night?, Magnificent Obsession* 1935; *Modern Times, My Man Godfrey, Show Boat* 1936; *The Road Back* 1937; *Merrily We Live, There Goes My Love* 1938; *Topper Takes a Trip* 1939; *One Million B.C., Captain Fury* 1940; *Red Planet Mars* 1952; *Shield for Murder* 1954.

Hall, Conrad. Director of photography. Born in 1926, in Tahiti. The son of James Norman Hall, co-author of *Mutiny on the Bounty,* he studied filmmaking at USC. With two classmates, he formed a small production company, entering the business by selling a prize-winning class project, *Sea Theme,* to TV. He subsequently made industrial and TV films and commercials, and shot bits of footage for various feature films, including Disney's *The Living Desert* (1953). In the early 60s he worked as camera assistant and camera operator on various features, getting his first sole credit as director of photography in 1965. In just a few years he acquired a considerable reputation for his color cinematography and won an Academy Award for his work on *Butch Cassidy and the Sundance Kid* (1969). After a decade's absence, he returned to feature films in the late 80s and was promptly nominated for an Oscar for the cinematography of *Tequila Sunrise.*

FILMS INCLUDE: *Edge of Fury* (co-phot.) 1958; *The Wild Seed, Morituri* 1965; *Harper, The Professionals* 1966; *Divorce American Style, Cool Hand Luke, In Cold Blood* 1967; *Hell in the Pacific* 1968; *Butch Cassidy and the Sundance Kid, The Happy Ending, Tell Them Willie Boy Is Here* 1969; *Fat City* 1972; *Electra Glide in Blue* 1973; *Catch My Soul* 1974; *Smile, The Day of the Locust* 1975; *Marathon Man* 1976; *Black Widow* 1987; *Tequila Sunrise* 1988; *Class Action* 1991; *Jennifer Eight* 1992; *Searching for Bobby Fischer* 1993; *Love Affair* 1994.

Hall, Huntz. Actor. Born Henry Hall, in 1920, in New York City. One of 14 children of an Irish-born engineer, he attended New York's Professional Children's School and appeared on radio serials from early boyhood. He went to Hollywood in 1937 with the cast of Broadway's hit play 'Dead End' as one of the gang of slum boys who were later to form the nucleus of the wisecracking, tough-talking young hoodlum screen team known as the Dead End Kids, later as the East Side Kids, and eventually as the Bowery Boys. Rubber-faced and smash-nosed, he played Dippy, the gang's dumbbell and the sidekick of gang leader Spit (Leo GORCEY). After the group broke up, Hall appeared in occasional films and more frequently on TV and the nightclub circuit. He also co-directed a TV movie, 'Lost Island.'

FILMS INCLUDE: *Dead End* 1937; *Crime School, Little Tough Guys, Angels with Dirty Faces* 1938; *They Made Me a Criminal, Hell's Kitchen, Angels Wash Their Faces, The Return of Dr. X* 1939; *You're Not So Tough, Give Us Wings* 1940; *Hit the Road, Bowery Blitzkrieg, Mob Town* 1941; *Mr. Wise Guy, Private Buckaroo* 1942; *Kid Dynamite* 1943; *Bowery Champs* 1944; *Wonder Man* 1945; *A Walk in the Sun* 1946; *News Hounds* 1947; *Master Minds* 1949; *Tell It to the Marines* 1952; *Bowery to Bagdad* 1955; *Spook Chasers* 1957; *Gentle Giant* 1967; *Herbie Rides Again* 1974; *The Manchu Eagle Murder Caper Mystery* 1975; *Valentino* (as Jesse Lasky; UK) 1977; *The Escape Artist* 1982; *Cyclone* 1987.

Hall, James. Actor. *b.* James Brown, Oct. 22, 1900, Dallas. *d.* 1940. Handsome leading man of Hollywood films of the 20s and early 30s, following stage experience from boyhood. He is best remembered as the pure-hearted hero of Howard Hughes's *Hell's Angels* (1930), whose fiancée (Jean Harlow) seduces his cowardly brother (Ben Lyon).

FILMS INCLUDE: *The Man Alone* 1923; *The Campus Flirt, Stranded in Paris* 1926; *Hotel Imperial, Love's Greatest Mistake, Senorita, Ritzy, Rolled Stockings, Silk Legs* 1927; *Four Sons, The Fifty-Fifty Girl, Just Married, The Fleet's In* 1928; *The Case of Lena Smith, The Canary Murder Case, This Is Heaven, Smiling Irish Eyes, The Saturday Night Kid* 1929; *Dangerous Nan McGrew, Hell's Angels, Let's Go Native, Maybe It's Love, The Third Alarm, Divorce Among Friends* 1930; *Millie, The Good Bad Girl, Mother's Millions/The She-Wolf, Sporting Chance* 1931; *Manhattan Tower* 1932.

Hall, Jon. Actor. *b.* Charles Hall Loeher, Feb. 23, 1913, Fresno, Calif. *d.* 1979. He began his film career in 1935 as Charles Locher, then changed his name to Lloyd Crane in 1936, and then to Jon Hall in 1937. He became a popular screen hero of the 40s after playing the lead in John Ford's *The Hurricane* (1937). Muscular and athletic, he was often seen in a loincloth in South Seas films as a male counterpart of Dorothy LAMOUR or in Bedouin robes in Arabian Nights films as a sort of male version of Maria Montez, and sometimes thankfully unseen in Invisible Man roles. In 1952–54 he brought his elementary acting style to TV's 'Ramar of the Jungle.' He invested his profits from the show in specialized underwater camera equipment, which he rented out to filmmakers after retiring from the screen. He also ran a flying school and operated a fleet of small airplanes. In 1969 he co-produced and photographed a low-budget film, *Five the Hard Way/The Sidehackers.* In rapidly deteriorating health after months of treatment for bladder cancer, he shot himself to death. His second (1938–55) of three wives was actress Frances LANGFORD. The third (from 1959) was actress Raquel TORRES.

FILMS INCLUDE: *Charlie Chan in Shanghai* 1935; *The Clutching Hand* (serial), *The Mysterious Avenger* 1936; *Girl from Scotland Yard, The Hurricane* 1937; *South of Pago Pago, Kit Carson* 1940; *Aloma of the South Seas* 1941; *The Tuttles of Tahiti, Eagle Squadron, Invisible Agent, Arabian Nights* 1942; *White Savage* 1943; *Ali Baba and the Forty Thieves, Lady in the Dark, Invisible Man's Revenge, Cobra Woman, Gypsy Wildcat, San Diego I Love You* 1944; *Sudan, Men in Her Diary* 1945; *Last of the Redmen, The Vigilantes Return* 1947; *The Prince of Thieves* 1948; *The Mutineers, Zamba, Deputy Marshal* 1949; *On the Isle of Samoa* 1950; *When the Redskins Rode, Hurricane Island* 1951; *Last Train from Bombay* 1952; *Hell Ship Mutiny* 1957; *Forbidden Island* 1959; *The Beach Girls and the Monster* 1965.

Hall, Sir Peter. Director. Born on Nov. 22, 1930, in Bury St. Edmunds, Suffolk, England. A stationmaster's son, he began directing stage plays while studying at Cambridge and quickly rose to prominence as a leading force in the British theater, both as a play director and as a managing director of the Royal Shakespeare Company. His work as a film director from the late

60s has been less accomplished and he is still primarily recognized for his achievements in the theater. He directed a sequence featuring members of the Royal Shakespeare Company for Sidney Lumet's *The Deadly Affair* (1967), designed the costumes for Richard Burton's *Doctor Faustus* (also 1967), and appeared as an actor in Maximilian Schell's film *The Pedestrian* (1974). In 1973 he was appointed director of London's newly formed National Theatre, with which his name became synonymous for nearly two decades. He returned to filmmaking in 1989, after a 15-year absence. Formerly (1956–66) married to Leslie CARON. Their daughter Jenny is a budding actress. He was knighted in 1977. Author: *Peter Hall's Diaries* (1983).

FILMS. *Work Is a Four-Letter Word, A Midsummer Night's Dream* 1968; *Three Into Two Won't Go* 1969; *Perfect Friday* 1970; *The Homecoming* 1973; *Akenfield* 1974; *She's Been Away* 1989.

Hall, Porter. Actor. *b.* 1888, Cincinnati. *d.* 1953. *ed.* U. of Cincinnati. A former steel-mill worker and itinerant Shakespearean stage player, he entered films in the mid-30s and subsequently played scores of character roles in a variety of Hollywood productions, most often as a shifty, cowardly little man.

FILMS INCLUDE: *Secrets of Secretary* 1931; *The Thin Man* 1934; *The Case of the Lucky Legs* 1935; *The Story of Louis Pasteur, The Petrified Forest, The General Died at Dawn, The Plainsman* 1936; *Make Way for Tomorrow, Souls at Sea, Wells Fargo* 1937; *King of Alcatraz, Stolen Heaven* 1938; *Mr. Smith Goes to Washington* 1939; *His Girl Friday, Dark Command* 1940; *Sullivan's Travels* 1941; *The Miracle of Morgan's Creek, Double Indemnity, Going My Way* 1944; *Murder He Says, Blood on the Sun* 1945; *Miracle on 34th Street, Unconquered* 1947; *Intruder in the Dust* 1949; *The Big Carnival* 1951; *Carbine Williams* 1952; *Vice Squad* 1953; *Return to Treasure Island* 1954.

Hall, Thurston. Actor. *b.* 1882, Boston. *d.* 1958. He toured with various New England stage companies during his teens, then went to London, where he formed a small stage troupe with which he toured New Zealand and South Africa. After returning to the US, he entered films in 1915 and played, among other lead roles, Marc Antony to Theda Bara's Cleopatra (1917). He left the screen early in the 20s and spent the next 15 years on the Broadway stage. He returned to films in the mid-30s as a character player, typically portraying hard-boiled business executives or influential politicians. In all he appeared in hundreds of Hollywood productions.

FILMS INCLUDE: *Cleopatra* (as Marc Antony), *The Price Mark* 1917; *An Alien Enemy, Tyrant Fear, We Can't Have Everything, The Kaiser's Shadow, The Brazen Beauty, The Midnight Patrol* 1918; *The Exquisite Thief, The Spitfire of Seville* 1919; *The Scarlet Dragon* 1920; *Idle Hands, The Iron Trail, Mother Eternal* 1921; *Fair Lady, Wilderness of Youth* 1922; *Metropolitan, Crime and Punishment* 1935; *The Lone Wolf Returns, Theodora Goes Wild* 1936; *Professor Beware, The Amazing Dr. Clitterhouse* 1938; *You Can't Cheat an Honest Man, Each Dawn I Die* 1939; *The Blue Bird, City for Conquest* 1940; *The Great Lie* 1941; *The Hard Way, This Land Is Mine* 1943; *Cover Girl, Wilson* 1944; *Brewster's Millions, Lady on a Train* 1945; *One More Tomorrow* 1946; *The Farmer's Daughter, The Secret Life of Walter Mitty, Mourning Becomes Electra* 1947; *Bright Leaf* 1950; *Affair in Reno* 1957.

Haller, Daniel. Director, art director. Born in 1926, in Glendale, Calif. A long-time associate of Roger CORMAN, he designed the sets for many of the latter's films from 1957, then for a brief time turned to directing in the late 60s.

FILMS (as director): *Die Monster Die!/Monster of Terror* (US/UK) 1965; *Devil's Angels* 1967; *The Wild Racers* 1968; *The Dunwich Horror, Paddy/Goodbye to the Hill* (Ire.), *Pieces of Dreams* 1970; *Little Mo* (orig. for TV) 1978; *Buck Rogers in the 25th Century* 1979.

Haller, Ernest. Director of photography. *b.* May 31, 1896, Los Angeles. *d.* 1970. He entered films in 1914 as an actor at Biograph, occasionally doubling as cameraman until 1920, when he became director of photography. He soon distinguished himself as one of Hollywood's most sensitive lighting cameramen, equally expressive in black and white and color. He shared an Academy award for the cinematography of *Gone With the Wind* (1939). He died in an automobile accident.

FILMS INCLUDE: *Such a Little Queen* 1914; *The Hazards of Helen* (serial) 1915; *Wolves of the Rail* 1918; *Yes or No* 1920; *The Gilded Lily* 1921; *Homeward Bound* 1923; *Any Woman, Stella Dallas* (2nd-unit) 1925; *The Dancer of Paris* 1926; *Convoy, For the Love of Mike* 1927; *Wheel of Chance, Harold Teen* 1928; *House of Horror* (co-phot.) 1929; *The Dawn Patrol* 1930; *Scarlet Dawn* 1932; *Emperor Jones, The House on 56th Street* 1933; *British Agent* 1934; *Escapade* 1935; *The Great Garrick* 1937; *Jezebel, Four Daughters, Brother Rat* 1938; *Gone With the Wind* (co-phot.), *Dark Victory, The Roaring Twenties* 1939; *All This and Heaven Too* 1940; *Manpower* 1941; *In This Our Life* 1942; *Mr. Skeffington* 1944; *Mildred Pierce, Rhapsody in Blue* (co-phot.), *Saratoga Trunk* 1945; *Deception, The Verdict, Devotion* 1946; *A Stolen Life* (co-phot.), *Humoresque* 1947; *The Unfaithful* 1948; *Rebel Without a Cause* 1955; *Men in War* 1957; *God's Little Acre, Man of the West* 1958; *What Ever Happened to Baby Jane?, Pressure Point* 1962; *Lilies of the Field* 1963; *Dead Ringer* 1964.

Halliday, John. Actor. *b.* Sept. 14, 1880, Brooklyn, N.Y. *d.* 1947. *ed.* Cambridge. A suave leading man of the American stage and screen, he trained as a mining engineer in Scotland and later studied at Cambridge but finally chose acting as a career. He appeared in many Broadway plays and had his first film role in 1916. After a long absence, he returned to the screen in 1929 and played leads and second leads in Hollywood productions of the 30s. He was married to actress Eleanor Griffith.

FILMS INCLUDE: *The Devil's Toy* 1916; *The Love Expert, The Woman Gives* 1920; *East Side Sadie* 1929; *Recaptured Love, Scarlet Pages* 1930; *Once a Sinner, Millie, Father's Son, Fifty Million Frenchmen, Transatlantic, Consolation Marriage* 1931; *The Impatient Maiden, Week Ends Only, The Age of Consent, Bird of Paradise* 1932; *Perfect Understanding, The Woman Accused, Bed of Roses, The House on 56th Street* 1933; *A Woman's Man, The Witching Hour, Return of the Terror, Housewife, Desirable, Happiness Ahead* 1934; *The Dark Angel, Peter Ibbetson* 1935; *Desire, Fatal Lady, Hollywood Boulevard* 1936; *Arsene Lupin Returns, Blockade* 1938; *Hotel for Women, Intermezzo—A Love Story* 1939; *The Philadelphia Story* 1940; *Lydia* 1941.

Halliwell, Leslie. Author, critic. *b.* 1929, England. *d.* 1989. Creator of *Halliwell's Filmgoer's Companion* and *Halliwell's Film Guide*, two of the most wide-ranging and idiosyncratic reference books on film. "This book is for people who like movies," he wrote in the preface to the first edition of the *Companion*, in 1965.

Hallström, Lasse. Director. Born in 1946, in Stockholm. A cinema fanatic from childhood, he progressed from 8 mm through 16 mm into feature films, specializing in comedy. The huge success in the US of his engaging story of childhood, *My Life as a Dog* (1985), led to his first American film assignment, *Once Around* (1991). He usually writes and/or collaborates on his own scripts.

FEATURE FILMS: *A Lover and His Lass* 1975; *ABBA—The Movie* 1977; *Father to Be* 1979; *The Rooster* 1981; *My Life as a Dog* 1985; *The Children of Bullerby Village* 1986; *More*

About the Children of Bullerby Village 1987; *Once Around* (US) 1991; *What's Eating Gilbert Grape* 1993; *Something to Talk About* 1995.

Halop, Billy. Actor. *b.* Feb. 11, 1920, New York City. *d.* 1976. A radio performer since childhood, he was the original leader, as well as the most personable member, of the Dead End Kids on stage and later in several films. He broke away from the gang in the early 40s, hoping for a starring career on his own, but landed only routine secondary film roles, and finally bit parts. In addition to having career woes he suffered through marital problems and a long bout with alcoholism, which he won. He told of these in his autobiography, *There's No Dead End.* During the late 60s he made a living as an appliance salesman, then as a male nurse. But his career was resurrected in the 70s by a regular role (as Bert Munson, 1972–76) in the TV series 'All in the Family.' His sister, Florence Halop (*b.* Jan. 23, 1923, Queens, N.Y. *d.* 1986), was also an actress, mainly on radio and TV.

FILMS INCLUDE: *Dead End* 1937; *Crime School, Little Tough Guy, Angels with Dirty Faces* 1938; *They Made Me a Criminal, You Can't Get Away with Murder, Hell's Kitchen, Angels Wash Their Faces, Dust Be My Destiny, Dress Parade* 1939; *Tom Brown's School Days, You're Not So Tough, Give Us Wings* 1940; *Mob Town, Blues in the Night* 1941; *Junior Army* 1942; *Gas House Kids* 1946; *Dangerous Years* 1947; *Air Strike* 1955; *For Love or Money, Move Over Darling* 1963; *A Global Affair* 1954; *Mister Buddwing* 1966; *Fitzwilly* 1967.

Halperin, Victor Hugo. Director. *b.* Aug. 24, 1895, in Chicago. Deceased. *ed.* U. of Wisconsin; U. of Chicago. A former stage actor and director, he directed and often co-produced (with brother Edward) many low-budget films of no distinction but left his mark on the horror films genre with *White Zombie* (1932). He has since died, though his date of death is uncertain.

FILMS: *When a Girl Loves* (also prod., sc.), *Greater Than Marriage* (also sc.) 1924; *School for Wives* (also co-prod., sc.), *The Unknown Lover* (also co-prod., sc.) 1925; *In Borrowed Plumes* 1926; *Dance Magic* 1927; *Party Girl* (also co-prod., co-sc.), *Ex-Flame* (with dial. dir. Herbert Farjeon; also story) 1930; *White Zombie* 1932; *Supernatural* 1933; *I Conquer the Sea, Revolt of the Zombies* (also co-sc.) 1936; *Nation Aflame* (also co-prod.) 1937; *Torture Ship* 1939; *Buried Alive* 1940; *Girls Town* 1942.

Halton, Charles. Actor. *b.* 1876, Washington, D.C. *d.* 1959. A veteran of the stage, including many Broadway performances, he played character parts in more than 150 films, typically as an indignant or shifty bespectacled official.

FILMS INCLUDE: *Honor Among Lovers* 1931; *Storm at Daybreak* 1933; *Dodsworth, Come and Get It* 1936; *Black Legion, Dead End, The Prisoner of Zenda* 1937; *Room Service* 1938; *Jesse James, Young Mr. Lincoln, Dodge City, Juarez* 1939; *Dr. Cyclops, The Shop Around the Corner, They Drive by Night, Dr. Ehrlich's Magic Bullet, Lillian Russell, The Westerner* 1940; *Tobacco Road, H. M. Pulham Esq.* 1941; *To Be or Not to Be, The Spoilers, Across the Pacific* 1942; *Address Unknown, Up in Arms, Wilson* 1944; *Rhapsody in Blue, A Tree Grows in Brooklyn* 1945; *The Best Years of Our Lives* 1946; *Three Godfathers* 1949; *When Willie Comes Marching Home* 1950; *Carrie* 1952; *Friendly Persuasion* 1956.

Hamel, Veronica. Actress. Born on Nov. 20, 1943, in Philadelphia. Pretty, intelligent-looking brunette leading lady of American films and TV. A carpenter's daughter, she began modeling while attending Temple University and later pursued a successful modeling career in New York. Moving to Los Angeles in 1975, she began appearing sporadically in films and in 1981 landed the TV role with which she became most closely identified, that of a stunning lawyer in the long-running series 'Hill Street Blues.'

FILMS: *Cannonball* 1976; *Beyond the Poseidon Adventure* 1979; *When Time Ran Out* 1980; *A New Life* 1988; *Taking Care of Business* 1990.

Hamer, Robert. Director. *b.* Mar. 31, 1911, Kidderminster, England. *d.* 1963. A graduate of Cambridge, he entered British films in 1934 as a clapper boy and became a film editor the following year. As an editor he worked on such films as *Vessel of Wrath* (1938), *Jamaica Inn* (1939), *Ships with Wings* (1941), and *The Foreman Went to France* (1942). He became an associate producer in 1943 and made an auspicious debut as a director in 1945 with the celebrated "The Haunted Mirror" episode from *Dead of Night.* He followed this with an authentically atmospheric drama of the London underworld, *It Always Rains on Sunday* (1947), and one of the prime examples of British screen humor, the witty black comedy *Kind Hearts and Coronets* (1949). But his subsequent films were variable in quality and his career suffered a setback in the late 50s as he seemed to be losing his bout with alcoholism. After his directing career ended in 1960, he contributed to the screenplays of *55 Days at Peking* (1963) and *A Jolly Bad Fellow* (1965).

FILMS: *Dead of Night* ("The Haunted Mirror" episode; also sc.), *Pink String and Sealing Wax* 1945; *It Always Rains on Sunday* (also co-sc.) 1947; *Kind Hearts and Coronets* (also co-sc.), *The Spider and the Fly* 1949; *His Excellency* (also co-sc.), *The Long Memory* (also co-sc.) 1952; *Father Brown/The Detective* (also sc.) 1954; *To Paris with Love* 1955; *The Scapegoat* (also sc.) 1959; *School for Scoundrels* 1960.

Hamill, Mark. Actor. Born on Sept. 25, 1951, in Oakland, Calif. The son of a US Navy captain, he grew up in California, Virginia, New York, and Japan. While still a student at the Los Angeles City College, majoring in drama, he made his professional acting debut in an episode of 'The Bill Cosby Show' in 1970. He later appeared on numerous TV programs and in several TV movies, was a regular on the daytime soap opera 'General Hospital,' and co-starred in the critically acclaimed but short-lived action-comedy series 'The Texas Wheelers' (1974–75). In 1977, the boyish, fair-haired, blue-eyed Hamill rose to sudden film stardom as Luke Skywalker, the gallant hero of the blockbuster box-office hit *Star Wars* and its sequels. After he overcame the effects of a disfiguring motor crash, he later appeared in several Broadway plays, including a brief stint as Mozart in 'Amadeus.' In 1989 he returned to the screen after a six-year interval.

FILMS: *Wizards* (v/o), *Star Wars* 1977; *Corvette Summer* 1978; *The Empire Strikes Back, The Big Red One* 1980; *The Night the Lights Went Out in Georgia* 1981; *Britannia Hospital* (bit; UK) 1982; *Return of the Jedi* 1983; *Slipstream* (UK) 1989; *Black Magic Woman, Midnight Ride* 1991; *In Exile* 1992; *Batman: Mask of the Phantasm* (v/o) 1993; *Village of the Damned* 1995; *Star Wars, The Empire Strikes Back, Return of the Jedi* (all re-released special editions) 1997.

Hamilton, George. Actor. Born on Aug. 12, 1939, in Memphis, Tenn. Tall, darkly handsome, perpetually tanned leading man of Hollywood films and television. The son of an oft-married Southern belle and the second of her four husbands, a bandleader, Hamilton was active in high school dramatics before going to Hollywood in the late 50s. He showed promise with his first few films but his career never blossomed. Typecast in real life as a dashing escort of the rich and famous, he made headlines in 1966 as the companion of President Lyndon Johnson's daughter, Lynda Bird. After a long string of unsuccessful films, he made a nice comeback in the role of a modern-day Dracula in *Love at First Bite* (1979). In the 1980s, he became the frequent escort of a rejuvenated Elizabeth TAYLOR. His name synonymous with suntans, Hamilton started a line of skin-care products in 1989, and the next year launched a nationwide chain of tanning salons. He has a son, Ashley, by his former wife, Alana.

FILMS: *Crime and Punishment U.S.A.* 1959; *Home from the Hill, All the Fine Young Cannibals, Where the Boys Are* 1960; *Angel Baby, By Love Possessed, A Thunder of Drums* 1961; *Light in the Piazza, Two Weeks in Another Town* 1962; *The Victors, Act One* (as Moss Hart) 1963; *Looking for Love, Your Cheatin' Heart* 1964; *Viva Maria!* (Fr./It.) 1965; *L'Homme de Marrakech/Our Man George/Our Man in Marrakesh* (Fr./It./Sp.) 1966; *Doctor You've Got to Be Kidding, Jack of Diamonds* 1967; *A Time for Killing, The Power* 1968; *Togetherness* 1970; *Evel Knievel* (title role; also co-prod.) 1971; *The Man Who Loved Cat Dancing* 1973; *Once Is Not Enough* 1975; *The Happy Hooker Goes to Washington* 1977; *Sextette* 1978; *Love at First Bite* (as Count Dracula; also co-exec. prod.), *Da Dunkerque alla Vittoria/From Hell to Victory* (It./Fr.) 1979; *Zorro the Gay Blade* 1981; *The Godfather Part III* 1990; *Doc Hollywood* 1991; *Once Upon a Crime* 1992.

Hamilton, Guy. Director. Born in September, 1922, in Paris, to British parents. He entered films as an apprentice in a Nice, France, studio in 1939. After WW II service with the British Navy (1940–45) he worked as assistant director on a number of distinguished British productions, including *Fallen Idol, The Third Man,* and *The African Queen.* A director since the early 50s, he is among England's most technically proficient craftsmen. His films include several of the slick James Bond adventures. Divorced from actress Naomi Chance, he later married KERIMA.

FILMS: *The Ringer* 1952; *The Intruder* 1953; *An Inspector Calls* 1954; *The Colditz Story* (also co-sc.) 1955; *Charley Moon* 1956; *Manuela/Stowaway Girl* (also co-sc.) 1957; *The Devil's Disciple, A Touch of Larceny* (also co-sc.) 1959; *I Due Nemici/The Best of Enemies* (It./UK) 1961; *Man in the Middle* (UK/US), *Goldfinger* 1964; *The Party's Over* (release delayed from 1963 because of censorship problems) 1965; *Funeral in Berlin* 1966; *Battle of Britain* 1969; *Diamonds Are Forever* 1971; *Live and Let Die* 1973; *The Man with the Golden Gun* 1974; *Force 10 from Navarone* (also prod.) 1978; *The Mirror Crack'd* 1980; *Evil Under the Sun* 1982; *Remo Williams: The Adventure Begins* 1985; *Try This on for Size* (also co-sc.; Fr.) 1989.

Hamilton, Linda. Actress. Born on Sept. 26, 1957, in Salisbury, Md. Sensual leading lady of American TV and films who gained fame for her athletic build in *Terminator 2.* The twin daughter of a physician who died when she was five, and stepdaughter of her hometown's police chief, she began with children's theater groups and majored in drama at Maryland's Washington College. After further training in New York, with Nicholas RAY and at the Lee Strasberg Institute, she appeared briefly in a daytime soap opera, then moved in 1979 to the West Coast, where she began appearing in TV movies and series, and low-budget feature films. Her career was boosted by co-starring roles in the box-office hits *The Terminator* (1984) and *Terminator 2: Judgment Day* (1991) and in the short-lived TV series and cult favorite 'Beauty and the Beast.'

FILMS: *Night-Flowers* 1979; *T.A.G.: The Assassination Game* 1982; *Children of the Corn, The Stone Boy, The Terminator* 1984; *Black Moon Rising, King Kong Lives* 1986; *Mr. Destiny* 1990; *Terminator 2: Judgment Day* 1991; *Silent Fall* 1994; *The Shadow Conspiracy, Dante's Peak* 1997.

Hamilton, Lloyd. Actor. *b.* Aug. 19, 1891, Oakland, Calif. *d.* 1935. A veteran of burlesque and musical comedy, he entered films in 1914 and teamed successfully with Bud Duncan (1886–1960) in some 200 one-reel "Bud and Ham" comedies at Kalem. He later developed into a popular comedy star in Fox's Sunshine Comedies. In 1924 he started his own company and starred in numerous successful two-reelers, which he released through Educational. He also appeared in occasional feature films.

FILMS INCLUDE: *Ham the Lineman, Ham the Piano Mover, Ham and the Villain Factory, Ham the Iceman* 1914; *Ham and the Jitney Bus, Ham Among the Redskins, Ham the Detective, Ham in the Harem, Ham at the Garbage Gentlemen's Ball, Ham at the Beach* 1915; *A Twilight Baby* 1918; *Occasionally Yours/The Mischief Man* 1920; *His Darker Self, A Self-Made Failure* 1924; *Rolling Stones* 1925; *The Rainmaker* 1926; *Robinson Crusoe Ltd.* 1928; *Tanned Legs, The Show of Shows* 1929; *Are You There?* 1931; *False Impressions* 1932; *Too Many Highballs* 1933.

Hamilton, Margaret. Actress. *b.* Dec. 9, 1902, Cleveland. *d.* 1985. A former kindergarten teacher, she arrived in Hollywood in 1933 after unrewarding roles on the stage. She is best remembered as the Wicked Witch of the West in *The Wizard of Oz* (1939). She also played a variety of amusing character roles in scores of other films, often as a gossipy spinster, prying housekeeper, or, in her own words, "women with a heart of gold and a corset of steel." After retiring from the screen, she remained active on the stage. She was seen frequently in commercials, most memorably as the kindly Cora in a Maxwell House coffee campaign.

FILMS INCLUDE: *Another Language* 1933; *Broadway Bill* 1934; *The Farmer Takes a Wife, Way Down East* 1935; *These Three, The Moon's Our Home* 1936; *You Only Live Once, Mountain Justice, Nothing Sacred* 1937; *A Slight Case of Murder, The Adventures of Tom Sawyer, Stablemates, Four's a Crowd* 1938; *The Wizard of Oz, Angels Wash Their Faces, Babes in Arms* 1939; *The Villain Still Pursued Her, My Little Chickadee* 1940; *The Invisible Woman* 1941; *Meet the Stewarts* 1942; *The Ox-Bow Incident, Johnny Come Lately* 1943; *George White's Scandals* 1945; *Janie Gets Married* 1946; *Mad Wednesday* 1947; *State of the Union* 1948; *The Red Pony, The Beautiful Blonde from Bashful Bend* 1949; *Riding High, Wabash Avenue* 1950; *People Will Talk, Comin' Round the Mountain* 1951; *13 Ghosts* 1960; *Paradise Alley* 1962; *The Daydreamer* 1966; *Rosie!* 1967; *Brewster McCloud* 1970; *The Anderson Tapes* 1971; *Journey Back to Oz* (v/o) 1974.

Hamilton, Murray. Actor. *b.* Mar. 24, 1923, Washington, N.C. *d.* 1986, of lung cancer. Versatile character player of the American stage, TV, and films, often cast as an ambitious or conniving figure. He won a Tony Award for his performance in Broadway's 'Absence of a Cello' (1964). His wife, Terry, was one of the DeMarco Sisters. Their son, David Hamilton, became an actor.

FILMS INCLUDE: *The Whistle at Eaton Falls* 1951; *Bright Victory* 1952; *Toward the Unknown* 1956; *The Spirit of St. Louis* 1957; *No Time for Sergeants, Houseboat* 1958; *Anatomy of a Murder, The FBI Story* 1959; *Tall Story* 1960; *The Hustler* 1961; *Thirteen Frightened Girls, The Cardinal* 1963; *Seconds* 1966; *The Graduate* 1967; *The Brotherhood, No Way to Treat a Lady, The Boston Strangler* 1968; *If It's Tuesday This Must Be Belgium* 1969; *The Way We Were* 1973; *Jaws* 1975; *Jaws 2* 1978; *1941, The Amityville Horror* 1979; *Brubaker* 1980; *Hysterical* 1983; *Too Scared to Scream* (released delayed from 1982) 1985.

Hamilton, Neil. Actor. *b.* James Neil Hamilton, Sept. 9, 1899, Lynn, Mass. *d.* 1984. A pleasant, husky, highly popular silent star, a former stock actor and shirt model, he played occasional film roles beginning in 1918 but received his first big opportunity in D. W. GRIFFITH's *The White Rose* (1923). He starred in a couple of other Griffith pictures, then became Paramount's most popular leading man of the late 20s. Active through the early 70s, he played character roles from the mid-30s, occasionally as a heavy. He played Police Commissioner Gordon in TV's 'Batman' series of the late 60s.

FILMS INCLUDE: *The Beloved Impostor* 1918; *The Great Romance* 1919; *The White Rose* 1923; *America, The Side Show of Life, Isn't Life Wonderful?* 1924; *Men and Women, The Little French Girl, The Street of Forgotten Men, The Golden Princess, New Brooms, The Splendid Crime* 1925; *Desert Gold, Beau Geste* (as Digby Geste), *Diplomacy, The Great Gatsby* (as Nick Carraway) 1926; *The Music Master, Ten Modern Commandments, The Joy Girl, The Spotlight, The Shield of Honor* 1927; *The Showdown, Mother Machree, Something Always Happens, Don't Mary, The Grip of the Yukon, Hot News, The Patriot* (as Crown Prince Alexander of Russia), *Take Me Home, Three Week-Ends, What a Night!* 1928; *Why Be Good, A Dangerous Woman, The Studio Murder Mystery, The Mysterious Dr. Fu Manchu, The Love Trap, Darkened Rooms* 1929; *The Kibitzer, The Return of Dr. Fu Manchu, Anybody's War, The Dawn Patrol, Ladies Must Play, The Cat Creeps, The Widow from Chicago, Ex-Flame* 1930; *Strangers May Kiss, Laughing Sinners, The Great Lover, This Modern Age, The Sin of Madelon Claudet* 1931; *Tarzan the Ape Man, The Wet Parade, The Woman in Room 13, What Price Hollywood, Two Against the World, Payment Deferred, The Animal Kingdom* 1932; *Terror Abroad, The World Gone Mad, The Silk Express* 1933; *Tarzan and His Mate, Blind Date* 1934; *The Keeper of the Bees* 1935; *Lady Behave!, The Stadium Murders* 1938; *The Saint Strikes Back* 1939; *Queen of the Mob* 1940; *King of the Texas Rangers* (serial) 1941; *X Marks the Spot* 1942; *All by Myself* 1943; *Brewster's Millions* 1945; *The Little Shepherd of Kingdom Come* 1961; *The Patsy, Good Neighbor Sam* 1964; *The Family Jewels* 1965; *Batman* 1966; *Strategy of Terror* 1969; *Which Way to the Front?* 1970.

Hamlin, Harry. Actor. Born on Oct. 30, 1951, in Pasadena, Calif. *ed.* U. of California; Yale. Square-jawed leading man of the American stage, TV, and films. He trained for two years at the American Conservatory Theatre in San Francisco before starting his professional career in the late 70s. His feature film career started strongly, gaining momentum from the heroic role of Perseus in *Clash of the Titans* (1981). But it was soon overshadowed by his TV work, which included the title role in the miniseries 'Studs Lonigan' (1979) and a co-starring part (beginning in 1986) in the popular series 'L.A. Law.' He is the father of a son by onetime companion actress Ursula ANDRESS, many years his senior, and was married for a short time to actress Nicolette Sheridan.

FILMS: *Movie Movie* 1978; *King of the Mountain, Clash of the Titans* (as Perseus) 1981; *Making Love* 1982; *Blue Skies Again* 1983; *Maxie* 1985; *Save Me* 1994.

Hamlisch, Marvin. Composer, arranger. Born on June 2, 1944, in New York City. The son of a Vienna-born accordionist, at seven he was the youngest student ever admitted to Manhattan's Juilliard School of Music. While attending Queens College at night (he graduated *cum laude*), he worked days on Broadway as a rehearsal pianist and eventually began composing for the stage. A chance meeting with producer Sam Spiegel at a Broadway party resulted in his first film score in 1968. He quickly adapted to the specialized techniques of film scoring and caused a minor sensation at the 1974 Academy Award ceremony (for films of 1973) by becoming the first individual ever to win three Oscars in one night—one for the score of *The Sting,* a hit adaptation of Scott Joplin's ragtime music; and two for *The Way We Were,* one for the score and one for the title song (sung by Barbra Streisand). He won a Tony Award in 1976 for the score of Broadway's hit musical 'A Chorus Line.'

FILMS INCLUDE: *Ski Party* (co-songs only), *The Swimmer* 1968; *The April Fools, Take the Money and Run* 1969; *Move, Flap* 1970; *Bananas, Kotch, Something Big* 1971; *The War Between Men and Women, Fat City* 1972; *Save the Tiger, The Way We Were, The Sting* 1973; *The Prisoner of Second Avenue, The Entertainer* (also co-prod.) 1975; *The Spy Who Loved Me* 1977; *Same Time Next Year, Ice Castles, Chapter Two* 1979; *Ordinary People, Seems Like Old Times* 1980; *The Fan* (songs), *Pennies from Heaven* 1981; *Sophie's Choice, I Ought to Be in Pictures* 1982; *Romantic Comedy* 1983; *A Chorus Line, D.A.R.Y.L.* 1985; *Shy People, Three Men and a Baby* 1987; *Big, Little Nikita* 1988; *The Experts, The January Man, Shirley Valentine, Troop Beverly Hills* 1989; *Frankie and Johnny* 1991; *Angie* 1994; *The Mirror Has Two Faces, Open Season* 1996.

Hammer Films. The most successful film company, from a financial viewpoint, in the history of British cinema. Founded in 1948 by Will Hammer and Sir John Carreras, a former exhibitor, Hammer started out as a distribution company and in the same year also turned to production. Its success story began in 1956, when the company launched a cycle of low-budget horror movies that quickly captured wide markets in Britain and the US. Emphasizing blood and gore, in vivid color, over plot and atmosphere, Hammer revived such horror figures from the American movie past as Frankenstein, Dracula, the Mummy, and the Werewolf. The Hammer formula called for top budgets of $500,000, a maximum of 25 shooting days, and relatively high promotion budgets. Over the years, Hammer expanded into other genres, such as science fiction, psychological thrillers, and costume spectaculars, but its mainstay into the 1970s, when it went into decline, was still the horror film. With Sir John's son, Michael Carreras, at the helm as executive producer, the company occasionally attracted such directors as Joseph Losey, Guy Green, and Ken Hughes. The actors most readily identified with the horror series were Peter Cushing and Christopher Lee. Sex goddesses Ursula Andress and Raquel Welch started their careers in Hammer films.

Hammerstein, Elaine. Actress. *b.* 1897, Philadelphia. *d.* 1948, in a Mexico car crash. The daughter of noted stage producer Arthur Hammerstein, she made her screen debut in 1915, following a brief career in the theater. She starred in many Hollywood productions, typically melodramas, until 1926, when she retired to marry an insurance executive. Her first husband was director Alan CROSLAND.

FILMS INCLUDE: *The Moonstone* 1915; *The Mad Lover, The Argyle Case* 1917; *Wanted for Murder, Her Man, Accidental Honeymoon* 1918; *The Country Cousin* 1919; *Greater Than Fame/Love or Fame, The Woman Game, Whispers, The Pleasure Seekers* 1920; *Poor Dear Margaret Kirby, The Miracle of Manhattan* (dual role), *The Girl from Nowhere, Handcuffs or Kisses, Remorseless Love, The Way of a Maid* 1921; *Reckless Youth, Evidence, Under Oath, One Week of Love* 1922; *Broadway Gold, Rupert of Hentzau, The Drums of Jeopardy* 1923; *Daring Love, The Foolish Virgin, The Midnight Express, One Glorious Night* 1924; *Every Man's Wife, Parisian Nights, After Business Hours, The Unwritten Law, Paint and Powder, S.O.S. Perils of the Sea* (dual role) 1925; *The Checkered Flag, Ladies of Leisure* 1926.

Hammerstein, Oscar II. Lyricist, screenwriter. *b.* July 12, 1895, New York City. *d.* 1960. *ed.* Columbia. He spent a year in a law office before turning to his uncle, producer Arthur Hammerstein, for a job in the theater. He wrote the book and lyrics for many famous Broadway musicals and later also films, collaborating with Jerome Kern and George Gershwin, among other composers. His early stage musicals include 'Rose Marie,' 'Sunny,' 'Show Boat,' and 'New Moon,' which were later made into films. He also contributed a number of original screenplays. In the early 40s he began a long and productive collaboration with composer Richard RODGERS, which resulted in many successful musical plays and films. His best-known song is probably 'Ol' Man River.' He won Academy Awards for the song 'The Last Time I Saw Paris' from the film *Lady Be Good* (1941) and for 'It Might As Well Be Spring' from *State Fair* (1945). Appeared as himself in *Main Street to Broadway* (1953).

FILMS INCLUDE (as songwriter): *New Toys* (co-play basis only) 1925; *The Desert Song, Show Boat* 1929; *Song of the West, Song of the Flame, Golden Dawn, Viennese Nights* (also sc.), *Sunny, New Moon* 1930; *Children of Dreams* (also sc.) 1931; *Music in the Air* 1934; *Sweet Adeline, Reckless, The Night Is Young* 1935; *Rose Marie, Give Us This Night, Show Boat* 1936; *Swing High Swing Low* (sc. only), *High Wide and Handsome* (sc. only), *I'll Take Romance* 1937; *The Lady Objects, The Great Waltz* 1938; *The Story of Vernon and Irene Castle* (sc. only) 1939; *New Moon, One Night in the Tropics* 1940; *Sunny, Lady Be Good* 1941; *The Desert Song* 1943; *Broadway Rhythm* 1944; *State Fair* (also sc.) 1945; *Show Boat* 1951; *The Desert Song* 1953; *Rose Marie, Carmen Jones* 1954; *Oklahoma!* 1955; *Carousel, The King and I* 1956; *South Pacific* 1958; *Flower Drum Song* 1961; *State Fair* 1962; *The Sound of Music* 1965.

Hammett, Dashiell. Novelist, screenwriter. *b.* May 27, 1894, St. Mary's County, Md. *d.* 1961. He quit school at 13 to become a messenger boy, then a stevedore, and finally a Pinkerton detective. In the latter capacity, he investigated the "Fatty" ARBUCKLE case and the affairs of gambler Nick Arnstein. In the late 20s and early 30s he wrote five mystery novels, three of which have been made into films: *The Maltese Falcon* (1931, 1941, and as *Satan Met a Lady* in 1936); *The Glass Key* (1935, 1942); and *The Thin Man,* which provided the basis for a series of five mystery movies from 1934 to 1947 starring William Powell and Myrna Loy. The influence of these five novels on the private-eye-thriller genre in American fiction was considerable. Excluding the gay, debonair Nick Charles in *The Thin Man,* the Hammett hero was typically as tough and brutal as the criminals he pursued and his universe was a pessimistic one, filled with raw sensuality and devoid of emotion.

In 1931, Hammett was put on contract by Paramount to write original stories directly for the screen. The first of these provided the basis for Rouben Mamoulian's memorable gangster melodrama *City Streets* (1931). Hammett's few other original screen stories were rather routine. But in 1943 he wrote an excellent screenplay for *Watch on the Rhine,* from the Lillian Hellman play. In 1951 he was identified as a Communist in testimony before the House Un-American Activities Committee, and the same year he was jailed for six months for refusing to divulge the source of the funds he was holding as trustee of the Civil Right Congress, an alleged Communist-dominated organization. He was later charged with tax delinquency by the Bureau of Internal Revenue and never resumed writing. Hammett was portrayed by Jason Robards, Jr., in the film *Julia* (1977).

Hammid, Alexander. See DEREN, Maya.

Hammond, Kay. Actress. *b.* Dorothy Katherine Standing, Feb. 18, 1909, London. *d.* 1980. *ed.* RADA. The daughter of the distinguished actor Sir Guy STANDING, she began her stage career in London in 1927 but made her screen debut in Hollywood. She played leads in early US talkies, notably as Mary Todd Lincoln in Griffith's *Abraham Lincoln,* then returned to England, where she resumed her stage career while also appearing in occasional films. She was the mother of actor John Standing (*b.* 1934) by her first marriage. Her second husband (from 1946) was actor Sir John CLEMENTS.

FILMS INCLUDE: *Her Private Affair* (US), *The Trespasser* (US) 1929; *Abraham Lincoln* (as Mary Todd Lincoln; US), *Children of Chance* 1930; *Fascination, Carnival/Venetian Nights, A Night in Montmartre* 1931; *Out of the Blue, A Night Like This, Sally Bishop* 1932; *Sleeping Car, Bitter Sweet, Racetrack* (US), *Double Harness* (US) 1933; *Bypass to Happiness* 1934; *Two on a Doorstep* 1936; *Jeannie/Girl in Distress* 1941; *Blithe Spirit* 1945; *Call of the Blood* 1948; *Five Golden Hours* 1961.

Hampden, Walter. Actor. *b.* June 30, 1879, Brooklyn, N.Y. *d.* 1955. A graduate of Harvard, he made his stage debut in 1901 and rose to prominence on Broadway in Shakespearean and classical roles, notably as Cyrano in Rostand's 'Cyrano de Bergerac' (1923). His film career was sporadic. He played leads in a number of silent productions and a variety of character roles in talkies of the 40s and 50s.

FILMS INCLUDE: *The Dragon's Claw* 1915; *The Warfare of the Flesh* 1917; *The Hunchback of Notre Dame* 1939; *All This and Heaven Too, North West Mounted Police* 1940; *They Died with Their Boots On* 1941; *Reap the Wild Wind* 1942; *The Adventures of Mark Twain* 1944; *All About Eve* 1950; *The First Legion* 1951; *Five Fingers* 1952; *Sombrero* 1953; *Sabrina, The Silver Chalice* 1954; *The Prodigal* 1955; *The Vagabond King* 1956.

Hampshire, Susan. Actress. Born on May 12, 1938, in London. On the British stage since childhood, she made her initial impact on London's West End audiences in 1958 with a show-stopping cameo in 'Expresso Bongo.' Apart from a single screen appearance at age six, she made her film debut in 1959. At first she played sweet, innocent debutante roles but eventually emerged as a mature leading lady in the French film *Paris in the Month of August,* in which she appeared in a nude scene. She married the film's director, Pierre Granier-Deferre in 1967 but divorced him seven years later. In 1981 she married a Greek shipowner-impresario. She won American Emmy Awards for her performances in the British TV series 'The Forsyte Saga' (as Fleur), 'The First Churchills' (as Sarah, Duchess of Marlborough), and 'Vanity Fair' (as Becky Sharp). She is the author of *Susan's Story* (1982), an autobiographical account of her lifelong struggle with dyslexia. In another book, *The Maternal Instinct,* she tells of her pilgrimage to Lourdes to pray for a child.

FILMS: *The Woman in the Hall* 1947; *Idol on Parade* (bit), *Upstairs and Downstairs* 1959; *During One Night/Night of Passion, The Long Shadow* 1961; *The Three Lives of Thomasina* (US/UK), *Night Must Fall, Wonderful Life/Swingers' Paradise* 1964; *Paris au Mois d'Août/Paris in the Month of August* (Fr.), *The Fighting Prince of Donegal* 1966; *The Trygon Factor* 1967; *Monte Carlo or Bust/Those Daring Young Men in Their Jaunty Jalopies* (UK/Fr./It.) 1969; *David Copperfield* 1970; *Living Free* 1971; *A Time for Loving, Malpertius/The Legend of Doom House* (Bel./Fr.) 1972; *Neither the Sea nor the Sand* 1973; *Roses rouges et Piments verts/The Lonely Woman* (Fr./It./Sp.) 1975; *Bang!* (Sw.) 1977.

Hampton, Christopher. Playwright, screenwriter. Born on Jan. 26, 1946, in Fayal, Azores, to British parents. *ed.* Oxford. He had his first play produced at 18. In 1968–70 he was resident dramatist at the London's Royal Court, and later went on to write several successful plays and adapt translated works of Chekhov and Ibsen, among others, to the stage. Sporadically involved in screenwriting, he won an Academy Award and the Writers Guild Award for the screenplay of *Dangerous Liaisons* (1988), which he adapted from his own stage play.

FILMS: *A Doll's House* (from his own stage adaptation) 1973; *Tales from the Vienna Woods* (co-sc., from his own play) 1981; *Beyond the Limit* 1983; *The Wolf at the Door* 1986; *The Good Father* 1987; *Dangerous Liaisons* (from his own play, also co-prod.) 1988; *Carrington* (sc., dir.), *Total Eclipse* (sc. only, from his play) 1995; *Mary Reilly* (sc. only), *The Secret Agent* (co-sc., dir.) 1996.

Hanbury, Victor. Director, producer. *b.* 1897, London. *d.* 1954. He entered British films as a salesman in 1919, after completing his WW I service with the Royal Navy. He began directing in the early 30s and switched to producing in the early 40s. Joseph Losey used Hanbury's name as a pseudonym to evade blacklisting in 1954.

FILMS INCLUDE: As director—*Where Is This Lady?* (co-dir. with Ladislao Vajda), *No Funny Business, Dick Turpin* 1933; *Spring in the Air* 1934; *The Crouching Beast* 1935; *Ball at Savoy, Beloved Impostor, The Avenging Hand, Second Bureau* 1936; *Return of a Stranger* 1937. As producer—*A Gentleman of Venture/It Happened to One Man* 1940; *They Flew Alone, Squadron Leader X* 1942; *Escape to Danger* 1943; *Hotel Reserve* 1944; *Great Day* 1945; *Daughter of Darkness* 1949; *Noose for a Lady* 1953; *The Sleeping Tiger* (credited as producer-director but film was actually made by blacklisted Joseph Losey, who used Hanbury's name as a front) 1954.

Hancock, John. Director. Born on Feb. 9, 1939, in Kansas City, Mo. *ed.* Harvard. A graduate of the American Film Institute's Center for Advanced Film Studies, he was a musician and theater director before turning to films. He was nominated for an Academy Award for one of his shorts, *Sticky My Fingers—Fleet My Feet.* His first feature film, *Let's Scare Jessica to Death* (1971), was a standard little horror film, but his next, *Bang the Drum Slowly* (1973), was a touching, sensitively told story of human relations within the unlikely milieu of baseball.

FEATURE FILMS: *Let's Scare Jessica to Death* 1971; *Bang the Drum Slowly* 1973; *Baby Blue Marine* 1976; *California Dreaming* 1979; *Weeds* (also co-sc.) 1987; *Prancer* 1989.

Hand, David. Animator. *b.* Jan. 23, 1900, Plainfield, N.J. *d.* 1986. *ed.* Academy of Fine Arts (Chicago). He entered the film industry in 1919 and worked for various US animation producers, including BRAY, Dave and Max FLEISCHER, and DISNEY. In 1945 he formed G.B.—Animation in England as a cartoon unit for the Rank Organisation and subsequently produced and directed many instructional, advertising, and entertainment animated films through 1950, when he returned to the US.

FILMS INCLUDE: In the US—*Snow White and the Seven Dwarfs* (supervising dir.) 1937; *Bambi* (supervising dir.) 1942; *Victory Through Air Power* (animation supervisor) 1943. In the UK—*Animaland* (series), *Musical Paintbox* (series) 1946–47; *The Lion, The Thames, The House Cat* 1948; *Wales, A Fantasy on Ireland, Sketches from Scotland, Canterbury Road* 1949; *A Fantasy on London Life, Ginger Nutt's Forest Dragon* 1950.

hand-held camera. See CAMERA, HAND-HELD.

Handke, Peter. Novelist, screenwriter, playwright. Born in 1942 in Austria. A leading figure in postwar European avant garde writing, he began writing for film in 1972, often adapting his own works. Best known for co-writing the haunting, meditative *Wings of Desire*, which has become an art-house favorite.

FILMS INCLUDE (as screenwriter): *Die Angst des Tormanns beim Elfmeter/The Goalkeeper's Fear of the Penalty Kick* 1972; *Falsche Bewegung/Wrong Move* 1975; *Die Linkshädinge Frau/The Left-Handed Woman* (also dir.) 1977; *Das Mal des Todes* 1985; *Der Himmel über Berlin* (co-wrote) 1987; *Ville étrangere* 1988.

Handl, Irene. Actress. *b.* Dec. 27, 1901, London. *d.* 1987. Delightful character comedienne of the British stage, films, and TV. She made her stage and screen debuts in 1937 and later appeared in many plays and films. She was the author of two successful novels.

FILMS INCLUDE: *Missing—Believed Married* 1937; *Mrs. Pym of Scotland Yard, On the Night of the Fire/The Fugitive* 1939; *Night Train/Night Train to Munich, The Girl in the News* 1940; *Pimpernel Smith/Mister V* 1941; *Mr. Emmanuel* 1944; *Brief Encounter* 1945; *Temptation Harbor* 1947; *Silent Dust, The Perfect Woman* 1949; *Stage Fright* 1950; *Top Secret/Mr. Potts Goes to Moscow* 1952; *The Belles of St. Trinian's* 1954; *A Kid for Two Farthings* 1955; *Brothers in Law* 1957; *The Key* 1958; *I'm All Right Jack* 1959; *School for Scoundrels, Doctor in Love, Two-Way Stretch, Make Mine Mink, A French Mistress* 1960; *Double Bunk, A Weekend with Lulu, The Pure Hell of St. Trinian's, The Rebel/Call Me Genius* 1961; *Heavens Above!* 1963; *You Must Be Joking!* 1965; *Morgan, The Wrong Box* 1966; *Smashing Time* 1967; *The Italian Job* 1969; *On a Clear Day You Can See Forever* (US), *The Private Life of Sherlock Holmes* (US/UK) 1970; *The Last Remake of Beau Geste* (US) 1977; *The Hound of the Baskervilles* 1978; *The Great Rock 'n' Roll Swindle* 1979; *Absolute Beginners* 1986.

hand props. Small props for personal use by individual players, such as a sword or an umbrella.

Hani, Susumu. Director. Born on Oct. 10, 1926, in Tokyo. The son of a noted Japanese historian and himself a former journalist, he was among the founders of Iwanami Productions, through which he turned out a number of quality shorts and medium-length documentaries in the early 60s. His films about children won several international awards. His best-known short, *Children Who Draw* (1956), won the Educational Prize at the Venice Film Festival. *Children Hand in Hand* (1962) took the Special Jury Prize for best direction at the 1965 Moscow Festival. In the early 60s he began directing feature films, but in the mid-70s he returned to the documentary format with a series of African wildlife films for TV. Hani's features typically deal with contemporary problems, social and emotional. Faithful to his documentary background, he prefers to work on location with nonprofessional actors. He usually collaborates on the scripts of his films. His books include *The Non-Professional Actor* (1958), *The Aesthetics of Camera and Microphone* (1960), and two diaries about filming in Africa and in the Andes.

FILMS: Documentaries—*Water* 1952; *Snow Festival* 1953; *Children in the Classroom* 1954; *Children Who Draw, Twin Sisters* 1956; *Zoo Diary* 1957; *The Living Sea* 1958; *Dance in Japan* 1960. Features (complete)—*Bad Boys* 1961; *A Full Life, Children Hand in Hand* 1962; *She and He* 1963; *Bwana Toshi* 1965; *Bride of the Andes* 1966; *Nanami: Inferno of First Love* 1968; *Aido—Slave of Love* 1969; *Mio* (Fr./It./Jap.) 1972; *Timetable* 1973; *A Tale of Africa* 1981.

Hanin, Roger. Actor, director. Born on Oct. 23, 1925, in Algiers, to French parents. He studied law and pharmaceutics but was drawn to acting and after some experience in amateur dramatics began appearing professionally on the Paris stage. He entered films in the early 50s and was immediately typecast in tough-guy roles, both in leads and supporting roles, in crime, mystery, and espionage films. He played the title role of The Tiger in two Claude Chabrol parodies of secret-agent action productions, *Le Tigre aime la Chair fraiche/The Tiger Likes Fresh Blood* (1964) and *Le Tigre se parfume à la Dynamite/An Orchid for the Tiger* (1965). In 1974 he turned out a first film as director, *Le Protecteur.*

FILMS INCLUDE: As actor—*Le Chemin de Damas* 1952; *Série noire* 1954; *Gas-Oil* 1955; *Celui qui doit mourir/He Who*

Must Die 1957; *Tamango, Le Désordre et la Nuit/Night Affair, Sois Belle et tais-toi/Be Beautiful and Shut Up, La Chatte/The Cat, Un Drôle de Dimanche* 1958; *Ramuntcho, Du Rififi chez les Femmes/Riff Raff Girls, Le Flic, La Sentence, La Valse du Gorille* 1959; *L'Affaire d'une Nuit, Rocco e i suoi Fratelli/ Rocco and His Brothers* (It./Fr.) 1960; *Vive Henri IV vive l'Amour, Le Miracle des Loups* 1961; *Le Tigre aime la Chair fraiche/The Tiger Likes Fresh Blood* 1964; *Marie-Chantal contre le Docteur Kha, Le Tigre se parfume à la Dynamite/An Orchid for the Tiger* 1965; *The Brides of Fu Manchu* (UK) 1966; *Las Vegas 500 Millones/They Came to Rob Las Vegas* (Sp./Fr./It./Ger.) 1968; *Les Aveux les plus Doux* 1970; *The Revengers* (US) 1972; *Le Sucre* 1978; *Le Coup de Sirocco* 1979; *La Baraka* 1982; *Attention—une Femme peut en cacher une autre!/My Other "Husband"* 1983; *Dernier Eté à Tangier* 1987; *L'Orchestre rouge* 1989. As director—*Le Protecteur* (also sc.) 1974; *Le Faux-Cul* (also sc., act.) 1975; *Train d'Enfer* (also co-sc., act.) 1985.

Hanks, Tom. Actor. Born on July 9, 1956, in Concord, Calif. *ed.* Calif. State U. Highly talented, boyishly charming comedy star of the American screen. His parents having divorced when he was five, he was raised by his father, an itinerant cook, who moved about northern California before settling in Oakland. He began acting in high school, then majored in drama at college. Invited to join the Great Lakes Shakespeare Festival, near Cleveland, he played roles of the classic repertoire for three summer seasons, before heading to New York, where he continued playing the classics with the Riverside Theater company. He first national exposure came in the TV comedy series 'Bosom Buddies' (1980–82), a twist on *Some Like It Hot* featuring two men who must pretend to be women in order to live in all-female housing. Following an unmemorable screen debut in a horror movie, Hanks soared to sudden stardom with his second film, the comedy box-office hit *Splash* (1984). His appealing personality, natural ease, and comic precision combined to accelerate his popularity in the coming years. He scored a huge hit in *Big* (1988), gaining an Academy Award nomination for his disarming portrayal of a boy trapped in a man's body. After a succession of flops, he regained momentum with his performance as a burned-out ex-ballplayer coaching an all-female baseball team in *A League of Their Own* (1992), and with the romantic comedy *Sleepless in Seattle* (1993). His most challenging dramatic role came in 1993 with *Philadelphia*, as a gay lawyer dying of AIDS in the early 80s. The following year, Hanks returned with a triumphant performance as the title character in the blockbuster *Forrest Gump,* receiving back-to-back Academy Awards as best actor for the latter films. In 1996 Hanks tried his hand at directing his own screenplay, *That Thing You Do*, to modest success. He is now considered one of the top box-office stars in American cinema. Divorced from actress-producer Samantha Lewes, Hanks is now married to actress Rita Wilson.

FILMS: *He Knows You're Alone* 1980; *Splash, Bachelor Party* 1984; *The Man with One Red Shoe, Volunteers* 1985; *The Money Pit, Nothing in Common, Every Time We Say Goodbye* (Isr.) 1986; *Dragnet* 1987; *Big, Punchline* 1988; *The 'burbs, Turner & Hooch* 1989; *Joe Versus the Volcano, The Bonfire of the Vanities* 1990; *Radio Flyer* 1991; *A League of Their Own* 1992; *Sleepless in Seattle, Philadelphia* 1993; *Forrest Gump* 1994; *Apollo 13, The Celluloid Closet, Toy Story* (v/o) 1995; *That Thing You Do* (also dir., sc.) 1996.

Hanley, Jimmy. Actor. *b.* Oct. 22, 1918, Norwich, England. *d.* 1970. A child star in British films from age six, he later played boy-next-door-type of roles in films of the 40s and early 50s. At one time (1942–53) married to actress Dinah Sheridan. A daughter, born in 1947, is actress Jenny Hanley.

FILMS INCLUDE: *Red Wagon, Little Friend* 1934; *Forever England/Born to Glory, Boys Will Be Boys* 1935; *The Tunnel/Transatlantic Tunnel* 1936; *Coming of Age, Housemaster* 1938; *Gaslight/Angel Street* 1940; *The Gentle Sex* 1943; *The Way Ahead* 1944; *29 Acacia Avenue/The Facts of Love, Henry V, Murder in Reverse* 1945; *The Captive Heart* 1946; *Holiday Camp, Master of Bankdam, It Always Rains on Sunday* 1947; *It's Hard to Be Good* 1948; *Boys in Brown, The Blue Lamp* 1949; *The Galloping Major* 1951; *The Deep Blue Sea* 1955; *Satellite in the Sky* 1956; *The Lost Continent* 1968.

Hanna, William. Animator, production executive. Born on July 14, 1910, in Melrose, N.M. At 20 he joined the story department of the Harman-Ising studios, where he worked for seven years as a story editor, lyricist, and composer. In 1937 he moved over to MGM, where he collaborated with Joseph BARBERA and producer Fred QUIMBY in creating the cartoon characters of Tom and Jerry. He and Barbera produced more than 100 cartoons for MGM, then set up their own production company, Hanna-Barbera, in 1957. For film and TV credits, see BARBERA, Joseph.

Hannah, Daryl. Actress. Born in 1960, in Chicago. Tall, blonde, physically fit leading lady of Hollywood movies, often comedies. While still at high school, she studied ballet with Maria Tallchief and trained and performed at the Goodman Theatre. Before her graduation she made her debut in a small role in Brian De Palma's *The Fury* (1978). Moving to Los Angeles, she attended UCLA while receiving drama training from Stella ADLER. Her striking appearance helped her secure roles in several films. She first attracted attention in Ridley Scott's futuristic cult classic *Blade Runner* (1982), then got her big break in 1984, in a tailor-made part as a mermaid in Ron Howard's hit romantic comedy *Splash,* opposite Tom HANKS. More recently, she starred in the made-for-cable remake of *Attack of the 50-Foot Woman.* Following a turbulent relationship with singer/songwriter Jackson Browne, she was romantically linked for a time with John F. Kennedy, Jr. Hannah is a niece of cinematographer Haskell WEXLER. Her younger sister, Page Hannah (*b.* Apr. 13, 1964, Chicago), is also a TV and film actress.

FILMS: *The Fury* 1978; *The Final Terror, Hard Country* 1981; *Blade Runner, Summer Lovers* 1982; *Splash, Reckless, The Pope of Greenwich Village* 1984; *The Clan of the Cave Bear, Legal Eagles* 1986; *Roxanne, Wall Street* 1987; *High Spirits* 1988; *Crimes and Misdemeanors* (uncredited bit), *Steel Magnolias* 1989; *Crazy People* 1990; *At Play in the Fields of the Lord* 1991; *Memoirs of an Invisible Man* 1992; *Grumpy Old Men* 1993; *The Little Rascals* 1994; *Grumpier Old Men, The Tie That Binds* 1995; *Two Much* 1996.

Hanson, Curtis. Writer, director. Born in Los Angeles, Calif. Originally the editor of *Cinema* magazine, he turned to screenwriting in the late 70s and directing in the late 80s.

FILMS INCLUDE (as screenwriter): *The Silent Partner* 1978; *White Dog* 1982; *Never Cry Wolf* 1983; *The Bedroom Window* (also dir.) 1987; *Bad Influence* (dir. only) 1990; *The Hand That Rocks the Cradle* (dir. only) 1992; *The River Wild* 1994; *L.A. Confidential* (also co-prod.) 1997.

Hanson, Lars. Actor. *b.* July 26, 1886, Göteborg, Sweden. *d.* 1965. Tall, blond, handsome leading man of Swedish silent films. After the international success of *The Legend of Gösta Berling* (also known as *The Saga of Gösta Berling, The Story of Gösta Berling,* or *The Atonement of Gösta Berling,* 1924), in which he starred opposite Greta GARBO, he was invited by MGM to Hollywood, where he starred in a number of films with Garbo, Lillian GISH, and others. With the advent of sound, he returned to Europe, where he continued appearing in films through the mid-40s. He was married to actress Karin MOLANDER.

FILMS INCLUDE: In Sweden—*Ingeborg Holm* 1913; *The Dagger* 1915; *The Wings* 1916; *The Girl from the Marsh Croft* 1917; *Song of the Scarlet Flower* 1919; *Erotikon* 1920; *The Exiles* 1921; *The Legend of Gösta Berling* 1924; *The Ingmar Inheritance* 1925; *To the Orient* 1926. In the US—*The Scarlet Letter* (as the Rev. Arthur Dimmesdale) 1926; *Flesh and the Devil, Captain Salvation, Buttons* 1927; *The Divine Woman, The Wind* 1928. In Germany—*Heimkehr/Homecoming* 1928. In the UK—*The Informer* 1929; *Abdul the Damned* 1935. In Sweden—*Walpurgis Night* 1935; *Conflict, On the Sunny Side* 1936; *First Division* 1941; *Ride Tonight* 1942; *His Excellency* 1944; *Unto the Gates of Hell* 1948; *491* 1964.

Hara, Setsuko. Actress. Born in 1920, in Yokohama. The sister-in-law of director Hisatora Kumagai, she made her screen debut at 17 and subsequently played leads in many Japanese films. She had some of her best roles in the works of Yasujiro Ozu, for whom she typically portrayed modern, independent-minded heroines. She retired from the screen shortly after the director's death.

FILMS INCLUDE: *New Earth/The Samurai's Daughter* (Jap./Ger.) 1937; *Pastoral Symphony* 1938; *Hot Wind* 1943; *No Regrets for Our Youth* 1946; *Temptation* 1948; *Late Spring, Blue Mountains* 1949; *The Idiot, Early Summer, Repast* 1951; *Tokyo Story* 1953; *Shower* 1956; *Tokyo Twilight* 1957; *A Woman's Secret* 1959; *Late Autumn* 1960; *The Loyal Forty-seven Ronin* 1962.

Harareet, Haya. Actress. Born in 1931, in Haifa, Israel. A stage actress with Israel's Cameri (Chamber) Theater, she became world famous as the female lead in *Ben-Hur* (1959) but was later seen only in minor films, mostly in Europe.

FILMS INCLUDE: *Hill 24 Doesn't Answer* (Isr.) 1955; *La Donna del Giorno/The Doll That Took the Town* (It.) 1957; *Ben-Hur* (as Esther; US) 1959; *Antinea l'Amante della Città Sepolta/L'Atlantide/Journey Beneath the Desert* (It./Fr.), *The Secret Partner* (UK) 1961; *The Interns* (US), *La Legenda di Fra' Diavolo* (It.) 1962; *The Last Charge* 1964; *Our Mother's House* (co-sc. only; UK/US) 1967.

Harbou, Thea von. Screenwriter, director. *b.* Dec. 12, 1888, Tauperlitz, Bavaria. *d.* 1954. A best-selling novelist, she began collaborating with Fritz Lang on the scripts of his films in 1920. She married the director in 1924, following her divorce from one of his prime stars, Rudolf Klein-Rogge, famous for the title role in Lang's *Dr. Mabuse.* She worked with Lang on all his subsequent German films and also collaborated with Murnau, Joe May, Dreyer, and other directors, playing an important role in the German expressionist movement of the 20s. She also directed two films in the early 30s. With the advent of Nazism, she joined the party, took to glorifying the new regime, and was appointed an official screenwriter. This resulted in a split, both personal and professional, with Lang and led to their divorce. Lang went to Hollywood and von Harbou continued working in Germany with diminishing success.

FILMS INCLUDE (as screenwriter, alone or in collaboration): *Die heilige Simplizia, Das wandernde Bild, Vier um die Frau* 1920; *Das indische Grabmal/The Indian Tomb, Der müde Tod/Between Two Worlds/Beyond the Wall* 1921; *Der brennende Acker/Burning Soil, Dr. Mabuse der Spieler/Dr. Mabuse, Phantom* 1922; *Die Finanzen des Grossherzogs/The Grand Duke's Finances* 1923; *Mikael, Die Nibelungen* 1924; *Zur Chronik von Grieshaus/At the Grey House* 1925; *Metropolis* 1927; *Spione/Spies* 1928; *Die Frau im Mond/By Rocket to the Moon* 1929; *M* 1931; *Das Testament des Dr. Mabuse/The Last Will of Dr. Mabuse* 1932; *Elisabeth und der Narr* (dir. only), *Der Läufer von Marathon* 1933; *Hanneles Himmelfahrt* (also dir.), *Prinzessin Tourandot* 1934; *Der alte und der junge König* 1935; *Eine Frau ohne Bedeutung/A Woman of No Importance, Eskapade* 1936; *Der Herrscher/The Ruler, Mutterlied* 1937; *Jugend/Youth* 1938; *Lauter Liebe* 1940; *Die Gattin* 1943; *Fahrt ins Glück, Via Mala* 1945; *Dr. Holl* 1951; *Dein Herz ist meine Heimat* 1953.

Harburg, E. Y. ("Yip"). Lyricist, librettist. *b.* Isidore Hochberg, Apr. 8, 1896, New York City. *d.* 1981. *ed.* CCNY. He ran an electrical appliance business before turning to writing songs and librettos for the stage and films in 1929. Working in collaboration with such composers as Vernon Duke, Arthur Schwartz, Jerome Kern, and especially Harold Arlen, he contributed numerous memorable songs and entire musicals to Broadway and Hollywood. Among his hit songs are 'I'm Yours,' 'Brother, Can You Spare a Dime?,' 'Thrill Me,' 'April in Paris,' 'It's Only a Paper Moon,' 'Last Night When We Were Young,' 'God's Country,' 'Lydia, the Tattooed Lady,' 'Happiness Is a Thing Called Joe,' 'Can't Help Singing,' 'How Are Things in Glocca Morra?,' 'Old Devil Moon,' 'When I'm Not Near the Girl I Love,' 'If I Only Had a Brain,' 'Ding Dong the Witch Is Dead,' and 'Over the Rainbow.' He won an Academy Award for the lyrics of 'Over the Rainbow' from the film *The Wizard of Oz* (1939). In 1943 he married Edelaine Gorney, a silent film starlet and former wife of composer Jay Gorney, his collaborator on 'Brother, Can You Spare a Dime?' Author: *Rhymes for the Irreverent.*

FILMS INCLUDE: *Rio Rita, Applause, Glorifying the American Girl* 1929; *Roadhouse Nights, The Sap from Syracuse, Follow the Leader* 1930; *Moonlight and Pretzels, Take a Chance* 1933; *Broadway Gondolier* (co-story only) 1935; *The Singing Kid, Stage Struck, The Gold Diggers of 1937* 1936; *The Wizard of Oz, Babes in Arms, At the Circus* 1939; *Babes on Broadway, Rio Rita, Ship Ahoy, Panama Hattie, Cairo* 1942; *Presenting Lily Mars, Cabin in the Sky, Du Barry Was a Lady, Thousands Cheer* 1943; *Song of Russia, Meet the People* (also prod.), *Can't Help Singing* 1944; *California* 1947; *April in Paris* 1953; *Gay Purr-ee* 1962; *I Could Go on Singing* (UK) 1963; *Finian's Rainbow* 1968; *Alex in Wonderland* 1970.

Harden, Marcia Gay. Actress. Born in 1960 in La Jolla, Calif. *ed.* University of Texas, Austin; NYU's Tisch School of the Arts, New York City. Gaining stature on both the Broadway stage and in feature films, notably with her auspicious debut in fellow NYU graduates Joel and Ethan Coen's *Miller's Crossing* (1990), she has become a solid, dependable performer in a number of varying film roles. Frequently returning to the stage, she soared on Broadway as the prescription pill–popping wife in Tony Kushner's Pulitzer Prize–winning epic 'Angels in America.'

FILMS: *Miller's Crossing* 1990; *Late For Dinner* 1991; *Crush* (NZ), *Used People* 1992; *Convict Cowboy, Safe Passage* 1995; *Spitfire Grill, Spy Hard* 1996.

Hardin, Ty. Actor. Born Orson Whipple Hungerford II, on Jan. 1, 1930, in New York City. Virile leading man and supporting player of Hollywood films of the 60s. He also starred in such short-lived TV series as 'Bronco' (1959–60) and 'Riptide' (1965). With his career in eclipse in the late 60s, he moved to Spain and began appearing in locally made action pictures. When these also became scarce, he operated a bar and a chain of laundromats on the Costa Brava. In 1974 he was arrested by Spanish authorities for dealing hashish and was forced to leave the country. Back in the US, he became a roving TV evangelist, then settled in Arizona, where he became involved in right-wing politics. In 1984 he announced his intention to run for president on the Populist Party ticket. The six-times married Hardin has since returned to acting.

FILMS INCLUDE: *I Married a Monster from Outer Space* (billed as Ty Hungerford) 1958; *Merrill's Marauders, The*

Chapman Report 1962; *PT 109, Wall of Noise, Palm Springs Weekend* 1963; *Battle of the Bulge* 1965; *Pampa salvaje/Savage Pampas* (Sp./Arg./US) 1966; *Berserk* (UK) 1967; *Custer of the West, Rey de Africa/One Step to Hell* (Sp./It./US) 1968; *The Last Rebel* 1971; *Drums of Vengeance* 1974; *Bad Jim* 1990.

Harding, Ann. Actress. *b.* Dorothy Walton Gatley, Aug. 7, 1901, Fort Sam Houston, Tex. *d.* 1981. The daughter of a career Army officer, she spent much of her youth moving around military bases through the US and Cuba. She dropped out of Bryn Mawr College after one year, and when the family moved to New York, she took a job as an insurance clerk, supplementing her income as a freelance script reader for the Famous Players-Lasky company. She made her stage acting debut in 1921 with the Provincetown Players of Greenwich Village and made her first Broadway appearance later that year. She soon became established as a highly regarded leading lady on Broadway and in stock and her growing reputation resulted in a movie contract with Pathé in 1929. Within a year she was a Hollywood star, typically playing gentle, refined, patrician heroines. She handled her roles with grace and assurance, but in the long run her career suffered from typecasting, as she was seen time and again in a long string of tearjerkers in the part of the noble lady sacrificing all with pride and magnanimity. She was nominated for a best actress Oscar for her performance in *Holiday* (1930). Miss Harding, who had been married to actor Harry Bannister from 1926 to 1932, retired from the screen in 1937 after marrying symphony conductor Werner Janssen but returned to films in 1942 and through the mid-50s played dignified ladies for various studios. Divorced from Janssen in 1962, she lived in retirement in Westport, Conn.

FILMS: *Paris Bound, Her Private Affair, Condemned* 1929; *Holiday, The Girl of the Golden West* 1930; *East Lynne, Devotion* 1931; *Prestige, Westward Passage, The Conquerors, The Animal Kingdom* 1932; *When Ladies Meet, Double Harness, The Right to Romance* 1933; *Gallant Lady, The Life of Vergie Winters, The Fountain* 1934; *Biography of a Bachelor Girl, Enchanted April, The Flame Within, Peter Ibbetson* 1935; *The Lady Consents, The Witness Chair* 1936; *Love from a Stranger* 1937; *Eyes in the Night* 1942; *Mission to Moscow, The North Star/Armored Attack* 1943; *Janie, Nine Girls* 1944; *Those Endearing Young Charms* 1945; *Janie Gets Married* 1946; *It Happened on Fifth Avenue, Christmas Eve* 1947; *Two Weeks with Love* 1950; *The Magnificent Yankee, The Unknown Man* 1951; *The Man in the Gray Flannel Suit, I've Lived Before, Strange Intruder* 1956.

Hardwicke, Sir Cedric. Actor. *b.* Feb. 19, 1893, Lye, England. *d.* 1964. He trained for the stage at the Royal Academy of Dramatic Art and made his London debut in 1912, gaining in reputation after returning from WW I service. By 1934 he was distinguished enough as a stage and screen character star to be knighted. He subsequently took his reputation and title to Hollywood, where he became established as a leading character actor, typically in authoritative or villainous roles, often during WW II as a high-ranking Nazi. After the war, he occasionally shuttled back and forth across the Atlantic, alternating between stage and screen and between British and American plays and films. In 1960 he wrote an autobiography, *A Victorian in Orbit,* a revised and expanded version of his 1932 memoir *Let's Pretend.*

FILMS: In the UK—*Riches and Rogues* (short) 1913; *Nelson* 1926; *Dreyfus/The Dreyfus Case* (title role) 1931; *Rome Express* 1932; *Orders Is Orders, The Ghoul* 1933; *The Lady Is Willing, Bella Donna, Nell Gwyn* (as Charles II), *Jew Suss/Power, King of Paris* 1934; *Peg of Old Drury* (as David Garrick), *Les Misérables* (US), *Becky Sharp* (as Lord Steyne; US) 1935; *Things to Come, Tudor Rose/Nine Days a Queen* (as the Earl of Warwick), *Laburnum Grove, Calling the Tune* 1936; Green Light (US), *King Solomon's Mines* (as Allan Quatermain) 1937. In the US—*On Borrowed Time* (as Death), *Stanley and Livingstone* (as Livingstone), *The Hunchback of Notre Dame* (as Frollo) 1939; *The Invisible Man Returns, Tom Brown's School Days* (as Dr. Thomas Arnold), *The Howards of Virginia, Victory* (as Mr. Jones) 1940; *Suspicion, Sundown* 1941; *Valley of the Sun, The Ghost of Frankenstein* (as Dr. Frankenstein), *Invisible Agent* 1942; *The Commandos Strike at Dawn, Forever and a Day, The Moon Is Down, The Cross of Lorraine* 1943; *The Lodger, Wilson* (as Henry Cabot Lodge), *Wing and a Prayer* 1944; *The Keys of the Kingdom* 1945; *Sentimental Journey, Beware of Pity* (UK) 1946; *The Imperfect Lady, Ivy, Lured, Nicholas Nickleby* (as Ralph Nickleby; UK), *Tycoon* 1947; *Song of My Heart, A Woman's Vengeance, I Remember Mama, Rope, The Winslow Boy* (UK) 1948; *A Connecticut Yankee in King Arthur's Court* (as King Arthur), *Now Barabbas* (UK) 1949; *The White Tower* 1950; *Mr. Imperium, The Desert Fox* 1951; *The Green Glove, Caribbean* 1952; *Salome* (as Tiberius), *Botany Bay* 1953; *Bait* 1954; *Richard III* (as Edward IV; UK) 1955; *Diane, Helen of Troy* (as Priam; US/It.), *Gaby, The Vagabond King, The Power and the Prize, Around the World in 80 Days, The Ten Commandments* 1956; *The Story of Mankind, Baby Face Nelson* 1957; *The Magic Fountain* 1961; *Five Weeks in a Balloon* 1962; *The Pumpkin Eater* (UK) 1964.

Hardy, Oliver. Actor. *b.* Norvell Hardy, Jan. 18, 1892, Harlem, Ga. *d.* 1957. He began his career as a performer at age eight, singing professionally with a minstrel show. He later appeared in stock and formed his own singing act, with which he toured the South. The son of a lawyer, he enrolled at the University of Georgia, intending to pursue law studies, but soon left school and in 1910 opened a small movie theater. In 1913 he joined the Lubin company in Jacksonville, Fla., beginning his film career as a supporting player, usually a villain, in one- and two-reel comedies. He played second banana to such silent screen comics as Harry Myers, Billy West, and Larry Semon, occasionally doubling as director and gag writer. His heavy frame made him ideally suited for comic villainy. In the 20s he also played occasional character parts in feature films, including Buster Keaton's *The Three Ages* and several Buck Jones Westerns.

Hardy's comic talents were largely wasted on minor roles in Hal Roach comedies until 1926, when he was teamed with Stan LAUREL to form the most fabulously successful comedy duo the screen has ever known. Laurel and Hardy were first cast in the same film, *Lucky Dog,* in 1917, but the crossing of their paths at that point was a mere accident. Hardy, "the fat one," was perhaps less creative than his partner, contributing fewer of the ideas that made the team's formula successful, but his comic characterizations were superb, and he made the most of his bulky figure, cherubic face, and expressive eyes to bring hours of laughter to millions.

A selection of Hardy's films before and after his partnership with Laurel appears below. For the team's full film credits and a survey of their joint work see LAUREL AND HARDY.

FILMS INCLUDE (without Laurel): *Outwitting Dad* 1914; *Spaghetti and Lottery/Spaghetti a la Mode, Charley's Aunt, Paperhanger's Helper, Mixed Flats* 1915; *Dreamy Knights, The Serenade, Aunt Bill, Human Hounds, The Heroes, Love and Duty, Better Halves* 1916; *Backstage, The Villain, The Millionaire, The Fly Cop, The Pest, The Hobo* 1917; *His Day Out, The Handyman, The Chef, Hello Trouble, Playmates* 1918; *Mules and Mortgages* 1919; *Married to Order* 1920; *The Blizzard* 1921; *Little Wildcat, Fortune's Mask* 1922; *One Stolen*

Night, The Three Ages 1923; *King of the Wild Horses* 1924; *The Wizard of Oz* (as the Tin Woodsman) 1925; *Stop Look and Listen* (also asst. dir.), *Madame Mystery, The Gentle Cyclone, The Perfect Clown* 1926; *No Man's Law, Fluttering Hearts* 1927; *Zenobia* 1939; *The Fighting Kentuckian* 1949; *Riding High* 1950.

Hare, David. Playwright, screenwriter, director. Born David Rippon, on June 5, 1947, in Sussex, England. After graduating from Cambridge in 1968, he co-founded the Portable Theatre, a traveling experimental company. He later served as literary manager and resident dramatist at the Royal Court and Nottingham Playhouse, then became the director of the Joint Stock Theatre Group. His many plays include 'Slag' (1970), 'Knuckle' (1974), 'Licking Hitler' (teleplay, 1978), 'Plenty' (1978), 'Saigon: Year of the Cat' (1981), and 'Secret Rapture (1983).' Turning to cinema as director and screenwriter in the mid-80s, he shared the Golden Bear at the 1985 Berlin Festival for his debut film *Wetherby.*

FILMS: *Wetherby* (dir., sc.) 1985; *Plenty* (sc., from own play) 1986; *Paris by Night* (dir., sc.) 1989; *Strapless* (dir., sc.) 1990; *Damage* (sc.) 1992; *The Secret Rapture* (assoc. prod., sc.) 1994; *The Designated Mourner* (dir.) 1997.

Harewood, Dorian. Actor. Born on Aug. 6, 1950, in Dayton, Oh. *ed.* U. of Cincinnati. He began his career on the stage, appearing in the road company of 'Jesus Christ Superstar,' then began delivering strong support performances on film. He was most memorable as the marine killed slowly by sniper fire in *Full Metal Jacket.* He has appeared frequently in TV movies and miniseries, notably as Alex Haley's father in *Roots: The Next Generation* (1979). Married actress Ann McCurry.

FILMS: *Sparkle* 1976; *Gray Lady Down* 1978; *Looker* 1981; *Against All Odds, Tank* 1984; *The Falcon and the Snowman* 1985; *Full Metal Jacket* 1987; *Pacific Heights, Solar Crisis* 1990; *The Pagemaster* (v/o) 1994; *Sudden Death* 1995.

Hargreaves, John. Actor. Solid, award-winning leading man of Australian films. One of his country's top stars since the mid-70s. Another John Hargreaves (*b.* 1921) is a British producer and production executive, also active in US and Australia.

FILMS INCLUDE: *The Removalists* 1975; *Mad Dog Morgan, Don's Party, Deathcheaters* 1976; *Long Weekend* 1977; *The Odd Angry Shot* 1979; *Beyond Reasonable Doubt* 1980; *Hoodwink, The Killing of Angel Street* 1981; *Careful, He Might Hear You* 1983; *My First Wife* 1984; *Sky Pirates* 1985; *Malcolm* 1986; *Comrades, Cry Freedom* (UK) 1987; *Emerald City* 1988.

Harker, Gordon. Actor. *b.* Aug. 7, 1885, London. *d.* 1967. Cockney comic of numerous British films, often low-budget mysteries.

FILMS INCLUDE: *The Ring* 1927; *The Farmer's Wife, Champagne, The Wrecker* 1928; *The Return of the Rat* 1929; *Elstree Calling, The W Plan, The Squeaker, Escape* 1930; *The Calendar/Bachelor's Folly, The Ringer* 1931; *Condemned to Death, The Frightened Lady/Criminal at Large, Rome Express* 1932; *Friday the 13th* 1933; *Boys Will Be Boys* 1935; *The Amateur Gentleman* 1936; *The Frog* 1937; *Inspector Hornleigh* 1939; *Warn That Man* 1942; *29 Acacia Avenue/The Facts of Love* 1945; *Things Happen at Night* 1948; *Her Favorite Husband* 1950; *Derby Day* 1952; *Out of the Clouds* 1955; *Small Hotel* 1957; *Left Right and Centre* 1958.

Harlan, Kenneth. Actor. *b.* July 26, 1895, Boston. *d.* 1967. A matinee idol of silent days, he was signed by D. W. Griffith following a successful career on stage from age seven. Retiring in the early 40s, after numerous film roles and seven marriages, he became a theatrical agent and a restaurateur. His uncle, Otis Harlan (*b.* Dec. 29, 1865, Zanesville, Ohio. *d.* 1940), was a plump character player of Hollywood silent films and talkies who was typically seen in mischievous roles.

FILMS INCLUDE: *Betsy's Burglar, Cheerful Givers, The Flame of the Yukon, The Lash of Power* 1917; *A Man's Man, Midnight Madness, Bread* 1918; *The Microbe, The Hoodlum* 1919; *Dangerous Business, The Penalty* 1920; *Nobody, Dawn of the East, Woman's Place* 1921; *Polly of the Follies, I Am the Law, The Married Flapper, The Primitive Lover, The Toll of the Sea, The Beautiful and the Damned* 1922; *The Virginian, East Side—West Side, The Broken Wing* 1923; *For Another Woman, Butterfly, Poisoned Paradise* 1924; *The Crowded Hour, The Marriage Whirl, Ranger of the Big Pines, Bobbed Hair* 1925; *The Sap, The Ice Flood, Twinkletoes* 1926; *Easy Pickings, Cheating Cheaters* 1927; *Streets of Shanghai, United States Smith, Midnight Rose, Code of the Air* 1928; *Man Woman and Wife* 1929; *Paradise Island, Under Montana Skies* 1930; *Danger Island* (serial), *Finger Prints* (serial), *Women Men Marry, Air Police* 1931; *Widow in Scarlet* 1932; *Wanderer of the Wasteland* 1935; *Man Hunt, San Francisco, China Clipper, The Case of the Velvet Claws, The Walking Dead* 1936; *Marked Woman* 1937; *The Duke of West Point* 1938; *Dick Tracy's G-Men* (serial) 1939; *Slightly Honorable* 1940; *Pride of the Bowery* 1941; *The Masked Marvel* (serial), *Hitler—Dead or Alive* 1943; *Death Valley Rangers* 1944.

Harlan, Russell. Director of photography. *b.* Sept. 16, 1903, Los Angeles. *d.* 1974. A former stuntman and double, he worked behind the cameras beginning in the mid-30s and had a number of distinguished films to his credit after the mid-40s, including several Howard Hawks productions.

FILMS INCLUDE: *Bar 20 Rides Again* 1935; *Hopalong Rides Again* 1937; *Sunset Trail* 1938; *Heritage of the Desert* 1939; *The Light of Western Stars* 1940; *The Parson of Panamint* 1941; *Tombstone, Silver Queen, American Empire* 1942; *Tarzan's Desert Mystery* 1943; *Mystery Man* 1944; *A Walk in the Sun* 1946; *Ramrod* 1947; *Four Faces West, Red River* 1948; *Guilty Bystander* 1950; *The Thing* 1951; *The Big Sky* 1952; *Ruby Gentry* 1953; *Riot in Cell Block 11* 1954; *The Blackboard Jungle, Land of the Pharaohs* (co-phot.) 1955; *The Last Hunt, Lust for Life* (co-phot.) 1956; *Something of Value, Witness for the Prosecution* 1957; *Run Silent Run Deep, King Creole* 1958; *Rio Bravo* 1959; *Pollyanna, Sunrise at Campobello* 1960; *Hatari!* (co-phot.) 1962; *To Kill a Mockingbird, A Gathering of Eagles* 1963; *The Great Race* 1965; *Hawaii* 1966; *Tobruk* 1967; *Darling Lili* 1970.

Harlan, Veidt. Director. *b.* Sept. 22, 1899, Berlin. *d.* 1964. A former stage actor and director, he entered German films as an actor in 1927, becoming a director in 1934. With wife Kristina Söderbaum as his frequent star, he became the foremost propagator of Nazi ideology on the screen. Under the personal aegis of Goebbels, he turned out pretentiously fanatic propaganda films, including the infamous *Jud Süss/Jew Suess* (1940), a vicious anti-Semitic distortion of an anti-Fascist book by a Jewish author. Other films, typically sugar-coated historical sagas, exalted Prussian militarism and the German soul. Ever present at Nazi social functions during the war, he was tried and acquitted of the charge of disseminating Nazi propaganda. He disappeared from public view in 1945 but resumed directing activity in 1950. Autobiography: *Im Schatten meiner Filme* (1966).

FILMS (as director): *Die Pompadour* (co-dir., co-sc.), *Krach im Hinterhaus/Trouble Back Stairs* 1935; *Der. müde Theodor, Maria die Magd* (also co-sc.), *Kater Lampe, Alles für Veronika* 1936; *Mein Sohn der Herr Minister, Die Kreutzersonate/The Kreutzer Sonata, Der Herrscher/The Ruler* 1937; *Verwehte*

Spuren (also co-sc.), *Jugend/Youth* 1938; *Die Reise nach Tilsit* (also sc.), *Das unsterbliche Herz* (also co-sc.) 1939; *Jud Süss/Jew Suess* (also co-sc.) 1940; *Pedro soll hängen* (also co-sc.) 1941; *Die goldene Stadt* (also co-sc.), *Der Grosse König* (also sc.) 1942; *Immensee* (also co-sc.) 1943; *Opfergang* (also co-sc.) 1944; *Kolberg* (also co-sc.) 1945; *Unsterbliche Geliebte* (also sc.) 1950; *Hanna Amon* (also sc.) 1951; *Die blaue Stunde* (also sc.) 1953; *Sterne über Colombo, Die Gefangene des Maharadscha* 1954; *Verrat an Deutschland* (also co-sc.) 1955; *Anders als Du und Ich/The Third Sex* 1957; *Ich werde Dich auf Händen tragen* (also co-sc.), *Liebe kann wie Gift sein* 1958; *Die blonde Frau des Maharadscha* 1962.

Harlin, Renny. Director. Born in 1958, in Helsinki. The son of a doctor and nurse, he became infatuated with cinema in childhood and began making amateur films as a juvenile. After graduating from a film school, he set up his own production company and turned out a number of shorts and documentaries. Repeatedly frustrated in his attempt to make a feature film with the necessary financial support of the Finnish government, he set out for Hollywood, where after much maneuvering he was able to secure a low budget for his debut feature in 1986. He scored a box-office hit in 1990 with the action picture *Die Hard 2* (1990), but couldn't repeat that success with the disastrous *Cutthroat Island* (1995), one of the worst box-office deaths in film history. He is married to actress Geena DAVIS who produced and starred in Harlin's next film, a well-received actioner *The Long Kiss Goodnight*.

FILMS: *Born American* (also co-sc.)(US/Finn.) 1986; *Prison, A Nightmare on Elm Street 4: The Dream Master* 1988; *Die Hard 2, The Adventures of Ford Fairlane* 1990; *Rambling Rose* (prod. only) 1991; *Cliffhanger* 1993; *Speechless* (co-prod. only) 1994; *Cutthroat Island* (also prod.) 1995; *The Long Kiss Goodnight* (also prod.) 1996.

Harline, Leigh. Composer. *b.* Mar. 26, 1907, Salt Lake City. *d.* 1969. He worked for various radio stations before joining the Walt Disney studios in 1932 as arranger and scorer, and won an Academy Award for the song 'When You Wish Upon a Star' from Disney's *Pinocchio.* He left Disney in 1941 and free-lanced for various studios.

FILMS INCLUDE: *Snow White and the Seven Dwarfs* 1938; *Pinocchio* 1940; *The Pride of the Yankees* 1942; *The More the Merrier* 1943; *George White's Scandals* 1945; *From This Day Forward, Nocturne, Road to Utopia, Till the End of Time* 1946; *The Bachelor and Bobby-Soxer, The Farmer's Daughter* 1947; *The Miracle of the Bells, The Velvet Touch, The Boy with Green Hair* 1948; *It Happens Every Spring, The Big Steal* 1949; *Monkey Business* 1952; *Broken Lance* 1954; *23 Paces to Baker Street* 1956; *The Wayward Bus* 1957; *Ten North Frederick* 1958; *The Wonderful World of the Brothers Grimm* 1962; *The Seven Faces of Dr. Lao* 1964; *Strange Bedfellows* 1965.

Harlow, Jean. Actress. *b.* Harlean Carpenter, Mar. 3, 1911, Kansas City, Mo. *d.* 1937. The daughter of a dentist, she eloped at 16 with a young businessman. The newlyweds settled in Los Angeles, where the bride soon found work as an extra in films (*Moran of the Marines,* 1928; *Love Parade,* 1929; *City Lights,* 1931, etc.). In between such parts in features, she was displayed more prominently in Hal Roach comedy shorts, notably *Double Whoopee* (1928). She had a featured part in Paramount's *The Saturday Night Kid* but went unnoticed and returned to shorts, working for Al Christie. She disposed of her real name and took her mother's maiden name, Jean Harlow. In 1929 she obtained a divorce. Opportunity knocked in the person of Howard HUGHES, who was converting his WW I aviation saga, *Hell's Angels,* to sound. The film had been started in 1927 and now had to be largely reshot, with an English-speaking girl to take the place of the heavy-accented Swede Greta Nissen. Hughes signed Harlow to a contract and after the film's completion began loaning her out to other studios at a profit.

Harlow's early career was far from spectacular. But the public began responding to her vulgar platinum-blonde glamour in such films as Warner's *The Public Enemy* and Columbia's *Platinum Blonde.* The turning point was provided by a contractual switch to MGM in 1932. Now she worked for a permanent studio with a vested interest in developing her career and star image. In just months the coarse, flashy, whorish sexpot underwent a transformation into a subtle actress with a natural flair for comedy. Cast opposite Clark Gable and Spencer Tracy, Harlow quickly developed into a superstar. Film critics praised her vitality and comic talent in such career highlights as *Red Dust, Bombshell, Dinner at Eight, China Seas, Riffraff,* and *Libeled Lady.*

The private life of America's sex symbol of the 30s was unhappy. In July of 1932 she married Paul BERN, a former director and right-hand man of Irving Thalberg, MGM's production genius. Several months later Bern committed suicide. His suicide note, widely interpreted as hinting at impotence on his part, caused Miss Harlow much adverse publicity, which somehow failed to affect her career. In 1933 she married Harold Rosson, the director of photography on several of her films, but the union lasted only one year. She then became engaged to her sometime co-star William Powell. They ran away but never married. Harlow became quite ill during the filming of *Saratoga* in 1937. She was hospitalized and treated for uremic poisoning. She died on June 7 of that year, of cerebral edema, at age 26. Her short life was the subject of a rather sensational 1964 biography and two quickie 1965 films, one starring Carroll Baker, the other Carol Lynley. Neither star could even remotely capture Harlow's legendary sparkle and glamour.

FEATURE FILMS: *The Saturday Night Kid* 1929; *Hell's Angels* 1930; *The Secret Six, The Iron Man, The Public Enemy, Goldie, Platinum Blonde* 1931; *Three Wise Girls, The Beast of the City, Red-Headed Woman, Red Dust* 1932; *Hold Your Man, Bombshell* 1933; *Dinner at Eight, The Girl from Missouri* 1934; *Reckless, China Seas* 1935; *Riffraff, Wife vs. Secretary, Suzy, Libeled Lady* 1936; *Personal Property, Saratoga* 1937.

Harman, Hugh. Animator. *b.* Aug. 31, 1908, Pagosa Springs, Colo. *d.* 1982. In films from the early 20s, he worked for DISNEY, then formed the Harman-Ising Company, with Rudolph Ising, to rival his former boss. He produced the first synchronized talking cartoon, *Bosco the Talking Kid,* and originated the "Merrie Melodies" and "Looney Tunes" cartoon series. He was cited by the Nobel Prize jury for his animated film *Peace on Earth* (1940).

Harmon, Mark. Actor. Born on Sept 2, 1951, Burbank, Calif. Handsome, blue-eyed leading man of American TV and films. The son of legendary Michigan football hero (later sportscaster) Tom Harmon and actress Elyse KNOX, he followed in his father's footsteps as an all-American quarterback at UCLA, where he graduated in 1974. He turned to acting and began appearing with increasing frequency in TV series and mini-series, in TV movies, and in occasional films. His popularity reached a peak in the 80s, thanks to starring roles in the series 'Flamingo Road,' 'St. Elsewhere,' and 'Moonlighting,' and several big-budget TV movies; but his impact on the big screen remained marginal. In 1987 he married television actress Pam Dawber. His sisters, Kristine (wife of Rick Nelson) and Kelly Harmon, are actresses, as is his niece, Tracy Nelson.

FILMS: *Comes a Horseman* 1978; *Beyond the Poseidon Adventure* 1979; *Let's Get Harry* 1986; *Dear America* (doc.; v/o), *Summer School* 1987; *The Presidio, Stealing Home* 1988;

Worth Winning 1989; *Till There Was You* 1991; *Cold Heaven* 1992; *Wyatt Earp* 1994; *Magic in the Water* 1995; *The Last Supper* 1996.

Harper, Jessica. Actress. Born on Oct. 10, 1949, in Chicago. *ed.* Sarah Lawrence Coll. Brunette leading lady of the American stage, TV, and films. She began her career as an understudy in the Broadway production of 'Hair.' She later appeared in a number of off-Broadway plays before making her screen debut in 1974. She married producer Thomas E. Rothman, a top executive at Columbia and later worldwide production chief at Goldwyn.

FILMS: *Phantom of the Paradise* 1974; *Love and Death* 1975; *Inserts* (UK) 1976; *Suspiria* (It.) 1977; *The Evictors* 1979; *Stardust Memories* 1980; *Shock Treatment, Pennies from Heaven* 1981; *My Favorite Year* 1982; *The Imagemaker, Once Again* 1986; *The Blue Iguana* 1988; *Big Man on Campus/The Hunchback of UCLA* 1989.

Harper, Tess. Actress. Born in 1952, in Mammoth Springs, Ark. *ed.* Southwest Missouri State Coll. (Springfield). Leading lady and supporting player of American TV and films. She performed with a children's company and in dinner theaters before breaking into television via commercials in the late 70s. In feature films from 1982, she was nominated for an Academy Award as best supporting actress for *Crimes of the Heart* (1986).

FILMS: *Tender Mercies* 1982; *Amityville 3-D, Silkwood* 1983; *Flashpoint* 1984; *Crimes of the Heart* 1986; *Ishtar* 1987; *Far North* 1988; *Her Alibi, Criminal Law* 1989; *Daddy's Dyin'. . . Who's Got the Will?* 1990; *My Heroes Have Always Been Cowboys* 1991; *Man in the Moon, My New Gun, The Turning* 1992.

Harper, Valerie. Actress. Born on Aug. 22, 1940, in Suffern, N.Y. Spunky, green-eyed, brunette leading lady of American TV and films. She enjoyed great success in the role of the feisty Rhoda Morgenstern in TV's 'The Mary Tyler Moore Show' (1970–74) for which she won three successive Emmy Awards, and later starred in the hit spin-off comedy series 'Rhoda' (1974–78), copping another Emmy, and 'Valerie' (1986). She later tackled dramatic as well as comic roles in TV movies.

FILMS: *Freebie and the Bean* 1974; *Chapter Two* 1979; *The Last Married Couple in America* 1980; *Blame It on Rio* 1984.

Harrelson, Woody. Actor. Born on July 23, 1961 in Midland, Tex. *ed.* Hanover College. Rangy lead of television and film. A former Broadway understudy for 'Biloxi Blues,' he became nationally known as the clueless barkeep Woody on the TV sitcom 'Cheers.' He has gone on to enjoy a thriving career in feature films, earning an Academy Award nomination as best actor for the title role in the controversial *The People vs. Larry Flynt* (1996).

FILMS INCLUDE: *Harper Valley P.T.A.* 1978; *Wildcats* 1986; *L.A. Story, Doc Hollywood, Ted and Venus* 1991; *White Men Can't Jump* 1992; *Indecent Proposal* 1993; *I'll Do Anything, Natural Born Killers* 1994; *The Cowboy Way, Money Train* 1995; *Kingpin, The People vs. Larry Flynt, Sunchaser* 1996; *Welcome to Sarajevo* 1997.

Harrington, Curtis. Director. Born on Sept. 17, 1928, in Los Angeles. *ed.* USC. He took an interest in filmmaking during his early teens and made many experimental shorts in 8 mm and 16 mm, including *The Fall of the House of Usher* (1942), *Fragment of Seeking* (1946), *Picnic* (1948), *On the Edge* (1949), *Dangerous Houses* (1952), *The Assignation* (1953), and *The Wormwood Star* (1955). He entered the industry as executive assistant to producer Jerry Wald, became an associate producer at Fox in 1955, and turned out his first feature film as a director in 1963. He has specialized in horror-thrillers.

FEATURE FILMS: *Night Tide* (also sc.) 1963; *Queen of Blood/Planet of Blood* (also sc.) 1966; *Games* (also co-story) 1967; *What's the Matter with Helen?, Who Slew Auntie Roo?* 1971; *The Killing Kind* 1973; *Ruby* 1977.

Harris, Barbara. Actress. Born Sandra Markowitz, on July 25, 1935, in Evanston, Ill. *ed.* Goodman School of the Theatre; U. of Chicago. Fetching leading lady of the American stage and occasional films. She came to New York in 1961 with Chicago's famous Second City improvisation troupe and went on to star in off-Broadway and Broadway productions, winning a Tony Award in 1967 for her performance in Broadway's 'The Apple Tree.' She also directed one Broadway production. Her screen appearances have been infrequent but usually rewarding.

FILMS: *A Thousand Clowns* 1965; *Oh Dad Poor Dad—Mama's Hung You in the Closet and I'm Feeling So Sad* 1967; *Plaza Suite, Who Is Harry Kellerman and Why Is He Saying Those Terrible Things About Me?* 1971; *The War Between Men and Women* 1972; *Mixed Company* 1974; *The Manchu Eagle Murder Caper Mystery, Nashville* 1975; *Family Plot* 1976; *Freaky Friday* 1977; *Movie Movie* 1978; *The North Avenue Irregulars, The Seduction of Joe Tynan* 1979; *Second-Hand Hearts/The Hamster of Happiness* (released delayed from 1979) 1981; *Peggy Sue Got Married* 1986; *Nice Girls Don't Explode* 1987; *Dirty Rotten Scoundrels* 1988.

Harris, Ed. Actor. Born on Nov. 28, 1950, in Tenafly, N.J. Diverse, balding leading man of the American stage, TV, and films. After a two-year attendance, he dropped out of Columbia University, where he focused on football, and enrolled in acting classes at Oklahoma State University. He was 25 by the time he got a B.F.A. degree in drama from the California Institute of the Arts. Remaining on the West Coast, he performed in stock and made his screen debut in 1978. His career took an important turn in 1983, when he basked in the portrayal of astronaut John Glenn in the film *The Right Stuff* and won an Obie Award for his performance in the play 'Fool for Love,' his off-Broadway debut. It was also the year in which he married his sometime co-star Amy MADIGAN. He was nominated for an Academy Award as best supporting actor for his role in *Apollo 13* (1995).

FILMS: *Coma* 1978; *Borderline* 1980; *Knightriders, Dream On* 1981; *Creepshow* 1982; *The Right Stuff* (as John Glenn), *Under Fire* 1983; *Swing Shift, Places in the Heart* 1984; *Alamo Bay, A Flash of Green, Code Name: Emerald, Sweet Dreams* 1985; *Walker* 1987; *To Kill a Priest* 1988; *Jacknife, The Abyss* 1989; *State of Grace* 1990; *China Moon, Glengarry Glen Ross* 1992; *Needful Things, The Firm* 1993; *China Moon, Milk Money, Nostradamus* 1994; *Apollo 13, Just Cause, Nixon* 1995; *Eye for an Eye, The Rock* 1996; *Absolute Power* 1997.

Harris, James B. Producer, director. Born on Aug. 3, 1928, in New York City. *ed.* Juilliard. He formed a partnership with Stanley KUBRICK and produced several of the director's films, then went his own way as both producer and director.

FILMS: *The Killing* (prod.) 1956; *Paths of Glory* (prod.) 1957; *Lolita* (prod.) 1962; *The Bedford Incident* (prod., dir.) 1965; *Some Call It Loving* (prod., dir., sc.) 1973; *Telefon* (prod.) 1977; *Fast-Walking* (prod., dir., sc.) 1982; *Cop/Blood on the Moon* (co-prod., dir., sc.) 1988; *Boiling Point* (dir., sc.) 1993.

Harris, Julie. Actress. Born Julia Ann Harris, on Dec. 2, 1925, in Grosse Pointe, Mich. The daughter of an investment banker, she was educated at a finishing school and received her stage training at the Yale Drama School and at the Actors Studio. She made her Broadway debut in 1945 and almost immediately won recognition for her sensitive and subtle portrayal of complex roles. She established herself as a star in 1950 in 'The Member of the Wedding,' a role she would later repeat in her 1952 Oscar-nominated screen debut. Miss Harris went on to make many distinguished stage and TV appearances, winning several Tony and Emmy awards in the process. Her sporadic film appearances include memorable roles in *East of Eden, I Am a Camera* (both 1955), *Requiem for a Heavyweight* (1962), *The Haunting* (1963), and *Harper* (1966). During much of the 80s (1981–88) she played a regular supporting role in the TV series 'Knots Landing.' In 1988 she returned to the screen after a decade's absence. Her third husband (from 1977) is writer William Carroll. Another Julie Harris (*b.* 1921, London) is a costume designer with numerous major films to her credit and an Oscar for *Darling* (1965).

FILMS: *The Member of the Wedding* 1952; *East of Eden, I Am a Camera* 1955; *The Truth About Women* (UK), *Sally's Irish Rogue/The Poacher's Daughter* (Ire.) 1958; *Requiem for a Heavyweight* 1962; *The Haunting* (US/UK) 1963; *Harper* 1966; *You're a Big Boy Now, Reflections in a Golden Eye* 1967; *The Split* 1968; *The People Next Door* 1970; *The Hiding Place* 1975; *Voyage of the Damned* (UK) 1976; *The Bell Jar* 1979; *Gorillas in the Mist* 1988; *The Dark Half* 1991; *Housesitter* 1992; *Carried Away* 1996.

Harris, Mildred. Actress. *b.* Nov. 29, 1901, Cheyenne, Wyo. *d.* 1944. In films from age nine, she starred at 13 as Dorothy in *The Patchwork Girl of Oz* and played different roles in two other Oz features of 1915. She later played juvenile and ingenue leads in many silent and several early talkies. She continued playing bits in occasional films until her death of pneumonia at 43, following surgery. She had also appeared in vaudeville and burlesque and on the legitimate stage and was the first wife of Charlie CHAPLIN. In several of her films she was billed as Mildred Harris Chaplin.

FILMS INCLUDE: *The Patchwork Girl of Oz, The Magic Cloak of Oz, His Majesty the Scarecow of Oz/The New Wizard of Oz* 1914; *Enoch Arden, The Warrens of Virginia* 1915; *Intolerance, Hoodoo Ann, Old Folks at Home* 1916; *The Price of a Good Time, Bad Boy, A Love Sublime* 1917; *For Husbands Only, Cupid by Proxy, Borrowed Clothes* 1918; *When a Girl Loves, Forbidden, Home* 1919; *Polly of the Storm Country, Old Dad, The Woman in His House, The Inferior Sex* 1920; *A Prince There Was, Old Dad, Habit, Fool's Paradise* 1921; *The First Woman* 1922; *The Daring Years, Fog* 1923; *One Law for the Woman, Unmarried Wives* 1924; *The Dressmaker from Paris, Private Affairs, My Neighbor's Wife* 1925; *Isle of Retribution, The Mystery Club, The Wolf Hunters* 1926; *The Girl from Rio, Out of the Past, The Show Girl* 1927; *The Adventurous Soul, Lingerie, The Heart of a Follies Girl, The Power of the Press, Hearts of Men, Melody of Love* 1928; *Side Street, Sea Fury* 1929; *No No Nanette* 1930; *Lady Tubbs, Never Too Late* 1935; *Reap the Wild Wind* 1942; *The Story of Dr. Wassell* 1944.

Harris, Phil. Actor, musician. Born on June 24, 1904, in Linton, Ind. The son of a musician, he grew up in Nashville, Tenn. He began his career as a drummer, forming his own band in 1931. In the early 30s he began appearing in films, at first with his band and later as a comedian and dramatic actor. In 1941 he married film star Alice FAYE and teamed with her in popular radio shows of the 40s.

FILMS INCLUDE: *Melody Cruise* 1933; *Turn Off the Moon* 1937; *Man About Town* 1939; *Buck Benny Rides Again* 1940; *I Love a Bandleader* 1945; *Wabash Avenue* 1950; *Here Comes the Groom, The Wild Blue Yonder* 1951; *The High and the Mighty* 1954; *Anything Goes, Goodbye My Lady* 1956; *The Wheeler Dealers* 1963; *The Patsy* 1964; *The Jungle Book* (v/o), *The Cool Ones* 1967; *The Aristocats* (v/o) 1970; *Robin Hood* (v/o) 1973.

Harris, Richard. Actor. Born on Oct. 1, 1930, in Limerick, Ireland. *ed.* Sacred Heart Jesuit Coll. A miller's son, he trained at the London Academy of Music and Dramatic Art; made his stage debut in 1956 and his first appearance in British films in 1958. He was propelled into international stardom by his robust performance in *This Sporting Life,* for which he won the Cannes Festival acting award and was nominated for an Oscar. After enjoying great success as King Arthur in the screen musical *Camelot* (1967), Harris pursued a parallel career as a singer, often combining songs and his own poetry in concert tours. In 1971 he took a stab at directing with *Bloomfield,* which he shot in Israel. A powerful presence on screen, Harris earned a reputation for his robust, bawdy appetites in private life, especially heavy boozing (combined with cocaine consumption) which ravaged his health. With his career flagging by the early 80s, the reclusive actor retreated to Paradise Island in the Bahamas, where he rediscovered religion, swore off drinking, and adhered to a strict diet to ward off hypoglycemia. Devoting much of his time to the writing of poetry and short stories, he also published a thriller novel, *Honor Bound,* in 1982. After a long hiatus, he revived his screen career late in the decade. His second wife (1974–82) was New York–based actress Ann Turkel. Another Richard Harris, also billed as Richard A. Harris, is a Hollywood film editor.

FILMS: *Alive and Kicking* 1958; *Shake Hands with the Devil* (Ire.), *The Wreck of the Mary Deare* (US) 1959; *A Terrible Beauty/The Night Fighters* 1960; *The Guns of Navarone* (UK/US), *The Long and the Short and the Tall/The Jungle Fighters* 1961; *Mutiny on the Bounty* (US) 1962; *This Sporting Life* 1963; *Il Deserto Rosso/The Red Desert* (It./Fr.) 1964; *I Tre Volti/Three Faces of a Woman (It.), Major Dundee* (US), *The Heroes of Telemark* 1965; *La Bibbia/The Bible* (as Cain; It./US), *Hawaii* (US) 1966; *Caprice* (US), *Camelot* (as King Arthur; US) 1967; *The Molly Maguires* (US), *A Man Called Horse* (US), *Cromwell* (title role), *La Dame dans l'Auto avec des Lunettes et un Fusil/The Lady in the Car with Glasses and a Gun* (co-sc. only; Fr./US) 1970; *Bloomfield/The Hero* (also dir.; Isr./UK), *Man in the Wilderness* 1971; *The Deadly Trackers* (US) 1973; *99 44/100% Dead* (US), *Juggernaut* 1974; *Echoes of a Summer/The Last Castle* (also co-exec. prod., co-song; US/Can.) 1975; *Robin and Marian* (as King Richard the Lion-Hearted), *The Return of a Man Called Horse* (also co-exec. prod.; US) 1976; *The Cassandra Crossing* (US), *Gulliver's Travels* (UK/Bel.), *Orca* (US), *Golden Rendezvous* (US) 1977; *The Wild Geese* 1978; *Ravagers* (US), *The Number, Game for Vultures* 1979; *The Last Word* (US), *Highpoint* (Can.) 1980; *Tarzan the Ape Man* (US) 1981; *Au-dela de cette Limite votre Ticket n'est plus valable/ Your Ticket Is No Longer Valid* (Can./Fr.) 1982; *Triumphs of a Man Called Horse* (US/Mex.) 1983; *Martin's Day* (Can.) 1984; *Mack the Knife* (as Mr. Peachum) 1989; *The Field* 1990; *Patriot Games, Undefeated* 1992; *Wrestling Ernest Hemingway* 1993; *Silent Tongue* 1994; *Cry the Beloved Country* 1995; *Smilla's Sense of Snow, Trojan Eddie* 1997.

Harris, Timothy. Screenwriter, novelist. Born on July 21, 1946, in Los Angeles. Graduating from Cambridge with a master's degree (with honors) in English literature, he published several novels, then teamed up with Herschel Weingrod to write lowbrow screenplays for a number of popular Hollywood comedies. He also churned out a number of film novelizations, including *Steelyard Blues* and *American Gigolo.*

FILMS: *Cheaper to Keep Her* 1980; *Trading Places* 1983; *My Stepmother Is an Alien, Twins* 1988; *Kindergarten Cop* 1990; *Pure Luck* 1991.

Harrison, Doane. American film editor. *d.* 1968. In films from the early 20s, he worked mainly for Paramount, cutting some of that studio's prime films of the 40s and early 50s. A favorite of Mitchell LEISEN and Billy WILDER, he later became the latter's associate producer.

FILMS INCLUDE: *Youth and Adventure* 1925; *Show Folks* 1928; *The Racketeer* 1929; *Her Man* 1930; *Annapolis Farewell* 1935; *Easy Living* 1937; *Midnight* 1939; *Remember the Night, Arise My Love* 1940; *Hold Back the Dawn* 1941; *The Major and the Minor, Take a Letter, Darling* 1942; *Five Graves to Cairo* 1943; *Double Indemnity, The Uninvited* 1944; *The Long Weekend, The Unseen* 1945; *The Emperor Waltz, A Foreign Affair* 1948; *Sunset Boulevard* (co-edit.) 1950; *Stalag 17* 1953.

Harrison, George. See BEATLES, The.

Harrison, Joan. Screenwriter, producer. Born in 1911, in Guildford, England. *ed.* Sorbonne; Oxford. Longtime assistant to Alfred HITCHCOCK, she collaborated on the screenplays of several of his notable films and later acted as producer or associate producer on a number of Hollywood productions. She produced the TV series 'Alfred Hitchcock Presents.'

FILMS INCLUDE: As screenwriter—*Jamaica Inn* 1939; *Rebecca, Foreign Correspondent* 1940; *Suspicion* 1941; *Saboteur* 1942; *Dark Waters* 1944. As producer—*Phantom Lady* 1944; *Uncle Harry* 1945; *Nocturne* 1946; *Ride the Pink Horse* 1947; *Once More My Darling* 1949; *Eye Witness* 1950; *Circle of Danger* 1951.

Harrison, Kathleen. Actress. Born on Feb. 23, 1898, in Blackburn, England. *ed.* RADA. Character star of British stage, screen, and television, typically in cockney portrayals. Enormously popular in Britain during the 40s and 50s.

FILMS INCLUDE: *Our Boys* 1915; *Hobson's Choice* 1931; *Happy Ever After* 1932; *The Ghoul* 1933; *Broken Blossoms* 1936; *Night Must Fall* (US) 1937; *Bank Holiday/Three on a Weekend, Convict 99* 1938; *The Outsider* 1939; *Gaslight/Angel Street, The Girl in the News* 1940; *The Ghost Train, Kipps/The Remarkable Mr. Kipps, Major Barbara* 1941; *In Which We Serve* 1942; *Dear Octopus/The Randolph Family* 1943; *Caesar and Cleopatra* 1945; *I See a Dark Stranger/The Adventuress* 1946; *Holiday Camp* 1947; *The Winslow Boy, Oliver Twist* 1948; *Here Come the Huggetts, Now Barabbas. . .* 1949; *Waterfront/Waterfront Women* 1950; *Scrooge* 1951; *The Pickwick Papers* 1952; *Turn the Key Softly* 1953; *Lilacs in the Spring/Let's Make Up* 1954; *Cast a Dark Shadow* 1955; *All for Mary* 1956; *A Cry from the Streets, Alive and Kicking* 1958; *The Fast Lady* 1962; *Lock Up Your Daughters* 1969; *The London Connection/The Omega Connection* 1979.

Harrison, Michael. See CARSON, Sunset.

Harrison, Sir Rex. Actor. *b.* Reginald Carey Harrison, Mar. 5, 1908, Hyton, England. *d.* 1990. *ed.* Liverpool Coll. Suave, urbane leading man of the British and American stage and screen. The son of a cotton broker, he made his stage debut at 16 with the Liverpool Repertory Theatre, with which he remained for three years. In 1930 he first appeared on the London stage as well as in British films. In 1936 he made the first of many appearances on Broadway, in 'Sweet Aloes,' and later that year became a London stage star in 'French Without Tears,' a play that established him as an adroit master of black-tie comedy. His rising stage and screen career was interrupted by WW II, in which he served as flight lieutenant in the RAF, but was resumed triumphantly in 1945 with such British films as *Blithe Spirit* and *The Rake's Progress.* Later that year he went to Hollywood, where he starred in a number of films, notably *Anna and the King of Siam.*

His remarkable stage and screen career on both sides of the Atlantic culminated in the mid-50s with a Tony Award–winning portrayal of Professor Henry Higgins in Broadway's 'My Fair Lady.' He won the Academy Award in 1964 for repeating the role in the film version. He had been nominated for an Oscar the year before for his portrait of Julius Caesar in *Cleopatra.* The elegant, charming, and blasé actor was married six times. His first marriage (1934–42), to one Marjorie Thomas, produced actor Noel Harrison (*b.* Jan. 29, 1936, London); his second (1943–57) was to actress Lilli PALMER; his third (1957–59) to actress Kay KENDALL; his fourth (1962–71) to actress Rachel ROBERTS; his fifth (in 1971) to Elizabeth Harris, the ex-wife of actor Richard Harris; and his sixth (in 1978) to one Mercia Tinker. In 1948, Harrison's name was mentioned in connection with the suicide of Hollywood actress Carole Landis. Gossip columnists nicknamed him teasingly "Sexy Rexy." Knighted by the Queen for his achievements in 1989, Harrison remained a dedicated actor to the last. Only a month before his death at 82 of pancreatic cancer, he was starring on Broadway, opposite Glynis JOHNS and Stewart GRANGER, in a revival of Somerset Maugham's play 'The Circle.' In addition to an autobiography, *Rex* (1975), he published *If Love Be Love* (1979), an anthology of romantic poems which he edited.

FILMS: In the UK—*The Great Game, School for Scandal* 1930; *Get Your Man, Leave It to Blanche* 1934; *All at Sea* 1935; *Men Are Not Gods* 1936; *Storm in a Teacup, School for Husbands, Over the Moon* 1937; *St. Martin's Lane/Sidewalks of London, The Citadel, The Silent Battle/Continental Express* 1939; *Ten Days in Paris/Missing Ten Days, Night Train to Munich/Night Train* 1940; *Major Barbara* (as Adolphus Cusins) 1941; *Blithe Spirit, I Live in Grosvenor Square/A Yank in London, The Rake's Progress/Notorious Gentleman* 1945. In the US—*Anna and the King of Siam* (as the King) 1946; *The Ghost and Mrs. Muir, The Foxes of Harrow* 1947; *Escape* (UK), *Unfaithfully Yours* 1948; *The Long Dark Hall* (UK) 1951; *The Four Poster* 1952; *Main Street to Broadway* 1953; *King Richard and the Crusaders* (as Saladin; US/UK) 1954; *The Constant Husband* (UK) 1955; *The Reluctant Debutante* 1958; *Midnight Lace* 1960; *The Happy Thieves* 1962; *Cleopatra* (as Julius Caesar; US/UK) 1963; *The Yellow Rolls-Royce* (UK), *My Fair Lady* (as Henry Higgins) 1964; *The Agony and the Ecstasy* (as Pope Julius II) 1965; *The Honey Pot/It Comes Up Murder* (US/UK/It.), *Doctor Dolittle* (title role) 1967; *A Flea in Her Ear* (US/Fr.) 1968; *Staircase* (UK) 1969; *The Prince and the Pauper/Crossed Swords* (as the Duke of Norfolk; UK), *Behind the Iron Mask/The Fifth Musketeer* (Aus.) 1977; *Shalimar* (Ind.) 1978; *Ashanti* (Switz./US) 1979; *Seven Graves for Rogan/A Time to Die* (release delayed from 1979) 1983.

Harrold, Kathryn. Actress. Born on Aug. 2, 1950, in Tazewell, Va. *ed.* Mills Coll. Leading lady of the American stage, TV, and a handful of films. Trained at New York's Neighborhood Playhouse and by Uta HAGEN, she performed in off-Broadway plays and with an experimental group and taught drama at Connecticut College and NYU before her screen debut in 1979.

FILMS: *Nightwing* 1979; *The Hunter* 1980; *Modern Romance, The Pursuit of D. B. Cooper* 1981; *Yes Giorgio, The Sender* (UK) 1982; *Heartbreakers* 1984; *Into the Night* 1985; *Raw Deal* 1986; *Someone to Love* 1987.

Harron, John (Johnnie). Actor. *b.* Mar. 31, 1903, New York City. *d.* 1939. The younger brother of Robert (Bobby) HARRON, he began his screen career shortly after the death of his more famous sibling. He played wholesome romantic leads in many silents of the 20s but was reduced to minor roles or minor films after the advent of sound.

FILMS INCLUDE: *Hearts of the World* (bit) 1920; *Through the Back Door, The Fox* 1921; *Penrod, Love in the Dark* 1922; *Dulcy, The Gold Diggers, The Supreme Test* 1923;

What Shall I Do?, Behind the Curtain, The Painted Flapper 1924; *Learning to Love, Old Shoes, My Wife and I, The Woman Hater, Below the Line, Satan in Sables* 1925; *Bride of the Storm, The Night Cry, The Gilded Highway, Hell-Bent for Heaven, The Boy Friend, The False Alarm, Rose of the Tenements* 1926; *Closed Gates, Naughty, Once and Forever, Silk Stockings, Night Life* 1927; *Finders Keepers, Their Hour, Green Grass Widows* 1928; *Street Girl* 1929; *The Czar of Broadway, Big Boy* 1930; *Laugh and Get Rich* 1931; *White Zombie* 1932; *Sister to Judas* 1933; *Murder in the Private Car* 1934; *Symphony of Living* 1935; *Missing Witness* 1937; *The Invisible Menace, Torchy Gets Her Man* 1938; *Secret Service of the Air, Indianapolis Speedway* 1939.

Harron, Robert (Bobby). Actor. *b.* Apr. 24, 1894, New York City, to a large, poor family of Irish immigrants. *d.* 1920. In 1907 he began working for the American Biograph studio on New York's East 14th Street as a messenger boy and soon began playing bit roles in films. The following year he struck up a friendship with newcomer D. W. GRIFFITH and subsequently played leading roles in many of the latter's films, often starring opposite Mae MARSH and the GISH sisters. Boyish, charming, and sincere, he enjoyed considerable popularity with movie audiences. He was planning to set up his own production company in 1920 when an accidentally discharged pistol bullet ended his life. He was the brother of John (Johnnie) HARRON.

FILMS INCLUDE: *Dr. Sinkum* 1907; *The Valet's Wife, The Test of Friendship* 1908; *The Hindoo Dagger, A Burglar's Mistake, Two Memories, The Lonely Villa, The Little Darling* 1909; *Ramona, A Summer Idyll* 1910; *Enoch Arden, Bobby the Coward, The Unveiling, The Battle* 1911; *Man's Genesis, An Unseen Enemy, The New York Hat, My Hero, Home Folks, A Cry for Help, Oil and Water, The Burglar's Dilemma, The Musketeers of Pig Alley, The Informer* 1912; *Fate, A Misunderstood Boy, The Lady and the Mouse, The Adopted Brother, The Reformers, The Primitive Man* 1913; *Judith of Bethulia, The Battle of the Sexes, The Massacre, Brute Force, The Battle at Elderbush Gulch, The Escape, Home Sweet Home, The Avenging Conscience, Sands of Fate* 1914; *The Birth of a Nation* (as Tod Stoneman and three other minor roles), *The Outcast, The Outlaw's Revenge* 1915; *Hoodoo Ann, A Child of the Paris Streets, Intolerance* (as the Boy, in "The Modern Story"), *Wharf Rat* 1916; *The Bad Boy, An Old-Fashioned Young Man* 1917; *Hearts of the World, The Great Love, The Greatest Thing in Life* 1918; *A Romance of Happy Valley, The Girl Who Stayed at Home, True Heart Susie, The Greatest Question* 1919; *Coincidence* 1921.

Harryhausen, Ray. Special effects master, model animator. Born in 1920, in Los Angeles. *ed.* Los Angeles City College (drama, photography, sculpture); USC (drama, art direction, film editing). A photography enthusiast since adolescence, he was inspired after viewing *King Kong* (1933) to experiment in the family garage with three-dimensional STOP MOTION animation, a hobby which led to his first job as a model animator on George Pal's "Puppetoons" shorts. Following WW II service with the Signal Corps, he made a series of puppet-animated fairy tale shorts, and late in 1946 went to work for the legendary special-effects artist Willis O'BRIEN, whom he assisted on the Oscar-winning effects of *Mighty Joe Young* (1949). Before long, Harryhausen was gaining a reputation as one of the most inventive craftsmen in the field. His spectacular effects include the famous dueling-skeletons scenes in *The Seventh Voyage of Sinbad* (1958) and *Jason and the Argonauts* (1963), pitching live actors in battle against animated models through an intricate process of his own invention he called "Dynamation" and later "Superdynamation." Most of his work, in the UK as well as in the US, has been with producer Charles H. SCHNEER. He played a cameo role in John Landis's *Spies Like Us* (1985). At the 1992 Academy Awards, he received the Gordon E. Sawyer Award for Technical Achievement. Author: *Film Fantasy Scrapbook* (1972).

FILMS INCLUDE: *Mighty Joe Young* (assistant only) 1949; *The Beast from 20,000 Fathoms* 1953; *It Came from Beneath the Sea* 1955; *Earth vs. the Flying Saucers* 1956; *20 Million Miles to Earth* 1957; *The Seventh Voyage of Sinbad* 1958; *The Three Worlds of Gulliver* 1960; *Mysterious Island* 1961; *Jason and the Argonauts* 1963; *First Men in the Moon* 1963; *One Million Years B.C.* 1967; *The Valley of Gwangi* 1969; *Trog* 1970; *The Golden Voyage of Sinbad* 1974; *Sinbad and the Eye of the Tiger* 1977; *Clash of the Titans* (also co-prod.) 1981.

Hart, Dolores. American actress. Born Dolores Hicks, in 1938. A popular starlet in the late 50s, as Elvis Presley's screen partner, and an established leading lady in the early 60s, she stunned Hollywood in 1963 by announcing she was giving up her career to become a Roman Catholic nun. She spent seven probationary years in a Bethlehem, Conn., convent and in 1970 took her vows as a full-fledged member of the Benedictine Order. She is now called Mother Dolores.

FILMS: *Loving You, Wild Is the Wind* 1957; *King Creole* 1958; *Lonelyhearts* 1959; *The Plunderers, Where the Boys Are* 1960; *Francis of Assisi* 1961; *Sail a Crooked Ship, The Inspector/Lisa* (UK/US) 1962; *Come Fly with Me* 1963.

Hart, Harvey. Director. *b.* Mar. 19, 1928, Toronto. *d.* 1989, of a heart attack. *ed.* U. of Toronto. He began his career in Canadian TV in a production unit that also included Norman Jewison, Paul Almond, and Arthur Hiller. From 1963 to 1970 he worked in the US, directing episodes for TV series and a number of interesting low-budget action features.

FILMS: In the US—*Bus Riley's Back in Town, Dark Intruder* 1965; *Sullivan's Empire* (co-dir. with Thomas Carr) 1967; *The Sweet Ride* 1968. In Canada—*Fortune and Man's Eyes* (Can./US) 1971; *Mahoney's Estate* 1972; *The Pyx* 1973; *Shoot* 1976; *Goldenrod* 1977; *The Mad Trapper* 1979; *The Aliens Are Coming* 1980; *The High Country* 1981; *Utilities* 1983.

Hart, Mary. See ROBERTS, Lynn.

Hart, Moss. Playwright, screenwriter. *b.* Oct. 24, 1904, the Bronx, N.Y. *d.* 1961. Poverty forced him to leave school and go to work at age ten. At 17 he wrote his first play, which closed out of town. Discouraged, he became a floorwalker for Macy's but the following year returned to the stage as an actor. He spent his summers as a social director in the Catskills. He eventually became a highly successful playwright, often in collaboration with George S. KAUFMAN. Among his plays that were made into films are *Once in a Lifetime* (1932), *You Can't Take It with You* (1938), *The Man Who Came to Dinner* (1942), *George Washington Slept Here* (1942), *Lady in the Dark* (1944), and *The Decision of Christopher Blake* (1948). His autobiography, *Act One,* was made into a film in 1963. George Hamilton impersonated Hart. He also wrote several screenplays directly for films. Hart, who was married to actress-singer Kitty CARLISLE, won a Tony Award in 1957 for directing 'My Fair Lady' on Broadway.

FILMS INCLUDE (screenplays): *Flesh* (dial. only) 1932; *Broadway Melody of 1936* (orig. story) 1935; *Frankie and Johnnie* 1936; *Winged Victory* (from his own play) 1944; *Gentleman's Agreement* 1947; *Hans Christian Andersen* 1952; *A Star Is Born* 1954; *Prince of Players* 1955.

Hart, William S. Actor, director. *b.* Dec. 6, 1865, Newburgh, N.Y. *d.* 1946. The son of an itinerant laborer, he spent much of his youth traveling about the country and developed a deep attachment to the American West. Returning to New York, he became a postal clerk at 19 and after some training made his debut as a stage actor at 24 and soon gained a reputation as a Shakespearean actor on Broadway (hence the apocryphal story that his middle initial stood for Shakespeare; it was actually Surrey). He scored a popular success as Messala in the 1899 Broadway production of 'Ben-Hur' and in the stage versions of the Western dramas 'The Squaw Man,' 'The Virginian,' and 'The Trail of the Lonesome Pine.' Hart was a mature man of 49 when he entered films in 1914 and began working for his friend Thomas H. INCE. Following a couple of villainous parts in two-reelers, he moved into starring roles and soon began directing his own films and occasionally writing his own scripts. His genuine love for the West and his memory of real cowboys and Indians he had known in his youth were to set his Westerns apart from any other films of the genre before or after.

Resenting the artificial, glamorized depiction of the West in films, Hart insisted on stark realism and careful re-creation of sets and costumes for his own productions. His unadorned oaters were the first real "adult" Westerns, not only for their documentary-like realism but also for their down-to-earth plots. Hart introduced to the screen the "good-bad man" character, the fellow who starts out with bad intentions but is redeemed at the end by some good and noble deed. Hart's Westerns were as popular with film audiences as they were critically successful, and their influence on the development of the genre cannot be overstated. But stagnation soon reversed Hart's fortunes. Despite changing public taste and the emergence of such cowboy stars as Tom MIX and Buck JONES, who emphasized spectacular action in their films, Hart stubbornly refused to change his formula.

By 1920, Hart's popularity was fading fast. He persisted valiantly at his brand of Western through 1925, when he turned out his final film, *Tumbleweeds,* a critical and commercial success that somehow did not live up to its fullest box-office potential. Hart sued United Artists for what he believed was negligent handling of distribution. He eventually won his case and $278,000 in damages, but meanwhile the court litigation spelled the end of his career. He went into retirement and wrote several Western novels and an autobiography, *My Life—East and West* (1929). Hart, who had a strange habit of proposing to his leading ladies, was married briefly to one of them, Winifred Westover (1899–1978).

FILMS (as actor): *His Hour of Manhood, Jim Cameron's Wife, The Bargain, The Passing of Two-Gun Hicks/Taming the Four-Flusher* (also dir.), *In the Sage Brush Country/Mr. Nobody* (also dir.), *The Scourge of the Desert* (also dir.), *Mr. Silent Haskins* (also dir.), *The Sheriff's Streak of Yellow* (also dir.), *The Grudge* (also dir.), *The Roughneck/The Gentleman from Blue Gulch* (also dir.), *On the Night Stage, The Taking of Luke McVane/The Fugitive* (also dir.), *The Man from Nowhere/The Silent Stranger* (also dir.), *The Bad Buck of Santa Ynez/The Bad Man/Revolver Bill/A Desperate Chance* (also dir.), *The Darkening Trail/Hell Hound of Alaska* (also dir.), *The Conversion of Frosty Blake/The Convert/Staking His Life* (also dir.), *Tools of Providence/Dakota Dan/Every Inch a Man/The Struggle in the Steeple* (also dir.), *The Ruse/Square Deal Man/A Square Deal* (also dir.), *Cash Parrish's Pal/Double Crossed* (also dir.), *Pinto Ben/Horns and Hoofs* (also dir., sc. from own poem), *A Knight of the Trails/Prowlers of the Plains* (also dir.), *Keno Bates—Liar The Last Card* (also dir.), *The Disciple* (also dir.) 1915; *Between Men* (also dir.), *Hell's Hinges* (also co-dir. with Charles Swickard), *The Aryan* (also dir.), *The Primal Lure* (also dir.), *The Apostle of Vengeance* (also dir.), *The Captive God, The Dawn Maker* (also dir.), *The Return of Draw Egan/The Fugitive* (also dir.), *The Patriot* (also dir.), *The Devil's Double* (also dir.), *Truthful Tulliver* (also dir.) 1916; *The Gun Fighter* (also dir.), *The Square Deal Man* (also dir.), *The Desert Man* (also dir.), *Wolf Lowry* (also dir.), *The Cold Deck* (also dir.), *War Relief* (Liberty Loan short), *The Silent Man* (also dir., exec. prod.), *The Narrow Trail* (also story exec. prod.) 1917; *Wolves of the Rail* (also dir., story, exec. prod.), *Blue Blazes Rawden* (also dir., exec. prod.), *The Tiger Man* (also dir., exec. prod.), *Selfish Yates* (also dir., exec. prod.), *Shark Monroe* (also dir., exec. prod.), *Riddle Gawne* (also dir., exec. prod.), *A Bullet for Berlin* (propaganda short; also dir., prod.), *The Border Wireless* (also dir., exec. prod.), *Branding Broadway* (also dir., exec. prod.) 1918; *Breed of Men* (also sc., exec. prod.), *The Poppy Girl's Husband* (also dir., exec. prod.), *The Money Corral* (also dir., story ['Somebody's Fool']), *Square Deal Sanderson* (also co-dir. with Lambert Hillyer, exec. prod.), *Wagon Tracks* (also exec. prod.), *John Petticoats* (also exec. prod.) 1919; *The Toll Gate* (also co-sc., story ['By Their Fruits Ye Shall Know Them'], exec. prod.), *Sand* (also exec. prod.), *The Cradle of Courage* (also exec. prod.), *The Testing Block* (also story, exec. prod.) 1920; *O'Malley of the Mounted* (also story, exec. prod.), *The Whistle* (also exec. prod.), *Three World Brand* (also exec. prod.), *White Oak* (also story ['Single Handed'], exec. prod.) 1921; *Travelin' On* (also story ['J.B. the Unbeliever'], exec. prod.) 1922; *Wild Bill Hickok* (title role; also story) 1923; *Singer Jim McKee* (also story, exec. prod.) 1924; *Tumbleweeds* (also exec. prod.) 1925 (reissued in 1939 with sound effects and prologue spoken by Hart).

Hartl, Karl. Director. Born in 1899, in Vienna. He entered Austrian films in 1917 as a cameraman. A director from 1930, he turned out many films of all genres in Austria and Germany. He is best known for *F.P.I.* (1932), a fantastic thriller, from a story by Kurt Siodmak, about the construction of a floating ocean platform for the landing of aircraft, then considered a novel science-fiction notion. The hugely successful film was made in German, French, and English versions with different casts. Steering clear of political themes, Hartl's career continued uninterrupted through the Nazi and postwar eras, ending in the late 50s.

FILMS INCLUDE: *Ein Burschenlied aus Heidelberg* 1930; *Berge in Flammen/The Doomed Battalion* (co-dir., co-sc. with Luis Trenker) 1931; *Die Gräfilm von Monte-Cristo/The Countess of Monte Cristo, F.P.I. antwortet nicht/F.P.I. Doesn't Answer/F.P.I.* 1932; *Gold* 1934; *Zigeunerbaron/The Gypsy Baron* 1935; *Ritt in der Freiheit* 1936; *Der Mann der Sherlock Holmes war/The Man Who Was Sherlock Holmes* 1937; *Wen die Götter lieben/Whom the Gods Love/The Mozart Story* 1942; *Der Engel mit der Posaune/The Angel with the Trumpet* (also sc.) 1948; *Eroica/The Beethoven Story* 1949; *The Wonder Kid/Wonder Boy* (also prod., story; UK) 1951; *Haus des Lebens/House of Life* (also sc.) 1952; *Der Weg in die Vergangenheit/Journey into the Past* 1954; *Reich mir di Hand mein Leben/Mozart/The Life and Loves of Mozart* (also co-sc.) 1955; *Rot ist die Liebe/Love Is Red* (also co-sc.) 1957.

Hartley, Hal. Director, screenwriter. Born in 1960. *ed.* The Massachusetts Institute of Art; SUNY (Purchase, N.Y.). This versatile director-screenwriter is also a film producer and editor. His offbeat approach to each film has given him critical status as an independent filmmaker. He primarily concentrates on oddball characters and situations, combining humor with a rather funky stylishness.

FILMS: *The Unbelievable Truth* (prod., dir., sc., ed.) 1990; *Ambition* (dir. only), *Trust* (dir., sc.) 1991; *Simple Men* (co-prod., ed.) 1992; *Amateur* (sc.) 1994; *Flirt* (dir., sc.) 1995.

Hartley, Mariette. Actress. Born on June 21, 1940, in New York City. *ed.* Carnegie Tech. Elegant, appealing leading lady of the American stage, TV, and scattered films. The granddaughter of psychiatrist John B. Watson, the famous behaviorist, she trained with Eva LE GALLIENNE, and was still a teenager when she began performing on stage with the Shakespeare Festivals of New York and Stratford, Connecticut. She was a seasoned veteran by the time she made her screen debut at 21. But despite leads in a couple of major films and numerous TV appearances, including the 'Peyton Place' (1965) series and an Emmy-winning performance in 'The Incredible Hulk,' the pivotal role in her career proved to be in a series of award-winning Polaroid commercials opposite James GARNER. She wrote a memoir about dealing with an alcoholic parent, *Breaking the Silence* (1990). Married to French producer-director Patrick Boyriven.

FILMS: *Ride the High Country* 1962; *Drums of Africa* 1963; *Marnie* 1964; *Marooned* 1969; *Barquero* 1970; *The Return of Count Yorga* 1971; *Skyjacked, The Magnificent Seven Ride* 1972; *Improper Channels* (Can.) 1981; *O'Hara's Wife* 1983; *1969* 1988; *Encino Man* 1992.

Hartman, Don. Screenwriter, director, producer, songwriter. *b.* Samuel Donald Hartman, Nov. 18, 1900, New York City. *d.* 1958. *ed.* Baylor U. Formerly an actor in repertory and summer stock, he began writing books and lyrics for musical plays and special material for radio and stage performers. He entered films in 1930 as a lyricist and in 1935 switched to screenwriting, specializing in light, comic scripts, often for Hope and Crosby and later Danny Kaye vehicles. From 1947, Hartman was also a producer and director. In 1951 he was put in charge of production at Paramount, a post he left to establish his own company in 1956.

FILMS INCLUDE (as screenwriter): *The Gay Deception, Coronado* 1935; *The Princess Comes Across* 1936; *Champagne Waltz, Waikiki Wedding* (also songs) 1937; *Tropic Holiday* 1938; *Paris Honeymoon, Never Say Die, The Star Maker* 1939; *Road to Singapore* 1940; *Road to Zanzibar, Nothing but the Truth* 1941; *My Favorite Blonde, Road to Morocco* 1942; *True to Life* 1943; *Up in Arms, The Princess and the Pirate* 1944; *Wonder Man* 1945; *The Kid from Brooklyn* 1946; *Down to Earth* (also prod.), *It Had to Be You* (also dir., prod.) 1947; *Every Girl Should Be Married* (also dir., prod.) 1948; *Mr. Imperium* (also dir.) 1951; *It's a Big Country* (co-dir. only) 1952; *Desire Under the Elms* (prod. only), *The Matchmaker* (prod. only) 1958.

Hartman, Elizabeth. Actress. *b.* Dec. 23, 1941, Youngstown, Ohio. *d.* 1987. *ed.* Carnegie Tech. Fragile, high-strung, red-headed leading lady of stage and screen. Usually in sensitive roles. Nominated for an Academy Award for her very first movie role, as a blind woman in *A Patch of Blue* (1965), she went on to appear in several major films. But her early promise was never fulfilled. Increasingly depressed over her declining career, she became a recluse in her Manhattan apartment and eventually an outpatient at a Pittsburgh psychiatric hospital. She died at 45 in a fall from her nearby fifth-floor apartment, an apparent suicide.

FILMS: *A Patch of Blue* 1965; *The Group* 1966; *You're a Big Boy Now* 1967; *The Fixer* 1968; *The Beguiled* 1971; *Walking Tall* 1973; *Full Moon High* 1981; *The Secret of Nimh* (v/o) 1982.

Hartman, Phil. Actor, comedian, screenwriter. Born Sept. 28, 1948, in Ontario, Canada. *ed.* Santa Monica College; California State University, Northridge. Starting out as a graphic designer, he eventually found his true calling as a comedian/actor. Following a long, successful stint on television's 'Saturday Night Live,' where impersonations became his calling card, he moved to another TV show, NBC's 'News Radio,' while maintaining an active feature film career.

FILMS: *Cheech and Chong's Next Movie* 1980; *Weekend Pass* 1984; *Pee-wee's Big Adventure* (also sc.) 1985; *Jumpin' Jack Flash, Last Resort, Three Amigos* 1986; *Amazon Women on the Moon, Blind Date, The Brave Little Toaster* (v/o) 1987; *Fletch Lives, How I Got Into College* 1989; *Quick Change* 1990; *CB4, Coneheads, National Lampoon's Loaded Weapon I, So I Married an Axe Murderer* 1993; *Greedy, The Pagemaster* 1994; *Houseguest* 1995; *Jingle All the Way, Sgt. Bilko* 1996.

Hartmann, Edmund L. Screenwriter. Born on Sept. 24, 1911, in St. Louis. *ed.* Washington U. A former songwriter for the "Ziegfeld Follies," etc., he switched to screenwriting in 1934 and has since written numerous screenplays, alone and in collaboration, mostly adventure and comedy material, often for Abbott and Costello and later Bob Hope. He produced several films in the mid-40s but since the mid-50s has been active mostly in TV. In the 60s he was national chairman of the Writers Guild of America.

FILMS INCLUDE: *Helldorado* 1934; *Without Orders* 1936; *China Passage, Behind the Headlines* 1937; *Law of the Underworld, The Last Warning* 1938; *Big Town Czar* 1939; *Enemy Agent, San Francisco Docks* 1940; *The Feminine Touch* 1941; *Sherlock Holmes and the Secret Weapon* 1943; *Ali Baba and the Forty Thieves, In Society* (also prod.) 1944; *See My Lawyer, The Naughty Nineties* (both also prod.), *Sudan* 1945; *Variety Girl* 1947; *The Paleface* 1948; *Sorrowful Jones* 1949; *Fancy Pants* 1950; *The Lemon Drop Kid* 1951; *The Caddy* 1953; *Casanova's Big Night* 1954; *The Sword of Ali Baba* 1965; *The Shakiest Gun in the West* 1968.

Hartnell, William (Billy). Actor. *b.* Jan. 8, 1908, London. *d.* 1975. A former jockey's apprentice, he made his stage debut in 1924. In films from the early 30s, he played some light leads and many character parts, frequently in tough military or law-enforcement roles but also in amiable parts. He enjoyed a career revival in the 60s as British TV's original Dr. Who.

FILMS INCLUDE: *The Lure* 1933; *Seeing Is Believing* 1934; *Farewell Again* 1937; *Murder Will Out* 1939; *They Came by Night* 1940; *Suspected Person* 1942; *The Way Ahead* 1944; *The Agitator, Murder in Reverse* 1945; *Appointment with Crime* 1946; *Odd Man Out, Temptation Harbor, Brighton Rock/Young Scarface* 1947; *Escape* 1948; *Now Barabbas, The Lost People* 1949; *Double Confession* 1950; *The Magic Box* 1951; *The Holly and the Ivy, The Ringer, The Pickwick Papers* 1952; *Will Any Gentleman?* 1953; *Private's Progress* 1955; *Yangtse Incident/Battle Hell* 1957; *Carry on Sergeant* 1958; *The Mouse That Roared* 1959; *This Sporting Life, Heavens Above!* 1963.

Harvey, Anthony. Director, former film editor. Born on June 3, 1931, in London. Trained as an actor at the Royal Academy of Dramatic Art, he appeared in several stage plays and in the picture *Caesar and Cleopatra* (1945). A film editor since 1949, he worked on many distinguished British productions before turning director in the late 60s. As a director, he impressed with his initial three films but disappointed with his subsequent work.

FILMS INCLUDE: As editor—*Private's Progress* 1956; *Brothers in Law* 1957; *I'm All Right Jack* 1959; *Lolita, The L-Shaped Room* 1962; *Dr. Strangelove* 1963; *The Spy Who Came in from the Cold* 1965; *The Whisperers* 1967. As director (complete)—*Dutchman* (also edit.) 1967; *The Lion in Winter* 1968; *They Might Be Giants* (US) 1971; *The Abdication* 1974; *Players* (US), *Eagle's Wing* 1979; *Richard's Things* 1981; *The Ultimate Solution of Grace Quigley/Grace Quigley* (US) 1984.

Harvey, Laurence. Actor. *b.* Lauruska Mischa Skikne, Oct. 1, 1928, Yomishkis, Lithuania. *d.* 1973. As a child he emigrated with his Jewish parents to South Africa. At 14, lying about his age, he enlisted in the South African navy but was discovered and returned home. At 15 he made his stage debut with the Johannesburg Repertory Theatre. The same year, 1943, he joined the army and served for the duration of WW II. In 1946 he went to England, where he enrolled at the Royal Academy of Dramatic Art. After three months he joined a Manchester repertory company and quickly moved into lead parts. Bright and ambitious, he made his screen debut in 1948 and played his first lead the following year. Meanwhile, he continued his rise on the stage both in London and in New York, scoring a personal triumph in the title part of *Henry V* in the 1958–59 Old Vic tour of the US. At the same time, he became established as a screen star with his perceptive performance as a ruthlessley ambitious young man in the British film *Room at the Top.* He subsequently starred in many top-budget Hollywood productions as well as in important British films. Harvey married and divorced actress Margaret LEIGHTON (1957–61) and Joan Perry Cohn (1968–72), the widow of Columbia's late boss—the first two of three marriages. He died of cancer at 45.

FILMS: In the UK—*House of Darkness* 1948; *Man on the Run, Landfall, The Man from Yesterday* 1949; *Cairo Road, The Black Rose* (US/UK) 1950; *There Is Another Sun, The Scarlet Thread/Wall of Death* 1951; *I Believe in You, A Killer Walks, Women of Twilight* 1952; *Innocents in Paris* 1953; *The Good Die Young, King Richard and the Crusades* (US), *Giulietta e Romeo/Romeo and Juliet* (as Romeo; It./UK) 1954; *I Am a Camera, Storm Over the Nile* 1955; *Three Men in a Boat* 1956; *After the Ball* 1957; *The Truth About Women, The Silent Enemy, Room at the Top* 1958; *Expresso Bongo* 1959. In the US—*The Alamo* (as Col. William Travis), *Butterfield 8* 1960; *Two Loves, Summer and Smoke, The Long and the Short and the Tall/The Jungle Fighters* (UK) 1961; *Walk on the Wild Side, The Wonderful World of the Brothers Grimm* (as Wilhelm Grimm), *The Manchurian Candidate* 1962; *A Girl Named Tamiko, The Running Man* (UK), *The Ceremony* (also prod., dir.; US/Sp.) 1963; *Of Human Bondage* (as Philip Carey; UK), *The Outrage* 1964; *Darling* (UK), *Life at the Top* (UK) 1965; *The Spy with the Cold Nose* (UK) 1966; *A Dandy in Aspic* (completed direction of film, uncredited, after Anthony Mann's death; UK), *Kampf um Rom* (Ger./It./Fr.) 1968; *L'Assoluto Naturale* (also prod.; It.), *The Magic Christian* (as Hamlet; UK) 1969; *WUSA* 1970; *Escape to the Sun* (Isr.) 1972; *Night Watch* 1973; *Welcome to Arrow Beach/Tender Flesh* (also dir.) 1974.

Harvey, Lilian. Actress. *b.* Helene Lilian Muriel Pape, Jan. 19, 1906, Edmonton, England. *d.* 1968. When she was eight, her British parents moved to Berlin. Soon after, WW I broke out and she was sent to Switzerland for safety. Returning to Germany, she studied ballet and when she reached 17 made her debut in a musical in Vienna. A lovely, lively blonde with energy to spare, she began appearing in films in 1925 and soon became the most popular star of her day in the screen operetta genre. Frequently teaming with Willy FRITSCH, she reached a career peak in the early 30s in such internationally successful musicals as *Die Drei von der Tankstelle* and *Der Kongess tanzt/The Congress Dances.* In 1933 she went to Hollywood, where she starred in a number of films, none of which were too successful. She returned to Los Angeles during WW II, this time no longer a movie star, and found employment as a nurse. After the war she lived in retirement on the French Riviera but returned to the German stage in the 60s.

FILMS INCLUDE: *Der Fluch* (Aus.), *Liebe und Trompetenblasen* 1925; *Prinzessin Tralala* 1926; *Die tolle Lola* 1927; *Du sollst nicht stehlen/The Love Commandment, Eine Nacht in London* (and UK version, *A Knight in London*) 1928; *Hokuspokus/Hocuspocus* (and UK version, *Temporary Widow*), *Die Drei von der Tankstelle* (German- and French-language versions), *Liebeswalzer* (and English-language version, *The Love Waltz*) 1930; *Nie wieder Liebe* (German- and French-language versions), *Der Kongress tanzt* (and English-language version, *The Congress Dances,* and French-language version, *Le Congres s'amuse*) 1931; *Quick* (German- and French-language versions), *Ein blonder Traum/A Blonde Dream* (German-, English-, and French-language versions) 1932; *Ich und die Kaiserin* (and UK version, *The Only Girl/Heart Song), My Weakness* (US), *My Lips Betray* (US) 1933; *I Am Suzanne* (US) 1934; *Let's Live Tonight* (US), *Schwarze Rosen* (German- and French-language versions), *Glückskinder* 1935; *Sieben Ohrfeigen, Invitation to the Waltz* (UK) 1937; *Capriccio, Castelli in Aria/Ins blaue Leben* (It./Ger.) 1938; *Sérénade/ Schubert's Serenade* (Fr.), *Miquette et sa Mère/Miquette* (Fr.) 1940; *Herrliche Zeiten* 1950; *Da kommt nicht wieder* 1960.

Harwood, Ronald. Screenwriter, playwright. Born on Nov. 9, 1934, in Capetown, South Africa. Trained at London's Royal Academy of Dramatic Art, he gave up acting to become the devoted dresser of imperious Shakespearean actor Donald WOLFIT, an experience he would commemorate in his brilliant 1980 play 'The Dresser.' A screenwriter since the early 60s, Harwood was nominated for an Academy Award for his 1983 screen adaptation of that play. He was portrayed in the film by Tom COURTENAY.

FILMS INCLUDE: *Private Potter* (from his own teleplay) 1962; *High Wind in Jamaica* 1965; *Drop Dead, Darling/ Arrivederci, Baby!* 1966; *Diamonds for Breakfast* 1968; *Eyewitness/Sudden Terror* 1970; *One Day in the Life of Ivan Denisovich* 1971; *Operation Daybreak/Price of Freedom* 1976; *The Dresser* (from his own play) 1983; *The Doctor and the Devils* 1985; *Cry the Beloved Country* 1995.

Has, Wojciech. Director. Born on April 1, 1925, in Krakow, Poland. A graduate of the Krakow Film Institute and of a school of fine arts, he made his debut as a director of shorts with *Harmonica,* in 1948. During the next decade he turned out many short and medium-length fiction, documentary, and scientific films. He scored an immediate success with his first feature, *The Noose* (1958), an adaptation of Marek Hlasko's story about a day in the life of an alcoholic. Has gradually taken his place among Poland's leading film directors although he adhered to no particular contemporary school and followed his own course in selecting his themes and developing his style. His films are often evocative and nostalgic and have often dealt with an individual's "Odyssey" through a stretch of time. Has's early productions were intimate but from the mid-60s he has tackled large-scale themes of near-epic proportions, usually deriving from periods of the past. His best-known film in the West remains *The Saragossa Manuscript* (1964), a dreamlike, complex story-within-a-story visual labyrinth adapted from an 1804 novel. His most ambitious work to date is, however, *The Sandglass* (1973), an imaginative, stream-of-consciousness film dealing with memory and the immortality of the spirit of man. In 1981 he was appointed director of the Leon Schiller Lodz Film School.

FEATURE FILMS: *The Noose* (also co-sc.) 1958; *Farewells/Lydia Ate the Apple* (also co-sc.) 1959; *One-Room Tenants* (also sc.) 1960; *Goodbye to the Past* 1961; *Gold/Golden Dreams* 1962; *How to Be Loved* 1963; *The Saragossa Manuscript* 1964; *The Code* 1966; *The Doll* (also sc.) 1968; *The Sandglass/The Hourglass Sanatorium* (also sc.) 1973.

Hasegawa, Kazuo. Actor. *b.* Feb. 27, 1908, Kyoto, Japan. *d.* 1984. One of the most popular performers of the Japanese stage and a former Kabuki star, he appeared in hundreds of films from 1927, typically as a warrior hero. His popularity was so great and market value so high that when, in 1937, he left one studio for another, he was attacked by a hired thug with a knife allegedly at the instigation of his infuriated former employer. He retired from the screen in the early 60s, but continued performing on stage.

FILMS INCLUDE: *Childish Sword Master* 1927; *Before Dawn* 1931; *Loyal Forty-seven Ronin* 1932; *Yukinojo's Disguise* 1936; *Song of the White Orchid* 1939; *Fire Bird* 1948; *A Tale of Genji* 1951; *Saga of the Great Buddha* 1952; *Gate of Hell* 1953; *Chikimatsu Monogatari/The Crucified Lovers* 1954; *A Fantastic Tale of Naruto* 1957; *Utamaro Painter of Women* 1959; *The Last Betrayal* 1960; *Clear Weather* 1961; *The Great Wall* 1962; *An Actor's Revenge/The Revenge of Okenojo* 1963.

Haskin, Byron. Director, director of photography, special effects artist. *b.* Apr. 22, 1899, Portland, Ore. *d.* 1984. The descendant of a family line that traces back to pre-Revolutionary America, he moved with his family to San Francisco as a child. He attended the University of California at Berkeley for three years before enlisting as a naval aviation cadet during WW I. On demobilization, he worked briefly as a newspaper cartoonist and advertising man before entering films as a newsreel cameraman in 1918. The following year he went to Hollywood and entered the industry as an assistant cameraman and assistant director. As director of photography from 1922, he was behind the camera on several John Barrymorre pictures late in the silent period. In 1927–28 he was assigned to direct four films, but then resumed his work as a cinematographer. In 1929 he went to England, where he spent three years as a production executive and technical advisor to Herbert Wilcox. Back in Hollywood, he joined the special effects department of Warner Bros. In 1937 he succeeded Fred Jackman as the department's head, a position he held until 1945. In 1938 Haskin and his group were awarded a special Oscar for the development and first application of the triple head background projector. He was subsequently nominated for Academy Awards for the special effects for four films. In 1945 he followed Hal WALLIS to Paramount, where he resumed his career as a director. In that capacity, he worked in a variety of genres, from *film noir* to Westerns, but was most admired for his lively science-fiction and adventure yarns.

FILMS INCLUDE: As director of photography—*The World's a Stage* 1922; *Slander the Woman* 1923; *Bobbed Hair, On Thin Ice* 1925; *Across the Pacific, Don Juan, The Sea Beast* 1926; *When a Man Loves* 1927; *The Singing Fool* 1928; *The Glad Rag Doll* 1929; *The Guilty Generation* 1931; *Black Fury* 1935; *Stage Struck* 1936; *Green Light* 1937. As special effects artist—*A Midsummer Night's Dream* 1935; *Submarine D–1, Slim* 1937; *The Private Lives of Elizabeth and Essex, Dodge City, The Roaring Twenties, We Are Not Alone* 1939; *The Fighting 69th, A Dispatch from Reuters, Brother Orchid, The Santa Fe Trail, The Sea Hawk, They Drive by Night* 1940; *City for Conquest, Dive Bomber, The Great Lie, High Sierra, The Sea Wolf* 1941; *Across the Pacific* 1942; *Arsenic and Old Lace, Passage to Marseilles* 1944. As director (complete)—*Matinee Ladies, Irish Hearts, Ginsberg the Great* 1927; *The Siren* 1928; *I Walk Alone* 1947; *Man Eater of Kumaon* 1948; *Too Late for Tears* 1949; *Treasure Island* (US/UK) 1950; *Tarzan's Peril, Warpath, Silver City* 1951; *The Denver and Rio Grande* 1952; *The War of the Worlds, His Majesty O'Keefe* 1953; *The Naked Jungle* 1954; *Long John Silver, Conquest of Space* 1955; *The First Texan, The Boss* 1956; *From the Earth to the Moon* 1958; *The Little Savage* 1959; *Jet Over the Atlantic, September Storm* 1960; *Armored Command* 1961; *Captain Sinbad* 1963; *Robinson Crusoe on Mars* 1964; *The Power* 1968.

Hasse, O. E. Actor. *b.* Otto Eduard Hasse, July 11, 1903, Obersitzka (Posen), Germany. *d.* 1978. Impressive character player of stage and screen whose commanding presence and typically Teutonic features figured prominently in many German and international productions. The holder of a law degree, he received his stage training under Max Reinhardt and established his reputation at Munich's Kammerspiele and Berlin's Deutsches Theater. On screen from the early 30s, he established an international reputation after WW II.

FILMS INCLUDE: *Peter Voss—der Milionendieb* 1932; *Fräulein Hoffmanns Erzählungen* 1933; *Peer Gynt* 1934; *Ein ganzer Kerl* 1935; *Illusion* 1941; *Dr. Crippen an Bord, Rembrandt* 1942; *Philharmoniker* 1944; *Berliner Ballade/The Berliner* 1948; *The Big Lift* (US), *Epilog* 1950; *Decision Before Dawn* (US) 1951; *I Confess* (US), *Der letzte Walzer/The Last Waltz* 1953; *Betrayed* (US), *Canaris/Deadly Decision* (as Admiral Canaris) 1954; *Alibi, Above Us the Waves* (UK) 1955; *Les Aventures d'Arsène Lupin* (Fr.), *Sait-on jamais?/No Sun in Venice* (Fr.), *Les Espions* (Fr.), *Der gläserne Turm/The Glass Tower* 1957; *Der Arzt von Stalingrad* 1958; *Le Caporal epinglé/The Elusive Corporal* (Fr.) 1962; *Le Vice et la Vertu/Vice and Virtue* (Fr./It.) 1963; *Die Todesstrahlen des Dr. Mabuse* 1964; *Trois Chambres à Manhattan* (Fr.) 1965; *Etat de Siège/State of Siege* (Fr./It.) 1973.

Hassett, Marilyn. Actress. Born on Dec. 17, 1947, in Los Angeles. Sincere leading lady of Hollywood films of the 70s. She received good notices for her portrayal of paralyzed Olympics-bound skier Jill Kinmont in *The Other Side of Midnight* (1975) and a sequel, but her potential starring career never materialized.

FILMS: *They Shoot Horses Don't They?* 1972; *The Other Side of the Mountain* 1975; *The Shadow of the Hawk* (Can.), *Two-Minute Warning* 1976; *The Other Side of the Mountain: Part 2* 1978; *The Bell Jar* 1979; *Massive Retaliation* 1984; *Messenger of Death* 1988; *Twenty Dollar Star* 1991.

Hasso, Signe. Actress. Born Signe Larsson on Aug. 15, 1910, in Stockholm. On the Swedish stage from her teens, she starred in Swedish films of the 30s, then played strong-willed leading ladies in Hollywood films of the 40s. She was later active on stage and screen in both the US and Europe. A capable actress of cool, strong personality, she has also made many appearances on American TV and has written lyrics for Swedish songs.

FILMS INCLUDE: In Sweden—*House of Silence* 1933; *Witches' Night* 1937; *Career, Geld fällt vom Himmel* (Ger./Sw.) 1938; *Us Two* 1939; *Steel* 1940. In the US—*Journey for Margaret* 1942; *Assignment in Brittany, Heaven Can Wait* 1943; *The Story of Dr. Wassell, The Seventh Cross* 1944; *Dangerous Partners, Johnny Angel, The House on 92nd Street* 1945; *Strange Triangle, A Scandal in Paris* 1946; *Where There's Life* 1947; *To the Ends of the Earth, A Double Life* 1948; *This Can't Happen Here/High Tension* (Sw.), *Outside the Wall, Crisis* 1950; *Maria Johanna* (Sw.) 1953; *Taxi 13* (Ger./Sw.) 1954; *The True and the False* 1955; *Picture Mommy Dead* 1966; *The Black Bird* 1975; *I Never Promised You a Rose Garden* 1977.

Hatcher, Teri. Actress. Born December 8, 1964, in Sunnyvale, Calif. *ed.* De Anza College; American Conservatory Theatre. Slim, lovely leading lady of television and films. Known primarily for her TV role as Lois Lane in ABC's 'Lois and Clark,' she spent a number of her early years working in sitcoms until her star rose with a succession of feature films, namely her acclaimed performance in *Heaven's Prisoners* (1996).

FILMS: *The Big Picture, Tango and Cash* 1989; *Soapdish* 1991; *Straight Talk* 1992; *Heaven's Prisoners* 1996.

Hatfield, Hurd. Actor. Born William Rukard Hurd Hatfield, on Dec. 7, 1918, in New York City. *ed.* Columbia. He won a scholarship to the Chekhov Drama School in Devonshire, England, and made his professional debut on the London stage. He later appeared on Broadway and made his first film appearance in 1944. Darkly handsome, he seemed to be headed for screen stardom after playing the title role in *The Picture of Dorian Gray* (1945), but somehow his film career never took off. He continued appearing intermittently in films, but his best roles have been on the stage.

FILMS: *Dragon Seed* 1944; *The Picture of Dorian Gray* (title role) 1945; *Diary of a Chambermaid* 1946; *The Beginning or the End, The Unsuspected* 1947; *The Checkered Coat, Joan of Arc* 1948; *Chinatown at Midnight* 1949; *Tarzan and the Slave Girl, Destination Murder* 1950; *The Left-Handed Gun* 1958; *El Cid, King of Kings* (as Pontius Pilate) 1961; *Mickey One, Harlow* (as Paul Bern, in Carol Lynley version) 1965; *The Boston Strangler* 1968; *Von Richthofen and Brown* 1971; *King David* 1985; *Crimes of the Heart* 1986; *Her Alibi* 1989.

Hathaway, Henry. Director. *b.* Henri Leopold de Fiennes, Mar. 13, 1898, Sacramento, Calif. *d.* 1985. The son of an actress and a stage manager, and grandson of a Belgian marquis who settled in San Francisco after failing to acquire the Sandwich Islands for his king, he entered films at ten as a child actor in Western shorts of the American Film Company, appearing frequently in the early films of Allan Dwan. After a stint as property boy for Universal, he returned to film acting in juvenile roles. Following military service (1918–19) he became an assistant director. His many years of experience in front of and behind the camera proved useful when he was given his chance to direct in 1932. Beginning with a series of low-budget Westerns starring Randolph Scott, he was an established director of prestige pictures by 1936. At first with Paramount and later with Fox, he gained the reputation of being a skilled craftsman who handled his material straightforwardly with few complications or pretensions. He was known as a studio workhorse who made the most of his assignments, and was within budget and on schedule. When working with quality scripts, he created superior productions, such as *The Lives of a Bengal Lancer, Kiss of Death,* and *Desert Fox.* Even his pedestrian films were usually well crafted and entertaining. In the mid-40s—with films like *The House on 92nd Street, 13 Rue Madeleine,* and *Call Northside 777*—he pioneered the postwar trend of shooting features on actual exterior locations in a semidocumentary style. He worked proficiently in a variety of genres, but was at his best with action footage, particularly Westerns and crime dramas. Occasionally also his own producer, Hathaway was the consummate Hollywood professional.

FILMS: *Heritage of the Desert, Wild Horse Mesa* 1932; *Under the Tonto Rim, Sunset Pass, Man of the Forest, To the Last Man, The Thundering Herd* 1933; *The Last Round-Up, Come on Marines!, The Witching Hour, Now and Forever* 1934; *The Lives of a Bengal Lancer, Peter Ibbetson* 1935; *The Trail of the Lonesome Pine, Go West Young Man* 1936; *Souls at Sea* (also prod.) 1937; *Spawn of the North* 1938; *The Real Glory* 1939; *Johnny Apollo, Brigham Young Frontiersman* 1940; *The Shepherd of the Hills, Sundown* 1941; *Ten Gentlemen from West Point* 1942; *China Girl* 1943; *Home in Indiana, Wing and a Prayer* 1944; *Nob Hill, The House on 92nd Street* 1945; *The Dark Corner* 1946; *13 Rue Madeleine, Kiss of Death* 1947; *Call Northside 777* 1948; *Down to the Sea in Ships* 1949; *The Black Rose* (US/UK) 1950; *You're in the Navy Now/USS Teakettle, Fourteen Hours, Rawhide, The Desert Fox* 1951; *Red Skies of Montana* (dir. some scenes, uncredited), *Diplomatic Courier, O Henry's Full House* ("The Clarion Call" episode) 1952; *Niagara, White Witch Doctor* 1953; *Prince Valiant, Garden of Evil* 1954; *The Racers* 1955; *The Bottom of the Bottle, 23 Paces to Baker Street* 1956; *The Wayward Bus* (directed part, uncredited), *Legend of the Lost* (also prod.) 1957; *From Hell to Texas* 1958; *Woman Obsessed* 1959; *Seven Thieves, North to Alaska* (also prod.) 1960; *How the West Was Won* ("The Rivers," "The Plains," "The Outlaws" episodes) 1962; *Rampage* (dir. some scenes, uncredited) 1963; *Of Human Bondage* (started, uncredited), *Circus World* 1964; *The Sons of Katie Elder* 1965; *Nevada Smith* (also prod.) 1966; *The Last Safari* 1967; *Five Card Stud* 1968; *True Grit* 1969; *Airport* (temporarily replaced ailing George Seaton, uncredited) 1970; *Raid on Rommel, Shootout* 1971; *Hangup/Superdude* 1974.

Hatton, Raymond. Actor. *b.* July 7, 1887, Red Oak, Iowa. *d.* 1971. In vaudeville and stock from age 12, he began appearing in films in 1912, usually in villainous or comic character roles. He was featured prominently in many C. B. De Mille silents. In the mid- to late 20s he costarred with Wallace BEERY in a series of slambang Paramount comedies. In the 30s he began playing the comic sidekick of Johnny Mack BROWN, Buck JONES, and other Western stars. In all, he appeared in hundreds of films.

FILMS INCLUDE: *The Circus Man* 1914; *The Girl of the Golden West, The Warrens of Virginia, The Unafraid, The Wild Goose Chase, The Arab, Chimmie Fadden, The Kindling, Armstrong's Wife* 1915; *The Golden Chance, Temptation, Oliver Twist* (as the Artful Dodger) 1916; *Joan the Woman* (as King Charles VII of France), *Romance of the Redwoods, The Little American, The Woman God Forgot* (as Montezuma) 1917; *We Can't Have Everything, The Source, The Firefly of France, The American Consul* 1918; *For Better for Worse, You're Fired, The Love Burglar, Male and Female, Everywoman* 1919; *The Dancin' Fool, The Sea Wolf, Jes' Call Me Jim* 1920; *The Concert, Salvage, Peck's Bad Boy, The Affairs of Anatol, The Ace of Hearts, Doubling for Romeo* 1921; *His Back Against the Wall, Manslaughter, Pink Gods, To Have and to Hold, Ebb Tide, The Hottentot* 1922; *Java Head, Three Wise Fools, The Hunchback of Notre Dame* (as Pierre Gringoire), *The Virginian, Big Brother* 1923; *Triumph, Cornered, The Mine with the Iron Door* 1924; *Contraband, The Devil's Cargo, The Thundering Herd, Adventure, A Son of His Father, Lord Jim* (as Cornelius) 1925; *Behind the Front, Silence, Born to the West, We're in the Navy Now* 1926; *Fashions for Women, Fireman Save My Child, Now We're in The Air* 1927; *Wife Savers, Partners in Crime, The Big Killing* 1928; *The Office Scandal, Trent's Last Case, The Mighty, Her Unborn Child* (co-sc. only) 1929; *Hell's Heroes, Murder on the Roof, Road to Paradise, The Silver Horde* 1930; *Woman Hungry, The Squaw Man* 1931; *Polly of the Circus, Uptown New York* 1932; *Terror Trail, Penthouse, Alice in Wonderland* (as the Mouse), *Lady Killer* 1933; *Rustlers of Red Gap* (serial), *G-Men, Steamboat 'Round the Bend* 1935; *Jungle Jim* (serial), *Exclusive Story* 1936; *Marked Woman, Roaring Timber, Torchy Blane* 1937; *Love Finds Andy Hardy, The Texans* 1938; *Paris Honeymoon, 6000 Enemies, Career* 1939; *Kit Carson* 1940; *The Ghost Rider* 1943; *Tall in the Saddle* 1944; *Gun Smoke* 1945; *Black Gold* 1947; *Frontier Agent* 1948; *Fast on the Draw* 1950; *The Golden Hawk* 1952; *Motorcycle Gang* 1957; *The Quick Gun* 1964; *Requiem for a Gunfighter* 1965; *In Cold Blood* 1967.

Hatton, Rondo. Actor. *b.* Apr., 22, 1894, Hagerstown, Md. *d.* 1946. Horrific character player of Hollywood films. Of normal birth, he was a handsome youth, but later became deformed by acromegaly. He developed monstrous bodily and facial features, which were exploited by producers for gruesome shock effect. In the year of his death of a heart attack, he played the title role in *The Brute Man,* a film inspired by the actor's own tragic story.

FILMS INCLUDE: *Hell Harbor* 1930; *In Old Chicago* 1938; *The Hunchback of Notre Dame* 1939; *Chad Hanna* 1940; *The Moon and Sixpence* 1942; *The Ox-Bow Incident* 1943; *The Pearl of Death, The Princess and the Pirate* 1944; *Jungle*

Captive 1945; *The Spider Woman Strikes Back, House of Horrors, The Brute Man* 1946.

Hauer, Rutger. Actor. Born on Jan. 23, 1944, in Breukelen, The Netherlands. Forceful, charismatic, blond, blue-eyed leading man of Dutch and international films. A six-year veteran of the Amsterdam stage, he made his screen debut in 1973 and before long developed into his country's top star, known as the "Dutch Paul Newman." A solid performance in Paul VERHOEVEN's *Soldier of Orange* (1977) paved his way to Hollywood films and a memorable incarnation of unearthly evil in both Ridley SCOTT's *Blade Runner* (1982) and *The Hitcher* (1986).

FILMS INCLUDE: *Turks Fruit/Turkish Delight* 1973; *Hard to Remember* 1974; *The Wilby Conspiracy, Keetje Tippel* 1975; *Max Havelaar* 1976; *Soldier of Orange* 1977; *Spetters* 1980; *Nighthawks, Chanel Solitaire* (UK/Fr.) 1981; *Blade Runner* 1982; *Eureka* (UK), *The Osterman Weekend* 1983; *A Breed Apart* 1984; *Ladyhawke, Flesh and Blood* 1985; *The Hitcher* 1986; *Wanted Dead or Alive* 1987; *Bloodhounds of Broadway, The Salute of the Jugger* (Austral.) 1989; *Blind Fury* 1990; *Ocean Point, On a Moonlit Night* 1991; *Split Second, Buffy the Vampire Slayer, Past Midnight* 1992; *The Beans of Egypt, Maine, Nostradamus, Surviving the Game* 1994.

Havelock-Allan, Anthony. Producer. Born on Feb. 28, 1905, in Darlington, England, into the British peerage. He entered films in 1933 and after working in the industry in various capacities produced his first picture in 1938. The many films he produced or co-produced in the following three decades included a number of distinguished British motion pictures, notably several directed by David LEAN. Formerly married to actresses Valerie HOBSON and Marguerite CHAPMAN.

FILMS INCLUDE: *This Man Is News* 1938; *The Lambeth Walk, The Silent Battle/Continental Express* 1939; *From the Four Corners* (doc.; also dir.) 1941; *In Which We Serve* (assoc. prod.) 1942; *This Happy Breed* (assoc. prod.; also co-adapt.) 1944; *Blithe Spirit* (assoc. prod.; also co-adapt.), *Brief Encounter* (co-exec. prod.; also co-sc.) 1945; *Great Expectations* (exec. prod.; also co-sc.) 1946; *Blanche Fury, Take My Life* 1947; *Oliver Twist* (exec. prod.) 1948; *Interrupted Journey* 1949; *Never Take No for an Answer* 1951; *Meet Me Tonight/Tonight at 8:30* 1952; *The Young Lovers* 1954; *Orders to Kill* 1958; *The Quare Fellow* 1962; *An Evening with the Royal Ballet* (also co-dir.) 1963; *Othello* 1966; *The Mikado* 1967; *Up the Junction, Romeo and Juliet* 1968; *Ryan's Daughter* 1970.

Haver, June. Actress. Born June Stovenour, on June 10, 1926, in Rock Island, Ill. On stage from age six, she sang and played the piano on radio and with various bands and appeared in a couple of musical shorts before her feature film debut in 1943. Groomed by Fox to succeed Betty GRABLE, she starred in musicals of the 40s without attaining the latter's popularity. In 1953 she announced her retirement and soon after entered a convent as a nun. Several months later she left the convent, married actor Fred MACMURRAY, and has since lived in retirement on their San Fernando Valley ranch.

FEATURE FILMS: *The Gang's All Here* 1943; *Home in Indiana, Irish Eyes Are Smiling* 1944; *Where Do We Go from Here?, The Dolly Sisters* 1945; *Three Little Girls in Blue, Wake Up and Dream* 1946; *I Wonder Who's Kissing Her Now* 1947; *Scudda-Hoo! Scudda-Hay!* 1948; *Oh You Beautiful Doll!, Look for the Silver Lining* 1949; *The Daughter of Rosie O'Grady, I'll Get By* 1950; *Love Nest* 1951; *The Girl Next Door* 1953.

Haver, Phyllis. Actress. *b.* Phyllis O'Haver, Jan. 6, 1899, Douglas, Kans. *d.* 1960. After graduating from high school, she became a pianist in a silent movie theater and, shortly after, broke into films as a Mack Sennett bathing beauty. A tall, vivacious blonde, she was elevated to leading lady within months and soon became one of Hollywood's most popular sex queens. She starred in many silent productions, notably as a thieving temptress in *The Way of All Flesh,* as murder suspect Roxie Hart in *Chicago* (both 1927), and as a vampish gold digger in D. W. Griffith's *The Battle of the Sexes* (1928). She retired from the screen in 1929 to marry a Manhattan millionaire. They divorced 16 years later, but she never returned to films. She died at 61 in her Connecticut home of barbiturate poisoning. It was ruled a suicide.

FILMS INCLUDE: (features complete): *A Bedroom Blunder, The Pullman Bride* (shorts) 1917; *Ladies First* (short) 1918; *The Foolish Age, Hearts and Flowers, Yankee Doodle in Berlin* (shorts) 1919; *Love Honor and Behave, Married Life* 1920; *A Small Town Idol, Home Talent* 1921; *The Christian, The Bolted Door, The Common Law, The Temple of Venus* 1923; *Lilies of the Field, The Fighting Coward, Singer Jim McKee, The Perfect Flapper, Single Wives, The Midnight Express, The Foolish Virgin, The Breath of Scandal, The Snob, One Glorious Night* 1924; *So Big, Her Husband's Secret, I Want My Man, After Business Hours, Rugged Water, The Golden Princess, New Brooms, A Fight to the Finish* 1925; *The Cave Man, Other Women's Husbands, Hard Boiled, Up in Mabel's Room, Don Juan, Three Bad Men, Fig Leaves, The Nervous Wreck, What Price Glory* 1926; *Nobody's Widow, No Control, The Little Adventuress, The Way of All Flesh, The Rejuvenation of Aunt Mary, The Fighting Eagle, Chicago, Your Wife and Mine, The Wise Wife* 1927; *Tenth Avenue, The Battle of the Sexes* 1928; *Sal of Singapore, The Shady Lady, The Office Scandal, Thunder* 1929.

Havers, Nigel. Actor. Born on Nov. 6, 1949, in London. *ed.* Leicester U. Charming, patrician leading man and second lead of British stage, TV, and films. The descendant of a five-century line of attorneys and judges, and the son of Britain's Solicitor General (now Lord Chancellor), he broke away from family tradition and trained for the stage at London's Arts Educational Trust. He first attracted international attention as one of the heroes of *Chariots of Fire* (1981). He enjoyed some success in 'Upstairs, Downstairs' and other British TV series and made his mark on the stage playing the title role in the mammoth production of 'Nicholas Nickleby.' He has also made numerous recordings of books for the blind.

FILMS INCLUDE: *Pope Joan* 1972; *Full Circle/The Haunting of Julia* 1976; *Who Is Killing the Great Chefs of Europe?* (US/Ger.) 1978; *Chariots of Fire* 1981; *A Passage to India* 1984; *Burke and Wills* (Austral.) 1986; *The Whistle Blower, Empire of the Sun* (US) 1987; *Farewell to the King* (US) 1989; *Quiet Days in Clichy* (Fr./It./Ger.) 1990.

Havoc, June. Actress. Born Ellen Evangeline Hovick, on Nov. 8, 1916, in Seattle, Wash. The younger sister of Gypsy Rose LEE, she too was driven by their ambitious stage mother and made her professional debut at the age of two, playing bits in silent film shorts. By age five she was a headliner in vaudeville, earning $1,500 a week. She married the first of three husbands at 13. In the early 30s, during the Depression and the demise of vaudeville, she worked as a model and participated in dance marathons. (She recalled that period of her life in her autobiography, *Early Havoc* [1959], and in the Broadway play 'Marathon '33' [1963], which she wrote and directed.) She later performed in Catskill Mountains resorts and appeared in stock before her Broadway debut in 1936. Her success in the 1940 production of 'Pal Joey' resulted in a Hollywood invitation. But despite solid performances as a leading lady or second lead in a number of films, the blonde, blue-eyed actress never became a top screen star and was cast mainly in routine productions. She had more success in her repeated appearances on the stage (she won a Donaldson Award for 'Mexican Hayride' in 1944) and later also on TV. She married TV and sometime film director William Spier. In 1985 she appeared on the London stage with a one-woman show, 'An Unexpected Evening with June Havoc.' She later toured England with a play.

FEATURE FILMS: *Four Jacks and a Jill* 1941; *Sing Your Worries Away, Powder Town, My Sister Eileen* 1942; *Hello Frisco Hello, Hi Diddle Diddle, No Time for Love* 1943; *Timber Queen, Casanova in Burlesque, Sweet and Low Down* 1944; *Brewster's Millions* 1945; *Gentleman's Agreement, Intrigue* 1947; *The Iron Curtain, When My Baby Smiles at Me* 1948; *Red Hot and Blue, Chicago Deadline, The Story of Molly X* 1949; *Mother Didn't Tell Me, Once a Thief* 1950; *Follow the Sun* 1951; *Lady Possessed* 1952; *Three for Jamie Dawn* 1956; *The Private Files of J. Edgar Hoover* 1977; *Can't Stop the Music* 1980; *Return to Salem's Lot* 1987.

Hawke, Ethan. Actor. Born on Nov. 6, 1970 in Austin, Tex. *ed.* NYU. Boyish lead. After training at Carnegie Mellon U. and the British Theatre Association, he debuted in Hollywood in 1985 and gained wide exposure in the prep-school drama *Dead Poets Society*.

FILMS INCLUDE: *Explorers* 1985; *Dead Poets Society, Dad* 1989; *White Fang, Mystery Date, A Midnight Clear* 1991; *Waterland, Alive* 1992; *Quiz Show* (cameo), *Reality Bites, White Fang II* 1994; *Before Sunrise, Search and Destroy* 1995; *The Eighth Day* 1997.

Hawkins, Jack. Actor. *b.* Sept. 1, 1910, London. *d.* 1973. On stage from age 13 and in British films from 1930, he developed into one of England's strongest screen personalities in both leads and character roles. He typically portrayed tough men of decision and action, both in and out of uniform. He was one of the busiest and most sought-after character actors around when he lost his voice in 1966 following an operation for cancer of the larynx. However, he continued appearing in films, with his speaking parts dubbed by others, until his death. His first wife was Jessica TANDY.

FILMS: *Birds of Prey/The Perfect Alibi* 1930; *The Lodger/Phantom Fiend* 1932; *The Good Companions, The Lost Chord, I Lived with You, The Jewel, A Shot in the Dark* 1933; *Autumn Crocus, Death at Broadcasting House* 1934; *Peg of Old Drury* 1935; *Beauty and the Barge, The Frog* 1937; *Who Goes Next?, A Royal Divorce* 1938; *Murder Will Out* 1939; *The Flying Squad* 1940; *Next of Kin* 1942; *The Fallen Idol, Bonnie Prince Charlie, The Small Back Room* 1948; *State Secret, The Black Rose* (US/UK), *The Elusive Pimpernel/The Fighting Pimpernel* 1950; *The Adventurers/The Great Adventure, No Highway/No Highway in the Sky* (UK/US), *Home at Seven/Murder on Monday* 1951; *Angels One Five, Mandy/The Story of Mandy/ Crash of Silence, The Planter's Wife/Outpost in Malaya* 1952; *The Cruel Sea, Twice Upon a Time, Malta Story, The Intruder* 1953; *Front Page Story, The Seekers/Land of Fury* 1954; *Land of the Pharaohs* (as the Pharaoh; US), *The Prisoner, Touch and Go* 1955; *The Long Arm/The Third Key, Man in the Sky* 1956; *Fortune Is a Woman, The Bridge on the River Kwai* 1957; *Gideon's Day/Gideon of Scotland Yard, The Two-Headed Spy* 1958; *Ben-Hur* (as Quintus Arrius; US) 1959; *The League of Gentlemen* 1960; *Two Loves* (US) 1961; *Lafayette* (as Gen. Cornwallis; Fr./It.), *Five Finger Exercise* (US), *Lawrence of Arabia* (as Gen. Allenby) 1962; *Rampage* (US) 1963; *Zulu, The Third Secret, Guns at Batasi* 1964; *Lord Jim* (as Marlow; UK/US), *Masquerade, The Party's Over* (co-exec. prod. only), *Judith* (US/Isr.) 1965; *The Poppy Is Also a Flower* (US) 1966; *Great Catherine, Shalako* 1968; *Oh! What a Lovely War* (as Emperor Franz Josef), *Monte Carlo or Bust!/Those Daring Young Men in Their Jaunty Jalopies* (UK/Fr./It.) 1969; *Waterloo* (It./USSR), *Jane Eyre, Twinky/Lola* (UK/It.), *The Adventures of Gerard* 1970; *When Eight Bells Toll, Kidnapped* (as Captain Hoseason), *Nicholas and Alexandra* 1971; *The Ruling Class* (co-prod. only), *Young Winston, Escape to the Sun* (Isr.) 1972; *The Last Lion, Theatre of Blood, Tales That Witness Murder* 1973.

Hawks, Howard. Director, screenwriter, producer. *b.* May 30, 1896, Goshen, Ind. *d.* 1977. Having moved to California with his family at age ten, he attended school at Pasadena and studied at the Philips-Exeter Academy in Massachusetts. He studied mechanical engineering at Cornell and during summer vacations worked in the property department of Famous Players-Lasky studios in Hollywood. A professional car and plane racer from age 16, he served as a pilot with the Army Air Corps during WW I and after his discharge worked in an aircraft factory, designing and flying planes. He decided, however, that he liked the movie business better and returned to Hollywood, working first as a cutter, then assistant director, story editor, and casting director. In 1922 he wrote and directed two comedy shorts, which he financed himself, and the following year he produced and wrote the screenplay for Jack Conway's feature *Quicksands.* After writing another screenplay, for *Tiger Love* (1924), and a couple of screen stories for Paramount films, Hawks sold a story, *The Road to Glory,* to Fox, in 1925, on the condition that he be assigned to direct it. He was. Thus began one of the longest, most versatile, and most professional directorial careers in American films.

In a period that spanned four and a half decades, Hawks tackled every possible film genre with equal facility—from screwball comedy (*Bringing Up Baby, Ball of Fire*) and musicals (*Gentlemen Prefer Blondes*) to gangster films (*Scarface*), private-eye thrillers (*The Big Sleep*), and Westerns (*Red River, Rio Bravo*), among others. Hawks was not an innovator. He did not establish his reputation by starting trends or originating styles (except for the overlapping dialogue perfected both by him and by Frank CAPRA in their 1930s comedies), but he made some of the best films in genres introduced by others. He was a practical, down-to-earth director, unburdened by self-conscious pictorial stylistics and technical razzle-dazzle. His handling of the camera was functional and direct. He was a storyteller first and foremost, in that old-fashioned tradition that has made American films universally popular.

Hawks employed technique to advance his story, not for its own sake. His framing, cutting, and camera movement were nearly "invisible," rarely calling attention to themselves. Yet he was among Hollywood's most proficient technicians, a master craftsman who constructed his films compactly and economically and had few peers in the ability to establish and sustain mood and atmosphere. He frequently was his own producer and had a hand in many of his scripts, and came as close as any other Hollywood director to what the French term an *auteur,* the complete filmmaker in control of his material from start to finish. Regardless of genre, certain themes (camaraderie between male proponents, for one) and a certain type of hero (often an achievement-oriented man in a risky situation) keep appearing in his films. Highly regarded among French film cultists since the early 30s, Hawks gained considerable stature among American critics in more recent years. He was awarded an honorary Oscar for his cumulative work during the Academy Award ceremony for 1974, held in 1975. Two of his brothers, director Kenneth Hawks (who was killed in a plane crash in 1930) and producer William Hawks, were also in films. Among the many studies of Hawks are *Hawks on Hawks* by Joseph McBride and *Howard Hawks: Storyteller* by Gerald Mast.

FILMS (as director): *The Road to Glory* (also story), *Fig*

Leaves (also story) 1926; *The Cradle Snatchers, Paid to Love* 1927; *A Girl in Every Port* (also story), *Fazil, The Air Circus* (co-dir. with Lewis Seiler) 1928; *Trent's Last Case* 1929; *The Dawn Patrol* (also co-sc.) 1930; *The Criminal Code* 1931; *The Crowd Roars* (also story), *Scarface: The Shame of a Nation* (also co-prod.), *Tiger Shark* 1932; *Today We Live* (also prod.) 1933; *Viva Villa!* (co-dir., co-sc.; completed by and credited to Jack Conway), *Twentieth Century* (also prod.) 1934; *Barbary Coast* 1935; *Ceiling Zero, The Road to Glory, Come and Get It* (co-dir. with William Wyler) 1936; *Bringing Up Baby* (also prod.) 1938; *Indianapolis Speedway* (story only), *Only Angels Have Wings* (also prod., story) 1939; *His Girl Friday* (also prod.) 1940; *The Outlaw* (removed in mid-production by Howard Hughes, who completed the film and assigned himself the credit; film completed in 1940, released in 1943, 1947, 1950); *Sergeant York* 1941; *Ball of Fire* 1942; *Air Force, Corvette K–225* (prod. only) 1943; *To Have and Have Not* (also prod.) 1944; *The Big Sleep* (also prod.) 1946; *Red River* (also prod.), *A Song is Born* 1948; *I Was a Male War Bride* 1949; *The Thing* (prod., co-sc. only) 1951; *The Big Sky* (also prod.), *O. Henry's Full House* ("The Ransom of Red Chief" episode), *Monkey Business* 1952; *Gentlemen Prefer Blondes* 1953; *Land of the Pharaohs* (also prod.) 1955; *Rio Bravo* (also prod.) 1959; *Hatari!* (also prod.) 1962; *Man's Favorite Sport?* (also prod.) 1964; *Red Line 7000* (also prod., co-sc.) 1965; *El Dorado* (also prod.) 1967; *Rio Lobo* (also prod.) 1970.

Hawley, Wanda. Actress. *b.* 1897, Pennsylvania. *d.* 1949. Blonde leading lady of Hollywood silents. Starting her career as Wanda Petit, she played the beautiful heroine of many silent films, opposite some of the leading stars of the period. Later she specialized in seductive vampy roles. She appeared in several De Mille and early Sam Wood productions and for a while rivaled Gloria Swanson at Paramount. Her career ended with the arrival of sound.

FILMS INCLUDE: As Wanda Petit—*The Derelict, The Broadway Sport, This Is the Life* 1917; *Cupid's Roundup* 1918. As Wanda Hawley—*Mr. Fix-It, Old Wives for New, The Border Wireless, The Way of a Man with a Maid* 1918; *For Better for Worse, Greased Lightning, The Lottery Man, Peg o' My Heart, Everywoman* 1919; *Double Speed, Miss Hobbes, Food for Scandal, Her Beloved Villain, Her First Elopement* 1920; *The Snob, The Affairs of Anatol, The House That Jazz Built, A Kiss in Time, The Love Charm, Her Face Value* 1921; *The Young Rajah, The Woman Who Walked Alone, Burning Sands, The Truthful Liar, Bobbed Hair, Thirty Days* 1922; *Brass Commandments, Masters of Men, The Man from Brodney's* 1923; *The Desert Sheik, Bread* 1924; *Barriers Burned Away, Smouldering Fires, Stop Flirting, Graustark, American Pluck* 1925; *A Desperate Moment, Midnight Limited, The Combat, Hearts and Spangles, The Last Alarm, The Midnight Message, The Smoke Eaters* 1926; *Eyes of the Totem, Pirates of the Sky* 1927.

Hawn, Goldie. Actress. Born on Nov. 21, 1945, in Washington, D.C. Comic star of American TV and films. Raised in suburban Takoma Park, Maryland, by a Presbyterian musician father and a Jewish mother who ran a dance studio and jewelry stores, she began taking ballet and tap-dancing lessons at three and made her professional acting debut at 16 playing Juliet in a production of the Virginia Stage Company. She then studied drama at the American University, paying her tuition by operating a dance studio. Dropping out of college at 18, she arrived in New York and landed her first job as a chorus-line cancan dancer at the 1964 World's Fair. Later she worked as a go-go dancer, appeared in occasional stock productions, and played a bit part in Disney's *The One and Only Genuine Original Family Band.* After appearing on TV in the aborted series 'Good Morning World' (1967–68) she won national popularity as a kooky blonde in the zany TV comedy show 'Laugh-In' (1968–70). She left the cast to make films and won a best supporting actress Academy Award for her first role, *Cactus Flower* (1969). She was nominated for another Oscar for her performance in *Private Benjamin* (1980), a film she also produced, and remained one of Hollywood's most popular screen personalities into the 90s. Divorced from actor-director Gus Trikonis and from Bill Hudson of the Hudson Brothers rock-comedy group, she has been sharing home since 1986 with actor Kurt RUSSELL and their children.

FILMS: *The One and Only Genuine Original Family Band* (bit) 1968; *Cactus Flower* 1969; *There's a Girl in My Soup* 1970; *$/Dollars* 1971; *Butterflies Are Free* 1972; *The Sugarland Express, The Girl from Petrovka* 1974; *Shampoo* 1975; *The Duchess and the Dirtwater Fox* 1976; *Foul Play* 1978; *Viaggio con Anita/Travels with Anita/Lovers and Liars* (It./Fr.) 1979; *Private Benjamin* (also exec. prod.), *Seems Like Old Times* 1980; *Best Friends* 1982; *Swing Shift, Protocol* (also exec. prod.) 1984; *Wildcats* 1986; *Overboard* 1987; *Bird on a Wire, My Blue Heaven* (co-exec. prod. only) 1990; *Deceived* 1991; *Crisscross* (also co-prod.), *Housesitter, Death Becomes Her* 1992; *Something to Talk About* (ex.-prod. only) 1995; *Everyone Says I Love You, First Wives Club* 1996.

Haworth, Jill. Actress. Born on Aug. 15, 1945, in Sussex, England. She showed early promise as an ingenue and young leading lady of Hollywood films of the early 60s and played the feminine lead in the Broadway musical 'Cabaret' (1966). But by the early 70s she was back in England, appearing in low-budget horror films.

FILMS INCLUDE: *Exodus* (US) 1960; *Ton Ombre est la mienne/Your Shadow Is Mine* (Fr./It.) 1962; *The Cardinal* (US) 1963; *In Harm's Way* (US) 1965; *It!* 1967; *The Haunted House of Horror/Horror House* 1970; *Tower of Evil/Horror on Snape Island/Beyond the Fog* 1972; *The Mutations* 1973.

Hawthorne, Nigel. Actor. Born April 5, 1929, in Coventry, England. *ed.* University of Capetown, South Africa. Established, respected British character actor, for years the darling of critics for his work on the English stage, in films and television. He gained exposure to American audiences primarily through the BBC sitcom 'Yes, Prime Minister,' widening his international reputation. He received the Tony Award for his bravura Broadway performance in 'Shadowlands' and was nominated for a best actor Oscar for his title role in *The Madness of King George* (1994).

FILMS INCLUDE: *Young Winston* 1972; *The Hiding Place* 1975; *Watership Down* 1978; *History of the World—Part I, Memoirs of a Survivor* 1981; *Firefox, Ghandi, The Plague Dogs* 1982; *The Black Cauldron, Dreamchild, Turtle Diary* 1985; *Freddie as F.R.O.7.* 1992; *Demolition Man* 1993; *The Madness of King George* 1994; *Richard III* 1995; *Amistad, Inside* 1997.

Hawtrey, Charles. Actor. *b.* George Frederick Joffre Hartree, 1914, London, of a theatrical family. *d.* 1988. Scrawny comic character player of the British screen, aptly described by a critic as a "thin wet hen in granny specs." In show business from childhood, he made his first film appearance at seven and his London stage debut at 13. He also cut several records as a boy soprano and in 1929 he began a long career in radio. In the late 30s and early 40s he played smart-aleck boys in Will Hay comedies. As an adult, he appeared in numerous British films, in a variety of campy character roles, memorably in many of the "Carry On" series.

FILMS INCLUDE: *Tell Your Children* 1922; *The Melody Maker* 1933; *Sabotage/The Woman Alone* 1936; *Good Morning*

Boys 1937; *Where's That Fire?* 1939; *The Goose Steps Out* 1942; *A Canterbury Tale* 1944; *Passport to Pimlico* 1949; *The Galloping Major* 1950; *Brandy for the Parson* 1951; *You're Only Young Twice* 1952; *Simon and Laura* 1955; *Carry on Sergeant* 1958; *Carry on Cleo* 1964; *Carry on Cowboy* 1965; *Carry on Up the Khyber* 1968; *Carry on Abroad* 1972.

Hay, Will. Actor. *b.* 1888, Stockton-on-Tees, England. *d.* 1949. A popular music hall comic from 1909, he was one of the top box-office stars of British film comedies of the 30s and early 40s, usually playing seedy characters in positions of authority.

FEATURE FILMS: *Those Were the Days, Radio Parade of 1935/Radio Follies* 1934; *Dandy Dick, Boys Will Be Boys* 1935; *Where There's a Will, Windbag the Sailor* 1936; *Good Morning Boys, Oh Mr. Porter* 1937; *Convict 99, Hey Hey USA, Old Bones of the River* 1938; *Ask a Policeman, Where's the Fire?* 1939; *The Ghost of St. Michael's* 1941; *The Black Sheep of Whitehall, The Big Blockade, The Goose Steps Out* (also co-dir.) 1942; *My Learned Friend* (also co-dir.) 1943.

Hayakawa, Sessue. Actor. *b.* Kintaro Hayakawa, June 10, 1889, Nanaura, Chiba, Japan. *d.* 1973. A descendant of a long aristocratic line, he enrolled at Japan's Naval Academy in 1908, but was forced to abandon plans for a naval career because of a partial loss of hearing. He turned to the Japanese stage and joined a troupe directed by an uncle. Shortly after, at age 19, he came to the US and enrolled at the University of Chicago, graduating in 1913 with a degree in political science. On his way home, he stopped in Los Angeles, where in a change of plans he joined a Japanese stage troupe. He was seen by Thomas INCE, who offered him a film contract. Exotic, expressive, and "different," Hayakawa was an instant success as a screen personality. After his triumph in *The Typhoon* (1914), in which he co-starred with his wife, Tsuru Aoki, his fan mail was as abundant as that of any big Hollywood star of the era. The following year he impressed critics with his restrained performance as a lecherous villain in De Mille's *The Cheat* (1915), which stood in marked contrast to the exaggerated gestures of actors of the silent screen. In 1918 he formed his own production company, Haworth Pictures, through which he produced more than 20 films in the next few years.

Hayakawa's acting has since been described as a blend of "the Method" and Zen. Playing both exotic heroes and charming villains, he remained in Hollywood until 1923, then left for Europe, where he starred in many films, mostly French, and made occasional sojourns to Japan. In the late 40s he made a Hollywood comeback in character parts. In 1957 he was nominated for an Oscar for his portrayal of a Japanese officer in *The Bridge on the River Kwai.* Hayakawa, who in the 50s was ordained a Zen Buddhist priest, authored several screen stories; a novel, *The Bandit Prince* (1926); a play, *The Life of the Buddha* (1949); and a spiritual memoir, *Zen Showed Me the Way* (1960).

FILMS INCLUDE: *The Ambassador's Envoy, The Wrath of the Gods, The Typhoon* 1914; *The Last of the Line, After Five, The Clue, The Secret Sin, The Cheat* 1915; *Temptation, Alien Souls, Honorable Friend, The Soul of Kura-San* 1916; *The Bottle Imp, The Jaguar's Claws, Forbidden Paths, Hashimura Togo, The Call of the East, The Secret Game* 1917; *The White Man's Law, The Honor of His House, The Bravest Way, The City of Dim Faces, His Birthright* (also prod., co-story), *The Temple of Dusk* (also prod.) 1918; *Bonds of Honor* (also prod.), *His Heart in Pawn* (also prod., unproduced play basis, 'Shadows'), *The Man Beneath* (also prod.), *The Dragon Painter* (also prod.), *The Illustrious Prince* (also prod.), *The Tong Man* (also prod.) 1919; *The Beggar Prince* (also prod.), *The Brand of Lopez* (also prod.), *The Devil's Claim* (also prod.), *Li Ting Lang* (also prod.), *An Arabian Knight* (also prod.) 1920; *The First Born* (also prod.), *Where Lights Are Low* (also prod.), *The Swamp* (also prod. story), *Black Roses* (also prod.) 1921; *The Vermilion Pencil, Five Days to Live* 1922; *La Bataille/The Danger Line* (Fr.) 1923; *Ja'i tué* (Fr.), *The Great Prince Shan* (UK), *Sen Yan's Devotion* (UK) 1924; *Daughter of the Dragon* 1931; *Yoshiwara* (Fr.) 1936; *Forfaiture* (remake of *The Cheat;* Fr.), *Die Tochter des Samurai/Daughter of the Samurai* (Ger./Jap.) 1937; *Tempête sur l'Asie/Storm Over Asia* (Fr.) 1938; *Macao l'Enfer du Jeu/Gambling Hell* (Fr.) 1940; *Le Soleil de Minuit* (Fr.) 1941; *Quartier Chinois* (Fr.) 1947; *Tokyo Joe* 1949; *Three Came Home, Les Miserables* 1950; *House of Bamboo* 1955; *The Bridge on the River Kwai* 1957; *The Geisha Boy* 1958; *Green Mansions* 1959; *The Swiss Family Robinson* 1960; *The Big Wave* (US/Jap.) 1962; *The Daydreamer* (v/o) 1966.

Hayden, Russell. Actor. *b.* Pate Lucid, June 12, 1912, Chico, Calif. *d.* 1981. He entered films as a grip, then worked as a sound recorder, film cutter, and assistant cameraman before making his acting debut in the mid-30s. He played Lucky Jenkins, one of a trio of heroes in many Hopalong Cassidy Westerns starring William BOYD. In the 40s he starred in his own Western series, then co-starred with James ELLISON in a number of Westerns that he also co-produced. From the early 50s he produced and directed TV Westerns, including the series '26 Men' and 'Judge Roy Bean.' He also produced and directed a low-budget feature, *When the Girls Take Over* (1962). Divorced from Jan Clayton, he married Lillian Porter, a Fox starlet.

FILMS INCLUDE: *Hills of Old Wyoming, Hopalong Rides Again* 1937; *Partners of the Plains, Heart of Arizona, In Old Mexico, The Mysterious Rider* 1938; *Heritage of the Desert, Range War* 1939; *Santa Fe Marshal, Three Men from Texas* 1940; *In Old Colorado* (also co-sc.) 1941; *The Lone Prairie* 1942; *Lucky Legs* 1943; *Marshal of Gunsmoke* 1944; *Albuquerque* 1948; *Apache Chief* 1949; *Sudden Death, Fast on the Draw* 1950; *Valley of Fire* 1951.

Hayden, Sterling. Actor. *b.* Sterling Relyea Walter, Mar. 26, 1916, Montclair, N.J. *d.* 1986. Tall (6' 5"), blond, ruggedly wholesome leading man of Hollywood films of the 40s and early 50s who later matured into a weathered, barrel-chested, solid character actor. Drawn to the sea from his early teens, he dropped out of school at 16 to become a mate on a schooner and was a ship's captain by the time he was 22. Needing money to buy his own vessel, he banked on his extreme good looks, accepting modeling assignments. In 1940 he signed with Paramount, making his debut the following year in *Virginia.* He gained further publicity from his 1942 marriage to film star Madeleine CARROLL, a union that lasted four years.

After only two productions, Hayden left Hollywood to join the Marines. Later in WW II he served with the OSS behind enemy lines in Greece and Yugoslavia, operating under the code name John Hamilton. Influenced by his underground associations in Europe, he joined the Communist Party in 1946 but terminated his membership after six months. He returned to Paramount in 1947 but after appearing in several inconsequential roles began freelancing and, to the surprise of many, proved himself a superior actor in the role of a hoodlum in John Huston's *The Asphalt Jungle* (1950). Despite the critical acclaim, however, Hayden's acting talent was rarely tapped in a long film career. In 1951, he admitted his past Communist affiliation before the House Un-American Activities Committee and named several Hollywood personalities as fellow travelers. The memory of the event left a lifelong scar on his psyche; but his career was saved. Nonetheless, with few notable exceptions—among them commanding performances in Stanley Kubrick's

The Killing (1956) and *Dr. Strangelove* (1964)—that career was strewn with poor opportunities and mediocre roles. He never seemed truly interested in the acting profession and periodically abandoned films to return to the sea. In 1959 he sailed on his schooner *The Wanderer* to the South Seas with his four children, in his custody after a second divorce. His obsessive affair with the sea and his adventurous voyages are depicted in his autobiography, *Wanderer* (1963). In 1976 he published a novel, *Voyage*. In 1983 he was the subject of a documentary film, *Lighthouse of Chaos*. He died at 70 of prostate cancer.

FILMS: *Virginia, Bahama Passage* 1941; *Variety Girl, Blaze of Noon* 1947; *El Paso, Manhandled* 1949; *The Asphalt Jungle* 1950; *Journey Into Light* 1951; *Flaming Feather, The Denver and Rio Grande, Hellgate, The Golden Hawk, Flat Top* 1952; *The Star, Take Me to Town, Kansas Pacific, Fighter Attack, So Big* 1953; *Crime Wave, Prince Valiant, Arrow in the Dust, Johnny Guitar, Naked Alibi, Suddenly* 1954; *Battle Taxi, Timberjack, Shotgun, The Eternal Sea, The Last Command, Top Gun* 1955; *The Come On, The Killing* 1956; *Crime of Passion, Five Steps to Danger, The Iron Sheriff, Valerie, Gun Battle at Monterey, Zero Hour* 1957; *Terror in a Texas Town, Ten Days to Tulara* 1958; *Dr. Strangelove* (UK) 1964; *Sweet Hunters* (Pan./Fr.), *Hard Contract* 1969; *Loving* 1970; *Le Saut de l'Ange/Cobra* (Fr.) 1971; *The Godfather* 1972; *The Long Goodbye, The Final Programme/Last Days of Man on Earth* (UK) 1973; *Deadly Strangers* (UK) 1974; *Cipola Colt/Cry Onion* (It.) 1975; *Novecento/1900* (It.) 1976; *King of the Gypsies* 1978; *Winter Kills, The Outsider* 1979; *9 to 5* 1980; *Gas* (Can.) 1981; *Venom* (UK) 1982.

Haydn, Richard. Actor, occasional director. *b.* 1905, London. *d.* 1985. He was an overseer of a Jamaica banana plantation and a comic star of British revues before coming to Hollywood in the early 40s. Highly amusing in prissy, eccentric, or neurotic character parts with his distinctive nasal voice, most memorably in *Sitting Pretty* (1948). He directed several enjoyable films in the late 40s. He also did some writing under the pseudonym Edwin Carp.

FILMS INCLUDE (as actor): *Charley's Aunt* 1941; *Ball of Fire* 1942; *Forever and a Day, No Time for Love* 1943; *And Then There Were None* 1945; *Adventure, The Green Years, Cluny Brown* 1946; *The Beginning or the End, The Late George Apley, Singapore, The Foxes of Harrow, Forever Amber* 1947; *Sitting Pretty, The Emperor Waltz* (as Emperor Franz Josef), *Miss Tatlock's Millions* (also dir.) 1948; *Dear Wife* (dir. only), *Mr. Music* (also dir.) 1950; *The Merry Widow* 1952; *Never Let Me Go* 1953; *Money from Home, Her Twelve Men* 1954; *Jupiter's Darling* 1955; *Twilight for the Gods* 1958; *The Lost World, Please Don't Eat the Daisies* 1960; *Five Weeks in a Balloon, Mutiny on the Bounty* 1962; *The Sound of Music, Clarence the Cross-Eyed Lion* 1965; *The Adventures of Bullwhip Griffin* 1967; *Young Frankenstein* 1974.

Hayes, Alfred. Poet, novelist, screenwriter. *b.* 1911, London. *d.* 1985. In the US from age three, he attended New York's City College, then worked as a reporter for *The Daily Mirror* and *The New York American,* before turning to writing fiction and poetry. After serving during WW II with the US Army Special Services in Europe, he remained in Rome and became involved with the work of Italian neorealist directors. He collaborated on Rossellini's *Paisa/Paisan* (1946), sharing an Oscar nomination for the film's US release in 1949, and worked uncredited on De Sica's *The Bicycle Thief.* He received another Academy Award nomination as the co-writer of the original story of Fred Zinnemann's *Teresa* (1951), a compassionate tale of an American soldier and his Italian bride, shot on location in Italy. His novel and play, *The Girl on the Via Flaminia,* provided the basis for the Franco-American production, *Act of Love* (1954). In addition to films, he also contributed scripts for episodes of TV series, including 'Alfred Hitchcock Presents' and 'Twilight Zone.' His many poems include the lyrics for the ballad 'Joe Hill,' popularized by Joan Baez, about the labor organizer who was executed in Utah in 1915.

FILMS: *Paisa/Paisan* 1946; *Ladri di Biciclette/The Bicycle Thieves/The Bicycle Thief* (uncredited) 1949; *Teresa* (co-story only) 1951; *Clash by Night* 1952; *Act of Love* (play basis only), *Human Desire* 1954; *The Left Hand of God* 1955; *Island in the Sun, A Hatful of Rain* 1957; *These Thousand Hills* 1959; *The Mountain Road* 1960; *Joy in the Morning* 1965; *The Double Man* 1968; *Lost in the Stars* 1974; *The Blue Bird* (US/USSR) 1976.

Hayes, Allison. Actress. *b.* Mary Jane Haynes Mar. 6, 1930, Charleston, W. Va. *d.* 1977, of blood poisoning. Statuesque leading lady of Hollywood films of the 50s and early 60s. A former concert pianist, she had an unremarkable career in mostly B productions, but became somewhat of a cult heroine posthumously, thanks to the title role in the hilariously awful science-fiction saga, *Attack of the 50-Foot Woman* (1958).

FILMS INCLUDE: *Francis Joins the WACS, Sign of the Pagan* 1954; *So This Is Paris, Chicago Syndicate, Count Three and Pray* 1955; *The Steel Jungle, Mohawk, The Gunslinger* 1956; *Zombies of Mora-Tau, The Undead, The Unearthly, The Disembodied* 1957; *Attack of the 50-Foot Woman, Wolf Dog, Hong Kong Confidential* 1958; *Counterplot* 1959; *The Hypnotic Eye* 1960; *The Crawling Hand/Strike Me Deadly, Who's Been Sleeping in My Bed?* 1963; *Tickle Me* 1965.

Hayes, George ("Gabby"). Actor. *b.* May 7, 1885, Wellsville, N.Y. *d.* 1969. Lovable toothless rascal of more than 200 Westerns. A former vaudevillian, he began his film career in the 20s playing villains, often in John Wayne vehicles. In the mid-30s he began playing comic sidekicks to William BOYD, Roy ROGERS, and other Western heroes, typically as a bewhiskered, fearless old-timer. In the 50s he had his own show on TV.

FILMS INCLUDE: *Why Women Marry?* 1923; *The Rainbow Man* 1929; *Rose of the Rio Grande* 1931; *Love Me Tonight* 1932; *Wild Horse Mesa* 1933; *Beggars in Ermine, The Lost Jungle* (serial), *In Old Santa Fe* 1934; *Hopalong Cassidy, Tumbling Tumbleweeds* 1935; *Mr. Deeds Goes to Town, The Lawless Nineties, Texas Rangers* 1936; *The Plainsman, Borderland* 1937; *Gold Is Where You Find It, The Frontiersman* 1938; *Let Freedom Ring, Man of Conquest* 1939; *Dark Command, Wagons Westward, Colorado* 1940; *Nevada City* 1941; *Man of Cheyenne* 1942; *In Old Oklahoma* 1943; *Tall in the Saddle* 1944; *The Big Bonanza, Don't Fence Me In* 1945; *Badman's Territory, Helldorado* 1946; *Wyoming* 1947; *Albuquerque* 1948; *El Paso* 1949; *The Cariboo Trail* 1950; *Pals of the Golden West* 1951.

Hayes, Helen. Actress. *b.* Helen Hayes Brown, Oct. 10, 1900, in Washington, D.C. *d.* 1993. The daughter of an actress, she made her stage debut at age five and her first Broadway appearance at nine in 'Old Hutch.' As a teenager, she appeared in many plays and occasional silent films and emerged as a Broadway star in 'Dear Brutus' in 1918. She went on to become a Broadway institution and over the years won acclaim as the "First Lady of the American Theater." In 1928 she married playwright Charles MACARTHUR. The marriage produced an actress daughter, Mary, who died of polio in 1949, and an adopted son, actor James MACARTHUR. She accompanied her husband to Hollywood when he signed a long-term contract as screenwriter for MGM and was coaxed by the studio to appear in their films. She won the best actress Academy Award for her very first role, in *The Sin of Madelon Claudet* (1931), and played leads in other films of the early 30s.

However, Miss Hayes was uncomfortable in the role of a movie star, lacking the sex appeal and the temperament of a Hollywood personality, so she returned to Broadway in 1935. She enjoyed the greatest triumph of her stage career in 'Victoria Regina' (1935–38) and subsequently appeared in numerous New York productions. She returned only occasionally to films and won a second Academy Award, this time as best supporting actress, for her portrayal of an eccentric lady passenger in *Airport* (1970). Miss Hayes ended her illustrious stage career in 1971, because of chronic asthmatic bronchitis, which was aggravated by the dusty environment of the theater. But she continued appearing sporadically in films and on television. In 1973–74 she co-starred with Mildred NATWICK in the TV series 'The Snoop Sisters.' She was the subject of a 90-minute feature documentary, *Helen Hayes: Portrait of an American Actress* (1974). To commemorate her contribution to American drama, a theater was named after her in 1959, on the occasion of her Broadway jubilee. The demolition of the Helen Hayes Theater in 1982, to make room for a new hotel near Times Square, caused such an uproar that another Broadway auditorium was renamed after her the following year. In 1984 the US Mint struck a commemorative gold coin bearing her likeness. A recipient of a Life Achievement Award from Washington's Kennedy Center, she was presented with the National Medal of Arts in 1988 by President Reagan. Memoirs: *A Gift of Joy* (1965), *On Reflection* (1969), *Twice Over Lightly* (with Anita Loos, 1971), *Loving Life* (1987), *Where the Truth Lies* (1988), *My Life in Three Acts* (1990).

FILMS: *Jean and the Calico Doll* (two-reeler) 1910; *The Weavers of Life* 1917; *Babs* 1920; *The Sin of Madelon Claudet, Arrowsmith* (as Leora Tozer) 1931; *A Farewell to Arms* (as Catherine Barkley), *The Son-Daughter* 1932; *The White Sister, Another Language, Night Flight* 1933; *Crime Without Passion* (unbilled cameo), *What Every Woman Knows* 1934; *Vanessa: Her Love Story* 1935; *Stage Door Canteen* (cameo) 1943; *My Son John* 1952; *Main Street to Broadway* (cameo) 1953; *Anastasia* (as the Dowager Empress) 1956; *Third Man on the Mountain* (unbilled cameo) 1959; *Airport* 1970; *Helen Hayes: Portrait of an American Actress* (feature-length documentary with Hayes narrating the story of her life), *Herbie Rides Again* 1974; *One of Our Dinosaurs Is Missing* 1975; *Candleshoe* 1978.

Hayes, John Michael. Screenwriter. Born on May 11, 1919, in Worcester, Mass. *ed.* U. of Massachusetts. He wrote scripts for many Hollywood films of the 50s and 60s, alone or in collaboration, notably several Hitchcock productions.

FILMS INCLUDE: *Red Ball Express* 1952; *Thunder Bay, Torch Song* 1953; *Rear Window* 1954; *To Catch a Thief, The Trouble with Harry, It's a Dog's Life* 1955; *The Man Who Knew Too Much* 1956; *Peyton Place* 1957; *The Matchmaker* 1958; *But Not for Me* 1959; *Butterfield 8* 1960; *The Children's Hour* 1962; *The Chalk Garden, The Carpetbaggers, Where Love Has Gone* 1964; *Harlow* (Carroll Baker version) 1965; *Judith, Nevada Smith* 1966.

Haymes, Dick. Singer, actor. *b.* Richard Benjamin Haymes, Sept. 13, 1916, Buenos Aires, of Scots-English-American descent. *d.* 1980. Raised by his singer mother after the separation of his parents, he was educated in France, Switzerland, and England before coming to the US in 1936. Here he began his show business career as a radio announcer, band vocalist, and occasional film extra and bit player. In the early 40s he became a highly successful nightclub and recording artist and soon developed into one of America's leading crooners. He was signed on a movie contract by 20th Century-Fox, but he proved much less effective as a screen actor than a vocal entertainer and never really clicked as a film star. Compounding his professional setbacks were marital and immigration problems. His six marriages and five divorces—his wives included actresses Joanne DRU, his second (1941–49); and Rita HAYWORTH, his fourth (1953–55)—proved a constant drain on his finances. In 1953 he left the country briefly with Miss Hayworth and when he returned he was held for illegal entry and ordered deported as an undesirable alien. His troubles dated back to WW II, when he avoided the draft by registering as a resident alien, waiving his right to become a US citizen. The deportation order was later revoked, but Haymes's career never fully recovered. He declared bankruptcy twice, in 1960 and in 1971. A resident and citizen of Ireland from the mid-60s, he made a modest comeback in the US in nightclubs and on occasional TV shows.

FILMS: *Dramatic School* 1938; *Du Barry Was a Lady* 1943; *Four Jills in a Jeep, Irish Eyes Are Smiling* 1944; *Diamond Horseshoe, State Fair* 1945; *Do You Love Me?* 1946; *The Shocking Miss Pilgrim, Carnival in Costa Rica* 1947; *Up in Central Park, One Touch of Venus* 1948; *St. Benny the Dip* 1951; *All Ashore, Cruisin' Down the River* 1953; *Won Ton Ton—The Dog Who Saved Hollywood* 1976.

Haynes, Todd. Director. Born in 1961. Creative, idiosyncratic, independent American filmmaker who gained attention with *Superstar: The Karen Carpenter Story*, in which he used Barbie dolls to tell the story of the singer's ultimately unhappy life. Has also directed *Dottie Gets Spanked*, a short for HBO.

FILMS: *Superstar: The Karen Carpenter Story* 1987; *Poison* 1991; *Swoon* 1992; *Safe* 1995.

Hays, Robert. Actor. Born on July 24, 1947, in Bethesda, Md. *ed.* Grossmont Coll., San Diego State U. Pleasant light leading man of the American screen and TV, following five years on the San Francisco stage. His numerous TV credits include the series 'Angie' (1979–80) and 'Starman' (1986).

FILMS INCLUDE: *Airplane!* 1980; *Take This Job and Shove It, Utilities* (Can.) 1981; *Airplane II: The Sequel* 1982; *Trenchcoat, Touched* 1983; *Scandalous* 1984; *Cat's Eye* 1985; *Honeymoon Academy* 1990; *Fifty Fifty, Homeward Bound: The Incredible Journey* 1992; *Raw Justice* 1994; *Homeward Bound II: Lost in San Francisco* 1996.

Hays, Will H. Executive. *b.* Nov. 5, 1879, Sullivan, Ind. *d.* 1954. A former lawyer, chairman of the Republican National Committee, and US Postmaster General in President Harding's cabinet, he was appointed by the major Hollywood studios in 1922 as the head of their new organization, Motion Picture Producers and Distributors of America, Inc. (MPPDA). It was created by the Hollywood moguls in an effort to improve the image of the industry after widely publicized scandals and increasing pressures to create some form of film censorship. In 1930 the MPPDA, by then known as the Hays Office, created the Motion Picture Production Code, a strict self-regulatory charter of do's and don'ts that became known as the Hays Code. Hays wielded much power over the industry during his years as head of the MPPDA, and his Code molded the content and image of Hollywood's films for many years. The Hays administration terminated in 1945, but the infamous Code remained unchanged until 1966. See also PRODUCTION CODE.

Hayter, James. Actor. *b.* Apr. 23, 1907, Lonuvla, India, to British parents. *d.* 1983. *ed.* Royal Academy of Dramatic Art. On stage since 1936, he made his film debut in 1936 and came to play numerous character roles, typically as a merry and congenial fellow, in numerous British and some US productions.

FILMS INCLUDE: *Sensation* 1936; *Sailors Three* 1941; *Nicholas Nickleby* (dual role, as both Cheeryble brothers), *The*

End of the River 1947; *The Fallen Idol* 1948; *The Blue Lagoon, Silent Dust* 1949; *Eye Witness* (US), *Trio* (lead in "The Verger" episode), *Morning Departure/Operation Disaster, The Woman with No Name/Her Panelled Door* 1950; *Tom Brown's School Days* 1951; *The Story of Robin Hood* (as Friar Tuck; UK/US), *The Crimson Pirate* (US/UK), *The Pickwick Papers* (as Mr. Pickwick) 1952; *Four Sided Triangle* (lead), *Always a Bride* 1953; *Beau Brummel* (US/UK) 1954; *Land of the Pharaohs* (US) 1955; *Port Afrique* (US/UK) 1956; *Seven Waves Away/ Abandon Ship!* 1957; *The Captain's Table* 1958; *The Thirty-nine Steps* 1959; *Stranger in the House/Cop-Out* 1967; *A Challenge for Robin Hood* (again as Friar Tuck) 1967; *Oliver!* 1968; *David Copperfield, Song of Norway* (US) 1970; *The Blood on Satan's Claw* 1971; *The Bawdy Adventures of Tom Jones* 1976.

Hayward, Leland. Producer. *b.* Sept. 13, 1902, in Nebraska City, Neb. *d.* 1971. A highly successful stage producer, talent agent, and airline executive, as well as one of the most colorful characters in American show business, early in his career he worked in the publicity department of United Artists and in the scenario department of First National. He produced three Hollywood films in the late 50s in addition to a long string of Broadway hits. His second wife was Margaret SULLAVAN.

FILMS: *Mister Roberts* 1955; *The Spirit of St. Louis* 1957; *The Old Man and the Sea* 1958.

Hayward, Lillie. Screenwriter. *b.* Sept. 12, 1892, St. Paul, Minn. *d.* 1978. A former musician, she entered films in 1919 as a script editor and subsequently worked for various studios as editor, original story writer, and screenwriter. At her best with adventure and action material.

FILMS INCLUDE: *Janice Meredith* 1924; *Every Man's Wife, The Fighting Heart* 1925; *My Own Pal, Ranson's Folly, The Amateur Gentleman* 1926; *Driftwood* 1928; *On the Border* 1930; *Frisco Jenny* (story only) 1933; *Housewife* (story only) 1934; *The White Cockatoo, Front Page Woman* 1935; *The Walking Dead* 1936; *Penrod and Sam, Ever Since Eve, Night Club Scandal* 1937; *Her Jungle Love, Sons of the Legion* 1938; *King of Chinatown* 1939; *The Biscuit Eater* 1940; *Aloma of the South Seas* 1941; *Margin for Error, My Friend Flicka* 1943; *Smoky, Black Beauty* 1946; *Blood on the Moon, Northwest Stampede* 1948; *Follow Me Quietly* 1949; *Cattle Drive* 1951; *The Raiders* 1952; *Tarzan and the Lost Safari* 1957; *The Proud Rebel* 1958; *The Shaggy Dog, Tonka* 1959; *Toby Tyler, The Boy and the Pirates* 1960; *Lad: A Dog* 1962.

Hayward, Louis. Actor. *b.* Seafield Grant, Mar. 19, 1909, Johannesburg, South Africa. *d.* 1985, of lung cancer. After the death of his father, a mining engineer, he was raised in London, where he discovered the theater and before long began acting on the stage and in films. Following a Broadway debut in 1935, he went to Hollywood, where for the next 20 years he played smooth, suave leads in many films, often as the swashbuckling hero of period adventure yarns. He performed some real-life heroics as a Marine during WW II and was awarded a Bronze Star. He returned to films after the war and was one of the first stars to get a percentage from the profits of his pictures. He also had an interest in his TV series 'The Lone Wolf' (1954). In the 60s he starred in two other TV series, 'The Pursuers' (1963) and 'Survivors' (1969–70). His first of three marriages was to Ida LUPINO.

FILMS INCLUDE: In the UK—*Self-Made Lady* 1932; *Chelsea Life* 1933; *Sorrell and Son* 1934. In the US—*The Flame Within, A Feather in Her Hat* 1935; *Absolute Quiet, Trouble for Two, Anthony Adverse* (as Denis Moore), *The Luckiest Girl in the World* 1936; *The Woman I Love* 1937; *Midnight Intruder, Condemned Women, The Saint in New York* (as the Saint), *The Rage of Paris, The Duke of West Point* 1938; *The Man in the Iron Mask* (in dual role, as Louis XIV/Philippe) 1939; *My Son My Son!, Dance Girl Dance, The Son of Monte Cristo* (as the Count of Monte Cristo) 1940; *Ladies in Retirement* 1941; *And Then There Were None* 1945; *Young Widow, The Strange Woman, The Return of Monte Cristo* (again as the Count of Monte Cristo) 1946; *Repeat Performance* 1947; *Ruthless, The Black Arrow* (as Richard Shelton), *Walk a Crooked Mile* 1948; *I Pirati di Capri/The Pirates of Capri* (in dual role) 1949; *House by the River, Fortunes of Captain Blood* (as Captain Peter Blood) 1950; *The Lady and the Bandit* (as Highwayman Dick Turpin), *The Son of Dr. Jekyll* (title role) 1951; *Lady in the Iron Mask* (as D'Artagnan), *Captain Pirate* 1952; *Duffy of San Quentin* 1954; *The Search for Bridey Murphy* 1956; *Joe Navidad/The Christmas Kid* (Sp./US) 1966; *Chuka* 1967; *Terror in the Wax Museum* 1973.

Hayward, Susan. Actress. *b.* Edythe Marrener, June 30, 1918, Brooklyn, N.Y. *d.* 1975. The daughter of a transit worker, she attended a commercial high school, where she studied stenography and dress design and began her working career as a photographer's model. A ravishing, husky-voiced redhead, she arrived in Hollywood in 1937 as one of the scores of candidates for the Scarlett O'Hara role in *Gone With the Wind.* After a discouraging beginning as a contract player in minor roles, she gradually reached star stature. In 1947 she received the first of five Oscar nominations, for *Smash-Up: The Story of a Woman,* a film in which she introduced the kind of role that would become her specialty, that of a fallen woman gutsily struggling to bounce back. Her other nominations were for *My Foolish Heart* (1950), *With a Song in My Heart* (as Jane Froman, 1952), *I'll Cry Tomorrow* (as Lillian Roth, 1956), and *I Want to Live* (1958). She won the best actress Academy Award for the last. Through a combination of determined courage, spunky energy, sexy good looks, and undeniable talent she maintained her status as one of Hollywood's leading stars through the late 50s, but became victimized by a string of poor tearjerkers early in the 60s and called it quits in 1964. She later returned to the screen in occasional roles. Her first husband (1944–54) was actor Jess Barker. She attempted suicide in 1955 following their bitter courtroom case over the custody of their twin sons. Following a two-year bout with a brain tumor, she died at 56.

FILMS: *Hollywood Hotel* 1937; *The Sisters, Comet Over Broadway, Girls on Probation* 1938; *Our Leading Citizen, Beau Geste, $1,000 a Touchdown* 1939; *Adam Had Four Sons, Sis Hopkins, Among the Living* 1941; *Reap the Wild Wind, The Forest Rangers, I Married a Witch, Star Spangled Rhythm* 1942; *Hit Parade of 1943, Young and Willing, Jack London* 1943; *The Fighting Seabees, The Hairy Ape, And Now Tomorrow* 1944; *Deadline at Dawn, Canyon Passage* 1946; *Smash-Up: The Story of a Woman, They Won't Believe Me, The Lost Moment* 1947; *Tap Roots, The Saxon Charm* 1948; *Tulsa, House of Strangers* 1949; *My Foolish Heart* 1950; *I'd Climb the Highest Mountain, Rawhide, I Can Get It for You Wholesale, David and Bathsheba* (as Bathsheba) 1951; *With a Song in My Heart* (as singer Jane Froman), *The Snows of Kilimanjaro, The Lusty Men* 1952; *The President's Lady* (as Rachel Jackson), *White Witch Doctor* 1953; *Demetrius and the Gladiators* (as Messalina), *Garden of Evil* 1954; *Untamed, Soldier of Fortune* 1955; *I'll Cry Tomorrow* (as Lillian Roth), *The Conqueror* 1956; *Top Secret Affair* 1957; *I Want to Live* 1958; *Woman Obsessed, Thunder in the Sun* 1959; *The Marriage-Go-Round, Ada, Back Street* 1961; *I Thank a Fool* 1962; *Stolen Hours* 1963; *Where Love Has Gone* 1964; *The Honey Pot, Valley of the Dolls* 1967; *The Revengers* 1972.

Hayworth, Rita. Actress. *b.* Margarita Carmen Cansino, Oct. 17, 1918, Brooklyn, N.Y. *d.* 1987. The daughter of Spanish-born dancer Eduardo Cansino and his 'Ziegfeld Follies' partner Volga Haworth, she began dancing professionally at age 12. At 13 she was dancing at Mexican night spots where she was eventually noticed by Fox production boss Winfield Sheehan. She made her screen debut in 1935, playing bits in a number of films under her real name, usually as a dancer. She was beginning to get leads in minor pictures when the merger of Fox with 20th Century resulted in Sheehan's removal from power and in her dismissal from the studio. She was drifting into obscurity in films of minor companies when, in 1937, she married Edward Judson, a shrewd businessman 22 years her senior who dropped his regular line of car sales to concentrate on his wife's talent. He won her a seven-year contract with Columbia. Under his guidance, she changed her name and was transformed from a raven-haired exotic into an auburn-haired sophisticate. But for the remainder of the 30s she was confined to leads in B pictures, typically on the action side.

Her first promising role was the second female lead in Howard Hawks's *Only Angels Have Wings* (1939), in which she played a philandering wife. She briefly returned to Bs but by the early 40s rapidly developed into a glamorous star through such career landmarks as *Blood and Sand* (as a stunning temptress), *You'll Never Get Rich* and *You Were Never Lovelier* (in both of which she sparkled as Fred Astaire's dancing partner), and *Cover Girl* (in which she teamed with Gene Kelly). Her picture in *Life* magazine was so much in demand as a pinup by American servicemen overseas that it was reproduced in millions of copies and adorned the atomic bomb that was dropped on Bikini. The film that more than any other confirmed Rita's position as Hollywood's "Love Goddess" was *Gilda* (1946), in which she oozed sexuality.

Through much of the 40s, Rita was the undisputed erotic queen of Hollywood films and naturally the hottest property of Columbia. Studio boss Harry COHN took personal charge of her career and tried, not too successfully, to direct her personal affairs as well. Her habit of falling in and out of love and into and out of marriage exasperated Cohn. In 1942 she fell in love with Victor MATURE, her co-star in *My Gal Sal,* and separated from her husband. The following year, when she obtained a divorce, she announced her engagement to Mature but instead married director-actor Orson WELLES. The marriage did not last.

In May of 1948, on her first visit to Europe, Rita met and fell in love with Aly Khan, the playboy son of the spiritual leader of millions of Moslems. Their romantic escapade took them all over Europe to the accompaniment of loud press coverage and indignant criticism, since the Prince was not legally divorced. In May of 1949, Aly and Rita were married in France. Two years later they were divorced.

Rita returned to Hollywood broke and asked Columbia to restore her contract. Harry Cohn obliged. She was back in films, but somehow the magic was gone. A bitter rift developed between her and Cohn. Her planned fourth marriage, to singer Dick HAYMES, took place in 1953 and was dissolved in 1955, beset by Dick's immigration and financial problems. Rita was absent from the screen for three years. She returned in 1957, now playing aging beauties. She gave a creditable performance in *Separate Tables* (1958) and in the same year married the film's co-producer, James HILL. They divorced in 1961. She later appeared in mostly routine films, some in Europe.

Miss Hayworth attempted a stage career in 1971, but it ended abruptly because she couldn't remember her lines. In 1977 a court-appointed administrator took charge of her affairs. In 1981 she was declared legally unable to care for herself and was put in the care of her second daughter, Yasmin Aga Khan. It was then revealed the star was suffering from Alzheimer's disease. She died at 68, a tragic remnant of the world's memory of her as Hollywood's epitome of glamour.

FILMS: As Rita Cansino—*Under the Pampas Moon, Charlie Chan in Egypt, Dante's Inferno, Paddy O'Day* 1935; *Human Cargo, Meet Nero Wolfe, Rebellion* 1936; *Trouble in Texas, Old Louisiana, Hit the Saddle* 1937. As Rita Hayworth—*Girls Can Play, The Game That Kills, Criminals of the Air, Paid to Dance, The Shadow* 1937; *Who Killed Gail Preston?, There's Always a Woman, Convicted, Juvenile Court* 1938; *Homicide Bureau, The Renegade Ranger, The Lone Wolf Spy Hunt, Only Angels Have Wings, Special Inspector* 1939; *Music in My Heart, Blondie on a Budget, Susan and God, The Lady in Question, Angels Over Broadway* 1940; *The Strawberry Blonde, Affectionately Yours, Blood and Sand, You'll Never Get Rich* 1941; *My Gal Sal, Tales of Manhattan, You Were Never Lovelier* 1942; *Cover Girl* 1944; *Tonight and Every Night* 1945; *Gilda* 1946; *Down to Earth* (in dual role) 1947; *The Lady from Shanghai, The Loves of Carmen* (as Carmen) 1948; *Champagne Safari* (doc.), *Affair in Trinidad* 1952; *Salome* (title role), *Miss Sadie Thompson* 1953; *Fire Down Below, Pal Joey* 1957; *Separate Tables* 1958; *They Came to Cordura* 1959; *The Story on Page One* 1960; *The Happy Thieves* (also prod.) 1962; *Circus World* 1964; *The Money Trap, The Poppy Is Also a Flower* 1966; *L'Avventurière/The Rover* (It.) 1967; *I Bastardi/Sons of Satan* (It.) 1969; *Sur la Route de Salina/The Road to Salina* (Fr./It.) 1970; *The Naked Zoo/The Grove* 1971; *The Wrath of God* 1972.

haze. A cloudy or foggy effect appearing in exterior long shots as a result of the scattering of light by dust and other particles in the atmosphere. It can be partly corrected by using a haze filter, which absorbs blue and ultraviolet light.

Head, Edith. Costume designer. *b.* Oct. 28, 1907, Los Angeles. *d.* 1981. *ed.* UCLA (B.A.); Stanford (M.A.). Hollywood's best known and most successful designer. A former language and art teacher, she served as head designer for Paramount from the late 30s and worked for Universal from 1967, fashioning outfits for some of the screen's most glamorous stars, including Barbara Stanwyck, Elizabeth Taylor, Grace Kelly, Bette Davis, Audrey Hepburn, Paul Newman, and Robert Redford. Among her design accomplishments were Dorothy Lamour's sarong, the off-the-shoulder dress worn by Bette Davis in *All About Eve* (which, she says, was born of a design miscalculation the night before shooting), and the natty suits worn by Newman and Redford in *The Sting*. She won eight Academy Awards (designated AA below) and received numerous Oscar nominations. She was married to art director Wiard IHNEN. Author: *Dress Doctor; How to Dress for Success.*

FILMS INCLUDE: *Love Me Tonight* 1932; *She Done Him Wrong* 1933; *Poppy* 1936; *Souls at Sea* 1937; *Her Jungle Love, If I Were King* 1938; *Beau Geste* 1939; *Remember the Night* 1940; *The Lady Eve, Birth of the Blues, Here Comes Mr. Jordan, Hold Back the Dawn, Ball of Fire, Road to Zanzibar, Sullivan's Travels* 1941; *The Major and the Minor, The Glass Key, I Married a Witch* 1942; *Five Graves to Cairo, Lady of Burlesque, Flesh and Fantasy* 1943; *Ministry of Fear, Miracle of Morgan's Creek, The Uninvited, Going My Way, Lady in the Dark, Double Indemnity, Hail the Conquering Hero* 1944; *The Lost Weekend, Love Letters* 1945; *The Blue Dahlia, Notorious, Blue Skies* 1946; *The Farmer's Daughter* 1947; *The Big Clock, Arch of Triumph, The Emperor Waltz, Sorry Wrong Number, A Foreign Affair* 1948; *The Great Gatsby, The Heiress* (AA), *My Foolish Heart* 1949; *Sunset Boulevard, All About Eve* (AA), *Samson and Delilah* (AA) 1950; *Detective Story, Come Back Little Sheba, A Place in the Sun* (AA) 1951; *Carrie, The Greatest Show on Earth* 1952; *War of the Worlds, Shane,*

Houdini 1953; *Rear Window, White Christmas, The Country Girl, Roman Holiday* (AA) 1953; *Sabrina* (AA) 1954; *To Catch a Thief* 1955; *The Man Who Knew Too Much, High Society, The Rose Tattoo, The Ten Commandments* 1956; *Funny Face, Gunfight at the OK Corral, Witness for the Prosecution* 1957; *Vertigo, Houseboat, Separate Tables* 1958; *A Hole in the Head* 1959; *The Facts of Life* (AA), *Pepe* 1960; *Breakfast at Tiffany's, Pocketful of Miracles* 1961; *The Man Who Shot Liberty Valance* 1962; *The Birds, Come Blow Your Horn, Hud* 1963; *The Carpetbaggers, Marnie* 1964; *The Great Race, Harlow* 1965; *Torn Curtain, The Oscar* (also personal appearance) 1966; *Barefoot in the Park, El Dorado* 1967; *Sweet Charity, Butch Cassidy and the Sundance Kid, Topaz* 1969; *Airport, Myra Breckinridge* 1970; *Sometimes a Great Notion* 1971; *Hammersmith Is Out, Pete 'n' Tillie* 1972; *A Doll's House* (UK), *The Sting* (AA) 1973; *Airport 1975* 1974; *Rooster Cogburn, The Man Who Would Be King* 1975; *Gable and Lombard, W. C. Fields and Me, Family Plot* 1976; *Airport '77* 1977; *The Big Fix* 1978; *The Last Married Couple in America* 1980; *Dead Men Don't Wear Plaid* 1982.

Headly, Glenne. Actress. Born on March 13, 1957 in New London, Conn. *ed.* High School of Performing Arts, N.Y., American College of Switzerland. Soulful stage-trained film lead who has appeared widely in films. She won several awards for work with Steppenwolf Theater in Chicago and appeared in the cable film 'And the Band Played On'. Formerly married to actor John MALKOVICH.

FILMS: *Four Friends* 1981; *Doctor Detroit* 1983; *Fandango, The Purple Rose of Cairo, Eleni* 1985; *Nadine, Making Mr. Right* 1987; *Paperhouse, Stars and Bars, Dirty Rotten Scoundrels* 1988; *Dick Tracy* (as Tess Trueheart) 1990; *Mortal Thoughts* 1991; *Grand Isle* 1992; *Getting Even with Dad* 1994; *Mr. Holland's Opus* 1995; *2 Days in the Valley, Sgt. Bilko* 1996.

head-on shot. A shot in which the action appears to come directly toward the camera.

head up (also **head out**). Film wound so that its opening frames are on the outside of the roll and hence ready for projection is said to be "head up," or "head out." When film is wound with its leader toward the core, it is said to be "tails up," or "tails out."

Heald, Anthony. Actor. Born on Aug. 25, 1944, in New Rochelle, N.Y. *ed.* Michigan State U. Reedy character actor seen often in role of obsequious heavy.

FILMS INCLUDE: *Silkwood* 1983; *Teachers* 1984; *Outrageous Fortune, Happy New Year, Orphans* 1987; *Postcards from the Edge* 1990; *The Silence of the Lambs* 1991; *Whispers in the Dark* 1992; *The Ballad of Little Jo, The Pelican Brief, Searching for Bobby Fischer* 1993; *The Client* 1994; *Bushwhacked, Kiss of Death* 1995.

Heard, John. Actor Born on Mar. 7, 1946, in Washington, D.C. *ed.* Clark U. Versatile, open-faced leading man and second lead of American films and stage. He was briefly married to actress Margot KIDDER.

FILMS: *Between the Lines, First Love* 1977; *On the Yard* 1978; *Head Over Heels/Chilly Scenes of Winter* (Can.) 1979; *Heart Beat* 1980; *Cutter's Way/Cutter and Bone* 1981; *Cat People* 1982; *C.H.U.D., Violated* 1984; *Too Scared to Scream* (release delayed from 1982), *Heaven Help Us, After Hours, The Trip to Bountiful* 1985; *The Telephone, The Milagro Beanfield War, The Seventh Sign, Big, Betrayed* 1988; *Beaches, The Package* 1989; *Mindwalk, The End of Innocence, Home Alone, Awakenings* 1990; *Rambling Rose, Mindwalk, Deceived* 1991; *Gladiator, Home Alone 2, Radio Flyer, Waterland* 1992; *In the Line of Fire, The Pelican Brief* 1993; *Before and After, My Fellow Americans* 1996.

Hearst, William Randolph. Publisher. *b.* Apr. 29, 1863, San Francisco. *ed.* Harvard; Oglethorpe U. *d.* 1951. The son of a US senator, he created a newspaper empire that made him a formidable force in the American political scene. Almost single-handedly he forced the US into the Spanish-American War as a circulation booster and his influence was instrumental in the elevation to the presidency of both Theodore and Franklin Delano Roosevelt. In 1917 he met and took an interest in the career of a struggling blonde starlet, Marion DAVIES. Vowing to make her Hollywood's greatest star, he formed Cosmopolitan Pictures for the sole purpose of producing her films and mobilized the resources of the Hearst press to publicize her personality and praise her film performances. From 1919 to 1923 the Cosmopolitan films were released by Paramount. Despite a good deal of publicity, they all lost money, largely because Hearst insisted on top production values for his protégée. But the Hearst patronage made Miss Davies one of the most famous of the Hollywood stars. In 1924, Cosmopolitan and Davies moved over to the Goldwyn company and in the following year the unit was absorbed into the newly formed MGM.

The Hearst-Davies romantic relationship, although widely known, was successfully shielded from newspaper publicity. Hearst wanted to marry his protégée but he was unable to obtain his wife's consent to a divorce. He and Miss Davies maintained several homes, including a 110-room palatial beach house in Santa Monica and their famous San Simeon castle-by-the-sea. In 1934, Hearst broke with MGM, and Cosmopolitan moved over to the Warners lot. Shortly after, when the Hearst empire suffered a financial setback, Miss Davies loaned her benefactor a million dollars to help him overcome his fiscal troubles. Despite the age difference, their relationship seemed deep and sincere. Only after Hearst's death, in 1951, did Miss Davies marry for the first time. Hearst's fascinating and enigmatic character and his long, costly affair with Miss Davies provided the inspiration for Orson Welles's film classic *Citizen Kane* (1941).

heavy. The character identified as the villain or the actor playing the role.

Hecht, Ben. Screenwriter, director, producer, playwright, novelist. *b.* Feb. 28, 1893, New York City. *d.* 1964. The son of Jewish immigrants from South Russia, he was raised in Racine, Wis., where he began showing promise as a violinist at age ten. At 12 he was a circus acrobat for a brief spell and at 17 he ran away to Chicago, where he began his writing career as a reporter. By the early 20s he was embroiled in the Chicago literary scene, much respected for his youthful achievements as a crack reporter, astute foreign correspondent, columnist, short-story writer, and budding novelist (his fictionalized reminiscences of the Chicago period provided the basis for Norman Jewison's 1969 film *Gaily Gaily*). The *Chicago Literary Times,* which he began publishing in 1923, brought him more prestige than monetary rewards, and in 1925 he arrived in New York penniless. A telegram from writer Herman Mankiewicz, an old friend, offering Hecht a Paramount contract, brought him to Hollywood in the following year.

A facile and prolific storyteller (he authored 35 books), Hecht turned out some of Hollywood's most entertaining screenplays with amazing ease. He never respected Hollywood and saw in films only a reliable source of quick money, accepting movie assignments only when he ran out of funds, which was quite often. Over a period of nearly 40 years Hecht received screen credit, alone or in collaboration, for the stories or screenplays of some 70 films, but he was also known to have collaborated on many more productions credited to other writers, notably *Back Street* (1932), *Topaze, Queen Christina* (1933), *The Hurricane* (1937), *Gone With the Wind* (1939), *Foreign*

Correspondent, The Shop Around the Corner (1940), *Roxie Hart* (1942), *The Outlaw, Lifeboat* (1943), *Gilda* (1946), *The Paradine Case* (1947), *Rope* (1948), and *Roman Holiday* (1953). His favorite collaborator was Charles MACARTHUR, with whom he also co-authored several stage plays, including 'The Front Page' and 'Twentieth Century,' and co-directed several films in the 30s.

Hecht later directed a number of films alone or with other collaborators, but his contribution to American cinema as a director was hardly comparable to the influence he exerted as a screenwriter. He received the best original story Academy Award in the first-ever Oscar ceremony for Von Sternberg's *Underworld* (1927) and another for *The Scoundrel* (1935), which he co-directed and co-wrote with MacArthur. In the late 40s Hecht was boycotted by British exhibitors for his outspoken criticism of British policies in Palestine and his active support of the Jewish resistance movement. He continued writing for the screen until his last day. He died in 1964 while working on the script of *Casino Royale* (1967), another collaboration for which he received no screen credit. An illegal immigrant ship of the rightist Irgun underground was named "Ben Hecht" in his honor.

FILMS (credited screenplays, alone or in collaboration; contributions of original story only are denoted by "S"): *Underworld* (S) 1927; *The Great Gabbo* (S), *The Unholy Night* (S) 1929; *Roadhouse Nights* (S) 1930; *The Front Page* (play basis only), *The Unholy Garden* 1931; *Scarface* 1932; *Hallelujah I'm a Bum* (S), *Turn Back the Clock, Design for Living* 1933; *Upper World* (S), *Twentieth Century* (from own play), *Shoot the Works* (play basis only, 'The Great Magoo'), *Crime Without Passion* (also co-dir., co-prod.), *Viva Villa!* 1934; *The Florentine Dagger* (novel basis only), *The Scoundrel* (also co-dir., co-prod., from own play 'All He Ever Loved'), *Barbary Coast, Spring Tonic* (play basis only, 'Man-Eating Tiger') 1935; *Once in a Blue Moon* (also co-dir., co-prod.), *Soak the Rich* (also co-dir., co-prod., from own play) 1936; *Nothing Sacred* 1937; *The Goldwyn Follies* 1938; *Gunga Din, Let Freedom Ring, Wuthering Heights, It's a Wonderful World, Some Like It Hot* (play basis only, 'The Great Magoo'), *Lady of the Tropics* 1939; *His Girl Friday* (play basis only, 'The Front Page'), *Angels Over Broadway* (also co-dir., prod.), *Comrade X* 1940; *Lydia* 1941; *Ten Gentlemen from West Point* (prod. only), *Tales of Manhattan, The Black Swan, China Girl* (also prod.) 1942; *Spellbound* 1945; *Specter of the Rose* (also co-dir., prod., from own short story), *Notorious* 1946; *Kiss of Death, Ride the Pink Horse, Her Husband's Affairs* 1947; *The Miracle of the Bells* 1948; *Whirlpool, Perfect Strangers* (play basis only, 'Ladies and Gentlemen'), *Where the Sidewalk Ends* 1950; *Actors and Sin* (also dir., prod.), *Monkey Business* 1952; *Living It Up* (musical play basis, 'Hazel Flagg,' and material from his screenplay for *Nothing Sacred)* 1954; *Ulysses, The Indian Fighter* 1955; *Miracle in the Rain* (from his own novel) 1956; *Legend of the Lost, A Farewell to Arms* 1957; *The Fiend Who Walked the West* (from his screenplay for *Kiss of Death), Queen of Outer Space* (S) 1958; *Jumbo* (play basis only) 1962; *Circus World* 1964; *Gaily Gaily* (book basis only) 1969; *The Front Page* (play basis only) 1974; *Scarface* (orig. screenplay basis only) 1983; *Switching Channels* (play basis only, 'The Front Page') 1988.

Hecht, Harold. Producer. *b.* June 1, 1907, New York City. *d.* 1985. He joined the American Laboratory Theater at 16, as an assistant to director Richard Boleslawski, and during a five-year period of study appeared on the New York stage in a number of classical productions. He later danced with the Metropolitan Opera and Martha Graham companies and in the early 30s became a dance director in films, working on such productions as *Horse Feathers* (1932) and *She Done Him Wrong* (1933). In 1934 he joined the Federal Theater Project, then returned to Hollywood as an agent. He "discovered" Burt LANCASTER on the New York stage and brought him to Hollywood. In 1947 they formed Norma Productions, opening a new era in Hollywood by breaking away from the studio system and independently handling all aspects of filmmaking, from project inception to product release. In 1952, they formed the Hecht-Lancaster company, releasing through United Artists. They were later joined by writer-producer James HILL, forming the Hecht-Hill-Lancaster company. The partnership, which produced a number of films of quality as well as commercial appeal, dissolved in the early 60s. Hecht then produced several successful films on his own. He continued developing projects—including sequels to *The Crimson Pirate* and *Cat Ballou*—right up to his death at 77 of complications from cancer.

FILMS INCLUDE: *Kiss the Blood Off My Hands* (exec. prod.) 1948; *The Flame and the Arrow* 1950; *Ten Tall Men* 1951; *The Crimson Pirate* 1952; *His Majesty O'Keefe, Apache, Vera Cruz* 1954; *Marty, The Kentuckian* 1955; *Trapeze* 1956; *The Bachelor Party, Sweet Smell of Success* (exec. prod.) 1957; *Run Silent Run Deep, Separate Tables* 1958; *The Devil's Disciple* 1959; *The Unforgiven* 1960; *The Young Savages* (exec. prod.) 1961; *Taras Bulba, Birdman of Alcatraz* (exec. prod.) 1962; *Wild and Wonderful* 1964; *Cat Ballou* 1965; *The Way West* 1967.

Heckart, Eileen. Actress. Born Anna Eckart Herbert, on Mar. 29, 1919, in Columbus, Ohio. *ed.* Ohio State; American Theatre Wing. Tall, slender, highly accomplished character actress of the American stage, TV, and films. On Broadway from the early 40s, she appeared in many important productions, winning the Drama Critics Award for 'The Dark at the Top of the Stairs' (1957–58). She also achieved eminence in many TV appearances and won an Emmy in 1967 for 'Win Me a Place at Forest Lawn.' Her film appearances have been sporadic but always impressive. She won an Academy Award as best supporting actress for her performance in *Butterflies Are Free* (1972). Earlier she had been nominated for an Oscar for *The Bad Seed* (1956). In 1976 she opened a one-woman play, 'Eleanor,' in which she portrayed Eleanor Roosevelt.

FILMS: *Miracle in the Rain, Somebody Up There Likes Me, Bus Stop, The Bad Seed* 1956; *Hot Spell* 1958; *Heller in Pink Tights* 1960; *My Six Loves* 1963; *Up the Down Staircase* 1967; *No Way to Treat a Lady* 1968; *The Tree* 1969; *Butterflies Are Free* 1972; *Zandy's Bride* 1974; *The Hiding Place* 1975; *Burnt Offerings* 1976; *Heartbreak Ridge, Seize the Day* 1986.

Heckerling, Amy. Director. Born on May 7, 1954, in New York City. A graduate of New York's Art and Design High School and the NYU Film School, she also trained at the American Film Institute and made a number of shorts before making a splendid debut as a feature director in 1982 with *Fast Times at Ridgemont High.* The unexpected box-office success of the film spawned a TV series which she helped produce. Her subsequent films of the 80s were commercially profitable comedies, particularly the *Look Who's Talking* entries. She also directed episodes of 'Twilight Zone' for TV. She married writer-director Neal ISRAEL.

FEATURE FILMS: *Fast Times at Ridgemont High* 1982; *Johnny Dangerously* 1984; *National Lampoon's European Vacation* 1985; *Look Who's Talking* (also sc.) 1989; *Look Who's Talking Too* (also co-sc.) 1990; *Look Who's Talking Now* (co-prod. only) 1993; *Clueless* (also sc.) 1995.

Heckroth, Hein. Art director. *b.* 1897, Giessen, Germany. *d.* 1970. A set and costume designer for German ballet, he left his country in 1933, with Hitler's rise to power, but during WW II he was interned in England as an enemy agent and sent to a concentration camp in Australia. After the war he designed imaginative fantasy sets and costumes for British films, often for Michael POWELL and Emeric PRESSBURGER. Academy Award for *The Red Shoes* (1948).

FILMS INCLUDE: *Caesar and Cleopatra* 1945; *A Matter of Life and Death/Stairway to Heaven* 1946; *Black Narcissus* 1947; *The Red Shoes, The Small Back Room* 1948; *The Elusive Pimpernel/The Fighting Pimpernel* 1950; *The Tales of Hoffman* 1951; *Gilbert and Sullivan* 1953; *Oh Rosalinda!* 1955; *The Battle of the River Plate/Pursuit of the Graf Spee* 1956; *Robinson soll nicht sterben/The Girl and the Legend* (co-art dir.; Ger.) 1957; *Die Dreigroschenoper/Threepenny Opera* (Ger./Fr.) 1963; *Torn Curtain* (US) 1966.

Hedren, Tippi. Actress. Born Nathalie Kay Hedren, on Jan. 19, 1931, in Lafayette, Minn. Leading lady of Hollywood films, a former model. Her screen career was launched by Alfred Hitchcock, in two of whose films she starred in the early 60s, but faltered thereafter. She is the mother of actress Melanie GRIFFITH.

FILMS INCLUDE: *The Petty Girl* (bit) 1950; *The Birds* 1963; *Marnie* 1964; *A Countess from Hong Kong* 1967; *Tiger by the Tail* 1968; *The Man with the Albatross* 1969; *Satan's Harvest* 1970; *Mr. Kingstreet's War, The Harrad Experiment* 1973; *Adonde muerte el Vineto* (Arg.) 1975; *Roar* 1981; *Pacific Heights* 1990; *In the Cold of the Night, Shadow of a Doubt* 1991; *Inevitable Grace* 1994; *Citizen Ruth* 1996.

Heerman, Victor. Director, screenwriter. *b.* Aug. 27, 1893, Surrey, England. *d.* 1977. In the US from boyhood, he was raised and educated in New York City and began acting on the stage as a child. He entered films in the mid-1910s and, after turning out a number of shorts for Mack Sennett and others, directed his first feature in 1920. During the 20s he directed a score of entertaining films, typically in the light vein, mainly for Famous Players and Paramount. He gave up directing in 1930, not long after completing his best-known film, *Animal Crackers,* starring the Marx Brothers. Thereafter he worked in films as a screenwriter, often in collaboration with his wife, Sarah Y. Mason (*b.* Mar. 31, 1896, Puma, Ariz.), who had also written the scripts for several of his earlier films as director. They won an Oscar for their screen adaptation of *Little Women* (1933).

FEATURE FILMS: As director—*Don't Ever Marry* (co-dir. with Marshall Neilan), *The Poor Simp* 1920; *A Divorce of Convenience* (also story), *The Chicken in the Case* (also story), *My Boy* (co-dir. with Albert Austin) 1921; *John Smith* (also story), *Love Is an Awful Thing* 1922; *Rupert of Hentzau, Modern Matrimony* (also story), *The Dangerous Maid* 1923; *The Confidence Man* 1924; *Old Home Week, Irish Luck* 1925; *For Wives Only* 1926; *Rubber Heels, Ladies Must Dress* (also story) 1927; *Love Hungry* (also co-story) 1928; *Personality, Paramount on Parade* (co-dir. with ten others), *Animal Crackers, Sea Legs* 1930. As screenwriter (mainly in collaboration; partial list)—*Little Women* 1933; *The Age of Innocence, The Little Minister* 1934; *Break of Hearts, Magnificent Obsession* 1935; *Stella Dallas* 1937; *Golden Boy* 1939; *Little Women* (remake) 1949; *Magnificent Obsession* (remake) 1954.

Heffron, Richard T. Director. Born on Oct. 6, 1930, in Chicago. A technically skilled craftsman, he has turned out a number of features in addition to his prolific work for TV. In 1989, French producers demonstrated their regard for his ability by selecting him to direct the first of two parts of their mammoth commemorative historical epic, *The French Revolution.*

FEATURE FILMS: *Fillmore* (rock documentary) 1972; *Newman's Law* 1974; *Trackdown, Futureworld* 1976; *Outlaw Blues* 1977; *Foolin' Around* 1980; *I, the Jury* 1982; *La Revolution Française: Les Années Terribles/The French Revolution: The Terrible Years* (also co-sc.; Fr./W. Ger./It./Can.) 1989.

Heflin, Van. Actor. *b.* Emmett Evan Heflin, Jr., Dec. 13, 1910, Walters, Okla. *d.* 1971. *ed.* U. of Oklahoma; Yale School of Drama. A restless youth, he frequently interrupted his university studies for overseas voyages as a merchant seaman and for occasional stage appearances. He made his first appearance on Broadway in 1928. Katharine Hepburn saw him in *End of Summer,* opposite Ina Claire, and persuaded RKO to cast him as her lover in the film *A Woman Rebels.* In 1939 he won acclaim as her stage co-star in Broadway's 'The Philadelphia Story.' Meanwhile, he continued asserting himself in films as a rugged second lead with a boyish countenance and won the best supporting actor Academy Award for his performance as an alcoholic intellectual in *Johnny Eager* (1942). He was subsequently promoted to leading man and turned in many fine performances as the star of both dramas and action films, memorably in *Shane* and *Patterns.* He also made some notable stage appearances, including 'A View From the Bridge' and 'A Case of Libel.' Not romantically handsome in the Hollywood mold, he played intelligent, determined, often complex heroes, and in the 60s character parts. His last role was that of a mad bomber in *Airport.* His second wife (1942–67) was a former bit player in movies, Frances Neal. He died of a heart attack while swimming in the pool of the Hollywood apartment building in which he lived. In accordance with his will his remains were cremated and scattered over the Pacific Ocean, where he loved to sail and fish.

FILMS: *A Woman Rebels* 1936; *The Outcasts of Poker Flat, Flight from Glory, Annapolis Salute, Saturday's Heroes* 1937; *Back Door to Heaven* 1939; *Santa Fe Trail* 1940; *The Feminine Touch, H. M. Pulham, Esq.* 1941; *Johnny Eager, Kid Glove Killer, Grand Central Murder, Seven Sweethearts, Tennessee Johnson* (as Andrew Johnson) 1942; *Presenting Lily Mars* 1943; *The Strange Love of Martha Ivers, Till the Clouds Roll By* 1946; *Possessed, Green Dolphin Street* 1947; *B. F.'s Daughter, Tap Roots, The Three Musketeers* (as Athos) 1948; *Act of Violence, Madame Bovary* (as Charles Bovary), *East Side West Side* 1949; *Tomahawk, The Prowler, Weekend with Father* 1951; *South of Algiers/The Golden Mask* (UK), *My Son John* 1952; *Shane, Wings of the Hawk* 1953; *Tanganyika, The Raid, Woman's World, Black Widow* 1954; *Battle Cry, Count Three and Pray* 1955; *Patterns* 1956; *3:10 to Yuma* 1957; *Gunman's Walk* 1958; *Tempest* (as Pugachev), *They Came to Cordura* 1959; *Jovanka e l'Altri/Five Branded Women* (It./Yug.), *Sotto dieci Bandiere/Under Ten Flags* (It./US) 1960; *Il Relitto/The Wastrel* (It.) 1961; *Cry of Battle/To Be a Man* 1963; *The Greatest Story Ever Told, Once a Thief* 1965; *Stagecoach* 1966; *The Man Outside* (UK), *Ognuno per sé/The Ruthless Four* (It./Ger.) 1968; *The Big Bounce* 1969; *Airport* 1970.

Heggie, O. P. Actor. *b.* 1879, Angaston, South Australia. *d.* 1936. *ed.* Adelaide Conservatory of Music; Whinham Coll. A veteran of the Australian and American stage, he made his screen debut in 1928 and for the remainder of his life played key character roles in Hollywood films. Among these were Inspector Nayland Smith in *The Mysterious Dr. Fu Manchu* (1929) and its sequel, and the part for which he is best remembered, that of the blind hermit in the horror classic, *Bride of Frankenstein* (1935).

FILMS INCLUDE: *The Actress* 1928; *The Letter, The Wheel of Life, The Mysterious Dr. Fu Manchu, The Mighty* 1929; *The Vagabond King* (as King Louis XI), *The Return of Dr. Fu Manchu, One Romantic Night/The Swan, The Bad Man, Playboy of Paris, Sunny* 1930; *East Lynne, Devotion* 1931; *Smilin' Through* 1932; *The King's Vacation, Zoo in Budapest* 1933; *Midnight, The Count of Monte Cristo, Peck's Bad Boy,*

Anne of Green Gables 1934; *Bride of Frankenstein* 1935; *The Prisoner of Shark Island* 1936.

Heifitz, Josef. Director. Born on Dec. 17 (or July 17), 1905, in Minsk, Russia, the son of a Jewish pharmacist. A graduate of the Leningrad School of Screen Arts, he collaborated on several scripts before turning director in 1928. Until 1950 he co-directed all his films with Alexander ZARKHI, notably *Baltic Deputy* (1937), a forerunner of the "historic realism" style in Soviet films. His best-known solo film is *The Lady with the Dog* (1960), an excellent screen adaptation of a Chekhov story.

FILMS: In collaboration with Alexander Zarkhi—*A Song of Steel* (also co-sc.) 1928; *Facing the Wind* 1930; *Noon* (also co-sc.) 1931; *My Country/My Fatherland* (also co-sc.) 1933; *Hectic Days/Red Army Days* (also co-sc.) 1935; *Baltic Deputy* (also co-sc.), *The Great Beginning* 1937; *A Member of the Government* 1940; *His Name Is Sukhe-Bator* 1942; *The Last Hill* (also co-sc.) 1944; *The Defeat of Japan* (doc.) 1946; *In the Name of Life* (also co-sc.) 1947; *The Precious Seeds* 1948; *Flames Over Baku* (release delayed from 1950) 1958. Alone—*Spring in Moscow* (filmed stageplay) 1953; *A Big Family* 1954; *The Rumiantsev Case* 1955; *My Beloved* (also co-sc.) 1958; *The Lady with the Dog* (also sc.) 1960; *Horizon* 1962; *A Day of Happiness* (also co-sc.) 1963; *In the Town of "S"* (also sc.) 1966; *Salute Maria!* 1970; *The Bad Good Man* 1973; *The Only One* (also co-sc.) 1976; *Asya* 1978; *First Marriage* 1980.

Heindorf, Ray. Conducter, arranger, composer. *b.* Aug. 25, 1908, Haverstraw, N.Y. *d.* 1980. For many years head of Warner Bros. music department, he arranged and conducted the musical scores for numerous films and occasionally wrote original scores and songs. He won Academy Awards for his orchestrations of *Yankee Doodle Dandy* (1942), *This Is the Army* (1943), and *The Music Man* (1962).

FILMS INCLUDE: *Big City Blues* 1932; *Captain Blood, Sweet Music* 1935; *Gold Diggers of 1937* 1936; *San Quentin* 1937; *The Roaring Twenties* 1939; *City of Conquest* 1941; *Yankee Doodle Dandy* 1942; *This Is the Army, The Desert Song* 1943; *Up in Arms* 1944; *Wonder Man, Rhapsody in Blue* 1945; *Night and Day* 1946; *Flamingo Road* 1949; *Young Man with a Horn, Tea for Two* 1950; *Strangers on a Train, A Streetcar Named Desire* 1951; *The Jazz Singer* 1953; *A Star Is Born* 1954; *Young at Heart* 1955; *The Pajama Game* 1957; *Damn Yankees* 1958; *The Music Man* 1962; *Finian's Rainbow* 1968; *1776* 1972.

Heisler, Stuart. Director. *b.* 1894, Los Angeles. *d.* 1979. He entered films in 1913 as a prop man, gradually working his way up to film editor (*Roman Scandals, Peter Ibbetson, Poppy,* etc.). He was second-unit director on John Ford's *The Hurricane* (1937) and one of several directors who were removed by Howard Hughes from the helm of his ill-fated production *Vendetta* (1946–50). As a director from the late 30s, he demonstrated an eye for visual action and was at his best with the thriller genre, but the overall quality of his output was uneven. Directed TV films in the 60s.

FILMS: *Straight from the Shoulder* 1936; *The Hurricane* (2nd-unit dir.) 1937; *The Biscuit Eater* 1940; *The Monster and the Girl, Among the Living* 1941; *The Remarkable Andrew, The Glass Key* 1942; *The Negro Soldier* (Army doc.) 1944; *Along Came Jones* 1945; *Blue Skies* 1946; *Smash-Up: The Story of a Woman* 1947; *Tulsa, Tokyo Joe* 1949; *Vendetta* (co-dir.; uncredited), *Chain Lightning, Dallas* 1950; *Storm Warning, Journey Into Light* 1951; *Saturday Island/Island of Desire* 1952; *The Star* 1953; *Beachhead, This Is My Love* 1954; *I Died a Thousand Times* 1955; *The Lone Ranger, The Burning Hills* 1956; *Hitler* 1962.

Heller, Lukas. Screenwriter. *b.* 1930, Kiel, Germany. *d.* 1988, of a heart attack. He began his career in England but before long moved to Hollywood, where he started a long and fruitful collaboration with Robert ALDRICH, providing him and other directors with gutsy, well-paced, often intelligent scripts.

FILMS INCLUDE (alone or in collaboration): *Sapphire* (addnl. dial. only; UK) 1959; *Victim* (uncredited; UK) 1961; *Candidate for Murder* (UK), *What Ever Happened to Baby Jane?* 1962; *Hot Enough for June/Agent 8¾* (UK) 1964; *Hush Hush. . . Sweet Charlotte* 1965; *The Flight of the Phoenix* 1966; *The Dirty Dozen* 1967; *The Killing of Sister George* 1968; *Too Late the Hero, Monte Walsh* 1970; *The Deadly Trackers* 1973; *Damnation Alley* 1977; *Force 110 from Navarone* (uncredited; UK) 1978; *Blue City* 1986; *Extreme Prejudice* (uncredited) 1988.

Heller, Paul M. Producer. Born on Sept. 25, 1927, in New York City. *ed.* Drexel Institute of Technology. Trained as an engineer, he served with a special branch of the Army's Signal Corps, then entered the theater as a set designer. He later worked in a similar capacity in TV and eventually in films, including *Happy Anniversary* (1959). He turned to producing in the early 60s. Working in both the US and England, he produced films ranging from great to awful.

FILMS INCLUDE (as producer alone or in collaboration): *David and Lisa* (also art dir.) 1962; *El Ojo de la Cerradura/The Eavesdropper* (Arg./US) 1964; *Secret Ceremony* (original developer) 1968; *Enter the Dragon* 1973; *The Ultimate Warrior* 1975; *Trial by Combat/Choice of Arms/Dirty Knight's Work* (also co-sc.) 1976; *The Pack* 1977; *The Promise* (also co-sc.) 1979; *First Monday in October* 1981; *Withnail and I* 1987; *My Left Foot* (co-exec. prod.) 1989.

Heller, Otto. Director of photography. *b.* Mar. 8, 1896, Prague. *d.* 1970. He began as a projectionist at a Prague motion picture theater and shot his first film footage, a record of Emperor Franz Josef's funeral procession, while serving in the Austrian army in 1916. He became a professional cameraman in 1918 and worked on many Czech and later also German productions, often for director Karel (Carl) LAMAÇ. He stayed away from Germany after the Nazi rise to power in 1933 and filmed in England, France, Holland, and Czechoslovakia. In 1940 he fled the Continent to England, where he joined the Czech air force. He remained in England, became a British citizen, and subsequently worked on many distinguished British films, showing remarkable skill in both black-and-white and color cinematography.

FILMS INCLUDE: In Czechoslovakia—*The Czech Baby Jesus* (co-phot.) 1918; *Beautiful Katya* 1920; *The Kreutzer Sonata, Werther* 1926. In Germany—*Der erste Kuss* 1928; *Die Kaviarprinzessin* 1929; *Das Mädel aus USA* 1930; *Die Fledermaus* 1931; *Kiki* 1932. In the UK—*The Amazing Quest of Mr. Bliss* 1936; *The High Command* (co-phot.) 1937; *Forty Years* (Holl.) 1939; *De Mayerling à Sarajevo* (co-phot.; Fr.) 1940; *Alibi* 1942; *Mr. Emmanuel* 1944; *I Live in Grosvenor Square/A Yank in London* 1945; *They Made Me a Fugitive/I Became a Criminal* 1947; *The Queen of Spades* 1949; *The Woman with No Name/Her Paneled Door* 1950; *Lucky Nick/I'll Get You for This* 1951; *The Crimson Pirate, The Man Who Watched the Trains Go By/Paris Express* 1952; *His Majesty O'Keefe* 1953; *The Divided Heart* 1954; *The Ladykillers, Richard III* 1955; *Manuela* 1957; *The Silent Enemy, The Sheriff of Fractured Jaw* 1958; *Ferry to Hong Kong* 1959; *Victim* 1961; *The Light in the Piazza* 1962; *Woman of Straw* 1964; *Masquerade, The Ipcress File* 1965; *Alfie, Funeral in Berlin* 1966; *Duffy* 1968; *In Search of Gregory* (co-phot.), *Bloomfield/The Hero* (UK/Isr.) 1971.

Hellinger, Mark. Producer, writer. *b.* Mar. 21, 1903, New York City. *d.* 1947. A noted journalist and columnist, he also wrote short stories and wrote and produced several Broadway revues and plays. The film *Night Court* (1932) was based on an unproduced play he had co-authored with Charles Beahan. He wrote the story for Frank Capra's racetrack comedy *Broadway Bill* (1934), which was remade in 1950 as *Riding High,* and the story for Raoul Walsh's Prohibition drama *The Roaring Twenties* (1939). He collaborated on the screenplay of Busby Berkeley's *Comet Over Broadway* (1938). He turned producer in the early 40s and characteristically presented hard-punching, masculine-oriented films. On some of his early films at Warner Bros. he was credited as associate producer under the supervision of Hal Wallis. A Broadway theater has been named after Hellinger.

FILMS INCLUDE: As associate producer—*It All Came True, Torrid Zone, Brother Orchid, They Drive by Night* 1940; *High Sierra, The Strawberry Blonde, Manpower* 1941. As producer—*Rise and Shine* 1941; *Moontide* 1942; *Thank Your Lucky Stars* 1943; *Between Two Worlds* 1944; *The Horn Blows at Midnight* 1945; *The Killers* 1946; *The Two Mrs. Carrolls, Brute Force* 1947; *The Naked City* 1948.

Hellman, Jerome. Producer. Born on Sept. 4, 1928, in New York City. *ed.* NYU. After a spell in the *New York Times* advertising department, he became an agent, eventually listing among his clients such movie directors as John Frankenheimer, George Roy Hill, Sidney Lumet, and Franklin Schaffner. Having gained some experience as a TV producer, he moved into feature films in the mid-60s. His films have been few but distinguished, including the Oscar-winning *Midnight Cowboy.* He took a first stab at directing in 1979.

FILMS: *The World of Henry Orient* 1964; *A Fine Madness* 1966; *Midnight Cowboy* 1969; *The Day of the Locust* 1975; *Coming Home* 1978; *Promises in the Dark* (also dir.) 1979; *The Mosquito Coast* 1986.

Hellman, Lillian. Playwright, screenwriter. *b.* June 20, 1905, New Orleans. *d.* 1984. *ed.* NYU; Columbia. One of the most important American dramatists, notable for the psychological intensity and liberal views expressed in her plays, she adapted a number of them to the screen and wrote several original screenplays, alone or in collaboration. In addition, several of her plays were adapted to the screen by others, including *Watch on the Rhine* (1943), *Another Part of the Forest* (1948), *The Children's Hour* (1962), and *Toys in the Attic* (1963). She recounted her life story and her long relationship with writer Dashiell HAMMETT in an autobiography, *An Unfinished Woman* (1969), and told of her experiences as an uncooperative witness during the House Un-American Activities Committee hearings in *Scoundrel Time* (1976). A chapter from her *Pentimento* (1973) provided the basis for the film *Julia* (1977), in which she was portrayed by Jane Fonda.

FILMS (as screenwriter): *The Dark Angel* (co-sc.) 1935; *These Three* (from her own play 'The Children's Hour') 1936; *Dead End* 1937; *The Little Foxes* (from her own play) 1941; *The North Star/Armored Attack* (also story) 1943; *The Searching Wind* (from her own play) 1946; *The Chase* 1966.

Hellman, Monte. Director. Born in 1932, in Greenpoint, Long Island, N.Y., to visiting Midwestern parents. Later raised in Albany. He studied drama at Stanford University and film at UCLA and began his career under the patronage of Roger CORMAN. For the most part, his films have been made with minuscule budgets at the fringe of the industry, and have enjoyed limited commercial distribution, yet he has gained a following among film aficionados for his keen visual sense and original ideas. He is held in special esteem for his Westerns, *The Shooting* and *Ride in the Whirlwind,* which were made simultaneously in Utah with skeleton crews with a combined budget of $150,000. To save on expenses he has shot some of his film in such remote locations as the Philippines and Hong Kong. His *Two-Lane Blacktop* (1971), about a car race across the Southwest, has become a lasting cult classic. In addition to his work as a director, he edited several films for Corman. He appeared as an actor in *Someone to Love* (1988). His 1989 comeback film as a director, after a decade-long hiatus, proved disappointing.

FILMS: *The Beast from Haunted Cave* 1959; *Creature from the Haunted Sea* (precredits sequence only) 1961; *The Terror* (2nd-unit dir.) 1962; *Back Door to Hell, Flight to Fury* (also co-story) 1965; *The Shooting, Ride in the Whirlwind* 1966; *Two-Lane Blacktop* 1971; *Cockfighter/Born to Kill* 1974; *Shatter* 1975; *China 9 Liberty 37/Clayton and Catherine* (It.) 1978; *Silent Night, Deadly Night III: Better Watch Out!* (also co-story), *Iguana* (US/Sp./Port.) 1989; *Reservoir Dogs* (ex.-prod.) 1992.

Helm, Brigitte. Actress. Born Gisele Eve Schittenhelm, on Mar. 17, 1906, in Berlin. Became a world-famous star after her film debut in Fritz Lang's *Metropolis* (1926). Appeared in many other German and some British and French films, but her acting range never matched her exceptional beauty, a fact that became more evident with sound. She retired in the mid-30s.

FILMS INCLUDE: *Metropolis, Am Rande der Welt/At the Edge of the World, Die Liebe der Jeanne Ney/The Loves of Jeanne Ney* 1927; *Alraune/Unholy Love, L'Argent* (Fr.), *Abwege* 1928; *Die wunderbare Lüge der Nina Petrowna/The Wonderful Lies of Nina Petrovna, Manolescu* 1929; *Die singende Stadt* 1930; *The City of Song* (UK version of latter film), *Gloria* (German and French versions), *Im Geheimdienst* 1931; *The Blue Danube* (UK), *Die Herrin von Atlantis/L'Atlantide, Die Gräfin von Monte Christo/The Countess of Monte Cristo* 1932; *Inge und die Millionen, Der Läufer von Marathon, Spione am Werk* 1933; *Die Insel, Gold* 1934; *Ein idealer Gatte* 1935.

Helmond, Katherine. Actress. Born on July 5, 1934, in Galveston, Tex. Character lead and supporting player of the American stage, TV, and films. For many years she toiled in the obscurity of provincial theater, summer stock, and off-off-Broadway, teaching drama to supplement her income. Finally receiving broader exposure in the 70s on the stage and in scattered films, she soared to sudden fame when she co-starred in the TV comedy series 'Soap' (1977–81) in the role of Jessica Tate. In 1983 she was accepted into the American Film Institute's Directing Workshop, and later directed a film, *Bankrupt,* as well as episodes of the series 'Who's the Boss,' in which she also appeared (1984–1990). On the big screen, she had some of her meatier roles in British films.

FILMS: *Believe in Me, The Hospital* 1971; *The Hindenburg* 1975; *Baby Blue Marine, Family Plot* 1976; *Time Bandits* (UK) 1981; *Brazil* (UK) 1985; *Shadey* (UK) 1986; *Overboard* 1987; *Lady in White* 1988.

Helpmann, Sir Robert. Dancer, choreographer, actor. *b.* Apr. 9, 1909, Mount Gambier, South Australia. *d.* 1986. In the Australian ballet from age 11, he later appeared in stage musicals and toured with Pavlova's dance company. He went to England in 1933, joined the Sadler's Wells Ballet, and soon became the principal dancer of that company. During the 40s he choreographed many of the company's productions and in 1950 directed the opera 'Madame Butterfly,' at Convent Garden. Long known for his mimicking skills as a dancer, he devoted most of the 50s to acting, appearing in Shakespearean roles with the Old Vic. He returned to ballet in the 60s and in 1965 was appointed co-director of the Australian Ballet company. He was knighted in 1968. He appeared sporadically in films starting in the early 40s, as both an actor and a dancer, most memorably in *The Red Shoes* (1948), which he also choreographed, and *The Tales of Hoffman* (1951). In 1973 he co-directed with Rudolf Nureyev and played the title role in the ballet-film *Don Quixote.*

FILMS: *One of Our Aircraft Is Missing* 1942; *Henry V* 1944; *Caravan* 1946; *The Red Shoes* (also chor.) 1948; *The Tales of Hoffman* 1951; *The Iron Petticoat* 1956; *The Big Money* 1958; *55 Days at Peking* (US) 1963; *The Soldier's Tale* (also chor.) 1964; *The Quiller Memorandum* 1966; *Chitty Chitty Bang Bang* 1968; *Alice's Adventures in Wonderland* (as the Mad Hatter) 1972; *Don Quixote* (title role; also co-dir. with Rudolf Nureyev) 1973; *The Mango Tree* 1977; *Patrick* 1978; *Second Time Lucky* (Austral./NZ) 1984.

Hemingway, Mariel. Actress. Born on Nov. 22, 1961, in Ketchum, Idaho. Tall (5' 11"), hale leading lady of American films. A granddaughter of novelist Ernest Hemingway, she made her screen debut at 15 and was nominated for an Academy Award as best supporting actress for her second feature, Woody Allen's *Manhattan.* She was the talk of Tinseltown's gossips when she agreed to breast augmentation before portraying Playboy centerfold Dorothy Stratten in *Star 80.* From 1991, she gained exposure playing a sexy divorce lawyer in TV's 'Civil Wars.' In one controversial episode, she appeared nude, though the scene was more the suggestion of nudity than an explicit portrayal. Nicknamed Sam, she was the owner of Sam's Restaurant in midtown Manhattan. Her older sister, Margaux Hemingway (*b.* Feb. 1955, Portland, Ore. *d.* 1996), a former model, also played leads in a number of films.

FILMS: *Lipstick* 1976; *Manhattan* 1979; *Personal Best* 1982; *Star 80* 1983; *The Mean Season, Creator* 1985; *Superman IV: The Quest for Peace* 1987; *Sunset, The Suicide Club* (also co-prod) 1988; *Falling from Grace* 1992; *Naked Gun 33⅓* 1994; *Bad Moon* 1996.

Hemmings, David. Actor. Born on Nov. 18, 1941, in Guildford, England, the only son of a cookie salesman. Entered show business at the age of nine, touring with the English Opera Group as a boy soprano. When his voice changed he took up painting and at 15 exhibited his art in a one-man show in London. Later he returned to singing, now in nightclubs, and after some roles on the stage and in TV began appearing in British films in the late 50s. He gained sudden international fame in 1966 portraying the ambiguous protagonist of Antonioni's *Blow-Up.* A small-framed man with sensitive eyes and blond, boyish good looks, he went on to play leads in other films and turned to directing and to novel-writing in the early 70s. His second wife (1968–74) was actress Gayle HUNNICUTT.

FILMS INCLUDE: *Saint Joan* 1957; *No Trees in the Street* 1959; *The Painted Smile/Murder Can Be Deadly, Some People* 1962; *Live It Up/Sing and Swing* 1963; *The System/The Girl-Getters* 1964; *Dateline Diamonds* 1965; *Blow-Up* (UK/It.) 1966; *Eye of the Devil, Camelot* (US) 1967; *Barbarella* (Fr./It.), *The Charge of the Light Brigade, The Long Day's Dying, Only When I Larf* 1968; *Alfred the Great* (title role), *The Best House in London* 1969; *The Walking Stick, Fragment of Fear* 1970; *Unman Wittering and Zingo, The Love Machine* (US) 1971; *Running Scared* (dir., co-sc. only) 1972; *The 14* (dir. only), *Voices* 1973; *Juggernaut* 1974; *Mr. Quilp* 1975; *Profondo Rosso/Deep Red* (It.) 1976; *The Squeeze, Islands in the Stream* (US), *The Prince and the Pauper/Crossed Swords, The Disappearance* (also co-prod.; Can.) 1977; *Les Liens de Sang/Blood Relatives* (Fr./Can.), *Squadra Antiruffa* (It.), *Power Play* (also co-prod.; Can./UK), *Schöner Gigolo—armer Gigolo/Just a Gigolo* (also dir.; Ger.) 1978; *Murder by Decree, Thirst* (Austral.) 1979; *Survivor* (dir. only; Austral.), *Beyond Reasonable Doubt* (NZ) *Harlequin* (Austral.) 1980; *Race for the Yankee Zephyr/Treasure of the Yankee Zephyr* (dir., prod. only; NZ/Austral.) 1981; *Man, Woman, and Child* (US) 1983; *Come the Day* (dir. only) 1985; *The Rainbow, Turn of the Screw* 1989; *Dark Horse* (dir. only) 1991.

Henabery, Joseph. Director. *b.* 1888, Omaha, Nebr. *d.* 1976. A former railroad worker, draftsman, and stage player, he entered films in 1913 as an actor, and among the films he appeared in were D. W. Griffith's *The Birth of a Nation* (1915, as President Lincoln) and *Intolerance* (1916, in "The French" episode). He also served as a researcher and production assistant on the latter film. Later that year he directed his first production, a Dorothy Gish vehicle, under the supervision of Griffith. He then moved over to Famous Players, where his first three assignments were Douglas Fairbanks productions. During the 20s he turned out many silent features for Paramount, First National, and other studios, often with the emphasis on humor, action, and suspense. He directed, among others, such stars as Fatty Arbuckle, Mary Miles Minter, Betty Compson, Richard Dix, and Rudolph Valentino. Henabery moved east in 1930 and subsequently directed comedy shorts and mystery featurettes at the Vitaphone studios in Brooklyn, venturing only once more into feature film direction, in 1943, with the low-budget action picture *The Leather Burners.* From the late 30s through his retirement in 1957 he worked mainly for the US Army Signal Corps, making training films and documentaries.

FEATURE FILMS: *Children of the Feud* 1916; *Her Official Fathers* (co-dir. with Elmer Clifton), *The Man from Painted Post* 1917; *Say! Young Fellow* (also story, sc.) 1918; *The Knickerbocker Buckaroo* (co-sc. only), *His Majesty the American* (also co-story, co-sc.) 1919; *The Inferior Sex, Love Madness, The Life of the Party, The 14th Man* 1920; *Brewster's Millions, The Traveling Salesman, Don't Call Me Little Girl, Her Winning Way, Moonlight and Honeysuckle, The Call of the North* 1921; *Her Own Money, The Man Unconquerable, While Satan Sleeps, Missing Millions, North of the Rio, Making a Man* 1922; *Sixty Cents an Hour, The Tiger's Claw, Stephen Steps Out, A Gentleman of Leisure* 1923; *The Stranger, The Guilty One, A Sainted Devil, Tongues of Flame* 1924; *Cobra, The Pinch Hitter* 1925; *The Broadway Boob, Meet the Prince, Shipwrecked* 1926; *Play Safe, See You in Jail, Lonesome Ladies* 1927; *Hellship Bronson, Sailors' Wives, United States Smith, The River Woman* 1928; *The Quitter, Light Fingers, Clear the Decks, Red Hot Speed* 1929; *The Love Trader* (also co-prod.) 1930; *The Leather Burners* 1943.

Henderson, Del(l). Director, actor. *b.* George Delbert Henderson, July 5, 1883, St. Thomas, Ontario, Canada. *d.* 1956. A stage actor in stock for several years, he joined Biograph in 1909 as a leading man in D. W. Griffith's early films and later became a close associate of Mack SENNETT. He worked for the latter in various capacities at Keystone, graduating to director by the end of 1913. He subsequently piloted numerous shorts and features for various studios, mainly melodramas emphasizing action, through 1927, when he returned to acting, in character roles. He was married to screen actress Florence Lee (1888–1962).

FILMS INCLUDE: As director—*As It Might Have Been* (also sc.), *Among the Mourners, Ambrose's First Falsehood* 1914; *Liberty Belles Divorçons* (also act.), *A Favorite Fool* (co-dir. with Edwin Frazee), *A Janitor's Wife's Temptation, That Springtime Feeling* 1915; *The Great Pearl Tangle, Because He Loved Her, Perils of the Park, A Coney Island Princess, Rolling Stones, The Kiss* 1916; *A Girl Like That, The Outcast, The Runaway, The Beautiful Adventure, Please Help Emily* 1917; *Her Second Husband, The Impostor, The Golden Wall, The*

Beloved Blackmailer, By Hook or Crook, The Road to France, Hitting the Trail 1918; *Love in a Harry, Courage for Two, Hit or Miss, Three Green Eyes, The Dead Line* 1919; *The Shark, The Plunger* 1920; *Dynamite Allen, Dead or Alive, The Girl from Porcupine* 1921; *The Broken Silence, Sure Fire Flint* 1922; *Jacqueline or Blazing Barriers* 1923; *Battling Brewster* (serial), *The Love Bandit, Gambling Wives* (also exec. prod.), *One Law for the Woman* 1924; *Defend Yourself, Quick Change* (also prod.), *Pursued, The Bad Lands, Rough Stuff* (also prod.), *Accused* 1925; *The Pay Off* 1926; *The Rambling Ranger* 1927. As actor—*Lines of White on the Sullen Sea* 1909; *The Purgation* 1910; *When a Man Loves, Comrades, In the Days of '49, The Crooked Road* 1911; *A String of Pearls* 1912; *The Clinging Vine* 1926; *Getting Gertie's Garter* 1927; *The Crowd, The Patsy, Show People, The Power of the Press, Riley the Cop* 1929; *The Laurel and Hardy Murder Case, Hit the Deck, Sins of the Children* 1930; *The Champ, Newly Rich* 1931; *From Hell to Heaven* 1933; *Bottoms Up, You're Telling Me, The Old-Fashioned Way, The Notorious Sophie Lang, It's a Gift* 1934; *Ruggles of Red Gap* 1935; *Our Relations, Poppy* 1936; *Make Way for Tomorrow* 1937; *Goodbye Broadway* 1938; *Frontier Marshal* 1939; *You Can't Fool Your Wife* 1940; *Nothing but Trouble* 1944; *Wilson* 1945.

Hendrix, Wanda. Actress. *b.* Dixie Wanda Hendrix, Nov. 3, 1928, Jacksonville, Fla. *d.* 1981. She joined the Jacksonville Little Theater directly out of junior high school and made her film debut at 16. She showed much promise with her early performances as an ingenue in such films as *Confidential Agent* (1945) and *Ride the Pink Horse* (1947) but then settled into routine lead roles, typically as a lady in distress, mainly in minor action films. Her first of three husbands (1949–50) was actor Audie MURPHY. She died at 52 of pneumonia.

FILMS: *Confidential Agent* 1945; *Nora Prentiss, Welcome Stranger, Variety Girl, Ride the Pink Horse* 1947; *Miss Tatlock's Millions* 1948; *My Own True Love, Prince of Foxes, Song of Surrender* 1949; *Captain Carey USA, Saddle Tramp, Sierra, The Admiral Was a Lady* 1950; *My Outlaw Brother, The Highwayman* 1951; *South of Algiers/The Golden Mask* (UK), *Montana Territory* 1952; *The Last Posse, Sea of Lost Ships* 1953; *Highway Dragnet, The Black Dakotas* 1954; *The Boy Who Caught a Crook* 1961; *Johnny Cool* 1963; *Stage to Thunder Rock* 1964.

Hendry, Ian. Actor. *b.* Jan. 13, 1931, Ipswich. England. *d.* 1984. Stalwart lead and character player of British TV and films, typically in sly, aggressive roles. He started as a stooge to a circus clown, but after military service, trained for the stage at the Central School of Speech and Drama. Appearances in provincial and London productions were followed by hundreds of TV roles and many films. His screen career showed promise in the 60s when he was cast in several starring and strong supporting roles. In 1971 he won the British Film Academy Award as best supporting actor for his part as an unscrupulous heavy in *Get Carter.* But his career suffered a steep decline in the 70s, and ended tragically in bankruptcy and ill health. His second (1963–71) of three wives was actress Janet MUNRO.

FILMS INCLUDE: *Simon and Laura* (bit) 1955; *Room at the Top* 1958; *Sink the Bismarck!, In the Nick* 1960; *Live Now, Pay Later* 1962; *The Girl in the Headlines/The Model Murder Case, Children of the Damned, This Is My Street* 1963; *The Beauty Judge/Contest Girl* 1964; *Repulsion, The Hill* 1965; *The Sandwich Man* 1966; *Casino Royale* 1967; *Cry Wolf* 1968; *Doppelganger/Journey to the Far Side of the Sun, The Southern Star* 1969; *The Mackenzie Break* 1970; *Get Carter* 1971; *The Jerusalem File, Tales from the Crypt* 1972; *Theatre of Blood, Assassin* 1973; *The Internecine Project* 1974; *Professione: Reporter/The Passenger* (It./Fr./Sp./US) 1975; *Damien—Omen II* (US) 1978; *The Bitch* 1979; *McVicar* 1980.

Henie, Sonja. Skater, actress. *b.* Apr. 8, 1910, Oslo, Norway. *d.* 1969. She began dancing at age four and ice skating at eight, going on to win Norway's skating championship at 14 and become the world champion at 15. She won gold medals and set world marks in three consecutive Winter Olympics: 1928, 1932, and 1936. She then turned professional, toured with an ice show, and set out for Hollywood and a successful film career. A charming blue-eyed blonde with a winning smile and a sense of showmanship, she combined a fetching personality and her athletic skill to become one of the leading stars of 20th Century-Fox in the late 30s. Her screen vehicles were typically light romantic affairs with sugar-coated, thin stories surrounding skating displays. By the early 40s, however, her popularity was waning and her screen career came to a frozen halt by the end of the decade. But she continued to draw huge audiences and reap enormous profits as the producer and star of the Hollywood Ice Revue extravaganzas at New York's Madison Square Garden and in other arenas from coast to coast. The thrice-married, twice-divorced Miss Henie retired from show business in 1960; nine years later she died of leukemia.

FILMS: *Svy Dager for Elisabeth* (Nor.) 1927; *One in a Million, Thin Ice* 1937; *Happy Landing, My Lucky Star* 1938; *Second Fiddle, Everything Happens at Night* 1939; *Sun Valley Serenade* 1941; *Iceland* 1942; *Wintertime* 1943; *It's a Pleasure* 1945; *The Countess of Monte Cristo* 1948; *Hello London/London Calling* (UK) 1958.

Henley, Beth. Playwright, screenwriter. Born Elizabeth Becker Henley (Caldwell), on May 8, 1952, in Jackson, Miss. *ed.* Southern Methodist U. (B.F.A.); U. of Illinois (postgrad). She had her first play produced when she was still a college sophomore, then went on to win a Pulitzer Prize for 'Crimes of the Heart' (1978). She was nominated for an Academy Award for her 1986 screen adaptation of the play. She played a cameo role as a Bible pusher in Jonathan Demme's *Swing Shift* (1984).

FILMS: *True Stories* (co-sc.), *Crimes of the Heart* (from her own play), *Nobody's Fool* 1986; *Miss Firecracker* (from her own play, 'The Miss Firecracker Contest') 1989.

Henner, Marilu. Actress. Born on Apr. 6, 1952, in Chicago. *ed.* U. of Chicago. Bubbly light leading lady of American TV and movies. She appeared in stage musicals before her screen debut in 1977. It was on TV that she first gained and, later, furthered her fame, as Elaine in the popular comedy series 'Taxi' and as the unflappable wife of Burt REYNOLDS in 'Evening Shade.'

FILMS: *Between the Lines* 1977; *Bloodbrothers* 1978; *Hammett* 1982; *The Man Who Loved Women* 1983; *Cannonball Run II, Johnny Dangerously* 1984; *Rustlers' Rhapsody, Perfect* 1985; *Chains of Gold* 1990; *L.A. Story* 1991; *Noises Off* 1992; *Chasers* 1994.

Henning, Eva. Actress. Born on May 10, 1920, in New York City. A graduate of the Royal Dramatic Theater in Stockholm, she appeared in Swedish films from the late 30s and became a popular star in the 40s. Since 1958 she has worked in Norway, mostly on stage. At one time she was married to Hasse Ekman, who directed some of her films. She reached her career peak in two Ingmar Bergman films in 1949, *The Devil's Wanton* and *Three Strange Loves.*

FILMS INCLUDE: *Gentleman for Hire* 1940; *Elvira Madigan* 1943; *The Royal Rabble* 1945; *One Swallow Doesn't Make a Summer* 1947; *The Banquet* 1948; *The Devil's Wanton/Prison, Three Strange Loves/Thirst* 1949; *Girl with Hyacinths* 1950; *The White Cat* 1951; *Gabrielle* 1954; *Black Palm Trees* 1968.

Henning-Jensen, Astrid and **Bjarne.** Danish husband-wife director-writer team. Bjarne (*b.* Oct. 6, 1908, Copenhagen), a former stage actor and playwright, turned to film directing in 1940, starting out with documentary shorts and moving on to feature films. He soon became established as one of the leading figures of the Danish cinema, although his only internationally well-known work is *Ditte: Child of Man* (1946). Astrid (*b.* Astrid Smahl, Dec. 10, 1914, Copenhagen), a former stage actress, began working with Bjarne as an assistant and script collaborator but soon joined him as co-director as well. In 1945 she made her first solo film as director and subsequently piloted quite a few documentaries and a number of feature films on her own in between collaborations with her husband. Bjarne has also collaborated in various capacities on his wife's films as director.

Astrid won the Catholic Film Office Award at the 1960 Cannes Festival for *Paw* and the best director prize at the 1979 Berlin Festival for *Winter Children.* She also appeared as an actress in several films, and played the pivotal role of the housekeeper in Lars von Trier's *The Element of Crime* (1984).

FILMS INCLUDE: Directed by Bjarne—*Christian IV: Master Builder, Carbon* 1941; *Sugar* 1942; *Corn, Horses Paper, To Be Young* 1943; *Danish Island* 1944; *Danish Brigade in Sweden, Freedom Committee* 1945; *Ditte: Child of Man* 1946; *Where Mountains Float* 1955; *Short Is the Summer* 1962; *The Ship and the Stars* 1975. Directed by both—*S.O.S. Molars* 1943; *Fugitives Find Shelter* 1945; *Those Blasted Kids* 1947; *Kristinus Bergman* 1948; *Boys from the West Coast* 1950; *Solstik* 1953; *Tivoli Garden Games* 1954. Directed by Astrid—*Denmark Grows Up* 1947; *Palle Alone in the World* 1949; *Krane's Bakery Shop* 1951; *Unknown Man* 1953; *Ballet Girl* 1954; *Love on Credit* 1955; *Paw/Boy of Two Worlds/The Lure of the Jungle* 1959; *Unfaithful* 1966; *Me and You* 1968; *Vinterboern/Winter Children* (also sc., edit.) 1978; *The Moment* 1980; *Hodja fra Pjort* 1985; *Street of My Childhood* 1986.

Henreid, Paul. Actor, director. *b.* Paul George Julius von Henreid, Jan. 10, 1908, in Trieste. *d.* 1992. The son of a Viennese baron banker, he began his working career in publishing. In 1933 he was discovered by Otto PREMINGER, then managing director for Max REINHARDT, and became a leading player with the latter's Vienna theater. In England from 1935, he appeared on stage and in films, then emigrated to the US in 1940 and became an American citizen. As a Hollywood star he was soon the object of the admiration of American women as a prototype of the Continental lover, aristocratic, elegant, and gallant, memorably opposite Bette Davis in *Now Voyager* and Ingrid Bergman in *Casablanca.* In the 50s he began doubling as director and directed a number of films and TV movies before his death in 1992. His daughter, Monika Henreid, became a screen actress. Autobiography: *Ladies Man* (1984).

FILMS (as actor): In Morocco—*Baroud/Love in Morocco* 1933. In Austria—*Morgenrot/Dawn* 1933; *Hohe Schule/Das Geheimnis des Carlo Cavelli/High School/The Secrets of Cavelli* 1934; *Nur ein Komödiant/Only a Comedian, Eva* 1935. In the UK—*Victoria the Great* 1937; *Goodbye Mr. Chips* (US/UK), *An Englishman's Home/Madmen of Europe* 1939; *Night Train to Munich/Night Train, Under Your Hat* 1940. In the US—*Joan of Paris, Now Voyager* 1942; *Casablanca* 1943; *In Our Time, Between Two Worlds, The Conspirators, Hollywood Canteen* 1944; *The Spanish Main* 1945; *Devotion, Of Human Bondage* (as Philip Carey), *Deception* 1946; *Song of Love* (as Robert Schumann) 1947; *Hollow Triumph/The Scar* (also prod.) 1948; *Rope of Sand* 1949; *So Young So Bad, Last of the Buccaneers* (as Jean Lafitte) 1950; *Pardon My French* 1951; *For Men Only* (also dir., prod.), *Thief of Damascus* 1952; *Siren of Bagdad* 1953; *Deep in My Heart* 1954; *Pirates of Tripoli* 1955; *A Woman's Devotion* (also dir.), *Meet Me in Las Vegas* 1956; *Ten Thousand Bedrooms* 1957; *Girls on the Loose, Live Fast Die Young* (both dir. only) 1958; *Holiday for Lovers, Never So Few* 1959; *The Four Horsemen of the Apocalypse* 1962; *Dead Ringer* (dir. only) 1964; *Operation Crossbow* (UK/It.), *Ballad in Blue/Blues for Lovers* (dir., co-story only; UK) 1965; *The Madwoman of Chaillot* (UK) 1969; *Exorcist II: The Heretic* 1977.

Henriksen, Lance. Actor. Born in New York City. *ed.* Actors Studio. Gaunt supporting player with striking eyes. He has acted on Broadway, notably in 'Richard III', but is best known to moviegoers for his roles in science fiction, horror, and suspense films, particularly as the sympathetic android Bishop in *Aliens.*

FILMS INCLUDE: *It Ain't Easy* 1972; *Dog Day Afternoon, The Terror of Dr. Chancey* 1975; *The Next Man* 1976; *Close Encounters of the Third Kind* 1977; *Damien: Omen II* 1978; *The Visitor* 1979; *The Dark End of the Street, Piranha II: The Spawning, Prince of the City* 1981; *Nightmares, The Right Stuff* 1983; *The Terminator* 1984; *Jagged Edge* 1985; *Aliens, Choke Canyon* 1986; *Near Dark* 1987; *Deadly Intent, Pumpkinhead* 1988; *Hit List, The Horror Show, Johnny Handsome, Survival Quest* 1989; *The Pit and the Pendulum, Stone Cold* 1992; *Alien 3, Jennifer Eight* 1992; *Excessive Force, Hard Target, Knights, Man's Best Friend, The Outfit, Super Mario Brothers* 1993; *Color of Night, No Escape* 1994; *Powder, The Quick and the Dead* 1995.

Henrikson, Anders. Director, actor. *b.* June 13, 1896, Stockholm. *d.* 1965. A stage and screen actor from the 20s, he began directing pictures in 1933. Although most of his films were not of exceptional caliber, during the early 40s he played an important role in the rejuvenation of the Swedish cinema, notably with *A Crime* (1940). He often appeared in his own films and in those of other Swedish directors.

FILMS INCLUDE: As director—*The Girl from the Department Store* (co-dir.) 1933; *It Pays to Advertise* (also act.) 1936; *The Great Love* (also co-sc., act.) 1938; *Whalers* 1939; *A Crime* (also co-sc., act.) 1940; *Only a Woman, Life Goes On* (both also co-sc., act.) 1941; *Dangerous Roads* (also act.) 1942; *Blood and Fire* (also act.) 1945; *The Key and the Ring* (also act.) 1947; *The Girl from the Mountain Village* 1948; *Giftas/Of Love and Lust/Married Life* (also act.) 1951. As actor only—*The Strongest* 1929; *Walpurgis Night* 1935; *Intermezzo* 1936; *Himlaspelet/The Road to Heaven* 1942; *The Devil's Wanton* 1949; *Morianna* 1965.

Henry, Buck. Screenwriter, actor. Born Buck Henry Zuckerman, in 1930, in New York City. *ed.* Dartmouth. The son of former Mack Sennett bathing beauty Ruth Taylor, and an Air Force general later turned prominent Wall Street stockbroker, he broke into show business at 16 as a minor member of the cast of the Broadway production of 'Life with Father.' He spent his military service years during the Korean War touring Germany with the Seventh Army Repertory Company in a musical comedy that he wrote, directed, and starred in. When he returned to civilian life, he found acting and writing jobs elusive but gained some fame in the 50s as a hoaxer when, with a friend, he formed SINA, the Society for Indecency to Naked Animals, and appeared on TV talk shows to promote his philosophical joke about the link between the nudity of animals and the moral decline of man. In 1960 he joined The Premise, the off-Broadway improvisational theater group, then moved to Hollywood, where he began writing comedy material for the TV shows of Steve Allen and Garry Moore and for the weekly satirical show 'That Was the Week That Was.' He hit the jackpot in

1964 as co-writer with Mel Brooks of the pilot for the highly successful 'Get Smart' TV comedy series. That same year he collaborated on the script of, and acted in, the hilariously offbeat film *The Troublemaker* and three years later became one of Hollywood's most sought-after comedy screenwriters after collaborating on the script of the hit film *The Graduate* and appearing as the hotel clerk. He also appears in films as an actor, and in 1978 made his directorial debut, collaborating with Warren BEATTY on *Heaven Can Wait,* for which both were nominated for an Oscar.

FILMS: *The Troublemaker* (story, co-sc., act.) 1964; *The Graduate* (co-sc., act.) 1967; *The Secret War of Harry Frigg* (act.), *Candy* (sc.) 1968; *Catch-22* (sc., act.), *The Owl and the Pussycat* (sc., act. in bit role) 1970; *Taking Off* (act.), *Is There Sex After Death?* (act.) 1971; *What's Up Doc?* (co-sc.) 1972; *The Day of the Dolphin* (sc.) 1973; *The Man Who Fell to Earth* (act.; UK) 1976; *Heaven Can Wait* (co-prod., co-dir. with Warren Beatty, act.) 1978; *Old Boyfriends* (act.) 1979; *Gloria* (act.), *First Family* (dir. sc., act.) 1980; *Strong Medicine* (act.) 1981; *Eating Raoul* (act.) 1982; *Protocol* (sc.) 1984; *Aria* (act., 'Rigoletto' segment; UK) 1987; *Dark Before Dawn* (act.) 1988; *Rude Awakening* (act.) 1989; *Tune in Tomorrow* (act.) 1990; *Defending Your Life* (act.) 1991; *The Player* (act.), *The Linguini Incident* (act.) 1992; *Grumpy Old Men* (act.), *Short Cuts* (act.) 1993; *Even Cowgirls Get the Blues* 1994; *To Die For* (act.) 1995.

Henry, Charlotte. Actress. *b.* Mar. 3, 1913, Brooklyn, N.Y. *d.* 1980. On stage from the age of five, she made her screen debut in 1930, repeating her Broadway role in *Courage.* She played juvenile leads in Paramount films of the early 30s, notably in the title role of the all-star-cast production of *Alice in Wonderland* (1933) and as Bo Beep in the Laurel and Hardy vehicle *Babes in Toyland* (1934). She later played a number of leading-lady roles but could not get past low-grade B productions and in the early 40s retired from the screen.

FILMS INCLUDE: *Harmony at Home, Courage* 1930; *Huckleberry Finn* (as Mary Jane), *Arrowsmith* 1931; *Forbidden, Lena Rivers, Rebecca of Sunnybrook Farm* 1932; *Alice in Wonderland* (title role) 1933; *The Human Side, The Last Gentleman, Babes in Toyland* 1934; *Laddie, Three Kids and a Queen* 1935; *Hearts in Bondage, The Mandarin Mystery, Charlie Chan at the Opera* 1936; *Jungle Menace* (serial) 1937; *Bowery Blitzkrieg* 1941; *She's in the Army* 1942.

Henry, Justin. Actor. Born on May 25, 1971, in Rye, N.Y. He was only eight when he captivated filmgoers with his spontaneous performance as the boy over whose custody Dustin HOFFMAN and Meryl STREEP were battling in *Kramer vs. Kramer* (1979). He won an Academy Award nomination for the role, the youngest performer so honored. He appeared in films during the 80s but hasn't been seen on screen since 1988.

FILM: *Kramer vs. Kramer* 1979; *Sixteen Candles, Martin's Day* (Can.) 1984; *Sweet Hearts Dance* 1988.

Henry, William (Bill). Actor. Born in 1918, in Los Angeles. In films from age eight, he played mostly bit roles while attending elementary and high schools. Subsequently he appeared in more than 100 films, both as the hero of B action pictures and as the second lead or a character player in a variety of film genres.

FILMS INCLUDE: *Lord Jim* 1926; *Adorable* 1933; *The Thin Man* 1934; *China Seas* 1935; *Tarzan Escapes* 1936; *Double or Nothing, Madame X* 1937; *Four Men and a Prayer, Yellow Jack, Campus Confessions* 1938; *Ambush* 1939; *Parole Fixer, The Way of All Flesh* 1940; *Blossoms in the Dust* 1941; *Sweater Girl* 1942; *Johnny Come Lately, Tornado* 1943; *Women in Bondage, The Adventures of Mark Twain* 1944; *The Invisible Informer* 1946; *Gun Talk* 1947; *Women of the Night, The Denver Kid* 1948; *Federal Man* 1950; *Valentino* 1951; *Canadian Mounties vs. the Atomic Invaders* (serial) 1953; *Secret of the Incas* 1954; *Mister Roberts* 1955; *Wings of Eagles* 1957; *The Last Hurrah* 1958; *The Horse Soldiers* 1959; *Sergeant Rutledge, The Alamo* 1960; *Two Rode Together* 1961; *The Man Who Shot Liberty Valance* 1962; *Cheyenne Autumn* 1964; *El Dorado* 1967.

Henson, Jim. Puppeteer, director, producer. *b.* Sept. 24, 1936, Greenville, Mass. *d.* 1990. As a youngster, he moved with his family to Hyattsville, Maryland, when his father, an agronomist, was reassigned by the US Department of Agriculture to Washington, D.C. As a high school senior in 1954 he landed a job as a puppeteer on a local TV show, 'Sam and His Friends.' He continued with the show while studying theater arts at the University of Maryland. Deciding to make puppeteering his career, he began creating the characters that would one day make him famous, starting with Kermit the Frog, whom he fashioned in 1959 from his mother's old coat. Other puppet characters followed. He called them Muppets. At the same time, he began experimenting with film. In 1965, his short *Time Piece* was nominated for an Academy Award. Henson's big break came in 1969, when the Children's Television Workshop launched on public TV the preschoolers' program 'Sesame Street.' The beloved Muppets became the show's heart and soul. Kermit the Frog, Oscar the Grouch, the Cookie Monster, Big Bird, Bert and Ernie, and other Henson creatures became the teachers and playmates of millions of children in the US and in 80 countries around the world. The affable, bearded Henson not only created and orchestrated the puppet gang but was himself the voice and manipulator of Kermit, Ernie, and game-show host Guy Smiley. The program's enormous success spawned others, including 'The Muppet Show' and 'Fraggle Rock.' He won a Peabody Award as well as several Emmys.

In 1979, Henson broke into feature films with *The Muppet Movie.* He made his debut as a feature director in 1981 with *The Great Muppet Caper* and went on to direct or produce several other films, some in collaboration with longtime associate Frank Oz. The Muppet enterprise had grown into a mammoth empire by 1989, when the Disney company was set to acquire it for a reported $150 million. In the prime of his career, the 53-year-old Henson fell suddenly ill with acute respiratory distress. When he died of streptococcus pneumonia, he was mourned by millions of fans. The Henson organization is now run by son Brian Henson, and a deal with Disney, different from the one planned before Henson's death, was effected. Daughter Lisa Henson is a film executive.

FEATURE FILMS: *The Muppet Movie* (prod., act.) 1979; *The Great Muppet Caper* (dir., act.) 1981; *The Dark Crystal* (co-dir., co-prod., story, voice) 1982; *The Muppets Take Manhattan* (exec. prod. act.) 1984; *Into the Night* (cameo), *Sesame Street Presents: Follow That Bird* (act.), *Dreamchild* (creature des.) 1985; *Labyrinth* (dir., co-story) 1986; *The Bear* (creature des.) 1989; *Teenage Mutant Ninja Turtles* (creature des.), *The Witches* (exec. prod.) 1990.

Hepburn, Audrey. Actress. *b.* Audrey Hepburn-Ruston, May 4, 1929, near Brussels, Belgium. *d.* 1993. The daughter of an English banker and a Dutch baroness, she was sent to a girls' school near London after her parents' divorce. She was vacationing with her mother in Arnhem, Holland, when WW II broke out. She spent the war years in the Nazi-occupied town, attending a local public school and receiving ballet training at the Arnhem Conservatory. After the war she went to London on a ballet scholarship. Graceful, slender, and long-legged, she soon began winning modeling assignments from fashion photographers. In the early 50s she joined Felix Aylmer's acting classes and began playing bit parts in British movies. While filming

Monte Carlo Baby on the French Riviera, in 1951, she met Colette, the French novelist, who insisted that Audrey play the lead in the forthcoming Broadway adaptation of her *Gigi.*

Fragile and radiant, projecting both childlike and feminine qualities, Miss Hepburn was an ideal Colette heroine. Her success in the play led to a starring part opposite Gregory Peck in the film *Roman Holiday,* for which she won an Academy Award (she would later be nominated for Oscars for *Sabrina, The Nun's Story, Breakfast at Tiffany's,* and *Wait Until Dark*). Six weeks after the Oscar ceremonies she won the Tony Award for her performance in the Broadway play 'Ondine.' Later in 1954 she married Mel FERRER, her co-star in the play. They also co-starred in King Vidor's *War and Peace,* she as Natasha and he as Andrei. Ferrer later directed her in *Green Mansions* and produced her last picture of the 60s, *Wait Until Dark* (1967), for which she received her fifth Oscar nomination, for her portrayal of a terrorized blind woman. But Ferrer had no part in the real highlights of her career, notably *Funny Face, Love in the Afternoon, The Nun's Story, Breakfast at Tiffany's, Charade,* and *My Fair Lady.* They divorced in 1968. The following year she married an Italian psychiatrist nine years her junior and made her home in Rome and later in Switzerland. She was named a Special Ambassador for UNICEF and devoted much of her free time to charity. She returned to the screen in 1976 after a nine-year absence as a luminous Maid Marian in *Robin and Marian*, but her subsequent film appearances were few and far between. Shortly after a highly publicized 1992 mission of mercy to famine- and war-torn Somalia, she was diagnosed with colon cancer. She succumbed after a brief struggle with the disease. Her death was mourned internationally as the loss of one of the favorite film actresses of all time, an icon to style, elegance, dignity, and charity.

FILMS: In the UK—*One Wild Oat, Young Wives' Tale, Laughter in Paradise, The Lavender Hill Mob, Nous irons à Monte Carlo/Monte Carlo Baby* (Fr.) 1951; *The Secret People* 1952. In the US—*Roman Holiday* 1953; *Sabrina* 1954; *War and Peace* (as Natasha; US/It.) 1956; *Funny Face, Love in the Afternoon* 1957; *Green Mansions, The Nun's Story* 1959; *The Unforgiven* 1960; *Breakfast at Tiffany's* 1961; *The Children's Hour* 1962; *Charade* 1963; *Paris When It Sizzles, My Fair Lady* (as Eliza Doolittle) 1964; *How to Steal a Million* 1966; *Two for the Road* (US/UK), *Wait Until Dark* 1967; *Robin and Marian* (as Maid Marian; UK) 1976; *Bloodline/Sidney Sheldon's Bloodline* 1979; *They All Laughed* 1981; *Always* 1989.

Hepburn, Katharine. Actress. Born on Nov. 9, 1907, in Hartford, Conn. *ed.* Bryn Mawr. The second of six children of a distinguished New England family (her father was a noted surgeon and her mother a dedicated suffragette and early crusader for birth control), she was brought up in an atmosphere of complete spiritual freedom and Spartan physical discipline. Drawn to the stage at an early age, she began acting in amateur productions at age 12 and later gained much experience in college dramatics. In June of 1928, she arrived in Baltimore with a letter of recommendation to Edwin Knopf, who was casting for his stock company's production of 'Czarina.' She made her professional debut in a minor role in that play. Before the year was out she was playing bits on Broadway and the leading lady part in the life of a Philadelphia socialite broker, Ludlow Ogden Smith, whom she married that year and divorced in 1934.

Strong-minded and outspoken, Hepburn got herself into constant trouble with Broadway and summer-stock producers and directors. She was hired, fired, then rehired for the leading part in Broadway's 'The Warrior's Husband' (1932), in which she scored her first critical success. RKO offered her a film contract. Not really interested, she named a ridiculous fee, but to her astonishment the studio accepted her terms. Her screen debut in *A Bill of Divorcement,* opposite John Barrymore, was an unqualified hit, the first of a long succession of memorable film appearances that won for her three Academy Awards (for *Morning Glory, Guess Who's Coming to Dinner,* and *The Lion in Winter*), eight more Oscar nominations (for *Alice Adams, The Philadelphia Story, Woman of the Year, The African Queen, Summertime, The Rainmaker, Suddenly Last Summer,* and *Long Day's Journey Into Night*), and the unanimous admiration of the critics and the public.

From the moment she arrived in Hollywood, Hepburn projected an image quite different from that of the usual Hollywood star. She strode through town in slacks, refused to grant interviews, shunned autograph hounds, and kept her private life tightly sealed. She didn't mingle with the Hollywood crowd, preferring the company of a select group of intellectuals. Dignified and arrogant, she demanded and commanded the respect of studio executives, who were quite unaccustomed to her style and didn't know how to handle her. She won her first Academy Award for her third picture, *Morning Glory,* and scored another personal triumph with her fourth, *Little Women* (both 1933). Fortified with her newly won acclaim, she returned to the Broadway stage in 'The Lake.' But her stage comeback was a disaster and provoked Dorothy Parker's famous remark that Hepburn "ran the gamut of emotions from A to B." Returning to RKO, a little subdued, she appeared in a mixture of good and mediocre productions, then capped her screen achievements of the 30s with sparkling performances in the hilarious screwball comedy *Bringing Up Baby* and the film version of the Broadway hit 'Holiday' (both 1938, opposite Cary Grant).

Despite the critical and popular success of these films, Hepburn was branded "box office poison" by a leading exhibitor, and true to character, she stormed out of Hollywood, vowing to return only under the most favorable circumstances.

After turning down several stage and screen projects, and being in turn rejected for the role of Scarlett O'Hara in *Gone With the Wind,* for which she tested, Hepburn agreed to play the lead in the Broadway play 'The Philadelphia Story,' by Philip Barry, the author of 'Holiday.' Wisely, she waived salary for a cut of the profits and secured the movie rights of the play. It enjoyed tremendous success in New York and on the road. She now returned to Hollywood holding a trump. She sold the movie rights to MGM for a neat sum and dictated the choice of director (George Cukor) and co-stars (Cary Grant and James Stewart). The film version broke attendance records and brought Hepburn the New York Film Critics Award as well as her third Oscar nomination.

Her next film at MGM, *Woman of the Year* (1942), brought into her life the man who was to become a lifelong intimate friend, Spencer TRACY. The Tracy-Hepburn relationship (he always insisted on first billing) has long been a Hollywood legend. Extreme opposites in background, taste, and acting techniques, yet both strong-willed and eccentric by Hollywood standards, they formed a most remarkable screen team in nine films. Their 25-year-long romance, an open secret from its inception, was a tender, dignified, and very private affair. Even the notorious Hollywood columnists laid off the affair, in deference to the respected couple. Writer-director Garson Kanin, who was instrumental in getting Tracy and Hepburn together for their first screen collaboration, wrote a touching tribute to their romance, *Tracy and Hepburn: An Intimate Memoir* (1971), which became a best-seller.

Two memorable portrayals of spinsters, in *The African Queen* (1951) and *Summertime* (1955), as well as a remarkable performance as a Southern matriarch in *Suddenly Last Summer*

(1959), highlighted Hepburn's career in the 50s. In 1962 she won the best actress award at the Cannes Film Festival for *Long Day's Journey Into Night.* She wasn't to make another film or stage appearance for the next five years, during which she spent much of her time with the ailing Tracy. At one point of crisis, in 1965, she alternated with Tracy's wife (since 1928), Louise, in keeping vigil at his bedside.

Hepburn and a gravely ill Tracy were reunited on the screen for the last time in *Guess Who's Coming to Dinner* (1967). A few weeks after the film's completion he died. Hepburn won her second Academy Award for that film. The following year, she received her third Oscar, in a tie with Barbra Streisand, for *The Lion in Winter.* After a long absence, she returned to Broadway, in 1969, in 'Coco' and again in 1976, in 'A Matter of Gravity.' Undaunted by deteriorating health, she continued appearing in occasional films. She won a fourth Oscar and the British Academy Award for her performance in *On Golden Pond* (1981). In 1987 she published a memoir, *The Making of the African Queen,* recollecting the harrowing events surrounding the production of one of her finest films. Her 1992 memoir, *Me*, was an international best-seller.

FILMS: *A Bill of Divorcement* 1932; *Christopher Strong, Morning Glory, Little Women* 1933; *Spitfire, The Little Minister* 1934; *Break of Hearts, Alice Adams* 1935; *Sylvia Scarlett, Mary of Scotland, A Woman Rebels* 1936; *Quality Street, Stage Door* 1937; *Bringing Up Baby, Holiday* 1938; *The Philadelphia Story* 1940; *Woman of the Year, Keeper of the Flame* 1942; *Stage Door Canteen* 1943; *Dragon Seed* 1944; *Without Love* 1945; *Undercurrent* 1946; *The Sea of Grass, Song of Love* 1947; *State of the Union* 1948; *Adam's Rib* 1949; *The African Queen* 1951; *Pat and Mike* 1952; *Summertime* 1955; *The Rainmaker, The Iron Petticoat* 1956; *Desk Set* 1957; *Suddenly Last Summer* 1959; *Long Day's Journey Into Night* 1962; *Guess Who's Coming to Dinner* 1967; *The Lion in Winter* 1968; *The Madwoman of Chaillot* 1969; *The Trojan Women* 1971; *A Delicate Balance* 1973; *Love Among the Ruins* (TV) 1975; *Rooster Cogburn* 1976; *Olly Olly Oxen Free* 1978; *The Corn Is Green* (TV) 1979; *On Golden Pond* 1981; *The Ultimate Solution of Grace Quigley/Grace Quigley* 1984; *Mrs. Delafield Wants to Marry* (TV) 1986; *Love Affair* 1994.

Hepworth, Cecil. Director, producer, inventor, pioneer of British films. *b.* Mar. 19, 1874, Lambeth, London. *d.* 1953. As a boy he accompanied his father, noted magic-lantern lecturer T. C. Hepworth, on his lecture tours and developed an interest in the potential of motion pictures. He patented a number of photographic inventions, including a projection lamp (1895) and an automated developing and printing system and in 1898 wrote a handbook on film, *Animated Photography,* one of the earliest and possibly *the* earliest published work on the newly emerging medium. The following year, he began producing, directing, and photographing a variety of short films, on both factual and fictional subjects, in some of which he also appeared as an actor. In 1904 he founded the Hepworth Manufacturing Company. Both as a showman and an artist, Hepworth helped lay the foundations of the British film industry. His six-minute long *Rescued by Rover* (1905), featuring his own family, is a landmark in cinema history, one of the earliest films to employ advanced continuity and narrative techniques through sophisticated cutting.

After 1905, Hepworth concentrated on his functions as a producer and businessman and the running of his own studio, which he had set up in 1903. In 1910 he patented the Vivaphone, a rather primitive sound system involving synchronization of film with a phonograph. He returned to directing in 1914, when he turned out the first of many feature films. They were mainly routine productions with a commercial appeal to the average taste. But the man whose early work had often been well in advance of its times, soon found himself falling behind new developments in the industry and gradually drifting into the background. Some of his post–WW I films were failures and in 1924 he went bankrupt. He ended his career as a director of trailers and advertising shorts. Autobiography: *Came the Dawn* (1951).

FILMS INCLUDE: Shorts—*Express Train in a Railway Cutting* 1899; *How It Feels to Be Run Over, The Eccentric Dancer, The Kiss, The Explosion of a Motor Car* 1900; *Funeral of Queen Victoria, Coronation of King Edward VII, How the Burglar Tricked the Bobby, The Glutton's Nightmare* 1901; *The Call to Arms, How to Stop a Motor Car* 1902; *Alice in Wonderland, Firemen to the Rescue* 1903; *The Jonah Man* 1904; *Rescued by Rover, Falsely Accused, The Alien's Invasion, A Den of Thieves* 1905; *A Seaside Girl* 1907; *John Gilpin's Ride* 1908; *Tilly the Tomboy* 1909; *Rachel's Sin* 1911. Features—*The Basilisk, Time the Great Healer, The Canker of Jealousy, The Battle, The Man Who Stayed at Home, The Outrage, Iris, Sweet Lavender* 1915; *Annie Laurie, Comin' Thro' the Rye, Sowing the Wind, The Cobweb* 1916; *The American Heiress, Nearer My God to Thee* 1917; *The Blindness of Fortune, Boundary House* 1918; *The Nature of the Beast, The Forest on the Hill, Sheba* 1919; *Anna the Adventuress, Alf's Button, Helen of Four Gates* 1920; *Tinted Venus, Narrow Valley, Wild Heather* 1921; *The Pipes of Pan, Mist in the Valley, Comin' Thro' the Rye* (new version) 1922; *The House of Marney* 1927.

Herbert, F(rederick) Hugh. Screenwriter. *b.* May 29, 1897, Vienna. *d.* 1958. *ed.* London U. He wrote screenplays, alone or in collaboration, for numerous Hollywood silents and talkies, occasionally directing his own scripts. He also authored several plays and many short stories. At his best with comedy material. *Sitting Pretty* (1948) was one of the funniest films of the 40s. His screen adaptation of his own play, *The Moon Is Blue* (1953), was a *cause célèbre* in the 50s for its then-daring use of the word "virgin," in defiance of the Legion of Decency and the censorship code.

FILMS INCLUDE: *The Waning Sex, There You Are!* (from own novel) 1926; *The Demi-Bride, On Ze Boulevard* (co-story only), *Adam and Evil, Tea for Three* 1927; *Baby Mine, The Cardboard Lover, The Air Circus* (dial. only), *The Baby Cyclone, Beau Broadway* (adapt. only) 1928; *A Single Man, The Great Gabbo* 1929; *Murder on the Roof, Second Wife, Vengeance, He Knew Women* (also dir.), *Road to Paradise, Danger Lights* (dial. dir., act. only) 1930; *X Marks the Spot* 1931; *Vanity Fair, Hotel Continental* 1932; *The Constant Woman, By Candlelight* 1933; *Fashions of 1934, Journal of a Crime* 1934; *The Secret Bride, Traveling Saleslady* 1935; *Colleen, The Case of the Black Cat* 1936; *As Good as Married* 1937; *That Certain Age* (story only) 1938; *Dark Command, Three Faces West* 1940; *West Point Widow* 1941; *Together Again* 1944; *Kiss and Tell* (from his own play) 1945; *Home Sweet Homicide, Margie* 1946; *Scudda-Hoo! Scudda-Hay!* (also dir.), *Sitting Pretty* 1948; *Our Very Own* 1950; *Let's Make It Legal* 1951; *The Girls of Pleasure Island* (also co-dir. with Alvin Ganzer), *The Moon Is Blue* (from own play) 1953; *The Little Hut* 1957; *This Happy Feeling* (play basis only, 'For Love or Money') 1958.

Herbert, Holmes. Actor. *b.* Edward Sanger, July 3, 1882, Mansfield, England. *d.* 1956. On the British stage from age eight, he came to Hollywood toward the end of WW I and played romantic leads in many films before graduating into character parts by the late 20s. Tall and dignified, he played distinguished supporting roles in scores of talkies through the early 50s. Early in his career he was billed as Holmes E. Herbert or H. E. Herbert. His second wife was actress Beryl MERCER.

FILMS INCLUDE: *His Wife* 1915; *The Man Without a Country* 1917; *The Death Dance, A Doll's House* (as Torvald Helmer), *The Whirlpool* 1918; *The Divorcee, The A.B.C. of Love, The White Heather, Market of Souls* 1919; *Black Is White, His House in Order, My Lady's Garter, The Right to Love, Lady Rose's Daughter, Dead Men Tell No Tales* 1920; *Heedless Moths, Her Lord and Master, The Family Closet, The Wild Goose* 1921; *Any Wife, A Stage Romance* (as the Prince of Wales), *Divorce Coupons, A Woman's Woman* 1922; *Toilers of the Sea* 1923; *The Enchanted Cottage, Sinners in Heaven, Love's Wilderness* 1924; *Daddy's Gone a-Hunting, Wildfire, Wreckage, The Wanderer, A Woman of the World* 1925; *Josselyn's Wife, The Fire Brigade* 1926; *When a Man Loves, Mr. Wu, The Heart of Salome, The Nest, East Side West Side, Slaves of Beauty* 1927; *Gentlemen Prefer Blondes, The Sporting Age, Through the Breakers* 1928; *The Charlatan, Madame X, The Careless Age, Her Private Life, Untamed* 1929; *The Ship from Shanghai* 1930; *Chances, Daughter of the Dragon* 1931; *Dr. Jekyll and Mr. Hyde* 1932; *The Mystery of the Wax Museum, The Invisible Man* 1933; *The House of Rothschild, The Count of Monte Cristo, The Pursuit of Happiness* 1934; *Mark of the Vampire, Accent on Youth, Captain Blood* 1935; *Lloyds of London* 1936; *Slave Ship* 1937; *The Buccaneer, Say It in French* 1938; *The Little Princess, Juarez, Stanley and Livingstone, The Adventures of Sherlock Holmes, We Are Not Alone* 1939; *Man Hunt* 1941; *The Ghost of Frankenstein, This Above All, Invisible Agent* 1942; *Corvette K-225* 1943; *Our Hearts Were Young and Gay* 1944; *The Mummy's Curse, Confidential Agent* 1945; *Three Strangers, The Verdict* 1946; *Singapore, This Time for Keeps* 1947; *Johnny Belinda* 1948; *David and Bathsheba* 1951; *The Brigand* 1952.

Herbert, Hugh. Actor. *b.* Aug. 10, 1887, Binghamton, N.Y. *d.* 1952. Originally a vaudeville and stage comic with author's credit for some plays, playlets, and sketches, he appeared in more than 100 films from the late 20s, mainly in supporting comedy roles but often also in leads. Fidgety movements and an excited "woo-woo" sound were the trademarks of his zany comedy style. His brother, Thomas F. Herbert (1888–1946), was also a stage and screen actor.

FILMS INCLUDE: *Husbands for Rent, Lights of New York* 1928; *Hook Line and Sinker* 1930; *Laugh and Get Rich, Friends and Lovers* 1931; *The Lost Squadron, Million Dollar Legs, Faithless* 1932; *Bureau of Missing Persons, Footlight Parade, College Coach, From Headquarters, Convention City* 1933; *Fashions of 1934, Wonder Bar, Fog Over Frisco, Dames* 1934; *Sweet Adeline, Gold Diggers of 1935, A Midsummer Night's Dream* (as Snout), *To Beat the Band* (lead), *Miss Pacific Fleet* 1935; *Colleen, One Rainy Afternoon, We Went to College* 1936; *Top of the Town, That Man Is Here Again* (lead), *The Singing Marine, Marry the Girl* (lead), *The Perfect Specimen, Sh! The Octopus* (lead) 1937; *Hollywood Hotel, Gold Diggers in Paris, Four's a Crowd, The Great Waltz* 1938; *The Family Next Door* (lead), *Eternally Yours, Little Accident* (lead) 1939; *La Conga Nights* (lead), *Slightly Tempted* (lead), *A Little Bit of Heaven* 1940; *Meet the Chump* (lead), *The Black Cat, Hellzapoppin* 1941; *Kismet, Music for Millions* 1944; *A Miracle Can Happen, A Song Is Born* 1948; *The Beautiful Blonde from Bashful Bend* 1949; *Havana Rose* 1951.

Herek, Stephen. Director. Born on Nov. 10, 1958, in San Antonio, Tex. Director of youth-oriented films that are often derided by mainstream critics but successful at the box office and admired by cult followers.

FILMS INCLUDE: *Critters* 1986; *Bill & Ted's Excellent Adventure* 1989; *Don't Tell Mom the Babysitter's Dead* 1991; *The Mighty Ducks* 1992; *The Three Musketeers* 1993.

Herlie, Eileen. Actress. Born Eileen Herlihy on Mar. 8, 1919, in Glasgow. British stage actress in occasional, but striking, film roles.

FILMS: *Hungry Hill* 1946; *Hamlet* (as Queen Gertrude) 1948; *Angel with the Trumpet* 1949; *The Story of Gilbert and Sullivan/Gilbert and Sullivan, Isn't Life Wonderful?* 1953; *For Better for Worse/Cocktails in the Kitchen* 1954; *She Didn't Say No* 1958; *Freud* (US) 1962; *Hamlet* (filmed Broadway stage production starring Richard Burton; again as Queen Gertrude; US) 1964; *The Sea Gull* (as Polina; US/UK) 1968.

Herlth, Robert. Art director. *b.* May 2, 1893, Wriezen, Germany. *d.* 1962. One of the leading set designers of the expressionist movement in the German theater and films of the 20s, often in collaboration with Walter RÖHRIG. However, the brilliant baroque sets for which he was noted were not much in demand in the German cinema of the 30s and after, and he settled into a routine career as a prolific art director of numerous routine productions. His younger brother, Kurt, is also an art director of German films.

FILMS INCLUDE: *Das lachende Grauen, Das Geheimnis von Bombay, Die Toteninsel* 1920; *Der Idiot, Der müde Tod/Between Two Worlds, Satansketten* 1921; *Pariserinnen, Fräulein Julie* 1922; *Der Schatz/The Treasure* 1923; *Komödie des Herzens, Der letzte Mann/The Last Laugh* 1924; *Zur Chronik von Grieshuus/At the Grey House, Tartüff* 1925; *Faust* 1926; *Luther* 1927; *Looping the Loop* 1928; *Die wunderbare Lüge der Nina Petrowna/The Wonderful Lie of Nina Petrovna, Manolescu* 1929; *Hokuspokus/Hocuspocus* 1930; *Im Geheimdienst, Der Kongress tanzt/The Congress Dances* 1931; *Die Gräfin von Monte Christo, Mensch ohne Namen/Man Without a Name, Der schwarze Husar/The Black Hussar* 1932; *Walzerkrieg/Waltz Time in Vienna* 1933; *Prinzessin Tourandot* 1934; *Barcarole, Das Mädchen Johanna, Amphytrion* 1935; *Hans in Glück* (also dir., sc.) 1936; *Der Herrscher/The Ruler* 1937; *Der Spieler* 1938; *Opernball* 1939; *Die Fledermaus* 1945; *Film ohne Titel/Film Without Title* 1948; *Alraune* 1952; *Der letzter Mann* 1955; *Teufel in Seide/Devil in Silk* 1956; *Bekenntnisse des Hochstaplers Felix Krull/The Confessions of Felix Krull* 1957; *Buddenbrooks* 1959; *Gustav Adolfs Page* 1960.

Herman, Pee-Wee. Actor. Born Paul Rubenfeld, in July, 1952, in Peekskill, N.Y. Eccentric comedian of nightclubs, TV, and films. Raised in Sarasota, Florida, where his parents ran a retail lamp store, he began performing on stage at 11. He kept on acting while attending high school, Boston University (one year), and the California Institute of the Arts at Valencia. Following graduation, he joined the Groundlings, a Los Angeles improvisational troupe and changed his professional name to Paul Reubens. His big breakthrough came in 1978, when he developed the manic comic character Pee-Wee Herman, a baby-faced innocent resembling in appearance and manner silent-screen comedian Harry LANGDON. With his popularity rapidly growing, he became the star of the 'Pee-Wee Herman Show,' which ran for months to packed houses in a large Los Angeles nightclub. Success on Saturday morning TV with 'Pee-Wee's Playhouse' led to his first film, *Pee-Wee's Big Adventure,* a surrealistic fantasy that baffled but was admired by others and proved attractive to moviegoers. In 1991, he announced the end of his series. Shortly thereafter, he was arrested in a routine raid of a Florida adult entertainment center for "exposing himself" during a screening of *Naughty Nurses*. The scandal was more of a humiliation than a fall from grace, but his character had run its course, and his career went into abeyance. He uses the names Pee-Wee Herman and Paul Reubens interchangeably in screen credits.

FILMS: *The Blues Brothers* (bit) 1980; *Cheech and Chong*

Nice Dreams 1981; *Pee-Wee's Big Adventure* (also co-sc.) 1985; *Back to the Beach* (cameo; song) 1987; *Big Top Pee-Wee* (also co-prod., co-sc.) 1988; *Batman Returns, Buffy the Vampire Slayer* 1992; *Buddy* 1997.

Hernandez, Juano. Actor. *b.* Juan G. Hernandez, 1896, San Juan, Puerto Rico. *d.* 1970. He quit boxing in the early 20s to go on the road with circuses, carnivals, and minstrel shows. He later made the vaudeville and stage circuit before coming into his own as scriptwriter in radio and actor on Broadway. Among the first black actors to play prominent straightforward dramatic roles on stage and in films, he is best remembered as the intended lynching victim in *Intruder in the Dust,* his very first film role.

FILMS INCLUDE: *Intruder in the Dust* 1949; *Young Man with a Horn, The Breaking Point, Stars in My Crown* 1950; *Trial* 1955; *Ransom* 1956; *Something of Value* 1957; *The Mark of the Hawk, St. Louis Blues* 1958; *Sergeant Rutledge* 1960; *The Sins of Rachel Cade, Two Loves* 1961; *Hemingway's Adventures of a Young Man* 1962; *The Pawnbroker* 1965; *The Extraordinary Seaman, The Reivers* 1969; *They Call Me Mister Tibbs* 1970.

Herrmann, Bernard. Composer. *b.* June 29, 1911, New York City. *d.* 1975. *ed.* NYU; Juilliard. The winner of a composition prize at age 13, he founded and conducted a chamber orchestra at age 20. In 1934 he joined CBS radio as a composer-conductor and later was a guest conductor with the New York Philharmonic, BBC, etc. The composer of several operas (*Wuthering Heights,* etc.) and ballets, as well as a cantata, *Moby Dick,* he is noted for his imposing film scores, often achieved by limited orchestral means, primarily string instruments. Also known as a pedantic autocrat and uncompromising perfectionist. Best work for Orson WELLES and Alfred HITCHCOCK. Academy Award for score of *All That Money Can Buy* (1941). He died in his sleep shortly after completing the recording sessions for his score of *Taxi Driver* (1976). Director Martin SCORSESE dedicated the film to the memory of the composer.

FILMS: *Citizen Kane, All That Money Can Buy/The Devil and Daniel Webster* 1941; *The Magnificent Ambersons* 1942; *Jane Eyre* 1944; *Hangover Square* 1945; *Anna and the King of Siam* 1946; *The Ghost and Mrs. Muir* 1947; *The Day the Earth Stood Still* 1951; *On Dangerous Ground, Five Fingers* 1952; *Snows of Kilimanjaro, White Witch Doctor, Beneath the 12-Mile Reef* 1953; *King of the Khyber Rifles, Garden of Evil, The Egyptian* 1954; *Prince of Players, The Kentuckian* 1955; *The Trouble with Harry, The Man Who Knew Too Much, The Man in the Gray Flannel Suit* 1956; *A Hatful of Rain, The Wrong Man* 1957; *Vertigo, The Naked and the Dead, The Seventh Voyage of Sinbad* 1958; *North by Northwest, Blue Denim, Journey to the Center of the Earth* 1959; *Psycho, The Three Words of Gulliver* 1960; *Mysterious Island* 1961; *Tender Is the Night, Cape Fear* 1962; *The Birds* (sound consultant), *Jason and the Argonauts* 1963; *Marnie* 1964; *Joy in the Morning* 1965; *Fahrenheit 451* 1966; *La Mariée était en Noir/The Bride Wore Black* 1967; *Twisted Nerve* 1969; *Battle of Neretva, The Night Digger* 1971; *Endless Night* 1972; *Sisters* 1973; *It's Alive* 1974; *Taxi Driver, Obsession* 1976; *It's Alive Again* (theme music only) 1978; *It's Alive III: Island of the Alive* (theme only) 1987; *Cape Fear* 1991.

Herrmann, Edward. Actor. Born on July 31, 1943, in Washington, D.C. Tall, stalwart character lead and supporting player of the American stage, TV, and films. Typically in dignified, reserved roles. A graduate of Bucknell, he studied on a Fulbright Scholarship at London's Academy of Music and Dramatic Art. After several years with the Dallas Theater Center, he began appearing in films in the early 70s. His numerous television roles included outstanding portrayals of President Franklin Delano Roosevelt in the TV movie *Eleanor and Franklin* (1976) and its 1977 sequel, a part he also played in the film *Annie.* Also memorable as Lou Gehrig in the TV movie *A Love Affair: The Eleanor and Lou Gehrig Story* (1978). On Broadway, he won a Tony for 'Mrs. Warren's Profession.'

FILMS: *La Mortadella/Lady Liberty* (It.) 1971; *The Paper Chase, The Day of the Dolphin* 1973; *The Great Gatsby* 1974; *The Great Waldo Pepper* 1975; *The Betsy, Brass Target* 1978; *Take Down, The North Avenue Irregulars* 1979; *Harry's War, Reds* 1981; *A Little Sex, Annie* (as Franklin Delano Roosevelt), *Death Valley* 1982; *Mrs. Soffel* 1984; *The Purple Rose of Cairo, Compromising Positions, The Man with One Red Shoe* 1985; *The Lost Boys, Overboard* 1987; *Big Business* 1988; *Hero* 1992; *Born Yesterday, My Boyfriend's Back* 1993; *Forever Student* 1994; *Richie Rich* 1995.

Hershey, Barbara. Actress. Born Barbara Herzstein, on Feb. 5, 1948, in Hollywood, Calif. Good-looking brunette of the American screen. As a teenager, she was a regular in 'The Monroes' series (1966–67) on TV. In films since the late 60s, she registered strongly as star prospect with a fresh and fetching lead in *Last Summer* (1969). In 1973, after accidentally killing a seagull, she changed her name to Barbara Seagull; but she reverted to Hershey in 1975. After meandering through mediocre opportunities, her career blossomed in the 80s. She played a pivotal role in Woody Allen's *Hannah and Her Sisters* (1986). In 1987 she won the best actress prize at Cannes for *Shy People.* She shared the same award the following year for *A World Apart.* She received her first Academy Award nomination as a supporting actress for her exquisite performance in Jane Campion's *The Portrait of a Lady* (1996). The independent, free-spirited actress had a stormy six-year (1969–75) relationship with David CARRADINE that produced a son, Free.

FILMS: *With Six You Get Eggroll* 1968; *Heaven with a Gun, Last Summer* 1969; *The Liberation of L. B. Jones, The Baby Maker* 1970; *The Pursuit of Happiness* 1971; *Dealing, Boxcar Bertha* 1972; *The Crazy World of Julius Vrooder* 1974; *Love Comes Quietly* (Hol.) 1975; *You and Me* (release delayed from 1972), *Diamonds* (Isr./US/Switz.) 1975; *Trial by Combat/ Choice of Weapons/Dirty Knight's Work* (UK), *The Last Hard Men* 1976; *The Stunt Man* 1980; *Take This Job and Shove It* 1981; *The Entity, Americana* (release delayed from 1981), *The Right Stuff* 1983; *The Natural* 1984; *Hannah and Her Sisters, Hoosiers* 1986; *Tin Men, Shy People* 1987; *A World Apart* (UK), *The Last Temptation of Christ* (as Mary Magdalene), *Beaches* 1988; *Tune in Tomorrow* 1990; *Defenseless, Paris Trout, The Public Eye* 1991; *Swing Kids* 1992; *A Dangerous Woman, Falling Down, Splitting Heirs* 1993; *Last of the Dogmen* 1995; *The Pallbearer, The Portrait of a Lady* 1996.

Hersholt, Jean. Actor. *b.* July 12, 1886, Copenhagen. *d.* 1956. The son of a famous Danish actor and actress, he appeared in stage plays throughout Scandinavia before coming to the US in 1914. He made his film debut with Thomas Ince's studio the following year and in the 20s developed into one of the leading character stars of the American silent screen. Because of his foreign accent, the range of his roles became more limited after the coming of sound, but he continued playing character leads and supporting roles in many films, eventually becoming typecast in kindly-country-doctor parts. He is most closely associated with the character of Dr. Paul Christian, which he portrayed in the long-running radio series and in several films. In 1944 he became a partner of producer Sol Lesser and an executive of the independent Principal Pictures. Offscreen, Hersholt was known for his humanitarian activities. In 1939 he received a special Academy Award for services to the industry by the Motion Picture Relief Fund, which he had founded and of which he was president, and in 1949 he was awarded another special Oscar "for distinguished service to the motion picture industry." In 1956, the year of his death from cancer, the Academy of Motion Picture Arts and Sciences, of which he had been president, instituted the Jean Hersholt Humanitarian Award, a special Oscar that has since been awarded each year to film personalities for humanitarian achievements. Hersholt co-authored a novel, *Dr. Christian's Office* (1944). He edited *Hans Christian Andersen, The Maker of Fairy Tales* (1942) and published two volumes of Andersen translations.

FILMS INCLUDE: *The Disciple* 1915; *The Aryan, Hell's Hinges, The Deserter* 1916; *The Terror, Love Aflame, Southern Justice, The Greater Law* 1917; *Princess Virtue, Madame Spy* 1918; *Whom the Gods Would Destroy, In the Land of the Setting Sun/Martyrs of Yesterday* 1919; *The Servant in the House, The Golden Trail* (also co-sc.), *The Deceiver* 1920; *The Servant in the House, The Four Horsemen of the Apocalypse, Man of the Forest* 1921; *Golden Dreams, The Gray Dawn, Tess of the Storm Country* 1922; *Jazzmania, Quicksands, Red Lights* 1923; *Greed, Torment, The Woman on the Jury, Sinners in Silk, The Goldfish, Her Night of Romance* 1924; *So Big, Fifth Avenue Models, If Marriage Fails, Dangerous Innocence, A Woman's Faith, Don Q Son of Zorro, Stella Dallas* 1925; *The Greater Glory, It Must Be Love, Flames, The Old Soak* 1926; *Alias the Deacon, The Wrong Mr. Wright, The Student Prince* 1927; *13 Washington Square, The Secret Hour, Abie's Irish Rose, The Battle of the Sexes, Jazz Mad* 1928; *The Girl on the Barge, The Younger Generation, Modern Love* 1929; *The Climax, The Case of Sergeant Grischa, Mamba, Hell Harbor, The Cat Creeps, Viennese Nights, A Soldier's Plaything, The Third Alarm* 1930; *Daybreak, Transatlantic, Susan Lenox: Her Fall and Rise, The Sin of Madelon Claudet, The Phantom of Paris, Private Lives* 1931; *Emma, The Beast of the City, Grand Hotel, Hearts of Humanity, The Mask of Fu Manchu, Flesh* 1932; *The Crime of the Century, Dinner at Eight, Christopher Bean* 1933; *The Cat and the Fiddle, Men in White, The Fountain, The Painted Veil* 1934; *Mark of the Vampire, Break of Hearts* 1935; *The Country Doctor, Sins of Man, Reunion* 1936; *One in a Million, Seventh Heaven, Heidi* 1937; *Happy Landing, Mr. Moto in Danger Island, I'll Give a Million, Alexander's Ragtime Band, Five of a Kind* 1938; *Meet Dr. Christian* 1939; *The Courageous Dr. Christian, Remedy for Riches* 1940; *Melody for Three* 1941; *Dancing in the Dark* 1949; *Run for Cover* 1955.

Hertz, Aleksander. Director, film pioneer. *b.* 1879, Warsaw. *d.* 1928. The founder of his country's first film production house, The Sphynx, in 1911, he is considered the father of Polish cinema. He is also credited with the discovery of Pola NEGRI and other future stars.

FILMS INCLUDE: *The Married Ones* 1913; *Meir Ezofewicz* 1914; *The Beast* 1915; *Students, Arabella, The Mysteries of Warsaw* 1916; *The Daughter of Madame X* 1917; *I Want a Husband* 1919; *The Czar's Favorite* 1920; *The Promised Land* 1928.

Hervey, Irene. Actress. Born Irene Herwick, on July 11, 1910, in Los Angeles. Attractive, dimpled leading lady of Hollywood films of the 30s and 40s, mainly in second features. Later in occasional supporting roles through the early 70s as well as much TV. Her second husband (1936–57) was actor-singer Allan JONES. Their son is singer Jack Jones.

FILMS INCLUDE: *The Stranger's Return* 1933; *Let's Try Again, The Count of Monte Cristo, The Dude Ranger* 1934; *The Winning Ticket, Charlie Chan in Shanghai, His Night Out* 1935; *The Three Godfathers, Absolute Quiet, Along Came Love* 1936; *Woman in Distress, The League of Frightened Men, The Girl Said No* 1937; *Say It in French* 1938; *Society Smugglers, East Side of Heaven, House of Fear, Missing Evidence, Destry Rides Again* 1939; *Three Cheers for the Irish, The Crooked Road, The Boys from Syracuse* 1940; *San Francisco Docks, Mr. Dynamite* 1941; *Bombay Clipper, Frisco Lil, Destination Unknown, Night Monster* 1942; *He's My Guy, Half Way to Shanghai* 1943; *Mickey, Mr. Peabody and the Mermaid* 1948; *The Lucky Stiff, Manhandled, Chicago Deadline* 1949; *A Cry in the Night, Teenage Rebel* 1956; *Going Steady, Crash Landing* 1958; *Cactus Flower* 1969; *Play Misty for Me* 1971.

Herzog, Werner. Director. Born Werner Stipetic, on Sept. 5, 1942, in Munich, Germany. Raised in Sachrang, a small Bavarian village, at age 12 he returned to Munich with his divorced Yugoslav-born mother, where they lived in abject poverty. He developed a strong passion for cinema and at age 14 began submitting ideas for film projects to local producers. None materialized. While still in high school, he worked nights as a welder in a steel factory and invested his entire income in the production of amateur shorts. He shot the first, *Herakles,* in 1962, admittedly with a stolen camera, during his freshman year at the University of Munich. Two other shorts followed. In 1966, Herzog traveled to the US, where he attended Duquesne University in Pittsburgh, and, according to his own account, worked at a local TV station and later was briefly a filmmaker for the US National Aeronautics and Space Administration (NASA). Returning to Germany, he directed a fourth short, *Letzte Worte* (1967), a major prize winner at the Oberhausen Festival.

Herzog shot his first feature film, *Signs of Life* (1968), in Greece. Exploring the effect of an alien landscape on the mind, it told the story of three bored German soldiers assigned to guard a munitions dump on the Greek island of Cos, off Crete, and the gradual descent into madness of one of them. It won the German Film Prize, as well as a Silver Bear for best first film at the 1968 Berlin Film Festival. Maddening loneliness and alienation amidst unfamiliar environments would become recurring Kafkaesque motifs in several of the director's subsequent films. Herzog's next feature, *Even Dwarfs Started Small,* was a truly disturbing parable, using an uprising in an asylum for dwarfs as a microcosm of crumbling bourgeois values.

With his next feature, *Aguirre, the Wrath of God* (1972), Herzog vaulted to the forefront of the New German Cinema. A haunting film of powerful imagery, it was shot on a grand scale in the Peruvian jungles, unfolding the saga of a power-mad Spanish conquistador destructively intent on discovering the legendary city of gold, Eldorado. Like several of the director's films, it starred Klaus KINSKI. The performance of Bruno S. provided the forceful core of Herzog's next film, *Every Man for Himself and God Against All/The Mystery of Kasper Hauser,* a haunting, true 19th-century story of a man who is trying to reclaim his place in society, after having been confined from birth in a solitary room. The stunningly shot film won the Jury Prize at the 1975 Cannes Festival. Far less accessible to general audiences was *Heart of Glass* (1976), a bizarre drama of metaphysical concerns. To achieve a stylized portrayal of hallucination and madness in this film, Herzog had his actors put under hypnosis.

Herzog's own obsession with the theme of obsession took a formidable shape in *Fitzcarraldo,* winner of the best director award at Cannes in 1982. In the process of telling this story about a man so determined to bring grand opera to the Amazons that he attempt to haul a ship over mountains, Herzog proved himself no less consumed by mad tenacity than his protagonist. He and his crew endured incredible hardships, facing mortal danger and plagued by every imaginable natural and man-made disaster during three years of preparation and nine months of actual shooting. Their trials and tribulations and the madness of it all were persuasively recorded in the Les BLANK documentary *Burden of Dreams* (1983), in which an exasperated Herzog concedes. But of course he was back, winning more admirers and prizes with *Nosferatu: The Vampyre* (1979) and other films. In the late 70s he was the subject of a documentary, *I Am My Films: A Portrait of Werner Herzog*. Married since 1966, he is the father of a son, Rudolph Amos Achmed.

Herzog exerts total control over his work, which he also produces and writes. His films are deeply personal and thoroughly uncompromising. But he is increasingly admired as one of the most creative and exhilarating artists on the international film scene today.

FEATURE FILMS (as director-producer-screenwriter): *Lebenzeichen/Feuerzeichen/Signs of Life* 1968; *Auch Zwerge haben klein angefangen/Even Dwarfs Started Small* 1970; *Fata Morgana Behinderte Zukunft/Frustrated Future* (doc.) 1971; *Land des Schweigens und der Dunkelheit/Land of Silence and Darkness* (doc.) 1972; *Aguirre der Zorn Gottes/Aguirre the Wrath of God* 1973; *Jeder für sich und Gott gegen Alle/Every Man for Himself and God Against All/The Mystery of Kasper Hauser/The Enigma of Kasper Hauser* 1975; *Herz aus Glas/Heart of Glass* 1976; *Stroszek* 1977; *Nosferatu: Phantom der Nacht/Nosferatu: The Vampyre* (also act. in bit as monk), *Woyzek* 1979; *Fitzcarraldo* 1982; *The Ballad of the Little Soldier, Where the Green Ants Dream* (Austral.) 1984; *Stroszek* 1987; *Cobra Verde, Herdsmen of the Sun* 1988; *Es ist nicht leicht ein Gott zu sein/It Isn't Easy Being God* (Ger./It./USSR/Fr./Switz.) 1989; *Echos Aus Einem Dusteren Reich/Echoes from a Somber Empire* (doc.; Ger./Fr.) 1990; *Scream of Stone/Schrei aus Stein* 1991; *Lessons in Darkness/Lektionen in Finsternis* 1992.

Hesperia. See NEGRONI, Baldassare.

Hessler, Gordon. Director. Born in 1930, in Berlin. Raised in Britain, he attended Reading University and began making shorts and documentary films in 1950. In 1960 he became a story editor for the TV series 'Alfred Hitchcock Presents' and later served as a producer and director on the 'Alfred Hitchcock Hour.' Making his debut as feature director in 1964, he has specialized in horror and adventure thrillers. He also has a good number of TV movies to his credit.

FEATURE FILMS: *Catacombs/The Woman Who Wouldn't Die* 1964; *The Last Shot You Hear, The Oblong Box* (also prod.) 1969; *Scream and Scream Again, Cry of the Banshee* (also prod.) 1970; *Murders in the Rue Morgue* 1971; *Embassy* 1972; *The Golden Voyage of Sinbad* 1974; *Puzzle* (Austral.) 1978; *Pray for Death* 1985; *Rage of Honor, Wheels of Terror/The Misfit Brigade* 1987; *The Girl in a Swing* (also sc.) 1988; *Out on Bail* 1989; *Mayeda* 1991.

Hessling, Catherine. Actress. Born Andrée Madeleine Heuchling, in 1900, in Morionvilliers, Alsace. The ravishingly beautiful redhead model of painter Auguste Renoir in the last two years of his life (1917–19), she married his son, Jean RENOIR, in 1920 and starred in his early films as a director. After her striking appearance in *Nana* (1926) she was compared by some critics with Garbo and Asta Nielsen. She also appeared in a couple of Cavalcanti films. But her film career came to an end shortly after her separation from Renoir in the early 30s.

FILMS INCLUDE: *Une Vie sans Joie/Catherine, La Fille de l'Eau* 1924; *Nana* (title role) 1926; *Charleston, En Rade/Sea-Fever* 1927; *La Petite Marchande d'Allumettes/The Little Match Girl, Yvette* 1928; *Le Petit Chaperon Rouge, La Petite Lili* 1929; *Du Haut en Bas* 1924; *Crime et Châtiment/Crime and Punishment* 1935.

Heston, Charlton. Actor. Born Charles Carter, on Oct. 4, 1923, in Evanston, Ill. After speech and drama studies at Northwestern University, during which he starred in an amateur student film production of *Peer Gynt* (1942) and performed on Chicago radio stations, he served three years with the Air Force. Returning to civilian life, he made his stage debut in stock and his first Broadway appearance as a member of the cast of Katharine Cornell's production of 'Anthony and Cleopatra' in 1947. He then began gaining national notice in a succession of TV specials, playing such roles as Antony in 'Julius Caesar,' Heathcliff in 'Wuthering Heights,' and Petruchio in 'The Taming of the Shrew.' He also appeared in another amateur film production, playing Mark Antony in *Julius Caesar* (1949), before making his professional film debut in 1950. Tall and muscular, with a dominant physical presence and a strong-jawed, patrician facial bone structure suggesting intelligence and dignity, he started out his film career in tough but down-to-earth roles, but before long he developed into Hollywood's resident epic hero, portraying larger-than-life characters, from Moses to Michelangelo, in a long string of screen superspectacles. He won an Academy Award for the lead role in *Ben-Hur* (1959). A leader offscreen as well as on, he served six terms as president of the Screen Actors Guild and is chairman of the American Film Institute. He received the Jean Hersholt Humanitarian Award during the Oscar ceremony for 1977. As a political activist of conservative persuasions, he often engaged in vocal battles with liberal Ed ASNER over Actors Guild policies. He took a first stab at directing in 1982 with *Mother Lode*. His son Fraser Heston (who portrayed the infant Moses in *The Ten Commandments*) is a film director. Author: *The Actor's Life: Journals* 1956–1976 (1978).

FILMS: *Peer Gynt* (title role; 16 mm) 1942; *Julius Caesar* (as Antony; 16 mm) 1949; *Dark City* 1950; *The Greatest Show on Earth, The Savage, Ruby Gentry* 1952; *The President's Lady* (as Andrew Jackson), *Pony Express* (as Buffalo Bill Cody), *Arrowhead, Bad for Each Other* 1953; *The Naked Jungle, Secret of the Incas* 1954; *The Far Horizons* (as Bill Clark of the Lewis and Clark expedition), *The Private War of Major Benson, Lucy Gallant* 1955; *The Ten Commandments* (as Moses) 1956; *Three Violent People* 1957; *Touch of Evil, The Big Country, The Buccaneer* (as Andrew Jackson) 1958; *The Wreck of the Mary Deare, Ben-Hur* (title role) 1959; *El Cid* (title role) 1961; *The Pigeon That Took Rome* 1962; *Diamond Head, 55 Days at Peking* 1963; *The Greatest Story Ever Told* (as John the Baptist), *Major Dundee, The Agony and the Ecstasy* (as Michelangelo), *The War Lord* 1965; *Khartoum* (as General Gordon) 1966; *Counterpoint, Planet of the Apes, Will Penny* 1968; *Number One* 1969; *Julius Caesar* (as Antony; UK), *Beneath the Planet of the Apes, The Hawaiians* 1970; *The Omega Man* 1971; *Call of the Wild* (UK/Ger./Fr./It./Sp.), *Anthony and Cleopatra* (as Anthony; also adapt., dir.; UK), *Skyjacked* 1972; *Soylent Green* 1973; *The Three Musketeers* (as Cardinal Richelieu; UK), *Airport 1975, Earthquake* 1974; *The Four Musketeers* (as Richelieu; UK) 1975; *The Last Hard Men, Midway, Two-Minute Warning* 1976; *The Prince and the Pauper/Crossed Swords* (as Henry VIII; UK) 1977; *Gray Lady Down* 1978; *Mountain Men, The Awakening* 1980; *Mother Lode/The Search for the Mother Lode: The Last Great Treasure* (also dir.) 1982; *Solar Crisis* (Jap.), *Almost An Angel* 1990; *Wayne's World 2, Tombstone* 1993; *True Lies* (cameo) 1994; *In the Mouth of Madness* 1995; *Alaska, Hamlet* 1996; *Hercules* (v/o) 1997.

Heydt, Louis Jean. Actor. *b.* Apr. 17, 1905, Montclair, N.J. *d.* 1960. Formerly a reporter for the New York *World*, he came to films in the mid-30s with ten years of stage experience. He played numerous, sometimes shifty, character roles in films and on TV.

FILMS INCLUDE: *Before Morning* 1933; *Make Way for Tomorrow* 1937; *Test Pilot, I Am the Law* 1938; *They Made Me a*

Criminal, Each Dawn I Die, Charlie Chan of Treasure Island, Gone With the Wind 1939; *Abe Lincoln in Illinois, The Great McGinty, Dr. Ehrlich's Magic Bullet* 1940; *High Sierra, Dive Bomber* 1941; *Captains of the Clouds, Tortilla Flat* 1942; *Mission to Moscow, The Commandos Strike at Dawn, Captains of the Clouds* 1942; *Gung Ho!* 1943; *30 Seconds Over Tokyo* 1944; *They Were Expendable* 1945; *The Big Sleep* 1946; *I Cover the Big Town* 1947; *Paid in Full, The Furies* 1950; *Rawhide* 1951; *Island in the Sky* 1953; *The Eternal Sea* 1955; *The Wings of Eagles* 1957; *The Man Who Died Twice* 1958; *Inside the Mafia* 1959.

Heymann, Werner Richard. Composer. Born on Feb. 14, 1896, in Koenigsberg, Germany. After WW I service with the Prussian army, he worked for the Vienna and Berlin philharmonics and Max REINHARDT's theater. In 1925 he became assistant to the musical director of UFA, the German film company. He later became the company's musical director. In 1933 he came to the US, where he scored numerous Hollywood films before returning to Germany in the early 50s.

FILMS INCLUDE: In Germany—*Melodie des Herzens/Melody of the Heart* 1929; *Die Drei von der Tankstelle/The Three from the Filling Station, Liebeswalzer* 1930; *Der Kongress tanzt/The Congress Dances* 1931; *Ein Blonder Traum/A Blonde Dream, Quick* 1932. In the US—*Adorable* 1933; *Caravan* 1934; *The King and the Chorus Girl* 1937; *Bluebeard's Eighth Wife* 1938; *Ninotchka* 1939; *The Shop Around the Corner* 1940; *Bedtime Story* 1941; *To Be or Not to Be* 1942; *Hail the Conquering Hero, Knickerbocker Holiday, Together Again* 1944; *Kiss and Tell* 1945; *Mad Wednesday* 1947; *Tell It to the Judge* 1949; *A Woman of Distinction* 1950; *Heidelberg Romanze* 1951; *Der Kongress tanzt/The Congress Dances* (remake) 1955.

Heywood, Anne. Actress. Born Violet Pretty, on Dec. 11, 1932, in Handsworth, England. Leading lady of British and international films. A former beauty queen, she has appeared mainly in decorative roles in routine productions. Married to producer Raymond Stross.

FILMS INCLUDE: *Lady Godiva Rides Again* 1951; *Checkpoint* 1956; *Doctor at Large, Dangerous Exile* 1957; *Violent Playground* 1958; *Upstairs and Downstairs* 1959; *Cartagine in Fiamme/Carthage in Flames* (It./Fr.), *A Terrible Beauty/The Night Fighters* 1960; *Stork Talk, Vengeance/The Brain* (UK/Ger.) 1962; *The Very Edge* 1963; *90 Degrees in the Shade* (Czech./UK) 1965; *The Fox* (US) 1968; *The Chairman/The Most Dangerous Man in the World* (US/UK), *Midas Run* (US), *La Monaca di Monza/The Lady of Monza* (It.) 1969; *I Want What I Want* 1972; *Trader Horn* (US) 1973; *Love Under the Elms* 1975; *Good Luck Miss Wyckoff* 1979; *Secrets of the Phantom Caverns* 1984.

h.i. A high-intensity arc emitting a very bright, white light.

Hibbs, Jesse. Director. *b.* Jan. 11, 1906, Normal, Ill. *d.* 1985. An all-American football player at USC in 1927–28, he played one professional season with the Chicago Bears before joining Warner Bros. as an assistant director in the early 30s. He began directing in 1953 and gained attention among some critics for the flair with which he handled his films, mostly poorly scripted, low-budget Westerns and crime and action pictures. But he abandoned motion picture directing for TV work in the late 50s. He turned out numerous episodes of the 'Perry Mason,' 'The FBI,' and 'Ironside' series.

FILMS: *The All-American* 1953; *Ride Clear of Diablo, Black Horse Canyon, Rails Into Laramie, The Yellow Mountain* 1954; *To Hell and Back, The Spoilers* 1955; *World in My Corner, Walk the Proud Land* 1956; *Joe Butterfly* 1957; *Ride a Crooked Trail* 1958.

Hickey, William. Actor. *b.* 1928, in Brooklyn, N.Y. *d.* 1997. Versatile character player of Hollywood films. He was nominated for an Academy Award as best supporting actor for his portrayal of Mafia Don Corrado Prizzi in *Prizzi's Honor* (1985).

FILMS INCLUDE: *A Hatful of Rain* 1957; *Something Wild* 1961; *Invitation to a Gunfighter* 1964; *The Boston Strangler, The Producers* 1968; *Little Big Man* 1970; *Happy Birthday, Wanda June* 1971; *92 in the Shade* 1975; *Mickey and Nicky* 1976; *The Sentinel* 1977; *Nunzio* 1968; *Prizzi's Honor, Remo Williams, Flanagan* 1985; *The Name of the Rose* (It./Fr./Ger.) 1986; *Bright Lights Big City, Da* 1988; *Pink Cadillac, Puppet Master* (title role), *Sea of Love, It Had to Be You, National Lampoon's Christmas Vacation* 1989; *Tales from the Darkside: The Movie, Any Man's Death, Mob Boss, My Blue Heaven* 1990; *Tim Burton's The Nightmare Before Christmas* (v/o) 1993; *Forget Paris, Jerky Boys* 1995; *Love Is All There Is* 1996.

Hickman, Darryl. Actor. Born on July 28, 1931, in Hollywood, Calif. Driven by a "stage mother," he began taking dancing lessons at three, joined a kiddie troupe when he was five, and made his film debut at seven. He played child roles, then juvenile leads in many Hollywood productions of the 40s, later gradually evolving into a character player. With his film career in decline in the late 50s, he began appearing in TV dramas and for one season (1959–60) played a supporting role in the comedy series 'The Many Loves of Dobie Gillis,' which starred his brother, Dwayne HICKMAN. He soon became involved in the production end of the business. In the late 60s and early 70s he served as executive producer of daytime programming at CBS-TV and later as executive producer of the TV soap opera 'Love of Life.' In 1976 he played a supporting part in the film *Network*, his first screen role in 17 years.

FILMS INCLUDE: *If I Were King* 1938; *The Star Maker* 1939; *The Grapes of Wrath, The Way of All Flesh, Untamed, Young People* 1940; *Men of Boys Town, Mob Town* 1941; *Joe Smith—American, Jackass Mail, Keeper of the Flame* 1942; *The Human Comedy, Assignment in Brittany* 1943; *Song of Russia, And Now Tomorrow, Meet Me in St. Louis* 1944; *Captain Eddie* (as Eddie Rickenbacker as a child), *Rhapsody in Blue* (as Ira Gershwin as a boy), *Leave Her to Heaven* 1945; *The Strange Love of Martha Ivers, Boys' Ranch, Two Years Before the Mast* 1946; *The Devil on Wheels, Dangerous Years* 1947; *The Sainted Sisters, Fighting Father Dunne* 1948; *Alias Nick Beal, The Set-Up, Any Number Can Play* 1949; *The Happy Years* 1950; *Lightning Strikes Twice, Submarine Command* 1951; *Destination Gobi, Sea of Lost Ships* 1953; *Southwest Passage* 1954; *Tea and Sympathy* 1956; *The Iron Sheriff* 1957; *The Tingler* 1959; *Network* 1976; *Looker* 1981; *Sharkey's Machine* 1982.

Hickman, Dwayne. Actor. Born on May 18, 1934, in Los Angeles. The younger brother of Darryl HICKMAN, he appeared as a child in Hollywood films of the 40s. In 1955–59 he was a regular on TV's 'The Bob Cummings Show,' then starred in his own series, 'The Many Loves of Dobie Gillis' (1959–63). In the late 60s he played leads in a number of teen-oriented beach films, then retired from the screen to run a Las Vegas public relations firm. In 1979, he joined brother Darryl at CBS, serving there as a supervisor of comedy series.

FILMS INCLUDE: *Captain Eddie* 1945; *The Return of Rusty, The Secret Heart* 1946; *The Boy with Green Hair* 1948; *Rally 'Round the Flag Boys!* 1958; *Cat Ballou, How to Stuff a Wild Bikini, Ski Party, Dr. Goldfoot and the Bikini Machine* 1965; *Doctor You've Got to Be Kidding* 1967.

Hickox, Douglas. Director. *b.* 1929, London. *d.* 1988. He entered British films at 16 as a production assistant on *Black Narcissus* (1946) and was later employed as assistant director on many films and TV programs. In the late 50s he worked on several features as a second-unit director and was credited as co-director on Eugene Lourie's *The Giant Behemoth* (1959). During the 60s he developed a reputation as one of Britain's top directors of TV commercials, winning many international awards for his own company, Illustra Films. His career as a feature director took off in the 70s, when he turned out several entertaining films, including *Theatre of Blood,* a cult favorite about an actor (Vincent Price) who murders his critics; *Brannigan,* a John Wayne vehicle; and *Zulu Dawn,* a lavish war drama. He then turned to miniseries and TV movies, including a well-crafted version of *The Hound of the Baskervilles* (1983). He died at 59 of a heart attack, following bypass surgery. He was married to film editor Anne V. COATES. His son, Anthony Hickox, became a film director.

FEATURE FILMS: *The Giant Behemoth/Behemoth, The Sea Monster* (co-dir.) 1959; *It's All Over Town* (medium-length) 1963; *Just for You* (also co-sc.) 1964; *Les Bicyclettes de Belsize* 1969; *Entertaining Mr. Sloane* 1970; *Sitting Target* 1972; *Theatre of Blood* 1973; *Brannigan* 1975; *Sky Riders* 1976; *Zulu Dawn* 1979.

Hickox, Sidney. Director of photography. Born on July 15, 1895, in New York City. Entered films in 1915 as an assistant cameraman with American Biograph and the following year made his first film as a cinematographer, the serial *Gloria's Romance.* His career was then interrupted by WW I service, but he returned behind the camera in the early 20s and subsequently worked on many Hollywood productions, including many Warner Bros. films of the 30s and 40s, both minor and major. He switched from feature films to TV cinematography in the mid-50s.

FILMS INCLUDE: *Gloria's Romance* (serial) 1916; *School Days* 1921; *The Little Giant* 1926; *The Private Life of Helen of Troy* 1927; *Lilac Time* 1928; *Footlights and Fools* 1929; *Those Who Dance* 1930; *The Gorilla, The Last Flight, Pleasure* 1931; *Blonde Crazy, The Crowd Roars, So Big, A Bill of Divorcement* 1932; *Female, Frisco Jenny* 1933; *Dames, Registered Nurse* 1934; *Special Agent* 1935; *The Case of the Velvet Claws* 1936; *Confession, Slim, San Quentin* 1937; *A Slight Case of Murder* 1938; *King of the Underworld, The Return of Dr. X* 1939; *Flowing Gold* 1940; *The Wagons Roll at Night, Underground* 1941; *All Through the Night, Always in My Heart, The Big Shot, Gentleman Jim* 1942; *The Edge of Darkness, Northern Pursuit* 1943; *Uncertain Glory, To Have and Have Not* 1944; *God Is My Co-Pilot, The Horn Blows at Midnight* 1945; *The Big Sleep* 1946; *The Man I Love, Dark Passage* 1947; *Silver River* 1948; *Colorado Territory, White Heat* 1949; *Three Secrets* 1950; *Lightning Strikes Twice, Along the Great Divide, Distant Drums* 1951; *Blowing Wild* 1953; *Them* 1954; *Battle Cry* 1955.

Hicks, Catherine. Actress. Born on Aug. 6, 1951, in Scottsdale, Ariz. *ed.* St. Mary's Notre Dame; Cornell. Leading lady and second lead of Hollywood films. She began performing on the stage and co-starred in the TV series 'The Bad News Bears' (1979–80) and 'Tucker's Witch' (1982–83) before embarking on her screen career.

FILMS: *Death Valley* 1982; *Better Late Than Never* 1983; *Garbo Talks* 1984; *Fever Pitch* 1985; *Peggy Sue Got Married, Star Trek IV: The Voyage Home* 1986; *Like Father Like Son* 1987; *Child's Play* 1988; *Souvenir* (UK), *She's Out of Control* 1989; *Running Against Time* 1990.

Hicks, Russell. Actor. *b.* Edward Hicks, June 4, 1895, Baltimore. *d.* 1957. One of Hollywood's busiest character actors, he had entered the industry as an assistant casting director for Famous Players in 1920. After gaining acting experience in stock, he returned to films as an actor in the mid-30s. Appeared in more than 200 pictures, typically in executive or leading-citizen parts.

FILMS INCLUDE: *Happiness Ahead, Babbitt* 1934; *Devil Dogs of the Air, Living on Velvet, Cardinal Richelieu, Lady Tubbs, Charlie Chan in Shanghai* 1935; *Follow the Fleet* 1936; *The Toast of New York* 1937; *The Big Broadcast of 1938, Kidnapped, Hold That Co-Ed, Kentucky* 1938; *The Three Musketeers* (as Porthos), *The Story of Alexander Graham Bell, Stanley and Livingstone, The Real Glory, Hollywood Cavalcade, Swanee River* 1939; *The Blue Bird* (as Daddy Tyl), *Johnny Apollo, Virginia City, The Mortal Storm, The Return of Frank James, The Bank Dick, No No Nanette* 1940; *Western Union, The Great Lie, The Big Store, Hold That Ghost, Great Guns, The Little Foxes, Blood and Sand* 1941; *To the Shores of Tripoli, We Were Dancing, Tennessee Johnson* 1942; *Air Raid Wardens* 1943; *Flame of the Barbary Coast, Scarlet Street* 1945; *The Bandit of Sherwood Forest* (as aging Robin Hood) 1946; *The Sea of Grass* 1947; *The Black Arrow* 1948; *Samson and Delilah* 1949; *The Big Hangover* 1950; *Man of Conflict* 1953; *The Seventh Cavalry* 1956.

Hicks, Sir Seymour. Actor, screenwriter, occasional director. *b.* Jan. 30, 1871, St. Helier, England. *d.* 1949. On British stage from 1887 as actor, producer, and playwright. He also appeared intermittently in British films, often with his wife, Ellaline Terriss. Wrote the screenplays for many of his films and several books about the stage. In 1922 he collaborated with Alfred Hitchcock on completing the direction of *Always Tell Your Wife,* a film Hicks also produced. He was knighted in 1934.

FILMS INCLUDE (as actor): *Scrooge* (title role; also sc.), *David Garrick* (title role) 1913; *Sleeping Partners* (also dir., sc.) 1930; *Glamour* (also co-dir., sc.), *The Love Habit* (also sc.) 1931; *Money for Nothing* (also sc.) 1932; *Vintage Wine* (also sc.), *Scrooge* (remake; also sc.), *Royal Cavalcade* 1935; *Change for a Sovereign* (also sc.) 1937; *The Lambeth Walk* 1939; *Busman's Honeymoon/Haunted Honeymoon, Pastor Hall* 1940; *Fame Is the Spur* 1947; *Silent Dust* 1948.

Higgins, Colin. Director, screenwriter. *b.* 1941, New Caledonia, South Pacific, to American and Australian parents. *d.* 1988. He was a 28-year-old student at the UCLA film department when he wrote a 20-minute drama as part of a master's thesis. The expanded version of it became the basis for Hal Ashby's *Harold and Maude* (1971), a hugely popular cult classic about a quirky love affair between a 20-year-old young man obsessed with death (Bud CORT) and a 79-year-old swinger (Ruth GORDON). The film failed with the critics and at the box office when it was originally released and Higgins had to endure five lean years before he scored a commercial success with his screenplay for the comedy-adventure *Silver Streak.* He agreed to sell his next screenplay to Paramount at a cut rate in exchange for the opportunity to direct it. *Foul Play* (1978) proved a hit at the box office, paving the way for his even greater success, *9 to 5.* But he flopped badly with the screen adaptation of the musical *The Best Little Whorehouse in Texas* (1982), his last film. At age 47 he died of AIDS.

FILMS: *Harold and Maude* (sc., co-prod.) 1971; *Silver Streak* (sc.) 1976; *Foul Play* (dir., sc.) 1978; *9 to 5* (dir., co-sc.) 1980; *The Best Little Whorehouse in Texas* (dir., co-sc.) 1982.

high-angle shot. A shot taken from an elevated position looking down on the subject or the action. See also ANGLE, CAMERA; LOW-ANGLE SHOT.

high hat. Also "top hat." A small, low camera mount used instead of a tripod in filming low-angle shots.

high key lighting. A lighting arrangement designed to produce an overall light tone in a scene. The use of a high level of illumination emphasizes the lighter tones of the gray scale at the expense of the darker ones and results in a picture with a low lighting contrast, often suggesting brightness or cheerfulness.

highlights. The brightest areas of a photographed image. They appear as the densest parts of the negative image and, conversely, as the lightest areas on the positive print. The emphasis of a part of the subject matter by means of tone variation is known as "highlighting."

high-speed cinematography. Motion picture photography of moving objects taken at a rate of speed greater than that possible with the normal intermittent-action camera. Since intermittent action does not permit photography at speeds greater than several hundreds of frames per second without causing the film to break, special cameras must be used to obtain higher speeds. These cameras work on the principle of continuous rather than intermittent motion. Exposure is made with the aid of rotating prisms, mirrors, and synchronized flash lamps. Other types have components that move continuously in relation to stationary film. Either type of camera makes possible motion picture photography at a rate of thousands of frames per second. When the resultant film is projected at normal speed, a slow-motion effect is produced on the screen. High-speed cinematography has proved extremely useful in analyzing movement and action in such diverse matters as scientific research and post mortems of football games.

Hildyard, Jack. Director of photography. Born in 1915, in London. Entered British films as a clapper boy in 1932 and worked as a camera operator on such films as *The Divorce of Lady X* (1938), *Pimpernel Smith* (1941), *Henry V* (1945), and *Caesar and Cleopatra* (1946). Became a lighting cameraman in 1946 and subsequently worked on British and US productions. His work is noted for its slickness and rich color. He won an Academy Award for the cinematography of *The Bridge on the River Kwai* (1957).

FILMS INCLUDE: *School for Secrets/Secret Flight* 1946; *Vice Versa* 1948; *The Sound Barrier/Breaking Through the Sound Barrier* 1952; *Hobson's Choice* 1954; *Summer Madness/Summertime* 1955; *Anastasia* 1956; *The Bridge on the River Kwai* 1957; *Another Time Another Place* 1958; *The Journey, The Devil's Disciple* 1959; *Suddenly Last Summer, The Millionairess, The Sundowners* 1960; *The Road to Hong Kong* 1962; *Cleopatra* (some sequences only), *55 Days at Peking, The V.I.P.'s* 1963; *Circus World, The Yellow Rolls-Royce* 1964; *Battle of the Bulge* 1965; *Modesty Blaise* 1966; *Casino Royale, The Long Duel* 1967; *Villa Rides* 1968; *Hard Contract, Topaz* 1969; *Puppet on a Chain* 1971; *The Beast Must Die* 1973; *The Message, Emily* 1976; *Lion of the Desert* 1981.

Hill, Arthur. Actor. Born on Aug. 1, 1922, in Melfort, Saskatchewan, Canada. ed. U. of British Columbia. Began acting in college and in Seattle, then moved in 1948 to England, where he developed a reputation as a fine actor on the stage and in occasional films. He impressed Broadway audiences with a number of appearances in the late 50s and won a Tony Award in 1962 for his performance in 'Who's Afraid of Virginia Woolf?' From the early 60s he has been playing intelligent, often introspective leads and key supporting roles in occasional Hollywood films. He starred in numerous television productions, including the series 'Owen Marshall, Counselor at Law' (1971–74), as well as many TV movies.

FILMS INCLUDE: *Miss Pilgrim's Progress* 1950; *The Deep Blue Sea* 1955; *The Young Doctors* 1961; *The Ugly American, In the Cool of the Day* 1963; *Moment to Moment, Harper* 1966; *Petulia* 1968; *The Chairman/The Most Dangerous Man in the World* 1969; *Rabbit Run* 1970; *The Pursuit of Happiness, The Andromeda Strain* 1971; *The Killer Elite* 1975; *Futureworld* 1976; *A Bridge Too Far* 1977; *A Little Romance, The Champ* 1979; *Dirty Tricks* 1981; *Making Love, The Amateur* 1982; *Something Wicked This Way Comes* (narrator) 1983; *One Magic Christmas* 1985.

Hill, Benny. Comedian. *b.* Alfred Hawthorne Hill, Jan. 21, 1925, Southhampton, England. *d.* 1992. The popular comic star of bawdy slapstick shows on British TV, often bordering on vulgarity. Made occasional appearances in movies.

FEATURE FILMS: *Who Done It?* 1956; *Light Up the Sky* 1960; *Those Magnificent Men in Their Flying Machines* 1965; *Chitty Chitty Bang Bang* 1968; *The Italian Job* 1969; *The Best of Benny Hill* (compilation) 1974; *Benny and Friends* (video) 1984.

Hill, Bernard. Actor. Born on Dec. 17, 1944 in Manchester, England. *ed.* Manchester Art College, England. Versatile stage-trained character actor seen widely in British films of the 80s and 90s. Known for role as insensitive husband in *Shirley Valentine*.

FILMS INCLUDE: *It Could Happen to You* 1975; *A Choice of Weapons* 1976; *The Black Stuff, The Sailor's Return* 1978; *Gandhi* 1982; *Runners, Squaring the Circle* 1983; *The Bounty* 1984; *The Chain, Restless Natives* 1985; *Milwr Bychan, New World, No Surrender* 1986; *Bellman & True* 1987; *Drowning by Numbers* 1988; *Shirley Valentine* 1989; *Mountains of the Moon* 1990; *Double X* 1992; *Madagascar Skin* 1996.

Hill, Debra. Producer. Born in Haddonfield, N.J. She started her career as a production assistant on adventure documentaries. Entering feature films as a script girl, she gradually moved up to assistant director and second-unit director. In 1978 she made a fortuitous debut as a producer with John Carpenter's low-budget chiller, *Halloween,* a huge hit at the box office. Two sequels followed, as well as other productions designed to appeal to youngsters, maximizing profit through economical budgeting.

FILMS INCLUDE: *Halloween* (also co-sc.) 1978; *The Fog* (also co-sc.) 1980; *Escape from New York* 1981; *The Dead Zone* 1983; *Head Office* 1985; *Adventures in Babysitting* 1987; *Big Top Pee-Wee, Heartbreak Hotel* 1988; *Gross Anatomy* 1989; *The Fisher King* 1991; *Escape from L.A.* 1996.

Hill, George Roy. Director. Born on Dec. 20, 1922, in Minneapolis. He studied music at Yale and at Dublin's Trinity College. He began his professional career as an actor with Cyril Cusack's repertory company in Dublin and later toured the US with a Shakespearean company and performed in off-Broadway productions. Following WW II service as a Navy pilot in the Pacific, he directed his first stage production in Dublin in 1948. He served again as a pilot in the Korean War, and after his discharge with the rank of major began writing and directing for TV and in 1957 directed the first of several Broadway plays. He was 40 years old by the time he made his debut as a motion picture director in 1962. But he has demonstrated youthful zest and a vigorous sense of humor with such commercially and critically successful films as *The World of Henry Orient* (1964), *Butch Cassidy and the Sundance Kid* (1969), and *The Sting* (1973). He won the best director Academy Award for the last (which was also voted best film) and was awarded the special jury prize at the 1972 Cannes Festival for his screen handling of Kurt Vonnegut's unconventional fantasy novel *Slaughterhouse Five.*

FILMS: *Period of Adjustment* 1962; *Toys in the Attic* 1963; *The World of Henry Orient* 1964; *Hawaii* 1966; *Thoroughly Modern Millie* 1967; *Butch Cassidy and the Sundance Kid* 1969; *Slaughterhouse Five* 1972; *The Sting* 1973; *The Great Waldo Pepper* (also prod., story) 1975; *Slap Shot* 1977; *A Little Romance* (also co-exec. prod.) 1979; *The World According to Garp* (also co-prod.) 1982; *The Little Drummer Girl* 1984; *Funny Farm* 1988.

Hill, George W(illiam). Director. *b.* Apr. 25, 1895, Douglass, Kans. *d.* 1934. He began his career at age 13 as a stagehand for D. W. Griffith, then worked as cameraman and screenwriter before turning to direction early in the 20s. Imaginative and inventive, he directed several starkly realistic pictures for MGM, capped by his masterpiece, *The Big House.* His experience as cameraman (including *The Sea Wolf,* 1913; *Martin Eden,* 1914; *Macbeth,* 1916; and *Polly of the Circus,* 1917) is evident in his original handling of lighting and visual atmosphere. He often collaborated with his wife, screenwriter Frances MARION. He was found dead at his beach house, apparently a suicide, while preparing the production of *The Good Earth* (which was eventually handed over to Sidney Franklin).

FILMS: *While the Devil Laughs* (also story, sc.), *Get Your Man* (co-dir. with William K. Howard) 1921; *Through the Dark, The Hill Billy, The Midnight Express* (also sc.), *The Foolish Virgin* 1924; *Zander the Great, The Limited Mail* 1925; *The Barrier* 1926; *Tell It to the Marines, The Callahans and the Murphys, Buttons* (also story) 1927; *The Cossacks* 1928; *The Flying Fleet* 1929; *The Big House, Min and Bill* 1930; *The Secret Six* 1931; *Hell Divers* 1932; *Clear All Wires* 1933.

Hill, James. Producer. Born on Aug. 1, 1916, in Jeffersonville, Ind. *ed.* U. of Washington. A former page boy at NBC, he formed a partnership with Burt LANCASTER and Harold HECHT and produced a number of films in the 50s. He was the fifth husband (1958–61) of Rita HAYWORTH. Author: *Rita Hayworth, a Memoir.*

FILMS INCLUDE: *Vera Cruz* 1954; *The Kentuckian* 1955; *Trapeze* 1956; *Sweet Smell of Success* 1957; *The Unforgiven* 1960; *The Happy Thieves* (exec. prod.) 1961.

Hill, James. Director. Born in 1919 in England. At first a documentary filmmaker, he won several international prizes for his shorts, including an Academy Award for *Giuseppina* (1961). He has directed occasional feature films since the early 50s and many TV episodes ('The Saint,' 'The Avengers'). At his best with adventure and nature films.

FEATURE FILMS: *The Stolen Plans* (also sc.) 1952; *Gibraltar Adventure/The Clue of the Missing Ape* (also sc.) 1953; *Peril for the Guy* 1956; *Mystery in the Mine* (serial; also co-sc.) 1959; *The Kitchen* 1961; *The Dock Brief/Trial and Error, Lunch Hour* 1962; *Every Day's a Holiday/Seaside Swingers, A Study in Terror/Fog* 1965; *Born Free, Il Sigillo de Pechino/Die Hölle von Macao/Les Corrompus/The Corrupt Ones/The Peking Medallion/Hell to Macao* (co-dir. with Bill Catching; It./Ger./Fr.) 1966; *Captain Nemo and the Underwater City* 1969; *An Elephant Called Slowly* (also co-prod., so-sc.) 1970; *Black Beauty* 1971; *The Belstone Fox* (also sc.), *Christian the Lion* (co-dir., co-prod., co-sc.) 1976.

Hill, Robert F. Director. *b.* Apr. 14, 1886, in Port Rohen, Ontario, Canada. *d.* 1966. Entering films as an actor and screenwriter, he directed numerous serials and low-budget features, mainly action dramas, from 1916 through 1941. He directed the screen's first Tarzan, Elmo Lincoln, in the serial *The Adventures of Tarzan* (1921) and the seventh, Buster Crabbe, in *Tarzan the Fearless* (1933) as well as Crabbe's *Flash Gordon's Trip to Mars* (1938). His screenplays, alone or in collaboration, included Clarence Badger's *Jubilo* (1919) and other Will Rogers silent vehicles, and Paul Leni's *The Cat and the Canary* (1928) and *The Last Warning* (1930).

FILMS INCLUDE: *Temptation and the Man* 1916; *The Great Radium Mystery* (serial; co-dir. with Robert Roadwell) 1919; *The Flaming Disc* (serial) 1920; *The Adventures of Tarzan* (serial) 1921; *The Adventures of Robinson Crusoe* (serial), *The Radio King* (serial) 1922; *The Phantom Fortune* (serial), *The Social Buccaneer* (serial), *Shadows of the North, Crooked Alley* (also adapt.), *His Mystery Girl* 1923; *The Breathless Moment, Excitement, The Dangerous Blonde, Dark Stairways, Young Ideas* 1924; *Idaho* (serial), *The Wild West* (serial) 1925; *The Bar-C Mystery* (serial and feature versions) 1926; *Blake of Scotland Yard* (serial) 1927; *Haunted Island* (serial), *A Million for Love, Life's Mockery* 1928; *Silks and Saddles, Melody Lane* (also co-sc.) 1929; *Spell of the Circus* (serial) 1931; *The Cheyenne Kid, Tarzan the Fearless* 1933; *Frontier Days, Inside Information* 1934; *Cyclone Ranger, Texas Rambler* 1935; *Shadow of Chinatown* (serial), *Idaho Kid, Kelly of the Secret Service, Face in the Fog, Rio Grande Romance* 1936; *Million Dollar Racket, Two Minutes to Play* 1937; *Flash Gordon's Trip to Mars* (serial; co-dir. with Ford Beebe; and feature version, *Mars Attacks the World*), *Man's Country, The Painted Trail* 1938; *Wild Horse Canyon, Overland Mail* 1939; *East Side Kids, Wanderers of the West* 1941.

Hill, Sinclair. Director. *b.* June 10, 1894, London. *d.* 1945. Prominent director of British films of the 20s, he received his training at Italy's Turin studios, then among the most active in Europe. Also wrote several screenplays.

FILMS INCLUDE: *The Tidal Wave* 1920; *The Experiment* 1922; *Indian Love Lyrics* 1923; *The Conspirators* 1924; *The Secret Kingdom* 1925; *The Chinese Bungalow* 1926; *The King's Highway* 1927; *The Guns of Loos, The Price of Divorce, Boadicea* 1928; *The Unwritten Law* 1929; *Greek Street* 1930; *A Gentleman of Paris* 1931; *The Man from Toronto, The First Mrs. Fraser* 1932; *My Old Dutch* 1934; *Hyde Park Corner* 1935; *The Cardinal* 1936; *Command Performance* 1937; *Follow Your Star* 1938.

Hill, Terence. Actor. Born Mario Girotti, on Mar. 29, 1939, in Venice, of German descent. *ed.* U. of Rome. Handsome, blue-eyed, blond hero of Italian action pictures and spaghetti Westerns. One of his country's most popular and highest paid stars. He began his career in the early 50s as a dark-haired adolescent and in the following 15 years played supporting parts and occasional leads in numerous films under his real name. The changing of his screen persona from Mario Girotti to the Anglo-Saxon Terence Hill, and his hair color from brunet to blond, coincided with his rise to stardom in the late 60s in imitation horse operas, which often co-starred another transformed Italian, Bud Spencer (born in 1931 as Carlo Pedersoli). Hill, who runs his own production company, Paloma Films, took an occasional stab at directing in the 80s. In his debut film, he absurdly cast himself in the title role of *Don Camillo* (1983), an awfully poor remake of the Fernandel classic of the early 50s.

FILMS INCLUDE: As Mario Girotti—*Vacanze col Gangster, La Voce del Silenzio* 1952; *Villa Borghese* 1954; *Gli Sbandati* 1955; *Guaglione, La Grande Strada Azzurra* 1957; *Annibale/Hannibal, Fiamme/Carthage in Flames, Giuseppe venduto dai Fratelli/The Story of Joseph and His Brethren* (as Benjamin) 1960; *Le Meraviglie di Aladino/The Wonders of Aladdin* 1962; *Il Gattopardo/The Leopard* 1963; *Winnetou II/Last of the Renegades* (Ger./It./Fr./Yug.) 1964; *Old Surehand/Flaming Frontier* (Ger./Yug.) 1965; *Die Nibelungen* (Ger./Yug.) 1966–67. As Terence Hill—*Dio perdona... io no/God Forgives—I Don't* 1967; *I Quattro dell'Ave Maria/Ace High* 1968; *La Collina degli Stivali/Boot Hill Barbagia* 1969; *Lo chiamavano Trinità/They Call Me Trinity, Continuavano a chiamarlo Trinità/Trinity Is Still My Name, La Collera del Vento* 1971; *Il Vero e il Falso, E poi lo chiamarono il Magnifico/A Man from the East* 1972; *Più forte Ragazzi!/All the Way Boys, My Name Is Nobody* 1973; *Mr. Billion* (US), *March or Die* (UK) 1977; *Deux Super Flics/Two Super Cops* (Fr./It.) 1978; *Super Snooper/Super Fuzz* 1981; *Don Camillo* (title role; also dir., prod.) 1983; *The Crew* 1984; *Don Camillo II* 1985; *Renegade Luke* 1987; *Lucky Luke* 1991.

Hill, Walter. Director, screenwriter. Born on Jan. 10, 1942, in Long Beach, Calif. The son of a dockyard riveter, he enrolled briefly in the arts program at the University of the Americas, in Mexico City, intending to become a cartoonist. Deciding instead on a career in journalism, he transferred to Michigan State University. After graduating with a degree in English, he drifted about, then worked in construction and oil drilling. In 1967, following marginal experience as a writer for educational documentaries, he entered films as a second assistant director and worked in that capacity on such films as *Bullitt* (1968), *The Thomas Crown Affair* (1968), and *Take the Money and Run* (1969). Driven by the experience with a desire to become a director, he began writing screenplays, hoping they would provide a shortcut to his goal. They eventually did, starting with *Hard Times* (1975), a virile tale about the lives and times of a tough bareknuckle streetfighter and his sharp manager. The film set the tone for Hill's subsequent work a director: masculine themes, vivid storytelling, plenty of action, and a broad appeal extending from discriminating critics to general audiences. His stylized but riveting drama *The Warriors* (1979), about New York street gangs, became notorious for allegedly instigating gang violence in its wake. His exciting Jesse James epic *The Long Riders* (1980) revived the long-dormant Western genre on the American screen. Hill reached a peak of commercial success with the highly entertaining, action-packed comedy *48 Hours* (1982), a huge box-office hit. Thereafter, beset by a string of relative failures, his reputation gradually declined.

FILMS: As screenwriter—*Hickey and Boggs, The Getaway* 1972; *The Thief Who Came to Dinner, The Mackintosh Man* (UK) 1973; *The Drowning Pool* (co-sc.) 1975; *The Getaway* (co-sc.) 1994. As director—*Hard Times* (also co-sc.) 1975; *The Driver* (also sc.) 1978; *The Warriors* (also co-sc.), *Alien* (co-prod. only) 1979; *The Long Riders* 1980; *Southern Comfort* (also co-sc.) 1981; *48 Hours* (also co-sc.) 1982; *Streets of Fire* (also co-sc.) 1984; *Brewster's Millions* 1985; *Crossroads, Blue City* (co-prod., co-sc. only), *Aliens* (co-exec prod., co-story only) 1986; *Extreme Prejudice* 1987; *Red Heat* (also co-prod., story, co-sc.) 1988; *Johnny Handsome* 1989; *Another 48 Hours* 1990; *Aliens 3* (prod. only) 1992; *Geronimo: An American Legend* 1993; *Tales from the Crypt Presents Demon Knights* (ex-prod.), *Wild Bill* (also sc.) 1995; *Last Man Standing* 1996.

Hiller, Arthur. Director. Born on Nov. 22, 1923, in Edmonton, Alberta, Canada. *ed.* U. of Toronto (B.A.); U. of British Columbia (one year of law); U. of Alberta (M.A. in psychology). Following WW II service as a navigator with the Royal Canadian Air Force in Britain, he began his career in Canadian radio. He began directing for CBC-Television in 1954, and shortly after moved to the US, where he worked on such prestigious live and film television series as 'Playhouse 90,' 'Alfred Hitchcock Presents,' 'Gunsmoke,' and 'Naked City' before launching his big-screen career in the late 50s. Several of his films, both comedies and dramas, have enjoyed commercial success and he had a big box-office hit with the maudlin *Love Story* (1970). But with the notable exception of *The Americanization of Emily* (1964) and *The Hospital* (1971), his work has offered little excitement beyond its surface gloss. Named president of the Academy of Motion Picture Arts and Sciences in 1993.

FILMS: *The Careless Years* 1957; *Miracle of the White Stallions, The Wheeler Dealers* 1963; *The Americanization of Emily* 1964; *Promise Her Anything, Penelope* 1966; *Tobruk, The Tiger Makes Out* 1967; *Popi* 1969; *The Out-of-Towners, Love Story* 1970; *Plaza Suite, The Hospital* 1971; *Man of La Mancha* 1972; *The Crazy World of Julius Vrooder* (also co-prod.) 1974; *The Man in the Glass Booth* 1975; *W. C. Fields and Me, Silver Streak* 1976; *The In-Laws* (also co-prod.), *Nightwing* 1979; *Making Love, Author! Author!* 1982; *Romantic Comedy* 1983; *The Lonely Guy* (also prod.), *Teachers* 1984; *Outrageous Fortune* 1987; *See No Evil Hear No Evil* 1989; *Taking Care of Business* 1990; *Married To It* 1991; *The Babe* 1992.

Hiller, Dame Wendy. Actress. Born on Aug. 15, 1912, in Bramshall, Cheshire, England. On stage from the age of 18, she became an instant star with her London debut in 'Love on the Dole' in 1935, and the following year repeated her success on Broadway. In 1937 she married the play's author, Ronald Gow, and made her first British film. She remained primarily a stage actress, appearing only sporadically in films, but several of her film roles have made her a notable screen personality. She is best remembered for her captivating, Oscar-nominated performance as Eliza Doolittle opposite Leslie Howard in *Pygmalion* (1938), but she also did remarkably well with another screen adaptation of a Shaw play, *Major Barbara* (1941), and won an Academy Award as best supporting actress for her delicate portrayal of a dejected, lonely woman in *Separate Tables* (1958). She was nominated again for an Oscar for *A Man for All Seasons* (1966). She was created Dame in 1975.

FILMS: *Lancashire Luck* 1937; *Pygmalion* (as Eliza Doolittle) 1938; *Major Barbara* (title role) 1941; *I Know Where I'm Going* 1945; *An Outcast of the Islands, Single-handed/Sailor of the King* 1951; *Something of Value, How to Murder a Rich Uncle* 1957; *Separate Tables* 1958; *Sons and Lovers* (as Gertrude Morel) 1960; *Toys in the Attic* 1963; *A Man for All Seasons* (as Alice More) 1966; *David Copperfield* (as Mrs. Micawber) 1970; *Murder on the Orient Express* 1974; *Voyage of the Damned* 1976; *The Cat and the Canary* 1978; *The Elephant Man* 1980; *Making Love* 1982; *The Lonely Passion of Judith Hearne* 1987.

Hilliard, Harriet. Actress, singer. Born on July 18, 1914, in Des Moines. A daughter of show people, she began her career as vocalist with the band of Ozzie NELSON, whom she married in 1935. She played lead roles in mostly low-budget musical and action films from the mid-30s to mid-40s, using her maiden name, and with her husband, as Harriet Nelson, starred on radio and in the long-running 'Ozzie and Harriet' (1952–66) TV show.

FILMS INCLUDE: *Follow the Fleet* 1936; *New Faces of 1937, The Life of the Party* 1937; *She's My Everything, Cocoanut Grove* 1938; *The Letter* 1940; *Confessions of Boston Blackie* 1941; *Canal Zone, Juke Box Jenny* 1942; *Honeymoon Lodge, The Falcon Strikes Back, Gals Inc.* 1943; *Swingtime Johnny* 1944; *Here Come the Nelsons* 1952.

Hillier, Erwin. Director of photography. Born in 1911, in Germany. In Britain since 1929. A dependable craftsman, he was behind the camera on many British productions from the early 40s to the late 60s.

FILMS INCLUDE: *The Lady from Lisbon* 1942; *I Know Where I'm Going* 1945; *London Town* 1946; *The October Man* 1947; *Private Angelo* 1949; *Where's Charley?* 1952; *The Dam Busters* 1955; *Chase a Crooked Shadow* 1958; *Shake Hands with the Devil* 1959; *The Naked Edge* 1961; *A Matter of Who* 1962; *Operation Crossbow, Sands of Kalahari* 1965; *Eye of the Devil, The Quiller Memorandum* 1966; *The Shoes of the Fisherman* (US) 1968; *The Valley of Gwangi* (US) 1969.

Hillyer, Lambert. Director. *b.* July 8, 1889, South Bend, Ind. Deceased. A former newspaperman, short-story writer, vaudevillian, and stock actor, he entered films during WW I and over three decades directed hundreds of low-budget Hollywood productions, many from his own scripts. One of the American cinema's most prolific and least pretentious directors, he wrote and directed many of the silent Westerns of William S. Hart and later Tom Mix, Buck Jones, and other cowboy stars. In the mid-20s he expanded his range to include B-grade romantic and crime melodramas and in 1936 delighted horror fans with two well-executed chillers, *The Invisible Ray* and *Dracula's Daughter.* In the early 40s, however, he returned to his old specialty, economical Westerns, and ended his career with Monogram, with ever-decreasing budgets at his command. He directed the serial *Batman* (1943).

FILMS INCLUDE: *An Even Break* (also sc.), *The Narrow Trail, Strife* 1917; *Riddle Gawne* (assoc. dir.) 1918; *Breed of Men* (assoc. dir.), *The Poppy Girl's Husband* (co-dir.), *The Money Corral* (also co-sc.), *Square Deal Sanderson* (co-dir., sc.), *Wagon Tracks, John Petticoats* 1919; *The Cradle of Courage* (also sc.), *The Testing Block* (also sc.) 1920; *The Toll Gate* (also co-sc.), *Sand* (also sc.) 1920; *O'Malley of the Mounted* (also sc.), *Three Word Brand, White Oak* 1921; *White Hands* (also sc.), *Travelin' On* (also sc.), *Caught Bluffing, Skin Deep, The Super-Sex* (also sc.), *The Altar Stairs* 1922; *Scars of Jealousy* (also sc.), *The Shock, Temporary Marriage* (also sc.), *The Spoilers, The Lone Star Ranger* (also sc.), *Mile-a-Minute Romeo, Eyes of the Forest* 1923; *Those Who Dance* (also co-sc.), *Barbara Frietchie* (also co-sc.), *Idle Tongues* 1924; *I Want My Man, The Making of O'Malley, The Knockout, The Unguarded Hour* 1925; *Her Second Chance, Miss Nobody, 30 Below Zero* (co-dir. with Robert P. Kerr) 1926; *The War Horse* (also sc.), *Hills of Peril, Chain Lightning* (also sc.) 1927; *The Branded Sombrero* (also sc.), *Fleetwing* (also co-story) 1928; *Beau Bandit* 1930; *One Man Law* (also sc.) 1931; *The Deadline* (also sc.), *The Fighting Fool, South of the Rio Grande, White Eagle, Hello Trouble* (also prod., sc.), *The Forbidden Trail* 1932; *Police Car 17, Unknown Valley, Dangerous Crossroads, The Sundown Rider, Before Midnight, Master of Men* 1933; *Once to Every Woman, One Is Guilty, The Man Trailer, The Defense Rests, The Most Precious Thing in Life, Against the Law, Men of the Night* (also sc.) 1934; *Behind the Evidence, Men of the Hour, Superspeed, Guard That Girl* (also sc.) 1935; *The Invisible Ray, Dangerous Waters, Dracula's Daughter* 1936; *Speed to Spare, Girls Can Play, All-American Sweetheart* 1937; *Women in Prison, My Old Kentucky Home, Extortion* 1938; *Convict's Code, Should a Girl Marry?, The Girl from Rio* 1939; *The Durango Kid* 1940; *The Wildcat of Tucson, The Return of Daniel Boone, The Son of Davy Crockett, King of Dodge City, The Royal Mounted Patrol* 1941; *The Devil's Trail, Vengeance of the West* 1942; *Batman* (serial), *The Texas Kid* 1943; *Law Men, Ghost Guns* 1944; *South of the Rio Grande* 1945; *Under Arizona Skies, Trigger Fingers* 1946; *Valley of Fear, Land of the Lawless, The Hat Box Mystery, The Case of the Baby Sitter* 1947; *Oklahoma Blues, Frontier Agent* 1948; *Gun Runner, Range Land, Trail's End* 1949.

Hilton, James. Novelist, screenwriter. *b.* Sept. 9, 1900, Leigh, England. *d.* 1954. *ed.* Cambridge. Several of the works of this best-selling British novelist were adapted to the screen by others, including *Knight Without Armor* (1937), *Lost Horizon* (1937 and 1973), *Goodbye Mr. Chips* (1939 and 1969), *Rage in Heaven* (1941), and *So Well Remembered* (1947). In addition, he wrote a number of screenplays directly for films (listed below) alone or in collaboration. A resident of Hollywood from 1935, he was a member of the governing board of the Academy of Motion Picture Arts and Sciences and vice president of the Screen Writers Guild.

FILMS INCLUDE (screenplays): *Camille* 1937; *We Are Not Alone* (from his own novel) 1939; *Foreign Correspondent* (dialogue only) 1940; *Mrs. Miniver, The Tuttles of Tahiti* 1942; *Forever and a Day* 1943.

Hinds, Samuel S. Actor. *b.* Apr. 4, 1875, Brooklyn, N.Y. *d.* 1948. A graduate of Harvard, he practiced law and participated in amateur dramatics for 35 years before becoming a professional stage and screen actor in the early 30s. He was among the founders of the Pasadena Community Playhouse. On the screen, he played more than 150 character roles, typically as a wise, kind gentleman. He played Lew Ayres's doctor father in many films of the "Dr. Kildare" series.

FILMS INCLUDE: *If I Had a Million* 1932; *The Crime of the Century, Gabriel Over the White House, Berkeley Square, Little Women* (as Mr. March) 1933; *No Greater Glory, Men in White* 1934; *Sequoia, Rumba, Private Worlds, The Raven, She* (as John Vincey), *Dr. Socrates, Rendezvous* 1935; *Rhythm on the Range* 1936; *Black Legion, Top of the Town, The Road Back, Stage Door, Navy Blue and Gold* 1937; *Test Pilot, The Rage of Paris, You Can't Take It with You, Young Doctor Kildare* 1938; *Calling Dr. Kildare, Career, The Under-Pup, First Love, Destry Rides Again* 1939; *The Boys from Syracuse, Spring Parade, Seven Sinners* 1940; *Back Street, Buck Privates, Blossoms in the Dust, The Shepherd of the Hills, Dr. Kildare's Wedding Day* 1941; *The Spoilers, Lady in a Jam, Pittsburgh* 1942; *Son of Dracula* 1943 *Cobra Woman* 1944; *Uncle Harry, Lady on a Train, Weekend at the Waldorf* 1945; *Scarlet Street, It's a Wonderful Life* 1946; *The Egg and I* 1947; *The Boy with Green Hair* 1948; *The Bride* 1949.

Hines, Gregory. Dancer, actor. Born on Feb. 14, 1946, in New York City. Tap dancing from the age of two, he teamed up when he was five with brother, Maurice Jr., to form "The Hines Kids" and began performing in nightclubs and theaters around the country. They became "The Hines Brothers" in 1955 and "Hines, Hines, and Dad" in 1963, when their father, Maurice, joined the act. In 1973, Gregory quit the team and formed a jazz-rock band, "Severance," in Venice, California. He later began appearing on Broadway and was nominated for a Tony for his performance in the musical 'Eubie!' (1978). He first brought his considerable talent and warm personality to the screen in 1981. He won a Tony for his performance as Jelly Roll Morton in *Jelly's Last Jam*.

FILMS: *History of the World: Part I, Wolfen* 1981; *Deal of the Century* 1983; *The Muppets Take Manhattan* (cameo), *The Cotton Club* 1984; *White Nights* 1985; *Running Scared* 1986; *Off Limits/Saigon* 1988; *Tap* 1989; *Eve of Destruction* 1990; *A Rage in Harlem, White Lie* 1991; *Renaissance Man* 1994; *Waiting to Exhale* 1995; *Mad Dog Time* 1996.

Hines, Johnny. Actor. *b.* July 25, 1895, Golden, Col. *d.* 1970. *ed.* CCNY. Star comedian of Hollywood silents. Entering films in 1913, he played supporting roles and some leads in numerous early features and became highly popular in the 20s. Many of his films were directed by his brother, Charles Hines (*b.* 1893, Pittsburgh; deceased), who was also an actor. Johnny's career faltered after the arrival of sound.

FILMS INCLUDE: *The Man of the Hour, The Wishing Ring* 1914; *Alias Jimmy Valentine, The Cub* 1915; *The Pawn of Fate, Miss Petticoats* 1916; *Tillie Wakes Up, Yankee Pluck, Youth* 1917; *Neighbors, The Power and the Glory, Just Sylvia* 1918; *What Love Forgives, Heart of Gold* 1919; *Burn 'Em Up Barnes* 1921; *Sure Fire Flint* 1922; *Luck, Little Johnny Jones* 1923; *The Speed Spook* 1924, *The Crackerjack, The Live Wire* 1925; *Rainbow Riley, The Brown Derby* 1926; *All Aboard, Home Made* 1927; *Chinatown Charlie* 1928; *The Runaround* 1931; *Whistling in the Dark, Her Bodyguard* 1933; *Society Doctor* 1935; *Too Hot to Handle* 1938.

Hingle, Pat. Actor. Born Martin Patterson Hingle, on July 19, 1923, in Denver. *ed.* U. of Texas. A former laborer, waiter, and construction worker, he studied drama at the Theatre Wing, the Berghof Studio, and the Actors Studio, making his professional stage debut in 1950 and his first Broadway appearance in 1953. He has since gained a reputation as a solid character actor on stage, on TV, and in films.

FILMS INCLUDE: *On the Waterfront* 1954; *The Strange One, No Down Payment* 1957; *Splendor in the Grass* 1961; *The Ugly American, All the Way Home* 1963; *Invitation to a Gunfighter* 1964; *Nevada Smith* 1966; *Jigsaw, Sol Madrid, Hang 'em High* 1968; *Bloody Mama, WUSA, Norwood* 1970; *The Carey Treatment* 1972; *Running Wild, One Little Indian, Happy as the Grass Was Green/Hazel's People* 1973; *The Super Cops, Deadly Honeymoon* 1974; *Independence* (short; as John Adams) 1976; *The Gauntlet* 1979; *When You Comin' Back Red Ryder?, Norma Rae* 1979; *Running Brave* (Can.), *Going Berserk, Sudden Impact* 1983; *The Falcon and the Snowman, Brewster's Millions* 1985; *Maximum Overdrive* 1986; *Baby Boom* 1987; *Batman* (as Commissioner Gordon) 1989; *The Grifters* 1990; *Batman Returns* 1992; *Lightning Jack* 1994; *Batman Forever, The Quick and the Dead* 1995; *Larger Than Life* 1996; *A Thousand Acres* 1997.

Hird, Thora. See SCOTT, Janette.

Hirsch, Judd. Actor. Born on Mar. 15, 1935, in New York City. *ed.* CCNY. Trained as an engineer, he found the profession ungratifying and in 1962 turned to acting with a stock company in Colorado. Off-Broadway and Broadway roles followed. His big break came on television, however, with a leading role in the TV movie, *The Law* (1974). He went on to play the title role in the police series 'Delvecchio' (1976–77), then starred in the hit comedy series 'Taxi' (1978–83), for which he won two Emmy Awards. He started another series, 'Dear John,' in 1988. Onstage, he won an Obie for 'Talley's Folley' and a Tony for 'I'm Not Rappaport.' His busy TV schedule limited his feature film appearances.

FILMS: *King of the Gypsies* 1978; *Ordinary People* 1980; *Without a Trace* 1983; *Teachers, The Goodbye People* 1984; *Running on Empty* 1988; *Independence Day* 1996.

Hirschfeld, Gerald. Director of photography. Born on Apr. 25, 1921, in New York City. *ed.* Columbia U. In films from the late 40s, he disappeared from features in the early 50s but returned prestigiously in the mid-60s.

FILMS INCLUDE: *Shades of Gray* 1948; *Guilty Bystander* 1950; *Gail Safe* 1964; *The Incident* 1967; *Goodbye Columbus, Last Summer* 1969; *Cotton Comes to Harlem, Diary of a Mad Housewife* 1970; *Doc* 1971; *Summer Wishes, Winter Dreams, Two People* 1973; *Young Frankenstein* 1974; *Two-Minute Warning* 1976; *The World's Greatest Lover* 1977; *Coma* 1978; *The Bell Jar* 1979; *Neighbors* 1981; *My Favorite Year* 1982; *To Be or Not to Be* 1983; *Head Office* 1985; *Malone* 1987.

Hiscott, Leslie. Director. *b.* July 25, 1894, London. *d.* 1968. His law studies at Cambridge were interrupted by WW I service on the western front. Began in 1919 as assistant to various directors in Italy, France, England, and elsewhere. He became a director in 1925 and turned out numerous quickie films to take advantage of the quota provisions of the British government's film production policy of the early 30s.

FILMS INCLUDE: *This Marriage Business* 1927; *S.O.S.* 1928; *The Feather* 1929; *At the Villa Rose/Mystery at the Villa Rose, The House of the Arrow, The Call of the Sea* 1930; *The Sleeping Cardinal/Sherlock Holmes's Fatal Hour, Alibi, A Night in Montmartre* 1931; *The Missing Rembrandt, Murder at Covent Garden, The Crooked Lady, When London Sleeps, The Face at the Window* 1932; *The Iron Stair, The Stolen Necklace, Marooned* 1933; *The Man I Want, Passing Shadows, Crazy People* 1934; *The Triumph of Sherlock Holmes, Death on the Set, Three Witnesses, She Shall Have Music* 1935; *Fame, The Interrupted Honeymoon* 1936; *Fine Feathers* 1937; *Tilly of Bloomsbury* 1940; *Sabotage at Sea* 1942; *The Butler's Dilemma* 1943; *The Time of His Life* 1955; *Tons of Trouble* 1956.

Hitchcock, Alfred. Director. *b.* Aug. 13, 1899, London, the son of a poultry dealer and fruit importer. *d.* 1980. The family was Catholic, and Alfred was enrolled at a Jesuit school, London's St. Ignatius College, at a young age. In 1920 he entered the film industry as a designer of titles for the newly formed London branch of Hollywood's Famous Players-Lasky (Paramount). Before long he was the head of the title department, working closely with the screenwriters of the editorial department. Occasionally he was even permitted to direct an unimportant scene that did not involve acting. In 1922 the Famous Players studios were taken over by a British production company formed by Michael Balcon, and Hitchcock was retained as an assistant director; but he soon took on other functions as well, working as an art director and screenwriter on *Woman to Woman* and *The White Shadow* (both 1923), *The Passionate Adventure* (1924), and *The Blackguard* and *The Prude's Fall* (both 1925).

In 1925, Hitchcock was promoted to director, getting as his first assignment an Anglo-German production, *The Pleasure Garden.* Back in 1922 he had collaborated with actor Seymour Hicks on completing the final scenes of *Always Tell Your Wife* for an ailing director. In the same year he had also directed a two-reel fiction film, *Number Thirteen,* but the production was never completed. *The Pleasure Garden* was his first real stab at directing, and it proved an impressive debut. Hitchcock, however, considers his third production, *The Lodger* (titled in the US *The Case of Jonathan Drew;* 1926), as his first true film. A suspense drama about a landlady who suspects her new tenant is Jack the Ripper, it contained some bold special effects and introduced a theme that was to reappear in many of the director's films, that of a man accused of a crime he did not commit, an ordinary man caught in a web of extraordinary events. It was also the first film in which Hitchcock made a personal appearance as an extra, needing one more body to fill the screen. The momentary personal appearance later became a Hitchcock trademark.

In 1926, Hitchcock married Alma REVILLE, a film editor and script girl who had been working with him for several years. She would later collaborate as a screenwriter on many of his films. Hitchcock failed to match the commercial success of *The Lodger* with any of his next few productions, although *The Ring* (1927), a romantic triangle melodrama with a boxing background, gained the esteem of critics. Hitchcock's next major production was *Blackmail* (1929), the British cinema's first feature film with synchronous sound, although it had been started as a silent film. *Blackmail* contained some innovations in the use of sound and a number of striking special effects, highlighted by the use of the SCHÜFFTAN PROCESS for the climactic chase sequence through the halls and over the roofs of the British Museum. Similar chases were to highlight many of Hitchcock's films.

The director's next few productions were for the most part unexceptional adaptations of novels and plays, among them *Elstree Calling* (1930), a musical spoof of Shakespeare's 'The Taming of the Shrew'; *Juno and the Paycock* (1930), a straightforward screen adaptation of the Sean O'Casey play; and *Waltzes from Vienna* (*Strauss's Great Waltz* in the US; 1933), a rickety low-budget musical. His only truly interesting film of this ebb period was *Murder* (1930), a slow-paced but still intriguing whodunit thriller with a backstage background and daring—for that time—homosexual motif.

The year 1934 signaled the beginning of Alfred Hitchcock's international reputation as the master of the thriller genre. During a period spanning five years he turned out a cycle of superb suspense dramas that established him as England's foremost director. First came *The Man Who Knew Too Much* (1934), a suspense story about a British couple touring in Switzerland who become accidentally involved in international intrigue. The film introduced such Hitchcockian hallmarks as the sudden-shock effect and the lurking of sinister jeopardy beneath a surface of commonplace serenity. A huge commercial success both in England and abroad, *The Man Who Knew Too Much* was remade by Hitchcock in the US in 1956 as a more elaborate and in many ways more accomplished color production.

The 39 Steps (1935) was an even greater success, both commercially and critically. A free adaptation of a John Buchan novel, it was a delightful combination of hair-raising suspense and diverting romantic and comic relief that served to heighten rather than diminish the tension. Hitchcock had less success with *The Secret Agent* (1936), an adaptation of two of Somerset Maugham's Ashenden stories; *Sabotage* (US title, *The Woman Alone;* 1937), which was adapted from the Joseph Conrad novel *The Secret Agent*; and the much underrated *Young and Innocent* (*The Girl Was Young* in the US; 1937). But these films too were among the finest produced in England in the 30s.

Hitchcock capped his so-called British period with *The Lady Vanishes* (1938), a superb thriller noted for its technical inventiveness and breezy, often humorous suspenseful action. It won the best director award from the New York Film Critics. As soon as the picture was completed, Hitchcock was signed by producer David O. Selznick to direct in America. Before leaving England, he regrettably made a final British film, *Jamaica Inn* (1939), an unmemorable production not at all typical of the style or quality of his work.

Ever since he began directing, Hitchcock had been aware of the technical superiority of American films over the standards prevailing in the British industry during the 20s and early 30s. Thus, in 1939, Hitchcock was eagerly looking forward to working with the technical facilities of a Hollywood studio, although by making the move he was clearly risking a career that had just reached a peak of reputation and prestige.

Hitchcock's first American movie, *Rebecca* (1940), was not typical of his previous work. It was an adaptation of a Daphne du Maurier romantic novel that he successfully turned into a suspenseful psychological drama. Stylistically, too, the continuity relied more on camera movement than on the more familiar Hitchcockian cutting techniques. *Rebecca* won the best picture Academy Award for 1940. Hitchcock was nominated for an Oscar as best director.

Following two entertaining but minor productions, *Foreign Correspondent* (1940), an espionage adventure, and *Mr. and Mrs. Smith* (1941), a diverting romantic comedy starring Carole Lombard, Hitchcock came back with another well-acted glossy suspense drama, *Suspicion* (1941). Joan Fontaine won an Oscar for her portrayal of a woman who suspects that her husband is scheming to murder her. The husband was played by Cary Grant, his first of several solid appearances in Hitchcock films.

Saboteur (1942) was a virtuoso exercise in the techniques and gimmickry of the thriller genre, a chock-full-of-fun compilation of Hitchcock's bag of old tricks. *Shadow of a Doubt* (1943) was Hitchcock's first serious attempt at creating suspenseful drama through subtle characterization, understated plot, and the careful authentic re-creation of the flavor of a small American town. In *Lifeboat* (1944) he demonstrated his technical mastery by confining the entire action to the space of a tiny vessel, and he continued to flaunt his virtuosity with film technique with such films as *Spellbound* (1945), a thriller with a psychiatric background and a memorable Salvador Dali dream sequence; the lavish romantic thriller *Notorious* (1946); and with *Rope* (1948), an experiment in continuous shooting in which unusually long takes were interrupted only when the camera had to be reloaded. *The Paradine Case* (1948) was a lavish but talky and empty court drama, totally unrecognizable as a Hitchcock production, and *Stage Fright* (1950), which he made in England, was one of Hitchcock's less convincing and least successful thrillers.

After a decade marked by hits and misses, the 50s signaled a return to greatness for Hitchcock. *Strangers on a Train* (1951), a superb achievement in suspense buildup and audience manipulation, was but the first of several films many consider the director's richest and most rewarding. Hitchcock's art reached its full maturity with such superior thrillers as *Rear Window* (1954), *Vertigo* (1958), *North by Northwest* (1959), and *Psycho* (1960). These films culminated one of the most illustrious directorial careers in the history of the cinema.

Although he chose to limit his thematic range to the genre of suspenseful melodrama and has disappointed some high-minded critics with his lack of seriousness or interest in important social issues, Hitchcock is without question among the few most gifted directors who ever worked in the film medium. A supreme technician and stylist with an unmistakable personal imprint and a great visual artist, he is impossible to dismiss as just the "Master of Suspense," as he has been frequently described.

Among all film directors, Hitchcock is probably the best known to the general public not only by name but also by appearance and area of specialty. This is not only because of the great popular appeal of his films, or his brief cameo appearances, but also because of the two anthology mystery series he produced and hosted for TV, 'Alfred Hitchcock Presents' (1955–62) and 'The Alfred Hitchcock Hour' (1962–1965). Several book anthologies and a mystery magazine have also used Hitchcock's name as part of their title. The man and his work have been the subject of numerous articles and several books, including three by noted directors François Truffaut, Peter Bogdanovich, and a collaborative volume by Claude Chabrol and Eric Rohmer. Hitchcock was the recipient of the American Film Institute's Life Achievement Award in 1979.

Hitchcock was a meticulous director who planned each shot in his films with great care and rarely deviated from his script and storyboard sketches once the cameras began to roll. He regarded acting as just another element of his *mise-en-scène* and alienated many actors with fragile egos by treating them with the same close attention but aloof detachment as he did the inanimate objects on a set. His ability to manipulate the minds and emotions of audiences is legendary, but audiences didn't seem to mind at all. They continued to flock to every Hitchcock film, expecting and getting exhilarating entertainment from the grandest wizard of cinema magic the screen has ever known.

FILMS: As art director and assistant director—*Woman to Woman* (also co-sc.), *The White Shadow* (also co-sc., edit.) 1923; *The Passionate Adventure* (also co-sc.) 1924; *The Blackguard* (also sc.), *The Prude's Fall* (also sc.) 1925. As director: in the UK—*Number Thirteen* (unfinished two-reeler), *Always Tell Your Wife* (completed in collaboration with Seymour Hicks) 1922; *The Pleasure Garden* (UK/Ger.) 1925; *The Mountain Eagle/Fear o' God* (UK/Ger.), *The Lodger/The Case of Jonathan Drew* (also co-sc.) 1926; *Downhill/When Boys Leave Home, Easy Virtue, The Ring* (also co-sc.) 1927; *The Farmer's Wife* (also sc.), *Champagne* 1928; *Harmony Heaven* (co-dir. with Eddie Pola and Edward Brandt), *The Manxman, Blackmail* (also co-sc.) 1929; *Elstree Calling* (co-dir. with Andre Charlot, Jack Hulbert, and Paul Murray under supervision of Adrian Brunel), *Juno and the Paycock* (also co-sc.),

Murder (also co-adapt.; and German-language version, *Mary/Sir John greift ein!*) 1930; *The Skin Game* (also co-sc.) 1931; *Rich and Strange/East of Shanghai* (also adapt.), *Number Seventeen* (also co-sc.) 1932; *Waltzes from Vienna/Strauss's Great Waltz* 1933; *The Man Who Knew Too Much* 1934; *The 39 Steps* 1935; *The Secret Agent* 1936; *Sabotage/The Woman Alone, Young and Innocent/The Girl Was Young* 1937; *The Lady Vanishes* 1938; *Jamaica Inn* 1939. In the US—*Rebecca, Foreign Correspondent* 1940; *Mr. and Mrs. Smith, Suspicion* 1941; *Saboteur* (also story) 1942; *Shadow of a Doubt* 1943; *Lifeboat, Bon Voyage* (four-reel doc. for British Ministry of Information), *Adventure Malagache* (doc. short for British M.O.I.; never released) 1944; *Spellbound* 1945; *Notorious* (also prod., story) 1946; *The Paradine Case, Rope* (also co-prod.) 1948; *Under Capricorn* (also co-prod.; UK) 1949; *Stage Fright* (also prod.) 1950; *Strangers on a Train* (also prod.) 1951; *I Confess* (also prod.) 1953; *Dial M for Murder* (also prod.), *Rear Window* (also prod.) 1954; *To Catch a Thief* (also prod.), *The Trouble with Harry* (also prod.) 1955; *The Man Who Knew Too Much* (also prod.; remake of 1934 film) 1956; *The Wrong Man* (also prod.) 1957; *Vertigo* (also prod.) 1958; *North by Northwest* (also prod.) 1959; *Psycho* (also prod.) 1960; *The Birds* (also prod.) 1963; *Marnie* (also prod.) 1964; *Torn Curtain* (also prod.) 1966; *Topaz* (also prod.) 1969; *Frenzy* (also prod.; UK) 1972; *Family Plot* (also prod.) 1976.

Hobart, Rose. Actress. Born Rose Kefer, on May 1, 1906, in New York City. On the stage from age 15, she was brought to Hollywood in 1930 to play the feminine lead in *Liliom.* Played leads in several other films of the early 30s before returning to the stage, then reappeared on the screen mainly in second leads, typically as "the other woman."

FILMS INCLUDE: *Liliom, A Lady Surrenders* 1930; *Chances, East of Borneo, Compromised* 1931; *Dr. Jekyll and Mr. Hyde, Scandal for Sale* 1932; *The Shadow Laughs* 1933; *Convention Woman* 1935; *Tower of London* 1939; *Susan and God* 1940; *Ziegfeld Girl, Lady Be Good, Nothing but the Truth* 1941; *Mr. and Mrs. North, Prison Girls, Dr. Gillespie's New Assistant* 1942; *The Mad Ghoul, Salute to the Marines* 1943; *The Soul of a Monster* 1944; *The Brighton Strangler, Conflict* 1945; *The Cat Creeps, Canyon Passage, Claudia and David* 1946; *The Farmer's Daughter, The Trouble with Women, Cass Timberlane* 1947; *Mickey* 1948; *Bride of Vengeance* 1949.

Hobbes, Halliwell. Actor. *b.* Herbert Halliwell Hobbes Nov. 16, 1877, Stratford-on-Avon, England. *d.* 1962. On British stage from 1898, he came to the US in 1923. After appearing on Broadway, he became a permanent fixture in Hollywood films, playing English types, from aristocrats to butlers, in more than 100 movies.

FILMS INCLUDE: *Jealousy* 1929; *Grumpy, Scotland Yard, Charley's Aunt* 1930; *The Sin of Madelon Claudet* 1931; *Dr. Jekyll and Mr. Hyde* 1932; *A Study in Scarlet, The Masquerader* 1933; *Riptide, Bulldog Drummond Strikes Back, Madame Du Barry* 1934; *Cardinal Richelieu* 1935; *The Story of Louis Pasteur, Dracula's Daughter* 1936; *Maid of Salem, The Prince and the Pauper* 1937; *Kidnapped, You Can't Take It with You* 1938; *Nurse Edith Cavell, Remember?* 1939; *The Sea Hawk* 1940; *That Hamilton Woman, Here Comes Mr. Jordan* 1941; *To Be or Not to Be, Journey for Margaret* 1942; *Forever and a Day* 1943; *The Invisible Man's Revenge, Gaslight, Mr. Skeffington* 1944; *If Winter Comes* 1947; *That Forsyte Woman* 1949; *Miracle in the Rain* 1956.

Hobson, Valerie. Actress. Born on Apr. 14, 1917, in Larne, Northern Ireland. *ed.* RADA. The daughter of a British army officer, she entered films at 16, shortly after making her debut on the London stage. She was invited to Hollywood in 1934 but returned disappointed to England two years later after playing leads in a number of horror and thriller films. She then developed into one of the prime leading ladies of the British screen, gentle, graceful, and elegant, the personification of the well-bred upper-crust English lady. In 1939 she married Anthony Havelock-Allan, the producer of several of her films. They divorced in 1952, and she retired from the screen in 1954 following her marriage to politician John Profumo. She stood faithfully by her husband during the famous Christine Keeler sex scandal, which toppled the British cabinet in 1963 and in which Profumo was a central figure.

FILMS: *Eyes of Fate* 1933; *Path of Glory, Two Hearts in Waltz Time, Badger's Green, Strange Wives* (US), *The Man Who Reclaimed His Head* (US) 1934; *Oh What a Night!, The Mystery of Edwin Drood* (US), *The Werewolf of London* (US), *The Bride of Frankenstein* (US), *Chinatown Squad* (US), *Rendezvous at Midnight* (US), *The Great Impersonation* (US) 1935; *Tugboat Princess* (US), *The Secret of Stamboul, No Escape* 1936; *Jump for Glory/When Thief Meets Thief* 1937; *The Drum/Drums, This Man Is News* 1938; *Q Planes/Clouds Over Europe, The Spy in Black/U-Boat 29, The Silent Battle/Continental Express, This Man in Paris* 1939; *Contraband/Blackout* 1940; *Atlantic Ferry* 1941; *Unpublished Story* 1942; *The Adventures of Tartu* 1943; *The Years Between, Great Expectations* (as Estella) 1946; *Blanche Fury* 1947; *The Small Voice/Hideout* 1948; *Kind Hearts and Coronets, The Rocking Horse Winner, The Interrupted Journey, Train of Events* 1949; *The Card/The Promoter* 1951; *Who Goes There?/The Passionate Sentry, Meet Me Tonight/Tonight at 8:30, The Voice of Merrill/Murder Will Out* 1952; *Background/Edge of Divorce* 1953; *Knave of Hearts/Monsieur Ripois/Lovers Happy Lovers* 1954.

Hoch, Winton C. Director of photography. *b.* 1907, Iowa. *d.* 1979. *ed.* California Inst. of Technology. A research physicist, he spent 20 years with the Technicolor corporation as a color specialist and helped develop the company's three-color system. While still on the payroll of Technicolor as a consultant, he began freelancing as a cinematographer in the early 40s, but his early career was interrupted by WW II service with the Navy's Photographic Science Lab. He later worked on several visually exquisite John Ford films, won an Academy Award for the cinematography of *She Wore a Yellow Ribbon* (1950), and shared two other Oscar honors, for *Joan of Arc* (1948) and *The Quiet Man* (1952). He was responsible for the quality of color photography of several successful TV series in addition to many films.

FILMS INCLUDE: *Dr. Cyclops* (co-phot.) 1940; *Dive Bomber* (co-phot.) 1941; *Captains of the Clouds* (co-phot.) 1942; *Joan of Arc* (co-phot.), *Three Godfathers, Tap Roots* (co-phot.) 1948; *She Wore a Yellow Ribbon, Tulsa* 1949; *Bird of Paradise, The Sundowners* 1950; *Halls of Montezuma* (co-phot.) 1951; *The Quiet Man* (co-phot.) 1952; *Mister Roberts* 1955; *The Searchers* 1956; *Jet Pilot* 1957; *Darb O'Gill and the Little People, This Earth Is Mine, The Big Circus* 1959; *The Lost World* 1960; *Voyage to the Bottom of the Sea* 1961; *Sergeants 3, Five Weeks in a Balloon* 1962; *Robinson Crusoe on Mars* 1964; *The Green Berets* 1968; *Necromancy* 1972.

Hodges, Mike. Director. Born in 1932, in England. A veteran director-producer-writer for British TV, he turned to features in the early 70s, demonstrating a taste for action and a dash of technical flash. His output has been meager.

FILMS: *Get Carter* (also sc.) 1971; *Pulp* (also sc.) 1972; *The Terminal Man* (also prod., sc.; US) 1974; *Damien—Omen II* (co-sc. only) 1979; *Flash Gordon* 1980; *Morons from Outer Space* 1985; *A Prayer for the Dying* 1987; *Black Rainbow* (also sc.) 1990.

Hodiak, John. Actor. *b.* Apr. 16, 1914, Pittsburgh, of Ukrainian-Polish descent. *d.* 1955. *ed.* Northwestern. A former Chevrolet stock clerk, he began his acting career in radio and entered films during WW II, when Hollywood leading men were in short supply (he was excused from service because of hypertension). Square-jawed and sad-eyed, he became a mildly popular Hollywood personality thanks to such vehicles as *Lifeboat, Sunday Dinner for a Soldier, A Bell for Adano,* and *The Harvey Girls.* But he never became a leading star and after the war ended was reduced to secondary roles or leads in minor films, playing both sensitive protagonists and callous heels. He received good notices for his role as Lt. Maryk in the Broadway production of 'The Caine Mutiny Court-Martial' in 1953. He was married to Anne BAXTER from 1946 to 1953. He died of a heart attack at 41.

FILMS: *A Stranger in Town, Swing Shift Maisie, I Dood It* 1943; *Lifeboat, Song of Russia, Maisie Goes to Reno, Marriage Is a Private Affair, Sunday Dinner for a Soldier* 1944; *A Bell for Adano* 1945; *The Harvey Girls, Somewhere in the Night, Two Smart People* 1946; *The Arnelo Affair, Desert Fury, Love from a Stranger* 1947; *Homecoming* 1948; *Command Decision, The Bribe, Battleground* 1949; *Ambush, Malaya, Lady Without a Passport, The Miniver Story* 1950; *Night Into Morning, The People Against O'Hara, Across the Wide Missouri* 1951; *The Sellout, Battle Zone* 1952; *Mission Over Korea, Conquest of Cochise, Ambush at Tomahawk Gap* 1953; *Dragonfly Squadron* 1954; *Trial* 1955; *On the Threshold of Space* 1956.

Hodkinson, W. W. Motion picture pioneer. *b.* 1881, Pueblo, Colo. *d.* 1971. A former railroad telegrapher and correspondence-school salesman, he entered the film business by opening one of the nation's first movie theaters, in Ogden, Utah, in 1907. Later the same year he opened a film exchange in that town and convinced other exhibitors in the region to switch from shabby nickelodeons to clean motion picture theaters and to charge customers more for a better product. Soon a leading West Coast distributor, he came to New York in 1914 to negotiate film deals and remained to rise to a position of leadership among East Coast distributors. That same year he founded the PARAMOUNT company as a distributing arm for the films of Adolph ZUKOR's FAMOUS PLAYERS company. He hit upon the name Paramount when he passed by a building complex by the same name on his way to a meeting establishing the company. During that meeting he drew on a blotter the snow-capped peak that was to become the Paramount trademark. After Paramount merged with Famous Players-Lasky and other companies to form the Paramount Picture Corporation, Hodkinson organized a national distribution network for independent productions and sponsored the films of James CRUZE, among others. In 1929 he left the motion picture business and became an aircraft manufacturer. In 1936 he started an airline in Central America.

Hoey, Dennis. Actor. *b.* Samuel David Hyams, Mar. 30, 1893, London. *d.* 1960. On the stage from 1918, he played character parts in British films from 1927 and in Hollywood from the late 30s. He portrayed Inspector Lestrade in several Sherlock Holmes films of the 40s.

FILMS INCLUDE: In the UK—*Tiptoes* 1927; *Tell England/The Battle of Galipoli, Baroud/Love in Morocco* (Fr.), *Love Lies* 1931; *The Good Companions, The Wandering Jew* 1933; *Lily of Killarney/The Bride of the Lake, Chu Chin Chow* 1934; *Brewster's Millions, Maria Marten/Murder in the Old Red Barn* 1935; *Uncivilized* (Austral.) 1936. In the US—*How Green Was My Valley* 1941; *Son of Fury, This Above All, Cairo* 1942; *Sherlock Holmes and the Secret Weapon* (as Inspector Lestrade), *Frankenstein Meets the Wolf Man, Sherlock Holmes Faces Death* (as Lestrade) 1943; *Spider Woman* (as Lestrade), *Uncertain Glory, Pearl of Death* (as Lestrade), *National Velvet* 1944; *The House of Fear* (as Lestrade), *A Thousand and One Nights* 1945; *Terror by Night* (as Lestrade), *Kitty, Anna and the King of Siam* 1946; *The Strange Woman* (lead), *The Foxes of Harrow, Golden Earrings* 1947; *If Winter Comes, Joan of Arc* 1948; *The Kid from Texas* 1950; *David and Bathsheba* 1951; *Caribbean* 1952.

Hoffenstein, Samuel. Screenwriter. *b.* 1889, Russia. *d.* 1947. Drama critic for the New York *Evening Sun,* essayist and poet, he collaborated on a number of distinguished Hollywood screenplays in the 30s and 40s.

FILMS INCLUDE: *An American Tragedy* 1931; *Dr. Jekyll and Mr. Hyde, Love Me Tonight* 1932; *Song of Songs* 1933; *The Gay Divorcee* (music adapt. only), *Marie Galante* 1934; *Desire, Piccadilly Jim* 1936; *Conquest* 1937; *The Great Waltz* 1938; *Lydia* 1941; *Tales of Manhattan, The Loves of Edgar Allan Poe* 1942; *The Phantom of the Opera, Flesh and Fantasy, His Butler's Sister* 1943; *Laura* 1944; *Cluny Brown, Sentimental Journey* 1946; *Carnival in Costa Rica* 1947; *Give My Regards to Broadway* 1948.

Hoffman, Charles. Screenwriter. *b.* Sept. 28, 1911, San Francisco. *d.* 1972. *ed.* Stanford; Columbia. A freelance fiction writer, he began selling short stories and novels to Hollywood in the late 30s. Films based on his works include *The Affairs of Annabel* (1938), *It Could Happen to You* (1939), *Somewhere I'll Find You* (1942), and *Her Kind of Man* (1946). In the mid-40s he became a contract screenwriter for Warner Bros. and subsequently wrote many screenplays, alone or in collaboration, for that and other studios, occasionally doubling as a producer. In the late 50s he turned to TV as a producer-writer for 'Hawaiian Eye' and other series and ended his career as a story editor on such TV series as 'Batman' and 'The Brady Bunch.'

FILMS INCLUDE: *Janie* 1944; *Pillow to Post* 1945; *Cinderella Jones, One More Tomorrow, Night and Day, Two Guys from Milwaukee* 1946; *That Way with Women, The Unsuspected* (both prod. only), *The Voice of the Turtle* (prod., addnl. dial. only), *That Hagen Girl* 1947; *A Woman of Distinction, The West Point Story* 1950; *The Blue Gardenia* 1953; *So This Is Paris, The Spoilers* 1955; *The Second Greatest Sex, Never Say Goodbye* 1956.

Hoffman, Dustin. Actor. Born on Aug. 8, 1937, in Los Angeles. Antiheroic, unlikely superstar of Hollywood films. The son of a furniture designer, he dropped out of Santa Monica City College, where he studied music, intending to become a concert pianist, to attend the Pasadena Playhouse and began acting at 19. He went to New York, hoping for a career on the stage, but for several years struggled along as a janitor and an attendant in a hospital mental ward and in other menial jobs. On many nights his bed was Gene Hackman's kitchen floor. Eventually, he began getting occasional small roles on TV and in summer stock, but it wasn't until 1965 that he was able to crash even off Broadway. He received his first big break the following year when he won the Obie Award as best off-Broadway actor of the year for his performance in 'The Journey of the Fifth Horse.' He received much critical praise later in 1966 for his performance in a British farce, 'Eh?' Director Mike NICHOLS, who saw the play, insisted the then little-known Hoffman play the lead role in his upcoming film *The Graduate* (1967).

The great commercial success of *The Graduate* catapulted Hoffman into instant stardom. It wasn't Hoffman's first movie. Some months earlier he had appeared in a low-budget Spanish-Italian co-production, *Madigan's Millions,* but that film wasn't released in Europe or the US until after *The Graduate.* He had also played a minor role in *The Tiger Makes Out.* After appearing on Broadway in 'Jimmy Shine,' Hoffman returned to the screen in John Schlesinger's *Midnight Cowboy* (1969), giving a memorable performance as the pathetic Ratso Rizzo. He has since demonstrated a remarkable range of screen characterizations, drawing accolades for his effective performances in widely diverse roles. He played an Indian-adopted white man who ages on screen from adolescence to 121 in *Little Big Man* (1970), portrayed a doomed ugly little Frenchman on Devil's Island in *Papillon* (1973), impersonated tragic comedian Lenny Bruce in *Lenny* (1974), and was Washington *Post* reporter Carl Bernstein in *All the President's Men* (1976). He was nominated for Academy Awards for his performances in *The Graduate, Midnight Cowboy,* and *Lenny.* He won his first Oscar for his role as a beleaguered, custody-battling father in *Kramer vs. Kramer* (1979) and a second for a stunning performance as an autistic brother to Tom CRUISE in *Rain Man* (1988). In between, he received another nomination for the hilarious performance in drag in *Tootsie* (1982). Hoffman returned triumphantly to the stage in 1984, winning a Drama Desk Award for his portrayal of Willy Loman in a Broadway revival of Arthur Miller's 'Death of a Salesman.' He won an Emmy for the TV replication of the play, which was screened in movie theaters abroad. He later played Shylock in the 1989 London and 1990 Broadway productions of Shakespeare's 'The Merchant of Venice.'

FILMS: *The Tiger Makes Out, The Graduate* 1967; *El Millon de Madigan/Un Dollaro per 7 Vigliacchi/Madigan's Millions* 1968; *Midnight Cowboy, John and Mary* 1969; *Little Big Man* 1970; *Who Is Harry Kellerman and Why Is He Saying Those Terrible Things About Me?, Straw Dogs* (UK) 1971; *Alfredo Alfredo* (It.) 1972; *Papillon* 1973; *Lenny* (as Lenny Bruce) 1974; *All the President's Men* (as reporter Carl Bernstein), *Marathon Man* 1976; *Straight Time* 1978; *Agatha, Kramer vs. Kramer* 1979; *Tootsie* 1982; *Death of a Salesman* (TV movie in US; theatrically released abroad) 1985; *Ishtar* 1987; *Rain Man* 1988; *Family Business* 1989; *Dick Tracy* (as Mumbles) 1990; *Billy Bathgate, Hook* 1991; *Hero* 1992; *Outbreak* 1995; *American Buffalo, Sleepers* 1996; *Mad City* 1997.

Hoffman, Gaby. Actress. Born January 8, 1961, in New York City. The daughter of Andy Warhol contemporary Viva, this striking young actress was making films by the age of eight while, at the same time, appearing on television, notably on NBC's 'Someone Like Me.' She is now an established actress featured in many of Hollywood's major motion pictures.

FILMS: *Field of Dreams, Uncle Buck* 1989; *This Is My Life, The Man Without a Face, Sleepless in Seattle* 1993; *Now and Then* 1995; *Everyone Says I Love You* 1996; *Volcano* 1997.

Hoffman, Jerzy. Director. Born in 1932, in Poland. A graduate of Moscow's State Film Institute, he began a long-term collaboration with Edward Skorzewski in the mid-50s on many prize-winning Polish documentaries and feature films, some made in Cuba. He has worked alone since 1966.

FILMS INCLUDE: Documentaries—*Are You Among Them?* 1954; *Attention Hooligans* 1955; *A Souvenir from Calvary* 1958; *The Rail* 1959; *Two Faces of God* 1960; *They Met in Havana, Patria o Muerte* 1961; *Visit Zakopane* 1963; *Market of Miracles* 1966. Feature films—*Gangsters and Philanthropists* 1962; *The Law and the Fist* 1964; *Three Steps on Earth* 1965; *Colonel Wolodyjowski* 1969; *The Deluge* 1974; *Leper* 1976.

Hoffmann, Carl. Director of photography. *b.* 1881, Neisse an der Wobert, Silesia, Germany (now Nysa, Poland). *d.* 1947. One of the most important cameramen of the silent era, he photographed several of Germany's most distinguished expressionist films in the 20s, notably for Fritz LANG, as well as many of the country's commercially successful light films of the 30s. He worked on more than 200 productions between 1908 and 1912. His son, Kurt Hoffmann (*b.* Nov. 12, 1910, Freiburg, Germany), has been a successful director and producer since 1939; his credits include *The Confessions of Felix Krull* (1957).

FILMS INCLUDE: *Piesco* 1913; *Homunculus* (serial) 1916; *Die Hochzeit in Ekzentrik Klub* 1917; *Halbblut, Harakiri* 1919; *Der Januskopf* (co-phot.) 1920; *Uriel Acosta* 1921; *Lady Hamilton, Dr. Mabuse der Spieler* 1922; *Die Nibelungen* (co-phot.), *Die Andere* 1924; *Faust* (co-phot.) 1926; *Der geheimnisvolle Spiegel* (also co-dir.) 1927; *Looping the Loop* 1928; *Die Wunderbare Lüge der Nina Petrowna/The Wonderful Lies of Nina Petrovna, Ungarische Rhapsodie/Hungarian Rhapsody* 1929; *Hokuspokus/Hocuspocus* 1930; *Der Kongress tanzt/The Congress Dances* 1931; *Der Tunnel, Walzerkrieg/Waltz War* 1933; *Die lustigen Weiber, Viktoria* (both dir. only), *Peer Gynt* 1934; *Ab Mitternacht* (dir. only) 1938; *Symphonie eines Lebens* (co-phot.) 1942; *Via Mala* 1945.

Hogan, James P. Director. *b.* 1891, Lowell, Mass. *d.* 1943. Entering films in 1916, he worked as an assistant director and set designer on several Douglas Fairbanks and Allan Dwan productions before becoming a director in 1920. He turned out many silents and talkies, often melodramas with emphasis on action, only a few of which are better than routine. He gave up directing after the advent of sound but after a period of retraining returned to the helm in 1936. He worked mainly for tight-budget studios, but in the late 30s and early 40s his films enjoyed the superior production values of Paramount.

FILMS: *The Swayman, The Little Grey Mouse* (also sc.) 1920; *Bare Knuckles* (also sc.) 1921; *Where Is My Wandering Boy Tonight?* (co-dir. with Millard Webb) 1922; *Unmarried Wives* (also prod.), *Black Lightning* 1924; *Women and Gold* (also story), *Capital Punishment, The Mansion of Aching Hearts, Jimmie's Millions, My Lady's Lips, S.O.S. Perils of the Sea, The Bandit's Baby, Steel Preferred* 1925; *The King of the Turf, The Isle of Retribution, Flaming Fury* 1926; *The Final Extra, The Silent Avenger, Mountains of Manhattan, Finnegan's Ball* 1927; *Top Sergeant Mulligan, The Broken Mask, Hearts of Men, Burning Bridges, Code of the Air, The Border Patrol* 1928; *The Sheriff's Secret* (also story, sc.) 1931; *Desert Gold, The Arizona Raiders, The Accusing Finger* 1936; *Arizona Mahoney, Bulldog Drummond Escapes, The Last Train from Madrid, Ebb Tide* 1937; *Scandal Street, Bulldog Drummond's Peril, The Texans, Sons of the Legion* 1938; *Arrest Bulldog Drummond, Bulldog Drummond's Secret Police, Grand Jury Secrets, Bulldog Drummond's Bride, $1,000 a Touchdown* 1939; *The Farmer's Daughter, Queen of the Mob, Texas Rangers Ride Again* 1940; *Ellery Queen's Penthouse Mystery, Power Dive, Ellery Queen and the Perfect Crime, Ellery Queen and the Murder Ring* 1941; *Enemy Agents Meet Ellery Queen* 1942; *No Place for a Lady, The Strange Death of Adolf Hitler, The Mad Ghoul* 1943.

Hogan, Paul. Actor. Born on Oct. 8, 1941, in Lightning Ridge, New South Wales, Australia. Nonchalant, wiry, blond, leather-faced star of Australian TV and films. Raised in a blue-collar suburb of Sydney, he dropped out of school at 15 and earned a living in a variety of menial occupations, including chauffeur, boxer, and bridge rigger. On a dare by co-workers on the Sydney Harbour Bridge, he appeared on 'New Faces,' a TV talent show designed to stump and embarrass its guests. He turned the tables around on the panel of judges with his off-the-cuff humor and suddenly became the talk of the town. He began appearing regularly on television and before long became the star of his own comedy program, 'The Paul Hogan Show.' The ratings were phenomenal. The show ran for nine years and was syndicated in 30 countries. A popular national hero, he began appearing in TV commercials encouraging tourism to Australia.

On a trip to the US, Hogan conceived the idea for the feature film that would make him an international star and earn a fortune for himself and his partner, producer John Cornell. Depicting the adventures of a rugged, bush-country Aussie in the urban jungle of New York, *Crocodile Dundee* (1986) became a sensational box-office hit and promptly spawned a sequel. Having divorced the mother of his three sons, Hogan married his co-star, Linda Kozlowski.

FILMS: *Crocodile Dundee* (also story, co-sc.) 1986; *Crocodile Dundee II* (also exec. prod., co-sc.) 1988; *Almost an Angel* (US) 1990; *Lightning Jack* 1994; *Flipper* 1996.

Holbrook, Hal. Actor. Born Harold Rowe Holbrook, Jr., on Feb. 17, 1925, in Cleveland. Abandoned by his parents at the age of two, he was raised by relatives. He came to New York in the late 50s via San Francisco's Purple Onion club, and after performing at a Greenwich Village nightclub and appearing in a daytime TV soap opera he became an overnight hit off Broadway with his one-man show 'Mark Twain Tonight!' Over the years, he has portrayed the humorist on the stage some 2,000 times, to much acclaim both in the US and abroad. He has also performed with distinction in many Broadway and Lincoln Center Repertory productions and on TV. He starred in the series 'The Senator' (1970–71), for which he won the first of several Emmys, and impersonated Abraham Lincoln in the miniseries, 'Sandburg's Lincoln' (1976) and 'North and South' (1985). His film appearances, mostly in character roles, have been sporadic. Twice divorced, he married actress Dixie Carter in 1984.

FILMS: *The Group* 1966; *Wild in the Streets* 1968; *The People Next Door, The Great White Hope* 1970; *They Only Kill Their Masters* 1972; *Jonathan Livingston Seagull* (v/o), *Magnum Force* 1973; *The Girl from Petrovka* 1974; *All the President's Men* (as "Deep Throat"), *Midway* 1976; *Julia* 1977; *Rituals/The Creeper* (Can.), *Capricorn One* 1978; *Natural Enemies* 1979; *The Fog, The Kidnapping of the President* 1980; *Creepshow* 1982; *The Star Chamber* 1983; *Girls Nite Out* 1984; *Wall Street* 1987; *The Unholy* 1988; *Fletch Lives* 1989; *The Firm* 1993; *Eye of God, Hercules* (v.o) 1997.

hold. In animation, the equivalent of FREEZE FRAME in live-action film. One drawing is photographed over several frames so that it appears as a still on the screen.

Holden, Fay. Actress. *b.* Dorothy Fay Hammerton, Sept. 26, 1895, Birmingham, England. *d.* 1973. On the British stage from age nine, initially as a dancer, she was 40 years old by the time she made her screen debut in Hollywood in the mid-30s. At the outset of her film career, she used her stage name, Gaby Fay, but soon changed it to Fay Holden. She played supporting roles in many films, often as a warm, devoted mother. Best remembered as Mickey Rooney's model mother in the popular "Andy Hardy" series. She was married to David Clyde, the actor brother of screen comedian Andy Clyde.

FILMS INCLUDE: *I Married a Doctor, Wives Never Know, Polo Joe* 1936; *Bulldog Drummond Escapes, Exclusive, Double or Nothing* 1937; *You're Only Young Once, Love Is a Headache, Judge Hardy's Children, Hold That Kiss, Sweethearts* 1938; *Sergeant Madden, Andy Hardy Gets Spring Fever* 1939; *Bitter Sweet* 1940; *Ziegfeld Girl, Washington Melodrama, I'll Wait for You, Blossoms in the Dust, H. M. Pulham Esq.* 1941; *The Courtship of Andy Hardy* 1942; *Andy Hardy's Blonde Trouble* 1944; *Canyon Passage* 1946; *Whispering Smith, Samson and Delilah* 1949; *The Big Hangover* 1950; *Andy Hardy Comes Home* 1958.

Holden, Gloria. Actress. Born on Sept. 5, 1908, in London. A former model and stage actress, she played leads and supporting roles in Hollywood films from the late 30s through the late 50s, often as a femme fatale type. Best remembered for the title role in *Dracula's Daughter* (1936).

FILMS INCLUDE: *Wife vs. Secretary, Dracula's Daughter* (title role) 1936; *The Life of Emile Zola* 1937; *Test Pilot, Hawaii Calls* 1938; *Dodge City, Miracles for Sale* 1939; *A Child Is Born* 1940; *This Thing Called Love, The Corsican Brothers* 1941; *A Gentleman After Dark, Miss Annie Rooney* 1942; *Behind the Rising Sun* 1943; *Strange Holiday, Adventures of Rusty* 1945; *Hit the Hay* 1946; *The Hucksters* 1947; *Killer McCoy* 1948; *A Kiss for Corliss* 1949; *Dream Wife* 1953; *The Eddie Duchin Story* 1956; *This Happy Feeling* 1958.

Holden, William. Actor. *b.* William Franklin Beedle, Jr., Apr. 17, 1918, O'Fallon, Ill. *d.* 1981. The product of a wealthy family in the chemical business, he began acting as a student at the Pasadena Junior College in California and was spotted by a Paramount talent scout and signed to a film contract. After appearing as an extra in *Prison Farm* (1938) and playing a one-line bit in *Million Dollar Legs* (1939) he became a star with his very first real screen role, as the boxer-violinist hero of *Golden Boy*. Clean-cut and pleasantly handsome, he was subsequently typecast in innocuous nice-boy-next-door roles, the epitome of young American manhood. His screen image ripened somewhat after his return from WW II service as an Army lieutenant, and in 1949 he was cast against type as a psychotic killer in *The Dark Past*. He followed this with creditable performances in two choice roles, playing the writer-gigolo in Billy Wilder's drama *Sunset Boulevard* and Judy Holliday's tutor in George Cukor's comedy *Born Yesterday* (both 1950). But the real turning point in his career was the role of the tough maverick hero of Wilder's *Stalag 17* (1953), a role for which he won a best actor Academy Award. Throughout the 50s he remained one of Hollywood's most dependable and sexually charged stars of box-office attractions, most notably *Picnic*. In the 50s he also began traveling extensively for filming and multimillion dollar business ventures. After a long sojourn in the Far East, he became a resident of Geneva, Switzerland, but spent much of his time in Africa, where he was the co-owner of the 1,260-acre Mount Kenya Safari Club. He was once (1941–70) married to actress Brenda MARSHALL. Their son, Scott Holden, began appearing in films in the early 70s. Another actor named William Holden (1872–1932) played character roles in late silent and early sound Hollywood films.

FILMS: *Prison Farm* (extra) 1938; *Million Dollar Legs* (bit), *Golden Boy* (as Joe Bonaparte) 1939; *Invisible Stripes, Our Town* (as George Gibbs), *Those Were the Days, Arizona* 1940; *I Wanted Wings, Texas* 1941; *The Remarkable Andrew, The Fleet's In, Meet the Stewarts* 1942; *Young and Willing* 1943; *Blaze of Noon, Dear Ruth, Variety Girl* (cameo) 1947; *Rachel and the Stranger, Apartment for Peggy, The Man from Colorado* 1948; *The Dark Past, Streets of Laredo, Miss Grant Takes Richmond* 1949; *Dear Wife, Father Is a Bachelor, Sunset Boulevard, Union Station* 1950; *Born Yesterday, Force of Arms, Submarine Command* 1951; *Boots Malone, The Turning Point* 1952; *Stalag 17, The Moon Is Blue, Escape from Fort Bravo* 1953; *Forever Female, Executive Suite, Sabrina* 1954; *The Country Girl, The Bridges at Toko-Ri, Love Is a Many-Splendored Thing* 1955; *Picnic, The Proud and the Profane, Toward the Unknown* 1956; *The Bridge on the River Kwai* (UK) 1957; *The Key* (UK) 1958; *The Horse Soldiers* 1959; *The World of Suzie Wong* 1960; *Satan Never Sleeps, The Counterfeit Traitor, The Lion* (UK) 1962; *Paris When It Sizzles, The 7th Dawn* (US/UK) 1964; *Alvarez Kelly* 1966; *Casino Royale* (UK) 1967; *The Devil's Brigade* 1968; *The Wild Bunch, L'Arbre de Noël/The Christmas Tree* (Fr./It.) 1969; *Wild Rovers* 1971; *The Revengers* 1972; *Breezy* 1973; *Open Season, The Towering Inferno* 1974; *Network* 1976; *Damien—Omen II, Fedora* (Ger./Fr.) 1978; *Ashanti* 1979; *When Time Ran Out, The Earthling* (Austral.) 1980; *S.O.B.* 1981.

Holger-Madsen, Forest. Director. *b.* Holger Madsen, Apr. 11, 1878, Copenhagen. *d.* 1943. A stage actor from age 18, he began appearing in films in 1907 and became a screen director in 1913. The leading creative director of the Scandinavian cinema up to the end of WW I, he is credited with many innovations of style and technique. He experimented with lighting, décor, composition, and variable shooting angles, and his stylized films, often fantastic and mystical, were precursors of the later work of such German expressionist directors as LANG and MURNAU and his fellow countryman Carl DREYER. During the 20s he worked mainly in Germany. He ended his career as a part-time actor and manager of a small movie theater in Copenhagen.

FILMS INCLUDE: *Kun en Tigger* 1912; *In the Bonds of Passion, During the Plague, The White Woman?, The White Ghost, Voice of the Heart* 1913; *A Marriage of Convenience, Opium Dreams, A Deal with the Devil, Without a Country, The Candle and the Moth, Love and War, A Voice from the Past* 1914; *A Terrible Ordeal, The Dancer's Revenge, The Beggar Princess, The Crossroads of Life, The Man Without a Future, The Buried Secret* 1915; *His Father's Guilt/The Veiled Lady,, The Sins of the Children, An Impossible Marriage, The Road to Happiness, The Pastor's Daughter* 1916; *A Trip to Mars, Justice Victorious* 1917; *A Friend of the People, Toward the Light* 1918; *The Penalty of Fame, Flight from Life* 1919; *Tobias Buntschuh* (co-dir. with Joe May; also act.; Ger.) 1921; *Der Evangelimann/The Evangelist* (Ger.) 1923; *Der Mann um Mitternacht/The Midnight Man* (Ger.) 1924; *Ein Lebenkünstler* (Ger.) 1925; *Spitzen* (Ger.) 1926; *Die heilige Lüge/The Sacred Lie* (Ger.) 1927; *Die seltsame Nacht der Helga Wangen* (Ger.) 1928; *Sun Over Denmark* 1936.

Holland. See NETHERLANDS, THE.

Holland, Agnieszka. Director. Born in 1948, in Poland. Returning home after graduating from the Prague Film School in 1971, she began her career as an assistant to director Krzysztof ZANUSSI on *Illumination* (1973). She made her debut as a director in 1974 and within several years thrust herself to the forefront of the Polish New Wave. Her *Provincial Actors,* using a stage company as a microcosm of society and its ills, won the International Critics Prize at the 1980 Cannes Festival, in a tie with Alain Resnais's *Mon Oncle d'Amérique.* Stifled by the imposition of martial law in Poland late in 1981, she moved to Paris and made documentaries for French TV. Her German-made feature, *Angry Harvest,* an exploration of an odd relationship between a gentile farmer and a hunted Jewish woman he hides, was nominated for an Oscar as best foreign language film of 1985. She was less successful with her American-French co-production, *To Kill a Priest* (1988), a true story of a courageous Polish clergyman who paid with his life for his support of the Solidarity movement. The movement's victory in 1989 paved the way for Holland's return to Poland. Her *Europa, Europa* (1991) was a great success on the American art-house circuit, winning great acclaim and also inviting controversy with its subject matter: the sympathetic treatment of a young Jewish man who pretends to be an Aryan Nazi in order to survive World War II. She writes, or collaborates on, all of her own scripts. In addition, she has worked as a screenwriter on the films of other directors, especially Andrzej WAJDA.

FILMS: As director-screenwriter—*Evening at Abdon's* 1974; *Sunday Children* 1976; *Something for Something, Screen Test* (co-dir.) 1977; *Provincial Actors* 1979; *Fever* 1980; *A Woman Alone* 1982; *Bittere Ernte/Angry Harvest* (Ger.) 1984; *To Kill a Priest* 1988. As screenwriter (incomplete)—*Without Anesthesia/Rough Treatment* 1978; *Man of Iron* 1981; *Danton* (Fr./Pol.) 1983; *Ein Liebe in Deutschland/Love in Germany* (Ger.Fr.) 1984; *Anna* (US) 1987; *Korczak* 1990; *Europa, Europa* 1991; *The Secret Garden* 1993; *Total Eclipse* 1995; *Washington Square* 1997.

Holland, Tom. American screenwriter-turned-director. At his best with gripping horror. As a director, he started well with *Fright Night* (1985), a competent thriller, faltered badly with *Fatal Beauty,* a silly Whoopi Goldberg vehicle, then scored a critical and commercial hit with *Child's Play* (1988), a clever shocker about a murderous doll.

FILMS: As screenwriter—*The Beast Within* 1982; *Psycho II* 1983; *Class of '84, Cloak and Dagger, Scream for Help* 1984. As director—*Fright Night* (also sc.) 1985; *Fatal Beauty* 1987; *Child's Play* (also co-sc.) 1988; *The Temp* 1993; *Thinner* 1996.

Hollander, Frederick. Composer. *b.* Friedrich Holländer, Oct. 18, 1896, London, to German parents. *d.* 1976. Composed for Max REINHARDT and for his own theater in Berlin. Wrote scores and songs for German (including the famous 'Falling in Love Again' from *The Blue Angel*) and later many Hollywood films. He often wrote his own lyrics. Directed (and wrote the music for) the German film *Ich und die Kaiserin* (1933). Returned to Germany in 1956.

FILMS INCLUDE: In Germany—*Der blaue Engel/The Blue Angel* (Ger.), *Der Andere* 1930; *Das Lied vom Leben/Song of Life* 1931; *Ich und die Kaiserin/The Empress and I/Heart Song* (also dir.) 1931. In the US—*I Am Suzanne* 1934; *Millions in the Air* 1935; *Desire, Poppy, Anything Goes, Rhythm on the Range* 1936; *Champagne Waltz, Artists and Models, Angel, 100 Men and a Girl* 1937; *Bluebeard's Eighth Wife* 1938; *Destry Rides Again, Hotel Imperial* 1939; *Seven Sinners, Victory, The Farmer's Daughter, Typhoon* 1940; *Here Comes Mr. Jordan* 1941; *The Man Who Came to Dinner, Talk of the Town* 1942; *Princess O'Rourke* 1943; *Conflict, Once Upon a Time* 1945; *The Time the Place and the Girl, The Verdict* 1946; *Stallion Road* 1947; *Berlin Express, That Lady in Ermine, Foreign Affair* 1948; *Caught, Adventure in Baltimore* 1949; *Born Yesterday* 1951; *Androcles and the Lion, The 5,000 Fingers of Dr. T.* 1953; *It Should Happen to You, Sabrina, Phffft* 1954; *We're No Angels* 1955. In Germany—*Das Spukschloss im Spessart* 1959.

Holliday, Judy. Actress. *b.* Judith Tuvim, June 21, 1922, New York City. *d.* 1965. She began her association with the theater as a backstage switchboard operator for Orson Welles's Mercury Theater and made her debut with The Revuers, a cabaret group she formed with Betty COMDEN and Adolph GREEN. This led to minor roles in three Hollywood films in 1944 and to eventual stardom on Broadway as Billie Dawn, the shrewd dumb blonde in 'Born Yesterday' (1946). She repeated the role with hilarious success in the 1950 screen version, winning an Academy Award in the process, the year after stealing the show from Katharine Hepburn and Spencer Tracy in the role of a bird-brained attempted-murder suspect in the film *Adam's Rib* (1949). A comedienne of great intelligence who handled her art with intuitive precision and exuberant talent, she went on to display her unique comic style and voice inflection in a number of other plays and films before being stricken by cancer at 43.

FILMS: *Greenwich Village, Something for the Boys, Winged Victory* 1944; *Adam's Rib* 1949; *Born Yesterday* 1950; *The Marrying Kind* 1952; *It Should Happen to You, Phffft* 1954; *The Solid Gold Cadillac* 1956; *Full of Life* 1957; *Bells Are Ringing* 1960.

Holliman, Earl. Actor. Born on Sept. 11, 1928, in Tennesas Swamp, Delhi, La. *ed.* Louisiana State U.; UCLA. Rugged supporting player of Hollywood films from the early 50s, following a stint in the Navy. Typically in action-based, sometimes impetuous or simple-minded roles, occasionally in leads. Co-star of the 'Police Woman' (1974–78) and numerous other TV series, miniseries, and movies.

FILMS INCLUDE: *Scared Stiff, Destination Gobi* 1953; *Broken Lance* 1954; *The Bridges of Toko-Ri, The Big Combo, I Died a Thousand Times* 1955; *Forbidden Planet, Giant, The Burning Hills, The Rainmaker* 1956; *Don't Go Near the Water, Gunfight at the O.K. Corral* 1957; *Hot Spell* 1958; *Last Train from Gun Hill* 1959; *Visit to a Small Planet* 1960; *Armored Command, Summer and Smoke* 1961; *The Sons of Katie Elder* 1965; *A Covenant with Death* 1967; *Lo Sbarco di Anzio/Anzio* (It.), *The Power* 1968; *The Biscuit Eater* 1972; *Good Luck Miss Wyckoff* 1979; *Sharkey's Machine* 1982.

Holloway, Stanley. Actor, singer, *b.* Oct. 1, 1890, London. *d.* 1982. Spirited performer of British music halls and legitimate stage since 1919, he also appeared in numerous films from 1921 in fine comic characterizations. Most memorable as Alfred Doolittle in *My Fair Lady,* both on stage and screen. He was nominated for an Oscar for that role. Autobiography: *Wiv' a Little Bit of Luck* (1969).

FILMS INCLUDE: *The Rotters* 1921; *The Co-Optimists* 1930; *Lily of Killarney/The Bride of the Lake, Sing As We Go* 1934; *Squibs* 1935; *The Vicar of Bray* 1936; *Major Barbara* 1941; *Salute John Citizen* 1943; *The Way Ahead, This Happy Breed, Champagne Charlie* 1944; *The Way to the Stars/Johnny in the Clouds, Brief Encounter, Caesar and Cleopatra* 1945; *Meet Me at Dawn* 1946; *Nicholas Nickleby* (as Vincent Crummles) 1947; *The Winslow Boy, Hamlet, Another Shore* 1948; *Passport to Pimlico, The Perfect Woman* 1949; *Midnight Episode* 1950; *The Lavender Hill Mob, The Magic Box* 1951; *The Happy Family/Mr. Lord Says No!, Meet Me Tonight/Tonight at 8:30, The Titfield Thunderbolt* 1952; *The Beggar's Opera* (as Lockit), *Meet Mr. Lucifer* 1953; *An Alligator Named Daisy* 1955; *Hello London, No Tree in the Street* 1959; *No Love for Johnnie* 1961; *My Fair Lady* (as Alfred Doolittle; US) 1964; *In Harm's Way* (US) 1965; *Ten Little Indians* 1966; *Mrs. Brown You've Got a Lovely Daughter* 1968; *How to Make It* (US) 1969; *The Private Life of Sherlock Holmes* (US/UK) 1970; *Flight of the Doves* 1971; *Up the Front* 1972; *Journey Into Fear* 1975.

Holloway, Sterling. Actor. *b.* Jan. 4, 1905, in Cedartown, Ga. *d.* 1992. *ed.* AADA. Played hillbillies, country bumpkins, delivery boys, and soda jerks in some 100 films. Originally a stage comic and singer, he also provided the backscreen voice for many Walt Disney animal characters. Appeared in a number of two-reelers and a feature during the silent days but made the bulk of his films in the 30s and 40s. Also on TV: 'The Baileys of Balboa,' etc.

FILMS INCLUDE: *Casey at the Bat* 1927; *Hell Below, Elmer the Great, Gold Diggers of 1933, Dancing Lady, Advice to the Lovelorn, Alice in Wonderland* (as The Frog) 1933; *Strictly Dynamite, The Merry Widow* 1934; *Life Begins at 40, Doubting Thomas* 1935; *Maid of Salem, The Woman I Love, Varsity Show* 1937; *Of Human Hearts, Doctor Rhythm, Professor Beware, Spring Madness* 1938; *Nick Carter—Master Detective* 1939; *Remember the Night, The Blue Bird, Little Men* 1940; *Meet John Doe, Cheers for Miss Bishop* 1941; *New Wine, Iceland* 1942; *A Walk in the Sun* 1946; *Addio Mimi/Her Wonderful Lie* (It.), *Sioux City Sue* 1947; *The Beautiful Blonde from Bashful Bend* 1949; *Shake Rattle and Rock* 1956; *The Adventures of Huckleberry Finn* 1960; *It's a Mad Mad Mad Mad World* 1963; *Batman* 1966; *Live a Little Love a Little* 1968; *The Aristocats* (v/o) 1970; *Thunder and Lightning* 1977.

Hollywood. A section of Los Angeles, California, and for many years the center of the American motion picture and television industries. It was named by a Mrs. Deida Wilcox, the wife of a Kansas City real estate man, who in 1886 retired with her husband to a huge ranch that stood on the site. In 1891 they began dividing their land and in 1903 the growing community was incorporated as a village, retaining the original name of the ranch, Hollywood. In 1910, Hollywood was annexed to Los Angeles so that it could avail itself of the city's water supply and sewage system.

In the early days of American cinema, the center of film production was New York City (Westerns were shot in the wilderness of New Jersey), with some activity taking place in Chicago and other American cities. Southern California, with its eternal sunshine and variety of terrain, attracted occasional film production. In 1907, Col. William N. Selig, Edison's chief rival, moved part of his company from Chicago to Los Angeles, soon to become the first producer to make films regularly on the West Coast. In 1909 he opened California's first large motion picture studio, on Los Angeles's Mission Road. But the greatest impetus to the growth of Hollywood was provided in 1913 by a man named Cecil B. De Mille. Earlier that year he had entered a partnership with Jesse L. Lasky and glove salesman Samuel Goldfish (later Sam Goldwyn), forming the Jesse L. Lasky Feature Play Company. They purchased the rights to a Western novel, *The Squaw Man,* and De Mille and co-director Oscar C. Apfel were dispatched to Flagstaff, Ariz., to do the shooting on location.

Finding the snow-capped Arizona mountains unsuitable for their story, De Mille and Apfel got back on the train and continued to the end of the line. And that's how they stumbled upon Hollywood. They found the small town to be peaceful and pastoral, surrounded by acres of citrus and avocado groves. They converted a large stable into a studio and began their production, shooting the exteriors in the nearby countryside. Within months, other producers followed, partly because of the inviting climate but largely to escape the long reach of the Motion Picture Patents Company, the huge eastern trust that tried to force all small, independent producers out of the film business. In 1917 the Patents Company was disbanded by government antitrust action, and Hollywood was well on its way to becoming the movie capital of America and a cosmopolitan Mecca of a rapidly growing show business industry. By 1920, thanks to the phenomenal growth of several major studios and the emergence of the star system, Hollywood was turning out nearly 800 films annually, and its name became a synonym for luxury, glamour, and illusory magic.

Hollywood remained the world's greatest dream factory through the late 40s, when its supremacy began to be threatened by a growing tendency of producers and stars to seek tax shelters by filming abroad. At the same time, the emergence of television as a competitor drastically cut into cinema audiences. This and government antitrust action that forced major studios to divest themselves of their chains of motion picture theaters combined to undermine the financial basis of many large companies. By the early 60s, the era of independent production, based on individual packaging, was firmly established. More often than not, films were being shot away from Hollywood and an increasing number of resident actors and technicians found themselves out of work.

If it hadn't been for the regular production of TV films, the impact would have been even greater and perhaps would have knocked Hollywood off the motion picture production map.

Hollywood has no set physical boundaries. Many of the studios are located in other communities, some many miles away. It has always been and will continue to be a state of mind, a dream shared by millions, rather than a mere place where movies are made. And that's probably why it will never die. (See also United States.)

Hollywood Canteen. A place of hospitality for members of the armed forces during World War II, co-founded by Bette

Davis, John Garfield, Carroll Hollister, and J. K. "Spike" Wallace. In addition to meals, visiting servicemen received entertainment from most of Hollywood's top stars, with the notable exceptions of Charlie Chaplin and Greta Garbo. Founded on the model of the Stage Door Canteens that provided food and entertainment for servicemen in New York and other cities, the Hollywood Canteen opened its doors on Oct. 17, 1942 and closed on Nov. 22, 1945. The star-studded Warner Bros. musical *Hollywood Canteen* (1944) helped raise funds for the organization, which survived the war as the Hollywood Canteen Foundation and continues to perform charitable work.

Hollywood Foreign Press Association. Organization of journalists and photographers who cover Hollywood film and television for foreign publications. It was founded in 1943 as the Hollywood Foreign Correspondents Association, with William Mooring as its first president. Since 1944, it has presented annual awards that became known as the Golden Globes; the first best motion picture award went to *The Song of Bernadette* (1943). In 1950, dissension caused the organization to split in two: as the Hollywood Foreign Correspondents Association, it continued to present the Golden Globes, while the Foreign Press Association of Hollywood presented awards called Henriettas. The two groups were reunited in 1955 as the Hollywood Foreign Press Association.

Hollywood Pictures. See DISNEY COMPANY, THE WALT.

Hollywood Ten, The. A group of creative Hollywood artists who, in the fall of 1947, were subpoenaed to appear before the House Committee on Un-American Activities investigating "the extent of Communist infiltration in the Hollywood motion picture industry." The ten filmmakers—producer-director Herbert Biberman, director Edward Dmytryk, producer-writer Adrian Scott, and screenwriters Alvah Bessie, Lester Cole, Ring Lardner, Jr., John Howard Lawson, Albert Maltz, Samuel Ornitz, and Dalton Trumbo—were cited for contempt of Congress for their refusal to divulge their political affiliations past or present. In April of 1948 they were tried at the Federal Court of Washington, D.C., convicted of contempt of Congress, and given the maximum sentence of a year in jail and a fine of one thousand dollars. They were also blacklisted by the American film industry and were able to find work only by going abroad or using pseudonyms.

Director Edward Dmytryk subsequently agreed to cooperate with the committee, admitted past membership in the Communist party, was released early from jail, and resumed his career as a Hollywood director. He was the star witness in the committee's second round of investigation of the "Communist infiltration of Hollywood" in 1951. Among other celebrities who confessed to past membership in the Communist party and identified colleagues as members were Lloyd Bridges, Sterling Hayden, Elia Kazan, Marc Lawrence, Isobel Lennart, Clifford Odets, Larry Parks, Budd Schulberg, and Frank Tuttle. Committee witnesses in 1951 aired the names of more than 300 Hollywood personalities as past or present members of the Communist party. Among them were Ben Barzman, John Berry, Henry Blankfort, Sidney Buchman, Abe Burrows, Morris Carnovsky, Edward and Jerome Chodorov, Dorothy Comingore, Jeff Corey, Howard DaSilva, Jules Dassin, Cy Endfield, Carl Foreman, Will Geer, Michael Gordon, Dashiell Hammett, Lillian Hellman, Joris Ivens, Joseph Losey, Karen Morley, Dorothy Parker, Abraham Polonsky, Ann Revere, Robert Rossen, Gale Sondergaard, Lionel Stander, Mrs. Lee Strasberg (Paula Miller), and Dorothy Tree.

Most of the above named, as well as many other producers, directors, writers, and actors, were blacklisted by the industry, draining Hollywood of much of its creative talent. Some appeared on the list (an actual blacklist was compiled by a self-appointed vigilante group, Aware, and circulated by the American Legion) merely on the basis of some vague statement concerning unspecified links to left-wing causes, such as the Loyalist side in the Spanish Civil War. Directors like Dassin and Losey were forced into exile in Europe; most of the actors sought employment on the stage or went into retirement. Many of the writers were able, however, to continue their work under various guises. Thus, the "Robert Rich" who won an Academy Award in 1956 for the screenplay of *The Brave One* turned out later to be, to the embarrassment of the industry, none other than Dalton Trumbo, one of the Hollywood Ten.

Blacklisting began dying out in the late 50s, along with the other vestiges of the McCarthy Red-scare hysteria. But this dark chapter in the Hollywood story left deep scars upon many who had lived and suffered through the madness.

Holm, Celeste. Actress. Born on Apr. 29, 1919, in New York City. The daughter of a Norwegian-born insurance executive and a portrait-artist mother, she was educated in Holland, France, and the US and took ballet and drama classes as a child. She studied drama at the University of Chicago while attending high school in that city and made her professional stage debut with a Pennsylvania stock company at 17. She made her first Broadway appearance in 1938 and scored a triumph in 1943 in the role of Ado Annie in the long-running Rodgers and Hammerstein musical 'Oklahoma!' She signed a long-term contract with 20th Century-Fox, making her screen debut in 1946 and winning an Academy Award as best supporting actress for her third film, *Gentleman's Agreement* (1947). An intelligent and remarkably versatile actress, she was twice more nominated for Oscars (for *Come to the Stable* and *All About Eve*) and made many memorable appearances, in a wide range of roles, both in leads and supporting parts, in films, on the stage, radio, and television, and in nightclubs. She was knighted by King Olav V of Norway in 1979. In 1982 she was named by President Reagan to the National Council for the Arts and in the following year was appointed chairman of the New Jersey Motion Picture and Television Development Commission. Her first husband was director Ralph NELSON; her fourth is actor Wesley Addy.

FILMS: *Three Little Girls in Blue* 1946; *Carnival in Costa Rica, Gentleman's Agreement* 1947; *Road House, The Snake Pit* 1948; *Chicken Every Sunday, A Letter to Three Wives* (off-screen v/o), *Come to the Stable, Everybody Does It* 1949; *Champagne for Caesar, All About Eve* 1950; *The Tender Trap* 1955; *High Society* 1956; *Bachelor Flat* 1961; *Doctor You've Got to Be Kidding!* 1967; *Tom Sawyer* (as Aunt Polly) 1973; *Bittersweet Love* 1976; *The Private Files of J. Edgar Hoover* 1978; *Three Men and a Baby* 1987; *Still Breathing* 1996.

Holm, Ian. Actor. Born Ian Holm Cuthbert, on Sept. 12, 1931, in Goodmayes, England. *ed.* RADA. On the London stage since the mid-50s, he made a late entry into films in the late 60s. He won the British Film Academy (BFA) Award as best supporting actor for his performance in *The Bofors Gun* (1968), his screen debut, and again for *Chariots of Fire* (1981). He was Oscar-nominated for the latter.

FILMS: *The Bofors Gun, The Fixer, A Midsummer Night's Dream* (as Puck) 1968; *Oh! What a Lovely War* (as France's President Poincaré) 1969; *A Severed Head, Nicholas and Alexandra, Mary Queen of Scots* 1971; *Young Winston* 1972; *The Homecoming* 1973; *Juggernaut* 1974; *Robin and Marian* (as King John), *Shout at the Devil* 1976; *March or Die* 1977; *Alien* 1979; *Chariots of Fire, Time Bandits* (as Napoleon) 1981; *The Return of the Soldier* 1983; *Greystoke: The Legend of Tarzan, Lord of the Apes, Laughter House* 1984; *Brazil, Dance with a Stranger, Wetherby, Dreamchild* 1985; *Another Woman* 1988; *Henry V* (as Fluellen) 1989; *Hamlet* (as Polonius) 1990; *Naked Lunch* 1991; *Blue Ice, Kafka* 1992; *The Advocate, The Madness of King George, Mary Shelley's Frankenstein* 1994; *Big Night* 1996; *The Fifth Element, A Life Less Ordinary, Night Falls on Manhattan, The Sweet Hereafter* 1997.

Holmes, Helen. Actress. *b.* 1892, Chicago. *d.* 1950. Athletic heroine of many Hollywood silent serials and action pictures, many of which were directed by her husband, J. P. McGowan. She entered films with Mack Sennett in 1912 but the following year moved over to Kalem, where she scored a huge success in 1914–15 as the original star of the serial *The Hazards of Helen.* She quit Kalem in 1915, dropping out of the cast of that serial, which continued running successfully through February of 1917 (119 chapters!) with a succession of other actresses in the title role. After a brief stay at Universal, Miss Holmes joined Signal, a subsidiary of Mutual, where she starred in another highly successful serial, *The Girl and the Game.* For several years she had a huge following, trailing only Pearl White and Ruth Roland for popularity as the screen's "serial queen." Her serials typically had a railroad background, and her specialty was chasing villains along the top of a moving train and leaping from train to horse or horse to train with both in motion. After the debacle of Mutual around 1919, she began freelancing and her career gradually declined. She retired from the screen in 1926 but later returned for a few minor roles in talkies.

FILMS INCLUDE: *The Alibi* 1913; *The Operator at Black Rock, The Car of Death* 1914; *The Hazards of Helen* (serial) 1914–15; *The Girl and the Game* (serial; also co-sc.) 1915–16; *Judith of the Cumberlands, The Diamond Runners, Whispering Smith, Medicine Bend* 1916; *A Lass of the Lumberland* (serial), *The Lost Express* (serial), *The Railroad Raiders* (serial), *Danger Trail* 1917; *The Fatal Fortune* (serial) 1919; *The Tiger Band* (serial) 1920; *Ghost City* 1921; *The Lone Hand* 1922; *One Million in Jewels, Stormy Seas* 1923; *Battling Brewster* (serial), *The Riddle Rider* (serial), *Fighting Fury* 1924; *Barriers of the Law, Blood and Steel, Duped, Outwitted, The Sign of the Cactus, The Train Wreckers, Webs of Steel* 1925; *Crossed Signals, The Lost Express, Peril of the Rail* 1926; *Poppy* 1936; *The Californian* 1937; *Dude Cowboy* 1941.

Holmes, Phillips. Actor. *b.* July 22, 1907, Grand Rapids, Mich. *d.* 1942. *ed.* Princeton; Trinity Coll.; Paris. Blond, blue-eyed leading man of Hollywood films of the 30s. The son of veteran character actor Taylor Holmes (*b.* 1872, Newark, N.J. *d.* 1959), he entered films at 19 and played young leads in a number of important productions, memorably Von Sternberg's *An American Tragedy,* Lubitsch's *The Man I Killed/Broken Lullaby,* and Dorothy Arzner's *Nana.* His career declined sharply in the mid-30s. He was killed in an air collision aboard a Royal Canadian Air Force plane during his WW II service. His brother, Ralph Holmes (1915–45), played supporting roles in several films before committing suicide.

FILMS INCLUDE: *Varsity* 1928; *The Wild Party, Stairs of Sand, The Return of Sherlock Holmes, Pointed Heels* 1929; *Only the Brave, The Devil's Holiday, Grumpy, Her Man, The Dancers, Man to Man* 1930; *The Criminal Code, Stolen Heaven, Confessions of a Co-Ed, An American Tragedy* (as Clyde Griffiths) 1931; *Two Kinds of Women, The Man I Killed/Broken Lullaby, Night Court, 70,000 Witnesses* 1932; *The Secret of Madame Blanche, Men Must Fight, Looking Forward, Storm at Daybreak, The Big Brain, Dinner at Eight, Penthouse, Beauty for Sale, Stage Mother* 1933; *Nana, Private Scandal, Caravan, Great Expectations* (as Pip) 1934; *Ten Minute Alibi* (UK), *The Divine Spark* (as composer Vincenzo Bellini; UK/It.), *Chatterbox* 1935; *The House of a Thousand Candles, General Spanky* 1936; *The Dominant Sex* (UK) 1937; *Housemaster* (UK) 1938.

Holmes, Stuart. Actor. *b.* Mar. 10, 1887, Chicago. *d.* 1971. A veteran of the stage, he starred in early silent films, including several Theda Bara vehicles, but in the 20s gradually moved into character roles. He appeared in numerous Hollywood productions through the early 60s, usually in suave, aristocratic parts.

FILMS INCLUDE: *How Mrs. Murray Saved the Army* 1911; *Oliver Twist* (as Mr. Bumble) 1912; *In the Stretch* 1913; *The Criminal Path, Thou Shalt Not, Life's Shop Window, The War of Wars* 1914; *The Clemenceau Case, Princess, The Blindness of Devotion, The Galley Slave* 1915; *Sins of Men, East Lynne, Under Two Flags, Her Double Life, A Daughter of the Gods, Love and Hate* 1916; *The Scarlet Letter* (as Arthur Dimmesdale), *Tangled Lives, The Derelict, A Broadway Sport* 1917; *The Ghosts of Yesterday, A Romance of the Air, The Poor Rich Man* 1918; *The New Moon, The Other Man's Wife* 1919; *Trailed by Three* (serial), *The Evil Eye* (serial), *Body and Soul* 1920; *Passion Fruit, The Four Horsemen of the Apocalypse* 1921; *Her Husband's Trademark, The Prisoner of Zenda* (as the Black Duke), *Under Two Flags* 1922; *The Scarlet Lily, Tea—With a Kick, The Unknown Purple* 1923; *Three Weeks, On Time, Tess of the D'Urbervilles* (as Alec D'Urberville), *The Siren of Seville, Vanity's Price, The Beloved Brute* 1924; *A Fool and His Money, The Salvation Hunters, Friendly Enemies, The Primrose Path, North Star* 1925; *The Shadow of the Law, The Hurricane, Good and Naughty, Broken Hearts of Hollywood, Everybody's Acting, My Official Wife* 1926; *When a Man Loves* (as Louis XV), *Your Wife and Mine, Polly of the Movies* 1927; *Beware of Married Men, The Man Who Laughs, The Hawk's Nest, Danger Trail, The Cavalier* 1928; *The Heroic Lover* 1929; *Captain of the Guard* (as Louis XVI) 1930; *My Pal the King* 1932; *Are We Civilized?, Belle of the Nineties* 1934; *Murder by an Aristocrat, The Case of the Velvet Claws* 1936; *Her Husband's Secretary* 1937; *British Intelligence* 1940; *The Adventures of Mark Twain* 1944; *Moss Rose* 1947; *A Letter to Three Wives* 1948; *The Cobweb* 1955; *The Man Who Shot Liberty Valance* 1962.

Holt, Jack. Actor. *b.* Charles John Holt, May 31, 1888, Winchester, Va. *d.* 1951. Rugged, virile, tight-lipped hero of numerous Hollywood silents and talkies. A dropout from the Virginia Military Institute, he was a sandhog, gold prospector, and cowpuncher, among other itinerant pursuits, before beginning his screen career in 1913. Initially, he was cast in villainous roles, but before long he moved into lead parts, starring in both action-adventure pictures as a two-fisted hero and in society dramas as a suave, romantic leading man. Tall and slim, with an angular face and jutting jaw, and sporting a dapper moustache, he continued playing leads well into his 50s, mainly in B pictures. After returning from WW II service, during which he rose in rank to major, he went on playing supporting roles in films until his death of a heart attack. He was the father of Jennifer Holt, and Tim Holt, and supporting player David Holt.

FILMS INCLUDE: *Salomy Jane* (bit) 1914; *The Broken Coin* (serial; bit), *Jewel* 1915; *The Dumb Girl of Portici, Naked Hearts, Liberty—A Daughter of the USA* (serial) 1916; *Sacrifice, The Little American, The Call of the East, The Secret Game* 1917; *Love Me, The White Man's Law, Green Eyes, The Marriage Ring, The Road Through the Dark, The Squaw Man* 1918; *Cheating Cheaters, A Midnight Romance, For Better for Worse, The Woman Thou Gavest Me, The Life Line, Victory* 1919; *Held by the Enemy, The Best of Luck, Midsummer Madness* 1920; *All Souls' Eve, Ducks and Drakes, The Mask, The Lost Romance, After the Show, The Grim Comedian, The Call of the North* 1921; *Bought and Paid for, While Satan Sleeps, North of the Rio Grande, The Man Unconquerable, On the High Seas, Making a Man* 1922; *Nobody's Money, The Tiger's Claw, A Gentleman of Leisure, The Cheat, The Marriage Maker, Don't Call It Love* 1923; *Wanderer of the Wasteland, The Lone Wolf, Empty Hands* 1924; *The Thundering Herd, Eve's Secret, The Light of Western Stars, Wild Horse Mesa, The Ancient Highway* 1925; *The Enchanted Hill, Sea Horses, The Blind Goddess, Born to the West, Forlorn River, Man of the Forest* 1926; *The Mysterious Rider, The Tigress, The Warning* 1927; *The Smart Set, The Vanishing Pioneer, Court-Martial, The Water Hole, Avalanche, Submarine* 1928; *Sunset Pass, The Donovan Affair, Father and Son, Flight* 1929; *Vengeance, The Border Legion, Hell's Island, The Squealer* 1930; *The Last Parade, Dirigible, Subway Express, White Shoulders, Fifty Fathoms Deep, A Dangerous Affair, Maker of Men* 1931; *Behind the Mask, War Correspondent, This Sporting Age, Man Against Woman* 1932; *When Strangers Marry, The Woman I Stole, The Wrecker, Master of Men* 1933; *Whirlpool, Black Moon, The Defense Rests* 1934; *Best Man Wins, The Littlest Rebel* 1935; *Dangerous Waters, San Francisco, Crash Donovan* 1936; *Trouble in Morocco, Roaring Timber, Outlaws of the Orient, Trapped by G-Men, Under Suspicion* 1937; *Making the Headlines, Flight Into Nowhere, Reformatory, Crime Takes a Holiday* 1938; *Hidden Power, Fugitive at Large* 1939; *Passport to Alcatraz, Prison Camp, The Great Plane Robbery* 1940; *Holt of the Secret Service* (serial), *The Great Swindle* 1941; *Thunder Birds, Cat People* 1942; *They Were Expendable* 1945; *My Pal Trigger, The Chase* 1946; *The Wild Frontier* 1947; *The Treasure of the Sierra Madre* (bit) 1948; *The Last Bandit, Task Force* 1949; *Return of the Frontiersman* 1950; *Across the Wide Missouri* 1951.

Holt, Jennifer. Actress. Born Elizabeth Marshall Holt, on Nov. 10, 1920, in Hollywood, Calif. Daughter of Jack HOLT and sister of Tim HOLT, and David Holt, she played leading lady to several cowboy stars (Johnny Mack Brown, Rod Cameron, etc.) in low-budget Westerns of the 40s. Early in her career she was billed as Jacqueline Holt.

FILMS INCLUDE: *San Francisco Docks* 1941; *Deep in the Heart of Texas, Cowboy Buckaroo* 1942; *Lone Star Trail, Cowboy in Manhattan* 1943; *Oklahoma Raiders* 1944; *Gun Smoke, Under Western Skies* 1945; *Hop Harrigan* (serial), *Moon Over Montana* 1946; *Buffalo Bill Rides Again, The Fighting Vigilantes* 1947; *The Hawk of Powder River, Range Renegades* 1948.

Holt, Seth. Director. *b.* 1923, Palestine, to British parents. *d.* 1971. He started out as an actor in repertory and entered British films as assistant editor of documentaries in 1942. Two years later he joined Ealing as assistant editor of features at the invitation of his brother-in-law, Robert HAMER. He worked on many important films in that capacity and later as a full editor (*The Lavender Hill Mob, Mandy, The Titfield Thunderbolt,* etc.). In 1955 he was appointed associate producer and in 1958 made his debut as a director, although he later returned to editing with *Saturday Night and Sunday Morning* (1960). His career was marred by a persistent battle with alcoholism and he was forced to abandon a number of projects. He had a keen eye for visual dynamics and intermittently demonstrated flashes of talent, but on the whole his work failed to achieve a consistent level of excellence.

FILMS: *Nowhere to Go* (also co-sc.) 1958; *Taste of Fear/Scream of Fear* 1961; *Station Six—Sahara* (UK/Ger.) 1964; *The Nanny* 1965; *Danger Route* 1967; *Blood from the Mummy's Tomb* (completed by Michael Carreras after Holt's death) 1971.

Holt, Tim. Actor. *b.* Charles John Holt, Jr., Feb. 5, 1918, Beverly Hills, Calif. *d.* 1973. *ed.* Culver Military Acad. The son of Jack HOLT and brother of Jennifer HOLT and David Holt, he appeared as a child in several of his famous father's silent films. He later played juveniles and boyish Western heroes in numerous B pictures, occasionally getting meatier parts in high-quality films, like Orson Welles's *The Magnificent Ambersons* (1942). Probably the best role of his career was that of Curtin, Humphrey Bogart's conscientious partner, in John Huston's *The Treasure of the Sierra Madre* (in which his father played a bit part). He retired from the screen to go into business in the mid-50s but returned in 1971 for a last, embarrassing role. At the time of his death, of cancer, he was manager of an Oklahoma radio station.

FILMS INCLUDE: *The Vanishing Pioneer* 1928; *History Is Made at Night, Stella Dallas* 1937; *Gold Is Where You Find It, The Law West of Tombstone* 1938; *The Renegade Ranger, Spirit of Culver, Stagecoach, Fifth Avenue Girl* 1939; *Swiss Family Robinson, Laddie* 1940; *Back Street, Dude Cowboy* 1941; *The Magnificent Ambersons* 1942; *The Avenging Rider, Hitler's Children* 1943; *My Darling Clementine* 1946; *Under the Tonto Rim* 1947; *The Treasure of the Sierra Madre* 1948; *The Mysterious Desperado* 1949; *Law of the Badlands* 1950; *His Kind of Woman* 1951; *Road Agent* 1952; *The Monster That Challenged the World* 1957; *This Stuff'll Kill Ya!* 1971.

Homeier, Skip. Actor. Born George Vincent Homeier, on Oct. 5, 1929, in Chicago. *ed.* UCLA. A radio performer from age six, he entered films at 14, repeating his Broadway role as a Nazi brat in *Tomorrow the World.* Afterward, often typecast as a juvenile delinquent. Since the 50s, mostly in Westerns, often as a villain. He played positive parts in the TV series 'Dan Raven' (title role, 1960–61) and 'The Interns' (1970–71).

FILMS INCLUDE: *Tomorrow the World* 1944; *Boys' Ranch* 1946; *Mickey* 1948; *The Big Cat* 1949; *The Gunfighter* 1950; *The Halls of Montezuma, Sealed Cargo, Fixed Bayonets* 1951; *Sailor Beware* 1952; *Beachhead, The Black Widow* 1954; *Cry Vengeance, At Gunpoint* 1955; *The Burning Hills* 1956; *The Tall T* 1957; *The Day of the Badman* 1958; *Comanche Station* 1960; *Stark Fear, Showdown* 1963; *Bullet for a Badman* 1964; *The Ghost and Mr. Chicken* 1966; *Tiger by the Tail* 1970; *Starbird and Sweet William* 1976; *The Greatest* 1977.

Homes, Geoffrey. See MAINWARING, Daniel.

Homolka, Oscar (Oskar). Actor. *b.* Aug. 12, 1898, Vienna. *d.* 1978. A graduate of Vienna's Royal Dramatic Academy, he performed on the Austrian and German stage and appeared in many German silent and sound films. He went to England after Hitler's rise to power and continued to the US in 1936. He played imposing character roles in many Hollywood films, as well as on Broadway, sometimes sympathetic or humorous but mostly scheming or villainous. He was nominated for an Oscar for his role as Uncle Chris in *I Remember Mama* (1948), in which he repeated his 1944 stage success. His coarse, houndlike Slavic features, thick accent, and bushy eyebrows made him an ideal heavy in films about foreign intrigue. In the mid-60s he returned to England, intending to retire, but he continued appearing in films for another decade. His last (1949–77) of four or five marriages was to actress Joan Tetzel (1924–1977).

FILMS INCLUDE: In Germany—*Die Abenteuer eines Zehnmarkscheines/Uneasy Money, Brennende Grenze/Aftermath* 1926; *Dirnentragödie/Women Without Men/Tragedy of the Street, Die heilige Lüge, Schinderhannes/The Prince of Rogues* 1927; *Masken* 1929; *Dreyfus/The Dreyfus Case* (as Esterhazy) 1930; *Hokuspokus/Hocuspocus 1914: Die letzte Tage vor dem Weltbrand/1914: The Last Days Before the War, Im Geheimdienst/In the Employ of the Secret Service* 1931; *Spione am Werk* 1933. In the UK—*Rhodes of Africa/Rhodes, Sabotage/The Woman Alone* 1936. In the US—*Ebb Tide* 1937; *Seven*

Sinners, Comrade X 1940; *The Invisible Woman, Rage in Heaven* 1941; *Ball of Fire* 1942; *Mission to Moscow* (as Litvinoff), *Hostages* 1943; *I Remember Mama* 1948; *Anna Lucasta* 1949; *The White Tower* 1950; *Top Secret/Mr. Potts Goes to Moscow* (UK) 1952; *Prisoner of War* 1954; *The Seven Year Itch* 1955; *War and Peace* (as General Kutuzov) 1956; *A Farewell to Arms* 1957; *The Key* (UK) 1958; *La Tempesta/ Tempest* (It.) 1959; *Mr. Sardonicus* 1961; *Boys' Night Out, The Wonderful World of the Brothers Grimm* 1962; *The Long Ships* (UK/Yug.) 1964; *Joy in the Morning* 1965; *Funeral in Berlin* (UK) 1966; *The Happening, Billion Dollar Brain* (UK) 1967; *Assignment to Kill, The Madwoman of Chaillot* (UK) 1969; *Song of Norway, The Executioner* (UK) 1970; *The Tamarind Seed* (UK) 1974.

Honda, Inoshiro (Ishiro). Director. Born 1911. Japanese director who brought the world Godzilla, Rodan, Mothra, and Ghidrah the Three-Headed Monster. The worldwide craze for Japanese monster films began with Honda's *Gojira*, known in the US as *Godzilla, King of the Monsters*, which established the formula of giant creatures set loose to destroy Japanese cities and threaten civilization. In this and many subsequent films made at Toho Studios, Honda worked closely with special effects artist Eiji Tsuburaya, who used miniature sets and high-speed filming of actors in monster costumes to create his illusions. *Godzilla*'s American release also set the pattern of adding scenes with American actors to make the dubbed Japanese films more palatable to US audiences. Honda co-scripted several of his films, including *Godzilla*. Though other directors took over the *Godzilla* franchise, Honda continued to make monster films into the 1970s, when the Toho monster cycle petered out. Honda's films are now perennial cult favorites on television.

FILMS INCLUDE: *Half-Human* 1955; *Gigantis the Fire Monster, Gojira/Godzilla, King of the Monsters* (also co-sc.) 1956; *Rodan* 1957; *The H-Man* 1959; *Battle in Outer Space* 1960; *Mothra* 1962; *King Kong vs. Godzilla* 1963; *Godzilla vs. Mothra, Attack of the Mushroom People, Dagora the Space Monster, Frankenstein Conquers the World* 1964; *Ghidrah the Three-Headed Monster* 1965; *King Kong Escapes* 1968; *Destroy All Monsters!* (also co-sc.), *Godzilla's Revenge* 1969; *Monster Zero, The War of the Gargantuas* (also co-sc.) 1970; *Yog—Monster from Space* 1971; *Monsters from the Unknown Planet* 1975.

Honegger, Arthur. Composer. *b.* Mar. 10, 1892, Le Havre, France, of Swiss origin. *d.* 1955. The celebrated composer of the *King David* oratorio and other symphonic works also scored a considerable number of French films as well as some British and Italian. He wrote musical accompaniment for some silent films, notably those of Abel GANCE, then scores for numerous talkies. A documentary film on his life and work, directed by Georges Rouquier, was released in France in 1955.

FILMS INCLUDE: *La Roue* 1923; *Fait Divers* 1924; *Napoléon, L'Idée* 1926; *Pacific 231* 1931; *Les Misérables* 1933; *Rapt, Cease Fire* 1934; *Crime and Punishment, L'Equipage* 1935; *Nitchevo, Mayerling* 1936; *Mademoiselle Docteur, Regain, Le Citadelle de Silence* 1937; *Pygmalion* (UK) 1938; *Je t'attendrai, Cavalcade d'Amour* 1939; *Le Capitaine Fracasse, Secrets* 1942; *Un seul Amour* 1943; *Un Ami viendra ce Soir* 1945; *Un Revenant* 1946; *Giovanna al Rogo* (from his oratorio *Joan of Arc at the Stake;* It.) 1954.

Hong Kong. Despite its small size and population, this former British crown colony of 5.7 million inhabitants, situated on the southern coast of China, boasts the world's third largest movie industry (after the US and India), producing over 2,000 films in the 1980s, and is one of the few places in the world where the locally produced movies are more popular than the American product. In the 1920s and 30s the industry enjoyed a two-way exchange of talent with the Shanghai studios. After World War II and the Communist takeover of China it became the main source of Chinese-language films for the Asian market. Opulent historical adventures, a specialty of the Shaw Bros. studio, dominated production in the 1960s. In the early 70s Hong Kong became the main source of martial-arts action films. One of these, *A Touch of Zen*, won the Grand Prix at the Cannes Festival in 1975, focusing attention on the qualitative aspect of Hong Kong's thriving industry. The film was directed by King Hu, who stresses the philosophical rather than the physically spectacular manifestations of the martial arts.

In the 1980s a "New Wave" of Hong Kong directors, many Western-trained, brought an Asian approach to such American genres as action films, gangster movies, ghost stories, historical epics, and comedies. Such directors as John WOO and TSUI Hark and such stars as the action comedian Jackie CHAN and the suave and versatile Chow Yun-Fat began to draw international attention on the art-house and festival circuits. The future of the industry is up in the air now that control of the colony has been returned to the Chinese. Many prominent filmmakers, notably Woo, emigrated well before the 1997 handover. Another sign of Hong Kong's anticipation of the takeover was an increase in the number of Hong Kong–China co-productions.

Hood, Darla. Child actress. *b.* Nov 4, 1931, Leedey, Okla. *d.* 1979. The "leading lady" of the popular "Our Gang" comedy shorts. She joined the series in 1935, at the age of four, and appeared in more than 150 segments through 1945, singing as well as providing the romantic interest of Carl "Alfalfa" Switzer. She also appeared in occasional features. After retiring from the screen at the ripe age of 14, she was heard periodically singing jingles for TV commercials and was seen in bit roles in several movies.

FILMS: *The Bohemian Girl,, Neighborhood House* 1936; *Ice Follies of 1939* 1939; *Born to Sing* 1942; *Happy Land* 1943; *Calypso Heat Wave* 1957; *The Bat* 1959.

Hooks, Kevin. Actor, director. Handsome, gifted film actor since the 70s. The product of a prominent theatrical family, he carries his heritage with great success. He switched gears in 1988 to his first directing effort, the TV movie *Roots: The Gift,* and from there went on to features, proving himself a provocative, proficient filmmaker. His father is actor Robert HOOKS.

FILMS: As actor—*Sounder* 1972; *Aaron Loves Angela* 1975; *Just an Old Sweet Song* 1976; *The Greatest Thing That Almost Happened* 1977; *A Hero Ain't Nothin' But a Sandwich* 1978; *Take Down* 1978; *Innerspace* 1987. As director—*Heat Wave* 1990; *Strictly Business* 1991; *Passenger 57* 1992.

Hooks, Robert. Actor. Born on Apr. 18, 1937, in Washington, D.C. *ed.* Temple U. Handsome leading man of American films and television. On screen from the late 60s, usually in tough, assertive roles. Among his TV appearances, he co-starred in the police series 'N.Y.P.D.' (1967–69). His son is actor-director Kevin HOOKS.

FILMS INCLUDE: *Sweet Love Bitter, Hurry Sundown* 1967; *The Last of the Mobile Hotshots* 1970; *Trouble Man* 1972; *Aaron Loves Angela* 1975; *Airport '77* 1977; *Fast Walking* 1982; *Star Trek III: The Search for Spock* 1984.

Hooper, Tobe. Director. Born in 1943, in Austin, Tex. He began his career making documentaries, industrial films, and commercials in Texas. Appointed an assistant director of the film program at the University of Texas, he continued making films with the help of students. He made a sensational feature debut in 1974 with *The Texas Chainsaw Masscare,* a violent, low-budget horror film of eerie, nightmarish quality. It won the top prize at the Avoriaz Horror Film Festival and went on to become a huge cult favorite, spawning two weak sequels, a video game, and numerous imitations. After some more work at the fringe of the industry, Hooper got to direct the prestigious Steven Spielberg horror venture *Poltergeist* (1982), but despite its success he then reverted to lower-budget thrillers. He has also done some stylish work for television, including the TV movie *Salem's Lot* (1979) and episodes for 'The Equalizer' series.

FILMS: *The Texas Chainsaw Massacre* (also prod., co-sc.) 1974; *Eaten Alive/Starlight Slaughter/Death Trap/Horror Hotel Massacre* 1976; *The Funhouse* 1981; *Poltergeist* 1982; *Lifeforce* 1985; *Invaders from Mars, The Texas Chainsaw Massacre: Part 2* (also co-prod., co-mus.) 1986; *Spontaneous Combustion* 1990; *Sleepwalkers* (act. only) 1992; *The Mangler* (also sc.) 1994.

Hopalong Cassidy. See BOYD, William (Bill)

Hope, Bob. Actor. Born Leslie Townes Hope, on May 29, 1903, in Eltham, England. In the US from age four, he grew up in Cleveland, where he won a Chaplin-imitation contest at ten. In his teens he was a newsboy, a soda jerk, and briefly a boxer before trying his hand at amateur show business in an act of "song, patter, and eccentric dancing." He later hit the road in vaudeville, in which he added comedy to his routine. In 1929 he made it to New York and in 1933 he got a solid comedy part in the Broadway musical *Roberta*. Between 1934 and 1936 he appeared in eight comedy shorts, all filmed in New York. But it was his success on radio that brought him a Hollywood invitation to appear in *The Big Broadcast of 1938*. In this loosely knit comedy-variety film, he sang for the first time the tune that was to become his theme song, 'Thanks for the Memory.' He scored his first popular screen hit with *The Cat and the Canary* (1939) and struck it rich with *Road to Singapore* (1940), the first of seven highly successful "Road" pictures he was to make over the years with Bing CROSBY and Dorothy LAMOUR.

Hope's style of screen comedy, relying heavily on rapid quips and topical wisecracks, thrived through the 40s, reaching a peak in the Western parody *The Paleface* (1948). His films of the 50s were a mixed bag and those of the 60s increasingly less entertaining. But the indefatigable Hope continued bombarding the public with laughs not only in films but also in frequent TV specials and worldwide personal appearances. He frequently emceed the Oscar ceremonies and he won "Special" Academy Awards five times (1940, 1944, 1952, 1959, and 1965), not for his acting, but for humanitarian action and contribution to the industry.

From 1941 to 1953, Hope ranked each year (except for 1948) among Hollywood's top ten money-making stars. While enriching Paramount, he became one of the world's wealthiest entertainers, his worth estimated at hundreds of millions. In spite of his busy professional schedule, Hope allowed generous chunks of time for annual trips to entertain troops overseas, a ritual that spanned several major wars, from WW II, through Korea and Vietnam, to the Persian Gulf (1990–91), on the eve of operation Desert Storm. For many years an avid golfer, his name became associated with the Bob Hope Desert Classic, an annual event that produced millions of dollars for charity. His numerous awards and citations for humanitarian endeavors included the Presidential Medal of Freedom. His lifetime professional achievements were ratified by Kennedy Center honors in 1985. Hope, who over the years has assumed the stature of a national institution, authored several humorous books about his career and travels, some in collaboration: *They Got Me Covered* (1941), *I Never Left Home* (1944), *So This Is Peace* (1946), *Have Tux, Will Travel* (1954), *I Owe Russia $1,200* (1963), *Five Women I Love: Obit Hope's Vietnam Story* (1966), *The Last Christmas Show* (1974), *The Road to Hollywood: My 40-Year Love Affair with the Movies* (1977), *Confessions of a Hooker: My Lifelong Love Affair with Golf* (1985), *Don't Shoot, It's Only Me* (1990).

FEATURE FILMS: *The Big Broadcast Of 1938, College Swing, Give Me A Sailor, Thanks for the Memory* 1938; *Never Say Die, Some Like It Hot, The Cat and the Canary* 1939; *Road to Singapore, The Ghostbreakers* 1940; *Road to Zanzibar, Caught in the Draft, Nothing But the Truth, Louisiana Purchase* 1941; *My Favorite Blonde, Road to Morocco, Star Spangled Rhythm* 1942; *They Got Me Covered, Let's Face It* 1943; *The Princess and the Pirate* 1944; *Road to Utopia, Monsieur Beaucaire* 1946; *My Favorite Brunette, Where There's Life, Variety Girl* (cameo) 1947; *Road to Rio, The Paleface* 1948; *Sorrowful Jones, The Great Lover* 1949; *Fancy Pants* 1950; *The Lemon Drop Kid, My Favorite Spy* 1951; *The Greatest Show on Earth* (cameo), *Son of Paleface* 1952; *Road to Bali, Off Limits, Scared Stiff* (cameo), *Here Come the Girls* 1953; *Casanova's Big Night* 1954; *The Seven Little Foys* 1955; *That Certain Feeling, The Iron Petticoat* (UK) 1956; *Beau James* 1957; *Paris Holiday* (also prod., orig. story) 1958; *The Five Pennies* (cameo), *Alias Jesse James* (also Prod.) 1959; *The Facts of Life* 1960; *Bachelor in Paradise* 1961; *The Road to Hong Kong* 1962; *Critic's Choice, Call Me Bwana* 1963; *A Global Affair* 1964; *I'll Take Sweden* 1965; *The Oscar* (cameo), *Not with My Wife You Don't* (cameo), *Boy Did I Get the Wrong Number, The Bob Hope Vietnam Christmas Show* (feature-length TV Special, later shown theatrically; also exec. prod.) 1966; *Eight on the Lam* 1967; *The Private Navy of Sgt. O'Farrell* 1968; *How to Commit Marriage* 1969; *Cancel My Reservation* (also exec. prod.) 1972; *The Muppet Movie* (cameo) 1979; *Spies Like Us* (cameo) 1985.

Hopkins, Sir Anthony. Actor. Born On Dec. 31, 1937, in Port Talbot, South Wales. Impressive character lead of British and American stage, TV, and films. Of blue-collar descent, he showed little aptitude for formal education. Deciding on an acting career, following two years of military service, he attended the Cardiff College of Drama, then transferred to London's Royal Academy of Dramatic Art. Making his stage debut in 1960 and his first London appearance in 1964, he was soon recognized as a major talent. In the late 60s and early 70s he was a leading star of the National Theatre, specializing in Shakespeare and the classics. He came to America in 1974 to play on Broadway in 'Equus' and stayed for ten years, appearing in occasional feature films and numerous TV movies and miniseries, impersonating characters from Quasimodo (in *The Hunchback of Notre Dame*) to Adolf Hitler (in *The Bunker*) and Yitzhak Rabin (in *Victory at Entebbe*). He won the Oscar in 1992 for his mesmerizing portrayal of cannibalistic serial killer Hannibal Lecter, a performance that re-ignited his career and made him one of the most sought-after prestige actors of the 90s. He maintains homes in London and Beverly Hills with his second wife, a former production assistant.

FILMS: *The White Bus* (medium-length) 1967; *The Lion in Winter* (as Richard the Lionheart) 1968; *Hamlet* (as Claudius) 1969; *The Looking Glass War* 1970; *When Eight Bells Toll* 1971; *Young Winston* (as Lloyd George) 1972; *A Doll's House* (as Torvald Helmer) 1973; *The Girl from Petrovka, Juggernaut* 1974; *All Creatures Great and Small* (TV in US) 1975; *Audrey Rose, A Bridge Too Far* 1977; *International Velvet, Magic* 1978; *The Elephant Man, A Change of Seasons* 1980; *The Bounty* (as Captain Bligh) 1984; *The Good Father, Blunt* 1986; *84 Charing Cross Road* 1987; *The Dawning* 1988; *A Chorus of Disapproval* 1989; *Desperate Hours* 1990; *The Silence of the Lambs* 1991;

Freejack, Howards End, Bram Stoker's Dracula, The Trial, The Innocent 1992; *The Remains of the Day, Shadowlands* 1993; *Legends of the Fall, The Road to Wellville* 1994; *Nixon* 1995; *August* (dir. only), *Surviving Picasso* 1996; *Amistad, The Edge* 1997.

Hopkins, Bo. Actor. Born on Feb. 2, 1942, in Greenwood, S.C. Trained by Uta Hagen in New York and later at the Desilu Playhouse School in Hollywood, he made his screen debut in Sam Peckinpah's *The Wild Bunch* (1969). He has since played leads, second leads, and major supporting roles in numerous films, often as a tough, adventurous macho youth, and later as a rugged westerner or small-town sheriff.

FILMS INCLUDE: *The Wild Bunch, The Bridge at Remagen* 1969; *Macho Callahan, Monte Walsh* 1970; *The Culpepper Cattle Company, The Only Way Home, The Getaway* 1971; *The Man Who Loved Cat Dancing, White Lightning, American Graffiti* 1973; *The Nickel Ride* 1974; *The Day of the Locust, Posse, The Killer Elite* 1975; *A Small Town in Texas* 1976; *Tentacles* (It.) 1977; *Midnight Express* (UK) 1978; *More American Graffiti* 1979; *The Fifth Floor* 1980; *Sweet Sixteen* 1983; *Night Shadows* 1984; *Sex Appeal* 1986; *The Bounty Hunter* 1989; *Big Bad John* 1990; *Center of the Web, Inside Monkey Zetterland* 1992; *The Ballad of Little Jo* 1993; *Radioland Murders* 1994.

Hopkins, Miriam. Actress. *b.* Ellen Miriam Hopkins, Oct. 18, 1902, Bainbridge, Ga. *d.* 1972. *ed.* Syracuse U. Studied ballet, but after breaking an ankle settled for a career as a chorus girl and made her professional debut in 1921 in 'The Music Box Revue.' Two years later she switched to drama and by the late 20s was an established Broadway actress. In 1930 she signed a Paramount screen contract and almost immediately became an important star, thanks to leads in Lubitsch's *The Smiling Lieutenant, Trouble in Paradise,* and *Design for Living,* and Mamoulian's *Dr. Jekyll and Mr. Hyde* and *Becky Sharp.* A seductive, blue-eyed blonde, she played well-bred ladies and floozies alike, often bitchy. In 1935 she moved over to Goldwyn and in 1939 to Warners, where she was engaged in a publicity-inspired feud with Bette Davis, her co-star in several films. Her starring career, faltering since the late 30s, ended in the early 40s. She returned to Broadway and later appeared in summer stock and with touring companies. Beginning in the early 50s she was seen in character parts in occasional films. Her first of four husbands (1926–31) was actor Brandon Peters; her third was director Anatole LITVAK.

FILMS: *Fast and Loose* 1930; *The Smiling Lieutenant* (and French-language version, *Le Lieutenant souriant), Twenty-Four Hours* 1931; *Dr. Jekyll and Mr. Hyde, Two Kinds of Women, Dancers in the Dark, The World and the Flesh, Trouble in Paradise* 1932; *The Story of Temple Drake, The Stranger's Return, Design for Living* 1933; *All of Me, She Loves Me Not, The Richest Girl in the World* 1934; *Becky Sharp* (title role), *Barbary Coast, Splendor* 1935; *These Three* 1936; *Men Are Not Gods* (UK), *The Woman I Love, Woman Chases Man, Wise Girl* 1937; *The Old Maid* 1939; *Virginia City, Lady with Red Hair* (as actress Mrs. Leslie Carter) 1940; *A Gentleman After Dark* 1942; *Old Acquaintance* 1943; *The Heiress* 1949; *The Mating Season* 1951; *Outcasts of Poker Flat, Carrie* 1952; *The Children's Hour* 1962; *Fanny Hill* (Ger./US) 1964; *The Chase* 1966; *Comeback* (unreleased).

Hopper, Dennis. Actor, director. Born on May 17, 1936, in Dodge City, Kans. A screen actor since the mid-50s, he was profoundly influenced by the personality of James DEAN, whom he supported in the films *Rebel Without a Cause* and *Giant.* He typically played minor roles in major films but soon developed a reputation as a difficult and rebellious young character actor with a violent temper who wouldn't take direction, and he found it increasingly difficult to get good movie parts. He began playing major roles in minor films. Hopper shook up the Hollywood establishment with the phenomenal success *Easy Rider,* which he directed and co-authored and in which he co-starred with his partner to the venture, Peter FONDA. The film, made for less than $400,000, reaped more than $19 million in North American rentals ($40 million in worldwide box-office grosses), while assuming the stature of a counterculture anthem. But critics turned thumbs down on his second venture as director-writer-star, *The Last Movie,* which he shot in Peru. The box-office failure of the film led Hopper into a decade-long hiatus from the director's chair and the Hollywood scene. He moved to Taos, New Mexico, where he lived in semi-oblivion, drinking and using drugs, and sporadically emerging for screen roles, mainly in obscure foreign films. His next crack at directing came accidentally, when he was asked to take the helm on *Out of the Blue* (1980), a small Canadian film in which he was appearing. Working on a tight schedule and even tighter budget, he came up with a reasonably accomplished film of brooding atmosphere. It signaled the start of a gradual recovery of Hopper's life and career, which culminated with critically acclaimed roles in *Blue Velvet* and *Hoosiers* (both 1986), then in his direction of *Colors* (1988). Also in 1988 he wrote *Out of the Sixties,* a selection of his photographs. A postproduction dispute with producers over the cutting of *Backtrack,* a film he began shooting in 1988, however, resulted in messy delays. It was finally released in 1991 as *Catchfire,* with Hopper removing his name from the credits and taking the Directors Guild moniker "Alan Smithee."

FILMS: *Rebel Without a Cause, I Died a Thousand Times* 1955; *The Steel Jungle, Giant* 1956; *Gunfight at the O.K. Corral, The Story of Mankind* 1957; *From Hell to Texas* 1958; *The Young Land* 1959; *Key Witness* 1960; *Night Tide* 1963; *Tarzan and Jane Regained Sort Of* 1964; *The Sons of Katie Elder* 1965; *Queen of Blood/Planet of Blood* 1966; *Cool Hand Luke, The Trip, The Glory Stompers* 1967; *Panic in the City, Hang 'Em High* 1968; *Easy Rider* (also dir., co-sc.), *True Grit* 1969; *The American Dreamer* (doc.; also sc.), *The Last Movie/Chinchero* (also dir., sc.) 1971; *Crush Proof* 1972; *Kid Blue/Dime Box* 1973; *The Sky Is Falling* (Sp.) 1975; *Mad Dog/Mad Dog Morgan* (Austral.), *Tracks* 1976; *Les Apprentis Sorciers* (cameo; Fr.), *Der amerikanische Freund/The American Friend* (Ger./Fr.), *Couleur chair* (Belg./Fr.) 1977; *L'Ordre et la Securité du Monde* 1978; *Apocalypse Now* 1979; *Out of the Blue* (also dir.; Can.) 1980; *Renacida/Reborn* (Sp.), *King of the Mountain* 1981; *White Star, Human Highway* 1982; *The Ostermann Weekend, Rumble Fish* 1983; *Slagskampen* 1984; *My Science Project* 1985; *The Texas Chainsaw Massacre: Part 2, Blue Velvet, Hoosiers, The American Way/Riders of the Storm* (UK) 1986; *Black Widow, River's Edge, Straight to Hell, O. C. and Stiggs, The Pick-Up Artist* 1987; *Colors* (also dir.) 1988; *Blood Red, Chattahoochee* 1989; *The Hot Spot* (dir. only), *Flashback* 1990; *Catchfire/Backtrack* (also dir.; release delayed from 1989), *Superstar: The Life and Times of Andy Warhol* (interview subject), *The Indian Runner, Hearts of Darkness: A Filmmaker's Apocalypse, Eye of the Storm, Double-Crossed* 1991; *Midnight Heat* 1992; *True Romance, Boiling Point, Red Rock West, Super Mario Bros.* 1993; *Chasers* 1994; *Search and Destroy, Waterworld* 1995; *Basquiat, Carried Away* 1996.

Hopper, E. Mason. Director. *b.* Dec. 6, 1885, Enosburg, Vt. *d.* 1966. On stage from age 14 in vaudeville and summer stock, he briefly assisted his father in the manufacture of processed food after graduating from the University of Maryland and for a while played semipro baseball. He later studied art in Europe and became a syndicated cartoonist.

However, he remained attracted to the stage and continued in vaudeville and stock musicals as actor and director. He directed his first film for Essenay in 1911 and subsequently turned out numerous silents and early talkies, for various studios specializing in frothy romantic comedies and dramas. He retired from film work in the mid-30s.

FILMS INCLUDE: *Mr. Wise—Investigator* (also sc.) 1911; *Alkali Ike in Jayville* 1913; *The Labyrinth* 1915; *The Selfish Woman/The Taming of Helen* (co-dir.), *Gloriana* (also prod., story) 1916; *The Spirit of Romance, The Wax Model, The Prison Without Walls, As Men Love, The Hidden Spring/The Secret Spring, The Firefly of Tough Luck, Without Honor* 1917; *The Answer, The Love Brokers, Boston Blackie's Little Pal, Mystic Faces/Unexpected Places* 1918; *Come Again Smith, As the Sun Went Down* 1919; *It's a Great Life* 1920; *Hold Your Horses, All Is Fair in Love, Dangerous Curve Ahead, From the Ground Up* 1921; *The Glorious Fool, Brothers Under the Skin, Hungry Hearts* 1922; *Daddy, The Love Piker* 1923; *The Great White Way, Janice Meredith* 1924; *The Crowded Hour* 1925; *Up in Mabel's Room, Paris at Midnight, Almost a Lady* 1926; *Getting Gertie's Garter, The Night Bride, The Wise Wife, The Rush Hour* 1927; *A Blonde for a Night, My Friend from India* 1928; *The Carnation Kid, Square Shoulders, Wise Girls, Their Own Desire* 1929; *Temptation* 1930; *Shop Angel, Midnight Morals, Alias Mary Smith, No Living Witness, Her Mad Night* 1932; *Sister to Judas, Malay Nights, One Year Later* 1933; *Curtain at Eight* 1934.

Hopper, Hedda. Gossip columnist, actress. *b.* Elda Furry, June 2, 1890, Hollidaysburg, Pa., a butcher's daughter. *d.* 1966. As a Broadway chorine she met and married in 1913 matinee idol DeWolf Hopper (*b.* William DeWolf Hopper, Mar. 30, 1858, New York City. *d.* 1935). In 1915 they took their newborn son, William Hopper (*b.* William DeWolf Hopper, Jr., Jan. 26, 1915, *d.* 1970) to Hollywood, where Hopper Senior became a star for the newly formed Triangle Company, in such films as *Don Quixote* (1915), *Casey at the Bat,* and *Macbeth* (both 1916). Hedda, too, began appearing in films, initially as a star in "vampy" roles, later as a supporting player, and Hopper Junior was featured prominently in one of his father's films before he was a year old (William Hopper later played leads and character parts in films, becoming famous as Detective Paul Drake in the 'Perry Mason' series on TV). The Hoppers divorced in 1922. Hedda became a Hollywood fixture, both as a supporting actress and a social butterfly. She appeared in scores of films and became known as "Queen of Quickies." In 1936 she started a chitchat radio show and in 1938 began a 28-year career as a Hollywood columnist. She became famous for her rivalry with gossip columnist Louella Parsons; her lifelong feuds with Constance Bennett and Elsa Maxwell, among others; and her collection of hats. Well aware of the great power she wielded over Hollywood lives and careers, she sarcastically called her home "the house that fear built."

FILMS INCLUDE: *Battle of Hearts* 1916; *Her Excellency the Governor, Seven Keys to Baldpate, Nearly Married, Virtuous Wives* 1917; *The Beloved Traitor* 1918; *The Third Degree, Isle of Conquest* 1919; *The Man Who Lost Himself, The New York Idea* 1920; *Heedless Moths, Conceit* 1921; *Sherlock Holmes, Women Men Marry* 1922; *Has the World Gone Mad!, Reno* 1923; *Why Men Leave Home, Happiness, Miami, Sinners in Silk, The Snob* 1924; *Déclassée, Raffles the Amateur Cracksman, Zander the Great, The Teaser* 1925; *The Caveman, Dance Madness, Lew Tyler's Wives, Don Juan, Fools of Fashion* 1926; *Children of Divorce, Matinee Ladies, Orchids and Ermine, The Cruel Truth, Adam and Evil, Wings, A Reno Divorce* 1927; *Love and Learn, The Whip Woman, The Port of Missing Girls, Harold Teen, Undressed* 1928; *Girls Gone Wild, The Last of Mrs. Cheyney, His Glorious Night* 1929; *Such Men Are Dangerous, High Society Blues, Holiday, Our Blushing Brides, Let Us Be Gay, War Nurse* 1930; *Men Call It Love, The Prodigal, The Common Law, Rebound* 1931; *The Man Who Played God, As You Desire Me, Skyscraper Souls, Speak Easily, Downstairs* 1932; *The Barbarian, Pilgrimage* 1933; *Little Man What Now?* 1934; *Lady Tubbs, Alice Adams* 1935; *Dracula's Daughter* 1936; *Artists and Models, Topper* 1937; *Tarzan's Revenge, Thanks for the Memory* 1938; *Midnight, The Women, What a Life* 1939; *Queen of the Mob* 1940; *Life with Henry* 1941; *Reap the Wild Wind* 1942; *Breakfast in Hollywood* (as herself) 1946; *Sunset Boulevard* (as herself) 1950; *Pepe* (cameo) 1960; *The Oscar* (as herself) 1966.

Hopper, Jerry. Director. Born on July 29, 1907, in Guthrie, Okla. A former radio writer, he worked in films in various capacities, including casting and editing, before becoming a director early in the 50s. His films typically emphasize action. Since the 60s he has worked mostly for TV.

FILMS: *The Atomic City, Hurricane Smith* 1952; *Pony Express* 1953; *Alaska Seas, Secret of the Incas, Naked Alibi* 1954; *Smoke Signal, The Private War of Major Benson, One Desire, The Square Jungle* 1955; *Never Say Goodbye, Toy Tiger* 1956; *The Missouri Traveler* 1958; *Blueprint for Robbery* 1961; *Madron* (US/Isr.) 1970.

Hopper, Victoria. Actress. Born in 1909, in Vancouver, B.C., Canada. Popular leading lady of British films of the 30s. Married to Basil DEAN.

FILMS: *The Constant Nymph* 1933; *Lorna Doone* 1935; *Laburnum Grove, Whom the Gods Love/Mozart, The Lonely Road/Scotland Yard Commands* 1936; *The Mill on the Floss* 1937; *Escape from Broadmoor* 1948.

Hordern, Sir Michael. Actor. Born on Oct. 3, 1911, in Berkhampstead, England. *ed.* Brighton Coll. Balding, intelligent-looking character actor of many British and some American films, often typecast as a world-weary political or military leader. He was a teacher, textbook salesman, and amateur actor before his untutored professional stage debut in 1937. In films, with increasing prominence, from 1939. Knighted in 1983.

FILMS INCLUDE: *A Girl Must Live* 1939; *The Girl in the News* 1940; *School for Secrets* 1946; *Mine Own Executioner* 1947; *Passport to Pimlico* 1949; *Trio* 1950; *Scrooge/A Christmas Carol* (as Jacob Marley), *Tom Brown's School Days* 1951; *The Story of Robin Hood, The Card/The Promoter* 1952; *The Heart of the Matter* 1953; *The Beachcomber* 1954; *The Warriors/The Dark Avenger* (as Edward III; US/UK), *Storm Over the Nile, The Constant Husband* 1955; *Alexander the Great* (as Demosthenes; US), *The Man Who Never Was, The Baby and the Battleship, The Spanish Gardener* 1956; *Windom's Way* 1958; *Sink the Bismark!, Moment of Danger/Malaga, Man in the Moon* 1960; *El Cid* (US/It.) 1961; *Macbeth* (as Banquo; orig. shown on TV in 1960; US/UK), *Cleopatra* (as Cicero; US/UK), *The V.I.P.s* 1963; *The Yellow Rolls-Royce* 1964; *Genghis Khan* (US/UK/Ger.), *The Spy Who Came in from the Cold* 1965; *Cast a Giant Shadow* (US), *Khartoum, A Funny Thing Happened on the Way to the Forum* (US) 1966; *The Taming of the Shrew* (as Baptista; US/It.), *How I Won the War, The Jokers, I'll Never Forget What's 'is Name* 1967; *Where Eagles Dare, The Bed Sitting Room, Anne of the Thousand Days* 1969; *Girl Stroke Boy* 1971; *The Pied Piper, The Possession of Joel Delaney* (US) 1972; *Theatre of Blood, The Mackintosh Man, England Made Me* 1973; *Demons of the Mind, Up Pompeii* 1974; *Royal Flash, Mr. Quilp, Barry Lyndon* (off-screen narrator only), *Lucky Lady* (US) 1975; *The Slipper and the Rose* (as The King) 1976; *Joseph Andrews* 1977; *The*

Medusa Touch 1978; *Gandhi, The Missionary* 1982; *Yellowbeard* 1983; *Lady Jane, Labyrinth* 1986; *Comrades, The Trouble with Spies* (release delayed from 1984) 1987; *Dark Obsession/Diamond Skulls* 1989.

Horn, Camilla. Actress. Born on Apr. 25, 1906, in Frankfurt am Main, Germany. Beautiful blonde star of silent and sound German films. A former dancer, she was discovered by MURNAU and made her screen debut as Gretchen in his production of *Faust* (1926). She starred in several Hollywood films of the late 20s and later also appeared in British and Italian productions.

FILMS INCLUDE: *Faust* 1926; *Jugendrausch/Eva and the Grasshopper* 1927; *Tempest* (US) 1928; *Eternal Love* (US), *The Royal Box* (US) 1929; *Sonntag des Lebens* (German version of US film *The Devil's Holiday,*) *Die grosse Sehnsucht* 1930; *Das Lied der Nationen* 1931; *The Return of Raffles* (UK), *Der Frechedachs* 1932; *Matinee Idol* (UK), *The Love Nest* (UK), *Moral and Liebe, Rakoczy Marsch* 1933; *Luck of a Sailor* (UK), *Die grosse Chance, Der letzte Walzer, Wenn ich König wär/If I Were King, Ein Walzer für Dich* 1934; *Weisse Sklaven* 1936; *Fahrendes Volk, Rote Orchideen/Red Orchids* 1938; *Die letzte Runde* 1939; *Friedemann Bach* 1941; *Tragödie einer Liebe* 1942; *Intimitäten* 1944; *Vatti macht Dummheiten* 1953; *Heisses Spiel für harte Männer* 1968.

Hornbeck, William. Film editor. *b.* Aug. 23, 1901, Los Angeles. *d.* 1983. He entered films at age 15 as a lab assistant at Keystone and worked his way up to supervising editor of Mack Sennett's comedies. In 1934 he went to England, where he was put in charge of editing Alexander Korda productions. In this capacity he edited or supervised the editing of some of Britain's most prestigious films of the period. Returning to the US after the outbreak of WW II, he joined the US Army Pictorial Service of the Signal Corps with the rank of lieutenant colonel and, among other duties, supervised the editing of the entries in the famed "Why We Fight" series, which were made by such Hollywood directors as Frank Capra and Anatole Litvak. After the war, he edited a number of notable Hollywood productions, including George Stevens's *A Place in the Sun* (1951), for which he received an Academy Award. Named a Universal executive in 1960, he was appointed vice president in 1966.

FILMS INCLUDE (as editor or supervisor, alone or in collaboration): In the US—*Home Talent* 1921; *The Extra Girl* 1923; *The Goodbye Kiss* 1928; *Midnight Daddies* 1929; *Hypnotized* 1932. In the UK—*The Scarlet Pimpernel* 1934; *Sanders of the River* 1935; *The Ghost Goes West, Things to Come, Rembrandt* 1936; *The Man Who Could Work Miracles, Elephant Boy, Knight Without Armour, Dark Journey* 1937; *The Divorce of Lady X, The Drum/Drums* 1938; *The Four Feathers* 1939; *The Thief of Bagdad* (UK/US) 1940. In the US—*Jungle Book* 1942; *It's a Wonderful Life* 1946; *Singapore* 1947; *State of the Union* 1948; *The Heiress* 1949; *Riding High* 1950; *A Place in the Sun* 1951; *Something to Live For* 1952; *Shane* 1953; *The Barefoot Contessa* 1954; *Giant* 1956; *I Want to Live!, The Quiet American* 1958; *A Hole in the Head* 1959; *Suddenly Last Summer* 1960.

Hornblow, Arthur, Jr. Producer. *b.* Mar. 15, 1893, New York City. *d.* 1976. *ed.* Dartmouth Coll.; New York Law School. Shortly after being admitted to the New York bar in 1917, he saw WW I service as a lieutenant with counterespionage for US Intelligence. Upon discharge he began writing and producing for Broadway. In 1927 he went to Hollywood as a production supervisor for Sam Goldwyn and was appointed producer at Paramount in 1933. He moved to MGM in 1942 and became an independent producer in the mid-50s. He was the first husband (1936–42) of Myrna LOY. He authored six popular children's books in collaboration with his third wife, the former Leonora Schinasi.

FILMS INCLUDE: *The Pursuit of Happiness* 1934; *Mississippi, Ruggles of Red Gap* 1935; *The Princess Comes Across* 1936; *Easy Living, High Wide and Handsome* 1937; *Artists and Models Abroad* 1938; *Midnight, The Cat and the Canary* 1939; *The Ghost Breakers, Arise My Love* 1940; *Nothing But the Truth, Hold Back the Dawn, I Wanted Wings* 1941; *The Major and the Minor* 1942; *The Heavenly Body* 1943; *Gaslight* 1944; *Weekend at the Waldorf* 1945; *Desire Me, The Hucksters* 1947; *Cass Timberlane* 1948; *Conspirator, The Asphalt Jungle* 1950; *Remains to Be Seen* 1953; *Oklahoma!* 1955; *Witness for the Prosecution* 1957; *The War Lover* 1962.

Horne, James W. Director. *b.* Dec. 14, 1880, San Francisco. *d.* 1942. He entered films with Kalem in 1911, following stage experience as actor and director, and piloted features, serials, and a great many two-reelers, including Charlie Chase and Laurel and Hardy comedies for Hal Roach. Among his features were one Buster Keaton and three Laurel and Hardy vehicles. He ended his career as he had started it, as a serial specialist.

FILMS INCLUDE (complete from 1921): *The Accomplice, The Barnstormers, The Pitfall* (also act.) 1915; *Stingaree* (serial; also sc., act.) 1915–16; *Mystery of the Grand Hotel, Social Pirates* 1916; *Bull's Eye* (serial), *Hands Up* (serial) 1918; *The Midnight Man* (serial) 1919; *The Third Eye* (serial), *Occasionally Yours* 1920; *The Bronze Bell, Dangerous Pastime* 1921; *Don't Doubt Your Wife, The Forgotten Law, The Hottentot* 1922; *Can a Woman Love Twice, The Sunshine Trial, A Man of Action, Itching Palms, Blow Your Own Horn* 1923; *Alimony, The Yankee Consul, American Manners, Hail the Hero, In Fast Company, Stepping Lively, Laughing at Danger* 1924; *Youth and Adventure* 1925; *Kosher Kitty Kelly, The Cruise of the Jasper B* 1926; *College* 1927; *The Big Hop, Black Butterflies* 1928; *Big Business* (short) 1929; *Laughing Gravy* (short), *Our Wife* (short), *Beau Chumps* (short) 1931; *Any Old Port* (short), *Love Pains* (short) 1932; *Bonnie Scotland* 1935; *The Bohemian Girl* (co-dir. with Charles Rogers) 1936; *Way Out West, All Over Town* 1937; *The Spider's Web* (serial; co-dir. with Ray Taylor) 1938; *Flying G-Men* (serial; co-dir. with Taylor) 1939; *Deadwood Dick* (serial), *The Green Archer* (serial), *The Shadow* (serial), *Terry and the Pirates* (serial) 1940; *Holt of the Secret Service* (serial), *The Iron Claw* (serial), *The Spider Returns* (serial), *White Eagle* (serial) 1941; *Captain Midnight* (serial), *Perils of the Royal Mounted* (serial) 1942.

Horne, Lena. Singer, actress. Born on June 30, 1917, in Brooklyn, N.Y. Raised by her divorced actress mother, she spent much of her childhood on the road or with relatives. She dropped out of school at 16 to join the chorus at the Cotton Club in Harlem and eventually rose to stardom on the nightclub circuit as a popular singer of blues and ballads. An exotic, stunning-looking woman with a vibrant voice and electrifying personality, she was the first black performer to sign a long-term contract with a major Hollywood studio (MGM). But the studio carefully cast her in isolated guest spots in its musicals which could be easily excised when the films made the rounds in Southern markets. In the early 50s she found herself blacklisted by the movie and TV industries, possibly because of her close relationship with Paul ROBESON. She returned to the screen after a long absence in 1969, playing her first dramatic role, opposite Richard Widmark, in the Western *Death of a Gunfighter.* In the 80s she appeared on Broadway (Tony Award), then toured the globe with a triumphant one-woman show, 'Lena Horne: The Lady and Her Music.' In 1984 she was honored with a Lifetime Achievement ceremony at the Kennedy Center. In 1989 she made a rare television appearance on 'The Cosby Show.' Her daughter, actress Gail Jones, was at one time married to director Sidney LUMET. Memoirs (in collaboration): *In Person* (1951), *Lena* (1965).

FILMS: *The Duke Is Tops* 1938; *Panama Hattie* 1942; *Cabin in the Sky, Stormy Weather, I Dood It, Thousands Cheer, Swing Fever* 1943; *Broadway Rhythm, Two Girls and a Sailor* 1944; *Ziegfeld Follies, Till the Clouds Roll By* 1946; *Words and Music* 1948; *Duchess of Idaho* 1950; *Meet Me in Las Vegas* 1956; *Death of a Gunfighter* 1969; *The Wiz* (as Glinda) 1978.

Horner, Harry. Art director, director. *b.* July 24, 1910, in Holic, Czechoslovakia. *d.* 1994. Formerly an assistant to Max REINHARDT, he came to the US with the master and stayed to become a prominent art director and production designer, winning Academy Awards (in collaboration) for *The Heiress* (1949) and *The Hustler* (1961). As part of his WW II service he designed the Air Force spectacle 'Winged Victory.' His work as director is less impressive. Since the 60s, he has been active as a TV producer-director.

FILMS INCLUDE: As art director—*Our Town* 1940; *The Little Foxes* 1941; *Stage Door Canteen* 1943; *Winged Victory* 1944; *A Double Life* 1948; *The Heiress* 1949; *Born Yesterday* 1950; *He Ran All the Way* 1951; *Separate Tables* 1958; *The Wonderful Country* 1959; *The Hustler* 1961; *They Shoot Horses Don't They?* 1969; *Audrey Rose* 1977; *The Driver* 1978; *The Jazz Singer* 1980. As director—*Red Planet Mars, Beware My Lovely* 1952; *Vicki* 1953; *New Faces* 1954; *Life in the Balance* 1955; *Man from Del Rio, The Wild Party* 1956.

Horner, James. Composer. Born c. 1954 in Los Angeles, Calif. *ed.* Royal College of Music, London; USC; UCLA. Prolific composer/scorer of Hollywood films beginning in 1979 with sci-fi and thriller genres. He has developed into one of the leading film composers in Hollywood. His talent for creating arresting, memorable music continues to generate critical praise, earning five Academy Award nominations for the films *Aliens* (1986), *An American Tail* (1986), *Field of Dreams* (1989), *Apollo 13* (1995), and *Braveheart* (1995).

FILMS INCLUDE (partial list): *The Lady in Red* 1979; *Battle Beyond the Stars, Humanoids of the Deep* 1980; *Wolfen* 1981; *Star Trek II: The Wrath of Khan, 48 Hours* 1982; *Krull, Gorky Park, The Dresser, Testament, Uncommon Valor* 1983; *The Stone Boy* 1984; *Heaven Help Us, Cocoon, Commando, The Journey of the Natty Gann* 1985; *Aliens, The Name of the Rose* (W. Ger./It./Fr.)., *An American Tail* 1986; *Project X* 1987; *Willow, Red Heat* 1988; *Field of Dreams, Honey I Shrunk the Kids, Glory* 1989; *I Love You to Death* 1990; *Once Around, My Heroes Have Always Been Cowboys, Another 48 Hours, Class Action, The Rocketeer* 1991; *Thunderheart, Patriot Games, Sneakers, Unlawful Entry* 1992; *Bopha!, Hocus Pocus, Jack the Bear, The Man Without a Face, The Pelican Brief* 1994; *Clear and Present Danger, Pagemaster* 1994; *Apollo 13, Balto, Jumanji, Legends of the Fall* 1995; *Spitfire Grill, To Gillian on Her 37th Birthday, Ransom* 1996.

Horner, William George. Mathematician, inventor. *b.* 1786, Bristol, England. *d.* 1837. In 1834 he demonstrated his Daedalum (later to be known as Zoötrope or Zoetrope), a revolving drum with mounted stills which gave viewers the illusion of continuous motion.

horse. A simple device for racking up reels of film in the cutting room in order to wind or feed the film through the synchronizer or the viewing machine.

horse opera. Slang for a Western movie, usually applied to a standard B picture. Also known as "horse opry," "oater," or "sagebrusher."

Horton, Edward Everett. Actor. *b.* Mar. 18, 1886, Brooklyn, N.Y. *d.* 1970. *ed.* Oberlin Coll.; Columbia. The son of a *New York Times* proofreader, he made his professional stage debut in 1908 while a student at Columbia University, then sang with choruses and appeared in stock with increasing success. On screen from the early 20s, he played delightful comedy leads and character parts in some 150 films, typically as a jittery, befuddled, fussbudget with inimitable "Oh, dear!" doomsday utterances. He is fondly remembered as Fred ASTAIRE's sidekick in several musicals of the 30s and in Lubitsch's sophisticated comedies. Like the characters he often played, Horton never married.

FILMS INCLUDE: *Leave It to Me* (uncredited bit), *Too Much Business, The Ladder Jinx, A Front Page Story* 1922; *Ruggles of Red Gap* (title role), *To the Ladies* 1923; *Flapper Wives, Try and Get It* 1924; *Marry Me, Beggar on Horseback, The Business of Love* 1925; *La Boheme* (as Colline), *The Nut-Cracker, Poker Faces, The Whole Town's Talking* 1926; *Taxi! Taxi!* 1927; *The Terror* 1928; *Sonny Boy, The Hottentot, The Sap* 1929; *The Aviator, Take the Heir, Holiday, Once a Gentleman* 1930; *Reaching for the Moon, Kiss Me Again, Lonely Wives, The Front Page, Six Cylinder Love, Smart Woman, The Age for Love* 1931; *But the Flesh Is Weak, Trouble in Paradise* 1932; *A Bedtime Story, The Way to Love, Design for Living, It's a Boy* (UK), *Soldiers of the King/The Woman in Command* (UK), *Alice in Wonderland* (as the Mad Hatter) 1933; *Easy to Love, Kiss and Make-Up, Ladies Should Listen, The Merry Widow, The Gay Divorcee* 1934; *Biography of a Bachelor Girl, The Devil Is a Woman, In Caliente, Top Hat, His Night Out, Your Uncle Dudley* 1935; *The Singing Kid, The Man in the Mirror, Nobody's Fool, Hearts Divided* 1936; *Lost Horizon, The King and the Chorus Girl, Shall We Dance, Oh Doctor!, The Great Garrick, The Perfect Specimen, Angel* 1937; *Bluebeard's Eighth Wife, Holiday* 1938; *Paris Honeymoon* 1939; *Ziegfeld Girl, Sunny, Bachelor Daddy, Here Comes Mr. Jordan* 1941; *The Body Disappears, The Magnificent Dope, I Married an Angel, Springtime in the Rockies* 1942; *Thank Your Lucky Stars, The Gang's All Here* 1943; *Arsenic and Old Lace, Summer Storm, Brazil* 1944; *Lady on a Train* 1945; *Cinderella Jones* 1946; *Down to Earth, Her Husband's Affairs* 1947; *The Story of Mankind* (as Sir Walter Raleigh) 1957; *Pocketful of Miracles* 1961; *It's a Mad Mad Mad Mad World* 1963; *Sex and the Single Girl* 1964; *The Perils of Pauline* 1967; *2000 Years Later* 1969; *Cold Turkey* 1971.

Horton, Robert. Actor. Born on July 29, 1924, in Los Angeles. *ed.* U. of Miami; UCLA. Square-jawed, rugged TV star who had much less impact on films. He began appearing on stage following WW II service with the Coast Guard, then performed on radio and in live TV in the early days of the medium. He showed promise as a leading man and second lead of action-oriented films of the 50s, but his screen career never took off. First attracting attention in the short-lived series 'Kings Row' (1955–56), he soared in popularity as the star of the Western series 'Wagon Train' (1957–62) and 'A Man Called Shenandoah' (1965–66). His career evaporated in the 70s but in the 80s he appeared for a stint on the daytime soaper 'As the World Turns.' His first wife was actress Barbara Ruick.

FILMS: *The Tanks Are Coming* 1951; *Return of the Texan, Pony Soldier, Apache War Smoke* 1952; *Code Two, Bright Road, The Story of Three Loves, Arena* 1953; *Men of the Fighting Lady, Prisoner of War* 1954; *The Man Is Armed* 1956; *The Green Slime* 1969.

Hoskins, Bob. Actor. Born on Oct. 26, 1942, in Bury St. Edmunds, Suffolk, England. Squat (5' 6"), barrel-chested, plebeian-seeming, dynamic character star of British and international films. Raised in a cockney section of London, the son of a bookkeeper and a nursery-school aide, he dropped out of school at 15 and for nearly a decade wandered about, supporting himself with an odd variety of occupations, including a chimney sweep, nightclub bouncer, circus fire-eater, and fruit picker in an Israeli kibbutz. He later trained to become an accountant, but was panicked by the drudgery and turned to sculpting, painting, and poetry-writing. Accidentally stumbling on a theatrical audition, he amazingly got the part with no previous training or preparation, and before long found himself performing in prestigious productions of London's Royal Court and National Theatres, alongside John Gielgud and other thespian legends. A natural, spontaneous actor, he slipped into films with ease and rapidly worked his way up from supporting roles as a toughie to character leads of complexity and range. A keen ability to observe behavior and imitate accents allowed him to impersonate American characters in such Hollywood productions as *The Cotton Club* (1984), *Sweet Liberty* (1986), and *Who Framed Roger Rabbit* (1988). He was nominated for an Academy Award as best actor for his deeply moving portrayal of a romantic, small-time hood in *Mona Lisa* (1986). He directed his first film in 1989.

FILMS: *The National Health* 1973; *Royal Flash, Inserts* 1975; *Zulu Dawn* 1979; *The Long Good Friday* 1980; *Pink Floyd—The Wall* 1982; *The Honorary Consul/Beyond the Limit* 1983; *Lassiter, The Cotton Club* 1984; *Brazil* 1985; *Sweet Liberty, Mona Lisa* 1986; *A Prayer for the Dying, The Lonely Passion of Judith Hearne* 1987; *Who Framed Roger Rabbit?* 1988; *Raggedy Rawney* (also dir., co-sc.) 1989; *Heart Condition, Mermaids* 1990; *Shattered, Hook, The Inner Circle* 1991; *Blue Ice, The Favor the Watch and the Very Big Fish, Passed Away* 1992; *Super Mario Bros.* 1993; *Balto* (v/o), *Nixon* 1995; *Michael, The Secret Agent, Rainbow* (dir. only) 1996.

Hossein, Robert. Actor, director, screenwriter. Born Robert Hosseinoff, on Dec. 30, 1927, in Paris. Formerly a stage actor-director, he entered films in 1953 as actor and soon stepped in to fill the vacuum created by the absence of new directorial talent in French films of the mid-50s. He directed a number of violent melodramas, in all of which he also starred. His father, composer André Hossein, scored some of these films. Robert's earlier films showed some creative originality, but he later settled for commercial routine. His work as an actor, typically as a dark-souled villain, has been more consistent in quality.

FILMS INCLUDE: As actor—*Quai des Blondes* 1954; *Série noire, Du Rififi chez les Hommes/Rififi* 1955; *Crime et Châtiment/Crime and Punishment* (as Raskolnikov) 1956; *Sait-on jamais, Méfiez-vous Fillettes/Young Girls Beware* 1957; *La Sentence, Du Rififi chez les Femmes/Riff Raff Girls, Les Canailles* 1959; *La Menace* 1960; *Les Petits Matins, Madame Sans-Gêne/Madame* 1961; *Le Repos du Guerrier/Love on a Pillow* 1962; *Le Vice et la Vertu/Vice and Virtue, Le Meurtrier/Enough Rope, Les Grands Chemins/Of Flesh and Blood, Chair de Poule/Highway Pickup* 1963; *Angélique Marquise des Anges* 1964; *Guerre secrète/The Dirty Game, La Fabuleuse Aventure de Marco Polo/Marco the Magnificent* 1965; *La Longue Marche, La Musica* 1966; *Le Casse/The Burglar* 1971; *Helle* 1972; *Don Juan 1973/Si Don Juan était une Femme/Ms. Don Juan, Le Prolecteur, Un Officier de Police sans Importance* 1973; *Démons de Midi* 1979; *Les Uns et les Autres/Bolero* 1981; *Un Homme et une Femme: Vingt Ans Déja/A Man and a Woman: 20 Years Later* 1986; *Levy et Goliath* 1987; *Children of Chaos* 1989. As director-screenwriter-actor—*Les Salauds vont en Enfer/The Wicked Go to Hell* 1955; *Pardonnez-nous nos Offenses* 1956; *Toi le Venin/Nude in a White Car, La Nuit des Espions/Night Encounter* 1959; *Les Scélérats* 1960; *Le Goût de la Violence, Le Jeu de la Vérité* 1961; *La Mort d'un Tueur* 1963; *Les Yeux cernés, Le Vampire de Düsseldorf* 1964; *J'ai tué Raspoutine/I Killed Rasputin* 1967; *Une Corde... un Colt* 1968; *Point de Chute* 1970; *Les Misérables* (also co-sc.) 1982; *Le Caviar Rouge* (also co-sc. from co-novel, act.) 1985; *L'Affaire* 1994.

hot frame. A frame at the beginning or end of a shot deliberately overexposed to produce a cue mark for synchronization with sound.

hot splice. A method of film splicing in which two clips of film are joined by use of cement and pressure contact with a splicer device. The emulsion on at least one of the clips must be scraped off to permit a strong bond. Hot splicing assures a permanent joint and is therefore used for splicing original negatives and release prints. An alternate method, called "tape splicing," utilizes clear adhesive tape and is used mostly for splicing clips of a work print during editing, when temporary splices are desired. The hot splice method results in the loss of half a frame when the two overlapping pieces of film are joined together. The tape splice, on the other hand, joins the two clips at the frame line.

hot splicer. A heavy-duty precision splicing machine that utilizes thermostatically controlled heat to obtain rapid drying of the cement in the splice.

hot spot. An area in a scene which is excessively lighted. It appears as an overexposed patch on the film image during projection.

Houdini, Harry. Magician, actor. *b.* Erich Weiss, Mar. 24, 1874, Budapest. *d.* 1926. The celebrated escape artist starred in several Hollywood silent action films, some of which he also produced. A romanticized version of his life story was told in the film *Houdini* (1953), starring Tony Curtis.

FILMS INCLUDE: *Deep Sea Loot* (?), *The Master Mystery* (serial), *The Grim Game* 1919; *Terror Island* 1920; *The Soul of Bronze* (also prod.) 1921; *The Man from Beyond* (also prod., story) 1922; *Haldane of the Secret Service* (also prod.) 1923.

Hough, John. Director. Born on Nov. 21, 1941, in London. Entering British films in 1960, he worked in the industry in several capacities, then began directing for TV, including episodes for the popular 'The Avengers' series. He turned out his first feature in 1971 and two years later moved to Hollywood, where, after a promising start, he became trapped in the minibudget rut.

FILMS: In the UK—*Wolfshead: The Legend of Robin Hood* (orig. intended as TV pilot) 1969; *Eyewitness/Sudden Terror, The Practice, Twins of Evil* 1971; *Treasure Island* 1972. In the US—*The Legend of Hell House* 1973; *Dirty Mary Crazy Larry* 1974; *Escape to Witch Mountain* 1975; *Return from Witch Mountain, Brass Target* 1978; *The Watcher in the Woods* 1980; *The Incubus* (Can.) 1982; *Triumphs of a Man Called Horse* 1983; *Biggles/Biggles Adventure in Time* (UK) 1986; *American Gothic* 1988; *Howling IV—The Original Nightmare* 1990.

Hou Hsiao-Hsien. Director. Born in 1947 in Meixiam Kuangtung Province, China. His family joined the exodus to Taiwan in 1948, and he spent his childhood in Hualien. After his discharge from the military in 1969 he studied film at the National Taiwan Arts Academy. In 1973 he began work as continuity director and later assistant director to Li Hsin, Lai Cheng-ying, and Chen Kun-hou, for whom he also wrote scripts. He made his directorial debut in 1980 with *Cute Girls. The Time to Live and the Time to Die* (1985), an autobiographical story of his family's adjustment to life in Taiwan, filmed at his childhood home and neighborhood, won the International Critics Award at the 1986 Berlin Film Festival. Hou continued exploring his concern over the displacement between city and country in 1986's *Dust in the Wind*, about a young couple who quit high school and move to Taipei, and 1987's *Daughter of the Nile*, about the disintegration of a family on the edge of Taipei as seen through the eyes of the daughter (which won a special jury award at the Torino Film Festival). Hou's international reputation rose even more with 1989's *A City of Sadness*, a national epic about the birth of Taiwan set between the end of World War II and mainland China's fall to the Communists in 1949, starring Hong Kong star Tony Leung.

FILMS INCLUDE: *Cute Girls* 1980; *Cheerful Wind* 1981; *Growing Up* 1982; *The Sandwich Man* ("The Son's Big Doll" episode) 1983; *The Boys from Fengkuei* 1983; *A Summer at Grandpa's, Taipei Story* (prod. and act. only) 1984; *The Time to Live and the Time to Die* 1985; *Dust in the Wind, Soul* (act. only) 1986; *Daughter of the Nile* 1987; *A City of Sadness* 1989.

Houseman, John. Producer, actor, stage and film writer, stage director. *b.* Jacques Haussmann, Sept. 22, 1902, in Bucharest, to an Alsatian father and an English mother. *d.* 1988. *ed.* Clifton Coll. (England). At 21 he went to Argentina as a representative of his father's grain business and two years later arrived in the US on a similar mission. But before long he began writing for magazines and translating plays for the stage from German and French. Financially broke after the Depression had ruined his grain business, he exploited social contacts to get to direct the Gertrude Stein–Virgil Thomson avant-garde opera 'Four Saints in Three Acts,' which he turned into a hit on Broadway in 1934. In the following year, he began a fruitful but stormy creative partnership with the brash, enormously talented Orson WELLES, then barely 20 years old. Together they formed WPA's Negro Theater Project (1935) and the Classical Theater (1936), which folded after their controversial production of Marc Blitzstein's proletarian musical 'The Cradle Will Rock.' Their most famous collaboration was the Mercury Theater, founded in 1937. Houseman directed or produced many of its productions, as well as programs for its offspring radio program 'Mercury Theater of the Air,' while at the same time teaching at Vassar. He was associated with Welles on the famous radio broadcast of 'War of the Worlds' and producer of Welles's never-completed first film, *Too Much Johnson* (1938). He was also instrumental in the packaging of Welles's masterpiece, *Citizen Kane* (1941). Although he received no screen credit for the effort, Houseman claimed to have developed the original story for the film with Herman MANKIEWICZ. The claim infuriated Welles and led to a lifelong rift between the two artists.

Following the breakup with Welles, Houseman joined David O. Selznick Productions. But within days after Pearl Harbor he quit to become chief of the overseas radio division of the OWI. Upon his return to Hollywood he became the producer of a long list of distinguished films and commuted to New York to produce and direct Broadway plays as well as TV specials, winning three Emmy Awards. In 1956–59 he was the artistic director of the American Shakespeare Festival, then of UCLA's Professional Theater Group. In 1967 he became director of the drama division at Juilliard, and in the early 70s he enjoyed great success with his touring repertory troupe, the Acting Company, of which he was the artistic director. Houseman, who played small roles in the unfinished *Too Much Johnson* (1938), *Ill Met by Moonlight* (1957), and *Seven Days in May* (1964), emerged surprisingly as a strong film actor in the early 70s, winning an Oscar as best supporting player for his portrayal of a stern Harvard law professor in *Paper Chase* (1973). He went on to re-create the character in the TV series of the same name (1978–79 and 1983–84) and performed admirably in many other films and television programs. An off-Broadway, Times Square–area theater was named after him in 1986. His first wife was actress Zita JOHANN. Houseman published three volumes of memoirs, *Run-Through* (1972), *Front and Center* (1979), and *Final Dress* (1983). A fourth volume, *Unfinished Business,* a distillation of the earlier books with new material, was published posthumously in 1988. He also authored *Entertainers and the Entertained* (1986).

FILMS: As screenwriter—*Citizen Kane* (uncredited co-story, script superv. only) 1941; *Jane Eyre* (co-sc.) 1944. As producer—*The Unseen* 1945; *Miss Susie Slagle's, The Blue Dahlia* 1946; *Letter from an Unknown Woman* 1948; *They Live by Night* 1949; *The Company She Keeps* 1951; *On Dangerous Ground, Holiday for Sinners, The Bad and the Beautiful* 1952; *Julius Caesar* 1953; *Executive Suite, Her Twelve Men* 1954; *Moonfleet, The Cobweb* 1955; *Lust for Life* 1956; *All Fall Down, Two Weeks in Another Town* 1962; *In the Cool of the Day* 1963; *This Property Is Condemned* 1966. As actor—*Ill Met by Moonlight/Night Ambush* (UK) 1957; *Seven Days in May* 1964; *Paper Chase* 1973; *I'm a Stranger Here Myself* (doc.), *Rollerball, Three Days of the Condor* 1975; *St. Ives* 1976; *The Cheap Detective* 1978; *Old Boyfriends* 1979; *The Fog, Wholly Moses, My Bodyguard, Bells/Murder by Phone* (Can.) 1980; *Ghost Story* 1981; *Bright Lights Big City, Another Woman, Scrooged* (as himself) 1988.

Houston, Donald. *b.* Nov. 6, 1923, in Tonypandy, South Wales. *d.* 1991. Blond, thickly built leading man and second lead of British films. In character roles from the early 70s. He married actress Brenda Hogan (*b.* 1928). His brother, Glyn Houston (*b.* Oct. 23, 1926, Tonypandy, South Wales), played character roles in numerous British films.

FILMS INCLUDE: *The Blue Lagoon, A Run for Your Money, Dance Hall* 1949; *The Red Beret/Paratrooper* 1953; *Doctor in the House* 1954; *Yangtse Incident/Battle Hell* 1957; *The Man Upstairs, Room at the Top* 1958; *The Mark* 1961; *The 300 Spartans* (US), *The Longest Day* (US) 1962; *Maniac, Doctor in Distress, Carry on Jack* 1963; *633 Squadron* (US/UK) 1964; *A Study in Terror/Fog* 1965; *The Viking Queen* 1967; *Where Eagles Dare* 1969; *My Lover My Son* (US/UK), *The Bushbaby* 1970; *Tales That Witness Murder* 1973; *Voyage of the Damned* 1976; *The Sea Wolves* 1980; *Clash of the Titans* 1981.

Houston, George. Actor, singer. *b.* 1898, Hampton, N.J. *d.* 1944. A graduate of Rutgers and Juilliard, he sang with the American Opera Company and in Broadway musicals before making his screen debut in 1935. He starred in a number of inexpensive musical films and played supporting roles in several major Hollywood dramas. In a sudden change of pacc, he donned cowboy garb in 1940 and for the next two years starred as "The Lone Rider" in a series of action-packed low-budget Westerns for PRC. He died of a heart attack shortly after the series ran its course.

FILMS INCLUDE: *The Melody Lingers On* 1935; *Let's Sing Again, Captain Calamity* 1936; *Wallaby Jim of the Islands, Conquest* 1937; *Blockade, Frontier Scout, The Great Waltz* 1938; *Laughing at Danger, The Howards of Virginia* 1940; *The Lone Rider in Ghost Town* 1941; *The Lone Rider in Cheyenne* 1942.

Houston, Whitney. Singer, actress. Born August 8, 1963, in Newark, N.J. An international popular music icon, this former model began an overwhelmingly successful singing career in the 80s, becoming one of the top-selling vocalists of all time. In her youth she was surrounded by music, singing in church with her mother, legendary gospel singer Cissy Houston, as well as growing up in the shadow of cousin Dionne Warwick's sensational rise to pop music stardom. With designs on becoming an actress, Houston started training and pursuing film roles. Greeted with tremendous box-office success for her first outing *The Bodyguard* (1992), she portrayed, appropriately enough, a pop music diva stalked by an obsessed fan. The combination of her raw talent as an actress with her undeniable vocal gifts and screen presence, put her on the map and opened the door to starring roles in major Hollywood films.

FILMS: *Perfect* (song only) 1985; *The Bodyguard* (also songs) 1992; *Waiting to Exhale* (also songs) 1995; *The Preacher's Wife* (also songs) 1996.

Hovick, Louise. See LEE, Gypsy Rose.

Howard, Cy. Screenwriter, director. *b.* Sept. 27, 1915, in Milwaukee. *d.* 1993. *ed.* U. of Minnesota; U. of Wisconsin. A former radio producer-director and writer of comedy material for the radio shows of Jack Benny, Danny Thomas, Milton Berle, and others, he entered films as co-scripter of the screen version of his play 'My Friend Irma' and its sequels. Later was executive producer with Desilu TV studios. Made his directorial debut in 1970 with an entertaining marital comedy, *Lovers and Other Strangers*. Once (1954–57) married to Gloria GRAHAME.

FILMS: As screenwriter—*My Friend Irma* 1949; *My Friend Irma Goes West* 1950; *That's My Boy* 1951; *Marriage on the Rocks* 1965; *Won Ton Ton—The Dog Who Saved Hollywood* 1976. As director—*Lovers and Other Strangers* 1970; *Every Little Crook and Nanny* (also co-sc.) 1972.

Howard, James Newton. Composer. A prolific musician, he has composed scores for over two dozen films in less than ten years. His original scores for *The Prince of Tides* (1991) and *The Fugitive* (1993) were nominated for Academy Awards, as were his music and lyrics for *Junior* (1994).

FILMS INCLUDE: *Tough Guys* 1988; *Everybody's All-American, Five Corners, Promised Land* 1988; *Major League, Tap* 1989; *Flatliners, Pretty Woman, Three Men and a Little Lady* 1990; *Grand Canyon, King Ralph, The Man in the Moon, My Girl, The Prince of Tides* 1991; *Diggstown, Glengarry Glen Ross, Night and the City* 1992; *Alive, American Heart, Dave, The Fugitive, The Saint of Fort Washington* 1993; *Junior, Wyatt Earp* 1994; *One Fine Day, Space Jam* 1996; *Father's Day, My Best Friend's Wedding, The Devil's Advocate* 1997.

Howard, John. Actor. *b.* John R. Cox, Jr., on Apr. 14, 1913, in Cleveland. *d.* 1995. The hero of many low-budget action films of the 30s and 40s, including several well-made Bulldog Drummond episodes in the late 30s. A Phi Beta Kappa graduate of Ohio's Western Reserve University, he appeared on the stage in Cleveland before his 1935 screen debut. In addition to the many B pictures in which he starred, he appeared occasionally in secondary roles in major productions, memorably as Ronald Colman's brother in *Lost Horizon* (1937) and as Katharine Hepburn's rich fiancé in *The Philadelphia Story* (1940). Since the 50s mostly on TV and in character roles. A real-life hero in WW II, he was awarded the Navy Cross and the Croix de Guerre for valor. Not to be confused with an American film editor or an Australian actor who go by the same name.

FILMS INCLUDE: *Annapolis Farewell, Four Hours to Kill* 1935; *Soak the Rich, 13 Hours by Air, Border Flight, Valiant Is the Word for Carrie* 1936; *Let Them Live, Lost Horizon, Bulldog Drummond Comes Back, Hold 'em Navy* 1937; *Penitentiary, Bulldog Drummond's Peril, Touchdown Army* 1938; *Arrest Bulldog Drummond!, Grand Jury Secrets* 1939; *Green Hell, The Man from Dakota, The Philadelphia Story* 1940; *The Invisible Woman, The Mad Doctor, Texas Rangers Ride Again* 1941; *Submarine Raider, The Undying Monster, Isle of Missing Men* 1942; *Love from a Stranger* 1947; *I Jane Doe* 1948; *The Fighting Kentuckian* 1949; *Radar Secret Service* 1950; *Models Inc.* 1952; *The High and the Mighty* 1954; *The Unknown Terror* 1957; *Destination Inner Space* 1966; *The Destructors* 1968; *Buck and the Preacher* 1972.

Howard, Kathleen. Actress. *b.* 1879, Canada. *d.* 1956. Sang with the Metropolitan Opera (1916–28) and other opera companies throughout the world. A contributor to major magazines, she became fashion editor of *Harper's Bazaar* in 1928, also serving as president of the magazine publisher's "Fashion Group." In films from 1934, she played many character roles. Best remembered as W. C. FIELDS's mate in *It's a Gift* (1934) and *The Man on the Flying Trapeze* (1935).

FILMS INCLUDE: *Death Takes a Holiday, You're Telling Me, One More River, It's a Gift* 1934; *The Man on the Flying Trapeze* 1935; *Stolen Holiday* 1937; *First Love* 1939; *Young People, Mystery Sea Raider, One Night in the Tropics* 1940; *Blossoms in the Dust* 1941; *Ball of Fire, You Were Never Lovelier* 1942; *Crash Dive* 1943; *Laura* 1944; *Shady Lady* 1945; *Centennial Summer* 1946; *The Late George Apley, Cynthia* 1947; *The Bride Goes Wild, Cry of the City* 1948; *The Petty Girl, Born to Be Bad* 1950.

Howard, Ken. Actor. Born on Mar. 28, 1944, in El Centro, Calif. *ed.* Yale. Handsome blond leading man of Hollywood films of the 70s. He began appearing on Broadway in 1967, while still attending the Yale Drama School, and won a Tony Award as best supporting actor for 'Child's Play' in 1970, the year of his screen debut. He portrayed Thomas Jefferson in both the stage and screen versions of the musical '1776.' But it was on TV that he has enjoyed his best success, primarily in the series 'The White Shadow' (1978–81), in which he banked on his height and athletic experience at high school and college to play the role of a basketball coach.

FILMS INCLUDE: *Tell Me That You Love Me Junie Moon* 1970; *Such Good Friends* 1971; *The Strange Vengeance of Rosalie, 1776* (as Thomas Jefferson) 1972; *Independence* (Bicentennial short; again as Jefferson) 1976; *Second Thoughts* 1983; *Challenge the Wind* (also co-prod., co-sc.) 1990; *Oscar* 1991; *The Net* 1995.

Howard, Leslie. Actor, director, producer. *b.* Leslie Howard Stainer, Apr. 24, 1893, in London, to Hungarian immigrants. *d.* 1943. *ed.* Dulwich Coll. Suffering from shell shock during WW I action on the Western front, he was encouraged to take up acting as therapy. Having appeared in a short film, *The Heroine of Mons,* in 1914, he made his professional stage debut in London. But it was in the US, first on the stage, then in films, that he became established as a star. Blond, blue-eyed, and extremely charming, he represented the perfect Englishman to American audiences, a combination of romantic poet and incisive intellectual. During the 30s he co-starred with some of Hollywood's most glamorous leading ladies in a succession of popular films, occasionally also appearing in British pictures. At the outbreak of WW II he returned to England, where he began directing and producing films in addition to his acting. In 1943, while he was flying back to London from a secret mission to Lisbon, his plane was shot down by Nazi raiders, who erroneously had suspected that Winston Churchill was among its passengers. He was the father of Ronald HOWARD. A brother, Arthur Howard (*b.* 1910), played character roles in British films. His daughter, Leslie Ruth Howard, wrote a loving biography, *A Quite Remarkable Father* (1959).

FEATURE FILMS (as actor): In the UK—*The Happy Warrior* 1917; *The Lackey and the Lady* 1919. In the US—*Outward Bound* 1930; *Never the Twain Shall Meet, A Free Soul, Five and Ten, Devotion* 1931; *Service for Ladies/Reserved for Ladies* (UK), *Smilin' Through, The Animal Kingdom* 1932; *Secrets, Captured, Berkeley Square* 1933; *The Lady Is Willing* (UK), *Of Human Bondage* (as Philip Carey), *British Agent* 1934; *The Scarlet Pimpernel* (UK) 1935; *The Petrified Forest, Romeo and Juliet* (as Romeo) 1936; *It's Love I'm After, Stand-In*

1937; *Pygmalion* (as Henry Higgins; also co-dir. with Anthony Asquith; UK) 1938; *Intermezzo—A Love Story* (also assoc. prod.), *Gone With the Wind* (as Ashley Wilkes) 1939. In the UK—*Pimpernel Smith/Mister V* (also dir., prod.), *The 49th Parallel/The Invaders, From the Four Corners* (short) 1941; *The First of the Few/Spitfire* (also dir., prod.) 1942; *The Lamp Still Burns* (prod. only), *The Gentle Sex* (co-dir. only, with Maurice Elvey) 1943.

Howard, Moe, Shemp, and **Curly.** See STOOGES, THE THREE.

Howard, Ron. Actor, director, producer. Born on Mar. 1, 1953, in Duncan, Okla. *ed.* USC. Child star of TV and films who went on to become one of Hollywood's hottest directors. He made his professional debut as Ronny Howard at age two, appearing with his parents, Rance and Jean Howard, in a Baltimore stage production of 'The Seven Year Itch.' He made his first screen appearance in *Frontier Woman* (1956) and in the next few years played child roles in several other Hollywood productions. Although he rated himself as "kind of dull," the blond, clean-cut youngster won great popularity on TV, playing Opie Taylor in the series 'The Andy Griffith Show' (1960–68) and Richie Cunningham in 'Happy Days' (1974–80). He returned to the screen in the early 70s as a young leading man and played a memorable role in George Lucas' *American Graffiti* (1973). It was his last film as Ronny Howard. Thereafter he would be billed as Ron. In 1977 he directed his first film, *Grand Theft Auto,* from a script co-written with his father. He turned to directing full time in the 80s and in the second half of the decade scored a string of box-office hits, including *Splash* and *Parenthood.* With longtime friend Brian GRAZER, he formed Imagine Films Entertainment, one of the most successful independent production companies in the business. Married to his high-school sweetheart, Cheryl, and a father of four, Howard now lives and edits his films in Connecticut, far from the Hollywood glare. His younger brother, Clint Howard (*b.* Apr. 20, 1959, Burbank, Calif.) is a TV and film actor from early childhood.

FILMS: As actor—*Frontier Woman* 1956; *The Journey* 1959; *Five Minutes to Live* 1961; *The Music Man* 1962; *The Courtship of Eddie's Father* 1963; *Village of the Giants* 1965; *The Wild Country* 1971; *American Graffiti, Happy Mother's Day—Love George* 1973; *The Spikes Gang* 1974; *Eat My Dust!, The Shootist* 1976; *More American Graffiti* 1979. As director—*Grand Theft Auto* (also co-sc., act.) 1977; *Leo and Loree* (exec. prod. only) 1980; *Night Shift* 1982; *Splash* 1984; *Cocoon* 1985; *Gung Ho* (also exec. prod.) 1986; *No Man's Land* (co-exec. prod only) 1987; *Willow, Vibes* (exec. prod. only), *Clean and Sober* (exec. prod. only) 1988; *The 'Burbs* (co-exec. prod. only), *Parenthood* (also co-story) 1989; *Kindergarten Cop* (co-exec. prod. only), *Closet Land* (exec. prod. only) 1990; *Backdraft* 1991; *Far and Away* (also co-prod., co-sc.) 1992; *The Paper* 1994; *Apollo 13* 1995; *Ransom* 1996.

Howard, Ronald. Actor. Born on Apr. 7, 1918, in Anerley, England. The son of Leslie HOWARD, to whom he bears a remarkable resemblance, he was a journalist and sailor before embarking on a career as a leading man in British films in the mid-40s. Later also Hollywood. Played Sherlock Holmes in a TV series.

FILMS INCLUDE: *Pimpernel Smith/Mister V* (bit) 1941; *While the Sun Shines, Night Beat* 1947; *Bond Street, My Brother Jonathan* 1948; *The Queen of Spades, Now Barabbas* 1949; *Double Confession, Portrait of Clare, Flesh and Blood* 1950; *The Browning Version* 1951; *Street Corner/Both Sides of the Law* 1952; *Drango* (US) 1957; *I Accuse!, Gideon's Day/Gideon of Scotland Yard* 1958; *No Trees in the Street, Babette s'en va-t-en Guerre/Babette Goes to War* (Fr.) 1959; *The Spider's Web* 1960; *The Naked Edge* (UK/US), *Come September* (US), *Murder She Said* 1961; *Bomb in the High Street, Siege of the Saxons* (as Edmund of Cornwall) 1963; *Week-end a Zuydcoote/ Weekend at Dunkirk* (Fr./It.), *The Curse of the Mummy's Tomb* 1964; *Africa—Texas Style!* (UK/US) 1967; *The Hunting Party* 1971; *Take a Hard Ride* (US) 1975.

Howard, Sidney. Playwright, screenwriter. *b.* 1891, Oakland, Calif. *d.* 1939. A Pulitzer Prize–winning dramatist, he wrote Hollywood screenplays alone and in collaboration from 1929. Several film versions were made from his play 'They Knew What They Wanted' (1928, 1930, 1940). It was also made into a successful Broadway musical, 'The Most Happy Fella' (1956).

FILMS INCLUDE: Based on his plays—*We're All Gamblers* 1927; *The Secret Hour* (from 'They Knew What They Wanted') 1928; *Ned McCobb's Daughter* 1929; *Free Love* (from 'Half Gods') 1930; *The Silver Cord, Christopher Bean* (from 'The Late Christopher Bean') 1933; *Yellow Jack* 1938; *They Knew What They Wanted* 1940. As screenwriter (alone or in collaboration)—*Bulldog Drummond, Condemned* 1929; *A Lady to Love* (from his own play 'They Knew What They Wanted'), *Raffles* 1930; *One Heavenly Night, Arrowsmith* 1931; *The Greeks Had a Word for Them* 1932; *Dodsworth* 1936; *Gone With the Wind, Raffles* (remake) 1939.

Howard, Trevor. Actor. *b.* Sept. 29, 1916, Cliftonville, Margate, England. *d.* 1988. *ed.* Clifton Coll. He made his London stage debut in 1934 while still training at the Royal Academy of Dramatic Art but did not gain much prominence until the mid-40s, after being invalided out of WW II service with the Royal Artillery. He made his first screen appearance in 1944, gaining stardom in the following year as the restrained romantic lead in David Lean's *Brief Encounter.* He rapidly developed a reputation as a reliable, polished performer whose understated style created believable, if often unexciting, characters. At first playing romantic leads, he gradually moved to heroic parts and finally to character roles with equal success. From the mid-50s he was seen frequently in Hollywood as well as British productions. He was nominated for an Oscar for his performance in *Sons and Lovers* (1960). He was married from 1944 to Helen Cherry (*b.* Nov. 24, 1915, Manchester, England), a gentle-mannered stage and screen actress who played leads and supporting roles in British and some American films from the late 40s.

FILMS: *The Way Ahead* 1944; *The Way to the Stars/ Johnny in the Clouds, Brief Encounter* 1945; *I See a Dark Stranger/The Adventuress, Green for Danger* 1946; *They Made Me a Fugitive/I Became a Criminal, So Well Remembered* 1947; *The Passionate Friends/One Woman's Story* 1948; *The Third Man, The Golden Salamander* 1949; *Odette, The Clouded Yellow* 1950; *Outcast of the Islands* 1951; *The Gift Horse/Glory at Sea* 1952; *The Heart of the Matter, La Mano dello Straniero/ The Stranger's Hand* (It./UK) 1953; *Les Amants du Tage/ Lovers' Net* (Fr.), *The Cockleshell Heroes* 1955; *Run for the Sun* (US), *Around the World in 80 Days* (US) 1956; *Interpol/Pickup Alley, Manuela/Stowaway Girl* 1957; *The Key, The Roots of Heaven* (US) 1958; *Moment of Danger/Malaga, Sons and Lovers* (as Walter Morel) 1960; *The Lion, Mutiny on the Bounty* (as Captain Bligh; US) 1962; *Man in the Middle* (UK/US) 1963; *Father Goose* (US) 1964; *Operation Crossbow* (UK/It.), *Von Ryan's Express* (US) *Morituri/The Saboteur: Code Name Morituri* (US) 1965; *The Poppy Is Also a Flower* (UK/US), *The Liquidator, Triple Cross* (UK/Fr.) 1966; *The Long Duel, Pretty Polly/A Matter of Innocence* 1967; *The Charge of the Light Brigade* (as Lord Cardigan) 1968; *Battle of Britain* 1969;

Twinky/Lola (UK/It.), *Ryan's Daughter* 1970; *The Night Visitor, Catch Me a Spy, Kidnapped, Mary Queen of Scots* (as William Cecil, Lord Burleigh) 1971; *Pope Joan* (as Pope Leo), *Something Like the Truth* 1972; *Ludwig* (as Richard Wagner; It.), *The Offence/The Offense, A Doll's House* (as Dr. Rank) 1973; *Craze, 11 Harrowhouse, Persecution/The Terror of Sheba* 1974; *Who?* (US), *Hennessy, Conduct Unbecoming* 1975; *The Bawdy Adventures of Tom Jones* (as Squire Western), *Whispering Death* (Ger./S. Afr.), *The Count of Monte Cristo, Aces High, Eliza Fraser* (Austral.) 1976; *Slavers* (Ger.), *The Last Remake of Beau Geste* (US) 1977; *Meteor* (US), *Stevie, Superman* (US) 1978; *Hurricane* (US) 1979; *Sir Henry at Rawlinson End, The Sea Wolves, The Shillingbury Blowers, Windwalker* (US) 1980; *Les Années Lumière/Light Years Away* (Fr./Switz.) 1981; *The Missionary, Gandhi* 1982; *Sword of the Valiant* (as King Arthur) 1984; *Dust* (Bel./Fr.) 1985; *Foreign Body* 1986; *White Mischief* 1987; *The Unholy, The Dawning* 1988.

Howard, William K. Director. *b.* June 16, 1899, St. Mary's, Ohio, the son of Irish immigrants. *d.* 1954. *ed.* Ohio State (engineering and law). A former film salesman and movie theater manager, he went to Hollywood after returning from WW I service, and after a brief period of apprenticeship, he began directing movies in 1921. His silent films were mostly routine melodramas, light romances, Westerns, and action pictures, but following the critical success of the atmospheric *White Gold* (1927), he moved on to more ambitious productions. He was intermittently very successful with his sound films of the early 30s, notably with a solid version of *Sherlock Holmes* (1932); a well-handled flashback story of the rise and fall of a tycoon, starring Spencer Tracy, *The Power and the Glory* (1933), which is considered by many a forerunner of and model for *Citizen Kane;* and the breezy mystery-comedy *The Princess Comes Across* (1936), starring Carole Lombard. But many of his other films were less inspired. He directed two pictures in England in 1937 and after returning to Hollywood found major film assignments difficult to line up. After directing a number of low-budget productions he retired from the screen in the mid-40s.

FILMS: *Get Your Man* (co-dir. with George W. Hill), *Play Square, What Love Will Do* 1921; *Deserted at the Altar* (co-dir. with Al Kelley), *Extra! Extra!, Lucky Dan, Captain Fly-by-Night* 1922; *The Fourth Musketeer, Danger Ahead, Let's Go* 1923; *The Border Legion, East of Broadway* 1924; *The Thundering Herd, Code of the West, The Light of Western Stars* 1925; *Red Dice, Bachelor Brides, Volcano, Gigolo* 1926; *White Gold, The Main Event* 1927; *A Ship Comes In, The River Pirate* 1928; *The Valiant, Love Live and Laugh, Christina* 1929; *Good Intentions* (also story, co-dial.), *Scotland Yard* 1930; *Don't Bet on Women, Transatlantic, Surrender* 1931; *The Trial of Vivienne Ware, The First Year, Sherlock Holmes* 1932; *The Power and the Glory* 1933; *This Side of Heaven, The Cat and the Fiddle, Evelyn Prentice* 1934; *Vanessa: Her Love Story, Rendezvous, Mary Burns—Fugitive* 1935; *The Princess Comes Across* 1936; *The Squeaker/Murder on Diamond Row* (UK), *Fire Over England* (UK) 1937; *Back Door to Heaven* (also prod., sc.) 1939; *Money and the Woman* 1940; *Bullets for O'Hara* 1941; *Klondike Fury* 1942; *Johnny Come Lately* 1943; *When the Lights Go on Again* 1944; *A Guy Could Change* (also assoc. prod.) 1946.

Howe, James Wong. Director of photography. *b.* Wong Tung Jim, Aug. 28, 1899, Kwantùng (Canton), China. *d.* 1976. In the US from age five, he was raised in the Northwest and for a while pursued a career as a professional boxer. Moving to Los Angeles, he became a delivery boy for a commercial photographer. He entered films in 1917, quickly graduating from cutting-room helper to slate boy (for De Mille) and assistant cameraman. He became a director of photography in 1922 and soon gained a reputation as an inventive and meticulous lighting cameraman. He was initially known as James Howe until MGM Publicity decided to add an exotic note to his image by putting the Chinese name Wong in the credits. In industry circles, he was nicknamed Low Key for his penchant for low-key photography. His low-key style helped establish the distinctive look of Warner Bros. pictures of the 40s. Howe, who hand-held cameras and used deep focus long before these techniques became fashionable, is one of the few Hollywood cameramen known by name to the general public. He won Academy Awards for the photography of *The Rose Tattoo* and *Hud.* He directed, but did not photograph, *Go, Man, Go* (1954), a feature film about the Harlem Globetrotters, and co-directed *The Invisible Avenger* (1958) with John Sledge.

FILMS INCLUDE: *Drums of Fate, The Trail of the Lonesome Pine, The Spanish Dancer, The Call of the Canyon* 1923; *The Alaskan, The Breaking Point, Peter Pan* 1924; *The Charmer, The Best People* 1925; *Sea Horses, Mantrap* 1926; *The Rough Riders, Sorrell and Son* 1927; *Laugh Clown Laugh, Four Walls* 1928; *Desert Nights* 1929; *Today* 1930; *Transatlantic, The Criminal Code, The Spider, The Yellow Ticket* 1931; *After Tomorrow, Chandu the Magician* 1932; *Hello Sister/Walking Down Broadway, The Power and the Glory* 1933; *Viva Villa!* (co-phot.), *The Thin Man, Manhattan Melodrama* 1934; *Mark of the Vampire* 1935; *Fire Over England* (UK), *Under the Red Robe* (UK), *The Prisoner of Zenda* 1937; *The Adventures of Tom Sawyer, Algiers* 1938; *They Made Me a Criminal, The Oklahoma Kid, Daughters Courageous* 1939; *Abe Lincoln in Illinois, Dr. Ehrlich's Magic Bullet, Torrid Zone, City for Conquest, A Dispatch from Reuters* 1940; *Strawberry Blonde, Shining Victory* 1941; *Kings Row, Yankee Doodle Dandy* 1942; *Hangmen Also Die, Air Force* 1943; *Passage to Marseilles* 1944; *Objective Burma!, Confidential Agent* 1945; *Nora Prentiss, Pursued, Body and Soul* 1947; *The Baron of Arizona* 1950; *The Brave Bulls* (co-phot.), *He Ran All the Way* 1951; *Come Back Little Sheba* 1953; *The Rose Tattoo* 1955; *Picnic* 1956; *The Sweet Smell of Success* 1957; *The Old Man and the Sea* 1958; *Bell Book and Candle, The Last Angry Man* 1959; *Song Without End* 1960; *Hud* 1963; *The Outrage* 1964; *Seconds* 1966; *Hombre* 1967; *The Heart Is a Lonely Hunter* 1968; *The Molly Maguires* 1970; *Funny Lady* 1975.

Howell, C. Thomas. Actor. Born on Dec. 7, 1966, in Los Angeles. Sincere, clean-cut, all-American-type juvenile player, then young leading man of Hollywood films. A former child performer and junior rodeo circuit champion. Billed as Tom Howell in his 1982 debut film, *E.T.* Married to actress Rae Dawn CHONG.

FILMS: *E.T.: The Extra Terrestrial* 1982; *The Outsiders* 1983; *Grandview U.S.A., Red Dawn, Tank* 1984; *Secret Admirer* 1985; *The Hitcher, Soul Man* 1986; *A Tiger's Tale, Young Toscanini* (It.) 1988; *Side Out, Far Out Man* (as himself), *Kid* 1990; *Breaking the Rules, First Force, One Hot Summer* 1991; *Nickel & Dime* 1992; *Gettysburg, That Night* 1993; *Acting on Impulse, Jailbait, Playback, Treacherous* 1994; *Mad Dogs and Englishmen* 1995.

Howerd, Frankie. Actor. *b.* Francis Howard, Mar. 6, 1921, in York, England. *d.* 1992. Eccentric comedy star of the British stage, TV, and films. A former insurance clerk, he first exercised his comic talent entertaining troops during his WW II service with the Royal Artillery. After returning to civilian life, he began performing professionally in London revues and light stage plays, gained popularity in radio and later on TV and in films. He starred in his own TV program, 'The Frankie Howerd Show,' and was a regular on such shows as 'That Was the Week That Was' and 'Up Pompeii.' He was said to be the favorite comedian of Britain's Queen Mother. Autobiography: *On My Way I Lost It* (1977).

FILMS INCLUDE: *The Runaway Bus* 1954; *The Ladykillers* 1955; *A Touch of the Sun* 1956; *Further Up the Creek* 1958; *The Cool Mikado* 1963; *The Great St. Trinian's Train Robbery* 1966; *Carry on Doctor* 1968; *Up Pompeii* 1970; *Up the Chastity Belt* 1971; *The House in Nightmare Park/Crazy House* 1973; *Sgt. Pepper's Lonely Hearts Club Band* (US) 1978.

Howes, Bobby. See HOWES, Sally Ann.

Howes, Reed. Actor. *b.* 1900, Washington, D.C. *d.* 1964. One of the silent screen's handsomest heroes who turned villain in Westerns and serials of the sound era. After studies at the University of Utah, he attended courses at Harvard and in the early 20s became famous as the "Arrow Collar Man" for his many modeling assignments for the shirt company. He made his film debut in 1923 and for a decade played dashing romantic heroes, often in action melodramas, opposite some of the screen's most glamorous stars. His popularity declined after the advent of sound and after leads in a number of low-budget productions he was reduced to supporting roles.

FILMS INCLUDE: *The Broken Violin, High Speed Lee* 1923; *The Cyclone Rider, Lightning Romance* 1924; *The Snob Buster, Courageous Fool, Youth's Gamble, Bobbed Hair, Bashful Buccaneer* 1925; *Danger Quest, The Self Starter, Racing Romance, Moran of the Mounted, The High Flyer, Kentucky Handicap, Wings of the Storm, The Night Owl* 1926; *The Scorcher, Rough House Rosie, Romantic Rogue, The Royal American* 1927; *A Million for Love, Ladies' Night in a Turkish Bath, Hellship Bronson, The Sawdust Paradise, The Singing Fool, Fashion Madness* 1928; *Stolen Kisses, Come Across* 1929; *Clancy in Wall Street, Terry of the Times* (serial), *Sheer Luck* 1930; *Anybody's Blonde, Hell Divers* 1931; *Devil on Deck* 1932; *Paradise Canyon, Dawn Rider* 1935; *The Clutching Hand* (serial), *Custer's Last Stand* (serial) 1936; *Zorro Rides Again* (serial) 1937; *Dick Tracy Returns* (serial) 1938; *Six-Gun Rhythm, Buck Rogers* (serial) 1939; *Texas Terrors* 1940; *Fugitive Valley* 1941; *Wild Horse Stampede* 1943; *Under Arizona Skies* 1946; *My Dog Shep* 1948; *The Walking Hills* 1949; *Gunslingers* 1950; *Stage to Tucson* 1951; *Hangman's Knot* 1952; *The Stranger Wore a Gun* 1953; *Sierra Baron* 1958; *Gunfighters of Abilene* 1960; *The Sinister Urge* 1961.

Howes, Sally Ann. Actress, singer. Born on July 20, 1930, in London. Daughter of Bobby Howes (1895–1972). Bouncy star of British film musicals of the 30s, she started her career as a child star in the 40s. She returned to films in occasional adult roles after success on the stage and on TV in both the UK and the US.

FILMS: *Thursday's Child* 1943; *Halfway House* 1944; *Pink String and Sealing Wax, Dead of Night* 1945; *Nicholas Nickleby* (as Kate Nickleby) 1947; *Anna Karenina* (as Kitty Shtcherabatskaya), *The History of Mr. Polly, My Sister and I* 1948; *Fools Rush In* 1949; *Stop Press Girl* 1950; *Honeymoon Deferred* 1951; *The Admirable Crichton/Paradise Lagoon* 1957; *Chitty Chitty Bang Bang* 1968; *Death Ship* (Can.) 1980.

Hoxie, Jack. Actor. *b.* Jan. 24, 1885, Kingfish Creek, near Guthrie, Okla. *d.* 1965. Popular cowboy star of numerous Hollywood silents and a number of early talkies. A former rodeo performer, he entered films in 1914 as an extra and bit player and began playing leads in serials and Westerns two years later. Tall, husky, and square-jawed, he looked impressive in his role as a cowboy hero, but contemporary critics thought little of his acting ability. His popularity reached its peak in the mid-20s, when he starred in many fast-paced oaters for Universal, but his career had declined sharply by the advent of sound. His wife, Marin Sais, co-starred in many of his films. His brother, Al Hoxie, also starred in Westerns but never attained Jack's success.

FILMS INCLUDE: *Captain Courtesy* 1915; *Nan of Music Mountain* 1917; *Lightning Bryce* (serial) 1919; *Thunderbolt Jack* (serial), *The Man from Nowhere* 1920; *Dead or Alive, The Sheriff of Hope Eternal, Cupid's Brand, Devil Dog Dawson, Hills of Hate* 1921; *Two-Fisted Jefferson, A Desert Bridegroom, The Crow's Nest, Back Fire, Riders of the Law* 1922; *The Forbidden Trail, Don Quickshot of the Rio Grande, Where Is This West?, Men in the Raw, The Red Warning* 1923; *The Man from Wyoming, The Phantom Horseman, Fighting Fury, The Western Wallop* 1924; *The Sign of the Cactus, A Roaring Adventure, Don Dare Devil, The Red Rider* 1925; *The Demon, The Border Sheriff, The Fighting Peacemaker, The Last Frontier* (as Buffalo Bill) 1926; *Rough and Ready, The Western Whirlwind, Grinning Guns, Heroes of the Wild* (serial), *The Fighting Three* 1927; *The Phantom Express* 1932; *Trouble Buster, Gun Law* 1933.

Hoyt, Harry O. Director, screenwriter *b.* Aug. 6, 1891, Minneapolis. *d.* 1961. *ed.* U. of Minnesota; Columbia; Yale. Began writing original stories for the screen while still a student at Yale and continued collaborating on screenplays after becoming a lawyer. He turned to screenwriting full time in 1916. Making his debut as a director early in 1919, he continued writing for other filmmakers throughout his career. The many silent films and few early talkies he piloted were mostly routine melodramas. He remains best known as the director of *The Lost World* (1925), an influential science-fiction adventure saga famous for its pioneering stop-motion animation and other special effects.

FILMS INCLUDE (as director): *The Hand Invisible, Through the Toils* (also sc.), *Broadway Saint, The Forest Rivals* (also sc.) 1919; *The Rider of the King Log* 1921; *The Curse of Drink* (also sc.), *That Woman* 1922; *The Woman of the Jury, The Law Demands, Fangs of the Wolf, Sundown* (co-dir. with Laurent Trimble), *The Radio Flyer, The Fatal Plunge* 1924; *When Love Grows Cold* (also sc.), *The Lost World, The Primrose Path, The Unnamed Woman* 1925; *The Belle of Broadway* 1926; *Bitter Apples* (also sc.), *The Return of Boston Blackie* 1927; *The Passion Song* 1928; *Darkened Skies* (co-dir. with Harry Webb) 1930; *Jungle Bride* (co-dir. with Albert Kelly) 1933.

Hoyt, John. Actor. *b.* Oct. 5, 1904, in Bronxville, N.Y. *d.* 1991. Assertive, gaunt character player of the American screen. A former history and drama teacher, he entered films following WW II military service. He typically played Nazis, master criminals, and mad scientists, but occasionally gentler, thoughtful men. In the 80s he played Grandpa Stanley Kanisky in the TV series 'Gimme a Break.'

FILMS INCLUDE: *O.S.S.* 1946; *My Favorite Brunette, The Unfaithful, Brute Force* 1947; *To the Ends of the Earth, Winter Meeting, Sealed Verdict* 1948; *The Bribe, The Lady Gambles, Everybody Does It, Trapped* 1949; *The Lawless* 1950; *The Desert Fox* (as Field Marshal Keitel) 1951; *When Worlds Collide* 1951; *Loan Shark* 1952; *Androcles and the Lion* (as Cato), *Julius Caesar* (as Decius Brutus), *Sins of Jezebel* (as the Prophet Elijah) 1953; *The Student Prince, Desiree* (as Talleyrand) 1954; *The Blackboard Jungle, The Big Combo, Moonfleet, Trial, The Girl in the Red Velvet Swing* 1955; *The Conqueror, Death of a Scoundrel* 1956; *Never So Few, Spartacus* 1960; *Cleopatra* (as Cassius), *X—The Man with the X-Ray Eyes* 1963; *Young Dillinger* 1965; *Duel at Diablo* 1966;

Panic in the City 1968; *Flesh Gordon* (soft-core porno) 1972; *In Search of Historic Jesus* 1980.

Hruba, Vera. See RALSTON, Vera Hruba.

Hrusinsky, Rudolf. Actor. Born Oct. 17, 1920, in Etynk, Czechoslovakia. Juvenile player, then leading man and character star of Czech stage and screen in a career spanning more than five decades. He directed the film, *Jarni Pisen* (1944), and co-directed *Pancho Takes a Wife* (1946).

FILMS INCLUDE: *Lizin le do Nebe* 1937; *Humoresque* 1939; *Night Moth* 1941; *Barara Hlasová* 1943; *Presentiment* 1947; *Unos* 1952; *Jan Hus* 1955; *Jan Zizka* 1956; *The Good Soldier Schweick* (title role) 1957; *A Compact with Death, Night Guest* 1960; *Fear, Hope, The Death of Tarzan* 1963; *90 Degrees in the Shade, How to Steal a Million* 1966; *Murder Czech Style* 1967; *Capricious Summer, The Cremators* 1968; *Those Wonderful Men with a Crank, Dinner for Adele/Nick Carter in Prague* 1978; *Short Cuts, Watch Out* 1980; *My Sweet Little Village* 1985; *It's All Right, Dear Comrades* 1990.

Hu, King. Director. *b.* Hu Chin-ch'üan, on Apr. 29, 1931, in the County of Yung-Nien, near Peking. *d.* 1997. *ed.* National Art Institute, Peking. The son of a mining engineer and an artist, he was visiting Hong Kong during the Communist takeover of China. With the borders closed, he was unable to return home and had to scrape for a living as a tutor, proofreader, and graphic artist. His painting of a poster for a movie theater led to his being hired as an art director by a Hong Kong film company. Before long, he was acting in films and eventually also writing screenplays. When the studio shut down, he moved on to broadcasting and during the mid-50s produced, wrote, and presented programs for the Voice of America. In 1958 he went to work as an actor and screenwriter for the Shaw Brothers (Run Run and Runme Shaw), Hong Kong's leading producers, whose company is among the world's most prolific and prosperous, a virtual factory of cheap, conventional melodramas and action pictures. Turning director in the early 60s, King Hu soon brought intelligence, imagination, and invention into some of these films. He helped popularize the martial arts genre by interjecting humor into the drama and pacing the action with the help of a choreographer. The brilliant images, authentic sets, and carefully orchestrated battle scenes attracted international attention to his best known period piece, *A Touch of Zen* (1969), winner of the technical superiority prize at the Cannes Festival.

FILMS (as director-screenwriter): *The Story of Sue Sen* (exec. dir. only) 1962; *Eternal Love* (assoc. dir. only) 1963; *Sons of the Good Earth* 1964; *Come Drink with Me* 1965; *Dragon Gate Inn* 1966; *A Touch of Zen* 1969; *The Four Moods* ("Anger" episode) 1970; *The Fate of Lee Khan* 1972; *The Valiant Ones* 1975; *Raining in the Mountains, Legend in the Mountains* 1979; *The Juvenizer* 1981; *All the King's Men, The Wheel of Life* (one episode) 1983; *The Boiling Sea* (anim.) 1985; *Swordsman* 1990.

Hubert, Jean-Loup. Director. Born on Oct. 4, 1949, in France. Up-and-coming director of French films. He made his debut in 1981 and scored his first critical and commercial success with *The Grand Highway* (1987), the touching story of a sensitive Parisian boy and his experiences in a rural household while his mother is hospitalized, giving birth. The boy was portrayed by the director's own son, Antoine, who was also featured in Hubert's next film, *After the War,* as was the director's younger son, Julien. Hubert writes his own scripts.

FILMS: *L'Année prochaine si tout va bien* 1981; *La Smala* 1984; *Le Grand Chemin/The Grand Highway* 1987; *Après la Guerre/After the War* 1983; *La Reine Blanche* 1991; *À Cause d'Elle* 1993.

Hubert, Roger. Director of photography. *b.* Mar. 30, 1903, Montreuil-sous-Bois, France. *d.* 1964. One of France's most highly regarded cameramen, he entered the motion picture industry in 1923 and collaborated with such directors as Gance, Feyder, Carné, and Cocteau, adapting his style to their individual aesthetic preferences.

FILMS INCLUDE: *Le Retour à la Vie* (also dir.) 1923; *Napoléon* (co-phot.) 1927; *La Chienne* 1931; *Fanny, Mater Dolorosa* 1932; *La Bataille/The Battle* 1933; *Pension Mimosas* 1934; *Jenny* 1936; *J'accuse* 1937; *Volpone, La Loi du Nord* 1939; *Les Visiteurs du Soir/The Devil's Envoy* 1942; *L'Eternel Retour/The Eternal Return* 1943; *Les Enfants du Paradis/Children of Paradise* 1944; *Gli Ultimi Giorni di Pompei/The Last Days of Pompeii* (It.) 1948; *Les Amants de Bras-Mort* 1950; *Nez-de-Cuir* 1951; *La Fête à Henriette/Holiday for Henrietta* 1952; *Thérèse Raquin/The Adulteress, La Rage au Corps/Tempest in the Flesh* 1953; *L'Air de Paris* 1954; *Thérèse Etienne* 1957; *La Fayette/La Fayette* (co-phot.) 1961; *La Bonne Soupe* 1964.

Hubley, John. Animator. *b.* May 21, 1914, Marinette, Wisc. *d.* 1977. *ed.* Art Center at Los Angeles. Began his film career in the employ of Walt Disney, working on such cartoon features as *Snow White, Pinocchio, Fantasia,* and *Bambi.* He made training films for the US Navy during WW II. He later joined UPA, where his work stood out for its superior quality. In 1949 he helped create the Mr. Magoo cartoon character, based on an uncle, and directed the first Magoo cartoon, *Ragtime Bear.* Gaining an international reputation as one of the most creative figures in the world of animation, he set up his own company, Storyboard Productions, in 1955 and created many intelligent, educational, and entertaining cartoons, for theatrical release as well as TV commercials. He won Oscars for the animated shorts *Moonbirds* (1959) and *The Hole* (1962). He directed the cartoon sequences in the feature *The Four Poster* (1952) as well as animated title sequences for several other features. His wife, Faith Hubley, has often collaborated on his films as producer, writer, and animator.

FILMS INCLUDE: *The Magic Fluke* 1945; *Robin Hoodlum* 1946; *Fuddy Duddy Buddy* 1949; *Trouble Indemnity* 1950; *Sloppy Jalopy* 1951; *The Four Poster* (animation sequence), *Rooty Toot Toot* 1952; *Adventures of an Asterisk* 1956; *Harlem Wednesday* 1958; *Seven Lively Arts* 1959; *Moonbird* 1960; *Of Stars and Men, The Hole* 1962; *The Hat* 1964; *The Year of the Horse* (animation sequences), *Gulliver's Troubles* 1967; *Uptight* (titles), *Of Men and Demons* 1971; *The Cosmic Eye* (anim.) 1985.

Hubley, Season. Actress. Born on May 14, 1951, in New York City. Blonde leading lady of American TV and scattered films. Formerly married to Kurt RUSSELL.

FILMS INCLUDE: *Lolly-Madonna Thirty/The Lolly Madonna War* 1973; *Catch My Soul* 1974; *Hardcore* 1979; *Escape from New York* 1981; *Vice Squad* 1982; *Prettykill* 1987; *Child in the Night* 1991.

Hubschmid, Paul. Actor. Born on July 20, 1917, in Schoenenwerd, Switzerland. Leading man of Swiss, German, and Austrian stage and screen since the late 30s, he also appeared in several Hollywood films in the late 40s and early 50s, using the name Paul Christian. Recently in character parts.

FILMS INCLUDE: *Füsilier Wipf* (Switz.) 1938; *Maria Ilona* (Ger.) 1939; *Der Fall Rainer* (Ger.) 1942; *Liebesbriefle* (Ger.) 1943; *Das Gesetz der Liebe* (Ger.) 1944; *Bagdad* (US), *The Thief of Venice* (US/It.) 1949; *No Time for Flowers* (US) 1952; *The Beast from 20,000 Fathoms* (US) 1953; *Ingrid* (Ger.) 1955; *Du bist Musik* (Ger.) 1956; *Scampolo* (Ger.), *La Morte viene dallo Spazio/The Day the Sky Exploded* (It./Fr.) 1958; *Heldinnen* (Ger.) 1960; *Il Tesoro di Rommel/Rommel's Treasure* (It.) 1962; *Das grosse Liebesspiel/And So to Bed* (Aus./Ger.)

1963; *Die Lady/Games of Desire* (Ger./Fr.) 1964; *Mozambique* (UK) 1965; *Playgirl/That Woman* (Ger.), *Funeral in Berlin* (UK) 1966; *Skullduggery* (US) 1970; *Versuchung in Sommerwind* (Ger.) 1973; *Klassezämekunft* (Switz.) 1988.

Hudlin, Reginald. Actor, director, screenwriter. Born December 15, 1961, in Centerville, Mo. *ed.* Harvard. Shortly after graduating from college, this bright filmmaker earned an Academy Award for his senior film project *House Party,* which later became his first full feature as a director. His obvious flair for comedy is fresh and evident in films such as *Boomerang* (1992) starring Eddie MURPHY. He and his brother Warrington Hudlin (*b.* 1953, in East St. Louis, Ill.) have their own production company.

FILMS: *She's Gotta Have It* (act. only) 1986; *House Party* (dir., sc., act.) 1990; *Boomerang* (dir., act.) 1992; *Posse* (act. only) 1993; *Bebe's Kids* (sc.), *The Great White Hype* (dir.) 1996.

Hudson, Ernie. Actor. Born December 17, 1945, in Benton Harbor, Mich. *ed.* Wayne State University; Yale School of Drama; University of Minnesota. Distinguished, solid player of the American stage, television, and film. With numerous guest starring roles on television, he is at his best on the big screen where his quiet strength and versatility have been used to their full potential.

FILMS: *The Main Event* 1979; *The Jazz Singer, The Octagon, Joni* 1980; *Penitentiary II* 1982; *Going Berserk, Spacehunter: Adventures in the Forbidden Zone, Two of a Kind* 1983; *Ghostbusters, The Joy of Sex* 1984; *Love on the Run, The Last Precinct* 1986; *Collision Course, Weeds* 1987; *The Wrong Guys* 1988; *Ghostbusters II, Leviathan* 1989; *The Hand That Rocks the Cradle* 1992; *Heart and Souls* 1993; *Airheads, The Cowboy Way, The Crow, No Escape, Speechless, Sugar Hill* 1994; *The Basketball Diaries, Congo* 1995; *The Substitute* 1996.

Hudson, Hugh. British director. An Eton graduate, he began his career as the head of the casting department of a London advertising agency. Later went to Paris, where he became a film editor. Returning to London, he established a partnership through which he turned out award-winning documentaries. In 1970 he teamed up with Ridley SCOTT in the production of TV commercials and in 1975 established his own production company, Hudson Films. He made an auspicious debut as a feature director with *Chariots of Fire,* an absorbing drama of drive, dedication, honor, and bigotry set against the background of the 1924 Summer Olympics. It won the Academy Award as best picture of 1981. After scoring a lesser success with a solemn, visually gratifying version of the Tarzan legend, Hudson seemed to be reaching an impasse in his career.

FILMS: *Chariots of Fire* 1981; *Greystoke: The Legend of Tarzan, Lord of the Apes* (also prod.) 1984; *Revolution* 1985; *Lost Angels* (US) 1989.

Hudson, Rochelle. Actress. *b.* Mar. 6, 1914, Oklahoma City, Okla. *d.* 1972. Sweet, innocent ingenue, then increasingly hard-boiled leading lady of Hollywood films of the 30s and early 40s, mostly B pictures. Later in occasional films. During WW II she worked for Naval Intelligence in Mexico and Central America with her first husband, a reserve officer. She married and divorced twice more and was a prosperous real estate broker.

FILMS INCLUDE: *Fanny Foley Herself, Are These Our Children?* 1931; *Hell's Highway, The Savage Girl* 1932; *She Done Him Wrong, Wild Boys of the Road, Love Is Dangerous, Doctor Bull, Mr. Skitch* 1933; *Judge Priest, Imitation of Life, The Mighty Barnum* 1934; *Life Begins at 40, Les Misérables* (as Cosette), *Curly Top, Way Down East, Show Them No Mercy* 1935; *The Music Goes 'Round, The Country Beyond, Poppy, Reunion* 1936; *Woman Wise, That I May Live, She Had to Eat, Born Reckless* 1937; *Rascals, Mr. Moto Takes a Chance, Storm Over Bengal* 1938; *Pride of the Navy, Missing Daughters* 1939; *Convicted Woman, Men Without Souls, Island of Doomed Men, Babies for Sale* 1940; *Meet Boston Blackie, The Officer and the Lady* 1941; *Rubber Racketeers* 1942; *Queen of Broadway* 1943; *Bush Pilot* 1947; *Devil's Cargo* 1948; *Rebel Without a Cause* 1955; *Strait-Jacket* 1964; *The Night Walker* 1965; *Dr. Terror's Gallery of Horrors/The Blood Suckers/Return from the Past* 1967.

Hudson, Rock. Actor. *b.* Roy Harold Scherer, Jr., Nov. 17, 1925, Winnetka, Ill. *d.* 1985. Tall (6' 4"), square-jawed, engagingly handsome star of Hollywood films of the 50s and 60s. The son of an auto mechanic and a telephone operator who divorced when he was eight, he tried out for roles in school plays but failed to win any. After graduating from high school, he was a Navy airplane mechanic during WW II. Returning to civilian life, he drove a truck, among other odd jobs, before breaking into films through the efforts of a persistent agent. He had never acted before, but his height and manly good looks made him a promising prospect. His name was changed from Roy Fitzgerald to the more vigorous-sounding Rock Hudson. His teeth were capped and he was coached intensively in acting, singing, dancing, fencing, and riding. He learned on the job. No less than 38 takes had to be filmed before he could successfully complete one line in his first picture, *Fighter Squadron* (1948). But he prevailed and by the mid-50s, after *Magnificent Obsession,* was among the leading stars on the Universal lot. In 1956 he was nominated for an Oscar for *Giant* and in 1958 he won *Look* magazine's award as Star of the Year. He was twice voted Hollywood's top box-office draw. In the 60s Hudson displayed a surprising gift for comedy, supplementing his repertoire of tearful melodramas and adventure films with glossy bedroom farces, often opposite Doris Day. In the 70s he starred on TV in the popular light police series 'McMillan and Wife' (1971–77). He started another series, 'The Devlin Connection,' in 1981, but its production was suspended for a year while Hudson was recovering from quintuple-bypass heart surgery. In 1984–85 he played a recurring role on the television series 'Dynasty.'

Throughout his career, Hudson epitomized wholesome manliness. In 1955 he married Nancy Gates, the secretary of his agent, Henry Wilson. The union lasted three years. His death at 59 of complications from AIDS astounded many of his fans, who were unaware of his homosexuality. His search for a cure focused worldwide attention on AIDS. He was the first major public figure to acknowledge openly that he was suffering from the disease. Posthumously published autobiography (in collaboration): *Rock Hudson: His Story* (1986).

FILMS: *Fighter Squadron* 1948; *Undertow* 1949; *I Was a Shoplifter, One Way Street, Winchester '73, Peggy, The Desert Hawk, Shakedown, Double Crossbones* 1950; *Tomahawk, Air Cadet, The Fat Man, The Iron Man, Bright Victory* 1951; *Here Come the Nelsons, Bend of the River, Scarlet Angel, Has Anybody Seen My Gal?, Horizons West* 1952; *The Lawless Breed, Seminole, Sea Devils* (UK), *The Golden Blade, Gun Fury, Back to God's Country* 1953; *Taza Son of Cochise, Magnificent Obsession* (as Bob Merrick), *Bengal Brigade* 1954; *Captain Lightfoot, One Desire* 1955; *All That Heaven Allows, Never Say Goodbye, Giant* 1956; *Written on the Wind, Battle Hymn, Something of Value, A Farewell to Arms* (as Lt. Frederic Henry) 1957; *The Tarnished Angels, Twilight for the Gods* 1958; *This Earth Is Mine, Pillow Talk* 1959; *The Last Sunset, Come September* 1961; *Lover Come Back, The Spiral Road* 1962; *Marilyn* (compilation film; narrator), *A Gathering of Eagles* 1963; *Man's Favorite Sport?, Send Me No Flowers* 1964; *Strange Bedfellows, A Very Special Favor* 1965; *Blindfold, Seconds* 1966; *Tobruk* 1967; *Ice Station Zebra* 1968; *Ruba al*

Prossimo Tuo/A Fine Pair (It.), *The Undefeated* 1969; *The Hornet's Nest, Darling Lili* 1970; *Pretty Maids All in a Row* 1971; *Showdown* 1973; *Embryo* 1976; *Avalanche* 1978; *The Mirror Crack'd* (UK) 1980; *The Ambassador* 1984.

Huggins, Roy. Screenwriter. Born on July 18, 1914, in Litelle, Wash. *ed.* U. of California (B.A., M.A.). A former industrial engineer, in the mid-40s he turned to writing novels, short stories, and screenplays. In 1952 he directed a quality Western, *Hangman's Knot,* starring Randolph Scott, then returned to writing. Beginning in the mid-50s, he created and produced several successful TV series, including '77 Sunset Strip,' 'Maverick,' 'The Fugitive,' and 'Run for Your Life.' Married Adele MARA.

FILMS INCLUDE: *I Love Trouble* 1947; *The Fuller Brush Man* (story basis) 1948; *The Lady Gambles, Too Late for Tears* 1949; *Sealed Cargo* 1951; *Hangman's Knot* (also dir.) 1952; *Gun Fury* 1953; *Pushover, Three Hours to Kill* 1954; *A Fever in the Blood* (also prod.) 1961.

Hughes, Allen and **Albert (The Hughes Brothers).** Directors. Born in Detroit, Mich. *ed.* Los Angeles City College (Albert). Twin-brother filmmaking team who were raised in Pomona, Calif., and have made movies since their mother gave them a video camera when they were 12. At age 21 they gained attention with their unsparing look at Watts urban life, *Menace II Society*, with a visceral approach and vibrant cinematography inspired by the work of director Martin Scorsese.

FILMS: *Menace II Society* 1993; *Dead Presidents* 1995.

Hughes, Barnard. Actor. Born on July 16, 1915, in Bedford Hills, N.Y. Character lead of the American stage, television, and scattered films. He starred in the TV comedy series 'Doc' (1975–76) and 'Mr. Merlin' (1981–82) and won an Emmy in 1978 for an episode of 'Lou Grant.' He won a Tony for his performance in the Broadway play 'Da' (1978), a role he later transported to the screen.

FILMS: *The Young Doctors* 1961; *Hamlet* 1964; *Midnight Cowboy* 1969; *Where's Poppa?* 1970; *The Pursuit of Happiness, Cold Turkey, The Hospital* 1971; *Deadhead Miles, Rage* 1972; *Sisters* 1973; *Oh God!* 1977; *First Monday in October* 1981; *Tron, Best Friends* 1982; *Maxie* 1985; *Where Are the Children?* 1986; *The Lost Boys* 1987; *Da* 1988; *Doc Hollywood* 1991; *Sister Act 2: Back in the Habit* 1993.

Hughes, Howard. Producer, director, industrialist, aviator. *b.* Dec. 24, 1905, Hodston, Tex. *d.* 1976. *ed.* Rice Inst.; California Inst. of Technology. At age 18 he inherited and took over the management of the Hughes Tool Company, a prosperous manufacturer of oil-drilling equipment which had been founded by his father. At 20, he began investing part of his profits in Hollywood films such as *Two Arabian Knights, The Front Page,* and *Scarface.* But he made his name as the producer-director of *Hell's Angels* (1930), notable for its opulent aerial action scenes and for launching the career of Jean HARLOW.

Miss Harlow was only one of many starlets that Hughes habitually put on personal long-term contracts. Some were known to be on his payroll for years without ever appearing in a film or even seeing their employer. During his first Hollywood phase, Hughes was seen in the company of many of the movie colony's most beautiful stars and was variously rumored to be engaged to some of the most glamorous, such as Ava Gardner, Ginger Rogers, and Katharine Hepburn. He also became known as an impulsive eccentric. One day in 1932, the young millionaire, an aviation enthusiast since his early teens, suddenly left Hollywood. Under the assumed name of Charles Howard, he took a $250-a-month job as a co-pilot with American Airways. He stayed long enough to learn all he wanted to know about commercial aviation, then walked out on the job and began a new phase in his remarkable, adventure-filled career, that of a designer, builder, and daring pilot of advanced aircraft.

In 1935, flying a machine of his own design, he broke the world's speed record and was forced to crash-land in the process. The following year he broke the transcontinental speed record; in 1937 he bettered his own mark. And in 1938 he flew around the world in the record-breaking time of just over 91 hours. He then returned to filmmaking as suddenly as he had left, launching Jane RUSSELL's famous cleavage in the first sexy Western, *The Outlaw,* which he produced and directed. The film wasn't much, but it became a landmark in the annals of Hollywood's self-censorship and gained much publicity in the process. It premiered in 1943, was almost immediately recalled, was re-released in 1946 and again in the early 50s.

Meanwhile, Hughes was making his contribution to the war effort by designing and building the Hercules, nicknamed the Spruce Goose, a huge wooden seaplane, the largest aircraft ever flown. It took him five years to build the plane, at the cost of $18 million to the taxpayers. When it was finally completed in 1947, it was flown only once, by Hughes himself. But this ill-fated venture provided much essential technical knowledge for the future development of the American aerospace industry.

In July of 1946, while test-flying an XF–11 photoreconnaissance plane of his own design, Hughes crashed into a Beverly Hills home. His injuries were severe—a crushed chest, nine broken ribs, a collapsed lung, and a lacerated skull, among others—and he was not expected to live. However, he recovered and resumed his business activity, including the production of films. But he was a changed man. No longer was he Hollywood's flamboyant playboy. Gradually he turned recluse, surrounding himself with a few trusted employees and shutting himself away from the world. His last public appearance was as a witness before a US Senate committee investigating the Hercules fiasco of 1947, and thereafter Hughes began conducting his business affairs from a safe distance.

In 1948, Hughes acquired a controlling interest in the RKO studios and theater chain for a reported $9 million. His inexplicable policies caused most of the RKO staff to resign within months. RKO, once one of Hollywood's major studios, began to resemble a ghost town. By 1954 it had lost nearly $40 million under Hughes's remote-control management. To everyone's surprise, he offered to buy all the outstanding stock of the company from the shareholders. This accomplished, he then sold the studio at a $10 million profit. He surpassed this financial coup in 1966 when he sold his holdings in TWA for over half a billion dollars.

In November of 1966, Hughes cut himself off entirely from the outside world. Under cover of darkness, he moved into the penthouse suite of the Desert Inn in Las Vegas. Not even his wife since 1957, beautiful screen star Jean PETERS, saw him afterward (they were officially divorced in 1971). Served and protected by five trusted Mormon male nurses, he saw practically no one. With the aid of an electronic communications network, he continued to command the affairs of his $2.5 billion empire (Hughes Tool, Hughes Aircraft, the Hughes Medical Institute, etc.) and proceeded to buy a cluster of hotels and gambling casinos and large chunks of land in Las Vegas, as well as a local airline and a TV station, thus acquiring control over much of the economy of the city. In November of 1970, mystery man Hughes left Las Vegas as he entered it, suddenly and under the cover of darkness.

The Howard Hughes puzzle now loomed larger than ever and he was reported moving from one foreign haven to another. Even his death in 1976 offered more questions than answers and precipitated a battle for his multimillion-dollar fortune, highlighted by an avalanche of fake wills. One such claim was the subject of Jonathan Demme's film *Melvin and Howard* (1980), in which Hughes was portrayed by Jason Robards.

FILMS (as producer): *Everybody's Acting* 1926; *Two Arabian Knights* 1927; *The Mating Call, The Racket* 1928; *Hell's Angels* (also dir.) 1930; *The Front Page* 1931, *The Age for Love; Cock of the Air, Sky Devils, Scarface* 1932; *Bombshell* (co-exec. prod. only) 1933; *The Outlaw* (also dir., with uncredited help from Howard Hawks) 1941, '43, '47, '50; *Vendetta* (also dir., with uncredited participation of several other directors) 1946–50; *Mad Wednesday* 1947; *His Kind of Woman* (co-prod.), *Two Tickets to Broadway* 1951; *Affair with a Stranger* (exec prod.) 1953.

Hughes, John. Director, producer, screenwriter. Born on Feb. 18, 1950, in Lansing, Mich. A salesman's son, he moved at 13 with his family to Chicago, a city whose landscape would figure prominently in several of his films. After dropping out of the University of Arizona in his junior year, Hughes, now married, became an advertising copywriter. He also wrote short stories, magazine articles, unpublished novels, and jokes for stand-up comedians before joining *National Lampoon* as an editor in 1979. In the early 80s he became involved in the magazine's profitable movie projects as a screenwriter and from 1984 also as a director. In 1985 he entered a multiple-picture deal with Paramount, under which he produced his films under his own banner, the John Hughes Company. In 1988 his Hughes Entertainment became associated with Universal. His films, typically broad comedies and teen romances, have been aimed mainly at the youth market. Several were box-office hits, particularly the two *Home Alone* entries, both of which landed high on the list of all-time moneymakers.

FILMS: As screenwriter—*National Lampoon's Class Reunion* 1982; *National Lampoon's Vacation* (also co-lyr.), *Mr. Mom, Nate and Hayes* 1983. As director-screenwriter—*Sixteen Candles* 1984; *The Breakfast Club, Weird Science, National Lampoon's European Vacation* 1985; *Pretty in Pink* (sc., co-exec. prod. only), *Ferris Bueller's Day Off* (also co-prod.) 1986; *Some Kind of Wonderful* (also prod.), *Planes Trains, and Automobiles* (also prod.) 1987; *She's Having a Baby* (also prod.), *The Great Outdoors* (also exec. prod.) 1988; *Uncle Buck* (also co-prod.), *National Lampoon's Christmas Vacation* (sc., co-prod. only) 1989; *Home Alone* (sc., prod. only) 1990; *Career Opportunities* (sc., prod. only), *Only the Lonely* (co-prod. only), *Dutch* (sc., prod. only), *Curly Sue* (dir., sc., prod.) 1991; *Home Alone 2* (prod., sc. only) 1992; *Dennis the Menace* (co-prod., sc. only) 1993; *Baby's Day Out* (co-prod., sc.), *Miracle on 34th Street* (prod., sc.) 1994; *101 Dalmations* (sc. only) 1996.

Hughes, Kathleen. Actress. Born Betty von Gerkan, on Nov. 14, 1928, in Hollywood, Calif. *ed* Los Angeles City College; UCLA. Leading lady of Hollywood films of the 50s. Groomed as a starlet by Fox, she later signed with Universal. Married to producer Stanley Rubin, she is the mother of juvenile actor Michael Hughes.

FILMS INCLUDE: *Mother Is a Freshman, Mr. Belvedere Goes to College* 1949; *Where the Sidewalk Ends, Mister 880, I'll Get By* 1950; *Take Care of My Little Girl* 1951; *For Men Only/The Tall Lie* 1952; *It Came from Outer Space, The Golden Blade, The Glass Web* 1953; *Dawn at Socorro* 1954; *Cult of the Cobra* 1955; *Three Bad Sisters* 1956; *Unwed Mother* 1958; *The President's Analyst* 1967.

Hughes, Ken. Director. Born in 1922, in Liverpool, England. At age 14 he won an amateur filmmaking contest, but the closest he was able to come to professional work in the industry was as a projectionist at a London cinema. At 16 he joined the BBC, where he worked his way up to sound engineer. During his military service he was assigned to a unit making training films and it was here that he learned the rudiments of the craft. Out of uniform, he began directing documentary shorts and half-hour crime films, for most of which he also wrote the scripts. He made his first feature in 1952 and soon acquired a reputation as a reliable director of B pictures who utilized dynamic American techniques and often employed former Hollywood stars to enliven otherwise routine films. He moved into the big time in 1960 with *The Trials of Oscar Wilde* and subsequently directed several large-budget high-gloss films, culminating with *Cromwell*. His career then entered a steep decline from which it never recovered. He usually wrote his own scripts and occasionally collaborated as a screenwriter on films of other directors.

FEATURE FILMS (as director-screenwriter): *Wide Boy* 1952; *The House Across the Lake/Heat Wave* (from own novel), *Black 13* (dir. only) 1954; *The Brain Machine, Little Red Monkey/Case of the Red Monkey, Confession/The Deadliest Sin, Timeslip/The Atomic Man, Joe Macbeth* 1955; *Wicked as They Come* 1956; *The Long Haul* 1957; *Jazzboat, In the Nick, The Trials of Oscar Wilde* 1960; *The Small World of Sammy Lee* (from own teleplay) 1963; *Of Human Bondage* (dir. only; addnl. scenes by Henry Hathaway) 1964; *Drop Dead Darling/Arrivederci Baby* (also prod.) 1966; *Casino Royale* (co-dir. with several others) 1967; *Chitty Chitty Bang Bang* 1968; *Cromwell* 1970; *The Internecine Project* 1974; *Alfie Darling/Oh! Alfie* 1975; *Sextette* (dir. only; US) 1978; *Night School/Terror Eyes* (US) 1981.

Hughes, Lloyd. Actor. *b.* Oct 21, 1896, Bisbee, Ariz. *d.* 1958. Tall, slim, masculine star of Hollywood silents and early talkies. He played leads in many major films, opposite some of the screen's most glamorous sirens. His career reached its peak in the 20s and spilled over well into the 30s, where he appeared mainly in low-budget action pictures. At one time married to actress Gloria Hope.

FILMS INCLUDE: *Impossible Susan* 1918; *The Turn in the Road, The Haunted Bedroom* 1919; *Dangerous Hours, The False Road, Homespun Folks* 1920; *Beau Revel, Love Never Dies, Hail the Woman* 1921; *Tess of the Storm Country* 1922; *Scars of Jealousy, The Huntress* 1923; *Heritage of the Desert, The Sea Hawk* 1924; *The Lost World, Sally, Déclassée, The Desert Flower* 1925; *Irene, Ella Cinders, Ladies at Play/Loose Ankles, Valencia* 1926; *An Affair of the Follies, The Stolen Bride, American Beauty, No Place to Go/Her Primitive Man* 1927; *Sailors' Wives, Heart to Heart* 1928; *Where East Is East, The Mysterious Island* 1929; *Love Comes Along, Moby Dick, Big Boy* 1930; *Hell Bound, The Deceiver* 1931; *The Miracle Man* 1932; *The Man Who Reclaimed His Head* 1934; *Harmony Lane* 1935; *A Face in the Fog, Kelly of the Secret Service* 1936; *Romance of the Redwoods* 1939; *Vengeance of the Deep* 1940.

Hughes, Mary Beth. Actress. Born on Nov. 13, 1919, in Alton, Ill. Spurred by an ex-actress grandmother, she began playing in repertory while still in high school. Late in 1938 she broke into films and the following year played supporting parts in several MGM movies. Moving over to Fox in 1940, she began playing leading ladies, usually in low-budget films. She was typically cast as a hardened blonde, frequently a floozie or gang moll. Her never-spectacular screen career reached an impasse in the late 40s and ended in the mid-50s. She returned to the screen in the early 70s in occasional potboilers and still appears in suburban and small-town night spots, singing and strumming the electric bass. In later years she enjoyed some cult following among nostalgia fans.

FILMS INCLUDE: *Broadway Serenade, The Women, These Glamour Girls, Dancing Co-Ed, Fast and Furious* 1939;

Free Blonde and 21, Star Dust, Lucky Cisco Kid, Four Sons, The Great Profile 1940; *Sleepers West, The Great American Broadcast, The Cowboy and the Blonde, Dressed to Kill, Charlie Chan in Rio, Design for Scandal* 1941; *Orchestra Wives* 1942; *Over My Dead Body, The Ox-Bow Incident, Follow the Band* 1943; *Never a Dull Moment, Timber Queen* 1944; *The Great Flamarion, The Lady Confesses* 1945; *Caged Fury, Waterfront at Midnight, Inner Sanctum* 1948; *El Paso, The Devil's Henchman, Grand Canyon* 1949; *Young Man with a Horn, Holiday Rhythm* 1950; *Close to My Heart* 1951; *Highway Dragnet, Loophole* 1954; *Las Vegas Shakedown* 1955; *Gun Battle at Monterey* 1957; *The Working Girls* 1974; *How's Your Love Life?* 1977.

Hughes, Wendy. Actress. Born *c.* 1952, in Melbourne. Accomplished leading lady of the Australian stage, TV, radio, and films. Trained early as a ballet dancer, she then attended the National Institute of Dramatic Arts, graduating in 1970. After several prolific years on the stage and in TV, she made her film debut in 1974. She soon emerged as a glowing screen personality, one of Australia's best.

FILMS INCLUDE: *Petersen* 1974; *Sidecar Racers* 1975; *High Rolling* 1977; *My Brilliant Career, Kostas* 1979; *Touch and Go* 1980; *Hoodwink* 1981; *Duet for Four, Lonely Hearts* 1982; *Careful, He Might Hear You* 1983; *My First Wife* 1984; *An Indecent Obsession, I Can't Get Started, An Old Acquaintance* 1985; *Promises to Keep* 1986; *Shadows of the Peacock/Echoes of Paradise, Happy New Year* (US) 1987; *Boundaries of the Heart* 1988; *Luigi's Ladies* (also co-sc.) 1989; *Wild Orchid II: Two Shades of Blue* 1992; *Princess Caraboo* 1994.

Hughes Brothers, The. See Allen and Albert HUGHES.

Hui, Ann. Director. Born 1947 in Manchuria. *ed.* Hong Kong Univ. (comp. lit.). After two years at the London Film Institute she returned to Hong Kong in 1975 to work as an assistant to the director King HU. She then directed episodes of a drama series and documentaries for television. In 1977 she produced and directed six one-hour films for Hong Kong's Independent Commission Against Corruption. Her first feature, *The Secret* (1979) was based on the true-life murder case of a young couple. She followed that with 1980's *The Spooky Bunch*, a ghost movie, and 1982's *Story of Woo Viet*, about Vietnam refugees in Manila, before directing her most acclaimed film, *Boat People* (1982), a documentary-style story of a family's escape from Vietnam that received much attention at the Cannes and New York festivals. Her 1987 *Romance of Book and Sword* was an epic of the struggle between Han Chinese and Manchu warlords, based on Jin Yung's oft-filmed novel. Hui won critical praise abroad for *Song of the Exile* (1990), the semiautobiographical tale of a film student who returns to Hong Kong, where she re-assesses her relationship with her Japanese mother; but the film was unsuccessful at home. After *My American Grandson* (1991), Hui turned to working on genre pictures in Hong Kong's commercial mainstream.

FILMS INCLUDE: *The Secret* 1979; *The Spooky Bunch* 1980; *The Story of Woo Viet* 1982; *Boat People* 1982; *Love in a Fallen City* 1984; *Starry Is the Night* 1987; *Romance of Book and Sword* 1987; *Song of the Exile* 1990; *My American Grandson* 1991.

Hui, Michael. Director, actor, writer. Born in 1942 in Canton, China. *ed.* Chinese Univ. (social science). Taught high school and managed an ad agency before hosting an after-school TV quiz show, then variety shows. In 1972 he took the title role in the comedy *The Warlord*, directed by Li Hanxiang. He starred in three more films by Li before directing (as well as writing and starring in) *Games Gamblers Play* in 1973. His next three features, *The Private Eyes, The Contract*, and *Security Unlimited*, solidified his comic persona of the greedy but self-defeating boss, and established him as one of Hong Kong's most popular comedians. Beginning in 1987 he produced and starred in a series of films directed by others, often teamed with brothers Sam and Ricky, and in 1992 he returned to directing with *The Magic Touch*.

FILMS INCLUDE: (director-actor-writer-producer unless otherwise indicated): *The Warlord* (act. only), *The Happiest Moment* (act. only) 1972; *The Four Tales* (act. only), *The Scandal* (act. only) 1973; *Games Gamblers Play* 1974; *The Last Message* 1975; *The Private Eyes (Mr. Boo)* 1977; *The Contract* 1978; *Security Unlimited, The Cannonball Run* (act. only) 1981; *Teppanyaki* 1983; *Happy Ding Dong, Mr. Boo Meets Pom Pom* (act. only) 1985; *Inspector Chocolate* 1986; *Chicken and Duck Talk* (act., sc., exec. prod. only) 1988; *Mr. Coconut* (act., sc., exec. prod. only) 1989; *Front Page* (act., sc., exec. prod. only) 1990; *The Magic Touch* 1992.

Huillet, Danièle. See STRAUB, Jean-Marie.

Hulbert, Jack. Actor. *b.* Apr. 24, 1892, Ely, England. *d.* 1978. Long-chinned, prominent-nosed, highly popular comic star of the British stage and screen. He began performing professionally while studying at Cambridge and went on to become a favorite of London audiences, often in plays co-starring Cicely COURTNEIDGE, his wife from 1916. He enjoyed great popularity in British films of the 30s. His brother, Claude Hulbert (1900–64), was also a successful screen comedian. Autobiography: *The Little Woman's Always Right* (1976).

FILMS: *Elstree Calling* 1930; *The Ghost Train, Sunshine Susie/The Office Girl* 1931; *Jack's the Boy/Night and Day, Love on Wheels, Happy Ever After* 1932; *Falling for You* 1933; *Jack Ahoy!, The Camels Are Coming* 1934; *Bulldog Jack/Alias Bulldog Drummond* 1935; *Jack of All Trades/The Two of Us* 1936; *Take My Tip, Paradise for Two/The Gaiety Girls* 1937; *Kate Plus Ten* 1938; *Under Your Hat* 1940; *Into the Blue/The Man in the Dinghy* 1950; *The Magic Box* 1951; *Miss Tulip Stays the Night* 1955; *The Spider's Web* 1960; *Not Now Darling, The Cherry Picker* 1972.

Hulce, Tom. Actor. Born on Dec. 6, 1953, in White Water, Wis. *ed.* North Carolina School of the Arts. Youthful leading man of the American stage and screen. A surprise selection for the title role in *Amadeus* (1984), he was nominated for an Academy Award and won Italy's David Di Donatello best actor award for that performance. He has since appeared in a number of less showy, but distinctive, roles.

FILMS: *September 30, 1955/24 Hours of the Rebel* 1977; *National Lampoon's Animal House* 1978; *Those Lips Those Eyes* 1980; *Amadeus* (as Wolfgang Amadeus Mozart) 1984; *Echo Park* (Aus./US) 1986; *Slamdance* 1987; *Dominick and Eugene* 1988; *Parenthood* 1989; *Shadow Man* 1990; *The Inner Circle* 1991; *Fearless* 1993; *Mary Shelley's Frankenstein* 1994; *Wings of Courage* 1995; *Hunchback of Notre Dame* (v/o) 1996.

Hull, Henry. Actor. *b.* Oct. 3, 1890, Louisville. Ky. *d.* 1977. *ed.* CCNY; Cooper Union; Columbia. The son of a drama critic, he made his stage debut in 1911 but later pursued a career as a mining engineer and prospector in Quebec. He made his first film appearance in 1916 and subsequently alternated between stage and screen. A leading man during the silent era, he developed into an excellent character player in talkies, memorably in the title role of *The Werewolf of London.* As a stage player he is best known for creating the role of Jeeter Lester in the original Broadway production of 'Tobacco Road.' He wrote several plays, including 'Manhattan' (co-author, 1922) and 'Congratulations' (1929).

FILMS INCLUDE: *The Man Who Came Back* 1916;

Rasputin the Black Monk (as Alexander Kerensky); *The Volunteer* 1917; *Little Women* 1919; *One Exciting Night* 1922; *The Last Moment, A Bride for a Knight* 1923; *Roulette, The Hoosier Schoolmaster, For Woman's Favor* 1924; *The Wrongdoers* 1925; *Midnight, Great Expectations* 1934; *Transient Lady, The Werewolf of London* (title role) 1935; *Paradise for Three, Yellow Jack, Three Comrades, Boys Town, The Great Waltz* (as Emperor Franz Josef) 1938; *Jesse James, Spirit of Culver, The Return of the Cisco Kid, Stanley and Livingstone, Miracles for Sale, Babes in Arms, Nick Carter—Master Detective* 1939; *My Son My Son!, The Return of Frank James* 1940; *High Sierra* 1441; *Lifeboat, The Woman of the Town* 1944; *Objective Burma!* 1945; *High Barbaree, Deep Valley, Mourning Becomes Electra* (as Seth Beckwith) 1947; *The Walls of Jericho, Fighter Squadron* 1948; *El Paso, Portrait of Jennie, The Fountainhead, Colorado Territory, The Great Gatsby* 1949; *Hollywood Story* 1951; *Inferno* 1953; *Man with the Gun* 1955; *The Proud Rebel, The Buccaneer* 1958; *The Oregon Trail* 1959; *Master of the World* 1961; *The Fool Killer* 1965; *The Chase* 1966.

Hull, Josephine. Actress. *b.* Josephine Sherwood, 1884, Newton, Mass. *d.* 1957. A celebrated stage character actress, she appeared in only a handful of films but left a lasting memory in two—*Arsenic and Old Lace* and *Harvey.* She won an Academy Award as best supporting actress for the latter. She was married to Henry Hull's brother, actor Shelley Hull, who died in 1919.

FILMS: *After Tomorrow, Careless Lady* 1932; *Arsenic and Old Lace* 1944; *Harvey* 1950; *The Lady from Texas* 1951.

Hull, Warren. Actor. *b.* Jan. 17, 1903, Gasport, N.Y. *d.* 1974. He dropped out of college (NYU) to study voice at the Eastman School of the University of Rochester and made his professional debut in the chorus of operettas. He later played leading roles in 'The Student Prince' and other musical stage presentations. In the late 30s and early 40s he played leads in many low-budget Hollywood productions, including a number of popular serials in which he portrayed such comic-strip heroes as the Spider, Mandrake the Magician, and the Green Hornet. But it was as a master of ceremonies of radio and television that he became most successful. He had started in radio as an announcer and MC in 1923 and continued in broadcasting while appearing on the stage and in films. He was the announcer for the 'Hit Parade' show from 1935 and in the early 40s was a co-interviewer on the 'Vox Populi' programs. He was best known as the host of the long-running 'Strike It Rich' quiz program on radio and later (1951–55) on TV.

FILMS INCLUDE: *Personal Maid's Secret, Miss Pacific Fleet* 1935; *Freshman Love, The Walking Dead, The Law in Her Hands, The Big Noise, Bengal Tiger, Love Begins at 20* 1936; *Fugitive in the Sky, Her Husband's Secretary, Night Key, Rhythm in the Clouds, Paradise Isle* 1937; *The Spider's Web* (serial), *Hawaii Calls* 1938; *Mandrake the Magician* (serial), *Star Reporter, Smashing the Spy Ring, Should a Girl Marry?* 1939; *The Green Hornet Strikes Again* (serial), *The Last Alarm, The Lone Wolf Meets a Lady, Wagons Westward, Marked Men* 1940; *The Spider Returns* (serial), *Bowery Blitzkrieg* 1941.

Humberstone, H. Bruce ("Lucky"). Director. *b.* Nov. 18, 1903, Buffalo, N.Y. *d.* 1984. *ed.* Miami (Fla.) Military Academy. He entered films in his teens as a script clerk; then later played some juvenile roles and was assistant director to King Vidor, Edmund Goulding, and Allan Dwan, among others. A director since the early 30s, he specialized in adventure thrillers and light musical films, mostly minor, which he usually handled with verve and skill. Among his better films were the Sonja Henie musical, *Sun Valley Serenade,* the Victor Mature-Betty Grable crime melodrama, *I Wake Up Screaming,* and the delightful Danny Kaye comedy, *Wonder Man.* He also directed many episodes for TV series.

FILMS: *Strangers of the Evening, The Crooked Circle, If I Had a Million* (one episode) 1932; *King of the Jungle* (co-dir. with Max Marcia), *Goodbye Love* 1933; *The Merry Wives of Reno, The Dragon Murder Case* 1934; *Silk Hat Kid, Ladies Love Danger* 1935; *Three Live Ghosts, Charlie Chan at the Race Track, Charlie Chan at the Opera* 1936; *Charlie Chan at the Olympics* 1937; *Checkers, In Old Chicago* (fire sequence only), *Rascals, Time Out for Murder, While New York Sleeps, Charlie Chan in Honolulu* 1938; *Pack Up Your Troubles* 1939; *Lucky Cisco Kid, The Quarterback* 1940; *Tall Dark and Handsome, Sun Valley Serenade, I Wake Up Screaming* 1941; *To the Shores of Tripoli, Iceland* 1942; *Hello Frisco Hello* 1943; *Pin Up Girl* 1944; *Wonder Man, Within These Walls* 1945; *Three Little Girls in Blue* 1946; *The Homestretch* 1947; *Fury at Furnace Creek* 1948; *South Sea Sinner* 1950; *Happy Go Lovely* (UK) 1951; *She's Working Her Way Through College* 1952; *The Desert Song* 1953; *The Purple Mask, Ten Wanted Men* 1955; *Tarzan and the Lost Safari* 1957; *Tarzan's Fight for Life, Tarzan and the Trappers* 1958; *Madison Avenue* (also prod.) 1962.

Hume, Alan. Director of photography. Born on Oct. 16, 1924, in London. In British films from age 17, he rose from apprentice and assistant cameraman to full-fledged lighting cinematographer in the early 60s. After paying his dues with prolific work on numerous "Carry On" films and other quickies, he was rewarded with major productions.

FILMS INCLUDE: *Carry on Constable* 1960; *The Kiss of the Vampire* 1963; *Carry on Cleo* 1964; *Dr. Terror's House of Horrors* 1965; *The Bofors Gun* 1968; *Captain Nemo and the Underwater City* 1969; *Perfect Friday* 1970; *Zeppelin* 1971; *The Legend of Hell House* 1973; *The Land That Time Forgot* 1974; *Gulliver's Travels* 1977; *Arabian Adventure, The Legacy* 1978; *The Watcher in the Woods* 1980; *Caveman, For Your Eyes Only, Eye of the Needle* 1981; *Return of the Jedi, Octopussy* 1983; *Supergirl* 1984; *A View to a Kill, Runaway Train* 1985; *A Fish Called Wanda, Without a Clue* 1988; *Shirley Valentine* 1989; *Eve of Destruction* 1990.

Hume, Benita. Actress. *b.* Oct. 14, 1906, London. *d.* 1967. On stage from age 17, she made her British screen debut at 19 and subsequently played ladylike leads in both British and Hollywood films. She retired from the screen following her marriage to Ronald COLMAN in 1938. Widowed in 1958, she then married George SANDERS.

FILMS INCLUDE: In the UK—*The Happy Ending* 1925; *Easy Virtue, The Constant Nymph, The Wrecker, The Lady of the Lake* 1928; *High Treason* 1929; *Balaclava/Jaws of Steel* 1930; *The Flying Fool, A Honeymoon Adventure* 1931; *Service for Ladies/Reserved for Ladies, Men of Steel, Diamond Cut Diamond/Blame the Woman* 1932. In the US—*Clear All Wires, Looking Forward/The New Deal, Gambling Ship, Only Yesterday, The Worst Woman in Paris?* 1933; *The Private Life of Don Juan* (UK), *Jew Suss/Power* (UK) 1934; *The Gay Deception* 1935; *The Garden Murder Case, Moonlight Murder, Suzy, Tarzan Escapes, Rainbow on the River* 1936; *The Last of Mrs. Cheyney* 1937; *Peck's Bad Boy with the Circus* 1938.

Humphrey(s), William. Actor, director. *b.* Jan. 2, 1874, Chicopee Falls, Mass. *d.* 1942. Following extensive stage experience on tour, in summer stock, and on Broadway, during which he became famous for his portrayals of Napoleon, he joined the Vitagraph company in Brooklyn, N.Y., in 1909. He played his specialty in his film acting debut, in J. Stuart Blackton's one-reel *Napoleon—The Man of Destiny,* and again later that year in *Napoleon Bonaparte and Empress Josephine of France.* He stayed with the company as both actor and director and remained an important character player through the early 30s. His name appears as Humphreys in early screen credits, and later as Humphrey.

FILMS INCLUDE: As director—*A Tale of Two Cities* 1911; *The Snare of Fate* 1913; *An Affair for the Police* 1914; *On Her Wedding Night, To Cherish and Protect* 1915; *Fathers of Men, The Footlights of Fate* 1916; *Two Men and a Woman* (also co-sc.), *Babbling Tongues* (also co-story) 1917; *Joan of Plattsburg* (co-dir.), *The Unchastened Woman* (also co-sc.) 1918; *Atonement* (also co-sc.) 1919; *The Midnight Bride* 1920; *Foolish Monte Carlo* (also sc.) 1922. As actor—*Napoleon—The Man of Destiny* (title role), *Napoleon Bonaparte and Empress Josephine of France* (again as Napoleon) 1909; *The Prejudice of Pierre Marie* 1911; *The Spirit of Christmas* 1913; *Mr. Barnes of New York* 1914; *A House Divided* 1919; *The Stranger's Banquet* 1922; *Vanity Fair* (as John Sedley), *Scaramouche* 1923; *Abraham Lincoln* (as Stephen Douglas), *Beau Brummel* 1924; *Drusilla with a Million, Dangerous Innocence, The Unholy Three* 1925; *Midnight Limited, The Silent Lover* 1926; *The Dice Woman* 1927; *The Actress* 1928; *Devil-May-Care* (again as Napoleon) 1929; *Murder at Midnight, Manhattan Parade* 1931; *The Vampire Bat, Cheating Blondes* 1933; *Are We Civilized?* 1934.

Hunebelle, André. Director, producer. *b.* Sept. 1, 1896, Meudon, France. *d.* 1985. Formerly a glassmaker, he entered French films as a producer in 1941 and turned director in 1948. He directed numerous commercially oriented films, both comedies and dramas, with few artistic pretensions.

FILMS (as director): *Métier de Fous* 1948; *Mission à Tanger* 1949; *Millionnaires d'un Jour/A Simple Case of Money, Méfiez-vous des Blondes* 1950; *Ma Femme est formidable* 1951; *Massacre en Dentelles, Monsieur Taxi* 1952; *Mon Mari est merveilleux, Les Trois Mousquetaires/The Three Musketeers* 1953; *Cadet Rousselle* 1954; *L'Impossible Monsieur Pipelet* 1955; *Treize à Table, Mannequins de Paris* 1956; *Les Collégiennes/The Twilight Girls, Casino de Paris* 1957; *Les Femmes sont marrantes, Ami Ami, Taxi Roulotte et Corrida* 1958; *Arrêtez le Massacre, Le Bossu* 1959; *Le Capitan* 1960; *Le Miracle des Loups* 1961; *Les Mystères de Paris* 1962; *Méfiez-vous Mesdames* 1963; *Banco à Bangkok/Shadow of Evil, Fantômas* 1964; *Furia à Bahia pour OSS 117/OSS 117—Mission for a Killer, Fantômas se déchaîne* 1965; *Fantômas contre Scotland Yard* 1967; *Pas de Roses pour OSS 117* 1968; *Sous le Signe de Monte-Cristo* 1969; *Les Quatre Charlots Mousquetaires* 1974.

Hung, Samo (Hung Jinbao). Director and actor. Rotund Hong Kong filmmaker and star of martial arts comedies. Studied martial arts and acrobatics at the Peking Opera School with future film stars Jackie CHAN and Yuen Biao. Worked as martial arts coordinator for Bruce LEE. Directed and costarred with Chan in several action comedies in the early 1980s. His *Eastern Condors*, a 1987 *Dirty Dozen*–inspired story of convicts recruited to carry out a mission for the US military in Vietnam, was among the first Hong Kong "New Wave" films to receive notice abroad.

FILMS INCLUDE (director and actor): *The Magnificent Butcher* 1980; *Encounter of the Spooky Kind* 1981; *Winners and Sinners, Project A, Wheels on Meals* 1984; *Heart of the Dragon* 1985; *Eastern Condors* 1987; *Eight Taels of Gold* (actor only) 1990; *The Prisoner* 1991; *Eagle Shooting Heroes* (dir.) 1993.

Hungary. This enclave of ten million Magyars in a part of Europe dominated by Slavs has maintained a distinct national culture in the face of continually adverse political conditions and frequently changing frontiers. Film production in Hungary began early but for many years led nowhere. A newsreel was shot as early as 1896 and the first documentary in 1901, but it was not until 1905 that the first motion picture theater opened in Budapest, the capital. Regular feature production began in 1912, after the completion of the country's first studio, also in Budapest. However, films produced during this period were light comedies or heavy melodramas of little artistic or commercial appeal. During the brief Communist regime of 1919, following the collapse of the monarchy, Hungary became the first country to nationalize its film industry, doing so several months before the Soviet Union. During a four-month burst of activity, more than 30 films were produced by the state.

The industry was restored to private ownership under the regency of Admiral Horthy, but the repressive new regime forced such leading filmmakers as Alexander KORDA, Michael CURTIZ, and Paul FEJOS and film theoretician-screenwriter Béla BALÁZS to flee the country and seek employment abroad. Among the actors who left were Peter LORRE, Mischa AUER, Bela LUGOSI, Paul LUKAS, and Marta EGGERTH. The number of Hungarian films produced annually dwindled to almost zero by the mid-20s. In the 30s and early 40s production was high in quantity, reaching an annual average of some 40 features, but quite poor in quality and rarely screened abroad. Quality reached its lowest ebb during Hungary's WW II alliance with the Axis powers.

Postwar reconstruction was slow. Yet in 1947 Hungarian cinema scored its first important international success in many years with Geza von RADVÀNYI's *Somewhere in Europe/It Happened in Europe.* In 1948 the industry was again nationalized by the Communist regime. Production of feature films gradually increased in the 50s and reached an annual average of 20 in the 60s and 70s, in addition to some 50 documentaries and 35 animated films. The 60s and 70s also saw the emergence of an enthusiastic and talented New Wave of directors with a zeal for "relevant" contemporary themes, largely as a result of the establishment of the Béla Balázs Studio, a training ground for young filmmakers, most of whom were graduates of Budapest's Academy for Cinematographic Art. By the 70s, Hungarian films were doing well in international film festivals, fetching prizes at a rate far exceeding the country's share in global feature production. Among the leading directors of this period were Zoltán FÁBRI, János Herskó, Károly MAKK, Imre Fehér, György Révész, Miklós JANCSÓ, András KOVÁCS, István SZABÓ, and István GAÁL.

Since then, Hungarian cinema has gone into decline. Only 14 features, four documentaries, and one animated feature were produced in 1991. Cinema attendances have fallen, and Hungarian films capture a shrinking portion of the box office, which is dominated by American films. Following the collapse of Hungary's Communist government, the local film industry, once completely state-subsidized, must now face the pressures of the free market. Even so, the government (through the Motion Picture Foundation of Hungary) continues to give partial subsidies to native filmmakers and to native art houses that exhibit their films. Recent Hungarian directors of note include Janos Rozsa, Andras Salamon, Ferenc Grunwalsky, Andras Szoke, Gabor Koltay, and Can Togay.

Hunnicutt, Arthur. Actor. *b.* Feb. 17, 1911, Gravelly, Ark. *d.* 1979. *ed.* Arkansas State Teachers Coll. A veteran of the stage, he entered films early in the 40s and played numerous character parts, typically as a country bumpkin or Western oldtimer. He was nominated for an Academy Award as best supporting actor for *The Big Sky* (1952).

FILMS INCLUDE: *Wildcat* 1942; *Johnny Come Lately* 1943; *Abroad with Two Yanks* 1944; *Lust for Gold, Pinky* 1949; *Broken Arrow, A Ticket to Tomahawk, Two Flags West, Stars in My Crown* 1950; *The Red Badge of Courage, Distant Drums*

1951; *The Big Sky, The Lusty Men* 1952; *The Devil's Canyon* 1953; *The Last Command* 1955; *The Kettles in the Ozarks* 1956; *Born Reckless* 1959; *The Cardinal* 1963; *Cat Ballou* 1965; *Apache Uprising* 1966; *El Dorado* 1967; *Shoot-Out* 1971; *The Revengers* 1972; *Harry and Tonto, The Spikes Gang, Moonrunners* 1974; *Winter Hawk* 1975.

Hunnicutt, Gayle. Actress. Born on Feb. 6, 1942, in Fort Worth, Tex. *ed.* UCLA. Leading lady of American and European films, following stage experience in community theaters. Formerly (1968–74) married to actor David HEMMINGS.

FILMS INCLUDE: *The Wild Angels* 1966; *P.J.* 1968; *Eye of the Cat, Marlowe* 1969; *Fragment of Fear* (UK) 1970; *The Love Machine* 1971; *Running Scared* (UK) 1972; *The Legend of Hell House, Scorpio* 1973; *L'Homme sans Visage/Shadowman* (Fr./It.) 1974; *The Sell Out* (UK), *Tony Saitta/Tough Tony* (It.) 1976; *Strange Shadows in an Empty Room* (It.) 1977; *Once in Paris* 1979; *Target* 1985; *Dream Lover* 1986; *Turnaround* 1987; *Silence Like Glass* 1990.

Hunt, Helen. Actress. Born on June 15, 1963, in Los Angeles. Performing professionally from early childhood, she appeared in various TV series ('Swiss Family Robinson,' etc.) from age ten and in an isolated film at 13. After co-starring as a juvenile in the series 'It Takes Two' (1982–83), she returned to the big screen as a young lead. Her return to television was, from 1992, on 'Mad About You,' receiving numerous Emmys. She made the crossover to box-office success in 1996 with the blockbuster *Twister*. She is married to actor Hank AZARIA.

FILMS: *Rollercoaster* 1977; *Girls Just Want to Have Fun, Future Cop* 1985; *Peggy Sue Got Married* 1986; *Project X* 1987; *Stealing Home, Miles from Home* 1988; *Next of Kin* 1989; *Queens Logic, Trancers 2: The Return of Jack Deth* 1991; *Bob Roberts, Only You, Mr. Saturday Night, The Waterdance, Into the Badlands, Trancers 3: Deth Lives* 1992; *Kiss of Death* 1995; *Twister* 1996.

Hunt, Linda. Actress. Born on Apr. 2, 1945, in Morristown N.J. *ed.* Interlochen Arts Academy, Michigan; Goodman Theater School of Drama, Chicago. Formidable though diminutive (4' 9") character player of the American stage and screen. She won an Academy Award as best supporting actress for her amazing portrayal of a man in *The Year of Living Dangerously* (1983). On Broadway, she was nominated for a Tony for 'End of the World' and won off-Broadway Obies for 'A Metamorphosis in Miniature' and 'Top Girls.'

FILMS: *Popeye* 1980; *The Year of Living Dangerously* (1983); *The Bostonians, Dune* 1984; *Silverado, Eleni* 1985; *Waiting for the Moon* (as Alice B. Toklas) 1987; *She-Devil* 1989; *Kindergarten Cop* 1990; *If Looks Could Kill, 20 Bucks* 1991; *Ready to Wear* 1994; *Pocahontas* (v/o) 1995; *Younger and Younger* 1996.

Hunt, Marsha. Actress. Born Marcia Virginia Hunt, on Oct. 17, 1917, in Chicago. The daughter of an insurance executive and a former operatic soprano and vocal coach, she was raised in New York and attended the Theodore Irving School of Dramatics. She was a Powers model before beginning her film career in the mid-30s. An intelligent person of pleasant if not striking looks, she had her best roles with MGM in the early 40s, playing leads in second features and second leads and supporting roles in major productions. Her career suffered a setback in the early 50s when she was blacklisted by the studios in the wake of the House Un-American Activities hearings, but she returned to the screen later in the decade for a number of roles. She has since been seen on numerous TV programs. Formerly (1938–43) married to then-editor, now-director Jerry HOPPER, she has been the wife of screenwriter Robert Presnell, Jr., since 1946. She is very active in liberal, civic, and charitable causes. Another Marsha Hunt appeared in *Britannia Hospital* and other British films of the 80s.

FILMS INCLUDE: *The Virginia Judge* 1935; *Hollywood Boulevard, Gentle Julia, The Accusing Finger, Desert Gold, College Holiday, Easy to Take* 1936; *Easy Living, Annapolis Salute, Born to the West* 1937; *Come on Leathernecks* 1938; *These Glamour Girls, The Star Reporter* 1939; *Irene, Pride and Prejudice* (as Mary Bennet) 1940; *I'll Wait for You, The Trial of Mary Dugan, The Penalty, Blossoms in the Dust, Unholy Partners* 1941; *Joe Smith—American, Kid Glove Killer, Panama Hattie, Seven Sweethearts* 1942; *The Human Comedy, Thousands Cheer, Cry Havoc* 1943; *Lost Angel, None Shall Escape, Music for Millions* 1944; *The Valley of Decision* 1945; *A Letter for Evie* 1946; *Smash-Up, Carnegie Hall* 1947; *Raw Deal* 1948; *Take One False Step* 1949; *Mary Ryan—Detective* 1950; *Actors and Sin, The Happy Time* 1952; *No Place to Hide* 1956; *Bombers B-52* 1957; *Blue Denim* 1959; *The Plunderers* 1960; *Johnny Got His Gun* 1971; *Rich and Famous* (cameo) 1981.

Hunt, Martita. Actress. *b.* Jan. 30, 1900, Argentina, to British parents. *d.* 1969. On the English stage from 1921, she went on to become a leading dramatic character actress on the West End and Broadway. Aside from an isolated appearance in a two-reel film of 1920, she began her screen career in the early 30s and went on to play memorable character parts in numerous British and some Hollywood films, typically as a slovenly shrew or eccentric dowager.

FILMS INCLUDE: *A Rank Outsider* 1920; *Service for Ladies/Reserved for Ladies* 1932; *Friday the 13th, I Was a Spy* 1933; *When Knights Were Bold, Tudor Rose/Nine Days a Queen* 1936; *Farewell Again/Troopship, The Mill on the Floss* 1937; *Prison Without Bars* 1938; *They Flew Alone/Wings and the Woman* 1942; *The Man in Grey* 1943; *The Wicked Lady* 1945; *Great Expectations* (as Miss Havisham) 1946; *Anna Karenina* (as Princess Betsy), *So Evil My Love* (US/UK) 1948; *The Fan* (as the Duchess of Berwick; US) 1949; *The Story of Robin Hood, It Started in Paradise, Folly to Be Wise* 1952; *Melba* 1953; *Anastasia* (UK/US) 1956; *The Admirable Crichton* 1957; *Bonjour Tristesse, Me and the Colonel* (US) 1958; *Song Without End* (US), *The Brides of Dracula* 1960; *Mr. Topaze/I Like Money* 1961; *The Wonderful World of the Brothers Grimm* (US) 1962; *Becket* (as Queen Matilda; UK/US), *The Unsinkable Molly Brown* (US) 1964; *Bunny Lake Is Missing* 1965; *The Best House in London* 1967.

Hunt, Peter. Director. Born on Mar. 11, 1928, in London. Studied the violin at the London College of Music and art history at the University of Rome before entering British films as a clapper boy in 1947. He became a film editor in the mid-50s and served in that capacity in the 60s on many of the James Bond films as well as other glossy productions. He made his debut as a director in 1969 with another James Bond adventure, *On Her Majesty's Secret Service.*

FILMS: As editor (partial list)—*A Hill in Korea/Hell in Korea* 1956; *The Admirable Crichton/Paradise Lagoon* 1957; *Sink the Bismarck* 1960; *H.M.S. Defiant/Damn the Defiant, Dr. No* 1962; *From Russia with Love* 1963; *Goldfinger* 1964; *The Ipcress File, Thunderball* 1965; *You Only Live Twice* 1967. As director (complete)—*On Her Majesty's Secret Service* 1969; *Gold* 1974; *Shout at the Devil* 1976; *Gulliver's Travels* (animation/live action; UK/Belg.) 1977; *Death Hunt* 1981; *Wild Geese II* 1985; *Hyper Sapien* 1986; *Assassination* 1987; *Desperate Hours* (superv. edit. only) 1990.

Hunt, Peter H. Director. Born on Dec. 19, 1938, in Pasadena, Calif. *ed.* Yale. Primarily a stage director, he also piloted a number of TV programs and in 1972 turned out his first feature film, *1776,* a screen adaptation of the musical he had earlier directed on Broadway and on the London stage.

FILMS: *1776* 1972; *Bully* 1978; *Adventures of Huckleberry Finn* (orig. for TV) 1985.

Hunte, Otto. Art director. *b.* 1881, Hamburg, Germany. *d.* 1947. Deceased. One of the leading artists of the German expressionist cinema of the 20s, he headed the team that designed the sets for Fritz Lang's films and collaborated on the imaginative design of other important films of the period, notably *The Blue Angel.* During WW II he worked on the Nazi propaganda film *Jud Süss/Jew Suess* but later about-faced and collaborated on the set of the postwar anti-Nazi film *The Murderers Are Among Us.* He died in the late 40s.

FILMS INCLUDE: *Die Spinnen/The Spiders, Die Herrin der Welt/Mistress of the World* 1919–20; *Das indische Grabmal/The Indian Tomb* 1921; *Dr. Mabuse der Spieler* 1922; *Die Nibelungen* 1924; *Die Liebe der Jeanne Ney/The Loves of Jeanne Ney* 1927; *Die Frau im Mond/Woman on the Moon/By Rocket to the Moon* 1929; *Der blaue Engel/The Blue Angel* 1930; *Gold* 1934; *Die Kreutzersonate/The Kreutzer Sonata* 1937; *Jud Süss/Jew Suess* 1940; *Die Mörder sind unter uns/The Murderers Are Among Us* 1946; *Razzia* 1947.

Hunter, Holly. Actress. Born on Mar. 20, 1958, in Conyers, Ga. Petite (5' 2"), accomplished leading lady of the American stage, TV, and films. She began acting in her freshman year in high school, and appeared in upstate New York summer stock when she was 16. Formally trained at Carnegie Mellon University, she made both her screen and off-Broadway debuts in 1981. Onstage, she established her reputation in four Beth Henley plays, getting her big break when she took over Mary Beth Hurt's role in 'Crimes of the Heart.' On-screen, she scored big in *Broadcast News* (1987) for which she was named the year's best actress at the Berlin Film Festival and by the New York as well as the Los Angeles film critics. Joel and Ethan COEN are said to have written *Raising Arizona* specifically with her in mind. She scored another personal triumph in *Miss Firecracker* (1989), reprising her stage success. In 1993 she reinvigorated her film career with her critically acclaimed, Academy Award–winning performance as a mute woman in Jane CAMPION's *The Piano*. On TV she won an Emmys for 'Roe vs. Wade' and 'The Positively True Adventures of the Alleged Texas Chearleader-Murdering Mom.'

FILMS: *The Burning* 1981; *Swing Shift* 1984; *Raising Arizona, End of the Line, Broadcast News* 1987; *Miss Firecracker, Animal Behavior, Always* 1989; *Once Around* 1991; *The Firm, The Piano* 1993; *Copycat, Home for the Holidays* 1995; *Crash, A Life Less Ordinary* 1997.

Hunter, Ian. Actor. *b.* June 13, 1900, Kenilworth, South Africa. *d.* 1975. Genial leading man of British and American films. He went to England in his teens and in 1917 joined the army and served in France. He made his stage debut in 1919, played his first screen role in 1924, and alternated as a leading man of stage and screen until 1934, when he left for Hollywood. He usually played devoted, dependable husbands, lovers, or friends, often opposite Kay FRANCIS. In 1942 he returned to England for war service. He subsequently appeared in numerous British plays and films. On both sides of the Atlantic, he has close to 100 films to his credit.

FILMS INCLUDE: In the UK—*Not for Sale* 1924; *Confessions* 1925; *The Ring* 1927; *Easy Virtue* 1928; *Syncopation* (US) 1929; *Escape* 1930; *Cape Forlorn/Love Storm* 1931; *The Sign of Four* 1932; *Orders Is Orders* 1933; *No Escape* 1934; *The Morals of Marcus* 1935. In the US—*The Girl from Tenth Avenue, Jalna* (as Renny Whiteoak), *A Midsummer Night's Dream* (as Theseus), *I Found Stella Parish* 1935; *The White Angel, To Mary—With Love, The Devil Is a Sissy* 1936; *Stolen Holiday, Call It a Day, Another Dawn, Confession, That Certain Woman, 52nd Street* 1937; *The Adventures of Robin Hood* (as King Richard the Lion-Heart), *Always Goodbye, Secrets of an Actress, The Sisters, Comet Over Broadway* 1938; *Yes My Darling Daughter, The Little Princess, Broadway Serenade, Tarzan Finds a Son, Maisie, Tower of London* (as Edward IV) 1939; *Broadway Melody of 1940, Strange Cargo, The Long Voyage Home, Bitter Sweet, Dulcy, Gallant Sons* 1940; *Come Live with Me, Andy Hardy's Private Secretary, Ziegfeld Girl, Billy the Kid, Dr. Jekyll and Mr. Hyde* (as Dr. Lanyon), *Smilin' Through* 1941; *A Yank at Eton* 1942; *If Winter Comes, Forever and a Day* 1943. In the UK—*Bedelia* 1946; *White Cradle Inn, The White Unicorn/Bad Sister* 1947; *Edward My Son* (UK/US) 1949; *Hunted* 1951; *It Started in Paradise* 1952; *Appointment in London* 1953; *Eight O'Clock Walk* 1954; *The Battle of the River Plate/Pursuit of the Graf Spee* 1956; *Rockets Galore/Mad Little Island* 1958; *North West Frontier/Flame Over India* 1959; *Doctor Blood's Coffin, The Treasure of Monte Cristo/The Secret of Monte Cristo* 1961; *Guns of Darkness* 1962.

Hunter, Jeffrey. Actor. *b.* Henry Herman McKinnies, Jr., Nov. 25, 1925, New Orleans. *d.* 1969. Pretty-boy star of Hollywood films of the 50s. The son of a sales engineer, he was raised in Milwaukee, where he began performing on radio during his senior year in high school and later appeared in summer stock. After Navy service (1945–46) he enrolled at Northwestern University, then went on to graduate courses at UCLA, where he made his first screen appearance in 1950, playing a bit in a college production of *Julius Caesar,* starring Charlton Heston. He made his professional film debut the following year. Rugged and boyishly handsome, he played leads in many Hollywood films mainly for Fox, often of the action genre; but he was atypically unaggressive in his most famous role, that of Jesus Christ in Nicholas Ray's *King of Kings* (1961). His career faded in the 60s, when he appeared mainly in cheap European productions. He died at 43 after brain surgery following an accidental fall. His first wife (1950–55) was actress Barbara RUSH.

FILMS: *Call Me Mister, Fourteen Hours, The Frogmen, Take Care of My Little Girl* 1951; *Red Skies of Montana/Smoke Jumpers, Belles on Their Toes, Dreamboat, Lure of the Wilderness* 1952; *Singlehanded/Sailor of the King* (UK) 1953; *Princess of the Nile* 1954; *White Feather, Seven Angry Men, Seven Cities of Gold* 1955; *The Searchers, The Great Locomotive Chase, The Proud Ones, A Kiss Before Dying* 1956; *Gun for a Coward, The True Story of Jesse James* (as Frank James), *The Way to the Gold, No Down Payment* 1957; *Count Five and Die, The Last Hurrah, In Love and War* 1958; *Sergeant Rutledge, Hell to Eternity, Key Witness* 1960; *Man Trap, King of Kings* (as Jesus Christ) 1961; *No Man Is an Island, The Longest Day* 1962; *Oro per i Cesari/Gold for the Caesars* (It./Fr.) 1963; *The Man from Galveston* 1964; *Joaquin Murrieta/Murieta* (title role; Sp.), *Brainstorm* 1965; *Dimension 5, Joe Navidad/The Christmas Kid* (Sp./US), *Una Bruja sin Escoba/A Witch Without a Broom* (Sp./US) 1966; *A Guide for the Married Man* 1967; *Custer of the West, The Private Navy of Sgt. O'Farrell, Frau Wirtin hat auch einen Grafen/Sexy Susan at the King's Court* (Aus./It./Ger.) 1968; *Joe! Cercati un Posto per morire/Joe Find a Place to Die* (It.) 1969; *Viva America* (Sp.) 1970.

Hunter, Kim. Actress. Born Janet Cole, on Nov. 12, 1922, in Detroit. *ed.* Actors Studio. On stage from age 17, she made an auspicious screen debut in the quality thriller *The Seventh Victim* (1943), but her subsequent Hollywood films were minor. Audiences rediscovered her in the British fantasy *A Matter of Life and Death* (titled *Stairway to Heaven* in the US). Returning from England in 1947, she was cast in the role of Stella Kowalski in Broadway's 'A Streetcar Named Desire.' She repeated the role in the 1951 film version, a performance for which she won an Academy Award in the best supporting actress category. But shortly after, her name appeared in *Red Channels,* the Red-scare pamphlet, and she was blacklisted by the industry for several years. Her screen career was temporarily damaged and her subsequent film appearances have been sporadic, but she has been seen frequently on TV. Author: *Loose in the Kitchen* (1975), an "autobiographical cookbook."

FILMS: *The Seventh Victim* 1943; *Tender Comrade, A Canterbury Tale* (UK), *When Strangers Marry* 1944; *You Came Along* 1945; *A Matter of Life and Death/Stairway to Heaven* (UK) 1946; *A Streetcar Named Desire* (as Stella Kowalski) 1951; *Deadline U.S.A., Anything Can Happen* 1952; *Storm Center* 1956; *The Young Stranger, Bermuda Affair* 1957; *Money Women and Guns* 1958; *Lilith* 1964; *Planet of the Apes, The Swimmer* 1968; *Beneath the Planet of the Apes* 1970; *Escape from the Planet of the Apes* 1971; *Dark August* 1976; *The Kindred* 1987; *Due Occhi diabolici/Two Evil Eyes* (It.) 1990.

Hunter, Ross. Producer. Born Martin Fuss, on May 6, 1916, in Cleveland. *ed.* Western Reserve U. (M.A.). A former schoolteacher, he entered films as an actor in the mid-40s and played leads in such B pictures as *Louisiana Hayride* (1944), *A Guy a Girl and a Pal* (1945), *Hit the Hay,* and *Sweetheart of Sigma Chi* (both 1946). He then returned to teaching, and after gaining some experience as stage producer and director, he returned to films in the early 50s as a producer. Produced numerous expensive-looking tearjerkers as well as comedies and thrillers for Universal until 1971, when he moved over to Columbia. He switched to Paramount in 1974 and subsequently restricted his output to TV movies.

FILMS INCLUDE: *Take Me to Town* 1953; *Magnificent Obsession* 1954; *The Spoilers, Captain Lightfoot* 1955; *All That Heaven Allows* 1956; *Battle Hymn, Tammy and the Bachelor, My Man Godfrey* 1957; *This Happy Feeling* 1958; *Imitation of Life, Pillow Talk* 1959; *Portrait in Black, Midnight Lace* 1960; *Back Street, Flower Drum Song* 1961; *The Thrill of It All* 1963; *The Chalk Garden* 1964; *The Art of Love* 1965; *Madame X, The Pad* 1966; *Thoroughly Modern Millie* 1967; *Airport* 1970; *Lost Horizon* 1973.

Hunter, Tab. Actor. Born Arthur Gelien, on July 1, 1931, in New York City. At 15 he lied about his age and joined the Coast Guard. At 18 he made his film debut with no previous acting experience. He did not score well with the critics, but his wholesome personality and all-American blond, athletic looks made him an idol to teenagers in the 50s. Has since appeared in many movies, mainly minor productions, including three campy pairings with female impersonator Divine. He has also appeared on TV and on Broadway in recent years. In 1960–61 he starred briefly in his own TV program, 'The Tab Hunter Show.' He later appeared regularly in the comedy series 'Mary Hartman, Mary Hartman' (1977–78).

FILMS INCLUDE: *The Lawless* 1950; *Saturday Island/Island of Desire* (UK) 1952; *Gun Belt* 1953; *Track of the Cat* 1954; *Battle Cry, The Sea Chase* 1955; *The Burning Hills, The Girl He Left Behind* 1956; *Lafayette Escadrille, Gunman's Walk, Damn Yankees* 1958; *That Kind of Woman, They Came to Cordura* 1959; *The Pleasure of his Company* 1961; *La Freccia d'Oro/The Golden Arrow* (It.) 1962; *Operation Bikini* 1963; *Ride the Wild Surf* 1964; *War Gods of the Deep, The Loved One* 1965; *Birds Do It* 1966; *Hostile Guns* 1967; *The Life and Times of Judge Roy Bean* 1972; *The Arousers* 1973; *Timber Tramps* 1975; *Polyester* 1981; *Pandemonium, Grease 2* 1982; *Lust in the Dust* (also co-pro.) 1985; *Grotesque, Cameron's Closet* 1988; *Out of the Dark* 1989; *Dark Horse* (story) 1992.

Hunter, T(homas) Hayes ("Happy"). Director. *b.* Dec. 1, 1896, Philadelphia. *d.* 1944. A Hollywood director from his teens, he turned out a good number of silent films before settling in England in 1927. He is best known for *The Ghoul* (1933), a nifty British horror thriller starring Boris KARLOFF and featuring Ralph RICHARDSON in his screen debut.

FILMS INCLUDE: In the US—*The Vampire* (co-dir. with Sidney Olcott; also co-sc.) 1913; *Fire and Sword, The Vampire's Trail* (co-dir., co-sc. with Robert Vignola), *The Seats of the Mighty* 1914; *Judy Forgot* 1915; *Father and Son, The Crimson Stain Mystery* (serial) 1916; *The Border Legion* (also prod.) 1918; *Once to Every Man, Desert Gold* 1919; *Cup of Fury, Earthbound* 1920; *The Light in the Clearing* 1921; *Damaged Hearts* (also prod.), *The Recoil, Trouping with Ellen* 1924; *The Sky Raider, Wildfire* 1925. In the UK—*One of the Best* 1927; *A South Sea Bubble, The Triumph of the Scarlet Pimpernel* 1928; *The Silver King* 1929; *The Man They Couldn't Arrest, The Calendar* 1931; *The Frightened Lady/Criminal at Large, White Face, Sally Bishop* 1932; *The Ghoul* 1933; *Warn London* 1934.

Hunter, Tim. American director. After collaborating on the screenplay of Jonathan Kaplan's *Over the Edge* (1979), a poignant drama of youthful alienation, he made an auspicious debut as a director with *Tex* (1982), an appealing story of rural youth, which he also wrote in collaboration with Charlie HAAS. His subsequent output, limited in quantity, varied in quality.

FILMS (as director): *Over the Edge* (co-sc. only) 1979; *Tex* (also co-sc.) 1982; *Sylvester* 1985; *River's Edge* 1987; *Paint It Black* 1990; *The Saint of Fort Washington* 1992.

Huntington, Lawrence. Director. *b.* 1900, London. *d.* 1968. He directed numerous British films and TV episodes, mainly suspense thrillers. Often wrote his own scripts.

FILMS INCLUDE: *After Many Years* 1929; *Strange Cargo, Bad Boy* (also sc.) 1936; *Passage to London* 1937; *Dial 999, Twin Faces* 1938; *This Man Is Dangerous/The Patient Vanishes* (also co-sc.), *Tower of Terror* 1941; *Suspected Person* (also sc.) 1942; *Night Boat to Dublin, Wanted for Murder* 1946; *The Upturned Glass* 1947; *Mr. Perrin and Mr. Traill* 1948; *Man on the Run* (also sc.) 1949; *The Franchise Affair* (also co-sc.) 1951; *There Was a Young Lady* (also sc.) 1953; *Contraband Spain* (also sc.) 1955; *Strangehold* (also sc.), *The Fur Collar* (also sc.) 1962; *The Vulture* (also prod., sc.) 1967; *The Oblong Box* (sc. only) 1969.

Huppert, Isabelle. Actress. Born on Mar. 16, 1955, in Paris. *ed.* Conservatoire National d'Art Dramatique. Fragile, freckle-faced leading lady of French and international films. On screen from age 16, she developed in the late 70s into one of Europe's foremost film personalities, a versatile interpreter of a wide range of roles, from delicate, innocent demoiselles to hardened mystery women. After gaining international fame in Claude Goretta's *The Lacemaker* (1977), she solidified her position with a best actress prize (in a tie) at Cannes for Claude Chabrol's *Violette Noziére* (1978) and went on to play the principal female role in Michael Cimino's notorious *Heaven's Gate* (1979). In the 80s she displayed a growing maturity and assurance in her roles, memorably in *Coup de Foudre/Entre Nous* (1983) and *Une Affaire de Femmes/Story of Women* (1988). She shared the best actress prize at Venice for the latter. Her busy schedule also includes many stage and TV appearances.

FILMS INCLUDE: *Faustine et le Bel Eté/Faustine and the Beautiful Summer/Growing Up* 1971; *Le Bar de la Fourche, César et Rosalie/Cesar and Rosalie* 1972; *L'Ampélopède* 1973; *Les Valseues/Going Places, Glissements progressifs du Plaisir,*

Aloïse 1974; *Rosebud* (US), *Le Grand Délire Sérieux comme le Plaisir, Dupont Lajoie/Rape of Innocence, Docteur Françose Gailland/No Time for Breakfast* 1975; *Je suis Pierre Rivière, Le Petit Marcel, Le Juge et l'Assasin/The Judge and the Assassin* 1976; *La Dentellière/The Lacemaker, Les Indiens sont encore loin, Des Enfants gâtés* 1977; *Violette Nozière/Violette* 1978; *Les Soeurs Brontë/The Brontë Sisters* (as Ann Brontë), *Retour à la bien-aimée* 1979; *Heaven's Gate* (US), *Orökseg/Les Héritières/The Heiresses* (Hung./Fr.), *Loulou, Sauve qui peut (la Vie)/Every Man for Himself* 1980; *La Vera Storia della Signora delle Camelie/La Dame aux Camélias* (It./Fr.), *Les Ailes de la Colombe, Coup de Torchon, Eaux profondes* 1981; *Passion, La Truite/The Trout* 1982; *Coup de Foudre/Entre Nous, Storia de Piera/L'Histoire de Pierra* (It./Fr.), *La Femme de mon Pote/My Best Friend's Girl* 1983; *La Garce* 1984; *Sac de Noeuds/All Mixed Up* 1985; *Signé Charlotte/Sincerely Charlotte; Cactus* (Austral.) 1986; *The Bedroom Window* (US) 1987; *Une Affaire de Femmes/Story of Women* 1988; *La Vengeance d'une Femme/A Woman's Revenge* 1990; *Malina, Madame Bovary* 1991; *Amateur, Love After Love* 1994; *The Ceremony; Love's Debris* 1996.

Hurd, Gale Anne. Producer. Born on Oct. 25, 1955, in Los Angeles. After graduating Phi Beta Kappa from Stanford in 1977, she joined New World Pictures as executive assistant to the company president, Roger CORMAN. She worked her way up through various administrative positions and eventually became involved in production. In 1982 she formed her own company, Pacific Western Productions, then went on to produce a number of box-office blockbusters. An active member of the Hollywood Women's Political Committee, she created a grant bearing her own name to encourage talent in the American Film Institute's Directing Workshop for Women. Was married to James Cameron.

FILMS: *Smokey Bites the Dust* (co-prod.) 1981; *The Terminator* (also co-sc.) 1984; *Aliens* 1986; *Bad Dreams, Alien Nation* (co-prod.) 1988; *The Abyss* 1989; *Downtown* (exec. prod.), *Tremors* (exec. prod.) 1990; *Terminator II: Judgement Day* (exec. prod.) 1991; *The Waterdance, Raising Cain* 1992; *Safe Passage, No Escape* 1994; *The Ghost and the Darkness, Going West in America* 1996; *Dante's Peak, The Relic* (co-prod.) 1997.

Hurst, Brandon. Actor *b.* 1866, London. *d.* 1947. Tall, gaunt, evil-eyed character player of Hollywood silents and talkies. Philology studies led him to acting on the stage and later in films. Memorable as Sir George Carewe in the John Barrymore version of *Dr. Jekyll and Mr. Hyde* (1920), as Quasimodo's cruel master, Jehan, in the Lon Chaney version of *The Hunchback of Notre Dame* (1923), and as the villainous caliph in the Douglas Fairbanks version of *The Thief of Bagdad* (1924).

FILMS INCLUDE: *Via Wireless* 1915; *Dr. Jekyll and Mr. Hyde* 1920; *The Hunchback of Notre Dame* 1923; *The Thief of Bagdad, Cytherea, He Who Gets Slapped, The Lover of Camille* 1924; *The Lady, Lightnin'* 1925; *The Grand Duchess and the Waiter* 1926; *The King of Kings, Seventh Heaven, Love* 1927; *The Man Who Laughs* 1928; *The Greene Murder Case* 1929; *A Connecticut Yankee* (as Merlin) 1931; *Murders in the Rue Morgue, White Zombie, Sherlock Holmes* 1932; *The Lost Patrol, Viva Villa* 1934; *The Charge of the Light Brigade, Mary of Scotland* 1936; *The Plough and the Stars, Wee Willie Winkie* 1937; *Suez* (as Franz Lizst) 1938; *Stanley and Livingstone* 1939; *The Blue Bird, Rhythm on the River* 1940; *The Remarkable Andrew* 1942; *Jane Eyre, The Man in Half Moon Street* 1944; *The Princess and the Pirate, Road to Utopia* 1945; *Monsieur Beaucaire* 1946; *My Favorite Brunette* 1947.

Hurst, Brian Desmond. Director. *b.* Feb. 12, 1900, Castle Reagh, Ireland. *d.* 1986. *ed.* École des Beaux-Arts, Paris. In 1925 he went to Hollywood, where he learned the cinema craft as assistant to director John FORD. Returning to England, he began directing British films in 1934. He worked in a variety of genres, turning out several fine films among many routine ones.

FEATURE FILMS: *The Tell-Tale Heart, Irish Hearts/Norah O'Neale* (Ire.) 1934; *Riders to the Sea* 1935; *Ourselves Alone, The Tenth Man* 1936; *Sensation, Glamorous Night* 1937; *Prison Without Bars* 1938; *The Lion Has Wings* (co-dir. with Michael Powell and Adrian Brunel), *On the Night of the Fire/The Fugitive* (also co-sc.) 1939; *Dangerous Moonlight/Suicide Squadron* 1941; *Alibi* 1942; *The £100 Window* 1944; *Caesar and Cleopatra* (dir. some scenes; uncredited) 1945; *Hungry Hill* 1946; *Mark of Cain* 1948; *Trottie True/The Gay Lady* 1949; *Tom Brown's School Days* (prod. only) 1950; *Scrooge/A Christmas Carol* 1951; *The Malta Story* 1953; *Simba* 1955; *The Black Tent* 1956; *Dangerous Exile* 1957; *Behind the Mask* 1958; *His and Hers* 1961; *The Playboy of the Western World* (also sc.; Ire.) 1962.

Hurt, John. Actor. Born on Jan. 22, 1940, in Chesterfield, England. Solemn, frail, craggy-faced character star of British stage, screen, and television, often in vulnerable, offbeat roles. Trained to become a painter at Grimsby Art School and St. Martin's School of Art, he then attended the Royal Academy of Dramatic Art and made both his stage and screen debuts in 1962. He first gained international recognition in 1975 with a heart-wrenching portrayal of a tormented homosexual in the TV play 'The Naked Civil Servant,' for which he won the British Academy Award. He later won that award in the feature category for *Midnight Express* (1978) and *The Elephant Man* (1980), films for which he was also nominated for Hollywood Oscars. He appeared in many American films in the 80s. Divorced from actresses Annette Robertson (in 1964) and Donna Peacock (in 1990), he married Jo Dalton, a production assistant on one of his films, in 1990.

FEATURE FILMS: *The Wild and the Willing/Wild and Willing* 1962; *This Is My Street* 1963; *A Man for All Seasons* 1966; *The Sailor from Gibraltar* 1967; *Before Winter Comes, Sinful Davey* 1969; *In Search of Gregory* 1970; *10 Rillington Place, Mr. Forbush and the Penguins/Cry of the Penguins* 1971; *The Pied Piper* 1972; *Little Malcolm and His Struggle Against the Eunuchs/Little Malcolm* 1974; *The Ghoul* 1975; *East of Elephant Rock, La Linea el Fiume/Stream Line* (Sp.) 1976; *The Disappearance* (Can.) 1977; *The Shout, Watership Down* (v/o), *Midnight Express, Lord of the Rings* (v/o; US) 1978; *Alien* (US) 1979; *The Elephant Man* (US), *Heaven's Gate* (US) 1980; *History of the World: Part I* (as Jesus; US) 1981; *Night Crossing* (UK/US), *Partners* (US), *The Plague Dogs* (v/o; UK/US) 1982; *The Osterman Weekend* (US) 1983; *Champions, 1984* (as Winston Smith), *The Hit, Success Is the Best Revenge* 1984; *The Black Cauldron* (v/o; US) 1985; *Jake Speed* (US), *Rocinante* 1986; *White Mischief, From the Hip* (US), *Spaceballs* (US), *Aria* ('I Pagliacci' segment) 1987; *Vincent: The Life and Death of Vincent Van Gogh* (doc.; narr. only; Austral.) 1988; *Scandal* (as Dr. Stephen Ward of Profumo Affair notoriety) 1989; *Romeo-Juliet* (Belg.), *The Field, Frankenstein Unbound* 1990; *King Ralph, Resident Alien* 1991; *I Dreamt I Woke Up, Lapse of Memory, Dark at Noon* 1992; *Even Cowgirls Get the Blues, Monolith, Thumbelina* (v/o) 1994; *Rob Roy, Wild Bill* 1995; *Dead Man* 1996; *Contact* 1997.

Hurt, Mary Beth. Actress. Born Mary Beth Supinger, on Sept. 26, 1948, in Marshalltown, Iowa. *ed.* U. of Iowa; NYU. Leading lady of the American stage and screen. She made her professional debut in 1973 with New York's Shakespeare

Festival in Central Park and her first film appearance in 1978 in Woody Allen's *Interiors.* Divorced from actor William HURT, she married director Paul SCHRADER.

FILMS: *Interiors* 1978; *Head Over Heels/Chilly Scenes of Winter* 1979; *A Change of Seasons* 1980; *The World According to Garp* 1982; *D.A.R.Y.L., Compromising Positions* 1985; *Parents, Slaves of New York* 1989; *Defenseless* 1991; *Light Sleeper* 1992; *The Age of Innocence, My Boyfriend's Back, Six Degrees of Separation* 1993; *From the Journals of Jean Seberg* 1996; *Boy's Life 2* 1887.

Hurt, William. Actor. Born on Mar. 20, 1950, in Washington, D.C. Big, rangy (6' 3"), blond star of the American stage and screen. He spent much of his early childhood in the South Pacific, mainly in Guam, where his father was stationed on a State Department assignment. When he was six his parents divorced. He moved with his mother to Manhattan but continued to spend vacations with his father in faraway places. He was ten when his mother married Henry Luce III, heir to the Time-Life fortune. Bewildered by the sudden wealth and change in lifestyle, Hurt was sent off to the Middlesex prep school where he found some solace from alienation in school dramatics. Under the influence of his stepfather, he enrolled at Tufts University, majoring in theology. Again, he found himself drawn to the school's drama program, where, in his junior year, he met and married aspiring actress Mary Beth HURT (née Supinger). They moved to London, where he spent his senior year studying drama, then back to New York, where he enrolled at the drama wing of Juilliard. Just before graduating, with his life at an impasse and his marriage on the rocks, he motorbiked cross-country to Ashland, Oregon, where he made his professional stage debut during a regional Shakespeare festival. His real career began in 1976, after he joined New York's Circle Repertory Company. A string of successes, capped by an Obie Award for 'My Life' (1977) led to growing recognition and eventually to his auspicious screen debut in Ken Russell's *Altered States* (1980).

During the 80s Hurt developed into one of Hollywood's premier leading men, gaining audience popularity with his appealing screen presence and the growing approval of critics for his steadily maturing skills as an interpreter of complex roles. He won both the Academy Award and the Cannes Festival best actor awards for his exceptional portrayal of a homosexual prisoner in Hector Babenco's *Kiss of the Spider Woman* (1985). He was nominated for Oscars twice more in a row for *Children of a Lesser God* (1986) and *Broadcast News* (1987). Less successful in his personal affairs, he became involved with ballet dancer Sandra Jennings, who bore his child, Alex. In 1989, she sued the actor in a landmark "divorce" case, maintaining that she was, in fact, his common-law wife. By the time of the suit, Hurt was married to Heidi Henderson, daughter of bandleader Skitch Henderson.

FILMS: *Altered States* 1980; *Eyewitness, Body Heat* 1981; *The Big Chill, Gorky Park* 1983; *Kiss of the Spider Woman* 1985; *Children of a Lesser God* 1986; *Broadcast News* 1987; *A Time of Destiny, The Accidental Tourist* 1988; *I Love You to Death, Alice* 1990; *The Doctor* 1991; *Until the End of the World, The Plague* 1992; *Mr. Wonderful* 1993; *Second Best, Trial by Jury* 1994; *Smoke* 1995; *Jane Eyre, Michael* 1996.

Hurwitz, Leo. Documentary filmmaker. *b.* 1909, Brooklyn, N.Y. *d.* 1991. *ed.* Harvard. A leading figure in the development of the American documentary since the early 30s, he participated in the pioneering activities of the Film and Photo League and in 1937 co-founded Pioneer Films, America's first independent production company of documentary films. He collaborated with Pare Lorenz, Willard Van Dyke, Ralph Steiner, Paul Strand, and other leading American documentarians on several major landmarks in the history of American fact film. During WW II he worked on films for the Office of War Information and the British Information Service. He then became a producer-director and chief of news and special events at CBS-TV in its infancy. His *Strange Victory* (1948), a documentary about postwar racism in America, won prizes at the Karlovy-Vary and Venice festivals. Because of his left-wing leanings, he was blacklisted in the 50s and early 60s but continued working independently and directed, co-produced, and edited several segments for the CBS 'Omnibus' series without receiving screen credit. His *Verdict for Tomorrow* (1961), a documentary compiled from TV coverage of the Eichmann trial, won Emmy and Peabody Awards. From 1969 to 1974 Hurwitz was professor of film and Chairman of the Graduate Institute of Film and Television at NYU. In 1981 he won an International Film Critics Prize for *Dialogue with a Woman Departed,* a four-hour visual poem to his late second wife and collaborator, Peggy Lawson, who had passed away in 1971.

FILMS INCLUDE: *Hunger* (dir.) 1932; *Scottsboro* (dir.) 1934; *The Plow That Broke the Plains* (phot., co-sc.) 1935; *Pay Day* (co-dir. with Paul Strand), *Heart of Spain* (co-prod., edit.) 1938; *Native Land* (co-dir., with Strand, co-sc., edit.) 1942; *Strange Victory* (dir., edit.) 1948; *The Museum and the Fury* (dir.) 1956; *Here at the Water's Edge* (dir.) 1960; *Verdict for Tomorrow* (dir.) 1961; *Dialogue with a Woman Departed* 1981.

Hussein, Waris. Director. Born on Dec. 9, 1938, in Lucknow, U.P., India. Based in England, he turned out several quality features there and in the US, as well as numerous TV movies and plays.

FEATURE FILMS: *A Touch of Love/Thank You All Very Much* 1969; *Quackser Fortune Has a Cousin in the Bronx* (US; filmed in Ireland) 1970; *Melody* 1971; *The Possession of Joel Delaney* (US) 1972; *Henry VIII and His Six Wives* 1973.

Hussey, Olivia. Actress. Born on Apr. 17, 1951, in Buenos Aires, to British parents. Ingenue and leading lady of British and international films. Memorable as Juliet in Franco Zeffirelli's *Romeo and Juliet* (1968). The remainder of her career, comprising low-budget features and several expensive TV movies, was anticlimactic. Having divorced Dean Paul Martin, Dean Martin's now-deceased son, she married Japanese pop star Akira Fuse. They live in California.

FILMS: *The Battle of the Villa Fiorita* (UK/US), *Cup Fever* 1965; *Romeo and Juliet* (UK/It.) 1968; *All the Right Noises* 1971; *Lost Horizon* (US), *Summertime Killer* (US) 1973; *Black Christmas* 1974; *Death on the Nile, The Cat and the Canary* 1978; *The Man with Bogart's Face/Sam Marlowe, Private Eye* (US), *Virus* (Jap.) 1980; *Turkey Shoot/Escape 2000* (Austral.) 1981; *The Jeweller's Shop* (Fr.) 1989; *Psycho IV: The Beginning* 1990; *Undeclared War* 1991; *Quest of the Delta Knights, Save Me* 1994.

Hussey, Ruth. Actress. Born Ruth Carol O'Rourke, on Oct. 30, 1914, in Providence, R.I. *ed.* Pembroke Women's Coll.; Brown U.; U. of Michigan School of Drama. Leading lady of Hollywood films of the 40s. She started out as fashion commentator on a local radio station and later worked in New York as a Powers model. After several stage roles with touring companies she was signed by MGM to a five-year movie contract and made her film debut in 1937. Following a number of minor roles, she became established in the early 40s as one of the studio's second-rung leading ladies, typically playing elegant, sophisticated, knowing women. She was nominated for an Oscar for her supporting role as a cynical magazine photographer in *The Philadelphia Story* (1940) but enjoyed her greatest success on the stage in 1945, when she starred opposite Ralph

Bellamy in the Broadway production of 'State of the Union.' She subsequently returned to the screen in only occasional roles.

FILMS INCLUDE: *The Big City, Madame X* 1937; *Judge Hardy's Children, Rich Man Poor Girl, Spring Madness* 1938; *Honolulu, Within the Law, Maisie, Blackmail, The Women, Fast and Furious, Another Thin Man* 1939; *Northwest Passage, Susan and God, The Philadelphia Story* 1940; *Flight Command, Free and Easy, Our Wife, Married Bachelor, H. M. Pulham Esq.* 1941; *Pierre of the Plains* 1942; *Tennessee Johnson* 1943; *Tender Comrade, The Uninvited, Marine Raiders* 1944; *Bedside Manner* 1945; *I Jane Doe* 1948; *The Great Gatsby* 1949; *Louisa, Mr. Musica* 1950; *That's My Boy* 1951; *Stars and Stripes Forever* 1952; *The Lady Wants Mink* 1953; *The Facts of Life* 1960.

Huston, Anjelica. Actress. Born in 1952, in Los Angeles. Tall, imposing character lead of the American stage, TV, and films. The daughter of director John HUSTON and his fourth wife, ballerina Enrica (Ricki) Soma, and granddaughter of actor Walter HUSTON, she was raised in Ireland during the European phase of her father's career and after her parents separated when she was 11. Living in total obscurity, she was suddenly tossed into the limelight playing the lead, as a star-crossed young lover (opposite Assaf Dayan, son of Israel's famous one-eyed general), in the historic drama *A Walk with Love and Death* (1969), one of her father's weakest films. She returned to obscurity, but years later returned to the screen in sporadic supporting roles. It was not until the late 80s that she suddenly emerged as a formidable screen presence, true to the Huston tradition. After winning an Academy Award as best supporting actress for the role of a sly Mafia-family woman in her father's *Prizzi's Honor* (1985), she went on to portray a rich gallery of colorful lead characters in other films. She was nominated for Oscars twice in succession, for *Enemies, a Love Story* (1989) and *The Grifters* (1990). Her 17-year relationship with actor Jack NICHOLSON ended in 1990. Like her father before her, she turned her attention to directing with a critically hailed, if not controversial, television movie *Bastard Out of Carolina* (1996).

FILMS: *Sinful Davey* (bit), *A Walk with Love and Death, Hamlet* (bit) 1969; *Swashbuckler, The Last Tycoon* 1976; *The Postman Always Rings Twice* 1981; *This Is Spinal Tap, The Ice Pirates* 1984; *Prizzi's Honor* 1985; *Gardens of Stone, The Dead* 1987; *A Handful of Dust, Mr. North* 1988; *Crimes and Misdemeanors, Enemies, a Love Story* 1989; *The Witches, The Grifters* 1990; *The Addams Family* 1991; *The Player* (cameo) 1992; *Manhattan Murder Mystery, Addams Family Values* 1993; *The Crossing Guard, The Perez Family* 1995.

Huston, John. Director, screenwriter, actor. *b.* Aug. 5, 1906, Nevada, Mo., a town that family legend claims was won by his grandfather in a poker game. *d.* 1987. The son of Walter HUSTON, he made his first stage appearance at age three and spent much of his childhood traveling with his parents. After their divorce in 1913, he began traveling with each separately—on the vaudeville circuit with his father and the racetrack route with his mother. At age 12 he was placed in a sanitarium to rest an enlarged heart and cure a kidney ailment. The frail boy's recovery was so complete that when he was 14 he quit a Los Angeles high school to become a boxer. Eventually he won the amateur lightweight boxing championship of California at the price of a broken nose.

Huston made his professional stage debut at 19, playing a leading role off Broadway. At about the same time he married a high-school sweetheart. But he soon grew discontented with both acting and marriage and took off to Mexico, where he became an officer in the cavalry. Resigning his commission in 1928, he brought back home 'Frankie and Johnny,' a musical play he had written in Mexico. It was performed by puppets in 1929 and published in book form in 1930. Meanwhile, Huston was engaged by his father's friend, William WYLER, to play small parts in three of the director's films. Still restless and groping for direction, he began submitting short stories to the *American Mercury,* then joined the staff of the New York *Graphic* as a reporter. But his casual treatment of facts soon led to his being fired.

Huston's next stop was again Hollywood, where he was hired by Sam Goldwyn as a screenwriter, drawing a regular salary but being assigned no work. Thanks to his father's star status, he was able to switch over to Universal, for which he wrote dialogue for three films, two of them starring Huston, Sr. In 1932, John left Hollywood to lead a nomadic existence, on the verge of starvation, in London and Paris. Back home, he briefly edited an illustrated magazine called *Mid-Week Pictorial.* In 1933 he headed for Chicago to play the title role in the WPA production of 'Abraham Lincoln' three years after his celebrated father had played the same part in a D. W. Griffith film.

In 1937, John Huston remarried and the following year went to Hollywood to take a second stab at screenwriting, this time in a serious and regular manner that was soon to lead to his career as director. After collaborating on several notable Warner Bros. scripts, he was given his first chance to direct in 1941, on Dashiell Hammett's winning private-eye melodrama, *The Maltese Falcon,* still considered by many the best detective movie ever made. Huston was to direct two other films (and two Broadway plays, one of which he co-authored) before donning the uniform of a Signal Corps lieutenant late in 1942. While in uniform he turned out three of the finest and most realistic and human documentaries to come out of WW II. He was promoted to major and awarded the Legion of Merit for his courageous work under battle conditions on the Pacific and European fronts.

Huston returned to Hollywood in 1945, divorced his second wife, and after an ardent courtship of Olivia de Havilland, married actress Evelyn KEYES in 1946. This marriage, too, was to end in divorce, in 1950. Huston, who by this time had established what became his lifelong reputation as a colorful, impulsive, and unpredictable individual, next took another of his frequent gambles by bringing to Broadway Jean-Paul Sartre's existential play 'No Exit.' It won the New York Drama Critics Award as the best foreign play of 1946 but bombed at the box office. Huston's first postwar film, *The Treasure of the Sierra Madre,* brought him back to the Mexico of his cavalry days and was an astounding critical success. The New York Film Critics named Huston best director for this ruggedly masculine drama of greed and human relationships. He also won two Academy Awards, best director and best screenplay, for the film. Another Oscar, for best supporting actor, went to his father, Walter Huston.

In 1947, with director William Wyler and several others, a courageous Huston formed the Committee for the First Amendment, aiming to counter the industry witchhunt by the House Un-American Activities Committee (HUAC). In 1948, after the expiration of his contract with Warner Bros., Huston formed Horizon Pictures, with independent-minded producer Sam SPIEGEL. After getting out of a commitment to direct *Quo Vadis,* Huston directed what many consider his best film, *The Asphalt Jungle,* a big-city crime drama that became a classic of its genre for its intricate handling of plot, atmosphere, and characterization. He scored another critical success, but commercial failure, with his next, *The Red Badge of Courage,* and an unqualified triumph with *The African Queen.* He recreated brilliantly the colorful palette of crippled painter Toulouse-Lautrec in the visually splendid *Moulin Rouge* (1952). But from then on his misfires became more numerous than his hits and critics began to resist and often undervalue even the best of his efforts, such fine if flawed films as *Moby Dick* (1956), *The Unforgiven* (1960), *The Misfits* (1961), *Freud* (1962), and *Night of the Iguana* (1965).

His private life, too, seesawed between success and failure. In 1950, a day after divorcing Evelyn Keyes, he married ballet dancer Enrica (Ricki) Soma. In 1952, angered by the HUAC investigations and the Hollywood blacklisting, he moved with her and their children, including the newborn Anjelica, into St. Clerans, a 100-acre estate in Ireland's County Galway. They separated a decade later, after he became the father of future director Danny Huston (*b.* May 14, 1962), by the unwed actress Zoë Sallis, and remained apart until Ricki's death in 1969. In 1972 he took up residence in Las Caletas, near Puerto Vallarta, Mexico, and married Celeste Shane, his fifth and last wife. They divorced in 1977.

Professionally, Huston reached the nadir of his reputation with *A Walk with Life and Death* (1969), a debutante vehicle for his teenaged daughter, Angelica HUSTON. But the 70s saw him resurfacing as an admired director with the atmospheric boxing drama, *Fat City* (1972), the rousing Kipling epic, *The Man Who Would Be King* (1975), and the searing satire of Southern-style religion, *Wise Blood* (1979). His films of the early 80s were truly disappointing, especially the musical, *Annie* (1982). But he made remarkable final bows with *Prizzi's Honor* (1985), an offbeat black comedy of Mafia mores, which earned his daughter, Angelica, an Oscar, and *The Dead* (1987), an elegant adaptation (scripted by his son, Tony) of a James Joyce story. Huston, who began his career as an actor, resumed performing in films in the 60s and remained a formidable craggy-faced presence on the screen, in between directing assignments, for the remainder of his years. His toughness was tested the most in the last two decades of his life, when he suffered from chronic emphysema but continued working at an amazing pace, occasionally taking breaks for resuscitation with the aid of an oxygen machine. His condition so worsened toward the end of his career that insurance companies refused to cover his last production, *The Dead.* He was supposed to play a cameo role in *Mr. North* (1988), the directorial debut of his son, Danny Huston, but fell gravely ill with pneumonia and died on location, at 81. Autobiography: *An Open Book* (1980).

FILMS: As actor only—*The Shakedown, Two Americans* (short) 1929; *Hell's Heroes, The Storm* 1930; *The Cardinal* 1963; *Candy, The Rocky Road to Dublin* (doc.) 1968; *De Sade* 1969; *Myra Breckinridge* 1970; *The Bridge in the Jungle, Man in the Wilderness, The Deserter* 1971; *Battle for the Planet of the Apes* 1973; *Chinatown* 1974; *Breakout, The Wind and the Lion* 1975; *Tentacles, Il Grande Attacco/The Biggest Battle* (It.), *Angela* (Can.) 1977; *El Triangulo diabolico de la Bermudas/The Bermuda Triangle* (Mex./It.) 1978; *Il Visitatore/The Visitor, Jaguar Lives, Winter Kills* 1979; *Head On* (Can.), *Agee* (interview) 1980; *Cannery Row* (narrator only) 1982; *Lovesick, A Minor Miracle/Young Giants* 1983; *George Stevens: A Filmmaker's Journey* (interview) 1985. As screenwriter (in collaboration)—*A House Divided* (dial.) 1931; *Law and Order, Murders in the Rue Morgue* (dial.) 1932; *Death Drives Through* (co-story; UK); *It Happened in Paris* (UK) 1935; *Jezebel, The Amazing Dr. Clitterhouse* 1938; *Juarez* 1939; *Dr. Ehrlich's Magic Bullet* 1940; *High Sierra, Sergeant York* 1941; *The Killers, The Stranger* (both not credited), *Three Strangers* 1946; *Mr. North* (also exec. prod.) 1988. As director—*The Maltese Falcon* (also sc.) 1941; *In This Our Life* (also co-sc., uncredited), *Across the Pacific* 1942; *Report from the Aleutians* (also sc., narrator; doc.) 1943; *The Battle of San Pietro* (also sc., narrator; doc.) 1945; *Let There Be Light* (also co-sc., co-phot., narrator; doc.) 1946; *The Treasure of the Sierra Madre* (also sc., act.), *Key Largo* (also co-sc.) 1948; *We Were Strangers* (also co-sc.) 1949; *The Asphalt Jungle* (also prod., co-sc.) 1950; *The Red Badge of Courage* (also sc.), *The African Queen* (also co-sc.) 1951; *Moulin Rouge* (also co-sc.) 1952; *Beat the Devil* (also prod., co-sc.) 1954; *Moby Dick* (also prod., co-sc.) 1956; *Heaven Knows Mr. Allison* (also co-sc.) 1957; *The Barbarian and the Geisha, The Roots of Heaven* 1958; *The Unforgiven* 1960; *The Misfits* 1961; *The List of Adrian Messenger* (also act.) 1963; *The Night of the Iguana* (also co-sc.) 1964; *La Bibbia/The Bible. . . In the Beginning* (also act. as Noah) 1966; *Casino Royale* (co-dir., also act.), *Reflections in a Golden Eye* 1967; *Sinful Davey, A Walk with Love and Death* (also act.) 1969; *The Kremlin Letter* (also co-sc., act.) 1970; *Fat City, The Life and Times of Judge Roy Bean* (also act.) 1972; *The Mackintosh Man* 1973; *The Man Who Would Be King* (also co-sc.) 1975; *Independence* (28-minute short) 1976; *Wise Blood* (also act.) 1979; *Phobia* (Can.) 1980; *Victory* 1981; *Annie* 1982; *Under the Volcano* 1984; *Prizzi's Honor* 1985; *The Dead* 1987.

Huston, Walter. Actor. *b.* Walter Houghston, Apr. 6, 1884, Toronto. *d.* 1950. He studied engineering but was drawn to the stage and joined a road show. By 1905 he was quite successful in vaudeville and was even cast in a New York play, but after his marriage that year (to newspaperwoman Rhea Gore) and the birth of his son John (director-to-be John HUSTON) in 1906, he decided to meet his responsibilities as a husband and father by abandoning the stage and working as an engineer at water and electrical plants in Nevada and then St. Louis, Mo. However, he returned to the stage in 1909 and soon became a popular headliner in the vaudeville circuit. In 1913 he divorced and later married twice more. In 1924 he switched to drama and starred in the Broadway plays 'Mr. Pitt' and 'Desire Under the Elms'; then, in 1929, he joined the mass exodus of Broadway players to the movies, which were just then switching to sound.

In his mid-40s by the time he crossed to films, Huston was nonetheless cast in some romantic leads as well as character parts and received enthusiastic press notices for his portrayal of the title role in D. W. Griffith's *Abraham Lincoln* (1930). After becoming a film actor, he occasionally returned to Broadway, where he scored personal triumphs in 'Dodsworth,' a role he later repeated on the screen, and 'Knickerbocker Holiday,' in which he gave his now-famous rendition of 'September Song.' The New York Film Critics voted Huston best actor of 1936 for his performance in the screen version of *Dodsworth.* He received even greater accolades for his portrayal of the Devil in *All That Money Can Buy,* a delightful screen adaptation of Benét's 'The Devil and Daniel Webster.' Other memorable characterizations followed, culminating in his superb performance in his son's *The Treasure of the Sierra Madre,* for which he won the best supporting actor Academy Award for 1948.

FILMS: *Gentlemen of the Press, The Lady Lies, The Virginian* 1929; *Abraham Lincoln* (title role), *The Bad Man, The Virtuous Sin* 1930; *The Criminal Code, The Star Witness, The Ruling Voice* 1931; *The Woman from Monte Carlo, A House Divided, Law and Order, The Beast of the City, The Wet Parade, Night Court, American Madness, Rain, Kongo* 1932; *Gabriel Over the White House, Hell Below, Storm at Daybreak, Ann Vickers, The Prizefighter and the Lady* 1933; *Keep 'Em Rolling* 1934; *The Tunnel/Transatlantic Tunnel* (UK) 1935; *Rhodes of Africa/Rhodes* (title role, UK), *Dodsworth* (as Samuel Dodsworth) 1936; *Of Human Hearts* 1938; *The Light That Failed* 1940; *All That Money Can Buy, Swamp Water, The Maltese Falcon* (bit) 1941; *In This Our Life* (bit), *The Shanghai Gesture, Always in My Heart, Yankee Doodle Dandy* 1942; *The*

Outlaw (also re-released 1947, 1950), *Edge of Darkness, Mission to Moscow* (as Ambassador Joseph E. Davies), *The North Star/Armored Attack* 1943; *Dragon Seed* (as Ling Tau) 1944; *And Then There Were None* 1945; *Dragonwyck* 1946; *Duel in the Sun* 1947; *The Treasure of the Sierra Madre, Summer Holiday* 1948; *The Great Sinner* 1949; *The Furies* 1950.

Hutchinson, Josephine. Actress. Born on Oct. 12, 1904, in Seattle, Wash. *ed.* Cornish School of Music and Drama. As a child, she appeared in Mary Pickford's film *The Little Princess.* She played in stock and on Broadway and gained a reputation as a fine actress with Eva Le Gallienne's Civic Repertory Company before making her adult screen debut in 1934. In films she typically played mature, understanding leading ladies and devoted wives and later kindly character parts.

FILMS INCLUDE: *Happiness Ahead* 1934; *The Right to Live, Oil for the Lamps of China, The Melody Lingers On* 1935; *The Story of Louis Pasteur* (as Marie Pasteur), *I Married a Doctor* 1936; *Mountain Justice* 1937; *The Crime of Dr. Hallet* 1938; *The Son of Frankenstein* 1939; *My Son My Son!, Tom Brown's School Days* (as Mrs. Arnold) 1940; *Somewhere in the Night* 1946; *Cass Timberlane* 1947; *Adventure in Baltimore* 1949; *Love Is Better Than Ever, Ruby Gentry* 1952; *Many Rivers to Cross* 1955; *Miracle in the Rain* 1956; *Gun for a Coward* 1957; *North by Northwest* 1959; *The Adventures of Huckleberry Finn* (as Widow Douglas) 1960; *Baby the Rain Must Fall* 1965; *Nevada Smith* 1966; *Rabbit Run* 1970.

Hutton, Betty. Actress, singer. Born Betty June Thornburg, on Feb. 26, 1921, in Battle Creek, Mich. After the death of her father, she sang on street corners as a child to help support the family. At 13 she began singing with bands and soon made the big time as vocalist for the Vincent Lopez orchestra. An exuberant performer of boundless energy, she became known as "The Blonde Bombshell." In 1940 she made it to Broadway in 'Two for the Show' and the following year she signed a movie contract with Paramount. Playing uninhibited comedy and occasional dramatic roles, she exploded through a dozen or so tailor-made roles before getting her best opportunity as a replacement for the ailing Judy Garland in MGM's blockbuster musical *Annie Get Your Gun.* She subsequently played the lead in De Mille's *The Greatest Show on Earth.* Shortly after the release of the film in 1952, she walked out on her Paramount contract after the studio refused her demand that her second husband, choreographer Charles O'Curran, be assigned to direct her films. She has since returned to the screen only once, in a minor 1957 picture. She made occasional appearances on stage and in nightclubs and in 1965 replaced Carol Burnett in Broadway's 'Fade In Fade Out.' The following year she walked out on a B Western, *Red Tomahawk,* and in 1967 she filed for bankruptcy.

Miss Hutton subsequently appeared in occasional stage productions but time and again was forced to cancel performances because of the effects of an old shoulder injury and persistent personal problems. She had all but disappeared from public view when she re-emerged in the headlines in 1974. The former star, who had been married and divorced five times and during her Hollywood heyday made and spent close to $10 million, was discovered lonely and broke in a Rhode Island Catholic rectory, where she lived and worked as a cook and housekeeper. She left the rectory several months later to enter a hospital for intensive psychiatric care. She later announced plans to revive her career but returned to the rectory in mid-1975. In 1978 she was hired as an official greeter at a Connecticut jai-alai establishment.

Her sister, Marion Hutton (*b.* Marion Thornburg, 1919, Battle Creek., Mich. *d.* 1986), also appeared in a number of musical films but was best known as a big-band vocalist, most notably with the Glenn Miller orchestra.

FILMS: *The Fleet's In, Star Spangled Rhythm* 1942; *Happy Go Lucky, Let's Face It* 1943; *The Miracle of Morgan's Creek, And the Angels Sing, Here Come the Waves* 1944; *Incendiary Blonde* (as nightclub queen Texas Guinan), *Duffy's Tavern, The Stork Club* 1945; *Cross My Heart* 1946; *The Perils of Pauline* (as silent serial star Pearl White) 1947; *Dream Girl* 1948; *Red Hot and Blue* 1949; *Annie Get Your Gun* (as Wild West show star Annie Oakley), *Let's Dance* 1950; *Sailor Beware* (cameo), *The Greatest Show on Earth, Somebody Loves Me* (as vaudeville star Blossom Seely) 1952; *Spring Reunion* 1957.

Hutton, Brian G. Director. Born in 1935, in New York City. A former bit actor (*Fear Strikes Out, Gunfight at the O.K. Corral, The Big Fisherman, The Interns,* etc.), he directed TV films before switching to the big screen in the mid-60s. Handles action with flair.

FILMS: *Wild Seed* 1965; *The Pad (. . . And How to Use It)* 1966; *Sol Madrid* 1968; *Where Eagles Dare* (UK) 1969; *Kelly's Heroes* (US/Yug.) 1970; *Zee & Co./X Y & Zee* (UK) 1971; *Night Watch* (UK) 1973.

Hutton, Jim. Actor. *b.* Dana James Hutton, May 31, 1933, Binghamton, N.Y. *d.* 1979. Tall, affable leading man of Hollywood films. He was discovered by director Douglas SIRK, who saw him performing with a military troupe in Germany, where he was stationed during his Army service. Especially adept at comedy roles but also played rugged types in action films. He was the father of actor Timothy HUTTON.

FILMS INCLUDE: *A Time to Love and a Time to Die* 1958; *Ten Seconds to Hell* 1959; *The Subterraneans, Where the Boys Are* 1960; *The Honeymoon Machine, Bachelor in Paradise* 1961; *The Horizontal Lieutenant, Period of Adjustment* 1962; *Looking for Love* 1964; *Major Dundee, The Hallelujah Trail, Never Too Late* 1965; *The Trouble with Angels, Walk Don't Run* 1966; *Who's Minding the Mint?* 1967; *The Green Berets* 1968; *Hellfighters* 1969; *Psychic Killer* 1975.

Hutton, Lauren. Actress. Born Mary Laurence Hutton, on Nov. 17, 1943, in Charleston, S.C. Raised from early childhood near the Florida swamps, she briefly attended the University of Southern Florida and the Sophie Newcombe College in New Orleans. She started her working career as a waitress at Al Hirt's jazz club on Bourbon Street, then came to New York, where she became a Playboy bunny. A stunning beauty, she soon began modeling and within several years was one of fashion row's best known and highest paid cover girls and TV hucksters. She began playing decorative leads in films in the late 60s and gradually improved her acting ability and the quality of her roles in the 70s. In 1983 she made an impressive stage debut in the role of a rape victim in a Los Angeles Public Theater production of 'Extremities.' In the 90s, her modeling career was rejuvenated as she and several other over-50, still-gorgeous models suddenly became all the rage.

FILMS: *Paper Lion* 1968; *Pieces of Dreams, Little Fauss and Big Halsy* 1970; *Permette?—Rocco Papaleo/Rocco Papaleo* (It./Fr.) 1971; *The Gambler* 1974; *Gator* 1976; *Welcome to L.A., Viva Knievel!* 1977; *A Wedding* 1978; *American Gigolo* 1980; *Paternity, Zorro The Gay Blade* 1981; *Tout Feu tout Flamme, Hécate (Maîtresse de la Nuit)/Hecate* (Fr./Switz.) 1982; *Lassiter* 1984; *Once Bitten* 1985; *Flagrant Désir* (Fr.) 1986; *Malone* 1987; *Bulldance/Forbidden Sun* (UK) 1989; *Blue Blood, Run for Your Life, Billions* 1990; *Guilty as Charged, Missing Pieces* 1991; *Mom and Dad Save the World* 1992; *My Father the Hero* 1994.

Hutton, Robert. Actor. *b.* Robert Bruce Winne, on June 11, 1920, in Kingston, N.Y. *d.* 1994. Sincere-looking leading man of Hollywood films, following some experience in stock. In the late 60s he worked mainly in low-budget British films and in the early 70s took a single stab at screenwriting.

FILMS INCLUDE: *Destination Tokyo, Janie, Hollywood Canteen* 1944; *Roughly Speaking, Too Young to Know* 1945; *Janie Gets Married* 1946; *Time Out of Mind, Love and Learn* 1947; *Always Together, Wallflower* 1948; *The Younger Brothers, And Baby Makes Three* 1949; *The Man on the Eiffel Tower, Beauty on Parade* 1950; *The Steel Helmet, New Mexico, The Racket* 1951; *Casanova's Big Night* 1954; *The Big Bluff* 1955; *Yaqui Drums* 1956; *The Colossus of New York* 1958; *Invisible Invaders* 1959; *Cinderfella* 1960; *Wild Youth* 1961; *The Slime People* (also dir., co-exec. prod.) 1963; *The Secret Man/The Secret Door* (also assoc. prod.; UK/US) 1964; *Finders Keepers* (UK) 1966; *The Vulture* (US/UK/Austral.), *They Came from Beyond Space* (UK), *You Only Live Twice* (UK), *Torture Garden* (UK) 1967; *Cry of the Banshee* (UK), *Trog* (UK) 1970; *Tales from the Crypt* (UK) 1971; *Persecution/The Terror of Sheba* (story, sc. only) 1974.

Hutton, Timothy. Actor. Born on Aug. 16, 1960, in Malibu, Calif. Earnest, sensitive, lanky, blue-eyed leading man of the American screen. The son and look-alike of the late Jim HUTTON, he began performing in high school plays and later toured with his father in a production of 'Harvey.' After appearing in several TV movies, he made a fortuitous feature film debut in *Ordinary People* (1980), winning an Academy Award as best supporting actor for his portrayal of a guilt-ridden youth. Sidney LUMET, who directed him in *Daniel* (1983), compared Hutton to a young Henry FONDA. He married actress Debra WINGER in 1986. They divorced in 1990.

FILMS: *Ordinary People* 1980; *Taps* 1981; *Daniel* 1983; *Iceman* 1984; *The Falcon and the Snowman, Turk 182!* 1985; *Made in Heaven* 1987; *Betrayed, A Time of Destiny, Everybody's All-American* 1988; *Torrents of Spring* (It./Fr./UK), *Q & A* 1990; *The Dark Half, The Temp* 1993; *French Kiss* 1995; *Beautiful Girls, The Substance of Fire* 1996.

Huxley, Aldous. Novelist, essayist, screenwriter, *b.* July 26, 1894, Godalming, England. *d.* 1963. *ed.* Oxford. The celebrated author of *Brave New World, Point Counter Point,* and many other novels and short stories, resided in Hollywood from the late 30s to the mid-40s and collaborated on a number of screenplays.

FILMS: *Pride and Prejudice* 1940; *Madame Curie* (treatment only) 1943; *Jane Eyre* 1944; *A Woman's Vengeance* 1948; *Prelude to Fame* (story basis only, UK) 1950.

Huyck, Willard. American screenwriter, director. After graduating from USC, he joined American-International Pictures as a reader, soon rising to executive assistant and script rewriter. Following a script collaboration with John MILIUS in 1969, he quit the company and joined forces with Gloria Katz, who became his regular collaborator on many future screenplays. They were signed as a team by Francis Ford COPPOLA to develop writing-directing projects for his American Zoetrope but none of these materialized. They then celebrated their first fruitful collaboration with an Academy Award nomination for their screenplay of George Lucas's *American Graffiti* (1973). They enjoyed another success with Steven Spielberg's *Indiana Jones and the Temple of Doom* (1984) but fared poorly with several films that Huyck himself directed.

FILMS: As co-screenwriter—*The Devil's Eight* 1969; *American Graffiti* 1973; *Lucky Lady* 1975; *Indiana Jones and the Temple of Doom* 1984; *Radioland Murders* 1994. As director/co-screenwriter—*Dead People/Messiah of Evil/Return of the Living Dead/Revenge of the Screaming Dead/The Second Coming* 1974; *French Postcards* 1979; *Best Defense* 1984; *Howard the Duck* 1986.

Hyams, Leila. Actress. *b.* May 1, 1905, New York City. *d.* 1977. Green-eyed blonde leading lady of Hollywood films of the 20s and 30s. The daughter of vaudevillians, she joined her parents' act while still a child and later appeared on the legitimate stage. She then turned to modeling with great success and her photographs adorned ad campaigns for several products. She made her screen debut in 1924 and subsequently appeared in many late silents and early talkies, mainly for Warner Bros. and MGM, typically as a wholesome ingenue. Memorable as the heroine of Tod Browning's *Freaks* (1932). In 1927 she married Phil Berg, who later became a top talent agent. She retired from the screen in 1936.

FILMS INCLUDE: *Sandra* 1924; *The Kick-Off, Summer Bachelors* 1926; *The Brute, The Bush Leaguer, The Wizard* 1927; *The Branded Sombrero, A Girl in Every Port, Honor Bound, The Crimson City* 1928; *Alias Jimmy Valentine, Spite Marriage, The Far Call, The Idle Rich, Masquerade, Wonder of Women, Hurricane, The Thirteenth Chair* 1929; *The Bishop Murder Case, The Girl Said No, The Big House, Sweethearts and Wives, Sins of the Children, The Flirting Widow, Way Out West, Way for a Sailor, Part Time Wife* 1930; *Men Call It Love, A Gentleman's Fate, The New Adventures of Get-Rich-Quick Wallingford, The Phantom of Paris, Surrender* 1931; *Red Headed Woman, Freaks, The Big Broadcast, Island of Lost Souls* 1932; *The Constant Woman/Auction in Souls, Sing Sinner Sing, Saturday's Millions, Horse Play* 1933; *The Poor Rich, Affairs of a Gentleman* 1934; *Ruggles of Red Gap, People Will Talk* 1935; *Yellow Dust* 1936.

Hyams, Peter. Director, screenwriter. Born on July 26, 1943, in New York City. *ed.* Hunter Coll.; Syracuse U. A former TV newscaster, he began directing and writing TV movies and feature films in the early 70s. His films, often quite entertaining, are typically visually slick but emotionally remote and curiously uninvolving. His most spectacular effort was *2010* (1984), the much anticipated but disappointing sequel to Stanley Kubrick's *2001: A Space Odyssey.* He acted as his own cinematographer on that film, as well as on several of his other recent productions.

FILMS (as director): *T. R. Baskin* (prod., sc. only) 1971; *Busting* (also sc.), *Our Time* (also sc.) 1974; *Peeper* 1976; *Telefon* (co-sc. only) 1977; *Capricorn One* (also sc.) 1978; *Hanover Street* 1979; *The Hunter* (also co-sc.) 1980; *Outland* (also sc.) 1981; *The Star Chamber* (also co-sc.) 1983; *2010* (also prod., sc., phot.) 1984; *Running Scared* (also exec. prod., phot.) 1986; *The Monster Squad* (co-exec. prod. only) 1987; *The Presidio* (also phot.) 1988; *Narrow Margin* (also sc., phot.) 1990; *Stay Tuned* (also phot.) 1992; *Timecop* 1994; *Sudden Death* 1995; *The Relic* (also phot.) 1997.

Hyde-White, Wilfrid. Actor. *b.* May 12, 1903, in Bourton-on-the-Water, England, *d.* 1991. *ed.* Marlborough Coll.; RADA. On stage and screen from the mid-30s, he delighted audiences on both sides of the Atlantic with his wry humor and mischievous twinkle in numerous character parts.

FILMS INCLUDE: *Josser on the Farm* 1934; *Night Mail* 1935; *Rembrandt* 1936; *Elephant Boy* 1937; *The Demi-Paradise/Adventure for Two* 1943; *Meet Me at Dawn, Night Boat to Dublin* 1946; *The Winslow Boy* 1948; *The Passionate Friends/One Woman's Story, The Third Man* 1949; *The Man on the Eiffel Tower, Trio, The Browning Version, Last Holiday* 1950; *Outcast of the Islands* 1952; *The Million Pound Note/Man with a Million* 1953; *The Story of Gilbert and Sullivan* 1954; *The Adventures of Quentin Durward* 1955; *The Silken Affair* 1956; *Tarzan and the Lost Safari* 1957; *Libel* 1959; *Two Way Stretch, Let's Make Love* 1960; *On the Double* (US), *Ada* (US) 1961; *Crooks Anonymous, In Search of the Castaways* 1962;

Aliki My Love (US/Gr.), *My Fair Lady* (US) 1964; *Ten Little Indians, The Liquidator, Chamber of Horrors* (US) 1966; *P.J.* (US) 1968; *Gaily Gaily* (US) 1969; *Skullduggery* (US), *The Magic Christian* 1970; *Fragment of Fear* 1971; *No Longer Alone* (US), *The Cat and the Canary* 1978; *Battlestar Gallactica* (US) 1979; *In God We Trust* (US), *Oh God!: Book II* (US) 1980; *Tarzan the Ape* (US) 1981; *The Toy* (US) 1982; *Fanny Hill* 1983.

Hyer, Martha. Actress. Born on Aug. 10, 1924, in Fort Worth, Tex. *ed.* Northwestern; Pasadena Playhouse. Brunette, then blonde leading lady and second lead of Hollywood films, usually in refined roles. She was nominated for a best supporting actress Oscar for her performance in *Some Came Running* (1959). In 1966 she married producer Hal WALLIS, her second husband. Autobiography (as Martha Hyer Wallis): *Finding My Way* (1990).

FILMS INCLUDE: *The Locket* 1946; *Thunder Mountain* 1947; *Roughshod* 1949; *The Lawless* 1950; *Abbott and Costello Go to Mars, So Big* 1953; *Riders to the Stars, Lucky Me, Down Three Dark Streets, Sabrina, Cry Vengeance* 1954; *Francis in the Navy, Kiss of Fire* 1955; *Red Sundown* 1956; *Battle Hymn, Mister Cory, The Delicate Delinquent, My Man Godfrey* 1957; *Paris Holiday, Houseboat* 1958; *Some Came Running, The Big Fisherman, The Best of Everything* 1959; *Ice Palace, Desire in the Dust* 1960; *The Right Approach* 1961; *A Girl Named Tamiko, The Man from the Diners Club, Wives and Lovers* 1963; *The Carpetbaggers, First Men in the Moon* (UK), *Blood on the Arrow* 1964; *The Sons of Katie Elder* 1965; *The Chase, The Night of the Grizzly, Picture Mommy Dead* 1966; *The Happening, Das Hausder tausend Freuden/The House of 1,000 Dolls* (Ger./Sp.) 1967; *Lo Scatenato/Catch as Catch Can* (It.), *Once You Kiss a Stranger* 1969; *Day of the Wolves* 1973.

hyperfocal distance. The distance between the lens and the object nearest to it that is in acceptable focus when the lens is focused at infinity.

Hypergonar. Trade name of the anamorphic lens developed by Henri CHRÉTIEN of France during the late 20s which eventually became the basis of the CinemaScope process.

hyphenates. Film industry jargon for persons performing more than one creative role in the production of a film, such as writer-producer, actor-director, or director-producer-writer. Hyphenates have proliferated since the demise of the studio system as more and more films are being packaged individually and certain directors and actors are able not only to name their price but also to set conditions for their participation in a film. Thus, popular actors cannot be persuaded to appear in a film unless they have a hand in production. Top directors may insist on complete control over their productions by writing and producing, as well as directing, their films.

I

IATSE. The International Alliance of Theatrical Stage Employees (and Moving Picture Machine Operators of the US and Canada), the parent organization encompassing some 800 local unions in North America. Organized in the US in 1893 and expanded into Canada in 1902, it has affiliated union locals representing members in every branch of production—property craftsmen, art directors, cameramen, sound and lab technicians, makeup artists, script supervisors, set painters, screen cartoonists, gaffers, grips, set designers, etc.—as well as employees in film distribution and exhibition. It is affiliated with the AFL-CIO.

Ibbetson, Arthur. Director of photography. Born on Sept. 8, 1922, in England. After a long period of apprenticeship as a camera assistant and camera operator (from 1944), he became a lighting cameraman in the late 50s and has since been responsible for the cinematography of a number of major productions.

FILMS INCLUDE: *The Horse's Mouth* 1958; *The Angry Silence, The League of Gentlemen, Tunes of Glory* 1960; *Whistle Down the Wind* 1961; *Lisa/The Inspector* (US/UK) 1962; *I Could Go On Singing, Nine Hours to Rama* (US/UK) 1963; *The Chalk Garden* 1964; *A Countess from Hong Kong* 1967; *Inspector Clouseau* 1968; *Where Eagles Dare, Anne of the Thousand Days* 1969; *The Walking Stick* 1970; *The Railway Children, Willy Wonka and the Chocolate Factory* (US) 1971; *A Doll's House* 1973; *Out of Season* 1975; *The Sell Out* 1976; *A Little Night Music* (Aus./Ger./US) 1977; *The Medusa Touch* 1978; *The Prisoner of Zenda* 1979; *Hopscotch* 1980; *The Bounty* 1984; *Santa Claus: The Movie* 1985.

Ibert, Jacques. Composer. *b.* Aug. 15, 1890, Paris. *d.* 1962. This noted classical composer, known for his colorful orchestral compositions, also scored many French films, for Pabst, Duvivier, Tourneur, L'Herbier, and other directors. In addition, he provided the music for two American films, Orson Welles's *Macbeth* and Gene Kelly's *Invitation to the Dance*.

FILMS INCLUDE: *Les Cinq Gentlemen maudits* 1931; *Don Quichotte/Don Quixote* 1933; *Golgotha, Maternité, Koenigsmark* 1935; *Le Coupable* 1936; *L'Homme de Nulle Part* 1937; *Le Patriote* 1938; *La Charrette fantôme/The Phantom Carriage* 1939; *La Comédie du Bonheur* 1940; *La Vie de Bohème* 1942; *Le Père Serge* 1945; *Panique, L'Affaire du Collier de la Reine* 1946; *Macbeth* (US) 1948; *Marianne de ma Jeunesse* 1954; *Invitation to the Dance* (US) 1956.

Ichikawa, Kon. Director. Born on Nov. 20, 1915, in Uji Yamda, Japan. After graduating from a commercial school, he studied animation and made his entry into Japanese cinema in 1946 with a puppet film, *A Girl of Dojo Temple,* the negative of which was confiscated and destroyed by the American Occupation authorities. His early feature films were often satirical comedies, a rarity in Japanese cinema, and revealed a wry sense of humor that prompted some local critics to call him the "Japanese Frank Capra." He continued injecting doses of black humor into many of his later films but made his greatest impact on Western audiences with a number of rather bleak dramas of the late 50s and early 60s, which were typically peopled with obsessional characters at odds with a spiritually aberrant environment. Especially noteworthy are his two powerful antiwar films, *The Burmese Harp* (1956), in which a soldier experiences a Buddhist spiritual awakening and becomes obsessed with the need to bury the war dead, and *Fires on the Plain* (1959), which depicts the horrors of war in graphic, chilling terms, showing cannibalism among defeated Japanese soldiers.

Among his other major films are *Enjo/Conflagration* (1958), about a student priest who burns down his temple to save it from becoming contaminated by industrial pollution; *Odd Obsession* (1959), which deals with the sexual aspect of obsession; *Alone on the Pacific/My Enemy the Sea* (1963), which explores heroism with a light touch; and *An Actor's Revenge* (also 1963), the story of a Kabuki impersonator in which Ichikawa surpasses his own high standards of technical brilliance. Ichikawa is a highly proficient film craftsman with a keen eye for visual texture. He is a meticulous technician who labors long and carefully on every scene in advance of production. Even though few of his films have been widely exhibited in the West, his reputation as one of the leading directors of Japanese and world cinema is secure. His wife (from 1948), Natto Wada (*b.* 1920), collaborated on many of his early scripts.

FILMS: *A Girl at Dojo Temple* (puppet film; never released) 1946; *A Thousand and One Nights with Toho* (co-dir.; unfinished) 1947; *A Flower Blooms, 365 Nights* (in two parts) 1948; *Design of a Human Being, Endless Passion* 1949; *Sanshiro at Ginza, The Hot Marshland, Pursuit at Dawn* 1950; *Nightshade Flower, The Lover, The Man Without Nationality, Stolen Love, River Solo Flows, Wedding March* 1951; *Mr. Lucky, The Young Generation, The Woman Who Touched the Legs, This Way—That Way* 1952; *Mr. Poo, The Blue Revolution, The Youth of Heiji Senigata, The Lovers* 1953; *All of Myself, A Billionaire, Twelve Chapters About Women* 1954; *Ghost Story of Youth, The Heart* 1955; *The Burmese Harp, Punishment Room, Bridge of Japan* 1956; *The Crowded Train, The Hole, The Men of Tohoku* 1957; *Enjo/Conflagration/Flame of Torment, Money and Three Bad Men* 1958; *Goodbye—Good Day, Odd Obsession/The Key, Fires on the Plain, Police and Small Gangsters* 1959; *A Ginza Veteran, Bonchi, A Woman's Testament/Code of Women* (one episode), *Her Brother* 1960; *Ten Black Women* 1961; *The Sin, Being Two Isn't Easy* 1962; *An Actor's Revenge/The Revenge of Ukeno-Jo, Alone on the Pacific/My Enemy the Sea* 1963; *Money Talks* 1964; *Tokyo Olympiad* (doc.) 1965; *The Tale of Genji* (made as 26-part TV series) 1966; *Topo Gigio and the Missile War* (part animated; Jap./It.) 1967; *Youth/Tournament* (doc.) 1968; *Kyoto* (doc.) 1969; *Japan and the Japanese* (doc.) 1970; *Dodes' ka-den* (prod. only), *To Love Again* 1972; *Visions of Eight* ("The Fastest" segment; doc.), *Manatabi/The Wanderers* 1973; *I Am a Cat* 1975; *Between Women and Wives* (co-dir. with Shiro Toyoda), *The Inugami Family* 1976; *The Devil's Bouncing Ball Song/A Rhyme of Vengeance, The Devil's Island/Island of Horrors/Hell's Gate Island* 1977; *Queen Bee* 1978; *Hi no Tori/Hinotori/The Phoenix/The Firebird, The House of Hanging* 1979; *Koto The Ancient City* 1980; *Kofuku/Lonely Hearts/Happiness* 1981; *The Makica Sisters/Fine Snow* 1983; *Ohan* 1984; *The Burmese Harp* (remake) 1985; *Rokumiekan/High Society of Meiji/The Hall of the Crying Deer* 1986; *Film Actress/Movie Actress, Taketori Monogatari/Princess from the Moon* 1987; *Tenkawa Densetsu Satsujin Jiken/Noh Mask Murders* 1991; *47 Ronin* 1994.

ICM. See INTERNATIONAL CREATIVE MANAGEMENT.

IDHEC. Institut des Hautes Etudes Cinématographiques. Famed French film school, founded by Marcel L'HERBIER in 1943. All phases of film and television production have been taught at the school. Some of France's leading directors received their training at IDHEC.

idiot cards. See CUE CARDS.

Idle, Eric. Actor, screenwriter. Born Mar. 29, 1943, in South Shields, Durham, England. A Cambridge graduate, he performed in the school's Footlights revue, alongside John CLEESE and other students who later formed the core of the hit TV comedy series 'Monty Python's Flying Circus.' He later appeared in several of the group's feature films, also collaborating on their scripts. He co-wrote a number of Monty Python's books and wrote *Hello Sailor* and *The Rutland Dirty Weekend Book.* He has also appeared in stage productions and wrote the comedy 'Pass the Butler' (1982).

FILMS INCLUDE: *And Now for Something Completely Different* (also co-sc.) 1972; *Monty Python and the Holy Grail* (also co-sc.) 1975; *Monty Python's Life of Brian* (also co-sc.) 1979; *Monty Python Live at the Hollywood Bowl* 1981; *Monty Python's The Meaning of Life* (also co-sc.), *Yellowbeard* 1983; *National Lampoon's European Vacation* (bit; US) 1985; *The Transformers* (v/o) 1986; *Adventures of Baron Munchausen* 1989; *Nuns on the Run* (US) 1990; *Too Much Sun, Missing Pieces* 1991; *Mom and Dad Save the World* (US) 1992; *Splitting Heirs* (also ex-prod., scr., songs); *Casper* 1995.

Ihnen, Wiard. Art director. *b.* 1897, Jersey City, N.J. *d.* 1979. An architect's son, he studied architecture at Columbia University and at the Paris École des Beaux-Arts, and painting at New York's Art Students League. After designing several estates in the New York area, he entered films in 1919, initially working for Adolph ZUKOR at the Famous Players-Lasky Manhattan studios and at the dawn of the sound era at Paramount's Astoria studios in Long Island City. He later designed productions for RKO, Fox, and other Hollywood studios up to his retirement in the early 60s. He collaborated with Josef von Sternberg, Fritz Lang, and John Ford, among other leading directors, on numerous major productions, winning Academy Awards for *Wilson* (1944) and *Blood on the Sun* (1945). He was married to costume designer Edith HEAD.

FILMS INCLUDE: *On with the Show, Idols of Clay* 1920; *Potash and Perlmutter* 1923; *Monte Carlo* (unit art dir.) 1930; *City Streets* 1931; *Shanghai Express* (train interiors only), *Blonde Venus, If I Had a Million, Madame Butterfly* 1932; *Duck Soup, Cradle Song* 1933; *Thirty Day Princess, Good Dame* 1934; *Becky Sharp* 1935; *Dancing Pirate, Go West Young Man* 1936; *Every Day's a Holiday* 1938; *Stagecoach, Hollywood Cavalcade* 1939; *Johnny Apollo, Maryland, The Return of Frank James* 1940; *Hudson's Bay, Man Hunt, Western Union* 1941; *Roxie Hart, The Magnificent Dope, Iceland* 1942; *Crash Dive* 1943; *Jane Eyre, Wilson* 1944; *Along Came Jones, Blood on the Sun* 1945; *Tomorrow Is Forever* 1946; *The Time of Your Life, Kiss Tomorrow Goodbye* 1950; *Only the Valiant* 1951; *Rancho Notorious* 1952; *A Lion Is in the Streets* 1953; *The Indian Fighter* 1955; *The King and Four Queens* 1956; *The Gallant Hours* 1960.

illumination. Any light source, natural or artificial, with enough intensity to affect a film's sensitive layer of emulsion. In the stricter and more technical sense it is the density of the luminous flux on a surface.

ILM. See INDUSTRIAL LIGHT & MAGIC.

image. A likeness reproduced for viewing by means of photography, chemical processing, printing, and projection. The image is usually selected by the film director after consultation with the director of photography and is then captured on film by the camera operator. Some cinematographers (directors of photography) noted for their keen visual sense are more instrumental than others in influencing the director's selection of images. The choice is important because the image that is contained in each individual frame and the cumulative impact of these images, throughout a scene and an entire film, determine the visual quality of that particular film.

Imai, Tadashi. Director. Born on Jan. 8, 1912, in Tokyo, the son of a priest. He was arrested twice for subversive leftist activity during his studies at Tokyo's Imperial University. He entered films in 1934 as a screenwriter and began directing in

1939. He suspended his Marxist leanings for the duration of WW II, when his films glorified the ruling rightist regime, but joined the Communist party and resumed his attack on the establishment later on in his films. A highly controversial figure in Japanese cinema, both for his political beliefs and his unorthodox working methods, he was forced into freelancing after being discharged from the Toho studios for inciting a strike. Joseph L. Anderson and Donald Richie, in their book *The Japanese Film,* call him "at his best brilliant, at his worst incoherent." He has no doubt been hampered by his political commitment, but his films have often been inspired by his compassion for his protagonists, who are usually the poor and the oppressed. In 1963 he won first prize at the Berlin Festival for *Bushido: Samurai Saga,* and he won top prize at San Remo in 1975 for *Takiji Kobayashi.*

FILMS: *The Namazu Military Academy, Our Instructor* 1939; *The Village of Tajinko, Women's Town, The General* 1940; *Married Life* 1941; *The Suicide Troops of the Watch Tower* 1943; *The Angry Sea* 1944; *An Enemy of the People, Life Is Like a Somersault* 1946; *24 Hours of a Secret Life* (co-dir.) 1947; *Blue Mountains, A Woman's Face* 1949; *Until the Day We Meet Again* 1950; *And Yet We Live* 1951; *Pictures of the Atom Bomb* (doc.), *Echo School* 1952; *Muddy Waters, The Tower of Lilies* 1953; *Because I Love* (one episode), *Here Is a Spring, Yukiko* 1955; *Darkness at Noon* 1956; *Rice, A Story of Pure Love* 1957; *The Adulteress/Night Drum* 1958; *Kiku and Isamu* 1959; *The Cliff* 1960; *Pan Chopali* 1961; *The Old Women of Japan* 1962; *Bushido: Samurai Saga* 1963; *A Story for Echigo* 1964; *Revenge* 1965; *When the Cookie Crumbles* 1967; *The Time of Reckoning* 1968; *Bridge Across No River* 1969; *Takiji Kobayashi/The Life of a Communist Writer* 1974; *Ani Imoto/Mon and Ino/His Younger Sister* 1977; *Yoba/The Old Woman Ghost* 1978; *Himeyuri Lily Tower* 1982; *Senso to Seishun/War and Youth* 1991.

Imamura, Shohei. Director. Born on Sept. 15, 1926, in Tokyo, a doctor's son. *d.* 1997. After failing his entrance exams for agricultural studies at the university, he attended a technical school to avoid the draft, then majored in Occidental history at Tokyo's Waseda University. On graduating, in 1951, he went to work for the Ofuna Studios of the Sochiku film company as an assistant director, serving his apprenticeship under Yasijuro OZU and others. Frustrated by the company's rigid promotion system, which hindered his progress, he moved over in 1954 to the Nikkatsu studios, where he was finally given his first chance to direct in 1958. From the start, Imamura's films displayed some of the qualities that would later characterize his work: robust energy, sensuous earthiness, and a ribald, often outrageously off-color, sense of humor. Gradually he emerged as one of the leading figures of postwar Japanese cinema, an insightful, creative artist with a near-scientific interest in Japanese culture and society, new and old, and a flair for depicting the human condition audaciously and entertainingly. He is known as a slow and meticulous worker who spends a great deal of time researching and planning his projects. His films are often peopled with strong female protagonists who outperform males in the battle for survival. Bold eroticism, even incest, are recurring elements. But his films vary widely in theme and style. He collaborated on his own scripts and on several films by other directors. In 1965 he formed his own company, Imamura Productions, and subsequently served often as his own producer. Imamura won the Palme d'Or at Cannes for *The Ballad of Narayama* (1983). In recent years, he has focused much of his attention on administering and teaching at the Broadcast and Film Institute, which he founded in Yokohama in 1975.

FILMS: *Stolen Desire, Nishi Ginza Station/Lights of Night, Endless Desire* 1958; *My Second Brother/The Diary of Sueko* 1959; *Pigs and Battleships/Hogs and Warships/The Flesh Is Hot* 1961; *The Insect Woman* 1963; *Intentions of Murder/Unholy Desire* 1964; *The Pornographer/The Pornographers: An Introduction to Anthropology* 1966; *A Man Vanishes* 1967; *Kurageshima: Legends from a Southern Island/The Profound Desire of the Gods* 1968; *History of Postwar Japan as Told by a Bar Hostess* (doc.) 1970; *In Search of Unreturned Soldiers* (doc.) 1971; *Pirates of Bubuan* (doc.) 1972; *Muhomatsu Returns Home* (doc.) 1973; *Karayuki-san: The Making of a Prostitute* (doc.) 1974; *Still in Search of Unreturned Soldiers* (doc.), *Report on Two People Named Yoshinobu* (doc.) 1975; *Vengeance Is Mine* 1979; *Eijanaika/Why Not* 1981; *The Ballad of Narayama* 1983; *Zegen/The Lord of the Brothels* 1987; *Black Rain* 1989.

Imax. A wide-screen camera-projection system developed in Canada by William C. Shaw and P. R. W. Jones and first exhibited in 1970 at Expo 70 in Osaka, Japan. In this system, 70 mm film is advanced through the camera horizontally and projected horizontally on a curved screen. The result is an image of unusual height and depth, valuable in presenting documentaries on such subjects as nature and air-and-space travel. See also WIDE-SCREEN PROCESSES.

Im Quon Taek. Director. Born in 1937 (?). One of South Korea's most serious and prolific directors, able to combine commercial success with complex themes relevant to many aspects of Korean life. In a country whose film preferences are dominated by features made in America and Hong Kong, his films command large audiences.

FILMS INCLUDE: *Ticket* 1987; *Come Come to a Higher Place* 1989; *General's Son* 1990; *General's Son II, Kae Byok/Fly High Run Far* 1991.

IMP (Independent Motion Picture Company; also known as **Independent Moving Pictures Company**). A film production company founded in 1909 by Carl LAEMMLE, the owner of a chain of cinemas in Chicago, in defiance of the MOTION PICTURE PATENTS COMPANY. At first operating from a studio on Manhattan's Eleventh Avenue and 53rd Street, IMP quickly developed into a prosperous little company, thanks largely to star-piracy coups engineered by Laemmle. He lured away from American Biograph members of the Patents Company Florence Lawrence and Mary Pickford. He also recruited Thomas Ince and other talented directors. For fear of the long reach of the Patents Company, Laemmle sent Ince and Pickford to Cuba to make IMP's films there. IMP was absorbed into Universal in 1912.

impressionism. A style of artistic expression developed in France in the last third of the 19th century, in reaction to the dominant romantic and academic art of the period. The term was coined after Monet's painting "Impressions." In painting, the style is characterized by short brush strokes of bright colors through which the artist re-creates his impressions of the world, as in the works of Monet, Manet, Renoir, and Degas. As a film technique, it is characterized by the building of a sequence from a succession of brief shots, often seemingly unrelated. The early works of René CLAIR and the montage films of Sergei EISENSTEIN are examples of impressionism in the cinema.

Inagaki, Hiroshi. Director. Born on Dec. 30, 1905, in Tokyo. Formerly a child actor in Japanese films, he began directing in 1928, starting with serious social themes. However, he soon gained a reputation for his expert handling of large-scale period films. His *Musashi Miyamoto* (1940) met with great popular success when it was released in the US after WW II as *Samurai.* His *Rickshaw Man,* a remake of his 1943 *The Life of Matsu the Untamed,* won first prize at the 1958 Venice Festival. A prolific director, he turned out nearly 100 other films, for many of which he also wrote the scripts.

FILMS INCLUDE (as director and co-screenwriter):

Peace on Earth, The Wandering Gambler 1928; *Elegy of Hell, A Samurai's Career* 1929; *The Image of a Mother, A Sword and the Sumo Ring* 1931; *Travels Under the Blue Sky* 1932; *Chuji Kunishada* (trilogy) 1933; *Bad Luck* (trilogy) 1933–34; *White Snows of Fuji, The White Hood* 1935; *Journey of a Thousand and One Nights* 1936; *Spirit of the Wilderness* 1937; *A Great World Power Rising, Shadows of Darkness* 1938; *Mazo* 1939; *Musashi Miyamoto/Samurai* (trilogy) 1940; *The Last Days of Edo* 1941; *One-Eyed Dragon* 1942; *The Life of Matsu the Untamed* 1943; *Signal Fires of Shanghai* 1944; *The Last Abdication* 1945; *Children Hand in Hand* 1948; *Forgotten Children* 1949; *Kojiro Sasaki* (trilogy) 1950–51; *Pirates* 1951; *Sword for Hire* 1952; *Musashi Miyamoto/Samurai* (trilogy; remake) 1954–56; *The Lone Journey* 1955; *The Storm* 1956; *A Geisha in the Old City* 1957; *Secret Scrolls* (two parts) 1957–58; *The Rickshaw Man, Ninjutsu* 1958; *Samurai Saga* 1959; *Life of a Country Doctor/The Country Doctor* 1960; *Daredevil in the Castle, The Youth and His Amulet, Bandits on the Wind* 1961; *Chushingura/The Loyal 47 Ronin* (two parts), *Tatsu* 1962; *Young Swordsman* 1963; *Whirlwind, The Rabble* 1964; *Rise Against the Sword* 1966; *Kojiro* 1967; *Under the Banner of Samurai/Samurai Banners* 1969; *Machibuse/The Ambush* 1970.

in-betweens. In animation, the intermediate drawings prepared by assistants, known as "in-betweeners," to complete gaps in a sequence of movement between key positions of action drawn by the animation artist.

in camera. 1. Said of part of a set or action that is within the field of view of a camera at a particular moment. 2. A special effect that is carried out exclusively within the camera prior to developing the film. For example, one side of the lens might be blocked with a MATTE as an actor is photographed through the unobstructed side; the film is rewound and exposed again, but this time only the previously exposed side is blocked while the actor stands on the other side. The resulting image has the actor talking to an identical twin. Such "in-camera" or "in-the-camera" effects were common in the early days of special effects, before the introduction of OPTICAL PRINTERS.

Ince, John. Director, actor. *b.* 1879, New York City. *d.* 1947. The brother of Ralph INCE and Thomas H. INCE, he too began his career on the stage as a boy (at the age of eight) and became active in films both as actor and director, but achieved far less success or fame than his younger brothers, particularly Thomas. He entered films as a leading man in 1913 and began directing his own vehicles late that year. He gave up acting in 1915 but returned to the screen in character parts after ending his career as director at the end of the sound era.

FILMS INCLUDE: As actor-director—*The Price of Victory* 1913; *The Puritan, A Cruel Revenge, The House of Fear* 1914; *Road o' Strife* (serial; co-dir. with Howell Hansel) 1915. As director—*Sealed Lips, The Urchin, The Cowardly Way* 1915; *The Struggle, The Crucial Test* (co-dir.) 1916; *Her Man* (co-dir., sc.), *Secret Strings* 1918; *Blind Man's Eyes, Should a Woman Tell?* 1919; *Old Lady 31, Held in Trust* 1920; *Passion Fruit* 1921; *The Love Trap* 1923; *Cheap Kisses* 1924; *The Girl of Gold, If Marriage Fails* 1925; *The Great Jewel Robbery* (also prod.), *Her Big Adventure* 1926; *Wages of Conscience* (also act.), *The Hour of Reckoning* (also prod., act.) 1927; *Black Feather* 1928. As actor—*The Battle of Shiloh* 1913; *Fate* 1921; *Hate* 1922; *Alias French Gertie, Hot Curves, Moby Dick* 1930; *The Penal Code* 1932; *In Old Kentucky* 1935; *Don't Turn 'Em Loose* 1936; *The Miracle Kid* 1941; *Wilson* 1944; *The Last Frontier Uprising* 1947.

Ince, Ralph. Director, actor. *b.* Jan. 16, 1887, Boston, Mass. *d.* 1937. Like his brothers John INCE and Thomas H. INCE, he began his career on stage while still a child. After a succession of failures in stock, he turned commercial artist and entered films with Vitagraph in 1906 as a cartoonist. He soon switched to acting and achieved some fame in Lincoln impersonations. He made his debut as director in 1912 but continued acting in his own films as well as those of others. By 1914 he was reported to have appeared in no fewer than 500 films and directed 150. He was quite successful as a director, although his reputation never achieved that of his brother Thomas. In 1917 he set up his own company with brother John, but the enterprise was not successful. After the change-over to sound, he was given few opportunities to direct and instead asserted himself as a character actor, memorably in *Little Caesar.* In 1934 he went to England, where he was active again as director-actor until his death in a traffic accident.

FILMS INCLUDE: As actor—*The Battle Hymn of the Republic, One Flag at Last* 1911; *The Seventh Son, The Serpents, Lincoln's Gettysburg Address* (as Lincoln), *The Lady of the Lake* 1912; *Land of Opportunity* 1920; *Yellow Fingers* 1926; *Wall Street* 1929; *The Big Fight* 1930; *Little Caesar* 1931; *Law and Order* 1932. As director—*The Godmother* 1912; *A Regiment of Two* (also act.), *A Million Bid, The Call, A Prince of Evil, The Wreck, His Last Fight* (also sc., act.) 1913; *A Million Bid, Shadows of the Past* (also act.), *Lincoln the Lover* (also sc., act. as Lincoln), *The Girl from Prosperity, He Danced Himself to Death* (also act.), *Uncle Bill* 1914; *The Goddess* (serial), *The Awakening,* (also co-sc.), *Two Women, From Headquarters, The Juggernaut* (also co-sc.), *Sins of the Mothers* 1915; *Conflict, The Combat, The Destroyers, My Lady's Slipper* 1916; *The Argyle Case, Today,* (also sc.), *The Co-Respondent* 1917; *Tempered Steel, The Panther Woman, Her Man* (co-dir., prod.), *Our Mrs. McChesney, Fields of Honor, The Eleventh Commandment* 1918; *The Wreck, Virtuous Men. A Stitch in Time, Too Many Crooks, The Perfect Lover, Sealed Hearts, Out Yonder, Two Women* (expanded vers. of 1915 film) 1919; *Out of the Snows/The Law Bringers* (also act.), *His Wife's Money, Red Foam* 1920; *The Highest Law,* (also prod., act. as Lincoln), *Wet Gold* (also act.), *After Midnight, Remorseless Love, Tropical Love, The Last Door, A Man's Home* 1921; *Channing of the Northwest, Reckless Youth, A Wide-Open Town, The Referee* 1922; *Counterfeit Love* (co-dir. with Roy Sheldon), *Success, Homeward Bound* 1923; *The Moral Sinner, The Uninvited Guest, The House of Youth, Dynamite Smith, The Chorus Lady* 1924; *Playing with Souls, Smooth as Satin, Alias Mary Flynn, Lady Robinhood* 1925; *Bigger Than Barnum's* (also act.), *The Lone Wolf Returns/The Return of the Lone Wolf, Breed of the Sea* (also act.), *The Sea Wolf* (also exec. prod., act. as "Wolf" Larsen), *The Better Way* (also act.) 1926; *Wandering Girls, Moulders of Men, Home Struck, Not for Publication* (also prod., act.), *Shanghaied* (also exec. prod., act.) 1927; *South Sea Love, Coney Island, Chicago After Midnight* (also act.), *Hit of the Show, Danger Street, The Singapore Mutiny* (also co-titles, act.) 1928; *Hardboiled* (also titles), *Hurricane* 1929; *Men of America, Lucky Devils* 1933; *Flaming Gold, No Escape* (UK) 1934; *Murder at Monte Carlo, Crime Unlimited, The Black Mask, Blue Smoke* (all UK) 1935; *Jury's Evidence, Jail Break, Twelve Good Men, Hail and Farewell* (all UK) 1936; *The Vulture, Side Street Angel, It's Not Cricket, The Perfect Crime, The Man Who Made Diamonds* (all UK) 1937.

Ince, Thomas H(arper). Producer, director, screenwriter, actor. *b.* Nov. 6, 1882, Newport, R.I. *d.* 1924. The second of three sons (the others: John INCE, Ralph INCE) of a traveling actor and actress, he made his stage debut at age six and subsequently made numerous appearances on Broadway and on the road. He was often out of work and occasionally consented to appear in films, although they were still held in low regard by serious actors. In 1910, idle and broke, he decided to switch to films altogether. He appeared in several Biograph pictures, thanks to the connections of his wife, actress Alice Kershaw, then joined Carl Laemmle's IMP (Independent Motion Pictures) Company, where he was given a chance to direct the films of Mary PICKFORD, the company's new recruit from Biograph. Some were made in Cuba, out of the legal reach of the Motion Picture Patents Company. In September 1911, he left IMP to join Kessel and Bauman's NYMP (New York Motion Pictures).

Operating from the company's studio in Los Angeles, Ince soon gained a reputation for the quality of his films, many of which were Westerns. He insisted on detailed, tightly structured shooting scripts, which he often wrote himself, and high standards of production. To achieve the kind of spectacular action he found lacking in the Westerns of the day, he put a whole Wild West show on the payroll, thus obtaining the services of trained horses and buffaloes, as well as authentic cowboys and Indians and real props. He also acquired nearly 20,000 acres of land on which to shoot his Westerns. The studio he built on the property was to become soon known as Inceville.

Ince was at once a clever entrepreneur and an inspired visionary. A contemporary of D. W. GRIFFITH, he contributed as much to the art and craft of the film producer as Griffith did to the art of the director. By mid-1912 he gave up trying to direct the growing output of NYMP all by himself and began dividing the chores with Francis FORD, the brother of John. But he insisted that Ford stick closely to his, Ince's, scripts and supervised the production of every one of his films. By 1916 he gave up directing altogether and devoted his energies to writing his detailed shooting scripts and supervising the work of his growing stable of directors and stars. One of his most profitable acquisitions was actor-director William S. HART, an old friend of his from his days as an actor on Broadway. Hart's Westerns were famous for their authenticity and high quality and were immensely popular with the public. Another popular Ince star was Charles RAY. Among the directors Ince developed were Reginald BARKER, Jack CONWAY, Frank BORZAGE, and Fred NIBLO.

In 1915, in the midst of a corporate shuffle, Ince found himself working side by side with Griffith in the new Triangle Film Corporation. The following year Ince turned out his most ambitious and best-known work, *Civilization,* a pacifist allegory in support of President Wilson's international policy, which competed with Griffith's *Intolerance* of the same year for the critics' and public's attention. Ince received screen credit as director, but some film historians claim he only supervised the work of several of his choice directors.

Ince was a dynamic and often ruthless person and not always easy to get along with. In 1918 he quarreled with Henry Aitken, his boss at Triangle, and formed his own company. He built new studios at Culver City and distributed his films through Paramount-Artcraft and later Metro. Ince soon also clashed with Hart, his big moneymaking star, and they parted company. Still Ince continued making highly profitable pictures and in 1919 he joined with other producers and directors (including Mack Sennett, Allan Dwan, Marshall Neilan, and Maurice Tourneur) to form Associated Producers, Inc., an independent releasing company, which merged with First National in 1922. Then, on the night of November 19, 1924, Thomas Harper Ince was mysteriously and fatally injured aboard William Randolph Hearst's yacht, on which he had gone for a weekend of fun and frolic with several other distinguished guests. He died before regaining consciousness. The death was officially attributed to heart failure as a result of acute indigestion. But scandalous rumors persisted in Hollywood that Ince was shot by Hearst, who suspected him of carrying on an affair with his protégée, Marion DAVIES.

Ince was one of the most important and influential figures in the history of the American cinema. His combined output as director, producer, and screenwriter extended to thousands of films during the formative years of the industry. He introduced production procedures and quality standards that set the model and helped mold the distinct image of Hollywood cinema for many years to come. The French cinéaste Louis Delluc wrote in 1920: "Ince is the man of today. . . . Griffith is cinema's first director. Ince is its first prophet."

FILMS INCLUDE: As actor—*Seven Ages* 1906; *Richard III, Macbeth* 1908; *The Cardinal's Conspiracy* 1909; *The Englishman and the Girl, His New Lid* 1910. As director—*Little Nell's Tobacco* (also sc.) 1910; *Their First Misunderstanding* (co-dir. with George Loane Tucker), *The Dream* (co-dir. with Tucker), *Artful Kate, Behind the Stockade* (co-dir. with Tucker), *Her Darkest Hour, A Manly Man, In Old Madrid, Sweet Memories, The Aggressor* (co-dir. with Tucker) 1911; *The Indian Massacre, The Deserter, The War on the Plains* (also co-sc.), *The Crisis, The Hidden Trail, On the Firing Line, Custer's Last Raid, The Colonel's Ward, The Battle of the Red Men, When Lee Surrenders, The Invaders* (co-dir. with Francis Ford), *The Law of the West, A Double Reward* 1912; *A Shadow of the Past, The Mosaic Law, With Lee in Virginia, Bread Cast Upon the Waters, The Drummer of the Eighth, The Boomerang, The Seal of Silence, Days of '49, The Battle of Gettysburg 1913; Love's Sacrifice* (co-dir. with William Clifford), *A Relic of Old Japan, The Golden Goose* (co-dir. with Clifford), *One of the Discard* (co-dir. with C. Gardner Sullivan) 1914; *The Last of the Line* (also co-sc.), *The Devil, The Alien* 1915; *Civilization* 1916. As producer or production supervisor—*The Military Judas* 1913; *The Gringo* (also co-sc.), *The Wrath of the Gods/The Destruction of Sakura Jima, The Gangsters and the Girl, The Typhoon, The Bargain* 1914; *The Italian* (also co-sc.), *The Reward* (also co-sc.), *On the Night Stage* (also co-sc.), *The Cup of Life, Rumpelstiltskin* (also sc.), *The Darkening Trail, The Iron Strain, The Coward* (also co-sc.), *The Golden Claw, The Disciple* (also co-sc.), *Matrimony, Aloha Oe, The Winged Idol, The Painted Soul* 1915; *Peggy, D'Artagnan/The Three Musketeers, Hell's Hinges, The Moral Fabric, The Aryan, The Deserter, The Dividend, The Patriot, Home, Plain Jane* 1916; *Paddy O'Hara, The Desert Man, Golden Rule Kate, Her Fighting Chance* 1917; *The Narrow Trail, Madam Who?, Those Who Pay, Carmen of the Klondike, The Vamp, The Midnight Patrol, Within the Cup, Fuss and Feathers, String Beans* 1918; *The False Faces, The Home Breaker, The Busher, Stepping Out* 1919; *Behind the Door, Black Is White, Sex, Let's Be Fashionable, Homer Comes Home, Hairpins, Home Spun Folks* 1920; *Lying Lips, Beau Revel, Mother o' Mine, The Cup of Life* (remake), *Hail the Woman* 1921; *Skin Deep, Lorna Doone, The Hottentot* 1922; *Scars of Jealousy, Soul of the Beast, Human Wreckage, Her Reputation, Anna Christie* 1923; *The Marriage Cheat, Those Who Dance, Barbara Frietchie, Christine of the Hungry Heart, Idle Tongues* 1924; *Enticement, Percy, Playing with Souls* 1925.

incident light. The light falling directly upon a surface, as distinct from reflected light. An incident-light meter is a type of exposure meter that measures the intensity of light falling on an object as opposed to a reflected-light meter, which reads the amount of light reflected from an object.

independent. 1. A filmmaker or film producer who operates outside the major Hollywood STUDIOS, obtaining financing from other sources and retaining a greater degree of artistic control. 2. A film distribution and/or production company that is not one of the major studios. Since the collapse in the 50s of the STU-

DIO SYSTEM that had dominated the American film industry, independent companies ("indies") have come to enjoy a significant share of the market. Some are producers of film, others acquire films for distribution to theaters (including films made by independent filmmakers), while others carry out both functions. Most independents achieve success by keeping costs low and concentrating on "niche" markets neglected by the majors, such as foreign language, art-house, horror, and exploitation films. The independent sector flourished in the early 80s with the boom in sales to home video, but later ran into financial difficulties that winnowed the field. Notable independents of the past few decades (some of which have since gone out of business) include American International Pictures (AIP), Atlantic, Cannon, Carolco, Castle Hill, Cinecom, the Samuel Goldwyn Company, Island/Alive, Miramax, New Line Cinema, New World Pictures, Skouras, and Vestron.

India. This underdeveloped massive Asian land of nearly 900 million inhabitants is the world's most prolific film-producing country. More than 900 feature films and numerous shorts and documentaries are turned out each year by a vast assortment of studios and independent producers. The films are exhibited domestically at about 13,000 theaters and exported to Britain, Canada, the US, and numerous Asian and African countries with large Indian populations. Distribution and exhibition problems arise because Indians speak some 1,600 different dialects, with 16 languages officially recognized in the constitution. The diversity of religions, cultures, customs, and even racial types adds to the difficulty of creating mass art and entertainment for all the people to enjoy or even understand. As a result, two distinct film industries have developed: the so-called All-India film, produced in Hindi or Hindustani and distributed nationally; and regional films produced in a variety of languages for local consumption. The largest centers for All-India film are in Bombay and Madras, while regional film production is scattered across the country. The most important of the latter is the Bengali industry, centered at Calcutta. Other leading regional industries include the Marathi, the Oriya, and the Assamese.

Newsreel footage was shot in India as early as 1898 (*Train Arriving at Bombay Station,* etc.). But it wasn't until 1913 that the first feature-style film, *Rajah Harishandra,* was made, by D. G. PHALKE. The great commercial success of the film enabled him to found a studio in Bombay, the first of many that were to proliferate in the city. The most important silent Indian film, *Light of Asia* (a life of Buddha), was made in 1925 by a German director, Franz Osten. By the end of the silent era, India was producing some 100 films annually. The coming of sound signaled the beginning of the division between national and regional production. The first talkie, *Alam Ara* (1931), contained a dozen song and dance numbers. Since it was a huge financial success, it established a formula that is still very much a part of almost every All-India film, comedies and dramas alike. At regular intervals, the action of a film is stopped for a musical number, which may have nothing to do with the plot. At least six such intermezzos are inserted into every production, to the delight of the rupee-paying public.

However, in the mid-30s, a modest trend started in the rapidly growing regional industries toward the production of realistic films on contemporary social issues. The pace-setters in this trend were Bengali directors Debaki Bose (*Chandidas,* 1932; *Seeta,* 1934, etc.) and P. D. Barua (*Devdas,* 1935, etc.). A Marathi film, *Saint Tukaram,* was the first Indian film to win an international award (at the Venice Festival in 1937). The influence of this trend even reached the All-India industry in Bombay, and themes of social significance began infiltrating the product of such companies as Bombay Talkies, Ltd., the standard product of which was garish imitation of Hollywood entertainment.

The Indian film industry enjoyed a period of prosperity during WW II. One of the leading filmmakers of the period was Khwaja Ahmad Abbas, several of whose socially conscious films have been internationally distributed. The 50s saw the emergence in the Bengali film of Satyajit RAY. India's only great filmmaker by international standards. His "Apu Trilogy" (*Pather Panchali, Aparajito,* and *The World of Apu*) is among the great classics of world cinema. Another director of some international reputation who emerged during this period is Bimal ROY. Raj KAPOOR, a popular star and a respected director, infuses his films with social concern in the guise of pure entertainment. Indian producer Ismail MERCHANT, working with American director James IVORY and German-born screenwriter Ruth Prawer JHABVALA, has made a number of films with Indian themes, including *Shakespeare Wallah* (1965) and *Heat and Dust* (1983).

Films of social or moral significance, however, remain the exception rather than the rule in Indian cinema. The wartime prosperity and the consolidation of the industry in the years following independence have brought in their wake an outpouring of gaudy commercial films that have remained models for the standard Indian film of today. They are typically long, glossy, semiliterate, and replete with stock situations and moralistic clichés. One film resembles another to the extent that it becomes difficult to classify Indian films by genres.

The source of potential quality production for worldwide distribution remains the regional film industries. But the most important among these, the Bengali industry, suffered the loss of more than half its natural market following the India-Pakistani war of 1965, when Pakistani authorities refused to show Indian films in East Pakistan. The crisis that threatened the existence of the Bengali industry seemed over at the end of 1971, when a potential audience of 50 million filmgoers was regained by East Pakistan's declaration of independence and the establishment of the Republic of Bangladesh.

Over the last twenty years, Indian cinema has continued to expand, capitalizing on new distribution strategies to reach the largest possible audience. The art film has remained in decline, taken over by epic tales of teenage romance, often accompanied by musical scores more popular than the films themselves. It is the age of the teen star, an age when fortunes are made simply by reworking existing stories. In fact, one film, *Maine Pyarkiya/I Fell in Love* (directed by Sooraj Bharjatiya) remained the number one box-office draw for several years in the early 90s. It was simply re-cut and re-edited every few months with new bits and pieces, and then re-distributed to an adoring public.

In the early 90s, the Indian government liberalized its trade policies, relaxing its formerly strict control of foreign film imports and allowing Indians to see the latest American and European releases. Movie audiences in India responded enthusiastically, though cinema attendances continued a gradual decline.

India lost its most acclaimed and beloved serious filmmaker, Satyajit Ray, in 1992, but other directors have been striving to preserve Indian cinema's artistic strain. Among India's most successful and best known contemporary directors are Sandip Ray (Satyajit's son, who took over directing honors on what was to have been his father's final film, *The Broken Journey*, 1992), Raj Kapoor (*Henna*, 1991), Sai Paranjpe (*Disha/The Uprooted*, 1991), Ketan MEHTA, Shyam Zaidi, and Mani Kaul (*The Idiot*, 1991).

indie. An INDEPENDENT film distribution and/or production company.

Industrial Light & Magic (ILM). SPECIAL EFFECTS company. It was founded in 1975 by director George LUCAS to create the revolutionary visual effects for his film *Star Wars*. Headed by effects artist John DYKSTRA, the operation was set up in a warehouse in Van Nuys, Calif. There the artists, most of them quite young, used the innovative method of computerized MOTION CONTROL to create realistic scenes of fast-moving spaceships clashing in dogfights; the film's many other effects ranged from light sabers to animated chess pieces. After the year and a half it took to complete the project, ILM closed down, apparently for good. But the phenomenal success of *Star Wars* (1977) ensured that funding could be obtained for a sequel, *The Empire Strikes Back* (1980). It also opened the door for a flood of fantasy and science-fiction films that were even more laden with special visual effects.

To create the cinematic illusions in the *Star Wars* sequel, Lucas re-established ILM in San Rafael, near his home in northern California. As a division of Lucasfilm Ltd., ILM went on to become Hollywood's premier effects house, hired by studios to realize the fantastic visions of screenwriters and directors. ILM's effects artists and designers (some of whom have gone on to work independently) have included Richard Edlund, Dennis Muren, Joe Johnston, Ralph McQuarrie, Phil Tippett, Jon Berg, and Ken Ralston. Numerous processes and devices have been pioneered or perfected at ILM, including FRONT PROJECTION, GO-MOTION, MORPHING, and DIGITAL EFFECTS. Among the films for which ILM has provided effects are the *Star Trek* series, the *Indiana Jones* series, *E.T.: The Extraterrestrial*, the *Back to the Future* series, *Poltergeist*, *Cocoon*, *Ghost*, *Jurassic Park*, *Dragonheart*, and *Mars Attacks!*.

Inescort, Frieda. Actress. *b.* Frieda Wightman, June 29, 1900, Edinburgh, Scotland. *d.* 1976. The daughter of a journalist and an actress (Elaine Inescort), she worked in London as personal secretary to Lady Astor and in New York at the British consulate before making her Broadway debut in 1922. She appeared in many stage productions before making her first screen appearance in 1935. She played leads and supporting parts in many Hollywood films, usually in dignified roles, through the late 50s, when she retired. She finally succumbed after a long bout with multiple sclerosis.

FILMS INCLUDE: *The Dark Angel* 1935; *The Garden Murder Case, The King Steps Out, Mary of Scotland, Give Me Your Heart, Hollywood Boulevard* 1936; *The Great O'Malley, Call It a Day, Another Dawn, Portia on Trial* 1937; *Beauty for the Asking, Woman Doctor, Tarzan Finds a Son, The Zero Hour, A Woman Is the Judge* 1939; *Convicted Woman, Pride and Prejudice* (as Miss Bingley), *The Letter* 1940; *Father's Son, The Trial of Mary Dugan, Sunny, You'll Never Get Rich, Remember the Day* 1941; *The Courtship of Andy Hardy, Street of Chance* 1942; *It Comes Up Love, The Return of the Vampire* 1943; *Heavenly Days* 1944; *The Judge Steps Out* 1949; *The Underworld Story* 1950; *A Place in the Sun* 1951; *Never Wave at a WAC* 1953; *Casanova's Big Night* 1954; *Foxfire* 1955; *The Eddy Duchin Story* 1956; *Darby's Rangers* 1958; *The Alligator People* 1959; *The Crowded Sky* 1960.

infinity. A distance far enough away from a camera lens to cause rays of light to seem parallel. At such a distance, focal adjustments for sharp photography are no longer necessary, since all objects within view will be in focus.

infrared. The portion of the light spectrum having wavelengths greater than those of visible light. If a special filter and a special photographic emulsion sensitive to infrared light are used, objects may be photographed through haze and mist and even apparent darkness. Infrared photography is seldom employed in normal filming but is very useful in conditions of low illumination and for achieving a variety of special effects, including the simulation of a night scene while filming in broad daylight. Infrared photography is especially useful in aerial photography, in TRAVELING MATTE work, and in scientific research.

Inge, William. Playwright, screenwriter. *b.* May 3, 1913, Independence, Kans. *d.* 1973, a suicide. Several of the plays of this Pulitzer Prize–winning author have been adapted to the screen by others, including *Come Back Little Sheba* (1952), *Picnic, Bus Stop* (both 1956), and *The Stripper* (from his play 'A Loss of Roses,' 1963). The film *Bus Riley's Back in Town* (1965) was based on his story. He wrote only twice directly for the screen, winning an Academy Award for his original screenplay of *Splendor in the Grass* (1961), a film on which he was also the associate producer.

FILMS (as screenwriter): *Splendor in the Grass* (also assoc. prod.) 1961; *All Fall Down* 1962; *Bus Riley's Back in Town* (under pseudonym Walter Gage) 1965.

ingenue. A young female lead in the cast of a film or play.

Ingraham, Lloyd. Director, actor. *b.* 1885(?), Rochelle, Ill. *d.* 1956. A former stage actor and director, he entered films in 1912. Directed numerous features during the silent era, often melodramas featuring heroines and later robust Westerns, and at the same time played character roles in films of other directors. His career as a director ended with the transition to sound, but he continued acting in films through 1950.

FILMS INCLUDE: As director (complete)—*The Fox Woman, The Sable Lorcha, The Missing Links* 1915; *American Aristocracy, Casey at the Bat, A Child of the Paris Streets, Stranded, The Little Liar, The Children Pay, Hoodoo Ann* 1916; *Charity Castle, Nina the Flower Girl, An Old-Fashioned Young Man, Her Country's Call, Peggy Leads the Way, Miss Jackie of the Army* 1917; *Jilted Janet, Molly Go Get 'Em, Ann's Finish, The Primitive Woman, A Square Deal, Impossible Susan, The Eyes of Julia Deep, Rosemary Climbs the Heights, Wives and Other Wives* 1918; *The Amazing Imposter, The Intrusion of Isabel, Man's Desire, The House of Intrigue* 1919; *Mary's Ankle, What's Your Husband Doing? Let's Be Fashionable, Twin Beds, The Jailbird, Old Dad* 1920; *The Girl in the Taxi, Keeping Up with Lizzie, Lavender and Old Lace, My Lady Friends, Marry the Poor Girl* 1921; *At the Sign of Jack O' Lantern* (also sc.), *Second Hand Rose, The Veiled Woman, The Danger Point* 1922; *Going Up* 1923; *No More Woman, The Lightning Rider, The Wise Virgin, The Beauty Prize* 1924; *Soft Shoes, Midnight Molly* 1925; *The Nut-Cracker, Hearts and Fists, Oh! What A Night* 1926; *Don Mike, Silver Comes Through* (also sc.), *Arizona Nights, Jesse James* 1927; *Kit Carson* (co-dir. with Alfred L. Werker), *The Pioneer Scout, The Sunset Legion* (co-dir. with Werker) 1928; *Take the Heir* 1930. As actor—*The Spanish Jade* 1915; *Intolerance* 1916; *A Front Page Story* 1922; *Scaramouche* 1923; *The Chorus Lady* 1924; *The Rainbow Man, Night Parade, Untamed* 1929; *Montana Moon, Last of the Duanes, The Spoilers* 1930; *The Crusader* 1932; *Sixteen Fathoms Deep* 1934; *Modern Times* 1936; *Painted Desert* 1938; *My Little Chickadee* 1940; *Never Give a Sucker an Even Break* 1941; *The Merry Monahans* 1944; *The Caravan Trail* 1946; *The Savage Horde* 1950.

Ingram, Rex. Director. *b.* Reginald Ingram Montgomery Hitchcock, Jan. 15, 1892, Dublin. *d.* 1950. The son of a clergyman, and grandson of Dublin's fire chief, he studied law at Dublin's Trinity College before emigrating to the US in 1911. Here he took up sculpture at Yale's School of Fine Arts, supporting himself as a freight clerk in New Haven's railroad yards. A chance meeting with Charles Edison, son of the inventor, led to Ingram's entry into films in 1913 as a combination actor-writer-set designer for the Edison company in Manhattan. He later performed similar tasks for Vitagraph in Brooklyn and for the Fox studios and in 1916 switched over to Universal/Bluebird as a director-writer-producer. He began rising to prominence after joining Metro in 1920, following WW I service as a second lieutenant with Canada's Royal Flying Corps, during which he was badly injured in an air crash.

Ingram got his big break thanks to influential screenwriter June MATHIS, who insisted that he be assigned to direct her adaptation of *The Four Horsemen of the Apocalypse* (1921), a highly praised screen version starring Valentino. The enormous critical and commercial success of the film established Ingram as a leading Hollywood director and he went on to direct a number of other major productions noted for their ambitious scope and superb visual values. He was allowed much creative freedom from interference by the studio and set up his own production unit, which developed into a virtual stock company. Among Ingram's frequent collaborators were director of photography John F. SEITZ, screenwriter Willis GOLDBECK, and his own wife, Alice TERRY, who starred in many of his films. However, Ingram suffered a great personal disappointment when, despite studio promises, he was not assigned to direct the sumptuous *Ben-Hur,* and threatened to retire. He was talked out of his threat by a close friend, Erich von STROHEIM, who considered him "the world's greatest director," and Ingram later returned the favor by cutting von Stroheim's *Greed* from 24 to 18 reels when the controversial film ran afoul of studio management.

Although Ingram returned to the MGM fold, his rift with studio boss Louis B. Mayer never healed. In 1924 he and Terry left for Europe and set up their own studio in Nice, on the French Riviera, where he continued turning out films for MGM. But the advent of sound presented an insurmountable technical problem for Ingram's tiny studio and he retired from films in the early 30s after directing only one talkie in Morocco. Fascinated by exotic North Africa, he made it his home for a while and rumor says he even converted to Islam. But he eventually returned to the US and spent his remaining years as a writer and sculptor.

FILMS: *The Great Problem* (also prod., sc.), *Broken Fetters* (also prod., sc.), *The Chalice of Sorrows* (also adapt.) 1916; *Black Orchids* (also sc.), *The Reward of the Faithless* (also sc.), *The Pulse of Life* (also sc.), *The Flower of Doom* (also sc.), *The Little Terror* (also sc.) 1917; *His Robe of Honor, Humdrum Brown* 1918; *The Day She Paid* 1919; *Under Crimson Skies, Shore Acres, Hearts Are Trumps* 1920; *The Four Horsemen of the Apocalypse, The Conquering Power* (also prod.) 1921; *Turn to the Right, The Prisoner of Zenda* (also prod.), *Trifling Women* (also prod., story) 1922; *Where the Pavement Ends* (also prod., adapt.), *Scaramouche* (also prod.) 1923; *The Arab* (also sc.) 1924; *Mare Nostrum* (also prod.), *The Magician* (also adapt.) 1926; *The Garden of Allah* (also prod.) 1927; *The Three Passions* (also prod., sc.) 1929; *Baroud/Love in Morocco* (also prod., co-story, co-sc., act.) 1931.

Ingram, Rex. Actor. *b.* Oct. 20, 1895, aboard riverboat *Robert E. Lee,* near Cairo, Ill. *d.* 1969. The son of a ship's stoker, he attended military school in Chicago, then graduated from the Medical School of Northwestern University. But inexplicably, instead of practicing medicine, he wound up in Hollywood, playing a bit as an African native in the silent film *Tarzan of the Apes* (1918), starring Elmo Lincoln. He reputedly appeared in other silent films, including *The Ten Commandments* (1923), *The Big Parade* (1926), and *The King of Kings* (1927), but his name is found nowhere in their credits. An imposing, powerful black performer, he appeared in West Coast stage productions and in the early 30s began playing roles of increasing prominence on Broadway. He made a bid for film stardom with a magnificent performance as De Lawd in the screen version of Marc Connelly's *The Green Pastures* (1936), but leading roles for black actors were scarce in Hollywood and he never successfully capitalized on his triumph. He went on to play supporting roles in many films, most memorably as Jim, the runaway slave, in *The Adventures of Huckleberry Finn* (1939), as the giant genie in *The Thief of Bagdad* (1940), and as Lucifer in the all-black cast of *Cabin in the Sky* (1943).

FILMS INCLUDE: *Tarzan of the Apes* (bit) 1918; *The Green Pastures* 1936; *The Adventures of Huckleberry Finn* 1939; *The Thief of Bagdad* 1940; *The Talk of the Town* 1942; *Cabin in the Sky, Sahara* 1943; *Dark Waters* 1944; *A Thousand and One Nights* 1945; *Moonrise* 1948; *Tarzan's Hidden Jungle* 1955; *Congo Crossing* 1956; *Hell on Devil's Island* 1957; *God's Little Acre, Anna Lucasta* 1958; *Watusi* 1959; *Elmer Gantry* 1960; *Your Cheatin' Heart* 1964; *Hurry Sundown* 1967; *Journey to Shiloh* 1968.

inker. In animation, the artist who traces on CELS the lines previously drawn by the animator.

inkies. Incandescent lamps for studio LIGHTING.

in phase. The condition in which an intermittent shutter and the transport mechanism of motion picture equipment (camera, projector, printing machine) operate synchronously, so that film is exposed only when it is stationary.

in register. See REGISTRATION.

insert. A shot, usually a close-up or extreme close-up, intercut within a scene to help explain the action, emphasize a point, or facilitate continuity. A typical insert may consist of a close-up shot of a newspaper item, a hand holding a gun, or a clock on a wall.

insurance take. See COVER SHOT.

INT. An abbreviation used in film scripts to indicate an interior scene, either on location or in the studio, and requiring artificial lighting. Opposite of EXT.

integral tripack. In color photography, film with three layers of emulsion all differently sensitive. It is used in the production of separation negatives.

intensification. A chemical process for increasing the density or contrast of a photographic image. Useful for improving the quality of underexposed negatives.

intensity. The power of a light source. Its unit of measurement is the CANDELA.

interchangeable lenses. Lenses of any given focal length which can be dismounted and interchanged with those of other focal lengths.

intercutting. An editing technique by which two different sequences of action are alternated to suggest simultaneous action. This method allows an editor to enrich the narrative continuity of a film and also to manipulate time by accelerating or retarding the main action. For example, a girl is seen walking down a street to a corner flower shop. By intercutting this action with a shot of a man's face watching her go by and then showing her entering the shop, the editor can "condense" a two-minute walk into a few seconds of screen time. By distracting the audience momentarily from the main action of her walking, he can get the girl to the flower shop without showing us the entire span of the walk. Conversely, the editor can prolong the walk, if he so wishes, by introducing a number of intercuts, back and forth from her walk to the man watching, that would make her walk longer in screen time than it would normally take in real time.

Interlenghi, Franco. Actor. Born on Oct. 29, 1931, in Rome. He began his film career as a juvenile in De Sica's

Shoeshine in the 50s and developed into a sought-after leading man in Italian films, especially after his appearance in Fellini's *I Vitelloni.* He also scored a number of stage successes, notably in 'Death of a Salesman' under the direction of Visconti. For a while he rivaled Marcello MASTROIANNI as the leading star of the Italian screen but never achieved the latter's popularity outside Italy. He is married to Antonella LUALDI.

FILMS INCLUDE: *Sciuscia/Shoeshine* 1946; *Fabiola* 1948; *Una Domenica d'Agosto/Sunday in August* 1950; *Teresa* (US) 1951; *Le Petit Monde de Don Camillo* (Fr./It.), *Processo alla Città* 1952; *I Vinti, I Vitelloni, La Provinciale/The Wayward Wife* 1953; *The Barefoot Contessa* (US), *Ulisse/Ulysses* (as Telemachus) 1954; *Gli Inamorati/Wild Love* 1955; *Padri e Figli, A Farewell to Arms* (US) 1957; *Giovani Mariti/Young Husbands* 1958; *Il Generale della Rovere/General della Rovere, La Notte Brava/On Any Street/Bad Girls Don't Cry* 1959; *Chronache del '22* 1962; *Una Notte per 5 Rapine* 1968.

interlock. A system by which a picture reel and a soundtrack reel (or any two interdependent motors) are kept in phase to assure SYNCHRONIZATION.

intermittent movement. The stop-and-go action allowing the film to advance through a motion picture camera, projector, or printer, frame by frame, so that each frame is held momentarily motionless during exposure or projection. This action proceeds at such a speed that the film seems to be moving continuously through the camera, but in reality each frame is stopped long enough to be exposed in a manner similar to the exposure of a still photograph.

International Creative Management (ICM). Hollywood talent agency. It was founded in 1975 from two former companies, Creative Management Associates and International Famous Agency. In the 80s, it acquired other talent agencies, becoming one of the two most powerful agencies in Hollywood (the other being CREATIVE ARTISTS AGENCY, or CAA). In addition to representing film and television talent, ICM also markets movies and represents syndicated television shows. Its chairman and CEO is Jeff Berg.

internegative. A negative derived directly from an original color reversal film. Negatives derived from a source other than reversal film, regardless of generation, are known as "duplicate color negatives."

interpositive. A denser-than-usual color print used as intermediate film for making duplicate negatives. It can be recognized by its orange-colored base.

intervalometer. A timing device used in TIME LAPSE photography. It can be set to control the operation of a camera at predetermined intervals.

"in the can." A general term meaning that a film has been completed. More precisely, it is a term employed by production crews to indicate that a film or a sequence of film has been exposed or completed and is contained in cans for shipping to the lab.

inverse-square law. A rule stating that the efficiency of illumination is inversely proportional to the square of the distance between a subject and a source of light. In simple terms, it means that the illumination of an object falls off sharply as it is moved back farther from a light source, at a rate greater than the distance would indicate. At twice the distance, for example, the object receives only one fourth the original illumination.

invisible splices. Splices prepared for A and B roll printing. The film is placed in the splicer in such a way that one cut is made on the frame line and the other in the picture area. After the scene is spliced to a black leader, cut and scrape marks are concealed and the splice is invisible in the subsequent print.

Ioseliani, Otar [also Iosseliani, Otar]. Director. Born on Feb. 2, 1934, in Georgia, USSR. Trained as a musician at the Tbilisi Conservatory, he later studied graphic art and majored in mathematics at Moscow University before finally deciding on a career in films. He attended Moscow's film school, where he was tutored by Alexander DOVZHENKO, and directed his first film, a short, in 1958. When his first feature, *April,* completed in 1961, was withheld from distribution by the authorities, Ioseliani gave up in disgust and for a while sought employment as a sailor and factory worker. But he later returned, making his official feature debut in 1966. Because of continuing clashes with the authorities, his subsequent output was sparse. Yet before long he became established as the foremost figure in Georgian cinema and one of the most respected of contemporary Soviet directors. An uncompromising maverick who disdains plot and focuses instead on capturing moments of life through affectionate, sardonic character observation, he prefers working with amateur rather than professional performers. His long-suppressed *Pastoral,* completed in 1976, won the International Critics Prize at the 1982 Berlin Festival. In the 80s he worked mainly in France, where he is widely admired as a film poet. He was awarded the Grand Jury Special Prize at Venice for his French film, *Favorites of the Moon* (1984).

FEATURE FILMS: *April/Stories About Things* (unreleased) 1964; *Falling Leaves/When Leaves Fall* 1966; *There Was a Singing Blackbird* (also co-sc.) 1972; *Pastoral* (also co-sc.) 1976–82; *Les Favoris de la Lune/Favorites of the Moon* (also co-sc.; Fr.) 1984; *Et la Lumière fut/Let There Be Light* (also sc., co-edit.; Fr./Ger./It.) 1989.

i.p.s. Inches per second. A unit of measurement indicating the speed at which a recording is being taped. Slower speeds are usually sufficient for speech reproduction, but speeds of 7½ i.p.s. and higher are required for high fidelity in music.

Iran. The film industry in this Persian Gulf country of 60 million people dates back to about 1930. By the 60s, cinematography and production values had reached high professional standards, and a number of Iranian directors were creating original and interesting works, some of which won international recognition. Directors who worked in this period included Bahram Bayzai (*Downpour*, 1971; *The Crow*, 1977), Massoud Kimiai (*Come Stranger!*, 1969; *Stags*, 1975), Dariush Mehrjui (*Diamond 33*, 1967; *The Postman*, 1970), and Amir Naderi (*Goodbye My Friend,* 1971). However, the future of this industry, which at its peak in the early 70s was producing 90 features a year, was thrown into serious question in 1979, when Shah Mohammed Reza Pahlavi, who had ruled Iran since 1941, was deposed by the Islamic Revolution that brought the Ayatollah Ruhollah Khomeini into power. For several years, the film industry ground to a virtual halt, battered by economic recession, war with Iraq, and uncertainty about the fit between the cinematic art and Islamic fundamentalist ideals.

In 1983, the Islamic government resolved that uncertainty by creating the Farabi Cinema Foundation. The Foundation sought to develop a distinctively Iranian national cinema with both ethical substance (as defined by the Islamic state) and artistic merit. The result was a mix of censorship and encouragement. Farabi banned some existing works of established directors, forcing a number of them to retire or leave the country. Many producers, screenwriters, and actors found it impossible to work under the new conditions, and Iranian actresses who were deemed too seductively beautiful were forbidden to appear on-screen at all. At the same time, Farabi helped recruit and train a new generation of filmmakers, production personnel, and actors. By generously funding domestic cinema and severely restricting foreign imports, Farabi succeeded in boosting Iranian film production and reviving audience interest. By the 1990s, Iran was producing about 45 features a year, cinema attendances were high, and Iranian films were winning international prizes. Iranian cinema has been spotlighted annually at the Fajr International Film Festival, which replaced the Teheran film festival held during the Shah's reign.

The directors noted above have continued to work in postrevolutionary Iran, producing such acclaimed works as Bayzai's *Travellers* (1992), Kimiai's *Snake Fang* (1990), Mehrjui's *Hamoon* (1990), and Naderi's *The Runner* (1991). Naderi moved to New York in 1990, where he filmed *Manhattan by Numbers* (1992). Other important directors of the 80s and 90s include Kianoush Ayyari (*Beyond the Fire*, 1988), Alireza Davudnezhad (*The Need*, 1991), Abbas Kiarostami (*Where is the Friend's Home?*, 1987; *And Life Goes On. . .*, 1992), and Mohsen Makhmalbaf (*The Peddler*, 1987; *The Cyclist*, 1989). The themes, content, and style of this cinema vary greatly. *Travellers* is an allegorical story of a wedding that becomes a funeral; *The Runner* depicts the aspirations of a boy living on an abandoned ship; *Beyond the Fire* is a visually stark tale of fraternal rivalry in the desert. The two films of Kiarostami noted above present a documentary-style look at mountain life before and after a major earthquake; those of Makhmalbaf fuse realism and surrealism in sardonic stories of the grotesque.

Despite the obstacles posed by patriarchal tradition, a small number of women have succeeded in becoming directors. Of these, Puran Derakhshandeh has been the most outspoken in her criticism of patriarchy (notably in *Lost Time*, 1990, an account of a sterile woman who cares for an orphan girl); other women directors include Rakhshan Bani-Etemad (*Nargess*, 1992) and Ferial Behzad (*Kakoli/The Crested Hen* 1990).

Ireland. Ireland received motion pictures the same year England did, on April 20, 1896, with the first exhibition taking place at Dan Lowry's Star of Erin Theater of Varieties. Ireland was at that time a reluctant part of the UNITED KINGDOM, with many Irish straining for independence or home rule. Early Irish films were shown in music halls until 1909, when the first proper theater opened in Dublin (co-founded by novelist James Joyce, who then lost interest and faded from the scene).

Though many early efforts were nationalistic in theme, Irish cinema of this period was peppered with half-Irishmen and foreign-born participants. Robert PAUL, the British inventor, directed the first Irish documentary (*A Cattle Drive in Galway*, 1908), and British Arthur Melbourne-Cooper directed what was probably the first Irish fiction film, *Irish Wives and English Neighbors* (1907). Irish-Canadian director Sidney OLCOTT, working for the American production company Kalem, directed scores of films on location in Ireland for consumption at home and in Irish-population centers abroad.

The British government considered some early Irish films too inflammatory to be shown in Ireland. Walter McNamara's *Ireland, A Nation* (1914) was banned for several years in Ireland but played to packed houses in Chicago. The Film Company of Ireland managed to launch itself in 1916 despite the havoc of the Easter Rebellion. After Ireland succeeded in throwing off British rule in 1922 (with the founding of the Irish Free State), a period of filmic isolationism ensued. American features were all but banned. Alfred Hitchcock's British *Juno and the Paycock* (1935) was seized and burned at screening. Sound did not come to Irish film until 1933, with *The Voice of Ireland*, a lush musical by Col. Victor Haddick.

The Irish film industry languished for decades, hampered by foreign competition, lack of private capital or government support, and repressive censorship. However, as location filming became a vogue, foreign-born directors began coming to Ireland to make films. In the 50s, American John Ford filmed *The Quiet Man* in Ireland; in the 60s, American Tay Garnett filmed *The Night Fighters*, American Joseph Strick filmed *Ulysses*, and British David Lean filmed *Ryan's Daughter*. The Irish struggles against Britain (whether in the pre-1922 past or in the counties of Northern Ireland that remain part of the United Kingdom) provided dramatic grist for many of these films, while other films focused on romantic, folkloric, or literary views of Ireland.

Not until the 80s did a number of Irish-born directors, sometimes working abroad, begin to catch the attention of international audiences. Pat O'CONNOR's *Cal* (1984), Neil JORDAN's *Mona Lisa* (1986), and Jim SHERIDAN's *My Left Foot* (1989) were among the films that brought about a renaissance of Irish cinema, while Irish actors like Gabriel BYRNE and Brenda FRICKER became known to worldwide audiences. In 1985, the Dublin Film Festival was founded, attracting visitors from throughout the film world.

In the 90s, the Irish Film Centre was established to promote Irish cinema and preserve the heritage of its past. An Irish Film School was founded and the government announced increased support for film production. As the number of cinema screens grew, Irish audiences became more interested in seeing domestic films. The all-time box office champion in Ireland, *The Commitments* (1991), was filmed in Ireland with an all-Irish cast, though its director is British Alan Parker. Other prominent Irish films of the 90s are Jordan's *The Crying Game* (1992), Sheridan's *The Field* (1990), and Gillies MacKinnon's *The Playboys* (1992).

Ireland, Jill. Actress. *b.* Apr. 24, 1936, London. *d.* 1990. Leading lady of British, American, and international films. Trained as a dancer, she began performing professionally at 15 and for a while appeared with the Monte Carlo Ballet. She made her screen debut as a dancer, in *Oh Rosalinda!* (1955), but soon after switched to acting and began playing dramatic roles in a variety of British films and TV productions. In 1957 she married actor David MCCALLUM. They divorced in 1967 and the following year she married Charles BRONSON, her co-star in many subsequent films. After losing a breast to cancer in 1984, she became a spokeswoman for the American Cancer Society, urging afflicted women to fight on. Despite her own deteriorating condition, she continued working in films for several years. She told the story of her ordeal and self-discovery in the book *Life Wish* (1987). In a follow-up book, *Life Lines* (1989), she discussed her parallel struggle to save her 27-year-old adopted son, Jason McCallum Bronson, from drug addiction. He died of an overdose that year. She is survived by six other children. At the time of her death, she was writing a third book, *Life Times*.

FILMS INCLUDE: *Oh Rosalinda!* 1955; *Three Men in a Boat* 1956; *There's Always a Thursday, Hell Drivers, Robbery Under Arms* 1957; *The Big Money* 1958; *Carry on Nurse* 1959; *Raising the Wind/Roommates, Jungle Street/Jungle Street Girls* 1961; *Twice Round the Daffodils* 1962; *Villa Rides* (bit; US) 1968; *Le Passager de la Pluie/Rider on the Rain* (Fr./It.), *Città Violenta/Violent City/The Family* (It./Fr.), *De la part des Copains/Cold Sweat* (It./Fr.) 1970; *Quelqu'un derrière la Porte/Someone Behind the Door* (Fr./It.) 1971; *The Mechanic* (US) 1972; *Valdez il Mezzosangue/Chino* (It./Sp./Fr.) 1973; *Breakout* (US), *Hard Times* (US) 1975; *Breakheart Pass* (US), *From Noon Till Three* (US) 1976; *Love and Bullets* 1979; *Death Wish II* (US) 1982; *The Evil That Men Do* (co-prod. only; US) 1984; *Murphy's Law* (co-prod. only; US) 1986; *Assassination* (US), *Caught* (US) 1987.

Ireland, John. Actor. *b.* Jan. 30, 1914, Vancouver, B.C., Canada. *d.* 1992. A New Yorker from childhood, he began his show business career as a professional swimmer in a water carnival, then went on to play in the legitimate theater, appearing in many productions in stock and on Broadway, including much Shakespeare. In films from the mid-40s, he played many leads, frequently on the introspective side, early on in his screen career despite a less-than-handsome appearance. But he gradually drifted into secondary roles, frequently as a cynical heavy. He was nominated for an Oscar for his supporting role in *All the King's Men* (1949). His career declined in the 60s, when he appeared in a great many quickie Italian productions. He co-directed and co-produced (with cameraman Lee Garmes) one film, *Outlaw Territory* (1953). His second wife (1949–56) was actress Joanne DRU, who co-starred in several of his films.

FILMS INCLUDE: *A Walk in the Sun, My Darling Clementine* 1946; *Railroaded, The Gangster* 1947; *Open Secret, Raw Deal, Red River, Joan of Arc, A Southern Yankee* 1948; *I Shot Jesse James* (as Bob Ford, who shot James), *Roughshod, Anna Lucasta, The Doolins of Oklahoma, All the King's Men* 1949; *Cargo to Capetown, The Return of Jesse James* 1950; *Vengeance Valley, The Scarf, Little Big Horn, The Basketball Fix, The Bushwhackers* 1951; *Red Mountain, Hurricane Smith* 1952; *The 49th Man, Outlaw Territory* (also co-prod., co-dir.), *Combat Squad* 1953; *Security Risk, Southwest Passage, The Fast and the Furious, The Steel Cage* 1954; *Queen Bee, Hell's Horizon* 1955; *Gunslinger* 1956; *Gunfight at the O.K. Corral* 1957; *Party Girl* 1958; *Faces in the Dark* (UK), *Spartacus* 1960; *Wild in the Country, No Time to Kill* (UK/Sw./Ger.) 1961; *Brushfire!* 1962; *55 Days at Peking, The Ceremony* 1963; *The Fall of the Roman Empire* 1964; *Day of the Nightmare, I Saw What You Did* 1965; *Fort Utah* 1967; *Arizona Bushwhackers* 1968; *El Che Guevara* (It.) 1969; *The Adventurers* 1970; *Una sull'altra/One on Top of the Other* (It./Fr./Sp.) 1971; *Escape to the Sun* (Isr.) 1972; *The House of Seven Corpses, Welcome to Arrow Beach/Tender Flesh, The Mad Butcher* 1974; *Farewell My Lovely* 1975; *Il Letto in Piazza* (It.), *Salon Kitty/Madam Kitty* (It./Ger./Fr.) 1976; *Satan's Cheerleaders, The Swiss Conspiracy, Maniac/Assault on Paradise, Verano Sangriento* (Sp./It.) 1977; *Tomorrow Never Comes* (UK/Can.), *Love and the Midnight Auto Supply* 1978; *The Shape of Things to Come* (Can.), *Delta Fox* 1979; *Guyana, Cult of the Damned* (Mex./Sp./Pan.) 1980; *The Incubus* (Can.) 1982; *El Tesoro de la Amazona/The Treasure of the Amazon* (Mex./US) 1983; *Martin's Day* (Can.) 1984; *Thunder Run* (Austral.) 1985; *Messenger of Death* 1988; *Sundown: The Vampire in Retreat* 1990; *Waxwork II: Lost in Time* 1992.

Irene. Costume designer. *b.* Irene Lentz, 1901, Brookings, S.D. *d.* 1962. A graduate of the Wolf School of Design, she opened a dress shop in Los Angeles in the late 20s, with some well-known stars as customers. In 1933 she began designing gowns for films and in 1942 joined MGM, where she was chief costume designer throughout the 40s. In 1949 she formed her own fashion business for the design, manufacturing, and distributing of her styles. She returned briefly to films in the early 60s. She was nominated for an Academy Award for *B.F.'s Daughter* and *Midnight Lace*. Among her better-known designs were the arresting all-white outfits worn by Lana Turner in *The Postman Always Rings Twice*.

FILMS INCLUDE (alone or in collaboration): *Flying Down to Rio* 1933; *Merrily We Live, Shall We Dance, Topper* 1937; *Vivacious Lady, Algiers, You Can't Take It with You* 1938; *Midnight, Intermezzo: A Love Story, Bachelor Mother* 1939; *Waterloo Bridge, Seven Sinners* 1940; *That Uncertain Feeling, Bedtime Story* 1941; *To Be or Not to Be, Take a Letter, Darling, The Talk of the Town, You Were Never Lovelier, The Palm Beach Story, Tales of Manhattan* 1942; *Cabin in the Sky, The Human Comedy, DuBarry Was a Lady, Thousands Cheer, Madame Curie, A Guy Named Joe, The Heavenly Body* 1943; *The White Cliffs of Dover, Bathing Beauty, Gaslight, Kismet, National Velvet, Music for Millions* 1944; *The Picture of Dorian Gray, The Clock, The Valley of Decision, Anchors Aweigh, Weekend at the Waldorf, Yolanda and the Thief, Ziegfeld Follies* 1945; *The Harvey Girls, The Postman Always Rings Twice, Holiday in Mexico, The Dark Mirror, Undercurrent, Till the Clouds Roll By, The Yearling* 1946; *Lady in the Lake, The Hucksters, Merton of the Movies, Song of Love, Green Dolphin Street, Cass Timberlane* 1947; *B.F.'s Daughter, Summer Holiday, State of the Union, Easter Parade* 1948; *The Barkleys of Broadway, Neptune's Daughter, The Great Sinner* 1949; *Key to the City, Please Believe Me* 1950; *Midnight Lace* 1960; *Lover Come Back* 1961; *A Gathering of Eagles* 1963.

iris. 1. In a camera, an adjustable circular opening, consisting of a series of overlapping leaves, which is positioned directly in front of a lens to control the amount of light passing through the lens. Also known as a "diaphragm." 2. In lighting equipment, a similar device placed in front of a lamp to control the spread of the beam of light.

iris-in/iris-out. A transition effect, now seldom used, made in the camera by varying the aperture to or from zero, or by an optical printer. In the iris-in, sometimes also known as "circle-in," the image first appears in the middle of the screen as a pinpoint circle of light surrounded by black. The circle increases gradually in size until the picture fills the entire screen. The iris-out, also known as "circle-out," reverses the procedure; the picture, at first occupying the entire screen, diminishes in size until it becomes a pinpoint circle and the frame is turned completely black. Somewhat related to the WIPE, this fading process was employed effectively by D. W. Griffith in *The Birth of a Nation* and was commonly seen in later silent films.

Irons, Jeremy. Actor. Born on Sept. 19, 1948, in the Isle of Wight. Lanky, brooding leading man of British and international films. An accountant's son, he wanted to be a veterinarian but failed his qualification exams at Sherborne because of his involvement in a school play. After training at the Bristol Old Vic school, he joined the company, then moved to London, where he tended gardens, scrubbed floors, and installed bathroom tiles while scraping for stage roles. He got his first break in the role of John the Baptist in the West End production of the musical 'Godspell.' On Broadway, he later won rave reviews and a Tony Award for his performance in Tom Stoppard's 'The Real Thing.' On-screen from 1980, he made a strong impression in *The French Lieutenant's Woman* (1981) and, selecting his roles carefully, enjoyed great success in subsequent films and in the TV miniseries 'Brideshead Revisited.' His Byronic good looks and mellifluous voice soon made him the darling of the female intellectual set and one of the most widely respected performers of the decade. He was named Best Actor by the New York critics for his dual role as twin gynecologists in *Dead Ringers* (1988) and won an Academy Award as best actor for his remarkable portrayal of Claus von Bülow in *Reversal of Fortune* (1990). Divorced from actress Julie Hallam, he married actress Sinead Cusack in 1978.

FILMS: *Nijinsky* 1980; *The French Lieutenant's Woman* 1981; *Moonlighting* 1982; *Betrayal, The Wild Duck* (Austral.) 1983; *Un Amour de Swann/Swann in Love* (Fr.) 1984; *The Mission* 1986; *Dead Ringers* 1988; *A Chorus of Disapproval* 1989; *Reversal of Fortune* (US) 1990; *Kafka* 1991; *Damage* (Fr.) 1992; *Waterland* 1992; *The House of the Spirits, M. Butterfly* 1993; *The Lion King* (v/o) 1994; *Die Hard with a Vengeance* 1995; *Stealing Beauty* 1996.

Ironside, Michael. Actor. Born on Feb. 12, 1950, in

Toronto, Ont., Canada. *ed.* Ontario College of Art. Steely-eyed, thin-lipped supporting player best known for villainous roles, including the murderous leader of the *Scanners* in David Cronenberg's 1981 film.

FILMS INCLUDE: *Scanners* (Can.) 1981; *Visiting Hours* (Can.) 1982; *Cross Country* (Can.), *Spacehunter: Adventures in the Forbidden Zone* (Can./US) 1983; *The Falcon and the Snowman* 1985; *Jo Jo Dancer Your Life Is Calling, Top Gun* 1986; *Extreme Prejudice, Nowhere to Hide, Hello Mary Lou: Prom Night II* (Can./US) 1987; *Mindfield, Watchers* 1988; *Total Recall* 1990; *Highlander II: The Quickening* (UK/US), *McBain, The Vagrant* 1991.

Irvin, John. Director. Born on May 7, 1940, in England. He entered films as an apprentice cutter for the Rank Organisation. After making his first film, the documentary *Gela Day,* on a grant from the British Film Institute, he continued for a while with fact films, then turned to features in 1980. He established a reputation as a skilled, reliable craftsman.

FEATURE FILMS: *Dogs of War* 1980; *Ghost Story* (US) 1981; *Champions* 1984; *Turtle Diary* 1985; *Raw Deal* (US) 1986; *Hamburger Hill* (US) 1987; *Next of Kin* (US) 1989; *Eminent Domain* (Can./Isr./Fr.), *Robin Hood* (originally a feature, scaled down for cable) 1991; *Freefall, Widow's Peak* 1994; *A Month by the Lake* 1995; *City of Industry* 1997.

Irving, Amy. Actress. Born on Sept. 10, 1953, in Palo Alto, Calif. Gentle, appealing, intelligent leading lady of American stage, TV, and films. The daughter of theater director Jules Irving and actress Priscilla Pointer (and sister of director-screenwriter David Irving), she trained at San Francisco's American Conservatory Theatre, then at the London Academy of Dramatic Art. She made her screen debut playing a secondary role in Brian De Palma's horror classic *Carrie* (1976), in which her mother also appeared. Later played down-to-earth, believable leads as a piano prodigy in *The Competition* (1980) and a liberated Lower East Side Jewish intellectual in *Crossing Delancey* (1988), among other roles. She was nominated for a Best Supporting Actress Oscar for *Yentl,* in which she played Barbra Streisand's wife. On Broadway, she played Mozart's wife in 'Amadeus' (1982) and later appeared in several other productions. Her career in the late 80s was overshadowed by her marriage in 1985 to director Steven SPIELBERG and her role as a mother to their son, Max. They endured an especially antagonistic divorce in 1989. In the following year she bore a son, Gabriel, to Bruno BARRETO, the Brazilian director of her film, *A Show of Force* (1990).

FILMS: *Carrie* 1976; *The Fury* 1978; *Voices* 1979; *Honeysuckle Rose, The Competition* 1980; *Yentl* 1983; *Micki and Maude* 1984; *Rumpelstiltskin* 1987; *Who Framed Roger Rabbit* (singing v/o), *Crossing Delancey* 1988; *A Show of Force* 1990; *An American Tail: Fievel Goes West* (v/o) 1991; *Benefit of the Doubt* 1993; *Carried Away, I'm Not Rappaport* 1996.

Irving, George. Actor, director. *b.* 1874, New York City. *d.* 1961. A graduate of New York's City College and of the American Academy of Dramatic Arts, he played leads on the stage before entering films in 1913. He directed numerous films, some quite prestigious, in the following decade. But when his assignments dwindled to a few in the early 20s, he settled for acting and played a wide variety of character roles in scores of films through the mid-40s.

FILMS INCLUDE: As director—*The Jungle* (co-dir., act.) 1914; *The Builder of Bridges, Body and Soul* (also act.), *Just Out of College* 1915; *Then I'll Come Back to You, Jaffrey* (also act.), *The Conquest of Canaan, The Witching Hour* 1916; *God's Man, Daughter of Destiny, Raffles, The Amateur Cracksman* 1917; *Her Boy, The Landloper, Back to the Woods, To Hell with the Kaiser, Hidden Fires* 1918; *The Silver King, As a Man Thinks, The Volcano, The Glorious Lady* 1919; *The Capitol, The Blue Pearl, Children of Destiny, The Misleading Lady* 1920; *Just Outside the Door, The Wakefield Case* 1921; *Her Majesty* 1922; *Lost in a Big City* 1923; *Floodgates* 1924. As actor—*For Sale, The Wanderer of the Wasteland, The Man Who Fights Alone, Madonna of the Streets* 1924; *The Goose Hangs High, The Air Mail, Wild Horse Mesa* 1925; *The King of the Turf, The Midnight Kiss, Desert Gold, Eagle of the Sea* (as Andrew Jackson), *The City* 1926; *Wings, Shanghai Bound, Two Flaming Youths* 1927; *Craig's Wife* 1928; *The Godless Girl, Coquette, Thunderbolt, Paris Bound, The Last Performance* 1929; *Puttin' on the Ritz, The Divorcée, The Spoilers* 1930; *Resurrection, Free Soul* 1931; *Merrily We Go to Hell, Island of Lost Souls* 1932; *42nd Street* 1943; *Manhattan Melodrama, George White's Scandals* 1934; *Dante's Inferno, A Night at the Opera, Dangerous* 1935; *Captain January, Sutter's Gold* 1936; *The Toast of New York* 1937; *Bringing Up Baby* 1938; *New Moon* 1940; *Hangmen Also Die, Son of Dracula* 1943; *Christmas Holiday* 1944; *Magic Town* 1947.

Irwin, May. Actress. *b.* May Campbell, June 27, 1862, Whitby, Ont., Canada, of Scots descent. *d.* 1938. A celebrated stage comedienne at the turn of the century, she had started her professional career at 13, singing duets with her sister Flo at a Buffalo theater. A plump, jolly blonde, she became a Broadway star in 1895 in 'The Widow Jones' and in the following year made screen history when she repeated for the Edison cameras a kissing scene from that play with her stage partner John C. Rice. *The Kiss,* although just a brief episode from the play, became one of the most famous of the early American films, gaining much notoriety after being denounced as immoral by members of the clergy. As far as is known, Miss Irwin starred in only one other film, the four-reeler *Mrs. Black Is Back* (1914).

Ishii, Sogo. Director, writer. Born in 1957 (?) in Japan. One-time leader of a heavy-metal band and director of rock videos, he became known for his manic, comedic depictions of postwar Japanese life, filled with characters so obsessed with order and success that chaos becomes an unavoidable fate.

FILMS INCLUDE: *The Crazy Family/Gyakufunsha Kazoku* (also co-sc.) 1984.

Isley, Phyllis. See JONES, Jennifer.

Israel. Early in the development of cinema, the historic and religious sites of Israel attracted traveling cameramen to the Holy Land, then part of the Ottoman empire. The first known feature made in Turkish-ruled Palestine, *From the Manger to the Cross* (1912), was directed by Sidney OLCOTT for the Kalem company in New York. Irregular newsreel production by Jewish settlers began shortly after the British conquest of Jerusalem in 1917. Zionist propaganda shorts were also occasionally produced. But it wasn't until 1927 that the first permanent production company, Moledet, was established by Nathan Axelrod, an immigrant from Russia. In 1929 Axelrod launched the Moledet newsreel, which several years later became known as the Carmel newsreel, and in 1933 he produced the country's first fiction feature, *Oded Hanoded (Oded the Wanderer).* His only competitor was Baruch Agadati, who produced occasional newsreels and in 1934 turned out a feature-length semidocumentary, *This Is the Land.* But production facilities and techniques remained primitive for nearly two more decades, and filmmakers from the US and other countries had to be brought in to direct some of the country's more ambitious films in the years immediately preceding and following the establishment of the State of Israel in 1948.

Shortly after independence was won, two film studios, Geva and Herzeliyyah, were established to handle the growing demand of the government's information services for documentary material for both propagandistic and educational purposes. But feature production continued to lag behind international standards, and the only film of note made during that period was *Hill 24 Doesn't Answer* (1955), which was directed by Britain's Thorold DICKINSON, assisted by local talent.

The Knesset, Israel's parliament, passed the Encouragement of Israel Film Law in 1954, which provided substantial governmental financial aid and tax abatements to films produced locally by Israelis or foreign filmmakers. Still, progress in the development of the feature film was painfully slow. Directors came from the local stage, from among immigrants with some film experience abroad, or from among returning students who had attended film schools in the US and Europe. Local technicians gained important experience from working on Hollywood productions made in Israel, like Edward Dmytryk's *The Juggler* (1953), Otto Preminger's *Exodus* (1960), and Melville Shavelson's *Cast a Giant Shadow* (1966). As a result, the technical quality of Israeli film progressed more rapidly than its artistic merit.

Still, the Israeli film steadily improved. Feature production rose from an annual average of five in the early 60s to about 20 in the 70s. Israeli producer-director Menahem GOLAN became internationally known for turning out successful local films and international co-productions, many with producing partner Yoram Globus. Other leading Israeli directors include humorist Ephraim Kishon, former comic actor Uri Zohar, Boaz Davidson, Dan Wolman, and Moshe Mizrahi, who enjoyed his best success in France as the director of *La Vie devant soi/Madame Rosa* (1977). Several Israeli actors went on to success in international films. Per capita film attendance in Israel was among the highest in the world.

By the early 90s, the Israeli film industry was in the throes of an economic crisis, with film production falling to a low of five features in 1991. However, the industry has begun to bounce back, thanks in part to the assistance of the government's Fund for the Promotion of Quality Israeli Films and in part to a group of young producers with an abiding love for and knowledge of film. Producers like Ehud Bleiberg and Marek Rosenbaum have helped to revive the Israeli cinema, and young directors like Dalia Hager (*Summer with Erika*, 1991) and Ayeleth Menahemi (*Tel Aviv Stories*, 1992) have infused Israeli films with new creativity and energy.

Israel, Neal. American director and screenwriter specializing in sophomoric humor. Married to director Amy HECKERLING.

FILMS: As director—*Tunnelvision* (also exec. prod., co-sc., act.) 1976; *Americathon* (dir., sc.) 1979; *Bachelor Party* (also co-sc.) 1984; *Moving Violations* (also co-sc.) 1985; *Breaking the Rules* 1992; *Surf Ninjas* (also act.) 1993. As screenwriter (alone or in collaboration)—*Cracking Up* (also act.) 1977; *Police Academy* 1984; *Real Genius* 1985; *Look Who's Talking Too, Sketches* 1990; *Spurting Blood* (also exec. prod.) 1991; *All I Want for Christmas* (co-sc.) 1992. As actor—*Johnny Dangerously* 1984.

Italy. Technically, Italy was equipped to start a film industry as early as November 11, 1895, when Filoteo ALBERINI patented his Kinetograph, a device for making, printing, and projecting films. But it wasn't until 1905 that production of any consequence began. In the interim, representatives of France's Lumiére organization dominated the field. Several Lumiére trainees and local imitators recorded scenes of everyday life, and Leopoldo Fregoli, a music-hall impersonator, added brief comic film strips to his bag of tricks. A passion play, photographed from the stage performance, was produced by a small Franco-Italian company in 1900. The first Italian newsreel footage was shot in Turin in 1904 by Roberto Omegna under the auspices of optics dealer Arturo AMBROSIO. The turning point came in 1905, during which Alberini and a partner, Dante Santoni, built Italy's first studio in Rome and turned out the country's first ambitious story film, *La Presa di Roma.* It was also the first production of what would become a traditional genre of the Italian cinema, the historic spectacle. The Alberini-Santoni company was incorporated in 1906 at Cines, a name that remained prominent in Italian film production through the late 30s.

It was Turin, however, not Rome, that was to reign as Italy's most important film-production center in the early years. Ambrosio led the way when he built a glass-roofed studio there and started feature production in 1906. The catalogue consisted mainly of melodramas and comedies, some of the latter starring French comic André DEED (known as Cretinetti), and in 1908 boasted the first of many Italian screen versions of *Gli Ultimi Giorni di Pompei/The Last Days of Pompeii.* Ambrosio's biggest competitor in Turin was Giovanni PASTRONE's Itala-Film. Production companies in Turin, Milan, Rome, and even Naples proliferated in 1907–8, and by the end of the first decade of the 20th century a solid foundation for a national film industry had been built. The trend toward historical costume films became increasingly apparent. At Cines in Rome director Mario CASERINI led the way with opulent screen versions of *Othello* and *Garibaldi* (both 1907); *Marco Visconti* and *Romeo and Juliet* (both 1908); *Beatrice Cenci, Joan of Arc,* and *Macbeth* (all 1909); *Hamlet, Anna Garibaldi, El Cid, Federico Barbarossa,* and *Lucrezia Borgia* (all 1910); *Dante and Beatrice, Parsifal,* and *Siegfried* (all 1912), and yet another version of *The Last Days of Pompeii* (1913). Enrico GUAZZONI directed an eight-reel first version of *Quo Vadis?* in 1912. It was a monumental production with enormous sets, thousands of extras, and real lions.

The ambition and grandeur of the costume epic reached its peak with *Cabiria* (1914), directed by Pastrone under the pseudonym Piero Fosco. Nothing like it had been produced anywhere before. It was made at a record-setting budget of more than a million dollars and took nearly two years to complete from inception through editing. The Turin studio sets were sumptuous, even by today's standards, while exteriors were shot in Tunisia, Sicily, and the Alps. Impressive scenes included the siege of Syracuse and the crossing of the Alps by Hannibal's armies and elephants. Traveling shots and other advanced camera techniques made this film a truly remarkable achievement of its time. It had an enormous international box-office success and in the US influenced the work of both Cecil B. DE MILLE and D. W. GRIFFITH. *Cabiria*'s script was partly written by the famous poet-novelist-soldier Gabriele D'Annunzio, whose works were frequently adapted to the screen during that period. He was not the only literary figure recruited for cinema at the time. For unlike typically self-made moguls of the early American movies, Italian production companies were characteristically headed by cultivated members of the aristocracy with a taste for literature and drama.

The international success of the Italian cinema in the early 1910s was accompanied by the rapid development of a thriving star system. Most popular were the actresses who starred in the grand melodramas and costume epics. Like their counterparts in the opera, they were known as *dive* (divas). Among the most admired were Italia Almirante Manzini, Francesca Bertini, Lyda Borelli, Lina Cavalieri, HESPERIA, and Maria JACOBINI. Among the most popular male actors were Emilio GHIONE, the hero of the "Za la Mort" series, and Bartolomeo Pagano (the latter better known as Maciste, after the role he had played in *Cabiria*). The rising financial demands of the stars and the increasing costs of producing spectacular epics led to a gradual decrease in the number of costume films, but the genre has remained a popular staple of the Italian cinema to this day.

The Italian cinema of the period also boasted several fine adaptations of stage plays, notably Count Baldassare NEGRONI's *Storia di un Pierrot* (1913), a production noted for the realism of its exteriors. A trend toward a realistic style could be discerned in several successful films of the WW I years. The most highly regarded of these was Nino Martoglio's *Speduti nel Buio/Lost in Darkness* (1914), which contrasted palace and slum life in Naples with a degree of social concern and attention to real detail that has qualified it in the eyes of film historians as a true precursor of the neorealist film of the late 40s. Another impressive production with a realistic setting was Febo Mari's *Cenere/Ashes/Madre* (1916), which was filmed in Sardinia and featured the great Eleanora DUSE in her only screen role.

The prosperity the Italian cinema had enjoyed in the early 1910s appeared to continue through the war years and briefly after the Armistice, although on a diminished scale. Characteristic of the continued optimism, despite evident signs of a brewing crisis, was the establishment of several new production companies immediately after the war. Among these was Tespi, founded in 1919 by dramatist Luigi Pirandello and two partners. But within a year or two the industry began to feel the full impact of growing competition from abroad, especially from the US and Germany. By 1922 the industry found itself hopelessly crippled, its output reduced to only 6 percent of the fare shown on the Italian screens. A belated attempt to combat the competition through the amalgamation of the resources of several production companies into the Unione Cinematografica Italiana (UCI) proved futile.

As the crisis deepened, it became nearly impossible to raise funds for local production, and by the mid-20s average annual output had declined to about ten features. Quality as well as quantity reached its nadir. Hopes for a revival were raised briefly when American companies began filming some prestigious productions in Italian locations, among them Henry King's *The White Sister* (1923) and *Romola* (1924), but the colossal fiasco of the on-location phase of Hollywood's *Ben-Hur* (1926)—staggering expenditures, production delays, fatal accidents, which resulted in the switching of the production to a Hollywood studio—dealt these hopes a disastrous blow. Toward the end of the silent era there was a sudden mild awakening, led by such films as Mario CAMERINI's *Kiff Tebbi* (1927), which was shot on location in Africa, and *Rotaie* (1929), which dealt seriously with current social problems; and Alessandro BLASETTI's *Sole* (1929), which told of the reclamation of marshes and wasteland and was later hailed by the Fascists as the first true expression of the nationalist spirit.

Mussolini's Fascist regime interfered little with the affairs of the cinema during the silent era, but Fascist intervention increased considerably after the advent of sound.

Sound came slowly to Italy. It was not until 1930 that the country's first talkie, Gennaro Righelli's *La Canzone dell'Amore,* was released. As was the case elsewhere in the industry, the early talkies were cumbersome and talkative, often resembling photographed stage plays. Among the directors, only Blasetti and Camerini achieved acceptable results, the former with *Terra Madre* (1930) and *Resurrectio* (1931) and the latter with *Figaro e la sua Gran Giornata* (1931) and *Gli Uomini che Mascalzoni* (1932). *Gli Uomini* starred the dashing Vittorio DE SICA, one of Italy's most popular screen personalities of the 30s and later one of the country's greatest directors.

The genre that best characterized the Italian film of the 30s was the glossy, sentimental comedy or drama set against a glamorous background, which came to be sneeringly known as *telefoni bianchi* (or "white telephone") films. Typical of these were Guido Brignone's *Paradiso* (1932), Gennaro Righelli's *Al Buio insieme* (1933), and Carlo Bragaglia's *O la Borsa o la Vita* (1933). Such escapist films were made mainly in response to public taste but also because they embodied a way of avoiding serious topics that might incur the wrath of the Fascist censor. Italy's first blatantly propagandistic Fascist feature was Righelli's *L'Armata azzurra* (1932), a tribute to Mussolini's air force. Many others followed, including Giovacchino Forzano's *Camicia nera* (1933) and Blasetti's *Vecchia Guardia* (1935). Other officially sanctioned films drew on historic events to infuse the public with national pride. Among these were Blasetti's *1860* (1934) and Carmine GALLONE's *Scipione l'Africano* (1937).

The mid-30s saw a massive effort on the part of Mussolini's dictatorship to encourage the expansion of Italy's film industry for the service of the state. In 1935 the government established the Direzione Generale per le Cinematografia as part of the Ministry of Popular Culture to co-ordinate film industry affairs. At about the same time, a special cinematographic section was attached to one of Italy's leading banks through which funding was funneled to state-approved productions. Also in 1935, the government established the famed film school CENTRO SPERIMENTALE DI CINEMATOGRAFIA. Two years later the CINECITTÀ studios were opened near Rome, boasting Europe's most advanced production facilities with 16 stages and modern equipment. By the outbreak of WW II the government had taken firm control of the film industry through these and other measures, including a system of rebates that benefited successful producers and the virtual control of the importation of films under the aegis of a special screening organization, the Ente Nazionale Importazione Pellicole Estere. The infiltration of undesirable ideas from the outside world was effectively blocked by an ingenious scheme that made it illegal to show foreign films in their original language versions or subtitled: they had to be completely dubbed into Italian, a process that made it easy to substitute whole sections of dialogue, thus purging the films of any "harmful" ingredients. The practice lingered after the war, and to this day most films shown in Italy, whether local or foreign, are usually dubbed, although the reason is no longer political. (See DUBBING.)

The combined effect of the government's import protective measure and financial subsidies and rebates for local productions was to dramatically increase the quantity, if not the quality, of the Italian film. The system especially rewarded friends of the regime, among them the Duce's own son, Vittorio Mussolini, who founded Europa, a large production and distribution company. One of Europa's stars was Myria di San Servolo, sister of the Duce's mistress Clara Petacci. The system encouraged mediocrity, but certain directors began to assert their talents during the war years, among them Renato CASTELLANI (*Un Colpo di Pistola,* 1941); Vittorio De Sica (*Rose scarlatte,* 1940; *I Bambini ci Guardano,* 1943); Alberto LATTUADA (*La Freccia nel Fianco,* 1945); Roberto ROSSELLINI (*La Nave Bianca,* 1941; *Un Pilota Ritorna,* 1942); Mario SOLDATI (*Dora Nelson,* 1939; *Piccolo Mondo Antico,* 1941); and Luigi ZAMPA (*L'Attore Scomparso,* 1941). The most remarkable screen production of the period was Luchino VISCONTI's *Ossessione* (1942), a film freely adapted from James Cain's *The Postman Always Rings Twice* which heralded neorealism through its real-life plot, authentic settings, and personal lyricism.

Although the circulation of the uncut version of *Ossessione* was confined to limited audiences in clandestine showings, it acted as a catalyst on a group of filmmakers who in the years immediately following WW II gave the Italian cinema a new vitality and worldwide recognition. The term "neorealism" was first used by Italian critics to describe Visconti's film, but it was Rossellini's *Roma Città aperta/Open City* (1945) that gave the term international currency. The film was made under most difficult conditions, with the planning, scouting, and the early shooting taking place secretly while the Nazis still occupied Rome. The budget was minimal, and filming was executed with bits and pieces of available raw stock, combining the product of different manufacturers and varying speed rates. The raw reality of this story of Resistance heroism and the artless performances by Aldo Fabrizzi, Anna Magnani, and a cast of nonprofessionals were a revelation to audiences accustomed to the artificial gloss of the typical movie, and the film became an international box-office success.

Other neorealist productions came in quick succession, reflecting the tribulations of the postwar reconstruction. Among these were Rossellini's own *Paisà/Paisan* (1946) and *Germania Anno Zero/Germany Year Zero* (1947); De Sica's *Sciuscia/Shoeshine* (1946) and *Ladri di Biciclette/The Bicycle Thief* (1948); Aldo VERGANO's *Il Sole Sorge ancora/Outcry* (1947); Lattuada's *Senza Pietà/Without Pity* (1948); Visconti's *La Terra trema* (1948); and Pietro GERMI's *In Nome della Legge/Mafia* (1949) and *Il Cammino della Speranza/The Path of Hope* (1950). Giuseppe DE SANTIS's *Riso amaro/Bitter Rice* (1949) sprinkled neorealism with generous doses of earthy sensuality and turgid melodrama. The film launched the international starring careers of Silvana MANGANO, Vittorio GASSMAN, and Raf VALLONE.

The rapid decline of neorealism in the early 50s was accompanied by an industrywide return to the genres that had made the Italian film popular in the early silent days—comedies, melodramas, and costume epics. Commercial success on an international scale was achieved by a series of earthy comedies starring two new screen sirens, Gina LOLLOBRIGIDA (Luigi COMENCINI's *Pane Amore e Fantasia/Bread Love and Dreams,* 1953, etc.) and Sophia LOREN (De Sica's *L'Oro di Napoli/Gold of Naples,* 1954, etc.). But the international successes were by far outnumbered by routine productions for local consumption, often geared to the unsophisticated taste of the small-town populace.

With the increasing emphasis on commercialism, it became more and more difficult for individual directors to get backing for worthy but financially risky personal projects. Yet a number of determined filmmakers persisted in having their voices heard. Michelangelo ANTONIONI made his feature debut with *Cronaca di un Amore/Story of a Love Affair* (1950) and went on to establish his reputation as a profound explorer of alienation and personal anguish in such films as *Le Amiche/The Girl Friends* (1955), *Il Grido/The Outcry* (1957), *L'Avventura* (1960), *La Notte* (1961), *L'Eclisse/Eclipse* (1962), and *Deserto rosso/Red Desert* (1964). Federico FELLINI flaunted his exuberant, highly personal style in *Lo Sceicco bianco/The White Sheik* (1952), *I Vitelloni* (1953), *La Strada* (1954), *Il Bidone/The Swindle* (1955), *Le Notti di Cabiria/The Nights of Cabiria/Cabiria* (1957), *La Dolce Vita* (1960), *8½* (1963), *Giulietta degli Spiriti/Juliet of the Spirits* (1965), *Roma* (1972), and *Amarcord* (1974), among other films. De Sica's reputation declined after peaking with *Miracolo a Milano/Miracle in Milan* (1951) and *Umberto D* (1952) but revived with *La Ciociara/Two Women* (1960) and again with *Il Giardino dei Finzi-Contini/The Garden of the Finzi-Continis* (1971) and *Una Breve Vacanza/A Brief Vacation* (1973). Similarly, Rossellini went through a long dry period until *Il Generale della Rovere* (1959). Visconti continued to exert his mastery with *Senso/The Wanton Contessa* (1954), *Le Notti bianche/White Nights* (1957), *Rocco e i suoi Fratelli/ Rocco and His Brothers* (1960), *Il Gattopardo/The Leopard* (1963), *La Caduta degli Dei/Götterdämmerung/The Damned* (1969), *Morte a Venezia/Death in Venice* (1971), and *L'Innocente/The Innocent* (1976), his last film.

Lesser luminaries who from time to time illumed the vast wasteland of the Italian cinema during the 50s, 60s, and 70s with refreshing originality have included Marco BELLOCCHIO (*I Pugni in Tasca/Fist in His Pocket,* 1966; *La Cina e Vicina/China Is Near,* 1967), Bernardo BERTOLUCCI (*Prima della Rivoluzione/Before the Revolution,* 1964; *La Strategia del Ragno/The Spider's Stratagem,* 1970; *Il Conformista/The Conformist,* 1970; *1900,* 1976), Mauro BOLOGNINI (*Il Bell'Antonio,* 1960), Vittorio De Seta (*Banditi a Orgosolo/Bandits of Orgosolo,* 1961), Luciano EMMER (*Domenica d'Agosto,* 1950), Marco FERRERI (*L'Ape Regina/The Conjugal Bed,* 1963), Pietro GERMI (*Divorzio all'Italiana/Divorce Italian Style,* 1961), Carlo LIZZANI (*Cronache di Poveri Amanti,* 1954), Francesco MASELLI (*Gli Sbandati,* 1954), Mario MONICELLI (*I Soliti Ignoti/Big Deal on Madonna Street,* 1958; *La Grande Guerra/The Great War,* 1959; *I Compagni/The Organizer,* 1963), Ermanno OLMI (*Il Posto/The Job/The Sound of Trumpets,* 1961; *Un Certo Giorno/One Fine Day,* 1968; *The Tree of Wooden Clogs*, 1978), Pier Paolo PASOLINI (*Accatone,* 1961; *Il Vangelo Secondo Matteo/The Gospel According to St. Matthew,* 1964; *Edipo Re/Oedipus Rex,* 1967; *Teorema,* 1968; *Porcile/Pigsty/Pig Pen,* 1969), Elio PETRI (*L'Assassino/The Lady Killer of Rome,* 1961; *Un Tranquillo Posto di Campagna/A Quiet Place in the Country,* 1968; *La Classe Operaia va in Paradiso/Lulu the Tool/The Working Class Goes to Heaven,* 1971), Gillo PONTECORVO (*La Battaglia di Algeri/The Battle of Algiers,* 1966), Dino RISI (*Il Sorpasso/The Easy Life,* 1962), Francesco ROSI (*Salvatore Giuliano,* 1962; *Le Mani sulla Città/Hands Over the City,* 1963; *Cadaveri Eccelenti,* 1976), Franco Rossi (*Amici per la Pelle/Friends for Life/The Woman in the Painting,* 1955), Ettore SCOLA (*Se Permettete parliamo di Donne/Let's Talk About Women* 1964; *Brutti Sporchi e Cattivi* 1976), Paolo and Vittorio TAVIANI (*Un Uomo da bruciare/A Man for Burning,* 1962; *Padre Padrone,* 1977), and Valerio ZURLINI (*L'Estate violenta/Violent Summer,* 1959; *La Ragazza con la Valigia/Girl with a Suitcase,* 1961; *Cronaca Familiare/Family Diary,* 1962).

If the list of films in the preceding paragraphs seems long, it is also nearly exhaustive, comprising virtually the entire catalogue of superior-quality films produced in Italy in three full decades. Optimism ran the highest in the mid-50s when a grandiose scheme to build a "Hollywood on the Tiber" apparently materialized with a surge of activity by American producers on Italian locations and in the well-equipped Cinecittà studios. Among the sumptuous international productions made during that period were *Ulysses* (1954), *The Barefoot Contessa* (1954), *Helen of Troy* (1956), *War and Peace* (1956), and *Sodom and Gomorrah* (1961). However, American interest in foreign production, stemming mainly from the need to use up surpluses of frozen foreign currency, soon slackened and the dream of a Hollywood on the Tiber quietly faded away.

The optimism of the late 50s was enhanced in the early 60s by the international box-office success of certain films, mainly pseudosocial comedies that banked on the popularity of such stars as Marcello MASTROIANNI, Sophia Loren, and Claudia CARDINALE. Another source of sure revenue was the pseudohistoric action spectacles that proliferated during this period, echoing the silent-days exploits of Maciste in the heroics of Hercules, Samson, and other muscular giants. Mario BAVA was among several directors who attempted to embellish some of these inane productions with a bold, striking visual style.

But despite the isolated box-office successes, it soon became evident that all was not well in the economy of the

Italian film. Things nearly reached a state of panic by the mid-60s, when two industry giants, Titanus and Galatea, collapsed. Two producers who continued to thrive through the 50s and 60s were Dino DE LAURENTIIS and Carlo PONTI, but by the mid-70s they had both left Italy, the former coming to the US and the latter going to France. One lucrative formula was the "spaghetti Western," which during the late 60s enjoyed a measure of temporary popularity in the international market. Two directors who excelled in this genre were Sergio LEONE and Sergio CORBUCCI, who adorned their films with visual stylishness and ruthless sadism. The spaghetti Western vogue was replaced in the early 70s with a trend for equally stylish erotic thrillers modeled after Dario ARGENTO'S box-office hit *L'Uccello dalle Piume di Cristallo/The Bird with the Crystal Plumage* (1970).

Apart from the work of the veteran directors and such promising new filmmakers as Bellochio, Bertolucci, and the Taviani brothers, the Italian cinema was heading toward a creative drought in the early 70s, with the progressively diminishing number of films of personal or political statement virtually drowning in the sea of mediocre production. Italy had until then maintained a leadership position in Europe in terms of annual film output, averaging more than 200, and per capita attendance in movie theaters. But as the decade drew to a close, attendance began dropping sharply and the profit structure of the entire film industry was on the verge of collapse.

By the early 90s, American films had come to dominate the Italian market, while competition from television had cut severely into cinema attendance. Though the latter trend diminished box-office grosses, it also created an elite atmosphere among audiences who only went to the cinema in search of specialized, artistic fare not available on television. Supported at home by these audiences, the best productions of Italian cinema in the 80s and 90s enjoyed international acclaim and frequent prizes at festivals, as a number of new directors contributed to a creative revitalization of the industry. At the same time, only a few Italian films experienced major commercial success, notably those of director and comic movie actor Roberto Benigni, including *Il piccolo diavolo/The Little Devil* (1987) and *Johnny Stecchino* (1991).

The old master Fellini made several films in the 80s, including *City of Women* (1981) and *Ginger and Fred* (1985), while Bertolucci's Italian-British-Chinese co-production *The Last Emperor* (1987) earned him nine Oscars. Other Italian directors who won critical attention in the 80s and 90s include the inspired innovator Maurizio Nichetti (*Ladridi saponette/The Icicle Thief*, 1988; *Volere Volare/To Wish to Fly*, 1991); master comic Francesco Nuti (*Willy Signori, e vengo da lontano/Willy Signori, I'm Coming Home*, 1989); traditionalists Dimenticare Palermo (*To Forget Palermo*, 1990) and Marco Risi (*Boys*, 1990); Gabriele Salvatore (*Mediterraneo*, 1991—best foreign film Oscar); Giuseppe Tornatore (*Cinema Paradiso*, 1990—best foreign film Oscar); the "Italian Woody Allen" Massimo Troisi (*Ricominci da tre/I Am Starting Again from Three*, 1981; *Seusate il ritardi/Sorry I'm Late*, 1983; *Le vie del signore sono finite/The Lord's Ways Are Ended*, 1987).

Itami, Juzo. Director, screenwriter, actor. Born in 1933, in Kyoto, Japan. Inventive chronicler of modern-day Japanese culture, known for his robust satires of sacred national topics such as burial rites (*The Funeral*), food (*Tampopo*), and money (*A Taxing Woman*). A descendant of Samurai and the son of Mansaku Itami, a pioneer Japanese film director, he was an accomplished artist, essayist, talk-show host, and actor, before he first dared, at age 50, to follow in his father's footsteps. He scored a huge critical and commercial success with his debut film, *The Funeral* (1984), and an international triumph with *Tampopo* (1986). His works, which are highly popular in Japan and in Western art-house circles, are both highly artful and entertaining. Their structure may be influenced by such diverse sources as Luis Buñuel and Akira Kurosawa, while the attention to Japanese family life recalls Yasujiro Ozu. A few days after the premiere of *The Gangster's Moll*, a satire of the Japanese *yakuza* or crime syndicate, he made international headlines when his face and neck were slashed by alleged members of the *yakuza*. Itami writes his own scripts. His actress wife, Nobuko Miyamoto, is his favorite interpreter.

FILMS INCLUDE: As director-screenwriter—*The Funeral/Death Japanese Style* 1984; *Tampopo/Maruso no Onna* 1986; *A Taxing Woman* 1987; *A Taxing Woman's Return* 1988; *A-Ge-Man: Tales of a Golden Geisha* 1990; *The Gangster's Moll/Mimbo no Onna* 1992. As actor—*55 Days at Peking* 1963; *Lord Jim* 1965; *The Family Game* 1984; *The Makioka Sisters* 1985.

Ito, Daisuke. Director. Born on Oct. 13, 1898, in Tokyo. After studies at the Shochiku Cinema Institute, he entered Japanese films in 1923 as a screenwriter and production manager. The following year he began a prolific career as a director. His films, especially those of the silent period, are noted for their violent naturalism. From the 30s he specialized in period dramas, often involving the Samurai tradition. He has written scripts for films of other directors as well as for his own productions.

FILMS INCLUDE: *Jogashima* 1924; *Smoke* 1925; *The First Shrine* 1926; *The Servant, Evil Spirit* 1927; *A Diary of Chuji's Travels* (Pt. I–III) 1927–28; *Man-Slashing Horse-Piercing Sword* 1929; *The Rise and Fall of Shinsengumi* (Pt. I, II) 1930; *Samurai Nippon* (Pt. I, II) 1931; *The First Year of the Meiji Era* 1932; *The Loyal 47 Ronin* (Pt. I, II) 1934; *The 48th Comrade* 1936; *The Swordsman* 1938; *The Eagle's Tail* 1941; *Duel at Hannya-zaka* 1943; *International Smugglers* 1944; *King of Chess* 1948; *Les Misérables* 1950; *Five Men of Edo* 1951; *Lion's Dance* 1953; *The Story of Shunkin, Samurai's Love* 1954; *The Life of a Woman in the Meiji Era* 1955; *Flowers of Hell* 1957; *The Gay Masquerade* 1958; *The Woman and the Pirates* 1959; *The Conspirator* 1961; *Tokugawa Ieyasu* 1965; *The Ambitious* 1970.

Iturbi, José. Pianist, conductor. *b.* Nov. 28, 1895, Valencia, Spain, of Basque ancestry. *d.* 1980. *ed.* Conservatoire de Musique (Paris). As a child, he played piano accompaniment for silent movies. He later appeared in night spots and taught piano at the Conservatory of Geneva. Coming to the US in 1929, he appeared as a piano soloist and guest conductor with various orchestras and for several years was the conductor of the Rochester Philharmonic. His appearances in Hollywood films of the 40s (usually as himself) helped popularize classical music in America. His recording of the Chopin "Polonaise in A Flat" for the film *A Song to Remember* (1945) sold a million copies. He was occasionally called upon to act and played a straight lead opposite Jeanette MacDonald in *Three Daring Daughters*.

FILMS: *Thousands Cheer, Adventures in Music, Two Girls and a Sailor, Music for Millions* 1944; *Anchors Aweigh* 1945; *Holiday in Mexico* 1946; *Three Daring Daughters* 1948; *That Midnight Kiss* (also music superv.) 1949.

Ivan, Rosalind. Actress. *b.* 1884, England. *d.* 1959. A musical prodigy, she gave London piano recitals at ten and later developed into a fine character actress on the British stage. She made her New York debut in 1912 and subsequently appeared in many Broadway as well as London plays. She also pursued a subcareer as a writer, turning out magazine articles, writing book reviews, and translating *The Brothers Karamazov* for the 1927 Theatre Guild production starring the Lunts. Her film career was brief but memorable, notably in her convincing portrayal of Charles Laughton's nagging, shrewish wife and the victim of his murder scheme in *The Suspect* (1945). She played similar unsympathetic roles in several other films, leading some in Hollywood to nickname her "Ivan the Terrible."

FILMS: *The Garden Murder Case* (bit) 1936; *None but the Lonely Heart* 1944; *The Suspect, The Corn Is Green, Pursuit to Algiers, Pillow of Death, Scarlet Street* 1945; *Three Strangers, The Verdict, That Brennan Girl, Alias Mr. Twilight* 1946; *Ivy* 1947; *Johnny Belinda* 1948; *The Robe* 1953; *Elephant Walk* 1954.

Ivanov-Vano, Ivan. Animator. Born in 1900, in Moscow. A pioneer of animated films in the Soviet Union, since 1929 he has adapted many Russian folk tales for the screen. His films are directed primarily at the children's market.

FILMS INCLUDE: *Soviet Toys* 1923; *Senka the African* 1927; *The Adventures of Baron Munchhausen* 1929; *Black and White* 1931; *The Czar Durandai* 1934; *The Three Musketeers* 1938; *The Little Humpbacked Horse* 1947; *The Snow Maiden* 1952; *The Brave Hare* 1955; *The Mechanical Flea, The Left Hander* 1964; *Go to Nowhere* 1966; *Legend of a Cruel Giant* 1968; *Seasons* 1970; *Battle Under the Walls of Kerchenetz* 1971; *The Humpbacked Horse* 1976.

Ivens, Joris. Documentary director. *b.* Georg Henri Anton Ivens, Nov. 18, 1898, Nijmegen, Holland. *d.* 1989. His grandfather was a pioneer Dutch photographer and his father owned a chain of camera shops. To no one's surprise he made a cowboys-and-Indians film, *Flaming Arrow,* featuring his entire family, when he was 13. He was sent to the Rotterdam College of Economics so he could better run the family business, but his studies were interrupted by WW I service as a reserve field artillery lieutenant. Returning to school, he became involved in student foment and in the politics of the international student movement. In 1922 he went to Berlin to study photochemistry at the University of Charlottenburg, then served his apprenticeship at the German camera factories in Dresden and Jena (with Zeiss). While there, he participated in workers' demonstrations, which strengthened his formerly tentative leftist leanings. Returning to Holland in 1926, he became manager of his father's Amsterdam branch but continued to associate with student groups. In 1927 he was instrumental in establishing Filmliga, one of the earliest film societies.

Ivens's 1928 documentary, *The Bridge,* a rhythmically flowing cinematographic study of the structure and functions of a Rotterdam drawbridge, was enthusiastically received in European avant-garde circles. It is considered a landmark in the development of the Dutch cinema. In his subsequent films, Ivens moved away from the experimental toward a realistic, though technically stylized, format. In December of 1929 he went on a three-month lecture tour of the Soviet Union, at the personal invitation of Pudovkin. Following another visit to Russia in 1932, during which he shot the documentary *Song of Heroes,* Ivens began de-emphasizing technique in his films for the sake of social awareness and political polemics. At the same time, he moved out of the limited Dutch arena into international documentary projects.

Over the next three decades Ivens became the most cosmopolitan and most widely traveled of all film directors, working under many flags on every continent. In 1936 he arrived in the US to make an educational film for the Rockefeller Foundation. Instead, he set out for Spain, with American backing, to record the sorry plight of villagers near Madrid during the Spanish Civil War. Ernest Hemingway, who helped in the production by doing menial chores, wrote and narrated the commentary. Ivens next spent nine months in China, again with American backing, and came back with *The 400 Million,* a plea for the cause of the Chinese people, whose land had been invaded by Japan. Fredric March spoke the commentary for *The Spanish Earth* (1937). Then came *The Power and the Land,* a film for the US Department of Agriculture, which exalted the virtues of rural electrification.

During the WW II years Ivens made several anti-Fascist propaganda films in the US and one in Canada. He went to Hollywood, hoping to make feature films about the war, but nothing came of several projects. He spent months writing a script for a film vehicle for Greta Garbo, but the star turned it down. In 1944 he was named by the Dutch government as Film Commissioner for the Netherlands East Indies. But when Indonesian nationalists seeking independence clashed with the Dutch army he resigned his post and instead made a pro-Indonesian documentary, *Indonesia Calling!,* in Australia. Ivens, who was identified as a Communist in the 1951 hearings of the House Un-American Activities Committee, never returned to America.

Most of Ivens's films from the early 50s were made in the Communist world, including North Vietnam and Cuba. He operated out of Prague until 1957, when he established permanent residence in Paris. His love poem to the city, *La Seine a rencontré Paris* (1957), from a narrative by Jacques PRÉVERT, was named best documentary at the 1958 Cannes and San Francisco Film Festivals. His only feature film, *The Adventures of Till Eulenspiegel,* which he co-directed with the film's star, Gérard Philipe, was made in East Germany as a co-production with France. In the late 60s he returned briefly to Holland after an absence of 30 years and was given a welcome befitting a national artist. A Joris Ivens archive is now part of the Dutch Film Museum. His autobiography, *The Camera and I,* was published in 1969. A follow-up memoir, *Joris Ivens ou La Mémoire d'un Regard,* was published in Paris in 1982. Ivens continued working vigorously, defying his advancing age, aided since the late 60s by Marceline Loridan. Listed in the *Guinness Book of World Records* as the oldest active filmmaker, at age 89 he completed the film, *The Wind,* a lyrical evocation of his lifelong love of China, in which he also appeared. During the film's 1988 premiere at the Venice Festival, the director was honored with a life achievement award. He died of a heart attack the following year. Although his reputation in the West suffered as a result of his self-limiting political commitments, Ivens is still regarded as the most important documentarist of his period.

FILMS: In Holland (as director-screenwriter-cinematographer-editor)—*Flaming Arrow* (amateur) 1911; *Zeedijk Film Study* 1927; *Etudes des Mouvements* (Fr.), *The Bridge* 1928; *Breakers* (co-dir., phot., edit. only), *Rain, Skating* (unfinished), *'I' Film* (unfinished), *We Are Building, Pile Driving, New Architecture, Caissonbouw Rotterdam, South Limbuyrg, Day of Youth* (co-edit. only), *NVV Congress, Poor Drenthe* 1929; *Zuidersee* (dir., sc., co-phot. only), *The Tribune Film: Break and Build, News from the Soviet Union* (dir., edit. only), *Demonstration of Proletarian Solidarity* (dir., edit. only) 1930; *Philips Radio/Industrial Symphony, Creosote* (dir., sc., edit. only) 1931. Abroad (as director)—*Song of Heroes/Komsomol* (also edit.; USSR) 1932; *Misère au Borinage/Borinage* (co-dir., co-sc., co-phot, co-edit.; Belg.), *New Earth* (also cosc., co-phot., co-edit., narrator) 1934; *The Spanish Earth* (also sc., co-phot.; US) 1937; *The 400 Million* (also sc.; US) 1938; *The Power and the Land* (also co-sc.; US) 1940; *Our Russian Front* (co-dir. with Lewis Milestone; US) 1941; *Oil for Aladdin's Lamp* (US) 1942; *Action Stations!* (also sc., edit.; Can.) 1943; *Indonesia Calling* (also sc., edit.; Austral.) 1946; *The First Years* (also co-edit.; Czech./Bul./Pol.) 1949; *Peace Will Win* (co-dir.; Pol.) 1951;

Freundschaft Sieft/Friendship Triumphs (co-dir.; USSR/E. Ger.), *Friedensfahrt/Peace Tour* (also sc.; Pol./E. Ger.) 1952; *Lied der Ströme/Song of the Rivers* (also co-sc.; E. Ger.) 1954; *Die Windrose/The Wind Rose* (co-superv.; E. Ger.), *Les Aventures de Till l'Espiègle/The Adventures of Till Eulenspiegel* (co-dir.; Fr./E. Ger.) 1956; *La Seine a rencontré Paris* (also sc.; Fr.) 1957; *Early Spring, 600 Million People Are with You* (both also sc., edit.; China) 1958; *L'Italia non e un Paese Povere/Italy Is Not a Poor Country* (also co-sc., co-edit.; It.), *Demain à Nanguila/Nanguila Tomorrow* (Mali) 1960; *Carnet de Viaje/Travel Notebook, Cuba Pueblo Armado/An Armed Nation* (both also sc.; Cuba) 1961; *A Valparaiso* (also sc.), *Le Petit Chapiteau/The Little Circus* (both Chile/Fr.) 1963; *El Tren de la Victoria/The Victory Train* (Chile) 1964; *Le Ciel la Terre/The Threatening Sky* (also comment., personal appearance; Viet./Fr.) 1965; *Pour le Mistral/Mistral* (also co-sc.; Fr.), *Rotterdam-Europort* (Holl.) 1966; *Loin du Viêtnam/Far from Vietnam* (co-dir. with several others; Fr.) 1967; *Le 17e Parallèle: Le Viêtnam en Guerre/17th Parallel: Vietnam in War* (co-dir.; Fr.) 1968; *Le Peuple et ses Fusils/The People and Their Guns* (co-dir.; Laos), *La Guerre populaire au Laos* (co-dir.; Laos), *Recontre avec le Président Ho Chi Minh* (co-dir.; N. Viet.) 1970; *Comment Yukong deplace les Montagnes* (six-part doc. on China; 720 minutes long in all; co-dir.; Fr.) 1976; *Les Kazaks—Minorité nationale—Sinkiano* (co-dir.); *Les Quigours—Minorité nationale—Sinkiano* (co-dir.) 1977; *Le Vent/The Wind* (co-dir., also act. sc.) 1988.

Ives, Burl. Actor, folk singer. *b.* Burle Icle Ivanhoe, on June 14, 1909, in Hunt, Ill. *d.* 1995. *ed.* Charleston (Ill.) Teachers Coll. A former professional football player and itinerant worker, he became known as one of America's top balladeers and an authority on the country's folk music. A man of immense dimensions, the bearded Ives appeared in several outdoor films, singing and playing his guitar, before being discovered as a powerful dramatic actor in the mid-50s. He won an Academy Award as best supporting actor for *The Big Country* but is best remembered as Big Daddy in *Cat on a Hot Tin Roof* and in other Southern-patriarch roles.

FILMS: *Smoky* 1946; *Green Grass of Wyoming, Station West, So Dear to My Heart* 1948; *Sierra* 1950; *East of Eden* (as Sam Hamilton) 1955; *The Power and the Prize* 1956; *Desire Under the Elms* (as Ephraim Cabot), *The Big Country, Wind Across the Everglades, Cat on a Hot Tin Roof* (as Big Daddy) 1958; *Day of the Outlaw, Our Man in Havana* (UK) 1959; *Let No Man Write My Epitaph* 1960; *The Spiral Road, Flying Clipper—Traumreise unter weissen Segeln/Mediterranean Holiday* (feature-length Cinerama travelog; songs, narrator of English version only; Ger.) 1962; *Summer Magic* 1963; *The Brass Bottle, Ensign Pulver* 1964; *The Daydreamer* (v/o) 1966; *Jules Verne's Rocket to the Moon/Those Fantastic Flying Fools/Blast-Off* (UK) 1967; *The Other Side of Bonnie and Clyde* (narrator only) 1968; *The McMasters, The Only Way Out Is Dead* (Can.) 1970; *Hugo the Hippo* (v/o), *Baker's Hawk* 1976; *Just You and Me Kid* 1979; *Earthbound* 1981; *White Dog* 1982; *Uphill All the Way* 1984; *Two Moon Junction* 1988.

Ivey, Judith. Actress. Born on Sept. 4, 1951, in El Paso, Tex. *ed.* Illinois State U. Talented leading lady and supporting player of the American stage and screen. She began her stage career in 1974 with the Goodman Theatre in Chicago and made her name on Broadway, where she won both Tony and Drama Desk Awards for 'Steaming' and 'Hurlyburly.' On-screen from 1984, she has been cast to best advantage in slightly wacky roles, but her talent has yet to be fully tapped.

FILMS: *The Lonely Guy, Harry and Son, The Woman in Red* 1984; *Compromising Positions* 1985; *Brighton Beach Memoirs* 1986; *Sister Sister, Hello Again* 1987; *Miles from Home* 1988; *In Country* 1989; *Everybody Wins* (UK/US), *Alice* 1990; *Love Hurts* 1991; *There Goes the Neighborhood* 1992; *The Devil's Advocate* 1997.

Ivory, James. Director. Born on June 7, 1928, in Berkeley, Calif. Raised in Kamath Falls, Oregon, where his Irish-born father ran a sawmill, he studied fine arts at the University of Oregon, intending to become a set designer, but was attracted by the idea of directing and later enrolled at the film department of the University of Southern California. As a student he directed a ten-minute short, then went to Europe, where he shot the half-hour documentary *Venice: Theme and Variations* with financial aid from USC. His fledgling momentum was then interrupted by the draft, and he spent the next year and a half in Germany, helping organize entertainment programs for GIs. As soon as he shed his uniform, he eagerly resumed filmmaking. After filming another documentary in New York and San Francisco, *The Sword and the Flute,* which dealt with Indian art objects, he was commissioned by the Asia Society in 1960 to make a documentary about India on location. He remained in India for several years, formed a partnership with local producer Ismail MERCHANT, and turned out several intelligent comedy-of-manners films that characteristically parodied the East-West paradox of Indian culture. The scripts of these films were written by Ivory in collaboration with Ruth Prawer JHABVALA, a German-born author of Polish-Jewish descent who became an Indian by marriage. Their first international success was *Shakespeare Wallah* (1965), which explored the vanishing British lifestyle in postcolonial India. Following setbacks with *The Guru* (1969) and *Bombay Talkie* (1970), Ivory abandoned the Indian setting, but not his basic theme of conflicting lifestyles, in the early 70s with the US-made feature *Savages* (1972), an allegory about people at odds with an unfamiliar environment. But he seemed way off his stride with the shrill commercial Hollywood production *The Wild Party* (1975), which was loosely inspired by the Fatty Arbuckle tragedy.

Ivory was back in his Indian element with the small but appealing *An Autobiography of a Princess* (1975) and *Hullabaloo Over Georgie and Bonnie's Pictures* (1978) and achieved a measure of success with his New York-based *Roseland* (1977). But it was with *The Europeans* (1979), the visually striking adaptation of the Henry James novel, that he re-established his reputation as a director of distinction and elegance of style. After two other fine productions, *Quartet* (1981) and *Heat and Dust* (1983), Ivory and his team returned to Henry James with *The Bostonians* (1984). But it was with the graceful and witty E. M. Forster adaptation *A Room with a View* (1986) that they enjoyed their greatest unqualified success. The film won Academy Awards for screenplay, art direction, and costumes, and was nominated for several others, including best picture, best director, and best cinematography. Ivory's next film, *Maurice,* shared a Silver Lion at the 1987 Venice Festival. But it was *Howards End* (1992) that became Merchant-Ivory's greatest success, both at the box office and in awards circles. The film was one of the highest grossing of the year, and was nominated for the Academy Award. The string of successful Merchant-Ivory productions established the duo as makers of high-quality, tasteful, and well-acted films. In the 1990s, they signed a three-picture deal with the Walt Disney Co.

FILMS: *Four in the Morning* (16 mm short; also sc., phot., edit.) 1953; *Venice: Theme and Variations* (16 mm short, also sc., phot.) 1957; *The Sword and the Flute* (16 mm short; also sc., edit.) 1959; *The Householder* 1963; *The Delhi Way* (16 mm medium-length; also prod., sc., phot., edit.) 1964; *Shakespeare Wallah* (also co-sc.) 1965; *The Guru* (also co-sc.) 1969; *Bombay Talkie* (also co-sc.) 1970; *Adventures of a Brown Man in Search of Civilization* (16 mm medium-length; also sc.) 1971; *Savages* (also co-sc.) 1972; *Helen—Queen of the Nautch Girls, Mahatma and the Mad Boy* 1973; *The Wild Party, Autobiography of a Princess* 1975; *Sweet Sounds* 1976; *Roseland* 1977; *Hullabaloo Over Georgie and Bonnie's Pictures* 1978; *The Europeans* (also bit act.), *The 5:48* (orig. for TV) 1979; *Jane Austen in Manhattan* 1980; *Quartet* 1981; *The Courtesans of Bombay* (doc.; co-sc. only) 1982; *Heat and Dust* 1983; *The Bostonians* 1984; *A Room with a View* 1986; *Maurice* (also co-sc.) 1987; *Slaves of New York* 1989; *Mr. & Mrs. Bridge* 1990; *Howards End* 1992; *The Remains of the Day* 1993; *Jefferson in Paris* 1995; *Surviving Picasso, The Proprietor* 1996.

Iwashita, Shima. Actress. Born on Jan. 3, 1941, in Tokyo. Pretty, sensuous heroine of numerous Japanese films since the early 60s. The daughter of actors, she got off to a quick start in her film career, and rose to great popularity following her memorable performance in Ozu's *An Autumn Afternoon* (1962). In 1967 she married director Masahiro SHINODA, became his partner in an independent production company, and starred in many of his films, as well as in those of other directors.

FILMS INCLUDE: *Youth in Fury, Late Autumn* 1960; *Killers on Parade, Epitaph to My Love* 1961; *Her Last Pearl, Harakiri, An Autumn Afternoon* 1962; *The Hidden Profile, Twin Sisters of Kyoto* (dual role) 1963; *The Assassin, Samurai from Nowhere* 1964; *Snow Country/Love in the Snow, The Scarlet Camellia* 1965; *Springtime, Punishment Island* 1966; *Rebellion of Japan, Portrait of Chieko, Clouds of Sunset* 1967; *Gion Matsuri/The Day the Sun Rose* 1968; *Through Days and Months, Double Suicide, Red Lion, The Song from My Heart* 1969; *The Scandalous Adventures of Buraikan* 1970; *Silence* 1971; *The Petrified Forest* 1973; *Himiko* 1974; *Under the Fall of the Cherry Blossoms* 1975; *The Ballad of Orin/Banished* 1977; *Giwaku* 1982; *MacArthur's Children* 1984; *Gonza, the Spearman* 1985.

Iwerks, Ub. Animator, special effects artist. *b.* Mar. 24, 1901, Kansas City, Mo. *d.* 1971. While working at a Kansas City commercial art studio in 1919, he befriended a young fellow worker named Walt DISNEY. The following year they both quit their jobs and went into business for themselves. But the enterprise was not a success and several months later the two aspiring artists went to work for the Kansas City Film Ad Company. Disney, dynamic, ambitious, and business-oriented, soon left to pursue his dream of independent grandeur, while the hard-working Iwerks stayed behind to apply his technical genius to improving animation techniques. However, they were reunited in 1923 when Disney, now in Hollywood, sent for Iwerks to help him draw his fledgling cartoon series, "Alice in Cartoonland." He was present, and probably quite instrumental, in the creation of Mickey Mouse and received "drawn by" screen credit on the early Mickey Mouse and Silly Symphonies cartoons.

In 1930, Iwerks was lured away from the Disney studios and started his own cartoon series, "Flip the Frog" and "Willie Whopper." But several years later he was back with Disney, where he supervised special effects on many of the studio's major productions. He developed and perfected many animation techniques, including the multiplane camera and an improved matte process for blending live action with animation which was used successfully in a number of films, notably in *Mary Poppins.* He also acted as special-effects advisor on a number of films produced outside the Disney organization, including Hitchcock's *The Birds.* He won Academy Awards in 1959 and 1965 for his technical contributions to motion pictures.

FILMS INCLUDE: As animator—*Alice in Cartoonland* (series) 1923–26; *Steamboat Willie, Plane Crazy* 1928; *The Jazz Fool, Barnyard Battle, The Karnival Kid, The Opry House* 1929; *Flip the Frog* (series) 1931–33; *Willie Whopper* (series) 1933–34; *Don Quixote* 1934; *Merry Mannequins, Skeleton Frolic* 1937; *The Frog Pond, Midnight Frolics* 1938; *Crop Chasers, Gorilla Hunt* 1939. As special-effects supervisor—*The Reluctant Dragon* 1941; *The Three Caballeros* 1945; *Make Mine Music, Song of the South* 1946; *Fun and Fancy Free* 1947; *Melody Time* 1948; *Ichabod and Mr. Toad* 1949; *Cinderella* 1950; *The Living Desert* 1953; *The Vanishing Prairie, 20,000 Leagues Under the Sea* 1954; *Davy Crockett King of the Wild Frontier, Lady and the Tramp, The African Lion* 1955; *The Great Locomotive Chase, Davy Crockett and the River Pirates* 1956; *101 Dalmations, The Parent Trap* 1961; *The Birds* 1963; *The Three Lives of Thomasina 1964.*

J

Jackson, Anne. Actress. Born on Sept. 3, 1926, in Allegheny, Pa., of Yugoslav-Irish descent. *ed.* Neighborhood Playhouse; Actors Studio. Primarily a stage actress (from 1944), she has appeared only sporadically in films, usually in comic and somewhat eccentric middle-age-blues characterizations. She married Eli WALLACH in 1948.

FILMS: *So Young So Bad* 1950; *The Journey* 1959; *Tall Story* 1960; *The Tiger Makes Out* 1967; *How to Save a Marriage and Ruin Your Life, The Secret Life of an American Wife* 1968; *Zigzag, The Angel Levine* (cameo), *Lovers and Other Strangers, Dirty Dingus Magee* 1970; *Independence* (Bicentennial short; as Abigail Adams), *Nasty Habits* (UK) 1976; *The Bell Jar* 1979; *The Shining* 1980; *Sam's Son* 1984; *Sanford Meisner* (doc.) 1985; *Funny About Love* 1989; *Folks!* 1992.

Jackson, Freda. Actress. *b.* Dec. 29, 1909, Nottingham, England. *d.* 1990. *ed.* University Coll. (Nottingham). A veteran of the English stage (from 1934) in both lead and character roles, she also appeared in a supporting capacity in occasional British films, often in shrewish roles.

FILMS INCLUDE: *Mountains o' Mourne* 1938; *A Canterbury Tale, Henry V* (as Nell Quickly) 1944; *Beware of Pity, Great Expectations* (as Mrs. Joe Gargery) 1946; *No Room at the Inn* 1948; *The Crowded Day* 1954; *Bhowani Junction* 1956; *The Flesh Is Weak* 1957; *A Tale of Two Cities* (as Vengeance) 1958; *The Brides of Dracula* 1960; *The Shadow of the Cat* 1961; *Tom Jones* (as Mrs. Seagrim) 1963; *The Third Secret* 1964; *Monster of Terror/Die Monster Die!* 1965; *The Jokers* 1967; *The Valley of Gwangi* (US) 1969; *Clash of the Titans* 1981.

Jackson, Glenda. Actress. Born in May 9, 1936, in Birkenhead, England. *ed.* RADA. A bricklayer's daughter, she left school at 16 to join an amateur theater group. For a decade she alternated between repertory plays and odd jobs as a waitress, receptionist, and pharmacy assistant. Her break came in 1964 when she was invited by Peter Brook to join his Theater of Cruelty revue, which was sponsored by the Royal Shakespeare Company. This led to her triumphant portrayal of the mad Charlotte Corday on both the London and the New York stage in Brook's haunting 'The Persecution and Assassination of Jean-Paul Marat as Performed by the Inmates of the Asylum of Charenton Under the Direction of the Marquis De Sade' ('Marat/Sade' for short). She made her film debut in the same role and later established herself as an intriguing screen personality in two Ken Russell films, *Women in Love* and *The Music Lovers.* She won the best actress Academy Award for the former as well as the New York Film Critics Award. In *Sunday Bloody Sunday* she finally broke away from the mold in which she had been typecast in her early films, that of a bitchy, neurotic nymphomaniac. She won a second Oscar for her performance in *A Touch of Class* (1973) and an Emmy Award in 1972 for the role of Elizabeth I in a six-part BBC-TV drama series. She was also nominated for Oscars for *Sunday Bloody Sunday* (1971) and *Hedda* (1975). Defying the advancing years, she continued in the 80s to play leading-lady roles on the stage ('Strange Interlude' in 1985 and 'Macbeth' in 1988 on Broadway), TV movies (title role in *The Patricia Neal Story* in 1981, Dr. Elena Bonner in *Sakharov* in 1984), and in films. She announced her retirement from acting in 1992 when she ran for election as a member of parliament and won a seat in the British House of Commons.

FILMS: *The Persecution and Assassination of Jean-Paul Marat as Performed by the Inmates of the Asylum of Charenton Under the Direction of the Marquis de Sade* (as Charlotte Corday) 1967; *Tell Me Lies, Negatives* 1968; *Women in Love* (as Gudrun Brangwen) 1969; *The Music Lovers, Sunday Bloody Sunday, Mary Queen of Scots* (as Queen Elizabeth I), *The Boy Friend* 1971; *Triple Echo, A Bequest to the Nation/The Nelson Affair* (as Lady Hamilton), *A Touch of Class* 1973; *The Maids* 1974; *The Romantic Englishwoman, The Devil Is a Woman* (UK/It.), *Hedda* (as Ibsen's Hedda Gabler) 1975; *The Incredible Sarah* (as Sarah Bernhardt), *Nasty Habits* 1976; *House Calls* (US), *Stevie* (Can.), *The Class of Miss MacMichael* 1978; *Lost and Found* (US) 1979; *Hopscotch* (US) 1980; *Giro City/And Nothing But the Truth* 1982; *Return of the Soldier* 1983; *Turtle Diary* 1985; *Beyond Therapy* (US), *Business as Usual* 1987; *Salome's Last Dance* 1988; *The Rainbow* 1989; *Doombeach* 1990.

Jackson, Gordon. Actor. *b.* Dec. 19, 1923, Glasgow, Scotland. *d.* 1990. Versatile character player of many British and some American films from the early 40s. Also on TV, including the 'Upstairs Downstairs' series, for which he won a British Actor of the Year Award in 1974 and Emmy in 1976 for his portrayal of Hudson, a stiff-upper-lipped butler. He was married (from 1951) to actress Rona Anderson.

FILMS INCLUDE: *The Foreman Went to France/Somewhere in France* 1942; *Millions Like Us* 1943; *Pink Strings and Sealing Wax* 1945; *The Captive Heart* 1946; *Against the Wind, Eureka Stockade/Massacre Hill* 1948; *Whisky Galore/Tight Little Island* 1949; *Happy Go Lovely* 1951; *Sailor Beware/Panic in the Parlor* 1956; *Seven Waves Away/Abandon Ship!* 1957; *Rockets Galore/Mad Little Island* 1958; *The Bridal Path, Yesterday's Enemy, Blind Date/Chance Meeting* 1959; *Tunes of Glory* 1960; *Mutiny on the Bounty* (US) 1962; *The Great Escape* (US) 1963; *The Long Ships* 1964; *The Ipcress File, Those Magnificent Men in Their Flying Machines* 1965; *Cast a Giant Shadow* (US) 1966; *The Night of the Generals, Danger Route* 1967; *The Prime of Miss Jean Brodie, Run Wild Run Free, Hamlet* (as Horatio) 1969; *Scrooge* 1970; *Kidnapped* 1971; *Russian Roulette* (US) 1975; *Golden Rendezvous* (US) 1977; *The Shooting Party* 1985; *The Whistle Blower* 1987.

Jackson, Kate. Actress. Born on Oct. 29, 1948, Birmingham, Ala. *ed.* U. of Mississippi; Birmingham Southern U. Pretty leading lady of TV and films. She performed in summer stock before going to New York, where she attended the American Academy of Dramatic Arts, modeled, and worked as a tour guide at NBC. In 1970 she made her TV debut in the Gothic soap opera series 'Dark Shadows,' then appeared regularly in several TV series, including 'Charlie's Angels' (1976–79). She had a far lesser impact in her scattered film appearances. In 1990, she successfully fought breast cancer. Divorced from actor Andrew STEVENS, she married plastics mogul David Greenwald.

FILMS INCLUDE: *Night of Dark Shadows* 1971; *Limbo/Women in Limbo* 1972; *Thunder and Lightning* 1977; *Dirty Tricks* (Can.) 1981; *Making Love* 1982; *Loverboy* 1989.

Jackson, Pat. Director. Born in 1916, in London. He joined Britain's GPO Film Unit at 18 and within two years began directing documentaries, initially in collaboration. He achieved international repute with *Western Approaches/The Raider* (1944), a semidocumentary re-enactment of the heroic feats of men aboard Atlantic Ocean cargo convoys during WW II. After the war he graduated into feature films, but his career as a feature director, including a brief stay in Hollywood (1949–50), produced uneven results. Since the early 60s he has been mainly involved in TV production.

FILMS: Shorts—*Big Money* (co-dir. with Harry Watt) 1936; *Men in Danger, Happy in the Morning* 1938; *The First Days* (co-dir. with Watt and Humphrey Jennings) 1939; *Health in War* 1940; *Ferry Pilot* 1941; *Builders* 1942. Features—*Western Approaches/The Raider* (semidoc.) 1944; *Shadow on the Wall* (US) 1950; *Encore* (co-dir. with Harold French and Anthony Pelissier), *White Corridors* (also co-sc.) 1951; *Something Money Can't Buy* (also co-sc.) 1952; *The Feminine Touch* 1956; *The Birthday Present* 1957; *Virgin Island* 1958; *Snowball* 1960; *What a Carve Up!/No Place Like Homicide* 1961; *Seven Keys, Don't Talk to Strange Men* 1962; *Seventy Deadly Pills* (also sc.), *Dead End Creek* (also co-sc.) 1964.

Jackson, Peter. Director, producer, screenwriter. Born 1961, in New Zealand. With a fascination of film from boyhood, this offbeat, fiercely individualistic filmmaker has carved a career out of the bizarre, leading to the critically acclaimed, disquieting drama *Heavenly Creatures* (1994) and the more mainstream, special effects horror flick *The Frighteners* (1996).

FILMS: *Bad Taste* (prod., dir., sc., ed., cin., act.) 1988; *Dead Alive* (dir., sc., act.) 1992; *Heavenly Creatures* (co-prod., dir., sc.) 1994; *The Frighteners* 1996.

Jackson, Samuel L. Actor. Born in 1949. *ed.* Morehouse Coll. Intense, stage-trained actor known for distinctive, thought-provoking portrayals. Named best supporting actor by the Cannes Film Festival and New York Film Critics Circle for his role as the mercurial drug-addicted brother in *Jungle Fever.* He is co-founder of the Atlanta-based Just Us Theatre Co. A popular figure with audiences and fellow performers alike, Jackson, with seemingly little effort, makes the transition between powerfully dramatic roles to highly comedic characters. He was nominated for his first Academy Award as a supporting actor in Quentin TARANTINO's wildly successful *Pulp Fiction* (1994). He is married to actress LaTanya Richardson.

FILMS INCLUDE: *Ragtime* 1981; *Eddie Murphy Raw* 1987; *Sea of Love, Do the Right Thing* 1989; *Def by Temptation, A Shock to the System, Betsy's Wedding, Mo' Better Blues, The Exorcist III, GoodFellas* 1990; *Johnny Suede, Jungle Fever, Strictly Business* 1991; *Patriot Games, White Sands, Juice,*

Jumpin' at the Boneyard, Fathers and Sons 1992; *Amos & Andrew, Jurassic Park, Menace II Society, National Lampoon's Loaded Weapon, True Romance* 1993; *Fresh, The New Age, Pulp Fiction* 1994; *Die Hard with a Vengeance, Fluke* (v/o), *Kiss of Death, Losing Isaiah* 1995; *The Great White Hype, The Long Kiss Goodnight, The Search for One-Eyed Jimmy, A Time to Kill, Trees Lounge* 1996; *Hard Eight* 1997.

Jacobi, Derek. Actor. Born on Oct. 22, 1938, in London. *ed.* Cambridge. Impressive character lead and supporting player of the British stage, TV, and films. He began his acting career with the National Youth Theatre and the Marlowe Society at Cambridge, then joined the Birmingham Repertory Theatre, making his professional debut in 1960. He established his reputation on the stage in roles from the Shakespearean and classic repertoire and gained wider exposure on TV with such memorable outings as 'I Claudius' (title role), 'The Hunchback of Notre Dame' (as Frollo), and 'Inside the Third Reich' (as Hitler).

FILMS INCLUDE: *Othello* (as Cassio) 1965; *Interlude* 1968; *Three Sisters* 1970; *The Day of the Jackal* 1973; *The Odessa File* 1974; *The Medusa Touch* 1978; *The Human Factor* 1979; *Enigma* 1982; *Little Dorrit* (as Arthur Clennam) 1987; *Henry V* (as Chorus) 1989; *Dead Again* 1991; *Hamlet, Looking for Richard* 1996; *Hard Eight* 1997.

Jacobi, Lou. Actor. Born on Dec. 28, 1913, in Toronto, Ont., Canada. In amateur plays since childhood, he began acting professionally in the later 40s, at first on the Canadian stage, then in London and on Broadway. He has also played character roles in a number of films. His TV appearances include the title role in the comedy series 'Ivan the Terrible' (1976).

FILMS INCLUDE: *The Good Beginning* 1953; *A Kid for Two Farthings* (UK) 1955: *The Diary of Anne Frank* 1959; *Song Without End* 1960; *Irma La Douce* 1963; *Penelope* 1966; *Cotton Comes to Harlem* 1970; *Little Murders* 1971; *Everything You Always Wanted to Know About Sex. . .* 1972; *Next Stop Greenwich Village* 1976; *Roseland* 1977; *The Magician* (Isr./Ger.) 1979; *The Lucky Star* (Can.) 1980; *Arthur* 1981; *My Favorite Year* 1982; *Isaac Littlefeathers* (Can.) 1984; *The Boss' Wife* 1986; *Amazon Women on the Moon* 1987; *Avalon* 1990; *I Don't Buy Kisses Anymore* 1992.

Jacobini, Maria. Actress. *b.* Feb. 17, 1890, Rome. *d.* 1944. The offspring of a distinguished Roman family (her uncle was Cardinal Jacobini, minister of state to Pope Leo XIII), she was attracted to the theater at an early age and after studies at Rome's Academy of Dramatic Arts made both her stage and screen debuts in 1910. She rapidly became established as one of the leading "divas" of the Italian silent screen and was considered by her contemporaries one of the most cultured, intelligent, and personable European stars of her day. Her film vehicles were for the most part historical spectacles and society dramas. In addition to making her many Italian films, she starred in a number of German, Austrian, and French productions in the late 20s and co-starred with Pudovkin in Fedor Ozep's Soviet screen adaptation of Tolstoy's *The Living Corpse* (1929). Her sisters, Bianca (*b.* 1888) and Diomira (*b.* 1896) Jacobini, also appeared in films.

FILMS INCLUDE: *Lucrezia Borgia, Beatrice Cenci* 1910; *La Fugitiva, Vampe di Gelosia* 1912; *Giovanna d'Arco* 1913; *La Corsara* 1915; *Resurrezione* 1917; *La Signora Arlecchino, Addio Giovinezza* 1918; *La Vergine Folle* 1919; *Il Viaggio* 1921; *Amore rosso* 1922; *La Vie de Bohème* 1923; *Oriente* 1924; *Transatlantico, Il Carnavale di Venezia* 1926; *Unfug der Liebe, Villa Falconieri* (both Ger.) 1928; *The Living Corpse* (USSR), *Maman Colbiri* (Fr.) 1929; *La Scala* 1931; *Giuseppe Verdi* 1938; *Melodie eterne/Eternal Melodies* 1940; *La Donna della Montagna* 1943.

Jacobs, Arthur P. Producer. *b.* Mar. 7, 1922, Los Angeles. *d.* 1973. A graduate of USC, he entered films as a messenger and became a publicist for MGM, then for Warners, and finally for his own publicity firm. Turning independent producer in the mid-60s, he had several commercial successes, notably *Planet of the Apes* and its sequels. But also had his share of box-office flops, headed by *Doctor Dolittle.*

FILMS: *What a Way to Go!* 1964; *Doctor Dolittle* 1967; *Planet of the Apes* 1968; *The Chairman, Goodbye Mr.* Chips (both exec. prod.) 1969; *Beneath the Planet of the Apes* 1970; *Escape from the Planet of the Apes* 1971; *Play It Again Sam, Conquest of the Planet of the Apes* 1972; *Tom Sawyer, Battle for the Planet of the Apes* 1973; *Huckleberry Finn* 1974.

Jacobsson, Ulla. Actress. *b.* May 23, 1929, Göteborg, Sweden. *d.* 1982. Originally a stage actress, she attracted worldwide attention in her second film, Arne Mattsson's *One Summer of Happiness.* Beginning in the early 60s, she also starred in British, French, and German films.

FILMS INCLUDE: *Rolling Sea, One Summer of Happiness* 1951; *All the Joy of the Earth* 1953; *Eternal Love, Sir Arne's Treasure* 1954; *Smiles of a Summer Night, The Sacred Lie* 1955; *Crime et Châtiment/Crime and Punishment* (Fr.), *Song of the Scarlet Flower* 1956; *Unruhige Nacht/The Restless Night* (Ger.), *The Phantom Carriage* 1958; *Riviera Story* 1961; *Love Is a Ball* (US) 1963; *Zulu* (UK) 1964; *The Heroes of Telemark* (UK), *Nightmare* 1965; *The Double Man* (UK) 1967; *Bamse/Teddy Bear* 1969; *The Servant* 1970; *Faustrecht der Freiheit/Fist-Right of Freedom/Fox and His Friends* (Ger.) 1975.

Jacopetti, Gualtiero. Documentary director. Born in 1919, in Barga, Italy. A veteran journalist and the editor-in-chief of a leading Italian magazine, he turned to films in the late 50s as a commentary writer and narrator of documentaries. In 1962 he turned out *Mondo Cane,* the first and commercially most successful of several sensational feature-length documentaries that focused on lurid and cruel aspects of life, sometimes fabricating situations to add impact to his theme.

FILMS INCLUDE (as director): *Mondo Cane/A Dog's Life* (also prod., sc.) 1962; *La Donna nel Mondo/Eva Sconsciuta/Women of the World* (also prod., co-sc., edit.), *Mondo Cane n. 2/Mondo Pazzo/Crazy World/Insane World/ Mondo Insanity* (co-dir., co-sc. with Franco Prosperi) 1963; *Africa Addio/Africa—Blood and Guts* (co-dir. co-sc., co-edit. with Prosperi) 1966, *Zio Tom/Farewell Uncle Tom* (co-dir., co-sc. with Prosperi) 1972.

Jaeckel, Richard. Actor. Born on Oct. 10, 1926, in Long Beach, N.Y. *ed.* Hollywood High. *d.* 1997. Compact, baby-faced utility player of Hollywood films, he began as a delivery boy at 20th Century-Fox. From 1943 he played a mixed variety of screen roles—combat cowards, heavies, pugnacious heroes, misguided youths, and even some romantic parts. He was nominated for a best supporting actor Oscar for *Sometimes a Great Notion/Never Give an Inch* (1971).

FILMS INCLUDE: *Guadalcanal Diary* 1943; *Wing and a Prayer* 1944; *City Across the River, Battleground, Sands of Iwo Jima* 1949; *The Gunfighter* 1950; *Hoodlum Empire, Come Back Little Sheba* 1952; *The Big Leaguer* 1953; *The Violent Men* 1955; *Attack!* 1956; *3:10 to Yuma* 1957; *Cowboy, The Naked and the Dead* 1958; *Platinum High School, The Gallant Hours* 1960; *Town Without Pity* 1961; *The Young and the Brave, Four for Texas* 1963; *Town Tamer* 1965; *The Dirty Dozen* 1967; *The Devil's Brigade* 1968; *The Green Slime* 1969; *Chisum* 1970; *Sometimes a Great Notion/Never Give an Inch* 1971; *Ulzana's Raid* 1972; *Pat Garrett and Billy the Kid, The Outfit* 1973; *Chosen Survivors* 1974; *The Drowning Pool, Walking Tall Part 2* 1975; *Grizzly, The Jaws of Death* 1976; *Twilight's Last*

Gleaming, Day of the Animals 1977; *The Dark* 1979; *Herbie Goes Bananas* 1980; *... All the Marbles* 1981; *Airplane II: The Sequel, Cold River* 1982; *Starman* 1984; *Black Moon Rising* 1986; *Delta Force 2: The Colombian Connection, Ghetto Blasters* 1990; *The King of the Kickboxers* 1991.

Jaeckin, Just. Director. Born in 1940, in Vichy, France. A graduate of L'Ecole des Arts Décoratifs, he was a magazine art director as well as a designer and sculptor, and a director of TV commercials before turning to features in the early 70s. After scoring an enormous box-office hit with the erotic extravaganza *Emmanuelle* (1973), he remained devoted to lavishly photographed soft-core amorous themes. He usually collaborates on his own scripts.

FILMS INCLUDE: *Emmanuelle* 1973; *Histoire d'O/The Story of O* 1975; *Madame Claude* 1977; *Le Dernier Amant romantique* 1978; *Collections privées* (one episode) 1979; *Girls* 1980; *L'Amant de Lady Chatterley/Lady Chatterley's Lover* 1981; *Gwendoline/The Perils of Gwendoline in the Land of the Yik Yak* 1984.

Jaenzon, Julius. Director of photography. *b.* 1885 Göteborg, Sweden. *d.* 1961. The leading cameraman of the so-called "golden age" of the Swedish silent cinema, he was responsible for the excellent camera work in many of the films of Sjöström, Stiller, and other notable directors of the era. He often used the pseudonym J. Julius and directed several films. His brother, Henryk Jaenzon, was also a respected lighting cameraman of the silent period.

FILMS INCLUDE: *Report from the US on President Theodore Roosevelt* (newsreel) 1907; *Opium Den* (also dir.), *Two Swedish Immigrants in America* (also dir.) 1911; *Condemned by Society* (also dir.), *Agaton and Fina* (also dir.), *Black Masks* 1912; *The Vampire, The Marriage Bureau, The Clergyman, Life's Conflicts* 1913; *People of the Border, The Chamberlain* 1914; *His Wife's Past, The Dagger* 1915; *Therese, Love and Journalism, The Wings, The Ballet Primadonna* 1916; *Terje Vigen, Alexander the Great* 1917; *The Outlaw and His Wife* 1918; *The Sons of Ingmar, Song of the Scarlet Flower, Sir Arne's Treasure* 1919; *The Downey Girl* (co-dir.) 1920; *The Phantom Carriage* 1921; *Love's Crucible* 1922; *Gunnar Hede's Saga* 1923; *The Story of Gösta Berling* 1924; *Ulla My Ulla* (also dir.) 1930; *Song of the Scarlet Flower* 1934; *Johan Ulfstjerna* 1936; *His Official Fiancee* 1944.

Jaffe, Herb. Producer. Born in New York City. *ed.* Brooklyn Coll.; Columbia. A former press agent, talent agent, and sales executive, he was in charge of production and West Coast operations for United Artists before becoming an independent producer in 1973.

FILMS INCLUDE: *The Wind and the Lion* 1975; *Demon Seed* 1977; *Who'll Stop the Rain* 1978; *Time After Time* 1979; *Those Lips Those Eyes* 1980; *Jinxed* 1982; *The Lords of Discipline* 1983; *Fright Night* 1985; *Dudes* 1987; *Pass the Ammo* 1988; *Remote Control* 1990.

Jaffe, Sam. Actor. *b.* Mar. 8, 1891, New York City. *d.* 1984. *ed.* CCNY; Columbia (Graduate School of Engineering). Big little character player of the American stage, screen, and TV. As a youngster, he appeared with his mother, Ada Steinberg Jaffe, on the Yiddish stage. He was a teacher, then dean of math at the Bronx Cultural Institute before resuming his stage career with the Washington Square Players in 1915. He subsequently appeared in numerous stage productions, making his film debut in 1934. A spunky, dynamic character player, he achieved enormous screen and stage presence despite his small, frail physique. He won the Venice Festival best actor award and was nominated for a best supporting role Oscar for his performance as a cool-headed crime mastermind in *The Asphalt Jungle* (1950). Also memorable as the ancient High Lama in *Lost Horizon* (1937) and in the title role of *Gunga Din* (1939). He played Dr. Zorba in the 'Ben Casey' TV series, which also featured his second wife, Bettye Ackerman (*b.* Feb. 28, 1928, Cottageville, S.C.). His first, actress Lillian Taiz Jaffe, died in 1941. Not to be confused with a talent agent by the same name (*b.* May 21, 1901, N.Y.C.) who has produced a number of films.

FILMS: *The Scarlet Empress* (as Grand Duke Peter of Russia), *We Live Again* 1934; *Lost Horizon* (as the High Lama) 1937; *Gunga Din* (title role) 1939; *Stage Door Canteen* (cameo) 1943; *13 Rue Madeleine, Gentleman's Agreement* 1947; *The Accused, Rope of Sand* 1949; *The Asphalt Jungle* 1950; *Under the Gun, I Can Get It for You Wholesale, The Day the Earth Stood Still* 1951; *Les Espions* (Fr.) 1957; *The Barbarian and the Geisha* 1958; *Ben-Hur* (as Simonides) 1959; *A Guide for the Married Man* (cameo) 1967; *Guns for San Sebastian* 1968; *The Great Bank Robbery* 1969; *The Dunwich Horror* 1970; *Bedknobs and Broomsticks* 1971; *Battle Beyond the Stars* 1980; *Nothing Lasts Forever, On the Line* (Sp.) 1984.

Jaffe, Stanley R. Producer. Born on July 31, 1940, in New Rochelle, N.Y. *ed.* U. of Pennsylvania (Wharton School of Finance). A former production executive with Paramount and Columbia, he became an independent producer, boasting a number of major motion pictures among his credits. He made an adequate first attempt at directing with *Without a Trace* in 1983. From 1984 he worked mainly in collaboration with producer Sherry Lansing. In the 1990s, he was president/CEO of Paramount Communications, again working with Lansing, who became chairman.

FILMS INCLUDE (as producer): *Goodbye Columbus* 1969; *Bad Company* 1972; *The Bad News Bears* 1976; *Kramer vs. Kramer* 1979; *Taps* 1981; *Without a Trace* (also dir.) 1983; *Racing with the Moon, Firstborn* 1984; *Fatal Attraction* 1987; *The Accused* 1988; *Black Rain* 1989.

Jagger, Dean. Actor. *b.* Nov. 7, 1903, Lima, Ohio. *d.* 1991. Raised on farms in Columbus Grove, Ohio, and rural Indiana, he taught elementary school for several semesters before deciding on an acting career. After attending the Lyceum Art Conservatory in Chicago, he joined a stock company in Grand Rapids, Michigan, replacing Spencer Tracy. He later appeared in vaudeville, on radio, and on Broadway, and made his screen debut in 1929, soon developing into a fine lead and character actor. Bald, robust, and personable, he played a variety of roles in scores of films, from men of action to men of dreams. Academy Award as best supporting actor for *Twelve O'Clock High* (1950). Also much on TV, including the 'Mr. Novak' series (1963–65). He won an Emmy for his role in a 1980 segment of the religious program 'This Is the Life.'

FILMS INCLUDE: *The Woman from Hell* 1929; *You Belong to Me* 1934; *Wings in the Dark, Home on the Range, People Will Talk, Men Without Names* 1935; *13 Hours by Air, Revolt of the Zombies* 1936; *Brigham Young—Frontiersman* (title role) 1940; *Western Union, The Men in Her Life* 1941; *Valley of the Sun* 1942; *The North Star/Armored Attack* 1943; *When Strangers Marry/Betrayed* 1944; *I Live in Grosvenor Square/A Yank in London* 1945; *Sister Kenny* 1946; *Pursued* 1947; *C-Man* 1949; *Twelve O'Clock High, Dark City* 1950; *Rawhide, Warpath* 1951; *My Son John, It Grows on Trees* 1952; *The Robe* 1953; *Executive Suite, White Christmas* 1954; *Bad Day at Black Rock, The Eternal Sea* 1955; *On the Threshold of Space* 1957; *The Great Man, Three Brave Men, X the Unknown, Bernadine, Forty Guns* 1957; *The Proud Rebel, King Creole* 1958; *The Nun's Story* 1959; *Cash McCall, Elmer Gantry* 1960; *Parrish* 1961; *Jumbo* 1962; *First to Fight* 1967; *Firecreek, Day of the Evil Gun* 1968; *Smith!* 1969; *Tiger by the Tail, The Kremlin Letter* 1970; *Vanishing Point* 1971; *The Great Lester Boggs, So Sad about Gloria* 1975; *God Bless Dr. Shagetz, End of the World* 1977; *The Game of Death* 1979; *Alligator* 1980.

Jagger, Mick. Singer, songwriter, actor. Born on July 26, 1943, in Dartford, England. *ed.* London School of Economics. The enduring rock 'n' roll superstar, one of the pop world's most popular idols, appeared in a number of films, with or without his Rolling Stones group.

FILMS: *1 + 1/One Plus One/Sympathy for the Devil* 1969; *Ned Kelly, Performance, Gimme Shelter* (doc.) 1970; *The London Rock 'N Roll Show* (concert doc.) 1973; *Ladies and Gentlemen The Rolling Stones* (doc.) 1975; *Let's Spend the Night Together* (concert doc.) 1982; *At the Max* 1991; *Freejack* 1992; *Bent* 1997.

Jaglom, Henry. Director, screenwriter, actor. Born on Jan. 26, 1943, in New York City. Trained at the University of Pennsylvania and the Actors Studio, he began his acting career in off-Broadway plays and in such TV series as 'Gidget' and 'The Flying Nun.' In 1967 he shot a three-hour, unreleased documentary on the Six-Day War in Israel. Returning home, he made his screen-acting debut in 1968 and his first feature as a director three years later. He writes his own scripts and occasionally appears in his own films, typically sincere, pleasant romantic comedies.

FILMS: As actor—*Psych-Out* 1968; *The 1,000 Plane Raid* 1969; *Drive He Said, The Last Movie* 1971. As director—*A Safe Place* (also sc., edit.) 1971; *Tracks* (also sc.) 1977; *Sitting Ducks* (also sc., act.) 1979; *Can She Bake a Cherry Pie?* (also sc.) 1983; *Always* (also sc., act.) 1985; *Someone to Love* (also sc., act.) 1988; *New Year's Day* (also sc., act.) 1989; *Eating* (also sc.) 1990; *Venice Venice* (also act.) 1991; *Lucky Ducks* 1992; *Baby Fever* 1994; *Last Summer in the Hamptons* (also co-prod., act., editor) 1995.

Jakubowska, Wanda. Director. Born on Nov. 10, 1907, in Warsaw. *ed.* Warsaw U. (art history). A founding member of START and a documentary filmmaker in the 30s, she shocked filmgoers in 1948 with *The Last Stop,* a revealing account of life in the concentration camps, a fate she had herself endured in Auschwitz and Ravensbruck during WW II. Her subsequent Polish films never matched the power of that document but nevertheless were influential in the development of post–WW II Polish cinema.

FEATURE FILMS: *The Last Stop* 1948; *Soldier of Victory* 1953; *An Atlantic Story* 1954; *Farewell to the Devil* 1956; *King Mathias I* 1957; *Encounters in the Dark, It Happened Yesterday* 1960; *The End of Our World* 1964; *The Hot Line* 1965; *At 150 Kilometers Per Hour* 1971; *Ludwik Warynski* 1978; *Dance in Chains* 1979; *Invitation* 1985; *Colors of Love* 1987.

James, Clifton. Actor. Born on May 29, 1921, in New York City. *ed.* U. of Oregon. Beefy, versatile character player of the American stage, TV, and films; a product of the Actors Studio. At his most natural in rural, redneck roles.

FILMS INCLUDE: *On the Waterfront* 1954; *The Strange One* 1957; *The Last Mile* 1959; *Something Wild* 1961; *Experiment in Terror, David and Lisa* 1962; *Black Like Me* 1964; *The Chase* 1966; *The Happening, Cool Hand Luke* 1967; *Will Penny* 1968; *The Reivers* 1969; *WUSA* 1970; *The Biscuit Eater, The New Centurions* 1972; *Kid Blue, The Iceman Cometh, Werewolf of Washington, The Last Detail, Live and Let Die* 1973; *Bank Shot, Juggernaut, The Man with the Golden Gun* 1974; *Rancho Deluxe* 1975; *Silver Streak* 1976; *The Bad News Bears in Breaking Training* 1977; *Superman II* 1980; *Where Are the Children?* 1986; *Whoops Apocalypse* (UK) 1987; *Eight Men Out* 1988; *The Bonfire of the Vanities* 1990.

James, Harry. Trumpeter, bandleader. *b.* Mar. 15, 1916, Albany, Ga. *d.* 1983. The son of circus performers (father a musician, mother a trapeze artist), he started his career at four in a contortionist act, billed as "The Human Eel." He later became an accomplished trumpet player, the leader of a circus band, and eventually an idol of the Big Band era of the 30s and 40s whose records sold by the millions. He made occasional film appearances, with or without his orchestra, often as himself. He was musical director of the film *Young Man with a Horn* (1950) and supplied the actual trumpet notes supposedly played in the film by Kirk Douglas. He was once married (1943–65) to Betty GRABLE.

FILMS INCLUDE: *Hollywood Hotel* 1937; *Syncopation, Private Buckaroo, Springtime in the Rockies* 1942; *Best Foot Forward* 1943; *Two Girls and a Sailor, Bathing Beauty* 1944; *Do You Love Me?, If I'm Lucky* 1946; *Carnegie Hall* 1947; *On Our Merry Way/A Miracle Can Happen* 1948; *I'll Get By* 1950; *The Benny Goodman Story, The Opposite Sex* 1956; *The Big Beat* 1958; *The Ladies' Man* 1961.

Jancsó, Miklós. Director. Born on Sept. 27, 1921, in Vác, Hungary. He studied law, ethnography, and art history, and after gaining a doctor-of-law degree in 1944 he did ethnological research in Transylvania for several years. He then enrolled at Budapest's Academy of Dramatic and Film Art. After graduating in 1950, he turned out newsreels and many documentary shorts before making his first feature film in 1958. From the start, Jancsó chose war and its bitter aftermath as a background for the exploration of his ideas. But while his first three films were rather ascetic in style and revealed a compassion toward characters entrapped in the confusion of historic events, Jancsó's subsequent work shows a progressive detachment from humane concerns and an increasing emphasis on visual style for its own sake. *The Round-Up* caused a sensation at the 1965 Cannes Festival and launched the director's international reputation. He was named best director at Cannes in 1972 for *Red Psalm/Red Song/People Still Ask.* The film flamboyantly flaunted the mastery of camera movement which became Jancsó's trademark in future productions. His near-schematic technique relies heavily on few camera setups and long, elaborate compositional scenes that compellingly use the integration of figures with the landscape. Once he has planned his sequences Jancsó works quickly, often completing a film in a little more than two weeks. He shot *Cantata* (1963), for example, in 11 days, using only 12 or 13 camera setups in the process. The results of his methods are often overly mechanical, but the impact is nearly always great. Jancsó was honored by the 1979 Cannes Film Festival for the body of his work. He married director Márta Mészáros. Their son, Miklós Jancsó, Jr., is a cameraman.

FEATURE FILMS: *The Bells Have Gone to Rome* 1958; *Three Stars* (co-dir.) 1960; *Cantata* 1963; *My Way Home* 1964; *The Round-Up* 1965; *The Red and the White* 1967; *Silence and Cry* 1968; *The Confrontation, Sirokko/Sirocco d'Hiver/Winter Wind* (Hung./Fr.) 1969; *Agnus Dei, La Pacifista/The Pacifist* (It./Fr./Ger.), *La Tecnica e il Rito/Il Giovane Attila* (It.) 1971; *Red Psalm/Red Song/People Still Ask* 1972; *Roma rivuole Cesare* (It.) 1973; *Elektreia/Electra* 1974; *Vizi Privati—Pubbliche Virtu/Private Vices—Public Virtue* (It./Yug.) 1976; *Hungarian Rhapsody, Allegro Barbaro* 1978; *The Tyrant's Heart/Boccaccio in Hungary* 1981; *Doctor Faustus* 1984; *Budapest* (doc.) 1985; *L'Aube/Dawn* (Fr./Isr.) 1986.

Janda, Krystyna. Actress. Born in 1952, in Starachowice, Poland. Tall, blonde, leading player of the new Polish cinema. A graduate of the Warsaw College of Drama, she made her professional stage and screen debuts in 1976 and soon asserted herself as a capable, versatile, and captivating performer. Her progress was so rapid that in 1978, just two years into her career, she became the subject of a Polish documentary film, *Actress.* In 1990 she won the best actress prize at Cannes for her performance in *Interrogation,* a film banned by the Polish authorities on its completion in 1982.

FILMS INCLUDE: *Man of Marble* 1976; *Madame Bovary—That's Me, The Frontier/The Border* 1977; *Without Anesthesia/Rough Treatment, White Harvest* 1978; *The Conductor/Orchestra Leader, Golem* 1979; *Man of Iron, Mephisto* (Hung./Ger.) 1981; *Espion lève-toi* (Fr.) 1982; *Bella Donna* (Ger.) 1983; *Suspended* 1986; *Inner State* (release delayed from 1982), *Dekalog/The Ten Commandments* 1989; *Interrogation* (release delayed from 1982) 1990.

Janni, Joseph. Producer. Born on May 21, 1916, in Milan, Italy. *ed.* Milan U.; Centro Sperimentale (Rome). In the UK since 1939, he entered films in 1941 and formed his own production company in 1947. He has produced a number of notable British films, including several John SCHLESINGER efforts.

FILMS INCLUDE: *The Glass Mountain* 1948; *White Corridors* 1951; *Something Money Can't Buy* 1952; *Romeo and Juliet* 1953; *A Town Like Alice* 1956; *The Captain's Table* 1958; *A Kind of Loving* 1962; *Billy Liar* 1963; *Darling* 1965; *Modesty Blaise* 1966; *Far from the Madding Crowd* 1967; *Poor Cow* 1968; *In Search of Gregory* 1970; *Sunday Bloody Sunday* 1971; *Made* 1972; *Deaf Smith and Johnny Ears* (co-prod.) 1973; *Yanks* (co-prod.) 1979.

Jannings, Emil. Actor. *b.* Theodor Friedrich Emil Janenz, July 23, 1884, Rorschach, Switzerland, to an American-born father and German mother. *d.* 1950. (Many reference works still give Jannings's birthplace as Brooklyn, N.Y., and in 1886.) Raised in middle-class comfort in the German town of Görlitz, Jannings ran away from home at 16 to become a sailor. After serving as an assistant cook on a Hamburg-London liner, he returned home disenchanted but shortly after found a new love—the stage. Becoming a professional actor at 18, he toured with various companies and played in many provincial towns before being invited to join Max REINHARDT's theater in Berlin in 1906. By the time he made his screen debut, in 1914, he was an established and important stage actor.

Jannings's early film career was rather uneventful. Not until 1919 did he begin acquiring an international reputation in a string of notable UFA pseudohistorical dramas with a Germanic slant, in which he played such imposing figures as Louis XV, Henry VIII, Danton, and Peter the Great. The best of these were directed by Jannings's friend from his theater days, Ernst LUBITSCH. Next came a series of literary adaptations (*Othello, Quo Vadis?, Tartüff, Faust*) that solidified his reputation as the most distinguished performer of the German screen.

A powerfully built man with an enormous screen presence, Jannings was an ideal tragic figure of King Lear stature. Following his *tours de force* in Murnau's *The Last Laugh* and Dupont's *Variety,* he was widely acclaimed as the world's greatest film actor, although his acting was more in the theatrical than the screen tradition. His international fame led to a Paramount contract in 1927. Jannings's Hollywood films were designed to accommodate his gift for tragedy. Like some of his German vehicles, they typically dealt with a solid citizen ruined by sin. In the first ever Academy Award ceremony, he won an Oscar for his combined efforts in the first two of his American films, *The Last Command* and *The Way of All Flesh.* But his thick German accent put an end to his American career when the industry switched to sound. In 1929 he returned to Germany, where the following year he gave his immortal portrayal of Professor Rath, the pompous solid citizen enslaved and degraded by his passion for Marlene Dietrich in Von Sternberg's *The Blue Angel.*

With the Nazi rise to power in 1933, Jannings was recruited by the propaganda-conscious regime to lend his talent and reputation to Goebbels's cultural onslaught. Although not a Party member, he was an enthusiastic supporter of the Nazi ideology and gladly accepted roles in anti-British and other propaganda films. In 1938 he was rewarded with a medal from Goebbels and an appointment as head of Tobis, the company that produced his films. In 1941 he was honored as Artist of the State. In December of 1944 he began his last film, *Wo ist Herr Belling?/Where Is Mr. Belling?,* but production was halted in January of 1945 when illness and anguish over the apparent Nazi defeat combined to drive Jannings into retirement. The film was never completed. Blacklisted by the Allied authorities, he never made another. He died lonely and bitter five years later at age 65. Autobiography: *Wie ich zum Film kamm* [How I Got into Movies] (1928).

FILMS INCLUDE: In Germany—*Arme Eva, Passionels Tagebuch* 1914; *Nächte des Grauens* 1916; *Lulu* 1917; *Führmann Henschel, Die Augen der Mumie Ma/The Eyes of the Mummy* 1918; *Madame Dubarry/Passion* (as Louis XV), *Rose Bernd* 1919; *Kölhiesels Töchter, Anna Boleyn/Deception* (as Henry VIII), *Die Brüder Karamasoff/The Brothers Karamazov* (as Dimitri Karamazov) 1920; *Danton/All for a Woman* (title role), *Das Weib des Pharao/Loves of Pharaoh* (title role), *Vendetta* 1921; *Die Gräfin von Paris, Othello* (title role), *Peter der Grosse/Peter the Great* (title role), *Tragödie der Liebe* 1922; *Alles für Geld/Fortune's Fool* (also prod.) 1923; *Quo Vadis?* (as Nero; It.), *Nju/Husbands or Lovers, Das Waschsfigurenkabinett/Waxworks/The Three-Way Works* (as Harun al-Rashid, in a rare comedy role), *Der letzte Mann/The Last Laugh* 1924; *Varieté/Variety* 1925; *Tartüff* (title role), *Faust* (as Mephistopheles) 1926. In the US—*The Way of All Flesh* 1927; *The Last Command, The Street of Sin, The Patriot* (as Czar Paul I), *Sins of the Fathers* 1928; *Betrayal, Fighting the White Slave Traffic* 1929. In Germany—*Der blaue Engel/The Blue Angel, Liebling der Götter/Der Grosse Tenor/Darling of the Gods* 1930; *Stürme der Leidenschaft/Storms of Passion* 1931; *Der alte und der junge König* 1935; *Traumulus* 1936; *Der zerbrochene Krug* 1937; *Robert Koch* (title role) 1939; *Ohm Krüger* (title role) 1941; *Die Entlassung* (as Bismarck) 1942; *Altes Herz wird wieder jung* 1943; *Wo ist Herr Belling?* (unfinished) 1945.

Janssen, David. Actor. *b.* David Meyer, Mar. 27, 1930, Naponee, Nebr. *d.* 1980. The son of a beauty queen-turned-actress, he began performing on stage as a child. During his teens he played juvenile roles in several films and later matured into a competent leading man, typically as a reserved, often cynical or curiously vulnerable man of action. He attained only modest success on the big screen, but was among the dominant male stars of television in the 60s and 70s in such series as 'Richard Diamond, Private Detective' (1957–60), 'The Fugitive' (1963–67), 'O'Hara, US Treasury' (1971–72), and 'Harry-O' (1974–76), as well as many TV movies. He died suddenly of a heart attack at age 49.

FILMS INCLUDE: *Swamp Fire* 1946; *Yankee Buccaneer* 1952; *Chief Crazy Horse, To Hell and Back* 1955; *Never Say Goodbye, Toy Tiger, Away All Boats* 1956; *Lafayette Escadrille* 1958; *Hell to Eternity* 1960; *Dondi, Ring of Fire, King of the Roaring Twenties* (as gangster Arnold Rothstein), *Man-Trap* 1961; *Belle Sommers* 1962; *My Six Loves* 1963; *Warning Shot* 1967; *The Green Berets, The Shoes of the Fisherman* 1968; *Where It's At, Generation, Marooned* 1969; *Jacqueline Susann's Once Is Not Enough* 1975; *Two-Minute Warning* 1976; *Warhead, The Swiss Conspiracy, Golden Rendezvous* 1977; *Sono stato un Agente CIA/Covert Action* (It.) 1978; *Inchon* (released posthumously) 1982.

Japan. Although it remained virtually unknown in the West until the early 50s, the Japanese cinema developed rapidly from the very earliest days of the invention of the medium. Following successful demonstrations of the Edison and Lumière products in 1896–97, local entrepreneurs began making their own short films, initially simple recordings of street scenes and photographed highlights of Kabuki plays. Production became centered mainly in two cities, Tokyo and the ancient capital of Kyoto. Generally, studios in Tokyo specialized in films about contemporary life, known collectively as *gendai-geki,* while in Kyoto the prevailing genre was *jidai-geki,* or period costume films.

Contrary to the experience of the US and Europe, where films were held in disrepute in the early silent days, Japanese cinema gained respectability from the start, drawing the intelligentsia as well as working-class audiences to the movie theaters. Ironically, this became a handicap rather than a blessing. While the Americans and Europeans were forced to develop a film style distinct from the tradition of the theater, Japanese filmmakers, appealing to basically the same audiences that frequented the theaters, found themselves compelled to adhere to the traditions of the stage play and the novel. It was not until the early 20s that the Japanese cinema began developing its own distinct style. One of the by-products of the theatrical tradition was the institution of the *benshi,* or storytellers, who narrated the early silent films as they unrolled. Another theatrical tradition that was incorporated into the early cinema was the employment of female impersonators (*oyama*) to play feminine roles. This fidelity to some of the conventions of the stage retarded the development of technical and stylistic innovations in the Japanese cinema.

A gradual change began to be discerned in the years following the end of WW I. One of the first filmmakers to break with the old traditions was Norimasa Kaeriyama, the author of the book *The Production and Philosophy of Motion Picture Drama,* who in his films replaced female impersonators with real women. He also introduced into his productions a greater sense of realism by filming on location, rather than in the confines of a studio, and a greater variety of shots and camera setups which set his films apart from the stagy Japanese movies of the period. But he met with great resistance when he tried to do away with the narrating services of the *benshi,* who managed to hang on to their jobs in the Japanese cinema even after the advent of sound.

It took an earthquake to shake the foundations of the early Japanese cinema and bring about some crucial changes. The quake of September 1923 leveled a third of Tokyo and most of Yokohama, devastating many of Japan's studios and movie theaters. The immediate result was the suspension of production, followed by the dispersal of some film companies to other cities, especially Kyoto. During the lull in production, many foreign films were shown in the theaters, influencing the tastes of audiences and encouraging filmmakers to try new ways. The impact of the earthquake on peoples' lives also created a new moral atmosphere that made the public susceptible to modern social ideas. This gave the impetus to the rise of a new film genre, the *shomin-geki,* the motion picture dealing with lower-middle-class life. Among the leading proponents of the *shomin-geki* during the silent period were Minoro Murata (*Seisaku's Wife,* 1924; *The Street Juggler,* 1925), Kenji MIZOGUCHI (*In the Ruins,* 1923; *Street Sketches,* 1925; *Tokyo March,* 1929), Heinosuke GOSHO (*Tricky Girl, The Village Bride,* both 1927), Yasujiro Shimazu (*Father,* 1923), Yasujiro OZU (*Dreams of Youth,* 1928), and Teinosuke KINUGASA (*Jujiro/Crossroads/Crossways/The Shadows of the Yoshiwara,* 1928). Kinugasa's film was the first Japanese production to be commercially exploited in Europe.

One essential characteristic of Japanese culture, including cinema, is the tendency to regard history as a living phenomenon and to contemplate and show events of the past as though they were contemporary. It was thus possible for socially committed directors to express their criticism of certain aspects of the current established order under the guise of historic themes, as Daisuke ITO did in such films as *The Servant* (1927), *Ooka's Trial* (1928), and *Man-Slashing Horse-Piercing Sword* (1929).

The transition to sound was slow and gradual in Japan. One of the main reasons was the resistance of the *benshi,* who sometimes resorted to violence in their battle to protect their jobs. It was not until 1931 that the first full talkie, Gosho's *The Neighbor's Wife and Mine,* was released. For several years after the introduction of sound, many silent films continued to be made, with the *benshi* providing the narrative from behind the screen. During the 30s the Japanese cinema developed into a thriving industry, with annual feature output reaching some 400 by 1931 and 500 by 1940. This astonishingly high rate of production, unparalleled by any industry but Hollywood's, was largely the result of Japan's cultural and linguistic isolation in the family of nations. Few Japanese films reached foreign screens, and only a small proportion of films shown in Japan were of Western origin. This isolation forced the national industry into self-sufficiency, demanding a constant local supply for the approximately 2,500 motion picture theaters that existed in Japan at the outbreak of WW II.

Humanism and social realism were becoming increasingly important features of the Japanese cinema of the 30s. Notable examples were Mizoguchi's *And Yet They Go On* (1931), *Osaka Elegy* (1936), and *Sisters of the Gion* (1936); Ozu's *The Only Son* (1936); and Tomu UCHIDA's *Theater of Life* (1936), *The Naked Town* (1937), and *The Earth* (1939). Impressive achievements during the 30s in the historical costume genre included Kinugasa's *Before Dawn* (1931), *The Loyal 47 Ronin* (1932), and *Two Stone Lanterns* (1933); INAGAKI's *A Sword and the Sumo Ring* (1931) and *Musashi Miyamoto/Samurai* (1940); Mansaku Itami's *Kakita Akanishi* (1936); and Sadao Yamanaka's *The Life of Bangoku* (1932) and *Humanity and Paper Balloons* (1937).

Both the realist and period films shared a trait that has probably been the most characteristic feature of the Japanese cinema: the knack of capturing mood and atmosphere, of presenting the environment as an extension of man. Another national characteristic, the tendency to accept the world as it is, made it difficult for the Japanese to utilize film to advantage as a tool of propaganda before and during WW II. Kimisaburo YOSHIMURA's *The Story of Tank Commander Nishizumi* (1940) is considered Japan's most successful war film.

During the 30s the Japanese film industry was consolidated into a monolithic structure, with only five companies virtually controlling the country's entire output. After the outbreak of the war in the Pacific the number of companies authorized to produce films was reduced to three, each restricted to the production of only two features a month. The devastation of the war and shortage of films forced many motion picture theaters to close, reducing the number from 2,500 in 1940 to 850 at the end of hostilities. Considering the difficulties, postwar recovery was remarkably rapid. After Japan's surrender, production was briefly at a virtual standstill. During the last five months of 1945 only 12 features were turned out by the three major studios, Shochiku, Toho, and Daiei. Motion pictures had to be submitted to censorship by the Allied Authorities, who banned films reflecting the feudal spirit of old Japan and imposed on the industry themes of peace and democracy. The unstable economic conditions also discouraged recovery. Fortunately, however, there was not much else available in terms of entertainment, and the public began streaming to the cinemas as it never had before. Attendance in 1946 reached 733 million, compared to the prewar annual average of 400 million. Many of the old theaters reopened, and new ones were built to accommodate the crowds. By 1950 the number of operating theaters had nearly reached its prewar mark of 2,500.

Recovery was also impeded by the purge of some 40 film industry leaders as war criminals in 1947 (they were restored to their posts in 1950) and by recurrent labor unrest, which at one point resulted in suspension of production at Toho. But by 1950 two additional major production companies had entered the business, Shin-Toho and Toei. By the mid-50s annual feature output had reached its prewar level of 500. The many American films shown in Japan during the Occupation and its process of "democratizing" the country had some influence on local filmmakers, some of whom even began introducing the Western kiss into their films. The younger directors were the more susceptible to foreign influences. But on the whole the Japanese cinema has retained its unique flavor and traditional style. Postwar problems of reconstruction were depicted realistically by such veterans as Mizoguchi, Ozu, and Gosho as well as by such newcomers as Akira KUROSAWA, Keisuke KINOSHITA, Kozaburo YOSHIMURA, Tadashi IMAI, Heideo Sekigawa, Kaneto SHINDO, and Kon ICHIKAWA. Before long, the period films once again enjoyed a revival, capped by the great international success of Kurosawa's *Rashomon* (1950).

The visually striking *Rashomon,* winner of the top prize at the 1951 Venice Film Festival, astonished Western audiences with its rich imagery, psychological insight, intriguing ambiguity, and the excellent performances by Toshiro Mifune, Machiko Kyo, Masayuki Mori, and Takashi Shimura. Its commercial as well as critical success opened Western theaters to a steady stream of other Japanese productions, exposing uninitiated audiences to the surprising wealth of a culture about which they had known little or nothing.

Among the many Japanese films that have since been exhibited widely in the West are Kurosawa's *The Idiot* (1951), *Ikiru/To Live* (1952), *Seven Samurai/The Magnificent Seven* (1954), *The Throne of Blood* (1957), *The Lower Depths* (1957), *The Hidden Fortress* (1958), *The Bad Sleep Well* (1960), *Yojimbo* (1961), *Sanjuro* (1962), *High and Low* (1963), *Red Beard* (1965), and *Dersu Uzala* (1975); Susumu HANI's *Children Who Draw* (doc., 1956), *She and He* (1963), and *Bwana Toshi* (1965); Kon Ichikawa's *The Burmese Harp* (1956), *Enjo* (1958), *Odd Obsession* (1959), *Fires on the Plain* (1959), *An Actor's Revenge* (1963), *Alone on the Pacific* (1963), and *Tokyo Olympiad* (1965); Imai's *Bushido* (1963) and *The Time of Reckoning* (1968); Hiroshi Inagaki's *Samurai* (1954), *Secret Scrolls* (1957), *Rickshaw Man* (1958), *Young Swordsman* (1963), *The Rabble* (1964), *Whirlwind* (1964), *Kojiro* (1967), and *The Ambush* (1970); Keisuke Kinoshita's *Carmen Comes Home* (1951), *She Was Like a Wild Chrysanthemum* (1955), and *Ballad of Narayama* (1958); Teinosuke Kinugasa's *Gate of Hell* (1953); Masaki KOBAYASHI's *The Human Condition* trilogy (1959–61), *Harakiri* (1962), *Kwaidan* (1964), and *Rebellion* (1967); Yasuzo MASUMURA's *Passion* (1964) and *The Wife of Seishu Hanaoka* (1967); Zenzo Matsumaya's *My Hobo* (1960), *Happiness of Us Alone* (1961) and *Could I but Live* (1964); Kenji Misumi's *Buddha* (1963), *Showdown for Zatoichi* (1967), and *Devil's Temple* (1969); Kenji Mizoguchi's *The Life of Oharu* (1952), *Ugetsu* (1953), *Sansho the Bailiff* (1954), *Yang Kwei-Fei* (1955), and *Street of Shame* (1956); Ko Nakahira's *The Hunter's Diary* (1964); Mikio NARUSE's *When a Woman Ascends the Stairs* (1960), *Lonely Lane* (1962), *A Woman's Life* (1963), *Yearning* (1964), and *Moment of Terror* (1966); Nagisa OSHIMA's *Naked Youth* (1960), *Boy* (1969), and *In the Realm of the Senses* (1976); Yasujiro Ozu's *Early Summer* (1951), *Tea and Rice* (1952), *Tokyo Story* (1953), *Early Spring* (1956), *Ohayo/Good Morning* (1959), *Floating Weeds* (1959), *Early Autumn* (1961), and *An Autumn Afternoon* (1962); Hideo Sekigawa's *Hiroshima* (1953); Minoru Shibuya's *Mr. Radish and Mr. Carrot/Twilight Path* (1964); Kaneto Shindo's *Children of Hiroshima* (1952), *The Island* (1961), *Onibaba/The Demon/The Hole* (1964), and *Lost Sex* (1966); Masahiro SHINODA's *Youth in Fury* (1960), *The Assassin* (1964), *Double Suicide* (1969), and *Buraikan* (1970); Hiroshi TESHIGHARA's *Woman in the Dunes* (1964) and *The Face of Another* (1966); Shiro TOYODA's *Wild Geese/The Mistress* (1953), *The Twilight Story* (1960), *The Diplomat's Mansion* (1961), *Illusion of Blood* (1965), and *Portrait of Hell* (1969); and Kozaburo Yoshimura's *Before Dawn* (1953) and *The House of Sleeping Virgins* (1968).

A genre of Japanese postwar cinema that enjoyed some box-office success in the West is the science-fiction action film, noted for its imaginative special effects. Popular films in this genre include Ishiro Honda's *Godzilla* (1954) and its sequels, *Rodan* (1957), *The Mysterians* (1957), *Mothra* (1961), *Gorath* (1962), *Ghidrah* (1965), and *Destroy All Monsters* (1968). These films owed their inventiveness to effects specialist Eiji TSUBURAYA.

After a decade of unparalleled prosperity, the Japanese film industry began a retrenchment in the 60s which escalated in the 70s into a full-scale crisis. The main villain was TV, the competition of which progressively diminished attendance at the movies. In a futile attempt to reverse the trend, the major production companies retreated into the safety of formula entertainment films, while serious filmmaking became more and more the realm of the smaller independent companies that were now entering the field in large numbers. In 1975 the share of imported films on the Japanese screens for the first time reached the 50 percent mark, with American productions leading the invasions, especially with spectacular disaster movies, which found appreciative audiences in Japan.

The alarming scarcity of locally made high-quality films induced the Japanese government to create in 1972 a fund for monetary rewards to productions of artistic merit. By the 80s and 90s, Japanese cinema was back on the upswing, with new films by the ageless master Kurosawa (*Ran*, 1985; *Akira Kurosawa's Dreams*, 1990) and contributions from a host of newcomers, including Sogo ISHII (*The Crazy Family/Gyakufunsha Kazoku*, 1984), Juzo ITAMI (*Tampopo*, 1986; *Minbo-no onna/The Gangster's Moll* 1992), Fran Rubel Kuzui (*Tokyo Pop*, 1988), Takehiro Nakajima (*Kyoshu*, 1988), Totsuke Sato (*Banana Shoot*, 1989), Shinya Tsukamoto (*Tetsuo: The Iron Man*, 1992), Yoji Yamada (*Musoko/My Sons*, 1992), and Kiju Yoshida (*Arashi Ga Oka*, 1988). The Japanese tradition of animation has continued with such diverse animated features as the World War II drama *A Tombstone for the Fireflies* (Isao Takahata, 1988), the comic-book-based *Akira* (Katsuhiro Otomo, 1989) and the erotic action film *The Professional* (Osamu Dezaki and Carl Macek, 1992). Still, American imports dominate the Japanese box office.

Jarman, Claude, Jr. Actor. Born on Sept. 27, 1934, in Nashville, Tenn. *ed.* Vanderbilt U. A child star of the late 40s, he won a special Academy Award for his film debut in *The Yearling* (1946). He also played a memorable role in *Intruder in the Dust* (1949) but gradually faded into obscurity. As an adult, he served as executive director of the San Francisco Film Festival and was executive producer of the rock-concert feature film *Fillmore* (1972). He is also the manager of the San Francisco Opera House.

FILMS: *The Yearling* 1946; *High Barbaree* 1947; *The Sun Comes Up, Roughshod, Intruder in the Dust* 1949; *The Outriders, Rio Grande* 1950; *Inside Straight* 1951; *Hangman's Knot* 1952; *Fair Wind to Java* 1953; *The Great Locomotive Chase* 1956.

Jarman, Derek. Director. *b.* 1942, England. *d.* 1994 of AIDS. Innovative, outspoken British filmmaker whose homosexuality was central to his work. An irreverent maverick, he took on the establishment with abandon through vivid imagery. He exemplified the "queer film" movement with his confrontational themes and eroticized portrayals of male-to-male sex (see GAY AND LESBIAN CINEMA). He wrote or collaborated on his own scripts. His books include *Dancing Ledge* and *The Last of England* and two memoirs, *Modern Nature* and *At Your Own Risk.*

FILMS: *Sebastiane* (co-dir.) 1976; *Jubilee* 1978; *The Tempest* 1979; *In the Shadow of the Sun* (medium-length) 1980; *The Angelic Conversation* 1985; *Caravaggio* 1986; *Aria* ("Louise" segment), *The Last of England* (also co-phot.) 1987; *War Requiem* 1989; *The Garden* 1990; *Edward II* 1991; *Blue, Glitterbug, There We Are John, Wittgenstein* 1993; *Love Undefeated: Conversations with Derek Jarman* (as himself), *Memorial Tribute* 1994.

Jarmusch, Jim. Director. Born on Jan. 22, 1953, in Akron, Ohio, of Czech-German-French-Irish extraction. After his junior year at Columbia, he completed his undergraduate studies in Paris, then attended the NYU Film School, where he was a student and teaching assistant of director Nicholas RAY in a directing workshop. He made a promising, if awkward, directing debut with *Permanent Vacation* (1981), a 16 mm small-budget minisaga of an alienated youth in Manhattan. He achieved much greater success with his next feature, *Stranger Than Paradise* (1984), an eccentric comedy he had expanded from his 30-minute prize-winning short, *New World.* It won the Camera d'Or prize for best new director at Cannes and the Golden Leopard as best film at the Locarno Festival. Jarmusch was awarded the best artistic contribution prize at Cannes for *Mystery Train* (1989), another slice-of-life comedy typical of his quirky style. He writes his own scripts and occasionally appears as an actor in the films of other directors.

FEATURE FILMS: *Underground U.S.A.* (sound only) 1980; *Permanent Vacation* (also prod., sc., edit.) 1981; *Stranger Than Paradise* (also sc., edit.), *American Autobahn* (act. only) 1984; *Down by Law* (also sc.) 1986; *Candy Mountain* (act. only), *Straight to Hell* (act. only) 1987; *Mystery Train* (also sc.), *Leningrad Cowboys Go America* (act. only) 1989; *Night on Earth* 1991; *In the Soup* (act. only) 1992; *Blue in the Face* (act. only) 1994; *Dead Man* (dir., sc.), *Sling Blade* (act. only) 1996; *Year of the Horse* 1997.

Jarre, Maurice. Composer. Born on Sept. 13, 1924, in Lyons, France. *ed.* Paris Conservatoire. He wrote music for the concert hall and served as musical director of the Théâtre National Populaire in Paris before beginning his association with the cinema, scoring the short films of RESNAIS, FRANJU, and other French directors. Working on feature films since the late 50s, he has been noted for his restrained sound, even for epic films with stereophonic reproduction. Jarre favors the guitar and other stringed instruments. During his earlier period in France, he successfully blended natural noises into his scores. Since the early 60s he has been working on major international films. In the 80s he worked mainly in Hollywood. Winner of Academy Awards for the scores of *Lawrence of Arabia* (1962), *Doctor Zhivago* (1965), and *A Passage to India* (1984), all composed for director David Lean. Formerly married to actress Dany SAVAL. His son, Jean-Michel Jarre, is a popular composer of synthesizer music.

FILMS INCLUDE: Shorts—*Hôtel des Invalides* 1952; *Toute la Mémoire du Monde* 1956. Features—*La Tête contre les Murs/The Keepers* 1959; *Les Yeux sans Visage/The Horror Chamber of Dr. Faustus, Crack in the Mirror* (US) 1960; *The Big Gamble* (US), *Le Temps du Ghetto/The Witnesses* 1961; *Les Oliviers de la Justice/The Olive Trees of Justice, Thérèse Desqueyroux/Therese, The Longest Day* (US), *Cybèle ou les Dimanches de Ville d'Avray/Sundays and Cybele, Lawrence of Arabia* (US) 1962; *Mourir à Madrid/To Die in Madrid* 1963; *Judex, Behold a Pale Horse* (US), *Le Train/The Train* (Fr./US/It.) 1964; *The Collector* (US/UK), *Doctor Zhivago* (US) 1965; *Paris Brûle-t-il?/Is Paris Burning?* (Fr./US), *The Professionals* (US), *Grand Prix* (US), *Gambit* (US) 1966; *La Nuit des Generaux/The Night of the Generals* (Fr./UK) 1967; *Villa Rides* (US), *5 Card Stud* (US), *Barbarella, The Fixer* (US), *Isadora/The Loves of Isadora* (UK) 1968; *The Extraordinary Seaman* (US), *La Cauduta degli Dei/Götterdämmerung/The Damned* (It./Ger.), *Topaz* (US) 1969; *The Only Game in Town* (US), *El Condor* (US), *Ryan's Daughter* (UK) 1970; *Plaza Suite* (US), *Soleil rouge/Red Sun* 1971; *Pope Joan* (UK), *The Effect of Gamma Rays on Man-in-the-Moon Marigolds* (US), *The Life and Times of Judge Roy Bean* (US) 1972; *The Mackintosh Man* (UK), *Ash Wednesday* (US/UK) 1973; *The Island at the Top of the World* (US) 1974; *Mandingo* (US), *Posse* (US), *The Man Who Would Be King* (UK) 1975; *Shout at the Devil* (UK), *The Message/Mohammed Messenger of God* (UK), *The Last Tycoon* (US) 1976; *The Prince and the Pauper/Crossed Swords* (UK), *March or Die* (UK) 1977; *Die Blechtrommel/The Tin Drum* (Ger./Fr./Yug./Pol.) 1979; *Resurrection* (US) 1980; *Lion of the Desert* (Lyb./UK), *Die Falschung/Circle of Deceit* (Ger./Fr.), *Taps* (US) 1981; *Firefox* (US) 1982; *The Year of Living Dangerously* (Austral.) 1983; *Top Secret!* (US), *Dreamscape* (US), *A Passage to India* (UK) 1984; *Mad Max: Beyond Thunderdome* (Austral.), *Witness* (US), *The Bride* (US), *Enemy Mine* (US) 1985; *The Mosquito Coast* (US) 1986; *No Way Out* (US), *Fatal Attraction* (US) 1987; *Moon Over Parador* (US), *Gorillas in the Mist* (US) 1988; *Chances Are* (US), *Dead Poets Society* (US), *Enemies, a Love Story* (US) 1989; *Jacob's Ladder* (US), *Almost an Angel* (US), *Ghost* (US), *After Dark My Sweet* (US) 1990; *Fires Within, Only the Lonely* (US) 1991; *School Ties* (US), *Wildfire* 1992; *Fearless* (US), *Mr. Jones* (US), *A Walk in the Clouds* (US) 1995; *Sunchaser* (US) 1996.

Järrel, Stig. Actor. Born in 1910, in Malmberget, Sweden. A veteran of Swedish stage, radio, and TV, he appeared in scores of Swedish films but is still best remembered for his masterful portrayal of the sadistic schoolmaster in Sjöberg's *Torment/Frenzy* (1944). In 1947 he directed two films, *Evil Eyes* and *The Sixth Commandment,* appearing in both.

FILMS INCLUDE: *Walpurgis Night* 1935; *We Two* 1939; *Torment/Frenzy* 1944; *In the Waiting Room of Death/Interlude, Bad Eggs/Incorrigible* 1946; *It's My Model/Affairs of a Model, Evil Eyes* (also dir.), *The Sixth Commandment* (also dir.) 1947; *Sin* 1948; *Pippi Longstocking, The Street* 1949; *Helen of Troy* 1951; *Defiance, Say It with Flowers* 1952; *Paradise* 1955; *Seventh Heaven, Children of the Night* 1956; *The Devil's Eye* 1960; *Pleasure Garden* 1961.

Jarrico, Paul. Screenwriter. Born on Jan. 12, 1915, in Los Angeles. In Hollywood from the late 30s, he was nominated for an Academy Award for his original screenplay for *Tom, Dick, and Harry* (1941). His career was cut short by blacklisting after he was identified as a member of the Communist Party in the hearings by the House Un-American Activities Committee. He then produced *Salt of the Earth* (1954) a union-sponsored drama about the appalling conditions of striking coal miners in New Mexico.

FILMS INCLUDE: *No Time to Marry* 1938; *Beauty for the Asking* 1939; *The Face Behind the Mask, Tom Dick and Harry* 1941; *Thousands Cheer* 1943; *Song of Russia* 1944; *The Search* 1948; *Not Wanted* 1949; *The White Tower* 1950; *Salt of the Earth* (prod. only) 1954; *The Girl Most Likely* (uncredited screenplay basis, *Tom, Dick, and Harry*) 1957; *Le Rouble a Deux Faces/The Day the Hot Line Got Hot/The Hot Line* (Fr./Sp.) 1969; *The Day That Shook the World* (Yug./Czech.) 1976; *Messenger of Death* 1988.

Jarrott, Charles. Director. Born on June 6, 1927, in London. The son of a businessman and a former singer-dancer, he entered show business after returning from WW II service in the Far East. In 1949 he joined the Nottingham Repertory Theatre as a stage director and juvenile lead. In 1953 he went with another company on a tour of Canada and remained there as a resident leading actor of the Ottawa Theatre. In 1955 he moved to Toronto, where he made his TV acting debut opposite Katharine Blake, whom he later married. Two years later he began directing for Canadian TV, then worked also in Britain as a stage, TV, and eventually film director. After scoring impressive successes with the historical pageants *Anne of the Thousand Days* (1969) and *Mary, Queen of Scots* (1972), he faltered badly with the expensive Hollywood remake of *Lost Horizon* (1973) and his career never fully recovered from the setback.

FILMS: *Time to Remember* 1962; *Anne of the Thousand Days* 1969; *Mary Queen of Scots* 1971; *Lost Horizon* 1973; *The Dove* 1974; *Escape from the Dark/The Littlest Horse Thieves* 1976; *The Other Side of Midnight* 1977; *The Last Flight of Noah's Ark* 1980; *Condorman* 1981; *The Amateur* 1982; *The Boy in Blue* 1986.

Jasny, Wojtech. Director. Born on Nov. 30, 1925, in Kelc, Moravia, Czechoslovakia. A leading figure of the postwar Czech cinema. The son of a rural school principal and a math teacher, he attended Charles University in Prague, where he studied philosophy and Russian, but after one year transferred to the film school of the Prague Academy of Music and Performing Arts (FAMU), becoming one of the department's first graduates. After turning out a graduation feature in 1950, in collaboration with classmate Karel KACHYŇA, Jasny was assigned to the Army Film School in Prague as a director-cameraman of documentary shorts. In that capacity, he traveled to China, where he shot several films (again teaming up with Kachyňa), for which he won a Mao Tse-tung award as well as the Czechoslovak State prize. Demobilized after six years with the rank of major, Jasny joined the Barrandov Studios as a feature director. During the 60s he established an international reputation with a number of freshly styled, intimately personal films. His *That Cat/When the Cat Comes/Cassandra Cat* won a Special Jury Prize at the 1963 Cannes Festival, among other awards. *All Good Citizens/All My Countrymen,* banned in Czechoslovakia, shared the *mis-en-scène* prize at Cannes in 1969. That year he bid farewell to his native country with the 22-minute silent short *Czech Rhapsody,* designed for exhibition at the Osaka World's Fair. Stifled by the oppressive mood that hindered creativity in the wake of the "Prague Spring," Jasny uprooted his family and migrated to Yugoslavia in 1970. He then moved on to Salzburg, becoming an Austrian citizen in 1972. He continued directing films and TV programs, mainly in Germany, but his work in exile lacked the warmth and spark of his best native films. He also taught film at various European cities and in 1984 became a visiting professor at Columbia University in New York.

FEATURE FILMS: *It's Not Always Cloudy* (graduation film; co-dir. with Karel Kachyňa) 1950; *Everything Ends Tonight* (co-dir. with Kachyňa) 1954; *September Nights* 1957; *Desire* 1958; *I Survived Certain Death* 1960; *Pilgrimage to the Virgin Mary* 1961; *That Cat/One Day a Cat/Cassandra Cat/When the Cat Comes* 1963; *The Pipes* 1965; *All Good Citizens/All My Good Countrymen/Moravian Chronicle* 1968; *Ansichten eines Clowns/The Clown/The Clown's Opinions* (Ger.) 1975; *Fluchtversch/Escape Attempt* (Aus./Ger.) 1976; *Die Rücehr/The Return* (Aus.) 1978; *Sebevrah/The Suicide* 1984.

Jason, Leigh. Director. *b.* Leigh Jacobson, July 26, 1904, New York City. *d.* 1979. *ed.* Columbia. Taught at UCLA before entering films as an electrician in 1924, becoming a screenwriter in 1926. Changing his name from Jacobson to Jason, he began directing in 1928. He turned out many shorts and routine B features, mainly thrillers and light romances, through the early 50s, when he moved on to TV.

FEATURE FILMS: *The Price of Fear* 1928; *Wolves of the City, Eyes of the Underworld* (also co-story, co-sc.), *The Tip-Off, The Body Punch* 1929; *High Gear* (also co-story, co-sc.) 1933; *Love on a Bet, The Bride Walks Out* 1936; *That Girl from Paris, New Faces of 1937, Wise Girl* 1937; *The Mad Miss Manton* 1938; *The Flying Irishman, Career* 1939; *Model Wife* (also prod., story), *Three Girls About Town* 1941; *Lady for a Night* 1942; *Dangerous Blondes* 1943; *Nine Girls, Carolina Blues* 1944; *Meet Me on Broadway* 1946; *Lost Honeymoon, Out of the Blue, Man from Texas* 1947; *Okinawa* 1952.

Jason, Will. Director. *b.* June 23, 1910, New York City. *d.* 1970. In films in various capacities from age 13, he wrote the musical score for several screen productions before turning director of B pictures. Also produced some of his films.

FILMS INCLUDE (as director): *The Soul of a Monster* 1944; *Eve Knew Her Apples, Ten Cents a Dance* 1945; *Blonde Alibi* 1946; *Rusty Leads the Way* 1948; *Kazan* 1949; *Everybody's Dancing* 1950; *Chain of Circumstances, Harlem Globetrotters* 1951; *Thief of Damascus* 1952.

Jasset, Victorin. Director. *b.* 1862, Fumay, France. *d.* 1913. Formerly a sculptor-painter and stage designer and impresario, he began making French films in 1905, preceding FEUILLADE as a pioneer of the serial film. His most important contributions were as associate director to Alice GUY-BLACHÉ in *La Vie du Christ/The Life of Christ* (in 25 scenes; 1905) and as director of the serials *Nick Carter* (1906, 1909, 1911), *Rifle Bill—Le Roi de la Prairie* (1908), and *Zigomar* (1911). He was criticized for introducing female nudity into his pictures. Most of his films have been lost.

FILMS INCLUDE: *La Vie du Christ/The Life of Christ* (assoc. dir.), *La Esmeralda* 1906; *Rêve d'un Fumeur d'Opium, Nick Carter* (serial) 1906; *Rifle Bill—Le Roi de la Prairie* (serial) 1908; *Morgan le Pirate* 1909; *Herodiade* 1910; *Zigomar* (serial), *La Passante* 1911; *Les Batailles de la Vie* (serial) 1912; *Protea* (serial) 1913.

Jaubert, Maurice. Composer. *b.* Jan. 3, 1900, Nice, France. *d.* 1940. The most important creator of music for French films in the 30s. A former lawyer, he composed bright and sensitive scores for many of the major films of the period. He was killed in action in WW II.

FILMS INCLUDE: *Le Petit Chaperon Rouge* 1929; *Zero de Conduite, L'Affaire est dans le Sac, Quatorze Juillet* 1932; *L'Atalante* 1933; *Le Dernier Milliardaire* 1934; *Mayerling* 1936; *Drôle de Drame, Un Carnet de Bal* 1937; *Altitude 3200, Quai des Brumes, La Fin du Jour, Hôtel du Nord* 1938; *Le Jour se lève* 1939.

Jayston, Michael. Actor. Born Michael James, on Oct. 29, 1935, in Nottingham, England. *ed.* Nottingham U. Leading man and supporting player of the British stage, TV, and films.

Formerly an apprentice accountant, he trained for the stage at the Guildhall School of Music and Drama, and made his professional debut in 1962. In films sporadically since the late 60s. His film appearances have been few but distinguished.

FILMS INCLUDE: *A Midsummer Night's Dream* (as Demetrius) 1968; *Cromwell* 1970; *Nicholas and Alexandra* (as Czar Nikolai II of Russia) 1971; *Follow Me/The Public Eye, Alice's Adventures in Wonderland* 1972; *Bequest to the Nation/The Nelson Affair, Tales That Witness Madness, The Homecoming* 1973; *Craze, The Internecine Project* 1974; *Dominique* 1978; *Zulu Dawn* 1979.

Jeakins, Dorothy. Costume designer. Born in 1914, in California. *ed.* Otis Art Institute. In Hollywood from the late 40s, following stage experience, she designed gowns and costumes for many major films, sharing Academy Awards for *Joan of Arc* (1948), *Samson and Delilah* (1950), and *The Night of the Iguana* (1964).

FILMS INCLUDE: *Joan of Arc* 1948; *Samson and Delilah* 1949–50; *The Greatest Show on Earth, My Cousin Rachel, The Outcasts of Poker Flat* 1952; *Niagara, Titanic* 1952; *Three Coins in the Fountain* 1954; *Friendly Persuasion, The Ten Commandments* 1956; *South Pacific* 1958; *Let's Make Love* 1960; *The Children's Hour* 1961; *All Fall Down, The Music Man* 1962; *The Best Man, The Night of the Iguana* 1964; *The Sound of Music* 1965; *Hawaii* 1966; *Reflections in a Golden Eye* 1967; *Finian's Rainbow* 1968; *True Grit* 1969; *Little Big Man* 1970; *Fat City* 1972; *The Way We Were* 1973; *Young Frankenstein* 1974; *The Hindenburg, The Yakuza* 1975; *Audrey Rose* 1977; *The Betsy* 1978; *North Dallas Forty* 1979; *The Postman Always Rings Twice, On Golden Pond* 1981; *The Dead* 1987.

Jean, Gloria. Actress, singer. Born Gloria Jean Schoonover, on Apr. 14, 1926, in Buffalo, N.Y. A professional vaudeville and radio vocalist from age three, she was signed by Universal in 1939 and groomed as a successor to the studio's singing child star, Deanna DURBIN, who was gradually being switched to ingenue roles. Jean had a considerable following among young film fans in the early 40s but never quite achieved Durbin's popularity and fared poorly when she later attempted a transition to adult roles. After retiring from the screen in the early 60s she was employed as a receptionist and switchboard operator with a California cosmetics firm. Her sister, Lois Schoonover (1928–85), was her double and stand-in in several films.

FILMS: *The Under-Pup* 1939; *If I Had My Way, A Little Bit of Heaven* 1940; *Never Give a Sucker an Even Break* 1941; *What's Cookin', Get Hep to Love* 1942; *When Johnny Comes Marching Home, It Comes Up Love, Mister Big, Moonlight in Vermont* 1943; *Follow the Boys, Pardon My Rhythm, Ghost Catchers, The Reckless Age, Destiny* 1944; *I'll Remember April, River Gang, Easy to Look At* 1945; *Copacabana* 1947; *I Surrender Dear* 1948; *An Old-Fashioned Girl, Manhattan Angel* 1949; *There's a Girl in My Heart* 1950; *Air Strike* 1955; *The Ladies' Man* 1961; *The Madcaps* 1963.

Jeanmaire, Zizi (Renée). Dancer, actress. Born on Apr. 29, 1924, in Paris. A ballet dancer from age nine, she later became prima ballerina of Les Ballets des Champs Elysées and wife of its leader, Roland Petit. She had a brief career as a leading lady in American and French musical films.

FILMS INCLUDE: *Hans Christian Andersen* (US) 1952; *Anything Goes* (US), *Folies-Bergère* 1956; *Charmants Garçons* 1957; *Guinguette* 1958; *Un Deux Trois/Les Collants noirs/Black Tights* 1960.

Jeans, Isabel. Actress. *b.* Sept. 16, 1891, London. *d.* 1985. On the London stage from 1909, she also appeared in several UK and US films, usually playing refined ladies, initially in leads and later character roles. Once married to Claude RAINS, then to playwright-screenwriter Gilbert Wakefield.

FILMS INCLUDE: In the UK—*The Profligate* 1917; *Tilly of Bloomsbury* 1921; *The Triumph of the Rat* 1926; *Downhill* 1927; *Easy Virtue* 1928; *Sally Bishop* 1932; *The Love Affair of the Dictator/Loves of a Dictator, The Crouching Beast* 1935. In the US—*Tovarich* 1937; *Fools for Scandal, Garden of the Moon, Secrets of an Actress, Youth Takes a Fling, Hard to Get* 1938; *Good Girls Go to Paris, Man About Town* 1939; *Suspicion* 1941; *Great Day* (UK) 1945; *Gigi* 1958; *A Breath of Scandal* 1960; *Heavens Above!* (UK) 1963; *The Magic Christian* (UK) 1969.

Jeans, Ursula. Actress. *b.* Ursula McMinn, May 5, 1906, Simla, India, to British parents. *d.* 1973. Primarily a stage actress, she appeared sporadically in British films from the early 20s. Her second husband was actor Roger LIVESEY.

FILMS INCLUDE: *The Gypsy Cavalier* 1922; *The Virgin Queen* 1923; *S.O.S.* 1928; *The Love Habit* 1931; *The Crooked Lady* 1932; *Cavalcade, Friday the 13th* 1933; *Dark Journey, Storm in a Teacup* 1937; *The Life and Death of Colonel Blimp* 1943; *Mr. Emmanuel* 1944; *Gaiety George/Showtime* 1946; *The Woman in the Hall* 1947; *The Weaker Sex* 1948; *The Dam Busters* 1955; *North West Frontier/Flame Over India* 1959; *The Green Helmet* 1961; *The Battle of the Villa Fiorita* 1965.

Jeanson, Henri. Screenwriter. *b.* Mar. 6, 1900, Paris. *d.* 1970. A former actor, journalist, film critic, and playwright, he wrote witty dialogue and screenplays for French films from the early 30s. Also directed one film, *Lady Paname* (1950).

FILMS INCLUDE: *La Dame de chez Maxim's* 1933; *Mister Flow/Compliments of Mr. Flow* 1936; *Pépé le Moko, Un Carnet de Bal* 1937; *Entrée des Artistes/The Curtain Rises, Le Patriote/The Mad Emperor, Hôtel du Nord* 1938; *La nuit fantastique* 1942; *Carmen* (release delayed from 1943), *Boule de Suif/Angel and Sinner* 1945; *Un Revenant/A Lover's Return* 1946; *Les Maudits/The Damned* 1947; *Les Amoureux sont seuls au Monde/Monelle, La Vie en Rose/Loves of Colette* 1948; *Aux Yeux du Souvenir/Souvenir, Aux Royaume des Cieux/The Sinners* 1949; *Lady Paname* (also dir.), *Meurtres/Three Sinners* 1950; *Le Garçon sauvage/Savage Triangle* 1951; *Fanfan la Tulipe/Fanfan the Tulip, La Minute de Vérité/The Moment of Truth, La Fête à Henriette/Holiday for Henrietta* 1952; *Madame Du Barry* 1954; *Nana* 1955; *Marguerite de la Nuit* 1956; *Pot-Bouille* 1957; *Montparnasse 19/Modigliani of Montparnasse, Maxime* 1958; *Marie Octobre, La Vache et le Prisonnier/The Cow and I* 1959; *Vive Henri IV. . . Vive l'Amour, Madame Sans-Gêne/Madame* 1961; *Le Diable et les Dix Commandments/The Devil and the Ten Commandments* 1962; *La Glaive et la Balance/Two Are Guilty, Les Bonnes Causes/Don't Tempt the Devil* 1963; *Paris When It Sizzles* (based on his co-script for *La Fête à Henriette;* US) 1964; *Paris au Mois d'Août/Paris in the Month of August* 1966.

Jefferson, Thomas. Actor. *b.* 1857. *d.* 1932. Slight (5' 6", 115 pounds) character lead of the American silent screen. The son of actor-playwright Joseph Jefferson (1829–1905), the American theater's most popular comedian of the 19th century, and actress Margaret Lockyer, he made his stage debut as a child. He began his film career in 1909 as a member of D. W. Griffith's stock company, but came into his own in 1914, when he played the lead role in the screen adaptation of 'Rip Van Winkle,' his father's most famous play. He was married to stage and silent screen actress Daisy Robinson.

FILMS INCLUDE: *Classmates, Rip Van Winkle* (title role), *The Seats of the Mighty* 1914; *The Shadow of the Great City, The Old Chemist, Ghosts, The Americano, The Sable*

Lorcha, The Missing Links 1915; *The Beloved Liar, The Mainspring, A Child of Mystery* 1916; *An Old Fashioned Young Man* 1917; *Hands Up* (serial), *Tarzan of the Apes, A Hoosier Romance* 1918; *Sis Hopkins, The Grim Game, Deliverance* (as his father, Joseph Jefferson), *The Other Half, Lombardi Ltd.* 1919; *The Forged Bride, A Splendid Hazard, White Youth* 1920; *My Lady's Latchkey, Rip Van Winkle* (remake; title role), *The Idle Rich* 1921; *The Vermilion Pencil, The Son of the Wolf, Good Men and True* 1922; *The Thoroughbred* 1925; *Paid to Love, The Fortune Hunter* 1927; *Soft Living* 1928; *On with the Show* 1929; *Lightnin'* 1930; *Ten Nights in a Barroom* 1931; *Forbidden* 1932.

Jeffreys, Anne. Actress, singer. Born Anne Carmichael, on Jan. 26, 1923, in Goldsboro, N.C. *ed.* Anderson Coll. Leading lady of many B pictures of the 40s. A former opera singer and Powers model, she also appeared on the Broadway stage and in stock and has been seen frequently on TV, notably in the series 'Topper' (1953–55), in which she co-starred with her husband (from 1951), Robert STERLING.

FILMS INCLUDE: *X Marks the Spot, I Married an Angel* 1942; *Chatterbox, Wagon Tracks West* 1943; *Hidden Valley Outlaws, Step Lively* 1944; *Nevada, Dick Tracy, Zombies on Broadway, Dillinger* 1945; *Genius at Work* 1946; *Trail Street, Riff-Raff* 1947; *Return of the Badmen* 1948; *Boys' Night Out* 1962; *Panic in the City* 1968; *Southern Double Cross* 1991; *Clifford* 1992.

Jeffries, Lionel. Actor, director. Born in 1926, in London. *ed.* RADA. Gaunt, baldheaded character player of British and occasional Hollywood films; at his best in bumbling comic roles but also effective in straight menacing parts. He turned director early in the 70s while continuing to appear as an actor in films directed by others.

FILMS INCLUDE: As actor—*Stage Fright* 1950; *Will Any Gentleman?* 1953; *The Colditz Story, Windfall, The Quatermass Experiment/The Creeping Unknown* 1955; *The Baby and the Battleship, Bhowani Junction* (US/UK), *Lust for Life* (US) 1956; *Doctor at Large, The Vicious Circle/The Circle, Blue Murder at St. Trinian's* 1957; *Law and Disorder, Up the Creek, Orders to Kill* 1958; *The Nun's Story* (US) 1959; *Two-Way Stretch, The Trials of Oscar Wilde* (as the Marquis of Queensberry), *First Men in the Moon, Tarzan the Magnificent* 1960; *Fanny* (US), *The Hellions* 1961; *Operation Snatch, The Notorious Landlady* (US), *Kill or Cure* 1962; *The Wrong Arm of the Law, Call Me Bwana* 1963; *The Long Ships, Murder Ahoy* 1964; *The Truth About Spring, You Must Be Joking!, The Secret of My Success* 1965; *Drop Dead Darling/Arrivederci Baby, The Spy with a Cold Nose* 1966; *Oh Dad Poor Dad. . .* (US), *Jules Verne's Rocket to the Moon/Those Fantastic Flying Fools/Blast-Off, Camelot* (US) 1967; *Chitty Chitty Bang Bang* 1968; *Twinky/Lola* (UK/It.) 1970; *Eyewitness/Sudden Terror, Who Slew Auntie Roo?* 1971; *Royal Flash, What Changed Charley Farthing?* 1975; *The Prisoner of Zenda* (US) 1979; *Ménage à Trois/Better Late Than Never* 1982; *A Chorus of Disapproval* 1989. As director—*The Railway Children* (also sc.) 1971; *The Amazing Mr. Blunden* (also sc.), *Baxter* 1972; *Wombling Free* 1977; *The Water Babies* (part animated; also voice) 1978.

jelly. Short for "gelatin." 1. A diffuser placed in front of a studio lamp to soften its light. 2. A color transparency placed before a light source to change its color value.

Jenkins, Allen. Actor. *b.* Alfred McConegal, Apr. 9, 1900, New York City. *d.* 1974. The son of musical comedy performers, he entered the theater as a stage mechanic following employment in the shipyards during WW I. But he soon switched to acting and after studies at the American Academy of Dramatic Arts he appeared frequently on Broadway. In films from 1931, he played character roles in more than 175 productions, typically as a numbskulled, small-time gangster, memorably in Warner's crime-film cycle of the 30s. But he also portrayed many droll, Brooklynese, blue-collar types, from cab drivers and stoolies to fight managers and cops. In later years he appeared frequently on TV and was a regular on the series 'Hey, Jeannie.'

FILMS INCLUDE: *The Girl Habit* 1931; *Blessed Event, Three on a Match, I Am a Fugitive from a Chain Gang* 1932; *Hard to Handle, 42nd Street, The Mayor of Hell, Bureau of Missing Persons* 1933; *The Big Shakedown, Jimmy the Gent, The St. Louis Kid* 1934; *The Case of the Curious Bride, The Irish in Us* 1935; *The Singing Kid, Cain and Mabel, Three Men on a Horse* 1936; *Marked Woman, Ever Since Eve, Dead End* 1937; *A Slight Case of Murder, Fools for Scandal, The Amazing Dr. Clitterhouse, Racket Busters, Hard to Get* 1938; *Naughty but Nice, Destry Rides Again* 1939; *Brother Orchid, Tin Pan Alley* 1940; *Footsteps in the Dark, Dive Bomber* 1941; *Ball of Fire, Tortilla Flat, The Falcon Takes Over, They All Kissed the Bride* 1942; *Wonder Man, Lady on a Train* 1945; *Easy Come Easy Go, The Senator Was Indiscreet* 1947; *Bodyhold* 1949; *Behave Yourself* 1951; *Pillow Talk* 1959; *Doctor—You've Got to Be Kidding* 1967; *The Front Page* 1974.

Jenkins, Charles Francis. Inventor. *b.* 1867, near Dayton, Ohio. *d.* 1934. The holder of some 400 patents, he began his career as an inventor at 23. In 1892 he demonstrated a device for showing pictures in motion, and in 1894, in association with Thomas ARMAT, he developed the Phantascope, a primitive projector for showing a succession of still pictures on a screen. In 1913 he envisioned and primitively experimented with wireless transmission of newsreel film. In 1916 he founded the Society of Motion Picture Engineers, of which he was the first president. He is credited with the first demonstration of television in the US. In 1923 he radioed pictures of President Harding from Washington to Philadelphia and the following year transmitted Herbert Hoover's signature from Washington to Boston. In 1925 he demonstrated mechanical television and in 1929 he established a company to capitalize on his discovery.

Jenkins, George. Art director. Born on Nov. 19, 1908, in Baltimore. *ed.* U. of Pennsylvania. A leading set designer and lighting director of Broadway plays and musicals from the early 40s, he has also designed sets for major Hollywood productions as well as many TV specials. He won an Oscar for the production design of *All the President's Men* (1976). In 1985–89 he taught motion picture design at UCLA.

FILMS INCLUDE: *The Best Years of Our Lives* 1946; *The Secret Life of Walter Mitty* 1947; *A Song Is Born* 1948; *Roseanna McCoy* 1949; *The Miracle Worker* 1962; *Mickey One* 1965; *Up the Down Staircase, Wait Until Dark* 1967; *No Way to Treat a Lady, The Subject Was Roses* 1968; *Me Natalie* 1969; *The Angel Levine* 1970; *The Pursuit of Happiness, Klute* 1971; *1776* 1972; *Paper Chase* 1973; *The Parallax View* 1974; *Night Moves, Funny Lady* 1975; *All the President's Men* 1976; *Comes a Horseman* 1978; *The China Syndrome* 1979; *The Postman Always Rings Twice* 1981; *Sophie's Choice* 1982; *Dream Lover* 1986; *Orphans* 1987; *See You in the Morning* 1989; *Presumed Innocent* 1990.

Jenkins, Jackie ("Butch"). Child star. Born on Aug. 19, 1937, in Los Angeles. Freckled little charmer of MGM movies of the 40s, son of stage and screen actress Doris Dudley. He was forced to quit films after developing a stutter. He later supervised the East Texas Water System and ran a chain of car wash establishments.

FILMS: *The Human Comedy* (as Ulysses) 1943; *An American Romance, National Velvet* 1944; *Abbott and Costello in Hollywood* (unbilled cameo), *Our Vines Have Tender Grapes*

1945; *Boys' Ranch, Little Mr. Jim* 1946; *My Brother Talks to Horses* 1947; *Big City, Summer Holiday, The Bride Goes Wild* 1948.

Jenks, Frank. Actor. *b.* 1902, Des Moines, Iowa. *d.* 1962. A former vaudeville musician, he played light character parts in films, often as an easy-going Runyonesque type. Co-starred in TV series 'Colonel Humphrey Flack.'

FILMS INCLUDE: *College Humor* 1933; *Follow the Fleet* 1936; *100 Men and a Girl* 1937; *The Lady in the Morgue, Goodbye Broadway, Youth Takes a Fling, The Last Warning* 1938; *Big Town Czar, The Under-Pup, First Love* 1939; *His Girl Friday, Three Cheers for the Irish, A Little Bit of Heaven* 1940; *Tall Dark and Handsome, Back Street, The Flame of New Orleans* 1941; *Syncopation, Seven Miles from Alcatraz* 1942; *Corregidor, Thousands Cheer, His Butler's Sister* 1943; *Roger Touhy—Gangster, Two Girls and a Sailor, Follow the Boys, The Impatient Years* 1944; *Zombies on Broadway, Christmas in Connecticut* 1945; *That Brennan Girl* 1946; *Blonde Savage* 1947; *Family Honeymoon* 1948; *The Petty Girl, To Please a Lady, Woman on the Run* 1950; *The Scarf* 1951; *Highway Dragnet* 1954; *Artists and Models, The She-Creature* 1956; *The Amazing Colossal Man* 1957.

Jennings, Al. Outlaw, actor. *b.* 1864, Virginia. *d.* 1961. Real-life Old West gunslinging badman, a convicted cattle rustler and train robber, who banked on his notoriety to appear in a handful of Hollywood films. He later co-authored a pseudo-autobiography, *Al Jennings of Oklahoma,* which was adapted to the screen in 1951 with Dan Duryea in the title role.

FILMS INCLUDE: *Beating Back* (as himself; based on his own story) 1914; *Hands Up!* (story only), *The Captain of the Gray Horse Troop* 1917; *The Lady of the Dugout* 1918; *The Sea Hawk, Fighting Fury* 1924; *The Demon, The Ridin' Rascal* 1926; *Loco Luck* 1927; *The Land of Missing Men* 1930.

Jennings, Gordon. Special effects expert. Salt Lake City. *d.* 1953. Trained as an engineer in Europe and at the University of Utah, he entered films as an assistant cameraman for the Lois Weber production company in 1919. He invented the first moving titles by painting them on glass and sliding them over painted backdrops. He spent most of his film career at Paramount, where he served as head of the special effects department from the mid-1930s until his death in the mid-1950s. He won Academy Awards for his inventive work on *Spawn of the North* (1938), *I Wanted Wings* (1941), *Reap the Wild Wind* (1942), *When Worlds Collide* (1951), and *War of the Worlds* (1953), and special technical-scientific achievement Oscars in 1944 for the design and construction of the Paramount nodal point tripod and in 1951 for the design, construction, and application of a servo-operated recording and repeating device. He worked frequently with director Cecil B. DeMille, who called him "the best special effects man I have ever been privileged to work with."

FILMS INCLUDE: *Alice in Wonderland, Island of Lost Souls* 1933; *The Scarlet Empress* 1934; *The Crusades, Peter Ibbetson* 1935; *The General Died at Dawn* 1936; *High, Wide, and Handsome, Make Way for Tomorrow, The Plainsman, Souls at Sea* 1937; *If I Were King, Spawn of the North* 1938; *Union Pacific* 1939; *North West Mounted Police, Typhoon* 1940; *Aloma of the South Seas, I Wanted Wings* 1941; *I Married a Witch, Reap the Wild Wind* 1942; *Frenchman's Creek, Going My Way, Lady in the Dark* 1944; *The Lost Weekend, Murder, He Says* 1945; *Two Years Before the Mast, The Virginian* 1946; *My Favorite Brunette, Road to Rio* 1947; *The Big Clock, The Emperor Waltz* 1948; *The Heiress, Samson and Delilah* 1949; *Sunset Boulevard* 1950; *A Place in the Sun, When Worlds Collide* 1951; *The Greatest Show on Earth* 1952; *Stalag 17, Shane, War of the Worlds* 1953.

Jennings, Humphrey. Documentary filmmaker. *b.* 1907, Walberswick, Suffolk, England. *d.* 1950. *ed.* Cambridge. A former surrealist painter and critic, he joined Britain's GPO Film Unit in 1934. A keen observer and sensitive artist, in the early 40s he created some of the warmest, most lyrical documentaries ever produced in England or elsewhere. His films of the war years brilliantly reflected the mood and the sense of London during the Blitz. He died in Greece after falling off a cliff while scouting locations for a film.

FILMS: *Post Haste, The Story of the Wheel* 1934; *Locomotives* 1935; *The Birth of a Robot* (assoc. dir. to Len Lye) 1936; *Penny Journey* 1938; *English Harvest, Spare Time* (also sc.), *Speaking from America, The First Days/A City Prepares* (co-dir. with Harry Watt and Pat Jackson), *Her Last Trip/SS Ionian* 1939; *An Unrecorded Victory/Spring Offensive, London Can Take It* (co-dir. with Harry Watt), *Welfare of the Workers* 1940; *The Heart of Britain* (and longer US version, *This Is England), Words for Battle* (also sc.), *Listen to Britain* (co-dir., co-sc. with Stewart McAllister) 1941; *The Silent Village* (also prod., sc.), *Fires Were Started/I Was a Fireman* (also sc.) 1943; *The True Story of Lilli Marlene* (also sc., act.) 1944; *The 80 Days* (also prod.), *A Diary for Timothy* (also sc.) 1945; *A Defeated People* (also sc.) 1946; *The Cumberland Story* (also sc.) 1947; *Dim Little Island* (also prod.) 1949; *Family Portrait* (also sc.) 1950.

Jennings, Talbot. Screenwriter. *b.* 1896, Shoshone, Idaho. *d.* 1985. *ed.* Harvard (M.A.); Yale Drama School. He wrote several plays and many screenplays, alone or in collaboration. He shared Academy Award nominations for *Mutiny on the Bounty* (1935) and *Anna and the King of Siam* (1946).

FILMS INCLUDE: *Mutiny on the Bounty* 1935; *Romeo and Juliet* 1936; *The Good Earth* 1937; *Marie Antoinette* 1938; *Rulers of the Sea, Spawn of the North* 1939; *Northwest Passage, Edison the Man* 1940; *So Ends Our Night* 1941; *Frenchman's Creek* 1944; *Anna and the King of Siam* 1946; *The Black Rose* 1950; *Across the Wide Missouri* 1951; *Knights of the Round Table* 1954; *Untamed* 1955; *La Maja Desnuda/The Naked Maja* (co-story only; It.) 1959; *The Sons of Katie Elder* (story only) 1965.

jenny. Production crew nickname for a generator used as an electric power source on location.

Jens, Salome. Actress. Born on May 8, 1935, in Milwaukee. *ed.* U. of Wisconsin; Northwestern U. Mannered leading lady of the American stage, TV, and occasional films. A former secretary, she trained with Herbert Berghof and at the Actors Studio, making her New York stage debut in 1956 and her first screen appearance in 1961.

FILMS: *Angel Baby* 1961; *The Fool Killer* 1965; *Seconds* 1966; *Me Natalie* 1969; *Savages* 1972; *Cloud Dancer* 1980; *Harry's War* 1981; *Just Between Friends* 1986.

Jergens, Adele. Actress. Born on Nov. 28, 1917, in Brooklyn, N.Y. A former chorine and top model, she gained some publicity as the winner of the "Miss World's Fairest" contest at New York's 1939 World's Fair and subsequently decorated a number of Broadway shows. A brassy platinum blonde, she played leads and second leads in some 50 films of the 40s and 50s, mostly low-budget productions, often portraying sarcastic showgirls or sometimes a hardened gang moll. Since 1949 married to actor Glenn Langan.

FILMS INCLUDE: *Black Arrow* (serial) 1944; *A Thousand and One Nights, She Wouldn't Say Yes* 1945; *The Corpse Came C.O.D., Down to Earth, Woman from Tangiers* 1947; *The Fuller Brush Man, The Prince of Thieves, The Dark Past* 1948; *The Treasure of Monte Cristo, Slightly French, The Mutineers* 1949; *Side Street, Edge of Doom, Armored Car*

Robbery 1950; *Show Boat, Sugarfoot, Abbott and Costello Meet the Invisible Man* 1951; *Aaron Slick from Punkin Creek, Somebody Loves Me* 1952; *The Miami Story* 1954; *Strange Lady in Town, The Cobweb* 1955; *Girls in Prison* 1956; *The Lonesome Trail* 1958.

Jessel, George. Entertainer, actor, singer, songwriter, producer. *b.* Apr. 3, 1898, New York City. *d.* 1981. The son of a playwright–stage producer, he began singing professionally at age nine and at 11 teamed up with Eddie CANTOR in vaudeville. He appeared occasionally in silent and sound films, but it was in nightclubs and on Broadway ('The Jazz Singer,' etc.), and later on radio and in TV, that he achieved a reputation as an entertainer and songwriter. In the late 40s and early 50s he produced musical films for Fox. He traveled extensively, speaking, entertaining, and raising funds on behalf of various causes and won a special Oscar, the Jean Hersholt Humanitarian Award, in 1969, for this activity. He also frequently entertained US troops overseas. A compulsive teller of jokes and anecdotes, he was known as America's "Toastmaster General." His second of four wives was silent movie star Norma TALMADGE. Memoirs: *So Help Me* (1943), *This Way, Miss* (1955).

FILMS INCLUDE: As actor—*Widow at the Races* 1911; *The Other Man's Wife* 1919; *Private Izzy Murphy* 1926; *Sailor Izzy Murphy, Ginsberg the Great* 1927; *George Washington Cohen* 1928; *Lucky Boy, Love Live and Laugh* 1929; *Happy Days* 1930; *Stage Door Canteen* 1943; *Four Jills in a Jeep* 1944; *The Busy Body* 1967; *Can Heironymous Merkin. . .* 1969; *The Phynx* (cameo) 1970. As producer—*The Dolly Sisters* 1945; *Do You Love Me?* 1946; *I Wonder Who's Kissing Her Now* (also songs), *Nightmare Alley* 1947; *When My Baby Smiles at Me* 1948; *Oh You Beautiful Doll, Dancing in the Dark* 1949; *Meet Me After the Show, Anne of the Indies, Golden Girl* (also songs) 1951; *Wait Till the Sun Shines Nellie, Bloodhounds of Broadway* 1952; *Tonight We Sing* 1953; *Beau James* 1957; *Juke Box Rhythm* 1959; *The Busy Body, Valley of the Dolls* 1967; *The Phynx* (cameo) 1970; *Won Ton Ton—The Dog Who Saved Hollywood* (cameo) 1976; *Reds* (cameo) 1981.

Jessua, Alain. Director. Born on Jan. 16, 1932, in Paris. Formerly an assistant to BECKER, OPHÜLS, CARNÉ, and Yves ALLÉGRET, he won the Prix Jean Vigo for his first effort as a director, the short *Léon la Lune* (1957). He made his debut as a feature director in 1964 but has since tackled only a handful of assignments. His limited output reveals a director with intelligence and a light, witty, and personal style that reflects a serious interest in the psychology of reality. He writes all his own scripts.

FILMS (as director-writer): *Léon la Lune* (short) 1957; *La Vie à l'Envers/Life Upside Down/Inside Out* 1964; *Jeu de Massacre/The Killing Game* 1967; *Les Panthères blanches* 1971; *Traitement de Shoc/Shock Treatment* 1973; *Armaguedon/Armageddon* 1977; *Les Chiens/The Dogs* 1979; *Paradis pour tous* 1982; *Frankenstein 90* 1984; *En Toute Innocence* 1988.

Jewell, Isabel. Actress. *b.* July 1909, Shoshone, Wyo. *d.* 1972. The daughter of a doctor and medical researcher, she attended Hamilton College in Kentucky and made her stage debut as an ingenue with a Lincoln, Nebr., stock company. After several years in stock, she made her Broadway debut in a dramatic fashion when she stepped into a role in 'Up Pops the Devil' (1930) with only three hours of rehearsal and won critical acclaim for her performance. She went to Hollywood in 1932 to repeat her stage role in *Blessed Event* and remained in the film colony as a leading lady and second lead of many screen productions. She was most memorable as a simpleminded seamstress who accompanies Ronald Colman to the guillotine in *A Tale of Two Cities* (1935) and as a prostitute in another Colman vehicle, *Lost Horizon* (1937). Her career declined in the 40s, but she continued appearing in occasional films and stage productions. She was out of work in the late 50s. In 1959 she was arrested in Las Vegas on bad-check charges and in 1961 she was sentenced to five days in jail and a year's probation for drunk driving.

FILMS INCLUDE: *Blessed Event* 1932; *Bondage, Bombshell, Design for Living, Counsellor-at-Law* 1933; *The Women in His Life, Manhattan Melodrama, Here Comes the Groom, Evelyn Prentice* 1934; *Shadow of Doubt, Times Square Lady, The Casino Murder Case, A Tale of Two Cities, Mad Love* 1935; *Ceiling Zero, The Leathernecks Have Landed, Small Town Girl, Big Brown Eyes, Valiant Is the Word for Carrie, The Man Who Lived Twice, Go West Young Man* 1936; *Lost Horizon, Marked Woman* 1937; *The Crowd Roars* 1938; *Gone With the Wind* 1939; *Northwest Passage, Irene, Little Men* 1940; *High Sierra* 1941; *The Leopard Man, The Seventh Victim* 1943; *The Merry Monahans* 1944; *Badman's Territory* 1946; *Born to Kill* 1947; *Belle Starr's Daughter, Unfaithfully Yours, The Snake Pit* 1948; *Man in the Attic* 1954; *Bernadine* 1957.

Jewison, Norman. Director, producer. Born on July 21, 1926, in Toronto, Ont., Canada. *ed.* U. of Toronto. The son of a third-generation Canadian storekeeper and an English-born mother, he showed an early gift for acting. Following a brief stint in the Canadian Navy towards the end of WW II, he completed his college studies, then drove a cab for several months to pay for ocean passage to England. He began his career at London's BBC-TV as an actor and writer. After gaining directing experience in Canadian TV, he moved to the US and joined CBS-TV, for which he produced and directed a number of musical specials, starring Judy Garland, Harry Belafonte, and others. As a film director from 1963, he progressed from glittering Doris Day romantic comedies (*The Thrill of It All,* 1963, and *Send Me No Flowers,* 1964) to timely satire (*The Russians Are Coming, the Russians Are Coming,* 1966) and topical drama (*In the Heat of the Night,* 1967), with an accent on cinematic effect. The latter film, a gripping crime thriller with racial overtones, won the best picture Academy Award, as well as several other Oscars, catapulting Jewison to the top rank of Hollywood's directors. He returned to the musical scene of his TV days with two sumptuous but only mildly successful musical films, *Fiddler on the Roof* (1971) and *Jesus Christ Superstar* (1973), which he filmed on location in Israel. In the following years, Jewison's career zigzagged between mediocrity and excellence, meandering in no apparent pattern between the light and the serious, between the trivial and the worthy, between the pretentious and the sincere. But regardless of particular merit, his output always sustained the mark of the director's superior craftsmanship. In 1987 he won the best director prize at the Berlin Film Festival for *Moonstruck,* a delightful, ethnically flavored romantic comedy that triumphed both critically and commercially. Although he works mainly out of Hollywood and maintains a home in Malibu and offices in London, Jewison's principal residence is a farm near Toronto, where he lives with his wife and three children, all of whom are involved in some capacity in filmmaking. He is a founder and co-chairman of the Canadian Center for Advanced Film Studies.

FILMS (as director): *40 Pounds of Trouble, The Thrill of It All* 1963; *Send Me No Flowers* 1964; *The Art of Love, The Cincinnati Kid* 1965; *The Russians Are Coming the Russians Are Coming* (also prod.) 1966; *In the Heat of the Night* 1967; *The Thomas Crown Affair* (also prod.) 1968; *Gaily Gaily* (also prod.) 1969; *The Landlord* (prod. only) 1970; *Fiddler on the Roof* (also prod.) 1971; *Jesus Christ Superstar* (also co-prod.)

1973; *Billy Two Hats* (prod. only) 1974; *Rollerball* (also prod.) 1975; *F.I.S.T.* (also prod.) 1978; . . . *And Justice for All* (also co-prod.) 1979; *Best Friends* (also co-prod.) 1982; *Iceman* (co-prod. only), *A Soldier's Story* (also co-prod.) 1984; *Agnes of God* (also co-prod.) 1985; *Moonstruck* (also co-prod.) 1987; *January Man* (co-exec. prod. only), *In Country* (also co-prod.) 1989; *Other People's Money* 1991; *Only You* 1994; *Bogus* (also co-prod.) 1996.

Jhabvala, Ruth Prawer. Novelist, screenwriter. Born Ruth Prawer, on May 7, 1927, in Cologne, Germany, of Polish-Jewish parents. Raised in England, where her family settled as refugees in 1939, she majored in English at London University. In 1951 she married Indian architect C. S. H. Jhabvala and moved with him to New Delhi, where she began writing novels and short stories, several of which were published in England starting in 1955. In the mid-60s she turned also to screenwriting, beginning a long and fruitful association with director James Ivory and producer Ismail Merchant. She sometimes serves as co-producer. She won an Academy Award for her screenplay for *A Room with a View* (1986).

FILMS (alone or in collaboration): *The Householder* (from her own novel) 1963; *Shakespeare Wallah* 1965; *The Guru* 1969; *Bombay Talkie* 1970; *Autobiography of a Princess* 1975; *Roseland* 1977; *Hullabalo Over Georgie and Bonnie's Pictures* 1978; *The Europeans* 1979; *Jane Austen in Manhattan* 1980; *Quartet* 1981; *The Courtesans of Bombay* (doc.) 1982; *Heat and Dust* 1983; *The Bostonians* 1984; *A Room with a View* 1986; *Madame Sousatzka* 1988; *Slaves of New York* 1989; *Mr. & Mrs. Bridge* 1990; *Howards End* 1992; *The Remains of the Day* 1993; *Surviving Picasso, The Proprietor* 1996.

Jires, Jaromil. Director. Born on Dec. 10, 1935, in Bratislava, Czechoslovakia. Trained in film technique at the Cmelice vocational school, he later studied cinematography and direction at Prague's FAMU and began his career in 1960 making shorts and experimenting with multiscreen and Magic Lantern projects. His first feature, *The Cry/The First Cry* (1963), attracted wide approval for its bold imagination and freshness of style. But the prevailing political winds of the 60s denied him opportunities for further major contributions during the decade, which he spent mostly as the chief of a documentary film unit. He reasserted himself as a feature director in 1970–71—bleak years during which other leading Czech directors worked in exile abroad—with two admirable, politically safe films, *Valerie and the Week of Wonders,* a poetic fantasy film, and *And Give My Love to the Swallows,* a lyrical recreation of the life and death by execution of a 17-year-old girl and anti-Nazi fighter. Much of his subsequent work consisted of documentary and TV films. He usually collaborates on his own scripts.

FEATURE FILMS: *The Cry/The First Cry* 1963; *Pearls in the Deep* ("Romance" episode) 1965; *Bitter Almonds* (unfinished) 1966; *The Joke* 1969; *Valerie and the Week of Wonders* 1970; *And Give My Love to the Swallows* 1971; *The Safecracker* 1973; *People from the Metro* 1974; *The Island of Silver Herons* 1976; *Flying Saucers Over Our Town* 1977; *The Young Man and the White Whale* 1978; *The Rabbit Case* 1979; *Escapes Home* 1980; *Partial Eclipse* 1982; *Lev S Bilou Hrivou* 1986.

Joannon, Léo. Director. *b.* Aug. 21, 1904, Aix-en-Provence, France. *d.* 1969. After studying law he turned to writing film articles, short stories, and a novel (*Nostalgie,* 1929) and entered French films in the mid-20s as a cameraman and assistant director. A director from 1930, he turned out many routine commercial productions, occasionally surprising with an above-average film. He had the dubious distinction of directing Laurel And Hardy's last, and poorest, film, *Atoll K* (1951), in France. It was released in the US in 1954 as *Utopia.*

FILMS INCLUDE: *Adieu les Copains* (also sc.) 1930; *Suzanne* (co-dir. with Raymond Rouleau) 1932; *Six Cents Mille Francs par Mois* 1933; *Bibi la Purée* 1934; *Quelle Drôle de Gosse* 1935; *Train de Plaisir, Quand Minuit sonnera* 1936; *Vous n'avez rien à déclarer?* (co-dir. with Yves Allégret), *L'Homme sans Coeur, Le Chanteur de Minuit* 1937; *Alerte en Méditerranée/SOS Mediterranean* (also sc.) 1938; *L'Emigrante* 1939; *Caprices* 1942; *Le Camion blanc, Lucrèce, Le Carrefour des Enfants perdus/Children of Chaos* 1943; *Documents Secrets* 1945; *Le 84 prend des Vacances* 1950; *Atoll K/Utopia* (also story) 1951; *Drôle de Noce* (also co-prod., co-sc.) 1952; *Le Défroqué* (also co-sc., act.) 1954; *Le Secret de Soeur Angèle* (also co-sc.), *L'Homme aux Clefs d'Or* (also co-sc., act.) 1956; *Le Désert de Pigalle* (also co-sc., act.), *Tant d'Amour perdu* (also co-sc.) 1958; *L'Assassin est dans l'Annuaire* 1961; *Fort du Fou* (also co-adapt.) 1962; *Trois Enfants dans le Désordre* (also co-sc.) 1966; *Les Arnaud* (also co-sc.) 1967.

Joanou, Phil. Director. Born in 1962. A graduate of the USC Film School, he became a protégé of Steven Spielberg and began his career as the director of two episodes in the latter's 'Amazing Stories' TV series. Venturing into features in the late 80s, he exhibited a flashy command of camera technique.

FEATURE FILMS: *Three O'Clock High* 1987; *U2: Rattle and Hum* (concert film; also edit.) 1988; *State of Grace* 1990; *Final Analysis* 1992; *Heaven's Prisoners* 1995.

Jobert, Marlène. Actress. Born in 1943, in Algeria. Freckle-faced, redheaded leading lady of French films and European co-productions.

FILMS INCLUDE: *Masculin-Féminin/Masculine Feminine* 1966; *Le Voleur/The Thief of Paris* 1967; *Alexandre le Bienheurex/Very Happy Alexander/Alexander* 1968; *Le Passanger de la Pluie/Rider on the Rain, Dernier Domicile connu/Last Known Address* 1970; *Le Poudre de l'Escampette/Touch and Go, Catch Me a Spy* (UK/Fr.) 1971; *La Décade prodigieuse/Ten Days' Wonder, Nous ne vieillrons pas ensemble/We Won't Grow Old Together* 1972; *Docteur Popaul* 1973; *Le Secret* 1974; *Pas si Méchant que ca/The Wonderful Crook* 1975; *Le Bon et les Méchants/The Good and the Bad* 1976; *L'Imprecateur, Julie Pot de Colle/Chains of Pity* 1977; *Voir Maman. . . Papa travaille/Your Turn, My Turn* 1978; *La Guerre des Polices* 1979; *Une Salle Affaire, L'Amor nu* 1981; *Effraction* 1983; *Les Cavaliers de l'Orage* 1984; *Les Cigognes n'en font qu'a leur Tête* 1989.

Jodorowsky, Alexandro. Director. Born in 1930, in Chile, to Russian-Polish circus performers. A flamboyant, egocentric man of stage and screen. He studied pantomime in Paris with Marcel Marceau, then became a prolific theater director-writer in Europe and in Mexico, where he settled in the 60s. Turning to films, he created a sensation in 1970 with *El Topo,* a wildly eclectic, ultraviolent religious allegory starring the director, that developed a cult following and became, in January of 1971, the first major midnight movie at a small New York theater, where it ran for about a year. It was admired as a masterpiece by a large group of dedicated repeat viewers, but confused or disgusted many others with its structural absurdities and graphic savagery, and was dismissed by most serious critics as a self-indulgent, pretentious mishmash. After the release of *The Holy Mountain* in 1973, Jodorowsky dissolved his production company, Producciones Panicas, and withdrew from films. Settling in Paris, he returned to filmmaking in 1980 with the French-produced *Tusk,* a tame elephant-hunt story, set in the south of India in 1911. It wasn't until 1989 that he made yet another comeback with *Santa Sangre/Holy Blood,* an Oedipal tale about a madman who becomes the arms of his mutilated mother. *Variety* predicted the film would become another cult classic. It starred Axel

Jodorowsky and featured three of the director's four children. Author: *El Topo: A Book of the Film* (1971).

FILMS: *Fando and Lis* 1968(?); *El Topo* (also sc., mus., act.; Mex.) 1970; *The Holy Mountain* (also sc., co-mus., act.; Mex.) 1973; *Tusk* (Fr.) 1980; *Santa Sangre/Holy Blood* (It.) 1989; *The Rainbow Thief* (UK) 1990.

Joffe, Charles H. Producer. Born on July 16, 1929, in Brooklyn, N.Y. *ed.* Syracuse U. With Jack Rollins and others, he set up a talent management organization which numbered Woody ALLEN among its clients. Branching into production, Joffe became the producer, and later executive producer of Allen's films and occasionally those of other directors.

FILMS INCLUDE (as producer or executive producer or executive producer, alone or in collaboration): *Don't Drink the Water, Take the Money and Run* 1969; *Bananas* 1971; *Play It Again Sam, Everything You Always Wanted to Know About Sex But Were Afraid to Ask* 1972; *Sleeper* 1973; *Love and Death* 1975; *The Front* 1976; *Annie Hall* 1977; *Interiors* 1978; *Manhattan* 1979; *Arthur* 1981; *A Midsummer Night's Sex Comedy* 1982; *Broadway Danny Rose* 1984; *The Purple Rose of Cairo* 1985; *Hannah and Her Sisters* 1986; *Radio Days, September* 1987; *Another Woman* 1988; *Crimes and Misdemeanors* 1989; *Alice* 1990; *Shadows and Fog* 1992; *Manhattan Murder Mystery* 1993; *Bullets Over Broadway* 1994; *Everyone Says I Love You* 1996.

Joffé, Roland. Director. Born on Nov. 17, 1945, in London. *ed.* Manchester. He began his career in the theater, with the Young Vic, then directed at the National Theatre and the Old Vic. In 1978 he moved on to television as a director of documentaries and dramatic series. The documentary background served him extremely well on his first feature film, *The Killing Fields* (1984), a harrowingly realistic recreation of the chaos of the fall of Phnom Penh and the horrors of the Khmer Rouge takeover of Cambodia in 1975. The film, its director, and screenwriter were nominated for Academy Awards and won Oscars for best cinematography, best editing, and best supporting actor (Dr. Haing S. NGOR). Joffé was again nominated for best picture and best director Oscars for his next film, *The Mission* (1986), a visually magnificent drama of passion, religion, and politics in the 18th-century Brazilian jungle. The film won the Academy Award for best cinematography and took the Palme d'Or at the Cannes Festival. He was less successful with *Fat Man and Little Boy* (1989), an interesting but curiously flat dramatization of events leading to the creation of the atomic bomb in WW II.

FEATURE FILMS: *The Killing Fields* 1984; *The Mission* 1986; *Fat Man and Little Boy* (also co-sc.) 1989; *Made in Bangkok* (prod. only) 1991; *The City of Joy* (also co-prod.) 1992; *Super Mario Bros.* 1993; *The Scarlet Letter* 1995.

Johann, Zita. Actress. *b.* July 14, 1904, near Temesvar, Hungary. *d.* 1993. The daughter of a Hussar officer, she came to the US with her family at age seven and began showing promise for an acting career in high school dramatics. She made her Broadway debut in a Theatre Guild production in 1924 and was an established leading lady on the stage by the time she made her first screen appearance, in D. W. Griffith's last film, *The Struggle* (1931). She played competent leads in several other Hollywood films, memorably as the object of Boris Karloff's love in *The Mummy* (1932), but was hampered by poor roles and in 1934 returned to Broadway. Her first husband was producer-actor John HOUSEMAN.

FILMS: *The Struggle* 1931; *Tiger Shark, The Mummy* 1932; *Luxury Liner, The Man Who Dared, The Sin of Nora Moran* 1933; *Grand Canary* 1934; *Raiders of the Living Dead* 1989.

John, Rosamund. Actress. Born Nora Rosamund Jones, on Oct. 19, 1913, in Tottenham, England. Redheaded leading lady of British films, usually in refined roles.

FILMS INCLUDE: *The Secret of the Loch* 1934; *The First of the Few/Spitfire* 1942; *The Gentle Sex, The Lamp Still Burns* 1943; *Tawny Pipit* 1944; *The Way to the Stars/Johnny in the Clouds* 1945; *Green for Danger* 1946; *The Upturned Glass, Fame Is the Spur* 1947; *No Place for Jennifer* 1949; *She Shall Have Murder* 1950; *Street Corner/Both Sides of the Law* 1952; *Operation Murder* 1956.

Johns, Glynis. Actress. Born on Oct. 5, 1923, in Pretoria, South Africa. Charming, husky-voiced leading lady of the British stage and screen. The daughter of Mervyn JOHNS, she made her London stage debut at 12 and her first film appearance at 15. She gradually moved on from impish schoolgirl and naughty ingenue roles to leading lady parts, attracting a following among filmgoers thanks to her bright personality, alluring prettiness, and the unique quality of her voice. Especially adept at comedy roles, she began appearing in Hollywood films in the mid-50s and in 1963 starred in her own US-made TV series 'Glynis.' A familiar face on the New York stage since the early 50s, she scored a hit and won a Tony for her performance in the 1973 Broadway production of 'A Little Night Music.' She was nominated for an Oscar as supporting actress for *The Sundowners* (1960).

FILMS: *South Riding, Murder in the Family, Prison Without Bars* 1938; *On the Night of the Fire/The Fugitive, The Briggs Family, Under Your Hat* 1939; *The Prime Minister* 1940; *The 49th Parallel/The Invaders* 1941; *The Adventures of Tartu* 1942; *Half-Way House* 1944; *Perfect Strangers/Vacation from Marriage* 1945; *This Man Is Mine* 1946; *Frieda, An Ideal Husband* (as Mabel Chiltern) 1947; *Miranda, Third Time Lucky* 1948; *Dear Mr. Prohack* 1949; *State Secret/The Great Manhunt* 1950; *Flesh and Blood, No Highway/No Highway in the Sky, Appointment with Venus/Island Rescue, Encore, The Magic Box* 1951; *The Card/The Promoter* 1952; *The Sword and the Rose* (as Mary Tudor; UK/US), *Rob Roy the Highland Rogue/Rob Roy* (UK/US), *Personal Affair* 1953; *The Weak and the Wicked, The Seekers/Land of Fury, The Beachcomber, Mad about Men* 1954; *Josephine and Men* 1955; *The Court Jester* (US), *Loser Takes All, Around the World in 80 Days* (US) 1956; *All Mine to Give* (US) 1957; *Another Time Another Place* (US/UK) 1958; *Shake Hands with the Devil* (US/Ire.) 1959; *The Spider's Web, The Sundowners* 1960; *The Cabinet of Caligari* (US), *The Chapman Report* (US) 1962; *Papa's Delicate Condition* (US) 1963; *Mary Poppins* (US) 1964; *Dear Brigitte* (US) 1965; *Don't Just Stand There!* (US) 1968; *Lock Up Your Daughters* 1969; *Under Milk Wood* 1971; *Vault of Horror* 1973; *Zelly and Me* 1988; *Nuckie* 1992; *The Ref* 1994; *While You Were Sleeping* 1995.

Johns, Mervyn. Actor. *b.* Feb. 18, 1899, Pembroke, South Wales. *d.* 1992. *ed.* RADA. Father of Glynis JOHNS. Veteran character actor of numerous British plays and films. Widowed, he married actress Diana Churchill in 1976.

FILMS INCLUDE: *Lady in Danger* 1934; *Storm in a Teacup* 1937; *Jamaica Inn* 1939; *Convoy, The Girl in the News* 1940; *Next of Kin, Went the Day Well/48 Hours* 1942; *Half-Way House* 1944; *Pink String and Sealing Wax, Dead of Night* 1945; *The Captive Heart* 1946; *Captain Boycott* 1947; *Easy Money, Counterblast/Devil's Plot* 1948; *Quartet, Edward My Son* 1949; *Tony Draws a Horse* 1950; *Scrooge/A Christmas Carol* (as Bob Cratchit), *The Magic Box* 1951; *The Master of Ballantrae* 1953; *Romeo and Juliet* (as Friar Lawrence) 1954; *1984, Moby Dick* (as Captain Peleg) 1956; *The Devil's Disciple* 1959; *Once More with Feeling* (US), *Never Let Go* 1960; *No Love for Johnnie,*

Francis of Assisi (US), *The Rebel/Call Me Genius* 1961; *The Day of the Triffids, 55 Days at Peking* (US), *The Old Dark House* (UK/US), *The Victors* (UK/US) 1963; *A Jolly Bad Fellow/They All Died Laughing* 1964; *The Heroes of Telemark* 1965; *House of Mortal Sin/The Confessional* 1975; *Kill and Kill Again* 1981; *Ingrid* (UK) 1989.

Johnson, Arthur. Actor. *b.* 1876, Davenport, Iowa. *d.* 1916. The son of an Episcopal minister, he ran away from home to join a touring stage company and later played leads in New York productions. A big, handsome man, he made a strong impression on D. W. GRIFFITH, who chanced upon him on a Manhattan street and asked him to play the lead in *The Adventures of Dollie* (1908), Griffith's first film as a director. Although Johnson, like other screen players of the period, did not become publicly known by name for several years, he soon was a favorite of film audiences and was probably the first true matinee idol of the American screen. He starred in many of Griffith's early films, often opposite the famous "Biograph Girl," Florence Lawrence, and Griffith's wife, Linda Arvidson, and later was the top leading man of the Philadelphia-based Lubin organization.

FILMS INCLUDE: *The Adventures of Dollie, The Taming of the Shrew, After Many Years, The Valet's Wife, The Song of the Shirt, The Test of Friendship, The Helping Hand* 1908; *A Drunkard's Reformation, Pippa Passes, Resurrection, The Mills of the Gods, The Gibson Goddess, And a Little Child Shall Lead Them* 1909; *In Old California, The Unchanging Sea, Two Brothers, A Romance of the Western Hills, The Armorer's Daughter, Faithful* 1910; *The Actress and the Singer, Her Two Sons* 1911; *The Amateur Iceman, An Antique Ring* 1912; *Annie Rowley's Fortune* (also dir.), *The Artist's Romance* (also dir.) 1913; *The Beloved Adventurer* (serial) 1914.

Johnson, Ben. Actor. Born on June 13, 1918, in Foraker, near Pawhuska, Okla. A champion rodeo performer, he first arrived in Hollywood in the early 40s as a horse wrangler for Howard Hughes's *The Outlaw* and was later employed as a double and stuntman in Westerns. He was then discovered by John FORD, who cast him as a cavalry sergeant in two of his films and gave him the star part in *The Wagonmaster.* He also starred in *Mighty Joe Young* and other films but has been used for the most part in supporting roles, mainly in Westerns. He won the Academy Award as best supporting actor and the New York Film Critics Award for his performance in *The Last Picture Show* (1971).

FILMS INCLUDE: *Three Godfathers, She Wore a Yellow Ribbon, Mighty Joe Young* 1949; *The Wagonmaster, Rio Grande* 1950; *Fort Defiance* 1951; *Shane* 1953; *War Drums* 1957; *One-Eyed Jacks* 1961; *Major Dundee* 1965; *The Rare Breed* 1966; *Will Penny* 1968; *The Wild Bunch, The Undefeated* 1969; *Chisum* 1970; *The Last Picture Show, Something Big* 1971; *Junior Bonner, The Getaway* 1972; *The Train Robbers, Kid Blue, Dillinger* 1973; *The Sugarland Express* 1974; *Bite the Bullet, Hustle* 1975; *Breakheart Pass* 1976; *The Town That Dreaded Sundown, The Greatest, Grayeagle* 1977; *The Swarm* 1978; *The Hunter, Terror Train* (Can.) 1980; *Ruckus* 1981; *Tex* 1982; *Champions* (UK), *Red Dawn* 1984; *Let's Get Harry* 1986; *Cherry 2000, Dark Before Dawn* 1988; *Back to Back* 1990; *My Heroes Have Always Been Cowboys, Radio Flyer* 1991; *Angels in the Outfield* 1994; *The Evening Star* 1996.

Johnson, Dame Celia. Actress. *b.* Dec. 18, 1908, Richmond, England. *d.* 1982. *ed.* RADA. Primarily a stage actress (from 1928), she gave several remarkable film performances, most memorably as the refined, restrained romantic heroine of *Brief Encounter* (1945), for which she received an Oscar nomination as best actress, and as the heroine of two other filmed Noel Coward works, *In Which We Serve* (1942) and *This Happy Breed* (1944). She won the British Film Academy Award as best supporting actress for her last screen appearance, in *The Prime of Miss Jean Brodie* (1969).

FILMS: *In Which We Serve* 1942; *Dear Octopus/Randolph Family* 1943; *This Happy Breed* 1944; *Brief Encounter* 1945; *The Astonished Heart* 1949; *I Believe in You* 1951; *The Holly and the Ivy* 1952; *The Captain's Paradise* 1953; *A Kid for Two Farthings* 1955; *The Good Companions* 1957; *The Prime of Miss Jean Brodie* 1969.

Johnson, Chic. Comic actor. *b.* Harold Ogden Johnson, Mar. 5, 1891, Chicago. *d.* 1962. A former ragtime pianist, he teamed in 1914 with Ole OLSEN in a comedy act that eventually made them into popular vaudeville stars. Olsen and Johnson appeared in a number of films of the 30s and the 40s but had their one big success in 1941 with *Hellzapoppin,* a lunatic, near-surrealistic screen version of their hilarious 1938–40 Broadway hit.

FEATURE FILMS: *Oh Sailor Behave!* 1930; *Fifty Million Frenchmen, Gold Dust Gertie* 1931; *Country Gentlemen* 1936; *All Over Town* 1937; *Hellzapoppin* 1941; *Crazy House* 1943; *Ghost Catchers* 1944; *See My Lawyer* 1945.

Johnson, Don. Actor. Born on Dec. 15, 1949, in Flat Creek, Mo. *ed.* U. of Kansas; American Conservatory Theater, San Francisco. Muscular, dimple-cheeked leading man of American TV and films. On screen from the late 60s, he played routine leads in relative obscurity until 1984, when he soared in popularity as the macho star of the TV police series 'Miami Vice.' His unshaven, nonchalant appearance in the series helped start a casual chic fashion trend among men. Through his involvement in the series, Johnson became a motor-boating enthusiast. In a 1988 race, he captured the title of the world's offshore powerboat champion. In 1986 he released a first singing album, 'Heart Beat.' His second wife was actress Melanie GRIFFITH, whom he married in 1976, divorced shortly after, and remarried in 1989 only to divorce from her again in 1995. His long relationship in the interim with actress Patti D'ARBANVILLE produced a son in 1982.

FILMS: *Good Morning and Goodbye!* 1968; *The Magic Garden of Stanley Sweetheart* 1970; *Zachariah* 1971; *The Harrad Experiment* 1973; *A Boy and His Dog, Return to Macon County* 1975; *Melanie* (Can.), *Soggy Bottom USA* 1982; *Cease Fire* 1985; *Sweet Hearts Dance* 1988; *Dead-Bang* 1989; *The Hot Spot* 1990; *Harley Davidson and the Marlboro Man, Paradise* 1991; *Born Yesterday, Guilty as Sin* 1993; *Tin Cup* 1996.

Johnson, Edith. See DUNCAN, William.

Johnson, Kay. Actress. *b.* Catherine Townsend, Nov. 29, 1904, Mount Vernon, N.Y. *d.* 1975. *ed.* AADA. An architect's daughter, she made her Broadway debut in 1923 and went on to play leads in a number of stage productions before joining the swarm of Broadway actors to Hollywood with the switch to sound. She played competent leads in early talkies but really came into her own as a screen actress after being demoted to supporting roles later on. Formerly (1928–48) married to John CROMWELL.

FILMS: *Dynamite* 1929; *The Ship from Shanghai, This Mad World, The Spoilers, Billy the Kid, Madam Satan, The Passion Flower* 1930; *The Single Sin, The Spy* 1931; *American Madness, Thirteen Women* 1932; *Eight Girls in a Boat, This Man Is Mine, Of Human Bondage, Their Big Moment* 1934; *Jalna, Village Tale* 1935; *White Banners* 1938; *Real Glory* 1939; *Son of Fury* 1942; *Mr. Lucky* 1943; *The Adventures of Mark Twain* 1944; *Jivaro* 1954.

Johnson, Lamont. Director. Born on Sept. 30, 1922, in

Stockton, Calif. *ed.* UCLA. A former actor, he began directing for the stage in the late 40s and piloted many TV dramas and series episodes in the 60s before graduating to feature films in 1967. He appeared as an actor in several films of the 50s.

FILMS: *A Covenant with Death* 1967; *Kona Coast* 1968; *My Sweet Charlie, The McKenzie Break* 1970; *A Gunfight* 1971; *The Groundstar Conspiracy, You'll Like My Mother* 1972; *The Last American Hero* 1973; *Visit to a Chief's Son* 1974; *Lipstick* 1976; *One on One* (also act.) 1977; *Somebody Killed Her Husband* 1978; *Cattle Annie and Little Britches* 1981; *Spacehunter: Adventures in the Forbidden Zone* 1983; *Escape* 1990.

Johnson, Martin E. Explorer, documentary filmmaker. *b.* Oct. 9, 1884, Rockford, Ill. *d.* 1937. In 1906 he set out on a round-the-world cruise with Jack London. In 1910 he opened a chain of nickelodeons in which he exhibited his films of that expedition. In 1912, with his wife Osa (*née* Leighty, Mar. 14, 1894, Chanute, Kans. *d.* 1953), he began a series of explorations of remote places which resulted in many feature-length documentary films of scientific and social as well as entertainment value. He also wrote and lectured extensively on his travels, but his career was cut short by a fatal airplane crash. Osa, who was badly injured in the crash, later assisted Henry King on the production of *Stanley and Livingstone* (1939). In 1940 she produced *I Married Adventure,* a screen biography of her life with Martin, and in 1942 *African Paradise.*

FILMS INCLUDE: *Cannibals of the South Seas* 1912; *Among the Cannibal Isles of the South Pacific* 1918; *Jungle Adventures* 1921; *Head Hunters of the South Seas* 1922; *Trailing African Wild Animals* 1923; *East of Suez* 1925; *Simba the King of Beasts* 1928; *Across the World with Mr. and Mrs. Johnson* 1930; *Wonders of the Congo* 1931; *Congorilla* 1932; *Baboona* 1935; *Borneo* 1937.

Johnson, Noble. Actor. *b.* Apr. 18, 1881, Colorado Springs, Colo. Deceased. Imposing (6' 2", 225 pounds) black character player of the American screen. He quit school at 15 to join his father, a horse trainer, on the racing circuit. As a young adult, he worked as a rancher and a miner, among other occupations before making his film debut in 1909. In 1916 he was among the founders of the Lincoln Motion Picture Company in Los Angeles, a modest producer of black films. He left the company two years later and in the following three decades appeared in scores of Hollywood productions, portraying Indians, Mexicans, and other off-white characters, as well as blacks. Little was heard of him after his retirement from the screen in 1950.

FILMS INCLUDE: *Mr. Carlson from Arizona, A Western Governor's Humanity* 1915; *The Caravan, Eagle's Wings, Kincaid Gambler, 20,000 Leagues Under the Sea* 1916; *The Terror, The Hero of the Hour, Mr. Dolan of New York, The Realization of a Negro's Ambition* 1917; *The Red Ace* (serial) 1917–18; *The Bull's Eye* (serial) 1918; *The Lure of the Circus* (serial) 1918–19; *The Adorable Savage, Under Crimson Skies, The Leopard Woman* 1920; *Serenade, The Four Horsemen of the Apocalypse* 1921; *Drums of Fate, The Ten Commandments* 1923; *The Thief of Bagdad, Little Robinson Crusoe, The Navigator, The Midnight Express* 1924; *The Dancers, Adventure* 1925; *Hands Up, The Flaming Frontier* (as Chief Sitting Bull) 1926; *When a Man Loves, The King of Kings, Topsy and Eva* 1927; *The Gateway of the Moon, West of Zanzibar, Noah's Ark* 1928; *Redskin, The Four Feathers, The Mysterious Dr. Fu Manchu* 1929; *Moby Dick* (as Queequeg), *Kismet* 1930; *East of Borneo* 1931; *Murders in the Rue Morgue, The Most Dangerous Game, The Mummy* 1932; *Nagana, King Kong, Son of Kong, White Woman* 1933; *Kid Millions* 1934; *The Lives of a Bengal Lancer, She* 1935; *The Plainsman, Conquest, Wee Willie Winkie, Lost Horizon* 1937; *Four Men and a Prayer* 1938; *Union Pacific, Juarez, Drums Along the Mohawk* 1939; *Green Hell, The Ghost Breakers* 1940; *The Road to Zanzibar, Aloma of the South Sea* 1941; *Jungle Book* 1942; *The Desert Song* 1944; *A Game of Death* 1945; *The Plainsman and the Lady* 1946; *Unconquered* 1947; *She Wore a Yellow Ribbon* 1949; *North of the Great Divide* 1950.

Johnson, Nunnally. Screenwriter, producer, director. *b.* Dec. 5, 1897, Columbus, Ga. *d.* 1977. He started out as a reporter on the Columbus *Enquirer Sun,* then wrote for the Savannah (Ga.) *Press,* the Brooklyn *Daily Eagle, P.M.,* and the New York *Herald Tribune.* He later wrote short stories for *The Saturday Evening Post* and other magazines, some of which were published in 1930 as a book, *There Ought to Be a Law.* One of his *Post* stories provided the basis for the 1927 film *Rough House Rosie,* starring Clara Bow. Johnson went to Hollywood in 1932 and began writing for the screen the following year. Joining 20th Century-Fox, he became one of the screen's most prolific and highly respected writers, the author of intelligent scripts for many memorable films, among them John Ford's celebrated *The Grapes of Wrath* (1940). Johnson wrote most of his scripts alone, collaborating on only a handful. In 1935 he began producing as well as writing for the screen. In 1943 he formed International Pictures, which was eventually absorbed by Universal, but he later returned to Fox and in the 50s ventured into directing, as well as producing and writing, with mixed results. He retrenched into screenwriting only in the 60s. He was married to onetime screen actress Dorris Bowdon.

FILMS (as screenwriter unless otherwise noted): *Rough House Rosie* (story basis only) 1927; *A Bedtime Story* (co-adapt., uncredited), *Mama Loves Papa* (co-story only) 1933; *Moulin Rouge* (story basis only), *The House of Rothschild, Bulldog Drummond Strikes Back, Kid Millions* 1934; *Cardinal Richelieu* (assoc. prod. only), *Baby Face Harrington, Thanks a Million, The Man Who Broke the Bank at Monte Carlo* (also assoc. prod.) 1935; *The Prisoner of Shark Island* (also assoc. prod.), *The Country Doctor* (assoc. prod. only), *The Road to Glory* (assoc. prod. only), *Dimples* (assoc. prod. only), *Banjo on My Knee* 1936; *Nancy Steele Is Missing* (prod. only), *Cafe Metropole* (prod. only), *Slave Ship* (prod. only), *Love Under Fire* (prod. only) 1937; *Jesse James* (also assoc. prod.), *Wife Husband and Friend, Rose of Washington Square* (also prod.) 1939; *The Grapes of Wrath* (also assoc. prod.), *Chad Hanna* (also assoc. prod.) 1940; *Tobacco Road* 1941; *Roxie Hart* (also prod.), *The Pied Piper* (also prod.), *Life Begins at 8:30* (also prod.) 1942; *The Moon Is Down* (also prod.), *Holy Matrimony* (also prod.) 1943; *Casanova Brown* (also prod.), *The Woman in the Window* (also prod.) 1944; *The Keys of the Kingdom, Along Came Jones* 1945; *The Dark Mirror* (also prod.) 1946; *The Senator Was Indiscreet* (prod. only), *Mr. Peabody and the Mermaid* (also prod.) 1948; *Everybody Does It* (also prod.) 1949; *Three Came Home* (also prod.), *The Gunfighter* (prod. only), *The Mudlark* (also prod.) 1950; *The Long Dark Hall, The Desert Fox* (also prod.) 1951; *Phone Call from a Stranger* (also prod.), *We're Not Married* (also prod.), *O. Henry's Full House* ("The Ransom of Red Chief" episode), *My Cousin Rachel* (also prod.) 1952; *How to Marry a Millionaire* (also prod.) 1953; *Night People* (also prod., dir.), *Black Widow* (also prod., dir.) 1954; *How to Be Very Very Popular* (also prod., dir.) 1955; *The Man in the Gray Flannel Suit* (also dir.) 1956; *The True Story of Jesse James* (based on his screenplay for Jesse James), *Oh Men! Oh Women!* (prod., dir. only), *The Three Faces of Eve* (also prod., dir.) 1957; *The Man Who Understood Women* (also prod., dir.) 1959; *The Angel Wore Red* (also dir.), *Flaming Star* 1960;

Mr. Hobbs Takes a Vacation 1962; *Take Her She's Mine* 1963; *The World of Henry Orient* 1964; *The Dirty Dozen* 1967.

Johnson, Richard. Actor. Born on July 30, 1927, in Upminster, England. *ed.* RADA. Darkly handsome, saturnine leading man and second lead of the British stage and screen. He joined John Gielgud's repertory company in 1944 and after serving with the Royal Navy (1945–48) appeared in many films and stage productions on both sides of the Atlantic in increasingly more important roles. He frequently appeared with the Royal Shakespeare Company. In the late 70s his career slipped into low-budget Italian horror concoctions but it showed signs of recovery in the mid-80s, when he began producing some of his own vehicles. He was married briefly (1965–66) to Kim NOVAK.

FILMS INCLUDE: *Captain Horatio Hornblower* 1951; *Saadia* 1953; *Never So Few* 1959; *Cairo, The Haunting* 1963; *The Pumpkin Eater* 1964; *The Amorous Adventures of Moll Flanders, Operation Crossbow* 1965; *Khartoum, Deadlier Than the Male* 1966; *Danger Route, L'Avventuriero/The Rover* (It.) 1967; *Oedipus the King* (as Creon), *Some Girls Do, Les Amours de Lady Hamilton/Lady Hamilton/The Making of a Lady* (as Lord Nelson; Fr./It./Ger.), *A Twist of Sand* 1968; *Julius Caesar* (as Cassius) 1970; *Perche?!* (It.), *Beyond the Door* 1975; *Night Child, Aces High* 1976; *Take All of Me* (It.), *The Four Feathers, The Comeback* 1978; *L'Isola degli Uomini Pesci/Island of the Fishmen/The Island of Mutations/Screamers* (It.) 1979; *Zombi 2/Zombie* (It.), *The Monster Club* 1980; *Turtle Diary* (also prod.) 1985; *Lady Jane* 1986; *Castaway* (also co-exec. prod.), *The Lonely Passion of Judith Hearne* (co-prod. only) 1987; *Diving In* 1991; *Foreign Student* 1993.

Johnson, Rita. Actress. *b.* Rita McSean, Aug. 13, 1912, Worcester, Mass. *d.* 1965. Trained as a pianist, she veered toward acting in her late teens and after gaining experience on radio and in stock made her Broadway debut in 1935. Two years later she was signed as a contract player by MGM. For four years she played the heroine of many of the studio's second features, then freelanced with other studios, often playing "other woman" types. Her career was abruptly interrupted in 1948 as a result of a freak accident that required surgery for brain damage. She later returned to films in minor roles. She died of a brain hemorrhage at 53.

FILMS INCLUDE: *London by Night* 1937; *Man-Proof, Rich Man Poor Girl, Letter of Introduction* 1938; *Honolulu, Broadway Serenade, 6000 Enemies, They All Come Out, Nick Carter—Master Detective* 1939; *Congo Maisie, Forty Little Mothers, Edison the Man, The Golden Fleecing* 1940; *Here Comes Mr. Jordan, Appointment for Love* 1941; *The Major and the Minor* 1942; *My Friend Flicka* 1943; *Thunderhead, The Affairs of Susan, The Naughty Nineties* 1945; *Pardon My Past* 1946; *The Perfect Marriage, The Michigan Kid, They Won't Believe Me* 1947; *Sleep My Love, The Big Clock, An Innocent Affair* 1948; *Family Honeymoon* 1949; *The Second Face* 1950; *Susan Slept Here* 1954; *Emergency Hospital* 1956; *All Mine to Give* 1957.

Johnson, Van. Actor. Born Charles Van Johnson, on Aug. 25, 1916, in Newport, R.I., the son of a plumbing contractor. A former Broadway chorus boy, he zoomed to Hollywood popularity during the WW II years in the absence of the established stars. A freckled, red-haired, blue-eyed boy-next-door type, he captivated audiences of many MGM productions of the period with his air of innocent charm. Throughout the 40s he was idolized by hordes of screaming and swooning bobby-soxers, a phenomenon that earned him the label "The Voiceless Sinatra." From time to time, Johnson attempted serious acting but for many years was unable to shake off his boyish image. He remained with MGM through the mid-50s, then freelanced with various studios and occasionally worked in Europe. He was only sporadically active in films in the 60s and hardly at all in the 70s and 80s, but he still appears frequently on the stage, mainly on the dinner-theater circuit, and in TV movies. In 1985 he returned to Broadway, replacing Gene Barry in the hit musical 'La Cage aux Folles.' Long divorced, he lives in a Manhattan penthouse with his cat, Fred, and spends much of his free time painting acrylics.

FILMS: *Too Many Girls* (bit), *Murder in the Big House, Somewhere I'll Find You, The War Against Mrs. Hadley, Dr. Gillespie's New Assistant* 1942; *The Human Comedy* (as Marcus), *Pilot No. 5, Madame Curie, A Guy Named Joe* 1943; *The White Cliffs of Dover, Three Men in White, Two Girls and a Sailor, Thirty Seconds Over Tokyo* 1944; *Between Two Women, Thrill of a Romance, Weekend at the Waldorf* 1945; *Ziegfeld Follies* (cameo), *Easy to Wed, No Leave No Love, Till the Clouds Roll By* 1946; *High Barbaree, The Romance of Rosy Ridge* 1947; *State of the Union, The Bride Goes Wild* 1948; *Command Decision, Mother Is a Freshman, Scene of the Crime, In the Good Old Summertime, Battleground* 1949; *The Big Hangover, Duchess of Idaho* 1950; *Grounds for Marriage, Three Guys Named Mike, Go for Broke, Too Young to Kiss* 1951; *It's a Big Country, Invitation, When in Rome, Washington Story, Plymouth Adventure* 1952; *Confidentially Connie, Remains to Be Seen, Easy to Love* 1953; *The Siege at Red River, Men of the Fighting Lady, The Caine Mutiny* (as Lt. Maryk), *Brigadoon, The Last Time I Saw Paris* 1954; *The End of the Affair* 1955; *The Brass Bottle, Miracle in the Rain, 23 Paces to Baker Street* 1956; *Slander, Kelly and Me, Action of the Tiger* 1957; *The Last Blitzkrieg, Subway in the Sky* (UK), *Beyond This Place/Web of Evidence* (UK) 1959; *The Enemy General* 1960; *The Pied Piper of Hamelin* (originally shown on TV in 1957) 1961; *Wives and Lovers* 1963; *Divorce American Style* 1967; *Yours Mine and Ours, Where Angels Go... Trouble Follows* 1968; *La Battaglia d'Inghilterra/Battle Squadron/Eagle Over London* (It./Sp./Fr.), *Il Prezzo del Potere/The Price of Power* (It.) 1969; *Company of Killers* 1970; *L'Occhio del Ragno/The Eye of the Spider* 1971; *The Kidnapping of the President* (Can./US) 1980; *The Purple Rose of Cairo* 1985; *Laggiu Nella Giungla* (It.) 1988; *Fuga dal Paradiso/Escape from Paradise* (It./Fr./Ger.), *Delta Force Commando 2* (It.) 1990.

Johnston, Eric A. Executive. *b.* Dec. 21, 1896, Washington, D.C. *d.* 1962. The successor of Will HAYS as president of the Motion Picture Association of America, his rule as Hollywood's czar of censorship (1945–61) was somewhat less formidable than his predecessor's but was still marked by strict adherence to an inflexible code of self-censorship. A highly successful businessman and manufacturer, he held chairmanships and directorships in many companies and headed several government agencies. In 1953 he acted as President Eisenhower's special emissary to the Middle East with the rank of ambassador.

Johnston, Johnny (also **Johnnie**). Singer, actor. Born on Dec. 1, 1915, in St. Louis, Mo. A popular radio vocalist-guitarist, he played light leads in several Hollywood musicals of the 40s but fared better later as nightclub and stage star. Now retired from show business, he manufactures sporting goods in Phoenix, Arizona. He was briefly (1947–51) married to Kathryn GRAYSON.

FILMS: *Sweater Girl, Priorities on Parade, Star Spangled Rhythm* 1942; *You Can't Ration Love* 1944; *Till the Clouds Roll By* 1946; *This Time for Keeps* 1947; *Man from Texas* 1948; *Unchained* 1955; *Rock Around the Clock* 1956.

Johnston, Julanne. Actress. *b.* 1900, Indianapolis. *d.* 1988. Beautiful, exotic leading lady of Hollywood silents following a brief career as a dancer. Memorable as the Princess in the 1924 version of *The Thief of Bagdad,* opposite Douglas Fairbanks.

FILMS INCLUDE: *Better Times* 1919; *Miss Hobbs, Fickle Women* 1920; *The Brass Bottle, Madness of Youth* 1923; *The Thief of Bagdad* 1924; *Big Pal* 1925; *Aloma of the South Seas, Dame Chance, Twinkletoes* 1926; *Venus of Venice, Good Time Charley* 1927; *Name the Woman, The Olympic Hero, Oh Kay!* 1928; *The Younger Generation, Prisoners, Smiling Irish Eyes, City of Temptation, General Crack* 1929; *Strictly Modern, Madam Satan* 1930; *Stepping Sisters* 1932.

Johnston, Margaret. Actress. Born on Aug. 10, 1918, in Sydney, Australia. *ed.* RADA. Primarily a stage actress, she played lead roles in British films of the 40s and early 50s, character parts in the 60s.

FILMS INCLUDE: *The Prime Minister* 1940; *The Rake's Progress/The Notorious Gentleman* 1945; *A Man About the House* 1947; *Portrait of Clare* 1950; *The Magic Box* 1951; *Monsieur Ripois/Knave of Hearts/Lovers Happy Lovers* (Fr./UK) 1954; *Touch and Go* 1955; *Night of the Eagle/Burn Witch Burn!* 1962; *Girl in the Headlines/The Model Murder Case* 1963; *Life at the Top* 1965; *The Psychopath* 1966; *Sebastian* 1968.

Joker. Film company formed in 1913 by Carl LAEMMLE exclusively for the production of comedies. It specialized in lowbrow knockabout humor and through 1918 turned out numerous one-reel comedies for release through its parent company, Universal. Among Joker's stars were Max Asher, Louise Fazenda, and Bobby Vernon.

Jolson, Al. Singer, actor, entertainer. *b.* Asa Yoelson, May 26, 1886, St. Petersburg, Russia. *d.* 1950. In America from childhood, he sang in a synagogue, where his father was a cantor, then sought a show business career, at first with a circus, then as a black-faced café and vaudeville singer-entertainer. He rose to stardom on the New York stage and before long became America's most popular recording artist. Some still consider him the greatest entertaining talent of all time. His association with films started tentatively in 1923 when he was signed to star in a D. W. Griffith film, *Mammy's Boy.* But the film was never completed. In 1926 he sang three songs in a Warner Bros. experimental sound short, *April Showers.* Jolson made film history the following year as the star of the world's first talkie feature, *The Jazz Singer,* in which he spoke several sentences, including the immortal phrase "You ain't heard nothin' yet." He went on to star in several other successful formula musicals, but his popularity gradually declined as a result of changing public taste.

Jolson regained some of his old magic singing for the troops in WW II and found a new generation of admirers when his life story was told in the film *The Jolson Story* (1946); Larry Parks played Jolson, but Jolson provided the dubbed songs. The immense commercial success of the film prompted Columbia to produce a sequel, *Jolson Sings Again* (1949), in which the ailing singer was seen briefly, face to face with his impersonator. Jolson's third wife (among four) was Ruby KEELER. They married in 1928 and divorced in 1940. He died of a heart attack shortly after returning from entertaining US troops in Korea. Memoirs: *Mistah Jolson* (1951).

FEATURE FILMS: *The Jazz Singer* 1927; *The Singing Fool* 1928; *Sonny Boy* (unbilled cameo), *Say It with Songs, New York Nights* (song only) 1929; *Mammy, Big Boy* 1930; *Hallelujah I'm a Bum* 1933; *Wonder Bar* 1934; *Go Into Your Dance* 1935; *The Singing Kid* 1936; *Alexander's Ragtime Band* (unbilled cameo) 1938; *Rose of Washington Square, Hollywood Cavalcade* (as himself) 1939; *Swanee River* 1940; *Rhapsody in Blue* (as himself) 1945; *The Jolson Story* (v/o) 1946; *Jolson Sings Again* (voice, cameo) 1949.

Jones, Allan. Singer, actor. *b.* Oct. 14, 1907, in Scranton, Pa. *d.* 1992. The son of a coal miner, he worked in the mines as a boy and after graduating from high school used his savings and a scholarship to study music at the University of Syracuse and in Paris. Returning to the US, he appeared in musicals on the road and on Broadway before heading to Hollywood in the mid-30s. He became popular as a singing romantic lead in such films as *Show Boat* (1936), opposite Irene Dunne, and *The Firefly* (1937), opposite Jeanette MacDonald. In the latter he sang Rudolf Friml's 'Donkey Serenade,' a song with which he remained closely associated for the rest of his career. He also provided the rather wooden romantic interest for two Marx Brothers comedies, *A Night at the Opera* (1935) and *A Day at the Races* (1937). Once married to actress Irene HERVEY. Their son, Jack Jones, is a popular nightclub, TV, and recording singer.

FILMS: *Reckless, A Night at the Opera* 1935; *Rose Marie, Showboat* 1936; *A Day at the Races, The Firefly* 1937; *Everybody Sing* 1938; *Honeymoon in Bali, The Great Victor Herbert* 1939; *The Boys from Syracuse, One Night in the Tropics* 1940; *The Hard-Boiled Canary/There's Magic in Music* 1941; *Moonlight in Havana, True to the Army* 1942; *When Johnny Comes Marching Home, Crazy House* (cameo), *Larceny with Music, You're a Lucky Fellow Mr. Smith, Rhythm of the Islands* 1943; *The Singing Sheriff* 1944; *The Senorita from the West, Honeymoon Ahead* 1945; *Stage to Thunder Rock* 1964; *A Swingin' Summer* 1965.

Jones, Amy Holden. Director, screenwriter, former film editor. Born on Sept. 17, 1953, in Philadelphia. A graduate of Wellesley College, she got her film training at MIT and in 1973 won the top prize at the American Film Institute's National Student Film Festival. After working as an assistant on Martin Scorsese's *Taxi Driver* (1976) she became a film editor for Roger CORMAN. Anxious to direct, she invested $1,000 of her own money to make a seven-minute segment of a proposed horror film and persuaded Corman to finance its completion. It became her directorial debut, *Slumber Party Massacre* (1982). She is yet to emerge from the confinement of small budgets and flimsy story ideas. She married cinematographer Michael CHAPMAN.

FILMS: As editor—*Hollywood Boulevard* 1976; *Corvette Summer* 1978; *Second-Hand Hearts* (billed as Amy Holden Jones) 1981. As director—*Slumber Party Massacre* (also prod.) 1982; *Love Letters/My Love Letters* (also sc.) 1983; *Maid to Order* (also co-sc.) 1987; *Mystic Pizza* (story, co-sc. only) 1988; *It's Hard to Be Steve* (also co-sc.) 1992; *The Getaway* (scr.) 1994.

Jones, Barry. Actor. *b.* Mar. 6, 1893, Guernsey, Channel Islands. *d.* 1981. Bald character player of the British stage (from 1921) and screen (from 1932), typically in timid, jittery roles. Memorable as the mad bomber in *Seven Days to Noon* (1950), a superior lead role that led to his appearance in several Hollywood productions.

FILMS INCLUDE: *Number Seventeen, Arms and the Man* (as Bluntschli) 1932; *The Gay Adventure* 1936; *Murder in the Family* 1938; *Squadron Leader X* 1942; *Dancing with Crime, Frieda* 1947; *The Calendar* 1948; *The Bad Lord Byron* 1949; *Madeleine, Seven Days to Noon, The Clouded Yellow* 1950; *White Corridors, Appointment with Venus/Island Rescue* 1951; *Plymouth Adventure* (US) 1952; *Return to Paradise* (US) 1953; *Prince Valiant* (US), *Demetrius and the Gladiators* (US) 1954; *Brigadoon* (US) 1955; *The Glass Slipper* (US) 1955; *Alexander the Great* (US), *War and Peace* (US) 1956; *Saint Joan* (US) 1957; *The Safecracker* 1958; *The 39 Steps* 1959; *The Heroes of Telemark, A Study in Terror* 1965.

Jones, Buck. Actor. *b.* Charles Frederick Gebhart, Dec. 4, 1889, Vincennes, Ind. *d.* 1942. One of Hollywood's most popular cowboy stars, he had been an expert rider since childhood. At 17 he joined the US Cavalry and saw action in Mexico and the Philippines. After his discharge in 1913 he appeared in Wild West shows and circuses. He began his film career as an extra and stuntman in 1917. By 1919 he was playing lead roles and by 1921 he was a popular star. He appeared in numerous Westerns in the 20s and 30s, usually with his horse Silver, averaging eight productions a year. But his popularity had waned by 1941, when he signed with Monogram to co-star in the "Rough Rider" series. In December 1942, while on a campaign tour to sell US Bonds, he perished in a Boston nightclub fire.

FILMS INCLUDE: *Blood Will Tell* 1917; *True Blue, Riders of the Purple Sage, The Rainbow Trail* 1918; *The Sheriff's Son, The Speed Maniac* 1919; *The Last Straw, Forbidden Trails, The Square Shooter, Firebrand Trevison, Just Pals* 1920; *Riding with Death, Get Your Man* 1921; *Pardon My Nerve!, Western Speed* 1922; *Second-Hand Love, Big Dan* 1923; *The Vagabond Trail, The Circus Cowboy, The Desert Outlaw* 1924; *The Arizona Romeo, Hearts and Spurs, Lazybones* 1925; *The Fighting Buckaroo* 1926; *Black Jack, Blood Will Tell, The War Horse* 1927; *The Branded Sombrero, The Big Hop* 1928; *The Lone Rider* 1930; *The Avenger* 1931; *White Eagle, Riders of Death Valley* 1932; *Gordon of Ghost City* (serial), *Child of Manhattan* 1933; *Red Rider* (serial), *The Man Trailer, Texas Ranger* 1934; *The Roaring West* (serial), *Stone of Silver Creek* 1935; *Phantom Rider* (serial), *For the Service* (also dir.) 1936; *Law for Tombstone* (also dir.), *Black Aces* (also dir.), *Pony Express* 1937; *Headin' East, Hollywood Round-Up, Stranger from Arizona* 1938; *Unmarried* 1939; *Wagons Westward* 1940; *Riders of Death Valley* (serial), *White Eagle* (serial) 1941; *Down Texas Way, Dawn on the Great Divide* 1942.

Jones, Carolyn. Actress. *b.* Apr. 28, 1929, Amarillo, Tex. *d.* 1983. *ed.* Pasadena Playhouse. Versatile leading lady and second lead of Hollywood films with distinctive looks and offbeat style. A former disc jockey and stage player in stock, she gained wide popularity in the mid-60s in the role of Morticia in 'The Addams Family' (1964–66) TV series. On the big screen, she is perhaps best remembered as Vincent Price's embalmed victim in *House of Wax* (1953). She was nominated for an Oscar for her supporting role in *The Bachelor Party* (1957). Once married to producer Aaron Spelling, she died of cancer at 54.

FILMS INCLUDE: *The Turning Point, Road to Bali* 1952; *Off Limits, House of Wax, The Big Heat* 1953; *The Saracen Blade, Three Hours to Kill, Desiree* 1954; *The Seven Year Itch, The Tender Trap* 1955; *Invasion of the Body Snatchers, The Man Who Knew Too Much, The Opposite Sex* 1956; *The Bachelor Party, Baby Face Nelson* 1957; *Marjorie Morningstar, King Creole* 1958; *The Last Train from Gun Hill, A Hole in the Head, The Man in the Net, Career* 1959; *Ice Palace* 1960; *Sail a Crooked Ship, How the West Was Won* 1962; *A Ticklish Affair* 1963; *Color Me Dead, Heaven with a Gun* 1969; *Eaten Alive/Death Trap* 1977; *Good Luck, Miss Wyckoff* 1979.

Jones, Chuck (Charles M.). Animator. Born on Sept. 21, 1912, in Spokane, Wash. *ed.* Chouinard Art Inst. He worked at a variety of jobs, including seaman and portrait painter, before entering the industry in the early 30s as an assembly-line animator for Ub IWERKS, then Walter LANTZ. He later joined the Warner Bros. cartoon department and helped create such popular cartoon characters as Bugs Bunny, Porky Pig, Daffy Duck, Tweetie Pie, Speedy Gonzalez, Road Runner, Wile E. Coyote, and Private Snafu. His cartoons are noted for their speed, crazed action, and dynamic verve. Three of them won Academy Awards (designated AA below) and nine more were nominated for Oscars. In the early 50s he worked briefly for Walt DISNEY and was a leader in the famous strike that lead to the creation of UPA. After the dissolution of the Warner Bros. cartoon department in the early 60s he produced Tom and Jerry cartoons for MGM, then formed his own company and began creating many animation specials for TV. Widely recognized for his contributions to the art of animation, he was honored during the 70s and 80s with retrospectives of his work and showered with life achievement awards in the US and in international film festivals. Autobiography: *Chuck Amuck: The Life and Times of an Animated Cartoonist* (1989).

FILMS INCLUDE: *The Night Watchman* 1938; *Robin Hood Makes Good, Daffy Duck and the Dinosaur, Naughty but Mice, Little Brother Rat* 1939; *Elmer's Candid Camera, Sniffles Takes a Trip, Tom Thumb in Trouble* 1940; *Inki and the Lion, Porky's Midnight Matinee* 1941; *To Duck or Not to Duck, The Case of the Missing Hare* 1942; *The Aristo Cat* 1943; *From Hand to Mouse* 1944; *Hare Conditioned, The Eager Beaver* 1945; *Roughly Squeaking, Scenti-Mental Over You* 1946; *Mouse Wreckers, Scaredy Cat* 1948; *Frigid Hare, For Scent-imental Reasons* (AA), *So Much, So Little* (anim. doc.; AA) 1949; *The Scarlet Pumpernickel, The Rabbit of Seville* 1950; *The Wearing of the Grin* 1951; *Mousewarming, Little Beau Pepe, Kiss Me Cat* 1952; *Duck Amuck* 1953; *Punch Trunk* 1954; *Claws for Alarm, Lumber Jack Rabbit* (in 3-D) 1955; *Heaven Scent* 1956; *To Hare Is Human* 1957; *Hook, Line, and Stinker* (also sc.), *To Itch His Own* (also sc.) 1958; *Wild About Hurry* (also sc.) 1960; *Hopalong Casualty* (also sc.), *The Mouse on 57th Street* (also sc.) 1961; *Louvre, Come Back to Me* (also sc.), *Gay Purr-ee* (feature; story, co-sc. only) 1962; *Martian Thru Georgia* (also sc.), *I Was a Teenage Thumb* (also sc.) 1963; *The Cat Above the Mud Below, Snowbody Loves Me, The Unshrinkable Jerry Mouse* 1964; *The Dot and the Line* (AA), *Bad Day at Cat Rock* 1965; *Duel Personality* 1966; *The Phantom Toll Booth* (feature; co-dir.) 1971; *The Bugs Bunny-Roadrunner Movie/The Great American Chase* (compilation feature; also prod., co-sc.) 1979; *Gremlins* (cameo only, as himself) 1984; *Gremlins 2: The New Batch* (anim., dir., co-sc.) 1990; *Stay Tuned* (anim.) 1992.

Jones, David. Director. Born on Feb. 19, 1934, in Poole, England. *ed.* Cambridge (B.A., 1954; M.A. 1957). He began his career in 1958 as a producer and director for BBC-TV. In 1964 he became the artistic controller, and later associate director, of the Royal Shakespeare Company. In 1979 he moved to New York and for the next two years served as the artistic director of the Brooklyn Academy of Music. After teaching at the Yale School of Drama in 1981, he returned to England, where he directed a Shakespeare series for BBC-TV, before making his debut as a feature director in 1983. Although his initial offering, *Betrayal,* seemed too stagy for the screen, his subsequent film work proved literate, intelligent, and imaginative.

FILMS: *Betrayal* 1983; *84 Charing Cross Road* 1987; *Jacknife* 1989; *The Trial* 1993.

Jones, Dean. Actor, singer. Born on Jan. 25, 1931, in Morgan County, Ala. Light leading man of Hollywood films, seen often in kiddie-oriented Disney features. A former blues singer, he made frequent appearances on TV as a vocalist-entertainer and starred in such TV series as 'Ensign O'Toole' (1962–63), 'Chicago Teddy Bears' (1971), and 'Herbie, The Love Bug' (1982). He occasionally also appeared on the stage.

FILMS INCLUDE: *Tea and Sympathy* 1956; *Ten Thousand Bedrooms, Jailhouse Rock* 1957; *Imitation General, Torpedo Run* 1958; *Night of the Quarter Moon, Never So Few* 1959; *Under the Yum Yum Tree* 1963; *The New Interns* 1964; *Two on a Guillotine, That Darn Cat* 1965; *The Ugly Dachshund, Any Wednesday* 1966; *Monkeys Go Home!* 1967; *Blackbeard's*

Ghost, The Horse in the Gray Flannel Suit 1968; *The Love Bug* 1969; *The $1,000,000 Duck* 1971; *Snowball Express* 1972; *Mr. Superinvisible* 1973; *The Shaggy D.A.* 1976; *Herbie Goes to Monte Carlo* 1977; *Born Again* (as Charles Colson) 1978; *Other People's Money* 1991; *Beethoven* 1992; *Clear and Present Danger* 1994.

Jones, Freddie. Actor. Born on Sept. 12, 1927, in Stoke-on-Trent, England. Hammy, roguish character player of the British stage, screen, and TV, often seen in eccentric, offbeat roles, at times bordering on caricatures. A former laboratory assistant, he got into acting after winning a scholarship to the Rose Buford College of speech and drama. He appeared in many plays in rep and on the London stage before his screen debut in the mid-60s. He received accolades for his portrayal of Claudius in the British TV series 'The Caesars,' for which he was named the World's Best TV Actor at the 1969 Monte Carlo Festival. His growing reputation eventually led to roles in American and Continental films.

FILMS INCLUDE: *Marat/Sade* 1966; *Accident, Far from the Madding Crowd* 1967; *The Bliss of Mrs. Blossom, Otley* 1968; *Frankenstein Must Be Destroyed* 1969; *The Man Who Haunted Himself, Goodbye Gemini* 1970; *Kidnapped* 1971; *Antony and Cleopatra, Sitting Target* 1972; *The Satanic Rites of Dracula/Count Dracula and His Vampire Bride* 1973; *All Creatures Great and Small, Juggernaut, Vampira/Old Dracula* 1974; *Zulu Dawn* (US/Hol.) 1979; *The Elephant Man* 1980; *Firefox* (US) 1982; *E la Nave va/And the Ship Sails On* (It.), *Krull* 1983; *Firestarter* (US), *Dune* (US) 1984; *Consuming Passions* (UK/US) 1988; *Erik the Viking* (UK/Sw.) 1989; *Wild at Heart* (US) 1990; *The Last Butterfly* (Fr./Czech.) 1991; *Mystery of Edwin Drood* (UK) 1993; *The Neverending Story III* 1994; *Cold Comfort Farm* 1995.

Jones, F. Richard (Dick). Director. *b.* 1890(?), in St. Louis, Mo. Deceased. One of the prime directors of early American screen comedy, he made many hilarious two-reelers for Mack SENNETT in the years 1915–20, starring such comics as Charles Murray, Slim Summerville, Louise Fazenda, Edgar Kennedy, Chester Conklin, Ben Turpin, and Polly Moran. He then moved on to feature films for Sennett and other producers and proved himself equally at home with romances and adventure dramas. His last film, and only talkie, *Bulldog Drummond* (1929), starring Ronald Colman, was a superior early sound thriller.

FILMS INCLUDE: Shorts—*A Game Old Knight, Her Painted Hero, The Great Vacuum Robbery* 1915; *His Hereafter, A Love Riot* 1916; *It Pays to Exercise, Saucy Madeline, His Smothered Love, The Battle Royal, Mickey, Sleuths* 1918; *Never Too Old, The Foolish Age, Love's False Faces, The Dentist, The Speakeasy* 1919; *Down on the Farm* (also co-sc.), *Down on the Farm* (co-dir. with Erle Kenton and Ray Gray), *Gee Whiz!* 1920; *The First 100 Years, Little Robinson Corkscrew* 1924. Features—*Mickey* (co-dir. with James Young) 1918; *Yankee Doodle in Berlin* 1919; *Love Honor and Behave* (co-dir. with Erle Kenton) 1920; *The Ghost in the Garret, Molly O* 1921; *The Crossroads of New York, The Country Flapper* 1922; *Suzanna, The Shriek of Araby, The Extra Girl* 1923; *The Gaucho* 1927; *The Water Hole, The Big Killing, Someone to Love* 1928; *Bulldog Drummond* 1929.

Jones, Grace. Singer, actress. Born on May 19, 1952, in Spanishtown, Jamaica. Tall, slick, androgynous black singer and performance artist. She made a forgettable debut in 1973, then appeared in several obscure Italian films, before making her first screen impact as a bald warrior in *Conan the Destroyer* (1984).

FILMS INCLUDE: *Gordon's War* 1973; *Conan the Destroyer* 1984; *A View to a Kill* 1985; *Vamp* 1986; *Straight to Hell, Siesta* 1987; *Boomerang, Freddie as F.R.O.7* (song only) (UK) 1992.

Jones, Griffith. Actor. Born on Nov. 19, 1910 in London. *ed.* University Coll.; RADA (gold medalist). Appealing leading man of the British stage and screen, with several impressive film roles to his credit in the 30s and 40s. Later in diminishing character parts. His daughter, Gemma Jones (*b.* Dec. 4 1932, London), and son, Nicholas Jones, are also actors.

FILMS INCLUDE: *The Faithful Heart* 1932; *Catherine the Great* 1934; *Escape Me Never* 1935; *The Mill on the Floss* 1936; *A Yank at Oxford* 1938; *The Four Just Men/The Secret Four, Young Man's Fancy* 1939; *Atlantic Ferry/Sons of the Sea* 1941; *The Day Will Dawn/The Avengers* 1942; *Henry V* 1944; *The Wicked Lady, The Rake's Progress/Notorious Gentleman* 1945; *They Made Me a Fugitive/I Became a Criminal* 1947; *Good Time Girl, Miranda, Look Before You Love* 1948; *Once Upon a Dream* 1949; *Honeymoon Deferred* 1951; *Star of My Night* 1954; *Face in the Night/Menace in the Night* 1957; *The Truth About Women* 1958; *Kill Her Gently* 1959; *Strangler's Web* 1963; *Decline and Fall* 1968.

Jones, Harmon. Director, editor. *b.* June 3, 1911, Canada. *d.* 1972. A highly accomplished film editor at Fox in the 40s, he achieved only modest distinction as a director in the 50s, and was relegated mostly to TV work in the 60s.

FILMS INCLUDE: As editor—*Home in Indiana* 1944; *The House on 92nd Street* 1945; *13 Rue Madeleine* 1946; *Boomerang, Gentleman's Agreement* 1947; *Sitting Pretty, Cry of the City, Yellow Sky* 1948; *House of Strangers, Pinky* 1949; *Panic in the Streets* 1950. As director (complete)—*As Young As You Feel* 1951; *The Pride of St. Louis, Bloodhounds of Broadway* 1952; *The Silver Whip, City of Bad Men, The Kid from Left Field* 1953; *Gorilla at Large, Princess of the Nile* 1954; *Target Zero* 1955; *Day of Fury, Canyon River* 1956; *The Beast of Budapest, Bullwhip, Wolf Larsen* 1958; *Don't Worry—We'll Think of a Title* 1966.

Jones, Henry. Actor. Born on Aug. 1, 1912, in Philadelphia. *ed.* St. Joseph's Coll. Fine, versatile character player of the American stage and screen whose bulldog-like expressive features ranged from the friendly and reliable to the menacing and the perverse. A Tony winner for 'Sunrise at Campobello' (1958) on Broadway, he also appeared in numerous dramas and comedies on TV.

FILMS INCLUDE: *The Lady Says No* 1951; *The Bad Seed, The Girl Can't Help It* 1956; *Will Success Spoil Rock Hunter?, 3:10 to Yuma* 1957; *Vertigo* 1958; *Cash McCall* 1959; *The Bramble Bush* 1960; *Angel Baby* 1961; *Never Too Late* 1965; *Le Scandale/The Champagne Murders* (Fr.) 1967; *Project X, Stay Away Joe* 1968; *Support Your Local Sheriff, Butch Cassidy and the Sundance Kid* 1969; *Dirty Dingus Magee, Rabbit Run* 1970; *Support Your Local Gunfighter* 1971; *Pete 'n' Tillie* 1972; *Tom Sawyer* 1973; *The Outfit* 1974; *9 to 5* 1980; *Deathtrap* 1982; *Nowhere to Run* 1989; *Dick Tracy* 1990.

Jones, James Earl. Actor. Born on Jan. 17, 1931, in Arkabutla, Miss. Imposing character lead of the American stage, screen, and television. The son of prizefighter-turned-actor Robert Earl Jones, he was raised by his maternal grandparents on a Michigan farm. He planned to study medicine at the University of Michigan but switched to drama and, following a stint with the Army, enrolled at New York's American Theatre Wing. He and his father waxed floors while pursuing their theatrical ambitions. He made his Broadway debut in 1957 and subsequently appeared in many stage productions, including several seasons with Joseph Papp's New York Shakespeare Festival. A sturdy black performer, he was impressive in such productions as 'Othello' and 'The Emperor Jones' (both 1964) and scored his greatest triumph as the Tony Award–winning star of Broadway's 'The Great White Hope' (1966–68). Meanwhile he had appeared as an African chieftain in the TV 'Tarzan' series and made his big-screen debut in 1964. He was nominated for an Oscar for repeating his stage role in the 1970 film version of *The Great White Hope* and portrayed the "first black President of the US" in *The Man* (1972). Jones's other memorable portrayals included the title role in the Broadway play 'Paul Robeson' (1977) and author Alex Haley in the TV miniseries 'Roots: The Next Generation' (1979). His rich, rumbling voice added a dimension of mysterious menace to the masked figure of Darth Vader in the space fantasy *Star Wars* (1977) and its sequels. While sustaining a strong presence on the big screen, Jones starred in his own TV series 'Paris' (1979–80) and 'Gabriel's Fire' (1990–91), appeared in a number of TV movies, and won another Tony for his performance on Broadway in 'Fences' (1986). He was notable as the reclusive writer Terence Mann in *Field of Dreams*.

FILMS: *Dr. Strangelove* 1964; *The Comedians* 1967; *King* (doc.), *End of the Road, The Great White Hope* 1970; *Malcolm X* (doc.; narr.), *The Man* 1972; *Claudine* 1974; *Deadly Hero, The River Niger, The Bingo Long Traveling All-Stars and Motor Kings, Swashbuckler* 1976; *The Greatest, Exorcist II: The Heretic, The Last Remake of Beau Geste, Star Wars* (voice of Darth Vader only; uncredited), *A Piece of the Action* 1977; *The Bushido Blade* (Jap.) 1979; *The Empire Strikes Back* (v/o) 1980; *Conan the Barbarian, Blood Tide* 1982; *Return of the Jedi* (v/o) 1983; *My Little Girl, Soul Man* 1986; *Allan Quartermain and the Lost City of Gold, Will Vinton's Festival of Claymation* (v/o), *Gardens of Stone, Pinocchio and the Emperor of the Night* (v/o), *Matewan* 1987; *Coming to America* 1988; *Three Fugitives, Best of the Best, Field of Dreams, Grim Prairie Tales* 1989; *The Hunt for Red October, Terrorgram* (narr.), *The Ambulance* 1990; *True Identity, Convicts* 1991; *Scorchers, Patriot Games* 1992; *Sommersby, Meteor Man* 1993; *Clean Slate, Clear and Present Danger, The Lion King* (v/o) 1994; *Cry the Beloved Country, Jefferson in Paris, Judge Dredd* (v/o) 1995; *A Family Thing, Looking for Richard* 1996.

Jones, Jeffrey. Actor. Born on Sept. 28, 1947, in Buffalo, N.Y. Busy, sharp-featured character player of the American stage, TV, and films. He became involved in school dramatics while attending Lawrence U. (Wisconsin) as a premed student, then joined Sir Tyrone Guthrie's Theatre in Minneapolis. After a sojourn in South America, and studies on a full scholarship at London's Academy of Music and Dramatic Arts, he performed for a couple of years in Canada before returning to the US in the mid-70s.

FILMS INCLUDE: *A Wedding* 1978; *The Soldier* 1982; *Easy Money* 1983; *Amadeus* (as Emperor Joseph II) 1984; *Transylvania 6–5000* 1985; *Ferris Bueller's Day Off, Howard the Duck* 1986; *Hanoi Hilton* 1987; *Beetlejuice, Without a Clue* (as Inspector Lestrade; UK) 1988; *Who's Harry Crumb?, Valmont* (Fr./UK) 1989; *The Hunt for Red October, Enid Is Sleeping* 1990; *Over Her Dead Body, Mom and Dad Save the World, Stay Tuned, Out on a Limb* 1992.

Jones, Jennifer. Actress. Born Phyllis Isley, on Mar. 2, 1919, in Tulsa, Okla. As a child she toured with her parents in vaudeville tent shows and later performed in stock. While attending the American Academy of Dramatic Arts in New York, she met another aspiring actor, Robert WALKER. They married in 1939 and together headed for Hollywood, where she began her screen career that same year playing leads in minor action films—a Western and a serial—under her real name, Phyllis Isley. She then attracted the attention of David O. SELZNICK, who signed her to a long-term contract, changed her name to Jennifer Jones, and groomed her for stardom. After three years of training and hit-and-run publicity tactics, he unveiled his new discovery in a carefully chosen role as the star of *The Song of Bernadette* (1943). She won an Academy Award for her effort and went on to star in many other high-budget productions, in roles judiciously selected by Selznick, who became her husband in 1949 (she had divorced Walker in 1945). In looks and personality she was not the typical Hollywood leading lady, and although hardly a formidable actress, she could turn out a creditable performance in the right vehicle and under the right directorial tutelage. She was nominated for Oscars as best supporting actress for *Since You Went Away* (1944) and as best actress for *Love Letters* (1945), *Duel in the Sun* (1946), and *Love Is a Many Splendored Thing* (1955). She carefully avoided typecasting and played roles ranging from the innocent and placid to the sensuous and tempestuous. She was widowed in 1965, and in 1971 married industrialist Norton Simon. She is president of the Norton Simon Museum in Pasadena, California. Her son by Robert Walker, Robert Walker, Jr. (*b.* 1941), is a film and TV actor.

FILMS: As Phyllis Isley—*New Frontier, Dick Tracy's G-Men* (serial) 1939. As Jennifer Jones—*The Song of Bernadette* (as Bernadette Soubirous), *Since You Went Away* 1944; *Love Letters* 1945; *Cluny Brown* 1946; *Duel in the Sun* 1947; *Portrait of Jennie, We Were Strangers, Madame Bovary* (title role) 1949; *Gone to Earth/The Wild Heart* (UK) 1950; *Carrie* (as Dreiser's Sister Carrie) 1952; *Ruby Gentry* 1953; *Stazione Termini/Indiscretion of an American Wife* (It./US), *Beat the Devil* (UK/US) 1954; *Love Is a Many Splendored Thing, Good Morning Miss Dove* 1955; *The Man in the Gray Flannel Suit* 1956; *The Barretts of Wimpole Street* (as Elizabeth Barrett), *A Farewell to Arms* (as Nurse Catherine Barkley) 1957; *Tender Is the Night* (as Nicole Diver) 1962; *The Idol* 1966; *Angel Angel Down We Go/Cult of the Damned* 1969; *The Towering Inferno* 1974.

Jones, L. Q. Actor. Born Justice Ellis McQueen, on Aug. 19, 1927, in Beaumont, Tex. *ed.* Lamar Jr. Coll.; Lon Morris Coll.; U. of Texas. Tall, broad-shouldered, rugged supporting player of numerous Hollywood Westerns and action pictures, since the mid-50s. He directed *A Boy and His Dog* (1975), a futuristic black comedy that has attracted a cult following. Also quite busy on TV.

FILMS INCLUDE: *An Annapolis Story, Target Zero* 1955; *Santiago, Toward the Unknown, Love Me Tender* 1956; *Men in War, Operation Mad Ball* 1957; *The Young Lions, The Naked and the Dead, Torpedo Run* 1958; *Hound Dog Man* 1959; *Flaming Star* 1960; *Ride the High Country* 1962; *Major Dundee* 1965; *The Counterfeit Killer* 1968; *The Wild Bunch* 1969; *The Ballad of Cable Hogue* 1970; *The Hunting Party* (UK), *The Brotherhood of Satan* (also co-prod.) 1971; *Pat Garrett and Billy the Kid* 1973; *White Line Fever, A Boy and His Dog* (dir., sc. only) 1975; *Mother Jugs & Speed* 1976; *Fast Charlie, The Moonbeam Rider* 1979; *The Beast Within* 1982; *Lone Wolf McQuade* 1983; *Bulletproof* 1988; *River of Death* 1989.

Jones, Marcia Mae. Actress. Born on Aug. 1, 1924, in Los Angeles. She made her film debut at the age of two, playing Dolores Costello as a baby in *Mannequin* (1926), and during the 30s played child roles in many Hollywood films. She was not particularly pretty or cute and never developed into a popular child star. But she had an expressive face that was occasionally used to advantage in young "character" roles, most memorably in *These Three* (1936), a screen adaptation of Lillian Hellman's 'The Children's Hour,' in which she gave a convincing portrayal of a terrorized little girl. Her career declined sharply in the 40s following a succession of poor ingenue roles, and she retired from the screen early in the 50s. However, she came out of retirement in the late 60s and has since been seen occasionally in supporting roles on TV and in films, sometimes using the name Marsha Jones.

FILMS INCLUDE: *Mannequin* 1926; *The Champ* 1931; *These Three, The Garden of Allah* 1936; *The Life of Emile Zola, Heidi* 1937; *The Adventures of Tom Sawyer, Mad About Music* 1938; *The Little Princess, First Love, Meet Doctor Christian* 1939; *Tomboy, Anne of Windy Poplars, The Haunted House* 1940; *Nice Girl?, Let's Go Collegiate* 1941; *Secrets of a Co-Ed* 1942; *The Youngest Profession, Top Man* 1943; *Snafu* 1945; *Arson Inc.* 1949; *Hi-Jacked, The Daughter of Rosy O'Grady* 1950; *Chicago Calling* 1952; *Rogues' Gallery* 1968; *The Spectre of Edgar Allan Poe, The Way We Were* 1973.

Jones, Paul. American producer. *b.* 1901. *d.* 1968. He began as an assistant director in 1929, became a writer and associate producer in 1934, and produced many successful light Paramount films from 1939, including several Preston Sturges sparklers and Bob Hope and Martin and Lewis comedies.

FILMS INCLUDE: *Poppi* (assoc. prod.) 1936; *Never Say Die* 1939; *The Great McGinty* 1940; *The Lady Eve, Road to Zanzibar, Sullivan's Travels, Kiss the Boys Goodbye* 1941; *My Favorite Blonde, The Palm Beach Story, The Road to Morocco* 1942; *A Medal for Benny, Hold That Blonde* 1945; *Monsieur Beaucaire, Road to Utopia, The Virginian* 1946; *Dear Ruth, Where There's Life* 1947; *A Southern Yankee* 1948; *My Favorite Spy* 1951; *The Caddy* 1953; *Casanova's Big Night* 1954; *You're Never Too Young* 1955; *Pardners* 1956; *It's Only Money* 1962; *Who's Minding the Store?* 1963; *The Disorderly Orderly* 1964.

Jones, Quincy. Composer, producer. Born on Mar. 14, 1933, in Chicago. *ed.* Seattle U.; Berklee School of Music; Boston Conservatory. He started his professional music career at 17 as a trumpeter and arranger for Lionel Hampton. He later played and arranged for Dizzy Gillespie, Count Basie, and other jazz greats, then formed his own band, with which he toured Europe. After holding executive positions with recording companies, he began composing for films in the mid-60s, soon drawing praise for his colorful jazz scores. He was nominated for an Academy Award for *In Cold Blood* (1967) and won an Emmy for the score of the TV miniseries 'Roots' (1977). Along with his prolific career as a composer, Jones remained active as an arranger, conductor, and recording producer under his own label; he produced much of Michael Jackson's most memorable material in the mid-80s. In 1991 he won six Grammy Awards for his album 'Back on the Block,' bringing his lifetime total to 25, the most for any nonclassical musician. The artist and his work were the subject of the documentary *Listen Up: The Lives of Quincy Jones* (1990).

FILMS INCLUDE: *The Pawnbroker, Mirage* 1965; *In the Heat of the Night, Banning, In Cold Blood* 1967; *Jigsaw* 1968; *The Lost Man, Bob & Carol & Ted & Alice, Cactus Flower* 1969; *The Out-of-Towners* 1970; *Brother John, The Anderson Tapes* 1971; *The Hot Rock, The New Centurions, The Getaway* 1972; *The Wiz* 1978; *The Color Purple* (also co-prod.) 1985; *Listen Up: The Lives of Quincy Jones* (music, perf.) 1990; *Boyz N the Hood* (song) 1991; *The Getaway, A Great Day in Harlem* (narr.) 1994; *A Family Thing* 1996.

Jones, Sam J. Actor. Born on Aug. 12, 1954, in Chicago. Athletic, blond leading man of Hollywood films. Best known for the title role of *Flash Gordon* (1980). Later seen mostly in low-budget productions. His TV appearances included the lead in the series 'Code Red' (1981–82).

FILMS INCLUDE: *10* 1979; *Flash Gordon* 1980; *My Chauffeur* 1986; *Jane and the Lost City* (UK) 1987; *Silent Assassins* 1988; *One Man Force* 1989; *Driving Force* (Austral.) 1990; *In Gold We Trust* 1991; *DaVinci's War, Fist of Honor* 1992.

Jones, Shirley. Actress, singer. Born on Mar. 31, 1934, in Smithton, Pa. A former Miss Pittsburgh, then a musical comedy star, she became typecast in films as a sweet, wholesome young lady but won an Academy Award as best supporting actress for her role as a prostitute in *Elmer Gantry.* Often appeared on the stage, on TV, and in nightclubs with her onetime husband, the late singer Jack Cassidy. She co-starred with her stepson, David Cassidy, in the TV series 'The Partridge Family' (1970–74) and later starred in 'Shirley Miller' (1979–80). Her own son, Shaun Cassidy (*b.* Sept. 27, 1958, Los Angeles), was a popular TV actor throughout the 70s. She married actor Marty Ingels (*b.* Mar. 9, 1936, Brooklyn, N.Y.). She is the national chairman of the Leukemia Foundation.

FILMS: *Oklahoma!* 1955; *Carousel* 1956; *April Love* 1957; *Never Steal Anything Small* 1959; *Bobbikins* (UK), *Elmer Gantry, Pepe* 1960; *Two Rode Together* 1961; *The Music Man* 1962; *The Courtship of Eddie's Father, A Ticklish Affair* 1963; *Dark Purpose, Bedtime Story* 1964; *Fluffy, The Secret of My Success* 1965; *The Happy Ending* 1969; *The Cheyenne Social Club* 1970; *Beyond the Poseidon Adventure* 1979; *Tank* 1984.

Jones, Terry. Director, screenwriter, actor. Born in 1942, in Colwyn Bay, North Wales. He worked with various repertory groups before joining BBC-TV's writing staff in 1965. In 1969 he became part of the hit comedy TV show 'Monty Python's Flying Circus' as a performer, writer, and director, and collaborated in all three capacities on several of the group's feature films. He later continued directing on his own.

FILMS: *And Now for Something Completely Different* (co-sc., act.) 1972; *Monty Python and the Holy Grail* (co-dir., co-sc. act.) 1975; *Monty Python's Life of Brian/Life of Brian* (dir., co-sc., act.) 1979; *Monty Python's The Meaning of Life* (dir., co-sc., act.) 1983; *Labyrinth* (sc.) 1986; *Personal Services* (dir.) 1987; *Consuming Passions* (co-play basis only) 1988; *Erik the Viking* (dir. sc., act.; UK/Sw.) 1989.

Jones, Tommy Lee. Actor. Born on Sept. 15, 1946, in San Saba, Tex. Intense, tough-looking leading man of the American stage, TV, and films, often in troubled or troublesome roles. He worked in the oil fields as a youth and became involved in acting at Harvard, where he majored in English. He made his Broadway debut in 1969 and his first screen appearance the following year. He returned to Broadway for several plays of the early 70s before resuming his film career in 1976. He won an Emmy Award for his portrayal of a convicted killer in the TV movie 'The Executioner's Song' (1982). Always a respected actor, he became a box-office draw in the 1990s with a spate of well-drawn performances, notably that of the smart, sardonic investigator in *The Fugitive,* for which he was awarded 1993's Oscar for best supporting actor. He is married to photojournalist Kimberlea Jones.

FILMS: *Love Story* 1970; *Jackson County Jail* 1976; *Rolling Thunder, Eliza's Horoscope* 1977; *The Betsy, Eyes of Laura Mars* 1978; *Coal Miner's Daughter* 1980; *Back Roads* 1981; *Nate and Hayes* (US/NZ) 1983; *The River Rat* 1984; *Black Moon Rising* 1986; *The Big Town* 1987; *Stormy Monday* (UK) 1988; *The Package* 1989; *Fire Birds* 1990; *JFK* 1991; *Under Siege* 1992; *The Fugitive, Heaven and Earth, House of Cards* 1993; *Blown Away, Blue Sky, The Client, Cobb, Natural Born Killers* 1994; *Batman Forever* 1995; *Men in Black, Volcano* 1997.

Jones, Trevor. Composer. Born on March 23, 1949, in Cape Town, South Africa. Composer of British and American film and television scores of the 80s and 90s. His work has enhanced epics such as *Excalibur* and thrillers such as *Mississippi Burning*.

FILMS INCLUDE: *Brothers and Sisters* (UK) 1980; *Excalibur, Time Bandits* 1981; *The Dark Crystal* (UK), *The Sender* (UK) 1982; *Nate and Hayes* (US/NZ), *Those Glory Glory Days* 1983; *Aderyn Papur* (UK) 1984; *Runaway Train* 1985; *Labyrinth* 1986; *Angel Heart* 1987; *Dominick and Eugene, Just Ask for Diamond, Mississippi Burning* 1988; *A Private Life, Sea of Love, Sweet Lies* 1989; *Arachnophobia, Bad Influence* 1990; *True Colors* 1991; *Freejack, Blame It on the Bellboy, Chains of Gold, Crisscross, The Last of the Mohicans* 1992.

Jordan, Dorothy. Actress. *b.* Aug. 9, 1906, Clarksville, Tenn. *d.* 1988. *ed.* Southwestern U.; AADA. Trained as a ballet dancer, she appeared in several Broadway musicals before moving to Hollywood during the switch to sound. She co-starred with Ramon NOVARRO in several of his early talkies and played routine leads in a variety of film productions of the early 30s, then retired to marry Merian C. COOPER. She made a brief comeback in the 50s, playing small roles in three John FORD films, particularly the wife still in love with John Wayne in *The Searchers*.

FILMS INCLUDE: *Words and Music* (bit as dancer), *Black Magic, The Taming of the Shrew* (as Bianca), *Devil-May-Care* 1929; *In Gay Madrid, Call of the Flesh, Love in the Rough, Min and Bill* 1930; *A Tailor-Made Man, Young Sinners, Shipmates, The Beloved Bachelor, Hell Divers* 1931; *The Lost Squadron, The Wet Parade, Roadhouse Murder, Down to Earth, 70,000 Witnesses, Cabin in the Cotton, That's My Boy* 1932; *Strictly Personal, Bondage, One Man's Journey* 1933; *The Sun Shines Bright* 1953; *The Searchers* 1956; *The Wings of Eagles* 1957.

Jordan, Glenn. Director. Born on Apr. 5, 1936, in San Antonio, Tex. *ed.* Harvard; Yale Drama School. A veteran of the stage, he directed and produced extensively for TV before a brief foray into features in the early 80s. Since then, he has been steadily involved in topical made-for-TV films, and also directed *O Pioneers!* (starring Jessica Lange) and *Sarah, Plain and Tall* (starring Glenn Close), Hallmark Hall of Fame presentations that were extremely popular among viewers and critics. The latter film received nine Emmy nominations.

FILMS: *Only When I Laugh* 1981; *The Buddy System, Mass Appeal* 1984.

Jordan, Neil. Director, screenwriter. Born on Feb. 25, 1950, in Sligo, Ireland. *ed.* University College, Dublin (Irish history, English). A successful novelist and short story writer (*Night in Tunisia*), he first became involved in film in 1980 when he was hired by John BOORMAN as a script consultant on *Excalibur* (1981) and made a documentary on the making of that film. He stunned critics with his Buñuelesque debut film, *Angel* (1982), a surrealistic trip into the netherworld of murder, revenge, and violence. He gained a widening circle of admirers with *The Company of Wolves* (1984), a fanciful, erotically charged exploration of the realm of fairy tales, and won international accolades for *Mona Lisa* (1986), a fascinating descent into the dark recesses of the dark domain of London's tarts and pimps, brightened by the persistent romantic naiveté of a petty hood. The latter film's commercial success led to two big-budget Hollywood assignments, both of which flopped, at least partly because of destructive studio interference. Jordan then returned to Ireland, where he made *The Crying Game*, a clever, emotionally charged film, based on a short story he had written years earlier. The film won international accolades, including nominations in the top six categories at the Oscars, and became the biggest surprise hit of 1992 with one of the most startling plot twists in film history. Separated from his wife, with whom he has two daughters, he is romantically involved with his assistant Brenda Rawn, with whom he has two sons.

FILMS (as director-screenwriter): *Traveller* (sc. only) 1981; *Angel* (Ire.) 1982; *The Company of Wolves* 1984; *Mona Lisa* 1986; *High Spirits* (US) 1988; *We're No Angels* (dir. only; US) 1989; *The Miracle* (Ire.) 1991; *The Crying Game* (UK) 1992; *Interview with a Vampire* 1994; *Michael Collins* 1996.

Jordan, Richard. Actor. *b.* July 19, 1938, in New York City. *d.* 1993. *ed.* Harvard. Rugged, good-looking leading man and supporting player of the American stage, screen, and TV. Starred in the miniseries 'Captains and the Kings' (1976). Once married to actress Kathleen Widdoes, he fathered a child with actress Blair BROWN.

FILMS: *Ready for the People* 1964; *Valdez Is Coming, Lawman* 1971; *Chato's Land, Trial of the Catonsville Nine* 1972; *Kamouraska* (Can./Fr.), *The Friends of Eddie Coyle* 1973; *Rooster Cogburn, The Yakuza* 1975; *Logan's Run, One Night Stand* (Fr.) 1976; *Interiors* 1978; *Old Boyfriends, A Nightingale Sang in Berkeley Square* 1979; *Raise the Titanic!* (UK) 1980; *A Flash of Green* (also prod.), *Dune* 1984; *The Mean Season* 1985; *The Men's Club, Solarbabies* 1986; *The Secret of My Success* 1987; *Romero* 1989; *The Hunt for Red October* 1990; *Heaven Is a Playground, Shout, Timebomb* 1991; *Primary Motive* 1992; *Posse* 1993.

Jory, Victor. Actor. *b.* Nov. 23, 1902, Dawson City, Alaska. *d.* 1982. *ed.* U. of California. Big and burly (he was boxing and wrestling champion of the Coast Guard), he played occasional leads, then numerous character parts in a variety of Hollywood films, mostly B pictures, typically as an evil-eyed heavy. Active on stage from 1929. Wrote a Broadway play, 'Five Who Were Mad.' His wife, Jean Innes (1902–78), also appeared in films.

FILMS INCLUDE: *Renegades* 1930; *Pride of the Legion* 1932; *State Fair, Broadway Bad, Infernal Machine, Trick for Trick, I Loved You Wednesday, The Devil's in Love* (lead), *My Woman* (lead), *Smoky* (lead) 1933; *I Believed in You* (lead), *Murder in Trinidad, He Was Her Man, Madame Du Barry* 1934; *A Midsummer Night's Dream* (as King Oberon), *Escape from Devil's Island* (lead) 1935; *The King Steps Out, Meet Nero Wolfe* 1936; *First Lady* 1937; *The Adventures of Tom Sawyer* (as Injun Joe) 1938; *Blackwell's Island, Dodge City, Man of Conquest* (as William Travis), *Susannah of the Mounties, Each Dawn I Die, Gone With the Wind* 1939; *The Shadow* (serial), *The Light of Western Stars, River's End, Give Us Wings* 1940; *Charlie Chan in Rio, Bad Men of Missouri* 1941; *Tombstone* 1942; *The Kansan* 1943; *The Loves of Carmen* (as Garcia), *Gallant Blade* 1948; *South of St. Louis, Canadian Pacific* 1949; *The Capture* 1950; *Son of Ali Baba* 1952; *The Man from the Alamo* 1953; *Valley of the Kings* 1954; *Death of a Scoundrel* 1956; *The Fugitive Kind* 1960; *The Miracle Worker* 1962; *Cheyenne Autumn* 1964; *Jigsaw* 1968; *Flap* 1970; *A Time for Dying* 1971; *Papillon* 1973; *The Mountain Men* 1980.

José, Edward. Director. *b.* 1880(?), Antwerp. Deceased. In the US from youth, he entered the film industry as an actor and gained some fame in the title role of *A Fool There Was* (1915) opposite Theda Bara. He then turned to directing, and in addition to piloting several early Pearl WHITE serials, he supervised many silent Hollywood features of the late 1910s and early 20s. His 1915 version of *The Beloved Vagabond,* six reels long and tinted in color, was among the most ambitious productions of the early American Cinema. In 1922 he went to France, where he continued directing through 1926.

FILMS INCLUDE: *The Beloved Vagabond, Simon the Jester, Nedra, The Closing Net* 1915; *The Iron Claw* (serial), *Pearl of the Army* (serial), *The Light That Failed, Ashes of*

Embers 1916; *Poppy, May Blossom, The Moth, Hungry Heart, The Slave Market* 1917; *Her Silent Sacrifice, Woman and Wife, La Tosca, Resurrection, Love's Conquest, Fedora, Private Peat, A Woman of Impulse, My Cousin* 1918; *Two Brides, Fires of Faith, The Isle of Conquest, The Peace of Roaring River* 1919; *The Fighting Shepherdess, The Riddle Woman, Yellow Typhoon, Mothers of Men* 1920; *Her Lord and Master, What Woman Will Do, The Scarab Ring, The Inner Chamber, The Matrimonial Web, Rainbow* 1921; *The Prodigal Judge, The Girl in His Room, The Man from Downing Street* 1922; *Terreur/Perils of Paris* (Fr.) 1924; *Le Puits de Jacob/A Daughter of Israel* (Fr.) 1926.

Josephson, Erland. Actor. Born on June 15, 1923, in Stockholm. Character lead of the Swedish stage and screen, notable for his portraits of egotistical males in the films of Ingmar BERGMAN. He became associated with Bergman while still in his teens and became his lifelong friend. He replaced the director in 1966 as head of Stockholm's Royal Dramatic Theater, a position he held through 1975. Josephson directed and performed in scores of plays and appeared in numerous films in Sweden and abroad. He made his American stage debut in a 1988 production of 'The Cherry Orchard.' He is the author of published poems, six novels, and several plays and screenplays.

FILMS INCLUDE: *To Joy* 1950; *Brink of Life/So Close to Life* 1958; *The Devil's Eye* 1960; *Pleasure Garden* (also co-sc. with Bergman) 1961; *All These Women/Now About These Women* (co-sc. with Bergman only) 1964; *The Hour of the Wolf, The Girls* 1968; *The Passion of Anna/Passion* 1969; *Scenes from a Marriage* 1973; *Face to Face* 1976; *Oltre il Bene e il Male/Beyond Good and Evil* (as Friedrich Nietzsche) 1977; *Herbstsonate/Autumn Sonata* (Ger.) 1978; *Dimenticare Venezia/To Forget Venice* (It./Fr.), *Montenegro* (Sw./UK) 1981; *Fanny and Alexander, Nostalghia/Nostalgia* (It./USSR) 1983; *After the Rehearsal* 1984; *Le Mal d'Aimer* (Fr./It.) *Amorosa, The Sacrifice* (Sw./Fr.), *Saving Grace* (US) 1986; *The Unbearable Lightness of Being* (US), *Hanussen* (Hung./Ger.) 1988; *Il Sole buio/The Dark Sun* (It.), *Good Evening, Mr. Wallenberg* 1990; *Meeting Venus, Prospero's Books* (UK/Neth./Fr./It.) 1991; *The Ox, Sofie/Sophie* 1992; *Dreamplay* 1994; *The Forbidden Fruit, Vendetta* 1995; *Ulysses' Gaze* 1997.

Joslyn, Allyn. Actor. *b.* July 21, 1901, Milford, Pa. *d.* 1981. Character comedian of American stage and screen. The son of a mining engineer, he worked briefly as an office boy before making his stage debut at 17. By the early 20s he was appearing regularly on Broadway and after scoring a hit in 'Boy Meets Girl' (1936) headed for Hollywood. In films, he often played pompous snobs, sometimes as a persistent suitor who loses the girl to the hero in the final scene. In addition to appearing in many films and Broadway plays (notably 'Arsenic and Old Lace' in 1941), Joslyn performed on some 3,000 radio shows and numerous TV programs.

FILMS INCLUDE: *They Won't Forget* 1937; *Hollywood Hotel, Sweethearts, The Shining Hour* 1938; *Cafe Society, Only Angels Have Wings* 1939; *If I Had My Way, The Great McGinty, No Time for Comedy, Spring Parade* 1940; *This Thing Called Love, Bedtime Story* 1941; *I Wake Up Screaming, The Wife Takes a Flyer, My Sister Eileen* 1942; *Immortal Sergeant, Heaven Can Wait* 1943; *The Imposter/Strange Confession* 1944; *The Horn Blows at Midnight, Junior Miss* 1945; *The Thrill of Brazil, It Shouldn't Happen to a Dog* 1946; *The Shocking Miss Pilgrim* 1947; *If You Knew Susie, Moonrise* 1948; *Harriet Craig* 1950; *As Young As You Feel* 1951; *The Jazz Singer, I Love Melvin, Titanic* 1953; *The Fastest Gun Alive* 1956; *Nightmare in the Sun* 1965; *The Brothers O'Toole* 1973.

Jost, Jon. American filmmaker. Born in 1943 in Chicago. Independent filmmaker whose work has critiqued American society and ideology since the early 60s. During the Vietnam War, he served two years in prison for refusing to accept military induction (1965–67). He went on to create a series of politically charged shorts and features that employed improvised dialogue and unconventional narrative. In addition to directing, producing, writing, and photographing his films, he often composes music for and edits them. His work includes a ten-part documentary series on America, *Plain Talk and Common Sense (uncommon senses)*.

FILMS INCLUDE (as director-producer-writer-director of photography): *Speaking Directly: Some American Notes* (also ed., comp.) 1973; *Angel City* (also ed.), *Last Chants for a Slow Dance* (also ed., song) 1977; *Chameleon* 1978; *Nightshift* (act., phot. only) 1982; *Slow Moves* (also ed., comp.) 1984; *Bell Diamond* (also ed.) 1987; *Rembrandt Laughing* (also art dir., ed.) 1989; *All the Vermeers in New York* (also art dir., ed.), *Sure Fire* (also ed.) 1990; *The Bed You Sleep In, Frameup* 1993; *One for Me One for You and One for Raffaelo* 1994.

Jourdan, Louis. Born Louis Gendre on June 19, 1919, in Marseilles, France. The son of a hotelman, he was educated in France, England, and Turkey, and received his dramatic training with René Simon at the Ecôle Dramatique in Paris. His cultivated polish and uncommon good looks were ideal ingredients for a career in films, and following his screen debut in 1939 he played dashing young leads in a number of French romantic comedies and dramas. But his new career was soon interrupted by WW II. His father was arrested by the Gestapo, and Louis and his two brothers joined the Underground. After the war he was lured to Hollywood by David O. SELZNICK to appear in *The Paradine Case* (1948) and stayed to star in a number of films, most memorably as the object of Joan Fontaine's secret longings in Max Ophüls's *Letter from an Unknown Woman* (1948). His looks captivated the admiration of American female audiences, but the sameness of his roles in American and international films as an old-fashioned Continental lover à la Charles Boyer limited his range and hampered his career. Character roles later in his career eventually offered him a somewhat broader range.

FILMS INCLUDE: In France—*Le Corsaire* 1939; *Premier Rendez-Vous/Her First Affair* 1941; *L'Arlésienne, Félicie Nanteuil, La Vie de Bohème* 1942; *Untel Père et Fils/The Heart of a Nation* 1943; *La Belle Aventure/Twilight* 1945. In the US—*The Paradine Case, Letter from an Unknown Woman, No Minor Vices* 1948; *Madame Bovary* (as Rodolphe) 1949; *Bird of Paradise, Anne of the Indies* 1951; *The Happy Time* 1952; *Rue de l'Estrapade* (Fr.), *Decameron Nights* (in four roles) 1953; *Three Coins in the Fountain* 1954; *La Mariée est trop Belle/The Bride Is Much Too Beautiful* (Fr.), *The Swan, Julie* 1956; *Dangerous Exile* (UK) 1957; *Gigi* 1958; *The Best of Everything* 1959; *Can-Can* 1960; *Le Vegini di Roma/Amazons of Rome* (It./Fr.), *Le Comte de Monte Cristo/The Story of Monte Cristo* (as Edmond Dantes; Fr./It.) 1961; *Il Disordine/Disorder* (It./Fr.) 1962; *The V.I.P.s* (UK) 1963; *Made in Paris* 1966; *Peau d'Espion/To Commit a Murder* (Fr./It./Ger.) 1967; *Cervantes/The Young Rebel* (Sp./Fr./It.), *A Flea in Her Ear* (US/Fr.) 1968; *The Count of Monte Cristo* (UK) 1976; *Silver Bears* 1977; *Swamp Thing* 1982; *Octopussy* (UK) 1983; *The Return of Swamp Thing* 1989; *Year of the Comet* 1992.

Jouvet, Louis. Actor. *b.* Dec. 24, 1887, Corzon, France. *d.* 1951. Trained as a druggist, he began his working life as a pharmacy assistant but kept on trying for an acting career. Despite three rejections by the Paris Conservatoire, he persisted and, after joining a stage company as an administrator in 1908, made his acting debut in 1910. He made a solitary silent film appearance in *Shylock,* in 1913, and that same year was appointed director of the Théâtre du Vieux-Colombier in Paris. Following combat service at the front during WW I, he came with his troupe to New York, where they played a repertory of productions to much acclaim from 1919 to 1921. Returning to France, he became the director of the Théâtre de Champs Elysées and was soon on his way to becoming one of the leading actors of the Paris stage.

Although he began appearing regularly in films in 1933, Jouvet remained primarily a man of the theater and often claimed he performed in films for money so that he could sponsor additional stage productions with his earnings. Just the same, he contributed a number of outstanding performances to the French cinema of the 30s, often overcoming even mediocre productions with his forceful screen personality. In films of high quality he was simply superb, handling complex roles with great subtlety and wit. He spent the WW II years touring South America with his company and after the war returned to Paris and resumed his work on the stage and in films. But he never recaptured the heights of his earlier screen achievements. His daughter, Lisa Jouvet, is a stage and screen actress.

FILMS: *Shylock* 1913; *Topaze* (title role), *Knock/Dr. Knock* (also co-dir. with Roger Goupilleres), *Du Haut en Bas* (participation unconfirmed) 1933; *La Kermesse héroïque* 1935; *Mister Flow/Compliments of Mr. Flow, 27 Rue de la Paix* (participation unconfirmed), *Les Bas-Fonds/The Lower Depths* (as The Baron) 1936; *Mademoiselle Docteur/Street of Shadows, Un Carnet de Bal, Drôle de Drame/Bizarre Bizarre, Forfaiture, L'Alibi* 1937; *La Marseillaise, Ramuntcho, La Maison du Maltais/Sirocco, Entrée des Artistes/The Curtain Rises, Education de Prince/The Barge-Keeper's Daughter, Le Drame de Shanghai/The Shanghai Drama, Hôtel du Nord* 1938; *La Fin du Jour/The End of a Day, La Charrette fantôme* 1939; *Sérénade/Schubert's Serenade* 1940; *Volpone* (as Mosca; release delayed from 1939) 1941; *Untel Père et Fils/The Heart of a Nation* (release delayed from 1939; not shown in Paris until 1945; first released in the US) 1943; *Un Revenant/A Lover's Return* 1946; *Copie conforme/Confessions of a Rogue, Quai des Orfèvres/Jenny Lamour* 1947; *Les Amoureux sont seuls au Monde/Monelle* 1948; *Entre Onze Heures et Minuit/Between Eleven and Midnight, Retour à la Vie* (Clouzot's episode) 1949; *Miquette et sa Mère/Miquette, Lady Paname* 1950; *Knock/Dr. Knock* (remake), *Une Histoire d'Amour* 1951.

Joy, Leatrice. Actress. *b.* Leatrice Joy Zeidler, Nov. 7, 1893, New Orleans. *d.* 1985. One of Hollywood's leading stars of the 20s, she made her debut as an extra in 1915. By 1918 she was leading lady in the comedies of Billy WEST and Oliver HARDY. A favorite of Cecil B. DE MILLE, she later starred in many of his silent films. Typically, she played a career girl attired in man-tailored clothes or a sophisticated, extracool society girl. One of the most elegant stars of the silent screen, she is credited with popularizing bobbed hair in the 20s. She retired shortly after the advent of sound but later returned periodically to the screen in supporting roles. Her first husband (1922–24) was matinee idol John GILBERT. Shortly before her death of acute anemia, she performed in 1985 in the 'Night of One Hundred Stars' extravaganza at Radio City Music Hall. Her daughter, Leatrice Gilbert Fountain, authored *Dark Star,* a biography of her father, John Gilbert.

FILMS INCLUDE: *His Turning Point* 1915; *The Folly of Revenge* 1916; *A Girl's Folly, The Pride of the Clan, The Slave* 1917; *Wedlock, City of Tears* 1918; *The Man Hunter, The Water Lily* 1919; *Just a Wife, Blind Youth, The Invisible Divorce, Smiling All the Way, Down Home* 1920; *Bunty Pulls the Strings, A Tale of Two Worlds, The Night Rose/Voices of the City, The Ace of Hearts, Ladies Must Live, The Poverty of Riches* 1921; *Saturday Night, The Bachelor Daddy, Manslaughter, Minnie* 1922; *Java Head, You Can't Fool Your Wife, The Silent Partner, The Ten Commandments* 1923; *The Marriage Cheat, Triumph, Changing Husbands* 1924; *The Dressmaker from Paris, Hell's Highroad, The Wedding Song* 1925; *Made for Love, Eve's Leaves, The Clinging Vine, For Alimony Only* 1926; *Nobody's Widow, Vanity, The Angel of Broadway* 1927; *The Blue Danube, Man-Made Women, Tropic Madness* 1928; *The Bellamy Trial, Strong Boy, A Most Immoral Lady* 1929; *The Love Trader* 1930; *Of Human Hearts* 1938; *First Love* 1939; *Air Hostess* 1949; *Love Nest* 1951.

Joy, Robert. Actor. Born on Aug. 17, 1951, in Montreal, Que., Canada. *ed.* Memorial U. of Newfoundland. Prolific stage-trained character player. A Rhodes Scholar, he began his acting career in regional and off-Broadway productions and became part of New York Shakespeare Festival and Broadway productions. His film appearances have spanned a variety of genres, including drama, comedy, and horror.

FILMS INCLUDE: *Atlantic City, Ragtime, Threshold* (Can.), *Ticket to Heaven* (Can.) 1981; *Amityville 3-D* 1983; *Terminal Choice* (Can.), *Joshua Then and Now* (Can.), *Desperately Seeking Susan* 1985; *Radio Days, Big Shots* 1987; *Millennium* 1989; *Longtime Companion* 1990; *Shadows and Fog, The Dark Half* 1992; *Waterworld* 1994.

Joyce, Alice. Actress. *b.* Oct. 1, 1889, Kansas City, Mo. *d.* 1955. She worked as a telephone operator from age 13, then later took up modeling. In 1910 she joined the KALEM company, with which she gained rapid popularity as a charming, well-mannered leading lady of numerous silent shorts. She married one of the company's leading stars and her frequent screen partner, Tom MOORE, but they later divorced. When Kalem was absorbed by Vitagraph in 1916, Joyce began starring in feature films and her popularity soared. She was still playing ingenue parts in the 20s but gradually switched to mature roles. Among other parts, she played the second Mrs. Dallas in *Stella Dallas* and Clara Bow's mother in *Dancing Mothers.* At the height of her fame she was called "The Madonna of the Screen." She retired after appearing in several early talkies. In 1933 she married director Clarence BROWN. They divorced in 1945.

FILMS INCLUDE: *The Engineer's Sweetheart* 1910; *The Bell of Penance, The Alcalde's Conspiracy, An American Invasion, The Spanish Revolt of 1836, The Street Singer, A Daughter's Sacrifice, A Race with Time* 1912; *The American Princess, The Artist's Sacrifice, The Adventure of an Heiress, The Heart of an Actress, An Unseen Terror, The Hunchback, The Shadow* 1913; *The Cabaret Dancer, A Celebrated Case, The Dance of Death, Nina of the Theatre, The Vampire Trail, The Brand, The Beast, Mystery of the Sleeping Death, The School for Scandal* 1914; *The White Goddess* 1915; *Whom the Gods Destroy* 1916; *The Courage of Silence, Within the Law, Womanhood, The Alabaster Box, The Fettered Woman* 1917; *A Woman Between Friends, To the Highest Bidder, The Song of the Soul, Triumph of the Weak, Find the Woman, Everybody's Girl, The Business of Life* 1918; *The Lion and the Mouse, The Cambric Mask, The Third Degree, The Spark Divine, The Winchester Woman* 1919; *Slaves of Pride, The Sporting Duchess, Dollars and the Woman, The Prey, The Vice of Fools* 1920; *Cousin Kate, Her Lord and Master, The Scarab Ring, The Inner Chamber* 1921; *The Green Goddess* (remake) 1923; *White Man* 1924; *Daddy's Gone a-Hunting, The Little French Girl, Headlines, The Home Maker, Stella Dallas* 1925; *Mannequin, Dancing Mothers, Beau Geste, So's Your Old Man, The Ace of Cads* 1926; *Sorrell and Son* 1927; *The Noose, 13 Washington Square* 1928; *The Squall* 1929; *The Green Goddess* (2nd remake), *Song of My Heart, He Knew Women, Midnight Mystery* 1930.

Joyce, Brenda. Actress. Born Betty Graffina Leabo, on Feb. 25, 1915, in Kansas City, Mo. *ed.* USC; UCLA. Blonde, fresh-faced, outdoorsy leading lady of Hollywood films of the 40s. A former model, she adorned the screen in a variety of decorative, often athletic, roles, mainly in second features. She played Jane opposite Johnny Weismuller and Lex Barker successively in a number of Tarzan pictures. Retired in 1949.

FILMS INCLUDE: *The Rains Came, Here I Am a Stranger* 1939; *Little Old New York, Maryland, Public Deb No. 1* 1940; *Private Nurse* 1941; *Whispering Ghosts, Little Tokyo USA* 1942; *Tarzan and the Amazons, Strange Confession, The Enchanted Forest, Pillow of Death* 1945; *Tarzan and the Leopard Woman, The Spider Lady Strikes Back, Little Giant* 1946; *Tarzan and the Huntress* 1947; *Tarzan and the Mermaids* 1948; *Tarzan's Magic Fountain* 1949.

Joyeux, Odette. Actress, screenwriter. Born on Dec. 5, 1917, in Paris. Trained as a dancer, she made her screen debut at 14 but for several years her important roles were limited to the Paris stage. Her first significant film role came in Marc Allégret's *Entrée des Artistes/The Curtain Rises* (1938). She was among the leading stars of the French cinema in the early 40s. Her first husband was Pierre BRASSEUR; her second is Philippe AGOSTINI. She has written a play and several novels and collaborated on a number of film scripts.

FILMS INCLUDE: As actress—*Jean de la Lune* 1931; *Lac aux Dames* 1934; *Hélène* 1936; *Entrée des Artistes/The Curtain Rises, Altitude 3200/Youth in Revolt* 1938; *Le Mariage de Chiffon, Lettres d'Amour* 1942; *Douce/Love Story* 1943; *Sylvie et le Fantôme/Sylvie and the Phantom* 1946; *Pour une Nuit d'Amour/Passionnelle* 1947; *Scandale* 1948; *La Ronde* 1950; *Si Paris nous était conté* 1955; *La Petite Fille à la recherche du printemps* 1971. As screenwriter—*La Mariée est trop Belle/The Bride Is Much Too Beautiful* (dial., from her own novel) 1956; *Sois Belle et tais-toi/Be Beautiful and Shut Up* (co-sc., co-dial.) 1958; *Rencontres* (co-sc., co-dial.) 1962.

Judd, Ashley. Actress. Born April 19, 1968, in Los Angeles. *ed.* University of Kentucky. Lovely, intelligent performer of stage and screen. The daughter and half sister of country music superstars Naomi and Wynonna Judd, respectively, this young leading lady chose acting over music and has proven herself a capable and sensitive actress, notably as the vulnerable drug addict in *Smoke* (1995).

FILMS: *Kuffs* 1992; *Ruby in Paradise* 1993; *Heat, Smoke* 1995; *Normal Life, A Time to Kill* 1996; *Kiss the Girls* 1997.

Judd, Edward. Actor. Born on Oct. 4, 1932, in Shanghai, to English parents. Leading man and supporting player of British films, often in science-fiction and horror pictures. Also on stage and in much TV. Raised and educated in the Far East, he began performing at age 16, supporting himself with various odd jobs until he established himself professionally in England. Although he entered films in 1940, he languished in small roles until the early 60s. Widowed by actress Gene Anderson (1932–65), he married actress Norma Ronald.

FILMS INCLUDE: *The Small Voice/Hideout, The Guinea Pig/The Outsider* 1948; *Boys in Brown* 1949; *The Good Die Young* 1954; *X the Unknown, Battle of the River Plate/Pursuit of the Graf Spee* 1956; *I Was Monty's Double/Hell Heaven and Hoboken, Subway in the Sky* 1958; *The Criminal/The Concrete Jungle* 1960; *The Day the Earth Caught Fire* 1961; *Mystery Submarine/Decoy, The Stolen Hours* (US) 1963; *The Long Ships, First Men in the Moon* 1964; *Strange Bedfellows* (US) 1965; *Invasion, Island of Terror* 1966; *The Vengeance of She* 1968; *Universal Soldier* 1971; *Living Free* 1972; *Vault of Horror, O Lucky Man!, Assassin* 1973; *The Incredible Sarah* 1976; *The Hound of the Baskervilles* 1983; *The Kitchen Toto* 1988.

Judge, Arline. Actress. *b.* Feb. 21, 1912, Bridgeport, Conn. *d.* 1974. Convent-educated. She started out as a dancer and appeared in the nightclub act of Jimmy DURANTE. On a train trip she met film director Wesley RUGGLES, who gave her her start in films and married her in 1931. They divorced in 1937. She played leads in many Hollywood B productions of the 30s and 40s but became more famous for her seven marriages and divorces than for her routine movie roles.

FILMS INCLUDE: *Bachelor Apartment, An American Tragedy* (as Bella Griffiths), *Are These Our Children?* 1931; *Girl Crazy, Love Starved, Roar of the Dragon, The Age of Consent* 1932; *Flying Devils* 1933; *Looking for Trouble, Shoot the Works, Sensation Hunters* 1934; *The Mysterious Mr. Wong, George White's Scandals, Million Dollar Baby* 1935; *King of Burlesque, It Had to Happen, Star for a Night, Valiant Is the Word for Carrie, Pigskin Parade* 1936; *One in a Million* 1937; *The Lady Is Willing, Law of the Jungle, Wildcat* 1942; *Song of Texas, Girls in Chains* 1943; *The Contender* 1944; *From This Day Forward* 1946; *Mad Wednesday* 1947; *Two Knights in Brooklyn* 1949.

juicer. A slang term for a film crew's lamp operator, the person who installs and activates lighting units on a set.

Julia, Raul. Actor. *b.* Mar. 9, 1940, in San Juan, Puerto Rico. *d.* 1994. *ed.* U. of Puerto Rico. Darkly handsome, talented leading man and character player of the American stage and screen. Receiving his stage training from Wynn Handman, he made his New York debut in 1964 in a Spanish-language play and his first appearance in English at the New York Shakespeare Festival in 1966. He was an established Broadway player by the time he entered films in 1971. He won a Tony Award for his portrayal of MacHeath in a Broadway production of 'The Threepenny Opera,' a role he would later repeat on the screen in *Mack the Knife*. In the 80s and 90s, his roles in films varied in range from suavely demonic in *Tequila Sunrise* to broadly comic in *The Addams Family*. Tragically, Julia died prematurely at the age of 54 of a sudden stroke.

FILMS: *The Panic in Needle Park, Been Down So Long It Looks Like Up to Me, The Organization* 1971; *The Gumball Rally* 1976; *Eyes of Laura Mars* 1978; *Strong Medicine* 1979; *One from the Heart, The Escape Artist, Tempest* 1982; *Kiss of the Spider Woman* (Braz./US), *Compromising Positions* 1985; *The Morning After* 1986; *Trading Hearts, La Gran Fiesta* (P.R.) 1987; *Tango Bar* (P.R./Arg.), *The Penitent, Moon Over Parador, Tequila Sunrise* 1988; *Romero* (as El Salvador's Archbishop Oscar Romero), *Mack the Knife* (as MacHeath) 1989; *Presumed Innocent, Frankenstein Unbound, The Rookie, Havana* 1990; *The Addams Family* 1991; *The Plague* 1992; *Addams Family Values* 1993; *Street Fighter* 1994.

Julian, Rupert. Director. *b.* Jan. 25, 1889. Auckland, New Zealand. *d.* 1943. In the US from 1913, he entered films as an experienced stage actor the following year, making his debut in the role of Antonio in *The Merchant of Venice* (1914). He began directing his own films late in 1915 and rose to prominence after being assigned to complete von Stroheim's *Merry-Go-Round* in 1923. He subsequently directed *The Phantom of the Opera,* starring Lon Chaney, but his career soon declined and he faded into obscurity shortly after the advent of sound.

FILMS: As director-actor—*The Water Clue* (short) 1915; *The Dumb Girl of Portici, Naked Hearts, Bettina Loved a Soldier, The Evil Women Do, The Bugler of Algiers/We Are French, The Turn of the Wheel* (short), *The Right to Be Happy* (as Ebenezer Scrooge) 1916; *The Gift Girl, The Circus of Life* (dir. only), *A Kentucky Cinderella, Mother o' Mine* (also story), *The Mysterious Mr. Tiller, The Desire of the Moth, The Savage* (dir. only), *My Little Boy* (story only), *The Door Between* (dir.

only) 1917; *Hands Down, The Kaiser—The Beast of Berlin* (as Kaiser Wilhelm II; also prod., sc.) *Hungry Eyes, Midnight Madness* (dir. only), *Fires of Youth* (dir., co-story only) 1918. As director—*Creaking Stairs* (also sc.), *The Millionaire Pirate, The Fire Flingers* (also act.), *The Sleeping Lion* 1919; *The Honey Bee* (also sc.) 1920; *The Girl Who Ran Wild* (also co-sc.) 1922; *Merry-Go-Round* (completed film begun by Erich von Stroheim) 1923; *Love and Glory* (also co-sc.) 1924; *Hell's Highroad, The Phantom of the Opera* 1925; *Three Faces East, Silence* 1926; *The Yankee Clipper, The Country Doctor* 1927; *The Leopard Lady, Walking Back* 1928; *Love Comes Along, The Cat Creeps* 1930.

Julien, Max. African-American actor, writer, producer. He first gained fame playing the lead in *The Mack* (1973), a "blaxploitation" film about a violent, high-living pimp. He also wrote and co-produced the equally successful *Cleopatra Jones* (1973), which starred Tamara Dobson as a government agent pursuing drug dealers.

FILMS INCLUDE: *The Black Klansman* 1966; *Psych-Out, The Savage Seven, Uptight* 1968; *Getting Straight* 1970; *The Mack, Cleopatra Jones* (sc. and co-prod. only) 1973; *Thomasine and Bushrod* (also sc. and co-prod.) 1974.

jump cut. A noticeably abrupt movement of a subject on the screen, resulting either from cutting out a section of film from the middle of a shot and joining the remaining ends together, or from stopping the camera, moving closer to the subject, and beginning to film again without changing the angle. Either way, a man seen walking across a room would seem to be jumping abruptly from one position to another rather than walking smoothly. Traditionally, such breaks in continuity and smooth transition have been considered intolerable, but some modern filmmakers employ jump cuts freely and deliberately.

junction box. See SPIDER BOX.

June, Ray. Director of photography. *b.* 1898, Ithaca, N.Y. *d.* 1958. *ed.* Cornell. He entered the film industry following WW I service, during which he gained experience as a cameraman for the Signal Corps. He subsequently worked on numerous Hollywood productions, displaying meticulous craftsmanship in the cinematography of both major and minor films. He did some of his best work for MGM from the mid-30s to the mid-50s.

FILMS INCLUDE: *Scrambled Wives* (co-phot.) 1921; *Penrod* (co-phot.) 1922; *Penrod and Sam* (co-phot.) 1923; *Wandering Husbands, Cornered* 1924; *A Broadway Butterfly, The Shadow on the Wall* 1925; *The Phantom of the Forest, The Golden Web, Racing Blood* 1926; *The Warning, The Satin Woman* 1927; *So This Is Love, The Sporting Age, Midnight Life* 1928; *New York Nights, Alibi* 1929; *Puttin' on the Ritz, The Lottery Bride, The Bat Whispers* 1930; *Reaching for the Moon* (co-phot.), *Indiscreet* (co-phot.), *Arrowsmith* 1931; *Cynara, Horse Feathers* 1932; *I Cover the Waterfront, Secrets, When Ladies Meet* 1933; *The Girl from Missouri, Riptide, Treasure Island* (co-phot.), *The Gay Bride* 1934; *China Seas, Barbary Coast* 1935; *Riffraff, Wife vs. Secretary, The Great Ziegfeld* (co-phot.), *Born to Dance* 1936; *Espionage, Night Must Fall, Saratoga* 1937; *Test Pilot* 1938; *Honolulu, Babes in Arms* 1939; *The Earl of Chicago, Strike Up the Band, Little Nellie Kelly* 1940; *Ziegfeld Girl, H. M. Pulham Esq., Love Crazy, The Feminine Touch* 1941; *Cairo, Journey for Margaret* 1942; *I Dood It* 1943; *Three Men in White* 1944; *The Hoodlum Saint* 1946; *The Beginning or the End* 1947; *Three Daring Daughters, A Southern Yankee, The Sun Comes Up* 1948; *The Secret Garden* 1949; *Shadow on the Wall, Crisis, Nancy Goes to Rio* 1950; *It's a Big Country* (co-phot.), *Callaway Went Thataway* 1951; *Invitation, Above and Beyond* 1952; *Easy to Love, Sombrero* 1953; *Hot Blood, The Court Jester* 1956; *Funny Face* 1957; *Houseboat* 1958.

Junge, Alfred. Art director. *b.* Jan. 29, 1886, Görlitz, Germany. *d.* 1964. He designed sets for the Berlin State Opera and State Theater before joining UFA as an art director in 1920. Toward the end of the decade he began working for E. A. Dupont in Britain and eventually settled there. His creative décor contributed greatly to the success of many British films, particularly those of Michael POWELL and Emeric PRESSBURGER in the 40s. He won an Academy Award for the stunning design of *Black Narcissus* (1947). From the late 40s till the late 50s he was head of the art department of MGM's British studios.

FILMS INCLUDE: In Germany—*Die Hintertreppe/Backstairs* 1921; *Die grüne Manuela* 1923; *Das Wachsfigurenkabinett/Waxworks/Three-Way Works* (co-art dir.) 1924; *Athleten* 1925; *Mata Hari* 1927. In the UK—*Moulin Rouge* 1928; *Piccadilly* 1929; *Two Worlds* 1930; *Ariane, Salto Mortale* (both Ger.), *Marius* (Fr.), *Cape Forlorn* 1931; *The Good Companions, The Constant Nymph, I Was a Spy, The Ghoul* 1933; *Jack Ahoy, The Man Who Knew Too Much* 1934; *The Iron Duke, Bulldog Jack* 1935; *King Solomon's Mines* 1937; *The Citadel* 1938; *Goodbye Mr. Chips* 1939; *Gaslight, Contraband* 1940; *The Life and Death of Colonel Blimp* 1943; *A Canterbury Tale* 1944; *I Know Where I'm Going* 1945; *A Matter of Life and Death/Stairway to Heaven* 1946; *Black Narcissus* 1947; *Edward My Son* 1949; *The Miniver Story* 1950; *Ivanhoe* 1952; *Mogambo* 1953; *Knights of the Round Table, Beau Brummel* 1954; *Quentin Durward* 1955; *Invitation to the Dance* 1956; *The Barretts of Wimpole Street, A Farewell to Arms* 1957.

junior. A 1,000- to 2,000-watt spot light. See also SENIOR.

Jurado, Katy. Actress. Born Maria Cristina Jurado Garcia, on Jan. 16, 1927, in Guadalajara, Mexico. In Hollywood as a columnist for Mexican publications following a Mexican film career, she played sensuous, exotic leads and supporting roles in a variety of films, most memorably in *High Noon* (1952) and *One-Eyed Jacks* (1961). She was nominated for an Oscar for her supporting role in *Broken Lance* (1954). Formerly (1959–64) wed to Ernest BORGNINE.

FILMS INCLUDE: In Mexico—*No Maturas* 1943; *El Museo del Crimen* 1945; *Rosa del Caribe* 1946; *Mujer e Medica Noche* 1949; *Cabellera blanca* 1950. In the US—*The Bullfighter and the Lady* 1951; *High Noon* 1952; *Arrowhead* 1953; *Broken Lance* 1954; *The Racers, Trial* 1955; *Trapeze, The Man from Del Rio* 1956; *The Badlanders* 1958; *One-Eyed Jacks, Barabba/Barabbas* (It.) 1961; *Un Hombre Solo* (Sp.) 1964; *Smoky* 1966; *A Covenant with Death* 1967; *Stay Away Joe* 1968; *Pat Garrett and Billy the Kid* 1973; *El Elegido* (Mex.), *Los Albaniles* (Mex.) 1977; *The Children of Sanchez* 1978; *La Viuda de Montiel* (Mex.) 1979; *Under the Volcano* 1984; *Fearmaker* 1989.

Juran, Nathan H(ertz). Director, former art director. Born on Sept. 1, 1907, in Austria. *ed.* U. of Minnesota; MIT. In the US from infancy, he was an architect before becoming a Hollywood art director in 1937. His design credits include *How Green Was My Valley* (Academy Award, 1941), *The Razor's Edge* (1946), *Body and Soul* (1947), and *Kiss the Blood Off My Hands* (1948). He served with the OSS in WW II. Turning to directing in the 50s, he has competently handled American and European productions, mainly low- to medium-budget action pictures. His best all-round film is the fantasy-adventure yarn *The Seventh Voyage of Sinbad* (1958).

FILMS (as director): *The Black Castle* 1952; *Gunsmoke, Law and Order, The Golden Blade, Tumbleweed* 1953; *Highway Dragnet, Drums Across the River* 1954; *The Crooked Web* 1955; *The Deadly Mantis, Hellcats of the Navy, Twenty Million Miles to Earth* 1957; *The Seventh Voyage of Sinbad, Good Day for a Hanging* 1959; *Flight of the Lost Balloon* (also assoc. prod., story, sc.) 1961; *Jack the Giant Killer* (also co-sc.) 1962; *Siege of the Saxons* (UK) 1963; *First Men in the Moon* (UK), *East of Sudan* (also prod.; UK) 1964; *Land Raiders* 1970; *The Boy Who Cried Werewolf* 1973.

Jurgens, Curt (in Europe **Curd Jürgens).** Actor. *b.* Dec. 13, 1912, Munich. *d.* 1982. A journalist, he turned to acting under the influence of his first wife, actress Louise Basler. On the German stage and screen from 1935, he was making steady gains when, in 1944, he was deported to a concentration camp for political unreliables in Hungary by special order of Dr. Göebbels. Jurgens first gained recognition abroad in *The Devil's General* (1955) and soon became a leading star of the European stage and international films. One of the screen's busiest actors, he appeared in well over 100 films but still considered himself primarily a stage actor. His occasional attempts at directing did not turn out well. His five marriages included a brief one to Eva BARTOK. Autobiography: *Sixty and Not Yet Wise* (1976).

FILMS INCLUDE: *Königswalzer/The Royal Waltz* 1935; *Die Unbekannte* 1936; *Zu neuen Ufern* 1937; *Herz ohne Heimat, Operette/Operetta* 1940; *Wen die Götter lieben/The Mozart Story* 1942; *Der Engel mit der Posaune* 1948; *Hexen* 1949; *Prämien auf den Tod* (also dir, co-sc.) 1950; *Gangsterpremiere* (also dir., co-sc.) 1951; *Haus des Lebens* 1952; *Der letzte Walzer/The Last Waltz* 1953; *Rummelplatz der Liebe/Circus of Love, Das Bekenntnis der Ina Kahr/The Confession of Ina Kahr, Orient Express* (It./Ger.) 1954; *Des Teufels General/The Devil's General, Die Ratten, Les Héros sont fatigués/Heroes and Sinners* (Fr.) 1955; *Teufel in Seide/Devil in Silk, Ohne Dich wird es Nacht* (also dir.), *Londra chiama Polo Nord/The House of Intrigue* (It.), *Et Dieu créa la Femme/And God Created Woman* (Fr.) 1956; *Michel Strogoff/Michael Strogoff* (title role; It./Fr./Yug.), *Oeil pour Oeil/An Eye for an Eye* (Fr./It.), *Les Espions* (Fr./It.), *Amère Victoire* (Fr.), *The Enemy Below* (US) 1957; *Tamango* (Fr./It.), *Der Schinderhannes, This Happy Feeling* (US), *Me and the Colonel* (US), *The Inn of the Sixth Happiness* (UK/US) 1958; *Le Vent se lève/Time Bomb* (Fr./It.), *Ferry to Hong Kong* (UK), *The Blue Angel* (US) 1959; *Katia/Magnificent Sinner* (as Czar Alexander II; Fr.), *Die Schachnovelle/Brainwashed/The Royal Game, I Aim at the Stars* (as rocket scientist Wernher von Braun; US/Ger.) 1960; *Il Disordine/Disorder* (It./Fr.), *The Longest Day* (US) 1962; *Die Dreigroschenoper/The Threepenny Opera* (as MacHeath; Ger./Fr.), *Miracle of the White Stallions* (US), *Of Love and Desire* (US), *Château en Suède/Nutty Naughty Chateau* (Fr./It.) 1963; *Hide and Seek* (UK), *Psyche 59* (UK) 1964; *Lord Jim* (UK/US) 1965; *Dalle Ardenne all'Inferno/Dirty Heroes* (It./Fr./Ger.) 1968; *The Assassination Bureau* (UK), *Battle of Britain* (UK) 1969; *The Invisible Six* (US)/Iran), *Hello-Goodbye* (US), *Battle of Neretva* (Yug./It./Fr.) 1970; *The Mephisto Waltz* (US), *Nicholas and Alexandra* (UK) 1971; *The Vault of Horror* (UK) 1973; *Soft Beds Hard Battles/Undercovers Hero* (UK) 1974; *Povero Cristo* (It.) 1975; *Domani saremo Ricchi e Onesti* (It./Ger.); *Folies bourgeoises* (Fr.); *Auch Mimosen wollen blüuhen* 1976; *The Spy Who Loved Me* (UK) 1977; *Schöner Gigolo—armer Gigolo/Just a Gigolo* 1978; *Sergeant Steiner/Breakthrough, Goldengirl* (US) 1979; *Die Partiotin* 1980; *Teheran 43* (USSR) 1981.

Justice, James Robertson. See ROBERTSON-JUSTICE, James.

Justin, John. Actor. Born on Nov. 24, 1917, in London. Dashingly handsome leading man of the British stage and screen. His first (1952–64) of two marriages was to actress Barbara Murray. Primarily a stage actor (since 1933), he flirted with film stardom as the hero of the popular *The Thief of Bagdad* but has since appeared only occasionally in films. He was an RAF pilot in WW II.

FILMS INCLUDE: *Dark Journey* 1937; *The Thief of Bagdad* 1940; *The Gentle Sex* 1943; *Journey Together* 1945; *Call of the Blood* 1947; *Angel with the Trumpet* 1949; *The Sound Barrier/Breaking Through the Sound Barrier, Unser Dorf/The Village* (Switz.) 1952; *Melba* (US), *King of the Khyber Rifles* (US) 1953; *Seagulls Over Sorrento/Crest of the Wave, The Teckman Mystery* 1954; *The Man Who Loved Redheads, Untamed* (US) 1955; *Safari* 1956; *Island in the Sun* 1957; *The Spider's Web* 1960; *Candidate for Murder* 1962; *Savage Messiah* 1972; *Lisztomania* 1975; *Valentino* 1977; *The Big Sleep* 1978; *Trenchcoat* 1983.

Jutra, Claude. Director. *b.* Mar. 11, 1930, Montreal, Que., Canada. *d.* 1986/87. The son of a noted radiologist, and a descendent of a line of physicians, he studied medicine at the University of Montreal, and after graduating worked for a year as an intern. But his regard for family tradition was overshadowed by his lifelong passion for film. He had begun making amateur shorts while still in his teens and was only 19 when he won a top prize for his surrealistic short *Movement perpétuel.* Forsaking plans for a future in medicine, he studied drama at Montreal's Théâtre du Nouveau Monde, began his professional career in 1953 as a writer in regional TV, and in 1954 joined Canada's National Film Board as an assistant director. Graduating to director in 1956, he shared with Norman MCLAREN the First Prize for experimental films at the Venice Film Festival for the brightly comic short, *A Chairy Tale* (1957). Rapidly establishing himself as a promising filmmaker, he traveled to France, then followed Jean ROUCH on a filming trip to Africa, where Jutra eventually shot his own feature-length documentary, *Le Niger—Jeune République* (1961), the winner of a special prize at Florence. He used his documentary background to advantage to lend authenticity and spontaneity to his semiautobiographical fiction feature, *A tous prendre/Take It All* (1963). The film was named best picture at the Canadian Film Awards, garnered a number of international prizes, and was widely praised by critics. But despite its minimal cost, it proved a financial failure, causing Jutra to abandon filmmaking for several years. It wasn't until 1971 that the director re-established his reputation with *Mon Oncle Antoine,* a film many consider his masterpiece and one of the finest achievements of the Canadian cinema. It swept the Canadian Film Awards for that year, winning eight of the prizes, including best picture and best director. In 1984 it was voted by a panel of Canadian critics and historians as the best Canadian film of all time. Jutra enjoyed far less success with his subsequent films and he got increasingly disappointed and depressed. By the mid-80s he was diagnosed as suffering from Alzheimer's disease. His memory fading and health deteriorating, he left his Montreal home one day in November of 1986 and simply disappeared. The mystery was solved in March of 1987, when his badly decomposed body was found floating amidst the thawing ice on the St. Lawrence River. He was identified by a note in his pocket: "I am Claude Jutra."

FEATURE FILMS: *Les Mains nettes* 1958; *Le Niger—Jeune République* (doc.; also edit.) 1961; *A tous prendre/Take It All* (also sc., edit., act.) 1963; *Wow!* (doc.; also sc., co-edit.) 1969; *Mon Oncle Antoine* (also act.) 1971; *Kamouraska* 1972; *Por le Meilleur et pur le Pire/For Better or for Worse* 1975; *Ada* (orig. for TV), *Québec Fête* (TV doc.; co-dir. with Jean-Clade Labrecque) 1976; *Dreamspeaker* (orig. for TV) 1977; *Surfacing* 1979; *By Design* 1982; *La Dame en Couleurs/Our Lady of the Paints* 1985.

Jutzi, Phil (Piel). Director, director of photography. *b.* 1894, Rheinpflaz, Germany. Deceased. Primarily a cinematographer, he began directing occasionally in 1919 and came to the fore in the late 20s as one of the leading directors of the short-lived realist period of the German cinema during the late silent and early sound era. Among his notable films of the period were three semidocumentaries on working-class themes: *Kindertragödie* (1927), *Unsertäglisches Brot/Our Daily Bread/Hunger in Waldenburg* (1928), and *Mutter Krausens Fahrt ins Glück/Mother Krause's Journey to Happiness* (1929). He scored a success in 1931 with a strong dramatic adaptation of the Alfred Döblin's novel, *Berlin-Alexanderplatz,* which 53 years later would provide the basis for a mammoth remake by Rainer Werner FASSBINDER. Jutzi was the cameraman on many of his own films and continued to work as a cinematographer during and after his career as a director. He stopped directing shortly after Hitler's rise to power but remained in German films as a director of photography through the early 40s.

FILMS INCLUDE (as director): *Die Rache des Banditen* 1919; *Der maskierte Schrecken* (also sc.) 1920; *Klaus und Datsch die Pechvögel* (also sc., phot., art dir.) 1926; *Kindertragödie* 1927; *Unser täglisches Brod/Our Daily Bread/Hunger in Waldenburg* (doc., also phot.) 1928; *Mutter Krausens Fahrt ins Glück/Mother Krause's Journey to Happiness* (also phot.) 1929; *Berlin-Alexanderplatz* 1931; *Der Kosak und die Nachtigall, Lockspitzel Asew* 1935.

juvenile. One who plays a youthful role in a film or a play, roughly in the age range of 16 to 20.

K

Kaboré, Gaston. Director. Born in 1951 in Bobo Dioulasso, Burkina Faso. A leading filmmaker in the small African nation of Burkina Faso, he has done much to develop the reputation of his country's film industry. He studied cinematography at the Ecole Supérieure d'Etudes Cinématographiques in Paris and earned a degree in history at the Sorbonne. He went on to make many documentaries and several feature films that won international acclaim. His debut feature was *Wend Kuuni—The Gift of God* (1981), a story of a rural child's moral education. Kaboré's later film *Zan Boko* (1988) studied the conflict between traditional African culture and the onslaught of industrialization and television. Since 1985, Kaboré has presided over FEPACI, the Pan-African Federation of Filmmakers, based in Ouagadougou.

FILMS INCLUDE: *Wend Kuuni—The Gift of God* 1981; *Zan Boko* 1988; *Rabi* 1991.

Kachyňa, Karel. Director. Born on May 1, 1924, in Vyskov, Czechoslovakia. One of the first graduates of the Prague cinema school, he collaborated with Vojtech JASNY on a number of short documentaries and one feature film. Working alone since 1956, he has specialized in psychological themes, frequently involving children and adolescents. He usually writes his own scripts, often in collaboration with Jan Procjáska. Banned in 1979, his film *The Ear* emerged to plaudits at the 1990 Cannes Festival.

FEATURE FILMS: *Everything Ends Tonight* (co-dir. with Vojtech Jasny) 1954; *The Lost Trail* 1956; *That Christmas* 1958; *Smugglers of Death* 1959; *The Slinger* 1960; *Fetters, Trials of Youth* 1961; *Vertigo* 1962; *Hope* 1963; *The High Wall* 1964; *Long Live the Republic!* 1965; *Coach to Vienna* 1966; *The Night of the Bride* 1967; *Christmas with Elizabeth* 1968; *Our Foolish Family* 1969; *Jumping Over Puddles Again* 1971; *Love* 1972; *The Little Mermaid* 1977; *Meeting in July, Waiting for the Rain* 1978; *Carriage to Vienna* (unreleased), *Love Between the Raindrops* 1979; *Sugar Hut* 1980; *Visit/Doctor's Rounds* 1981; *Fandy & Fandy* 1982; *Nursing Sisters* 1983; *Forbidden Dreams* 1987; *The Ear* (release delayed from 1979), *The Last Butterfly* (Czech./Fr.) 1990.

Kaczender, George. Director. Born in 1933, in Budapest. He was an assistant director in his native Hungary before emigrating to Canada, where he joined the National Film Board as an editor in 1957. He began directing shorts in 1963 and turned out his first feature in 1968. He co-founded International Cinemedia Center in 1969 and established George Kaczender Productions in 1971. His attempts at breaking through the Hollywood barrier have been largely unsuccessful.

FEATURE FILMS: *Don't Let the Angels Fall* (also edit.) 1968; *U-Turn* 1973; *The Girl in Blue* (also prod.; US) 1974; *In Praise of Older Women* (also edit.) 1978; *Agency, Chanel Solitaire* (UK/Fr.) 1981; *The Finishing Touch* 1983; *Prettykill* (US) 1987.

Kadár, Ján(os). Czech director. *b.* Apr. 1, 1918, Budapest, of Slovakian Jewish parents. *d.* 1979. As a youth he switched from law studies at Prague's Charles University to cinema studies at the Bratislava Film School in Czechoslovakia, but his schooling was interrupted by WW II, which he spent in a Nazi labor camp. His parents and sister perished in Auschwitz. After the Liberation he returned to Bratislava, where he directed his first film, *Life Is Rising from the Ruins* (1945), a documentary short, then went to Prague, where he began working as a screenwriter and assistant director at the Barrandov studios. In 1950 he directed his first feature, *Katka/Katya,* a comedy that met with some disapproval by the Czech authorities. In 1952 he began a long and fruitful collaboration with Elmar Klos (*b.* Jan. 26, 1910, Brno, Czechoslovakia. *d.* 1993), another law school dropout whose association with film had dated back to the late 20s. Working as a well-harmonized team, they co-directed and co-scripted a succession of documentaries and feature films that were noted for their sincere social concern and skilled technical handling. However, the political undertones of some of these films brought the two men into frequent clashes with the authorities and at one point resulted in a two-year suspension of their activity. Several of their films won international awards and their *The Shop on Main Street* received the 1965 best foreign film Academy Award. In 1968 they started *Adrift,* a Czech-American co-production, but shooting was interrupted by the Russian invasion and the film was not released until 1971, with Kadár getting sole director's credit. The collaboration had ended in 1969, when Kadár left Czechoslovakia to work in the US. But his first American film, *The Angel Levine* (1970), was a disappointment and he had difficulty securing further American assignments. Then he scored in 1975 with a tender, Canadian-made boyhood story, *Lies My Father Told Me.* He made five more films—all for TV—before his sudden death at age 61.

FILMS: Alone—*Life Is Rising from the Ruins* (doc. short) 1945; *Katka/Katya* (also co-sc.) 1950. Co-dir., co-sc. with Elmar Klos—*Kidnap/Hijack* 1952; *Music from Mars* 1954; *The House at the Terminus* (co-dir. only) 1957; *Three Wishes* 1958; *Magic Lantern II* (mixed-media presentation; co-dir. with several others), *Youth* (episode in Polyécran presentation; dir. segment alone), *Spartakiade* (doc.; co-dir. with several others) 1960; *Death Is Called Engelchen/Because We Don't Forget* 1963; *The Defendant/The Accused* 1964; *The Shop on Main Street/Shop on the High Street* 1965. Alone—*The Angel Levine* (US) 1970; *Adrift/Something Adrift in the Water* (Klos as assoc. dir.; completed in 1969; Czech./US) 1971; *The Blue Hotel* (for TV) 1973; *Mandelstam's Witness/Hope Against Hope* (for TV) 1974; *The Case Against Milligan* (for TV), *Lies My Father Told Me* (Can.) 1975; *The Other Side of Hell* (for TV) 1978; *Freedom Road* (for TV) 1979.

Kael, Pauline. Film critic. Born on June 19, 1919, in Petaluma, Calif. Provocative, often controversial doyenne of American film criticism. After graduating in 1940 from the University of California at Berkeley, where she majored in philosophy, she managed two movie theaters and developed a deep affection for the art. She later made experimental shorts and talked about film on a weekly radio show on the Pacifica network. She began writing film reviews for various publications in the 40s, and in 1968 became the film critic of *The New Yorker.* Despite a relatively small readership, she soon became the most influential of American critics among the cognoscenti, with firmly voiced opinions that helped establish reputations and puncture myths. She often found herself at odds with fellow critics but even her detractors acknowledged her genuine passion for the movies. In 1979 she took a leave of absence and went briefly to Hollywood as a producer for Warren BEATTY. In 1991 she announced her retirement from regular reviewing. Since 1965 her film reviews have been collected, in full or in condensed form, in a series of popular books, including *I Lost It at the Movies, Kiss Kiss Bang Bang, Going Steady, Deeper Into Movies, Reeling, When the Lights Go Down, 5001 Nights at the Movies, Taking It All In, State of the Art,* and *Hooked.* She also authored *The Citizen Kane Book* (1971).

Kagan, Jeremy Paul. Director. Born on Dec. 14, 1945, in Mount Vernon, N.Y. *ed.* Harvard; NYU. He started his film career in 1968 as an animator and helped design a multimedia show for the White House Conference on Youth and Education. After training at the American Film Institute, he began directing episodes for 'Columbo' and other TV series, making his feature debut in 1977. He won first prize at the 1981 Montreal World Film Festival for *The Chosen* and a Gold Prize at the 1987 Moscow Film Festival for *The Journey of Natty Gann.* Also directs above-average made-for-cable films, such as *Descending Angel* (1990).

FILMS: *Scott Joplin* (orig. for TV), *Heroes* 1977; *The Big Fix* 1978; *The Chosen* 1982; *The Sting II* 1983; *The Journey of Natty Gann* 1985; *Someone to Love* 1988; *Big Man on Campus/The Hunchback of UCLA* 1989; *By the Sword* 1991.

Kahn, Gus. Lyricist. *b.* Nov. 6, 1886, Coblenz, Germany. *d.* 1941. In the US from age four, he was raised and educated in Chicago and began his career writing special material for vaudeville acts. From the mid-20s he contributed songs to Broadway and Hollywood musicals, in collaboration with such composers as Walter Donaldson, George Gershwin, Sigmund Romberg, Victor Schertzinger, and Bronislaw Kaper. His best-known songs include 'Pretty Baby,' 'Some Sunday Morning,' 'Ain't We Got Fun?,' 'My Buddy,' 'Carolina in the Morning,' 'Side by Side,' 'Toot Toot Tootsie, Goodbye,' 'Nobody's Sweetheart,' 'I'll See You in My Dreams,' 'Charley My Boy,' 'It Had to Be You,' 'Yes Sir, That's My Baby,' 'Love Me or Leave Me,' 'Makin' Whoopee,' 'Beloved,' 'Coquette,' 'Flying Down to Rio,' 'The Carioca,' 'Orchids in the Moonlight,' and 'San Francisco.' Kahn's story was told in the biographic film *I'll See You in My Dreams* (1952), in which he was portrayed by Danny Thomas. Doris Day played his wife and sometime collaborator Grace LeBoy Kahn.

FILMS INCLUDE: *The Jazz Singer* 1927; *Hit of the Show* 1928; *Whoopee!* 1930; *Big City Blues* 1932; *Storm at Daybreak, Flying Down to Rio* 1933; *Bottoms Up, Stingaree, Hollywood Party, One Night of Love, Caravan, The Merry Widow, Kid Millions* 1934; *Reckless, Naughty Marietta, Love Me Forever, Escapade, Thanks a Million* 1935; *Rose Marie, Let's Sing Again, San Francisco, Three Smart Girls* 1936; *Captains Courageous, A Day at the Races, The Firefly, Music for Madame* 1937; *Everybody Sing, The Girl of the Golden West* 1938; *Honolulu, Broadway Serenade, Let Freedom Ring, Balalaika* 1939; *Lillian Russell, Spring Parade, Bitter Sweet, Go West* 1940; *Ziegfeld Girl, The Chocolate Soldier* 1941; *Broadway Rhythm, Show Business* 1944; *I'll See You in My Dreams* 1952.

Kahn, Madeline. Actress. Born on Sept. 29, 1942, in Boston. *ed.* Hofstra U. Delightfully funny, offbeat comedienne of the American stage, TV, and films. Trained as an opera singer, she sang and acted on and off Broadway and in nightclubs before her screen debut in the early 70s. She was nominated for best supporting actress Oscars for her performances in *Paper Moon* (1973) and *Blazing Saddles* (1974) and brightened many other films with her animated comic presence, often in feverishly lusty roles, most effectively in the zany farces of Mel BROOKS. She starred on TV in two series, 'Oh Madeline' (1983–84) and 'Mr. President' (1989) and in the telefilm *Wanted: The Perfect Guy* (1990). She co-starred with Ed ASNER in the 1989 Broadway revival of 'Born Yesterday,' a prelude to her Tony-winning performance as sister Gorgeous in Wendy Wasserstein's 'The Sisters Rosensweig' (1992).

FILMS: *The Dove* (short) 1968; *What's Up Doc?* 1972; *Paper Moon, From the Mixed-Up Files of Mrs. Basil E. Frankweiler* 1973; *Blazing Saddles, Young Frankenstein* 1974; *At Long Last Love, The Adventure of Sherlock Holmes' Smarter Brother* 1975; *Won Ton Ton—The Dog Who Saved Hollywood* 1976; *High Anxiety* 1977; *The Cheap Detective* 1978; *The Muppet Movie* (cameo) 1979; *Simon, Happy Birthday Gemini, Wholly Moses!, First Family* 1980; *History of the World: Part I* 1981; *Yellowbeard* 1983; *Slapstick of Another Kind, City Heat* 1984; *Clue* 1985; *My Little Pony* (voice only), *An American Tail* (voice only) 1986; *Betsy's Wedding* 1990; *Mixed Nuts* 1994; *Nixon* 1995.

Kahn, Michael. American film editor. After a period of apprenticeship, he began cutting low-budget features in the early 70s. Gaining stature in the latter part of the decade, through his work for Steven SPIELBERG, he became firmly established as one of Hollywood's prime editors after winning an Academy Award for *Raiders of the Lost Ark* (1981), a film noted for its breathtaking pace.

FILMS INCLUDE: *Rage* 1972; *Black Jack* 1973; *Golden Needles* 1974; *The Devil's Rain* 1975; *Return of a Man Called Horse* 1976; *Close Encounters of the Third Kind* 1977; *Eyes of Laura Mars* 1978; *Ice Castles, 1941* 1979; *Used Cars* 1980; *Raiders of the Lost Ark* 1981; *Poltergeist* 1982; *Table for Five, Twilight Zone—The Movie* 1983; *Indiana Jones and the Temple of Doom* 1984; *The Goonies, The Color Purple* 1985; *Wisdom* 1986; *Fatal Attraction* (co-edit.), *Empire of the Sun* 1987; *Arthur 2 on the Rocks* 1988; *Indiana Jones and the Last Crusade, Always* 1989; *Arachnophobia* 1990; *Hook, Toy Soldiers* 1991; *Alive, Jurassic Park, Schindler's List* 1993; *Twister* 1996; *Amistad, The Lost World* 1997.

Kalatozov, Mikhail. Director. *b.* Mikhail Konstantinovich Kalatozishvili, Dec. 23, 1903, Tiflis (now Tibilisi), Russia. *d.* 1973. Trained as an economist but entered Soviet films in 1925 as an actor, then became a cutter and cameraman in the Georgian studios. In 1928 he collaborated with Nutsa Gagoberidze on putting together a compilation film, *18–28,* about the counter-revolutionary activities of Georgia's Menshiviks between the years 1918 and 1928. Kalatazov's first important feature, the semidocumentary *Salt for Svanetia* (1930), was a lyrical, beautifully photographed (partly by himself) portrait of a remote Caucasian village and its primitive inhabitants. But the film, which is now considered among the foremost works of the Soviet cinema of the period, was criticized by the authorities for "negativism." So was Kalatozov's next film, *A Nail in the Boot* (1932), which was banned by the military commissars and never released. Kalatozov was then confined to administrative positions in the Georgian film industry and did not return to directing until 1939. During WW II he served as chief administrator of Soviet feature film production and spent some time in Los Angeles as a Soviet cultural representative. After the war he was appointed deputy minister of film production and again returned to directing in 1950. He was little known abroad until 1957, when he became internationally famous for *The Cranes Are Flying,* a rarity among Soviet films in its deeply felt romanticism and the absence of propaganda. It shared the 1958 Cannes Festival best picture award and was widely seen in the US and elsewhere. At home, however, it was criticized for "formalism" and "naturalism." Kalatazov's subsequent films, including co-productions with Cuba and Italy, were far less successful.

FILMS: *18–28* (compilation film; co-dir.) 1928; *Blind, Salt for Svanetia* (also sc., co-phot., 1930); *A Nail in the Boot* (censored, never released, 1932); *Manhood/Courage* 1939; *Valeri Chkalov/Wings of Victory* 1941; *Invincible* (co-dir., co-sc. with Sergei Gerasimov) 1943; *Moscow Music-Hall* 1945; *Conspiracy of the Doomed* 1950; *True Friends* 1954; *The First Echelon, The Hostile Wind, The Woman from Warsaw* 1956; *The Cranes Are Flying* 1957; *The Letter That Was Never Sent* 1960; *Soy Cuba/I Am Cuba!* (Cuba/USSR) 1963–66; *Krasnaya Palatka/The Red Tent* (It./USSR) 1971.

Kalem. A film production company founded in 1907 by George Kleine, Samuel Long, and Frank Marion and named for their initials (K-L-M). The company began production in a New York City loft but later expanded to branches in Florida and California. Its most famous early production was a quickie "spectacular," a one-reel version of *Ben-Hur,* shot during a Manhattan Beach fireworks show that featured a chariot race. (Heirs to the Lew Wallace estate sued Kalem for violation of the late author's copyright. After several years of litigation, Kalem paid them $25,000 in damages.) The film was co-directed by Sidney Olcott, who directed much of the Kalem product until leaving the company in 1912. The script was written by Gene Gauntier, the company's star actress (known as the "Kalem Girl") and busiest screenwriter.

Since Kalem had no indoor studios on any of its three lots, the company shot much of its product outdoors on locations throughout the United States and extending as far as Ireland, Italy, and Palestine. It was on the last location that Kalem's most prestigious and only feature-length film was shot. It was *From the Manger to the Cross* (1912), a story of Christ, directed by Olcott and written by Gauntier, who also played the Virgin Mary. Location shooting and careful photography made the Kalem product famous for quality. The company turned out an annual average of 200 films, all shorts with the exception of *From the Manger to the Cross.* Kalem was bought up by Vitagraph in 1916.

Kalmar, Bert. Lyricist, screenwriter. *b.* Feb. 16, 1884, New York City. *d.* 1947. He began his career as a child magician in tent shows, later appearing in vaudeville. In 1923 he teamed with composer Harry Ruby (*b.* Harry Rubinstein, Jan. 27, 1895, New York City; *d.* 1974) in a creative partnership that produced words and music for nine Broadway musicals and several films, including three Marx Brothers vehicles. They also collaborated on many of the scripts. In the romanticized film biography of the duo, *Three Little Words* (1950), Kalmar was portrayed by Fred Astaire and Ruby by Red Skelton.

FILMS INCLUDE: (songs or scripts or both): *The Cuckoos, Animal Crackers, Top Speed, Check and Double Check* 1930; *Broad Minded* 1931; *Horse Feathers, The Kid from Spain* 1932; *Duck Soup* 1933; *Hips Hips Hooray, The Circus Clown, Happiness Ahead, Kentucky Kernels* 1934; *Bright Lights, Thanks a Million, The Man Who Broke the Bank at Monte Carlo* 1935; *Walking on Air* 1936; *The Life of the Party* 1937; *Everybody Sing* 1938; *Ship Ahoy* 1942; *Look for the Silver Lining* 1949; *Three Little Words* 1950.

Kalmus, Dr. Herbert T. Inventor, film pioneer. *b.* Nov. 9, 1881, Chelsea, Mass. *d.* 1963. A graduate of MIT and the University of Zurich (Ph.D.), he was a college professor when he began experimenting with film color processes. In 1912 he formed the Technicolor Company, which he incorporated in 1915. In 1917 he turned out the first Technicolor film, *The Gulf Between,* a one-reeler, by superimposing two colored images on the screen at the same time. *The Black Pirate* (1926) was the first Technicolor film utilizing a true two-color process, and *Becky Sharp* (1935), the first to use today's three-color process. Kalmus's first wife, Natalie Kalmus (*b.* Natalie Dunfee, 1892, Boston; *d.* 1965), insisted on being credited as "color consultant" on all Technicolor films from 1933 till 1949, the expiration date of their patent.

Kamen, Michael. Composer. Prolific scorer of American and British films since the late 70s.

FILMS INCLUDE: *The Next Man* 1976; *Between the Lines* 1977; *Polyester* 1981; *Venom* 1982; *The Dead Zone* 1983; *Brazil* 1985; *Mona Lisa* 1986; *Lethal Weapon,* (co-mus.), *Adventures in Babysitting, Someone to Watch Over Me, Suspect* 1987; *Die Hard* 1988; *Lethal Weapon 2* (co-mus.), *Road House, Renegades* 1989; *Die Hard 2* 1990; *Circle of Friends, Die Hard with a Vengeance, Don Juan DeMarco, Mr. Holland's Opus* 1995; *101 Dalmatians, Jack* 1996; *Event Horizon, Inventing the Abbotts, The Winter Guest* 1997.

Kaminska, Ida. Actress. *b.* Ida Kaminski, Sept. 4, 1899, Odessa, Russia. *d.* 1980. The daughter of a celebrated actor and actress of the Yiddish theater, she began her stage career as a child of five and later played numerous leading roles at the Kaminski Theater in Warsaw. After touring the Soviet Union for three years, she established her own troupe in Warsaw, the Ida Kaminska Theater, and directed many of the productions in which she starred. She spent WW II in Russia and after returning to Warsaw in 1945 she founded the Jewish State Theater of Poland, with which she toured the US in 1967. She remained in this country and later emigrated to Israel. Kaminska, who had appeared in several Polish films from the mid-20s to the mid-30s, was nominated for a best actress Oscar for her moving performance in the Czech film *The Shop on Main Street* (1965).

FILMS INCLUDE: *A Vilna Legend* (Pol.) 1924; *Without a Home* (Pol.) 1936; *The Shop on Main Street* (Czech.) 1965; *The Angel Levine* (US) 1970.

Kane, Carol. Actress. Born on June 18, 1952, in Cleveland. Petite, animated leading lady and featured player of the stage and screen. An architect's daughter, she began acting professionally on the stage at age 14. She played a variety of interesting screen cameos before landing the lead role in *Hester*

Street (1975), for which she was nominated for an Oscar. She won an Emmy Award for her performance in the TV series 'Taxi' (1981–83).

FILMS: *Is This Trip Really Necessary?* 1970; *Carnal Knowledge, Desperate Characters* 1971; *Wedding in White, The Last Detail* 1973; *Dog Day Afternoon, Hester Street* 1975; *Harry and Walter Go to New York* 1976; *Annie Hall, Valentino* (UK), *The World's Greatest Lover* 1977; *The Mafu Cage* 1978; *The Muppet Movie* (cameo), *When a Stranger Calls, La Sabina/The Sabina* (Sp./Swed.) 1979; *Les Jeux de la Comtesse Dolingen de Gratz* (Fr.), *Norman Loves Rose* (Austral.), *Pandemonium/Thursday the 12th* 1982; *Racing with the Moon, Over the Brooklyn Bridge, The Secret Diary of Sigmund Freud* 1984; *Transylvania 6–5000* 1985; *Jumpin' Jack Flash* 1986; *Ishtar, The Princess Bride* 1987; *Sticky Fingers, License to Drive, Scrooged* (as Ghost of Christmas Present) 1988; *Joe Versus the Volcano* (uncredited cameo), *My Blue Heaven, The Lemon Sisters* 1990; *Ted and Venus, In the Soup* 1992; *Addams Family Values* 1993; *Even Cowgirls Get the Blues* 1994; *American Strays, Big Bully, The Pallbearer, Trees Lounge* 1996.

Kane, Helen. Actress, singer. *b.* Helen Schroeder, Aug. 4, 1903, the Bronx, N.Y. *d.* 1966. Onstage professionally from age 17, she began her career in vaudeville with the Marx Brothers and made her Broadway debut in the musical 'A Night in Spain' in 1927. The following year she created a sensation with her squeaky, childlike "boop-boop-a-doop" rendition of the song 'I Wanna Be Loved by You' in the musical 'Good Boy.' Her popularity led to a film contract and to a brief career as a leading lady in early Paramount talkies. She was portrayed by Debbie Reynolds in *Three Little Words* (1950), the film biography of the songwriting team of Kalmar and Ruby and provided the off-screen voice for Reynolds's "singing" of 'I Wanna Be Loved by You.'

FILMS: *Nothing but the Truth, Sweetie, Pointed Heels* 1929; *Paramount on Parade, Dangerous Nan McGrew, Heads Up* 1930.

Kane, Joseph (Joe). Director. *b.* Mar. 19, 1897, San Diego, Calif. *d.* 1975. A former cellist, he became a film editor in 1926 and a director in 1934. In the next decade, he turned out numerous low-budget action pictures for Republic, mostly Westerns, including some of John Wayne's vehicles and many of Gene Autry's and Roy Rogers's. In 1945 he was promoted by the studio to director of its medium-budget Westerns and action pictures. He was also credited as associate producer or co-producer of many of his films. From the late 50s he worked mostly in TV.

FILMS INCLUDE (complete from 1945): *Fighting Marines* (serial; co-dir. with Reeves Eason), *Tumbling Tumbleweeds, Melody Trail* 1935; *Darkest Africa* (serial; co-dir. with Eason), *The Lawless Nineties, The Lonely Trail, Guns and Guitars, Oh Susannah!* 1936; *Paradise Express, Come on Cowboys!, Boots and Saddles, Springtime in the Rockies* 1937; *Born to Be Wild, Arson Racket Squad, Under Western Stars, Man from Music Mountain, Billy the Kid Returns, Shine on Harvest Moon* 1938; *Southward Ho!, In Old Monterey, Wall Street Cowboy, The Arizona Kid, Days of Jesse James, Saga of Death Valley* 1939; *Young Buffalo Bill, The Ranger and the Lady, Colorado, The Border Legion* 1940; *Robin Hood of the Pecos, Sheriff of Tombstone, The Great Train Robbery, Nevada City, Rags to Riches, Red River Valley* 1941; *Sunset on the Desert, Romance of the Range, Sons of the Pioneers, Heart of the Golden West* 1942; *Idaho, King of the Cowboys, Song of Texas, Hands Across the Border* 1943; *The Cowboy and the Senorita, The Yellow Rose of Texas, Song of Nevada* 1944; *Flame of the Barbary Coast, The Cheaters, Dakota* 1945; *In Old Sacramento, The Plainsman and the Lady* 1946; *Wyoming* 1947; *Old Los Angeles, The Gallant Legion, The Plunderers* 1948; *The Last Bandit, Brimstone* 1949; *Rock Island Trail, The Savage Horde, California Passage* 1950; *Oh Susannah!, Fighting Coast Guard, The Sea Hornet* 1951; *Hoodlum Empire, Woman of the North Country* 1952; *Ride the Man Down, San Antone, Fair Wind to Java* 1953; *Sea of Lost Ships, Jubilee Trail* 1954; *Hell's Outpost, Timberjack, The Road to Denver, The Vanishing American* 1955; *The Maverick Queen, Thunder Over Arizona, Accused of Murder* 1956; *Duel at Apache Wells, Spoilers of the Forest, Last Stagecoach West, The Crooked Circle* 1957; *Gunfire at Indian Gap, The Notorious Mr. Monks, The Lawless Eighties, The Man Who Died Twice* 1958; *Beau Geste* (2nd-unit dir.), *Country Boy/Here Comes That Nashville Sound* 1966; *Tobruk* (2nd-unit dir.), *Track of Thunder* 1967; *In Enemy Country* (2nd-unit dir.) 1968; *Smoke in the Wind* (release delayed from 1971) 1975.

Kanew, Jeff. American director with experience in film editing. Typically handling lowbrow juvenile material, he scored a box-office hit with *Revenge of the Nerds* (1984). Also directed for TV.

FILMS: *The Wicked Die Slow* (sc., act.) 1968; *Black Rodeo* (dir., prod., edit.) 1972; *Natural Enemies* (dir., sc., edit.) 1979; *Ordinary People* (edit.) 1980; *Eddie Macon's Run* (dir., sc., edit.) 1983; *Revenge of the Nerds* (dir.) 1984; *Gotcha!* (dir.) 1985; *Tough Guys* (dir.) 1986; *Troop Beverly Hills* (dir.) 1989; *V. I. Warshawski* (dir.) 1991.

Kanin, Garson. Director, screenwriter, playwright. Born on Nov. 24, 1912, in Rochester, N.Y. Brother of Michael KANIN. He dropped out of high school after the 1929 Wall Street crash to help the family finances, at first as a jazz clarinetist and saxophonist, then as a vaudeville and burlesque comedian. After studies at the American Academy of Dramatic Arts, he turned to the legitimate stage, making his Broadway debut as an actor in 1933. He directed his first play in 1937 and the following year went to Hollywood, where he piloted a succession of entertaining films. His career was interrupted by WW II, during which he produced and directed documentaries for the Office of Emergency Management and collaborated with Sir Carol REED on the Oscar-winning *The True Glory* (1945), a film record of Operation Overlord, the last phase of the war in Europe from the invasion of Normandy to D day. After the war he returned to Broadway as a playwright and director and scored a big hit with the comedy 'Born Yesterday' (1946), which was later adapted to the screen. In between theatrical engagements he worked in Hollywood, writing several hilarious screenplays for George CUKOR, usually in collaboration with his wife, Ruth GORDON. He returned briefly to film directing in the late 60s. His several books include *Tracy and Hepburn* (1971), an intimate memoir of his relationship with the famed screen stars. Other books include: *Remembering Mr. Maugham* (1966), *Cast of Characters: Stories of Broadway and Hollywood* (1969), *A Thousand Summers* (1973), *Hollywood* (1974), *One Hell of an Actor* (1977), *It Takes a Long Time to Become Young* (1978), *Moviola* (1979), *Smash* (1980), *Together Again: Hollywood's Great Movie Teams* (1981), and *Cordelia* (1982). Kanin, who served as president of the Authors League, shared with his brother, Michael, in 1989 the Valentine Davies Award of the Writers Guild. In 1990 he married stage (and occasional movie) actress Marian Seldes (*b.* Aug. 23, 1928, New York City).

FILMS: As director—*A Man to Remember, Next Time I Marry* 1938; *The Great Man Votes, Bachelor Mother* 1939; *My Favorite Wife, They Knew What They Wanted* 1940; *Night Shift* (doc. short), *Tom Dick and Harry* 1941; *Fellow Americans, Ring of Steel* (both docs.) 1942; *Night Stripes* (doc. short) 1944; *The True Glory* (doc.; co-dir. with Carol Reed) 1945; *Salute to France* (doc. short; co-dir. with Jean Renoir) 1946; *Where It's At, Some Kind of a Nut* (both also sc.) 1969. As screenwriter—

From This Day Forward (adapt.) 1946; *A Double Life* 1948; *Adam's Rib* 1949; *Born Yesterday* (play basis only) 1951; *The Marrying Kind, Pat and Mike* 1952; *It Should Happen to You* 1954; *The Girl Can't Help It* (story basis only) 1956; *The Rat Race* (from own play), *High Time* (play basis only, 'The Live Wire.') 1960; *The Right Approach* (story basis only) 1961.

Kanin, Michael. Screenwriter. *b.* Feb. 1, 1910, Rochester, N.Y. *d.* 1993. Brother of Garson KANIN. A former commercial artist and musician, he began writing screenplays in the late 30s, winning an Academy Award for his collaboration with Ring Lardner, Jr., on *Woman of the Year* (1942). He often collaborated with his wife, Fay (née Mitchell, *b.* May 9, 1917, N.Y.C.), and directed one rather good film, *When I Grow Up* (1951). He also produced *A Double Life* (1948). Fay Kanin, who also wrote plays, screenplays, and award-winning teleplays on her own, served long stints as president of the Writers Guild of America, then of the Academy of Motion Pictures Arts and Sciences, and was a board member of the American Film Institute.

FILMS INCLUDE: *They Made Her a Spy* 1939; *Anne of Windy Poplars* 1940; *Woman of the Year, Sunday Punch* 1942; *The Cross of Lorraine* 1944; *Centennial Summer* 1946; *Honeymoon* 1947; *My Pal Gus* 1952; *Rhapsody* 1954; *The Opposite Sex* 1956; *Teacher's Pet* 1958; *The Right Approach* 1961; *Le Mercenaire/Swordsman of Siena* (Fr./It.) 1962; *The Outrage* 1964; *How to Commit Marriage* 1969.

Kanter, Hal. Screenwriter, occasional director. Born on Dec. 18, 1918, in Savannah, Ga. The writer of light material for top-rated early-day TV revues, he began writing screenplays in the early 50s, specializing in comedy but occasionally turning to drama. His several jabs at directing produced mediocre results. In the late 60s he returned to television and in the 70s was executive producer of the popular 'All in the Family' series. During the 80s he was involved as a writer or producer or both with numerous TV programs. In 1989 he received the Writers Guild's prestigious Paddy Chayefsky Laurel Award.

FILMS INCLUDE (as screenwriter): *My Favorite Spy* (dial. only), *Two Tickets to Broadway* 1951; *Road to Bali, Off Limits* 1953; *Money from Home, Casanova's Big Night, About Mrs. Leslie* 1954; *The Rose Tattoo, Artists and Models* 1956; *Loving You* (also dir.) 1957; *I Married a Woman* (dir. only), *Once Upon a Horse* (also dir., prod.) 1958; *Bachelor in Paradise, Pocketful of Miracles, Blue Hawaii* 1961; *Move Over Darling* 1963; *Dear Brigitte* 1965.

Kaper, Bronislaw (also **Bronislau**). Composer. *b.* Feb. 5, 1902, Warsaw. *d.* 1983. A graduate of the Warsaw Conservatory, he wrote concert music and scored early German sound films, usually in collaboration with Austrian composer Walter Jurmann. After Hitler came to power, Kaper emigrated to the US via France and began contributing songs for Hollywood films in the mid-30s, often in collaboration with lyricist Gus KAHN. He later signed a long-term contract with MGM and composed scores for many of the studio's major films, notably *Lili* (1953), for which he won an Academy Award.

FILMS INCLUDE: In Germany—*Die lustigen Musikanten, Alraune* 1930; *Die grosse Attraktion* 1931; *Melodie der Liebe* 1932; *Ein Lied für Dich, Madame wünscht keine Kinder* 1933. In the US—*Mutiny on the Bounty, A Night at the Opera* (songs only) 1935; *San Francisco* (songs only) 1936; *Three Smart Girls, A Day at the Races* (songs only) 1937; *Lillian Russell* (songs only), *Comrade X* 1940; *Go West, The Chocolate Soldier* (songs only), *Two-Faced Woman* 1941; *Keeper of the Flame* 1942; *Bataan, The Cross of Lorraine* 1943; *Gaslight, Mrs. Parkington* 1944; *Without Love, Our Vines Have Tender Grapes* 1945; *The Stranger, The Courage of Lassie* 1946; *Song of Love, Green Dolphin Street* 1947; *Homecoming, Act of Violence* 1948; *The Great Sinner, The Secret Garden, That Midnight Kiss, That Forsyte Woman* 1949; *A Life of Her Own, Key to the City* 1950; *The Red Badge of Courage* 1951; *Lili, The Actress* 1953; *Them!* 1954; *The Glass Slipper* 1955; *Somebody Up There Likes Me, The Swan* 1956; *The Barretts of Wimpole Street* 1957; *The Brothers Karamazov, Auntie Mame* 1958; *Butterfield 8, Home from the Hill* 1960; *Mutiny on the Bounty* 1962; *Lord Jim* 1965; *Tobruk, The Way West* 1967; *A Flea in Her Ear* 1968.

Kaplan, Jonathan. Director. Born on Nov. 25, 1947, in Paris. *ed.* U. of Chicago (B.A.); NYU (M.F.A.). After apprenticeship at Roger Corman's New World Pictures, he began directing features in the early 70s and, while working with limited budgets, turned out well-paced, technically proficient films. He was later rewarded with more generous budgets and better opportunities to flaunt his considerable skills. He also appeared in several productions and a couple of Broadway plays.

FILMS: *The Student Teachers, The Slams* 1973; *Truck Turner, Night Call Nurses* 1974; *White Line Fever* (also co-sc.) 1975; *Mr. Billion* (also co-sc.) 1977; *Over the Edge* 1979; *Heart Like a Wheel* 1983; *Project X* 1987; *The Accused* 1988; *Immediate Family* 1989; *Love Field, Unlawful Entry* 1992; *Bad Girls* 1994.

Kaplan, Nelly. Director, writer. Born in 1931, in Buenos Aires. *ed.* U. of Buenos Aires (economics). A cinema enthusiast, she went to Paris in the early 50s as a representative of an Argentinian cinematheque to an international congress of film archivists and stayed in France as a correspondent of Argentinian film magazines. Soon after her arrival she met director Abel GANCE and became his assistant and close collaborator. In 1961 she began directing shorts and in 1967 won a Golden Lion award in Venice for a medium-length film, *Le Regard Picasso.* Soon after, she turned to feature films. She has written a number of books, including a collection of short stories and a collection of erotic poems under the pseudonym Belen.

FEATURE FILMS (as director and co-screenwriter): *La Fiancée du Pirate/A Very Curious Girl/Dirty Mary* 1969; *Papa les Petits Bateaux* (also act.) 1971; *Néa/A Young Emmanuelle* 1976; *Le Satellite de Vénus* 1977; *Charles et Lucie/Charles and Lucie* 1979.

Kapoor, Raj. Actor, director, producer. *b.* Dec. 14, 1924, Peshawar, India (now in Pakistan). *d.* 1988. For many years India's most popular screen personality, he began directing many of his own films in the late 40s, soon rising to a prominent position in the industry. Kapoor had started his career as an apprentice to his father, veteran stage and silent screen star Prithviraj Kapoor (1906–72). He appeared in scattered films as a child and before maturing to adult roles was employed on the set as a clapper boy. His popularity soared with the release of *Awara/The Vagabond* (1951), a captivating, if simple-minded, melodrama sprinkled with songs, which he also directed and produced. It was dubbed into Turkish, Persian, and Arabic, broke all box-office records in the Middle East, and became a runaway hit in the Soviet Union. It was typical of Kapoor's films—naive but sincere and entertaining explorations of good versus evil and wealth versus poverty, in which the hero portrayed a Chaplinesque "little fellow" who confronted social injustice and overcame great odds with fervor and conviction. In his later films, Kapoor introduced a measure of sensuality into Indian cinema, an industry which usually shuns even kissing on the screen. His death at 64 of complications from an asthma attack was mourned by millions of Indian fans. His younger brother, Shashi KAPOOR, starred in many Indian and some British productions.

FILMS INCLUDE (as actor): *Inquilab* 1935; *Hamari Baat* 1943; *Valmiki* 1946; *Neel Kamal* 1947; *Aag/Fire* (also dir., prod.)

1948; *Barsaat* (also dir.), *Parivartan* 1949; *Awara/The Vagabond* (also dir., prod.) 1951; *Shri 420/Mister 420* (also dir., prod.) 1954; *Jagte Raho* (also prod.) 1956; *Sharada* 1958; *Anadi* 1959; *Where the Ganges Flows* (also prod.) 1960; *Nazraana* 1961; *Sangam* (also dir., prod.) 1964; *Around the World* 1967; *My Name Is Joker* (also dir., prod.) 1970; *Do Jasoos* 1975; *Chandi Sona* 1977; *Abdullah* 1981; *Prem Rog* (also dir., prod.) 1982.

Kapoor, Shashi. Actor, producer. Born on March 18, 1938, in Calcutta, India. Prolific stage-trained Indian actor known to Western audiences for his performances in British productions of, among others, Merchant-Ivory and Stephen Frears. Early in his career, he performed in his actor-director father Prithviraj Kapoor's company and appeared in actor-director brother Raj KAPOOR's films. Has over 200 Indian films to his credit.

FILMS INCLUDE: *The Householder* 1963; *Shakespeare Wallah* 1965; *Pretty Polly/A Matter of Innocence* 1967; *Bombay Talkie* 1970; *Siddhartha* 1972; *Junoon/Obsession* (also prod.) 1978; *Heat and Dust, Vijeta/Conquest* (also prod.) 1983; *Utsav/Festival* (also prod.) 1984; *The New Delhi Times* 1986; *Anjaam, Sammy and Rosie Get Laid* 1987; *The Deceivers* 1988; *In Custody* 1993.

Karina, Anna. Actress. Born Hanne Karin Blarke Bayer, on Sept. 22, 1940, in Copenhagen. A former model, she appeared in several Danish advertising films and arrived in France as the star of a Danish short that won a prize at the Cannes Festival. Her career in French films was launched by Jean-Luc GODARD, who married her in 1961 and divorced her in 1964. Her impulsive personality was highlighted in several of his films, as well as in those of other French New Wave directors. In 1973 she wrote, directed, and starred in *Vivre Ensemble.* In 1978 she married director Daniel-Georges Duval.

FILMS INCLUDE: *Le Petit Soldat* (release delayed until 1976), *Ce Soir ou jamais* 1960; *Une Femme est une Femme/A Woman Is a Woman* 1961; *She'll Have to Go/Maid for Murder* (UK), *Vivre sa Vie/My Life to Live, Les Quatre Vérités/Three Fables of Love* 1962; *Shéherazade/Scheherazade* (title role), *Dragées au Poivre/Sweet and Sour* 1963; *Bande à Part/Band of Outsiders, La Ronde/Circle of Love* 1964; *De l'Amour, Alphaville, Pierrot le Fou, La Religieuse/The Nun* 1965; *Made in USA* 1966; *Lo Straniero/The Stranger* (It./Fr./Alg.), *Le plus Vieux Métier du Monde/The Oldest Profession* 1967; *The Magus* (UK) 1968; *Before Winter Comes* (UK), *Laughter in the Dark* (UK/Fr.), *Justine* (US) 1969; *Rendez-vous à Bray* 1971; *The Salzburg Connection* (US/Ger.) 1972; *Vivre Ensemble* (also dir., sc.), *Pane e Cioccolata/Bread and Chocolate* (It.) 1973; *L'Invenzione di Morel* (It.) 1974; *Les Oeufs brouilles, Chinesisches Roulett/Chinese Roulette* (Ger.) 1976; *Also es war so* (Ger./Aus.) 1977; *Just Like at Home* (Hung.), *Chaussette Surprise* 1978; *The Story of a Mother* (Den.) 1979; *L'Ami de Vincent* 1983; *Ave Maria* 1984; *Dernier Eté à Tangiers, Cayenne Palace* 1987; *The Man Who Would Be Guilty* (Den./Fr.) 1990; *Haut bas Fragile/Up, Down/Fragile* 1997.

Karloff, Boris. Actor. *b.* William Henry Pratt, Nov. 23, 1887, Dulwich, England. *d.* 1969. *ed.* London U. The youngest of the eight children of a civil servant in the British foreign service, he was intended for a diplomatic career but in 1909 emigrated to Canada, where he found employment as a farmhand. Attracted to the stage, he joined one touring company, then another, and for the next decade played supporting parts in plays all over Canada and the US. In 1916, during a brief stay in Los Angeles, he made his screen debut as an extra in *The Dumb Girl of Portici,* starring Anna Pavlova. Out of a job three years later, he returned to Hollywood and began appearing regularly in films, in extra and bit parts. Unable to support himself as an actor, he alternated as a truck driver until the mid-20s, when his screen roles became more substantial. He was typically cast as a stock villain and failed to gain much recognition through the rest of the silent era, although he appeared in no less than 40 silent films.

Despite a pronounced lisp, Karloff's stage-trained voice became an asset during the transition to sound. He scored his first success in *The Criminal Code* (1931), in which he repeated a previous stage role. But the real turning point in his career came later that year, when he was cast by James WHALE in the role of the Monster in *Frankenstein,* a role that had been turned down by Bela LUGOSI, the star of an earlier horror classic, *Dracula.* Even the heavy makeup applied by Jack Pierce to Karloff's face could not hide the nuances of his performance. The film was a great success and assured Karloff a permanent niche in the horror film genre. During the Universal horror cycle of the early 30s and in many such films to follow, he and his now frequent screen partner Lugosi formed the most formidable duo of the macabre in film history. Karloff also played many supporting parts out of character, notably as a religious fanatic in John Ford's *The Lost Patrol* (1934), but he remained identified in the public mind exclusively with his roles as a scarred, tormented, humanely vulnerable monster or a deranged scientist.

In contrast, Karloff himself was known to be a mild-mannered, amiable gentleman who performed many acts of charity for needy children. He narrated a Mother Goose kiddie story record and played the kindly Colonel March of Scotland Yard on TV. He also hosted and occasionally starred in a suspense TV series called 'Thriller.' Throughout his busy screen career (some 140 films in all) Karloff continued to return to the stage. He scored a great success in 1941 as Jonathan Brewster in the Broadway production of 'Arsenic and Old Lace' and another in 1950 as Captain Hook in 'Peter Pan.' He gave one of his best performances in one of his last screen roles, virtually playing himself, as an aging star of horror movies, in Peter Bogdanovich's *Targets* (1968).

FILMS: *The Dumb Girl of Portici* (extra) 1916; *The Lightning Raider* (serial; bit), *The Masked Rider* (serial; bit), *His Majesty the American, The Prince and Betty* 1919; *The Deadlier Sex, The Courage of Marge O'Doone, The Last of the Mohicans* 1920; *The Hope Diamond Mystery* (serial), *Without Benefit of Clergy, Cheated Hearts, The Cave Girl* 1921; *The Man from Downing Street, The Infidel, The Altar Stairs, Omar the Tentmaker, The Woman Conquers* 1922; *The Prisoner* 1923; *The Hellion, Dynamite Dan* 1924; *Parisian Nights, Forbidden Cargo, The Prairie Wife, Lady Robinhood, Never the Twain Shall Meet* 1925; *The Greater Glory, Her Honor the Governor, The Nicklehopper* (short), *The Bells, Eagle of the Sea, Flames, The Golden Web, Flaming Fury, Valencia* (bit), *Man in the Saddle, Old Ironsides* 1926; *Tarzan and the Golden Lion, Let It Rain, The Meddlin' Stranger, The Princess from Hoboken, The Phantom Buster, Soft Cushions, Two Arabian Knights, The Love Mart* 1927; *Vultures of the Sea* (serial), *The Little Wild Girl* 1928; *The Fatal Warning* (serial), *Devil's Chaplain, Two Sisters, The Phantom of the North, Anne Against the World, King of the Kongo* (serial), *Behind That Curtain, The Unholy Night, Burning the Wind* 1929; *The Band One* (bit), *The Sea Bat, The Utah Kid* 1930; *Mother's Cry* (bit), *The Criminal Code, Cracked Nuts, Donovan's Kid, King of the Wild* (serial), *Smart Money, The Public Defender, I Like Your Nerve, Five Star Final, Pardon Us* (in French-language version only), *Graft, The Mad Genius, The Yellow Ticket, The Guilty Generation, Frankenstein* (as the Monster), *Tonight or Never* 1931; *Business and Pleasure, Alias the Doctor, Behind the Mask/The Man Who Dared, Scarface, The Miracle Man, The Cohens and Kellys in Hollywood* (cameo), *Night World, The Old Dark House, The Mask of Fu*

Manchu (title role), *The Mummy* (title role) 1932; *The Ghoul* (title role; UK) 1933; *The Lost Patrol, The House of Rothschild, The Black Cat, The Gift of Gab* (cameo) 1934; *The Bride of Frankenstein* (as the Monster), *The Black Room* (dual role), *The Raven* 1935; *The Invisible Ray, The Walking Dead, The Man Who Lived Again* (UK), *Juggernaut* (UK) 1936; *Charlie Chan at the Opera, Night Key, West of Shanghai* 1937; *The Invisible Menace, Mr. Wong—Detective* (title role) 1938; *Son of Frankenstein* (as the Monster), *The Mystery of Mr. Wong* (title role), *Mr. Wong in Chinatown* (title role), *The Man They Could Not Hang, Tower of London* 1939; *The Fatal Hour* (as Mr. Wong), *British Intelligence, Black Friday, The Man with Nine Lives, Devil's Island, Doomed to Die* (as Mr. Wong), *Before I Hang, The Ape, You'll Find Out* 1940; *The Devil Commands* 1941; *The Boogie Man Will Get You* 1942; *The Climax, House of Frankenstein* 1944; *The Body Snatcher, Isle of the Dead* 1945; *Bedlam* 1946; *The Secret Life of Walter Mitty, Lured, Unconquered, Dick Tracy Meets Gruesome* (as Gruesome) 1947; *Tap Roots* 1948; *Abbott and Costello Meet the Killer—Boris Karloff* 1949; *The Strange Door* 1951; *The Black Castle* 1952; *Colonel March of Scotland Yard/Colonel March Investigates* (orig. for UK TV), *Abbott and Costello Meet Dr. Jekyll and Mr. Hyde* (as Jekyll/Hyde), *Il Mostro dell'Isola/Monster of the Island* (It.), *The Hindu* 1953; *Voodoo Island* 1957; *Grip of the Strangler/The Haunted Strangler* (UK), *Frankenstein 1970* (as Baron Frankenstein) 1958; *Corridors of Blood* (UK) 1962; *The Raven, The Terror, I Tre Volti della Paura/Black Sabbath* (It./Fr./US), *The Comedy of Terrors/The Graveside Story* 1963; *Bikini Beach* (cameo) 1964; *Die Monster Die!/Monster of Terror* (US/UK) 1965; *The Ghost in the Invisible Bikini, The Daydreamer* (voice only) 1966; *The Venetian Affair, The Sorcerers* (UK), *Mad Monster Party* (voice of Baron Frankenstein) 1967; *Targets, Curse of the Crimson Altar/The Crimson Altar/The Crimson Cult* (UK) 1968; *The Snake People* (release delayed from 1968; US/Mex.), *The Incredible Invasion* (release delayed from 1968; US/Sp.), *Cauldron of Blood/Blind Man's Bluff* (release delayed from 1967) 1971; *House of Evil* (Mex./US; unreleased) 1972.

Karlson, Phil. Director. *b.* Philip N. Karlstein, July 2, 1908, Chicago, of Jewish-Irish parentage. *d.* 1985. His mother was actress Lillian O'Brien, who began her career with Dublin's Abbey Players and became a star of the Yiddish theater in Chicago. After completing high school, he took up painting at the Chicago Art Institute and made a tentative bid for a career as a song-and-dance man, finally acceding to his father's wish that he become a lawyer. While studying law at Loyola Marymount University in California, he worked in various capacities at the Universal studios and gradually moved up from prop man to second assistant director, first assistant, cutter, film editor, associate producer, short-subject director, and finally feature director in 1944. From the start he was confined to low-budget productions. Although his films of the 40s were mainly minor, run-of-the-mill B features, he made his mark in the 50s with a number of modest but hard-hitting crime films noted for their realism and uninhibited violence. Foremost among these were *Scandal Sheet* (1952), *99 River Street* (1953), *Tight Spot, Five Against the House,* and *The Phenix City Story* (all 1955), and *The Brothers Rico* (1957).

Karlson shot *The Phenix City Story* on location in Alabama while the trial for the murder it depicted was still in progress. During the course of filming he uncovered new evidence that helped convict the murder suspects. His dedication to authenticity could be great—for example, in filming *The Phenix City Story* he had John McIntire, who played the film's protagonist and murder victim, wear the same clothes the dead man had actually worn at the time of the murder. But despite the admiration of a few critics and a certain cult following, Karlson remained a B picture director, limited by small budgets to mainly unambitious projects. However, in 1973, at the age of 65 and after 30 years of relative anonymity and modest financial gains, he scored his first big commercial hit, *Walking Tall,* a fictionalized account of the true story of a Tennessee town sheriff, in which Karlson had a hefty financial stake.

FILMS: *A Wave a Wac and a Marine* 1944; *There Goes Kelly, G.I. Honeymoon, The Shanghai Cobra* 1945; *Live Wires, Swing Parade of 1946, Dark Alibi, The Missing Lady, Behind the Mask, Bowery Bombshell, Wife Wanted* 1946; *Black Gold, Kilroy Was Here, Louisiana* 1947; *Rocky, Adventure in Silverado, Thunderhoof* 1948; *Ladies of the Chorus, The Big Cat, Down Memory Lane* 1949; *The Iroquois Trail* 1950; *Mask of the Avenger, The Texas Rangers, Lorna Doone* 1951; *Scandal Sheet, The Brigand, Kansas City Confidential* 1952; *99 River Street* 1953; *Tight Spot, Hell's Island, Five Against the House, The Phenix City Story* 1955; *The Brothers Rico* 1957; *Gunman's Walk* 1958; *Hell to Eternity, Key Witness* 1960; *The Secret Ways, The Young Doctors* 1961; *The Scarface Mob* (fused into a feature from two segments of 'The Untouchables' TV series, originally made in the late 50s), *Kid Galahad* 1962; *Rampage* 1963; *The Silencers* 1966; *A Time for Killing* 1967; *The Wrecking Crew* 1968; *Hornets' Nest* 1970; *Ben* 1972; *Walking Tall* 1973; *Framed* 1975.

Karmen, Roman. Documentary filmmaker. *b.* 1906, Odessa, Russia. *d.* 1978. Formerly a magazine photographer, he made himself a name in the Soviet Union as a combat newsreel cameraman in such action spots as Spain (the Civil War), China (1938, 1941), and Leningrad (1943). He also covered the Nuremberg trials. He assembled much-admired compilation documentaries from his own footage.

FILMS INCLUDE: *Moscow* 1933; *Spain* 1937; *China Defends Herself* 1938; *Sedov's Expedition, One Day in the New World* 1940; *In China* 1941; *Days and Nights of Leningrad* 1943; *Albania* 1945; *Judgment of the People* 1947; *Caspian Story* 1953; *Vietnam* 1954; *Great Is My Country* (in 70 mm) 1958; *Dawn of India, Conquered Seas* 1959; *September 16th* 1960; *Island of Flame* (Cuba) 1961; *The Great Patriotic War* 1965; *Cinerama's Russian Adventure* (co-dir.; compiled from films made in 1959–61), *Death of a Commissar* 1966–68; *Granada My Granada* 1967; *Comrade Berlin* 1968; *Continent Aflame* 1970; *Chile Happenings* 1973.

Karns, Roscoe. Actor. *b.* Sept. 7, 1893, San Bernardino, Calif. *d.* 1970. *ed.* USC. A stage actor at age 15, he played light supporting parts in scores of Hollywood films from the early 20s through the mid-60s, most actively in the 30s, typically as a crusty but genial character, often a hustling newspaper reporter.

FILMS INCLUDE: *Poor Relations* 1919; *The Life of the Party* 1920; *Too Much Married* (lead) 1921; *Conquering the Woman* 1922; *Other Men's Daughters* 1923; *Bluff, The Midnight Express* 1924; *Dollar Down* 1925; *Ritzy, Ten Modern Commandments, The Jazz Singer* 1927; *Beau Sabreur, Beggars of Life, Moran of the Marines, Jazz Mad* 1928; *The Shopworn Angel, This Thing Called Love, New York Nights* 1929; *Troopers Three, Safety in Numbers, The Costello Case* 1930; *Dirigible, Laughing Sinners* 1931; *I Am a Fugitive from a Chain Gang, Night After Night, If I Had a Million* 1932; *Today We Live, Gambling Ship, Alice in Wonderland* (as Tweedledee) 1933; *It Happened One Night, Come on Marines!, Twentieth Century, Elmer and Elsie* 1934; *Wings in the Dark, Front Page Woman, Alibi Ike, Two Fisted* 1935; *Cain and Mabel* 1936; *Clarence* (lead) 1937; *Scandal Street, Tip-Off Girls, You and Me, Thanks for the Memory* 1938; *Everything's on Ice* (lead) 1939; *His Girl*

Friday, Saturday's Children, They Drive by Night, Ladies Must Live 1940; *Footsteps in the Dark* 1941; *Woman of the Year* 1942; *Old Acquaintance* 1943; *The Navy Way* 1944; *Avalanche* 1946; *It's a Wonderful Life, That's My Man* 1947; *Texas Brooklyn and Heaven* 1948; *Onionhead* 1958; *Man's Favorite Sport?* 1964.

Kasdan, Lawrence. Director, screenwriter, producer. Born on Jan. 14, 1949, in Miami Beach, Fla. Raised in West Virginia, he earned a master's degree in education at the University of Michigan, intending to become an English teacher. But he wound up in advertising as a Clio Award–winning copywriter of TV commercials. In his spare time he was writing screenplays. Undaunted by dozens of rejections, he finally broke through with a bang as the co-scripter of the sci-fi epic, *The Empire Strikes Back* (1980). His career further boosted by his solo screenplay in 1981 for Steven SPIELBERG's *Raiders of the Lost Ark,* he was in a position to demand a first opportunity to direct, making an impressive debut that same year with the lusty film noir, *Body Heat.* In the following years he enhanced his growing reputation with such diverse films as *The Big Chill* (1983), a retrospective on the radical 60s generation, and *Silverado* (1985), a sprawling Western epic. His *The Accidental Tourist* was nominated for an Academy Award and was named by the New York Film Critics as best picture of 1988. Married and a father of two, he lives in Los Angeles.

FILMS: *The Empire Strikes Back* (co-sc.) 1980; *Raiders of the Lost Ark* (sc.), *Body Heat* (dir., sc.), *Continental Divide* (sc.) 1981; *Return of the Jedi* (co-sc.), *The Big Chill* (dir., co-sc, co-exec. prod.) 1983; *Into the Night* (act.), *Silverado* (dir., co-sc., prod.) 1985; *Cross My Heart* (prod.) 1987; *The Accidental Tourist* (dir., co-sc., co-prod.) 1988; *Immediate Family* (exec. prod.) 1989; *I Love You to Death* (dir., act.) 1990; *Grand Canyon* (dir., co-sc.) 1991; *The Bodyguard* (sc., co-prod.), *Jumpin' at the Boneyard* (story) 1992; *Wyatt Earp* (co-prod., dir., sc.) 1994; *French Kiss* (dir.) 1995.

Kashfi, Anna. Actress. Born on Sept. 30, 1935, in Calcutta, India, of part-British descent. She played exotic roles in four Hollywood films of the mid- and late 50s but remains best known for her brief and unharmonious marriage to actor Marlon BRANDO. In 1979 she authored an unflattering memoir of their relationship, *Breakfast with Brando,* and returned to the screen in *The Violent Women.*

FILMS: *The Mountain* 1956; *Battle Hymn* 1957; *Cowboy* 1958; *Night of the Quarter Moon* 1959; *The Violent Women* 1979.

Kast, Pierre. Director. *b.* Dec 22, 1920, Paris. *d.* 1984. *ed.* Sorbonne. An active member of the French Resistance in WW II, he began his association with film after the Liberation as one of the founders of the Paris University Ciné-Club in 1945. The following year he went to work for the Cinémathèque Française and in 1948 became an assistant to director Jean GRÉMILLON. Kast collaborated with Grémillon on the former's first short, *Les Charmes de l'Existence* (1949), and subsequently directed many other short subjects on his own, notably *Les Désastres de la Guerre* (1951), in which he used etchings by Goya to powerful effect. Several of his shorts won international awards. While solidifying his reputation as a director of shorts, Kast also worked as an assistant director on feature films and wrote essays and film criticism for *Cahiers du Cinéma* and other publications. He made his first feature film in 1957 and subsequently turned out a number of sensitive, intimate, intelligent features as well as other shorts and TV films. Kast wrote several novels, including *Les Vampires de l'Alfama* and *Le Bonheur ou le Pouvoir.* He died of a heart attack at 63, during a flight back from Rome, where he had been shooting a TV film.

FEATURE FILMS: *Un Amour de Poche/Nude in His Pocket* 1957; *Le Bel Age* (also co-sc.), *Merci Natercia* 1960; *La Morte-Saison des Amours/The Season for Love* (also co-sc.) 1961; *Vacances portugaises* 1963; *Le Grain de Sable, La Naissance de l'Empire Romain* (both originally made for TV) 1965; *La Chute de l'Empire Romain* (made for TV) 1967; *Carnets Brésiliens* (made for TV), *Drôle de Jeu* (also co-sc.) 1968; *Le Drapeau blanc d'Oxala/Macumba* (doc.; also co-sc.) 1969; *Le Petit Matin* (co-sc. only) 1971; *Les Soleils de l'Ile de Pâques* 1972; *L'Amérique* (for TV) 1973; *An Animal Gifted with Reason* 1975; *Le Soleil en face* 1980; *La Guerillera* 1982; *L'Herbe rouge* (for TV; unfinished) 1984.

Kastner, Elliott. Producer. Born on Jan. 7, 1930, in New York City. A former talent agent, he ventured into packaging and producing motion pictures in the mid-60s and has since turned out many commercially successful films. His base of operations is London, but the scope of his business activity is international.

FILMS INCLUDE: *Bus Riley's Back in Town* 1965; *Harper, Kaleidoscope* 1966; *The Bobo* 1967; *Sweet November* 1968; *The Night of the Following Day, Where Eagles Dare* 1969; *A Severed Head* (exec. prod.), *Villain* (exec. prod.) 1971; *Zee and Co./X Y & Zee* (exec. prod.) 1972; *The Long Goodbye* (exec. prod.), *Jeremy* (exec. prod.), *Cops and Robbers* 1973; *11 Harrowhouse* 1974; *Farewell My Lovely* (co-exec. prod.), *92 in the Shade* (exec. prod.), *Russian Roulette* (exec. prod.), *Rancho Deluxe* 1975; *Breakheart Pass* (exec. prod.), *The Missouri Breaks* (co-prod.), *Swashbuckler* (exec. prod.) 1976; *A Little Night Music, Equus* (co-prod.) 1977; *The Medusa Touch* (co-prod.), *The Big Sleep* (co-prod.), *The Stick Up* (co-exec. prod.) 1978; *Goldengirl* (exec. prod.), *North Sea Hijack/Ffolkes* 1979; *The First Deadly Sin* (co-exec. prod.) 1980; *Absolution* (co-prod.; release delayed from 1978) 1981; *Death Valley* 1982; *Man Woman and Child* (co-prod.) 1983; *Oxford Blues* (co-prod.), *Garbo Talks* (co-dir.) 1984; *Black Joy, Nomads* (co-prod.) 1986; *Heat, Angel Heart* (co-prod.), *Jack's Back* (exec. prod.), *Zombie High (The School That Ate My Brain)* 1987; *The Blob, White of the Eye* (co-prod.), *Never on Tuesday, Homeboy* 1988; *A Chorus of Disapproval* (exec. prod.) 1989.

Kasznar, Kurt. Actor. *b.* Kurt Serwischer, Aug. 13, 1913, Vienna. *d.* 1979. *ed.* Minerva U. (Zurich). He made an isolated screen appearance as a child of 11 in *Der Zirkuskönig/Max, King of the Circus* (1924), the last film of French comedy star Max LINDER, which was shot in Vienna. On the Austrian stage from 1931, he arrived in the US in 1937 with the REINHARDT company. He appeared in many stage plays and from the early 50s also in films, typically playing exuberant, somewhat eccentric character roles. Memorable in *My Sister Eileen* (1955). He starred in the TV series 'Land of the Giants' (1968–70). His second wife (divorced) was actress Leora Dana.

FILMS INCLUDE: *Der Zirkuskönig/Max, King of the Circus* 1924; *The Light Touch* 1951; *Anything Can Happen, The Happy Time* 1952; *Lili, Sombrero, Ride Vaquero!, Kiss Me Kate* (as Baptista), *All the Brothers Were Valiant* 1953; *Valley of the Kings, The Last Time I Saw Paris* 1954; *My Sister Eileen* 1955; *Anything Goes* 1956; *Timbuctu/Legend of the Lost* (It./US), *A Farewell to Arms* 1957; *The Journey, For the First Time* (It./Ger.), *Helden/Arms and the Man* (Ger.) 1959; *55 Days at Peking* 1963; *Casino Royale* (UK), *The Perils of Pauline, The King's Pirate, The Ambushers* 1967.

Katch, Kurt. Actor. *b.* Isser Kac (Katz), Jan. 28, 1896, Grodno, Poland. *d.* 1958. A student of Max REINHARDT, he was active in Jewish theaters throughout Europe before emigrating to the US in 1937. He played character parts in Hollywood films of the 40s and 50s, often as a shaven-headed heavy.

FILMS INCLUDE: *Tkies Khaf/The Vow* (in Yiddish) 1938; *Man at Large* 1941; *Berlin Correspondent, They Came to Blow Up America, Quiet Please Murder* 1942; *Mission to Moscow* (as

Marshal Timoshenko), *Background to Danger, Watch on the Rhine, Ali Baba and the Forty Thieves* 1943; *The Purple Heart, The Mask of Dimitrios, The Conspirators, The Seventh Cross, The Mummy's Curse* 1944; *Salome—Where She Danced* 1945; *Angel on My Shoulder* 1946; *Song of Love* 1947; *Secret of the Incas, The Adventures of Hajji Baba* 1954; *Abbott and Costello Meet the Mummy* 1955; *Pharaoh's Curse* 1957; *The Beast of Budapest, The Young Lions* 1958.

Katselas, Milton. Director. Born on Feb. 22, 1933, in Pittsburgh. A graduate of the drama department of Carnegie Tech, he directed for the New York stage before turning to films in the 70s.

FILMS: *Butterflies Are Free* 1972; *Forty Carats* 1973; *Report to the Commissioner* 1975; *When You Comin' Back Red Ryder?* 1979.

Katt, William. Actor. Born on Feb. 16, 1950, in Los Angeles. Curly-haired, blond leading man of the American stage, screen, and TV. The son of actors Bill WILLIAMS (Herman Katt) and Barbara HALE, he majored in music at Orange Coast College and began his career as a pianist and guitarist. He later performed in stock and with touring stage companies, making his film debut in 1976. On TV, he starred in 'The Greatest American Hero' (1981–83), among other series and programs. In the late 80s and early 90s, he co-starred with his mother and shared writing credits on several Perry Mason telefilms.

FILMS: *Carrie* 1976; *First Love* 1977; *Big Wednesday* 1978; *Butch and Sundance: The Early Days* (as the Sundance Kid) 1979; *Baby. . . Secret of the Lost Legend/Dinosaur. . . Secret of the Lost Legend* 1985; *House* 1986; *Naked Obsession* 1990; *Tollbooth* 1994.

Katz, Gloria. See HUYCK, Willard.

Katzenberg, Jeffrey. Executive. Born in 1950. He began his career in the film industry in 1975 as an assistant to Barry Diller, then chairman and CEO of Paramount. He stayed at Paramount for almost a decade, becoming president of production in 1982. In 1984, he left to become chairman of the Walt Disney Studios. With Michael EISNER, chairman and CEO of the WALT DISNEY COMPANY, he helped to revive Disney from its moribund state, making it a top-ranked producer of motion pictures, animated and otherwise. In the course of doing so, he gained a reputation for shrewd judgments of audience tastes, tight production control, and hard bargaining with Hollywood talent. Films made during his tenure include *Outrageous Fortune* (1987), *Honey I Shrunk the Kids* (1989), *Pretty Woman* (1990), *Beauty and the Beast* (1991), *Aladdin* (1992), and *The Lion King* (1994).

The year 1994 was significant for this Hollywood executive. The release of *The Lion King* and its subsequent success, generating boffo box-office receipts, all but confirmed Katzenberg's position within Disney's executive ranks. Surprisingly though, shortly after the film's release, he announced his resignation citing a desire to pursue other career opportunities. In the fall of that year, Katzenberg shocked Hollywood again with the announcement of his partnership with filmmaker Steven SPIELBERG and producer David GEFFEN in a venture that would create a new motion picture studio, DREAMWORKS SKG.

Katzin, Lee H. Director. Born on Apr. 12, 1935, in Detroit. *ed.* Harvard. In Hollywood briefly in the late 60s and early 70s, he occasionally demonstrated good storytelling skills, which were sometimes offset by overuse of camera gimmickry. Later worked mainly for TV.

FEATURE FILMS: *Heaven with a Gun, Whatever Happened to Aunt Alice?* 1969; *The Phynx* 1970; *Le Mans* 1971; *The Salzburg Connection* 1972; *World Gone Wild* 1988

Katzman, Sam. Producer. *b.* July 4, 1901, New York City. *d.* 1973. Entered films as a prop boy at age 13, working his way up to producer through various studio positions. He was involved in numerous productions, for the most part low- and medium-budget pictures, stressing action and juvenile appeal. His son Jerry is also a producer.

FILMS INCLUDE: *Ship of Wanted Men* 1933; *Danger Ahead* 1934; *Blake of Scotland Yard* (serial) 1937; *East Side Kids* 1940; *Spooks Run Wild* 1941; *The Corpse Vanishes* 1942; *Voodoo Man* 1944; *Docks of New York* 1945; *High School Hero* 1946; *Last of the Redmen, Little Miss Broadway* 1947; *Jungle Jim* 1948; *Chinatown at Midnight* 1949; *Last of the Buccaneers* 1950; *The Golden Hawk, California Conquest* 1952; *Fort Ti* 1953; *The Miami Story* 1954; *Rock Around the Clock, Earth vs. the Flying Saucers* 1956; *Calypso Heat Wave, Escape from San Quentin* 1957; *Crash Landing* 1958; *The Last Blitzkrieg* 1959; *The Enemy General* 1960; *Twist Around the Clock* 1961; *The Wild Westerners* 1962; *Kissin' Cousins* 1964; *Harum Scarum* 1965; *Riot on the Sunset Strip* 1967; *The Young Runaways* 1968; *Angel Angel Down We Go/Cult of the Damned* 1969; *How to Succeed with Sex* (exec. prod.), *The Loners* (exec. prod.) 1972.

Kaufman, Boris. Director of photography. *b.* 1906, Bialystok, Poland. *d.* 1980. *ed.* Sorbonne. The brother of Dziga VERTOV and Mikhail KAUFMAN, he emigrated in 1927 to France, where he befriended Jean VIGO and acted as cameraman on all four of the director's films. After serving in the French army (1939–41), he settled in the US in 1942. He worked on National Film Board of Canada shorts and US propaganda documentaries prior to his Hollywood feature film debut in the mid-50s. He was particularly effective with black-and-white photography in controlled situations. Winner of an Academy Award for the cinematography of *On the Waterfront* (1954).

FILMS INCLUDE: In France—*La Marche des Machines* (short) 1928; *A Propos de Nice* 1930; *Taris Champion de Natation* (short) 1931; *Zéro de Conduite/Zero for Conduct* 1933; *L'Atalante* (co-phot.) 1934; *Lucrèce Borgia* (co-phot.) 1935; *Fort Dolores* 1937; *Sérénade* 1938. In the US—*Better Tomorrow* (doc.) 1945; *Journey Into Medicine* (doc.) 1947; *The Tanglewood Story* (doc.) 1950; *On the Waterfront* 1954; *Patterns, Baby Doll* 1956; *12 Angry Men* 1957; *That Kind of Woman* 1959; *The Fugitive Kind* 1960; *Splendor in the Grass* 1961; *Long Day's Journey Into Night* 1962; *All the Way Home, Gone Are the Days* 1963; *The World of Henry Orient* 1964; *The Pawnbroker* 1965; *The Group* 1966; *Bye Bye Braverman, The Brotherhood, Uptight* 1968; *Tell Me That You Love Me Junie Moon* 1970.

Kaufman, George S. Playwright. *b.* Nov. 14, 1889, Pittsburgh. *d.* 1961. Many of the plays of this Pulitzer Prize–winning author (written in collaboration with Moss Hart, Marc Connelly, Ring Lardner, Edna Ferber, or Morrie Ryskind, among others) have been adapted to the screen. Films adapted by others from his works include: *Dulcy* (1923, 1940), *Merton of the Movies* (1924, 1947), *Beggar on Horseback* (1925), *The Cocoanuts* (1929), *Animal Crackers* (1930), *The Royal Family of Broadway* (1931), *Dinner at Eight* (1933), *Stage Door* (1937), *You Can't Take It with You* (1938), *The Man Who Came to Dinner* (1942), and *The Solid Gold Cadillac* (1956). Kaufman steadfastly resisted offers to work in Hollywood. He disliked the town and resented the manner in which writers were treated by studio bosses. But he finally succumbed to an offer by Samuel Goldwyn to write a comedy script as a vehicle for Eddie Cantor. (It turned out to be *Roman Scandals,* 1933.) He did a first draft in collaboration with Robert E. Sherwood but quit the project because of interference by the film's star and was credited only as co-author of the original story.

In 1935, Kaufman collaborated with Morrie Ryskind on what was to remain his only original film script, *A Night at the Opera,* the best and funniest of the Marx Brothers films. It was not until 1947 that he reappeared professionally in Hollywood, this time as a director of *The Senator Was Indiscreet,* a hilarious political comedy starring William Powell, which turned out extremely well. But Kaufman, who had directed many Broadway productions, felt uncomfortable with the technical aspects of motion pictures and never directed another film. Kaufman's name figured prominently in the famous Mary ASTOR diary which made headlines during her child-custody court battle in the 30s.

FILMS: As screenwriter—*Roman Scandals* (co-story only) 1933; *A Night at the Opera* (co-story, co-sc.) 1935. As director—*The Senator Was Indiscreet* 1947.

Kaufman, Mikhail. Cameraman, documentary filmmaker. Born on Sept. 5, 1897, in Bialystok, Poland. Brother of Boris KAUFMAN and Dziga VERTOV, he was the latter's cameraman on the *cinéma vérité* film *Kino-Eye* and the modernistic *Man with a Movie Camera.* His own *Moscow* (1926) is probably the first documentary to utilize the dawn-to-dusk format that later became a standard technique of the film genre known as CITY SYMPHONIES. In 1930 Kaufman directed a highly esteemed feature-length documentary, *Spring.*

Kaufman, Millard. Screenwriter. Born on May 12, 1917, in New York City. In Hollywood from the late 40s, he did adequately in his single outing as a director in 1962.

FILMS INCLUDE: *Deadly Is the Female* 1949; *Gun Crazy* 1950; *Unknown World* 1951; *Take the High Ground* 1953; *Bad Day at Black Rock* 1954; *Raintree County* 1957; *Never So Few* 1959; *Convicts 4/Reprieve* (also dir.) 1962; *The War Lord* 1965; *Living Free* 1972; *The Klansman/The Burning Cross* 1974.

Kaufman, Philip. Director. Born on Oct. 23, 1936, in Chicago. The grandson of German-Jewish immigrants, he spent a year in Israel as a volunteer in a kibbutz. After graduating from the University of Chicago in 1958 with a degree in history, he went to Harvard Law School, but returned to his alma mater within a year for postgraduate work in history. Now married and a father of a baby son, he moved in 1960 to San Francisco, where he worked on a novel, then traveled to Europe, where he continued writing, supporting his new family by teaching at American schools. It was there that he became enchanted with film. Inspired by the vibrancy of the French New Wave and the New Italian Cinema, he resolved to become a filmmaker. On returning to Chicago in 1963, he learned all he could about movie technique. With $50,000 he raised from family and friends, he proceeded, in collaboration with pal Benjamin MANASTER, to produce, direct, and write *Goldstein,* a modest mystical-satirical film based on a Hassidic tale by Martin Buber. The film made a small splash at the 1964 Cannes Festival, sharing the Prix de la Nouvelle Critique. Jean RENOIR called it "the best American film I have seen in 20 years." But it was largely ignored during its US release in 1965. Kaufman misfired on both sides of the Atlantic with his next film, *Fearless Frank,* a rather forced satirical fable featuring members of the Second City group. It was shot in 1965, and shown at Cannes in 1967, but found no American distributor until 1969. Nonetheless, the director was able to get major studio backing and a substantial budget for his next venture, *The Great Northfield Minnesota Raid* (1972), a Western saga offering a revisionist view of the exploits of the James and Younger gangs. Following *The White Dawn* (1974), a whaling adventure shot on location in the wilds of the Arctic, Kaufman began shooting the Clint Eastwood vehicle, *The Outlaw Josey Wales,* but was replaced as director by the star after two weeks of filming, retaining credit only as co-screenwriter. Kaufman then scored his first box-office hit with the 1978 remake of Don Siegel's science-fiction horror classic, *Invasion of the Body Snatchers,* a film that was also rated highly by most critics. Pauline KAEL judged it "maybe the best movie of its kind ever made." Kaufman's growing reputation was further enhanced by *The Wanderers* (1979), a seemingly authentic look back at Bronx Italian-American street gangs in the early 60s. It became a cult favorite. Continuing his rise in the pantheon of Hollywood's directors, Kaufman next tackled *The Right Stuff* (1983), a three-hour megabudget epic of the birth and early breakthroughs of the American space program. It was nominated for eight Academy Awards, including best picture, but won only four, in lesser categories. After a five-year hiatus, Kaufman returned with a film many consider his masterpiece. Liberally adapted from the Milan Kundera novel, *The Unbearable Lightness of Being* (1988) was a stunning achievement, a perceptive, intelligent, sexually frank view of life and love in late-60s Czechoslovakia, set against the political turmoil of the period—a candid homage to sensuality as a life force. Strikingly photographed by Sven NYKVIST, the film handled emotional and sexual intimacy with a maturity and discretion uncommon in the American cinema. It was named best film and Kaufman best director by the National Society of Film Critics. Kaufman's next project, *Henry and June* (1990), based on the diarized accounts of Parisian Anaïs Nin's love affair with author Henry Miller and his wife, June, was bound to be anticlimactic, considering the anticipation. And it was. It was co-scripted by the director's college-sweetheart wife, Rose (Fisher) Kaufman, and produced by their son, Peter Kaufman. Kaufman turned back to mass-audience material with his next film, *Rising Sun* (1993), a thriller based on the Michael Crichton novel. The Kaufmans live in San Francisco, away from the Hollywood glare.

FILMS: *Goldstein* (co-dir., co-prod., co-sc. with Benjamin Manaster) 1964–65; *Fearless Frank/Frank's Greatest Adventure* (also prod., sc.) 1967–69; *The Great Northfield Minnesota Raid* (also sc.) 1972; *The White Dawn* 1974; *The Outlaw Josie Wales* (co-sc. only) 1976; *Invasion of the Body Snatchers* 1978; *The Wanderers* (also co-sc. with wife, Rose) 1979; *Raiders of the Lost Ark* (co-story only) 1981; *The Right Stuff* (also sc.) 1983; *The Unbearable Lightness of Being* (also co-sc.) 1988; *Henry and June* (also co-sc. with wife, Rose) 1990; *Rising Sun* (also co-sc.) 1993.

Kaufman, Robert. Screenwriter. *b. c.*1930, New York City. *d.* 1991. *ed.* Columbia. A comedy specialist, he wrote for TV as well as for light films. He was nominated for an Academy Award for his highly amusing screenplay of *Divorce, American Style* (1967) and scored nicely with the Dracula spoof, *Love at First Bite* (1979). But the level of humor in much of the rest of his material was painfully sophomoric.

FILMS INCLUDE: *Dr. Goldfoot and the Bikini Machine, Ski Party* 1965; *The Cool Ones, Divorce American Style* 1967; *I Love My Wife, Getting Straight* 1970; *Freebie and the Bean* 1974; *Harry and Walter Go to New York* 1976; *The Happy Hooker Goes to Washington* 1977; *Love at First Bite* (also co-exec. prod.) 1979; *Nothing Personal, How to Beat the High Cost of Living* (also co-prod.) 1980; *Split Image* 1982; *The Check Is in the Mail* (also co-prod.), *Separate Vacations* 1986.

Kaufmann, Christine. Actress. Born on Jan. 11, 1945, in Lengdorf, Austria. She developed from a child actress of German films of the 50s into a pretty leading lady of international productions in the 60s. Formerly (1963–67) married to Tony CURTIS, she spent several years in Hollywood, then returned to Germany.

FILMS INCLUDE: *Salto Mortale* 1953; *Der schweigende Engel* 1954; *Die Stimme der Sehnsucht* 1956; *Mädchen in*

Uniform, Der veruntreute Himmel/Embezzled Heaven 1958; *Gli Ultimi Giorni di Pompei/The Last Days of Pompeii* (It./Sp.) 1959; *Labbra Rosse/Red Lips* (It./Fr.) 1960; *Constantino il Grande/Constantine and the Cross, Stadt ohne Mitleid/Town Without Pity* (Ger./Switz./US) 1961; *Le Mercenaire/Lo Spadaccino di Siena/Swordsman of Siena* (Fr./It.), *Toller Hecht auf krummer Tour/The Phony American, Tunnel 28/Escape from East Berlin* (Ger./US), *Taras Bulba* (US) 1962; *Wild and Wonderful* (US) 1964; *Murders in the Rue Morgue* (US) 1971; *Auf biegen oder brechen* 1976; *Lili Marleen, Lola* 1981; *Out of Rosenheim/Bagdad Cafe* 1988; *Der Geschichtenerzähler* 1989; *Es ist nicht leicht ein Gott zu sein* 1990.

Kaurismäki, Aki and **Mika.** Independent, irreverent team of brother filmmakers. Born in Finland, Mika in 1955 and Aki in 1957, they began their collaboration in the early 80s, dividing their work according to a carefully observed schedule. To save scarce funds and optimize the use of time, equipment and crews, they alternated as directors, one starting a project as soon as the other was through. They usually collaborated on each other's scripts. They started out as thorns in the side of the established industry, with films full of robust humor and scornful invention that broke conventions and taboos. But their growing popularity eventually made them leading figures in the largely dormant local film business, helping put Finnish cinema on the international map. Aki, especially, has been gaining recognition abroad for his witty, absurd spoofs. In 1990 alone, seven of his films were shown in New York City, where his 1989 *Ariel* became a cult favorite. The brothers, who operate more and more independently of each other in various parts of the world but still meet regularly to coordinate their schedules, also run specialized movie theaters in Helsinki, for which they import art films. They also distribute noncommercial foreign films and run the annual Midnight Sun Film Festival.

FILMS INCLUDE: Mika directing—*The Worthless* 1982; *The Clan* 1984; *Rosso* 1985; *Helsinki-Naples All Night Long* 1987; *Amazon, Zombie and the Ghost Train* 1991; *The Last Border* 1993. Aki directing—*Crime and Punishment* 1983; *Calamari Union* 1985; *Shadows in Paradise* 1986; *Hamlet Gets Business* 1987; *Ariel* 1989; *The Match Factory Girl, I Hired a Contract Killer, Leningrad Cowboys Go America* 1990; *I Hired a Contract Killer* 1990; *Bohemian Life/La Vie de Bohème* 1992; *Total Balalaika Show, Leningrad Cowboys Meet Moses, Take Care of Your Scarf, Tatjana/Pidä Huivista Kiinni, Tatjana* 1994.

Käutner, Helmut. Director. *b.* Mar. 25, 1908, Düsseldorf, Germany. *d.* 1980. *ed.* Munich U. A former cabaret actor-writer, he entered German films as an actor in the early 30s, switched to screenwriting later in the decade, and made his first film as a director in 1939. During WW II he mostly directed minor light films, carefully avoiding subjects that might have subjected him to the scrutiny of the Nazi propaganda machine. But his postwar work—often original and humane—stood out amid the vast wasteland of contemporary German cinema, although he too, in response to the commercial pressures of a mediocre industry, had his share of mediocre films. His most successful film of the postwar period was *The Last Bridge* (1954), winner of the International Jury Prize at the Cannes Film Festival. His brief Hollywood stint in the late 50s resulted in two disappointing pictures for Universal. From the mid-60s he worked mainly for German television. He wrote most of his own scripts, alone or in collaboration, and contributed screenplays for films of other directors.

FILMS: *Kitty und die Weltkonferenz, Die acht Entfesselten* 1939; *Kleider machen Leute, Frau nach Mass* 1940; *Auf Wiedersehen Franziska* 1941; *Wir machen Musik, Anuschka* 1942; *Romanze in Moll* 1943; *Grosse Freiheit Nr. 7/La Paloma* 1944; *Unter den Brücken* 1945; *In jennen Tagen/Seven Journeys* 1947; *Der Apfel ist ab/The Original Sin* 1948; *Königskinder* 1949; *Epilog* 1950; *Weisse Schatten* 1951; *Käpt'n Bay-Bay* 1952; *Die letzte Brücke/The Last Bridge, Bildnis einer Unbekannten/Portrait of an Unknown Woman* 1954; *Des Teufels General/The Devil's General, Ludwig II, Himmel ohne Sterne/Sky Without Stars, Ein Mädchen aus Flandern* 1955; *Der Hauptmann von Köpenick/The Captain from Koepenick, Die Zürcher Verlobung, Monpti* 1956; *Der Schinderhannes, The Restless Years/The Wonderful Years* (US) 1958; *Stranger in My Arms* (US), *Der Rest ist Schweigen/The Rest Is Silence, Die Gans von Sedan* 1959; *Das Glas Wasser/A Glass of Water, Schwarzer Kies* 1960; *Der Traum von Lieschen Muller* 1961; *Die Rote/The Redhead* 1962; *Das Haus in Montevideo* 1963; *Lausbubengeschichten* 1964; *Die Feuerzangenbowle* 1970.

Kavner, Julie. Actress. Born on Sept. 7, 1951, in Los Angeles, Calif. Urban everywoman character player of screen and TV. After an Emmy-winning debut as younger sister Brenda Morgenstern in the TV sitcom 'Rhoda,' she has appeared widely on the small screen and, regularly, but with less notoriety, on film. Since 1983, she has been a semiregular in the films of Woody Allen. She is the voice of Marge Simpson on the TV animated series 'The Simpsons.'

FILMS INCLUDE: *National Lampoon Goes to the Movies* 1981; *Bad Medicine* 1985; *Hannah and Her Sisters* 1986; *Radio Days* 1987; *New York Stories ('Oedipus Wrecks')* 1989; *Awakenings, Alice* 1990; *This Is My Life* 1991; *Shadows and Fog* 1992; *I'll Do Anything* 1994; *Forget Paris* 1995.

Kawalerowicz, Jerzy. Director. Born on Jan. 15, 1922, in Gwozdziec (Gwózda), Poland (now part of the Ukraine). A graduate of the Kraków Film Institute, he was an assistant director and screenwriter for several years before making his directorial debut in 1950. In 1955 he was appointed artistic director of the "Kadr" production unit, which counts among its members such directors as WAJDA, MUNK, and Konwicki. He is considered among the most gifted and visually oriented directors of postwar Polish cinema. His work has comprised both intimate psychological dramas and elaborate period epics. He combined both these elements successfully in the historical drama *Mother Joan of the Angels?* (alternate US title: *Joan of the Angels?*), which won the Jury Prize at the Cannes Festival in 1961. Following the political unrest of 1968, Kawalerowicz lost his position as artistic director of Kadr; but he continued to serve as the president of Poland's screenwriters association through 1978. That year the director was awarded a Special Silver Prize at the Berlin Festival for *Death of a President* and the entire body of his work. He has collaborated on the scripts of virtually all his films. His wife, Lucyna Winnicka, has appeared in many of them.

FILMS: *Commune/Rural Community/The Village Mill* (co-dir. with Kazimierz Sumerski) 1950; *Cellulose/A Night of Remembrance* (also co-sc.), *Under the Phrygian Star* (sequel to former film; also co-sc.) 1954; *The Shadow* 1956; *The Real End of the Great War* (also co-sc.) 1957; *Night Train/Baltic Express* (also co-sc.) 1959; *Mother Joan of the Angels?/Joan of the Angels?* (also co-sc.) 1961; *Pharaoh* (also co-sc.) 1965; *The Game* 1969; *Maddalena* (also sc.; It./Yug.) 1971; *Death of the President* (also co-sc.) 1978; *Chance Meeting on the Atlantic* 1979; *Austeria* 1982.

Kaye, Danny. Actor. *b.* David Daniel Kaminski, Jan. 18, 1913, Brooklyn, N.Y. *d.* 1987. A garment center tailor's son, he dropped out of school at 13 to become a clowning busboy on the "Borscht Circuit" in New York's Catskill Mountains. He later worked intermittently as a soda jerk and insurance agent while slowly getting ahead in vaudeville and nightclubs as a singer-dancer-entertainer. During the 30s he appeared in several two-reel film shorts and made his Broadway debut in 'The Straw Hat Revue,' with Imogene Coca. Early in 1941, appearing in Broadway's 'Lady in the Dark,' he stopped the show nightly with a song called 'Tchaikovsky,' in which he reeled off the names of 54 Russian composers, real and imagined, in 38 seconds. This type of staccato delivery of tongue-twisting lyrics would be his trademark in many subsequent stage, film, and TV appearances. In 1943 he was signed by producer Samuel GOLDWYN and the following year starred in *Up in Arms,* the first of a highly successful string of lavish technicolor Goldwyn comedies that were tailor-made as showcases for the display of Kaye's versatile talents. Easygoing and personable, Kaye enjoyed enormous popularity in the late 40s. *The Secret Life of Walter Mitty* (1947) gave him the opportunity to caricature several different personalities. Kaye's popularity was even greater in Britain, where he enjoyed huge success with record-breaking engagements at the Palladium in 1948 and 1949 and made personal appearances at Buckingham Palace. But his popularity on either side of the Atlantic decreased in the late 50s, when he began devoting more and more of his time to worldwide travel on behalf of UNICEF, entertaining children in developing countries. In 1954 he was awarded a special Oscar. During the Oscar ceremonies for 1981 he was the recipient of the Jean Hersholt Humanitarian Award.

Kaye made only sporadic film appearances after 1960. From 1963 to 1967 he starred in his own hour-long TV variety program, 'The Danny Kaye Show,' for which he won both an Emmy and a Peabody Award. In 1970 he returned to Broadway in the musical 'Two by Two.' He appeared from time to time as a mock guest conductor with the New York Philharmonic and other symphony orchestras. He was a co-owner of the Seattle Mariners baseball club. Many of his songs and much of his comedy material were written by his wife since 1940, Sylvia Fine. He died at 74 of hepatitis and internal bleeding, the consequence of a transfusion of contaminated blood during quadruple bypass heart surgery in 1983.

FEATURE FILMS: *Up in Arms* 1944; *Wonder Man* 1945; *The Kid from Brooklyn* 1946; *The Secret Life of Walter Mitty* 1947; *A Song Is Born* 1948; *It's a Great Feeling* (unbilled cameo), *The Inspector General* 1949; *On the Riviera* 1951; *Hans Christian Andersen* (title role) 1952; *Knock on Wood, White Christmas* 1954; *The Court Jester* 1956; *Merry Andrew, Me and the Colonel* 1958; *The Five Pennies* (as bandleader Red Nichols) 1959; *On the Double* 1961; *The Man from the Diners' Club* 1963; *The Madwoman of Chaillot* 1969.

Kaye, Stubby. Actor, singer. Born on Nov. 11, 1918, in New York City. Heavyset comic supporting player of the American stage, TV, and films. He began his professional career in 1939 after winning the Major Bowes Amateur Hour radio contest. After touring in vaudeville and during WW II with the USO, he made his Broadway debut in 1950 as Nicely-Nicely Johnson in 'Guys and Dolls,' a role he later repeated in the 1955 screen version.

FILMS INCLUDE: *Taxi* 1953; *Guys and Dolls* 1955; *Li'l Abner* 1959; *40 Pounds of Trouble* 1963; *Sex and the Single Girl* 1964; *Cat Ballou* 1965; *The Way West* 1967; *Sweet Charity* 1969; *The Cockeyed Cowboys of Calico County* 1970; *The Dirtiest Girl I Ever Met* 1973; *Six Pack Annie* 1975; *Who Framed Roger Rabbit* 1988.

Kazan, Elia ("Gadge"). Director. Born Elia Kazanjoglou, on Sept. 7, 1909, in Constantinople (now Istanbul). He was four when his Greek parents emigrated to the US and settled in New York City, where his father became a rug merchant. After graduating from Williams College, young Kazan attended the drama department at Yale and in 1932 joined the Group Theatre as an actor and assistant stage manager. He directed his first stage play in 1935 and in the 40s became established as one of Broadway's finest directors with such productions as 'The Skin of Our Teeth' (1942), 'One Touch of Venus' (1943), 'Jacobowsky and the Colonel' (1944), 'All My Sons' (1947), 'A Streetcar Named Desire' (1947), and 'Death of a Salesman' (1949). He had made his last stage appearance as an actor in 1941, and in 1940 and 1941 respectively he played supporting roles in two films, *City for Conquest* and *Blues in the Night.*

Kazan's interest in the cinema dates to the 30s, when he appeared in Ralph Steiner's short *Pie in the Sky* (1934) and directed *The People of the Cumberland* (1937), a documentary short about Tennessee miners. Following a full-length documentary about food rationing, *It's Up to You* (1941), which he made for the US Department of Agriculture, Kazan began directing feature films in 1945. Although his early pictures were solidly staged dramas that were well received by critics and the public, they seemed too deeply rooted in Kazan's theatrical background and showed minimal use of the specific tools of the cinema. His debut film, *A Tree Grows in Brooklyn* (1945), a sensitive dramatization of the Betty Smith novel, boasted fine performances from everyone in the cast, including Oscar-winning stints by James Dunn and Peggy Ann Garner. Kazan himself won an Academy Award as best director for *Gentleman's Agreement* (1947), considered at the time a courageous breakthrough indictment of anti-Semitism but, viewed in retrospect, a benign, naïve little drama. *Gentleman's Agreement* also won the best film Oscar and best supporting actress for Celeste Holm. *Pinky* (1949) was similarly a pioneer racial drama considered daring at the time, about a light-skinned black girl (Jeanne Crain) passing for white. It too was marked by excellent performances under Kazan's guidance but seems static and tame in retrospect. *Boomerang* (1947), by contrast, was an obstruction-of-justice-by-political-considerations thriller energized by a semidocumentary style that indicated Kazan's growing awareness of the film medium. The same was true of *Panic in the Streets* (1950), a taut thriller with a social message beyond its ostensible plague-scare plot.

While carrying on this intensive activity as a film director, Kazan continued working in and influencing the American theater. In 1947 he co-founded the Actors Studio, the breeding ground of "the Method" and a nucleus of intense new actors, best personified by the studio's most famous student, Marlon BRANDO. Kazan, who had directed Brando in the highly successful 1947 Broadway production of 'A Streetcar Named Desire,' now thrust Brando's brooding, explosive talent onto filmgoers in the 1951 screen version of that play as well as in two other memorable films, *Viva Zapata!* (1952) and *On the Waterfront* (1954). Although powerful and electrifying, *Streetcar* was basically filmed theater, interesting mostly for the clash of acting styles between Brando's instinctive Kowalski and Vivien Leigh's traditional Blanche. *Zapata,* on the other hand, was in many ways a breakthrough for Kazan, a film that combined his long-established ability to handle actors with a suddenly found visual sensibility and an intense grasp of atmosphere and locale.

On the Waterfront provided another high point in Kazan's film career. This powerful, grim drama of corruption on the docks of New York successfully integrated the realism of the location photography with the naturalism of the acting to achieve a deeply felt and intensely moving motion picture. The brilliant acting brought to the screen some of the most memorable scenes in American film history. Brando won an Academy Award for his role as Terry Malloy; Eva Marie Saint received the best supporting actress Oscar for her tender portrayal of Edie Doyle; and Rod Steiger, Karl Malden, and Lee J. Cobb gave some of the best performances of their careers. *On the Waterfront* won the best film Oscar and Kazan was named best director. The film also reaped awards for best screenplay, cinematography, and art direction. There were some who saw in *On the Waterfront* an attempt by Kazan to defend the testimony he had given two years earlier to the House Un-American Activities Committee, in which he admitted past membership in the Communist party and named names, reversing a previous "unfriendly" stand.

Kazan's next film, *East of Eden* (1955), is considered by many to be his best. Again, he stunned filmgoers with the acting talent of a newcomer, this time James DEAN, who was nominated for an Academy Award for his performance in the film. Jo Van Fleet won the best supporting actress Oscar. Kazan handled the complex characters and complicated plot with meticulous care, exerting superb control over his first color and wide-screen production. In *Baby Doll* (1956), *A Face in the Crowd* (1957), *Wild River* (1960), and *Splendor in the Grass* (1961), Kazan kept on extracting great performances from his casts. Under his guidance, actresses like Carroll Baker and Natalie Wood achieved levels of performance they could not match before or after.

Until the early 60s, Kazan expressed his creative energy on both the stage and screen as a superb interpreter of such playwrights as Tennessee Williams, Robert Anderson, William Inge, and Arthur Miller. The film *America, America* (1963) signified a new juncture in his career, a first wholly original expression of his own world and personality. The film was based on his own 1961 novel depicting with nostalgic warmth the trials and tribulations of an uncle's odyssey from Turkey to the US. The early 60s also marked a decisive break with Kazan's association with the theater. During the 50s, along with his film work, he directed on Broadway such successful plays as 'Camino Real' (1953), 'Tea and Sympathy' (1953), 'Cat on a Hot Tin Roof' (1955), and 'The Dark at the Top of the Stairs' (1957). In 1963 he was named co-director of the Repertory Theatre of Lincoln Center for the Performing Arts and he directed several of the company's early productions, but in 1964 he turned his back on the theater altogether.

In 1969, Kazan made his second personal film, *The Arrangement,* from his own 1967 second novel. The novel was a success; the film a resounding failure. In 1972 he published his third novel, *The Assassins,* and returned to filmmaking with *The Visitors,* a film about the violent heritage of the Vietnam War which he made in and around his home, on a minuscule budget, from a script by his son, Chris. Kazan now devoted more of his time to writing, turning out three additional novels—*The Understudy* (1974), *Act of Love* (1978), and *The Anatolian* (1982)—and an autobiography: *Elia Kazan: A Life* (1988). In 1983 he was honored for his Life Achievement in a Kennedy Center ceremony.

Kazan's first wife (from 1932), Molly Day Thatcher, died in 1963; his second (from 1967) was actress-director Barbara Loden, who died in 1980. In 1982 he married Frances Rudge. His son from the first marriage, Nicholas Kazan, is a screenwriter.

FILMS: *The People of the Cumberlands* (two-reel doc.; also prod., sc.) 1937; *It's Up to You* (feature-length doc.) 1941; *A Tree Grows in Brooklyn* 1945; *The Sea of Grass, Boomerang, Gentleman's Agreement* 1947; *Pinky* 1949; *Panic in the Streets* 1950; *A Streetcar Named Desire* 1951; *Viva Zapata!* 1952; *Man on a Tightrope* 1953; *On the Waterfront* 1954; *East of Eden* (also prod.) 1955; *Baby Doll* (also prod.) 1956; *A Face in the Crowd* (also prod.) 1957; *Wild River* (also prod.) 1960; *Splendor in the Grass* (also prod.) 1961; *America America* (also prod., sc., from own novel) 1963; *The Arrangement* (also prod., sc., from own novel) 1969; *The Visitors* 1972; *The Last Tycoon* 1976.

Keach, Stacy. Actor. Born Walter Stacy Keach, Jr., on June 2, 1941, in Savannah, Ga. Square-jawed, virile leading man of the American stage and screen. The son of actor, drama teacher (he coached Maria MONTEZ, among others), dialogue director, and industrial film producer Stacy Keach (*b.* May 29, 1914, Chicago), he overcame four scarring childhood operations for a harelip to launch a solid acting career. After training at the University of California (Berkeley) and the Yale Drama School, he attended London's Royal Academy of Dramatic Art on a Fulbright Scholarship. He made his New York debut in 1964, playing Marcellus in a Shakespeare Festival production of 'Hamlet,' and rapidly established a reputation as a fine interpreter of both classic and modern roles. He won Obie Awards for the 1967 off-Broadway spoof 'McBird,' in which he impersonated LBJ, and for the 1971 revival of 'Long Days's Journey Into Night.' On Broadway he starred in 1969 as Buffalo Bill in 'Indians' and in the title role of 'Peer Gynt,' later excelling as 'Hamlet.' On-screen from 1968, he demonstrated versatility in a wide range of roles, ranging from thinkers and dreamers to macho men. He also wrote and directed a short, *The Repeater* (1972), which was shown on TV. Having starred in the short-lived TV series 'Caribe' (1975), Keach reached the peak of his popularity in the 1983–84 season as the star of the successful detective series, 'Mickey Spillane's Mike Hammer.' But in April of 1984, he was arrested at London's Heathrow Airport on the charge of smuggling cocaine for personal use. The following year he spent six months in a Reading jail. Once out, Keach joined an anti-drug campaign and began speaking publicly on the dangers of addiction. Within months he was back at work, resuming the Mike Hammer role in a string of TV movies. He returned to features in 1990 and in the same year triumphed on the Washington stage, playing the title role in 'Richard III.' In 1986 he married actress Malgosia Tomassi, his fourth wife. His brother, James Keach, is also a film and TV actor.

FILMS: *The Heart Is a Lonely Hunter* 1968; *End of the Road, The Traveling Executioner, Brewster McCloud* 1970; *Doc* (as "Doc" Holliday) 1971; *Fat City, The New Centurions, The Life and Times of Judge Roy Bean, Goodnight Mike* 1972; *Luther* (as Martin Luther; UK) 1973; *Gravy Train, Watched* 1974; *Conduct Unbecoming* (UK) 1975; *Gli Esecutori/Street People/The Sicilian Cross* (It.), *The Killer Inside Me* 1976; *The Squeeze* (UK), *The Duellists* (narrator only; UK) 1977; *Il Grande Attacco/The Great Battle/Battle Force* (It./Ger./Yug.), *Gray Lady Down, Two Solitudes, Up in Smoke, La Montagna di Dio Cannibale/Slave of the Cannibal God/Primitive Desires* (It.) 1978; *The Ninth Configuration/Twinkle Twinkle Killer Kane, The Long Riders* (as Frank James; also co-sc.) 1980; *Road Games* (Austral.), *Cheech and Chong's Nice Dreams* 1981; *Butterfly, That Championship Season* 1982; *False Identity* 1989; *Class of 1999* 1990; *New Crime City* 1994; *Escape from L.A.* 1996.

Keane, Constance. See LAKE, Veronica.

Keaton, Buster. Actor, director, producer, screenwriter. *b.* Joseph Francis Keaton, Oct 4, 1895, Piqua, Kans., to medicine show performers on the road. *d.* 1966. He was nicknamed Buster by Harry Houdini, who admired the way Keaton at the age of six months had survived unharmed a fall down a flight of stairs at a boardinghouse for show people. When he was three, Buster joined the family acrobatic comedy act as The Human Mop in a knockabout sketch that had the father literally sweep the floor with his child's outstretched body. They were known as The Three Keatons. He was by now an accomplished acrobat, capable of taking repeated dangerous falls without hurting himself, and an experienced comedian with a veteran's bag of tricks and sense of comic timing. He was so skilled at his craft that many believed he was actually a midget masquerading as a child.

The Keaton family act broke up early in 1917, when it became evident that father Joe's drinking problem was becoming a dangerous liability to a performance relying on physical precision. Buster, now 21 and a well-established name in vaudeville, was offered a starring role for a hefty salary in a Shubert revue at New York's Winter Garden, but he chose instead to enter films as a supporting player in a series of comedy shorts starring and directed by Roscoe "Fatty" ARBUCKLE. The first of these was *The Butcher Boy* (1917). Sources differ and confusion abounds over the titles of the rest, and a full, reliable list of Keaton credits for the Arbuckle period has never been compiled, since some of the films have been lost and some exist only under foreign titles. These films, all made between 1917 and 1919, were initially shot at studios on New York's West 48th St., then on 174th St., and finally in Long Beach, Calif. Keaton's work was interrupted for several months during this period for military service with the 40th Infantry in France in the waning days of WW I.

Late in 1919, Joseph M. SCHENCK, who had produced most of the Arbuckle-Keaton films, releasing through Paramount Famous Players-Lasky, set up a new company to produce a series of comedy shorts starring Keaton, releasing through Metro and later through First National. For this purpose, the former Chaplin studios were purchased and renamed the Buster Keaton Studio. The first of the shorts was released in September of 1920, followed a month later by the release of Keaton's first feature as a star, *The Saphead.* Although a prestigious, sumptuous seven-reel production and a success at the box office and with many critics, establishing Keaton as a major star, *The Saphead* was less typical and in many ways less entertaining than the Keaton shorts that preceded and followed it for several years. Especially appealing was *One Week* (1920), in which Keaton as a bridegroom spends seven exasperating days trying to put together a portable home for his bride from a do-it-yourself kit. Many consider it Keaton's first masterpiece. Other shorts followed at regular intervals of a month or two, with Keaton starring, co-directing, and co-scripting. By mid-1921, Schenck's production company had been renamed Buster Keaton Productions.

The year 1921 proved to be crucial in Keaton's personal life and artistic career. During the course of the year, he married Natalie Talmadge (1898–1969), the sister-in-law of producer Schenck, who had earlier married film star Norma TALMADGE. Natalie, who had had an undistinguished film career, co-starred in three of Keaton's films and for a while seemed a perfect choice as a wife and companion. But their relationship gradually deteriorated and after many unhappy moments they divorced in 1932.

Also in 1921, following a period of enforced rest because of a broken ankle he had suffered during the production of *The Electric House* (the film was abandoned and later remade), Keaton returned to the screen with a succession of comedy gems. *The Playhouse,* a surrealistic, dreamlike short, filled with images from Keaton's past as a vaudevillian, boasted tricky photographic effects and illusions, most memorably the opening scene, in which every face in a theater, in the audience, and backstage, is that of Keaton. The elaborate trick involving complicated multiple exposures, was accomplished by an inventive special-effects man, Fred Gabourie, who was also responsible for the camera sorcery in Keaton's next great comedy short, *The Boat,* in which the comedian is repeatedly frustrated in his effort to launch and sail a new boat. Another memorable comedy was *Cops* (1922), the last of Keaton's great shorts. Several other shorts followed, but most lacked the freshness and inventiveness of the aforementioned films.

By this time, Keaton's screen personality, manner, and style had become pretty well established. Keaton typically portrayed a dignified, remarkably restrained young man whose handsome deadpan "stone face" betrayed frustration or bewilderment only through the slightest of muscular contractions. A fixed gaze, a raised eyebrow, the outline of a frown—these are all the solitary, determined little man he impersonated on the screen ever needed in order to express defiance and resolve in adversity. Keaton exercised complete artistic control over his films, and although he was usually billed as co-director of his productions, he was actually in charge of all directorial decisions on the set.

In 1923, Keaton and producer Schenck decided to switch from shorts to the production of feature-length comedies. First came *The Three Ages.* A parody of the structural style of D. W. Griffith's *Intolerance, Ages* was composed of three episodes—Stone Age, Roman, and modern—and was basically more in the nature of three two-reelers combined than a true feature. Then came Keaton's first feature-length masterpiece, *Our Hospitality,* a film constructed with fluid dramatic logic and filled with suspenseful action, outrageous physical feats, and inventive visual gags. It was beautifully photographed in the vicinity of Lake Tahoe, Nev., and its solid comic-dramatic integrity strongly supports the contention of some historians that Keaton was not simply a comic genius as a performer but also a highly gifted director. As a director, he was clearly superior to Chaplin, whose films were rather casually constructed and derived their main strength from the comedian's performance.

Keaton's maturing virtuosity as a director is again demonstrated in *Sherlock, Jr.* (1924), which finds the comedian roaming between dream and reality in the role of a projectionist in a motion picture theater who hallucinates about becoming involved in the action on the screen. It was followed by Keaton's biggest commercial success, *The Navigator* (also 1924), a film in which he was able to derive a broad range of comic situations from a single prop, a deserted schooner. *Seven Chances* and *Go West* (both 1925) and *Battling Butler* (1926), which followed, were not among Keaton's best, but *The General* (1927) notched another high mark in his career. It is a brilliantly conceived and executed Civil War story in which the dramatic flow of action and the comic situations and gags complement one another in perfect harmony.

After only two more films for his own production company—*College* (1927) and *Steamboat Bill, Jr.* (1928)—Keaton made a move that he later considered the worst mistake of his career. He gave up his own studio and signed a contract with MGM to star in films on which he would no longer have artistic control. The first two of these—*The Cameraman* (1928) and *Spite Marriage* (1929)—still provided excellent showcases for Keaton's unique comic talent, but then his career rapidly deteriorated, as did his marriage to Natalie Talmadge and his mental and physical health. In 1937 he entered a psychiatric clinic but later returned to films as an actor and uncredited gag writer and assistant director. The features in which he appeared were mostly minor, his roles in them increasingly small. But then in 1947 came the first of a series of live appearances at the Cirque Medrano in Paris which signified the beginning of a revival of the Keaton legend. Another important step in that direction was a sequence in Charlie Chaplin's *Limelight* (1952) in which the two great comedians, appearing together for the first and only time, run into all sorts of obstacles in their attempt to give a violin-piano recital on a stage and wind up in the orchestra pit. Once the Keaton resurrection started, it never stopped. There were financially rewarding appearances on TV shows and in commercials, retrospectives of Keaton's silents by film societies and international festivals, and invitations for personal appearances from all over the world. Then came the release of *The Buster Keaton Story* in 1957, a rather weak screen biography in which the comedian was portrayed by Donald O'Connor. It was hardly a proper tribute to Keaton's talent, but the fee he received provided him with financial security for the rest of his life. There were also many big and small film roles and a working schedule he found increasingly difficult to keep up with. In September of 1965 he made a personal appearance at the Venice Film Festival and received the loudest and longest ovation ever accorded any artist there before or after. Several months later, on February 1, 1966, he died of cancer. His life and career were the subject of an excellent three-hour film tribute, *Buster Keaton: A Hard Act to Follow* (1987), by Kevin BROWNLOW and David GILL. Autobiography: *My Wonderful World of Slapstick* (1960).

FILMS (as actor; shorts are denoted by "s"; list for 1917–19 period may contain duplications or omissions; some guest appearances in talkie shorts are excluded): *The Butcher Boy* (s), *A Reckless Romeo* (s), *The Rough House* (s), *His Wedding Night* (s), *Oh Doctor!* (s), *Fatty at Coney Island* (s), *A Country Hero* (s) 1917; *Out West* (s), *The Bell Boy* (s), *Moonshine* (s), *Good Night Nurse* (s), *The Cook* (s) 1918; *A Desert Hero* (s), *Back Stage* (s), *The Hayseed* (s), *The Garage* (s) 1919; *One Week* (s; also co-dir., co-sc. with Eddie Cline), *Convict 13* (s; also co-dir., co-sc. with Cline), *The Saphead, The Scarecrow* (s; also co-dir., co-sc. with Cline), *Neighbors* (s; also co-dir., co-sc. with Cline) 1920; *The Haunted House* (s; also co-dir., co-sc. with Cline), *Hard Luck* (s; also co-dir., co-sc. with Cline), *The High Sign* (first short starring Keaton; made before *One Week,* in 1920, but not released until much later; also co-dir., co-sc. with Cline), *The Goat* (s; also co-dir., co-sc. with Mal St. Clair), *The Playhouse* (s; also co-dir., co-sc. with Cline), *The Boat* (s; also co-dir., co-sc. with Cline), *The Paleface* (s: also co-dir., co-sc. with Cline) 1921; *Cops* (s; also co-dir., co-sc. with Cline), *My Wife's Relations* (s; also co-dir., co-sc. with Cline), *The Blacksmith* (s; also co-dir., co-sc. with St. Clair), *The Frozen North* (s; also co-dir., co-sc. with Cline), *Day Dreams* (s; also co-dir., co-sc. with Cline), *The Electric House* (s; also co-dir., co-sc. with Cline) 1922; *The Balloonatic* (s; also co-dir., co-sc. with Cline), *The Love Nest* (s; also dir., sc.), *The Three Ages* (also co-dir. with Cline), *Our Hospitality* (also co-dir. with John G. Blystone) 1923; *Sherlock Jr.* (also dir.), *The Navigator* (also co-dir. with Donald Crisp) 1924; *Seven Chances* (also dir.), *Go West* (also dir., sc.) 1925; *Battling Butler* (also dir.) 1926; *The General* (also co-dir., co-sc. with Clyde Bruckman), *College* 1926; *Steamboat Bill Jr., The Cameraman* (also prod.) 1928; *Spite Marriage* (and French-language version, *Buster se marie*), *The Hollywood Revue* 1929; *Free and Easy* (and French-language version, *Le Metteur en Scène,* and Spanish-language version, *Estrellados), Dough Boys/The Big Shot* 1930; *Parlor Bedroom and Bath* (also prod.), *Sidewalks of New York* (also prod.) 1931; *The Passionate Plumber* (and French-language version, *Le Plombier amoureux*; also prod.), *Speak Easily* 1932; *What! No Beer?* 1933; *The Gold Ghost* (s), *Allez Oop* (short) 1934; *Palooka from Paducah* (s), *One-Run Elmer* (s), *Hayseed Romance* (s), *Le Roi des Champs-Elysées* (Fr.), *An Old Spanish Custom/The Invaders* (UK), *Tars and Stripes* (s), *The E-Flat Man* (s), *The Timid Young Man* (s) 1935; *Grand Slam Opera* (s; also co-sc.), *Three on a Limb* (s), *Blue Blazes* (s), *The Chemist* (s), *Three Men on a Horse* (cameo?; participation unconfirmed), *Mixed Magic* (s) 1936; *Jail Bait* (s), *Ditto* (s), *Love Nest on Wheels* (s) 1937; *Life in Sometown USA* (s; dir. only), *Hollywood Handicap* (s; dir. only), *Streamlined Swing* (s; dir. only) 1938; *Pest from the West* (s), *Mooching Through Georgia* (s), *The Jones Family in Hollywood* (also co-story), *The Jones Family in Quick Millions* (also co-story), *Hollywood Cavalcade* (as himself) 1939; *Nothing but Pleasure* (s), *Pardon My Berth Marks* (s), *The Taming of the Snood* (s), *The Spook Speaks* (s), *The Villain Still Pursued Her, Li'l Abner, His Ex Marks the Spot* (s) 1940; *So You Won't Squawk* (s), *She's All Mine* (s), *General Nuisance* (s) 1941; *Forever and a Day* 1943; *Bathing Beauty* (gag contributor only; uncredited), *San Diego I Love You* 1944; *That's the Spirit, That Night with You* 1945; *God's Country, El Moderno Barba Azul* (Mex.) 1946; *A Southern Yankee* (gag contributor only; uncredited) 1948; *The Lovable Cheat, Neptune's Daughter* (gag contributor only; uncredited), *In the Good Old Summertime, You're My Everything* 1949; *Sunset Boulevard* 1950; *Un Duel a Mort* (s; Fr.), *Limelight* 1952; *L'Incantevole Nemica* (It.) 1954; *Around the World in 80 Days* 1956; *The Adventures of Huckleberry Finn* 1960; *Ten Girls Ago* (Can.) 1962; *It's a Mad Mad Mad Mad World* 1963; *The Triumph of Lester Snapwill* (s), *Pajama Party* 1964; *The Railroader* (s; Can.), *Film* (s; Can.), *Beach Blanket Bingo* (as himself), *How to Stuff a Wild Bikini, Sergeant Deadhead* 1965; *Due Marines e un Generale/War Italian Style* (It.), *A Funny Thing Happened on the Way to the Forum, The Scribe* (Can.) 1966.

Keaton, Diane. Actress. Born Diane Hall, on Jan. 5, 1946, in Los Angeles. Offbeat leading lady of Hollywood films of the 70s. The daughter of a civil engineer and a photographer mother, at 19 she quit a Santa Ana junior college after three semesters to study acting at New York's Neighborhood Playhouse. Somewhere along the line, she sang and danced with a rock group. After several months of summer stock at Woodstock, she joined the cast of the Broadway musical 'Hair' as a supporting player and understudy for the lead and in 1968 took over the starring role. The following year she played the lead opposite Woody ALLEN in the Broadway production of 'Play It Again, Sam.' For several years, she was Allen's romantic companion and in the 70s played in a number of his films, notably *Annie Hall* (1977), for which she won the best actress Academy Award, and *Manhattan* (1979). In these films, which mirrored her offscreen relationship with Allen, she captured with fetching natural awkwardness the paradoxical personae of the modern urban American woman and helped set a fashion trend for thrown-together styles. She was also notable as Kay Corleone, the conscience-stricken wife in *The Godfather* (1972) and its sequels, as the lost, promiscuous heroine of Richard Brooks's *Looking for Mr. Goodbar* (1977); she received an Oscar nomination for her performance as the radical Louise Bryant in Warren Beatty's *Reds* (1981). The versatile Keaton (she chose her mother's maiden surname over her father's Hall) published two photography books, *Reservations* (1980) and *Still Life* (1983), and tried her hand in film directing with an offbeat documentary about heaven, titled *Heaven* (1987). She directed a music video for singer Belinda Carlisle's 'Heaven Is a Place on Earth,' and in 1990 she began directing for TV, her early efforts including an episode for the cult serial 'Twin Peaks.' She turned in a deft comic performance as the driven career woman in *Baby Boom* (1987). After Woody Allen's personal and professional split with Mia Farrow, Keaton took over what was to have been Farrow's role in *Manhattan Murder Mystery* (1993), recapturing some of the chemistry of their earlier collaborations.

Ever interested in directing, she took the helm for the first time with *Unstrung Heroes* (1995), a sensitive, tender look into the lives of a family of oddballs and a son who loses his mother to a tragic illness. While the film fared well enough critically, she again found herself in the spotlight as an actress in 1996 for the box-office giant *First Wives Club*, and earning a best actress

Academy Award nomination for her emotional turn as terminally ill matron in the late Scott McPherson's touching drama *Marvin's Room*.

FILMS: *Lovers and Other Strangers* 1970; *The Godfather, Play It Again Sam* 1972; *Sleeper* 1973; *The Godfather Part II* 1974; *Love and Death* 1975; *I Will I Will. . . for Now, Harry and Walter Go to New York* 1976; *Looking for Mr. Goodbar, Annie Hall* 1977; *Interiors* 1978; *Manhattan* 1979; *Reds* 1981; *What Does Dorrie Want?* (short; dir. only), *Shoot the Moon* 1982; *The Little Drummer Girl* 1983; *Mrs. Soffel* 1984; *Crimes of the Heart* 1986; *Radio Days, Heaven* (doc.; dir. only), *Baby Boom* 1987; *The Good Mother* 1988; *The Lemon Sisters* (also prod.), *The Godfather Part III* 1990; *Father of the Bride* 1991; *Manhattan Murder Mystery* 1993; *Father of the Bride II, Unstrung Heroes* (dir. only) 1995; *First Wives Club, Marvin's Room* 1996.

Keaton, Michael. Actor. Born Michael Douglas, on Sept. 9, 1951, in Coraopolis, Penn. Intense, mercurial lead with a flair for dark comedy. The youngest of seven children, he dropped out after two years from Kent State University, where he majored in speech. For a while, he bummed around Pittsburgh, then began performing in local coffeehouses, supplementing his income by driving a cab and an ice-cream truck. In 1972 he joined the technical crew of the city's Public Television station, WQED, and three years later moved to Los Angeles in search of a show business career. He started out with the improvisational Second City group, then wrote comedy material and performed in such TV series as 'All's Fair' (1977), 'Working Stiffs' (1979), and 'Report to Murphy' (1982). But it was only in the early 80s, when he began appearing in feature films, that he found his path to success. At first attracting attention in routine comic parts, he was eventually able to demonstrate a capacity for a widening range of roles. In 1988 he was named best actor by the National Society of Film Critics for his whimsical portrait of a mischievous ghoul in *Beetlejuice* and for his utterly believable portrayal of a drug addict in *Clean and Sober.* In the following year he achieved superstardom with a brooding interpretation of the title role in *Batman.* He turned in a bizarre character performance as Dogberry in Kenneth Branagh's *Much Ado About Nothing* (1993). He married actress Caroline MacWilliams in 1982. They separated in 1988 only to reunite in 1989.

FILMS: *Night Shift* 1982; *Mr. Mom* 1983; *Johnny Dangerously* 1984; *Gung Ho, Touch and Go* 1986; *The Squeeze* 1987; *Beetlejuice, Clean and Sober* 1988; *The Dream Team, Batman* (title role) 1989; *Pacific Heights* 1990; *One Good Cop* 1991; *Batman Returns* 1992; *Much Ado About Nothing, My Life* 1993; *The Paper, Speechless* 1994; *Multiplicity* 1996; *Desperate Measures* 1997.

Kedrova, Lila. Actress. Born in 1918, in Leningrad. Expressive, flamboyant character actress in occasional European and American films. A resident of France from 1928. She won an Academy Award as best supporting actress for her performance in *Zorba the Greek* (1964). She was awarded the Golden Mask (best performance) at Taormina for *Tell Me a Riddle* (1980).

FILMS INCLUDE: *Weg ohne Umkehr/No Way Back* (Ger.) 1953; *Le Defroqué* (Fr.) 1954; *Razzia sur la Chnouff/Razzia* (Fr.) 1955; *Des Gens sans Importance* (Fr.), *Calle Mayor/The Lovemaker* (Sp.) 1956; *Montparnasse 19/Modigliani of Montparnasse* (Fr.) 1958; *La Femme et la Pantin/The Female* (Fr./It.) 1959; *Zorba the Greek* (US/Gr.) 1964; *A High Wind in Jamaica* (US/UK) 1965; *Torn Curtain* (US), *Penelope* (US) 1966; *Tenderly/The Girl Who Couldn't Say No* (It.) 1968; *The Kremlin Letter* (US) 1970; *Escape to the Sun* (Isr./Fr./Ger.) 1972; *Soft Beds Hard Battles/Undercovers Hero* (UK) 1974; *Perchè?!* (It.), *Eliza's Horoscope* (Can.) 1975; *Le Locataire/The Tenant* (Fr.) 1976; *Moi Fleur bleue* (Fr.), *Widows' Nest* (US/Sp.) 1977; *Le Cavaleur/Practice Makes Perfect* (Fr.), *Clair de Femme* (Fr./Ger./It.) 1979; *Tell Me a Riddle* (US) 1980; *Sword of the Valiant* (UK) 1984; *Some Girls* (US) 1988.

Keel, Howard. Actor, singer. Born Harold Clifford Leek, on Apr. 13, 1917, in Gillespie, Ill. The son of a coal miner, he made his semiprofessional debut as a singing busboy in a Los Angeles café. Later, as an employee of Douglas Aircraft, he was named a roving entertainer in company plants, a job that eventually led to a singing stage debut in a West Coast production of 'Carousel' in 1945. In 1948, while appearing on the London stage in 'Oklahoma,' he made his film debut playing a secondary role in a minor British film. Two years later he made an impressive Hollywood debut in *Annie Get Your Gun.* Tall, good-looking, and self-assured, with a fine, untrained baritone, he starred in many musical films of the 50s, switching to straight acting parts, mostly in action films, in the 60s. Although inactive on the screen, he still makes stage and nightclub tours, occasionally teaming up with former co-star Kathryn GRAYSON. He was visible throughout the 80s as a member of the cast of the hit TV series 'Dallas.'

FILMS: *The Small Voice/Hideout* (UK) 1948; *Annie Get Your Gun, Pagan Love Song* 1950; *Three Guys Named Mike, Show Boat, Texas Carnival* 1951; *Callaway Went Thataway, Lovely to Look At, Desperate Search* 1952; *Ride Vaquero!, Fast Company, I Love Melvin, Calamity Jane, Kiss Me Kate* 1953; *Rose Marie, Seven Brides for Seven Brothers, Deep in My Heart* 1954; *Jupiter's Darling, Kismet* 1955; *Floods of Fear, The Big Fisherman* 1959; *Armored Command* 1961; *Day of the Triffids* (UK) 1963; *The Man from Button Willow* 1965; *Waco* 1966; *Red Tomahawk, The War Wagon* 1967; *Arizona Bushwhackers* 1968.

Keeler, Ruby. Actress, dancer, singer. *b.* Ethel Hilda Keeler, Aug. 25, 1909, in Halifax, N.S., Canada. *d.* 1993. When she was three, her family moved to New York City, where her father made a meager living delivering ice. Despite her family's near poverty, Ruby began taking dancing lessons before she was ten. At 13 she was an accomplished tap dancer and at 14 broke into the chorus line of a George M. Cohan Broadway production. For the next three years she danced in the chorus of theater-district night spots, returning to the Broadway stage in 1927 as a featured attraction in the musicals 'Bye Bye Bonnie' and 'The Sidewalks of New York.' She was seen by Florenz Ziegfeld, who offered her a sizable part in the musical 'Whoopee,' starring Eddie Cantor. But before rehearsals were scheduled to begin, she went to the West Coast for a brief stage engagement and an appearance in a Fox short. It was in Los Angeles that she met singer Al JOLSON. He followed her to New York, where they were married in 1928. She left the cast of 'Whoopee' during its out-of-town tryout. In 1929 she got star billing in Broadway's 'Show Girl' but left the show after four weeks to join her husband on the West Coast.

In the 30s, Miss Keeler starred in a string of Warner Bros. film musicals that have since become classics of sorts, thanks to the colossal, geometrically patterned dance routines engineered by Busby BERKELEY. In the naïve backstage plots of these films, she typically played a sweet-natured girl picked from the chorus line at the last possible moment to replace the temperamental, ailing star. Dick POWELL was her frequent co-star. In 1937, Miss Keeler left Warners at the insistence of Jolson, who had quarreled with the front office. In 1939 she and Jolson separated and the following year their divorce became final. Miss Keeler appeared in one RKO picture in 1938 and a Columbia film in 1941, then married a real estate broker and retired.

Apart from occasional brief TV spots in the 50s and early 60s, Miss Keeler made no public appearances until the late 60s, when she enjoyed a sentimental comeback thanks to the re-release of her Berkeley films. In 1970, after a 40-year absence, she returned triumphantly to Broadway, on the wings of nostalgia, in a revival of the 1925 musical 'No No Nanette.'

FILMS: *Show Girl in Hollywood* (bit) 1930; *42nd Street, Gold Diggers of 1933, Footlight Parade* 1933; *Dames, Flirtation Walk* 1934; *Go Into Your Dance, Shipmates Forever* 1935; *Colleen* 1936; *Ready Willing and Able* 1937; *Mother Carey's Chickens* 1938; *Sweetheart of the Campus* 1941; *The Phynx* (cameo) 1970.

Keen, Geoffrey. Actor. Born on Aug. 21, 1916, in London. Dependable character player of the British stage and screen. The son of distinguished actor Malcolm Keen (*b.* Aug. 8, 1887, Bristol; *d.* 1970), he attended the Royal Academy of Dramatic Art on scholarship, graduating as a gold medalist. Making his stage debut in 1932 and his first film appearance in 1946, he played a wide variety of supporting roles, typically in restrained, commanding characterizations. He took over the part of "M" from Bernard LEE in the James Bond films.

FILMS INCLUDE: *Odd Man Out* 1946; *The Fallen Idol* 1948; *The Small Back Room/Hour of Glory, The Third Man* 1949; *Treasure Island, Seven Days to Noon* 1950; *The Clouded Yellow, His Excellency, Cry the Beloved Country* 1951; *Genevieve* 1953; *Doctor in the House, The Divided Heart* 1954; *The Man Who Never Was, The Long Arm/The Third Key* 1956; *Sink the Bismarck!* 1960; *No Love for Johnnie* 1961; *The Spiral Road* 1962; *Doctor Zhivago, The Heroes of Telemark* 1965; *Born Free* 1966; *Cromwell, Taste the Blood of Dracula* 1970; *Doomwatch* 1972; *The Spy Who Loved Me* 1977; *Moonraker* 1979; *For Your Eyes Only* 1981; *Octopussy* 1983; *A View to a Kill* 1985; *The Living Daylights* 1987.

Keene, Tom. See DURYEA, George.

Keighley, William. Director. *b.* Aug. 4, 1889, Philadelphia. *d.* 1984. He dropped out of a vocational school at 17 and worked as a messenger boy and railroad clerk while attending the Ludlum School of Dramatic Art part time. In 1912 he joined a touring company, specializing in Shakespearean roles. He first acted on Broadway in 1915 and first directed a New York play in 1928. He entered films with the advent of sound, and, after a period of apprenticeship as an assistant director and dialogue director, began directing in 1932. Under contract to Warner Bros. for most of his career, he was assigned a varied mixture of the studio's films, ranging from second features to major productions through a broad spectrum of film genres. The results were mixed. At his best, especially with gangster and adventure films, Keighley handled his material dynamically and stylishly. *Each Dawn I Die* (1939), *G-Men* (1935), and *Bullets or Ballots* (1936) were well-paced, exciting examples of the genre. (Stalin reportedly told Roosevelt that *Each Dawn I Die* was his favorite film.) And Keighley directed a number of comedies—most notably *The Man Who Came to Dinner* (1942)—with flair. But a number of films in his prolific output were surprisingly sluggish. During WW II, Keighley headed the motion picture division of the Army Air Corps, organizing combat camera units, supervising the making of training films, and directing in England the feature-length documentary *Target for Today,* about the RAF's Bomber Command. Genevieve TOBIN, his wife from 1938, starred in several of his pictures. After his retirement in the early 50s they moved to Paris, where Keighley devoted himself to still photography, mainly of architectural edifices in Europe and the Near East. Much of his work was done under the auspices of New York's Metropolitan Museum of Art. He was decorated a Chevalier of the French Legion of Honor and in 1958 became an honorary citizen of Paris and a director of the Musée Carnavelt. In 1972, however, the Keighleys returned to New York and settled in a Fifth Avenue apartment, where the former director died 12 years later of stroke at the age of 94.

FILMS: *The Match King* (co-dir. with Howard Bretherton); *Ladies They Talk About* (co-dir. with Bretherton) 1933; *Easy to Love, Journal of a Crime, Dr. Monica, Kansas City Princess, Big Hearted Herbert, Babbitt* 1934; *The Right to Live, G-Men, Special Agent, Stars Over Broadway, Mary Jane's Pa* 1935; *The Singing Kid, Bullets or Ballots, The Green Pastures* (co-dir. with Marc Connelly) 1936; *God's Country and the Woman, The Prince and the Pauper, Varsity Show* 1937; *The Adventures of Robin Hood* (co-dir. with Michael Curtiz), *Valley of the Giants, Secrets of an Actress, Brother Rat* 1938; *Yes My Darling Daughter, Each Dawn I Die* 1939; *The Fighting 69th, Torrid Zone, No Time for Comedy* 1940; *Four Mothers, The Bride Came C.O.D.* 1941; *The Man Who Came to Dinner, George Washington Slept Here* 1942; *Target for Today* (doc.) 1944; *Honeymoon* 1947; *The Street with No Name* 1948; *Rocky Mountain* 1950; *Close to My Heart* (also sc.) 1951; *The Master of Ballantrae* 1953.

Keir, Andrew. Actor. Born on Apr. 3, 1926, in Scotland. Imposing character player of British films, usually in commanding roles.

FILMS INCLUDE: *The Lady Craved Excitement* 1950; *The Brave Don't Cry* 1952; *The Maggie/High and Dry* 1954; *A Night to Remember* 1958; *The Pirates of Blood River* 1961; *Cleopatra* 1963; *The Fall of the Roman Empire* 1964; *Lord Jim* 1965; *Dracula—Prince of Darkness, Daleks—Invasion Earth 2150 A.D.* 1966; *The Viking Queen, The Long Duel, Quatermass and the Pit/Five Million Miles to Earth* 1967; *The Royal Hunt of the Sun* 1969; *The Last Grenade* 1970; *Zeppelin, Blood from the Mummy's Tomb, Mary, Queen of Scots* 1971; *The 39 Steps* 1978; *Absolution* (release delayed from 1978), *Lion of the Desert* 1981; *Hunters of the Deep* 1984; *Rob Roy* 1995.

Keitel, Harvey. Actor. Born on May 13, 1941, in Brooklyn, N.Y. Powerful leading man and supporting player of Hollywood films. He joined the Marine Corps directly out of high school, then trained for the stage under Frank Corsaro, Stella Adler, and Lee Strasberg. A member of the Actors Studio, he began performing professionally in off-off-Broadway coffeehouses, finally making his off-Broadway debut in 1965. He made his screen debut in 1968 in director Martin Scorsese's thesis project *Who's That Knocking at My Door?* and later played key roles in Scorsese's *Mean Streets* (1973), *Alice Doesn't Live Here Anymore* (1975), and *Taxi Driver* (1976). He has fared best as tough, street-wise characters; he won acclaim for his intense, unflinching performance as a corrupt policeman in *Bad Lieutenant* (1992). In the 80s he worked frequently in Europe. Formerly married to actress Lorraine BRACCO.

FILMS: *Who's That Knocking at My Door?* 1968; *Mean Streets* 1973; *Alice Doesn't Live Here Anymore, That's the Way of the World* 1975; *Taxi Driver, Mother Jugs and Speed, Buffalo Bill and the Indians* 1976; *Welcome to L.A., Shining Star, The Duellists* (UK) 1977; *Fingers, Blue Collar* 1978; *Health, Eagle's Wing* (UK) 1979; *La Mort en Direct/Deathwatch, Bad Timing/A Sensual Obsession* (UK), *Saturn 3* (UK) 1980; *The Border, La Nuit de Varennes* (It./Fr.) 1982; *Exposed, L'Assassino dei Poliziotti/Corrupt/Order of Death/Cop Killers* (It.), *Une Pierre dans la Bouche/A Stone in the Mouth* (Fr.) 1983; *Falling in Love, Nemo/Dream One* (Fr./UK) 1984; *Un Complicato Intrigo di Donne Vicoli e Delitti/Camorra* (It.), *El Caballero del Dragon/The Knight of the Dragon* (Sp./It.) 1985; *La Sposa Americana/The American Wife* (It.), *Wise Guys, Off Beat, The Men's Club* 1986; *Corsa in Discesa* (It.), *Dear America* (doc.; voice only), *L'Inchiesta/The Inquiry/The Investigation* (as Pontius

Pilate; It.), *The Pick-Up Artist* 1987; *The Last Temptation of Christ* (as Judas), *Blindside* 1988; *The January Man* 1989; *The Two Jakes, Due Occhi diabolici/Two Evil Eyes/The Black Cat* (It.) 1990; *Mortal Thoughts, Thelma and Louise, Bugsy* 1991; *Sister Act, Reservoir Dogs, Bad Lieutenant* 1992; *Dangerous Game, The Piano, Point of No Return, Rising Sun, The Young Americans* 1993; *Imaginary Crimes, Monkey Trouble, Pulp Fiction* 1994; *Blue in the Face, Clockers, From Dusk Till Dawn, Get Shorty, Smoke* 1995; *Somebody to Love* 1996; *City of Industry, Cop Land, Head Above Water, Ulysses Gaze* 1997.

Keith, Brian. Actor. *b.* Robert Brian Keith, Jr., on Nov. 14, 1921, in Bayonne, N.J. *d.* 1997. The son of Robert KEITH, he made his first film appearance at age three, then appeared in stock and radio and served as a machine gunner in the Marines before making his adult film debut in 1953. A fine actor, much at home in Westerns, he gradually switched from heavy character parts to sympathetic, increasingly more important and versatile roles. He often starred in Disney films and other juvenile-market fare but his gruff appeal extended as well to adult audiences. His popularity was enhanced by starring roles in such TV series as 'Crusader' (1955–56), 'The Westerner' (1960), 'Family Affair' (1966–71), 'The Brian Keith Show' (1972–74), 'Lew Archer' (1975), and 'Hardcastle & McCormick' (1983–86).

FILMS INCLUDE: *Pied Piper Malone* 1924; *Arrowhead* 1953; *Alaska Seas* 1954; *The Violent Men, Tight Spot, Five Against the House* 1955; *Storm Center* 1956; *Nightfall, Run of the Arrow, Chicago Confidential* 1957; *Fort Dobbs, Sierra Baron* 1958; *The Young Philadelphians* 1959; *Ten Who Dared* 1960; *The Parent Trap, The Deadly Companions/Trigger Happy* 1961; *Moon Pilot* 1962; *Savage Sam* 1963; *The Raiders, A Tiger Walks* 1964; *The Pleasure Seekers, The Hallelujah Trail, Those Calloways* 1965; *The Russians Are Coming the Russians Are Coming, The Rare Breed, Nevada Smith* 1966; *Reflections in a Golden Eye* 1967; *With Six You Get Eggroll* 1968; *Krakatoa—East of Java, Gaily Gaily* 1969; *Suppose They Gave a War and Nobody Came, The McKenzie Break* 1970; *Something Big, Scandalous John* 1971; *The Yakuza, The Wind and the Lion* (as Teddy Roosevelt) 1975; *Joe Panther, Nickelodeon* 1976; *Hooper* 1978; *Moonraker, Meteor* 1979; *The Mountain Men* 1980; *Charlie Chan and the Curse of the Dragon Queen, Sharkey's Machine* 1981; *Death Before Dishonor* 1987; *Young Guns, After the Rain/The Passage* 1988; *Welcome Home* 1989.

Keith, David. Actor, director. Born on May 8, 1954, in Knoxville, Tenn. Rugged leading man of Hollywood films, often in contentious roles. A graduate in speech and drama of the University of Tennessee, he appeared in a Chicago musical and briefly on TV before his 1979 screen debut. He began directing in the late 80s.

FILMS (as actor): *The Rose, The Great Santini* 1979; *Brubaker* 1980; *Back Roads, Take This Job and Shove It* 1981; *An Officer and a Gentleman* 1982; *Independence Day, The Lords of Discipline* 1983; *Firestarter* 1984; *Gulag* (UK) 1985; *The Curse* (dir. only), *White of the Eye* (UK) 1987; *The Further Adventures of Tennessee Buck* (also dir.) 1988; *Heartbreak Hotel* (as Elvis Presley) 1989; *The Two Jakes* 1990; *Off and Running, Caged Fear* 1992; *Desperate Motive* 1993; *Born Wild, Lions of Darkness, Major League II, The Puppet Masters, Raw Justice, Running Wild, Temptation* 1994; *Gold Diggers: The Secret of Bear Mountain, The Indian in the Cupboard, Till the End of the Night* 1995; *A Family Thing* 1996.

Keith, Ian. Actor. *b.* Keith Ross, Feb. 27, 1899, Boston. *d.* 1960. A Broadway matinee idol in the early 20s, he was lured to Hollywood in 1924. He played romantic leads through the early sound era, and later character parts. He was at one time married to Blanche YURKA and later to Ethel CLAYTON.

FILMS INCLUDE: *Manhandled, Her Love Story, Christine of the Hungry Heart, Love's Wilderness* 1924; *Enticement, The Talker, My Son, The Tower of Lies* 1925; *The Greater Glory, The Lily, The Prince of Tempters* 1926; *The Love of Sunya, Convoy, A Man's Past, What Every Girl Should Know, Two Arabian Knights* 1927; *Street of Illusion* 1928; *The Divine Lady, Light Fingers, Prisoners, The Great Divide* 1929; *Prince of Diamonds, Abraham Lincoln* (as John Wilkes Booth), *The Boudoir Diplomat* 1930; *Susan Lennox: Her Fall and Rise, The Deceiver* 1931; *The Sign of the Cross* 1932; *Queen Christina* 1933; *Cleopatra* (as Octavian) 1934; *The Crusades* (as Saladin), *The Three Musketeers* (as De Rochefort) 1935; *Mary of Scotland* 1936; *The Buccaneer* 1938; *All This and Heaven Too, The Sea Hawk* 1940; *Five Graves to Cairo* 1943; *The Spanish Main* 1945; *Valley of the Zombies* 1946; *Nightmare Alley* 1947; *The Three Musketeers* (again as De Rochefort) 1948; *The Black Shield of Falworth* (as Henry IV) 1954; *Prince of Players* (as the King in 'Hamlet' sequence) 1955; *The Ten Commandments* (as Ramses I) 1956.

Keith, Robert. Actor. *b.* Feb. 10, 1896, Fowler, Ind. *d.* 1966. He made his stage debut at 16 in stock and later appeared in many Broadway productions and an occasional silent film. After writing a Broadway play ('The Tightwad,' 1927) he went to Hollywood as a dialogue writer for Universal and Columbia, and in the early 30s he played minor roles in a number of films. He then returned to the New York stage, wrote another play ('Singapore,' 1932), and appeared in many others. He was back in Hollywood to stay in the late 40s and his many film appearances included a number of richly detailed characterizations. He was the father of Brian KEITH.

FILMS INCLUDE: *The Other Kind of Love* 1924; *Just Imagine* 1930; *Bad Company* 1931; *Destry Rides Again* (co-sc. only), *Scandal for Sale* (co-sc. only), *Unexpected Father* (co-sc. only) 1932; *The Spirit of Culver* 1939; *Boomerang, Kiss of Death* 1947; *My Foolish Heart, Edge of Doom, Woman on the Run* 1950; *14 Hours, Here Comes the Groom, I Want You* 1951; *Somebody Loves Me* 1952; *Battle Circus* 1953; *The Wild One, Drum Beat* 1954; *Young at Heart, Love Me or Leave Me, Guys and Dolls* 1955; *Ransom, Between Heaven and Hell* 1956; *Written on the Wind, Men in War, My Man Godfrey* 1957; *The Lineup, La Tempesta/Tempest* (It.) 1958; *They Came to Cordura* 1959; *Cimarron* 1960; *Posse from Hell* 1961.

Kelber, Michel. Director of photography. Born on Apr. 9, 1908, in Kiev, Russia. After studying art and architecture at the École des Beaux-Arts in Paris, he entered French films as an assistant cameraman in 1928. As a cinematographer from 1933, he was behind the camera on many major film productions, working for Autant-Lara, Clair, Duvivier, and Renoir, among other French directors. He spent the WW II years working in Switzerland and Spain.

FILMS INCLUDE: *Incognito* 1933; *Zou-Zou, L'Or dans la Rue* 1934; *Sous les Yeux d'Occident/Razumov* 1936; *Un Carnet de Bal* (co-phot.), *Gribouille/Heart of Paris* (co-phot.), *L'Affaire du Courrier de Lyon/The Courier of Lyons* 1937; *Pièges/Personal Column* 1939; *Une Femme disparaît/Portrait of a Woman* (Fr./Switz.) 1943; *Le Diable au Corps/Devil in the Flesh, Ruy Blas* 1947; *Les Parents terribles/The Storm Within* 1948; *Jean de la Lune* 1949; *La Beauté du Diable/Beauty and the Devil* 1950; *Les Amants de Tolède/The Lovers of Toledo* 1953; *Le Grand Jeu/Flesh and the Woman, Le Rouge et le Noir/The Red and the Black* 1954; *French Cancan/Only the French Can* 1955; *Calle Mayor/The Lovemaker* (Sp.), *Notre Dame de Paris/The Hunchback of Notre Dame* 1956; *Pot-Bouille, Amère Victoire/Bitter Victory* 1957; *John Paul Jones* (US) 1959; *Katia/Magnificent Sinner* 1960; *Vue du Pont/A View from the Bridge* 1962; *In the French Style* (US/Fr.), *Lulu* 1963; *Mata Hari—Agent H-21, Le Journal d'une Femme en blanc* 1965; *Le Franciscain de Bourges* 1967; *Phèdre* 1969; *Les Patates* 1970; *Roses rouges et Piments verts/The Lonely Woman* (Fr./It./Sp.) 1975; *Fidélio* 1979; *Y'a-t-il un Français dans la Salle?* 1982.

Kellaway, Cecil. Actor. *b.* Aug. 22, 1891, Cape Town, South Africa. *d.* 1973. In Hollywood since the late 30s after extensive stage and screen activity in Australia, he appeared in well over 100 films, typically in roguish, twinkly-eyed, lovable character parts. He was nominated for an Oscar for his portrayal of a leprechaun in *The Luck of the Irish* (1948) and again for his performance in *Guess Who's Coming to Dinner* (1967).

FILMS INCLUDE: *It Isn't Done* 1937; *Tarnished Angel* 1938; *Wuthering Heights* (as Mr. Earnshaw), *Intermezzo, We Are Not Alone* 1939; *The Invisible Man Returns, The House of the Seven Gables, Brother Orchid, The Mummy's Hand, The Letter* 1940; *Appointment for Love, Bahama Passage* 1941; *Are Husbands Necessary?, I Married a Witch* 1942; *Forever and a Day* 1943; *Frenchman's Creek, Mrs. Parkington* 1944; *Love Letters, Kitty* 1945; *The Postman Always Rings Twice, The Cockeyed Miracle* 1946; *Unconquered* 1947; *The Luck of the Irish, Joan of Arc* 1948; *Portrait of Jennie, Down to the Sea in Ships* 1949; *Harvey, Kim* 1950; *Half Angel* 1951; *Young Bess* 1953; *The Prodigal* 1955; *Toy Tiger* 1956; *The Proud Rebel* 1958; *The Private Lives of Adam and Eve* 1960; *Francis of Assisi* 1961; *The Cardinal* 1963; *Hush Hush. . . Sweet Charlotte* 1965; *Fitzwilly, Guess Who's Coming to Dinner* 1967; *Getting Straight* 1970.

Keller, Harry. Director, producer. Born on Feb. 22, 1913, in Los Angeles. A film editor from 1936, he began directing in the late 40s and subsequently turned out many modest-budget films, mostly routine escapist entertainment, some of it handled with a certain flair. In the late 60s he also produced a number of films. He has been active in TV as well, directing 'The Loretta Young Show,' among other programs.

FILMS: As director—*The Blonde Bandit* 1949; *Tarnished* 1950; *Fort Dodge Stampede, Desert of Lost Men* 1951; *Rose of Cimarron, Leadville Gunslinger, Thundering Caravans, Black Hills Ambush* 1952; *Marshal of Cedar Rock, Bandits of the West, Savage Frontier, El Paso Stampede* 1953; *Red River Shore, Phantom Stallion* 1954; *The Unguarded Moment* 1956; *Man Afraid, Quantez* 1957; *The Female Animal, Day of the Badman, Voice in the Mirror, Step Down to Terror* 1958; *Seven Ways from Sundown* 1960; *Tammy Tell Me True* 1961; *Six Black Horses* 1962; *Tammy and the Doctor* 1963; *The Brass Bottle* 1964; *In Enemy Country* (also prod.) 1968. As producer—*Kitten with a Whip, Send Me No Flowers* 1964; *Mirage, That Funny Feeling* 1965; *Texas Across the River* 1967; *Skin Game* 1971; *Class of '44* (exec. prod.) 1973.

Keller, Marthe. Actress. Born in 1945, on a farm near Basle, Switzerland. Exotic, sad-eyed leading lady of international films. The daughter of a horse breeder, she trained for the ballet from the age of eight but was forced to give up dancing at 16 after a skiing accident. Switching to drama, she studied acting for three years at the Stanislavsky School in Munich, Germany, then joined a Heidelberg repertory group and worked her way up to the famous Schiller Theater in Berlin, where she played many leading roles in the classic repertoire. During that formative period of her acting career, she also appeared on German TV and played a supporting role in the British film about espionage *Funeral in Berlin* (1966), which was shot on location in Berlin. She then went to France, where, in addition to filling stage and TV roles, she began developing into a popular screen personality in such films as Philippe de Broca's *Le Diable par la Queue/The Devil by the Tail* (1969) and *Les Caprices de Marie/Give Her the Moon* (1970), and Claude Lelouch's *Toute une Vie/And Now My Love* (1974). She was romantically attached to both directors. De Broca is the father of her son, Alexandre. Her growing reputation as a fine actress and attractive screen personality led to an invitation from Hollywood and to starring roles in such films as *Marathon Man* (1976) and *Black Sunday* and *Bobby Deerfield* (both 1977). She was linked romantically with her co-star in the last film, Al PACINO. In the early 80s she returned to Europe.

FILMS INCLUDE: *Funeral in Berlin* (UK) 1966; *Le Diable par la Queue/The Devil by the Tail* (Fr.) 1969; *Les Caprices de Marie/Give Her the Moon* (Fr.) 1970; *La Vieille Fille* (Fr.) 1971; *Elle court Elle court la Banlieu* (Fr.), *La Raison du plus Fou* (Fr.) 1973; *Toute une Vie/And Now My Love* (Fr.) 1974; *Per le Antiche Scale/Down the Ancient Stairs* (It./Fr.) 1975; *Le Guepier* (Fr.), *Marathon Man* (US) 1976; *Black Sunday* (US), *Bobby Deerfield* (US) 1977; *Fedora* (Ger./Fr.) 1978; *The Formula* (US) 1980; *The Amateur* (Can.) 1982; *Wagner* (UK) 1983; *Femmes de Personne* 1984; *Rouge Baiser/Red Kiss* (Fr.) 1985; *Oci Ciornie/Dark Eyes* (It.) 1987; *Georg Elser/Seven Minutes* (Ger./US) 1990; *Lapse of Memory* 1992; *Mon Amie Max/My Friend Max* (Fr.) 1994.

Kellerman(n), Annette. Athlete, actress. *b.* 1887, Australia *d.* 1975. A champion swimmer and diver, famous in her time as "The Diving Venus," she starred in a number of stage productions and silent films in which her swimming skills were the chief attraction. (She was arrested in Boston in 1907 for wearing a then-shocking, limb-baring one-piece bathing suit on the beach.) She was portrayed by Esther WILLIAMS in a 1952 film biography, *Million Dollar Mermaid.*

FILMS INCLUDE: *Miss Annette Kellerman, Fancy Swimming and Diving Displays* (both reportage films) 1909; *Neptune's Daughter* 1914; *Isle of Love, A Daughter of the Gods* 1916; *The Honor System* 1917; *Queen of the Sea* 1918; *The Art of Diving* (reportage), *What Women Love* 1920; *Venus of the South Seas* 1924.

Kellerman, Sally. Actress. Born on June 2, 1936, in Long Beach, Calif. Offbeat leading lady of the American screen. Stagestruck after appearing in a high school play, she enrolled in acting classes at the Actors Studio West, then with Jeff Corey, but for more than a decade was unable to land other than occasional small parts in plays on TV and in films. A very tall siren-type comedienne, she was an "instant" smash as Major "Hot Lips" Houlihan, an uptight Army nurse, in the film *M*A*S*H*, a role for which she was nominated for an Academy Award, and went on to a successful career in other films. In 1970 she married TV director Rick Edelstein. Following their divorce, she married talent agent–movie producer Jonathan Krane.

FILMS: *Reform School Girl* 1959; *Hands of a Stranger* 1962; *The Third Day* 1965; *The Boston Strangler* 1968; *The April Fools* 1969; *M*A*S*H, Brewster McCloud* 1970; *Last of the Red Hot Lovers* 1972; *A Reflection of Fear* (UK), *Lost Horizon, Slither* 1973; *Rafferty and the Gold Dust Twins* 1975; *The Big Bus* 1976; *The Mouse and His Child* (voice only), *Welcome to L.A.* 1977; *She'll Be Sweet, It Rained All Night the Day I Left* (Can./Isr.) 1978; *A Little Romance* 1979; *Foxes, Serial, Loving Couples, Head On* (Can.) 1980; *Moving Violations, Sesame Street Presents. . . Follow That Bird* (voice only) 1985; *Back to School, KGB: The Secret War/Lethal, Meatballs III, That's Life!* 1986; *Three for the Road* 1987; *You Can't Hurry Love, Someone to Love, Paramedics* 1988; *All's Fair, Secret of the Ice Cave* 1989; *Happily Ever After* (voice only) 1990; *Boris and Natasha, The Player* 1992; *Ready to Wear* 1994; *It's My Party* 1996.

Kelley, Barry. Actor. *b.* 1908, Chicago. *d.* 1991. Bulky (6' 2", 230 pounds), tough-looking character player of the American stage and screen. Trained at the Goodman Theater School, he appeared in several Broadway productions before making his film debut in 1947. He specialized in shady, menacing roles, often as a corrupt official.

FILMS INCLUDE: *Boomerang* 1947; *Force of Evil* 1948; *Knock on Any Door, Undercover Man, Johnny Stool Pigeon* 1949; *Black Hand, The Capture, The Asphalt Jungle, Southside 1-1000, Right Cross* 1950; *The Great Missouri Raid, The Well* 1951; *Carrie* 1952; *The Long Wait* 1954; *New York Confidential* 1955; *Monkey on My Back* 1957; *The Buccaneer* 1958; *Elmer Gantry* 1960; *The Manchurian Candidate* 1962; *Rio Conchos* 1964; *The Love Bug* 1968.

Kelley, DeForest. Actor. Born on Jan. 20, 1920, in Atlanta. Supporting character player of many Hollywood films since the late 40s. He emerged from relative obscurity in the late 60s, thanks to his role as Dr. Leonard "Bones" McCoy in the popular TV series 'Star Trek' (1966–69) and its movie offshoots.

FILMS INCLUDE: *Fear in the Night* 1947; *Canon City* 1948; *House of Bamboo* 1950; *Taxi* 1953; *Illegal* 1955; *The Man in the Gray Flannel Suit* 1956; *Gunfight at the O.K. Corral, Raintree County* 1957; *The Law and Jake Wade, Warlock* 1959; *Where Love Has Gone* 1964; *Marriage on the Rocks* 1965; *Apache Uprising* 1966; *Night of the Lepus* 1972; *Star Trek: The Motion Picture* 1979; *Star Trek II: The Wrath of Khan* 1982; *Star Trek III: The Search for Spock* 1984; *Star Trek IV: The Voyage Home* 1986; *Star Trek V: The Final Frontier* 1989; *Star Trek VI: The Undiscovered Country* 1991.

Kelley, Sheila. Actress. Born in 1964, in Philadelphia. Spontaneous, sensitive, up-and-coming leading lady of the American screen. One of nine children of a coal industry employee, she trained as a dancer at NYU but switched to the acting program at the Film School after a hip injury. She made an impressive start in films in the late 80s.

FILMS: *Wish You Were Here* (UK) 1987; *Some Girls* 1988; *Breaking In, Staying Together* 1989; *Mortal Passions, Where the Heart Is* 1990.

Kelly, Gene. Dancer, actor, choreographer, director. *b.* Eugene Curran Kelly, on Aug. 23, 1912, in Pittsburgh, the son of a sales executive and a former stage actress. *d.* 1996. *ed.* Penn State; U. of Pittsburgh (economics). Dancing since childhood, he supported himself as a dance instructor, gas station attendant, and ditch digger before making it to Broadway in the chorus of 'Leave It to Me' in 1938. Two years later he choreographed 'Billy Rose's Diamond Horseshoe' and got the starring part in 'Pal Joey.' In 1941 he choreographed another successful Broadway musical, 'Best Foot Forward.' The following year he made his screen debut as Judy Garland's co-star in *For Me and My Gal.* Combining a pleasant, casual personality with a husky, caressing singing voice and a spontaneous, masculine dancing style, he became increasingly popular in the 40s.

Beginning with *Cover Girl* (1944), for which he was loaned out to Columbia, Kelly's free-flowing, imaginative dance routines revolutionized the Hollywood musical, infusing it with freshness and vitality. He was nominated for a best actor Oscar for *Anchors Aweigh* (1945). Following the success of *On the Town* (1949), the first of three sparkling musicals that Kelly also co-directed with Stanley DONEN, he succeeded Fred ASTAIRE as Hollywood's number one dancing master. He was less successful, however, in his several outings as a straight dramatic actor. In 1951 he received a Special Academy Award. His first effort as a solo director, *Invitation to the Dance* (1956), a musical with no dialogue, won the grand prize at the West Berlin Film Festival. His subsequent product as director was proficiently handled but far less inspired than his dancing and choreography. After choreographing the ballet 'Pas de Deux' for the Paris Opera in 1960, he was given the Chevalier of the Legion of Honor by the French government. He was honored with Life Achievement Awards from the Kennedy Center in 1982 and the American Film Institute in 1985. Still vital in his 80s, he survived the complete destruction of his home to a fire. Kelly's first wife (1940–57) was actress Betsy BLAIR. In 1960 he married former dancing assistant Jean Coyne, who died in 1973. In 1990 he married Patricia Ward, a young writer he had hired to collaborate on his memoirs.

FILMS (as actor): *For Me and My Gal* 1942; *Pilot No. 5, Du Barry Was a Lady, Thousands Cheer, The Cross of Lorraine* 1943; *Cover Girl* (also chor.), *Christmas Holiday* 1944; *Anchors Aweigh* (also chor.) 1945; *Ziegfeld Follies* 1946; *Living in a Big Way* (also chor.) 1947; *The Pirate* (also co-chor.), *The Three Musketeers* (as D'Artagnan), *Words and Music* 1948; *Take Me Out to the Ball Game* (also co-story, co-chor.), *On the Town* (also co-dir. with Stanley Donen, chor.) 1949; *Black Hand, Summer Stock* 1950; *An American in Paris* (also chor.) 1951; *It's a Big Country, Singin' in the Rain* (also co-dir. with Donen, co-chor.), *The Devil Makes Three* 1952; *Brigadoon* (also chor.), *Seagulls Over Sorrento/Crest of the Wave* (UK), *Deep in My Heart* (cameo) 1954; *It's Always Fair Weather* (also co-dir. with Donen, chor.) 1955; *Invitation to the Dance* (also dir., sc., chor.) 1956; *The Happy Road* (also dir., prod.), *Les Girls* 1957; *Marjorie Morningstar, Tunnel of Love* (dir. only) 1958; *Let's Make Love* (cameo), *Inherit the Wind* 1960; *Gigot* (dir. only) 1962; *What a Way to Go!* 1964; *Les Demoiselles de Rochefort/The Young Girls of Rochefort* (Fr.), *A Guide for the Married Man* (dir. only) 1967; *Hello Dolly!* (dir. only) 1969; *The Cheyenne Social Club* (dir., prod. only) 1970; *40 Carats* 1973; *That's Entertainment* (on-screen co-narr.) 1974; *That's Entertainment Part II* (on-screen co-narr.; also dir. of new sequences) 1976; *Viva Knievel!* 1977; *Xanadu* 1980; *Reporters* (doc.; Fr.) 1981; *That's Dancing!* 1985; *That's Entertainment III* 1994.

Kelly, Grace (Grimaldi; Princess Grace of Monaco). Actress. *b.* Nov. 12, 1928, Philadelphia. *d.* 1982. Gracefully exquisite star of Hollywood films of the 50s. The daughter of a former cover girl and a wealthy industrialist, former world champion oarsman Jack Kelly, and the niece of Pulitzer Prize–winning playwright ('Craig's Wife,' etc.) George Kelly, she made her stage debut as a child of ten in a Philadelphia production. After attending Raven Hall Academy, then the Stevens School, both in Philadelphia, she came to New York, where she took up modeling while attending acting classes at the American Academy of Dramatic Arts. She auditioned for many plays, but at first the only parts she could get were in cigarette commercials on TV. She finally made it to Broadway in 1949, in a revival of Strindberg's *The Father,* starring Raymond Massey. Her serene beauty attracted attention in Hollywood and she landed a bit part in the film *Fourteen Hours* (1951). The following year she got her first starring role, as the wife who ultimately did not forsake Gary Cooper in *High Noon.* She was nominated for a best supporting actress Oscar in 1953 for her portrayal of an adulteress in *Mogambo.* The following year she won the best actress Academy Award and the New York Film Critics Award for her performance as the embittered wife of an alcoholic actor-singer (Bing Crosby) in *The Country Girl.* The qualities that typed her as a star were an icy aloofness and haughty reserve underneath which lay dormant passions. A dash of humor was added to her screen personality in two of the three films she made for Alfred HITCHCOCK.

While working on her third Hitchcock film, *To Catch a Thief* (1955), the action of which takes place on the French Riviera, she met Prince Rainier III, the ruler of the tiny principality of Monaco.

They married in 1956 in a spectacular royal ceremony, and Grace retired from the screen. Instead of publicity photos, her delicate face now appeared on postage stamps. In 1962 she hosted a TV tour of Monaco. There was talk of a film comeback, but several announced projects did not materialize. She did narrate, however, *The Children of Theatre Street* (1978) and other documentaries. At 52, still one of the world's most beautiful and elegant women, she died of cerebral hemorrhages, one leading to and another resulting from a fatal accident, when the car she was driving on a treacherous Cote d'Azur mountain road plunged down a 45-foot embankment and burst into flames. The circumstances of the crash remain a mystery. Cheryl Ladd impersonated her in the TV movie *Grace Kelly* (1983).

FILMS: *Fourteen Hours* 1951; *High Noon* 1952; *Mogambo* 1953; *Dial M for Murder, Rear Window, The Country Girl, Green Fire* 1954; *The Bridges at Toko-Ri, To Catch a Thief* 1955; *The Swan, High Society* 1956.

Kelly, Jack. Actor. *b.* Sept. 16, 1927, Astoria, N.Y. *d.* 1992. The brother of Nancy KELLY, he performed as a child on stage, on radio, and in occasional movies, then played lead and supporting roles in films and TV from the early 50s. His TV appearances included the series 'Kings Row' (1955–56) and 'Maverick' (1957–62).

FILMS INCLUDE: *The Story of Alexander Graham Bell, Young Mr. Lincoln* 1939; *Where Danger Lives* 1950; *Submarine Command* 1951; *Red Ball Express* 1952; *Gunsmoke* 1953; *Drive a Crooked Road, The Country Girl* 1954; *The Night Holds Terror, To Hell and Back, Cult of the Cobra* 1955; *Forbidden Planet* 1956; *She-Devil* 1957; *The Hong Kong Affair* 1958; *A Fever in the Blood* 1961; *FBI Code 98* 1964; *Love and Kisses* 1965; *Young Billy Young* 1969; *Oh God! You Devil!* 1984.

Kelly, Moira. Actress. Born 1968, in Ronkonkoma, N.Y. *ed.* Marymount Manhattan College, New York City. Attractive, spirited young lead of American television and film. She got her start in television and quickly made a name for herself in her first feature film role, Robert BENTON's *Billy Bathgate* (1991). She has developed into an arresting performer with a serious flair for comedy.

FILMS: *Billy Bathgate, The Boy Who Cried Bitch* 1991; *Chaplin, The Cutting Edge, Twin Peaks: Fire Walk with Me* 1992; *Daybreak* 1993; *The Lion King* (voice only), *Little Odessa, With Honors* 1994; *The Tie That Binds* 1995; *Entertaining Angels* 1996; *The Bitter End, Changing Habits* 1997.

Kelly, Nancy. Actress. Born on Mar. 25, 1921, in Lowell, Mass. The daughter of actress Nan Kelly Yorke (1895–1978), she began modeling as a baby and later played child roles on the stage and in films of the late 20s. After a period of transition on radio, she returned to films as a young adult in 1938 and played competent leads in a variety of films, both A and B productions, mainly for Fox, through the mid-40s. In the mid-50s she returned to the screen in character roles. She also appeared in many Broadway productions, winning a Tony Award for the mother role in 'The Bad Seed,' a role she later repeated in the screen version. The sister of Jack KELLY, she was married briefly (1941–42) to Edmond O'BRIEN.

FILMS INCLUDE: *Untamed Lady, Mismates* 1926; *The Girl on the Barge* 1929; *Convention Girl* 1935; *Submarine Patrol* 1938; *Jesse James, Tail Spin, Frontier Marshal, Stanley and Livingstone* 1939; *He Married His Wife, Sailor's Lady, One Night in the Tropics* 1940; *Scotland Yard, Parachute Battalion* 1941; *To the Shores of Tripoli, Friendly Enemies* 1942; *Tarzan's Desert Mystery* 1943; *Show Business, Double Exposure* 1944; *Betrayal from the East, Song of the Sarong, Follow That Woman* 1945; *Murder in the Music Hall* 1946; *Crowded Paradise, The Bad Seed* 1956.

Kelly, Patsy. Actress. *b.* Sarah Kelly, Jan. 12, 1910, Brooklyn, N.Y. *d.* 1981. A dancer since childhood and a highly talented comedienne, she enjoyed great popularity in Broadway musicals of the early 30s, notably in 'Earl Carroll's Sketches' and in 'Wonder Bar,' the latter opposite Al Jolson. She was brought to Hollywood by Hal Roach in 1933 to replace ZaSu Pitts as the co-star of Thelma Todd in a popular series of two-reel comedies (she paired briefly with Lyda Roberti after Todd's mysterious death in 1936). Kelly's deadpan comedy style also proved ideal for her many roles as a wisecracking friend of the heroine in feature comedies and musicals as well as occasional leads. She retired in the early 40s but returned to the screen in the 60s, mostly in minor parts. In 1971 she returned triumphantly to the Broadway stage in a nostalgic hit revival of 'No No Nanette,' co-starring with her childhood friend Ruby Keeler. Kelly won a Tony Award for her performance and later appeared in another Broadway revival, 'Irene.'

FILMS INCLUDE: *Going Hollywood* 1933; *The Countess of Monte Cristo, The Girl from Missouri* 1934; *Go Into Your Dance, Every Night at Eight, Page Miss Glory, Thanks a Million* 1935; *Private Number, Sing Baby Sing, Kelly the Second, Pigskin Parade* 1936; *Wake Up and Live, Nobody's Baby, Pick a Star, Ever Since Eve* 1937; *Merrily We Live, There Goes My Heart, The Cowboy and the Lady* 1938; *The Gorilla* 1939; *Hit Parade of 1941* 1940; *Road Show, Topper Returns, Broadway Limited, Playmates* 1941; *Sing Your Worries Away, In Old California* 1942; *Ladies' Day* 1943; *Please Don't Eat the Daisies, The Crowded Sky* 1960; *The Naked Kiss* 1964; *The Ghost in the Invisible Bikini* 1966; *Rosemary's Baby* 1968; *The Phynx* (cameo) 1970; *Freaky Friday* 1977; *North Avenue Irregulars* 1979.

Kelly, Paul. Actor. *b.* Aug. 9, 1899, Brooklyn, N.Y. *d.* 1956. Onstage from age seven and in films from eight, he played child and juvenile roles in many early Vitagraph silents. He subsequently appeared in many Broadway plays and scores of Hollywood silent and sound films, playing leads in B pictures, mostly crime melodramas, and competent supporting roles in major productions. In the late 20s he spent two years in jail for manslaughter. The victim was stage actor Ray Raymond, the former husband of stage actress Dorothy MacKaye, who became Kelly's wife in 1931.

FILMS INCLUDE: *A Good Little Devil* 1908; *A Juvenile Love Affair, Captain Barnacle's Waif* 1912; *Buddy's First Call, Buddy's Downfall* 1914; *The Jarr Family Discovers Harlem* 1915; *Knights of the Square Table* 1917; *Fit to Fight* (WW I propaganda doc.) 1918; *Anne of Green Gables* 1919; *Uncle Sam of Freedom Ridge* 1920; *The Great Adventure, The Old Oaken Bucket* 1921; *The New Klondike* 1926; *Slide Kelly Slide, Special Delivery* 1927; *Girl from Calgary* 1932; *Broadway Thru a Keyhole* 1933; *Side Streets, Blind Date, The President Vanishes* 1934; *Star of Midnight, Public Hero No. 1* 1935; *The Song and Dance Man, The Country Beyond, The Accusing Finger, Murder with Pictures* 1936; *Parole Racket, It Happened Out West, Frame-Up, Navy Blue and Gold* 1937; *Torchy Blane in Panama, The Devil's Party, The Missing Guest, Juvenile Court, Adventure in Sahara* 1938; *Within the Law, The Flying Irishman, 6,000 Enemies, The Roaring Twenties, Invisible Stripes* 1939; *Queen of the Mob, The Howards of Virginia, Wyoming* 1940; *Flight Command, Ziegfeld Girl, Mystery Ship* 1941; *Mr. and Mrs. North, The Secret Code* (serial), *Tarzan's New York Adventure, Flying Tigers* 1942; *The Story of Dr. Wassell, Dead Man's Eyes, Faces in the Fog* 1944; *Allotment Wives, San Antonio, Grissly's Millions* 1945; *The Cat Creeps, Deadline for Murder* 1946; *Strange Journey, Fear in the Night, Crossfire, Adventure Island* 1947; *Thelma Jordan, Side Street, Guilty of Treason, The Secret Fury* 1950; *The Painted Hills* 1951; *Springfield Rifle* 1952; *Split Second, Gunsmoke* 1953; *The High and the Mighty, The Steel Cage* 1954; *The Square Jungle* 1955; *Storm Center* 1956; *Bailout at 43,000* 1957.

Kelton, Pert. Actress. *b.* Oct. 14, 1907, on a cattle ranch near Great Falls, Mont. *d.* 1968. The daughter of vaudevillians, she joined the family act at age three and began playing solo engagements at 12. She made her Broadway debut in 1925, in the musical 'Sunny,' in support of Marilyn Miller, and her first film appearance in 1929. On the screen, she proved to be a delightful comedienne, typically playing a blonde floozie, occasionally in a lead but more often as a friend of the heroine. A rare exception was her dramatic role as a stool pigeon who betrays Sylvia Sidney in *Mary Burns—Fugitive* (1935). She retired from the screen in 1939 but returned in the 60s in a number of character parts.

She was the original Alice, Jackie Gleason's wife, in TV's 'The Honeymooners' in 1950–52, when the popular series started as a segment of the variety show 'Cavalcade of Stars.' Her career was hampered by blacklisting after she was named in the scare publication *Red Channels* as a Communist sympathizer.

FILMS INCLUDE: *Sally* 1929; *Hot Curves* 1930; *Bed of Roses, The Bowery* 1933; *The Meanest Gal in Town, Sing and Like It, Bachelor Bait* 1934; *Hooray for Love, Mary Burns—Fugitive, Annie Oakley* 1935; *Kelly the Second, Sitting on the Moon, Cain and Mabel* 1936; *Women of Glamour, The Hit Parade* 1937; *Rhythm of the Saddle* 1938; *Whispering Enemies* 1939; *The Music Man* 1962; *Love and Kisses* 1965; *The Comic* 1969.

Kemp, Jeremy. Actor. Born Edmund Walker, on Feb. 3, 1934, near Chesterfield, England. Trained at London's Central School of Speech and Drama, he made his stage debut in 1957, joining the Old Vic company the following year. He has appeared in plays, TV productions, and films, both in leads and strong supporting roles.

FILMS INCLUDE: *Cleopatra* (bit) 1963; *Dr. Terror's House of Horrors, Operation Crossbow* 1965; *Cast a Giant Shadow* (US), *The Blue Max* 1966; *The Strange Affair, A Twist of Sand* 1968; *The Games, Darling Lili* (US) 1970; *Eyewitness/Sudden Terror* 1971; *Pope Joan* 1972; *The Belstone Fox* 1973; *Leopard in the Snow, Caravans* (US/Iran) 1978; *The Prisoner of Zenda* 1979; *The Return of the Soldier, Uncommon Valor* 1983; *Top Secret!* (US) 1984; *When the Whales Came* 1989; *Four Weddings and a Funeral* 1994; *Angels & Insects* 1995.

Kemper, Victor J. Director of photography. Born on Apr. 14, 1927, in Newark, N.J. *ed.* Seton Hell. He began his career in 1949 as a TV engineer with New York's Channel 13. In 1954 he moved on to Screen Gems as technical supervisor, and later served as an engineering executive with other companies before becoming a cinematographer in the early 70s.

FILMS INCLUDE: *Husbands* 1970; *They Might Be Giants, The Hospital* 1971; *The Candidate* 1972; *Shamus, The Friends of Eddie Coyle* 1973; *The Gambler* 1974; *The Reincarnation of Peter Proud, Dog Day Afternoon* 1975; *Stay Hungry, The Last Tycoon, Mikey and Nicky* 1976; *Slap Shot, Audrey Rose, Oh God!* 1977; *Coma, Eyes of Laura Mars* 1978; *. . . And Justice for All, The Jerk* 1979; *The Final Countdown, Xanadu* 1980; *The Four Seasons* 1981; *Author! Author!* 1982; *National Lampoon's Vacation, Mr. Mom* 1983; *The Lonely Guy, Cloak and Dagger* 1984; *Pee-Wee's Big Adventure* 1985; *Hot to Trot* 1988; *See No Evil, Hear No Evil* 1989; *Crazy People* 1990; *FX 2: The Deadly Art of Illusion* 1991; *Another You, Married To It, Beethoven* 1992; *Tommy Boy* 1995; *Eddie, Jingle All the Way* 1996.

Kemplen, Ralph. Film editor. Born in 1912, in England. In British films as an apprentice from the early 30s, he rose to prominence in the 50s, when he began working on major productions for John Huston and other directors. He was nominated for Oscars for the editing of *Moulin Rouge* (1952), *Oliver!* (1968), and *The Day of the Jackal* (1973). He directed one film, the absurd ghostly crime melodrama *The Spaniard's Curse* (1958).

FILMS INCLUDE: *The Saint's Vacation* 1941; *Carnival* 1946; *Trottie True/The Gay Lady* 1949; *Pandora and the Flying Dutchman, The African Queen* 1951; *Moulin Rouge* 1952; *Beat the Devil* 1953; *Alexander the Great* 1956; *The Spaniard's Curse* (dir. only) 1958; *Room at the Top* 1959; *Freud* 1962; *The Night of the Iguana* 1964; *A Man for All Seasons* 1966; *Oliver!* 1968; *Goodbye, Mr. Chips* 1969; *The Day of the Jackal* 1973; *The Odessa File* 1974; *The Great Muppet Caper* 1981; *The Dark Crystal* 1982.

Kempson, Rachel. See REDGRAVE, Sir Michael.

Kendall, Kay. Actress. *b.* Justine Kay Kendall McCarthy, May 21, 1926, Withernsea, near Hull, England. *d.* 1959. A third-generation show-business performer, she joined the chorus line at the London Palladium at 13. Later she toured with her sister Kim in a music hall act and began playing minor roles in minor British films in 1944. After an interim period onstage in provincial repertory, she returned to the screen in 1950, playing somewhat bigger roles but still in minor films. Not until 1953 did she finally get her big break, in a tailor-made role in the hit comedy *Genevieve.* She subsequently proved herself one of the most delightful contemporary screen comediennes in both British and American films, often enlivening mediocre productions with her vivacious personality and keen sense of comedy timing. She was married to Rex HARRISON from 1957 until her death of leukemia two years later.

FILMS: *Fiddlers Three, Champagne Charlie, Dreaming* 1944; *Waltz Time, Caesar and Cleopatra* 1945; *Spring Song/Spring Time, London Town/My Heart Goes Crazy* 1946; *Night and the City, Dance Hall* 1950; *Happy Go Lovely, Lady Godiva Rides Again* 1951; *Wings of Danger/Dead on Course, Curtain Up, It Started in Paradise* 1952; *Mantrap/Man in Hiding, Street of Shadows/Shadow Man, The Square Ring, Genevieve, Meet Mr. Lucifer* 1953; *Fast and Loose, Doctor in the House* 1954; *The Constant Husband, Simon and Laura, The Adventures of Quentin Durward/Quentin Durward* 1955; *Abdullah the Great/Abdullah's Harem* (Egypt) 1956; *Les Girls* (US) 1957; *The Reluctant Debutante* (US) 1958; *Once More with Feeling* (US) 1960.

Kendall, Suzy. Actress. Born Frieda Harrison, in 1944, in Belper, England. *ed.* Derby Art Coll. A former fashion model and fabric designer, she played lead roles in British as well as Continental and Hollywood films from the mid-60s to the mid-70s, mainly in routine productions. She married actor Dudley MOORE in 1968. They later divorced.

FILMS INCLUDE: *The Liquidator* 1966; *Circus of Fear/Psycho-Circus, To Sir with Love, The Penthouse* 1967; *30 Is a Dangerous Age Cynthia, Up the Junction* 1968; *Fräulein Doktor* (It./Yug.) 1969; *The Gamblers* (US), *L'Uccello dalle Piume di Cristallo/The Bird with the Crystal Plumage* (It./Ger.), *Darker Than Amber* (US) 1970; *Assault/In the Devil's Garden* 1971; *Fear Is the Key* (US), *Tales That Witness Murder, Storia di una Monaca di Clasura/Diary of a Cloistered Nun* (It.) 1973; *Craze, Torso* (It.) 1974; *Spasmo* (It.), *Bis zur bitteren Neige/To the Bitter End* (Aus./Ger.) 1975; *Adventures of a Private Eye* 1975.

Kennedy, Arthur. Actor. *b.* John Arthur Kennedy, Feb. 17, 1914, Worcester, Mass. a dentist's son. *d.* 1990. *ed.* Carnegie Inst. of Technology. Onstage from 1934, he was brought to Hollywood by James CAGNEY, who saw him perform in Los Angeles, and made his screen debut in the role of the prodigy brother for whom Cagney sacrifices all in *City for Conquest* (1940). Dividing his time between coasts, Kennedy began building himself a reputation for excellence of performance on Broadway and in films. He triumphed on the stage in two Arthur

Miller plays of the late 40s, 'All My Sons' (1947) and 'Death of a Salesman' (1949). He won a Tony Award for his portrayal of Biff in the latter. He later starred in two more Miller plays, 'The Crucible' (1953) and 'The Price' (1968). In films, meanwhile, he demonstrated great versatility in a wide range of supporting roles and occasional leads, portraying with admirable subtlety a broad array of character shades ranging from benevolent to villainous, from dreamy idealist to cynical heel. He was nominated for Academy Awards as best actor for *Bright Victory* (1951) and as best supporting actor for *Champion* (1949), *Trial* (1955), *Peyton Place* (1957), and *Some Came Running* (1958). In the 70s he appeared in numerous cheap European melodramas and in TV movies. He was absent from the screen for much of the 80s, during which he battled thyroid cancer and eye disease. He died of a brain tumor at 76, survived by a daughter, actress Laurie Kennedy, from his marriage to stage actress Mary Cheffey.

FILMS: *City for Conquest* 1940; *High Sierra, Strange Alibi, Knockout, Highway West, Bad Men of Missouri* (as outlaw Jim Younger), *They Died with Their Boots On* 1941; *Desperate Journey* 1942; *Air Force* 1943; *Devotion* 1946; *Boomerang, Cheyenne* 1947; *Champion, The Window, Too Late for Tears, Chicago Deadline, The Walking Hills* 1949; *The Glass Menagerie* (as Tom Wingfield) 1950; *Bright Victory* 1951; *Bend of the River, Red Mountain, Rancho Notorious, The Girl in White, The Lusty Men* 1952; *Crashout, The Man from Laramie, The Desperate Hours, Trial, The Naked Dawn* 1955; *The Rawhide Years* 1956; *Peyton Place* 1957; *Twilight for the Gods* 1958; *Some Came Running, A Summer Place* 1959; *Elmer Gantry* 1960; *Home Is the Hero, Claudelle Inglish, Murder She Said* (UK), *Barabba/Barabbas* (as Pontius Pilate; It.) 1961; *Hemingway's Adventures of a Young Man, Lawrence of Arabia* (UK) 1962; *Italiani Brava Gente/Italiano Brava Gente* (It./USSR), *Cheyenne Autumn* (as Doc Holliday) 1964; *Joaquin Murrieta/Murieta* (Sp.), *Joy in the Morning* 1965; *Nevada Smith, Fantastic Voyage* 1966; *Il Chica del Lunes/Monday's Child* (Argen.) 1967; *Un Minuto per Pregare un Instante per Morire/A Minute to Pray a Second to Die/Escondido/Dead or Alive* (It./US), *Day of the Evil Gun, Lo Sbarco di Anzio/Anzio* (It.) 1968; *Shark!* (US/Mex.), *Hail Hero!* 1969; *My Old Man's Place/Glory Boy* 1971; *Bacciamo le Mani/Ferrente/Kiss My Hand/Mafia War/Family Killer* (It.) 1973; *Rico/The Dirty Mob* (It.), *Fin de Semana para los Muertos/The Living Dead at Manchester Morgue/Open the Window* (Sp./It.), *L'Anticristo/The Antichrist/The Tempter* (It.) 1974; *La Polizia ha le Mani legate/The Police Can't Move/Killer Cop* (It.) 1975; *Roma a Mano armata/Brutal Justice* (It.), *Una Spiaggia chiamata desiderio/Emmanuelle on Taboo Island* (It.), *Nove Ospiti per un Delitto/Nine Guests for a Crime* (It.) 1976; *The Sentinel, Porco Mondo* (It.), *Ab Morgen sind wir reich und ehrlich/Rich and Respectable* (Aus./Ger.), *Gli Ultimi Ageli/The Last Angels* (It.), *Ciclon/Cyclone* (Sp./It.) 1977; *Sono stato un Agene CIA/Covert Action* (It.), *La Cueve de los Tiburones/Cave of Sharks* (Sp./It.) 1978; *L'Umanoide/The Humanoid* (It.) 1979; *Due nelle Stelle* (It.) 1980; *Signs of Life* 1989; *Grandpa* 1990.

Kennedy, Burt. Director, screenwriter. Born on Sept. 3, 1922, in Muskegon, Mich. The youngest son of vaudevillians, he was four when he joined the family act, "The Dancing Kennedys." After completing high school, he joined the Army in 1942 and served three years in the Pacific as an officer with the First Cavalry Division. Discharged in 1946 with a Silver Star, Bronze Star, and Purple Heart with Oak Leaf Cluster, he became a radio writer, specializing in Western comedies. He broke into films in the mid-50s, when he was put under contract as a screenwriter by John Wayne's Batjac Productions. His early screenplays provided a robust foundation for several highly regarded Westerns directed by Budd BOETTICHER and starring Randolph SCOTT, as well as for other spirited Westerns and action pictures of the period. Kennedy made an unsuccessful debut as a director in 1961 with *The Canadians,* a corny Indian vs. settler saga, then retreated into TV, directing and writing scripts for 'The Lawman,' 'The Virginian,' and 'Combat,' among other action series. He returned to the big screen in 1963, and in the following year had his first success with *The Rounders,* an agreeable, contemporary Western laced with humor. Kennedy had perhaps his strongest outing as a director with *Welcome to Hard Times* (1967), an intriguing, hard-hitting morality tale, adapted from an E. L. Doctorow novel. With few exceptions, his subsequent films were characteristically relaxed, casually paced near-parodies of the Western genre. His more recent output comprises many TV movies.

FILMS: As screenwriter—*Seven Men from Now, Gun the Man Down, Man in the Vault* 1956; *The Tall T* 1957; *Fort Dobbs* 1958; *Ride Lonesome, Yellowstone Kelly* 1959; *Comanche Station* 1960; *Six Black Horses* 1962; *Stay Away, Joe* 1968; *The Littlest Horsethiefs* 1977; *White Hunter, Black Heart* 1990. As director—*The Canadians* (also. sc.) 1961; *Mail Order Bride* (also sc.) 1964; *The Rounders* (also sc.) 1965; *The Money Trap, Return of the Seven* 1966; *Welcome to Hard Times* (also sc.), *The War Wagon* 1967; *Support Your Local Sheriff, Young Billy Young* (also sc.), *The Good Guys and the Bad Guys* 1969; *Dirty Dingus Magee* 1970; *Support Your Local Gunfighter* (also exec. prod.), *Hannie Caulder* (also sc. under pseudonym Z. X. Jones; UK), *La Spina Dorsale del Diavolo/The Deserter* (It./Yug.) 1971; *The Train Robbers* (also sc.) 1973; *The Killer Inside Me* 1976; *Wolf Lake* (also sc.) 1979; *The Trouble with Spies* (also prod., sc.; release delayed from 1984) 1987; *Big Bad John* (also sc.) 1990; *Suburban Commando* 1991; *All the Kind Strangers* 1992.

Kennedy, Douglas. Actor. *b.* Sept. 14, 1915, New York City. *d.* 1973. *ed.* Deerfield Acad.; Amherst. Character player and occasional leading man of Hollywood films. He made his screen debut in 1940 and played a number of supporting roles, some under the name Keith Douglas. His career was interrupted by WW II service as a major in the Signal Corps and later with the OSS and Army Intelligence. He then returned to films and played character roles, often villainous, in numerous productions, as well as isolated leads in low-budget pictures. He starred in the TV series 'Steve Donovan—Western Marshal.'

FILMS INCLUDE: *The Ghost Breakers, The Way of All Flesh, North West Mounted Police* 1940; *The Roundup* 1941; *Nora Prentiss, Possessed, The Unfaithful, Dark Passage* 1947; *To the Victor, Adventures of Don Juan, Whiplash* 1948; *South of St. Louis* 1949; *East Side West Side, Chain Gang, Montana* 1950; *Revenue Agent, I Was an American Spy, The Texas Rangers, Callaway Went Thataway* 1951; *Indian Uprising, Last Train from Bombay* 1952; *Gun Belt* 1953; *Sitting Bull* 1954; *The Eternal Sea* 1955; *The Last Wagon* 1956; *Chicago Confidential, Rockabilly Baby* 1957; *The Lone Ranger and the Lost City of Gold* 1958; *The Alligator People* 1959; *The Amazing Transparent Man* 1960; *Flight of the Lost Balloon* 1961; *The Fastest Guitar Alive* 1967; *The Destructors* 1968.

Kennedy, Edgar. Actor, director. *b.* Apr. 26, 1890, Monterey, Calif. *d.* 1948. After four years of clowning and singing in vaudeville and musical comedy, he began his film career in 1914 in Keystone comedies, playing second banana to Charlie CHAPLIN and other comedy stars. He remained with Mack SENNETT for several years. In the 20s he began playing comic character parts in feature films in addition to his appearances in comedy shorts. In 1928, he joined the Hal ROACH studio, where he gained popularity in a number of LAUREL AND HARDY comedies, two of which he directed, using the name E.

Livingston Kennedy. It was during this period that he perfected his trademark, the "slow burn," a delayed explosive reaction to frustrating situations. Before leaving Roach in 1930, Kennedy also appeared in several "Our Gang" comedies. Beginning in 1931 he starred in a popular two-reel comedy series, originally called "The Average Man" and later "The Edgar Kennedy series," depicting the everyday tribulations of the average Joe American, henpecked by wife, harassed by mother-in-law, and unable to cope with the pressures of modern living. The series lasted for 17 years, until Kennedy's death of throat cancer. Many of the films have been recently popping up on late night TV. He also appeared in scores of feature films up to his death.

FILMS INCLUDE: (shorts denoted by "s"): *Hoffmeyer's Legacy* (s) 1912; *The Star Boarder* (s), *Caught in a Cabaret* (s), *The Knockout* (s), *Tillie's Punctured Romance, Getting Acquainted* (s), *The Noise of Bombs* (s) 1914; *A Game Old Knight* (s), *The Great Vacuum Robbery* (s) 1915; *His Hereafter* (s), *His Bitter Pill* (s), *A Scoundrel's Toll* (s) 1916; *Her Fame and Shame* (s), *Her Torpedoed Love* (s), *Oriental Love* (s) 1917; *She Loved Him Plenty* (s) 1918; *Skirts* 1921; *The Night Message, The Battling Fool* 1924; *The Marriage Circus* (s; co-dir. with Reggie Morris only), *Cupid's Boots* (s; dir. only), *The Golden Princes, His People/Proud Heart* 1925; *My Old Dutch, The Better 'Ole, Across the Pacific, Going Crooked* 1926; *Finger Prints, The Wrong Mr. Wright, Wedding Bill$, The Chinese Parrot* 1927; *From Soup to Nuts* (s; dir. only), *You're Darn Tootin'* (s; dir. only), *Two Tars* (s), *A Pair of Tights* (s) 1928; *Trent's Last Case, They Had to See Paris, Perfect Day* (s), *Bacon Grabbers* (s), *Angora Love* (s), *Moan and Groan* (s) 1929; *Shivering Shakespeare* (s), *Night Owls* (s) 1930; *Rough House Rhythm* (s), *Lemon Meringue* (s), *Bad Company* 1931; *Bon Voyage* (s), *Carnival Boat, Mother-in-Law's Day* (s), *Hold 'Em Jail!, Parlor Bedroom and Wrath* (s) 1932; *Art in the Raw* (s), *The Merchant of Menace* (s), *Good House-wrecking* (s), *Professional Sweetheart, Tillie and Gus, Grin and Bear It* (s), *Duck Soup* 1933; *All of Me, Twentieth Century, Murder on the Blackboard, In-Laws Are Out* (s), *A Blasted Event* (s), *Kid Millions* 1934; *Bric-a-Brac* (s), *Living on Velvet, Edgar Hamlet* (s), *Little Big Shot, Happy Tho Married* (s), *The Bride Comes Home* 1935; *Gasoloons* (s), *The Robin Hood of El Dorado, Small Town Girl, High Beer Pressure* (s), *San Francisco, Dummy Ache* (s), *Yours for the Asking, Mad Holiday, Three Men on a Horse* 1936; *Bad Housekeeping* (s), *Locks and Bonds* (s), *A Star Is Born, Dumb's the Word* (s), *Super-Sleuth, Double Wedding, Edgar and Goliath* (s), *True Confession* 1937; *Hollywood Hotel, False Roomers* (s), *Kennedy's Castle* (s), *Fool Coverage* (s), *Beaux and Errors* (s) 1938; *Peck's Bad Boy with the Circus, Maid to Order* (s), *It's a Wonderful World, Kennedy the Great* (s) 1939; *Mutiny in the County* (s), *The Quarterback* 1940; *It Happened All Night* (s), *The Bride Wore Crutches* 1941; *Heart Burn* (s), *In Old California* 1942; *Hold Your Temper* (s), *The Falcon Strikes Back, Air Raid Wardens, Hitler's Madman, Crazy House* 1943; *Prunes and Politics* (s), *It Happened Tomorrow, The Kitchen Cynic* (s) 1944; *Anchors Aweigh, You Drive Me Crazy* (s), *Captain Tugboat Annie* 1945; *Trouble or Nothing* (s), *Wall Street Blues* (s), *Noisy Neighbors* (s) 1946; *Do or Diet* (s), *Host to a Ghost* (s), *Television Turmoil* (s), *Mad Wednesday, Heaven Only Knows* 1947; *No More Relatives* (s), *Unfaithfully Yours* 1948; *My Dream Is Yours* 1949.

Kennedy, George. Actor. Born on Feb. 18, 1925, in New York City. Brawny, hale character lead and supporting player of Hollywood films. The son of an orchestra leader and a ballet dancer, he began appearing onstage at two and spent many of his young years as a radio performer. He enlisted in the Army during WW II and served 16 years, both in combat and later as an armed forces radio and TV officer. He returned to civilian life as a technical adviser on the 'Sergeant Bilko' TV series and later began acting in various TV shows and in the early 60s also in films. Physically rugged (6' 4", 230 pounds), he started out as a heavy but gradually moved into more important, more subtle, often sympathetic roles. He won an Academy Award as best supporting actor for his performance in *Cool Hand Luke* (1967). He directed a short, *Two Songs* (1965).

FILMS INCLUDE: *The Little Shepherd of Kingdom Come* 1961; *Lonely Are the Brave, The Silent Witness* 1962; *The Man from the Diner's Club, Charade* 1963; *Island of the Blue Dolphins, Strait-Jacket, McHale's Navy* 1964; *Hush Hush... Sweet Charlotte, In Harm's Way, Mirage, Shenandoah, The Sons of Katie Elder* 1965; *The Flight of the Phoenix* 1966; *Hurry Sundown, The Dirty Dozen, Cool Hand Luke* 1967; *The Ballad of Josie, The Legend of Lylah Clare* (bit), *Bandolero!, The Pink Jungle, The Boston Strangler* 1968; *Guns of the Magnificent Seven, The Good Guys and the Bad Guys, Gaily Gaily* 1969; *Tick...Tick... Tick..., Airport, Zigzag, Dirty Dingus Magee* 1970; *Fools' Parade* 1971; *The Family* (It.) 1972; *Lost Horizon, Cahill—US Marshal* 1973; *Thunderbolt and Lightfoot, Airport 1975, Earthquake* 1974; *The Eiger Sanction, The Human Factor* 1975; *Airport '77, Proof of the Man* (Jap.) 1977; *Mean Dog Blues, Death on the Nile, Brass Target* (as Gen. George S. Patton, Jr.) 1978; *The Double McGuffin, The Concorde—Airport '79* 1979; *Death Ship* (Can.), *Steel/Look Down and Die/Men of Steel, Virus* (Jap.) 1980; *Modern Romance* 1981; *Rare Breed, Bolero, Chattanooga Choo Choo* 1984; *The Delta Force, Radioactive Dreams* 1986; *Creepshow 2* 1987; *Born to Race, The Naked Gun: From the Files of Police Squad* 1988; *The Terror Within, Brain Dead, Ministry of Vengeance* 1989; *Hangfire* 1990; *The Naked Gun 2½* 1991; *Driving Me Crazy, Distant Justice* 1992; *Naked Gun 33⅓: The Final Insult* 1994.

Kennedy, Joseph P. Financier. *b.* Sept. 6, 1888, Boston. *d.* 1969. A noted businessman and public servant, father of a US President and two senators, he was deeply involved in the film business in the 20s and 30s. In 1926 he bought out a film distribution and production company, Film Booking Offices of America (FBO), of which he became president and chairman of the board. In 1928 he became chairman of the Keith-Albee-Orpheum corporation. Later that year he sold out his interests to RCA and acquired an interest in Pathé Exchange, of which he was president and director until 1930, when the company merged into RKO. His activities included those of executive producer for the films of Gloria Swanson. In 1936 he served as special advisor to Paramount Pictures.

Kennedy, Kathleen. See MARSHALL, Frank.

Kennedy, Leon Isaac. Actor. Born in 1949, in Cleveland. Presentable, black leading man of the American screen. Occasionally writes his own material.

FILMS: *Penitentiary* 1979; *Body and Soul* (also sc.) 1981; *Penitentiary II* 1982; *Lone Wolf McQuade* 1983; *Too Scared to Scream* 1985; *Knights of the City* (also co-prod., co-story, sc.), *Hollywood Vice Squad* 1986; *Penitentiary III* (also co-prod.) 1987; *Skeleton Coast* 1989.

Kennedy, Madge. Actress. *b.* 1890, Chicago. *d.* 1987. A popular Broadway ingenue, she was recruited into films by Sam Goldwyn in 1917. She starred in many Hollywood silents, typically in reserved, ladylike roles, but kept her stage career alive with frequent Broadway appearances, notably in 'Poppy' (1923) with W. C. Fields. In the mid-20s she retired from the screen, returning briefly to Broadway. Little was heard of her in the 30s and 40s, but in the early 50s she returned to the screen in character parts and in 1965 she was seen on Broadway in 'A Very Rich Woman.' She died at 96, leaving no survivors.

FILMS INCLUDE: *Baby Mine, Nearly Married* 1917; *The Danger Game, The Fair Pretender, The Service Star, Friendly Husband, The Kingdom of Youth, A Perfect Lady* 1918; *Day Dreams, Leave It to Susan, Through the Wrong Door, Strictly Confidential* 1919; *The Blooming Angel, Dollars and Sense, The Truth* 1920; *Oh Mary Be Careful, The Girl with a Jazz Heart, The Highest Bidder* 1921; *The Purple Highway* 1923; *Three Miles Out* 1924; *Scandal Street, Bad Company, Lying Wives* 1925; *Oh Baby!* 1926; *The Marrying Kind* 1952; *The Rains of Ranchipur* 1955; *Three Bad Sisters, The Catered Affair, Lust for Life* 1956; *Let's Make Love* 1960; *They Shoot Horses Don't They?* 1969; *The Baby Maker* 1970; *The Day of the Locust* 1975.

Kennedy, Merna. Actress. *b.* Maude Kahler, Sept. 7, 1908, Kankakee, Ill. *d.* 1944. Onstage from age nine, she was discovered by Charlie Chaplin, who made her his leading lady in *The Circus.* She subsequently starred in early sound films but retired in 1934 to marry director Busby BERKELEY. They divorced the following year. She died of a heart attack at 35.

FILMS INCLUDE: *The Circus* 1928; *Broadway, Barnum Was Right, Skinner Steps Out* 1929; *The Rampant Age, Embarrassing Moments, The King of Jazz, Worldly Goods, The Midnight Special* 1930; *Stepping Out* 1931; *Lady with a Past, The Gay Buckaroo, Ghost Valley, The All American, Red-Haired Alibi* 1932; *Laughter in Hell, Emergency Call, Arizona to Broadway, Don't Bet On Love, Police Call, Easy Millions* 1933; *Wonder Bar, I Like It That Way, Jimmy the Gent* 1934.

Kennedy, Tom. Actor. *b.* 1884, New York City. *d.* 1965. A former amateur boxer, he entered films late in 1915 and played second bananas in Mack SENNETT's Keystone comedies for several years. Beefy and flat-nosed, he later played character roles in more than 100 silent and sound features as well as innumerable shorts, including several Laurel and Hardy comedies. He often played dumb but lovable cops, cabbies, or bartenders.

FILMS INCLUDE: *Double Trouble* 1915; *The Village Blacksmith, Hearts and Sparks* 1916; *The Pullman Bride* 1917; *Mickey, Sleuths* 1918; *Kismet* 1920; *Skirts, Serenade* 1921; *Our Leading Citizen, The Flirt* 1922; *With Naked Fists, Scaramouche* 1923; *Madonna of the Streets* 1924; *As Man Desires* 1925; *The Yankee Senor, Behind the Front, Mantrap, We're in the Navy Now, Man of the Forest* 1926; *Fireman Save My Child* 1927; *Alias the Deacon, Wife Savers, Tillie's Punctured Romance, The Cop* 1928; *Liberty, The Cohens and Kellys in Atlantic City, Big News, The Shannons of Broadway* 1929; *The Big House, See America Thirst* 1930; *The Gang Buster, It Pays to Advertise, Monkey Business* 1931; *Pack Up Your Troubles* 1932; *She Done Him Wrong* 1933; *Hollywood Party* 1934; *Bright Lights* 1935; *Poppy* 1936; *The Adventurous Blonde* 1937; *Torchy Blane in Panama* 1938; *Remember the Night* 1940; *Ladies' Day* 1943; *The Princess and the Pirate* 1945; *Bringing Up Father* 1946; *The Pretender* 1947; *The Paleface* 1948; *Invasion USA* 1952; *Gold Fever* 1953; *It's a Mad Mad Mad Mad World* 1963; *The Bounty Killer* 1965.

Kensit, Patsy. Actress. Born on Mar. 4, 1968, in London. Former child screen and TV star who established herself in films as an adult. Debuting on-screen at age four in *The Great Gatsby*, she also appeared in commercials directed by Adrian Lyne and Tony Scott.

FILMS INCLUDE: *The Great Gatsby* 1974; *Alfie Darling* 1975; *The Blue Bird* 1976; *Hanover Street* 1979; *Absolute Beginners* 1986; *A Chorus of Disapproval* 1988; *Lethal Weapon 2, Bullseye!* 1989; *Chicago Joe and the Showgirl* 1990; *Blame It on the Bellboy, Blue Tornado, Does This Mean We're Married?/Les Epoux Ripoux* (Fr.), *Prince of Shadows, Twenty-One, Timebomb* 1991; *The Turn of the Screw* (Fr./UK) 1992; *Bitter Harvest, Kleptomania* 1993; *Angels & Insects* 1995; *Grace of My Heart* 1996.

Kent, Barbara. Actress. Born Barbara Klowtman, on Dec. 16, 1906, in Gadsby, Canada. Leading lady of Hollywood films, she starred in some late silents and early talkies, often opposite Reginald DENNY and twice opposite Harold Lloyd.

FILMS INCLUDE: *Prowlers of the Night* 1926; *Flesh and the Devil, No Man's Law, The Drop Kick, The Lone Eagle, The Small Bachelor* 1927; *That's My Daddy, Stop That Man, Modern Mothers, Lonesome* 1928; *The Shakedown, Welcome Danger* 1929; *Night Ride, What Men Want, Dumbbells in Ermine, Feet First* 1930; *Indiscreet, Chinatown After Dark* 1931; *Emma, Vanity Fair* (as Amelia Sedley), *Exposed, Pride of the Legion* 1932; *The Big Pay-Off, Oliver Twist* (as Rose Maylie), *Marriage on Approval* 1933; *Old Man Rhythm, Swell Head* 1935; *Under Age* 1941.

Kent, Charles. American director, actor. *b.* 1852. *d.* 1923. He directed a number of prestigious early silents for Vitagraph, mainly literary adaptations, sometimes starring in his own productions. Among the first to use the close-up creatively on the screen, he was attacked by contemporary critics for "the pernicious habit of cutting characters off at the knees." While pursuing his career as a director, Kent appeared as an actor in many films made by others. In 1913 he retired from directing but remained in films as an actor until his death.

FILMS INCLUDE: As director—*Antony and Cleopatra* 1908; *A Midsummer Night's Dream* 1909; *Twelfth Night* (also act.) 1910; *Barnaby Rudge, A Christmas Carol, Vanity Fair* (also act.) 1911; *Fortunes of a Composer, Rip Van Winkle* (also act.) 1912; *The Tables Turned* 1913. As actor—*Uncle Tom's Cabin, A Dixie Mother* 1910; *A Tale of Two Cities, The Death of King Edward III, Daniel* 1911; *As You Like It* 1912; *The Doctor's Secret* 1913; *The Christian, A Million Bid* 1914; *The Battle Cry of Peace, On Her Wedding Night, A Price for Folly* 1915; *Kennedy Square, The Supreme Temptation, Tarantula, Rose of the South, The Enemy, Whom the Gods Destroy* 1916; *Soldiers of Chance* 1917; *Wild Primrose* 1918; *Gamblers* 1919; *Man and His Woman/Body and Soul, The Forbidden Valley* 1920; *The Charming Deceiver, Rainbow* 1921; *The Prodigal Judge* 1922; *The Leopardess, The Purple Highway* 1923.

Kent, Christopher. See KJELLIN, Alf.

Kent, Jean. Actress. Born Joan Summerfield, on June 21, 1921, in London. Onstage as a child dancer from age 11, she played leading roles in some British films of the 40s and 50s. For a time professionally known as Jean Carr.

FILMS INCLUDE: *Rocks of Valpre* 1935; *Hullo Fame* 1940; *It's That Man Again* 1942; *Fanny by Gaslight/Man of Evil, 2000 Women, Champagne Charlie, Madonna of the Seven Moons, Waterloo Road* 1944; *The Rake's Progress/Notorious Gentleman, The Wicked Lady* 1945; *Caravan, Carnival, The Magic Bow* 1946; *The Man Within/The Smugglers, Bond Street* 1947; *Sleeping Car to Trieste, Good Time Girl* 1948; *Trottie True/The Gay Lady* 1949; *The Reluctant Widow, The Woman in Question* 1950; *The Browning Version* 1951; *Before I Wake* 1954; *The Prince and the Showgirl* 1957; *Bonjour Tristesse, Grip of the Strangler/The Haunted Strangler* 1958; *Please Turn Over* 1959; *Bluebeard's Ten Honeymoons* 1960; *Shout at the Devil* 1976.

Kenton, Erle C. Director. *b.* Aug. 1, 1896, Norboro, Mont. *d.* 1980. He entered films in 1914 as actor and jack-of-all-trades with Mack SENNETT and by 1919 was directing two-reel shorts for the comedy king. He moved on to feature films in 1920 and subsequently directed scores of silent and sound films for various studios, mainly low- to medium-budget productions. His films include several rather interesting horror pictures and a number of Abbott and Costello comedies. In the 50s he switched to TV.

FEATURE FILMS: *Down on the Farm, Married Life, Love Honor and Behave* (co-dir. with Richard Jones) 1920; *A Small Town Idol* 1921; *Tea with a Kick* 1923; *The Danger Signal, A Fool and His Money, Red Hot Tires* 1925; *The Palm Beach Girl, The Sap, Love Toy, Other Women's Husbands* 1926; *The Girl in the Pullman, Wedding Bills$, The Rejuvenation of Aunt Mary* 1927; *Bare Knees, The Companionate Marriage, Golf Widows, Name the Woman, Nothing to Wear, The Side Show, The Sporting Age, The Street of Illusion* 1928; *Father and Son, Trial Marriage, The Song of Love, Mexicali Rose* 1929; *A Royal Romance* 1930; *The Last Parade, Lover Come Back, Leftover Ladies, X Marks the Spot* 1931; *Stranger in Town, Guilty as Hell, Island of Lost Souls* 1932; *From Hell to Heaven, Disgraced, Big Executive* 1933; *Search for Beauty, You're Telling Me* 1934; *Best Man Wins, Party Wire, The Public Menace, Grand Exit* 1935; *Devil's Squadron, Counterfeit, End of the Trail* (also cameo, as Teddy Roosevelt) 1936; *Devil's Playground, Racketeers in Exile, She Asked for It* 1937; *The Lady Objects, Little Tough Guys in Society* 1938; *Everything's on Ice, Escape to Paradise* 1939; *Remedy for Riches* 1940; *Petticoat Politics, Melody for Three, Naval Academy, They Meet Again, Flying Cadets* 1941; *Frisco Lil, North to the Klondike, The Ghost of Frankenstein, Pardon My Sarong, Who Done It?* 1942; *How's About It?, It Ain't Hay, Always a Bridesmaid* 1943; *House of Frankenstein, She Gets Her Man, House of Dracula* 1945; *The Cat Creeps, Little Miss Big* 1946; *Bob and Sally* 1948; *One Too Many* 1950.

Kenyon, Doris. Actress. *b.* Sept. 5, 1897, Syracuse, N.Y. *d.* 1979. The daughter of a clergyman-poet, she made her stage and screen debuts at 18. Played pleasant leads in many silent films opposite such stars as Rudolph Valentino, Thomas Meighan, Lewis Stone, and Milton SILLS, who became the first of her four husbands in 1926. She made a smooth transition to sound and continued playing leads and supporting roles through the late 30s. In 1964 she appeared in the TV series 'The Tycoon.'

FILMS INCLUDE: *The Rack* 1915; *The Feast of Life, The Ocean Waif, The Pawn of Fate* 1916; *A Girl's Folly, The Empress, The Great White Trail* 1917; *The Hidden Hand* (serial) 1917–18; *The Street of Seven Stars, The Inn of the Blue Moon* 1918; *Wild Honey, Twilight, The Bandbox* 1919; *The Harvest Moon* 1920; *The Conquest of Canaan, Get-Rich-Quick Wallingford* 1921; *The Ruling Passion, Shadows of the Sea* 1922; *You Are Guilty, The Last Moment, Bright Lights of Broadway* 1923; *Restless Wives, Monsieur Beaucaire, Idle Tongues* 1924; *If I Marry Again, A Thief in Paradise, I Want My Man, The Half-Way Girl, The Unguarded Hour* 1925; *Men of Steel, Ladies at Play, Mismates, The Blonde Saint* 1926; *The Valley of the Giants* 1927; *Burning Daylight, The Hawk's Nest, Interference, The Home Towners* 1928; *Beau Bandit* 1930; *The Bargain, Alexander Hamilton* (as Betsy Hamilton), *Road to Singapore, The Ruling Voice* 1931; *Young America, The Man Called Back* 1932; *No Marriage Ties, Voltaire* (as Madame Pompadour), *Counsellor-at-Law* 1933; *Whom the Gods Destroy, The Human Side* 1934; *Girls' School* 1938; *The Man in the Iron Mask* (as Queen Anne) 1939.

Kerima. Actress. Born in 1925, in Algiers. Exotic leading lady and supporting player of a number of international films of the 50s and early 60s. Most memorable in her screen debut as the feminine lead in Carol Reed's *An Outcast of the Islands* (1951).

FILMS INCLUDE: *An Outcast of the Islands* (UK) 1951; *La Lupa/The She-Wolf* (It.) 1952; *La Nave delle Donne Maledette/The Ship of Condemned Women* (It.), *Cavalleria Rusticana/Fatal Desire* (as Lola; It.) 1953; *Tam Tam Mayumbe* (It./Fr.), *Land of the Pharaohs* (US) 1955; *Fuga nel Sole* (It./Fr.) 1956; *The Quiet American* (US) 1958; *Il Mondo dei Miracoli* 1959; *Jessica* (US/Fr./It.) 1962.

Kern, Hal C. Film editor. *b.* July 14, 1894, Anaconda, Mont. *d.* 1985. He began his career in 1915, cutting shorts at Inceville. A nitrate fire that started in his cutting room during the editing of Thomas H. Ince's epic, *Civilization* (1916), destroyed the entire studio, forcing him to move to Culver City. He rose to prominence in the 20s, when he worked on a number of distinguished productions and was in charge of editing for Joseph M. SCHENCK at United Artists. In 1933 he joined MGM, and in the following year went to work for Selznick International, where he remained for more than a decade. He shared the Academy Award for editing *Gone With the Wind* (1939) and was nominated for Oscars for *Rebecca* (1940) and *Since You Went Away* (1944). He ended his career in a supervisory capacity at Paramount. His brother, Robert J. KERN, was a distinguished film editor for MGM, who was responsible for cutting many of the studio's top productions of the 30s and 40s and won an Academy Award for *National Velvet* (1945).

FILMS INCLUDE: *The Toll of the Sea* 1922; *Brass* 1923; *Her Night of Romance* 1924; *The Eagle* 1925; *The Bat* 1926; *The Dove* 1927; *The Woman Disputed* 1928; *Alibi, The Locked Door, New York Nights* 1929; *Puttin' on the Ritz, Abraham Lincoln* 1930; *The Bat Whispers, Corsair, Reaching for the Moon* 1931; *Night Flight* 1933; *The Garden of Allah* 1936; *A Star Is Born, The Prisoner of Zenda* 1937; *Little Lord Fauntleroy, The Young in Heart, The Adventures of Tom Sawyer* 1938; *Intermezzo: A Love Story, Made for Each Other, Gone With the Wind* 1939; *Rebecca* 1940; *Stage Door Canteen* 1943; *Spellbound* 1945; *Duel in the Sun* 1946; *The Paradine Case* 1947.

Kern, James V. Director. *b.* Sept. 22, 1909, New York City. *d.* 1966. A former lawyer, he directed a number of mediocre films and hundreds of TV shows. He also wrote a number of screenplays for the films of other directors.

FILMS WITH: (as director): *The Doughgirls* (also sc.) 1944; *Never Say Goodbye* (also sc.) 1946; *Stallion Road* 1947; *April Showers* 1948; *The Second Woman, Two Tickets to Broadway* 1951; *Lum and Abner Abroad* (also prod., sc.) 1956.

Kern, Jerome. Composer. *b.* Jan. 27, 1885, New York City. *d.* 1945. The celebrated creator of stage musicals and popular songs also contributed scores and songs, as well as screenplays, directly for the screen. The son of a furniture dealer, he composed his first song at 17, in 1902, and had his first of many hits in 1905. Early in his career he wrote songs mainly for incorporation into musical imports from Europe to Broadway, particularly operettas. But soon he began composing his own musicals, achieving considerable success with his melodious scores and songs. His most popular musical, 'Show Boat,' has been adapted to the screen three times, in 1929, 1936, and 1951. In 1930, Kern settled in Hollywood and began to write original scores and songs for many films, in addition to adaptations of his stage musicals. His first film score was an accompaniment to the silent serial *Gloria's Romance* (1916). He won Oscars for the song 'The Way You Look Tonight' from the film *Swing Time* (1936) and 'The Last Time I Saw Paris' from *Lady Be Good* (1941). Among his best-known songs are 'Ol' Man River,' 'Smoke Gets in Your Eyes,' 'Look for the Silver Lining,' 'They Didn't Believe Me,' and 'Why Do I Love You?' His life story was told in the film *Till the Clouds Roll By* (1946), in which he was portrayed by Robert Walker.

FILMS INCLUDE: *Gloria's Romance* (serial) 1916; *Sally, Show Boat* 1929; *The Three Sisters, Sunny* 1930; *The Cat and the Fiddle, Music in the Air, Sweet Adeline* 1934; *Roberta, Reckless, I Dream Too Much* 1935; *Show Boat, Swing Time*

1936; *When You're in Love, High Wide and Handsome* 1937; *Joy of Living* 1938; *One Night in the Tropics* 1940; *Sunny* (remake), *Lady Be Good* 1941; *You Were Never Lovelier* 1942; *Song of Russia, Cover Girl, Broadway Rhythm, Can't Help Singing* 1944; *Centennial Summer, Till the Clouds Roll By* 1946; *Show Boat* 1951; *Lovely to Look At* 1952.

Kerr, Deborah. Actress. Born Deborah J. Kerr-Trimmer, on Sept. 30, 1921, in Helensburgh, Scotland. Trained as a dancer at her aunt's drama school in Bristol, England, she won a scholarship to the Sadler's Wells ballet school and at 17 made her London debut in the *corps de ballet* of 'Prometheus.' However, she soon discovered that she was more interested in drama and began playing bits and walk-ons in various Shakespearean productions. In the early 40s she made her British film debut as a Salvation Army lass in *Major Barbara.* Other film roles followed in which she typically played cool and reserved well-bred ladies. In 1947, on the strength of her sensitive portrayal of a nun in *Black Narcissus,* she was brought to Hollywood by MGM to play the lead opposite Clark Gable in *The Hucksters.* She retained her serene, ladylike image on the American screen until 1953, when she was given the opportunity to play, on a loan-out to Columbia, a turbulent adulteress in *From Here to Eternity.* She has since played a wider variety of characters of a broader emotional range while maintaining a ladylike poise. She was nominated for a best actress Oscar six times, for *Edward My Son* (1949), *From Here to Eternity* (1953), *The King and I* (1956), *Heaven Knows Mr. Allison* (1957), *Separate Tables* (1958), and *The Sundowners* (1960). She remained a leading star throughout her screen career until her announced retirement in 1969. She has since returned occasionally to the stage, and appeared in a feature and several TV movies. Her second husband (since 1960) is novelist and screenwriter Peter Viertel. They make their home in Switzerland.

FILMS: In the UK—*Major Barbara* (as Jenny Hill), *Love on the Dole, Penn of Pennsylvania/Courageous Mr. Penn, Hatter's Castle* 1941; *The Day Will Dawn/The Avengers* 1942; *The Life and Death of Colonel Blimp* 1943; *Perfect Strangers/Vacation from Marriage* 1945; *I See a Dark Stranger/The Adventuress* 1946; *Black Narcissus* 1947. In the US—*The Hucksters* 1947; *If Winter Comes* 1948; *Edward My Son* 1949; *Please Believe Me, King Solomon's Mines* 1950; *Quo Vadis* (as Lygia) 1951; *The Prisoner of Zenda* (as Princess Flavia) 1952; *Thunder in the East, Young Bess* (as Catherine Parr), *Julius Caesar* (as Portia), *Dream Wife, From Here to Eternity* (as Karen Holmes) 1953; *The End of the Affair* (UK) 1954; *The Proud and the Profane, The King and I* (as Anna), *Tea and Sympathy* (as Laura Reynolds) 1956; *Heaven Knows Mr. Allison, An Affair to Remember* 1957; *Bonjour Tristesse* (UK), *Separate Tables* 1958; *The Journey, Count Your Blessings, Beloved Infidel* (as Sheilah Graham) 1959; *The Sundowners, The Grass Is Greener* 1960; *The Naked Edge* (UK/US), *The Innocents* (UK/US) 1961; *The Chalk Garden* (UK) 1963; *The Night of the Iguana* 1964; *Marriage on the Rocks* 1965; *Eye of the Devil* (UK), *Casino Royale* (UK) 1967; *Prudence and the Pill* (UK) 1968; *The Gypsy Moths, The Arrangement* 1969; *The Assam Garden* (UK) 1985.

Kerr, John. Actor. Born on Nov. 15, 1931, in New York City. The son of an actor and actress, he went onstage immediately after graduating from Harvard and played an important part in Broadway's 'Bernadine' (1952). The following year he made his mark as the shy, sensitive lead in 'Tea and Sympathy,' a role he was to repeat in the 1956 film version. He starred in a handful of films till early in the 60s. He played an assistant district attorney in the TV series 'Arrest and Trial' (1963–64) and a D.A. in 'Peyton Place' (1965–66). Now a practicing attorney, he still appears occasionally on TV. Both of his parents, Geoffrey Kerr (*b.* Jan. 25, 1895, London) and June Walker (*b.* June 14, 1904, N.Y.C.; *d.* 1966), were successful Broadway stars who appeared sporadically on the screen.

FILMS: *The Cobweb* 1955; *Gabby, Tea and Sympathy* (as Tom Robinson Lee) 1956; *The Vintage* 1957; *South Pacific* (as Lt. Cable) 1958; *Girl of the Night, The Crowded Sky* 1960; *The Pit and the Pendulum, Seven Women from Hell* 1961.

Kerrigan, J(ack) Warren. Actor. *b.* July 25, 1889, Louisville, Ky. *d.* 1947. A leading star of the silent American screen, one of the most popular screen personalities of his day. He entered films late in 1909 and before long became known as "The Gibson Man," to suggest that he was as handsome as the famous Gibson Girl was beautiful. Between 1910 and 1924 he appeared in hundreds of films, typically as a dashing hero. He retired from the screen at the height of his success, shortly after playing two of his most famous roles, as the hero of James Cruze's Western saga *The Covered Wagon* (1923) and the title role in the silent version of *Captain Blood* (1924).

FILMS INCLUDE: *A Voice from the Fireplace, The Hand of Uncle Sam* 1910; *The Genius, The Sheriff's Sisters* 1911; *The Agitator/The Cowboy Socialist, The Stranger at Coyote, The Animal Within* 1912; *Calamity Anne's Inheritance, Ashes of Three, Angel of the Canyons, The Wishing Seat, The Adventures of Jacques, Tom Blake's Redemption, For the Flag, In the Days of Trajan* 1913; *The Man Who Lied, Samson, His Heart His Hand and His Sword, The Widow's Secret* (also dir.), *Landon's Legacy* 1915; *The Gay Lord Waring, A Son of the Immortals, The Silent Battle, The Beckoning Trail, The Social Buccaneer* 1916; *A Man's Man* 1917; *One Dollar Bid, Prisoners of the Pines, Three X Gordon* 1918; *The End of the Game, The Best Man, The Drifters, The Joyous Liar* 1919; *The Dream Cheater, The Green Flame, House of Whispers, The Coast of Opportunity* 1920; *The Covered Wagon, The Girl of the Golden West, Thundering Dawn, The Man from Brodney's* 1923; *Captain Blood* 1924.

Kerrigan, J(oseph) M. Actor. *b.* Dec. 16, 1887, Dublin. *d.* 1964. A former reporter, he joined the Abbey Players in 1907 and appeared in many stage productions and occasional films in Ireland before coming to the US in 1917. He subsequently played many memorable character roles on Broadway and in Hollywood films, often portraying Irish types.

FILMS INCLUDE: *O'Neil of the Glen* (also dir.; Ire.) 1916; *Little Old New York* 1923; *Lucky in Love* 1929; *Song o' My Heart, Lightnin'* 1930; *Merely Mary Ann* 1931; *Careless Lady* 1932; *A Study in Scarlet* 1933; *The Lost Patrol, A Modern Hero, The Key, The Fountain, Happiness Ahead* 1934; *The Informer, The Werewolf of London, Barbary Coast* 1935; *Colleen, Laughing Irish Eyes, The General Died at Dawn, Lloyds of London, The Prisoner of Shark Island* 1936; *The Plough and the Stars, London by Night* 1937; *Ride a Crooked Mile* 1938; *The Great Man Votes, The Flying Irishman, Union Pacific, Gone With the Wind* 1939; *Three Cheers for the Irish, Young Tom Edison, Untamed, The Sea Hawk, No Time for Comedy, The Long Voyage Home* 1940; *Appointment for Love, The Wolf Man* 1941; *Captains of the Clouds* 1942; *Action in the North Atlantic, Mr. Lucky* 1943; *The Fighting Seabees, Wilson* 1944; *Tarzan and the Amazons, The Spanish Main* 1945; *Black Beauty, Abie's Irish Rose* 1946; *Call Northside 777, The Luck of the Irish* 1948; *The Fighting O'Flynn* 1949; *Sealed Cargo* 1951; *My Cousin Rachel* 1952; *20,000 Leagues Under the Sea* 1954; *The Fastest Gun Alive* 1956.

Kerry, Norman. Actor. *b.* Arnold Kaiser, June 16, 1889, Rochester, N.Y. *d.* 1956. Dashing hero and occasional villain of Hollywood films of the silent era. He often sported a fancy waxed mustache.

FILMS INCLUDE: *Manhattan Madness, The Black Butterfly* 1916; *The Little Princess* 1917; *Amarilly of Clothes-Line, Good Night Paul* 1918; *Toton, Getting Mary Married, Virtuous Sinners, The Dark Star, Soldiers of Fortune* 1919; *Passion's Playground, A Splendid Hazard* 1920; *Buried Treasure, The Wild Goose, Little Italy, Proxies, Get-Rich-Quick Wallingford* 1921; *Three Live Ghosts, The Man from Home, Brothers Under the Skin, Till We Meet Again, Find the Woman* 1922; *Merry-Go-Round, The Hunchback of Notre Dame* (as Capt. Phoebus), *The Spoilers, The Acquittal* 1923; *Between Friends, Cytherea, True as Steel, Tarnish* 1924; *Fifth Avenue Models, The Price of Pleasure, The Phantom of the Opera* 1925; *The Barrier, Mlle. Modiste, The Love Thief, Under Western Skies* 1926; *The Claw, Annie Laurie, The Unknown, The Irresistible Lover, Body and Soul* 1927; *Love Me and the World Is Mine, Affairs of Hannerl, The Foreign Legion, The Woman from Moscow, Man Woman and Wife* 1928; *The Bondsman, Trial Marriage* 1929; *Ex-Flame* 1930; *Bachelor Apartment, Air Eagles* 1931; *Phantom of Santa Fe* 1937; *Tanks a Million* 1941.

Kershner, Irvin. Director. Born on Aug. 29, 1923, in Philadelphia. Following WW II service with the Army Air Force as a flight engineer on B-24 bombers, he studied art and design at Temple University's Tyler School of Fine Arts and was further tutored in New York by painter Hans Hofmann. He then switched to USC, where he attended film courses and taught classes in photography. In 1950 he became a documentary film-maker for the USIS (United States Information Service), working in Iran and Jordan, and later for another agency in Greece and Turkey. Returning to Los Angeles in 1953, he worked for two years as a director-cameraman on the local TV documentary series 'Confidential File.'

It wasn't until 1958 that Kershner finally got his chance to become a feature director, with *Stakeout on Dope Street,* a minibudget ($30,000), Roger Corman project. His work in the next few years was characterized by location shooting of semi-documentary rawness and a sensitivity to human frailties and social alienation in the urban climate. *The Hoodlum Priest* (1961) won the Catholic Film Office Award at the Cannes Festival. *The Luck of Ginger Coffey* (1964), made in Canada, gained wide approval, and *Loving* (1970), regarded by many as the director's most accomplished film, was universally admired. In the 70s Kershner gradually submitted to the lure of studio-controlled commercial cinema, a tendency that culminated in his proficient handling of the high-budget, action-packed space epic *The Empire Strikes Back* (1980). A James Bond adventure naturally followed.

FILMS: *Stakeout on Dope Street* (also co-sc.) 1958; *The Young Captives* 1959; *The Hoodlum Priest* 1961; *A Face in the Rain* 1963; *The Luck of Ginger Coffey* (Can.) 1964; *A Fine Madness* 1966; *The Flim-Flam Man* 1967; *Loving* 1970; *Up the Sandbox* 1972; *S*P*Y*S* 1974; *The Return of a Man Called Horse* 1976; *Eyes of Laura Mars* 1978; *The Empire Strikes Back* 1980; *Never Say Never Again* 1983; *Wildfire* (exec. prod.) 1988; *Orders* 1989; *The White Crow, RoboCop II* 1990.

Keyes, Evelyn. Actress. Born on Nov. 20, 1919, in Port Arthur, Tex. A former nightclub chorus dancer, she broke into films in 1938 after repeated attempts. Following a succession of supporting roles at Paramount (under personal contract to C. B. De Mille) and other studios, she found a home at Columbia, where she ably played comely leads in a variety of the studio's films of the 40s, most memorably in *Here Comes Mr. Jordan* (1941) and *The Jolson Story* (1946). She freelanced in the early 50s and retired from the screen in 1956. Her marriages include those to directors Charles VIDOR (1943–45) and John HUSTON (1946–50) and bandleader Artie Shaw (his eighth wife, from 1957). She also lived with producer Mike TODD for three years (1953–56). In 1971 she published a first novel, *I Am a Billboard.* In 1977 she authored an autobiography, *Scarlett O'Hara's Younger Sister* (she played the role in *Gone With the Wind*) that told much about her sexual exploits with Hollywood's famous but little about her work in films. She followed it up in 1991 with a much tamer memoir, *I'll Think About That Tomorrow,* covering her post-career recollections of the past 20 years. She popped up on the screen twice in the late 80s, when she was also seen occasionally on television.

FILMS INCLUDE: *The Buccaneer, Men with Wings, Sons of the Legion, Artists and Models Abroad* 1938; *Union Pacific, Gone With the Wind* (as Suellen O'Hara), *Slightly Honorable* 1939; *Before I Hang, The Lady in Question* 1940; *The Face Behind the Mask, Here Comes Mr. Jordan, Ladies in Retirement* 1941; *The Adventures of Martin Eden, Flight Lieutenant, The Desperadoes, Dangerous Blondes* 1943; *Nine Girls, Strange Affair* 1944; *A Thousand and One Nights* 1945; *The Thrill of Brazil, Renegades, The Jolson Story* 1946; *Johnny O' Clock* 1947; *The Mating of Millie, Enchantment* 1948; *Mr. Soft Touch, Mrs. Mike* 1949; *The Killer That Stalked New York* 1950; *The Prowler, Iron Man* 1951; *Shoot First, 99 River Street* 1953; *Hell's Half Acre* 1954; *Top of the World, The Seven Year Itch* 1955; *Around the World in 80 Days* (cameo) 1956; *Across 110th Street* (cameo) 1972; *Return to Salem's Lot* 1987; *Wicked Stepmother* 1989.

key grip. The head GRIP on a film set, in charge of a group of people, usually numbering from five to fifteen.

key light. The principal and dominant source of light used in illuminating a motion picture set. It determines the tone and mood of a scene and is therefore established first by the director of photography, who later builds around it the FILL LIGHT and other compensating sources of illumination, such as the cross light and back light.

key numbers. See EDGE NUMBERS.

keys. Animation drawings of the principal positions of a figure or an object in motion, such as starting, stopping, or changing direction.

keystone. A distorted shape of a projected image on a screen, usually caused by improper angling of projector and screen but sometimes by an awkward camera angle during filming.

Keystone. American film production company founded in 1912 by Charles O. Bauman and Adam Kessel. With Mack Sennett as director and Mabel Normand, Fred Mace, and Ford Sterling as stars, the company started production in the fall of that year, turning out one split reel of frenzied comedy every week. The first program, *Cohen Collects a Debt* and *The Water Nymph* (released Sept. 23, 1912), set the pattern and the style that were soon to become the trademark of the Keystone comedies: irrational, unrestrained slapstick unfolding at a frantic pace, emphasizing constant movement and utilizing skilled editing techniques. By mid-1913, Keystone was joined by such talented comics as Roscoe "Fatty" Arbuckle and his wife Minta Durfee, Chester Conklin, Hank Mann, Charlie Chase, and Edgar Kennedy, to form a formidable stock company, a virtual powerhouse of laughter.

A favorite feature of the Sennett comedies was the Keystone Kops (or "Cops"), those clumsy, absurd policemen whose misadventures cast a hilarious image of the mechanics of the law, and the Bathing Beauties, those dizzy sexpots out of whose ranks emerged such stars as Phyllis Haver, Marie Prevost, and Louise Fazenda. The key to the madness was inventiveness, with one visual gag following another in dizzying succession. In 1914 the Keystone team was enriched by the arrival of Charlie Chaplin, who stayed with the company nearly a year, appearing in some 35 films, culminating in the six-reel *Tillie's Punctured Romance.*

In 1915, Keystone was absorbed by Triangle but continued to function as an autonomous unit under Sennett's direction. Late in 1917, Sennett pulled out of Keystone, taking his team along, to become an independent producer, releasing through Paramount. Like its parent company, Triangle-Keystone soon folded.

Khouri, Callie. Screenwriter, producer. Born 1958, in San Antonio, Tex. *ed.* Purdue University. Clever, skillful writer who burst onto the Hollywood scene with the sharp and witty film *Thelma and Louise* (1991) earning the Academy Award for best original screenplay.

FILMS: *Aria* 1987; *Thelma and Louise* (co-prod., sc.) 1991; *Something to Talk About* (sc. only) 1995.

Kibbee, Guy. Actor *b.* Mar. 6, 1882, El Paso, Tex. *d.* 1956. Pudgy, jolly, often foxy character player of numerous Hollywood films of the 30s and 40s. He began his show business career at 13 as an entertainer on Mississippi riverboats and later spent many years on the legitimate stage. On the screen, he played key supporting roles and occasional leads, in productions of Warner Bros. and other studios, often portraying small-town civic leaders. His son, Charles, was chancellor of the City University of New York.

FILMS INCLUDE: *Stolen Heaven, Man of the World, City Streets, Laughing Sinners, Blonde Crazy* 1931; *Union Depot, Play Girl, The Crowd Roars, So Big, The Dark Horse, Winner Take All, Rain, The Conquerors, Central Park* 1932; *42nd Street, Gold Diggers of 1933, Lilly Turner, The Silk Express, Lady for a Day, Footlight Parade, The World Changes, Havana Widows* 1933; *Wonder Bar, Dames, Big Hearted Herbert* (title role), *Babbitt* (title role) 1934; *While the Patient Slept* (lead), *Captain Blood* 1935; *Little Lord Fauntleroy, Captain January* (title role), *The Big Noise* (lead), *Three Men on a Horse* 1936; *Don't Tell the Wife* (lead), *The Big Shot* (lead) 1937; *Of Human Hearts, Joy of Living, Three Comrades* 1938; *Let Freedom Ring, It's a Wonderful World, Mr. Smith Goes to Washington, Babes in Arms* 1939; *Our Town* (as Mr. Webb, the editor), *Chad Hanna* 1940; *Scattergood Baines* (title role), *It Started with Eve* 1941; *Design for Scandal, Miss Annie Rooney, Whistling in Dixie* 1942; *Girl Crazy* 1943; *The Horn Blows at Midnight* 1945; *The Romance of Rosy Ridge* 1947; *Fort Apache* 1948; *Three Godfathers* 1949.

Kibbee, Roland. Screenwriter. *b.* Feb. 15, 1914, Monogahela, Pa. *d.* 1984. *ed.* L.A. City College. Briefly a stage actor, he began his writing career in radio, providing comedy material for Fred Allen, Groucho Marx, and Fanny Brice. After serving as a pilot in WW II, he began writing for the screen, but his most successful endeavors came later on TV. He won Emmys for 'The Bob Newhart Show,' 'Columbo,' and 'Barney Miller,' and contributed to 'The Bob Cummings Show,' 'The Virginian,' and 'Alfred Hitchcock Presents,' among other series. He co-directed (with Burt Lancaster) one feature, *The Midnight Man* (1974), his last.

FILMS INCLUDE: *A Night in Casablanca, Angel on My Shoulder* 1946; *Painting the Clouds with Sunshine, Ten Tall Men* 1951; *Pardon My French, The Crimson Pirate* 1952; *The Desert Song, Three Sailors and a Girl* 1953; *Vera Cruz* 1954; *Top Secret Affair* 1957; *The Devil's Disciple* 1959; *The Amorous Adventures of Moll Flanders* 1965; *The Appaloosa* 1966; *Valdez Is Coming* (also exec. prod.) 1971; *The Midnight Man* (also co-dir., co-prod.) 1974.

kicker. Illumination used to make the eyes and teeth of a performer appear brighter without an appreciable increase of light elsewhere. Also known as "eye light."

Kidd, Michael. Choreographer, dancer. Born on Aug. 12, 1919, in Brooklyn, N.Y. He trained for an engineering career but found the dance more appealing and presented his first ballet in 1945. Dynamic and inventive, he infused Broadway musicals with a new life, collecting five Tony Awards in the process, then turned to films with equal success. By his own account, he has been strongly influenced by the pantomime and pathos of Charlie CHAPLIN. He directed one film, *Merry Andrew* (1958), starring Danny Kaye.

FILMS INCLUDE (as choreographer): *Where's Charley?* 1952; *The Band Wagon* 1953; *It's Always Fair Weather* (act. only), *Knock on Wood, Seven Brides for Seven Brothers* 1954; *Guys and Dolls* 1955; *Merry Andrew* (also dir.) 1958; *Star!* 1968; *Hello Dolly!* 1969; *Smile* (act. only) 1975; *Movie Movie* (also act.) 1978; *Skin Deep* (act. only) 1989.

Kidder, Margot. Actress. Born Margaret Kidder, on Oct. 17, 1948, in Yellowknife, N.W.T., Canada. *ed.* U. of British Columbia. Attractive, unadorned brunette leading lady of the Canadian and American screen. The daughter of a mining engineer, she was raised in the Northwest Territories and gravitated toward acting when her family moved to Toronto. Although she appeared in many features and TV movies from the late 60s, typically as a sincere, unglamorous ingenue, she kept a low profile until she landed the part of reporter Lois Lane in *Superman* (1978) and its sequels. She suffered a debilitating injury on a Canadian movie set in the late 80s and spent several years recuperating. Formerly married to writer Thomas McGuane, actor John HEARD, and the French director Philippe de BROCA.

FILMS INCLUDE: *The Best Damn Fiddler from Calabogie to Kaladar* (medium-length) 1968; *Gaily Gaily* 1969; *Quackser Fortune Has a Cousin in the Bronx* 1970; *Sisters, A Quiet Day in Belfast* 1973; *Black Christmas, Gravy Train/The Dion Brothers* 1974; *The Great Waldo Pepper, The Reincarnation of Peter Proud, 92 in the Shade* 1975; *Superman* (as Lois Lane) 1978; *The Amityville Horror, Mr. Mike's Mondo Video* 1979; *Superman II, Willie and Phil* 1980; *Heartaches, Shoot the Sun Down* 1981; *Some Kind of a Nut* 1982; *Trenchcoat, Superman III* 1983; *Little Treasure* 1985; *Superman IV: The Quest for Peace* 1987; *Miss Right* (release delayed from 1980) 1988; *White Room* (bit) 1990; *The Pornographer* 1993.

Kidman, Nicole. Actress. Born in 1967 in Hawaii. Willowy actress known for early work in Australian films and later in major Hollywood fare. Raised in Australia, she made her film debut in Australia at age 14. Married to actor Tom CRUISE, with whom she has adopted a daughter and a son.

FILMS INCLUDE: *Prince and the Great Race* 1983; *BMX Bandits* 1984; *Windrider, Night Master* 1987; *Dead Calm, Flirting* 1989; *Days of Thunder* 1990; *Billy Bathgate, Emerald City* 1991; *Far and Away, Damages* 1992; *Malice, My Life* 1993; *Batman Forever, To Die For* 1995; *The Portrait of a Lady* 1996; *The Peacemaker* 1997.

Kiel, Richard. Actor. Born on Sept. 13, 1939, in Redford, Mich. Gigantic supporting player of Hollywood films. A former nightclub bouncer, he stands seven feet two, weighs about 330 pounds, and wears a shoe size 16 EEE. Memorable as the villainous, steel-toothed Jaws in the James Bond adventures *The Spy Who Loved Me* (1977) and *Moonraker* (1979).

FILMS INCLUDE: *The Phantom Planet* 1961; *The Magic Sword* 1962; *House of the Damned* 1963; *The Human Duplicators* 1965; *A Man Called Dagger* 1968; *The Longest Yard* 1974; *Silver Streak* 1976; *The Spy Who Loved Me* 1977; *They Went That-a-Way and That-a-Way* 1978; *L'Umanoide/The Humanoid* (It.), *Moonraker* 1979; *So Fine* 1981; *Hysterical* 1983; *Cannonball Run II* 1984; *Pale Rider* 1985; *Think Big* 1990; *The Giant of Thunder Mountain* (also co-sc., co-exec. prod.) 1992.

Kiepura, Jan. Actor, singer. *b.* May 16, 1902, Sosnowiec, Poland, *d.* 1966. A leading tenor with the Warsaw State Opera and later in Vienna and Milan, he became very popular in musical films of the 30s in which he often appeared with his wife, Marta EGGERTH. Late in the 30s they emigrated to the US, where his film career came to a virtual halt. He sang with New York's Metropolitan Opera and other establishments, appeared in some postwar European films, then retired in the mid-50s.

FILMS: *Die singende Stadt/La Ville qui chante/The City of Song/Farewell to Love* (German-, French-, English-language versions) 1931; *Das Lied einer Nacht/Tell Me Tonight/Be Mine Tonight* (German-, English-, French-language versions) 1932; *Ein Lied für Dich/My Song for You* (German-, English-, French-language versions) 1933; *Mein Herz ruft nach Dir/My Heart Is Calling/Mon Coeur t'appelle* (German-, English-, French-language versions) 1934; *Ich liebe alle Frauen* (German-, French-language versions) 1935; *Give Us This Night* (US), *Im Sonnenschein/Opernring/Thank You Madame* (Aus.) 1936; *Zauber der Bohème/The Charm of la Bohème* (Aus.) 1937; *Addio Mimi/Her Wonderful Lie* (It.) 1947; *La Valse brillante* (Fr.) 1948; *Das Land des Lächelns/Land of Smiles* (Ger.) 1952.

Kieslowski, Krzysztof. Director. *b.* June 27, 1941, in Warsaw. *d.* March 13, 1996. A leading figure in Eastern European cinema of the 70s and 80s. A graduate of the Lodz film school, he turned out his first film in 1969 and first captured international attention with *Camera Buff* (1979), a satirical critique of political movie censorship in his native land. Several of his earlier and subsequent films were banned or shelved for long periods. Some won awards at international film festivals, including *A Short Film About Killing* and *A Short Film About Love,* both feature versions of segments from his mammoth *Dekalog/The Ten Commandments* (1988)—a series of ten TV films, each representing a biblical commandment through a modern story reflecting the drab reality of Poland today. The screening of the entire cycle was the central event of the 1989 Venice Festival. He usually writes or collaborates on his own scripts.

FILMS INCLUDE: *Picture* 1969; *Workers* 1972; *First Love* 1974; *Personnel, Biography* 1975; *Scar, Politics* 1976; *Hospital, Calm* 1977; *Seen by the Night Porter, Station* 1978; *Amator/Camera Buff* 1979; *Talking Heads* 1980; *A Short Day's Work* (banned) 1982; *No End* 1984; *Blind Chance* (release delayed from 1982) 1987; *A Short Film About Killing/Thou Salt Not Kill, A Short Film About Love* (both parts of the *Dekalog/The Ten Commandments* series) 1988; *City Life* ("Seven Days a Week" [Warsaw] episode) 1990; *The Double Life of Veronique* (Fr./Pol.) 1991; *Blue* (also co-sc.; Fr./Pol./Switz.) 1993; *White* (also co-sc.; Fr.), *Red/Rouge* (also co-sc.; Fr./Pol./Switz.) 1994.

Kilbride, Percy. Actor. *b.* July 16, 1888, San Francisco. *d.* 1964. He had hundreds of stage roles in stock and on the road before reaching Hollywood. He assayed many character parts there, typically as a rascally country bumpkin. In 1947 he first played Pa Kettle, a drawling, peppery farmer, in the film *The Egg and I,* and subsequently became the costar of the "Ma and Pa Kettle" films featuring that character and his female counterpart, played by Marjorie MAIN. He died of injuries sustained in a car crash.

FILMS INCLUDE: *White Woman* 1933; *Soak the Rich* 1936; *George Washington Slept Here, Keeper of the Flame* 1942; *Crazy House* 1943; *The Adventures of Mark Twain, Knickerbocker Holiday* 1944; *State Fair* 1945; *The Well-Groomed Bride* 1946; *The Egg and I, Welcome Stranger* 1947; *Black Bart* 1948; *Ma and Pa Kettle* 1949; *Riding High* 1950; *Ma and Pa Kettle Back on the Farm* 1951; *Ma and Pa Kettle at the Fair* 1952; *Ma and Pa Kettle on Vacation* 1953; *Ma and Pa Kettle at Home* 1954; *Ma and Pa Kettle at Waikiki* 1955.

Kilburn, Terry. Actor. Born Terence Kilbourne, on Nov. 25, 1926, in London. Child player of Hollywood films of the late 30s and early 40s, following a stint on the Eddie Cantor radio show. Memorable in *A Christmas Carol* (1938) as Tiny Tim, and in *Goodbye Mr. Chips* (1939), in which he played four roles. He continued appearing in occasional films as a young adult but after drama studies at UCLA gradually phased out his waning film career in favor of the stage, initially as an actor and later as a director. He is artistic director of the Meadowbrook Theatre in Rochester, Michigan.

FILMS INCLUDE: *Lord Jeff, Sweethearts, A Christmas Carol* (as Tiny Tim) 1938; *Goodbye Mr. Chips, Andy Hardy Gets Spring Fever, They Shall Have Music, The Adventures of Sherlock Holmes* 1939; *The Swiss Family Robinson* 1940; *A Yank at Eton* 1942; *National Velvet* 1944; *Black Beauty* 1946; *Song of Scheherazade, Bulldog Drummond at Bay* 1947; *The Fan* 1949; *Only the Valiant* 1951; *Slaves of Babylon* 1953; *Fiend Without a Face* 1958; *Lolita* 1962.

Kiley, Richard. Actor, singer. Born on Mar. 31, 1922, in Chicago. *ed.* Loyola U. He began his professional career on radio and played character roles, often as a heavy, in Hollywood films of the 50s before becoming a successful star of Broadway plays and musicals, memorably in *Redhead* (1959) and *Man of La Mancha* (1965), both of which earned him Tony Awards. He won an Emmy as best supporting actor for the TV miniseries 'The Thorn Birds' (1983) and returned to Broadway powerfully in a 1987 revival of 'All My Sons.' An impressive participant in the TV miniseries 'Separate But Equal,' dramatizing the 1954 Brown vs. the Board of Education case that desegregated the American school system.

FILMS INCLUDE: *The Mob* 1951; *The Sniper, Eight Iron Men* 1952; *Pickup on South Street* 1953; *The Blackboard Jungle, The Phenix City Story* 1955; *The Spanish Affair* 1958; *Pendulum* 1969; *The Little Prince* 1974; *Looking for Mr. Goodbar* 1977; *Endless Love* 1981; *Howard the Duck* (voice only) 1986.

Kilian, Victor. Actor. *b.* Mar. 6, 1891, Jersey City, N.J. *d.* 1979. Tall, heavyset character player of numerous Hollywood films of the 30s and 40s, usually in angry, sometimes villainous roles. Drove a wagon for his father's laundry and played in vaudeville, in stock, and on Broadway before making his screen debut in 1929. McCarthy-era blacklisting forced his retirement from films in the early 50s but he continued appearing on the stage for another decade. He enjoyed a revival of his career in the mid-70s, playing the role of the grandfather, known to the local police as "the Fernwood Flasher," in the TV comic soap opera series 'Mary Hartman, Mary Hartman.' He was killed by intruders in his Hollywood apartment.

FILMS INCLUDE: *Gentlemen of the Press* (bit) 1929; *The Wiser Sex* 1932; *Air Hawks* 1935; *Riffraff, The Road to Glory, Ramona, Banjo on My Knee* 1936; *Seventh Heaven, The League of Frightened Men, It Happened in Hollywood, Tovarich* 1937; *The Adventures of Tom Sawyer, Boys Town* 1938; *Paris Honeymoon, Huckleberry Finn* (as Pap Finn), *Only Angels Have Wings, Dust Be My Destiny* 1939; *Little Old New York, Young Tom Edison, Dr. Cyclops, Torrid Zone, The Return of Frank James, They Knew What They Wanted* 1940; *Western Union, Blood and Sand, I Was a Prisoner on Devil's Island* 1941; *Reap the Wild Wind, This Gun for Hire, Atlantic Convoy* 1942; *The Ox-Bow Incident, Hitler's Madman* 1943; *Uncertain Glory* 1944; *Spellbound, The Spanish Main* 1945; *Little Giant, Smoky* 1946; *Gentleman's Agreement* 1947; *Northwest Stampede* 1948; *Yellow Sky* 1949; *The Flame and the Arrow* 1950; *The Tall Target* 1951.

Kilmer, Val. Actor. Born on Dec. 31, 1959, in Los Angeles.

ed. Hollywood Professional School; Juilliard. Tall, virile leading man of the American screen, following and preceding appearances on the New York stage. His performance as the late Jim Morrison in *The Doors* was eerily dead-on, gaining him notice and helping to make him a sensation among twentysomething moviegoers. Divorced from actress Joanne WHALLEY-KILMER.

FILMS: *Top Secret!* 1984; *Real Genius* 1985; *Top Gun* 1986; *Willow* 1988; *Kill Me Again* 1989, *The Doors* 1991; *Thunderheart* 1992; *True Romance, The Real McCoy, Tombstone* 1993; *Batman Forever, Heat, Wings of Courage* 1995; *The Ghost and the Darkness, The Island of Dr. Moreau* 1996; *The Saint* 1997.

Kimmins, Anthony. Director, screenwriter, producer, actor. *b.* Nov. 10, 1901, Harrow, England, *d.* 1963. After long service in the British navy, he entered films in 1933 as an actor, appearing in low-budget pictures. About the same time, he began writing comedy scripts for George FORMBY and others. A director from 1937, he often produced and wrote screenplays for his own films.

FILMS (as director): *Keep Fit* 1937; *I See Ice, It's in the Air* 1938; *Come on George, Trouble Brewing* 1939; *Mine Own Executioner* 1947; *Bonnie Prince Charlie* 1948; *Flesh and Blood* 1950; *Mr. Denning Drives North* 1951; *Who Goes There?/The Passionate Sentry* 1952; *The Captain's Paradise, Aunt Clara* 1954; *Smiley* 1956; *Smiley Gets a Gun* 1958; *The Amorous Prawn* 1962.

Kinemacolor. A color effect process obtained by rotating a filter wheel in front of the camera lens, exposing alternate frames of the negative to red, then to blue-green. Introduced in 1906, it was the world's first commercial motion picture color process. See SMITH, George Albert.

kinescope. A film recording made from a television picture. Usually of poor quality, kinescopes were indispensable as a method of transferring live TV shows to film to keep as a permanent record before the advent of videotape recording. Usually called "kine" (pronounced "kinny") for short.

Kinetograph. The world's first motion picture camera. It was developed in 1888 by Thomas Alva EDISON and W. K. L. DICKSON, first used in 1889 for making brief story film strips, and patented in 1891.

Kinetophone. See SOUND.

Kinetoscope. The apparatus invented by Thomas A. EDISON and W. K. L. DICKSON in 1889 for viewing the strips of films they made with their KINETOGRAPH. Both inventions were patented in 1891.

King, Alan. Comedian, actor. Born Irwin Alan Kinberg, on Dec. 26, 1927, in Brooklyn, N.Y. Began his professional career at 15 as a musician, later becoming a stand-up comedian in the Catskills and eventually reaching stardom on the supper-club circuit. He has appeared frequently on TV and played comic roles in a number of plays and films. American suburbia has been the target of many of his jokes. Author: *Anyone Who Owns a House Deserves It* and *Help! I'm a Prisoner in a Chinese Bakery.*

FILMS: *Hit the Deck* 1955; *Miracle in the Rain, The Girl He Left Behind* 1956; *The Helen Morgan Story* 1957; *Operation Snafu* 1965; *Bye Bye Braverman* 1968; *The Anderson Tapes* 1971; *Sunday in the Country* (Can.) 1974; *Just Tell Me What You Want, Happy Birthday Gemini* (exec. prod. only) 1980; *Cattle Annie and Little Britches* (co-prod. only) 1981; *Author! Author!, I, The Jury* 1982; *Lovesick* 1983; *Cat's Eye* 1985; *You Talkin' to Me?* (as himself) 1987; *Memories of Me* (also co-prod.) 1988; *Funny* (doc.), *Enemies: A Love Story* 1989; *The Bonfire of the Vanities* 1990.

King, Allan. Director. Born in 1930, in Vancouver, B.C., Canada. *ed.* U. of British Columbia (philosophy). He drove a cab and traveled in Europe before joining the film unit of the Canadian Broadcasting Corporation (CBC) in 1954. He began directing for TV two years later and in the 60s became an independent producer-director. He gained an international reputation with the feature-length documentary *Warrendale,* which he shot in 1966 at a home for emotionally disturbed adolescents. Both the CBC and London's BBC refused to air the film because of its harrowing scenes and foul language, but it was released theatrically in 1967 to unanimous critical acclaim. It shared the International Critics Prize (with Antonioni's *Blow-Up*) at the 1967 Cannes Film Festival. The material he shot for the film over a period of five weeks was later expanded into an 18-part TV series, 'Children in Conflict.' King went on to produce and direct other features and TV programs, establishing a position as one of Canada's leading filmmakers. He has also worked in England.

FILMS INCLUDE: *Skid Row* 1956; *Portrait of a Harbor* 1957; *Morocco* 1958; *Bull Fight* 1959; *Rickshaw* 1960; *A Matter of Pride* 1961; *The Pursuit of Happiness* 1962; *The Peacemakers* 1963; *Bjorn's Inferno, Coming of Age in Ibiza* 1964; *Warrendale* (also prod.) 1967; *The New Woman* 1968; *A Married Couple* (also prod.) 1969; *Come On Children* (also prod.) 1973; *Who Has Seen the Wind* (also prod.) 1977; *One-Night Stand* 1979; *Silence of the North* 1981.

King, Andrea. Actress. Born Georgette Barry, on Feb. 1, 1919, in Paris. She was educated in the US and, following stage experience, made her film debut in the mid-40s. She characteristically played cool, sometimes calculating women, in both leads and second leads. Since the late 50s seen mainly on TV.

FILMS: *The Very Thought of You, Hollywood Canteen* 1944; *Roughly Speaking, Hotel Berlin, God Is My Co-Pilot* 1945; *Shadow of a Woman* 1946; *The Beast with Five Fingers, The Man I Love, Ride the Pink Horse, My Wild Irish Rose* 1947; *Mr. Peabody and the Mermaid* 1948; *Song of Surrender* 1949; *Dial 1119, Southside 1-1000, Buccaneer's Girl, I Was a Shoplifter* 1950; *The Lemon Drop Kid, Mark of the Renegade* 1951; *Red Planet Mars, The World in His Arms* 1952; *Silent Fear* 1956; *Band of Angels* 1957; *Darby's Rangers* 1958; *House of the Black Death* 1965; *Daddy's Gone A-Hunting* 1969; *Blackenstein* 1973.

King, Charles. Actor. *b.* Oct. 31, 1889, New York City. *d.* 1944. A vaudeville song-and-dance man, he later starred in Broadway musicals and the Ziegfeld Follies. Sound brought him to Hollywood, where he starred in several early musicals. He is often confused with a character player by the same name (*b.* Feb. 21, 1895, Hillsboro, Tex.; *d.* 1957), who appeared mainly in Westerns and action pictures, including many serials, typically in villainous roles.

FILMS INCLUDE: *The Broadway Melody, The Hollywood Revue* 1929; *Chasing Rainbows, Oh Sailor Behave, Remote Control* 1930; *Crashing Broadway* 1933; *Mississippi* 1935.

King, Dennis. Actor, singer. *b.* Dennis Pratt, Nov. 2, 1897, Coventry, England. *d.* 1971. He began his stage career at 14 as a call boy and made his first stage appearance at 19. By the mid-20s he was a matinee idol in both London and New York and enjoyed equal success as a dramatic actor in Shakespearean and classical roles and as a baritone in stage operettas on both sides of the Atlantic. He appeared in numerous Broadway productions, both dramas and musicals, from the early 20s. In the early 30s he starred in a couple of early Hollywood musicals and later appeared occasionally in films. He became an American citizen in 1953. His two sons, Dennis, Jr., and John Michael King, were also actors.

FILMS: *The Vagabond King, Paramount on Parade* 1930; *Fra Diavolo/The Devil's Brother* 1931; *Between Two Worlds* 1937; *Some Kind of a Nut* 1969.

King, George. Director, producer. *b.* 1899, London. *d.*

1966. A prolific toiler, he turned out numerous cheap British films and became known in industry circles as "King of the Quickies."

FILMS INCLUDE (as director, often also producer): *Too Many Crooks* 1930; *Midnight* 1931; *Men of Steel* 1932; *Matinee Idol* 1933; *The Blue Squadron* 1934; *The Man Without a Face* 1935; *Reasonable Doubt* 1936; *Wanted* 1937; *Silver Top* 1938; *The Face at the Window* 1939; *The Chinese Bungalow/The Chinese Den, The Case of the Frightened Lady/Frightened Lady* 1940; *Tomorrow We Live/At Dawn We Die* 1942; *Candlelight in Algeria* 1943; *Gaiety George/Showtime, The Shop at Sly Corner* 1946; *Forbidden* 1948.

King, Henry. Director. *b.* June 24, 1888, Christiansburg, Va. *d.* 1982. One of the most durable and commercially viable of Hollywood's directors whose work in films spanned half a century. Raised on the family's plantation, he worked briefly in a railroad office and acted in road shows, vaudeville, and burlesque and on the legitimate stage before entering films as an actor in 1912. Among the films in which he appeared were *Love and War in Mexico* (1913), *The Moth and the Flame* (1913), and *Will o' the Wisp* (1914). He began directing late in 1915 but continued acting in his own films through 1920. His early films as director were mainly shorts and medium-length features and few if any of them survive.

King's first big commercial success was *23½ Hours Leave* (1919), an army comedy he made for producer Thomas Ince. In 1921 he established his own production company, Inspiration Films, in partnership with actor Richard BARTHELMESS and that same year created an early masterpiece, *Tol'able David,* a simple, evocative rural drama. The film revealed traits that were to become typical of King's later work, a nostalgic love of wide open spaces and a devotion to the re-creation of Americana, particularly rural settings of periods past.

A sure-handed craftsman, King went on to pursue a prolific, enduring, successful career through the early 60s, spending nearly his entire "talkie" years at Fox. He handled a wide variety of films with professional efficiency but rarely with deeper than surface interpretation of theme. His films, even his many adventure yarns, were typically leisurely paced with restrained camera movement and a prevalence of medium shots. Among his more successful sound-era films were *State Fair* (1933), *Lloyds of London* (1936), *In Old Chicago* (1938), *Jesse James* (1939), *Stanley and Livingstone* (1939), *Remember the Day* (1941), *The Song of Bernadette* (1943), and in particular *Twelve O'Clock High* (1949), an excellent WW II Air Force drama, and *The Gunfighter* (1950), a superior Western, both starring Gregory Peck. He was the brother of Louis KING.

FILMS (features complete): *Who Pays?* (serial; credit uncertain), *Nemesis/The Brand of Man* (short; also act.) 1915; *Little Mary Sunshine* (also act.), *The Oath of Hate* (short; also act.), *Pay Dirt* (also act.), *Shadows and Sunshine, Joy and the Dragon* 1916; *Twin Kiddies* (also act.), *Told at Twilight* (also act.), *Sunshine and Gold* (also sc., act.), *The Mainspring* (also act.), *Souls in Pawn, The Bride's Silence, The Climber, A Game of Wits, The Mate of the Sally Ann, New York Luck* (credit doubtful), *Scepter of Suspicion* (short) 1917; *Beauty and the Rogue, Powers That Prey, Hearts or Diamonds, Social Briars, Up Romance Road, The Ghost of Rosy Taylor* (credit doubtful), *The Locked Heart* (also act.), *No Children Wanted* (credit doubtful), *Hobbs in a Hurry, All the World to Nothing* 1918; *When a Man Rides Alone, Where the West Begins, Brass Buttons, Some Liar, A Sporting Chance, This Hero Stuff, Six Feet Four, 23½ Hours Leave, A Fugitive from Matrimony* 1919; *Haunting Shadows, The White Dove/Judge Not Thy Wife, Uncharted Channels, One Hour Before Dawn, Help Wanted—Male* (also act.), *Dice of Destiny* 1920; *When We Were 21, The Mistress of Shenstone, Salvage, The Sting of the Lash, Tol'able David* (also prod., co-sc.) 1921; *The Seventh Day* (also prod.), *Sonny* (also prod., co-sc.), *The Bond Boy* (also prod.) 1922; *Fury* (also prod.), *The White Sister* (also prod.) 1923; *Romola* (also prod.) 1924; *Sackcloth and Scarlet* (also prod.), *Any Woman* (also prod.), *Stella Dallas* 1925; *Partners Again, The Winning of Barbara Worth* 1926; *The Magic Flame* 1927; *The Woman Disputed* (co-dir. with Sam Taylor; also prod.) 1928; *She Goes to War* (also exec. prod.) 1929; *Hell Harbor* (also exec. prod.), *The Eyes of the World* (also exec. prod.), *Lightnin'* 1930; *Merely Mary Ann, Over the Hill* 1931; *The Woman in Room 13* 1932; *State Fair, I Loved You Wednesday* (co-dir. with William Cameron Menzies) 1933; *Carolina, Marie Galante* 1934; *One More Spring, Way Down East* 1935; *The Country Doctor, Ramona, Lloyds of London* 1936; *Seventh Heaven* 1937; *In Old Chicago, Alexander's Ragtime Band* 1938; *Jesse James, Stanley and Livingstone* 1939; *Little Old New York, Maryland, Chad Hanna* 1940; *A Yank in the R.A.F., Remember the Day* 1941; *The Black Swan* 1942; *The Song of Bernadette* 1943; *Wilson* 1944; *A Bell for Adano* 1945; *Margie* 1946; *Captain from Castile* 1947; *Deep Waters* 1948; *Prince of Foxes, Twelve O'Clock High* 1949; *The Gunfighter* 1950; *I'd Climb the Highest Mountain* 1951; *Wait Till the Sun Shines Nellie, The Snows of Kilimanjaro, O Henry's Full House* ("The Gift of the Magi" episode) 1952; *King of the Khyber Rifles* 1953; *Untamed, Love Is a Many-Splendored Thing* 1955; *Carousel* 1956; *The Sun Also Rises* 1957; *The Bravados* 1958; *This Earth Is Mine, Beloved Infidel* 1959; *Tender Is the Night* 1962.

King Hu. See HU, King.

King, John ("Dusty"). Actor. Born Miller McLeod Everson, on July 11, 1909, in Cincinnati. *ed.* Cincinnati U. Tall, lean leading man of Hollywood B pictures of the late 30s and early 40s, mainly Westerns and other action productions. A grain elevator stoker, lumberjack, radio announcer, and band vocalist before his film debut in 1935. After retiring from the screen, he operated a waffle shop in La Jolla, California.

FILMS INCLUDE: *Stolen Harmony* 1935; *Ace Drummond* (serial), *Love Before Breakfast, Crash Donovan* 1936; *Three Smart Girls, The Road Back* 1937; *State Police, The Crime of Dr. Hallet, Sharpshooters* 1938; *Charlie Chan in Honolulu, The Three Musketeers* (as Aramis), *The Hardys Ride High, Mr. Moto Takes a Vacation* 1939; *Midnight Limited, Half a Sinner, The Range Busters* 1940; *Fugitive Valley* 1941; *The Law of the Jungle, Texas to Bataan* 1942; *Two-Fisted Justice* 1943; *Renegade Girl* 1946.

King, Louis. Director. *b.* June 28, 1898, Christiansburg, Va. *d.* 1962. The younger brother of Henry KING, he entered films in 1917 as an actor, following studies at the University of Virginia. He played character roles in many films, often portraying rough types or drunks, before and shortly after becoming a director in 1927. Among the films in which he appeared, sometimes billed as Lewis King, were *The Secret of Black Mountain* (1917), *The Forbidden Room* (1919), *Ever Since Eve* (1921), *The Sin Flood* (1922), *Main Street* (1923), *The Devil's Cargo* (1925), *Mexicali Rose* (1929), and *The Way of All Men* (1930). He began his career as a director with FBO (Film Booking Offices), for which he turned out many low-budget Westerns starring Buzz Barton and other cowboy heroes. He joined Columbia in 1929 and, after directing several Buck Jones Westerns, he handled a variety of low-budget productions for various other studios, including Fox, Warner Bros., and Paramount. He shared his brother's love of rural Americana but not his commercial success.

FILMS: *Is Your Daughter Safe?* (co-dir. with Leon Lee), *The Boy Rider, The Slingshot Kid* 1927; *The Little Buckaroo,*

The Pinto Kid, The Fightin' Redhead, The Bantam Cowboy, Terror, Young Whirlwind, Rough Ridin' Red, Orphan of the Sage 1928; *The Vagabond Cub, The Freckled Rascal, The Little Savage, Pals of the Prairie* 1929; *The Lone Rider, Shadow Ranch, Men Without Law* 1930; *Desert Vengeance, The Fighting Sheriff, Border Law, The Deceiver* 1931; *Police Court, The County Fair, Fame Street, Arm of the Law, Drifting Souls* 1932; *Robbers' Roost, Life in the Raw* 1933; *La Ciudad de Carton* (in Spanish), *Murder in Trinidad, Pursued, Bachelor of Arts* 1934; *Julieta compra on Hijo* (in Spanish), *Charlie Chan in Egypt, Angelita* (in Spanish) 1935; *Road Gang, Special Investigator, Song of the Saddle, Bengal Tiger* 1936; *That Man's Here Again, Melody for Two, Draggerman Courage, Wild Money, Bulldog Drummond Comes Back, Wine Women and Horses, Bulldog Drummond's Revenge* 1937; *Tip-Off Girls, Hunted Men, Prison Farm, Bulldog Drummond in Africa, Illegal Traffic, Tom Sawyer—Detective* 1938; *Persons in Hiding, Undercover Doctor* 1939; *Seventeen, Typhoon, The Way of All Flesh, Moon Over Burma* 1940; *Young America* 1942; *Chetniks* 1943; *Ladies of Washington* 1944; *Thunderhead—Son of Flicka* 1945; *Smoky* 1946; *Thunder in the Valley* 1947; *Green Grass of Wyoming* 1948; *Sand, Mrs. Mike* 1949; *Frenchie* 1950; *The Lion and the Horse* 1952; *Powder River, Sabre Jet* 1953; *Dangerous Mission* 1954; *Massacre* 1956.

King, Perry. Actor. Born on Apr. 30, 1948, in Alliance, Ohio. *ed.* Yale. Trained by John Houseman at Juilliard, he played romantic leads, second leads, and supporting roles in television series, miniseries, and TV movies, as well as in feature films.

FILMS: *Slaughterhouse Five, The Possession of Joel Delaney* 1972; *The Lords of Flatbush* 1974; *Mandingo, The Wild Party* 1975; *Lipstick* 1976; *Andy Warhol's Bad, The Choirboys* 1977; *A Different Story* 1978; *Search and Destroy/Striking Back* 1981; *The Class of 1984, The Killing Hour/The Clairvoyant* 1982; *Switch* 1991.

King, Stephen. Novelist, screenwriter. Born on Sept. 21, 1947, in Portland, Maine. A former English teacher, he published his first novel, *Carrie,* in 1974, then rapidly became established as America's top-selling author of horror novels and tales, many of which were adapted—with wildly mixed results—to the screen. In the 80s he began writing his own scripts, and even tried his hand at directing with *Maximum Overdrive* (1986) and occasional acting.

FILMS: Novel/story basis only—*Carrie* 1974; *Salem's Lot* (TV movie shown theatrically abroad) 1979; *The Shining* 1980; *Cujo, The Dead Zone, Christine* 1983; *Children of the Corn, Firestarter* 1984; *Stand by Me* (from *The Body*) 1986; *The Running Man* (novel written under pseudonym Richard Bachman), *Creepshow 2, Return to Salem's Lot* (character creator only) 1987; *Graveyard Shift* 1990. As screenwriter (from own material)—*Creepshow* (also act.) 1982; *Cat's Eye, Silver Bullet* (from *Cycle of the Werewolf*) 1985; *Maximum Overdrive* (also dir., act.) 1986; *Pet Sematary* (also act.) 1989; *Sleepwalkers* (also act.), *The Lawnmower Man* (also act.), *Pet Sematary II* (based on first film, not on a written sequel) 1992; *Needful Things* (also act.) 1993; *The Shawshank Redemption* 1994; *Dolores Claiborne* 1995; *Thinner* (also cameo) 1996.

King, Zalman. Actor, director, writer, producer. Born Zalman King Lefkowitz in 1941 in Trenton, N.J. Creator of steamy feature films of the 80s and 90s. He began his acting career on the short-lived TV series 'The Young Lawyers' (1970–71) and in the ill-received feature film *The Ski Bum* (1971). After appearing in many TV movies and portraying Christ in *The Passover Plot* (1976), he made a greater impact behind the camera as co-screenwriter and co-producer of the erotic melodrama *9½ Weeks*, starring Mickey Rourke and Kim Basinger; he went on to direct *Wild Orchid*, again starring Rourke. King is also the executive producer, director, and co-writer of cable television's 'Red Shoes Diaries.' King's wife, Patricia Knop, often collaborates on his screenplays.

FILMS INCLUDE: *The Ski Bum* (act.), *You've Got to Walk It Like You Talk It or You'll Lose the Beat* (act.) 1971; *The Passover Plot* (act.) 1976; *Roadie* (exec. prod., co-story) 1980; *Endangered Species* (exec. prod.) 1982; *9½ Weeks* (co-sc., co-prod.) 1986; *Two-Moon Junction* (dir., sc.) 1988; *Wild Orchid* (dir., co-sc.) 1990; *Wild Orchid 2: Two Shades of Blue* (dir., co-sc.) 1992; *Boca* (ex-prod.), *Delta of Venus* 1994.

Kingsley, Ben. Actor. Born Krishna Banji, on Dec. 31, 1943 in Yorkshire, England. Intense, wiry character star of British and international films. The son of an Indian physician of South African origin and a British model-actress, he began his career with an amateur stage company in Manchester. Turning professional in London in 1966, he joined the Royal Shakespeare Company the following year and appeared in many productions of the classic repertoire. He made an isolated film appearance in 1972, then returned to the screen impressively a decade later in a tour-de-force performance in *Gandhi* (1982). He won the best actor Oscar and a British Academy Award for his stunning portrayal of the Indian leader, for which he prepared by losing 20 pounds. He went on to play strong, perceptive roles in other films, memorably *Betrayal* and *Turtle Diary,* as well as in such TV movies as *Murderers Among Us: The Simon Wiesenthal Story* (1989). He scored a hit in New York in 'Edmund Kean' (1983), a performance directed by his second wife (from 1978), Alison Sutcliffe. His first was actress Angela Morant.

FEATURE FILMS: *Fear Is the Key* 1972; *Gandhi* (title role) 1982; *Betrayal* 1983; *Harem* (Fr.), *Turtle Diary* 1985; *Maurice* 1987; *Testimony* (as Dimitri Shostakovich), *Pascali's Island, Without a Clue* (as Dr. Watson) 1988; *Slipstream* 1989; *Una Vita scellerata/A Violent Life* (It./Fr./Ger.), *Romeo-Juliet* (voice only; Bel.) 1990; *Bugsy* 1991; *Sneakers* 1992; *Dave, Schindler's List, Searching for Bobby Fischer* 1993; *Death and the Maiden* 1994; *Species* 1995; *Twelfth Night* 1996; *Children of the Revolution* 1997.

Kingsley, Dorothy. Screenwriter. Born on Oct. 14, 1909, in New York City. *d.* 1997. A former radio comedy writer for Bob Hope, Edgar Bergen, and others, she turned to screenwriting in the mid-40s and collaborated primarily on light films, including a number of MGM musicals. In the late 60s she created the TV series 'Bracken's World.'

FILMS INCLUDE: *Look Who's Laughing* 1941; *Girl Crazy* 1943; *Broadway Rhythm, Bathing Beauty* 1944; *Easy to Wed* 1946; *A Date with Judy* 1948; *Neptune's Daughter* 1949; *Two Weeks with Love* 1950; *Texas Carnival, Angels in the Outfield* 1951; *It's a Big Country* 1952; *Dangerous When Wet, Kiss Me Kate* 1953; *Seven Brides for Seven Brothers* 1954; *Jupiter's Darling* 1955; *Pal Joey, Don't Go Near the Water* 1957; *Green Mansions* 1959; *Can-Can, Pepe* 1960; *Valley of the Dolls, Half a Sixpence* (UK/US) 1967.

Kingston, Winifred. American actress. *b.* 1895. *d.* 1967. Leading lady of early Hollywood silents, often opposite Dustin FARNUM, whom she married.

FILMS INCLUDE: *The Squaw Man, Brewster's Millions, The Call of the North, The Virginian, Cameo Kirby* 1914; *The Love Route, Captain Courtesy, The Gentleman from Indiana* 1915; *The Call of the Cumberlands, David Garrick, Davy Crockett, The Parson of Panamint* 1916; *The Spy, Durand of the Bad Lands, The Scarlet Pimpernel* 1917; *The Light of Western Stars* 1918; *The Corsican Brothers* 1920; *Beyond* 1921; *The Trail of the Axe* 1922; *The Boy and the Bridge* (bit; UK) 1959.

Kino-Eye; Kino-Glaz; Kino-Oki. See VERTOV, Dziga.

Kinopanorama. A Soviet wide-screen system utilizing multiple cameras and projectors and split-screen effects over a 360-degree cylindrical screen surface.

Kino-Pravda. See VERTOV, Dziga.

Kinoshita, Keisuke. Director. Born on Dec. 5, 1912, in Hamamatsu, Japan, a grocer's son. Trained as a photographer, he entered Japanese films in 1933 as a lab and camera assistant. Three years later he became an assistant to director Yasujiro Shimazu and in 1943 turned out his own first film as director. He has worked in a variety of genres, ranging from comedy and satire to romantic drama and themes of social realism. Some critics have compared his satirical works with those of France's René CLAIR. Although little known outside Japan, Kinoshita is among the most respected directors in his native land. His films of the late 40s and early 50s helped resurrect Japanese cinema from the devastation it had suffered in the aftermath of WW II. He directed Japan's first color film, *Carmen Comes Home* (1951). His best-known films in the West are *She Was Like a Wild Chrysanthemum* (1955), a sentimental romantic drama, and *Ballad of Narayama* (1958), a Kabuki-style evocation of Japan's past. He has usually written his own scripts.

FILMS INCLUDE: *The Blossoming Port* 1943; *Army, Jubilation Street* 1944; *The Girl I Loved* 1946; *Marriage* 1947; *Woman, A Portrait* 1948; *The Yotsuya Ghost Story* (in two parts), *The Broken Drum* 1949; *Engagement Ring* 1950; *Carmen Comes Home, The Good Fairy, Youth, Sea of Fireworks* 1951; *Carmen's Pure Love* 1952; *A Japanese Tragedy* 1953; *The Eternal Generation, Twenty-Four Eyes* 1954; *Distant Clouds, She Was Like a Wild Chrysanthemum* 1955; *Clouds at Twilight, The Rose on His Arm* 1956; *The Lighthouse/Times of Joy and Sorrow, Candle in the Wind* 1957; *Ballad of Narayama, The Eternal Rainbow* 1958; *Snow Flurry* 1959; *Spring Dreams* 1960; *The Bitter Spirit/Immortal Love* 1961; *New Year's Love, Ballad of a Workman* 1962; *Sing Young People* 1963; *The Scent of Incense* 1964; *Lovely Flute and Drum/Eyes the Sea and a Ball* 1967; *Love and Separation in Sri Lanka* 1976; *My Son/The Impulsive Murder of My Son* 1979; *Parents Awake!* 1980; *Children of Nagasaki/Leaving These Children Behind* 1983; *Big Joys, Small Sorrows/The Lighthouse Keeper's Family* 1986.

Kinskey (sometimes **Kinsky), Leonid.** Actor. Born on Apr. 18, 1903, in St. Petersburg, Russia. He appeared with various European theaters and toured South America before settling in the US early in the 30s. He soon found a niche in Hollywood films as a light supporting player, portraying exaggerated character parts, often caricatures of foreign types. He retired from films in the late 40s, returning to the screen briefly in the mid-50s. He subsequently appeared occasionally on TV and later made his living as a director-producer of industrial shows. His late wife, Iphigenie Castiglioni, a noted Viennese beauty in her time, played distinguished cameos in a number of Hollywood films.

FILMS INCLUDE: *Trouble in Paradise* 1932; *Duck Soup, Girl Without a Room* 1933; *We Live Again* 1934; *Les Misérables, Peter Ibbetson* 1935; *Rhythm on the Range, The Road to Glory, The General Died at Dawn, The Garden of Allah* 1936; *Espionage, Cafe Metropole, Make a Wish* 1937; *Three Blind Mice, Algiers, The Great Waltz, Professor Beware* 1938; *The Story of Vernon and Irene Castle, Exile Express, On Your Toes, Daytime Wife, Everything Happens at Night* 1939; *He Stayed for Breakfast, Down Argentine Way* 1940; *So Ends Our Night, That Night in Rio, Week-End in Havana* 1941; *Ball of Fire, I Married an Angel, The Talk of the Town* 1942; *Casablanca, Presenting Lily Mars* 1943; *The Fighting Seabees, Can't Help Singing* 1944; *Monsieur Beaucaire* 1946; *Alimony* 1949; *The Man with the Golden Arm* 1955; *Glory* 1956.

Kinski, Klaus. Actor. *b.* Nikolaus (Claus) Günther Nakszynski, 1926, Sopot (Zoppot), Free State of Danzig (later Germany; now Gdansk, Poland). *d.* 1991. Compact, pugnacious, unbridled character player of German and international films. Raised in Berlin, he was drafted into the German army at 18 and spent the waning months of WW II as a British prisoner. After the war, he began acting in the theater, eventually establishing a reputation as a brilliant but unruly performer. On-screen from 1948, he appeared in scores of mostly routine productions, typically in eccentric villainous roles, before emerging as a powerful interpreter of ferociously obsessive characters in such Werner HERZOG films as *Aguirre, the Wrath of God* (1972), *Nosferatu: The Vampyre* (1979), *Fitzcarraldo* (1982), and *Cobra Verde.* He pulled out all the stops in his directorial debut, *Paganini* (1989), an excessive screen biography of the violinist-composer, in which he played the title role. He was the father of actress Nastassja KINSKI and her lesser known sister, Pola. Autobiography: *All I Need Is Love* (1989).

FILMS INCLUDE: *Morituri* 1948; *Decision Before Dawn* (US) 1951; *Ludwig II, Kinder Mütter und ein General, Sarajevo* (Aus.) 1955; *Waldwinter* 1956; *A Time to Love and a Time to Die* (US) 1958; *Der Rächer* 1960; *Die toten Augen von London/Dead Eyes of London, Das Geheimnis der gelben Narzissen/The Devil's Daffodil* (Ger./UK) 1961; *The Counterfeit Traitor* (US) 1962; *Scotland Yard jagt Dr. Mabuse* 1963; *Winnetou II. Teil/Last of the Renegades* 1964; *The Pleasure Girls* (UK), *Doctor Zhivago* (US), *La Geurre secrète/The Dirty Game* (Fr./It./Ger.) 1965; *Per qualche Dollaro in più/For a Few Dollars More* (It./Sp./Ger.), *Our Man in Marrakesh/Bang! Bang! You're Dead!* (UK) 1966; *Jules Verne's Rocket to the Moon/Those Fantastic Flying Fools* (UK), *Sumuru/The Million Eyes of Su-Muru* (UK), *Circus of Fear/Psycho-Circus* (UK), *Quien Sabe?/A Bullet for the General* (It.), *Ad ogni Costo/Grand Slam* (It./Sp./Ger.) 1967; *Ognuno per sè* (It./Ger.) 1968; *Paroxismus/Venus in Furs* (It./Ger./UK) 1969; *Vampir/Count Dracula* (Sp.), *L'Occhio del Ragno* (It.) 1971; *Aguirre der Zorn Gottes/Aguirre the Wrath of God* (title role) 1973; *L'Important c'est d'aimer/The Most Important Thing: Love* (Fr.) 1975; *Das Netz/The Web, Jack the Ripper* (It./Ger.), *Nuit d'Or* (Fr.) 1976; *Operation Thunderbolt* (Isr.), *Madame Claude* (Fr.), *Mort d'un Pourri* (Fr.) 1977; *Nosferatu: Phantom der Nacht/Nosferatu, The Vampyre* (as Nosferatu-Dracula), *Woyzeck* 1979; *La Femme Enfant* (Fr.), *Schizoid* (US) 1980; *Buddy Buddy* (US), *Les Fruits de la Passion/The Fruits of Passion* (Fr./Jap.) 1981; *Venom* (UK), *Love and Money* (US), *Fitzcarraldo, The Soldier* (US), *Android* (US) 1982; *The Secret Diary of Sigmund Freud* (US), *Codename: Wildgeese* (It./Ger.), *The Little Drummer Girl* 1984; *Cobra Verde* 1988; *Paganini* (title role; also dir., sc.; It.) 1989.

Kinski, Nastassja (also **Nastassia).** Actress. Born Nastassja Nakszynski, on Jan. 24, 1959, in West Berlin. Radiantly sensual, full-lipped, gray-green-eyed star of international films. The daughter of actor Klaus KINSKI from his first marriage, to poet Ruth Brigitte, she lost contact with her father after her parents separated when she was ten. A stunning nymphet in her teens, she made her screen debut in Wim Wenders's *Wrong Move* (1975), then met and fell in love with director Roman POLANSKI, 25 years her senior, who became her lover and mentor. Under his guidance, she went to Los Angeles for six months of training with Lee STRASBERG, then to London for additional coaching, and to a Dorchester farm for four months of hands-on experience, all in preparation for her first major starring role in Polanski's film, *Tess* (1980), which briefly established her as one of the screen's premier leading ladies. Admitting fleeting Trilby-like passions for her directors, she had a well-publicized affair with Frenchman Jean-Jacques (*Diva*)

BEINEIX who directed her in *Moon in the Gutter* (1983). When she gave birth to a son in 1984, the director was among eight paternity "suspects" listed by a sensational German magazine. The father was eventually officially identified as Egyptian-born producer-talent agent Ibrahiim Moussa, whom Kinski married later that year. Her film career since has been erratic and low-key.

FILMS: *Falsche Bewegung/The Wrong Move/Wrong Movement* (Ger.) 1975; *Reifezeugnis/For Your Love Only* (TV movie theatrically released in 1982; Ger.), *To the Devil a Daughter* (UK/Ger.) 1976; *Leidenschaftliche Blumchen/Virgin Campus/Passion Flower Hotel* (Ger.), *Cosi coe sei/Stay as You Are* (It.) 1978; *Tess* (Fr./UK) 1979; *One from the Heart* (US), *Cat People* (US) 1982; *Exposed* (US), *Frülingssinfonie/Spring Symphony* (as Robert Schumann's wife, pianist Clara Wieck; E. Ger./W. Ger.), *La Lune das le Canivaux/The Moon in the Gutter* (Fr./It.) 1983; *Unfaithfully Yours* (US), *The Hotel New Hampshire* (US), *Paris Texas* (US) 1984; *Maria's Lovers* (US), *Harem* (Fr.), *Revolution* (UK/Nor.) 1985; *Maladie d'Amour* (Fr.) 1987; *Magdalene* (US) 1988; *Torrents of Spring* (It./Fr./UK) 1989; *Il sole anche di notte/The Sun Also Shines at Night* (It./Fr./Ger.) 1990; *The Insulted and the Injured, On a Moonlit Night* (US), *The Secret* (US) 1991; *Night Sun* (US) 1992; *Faraway, So Close!* (Ger.) 1993; *The Blonde, Terminal Velocity* 1994; *Somebody Is Waiting* 1996; *Father's Day, One Night Stand* 1997.

Kinugasa, Teinosuke. Director. *b.* Teinosuke Kogame, Jan. 1, 1896, Mie Prefecture, Japan. *d.* 1982. A tobacconist's son, he ran away from home to Nagoya at 17, in quest of theatrical training. Making a dual debut onstage and on-screen two years later, he initially specialized in *oyama* roles, in which males impersonate females. He began directing in 1921, usually writing his own scripts. Almost from the start he played an important part in the emergence of Japanese cinema as an art while experimenting with novel modes of expression. In his impressionist *A Crazy Page/A Page of Madness* (1926), he deftly manipulated past and present, reality and hallucination, with inventiveness making up for budget limitations. The film was notable for its near absence of intertitles. So was Kinugasa's next important film, *Jujiro* (1928), variably known in the West as *Crossroads, Crossways,* or *The Shadows of the Yoshiwara.* More conventional in structure than its predecessor, it was nonetheless startlingly innovative and dramatically captivating. It was the first Japanese film to attempt commercial exploitation in Europe. In 1928, Kinugasa traveled to Russia, where he met Eisenstein and Pudovkin, then to Germany and France. His early work after his return to Japan showed the influence of Soviet montage and an interest in the spirit of revolution. But he soon adopted a formal visual style, specializing in period dramas. His brilliant use of color in *Gate of Hell* (1953) dazzled Western audiences. The film captured the Grand Prix at Cannes, as well as Academy Awards as best foreign language film and for best color costume design.

FILMS INCLUDE: *The Death of My Sister* (also act.) 1921; *Two Little Birds* 1922; *The Golden Demon, Beyond Decay* 1923; *She Has Lived Her Destiny, Secret of a Wife, Love Fog and Rain* 1924; *Love and the Warrior, The Sun* 1925; *A Crazy Page/A Page of Madness* 1926; *Epoch of Loyalty, Moonlight Madness* 1927; *Jujiro/Crossroads/Crossways/The Shadows of the Yoshiwara, The Gay Masquerade, Tales from a Country by the Sea* 1928; *Before Dawn* 1931; *The Loyal 47 Ronin* 1932; *Two Stone Lanterns* 1933; *The Sword and the Sumo Ring* 1934; *Yukinojo's Disguise* (trilogy) 1935–36; *The Summer Battle of Osaka* 1937; *Miss Snake Princess* (in two parts) 1940; *Rose of the Sea* 1945; *Lord for a Night* 1946; *Four Love Stories, Actress* 1947; *Koga Mansion* 1949; *The Face of a Murderer* 1950; *Saga of the Great Buddha/Dedication of the Great Buddha* 1952; *Gate of Hell* 1953; *Duel of a Snowy Night* 1954; *It Happened in Tokyo, The Romance of Yushima* 1955; *A Fantastic Tale of Naruto* 1957; *Symphony of Love, A Woman of Osaka, The White Heron* 1958; *Tormented Flame* 1959; *The Lantern* 1960; *Okoto and Sasuke* 1961; *The Sorcerer* 1963; *The Little Runaway* (co-dir. with Nkandrovich; Jap./USSR) 1967.

Kirby, Bruno. Actor. Born in 1949 in New York City. Open-faced supporting player, often cast in comic everyman roles. Billed early in his career as B. Kirby, Jr. and Bruno Kirby, Jr. Son of actor Bruce Kirby.

FILMS INCLUDE: *The Harrad Experiment, Cinderella Liberty* 1973; *The Godfather, Part II* 1974; *Baby Blue Marine* 1976; *Between the Lines* 1977; *Almost Summer* 1978; *Where the Buffalo Roam, Borderline* 1980; *Modern Romance* 1981; *This Is Spinal Tap, Birdy* 1984, *Flesh and Blood* 1985, *Tin Men, Good Morning Vietnam* 1987; *Bert Rigby You're a Fool, When Harry Met Sally. . . , We're No Angels* 1989; *The Freshman* 1990, *City Slickers* 1991, *Hoffa* (uncred.) 1992; *The Basketball Diaries, Golden Gate* 1994.

Kirk, Phyllis. Actress. Born Phyllis Kirkegaard, on Sept. 18, 1926, in Syracuse, N.Y. A former model, she played leads in Hollywood films of the 50s. A pretty, perky brunette, she was popular as Nora Charles in TV's 'The Thin Man' series (1957–59). With her acting career hampered by a hip injury, she turned to business, becoming a public relations executive.

FILMS: *Our Very Own, A Life of Her Own, Two Weeks with Love, Mrs. O'Malley and Mr. Malone* 1950; *Three Guys Named Mike* 1951; *About Face, The Iron Mistress* 1952; *House of Wax, Thunder Over the Plains* 1953; *Crime Wave, River Beat* 1954; *Johnny Concho, Back from Eternity* 1956; *That Woman Opposite/City After Midnight* (UK), *The Sad Sack* 1957.

Kirk, Tommy. Actor. Born on Dec. 10, 1941, in Louisville, Ky. Juvenile hero of Walt Disney film and TV productions of the late 50s and early 60s. He later played leads in "beach party" movies and other low-budget, teen-oriented films.

FILMS INCLUDE: *Old Yeller* 1957; *The Shaggy Dog* 1959; *Swiss Family Robinson* 1960; *The Absent-Minded Professor, Babes in Toyland* 1961; *Moon Pilot, Bon Voyage!* 1962; *Son of Flubber, Savage Sam* 1963; *The Misadventures of Merlin Jones* 1964; *The Monkey's Uncle, Village of the Giants* 1965; *The Ghost in the Invisible Bikini* 1966; *The Catalina Caper* 1967; *Track of Thunder* 1968; *Downhill Racer* 1969; *My Name Is Legend* 1976.

Kirkland, Sally. Actress. Born Sally Kirkland, Jr., on Oct. 31, 1944, in New York City. Maverick leading lady and supporting player of the American stage and screen. The daughter of a scrap-metal dealer and Sally Kirkland, the influential fashion editor of *Life,* she trained at the Actors Studio with Uta Hagen and Lee STRASBERG. She acquired early notoriety in the 60s for her nude appearances in such stage productions as 'Sweet Eros' and 'Futz.' She performed in experimental off-off-Broadway plays and underground films, and was an outspoken member of Andy Warhol's inner circle before settling down in the early 70s into a more conventional career, playing mostly small roles in Hollywood movies. She was nominated for an Academy Award as best actress for her portrayal of the title role in *Anna* (1987). In 1983 she founded the Sally Kirkland Acting Workshop, a traveling seminar in which she teaches yoga and transcendental meditation as well as drama. In 1990 she returned to the New York stage after a long absence, in 'Grotesque Lovesongs,' and has also appeared on television in small roles on such shows as "Roseanne."

FILMS: *The Thirteen Most Beautiful Women* 1964; *Blue* 1968; *Coming Apart, Futz* 1969; *Brand X* 1970; *Going Home*

1971; *The Young Nurses, The Way We Were, Cinderella Liberty, The Sting* 1973; *Candy Striped Nurses, Big Bad Mama* 1974; *Bite the Bullet, Crazy Mama* 1975; *Breakheart Pass, Pipe Dreams, A Star Is Born* 1976; *Hometown U.S.A.* 1979; *Private Benjamin* 1980; *The Incredible Shrinking Woman* 1981; *Human Highway* 1982; *Talking Walls, Double Exposure, Love Letters, Fatal Games* 1983; *Anna* 1987; *Crack in the Mirror* 1988; *Best of the Best, Bullseye!, Cold Feet* 1989; *Paint It Black, Revenge, Due Occhi Diabolici/Two Evil Eyes* (It.) 1990; *J.F.K.* 1991; *In the Heat of Passion* 1991; *The Player* (cameo), *Primary Motive, Forever* 1992; *Gunmen* 1994; *Body and Soul* 1997.

Kirkwood, James. Director, actor. *b.* Feb. 22, 1883, Grand Rapids, Mich. *d.* 1963. A veteran of the stage, he entered films in 1909 and played leading roles in many of the early pictures of D. W. GRIFFITH. In 1912 he turned to directing and during 1914 helmed nine films starring Mary PICKFORD. He played the romantic lead in three of these films. He also directed and co-starred in several productions featuring Lillian Gish or Blanche Sweet. A flamboyant, hard-drinking man of distinguished good looks, Kirkwood proved to be a facile, intelligent director, but he lacked the discipline and ambition usually associated with his position and before long found directing assignments hard to come by. He returned to acting and continued playing leading and supporting roles in films through the mid-50s. His first wife was silent screen actress Gertrude Robinson, and his second, Lila LEE. He was the father of actor-playwright-novelist James Kirkwood, Jr. (1930–89), the Pulitzer Prize–winning co-author of 'A Chorus Line.'

FILMS INCLUDE: As director—*Prince Charming* (co-dir. with George Loane Tucker; also act.) 1912; *The House of Discord* (also act.) 1913; *The Soul of Honor* (also act.), *Ashes of the Past* (also act.), *The Floor Above, The Gangsters, The Mountain Rat* (also act.), *Classmates, Strongheart* (also act.), *The Eagle's Mate* (also act.), *Men and Women, Behind the Scenes* (also act.), *Cinderella* 1914; *Mistress Nell, Fanchon the Cricket* (also sc.), *The Dawn of a Tomorrow, Little Pal, The Heart of Jennifer* (also act.), *Rags, Esmeralda, The Masqueraders, The Old Homestead* 1915; *The Lost Bridegroom, Saints and Sinners, Susie Snowflake, Dulcie's Adventure, Faith* (also sc.), *A Dream or Two Ago* 1916; *The Gentle Intruder, Environment* (also sc.), *Perriwinkle, Over There* 1917; *Eve's Daughter, A Romance of the Underworld* (also prod.), *Out of the Night* (also prod.), *Marriage, The Struggle Everlasting, I Want to Forget* (also sc.) 1918; *Bill Apperson's Boy* (also sc.), *In Wrong* (also sc.) 1919. As actor—*At the Altar, The Road to the Heart, The Renunciation, The Message, The Slave, The Mended Lute, A Convict's Sacrifice, The Seventh Day, The Indian Runner's Romance, The Better Way, Comata the Sioux, 1776 or the Hessian Renegades, Fools of Fate, Pippa Passes, The Gibson Goddess, Through the Breakers, The Redman's View* 1909; *The Rocky Road, The Honor of His Family, The Last Deal, The Final Settlement, A Victim of Jealousy, Winning Back His Love* 1910; *Home Sweet Home* 1914; *The Luck of the Irish, The Scoffer, The Forbidden Thing, Love* 1920; *Man—Woman—Marriage, Bob Hampton* 1921; *The Man from Home, Pink Gods, Under Two Flags, The Sin Flood, Ebb Tide* 1922; *Human Wreckage, Ponjola, The Eagle's Feather* 1923; *Love's Whirlpool, Wandering Husbands, Broken Barriers, Gerald Cranston's Lady, Circle the Enchantress* 1924; *The Top of the World* (dual role), *Secrets of the Night, Lover's Island, That Royle Girl* 1925; *The Reckless Lady, The Wise Guy, Butterflies in the Rain* 1926; *Million Dollar Mystery* 1927; *Someone to Love* 1928; *The Time the Place and the Girl, Hearts in Exile* 1929; *The Devil's Holiday, Worldly Goods, The Spoilers* 1930; *Young Sinners, A Holy Terror, Over the Hill* 1931; *Charlie Chan's Chance, The Rainbow Trail, She Wanted a Millionaire, Cheaters at Play, My Pal the King* 1932; *Hired Wife* 1934; *No Hands of the Clock* 1941; *Madame Curie* 1943; *Joan of Arc, The Untamed Breed* 1948; *Intruder in the Dust, Roseana McCoy* 1949; *Fancy Pants* 1950; *Stage to Tucson* 1951; *The Last Posse* 1953; *The Search for Bridey Murphy* 1956.

Kirsanoff, Dimitri. Director. *b.* Mar. 6, 1899, Dorpat, Estonia. *d.* 1957. In Paris from 1923, he directed several original, lyrical silent films, some experimental in nature, notably the personal and poetic *Menilmontant* (1926). His sound films are more conventional and far less interesting. His first wife, Nadia Sibirskaia (*b.* Jeanne Brunet 1901, Redon, France), starred in several of his films. His second, Monique Kirsanoff (*b.* 1913, Sussac, France), is the editor of numerous French films.

FILMS: *L'Ironie du Destin/The Irony of Fate* (also sc., act.) 1923; *Menilmontant* (also prod., sc., co-phot.) 1926; *Sylvie Destin/Destins* (also sc.), *Sables* 1927; *Brumes d'Automne* (also sc.) 1929; *Les Nuits de Port-Saïd* (co-dir.) 1931; *Rapt/The Mystic Mountain* (Switz.) 1934; *Les Berceaux* (short) 1953; *Visages de France* (doc.), *La Fontaine d'Aréthuse* (short), *Jeune Fille au Jardin* (short) 1936; *Franco de Port* (also sc.) 1937; *L'Avion de Minuit* (also co-dial.), *La plus Belle fille du Monde* (also sc.) 1938; *Quartier sans Soleil* (also sc.; release delayed from 1939) 1945; *Deux Amis* (short) 1946; *Faits divers à Paris* (short) 1949; *Arrière Saison* (short) 1950; *Une Chasse à Courre/La Mort du Cerf* (short) 1951; *Le Témoin de Minuit* 1952; *Le Craneur/La Vallée du Paradis* 1955; *Ce Soir les Jupons volent, Miss Catastrophe* 1956.

Kitt, Eartha. Singer, actress. Born on Jan. 26, 1928, in North, S.C. Feline, slinky, smoldering black star of nightclubs, the stage, and a handful of films. A resident of New York's Harlem from the age of eight, she attended the High School of Performing Arts and joined the Katherine Dunham dancers, with whom she went on a tour of Europe. At the end of the tour, she remained in Paris, where she appeared in a fashionable nightclub. Returning to the US, she performed in top Manhattan supper clubs and scored a personal triumph in the Broadway production of 'New Faces of 1952.' Two years later she made her film debut in the screen version of that show. She returned to the screen in 1975, after a decade's absence, in *Friday Foster,* and to the Broadway stage in 1978, after two decades, as the star of the musical 'Timbuktu,' a black-cast version of 'Kismet.' She was the subject of a 1982 feature-length documentary, *All by Myself.* Memoirs: *Thursday's Child* (1956), *A Tart Is Not a Sweet, Alone with Me* (1976), *I'm Still Here: Confessions of a Sex Kitten* (1992).

FILMS: *New Faces* 1954; *The Mark of the Hawk, St. Louis Blues* 1958; *Anna Lucasta* 1959; *The Saint of Devil's Island* 1961; *Onkel Toms Hütte/Uncle Tom's Cabin* (Ger./Fr./It./Yug.), *Synanon* 1965; *Up the Chastity Belt* (UK) 1971; *Friday Foster* 1975; *The Last Resort* 1979; *All By Myself* (doc.) 1982; *The Serpent Warriors* 1986; *The Pink Chiquitas* 1987; *Erik the Viking* (UK/Swed.) 1989; *Ernest Scared Stupid, Boomerang* 1992; *Harriet the Spy* 1996.

Kitzmiller, John. Actor. *b.* Dec. 4, 1913, Battle Creek, Mich. *d.* 1965. A US serviceman in Italy during the last phases of WW II, he was asked to appear in a couple of Italian neorealist films, then was given the lead role in *Senza Pietá/Without Pity* (1948). He stayed in Europe, appearing in many films, often stereotyped as a Negro fighting prejudice. He won the 1957 Cannes Festival Award as best actor for his performance in the Yugoslavian film *Dolina Miru/Peace Valley/Sergeant Jim.*

FILMS INCLUDE: *Vivere in Pace/To Live in Peace* 1947; *Senza Pietá/Without Pity* 1948; *Il Teneto Craig—Mio Marito/Lieutenant Craig—Missing* 1949; *Luci del Varietà/Variety*

Lights 1951; *Massacre en Dentelles* (Fr.), *A Fil di Spada* 1952; *La Peccatrice dell'Isola/The Island Sinner, Legione Staniera* 1953; *Quai des Blondes* (Fr.) 1954; *Dolina Miru/Peace Valley/Sergeant Jim* (Yug.) 1957; *Naked Earth* (UK), *Vite Perdute/Lost Souls* 1958; *I Pirati della Costa* 1960; *La Rivolta dei Mercenari/Revolt of the Mercenaries* (It./Sp.), *Il Figlio del Capitane Blood/The Son of Captain Blood* (It./Sp./US), *Dr. No* (UK) 1962; *La Tigre dei Sette Mari/Tiger of the Seven Seas* (It./Fr.) 1963; *Der Fluch der grünen Augen/Cave of the Living Dead* (Ger./Yug.) 1964; *Onkel Toms Hütte/Uncle Tom's Cabin* (as Uncle Tom; Ger./Fr./It./Yug.) 1965.

Kjellin, Alf. Actor, director. *b.* Feb. 28, 1920, Lund, Sweden. *d.* 1987. Tall, handsome, popular leading man of Swedish films of the 40s. Trained for the stage, he made only a few theater appearances before entering films and became internationally known as the young hero of Alf Sjöberg's *Hets* (1944), a film scripted by Ingmar Bergman which was released in the US as *Torment* and in the UK as *Frenzy.* In the wake of that film's success, Kjellin was imported by Hollywood, making his American debut in Vincente Minnelli's *Madame Bovary* (1949) under the pseudonym of Christopher Kent. He later reverted to his real name and appeared in several Hollywood films of the early 50s, but he continued working out of Sweden, directing as well as acting, until the early 60s, when he settled in Hollywood as a TV director and occasionally a feature film director or actor.

FILMS INCLUDE: As actor—*John Ericsson the Victor at Hampton Roads* 1937; *Rejoice While You're Young, Fellow Cadets* 1939; *His Grace's Will* 1940; *Night in the Harbor* 1943; *Appassionata, Torment/Frenzy* 1944; *Wandering with the Moon* 1945; *Sunshine Follows Rain, Iris and the Lieutenant* 1946; *A Girl from the Marsh Croft, Woman Without a Face* 1947; *Madame Bovary* (US) 1949; *Singoalla/The Wind Is My Lover* (Sw./Fr.), *This Can't Happen Here/High Tension, The White Cat* 1950; *Illicit Interlude, Rolling Sea, Divorced* 1951; *My Six Convicts* (US), *The Iron Mistress* (US) 1952; *The Juggler* (US), *No Man's Woman* 1953; *Playing on the Rainbow* 1958; *Two Living One Dead* (UK/Sw.) 1961; *The Victors* (UK/US), *My Love Is a Rose* 1963; *Ship of Fools* 1965; *Assault on a Queen* (US) 1966; *Ice Station Zebra* (US) 1968; *Zandy's Bride* (bit) 1974. As director—*Girl in the Rain* (also sc., act.), *Seventeen Years Old* (also co-sc.), *Encounters at Dusk* 1957; *Swinging at the Castle* 1959; *Only a Waiter* 1960; *Pleasure Garden* 1961; *Siska* 1962; *Midas Run* (US) 1969; *The McMasters* (US) 1970.

Klane, Robert. American screenwriter, noted for his offbeat, if sometimes silly, humorous style.

FILMS: *Where's Poppa?* 1970; *Every Little Crook and Nanny* 1972; *Fire Sale* 1977; *Thank God It's Friday* (also dir.) 1978; *Unfaithfully Yours* 1984; *The Man with One Red Shoe, National Lampoon's European Vacation* 1985; *Walk Like a Man* 1987; *Weekend at Bernie's* (also co-exec prod.) 1989; *Weekend at Bernie's 2* 1993.

Klein, William. Director. Born in 1926, in New York City. Remaining in Paris after his discharge from WW II service with the US Army, he studied painting with Fernand LÉGER and exhibited his own work in various European cities. He then took up photography, contributed regularly to *Vogue* magazine, and published several photo albums on various cities. In 1958 he made his first film, the short *Broadway by Light.* In 1960 he served as an artistic consultant on Louis Malle's *Zazie dans le Metro/Zazie* and subsequently directed a number of "protest" documentary shorts and features in the *cinéma vérité* style. His work for French TV included *Cassius le Grand* (1964), a documentary about boxer Muhammad Ali which he later expanded into the feature length film *Float Like a Butterfly—Sting Like a Bee* (1969). He had made his first feature-length film in 1966.

FEATURE FILMS: *Qui êtes-vous Polly Maggoo?/Who Are You Polly Maggoo?* (also sc.) 1966; *Loin du Vietnam/Far from Vietnam* (co-dir., co-prod., co-sc.) 1967; *Mister Freedom* (also sc.), *Float Like a Butterfly—Sting Like a Bee* (also prod., sc., phot., edit.) *Festival Panafricain* (also sc.) 1969; *Eldridge Cleaver* (also prod., sc., co-phot., co-edit) 1970; *Le Couple Témoin* (dir., sc.) 1977; *The French* (also sc., co-phot.) 1982.

Kleiner, Harry. Screenwriter. Born on September 10, 1916, in Tiflis, Russia. In the US from infancy, he was raised in Philadelphia and educated at Temple University (B.S.) and Yale (M.F.A.). In addition to writing Hollywood screenplays, alone or in collaboration, he has authored a number of stage plays and TV scripts. He has also produced several films.

FILMS INCLUDE: *Fallen Angel* 1945; *The Street with No Name* 1948; *Red Skies of Montana, Kangaroo* 1952; *Salome* 1953; *Miss Sadie Thompson, Carmen Jones* 1954; *The Violent Men* 1955; *The Garment Jungle* (also prod.) 1957; *Cry Tough* (also prod.), *The Rabbit Trap* (prod. only) 1959; *Ice Palace* 1960; *Fever in the Blood* 1961; *Fantastic Voyage* 1966; *Bullitt* 1968; *Le Mans* 1971; *Extreme Prejudice* 1987; *Red Heat* 1988.

Klein-Rogge, Rudolf. Actor. *b.* Nov. 24, 1888, Cologne, Germany. *d.* 1955. Played impressive character parts in expressionist German films of the 20s, notably the title roles in Fritz Lang's *Dr. Mabuse der Spieler/Dr. Mabuse the Gambler* (1922) and *Das Testament des Dr. Mabuse/The Testament of Dr. Mabuse/The Last Will of Dr. Mabuse* (1933). At his best in villainous roles. He married Thea von HARBOU and influenced her pro-Nazi leanings. They later divorced.

FILMS INCLUDE: *Morphium* 1919; *Das wandernde Bild* 1920; *Zirkus des Lebens, Der müde Tod/Destiny/Between Worlds* 1921; *Dr. Mabuse der Spieler/Dr. Mabuse the Gambler* 1922; *Die Nibelungen: Kriemhilds Rache/Kriemhild's Revenge, Pietro der Korsar/Peter the Pirate* 1924; *Metropolis* 1926; *Der Zigeunerbaron* 1927; *Spione/Spies, Wolga-Wolga* 1928; *Das Testament des Dr. Mabuse/The Testament of Dr. Mabuse/The Last Will of Dr. Mabuse, Elisabeth und der Narr* 1933; *Zwischen Himmel und Erde/Between Heaven and Earth* 1934; *Der alte und der junge Konig/The Old and the Young King* 1935; *Moral, Intermezzo* 1936; *Madame Bovary, Der Herrscher* 1937; *Robert Koch, Menschen vom Variete* 1939; *Hochzeit auf Barenhof* 1942.

Kleiser, Randal. American director. Born on July 20, 1946. A graduate of the University of Southern California (USC), he accumulated impressive television credits before making a sparkling entry into features with an energetic screen adaptation of the musical *Grease* (1978). His films are technically slick and typically marked by an unsophisticated, youthful appeal. *The Blue Lagoon*, his saga of sexual awakening on a desert island (starring Brooke SHIELDS), attracted both critical derision and a cult following.

FILMS: *Grease* 1978; *The Blue Lagoon* (also prod.) 1980; *Rich and Famous* 1981; *Summer Lovers* (also sc.) 1982; *Grandview U.S.A.* 1984; *Flight of the Navigator* 1986; *North Shore* (exec prod., co-story only) 1987; *Big Top Pee-Wee* 1988; *Getting It Right* (also co-prod.) 1989; *White Fang* 1990; *Return to the Blue Lagoon* (exec. prod. only), *Honey I Blew Up the Kid* 1992; *It's My Party* 1996.

Klemperer, Werner. Actor. Born on Mar. 20, 1920, in Cologne, Germany. After the Nazi takeover, he came to the US with his father, famed conductor Otto Klemperer, in 1933. He played character parts, typically as a ridiculous, bald, monocled Nazi, in a number of films, and twice (1968, 1969) won an Emmy Award for his portrayal of the camp commandant in the TV series 'Hogan's Heroes' (1965–71).

FILMS INCLUDE: *Death of a Scoundrel, Flight to Hong Kong* 1956; *Istanbul, Five Steps to Danger, Kiss Them for Me*

1957; *The Goddess* 1958; *Operation Eichmann* (title role), *Judgment at Nuremberg* 1961; *Escape from East Berlin* 1962; *Youngblood Hawke* 1964; *Ship of Fools* 1965; *The Wicked Dreams of Paula Schultz* 1968.

klieg lights. Powerful, open-arc floodlights used in motion picture production; named after their German-born American designers, the brothers J. H. and Anton Kliegl.

Klimov, Elem. Soviet director. Born in 1933. His early films, broad satires of the system, drew sharp criticism from the authorities. After turning out a successful semidocumentary history of sports, he directed *Agony,* a film about Rasputin and the disintegration of the Russian ruling class, in which he mixed black-and-white authentic and recreated documentary footage with color fiction material. The film, made in 1975, was deemed pointless and was shelved until its exhibition in 1981 at the Moscow Film Festival. His *Come and See* received the Grand Prix at the same event in 1985.

FILMS: *We Welcome You* 1964; *Adventures of a Dentist* 1967; *Sport Sport Sport* 1971; *Agony/Rasputin* (release delayed from 1975), *Farewell* 1981; *Larissa* (short) 1982; *Come and See* 1985.

Kline, Herbert. Documentary director. Born on Mar. 13, 1909, in Chicago. A former editor of the magazine *New Theatre* and a left-wing activist, he became associated with the New York Film and Photo League, a sociopolitical documentary movement, in the early 30s. He was one of the first Americans to arrive in Spain during the Civil War and he recorded on film the strife and agony there in the documentary *Heart of Spain* (1937; the film was edited in New York by Paul Strand and Leo Hurwitz). Kline subsequently directed a number of political documentaries, notably *Crisis* (1938), about Hitler's conquest of Czechoslovakia; *Lights Out in Europe* (1940), documenting the outbreak of WW II; and *The Forgotten Village* (1941), a remarkable documentary about Mexican life from a script by John Steinbeck. The latter film was honored as best feature documentary at the Brussels World Film Festival of 1947. In 1947, Kline directed *My Father's House,* an appealing feature-length film dramatizing the Jewish struggle for a homeland in Israel. He later attempted unsuccessfully to join the mainstream of Hollywood's commercial cinema as a director and a writer.

FILMS INCLUDE (as director unless otherwise noted): *Heart of Spain* (co-phot., assoc. prod. only) 1937; *Return to Life* (co-dir. with Cartier-Bresson), *Crisis* 1938; *Lights Out in Europe* 1940; *The Forgotten Village* 1941; *Youth Runs Wild* (story only) 1944; *My Father's House* (also prod.) 1947; *The Kid from Cleveland* (also story), *Illegal Entry* (story only) 1949; *The Fighter* (also sc.) 1952; *Prince of Pirates* (co-story only) 1953; *Walls of Fire* (also co-sc.) 1974; *The Challenge of Greatness/The Challenge: A Tribute to Modern Art* (also prod.) 1976; *Acting: Lee Strasberg and the Actors Studio* (also prod., sc.) 1981.

Kline, Kevin. Actor. Born on Oct. 24, 1947, in St. Louis. Bright, versatile, dynamic leading man of the American stage and screen. The product of a Jewish father, a musician who operated a record store, and a Catholic mother, he was educated in Catholic schools by Benedictine monks. He enrolled at Indiana University as a music major but later switched to drama, then went on to Juilliard's drama department. After four years on the road with John Houseman's Acting Company, he returned to New York, where he appeared in the TV daytime soaper 'Search for Tomorrow' (1976–77) and soon flourished on Broadway, winning Tony Awards for 'On the Twentieth Century' (1978) and 'The Pirates of Penzance' (1980). In a four-year span (1986–90) Kline starred in two lauded off-Broadway productions of 'Hamlet,' the latter under his own direction. On-screen from 1982, he won an Academy Award as best supporting actor for his eccentric role in the madcap crime caper *A Fish Called Wanda*. He also won acclaim for his comic portrayal of a US president and his double in *Dave*. Combining the range of a character actor with the dashing looks of a leading man, his diverse talent is yet to be fully tapped in films. In 1989 he married actress Phoebe CATES.

FILMS: *Sophie's Choice* 1982; *The Pirates of Penzance, The Big Chill* 1983; *Silverado* 1985; *Violets Are Blue* 1986; *Cry Freedom* 1987; *A Fish Called Wanda* 1988; *The January Man* 1989; *I Love You to Death* 1990; *Soapdish, Grand Canyon* 1991; *Dave* 1993; *Princess Caraboo* 1994; *French Kiss* 1995; *The Hunchback of Notre Dame, Looking for Richard* 1996; *Fierce Creatures, Ice Storm, In and Out* 1997.

Kline, Richard H. American director of photography. Born in 1926. Graduated to cinematographer in the late 60s after several years as a camera assistant and camera operator and has since worked effectively on a number of major productions.

FILMS INCLUDE: *Chamber of Horrors* 1966; *Camelot* 1967; *The Boston Strangler* 1968; *Gaily Gaily, A Dream of Kings* 1969; *The Moonshine War* 1970; *The Andromeda Strain, Kotch* 1971; *Hammersmith Is Out, When the Legends Die, The Mechanic* 1972; *Soylent Green, Battle for the Planet of the Apes, The Don Is Dead* 1973; *The Terminal Man, Mr. Majestyk* 1974; *Mandingo* 1975; *King Kong* 1976; *The Fury, Who'll Stop the Rain?* 1978; *Star Trek: The Motion Picture* 1979; *The Competition* 1980; *Body Heat* 1981; *Death Wish II* 1982; *Breathless* 1983; *All of Me* 1984; *The Man with One Red Shoe* 1985; *Howard the Duck* 1986; *Touch and Go* 1987; *My Stepmother Is an Alien* 1988.

Klos, Elmar. See KADÁR, Ján.

Kluge, Alexander. Director. Born on Feb. 14, 1932, in Halberstadt, Germany, a physician's son. A practicing lawyer and a published novelist and political writer, he entered German films in 1958 as an assistant to Fritz LANG. He began making shorts in 1960 and in 1962 became a leading spokesman for a group of young German filmmakers protesting at the Oberhausen Festival the stagnant state of the traditional German cinema. He turned out his first feature, *Abschied von Gestern/Yesterday Girl* in 1966. He adapted the screenplay from his own story, based on a real character about the unhappy ordeals of a young Jewish fugitive from East Germany (played brilliantly by Kluge's sister, Alexandra [née Karen]), who seeks a new life in the Federal Republic but encounters apathy and misery on her pitiable odyssey in the prosperous West. The film, which boasted unconventional stylistic devices, including direct speech to the camera, accelerated motion, and surrealistic scenes, was a watershed production in the development of the New German Cinema. It won several awards at Venice, including a Special Jury Prize (Silver Lion), giving the German film industry its first international recognition in years. With his subsequent films, Kluge further established himself as a guiding spirit and eminent voice of the new German Cinema. Paying him a disciple's homage, Rainer Werner FASSBINDER dedicated his *Lola* (1981) to Kluge. A capable craftsman as well a creative, intelligent artist, Kluge views filmmaking as an extension of his writing and pursues on celluloid the same social and political concerns that he does in print. His protagonists are frequently women (often portrayed by his sister, Alexandra), through whose tribulations he reflects on the human condition in contemporary society. His films are often ponderous and complex in style. He invariably writes his own scripts. He won the Golden Lion at Venice in 1968 for *Artists at the Top of the Big Top: Disoriented,* and the International Critics

Prize at Cannes in 1976 for *Strongman Ferdinand* and at Venice in 1983 for *The Power of Emotion.*

FEATURE FILMS (as director-screenwriter): *Abschied von Gestern/Yesterday Girl* (from own story 'Attendance List for a Funeral'; also prod., act.) 1966; *Die Artisten in der Zirkuskuppel: Ratlos/Artists at the Top of the Big Top: Disoriented* (also act.) 1968; *Die unbezähmbare Leni Peickert* 1969; *Der grosse Verhau* 1970; *Willi Tobler und der Untergang der 6. Flotte/Willi Tobler and the Demise of the Sixth Fleet* 1971; *Gelegenheitsarbeit einer Sklavin/Part-Time Work of a Domestic Slave* 1974; *In Gefahr und Gröster Not bringt der Mittelweg den Tod/The Middle of the Road Is a Very Dead End/Blind Alley* (also des.), *Augen aus einen anderen Land* 1975; *Der starke Ferdinand/Strongman Ferdinand* (also act.) 1976; *Zu böser Shlacht Schleich'ich heut'Nacht so bang* (revised vers. of *Willi Tobler,* 1971) 1977; *Deutschland im Herbst/Germany in Autumn* (one episode) 1978; *Die Patriotin/The Patriot* (also prod., act.) 1979; *Der Kandidat/The Candidate* 1980; *Krieg und Frieden/War and Peace, Die Macht der Gefühle/The Power of Emotion* (also prod., act.) 1983; *Der Angriff der Gegenwart auf die unbrige Zeit* 1986; *Vermischte Nachrichten* (also prod.) 1987; *Schweingeld—ein Märchen der Gebrüder Nimm* (prod. only) 1989.

Klugman, Jack. Actor. Born on Apr. 27, 1922, in Philadelphia. *ed.* Carnegie Tech. Versatile character player of the American stage, TV, and some films; capable of a broad range of roles, from the comic to the sinister. He worked in various menial occupations while training for the stage at the American Theatre Wing in New York. He made his stage debut in the Equity Library Theatre production of 'Stevedore' (1949) and his first film appearance in 1956. But it was on TV that he achieved his greatest fame, winning an Emmy Award for the 'Blacklist' segment (1964) of 'The Defenders' series and two Emmys (1971, 1973) for his portrayal of Oscar Madison in the popular comedy series 'The Odd Couple' (1970–75). He enjoyed further success playing the title role in the police series 'Quincy M.E.' (1976–83). In 1987 he co-starred in the Broadway comedy, 'I'm Not Rappaport.' In 1989, he was diagnosed with throat cancer, and lost his ability to speak for several years. During this time he made a series of appearances with his old 'Odd Couple' partner Tony Randall in television commercials for potato chips, all of which were cleverly arranged around his speechlessness. In 1993, he returned to TV in an 'Odd Couple' reunion, speaking (with effort) on film for the first time in years.

FILMS: *Timetable* 1956; *12 Angry Men* 1957; *Cry Terror* 1958; *Days of Wine and Roses* 1962; *I Could Go On Singing* (UK), *The Yellow Canary, Act One* 1963; *Je vous salue Maffia!/Hail Mafia!* (Fr./It.) 1966; *The Detective, The Split* 1968; *Goodbye Columbus* 1969; *Who Says I Can't Ride a Rainbow!* 1971; *Two-Minute Warning* 1976; *Dear God* 1996.

Knapp, Evalyn. Actress. *b.* June 17, 1908, Kansas City, Mo. *d.* 1981. Blonde leading lady of mostly routine Hollywood B pictures of the 30s, following some experience on the stage. She retired from the screen in the early 40s.

FILMS INCLUDE: *Sinners' Holiday, Mother's Cry, River's End* 1930; *Fifty Million Frenchmen, The Millionaire, Smart Money, The Bargain, Side Show* 1931; *High Pressure, Fireman Save My Child, The Strange Love of Molly Louvain, The Vanishing Frontier, Madame Racketeer, Big City Blues, A Successful Calamity, This Sporting Age, The Night Mayor* 1932; *Air Hostess, State Trooper, Corruption, His Private Secretary, Dance Girl Dance* 1933; *The Perils of Pauline* (serial), *Speed Wings* 1934; *Ladies Crave Excitement, Confidential* 1935; *Laughing Irish Eyes, Three of a Kind* 1936; *Rawhide, Wanted by the Police* 1938; *The Lone Wolf Takes a Chance* 1941; *Two Weeks to Live* 1943.

Knef, Hildegard. Actress. Born Hildegard Knef, Dec. 28, 1925, Ulm, Germany. Cool, intriguing blonde leading lady of international films, acclaimed by some as "the thinking man's Marlene Dietrich." A sickly, undernourished child of war, she began her career at UFA in propaganda-oriented films on the eve of the Nazi defeat. She fell in love with a top film official, a protégé of Goebbels. When he was sent to the front lines to fight against the invading Russians, she went with him disguised as a man. They were both captured by the Russians. She escaped and never saw him again. Her wartime memories and the story of her subsequent career onstage and in films were candidly and bitterly described in her best-selling autobiography *The Gift Horse* (American edition, 1971). In 1947, after appearing in two prominent postwar German films, she was brought to Hollywood by David O. Selznick, who suggested she change her name to Gilda Christian and present herself as Austrian-born. She refused. After two years of unemployment she was assigned by Fox to co-star with Montgomery Clift in *The Big Lift* but lost the part when her past was discovered. She returned to Germany, where she scandalized audiences with a nude scene in a film called *The Sinner.*

In 1951 Miss Knef was back in Hollywood, where her name was changed slightly to the more pronounceable Hildegard Neff, and she was finally launched in American films. But her stay was brief and within a year she was back in Europe, making British, then French, German, and Italian films. In between film appearances abroad, she journeyed to New York in 1955, where she scored a personal triumph on Broadway in 'Silk Stockings,' a musical adaptation of the film *Ninotchka.* In the 60s, she began a second career as a cabaret singer, writing her own lyrics to songs she delivered in her deep, bullfrog voice. But once again tragedy touched her life, this time in the form of cancer. She underwent 56 surgeries, fighting valiantly to survive. She told of the desperate years of her illness in her second book, *The Verdict* (1975).

FILMS INCLUDE: In Germany—*Fahrt ins Glück, Unter den Brücken* 1945; *Die Mörder sind unter uns/Murderers Among Us* 1946; *Zwischen Gestern und Morgen* 1947; *Film ohne Titel/Film Without a Name* 1948; *Die Sünderin/The Sinner* 1951. In the US—*Decision Before Dawn* 1951; *Diplomatic Courier, The Snows of Kilimanjaro, Night Without Sleep* 1952. In Europe—*Alraune/Mandrake* (Ger.), *Illusion in Moll* (Ger.) 1952; *La Fête à Henriette/Holiday for Henrietta* (Fr.), *The Man Between* (UK) 1953; *Svengali* (as Trilby; UK), *Eine Liebesgeschichte* 1954; *La Fille de Hambourg/Port of Desire* (Fr.), *Madeleine und der Legionär* (Ger.) 1958; *Subway in the Sky* (UK) 1959; *Caterina de Russia* (as Catherine the Great; It.), *Lulu* (Ger.) 1962; *Landru/Bluebeard* (Fr./It.), *Die Dreigroschenoper/ Threepenny Opera* (as Pirate Jenny; Ger./Fr.), *Das grosse Liebesspiel/And So to Bed* (Ger./Aus.) 1963; *Mozambigue* (UK) 1965; *The Lost Continent* (UK) 1968; *Jeder stirbt für sich allein* (Ger.) 1976; *Fedora* (Ger./Fr.) 1978; *Flügel und Fesseln/L'Avenir d'Emilie* (Ger./Fr.) 1984; *Offret/Sacrificatio/Le Sacrifice/The Sacrifice* (Swed./Fr.) 1986; *Witchery* (US) 1988.

Knight, David. Actor. Born David Mintz, on Jan. 16, 1927, in Niagara Falls, N.Y. A former teacher, he went to London for a stage career and eventually played leads in a number of British films. Another David Knight began appearing in films in the late 80s.

FILMS INCLUDE: *The Young Lovers/Chance Meeting* 1954; *Out of the Clouds* 1955; *Lost/Tears for Simon* 1956; *Across the Bridge* 1957; *Battle of the V-1* 1959; *Clue of the Twisted Candle* 1960; *The Story of David* 1961; *Nightmare* 1964.

Knight, Esmond. Actor. *b.* May 4, 1906, East Sheen, England. *d.* 1987. A veteran of the London stage, he appeared in numerous British films from the late 20s, in both leads and supporting roles. Memorable in Jean Renoir's *The River* (1951). He was temporarily blinded in WW II action with the Royal Navy against the *Bismarck* in 1941 but later partially regained his sight and returned to acting. He was married to Nora SWINBURNE.

FILMS INCLUDE: *The Blue Peter* 1928; *The Ringer* 1931; *Waltzes from Vienna* 1933; *Crime Unlimited* 1935; *Pagliacci/A Clown Must Laugh* (as Silvio) 1937; *The Drum/Drums* 1938; *The Arsenal Stadium Mystery* 1939; *Contraband/Blackout* 1940; *This England* 1941; *The Silver Fleet* 1943; *Half-Way House, A Canterbury Tale, Henry V* (as Fluellen) 1944; *Black Narcissus, Holiday Camp, Uncle Silas/The Inheritance, End of the River* 1947; *Hamlet* (as Bernardo), *The Red Shoes* 1948; *Gone to Earth/The Wild Heart* 1950; *The River* 1951; *The Steel Key* 1953; *Helen of Troy* 1955; *Richard III* (as Ratcliffe) 1956; *The Prince and the Showgirl* 1957; *Sink the Bismarck!, Peeping Tom* 1960; *The Spy Who Came in from the Cold* 1965; *Where's Jack?, Anne of the Thousand Days* 1969; *Robin and Marian* 1976; *The Element of Crime* (Den.) 1984.

Knight, Fuzzy. Actor. *b.* John Forrest Knight, May 9, 1901, in Fairmont, W.Va. *d.* 1976. *ed.* U. of West Virginia (law). A musician, singer, and bandleader in nightclubs and vaudeville and on stage, he was featured in early musical film shorts, then provided comic relief in more than 200 Westerns, playing an awkward, stuttering saddle partner to Johnny Mack BROWN, Tex RITTER, and other Western heroes. He also occasionally played straight dramatic roles.

FILMS INCLUDE: *Hell's Highway* 1932; *She Done Him Wrong* 1933; *Moulin Rouge, Music in the Air* 1934; *Home on the Range, Wanderer of the Wasteland* 1935; *Trail of the Lonesome Pine, And Sudden Death, The Plainsman* 1936; *Mountain Justice, Singing Outlaw, Spawn of the North, The Cowboy and the Lady* 1938; *Union Pacific* 1939; *My Little Chickadee, Brigham Young, Johnny Apollo* 1940; *Horror Island, The Shepherd of the Hills, Badlands of Dakota* 1941; *Juke Girl* 1942; *Corvette K-225* 1943; *The Singing Sheriff* 1944; *Frisco Sal, Frontier Gal* 1945; *The Egg and I* 1947; *Down to the Sea in Ships* 1949; *Kansas Territory* 1952; *The Naked Hills* 1956; *The Bounty Killer* 1965; *Waco* 1966; *Hostile Guns* 1967.

Knight, Shirley. Actress. Born on July 5, 1937, in Goessel, Kans. *ed.* U. of Wichita; U. of California. Luminous leading lady of stage and screen. Trained at the Pasadena Playhouse, she made her film debut in 1959 and in the following year was nominated for an Oscar as best supporting actress for her performance in Delbert Mann's *The Dark at the Top of the Stairs.* She received another Oscar nomination for her role of Heavenly, Paul Newman's childhood sweetheart in Richard Brooks's *Sweet Bird of Youth* (1962). Candid and outspoken, she expressed dissatisfaction with the Hollywood scene and in the mid-60s abandoned films for a while to devote her talent to the Broadway stage, where she scored a string of successes. In 1966 she went to London with her first husband, stage producer Gene Persson, to appear in his film *Dutchman,* for which she won the Volpi Prize as best actress at the 1967 Venice Festival. She later married British dramatist John Hopkins and remained in England for several years, appearing in films and TV plays. She returned to Broadway in the 1975–76 season, and later earned Emmy nominations for her television appearances on 'The Equalizer' and 'thirtysomething,' winning for the latter.

FILMS: *Five Gates to Hell* 1959; *Ice Palace, The Dark at the Top of the Stairs* 1960; *The Couch, Sweet Bird of Youth, House of Women* 1962; *Flight from Ashiya* (US/Jap.) 1964; *The Group* 1966; *Dutchman* (UK) 1967; *Petulia* (UK/US), *The Counterfeit Killer* 1968; *The Rain People* 1969; *Secrets* (UK) 1971; *Juggernaut* (UK) 1974; *Beyond the Poseidon Adventure* 1979; *Endless Love* 1981; *The Sender* (UK) 1982; *Prisoners* (US) 1991; *Hard Promises* (US) 1992; *Color of Night* 1994; *Someone is Waiting, Stuart Saves His Family* 1996.

Knopf, Edwin H. Producer, director, screenwriter. *b.* Nov. 11, 1899, New York City. *d.* 1981. He began his career in the editorial department of brother Alfred Knopf's publishing house; then, in 1920, he turned to acting, playing leads on Broadway and in Germany. In 1928, after producing several hit plays, he went to Hollywood as a director and screenwriter. In 1936 he was appointed head of MGM's scenario department. In the early 40s he became a producer. Once married to actress-singer Mary Ellis.

FILMS INCLUDE: As director (complete)—*Fast Company* (co-dir. with A. Edward Sutherland; uncredited) 1929; *Slightly Scarlet* (co-dir. with Louis Gasnier), *The Light of Western Stars* (co-dir. with Otto Brower), *Paramount on Parade* (co-dir. with ten others), *The Border Legion* (co-dir. with Brower), *The Santa Fe Trail* (co-dir. with Brower), *Only Saps Work* (co-dir. with Cyril Gardner) 1930; *Nice Women* 1931; *Der Rebell/The Rebel* (co-dir., co-story, co-sc. with Luis Trenker; Ger.) 1932; *The Law and the Lady* 1951. As producer—*The Trial of Mary Dugan* 1941; *Crossroads* 1942; *The Cross of Lorraine, Cry Havoc* 1944; *The Valley of Decision* 1945; *The Secret Heart* 1946; *Cynthia* 1947; *B.F.'s Daughter* 1948; *Edward My Son, Malaya* 1949; *Night Into Morning* 1951; *Lili* 1953; *The Glass Slipper* 1955; *Diane, Gaby* 1956; *The Vintage, Tip on a Dead Jockey* 1957.

Knotts, Don. Actor. Born on July 21, 1924, in Morgantown, W.Va. Fidgety, pop-eyed comic whose film career has been secondary to his great success on TV. A graduate of the University of West Virginia, he entered show business as a nightclub ventriloquist. After gaining some acting experience on radio, he appeared in the 1955 Broadway production of 'No Time for Sergeants' and achieved popularity as a regular on the Steve Allen TV show (1956–60). He made his screen debut in the film version of *No Time for Sergeants* (1958) and two years later began a long-running stint on TV in the role of Barney Fife, the jittery deputy sheriff on the popular 'Andy Griffith Show' (1960–68). Knotts won three successive Emmy Awards (1961, 1962, and 1963) and a string of two more (1966, 1967) for his frantic portrayal of that comic sidekick character and in 1970–71 starred on his own TV variety program, 'The Don Knotts Show' (1970–71). His success on TV extended into the 80s, when he played the quirky landlord in the sitcom 'Three's Company' (1979–84). Most of his film vehicles, however, have been rather limp.

FILMS INCLUDE: *No Time for Sergeants* 1958; *Wake Me When It's Over* 1960; *The Last Time I Saw Archie* 1961; *It's a Mad Mad Mad Mad World, Move Over Darling* 1963; *The Incredible Mr. Limpet* 1964; *The Ghost and Mr. Chicken* 1966; *The Reluctant Astronaut* 1967; *The Shakiest Gun in the West* 1968; *The Love God?* 1969; *How to Frame a Figg* (also co-story) 1971; *The Apple Dumpling Gang* 1975; *No Deposit No Return, Gus* 1976; *Herbie Goes to Monte Carlo* 1977; *Hot Lead and Cold Feet* 1978; *The Apple Dumpling Gang Rides Again, The Pie Fighter* 1979; *The Private Eyes* 1980; *Cannonball Run II* 1984; *Pinocchio and the Emperor of the Night* (voice only) 1987; *Big Bully* 1995.

Knowles, Bernard. Director, former director of photography. Born in 1900, in Manchester, England. An assistant cameraman in the early 20s, he became a lighting cameraman toward the end of the decade, working in that capacity on several Hitchcock classics. He was a director of mainly routine British films in the mid-40s. Also very active in British TV. In a famous one-word review, critic C. A. Lejeune of the London

Observer once dismissed his film biography of Paganini, *The Magic Bow,* with a single biting comment: "Fiddlesticks."

FILMS INCLUDE: As director of photography—*Dawn* 1928; *The Hound of the Baskervilles* 1930; *The Good Companions* 1932; *Jew Suss/Power, Jack Ahoy* 1934; *King of the Damned, The 39 Steps* 1935; *The Secret Agent, Sabotage Rhodes* 1936; *Young and Innocent/The Girl Was Young, King Solomon's Mines* 1937; *Jamaica Inn, The Mikado* 1939; *Quiet Wedding, Gaslight/Angel Street* 1940; *The Demi-Paradise/Adventure for Two* 1943. As director (complete)—*A Place of One's Own* 1945; *The Magic Bow* 1946; *The Man Within/The Smugglers, The White Unicorn/Bad Sister, Jassy* 1947; *Easy Money* 1948; *The Lost People, The Perfect Woman* (also co-sc.) 1949; *The Reluctant Widow* 1950; *Park Plaza 605* 1953; *Barbados Quest* 1955; *Der Fall X701/Frozen Alive* (Ger./UK) 1964; *Spaceflight IC-1* 1965; *Hell Is Empty* (Czech.) 1968.

Knowles, Patric. Actor. Born Reginald Lawrence Knowles, on Nov. 11, 1911, in Horsforth, England. A former stage player, he appeared in several British films before his Hollywood debut in 1936. He established his credentials as a romantic lead that same year in *The Charge of the Light Brigade,* in which he won Olivia de Havilland's heart away from screen-brother Errol Flynn. Knowles's patrician good looks and cultivated personality helped him along a busy screen career comprising scores of leads, second leads, and eventually character roles. He has authored a novel, *Even Steven.*

FILMS INCLUDE: In the UK—*Men of Tomorrow* 1932; *Irish Hearts/Norah O'Neale* 1934; *The Guv'nor/Mister Hobo, Abdul the Damned* 1935; *The Student's Romance* 1936. In the US—*Give Me Your Heart, The Charge of the Light Brigade* 1936; *It's Love I'm After, Expensive Husbands* 1937; *The Patient in Room 18, The Adventures of Robin Hood* (as Will Scarlet), *Four's a Crowd, The Sisters, Storm Over Bengal* 1938; *Beauty for the Asking, Five Came Back, Another Thin Man* 1939; *Married and in Love, Women in War, A Bill of Divorcement* 1940; *How Green Was My Valley, The Wolf Man* 1941; *The Strange Case of Dr. Rx, The Mystery of Marie Roget, Lady in a Jam, Sin Town, Who Done It?* 1942; *Frankenstein Meets the Wolf Man, All by Myself, Hit the Ice, Crazy House* 1943; *This Is the Life, Pardon My Rhythm* 1944; *Masquerade in Mexico* 1945; *Kitty, OSS, The Bride Wore Boots, Of Human Bondage, Monsieur Beaucaire* 1946; *Ivy* 1947; *Dream Girl, Isn't It Romantic?* 1948; *The Big Steal* 1949; *Three Came Home* 1950; *Quebec* 1951; *Mutiny, Tarzan's Savage Fury* 1952; *Jamaica Run, Flame of Culcutta* 1953; *World for Ransom, Khyber Patrol* 1954; *Band of Angels* 1957; *From the Earth to the Moon, Auntie Mame* 1958; *The Way West* 1967; *The Devil's Brigade* (as Admiral Lord Mountbatten) 1968; *Chisum* 1970; *The Man* 1972; *Terror in the Wax Museum, Arnold* 1973.

Knox, Alexander. Actor. Born on Jan. 16, 1907, in Strathroy, Ontario, Canada. *ed.* U. of Western Ontario. Distinguished character player of stage and screen. After his 1929 stage debut in Boston, he went to England, where he appeared on the London stage and in a couple of films. He returned to America at the outbreak of WW II and in the early 40s began a durable and prominent career as a character actor in Hollywood films. In the following three decades he played character leads and solid supporting parts in numerous screen productions, memorably in the title role of *Wilson* (1944), a performance that brought him a nomination for a best actor Academy Award. He has collaborated on several screenplays and authored a number of plays, novels, and mysteries. He and his wife, former actress Doris NOLAN, now live in England.

FILMS INCLUDE: In the UK—*The Ringer* 1931; *The Gaunt Stranger/The Phantom Strikes* 1938; *The Four Feathers* 1939. In the US—*The Sea Wolf* (as Humphrey Van Weyden) 1941; *This Above All* 1942; *The Commandos Strike at Dawn* 1943; *None Shall Escape, Wilson* (as President Wilson) 1944; *Over 21* 1945; *Sister Kenny* (also co-sc.) 1946; *The Sign of the Ram* 1948; *The Judge Steps Out* (also co-sc.), *Tokyo Joe* 1949; *I'd Climb the Highest Mountain, Saturday's Hero, The Son of Dr. Jekyll* 1951; *Paula, Europa '51/The Greatest Love* (It.) 1952; *The Sleeping Tiger* (UK), *The Divided Heart* (UK) 1954; *The Night My Number Came Up* (UK) 1955; *Reach for the Sky* (UK) 1956; *Chase a Crooked Shadow* (UK), *The Vikings, Intent to Kill* (UK), *The Two-Headed Spy* (UK) 1958; *The Wreck of the Mary Deare* 1959; *Oscar Wilde* (UK), *Crack in the Mirror* 1960; *The Damned/These Are the Damned* (UK) 1961; *The Longest Day* 1962; *In the Cool of the Day* 1963; *Man in the Middle* (UK/US), *Woman of Straw* (UK) 1964; *Crack in the World, Mister Moses* 1965; *Modesty Blaise* (UK), *Khartoum* (UK) 1966; *Accident* (UK), *La 25e Heure/The 25th Hour* (Fr./It./Yug.), *You Only Live Twice* (UK), *How I Won the War* (UK) 1967; *Villa Rides, Shalako* (UK) 1968; *Fräulein Doktor* (It./Yug.) 1969; *Skullduggery* 1970; *Nicholas and Alexandra* (UK), *Puppet on a Chain* (UK) 1971; *Holocaust 2000/The Chosen* (It./UK) 1977; *Gorky Park* 1983; *Joshua Then and Now* (Can.) 1985.

Knox, Elyse. Actress. Born on Dec. 14, 1917, in Hartford, Conn., the daughter of Frank (William Franklin) Knox, who became Secretary of the Navy under FDR during WW II. Trained as an artist, she began her career as a designer for *Vogue* and later worked as a photographer's model. A blonde beauty, she entered films in the late 30s and in the following decade played leads and second leads in a variety of screen productions, mainly routine B pictures. She married Michigan's famous halfback football hero Tom Harmon. Their son is actor Mark HARMON.

FILMS INCLUDE: *Wake Up and Live* 1937; *Free Blonde and 21, Lillian Russell, Youth Will Be Served* 1940; *Footlight Fever, Tanks a Million* 1941; *Night Monster, The Mummy's Tomb* 1942; *Mr. Big, Hit the Ice, Hy Ya Sailor!, So's Your Uncle* 1943; *A Wave a Wac and a Marine, Moonlight and Cactus* 1944; *Army Wives* 1945; *Joe Palooka—Champ, Sweetheart of Sigma Chi* 1946; *Black Gold, Linda Be Good* 1947; *Winner Take All* 1948; *Forgotten Women* 1949; *There's a Girl in My Heart* 1950.

Kobayashi, Masaki. Director. Born on Feb. 14, 1916, in Otaru, Hokkaido, Japan. Following philosophy and Oriental art studies at Tokyo's Waseda University, he entered films in 1941; but eight months later he was drafted into the Imperial Japanese Army and dispatched to Manchuria. In a courageous act of personal defiance, he refused promotion and remained a private for the duration of WW II. He spent the last year of the conflict as an American prisoner of war. He resumed his budding film career late in 1946 as an assistant to Keisuke KINOSHITA at the Shochiku company. It wasn't until 1952 that Kobayashi turned out his first film as a director. His early films showed the influence of his mentor. But gradually he carved his own path, and in 1959–61 asserted his mastery with a remarkable nine-hour trilogy, *Ningen no Joken/The Human Condition* (1959–61), a graphically vivid, uncompromising critique of the brutalities and horrors of the Second World War and their effect on the emotional lives of its participants. The trilogy's first part, *No Greater Love,* won the San Giorgio Prize at the 1960 Venice Film Festival. Kobayashi attracted wider admiration with *Sepukku/Harakiri* (1962), a Samurai period film many consider his masterpiece, and *Kaidan/Kwaidan* (1964), a harrowing anthology of ghost stories. Both of these films won the International Jury Prize at Cannes, in 1963 and 1965, respectively. Other personal triumphs in Kobayashi's sparse but rich repertoire were *Joiuchi/Rebellion/Samurai Rebellion* (1967) and

Kaseki/Fossil (1975), the latter a tautly edited feature version of his eight-hour TV drama.

FILMS: *My Son's Youth* 1952; *Sincere Heart, Room with Thick Walls* (release delayed to 1956) 1953; *Three Loves, Somewhere Beneath the Wide Sky* 1954; *Beautiful Days/The Beautiful Years* 1955; *The Fountainhead, I'll Buy You* 1956; *Black River* 1957; *No Greater Love/The Human Condition Part I, Road to Eternity/The Human Condition Part II* 1959; *A Soldier's Prayer/The Human Condition Part III* 1961; *The Inheritance, Harakiri* 1962; *Kwaidan* 1964; *Rebellion* 1967; *The Youth of Japan/Hymn to a Tired Man* 1968; *Inn of Evil/At the Risk of My Life* 1971; *Fossils* (213-minute feature version of eight-hour TV program) 1975; *Glowing Autumn* 1979; *The Tokyo Trials/The Far East Martial Court* (doc.) 1983; *The Empty Table* 1985.

Koch, Howard. Screenwriter. *b.* Dec. 12, 1902, in New York City. *d.* 1995. The holder of a Columbia law degree, he began writing plays in the late 20s and later wrote radio scripts, including the famous Orson Welles broadcast of H. G. Wells's *War of the Worlds.* In Hollywood from 1940, he contributed many literate screenplays to films, mostly alone, some in collaboration, and shared in the Academy Award for *Casablanca* (1942). In 1951 he was blacklisted by the industry under pressure from the House Un-American Activities Committee. He used the pseudonym Peter Howard for screen credit on Joseph Losey's (under pseudonym Joseph Walton) British-made *The Intimate Stranger/Finger of Guilt* (1956) but didn't resume screenwriting under his own name until the early 60s. Occasionally also a playwright, Koch wrote the books *The Panic Broadcast* and *As Time Goes By: Memoirs of a Writer in Hollywood, New York, and Europe.*

FILMS: *Virginia City* (co-story, uncredited), *The Sea Hawk* (co-story, co-sc.), *The Letter* 1940; *Shining Victory* (so-sc.), *Sergeant York* (co-sc.) 1941; *In This Our Life, Casablanca* (co-sc.) 1942; *Mission to Moscow* 1943; *In Our Time* (co-story, co-sc.) 1944; *Rhapsody in Blue* (co-sc.) 1945; *Three Strangers* (co-story, co-sc.), *The Best Years of Our Lives* (co-sc., uncredited) 1946; *Letter from an Unknown Woman* 1948; *No Sad Songs for Me* 1950; *The Thirteenth Letter* 1951; *The Intimate Stranger/Finger of Guilt* (as Peter Howard) 1956; *The Greengage Summer/Loss of Innocence* (UK) 1961; *The War Lover* (UK) 1962; *633 Squadron* (co-sc.; UK) 1964; *The Fox* (co-sc.; also assoc. prod.) 1967.

Koch, Howard W. Director, producer, production executive. Born on Apr. 11, 1916, in New York City. He started out as a runner on Wall Street, then entered films as an assistant cutter at Fox. Later he progressed from assistant director to second-unit director and finally, in the 50s, director and producer of low- and medium-budget films for various studios. He also produced and directed for TV. In the early 60s he acted as executive producer of Frank Sinatra Enterprises and in 1965 was appointed vice president in charge of production at Paramount and subsequently produced a number of expensive pictures. His son, Howard W. KOCH, Jr., entered films in the early 70s as an assistant director and worked his way up to producer later in the decade.

FILMS INCLUDE: As director (complete)—*Shield for Murder* (co-dir. with Edmond O'Brien) 1954; *Big House USA* 1955; *Untamed Youth, Bop Girl, Jungle Heat, The Girl in Black Stockings* 1957; *Fort Bowie, Violent Road, Frankenstein* 1970, *Andy Hardy Comes Home* 1958; *The Last Mile, Born Reckless* 1959; *Badge 373* (also prod.) 1973. As producer or executive producer—*War Paint* 1953; *Beachhead* 1954; *Emergency Hospital, The Black Sleep* 1956; *Sergeants 3, The Manchurian Candidate* 1962; *Come Blow Your Horn* 1963; *Robin and the 7 Hoods* 1964; *None but the Brave* 1965; *The President's Analyst* 1967; *The Odd Couple* 1968; *On a Clear Day You Can See Forever* 1970; *Plaza Suite* 1971; *Last of the Red Hot Lovers* 1972; *Once Is Not Enough* 1975; *Ghost* 1990. As producer or executive producer (complete)—*Beyond Reason, The Other Side of Midnight* 1977; *Heaven Can Wait* (also assis. dir.) 1978; *The Frisco Kid* 1979; *The Idolmaker* 1980; *Dragonslayer, Honky Tonk Freeway* 1981; *Airplane II: The Sequel, Some Kind of Hero* 1982; *Gorky Park, The Keep, A Night in Heaven* 1983; *Nothing in Common, Peggy Sue Got Married* 1986; *Collision Course, The Secret of My Success* 1987; *Rooftops* 1989; *The Long Walk Home* 1990; *Necessary Roughness* 1991; *Wayne's World* 1992; *Sliver, The Temp, Wayne's World 2* 1993; *Losing Isaiah, Virtuosity* 1995; *Primal Fear* 1996; *The Beautician and the Beast* 1997.

Koch, Marianne. Actress. Born in 1930 in Munich. Leading lady of German films, international co-productions, and occasional Hollywood movies. Often billed in the US and UK as Marianne Cook.

FILMS INCLUDE: *Der Mann der zweimal leben wollte* 1950; *Dr. Holl* 1952; *Night People* (US) 1954; *Ludwig II, Der Teufels General/The Devil's General, Königswalzer* 1955; *Four Girls in Town* (US) 1956; *Interlude* (US) 1957; *Pleins Feux sur l'Assassin* (Fr./Ger.), *Napoléon III* (Fr./Ger.) 1961; *Die Fledermaus* 1962; *Der Letzte Ritt nach Santa Cruz* 1963; *Frozen Alive, Per un Pugno di Dollari/A Fistful of Dollars* (It.), *Coast of Skeletons* (UK) 1964; *La Balada de Johnny Ringo* (Sp./It.) 1966; *Clint il Solitario* (It.) 1968; *España oltra vez* (sp.) 1969.

Koenekamp, Fred J. Director of photography. Born on Nov. 11, 1922, in Los Angeles. His father was Hans F. Koenekamp (1891–1992), pioneer special effects cinematographer whose credits include *Noah's Ark* (1929), *A Midsummer Night's Dream* (1935), and *Air Force* (1943). Hans's son Fred entered films as an apprentice cinematographer in the late 40s. A solid craftsman who demonstrated his skill with color cinematography in many Hollywood films of the 60s and 70s, following experience in TV. He shared an Academy Award with Joseph BIROC for *The Towering Inferno* (1974).

FILMS INCLUDE: *The Spy with My Face* 1966; *Sol Madrid* 1968; *Heaven with a Gun* 1969; *Patton* 1970; *Billy Jack* (co-phot.), *Happy Birthday Wanda June* 1971; *Kansas City Bomber, Rage* 1972; *Papillon* 1973; *Uptown Saturday Night, The Towering Inferno* (co-phot.) 1974; *Doc Savage the Man of Bronze, White Line Fever* 1975; *Embryo* 1976; *Islands in the Stream, Fun with Dick and Jane, The Domino Principle* (co-phot.), *The Other Side of Midnight* 1977; *The Swarm* 1978; *Love and Bullets* (co-phot.; UK), *The Champ, The Amityville Horror* 1979; *When Time Ran Out, The Hunter* 1980; *First Monday in October* 1981; *Wrong Is Right* 1982; *Two of a Kind* 1983; *The Adventures of Buckaroo Banzai Across the 8th Dimension* 1984; *Listen to Me, Welcome Home* 1989; *Flight of The Intruder* 1991.

Kohler, Fred. Actor. *b.* Apr. 20, 1889, Kansas City, Mo. *d.* 1938. Tall, brawny character player of innumerable Hollywood silents and talkies; one of the screen's nastiest, most brutal heavies. He made his film debut in 1911, following some experience in vaudeville and stock, and became established as an arch villain in Westerns and dramas of the 20s and 30s. His son, Fred Kohler, Jr., has been carrying on the villainous tradition on the screen since 1935. He was married to stage musical actress Maxine Marshall.

FILMS INCLUDE: *The Code of Honor* 1911; *Soldiers of Fortune* 1919; *The Stampede* 1921; *Yellow Men and Gold* 1922; *Three Who Paid, North of Hudson Bay, Anna Christie* 1923; *Abraham Lincoln, The Iron Horse* 1924; *Dick Turpin, Riders of the Purple Sage, Winds of Chance* 1925; *The Country Beyond,*

The Ice Flood, Old Ironsides 1926; *The Rough Riders, The Way of All Flesh, The Blood Ship, Underworld, Loves of Carmen, The City Gone Wild, The Gay Defender* 1927; *The Showdown, The Dragnet, The Vanishing Pioneer, Forgotten Faces, The Spieler* 1928; *The Case of Lena Smith, The Dummy, Tide of Empire, The Leatherneck, Thunderbolt, Broadway Babies, The River of Romance, Say It with Songs* 1929; *Hell's Heroes, Roadhouse Nights, Under a Texas Moon, The Light of Western Stars, A Soldier's Plaything, The Lash/Adios* 1930; *Fighting Caravans, The Right of Way, Corsair, X Marks the Spot* 1931; *Carnival Boat, Wild Horse Mesa* 1932; *Deluge* 1933; *The Last Round-Up, Little Man What Now?, West of the Pecos* 1934; *Times Square Lady, Mississippi, Goin' to Town, Frisco Kid* 1935; *The Accusing Finger* 1936; *The Plainsman, Daughter of Shanghai* 1937; *The Buccaneer, Gangs of New York, Blockade, Painted Desert* 1938.

Kohlmar, Fred. Producer. *b.* Aug. 10, 1905, New York City. *d.* 1969. A former actors' agent, for five years he was an executive assistant to Sam GOLDWYN before becoming a producer in the late 30s. Worked mainly for Fox, Paramount, and Columbia.

FILMS INCLUDE: *Coast Guard* 1939; *The Lone Wolf Strikes* 1940; *That Night in Rio* 1941; *Take a Letter Darling, The Glass Key, Lucky Jordan* 1942; *And Now Tomorrow* 1944; *The Dark Corner* 1946; *The Ghost and Mrs. Muir, The Late George Apley, Kiss of Death* 1947; *Fury at Furnace Creek, That Wonderful Urge* 1948; *When Willie Comes Marching Home* 1950; *Call Me Mister* 1951; *Les Misérables* 1952; *It Should Happen to You, Phffft* 1954; *My Sister Eileen,* 1955; *Picnic, The Solid Gold Cadillac* 1956; *Full of Life, Pal Joey* 1957; *The Last Angry Man* 1959; *The Devil at Four O'Clock* 1961; *The Notorious Landlady* 1962; *Bye Bye Birdie* 1963; *Dear Brigitte* 1965; *How to Steal a Million* 1966; *A Flea in Her Ear* 1968; *The Only Game in Town* 1970.

Kohner, Susan. Actress. Born on Nov. 11, 1936, in Los Angeles, the daughter of Mexican-born actress Lupita Tovar and Czech-born Hollywood agent Paul Kohner (1902–88). Leading lady of Hollywood films of the late 50s and early 60s, as well as the stage and TV. She was nominated for an Academy Award as best supporting actress for her performance in *Imitation of Life* (1959). She retired from acting after her 1964 marriage to fashion designer John Weitz. Later volunteered as hostess of a weekly radio show on Touch, a network for the blind, and became a member of the Board of Associates of the Juilliard School of Music.

FILMS: *To Hell and Back* 1955; *The Last Wagon* 1956; *Dino, Trooper Hook* 1957; *Imitation of Life, The Big Fisherman, The Gene Krupa Story* 1959; *All the Fine Young Cannibals* 1960; *By Love Possessed* 1961; *Freud* 1962.

Konchalovsky, Andrei. Director. Born Andrei Mikhalkov-Konchalovsky, on Aug. 20, 1937, in Moscow. The descendent of famous painters and the son of poets (his father wrote the lyrics for the Soviet national anthem), he trained as a pianist at the Moscow Conservatory and later studied filmmaking at the State Film School (VGIK) under Mikhail Romm. His thesis film, the 1961 short *The Boy and the Pigeon,* was awarded a prize at the 1962 Venice Film Festival. He entered the industry as a screenwriter and assistant to director Andrei TARKOVSKY, working on such films as *Ivan's Childhood* and *Andrei Rublev.* Making his own directorial feature debut in 1965, Konchalovsky (then still billed Andrei Mikhalkov-Konchalovsky) instantly attracted recognition for his mature skills and distinct gift for character observation. These qualities were validated by his subsequent films. He won a prize at San Sebastian for his version of *Uncle Vanya* (1971) and the Grand Prix at Karlovy Vary for *Romance for Lovers* (1974). He ran into trouble with Soviet authorities over *Asya's Happiness,* which was completed in 1967 but not released until 1988, but scored a domestic and international triumph with the panoramic epic *Siberiade* (1978), winner of the Special Jury Prize at the 1979 Cannes Festival. The film's success, coupled with a lobbying effort by actor Jon VOIGHT, opened Hollywood's gates for Konchalovsky. But, with the exception of *Runaway Train* (1985), an exhilarating psychological thriller based on a Kurosawa script, the Russian director's American phase has been sadly disappointing. His younger brother is actor-director Nikita MIKHALKOV.

FILMS (as director-screenwriter): In the USSR—*The Boy and the Pigeon* (short) 1961; *The First Teacher* 1965; *Asya's Happiness/The Story of Asya Klyachina* (release delayed to 1988) 1967; *A Nest of Gentry/A Nest of Gentlefolk* 1969; *Uncle Vanya* 1971; *Romance for Lovers* 1974; *Siberiade* 1978; *Assia and the Hen with the Golden Eggs, Ryaba My Chicken/Riaba Ma Poule* (also prod.) 1994. In the US—*Maria's Lovers, Runaway Train* (dir. only) 1985; *Duet for One* (US/UK) 1986; *Shy People* 1987; *Homer and Eddie* (dir. only), *Tango and Cash* (dir. only) 1989; *The Inner Circle* 1991.

Kopelson, Arnold. Producer, distributor. Born on Feb. 14, 1935, in New York City. *ed.* N.Y.U., New York Law School (J.D.). Producer or executive producer of numerous films who won recognition with the 1986 best picture award for *Platoon.* He is also a financier and distributor who has handled international distribution of such films as *Salvador*. His business partner is Anne Kopelson.

FILMS INCLUDE: *The Legacy* (exec. prod.), *Lost and Found* (exec. prod.) 1979; *Foolin' Around* (prod.), *Night of the Juggler* (exec. prod.), *Dirty Tricks* (exec. prod., US/Can.), *Final Assignment* (exec. prod., Can.) 1980; *Platoon* (prod.) 1986; *Triumph of the Spirit* (prod.) 1989; *Firebirds* (exec. prod.) 1990; *Out for Justice* (prod.), *Warlock* (exec. prod.) 1991; *Falling Down* (prod.), *The Fugitive* (prod.) 1993; *Outbreak, Seven* 1995; *The Devil's Advocate, Murder at 1600* 1997.

Kopple, Barbara. Filmmaker. Born on July 30, 1946, in New York City. Raised in Scarsdale, N.Y. Graduating from Northeastern University with a degree in psychology, she began using film for clinical studies. Armed with that experience, she started assisting documentary filmmakers as an editor, sound recordist, and camerawoman. She then spent four years (1972–76) in the coal fields of Harlan County, Ky., vividly recording in film the brewing struggle of unionized miners against wage cuts. The result was a stirring, openly militant film, *Harlan County, U.S.A.,* which went on to win the Academy Award as best feature-length documentary of 1976. The event later inspired her only fiction film, *Keeping On* (1981), originally shown on public TV.

FILMS (as director): *Richard III* (medium-length; co-dir. prod., edit., sound) 1970?; *Winter Soldier* (doc.; co-dir.) 1970?; *Harlan County U.S.A.* (also prod.) 1976; *No Nukes* (doc.; co-dir.) 1980; *Keeping On* (also exec. prod.) 1981; *American Dream* (doc.; also prod.) 1990.

Korda, Sir Alexander. Director, producer, executive. *b.* Sándor Laszlo Kellner, Sept. 16, 1893, Pusztaturpaszto, near Turkeve, Hungary, into an assimilated Jewish family. *d.* 1956. A precocious early reader, he enrolled at a local Hebrew school at five and was only nine when he began his secondary education. After the sudden death of his father, an estate manager and former Hussar officer, left the family destitute, he moved in with cousins in Budapest, where he became a journalist and a left-wing activist, writing under the pseudonym Sandor Korda. In 1912, following a sojourn to Paris, which included frequent visits to film studios, he entered the Hungarian film industry as a publicist and caption translator, among other diverse duties. He also started a film magazine that folded in less than a year. Becoming a director in 1914, Korda turned out many Hungarian films, none of which has survived. By 1917 he had established his own production company, in partnership with a friend, which specialized in the production of a selective list of quality films, several of which Korda directed. His influence steadily growing, he was appointed the postwar interim government's commissioner of film production late in 1918. The following year, as a member of the Communist Directory for the Arts, he was instrumental in the nationalization of the Hungarian film industry. But when the rightist Horthy government came to power he was forced to flee to Vienna, where he soon resumed making films for the Sacha company. He continued on to Germany, then to Hollywood, where he worked through 1930 with middling success. Returning to Europe, he worked briefly in France, then settled in England where he directed or produced some of Britain's most successful films commercially as well as artistically. As the founder and head of London Films, he infused the British film industry with much-needed creative and business energy. The quality and good taste that were the hallmarks of his product set a standard and a tradition for future film production in Britain. His *The Private Life of Henry VIII* (1933) was the first British talkie to capture sizeable revenues in the international box office. As a director, he provided such actors as Charles LAUGHTON and Robert DONAT with the roles that were to establish their future careers. He married two of his protégées, Maria Corda (1919–30) and Merle OBERON (1939–45). As a producer, he employed nepotism sensibly, utilizing the talents of his brothers, Zoltán and Vincent KORDA, and was largely responsible for the advancement of the careers of Carol REED and other British directors. In recognition of his achievements and his lasting contribution to British cinema, he was knighted in 1942.

FILMS: As director: In Hungary—*The Duped Journalist* (co-dir. with Gyula Zilhay), *Tutyu and Totyo* (co-dir. with Zilhay) 1914; *Lea Lyon* (co-dir. with Miklós Pásztory), *The Officer's Sword* (uncredited; also sc.) 1915; *White Nights/Fedora* (also sc.), *The Grandmother* (also sc.), *Tales of the Typewriter* (also sc.), *The Man with Two Hearts, The Million Pound Note* (also sc.), *Cyclamen, Battling Hearets, Laughing Sakia* (credit questionable), *Miska the Magnate* (credit questionable) 1916; *St. Peter's Umbrella* (also prod.), *The Stork Caliph* (also prod.), *Magic* (also prod.), *Harrison and Barrison* (also prod.) 1917; *Faun* (also prod.), *The Man with the Golden Touch* (also prod.), *Mary Ann* (also prod.) 1918; *Ave Caesar!* (also prod.), *White Rose* (also prod.), *Yamata* (also prod.), *Neither Home nor Abroad* (also prod.), *Number 111* (also prod.) 1919. In Austria—*Seine Majestät das Bettelkind/Prinz und Bettelknabe/The Prince and the Pauper* 1920; *Herren der Meere, Eine versunkene Welt, Samson und Delilah/Samson and Delilah* (also prod.) 1922. In Germany—*Das unbekannte Morgen/The Unknown Tomorrow* (also prod.) 1923; *Jedermanns Frau/Jedermanns Weib* (also prod.), *Tragödie im Hause Habsburg/Das Drama von Mayerling/Der Prinz der Legende* (also prod.) 1924; *Der Tänzer meiner Frau/Dancing Mad* 1925; *Madame wünscht keine Kinder/Madame Wants No Children* 1926; *Eine Dubarry von heute/A Modern du Barry* 1927. In the US—*The Stolen Bride, The Private Life of Helen of Troy* 1927; *The Yellow Lily, The Night Watch* 1928; *Love and the Devil, The Squall, Her Private Life* 1929; *Lilies of the Field, Women Everywhere, The Princess and the Plumber* 1930. In France—*Rive Gauche, Die Manner um Lucie* (French and German versions of Harry D'Arrast's *Laughter*), *Marius* (and its German version, *Zum goldenen Anker*) 1931. As director-producer: In the UK—*Service for Ladies/Reserved for Ladies, Wedding Rehearsal* 1932; *The Girl from Maxim's* (and French version, *La Dame de chez Maxim*), *The Private Life of Henry VIII* 1933; *The Private Life of Don Juan* 1934; *Rembrandt* 1936; *Lady Hamilton/That Hamilton Woman* 1941; *Perfect Strangers/Vacation from Marriage* 1945; *An Ideal Husband* 1948. As producer: In the UK (partial list)—*Men of Tomorrow* 1933; *Catherine the Great, The Scarlet Pimpernel* 1934; *Sanders of the River, Moscow Nights, The Ghost Goes West* 1935; *Things to Come, Knight Without Armor* 1936; *Elephant Boy* 1937; *The Divorce of Lady X, The Drum/Drums* 1938; *The Four Feathers, The Lion Has Wings* 1939; *The Thief of Bagdad* 1940; *Lydia* 1941; *Jungle Book, To Be or Not to Be* (co-prod.; US) 1942; *Sahara* (US) 1943; *Anna Karenina, The Fallen Idol* 1948. As executive producer: In the UK (partial list)—*The Winslow Boy* 1948; *The Small Back Room, The Third Man* 1949; *Seven Days to Noon, The Happiest Days of Your Life, The Wooden Horse* 1950; *The Tales of Hoffman, Outcast of the Islands* 1951; *Cry the Beloved Country, The Sound Barrier/Breaking Through the Sound Barrier* 1952; *Hobson's Choice, The Man Between* 1953; *The Constant Husband, A Kid for Two Farthings, Summertime/Summer Madness* (UK/US) 1955; *Richard III* 1956.

Korda, Vincent. Art director. *b.* Vincent Kellner, 1896, Pusztaturpaszto, near Turkeve, Hungary. *d.* 1979. A gifted artist, trained in Budapest, Vienna, Florence, and Paris, he often collaborated with his director brothers Alexander and Zoltán KORDA and created impressive sets for other directors as well. At his best with large-scale productions. He won an Academy Award for the sets of *The Thief of Bagdad* (1940) and Oscar nominations for *That Hamilton Woman* (1941), *Jungle Book* (1942), and *The Longest Day* (1962).

FILMS INCLUDE: *Marius* (co-art dir.) 1931; *Men of Tomorrow* 1932; *The Private Life of Henry VIII* 1933; *Catherine the Great, The Private Life of Don Juan* 1934; *The Scarlet Pimpernel, Sanders of the River* 1935; *The Ghost Goes West, Things to Come, Rembrandt* 1936; *Elephant Boy* 1937; *The Drum/Drums* 1938; *Q Planes/Clouds Over Europe, The Four Feathers, The Lion Has Wings* 1939; *21 Days/21 Days Together* (release delayed from 1937), *The Thief of Bagdad* 1940; *Lady Hamilton/That Hamilton Woman* 1941; *To Be or Not to Be* (US), *Jungle Book* 1942; *An Ideal Husband, The Fallen Idol, Bonnie Prince Charlie* 1948; *The Third Man* 1949; *An Outcast of the Islands* 1951; *The Sound Barrier/Breaking Through the Sound Barrier* 1952; *Summertime/Summer Madness* (US/UK) 1955; *Scent of Mystery* 1960; *The Longest Day* (co-art dir.; US) 1962; *The Yellow Rolls-Royce* (co-art dir.) 1964.

Korda, Zoltán. Director. *b.* Zoltán Kellner, May 3, 1895, Pusztaturpaszto, near Turkeve, Hungary. *d.* 1961. A younger brother of Alexander KORDA, he arrived in Budapest in 1908, attended a commercial high school, and had been working as a clerk for a coal company when he was drafted into the Austro-Hungarian Army at the outbreak of WW I. Fighting on the Galician front, he was felled by poisoned gas, which seriously damaged his lungs, rendering him susceptible to illness for the rest of his life. In 1918 he joined his brother's studio as an editor and in that same year co-directed his first film. He followed Alexander to Vienna, Berlin, and London, and in the 40s directed a number of films in Hollywood. His films typically took place in faraway, exotic places, evoking a strong sense of period and locale. For the creation of atmosphere, he was frequently aided by brother Vincent KORDA. His British-made *The Four Feathers* (1939) remains one of the grandest Empire adventures of all time; the American-made *Sahara* (1943) is a memorable WW II action picture starring Humphrey Bogart.

FILMS: In Hungary—*Karoly-Bakak* (co-dir. with Miklós Pasztory) 1918. In Germany—*Die Elf Teufel* 1927. In the UK—*Men of Tomorrow* (co-dir., uncredited, with Leontine Sagan)

1932; *Cash/For Love and Money* 1933; *Sanders of the River/Bosambo* 1935; *Forget Me Not/Forever Yours, Conquest of the Air* (doc.; co-dir. with several others) 1936; *Elephant Boy* (co-dir. with Robert Flaherty) 1937; *The Drum/Drums* 1938; *The Four Feathers* 1939. In the US—*Jungle Book* 1942; *Sahara* 1943; *Counter-Attack* 1945; *The Macomber Affair* 1947; *A Woman's Vengeance* (also prod.) 1948. In the UK—*Cry the Beloved Country/African Fury* (also co-prod.) 1951; *Storm Over the Nile* (co-dir. with Terence Young; also co-prod.) 1955.

Korjus, Miliza. Singer. *b.* Aug. 18, 1900, Warsaw. *d.* 1980. Voluptuous blonde coloratura soprano who starred with various European opera companies in the late 20s and early 30s, notably the Berlin Opera under the baton of Wilhelm Furtwangler. She was signed by MGM to co-star in the film biography of Johann Strauss, *The Great Waltz* (1938). But despite an Academy Award nomination for best supporting actress, she never made another Hollywood picture. She later appeared in Carnegie Hall and gave concerts in other American cities before retiring in the early 50s.

Korman, Harvey. Actor. Born on Feb. 15, 1927, in Chicago. Trained at Chicago's Goodman School of Drama, he played minor roles on Broadway and appeared in TV commercials before establishing himself as a successful TV comedian on 'The Danny Kaye Show' (1964–67). He later co-starred on 'The Carol Burnett Show' (1967–77) and other variety and comedy series, winning four Emmy Awards. In between television appearances he played light supporting roles in films.

FILMS INCLUDE: *Living Venus* 1961; *Gypsy* 1962; *Lord Love a Duck* 1966; *Three Bites of the Apple* 1967; *Don't Just Stand There!* 1968; *The April Fools* 1969; *Blazing Saddles, Huckleberry Finn* (as The King) 1974; *High Anxiety* 1977; *Americathon* 1979; *Herbie Goes Bananas, First Family* 1980; *History of the World: Part I* 1981; *The Trail of the Pink Panther* 1982; *The Curse of the Pink Panther* 1983; *The Longshot* 1986; *Munchies* 1987.

Korngold, Erich Wolfgang. Composer. *b.* May 29, 1897, Brno, Czechoslovakia (then Moravia). *d.* 1957. A child-prodigy composer and conductor in the concert halls of Vienna and Berlin, he came to the US in the 30s. He wrote scores for Warner Bros. films, winning Academy Awards for *Anthony Adverse* (1936) and *The Adventures of Robin Hood* (1938).

FILMS INCLUDE: *A Midsummer Night's Dream, Captain Blood* 1935; *Green Pastures, Anthony Adverse* 1936; *The Prince and the Pauper* 1937; *The Adventures of Robin Hood* 1938; *Juarez, The Private Lives of Elizabeth and Essex* 1939; *The Sea Hawk* 1940; *The Sea Wolf* 1941; *Kings Row* 1942; *The Constant Nymph* 1943; *Devotion, Deception, Of Human Bondage* 1946; *Escape Me Never* 1947; *Magic Fire* 1956.

Kortner, Fritz. Actor, director. *b.* Fritz Nathan Kohn, May 12, 1892, Vienna. *d.* 1970. A graduate of Vienna's Academy of Music and Dramatic Arts, he rose to prominence on the Berlin stage after WW I as an actor and director and became widely known in Europe for his unconventional interpretations of the classics. At the same time, he pursued a successful career in German films as an actor and occasional director. Fleeing Germany after the advent of the Nazis in 1933, he toured various European cities and in 1938 found refuge in the US. He wrote two Broadway plays, directing one, before going out to Hollywood as a screenwriter and character actor in the early 40s. Returning to Germany in 1947, he soon regained his prewar prestige as an actor and director of the stage and films.

FILMS INCLUDE (as actor): In Germany—*Police 1111* 1916; *Gregor Marold* (also dir.) 1918; *Else von Erlenhof* (also dir.), *Satanas* 1919; *Die Brüder Karamasoff/The Brothers Karamazov, Katherina die Grosse/Catherine the Great, Weltbrand* 1920; *Danton/All for a Woman, Die Hintertreppe/Backstairs* 1921; *Peter der Grosse/Peter the Great* 1922; *Schatten/Warning Shadows* 1923; *Orlacs Hände/The Hands of Orlac* 1924; *Beethoven/The Life of Beethoven* (title role; Aus.), *Maria Stuart* (as Bothwell), *Mata Hari/Mata Hari: The Red Dancer, Primanerliebe* 1927; *Marquis d'Eon der Spion der Pompadour/The Spy of Madame de Pompadour, Revolutionshochzeit/The Last Night, Die Frau auf der Folter/A Scandal in Paris, Die Büchse der Pandora/Pandora's Box* 1928; *Die Frau nach der Mann sich sehnt/Three Loves, Atlantik* 1929; *Dreyfus/The Dreyfus Case* (title role), *Menschen im Käfig/Love Storm, Der Andere* (in dual role), *Die grosse Sehnsucht* 1930; *Der Mörder Dimitri Karamasoff/The Murderer Dimitri Karamazov* (title role), *Danton* (title role), *Der Brave Sünder/The Upright Sinner* (dir., co-sc. only) 1931; *So ein Mädel vergisst man nicht* (dir., co-sc. only) 1932. In the UK—*Chu Chin Chow, Evensong* 1934; *Abdul the Damned, The Crouching Beast* 1935. In the US—*The Strange Death of Adolf Hitler* (also sc., from own co-story) 1943; *The Hitler Gang* 1944; *The Wife of Monte Cristo, Somewhere in the Night, The Razor's Edge* 1946; *The Brasher Doubloon* 1947; *Berlin Express, The Vicious Circle* 1948. In Germany—*Der Ruf/The Last Illusion* (also sc.) 1949; *Epilog* 1950; *Die Stadt ist voller Geheimnisse/City of Secrets/Secrets of the City* (dir., co-sc. only), *Sarajevo* (dir. only) 1955; *Die Sendung der Lysistrata* (dir. only, for TV) 1961.

Korty, John. Director. Born on June 22, 1936, in Lafayette, Ind. *ed.* Antioch Coll. The son of an industrial salesman. He began making amateur films at 16 and worked his way through college making animated TV commercials. Since the mid-60s he has been directing and producing solid independent low-budget feature films. He writes his own screenplays, handles his own photography, and typically employs unknown actors for his films. He has also directed several TV movies, winning much acclaim for 'The Autobiography of Miss Jane Pittman' (1974) and 'Eye on the Sparrow' (1991). He shared an Oscar for the feature-length documentary *Who Are the De Bolts?. . . And Where Did They Get 19 Kids?* (1977).

FEATURE FILMS: *Crazy Quilt* 1966; *Funnyman* 1967; *Riverrun* 1970; *Silence* 1974; *Alex and the Gypsy/Love and Other Crimes* 1976; *Who Are the De Bolts?. . . And Where Did They Get 19 Kids?* (doc.) 1977; *Oliver's Story* 1978; *Twice Upon a Time* 1983.

Korvin, Charles. Actor. Born Geza Korvin Karpathi, on Nov. 21, 1907, in Czechoslovakia. *ed.* Sorbonne. A former documentary director and cameraman, he arrived in the US in 1937 and played romantic leads and later supporting roles onstage and in films. He starred in the TV series 'Interpol Calling' (1959).

FILMS INCLUDE: *Enter Arsene Lupin* (title role) 1944; *This Love of Ours* 1945; *Temptation* 1946; *Berlin Express* 1948; *The Killer That Stalked New York* 1950; *Lydia Bailey* 1952; *Sangaree* 1953; *Thunderstorm* (Sp.) 1956; *Ship of Fools* 1965; *The Man Who Had Power Over Women* (UK) 1970; *Inside Out* (UK) 1975.

Koscina, Sylva. Actress. Born on Aug. 22, 1933, in Zagreb, Yugoslavia. Voluptuous leading lady of Italian films and international co-productions. In Italy since 1945, she started out in costume melodramas and quickie spectaculars but gradually worked her way into romantic comedies and dramas. In the late 60s she starred in several Hollywood productions.

FILMS INCLUDE: *Il Ferroviere/The Railroad Man* 1955; *Michel Strogoff/Michael Strogoff, Guendalina* 1956; *Le Fatiche di Ercole/Hercules, Gerusalemme Liberata/The Mighty Crusaders* 1957; *Ercole e la Regina di Lidia/Hercules Unchained, Racconti d'Estate/Love on the Riviera* 1958; *Erode il Grande* 1959; *L'Assedio di Siracusa/Siege of Syracuse* 1960; *Le Mercenaire/Swordsman of Siena* (Fr./It.), *Les Quatres*

Vérités/Three Fables of Love (Fr./It./Sp.), *Jessica, Copacabana Palace/Girl Game* (Braz./Fr./It.) 1962; *Le Monachine/The Little Nuns* 1963; *Judex* (Fr./It.), *Hot Enough for June/Agent 8¾* (UK) 1964; *Giulietta degli Spiriti/Juliet of the Spirits, Made in Italy* 1965; *Deadlier Than the Male* (UK) 1966; *Three Bites of the Apple* (US), *Johnny Banco* (Fr./It./Ger.) 1967; *The Secret War of Harry Frigg* (US), *A Lovely Way to Die* (US), *Johnny Banco* (Fr.) 1968; *Hornet's Nest* (US), *Battle of Neretva* (Yug./It./Fr.) 1970; *Homo Eroticus/Man of the Year* 1971; *Uccidere in Silenzio, La Mala Ordina* 1972; *Clara and Nora* (Sp.), *So Sweet So Dead, House of Exorcism* 1975; *Delitto d'Autore* 1976; *Casanova & Co.* (Ger./Aus./Fr.) 1977; *Sunday Lovers* 1980; *Stelle emigranti* 1983; *Cinderella '80* 1984; *Deadly Sanctuary* 1986.

Kosleck, Martin. Actor. *b.* Nicolai Yoshkin, on Mar. 24, 1907, Barkotzen, Pomerania (now Germany). *d.* 1994. A product of Max REINHARDT's Berlin theater, he played character roles, often sinister, in many Hollywood films from the late 30s. A specialist in nasty Nazis, despite his Jewish background, he impersonated Joseph Goebbels on the screen several times.

FILMS INCLUDE: *Alraune* (Ger.) 1930; *Confessions of a Nazi Spy* (as Goebbels), *Nurse Edith Cavell, Nick Carter—Master Detective* 1939; *Calling Philo Vance, Foreign Correspondent* 1940; *The Mad Doctor, Underground, International Lady* 1941; *All Through the Night, Nazi Agent, Berlin Correspondent* 1942; *Chetniks, Bomber's Moon, The North Star/Armored Attack* 1943; *The Hitler Gang* (again as Goebbels) 1944; *The Mummy's Curse, The Frozen Ghost, Strange Holiday, The Spider* 1945; *Crime of the Century, House of Horrors* 1946; *The Beginning or the End* 1947; *Half Past Midnight* 1948; *Something Wild* 1961; *Hitler* (again as Goebbels) 1962; *The Flesh Eaters* 1964; *36 Hours, Morituri* 1965; *Agent for H.A.R.M.* 1966; *Which Way to the Front?* 1970; *The Man with Bogart's Face* 1980.

Kosloff, Theodore. Actor, dancer. *b.* 1882, Moscow. *d.* 1956. In the US since WW I, he produced and choreographed Russian ballet for the stage and played both leads and supporting roles, often exotic, in many silent films, including several C. B. De Mille productions. He also choreographed a number of films.

FILMS INCLUDE: *The Woman God Forgot* 1917; *Why Change Your Wife?, The City of Masks, Something to Think About* 1920; *Forbidden Fruit, The Affairs of Anatol, Fool's Paradise* 1921; *The Lane That Had No Turning, The Green Temptation, The Dictator, Manslaughter* (choreographed only), *To Have and to Hold* 1922; *Adam's Rib, The Law of the Lawless, Children of Jazz, Don't Call It Love* 1923; *Triumph, Feet of Clay* 1924; *The Golden Bed, New Lives for Old, Beggar on Horseback* 1925; *The Volga Boatman* 1926; *The Little Adventuress, The King of Kings* 1927; *Woman Wise* 1928; *Madame Satan, Sunny* (choreographed only) 1930.

Kosma, Joseph. Composer. *b.* Jozsef Kozma, Oct. 22, 1905, Budapest. *d.* 1969. In France from 1933, he wrote melodic scores for many films, especially for Renoir and Carné, and composed numerous popular songs ("Autumn Leaves," etc.) as well as ballet and concert music. During WW II he masked his Jewish identity behind the pseudonym Georges Mouque.

FILMS INCLUDE: *Le Crime de Monsieur Lange/The Crime of Monsieur Lange* (song only), *Jenny, Une Partie de Campagne/A Day in the Country* 1936; *La Grande Illusion/ Grand Illusion* 1937; *La Marseillaise* (co-comp.), *La Bête humaine/The Human Beast* 1938; *La Règle du Jeu/The Rules of the Game* 1939; *Les Visiteurs du Soir/The Devil's Envoys* 1942; *Adieu Léonard* 1943; *Les Enfants du Paradis/ Children of Paradise* (co-comp.) 1945; *Les Portes de la Nuit/Gates of the Night* 1946; *Les Amants de Vèrone/The Lovers of Verona, Le Sang des Bêtes* 1949; *Juliette ou la Clef des Songes* 1951; *Les Fruits sauvages* 1953; *Huis clos/No Exit* 1954; *L'Amant de Lady Chatterley/Lady Chatterley's Lover* 1955; *Eléna et les Hommes/Paris Does Strange Things, Calle Mayor/The Lovemaker* (Sp.) 1956; *La Chatte/The Cat* 1958; *Le Déjeuner sur l'Herbe/Picnic on the Grass* 1959; *Katia/ Magnificent Sinner* 1960; *Le Caporal épinglé/The Elusive Corporal, La Poupée/He She or It* (co-comp.) 1962; *Un Drôle de Paroissien/Thank Heaven for Small Favors, In the French Style* (US/Fr.) 1963; *Le Petit Théâtre de Jean Renoir* 1969.

Kossoff, David. Actor. Born on Nov. 24, 1919, in London. A former interior designer and aircraft draftsman, he made his stage debut in 1942 and has played character parts in British films since the early 50s.

FILMS INCLUDE: *The Good Beginning* 1953; *The Young Lovers/Chance Meeting, Svengali* 1954; *The Angel Who Pawned Her Harp, A Kid for Two Farthings* 1955; *1984, The Bespoke Overcoat, The Iron Petticoat* 1956; *Count Five and Die* 1957; *Indiscreet* 1958; *The Journey* (US), *Jet Storm, The Mouse That Roared* 1959; *Conspiracy of Hearts, The Two Faces of Dr. Jekyll/House of Fright* 1960; *Freud* (US) 1962; *Summer Holiday, The Mouse on the Moon* 1963; *Ring of Spies/Ring of Treason* 1964; *The Private Life of Sherlock Holmes* (UK/US) 1970; *The London Connection/The Omega Connection* 1979.

Koster, Henry. Director. *b.* Hermann Kosterlitz, May 1, 1905, Berlin. *d.* 1988. *ed.* Acad. of Fine Arts (Berlin). A former painter, cartoonist, reporter, and film critic, he entered German films in 1925 as a screenwriter and had written a good number of scripts by 1931. In 1932, under the patronage of Joe PASTERNAK, he turned director, but the following year, with the Nazi rise to power, the Jewish Kosterlitz emigrated to France. In Hollywood since 1936, he directed many light films with considerable charm and flair, beginning with a succession of pictures with Deanna DURBIN, whose popularity saved Universal from bankruptcy. His attempts at drama were for the most part less successful but always visually pleasing. He was nominated for an Academy Award for directing *The Bishop's Wife* (1947). His reputation as a craftsman led to his assignment as director of the first film in CinemaScope, *The Robe* (1953).

FILMS (as director): In Europe (as Hermann Kosterlitz)—*Das Abenteuer der Thea Roland* (Ger.) 1932; *Das Hässliche Mädchen* (also co-sc.; Ger.) 1933; *Peter* (Aus./Hung.), *Kleine Mutti* (Aus./Hung.) 1934; *Katharina die Letzte* (Aus.) 1935; *Das Tagebuch der Geliebten/Il Diario di una Amata/Maria Baschkirtzeff/Affairs of Maupassant* (German-, Italian-, and French-language versions; Aus./It.) 1936. In the US (as Henry Koster)—*Three Smart Girls* 1936; *100 Men and a Girl* 1937; *The Rage of Paris* 1938; *Three Smart Girls Grow Up, First Love* 1939; *Spring Parade* 1940; *It Started with Eve* 1941; *Between Us Girls* (also prod.) 1942; *Music for Millions* 1944; *Two Sisters from Boston* 1946; *The Unfinished Dance, The Bishop's Wife,* 1947; *The Luck of the Irish* 1948; *Come to the Stable, The Inspector General* 1949; *Wabash Avenue, My Blue Heaven, Harvey* 1950; *No Highway/No Highway in the Sky* (UK), *Mr. Belvedere Rings the Bell, Elopement* 1951; *O. Henry's Full House* ("The Cop and the Anthem" episode), *Stars and Stripes Forever* 1952; *My Cousin Rachel, The Rope* 1953; *Desiree* 1954; *A Man Called Peter, The Virgin Queen, Good Morning Miss Dove* 1955; *D-Day the Sixth of June, The Power and the Prize* 1956; *My Man Godfrey* 1957; *Fraulein* 1958; *La Maja Desnuda/The Naked Maja* (It.) 1959; *The Story of Ruth* 1960; *Flower Drum Song* 1961; *Mr. Hobbs Takes a Vacation, Take Her She's Mine* (also prod.) 1963; *Dear Brigitte* (also prod.) 1965; *The Singing Nun* 1966.

Kotcheff, Ted. Director. Born William Theodore Kotcheff, on Apr. 7, 1931, in Toronto, Ont., Canada. A five-year veteran of

Canadian TV, he went to England in 1957 and there subsequently directed many TV productions and stage plays as well as several films. But it was back in Canada that he scored his biggest success as the director of the highly acclaimed film *The Apprenticeship of Duddy Kravitz* (1974), a funny-sad saga of a poor Jewish boy on the make in Montreal of the late 40s, based on the novel by Mordecai Richler. It was the first true international hit to come out of Canada since that country started turning out feature films in 1914. He later directed a number of Hollywood glossies, demonstrating assured technical skill if no particular distinction. It was again in Canada, and again in a Richler book, that he found the inspiration for *Joshua Then and Now* (1985), his most personal, and possibly best film of the 80s.

FILMS: In UK—*Tiara Tahiti* 1962; *Life at the Top* 1965; *Two Gentlemen Sharing* 1969; *Wake in Fright* 1970; *Outback* 1971; *Billy Two Hats* 1973; *The Apprenticeship of Duddy Kravitz* (Can.) 1974. In US—*Fun with Dick and Jane* 1977; *Who Is Killing the Great Chefs of Europe?* 1978; *North Dallas Forty* (also co-sc.) 1979; *Split Image* (also prod.), *First Blood* 1982; *Uncommon Valor* (also exec. prod.) 1983; *Joshua Then and Now* 1985; *Switching Channels* 1988; *Winter People, Weekend at Bernie's* (also act.) 1989; *Folks!* 1992; *Weekend at Bernie's 2* 1993; *The Shooter* 1995.

Koteas, Elias. Actor. Born in 1961, in Canada, of Greek descent. Intense, offbeat, versatile leading man and character player of the American screen. The son of a railway mechanic and a hatmaker, he began acting at Montreal's Vanier College, then moved to New York in the early 80s for training at the American Academy of Dramatic Arts. On-screen from 1985, he gradually moved from oddball supporting roles to leads.

FILMS: *One Magic Christmas* 1985; *Some Kind of Wonderful, Gardens of Stone* 1987; *Tucker: The Man and His Dream, Full Moon in Blue Water* 1988; *Malarek* (Can.), *Friends, Lovers, and Lunatics* 1989; *Desperate Hours, Teenage Mutant Ninja Turtles, Look Who's Talking Too, Almost an Angel* 1990; *Chain of Desire* 1993; *Camilla* 1993; *Exotica* 1994.

Kotto, Yaphet. Actor. Born on Nov. 15, 1937, in New York City. Leading man and supporting player of the American stage and screen, typically portraying assertive, aggressive, rebellious blacks. In 1972 he directed a first film, *Time Limit/Speed Limit 65*.

FILMS INCLUDE: *Nothing But a Man* 1964; *The Thomas Crown Affair, Five Card Stud* 1968; *The Liberation of L. B. Jones* 1970; *Man and Boy, Bone, Time Limit* (also prod., dir., story), *Across 110th Street* 1972; *Live and Let Die* 1973; *Truck Turner* 1974; *Report to the Commissioner, Sharks' Treasure, Friday Foster* 1975; *The Monkey Hustle* 1976; *Blue Collar* 1978; *Alien* 1979; *Brubaker* 1980; *Fighting Back* 1982; *The Star Chamber* 1983; *Warning Sign* 1985; *Eye of the Tiger* 1986; *Prettykill, The Running Man* 1987; *Midnight Run* 1988; *Ministry of Vengeance* 1989; *Hangfire* 1990; *Freddy's Dead: The Final Nightmare* 1991; *Extreme Justice* 1993; *The Favor, The Puppet Masters* 1994; *Two If by Sea* 1996.

Kovács, András. Director. Born on June 20, 1925, in Kide, Transylvania. Leading figure of the new Hungarian cinema. A graduate of Budapest's Academy of Theater and Film, he headed the screenplay department of the capital's studios from 1951 to 1957, all the while growing in prominence as a film critic and theorist. In a sudden career shift, he switched to directing, turning out his first film in 1960, when he was 35. He first drew international attention with his fourth film, *Difficult People* (1964), a quasi-documentary feature exploring the negative effects of professional jealousy and bureaucratic incompetence on the careers and lives of five inventors. The search for answers for moral issues and social phenomena of past and present was characteristic of much of his later work, typically polemic and imbued with sincerity and courage. He won the Silver Prize at the Moscow Film Festival for *Temporary Paradise* (1981). He has served as president of the Union of Hungarian Filmmakers.

FILMS: *Summer Rain* 1960; *The Rooftops of Budapest* 1961; *Autumn Star* 1962; *Difficult People* (semi-doc.; also sc.) 1964; *Two Portraits* (doc.), *Today or Tomorrow* (doc.) 1965; *Cold Days* (also sc.) 1966; *Walls* (also sc.) 1968; *Ecstasy from 7 to 10* (TV doc.) 1969; *Heirs* (doc.), *Relay Race* (also sc.) 1970; *Fallow Land* (also sc.), *Meeting György Lukács* (TV doc.) 1972; *My Life with Mihály Károlyi* (TV doc.) 1973; *Blindfold* (also sc.), *People and Art* (doc.) 1975; *Labyrinth* (also sc.) 1976; *The Stud Farm* (also sc.) 1978; *A Sunday in October* (also sc.) 1979; *Temporary Paradise* (also sc.) 1981; *Közelkép, An Afternoon Affair* 1983; *The Red Countess* (also sc.) 1985.

Kovacs, Ernie. Actor. *b.* Jan. 23, 1919, Trenton, N.J. *d.* 1962. A zany, creative TV comic, he brought his mustachioed, cigar-smoking, offbeat personality to films in the late 50s but died in an automobile accident before he could leave a lasting mark on the medium. He was married to Edie ADAMS.

FILMS: *Operation Mad Ball* 1957; *Bell Book and Candle* 1958; *It Happened to Jane* 1959; *Our Man in Havana, Strangers When We Meet, North to Alaska, Pepe, Wake Me When It's Over* 1960; *Five Golden Hours* 1961; *Sail a Crooked Ship* 1962.

Kovacs, Laszlo (Leslie). Director of photography. Born on May 14, 1933, in Hungary. A graduate of Budapest's Academy of Drama and Film Art, he came to the US in 1957 and became a naturalized citizen in 1963. A lighting cameraman from the late 60s, he asserted himself in the 70s as one of Hollywood's most gifted craftsmen, equally adept at creating subdued atmosphere and producing dazzling color effects. He has worked frequently for Peter BOGDANOVICH.

FILMS INCLUDE: *The Notorious Daughter of Fanny Hill* (co-phot.) 1966; *Hell's Angels on Wheels* 1967; *Targets* 1968; *Easy Rider* 1969; *Getting Straight, Five Easy Pieces, Alex in Wonderland* 1970; *Directed by John Ford* (doc.), *The Marriage of a Young Stockbroker, The Last Movie* 1971; *Pocket Money, What's Up Doc?, The King of Marvin Gardens* 1972; *Steelyard Blues, Slither, Paper Moon* 1973; *Huckleberry Finn, For Pete's Sake, Freebie and the Bean* 1974; *Shampoo, At Long Last Love* 1975; *Baby Blue Marine, Harry and Walter Go to New York, Nickelodeon* 1976; *New York New York, Close Encounters of the Third Kind* (co-phot.) 1977; *The Last Waltz* (co-phot.), *F.I.S.T., Paradise Alley* 1978; *Butch and Sundance: The Early Days* 1979; *Inside Moves* 1980; *The Legend of the Lone Ranger* 1981; *Frances* 1982; *Ghostbusters* 1984; *Mask* 1985; *Legal Eagles* 1986; *Little Nikita* 1988; *Say Anything* 1989; *Shattered, Radio Flyer* 1991; *Deception, Ruby Cairo, Sliver* 1993; *The Next Karate Kid, The Scout* 1994; *Copycat, Free Willy 2: The Adventure Home, Out of Sync* 1995; *Multiplicity* 1996; *My Best Friend's Wedding* 1997.

Kozintsev, Grigori. Director. *b.* Mar. 22, 1905, Kiev, Russia. *d.* 1973. While still a boy, he organized a mobile theater with several friends, including Leonid TRAUBERG and Sergei YUTKEVICH. In 1922 they founded FEX (Factory of the Eccentric Actor) and scandalized the theatrical establishment with an unconventional stage production of Gogol's 'Marriage' into which they blended several film sequences. In 1924, Kozintsev and Trauberg began a 20-year-long collaboration as film directors which culminated in their celebrated "Maxim Trilogy" of the late 30s (*The Youth of Maxim, The Return of Maxim,* and *The Vyborg Side,* or *New Horizons*), which dramatized the events of the Bolshevik Revolution through the synthetically devised "biography" of a typical party worker. The trilogy was awarded the Stalin Prize in 1941. Working alone since the end of WW II, Kozintsev has specialized in the adaptation of classics. He was awarded the Lenin Prize for *Hamlet* (1964). Author: *Shakespeare: Time and Conscience*; *The Deep Screen.*

FILMS: With Trauberg—*The Adventures of Oktyabrina* 1924; *Mishka Versus Yudenich* 1925; *The Devil's Wheel, The Cloak/The Overcoat* 1926; *Bratishka/Little Brother, S.V.D./The Club of the Big Deed* 1927; *The New Babylon* 1929; *Alone* 1931; *The Youth of Maxim* 1935; *The Return of Maxim* 1937; *The Vyborg Side/New Horizons* 1939; *Incident at the Telegraph Office* (short, alone) 1941; *Plain People 1945–56.* Kozintsev alone—*Pirogov* 1947; *Belinski* 1953; *Don Quixote* 1957; *Hamlet* 1964; *King Lear* 1972.

Krabbé, Jeroen. Actor. Born on Dec. 5, 1944, in Amsterdam. Imposing character lead of Dutch and international films. Trained for the stage at Amsterdam's De Toneelschool and the Academy of Fine Arts, he founded his own touring company and translated plays into Dutch. He began appearing in films in the early 70s and cracked the international barrier on the strength of his performances in such Paul Verhoeven films as *Soldier of Orange* and *The Fourth Man.* At his best in cynical or cruel characterizations. He is also a set designer and fine painter, and is the author of a cookbook.

FILMS INCLUDE: In the Netherlands—*The Little Ark* (bit; US/Holl.) 1972; *Alicia* 1974; *Soldier of Orange* 1979; *Spetters* 1980; *The Fourth Man* 1982. Abroad—*Turtle Diary* (UK) 1985; *Jumpin' Jack Flash* (US), *No Mercy* (US) 1986; *The Living Daylights* (UK) 1987; *A World Apart* (UK), *Crossing Delancey* (US) 1988; *Scandal* (UK) 1989; *The Punisher* (US/Austral.) 1990; *Till There Was You, The Prince of Tides* (US) 1991; *Kafka* (US) 1992; *The Fugitive* (US) *King of the Hill* (US) 1993; *Immortal Beloved* (US) 1994; *Farinelli* (Bel.) 1995; *The Disappearance of Garcia Lorca* 1997.

Kracauer, Siegfried. Film theoretician, sociologist, and historian. *b.* 1889, Frankfurt am Main, Germany. *d.* 1966. The holder of a Ph.D. from the Berlin University, he was on the editorial staff of the *Frankfurter Zeitung* from 1920 to 1933 and wrote a novel and several scholastic works. Immigrating to the US in 1941, he worked at New York's Museum of Modern Art for a couple of years, then was awarded a Guggenheim Foundation fellowship to write a history of the German film. The result was *From Caligari to Hitler* (1947), a critical study of the social and economic conditions and the psychological atmosphere that culminated in the rise of Hitler in Germany as they were reflected in German cinema between the World Wars. This thorough and often fascinating study has been criticized for a certain twisting and bending on the part of the author in postulating his premise.

Dr. Kracauer, who in the 50s was a senior member of the Bureau of Applied Social Research at Columbia University, wrote a second important cinema book, *Theory of Film,* in 1960. Stipulating that the one aim of cinema is the "redemption of physical reality," Kracauer proceeds to present a laborious and systematic argument to support his theory. Although weakened by dogmatism and by subjective aesthetic preferences, and again by the tendency to twist and bend ideas to fit the author's *a priori* stipulations, the book remains one of the few comprehensive theoretical works in the field of film.

Kräly, Hans. Screenwriter. *b.* 1885, Germany. *d.* 1950. A former stage and screen actor, he began writing scripts in 1912 and for several years supplied the screenplays for the German films of Urban GAD. In 1918 he started a long and fruitful collaboration with Ernst LUBITSCH and subsequently wrote, alone or in collaboration, most of the screenplays of the director's silent films. In 1923 he accompanied Lubitsch to Hollywood, where he continued his activity as screenwriter, for him and for Milestone, Wyler, and other directors.

FILMS INCLUDE: In Germany—*Die Kinder des Generals* 1912; *Engelein, Die Filmpromadonna* 1913; *Die ewige Nacht, Das Feuer, Weisse Rosen* 1914; *Die Augen der Mummie Ma/The Eyes of the Mummy, Carmen/Gypsy Blood* 1918; *Meine Frau die Film Schauspielerin, Die Austerprinzessin/The Oyster Princess, Rausch, Madame DuBarry/Passion, Die Puppe/The Doll* 1919; *Sumurun/One Arabian Night* (co-adapt. only), *Anna Boleyn/ Deception* 1920; *Die Bergkatze/The Wildcat* 1921; *Das Weib des Pharao/The Loves of Pharaoh* 1922; *Alles für Geld/Fortune's Fool, Die Flamme/Montmartre* 1923. In the US—*Rosita* 1923; *Black Oxen, Three Women, Forbidden Paradise, Her Night of Romance* 1924; *The Eagle, His Sister from Paris, Kiss Me Again* 1925; *So This Is Paris, The Duchess of Buffalo, Kiki* 1926; *The Student Prince, Quality Street* 1927; *The Patriot, The Garden of Eden* 1928; *Eternal Love, Betrayal, The Last of Mrs. Cheyney, The Kiss, Wild Orchids, Devil-May-Care* 1929; *Lady of Scandal* 1930; *Private Lives* 1931; *My Lips Betray, By Candlelight* 1933; *Broadway Gondolier* (co-story only) 1935; *100 Men and a Girl* 1937; *It Started with Eve* (co-story only) 1941; *The Mad Ghoul* 1943.

Kramer, Stanley. Producer, director. Born on Sept. 23, 1913, in New York City. *ed.* NYU. In films since the mid-30s, as researcher, film editor, and writer, he worked his way up to the position of associate producer by the early 40s. Following WW II military service with the Army Signal Corps, he formed an independent motion picture company, Screen Plays Inc., and produced a string of prestigious modest-budget "message" films which enjoyed a certain *succès d'estime.* In 1951, economic considerations forced him to sacrifice some of his independence by bringing his company as an autonomous unit under the banner of a large studio, Columbia Pictures. The arrangement did not work out well; all the films except one (*The Caine Mutiny*) that Kramer produced for Columbia lost money. In 1954 the arrangement was terminated by mutual consent.

After 1955, Kramer directed and produced films with increasing dependence on higher budgets and name stars. His pictures ranged from the overblown empty epic nonsense of *The Pride and the Passion* (1957) to the moving racial drama of *The Defiant Ones* (1958), and from the ominous end-of-the-world atmosphere of *On the Beach* (1959) to the Sennett-style, free-for-all slapstick of *It's a Mad Mad Mad Mad World* (1963). The common denominator of many of Kramer's films has been an unquenched penchant for the big social theme. He is aware of the prevailing critical opinion that has typed many of his films as shallow and pretentious. His "artistic" record notwithstanding, Kramer's sincerity cannot be questioned and he deserves recognition for bucking the Hollywood system as an independent producer long before others thought it possible or worthwhile. In 1961 he received a special Oscar, the Irving G. Thalberg Award, for "consistently high quality in filmmaking." Six of Kramer's films as director or producer earned Academy Award nominations: *High Noon* (for best picture, 1952); *The Caine Mutiny* (for best picture, 1954); *The Defiant Ones* (for best picture, best director, 1958); *Judgment at Nuremberg* (for best picture, best director, 1961); *Ship of Fools* (for best picture, 1965); and *Guess Who's Coming to Dinner* (best picture, best director, 1967). His output amassed 16 Oscars and some 80 nominations in other categories. In 1991 he was honored with the Producers Guild's David O. Selznick Award and a Life Achievement Award by the American Foundation for the Performing Arts.

FILMS: As producer—*So Ends Our Night* (assoc. prod.) 1941; *The Moon and Sixpence* (assoc. prod.) 1942; *So This Is New York* 1948; *Champion, Home of the Brave* 1949; *The Men, Cyrano de Bergerac* 1950; *Death of a Salesman* 1951; *The*

Sniper, High Noon, The Happy Time, My Six Convicts 1952; *The Four Poster, Eight Iron Men, The Juggler, The 5,000 Fingers of Dr. T* 1953; *The Wild One, The Caine Mutiny* 1954. As producer-director—*Not as a Stranger* 1955; *The Pride and the Passion* 1957; *The Defiant Ones* 1958; *On the Beach* 1959; *Inherit the Wind* 1960; *Judgment at Nuremberg* 1961; *Pressure Point* (prod. only) 1962; *A Child Is Waiting* (prod. only), *It's a Mad Mad Mad Mad World* 1963; *Invitation to a Gunfighter* (prod. only) 1964; *Ship of Fools* 1965; *Guess Who's Coming to Dinner* 1967; *The Secret of Santa Vittoria* 1969; *R.P.M.* 1970; *Bless the Beasts and the Children* 1971; *Oklahoma Crude* 1973; *The Domino Principle* 1977; *The Runner Stumbles* 1979.

Krampf, Günther. Director of photography. *b.* Feb. 8, 1899, Vienna. Deceased. He was lighting cameraman on several important expressionist German films. Settled in England early in the 30s.

FILMS INCLUDE: In Germany—*Nosferatu—eine Symphonie des Grauens/Nosferatu the Vampire* (asst. phot.) 1922; *Der verlorene Schuh/Cinderella* 1923; *Orlacs Hände/The Hands of Orlac* (co-phot.) 1925; *Der Student von Prag/The Student of Prague/The Man Who Cheated Life* (co-phot.) 1926; *Der Büchse der Pandora/Pandora's Box* 1929; *Die letzte Kompanie/13 Men and a Girl, Alraune* 1930; *Kühle Wampe* 1932. In the UK—*Rome Express* 1932; *The Tunnel/Transatlantic Tunnel* 1935; *Latin Quarter/Frenzy* 1945; *Fame Is the Spur* 1947; *Portrait of Clare* 1950; *The Franchise Affair* 1951.

Krasker, Robert. Director of photography. *b.* Aug. 21, 1913, Perth, Australia. *d.* 1981. He started his film career in France, then moved to England in 1930. There he worked as a camera operator (*Rembrandt, The Drum, The Four Feathers, The Thief of Baghdad*) before establishing himself as a leading lighting cameraman. A brilliant technician and a master of color photography, he was behind the lens on some of Britain's most important films beginning in the mid-40s, occasionally also working abroad. He won an Academy Award for *The Third Man* (1949).

FILMS INCLUDE: *The Gentle Sex* 1943; *Henry V (co-phot.)* 1944; *Brief Encounter, Caesar and Cleopatra* (co-phot.) 1945; *Odd Man Out* 1947; *The Third Man* 1949; *State Secret, Cry the Beloved Country* 1952; *Senso* (co-phot.; It.), *Romeo and Juliet* (It./UK) 1954; *Alexander the Great* (US), *Trapeze* (US) 1956; *The Story of Esther Costello* 1957; *The Quiet American* (US) 1958; *The Doctor's Dilemma, Libel* 1959; *The Criminal/The Concrete Jungle* 1960; *El Cid* (US/It.) 1961; *Billy Budd, Guns of Darkness, Birdman of Alcatraz* (co-phot.; US) 1962; *The Fall of the Roman Empire* (US) 1964; *The Heroes of Telemark, The Collector* (co-phot.; US/UK) 1965; *The Trap* (Can./UK) 1966.

Krasna, Norman. Playwright, screenwriter, producer, director. *b.* Nov., 7, 1909, Corona, Queens, N.Y. *d.* 1984. After studies at NYU, Columbia, and the Brooklyn Law School, he became a film critic and drama editor on various New York newspapers and later entered the film industry as a publicity director at Warners. He began writing plays for Broadway and stories and screenplays for Hollywood in the early 30s. His film work included some dramatic material, including the original stories for two Fritz Lang productions, *Fury* (1936) and *You and Me* (1938). But his forte was the comedy—more specifically, the comedy of mistaken identity—and it was in this area that he contributed the backbone of some of Hollywood's most delightful light films in the 30s and 40s. He received an Academy Award for the original screenplay of *Princess O'Rourke* (1943), one of three films he directed as well as scripted. With Norman Panama and Melvin Frank, he co-scripted the holiday perennial *White Christmas* (1954). He also produced a number of films.

FILMS (screenplays): *Hollywood Speaks* (story, co-sc.), *That's My Boy* 1932; *So This Is Africa, Parole Girl* (both story, adapt. only), *Meet the Baron* (co-story only), *Love Honor and Oh Baby!* (co-adapt. only) 1933; *The Richest Girl in the World* (also story), *Romance in Manhattan* (play basis only) 1934; *Four Hours to Kill* (from his own play, 'Small Miracle'), *Hands Across the Table* (co-sc.) 1935; *Wife vs. Secretary* (co-sc.), *Fury* (story only) 1936; *The King and the Chorus Girl* (co-story, co-sc.), *As Good as Married* (story only), *The Big City* (story, prod. only) 1937; *The First 100 Years* (story, prod. only), *You and Me* (story, co-adapt. only), *Three Loves Has Nancy* (prod. only) 1938; *Bachelor Mother* 1939; *It's a Date* 1940; *Mr. and Mrs. Smith* (also story), *The Devil and Miss Jones* (also story, co-prod.), *The Flame of New Orleans* (also story), *It Started with Eve* (co-sc.) 1941; *Princess O'Rourke* (also dir., story) 1943; *Bride by Mistake* (story only) 1944; *Practically Yours* (also story) 1945; *Dear Ruth* (play basis only) 1947; *John Loves Mary* (play basis only) 1949; *The Big Hangover* (also dir., co-prod., story) 1950; *The Blue Veil, Behave Yourself* (both prod. only) 1951; *White Christmas* (co-sc.) 1954; *The Ambassador's Daughter* (also dir., prod., story), *Bundle of Joy* (co-sc.; remake of *Bachelor Mother*) 1956; *Indiscreet* (from his own play 'Kind Sir') 1958; *Who Was That Lady?* (from his own play; also prod.), *Let's Make Love* (also story); *The Richest Girl in the World* (Danish remake) 1960; *My Geisha* (also story) 1962; *Sunday in New York* (from own play), *I'd Rather Be Rich* (remake of *It Started with Eve*) 1964.

Krasner, Milton. Director of photography. *b.* Feb. 17, 1904, Philadelphia. *d.* 1988. He entered films at 17 as an assistant cameraman and later worked as a camera operator at the Vitagraph and Biograph studios in New York. He graduated to lighting cameraman in 1933 but was not assigned major films until the mid-40s, when he excelled in black-and-white photography. In the 50s, working for 20th Century-Fox, he gained a reputation as a specialist in the cinematography of sumptuous color CinemaScope and other wide-screen productions and won an Academy Award for *Three Coins in the Fountain* (1954).

FILMS INCLUDE: *Strictly Personal* 1933; *Hold 'Em Yale* 1935; *The Crime of Dr. Hallet* 1938; *You Can't Cheat an Honest Man, House of Fear* 1939; *The Invisible Man Returns, The House of the Seven Gables, Hired Wife, The Bank Dick* 1940; *Buck Privates, The Lady from Cheyenne* 1941; *Paris Calling, The Ghost of Frankenstein* (co-phot.), *The Spoilers, Pardon My Sarong, Arabian Nights* 1942; *Gung Ho!* 1943; *The Invisible Man's Revenge, The Woman in the Window* 1944; *Scarlet Street, Along Came Jones* 1945; *Without Reservations, The Dark Mirror* 1946; *The Egg and I, A Double Life, The Farmer's Daughter* 1947; *The Accused* 1948; *The Set-Up, House of Strangers* 1949; *All About Eve, No Way Out* 1950; *Rawhide, I Can Get It for You Wholesale, People Will Talk* 1951; *The Model and the Marriage Broker, Monkey Business, Phone Call from a Stranger, Deadline USA* 1952; *Three Coins in the Fountain, Garden of Evil* (co-phot.), *Demetrius and the Gladiators, Desiree* 1954; *The Seven Year Itch, The Girl in the Red Velvet Swing, The Rains of Ranchipur* 1955; *Bus Stop* 1956; *Boy on a Dolphin, An Affair to Remember, Kiss Them for Me* 1957; *A Certain Smile* 1958; *The Man Who Understood Women* 1959; *Home from the Hill, Bells Are Ringing* 1960; *King of Kings* (co-phot.) 1961; *The Four Horsemen of the Apocalypse, Sweet Bird of Youth, How the West Was Won* (co-phot.), *Two Weeks in Another Town* 1962; *The Courtship of Eddie's Father, Love with the Proper Stranger* 1963; *Advance to the Rear, Fate Is the Hunter* 1964; *The Sandpiper, Red Line 7000* 1965; *The Singing Nun* 1966; *Hurry Sundown* (co-phot.), *The St. Valentine's Day*

Massacre 1967; *The Ballad of Josie* 1968; *The Sterile Cuckoo* 1969; *Beneath the Planet of the Apes* 1970.

Krauss, Werner. Actor. *b.* July 23, 1884, Gestunghausen, Germany. *d.* 1959. A distinguished performer of the German and Austrian stage, he entered films in 1914 and became a leading interpreter of German expressionist cinema, appearing in more than 100 silent films. In recognition of his appearance in several propaganda films during the Nazi era, he was made an Actor of the State.

FILMS INCLUDE: *Die Pagode* 1914; *Hoffmanns Erzählungen/Tales of Hoffmann, Nacht des Grauens, Zirkusblut* 1916; *Die Rache der Toten* 1917; *Es Werde Licht* (Pt. III), *Opium* 1918; *Das Kabinett des Dr. Caligari/The Cabinet of Dr. Caligari* (as Dr. Caligari), *Rose Bernd, Totentanz* 1919; *Die Brüder Karamasoff/The Brothers Karamazov, Das lachende Grauen* 1920; *Danton/All for a Woman* (as Robespierre), *Die Frau ohne Seele, Grausige Nächte, Das Medium, Scherben/ Shattered, Sappho, Zirkus des Lebens* 1921; *Der brennende Acker/Burning Soil, Josef und seine Brüder, Lady Hamilton, Die Nacht der Medici, Nathan der Weise, Othello* (as Iago), *Tragikomödie* 1922; *I.N.R.I./Crown of Thorns, Das alte Gesetz/The Ancient Law, Der Schatz/The Treasure* 1923; *Dekameron Nächte/ Decameron Nights* (as the Sultan), *Ein Sommernachtstraum/A Midsummer Night's Dream* (as Bottom), *Das Wachsfigurenkabinett/ Waxworks/The Three Wax Works* (as Jack the Ripper) 1924; *Eifersucht/Jealousy, Die freudlose Gasse/Streets of Sorrow/ Joyless Street* 1925; *Tartüff/Tartuffe* (as Orgon), *Geheimnisse einer Seele/Secrets of a Soul, Nana* (as Muffat), *Der Student von Prag/The Man Who Cheated Life* 1926; *Die Hose/A Royal Scandal* 1927; *Looping the Loop* 1928; *Napoleon auf St. Helena* 1929; *Yorck* (title role) 1931; *Mensch ohne Namen/The Man Without a Name* 1932; *Burgtheater/ Vienna Burgtheater* 1936; *Robert Koch* (as Dr. Rudolf Virchow) 1939; *Jud Süss* 1940; *Zwischen Himmel und Erde* 1942; *Paracelsus* 1943; *Der fallende Stern* 1950; *Sohn ohne Heimat* 1955.

Krech, Warren. See WILLIAM, Warren.

Kress, Harold F. Film editor, sometimes director. Born on June 26, 1913, in Pittsburgh. *ed.* UCLA. An editor since the late 30s, he directed a couple of documentaries in the early 40s and flirted briefly with directing features in the early 50s but soon returned to editing. He won an Academy Award for cutting *How the West Was Won* (1962) and shared another for *The Towering Inferno* (1974).

FILMS INCLUDE: As director (complete)—*Wardcare of Psychotic Patients* (doc.) 1941; *Purity Squad* (doc.) 1945; *No Questions Asked, The Painted Hills* 1951; *Apache War Smoke* 1952; *Cromwell* (2nd-unit dir. only) 1970. As editor—*Broadway Serenade, It's a Wonderful World* 1939; *Bitter Sweet, Comrade X, New Moon* 1940; *Dr. Jekyll and Mr. Hyde, H. M. Pulham Esq., Rage in Heaven, Unholy Partners* 1941; *Mrs. Miniver, Random Harvest* 1942; *Cabin in the Sky, Madame Curie* 1943; *Dragon Seed* 1944; *The Yearling* 1946; *Command Decision, East Side West Side* 1949; *Rose Marie, Valley of the Kings* 1954; *The Cobweb, I'll Cry Tomorrow* 1955; *The Teahouse of the August Moon* 1956; *Silk Stockings* 1957; *Imitation General, Merry Andrew* 1958; *The World the Flesh and the Devil* 1959; *Home from the Hill* 1960; *King of Kings* 1961; *How the West Was Won* 1962; *The Greatest Story Ever Told* (superv. edit.) 1965; *Alvarez Kelly* 1966; *Luv* 1967; *The Horsemen* 1971; *The Poseidon Adventure* 1972; *The Iceman Cometh* 1973; *The Towering Inferno* (co-edit.) 1974; *Gator* 1976; *The Other Side of Midnight* (co-edit.), *Viva Knievel!* 1977; *The Swarm* 1978.

Kreuger, Kurt. Actor. Born on July 23, 1916, in Michenberg, Germany. Handsome blond supporting performer who played an assortment of Nazis in Hollywood films of the 40s, as well as occasional romantic roles. Raised in Switzerland, he attended London University's School of Economics, then Columbia University in New York. He became an American citizen in 1944. During the 50s he worked mainly in European films but later returned to Hollywood in occasional supporting roles.

FILMS INCLUDE: *The Moon Is Down, Edge of Darkness, The Strange Death of Adolf Hitler, Sahara* 1943; *None Shall Escape, Mademoiselle Fifi* (lead) 1944; *Hotel Berlin, Escape in the Desert, The Spider, Paris Underground* 1945; *Sentimental Journey, The Dark Corner* 1946; *Unfaithfully Yours* 1948; *Spy Hunt* 1950; *The Enemy Below* 1957; *Legion of the Doomed* 1959; *What Did You Do in the War Daddy?* 1966; *The St. Valentine's Day Massacre* 1967.

Krige, Alice. Actress. Born on June 28, 1954, in Upington, South Africa. Pretty, refined brunette leading lady of British and American films. Moving to London at 22, she attended the School of Speech and Drama and began performing on TV. She made her screen and London stage debuts in 1981, appearing in a West End revival of Shaw's 'Arms and the Man' and in the Oscar-winning film *Chariots of Fire.* She has since been seen mostly in Hollywood productions and made-for-television movies.

FILMS: *Chariots of Fire, Ghost Story* 1981; *King David* (as Bathsheba) 1985; *Barfly* 1987; *Haunted Summer* 1988; *See You in the Morning* 1989; *S.P.O.O.K.S., Sleepwalkers* 1992; *The Institute Benjamenta* 1995; *Star Trek: First Contact* 1996.

Kristel, Sylvia. Actress. Born on Sept. 28, 1952, in Utrecht, Holland. The daughter of middle-class innkeepers, she had a strict Calvinist education, intending to become a teacher of English. But she soon rebelled against the family and ran away from home, supporting herself as a secretary, then as an attendant at an Amsterdam gas station. A slim beauty, she began modeling and before long became one of Europe's best-known mannequins. After winning the Miss TV Europe contest, she began appearing in Dutch films in 1972 and became internationally famous as the star of the erotic French film *Emmanuelle* (1974) and its sequels.

FILMS INCLUDE: In Holland—*Because of the Cats* 1972; *Living Apart Together* 1973. In France—*Emmanuelle* 1974; *Un Linceul n'a pas de Poches, Le Jeu avec le Feu, Julia/Julia: Innocence Once Removed* (Ger.) 1974; *Emmanuelle II/Emmanuelle—The Joys of a Woman* 1975; *La Marge, Alice ou la Dernière Fugue/Alice or the Last Escapade, Une Femme, Fidèle* 1976; *René la Canne, Behind the Iron Mask/The Fifth Musketeer* (Aus.), *Pastorale 1943* (Holl.) 1977; *Goodbye, Emmanuelle, Mysteries* (Holl.) 1978; *The Concorde—Airport '79* (US), *Letti selvaggi/Tigers in Lipstick* (It.) 1979; *Un Amore in Prima Classe* (It.), *The Nude Bomb* (US) 1980; *Private Lessons* (US), *L'Amant de Lady Chatterley/Lady Chatterley's Lover* 1981; *Private School* (US), *Emmanuelle 4* 1983; *Mata Hari* (US) 1985; *Dracula's Widow* 1987; *The Arrogant* 1989; *Hot Blood* 1990.

Kristofferson, Kris. Songwriter, singer, actor. Born on June 22, 1936, in Brownsville, Tex. *ed.* Pomona Coll. The son of an Army general, he majored in creative writing at Pomona College, then went to Oxford as a Rhodes Scholar. After a hitch with the Army as an officer in Germany and a period of teaching English at West Point, he began attracting attention as a songwriter-singer. Before long he became a top country-and-western concert and recording star. In the early 70s he manifested another aspect of his versatility, that of an actor and increasingly popular film personality. His original song score for *Songwriter* (1984) was nominated for an Academy Award. The second (1973–79) of his three marriages was to singer Rita Coolidge.

FILMS (as actor): *The Last Movie* (bit; also music) 1971; *Cisco Pike* (title role; also music) 1972; *Pat Garrett and Billy the Kid* (as Billy), *The Gospel Road* (singing own songs), *Blume in Love* (also song) 1973; *Bring Me the Head of Alfredo Garcia* 1974; *Alice Doesn't Live Here Anymore* 1975; *The Sailor Who Fell from Grace with the Sea* (UK), *Vigilante Force, A Star Is Born* 1976; *Semi-Tough* 1977; *Convoy* 1978; *Heaven's Gate* 1980; *Rollover* 1981; *Flashpoint, Songwriter* (also songs) 1984; *Trouble in Mind* 1985; *Big Top Pee-Wee* 1988; *Millennium, Welcome Home* 1989; *Sandino* (Sp./Chile), *Night of the Cyclone* 1990; *Original Intent, No Place to Hide* 1992; *Cheatin' Hearts* 1993; *Lone Star* 1996; *Fire Down Below* 1997.

Kruger, Alma. Actress. *b.* Sept. 13, 1868, Pittsburgh. *d.* 1960. On the stage from early childhood, she played character roles in some 50 Hollywood films of the late 30s and early 40s, typically as a woman of position or authority, memorably in the key part of the grandmother in *These Three* (1936). She also portrayed the head nurse in the "Dr. Kildare" film series.

FILMS INCLUDE: *These Three, Craig's Wife* 1936; *Vogues of 1938, 100 Men and a Girl* 1937; *The Toy Wife, Marie Antoinette* (as Empress Maria Theresa), *The Great Waltz* 1938; *Made for Each Other, Calling Dr. Kildare, Balalaika* 1939; *His Girl Friday* 1940; *The Trial of Mary Dugan, The People vs. Dr. Kildare* 1941; *Saboteur* 1942; *Three Men in White, Our Hearts Were Young and Gay* 1944; *A Scandal in Paris* 1946; *Forever Amber* 1947.

Krüger, Hardy. Actor. Born Eberhard Krüger, on Apr. 12, 1928, in Berlin. Popular blond leading man of German stage and films who has often been seen in international screen productions. Rumored to be a past member of Hitler's Youth Corps. He occasionally directs TV documentaries. His daughter Christiane Kruger is also a stage and screen actress.

FILMS INCLUDE: *Junge Adler* 1944; *Illusion in Moll* 1952; *Das letzte Sommer* 1954; *Alibi* 1955; *The One That Got Away* (UK) 1957; *Bachelor of Hearts* (UK); *Gestehen Sie Dr. Corda/Confess Dr. Korda* 1958; *Blind Date/Chance Meeting* (UK), *Der Rest ist Schweigen/The Rest Is Silence* 1959; *Bumerang/Cry Double Cross* 1960; *Un Taxi pour Tobrouk/Taxi for Tobruk* (Fr.) 1961; *Cybèle ou les Dimanches de Ville d'Avray/Sundays and Cybele* (Fr.), *Hatari!* (US) 1962; *The Flight of the Phoenix* (US) 1965; *L'Espion/The Defector* (Fr./Ger.) 1966; *The Secret of Santa Vittoria* (US), *La Monaca di Monza/The Lady of Monza* (It.) 1969; *The Battle of Neretva* (Yug./It./Fr.) 1970; *Krasnaya Palatka/The Red Tent* (USSR/It.) 1971; *Death of a Stranger* 1973; *Paper Tiger* (UK), *Barry Lyndon* (UK) 1975; *Potato Fritz* 1976; *A Chacun son Enfer* (Fr.), *A Bridge Too Far* (UK) 1977; *The Wild Geese* (UK), *Blue Fin* (Austral.) 1978; *Wrong Is Right/The Man with the Deadly Lens* (US) 1982; *The Inside Man* (UK) 1984.

Kruger, Otto. Actor. *b.* Sept. 6, 1885, Toledo, Ohio. *d.* 1974. A grandnephew of Oom Paul Kruger, South Africa's president during the Boer War, he trained for a musical career as a child but switched to acting after becoming a student at Columbia University. After several years in stock, repertory, and vaudeville, he made his Broadway debut in 1915 and by the 1920s was among the leading matinee idols of the American theater, a specialist in urbane, sophisticated leading roles. He made his first film appearance in 1915, but it wasn't until the early 30s that he became a Hollywood fixture and one of the screen's leading character actors. Always suave and polished, he played occasional leads and a variety of supporting roles, often as the worldly silver-haired "other man," but is best remembered for his portrayals of smooth, cynical villains or immoral professional men. He retired in the mid-60s following a series of strokes.

FILMS INCLUDE: *The Runaway Wife, A Mother's Confession* 1915; *Under the Red Robe* 1923; *Turn Back the Clock, Beauty for Sale, Ever in My Heart* 1933; *Gallant Lady, The Women in His Life, The Crime Doctor, Men in White, Treasure Island* (as Dr. Livesey), *Chained* 1934; *Vanessa: Her Love Story* 1935; *Lady of Secrets, Dracula's Daughter* 1936; *They Won't Forget, Counsel for Crime* 1937; *I Am the Law, Exposed* 1938; *Disbarred, Housemaster, The Zero Hour, Another Thin Man* 1939; *Dr. Ehrlich's Magic Bullet* (as 1st Nobel Prize–winner Dr. Emil Behring), *Seventeen, The Man I Married, A Dispatch from Reuters* 1940; *The Men in Her Life* 1941; *Saboteur* 1942; *Hitler's Children, Corregidor, Tarzan's Desert Mystery* 1943; *Cover Girl, Storm Over Lisbon, Murder My Sweet/Farewell My Lovely* 1944; *Wonder Man* 1945; *Duel in the Sun* 1947; *Payment on Demand, Valentino* 1951; *High Noon* 1952; *Magnificent Obsession, Black Widow* 1954; *The Colossus of New York* 1958; *The Young Philadelphians, Cash McCall* 1959; *The Wonderful World of the Brothers Grimm* 1962; *Sex and the Single Girl* 1964.

Kruschen, Jack. Actor. Born on Mar. 20, 1922, in Winnipeg, Man., Canada. Character player of the American stage, TV, and films, usually in comic support, but sometimes in menacing roles. He was nominated for a best supporting actor Oscar for his performance in *The Apartment* (1960).

FILMS INCLUDE: *Red Hot and Blue* 1949; *Confidence Girl* 1952; *A Blueprint for Murder, The War of the Worlds* 1953; *Money from Home* 1954; *Julie* 1956; *Cry Terror, The Decks Ran Red* 1958; *The Last Voyage, The Angry Red Planet, The Apartment, Studs Lonigan* 1960; *Lover Come Back, Cape Fear, Convicts 4/Reprieve* 1962; *McLintock!* 1964; *Dear Brigitte, Harlow* 1965; *The Happening, Caprice* 1967; *$1,000,000 Duck* 1971; *Freebie and the Bean* 1974; *Guardian of the Wilderness, Satan's Cheerleaders* 1977; *Sunburn* 1979; *Under the Rainbow* 1981; *Money to Burn* 1983; *Cheaters* 1984.

Kubrick, Stanley. Director. Born on July 26, 1928, in the Bronx, N.Y. As a child he was encouraged by his physician father to take up still photography as a hobby. By the time he reached 17 he was a staff photographer for *Look* magazine. A motion picture addict since his high school days, he had long had the urge to make films. In 1950 he quit his job at *Look* and set out to make his first film, *Day of the Fight,* a short documentary that he promptly sold to RKO-Pathé for a $100 profit. He made another documentary short for RKO before his debut as a feature director in 1953 with *Fear and Desire,* a low-budget film he financed with money he had borrowed from relatives and friends. It was virtually a one-man show. Kubrick wrote the script, directed, loaded and operated the camera, and did the physical editing and almost everything else but the acting. He made his second feature, *Killer's Kiss,* in much the same way. In 1954, Kubrick formed a production company with producer James B. Harris. Working with a larger budget and a professional cast headed by Sterling HAYDEN, he made *The Killing,* a tense crime drama that first brought his work to the attention of critics (it has since been elevated to the status of a minor classic by Kubrick devotees). With his next film, *Paths of Glory,* a powerful indictment of the hypocrisy of the military, Kubrick firmly established himself as the most promising of the postwar generation of Hollywood directors. Working for a percentage of the profits, he received no salary and no other remuneration for either of the two films, both of which were astounding critical hits but did rather poorly at the box office. After a two-year interlude during which he was not able to obtain any work, Kubrick was asked to replace Anthony Mann as the director of the high-budget multistar epic *Spartacus* (1960). He handled the assignment intelligently, turning the film into something a notch above the standard Hollywood super-spectacle while flawlessly controlling the technical aspects.

In 1961, Kubrick moved to England, in search of greater independence and greater creative control of his films, away from the Hollywood studio system. But he came back to the US the following year for location shooting for *Lolita* (1962), a reworked adaptation of the Nabokov novel in which Kubrick was able to sprinkle the bitter cynicism that had characterized some of his earlier work with a good dash of black humor. Kubrick's penchant for the macabre exploded into nightmarish satire in *Dr. Strangelove* (1964), subtitled *How I Learned to Stop Worrying and Love the Bomb,* in which he treated the possibility of nuclear catastrophe as a grim joke. Despite its abundant frivolity, the film reaffirmed Kubrick's innate pessimism and his deep distrust of social and political institutions.

His next film, *2001: A Space Odyssey* (1968), sharply polarized critical and popular opinion. To some, this science fiction journey into humanity's future was overblown, tedious, pretentious, and confusing; to others, especially members of the younger generation, it represented the ultimate audiovisual "trip," a psychedelic experience appropriate to the drug culture; to still others, it was a symbolically rich vision of a technology-dominated society and humanity's ultimate destiny. The film's serene visual beauty and breathtaking special effects were disputed by no one and over the years *2001* has assumed the status of a classic in the fantasy/science-fiction genre. Kubrick won an Academy Award for his design of the film's special effects, which set a new standard for the cinematic depiction of outer space.

A Clockwork Orange (1971), cited as the year's best by the New York Film Critics, who also voted Kubrick best director. Despite thematic flaws and narrative gaps, it is a striking, visually brilliant film that provides a chilling, near-nihilistic vision of a world dominated by anarchic, vicious violence and engulfed by utter cynicism—a perverse world of tomorrow which some say mirrors Kubrick's view of the world today.

Kubrick is a pedantic, meticulous filmmaker who takes months, and sometimes years, to prepare a single film. He stages every scene and plans every shot with utmost care, assigning great importance to each and every image that is captured by the camera. He took 300 shooting days to complete *Barry Lyndon* (1975), a visually magnificent, stunningly elegant, but often hollow and slow adaptation of a minor Thackeray novel. Equally exasperating for many Kubrick admirers was *The Shining* (1980), his eerie but not horrific, disturbing but not absorbing excursion into the horror-fantasy genre. With *Full Metal Jacket* (1987), an austere, unflinching adaptation of a Gustav Hasford novel, Kubrick returned to the theme of the inhumanity of militarism and war (Vietnam) and went a long way toward redeeming his reputation.

Few contemporary directors have divided critical opinion as Kubrick has. His detractors call him pretentious, fussy, unfeeling, and self-indulgent. But to many others he is a unique artist with personal vision and a brilliant visual style, one of the outstanding talents of today's cinema. He continues to work in the film industry today.

FILMS: *Day of the Fight* (doc. short; also prod., sc., phot., edit.) 1950; *Flying Padre* (doc. short; also prod., sc., phot., edit.) 1951; *Fear and Desire* (also prod., phot., edit.) 1953; *Killer's Kiss* (also co-prod., story, sc., phot., edit.) 1955; *The Killing* (also sc.) 1956; *Paths of Glory* (also co-sc.) 1957; *Spartacus* 1960; *Lolita* 1962; *Dr. Strangelove or How I Learned to Stop Worrying and Love the Bomb* (also prod., co-sc.) 1964; *2001: A Space Odyssey* (also prod., co-sc., sp. eff.) 1968; *A Clockwork Orange* (also prod., sc., addnl. phot.) 1971; *Barry Lyndon* (also prod., sc.) 1975; *The Shining* (also prod., sc.) 1980; *Full Metal Jacket* (also prod., co-sc.) 1987.

Kulèshov, Lev (Leo). Director, film theoretician. *b.* Jan. 14, 1899, Tambov, Russia. *d.* 1970. At the age of 15 he enrolled at the college-level School of Art, Architecture, and Sculpture in Moscow and began drawing fashion designs for a ladies' magazine. At 17 he was hired as a set designer on pre-Revolutionary Russian films, in several of which he also appeared. At 18 he directed his first film, *The Project of Engineer Prite,* a detective melodrama, and published his first articles on cinema theory. Strongly influenced by American films, and especially the work of D. W. GRIFFITH, he expounded in his articles the principles of "American editing," out of which he developed a theory of MONTAGE as the basic component of cinema. His ideas were later elaborated upon in theory and practice by his pupils, EISENSTEIN and PUDOVKIN.

While in Red Army uniform during the Revolutionary period, Kuleshov shot newsreel footage that he edited into a number of short documentaries. During this same period he was also put in charge of re-editing foreign feature films before their exhibition to Soviet audiences and a short time later he was appointed head of the newsreel section at the Moscow film studios. It was then that Kuleshov began his editing experiments, including the famous "Kuleshov effect." Using clips of old footage, he juxtaposed shots of the famous actor Ivan MOZHUKHIN with shots of various objects. The results were astounding: the very same expressions of the actor suggested a different meaning with each combination, proving the power of editing to alter reality. The significance was not so much in the shots themselves but in the way the editor chose to manipulate them. In 1919, Kuleshov participated in the founding of Moscow's First National Film School and the following year he began teaching there, while continuing his work as a director. Among his first pupils was Alexandra Khokhlova, a former screen extra. They married and she became his close collaborator and frequent star. In 1921, Kuleshov set up a film workshop, a stock company that began its existence with live stage shows simulating a cinematic style because of a shortage of raw film in the Soviet Union during the period. Not until 1924 could the company work with real film.

The workshop's first production was a fast-paced burlesque comedy, *The Extraordinary Adventures of Mr. West in the Land of the Bolsheviks.* Kuleshov directed this parody about a gullible American in Russia. His star pupil, Pudovkin, created the designs and played the main role of a Russian con man fleecing the American. The film was highly popular with Soviet audiences, as was Kuleshov's next, *The Death Ray.* But Soviet officialdom frowned upon the political content of the latter and stripped Kuleshov of his stock company and much of his budget.

Despite a minuscule budget Kuleshov scored a critical success with his next film, *By the Law* (also known as *Dura Lex*), a gripping psychological drama of the Klondike gold rush adapted from Jack London's *The Unexpected.* But Soviet officials found this film too lacking in ideological merit. After several years of declining prestige in the Soviet industry, Kuleshov's directing activity came to a complete halt in 1933. Instead, he devoted his energies to the writing of books on film theory, including *Fundamentals of Film Direction* (1941). During WW II he briefly resumed directing films and in 1944 he was appointed head of the Moscow Film Institute.

Until the publication of Jay Leyda's *Kino* in 1960, Kuleshov's contribution to cinema as a filmmaker, as a pioneer theorist of montage, and as the mentor of Pudovkin and other noted Soviet directors, was practically unknown in the West and all but forgotten in Russia. However, since the early 60s

Kuleshov has enjoyed a renaissance of sorts. Retrospectives of his films have been shown in Russia and Europe and in 1966 he sat on the jury of the Venice Film Festival.

FEATURE FILMS: *The Project of Engineer Prite* (also art dir.) 1918; *The Unfinished Love Song* (co-dir. with Vitold Polonsky, art dir.) 1919; *On the Red Front* (also sc., act.) 1920; *The Extraordinary Adventures of Mr. West in the Land of the Bolsheviks* 1924; *The Death Ray* (also act.) 1925; *Dura Lex/By the Law* (also co-sc.) 1926; *Your Acquaintance/Journalist* (also co-sc.) 1927; *The Gay Canary* 1929; *Two-Buldi-Two* (co-dir. with Nina Agadzhanova-Shutko) 1930; *Forty Hearts* 1931; *Horizon/Horizon—The Wandering Jew* (also co-sc.), *The Great Consoler* (also co-sc.) 1933; *The Siberians* 1940; *Incident in a Volcano* (co-dir. with three others) 1941; *Timur's Oath* 1942; *We Are from the Urals* 1944.

Kulijanov (also **Kulidzhanov), Lev.** Director. Born on Mar. 19, 1924, in Tiflis, Russia. A highly regarded representative of the middle generation of Soviet filmmakers, he has been hailed by critics for his intimate personal style. A graduate of the state film school, where he studied under Sergei Gerasimov, he acquired his master's interest in the lives of ordinary people and the penchant for discovering beauty in modest surroundings. He was named People's Artist of the USSR in 1977.

FILMS: *Ladies* (co-dir., co-sc. with G. Oganisian) 1955; *It Started Like This* (co-dir., co-sc. with Yakov Segel) 1956; *The House I Live In* (co-dir. with Segel) 1957; *Our Father's House/A Home for Tanya* 1959; *The Lost Photograph* (USSR/Czech.) 1960; *When the Trees Were Tall* 1962; *The Blue Notebook* (also sc.) 1963; *Crime and Punishment* (also co-sc.) 1969; *A Moment in the Stars* (also co-sc.) 1975.

Kulik, Buzz. Director. Born Seymour Kulik, 1923, in New York City. After WW II service with the Army, he joined an advertising agency as producer-director of video and film and later produced and directed many live dramas and filmed episodes for such prominent CBS-TV anthologies and series as 'You Are There,' 'Playhouse 90,' 'The Defenders,' and 'Twilight Zone.' He began directing feature films in the early 60s but continued working mainly in TV, for which he produced and directed a number of movies, including the highly acclaimed 'Brian's Song' (1971). He served as TV adviser to Senator Edmund Muskie of Maine during the 1971–72 presidential campaign.

FILMS: *The Explosive Generation* 1961; *The Yellow Canary* 1963; *Ready for the People* 1965; *Warning Shot* (also prod.) 1967; *Sergeant Ryker, Villa Rides* 1968; *Riot* 1969; *To Find a Man/Sex and the Teenager* 1972; *Shamus* 1973; *The Hunter* 1980.

Kuri, Emile. Set decorator. Born on June 11, 1907, in Cuernavaca, Mexico. *ed.* Chaminade Coll. After an early stint working on episodes of the movie serial "Hopalong Cassidy" (for producer Harry Sherman), he was signed to contracts with major production companies, including Selznick International and Liberty Films. Later, in his work for Walt Disney Productions, he oversaw all film and TV set design, as well as that of Disneyland and Disney World. Won Academy Awards for *The Heiress* and *20,000 Leagues Under the Sea*. With art director Jack Okey, he was responsible for the look of small town Bedford Falls in *It's a Wonderful Life*.

FILMS INCLUDE: *The Silver Queen* 1942; *I'll Be Seeing You* 1944; *Spellbound* 1945; *It's a Wonderful Life, Duel in the Sun* 1946; *The Paradine Case* 1948; *The Heiress* 1949; *Fancy Pants* 1950; *A Place in the Sun* 1951; *Carrie* 1952; *The War of the Worlds, Shane, The Actress* 1953; *Executive Suite, 20,000 Leagues Under the Sea* 1954; *Old Yeller* 1957; *The Absent Minded Professor, The Parent Trap* 1961; *Mary Poppins* 1964; *Bedknobs and Broomsticks* 1971.

Kurnitz, Harry. Screenwriter, playwright, novelist. *b.* Jan. 5, 1909, New York City. *d.* 1968. A former reporter, he went to Hollywood in 1938 to work on the screen adaptation of his own story, *Fast Company,* and stayed to collaborate on many other screenplays. He wrote novels under his own name and detective thrillers and some scripts under the pseudonym Marco Page.

FILMS INCLUDE: *Fast Company* (from own novel) 1938; *Fast and Furious* 1939; *I Love You Again* 1940; *Shadow of the Thin Man* 1941; *Pacific Rendezvous* 1942; *They Got Me Covered* 1943; *See Here Private Hargrove, The Heavenly Body* 1944; *Something in the Wind, The Web* 1947; *The Adventures of Don Juan, One Touch of Venus* 1948; *My Dream Is Yours, The Inspector General, A Kiss in the Dark* (also prod.) 1949; *Pretty Baby* 1950; *Of Men and Music* 1951; *Tonight We Sing, Melba, The Man Between* (UK) 1953; *Land of the Pharaohs* 1955; *The Happy Road* (US/Fr.) 1957; *Witness for the Prosecution* 1958; *Once More with Feeling* (from own play) 1960; *A Shot in the Dark* (play basis only), *Goodbye Charlie* 1964; *How to Steal a Million* 1966.

Kurosawa, Akira. Director. Born on Mar. 23, 1910, in the Omori district of Tokyo. The youngest of seven children of a veteran army officer who turned athletic instructor, he showed a talent for painting at an early age. At 17 he enrolled at an art school that emphasized Western styles. Failing to earn a living as a commercial artist, he responded in 1936 to a film studio's recruiting advertisement for assistant directors, and after passing a battery of tests he was assigned as assistant to director Kajiro YAMAMOTO. By 1941 he was writing scripts and directing whole sequences for Yamamoto's films. In 1943 he made his debut as director with *Judo Saga,* revealing himself from the start as a highly skillful craftsman with an eye for beauty and a knack for economy of expression.

Produced as they were during WW II, Kurosawa's early films had to conform to themes prescribed by official state propaganda policy. It is possible that this freedom from the responsibilities of story and thematic involvement allowed the novice director to concentrate on the technical aspects of his work and rapidly develop as a craftsman. Kurosawa entered the mature, personally expressive phase of his career with *Drunken Angel* (1948), a film that coincidentally represented his first collaboration with actor Toshiro MIFUNE, his frequent protagonist. "In this picture," he once said, "I finally discovered myself." From here on, he increasingly asserted his creative independence, eventually assuming complete control over the content as well as the form of his productions.

Kurosawa is a man of all genres, all periods, and all places, bridging in his work the traditional and the modern, the old and the new, the cultures of the East and the West. His period dramas have a contemporary significance and like his modern themes they are typified by a compassion for their characters, a deep humanism that mitigates the violence that often surrounds them, and a concern for the ambiguities of human existence.

Kurosawa's film *Rashomon* introduced the West to the wealth of Japanese cinema when it won the top prize at the 1951 Venice Film Festival and a Special Oscar as best foreign picture of that year. This powerful study in ambiguity, rich in symbolism and psychological insight, not only opened Western theaters to many subsequent Japanese productions but directly inspired two American remakes, the motion picture *The Outrage,* starring Paul Newman, and a feature-length TV production starring Ricardo Montalban. Another of Kurosawa's films, *Seven Samurai* (which was also called *The Magnificent Seven*), was openly imitated in the Hollywood production that even used the name *The Magnificent Seven,* and the Italian "spaghetti Western" *A Fistful of Dollars* was pirated from Kurosawa's

Yojimbo. The intercultural influence has been reciprocal. Kurosawa's *The Hidden Fortress,* winner of the International Critics Prize at the 1959 Venice Festival, seems to have been directly influenced by Hollywood Westerns in the John Ford tradition; and four of his major films have been adaptations of Western literary works, Dostoevsky's *The Idiot,* Gorky's *The Lower Depths,* Shakespeare's *Macbeth* (adapted into *Throne of Blood*), and *King Lear* (reworked as *Ran*).

Despite the international success of these and other of his films—ranging from the tender and deeply moving modern story *Ikiru/To Live/Doomed* (1952) to the spectacular Samurai tale *Sanjuro* (1962)—and his growing stature as a leading film-maker, Kurosawa suffered a deep personal setback in the late 60s and early 70s. Following the ambitious *Akahige/Red Beard* (1965), in which he invested two years of intensive work, the director entered a frustrating period of aborted projects and forced inactivity. When *Dodeska-den* (1970), his first film in five years, failed at the box office, a despairing Kurosawa attempted suicide by self-inflicted multiple slashes. But he fully recovered from his wounds and within months regained his spirits and sense of purpose when he was offered the opportunity to direct a Soviet-Japanese co-production, *Dersu Uzala.* Nearly four years in the making, much of it on location in Siberia, this survival saga won the Academy Award as best foreign language film of 1975 as well as a Gold Medal at the Moscow Film Festival. Kurosawa surpassed that achievement with *Kagemusha* (1980), a deeply humanistic historical epic that shared the Palme d'Or at the Cannes Festival and won the British Academy Award for best direction and the Italian David di Donatello Award as best foreign film. *Ran* (1985), his fascinating adaptation of *King Lear,* also gained multiple international awards. Two later films, *Akira Kurosawa's Dreams* (1990) and *Rhapsody in August* (1991), received less critical praise.

Kurosawa is a true *auteur* who has edited or closely supervised the editing of nearly all his films and collaborated on the scripts of most. He has also written screenplays for the films of others. (Konchalovsky's American thriller, *Runaway Train,* was based on a Kurosawa screenplay.) Powerfully expressive and highly versatile, a master craftsman and a virtuoso stylist, he ranks among the world's great living directors. Since 1945 he has been married to Yoko Yaguchi (née Kato Kiyo), the star of his early film, *The Most Beautiful.* Memoirs: *Something Like an Autobiography* (1982).

FILMS (as director): *Sanshiro Sugata/Judo Saga* (also sc.) 1943; *The Most Beautiful/Most Beautifully* (also sc.) 1944; *Sanshiro Sugata Part II/Judo Saga II* (also sc.), *The Men Who Tread on the Tiger's Tail/They Who Step on the Tiger's Tail* (also sc., release delayed until 1952) 1945; *Those Who Make Tomorrow* (co-dir. with Kajiro Yamamoto and Hideo Sekigawa), *No Regrets for Our Youth/No Regrets for My Youth* (also co-sc.) 1946; *One Wonderful Sunday/Wonderful Sunday* (also co-sc.) 1947; *Drunken Angel* (also co-sc.) 1948; *The Quiet Duel/A Silent Duel* (also co-sc.), *Stray Dog* (also co-sc.) 1949; *Scandal* (also co-sc.), *Rashomon* (also co-sc.) 1950; *The Idiot* (also co-sc.) 1951; *Ikiru/To Live/Doomed* (also co-sc.) 1952; *Seven Samurai/The Magnificent Seven* (also co-sc.) 1954; *I Live in Fear/Record of a Living Being/What the Birds Knew* (also co-sc.) 1955; *Throne of Blood/The Castle of the Spider's Web/Cobweb Castle* (also co-prod., co-sc.), *The Lower Depths* (also co-prod., co-sc.) 1957; *The Hidden Fortress/Three Bad Men in a Hidden Fortress* (also co-prod., co-sc.) 1958; *The Bad Sleep Well/The Worse You Are the Better You Sleep/The Rose in the Mud* (also co-prod., co-sc.) 1960; *Yojimbo/The Bodyguard* (also exec. prod., co-sc.) 1961; *Sanjuro* (also exec. prod., co-sc.) 1962; *High and Low/Heaven and Hell/The Ransom* (also exec. prod., co-sc.) 1963; *Red Beard* (also exec. prod., co-sc.) 1965; *Dodeska-Den* (also co-prod., co-sc.) 1970; *Dersu Uzala* (also co-sc.; USSR/Jap.) 1975; *Kagemusha* (also co-prod., co-sc.) 1980; *Ran* (also co-sc.; Jap./Fr.) 1985; *Akira Kurosawa's Dreams* (also sc.) 1990; *Rhapsody in August* (also sc.) 1991; *Madadayo* (also sc.; Jap.) 1993.

Kurtz, Gary. Producer. Born on July 27, 1940, in Los Angeles. He began his professional career while still a student at UCLA's film school, working as a cameraman, sound man, editor, production supervisor, and assistant director on documentaries and low-budget features for Roger CORMAN and others. After serving two years as a draftee in the Marines, he became involved in major productions as a George LUCAS associate.

FILMS INCLUDE: *American Graffiti* 1973; *Star Wars* 1977; *The Empire Strikes Back* 1980; *The Dark Crystal* (also 2nd-unit dir.) 1982; *Return to Oz* 1985; *Slipstream* 1989.

Kurtz, Swoosie. Actress. Born on Sept. 6, 1944, in Omaha, Neb. *ed.* USC; Academy of Music and Dramatic Art, London. Brassy, red-headed leading lady and supporting player of the American stage, TV, and films. Typically seen in earthy, goofy roles. She won Tony Awards for her performances on Broadway in 'Fifth of July' and 'House of Blue Leaves.' She won the Emmy for her supporting role on 'Carol and Company' in 1990 and took up residence on TV's 'Sisters' in 1991. Her unusual first name is derived from "Alexander the Swoose," a B-17D bomber her much-decorated hero-pilot father flew during WW II.

FILMS: *Slap Shot, First Love* 1977; *Oliver's Story* 1978; *The World According to Garp* 1982; *Against All Odds* 1984; *Wildcats, True Stories* 1986; *Vice Versa, Bright Lights Big City, Dangerous Liaisons* 1988; *A Shock to the System, Stanley and Iris* 1990; *Reality Bites, Storybook* 1994; *Citizen Ruth* 1996; *Liar Liar* 1997.

Kurys, Diane. Director. Born on Dec. 3, 1948, in Lyons, France, to Jewish immigrants from Russia. After her parents divorced, she moved with her mother and sister to Paris, where she attended a conservative, stifling lycée. Following graduation, she began acting onstage and in 1970 joined Jean-Louis Barrault's theater group. She also appeared in films, including Gérard Pirès's *Elle court elle court la Banlieu,* Fellini's *Casanova,* and Maurice Dugwson's *F comme Fairbanks.* Frustrated by acting, she began to write and won a government grant to direct an original screenplay. Her debut film, *Diabolo Menthe/Peppermint Soda* (1978), about a rebellious schoolgirl in a stuffy lycée, was a personal triumph, winner of the Prix Louis Delluc as France's film of the year and a big box-office draw at home and abroad. Like her subsequent films, it was largely autobiographical. After confirming her talent with *Cocktail Molotov* (1980), which drew on her experiences as a budding young woman during the May '68 Paris student revolt, she stunned audiences with *Coup de Foudre* (1983), a daringly frank, thoughtfully subtle and emotionally rich look at the tightening friendship between two women in the throes of divorce. Retitled *Entre Nous* in the US, the film, inspired by Kurys's painful memories of her parents' divorce, was nominated for an Academy Award as best foreign picture. The role of Lena, played by Isabelle HUPPERT, was patterned after the director's mother. Kurys would return to that scene in *La-Baule-les-Pins/C'est la Vie* (1990), this time looking at the breakup of the marriage from the point of view of the couple's two daughters. The mother role was this time played by Nathalie BAYE. Kurys completed the film in her eighth month of pregnancy. She is married to director-producer Alexandre Arcady (*b.* 1947, Algiers).

FILMS (as director-screenwriter): *Diabolo Menthe/Peppermint Soda* 1978; *Cocktail Molotov* 1980; *Coup de*

Foudre/Entre Nous 1983; *Un Homme amoureux/A Man in Love* 1987; *La-Baule-les-Pins/C'est la Vie* 1990; *6 Days 6 Nights, After Love* 1994.

Kusturica, Emir. Director. Born in 1955, in Sarajevo, Yugoslavia. A graduate of FAMU, the Prague film school, he began his career in Yugoslavian TV, then made an auspicious debut as a feature director with *Do You Remember Dolly Bell?* (1981), a delightful story of young love for which he won the Golden Lion in the first film category at the Venice Festival. He surpassed that achievement with his next film, *When Father Was Away on Business* (1985), a poignant depiction of the national political and bureaucratic scene in the 50s from the point of view of a little boy. It won the Palme d'Or and shared the International Critics Prize at Cannes, and was nominated for an Academy Award as best foreign language film. It was followed by *Time of the Gypsies* (1989), an exposé sprinkled with fantasy of the exploitation of gypsy children smuggled from Yugoslavia to Italy and put on the streets to beg and steal for their masters. Although the spoken dialogue in the film was authentic Gypsy Romany, it broke box-office records in Yugoslavia. It earned Kusturica the best director prize at Cannes and the Roberto Rossellini career achievement award in Rome. After completing the film, Kusturica headed for New York, where he began teaching a film directing course at Columbia. In addition to his work as a director, he has also written several scripts.

FEATURE FILMS (as director): *Do You Remember Dolly Bell?* 1981; *When Father Was Away on Business* 1985; *Time of the Gypsies* (also co-sc.) 1989; *Arizona Dream* 1993; *Once Upon a Time There Was a Country* 1994; *Underground* 1996.

Kwan, Nancy. Actress. Born on May 19, 1939, in Hong Kong. A beautiful Eurasian, she was trained for the dance with the British Royal Ballet before becoming a Hollywood leading lady. After making a big splash in *The World of Suzie Wong*, her career tapered off quickly. From the late 70s seen mainly in quickie Hong Kong productions, and in an early-90s series of infomercials hawking beauty products.

FILMS INCLUDE: *The World of Suzie Wong* 1960; *Flower Drum Song* 1961; *The Main Attraction* (UK) 1962; *Tamahine* (UK) 1963; *Honeymoon Hotel, Fate Is the Hunter* 1964; *The Wild Affair* (UK) 1965; *Lt. Robin Crusoe USN, Drop Dead Darling/Arrivederci Baby!* (UK) 1966; *Nobody's Perfect* 1968; *The Wrecking Crew, The Girl Who Knew Too Much* 1969; *The McMasters* 1970; *Wonder Women* 1973; *Supercock* 1975; *Project: Kill* 1976; *Devil Cat/Night Creature* 1978; *Streets of Hong Kong* 1979; *Angkor* 1981; *Walking the Edge* 1983; *Night of Children, Stickfighter* 1989; *Cold Dog Soup* 1990; *Dragon: The Bruce Lee Story* 1993.

Kyo, Machiko. Actress. Born on Mar. 25, 1924, in Osaka, Japan. A former dancer, she began her screen career in 1949 on the strength of her beauty and physical grace but displayed unexpected dramatic ability the following year as the feminine lead in Kurosawa's *Rashomon,* a film that brought her international fame. She went on to star in many other Japanese productions, notably Kinugasa's *Gate of Hell* (1953), Mizoguchi's *Ugetsu* (1953) and *Street of Shame* (1956), and Ichikawa's *Odd Obsession* (1959). She co-starred with Marlon Brando and Glenn Ford in the US film *The Teahouse of the August Moon* (1956).

FILMS INCLUDE: *Tengu-daoshi* (bit) 1944; *Final Laugh* 1949; *The Snake Princess* (Pts. I, II) 1949–50; *Resurrection, Rashomon* 1950; *Pier of Passion, The Enchantress, A Tale of Genji* 1951; *Beauty and the Bandits, Saga of the Great Buddha* 1952; *Ugetsu, Gate of Hell* 1953; *A Certain Woman, The Story of Shunkin, The Princess Sen, Bazoku Geisha, Whirlpool of Spring* 1954; *Yang Kwei Fei* 1955; *The Teahouse of the August Moon* (US), *Street of Shame* 1956; *Itohan Monogatari, Dancing Girl, A Woman's Skin, Flowers of Hell, Night Butterflies, The Hole* 1957; *Chance Meeting, The Loyal 47 Ronin, A Woman of Osaka* 1958; *The Makioka Sisters, Paper Pigeon, Odd Obsession/The Key, Floating Weeds* 1959; *A Wandering Princess, The Last Betrayal, Assault from Hell* 1960; *Fantastico, A Design for Dying* 1961; *The Black Lizard, The Life of a Woman, The Great Wall* 1962; *Buddha* 1963; *Sweet Sweat* 1964; *The Face of Another, Daphne* 1966; *The Little Runaway* 1967; *Thousand Cranes* 1969; *The Family* 1974; *Yoba, Tora's Pure Love* 1976; *Kesho* 1985.

Kyser, Kay. Bandleader. *b.* James Kern Kyser, June 18, 1897, Rocky Mount, N.C. *d.* 1985. Popular in the late 30s as the quizmaster of 'Kay Kyser's Kollege of Musical Knowledge' radio show, he was featured with his big band in a number of minor musical films of the WW II years, usually as the main attraction.

FILMS: *That's Right You're Wrong* 1939; *You'll Find Out* 1940; *Playmates* 1941; *My Favorite Spy* 1942; *Stage Door Canteen, Around the World* 1943; *Swing Fever, Carolina Blues* 1944.

L

Laage, Barbara. Actress. Born Claire Colombat, on July 30, 1925, in Menthon-Saint-Bernard, France. Blonde leading lady of French films of the 50s. A former stage actress and nightclub performer, she made her screen debut in 1948, playing a supporting role in a Hollywood film, *B.F.'s Daughter,* then returned home and achieved some prominence as the star of *La Putain Respectueuse/The Respectful Prostitute* (1952) and a number of other French, Italian, and German films. She costarred with Gene Kelly in the US/French co-production *The Happy Road* (1957).

FILMS INCLUDE: *B.F.'s Daughter* (US) 1948; *La Rose Rouge* 1951; *La Putain Respectueuse/The Respectful Prostitute* 1952; *Fille d'Amour, L'Esclave* 1953; *Quai des Blondes, Un Acte d'Amour/Act of Love* (Fr./US) 1954; *Crime passionel, Gil Blas, Les Assassins du Dimanche/Every Second Counts* 1956; *The Happy Road* (US/Fr.), *Miss Pigalle* 1957; *Una Parigina a Roma* (It./Fr.) 1958; *Bomben auf Monte Carlo* (Ger.) 1960; *Paris Blues* (US) 1961; *Vacances portugaises* 1963; *Therese and Isabelle* (US/Ger.) 1968; *Domicile conjugal/Bed and Board* 1970.

LaBadie, Florence. American actress. *b.* 1893. *d.* 1917. Beautiful leading lady of early American silents. A former model, she was introduced to D. W. Griffith by Mary Pickford and starred in many Biograph productions for Griffith and other directors, often opposite James Cruze. She was under contract to Pathé when she suddenly died at age 23.

FILMS INCLUDE: *Getting Even* 1909; *After the Ball* 1910; *Paradise Lost, The Broken Cross, How She Triumphed, Enoch Arden, The Thief and the Girl, The Primal Call, The Blind Princess and the Poet* 1911; *As It Was in the Beginning, The Arab's Bride, The Merchant of Venice, Lucille, Undine, The Star of Bethlehem* 1912; *Cymbeline, The Snare of Fate* 1913; *Adrift in a Great City, The Million Dollar Mystery* (serial), *Cardinal Richelieu's Ward* 1914; *All Aboard, The Adventures of Florence, The Country Girl, God's Witness, Monsieur Lecoq, The Price of Her Silence* 1915; *Divorce and the Daughter, The Fear of Poverty, The Fugitive, Master Shakespeare, Strolling Player, Saint Devil and Woman* 1916; *Her Life and His, The Man Without a Country, When Love Was Blind, The Woman in White, War and the Woman* 1917.

La Cava, Gregory. Director. *b.* Mar. 10, 1892, Towanda, Pa. *d.* 1952. *ed.* Chicago Inst. of Art; New York Art Students League. A former newspaper and magazine cartoonist, he entered films as an animator during WW I and worked with Walter LANTZ on such early animated cartoons as "The Katzenjammer Kids" and "Mutt and Jeff." He later served as editor in chief of Hearst International Comic Films, then switched to live-action films in the early 20s as a director-writer of two-reel comedy shorts and in 1922 became a director of feature films. It was after the advent of sound that he came into his own, acquiring a reputation for his light but firm touch in directing sophisticated comedies, notably the political fantasy *Gabriel Over the White House* (1933), the period satire *The Affairs of Cellini* (1934), the screwball social comedies *She Married Her Boss* (1935) and *My Man Godfrey* (1936), and the comedy-drama *Stage Door* (1937), which contemporary critics found superior to the stage play on which it was based. La Cava was known for his ability to overcome weak scripts with his vitality and comic instinct and for his knack of drawing superior performances from actors. However, his straight dramas are far less satisfying than his comedies. His career ended sadly, in a bitter dispute with the Mary Pickford company. Assigned by the company to direct the romantic fantasy *One Touch of Venus,* starring Ava GARDNER, he walked off the set after 11 days of production in a huff over the script. The film was completed by William A. SEITER, who received sole screen credit for the 1948 release. La Cava sued unsuccessfully for breach of contract and never directed another film.

FEATURE FILMS: *His Nibs* 1922; *Restless Wives, The New School Teacher* 1924; *Womanhandled* 1925; *Let's Get Married, So's Your Old Man, Say It Again* 1926; *Paradise for Two* (also prod.), *Running Wild* (also co-sc.), *Tell It to Sweeney* (also prod.), *The Gay Defender* 1927; *Feel My Pulse* (also prod.), *Half a Bride* 1928; *Saturday's Children, Big News* 1929; *His First Command* 1930; *Laugh and Get Rich* (also sc.), *Smart Woman* 1931; *Symphony of Six Million, The Age of Consent, The Half-Naked Truth* (also co-sc.) 1932; *Gabriel Over the White House, Bed of Roses* (also co-dial.), *Gallant Lady* 1933; *The Affairs of Cellini, What Every Woman Knows* 1934; *Private Worlds* (also co-sc.), *She Married Her Boss* 1935; *My Man Godfrey* (also prod.) 1936; *Stage Door* 1937; *Fifth Avenue Girl* (also prod.) 1939; *Primrose Path* (also prod., co-sc.) 1940; *Unfinished Business* (also prod.) 1941; *Lady in a Jam* (also prod.) 1942; *Living in a Big Way* (also story, co-sc.) 1947; *One Touch of Venus* (co-dir., uncredited) 1948.

Lachman, Ed. American director of photography. Born Edward Lachman, Jr., in 1948. *ed.* Ohio U. The son of a Morristown, N.J., movie theater owner, he showed an early interest in film and began his career in documentary production. Moving into features, he worked as an assistant and later camera operator under such distinguished cinematographers as Sven Nykvist, Vittori Storaro, and Roby Müller. He also collaborated with German directors Werner Herzog and Wim Wenders. At the same time, he slowly developed his own reputation as a lighting cameraman on smaller-scale productions.

FILMS INCLUDE (as director of photography): *The Lords of Flatbush* (co-phot.) 1974; *False Face/Scalpel* 1976; *Stroszek* (co-phot., asst. dir.; Ger.) 1977; *Lightning Over Water* (doc.; co-phot., personal appearance; Ger./Swed.), *Union City* 1980; *Say Amen Somebody* (doc.; co-phot.) 1982; *In Our Hands* (doc.; co-phot.) 1983; *The Little Sister, Ornette: Made in America* (doc.), *Tokyo-Ga/Tokyo Story* (co-phot.; Ger./Jap.), *Mother Teresa* (doc.; co-phot.), *Desperately Seeking Susan* 1985; *Stripper* (doc.), *True Stories* 1986; *Making Mr. Right, Less Than Zero* 1987; *Backtrack* 1990; *Catchfire, London Kills Me* 1991; *Light Sleeper, Mississippi Masala, My New Gun* 1992; *Theremin: An Electronic Odyssey* (doc.) 1993; *My Family/Mi Familia* 1995; *Touch* 1997.

Lachman, Harry. Director. *b.* June 29, 1886, La Salle, Ill. *d.* 1975. A graduate of the University of Michigan, he began as a magazine illustrator in Chicago. In 1911 he went to Paris, where he soon gained recognition as a postimpressionist painter and where his works were exhibited at various museums. He was decorated by the French government in 1922, the year he first became associated with film as a set designer at the studios in Nice, France. In 1925 director Rex INGRAM hired him as an assistant on *Mare Nostrum.* In 1928, at the age of 42, he gave up painting to begin his career as a film director in England. He later piloted several films in France before settling in Hollywood in 1933. His movies were mainly routine second features, but he handled them with polished craftsmanship, and occasionally his painter's eye would come to the fore with an imaginative scene, such as the frantic ten-minute hell sequence that highlighted his *Dante's Inferno* (1935). He also directed a good Laurel and Hardy vehicle, *Our Relations* (1936), although comedy was by no means his forte. He retired from films in the early 40s and later returned to painting. His work hangs in such museums as the Petit Palais, the Musée de Luxembourg, the Prado, and the Chicago Art Institute.

FILMS: In the UK—*The Compulsory Husband* (co-dir. with Monty Banks), *Weekend Wives* 1928; *Under the Greenwood Tree* 1929; *Song of Soho, The Yellow Mask* 1930; *The Love Habit, The Outsider* 1931; *Aren't We All?, Down Our Street, Insult* 1932. In France—*La Belle Marinière, Mistigri, La Couturière de Lunéville* 1932. In the US—*Face in the Sky, Paddy the Next Best Thing* 1933; *George White's Scandals* (co-dir. with George White and Thornton Freeland), *I Like It That Way, Nada mas que una Mujer* (Spanish version of *Pursued*), *Baby Take a Bow* 1934; *Dante's Inferno, Dressed to Thrill* 1935; *Charlie Chan at the Circus, Our Relations, The Man Who Lived Twice* 1936; *The Devil Is Driving, It Happened in Hollywood* 1937; *No Time to Marry* 1938; *They Came by Night* (UK), *Murder Over New York* 1940; *Dead Men Tell, Charlie Chan in Rio* 1941; *Castle in the Desert, The Loves of Edgar Allan Poe, Dr. Renault's Secret* 1942.

Lacombe, Georges. Director. *b.* Aug. 19, 1902, Paris. *d.* 1990. He made his debut with an excellent medium-length documentary, *La Zone* (1928). After assisting Grémillon and Clair, he began directing feature films in the early 30s, but only a few of these fulfilled his initial promise, notably *Le Dernier des Six* (1941), *L'Escalier sans Fin* (1943), and *La Nuit est mon Royaume/The Night Is My Kingdom* (1951). Throughout his career, he was considered a disciplined, efficient studio technician who worked well with actors and completed productions within schedule and budget, but with only rare flashes of brilliance.

FILMS INCLUDE: *La Zone* (doc.) 1928; *Boule de Gomme*

1931; *Un Coup de Téléphone* 1932; *La Femme invisible* 1933; *Jeunesse* 1934; *La Route Heureuse* 1936; *Café de Paris* (co-dir.) 1938; *Derrière La Façade/32 Rue de Montmartre* (co-dir. with Yves Mirande) 1939; *Les Musiciens du Ciel, Elles étaient Douze Femmes* 1940; *Le Dernier des Six, Montmartre-sur-Seine* 1941; *Le Journal tombe à Cinq Heures, Monsieur la Souris/Midnight in Paris* 1942; *L'Escalier sans Fin* 1943; *Le Pays sans Etoiles, Martin Roumagnac/The Room Upstairs* 1946; *Les Condamnés* 1947; *Prelude à la Gloire* 1950; *La Nuit est mon Royaume/The Night Is My Kingdom* 1951; *Les Sept Péchés capitaux/The Seven Deadly Sins* ("The Eighth Sin" episode) 1952; *Leur Dernière Nuit* 1953; *La Lumière d'en Face/The Light Across the Street* 1956; *Mon Coquin de Père, Cargaison blanche* 1958.

lacquering. Protective coating of film against abrasion during use.

Ladd, Alan. Actor. *b.* Sept. 3, 1913, Hot Springs, Ark. *d.* 1964. Raised in California, he excelled in sports at high school despite his small frame. He then worked in a variety of jobs, including that of lifeguard, gas station attendant, and hot-dog vendor, before reaching the fringes of Hollywood as a bit player in films, radio, and local theatrical productions. To make ends meet, he worked as a GRIP on the Warners lot for two years. Short in stature (5' 5"), his face devoid of emotional expression, he seemed to have lacked the necessary ingredients for a movie star; and, indeed, for several years he played nothing but minor parts, among them a brief appearance as a reporter in Welles's *Citizen Kane* (1941). But thanks to the persistence of an agent, former screen actress Sue CAROL, who became his second wife in 1942, Ladd began getting somewhat meatier roles. His big break came that same year when he was cast by Paramount as a paid killer in *This Gun for Hire.* The enthusiastic reaction of film fans propelled him into sudden stardom. His stolid, icy-eyed, blond good looks matched perfectly with the provocative coolness of that film's female star, Veronica LAKE, and the studio teamed them in a number of other productions. Fans voted their strong approval at the box office.

Ladd remained with Paramount through the mid-50s, playing hero roles tailored to his dynamic, two-fisted image. But with the notable exception of *Shane* (1953), in which he registered strongly as a mysterious stranger, few of his action-packed formula films could boast of a quality exceeding sheer entertainment. His films away from Paramount, at Warners and other studios, were even less distinguished and his career was in a decline at the time of his death at 50, which came as a result of an overdose of sedatives mixed with alcohol, possibly intentional. Fourteen months earlier he was nearly killed by an "accidental" self-inflicted gunshot wound. He was the father of Alan LADD, Jr., David LADD, and former child actress Alana Ladd.

FILMS: *Once in a Lifetime* 1932; *Pigskin Parade* 1936; *Last Train from Madrid, Souls at Sea, Hold 'Em Navy, Born to the West* 1937; *The Goldwyn Follies, Come on Leathernecks, Freshman Year* 1938; *Beasts of Berlin/Goose Step, Rulers of the Sea* 1939; *The Green Hornet* (serial), *Light of the Western Stars, Gangs of Chicago, In Old Missouri, The Howards of Virginia, Those Were the Days, Captain Caution, Wildcat Bus, Meet the Missus, Her First Romance* 1940; *Great Guns, Citizen Kane, Cadet Girl, Petticoat Politics, The Black Cat, The Reluctant Dragon, Paper Bullets/Gangs, Inc.* 1941; *Joan of Paris, This Gun for Hire, The Glass Key, Lucky Jordan, Star Spangled Rhythm* (cameo) 1942; *China* 1943; *And Now Tomorrow* 1944; *Salty O'Rourke, Duffy's Tavern* (cameo) 1945; *The Blue Dahlia, O.S.S., Two Years Before the Mast* 1946; *Calcutta, Variety Girl* (cameo), *Wild Harvest, My Favorite Brunette* (unbilled cameo) 1947; *Saigon, Beyond Glory, Whispering Smith* 1948; *The Great Gatsby* (title role), *Chicago Deadline* 1949; *Captain Carey U.S.A.* 1950; *Branded, Appointment with Danger* 1951; *Red Mountain, The Iron Mistress* (as Jim Bowie) 1952; *Thunder in the East, Desert Legion, Shane, Botany Bay* 1953; *The Red Beret/Paratrooper* (UK), *The Black Knight* (UK), *Saskatchewan, Hell Below Zero, Drum Beat* 1954; *The McConnell Story* (as ace airman Capt. Joseph McConnell), *Hell on Frisco Bay* 1955; *Santiago* 1956; *The Big Land, Boy on a Dolphin* 1957; *The Deep Six, The Proud Rebel, The Badlanders* 1958; *The Man in the Net* 1959; *Guns of the Timberland, All the Young Men, One Foot in Hell* 1960; *Orazi e Curiazi/Duel of Champions* (It./Sp.) 1961; *13 West Street* 1962; *The Carpetbaggers* 1964.

Ladd, Alan, Jr. Producer, studio executive. Born on Oct. 22, 1937, in Los Angeles. The son of Alan LADD, and half brother of David LADD, he started out in 1963 as a talent agent. He became an independent producer in the late 60s, initially operating out of England. He joined 20th Century-Fox in 1973 and was put in charge of the studio's feature production the following year. In 1977 he was promoted to the company's presidency. In 1979 he resigned his post to form The Ladd Company, an independent production organization. His growing stature in the industry led in 1985 to his appointment as president and COO of MGM/UA Entertainment, and the following year as chairman of the board of Metro-Goldwyn-Mayer Pictures. He resigned that post in 1988 and in 1989 became co-chairman of Pathé Communications and chairman and CEO of Pathé Entertainment. Following Pathé's acquisition of MGM in 1990, Ladd became chairman and CEO of MGM-Pathé Communications (1991–92). After a series of box office disappointments, he left MGM to become an independent producer at Paramount.

FILMS INCLUDE (as producer): *The Walking Stick* (UK) 1970; *Villain* (co-prod.; UK), *A Severed Head* (UK) 1971; *Zee & Co./X Y & Zee* (co-prod.; UK) 1972; *Fear Is the Key* (co-prod.) 1973; *Vice Versa* (exec. prod.) 1988; *The Brady Bunch Movie, Braveheart* 1995.

Ladd, David. Actor. Born on Feb. 5, 1947, in Los Angeles. The son of Alan LADD and Sue CAROL and half brother of Alan LADD, Jr., he enjoyed some success as a child star in the late 50s and early 60s. As a young adult, he played supporting roles in occasional films. He also produced TV programs and a feature film. Formerly married to TV and film actress Cheryl Ladd (*b.* 1951).

FILMS INCLUDE: *The Big Land* 1957; *The Proud Rebel* 1958; *The Sad Horse* 1959; *A Dog of Flanders, Raymie* 1960; *Misty* 1961; *R.P.M.* 1970; *Catlow* 1971; *Raw Meat* 1973; *The Klansmen* 1974; *The Day of the Locust* 1975; *Evil in the Deep* 1976; *The Wild Geese* (UK) 1978; *The Serpent and the Rainbow* (co-prod. only) 1988.

Ladd, Diane. Actress. Born Rose Diane Ladnier, on Nov. 29, 1932, in Meridian, Miss. A former secretary, model, and Copa showgirl, and a cousin of Tennessee WILLIAMS, she first gained notice as a stage actress in the 1959–60 Equity Library revival of the playwright's 'Orpheus Descending' and made her first film appearance in 1961. She played roles ranging from leads to bits in a number of films, mostly minor, before scoring as Flo, the tough-talking bleached-blonde waitress friend of Ellen Burstyn in *Alice Doesn't Live Here Anymore* (1975). She was nominated for a best supporting actress Academy Award for her robust performance in that film and later co-starred in its offshoot TV series 'Alice' (1980–81). She received another Oscar nomination in 1990 for her appropriately histrionic characterization in David Lynch's *Wild at Heart*, campaigning unsuccessfully in the trade papers to win the award. Her first husband was actor Bruce DERN. Their daughter is film star Laura DERN.

FILMS: *Something Wild* 1961; *The Wild Angels* 1966; *The Reivers* 1969; *Rebel Rousers, Macho Callahan, WUSA* 1970;

White Lightning 1973; *Chinatown* 1974; *Alice Doesn't Live Here Anymore* 1975; *Embryo* 1976; *All Night Long* 1981; *Something Wicked This Way Comes* 1983; *Black Widow* 1987; *Plain Clothes* 1988; *National Lampoon's Christmas Vacation* 1989; *Wild at Heart* 1990; *A Kiss Before Dying, Shadow of a Doubt* 1991; *The Cemetery Club, Rambling Rose, Forever, Hold Me Thrill Me Kiss Me* 1992; *Carnosaur, Forever* 1993; *The Haunted Heart, Raging Angels* 1995.

Laemmle, Carl. Motion picture tycoon. *b.* Jan. 17, 1867, Laupheim, Germany. *d.* 1939. The tenth of 13 children of a middle-class Jewish family, he became gainfully employed at age 13 and was an experienced bookkeeper and office manager at 17 when he decided to seek greater opportunities in the New World. Arriving in America in 1884, he became an errand boy for a New York drugstore, then went to Chicago, where he held a variety of jobs, from newspaper delivery to bookkeeping. Moving on to Oshkosh, Wisconsin, he worked his way up to clothing store manager and married the boss's daughter. Returning to Chicago, he decided to invest his savings in a nickelodeon. He opened one in January of 1906 and, encouraged by the quick returns on his investment, launched another within two months. Unsatisfied with the quality of service by the local film exchange, he set up his own exchange, the Laemmle Film Service, in 1907. He subsequently opened exchanges in several other American and some Canadian cities and before long was among the leading distributors in the business.

In 1909 Laemmle courageously defied the pressure tactics of the MOTION PICTURE PATENTS COMPANY, which had put many other exchanges out of business. Not only did Laemmle refuse to sell or fold his company, but he also announced that he was going into production in direct competition with the trust. He promptly founded the Independent Motion Picture Company of America (known in the business as Imp; see IMP) and released its first production, *Hiawatha.* He began an enormous publicity campaign to discredit the Patents Company and build an image for his own studio.

In 1910 he pulled the clever publicity stunt that launched the star system in American cinema. Having lured from Biograph its most popular player, Florence LAWRENCE (she was known then only as "The Biograph Girl," since Patents Company producers feared that naming their players would result in the upping of their salary demands), he planted a report in the newspapers indicating that "The Biograph Girl," had been killed in a streetcar accident. The following day he came out with an indignant advertisement denouncing the malicious report and announcing that Miss Lawrence, now "The Imp Girl," was alive and well and working for him. He also lured away Mary Pickford, announcing that "Little Mary is an Imp now."

Intent on glorifying his company's product (100 shorts by 1910), Laemmle glamorized his players and spent unprecedented amounts on publicity, regularly mentioning his stars by name. Meanwhile, he successfully blocked continual attempts by the Patents Company to put him out of business and in 1912 won a court battle that hastened the demise of that trust. In 1912 also, IMP merged with several smaller companies to form the Universal Film Manufacturing Company, a major Hollywood studio (later known simply as Universal). In another pioneering coup, Laemmle's company turned out a feature length exposé of white slavery, *Traffic in Souls* (1913), which proved to the industry that there was money to be made in feature films and in the exploitation of sensational subjects. The film cost a little over $5,000 and grossed close to half a million dollars.

The diminutive (5' 2") and notoriously eccentric Laemmle celebrated the high point of his career in 1915, when a crowd of 20,000 gathered to watch him officiate at the opening of Universal City, a 230-acre studio municipality in San Fernando Valley. Many famous stars, directors, and executives started their careers as Laemmle employees. Irving THALBERG and future magnate Harry COHN began as his personal secretaries. But the first allegiance of "Uncle Carl," as he was amiably called in Hollywood, was to members of his own family. He gave the key job of Universal's production chief to his son, Carl LAEMMLE, Jr., as soon as the latter turned 21, and placed 70 other relatives on his payroll in various capacities. Laemmle Jr.'s extravagances during the Depression years compounded the financial difficulties the company was experiencing at the time. In 1935, Laemmle Sr. was forced to sell Universal for a little over $5 million. He lived just long enough to see his former company bouncing back to health thanks to a singing teenager, Deanna DURBIN.

Laemmle, Carl, Jr. Producer, production executive. *b.* Apr. 28, 1908, Chicago. *d.* 1979. The son of Carl LAEMMLE, he supervised short products at Universal while still in his teens and was put in charge of the company's production on his 21st birthday. He initiated a new production policy calling for emphasis on higher-budget quality films. One of his earliest ventures, *All Quiet on the Western Front* (1930), won an Oscar and enhanced Universal's prestige. Under his regime, the studio turned out a number of other prestigious films and started its famous cycle of horror pictures. But his budget extravagances put the company in increasing financial difficulties during the Depression and he was forced to resign. In 1936 he went into independent production, with little success.

FILMS INCLUDE: *The Love Brand* 1923; *The Irresistible Lover* 1927; *We Americans, Lonesome* 1928; *The Last Warning, Broadway, College Love, The Last Performance* 1929; *All Quiet on the Western Front, The King of Jazz, A Lady Surrenders, The Boudoir Diplomat* 1930; *Dracula, Frankenstein* 1931; *Only Yesterday, The Invisible Man* 1933; *Imitation of Life* 1934; *The Good Fairy, The Bride of Frankenstein* 1935; *Show Boat* 1936.

Lafont, Bernadette. Actress. Born on Oct. 26, 1938, in Nîmes, France. A former dancer, she figured prominently in French New Wave films, particularly those of Claude Chabrol, to which she brought a touch of unglamorous openness. Still much in demand by certain directors, she has played leads as well as supporting roles in numerous French films and European co-productions. Her daughter, sensual rising star Pauline Lafont, was killed in a fall from a cliff in 1988, at age 26.

FILMS INCLUDE: *Les Mistons/The Mischief-Makers* (short), *Le Beau Serge* 1958; *A Double Tour/Leda/Web of Passion* 1959; *L'Eau à la Bouche/A Game for Six Lovers, Les Bonnes Femmes* 1960; *Les Godelureaux, Tire-au-Flanc/The Army Game* 1961; *La Chasse à l'Homme/Male Hunt* 1964; *Compartiment Tueurs/The Sleeping Car Murder* 1965; *Le Voleur/The Thief, Lost Generation/Walls* (Hun.) 1967; *Piège, La Fiancée du Pirate/A Very Curious Girl* 1969; *Valparaiso Valparaiso* 1970; *Catch Me a Spy* (UK/Fr.) 1971; *Une Belle Fille comme moi/Such a Gorgeous Kid Like Me* 1972; *La Maman et la Putain/The Mother and the Whore* 1973; *Tendre Dracula* 1974; *Zig Zig/Zig-Zag, Vincent mit l'Ane dans un Pré* 1975; *L'Ordinateur des Pompes funèbres, Un Type comme moi ne derrait jamais mourir, Le Trouble-Fesses* 1976; *Noroit* 1977; *La Tortue sur le Dos/Like a Turtle on Its Back, Violette Nozière/ Violette, Chaussette surprise* 1978; *Certaines Nouvelles, La Gueule de l'autre* 1979; *Il Ladrone/The Thief* (It./Fr.), *Retour en Force* 1980; *Le Roi des Cons* 1981; *Cap Canaille, La Bête Noire* 1983; *Gwendoline/The Perils of Gwendoline in the Land of the Yik Yak* 1984; *Le Pactole, L'Affrontée* 1985; *Inspecteur Lavardin* 1986; *Masques, Waiting for the Moon* (US) 1987; *Les Saisons du Plaisir/The Seasons of Pleasure, Prisonnières* 1988; *L'Air de rien* 1989; *Boom Boom* (Sp.) 1990.

LaGravenese, Richard. Screenwriter. Born 1960, in Brooklyn, N.Y. *ed.* Emerson College; New York University. From peddling food on the streets of New York to earning an Academy Award nomination for his screenplay *The Fisher King* (1991), this poignant, crackerjack writer has risen to the top rung of the Hollywood ladder. At one time a member of a nightclub comedy act, he is also credited with adapting into a touching screenplay the Robert James Waller novel *The Bridges of Madison County* (1995).

FILMS: *Rude Awakenings* (co-sc.) 1989; *The Fisher King* 1991; *The Ref* (also prod.) 1994; *The Bridges of Madison County, A Little Princess, Unstrung Heroes* 1995; *The Mirror Has Two Faces* 1996.

Lahr, Bert. Actor. *b.* Irving Lahrheim, Aug. 13, 1895, New York City. *d.* 1967. A veteran and highly popular comic of vaudeville, burlesque, and the legitimate stage, he also appeared in many films, most memorably as the Cowardly Lion in *The Wizard of Oz* (1939). Biography by his son John: *Notes on a Cowardly Lion* (1975).

FEATURE FILMS: *Flying High* 1931; *Mr. Broadway* 1933; *Merry-Go-Round of 1938, Love and Hisses* 1937; *Josette, Just Around the Corner* 1938; *Zaza, The Wizard of Oz* 1939; *Sing Your Worries Away, Ship Ahoy* 1942; *Meet the People* 1944; *Always Leave Them Laughing* 1949; *Mr. Universe* 1951; *Rose Marie* 1954; *The Second Greatest Sex* 1955; *The Night They Raided Minsky's* 1968.

Lahti, Christine. Actress. Born on Apr. 14, 1950, in Birmingham, Mich. Talented, unadorned leading lady and supporting player of the American stage and screen, often in unconventional, at times offbeat, characterizations. The daughter of a surgeon and a former health-care worker, she was stagestruck from early childhood and regularly performed in school plays. After graduating from the University of Michigan (Ann Arbor), where she majored in drama, she traveled through Europe with a pantomime troupe, then attended graduate classes at Florida State University. In 1973, she headed for New York, where she worked as a waitress while studying with Uta HAGEN and appearing occasionally in off-off-Broadway productions. Work in commercials eventually paved her way to TV and feature films. She was nominated for an Academy Award as best supporting actress and won the New York critics nod for her role in *Swing Shift* (1984), and was named best actress by the Los Angeles critics for *Running on Empty* (1988). She was also praised for her haunting performance in *Housekeeping* (1987). She won the Academy Award for her short film *Leiberman in Love* (1995). Lahti, who won an Obie Award for her off-Broadway performance in Jules Feiffer's 'Little Murders,' took over the lead in Wendy Wasserstein's 'The Heidi Chronicles' on Broadway in 1989. She lives in New York with her husband, director Thomas Schlamme.

FILMS: *. . . And Justice for All* 1979; *Ladies and Gentlemen: The Fabulous Stains, Who's Life Is It Anyway?* 1981; *Swing Shift* 1984; *Just Between Friends* 1986; *Stacking, Housekeeping* 1987; *Running on Empty* 1988; *Miss Firecracker* (cameo), *Gross Anatomy* 1989; *Funny About Love* 1990; *The Doctor* 1991; *Leaving Normal*, *The Fear Inside* 1992; *Hideaway, Les Misérables* 1995.

Lai, Francis. Composer. Born on Apr. 26, 1931, in France. He gained worldwide fame as a result of his melodious score for Claude Lelouche's *A Man and a Woman.* He subsequently composed successful scores for many other French and international films and won an Oscar for the music of *Love Story* (1970). He is also a prolific composer of pop songs.

FILMS INCLUDE: *Masculin-Feminin/Masculine Feminine* (co-comp.), *Un Homme et Une Femme/A Man and a Woman* 1966; *The Bobo* (UK), *Le Soleil des Voyous, Vivre pour Vivre/Live for Life* 1967; *Mayerling* (Fr./UK) 1968; *La Vie l'Amour la Mort/Life Love Death, Three Into Two Won't Go* (UK), *Hannibal Brooks* (UK), *House of Cards* (US), *Un Homme qui me plait/Love Is a Funny Thing* 1969; *Le Passager de la Pluie/Rider on the Rain, Le Voyou/The Crook, The Games* (UK), *Hello-Goodbye* (US), *Love Story* (US) 1970; *Smic Smac Smoc* (also act.), *Le Petit Matin* 1971; *L'Aventure c'est l'Aventure/Money Money Money* 1972; *Un Homme libre, La Bonne Année/Happy New Year* 1973; *Toute une Vie/And Now My Love, Visit to a Chief's Son* (US), *Un Amour de Pluie/Loving in the Rain* 1974; *Le Chat et la Souris/Cat and Mouse, Emmanuelle* 1975; *Les Bons et les Mechants/The Good and the Bad, Si c'était a refaire, Le Corps de mon Ennemi* 1976; *Anima Persa, Un autre Homme une autre Chance/Another Man Another Chance* (Fr./US), *Widows' Nest* (US/Sp.) 1977; *International Velvet* (UK), *Robert et Robert, Les Ringards, Oliver's Story* (US) 1978; *A Nous Deux* 1979; *Les Uns et les autres/Bolero* 1981; *Edith et Marcel* 1982; *Canicule, Les Ripoux/My New Partner/Le Cop* 1984; *Un Homme et une Femme: Vingt Ans déja/A Man and a Woman: 20 Years Later* 1986; *Attention Bandits!/Bandits, Oci Ciornie/Dark Eyes* (It.) 1987; *Bernadette, Itinéraire d'un Enfant gaté/Itinerary of a Spoiled Child* 1988; *Der Aten/The Spirit* (Ger.), *Trop Belle pour toi/Too Beautiful for You* 1989; *Earth Girls Are Easy* (song only; US), *Il y a Des Jours. . . Et Des Lunes/There Were Days and Moons* (co-mus.) 1990.

Laine, Frankie. Singer, actor. Born Frank Paul Lo Vecchio, on Mar. 30, 1913, in Chicago. The son of an immigrant barber from Sicily, he sang in a church choir as a boy and worked for many years in a variety of office and sales jobs without being able to crack into show business. During the Depression he eked out a living as a champion marathon dancer, setting an endurance record in 1932 for dancing 3,501 hours in a span of nearly five months, for a mere $500 in prize money. A chance meeting with Hoagy CARMICHAEL led to his discovery in 1947 and eventually to a highly successful career as a nightclub singer and recording artist with 16 Golden Records to his credit. In the 50s he played film leads, in both musical and straight dramatic roles, but failed to click as a screen personality. He supplied the background voice for the title songs of several films, including *Blowing Wild* (1953) and *Gunfight at the O.K. Corral* (1957). In 1950 he married actress Nan GREY.

FILMS: *Make-Believe Ballroom* 1949; *When You're Smiling* 1950; *Sunny Side of the Street* 1951; *Rainbow 'Round My Shoulder* 1952; *Bring Your Smile Along* 1955; *Meet Me in Las Vegas* (cameo), *He Laughed Last* 1956.

Lake, Alice. Actress. *b.* 1896, Brooklyn, N.Y. *d.* 1967. Brunette leading lady of Hollywood silents. She started her career in Mack SENNETT comedy shorts, often opposite Fatty Arbuckle. During the 20s she starred in numerous features of Metro and other studios but never attained great popularity and was reduced to supporting roles or minor films by the advent of sound. She continued appearing in talkies through 1934 but was never seen in a color film, thus missing the opportunity to display fully on the screen her very rare eyes, one brown, the other gray.

FILMS INCLUDE: *Playing Dead* 1915; *The Moonshiners, The Waiters' Ball, A Creampuff Romance/A Reckless Romeo* 1916; *Her Mature Dance, Come Through* 1917; *Cupid's Day Off, Full of Pep, Lombardi Ltd., The Lion's Den, Should a Woman Tell?* 1919; *Shore Acres, The Misfit Wife, Body and Soul* 1920; *The Greater Claim, Unchartered Seas, Over the Wire, The Infamous Miss Revell* (in dual role), *The Hole in the Wall* 1921; *The Golden Gift, Kisses, Hate, I Am the Law, Environment* 1922; *The Spider and the Rose, Broken Hearts of Broadway, Red Lights, The Marriage Market, Modern Matrimony, The Unknown Purple* 1923; *The Dancing Cheat, The Virgin, The*

Law and the Lady 1924; *The Lost Chord, The Overland Limited, The Price of Success* 1925; *The Wives of the Prophet, Broken Homes, The Hurricane* 1926; *Spider Webs, Roaring Fires, The Angel of Broadway* 1927; *Obey Your Husband, Women Men Like* 1928; *Twin Beds, Circumstantial Evidence, Frozen Justice* 1929; *Young Desire* 1930; *Wicked* 1931; *Skyway* 1933; *Wharf Angel, Glamour, The Mighty Barnum* 1934; *Frisco Kid* 1935.

Lake, Arthur. Actor. *b.* Arthur Silverlake, Apr. 17, 1905, Corbin, Ky. *d.* 1987. The son of a circus acrobat and an actress, he joined the family act in vaudeville at age three. He played child roles in films from age 12, then juvenile leads long after he reached maturity. The turning point of his career came in 1938, when he was cast as Dagwood Bumstead in *Blondie,* the first of a long series of light films co-starring Penny SINGLETON. The profitable series helped the financially strapped Columbia Pictures overcome a budget crisis. He later also portrayed the character on radio and TV.

FILMS INCLUDE: *Jack and the Beanstalk* 1917; *Where Was I?* 1925; *Skinner's Dress Suit* 1926; *The Cradle Snatchers, The Irresistible Lover* 1927; *The Count of Ten, Stop That Man, Harold Teen, The Air Circus* 1928; *On with the Show, Tanned Legs, Dance Hall* 1929; *Cheer Up and Smile, She's My Weakness* 1930; *Indiscreet* 1931; *Midshipman Jack* 1933; *The Silver Streak* 1934; *Orchids to You* 1935; *Topper, Annapolis Salute* 1937; *Double Danger, There Goes My Heart, Blondie* 1938; *Blondie Meets the Boss* 1939; *Blondie Plays Cupid* 1940; *Blondie Goes Latin* 1941; *Blondie for Victory* 1942; *Footlight Glamour* 1943; *Sailor's Holiday, The Ghost That Walks Alone, Three Is a Family* 1944; *The Big Show-Off, Life with Blondie* 1945; *Blondie Knows Best* 1946; *Blondie's Holiday* 1947; *16 Fathoms Deep* 1948; *Blondie Hits the Jackpot* 1949; *Beware of Blondie* 1950.

Lake, Harriet(te). See SOTHERN, Ann.

Lake, Ricki. Actress. Born on Sept. 21, 1968, in New York City. Irrepressibly appealing lead and character player who launched her career as the amply-sized Baltimore hairhopper-turned-beatnik in John Waters's *Hairspray*. Educated at children's professional schools, she appeared in off-Broadway productions in her youth. A regular on the TV drama 'China Beach,' she has also gone on to host her own very popular syndicated talk show while maintaining an active film career.

FILMS INCLUDE: *Hairspray, Working Girl* 1988; *Cookie, Last Exit To Brooklyn* 1989; *Cry-Baby* 1990; *Where The Day Takes You* 1992; *Inside Monkey Zetterland* 1993; *Cabin Boy, Serial Mom* 1994; *Mrs. Winterbourne* 1996.

Lake, Veronica. Actress. *b.* Constance Frances Marie Ockelman, Nov. 14, 1919, Brooklyn, N.Y. *d.* 1973. Sultry, provocative glamour star of Hollywood films of the 40s whose long blond hair falling over one eye started a "peek-a-boo" style craze among the women of America. So widespread was the fad that government officials asked her to stop wearing her hair long for the duration of WW II because women in war plants were catching their long hair in machines. The daughter of a seaman who was killed when she was 12, she had entered films in 1939 as Constance Keane (her stepfather's surname), changing her name to Veronica Lake in 1941, the year that marked the beginning of her meteoric starring career. She clicked best at the box office as the screen partner of Alan LADD in a matchup of cool, determined personalities. At the height of her popularity Miss Lake was courted by such magnates as Aristotle Onassis and Howard Hughes and was married to director André DE TOTH (1944–52), the first of her three husbands. But by the late 40s her career began to decline. In the early 50s, shortly after she and De Toth filed bankruptcy petitions in court, she disappeared from view, except for occasional headlines telling of her arrest for public drunkenness. She was rediscovered by a newsman early in the 60s working as a barmaid in a downtown New York hotel. Slowly she picked up the pieces, found work off Broadway, in stock, and in rare low-budget films, and settled in England. She told her story in her autobiography, *Veronica,* published in 1969. She died of hepatitis.

FILMS: As Constance Keane—*All Women Have Secrets, Sorority House Dancing Co-Ed* 1939; *Young as You Feel, Forty Little Mothers* 1940. As Veronica Lake—*I Wanted Wings, Hold Back the Dawn* 1941; *Sullivan's Travels, This Gun for Hire, The Glass Key, I Married a Witch* 1942; *Star Spangled Rhythm* (cameo), *So Proudly We Hail* 1943; *The Hour Before Dawn* 1944; *Bring On the Girls, Out of This World, Duffy's Tavern* (cameo), *Hold That Blonde* 1945; *Miss Susie Slagle's, The Blue Dahlia* 1946; *Ramrod, Variety Girl* (cameo) 1947; *Saigon, The Sainted Sisters, Isn't It Romantic?* 1948; *Slattery's Hurricane* 1949; *Stronghold* 1952; *Footsteps in the Snow* (Can.) 1966; *Flesh Feast* (also co-prod.) 1970.

Lamaç, Karel (also **Karl, Carl**). Director, producer, screenwriter, actor. *b.* 1897, Prague. *d.* 1952. The son of an opera singer turned pharmacist, he studied chemistry but was drawn to art and entertainment. During WW I he reported for newsreels from the front and after the Armistice he began his commercial film career as an actor. By 1919 he was a director and during the 20s he turned out numerous films as a director, producer, and writer through a company he formed with his wife, actress Anny ONDRA, who starred in many of these light productions. He later also worked extensively in Russia, Germany, France, and England. In all, he directed or produced some 250 films.

FILMS INCLUDE (as director): In Czechoslovakia—*Akord Smrti* (also act.) 1919; *Lucerna, The Crystal Princess* 1925; *The Good Soldier Schweik, Schweik at the Front* 1926; *Dcery Eviny* 1928; *Suzy Saxophone* (Czech./Aus.) 1929; *Versuchen Sie meine Schwester* (Czech./Ger.), *Der falsche Feldmarschall* (Czech./Ger.) 1930. In Germany—*Das Mädelaus USA, Eine Freundin so goldig wie Du, Die vom Rummelplatz* 1930; *Die Fledermaus, Der Zinker* (co-dir. with Martin Fric), *Mamsell Nitouche* (Ger./Fr.) 1931; *Kiki* (Ger./Fr.), *Baby* (Ger./Fr.), *Der Hexer* (Ger./Aus.), *Eine Nacht im Paradies* 1932; *Die Tochter des Regiments* (Ger./Aus.) 1933; *Klein Dorrit, Polenblut* (Ger./Czech.), *Frasquita* (Ger./Czech.), *Karneval und Liebe* (Ger./Aus.) 1934; *Knock-Out* (co-dir. with Hans Zerlett), *Ich liebe alle Frauen* (and French-language version, *J'aime toutes les Femmes*), *Der junge Graf* 1935; *Ein Mädel vom Ballett, Der schüchterne Casanova, Der Postillon von Lonjumeau* (Ger./Aus.) 1936; *Peter im Schnee* (Ger./Aus.) 1937; *Walzerlange/Immer wenn ich glücklich bin* (Aus./Ger.) 1938. In France—*Place de la Concorde* 1939. In the UK—*They Met in the Dark* 1943; *It Happened One Sunday* 1944. In France—*La Colère des Dieux, Une Nuit à Tabarin* 1947.

Lamarque, Libertad. Actress, singer. Born on Nov. 24, 1908, in Rosario, Argentina. On stage from the age of eight, she appeared in occasional silent films, becoming the most popular star of the Argentine screen after the advent of sound. She also appeared in many Mexican films, and for three decades was among the best-liked screen personalities in the Spanish-speaking world.

FILMS INCLUDE: *Tango* 1933; *Ayudame a vivir/Help Me to Live* 1936; *Besos brujos/Bewitching Kisses* 1937; *La Ley que olvidaron/The Law They Forgot, Madreselva/Honeysuckle* 1938; *Puerta cerrada/Closed Door, Caminato da Gloria* 1939; *El Alma del Bandoneon/The Soul of the Accordion, La Casa del Recuerdo* 1940; *Una Vez en la Vida* 1941; *Eclipse de Sol* 1943; *El Fin de la Noche* 1944; *Romance musical, Gran Casino* 1946; *Soledad* 1947; *Otra Primavera* 1949; *La Dama del Velo* 1950;

La Mujer sin Lagrimas 1951; *Rostros Olvidados* 1953; *Creo en Ti* 1959.

La Marr, Barbara. Actress. *b.* Rheatha Watson, July 28, 1896, Richmond, Va. *d.* 1926. A beautiful, voluptuous ex-dancer, she starred in many silents of the 20s, typically in exotic vamp roles, and was considered by many as the most exquisite beauty of her day. An overdose of narcotics tragically ended her stormy career and scandal-ridden private life when she was 29. She also wrote several screen stories and was billed early in her career as Barbara Deely or Barbara LaMarr Deely.

FILMS: *The Mother of His Children* (story only), *The Little Gray Mouse* (story only), *Rose of Nome* (story only), *Harriet and the Piper, The Land of Jazz* (co-story only), *Flame of Youth* (story only) 1920; *The Nut, Desperate Trails, The Three Musketeers* (as Milady de Winter), *Cinderella of the Hills* (billed as Barbara LaMarr Deely) 1921; *Arabian Love, Domestic Relations, The Prisoner of Zenda* (as Antoinette de Mauban), *Trifling Women* (in dual role), *Quincy Adams Sawyer* 1922; *The Brass Bottle, The Hero, Poor Men's Wives, Souls for Sale, St. Elmo, Mary of the Movies* (cameo), *Strangers of the Night, The Eternal Struggle* 1923; *The Eternal City, Thy Name Is Woman, The White Moth, Sandra, My Husband's Wives* (story only) 1924; *Heart of a Siren, The White Monkey* (as Fleur Forsyte) 1925; *The Girl from Montmartre* 1926.

Lamarr, Hedy. Actress. Born Hedwig Eva Maria Kiesler, on Nov. 9, 1913, in Vienna, the daughter of a banker. She was discovered by Max Reinhardt and entered Austro-German films in 1930 as script girl and bit player. She gained worldwide fame and notoriety in 1933 when she appeared completely nude in a ten-minute sequence of Gustav Machaty's 1933 Czech production *Extase/Ecstasy.* Shortly after, she married Austrian munitions magnate Fritz Mandl, who sought to buy up all existing prints of that film, but she divorced him before he completed his mission and the film was released time and again in theaters the world over. In 1938 she arrived in Hollywood, billed as the world's most beautiful woman. She was indeed an exquisite beauty, but her acting ability was quite limited. Frequently typecast as a woman of mystery, she starred in many MGM films of the 40s without creating a pandemonium at the box office. Her most successful film commercially was Paramount's *Samson and Delilah.* By the early 50s her screen career was almost nonexistent. In 1965 she made the headlines after being arrested on a shoplifting charge, of which she was later exonerated. The following year she published her autobiography, *Ecstasy and Me,* later suing her collaborators for misrepresentation. In 1992, she was again involved in a shoplifting charge. The second of her six husbands was writer Gene MARKEY; the third, actor John LODER. IN 1940 Lamarr, who had learned weaponry through her husband Mandl, worked with composer George Antheil to create an anti-jamming device for the Allies. Their creation used paper rolls with perforations that exactly matched the split-second hops of radio frequencies. It was only in 1997 that authorities revealed that the device was the foundation for today's secure military communications.

FILMS: In Europe—*Geld auf der Strasse* (short; Ger.) 1930; *Die Blumenfrau von Lindenau/Sturm in Wasserglas* (Ger./Aus.), *Man braucht kein Geld/His Majesty King Ballyhoo* (Ger.), *Die Koffer des Herrn O.F./The 13 Trunks of Mr. O. F.* (Ger.) 1931; *Extase/Symphonie der Liebe/Ecstasy* (Czech.) 1933. In the US—*Algiers* 1938; *Lady of the Tropics* 1939; *I Take This Woman, Boom Town, Comrade X* 1940; *Come Live with Me, Ziegfeld Girl, H. M. Pulham Esq.* 1941; *Tortilla Flat, Crossroads, White Cargo* 1942; *The Heavenly Body, The Conspirators, Experiment Perilous* 1944; *Her Highness and the Bellboy* 1945; *The Strange Woman* 1946; *Dishonored Lady* 1947; *Let's Live a Little* 1948; *Samson and Delilah* (as Delilah) 1949; *A Lady Without a Passport, Copper Canyon* 1950; *My Favorite Spy* 1951; *Eterna Femmina/L'Amante di Paride/Love of Three Queens/The Face That Launched a Thousand Ships* (It./Fr.) 1954; *The Story of Mankind* (as Joan of Arc) 1957; *The Female Animal* 1958; *Instant Karma* 1990.

Lamas, Fernando. Actor. *b.* Jan. 9, 1915, Buenos Aires. *d.* 1982. The star of Spanish-speaking films in his native country, he was imported to Hollywood by MGM and typecast as a sporty Latin Lover in a number of the studio's light films of the early 50s, occasionally displaying a rich baritone singing voice. He later freelanced in low-budget productions, two of which he also directed. In addition, he directed a number of TV episodes. His third wife (1954–60) was Arlene DAHL. His fourth (from 1967) was Esther WILLIAMS. His son by Dahl, Lorenzo Lamas (*b.* Jan. 20, 1958, Los Angeles), is a TV and film actor.

FILMS INCLUDE: In Argentina—*En el ultimo Piso* 1942; *Villa Rica del Espiritu Santo* 1945; *Evasion* 1947; *Historia de una Mala Mujer/Lady Windermere's Fan* 1948; *La Historia del Tango* 1949. In the US—*The Avengers* 1950; *Rich Young and Pretty, The Law and the Lady* 1951; *The Merry Widow* 1952; *The Girl Who Had Everything, Dangerous When Wet, Sangaree, The Diamond Queen* 1953; *Jivaro, Rose Marie* 1954; *The Girl Rush* 1955; *The Lost World* 1960; *The Magic Fountain* (also dir.; in Spain) 1961; *Die Hölle von Manitoba/A Place Called Glory* (co-sc. only; Ger./Sp.) 1966; *The Violent Ones* (also dir.), *Valley of Mystery, Kill a Dragon* 1967; *100 Rifles, Backtrack* 1969; *The Cheap Detective* 1978.

Lambert, Christophe(r). Actor. Born on Mar. 29, 1957, in New York City. Athletic, charismatic leading man of international films. The son of a UN-based French diplomat, he traveled extensively as a child and received his formal education in Geneva. After barely completing his baccalaureate and serving for a year in the French military, he toyed briefly with a career in high finance, then enrolled at the Paris Conservatory of Dramatic Art, deciding on a future as an actor. He became an international star on the strength of his portrayal of the title role in the British film *Greystoke: The Legend of Tarzan, Lord of the Apes* (1984). Lambert, who is married to actress Diane LANE, has dual citizenship. His first name is listed as Christophe in his French passport and as Christopher in his American documents.

FILMS: *Le Bar du Téléphone* (Fr.) 1980; *Putain d'Histoire d'Amour* (Fr.) 1981; *Légitime Violence/Legitimate Violence* (Fr.) 1982; *Greystoke: The Legend of Tarzan Lord of the Apes* (UK), *Paroles et Musique/Love Songs* (Can./Fr.) 1984; *Subway* (Fr.) 1985; *Highlander* (UK), *I Love You* (Fr./It.) 1986; *The Sicilian* (US) 1987; *Love Dream, To Kill a Priest/Popieluszko* (US/Fr.) 1988; *Un Plan d'Enfer* (Fr.) 1989; *Priceless Beauty, Why Me?* 1990; *Highlander 2—The Quickening* (UK) 1991; *Knight Moves* (US), *Fortress* (US) 1993; *Gunmen, Highlander III: The Sorcerer* 1994; *The Hunted, Mortal Kombat* 1995; *Adrenalin, North Star* 1996; *Nirvana* 1997.

Lambert, Jack. Actor. Born in 1920 in Yonkers, N.Y. Played standard heavies in numerous Hollywood films. Not to be confused with a British character actor (*b.* Dec. 29, 1899; *d.* 1976) of the same name.

FILMS INCLUDE: *The Cross of Lorraine* 1943; *The Harvey Girls, Abilene Town, The Killers* 1946; *Dick Tracy's Dilemma* 1947; *River Lady* 1948; *Big Jack* 1949; *The Enforcer* 1951; *Bend of the River* 1952; *Scared Stiff* 1953; *Vera Cruz* 1954; *Kiss Me Deadly* 1955; *Chicago Confidential* 1957; *Machine Gun Kelly* 1958; *Day of the Outlaw* 1959; *The George Raft Story* 1961; *Four for Texas* 1963.

Lambert, Mary. American director. Born in Arkansas. *ed.* U. of Denver. She began making shorts while attending the Rhode Island School of Design. After gaining professional experience in a variety of production capacities, she headed for Los Angeles, where she soon gained success as the director of commercials and music videos. Her stylish song illustrations included Madonna's 'Material Girl,' 'Like a Virgin,' and 'Like a Prayer,' and videos by Sting, Mick Jagger, and Janet Jackson. She made her feature debut with *Siesta* (1987), an oddly fascinating but confusing and seemingly pointless film, then scored an unexpected box-office hit with the horror film *Pet Sematary* (1989).

FILMS INCLUDE: *Siesta* 1987; *Pet Sematary* 1989; *Pet Sematary II* 1992.

Lamont, Charles. Director. *b.* May 5, 1898, San Francisco. *d.* 1993. A fourth-generation actor, he appeared on stage in his teens and in films from 1919. In 1922 he turned director and turned out a great number of comedy shorts for SENNETT, CHRISTIE, and others. He began directing features in the mid-30s, mostly low-brow Universal comedies, later including many Abbott and Costello and Ma and Pa Kettle features. However, several of his Westerns and exotic adventure films acquired a cult following because of their satirical overtones. Some French critics have been particularly enamored of his two Yvonne De Carlo-Rod Cameron films, *Salome, Where She Danced* and *Frontier Gal* (both 1945), which went practically unnoticed when first shown in the US.

FEATURE FILMS: *The Curtain Falls* 1934; *Tomorrow's Youth, The World Accuses, Son of Steel, False Pretenses, Gigolette, A Shot in the Dark, Circumstantial Evidence, The Girl Who Came Back, Happiness C.O.D., The Lady in Scarlet* 1935; *Ring Around the Moon, Little Red School House, Below the Deadline, August Week-End, The Dark Hour, Lady Luck, Bulldog Edition* 1936; *Wallaby Jim of the Islands* 1937; *International Crime, Shadows Over Shanghai, Slander House, Cipher Bureau* 1938; *The Long Shot, Verbena Trágica/Tragic Festival* (for Spanish market), *Pride of the Navy, Panama Patrol, Inside Information, Unexpected Father, Little Accident* (also prod.) 1939; *Oh Johnny How You Can Love!, Sandy Is a Lady, Love Honor and Oh Baby!, Give Us Wings* 1940; *San Antonio Rose, Sing Another Chorus, Moonlight in Hawaii, Melody Lane, Road Agent* 1941; *Don't Get Personal, You're Telling Me!, Almost Married, Hi Neighbor!, Get Hep to Love* 1942; *When Johnny Comes Marching Home, It Comes Up Love, Mr. Big, Hit the Ice, Fired Wife, Top Man* 1943; *Chip Off the Old Block, Her Primitive Man, The Merry Monahans, Bowery to Broadway* 1944; *Salome Where She Danced, That's the Spirit, Frontier Gal* 1945; *The Runaround, She Wrote the Book* 1946; *Slave Girl* 1947; *The Untamed Breed* 1948; *Ma and Pa Kettle, Bagdad* 1949; *Ma and Pa Kettle Go to Town, I Was a Shoplifter, Abbott and Costello in the Foreign Legion, Curtain Call at Cactus Creek* 1950; *Abbott and Costello Meet the Invisible Man, Comin' Round the Mountain, Flame of Araby* 1951; *Abbott and Costello Meet Captain Kidd* 1952; *Abbott and Costello Go to Mars, Ma and Pa Kettle on Vacation, Abbott and Costello Meet Dr. Jekyll and Mr. Hyde* 1953; *Ma and Pa Kettle at Home, Untamed Heiress, Ricochet Romance* 1954; *Carolina Cannonball, Abbott and Costello Meet the Keystone Kops, Abbott and Costello Meet the Mummy, Lay That Rifle Down* 1955; *The Kettles in the Ozarks, Francis in the Haunted House* 1956.

Lamorisse, Albert. Director. *b.* Jan. 13, 1922. Paris. *d.* 1970. A former photographer, he turned to directing short subjects in the late 40s, soon acquiring an international reputation for the poetic quality of his short and medium-length films involving the fantasy world of children. Both his *Crin blanc/White Mane* (1952) and *Le Ballon rouge/The Red Balloon* (1956) received a grand prize at the Cannes Festival, the latter also winning an American Academy Award. In the early 60s he turned to feature length films with considerably less success, then retreated to documentary shorts. He was killed in a helicopter crash while shooting a documentary near Teheran. That film, *The Lovers' Wind,* a visually stunning helicopter tour of Iran, was later edited from his notes and was nominated for an Oscar as best feature documentary for the Academy Award ceremonies of 1978.

FILMS: *Djerba* 1947; *Bim* 1949; *Crin blanc/White Mane* 1952; *Le Ballon rouge/The Red Balloon* 1956; *Le Voyage en Ballon/Stowaway in the Sky* (feature) 1960; *Fifi la Plume* (feature) 1965; *Versailles* 1967; *Paris jamais vu* 1968; *Le Vent des Amoureux/The Lovers' Wind* (released posthumously) 1978.

Lamour, Dorothy. Actress. *b.* Mary Leta Dorothy Kaumeyer, on Dec. 10, 1914, in New Orleans. *d.* 1996. A former Miss New Orleans (1931), Chicago elevator operator, band vocalist, and radio performer, she entered films in the mid-30s and soon became one of Hollywood's most popular stars. Her trademark was the sarong, in which she was often lightly clad in her line of duty as an exotic South Sea heroine. She played her best roles in the "Road" series as sultry-breezy foil to Bob Hope and Bing Crosby, but her acting range proved too limited for a broader variety of screen parts. Her first husband (1935–39) was band leader Herbie Kaye. Autobiography: *My Side of the Road* (1980).

FILMS: *The Jungle Princess* 1936; *Swing High Swing Low, College Holiday, The Last Train from Madrid, High Wide and Handsome, The Hurricane, Thrill of a Lifetime* 1937; *The Big Broadcast of 1938, Her Jungle Love, Spawn of the North, Tropic Holiday* 1938; *St. Louis Blues, Man About Town, Disputed Passage* 1939; *Johnny Apollo, Typhoon, Road to Singapore, Moon Over Burma, Chad Hanna* 1940; *Road to Zanzibar, Caught in the Draft, Aloma of the South Seas* 1941; *The Fleet's In, Beyond the Blue Horizon, Road to Morocco* 1942; *Star Spangled Rhythm, They Got Me Covered, Dixie, Riding High* 1943; *And the Angels Sing, Rainbow Island* 1944; *A Medal for Benny, Duffy's Tavern, Masquerade in Mexico* 1945; *Road to Utopia* 1946; *My Favorite Brunette, Road to Rio, Wild Harvest, Variety Girl* 1947; *On Our Merry Way/A Miracle Can Happen, Lulu Belle, The Girl from Manhattan* 1948; *Slightly French, Manhandled, The Lucky Stiff* 1949; *Here Comes the Groom* (cameo) 1951; *The Greatest Show on Earth* 1952; *Road to Bali* 1953; *The Road to Hong Kong* 1962; *Donovan's Reef* 1963; *Pajama Party* 1964; *The Phynx* (cameo) 1970; *Creepshow 2* 1987.

Lamoureux, Robert. Actor, occasional director. Born on Jan. 21, 1920, in Paris. Charming, energetic leading man of French light films. A former cabaret and music hall entertainer and a recording star, he enjoyed some popularity as a screen personality in the 50s. He has also directed several films.

FILMS INCLUDE (as actor): *Le Roi des Camelots, Chacun son Tour* 1951; *Allo je t'aime* 1952; *Lettre ouverte à un Mari, Virgile* 1953; *Papa Maman la Bonne et moi/Mama Papa the Maid and I* 1954; *Escalier de Service* 1955; *Les Aventures d'Arsène Lupin* 1957; *La Vie à Deux* 1958; *La Brune que voilà* (also dir., sc.), *La Française et l'Amour/Love and the Frenchwoman* 1960; *Ravissante* (also dir., sc.) 1961; *On a retrouvá la 7e Compagnie* (also dir., co-sc.) 1975; *L'Apprenti Salaud* 1977; *La Septième Compagnie au Clair de la Lune* (also dir.) 1978.

Lampert, Zohra. Actress. Born on May 13, 1937, in New York City. Intelligent, shyly breathless leading lady of Broadway and some films. She won an Emmy as best supporting actress for her performance in a 1975 episode of the TV series 'Kojak.'

FILMS INCLUDE: *Pay or Die* 1960; *Posse from Hell, Splendor in the Grass, Hey Let's Twist!* 1961; *A Fine Madness* 1966; *Bye Bye Braverman* 1968; *Some Kind of a Nut* 1969; *Let's Scare Jessica to Death* 1971; *Opening Night* 1978; *Alphabet City, Teachers* 1984; *American Blue Note* 1989; *Stanley and Iris* 1990; *Alan and Naomi* 1992.

Lamprecht, Gerhard. Director. Born on Oct. 6. 1897, in Berlin. *ed.* Berlin U. Entered German films as a screenwriter in 1914. A director from the early 20s, he did not participate in the expressionist movement and failed to gain recognition abroad until the 1930s. His reputation rests mainly on such films as *Emil und die Detektive/Emil and the Detectives* (1931), a successful adaptation of Erich Kästner's popular adventure story in which Lamprecht effectively directed untrained children; *Prinzessin Turandot* (1934), in which he proved his skill at exploiting the realm of fantasy; and a solid version of *Madame Bovary* (1937) starring Pola Negri. Earlier in his career he directed an ambitious adaptation of Thomas Mann's *Die Buddenbrooks* (1923) and two realistic films indicting social conditions in Berlin, *Die Verrufenen/Slums of Berlin* (1925) and *Die Unehelichen/Children of No Importance* (1926). Lamprecht is also a noted historian of the German cinema. He compiled a complete catalogue of German silent films from 1903 to 1931, *Deutsche Stummfilme 1903–1931,* which was published in multiple volumes by the Deutsche Kinemathek in Berlin. His huge private collection of material pertaining to the early days of the German cinema has provided the nucleus of the Kinemathek's archives.

FILMS INCLUDE: *Der Friedhof der Lebenden* (also co-sc.) 1921; *Fliehende Schatten* (also co-sc.) 1922; *Die Buddenbrooks* (also co-sc.), *Das Haus ohne Lachen* (also co-sc.) 1923; *Die Andere* 1924; *Hanseaten* (also co-sc.), *Die Verrufenen/Slums of Berlin* (also co-sc.) 1925; *Schwester Veronika* (also co-sc.), *Die Unehelichen/Children of No Importance* (also co-sc.) 1926; *Der alte Fritz* (also co-sc.), *Der Katzensteg* (also co-sc.) 1927; *Unter der Laterne* (also co-sc.) 1928; *Zweierlei Moral* (also sc.) 1930; *Zwischen Nacht und Morgen, Emil und die Detektive/Emil and the Detectives* 1931; *Der Schwarze Husar* 1932; *Spione am Werk* 1933; *Prinzessin Turandot, Einmal eine grosse Dame sein* 1934; *Einer zu viel an Bord, Barcarole* 1935; *Ein seltsamer Gast* 1936; *Die gelbe Flagge, Madame Bovary* 1937; *Der Spieler* 1938; *Die Geliebte, Frau im Strom* 1939; *Clarissa* 1941; *Diesel* (also co-sc.) 1942; *Kamerad Hedwig* 1945; *Irgendwo in Berlin/Somewhere in Berlin* (also sc.) 1946; *Madonna in Ketten* 1949; *Meines Vaters Pferde* 1954; *Menschen im Werk* (short) 1958.

Lancaster, Burt. Actor. *b.* Burton Stephen Lancaster, on Nov. 2, 1913, in New York City. *d.* 1994. The son of a postal clerk, he grew up in the tough East Harlem section of Manhattan's Upper East Side. Excelling in basketball and other high school sports, he enrolled at NYU on an athletic scholarship but soon after quit college to form the Lang and Cravat acrobatic team with his pint-sized childhood friend Nick Cravat. For several years they toured with circuses and appeared in vaudeville and nightclubs. Bookings were sparse and in 1941 Lancaster took a job as a salesman in a Chicago department store and later as a refrigerator repairman. Returning from WW II action in North Africa and Italy, with Special Services, he was discovered (or so his studio biographers claim) in an elevator by a stage producer who mistook him for an actor and asked him to read for a Broadway part. The play, 'The Sound of Hunting' (1945), ran for only three weeks, just long enough for him to be noticed by Hollywood scouts. He made a striking screen debut as Swede in Robert Siodmak's "sleeper" film adaptation of a Hemingway short story, *The Killers* (1946).

Immediately established as a star, Lancaster rapidly revealed a sensitive interior beneath his athletic prowess. As early as 1948 he was among the first film actors to become an independent producer, forming the Hecht-Lancaster company with his agent, Harold HECHT. Later they were joined by producer James HILL. In the 50s, Lancaster alternated acrobatic portrayals in adventure films and sensitive, sincere performances in such dramas as *Come Back Little Sheba, From Here to Eternity, The Rose Tattoo,* and *Sweet Smell of Success.* He also directed a single film, *The Kentuckian* (1955), starring himself. His company produced several notable films of the 50s, including *Marty.* In 1960 he won an Academy Award for the title role of a charlatan in *Elmer Gantry* and in 1962 the Venice Festival award for his performance in *Birdman of Alcatraz.* He received Oscar nominations for *From Here to Eternity* (1953), *Birdman of Alcatraz* (1962), and *Atlantic City* (1981) and won Italy's David Di Donatello Award as best foreign actor for the latter film. Lancaster extended his career successfully into the 80s, despite quadruple bypass open-heart surgery in 1983. Late in 1990 he was hospitalized for a stroke.

FILMS: *The Killers* 1946; *Variety Girl* (cameo), *Brute Force, Desert Fury* 1947; *I Walk Alone, All My Sons, Sorry Wrong Number, Kiss the Blood off My Hands* 1948; *Criss Cross, Rope of Sand* 1949; *The Flame and the Arrow, Mister 880* 1950; *Vengeance Valley, Jim Thorpe—All American* (title role), *Ten Tall Men* 1951; *The Crimson Pirate, Come Back Little Sheba* 1952; *South Sea Woman, From Here to Eternity* 1953; *His Majesty O'Keefe, Apache, Vera Cruz* 1954; *The Kentuckian* (also dir.), *The Rose Tattoo* 1955; *Trapeze, The Rainmaker* 1956; *Gunfight at the O.K. Corral* (as Wyatt Earp), *Sweet Smell of Success* 1957; *Run Silent Run Deep, Separate Tables* 1958; *The Devil's Disciple* (as Rev. Anthony Anderson; UK/US) 1959; *The Unforgiven, Elmer Gantry* (title role) 1960; *The Young Savages, Judgment at Nuremberg* 1961; *Birdman of Alcatraz* 1962; *A Child Is Waiting, The List of Adrian Messenger, Il Gattopardo/The Leopard* (It./Fr.) 1963; *Seven Days in May, Le Train/The Train* (Fr./It./US) 1964; *The Hallelujah Trail* 1965; *The Professionals* 1966; *The Scalphunters, The Swimmer* 1968; *Castle Keep, The Gypsy Moths* 1969; *King* (doc.), *Airport* 1970; *Lawman, Valdez Is Coming* 1971; *Ulzana's Raid* 1972; *Scorpio, Executive Action* 1973; *The Midnight Man* (also co-dir., co-prod., co-sc. with Roland Kibbee) 1974; *Gruppo di Famiglia in uno Intero/Conversation Piece* (It./Fr.) 1975; *Moses* (title role; UK/It.), *Novecento/1900* (It.), *Buffalo Bill and the Indians* 1976; *The Cassandra Crossing, Twilight's Last Gleaming, The Island of Dr. Moreau* 1977; *Go Tell the Spartans* 1978; *Zulu Dawn, Arthur Miller on Home Ground* (doc.) 1979; *Atlantic City* (Can./Fr.), *Cattle Annie and Little Britches, La Pelle/The Skin* (It.) 1981; *Local Hero* (UK), *The Osterman Weekend* 1983; *Little Treasure* 1985; *Tough Guys* 1986; *Il Giorno prima* (It.) 1987; *Rocket Gibraltar* 1988; *La Boutiqe de l'Orfèvre* (Fr.), *Field of Dreams* 1989; *The Jeweller's Shop* (UK; adapted from a short story written by Karol Wojtyla, Pope John Paul II) 1990.

Lanchester, Elsa. Actress. *b.* Elizabeth Sullivan, Oct. 28, 1902, Lewisham, England. *d.* 1986. Delightful, elfin character actress of British and Hollywood films. As a child she danced with Isadora Duncan's troupe in Paris and at 16 began acting with a children's theater in Soho. She made her first film appearance in 1927 and two years later married Charles LAUGHTON, with whom she went to Hollywood in 1934. In films, she played a wide range of character roles but was at her best in eccentric or comic parts. Among her many memorable portrayals were that of Anne of Cleves, opposite Laughton, in *The Private Life of Henry VIII* (1933) and of the weird mate created in the lab for Frankenstein's monster in *The Bride of Frankenstein* (1935).

She was nominated for Oscars for *Come to the Stable* (1949) and *Witness for the Prosecution* (1958).

FILMS: In the UK—*One of the Best* 1927; *The Constant Nymph* 1928; *Day Dreams* (short) 1929; *Comets, The Love Habit* 1930; *The Stronger Sex, Potiphar's Wife, The Officers' Mess* 1931; *The Private Life of Henry VIII* (as Anne of Cleves) 1933. In the US—*David Copperfield* (as Clickett), *Naughty Marietta, The Bride of Frankenstein* (title role) 1935. In the UK—*The Ghost Goes West, Rembrandt* 1936; *Vessel of Wrath/The Beachcomber* 1938. In the US—*Ladies in Retirement* 1941; *Son of Fury, Tales of Manhattan* 1942; *Forever and a Day, Thumbs Up, Lassie Come Home* 1943; *Passport to Adventure* 1944; *The Spiral Staircase, The Razor's Edge* 1946; *Northwest Outpost, The Bishop's Wife* 1947; *The Big Clock* 1948; *The Secret Garden, Come to the Stable, The Inspector General* 1949; *Buccaneer's Girl, Mystery Street, The Petty Girl* 1950; *Frenchie* 1951; *Dreamboat, Les Misérables* 1952; *Androcles and the Lion, The Girls of Pleasure Island* 1953; *Hell's Half Acre* 1954; *Three-Ring Circus, The Glass Slipper* 1955; *Witness for the Prosecution, Bell Book and Candle* 1958; *Honeymoon Hotel, Mary Poppins, Pajama Party* 1964; *That Darn Cat* 1965; *Easy Come Easy Go* 1967; *Blackbeard's Ghost* 1968; *Rascal, Me Natalie* 1969; *Willard* 1971; *Terror in the Wax Museum, Arnold* 1973; *Murder by Death* 1976; *Die Laughing* 1980.

Lanci, Giuseppe ("Beppe"). Director of photography. Born in 1942, in Rome. A graduate of Rome's Centro Sperimentale di Cinematografia, he entered the industry as an apprentice in the mid-60s. As a lighting cameraman from the late 70s, he worked frequently with Marco BELLOCHIO and contributed startling images to films of Andrei TARKOVSKY, the TAVIANI brothers, and Lina WERTMULLER, among other directors. He entered the 90s as one of Europe's leading cinematographers.

FILMS INCLUDE: *Maternale* 1978; *Salto nel Vuoto/Leap Into Void* 1980; *Gli Occhi la Bocca/The Eyes the Mouth, Piso Piselli/Swee' Pea* 1982; *Nostalghia/Nostalgia, Stelle emigranti* 1983; *Enrico IV/Henry IV, Kaos/Chaos* 1984; *Un Complicato intrigo di Donne vicoli e delitti/Camorra* 1985; *Il Diavolo in Corpo/Devil in the Flesh, Every Time We Say Goodbye* (Isr.) 1986; *Good Morning Babilonia/Good Morning Babylon* 1987; *Paura e Amore/Three Sisters, Zoo* 1988; *Francesco/St. Francis of Assisi, Il Prete bello/The Handsome Priest* 1989; *La-Baule-Les-Pins/C'est la Vie* 1990.

Landau, Ely A. Producer, production executive. Born on Jan. 20, 1920, in New York City. Following WW II service with the Air Force, he worked for various companies as a TV director and producer. In 1953 he organized National Telefilm Associates, later serving as its president and board chairman. Landau won a Peabody Award as the producer of 'Play of the Week,' a series of TV adaptations of distinguished plays. He began producing motion pictures in the 60s and in 1972 formed the American Film Theatre for the purpose of bringing to the screen notable productions of the American and British stage.

FILMS: *Long Day's Journey Into Night* (exec. prod.) 1962; *The Pawnbroker* (co-exec. prod.) 1965; *The Madwoman of Chaillot* 1969; *King* (doc.) 1970; *The Iceman Cometh, The Homecoming, A Delicate Balance* 1973; *Luther, Butley, Rhinoceros, Lost in the Stars* 1974; *Galileo, In Celebration, The Man in the Glass Booth* 1975; *The Three Sisters* 1977; *The Greek Tycoon* (co-exec. prod.) 1978; *Hopscotch* 1980; *Beatlemania* 1981; *The Chosen* 1982; *The Holcroft Covenant* 1985.

Landau, Martin. Actor. Born on June 20, 1928, in Brooklyn, N.Y. Formerly a cartoonist with the *New York Daily News,* he attended the Actors Studio for three years, then appeared on stage and TV. One of the early heroes of TV's 'Mission: Impossible' (1966–69), co-starring with his wife, Barbara Bain (*b.* Sept. 13, 1931), he has also played morose, often evil, character parts in occasional films. He reached a career milestone in the late 80s, when he was nominated successively for Academy Awards as best supporting actor for his roles in Francis Coppola's *Tucker: The Man and His Dream* (1988) and Woody Allen's *Crimes and Misdemeanors* (1989). He finally received the Oscar for his turn as Bela Lugosi in Tim BURTON's ode to "B Filmmaker" *Ed Wood* (1994).

FILMS INCLUDE: *Pork Chop Hill, North by Northwest* 1959; *The Gazebo* 1960; *Stagecoach to Dancers' Rock* 1962; *Cleopatra* (as Rufius) 1963; *The Greatest Story Ever Told* (as Caiaphas), *The Hallelujah Trail* 1965; *Nevada Smith* 1966; *They Call Me Mister Tibbs* 1970; *A Town Called Hell* (Sp.) 1971; *Black Gunn* 1972; *Tony Saitta/Tough Tony* (It.) 1976; *Strange Shadows in an Empty Room/Blazing Magnum* (Can./It.) 1977; *Meteor, The Fall of the House of Usher* 1979; *The Last Word, Without Warning* 1980; *Alone in the Dark* 1982; *The Being* 1983; *Cyclone, Sweet Revenge, Empire State* (UK) 1987; *Tucker: The Man and His Dream* 1988; *Trust Me, Crimes and Misdemeanors* 1989; *Paint It Black, Real Bullets, Firehead* 1990; *Eye of the Widow* 1991; *Tipperary, The Color of Evening, Mistress* 1992; *Sliver* 1993; *Ed Wood, Intersection* 1994; *City Hall, Pinocchio* 1996.

Landers, Lew. Director. *b.* Louis Friedlander, Jan. 2, 1901, New York City. *d.* 1962. He started out directing Universal serials in 1934, under his real name, Louis Friedlander, but five serials and three feature films later began using the pseudonym Lew Landers, which he retained for the rest of his long and prolific career. He made his debut as a feature director in 1935 with *The Raven,* a neat little thriller featuring horror masters Boris Karloff and Bela Lugosi. He subsequently turned out scores of routine low-budget Hollywood films, for Universal, RKO, Columbia, Monogram, and other studios, mostly mysteries, horror thrillers, Westerns, and action adventures, occasionally rising above his thin material with flashes of originality. He also directed for TV.

FILMS: As Louis Friedlander—*The Red Rider* (serial), *Tailspin Tommy* (serial), *The Vanishing Shadow* (serial) 1934; *The Call of the Savage* (serial), *Rustlers of Red Dog* (serial), *The Raven, Stormy* 1935; *Parole!* 1936. As Lew Landers—*Without Orders, Night Waitress* 1936; *They Wanted to Marry, The Man Who Found Himself, You Can't Buy Luck, Border Cafe, Flight from Glory, Living on Love, Danger Patrol* 1937; *Crashing Hollywood, Double Danger, Condemned Women, Law of the Underworld, Blind Alibi, Sky Giant, Smashing the Rackets, Annabel Takes a Tour* 1938; *Pacific Liner, Twelve Crowded Hours, Fixer Dugan, The Girl and the Gambler, Bad Lands, Conspiracy* 1939; *Honeymoon Deferred, Enemy Agent, Ski Patrol, La Conga Nights, Wagons Westward, Sing Dance—Plenty Hot, Girl from Havana, Slightly Tempted* 1940; *Ridin' on a Rainbow, Lucky Devils, Back in the Saddle, The Singing Hill, I Was a Prisoner on Devil's Island, Mystery Ship, The Stork Pays Off* 1941; *The Man Who Returned to Life, Alias Boston Blackie, Canal Zone, Harvard Here I Come, Not a Ladies' Man, Submarine Raider, Cadets on Parade, Atlantic Convoy, Sabotage Squad, The Boogie Man Will Get You, Smith of Minnesota, Stand By All Networks, Junior Army* 1942; *After Midnight with Boston Blackie, Redhead from Manhattan, Murder in Times Square, Power of the Press, Doughboys in Ireland, Deerslayer* 1943; *The Return of the Vampire, Cowboy Canteen, The Ghost That Walks Alone, Two-Man Submarine, Stars on Parade, The Black Parachute, U-Boat Prisoner, Swing in the Saddle, I'm From Arkansas* 1944; *Crime Inc., The Power of the Whistler, Trouble Chasers, Follow That Woman, Arson Squad, Shadow of Terror, The Enchanted Forest, Tokyo Rose*

1945; *The Mask of Dijon, A Close Call for Boston Blackie, The Truth About Murder, Hot Cargo, Secrets of a Sorority Girl* 1946; *Death Valley, Danger Street, Seven Keys to Baldpate, Under the Tonto Rim, Thunder Mountain, The Son of Rusty, Devil Ship* 1947; *My Dog Rusty, Adventures of Gallant Bess, Inner Sanctum* 1948; *Stagecoach Kid, Law of the Barbary Coast, Air Hostess, Barbary Pirate* 1949; *Davy Crockett—Indian Scout, Girls' School, Dynamite Pass, Tyrant of the Sea, State Penitentiary, Beauty on Parade, Chain Gang, Last of the Buccaneers, Revenue Agent* 1950; *Blue Blood, A Yank in Korea, When the Redskins Rode, The Big Gusher, Hurricane Island, The Magic Carpet, Jungle Manhunt* 1951; *Aladdin and His Lamp, Jungle Jim in the Forbidden Land, California Conquest, Arctic Flight* 1952; *Torpedo Alley, Tangier Incident, Man in the Dark, Run for the Hills, Captain John Smith and Pocahontas* 1953; *Captain Kidd and the Slave Girl* 1954; *The Cruel Tower* 1956; *Hot Rod Gang* 1958; *Terrified!* 1963.

Landi, Elissa. Actress. *b.* Elizabeth Marie Christine Kuehnelt, Dec. 6, 1904, Venice, Italy, to an Austrian cavalry officer. *d.* 1948. The stepdaughter of an Italian nobleman, Count Carlo Zanardi-Landi, and purportedly a descendant of Emperor Franz Josef of Austria on her mother's side, she was educated by private tutors in Canada and England and made her acting debut on the London stage in 1924. Subsequently played leads in many stage productions and several British films. Following her Broadway bow in 'A Farewell to Arms' (1930), she went to Hollywood, where she starred in many films of the 30s, memorably in De Mille's *The Sign of the Cross* (1932). A talented, intelligent actress of ethereal beauty, she was boosted energetically by studio publicity, but less effort was put into providing her with suitable screen vehicles and by the late 30s her career had faltered. She then returned to the Broadway stage, appearing in only one more film, in the early 40s. Died of cancer. She was the author of several novels.

FILMS INCLUDE: *London* (UK) 1926; *Underground* (UK), *Sin* (Sw.) 1928; *The Inseparables* (UK) 1929; *Knowing Men* (UK), *The Price of Things* (UK), *Children of Chance* (UK), *Mon Gosse de Père/The Parisian* (Fr.) 1930; *Body and Soul, Always Goodbye, Wicked, The Yellow Ticket* 1931; *Devil's Lottery, The Woman in Room 13, A Passport to Hell, The Sign of the Cross* 1932; *The Warrior's Husband, I Loved You Wednesday, The Masquerader* 1933; *By Candlelight, Man of Two Worlds, Sisters Under the Skin, The Great Flirtation, The Count of Monte Cristo* 1934; *Enter Madame* 1935; *The Amateur Gentleman* (UK), *After the Thin Man, Mad Holiday* 1936; *The Thirteenth Chair* 1937; *Corregidor* 1943.

Landis, Carole. Actress. *b.* Frances Lillian Mary Ridste, Jan. 1, 1919, Fairchild, Wis. *d.* 1948. A shapely blonde, she began competing in beauty contests at age 12. At 15 she eloped with a writer, but they separated after only three weeks. She subsequently married three more times. After working as a milliner, waitress, and usherette in her hometown, she went to San Francisco, where she made her debut at 16 as a singer–hula dancer at a plush night spot. She arrived in Hollywood at 18 and, thanks to her pretty face and "best legs in town," she was launched almost immediately in films. From 1940 on she got star billing, but her vehicles were never better than routine. *Four Jills in a Jeep* was based on her true adventures while entertaining WW II troops with Kay Francis and Martha Raye. On July 6, 1948, she was found dead of an overdose of sleeping pills. Heartbreak over breaking up with Rex HARRISON, who was married to Lilli Palmer at the time, was mentioned as the cause of her suicide.

FILMS INCLUDE: *A Star Is Born, A Day at the Races* 1937; *Four's a Crowd* 1938; *Daredevils of the Red Circle* (serial) 1939; *One Million B.C., Turnabout, Mystery Sea Raider* 1940; *Road Show, Topper Returns, Moon Over Miami, I Wake Up Screaming, Dance Hall, Cadet Girl* 1941; *It Happened in Flatbush, My Gal Sal, Orchestra Wives, Manila Calling* 1942; *Wintertime* 1943; *Four Jills in a Jeep, Secret Command* 1944; *Having Wonderful Crime* 1945; *Behind Green Lights, It Shouldn't Happen to a Dog, A Scandal in Paris* 1946; *Out of the Blue* 1947; *The Brass Monkey/Lucky Mascot, The Noose/The Silky Noose* 1948.

Landis, Cullen. Actor. *b.* 1895, Nashville, Tenn. *d.* 1975. Leading man of numerous Hollywood silents. Following stage experience, he entered films in 1916, intending to become a director, but instead launched a modestly successful acting career. Despite his small stature (5' 6"), he starred opposite some of Hollywood's most glamorous leading ladies in some 100 films, consisting of romantic and domestic melodramas as well as action programmers and serials. He had the dubious distinction of playing the male lead in the Warner Bros. first all-talking feature film, *Lights of New York*, a technical breakthrough but an artistic disaster. He retired from the screen shortly after and moved to Detroit, where he established himself as a producer-director of industrial films for automobile manufacturers. During WW II he made combat and training films for the Army in the South Pacific and later produced documentaries on the war and the Middle East.

FILMS INCLUDE: *Joy and the Dragon* 1916; *The Checkmate, The Mainspring* 1917; *Beware of Blondes* 1918; *Almost a Husband, The Outcasts of Poker Flat, Where the West Begins, Upstairs, The Girl from Outside* 1919; *Pinto, Going Some, It's a Great Life* 1920; *Bunty Pulls the String, Snowblind, The Old Nest* 1921; *Where Is My Wandering Boy Tonight?, Watch Your Step, Gay and Devilish, The Night Rose/Voices of the City, Youth to Youth, Remembrance, Love in the Dark, Forsaking All Others* 1922; *The Famous Mrs. Fair, The Soul of the Beast, Masters of Men, The Fog, The Midnight Alarm, Pioneer Trails, The Man Life Passed By* 1923; *The Fighting Coward, One Law for the Woman, Born Rich, Cheap Kisses* 1924; *Easy Money, A Broadway Butterfly, Pampered Youth, An Enemy of Men, Sealed Lips, Peacock Feathers, The Midnight Flyer* 1925; *Perils of the Coast Guard, My Old Dutch, Davy Crockett at the Fall of the Alamo* (title role), *The Dixie Flyer, Christine of the Big Tops, Frenzied Flames, Sweet Rosie O'Grady, The Smoke Eaters, The Fighting Failure* 1926; *On Guard!* (serial), *The Crimson Flash* (serial), *Heroes of the Night, We're All Gamblers, Broadway After Midnight* 1927; *On to Reno, The Broken Mask, The Devil's Skipper, A Midnight Adventure, Lights of New York, The Little Wild Girl* 1928; *The Convict's Code* 1930.

Landis, Jessie Royce. Actress. *b.* Jessie Royce Medbury, Nov. 25, 1904, Chicago. *d.* 1972. Primarily a stage actress, she appeared in numerous Broadway productions from the mid-20s. In between theatrical engagements she played key character roles in a score of films, typically as a society matron. Remembered as Grace Kelly's mother in *To Catch a Thief* and Cary Grant's mother in *North by Northwest*.

FILMS INCLUDE: *Derelict* 1930; *Mr. Belvedere Goes to College, It Happens Every Spring* 1949; *My Foolish Heart, Mother Didn't Tell Me* 1950; *Meet Me Tonight/Tonight at 8:30* (UK) 1952; *To Catch a Thief* 1955; *The Swan, The Girl He Left Behind* 1956; *My Man Godfrey* 1957; *I Married a Woman* 1958; *North by Northwest* 1959; *Aimez-vous Brahms?/Goodbye Again* (Fr./US) 1961; *Bon Voyage!, Boys' Night Out* 1962; *Critic's Choice, Gidget Goes to Rome* 1963; *Airport* 1970.

Landis, John. Director. Born on Aug. 3, 1950, in Chicago. Raised in the Westwood section of Los Angeles, he was a movie fanatic from early childhood. He dropped out of school at 17 to take a job at the mailroom of 20th Century-Fox, where he observed all he could about the business of filmmaking. After a stint in Europe as a production assistant and stuntman, he concocted a minibudget, monster-thriller parody, *Schlock,* that became a minor cult film upon its release in 1972 and went on to gross $6 million. It won the top prize at the Trieste Science Fiction Film Festival in 1973 and a special award at France's Chamrousse Comedy Film Festival in 1975. This modest success eventually led to his assignment by humorists Jim ABRAHAMS and the ZUCKER brothers to direct their spoof of TV shows and commercials, *The Kentucky Fried Movie* (1977). This was followed by *National Lampoon's Animal House* (1978), an utterly tasteless parody of college life that became one of the biggest box-office hits in the history of the movies. Made for less than $3 million, it grossed more than $160 million. It spawned a number of even poorer imitations and the short-lived TV series 'Delta House.' The centerpiece of that film, comedian John BELUSHI, was also the star of *The Blues Brothers* (1980), another off-the-wall comedy and commercial draw. The knack for humor helped give Landis's excursion into the horror genre, *An American Werewolf in London* (1981), a special edge.

On Landis's next project, disaster struck. During the filming of a scene for his segment in the omnibus film, *Twilight Zone—The Movie* (1983), debris from a special-effects explosion hit an oncoming helicopter which crashed, killing actor Vic MORROW and two Vietnamese child performers. The director and four others in the production unit were charged with involuntary manslaughter. At the end of a lengthy trial stretching from mid-1986 to mid-1987, Landis was found not guilty. But he did not escape admonishment for reckless endangerment and subsequent civil suits for damages. To add insult to injury, the film itself, and in particular the Landis segment, flopped with both the critics and the public. He continued making films with sure-handed technical control but varying degrees of accomplishment. One of his most celebrated products of the 80s was the 17-minute music video 'Thriller,' featuring Michael Jackson. Landis often writes his own scripts. He appeared as an actor in a number of his own films as well as several by other directors, including *Battle for the Planet of the Apes* (1973), *Death Race 2000* (1975), *1941* (1979), *Eating Raoul* (1982), *The Muppets Take Manhattan* (1984), *Spontaneous Combustion* (1989), *Darkman* (1990), and *Stephen King's Sleepwalkers* (1992).

FEATURE FILMS (as director): *Schlock/The Banana Monster* (also sc., stunts) 1972; *The Kentucky Fried Movie* (also act.) 1977; *National Lampoon's Animal House* 1979; *The Blues Brothers* (also co-sc., act.) 1980; *An American Werewolf in London* (also sc., act.) 1981; *Twilight Zone—The Movie* (Prologue & 'Back There' segment; also sc.), *Trading Places* 1983; *Into the Night* (also act.), *Clue* (co-exec. prod., co-story only), *Spies Like Us* 1985; *Three Amigos* 1986; *Amazon Women on the Moon* (also co-exec. prod.) 1987; *Coming to America* 1988; *Oscar* 1991; *Innocent Blood, Venice/Venice* (as himself) 1992; *Beverly Hills Cop III, The Silence of the Hams* (act. only) 1994; *The Stupids* 1996.

Landon, Michael. Actor. *b.* Eugene Maurice Orowitz, Oct. 31, 1936, in Forest Hills, Queens, N.Y. *d.* 1991. Pleasant, likable leading man of American TV and occasional films. The son of a Jewish movie publicist and former Broadway comedienne Peggy O'Neill, he was raised in Collingswood, N.J., where he became his high school's champion javelin thrower. He attended USC on an athletic scholarship, but turned to acting when a torn ligament ended his aspirations in sports. Before long he was landing parts in TV shows and teen-oriented films, including the title role in the infamous *I Was a Teenage Werewolf* (1957). He hit the jackpot in 1959, when he joined the cast of the immensely popular TV series 'Bonanza,' with which he stayed through 1973, playing the role of Little Joe Cartwright and occasionally also directing and writing. He achieved even greater popularity as the star of 'Little House on the Prairie' (1974–82), a series he created to reflect his love of old-fashioned sentiment and traditional American values. In 1984, he moved on to the series 'Highway to Heaven' as producer, director, writer, and star. Also in that year, he wrote, directed, and starred in the autobiographical feature *Sam's Son.* On July 1, 1991, just three months after having been diagnosed as having pancreatic and liver cancer, and after a highly public battle that included a memorable last appearance on 'The Tonight Show,' Landon died at 54, leaving behind nine children from three marriages.

FEATURE FILMS: *These Wilder Years* 1956; *I Was a Teenage Werewolf* 1957; *God's Little Acre, Maracaibo, High School Confidential* 1958; *The Legend of Tom Dooley* 1959; *The Errand Boy* 1961; *Sam's Son* (also dir., sc.) 1984.

Landres, Paul. Director. Born on Aug. 21, 1912, in New York City. *ed.* UCLA. He entered films as an assistant editor in 1931, progressing to film editor in 1937. Since 1949 he has directed numerous TV episodes for major series and a score of minor low-budget action features.

FILMS: *Grand Canyon, Square Dance Jubilee* 1949; *Hollywood Varieties, A Modern Marriage* (re-released in 1962 as *Frigid Wife*) 1950; *Navy Bound, Rhythm Inn* 1951; *Army Bound* 1952; *Eyes of the Jungle* 1953; *Hell Canyon Outlaws, Last of the Badmen, The Vampire, Chain of Evidence, Oregon Passage* 1957; *Man from God's Country, Johnny Rocco, The Return of Dracula, The Flame Barrier, Frontier Gun* 1958; *The Lone Texan, Miracle of the Hills* 1959; *Son of a Gunfighter* 1966.

landscape. Scenery, real, manufactured, or painted, providing a background for filming.

Lane, Allan ("Rocky"). Actor. *b.* Harold Albershart, Sept. 22, 1904, Mishawaka, Ind. *d.* 1973. *ed.* Notre Dame. A former football player, he appeared briefly on the stage before starting his film career in 1929. He played supporting roles in numerous films before becoming a Western star early in the 40s and in all appeared in more than 100 features and serials, often accompanied by his "wonder" horse Blackjack. He was also the voice of Mr. Ed, the talking horse, in the TV series.

FILMS INCLUDE: *Not Quite Decent, The Forward Pass* 1929; *Love in the Rough, Madam Satan* 1930; *Night Nurse, Honor of the Family* 1931; *Winner Take All, Miss Pinkerton* 1932; *Stowaway* 1936; *Charlie Chan at the Olympics, Fifty Roads to Town* 1937; *Maid's Night Out, Crime Ring, Fugitives for a Night* 1938; *Pacific Liner, They Made Her a Spy, Conspiracy* 1939; *King of the Royal Mounted* (serial) 1940; *Yukon Patrol* 1942; *Daredevils of the West* (serial), *The Dancing Masters* 1943; *The Tiger Woman* (serial) 1944; *Bells of Rosarita* 1945; *The Wild Frontier* 1946; *Oklahoma Badlands* 1948; *The Bandit King of Texas* 1949; *Desert of Lost Men* 1951; *Bandits of the West* 1953; *The Saga of Hemp Brown* 1958; *Hell Bent for Leather* 1960; *Posse from Hell* 1961.

Lane, Burton. Composer, songwriter. *b.* Burton Levy, on Feb. 2, 1912, in New York City. *d.* 1996. He began writing songs as a child and broke through professionally while working as a pianist for a music publisher. After contributing music and lyrics for the 1931 Broadway production of 'Earl Carroll's Vanities,' he went to Hollywood, where he composed scores and songs for many films. His best-known Broadway musicals are 'Finian's Rainbow' and 'On a Clear Day You Can See Forever.'

FILMS INCLUDE: *Dancing Lady* 1933; *Bottoms Up, Strictly Dynamite, Kid Millions* 1934; *Folies-Bergère, Reckless* 1935; *College Holiday* 1936; *Champagne Waltz, Artists and Models, Swing High—Swing Low, Double or Nothing* 1937;

College Swing, Spawn of the North 1938; *St. Louis Blues, Some Like It Hot, Cafe Society* 1939; *Las Vegas Nights, Dancing on a Dime* 1941; *Babes on Broadway, Ship Ahoy, Panama Hattie, Seven Sweethearts* 1942; *Du Barry Was a Lady, Presenting Lily Mars, Thousands Cheer* 1943; *Rainbow Island, Hollywood Canteen* 1944; *Pillow to Post* 1945; *Royal Wedding* 1951; *Give a Girl a Break* 1953; *Jupiter's Darling* 1955; *Finian's Rainbow* 1968; *On a Clear Day You Can See Forever* 1970; *Heidi's Song* 1982.

Lane (Levison), Charles. Actor. Born in 1905 in San Francisco. Comically severe, bespectacled character player who appeared in Hollywood films for six decades. Entering films in 1931, he worked for several years under two different names, Charles Lane and Charles Levison, before settling on Lane after 1936. With his angular features and nasal voice, he was typically seen as a crabby accountant, reporter, or salesman. In the 30s he performed Shakespeare and Chekhov at the Pasadena Playhouse, Calif.; he appeared on Broadway in 'Love in E-Flat' (1967). He was a frequent guest on TV sitcoms and a regular on several series, notably as railroad executive Homer Bedloe on 'Petticoat Junction' (1963–69). He is not to be confused with the actor Charles Lane who appeared in silent films such as *Dr. Jekyll and Mr. Hyde* (1920) and *Love's Penalty* (1921) and the filmmaker Charles Lane who directed *Sidewalk Stories* (1989).

FILMS INCLUDE: *Blonde Crazy, Smart Money* 1931; *Gold Diggers of 1933* 1933; *Broadway Bill, Twentieth Century* 1934; *Mr. Deeds Goes to Town, The Milky Way* 1936; *Internes Can't Take Money* 1937; *Cocoanut Grove, Kentucky, You Can't Take It with You* 1938; *The Cat and the Canary, Fifth Avenue Girl, Golden Boy, Lucky Night, Mr. Smith Goes to Washington* 1939; *Buck Benny Rides Again, Ellery Queen Master Detective, The Great Profile, Johnny Apollo, Primrose Path, Rhythm on the River* 1940; *Are Husbands Necessary, Ball of Fire, Friendly Enemies, The Great Man's Lady, The Lady Is Willing, Tarzan's New York Adventure* 1942; *Arsenic and Old Lace* 1944; *It's a Wonderful Life* 1946; *Apartment for Peggy, The Gentleman from Nowhere, State of the Union* 1948; *Mother Is a Freshman, You're My Everything* 1949; *Borderline, Riding High* 1950; *Here Comes the Groom, I Can Get It for You Wholesale* 1951; *The Sniper* 1952; *The Juggler* 1953; *Top Secret Affair* 1957; *Teacher's Pet* 1958; *But Not for Me, The Mating Game, The Thirty Foot Bride of Candy Rock* 1959; *The Music Man* 1962; *It's a Mad Mad Mad Mad World* 1963; *The Carpetbaggers, Good Neighbor Sam* 1964; *The Gnome-Mobile* 1967; *What's So Bad About Feeling Good?* 1968; *Get to Know Your Rabbit* 1972; *Movie Movie* 1978; *Strange Invaders* 1983; *Murphy's Romance* 1985; *Date with an Angel* 1987.

Lane, Charles. Director, actor, producer, writer. Born in New York City on Dec. 26, 1953. *ed.* SUNY-Purchase (B.F.A.). African-American *auteur* whose first feature film, *Sidewalk Stories* (1989), earned critical praise and several international awards, including the Prix du Publique at Cannes. The silent, black-and-white comedy about a Chaplinesque homeless artist (Lane) who cares for a lost child was shot for $200,000 on New York locations. An impressive independent debut, it led to offers from Hollywood, resulting in a less successful second film, *True Identity*.

FILMS (as director): *Sidewalk Stories* (also prod., sc., act., co-ed.) 1989; *True Identity* (also act.) 1991; *Posse* (act. only) 1993.

Lane, Diane. Actress. Born in January, 1965, in New York City. Sexy leading lady of the American screen. Despite a turbulent childhood, the result of her parents' divorce when she was merely 13 days old, she thrived as a teenaged actress in films and in classic plays staged at New York's experimental La Mama theater. Following stormy relationships with actors Tim HUTTON, Chris ATKINS, and Matt DILLON, she married French-American "Tarzan" Christophe(r) LAMBERT.

FILMS: *A Little Romance* 1979; *Touched by Love/To Elvis with Love* 1980; *Cattle Annie and Little Britches* 1981; *National Lampoon Goes to the Movies/National Lampoon's Movie Madness, Six Pack, Ladies and Gentlemen the Fabulous Stains* 1982; *The Outsiders, Rumble Fish* 1983; *Streets of Fire, The Cotton Club* 1984; *The Big Town, Lady Beware* 1987; *Priceless Beauty* (It.) 1988; *Vital Signs* 1990; *My New Gun* 1992; *Indian Summer, Knight Moves* 1993; *Judge Dredd, Wild Bill* 1995; *Mad Dog Time* 1996; *Murder at 1600* 1997.

Lane, Lola. Actress. *b.* Dorothy Mullican, May 21, 1909, Macy, Ind. *d.* 1981. One of a dentist's five daughters, three of whom were to find careers in films, she was raised in Iowa's corn belt and by age 12 was playing the piano, accompanying silent films in a local movie theater. After two years of study at a music conservatory, she joined her older sister, Leota, on a trip to New York, where they both appeared in the Gus Edwards vaudeville revue and made their Broadway debut in 'Greenwich Village Follies.' Following a starring role opposite George Jessel in Broadway's 'War Song' (1928), Lola was signed by Fox and began appearing in films. She was cast mainly in minor productions at Fox and at other studios until the late 30s, when she joined Warners and co-starred in a series of popular sentimental films with her sisters Priscilla and Rosemary LANE. She retired from the screen in 1946 to go into real estate. Her five marriages included those to actor Lew AYRES and directors Alexander HALL and Roland WEST.

FILMS INCLUDE: *Speakeasy, Fox Movietone Follies of 1929, The Girl from Havana* 1929; *Let's Go Places, The Big Fight, Good News, The Costello Case* 1930; *Hell Bound* 1931; *Public Stenographer* 1933; *Burn 'Em Up Barnes* (serial and feature) 1934; *Murder on a Honeymoon, Alias Mary Dow* 1935; *Marked Woman* 1937; *Hollywood Hotel, Four Daughters* 1938; *Daughters Courageous, Four Wives* 1939; *Convicted Woman, Zanzibar, Gangs of Chicago, Girls of the Road* 1940; *Four Mothers, Mystery Ship* 1941; *Miss V from Moscow* 1942; *Why Girls Leave Home* 1945; *They Made Me a Killer, Deadline at Dawn* 1946.

Lane, Lupino. Actor, director. *b.* Henry Lane George Lupino, June 16, 1892, London. *d.* 1959. Versatile, rubber-jointed acrobatic comic, a descendant of several generations of stage performers; brother of screen actor Wallace Lupino-Lane; a cousin of Stanley Lupino, father of Ida LUPINO. Entering films in 1915, he starred in many British comedy shorts but gained fame and popularity in Hollywood during the 20s as the star of numerous two-reelers and a number of feature films. In one film he played no fewer than 25 different roles. He returned to England in 1930 and for a decade continued appearing in films and occasionally also directing.

FILMS INCLUDE (as actor): In the UK—*His Cooling Courtship, Nipper's Busy Holiday, The Man in Possession* 1915; *The Dummy* 1916; *The Missing Link* 1917; *Unexpected Treasure, His Salad Days* 1918; *A Dreamland Frolic* 1919; *A Night Out and a Day In* 1920. In the US—*The Broker* (short), *The Reporter* (short) 1922; *A Friendly Husband* 1923; *Isn't Life Wonderful* 1924; *The Fighting Dude* (short) 1925; *Movieland* (short) 1927; *Hectic Days* (short) 1928; *The Love Parade, The Show of Shows* 1929; *Bride of the Regiment, Golden Dawn* 1930. In the UK—*The Yellow Mask* 1930; *Never Trouble Trouble* (also dir.), *No Lady* (also dir.), *The Love Race* (dir. only) 1931; *Innocents of Chicago* (dir. only) 1932; *Letting in the Sunshine* (dir. only) 1933; *Oh What a Duchess!* (dir. only) 1934; *Trust the Navy* 1935; *Hot News* 1936; *The Lambeth Walk/Me and My Gal* 1939.

Lane, Priscilla. Actress. *b.* Priscilla Mullican, on June 12, 1917, in Indianola, Iowa. *d.* 1995. The youngest and best looking of the three Lane sisters (the others: Lola LANE, Rosemary LANE), she attended Simpson College, a music conservatory in Des Moines, and along with Rosemary entered show business as a vocalist with Fred Waring's Pennsylvanians. The sisters toured with the band for several years, arriving in Hollywood in 1937 to appear with the Pennsylvanians in the Warner Bros. film *Varsity Show.* Both girls were signed by the studio on long-term contracts, joining sister Lola, by then a veteran of the screen. The trio achieved popularity in the late 30s and early 40s in a series of sentimental dramas that was launched with *Four Daughters* (1938). A vibrant blue-eyed, sweet-looking blonde, Priscilla enjoyed the most successful screen career among the sisters, starring in such major productions as *Brother Rat* (1938), *The Roaring Twenties* (1939), *Saboteur* (1942), and *Arsenic and Old Lace* (1944). She retired from the screen in 1948.

FILMS: *Varsity Show* 1937; *Love Honor and Behave, Men Are Such Fools, Cowboy from Brooklyn, Four Daughters, Brother Rat* 1938; *Yes My Darling Daughter, Daughters Courageous, Dust Be My Destiny, The Roaring Twenties, Four Wives* 1939; *Brother Rat and a Baby, Three Cheers for the Irish, Ladies Must Live* 1940; *Four Mothers, Million Dollar Baby, Blues in the Night* 1941; *Saboteur, Silver Queen* 1942; *The Meanest Man in the World* 1943; *Arsenic and Old Lace* 1944; *Fun on a Weekend* 1947; *Bodyguard* 1948.

Lane, Rosemary. Actress. *b.* Rosemary Mullican, Apr. 4, 1914, Indianola, Iowa. *d.* 1974. Kewpie-doll-faced sister of Lola and Priscilla LANE. After attending Simpson College, she and Priscilla toured with Fred Waring's Pennsylvanians and made their film debuts with the band in *Varsity Show* (1937). Rosemary remained in Hollywood until 1945, sharing the limelight with her sisters in the "Four Daughters" series and appeared in a number of insignificant films on her own. She was the least popular of the sisters but enjoyed personal success in 1941 when she starred in the Broadway musical 'Best Foot Forward.' She died as a result of complications caused by pulmonary obstruction and diabetes.

FILMS INCLUDE: *Varsity Show* 1937; *Hollywood Hotel, Gold Diggers in Paris, Four Daughters* 1938; *Blackwell's Island, The Oklahoma Kid, Daughters Courageous, The Return of Dr. X, Four Wives* 1939; *An Angel from Texas, The Boys from Syracuse, Ladies Must Live, Always a Bride* 1940; *Four Mothers, Time Out for Rhythm* 1941; *Chatterbox, All By Myself, Harvest Melody* 1943; *Trocadero* 1944; *Sing Me a Song of Texas* 1945.

Lanfield, Sidney. Director. *b.* Apr. 20, 1898, Chicago. *d.* 1972. A former vaudevillian and jazz musician, he went to Hollywood in 1926 as a gagman for Fox and began writing screen stories and screenplays two years later. He made his first film as director in 1930 and over the next two decades directed many mildly entertaining features, comprising mainly comedies and light romances and including several Bob Hope vehicles. Lanfield's most successful film was, however, a thriller, the suspenseful and atmospheric *The Hound of the Baskervilles* (1939), which launched Fox's popular "Sherlock Holmes" series with Basil Rathbone in the role of the famous detective. In the early 40s, Lanfield transferred to Paramount. In the early 50s he was among the first established film directors to move over to TV. He directed some 200 television shows in addition to 37 feature films. He died of a heart attack, leaving as a widow former film actress Shirley MASON.

FILMS: *Cheer Up and Smile* 1930; *Three Girls Lost, Hush Money* 1931; *Dance Team, Society Girl, Hat Check Girl* 1932; *Broadway Bad* 1933; *Moulin Rouge, The Last Gentleman* 1934; *Hold 'Em Yale, Red Salute* 1935; *King of Burlesque, Half Angel, Sing Baby Sing* 1936; *One in a Million, Wake Up and Live, Thin Ice, Love and Hisses* 1937; *Always Goodbye* 1938; *The Hound of the Baskervilles, Second Honeymoon, Swanee River* 1939; *You'll Never Get Rich* 1941; *The Lady Has Plans, My Favorite Blonde* 1942; *The Meanest Man in the World, Let's Face It* 1943; *Standing Room Only* 1944; *Bring On the Girls* 1945; *The Well Groomed Bride* 1946; *The Trouble with Women, Where There's Life* 1947; *Station West* 1948; *Sorrowful Jones* 1949; *The Lemon Drop Kid, Follow the Sun* 1951; *Skirts Ahoy!* 1952.

Lang, Charles B. Director of photography. Born on Mar. 27, 1902, in Bluff, Utah. *ed.* USC. He entered films in the early 20s as a lab assistant at the Paramount studios, and after a period of apprenticeship as an assistant cameraman, he was given his first assignment as a cinematographer in 1926. However, he did not work regularly as a lighting cameraman until 1929. Lang soon distinguished himself as one of Hollywood's finest craftsmen, providing many Paramount films of the 30s and 40s with subtle black-and-white cinematography. Freelancing from 1952, he worked for various studios, adding dazzling color to his arsenal of photographic skills. He won an Academy Award for the cinematography of *A Farewell to Arms* (1933). The holder of 18 Oscar nominations for cinematography, the most garnered by any artist in a single category, he received a Life Achievement Award from the Society of American Cinematographers in 1991.

FILMS INCLUDE: *The Night Patrol* (co-phot.) 1926; *Ritzy* 1927; *The Shopworn Angel, Innocents of Paris* 1929; *Behind the Make-Up, The Light of Western Stars, Street of Chance, Tom Sawyer* 1930; *The Vice Squad* 1931; *Thunder Below, The Devil and the Deep* 1932; *A Farewell to Arms, She Done Him Wrong, A Bedtime Story* 1933; *Death Takes a Holiday* 1934; *Mississippi, The Lives of a Bengal Lancer, Peter Ibbetson* (co-phot.) 1935; *Desire* (co-phot.) 1936; *Souls at Sea, Angel, Tovarich* 1937; *You and Me, Spawn of the North* 1938; *Zaza, Midnight, The Cat and the Canary* 1939; *Buck Benny Rides Again, The Ghost Breakers, Arise My Love* 1940; *The Shepherd of the Hills, Sundown* 1941; *The Uninvited* 1944; *Blue Skies* 1946; *Desert Fury* (co-phot.), *The Ghost and Mrs. Muir* 1947; *A Foreign Affair, Miss Tatlock's Millions* 1948; *Rope of Sand* 1949; *Fancy Pants* 1950; *September Affair, The Big Carnival/Ace in the Hole, Peking Express* 1951; *Red Mountain, Sudden Fear* 1952; *Salome, The Big Heat* 1953; *Sabrina, Phffft, It Should Happen to You* 1954; *The Man from Laramie, Female on the Beach, Queen Bee* 1955; *Autumn Leaves, The Solid Gold Cadillac* 1956; *The Rainmaker, Gunfight at the O.K. Corral, A Farewell to Arms* 1957; *Wild Is the Wind, The Matchmaker, Separate Tables* 1958; *Some Like It Hot, Last Train from Gun Hill* 1959; *Strangers When We Meet, The Magnificent Seven* 1960; *One-Eyed Jacks, Summer and Smoke* 1961; *How the West Was Won* (co-phot.) 1962; *Charade* 1963; *Father Goose, Sex and the Single Girl* 1964; *Inside Daisy Clover* 1965; *How to Steal a Million* 1966; *Hotel, The Flim Flam Man, Wait Until Dark* 1967; *Bob & Carol & Ted & Alice, Cactus Flower* 1969; *A Walk in the Spring Rain* 1970; *The Love Machine, Doctors' Wives* 1971; *Butterflies Are Free* 1972; *40 Carats* 1973.

Lang, Fritz. Director. *b.* Dec. 5, 1890, Vienna. *d.* 1976. Expected to become an architect, like his father, he attended a technical high school and later studied at the College of Technical Sciences of Vienna's Academy of Graphic Arts. He was unhappy, however, with the prospect of the career his family had chosen for him, and when he was 20 he ran away from home to study art in Munich and Paris. Returning to Paris in 1913, he painted watercolors, designed fashions, and drew cartoons for German newspapers. The following year, at the outbreak of WW I, he caught the last train to Vienna, evading

French police, and was conscripted as a private in the Austrian army. Wounded in action four times, he was discharged as a lieutenant in 1916. During his year-long convalescence in a Vienna hospital he acted in Red Cross stage productions and began writing short stories and screenplays. He sold several of these to Joe MAY and other German directors, and after leaving the hospital, he joined the Decla company in Berlin as a reader and story editor. Before long he had become a staff screenwriter and an occasional bit player, and in 1919 he turned out his first film as director, *Halbblut* (literally, "The Half-Breed"), from his own script about a man destroyed by the love of a woman, a theme to which he would repeatedly return in some of his later films.

Lang scored his first commercial success with his third film, *Die Spinnen/The Spiders* (1919 and 1920), a two-part adventure melodrama about master criminals aiming to dominate the world, a theme popular in German films of the period and another to which he would return several times. Because of his involvement with that film, Lang was unable to direct *Das Kabinett des Dr. Caligari/The Cabinet of Dr. Caligari,* a film assigned to him by producer Erich Pommer. Lang had participated in the preliminary script discussions and preproduction preparations, but the project was turned over to Robert Wiene. Lang's only contribution that was retained in the completed film, a classic of German expressionism, was the basic structural suggestion that the main expressionistic plot be sandwiched between a realistic prologue and epilogue. In 1920, Lang began collaborating on his screenplays with writer Thea von HARBOU, who became his wife in 1924. She would collaborate on all his films until 1932, often getting sole credit as screenwriter. In 1921, Lang scored his first critical success with *Der müde Tod,* variably released in the US as *Between Two Worlds* and *Beyond the Wall* and in the UK as *Destiny.* A three-episode allegory about a confrontation between Death and a girl's love and devotion, *Der müde Tod* (literally, "The Tired Death") revealed Lang's mastery of the film medium and especially his skill with architectural design and pictorial composition.

Lang scored another big success with his next film, *Dr. Mabuse der Spieler* (1922), also known as *Dr. Mabuse the Gambler,* or simply *Dr. Mabuse,* or *The Fatal Passions.* Shown on consecutive evenings in German theaters, in two parts each a full feature long, *Dr. Mabuse* was a darkly brooding thriller about an arch criminal who leads a gang of murderers and commits an assortment of dastardly deeds before shooting it out with the police in a climactic final sequence. It is inaccurate to describe *Dr. Mabuse* as representative of expressionism in films, although it did include some stylized action and painted sets. The film was shown in the US in a drastically cut version, as was the case with most of Lang's other German productions.

Die Nibelungen (1924), in two parts like *Dr. Mabuse,* derived its plot and inspiration from the 13th-century Siegfried legend that also inspired Richard Wagner's opera cycle 'Der Ring des Nibelungen.' According to Lang his film was an attempt to counteract the pessimistic spirit of the time by reaching out for Germany's legendary heritage and epic past. The first of the two parts, *Siegfried* (later re-released with sound as *Siegfrieds Tod*), enjoyed greater success than the second, *Kriemhilds Rache/Kriemhild's Revenge.*

In October of 1924, Lang came to the US for a visit of several weeks to observe motion picture production techniques in New York and Hollywood. He was detained for several hours aboard ship in New York Harbor. Gazing upon the towering Manhattan skyline, he conceived the idea for his next film, *Metropolis* (1927), a futuristic, visually compelling allegorical look at relations between capital and labor in a Big Brother society ruled by robots, antagonism, and fear. The concept and plot of *Metropolis* are rather naïve. Today many of the scenes seem silly and the ideas pretentious, but it is still an impressive monument to Lang's artistic vision and film craftsmanship, particularly his painter's eye for set design and pictorial composition and his ability to create and maintain atmosphere on the screen. *Metropolis* took nearly two years (1925–26) to complete, and by the time of its release early in 1927, it was the most expensive film ever produced in Germany. Its cost nearly bankrupted UFA, the country's largest film production company.

Lang formed his own company to produce his next film, *Spione/Spies* (1928), once again returning to the theme of a master criminal who aims to rule the world. The well-paced and visually exciting film reflected the spy scare that engulfed Europe in the years before WW II. He next tackled science fiction with *Die Frau im Mond* (1929), released in the US as *By Rocket to the Moon* and in the UK as *The Girl in the Moon* and also known as *The Woman on the Moon.* It was not a great success, but it anticipated a trend for space films. Lang refused to add a sound effects track to the film, and it was released as a silent production many months after the advent of sound. However, Lang used sound masterfully on his next production, *M* (1931), a psychological thriller based on the true case of a compulsive child murderer in Düsseldorf. Combining the elements of a crime melodrama and a factual documentary, and stylistically fusing expressionism and realism, *M* captured the terrifying atmosphere of a city besieged by fear and torn between the forces of order and mob violence. Many consider *M* Lang's greatest masterpiece.

Lang's social comment in *M* was followed by a political statement in *Das Testament des Dr. Mabuse/The Last Will of Dr. Mabuse/The Testament of Dr. Mabuse* (1933), an underrated sequel to *Dr. Mabuse der Spieler,* in which the director expressed his anti-Nazi feelings by thinly disguised means, including the feeding of Nazi slogans to the mouths of the film's most evil characters. Early in 1933 the film was banned by the Nazis. Lang was summoned to the office of Dr. Joseph Goebbels, Hitler's Minister of Propaganda, who apologetically informed Lang of the ban and to the director's utter astonishment extended him an offer from the Fuehrer himself to direct and supervise Nazi productions. But suspecting a trap and fearing that the Nazis would soon discover the Jewish background of his mother, Lang caught a train to France that very evening, leaving behind the bulk of his possessions and bank savings. Also left behind was Thea von Harbou, who divorced Lang in the same year and later wrote and directed films for the Third Reich's propaganda machine.

In Paris, Lang directed one film, an adaptation of Ferenc Molnar's *Liliom* (1934). In June of 1934 he was signed by producer David O. Selznick in London to a one-picture deal with MGM, and he sailed to the US, settling in Hollywood. In February of 1935, Lang received his first American citizenship papers. He spent more than a year at MGM doing virtually nothing professionally, but he used his enforced leisure to improve his command of English and his understanding of the American character and ways of life. His script for one project was rejected, but he turned his next, *Fury* (1936), into a relentlessly vivid drama about lynching which successfully penetrated the psychology of mob violence and personal vengeance. The critical success of the relatively low-budgeted film did not persuade MGM to extend the director's contract. Lang, who had been accustomed to exercising full authority on the set and to having nearly total control over his productions, found himself frequently at odds with the policymakers of the Hollywood studio system and in daily friction with hard-to-discipline American actors and crews.

Lang made his next film, *You Only Live Once* (1937), for independent producer Walter Wanger. Echoing *Fury*'s theme of social injustice and persecuted innocence, Lang expressed with uncharacteristically tender humanity the bitter irony of this story of a petty criminal who is accused of a crime he did not commit. Lang completed a three-film cycle on themes of social concern with *You and Me* (1938), which he produced himself for Paramount. Following two aborted projects, he signed with 20th Century-Fox and proved his versatility as a craftsman by directing two well-paced, entertaining Westerns. *The Return of Frank James* (1940) and *Western Union* (1941), and an exciting little thriller, *Man Hunt* (1941), about a British hunter who unsuccessfully stalks Hitler, then is himself hunted by the Gestapo.

Lang chose Berthold Brecht as his screenplay collaborator for *Hangmen Also Die* (1943), an anti-Nazi film he produced independently for release by United Artists. He then returned to another favorite theme, the ruinous effect of a man's lust for a woman, in *The Woman in the Window* (1944) and *Scarlet Street* (1945), the latter a remake of Renoir's *La Chienne. Ministry of Fear* (1944) was a gripping espionage thriller tingling with atmospheric suspense. But Lang's output in the following few years was disappointing. He returned to top form with *Rancho Notorious* (1952), which many consider his finest Western, and *The Big Heat* (1953), a tense and searing crime melodrama that brought Lang back to the familiar themes of sinister menace and personal revenge. The inexorability of fate and the destructive powers of lust were again dominant motifs in *Human Desire* (1954), Lang's somber remake of Renoir's *La Bête humaine/The Human Beast.* He first tackled CinemaScope with *Moonfleet* (1955), a high-seas period adventure about buccaneers, then returned to crime melodrama with *While the City Sleeps* (1956), Lang's favorite, next to *Fury,* among his own American films.

Lang's American period sadly ended with *Beyond a Reasonable Doubt* (1956), a crime drama with ironic plot twists. Production was fraught with frustration and bitter fights with the film's producers. For Lang it was the culmination of 20 years of endless clashes and bickering with studio heads, producers, actors, and crews.

In 1956, Lang went to India to prepare the groundwork for a period love story, *Taj-Mahal,* but the project was abandoned. In 1957 he accepted an offer from Germany to direct a two-part exotic adventure, *Der Tiger von Eschnapur* and *Das indische Grabmal* (1959), based on a script Lang and Thea von Harbou had written for Joe May back in 1921. The two parts, each an hour and 45 minutes long, were shown in the US as one mutilated, drastically abbreviated film, *Journey to the Lost City.* Lang remained in Germany, where he made his last film, *Die tausend Augen des Dr. Mabuse/The 1000 Eyes of Dr. Mabuse* (1960), an updated sequel to the adventures of his now-famous master criminal. In 1963, Lang played a substantial role, as himself, in Jean-Luc Godard's *Le Mépris/Contempt.* He later returned to the US and spent the rest of his years in retirement in his Beverly Hills home.

Fritz Lang brought to the screen a vision of a world largely populated by criminals, psychopaths, prostitutes, and maladjusted personalities, a deterministic world ruled by the inevitability of fate. It wasn't, however, his fascination with the psychopathology of violence, but the fascinating visual means he chose to express it that made him one of the creative giants in the history of both the German and American cinema.

FILMS: As screenwriter—*Die Hochzeit in Ekzentrik Klub, Hilde Warren und der Tod, Joe Debbs* (series) 1917; *Totentanz, Die Frau mit den Orchiden, Lilith und Ly* (Aus.), *Die Pest in Florenz* 1919; *Das indische Grabmal* (in two parts: *Die Sendung des Yoghi* and *Der Tiger von Eschnapur*; co-sc. with Thea von Harbou) 1921. As director: In Germany—*Halbblut* (also sc.), *Der Herr der Liebe* (also act.), *Die Spinnen/The Spiders* (Pt. I: *Der goldene See*; also sc.), *Harakiri* 1919; *Die Spinnen/The Spiders* (Pt. II: *Das Brillantenschiff*; also sc.), *Das wandernde Bild* (also co-sc. with Von Harbou), *Vier um die Frau* (also co-sc. with Von Harbou) 1920; *Der müde Tod/Between Two Worlds/Beyond the Wall/Destiny* (also co-sc. with von Harbou) 1921; *Dr. Mabuse der Spieler/Dr. Mabuse the Gambler/Dr. Mabuse/The Fatal Passions* (in two parts: *Spieler aus Leidenschaft/Ein Bild der Zeit* and *Inferno des Verbrechens /Inferno—Menschen der Zeit*; also co-sc. with von Harbou) 1922; *Die Nibelungen* (in two parts: *Siegfried/ Siegfrieds Tod* and *Kriemhilds Rache/Kriemhild's Revenge*; also co-sc. with von Harbou but uncredited as a screenwriter) 1924; *Metropolis* (also co-sc. with von Harbou but uncredited as a screenwriter) 1927; *Spione/Spies* (also co-sc. with von Harbou but uncredited as a screenwriter) 1928; *Die Frau im Mond/By Rocket to the Moon/The Girl in the Moon/The Woman on the Moon* (also co-sc. with von Harbou but uncredited as screenwriter) 1929; *M* (also co-sc. with von Harbou but uncredited as a screenwriter) 1931; *Das Testament des Dr. Mabuse/The Last Will of Dr. Mabuse/The Testament of Dr. Mabuse* (German- and French-language versions; also co-sc. with von Harbou but uncredited as a screenwriter) 1933. In France—*Liliom* (also co-sc. but uncredited as screenwriter) 1934. In the US—*Fury* (also co-sc.) 1936; *You Only Live Once* 1937; *You and Me* (also prod.) 1938; *The Return of Frank James* 1940; *Western Union, Man Hunt* 1941; *Hangmen Also Die* (also prod., co-sc.) 1943; *The Woman in the Window, Ministry of Fear* 1944; *Scarlet Street* (also prod.) 1945; *Cloak and Dagger* 1946; *Secret Beyond the Door* (also prod.) 1948; *House by the River, American Guerrilla in the Philippines* 1950; *Rancho Notorious, Clash by Night* 1952; *The Blue Gardenia, The Big Heat* 1953; *Human Desire* 1954; *Moonfleet* 1955; *While the City Sleeps, Beyond a Reasonable Doubt* 1956. In Germany—*Der Tiger von Eschnapur* and *Das indische Grabmal/Journey to the Lost City/Tiger of Bengal* (double feature released as one in the US and UK; also co-sc. but uncredited as screenwriter; Ger./Fr./It.) 1959; *Die tausend Augen des Dr. Mabuse/The 1000 Eyes of Dr. Mabuse* (also prod., co-sc.; Ger./Fr./It.) 1960.

Lang, Jennings. Producer, production executive. Born on May 28, 1915, in New York City. *ed.* St. John's U. A practicing lawyer, he went to Hollywood in 1938 and before long became established as one of the leading talent agents in the film industry. He joined the MCA agency in 1950 and became involved in the development and supervision of Universal's film and TV product. In the late 60s he was appointed executive producer of the company's features and has since produced or supervised several prestigious motion pictures. He married actress-singer Monica Lewis.

FILMS INCLUDE (as producer or executive producer): *Winning* 1969; *Tell Them Willie Boy Is Here, Puzzle of a Downfall Child* 1970; *Slaughterhouse Five, Pete 'n' Tillie* 1972; *Charley Varrick, Breezy* 1973; *Airport* 1975, *Earthquake, The Front* 1974; *Swashbuckler* 1976; *Airport '77, Rollercoaster* 1977; *House Calls, Nunzio* 1978; *Real Life, The Concorde—Airport '79* 1979; *Little Miss Marker, The Nude Bomb* 1980; *The Sting II* 1983; *Stick* 1985.

Lang, June. Actress. Born Winifred June Vlasek, on May 5, 1915, in Minneapolis. Decorative leading lady of Hollywood films of the 30s and early 40s, mainly for Fox. A former dancer, she began her film career in 1931 as June Vlasek, changing to June Lang in 1934. Her career was damaged by a brief marriage to convicted mobster John Roselli. She later married and divorced British actor Josh Ambler.

FILMS INCLUDE: As June Vlasek—*Young Sinners* 1931; *Chandu the Magician* 1932; *The Man Who Dared* 1933. As June Lang—*Music in the Air* 1934; *Bonnie Scotland* 1935; *The Country Doctor, Captain January, The Road to Glory, White Hunter* 1936; *Nancy Steele Is Missing, Wee Willie Winkie, Ali Baba Goes to Town* 1937; *International Settlement, Meet the Girls* 1938; *Zenobia, Captain Fury, For Love or Money* 1939; *Convicted Woman* 1940; *Redhead, The Deadly Game* 1941; *City of Silent Men, Footlight Serenade* 1942; *Flesh and Fantasy* 1943; *Lighthouse* 1947.

Lang, Matheson. Actor. *b.* May 15, 1879, Montreal, to Scottish parents. *d.* 1948. The son of a clergyman and a cousin of the Archbishop of Canterbury, he defied family tradition by becoming an actor in 1897, soon developing into a popular matinee idol on the London stage. He was one of the few prominent British theater personalities who ventured into films regularly in the silent days and played starring roles in many British productions from 1916 to the mid-30s. Autobiography: *Mr. Wu Looks Back* (1940).

FILMS INCLUDE: *The Merchant of Venice* 1916; *Masks and Faces, The Ware Case* 1917; *Victory and Peace* 1918; *Mr. Wu* 1919; *Carnival* 1921; *A Romance of Old Bagdad* 1922; *The Wandering Jew, Guy Fawkes* 1923; *Henry—King of Navarre, Slaves of Destiny* 1924; *The Secret Kingdom* 1925; *The Chinese Bungalow* 1926; *The King's Highway* 1927; *The Triumph of the Scarlet Pimpernel* 1928; *The Chinese Bungalow* (sound version) 1930; *Carnival* (sound version) 1931; *Channel Crossing* 1933; *Little Friend* 1934; *Royal Cavalcade, Drake of England, The Cardinal* 1935.

Lang, Stephen. Actor. Born July 11, 1952, in Queens, N.Y. *ed.* Swarthmore College. Powerful, emotionally charged leading and support player of stage, television, and film. His professional career began in 1976 at the Folger Theatre in Washington, D.C. He went on to gain critical acclaim in the 1984 Broadway revival of 'Death of a Salesman' as well as 'A Few Good Men'. Often seen on television, notably 'Crime Story' (1986–88), his numerous film roles have included the sexually confused labor leader in *Last Exit to Brooklyn* (1989).

FILMS INCLUDE: *Twice in a Lifetime* 1985; *Band of the Hand, Manhunter* 1986; *Project X* 1987; *Last Exit to Brooklyn* (W.Ger.) 1989; *The Hard Way, Another You* 1991; *Gettysburg, Guilty as Sin, Tombstone* 1993; *The Amazing Panda Adventure, Tall Tale* 1995; *Fire Down Below, The Shadow Conspiracy* 1997.

Lang, Walter. Director. *b.* Aug. 10, 1898, Memphis, Tenn. *d.* 1972. A former men's fashion illustrator and a supporting actor in stock, he produced and directed stage plays for a nitrate plant shortly after WW I and entered films in the early 20s as a clerk at the New York business office of a production company. After a period of apprenticeship as an assistant director at Hearst's Cosmopolitan Productions, he went to work for producer Mrs. Wallace Reid (Dorothy DAVENPORT), for whom he directed his first two films in 1925–26. Other silent films followed, mostly for small independent companies and Harry Cohn's fledgling studio, Columbia. Lang was a proficient director by the advent of the talkies but became discouraged by the technical imperfections of early sound and left films briefly for an unsuccessful art career in Paris. Back in Hollywood, he resumed directing for various companies and in the mid-30s became associated with 20th Century-Fox, the studio that would remain his home for the rest of his prolific career. During the 40s and 50s he directed some of the studio's glossiest family entertainment, including many lively musicals and amusing comedies. His films appealed to the popular taste and were often gaudy in their technicolor splendor, but they provided a generation of filmgoers with many hours of highly polished, unpretentious entertainment.

FILMS: *Red Kimono* 1925; *The Earth Woman, The Golden Web, Money to Burn* 1926; *The Ladybird, The Satin Woman* (also sc.), *Sally in Our Alley, By Whose Hand?, The College Hero* 1927; *The Night Flyer, Shadows of the Past, The Desert Bride* 1928; *The Spirit of Youth* 1929; *Hello Sister, Cock o' the Walk* (co-dir. with Roy William Neill), *The Big Fight, The Costello Case, Brothers* 1930; *Command Performance, Hell Bound, Women Go On Forever* 1931; *No More Orchids* 1932; *The Warrior's Husband* (also co-sc.), *Meet The Baron* 1933; *The Party's Over, Whom the Gods Destroy, The Mighty Barnum* 1934; *Carnival, Hooray for Love* 1935; *Love Before Breakfast* 1936; *Wife Doctor and Nurse, Second Honeymoon* 1937; *The Baroness and the Butler, I'll Give a Million* 1938; *The Little Princess* 1939; *The Blue Bird, Star Dust, The Great Profile, Tin Pan Alley* 1940; *Moon Over Miami, Weekend In Havana* 1941; *Song of the Islands, The Magnificent Dope* 1942; *Coney Island* 1943; *Greenwich Village* 1944; *State Fair* 1945; *Sentimental Journey, Claudia and David* 1946; *Mother Wore Tights, Sitting Pretty* 1947; *When My Baby Smiles at Me* 1948; *You're My Everything* 1949; *Cheaper By the Dozen, The Jackpot* 1950; *On the Riviera* 1951; *With a Song in My Heart* 1952; *Call Me Madam* 1953; *There's No Business Like Show Business* 1954; *The King and I* 1956; *Desk Set* 1957; *But Not for Me* 1959; *Can-Can* 1960; *The Marriage-Go-Round, Snow White and the Three Stooges* 1961.

Langan, Glenn. Actor. *b.* July 8, 1917, Denver. *d.* 1991. Tall, square-jawed leading man and second lead of Hollywood films of the 40s and 50s. In 1949 he married Adele JERGENS, his co-star in *The Treasure of Monte Cristo*.

FILMS INCLUDE: *The Return of Dr. X* 1939; *Riding High* 1943; *Four Jills in a Jeep, A Wing and a Prayer* 1944; *A Bell for Adano, Hangover Square* 1945; *Margie, Dragonwyck* 1946; *Forever Amber* 1947; *Fury at Furnace Creek, The Snake Pit* 1948; *The Treasure of Monte Cristo* 1949; *The Big Chase* 1954; *The Amazing Colossal Man* 1957; *Mutiny in Outer Space* 1965; *Chisum* 1970.

Langdon, Harry. Actor. *b.* June 15, 1884, Council Bluffs, Iowa. *d.* 1944. The son of Salvation Army officers, he had been a prop boy, a cartoonist, and a barber before joining a medicine show in Omaha. He spent the next 20 years traveling with minstrel shows, circuses, burlesque, and vaudeville, scoring a modest success with a comedy act called "Jimmy's New Car." Late in 1923 he joined Mack SENNETT and was immediately put to work in a rapid succession of two-reel comedies out of which gradually emerged his unique screen character. His baby face covered with the traditional white makeup of the pantomimist, Langdon represented naïveté at its most infantile. His screen character was that of the wide-eyed simpleton, clumsy in a childlike fashion and bewildered by the goings-on of the adult world surrounding him. He was even dressed like a kid, with a tightly buttoned outgrown jacket. At times, especially when confronted with an erotic situation, the babyish character assumed an eerie, almost depraved, quality.

Langdon's earliest films, handled by directors Erle Kenton and Roy Del Ruth, were quite routine, but several months after his debut his career received an enormous lift, thanks to the combined talents of director Harry EDWARDS and then-screenwriter and gagman Frank CAPRA. It was under their guidance that Langdon took his place among the Big Four of American silent screen comedy, along with Chaplin, Keaton, and Lloyd. In 1926, when Langdon moved over to Warner Bros., where he was given control over the production of his own films, he took Edwards and Capra along. Here he starred in three excellent feature-length comedies—*Tramp Tramp Tramp, The Strong Man,* and *Long Pants*—by far the best films of his career. The first was written by Capra and directed by Edwards; the last two were directed by Capra. But cocky with his own success, Langdon decided he could do without either Edwards or Capra and began writing and directing his own material, with disastrous results, and after several abortive ventures Warners terminated his contract.

At Warners, he managed to spend the entire budget of his first film ($150,000) before the first word of the script ever was written. Much of his own big salary went into alimony payments. But the most tragic aspect of Langdon's naïveté was his inability to comprehend the limitations of his own talent, and his stubborn refusal to vary his style to the requirements of changing tastes.

After the breakup with Warners, Langdon returned to vaudeville. When he went back to Hollywood, joining Hal Roach after a year-and-a-half absence from the screen, he found himself completely out of touch with the times. In his absence the sound era had begun and his pantomimic style of comedy was now sadly outdated. His stature and income rapidly declined, and he filed for bankruptcy in 1931. However, he continued to appear in films, both shorts and features, still dreaming of a spectacular comeback, until his death of a cerebral hemorrhage.

FILMS INCLUDE: *Picking Peaches, Smile Please, Shanghaied Lovers, The First 100 Years, The Luck of the Foolish, The Hansom Cabman, Feet of Mud* (all shorts) 1924; *The Sea Squaw, Boobs in the Woods, His Marriage Wow, Plain Clothes, Lucky Stars* (all shorts) 1925; *Saturday Afternoon* (short), *Soldier Man* (short), *Tramp Tramp Tramp, Ella Cinders* (bit), *The Strong Man* 1926; *Long Pants, His First Flame, Three's a Crowd* 1927; *The Chaser, Heart Trouble* 1928; *Skirt Shy* (short) 1929; *See America Thirst, A Soldier's Plaything* 1930; *The King* (short) 1932; *Hallelujah I'm a Bum, My Weakness* 1933; *Atlantic Adventure* 1935; *There Goes My Heart* 1938; *Zenobia* 1939; *Misbehaving Husbands* 1940; *Double Trouble* 1941; *House of Errors* 1942; *Block Busters, Hot Rhythm* 1944; *Swingin' on a Rainbow* 1945.

Lange, Hope. Actress. Born on Nov. 28, 1931, in Redding Ridge, Conn. The daughter of a musician and an actress, she made her Broadway debut at 12 in 'The Patriots' (1943). She later appeared in stock and on TV and made an auspicious screen debut in the role of Emma in *Bus Stop* (1956). The following year she was nominated for an Oscar for her performance in *Peyton Place.* An attractive blonde, she subsequently played leads in other films and TV dramas and starred in the TV series 'The Ghost and Mrs. Muir' (1968–70) and 'The New Dick Van Dyke Show' (1971–74). She won Emmys as best actress in a comedy in 1969 and 1970 for her performance in the former series. She returned to Broadway in 1977, after an absence of 34 years, in the bedroom comedy 'Same Time Next Year.' She returned to feature films, after a decade's absence, in 1983. Her first husband (1956–61) was actor Don MURRAY; her second is director Alan PAKULA. They married in 1963 and divorced in 1969, but remarried in 1986.

FILMS: *Bus Stop* 1956; *The True Story of Jesse James, Peyton Place* 1957; *The Young Lions, In Love and War* 1958; *The Best of Everything* 1959; *Wild in the Country, Pocketful of Miracles* 1961; *Love Is a Ball* 1963; *Jigsaw* 1968; *Death Wish* 1974; *I Am the Cheese* 1983; *The Prodigal* 1984; *A Nightmare on Elm Street Part 2: Freddy's Revenge* 1985; *Blue Velvet* 1986; *Tune in Tomorrow* 1990; *Clear and Present Danger* 1994; *Just Cause* 1995.

Lange, Jessica. Actress. Born on Apr. 20, 1949, in Cloquet, Minn. The daughter of a traveling salesman, she moved frequently in her youth. After attending the University of Minnesota for two years, she studied mime in Paris and danced for several months in the chorus of the Opera Comique. Returning to the US, she modeled in New York and was among many hopefuls screen-tested by producer Dino De Laurentiis for the lead feminine role in the remake of *King Kong* (1976). She got the part and was signed by De Laurentiis to a seven-year contract. A lovely, toothsome blonde, she emerged in the 80s as one of the American screen's finest actresses, a superb, intuitive interpreter of a wide range of roles. She won the best supporting actress Academy Award, as well as the New York Film Critics and National Society of Film Critics awards, for her performance in the comedy *Tootsie* (1982), and in the same year was nominated for another Oscar for her riveting portrayal of actress Frances Farmer in the film biography, *Frances.* In the following years, she was nominated for Academy Awards as best actress for *Country* (1984), *Sweet Dreams* (1985), and *Music Box* (1989). It was her performance as the neurotic, nymphomaniacal military wife in *Blue Sky* (1994) that brought yet another Academy Award, this time as best actress. She also excelled in a TV remake of 'Cat on a Hot Tin Roof'. In 1991, she starred on television in the acclaimed Hallmark Hall of Fame presentation *O Pioneers!* and, in 1992, made her Broadway debut as Blanche DuBois in 'A Streetcar Named Desire,' later recreating the role in London's West End in 1996–97. Early on, Lange was married briefly to Spanish photographer Paco Grande. She has a daughter by dancer-actor Mikhail BARYSHNIKOV and a daughter and son by playwright-actor Sam SHEPARD, with whom she shares a home.

FILMS: *King Kong* 1976; *All That Jazz* 1979; *How to Beat the High Cost of Living* 1980; *The Postman Always Rings Twice* 1981; *Frances* (as Frances Farmer), *Tootsie* 1982; *Country* 1984; *Sweet Dreams* 1985; *Crimes of the Heart* 1986; *Everybody's All-American* 1988; *Far North* 1988; *Music Box* 1989; *Men Don't Leave* 1990; *Cape Fear* 1991; *Night and the City* 1992; *Blue Sky* (release delayed from 1991) 1994; *Losing Isaiah, Rob Roy* 1995; *A Thousand Acres* 1997.

Langella, Frank. Actor. Born on Jan. 1, 1940, in Bayonne, N.J. Magnetic, versatile lead and character player of the American stage, screen, and TV. Addicted to acting from an early age, he studied drama at Syracuse University, and after performing in regional repertory and summer stock joined off-Broadway's Lincoln Center Repertory Company, making his New York debut in 'The Immoralist' (1963). Three successive Obie Awards in the mid-60s (for 'The Old Glory,' 'Good Day,' and 'The White Devil') led to roles in movies and on Broadway, where he won a Tony for his remarkable debut role as a slithering lizard in Edward Albee's 'Seascape' (1977). He became best known for the title role in the Broadway revival of 'Dracula', a role he reprised on film (1979). Primarily a man of the theater, he has had a sporadic but not unmemorable film career.

FILMS: *Diary of a Mad Housewife, The Twelve Chairs* 1970; *La Maison sur l'Arbre/The Deadly Trap* (Fr./It.) 1971; *The Wrath of the Gods* 1972; *Dracula* (title role) 1979; *Those Lips Those Eyes* 1980; *Sphinx* 1981; *The Men's Club* 1986; *Masters of the Universe* 1987; *And God Created Woman* 1988; *True Identity* 1991; *1492* 1992; *Dave* 1993; *Bad Company, Brain Scan, Junior* 1994; *Empire Records* 1995; *The Funeral, Trees Lounge* 1996.

Langford, Frances. Actress, singer. Born on Apr. 4, 1914, in Lakeland, Fla. A popular vocalist of the 30s and 40s, she played leads and supporting roles in many light Hollywood films, compensating for her limited acting ability with a caressing, melodious singing voice. She is best known for her radio work, as the star of her own show and as a regular on the Bob Hope WW II–period broadcasts. Her first husband (1938–55) was Jon HALL.

FILMS INCLUDE: *Every Night at Eight, Broadway Melody of 1936* 1935; *Collegiate, Palm Springs, Born to Dance* 1936; *The Hit Parade* 1937; *Hollywood Hotel* 1938; *Too Many Girls, Dreaming Out Loud* 1940; *All-American Co-Ed* 1941; *Mississippi Gambler, Yankee Doodle Dandy* 1942; *Cowboy in Manhattan, This Is the Army, Follow the Band, Never a Dull Moment* 1943; *The Girl Rush, Dixie Jamboree* 1944; *Radio Stars on Parade* 1945; *The Bamboo Blonde* 1946; *Beat the Band* 1947; *Make Mine Laughs, Deputy Marshal* 1949; *Purple Heart Diary* 1951; *The Glenn Miller Story* (as herself) 1954.

Langley, Noel. Playwright, screenwriter, director. *b.* Dec. 25, 1911, Durban, South Africa. *d.* 1980. The author of many stage plays, several of which have been produced on Broadway, he began writing Hollywood screenplays in the late 30s. After the conclusion of his WW II service, he settled in London, where he resumed writing screenplays and occasionally also directed.

FILMS INCLUDE (as screenwriter, alone or in collaboration): In the US—*Maytime* 1937; *The Wizard of Oz* 1939; *Florian* 1940; *Unexpected Uncle* 1941. In the UK—*They Made Me a Fugitive* 1947; *Edward My Son* (co-play basis only), *Adam and Evelyne/Adam and Evelyn* 1949; *Trio* 1950; *Scrooge/A Christmas Carol, Tom Brown's School Days* 1951; *Ivanhoe* (US/UK), *The Prisoner of Zenda* (US), *The Pickwick Papers* (also dir.) 1952; *Our Girl Friday/The Adventures of Sadie* (also dir.) 1953; *The Knights of the Round Table* (US/UK), *Svengali* (also dir.) 1954. In the US—*The Search for Bridey Murphy* (also dir.), *The Vagabond King* 1956; *Snow White and the Three Stooges* 1961.

Langlois, Henri. Archivist. *b.* Nov. 13, 1914, Smyrna (Izmir), Turkey. *d.* 1977. In Paris from childhood, he began collecting old films while still in high school. In 1935 he founded the Cercle du Cinéma, a small club devoted to viewing and discussing film classics. The following year he established, with Georges FRANJU, the CINÉMATHÈQUE FRANÇAISE, a film archive, with only ten feature films. With almost manic enthusiasm he began collecting further films from every available source, saving thousands of them from destruction or loss. A whole generation of *cinéastes* and filmmakers was brought up in the darkness of the Cinémathèque's screening rooms. Such New Wave directors as Godard, Truffaut, Chabrol, and Demy proudly call themselves "Children of the Cinémathèque."

Over the years, the Cinémathèque grew from a small private collection into a government-subsidized institution, with a collection of nearly 60,000 films, many of them rare, and three exhibition halls. Langlois's reputation spread worldwide. But his autocratic rule of the archives and his eccentric working methods irritated many influential Frenchmen, especially in government circles. In 1968, when French Minister of Culture André Malraux tried to replace him as head of the Cinémathèque, by canceling the government's subsidy to the archives, the city of Paris rallied to block the attempt, and police had to be called to quell street riots. Film directors in the US, the USSR, and many other countries on both sides of the Iron Curtain wired Langlois their support, and studios threatened to invoke their copyrights to restrain the archive from showing their films. The government of France finally gave in to the international pressure, and Langlois was reinstated. In 1970 he organized festive screenings at New York's Metropolitan Museum of 70 films from his collection, and announced plans for a permanent American branch of the Cinémathèque Française. In the following years, he spent much of his time in New York, attempting to set up the American Cinémathèque in association with the City Center, but he died of a heart attack before his ambitious plan could be realized. In the 1974 Oscar ceremonies (for 1973) Langlois received an Honorary Academy Award "for his devotion to the art of film, his massive contribution in preserving its past, and his unswerving faith in its future."

Lanoux, Victor. Actor. Born in 1936, in France. Leading man and character player of French films. A former cabaret, then stage performer, he has specialized on the screen in tough types, particularly mean cops and vicious criminals. But he is best remembered in the US as the romantic lead in Tachella's box-office hit, *Cousin, Cousine* (1976).

FILMS INCLUDE: *La Vieille Femme indigne/The Shameless Old Lady* 1964; *Tu seras terriblement gentile/You Only Love Once* 1968; *Elle court elle court la Banlieue* 1972; *Deux Hommes dans la Ville/Two Men in Town/Two Against the Law* 1973; *Folle á tuer, Adieu Poulet/The French Detective* 1975; *Cousin Cousine, Un Eléphant ça trompe enorment/Pardon Mon Affaire, Une Femme á sa Fenêtre/A Woman at Her Window* 1976; *Servante et Maîtresse/Servant and Mistress, La Passé simple, Nous irons tous au Paradis/We Will All Meet in Paradise, Un Moment d'égarement/One Wild Moment* 1977; *La Carapate* 1978; *Les Chiens, Un si joli Village/Investigation, Au bout du bout du Banc/Make Room for Tomorrow* 1979; *Retour en Force* 1980; *Une Sale Affaire, La Revanche* 1981; *Boulevard des Assassins, Y a-t-il un Français dans la Salle?* 1982; *Un Dimanche de Flic, Stella* 1983; *Louisiane, Canicule, Les Voleur de la Nuit/Thieves After Dark, La Smala, La Triche* 1984; *National Lampoon's European Vacation* (bit; US) 1985; *Le Lieu du Crime/Scene of the Crime* 1986; *Sale Destin* 1987; *Venezia Rosso Sangue* (It./Fr.) 1989.

Lansbury, Angela. Actress. Born on Oct. 16, 1925, in London. The granddaughter of a Labour Party leader and daughter of stage and screen actress Moyna MacGill, she began training for the stage in childhood. In 1940, with London under the German blitz, she continued her drama studies in New York, supporting herself as a salesgirl. In 1943, following a brief summer engagement in a Montreal nightclub, she went to Hollywood and was signed by MGM to a long-term contract. She was nominated for the best supporting actress Oscar for her first role, in *Gaslight* (1944), and subsequently received nominations twice more, for *The Picture of Dorian Gray* (1945) and *The Manchurian Candidate* (1962). Following the early years of her career, when she often played the second lead or vixenish other woman, she became typecast as a domineering woman, often much older than she really was. She seldom got top billing, but she won wide respect for her professionalism and has always been quite popular with the public. Later in her career she played mothers, often to actors her own age. One of her most memorable performances was in *The Manchurian Candidate,* in which she played the mother of Laurence Harvey, only three years her junior. Frequently on Broadway from the late 50s through the late 70s, she scored personal hits with 'A Taste of Honey' (1960) and won Tony Awards for 'Mame' (1966), 'Dear World' (1969), 'Gypsy' (1975), and 'Sweeney Todd' (1979).

In 1984, Miss Lansbury began a new phase in her successful career, when she undertook the role of Jessica Fletcher (patterned after Agatha Christie's Miss Marple) in the hit TV mystery series 'Murder, She Wrote.' It remained one of the most watched programs through the mid-90s, widely increasing her celebrity to the American public. She has often hosted the Tony Awards and also the Emmys, doing so with wit and grace. She created and produced *Positive Moves* (1988), an exercise and lifestyle videotape cassette accompanied by a book. Briefly (for nine months in 1945–46) married to actor Richard CROMWELL, Miss Lansbury has been married since 1949 to Peter Shaw, who manages her career. They have three children and a number of grandchildren. Her younger twin brothers, Edgar and Bruce Lansbury (*b.* Jan. 12, 1930, London), are producers.

FILMS: *Gaslight, National Velvet* 1944; *The Picture of Dorian Gray* (as Sybil Vane) 1945; *The Harvey Girls, The Hoodlum Saint, Till the Clouds Roll By* 1946; *The Private Affairs of Bel Ami* (as Clotilde de Marelle) 1947; *If Winter Comes, Tenth Avenue Angel, State of the Union, The Three Musketeers* (as Queen Anne) 1948; *The Red Danube, Samson and Delilah* 1949; *Kind Lady* 1951; *Mutiny* 1952; *Remains to Be Seen* 1953; *A Lawless Street, The Purple Mask* 1955; *Please Murder Me, The Court Jester* 1956; *The Key Man/A Life at Stake* (UK) 1957; *The Long Hot Summer, The Reluctant Debutante* 1958; *Summer of the 17th Doll/Season of Passion* (Austral./UK) 1959; *The Dark at the Top of the Stairs, A Breath of Scandal* 1960; *Blue Hawaii* 1961; *All Fall Down, The Manchurian Candidate* 1962; *In the Cool of the Day* 1963; *The World of Henry Orient* 1964; *Dear Heart, The Greatest Story Ever Told, The Amorous Adventures of Moll Flanders, Harlow* (Carroll Baker version) 1965; *Mister Buddwing* 1966; *Something for Everyone* 1970; *Bedknobs and Broomsticks* 1971; *Death on the Nile* (UK) 1978; *The Lady Vanishes* (UK) 1979; *The Mirror Crack'd* (UK) 1980; *The Last Unicorn* (v/o) 1982; *The Pirates of Penzance* 1983; *The Company of Wolves* (UK) 1985; *Beauty and the Beast* (voice) 1992.

Lansing, Joi. Actress. *b.* Joyce Wassmansdoff, Apr. 6, 1928, Salt Lake City. *d.* 1972. Busty blonde leading lady and supporting player of Hollywood films of the 50s; typically in provocative secondary roles. She died of cancer at 44. Her first (1951–53) husband was actor Lance Fuller.

FILMS INCLUDE: *The Counterfeiters, Easter Parade* 1948; *Take Me Out to the Ball Game, Neptune's Daughter, The Girl from Jones Beach* 1949; *On the Riviera, Two Tickets to Broadway* 1951; *Singin' in the Rain, The Merry Widow* 1952; *The French Line* 1954; *Son of Sinbad* 1955; *The Brave One, Hot Cars* 1956; *Touch of Evil* 1958; *A Hole in the Head, It Started with a Kiss* 1959; *The Atomic Submarine, Who Was That Lady?* 1960; *Marriage on the Rocks* 1965; *Hillbillys in a Haunted House* 1967; *Bigfoot* 1970.

Lansing, Robert. Actor. Born Robert Brown, on June 5, 1928, in San Diego. Husky leading man of Hollywood films. On screen from the late 50s. He also starred in such TV action series as '87th Precinct' (1961–62), 'Twelve O'Clock High' (1964–65), and 'The Man Who Never Was' (1966–67), and played supporting roles in 'Automan' (1983–84), and 'The Equalizer' (from 1985).

FILMS INCLUDE: *The 4-D Man* 1959; *The Pusher* 1960; *A Gathering of Eagles, Under the Yum Yum Tree* 1963; *An Eye for an Eye, Namu the Killer Whale* 1966; *It Takes All Kinds* (US/Austral.) 1969; *The Grissom Gang* 1971; *Wild in the Sky/Black Jack* 1972; *Bittersweet Love* 1976; *False Face, Empire of the Ants* 1977; *Acapulco Gold* 1978; *Island Claws* 1981; *The Nest, After School/Private Tutor* 1988; *Blind Vengeance* 1990.

Lansing, Sherry. Producer, executive. Born on July 31, 1944, in Chicago. A graduate of Northwestern University, she taught math, English, and drama in a Los Angeles high school before breaking into films as an actress in 1970. Although attractive enough to model and appear in a couple of features and many TV shows, her intelligence and ambition soon drove her behind the cameras. After two years as a reader at a small studio, she joined Talent Associates in 1974 as an executive in charge of West Coast development. A year later she moved to MGM as a story editor and within two years became the studio's vice president of creative affairs. Late in 1977 she joined Columbia as vice president in charge of production, and in that capacity oversaw the manufacture of such hits as *Kramer vs. Kramer* and *The China Syndrome.* In 1980 she reached the pinnacle of her career when she was appointed president of 20th Century-Fox, becoming the first woman ever to hold the venerable position of a studio head. But getting increasingly restless over distancing herself from the actual filmmaking process, she resigned the post in 1982 to form Jaffe-Lansing Productions, an independent company with Stanley R. JAFFE. They went on to produce several prestigious box-office hits. She is currently head of production at Paramount.

FILMS INCLUDE: As actress—*Loving, Rio Lobo* 1970. As producer (or executive producer, alone or in collaboration)—*Racing with the Moon, Firstborn* 1984; *Fatal Attraction* 1987; *The Accused* 1988; *Black Rain* 1989; *School Ties* 1992; *Indecent Proposal* 1993.

Lantz, Walter. Animator, cartoon film producer. *b.* Apr. 27, 1900, New Rochelle, N.Y. *d.* 1994. *ed.* Art Students League. A former newspaper cartoonist, he began his career as an animator at the BRAY studios in New York, working with Isadore Klein and Gregory LA CAVA on the "Katzenjammer Kids," "Mutt and Jeff," "Happy Hooligan," and "Krazy Kat" animated cartoons. He later worked for Disney, Universal, and his own production company and created several popular cartoon characters, most notably Woody Woodpecker. He received an honorary Academy Award in the 1979 Oscar ceremony "in recognition of his unique animated motion pictures and especially his creation of Woody Woodpecker."

Lanza, Mario. Singer, actor. *b.* Alfred Arnold Coccozza, Jan. 31, 1921, Philadelphia. *d.* 1959. The son of a disabled veteran and a seamstress, he readily took to singing lessons as a child but was less interested in academic studies and dropped out of high school to work in his grandfather's wholesale grocery business. In 1942 he gained an audition with conductor Serge Koussevitzky; this resulted in a scholarship and an appearance at the Berkshire Summer Festival in Tanglewood. He was signed by Columbia for a concert tour, but it was interrupted by WW II service. After his discharge he was signed to a film contract by MGM and starred in a number of tailor-made musical vehicles. For a while Lanza enjoyed great popularity, thanks to a combination of a muscular appearance and a powerful, if not truly disciplined, singing voice. He reached his peak in *The Great Caruso* (1951), in which he portrayed the legendary tenor. But his meteoric rise was soon followed by a rapid decline. A highly volatile personality, an alcohol and barbiturate problem, and a constant bout with obesity helped ruin his career. He was reduced to minor films at the time of his death at 38 of a heart attack at a Rome clinic. The city of Philadelphia named a park after him.

FILMS: *That Midnight Kiss* 1949; *The Toast of New Orleans* 1950; *The Great Caruso* (title role) 1951; *Because You're Mine* 1952; *The Student Prince* (v/o, dubbing Edmund Purdom) 1954; *Serenade* 1956; *The Seven Hills of Rome* (and Italian-language vers., *Arrivederci Roma*) 1958; *Serenade einer prossen Liebe/For the First Time* (Ger./It./US) 1959.

LaPaglia, Anthony. Actor. Born in 1959 in Adelaide, Australia. Likeable character actor and lead seen in ethnic urban roles, often policemen. Upon moving to the US in 1984, he left teaching to pursue an acting career. Since 1989, he has worked steadily in feature films and television.

FILMS INCLUDE: *Slaves of New York* 1989; *Betsy's Wedding, Mortal Sins, Dangerous Obsession, Killer, One Good Cop* 1990; *He Said/She Said, Keeper of the City, 29th Street* 1991; *Innocent Blood, Whispers in the Dark* 1992; *The Custodian, So I Married an Axe Murderer* 1993; *The Client,*

Lucky Break 1994; *Brilliant Lies, Commandments, Paperback Romance* 1997.

lap dissolve. See DISSOLVE.

La Plante, Laura. Actress. Born on Nov. 1, 1904, in St. Louis, Mo. She entered films at 15, playing bit parts in CHRISTIE Comedies. By the early 20s she was Universal's top feminine star, heading the cast of numerous films, initially in Westerns, opposite Hoot Gibson and other cowboy heroes, then in comedies and melodramas. Billed as the girl-next-door type, she was at her finest in social comedies but is best remembered as the heroine of the spooky gothic melodrama sprinkled with humor *The Cat and the Canary* (silent version, 1927) and the dramatic part of Magnolia in *Show Boat* (1929). After divorcing director William SEITER and marrying producer Irving Asher, she retired from the screen, in the early 30s, reappearing only twice in character parts.

FILMS INCLUDE: *The Great Gamble/The Big Plunge* (serial) 1919; *The Old Swimmin' Hole, 813, The Big Round-Up, Play Square* 1921; *Perils of the Yukon* (serial), *The Wall Flower* 1922; *The Ramblin' Kid, Dead Game, Burning Words, Shootin' for Love, Out of Luck* 1923; *Ride for Your Life, Sporting Youth, Excitement, The Dangerous Blonde, Young Ideas, Butterflies, The Last Worker* 1924; *Smouldering Fires, Dangerous Innocence, The Teaser* 1925; *The Beautiful Cheat, The Midnight Sun, Skinner's Dress Suit, Poker Faces, Her Big Night, Butterflies in the Rain* 1926; *The Love Thrill, Beware of Widows, The Cat and the Canary, Silk Stockings* 1927; *Thanks for the Buggy Ride, Finders Keepers, Home James* 1928; *The Last Warning, Scandal, Show Boat* (as Magnolia), *The Love Trap, Hold Your Man* 1929; *Captain of the Guard, The King of Jazz* 1930; *Lonely Wives, God's Gift to Women, Arizona/Men Are Like That* 1931; *Little Mister Jim* 1946; *Spring Reunion* 1957.

Lardner, Ring, Jr. Screenwriter. Born Ringgold Wilmer Lardner, Jr., on Aug. 19, 1915, in Chicago. Son of the celebrated humorist, he dropped out of Princeton to work briefly as a reporter with the New York *Daily Mirror.* Shortly after, he set out for Hollywood, where he worked in Selznick's publicity department. Gradually he moved into screenwriting, becoming first an uncredited script doctor. In 1942 he won an Academy Award for collaborating on *Woman of the Year.* A member of the HOLLYWOOD TEN, he was sentenced in the late 40s to a year's imprisonment for contempt of Congress for refusing to cooperate with the House Un-American Activities Committee. Blacklisted after his release, he was forced to work "underground" or abroad, using various pseudonyms. His official onscreen rehabilitation did not come until the mid-60s. In 1970 he provided the Oscar-winning script for the highly successful black-comedy film *M*A*S*H.* In 1976 he published a book of memoirs about his illustrious family, *The Lardners.* He wrote the novels *The Ecstacy of Owen Muir* and *All for Love.* In 1988 he received the Writers Guild's Laurel Award.

FILMS: *A Star Is Born, Nothing Sacred* (both co-sc. uncredited) 1937; *Meet Dr. Christian* (co-sc.) 1939; *The Courageous Dr. Christian* (co-story, co-sc.) 1940; *Arkansas Judge* (co-adapt.) 1941; *Woman of the Year* (co-story, co-sc.) 1942; *The Cross of Lorraine* (co-sc.) 1943; *Marriage Is a Private Affair, Laura* (both co-sc., uncredited), *Tomorrow the World* (co-sc.) 1944; *Cloak and Dagger* (co-sc.) 1946; *Forever Amber* (co-sc.) 1947; *Britannia Mews/The Forbidden Street* 1949; *Swiss Tour/Four Days Leave* (dial.) 1950; *The Big Night* (co-sc., uncredited) 1951; *Virgin Island* (co-sc., under pseudonym) 1959; *A Breath of Scandal* (co-sc., uncredited) 1960; *The Cardinal* (co-sc., uncredited) 1963; *The Cincinnati Kid* (co-sc.) 1965; *M*A*S*H* 1970; *La Maison sous les Arbres/The Deadly Trap* (co-sc., uncredited; Fr.), *La Mortadella* (co-sc., 1972 English-language vers. only, *Lady Liberty*) 1971; *The Greatest* 1977.

La Rocque, Rod. Actor. *b.* Roderick la Rocque de la Rour, Nov. 29, 1896, Chicago. *d.* 1969. Tall, dashing matinee idol of the silent screen, he starred in several De Mille social comedies. So great was his popularity in the 20s that his wedding to Vilma BANKY in 1927 was turned into a Hollywood spectacular personally supervised by his discoverer, producer Samuel GOLDWYN. La Rocque made a successful transition to talkies, playing leading, then supporting roles into the early 40s. He then retired from the screen for a successful career as a real estate broker.

FILMS INCLUDE: *The Alster Case* 1915; *Efficiency Edgar's Courtship, The Dream Doll* 1917; *Ruggles of Red Gap, Let's Get a Divorce, Money Mad, A Perfect Lady, Hidden Fires, The Venus Model* 1918; *Love and the Woman, Miss Crusoe* 1919; *Easy to Get, The Stolen Kiss, The Garter Girl, Life* 1920; *Paying the Piper, Suspicious Wives* 1921; *Slim Shoulders, What's Wrong with the Women?, Notoriety, The Challenge* 1922; *Jazzmania, The French Doll, The Ten Commandments* 1923; *Phantom Justice, A Society Scandal, Triumph, Code of the Sea, Feet of Clay, Forbidden Paradise* 1924; *The Golden Bed, Night Life of New York, The Coming of Amos, Wild Wild Susan, Braveheart* 1925; *Red Dice, Bachelor Brides, Gigolo, The Cruise of the Jasper B* 1926; *Resurrection* (as Prince Dimitri Nekhludoff), *The Fighting Eagle* 1927; *Stand and Deliver, Hold 'Em Yale!/At Yale, Captain Swagger, Love Over Night* 1928; *The One Woman Idea, The Man and the Moment, Our Modern Maidens, The Delightful Rogue, The Locked Door* 1929; *Beau Bandit, One Romantic Night, Let Us Be Gay* 1930; *S.O.S. Eisberg/S.O.S. Iceberg* (Ger./US) 1933; *Mystery Woman* 1935; *The Preview Murder Mystery, Till We Meet Again* 1936; *The Shadow Strikes* (as The Shadow) 1937; *Taming the Wild, International Crime* 1938; *The Hunchback of Notre Dame* 1939; *Beyond Tomorrow, Dark Streets of Cairo* 1940; *Meet John Doe* 1941.

Larsen, Keith. Actor. Born on June 17, 1925, in Salt Lake City. Square-jawed leading man and supporting player of American films and TV. A former tennis pro, he entered the industry in the early 50s and appeared mostly in action second features. He also co-starred in the TV adventure series 'The Hunter' (1954), 'Brave Eagle' (1955–56), 'Northwest Passage' (1958–59), and 'The Aquanauts' (1960–61). He occasionally also directed. In 1960 he married actress Vera MILES.

FILMS INCLUDE: *Operation Pacific* 1951; *Flat Top, Hiawatha* 1952; *Fort Vengeance, Son of Belle Starr* 1953; *Arrow in the Dust* 1954; *Chief Crazy Horse, Wichita, Desert Sands* 1955; *Last of the Badmen, Apache Warrior* 1957; *Women of the Prehistoric Planet* 1966; *Mission Batangas* (also dir., prod., sc.) 1968; *Trap on Cougar Mountain* (also dir.) 1972.

LaShelle, Joseph. Director of photography. *b.* 1905, Los Angeles. *d.* 1989. Although trained as an electrical engineer, he entered films in 1923, as a lab assistant, and in 1925 moved up to assistant cameraman. After working as a camera operator on such Fox productions as *How Green Was My Valley* (1941) and *The Song of Bernadette* (1943), he was promoted to director of photography in 1943 and won an Academy Award the following year for the cinematography of *Laura* (1944). He worked on many other major Hollywood productions, excelling in both black-and-white and color cinematography and gaining nine Oscar nominations.

FILMS INCLUDE: *Rocking Moon* (co-phot.) 1925; *Whispering Smith* (co-phot.) 1926; *Happy Land* 1943; *Laura* 1944; *Hangover Square, A Bell for Adano* 1945; *Cluny Brown, Claudia and David* 1946; *The Late George Apley, The Foxes of*

Harrow 1947; *Come to the Stable, The Fan* 1949; *Under My Skin, The Jackpot, Mister 880* 1950; *The 13th Letter* 1951; *Les Miserables* 1952; *My Cousin Rachel* 1953; *River of No Return* 1954; *Marty* 1955; *The Conqueror* 1956; *The Bachelor Party* 1957; *The Long Hot Summer, The Naked and the Dead* 1958; *Career* 1959; *The Apartment* 1960; *How the West Was Won* (co-phot.) 1962; *Kiss Me Stupid* 1964; *Seven Women* 1965; *The Fortune Cookie* 1966; *Barefoot in the Park* 1967; *80 Steps to Jonah* 1969.

Lasky, Jesse, Jr. Screenwriter. *b.* Sept. 19, 1908, New York City. *d.* 1988. The son of Jesse L. LASKY, he wrote several novels, volumes of poetry, and plays as well as many screenplays, often for C. B. DE MILLE. He divided the last 25 years of his life between residences in London and Salta de Agua, Spain, with his wife and frequent collaborator Barbara Carlton, who wrote under the pseudonym Pat Silver. Autobiography: *Whatever Happened to Hollywood?* (1974).

FILMS INCLUDE: *Coming Out Party, The White Parade* 1934; *Secret Agent* (co-dial. only; UK) 1936; *Land of Liberty* (doc.), *Union Pacific* 1939; *North West Mounted Police* 1940; *Reap the Wild Wind* 1942; *Attack!—The Battle of New Britain* (doc.) 1944; *Appointment in Tokyo* (doc.) 1945; *Unconquered* 1947; *Samson and Delilah* 1949; *Mask of the Avenger, Lorna Doone* 1951; *The Brigand* 1952; *Salome* (story only), *Mission Over Korea* 1953; *Hell and High Water* 1954; *The Ten Commandments* 1956; *The Buccaneer* 1958; *John Paul Jones* 1959; *Seven Women from Hell* 1961; *Land Raiders* 1970; *An Ace up My Sleeve* (UK) 1975; *Crime and Passion* 1976; *Bulldance/ Forbidden Sun* (UK) 1989.

Lasky, Jesse L. Production executive, producer. *b.* Sept. 13, 1880, San Francisco. *d.* 1958. He worked briefly as a reporter before starting an abortive adventure as a participant in the Alaska gold rush. A gifted musician, he next showed up in Hawaii as a bandleader. Returning to the mainland, he was joined by his sister Blanche in a cornet duo act in vaudeville. Gradually he moved into the business side of vaudeville as a promoter and impresario. In 1913 he joined with his brother-in-law Samuel Goldfish (later GOLDWYN) and a friend, Cecil B. DE MILLE, in the formation of the Jesse L. Lasky Feature Play Company, of which he became president. The company scored an immediate triumph with its first film, *The Squaw Man* (1914), the first large-scale Western, a milestone production that helped turn the sleepy town of Hollywood, Calif., into a household word. In 1916 the company merged with Adolph Zukor's FAMOUS PLAYERS to form the Famous Players–Lasky Corporation. Zukor was named president and Lasky vice president in charge of production. Eventually, following a number of mergers and corporate realignments, the company became Paramount, one of Hollywood's major studios.

An amiable and considerate man, Lasky was among Hollywood's better liked production executives. In 1932, when Paramount, like most other studios, felt the pinch of the Depression, he was ousted from his post and became an independent producer, working for Fox, Warners, and RKO, among other corporations. In 1935 he was Mary PICKFORD's partner in the short-lived Pickford-Lasky corporation, of which he was president. In the late 30s he produced a radio talent show. In the late 50s, heavily in debt to the Bureau of Internal Revenue, he returned to Paramount to produce a film that he hoped would straighten out his finances. But he died just before the project got under way. Autobiography: *I Blow My Horn.* He was the father of Jesse LASKY, Jr. and assistant director William Lasky (1922–85).

FILMS INCLUDE (as independent producer): *Berkeley Square, The Power and the Glory, Zoo in Budapest* 1933; *The White Parade* 1934; *Helldorado, The Gay Deception* 1935; *Sergeant York* 1941; *The Adventures of Mark Twain* 1944; *Rhapsody in Blue* 1945; *Without Reservations* 1946; *The Miracle of the Bells* 1948.

Lassally, Walter. Director of photography. Born on Dec. 18, 1926, in Berlin. He came to England as a refugee after the outbreak of WW II and after working briefly as a camera assistant on industrial films became a clapper boy on features in 1945. Active in Britain's Free Cinema movement of the 50s, he became the favorite cameraman of such directors as Lindsay Anderson, Karel Reisz, and Greece's Michael Cacoyannis. In the 60s he photographed with sensitivity and technical skill several of Tony Richardson's films. Lassally won an Academy Award for the cinematography of the Greek-American production *Zorba the Greek* (1964). Declining to take advantage of his growing prestige, Lassaly generally continued to shun big commercial ventures and lent his talent to smaller-budget independent productions, including a number of Merchant-Ivory films.

FILMS INCLUDE: *Sunday by the Sea* (short) 1953; *Thursday's Children* (short), *Bow Bells* (short), *A Girl in Black* (Gr.) 1956; *Every Day Except Christmas* (short), *A Matter of Dignity* (Gr.) 1957; *We Are the Lambeth Boys* (short) 1959; *Maddalena* (Gr.), *Beat Girl/Wild for Kicks* 1960; *Electra* (Gr.), *A Taste of Honey* 1961; *The Loneliness of the Long Distance Runner* 1962; *Tom Jones* 1963; *Psyche 59, Zorba the Greek* (US/Gr.) 1964; *The Day the Fish Came Out* (US/Gr.) 1967; *Oedipus the King, Joanna* 1968; *Three Into Two Won't Go, The Adding Machine* (US/UK) 1969; *Something for Everyone* (US) 1970; *Savages* (US/UK) 1972; *Visions of Eight* (Arthur Penn episode), *Happy Mother's Day—Love George* (US) 1973; *The Wild Party* (US) 1975; *Ansichten einer Clowns/The Clown* (Ger.), *Pleasantville* (doc.; US) 1976; *Shenanigans* (US) 1977; *Die Frau Gegenüber* (Ger.) 1978; *Hullabaloo Over Georgie and Bonnie's Pictures, The Pilot* (US) 1979; *The Blood of Hussain* 1980; *Engel aus Eisen* (Ger.), *Memoirs of a Survivor* 1981; *Heat and Dust, Private School* (US) 1983; *The Bostonians* 1984; *The Deceivers, The Perfect Murder* (Ind.) 1988; *Kamilla* (Den.) 1989; *The Ballad of the Sad Café* 1991.

Lasser, Louise. Actress. Born on Apr. 11, 1939, in New York City. Offbeat comedienne of the American stage, TV, and films. After three years of political science studies at Brandeis University, she trained for the stage under Sanford Meisner and in 1964 joined the cast of Elaine May's improvisational revue 'The Third Ear.' She later appeared in several Broadway and off-Broadway productions. In 1966 she married Woody ALLEN and appeared in several of his early films. They divorced in 1970. In 1976–77 she achieved great popularity as the flaky star of TV's hit parody of soap operas 'Mary Hartman, Mary Hartman.'

FILMS: *What's New Pussycat?* 1965; *What's Up Tiger Lily?* 1966; *Bananas, Such Good Friends* 1971; *Everything You Always Wanted to Know About Sex but Were Afraid to Ask* 1972; *Slither* 1973; *In God We Trust* 1980; *Crimewave, The Perils of P.K.* 1986; *Nightmare at Shadow Woods, Surrender* 1987; *Sing, Rude Awakening* 1989; *Modern Love, Frankenhooker* 1990; *Layin' Low* 1996.

Lassie. Canine star of the collie breed who had long been a favorite of young film and TV audiences. The original screen Lassie, an intelligent and good-looking male dog actually named Pal, was recruited from among 300 candidates to play the heroine of the 1943 screen adaptation of Eric Knight's novel *Lassie Come Home.* The great commercial success of the picture and the personal appeal of its canine star (one reviewer, apparently moved by Lassie's performance, called him/her "Greer Garson in Furs") led to six feature sequels through 1951, in which four different descendants of Pal played the lead role. All have been males, since in the dog kingdom males tend to be better looking if less intelligent than females. There was also a 'Lassie' radio show which premiered on ABC in 1947. The original Pal did the actual barking on the air, but the whining, panting, and growling were provided by a human imitator. Then came the long-running TV series, which was broadcast nationally in six different formats from 1954 through 1972, and finally an animated cartoon version from 1973 to 1975. In 1963 a four-episode TV program, 'The Journey,' was shown in movie theaters as a feature, *Lassie's Greatest Adventure.* Lassie (the sixth generation by now) made a successful big-screen comeback in 1978 in *The Magic of Lassie,* a big-budget feature costarring James Stewart. While in New York for personal appearances on the stage of Radio City Music Hall the dog stayed in a $380-a-day suite at the Plaza Hotel.

FEATURE FILMS: *Lassie Come Home* 1943; *Son of Lassie* 1945; *Courage of Lassie* 1946; *Hills of Home* 1948; *The Sun Comes Up* 1949; *Challenge to Lassie* 1950; *The Painted Hills* 1951; *Lassie's Great Adventure* (compiled from four TV episodes) 1963; *The Magic of Lassie* 1978.

Laszlo, Andrew (Andy). Director of photography. Born on Jan. 12, 1926, in Papa, Hungary. In the US from 1947, he started his career in television and developed into a competent lighting cameraman in features in the 60s, working frequently on productions shot on location in New York. By the 80s he was working mainly on the West Coast, on traditional glossy Hollywood fare.

FILMS INCLUDE: *One Potato Two Potato* 1964; *You're a Big Boy Now* 1966; *The Night They Raided Minsky's* 1968; *Popi* 1969; *The Owl and the Pussycat* (co-phot.), *The Out-of-Towners, Lovers and Other Strangers* 1970; *Jennifer on My Mind* 1971; *To Find a Man, The Effect of Gamma Rays on Man-in-the-Moon Marigolds* 1972; *Class of '44* 1973; *Countdown at Kusini* (US/Nigeria) 1976; *Thieves* (co-phot.) 1977; *Somebody Killed Her Husband* 1978; *The Warriors* 1979; *Shogun, Southern Comfort, I, the Jury* 1981; *First Blood* 1982; *Streets of Fire* 1984; *Remo Williams. . . the Adventure Begins* 1985; *Poltergeist II: The Other Side* 1986; *Innerspace* 1987; *Star Trek V: The Final Frontier* 1989; *Ghost Dad* 1990; *Newsies* 1992.

Laszlo, Ernest. Director of photography, *b.* Apr. 23, 1905, Yugoslavia, of Hungarian descent. *d.* 1984. In the US from 1926, he entered films in 1927 as an assistant cameraman, was promoted briefly to cinematographer the following year, and during the 30s and early 40s worked as a camera operator at Paramount on such films as *Hold Back the Dawn* (1941) and *The Major and the Minor* (1942). He subsequently photographed many major films for Paramount and other studios, winning an Academy Award for *Ship of Fools* (1965), out of eight Oscar nominations.

FILMS INCLUDE: *The Pace That Kills* 1928; *The White Outlaw* 1929; *Hell's Angels* (2nd-unit phot.) 1930; *The Hitler Gang* 1944; *Two Years Before the Mast* 1946; *Dear Ruth, Road to Rio* 1947; *On Our Merry Way/A Miracle Can Happen* (co-phot.) 1948; *Manhandled, D.O.A.* 1949; *Riding High* (co-phot.) 1950; *The Well, M* 1951; *The Steel Trap* 1952; *The Moon Is Blue, The Star, Stalag 17* 1953; *Vera Cruz, Apache, The Naked Jungle, About Mrs. Leslie* 1954; *Kiss Me Deadly, The Big Knife, The Kentuckian* 1955; *While the City Sleeps, Bandido* 1956; *The Restless Years* 1958; *Inherit the Wind* 1960; *The Last Sunset, Judgment at Nuremberg* 1961; *4 for Texas, It's a Mad Mad Mad Mad World* 1963; *Ship of Fools, Baby the Rain Must Fall* 1965; *Fantastic Voyage* 1966; *Luv* 1967; *Star!* 1968; *Daddy's Gone A-Hunting* 1969; *Airport* 1970; *Showdown* 1973; *Logan's Run* 1976; *The Domino Principle* (co-phot.) 1977.

latensification. A method for increasing the density of a photographic image by exposing a negative to extremely low-intensity light over a long period of time.

latent image. The invisible image chemically present on exposed film that has not yet been developed. Once rendered visible by chemical processing, it becomes a true image.

Laterna Magika. Literally "magic lantern," this is a multimedia presentation that originated in Czechoslovakia, and combines live action on stage with a background of projected films and slides.

Latham, Major Woodville. American inventor. *b.* 1838. *d.* 1911. Best known as the originator of the Latham Loop (1895), still fundamental to the threading of modern projectors. This device, as well as Latham's development of the Edison Kinetoscope, are erroneously attributed by many to Eugene LAUSTE, with whom Latham became associated in 1894.

Lathrop, Philip H. American director of photography. Born on Oct. 22, 1916. In Hollywood since 1934, he worked his way up from camera loader through assistant cameraman and operator, becoming a lighting cameraman in 1957. An impeccable craftsman, he has provided many quality productions with slick cinematography.

FILMS INCLUDE: *The Monster of Piedras Blancas* 1957; *Wild Heritage, The Saga of Henry Brown* 1958; *The Perfect Furlough* 1959; *Experiment in Terror, Lonely Are the Brave* 1962; *Days of Wine and Roses, Soldier in the Rain* 1963; *The Pink Panther, The Americanization of Emily* 1964; *36 Hours, The Cincinnati Kid* 1965; *What Did You Do in the War Daddy?* 1966; *The Happening, Point Blank* 1967; *Finian's Rainbow, I Love You Alice B. Toklas* 1968; *The Illustrated Man, The Gypsy Moths, They Shoot Horses Don't They?* 1969; *The Traveling Executioner, The Hawaiians, Rabbit Run* 1970; *Wild Rovers* 1971; *Every Little Crook and Nanny, Portnoy's Complaint* 1972; *The All-American Boy* 1973; *Airport 1975, Earthquake* 1974; *The Prisoner of Second Avenue, Hard Times, The Killer Elite, The Black Bird* 1975; *Swashbuckler* 1976; *Airport '77* 1977; *A Different Story, The Driver, Moment by Moment* 1978; *The Concorde—Airport '79* 1979; *Little Miss Marker, A Change of Seasons* 1980; *All Night Long* 1981; *Hammett, National Lampoon's Class Reunion* 1982; *Deadly Friend* 1986.

Latimore, Frank. Actor. Born Frank Kline, on Sept. 28, 1925, in Darien, Conn. Curly-haired leading man who enjoyed some popularity among film fans in the 40s, when he played romantic roles in several productions at Fox. Toward the end of the decade he settled in Italy, where he continued appearing in films, in both leads and supporting parts, in European productions as well as in Hollywood films shot on the Continent.

FILMS INCLUDE: *In the Meantime Darling* 1944; *The Dolly Sisters* 1945; *Shock, Three Little Girls in Blue, The Razor's Edge* 1946; *13 Rue Madeleine* 1947; *Black Magic, Yvonne la Nuit* (It.) 1949; *Il Camiano del Piave* (It.) 1951; *Core Ingrato* (It.), *Tre Storie Proibite/Three Forbidden Stories* (It.), *La Nemica* (It.), *A Fil di Spada* (It.) 1952; *Napoletani a Milano* (It.), *Capitan Fantasma* (It.) 1953; *La Figlia di Mata Hari* (It./Fr.) 1954; *Il Principe dalla Maschera Rossa* (It.) 1955; *Terrore sulla Città* (It.) 1957; *I Cavalieri del Diavolo* (It.) 1959; *Plein Soleil/Purple Noon* (Fr./It.), *Les Scélérats* (Fr.) 1960; *Then There Were Three* 1961; *Rosa de Lima* (Sp.), *La Venganza del Zorro* (Sp.) 1962; *Cuatreros* (Sp.) 1964; *Cast a Giant Shadow* 1966; *The Honey Pot/It Comes Up Murder* (US/UK/It.) 1967; *The Sergeant* 1968; *If It's Tuesday This Must Be Belgium* 1969; *Patton* 1970; *All the President's Men* 1976.

latitude. The range of lens apertures and shutter speeds in which a film will produce a satisfactory image. Generally, the faster the emulsion speed of the film, the greater the latitude the cameraman has in selecting his lens stops. However, much also depends on the tone range of the subject. Dark tones reduce the latitude, while lighter ones increase it.

Lattuada, Alberto. Director. Born on Nov. 13, 1914, in Milan. The son of a noted composer, he studied architecture and entered Italian films at 19 as a set decorator. His wide range of interests also encompassed literature and politics. During his late teens and early 20s he helped found controversial periodicals to which he contributed antifascist articles. He worked in the film industry in various minor capacities while completing his studies and in 1940 founded with Mario Ferrari and Luigi COMENCINI the Italian film archives, Cineteca Italiana. In 1940–41 he worked as assistant screenwriter and assistant director on two films, then directed his own first film in 1942. After WW II he adhered for a period to the then-current neorealist style and established his reputation with such films as *Il Bandito/The Bandit* (1946), *Senza Pietà/Without Pity* (1948), *Il Mulino del Po/The Mill on the Po* (1949), *Luci del Varietà/Variety Lights* (1950; in collaboration with Federico Fellini), and *Il Capotto/The Overcoat* (1952). In 1951 he scored a big commercial success with *Anna,* starring Silvana Mangano. Lattuada has since worked in a variety of cinema genres, ranging from problem films to costume spectacles, displaying considerable ability if not great originality. The author of published volumes of poetry and short stories, he has collaborated on the scripts of most of his own films. The music for many of his films was composed by his father, Felice Lattuada. He married actress Carla Del Poggio in 1945. They later divorced. Although rarely achieving great brilliance, Alberto Lattuada turned out a body of work of consistently high quality and undeniable elegance and vigor.

FILMS (as director/co-screenwriter): *Giacomo l'Idealista* 1943; *La Freccia nel Fianco, La Nostra Guerra* (doc. short) 1945; *Il Bandito/The Bandit* 1946; *Il Delitto fi Giovanni Episcopo/Flesh Will Surrender* 1947; *Senza Pietà/Without Pity* 1948; *Il Mulino del Po/The Mill on the Po* 1949; *Luci del Varietà/Variety Lights* (co-dir. with Federico Fellini) 1950; *Anna* 1951; *Il Cappotto/The Overcoat* 1952; *La Lupa/The She-Wolf, Amore in Città/Love in the City* ('Gli Italiani si voltano' episode) 1953; *La Spiaggia/The Beach* 1954; *Scuola elementare* 1955; *Guendalina* 1957; *La Tempesta/Tempest* 1958; *I Dolci Inganni/Les Adolescents, Lettere di una Novizia/Rita* 1960; *L'Imprevisto/L'Imprévu/The Unexpected* (dir. only) 1961; *Mafioso* (dir. only) 1962; *La Steppa/The Steppe* 1963; *La Mandragola/The Love Root* 1965; *Matchless, Don Giovanni in Sicilia* 1967; *Fräulein Doktor, L'Amica* 1969; *Venga a prendere il Caffé. . . da noi/Come Have Coffee with Us* 1970; *Bianco Rosso e. . . /White Sister* 1972; *Sono stato io* 1973; *Le Farò di Padre/Mambina* (also act.) 1974; *Curo di Cane, Oh Serafina!/Bruciati da Concente Passione* (also act.) 1976; *Cosi come sei/Stay as You Are/The Daughter* 1978; *La Cicala* 1980; *Cristoforo Colombo/Christopher Columbus* (for TV) 1985; *Una Spina nel Cuore/A Thorn in the Heart* 1986; *Sarafina* 1992; *The Bull* 1994.

Laughlin, Tom. Actor, director, producer, screenwriter. Born in 1938, in Minneapolis. *ed.* U. of Indiana; U. of Minnesota. Played secondary juvenile roles in a number of Hollywood films of the late 50s, then ran a Montessori school in Santa Monica before returning to the screen in the mid-60s, this time as actor-director-producer-writer of independent low-budget productions. Working at the fringes of the industry, he used different pseudonyms—T. C. Frank, Donald Henderson, and Lloyd E. James, among others—for his various functions behind the camera. In 1971 he struck it rich with *Billy Jack,* a film he produced, directed, wrote, and distributed himself outside the studio system. The film, which starred Laughlin and his wife, Delores Taylor, was made for a mere $800,000 and returned tens of millions of dollars at the box office. A naïve tale with a simplistic moral of a loner who fights the establishment, the film struck a responsive chord among disillusioned young audiences during the Vietnam era and quickly became a commercial phenomenon. A sequel followed and it too was highly successful at the box office despite devastating reviews. Laughlin's company, Billy Jack Enterprises, opened a huge office complex in the heart of Hollywood, hired top managerial talent, and in 1975 announced plans to expand into an entertainment conglomerate, with record and book subsidiaries, and intentions to acquire the CBS West Coast Production Center. But overexpansion, insufficient cash flow, and the failure of the film *The Master Gunfighter,* combined to topple Laughlin's empire as suddenly as it rose and bring it to the verge of bankruptcy in 1976. Following the debacle, Laughlin virtually disappeared from view. He resurfaced briefly in 1985 with announcements about filming *The Return of Billy Jack* and a plan to open a film school in Houston. Neither project materialized.

FILMS INCLUDE (as actor): *Tea and Sympathy* 1956; *South Pacific* 1958; *Gidget* 1959; *Tall Story* 1960; *The Young Sinner* (also prod., dir., sc., edit.) 1965; *The Born Losers* (also prod., dir., sc.) 1967; *Billy Jack* (also prod., dir., co-sc.) 1971; *The Trial of Billy Jack* (also prod., dir., co-sc.) 1974; *The Master Gunfighter* (also exec. prod., dir.) 1975; *Billy Jack Goes to Washington* (also dir., prod., co-sc.) 1977; *The Legend of the Lone Ranger* 1981.

Laughton, Charles. Actor. *b.* July 1, 1899, Scarborough, England. *ed.* Stonyhurst Coll. *d.* 1962. Following in his hotelman father's footsteps, he started out as a hotel clerk, but after returning from WW I service, found himself drawn to the stage and joined an amateur group. He later enrolled at the Royal Academy of Dramatic Art, and as a gold-medal-winning student he appeared in several of the school's productions in 1925. The following year he made his professional debut on London's West End. In the cast of one of his first plays was a young actress, Elsa LANCHESTER, who was also appearing in a series of two-reel comedy films. He teamed with her in two of these in 1928, and in the following year they married. It was also in 1929 that he made his debut in feature films. His parallel stage career brought Laughton (and Lanchester) to New York in 1931 with the play 'Payment Deferred.' The following year he launched his lengthy and remarkable career as a Hollywood character star.

Although Laughton gave some of his finest performances in British films, notably in *The Private Life of Henry VIII* (1933), for which he won an Academy Award, and *Rembrandt* (1936), the bulk of his films were made in the United States, and in 1950 he became an American citizen. Rotund and boisterous, Laughton was a brilliant performer with an astonishing range. He played sadists and kind men, butlers and rulers of state, murderers and jurists, artists and gray, prosaic men with the same convincing strength and insatiable relish. At times, when his roles were thankless or the films unimportant, he tended to "ham it up," frivolously carrying a part to its ludicrous extreme; but audiences rarely minded and seemed to savor the feast along with him. One of the most productive years of his career was 1935, when he played three of his most memorable roles: Ruggles in *Ruggles of Red Gap,* Javert in *Les Misérables,* and Captain Bligh in *Mutiny on the Bounty.* Other memorable film appearances were in *The Hunchback of Notre Dame* (as Quasimodo), *The Canterville Ghost, The Big Clock, Witness for the Prosecution,* and his last, *Advise and Consent.*

In 1955 Laughton directed *The Night of the Hunter,* a visually striking and dramatically gripping production that showed much promise for a new career as a filmmaker. But he never made another. Instead, he spent much of his later years touring with highly acclaimed readings of Shaw's 'Don Juan in Hell,' Stephen Vincent Benét's 'John Brown's Body,' and selections from the Bible. He also appeared frequently on radio and TV. Many delectable morsels of his remarkable career are contained in Elsa Lanchester's book, *Charles Laughton and I* (1939).

FILMS: In the UK—*Bluebottles* (short), *Day Dreams* (short) 1928; *Piccadilly* 1929; *Comets, Wolves/Wanted Men* 1930; Down River 1931. In the US—*Devil and the Deep, The Old Dark House, Payment Deferred, The Sign of the Cross* (as Nero), *If I Had a Million, Island of Lost Souls* 1932; *The Private Life of Henry VIII* (title role; UK), *White Woman* 1933; *The Barretts of Wimpole Street* (as Elizabeth Barrett's father) 1934; *Ruggles of Red Gap* (title role), *Les Misérables* (as Javert), *Mutiny on the Bounty* (as Captain Bligh) 1935; *Rembrandt* (title role; UK) 1936; *I Claudius* (title role; unfinished; UK) 1937; *Vessel of Wrath/The Beachcomber* (UK), *St. Martin's Lane/Sidewalks of London* (UK) 1938; *Jamaica Inn* (UK), *The Hunchback of Notre Dame* (as Quasimodo) 1939; *They Knew What They Wanted* 1940; *It Started with Eve* 1941; *The Tuttles of Tahiti, Tales of Manhattan, Stand By for Action* 1942; *Forever and a Day, This Land Is Mine, The Man from Down Under* 1943; *The Canterville Ghost* 1944; *The Suspect, Captain Kidd* (title role) 1945; *Because of Him* 1946; *The Paradine Case, Arch of Triumph, The Big Clock, The Girl from Manhattan* 1948; *The Bribe* 1949; *The Man on the Eiffel Tower* (as Inspector Maigret; US/Fr.) 1950; *The Blue Veil, The Strange Door* 1951; *O. Henry's Full House, Abbott and Costello Meet Captain Kidd* 1952; *Salome* (as Herod), *Young Bess* (as Henry VIII) 1953; *Hobson's Choice* (UK) 1954; *The Night of the Hunter* (dir. only) 1955; *Witness for the Prosecution* 1958; *Sotto Dieci Bandiere/Under Ten Flags* (It.), *Spartacus* (as Gracchus) 1960; *Advise and Consent* 1962.

Launder, Frank. Director, screenwriter, producer. *b.* 1907, in Hitchin, England. *d.* 1997. A former civil servant, he acted in Brighton repertory and wrote a play before entering British films as a screenwriter in 1928. In collaboration with Sidney GILLIAT, he wrote intelligent scripts for a number of British films of the 30s and early 40s, notably *The Lady Vanishes* (1938), *Night Train to Munich/Night Train* (1940), *Kipps* (1941), and *The Young Mr. Pitt* (1942). In 1942 he directed his first film, a short, in collaboration with Gilliat and in the following year his first feature film, *Millions Like Us,* again in collaboration with Gilliat. In 1944 he and Gilliat formed their own production company, Individual Pictures (later Launder and Gilliat Productions), and began a long partnership. They collaborated as writers but each directed his own set of films with the other often collaborating as a producer. Like Gilliat, Launder has been most at home with comedy and farce. One of his most successful films was *The Happiest Days of Your Life* (1950), which launched his popular "St. Trinian's" madcap farce series about a wacky school for girls.

FILMS (As screenwriter, alone or in collaboration; partial list): *Cocktails* (titles only) 1928; *Under the Greenwood Tree* 1929; *Song of Soho, The W Plan, The Middle Watch* 1930; *How He Lied to Her Husband, Hobson's Choice* 1931; *After Office Hours, Arms and the Man* (uncredited) 1932; *You Made Me Love You* 1933; *Those Were the Days* 1934; *Emil and the Detectives, Rolling Home* 1935; *Seven Sinners* 1936; *Oh Mr. Porter* (story only) 1937; *The Lady Vanishes* 1938; *A Girl Must Live, Inspector Hornleigh on Holiday* 1939; *They Came by Night, Night Train to Munich/Night Train* 1940; *The Young Mr. Pitt* 1942; *The Rake's Progress/The Notorious Gentleman* (also co-prod.) 1945; *The Green Man* (also co-prod.) 1956; *Fortune Is a Woman/She Played with Fire* 1957; *Ring of Spies* 1963; *The Lions Are Free* (doc.) 1967. As producer or executive producer, alone or in collaboration (partial list)—*Green for Danger* 1947; *London Belongs to Me/Dulcimer Street* 1948; *State Secret/The Great Manhunt* 1950; *The Story of Gilbert and Sullivan* 1953; *The Constant Husband* 1955; *Endless Night* (exec. prod. only), *Ooh. . . You Are Awful/Get Charlie Tully* (co-exec. prod. only). As director-screenwriter (complete)—*Partners in Crime* (short; co-dir. with Sidney Gilliat) 1942; *Millions Like Us* (co-dir. with Gilliat) 1943; *2,000 Women* 1944; *I See a Dark Stranger/The Adventuress* (also co-prod.) 1946; *Captain Boycott* (also co-prod.) 1947; *The Blue Lagoon* 1949; *The Happiest Days of Your Life* (also prod.) 1950; *Lady Godiva Rides Again* (also co-prod.) 1951; *Folly to Be Wise* (also co-prod.) 1952; *The Belles of St. Trinian's* (also co-prod.) 1954; *Geordie/Wee Geordie* (also co-prod.) 1955; *Blue Murder at St. Trinian's* (also co-prod.) 1957; *The Bridal Path* (also co-prod.) 1959; *The Pure Hell of St. Trinian's* (also co-prod.) 1960; *Joey Boy* (also co-prod.) 1965; *The Great St. Trinian's Train Robbery* (co-dir. with Gilliat) 1966; *Get Charlie Tully* (co-exec. prod. only) 1976; *The Wildcats of St. Trinian's* 1980.

Laure, Carole. Actress. Born in 1948, in Montreal. Sensual, brunette leading lady of Canadian and French films. Traumatized in early childhood by her mother's madness and suicide and her father's disappearance, she adjusted as well as she could to life at an adoptive home. She seemed destined for a career as a concert pianist in the early 70s when she was discovered by director Gilles Carle, who began casting her in his Quebec-based French-Canadian films. Later also working in France, she gained international exposure as the star of the Oscar-winning box-office hit *Get Out Your Handkerchiefs* (1978). She is also an accomplished vocalist.

FILMS INCLUDE: *Mon Enfance à Montréal* 1970; *La Vraie Nature de Bernadette* 1972; *La Mort d'un Bûcheron/Death of a Lumberjack, Fleur bleue, Les Corps célestes/The Heavenly Bodies* 1973; *Sweet Movie* 1974; *Born for Hell, Blazing Magnums/Strange Shadows in an Empty Room, La Tete de Normande Saint-Onge* 1975; *Milles Lunes* 1976; *L'Ange et la Femme, La Menace* 1977; *Préparez vos Mouchoirs/Get Out Your Handkerchiefs* 1978; *Au revoir à Lundi* 1979; *Fantastica, Asphalte* 1980; *Victory/Escape to Victory, Croque la Vie* 1981; *Maria Chapdelaine* 1983; *A Mort l'Arbitre!, Stress, The Surrogate Heartbreakers* 1984; *Night Magic* 1985; *Sweet Country* 1987.

Laurel, Stan. Actor. *b.* Arthur Stanley Jefferson, June 16, 1890, Ulverston, England. *d.* 1965. The son of an actress and an actor-director-producer-playwright-impresario, he made his own stage debut at 16 at a small Glasgow, Scotland, theater and for the next few years played both drama and comedy in plays and danced and clowned in British music halls. In 1910 he joined the famous Fred Karno company and became Charlie Chaplin's understudy in the troupe's first American tour that same year. He also played various roles in the company's feature attraction 'A Night in an English Music Hall.' He was Chaplin's understudy again during Karno's second US tour in 1912. When the troupe returned to England, he stayed behind and began a lengthy stint in American vaudeville, changing his name to Stan Laurel. In 1917 he made the first of 76 film appearances that preceded his fortuitous teaming with Oliver HARDY in 1927. The two comedians appeared in the same two-reel short, *Lucky Dog,* in 1917, but their pairing in that film was accidental, with Hardy playing a bit and Laurel starring.

Laurel's screen character in those early days was that of a clown, typically wearing oversized clothes and playing the misfit. He continued performing in vaudeville while pursuing a part-time film career in comedy shorts. He worked for various studios, including Universal, Vitagraph, Hal Roach-Pathé and Metro, where he performed for a unit supervised by G. M. ANDERSON of "Broncho Billy" fame. Many of these comedy shorts were spoofs of popular feature films of the period. Laurel wrote many of his own comedy routines and occasionally helped with the directing. In 1926 he signed a long-term contract with Hal ROACH as a gagman and director but shortly after was persuaded to return to acting, and to begin his long and auspicious partnership with Oliver Hardy.

The "thin man" of the fat-thin duo, Laurel was often also the funnier member of the team, with a wide array of mannerisms that endeared him to film audiences, among them a baby-like weep, a confused eye-blink, and a bewildered scratching of the top of the head. He was the creative mind behind many of the team's comedy routines, a master of comedy nuance and technique. Inconsolable after Hardy's death in 1957, he refused to resume performing although he continued writing until his own death in 1965. In the Academy Award ceremony for 1960, he received a special Oscar "for his creative pioneering in the field of cinema comedy."

Following is a partial list of films Laurel made on his own prior to his teaming with Hardy. For details of the partnership and a list of their joint films, see LAUREL AND HARDY.

FILMS INCLUDE (shorts): *Nuts in May* 1917; *Hickory Hiram, Huns and Hyphens, Frauds and Frenzies, It's Great to Be Crazy* 1918; *Hoot Man, Lucky Dog, Scars and Stripes* 1919; *Make It Snappy* 1921; *When Knights Were Cold, The Egg, Week End Party, Mud and Sand, The Pest* 1922; *The Handy Man, Under Two Jags, Collars and Cuffs, Kill or Cure, Oranges and Lemons, Short Orders, Man About Town, Roughest Africa, Frozen Hearts, The Whole Truth, The Soilers, Searching Sands* 1923; *The Smithy, Zeb vs. Paprika, Brothers Under the Chin, Rupert of Hee-Haw, Wide Open Spaces, Short Kilts, Detained, West of Hot Dog* 1924; *Twins, Pie-Eyed, Snow Hawk, Navy Blue Days, The Sleuth, Dr. Pickle and Mr. Pride, Half a Man* 1925; *Atta Boy, Get 'Em Young, On the Front Page* 1926.

Laurel and Hardy. The most successful comedy team in the history of the screen, a skinny-fatty duo whose numerous silent and sound shorts and feature films have brought laughter to generations of filmgoers through their inventive buffoonery and timeless universality. Stan LAUREL and Oliver (Ollie "Babe") HARDY had pursued separate careers before they were persuaded late in 1926 to join forces as a team by director Leo MCCAREY at the Hal Roach studios. A year went by before they emerged as a full-fledged team, but they stayed together for the next three decades, appearing in more than 100 films, 27 of them features. The plots of many of these films, the shorts as well as the features, were deceptively simple. They gained their subtlety from the methodical development and systematic exploitation of a single idea or a progressive string of gags. Sometimes this process was agonizingly slow, but at its best the Laurel and Hardy formula enriched film comedy with some of its funniest, most magical moments. Depending more on situation than on plot and more on physical expression than the spoken word, Laurel and Hardy made people laugh by representing a level of naïveté and stupidity that almost anyone in the audience could feel superior to. They would constantly get into trouble as a result of a brainless act, usually on the part of Laurel, and sink into a deeper and deeper mess as they tried to extricate themselves from the original jeopardy. Relatively mild confrontations would characteristically escalate into virtual mayhem through an intensifying exchange of insults and acts of destruction.

Presenting an obvious contrast in physical appearance, Laurel and Hardy complemented each other perfectly in their screen personalities and mannerisms. Laurel was the feather-brained one, who had trouble developing one idea from start to finish, characteristically scratching his head, blinking his eyes, and sobbing profusely at the first hint of trouble. Short-fused Hardy, a study in frustrated dignity, fancied himself the leader of the team and its smarter member, and as a result his fall from grace was doubly embarrassing, causing him to twiddle his tie nervously. His exasperation with Laurel's follies was typically registered by a frustrated, incredulous gaze into the camera. Both comedians typically wore derby hats, symbolizing their gentlemanly aspirations, and invariably introduced each other as "Mr. Laurel" or "Mr. Hardy."

Laurel and Hardy's successful association with Hal ROACH ended in 1940, when the comedians decided they needed more freedom to express themselves. But the decision proved to be an unfortunate one, for they soon discovered that they had even less control over their own productions at such studios as 20th Century-Fox and MGM, where they made several features in the early 40s, all among their lesser efforts. They stopped making films in 1945 and two years later toured the British Isles with a music hall revue. Their final film was a virtual disaster, a sloppy, unfunny French-Italian co-production, *Atoll K* (1950), which was released in the US as *Robinson Crusoe-Land* and later as *Utopia.* Following a second music hall tour of Britain in 1954, they planned a movie comeback with a series of color films, but preparations for actual production halted suddenly when Hardy suffered a stroke from which he never recovered. After his death in 1957, Laurel resolved never to perform again, but he continued writing comedy material until his own death in 1965. The memory of Laurel and Hardy has been kept alive by frequent TV revivals of their films and by a series of successful compilation films highlighting their work. Following is a list of their films together. For films made separately, see HARDY, Oliver; LAUREL, Stan.

FILMS: Shorts—*Lucky Dog* (isolated, fortuitous co-appearance in same film) 1917; *45 Minutes from Hollywood* (joint appearance but not as a team) 1926; *Duck Soup, Slipping Wives, Love 'Em and Weep, Why Girls Love Sailors, With Love and Hisses, Sugar Daddies, Sailors Beware, The Second Hundred Years, Call of the Cuckoos, Hats Off, Do Detectives Think?, Putting Pants on Philip, The Battle of the Century* 1927; *Leave 'Em Laughing, Flying Elephants, The Finishing Touch, From Soup to Nuts, You're Darn Tootin', Their Purple Moment, Should Married Men Go Home?, Two Tars, Habeas Corpus, We Faw Down* 1928; *Liberty, Wrong Again, That's My Wife, Big Business, Unaccustomed As We Are* (first talkie), *Double Whoopee, Berth Marks, Men o' War, Perfect Day, They Go Boom, Bacon Grabbers, The Hoose-Gow, Angora Love* 1929; *Night Owls, Blotto, Brats, Below Zero, Hog Wild, The Laurel-Hardy Murder Case, Another Fine Mess* 1930; *Be Big, Chickens Come Home, The Stolen Jools* (promotional short; cameo appearances), *Laughing Gravy, Our Wife, Come Clean, One Good Turn, Beau Hunks, On the Loose* (cameos) 1931; *Helpmates, Any Old Port, The Music Box, The Chimp, County Hospital, Scram!, Their First Mistake, Towed in a Hole* 1932; *Twice Two, Me and My Pal, The Midnight Patrol, Busy Bodies, Wild Poses* (cameos in "Our Gang" comedy), *Dirty Work* 1933; *Oliver the Eighth, Going Bye-Bye, Them Thar Hills, The Live Ghost* 1934; *Tit for Tat, The Fixer-Uppers, Thicker Than Water* 1935; *On the Wrong Trek* (cameos in Charlie Chase comedy) 1936; *The Tree in a Test Tube* (Forest Service doc. short) 1943. Features—*Hollywood Revue of 1929* 1929; *The Rogue Song* 1930; *Pardon Us* 1931; *Pack Up Your Troubles* 1932; *The Devil's Brother/Fra Diavolo, Sons of the Desert* 1933; *Hollywood Party, Babes in Toyland* 1934; *Bonnie Scotland*

1935; *The Bohemian Girl, Our Relations* (also prod. by Laurel) 1936; *Way Out West* (also prod. by Laurel), *Pick a Star* 1937; *Swiss Miss, Block-Heads* 1938; *The Flying Deuces* 1939; *A Chump at Oxford, Saps at Sea* 1940; *Great Guns* 1941; *A-Haunting We Will Go* 1942; *Air Raid Wardens, Jitterbugs, The Dancing Masters* 1943; *The Big Noise* 1944; *Nothing but Trouble, The Bullfighters* 1945; *Atoll K/Robinson Crusoe-Land/Utopia* 1950.

Laurents, Arthur. Playwright, screenwriter. Born on July 14, 1918, in New York City. *ed.* Cornell. The author of such plays as 'Home of the Brave,' 'The Time of the Cuckoo' (*Summertime*), 'West Side Story,' and 'Gypsy,' all of which have been adapted to the screen by others, he also wrote or collaborated on a number of original screenplays.

FILMS (screenplays): *Rope, The Snake Pit* 1948; *Anna Lucasta, Caught* 1949; *Anastasia* 1956; *Bonjour Tristesse* 1958; *The Way We Were* (from his own novel) 1973; *The Turning Point* (also co-prod.) 1977.

Laurie, John. Actor. *b.* Mar. 25, 1897, Dumfries, Scotland. *d.* 1980. A former architect and stage player, he played character parts in numerous British films. Usually portrayed angry or somber types.

FILMS INCLUDE: *Juno and the Paycock* 1930; *The 39 Steps* 1935; *Tudor Rose/Nine Days a Queen, As You Like It* (as Oliver) 1936; *The Edge of the World* (lead), *Farewell Again/Troopship* 1937; *The Four Feathers* (as the Mahdi) 1939; *Convoy* 1940; *Dangerous Moonlight/Suicide Squadron* 1941; *The Life and Death of Colonel Blimp* 1943; *The Way Ahead, Medal for the General/The Gay Intruders, Henry V, Fanny by Gaslight/Man of Evil* 1944; *I Know Where I'm Going, The Agitator, Caesar and Cleopatra* 1945; *School for Secrets/Secret Flight, Gaiety George/Showtime* 1946; *Jassy, The Brothers, Uncle Silas/The Inheritance, Mine Own Executioner* 1947; *Bonnie Prince Charlie, Hamlet* (as Francisco) 1948; *Treasure Island* (as Blind Pew; US/UK), *Madeleine, Trio, Happy Go Lovely* 1950; *Laughter in Paradise, Pandora and the Flying Dutchman, Encore* 1951; *Hobson's Choice* 1954; *Richard III* (as Lord Lovel) 1955; *Campbell's Kingdom* 1957; *Kidnapped* (as Ebenezer Balfour; UK/US) 1960; *Don't Bother to Knock/Why Bother to Knock* 1961; *Siege of the Saxons* (as Merlin) 1963; *The Reptile* 1966; *Dad's Army* 1971; *The Prisoner of Zenda* 1979.

Laurie, Piper. Actress. Born Rosetta Jacobs, on Jan. 22, 1932, in Detroit. Leading lady of Hollywood films of the 50s, typecast by Universal in "cute" ingenue roles, mainly in mindless comedies and costume adventures. She proved she could handle a dramatic part effectively in the role of Paul Newman's crippled girlfriend in *The Hustler* (1961), a part that earned her an Oscar nomination as best actress. But the following year she retired from the screen to marry film critic Joseph Morgenstern. She made an impressive comeback in 1976 playing Sissy Spacek's fanatic mother in Brian De Palma's *Carrie,* a role that earned her a second nomination for an Academy Award, this time for best supporting actress. She gained a third nomination for *Children of a Lesser God* (1986). From 1990–91, she appeared in a recurring role in David Lynch's phenomenally successful, if short-lived, *Twin Peaks* series, for which she was nominated for an Emmy.

FILMS: *Louisa, The Milkman* 1950; *The Prince Who Was a Thief, Francis Goes to the Races* 1951; *No Room for the Groom, Has Anybody Seen My Gal?, Son of Ali Baba* 1952; *The Mississippi Gambler, The Golden Blade* 1953; *Dangerous Mission, Johnny Dark, Dawn at Socorro* 1954; *Smoke Signal, Ain't Misbehavin'* 1955; *Kelly and Me, Until They Sail* 1957; *The Hustler* 1961; *Carrie* 1976; *Ruby* 1977; *The Boss's Son* 1978; *Tim* (Austral.) 1979; *Return to Oz* (as Aunt Em) 1985; *Children of a Lesser God* 1986; *Appointment with Death* (UK), *Tiger Warsaw* 1988; *Dream a Little Dream* 1989; *Mother Mother* 1990; *Other People's Money* 1991; *Storyville, Rich in Love* 1992; *Wrestling Ernest Hemingway* 1993; *The Crossing Guard* 1995; *The Grass Harp* 1996.

Lauste, Eugene. Inventor. *b.* 1856, Paris. *d.* 1935. After successfully developing a variety of products and inventions in his native France, he came to the US, joining the staff of Edison's West Orange, N.J., laboratory in 1887. As chief mechanical assistant to W. K. L. DICKSON, and later with the American Mutoscope and Biograph Company, he probably contributed more mechanically than any other single person to the development of motion pictures in the United States. As early as 1900 he began experimenting with sound recording and by 1904 he had built a sound-on-film recording device. See also LATHAM, Major Woodville.

Lauter, Ed. Actor. Born on Oct. 30, 1940, in Long Beach, N.Y. Big, bald supporting player of American films and TV, typically in tough-guy characterizations, often villainous. Formerly a stand-up comedian.

FILMS INCLUDE: *The Magnificent Seven Ride!, The New Centurions, Hickey and Boggs, Bad Company* 1972; *The Last American Hero, Lolly Madonna XXX/The Lolly-Madonna War* 1973; *The Longest Yard, The Midnight Man* 1974; *The French Connection II* 1975; *Breakheart Pass, Family Plot, King Kong* 1976; *The White Buffalo* 1977; *Magic* 1978; *Loose Shoes* 1980; *Death Hunt* 1981; *The Amateur* 1982; *Cujo, The Big Score, Timerider* 1983; *Lassiter, Finders Keepers* 1984; *Death Wish 3* 1985; *Youngblood, Raw Deal* 1986; *Gleaming the Cube, Fat Man and Little Boy, Born on the Fourth of July* 1989; *Judgment, Tennessee Waltz* 1992; *Trial by Jury, Wagons East!* 1994; *Leaving Las Vegas* 1995; *Mulholland Falls* 1996.

Lautner, Georges. Director. Born on Jan. 24, 1926, in Nice, France, the son of actress Renée SAINT-CYR. He studied law and attempted several other occupations before entering films as an assistant director in 1950. He began directing shorts in 1953 and turned out his first feature film in 1958. Specializing in light entertainment, he has enjoyed some commercial success, particularly with his spoofs on spy thrillers.

FILMS INCLUDE: *La Môme aux Boutons* 1958; *Marche ou Crève* 1960; *Arrêtez les Tambours/Women and War/Women in War, Le Monocle noir, En plain Cirage* 1961; *Le Septième Juré/The Seventh Juror, L'Oeil du Monocle* 1962; *Les Tontons flingueurs* 1963; *Le Monocle rit jaune, Les Barbouzes/The Great Spy Chase* 1964; *Galia/I and My Lovers/I and My Love* 1966; *La Grande Sauterelle/Sauterelle/Femmina, Fleur d'Oseille* 1967; *Le Pacha* 1968; *La Route de Salina/Road to Salina* 1970; *Laisse aller—C'est une Valse* 1971; *Il était un fois un Flic* 1972; *La Valise/The Girl in the Trunk, Quelque Messieurs trop tranquilles* 1973; *Les Seins de Glace/Icy Breasts* 1974; *On aura tout vu* 1976; *Mort d'un Pourri* 1977; *Il sont Fous ces Sorciers* 1978; *Flic ou Voyou* 1979; *Le Guignolo* 1980; *Le Professionel* 1981; *Attention! Une Femme peut en cacher une autre!* 1983; *Joyeuses Pâques* 1984; *Le Cowboy, La Cage aux Folles III ("Elles" se marient)/La Cage aux Folles 3: The Wedding* 1985.

lavaliere. In films and television, a small microphone designed to be worn around the user's neck. It is useful in recording the voices of individual performers whose hands need to be free. More commonly used in TV and documentary work than in feature films.

Laven, Arnold. Director. Born on Feb. 23, 1922, in Chicago. In films in various capacities from 1940, he directed some well-paced dramas in the 50s and 60s. He later concentrated on TV movies.

FILMS: *Without Warning* 1952; *Vice Squad* 1953; *Down Three Dark Streets* 1954; *The Rack* 1956; *The Monster That Challenged the World, Slaughter on Tenth Avenue* 1957; *Anna Lucasta* 1958; *Geronimo* (also prod., co-story) 1962; *The Glory Guys* (also co-prod.) 1965; *Clambake* (co-prod. only), *Rough Night in Jericho* 1967; *The Scalphunters* (co-prod. only) 1968; *Sam Whiskey* (also co-prod.) 1969; *Underground* (co-prod. only) 1970.

lavender. In studio and lab slang, a fine-grain master positive for black-and-white duplication, so called because in the past it came supplied with a lavender-tinted base.

Lavi, Daliah (also **Dahlia**). Actress. Born Daliah Levenbuch, in 1940, in Shavei Zion, Israel. Exotic brunette leading lady of international films. Trained as a dancer, she made her screen debut at 15 in a Swedish production, then performed locally. After completing her compulsory military service, she went to Europe and began playing decorative leads in films of various nations.

FILMS INCLUDE: *The People of Hemsö* (Swed.) 1955; *Blazing Sands* (Isr.) 1956; *Candide ou l'Optimisme au XXe Siècle/Candide* (as Cunegonde; Fr.) 1960; *Im Stahlnetz des Dr. Mabuse/The Return of Dr. Mabuse/Phantom Fiend* (Ger./Fr./It.), *La Fête espagnole/No Time for Ecstasy* (Fr.), *Le Jeu de la Vérité* (Fr.) 1961; *Two Weeks in Another Town* (US), *Cyrano et D'Artagnan* (Fr.) 1962; *La Frusta e il Corpo/Night Is the Phantom/What!* (It./Fr./UK), *Das grosse Liebesspiel/And So to Bed* (Aus./Ger.), *Il Demonio* (It.) 1963; *Old Shatterhand/Shatterhand* (Ger./It./Fr./Yug.) 1964; *Lord Jim* (US/UK) 1965; *The Silencers* (US), *Ten Little Indians* (UK), *The Spy with a Cold Nose* (UK) 1966; *Casino Royale* (UK), *Jules Verne's Rocket to the Moon/Those Fantastic Flying Fools/Blast-Off* (UK) 1967; *Some Girls Do* (UK), *Nobody Runs Forever/The High Commissioner* (UK/US) 1968; *Catlow* (Sp.) 1971.

Law, John Phillip. Actor. *b.* Sept. 7, 1937, in Hollywood, Calif. *ed.* U. of Hawaii (engineering). Initiated in college dramatics, he made his professional debut at New York's Lincoln Center Repertory Theater. Tall (6' 4"), blond, and handsome, he appeared in several Italian films before making his Hollywood debut in *The Russians Are Coming the Russians Are Coming* (1966). He has since starred in many international productions. In the 80s seen mostly in low-budget action pictures. According to some sources, he made an isolated film appearance at age 13 in *The Magnificent Yankee* (1950).

FILMS INCLUDE: *Alta Infedeltà/High Infidelity* (It.), *Tre Notti d'Amore/Three Nights of Love* (It.) 1964; *The Russians Are Coming the Russians Are Coming* 1966; *Hurry Sundown, Da Uomo a Uomo/Death Rides a Horse* (It.) 1967; *Diabolik/ Danger Diabolik* (Fr./It), *Barbarella* (Fr./It.), *Skidoo, The Sergeant* 1968; *The Hawaiians* 1970; *Von Richthofen and Brown* (as Manfred von Richthofen, "The Red Baron"), *The Love Machine, The Last Movie* 1971; *The Golden Voyage of Sinbad* (as Sinbad; UK) 1973; *Open Season* 1974; *Dr. Justice* (Fr.) 1975; *Tigers Don't Cry* (So. Africa), *Sussuri nel Buio* (It.) 1976; *Colpo Secco* (It.), *The Cassandra Crossing* 1977; *Der Schimmelreiter* (Ger.) 1978; *Attack Force Z* (Austral.), *Tarzan the Ape Man* 1981; *Tin Man* 1983; *Hitman/American Commandos* 1985; *Johann Strauss—Der Konig ohne Krone* (Austria/Ger./Fr.), *Rainy Day Friends* 1986; *Combat Force/Striker* (It.) 1987; *Space Mutiny, Thunder Warrior 3* 1988; *Alienator* 1989; *Cold Heat* 1990.

Lawford, Peter. Actor. *b.* Sept. 7, 1923, London. *d.* 1984. The son of a knighted WW I general who turned to acting after his retirement, he was educated in private schools and made his screen debut as a boy of eight in the British film *Poor Old Bill* (1931). During a visit to California in 1938 he played a supporting role as a cockney boy in *Lord Jeff,* but it wasn't until 1942 that his Hollywood career began in earnest. Following a maturation period in minor supporting roles, he became established as a breezy romantic star of MGM films of the late 40s and early 50s, capitalizing on a clipped accent, social poise, athletic good looks, and natural charm. Offscreen he developed a reputation as a playboy and jet-setter. For years a member of Frank Sinatra's "Rat Pack" gang, he gained additional social prestige in the 60s as a brother-in-law of President John F. Kennedy. He was divorced from Patricia Kennedy in 1966, after 12 years of marriage, and in 1971 married the daughter of comedian Dan Rowan, 27 years his junior. From the 60s Lawford played mainly character roles. In addition to his many film appearances, he was seen on numerous TV shows and in several TV movies. He starred in the TV series 'Dear Phoebe' (1954–55) and 'The Thin Man' (1957–59) and appeared regularly in 1971–72 on 'The Doris Day Show' as Day's romantic interest. His production company, Chrislaw, turned out several feature films in the 60s. He was credited as executive producer on *Johnny Cool* (1963), *Billie* (1965), *Salt and Pepper* (1968), and *One More Time* (1970), the last two in partnership with Sammy Davis, Jr. Lawford suffered from deteriorating health after the 1972 removal of a pancreatic tumor. He was often hospitalized for liver and kidney ailments and other problems associated with alcoholism. He died at 61 of cardiac arrest.

FILMS INCLUDE: *Poor Old Bill* (UK) 1931; *Lord Jeff* 1938; *Mrs. Miniver, A Yank at Eton, Random Harvest* 1942; *Girl Crazy, The Immortal Sergeant, Above Suspicion, Flesh and Fantasy, Sahara* 1943; *The White Cliffs of Dover, The Canterville Ghost, Mrs. Parkington* 1944; *The Picture of Dorian Gray, Son of Lassie* 1945; *Cluny Brown, Two Sisters from Boston* 1946; *It Happened in Brooklyn, My Brother Talks to Horses, Good News* 1947; *Easter Parade, On an Island with You, Julia Misbehaves* 1948; *Little Women, The Red Danube* 1949; *Please Believe Me* 1950; *Royal Wedding* 1951; *Just This Once, Kangaroo, You for Me, The Hour of 13* 1952; *Rogue's March* 1953; *It Should Happen to You* 1954; *Never So Few* 1959; *Ocean's 11, Exodus, Pepe* 1960; *Sergeants 3, Advise and Consent, The Longest Day* 1962; *Dead Ringer* 1964; *Sylvia, Harlow* (as Paul Bern, in the Carroll Baker version) 1965; *The Oscar, A Man Called Adam* 1966; *Salt & Pepper* (also co-exec. prod.; US/UK), *Skidoo* 1968; *Buona Sera Mrs. Campbell, Hook Line and Sinker, The April Fools* 1969; *One More Time* (also co-exec. prod.) 1970; *They Only Kill Their Masters* 1972; *That's Entertainment* (on-screen co-host) 1974; *Rosebud* 1975; *Seven from Heaven* (cameo) 1979; *Angel's Brigade* 1979; *Body and Soul* 1981; *Where Is Parsifal?* 1984.

Lawrance (also **Lawrence**), **Jody.** Actress. Born Josephine Lawrence Goddard, on Oct. 19, 1930, in Forth Worth, Tex. Leading lady of standard Hollywood adventure films of the 50s.

FILMS INCLUDE: *Mask of the Avenger, The Son of Dr. Jekyll, Ten Tall Men* 1951; *The Brigand* 1952; *All Ashore* 1953; *The Scarlet Hour, The Leather Saint* 1956; *Hot Spell* 1958; *The Purple Gang* 1960; *Stagecoach to Dancer's Rock* 1962.

Lawrence, Barbara. Actress. Born on Feb. 24, 1928, in Carnegie, Okla. *ed.* UCLA. A former child model, she played supporting parts and occasional leads in films of the 40s and 50s. She was often seen in comic roles, typically as a sharp-tongued friend of the heroine.

FILMS INCLUDE: *Diamond Horseshoe* 1945; *Margie* 1946; *Captain from Castile* 1947; *You Were Meant for Me, Give My Regards to Broadway, The Street with No Name, Unfaithfully Yours* 1948; *A Letter to Three Wives, Mother Is a Freshman, Thieves' Highway* 1949; *Peggy* 1950; *Two Tickets to Broadway* 1951; *The Star, Arena* 1953; *Her Twelve Men, Jesse*

James vs. the Daltons 1954; *Oklahoma!, Man with the Gun* 1955; *Kronos* 1957; *Man in the Shadow* 1958.

Lawrence, Florence. Actress. *b.* 1886, Hamilton, Ont., Canada. *d.* 1938. The most popular player at Biograph and one of the great stars of the early American screen. The daughter of stage actress Lotta Lawrence, she made her stage debut at three and developed into a successful ingenue in a touring company managed by her mother. When the company disbanded in 1907, mother and daughter entered films with the Edison company. Florence's rise was meteoric when she starred in D. W. Griffith's earliest productions. Since company policy discouraged promoting actors by names lest they demand more money, she was simply known as "The Biograph Girl." In 1910, film pioneer Carl LAEMMLE engineered a coup by luring Miss Lawrence away from Biograph and putting her under contract to IMP (Independent Motion Picture Company of America). He fabricated a newspaper story according to which she was killed by a streetcar. He then announced in an advertisement that "enemies" of IMP had circulated a lie concerning the death of Florence Lawrence, "The Imp Girl," formerly known as "The Biograph Girl." The ad said she was alive and well and appearing in his company's next film, *The Broken Oath.* Thus, Florence Lawrence became the first film star to be known to the public by name. Laemmle also hired away from Biograph her first husband (of three) and frequent co-star and director, Harry Salter. Miss Lawrence was seriously injured in 1914 while performing a dangerous stunt and was forced away from the screen for eight years, apart from an isolated appearance in a 1916 production. Her attempted comeback in the early 20s fizzled, and she was soon forgotten. In the 30s she was put on the MGM payroll, along with several other old-timers, as an act of charity, drawing a small salary and being used occasionally as an extra. At 52 she committed suicide by consuming ant paste.

FILMS INCLUDE: *Daniel Boone* 1907; *Macbeth, Romeo and Juliette* (as Juliet), *Salome* (title role), *The Heart of O Yama, A Smoked Husband, The Barbarian Ingomar, Romance of a Jewess, The Call of the Wild, The Devil, The Zulu's Heart, The Planter's Wife, Antony and Cleopatra* (as Cleopatra), *The Song of the Shirt, The Taming of the Shrew* (as Katharina), *The Ingrate, After Many Years, The Viking's Daughter, Richard III, The Valet's Wife, The Test of Friendship, An Awful Moment* 1908; *Mrs. Jones Entertains, The Sacrifice, The Salvation Army Lass, The Lure of the Gown, Deception, The Drunkard's Reformation, The Cardinal's Conspiracy, Mrs. Jones' Lover, Love's Stratagem, The Joneses Have Amateur Theatricals, At the Altar, Confidence, Resurrection* (as Katyusha), *The Right to Love, Jane and the Stranger, Mother Love, The Broken Oath, The Eternal Triangle, The Call of the Circus, Irony of Fate, All the World's a Stage* 1910; *The Test, Vanity and Its Cure, The Burglar, The Actress and the Singer, Her Artistic Temperament, The Wife's Awakening, The Little Rebel, The Gypsy, The Slavey's Affinity, The Maniac, A Blind Deception* 1911; *The Players, All for Love, Flo's Disipline, The Advent of Jane, The Angel of the Studio* 1912; *The Closed Door, The Spender, A Girl and Her Money* 1913; *The Romance of a Photograph, The False Bride, The Honeymooners, Pawns of Destiny, Disenchantment, A Singular Cynic* 1914; *Elusive Isabel* 1916; *The Way of a Man, The Mended Lute, The Slave* 1909; *The Unfoldment* 1922; *The Satin Girl* 1923; *Gambling Wives* 1924; *The Johnstown Flood, The Greater Glory* 1926; *Secrets* (as extra) 1933.

Lawrence, Gertrude. Actress. *b.* Alexandra Dagmar Lawrence-Klasen, July 4, 1898, London. *d.* 1952. Celebrated star of British revues and musicals, she was equally popular on Broadway. Made only occasional screen appearances. She was portrayed by Julie Andrews in *Star!* (1968).

FILMS: *The Battle of Paris* (US) 1929; *Aren't We All?, Lord Chamber's Ladies* 1932; *No Funny Business* 1933; *Mimi* 1935; *Rembrandt* 1936; *Men Are Not Gods* 1937; *Stage Door Canteen* (US) 1943; *The Glass Menagerie* (US) 1950.

Lawrence, Jody. See LAWRANCE, Jody.

Lawrence, Marc. Actor. Born Max Goldsmith, on Feb. 17, 1910, in New York City. *ed.* CCNY. Formerly onstage, he entered Hollywood films in 1933 and played more than 100 character parts. Swarthy and pock-marked, he specialized in portraying sinister Mafia hoods. In the early 50s he migrated to Europe, where he appeared in many Italian productions and directed a number of low-budget films.

FILMS INCLUDE: *White Woman* 1933; *Dr. Socrates, Little Big Shot* 1935; *Road Gang* 1936; *San Quentin, Racketeers in Exile, Charlie Chan on Broadway, The Shadow* 1937; *Penitentiary, Convicted, I Am the Law* 1938; *Homicide Bureau, Dust Be My Destiny, Invisible Stripes* 1939; *Johnny Apollo, Brigham Young, The Great Profile* 1940; *The Monster and the Girl, Blossoms in the Dust, The Shepherd of the Hills, Lady Scarface, Hold That Ghost* 1941; *This Gun for Hire, Nazi Agent, Eyes of the Underworld* 1942; *The Ox-Bow Incident, Hit the Ice* 1943; *Tampico, Rainbow Island* 1944; *The Princess and the Pirate, Dillinger* 1945; *The Virginian, Cloak and Dagger* 1946; *Unconquered, Captain from Castile* 1947; *I Walk Alone, Key Largo* 1948; *Jigsaw* 1949; *Black Hand, The Asphalt Jungle* 1950; *My Favorite Spy* 1951; *Helen of Troy* (US/It.) 1956; *Kill Her Gently* (UK) 1958; *Johnny Cool* 1963; *Nightmare in the Sun* (dir., co-prod., co-story only) 1965; *Pampa Salvaje/Savage Pampas* (Sp./Arg./US), *Johnny Tiger* 1966; *Custer of the West* 1968; *Krakatoa—East of Java* 1969; *The Kremlin Letter* 1970; *Pigs/Daddy's Deadly Darling* (also dir., prod.), *Frasier—The Sensuous Lion* 1973; *The Man with the Golden Gun* (UK) 1974; *Marathon Man* 1976; *A Piece of the Action* 1977; *Foul Play, Goin' Coconuts* 1978; *Hot Stuff* 1979; *Supersnooper/Super Fuzz* 1981; *Night Train to Terror* 1985; *The Big Easy* 1987; *Ruby, Newsies* 1992; *From Dusk Till Dawn* 1996.

Lawrence, Martin. Actor, comedian. Born April 16, 1965, in Germany. Sharp-witted, controversial comedian who got his break as a stand-up, eventually becoming the host of HBO's 'Def Comedy Jam' as well as his own comedy specials and the FOX television sitcom 'Martin.' His slam-dunk, in-your-face style of comedy has led to success on the big screen, particularly in the 1995 box office smash *Bad Boys.* In 1996 his TV series was marked with scandal when his co-star left the show amid rumors of sexual harassment and poor working conditions.

FILMS: *Hand in Hand* 1961; *Do the Right Thing* 1989; *House Party* 1990; *House Party 2, Talkin' Dirty, After Dark* 1991; *Boomerang* 1992; *You So Crazy* 1994; *Bad Boys* 1995; *A Thin Line Between Love and Hate* (also dir., co-sc.) 1996; *Nothing to Lose* 1997.

Lawrence, Viola. American film editor. *b.* 1894. *d.* 1973. She spent most of her career at Columbia, where for three decades she was entrusted with the cutting of many of the studio's finest productions.

FILMS INCLUDE: *This Is Heaven* 1929; *A Man's Castle* 1933; *No Greater Glory* 1934; *The Whole Town's Talking* 1935; *The King Steps Out, Craig's Wife* 1936; *I Am the Law* 1938; *Only Angels Have Wings* 1939; *Here Comes Mr. Jordan* 1941; *Bedtime Story, My Sister Eileen* 1942; *Cover Girl* 1944; *Tonight and Every Night* 1945; *Down to Earth* 1947; *The Dark Past, The Lady from Shanghai* 1948; *Knock on Any Door* 1949; *In a Lonely Place* 1950; *Affair in Trinidad* 1952; *Miss Sadie Thompson, Salome* 1953; *Chicago Syndicate* 1955; *The Eddy Duchin Story* 1956; *Jeanne Eagels, Pal Joey* 1957; *Who Was That Lady?, Pepe* 1960.

Lawson, John Howard. Screenwriter, playwright. *b.* Sept.

25, 1894, in New York City. *d.* 1977. *ed.* Williams Coll. During WW I he served in Europe as a volunteer ambulance driver for the Red Cross, along with Hemingway, Dos Passos, and e. e. cummings. After the Armistice, he settled in Rome, where he edited a newspaper and was a publicity director for the American Red Cross. In the 20s and 30s he wrote many plays, often on proletarian Marxist themes, nine of which were produced successfully on the Broadway stage. He made his first contact with film in 1920, when he sold an unproduced script to Paramount. In 1928 he went to Hollywood as a contract writer and subsequently wrote screenplays, original stories, and dialogue for a variety of films. He was a co-founder of the Screen Writers Guild and its first president in 1933. In addition to many features—which included such politically inspired films as *Blockade* (1938), about the Spanish Civil War, and *Counter-Attack* (1945), a salute to the US-USSR fighting alliance—he collaborated on the script of Paul Strand's documentary *The Heart of Spain* (1937). He was nominated for an Academy Award for the original story of *Blockade.* His career came to an abrupt halt in 1948 when, as one of the HOLLYWOOD TEN, he was sentenced to a year's imprisonment for refusing to co-operate with House Un-American Activities Committee investigators. Blacklisted by the film industry, he went into self-exile in Mexico. He authored several books on drama and film—including *Theory and Technique of Playwriting and Screenwriting* (1949), *Film in the Battle of Ideas* (1953), and *Film: The Creative Process* (1964)—and lectured on the theater and cinema at a number of American universities.

FILMS: *Dream of Love* (co-titles only) 1928; *The Pagan* (co-titles only), *Dynamite* (co-dial. only) 1929; *The Sea Bat, The Ship from Shanghai, Our Blushing Brides* (all co-sc.) 1930; *Bachelor Apartment* (story only) 1931; *Success at Any Price* (co-sc. from own play 'Success Story') 1934; *Party Wire* 1935; *The Heart of Spain* (doc.) 1937; *Blockade, Algiers* 1938; *They Shall Have Music* (co-sc.) 1939; *Earthbound* (co-sc.), *Four Sons* 1940; *Sahara* (co-sc.), *Action in the North Atlantic* 1943; *Counter-Attack* 1945; *The Jolson Story* (co-sc., uncredited) 1946; *Smash-Up* 1947; *The Hollywood Ten* (doc.; also personal appearance) 1950; *Cry the Beloved Country* (co-sc., uncredited) 1952; *Terror in a Texas Town* (co-sc., uncredited) 1958.

Lawson, Wilfrid. Actor. *b.* Wilfrid Worsnop, Jan. 14, 1900, Bradford, England. *d.* 1966. A veteran of the stage, he played character leads and supporting roles in many British and occasional American films, often in eccentric parts. His career was beset by a lifelong struggle with alcoholism.

FILMS INCLUDE: *East Lynne on the Western Front* 1931; *Strike It Rich* 1933; *The Turn of the Tide* 1935; *Ladies in Love, White Hunter* 1936; *Bank Holiday, Pygmalion* (as Doolittle) 1938; *Stolen Life, Allegheny Uprising* (US) 1939; *Pastor Hall* (title role), *The Long Voyage Home* (US), *A Gentleman of Venture/It Happened to One Man* 1940; *Tower of Terror, Jeannie* 1941; *The Night Has Eyes, The Great Mr. Handel* (as composer George Frederick Handel) 1942; *Thursday's Child* 1943; *Fanny by Gaslight/Man of Evil* 1944; *Make Me an Offer* 1954; *The Prisoner, An Alligator Named Daisy* 1955; *War and Peace* (as Prince Nikolai Bolkonsky; US/It.) 1956; *Room at the Top* 1958; *Expresso Bongo* 1959; *Naked Edge* (UK/US) 1961; *Tom Jones* (as Black George Seagrim) 1963; *Becket* (UK/US) 1964; *The Wrong Box* 1966; *The Viking Queen* 1967.

Lawton, Charles, Jr. Director of photography. *b.* 1904, Los Angeles. *d.* 1965. He entered films as an assistant to cameraman George FOLSEY in 1926 and after several years as a camera operator graduated to lighting cameraman in 1937. He worked best outdoors and in the 50s and early 60s captured exciting images for several top-notch Westerns.

FILMS INCLUDE *My Dear Miss Aldrich* 1937; *Miracles for Sale, Nick Carter—Master Detective* 1939; *Forty Little Mothers* 1940; *Fingers at the Window, The Big Store* 1941; *The Youngest Profession* 1943; *See Here Private Hargrove, Up in Mabel's Room, Abroad with Two Yanks* 1944; *Brewster's Millions, Getting Gertie's Garter* 1945; *The Walls Came Tumbling Down* 1946; *I Love Trouble, The Lady from Shanghai, The Black Arrow* 1948; *Shockproof, The Walking Hills, The Doolins of Oklahoma, Tokyo Joe* 1949; *The Nevadan* 1950; *Man in the Saddle, Mask of the Avenger* 1951; *Hangman's Knot, The Happy Time* 1952; *Miss Sadie Thompson* 1953; *They Rode West, Three Hours to Kill* 1954; *The Long Gray Line, My Sister Eileen* 1955; *Jubal* 1956; *Full of Life, 3:10 to Yuma, Operation Mad Ball* 1957; *Cowboy, The Last Hurrah, Gunman's Walk* 1958; *Ride Lonesome, It Happened to Jane* 1959; *Man on a String* (co-phot.), *Comanche Station* 1960; *A Raisin in the Sun, Two Rode Together* 1961; *Rome Adventure* 1962; *Spencer's Mountain* 1963; *Youngblood Hawke* 1964; *A Rage to Live* 1965.

Lawton, Frank. Actor. *b.* Frank Lawton Mokeley, Jr., Sept. 30, 1904, London. *d.* 1969. Leading man of the British stage and films, specializing in gentlemanly roles. During the 30s he also appeared frequently on Broadway and starred in several Hollywood screen productions. Later seen mainly in character roles. He was married (from 1934) to musical comedy (and occasional film) star Evelyn Laye (*b.* Elsie Evelyn Lay, 1900).

FILMS: *Young Woodley, Birds of Prey/The Perfect Alibi* 1930; *The Skin Game, The Outsider, Michael and Mary* 1931; *After Office Hours* 1932; *Cavalcade* (US), *Heads We Go/The Charming Deceiver, Friday the 13th* 1933; *One More River* (US) 1934; *David Copperfield* (as David as a grown man; US) 1935; *The Invisible Ray* (US), *The Devil Doll* (US) 1936; *The Mill on the Floss* (as Philip Wakem) 1937; *Four Just Men/The Secret Four* 1939; *Went the Day Well?/48 Hours* 1942; *The Winslow Boy* 1948; *Rough Shoot* 1952; *Double Cross* 1955; *The Rising of the Moon* 1957; *Gideon's Day/Gideon of Scotland Yard, A Night to Remember* 1958; *The Queen's Guards* 1961.

Laydu, Claude. Actor. Born on Mar. 10, 1927, in Brussels. Lean, sensitive leading man of French films of the 50s. Memorable in the title role in Robert Bresson's *Diary of a Country Priest* (1950).

FILMS INCLUDE: *Le Journal d'un Curé de Campagne/Diary of a Country Priest* 1950; *Le Voyage en Amérique/Voyage to America* 1951; *Nous sommes tous des Assassins/We Are All Murderers* 1952; *Le Bon Dieu sans Confession, La Route Napoléon* 1953; *Raspoutine, Attila* (It.) 1954; *Sinfonia d'Amore* (as Schubert; It.) 1955; *La Roue* 1956; *Le Dialogue des Carmelites* 1959.

layout. The prefilming plotting of action, camera angles, camera movement, décor, lighting scheme, etc. In animation, this also includes the plotting of characters in correct size relative to the background, the choice of colors, etc.

Lazenby, George. Actor. Born on Sept. 5, 1939, in Goulburn, Australia. Husky leading man of minor international films. He appeared in Australian and British TV commercials but couldn't capitalize on the opportunity to become a major star overnight when he was cast in the role of James Bond in *On Her Majesty's Secret Service* (1969).

FILMS INCLUDE: *On Her Majesty's Secret Service* 1969; *Universal Soldier* 1971; *The Man from Hong Kong/The Dragon Flies* 1975; *The Kentucky Fried Movie* 1977; *Saint Jack* 1979; *Never Too Young to Die* 1986; *Hell Hunters* 1987.

Leachman, Cloris. Actress. Born on Apr. 30, 1926, in Des Moines, Iowa. The daughter of a lumber manufacturer, she began performing as a child. She studied drama for a year at Northwestern, then entered a local beauty contest, eventually becoming Miss Chicago and a runner-up in the 1946 Miss America pageant. As part of her reward, she appeared as an extra in a New York–made movie, then began appearing in Broadway plays and live TV dramas. In 1955 she played the sexy feminine lead in Robert Aldrich's *Kiss Me Deadly,* a Mickey Spillane thriller, but despite several other film appearances remained an obscure screen personality until 1971, when she won the best supporting actress Oscar for her poignant performance as a desperate smalltown housewife in Peter Bogdanovich's *The Last Picture Show*, a role she reprised years later in *Texasville*. She has since turned in talented performances in many other films, sometimes self-effacingly striving for an "ugly" look, as when she played Frau Blucher in Mel Brooks's *Young Frankenstein* (1974). She won six Emmy Awards for her innumerable TV appearances, which included the role of the mother in 'Lassie' (1957–58), a memorable supporting part in 'The Mary Tyler Moore Show' (1970–75), and the title role in her own spin-off series, 'Phyllis' (1975–77). She also appeared on 'The Facts of Life.' She has five children by her former marriage to producer-director George H. ENGLUND.

FILMS: *Kiss Me Deadly* 1955; *The Rack* 1956; *The Chapman Report* 1962; *Butch Cassidy and the Sundance Kid* 1969; *Lovers and Other Strangers, The People Next Door, WUSA* 1970; *The Steagle, The Last Picture Show* 1971; *Charley and the Angel, Dillinger, Happy Mother's Day—Love George* 1973; *Daisy Miller, Young Frankenstein* 1974; *Crazy Mama* 1975; *High Anxiety, The Mouse and His Child* (v/o) 1977; *The North Avenue Irregulars, The Muppet Movie, Scavenger Hunt* 1979; *Foolin' Around, Yesterday, Herbie Goes Bananas* 1980; *History of the World: Part I* 1981; *My Little Pony* (v/o), *Shadow Play* 1986; *Walk Like a Man, Hansel and Gretel* 1987; *Prancer* 1989; *Texasville, Love Hurts* 1990; *The Beverly Hillbillies* (as Granny) 1993; *Now and Then* 1995.

Leacock, Philip. Director. *b.* Oct. 8, 1917, London. *d.* 1990. Brother of Richard LEACOCK. A documentary filmmaker since 1935, he was strongly influenced by John GRIERSON. He turned to feature films in the early 50s, at first specializing in themes involving children and young people. From the late 50s he also worked in Hollywood, where he produced and directed action series for TV ('Route 66,' 'The Defenders,' 'Gunsmoke,' etc.) as well as feature films.

FILMS: *Island People* (doc.), *The Story of Wool* (doc.) 1940; *Riders of the New Forest* 1946; *Out of True* (doc.), *Life in Her Hands* (doc.), *Festival in London* (doc.) 1951; *The Brave Don't Cry* 1952; *Appointment in London, The Kidnappers/The Little Kidnappers* 1953; *Escapade* 1955; *The Spanish Gardener* 1956; *High Tide at Noon* 1957; *Innocent Sinners* 1958; *The Rabbit Trap* (US) 1959; *Let No Man Write My Epitaph* (US), *Take a Giant Step* (US) 1960; *Hand in Hand* 1961; *Reach for Glory, 13 West Street* (US), *The War Lover* 1962; *Tamahine* 1963; *Firecreek* (prod. only; US) 1968; *Adam's Woman* (Austral.) 1970; *Baffled* 1971; *Escape of the Birdman* 1972.

Leacock, Richard (Ricky). Documentary filmmaker. Born on July 18, 1921, in the Canary Islands, to British parents. Brother of Philip LEACOCK. A filmmaker from age 14 and in the US from age 17, he was educated at Harvard (physics) and during WW II served as combat cameraman in the US Army. After the war he worked as associate producer and cameraman on Robert Flaherty's *Louisiana Story.* Later he collaborated with Louis DE ROCHEMONT, Willard VAN DYKE, and other noted documentarians. In the 60s, often in collaboration with Robert Drew, D. A. PENNEBAKER, and Al Maysles, he pioneered in the CINÉMA VÉRITÉ style documentary with a series of experimental TV films made with portable equipment. He is the founder and head of the film department at MIT.

FILMS INCLUDE: *Canary Island Bananas* (also phot.) 1935; *Galapagos Islands* (also phot.) 1938; *Louisiana Story* (assoc. prod., phot. only) 1948; *Pelileo Earthquake* (also phot.) 1949; *New Frontier* (phot., edit. only) 1950; *Toby and the Tall Corn* (also phot.) 1954; *Bernstein in Israel* (also phot.) 1958; *Crystals* 1959; *Primary* (co-dir., co-phot.) 1960; *Mooney vs. Fowle/Football* (co-dir.) 1961; *The Chair* (co-dir.), *Kenya* (co-dir.) 1962; *A Happy Mother's Day* (co-dir.), *Crisis* (co-dir.) 1963; *Ku Klux Klan—The Invisible Empire* (phot. only) 1965; *Portrait of Van Cliburn* (co-dir. co-phot.) 1966; *Don't Look Back* (co-phot. only) 1967; *A Journey to Jerusalem* (co-phot. only), *A Stravinsky Portrait* (co-dir., phot., edit.), *Monterey Pop* (co-dir., co-phot.) 1968; *Chiefs* (also phot.) 1969; *Queen of Apollo* (also phot.) 1970; *Maidstone* (co-phot. only), *Sweet Toronto* (co-phot. only) 1971; *One P.M.* (co-phot. only) 1972; *Keep On Rockin'* (co-phot. only) 1973; *Isabella Stewart Gardner* 1977; *Light Coming Through* 1980; *Lulu in Berlin* 1984; *Impressions del l'Ile des Morts* 1986; *Girl Talk* (addnl. phot. only) 1988.

lead. The principal part in a film or a play; also the actor or actress playing that part.

leader. A blank length of a film, transparent or opaque, used for connecting parts of a work print during editing or at the beginning and end of a reel in order to thread a release print in a projector. When used in the latter fashion, it is known as an ACADEMY LEADER and contains a series of descending numbers at one-foot intervals to guide the projectionist.

Lean, Sir David. Director. *b.* Mar. 25, 1908, Croydon, England. *d.* 1991. Undaunted by his Quaker parents' disapproval of his early passion for "sinful" films, he frequented movie houses stealthily while attending a Quaker boarding school in Reading. Soon dropping out of school, he worked for a year as an apprentice at his accountant father's office, but found the experience boring and was determined to pursue a movie career. He entered British films as a tea boy at Gaumont in 1927; later served as clapper boy and messenger, and worked his way up to editor of newsreel footage in 1930 and of feature films in 1934. Among the films he edited were *Pygmalion* (1938), *49th Parallel* (1941), and *One of Our Aircraft Is Missing* (1942). Lean began his career as a director in 1942 with an excellent war film, *In Which We Serve,* which he co-directed with Noel COWARD. His next three films were adaptations of Coward pieces. The crowning achievement of this phase of Lean's career is the intimate romantic gem *Brief Encounter,* notable for its disciplined structure and the superlative acting of Trevor Howard and Celia Johnson.

The next phase in Lean's work produced two extraordinary adaptations of Dickens novels, *Great Expectations* and *Oliver Twist.* These two films launched the film career of Alec Guinness, who was to appear in many of Lean's subsequent works. The opening sequence of *Great Expectations* contains a masterful example of cutting for suspense effect which is frequently shown in film schools. Lean next directed three films starring his second (1949–57) wife, Ann TODD (his first [1940–49], of six, was actress Kay WALSH). Of these three films, the most interesting is the documentary-style *The Sound Barrier/Breaking Through the Sound Barrier* with a memorable performance by Sir Ralph Richardson. Lean also extracted excellent performances from John Mills and Brenda De Banzie in *Hobson's Choice* and a marvelous spinster characterization from Katharine Hepburn in *Summer Madness/Summertime.* He won the New York Film Critics directing award for the latter.

With *The Bridge on the River Kwai* (1957), Lean turned abruptly from intimate drama to the sumptuous superproduction with which he then became identified. Vastly popular with the public and widely admired by critics, the film went on to win

Academy Awards for best picture and best director, as well as Oscars in five other categories, including best actor for its star, Guinness. Like Lean's subsequent spectacles, it was not merely a superbly crafted adventure epic but a carefully planned and beautifully designed blend of the exciting and the thoughtful—an intelligently balanced work meshing interior conflict with exterior action into a diverting and satisfying whole.

Perhaps more than any other film, *Lawrence of Arabia* (1962) represented Lean's unique capacity to capture the exhilaration of physical adventure without sacrificing narrative elegance or abandoning the human scale. This film, too, earned seven Academy Awards, including best picture and best director. It launched the careers of Peter O'Toole and Omar Sharif and marked the beginning of regular collaborations with screenwriter Robert Bolt and composer Maurice Jarre. It was re-released to great acclaim in 1989, in a stunning version that restored 20 minutes that had been removed without the director's consent a few days after the film's original release.

A meticulous craftsman who often took years to properly develop a project, Lean toiled three years to create *Dr. Zhivago* (1965), a lush visualization of the Boris Pasternak novel, and two more to complete the oozingly romantic *Ryan's Daughter* (1970), probably his least successful film. Fourteen years were to go by before he could garner the financing for what would turn out to be his last film, *A Passage to India* (1984), a sumptuous, literate adaptation of the E. M. Forster novel. It earned nine Academy Award nominations but was eclipsed for the major prizes by Milos Forman's *Amadeus*. However, it earned the New York Critics' award as best picture and restored Lean to popular and critical favor. In the year of the film's release, Lean was knighted by Queen Elizabeth. In 1990 the director received the American Film Institute's 18th annual Life Achievement Award.

FILMS: As editor—*Escape Me Never* 1935; *As You Like It* 1936; *Dreaming Lips* 1937; *Pygmalion* 1938; *French Without Tears* 1939; *49th Parallel/The Invaders, One of Our Aircraft Is Missing* 1942. As director—*In Which We Serve* (co-dir. with Noel Coward) 1942; *This Happy Breed* (also co-adapt.) 1944; *Blithe Spirit* (also co-adapt.), *Brief Encounter* (also co-sc.) 1945; *Great Expectations* (also co-sc.) 1946; *Oliver Twist* (also co-sc.) 1948; *The Passionate Friends/One Woman's Story* (also co-adapt.) 1949; *Madeleine* 1950; *The Sound Barrier/Breaking Through the Sound Barrier* (also prod.) 1952; *Hobson's Choice* (also prod., co-sc.) 1954; *Summer Madness/Summertime* (also co-sc.) 1955; *The Bridge on the River Kwai* 1957; *Lawrence of Arabia* 1962; *Doctor Zhivago* 1965; *Ryan's Daughter* 1970; *A Passage to India* (also sc., edit.) 1984.

Leander, Zarah. Actress, singer. *b.* Zarah Hedberg, Mar. 15, 1900, Karlstad, Sweden. *d.* 1981. She appeared on Swedish stage and screen before becoming a star of operetta-style German films, under the guidance of Douglas SIRK (then Detlef Sierck). A deep-voiced dark beauty, she reached the height of her popularity during WW II, when she reigned as UFA's top star and her films were widely distributed throughout occupied Europe. In 1943 she suddenly retired and returned to Sweden, despite pleas from an admiring Hitler and promises by Goebbels of a villa and special privileges. She returned to the screen in the 50s in undistinguished productions. Her career and enigmatic style inspired an American documentary film, *My Life for Zarah Leander* (1986), directed, produced, written, photographed, and edited by Christian Blackwood.

FILMS INCLUDE: In Sweden—*The Dante Mystery* 1930; *The False Millionaire* 1931; *The Marriage Game* 1935. In Germany—*Premiere, Zu neuen Ufern/To New Shores, La Habañera* 1937; *Der Blaufuchs/Blue Fox, Die Heimat ruft/Magda* 1938; *Das Lied der Wüste/Desert Song* 1939; *Das Herz einer Königin/Marie Stuart* 1940; *Der Weg ins Freie* 1941; *Die grosse Liebe* 1942; *Damals* 1943; *Gabriela* 1950; *Cuba Cubana* 1952; *Ave Maria* 1953; *Der blaue Nachtfalter* 1959; *Come Imparai ad Amare le Donne* (It./Fr./Ger.) 1967.

Lear, Norman. Producer, screenwriter, director. Born on July 27, 1922, in New Haven, Conn. *ed.* Emerson Coll. Returning from WW II service with the USAAF, he entered the TV industry as a comedy writer in 1945 and later wrote, produced, and directed many early television programs. In 1959 he entered a partnership with Bud Yorkin that resulted in a number of light feature films (usually with Yorkin directing and Lear producing and writing) and several highly successful TV series, including 'All in the Family.' Lear scored an unexpected success in 1976 with his innovative nighttime soap opera parody 'Mary Hartman, Mary Hartman.'

FILMS: *Come Blow Your Horn* (co-prod., sc.) 1963; *Never Too Late* (prod.) 1965; *Divorce American Style* (prod., sc.) 1967; *The Night They Raided Minsky's* (prod., co-sc.) 1968; *Start the Revolution Without Me* (exec. prod.) 1970; *Cold Turkey* (prod., dir., co-story, sc.) 1971; *The Princess Bride* (exec. prod.) 1987; *Fried Green Tomatoes* (co-exec. prod.) 1991.

Lease, Rex. Actor. *b.* Feb. 11, 1901, Central City, W. Va. *d.* 1966. He studied for the ministry at Ohio Wesleyan College but was attracted to acting and in 1922 went to Hollywood, where he worked as an extra before playing his first featured role in *A Woman Who Sinned* (1924), ironically portraying an evangelist minister. During the late 20s and early 30s he played romantic leads in numerous dramas and comedies, then starred in Westerns and action serials. By the late 30s he was playing supporting roles, typically villainous.

FILMS INCLUDE: *A Woman Who Sinned, Chalk Marks* 1924; *Easy Money, Before Midnight, The Last Edition* 1925; *Somebody's Mother, The Last Alarm, Race Wild* 1926; *Heroes of the Night, Moulders of Men, Not for Publication, The Cancelled Debt, Clancy's Kosher Wedding, The College Hero* 1927; *The Law of the Range, Phantom of the Turf, Queen of the Chorus, Broadway Daddies, Riders of the Dark, The Candy Kid* (also sc.), *Making the Varsity, The Speed Classic, Stolen Love* 1928; *When Dreams Come True, The Younger Generation, Two Sisters* 1929; *Troopers Three, Sunny Skies, Hot Curves, Borrowed Wives, Wings of Adventure, The Utah Kid* 1930; *Chinatown After Dark, The Monster Walks* 1931; *Cannonball Express* 1932; *Inside Information* 1934; *The Ghost Ride* 1935; *Custer's Last Stand* (serial), *The Clutching Hand* (serial) 1936; *The Mysterious Pilot* (serial), *The Silver Trail* 1937; *Heroes of the Alamo* (as William B. Travis) 1938; *The Lone Ranger Rides Again* (serial), *South of the Border* 1939; *A Chump at Oxford* 1940; *The Phantom Cowboy* 1941; *Daredevils of the West* (serial) 1943; *The Cowboy and the Senorita* 1944; *Flame of the Barbary Coast, Frontier Gal* 1945; *The Crimson Ghost* (serial), *Days of Buffalo Bill, The Time of Their Lives* 1946; *Helldorado, Slave Girl, The Wistful Widow of Wagon Gap* 1947; *Ma and Pa Kettle* 1949; *Singing Guns, Curtain Call at Cactus Creek* 1950; *Ride Vaquero!* 1953; *Perils of the Wilderness* (serial) 1956.

Léaud, Jean-Pierre. Actor. Born on May 5, 1944, in Paris. The son of screenwriter and assistant director Pierre Léaud (*b.* 1905, Rennes, France) and stage and screen actress Jacqueline Pierreux (*b.* 1922, Rouen, France), he made a memorable film debut as the misunderstood little hero of François TRUFFAUT's *The 400 Blows* (1959). He subsequently played the same character, Antoine Doinel, in four other Truffaut films that saw him develop from adolescence to maturity as a virtual alter ego of the director, *Love at Twenty* (1962), *Stolen Kisses* (1968), *Bed and Board* (1970), and *Love on the Run* (1979). He also played in a number of other Truffaut films. A favorite interpreter of the 'New Wave,' he also played pivotal roles in several Jean-Luc GODARD films, including *Masculine Feminine* (1966), *Made in USA* (1966), *La Chinoise* (1967), *Weekend* (1968), and *Le Gai Savoir* (1968). He was named best actor at the Berlin Festival for *Masculine Feminine.* In addition he has worked as an assistant to several directors, including Truffaut and Godard.

FILMS INCLUDE: *Les Quatre Cents Coups/The 400 Blows* 1959; *Le Testament d'Orphée/Testament of Orpheus* 1960; *L'Amour à Vingt Ans/Love at Twenty* 1962; *Pierrot le Fou* 1965; *Masculin-Féminin/Masculine Feminine, Le Départ* (Belg.) 1966; *Made in USA, La Chinoise, Le plus Vieux Méitier du Monde/The Oldest Profession* (Godard episode) 1967; *Le Week-End/Weekend, Dialogue* (Czech.), *Baisers volés/Stolen Kisses, Le Gai Savoir* 1968; *Porcile/Pigsty/Pig Pen* (It.), *Los Herederos/The Heirs* (Sp.) 1969; *Der Leone Have Sept Cabecas* (Br./Sp.), *Domicile conjugal/Bed and Board* 1970; *Les Deux anglaises et le Continent/Two English Girls* 1971; *Ultimo Tango a Parigi/Last Tango in Paris* (It.) 1972; *Une Aventure de Billy le Kid, La Maman et la Putain/The Mother and the Whore, La Nuit américaine/Day for Night, Spectre/Out One—Out Two* 1973; *Les Lolos de Lola, Umarmungen und andere Sachen* 1976; *L'Amour en fuite/Love on the Run* 1979; *Aiutami a sognare* (It.) 1981; *Parano* 1982; *Rebelote* 1983; *Détective* 1985; *Corps et biens* 1986; *Les Keufs* 1987; *36 Fillette/Virgin* 1988; *Bunker Palace Hotel, Femme di Papier/Front Woman* 1989; *I Hired a Contract Killer* 1990; *La Vie Bohème* 1992; *La Naissance de l'Amour* (Fr.) 1993; *Personne ne M'Aime/No One Loves Me* (Fr.) 1994; *Irma Vep* (Fr.), *Just for Laughs* 1996; *Diary of a Seducer* 1997.

Leavitt, Sam. Director of photography. *b.* Feb. 6, 1904, New Jersey. *d.* 1984. He entered films in the mid-20s as a general-purpose apprentice at Paramount's Astoria, Queens, N.Y., studios, then became an assistant cameraman. Graduating to camera operator, he worked in the 40s on such MGM productions as *Bathing Beauty* (1944), *Anchors Aweigh* (1946), *Holiday in Mexico* (1946), and *The Romance of Rosy Ridge* (1947). In the 50s he began working as a freelance cinematographer, and went on to provide striking images for a number of major Hollywood productions. Leavitt won an Academy Award for the cinematography of *The Defiant Ones* (1958).

FILMS INCLUDE: *The Thief* 1952; *China Venture* 1953; *Carmen Jones, A Star Is Born, The Court Martial of Billy Mitchell* 1955; *The Man with the Golden Arm, The Bold and the Brave, Crime in the Streets* 1956; *Time Limit* 1957; *The Defiant Ones, The Fearmakers* 1958; *Pork Chop Hill, Anatomy of a Murder* 1959; *Seven Thieves, Exodus* 1960; *Cape Fear, Advise and Consent* 1962; *Diamond Head, Johnny Cool* 1963; *Shock Treatment* 1964; *Major Dundee* 1965; *An American Dream* 1966; *Guess Who's Coming to Dinner* 1967; *The Wrecking Crew* 1968; *The Desperados* 1969; *The Grasshopper* 1970; *Star Spangled Girl* 1971; *The Man in the Glass Booth* 1975.

LeBaron, William. Producer, production executive. *b.* Feb. 16, 1883, Elgin, Ill. *d.* 1958. *ed.* Chicago U.; NYU. A former playwright and managing editor of *Collier's* magazine, he entered films in 1919 with Cosmopolitan Productions in New York as a writer, eventually rising to the position of the company's general director. In 1924 he joined the Famous Players-Lasky Corporation as associate producer at the company's East Coast studios in Long Island City. Late in 1927 he moved over to FBO (Film Booking Office) as vice president in charge of production and in 1929 assumed the same post with that company's successor, RKO. He returned to Paramount (formerly Famous Players-Lasky) in 1932, initially as an associate producer. He then became a producer and supervised, among other films, several Mae West and W. C. Fields vehicles. In 1936 he succeeded Ernst Lubitsch as Paramount's chief of production, a post he held through 1941, when he moved over to 20th Century-Fox as an independent producer, mainly of light musicals starring such personalities as Alice Faye, Betty Grable, and Carmen Miranda. He retired from films in the late 40s.

FILMS INCLUDE (as producer or associate producer): *Humoresque* 1920; *When Knighthood Was in Flower* 1922; *Manhandled* (superv. ed. only) 1924; *Let's Get Married, Beau Geste* (uncredited), *Tin Gods, Love 'Em and Leave 'Em* 1926; *Paradise for Two, New York, Love's Greatest Mistake, Rubber Heels, Stark Love* 1927; *The Perfect Crime* (adapt. only), *Sinners in Love* 1928; *The Very Idea* (story, sc. only), *Street Girl, Side Street, Half Marriage, Rio Rita* 1929; *The Case of Sergeant Grischa, Beau Bandit, Midnight Mystery, She's My Weakness, Conspiracy, Danger Lights, Dixiana, The Silver Horde, Hook Line and Sinker* 1930; *Cimarron* 1931; *She Done Him Wrong, College Humor, Too Much Harmony, I'm No Angel* 1933; *Belle of the Nineties, The Old-Fashioned Way, It's a Gift* 1934; *Rumba, Goin' to Town, The Man on the Flying Trapeze, Here Comes Cookie* 1935; *Rose of the Rancho, Klondike Annie, Give Us This Night, Poppy, The General Died at Dawn* 1936; *Rhythm on the River, Week-End in Havana* 1941; *Song of the Islands, Footlight Serenade, Orchestra Wives, Iceland, Springtime in the Rockies* 1942; *Stormy Weather, Wintertime, The Gang's All Here* 1943; *Pin Up Girl, Greenwich Village, Sweet and Low Down* 1944; *Don Juan Quilligan* 1945; *Carnegie Hall* 1947.

Lebedeff, Ivan. Actor. *b.* June 18, 1895, Uspolial, Lithuania. *d.* 1953. *ed.* U. of St. Petersburg; Military Acad. of St. Petersburg. An officer in the Czar's army, he fled to Germany after the Bolshevik revolution. He began playing character parts in films in 1922. In 1924 he moved on to France, where he appeared in a number of films, and in 1925 he arrived in Hollywood. Darkly handsome, he typically played unscrupulous Latin gigolos or suave villains.

FILMS INCLUDE: *Friedericus Rex* (Ger.) 1923; *The Sorrows of Satan* 1926; *The Love of Sunya, The Forbidden Woman, The Angel of Broadway* 1927; *Let 'Er Go Gallegher, Walking Back* 1928; *Sin Town, The Veiled Woman, Street Girl, They Had to See Paris* 1929; *The Cuckoos, Conspiracy, Midnight Mystery* 1930; *Bachelor Apartment, The Gay Diplomat* 1931; *Sweepings, Made on Broadway, Bombshell* 1933; *Moulin Rouge* 1934; *Goin' to Town, China Seas* 1935; *The Golden Arrow, Love on the Run* 1936; *History Is Made at Night, Conquest* 1937; *Wise Girl, Straight Place and Show* 1938; *You Can't Cheat an Honest Man, Hotel for Women* 1939; *Passport to Alcatraz* 1940; *The Shanghai Gesture* 1941; *Are These Our Parents?* 1944; *Rhapsody in Blue* 1945; *The Snows of Kilimanjaro* 1952.

LeBorg, Reginald. Director. *b.* Dec. 11, 1902, Vienna. *d.* 1988. *ed.* U. of Vienna; Sorbonne; Columbia. Following banking, then a stage career in Europe as a playwright and director, he settled in Hollywood in the mid-30s, first as a director of musical sequences, then as a director of MGM shorts. He wrote the script for the two-reel *Heavenly Music* (1943), winner of an Academy Award. A feature director from 1943, he turned out many routine B pictures for Universal, Monogram, and other studios.

FILMS: *She's for Me, Calling Dr. Death* 1943; *Adventure in Music* (classical music feature; co-dir.), *Weird Woman, The Mummy's Ghost, Jungle Woman, San Diego—I Love You* (also prod.), *Dead Man's Eyes, Destiny* 1944; *Honeymoon Ahead* 1945; *Joe Palooka—Champ, Little Iodine, Susie Steps Out* 1946; *Fall Guy, The Adventures of Don Coyote, Philo Vance's Secret Mission, Joe Palooka in the Knockout* 1947; *Port Said,*

Joe Palooka in Winner Take All, Fighting Mad, Trouble Makers 1948; *Fighting Fools, Hold That Baby, Joe Palooka in the Counterpunch* 1949; *Young Daniel Boone, Wyoming Mail* (also sc.), *Joe Palooka in the Squared Circle* 1950; *G.I. Jane, Joe Palooka in Triple Cross* 1951; *Models Inc.* 1952; *Bad Blonde, The Great Jesse James Raid, Sins of Jezebel, The Flanagan Boy* 1953; *The White Orchid* (also prod., co-sc.) 1954; *The Black Sleep* 1956; *Voodoo Island, War Drums, The Dalton Girls* 1957; *The Flight That Disappeared* 1961; *Deadly Duo* 1962; *Diary of a Madman* 1963; *The Eyes of Annie Jones* (US/UK) 1964; *So Evil My Sister* 1973.

Le Chanois, Jean-Paul. Director. *b.* Jean-Paul Dreyfus, Oct. 25, 1909, Paris. *d.* 1985. A former journalist and stage actor-director, he entered French films as a bit actor in the early 30s, later becoming an assistant director and film editor. WW II interrupted his debut as director. Serving in the French underground, he adopted Le Chanois as his undercover name, later keeping it as a professional pseudonym. Working secretly during the occupation, he shot remarkable footage of the activities of the Resistance, which he released after the war as *Au Coeur de l'Orage* ("The Heart of the Storm"). His films are traditionalist in style and humanist in content. He collaborated on the screenplays of most of his films. He was married to actress Sylvia Monfort.

FILMS: *La Vie d'un Homme* (doc.), *Le Temps des Cérises* 1938; *L'Irrésistible Rebelle/Une Idée à l'Eau* 1939; *Messieurs Ludovic* (also sc.) 1946; *Au Coeur de l'Orage* (doc., also sc.) 1948; *L'Ecole Buissonière/Passion for Life* (also sc.) 1949; *La Belle que voilà* (also dial.) 1950; *Sans laisser d'Adresse* (also co-sc.) 1951; *Agence matrimoniale* (also sc.) 1952; *Papa Maman la Bonne et Moi/Mama Papa the Maid and I* (also dial.) 1954; *Le Village magique* (also story, dial.), *Les Evadés* (also co-sc.) 1955; *Papa Maman la Femme et Moi* 1956; *Le Cas du Docteur Laurent/The Case of Dr. Laurent* (also co-sc.) 1957; *Les Misérables* (also co-sc.) 1958; *La Française et l'Amour/Love and the Frenchwoman* ("La Femme seule" episode; also sc.) 1960; *Par-dessus le Mur* (also co-sc.) 1961; *Mandrin* (also co-sc.) 1963; *Monsieur* 1964; *Le Jardinier d'Argenteuil* 1966.

Leclerc, Ginette. Actress. *b.* Geneviève Manut, Feb. 9, 1912, Paris. *d.* 1992. A voluptuous brunette, she starred in many French films of the 30s, most memorably in the title role in Marcel Pagnol's *The Baker's Wife.* She also impressed as the amoral crippled girl in Henri-Georges Clouzot's thriller, *Le Corbeau/The Raven* (1943), and seemed assured of a bright future. But after the liberation, she was accused (unjustly, many say) of collaborating with the Nazis and the roles she was later assigned were unremarkable. Memoirs: *Ma Vie Privée.*

FILMS INCLUDE: *L'Enfant du Miracle* 1932; *La Dame de Chez Maxim, Ciboulette* 1933; *Le Commissaire est Bon Enfant, Dédé* 1934; *Fanfare d'Amour* 1935; *Il Fu Mattia Pascal/L'Homme de nulle Part/The Late Mathias Pascal* (It./Fr.) 1937; *Prisons sans Barreaux/Prisons Without Bars, La Femme du Boulanger/The Baker's Wife* 1938; *Louise, Coup de Feu* 1939; *L'Empreinte du Dieu/Two Women* 1940; *Fièvres* 1941; *Vie privée, Le Mistral* 1942; *Le Corbeau/The Raven, Le Val d'Enfer* 1943; *Les Eaux troubles* 1949; *La Maison dans la Dune, Le Plaisir* 1952; *Les Amants du Tage/Lover's Net, Gas-Oil* 1955; *Les Magiciennes/Double Deception* 1960; *Le Cave se rebiffe/The Counterfeiters of Paris* 1961; *Le Chant du Monde* 1965; *Tropic of Cancer* (US), *Popsy Pop/The Butterfly Affair, Le Bal du Comte d'Orgel* 1970; *La Drapeau noir flotte sur la Marmite* 1971; *Le Rempart des Béguines/Rampart of Desire* 1972; *Spermula* 1976; *La Barricade du Point du Jour* 1978.

Lederer, Charles. Screenwriter, sometime director. *b.* Dec. 31, 1910, New York City. *d.* 1976. *ed.* U. of California, Berkeley. The son of a stage producer and of a sister of actress Marion DAVIES, he gave up journalism in 1931 to become a Hollywood screenwriter. He was a collaborator and intimate friend of Ben HECHT and was highly regarded in the industry for his quick wit and prankish humor. At his best with light fare, he wrote many highly entertaining screenplays, alone or in collaboration, as well as original stories and adaptations. He also ventured occasionally into film directing, with modest results. He was producer and co-author (with Luther Davis) of the Broadway hit musical 'Kismet' (1953–54), which he co-adapted to the screen in 1955. Lederer married Virginia Nicholson, Orson Welles's former wife, in 1940, and actress Anne SHIRLEY in 1949.

FILMS: As screenwriter—*The Front Page* (co-dial.) 1931; *Cock of the Air* (co-story, co-sc., co-dial.) 1932; *Topaze* (co-sc., uncredited) 1933; *Mountain Music* (co-sc.) *Double or Nothing* (co-sc.) 1937; *Within the Law, Broadway Serenade* 1939; *His Girl Friday, I Love You Again* (co-sc.), *Comrade X* (co-sc.) 1940; *Love Crazy* (co-sc.) 1941; *Slightly Dangerous, The Youngest Profession* (co-sc.) 1943; *Kiss of Death* (co-sc.), *Ride the Pink Horse* (co-sc.), *Her Husband's Affairs* (co-sc.) 1947; *I Was a Male War Bride* (co-sc.), *Red Hot and Blue* (story) 1949; *Wabash Avenue* (co-story, co-sc.) 1950; *The Thing* 1951; *Fearless Fagan, Monkey Business* (co-sc.) 1952; *Gentlemen Prefer Blondes* 1953; *Kismet* (co-sc. from his and Luther Davis's musical) 1955; *Gaby* (co-sc.) 1956; *The Spirit of St. Louis* (adapt.), *Tip on a Dead Jockey* 1957; *It Started with a Kiss* 1959; *Can-Can* (co-sc.), *Ocean's 11* (co-sc.) 1960; *Follow That Dream, Mutiny on the Bounty* 1962; *A Global Affair* (co-sc.) 1964. As director—*Fingers at the Window* 1942; *On the Loose* 1951; *Never Steal Anything Small* (also sc.) 1959.

Lederer, Francis. Actor. Born Frantisek (Franz) Lederer, on Nov. 6, 1906, in Prague. A graduate of Prague's Academy of Music and Academy of Dramatic Art, he began his stage career locally while still in his teens and by the late 20s had developed into a matinee idol in Berlin, Vienna, and other European capitals. He starred in a number of films in Germany and France—including G. W. Pabst's *Die Büchse der Pandora/Pandora's Box* and Julien Duvivier's *Maman Colibri* (both 1929)—before arriving in the US in 1932. His success on Broadway in 'Autumn Crocus' led to a Hollywood contract and to a promising career as a romantic leading man, typically as a Continental lover, sometimes with a mean streak. He played some interesting roles for various studios during the late 30s, but by the early 40s his film career was fizzling and he gradually eased into character parts. Long active in various civic affairs, he has been an energetic spokesman for world peace and was among the founders of the Hollywood Museum. He has served as president of the Southern California chapter of the American National Theatre and Academy (ANTA) and director of its Academy of Performing Arts. He rarely acts now, living prosperously off his extensive real-estate investments. His second of three wives (1937–40) was actress MARGO.

FILMS INCLUDE: In Europe—*Die Büchse der Pandora/Pandora's Box* (Ger.), *Atlantik/Atlantic* (Ger./UK), *Maman Colibri* (Fr.), *Die wunderbare Lüge der Nina Petrovna/The Wonderful Lies of Nina Petrova* (Ger.) 1929; *Hai-Tang/Flame of Love* (Ger./UK), *Susanne macht Ordnung* (Ger.) 1930; *Das Schicksal der Renate Langen* (Ger.), *Ihre Majestät die Liebe* (Ger.) 1931. In the US—*Man of Two Worlds, The Pursuit of Happiness, Romance in Manhattan* 1934; *One Rainy Afternoon, My American Wife* 1936; *It's All Yours, The Lone Wolf in Paris* 1938; *Midnight, Confessions of a Nazi Spy* 1939; *The Man I Married* 1940; *Puddin' Head* 1941; *The Bridge of San Luis Rey, Voice in the Wind* 1944; *The Madonna's Secret,*

The Diary of a Chambermaid 1946; *Million Dollar Weekend* 1948; *A Woman of Distinction, Captain Carey USA, Surrender* 1950; *The Ambassador's Daughter, Lisbon* 1956; *Maracaibo, The Return of Dracula* 1958; *Terror Is a Man* 1959.

Lederman, D(avid) Ross. Director. *b.* Dec. 11, 1895, Lancaster, Pa. *d.* 1972. He began in films in 1913 as an extra in Mack Sennett comedies, later working as Fatty Arbuckle's prop man. He eventually became an assistant director and second-unit director, specializing in trick and action scenes. Becoming a director in the late 20s, he turned out a number of Rin Tin Tin features, followed by serials and numerous low-budget Westerns and action pictures.

FILMS INCLUDE: *A Dog of the Regiment* 1927; *Shadows of the Night* (also sc.), *Rinty of the Desert* 1928; *The Million Dollar Collar* 1929; *The Man Hunter* 1930; *The Phantom of the West* (serial), *The Texas Ranger, Branded* 1931; *Two-Fisted Law, The End of the Trail, High Speed* 1932; *State Trooper, Soldiers of the Storm* 1933; *Hell Bent for Love, The Crime of Helen Stanley, A Man's Game, Murder in the Clouds* 1934; *Red Hot Tires, Dinky* (co-dir. with Howard Bretherton), *The Case of the Missing Man* 1935; *Hell Ship Morgan, Panic in the Air, Pride of the Marines, The Final Hour, Alibi for Murder* 1936; *Counterfeit Lady, Frame-Up, The Game That Kills* 1937; *Tarzan's Revenge, Juvenile Court, Adventure in Sahara* 1938; *Racketeers of the Range, North of Shanghai* 1939; *Military Academy, Glamour for Sale* 1940; *Father's Son, Strange Alibi, Shadows on the Stairs, Passage from Hong Kong* 1941; *Bullet Scars, The Body Disappears, I Was Framed, Busses Roar, Escape from Crime* 1942; *The Gorilla Man, Adventure in Iraq, Find the Blackmailer* 1943; *The Racket Man* 1944; *Out of the Depths* 1945; *The Phantom Thief, The Notorious Lone Wolf, Dangerous Business, Sing While You Dance, Boston Blackie and the Law* 1946; *The Lone Wolf in Mexico, Key Witness* 1947; *The Return of the Whistler* 1948; *Military Academy* 1950.

Ledoux, Fernand. Actor. *b.* Jan. 24, 1897, Tirlemont, Belgium. *d.* 1993. Versatile, forceful character player of the Paris stage and French films. For many years (1921–43) a distinguished member of the Comedie-Française, he appeared in a number of silent films but did not gain prominence on the screen until the late 30s.

FILMS INCLUDE: *Le Carnaval des Vérités* 1919; *L'Atlantide* 1921; *Villa Destin* 1923; *L'Homme à la Barbiche* 1932; *L'Homme de Folies-Bergère* (French-language version of *Folies-Bergère*; US) 1935; *Le Vagabond bien-aimé* (French-language version of *The Beloved Vagabond*; UK), *Mayerling* 1936; *Altitude 3200/Youth in Revolt, La Bête humaine/The Human Beast* 1938; *Volpone* (as Corvino; release delayed from 1939), *Remorques/Stormy Waters, Premier Rendez-vous/Her First Affair, L'Assassinat du Père Noël/Who Killed Santa Claus?* 1941; *Les Visiteurs du Soir/The Devil's Envoys* 1942; *Untel Père et Fils/The Heart of a Nation* (release delayed from 1940), *Goupi Mains-Rouges/It Happened at the Inn* (title role), *L'Homme de Londres* 1943; *Sortilèges/The Bellman* 1945; *La Fille du Diable/Devil's Daughter* 1946; *Danger de Mort* 1947; *L'Ombre* 1948; *Pattes blanches, Monseigneur* 1949; *Un Acte d'Amour/An Act of Love* (Fr./US), *Papa Maman la Bonne et moi/Mama Papa the Maid and I* 1954; *Les Hommes en blanc/The Doctors* 1955; *Till l'Espiègle* 1956; *Celui qui doit mourir/He Who Must Die* 1957; *Les Misérables* 1958; *La Vérité/The Truth* 1960; *The Big Gamble* (US) 1961; *The Longest Day* (US), *Freud* (US), *Le Procès/The Trial* 1962; *Le Glaive et la Balance/Two Are Guilty* 1963; *Up from the Beach* (US) 1965; *Peau d'Ane/Donkey Skin* 1971; *Alice ou la Dernière Fugue, A chacun son Enfer* 1977; *Mille Milliards de Dollars* 1982.

Lee, Ang. Director, screenwriter. Born in Taiwan. *ed.* University of Illinois, Urbana; Institute of Film and Television, New York University. Poignant, intelligent filmmaker whose father fled to Taiwan after the communist revolution in China. With a love for film from childhood, Lee came to America to study his chosen craft, eventually ending up at NYU and working with such notables as Spike LEE and Ernest DICKERSON. His highly acclaimed independent features, particularly *The Wedding Banquet* (1993), launched a promising career and led the way to his Academy Award nominated film *Sense and Sensibility* (1995).

FILMS: *Pushing Hands* (prod., dir., sc.) 1992; *The Wedding Banquet* (prod., dir., sc.) 1993; *Eat Drink Man Woman* (dir., sc.) 1994; *Sense and Sensibility* (dir. only) 1995; *Ice Storm* 1997.

Lee, Anna. Actress. Born Joanna Winnifrith, in 1913, in Ightham, England. Blonde, petite leading lady and supporting player of British, then Hollywood films, following brief experience on the London stage. Best remembered in *How Green Was My Valley* (1941). In 1978 she joined the cast of the TV daytime soaper 'General Hospital.' Formerly married to director Robert STEVENSON, she became the seventh wife of novelist-playwright-poet Robert Nathan in 1970. She is the mother of actress-turned-producer Venetia Stevenson.

FILMS INCLUDE: In the UK—*Ebb Tide* 1932; *Mannequin, Chelsea Life* 1933; *Faces* 1934; *Heat Wave, First a Girl, The Passing of the Third Floor Back* 1935; *The Man Who Changed His Mind/The Man Who Lived Again* 1936; *O.H.M.S./You're in the Army Now, King Solomon's Mines, Non-Stop New York* 1937; *Four Just Men/The Secret Four* 1938; *Return to Yesterday* 1939. In the US—*Seven Sinners* 1940; *How Green Was My Valley, My Life with Caroline* 1941; *Flying Tigers* 1942; *The Commandos Strike at Dawn, Hangmen Also Die, Flesh and Fantasy* 1943; *Summer Storm* 1944; *Bedlam* 1946; *The Ghost and Mrs. Muir* 1947; *Fort Apache* 1948; *Prison Warden* 1949; *Boots Malone* 1952; *Gideon's Day* (UK), *The Last Hurrah* 1958; *The Horse Soldiers, This Earth Is Mine* 1959; *The Big Night* 1960; *Two Rode Together* 1961; *The Man Who Shot Liberty Valance, Jack the Giant Killer, What Ever Happened to Baby Jane?* 1962; *The Unsinkable Molly Brown* 1964; *The Sound of Music* 1965; *Seven Women, Picture Mommy Dead* 1966; *In Like Flint* 1967; *Star!* 1968.

Lee, Belinda. Actress. *b.* June 15, 1935, Budleigh Salterton, England. *d.* 1961 in a car crash. Beautiful, sexy star of British, then French, German, and Italian films, in many of which her body provided the sole solid structure.

FILMS INCLUDE: *The Runaway Bus* 1953; *The Belles of St. Trinian's, Murder by Proxy/Blackout* 1954; *Footsteps in the Fog, Man of the Moment* 1955; *The Feminine Touch, Eyewitness* 1956; *Miracle in Soho, Dangerous Exile* 1957; *The Big Money, Nor the Moon by Night* 1958; *Ce Corps tant désiré* (Fr.), *Les Dragueurs/The Chasers* (Fr.), *Le Notti di Lucrezia/The Nights of Lucretia Borgia* (title role; It./Fr.), *Messalina* (title role; It.) 1959; *Femmine di Lusso/Love the Italian Way, Giuseppe venduto dai Fratelli/The Story of Joseph and His Brethren* (It.) 1960; *Constantino il Grande/Constantine and the Cross* (It.) 1961.

Lee, Bernard. Actor. *b.* Jan. 10, 1908, London. *d.* 1981. An actor's son, he made his first appearance on the stage as a child of six but later earned his living as a fruit salesman at Southampton. After dramatic training at the Royal Academy of Dramatic Art he toured England with various plays, making his London debut in 1928. Concurrent with his busy stage career, he played character roles in numerous British films, often as a military leader, police inspector, or master spy, memorably as "M" in the James Bond thriller series.

FILMS INCLUDE: *The Double Event* 1934; *The River*

House Mystery 1935; *The Terror* 1937; *Let George Do It* 1940; *Quartet, The Fallen Idol* 1948; *The Third Man* 1949; *Last Holiday, The Blue Lamp, Morning Departure/Operation Disaster, Odette, Cage of Gold* 1950; *Appointment with Venus/Island Rescue, Mr. Denning Drives North, White Corridors* 1951; *The Gift Horse/Glory at Sea* 1952; *Singlehanded/ Sailor of the King* 1953; *Beat the Devil, Father Brown/The Detective, Seagulls Over Sorrento/Crest of the Wave, The Purple Plain* 1954; *The Spanish Gardener, The Battle of the River Plate/Pursuit of the Graf Spee* 1956; *Fire Down Below, Across the Bridge* 1957; *The Key, Dunkirk, The Man Upstairs* 1958; *Danger Within/Breakout* 1959; *Cone of Silence/Trouble in the Sky, Kidnapped* (as Captain Hoseason; UK/US), *The Angry Silence, Clue of the Twisted Candle* 1960; *The Secret Partner, Whistle Down the Wind* 1961; *Dr. No* 1962; *From Russia with Love* 1963; *Ring of Spies/Ring of Treason, Saturday Night Out, Goldfinger* 1964; *Dr. Terror's House of Horrors, The Spy Who Came in from the Cold, Thunderball* 1965; *You Only Live Twice* 1967; *On Her Majesty's Secret Service* 1969; *The Raging Moon/Long Ago Tomorrow, Diamonds Are Forever* 1971; *Live and Let Die* 1973; *The Man with the Golden Gun* 1974; *The Spy Who Loved Me* 1977; *Moonraker* 1979.

Lee, Bruce. Actor. *b.* Lee Yuen Kam, 1940, San Francisco, of Chinese origin. *d.* 1973. He spent much of his childhood in Hong Kong, where he appeared in a number of films as Li Siu Lung. The adult phase of his career began after he completed philosophy studies at the University of Washington. On TV, he appeared in several episodes of 'Batman' and played Kato, the Oriental houseboy-chauffeur, in the 'Green Hornet' series. He played supporting roles in a couple of Hollywood films before emerging in the early 70s as the internationally popular star of a string of made-in-Hong-Kong action films featuring karate, kung fu, and other martial arts. He was a virtual cult figure among action-loving youths, with fan clubs around the world at the time of his sudden and mysterious death of brain edema at the age of 32. To capitalize on his popularity, three of his 'Green Hornet' episodes were re-edited posthumously into a feature-length film in 1974, and a fictionalized film biography was rushed into production the following year. Several imitators soon appeared upon the scene, but none seemed single-handedly capable of reviving the past glory of the real Bruce Lee. Finally Hong Kong producers came up with a quantitative solution, throwing into battle three Bruce Lee look-alikes—Bruce Li, Bruce Le, and Bruce Lei—in *The Clones of Bruce Lee*. The original Lee left behind an outline for a story that was turned into the film *The Silent Flute/Circle of Iron* (1979) with David Carradine playing the role Lee had intended for himself. The action-filled *Game of Death* offers a final glimpse of Lee. Its filming interrupted by the star's death, it was partly re-shot with the original featured players and with doubles filling in for Lee. Released in 1979, six years after the star's death, the film contains a long sequence of martial arts combat that delighted Bruce Lee fans. His son, Brandon Lee (*b.* 1965; *d.* 1993), was a rising action-adventure star following in his father's footsteps when, in an eerie coincidence, he too died young. While filming *The Crow*, Brandon was killed when a gun that was supposed to contain only blanks fired a bullet that had accidentally been left lodged in the barrel.

FILMS INCLUDE: *The Birth of Mankind* 1946; *Kid Cheung* 1950; *Infancy* 1951; *Blame It on Father, A Mother's Tears* 1953; *An Orphan's Tragedy* 1955; *Too Late for Divorce* 1956; *The Thunderstorm* 1957; *Alone in the World* 1961; *The Wrecking Crew* (karate advisor only), *Marlowe* 1969; *The Big Boss/Fists of Fury* 1971; *Fist of Fury/The Chinese Connection* 1972; *Enter the Dragon, Way of the Dragon/Return of the Dragon* (also dir., sc.) 1973; *The Green Hornet/Kato and the Green Hornet* (reshuffled compilation of three TV episodes plus footage from Lee's old screen test) 1974; *The Silent Flute/Circle of Iron* (story only), *Game of Death* (re-shot and released posthumously) 1979.

Lee, Canada. Actor. *b.* Leonard Lionel Cornelius Canegate, 1907. *d.* 1952. A childhood friend of politician Adam Clayton Powell, Jr., he grew up in the Harlem section of New York City and became a boxer, a profession that cost him an eye. In the mid-30s he turned to stage acting, and won critical notice as Bigger Thomas in Orson Welles's Broadway production of "Native Son" (1941). Skilled at portraying strong, dignified outsiders, he had a brief career in films, including Alfred Hitchcock's *Lifeboat* (1944), before it ended when he was blacklisted as an alleged Communist because of his outspokenness about the rights of African-Americans. His son Carl Lee is also an actor whose films include *Superfly* (1972) and *Gordon's War* (1973).

FILMS INCLUDE: *Keep Punching* 1939; *Lifeboat* 1944; *Body and Soul* 1947; *Lost Boundaries* 1949; *Cry the Beloved Country* (UK) 1952.

Lee, Christopher. Actor. Born on May 27, 1922, in London. *ed.* Wellington Coll. He played small parts in many British films from 1947 before taking advantage of his gaunt features to become the sinister star of countless horror films in Britain and on the Continent. With frequent co-star Peter CUSHING, he worked often in the productions of Hammer Films, most notably in the title role of its new cycle of Dracula films (beginning with *Dracula/Horror of Dracula* in 1958). Following in the footsteps of Basil RATHBONE, he took an occasional leave of his villainous image to play Sherlock Holmes or, in one case (*The Private Life of Sherlock Holmes*, 1970), Holmes's brother Mycroft. He was also an effective villain for James Bond in *The Man with the Golden Gun* (1974). Autobiography: *Tall, Dark and Gruesome* 1977.

FILMS INCLUDE: *Corridor of Mirrors, Hamlet* 1948; *Captain Horatio Hornblower* 1951; *The Crimson Pirate* 1952; *Moulin Rouge* 1953; *The Cockleshell Heroes, Storm Over the Nile* 1955; *Beyond Mombasa* 1956; *The Curse of Frankenstein* (as the Monster) 1957; *A Tale of Two Cities* (as the Marquis St. Evrémonde), *Dracula/Horror of Dracula* (title role) 1958; *The Hound of the Baskervilles, The Man Who Could Cheat Death, The Mummy* (title role) 1959; *The Two Faces of Dr. Jekyll/House of Fright/Jekyll's Inferno, Beat Girl/Wild for Kicks, The City of the Dead/Horror Hotel, Too Hot to Handle/ Playgirl After Dark* 1960; *Les Mains d'Orlac/The Hands of Orlac* (French- and English-language versions; Fr./UK), *Taste of Fear/Scream of Fear, The Terror of the Tongs* 1961; *The Pirates of Blood River, Corridors of Blood, The Longest Day* (US), *Sherlock Holmes und das Halsband des Todes/Sherlock Holmes and the Deadly Necklace* (Ger./It./Fr.) 1962; *La Frusta e il Corpo/Night Is the Phantom/What!* (It./Fr./UK) 1963; *La Vergine de Norimberga/Horror Castle/Terror Castle* (It.), *The Gorgon* 1964; *Dr. Terror's House of Horrors, She* (as Billali), *The Skull, The Face of Fu Manchu* (title role) 1965; *Rasputin—The Mad Monk* (title role), *The Brides of Fu Manchu* (again as Fu Manchu) 1966; *Circus of Fear/Psycho-Circus, Theatre of Death/Blood Fiend* 1967; *The Face of Eve* (US/UK/Sp.), *Dracula Has Risen from the Grave* (again as Count Dracula), *Curse of the Crimson Altar/The Crimson Cult* 1968; *The Oblong Box, The Magic Christian* (again as Dracula) 1969; *Scream and Scream Again, Taste the Blood of Dracula* (again as Dracula), *The Scars of Dracula* (again as Dracula), *Julius Caesar* (as Artemidorus), *The Private Life of Sherlock Holmes, The House That Dripped Blood* 1970; *Vampir/Count Dracula* (Sp.), *Hannie*

Caulder, I Monster 1971; *Dracula A.D. 1972* 1972; *Frankenstein and the Monster from Hell/Island of the Burning Damned, The Satanic Rites of Dracula/Count Dracula and His Vampire Bride* (as Dracula), *The Creeping Flesh* 1973; *Tendre Dracula* (Fr.), *The Three Musketeers* (as Rochefort), *The Man with the Golden Gun* 1974; *In Search of Dracula* (doc.), *The Four Musketeers* (again as Rochefort), *Killer Force* 1975; *To the Devil a Daughter* (UK/Ger.), *Dracula Père et Fils/Dracula and Son* (as Dracula) (Fr.), *The Keeper* (Can.) 1976; *Airport '77* (US), *Starship Invasions* (Can.), *End of the World* (US) 1977; *Return from Witch Mountain* (US), *Caravans* 1978; *The Silent Flute/Circle of Iron* (US), *The Passage, Arabian Adventure, Jaguar Lives!* (US), *1941* (US) 1979; *Bear Island, Serial* (US) 1980; *An Eye for an Eye* (US) 1981; *Safari 3000* (US) 1982; *The Return of Captain Invincible/Legend in Leotards* (Austral.), *The Salamander* (US/It./UK), *House of the Long Shadows* 1983; *The Rosebud Beach Hotel* (US) 1984; *Howling II. . . Your Sister Is a Werewolf* 1986; *Jocks, Mio in the Land of Faraway* (USSR/Nor./Swed.) 1977; *La Revolution Française/The French Revolution* (Fr./W Ger./It./Can.) 1989; *L'Avaro/The Miser* (It./Fr./Sp.), *Honeymoon Academy* (US), *Gremlins 2: The New Batch* (US), *The Rainbow Thief, Curse 3: Blood Sacrifice* 1990; *Funny Man, Police Academy VII: Mission to Moscow* 1994.

Lee, Gypsy Rose. Ecdysiast, actress, writer. *b.* Rose Louise Hovick, Feb. 9, 1914, Seattle. *d.* 1970. She made her stage debut at age four, later appearing on the vaudeville circuit with kid sister June HAVOC as "Madame Rose's Dancing Daughters." She grew up to become the burlesque queen of the 30s, the best-known stripper of her day. Among other things, she wrote two mystery novels, one of which, *The G-String Murders,* was adapted to the screen as *Lady of Burlesque* (1943). A play of hers provided the basis for the screenplay of the film *Doll Face* (1946). Her autobiography, *Gypsy* (1957), was turned into a Broadway musical hit (1959) and a Hollywood film (1962). She also appeared sporadically in films, initially as Louise Hovick.

FILMS (as actress): As Louise Hovick—*You Can't Have Everything, Ali Baba Goes to Town* 1937; *Sally Irene and Mary, The Battle of Broadway, My Lucky Star* 1938. As Gypsy Rose Lee—*Stage Door Canteen* 1943; *Belle of the Yukon* 1944; *Babes in Bagdad* 1952; *Screaming Mimi, Wind Across the Everglades* 1958; *The Stripper* 1963; *The Trouble with Angels* 1966.

Lee, Jack. Director. Born in 1913, in Stroud, England. He entered the documentary film field in 1938 as associate producer with the GPO Film Unit and later edited the famous wartime documentary *London Can Take It* (1940). He began directing documentaries in 1941 and feature films in 1947. In the early 60s he set up his own production company in Australia.

FILMS: Documentaries—*The Pilot Is Safe* 1941; *Ordinary People* (co-dir. with J. B. Holmes) 1942; *Close Quarters/Undersea Raider* (also sc.) 1943; *By Sea and Land* 1944; *The Eighth Plague* 1945; *Children on Trial* (semidoc.; also co-sc.) 1946. Feature films—*The Woman in the Hall* (also co-sc.) 1947; *Once a Jolly Swagman* (also co-sc.) 1948; *The Wooden Horse* (also co-sc.) 1950; *South of Algiers/The Golden Mask* 1952; *Turn the Key Softly* (also co-sc.) 1953; *A Town Like Alice* (also sc.) 1956; *Robbery Under Arms* 1957; *The Captain's Table* 1958; *Circle of Deception* 1961.

Lee, Lila. Actress. *b.* Augusta Appel, July 25, 1901, Union Hill, N.Y. *d.* 1973. A child performer in vaudeville from age five, she entered films at 17 and became a popular silent movie star after appearing opposite Valentino in *Blood and Sand* (1922). She played demure leads in many silent productions, co-starring with Wallace Reid and Thomas Meighan, among others. She was one of the few silent stars whose careers were virtually unaffected by the advent of sound and she continued playing leads in films well into the 30s. After retiring from the screen in 1937, she appeared on the stage but was forced to quit show business following several bouts with tuberculosis. She died of a stroke at 72. The former wife of actor-producer James KIRKWOOD, she was the mother of actor-playwright-novelist James Kirkwood, Jr.

FILMS INCLUDE: *The Cruise of the Make-Believe, Such a Little Pirate* 1918; *The Lottery Man, A Daughter of the Wolf, Puppy Love, The Secret Garden, Male and Female* 1919; *The Soul of Youth, Terror Island, Midsummer Madness* 1920; *The Charm School, The Easy Road, Crazy to Marry, Gasoline Gus, After the Show* 1921; *One Glorious Day, Is Matrimony a Failure?, The Dictator, Blood and Sand, The Ghost Breaker, Ebb Tide* 1922; *The Ne'er-Do-Well, Homeward Bound, Woman-Proof* 1923; *Love's Whirlpool, Wandering Husbands, Another Man's Wife* 1924; *Coming Through, The Midnight Girl* 1925; *Broken Hearts, The New Klondike* 1926; *Million Dollar Mystery* 1927; *You Can't Beat the Law, Just Married, A Bit of Heaven, The Adorable Cheat, The Little Wild Girl* 1928; *Queen of the Night Clubs, Honky Tonk, Drag, The Argyle Case, Flight, Dark Streets, Love Live and Laugh, The Sacred Flame* 1929; *Second Wife, Murder Will Out, The Unholy Three, Those Who Dance, Double Cross Roads* 1930; *The Gorilla, Woman Hungry, Misbehaving Ladies* 1931; *War Correspondent, Unholy Love, The Night of June 13th, False Faces, The Iron Master* 1932; *Face in the Sky, The Intruder* 1933; *Whirlpool, In Love with Life* 1934; *The People's Enemy* 1935; *The Ex-Mrs. Bradford* 1936; *Two Wise Maids* 1937.

Lee, Peggy. Singer, songwriter, actress. Born Norma Deloris Engstrom, on May 26, 1920, in Jamestown, N.D. She milked cows before making her singing debut on a local radio show and later became famous as a vocalist with the Benny Goodman band. She continued on her own to secure a place among America's top nightclub, TV, and recording stars. She appeared in only five films, playing dramatic leads in two, *The Jazz Singer* (1953) and *Pete Kelly's Blues* (1955). She was nominated for an Oscar for her performance in the latter. She also wrote lyrics for many of her songs and for three films. Bravely surviving personal tragedies and an assortment of grave illnesses culminating in double bypass open-heart surgery, Miss Lee continued dazzling club audiences into the 90s. In 1991 she won a multimillion dollar suit against the Disney company, in which the court recognized her right to collect royalties from the 1987 videocassette release of the animated classic *Lady and the Tramp* (1955) for which she had written several songs and provided voices. She had earned only $3,500 for her initial effort. Sales of the videocassette as the trial opened were estimated at $90 million. Her four husbands included actors Brad Dexter and Dewey Martin.

FILMS: *The Powers Girl* (as herself), *Stage Door Canteen* (guest singer) 1943; *Mr. Music* (guest singer-actress) 1950; *The Jazz Singer* (act., singer, lyricist) 1953; *Lady and the Tramp* (lyrics, v/o), *Pete Kelly's Blues* (act., singer) 1955; *Tom Thumb* (lyrics only) 1958; *Pieces of Dreams* (v/o) 1970.

Lee, Rowland V. Director. *b.* Sept. 6, 1891, Findlay, Ohio. *d.* 1975. *ed.* Columbia. His parents had been on the stage, and he began as a juvenile stage actor in stock and on Broadway. He later left the theater for a career as a Wall Street stockbroker but returned to the stage after two years. He entered films in 1915 as an actor for Thomas INCE and after WW I service in France returned to Ince as a director in 1920. He piloted numerous silent and sound films of varying quality through the mid-40s, including a number of horror and adventure thrillers that stand out for their pictorial composition and chilling atmosphere.

FILMS: *The Cup of Life, Blind Hearts, Cupid's Brand, The Sea Lion* 1921; *The Dust Flower, His Back Against the Wall, The Men of Zanzibar, Mixed Faces, Money to Burn, A Self-Made Man* (also co-sc.), *Shirley of the Circus* 1922; *Alice Adams* (also adapt.), *Desire, You Can't Get Away with It, Gentle Julia* 1923; *In Love with Love* 1924; *The Man Without a Country/As No Man Has Loved, Havoc* 1925; *The Outsider, The Silver Treasure* 1926; *The Whirlwind of Youth, Barbed Wire* 1927; *The Secret Hour* (also sc.), *Doomsday, Three Sinners, The First Kiss, Loves of an Actress* (also sc.) 1928; *The Wolf of Wall Street, A Dangerous Woman, The Mysterious Dr. Fu Manchu* 1929; *Paramount on Parade* (co-dir.), *The Return of Dr. Fu Manchu/The New Adventures of Dr. Fu Manchu, Ladies Love Brutes, A Man from Wyoming, Derelict* 1930; *The Ruling Voice* (also story), *The Guilty Generation* 1931; *That Night in London/Over Night* (UK) 1932; *Zoo in Budapest* 1933; *I Am Suzanne* (also co-story, co-sc.), *The Count of Monte Cristo* (also co-sc.), *Gambling* 1934; *Cardinal Richelieu, The Three Musketeers* (also co-sc.) 1935; *One Rainy Afternoon* 1936; *Love from a Stranger, The Toast of New York* 1937; *Mother Carey's Chickens, Service de Luxe* (also prod.) 1938; *Son of Frankenstein* (also prod.), *The Sun Never Sets* (also prod.), *Tower of London* (also prod.) 1939; *The Son of Monte Cristo* 1940; *Powder Town* 1942; *The Bridge of San Luis Rey* 1944; *Captain Kidd* 1945; *The Big Fisherman* (prod., co-sc. only) 1959.

Lee, Spike. Director, producer, screenwriter, actor. Born Shelton Jackson Lee, on Mar. 20, 1957, in Atlanta. The son of jazz bass player–composer Bill Lee and a schoolteacher, he moved with his family to Brooklyn before he turned three and attended public schools at various parts of the New York borough, completing his secondary education at John Dewey High in Coney Island. He took a serious interest in film while majoring in communications at Atlanta's Morehouse College. He attended movie screenings with growing frequency and shared with classmates his dream of making films that would "speak to black Americans." After graduation, he enrolled at New York University's film school, where his master's thesis film, *Joe's Bed-Stuy Barbershop: We Cut Heads* (1980), won the Student Award of the Motion Picture Academy. Following an aborted attempt to produce a semi-autobiographical first film titled *The Messenger,* Lee made an auspicious professional debut with *She's Gotta Have It* (1986). Made on a shoestring budget, this flawed but refreshingly bright, black-and-white (with one color sequence), funky comedy about three macho black guys vying for the attention of one woman, was a surprise commercial hit. Its success provided Lee with the means to make his next film, *School Daze* (1988). A robust satirical farce about life on a black college campus, it was but a mild prelude to Lee's first major film, *Do the Right Thing* (1989), an angry assault on racism, prompted by the brutal Howard Beach incident in which a young black man was killed after being chased by white youths. It earned an Academy Award nomination for best screenplay. As he had in his earlier films, Lee played a secondary but pivotal role in *Do The Right Thing*. Also, like the earlier films, it was photographed by Ernest DICKERSON, Lee's NYU schoolmate, and scored by Bill Lee, the director's father, both comprising the core of Lee's developing creative ensemble.

Following *Mo' Better Blues* (1990), a celebration of jazz and its black artists, Lee confronted the racial issue once more with *Jungle Fever* (1991), a fierce exploration of the cultural and social foundations of a sexual relationship between an African-American man and an Italian-American woman, inspired by the Yusuf Hawkins incident in which a black teenager was killed by a group of whites who suspected he had been having an affair with a young woman in their racially segregated Bensonhurst neighborhood. With the strong reactions to this film still echoing, Lee set about planning his most ambitious production yet, a biography of Malcolm X, the Black Muslim militant who was assassinated in 1965 and became a heroic symbol of African-American pride. *Malcolm X* (1992) was a commercial disappointment, and lacked some of the bite of Lee's earlier efforts, but it was his most ambitious work, an epic built around a powerful performance by Denzel Washington.

A controversial figure whose films explore the nature of American racism, Lee has often criticized the attitudes of the Hollywood establishment toward black filmmakers. His outspokenness has not endeared him to the Academy, which has generally denied Oscar nominations to his films. *Malcolm X,* a film as likely as any to appeal to the Academy's taste for epics, received only two nominations and no awards. Married to lawyer Tonya Lynette Lewis.

FILMS (as director-screenwriter-producer-actor): *Joe's Bed-Stuy Barbershop: We Cut Heads* (also edit.) 1980; *She's Got to Have It* (also edit.) 1986; *School Daze* 1988; *Do the Right Thing, Making "Do the Right Thing"* (doc.; personal appearance only) 1989; *Mo' Better Blues, Lonely In America* (act. only) 1990; *Jungle Fever* 1991; *Malcolm X* 1992; *Crooklyn, Drop Squad* (exec. prod.) 1994; *Clockers, New Jersey Drive, Tales from the Hood* (exec. prod.) 1995; *Get on the Bus* (exec. prod.), *Girl 6* (exec. prod., actor) 1996; *Four Little Girls* 1997.

Leeds, Andrea. Actress. *b.* Antoinette M. Lees, Aug. 18, 1913, Butte, Mont. *d.* 1984. *ed.* UCLA. Wholesome star of a handful of Hollywood films of the 30s. Specializing in sentimental romantic roles, she was nominated for an Academy Award as best supporting actress for her portrayal of an innocent would-be suicide in *Stage Door* (1937). The film's director, Gregory La Cava, called her "the best natural actress who has ever passed under my hands." She retired from the screen in 1939, after marrying millionaire sportsman Robert S. Howard, and became involved in breeding race horses.

FILMS: *Dante's Inferno* (bit, as a maid) 1935; *The Moon's Our Home* (bit, as salesgirl), *Come and Get It* 1936; *Stage Door, It Could Happen to You* 1937; *The Goldwyn Follies, Letter of Introduction, Youth Takes a Fling* 1938; *They Shall Have Music, The Real Glory, Swanee River* 1939; *Earthbound* 1940.

Leeds, Herbert I. Director. *b.* Herbert I. Levy, 1900(?), New York City. *d.* 1954. A former film editor, he turned to directing in 1937 and turned out competent low-budget action adventure and light family fare.

FILMS: *Love on a Budget, Island in the Sky, Keep Smiling, Five of a Kind, Arizona Wildcat* 1938; *Mr. Moto in Danger Island, The Return of the Cisco Kid, Chicken Wagon Family, Charlie Chan in City in Darkness, The Cisco Kid and the Lady* 1939; *Yesterday's Heroes* 1940; *Romance of the Rio Grande, Ride on Vaquero, Blue White and Perfect* 1941; *The Man Who Wouldn't Die, Just off Broadway, Manila Calling, Time to Kill* 1942; *It Shouldn't Happen to a Dog* 1946; *Let's Live Again* 1948; *Bunco Squad, Father's Wild Game* 1950.

Leenhardt, Roger. Director. *b.* July 23, 1903, Paris. *d.* 1985. *ed.* Sorbonne (literature and philosophy). An influential film critic for a number of French publications, he exerted profound intellectual influence, on André BAZIN and others, with his serious, pioneering essays on cinema in the 30s. He began making documentary shorts in the middle of that decade. They covered a wide range of cultural subjects and gained him a reputation for excellence. One of the better known of these, *Naissance du Cinéma* (1946), a brief prehistory of the movies, was selected best documentary at the 1947 Brussels World Film Festival. His series of biographical studies of prominent personalities in literature and the arts has also been of special interest. In between dozens of shorts, he directed two feature films of some quality. The first of these, *Les Dernières Vacances* (1948), is noted for its evocative expression of first love. In retrospect, the film is seen as having foreshadowed the French New Wave. In 1949, with BRESSON and COCTEAU, Leenhardt founded the film magazine *Objectif 49,* a precursor of *Cahiers du Cinéma.* Through his articles and enthusiastic presence, he continued exerting influence on young filmmakers, eventually attaining recognition as the spiritual father of the NOUVELLE VAGUE. Bazin dedicated his famous collection of essays, *What Is Cinema?,* to Leenhardt, who also appeared in Godard's *Une Femme Mariée/The Married Woman* (1964) and was seen in silhouette in Truffaut's *L'Homme qui aimait les Femmes/The Man Who Loved Women* (1977). Memoirs: *Les Yeux ouverts* (1979).

FILMS INCLUDE: Features (complete)—*Les Dernières Vacances* 1948; *Le Rendez-vous de Minuit* 1962. Shorts—*L'Orient qui vient* (co-dir. with René Zuber), *Le Vrai Jeu* 1934; *Fêtes de France* (co-dir. with Zuber) 1940; *A la Pour-suite du Vent* 1943; *Lettre de Paris* 1945; *Naissance du Cinéma* (in two parts: 1. *The Toy That Grew Up*; 2. *Biography of the Motion Picture Camera*) 1946; *La Côte d'Azur* 1948; *Métro, La Fugue de Mahmoud* 1950; *Victor Hugo* 1951; *La France est un Jardin* 1953; *François Mauriac* 1954; *La Conquête de l'Angleterre* 1955; *Jean-Jacques Rousseau* (co-dir. with Jean-Paul Vivet), *En Plein Midi* 1958; *Daumier* 1959; *Paul Valéry, Entre Seine et Mer* 1960; *L'Homme à la Pipe* 1962; *Des Femmes et des Fleurs, Monsieur de Voltaire* 1962; *Naissance de la Photo* 1965; *Le Coeur de la France* 1966; *Le Beatnik et le Minet* 1967; *Douze Mois en France* (co-dir.) 1970; *Abraham Bosse* 1972; *Pissarro* 1975; *Anjou* 1977; *Du Plaisir á la Joie* 1978; *Manet ou Le Novateur malgé lui* 1980.

Lee Thompson, J(ohn). Director. Born in 1914, in Bristol, England. A stage actor with the Nottingham Repertory Company from age 17, he had two of his plays produced in London before he reached 20. He began in films in 1934 as an actor, switched to screenwriting in 1939, and made his first film as a director in 1950. His films (mostly British but many American-made) are noted for their brisk pace and strong visual sense, seldom for profundity. He scored his biggest box-office success with the suspenseful WW II action drama *The Guns of Navarone* (1961). He runs his own film company, Jaylee Productions.

FILMS: *Murder Without Crime* (also story, sc.) 1950; *The Yellow Balloon* (also sc.) 1952; *The Weak and the Wicked* (also co-sc.), *For Better for Worse* (also sc.) 1954; *As Long as They're Happy, An Alligator Named Daisy* 1955; *Yield to the Night/Blonde Sinner* 1956; *The Good Companions* (also co-prod.), *Woman in a Dressing Gown* (also co-prod.) 1957; *Ice Cold in Alex/Desert Attack* 1958; *No Trees in the Street/No Tree in the Street* (also co-exec. prod.), *Tiger Bay, North West Frontier/Flame Over India* 1959; *I Aim at the Stars* (US/Ger.) 1960; *The Guns of Navarone* (UK/US) 1961; *Cape Fear* (US), *Taras Bulba* (US) 1962; *Kings of the Sun* (US) 1963; *What a Way to Go!* (US) 1964; *John Goldfarb Please Come Home!* (also co-exec. prod.; US), *Return from the Ashes* (also prod.; US/UK) 1965; *Eye of the Devil* 1967; *Before Winter Comes, The Chairman/The Most Dangerous Man in the World* (US/UK), *Mackenna's Gold* (US) 1969; *Country Dance/Brotherly Love* 1970; *Conquest of the Planet of the Apes* (US) 1972; *Battle for the Planet of the Apes* (US) 1973; *Huckleberry Finn* (US) 1974; *The Reincarnation of Peter Proud* (US) 1975; *St. Ives* (US) 1976; *The White Buffalo* (US) 1977; *The Greek Tycoon* (US) 1978; *The Passage* 1979; *Caboblanco* (US), *Happy Birthday to Me* (Can.) 1981; *10 to Midnight* (US) 1983; *The Evil That Men Do* (US) 1984; *The Ambassador* (US), *King Solomon's Mines* (US) 1985; *Murphy's Law* (US), *Firewalker* (US) 1986; *Death Wish 4: The Crackdown* (US) 1987; *Messenger of Death* (US) 1988; *Kinijite/Forbidden Subjects* 1989.

Lefebvre, Jean-Pierre. Director. Born on Aug. 17, 1941, in Montreal. *ed.* U. of Montreal (French literature). Leading figure of the Quebec branch of Canadian cinema. The son of a pharmacist, he was a movie enthusiast from boyhood and at 19 began writing film criticism for the now-defunct periodical *Objectif.* A director from 1964, he became one of French-Canada's most prolific filmmakers, usually writing his own scripts and producing his own films. His films have been described as visual poems laced with warmth and humor. He also encouraged the development of young Quebecois directors through his tenure as head of the Fiction Studio at the National Film Board, and later through his own production companies. His first wife, Marguerite Duprac, edited and co-produced many of his films. She died in 1982. His second wife, Barbara Easto, then became his script collaborator.

FILMS (as director-producer-screenwriter): *L'Homoman* (short) 1964; *La Révolutionaire/The Revolutionary, Patricia et Jean Baptiste* 1965; *Il ne faut pas mourir pour ca/Don't Let It Kill You* 1967; *Jusqu'au Coeur/Straight to the Heart* (dir., sc. only) 1968; *Mon Amie Pierrette* (dir., sc. only; release delayed from 1967), *La Chambre blanche/House of Light* 1969; *Un Succès commercial/Q-bec My Love/Struggle for Love* 1970; *Les Maudits Sauvages/Those Damned Savages, Mon Oeil/My Eye* 1971; *Ultimatum, Les Dernières Finançailles/The Last Betrothal, On n'engraisse pas les Cochons á l'Eau claire/Pigs Are Seldom Clean* 1973; *L'Amour blessé/Les Confidences de la Nuit/Confessions of the Night* 1975; *Les Gars des Vues* (unreleased) 1976; *Le Vieux Pays oú Rimbaud est mort/The Old Country Where Rimbaud Died* 1977; *Avoir 16 Ans/To Be 16* 1979; *Les Fleurs sauvages/Wild Flowers* 1982; *Au Rhythme de mon Coeur/To the Rhythm of My Heart* 1983; *Le Jour "S"/"S" as in. . .* 1984; *Alfred Aliberte—Sculpteur* 1987.

Lefebvre, Robert. Director of photography. Born on Mar. 19, 1907, in Paris. He entered films in 1923 as a camera assistant and advanced to lighting cameraman in 1932. He has since been responsible for the cinematography of scores of French films, a few of which stand out, most notably *Casque d'Or* (1952).

FILMS INCLUDE: *Sapho* 1932; *Tartarin de Tarascon* 1934; *Quelle Drôle de Gosse* 1935; *Un Grand Amour de Beethoven/The Life and Loves of Beethoven* 1936; *Le Coupable* 1937; *Katia, Ultimatum* 1938; *Battements de Coeur* 1940; *Le Dernier des Six, Premier Rendez-vous/Her First Affair* 1941; *Le Colonel Chabert, Voyage sans Espoir* 1943; *Clochemerle/The Scandals of Clochemerle* 1948; *Aux Yeux du Souvenir/Souvenir* 1949; *Dieu a besoin des Hommes/God Needs Men* 1950; *Edouard et Caroline/Edward and Caroline, Le Garçon sauvage/Savage Triangle* 1951; *Casque d'Or, La Minute de Vérité/The Moment of Truth* 1952; *Le Blé en Herbe/The Game of Love, L'Affaire Maurizius* 1954; *Les Mauvaises Recontres, Les Grandes Manoeuvres/The Grand Maneuver* 1955; *Michel Strogoff/Michael Strogoff, Porte de Lilas/Gates of Paris* 1957; *Le Dos au Mur/Back to the Wall* 1958; *Faibles Femmes/Women Are Weak, Marie-Octobre* 1959; *La Française et l'Amour/Love and the Frenchwoman, Candide ou l'Optimisme au XXe Siècle/Candide* 1960; *La Bride sur le Cou/Please Not Now* 1961; *Patate/Friend of the Family* 1964; *La Peur et le Désir/Torment* 1967; *La Nuit la plus chaude/The Night of the Three Lovers* 1968; *Claude et Greta/Her She and Him* 1970.

Lefèvre, René. Actor, screenwriter. Born René Lefebvre, on Mar. 6, 1898, in Nice, France. Charming leading man of

French films of the 30s and a solid character actor thereafter. Less impressive as a screenwriter and one-shot director in collaboration (*Opéra-Musette,* 1942). He is the author of a number of novels.

FILMS INCLUDE (as actor): *Knock* 1925; *Le Tourbillon de Paris* 1928; *Pas si Bête, Ces Dames aux Chapeaux verts* 1929; *Mon Ami Victor, Jean de la Lune, Le Million, Le Chemin du Paradis* 1931; *Les Cinq Gentlemen maudits/Sous la Lune du Maroc* 1932; *Paprika* 1933; *L'Amour en Cage, La Femme Idéale* 1934; *Le Crime de Monsieur Lange* 1936; *Gueule d'Amour* 1937; *Les Musiciens du Ciel* (also sc. from own novel) 1940; *Opéra Musette* (also co-dir. with Claude Renoir, sc.) 1942; *La Boite aux Rêves* 1945; *Le Bataillon du Ciel/They Are Not Angels* 1947; *Le Point du Jour* 1949; *Celui qui doit mourir/He Who Must Die, La Garçonne, Bel-Ami* 1957; *Sois Belle et tais-toi/Be Beautiful and Shut Up* 1958; *Le Gorille vous salue bien* 1959; *Le Doulos/Doulos—The Finger Man* 1963; *Angélique et le Roi* 1965; *Un Oursin dans la Poche* 1978.

Le Gallienne, Eva. Actress, stage director, and producer. *b.* Jan. 11, 1899, London. *d.* 1991. *ed.* RADA. The daughter of journalists who divorced when she was four, she was raised partly in Paris, where she decided to devote her life to the theater after seeing Sarah Bernhardt perform. She made her London stage debut in 1914 and the following year went to the US, where she soon became one of Broadway's leading stars. She founded the famed Civic Repertory Theatre in New York in 1926 and directed and starred in many of its productions through 1932, when it folded as a result of the Depression. She later directed or appeared in numerous other plays on Broadway and in stock, but her film appearances were rare. She was nominated for an Academy Award as best supporting actress for her performance in *Resurrection* (1980). She also received a special Tony Award in 1964 and numerous other prizes. In 1961 she was honored with the Norwegian Grand Cross of the Royal Order of St. Olav for her work in furthering the presentation of plays by Ibsen and in 1968 she received the National Medal of Arts from President Reagan. In addition to doing several play translations and stage adaptations, she wrote two volumes of memoirs, *At 33* (1934) and *With a Quiet Heart* (1953), a children's book, *Flossie and Bossie,* and a study of Eleonora Duse, *The Mystic in the Theatre* (1966).

FILMS: *Prince of Players* (as the Queen in 'Hamlet') 1955; *The Devil's Disciple* 1959; *Resurrection* 1979.

Léger, Fernand. Painter, filmmaker. *b.* Feb. 4, 1881, Argentan, France. *d.* 1955. The celebrated cubist artist's involvement with the cinema was more an extension of his art as a painter than a direct exploration of the film medium. Attracted to the expressive potential of film after seeing a Charlie Chaplin movie, he made his first contribution as set designer for L'Herbier's *L'Inhumaine* (1923). The following year, with the technical assistance of an American named Dudley Murphy, he made *Le Ballet mécanique,* an experimental short film exploring rhythm and motion, which has since become a landmark of avant-garde cinema. Next he designed imaginative costumes for the British film *Things to Come* (1936), based on the H. G. Wells fantasy. In the US throughout WW II, he was the subject of the documentary *The World of Fernand Léger,* which he helped direct. Later he contributed part of the scenario for Hans Richter's *Dreams That Money Can Buy* (1944–46). He was making plans to film *Le Ballet des Couleurs* at the time of his death.

Legg, Stuart. Documentary producer-director. Born on Aug. 31, 1910, in London. *ed.* Cambridge. He turned out a number of important British documentaries in the early 30s, then took up administrative duties in the documentary film industry in England, Canada, and the US. In 1957 he became chairman of Britain's Film Centre International.

FILMS INCLUDE: *The New Generation, The New Operator* 1932; *Telephone Workers, Telephone Ship, The Coming of the Dial* 1933; *BBC—The Voice of Britain* 1934; *Powered Flight* 1953.

Legion of Decency. A Catholic censorship board set up in 1934 by a committee of US bishops, with the announced purpose of arousing public opinion against objectionable motion pictures and urging Catholics to avoid patronizing such films. Its formation exerted enormous pressure on the motion picture industry, whose own self-regulatory PRODUCTION CODE lacked provisions for effective enforcement. The Legion instituted its own rating system, classifying films into several categories ranging from "morally unobjectionable for general patronage" (A–I) to "condemned" (C). The ratings were guided by the treatment of various subjects on the screen rather than by the film's artistic value or overall content. Whole or partial nudity or immoral behavior, actual or suggested, almost invariably caused a film to be condemned. As late as 1965, *The Pawnbroker,* a sincere and socially important film, was given a C rating merely for briefly showing a woman's breasts, in the context of the drama.

The Legion periodically reinforced the effect of its motion picture code by eliciting annual pledges of support on the part of churchgoers across the country. The threat of a boycott of a film forced most producers, distributors, and exhibitors to accept and publicly support the Legion's moral code. Studios regularly submitted their films to the Legion's judgment prior to their public release. Some went as far as submitting scripts for approval before production ever began. In the 60s the Legion felt increasing pressure to change its image in the face of rapidly changing public taste and a liberal interpretation of obscenity by Federal courts. This image was not enhanced by decisions to condemn such fine European films as Polanski's *Knife in the Water* (in 1961) "because of nudity in the treatment," and Bergman's *The Silence* (1963) because "his selection of images is sometimes vulgar, insulting to a mature audience, and dangerously close to pornography."

In 1966 the National Legion of Decency changed its official name to the National Catholic Office for Motion Pictures and, in line with Pope John XXIII's policy of updating Catholic thought, announced a more progressive attitude. The Catholic office initially supported the rating system of the Motion Picture Association of America's Production Code when it was announced in 1968, but in 1971 it withdrew its support, criticizing the system as ineffective.

Legrand, Michel. Composer. Born on Feb. 24, 1931, in Paris. A musical prodigy, he entered the Paris Conservatory at 11 and graduated as a first-prize winner. In the 50s he became a popular bandleader, singer, and songwriter and began composing for films. He gained an international reputation with his score for *Les Parapluies de Cherbourg/The Umbrellas of Cherbourg* (1964) and subsequently worked on many British and American productions. He won an Oscar for the song 'The Windmills of Your Mind' in the film *The Thomas Crown Affair* (1968), another for the score of *The Summer of '42* (1971), and a third for the song score of *Yentl* (1983). His scores and songs have been noted for their lyricism and assertive melodious flow. Legrand turned out a first film as a director in 1989. The film, *Cinq Jours en Juin/Five Days in June,* is an autobiographical tale of the composer's early teens during the final phases of WW II, particularly his loss of innocence, at 14, with a woman twice his age. His father, Raymond Legrand (*b.* 1908, Paris), also a composer, wrote less memorable scores for many French films of the 40s and 50s.

FILMS INCLUDE: *Les Amants du Tage/Lovers' Net* 1955; *Charmants Garçons* 1958; *L'Amérique insolite* 1960; *Lola, Une Femme est une Femme/A Woman Is a Woman* 1961; *Cléo de 5 a 7/Cleo from 5 to 7* (also act.), *Vivre sa Vie/My Life to Live, Eva* 1962; *Love Is a Ball* (US), *La Baie des Anges/Bay of Angels, Le Joli Mai* 1963; *Les Parapluies de Cherbourg/The Umbrellas of Cherbourg, Bande à part/Band of Outsiders* 1964; *La Vie de Château/A Matter of Resistance, Tendre Voyou/Tender Scoundrel* 1966; *Les Demoiselles de Rochefort/The Young Girls of Rochefort, Pretty Polly/A Matter of Innocence* (UK) 1967; *How to Save a Marriage—and Ruin Your Life* (US), *Sweet November* (US), *The Thomas Crown Affair* (US), *Ice Station Zebra* (US) 1968; *Castle Keep* (US), *The Happy Ending* (US) 1969; *Pieces of Dreams* (US), *Wuthering Heights* (UK) 1970; *Peau d'Ane/Donkey Skin, Summer of '42* (US), *Le Mans* (US), *The Go-Between* (UK), *Un Peu de Soleil dans l'Eau froide* 1971; *Les Feux de la Chandeleur, Portnoy's Complaint* (US), *Lady Sings the Blues* (US) 1972; *A Bequest to the Nation/The Nelson Affair* (UK), *L'Impossible Object/Impossible Object, A Doll's House* (UK), *40 Carats* (US), *Cops and Robbers* (US), *Breezy* (US) 1973; *The Three Musketeers* (UK), *Our Time* (US) 1974; *F for Fake* (Ger./Fr.), *Sheila Levine Is Dead and Living in New York* (US), *Le Sauvage/The Savage* 1975; *Gable and Lombard* (US), *Le Voyage de Noces, Ode to Billy Joe* (US) 1976; *The Other Side of Midnight* (US) 1977; *Les Routes du Sud, Lady Oscar* (Jap./Fr.) 1978; *The Hunter* (US), *Atlantic City* (Can./Fr.) 1980; *Les Uns et les autres/Bolero* (co-mus.) 1981; *Le Cadeau/The Gift, Best Friends* (US) 1982; *Never Say Never Again* (UK), *Yentl* (US) 1983; *Ein Liebe in Deutschland/Love in Germany* (Ger./Fr.), *Paroles et Musique/Love Songs* (Can./Fr.) 1984; *Partir revenir* 1985; *Club de Rencontres* 1987; *Switching Channels* 1988; *Cinq Jours en Juin/Five Days in June* (also dir., co-sc.) 1989; *Fuga Dal Paradiso/Escape from Paradise* (It./Fr./Ger.), *Eternity* 1990; *Dingo, The Pickle* 1991; *Ready to Wear* 1994; *The Truth About Cats and Dogs* 1996.

Leguizamo, John. Actor. Born 1965 in Bogotá, Colombia. *ed.* Lee Strasberg Institute; Herbert Berghoff Studio; New York University. Multitalented, hip, and personable actor of stage and screen. He first gained notice on the New York stage with his hit one-man shows 'Mambo Mouth' and 'Spic-o-Rama,' showcasing his writing talents and the uncanny ability to impersonate people from all walks of life, male and female. Except for a short-lived television series, he has worked primarily on film in a variety of roles, notably as a cross-dressing nymphet in the comedy *To Wong Foo, Thanks for Everything, Julie Newmar* (1995).

FILMS: *Mixed Blood* 1985; *Casualties of War* 1989; *Die Hard 2, Revenge* 1990; *Hangin' with the Homeboys, Regarding Henry* 1991; *Whispers in the Dark* 1992; *Carlito's Way, Super Mario Bros.* 1993; *Executive Decision, A Pyromaniac's Love Story, To Wong Foo Thanks for Everything Julie Newmar* 1995; *Romeo and Juliet* 1996; *The Pest* (also co-prod., co-sc.), *Spawn* 1997.

Lehman, Ernest. Screenwriter, producer, director. Born in 1920, in New York City. *ed.* CCNY. Originally a financial editor and short-story writer, he has to his credit a number of outstanding scripts and five Oscar nominations. Since the mid-60s he has also been a producer. In 1971 he made an inauspicious debut as director with a pallid film version of Philip Roth's *Portnoy's Complaint.* Novels: *The French Atlantic Affair* (1977), *Farewell Performance.* Nonfiction: *Screening Sickness* (1988).

FILMS (as screenwriter, alone or in collaboration): *The Inside Story* (co-story only) 1948; *Executive Suite, Sabrina* 1954; *Somebody Up There Likes Me, The King and I* 1956; *Sweet Smell of Success* (from own story) 1957; *North by Northwest* 1959; *From the Terrace* 1960; *West Side Story* 1961; *The Prize* 1963; *The Sound of Music* 1965; *Who's Afraid of Virginia Woolf?* (also prod.) 1966; *Hello Dolly!* (also prod.) 1969; *Portnoy's Complaint* (also prod., dir.) 1972; *Family Plot* 1976; *Black Sunday* 1977.

Lehmann, Michael. Director. Born in 1957, in San Francisco. The son of a psychoanalyst father and artist mother, he briefly studied painting at New York's School of Visual Arts, then enrolled at Columbia, where he majored in philosophy. Following a year of postgraduate studies at West Germany's University of Tübingen, he returned to San Francisco and began working in various capacities at Francis Coppola's Zoetrope Studios. Becoming hopelessly addicted to movies, he returned to school, enrolling at USC's film department. On the strength of his graduation film, *The Beaver Gets a Boner,* he got the opportunity to direct a first feature, *Heathers* (1989), an off-the-wall inside view of high-school hierarchies and teenage suicide. The film's outrageous black humor caught the attention of critics, who marked Lehmann as a director worth watching.

FILMS: *Heathers* 1989; *Meet the Applegates/The Applegates* (also co-sc.) 1990; *Hudson Hawk* 1991; *Airheads* 1994; *The Truth About Cats and Dogs* 1996.

Lehrman, Henry ("Pathé"). Director, actor, screenwriter. *b.* Mar. 30, 1886, Vienna. *d.* 1946. In the US from 1905, he was a trolley conductor before entering films in 1909, allegedly by falsely representing himself as an agent for the French Pathé company (hence his nickname). He appeared in some early Griffith films, then became Mack SENNETT's right hand man, appearing in many Keystone Comedies and directing many others. He has the distinction of having directed Charlie Chaplin's four first films, *Making a Living, Kid Auto Races at Venice, Mabel's Strange Predicament* (co-dir. with Sennett), and *Between Showers* (all 1914). Soon after he left Keystone and founded L-KO (for Lehrman Knock-Out) Comedies for release through Universal. Most of the product was imitative of the Keystone style. In 1917, Lehrman moved to Fox, where he directed many of the company's Sunshine Comedies. In the early 20s he was involved in the famous Fatty ARBUCKLE scandal. The victim in the case, starlet Virginia Rappe, was Lehrman's fiancée, and it was the director's fierce condemnation of Arbuckle that helped close the lid on that actor's career and opened the way for screen censorship. Lehrman continued as screenwriter and gagman until 1935, when he retired from work in films.

FILMS INCLUDE: As actor—*Nursing a Viper* 1909; *As the Bells Rang Out, The Iconoclast* 1910; *A Beast at Bay* 1912. As director—*Algy the Watchman* (also act.) 1912; *Cupid in a Dental Parlor, Help Help Hydrophobia!, Passions He Had Three, For Love of Mabel, The Peddler, Just Kids, The New Baby, Love and Rubbish, Get Rich Quick, Their Husbands, Fatty at San Diego* (also act.), *Fatty Joins the Force* (also act.), *The Woman Haters* (also act.), *Protecting San Francisco from Fire* (doc.), *The Champion* 1913; *Making a Living/A Busted Johnny* (also act.), *Kid Auto Races at Venice* (also act.), *Mabel's Strange Predicament* (co-dir. with Mack Sennett), *Between Showers, A Rural Demon* 1914; *After Her Millions* (also act.) 1915; *Who's Your Father?, Mongrels, The Fatal Marriage* 1918; *Reported Missing* 1922; *Double Dealing* (also co-story) 1923; *On Time* 1924; *The Fighting Edge* 1926; *For Ladies Only* (co-dir. with Scott Pembroke), *Sailor Izzy Murphy* 1927; *Husbands for Rent, Why Sailors Go Wrong, Chicken a la King, Homesick* 1928; *New Year's Eve* 1929. As screenwriter—*The Poor Millionaire* (co-story, co-sc.) 1930; *Moulin Rouge* (co-adapt.) 1934; *Show Them No Mercy* (adapt.) 1935.

Leiber, Fritz. Actor. *b.* Jan. 31, 1882, Chicago. *d.* 1949. A noted Shakespearean on stage, he played some leads in silents and numerous character roles in films during the latter part of his career. He portrayed Caesar in the 1917 film version of *Cleopatra* starring Theda Bara.

FILMS INCLUDE: *Romeo and Juliet* (as Mercutio) 1916; *The Primitive Call, Cleopatra* (as Julius Caesar) 1917; *If I Were King* (as Louis XI) 1920; *The Queen of Sheba* (as King Solomon) 1921; *A Tale of Two Cities* (as Gaspard) 1935; *The Story of Louis Pasteur, Under Two Flags, Sins of Man, Anthony Adverse* (as M. Ouvard) 1936; *Camille, Champagne Waltz, The Prince and the Pauper, The Great Garrick* 1937; *Gateway* 1938; *Nurse Edith Cavell, The Hunchback of Notre Dame* 1939; *All This and Heaven Too, The Sea Hawk* 1940; *Aloma of the South Seas* 1941; *Crossroads* 1942; *First Comes Courage, The Phantom of the Opera* (as Franz Liszt) 1943; *This Love of Ours, The Spanish Main* 1945; *Angel on My Shoulder, Humoresque* 1946; *Monsieur Verdoux, The Web* 1947; *To the End of the Earth, Another Part of the Forest* 1948; *Bride of Vengeance, Samson and Delilah* 1949; *Devil's Doorway* 1950.

Leibman, Ron. Actor. Born on Oct. 11, 1937, in New York City. *ed.* Ohio Wesleyan U. Leading man and second lead of the American stage, TV, and films, usually in offbeat roles. Trained at the Actors Studio, he made his New York stage debut in 1959 and was later seen in a number of off-Broadway and Broadway productions. He won an Obie Award and a Drama Desk Award for his performance in 'Transfers,' Drama Desk Award for 'We Bombed in New Haven,' and the Tony for his virtuoso Broadway performance in Tony Kushner's epic 'Angels in America.' He has been appearing sporadically in films since 1970. He won an Emmy for his portrayal of the title role in the TV series 'Kaz' (1978–79). Divorced from actress Linda Lavin, he married actress Jessica WALTER.

FILMS: *Where's Poppa?* 1970; *The Hot Rock, Slaughterhouse Five* 1972; *Your Three Minutes Are Up* 1973; *The Super Cops* 1974; *Won Ton Ton—The Dog Who Saved Hollywood* 1976; *Norma Rae* 1979; *Zorro, the Gay Blade* 1981; *Phar Lap* (Austral.), *Romantic Comedy* 1983; *Rhinestone* 1984; *Door to Door* 1975; *Seven Hours to Judgment* 1988; *Night Falls on Manhattan* 1997.

Leigh, Janet. Actress. Born Jeanette Helen Morrison, on July 6, 1927, in Merced, Calif. The daughter of an insurance and real estate agent, she was a twice-married student at the College of the Pacific, majoring in music, when she was signed to a film contract by MGM in 1947 as a personal discovery of Norma Shearer. A fresh-faced, wholesome beauty with no previous acting experience, she was cast in sweet ingenue roles in many of the studio's films of the late 40s and early 50s. She acquired a more mature, sexier screen image after her much-publicized marriage to Tony CURTIS, which lasted from 1951 to 1962, and gradually improved her acting ability. She demonstrated convincing dramatic talent in such films as Orson Welles's *Touch of Evil* (1958) and Alfred Hitchcock's *Psycho* (1960) but is at her best with fluffy comedy. Throughout the 50s she ranked among Hollywood's leading stars. She is the mother of actress Jamie Lee CURTIS. Autobiography: *There Really Was a Hollywood* (1984).

FILMS: *The Romance of Rosy Ridge* 1947; *If Winter Comes, Hills of Home, Words and Music* 1948; *Act of Violence, Little Women* (as Meg), *The Doctor and the Girl, That Forstye Woman/The Forsyte Saga* (as June Forsyte), *The Red Danube, Holiday Affair* 1949; *Strictly Dishonorable, Angels in the Outfield, Two Tickets to Broadway* 1951; *It's a Big Country, Just This Once, Scaramouche, Fearless Fagan* 1952; *The Naked Spur, Confidentially Connie, Houdini, Walking My Baby Back Home* 1953; *Prince Valiant, Living It Up, The Black Shield of Falworth, Rogue Cop* 1954; *Pete Kelly's Blues, My Sister Eileen* 1955; *Safari* 1956; *Jet Pilot* 1957; *Touch of Evil, The Vikings* 1958; *The Perfect Furlough* 1959; *Who Was That Lady?, Psycho, Pepe* 1960; *The Manchurian Candidate* 1962; *Bye Bye Birdie, Wives and Lovers* 1963; *Kid Rodelo, Harper, Three on a Couch, An American Dream* 1966; *Grand Slam* 1968; *Hello Down There* 1969; *One Is a Lonely Number, Night of the Lepus* 1972; *Boardwalk* 1979; *The Fog* 1980.

Leigh, Jennifer Jason. Actress. Born Jennifer Leigh Morrow, February 2, 1962, in Los Angeles. The daughter of actor Vic MORROW and TV writer Barbara Turner (and step-daughter of director Reza Badiyi), she dropped out of high school to train at the Lee Strasberg Institute and pursue a career in TV and films. Displaying admirable versatility, she has portrayed a wide range of lead roles, often in characterizations of sinners and misfits.

FILMS: *Eyes of a Stranger* 1981; *Wrong Is Right, Fast Times at Ridgemont High* 1982; *Easy Money* 1983; *Grandview U.S.A.* 1984; *Flesh and Blood* 1985; *The Hitcher, The Men's Club* 1986; *Under Cover* 1987; *Sister Sister* 1988; *Heart of Midnight, The Big Picture, Last Exit to Brooklyn* (Ger.) 1989; *Miami Blues* 1990; *Crooked Hearts* 1991; *Rush, Single White Female* 1992; *Short Cuts* 1993; *The Hudsucker Proxy, Mrs. Parker and the Vicious Circle* 1994; *Dolores Claiborne, Georgia* (also co-prod.) 1995; *Kansas City* 1996; *A Thousand Acres, Washington Square* 1997.

Leigh, Mike. Director, playwright, screenwriter. Born in 1943, in Salford, England. He trained briefly at RADA for an acting career but found the experience stultifying and switched to a succession of art schools before going on to the London Film School. His first stage work, 'The Box Play' (1966), demonstrated his interest in the observation of reality through a collaborative improvisational process with his performers. His first film, *Bleak Moments* (1971), an angst-filled adaptation of Leigh's play about repressed feelings, was modestly financed by actor Albert FINNEY. Although it won first prizes at both the Chicago and Locarno festivals of 1972, it led to no further film projects for Leigh. He focused instead on stage and TV work that found increasing favor with the British public and critics for its keen social observation and bold political critiques. More than a decade would go by before the director could find financing for another feature. In 1988 his brightly original slice-of-life drama, *High Hopes,* made a strong impression on audiences at the New York Film Festival, finally allowing Leigh's talent the broader exposure it deserves. At Cannes, he was named best director for *Naked.* In 1996 he received an Academy Award nomination as best director for the emotionally powerful *Secrets & Lies*.

FEATURE FILMS: *Bleak Moments* 1971; *Meantime* (orig. for TV) 1983; *Four Days in July* (orig. for TV) 1984; *High Hopes* 1988; *Life Is Sweet* 1991; *Naked* 1993; *Secrets and Lies* 1996; *Career Girls* 1997.

Leigh, Suzanna. Actress. Born in 1945, in Reading, England. Blonde, shapely leading lady of mostly mindless British and American films and TV.

FILMS INCLUDE: *Oscar Wilde* 1960; *Bomb in the High Street* 1963; *The Pleasure Girls, Boeing Boeing* (US) 1965; *Paradise Hawaiian Style* (US), *Deadlier Than the Male* 1966; *The Deadly Bees* 1967; *The Lost Continent* 1968; *Subterfuge* (UK/US) 1969; *Lust for a Vampire* 1971; *Son of Dracula* 1974.

Leigh, Vivien. Actress. *b.* Vivian Mary Hartley, Nov. 5, 1913, Darjeeling, India. *d.* 1967. Convent-educated in England and on the Continent, she made her British film debut in 1934, her London stage debut the following year. An appearance opposite Laurence OLIVIER in the film *Fire Over England* (1937) led to a well-publicized romance between the two married stars. They finally married each other in 1940, following simultaneous divorces from their respective spouses. The year before, Miss Leigh had achieved fame and worldwide popularity as Scarlett O'Hara in Hollywood's *Gone With the Wind,* a role for which she had been chosen from among hundreds of aspirants and for which she received her first Academy Award, as well as the New York critics' best actress prize. She won her second Oscar, as well as the British Academy Award and the Venice Festival prize, and was again the New York critics' winner for the role of Blanche du Bois in *A Streetcar Named Desire* (1951). Delicate and small-framed, she was plagued by tuberculosis and physical exhaustion through much of her career. She was also diagnosed as a manic-depressive. But she is remembered as one of the most exquisite beauties ever to grace the screen.

FILMS: *Things Are Looking Up* 1934; *The Village Squire, Gentleman's Agreement, Look Up and Laugh* 1935; *Fire Over England, Dark Journey, Storm in a Teacup* 1937; *A Yank at Oxford* (US/UK), *St. Martin's Lane/Sidewalks of London* 1938; *Guide Dogs for the Blind* (short), *21 Days/21 Days Together* (release delayed from 1937); *Gone With the Wind* (as Scarlett O'Hara; US) 1939; *Waterloo Bridge* (US) 1940; *That Hamilton Woman/Lady Hamilton* (title role; US) 1941; *Caesar and Cleopatra* (as Cleopatra) 1945; *Anna Karenina* (title role) 1948; *A Streetcar Named Desire* (as Blanche du Bois; US) 1951; *The Deep Blue Sea* 1955; *The Roman Spring of Mrs. Stone* (US/UK) 1961; *Ship of Fools* (US) 1965.

Leighton, Margaret. Actress. *b.* Feb. 26, 1922, Barnt Green, near Birmingham, England. *d.* 1976. Tall, distinguished, elegant leading lady of the British stage and screen. A businessman's daughter, she began training for the stage at 15 and played her first professional role at 16. She rose to prominence in the late 40s after joining the reborn Old Vic company, under the direction of Laurence Olivier and Ralph Richardson, and thereafter gained growing recognition by London and Broadway critics for the quality of her playing. She won Tony Awards for her performances on Broadway in 'Separate Tables' (1956) and 'The Night of the Iguana' (1962). She typically played fragile, sensitive, highly vulnerable women. Although her film career was only secondary to her stage achievements, she portrayed many memorable screen roles and was nominated for an Oscar as best supporting actress for *The Go-Between* (1971). Her first husband was publisher Max Reinhardt; her second, actor Laurence HARVEY; and her third and last, actor Michael WILDING. She died of multiple sclerosis.

FILMS: *Bonnie Prince Charlie, The Winslow Boy* 1948; *Under Capricorn* (UK/US) 1949; *The Astonished Heart, The Elusive Pimpernel/The Fighting Pimpernel* 1950; *Calling Bulldog Drummond, Home at Seven/Murder on Monday* 1951; *The Holly and the Ivy* 1952; *The Good Die Young* 1953; *The Teckman Mystery, Carrington V.C./Court-Martial* 1954; *The Constant Husband* 1955; *The Passionate Stranger/A Novel Affair* 1957; *The Sound and the Fury* (US) 1959; *Waltz of the Toreadors/The Amorous General* 1962; *The Third Secret, The Best Man* (US) 1964; *The Loved One* (US) 1965; *Seven Women* (US) 1966; *The Madwoman of Chaillot* (as Constance) 1969; *The Go-Between* 1971; *Zee & Co./X Y & Zee, Lady Caroline Lamb* 1972; *A Bequest to the Nation/The Nelson Affair* (as Lady Nelson) 1973; *Galileo* (US/UK), *From Beyond the Grave* 1975; *Dirty Knights' Work, Great Expectations* (TV movie) 1976.

Leisen, Mitchell. Director. *b.* Oct. 6, 1898, Menominee, Mich. *d.* 1972. The son of a brewery owner, he trained as an architect at Washington University at St. Louis and worked in the advertising art department of the Chicago *Tribune* and for a Chicago architectural film before going to Hollywood in 1919. He played a small role in one film, then began designing costumes for Cecil B. DE MILLE and other directors. Among the films for which he designed costumes were De Mille's *Male and Female* (1919) and *Forbidden Fruit* (1921), Allan Dwan's *Robin Hood* (1922), Ernst Lubitsch's *Rosita* (1923), and Raoul Walsh's *The Thief of Bagdad* (1924). Moving up to set decorator and art director, Leisen later designed sets for such sumptuous De Mille productions as *The Road to Yesterday* (1925), *The Volga Boatman* (1926), *The King of Kings* (1927), *The Godless Girl* (1929), *Madam Satan* (1930), *The Squaw Man* (1931), and *The Sign of the Cross* (1932). Leisen's sense of design remained evident in his own films when he began directing in 1933.

The films Leisen directed for Paramount and other studios have been noted for their visual luster and entertaining pace. His consistency of style was particularly impressive in view of the thematic weakness of many of the films he was assigned to direct. Leisen was known as a "woman's director" for the many romantic films he made and for the strong performances he elicited from actresses. But above all he was known in the business as a thorough professional who handled each film with a great deal of preparation and methodical care. Leisen's career declined in the late 40s and after several flops in the 50s, he began directing for TV and devoting much of his time to a second career as an interior decorator and co-owner of a stylish Beverly Hills tailor shop. He was also a talented sculptor.

FILMS: *Tonight Is Ours* (assoc. dir. only), *The Eagle and the Hawk* (assoc. dir. only), *Cradle Song* 1933; *Death Takes a Holiday, Murder at the Vanities* 1934; *Behold My Wife, Four Hours to Kill, Hands Across the Table* 1935; *13 Hours by Air, The Big Broadcast of 1937* 1936; *Swing High Swing Low, Easy Living* 1937; *The Big Broadcast of 1938, Artists and Models Abroad* 1938; *Midnight* 1939; *Remember the Night* (also prod.), *Arise My Love* 1940; *I Wanted Wings, Hold Back the Dawn* (also act.) 1941; *The Lady Is Willing* (also prod.), *Take a Letter Darling* (also costume design) 1942; *No Time For Love* (also prod.) 1943; *Lady in the Dark, Frenchman's Creek, Practically Yours* (also prod.) 1944; *Kitty, Masquerade in Mexico* 1945; *To Each His Own* 1946; *Suddenly It's Spring, Golden Earrings* 1947; *Dream Girl* 1948; *Bride of Vengeance, Song of Surrender* 1949; *Captain Carey USA, No Man of Her Own* 1950; *The Mating Season, Darling How Could You!, Young Man with Ideas* 1951; *Tonight We Sing* 1953; *Bedevilled* 1955; *The Girl Most Likely* 1957; *Spree* (feature-length doc. filmed in 1962–63 in Las Vegas as *Las Vegas by Night*; co-dir. with Walon Green) 1967.

Leiser, Erwin. Filmmaker. Born on May 16, 1923, in Berlin. At 15 he fled to Sweden in the wake of a Nazi-inspired pogrom and after graduating from the University of Lund became a journalist and a literary and drama critic. He turned to documentaries in the late 50s, making his debut with an impressive film compilation of the Nazi horrors, *Mein Kampf* (1959). The German past remained his recurrent theme.

FILMS INCLUDE: *Den Blodiga Tiden/Mein Kampf* 1960; *Eichmann und das dritte Reich/Eichmann and the Third Reich/ Murder by Signature* 1961; *Wähle das Leben/Choose Life* 1962; *Deutschland Erwache!* 1966; *Following the Fuhrer* (co-dir.) 1985; *Die Feuerprobe/Ordeal by Fire* 1990.

Leland, David. Director, screenwriter, actor. Born on Apr. 20, 1947, in Cambridge, England. Raised in the small village of Waterbeach, he apprenticed for his electrician father before pursuing an acting career at the Nottingham Playhouse. He later joined London's newly formed Royal Court Theatre, where he began writing and directing as well as acting in plays. He also appeared in several films, including *Julius Caesar* (1970), *One*

Brief Summer, The Pied Piper (1972), *The Missionary* and *Time Bandits* (both 1981). Following the success of his teleplay 'Made in Britain,' he was commissioned by director Neil Jordan to write the screenplay that provided the memorable basis for *Mona Lisa* (1986). The following year, Leland made his own auspicious debut as a director with *Wish You Were Here.* He received the British Academy Award for that film's script which, like his typical work, centered on aspects of sexuality. The director's first Hollywood film, *Checking Out* (1989), was less successful, however, in focusing on the American preoccupation with health and death.

FILMS: As screenwriter—*Mona Lisa* (co-sc.) 1986; *Personal Services* (also act.) 1987. As director—*Wish You Were Here* (also sc., lyrics) 1987; *Checking Out* (US) 1989; *The Big Man* 1990.

Lelouch, Claude. Director. Born on Oct. 30, 1937, in Paris, the son of a Jewish confectioner whose family had resided in Algeria for three generations after having been expatriated from Palestine. He became passionately involved with film at a young age, and his first short, *Le Mal du Siècle,* which he directed when he was 13, won a prize at the Cannes Amateur Film Festival. Becoming a professional filmmaker in 1956, he made shorts and TV commercials. He continued making films during his military service, turning out ten shorts for the French army's cinematographic unit from 1957 to 1960. With financial help from his family he made his first feature film in 1960, but unable to secure further feature assignments, he returned to the production of shorts for two more years. After several commercial failures, he finally established himself internationally with *Un Homme et une Femme/A Man and a Woman* (1966), a somewhat contrived but technically glowing romantic drama that derived much of its impact from the personalities and performances of Anouk Aimée and Jean-Louis Trintignant. The film shared the Grand Prize at the Cannes Festival and won two Oscars, as best foreign film and for best original story and screenplay. The stars later reprised their roles in another Lelouch film, *Un Homme et une Femme: Vingt Ans déjé/A Man and a Woman: 20 Years Later* (1986). In 1967, Lelouch scored another commercial success with *Vivre pour vivre/Live for Life,* also a glossy romantic drama, this one enhanced by the acting of Annie Girardot and Yves Montand.

Lelouch is an excellent technician who takes advantage of the compactness and lightness of modern film equipment to achieve spontaneity and freedom of movement. His actors, too, are allowed a good measure of freedom for reacting and improvising. He is his own producer, writes all his own scripts (often in collaboration with Pierre Uytterhoven), and frequently operates his own camera. Through his production company, Les Films 13, he has also produced films by other directors. Lelouch ranks among the leading directors of the contemporary French cinema, but he has yet to reach for a theme that can match the eloquence of his glossy, decorative style. His second wife is actress Marie-Sophie L.

FEATURE FILMS: *Le Propre de l'Homme/The Right of Man* (also prod., sc., act.) 1960; *L'Amour avec des Si* (also prod., sc.) 1963; *La Femme spectacle/Night Women* (full-length doc.; also prod., phot.) 1964; *Une Fille et des Fusils/To Be a Crook* (also prod., co-sc., co-edit.), *Les Grands Moments* (also co-prod.) 1965; *Un Homme et Une Femme/A Man and a Woman* (also prod., story, co-sc., phot., co-ed.) 1966; *Vivre pour vivre/Live for Life* (also co-sc., co-phot., edit.), *Loin du Viêtnam/Far from Vietnam* (film essay; one episode) 1967; *13 Jours en France/Grenoble* (winter Olympics, Grenoble, doc.; co-dir. with François Reichenbach; also co-sc.), *Les Gauloises bleues* (co-prod. only) 1968; *La Vie l'Amour la Mort/Life Love Death* (also co-sc.), *Un Homme qui me plaît/Love Is a Funny Thing* (also co-sc., phot.) 1969; *Le Voyou/The Crook* (also co-sc., co-phot.) 1970; *Smic Smac Smoc* (also prod., sc., phot., act. in cameo role) 1971; *L'Aventure c'est l'Aventure/Money Money Money* (also prod., sc., co-phot.) 1972; *La Bonne Année/Happy New Year* (also prod., sc., co-phot.), *Visions of Eight* (summer Olympics, Munich, doc.; "The Losers" episode) 1973; *Toute une Vie/And Now My Love* (also prod., co-sc.) 1974; *Mariage/Marriage* (also co-sc.), *Le Chat et la Souris/Cat and Mouse* (also sc.) 1975; *Le Bon et les Mechants/The Good and the Bad* (also sc., phot.), *Si c'etait à refaire/Second Chance* (also prod. sc.) 1976; *Un Autre Homme une Autre Chance/Another Man Another Chance* (also sc.) 1977; *Molière* (four-hr. TV drama; prod. only), *Robert et Robert* (also sc.) 1978; *A nous deux/An Adventure for Two* (Fr./Can.), *Alors heureux?* (prod. only) 1979; *Les uns et les autres/Bolero* (also prod., sc.) 1981; *Edith et Marcel/Edith and Marcel* (also prod., co-sc.) 1983; *Vive la Vie* (also prod., sc., phot.) 1984; *Partier revenir* (also prod., co-sc.) 1985; *Un Homme et une Femme: Vingt Ans déjé/A Man and a Woman: 20 Years Later* (also prod. co-sc.) 1986; *Attention Bandits!/Bandits* (also prod., co-sc.), *Happy New Year* (screenplay basis only, *La Bonne Année*) 1987; *Itinéraire d'un Enfant paté/Itinerary of a Spoiled Child* (also co-prod. sc.) 1988; *Il y a des Jours. . . et des Lunes/There Were Days and Moons* (also prod., co-sc.; Fr.) 1990; *Beautiful Stray* 1992; *All That for That* 1993; *Les Misérables* 1995; *Men and Women: An Owner's Manual* 1996.

LeMaire, Charles. Costume designer. *b.* 1897, Chicago. *d.* 1985. A former vaudeville performer, he began creating wardrobes for Broadway shows in 1921, and subsequently designed costumes for 'The Ziegfeld Follies,' 'George White's Scandals,' and 'Earl Carroll Vanities,' among other extravaganzas, and occasional silent films and early talkies. In the mid-40s he joined 20th Century-Fox as executive designer and wardrobe director. Working mostly in collaboration, he shared Academy Awards for *All About Eve* (1950), *The Robe* (1953), and *Love Is a Many-Splendored Thing* (1955), and garnered 13 other Oscar nominations.

FILMS INCLUDE: *The Heart of a Siren* 1925; *George White's Scandals* 1934; *The Men in Her Life* 1941; *The Razor's Edge, Boomerang, The Ghost and Mrs. Muir, Miracle on 34th Street, Kiss of Death, Nightmare Alley, Forever Amber* 1947; *The Captain from Castille, Sitting Pretty, Unfaithfully Yours* 1948; *A Letter to Three Wives, Pinky, The Fan* 1949; *When Willie Comes Marching Home, My Blue Heaven, All About Eve* 1950; *On the Riviera, Panic in the Streets, The Model and the Marriage Broker, David and Bathsheba, The Day the Earth Stood Still, People Will Talk* 1951; *My Cousin Rachel, With a Song in My Heart, Viva Zapata!, The Pride of St. Louis, Les Misérables, What Price Glory, O. Henry's Full House* 1952; *Niagara, The Robe, The President's Lady, How to Marry a Millionaire, Titanic, Gentlemen Prefer Blondes* 1953; *Desires, There's No Business Like Show Business* 1954; *Prince of Players, Love Is a Many-Splendored Thing, The Virgin Queen, The Girl in the Red Velvet Swing* 1955; *The Man in the Gray Flannel Suit, Teenage Rebel, The Girl Can't Help It* 1956; *An Affair to Remember, The Desk Set, The Sun Also Rises* 1957; *The Long Hot Summer, The Young Lions, Ten North Fredrick, The Fly* 1958; *The Diary of Anne Frank* 1959; *The Marriage-Go-Round* 1960; *A Walk on the Wild Side* 1962.

Le Mat, Paul. Actor. Born in 1952, in New Jersey. Husky leading man of American films, following extensive training for the stage at several schools. Best remembered for his role as Melvin Dummar, claimant to a slice of Howard Hughes's fortune, in Jonathan Demme's comedy *Melvin and Howard* (1980).

FILMS: *American Graffiti* 1973; *Aloha Bobby and Rose* 1975; *Citizens Band/Handle with Care* 1977; *More American Graffiti* 1979; *Melvin and Howard* 1980; *Death Valley, Jimmy the Kid* 1982; *Rock & Rule, Strange Invaders* 1983; *P.K. and the Kid* (release delayed from 1982), *The Hanoi Hilton, Private Investigations* 1987; *Easy Wheels, Veiled Threats, Puppet Master* 1989; *Grave Secrets* 1990; *Deuce Coups, Wishman* 1992.

LeMay, Alan. Novelist, screenwriter. *b.* June 3, 1899, Indianapolis. *d.* 1964. A noted author of Western novels, some of which have been adapted to the screen (*Along Came Jones, The Vanishing American, The Searchers, The Unforgiven*). He also wrote many screenplays, directed one film, *High Lonesome* (1950), and produced two.

FILMS INCLUDE (as screenwriter): *North West Mounted Police* 1940; *Reap the Wild Wind* 1942; *The Adventures of Mark Twain, The Story of Dr. Wassell* 1944; *San Antonio* 1945; *Gunfighters, Cheyenne* 1947; *Tap Roots* 1948; *The Walking Hills* 1949; *The Sundowners* (also prod.), *High Lonesome* (also dir.), *Rocky Mountain* 1950; *Quebec* (also prod.) 1951; *I Dream of Jeannie, Blackbeard the Pirate* 1952.

Lemmon, Jack. Actor. Born John Uhler Lemmon III, on Feb. 8, 1925, in Boston. The son of the president of a doughnut company, he was educated in prep schools and at Harvard, where he was active in the Dramatic Club. After serving in the Navy as an ensign, he began the uphill climb toward an acting career, playing piano in a New York City beer hall, appearing on radio and off Broadway, and finally on TV. After a brief Broadway exposure, he was introduced on the screen in two successive Judy Holliday vehicles. Shortly after, he scored a personal triumph as Ensign Pulver in *Mister Roberts,* for which he won an Academy Award as best supporting actor, and was on his way to stardom. He won the best actor Oscar for his performance in *Save the Tiger* (1973). The brand of comedy he has made famous sadly mocks the frustrations of a well-bred, well-meaning individual in a world governed by impersonal superstructures. A serious actor, completely dedicated to his art, Lemmon is capable of a broad range of portrayals, from slapstick to deeply moving drama. Lemmon's Oscar nominations reflected his versatile mastery of characterization, spanning the gamut of thespian emotion from cynical comedies like *Some Like It Hot* (1959) and *The Apartment* (1960) to sincere dramas like *Days of Wine and Roses* (1962), *The China Syndrome* (1979), *Tribute* (1980), and *Missing* (1982). He was named best actor at Cannes for *China Syndrome* and *Missing.* In 1971 he directed his first film, *Kotch,* a comedy starring Walter Matthau. In 1985 Lemmon returned to the New York stage in a revival of Eugene O'Neil's 'Long Day's Journey Into Night.' In 1988 he was honored with the American Film Institute's Life Achievement Award. He is the father of actor Chris Lemmon (*b.* Jan. 22, 1954, L.A.) from his first marriage (1950–56) to actress Cynthia Stone. His second wife is actress Felicia FARR.

FILMS: *It Should Happen to You, Phffft* 1954; *Three for the Show, Mister Roberts, My Sister Eileen* 1955; *You Can't Run Away from It* 1956; *Fire Down Below, Operation Mad Ball* 1957; *Cowboy* 1958; *Bell Book and Candle, Some Like It Hot, It Happened to Jane* 1959; *The Apartment, Pepe, The Wackiest Ship in the Army* 1960; *The Notorious Landlady, Days of Wine and Roses* 1962; *Irma La Douce, Under the Yum Yum Tree* 1963; *Good Neighbor Sam* 1964; *How to Murder Your Wife, The Great Race* 1965; *The Fortune Cookie* 1966; *Luv* 1967; *The Odd Couple* 1968; *The April Fools* 1969; *The Out-of-Towners* 1970; *Kotch* (dir. only) 1971; *The War Between Men and Women, Avanti!* 1972; *Save the Tiger* 1973; *The Front Page* 1974; *The Prisoner of Second Avenue* 1975; *The Entertainer, Alex and the Gypsy* 1976; *Airport '77* 1977; *The China Syndrome* 1979; *Tribute* (Can.) 1980; *Buddy Buddy* 1981; *Missing* 1982; *Mass Appeal* 1984; *Maccheroni/Macaroni* (It.) 1985; *That's Life!* 1986; *Dad* 1989; *JFK* 1991; *The Player* (cameo), *Glengarry Glen Ross* 1992; *Grumpy Old Men, Short Cuts* 1993; *Grumpier Old Men* 1995; *Getting Away with Murder, My Fellow Americans* 1996; *Out to Sea* 1997.

Leni, Paul. Director, art director. *b.* July 8, 1885, Stuttgart, Germany. *d.* 1929. In Berlin from age 15, he was a struggling avant-garde painter before becoming a set designer for the stage productions of Max REINHARDT and others. In German films from 1914 as art director and from 1916 also as director, he was prominent in the expressionist movement and directed two key films of the German silent cinema, *Hintertreppe/Backstairs* and *Das Wachsfigurenkabinett/Waxworks* (also known as *Three Wax Works* or *Three Wax Men*). The latter, a three-part study of tyranny, was one of the most celebrated films of the period. It featured Emil Jannings as Harun al-Rashid, Conrad Veidt as Ivan the Terrible, and Werner Krauss as Jack the Ripper. Future director William DIETERLE played four roles in the film. Leni was the art director, alone or in collaboration, on most of the German films he directed and continued to design sets for other directors through 1926.

In 1927, Leni came to Hollywood to direct for Universal at the invitation of Carl LAEMMLE. His first American production, *The Cat and the Canary,* was an excellent achievement in the horror-suspense genre, rich in visual mystery and macabre humor. The film was a forerunner of Universal's horror cycle of the 30s, and many of its eerie effects—clutching hands, sliding panels, etc.—were later copied in many screen thrillers. Leni made three other American films before his sudden death from blood poisoning, all memorable for their architectural style and strong sense of mood and mystery.

FILMS (as director): In Germany—*Das Tagebuch des Dr. Hart* 1916; *Das Ratsel von Bangalore* (assoc. dir., co-sc. only), *Dornröschen* (also sc.) 1917; *Die Platonische Ehe, Prinz Kuckuck* 1919; *Patience* (also sc.) 1920; *Fiesco/Die Verschwörung zu Genua, Das Gespensterschiff, Hintertreppe/Backstairs* (co-dir. with Leopold Jessner), *Komödie der Leidenschaften* 1921; *Das Wachsfigurenkabinett/Waxworks/Three Wax Works/Three Wax Men* 1924. In the US—*The Cat and the Canary, The Chinese Parrot* 1927; *The Man Who Laughs* 1928; *The Last Warning* 1929.

Lenica, Jan. Animator. Born on Jan. 4, 1928, in Poznan, Poland. The son of a noted painter, he studied music and architecture but soon turned to art. He made his entry into Polish films as a designer of cinema posters, then worked in collaboration with Walerian BOROWCZYK on a series of prize-winning cartoons before going his own way in Poland and abroad. In 1958 he moved to France and later acquired French citizenship. He also worked extensively in Germany. His drawing style is bold, simple, and easily recognizable, often utilizing collage, cutouts, and carved backgrounds. In both style and theme he sometimes approaches the surreal. He won numerous international awards for his films, designs, and posters.

FILMS: *Once Upon a Time, Love Rewarded* (both co-anim.) 1957; *Dom/House* (co-anim.) 1958; *Monsieur Tête* (co-anim.) 1960; *Italia '61* (co-anim.), *Solitude* (co-anim.), *Janko the Musician* 1961; *Labyrinth* 1962; *Rhinoceros* 1963; *La Féminin Fleur, A* 1965; *Adam II* 1968; *Nature morte* 1970; *Landscape* 1974; *Ubu Roi* 1976; *Ubu Et la Grande Gidouille* 1979.

Lennart, Isobel. Screenwriter. *b.* May 18, 1915, Brooklyn, N.Y. *d.* 1971. In Hollywood from the early 40s, she wrote many screenplays, mostly light, occasionally dramatic, alone or in collaboration, and received three Oscar nominations. She scored a big hit on Broadway in 1964 as the author of the musical 'Funny Girl,' which she later adapted to the screen. She was killed in a car accident.

FILMS INCLUDE: *Once Upon a Thursday* 1942; *Lost Angel* 1944; *Anchors Aweigh* 1945; *Holiday in Mexico* 1946; *It Happened in Brooklyn* 1947; *The Kissing Bandit* 1948; *Holiday Affair, East Side West Side* 1949; *A Life of Her Own* 1950; *It's a Big Country, Skirts Ahoy!* 1952; *Latin Lovers* 1953; *Love Me or Leave Me* 1955; *Meet Me in Las Vegas* 1956; *This Could Be the Night* 1957; *Merry Andrew, The Inn of the Sixth Happiness* 1958; *Please Don't Eat the Daisies, The Sundowners* 1960; *Period of Adjustment, Two for the Seesaw* 1962; *Fitzwilly* 1967; *Funny Girl* (from her own play) 1968.

Lennon, John. See BEATLES, THE.

lens. A shaped, transparent optical device, usually made of glass, which focuses light rays. In filming, it forms images of objects within its field of view by concentrating or dispersing rays of light refracted from the objects. Then, as light passes through the lens, the images are exposed on film inside the camera. The size of the image produced by a camera lens is regulated by its focal length. Lenses are made in a wide range of focal lengths and are generally classified as "normal," "wide angle," or "telephoto." A zoom lens combines some of the capabilities of all three. Normal lenses cover a medium field; the images they produce are similar in their relation to the frame to those produced by the human eye. Wide-angle lenses cover an extensive field of view but cause a reduction in the proportional size of the elements making up the image. Telephoto lenses, on the other hand, cover a limited field but considerably magnify elements in the image. Zoom lenses are unique in that they can vary focal length while keeping the image in focus.

Lenses of all focal lengths are manufactured in a variety of shapes and types and are divided into two main groups, positive and negative. Positive lenses converge light rays; negative lenses produce a divergence of light rays. Lenses can be convex, concave, or a combination of both. Each shape and type has its own specific characteristics as well as its own limitations. Modern lenses have reached a high level of optical accuracy, even in the simplest of cameras.

lens adapter. A device attached to the front of a camera to facilitate a rapid change of lenses.

lens barrel. A cylindrical mounting for lens elements.

lens cap. A plastic or metal cover for a lens, designed to protect it against damage when not in use.

lens coating. A solution of magnesium fluoride applied to lenses to neutralize unwanted reflection with little loss of light.

lens hood. A shield that can be placed around a camera lens to prevent undesirable light from striking its surface.

lens mount. A metal holder housing the optical elements that make up a complete lens. Lens mounts come in a variety of types (standard, spiral, focusing, micrometer, etc.).

lens speed. The relative capacity of a lens to admit light. The speed of a lens is related to the size of its aperture. The larger the aperture, the faster the lens. A fast lens is capable of capturing images on film in relatively poor lighting conditions and at relatively high shutter speeds.

lens turret. A rotating disc in front of a camera on which are mounted several (usually four) lenses. By rotating the turret any of the lenses can be quickly brought into position before the camera aperture. When a lens is correctly shifted, the turret locks firmly.

Lenya, Lotte. Actress, singer. *b.* Karoline Blamauer, Oct. 18, 1900, Hitzing, Austria. *d.* 1981. A tightrope walker at age eight and later a ballet chorine in Switzerland, she rose to fame in Berlin as the voice of the Bertolt Brecht–Kurt Weill musical collaborations, notably 'The Threepenny Opera,' in which she played a leading role both on stage and in Pabst's film version. She married Weill and when the Nazis came to power fled with him through Paris to New York. Here she retired, following several stage appearances, but after her husband's death she returned to acting, recreating her legendary Jenny in a long-running off-Broadway revival of 'The Threepenny Opera.' Other stage triumphs followed, including 'Cabaret.' She also appeared in a handful of films, most effectively as the lady villain with the lethal shoe in the James Bond thriller *From Russia with Love.*

FILMS: *Die Dreigroschenoper/The Threepenny Opera/ The Beggar's Opera* 1931; *The Roman Spring of Mrs. Stone* 1961; *From Russia with Love* 1963; *The Appointment* 1969; *Semi-Tough* 1977.

Lenz, Kay. Actress. Born on Mar. 4, 1953, in Los Angeles. Attractive leading lady of American TV and films. Married actor-singer David Cassidy.

FILMS: *American Graffiti, Breezy* 1973; *White Line Fever* (Can.) 1975; *The Great Scout and Cathouse Thursday, Moving Violations* 1976; *Mean Dog Blues* 1978; *The Passage* (UK) 1979; *Fast Walking* 1982; *House* 1986; *Stripped to Kill, Death Wish 4: The Crackdown* 1987; *Fear* 1988; *Physical Evidence* 1989; *Streets, Headhunter* 1990; *Falling from Grace* 1992; *Trapped in Space* 1994.

Leonard, Robert Sean. Actor. Born on Feb. 28, 1969, in Westwood, N.J. Dark, handsome stage-trained actor who made a screen impression as the prep school student with thwarted artistic aspirations in *Dead Poets Society*. Appeared on Broadway in 'Brighton Beach Memoirs' and 'Breaking the Code,' among others.

FILMS INCLUDE: *The Manhattan Project* 1986, *My Best Friend Is a Vampire* 1988, *Dead Poets Society* 1989; *Mr. and Mrs. Bridge* 1990, *Married to It* 1991, *Swing Kids* 1992, *Much Ado About Nothing* 1993; *Safe Passage* 1994; *Killer, I Love You, Love You a Lot* 1997.

Leonard, Robert Z(igler). Director. *b.* Oct. 7, 1889, Chicago. *d.* 1968. *ed.* U. of Colorado. A stage actor from age 14, he acted and sang with the California Light Opera Company before entering films as an actor with the Selig Polyscope Company in 1907. He starred in such early silents as *Code of Honor* (1907), *The Courtship of Miles Standish* (1910), and *Robinson Crusoe* (1913) and made his debut as director with the serial *The Master Key* (1914), in which he also played a role. Many of his early films starred his first wife, Mae MURRAY. His second wife, Gertrude OLMSTEAD, appeared in several of his films of the late 20s. Leonard directed scores of silent and sound Hollywood films over a period spanning four decades, working for such studios as Universal, Paramount, and his own company. But it was as an MGM director that he made his best-known films from the mid-20s through the mid-50s. His specialty was the high-gloss glamour film, and his pictures ranged from soggy melodramas and saccharine romances to lavish musicals. He worked with some of MGM's most glittering stars, including Norma Shearer, Greta Garbo, Joan Crawford, Jeannette MacDonald and Nelson Eddy, Clark Gable, Robert Taylor, and Fred Astaire. He wasn't too creative a director, neither did he claim to be, but he held his own among Hollywood's top craftsmen and turned out a good number of slick entertainment films.

FILMS: *The Master Key* (serial; also act.) 1914; *The Silent Command* (also sc., act.), *Heritage* (also story, act.), *The Woman of Mona Diggins* (also co-sc.), *Judge Not* 1915; *The Crippled Hand* (co-dir. with David Kirkland; also act.), *The Plow Girl, The Eagle's Wings, Little Eva Egerton, Secret Love* 1916; *The Little Orphan, At First Sight, The Primrose Ring, A Mormon*

Maid, Princess Virtue, Face Value (also co-story) 1917; *The Bride's Awakening, Her Body in Bond, Danger—Go Slow* (also co-sc.), *Modern Love* (also co-story) 1918; *The Delicious Little Devil, The Big Little Person, What Am I Bid?, The Scarlet Shadow, The Way of a Woman, Miracle of Love* 1919; *April Folly, The Restless Sex* 1920; *The Gilded Lily* (also prod.), *Heedless Moths* (also sc.), *Peacock Alley* (also prod.) 1921; *Fascination* (also prod.), *Broadway Rose* (also prod.) 1922; *Jazzmania* (also prod.), *The French Doll* (also prod.), *Fashion Row* (also prod.) 1923; *Mademoiselle Midnight* (also prod.), *Circe the Enchantress* (also prod.), *Love's Wilderness* 1924; *Cheaper to Marry, Bright Lights* (also prod.), *Time the Comedian* 1925; *Dance Madness, Mademoiselle Modiste, The Waning Sex* 1926; *A Little Journey* (also prod.), *The Demi-Bride* (also prod.), *Adam and Evil, Tea for Three* (also prod.) 1927; *Baby Mine* (also prod.), *The Cardboard Lover, A Lady of Chance* (also prod.) 1928; *Marianne* (also prod.) 1929; *The Divorcee* (also prod.), *In Gay Madrid* (also prod.), *Let Us Be Gay* (also prod.) 1930; *The Bachelor Father* (also co-prod.), *It's a Wise Child* (also co-prod.), *Five and Ten* (also co-prod.), *Susan Lennox: Her Fall and Rise* (also prod.) 1931; *Lovers Courageous* (also prod.), *Strange Interlude* (also prod.) 1932; *Peg o' My Heart* (also prod.), *Dancing Lady* 1933; *Outcast Lady* (also prod.) 1934; *After Office Hours* (also co-prod.), *Escapade* (also co-prod.) 1935; *The Great Ziegfeld* (also co-prod.), *Piccadilly Jim* (also co-prod.) 1936; *Maytime* (also co-prod.), *The Firefly* (also co-prod.) 1937; *The Girl of the Golden West* 1938; *Broadway Serenade* (also prod.) 1939; *New Moon* (also prod.), *Pride and Prejudice, Third Finger Left Hand* 1940; *Ziegfeld Girl, When Ladies Meet* (also co-prod.) 1941; *We Were Dancing* (also co-prod.), *Stand By for Action* (also co-prod.) 1942; *The Man from Down Under* (also co-prod.) 1943; *Marriage Is a Private Affair* 1944; *Weekend at the Waldorf* (also co-prod.) 1945; *The Secret Heart* 1946; *Cynthia* 1947; *B.F.'s Daughter* 1948; *The Bribe, In the Good Old Summertime* 1949; *Nancy Goes to Rio, Duchess of Idaho, Grounds for Marriage* 1950; *Too Young to Kiss* 1951; *Everything I Have Is Yours* 1952; *The Clown, The Great Diamond Robbery* 1953; *Her Twelve Men* 1954; *The King's Thief, La Donna più Bella del Mondo/Beautiful but Dangerous* (It.) 1955; *Kelly and Me* 1957.

Leonard, Sheldon. Actor. *b.* Sheldon Leonard Bershad on Feb. 22, 1907, in New York City. *d.* 1997. *ed.* Syracuse U. A former stage actor, he played character parts in dozens of films, typically as a Runyonesque gangster. He later became a highly successful TV producer-director, scoring hits with such programs as 'The Danny Thomas Show,' 'The Andy Griffith Show,' 'The Dick Van Dyke Show,' 'Gomer Pyle,' 'I Spy,' and 'My World and Welcome to It,' and winning several Emmy awards in the process. He also starred in his own TV series, 'Big Eddie' (1975).

FILMS INCLUDE: *Another Thin Man* 1939; *Tall Dark and Handsome, Private Nurse* (lead), *Buy Me That Town, Week-End in Havana, Rise and Shine* 1941; *Tortilla Flat, Street of Chance, Lucky Jordan* 1942; *Hit the Ice* 1943; *Uncertain Glory, To Have and Have Not, The Falcon in Hollywood* 1944; *Why Girls Leave Home* (lead), *Captain Kidd, Frontier Gal* 1945; *Somewhere in the Night, Decoy, It's a Wonderful Life* 1946; *Sinbad the Sailor, Violence, The Gangster* 1947; *If You Knew Susie* 1948; *My Dream Is Yours, Take One False Step* 1949; *The Iroquois Trail* 1950; *Behave Yourself, Come Fill the Cup* 1951; *Stop You're Killing Me* 1952; *The Diamond Queen* 1953; *Money from Home* 1954; *Guys and Dolls* 1955; *Pocketful of Miracles* 1961; *The Brink's Job* (as J. Edgar Hoover) 1978.

Leone, Sergio. Director. *b.* Jan. 23, 1921, Rome. *d.* 1989. The man most responsible for the vogue of Italian "spaghetti Westerns" in the 60s. The son of a film industry pioneer, Vincenzo Leone, and screen diva Francesca Bertini, he entered Italian films at 18 and for many years worked as an assistant to various Italian directors (Gallone, Comencini, Soldati, Camerini, among others) as well as American directors filming in Italy, including Mervyn LeRoy, Robert Wise, William Wyler, Raoul Walsh, and Fred Zinnemann. Among other American films, he served as an assistant on *Quo Vadis, Helen of Troy,* and *Ben-Hur.* He appeared in a bit as a priest in De Sica's *The Bicycle Thief* and from time to time played small roles in films. He also worked as a second-unit director on a number of sumptuous productions and collaborated as a screenwriter on such costume adventure films as *Nel Segno di Roma/Sign of the Gladiator* (1958) and *Gli Ultimi Giorni di Pompei/The Last Days of Pompeii* (1959). He took over the direction of the latter film from an ailing Mario Bonnard but received no screen credit for his effort. He also figured prominently in the production of Robert Aldrich's *Sodom and Gomorrah* (1961) on which he was billed as the second-unit director. He made his own official debut as a director with a pseudohistorical epic, *Il Colosso di Rodi/The Colossus of Rhodes* (1961) and scored a string of box-office hits several years later with a series of brutal but stylish made-in-Italy "Westerns," which he launched with the enormously popular *Per un Pugno di Dollari/A Fistful of Dollars* (1964), a remake of Kurosawa's *Yojimbo.* The film, noted for its explicit brutality, flamboyant visual style, and abundant use of extreme close-ups, gave an enormous boost to the then-stagnant career of Clint EASTWOOD, who was perfectly cast as the laconic "Man with No Name." So influenced was Eastwood by Leone's filmmaking style that Eastwood's Academy Award–winning Western *Unforgiven* (1992) was in part dedicated to him.

Leone improved on his formula in the sequel *For a Few Dollars More* (1965) and scored another huge international hit with *The Good, the Bad, and the Ugly* (1966), the last of the Man with No Name trilogy. The success of these films spawned a virtual avalanche of imitation spaghetti Westerns which helped provide employment for several fading American stars and character players. Now backed with a hefty budget from Paramount, Leone proceeded to make *Once Upon a Time in the West* (1968), an operatic-scale Western epic many consider his masterpiece. It was, however, a commercial failure, both in its original release version, running 165 minutes, and its mangled 140-minute studio cut. Disheartened, Leone functioned thereafter mostly as a producer. But in 1984 he returned to directing with his most ambitious film, the Hollywood-financed *Once Upon a Time in America* (1984), a gangster saga starring Robert DE NIRO, set mostly in New York and running nearly four hours. The much abbreviated ("butchered," according to Leone) American release version fared poorly at the box office and only modestly with the critics, but viewers of the full original cut admired many aspects of the production. At the time of his sudden death of a heart attack, Leone was planning an even more ambitious project, a $70-million Soviet-Italian co-production, again starring De Niro, about the WW II German siege of Leningrad.

FILMS (as director): *Gli Ultimi Giorni di Pompeii/The Last Days of Pompeii* (co-dir., uncredited; co-sc.) 1959; *Il Colosso di Rodi/The Colossus of Rhodes* (also co-sc.; It./Fr./Sp.), *Sodoma e Gomorra/Sodom and Gomorrah* (2nd-unit dir. only; according to some sources, co-dir. with Robert Aldrich; It./Fr./US) 1961; *Per un Pugno di Dollari/A Fistful of Dollars* (also co-story, co-sc.; It./Sp./Ger.) 1964; *Per qualche Dollaro in più/For a Few Dollars More* (also co-story, co-sc.; It./Sp./Ger.) 1965; *Il Buono il Brutto il Cattivo/The Good the Bad and the Ugly* (also co-story, co-sc.) 1966; *C'era una Volta il West/Once Upon a Time in the West* (also co-story, co-sc.;

It./US filmed in the US and Spain) 1968; *Giù la Testa/Duck You Sucker/A Fistful of Dynamite* (also co-sc.) 1972; *Il Mio Nome è Nessuno/My Name Is Nobody* (co-production company, story idea only) 1973; *Un Genio due compari e un Pollo* (exec prod. only) 1975; *Il Gatto* (prod. only) 1978 *Il Giocattolo* (exec. prod. only) 1979; *Un Sacco Bello* (exec. prod. only) 1980; *Bianco Rosso e Verdone* (exec. prod. only) 1981; *Once Upon a Time in America* (also co-sc.; US) 1984; *Troppo Forte* (superv. prod. only) 1985.

Leonetti, Matthew F. American director of photography. A lighting cameraman since the mid-70s, he became established in the 80s as a reliable craftsman.

FILMS INCLUDE: *The Bat People* 1974; *Mr. Billion* 1977; *Breaking Away* 1979; *Raise the Titanic* (UK) 1980; *Eyewitness* 1981; *Poltergeist* 1982; *The Buddy System, Ice Pirates* 1984; *Commando, Jagged Edge* 1985; *Jumpin' Jack Flash* 1986; *Extreme Prejudice, Dragnet* 1987; *Action Jackson, Red Heat* 1988; *Johnny Handsome* 1989; *Another 48 Hrs., Hard to Kill* 1990; *Dead Again* 1991; *Angels in the Outfield* 1994.

Léotard, Philippe. Actor. Born in 1940, in France. Reliable character lead and supporting player of French films; a discovery of TRUFFAUT. At his best in pugnacious roles. He won the César Award as best actor for Bob Swaim's *La Balance* (1982).

FILMS INCLUDE: *Domicile conjugal/Bed and Board* 1970; *Les Deux Anglaises et le Continent/Two English Girls* 1971; *Une Belle Fille comme moi/Such a Gorgeus Kid Like Me* 1972; *The Day of the Jackal* (UK/Fr.) 1973; *The French Connection II* (US), *Pas si méchant que ça, Le Chat et la Souris/Cat and Mouse* 1975; *Le Bon et les Méchants/The Good and the Bad* 1976; *Le June Fayard dit le Shérif* 1977; *La Mémoire courte* 1979; *L'Empreinte des Géants, La Petite Sirène* 1980; *Paradis pour tous, La Balance, Mora* 1982; *Tcaho Pantin* 1983; *Femmes de Personne, La Pirate* 1984; *Tangos el Exilio de Gardel/Tangos: The Exile of Gardel* (Arg./Fr.) 1985; *Le Paltoquet, L'Aube/Dawn, L'Etat de Grace* 1986; *Si le Soleil ne revenait pas* (also dir.) 1987; *Il y a des Jours... et des Lunes/There Were Days and Moons* 1990; *Gavre Princip Himmel unter Steinen/Death of a Schoolboy* (Aus.) 1991; *Les Misérables* 1995.

Lerner, Alan Jay. Playwright, lyricist, screenwriter. *b.* Aug. 31, 1918, New York City. *d.* 1986. The son of the owner of a chain of dress shops, he was educated at prep schools (Choate) and at Harvard. In 1943, with 'What's Up?' he began a long and fruitful collaboration with composer Frederick LOEWE, which enriched Broadway with such musicals as 'Brigadoon,' 'Paint Your Wagon,' 'My Fair Lady,' and 'Camelot.' Lerner also collaborated with other composers, notably Burton LANE, with whom he wrote 'On a Clear Day You Can See Forever' after Loewe's retirement in 1960. But he and Loewe reunited in 1974 for the film *The Little Prince.* Lerner adapted several of his own musicals to film and wrote screenplay and lyrics directly for the screen. He won an Academy Award for the story and screenplay of *An American in Paris* (1951), another for the screenplay of *Gigi* (1958), and shared a third Oscar with Loewe for the title song of the latter film. His third of eight wives was actress Nancy OLSON. His widow is English musical comedy actress Liz Robertson. At the time of his death of cancer, he was being sued for $1.4 million in back taxes and for hundreds of thousands in unpaid alimony. Autobiography: *The Street Where I Live* (1978).

FILMS: *Royal Wedding* (story, sc., lyrics), *An American in Paris* (story, sc., lyrics) 1951; *Brigadoon* (sc. lyrics, from own musical play) 1954; *Gigi* (sc., lyrics) 1958; *My Fair Lady* (sc., lyrics, from own musical play) 1964; *The Girl and the Bugler* (Soviet film featuring songs from *My Fair Lady*; USSR) 1965; *Camelot* (sc., lyrics from own musical play) 1967; *Paint Your Wagon* (prod., sc., lyrics) 1969; *On a Clear Day You Can See Forever* (sc., lyrics from own play) 1970; *The Little Prince* (sc., lyrics) 1974.

Lerner, Irving. Director. *b.* Mar. 7, 1909, in New York City. *d.* 1976. A research editor on Columbia University's *Encyclopedia of Social Sciences,* he began his association with film as a producer-director of anthropological shorts for Columbia, the Rockefeller Foundation, and other institutions. In the late 30s he became associated with the American documentary movement, working as an editor and second-unit director on Dudley Murphy's *One Third of a Nation* (1939) and on Willard Van Dyke's *Valley Town* and *The Children Must Learn* (both 1940), and was one of four cameramen on Flaherty's *The Land* (1941). During WW II, Lerner produced two documentaries for the Office of War Information, *Toscanini: Hymn of the Nations* and *A Place to Live* (both 1944). He later headed the Educational Film Institute at New York University and in 1948 co-directed with Joseph Strick the documentary short *Muscle Beach.* The following year he made the first of several starvation-budget feature films on near-impossible week-long shooting schedules. He achieved interesting results with two of these, *Murder by Contract* (1958) and *City of Fear* (1959), but remained on the fringes of the industry and during the long gaps between his own quickie films worked in such secondary capacities as a technical advisor on *The Savage Eye* (1959), a second-unit director and associate editor on *Spartacus* (1960), supervising editor on *Deathwatch* (1966), co-editor on *Executive Action* (1973), and editor on *Steppenwolf* (1974) and *The River Niger* (1976). He was executive producer on *Custer of the West* (1968), also directing the war sequences, and associate producer on *Captain Apache* (1971). As a director, he worked with larger budgets and more leisurely shooting schedules in the 60s, but the resulting films were less intriguing than his earlier minithrillers.

FEATURE FILMS (as director): *C-Man* (also prod.) 1949; *Suicide Attack* 1951; *Man Crazy* 1953; *Edge of Fury* (co-dir. with Robert Gurney, Jr.), *Murder by Contract* 1958; *City of Fear* 1959; *Studs Lonigan* 1960; *Cry of Battle/To Be a Man* (US/Philippines) 1963; *Custer of the West* (dir. action sequences only; also exec. prod.), *The Royal Hunt of the Sun* (US/UK) 1968.

Lerner, Michael. Actor. Born on June 22, 1941, in Brooklyn, N.Y. Versatile thinking man's character actor. Originally a professor of dramatic literature at San Francisco State College, he made his film debut in 1970. Winner of Fulbright Scholarship to study acting, he was also a member of the American Conservatory Theater (San Francisco). Nominated for Academy Award for performance as the studio mogul in *Barton Fink.*

FILMS INCLUDE: *Alex in Wonderland* 1970; *The Candidate* 1972; *Busting, Newman's Law, Hangup* 1974; *St. Ives* 1976; *The Other Side of Midnight, Outlaw Blues* 1977; *Goldengirl* 1979; *Borderline, Coast to Coast, The Baltimore Bullet* 1980; *The Postman Always Rings Twice, Threshold* (Can.) 1981; *National Lampoon's Class Reunion* 1982; *Strange Invaders* (Can.) 1983; *Movers and Shakers* 1985; *Anguish, Vibes, Eight Men Out* 1988; *Harlem Nights* 1989; *Barton Fink* 1991; *Newsies, Amos & Andrew* 1992; *The Penal Colony* 1993; *No Escape, Radioland Murders, The Road to Wellville* 1994; *A Pyromaniac's Love Story* 1995.

Le Roy, Acme. Inventor, photographer. *b.* Jean-Aimé Le Roy, Feb. 5, 1854, Bedford, Ky. Deceased. In 1876 he photographed two children in a series of 200 transparent plates, then projected the images in a program he called "Children's Waltz," creating the illusion of motion. But his projecting apparatus was crude and clumsy. It wasn't until 1894, after having seen Edison's Kinetoscope, that he perfected his machine, in collaboration with Eugene LAUSTE, renamed it the Cinematographe, and began presenting his "Pictures in life motion" in various exhibition halls. According to some historians he was more of an entrepreneur than an inventor.

LeRoy, Baby. See BABY LEROY.

LeRoy, Mervyn. Director, producer. *b.* Oct. 15, 1900, San Francisco. *d.* 1987. Only five when his Jewish parents divorced, he experienced another childhood trauma at six, when his father's small department store was destroyed by the San Francisco earthquake. To help make ends meet, he became a newsboy at ten and at 12 dropped out of school to become an actor, when a regular customer, actor Theodore ROBERTS, hired him to portray a newsboy in a West Coast production of 'Barbara Fritchie.' Bitten by the acting bug, he began entering amateur contests, billing himself as "The Singing Newsboy" and later as "The Boy Tenor of the Generation." After winning a contest in 1915 for the best imitation of Chaplin, he performed daily at the San Francisco Exposition and began appearing regularly in vaudeville. He arrived in Hollywood in 1919 with a letter of recommendation from a cousin, producer Jesse L. LASKY, and got his first job there in the wardrobe department of Famous Players-Lasky.

Before long, LeRoy was working in the lab, then was promoted to assistant cameraman. At the same time, he began appearing in films, at first as an extra bit player, then as a featured player. Because of his very small frame, he typically played juveniles, at times jockeys. Among the films in which he appeared were *Double Speed* (1920), *The Ghost Breaker* (1922), *Little Johnny Jones* (1923), *The Call of the Canyon* (1923), *Broadway After Dark* (1924), and *The Chorus Lady* (1924). In 1924 he moved behind the camera as a gag writer and comedy construction specialist. In these capacities he worked on such films as *In Hollywood with Potash and Perlmutter* (1924), *Sally* (1925), *Irene* (1926), and *Orchids and Ermine* (1927). He also co-scripted *Ella Cinders* (1926).

Turning director in 1927, LeRoy established his reputation in the 30s when he directed several powerful social dramas for Warner Bros. and their subsidiary First National, notably *Little Caesar* (1931), which launched both Warners' gangster cycle and Edgar G. Robinson's starring career; *Five Star Final* (1931), an exposé of yellow journalism and again a *tour de force* by Robinson; *I Am a Fugitive from a Chain Gang* (1932), a forceful indictment of the penal system boasting a striking performance by Paul Muni; and *They Won't Forget* (1937), a compelling drama about justice and politics with an excellent performance by Claude Rains.

LeRoy demonstrated his versatility by his light touch with a musical like *Gold Diggers of 1933* and a comedy like *Tugboat Annie* (both 1933). In 1938 he joined MGM, abandoning his former realistic style for such decorative romances as *Waterloo Bridge* (1940), *Blossoms in the Dust* (1941), and *Random Harvest* (1942), as well as an interesting biography, *Madame Curie* (1943), an exciting WW II action drama, *Thirty Seconds Over Tokyo* (1944), and a lavish costume spectacle, *Quo Vadis* (1951). He produced, but did not direct, several films for MGM, including a Marx Brothers comedy, *At the Circus* (1939), and the most successful children's screen fantasy of all time, *The Wizard of Oz* (also 1939). He also produced several of the films he directed.

LeRoy's reputation declined somewhat after WW II, when he turned out a string of mediocre entertainment films for MGM, but it revived when he returned to Warners in the mid-50s. He retired in the mid-60s, ending a long and on the whole distinguished career that was frequently studded with commercial and critical successes. He received a special Academy Award for *The House I Live In* (1945), a short documentary on intolerance which he directed and co-produced. In 1975 he was awarded another special Oscar, the Irving Thalberg Memorial Award, for his achievements over the years. His second wife (of three) was Doris Warner, daughter of one of his studio bosses, Harry M. Warner. Their son, Warner LeRoy, became a well-known, innovative New York restaurateur. Autobiography: *Mervyn LeRoy: Take One* (1974).

FILMS (as director): *No Place to Go/Her Primitive Mate* 1927; *Flying Romeos, Harold Teen, Oh Kay!* 1928; *Naughty Baby, Hot Stuff, Broadway Babies, Little Johnny Jones* 1929; *Playing Around, Showgirl in Hollywood, Numbered Men, Top Speed* 1930; *Little Caesar, Gentleman's Fate, Too Young to Marry, Broad Minded, Five Star Final, Local Boy Makes Good, Tonight or Never* 1931; *High Pressure, The Heart of New York, Two Seconds, Big City Blues, Three on a Match, I Am a Fugitive from a Chain Gang* 1932; *Hard to Handle, Elmer the Great, Gold Diggers of 1933, Tugboat Annie, The World Changes* 1933; *Hi Nellie!, Heat Lightning, Happiness Ahead* 1934; *Sweet Adeline, Oil for the Lamps of China, Page Miss Glory, I Found Stella Parish* 1935; *Anthony Adverse, Three Men on a Horse* 1936; *The King and the Chorus Girl* (also prod.), *They Won't Forget* (also prod.), *The Great Garrick* (prod. superv. only) 1937; *Fools for Scandal* (also prod.), *Dramatic School* (prod. only) 1938; *Stand Up and Fight* (prod. only), *The Wizard of Oz* (prod. only), *At the Circus* (prod. only) 1939; *Waterloo Bridge, Escape* (also prod.) 1940; *Blossoms in the Dust, Unholy Partners* 1941; *Johnny Eager, Random Harvest* 1942; *Madame Curie* 1943; *Thirty Seconds Over Tokyo* 1944; *The House I Live In* (doc. short; also co-prod.) 1945; *Without Reservation* 1946; *Homecoming* 1948; *Little Women* (also prod.), *Any Number Can Play* 1949; *East Side West Side* 1950; *Quo Vadis* 1951; *Lovely to Look At, Million Dollar Mermaid* 1952; *Latin Lovers* 1953; *Rose Marie* (also prod.) 1954; *Strange Lady in Town* (also prod.), *Mister Roberts* (completed for ailing John Ford) 1955; *The Bad Seed* (also prod.), *Toward the Unknown* (also prod.) 1956; *No Time for Sergeants* (also prod.), *Home Before Dark* (also prod.) 1958; *The FBI Story* (also prod.) 1959; *Wake Me When It's Over* (also prod.) 1960; *The Devil at 4 O'Clock* (also prod.) 1961; *A Majority of One* (also prod.), *Gypsy* (also prod.) 1962; *Mary Mary* (also prod.) 1963; *Moment to Moment* (also prod.) 1965.

Leslie, Joan. Actress. Born Joan Agnes Theresa Sadie Brodel, on Jan. 26, 1925, in Detroit. First onstage before her third birthday, she made her professional debut at nine, performing in a song-and-dance act with her two sisters as "The Three Brodels." She began modeling in New York in 1935 and in the following year went to Hollywood, where she made her first screen appearance in the role of Robert Taylor's little sister in *Camille* (released in 1937). She continued playing child roles for various studios through 1940, using the name Joan Brodel. Blossoming into a fresh, wholesome young beauty, she was signed by Warner Bros. in 1941 and for the next five years played girl-next-door type of ingenue roles in a variety of the studio's productions. Her popularity and career declined after she left the Warners fold in 1946 and she retired from the screen in the mid-50s. She has since become a successful dress designer and is active in health-related humanitarian causes.

FILMS: As Joan Brodel—*Camille* 1937; *Men with Wings* 1938; *Nancy Drew—Reporter, Love Affair, Winter Carnival, Two Thoroughbreds* 1939; *High School, Young as You Feel, Star Dust, Susan and God, Military Academy, Foreign Correspondent,*

Laddie 1940. As Joan Leslie—*High Sierra, The Great Mr. Nobody, The Wagons Roll at Night, Thieves Fall Out, Sergeant York, The Male Animal, Yankee Doodle Dandy* 1942; *The Hard Way, This Is the Army, The Sky's the Limit, Thank Your Lucky Stars* 1943; *Hollywood Canteen* 1944; *Where Do We Go from Here?, Rhapsody in Blue, Too Young to Know* 1945; *Cinderella Jones, Janie Gets Married, Two Guys from Milwaukee* 1946; *Repeat Performance* 1947; *Northwest Stampede* 1948; *The Skipper Surprised His Wife, Born to Be Bad* 1950; *Man in the Saddle* 1951; *Hellgate, Toughest Man in Arizona* 1952; *The Woman They Almost Lynched* 1953; *Flight Nurse, Jubilee Trail, Hell's Outpost* 1954; *The Revolt of Mamie Stover* 1956.

Lesser, Sol. Producer. *b.* Feb. 17, 1890, Spokane, Wash. *d.* 1980. A former exhibitor and president of a movie theater chain, he went into production in the 30s. He produced many serials, low-budget Westerns, and Tarzan pictures, as well as occasional quality films. In 1941 he joined RKO as executive in charge of feature production but resigned soon after to set up his own production company.

FILMS INCLUDE: *Blame the Woman* 1932; *Thunder Over Mexico* (unauthorized assemblage of footage from Eisenstein's unfinished *Que Viva Mexico!*), *Tarzan the Fearless* 1933; *The Dude Ranger* 1934; *When a Man's a Man* 1935; *King of the Royal Mounted* 1936; *Secret Valley, Make a Wish, Dick Tracy* (serial) 1937; *Tarzan's Revenge* 1938; *Way Down South* 1939; *Our Town* 1940; *That Uncertain Feeling* 1941; *The Tuttles of Tahiti* 1942; *Stage Door Canteen, Tarzan Triumphs* 1943; *The Red House* 1947; *Kon-Tiki* 1951; *Vice Squad* 1953; *Tarzan's Fight for Life* 1958.

Lester, Mark. Actor. Born on July 11, 1958, in Oxford, England. Cherubic blond child star of British films of the 60s who developed into a dependable juvenile player in the 70s. The offspring of an actor and actress, he appeared on several TV programs before making his big-screen debut at the age of six and gained international fame playing (and singing) the title role in the film version of the musical *Oliver!* (1968).

FILMS INCLUDE: *Allez France!/The Counterfeit Constable* 1964; *Spaceflight IC-1* 1965; *Fahrenheit 451* 1966; *Our Mother's House* (UK/US) 1967; *Oliver!* (as Oliver Twist) 1968; *Run Wild Run Free* 1969; *Eyewitness/Sudden Terror, Melody, Black Beauty, Who Slew Auntie Roo?* 1971; *Scalawag* (Yug./It./US) 1973; *The Prince and the Pauper/Crossed Swords* (in dual title role) 1977; *Night of the Running Man* 1994.

Lester, Mark L(eslie). Director. Born on Nov. 26, 1946, in Cleveland. *ed.* U. of California, Northridge. Low-budget, violent action specialist.

FILMS: *Steel Arena* (also co-prod., sc.) 1973; *Truck Stop Women* (also prod., co-sc.) 1974; *Bobbie Jo and the Outlaw* (also prod.) 1976; *Stunts* 1977; *Roller Boogie* 1979; *The Funhouse* (co-exec. prod. only) 1981; *Class of 1984* (also co-exec. prod. co-sc.) 1982; *Firestarter* 1984; *Commando* 1985; *Armed and Dangerous* 1986; *Class of 1999* (also prod., story) 1990; *Showdown in Little Tokyo* 1991.

Lester, Richard. Director. Born on Jan. 19, 1932, in Philadelphia. The son of a teacher and a nurse, he was a precocious child who started grade school in suburban Germantown at age three. While attending the University of Pennsylvania (B.S. in clinical psychology) he composed light music, sang with a vocal group, and began working as a stagehand in a TV studio. By the time he reached 20 he was a successful TV director with CBS. Two years later he left the US on a bum's ride through Europe, playing the piano or the guitar for a meal. In 1956 he settled in England, where he resumed his activity as a TV director. Briefly, he even hosted his own TV comedy program, 'The Dick Lester Show.' A fortuitous association with Peter SELLERS led to the production of several zany TV programs, culminating with 'The Goon Show' (1958). In 1956 he married Deirdre Smith, a British ballet dancer and choreographer.

Lester made his entry into films with *The Running, Jumping, and Standing Still Film* (1960), a fragmented but inventive slapstick short packed with surrealistic sight gags which featured and was produced by Sellers. It was nominated for an Academy Award. He was far less successful with his initial two features. But the director's exuberance and visual flair finally found their free expression in *It's a Hard Day's Night* (1964) and *Help!* (1965), wildly energetic, delightfully absurd comic romps featuring THE BEATLES. Proving he had more to offer than camera-and-cutting-room razzle-dazzle, Lester paid a breezy tribute to the youthful spirit of the Swinging Sixties with *The Knack* (1965). These successes led to a Hollywood assignment to direct the screen version of the Broadway musical *A Funny Thing Happened on the Way to the Forum* (1966). The result was entertaining, but not quite on the level audiences had come to expect of Lester. After the inventive *How I Won the War* (1967), an antiwar black satire, Lester surprised everyone with *Petulia* (1968), a mature, poignant, honestly observed drama of romantic relationships. Lester's subsequent films have added up to an eclectic assortment of themes and styles, ranging from black comedy (*The Bed-Sitting Room*) and chamber farce (*The Ritz*) to thriller (*Juggernaut*), swashbuckler movies (*The Three Musketeers, Royal Flash, Robin and Marian*), Western myth (*Butch and Sundance: The Early Days*), and blockbuster Hollywood hokum (*Superman II, III*). The director's early experience with live TV and commercials has had considerable influence on his film work. He often uses several cameras to shoot action simultaneously from several angles and relies a great deal on bewildering and dazzling cutting techniques.

FILMS: *The Running Jumping and Standing Still Film* (short; also co-phot., co-edit., music) 1960; *It's a Trad Dad!/Ring-a-Ding Rhythm* (also prod.) 1962; *The Mouse on the Moon* 1963; *A Hard Day's Night* 1964; *The Knack. . . And How to Get It/The Knack, Help!* 1965; *A Funny Thing Happened on the Way to the Forum* (US) 1966; *Mondo Teeno/Teenage Rebellion* (doc.; dir. British sequences only; US/UK), *How I Won the War* (also prod.) 1967; *Petulia* (UK/US) 1968; *The Bed Sitting Room* (also prod.) 1969; *The Three Musketeers, Juggernaut* 1974; *The Four Musketeers, Royal Flash* 1975; *Robin and Marian, The Ritz* (US) 1976; *Butch and Sundance: The Early Days* (US), *Cuba* (US) 1979; *Superman II* 1980; *Superman III* 1983; *Finders Keepers* (US) 1984; *The Return of the Musketeers* 1990; *Get Back* 1991.

Leterrier, François. Director, actor. Born on May 26, 1929, in Margny-lès-Compiègne, France. He was a student of philosophy at the Sorbonne when he was chosen by Robert Bresson to play the difficult role of the protagonist in the director's *Un Condamné a Mort s'est échappé/A Man Escaped* (1956). He later became Louis Malle's assistant on *Ascenseur pour l'Echafaud/Frantic* and *Les Amants* (both 1958) and made his own debut as a director in 1961 with *Les Mauvais Coups/Naked Autumn.* His films have been visually attractive but somewhat sluggish in their pace.

FILMS (as director): *Les Mauvais Coups/Naked Autumn* (also co-sc.) 1961; *Un Roi sans Divertissement* (also co-sc.) 1963; *La Chasse royale* (also co-sc.) 1968; *Projection privée* (also co-sc.) 1973; *Milady* (also co-sc.) 1975; *Va voir Maman. . . Papa travaille* (also co-sc.), *Goodbye Emmanuelle* (also co-sc.) 1978; *Je vais craquer* (also co-sc.) 1980; *Quand tu seras débloqué fais-moi Signe* (also co-sc.) 1981; *Le Garde du Corps* (also co-sc.) 1984; *Tranches de Vie* (also co-adapt.) 1985.

Letz, George. See MONTGOMERY, George.

Levant, Oscar. Pianist, composer, actor. *b.* Dec. 27, 1906, Pittsburgh. *d.* 1972. Neurotic, hypochondriacal, insomniac wit and self-declared genius, famous as a leading interpreter of the music of George Gershwin. The son of a watch repairman, he left home at 16 to study music in New York, supporting himself by giving piano lessons. While preparing himself for a career as a concert pianist, he worked sporadically with small dance bands. A minor part in the Broadway show 'Burlesque' led to his first film role in the screen version of that play, *The Dance of Life* (1929). He remained in Hollywood the next few years, writing scores and songs for movies. It was during this period that he met and befriended Gershwin, to whom he became extremely devoted, subjugating his own career as a composer to become Gershwin's interpreter and virtual alter ego. Levant began attracting public attention as a knowledgeable and witty participant on radio's 'Information Please' program. As a result of his growing popularity, he began appearing regularly in films, typically in cynical, mordantly witty supporting roles, sometimes as himself. He later appeared frequently on TV, particularly on late night talk shows, which he used as a virtual psychiatric couch for a public display of his social gripes and psychological hang-ups. His physical and mental health deteriorated gradually in the last 20 years of his life. He spent much of his time in hospitals, became addicted to pills and potions, and displayed increasingly erratic behavior in public. He died of a heart attack, leaving behind about 100 musical recordings and three autobiographical books: *A Smattering of Ignorance, The Importance of Being Oscar,* and *The Memoirs of an Amnesiac.*

FILMS INCLUDE: As composer of scores or songs—*My Man* 1928; *Side Street, The Delightful Rogue, Street Girl, Jazz Heaven, Tanned Legs* 1929; *Love Comes Along, Leathernecking* 1930; *Black Sheep, Music Is Magic, In Person* 1935; *The Smartest Girl in Town* 1936. As actor (complete)—*The Dance of Life* 1929; *Rhythm on the River* 1940; *Kiss the Boys Goodbye* 1941; *Rhapsody in Blue* 1945; *Humoresque* 1946; *You Were Meant for Me, Romance on the High Seas* 1948; *The Barkleys of Broadway* 1949; *An American in Paris* 1951; *O. Henry's Full House* (segment cut from most release prints) 1952; *The I Don't Care Girl, The Band Wagon* 1953; *The Cobweb* 1955.

level. 1. The positioning of a camera in relation to the horizontal plane. 2. In sound recording, the level of sound at which a recording can be made with the greatest fidelity, as determined by an electronic signal.

Leven, Boris. Art director, production designer. *b.* 1900, Moscow. *d.* 1986. In the US from boyhood, he studied painting at New York's Beaux Arts School of Design and Architecture at USC. He won several awards in architectural competitions, but was forced by the Depression to seek employment in films. He went to work at Paramount in 1933 as a sketch artist and in 1938 became an art director at Fox. Freelancing from the late 40s, he designed many outstanding productions, in a wide variety of genres and styles, for various studios over the span of half a century. He was nominated for nine Academy Awards, winning an Oscar for *West Side Story* (1961).

FILMS INCLUDE: *Alexander's Ragtime Band* 1938; *The Shanghai Gesture* 1941; *Tales of Manhattan* 1942; *Doll Face* 1945; *Shock* 1946; *I Wonder Who's Kissing Her Now* 1947; *Mr. Peabody and the Mermaid* 1948; *Criss Cross* 1949; *Woman on the Run* 1950; *Sudden Fear* 1952; *The Star* 1953; *The Silver Chalice* 1955; *Giant* 1956; *Anatomy of a Murder* 1959; *West Side Story* 1961; *Two for the Seesaw* 1962; *Strait-Jacket* 1964; *The Sound of Music* 1965; *The Sand Pebbles* 1966; *Star!* 1968; *The Andromeda Strain, Happy Birthday Wanda June* 1971; *The New Centurions* 1972; *Jonathan Livingston Seagull* 1973; *Mandingo* 1975; *New York New York* 1977; *The Last Waltz, Matilda* 1978; *The King of Comedy* 1983; *Fletch* 1985; *Wildcats, The Color of Money* 1986.

Levene, Sam. Actor. *b.* Aug. 28, 1907, New York City. *d.* 1980. On Broadway from 1927, he went to Hollywood in 1936 to repeat his stage role in *Three Men on a Horse.* He played supporting parts in many other films, typically as a soft-tough big-city character.

FILMS INCLUDE: *Three Men on a Horse, After the Thin Man* 1936; *Yellow Jack, The Shopworn Angel, The Mad Miss Manton* 1938; *Golden Boy* 1939; *Shadow of the Thin Man, Grand Central Murder, The Big Street* 1942; *Action in the North Atlantic, I Dood It, Gung Ho!* 1943; *Whistling in Brooklyn, The Purple Heart* 1944; *The Killers* 1946; *Boomerang, Brute Force, Crossfire, Killer McCoy* 1947; *The Babe Ruth Story* 1948; *Guilty Bystander, Dial 1119* 1950; *Three Sailors and a Girl* 1953; *The Opposite Sex* 1956; *Sweet Smell of Success, Designing Woman, A Farewell to Arms, Slaughter on Tenth Avenue* 1957; *Act One* 1963; *A Dream of Kings* 1969; *Such Good Friends* 1971; *The Money, God Told Me So* 1976; *Demon* 1977; *Last Embrace, And Justice for All* 1979.

Levien, Sonya. Screenwriter. *b.* Dec. 25, 1895, Russia. *d.* 1960. In the US from childhood, she practiced law briefly before becoming a magazine editor and fiction writer. After several of her stories were adapted to the screen, she became an active screenwriter in the early 20s. She wrote scores of screenplays, alone or in collaboration, for Fox, MGM, and other studios. She shared an Academy Award for the script of *Interrupted Melody* (1955).

FILMS INCLUDE (as screenwriter, alone or in collaboration): *Who Will Marry Me?* (story only) 1919; *Cheated Love* 1921; *The Top of New York* (story only), *Pink Gods* 1922; *The Snow Bride* (also co-story), *The Exciters* 1923; *Salome of the Tenements* 1925; *Christine of the Big Tops* (also story) 1926; *The Princess from Hoboken* (also story), *The Heart Thief, A Harp in Hock* 1927; *A Ship Comes In, The Power of the Press* 1928; *The Younger Generation, Trial Marriage* (also story), *Lucky Star, They Had to See Paris, Frozen Justice, South Sea Rose* 1929; *Song o' My Heart, So This Is London, Liliom, Lightnin'* 1930; *The Brat, Surrender, Delicious, Daddy Long Legs* 1931; *Rebecca of Sunnybrook Farm, Tess of the Storm Country, After Tomorrow* 1932; *State Fair, Cavalcade, Berkeley Square* 1933; *The White Parade* 1934; *Navy Wife* 1935; *The Country Doctor, Reunion* 1936; *In Old Chicago, Four Men and a Prayer, Kidnapped, The Cowboy and the Lady* 1938; *Drums Along the Mohawk, The Hunchback of Notre Dame* 1939; *Ziegfeld Girl* 1941; *The Valley of Decision, Rhapsody in Blue* (story only), *State Fair* (remake) 1945; *The Green Years* 1946; *Cass Timberlane* 1947; *Three Daring Daughters* 1948; *The Great Caruso, Quo Vadis* 1951; *The Merry Widow* 1952; *The Student Prince* 1954; *Hit the Deck, Interrupted Melody, Oklahoma!* 1955; *Bhowani Junction* 1956; *Jeanne Eagles* 1957; *Pepe* (co-story only) 1960; *State Fair* (from her 1933 and 1945 adaptations) 1962.

Levin, Henry. Director. *b.* June 5, 1909, Trenton, N.J. *d.* 1980. *ed.* U. of Pennsylvania. A former actor, stage manager, and director with the Theatre Guild and other groups, he arrived in Hollywood in 1943 as a dialogue director on such films as *Appointment in Berlin* and *Dangerous Blondes.* He made his debut as a full director the following year and subsequently turned out many entertaining, though often empty, films in a variety of genres for Columbia, Fox, MGM, and other studios. A facile, prolific, sure-handed director, he was at his best with adventure yarns, but his output also included many comedies and musical films. He typically worked with medium-range budgets. Among his more interesting productions was *The*

Lonely Man (1957), an offbeat psychological Western starring Jack Palance.

FILMS: *The Cry of the Werewolf, Sergeant Mike, Dancing in Manhattan* 1944; *I Love a Mystery, The Fighting Guardsman* 1945; *The Bandit of Sherwood Forest* (co-dir. with George Sherman), *Night Editor, The Unknown, The Devil's Mask, The Return of Monte Cristo* 1946; *The Guilt of Janet Ames, The Corpse Came C.O.D., The Mating of Millie, Gallant Blade, The Man from Colorado* 1948; *Mr. Soft Touch* (co-dir. with Gordon Douglas), *Jolson Sings Again, And Baby Makes Three* 1949; *Convicted, The Petty Girl, The Flying Missile* 1950; *Two of a Kind, The Family Secret* 1951; *Belles on Their Toes* 1952; *The President's Lady* (also assoc. prod.), *The Farmer Takes a Wife, Mister Scoutmaster* 1953; *Three Young Texans, The Gambler from Natchez* 1954; *The Warriors/Dark Avenger* 1955; *The Lonely Man, Let's Be Happy* (UK), *Bernadine, April Love* 1957; *A Nice Little Bank That Should Be Robbed* 1958; *The Remarkable Mr. Pennypacker, Holiday for Lovers, Journey to the Center of the Earth* 1959; *Where the Boys Are* 1960; *Le Meraviglie di Aladino/The Wonders of Aladdin* (It./Fr.) 1961; *The Wonderful World of the Brothers Grimm* (co-dir. with George Pal), *If a Man Answers* 1962; *Come Fly with Me* 1963; *Honeymoon Hotel* 1964; *Genghis Khan* (US/UK/Ger./Yug.) 1965; *Murderers' Row* 1966; *Se tutte le Donne del Mondo/Operazione Paradiso/Kiss the Girls and Make Them Die* (co-dir. with Dino Maiuri; It./US), *The Ambushers* 1967; *The Desperados* 1969; *That Man Bolt* (co-dir. with David Lowell Rich) 1973; *The Thoroughbreds/Run for the Roses* 1977.

Levine, Joseph E. Producer, executive. *b.* Sept. 9, 1905, Boston. *d.* 1987. The youngest of six children of a Russian immigrant tailor, he grew up in joyless poverty, hustling pennies as a newsboy, shoeshine boy, and luggage carrier, dropping out of school at 14 for a full-time job in a dress factory. Eventually, he started his own modest dress shop and operated a small restaurant. Shortly after his 1937 marriage to Rosalie Harrison, a vocalist with Rudy Vallee's band, he took over a movie theater in New Haven, Connecticut, then went into the distribution end of the film business in 1943. In the late 50s he formed Embassy Pictures and began reaping huge profits by buying Japanese-made science-fiction action pictures, like *Godzilla,* and Italian-made muscle epics, like *Hercules,* cheaply, and spending lavishly on their exploitation. He next moved into production, financially backing such notable Italian films as *Two Women, Boccaccio 70, 8½,* and *Divorce Italian Style,* and himself producing American and international productions. He rapidly rose to a position of power as sole showman-tycoon in an industry run by big corporations. In the late 60s he sold his interests in Embassy to the Avco corporation but remained as president of Avco-Embassy. He resigned in 1974 to once more form his own company, Joseph E. Levine Presents.

FILMS INCLUDE: As producer—*Le Mépris/Contempt* (co-prod.) 1963; *The Carpetbaggers, Where Love Has Gone* 1964; *Harlow* (Carroll Baker version) 1965. As executive producer—*Sands of Kalahari* (UK), *La Decima Vittima/The Tenth Victim* (It./Fr.) 1965; *The Oscar, The Idol, Nevada Smith* 1966; *Sette Volte Donna/Sept fois Femme/A Woman Times Seven* (It./Fr./US), *The Graduate* 1967; *The Producers, The Lion in Winter* (UK) 1968; *Stiletto, Don't Drink the Water, I Girasoli/Sunflower* (It./Fr.) 1969; *Soldier Blue, The People Next Door, La Promesse de l'Aube/Promise at Dawn* (Fr./US) 1970; *Carnal Knowledge* 1971; *Thumb Tripping* 1972; *The Day of the Dolphin* 1973; *A Bridge Too Far* (co-prod.; UK) 1977; *Magic* (co-prod.) 1978; *Tattoo* (co-prod.) 1981.

Levinson, Barry. Director, screenwriter. Born on April 6, 1942, in Baltimore. The son of a businessman who started Baltimore's first discount appliance warehouse, he sold encyclopedias and used cars while attending junior college in Baltimore. He took a part-time job at a TV station when he transferred to American University in Washington D.C., majoring in broadcast journalism. After seven years of dropping in and out of school without gaining a degree, he drove to Los Angeles and signed up for acting lessons. A stint as a stand-up comic writer led to work on network TV as a writer-performer for Carol BURNETT. This in turn led to screenwriting collaborations on such Mel Brooks comedies as *Silent Movie* (1976) and *High Anxiety* (1977), in both of which Levinson also appeared.

Levinson made his debut as a director with *Diner* (1982), a largely autobiographical, disarmingly affectionate evocation of coming-of-age in Baltimore in the late 50s. Following *The Natural* (1984), a baseball fable based on the Bernard Malamud novel, and *Young Sherlock Holmes* (1985), a "cute" adventure with an interesting premise, the director returned to his hometown of Baltimore as the setting for *Tin Men* (1987), a comedy-drama about the tangled lives of two aluminum-siding salesmen. *Good Morning, Vietnam* (1988), the story of an Armed Forces broadcaster, proved an ideal vehicle for the comic exuberance of its star, Robin WILLIAMS.

Levinson reached a milestone in his still-blossoming career with *Rain Man* (1988), a sensitively observed study of a developing relationship between a brash, self-centered young man and his autistic, "idiot savant" brother. The film, a huge commercial hit, won Academy Awards for best picture, best director, best screenplay, and best actor (Dustin HOFFMAN). It also won the Golden Bear at the Berlin film festival. Resisting the temptation to take advantage of the opportunities he now had as a bankable director, Levinson returned once more to Baltimore for *Avalon* (1990), his next, very personal project, lovingly recapping the story of his Jewish family's beginnings in America. With *Bugsy* (1991), he returned to the commercial fold with the glittery saga of gangster-entrepreneur Bugsy Siegel, masterfully played by Warren Beatty. The film was nominated for several Academy Awards, including best director and best picture. His grand-scale 1992 antiwar fantasy, *Toys,* was his first major disappointment. Deemed by critics as ambitious but confused, it was largely ignored by the public. In 1990 he formed Baltimore Productions with producer Mark Johnson. Levinson's first wife was actress Valerie CURTIN, who collaborated on several of his scripts. A longtime hometown supporter, he became part of a group of investors who purchased the Baltimore Orioles baseball team in the 1990s.

Another Barry Levinson (1932–87) was a New York–born, London-based producer-writer whose credits included *The Internecine Project* (1974) and other films sometimes erroneously assigned to the Baltimore-born director.

FILMS: As screenwriter—*Silent Movie* (also act.) 1976; *High Anxiety* (also act.) 1977; *. . . And Justice for All* 1979; *Inside Moves* 1980; *History of the World: Part I* (act. only) 1981; *Best Friends* 1982; *Unfaithfully Yours* 1984. As director—*Diner* (also sc.) 1982; *The Natural* 1984; *Young Sherlock Holmes* 1985; *Tin Men* (also sc.) *Good Morning Vietnam* 1987; *Rain Man* (also act.) 1988; *Avalon* (also sc.) 1990; *Bugsy* 1991; *Toys* (also co-sc.) 1992; *Wilder Napalm* (prod. only) 1993; *Disclosure* (also co-prod.), *Jimmy Hollywood* (also sc., co-prod., act.), *Quiz Show* (act. only) 1994; *Sleepers* (also sc., co-prod.) 1996; *Donnie Brasco* (co-prod. only) 1997.

Levy, Eugene. Actor. Born on Dec. 17, 1946, in Hamilton, Ont., Canada. *ed.* McMaster U. Hirsute, manic performer in comic supporting roles. After acting in college ensemble theater, he made his film debut in *Cannibal Girls* (1973), a low-budget comedy-horror film directed by college friend Ivan REITMAN.

He went on to join Toronto's Second City comedy troupe. This led to a successful stint as a writer-performer on 'Second City TV,' which ran under various names from 1977 to 1983, and for which Levy won writing Emmys in 1982 and 1983. His feature film career has been spottier, though his performances often steal the show.

FILMS INCLUDE: *Cannibal Girls* (Can.) 1972; *Running* (Can.) 1979; *Heavy Metal* (v/o; Can.) 1981; *Strange Brew, Going Berserk* (Can.), *National Lampoon's Vacation* 1983; *Splash* 1984; *Armed and Dangerous, Club Paradise* 1986; *Speed Zone!* 1989; *Father of the Bride* 1991; *Once Upon a Crime* (also dir.) 1992.

Lévy, Raoul J. Producer. *b.* Mar. 14, 1922, Antwerp, Belgium. *d.* 1966. After WW II service with the RAF, he began his film career as production assistant for RKO on a Mexican location. He returned to Europe as representative for American producer Edward Small and shortly after founded his own production company in Paris. His main contribution to French films was as the man who launched the lucrative careers of Roger VADIM and Brigitte BARDOT. Later errors in judgment led to financial ruin. He directed two films before taking his own life, *Hail Mafia* (1965) and *The Defector* (1966), Montgomery Clift's last picture. Lévy often collaborated on the script of his films.

FILMS INCLUDE: *Identité judiciaire* 1951; *Les Orgueilleux/The Proud and the Beautiful* 1953; *Et Dieu créa la Femme/And God Created Woman* (also co-sc.) 1956; *Sait-on jamais/No Sun in Venice* 1957; *En Cas de Malheur/Love Is My Profession* 1958; *Babette s'en va-t-en Guerre/Babette Goes to War* (also co-story) 1959; *Moderato Cantabile, La Vérité/The Truth* 1960; *Je vous salue Mafia/Da New York Maffia Uccide/Hail! Mafia* (also dir., sc.; Fr./It.), *La Fabuleuse Aventure de Marco Polo/Marco the Magnificent* 1965; *L'Espion/Lautlose Waffen/The Defector* (also dir., co-sc.; Fr./Ger.) 1966; *Deux ou Trois Choses je sais d'elle/Two or Three Things I Know About Her* 1967.

Lewin, Albert. Director, producer, screenwriter. *b.* on Sept. 23, 1894, in Newark, N.J. *d.* 1968. *ed.* NYU (B.A.); Harvard (M.A.). Taught English at the University of Missouri and after WW I service became an assistant national director of the American Jewish Relief Committee. He was a drama and film critic for the *Jewish Tribune* before entering films in the early 20s as a reader for Samuel Goldwyn. He worked as a script clerk for directors King Vidor and Victor Sjöström and in 1924 joined MGM as a screenwriter. He was then appointed head of the studio's script department and by the late 20s was Irving THALBERG's personal assistant and closest associate. Nominally credited as an associate producer, he produced several of MGM's most important films of the 30s and after Thalberg's death joined Paramount as a producer in 1937. He began directing in 1942, but his entire output as director over a period spanning 15 years was limited to six films. He wrote the screenplays for all his own films and produced several of them. As a director-writer he showed arty literary and cultural aspirations in the selection and treatment of his themes. The results were usually a curious but interesting mixture of the naïve and the sophisticated, the dilettantish and the fascinating, the vulgar and the refined. Novel: *The Unaltered Cat* (1966).

FILMS INCLUDE: As screenwriter—*Bread* 1924; *The Fate of a Flirt* 1925; *Ladies of Leisure, Blarney, Tin Hats* 1926; *A Little Journey, Quality Street, Spring Fever* 1927; *The Actress* 1928; *Call Me Mister, Alice in Wonderland* 1951; *Down Among the Sheltering Palms* 1953; *Boy—Did I Get a Wrong Number!* 1966; *Eight on the Lam* 1967; *The Wicked Dreams of Paula Schultz* 1968. As producer (often credited as associate producer)—*The Kiss* 1929; *The Devil May Care* 1930; *Cuban Love Song, The Guardsman* 1931; *Red-Headed Woman, What Every Woman Knows* 1934; *China Seas, Mutiny on the Bounty* 1935; *The Good Earth, True Confession* 1937; *Spawn of the North* 1938; *Zaza* 1939; *So Ends Our Night* 1941. As director-screenwriter (complete)—*The Moon and Sixpence* (also co-exec. prod.) 1942; *The Picture of Dorian Gray* 1945; *The Private Affairs of Bel Ami* (also co-exec. prod.) 1947; *Pandora and the Flying Dutchman* (also co-prod.) 1951; *Saadia* (also prod.) 1954; *The Living Idol* (also co-prod.) 1957.

Lewis, David. Producer. *b.* David Levy, Dec. 14, 1903, Trinidad, Col. *d.* 1987. A former stage actor, he entered films in the early 30s as a story reader and before long he was Irving THALBERG's personal assistant, producing *Riffraff, Camille,* and other MGM films with a screen credit of associate producer. After Thalberg's death in 1936, he produced several Warner Bros. films, again being nominally credited as associate producer, this time to Hal B. WALLIS. In the mid-40s he finally began getting full credit as producer.

FILMS INCLUDE: *Cross Fire* 1933; *Riffraff* 1936; *Camille* 1937; *Four's a Crowd, The Sisters* 1938; *Each Dawn I Die, Dark Victory* 1939; *Till We Meet Again, All This and Heaven Too* 1940; *Kings Row, In This Our Life* 1942; *Frenchman's Creek* 1944; *It's a Pleasure* 1945; *Tomorrow Is Forever* 1946; *The Other Love* 1947; *Arch of Triumph* 1948; *The End of the Affair* 1955; *Raintree County* 1957.

Lewis, Fiona. Actress. Born on Sept. 28, 1946, in Westcliff, England. Sensual, well-built leading lady of British films and TV. From the late 70s she worked mostly in Hollywood. She wrote a dozen unproduced screenplays.

FILMS INCLUDE: *Dance of the Vampires/The Fearless Vampire Killers* 1967; *Joanna, Otley* 1968; *Where's Jack?* 1969; *Villain* 1971; *Dr. Phibes Rises Again* 1972; *Lisztomania* 1975; *Drum* (US) 1976; *Stunts* (US) 1977; *The Fury* (US) 1978; *Wanda Nevada* (US) 1979; *Dead Kids* (Austral./NZ) 1981; *Strange Invaders* (US) 1983; *Innerspace* 1987.

Lewis, Geoffrey. Actor. Born in 1935 in San Diego, Calif. Versatile character actor, often seen in films of Clint Eastwood. Father of Juliette LEWIS.

FILMS INCLUDE: *Welcome Home Soldier Boys, The Culpepper Cattle Company, Bad Company* 1972; *High Plains Drifter, Dillinger* 1973; *Thunderbolt and Lightfoot, Macon County Line* 1974; *The Great Waldo Pepper, Smile, The Wind and the Lion, Lucky Lady* 1975; *The Return of a Man Called Horse* 1976; *Every Which Way But Loose, Tilt* 1978; *Human Experiments, Tom Horn, Bronco Billy, Heaven's Gate, Any Which Way You Can* 1980; *I the Jury* 1982; *Night of the Comet* 1984; *Lust in the Dust, Stitches* 1985; *Out of the Dark* 1988; *Fletch Lives, Pink Cadillac* 1989; *Disturbed, Double Impact* 1991; *The Lawnmower Man* 1992; *Joshua Tree, The Man Without a Face, Point of No Return* 1993; *Maverick, White Fang II: Myth of the White Wolf* 1994.

Lewis, Jay. Director, producer. *b.* 1914, Warwickshire, England. *d.* 1969. A former stage actor, he began his association with British films in 1933. The films he directed were routine.

FILMS (as director): *A Man's Affair* 1949; *The Baby and the Battleship* (also co-sc.) 1956; *Invasion Quartet* 1961; *Live Now Pay Later* (also co-exec. prod.) 1962; *A Home of Your Own* 1964.

Lewis, Jerry. Actor, director, producer. Born Joseph Levitch, on Mar. 16, 1926, in Newark, N.J. The son of show people, he spent much of his childhood with relatives while his parents were on the road. Summers he joined them in the Catskills, where they performed in resorts of the "Borscht Circuit." From the age of five he occasionally joined their act with a solo singing number. He quit high school after one year and began making the rounds of booking agents. To support himself, he worked as, among other things, a soda jerk, a shipping clerk, and a theater usher. By the time he reached 18 he was an experienced one-night-stand small-time comic, with an act that consisted of mimicking famous performers whose recordings would be played off stage. Having a wife to support (he had married Patty Palmer, a vocalist with the Jimmy Dorsey band, in 1944), he spent his summers entertaining in the Catskills.

In 1946, Lewis met another small-time entertainer, a baritone by the name of Dean MARTIN. Since neither was doing very well on his own, they decided to try working as a team. They scored an immediate hit in their first joint appearance at the 500 Club in Atlantic City and before long were playing to packed houses in nightclubs and theaters all over the country. Their basic routine had Martin singing and constantly being interrupted by Lewis's zany clowning. Spontaneous ad-libbing, spiced with the trading of insults, added tension and suspense to the act. By the end of the 40s, Martin and Lewis were the most popular comedy team in the nation, on stage, on TV, and in clubs.

In 1949, Martin and Lewis were signed by Hal Wallis to a Paramount contract. They made their screen debut in the supporting cast of a minor comedy, *My Friend Irma.* Their wacky antics provided the only entertaining moments in the film and its sequel. They subsequently starred as a team in 16 more films before splitting up in 1956. Their films together varied in plot and locale. Many were adapted from screen comedy hits of the past, with Lewis playing parts that had been previously played by such female stars as Ginger Rogers, Carole Lombard, and Betty Hutton. But the basic premise was nearly always the same: Martin playing the secure, calm, romantic singer and Lewis the frantic misfit. The films appealed mostly to unsophisticated audiences and were all big moneymakers.

Since going his own way, Lewis has been taking his comedy ever more seriously. He began producing, then also directing, his own films. American critics shrugged off or ignored his work, but in France he rapidly became a cultural hero. In 1971 he was given a rousing welcome in Paris and played to sellout crowds in 16 performances at the Olympia. The same year he published a book, *The Complete Film-Maker,* which includes observations on how films are made and how they ought to be made. Lewis is an indefatigable worker with an unrestrained nervous energy that drove him to the brink of an emotional breakdown in the 70s, when he battled painkiller drug dependency and a potentially fatal ulcer condition. With the help of heart specialist Michael DeBakey, Lewis overcame his addiction and resumed his maddening schedule, which has perennially included the Muscular Dystrophy Telethon and other charitable activities. Although absent from the screen throughout the 70s, Lewis's name appeared on the marquees of some 200 movie theaters as part of a chain that bore his name. He returned to films in the early 80s and scored a personal triumph in Martin Scorsese's *The King of Comedy* (1983), in the role of a TV personality haunted by a manic Robert DE NIRO. In the same year he underwent open-heart bypass surgery. The twice-married Lewis is a father of six. Autobiography: *Jerry Lewis in Person* (1982).

FILMS (as actor): With Martin—*My Friend Irma* 1949; *My Friend Irma Goes West* 1950; *At War with the Army, That's My Boy* 1951; *Sailor Beware, Road to Bali* (cameo), *Jumping Jacks* 1952; *The Stooge, Scared Stiff, The Caddy* 1953; *Money from Home, Living It Up, Three Ring Circus* 1954; *You're Never Too Young, Artists and Models* 1955; *Pardners, Hollywood or Bust* 1956. Alone—*The Delicate Delinquent* (also prod.), *The Sad Sack* 1957; *Rock-a-Bye Baby* (also prod.), *The Geisha Boy* (also prod.) 1958; *Don't Give Up the Ship* 1959; *Visit to a Small Planet, The Bellboy* (also dir., prod., sc.), *Cinderfella* (also prod.) 1960; *The Ladies' Man* (also dir., prod., sc.), *The Errand Boy* (also dir., prod., sc.) 1961; *It's Only Money* 1962; *It's a Mad Mad Mad Mad World* (cameo), *The Nutty Professor* (also dir., prod., sc.), *Who's Minding the Store?* 1963; *The Patsy* (also dir., sc.), *The Disorderly Orderly* 1964; *The Family Jewels* (also dir., prod., sc.), *Boeing Boeing* 1965; *Three on a Couch* (also dir., prod.), *Way. . . Way Out* 1966; *The Big Mouth* (also dir., prod., sc.) 1967; *Don't Raise the Bridge—Lower the River* 1968; *Hook Line and Sinker* (also prod.) 1969; *One More Time* (dir. only), *Which Way to the Front?* (also dir., prod.) 1970; *The Day the Clown Cried* (also dir., co-sc.; unreleased, legendary personal film about a clown living in Nazi Germany) 1972; *Hardly Working* (also dir., co-sc.) 1981; *The King of Comedy, Smorgasbord/Cracking Up* (also dir., co-sc.) 1983; *Retenez-moi. . . ou je fais un Malheur* (Fr.), *Par oú t'est rentré on t'a pas vu sortir* (Fr.), *Slapstick of Another Kind* 1984; *Cookie* (bit) 1989; *Mr. Saturday Night* 1992; *Arizona Dream* 1993; *Funny Bones* 1995; *The Nutty Professor* 1996.

Lewis, Joseph H. Director. Born on Apr. 6, 1900, in New York City. *ed.* DeWitt Clinton HS. He began as an MGM camera assistant, then became a film editor for Republic. After a period of apprenticeship as second-unit director, he began directing low-budget action pictures in 1937. Always an effective technician, he managed to elevate some of his films well above prevailing B standards through his sense of rhythm and his handling of players. He was rediscovered in the 60s, acquiring an *auteur*'s status among some critics both in the US and France. Directing for TV from the late 50s.

FILMS: *Navy Spy* (co-dir. with Crane Wilbur), *Courage of the West, Singing Outlaw* 1937; *The Spy Ring/International Spy, Border Wolves, The Last Stand* 1938; *Two-Fisted Rangers, Blazing Six-Shooters, Texas Stagecoach, The Man from Tumbleweeds, Boys of the City, The Return of Wild Bill, That Gang of Mine* 1940; *The Invisible Ghost, Pride of the Bowery, Criminals Within, Arizona Cyclone* 1941; *Bombs Over Burma, The Silver Bullet, Secrets of a Co-Ed/Silent Witness, The Boss of Hangtown Mesa, The Mad Doctor of Market Street* 1942; *Minstrel Man* 1944; *The Falcon in San Francisco, My Name Is Julia Ross* 1945; *The Jolson Story* (musical numbers only), *So Dark the Night* 1946; *The Swordsman* 1947; *The Return of October* 1948; *The Undercover Man* 1949; *Gun Crazy/Deadly Is the Female, A Lady Without Passport* 1950; *Retreat Hell!, Desperate Search* 1952; *Cry of the Hunted* 1953; *The Big Combo, A Lawless Street* 1955; *The Seventh Cavalry* 1956; *The Halliday Brand* 1957; *Terror in a Texas Town* 1958.

Lewis, Juliette. Actress. Born in 1975. Bright, provocative, emotionally charged actress who often projects an innocent vulnerability with a formidable sexual presence. Well represented in a variety of roles, she was nominated for a supporting actress Academy Award as the terrorized daughter in Martin SCORSESE's 1991 re-make of *Cape Fear*. She is the daughter of actor Geoffrey LEWIS.

FILMS INCLUDE: *My Stepmother Is an Alien* 1988; *Life on the Edge, National Lampoon's Christmas Vacation* 1989; *Cape Fear, Crooked Hearts* 1991; *That Night* 1992; *Kalifornia, What's Eating Gilbert Grape* 1993; *Mixed Nuts, Natural Born Killers, Romeo Is Bleeding* 1994; *From Dusk Till Dawn, Strange Days* 1995; *The Evening Star* 1996.

Lewton, Val. Producer, screenwriter, novelist. *b.* Vladimir Ivan Leventon, May 7, 1904, Yalta, Russia. *d.* 1951. He came to the US as a child of seven with his mother, a sister of Alla Nazimova, and was educated at Columbia. By the time he entered films as an editorial assistant to David O. Selznick in the early 30s, he was the published author of some ten novels, six books of nonfiction, a book of poetry, and a book of pornography (*Yasmine*), which sold under the counter. In writing his books and later his screenplays he sometimes used pseudonyms such as Carlos Keith and Cosmo Forbes. In 1942 he was put in charge of a special RKO production unit, formed to turn out low-budget horror films. The films, which he closely supervised, have since become minor classics. They all bear his personal stamp more than that of their individual directors, and their influence on the subsequent films of the genre has been considerable. He was less successful as a producer of a number of nonhorror B pictures. He died of a heart attack at the age of 46.

FILMS (as producer): *Cat People* 1942; *I Walked with a Zombie, The Leopard Man, The Seventh Victim, The Ghost Ship* 1943; *Mademoiselle Fifi, The Curse of the Cat People, Youth Runs Wild* 1944; *The Body Snatcher, Isle of the Dead* 1945; *Bedlam* 1946; *My Own True Love* 1949; *Please Believe Me* 1950; *Apache Drums* 1951.

L'Herbier, Marcel. Director, *b.* Apr. 23, 1888, Paris. *d.* 1979. He studied law and wrote poetry, essays, and plays before being introduced to films during WW I, when he was assigned to the Cinematographic Service of the French army. In the 20s he was prominent among the impressionist filmmakers of the French avant-garde and influenced a number of young directors of the period, notably CAVALCANTI and AUTANT-LARA. But his films of the sound period were for the most part routinely commercial. In 1943 he founded IDHEC, the famed French film school. From 1954 he directed numerous pictures for French TV.

FILMS: *Phantasmes* (experimental short) 1917; *Rose France, Le Bercail* (short) 1919; *Le Carnaval des Vérités, L'Homme du Large* 1920; *Villa Destin* 1921; *Eldorado* (also sc.), *Prométhée Banquier* 1922; *Don Juan et Faust, L'Inhumaine/The New Enchantment* (also co-sc.) 1923; *Feu Mathias Pascal/The Late Matthew Pascal/The Living Dead Man* (also sc.) 1925; *Le Vertige* 1926; *Le Diable au Coeur/L'Ex-Voto* 1928; *L'Argent* (also sc.) 1929; *Nuits de Prince, L'Enfant de l'Amour* 1930; *Le Mystère de la Chambre jaune, La Parfum de la Dame en Noir, La Femme d'une Nuit* (and Italian version, *La Donna d'una Notte*) 1931; *L'Epervier/Les Amoureux/Bird of Prey* (also sc.) 1933; *Le Scandale, L'Aventurier* 1934; *Le Bonheur, La Route impériale, Veilles d'Armes/Sacrifice d'Honneur* (also co-sc.) 1935; *Les Hommes nouveaux, La Porte du Large/The Great Temptation* (also sc.) 1936; *La Citadelle du Silence/The Citadel of Silence, Nuits de Feu/The Living Corpse* (also co-sc.), *Forfaiture* 1937; *Adrienne Lecouvreur, Terre de Feu, La Tragédie impériale/Rasputin* 1938; *Entente cordiale, La Brigade sauvage/Savage Brigade, La Mode rêvée* 1939; *Histoire de Rire/Foolish Husbands* 1941; *La Comédie du Bonheur* (release delayed from 1939), *La Nuit fantastique* 1942; *L'Honorable Catherine* 1943; *La Vie de Bohème* (release delayed from 1943) 1945; *Au Petit Bonheur, L'Affaire du Collier de la Reine/The Queen's Necklace* 1946; *La Révoltée/Stolen Affections* (also sc.), *Les Derniers Jours de Pompéi/Gli Ultimi Giorni di Pompei/The Last Days of Pompeii* (also co-sc.; Fr./It.) 1949; *Le Père de Mademoiselle* (co-dir. with Robert Paul Dagan) 1953; *Hommage á Debussy* (short) 1963; *Le Cinéma du Diable* 1967; *La Féerrie des Fantasmes* (unfinished) 1978.

Lhermite, Thierry. Actor. Born in 1957, in France. Juvenile player, then romantic leading man of French films. Onscreen from the early 70s.

FILMS INCLUDE: *L'An 01* 1972; *Les Valseuses/Going Places* 1974; *Que la Fête commence/Let Joy Reign Supreme* 1975; *Des Enfants pâtés* 1977; *Les Bronzé, Le Dernier Amant romantique* 1978; *La Banquière* 1980; *L'Anné prochaine si tout va bien* 1981; *Légitime Violence* 1982; *Stella, La Femme de Mon Pote/My Best Friend's Girl, La Fiancée qui venait du Froid* 1983; *Until September* (US), *Les Ripoux/My New Partner/Le Cop* 1984; *Le Marriage du Siècle* 1985; *Nuit d'Ivresse* (also co-sc.) 1986; *Dernier Eté à Tangier, Fucking Fernando* 1987; *Ripoux contre Ripoux/My New Partner 2* 1990; *Tango* 1993; *Seven Sundays, Elles N'Oublient Jamais* 1994; *Grosse Fatigue* 1995; *The Sun Sister* 1997.

Lhomme, Pierre. Director of photography. Born in 1930, in Boulogne-sur-Seine, Paris, France. Worked on shorts before graduating to feature films in 1960. He has since been responsible for the cinematography of many French films and European co-productions. He won a César Award for the cinematography of *Camille Claudel* (1988).

FILMS INCLUDE: *St. Tropez Blues* 1960; *Un nommé La Rocca* 1961; *Le Joli Mai* 1963; *La Vie de Château/A Matter of Resistance, Le Roi de Coeur/King of Hearts* 1966; *Le plus vieux Métier du Monde/The Oldest Profession* 1967; *La Chamade* 1968; *Mister Freedom* 1969; *Quelq'un derrière la Porte/Someone Behind the Door, Quatre Nuits d'un Rêveur/Four Nights of a Dreamer* 1971; *Le Sex Shop* 1972; *La Maman et la Putain/The Mother and the Whore* 1973; *Sweet Movie* 1974; *Le Sauvage/The Savage* 1975; *L'Ombre des Châteaux* 1976; *Les Enfants du Placard, Dites lui que je l'aime* 1977; *L'Etat sauvage, Judith Therpauve* 1978; *Retour à la Bien-Aimée* 1979; *Quartet* (UK/Fr.) 1981; *Tous Feu tout Flamme* 1982; *Mortelle randoné* 1983; *My Little Girl* (US) 1986; *Maurice* (UK) 1987; *Camille Claudel* 1988; *Cyrano de Bergerac* 1990; *First Love, Voyager* (Fr./W. Ger.) 1992; *Toxic Affair* 1993; *Dieu que les Femmes Sont Amoureusesi* 1994.

Li, Gong. Actress. Born in 1965, in Shanghai, China. *ed.* Central Academy of Drama, Beijing, China. Luminous, emotionally powerful actress of international films, most notably for her stunning performances for acclaimed director and former companion Zhang Yimou. After meeting in drama school, the two collaborated on numerous films together, but it was *Red Sorghum* (1987) that set her apart and launched a career that has captivated audiences and critics around the world.

FILMS: *Red Sorghum* 1987; *Ju-Dou* 1989; *Raise the Red Lantern* 1991; *The Stories of Qiu Ju* 1992; *Farewell, My Concubine* 1993; *To Live* 1994; *Shanghai Triad* 1995; *Temptress Moon* 1997.

Liberace. Pianist. *b.* Wladziu Valentino Liberace, May 16, 1919, Milwaukee. *d.* 1987. A flamboyant, elaborately costumed concert-hall, ballroom, and nightclub pianist and showman, he made several film appearances, among them in the starring role in *Sincerely Yours* (1955). He hosted his own TV variety program, 'The Liberace Show' in 1952–55 and again in 1969. Autobiographies: *Liberace* (1973); *The Things I Love* (1977).

FILMS: *South Sea Sinner* 1950; *Footlight Varieties* 1951; *Sincerely Yours* 1955; *The Loved One, When the Boys Meet the Girls* 1965.

Libertini, Richard. Actor. Born on May 21, 1940(?) in Cambridge, Mass. Character comedian of the American stage, TV, and films. An original member of Chicago's Second City troupe, he performed in cabaret and off Broadway before making his screen debut in the late 60s.

FILMS INCLUDE: *The Night They Raided Minsky's* 1968; *Don't Drink the Water* 1969; *Catch-22, The Out-of-Towners* 1970; *La Mortadella/Lady Liberty* (It./Fr.) 1971; *Fire Sale* 1977; *The In-Laws* 1979; *Popeye* 1980; *Sharky's Machine, Soup for One* 1982; *Deal of the Century* 1982; *Unfaithfully Yours, All of Me* 1984; *Fletch* 1985; *Big Trouble* 1986; *Betrayed* 1988; *Fletch Lives* 1989; *The Bonfire of the Vanities* 1990; *Nell* 1994.

library. In the context of cinema: 1. A film repository organized to serve a specific group or the general public. Depending on its particular purpose, it may store feature films, short subjects, instructional or industrial films, or stock footage and newsreel clippings. As with books in a regular library, film materials must be classified and cataloged, but film libraries should be equipped with temperature-controlled storage vaults and basic editing facilities. 2. Libraries also exist for the storage of pretaped and prerecorded background music and sound effects for films. See also ARCHIVES, FILM.

library shot. Also called "stock footage." A film sequence previously photographed and stored for possible future use. Library shots usually consist of footage too difficult, too expensive, or too common to shoot time and again, such as jungle scenes, aerial combat, spectacular explosions, a rainstorm, cars moving on a highway. An editor must match such sequences carefully with his "live" footage if the audience is not to be aware of their origin.

Lieven, Albert. Actor. *b.* Albert Fritz Liévin, 1906, Hohenstein, Germany. *d.* 1971. A Berlin stage actor from 1928, he began playing lead roles in German films in 1932 but was forced to find refuge in England during the Nazi regime. After WW II he continued appearing in British as well as German films. His fourth wife was actress Susan SHAW.

FILMS INCLUDE: In Germany—*Ich bei Tag und Du bei Nacht* 1932; *Reifende Jugend, Die vom Niederrhein* 1933; *Charleys Tante/Charley's Aunt, Glückspilze, Fräulein Liselott, Krach am Iolanthe* 1934; *Die klugen Frauen* (German version of Feyder's *La Kermesse héroïque*) 1935; *Kater Lampe* 1936. In the UK—*Night Train to Munich/Night Train* (bit), *Convoy* 1940; *Jeannie* 1941; *The Young Mr. Pitt* (as Talleyrand) 1942; *The Yellow Canary, The Life and Death of Colonel Blimp* 1943; *English Without Tears/Her Man Gilbey* 1944; *The Seventh Veil* 1945; *Beware of Pity* 1946; *Frieda* 1947; *Sleeping Car to Trieste* 1948; *Hotel Sahara* 1951; *Die Rose von Stambul* (Ger.), *Geliebtes Leben* (Ger.), *Desperate Moment* 1953; *Des Teufels General/The Devil's General* (Ger.), *Reifende Jugend* (remake; Ger.) 1955; *Londra chiama Polo Nord/The House of Intrigue* (It.) 1956; *Das Schachnovelle/Brainwashed/The Royal Game* (Ger.), *Conspiracy of Hearts, Foxhole in Cairo* (as Rommel) 1960; *Das Geheimnis der gelben Narzissen/The Devil's Daffodil* (Ger./UK), *The Guns of Navarone* (UK/US) 1961; *Death Trap* 1962; *Mystery Submarine, The Victors* (UK/US) 1963; *Das Verrätertor/Traitor's Gate* (Ger./UK) 1964; *Ride the High Wind* (S. Afr.), *City of Fear* 1965; *Der Gorilla von Soho/The Gorilla Gang* (Ger.) 1968.

light, artificial. Man-made illumination not originating from such natural sources as the sun, the moon, or the stars. The latter provide "natural light."

light, hard. Intense light producing sharply defined shadows. The opposite of "diffused" (or "soft") light.

light box. A transparent animation desk illuminated from below.

lighting. In film production, the art and craft of artificially illuminating a set to achieve a desired photographic image. The choice and pattern of lighting setups are crucial in determining the texture, "look," and mood of a particular film, and a director of photography (also known as a lighting cameraman) will spend a great deal of time and thought on planning the distribution and balance of his light sources. Lighting is, of course, essential to interior cinematography, but even when shooting outdoors, in direct sunlight, natural light is often augmented and "corrected" by artificial light sources or through such devices as reflectors, which are used to direct sunlight to the areas where it is most needed. Indoors or out, lighting can be used to simulate a "natural" look, by achieving a delicate balance among the available sources, or to create a striking effect by harsh contrasts of light and shadow.

Lighting equipment is the predominant physical feature of a film studio. Lighting units of varying size, shape, and intensity, often dozens of them, are suspended from above, rigged to sets or catwalks, or mounted on stands, and may surround the entire shooting area. The light units are the bulkiest and most cumbersome of a film unit's equipment when traveling for location photography. They basically fall into two categories, the top-heavy arc lamps (the largest are known as "brutes"), which are used to simulate sunlight and are essential for bright color cinematography, and the incandescent lamp family, which consists of flood lamps and spot lamps of various sizes, shapes, and intensities.

In lighting the set, the director of photography makes use of three basic sources of illumination which he must balance to achieve a desired effect: the key light, the fill (or filler) light, and back light. The key light provides the principal source of illumination on the set and establishes the overall lighting pattern and intensity. It is directed at the players or the main inanimate subjects being photographed, usually at a side angle. Brutes are usually used to do this job. Fill (or filler) lights are used as a supplementary light source to balance the effect of the key light, reduce unwanted shadows, and minimize contrast. Ideally, they should neutralize the impact of the key light without affecting its intensity. They are typically positioned at camera level and usually provide about half as much light as the key light. Back lights are intended to add depth to the photographed image in relation to the background against which the subject is being photographed. They are positioned behind the players, in the back of the set, facing the camera, and are usually suspended from above so that they do not interfere with the action or enter the camera's field of view. This latter group also includes kickers, or kicker lights, also known as "eye lights," which are used to highlight a performer's eyes or teeth.

It is essential that a constant balance among the various light sources be maintained not only throughout one shooting session but during the entire production of a film, so that scenes don't vary noticeably on the screen when they follow one another after being reshuffled in editing.

The overall look of a film on a screen is strongly influenced by the way it was lit during production. During the heyday of the Hollywood studio system, it was often possible to tell the actual source of a motion picture by simply viewing it. For example, Warner Bros. pictures of the 30s were distinguishable by their low-key photography, designed to heighten atmosphere and hide flaws in inexpensive sets. In the 40s the pictures took on a foggy, murky look to suit the dark mood of the *film noir* genre, which the studio then espoused. Conversely, the films of 20th Century-Fox boasted sharp, glossy photography that was intended to give the studio's product a polished, brassy look; and MGM flaunted its sterling image through brightly lit, glittering sets.

lighting cameraman. See DIRECTOR OF PHOTOGRAPHY.

light meter. See EXPOSURE METER.

Lightner, Winnie. Actress. *b.* Winifred Josephine Reeves, Sept. 17, 1899, Greenport, L.I. *d.* 1971. A popular vaudeville and musical stage comedienne, she scored hits on Broadway in 'George White's Scandals of 1923' and in 'Gay Paree' (1926). She starred in early sound musical films but retired in 1934 to marry her fourth husband, film director Roy DEL RUTH.

FILMS INCLUDE: *The Gold Diggers of Broadway, The Show of Shows* 1929; *She Couldn't Say No, Hold Everything, The Life of the Party* 1930; *Sit Tight, Gold Dust Gertie, Side Show* 1931; *Manhattan Parade, Play Girl* 1932; *She Had to Say Yes, Dancing Lady* 1933; *I'll Fix It* 1934.

Lilley, Edward. Director. *b.* Aug. 7, 1896, Chester, Pa. *d.* 1974. A former actor and a veteran director of Broadway musicals ('The International Revue,' 'Ziegfeld Follies,' etc.), he turned out a number of low-budget screen musical comedies at Universal in the early 40s.

FILMS INCLUDE: *Honeymoon Lodge, Larceny with Music, Moonlight in Vermont, Never a Dull Moment* 1943; *Babes on Swing Street* 1944; *Swing Out Sister* 1945.

Lillie, Beatrice (Bea). Actress. *b.* May 29, 1894, Toronto. *d.* 1989. Popular comedienne of British and American revues and light plays. The daughter of a Canadian government official, she left school at 15 to go onto the stage, forming a singing trio with her mother and sister. She made her London debut in a 1914 revue and her Broadway bow in the hit 'Charlot's Revue of 1924.' She soon became the "toast of two continents," the intimate friend of such personalities as Noel Coward, Winston Churchill, George Bernard Shaw, and Charlie Chaplin. At the height of her success she was often called "the funniest woman in the world." In 1920 she married Sir Robert Peel and became officially known as Lady Peel. He left her a widow in 1934. Despite her great popularity onstage and on radio, she made only a handful of film appearances, mainly in vehicles that failed to capitalize on her talent. Her autobiography, *Every Other Inch a Lady,* was published in 1972.

FEATURE FILMS: *Exit Smiling* 1926; *The Show of Shows* 1929; *Are You There?* 1930; *Dr. Rhythm* 1938; *On Approval* (UK) 1944; *Around the World in 80 Days* 1956; *Thoroughly Modern Millie* 1967.

lily. A display of various patches of color shot at the beginning or the end of a roll of film to provide the lab technician with a standard for checking color accuracy and tonal values.

limbo. A set with a neutral, vague, or blacked-out background, excluding all but the principal object or action and containing the barest necessary foreground settings and props.

Lincoln, Elmo. Actor. *b.* Otto Elmo Linkenhelter, 1899, Rochester, N.Y. *d.* 1952. A sturdy 200-pounder, he started his motion picture career playing featured roles in three D. W. Griffith classics: *Judith of Bethulia* (1914); as a blacksmith in *The Birth of a Nation* (1915); and as "the mighty man of valor" in the Babylonian episode of *Intolerance* (1916). In 1918 he made film history of sorts by portraying the screen's original Tarzan in *Tarzan of the Apes.* He repeated the role in two features and a serial and played leading and supporting parts in a variety of films of the early 20s. But like some of the players who followed him in the role of Tarzan, he was a rather awkward performer and found further film roles scarce. He retired from films in 1926 but returned to the screen in the late 40s in minor supporting roles, mainly as a heavy. Early in his career he was sometimes billed Oscar Linkenhelt. He is not to be confused with E. K. Lincoln, another actor of the silent period who played romantic leads, often playboys.

FILMS INCLUDE: *Judith of Bethulia* 1914; *The Birth of a Nation, The Absentee, Jordan Is a Hard Road* 1915; *Intolerance, Hoodoo Ann, Children of the Feud* 1916; *Might and the Man, Aladdin and the Wonderful Lamp* (as the Genie) 1917; *Tarzan of the Apes* (title role), *Treasure Island, The Kaiser, The Beast of Berlin, The Romance of Tarzan* (again as Tarzan), *The Greatest Thing in Life* 1918; *Elmo the Mighty* (serial), *Deliverance* 1919; *The Return of Tarzan* (again as Tarzan), *Elmo the Fearless* (serial), *The Flaming Disc* (serial), *Under Crimson Skies* 1920; *The Adventures of Tarzan* (serial) 1921; *Quincy Adams Sawyer* 1922; *Rupert of Hentzau, Women Men Marry* 1922; *Repert of Hentzau, The Rendezvous, Fashion Row* 1923; *My Neighbor's Wife* 1925; *Union Pacific, The Real Glory* 1939; *Tarzan's New York Adventure* 1942; *The Story of Dr. Wassell* 1944; *The Man Who Walked Alone* 1945; *Rolling Home* 1947; *A Double Life, Tap Roots* 1948; *Tarzan's Magic Fountain* (bit) 1949; *Hollywood Story* (cameo, as himself) 1951; *Carrie* (bit) 1952.

Lindblom, Gunnel. Actress. Born on Dec. 18, 1931, in Göteborg, Sweden. Leading lady of the Swedish stage and screen. Memorable in several Bergman films. She directed a first film in 1977.

FILMS INCLUDE: *Love* 1952; *Girl in the Rain, Song of the Scarlet Flower, The Seventh Seal* 1956; *Wild Strawberries* 1957; *The Virgin Spring* 1959; *Winter Light* 1962; *The Silence, My Love Is a Rose* 1963; *Loving Couples, Rapture* 1964; *Hunger, Woman of Darkness* 1966; *The Girls* 1968; *The Father* 1969; *Brother Carl* 1971; *Scenes from a Marriage* 1973; *Summer Paradise/Paradise Place* (dir., co-sc. only) 1977; *Bomsalva/Misfire* 1978; *Sally and Freedom* (dir. only) 1981; *Bakom Jalusin* 1984; *Summer Nights on the Planet Earth* (dir., sc. only) 1987.

Linden, Eric. Actor. Born on Sept. 15, 1909, in New York City. *ed.* Columbia. Slight, youthful leading man of Hollywood films of the 30s, usually in sincere romantic roles, mostly in minor productions.

FILMS INCLUDE: *Are These Our Children?* 1931; *The Crowd Roars, Young Bride/Love Starved, Roadhouse Murder, Life Begins, The Age of Consent, Big City Blues, Afraid to Talk/Merry-Go-Round* 1932; *Sweepings, The Past of Mary Holmes, The Silver Cord* 1933; *I Give My Love* 1934; *Ladies Crave Excitement, Ah Wilderness!* 1935; *The Voice of Bugle Ann, The Robin Hood of El Dorado, In His Steps, Old Hutch* 1936; *Girl Loves Boy, A Family Affair, Good Old Soak, Sweetheart of the Navy* 1937; *Romance of the Limberlost* 1938; *Everything's on Ice, Gone With the Wind* (bit) 1939; *Criminals Within* 1941.

Linder, Max. Actor, director. *b.* Gabriel-Maximilien Leuvielle, Dec. 16, 1883, Caverne, France. *d.* 1925. At 17 he left high school to study drama and soon after began an acting career on the Bordeaux stage. He moved to Paris in 1904 and started playing supporting parts in melodramas. In 1905 he embarked upon a parallel career in Pathé films. For three years he spent his days in the film studios and his evenings on the stage, using his real name in the theater and the pseudonym Max Linder on the screen. By 1908 he had given up the stage to concentrate on his increasingly successful screen career. By 1910 he was an internationally popular comedian, possibly the best-known screen comic on either side of the Atlantic in the years before WW I. Typically playing a dapper dandy of the idle class, he developed a style of slapstick silent screen comedy that anticipated Mack Sennett and Chaplin and set the premises of the genre for years to come. Ferdinand Zecca, Louis Gasnier, and Alberto Capelani were among the directors of his earliest films.

By 1910, Linder was writing and supervising, and from 1911 also directing, all his own films. His popularity was at its peak in 1914, when he was called to arms. Early in the war he was a victim of gas poisoning and suffered a serious breakdown. The injury was to have a lasting effect on his physical and mental well-being. He returned briefly to French films, but finding his popularity vanishing, he accepted a bid from Essanay and left for the US late in 1916.

Continuous ill health hampered the American phase of Linder's career from the start. In mid-1917, after only three films, he was felled by double pneumonia and spent nearly a year recovering in a Swiss sanitarium. When he returned to the US in 1921, he formed his own production unit, releasing through United Artists. But after making only three more American films, including the celebrated parody (of Fairbanks's *The Three Musketeers*) *The Three Must-Get-Theres,* he returned to Europe, where he married the daughter of a Paris restaurateur in 1923. Linder made two more film appearances, one in France, the other in Austria, but realized his career was finished. In 1925 he entered a suicide pact with his wife. Their bodies were discovered side by side in a Paris hotel. He remained forgotten for years, until the 60s, when many of his old films began turning up, affording film historians an opportunity to evaluate his career and his contributions to the evolution of screen comedy.

FILMS INCLUDE: As actor—*La Première Sortie d'un Collegien* 1905; *Le Poison* 1906; *Une Conquête* 1908; *Le Petit Jeune Homme, Un Mariage à l'Américain* 1909; *Max Aeronaute, Max Champion de Boxe, Max se marie* 1910. As actor-director—*Max dans sa Famille* 1911; *Max et les Femmes, Le Mal de Mer* 1912; *Max Asthmatique, Max Virtuose* 1913; *Max dans les Aires* 1914; *Max et l'Espion* 1915; *Max Comes Across, Max Wants a Divorce, Max in a Taxi* (all US) 1917; *Le Petit Café* 1919; *Le Feu sacré* (act. only) 1920; *Be My Wife, Seven Years Bad Luck* (both US) 1921; *The Three Must-Get-Theres* (US) 1922; *Au Secours!* (act. only) 1923; *Der Zirkuskönig/Le Roi du Cirque/King of the Circus* (co-dir. with E. E. Violet, Aus.) 1924.

Lindfors, Viveca. Actress. *b.* Elsa Viveca Torstensdotter Lindfors, on Dec. 29, 1920, in Uppsala, Sweden. *d.* 1995. Tall, dark, and extraordinarily talented, she trained at Stockholm's Royal Dramatic Theater for three years before entering Swedish films in 1940. She also appeared in many plays before leaving for the US in 1946. Here she signed with Warner Bros., making her screen debut in 1948. She subsequently appeared in many film productions in the US and Europe, only a few of which took full advantage of her personality and ability. She won acting honors at the Berlin Film Festival for her performances in *Die Vier im Jeep/Four in a Jeep* (1951) and *Huis clos/No Exit* (1962). She has also appeared in a number of TV productions and many stage plays, the latter notably including 'Anastasia' (1954), 'Miss Julie' (1955), 'Brecht on Brecht' (1961), and her one-woman show, 'I Am a Woman' (1973). She directed her first film, *Unfinished Business. . .*, in 1987. Formerly (1949–53) married to director Don SIEGEL, she became the wife (1954) of playwright-director George Tabori and mother of actor Kristoffer Tabori (*b.* Aug. 4, 1952, Los Angeles).

FILMS INCLUDE: In Sweden—*The Spinning Family* 1940; *In Paradise* 1941; *The Yellow Ward* 1942; *Anna Lans* 1943; *Appassionata* 1944; *Black Roses, Marie in the Windmill* 1945; *In the Waiting Room of Death/Interlude* 1946. In the US—*To the Victor, Adventures of Don Juan* 1948; *Night Unto Night* 1949; *Singoalla* (Sw./Fr.), *Backfire, No Sad Songs for Me, This Side of the Law, Dark City* 1950; *Die Vier im Jeep/Four in a Jeep* (Switz.), *The Flying Missile, Journey Into Light* 1951; *The Raiders, No Time for Flowers* 1952; *Run for Cover, Moonfleet* 1955; *The Halliday Brand* 1957; *I Accuse!* (UK), *La Tempesta/Tempest* (It./Fr./Yug.) 1958; *The Story of Ruth* 1960; *King of Kings, The Damned/These Are the Damned* (UK) 1961; *Huis Clos/No Exit* (Arg./US) 1962; *An Affair of the Skin* 1963; *Sylvia, Brainstorm* 1965; *Coming Apart* 1969; *Puzzle of a Downfall Child* 1970; *Cauldron of Blood* (US/Sp.) 1971; *The Way We Were* 1973; *La Casa sin Fronteras* (Sp.) 1972; *Welcome to L.A., Tabu/Taboo* (Sw.) 1977; *Girlfriends, A Wedding* 1978; *Voices, Natural Enemies* 1979; *The Hand* 1981; *Creepshow* 1982; *Silent Madness* 1984; *The Sure Thing* 1985; *Unfinished Business. . .* (also dir., sc.), *Rachel River* 1987; *Goin' to Chicago, Luba* (Holl.), *The Exorcist III* 1990; *Zandalee* 1991; *North of Pittsburgh, The Linguine Incident* 1992; *Stargate* 1994; *Last Summer in the Hamptons* 1995.

Lindon, Lionel. Director of photography. *b.* 1905, Balboa, Calif. *d.* 1971. He entered films in his teens as a lab assistant and before long moved up to assistant director, working on De Mille's *The Ten Commandments* (1923), among other productions. He became a camera operator in 1930 and graduated to lighting cameraman in 1943. He was behind the camera on many major films, mostly for Paramount, and won an Academy Award for the cinematography of *Around the World in 80 Days* (1956). From the late 50s he also worked frequently for TV, winning an Emmy for 'Ritual of Evil' (1970).

FILMS INCLUDE: *Let's Face It* 1943; *Going My Way* 1944; *A Medal for Benny* 1945; *The Blue Dahlia, Road to Utopia, OSS, Monsieur Beaucaire* 1946; *My Favorite Brunette, Welcome Stranger* 1947; *Tap Roots* 1948; *Alias Nick Beal, Top of the Mornin'* 1949; *Destination Moon* 1950; *Only the Valiant, Rhubarb, Submarine Command, Hong Kong* 1951; *The Turning Point* 1952; *Jamaica Run* 1953; *Casanova's Big Night, Secret of the Incas* 1954; *Conquest of Space, Hell's Island, A Man Alone, Lucy Gallant* 1955; *Around the World in 80 Days* 1956; *The Big Caper, The Lonely Man* 1957; *I Want to Live!* 1958; *Alias Jesse James* 1959; *The Young Savages* 1961; *Too Late Blues, All Fall Down, The Manchurian Candidate* 1962; *The Trouble with Angels, Grand Prix, Dead Heat on a Merry-Go-Round* 1966; *Three Guns for Texas* 1968; *Pendulum, The Extraordinary Seaman, Generation* 1969.

Lindsay, Margaret. Actress. *b.* Margaret Kies, Sept. 19, 1910, Dubuque, Iowa. *d.* 1981. Personable, appealing leading lady of Hollywood films of the 30s and 40s. Trained at New York's American Academy of Dramatic Arts, she gained some stage experience in London, having failed to secure roles in the US. Back in America, she made her film debut in 1932 at Universal and first gained attention the following year, in Fox's prestigious *Cavalcade.* It is said that she bluffed her way into that film's all-British cast by presenting herself to the studio as London-born. She was then signed by Warners and appeared in many of the studio's productions throughout the 30s. But despite her engaging personality and acting ability, she was assigned mainly leads in low-grade films and secondary roles in more important productions. She played the feminine lead in seven "Ellery Queen" mysteries, among other tight-budget films. She freelanced with various studios in the 40s, again appearing mostly in B pictures, and later played character roles in occasional films.

FILMS INCLUDE: *Okay America!, The Fourth Horseman* 1932; *Cavalcade, Christopher Strong, Baby Face, The House on 56th Street, Captured, Voltaire, The World Changes, Lady Killer* 1933; *Fog Over Frisco, The Dragon Murder Case, Gentlemen Are Born* 1934; *Bordertown, Devil Dogs of the Air, The Case of the Curious Bride, G-Men, Frisco Kid, Dangerous* 1935; *The Lady Consents, Public Enemy's Wife, Sinner Take All* 1936; *Green Light, Slim, Back in Circulation* 1937; *Gold Is Where You Find It, Jezebel, Garden of the Moon* 1938; *On Trial, Hell's Kitchen, The Under-Pup, 20,000 Men a Year* 1939; *British Intelligence, Double Alibi, The House of Seven Gables, Ellery Queen—Master Detective* 1940; *There's Magic in Music/The Hard-Boiled Canary* 1941; *The Spoilers* 1942; *Crime Doctor* 1943; *Alaska* 1944; *Scarlet Street, Club Havana* 1945; *Seven Keys to Baldpate, The Vigilantes Return, Cass Timberlane* 1947; *B.F.'s Daughter* 1948; *The Bottom of the Bottle, Emergency Hospital* 1956; *The Restless Years* 1958; *Please Don't Eat the Daisies* 1960; *Tammy and the Doctor* 1963.

Lindsay-Hogg, Michael. See FITZGERALD, Geraldine.

Lindtberg, Leopold. Director. *b.* June 1, 1902, Vienna, of Jewish parents. *d.* 1984. A stage actor from 1924 and director from 1928 in Austria and Germany, he settled in Switzerland after the Nazi rise to power and in the 40s developed into that country's most important film director. His most accomplished film, *The Last Chance* (1945), won a special Peace Prize at Cannes, and *Four in a Jeep* (1951) a first prize at the Berlin Film Festival. For the stage, he directed the world premieres of Bertolt Brecht's 'Mother Courage and Her Children,' Max

Frisch's 'Chinese Wall,' William Faulkner's 'Requiem for a Nun,' and Friedrich Dürrenmatt's 'The Meteor,' among scores of other productions. He also directed major operatic works for the Vienna State Opera and other companies.

FILMS INCLUDE: *Jasoo* (co-dir.) 1935; *Fusillier Wipf* (co-dir.) 1938; *Wachtmeister Studer* 1939; *Die Missbrauchten Liebesbriefe* 1940; *Marie-Louise* 1944; *Die letzte Chance/The Last Chance* 1945; *Swiss Tour/Four Days Leave* 1949; *Die Vier im Jeep/Four in a Jeep* 1951; *Unser Dorf/The Village* 1953; *Daughter of the Storm* 1954.

line test. In animation, a photographed sequence of pencil drawings projected in negative form to check the quality of the animation before proceeding with tracing the drawings onto cels.

lining up. The act of setting up for a shot by a cameraman, usually involving such preparatory steps as positioning the camera and adjusting the lights.

Linklater, Richard. Director. Born in 1961 in Austin, Tex. *ed.* Sam Houston State U. Inventive director known for pointed yet playful explorations of the post-postwar generation. After dropping out of college, he worked on an oil rig and parked cars before filming *Slacker*, a documentary-style look at the students, ex-students, and hangers-on in the college town of Austin where he grew up. Aided in founding of Austin Film Society.

FILMS INCLUDE: *Slacker* 1991; *Dazed and Confused* (also act.) 1993; *Before Sunrise* 1995; *Suburbia* 1997.

Linson, Art. Producer, director. Born in 1942, in Chicago. The holder of a law degree from UCLA, he started his career as a rock music manager and later operated his own recording company, the Spin Dizzy label. As a film producer from the mid-70s, he was responsible for a number of major Hollywood productions, but he fared poorly in his occasional outings as a director.

FILMS INCLUDE (as producer or executive producer, alone or in collaboration): *Rafferty and the Gold Dust Twins* 1974; *Car Wash* 1976; *American Hot Wax* 1978; *Where the Buffalo Roam* (also dir.), *Melvin and Howard* 1980; *Fast Times at Ridgemont High* 1982; *The Wild Life* (also dir.) 1984; *The Untouchables* 1987; *Scrooged* 1988; *Casualties of War, We're No Angels* 1989; *Dick Tracy* 1990; *Singles* 1992; *This Boy's Life* 1993; *Casino, Heat* 1995; *The Edge* 1997.

Liotta, Ray. Actor. Born on Dec. 18, 1955, in Newark, N.J., of an Italian father and Scottish-Irish mother. Handsome, athletic, blue-eyed leading man of Hollywood films. Raised in suburban Union Township, N.J., he starred in high school basketball and soccer but showed enough interest in acting to enroll at the University of Miami as a drama major. After graduating he headed for New York, where he landed a quickie commercial and a regular role (1978–81) in the TV soap opera 'Another World.' Things got tougher when he went west, but just when he was about to give up, Liotta was assigned the part of Melanie Griffith's brutal ex-husband in Jonathan Demme's *Something Wild* (1986). Better parts followed, culminating in the role of Shoeless Joe Jackson in *Field of Dreams* (1989) and a convincing portrayal of Mafia mobster Henry Hill in Martin Scorsese's *GoodFellas* (1990).

FILMS: *The Lonely Lady* 1983; *Something Wild* 1986; *Dominick and Eugene* 1988; *Field of Dreams* (as Shoeless Joe Jackson); *GoodFellas* (as gangster Henry Hill) 1990; *Article 99, Unlawful Entry* 1992; *Corrina Corinna, No Escape* 1994; *Operation Dumbo Drop* 1995; *Turbulence, Unforgettable* 1996; *Copland* 1997.

Lipman, Jerzy. Director of photography. Born in 1922, in Brest Litovsk, Poland (now Belarus). A graduate (1948–52) of the Lodz film school, he is the best-known Polish cameraman abroad and is respected for his individual style. He has worked much with WAJDA and POLANSKI.

FILMS INCLUDE: *A Generation* 1954; *The Shadow, Kanal* 1956; *The Eighth Day of the Week* 1958; *Lotna* 1959; *Love at 20* (co-phot.), *Knife in the Water* 1962; *The Murderer and the Girl* 1963; *The Law and the Fist* 1964; *Ashes* 1965; *Zozya* 1967; *Colonel Wolodyjowski* 1969; *Dead Pigeon on Beethoven Street* (Ger.) 1972; *The Martyr* (Ger./Isr.) 1975.

Lipscomb, W. P. Screenwriter. *b.* 1887, England. *d.* 1958. In British films from the late 20s, he worked in Hollywood from 1935 through the end of WW II, then returned to England. Occasionally he has also produced or directed.

FILMS INCLUDE: *French Leave* 1927; *The Good Companions, Channel Crossing* 1933; *Colonel Blood* (also dir.) 1934; *Cardinal Richelieu* (dial. only; US) *Clive of India* (US), *Les Misérables* (US), *A Tale of Two Cities* (US) 1935; *A Message to Garcia* (US), *Under Two Flags* (US), *The Garden of Allah* (US) 1936; *Pygmalion* 1938; *The Sun Never Sets* (US) 1939; *Forever and a Day* (US) 1943; *Beware of Pity* (also co-prod.) 1946; *Make Me an Offer* (also prod.) 1954; *A Town Like Alice* 1956; *Dunkirk* 1958.

Lipsky, Oldrich. Director. *b.* 1924, Czechoslovakia. *d.* 1986. After spending part of WW II in a forced labor camp, he studied philosophy at Prague's Charles University and began his career as an artistic director in that city's Satirical Theater. He entered Czech films as an actor and screenwriter, and became a director in 1954. He specialized in comedy and satire. His brother, Lubomir Lipsky (*b.* 1923), became a stage and screen actor.

FILMS INCLUDE: *The Show Is On* 1954; *The Circus Is Coming* 1960; *The Man from the First Century* 1961; *Lemonade Joe* 1964; *Happy End* 1966; *I Killed Einstein* 1969; *Six Bears and a Clown* (release delayed from 1972) 1976; *Adele Hasn't Had Her Supper Yet, Nick Carter in Prague* 1978; *Long Live Ghosts!* 1979; *Mysterious Castle in the Carpathians* 1981.

lip sync. Accurate synchronization of filmed lip movements with recorded speech sounds. In a broader sense, the term is used to describe simultaneous recording of voice and picture rather than shooting with no sound at all or with wild sound. See also WILD TRACK.

liquid gate. A laboratory device for coating film during printing to minimize scratches and abrasions.

Lisi, Virna. Actress. Born Virna Pieralisi, on Sept. 8, 1936, in Ancona, Italy. An exquisite blonde, she began appearing in Italian films at the age of 16 and after playing decorative roles in many cheap melodramas and quickie spectaculars, she emerged in the 60s as a glamorous leading lady of international productions, particularly romantic comedies.

FILMS INCLUDE: *La Corda d'Acciaio* 1953; *Desiderio e Sole, Violenza sul Lago* 1954; *Luna Nova, La Rossa, Vendicata* 1955; *La Donna del Giorno/The Doll That Took the Town* 1957; *Caterina Sforza, Vita perduta/Lost Souls* 1958; *Il Mondo dei Miracoli* 1959; *Romolo e Remo/Duel of the Titans* 1961; *Eva* (Fr./It.) 1962; *Les Bonnes Causes/Don't Tempt the Devil* (Fr./It.) 1963; *Bambole/The Dolls* (It./Fr.), *Casanova '70* (It./Fr.), *Una Vergine per il Principe/A Maiden for a Prince* (It./Fr.), *Oggi Domani e Dopodomani/Kiss the Other Sheik* (It./Fr.), *How to Murder Your Wife* (US) 1965; *Signore e Signori/The Birds the Bees and the Italians* (It./Fr.), *Assault on a Queen* (US), *Not with My Wife You Don't!* (US) 1966; *La Ragazza e il Generale/The Girl and the General* (It./Fr.), *Made in Italy* (It./Fr.), *Le 25e Heure/The 25th Hour* (Fr./It.), *Le Dolci Signore/Anyone Can Play, Arabella* 1967; *Meglio Vedova/Better a Widow* (It./Fr.), *Tenderly/The Girl Who Couldn't Say No* 1968; *L'Arbre de Noël/The Christmas Tree* (Fr./It.), *The Secret of Santa Vittoria* (US) 1969; *Temps des Loupes* (Fr./It.) 1970; *The Statue* (UK),

Roma Bene (It./Fr.) 1971; *Bluebeard* (Hung./Fr./It.) 1972; *Le Serpent/The Serpent* (Fr./Ger.) 1973; *Oltre il Bene e il Male/Between Good and Evil* 1977; *Ernesto* 1978; *La Cicala* 1980; *Miss Right* 1981; *Sapore di Mare, Stelle emigranti* 1983; *I Love New York* 1987; *I Ragazzi di Via Panisperna* 1989; *Buon Natale Buon Anno/Merry Christmas Happy New Year* 1990; *Queen Margot* 1994; *Follow Your Heart* 1997.

Lister, Moira. Actress. Born on Aug. 6, 1923, in Cape Town, South Africa. A stage actress from age six, she made her London debut in 1937. A patrician, blue-eyed blonde, she played leads and supporting roles in many British films from the early 40s, typically as a sensuous aristocrat.

FILMS INCLUDE: *The Shipbuilders* 1943; *Love Story/A Lady Surrenders* 1944; *Wanted for Murder* 1946; *So Evil My Love, Another Shore* 1948; *A Run for Your Money* 1949; *Pool of London* 1950; *White Corridors* 1951; *The Cruel Sea* 1952; *Trouble in Store* 1953; *The Deep Blue Sea* 1955; *Seven Waves Away/Abandon Ship!* 1957; *The Yellow Rolls-Royce* 1964; *The Double Man, Stranger in the House/Cop-Out* 1967; *Not Now Darling* 1972; *Ten Little Indians* 1989.

Litel, John. Actor. *b.* Dec. 30, 1894, Albany, Wis. *d.* 1972. *ed.* U. of Pennsylvania. During WW I he enlisted in the French army and was twice decorated for bravery. When he returned to the US, he took up acting at the American Academy of Dramatic Arts and toured with various companies. He made his screen debut in 1929 but did not make Hollywood his home until 1937, after winning acclaim for a number of portrayals on Broadway. A sturdy, dependable character actor, he appeared in some 200 films, in a wide range of roles, initially also some leads.

FILMS INCLUDE: *On the Border* 1930; *Wayward* 1932; *Black Legion, Midnight Court, Marked Woman, Slim, The Life of Emile Zola, Alcatraz Island, Missing Witness* 1937; *Gold Is Where You Find It, A Slight Case of Murder, Jezebel, My Bill, The Amazing Dr. Clitterhouse, Valley of the Giants, Broadway Musketeers, Comet Over Broadway* 1938; *Wings of the Navy, On Trial, Dodge City, One Hour to Live, The Return of Dr. X* 1939; *The Fighting 69th, Castle on the Hudson, Men Without Souls, Murder in the Air, They Drive by Night, Lady with Red Hair, Santa Fe Trail* 1940; *Father's Son, Henry Aldrich for President, They Died with Their Boots On* (as General Phil Sheridan) 1941; *Don Winslow of the Navy* (serial), *Kid Glove Killer, Men of Texas, Invisible Agent* 1942; *Crime Doctor* 1943; *Where Are Your Children?* 1944; *Brewster's Millions, Salome—Where She Danced* (as General Robert E. Lee), *San Antonio* 1945; *Night in Paradise, Sister Kenny* 1946; *The Beginning or the End, Cass Timberlane, Christmas Eve* 1947; *Pitfall* 1948; *Outpost in Morocco* 1949; *Woman in Hiding, Kiss Tomorrow Goodbye* 1950; *The Texas Rangers* 1951; *Scaramouche* 1952; *Sitting Bull* 1954; *The Kentuckian* 1955; *Houseboat* 1958; *Voyage to the Bottom of the Sea, Pocketful of Miracles* 1961; *The Gun Hawk* 1963; *The Sons of Katie Elder* 1965; *Nevada Smith* 1966.

Lithgow, John. Actor. Born on Oct. 19, 1945, in Rochester, N.Y. Tall (6' 4"), bulky character star of the American stage and screen. The son of a theatrical producer specializing in Shakespearean plays, he grew up immersed in the world of the stage and made his acting debut at age six. After graduating from Harvard in 1967, he used a Fulbright fellowship to study acting at the London Academy of Music and Dramatic Art, then worked with the Royal Shakespeare Company and the Royal Court Theatre as actor and director. Returning to New York, he soon made his mark on Broadway, winning a Tony Award as best supporting actor for 'The Changing Room' (1973). His screen career, starting in the early 70s, was slower in developing but took off dramatically in the early 80s, when he was nominated for Academy Awards for memorable portrayals in *The World According to Garp* (1982, as a transsexual football player) and *Terms of Endearment* (1983). He has since cemented his reputation with pivotal roles in many films, many of them as intelligent villains. He has also distinguished himself in stage and TV productions in the 1980s, particularly in 'M. Butterfly.' He won an Emmy for a 1987 performance in the 'Amazing Stories' series and more recently returned to television in the successful sitcom '3rd Rock From the Sun.'

FILMS INCLUDE: *Dealing: Or the Berkeley-to-Boston Forty-Brick Lost-Bag Blues* 1972; *Obsession* 1976; *The Big Fix* 1978; *Rich Kids, All That Jazz* 1979; *Blow Out* 1981; *I'm Dancing as Fast as I Can, The World According to Garp* 1982; *Twilight Zone—The Movie, Terms of Endearment* 1983; *Footloose, The Adventures of Buckaroo Banzai: Across the 8th Dimension, 2010* 1984; *Santa Claus: The Movie* 1985; *Mesmerized* (UK/Austral./NZ), *The Manhattan Project* 1986; *Harry and the Hendersons, Hollow Point* 1987; *Distant Thunder* 1988; *Out Cold* (release delayed from 1988) 1989; *Memphis Belle* 1990; *Ricochet, At Play in the Fields of the Lord* 1991; *Raising Cain* 1992; *Cliffhanger, The Pelican Brief* 1993; *A Good Man in Africa, Princess Caraboo, Silent Fall* 1994.

Littin, Miguel. Director. Born on Aug. 9, 1942, in Palmilla, Chile. *ed.* U. of Chile School of the Theatre, Santiago. A political activist since his teens, he began his professional career as an actor and playwright, and soon after produced and directed for Chilean TV. A film director since the late 60s, he was named by President Allende in 1970 as head of Chile Films, the national production organization. Following the 1973 coup d'etat that toppled the Communist regime, he emigrated to Mexico, where he continued making politically inspired films. He achieved international success with the allegorical *Alsino and the Condor* (1982). In 1990 he directed *Sandino,* a spectacular Spanish-Chilean screen biography of the legendary guerrilla leader Augusto C. Sandino, after whom Nicaragua's Sandinistas were named.

FILMS (as director-screenwriter): *Por la Tierra ajena/On Foreign Land* 1968; *El Chacal de Nahueltoro/The Jackal of Nahueltoro* 1969; *Compañero Presidente* 1971; *La Tierra prometida/The Promised Land* 1973; *El Recurso del Método/Reasons of State* 1975; *La Viuda de Montiel/Montiel's Widow* 1979; *Alsino y el Condor/Alsino and the Condor* 1982; *Sandino* 1990; *The Shipwrecked* 1994.

Little, Cleavon. Actor. *b.* June 1, 1939, Chickasha, Okla. *d.* 1992. *ed.* San Diego Coll.; AADA. Black character player of the American stage TV, and films, at his best in comedy roles. He won a Tony Award for his performance in the Broadway musical 'Purlie' (1970). His many TV credits included regular appearances on 'The David Frost Revue' (1971–73) and the comedy series 'Temperature's Rising' (1972–74). Onscreen he was memorable as the mild-mannered sheriff in the Mel Brooks Western spoof, *Blazing Saddles* (1974).

FILMS INCLUDE: *What's So Bad About Feeling Good?* 1968; *John and Mary* 1969; *Cotton Comes to Harlem* 1970; *Vanishing Point* 1971; *Blazing Saddles* 1974; *Greased Lightning* 1977; *FM* 1978; *Scavenger Hunt* 1979; *High Risk, The Salamander* 1981; *Double Exposure* 1982; *Jimmy the Kid* 1983; *Surf II, Toy Soldiers* 1984; *The Gig, Once Bitten* 1985; *Murder By Numbers, Fletch Lives* 1989; *Goin' to Chicago* 1990.

Littlefield, Lucien. Actor. *b.* Aug. 16, 1895, San Antonio, Tex. *d.* 1960. A versatile veteran character actor, he played a wide variety of supporting roles in hundreds of Hollywood silents and talkies from 1913. Over the years he also collaborated on a number of scripts and he wrote the original story of *Early to Bed* (1936).

FILMS INCLUDE: *Rose of the Range* 1913; *The Ghost Breaker* 1914; *The Warrens of Virginia, The Wild Goose Chase* 1915; *To Have and to Hold* 1916; *The Golden Fetter* 1917; *Everywoman* 1919; *Why Change Your Wife?* 1920; *Crazy to Marry, The Sheik, Too Much Speed* 1921; *Tillie, Manslaughter, To Have and to Hold, Our Leading Citizen* 1922; *Three Wise Fools, The French Doll, In the Palace of the King* 1923; *Name the Man, Babbitt* (as Mr. Littlefield), *True as Steel, Never Say Die* 1924; *Charley's Aunt, Gold and the Girl, The Rainbow Trail, Tumbleweeds* 1925; *The Torrent, Take It from Me, Twinkletoes* 1926; *The Cat and the Canary, Uncle Tom's Cabin,* (as Marks), *My Best Girl, Cheating Cheaters* 1927; *Harold Teen, Heart to Heart, A Ship Comes In, Mother Knows Best* 1928; *Saturday's Children, Drag, The Great Divide, Seven Keys to Baldpate* 1929; *No No Nanette, High Society Blues, Clancy in Wall Street, Tom Sawyer* 1930; *Reducing, Scandal Sheet, Young as You Feel* 1931; *Broken Lullaby/The Man I Killed, If I Had a Million* 1932; *The Bitter Tea of General Yen, Sweepings, Alice in Wonderland* 1933; *Sons of the Desert, Mandalay, 30-Day Princess, Kiss and Make-Up* 1934; *Ruggles of Red Gap, Man on the Flying Trapeze, Magnificent Obsession* 1935; *Rose Marie* 1936; *High Wide and Handsome, Souls at Sea, Wells Fargo* 1937; *Sabotage* 1939; *The Great American Broadcast, The Little Foxes* 1941; *Mr. and Mrs. North, Whistling in Dixie* 1942; *Scared Stiff* 1945; *Casanova's Big Night* 1954; *Wink of an Eye* 1958.

Littleton, Carol. Film editor. Born in Oklahoma. *ed.* U. of Oklahoma. Highly regarded creative cutter of Hollywood films from the 80s, following experience in TV commercials. She was nominated for an Academy Award for *E.T.* (1982).

FILMS: *Legacy* 1975; *The Mafu Cage* 1978; *French Postcards* 1979; *Roadie* 1980; *Body Heat* 1981; *E.T. the Extra-Terrestrial* 1982; *The Big Chill* 1983; *Places in the Heart* 1984; *Silverado* 1985; *Brighton Beach Memoirs* 1986; *Swimming to Cambodia* 1987; *The Accidental Tourist, Vibes* 1988; *White Palace* 1990; *Grand Canyon, The Search for Intelligent Signs of Life in the Universe* 1991; *Benny & Joon* 1993; *China Moon, Wyatt Earp* 1994; *Diabolique* 1996.

Litvak, Anatole. Director. *b.* Michael Anatol Litwak, May 10, 1902, Kiev, Russia. *d.* 1974. The son of a Jewish bank manager, he began working at 14 as a stagehand at an avant-garde theater in St. Petersburg (later Leningrad). Later studied philosophy at the University of St. Petersburg, attended a state dramatic school, and joined a Leningrad stage troupe as an actor and assistant director. He entered films in 1923 as an assistant director and set decorator at the Nordkino studios and the following year collaborated on several scripts and directed his first film, *Tatiana.* In 1925 he left Russia for Western Europe, and for the next ten years he worked in Germany, England, and France. In Germany he was an editor on G. W. Pabst's *Die freudlose Gasse/Street of Sorrow/ Joyless Street* (1925) and assistant director on several other productions before beginning to direct for UFA in 1930. During this period he was known as Anatol Lutwak.

A Jew, Litvak left Germany with the advent of the Nazis and, after directing one film in England, joined Pathé in Paris, for which he directed several films, notably *L'Equipage/Flight Into Darkness* (1935) and an internationally successful version of *Mayerling* (1936), starring Charles Boyer and Danielle Darrieux. He was invited to Hollywood in 1937, in the wake of the latter film's popularity in the US, and for the next 20 years enjoyed commercial success with many productions at Warners, Fox, and other studios. Critical acclaim for his work was less consistent and he received most of it for two films of the late 40s, *Sorry Wrong Number* (1948), a tense melodrama adapted from an excellent radio thriller about a woman overhearing a murder scheme on the telephone, and *The Snake Pit* (1948), a gripping account of conditions at a mental institution, in which Litvak effectively combined elements of the drama and the documentary. The latter film was nominated for Academy Award as best picture and for best director, and won an International Prize at the 1949 Venice Festival "for a daring inquiry into a clinical case dramatically performed." He received another best picture nomination for *Decision Before Dawn* (1951).

Soon after arriving in Hollywood, Litvak had applied for American citizenship and during WW II he served with the US armed forces, rising to the rank of colonel by the end of the war. He collaborated with Frank CAPRA on the Army's "Why We Fight" series and was put in charge of combat photography and motion picture operations during the Normandy invasion. He was awarded the Légion d'Honneur and the Croix de Guerre, among other war decorations. After the war, he returned to Hollywood, where he was now established as a proficient, if not too inspired, director. In the 50s he began working intermittently in Europe and in the early 60s adopted Paris as his permanent home. He was married to actress Miriam HOPKINS from 1937 to 1939.

FILMS: *Tatiana* (short) 1923; *Hearts and Dollars* (short) 1924. In Germany—*Dolly macht Karriere/Dolly's Way to Stardom* 1930; *Nie wieder Liebe/No More Love* (and French version, *Calais-Douvres*) 1931; *Das Lied einer Nacht* (and English version, *Be Mine Tonight*) 1932; In France—*Coeur de Lilas* 1932. In the UK—*Sleeping Car* 1933. In France—*Cette Vieille Canaille* (also co-sc.) 1933; *L'Equipage/Flight Into Darkness* (also co-sc.) 1935; *Mayerling* 1936. In the US—*The Woman I Love* (remake of *L'Equipage*), *Tovarich* 1937; *The Amazing Dr. Clitterhouse* (also prod.), *The Sisters* 1938; *Confessions of a Nazi Spy* 1939; *Castle on the Hudson, All This and Heaven Too* (also prod.), *City for Conquest* (also prod.) 1940; *Out of the Fog, Blues in the Night* 1941; *This Above All, The Nazis Strike* (WW II doc.; co-dir. with Frank Capra) 1942; *Divide and Conquer* (WW II doc.; co-dir. with Capra), *Operation Titanic* (WW II doc.), *The Battle of Russia* (WW II doc.) 1943; *The Battle of China* (WW II doc.; co-dir. with Capra) 1944; *War Comes to America* (WW II doc.; also co-sc.) 1945; *The Long Night* (also co-prod.) 1947; *Sorry Wrong Number* (also co-prod.), *The Snake Pit* (also co-prod.) 1948; *Decision Before Dawn* (also co-prod.) 1951; *Un Acte d'Amour/Act of Love* (also prod.; Fr./US) 1954; *The Deep Blue Sea* (also prod.; UK) 1955; *Anastasia* 1956; *Mayerling* (TV production) 1957; *The Journey* (also prod.) 1959; *Aimez-vous Brahms?/Goodbye Again* (also prod.; Fr./US) 1961; *Le Couteau dans la Plaie/Five Miles to Midnight* (also prod.; Fr./It./US) 1962; *La Nuit des Généraux/The Night of the Generals* (Fr./UK) 1967; *La Dame dans l'Auto avec des Lunettes et un Fusil/The Lady in the Car with Glasses and a Gun* (also co-prod.; Fr./US) 1970.

live action. A sequence of film utilizing images of real people and scenery rather than artificial effects—animation, titles, etc.

Livesey, Roger. Actor. *b.* June 25, 1906, Barry, South Wales. *d.* 1976. A distinguished character lead of British stage and films, he was memorable in the title role of *The Life and Death of Colonel Blimp* and as the surgeon-advocate in *A Matter of Life and Death/Stairway to Heaven.* His father, Sam Livesey (1873–1936), and his brothers, Jack Livesey (1901–61) and Barry Livesey (*b.* 1904), were also actors of the British stage and screen. He was married to actress Ursula JEANS.

FILMS INCLUDE: *The Old Curiosity Shop, The Four Feathers* 1921; *Married Love* 1923; *East Lynne on the Western Front* 1931; *Blind Justice* 1934; *Lorna Doone* 1935; *Rembrandt* 1936; *The Drum/Drums, Keep Smiling/Smiling Along* 1938; *Spies of the Air* 1939; *The Girl in the News* 1940; *The Life and*

Death of Colonel Blimp (title role) 1943; *I Know Where I'm Going* 1945; *A Matter of Life and Death/Stairway to Heaven* 1946; *Vice Versa* 1947; *That Dangerous Age/If This Be Sin* 1949; *The Master of Ballantrae* 1953; *The Intimate Stranger* 1956; *Es geschah am hellichten Tag/It Happened in Broad Daylight* (Ger./Switz.) 1958; *The League of Gentlemen, The Entertainer* 1960; *No My Darling Daughter* 1961; *Of Human Bondage* (as Thorpe Athelney) 1964; *The Amorous Adventures of Moll Flanders* 1965; *Oedipus the King* 1968; *Hamlet* 1969; *Futtock's End* 1970.

live sound. Also called "live recording." Sound, such as dialogue, simultaneously recorded at the time of shooting, in contrast to sound dubbed in after filming.

Living Cinema. See CINÉMA VÉRITÉ.

Livingston, Jay. Composer, songwriter. Born Jacob Harold Levison, on Mar. 28, 1915, in McDonald, Pa. He composed many movie songs, often in collaboration with lyricist Ray EVANS. Their hits include 'To Each His Own,' 'Golden Earrings,' and 'Tammy,' as well as Academy Award winners 'Buttons and Bows' (from *The Paleface,* 1948), 'Mona Lisa' (from *Captain Carey, USA,* 1950), and 'Que Sera Sera' (from *The Man Who Knew Too Much,* 1956). Livingston and Evans also wrote several popular themes for TV series, including 'Bonanza' and 'Mr. Ed.'

FILMS INCLUDE: *Footlight Glamour* 1943; *Swing Hostess* 1944; *Dream Girl, The Paleface* 1948; *Sorrowful Jones, My Friend Irma* 1949; *Captain Carey USA, Fancy Pants* 1950; *The Lemon Drop Kid, Here Comes the Groom* 1951; *The Stars Are Singing* 1953; *Red Garters* 1954; *The Man Who Knew Too Much* 1956; *Tammy and the Bachelor* 1957; *Houseboat* 1958; *A Private's Affair, The Blue Angel* 1959; *All Hands on Deck* 1961; *Tammy and the Doctor* 1963; *Dear Heart, Harlow, Never Too Late* 1965; *The Night of the Grizzly, This Property Is Condemned* 1966; *Wait Until Dark* 1967; *Foxtrot* 1976.

Livingston, Margaret. Actress. *b.* Nov. 25, 1896, Salt Lake City, Utah. *d.* 1985. Vivacious leading lady and second lead of Hollywood silents and early talkies, often in vamp roles. Memorable as the city temptress in Murnau's *Sunrise.* Early in her career she was also billed as Marguerite Livingston. She was the fourth and last wife of bandleader Paul Whiteman.

FILMS INCLUDE: *The Chain Invisible* 1916; *Alimony* 1917; *Within the Cup* 1918; *All Wrong, The Busher* 1919; *What's Your Husband Doing?, Water Water Everywhere* 1920; *Lying Lips, The Home Stretch, Colorado Pluck* 1921; *Divorce* 1923; *Wandering Husbands, Love's Whirlpool, Her Marriage Vow, Butterfly, The Chorus Lady* 1924; *Capital Punishment, Greater Than a Crown, After Marriage, Havoc, The Wheel, The Best People, Wages for Wives* 1925; *Hell's 400, A Trip to Chinatown, The Blue Eagle, Womanpower, Breed of the Sea* 1926; *Slaves of Beauty, Lightning, Married Alive, American Beauty, Sunrise* 1927; *Streets of Shanghai, A Woman's Way, The Scarlet Dove, The Way of the Strong, Say It with Sables, Through the Breakers, The Apache, His Private Life, Beware of Bachelors* 1928; *The Last Warning, The Bellamy Trial, The Office Scandal, The Charlatan, Innocents of Paris, Tonight at Twelve, Acquitted* 1929; *Seven Keys to Baldpate, For the Love o' Lil, What a Widow!, Big Money* 1930; *Kiki, God's Gift to Women, Smart Money* 1931; *Call Her Savage* 1932; *Social Register* 1934.

Livingston, Robert (Bob). Actor. *b.* Robert E. Randall, Dec. 9, 1906, Quincy, Ill. *d.* 1988. The son of a newspaper columnist, he was raised in California and began his own career as a reporter. He was drawn to acting, however, and in the late 20s began appearing in stage productions and occasional films, initially billed under his real name. Within several years he was working in films exclusively, acquiring a professional name in the process, and in 1936 began a long and successful career as a cowboy star in the popular "Three Mesquiteers" Western series, in which he played the role of Stoney Brooke, one of a trio of saddle heroes. The other two were portrayed by Max Terhune and Ray ("Crash") CORRIGAN. In 1939 he played the screen's second Lone Ranger in Republic's serial *The Lone Ranger Rides Again.* (Lee Powell was first to play the role in the serial *The Lone Ranger,* 1938.) Livingston remained popular through the early 40s, when he starred in PRC's "Lone Rider" series with sidekick Al ("Fuzzy") ST. JOHN and in a number of non-Westerns. He was later seen in occasional character roles. In 1947 he was briefly married to Margaret Roach, the starlet daughter of producer Hal Roach. His brother, Addison ("Jack") Randall (1907–45), was a minor romantic lead and later singing cowboy who died in a fall from a horse during filming on location.

FILMS INCLUDE: *Babbitt* 1924; *Sunny Skies* 1930; *Dance Fools Dance Enlighten Your Daughter, Death on the Diamond, The Band Plays On* 1934; *Mutiny on the Bounty, West Point of the Air, The Winning Ticket, Baby Face Harrington, Murder in the Fleet* 1935; *The Vigilantes Are Coming* (serial), *The Three Godfathers, Absolute Quiet, The Three Mesquiteers* 1936; *The Bold Caballero, Larceny on the Air, Circus Girl, Come on Cowboys!, Renfrew of the Royal Mounted* 1937; *Purple Vigilantes, Call of the Mesquiteers, Arson Racket Squad, Ladies in Distress, The Night Hawk, Orphans of the Street* 1938; *The Lone Ranger Rides Again* (serial), *Federal Man Hunt, The Kansas Terrors* 1939; *Cowboys from Texas* 1942; *Lone Rider in Death Rides the Plains, Pistol Packin' Mama* 1943; *Beneath Western Skies, The Laramie Trail, Goodnight Sweetheart, Storm Over Lisbon, Brazil, Lake Placid Serenade* 1944; *The Big Bonanza, Don't Fence Me In, The Cheaters, Tell It to a Star, Dakota* 1945; *Undercover Woman, Valley of the Zombies* 1946; *Daredevils of the Clouds, Grand Canyon Trail, The Feathered Serpent* 1948; *The Mysterious Desperado, Riders in the Sky* 1949; *Mule Train* 1950; *Night Stage to Galveston* 1952; *Winning of the West* 1953; *Once Upon a Horse* 1958; *Girls for Rent* 1974; *The Naughty Stewardesses, Blazing Stewardesses* 1975.

Lizzani, Carlo. Director. Born on Apr. 3, 1917, in Rome. A journalist and film critic, he contributed to the magazines *Cinema* and *Bianco e Nero* and was among the early theoreticians of Italy's neorealism. He entered films in 1946 as an assistant director and screenwriter on such productions as Vergano's *Il Sole Sorge Ancora/Outcry* (also act., 1946), De Santis's *Caccia Tragica/Tragic Hunt* (also act., 1947) and *Riso Amaro/Bitter Rice* (1948), Rossellini's *Germannia Anno Zero/Germany Year Zero* (1947), and Lattuada's *Il Mulino del Po/The Mill on the Po* (1949). He directed several documentaries before turning out his first feature film, *Achtung! Banditi!,* in 1951. The film, a WW II Resistance drama, which provided Gina Lollobrigida with her first major role, remains his most important work along with *Cronache di Poveri Amanti/Chronicle of Poor Lovers* (1954), a love story set against the background of the struggle between the Fascists and their political rivals in the mid-20s. Many of Lizzani's well-intentioned social dramas have been marred, however, by the director's overly dogmatic Marxist ideology on the one hand and by commercial requirements on the other. His *Fontamara* won the Grand Prix at the 1980 Montreal Festival. He wrote an important crucial survey of Italian film, *Il Cinema Italiano* (1953). He has collaborated on the scripts of most of his own films.

FEATURE FILMS: *Achtung! Banditi!* 1951; *Ai Margini della Metropoli* 1952; *Amore in Città* ("L'Amore che si Paga" episode) 1953; *Cronache di Poveri Amanti/Chronicle of Poor Lovers* 1954; *Lo Svitato* 1956; *La Muraglia Cinese/Behind the Great Wall* (full-length doc.) 1958; *Esterina* 1959; *Il Gobbo/The*

Hunchback of Rome 1960; *Il Carabiniere a Cavallo* 1961; *Il Processo di Verona* 1962; *La Vita Agra, La Celestina, Amori Pericolosi* ("La Ronda" episode) 1964; *La Guerra Segreta/Guerre secrète/The Dirty War* (co-dir. with Terence Young, Christian-Jaque, and Werner Klingler; Fr./It./Ger.), *Thrilling* ("L'Autostrada del Sole" episode) 1965; *Svegliati e Uccidi/Wake Up and Die, Un Fiume di Dollari/The Hills Run Red* (under pseudonym Lee W. Beaver) 1966; *Requiescant, Banditi a Milano/The Violent Four, L'Amante di Gramigna* 1968; *Amore e Rabbia/Vangelo '70/Love and Anger* ("L'Indifferenza" episode), *Barbagia* 1969; *Roma Bene* 1971; *Torino Nera* 1972; *Crazy Joe, Mussolini—Ultimo Atto/The Last Four Days* 1974; *Un Delitto gratuito, Uomini Merce* 1976; *San Babila Oro 20: un Delitto inutile, Kleinhoff Hotel* 1977; *Fontamara* 1980.

Lloyd, Christopher. Actor. Born on Oct. 22, 1938, in Stamford, Conn. Offbeat character player of the American stage, TV, and films. Trained at New York's Neighborhood Playhouse, he toiled in obscurity for years before attaining his first success in the off-Broadway production of 'Kaspar,' for which he won both the Drama Desk and Obie Awards. He made his screen debut as one of the inmates in *One Flew Over the Cuckoo's Nest* (1975), but it was on TV that he enjoyed his real breakthrough, as the spaced-out Reverend Jim in the comedy series 'Taxi' (1979–83), for which he won an Emmy Award and wide popularity. He remains most memorable, however, for the role of the eccentric Doc Emmett Brown in the film *Back to the Future* (1985) and its sequels.

FILMS INCLUDE: *One Flew Over the Cuckoo's Nest* 1975; *Goin' South* 1978; *Butch and Sundance: The Early Days, The Lady in Red, The Onion Field* 1979; *Schizoid* 1980; *The Postman Always Rings Twice, The Legend of the Lone Ranger* 1981; *Mr. Mom, To Be or Not to Be* 1983; *Star Trek III: The Search for Spock, The Adventures of Buckaroo Banzai: Across the 8th Dimension* 1984; *Back to the Future, Clue* 1985; *Walk Like a Man* 1987; *Who Framed Roger Rabbit?, Track 29* (UK), *Eight Men Out* 1988; *The Dream Team, Back to the Future: Part II* 1989; *Back to the Future: Part III, Duck Tales: The Movie—Treasure of the Lost Lamp* (v/o), *Why Me?* 1990; *Suburban Commando, The Addams Family* 1991; *Twenty Bucks* 1992; *Dennis the Menace, Addams Family Values* 1993; *Angels in the Outfield, Camp Nowhere, The Pagemaster* (v/o), *Radioland Murders* 1994; *Rent-a-Kid, Things to Do in Denver When You're Dead* 1995; *Cadillac Ranch, Changing Habits* 1997.

Lloyd, Doris. Actress. *b.* July 3, 1900, Liverpool, England. *d.* 1968. Originally a stage actress, she played supporting parts in numerous silent and sound Hollywood films for four decades, beginning in the mid-20s, typically as a society lady.

FILMS INCLUDE: *The Lady* 1925; *The Black Bird, The Midnight Kiss, Exit Smiling* 1926; *Is Zat So?, Lonesome Ladies* 1927; *The Careless Age, Disraeli* 1929; *Sarah and Son, Old English, Reno, Charley's Aunt* 1930; *The Bachelor Father, Waterloo Bridge, Devotion* 1931; *Tarzan the Ape Man, Back Street* 1932; *Secrets, Oliver Twist* (as Nancy), *Looking Forward/The New Deal, Peg o' My Heart, A Study in Scarlet, Voltaire* 1933; *Glamour, Sisters Under the Skin, Kiss and Make-Up, British Agent* 1934; *Clive of India, Becky Sharp, Peter Ibbetson* 1935; *Mary of Scotland* 1936; *The Plough and the Stars, Tovarich* 1937; *Barricade* 1939; *The Letter* 1940; *The Great Lie* 1941; *The Ghost of Frankenstein, Night Monster, Journey for Margaret* 1942; *Mission to Moscow* (as Mrs. Winston Churchill), *The Constant Nymph* 1943; *The Lodger, Phantom Lady* 1944; *Devotion, Holiday in Mexico, Of Human Bondage* 1946; *The Secret Life of Walter Mitty* 1947; *The Sign of the Ram* 1948; *Kind Lady* 1951; *Young Bess* 1953; *The Swan* 1956; *The Time Machine, Midnight Lace* 1960; *The Notorious Landlady* 1961; *Mary Poppins* 1964; *The Sound of Music* 1965; *Rosie* 1967.

Lloyd, Emily. Actress. Born in 1970, in North London. Spunky, blonde, young leading lady. The daughter of a stage actor and Harold Pinter's secretary who divorced when she was two, she appeared in school plays but was professionally inexperienced when she burst into the scene with a gusty virtuoso performance in David Leland's 1987 British film, *Wish You Were Here.* The American Society of Film Critics named her that year's best actress. When Hollywood beckoned, she startled filmgoers with her ability to affect a Brooklyn accent for her role as a mobster's daughter in her first American film, *Cookie* (1989).

FILMS: *Wish You Were Here* (UK) 1987; *Cookie, In Country* 1989; *Chicago Joe and the Showgirl* 1990; *A River Runs Through It, Scorchers* 1992; *A Hundred and One Nights, Under the Hula Moon* 1995; *Welcome to Sarajevo* 1997.

Lloyd, Frank. Director. *b.* Feb. 2, 1888, Glasgow, Scotland. *d.* 1960. The son of a musical comedy actor, he began his own career on the British stage at 15. He went to Canada in 1910, the US in 1913, entered films as an actor in the same year, and began directing the following year, starting with a string of shorts. In the next four decades he directed some 100 films, for Paramount, then Fox and other studios, many of them routine commercial productions but some truly meritorious. A highly skilled craftsman, he had few pretensions about the significance of film other than as a means for entertainment, or about his own role as a director, and blended easily into the Hollywood studio system. Accordingly, he is short-shrifted by many film historians. But films like *Cavalcade* (1933), *Mutiny on the Bounty* (1935), and *Wells Fargo* (1937) reveal not only technical mastery but also a cohesive style and a keen visual sense. Lloyd produced or co-produced many of his own films as well as a number of productions directed by others, and in the silent years he wrote many of his own scripts. He won Academy Awards as best director for *The Divine Lady* (1929) and *Cavalcade.* His *Mutiny on the Bounty* was awarded a best picture Oscar for 1935.

FILMS: Shorts—*A Prince of Bavaria, As the Wind Blows, The Link That Binds, The Vagabond, The Chorus Girl's Thanksgiving, Traffic in Babies, A Page from Life* (also sc.) 1914; *Pawns of Fate* (also act.), *The Temptation of Edwin Swayne, Wolves of Society* (also act.), *His Last Serenade* (also act.), *Martin Lowe—Financier* (also co-sc., act.), *An Arrangement with Fate, To Redeem an Oath* (also co-sc., act.), *The Bay of Seven Isles* (also act.), *His Last Trick* (also sc.), *The Pinch* (also sc.), *His Captive, Life's Furrow, When the Spider Tore Loose, Nature's Triumph/The Cure of the Mountains, A Prophet of the Hills, $100,000, The Little Girl of the Attic, The Toll of Youth, Fate's Alibi* (also sc.), *Trickery* (also co-sc., act.), *The Golden Wedding, From the Shadows* (also co-sc. act.), *Little Mr. Fixer/Billy's Cupidity* (also co-sc.), *Eleven to One* (also act.), *Billie's Baby, Marin Lowe—Fixer, For His Superior Honor* (also sc.), *According to Value* (also co-sc., act.), *Paternal Love* (also sc.), *The Source of Happiness, In the Grasp of the Law* (also sc.), *A Double Deal in Pork, Dr. Mason's Temptation* (also sc.) 1915. Features—*The Gentleman of Indiana, Jane, The Reform Candidate* 1915; *Tongues of Men, Madame la Presidente/Madame President, The Code of Marcia Gray* (also sc.), *David Garrick, The Making of Maddallena, An International Marriage, The Stronger Love, The Intrigue, Sins of Her Parent* (also sc.) 1916; *The Price of Silence* (also sc.), *A Tale of Two Cities* (also sc.), *American Methods* (also co-sc.), *When a Man Sees Red* (also sc.) 1917; *The Heart of a Lion* (also sc.), *The Blindness of Divorce* (also sc.), *True Blue* (also sc.), *Riders of the Purple Sage* (also sc.), *The Rainbow Trail* (also co-sc.), *Les*

Misérables (also sc.), *For Freedom* 1918; *The Loves of Letty, The Man Hunter* (also sc.), *Pitfalls of a Big City, The World and Its Woman* 1919; *The Woman in Room 13, The Silver Horde, Madame X* (also co-sc.), *The Great Lover* 1920; *A Tale of Two Worlds, Roads to Destiny, A Voice in the Dark, The Invisible Power* (also prod.), *The Man from Lost River, The Sin Flood* 1921; *The Grim Comedian, The Eternal Flame, Oliver Twist* (also co-sc.) 1922; *The Voice from the Minaret, Within the Law, Ashes of Vengeance* (also sc.) 1923; *Black Oxen* (also prod.), *The Sea Hawk, The Silent Watcher* 1924; *Winds of Chance* (also prod.), *Her Husband's Secret* (also sc.), *The Splendid Road* (also prod.) 1925; *The Wise Guy* (also prod.), *The Eagle of the Sea* 1926; *Children of Divorce* (also prod.) 1927; *Adoration* (also prod.) 1928; *Weary River, The Divine Lady* (also prod.), *Drag, Dark Streets* (also prod.), *Young Nowheres* (also prod.) 1929; *Son of the Gods* (also prod.), *The Way of All Men* (also prod.), *The Lash/Adios* (also prod.) 1930; *East Lynne, The Right of Way* (also prod.), *The Age for Love* 1931; *A Passport to Hell* 1932; *Cavalcade, Berkeley Square, Hoopla* 1933; *Servants' Entrance* 1934; *Mutiny on the Bounty* (also prod.) 1935; *Under Two Flags* 1936; *Maid of Salem* (also prod.), *Wells Fargo* (also prod.) 1937; *If I Were King* (also prod.) 1938; *Rulers of the Sea* (also prod.) 1939; *The Howards of Virginia* (also prod.) 1940; *The Lady from Cheyenne* (also prod.), *This Woman Is Mine* (also prod.) 1941; *The Spoilers* (prod. only), *Saboteur* (prod. only), *Invisible Agent* (prod. only) 1942; *Forever and a Day* (co-dir., co-prod.) 1943; *Blood on the Sun* 1945; *The Shanghai Story* 1954; *The Last Command* 1955.

Lloyd, Harold. Actor. *b.* Apr. 20, 1893, Burchard, Nebr. *d.* 1971. The son of an unsuccessful photographer who became a pool-hall proprietor after moving to San Diego, he worked at odd jobs around local theaters and gradually began playing small roles with touring companies and in stock. He made his film debut in 1912 with the Edison company, playing an extra part as a near-naked Indian. The following year he appeared in a couple of Keystone comedies and was hired as an extra and bit player at Universal, where he befriended another extra, Hal ROACH. Late in 1914, when Roach inherited $3,000 and formed his own company, he hired Lloyd to play a character called Willie Work in a series of one-reel comedies. But when Roach could find no buyers for his product, Lloyd moved over to Mack Sennett's Keystone. However, Sennett and Lloyd became mutually disillusioned with each other, and when Roach reorganized his company under the sponsorship of Pathé, Lloyd happily returned to his fold.

Roach and Lloyd created a new character for the comedian, Lonesome Luke, who, like many other comedy characters of the day, was patterned after Charlie Chaplin. Luke was only incidental to the plot, which, in turn, was only incidental to the wild chases and speedy action scenes that climaxed every film. Neither Roach nor Lloyd was satisfied with Lonesome Luke, but the series proved very popular with the public, and Roach produced some 100 shorts of the series in the years 1916–17, most of which he directed himself.

During a moment of inspiration in 1917, Roach experimented with a new character for Lloyd. Instead of the traditional comedy mustache and grotesque clothes, he had Lloyd wear the clothes and assume the manners of an average young man. The final touch was a pair of oversized black horn-rimmed glasses, which was to become Lloyd's trademark for the rest of his brilliant comic career. In addition, Roach began providing Lloyd with comedy vehicles in which story, construction, and characterization took precedence over slapstick visual gags. In just a few years Lloyd developed into one of the funniest—if not the funniest—man of the American silent screen. His zanily optimistic Everyman, who time and again triumphed over adversity by a combination of persistence and luck, struck a responsive chord in cinema audiences and before long Lloyd had become the highest-paid actor in Hollywood.

During the 20s Lloyd's films often outdrew at the box office those of his rivals, Charlie Chaplin and Buster Keaton, in the great triumvirate of American silent screen comedy. In addition to his considerable skill at comedy, Lloyd had another important asset, his athletic prowess. During the filming of *Haunted Spooks* (1920) he was severely injured by a property bomb that exploded in his hand. He lost his right thumb and forefinger and his right hand remained semiparalyzed. Despite this handicap, he was able to perform some spectacular stunts, which had audiences screaming and laughing at the same time. Characteristic of these was the famous scene in *Safety Last* (1923) in which he was seen dangling from atop a skyscraper with nothing to hold on to but the hand of a clock. Similar thrilling situations were inserted into several of his other films. No doubles were ever used.

Encouraged by the success of their comedy formula, Roach and Lloyd gradually moved from one- and two-reelers to three- and four-reelers, and finally to full feature-length films. In 1923, Lloyd married Mildred Davis, his leading lady in several films. They remained together until her death in 1969. Also in 1923, Lloyd parted amicably with Roach and began producing his own films, in association with Pathé, then Paramount. He owned his later films outright and accumulated a fortune from their release and re-release. His success waned during the sound era, when his brand of comedy proved less effective and less popular. He gradually eased out of films, making his last, *Mad Wednesday*, for Howard Hughes in 1947.

In 1952, Lloyd was awarded a special Oscar as a "master comedian and good citizen." In 1962 he issued a compilation of scenes from his old films under the title *Harold Lloyd's World of Comedy*. He was given a standing ovation when he presented it personally at the Cannes Festival. In 1963 he produced a sequel compilation film, *The Funny Side of Life*. When Lloyd died of cancer at the age of 77, he left more than $5 million to his heirs and bequeathed his luxurious Beverly Hills mansion and its surrounding grounds as a motion picture museum. But the 44-room Italian Renaissance villa was later sold at auction.

FILMS INCLUDE (complete from 1920): *Algy on the Force* 1913; *Samson* (extra), *His Heart His Hand His Sword* (extra), *Willie, Willie's Haircut* 1914; *Just Nuts, From Italy's Shores, Willie Goes to Sea, Lonesome Luke, Once Every Ten Minutes, Spit-Ball Sadie, Terribly Stuck Up, Some Baby, Fresh from the Farm, Giving Them Fits, Tinkering with Trouble, Rouses Rhymes and Roughnecks, Peculiar Patients' Pranks, Lonesome Luke—Social Gangster* 1915; *Luke Leans to the Literary, Luke Rolls in Luxury, Luke Foils the Villain, Lonesome Luke—Circus King, Luke's Double, Ice, An Awful Romance, Unfriendly Fruit, A Matrimonial Mixup, Caught in a Jam, Luke Joins the Navy, Luke and the Mermaids, Jailed, Luke Gladiator, Luke's Movie Muddle* 1916; *Drama's Dreadful Deal, Lonesome Luke—Lawyer, Lonesome Luke on Tin Can Alley, Lonesome Luke's Honeymoon, Lonesome Luke—Plumber, Stop! Luke! Listen!, Lonesome Luke's Wild Women, Over the Fence, Birds of a Feather, Lonesome Luke from London to Laramie, Rainbow Island, Love Laughter and Lather, The Flirt, Clubs Are Trump, We Never Sleep, Bashful* 1917; *The Big Idea, The Lamb, Here Come the Girls, It's a Wild Life, The Non-Stop Kid, Fireman Save My Child, The City Slicker, Somewhere in Turkey, Kicking the Germ Out of Germany, An Ozark Romance, Nothing but Trouble* 1918; *Look Out Below, A Sammy in Siberia, Young Mr. Jazz, Si Señor, The Marathon, Spring Fever, Billy Blazes Esq.,*

Just Neighbors, Chop Suey & Co., Be My Wife, The Rajah, Soft Money, Bumping Into Broadway, Captain Kidd's Kids, From Hand to Mouth, His Royal Slyness 1919; *Haunted Spooks, An Eastern Westerner, High and Dizzy, Get Out and Get Under, Number Please* 1920; *Now or Never, A Sailor-Made Man, I Do, Among Those Present, Never Weaken* 1921; *Grandma's Boy, Dr. Jack* 1922; *Safety Last, Why Worry?* 1923; *Girl Shy, Hot Water* 1924; *The Freshman* 1925; *For Heaven's Sake* 1926; *The Kid Brother* 1927; *Speedy* 1928; *Welcome Danger* 1929; *Feet First* 1930; *Movie Crazy* 1932; *The Cat's Paw* 1934; *The Milky Way* 1936; *Professor Beware* 1938; *Mad Wednesday/The Sins of Harold Diddlebock* 1947; *Harold Lloyd's World of Comedy* (compilation) 1962; *Harold Lloyd's Funny Side of Life* (compilation) 1963.

Lloyd, Norman. Actor. Born on Nov. 8, 1914, in Jersey City, N.J. *ed.* NYU. Character player of Hollywood films. Memorable as the evil Fry, the man who fell from the Statue of Liberty in the climax of Hitchcock's *Saboteur* (1942). A former stage actor, he played heavies in other films before becoming a TV producer ('Alfred Hitchcock Presents' among other series). From 1982 he was cast against character as a kindly doctor in the long-running TV series 'St. Elsewhere.'

FILMS INCLUDE: *Saboteur* 1942; *The Unseen, The Southerner, Spellbound* 1945; *A Walk in the Sun, The Green Years* 1946; *The Beginning or the End* 1947; *No Minor Vices* 1948; *Calamity Jane and Sam Bass, Scene of the Crime, The Black Book/Reign of Terror* 1949; *The Flame and the Arrow* 1950; *M, He Ran All the Way* 1951; *Limelight* 1952; *Audrey Rose* 1977; *FM* 1978 *The Nude Bomb* 1980; *Dead Poets Society* 1989; *Mayeda* 1992; *The Age of Innocence* 1993.

loading. The placing of film in a camera or camera magazine before filming.

Loach, Ken. Director. Born Kenneth Loach, on June 17, 1936, in Nuneaton, England. The son of a machine-tool factory laborer, he was drawn to drama at Oxford, where he studied law, and served as president of the university's Experimental Theatre Club. After graduating, he served a two-year stint as a typist with the Royal Air Force, then turned his back on a law career, and instead toured as an actor with a roving repertory company. He entered British TV around 1960 and soon distinguished himself as the director of a popular BBC police series 'Z-Cars.' With producer Tony Garnett, he then turned out 'The Wednesday Play' series, a remarkable anthology of docudramas that generated controversy over their socialist political orientation. A similar ultra-real style characterized Loach's first feature, *Poor Cow* (1967), a frank, grim slice-of-life depiction of the squalid life of a promiscuous wife of a London convict. Like *Poor Cow*, the director's subsequent films were motivated by social concern and by a call for radical change. High on merit but low on box-office appeal, these plays were no doubt the reason for Loach's sparse feature output. Most of his work has been for TV. His 1993 *Raining Stones* was awarded the Jury Prize at Cannes.

FEATURE FILMS: *Poor Cow* (also co-sc.), *Kes* (also co-sc.) 1969; *Family Life/Wednesday's Child* 1971; *The Gamekeeper* (also co-sc.; orig. for TV) 1978; *Black Jack* (also co-sc.) 1979; *Looks and Smiles* (also co-sc.) 1982; *Fatherland/Singing the Blues in Red* (Ger./UK/Fr.) 1986; *Hidden Agenda* 1990; *Raining Stones* 1993; *Ladybird, Ladybird* 1994; *Land and Freedom* 1995; *Carla's Song* 1996.

lobby cards. Reproductions of scenes from films displayed in the lobbies of movie theatres to promote current or upcoming films. First manufactured by Universal in 1913, lobby cards were originally printed in black and white or brown and white; color lobby cards were developed in 1917. In most cases, they were packaged in sets of eight, owing perhaps to the fact that eight cards equaled the size of a standard movie theatre poster.

location. Any locale away from the studio selected for shooting. Location filming presents obvious logistic problems, the provision of food and shelter for performers and crew, and the use of power generators and other specialized equipment. On the other hand, location filming lends authenticity to a picture, especially when a great deal of outdoor shooting is required.

Locke, Sondra. Actress, director. Born on May 28, 1947, Shelbyville, Tenn. A wiry blonde, she was nominated for an Academy Award as best supporting actress for her very first screen role, in *The Heart Is a Lonely Hunter* (1968). Her career meandered, however, until the late 70s, when she co-starred in several vehicles for Clint EASTWOOD, with whom she was romantically involved. In the mid-80s she turned to directing, with some success.

FILMS: As actress—*The Heart Is a Lonely Hunter* 1968; *Cover Me Babe* 1970; *Willard* 1971; *A Reflection of Fear* 1973; *The Second Coming of Suzanne* 1974; *The Outlaw Josie Wales* 1976; *Death Game/The Seducers, The Gauntlet* 1977; *Wishbone Cutter, Every Which Way But Loose* 1978; *Bronco Billy, Any Which Way You Can* 1980; *Sudden Impact* 1983. As director—*Ratboy* (also act.) 1986; *Impulse* 1990.

Lockhart, Calvin. Actor. Born in 1934 in Nassau, West Indies. Intense, handsome African-American leading and supporting player. A musician's son who came to New York at 18, he dropped out of engineering studies at Cooper Union to become an actor. He appeared on the New York stage in such shows as 'The Cool World' (1960), then moved to Europe, acted on British television, and made his feature debut in British films, including *Joanna* (1968). Returning to the US, he delivered strong performances in such films as *Halls of Anger* (1970), earning him comparisons to Sidney Poitier. However, his career as a lead peaked in the early 70s, and he has appeared afterward mostly in support roles. In the 80s he had a recurring role on television's 'Dynasty'.

FILMS INCLUDE: *A Dandy in Aspic* (UK), *Dark of the Sun* (UK), *Joanna* (UK), *Only When I Larf* (UK), *Salt & Pepper* (UK), *Nobody Runs Forever/The High Commissioner* (UK/US) 1968; *Leo the Last* (UK), *Halls of Anger, Myra Breckinridge, Cotton Comes to Harlem* 1970; *Melinda* 1972; *Honeybaby Honeybaby, The Beast Must Die, Uptown Saturday Night* 1974; *Let's Do It Again* 1975; *The Baltimore Bullet* 1980; *Three Days in Beirut* 1983; *Wild at Heart* 1990.

Lockhart, Gene. Actor. *b.* July 18, 1891, London, Ontario, Canada. *d.* 1957. A veteran vaudeville and stage actor and writer, he played strong character parts in well over 100 films. He was equally at ease in genial or treacherous parts. His wife, Kathleen Lockhart (1881–1978, *née* Arthur, in England), also appeared in many films, as did his daughter, June LOCKHART.

FILMS INCLUDE: *Smilin' Through* 1922; *Star of Midnight, Crime and Punishment* (as Lushin) 1935; *The Garden Murder Case, The Gorgeous Hussy, The Devil Is a Sissy* 1936; *Make Way for Tomorrow, Something to Sing About* 1937; *Of Human Hearts, Sinners in Paradise, Algiers, Listen Darling, Blondie, A Christmas Carol* (as Bob Cratchit), *Sweethearts* 1938; *I'm from Missouri, The Story of Alexander Graham Bell, Hotel Imperial, Tell No Tales, Our Leading Citizen, Blackmail* 1939; *His Girl Friday, Geronimo, Abe Lincoln in Illinois* (as Stephen Douglas), *Edison the Man, A Dispatch from Reuters* 1940; *Meet John Doe, The Sea Wolf, Billy the Kid, All That Money Can Buy, One Foot in Heaven* 1941; *They Died with Their Boots On, The Gay Sisters* 1942; *Hangmen Also Die, Mission to Moscow* (as Molotov), *Northern Pursuit, The Desert Song* 1943; *Going My Way* 1944; *The House on 92nd Street,*

Leave Her to Heaven 1945; *A Scandal in Paris* 1946; *The Strange Woman, Miracle on 34th Street, The Foxes of Harrow* 1947; *Apartment for Peggy, Joan of Arc, That Wonderful Urge* 1948; *Down to the Sea in Ships, Madame Bovary* (as Monsieur Homais), *The Inspector General* (as the mayor) 1949; *Riding High, The Big Hangover* 1950; *I'd Climb the Highest Mountain, Rhubarb* 1951; *A Girl in Every Port, Hoodlum Empire, Face to Face* 1952; *Androcles and the Lion* 1953; *World for Ransom* 1954; *Carousel, The Man in the Gray Flannel Suit* 1956; *Jeanne Eagels* 1957.

Lockhart, June. Actress. Born on June 25, 1925, in New York City. Daughter of Gene and Kathleen LOCKHART, she made her stage debut at eight, her film debut at 12, appearing with her parents in the 1938 version of *A Christmas Carol.* She later played supporting roles in A films and lead parts in B pictures before becoming a TV star in such series as 'Lassie' (1958–64), 'Lost in Space' (1965–68), and 'Petticoat Junction' (1968–70). Her daughter, Anne Lockhart, is also a TV and movie actress.

FILMS INCLUDE: *A Christmas Carol* 1938; *All This and Heaven Too* 1940; *Adam Had Four Sons, Sergeant York* 1941; *Miss Annie Rooney* 1942; *The White Cliffs of Dover, Meet Me in St. Louis* 1944; *Son of Lassie* 1945; *The She-Wolf of London* (title role) 1946; *The Yearling, T-Men, Bury Me Dead* 1947; *Time Limit* 1957; *Lassie's Great Adventure* (feature re-edited from four TV episodes) 1963; *Butterfly* 1982; *Strange Invaders* 1983; *Troll* 1986; *The Big Picture* 1989; *Dead Women in Lingerie* 1990; *Sleep with Me* 1994.

Lockwood, Gary. Actor. Born John Gary Yusolfsky, on Feb. 21, 1937, in Van Nuys, Calif. A former stuntman and stand-in for Anthony Perkins, he has been playing leads and supporting parts in Hollywood and international films since the early 60s. He starred in the TV series 'The Lieutenant' (1963–64) and was married to actress Stefanie POWERS.

FILMS INCLUDE: *Tall Story* 1960; *Wild in the Country, Splendor in the Grass* 1961; *The Magic Sword* 1962; *It Happened at the World's Fair* 1963; *Firecreek, 2001: A Space Odyssey* (US/UK), *Las Vegas 500 Millones/They Came to Rob Las Vegas* (Sp./It./Fr./Ger.) 1968; *The Model Shop* 1969; *R.P.M.* 1970; *Stand Up and Be Counted* 1972; *Project Kill* 1976; *The Wild Pair* 1987.

Lockwood, Harold. Actor. *b.* Apr. 12, 1887, Newark, N.J. *d.* 1918. Handsome romantic star of early American silents. A former salesman and vaudeville and stock player, he entered films in 1911 with Edwin S. Porter's Rex company and later worked for Nestor, Ince, Famous Players, and other studios. Among his leading ladies were Dorothy Davenport, Kathlyn Williams, Marguerite Clark, and Mary Pickford, but he was most popular as the screen lover of May ALLISON, with whom he formed one of the earliest romantic teams in American films. He appeared in more than 120 films before his death at the age of 31 of influenza complicated by pneumonia.

FILMS INCLUDE: *The White Redman, A True Westerner* 1911; *The Lost Address, The Deserter, Harbor Island* 1912; *A Mansion of Misery, The Child of the Sea, The Fighting Lieutenant, Phantoms* 1913; *Hearts Adrift, The Man from Mexico, Tess of the Storm Country, Such a Little Queen, The County Chairman, Wildflower, The Conspiracy, The Crucible* 1914; *David Harum, Are You a Mason?, The Love Route, The House of a Thousand Scandals, The End of the Road* 1915; *Life's Blind Alley, The Masked Rider, The River of Romance, Pidgin Island, Big Tremaine* 1916; *The Haunted Pajamas, The Hidden Children, Paradise Garden, The Promise* 1917; *The Avenging Trail, The Landloper, Broadway Bill, Pals First* 1918; *The Great Romance, Shadows of Suspicion, A Man of Honor* 1919.

Lockwood, Margaret. Actress. *b.* Margaret Day, Sept. 15, 1916 (possibly 1911), Karachi, India (now Pakistan), to British parents. *d.* 1990. The daughter of a railway clerk in the colonial service, she was sent to England to be educated. *ed.* RADA. A stage actress from the age of 12, she made her film debut at 18 and first came to prominence in Alfred Hitchcock's *The Lady Vanishes* (1938). During the 40s she ranked as one of Britain's top screen stars. She played a variety of leading roles but was at her best in the portrayal of calculating, wicked ladies. Her popularity diminished in the late 40s, and in 1955 she retired from the screen to return to the stage but reappeared in a film in 1976. Her brief Hollywood sojourn in the late 30s was unsuccessful. Her daughter, Julia Lockwood (*b.* Aug. 23, 1941, Bournemouth, Eng.), has been seen in British films from age five. Autobiography: *Lucky Star* (1955).

FILMS: *Lorna Doone, The Case of Gabriel Perry, Some Day, Honours Easy, Man of the Moment, Midshipman Easy/Men of the Sea* 1935; *Jury's Evidence, The Amateur Gentleman, The Beloved Vagabond, Irish for Luck* 1936; *The Street Singer, Who's Your Lady Friend?, Dr. Syn, Melody and Romance* 1937; *Owd Bob/To the Victor, Bank Holiday/Three on a Weekend, The Lady Vanishes* 1938; *A Girl Must Live, Susannah of the Mounties* (US), *Rulers of the Sea* (US) 1939; *The Stars Look Down, Night Train to Munich/Night Train, The Girl in the News* 1940; *Quiet Wedding* 1941; *Alibi* 1942; *The Man in Grey, Dear Octopus/The Randolph Family* 1943; *Give Us the Moon, Love Story/A Lady Surrenders* 1944; *A Place of One's Own, I'll Be Your Sweetheart, The Wicked Lady* 1945; *Bedelia, Hungry Hill* 1946; *Jassy, The White Unicorn/Bad Sister* 1947; *Look Before You Love* 1948; *Cardboard Cavalier* (as Nell Gwyn), *Madness of the Heart* 1949; *Highly Dangerous* 1950; *Trent's Last Case, Laughing Anne* 1953; *Trouble in the Glen* 1954; *Cast a Dark Shadow* 1955; *The Slipper and the Rose* (as Cinderella's stepmother) 1976.

Loder, John. Actor. *b.* John Muir Lowe, Jan. 3, 1898, London. *d.* 1988. The son of a British general, he was educated at Eton and at the Royal Military College and served with the 15th Hussars as a second lieutenant in Gallipoli in WW I, ending as a prisoner of war. He made his screen debut in 1926, appearing as an extra, along with Marlene Dietrich, in a dance-party scene in Alexander Korda's German-made film *Madame Wants No Children.* Tall and aristocratically handsome, he played leads and second leads in a number of early Hollywood talkies before developing into a popular star in British films of the 30s. He returned to Hollywood at the outbreak of WW II and for seven years played leads in second features and supporting roles in major productions without attaining the same prominent status he had held in England. He concluded the second American phase of his career with Broadway appearances in 1947 and 1950, then returned to England, where he appeared in several more films before retiring to his fifth wife's ranch in Argentina. His third (1943–47) of five wives was actress Hedy LAMARR. Autobiography: *Hollywood Hussar* (1977).

FILMS INCLUDE: In Germany—*Madame wünscht keine Kinder/Madame Wants No Children* 1926; *Alraune/Unholy Love* 1927. In the UK—*The Firstborn* 1928. In the US—*The Doctor's Secret, Sunset Pass, Her Private Affair, The Unholy Night, The Racketeer* 1929; *Rich People, Lilies of the Field, The Man Hunter, Sweethearts and Wives* 1930; *Seas Beneath* 1931. In the UK—*Wedding Rehearsal* 1932; *The Private Life of Henry VIII* 1933; *The Battle, Java Head* 1934; *Lorna Doone* 1935; *Whom the Gods Love/Mozart, Ourselves Alone/River of Unrest, The Man Who Changed His Mind/The Man Who Lived Again, Sabotage/The Woman Alone* 1936; *King Solomon's Mines* (as Sir Henry Curtis), *Dr. Syn, Non-Stop New York, Mademoiselle*

Docteur 1937; *Owd Bob/To the Victor, Katia* (as Czar Alexander II; Fr.) 1938; *The Silent Battle/Continental Express, Murder Will Out* 1939. In the US—*Adventure in Diamonds, Diamond Frontier, Tin Pan Alley* 1940; *Scotland Yard, One Night in Lisbon, How Green Was My Valley* 1941; *Now Voyager, Gentleman Jim* 1942; *The Gorilla Man, The Mysterious Doctor, Murder on the Waterfront, Old Acquaintance* 1943; *Passage to Marseille, The Hairy Ape, Abroad with Two Yanks* 1944; *Jealousy, The Brighton Strangler, A Game of Death* 1945; *The Wife of Monte Cristo, One More Tomorrow* 1946; *Dishonored Lady* 1947. In the UK—*The Story of Esther Costello* 1957; *Gideon's Day/Gideon of Scotland Yard* 1958; *The Firechasers* 1970.

Lodge, John (Davis). Actor, politician, diplomat. *b.* Oct. 20, 1903, Washington, D.C. *d.* 1985. Grandson of the late Senator Henry Cabot Lodge and a holder of a Harvard law degree, he gave up legal practice in 1932 to pursue an acting career in American, British, French, and Italian films, as well as on Broadway. The high point of his career was as Marlene Dietrich's leading man in Von Sternberg's *The Scarlet Empress.* During WW II he served as liaison officer between the American and French fleets with the rank of a Navy captain. Upon his discharge he decided to follow in the family tradition. He was elected a member of the House of Representatives (1946–48), then Governor of Connecticut (1950–54). In 1964 he made an unsuccessful run for the US Senate. Between 1955 and 1961 he served as US Ambassador to Spain and from 1969 to 1973 as Ambassador to Argentina. Several months before his death of a heart attack, he had been forced by President Reagan to resign as ambassador to Switzerland.

FILMS INCLUDE: *The Woman Accused, Murders in the Zoo, Little Women* 1933; *The Scarlet Empress* (as Count Alexei), *Menace* 1934; *The Little Colonel* 1935; *Koenigsmark/The Crimson Dynasty* (Fr.), *Ourselves Alone/River of Unrest* (UK), *The Tenth Man* (UK) 1936; *Sensation* (UK), *Bulldog Drummond at Bay* (title role; UK) 1937; *Bank Holiday* (UK), *Première* (UK), *Queer Cargo* (UK), *Batticuore* (It.) 1938; *L'Esclave blanche/The Pasha's Wives* (Fr.) 1939; *De Mayerling a Sarajevo/Mayerling to Sarajevo* (as Archduke Francis Ferdinand; Fr.) 1940.

Loesser, Frank. Composer, songwriter. *b.* June 29, 1910. New York City. *d.* 1969. The composer of such landmark Broadway musicals as 'Guys and Dolls,' 'The Most Happy Fella,' 'Where's Charley?,' and the Pulitzer Prize–winning 'How to Succeed in Business Without Really Trying,' he also scored a number of films and wrote many popular film songs. He won an Academy Award for the music and lyrics of the song 'Baby, It's Cold Outside' from the film *Neptune's Daughter* (1949). Among his many other songs are 'The Moon of Manakoora,' 'Small Fry,' 'Dolores,' 'I Don't Want to Walk Without You,' 'Says My Heart,' 'Jingle Jangle Jingle,' 'No Two People,' 'I've Never Been in Love Before,' 'If I Were a Bell,' 'Heart and Soul,' 'They're Either Too Young or Too Old,' 'Tallahassee,' and 'On a Slow Boat to China.'

FILMS INCLUDE: *Blossoms on Broadway, The Hurricane, Vogues of 1938* 1937; *College Swing, Sing You Sinners, Thanks for the Memory, Spawn of the North* 1938; *Destry Rides Again, Man About Town, St. Louis Blues, Some Like It Hot* 1939; *Johnny Apollo, Typhoon, Seven Sinners* 1940; *Las Vegas Nights, Manpower, Kiss the Boys Goodbye, Aloma of the South Seas, Sis Hopkins* 1941; *Priorities on Parade, Beyond the Blue Horizon, Seven Days' Leave, Sweater Girl, This Gun for Hire* 1942; *Happy Go Lucky, Thank Your Lucky Stars* 1943; *Something for the Boys, Christmas Holiday* 1944; *The Perils of Pauline, Variety Girl* 1947; *Neptune's Daughter, Red Hot and Blue* (also act. as gangster), *Roseanna McCoy* 1949; *Let's Dance* 1951; *Where's Charley?, Hans Christian Andersen* 1952; *Guys and Dolls* 1956; *How to Succeed in Business Without Really Trying* 1967.

Loew, Marcus. Executive, exhibitor. *b.* May 7, 1870, New York City. *d.* 1927. The son of Jewish immigrants from Austria, he dropped out of school at nine and tried his hand at various odd jobs and business enterprises before moving in 1905 into the peep-show business through the purchase of penny arcades in Manhattan and Cincinnati in partnership with Adolph ZUKOR. By 1907 he owned some 40 nickelodeons all over the country. He then began acquiring motion picture theaters and by 1912 his Loew's Theatrical Enterprises owned some 400 cinemas. In 1920, in a step designed to provide a constant supply of films for his growing chain of theaters, he bought Metro Pictures. In 1924 he acquired controlling interest in the Goldwyn company and Louis B. Mayer Pictures and consolidated his three production companies into Metro-Goldwyn-Mayer (MGM), with Loew's, Inc., as the parent company. His twin sons, Arthur M. and David L. Loew (*b.* Oct. 5, 1897, N.Y.C.; Arthur *d.* 1976; David *d.* 1973), were both involved in the motion picture business, the former as a Loew executive (president from 1957) and the latter as an independent producer and executive of various film corporations.

Loewe, Frederick. Composer. *b.* June 10, 1904 Berlin. *d.* 1988. The son of Edmund Loewe, a famous Viennese tenor who created the role of Prince Danilo in Franz Lehar's operetta 'The Merry Widow,' he was a skillful pianist at age four and at 13 became the youngest piano soloist to appear with the Berlin Symphony Orchestra. He also began composing at a very young age and at 15 wrote 'Katerina,' a song that became an enormous hit throughout Europe. In 1924 Loewe emigrated to the US, where he at first supplemented his income from occasional concerts with odd jobs as a busboy, riding instructor, and even prizefighter and cowpuncher. He later played piano in New York beer halls and the organ in movie houses. His breakthrough came in 1935 when he sold his first song to Broadway. But it wasn't until a chance meeting in 1942 with lyricist Alan Jay LERNER that he embarked on the fabulous musical odyssey that would produce such legendary Broadway shows as 'Brigadoon,' 'Paint Your Wagon,' 'My Fair Lady,' and 'Camelot,' all of which would later be transferred to the screen. The Lerner-Loewe partnership also created two original films, *Gigi* (1958) and *The Little Prince* (1974). He shared with Lerner an Academy Award for the former film's title song and Oscar nominations for the song score and title song of the latter.

FILMS: *Brigadoon* 1954; *Gigi* 1958; *My Fair Lady* 1964; *Camelot* 1967; *Paint Your Wagon* 1969; *The Little Prince* 1974.

Logan, Jacqueline. Actress. *b.* Nov. 30, 1901, Corsicana, Tex. *d.* 1983. The daughter of an architect and a prima donna of the Boston Opera Company, she worked briefly as a reporter before making her stage debut in a Broadway revival of 'Floradora' in 1920. Following a successful stint with the Ziegfeld Follies that same year, she set out for Hollywood, where she starred in many silent films of the 20s. She was among the prettiest and most popular leading ladies of the silent screen, but her career waned with the advent of sound. She tried to revive her career in England, but after appearing in one film and co-directing another she retired from the screen in 1932.

FILMS INCLUDE: *A Perfect Crime, White and Unmarried, Molly O, A Fool's Paradise* 1921; *Burning Sands, Ebb Tide, A Blind Bargain* 1922; *Java Head, Sixty Cents an Hour, Salomy Jane, The Light That Failed* 1923; *Flaming Barriers, The Dawn of a Tomorrow, The House of Youth, Manhattan* 1924; *A Man Must Live, Playing with Souls, If Marriage Fails, Thank You, Peacock Feathers, Wages for Wives* 1925; *White Mice, The Outsider, Out of the Storm, Tony Runs*

Wild, Footloose Widows 1926; *One Hour to Love, The King of Kings* (as Mary Magdalene), *The Blood Ship, For Ladies Only, The Wise Wife* 1927; *The Leopard Lady, Stocks and Blondes, The Cop, Midnight Madness, The Charge of the Gauchos, The River Woman, Nothing to Wear, Power* 1928; *Bachelor Girl, Stark Mad, Ships of the Night, The Faker* 1929; *General Crack, The Middle Watch* (UK) 1930; *Strictly Business* (co-dir. with Mary Field) 1932.

Logan, Joshua. Director, playwright. *b.* Oct. 5, 1908, Texarkana, Tex. *d.* 1988. He was three when his father, a lumberman, died, and was raised in Louisiana by his mother and a stepfather, an officer on the staff of the Culver Military Academy, which Logan eventually attended. He then went to Princeton, where he played football, boxed, and became active in school dramatics. In the late 20s he organized the University Players, a summer stock group (in Cape Cod) that inaugurated the acting careers of James Stewart, Henry Fonda, Margaret Sullavan, and Myron McCormick, among others. He married one of the members of the troupe, Barbara O'Neill, but they were later divorced.

Logan next gained a scholarship to the Moscow Art Theater and studied under Stanislavsky. Returning to the US in 1932, he directed and acted in many Broadway plays and was dialogue director in Hollywood on such films as *The Garden of Allah* (1936) and *History Is Made at Night* (1937). He then co-directed the film *I Met My Love Again* (1938). That same year he scored his first major hit as a Broadway director with 'On Borrowed Time.' This was followed by such a prolific output that by early 1940, suffering from exhaustion and insomnia, Logan had himself committed to a psychiatric hospital for more than a year. (He would suffer a similar collapse, the result of a severe attack of manic depression, in the late 50s. Starting in the late 60s, he, however, learned to control the condition with the help of the drug lithium carbonate.)

In 1945, Logan married actress Nedda Harrigan. Returning to Broadway after WW II service with the Air Force Combat Intelligence, he scored a succession of hits as the director of such plays and musicals as 'Annie Get Your Gun,' 'Mister Roberts' (also co-author), 'South Pacific' (also co-author), 'The Wisteria Trees' (also co-author), 'Picnic,' 'Fanny' (also co-author), and 'Middle of the Night.' It wasn't until 1955 that Logan turned seriously to the making of films. His first two productions, *Picnic* and *Bus Stop,* were unanimously acclaimed, and many consider Marilyn Monroe's performance in the latter the best of her career. But critics largely remained cool to much of Logan's subsequent, rather sparse, film work. He appeared as himself in the film *Main Street to Broadway* (1953). In 1977 he produced, directed, acted, and sang in his first nightclub show, at New York's Rainbow Grill. Autobiography: *Josh: My Up-and-Down In-and-Out Life* (1976). Memoirs: *Movie Stars, Real People and Me* (1978).

FILMS (as director): *I Met My Love Again* (co-dir. with Arthur Ripley) 1938; *Higher and Higher* (co-play basis only) 1944; *Mister Roberts* (co-sc. from co-play only) 1955; *Picnic, Bus Stop* 1956; *Sayonara* 1957; *South Pacific* 1958; *Tall Story* (also prod.) 1960; *Fanny* (also prod.) 1961; *Ensign Pulver* (also prod., co-sc.) 1964; *Camelot* 1967; *Paint Your Wagon* 1969.

Loggia, Robert. Actor. Born on Jan. 3, 1930, in Staten Island, N.Y., of Sicilian descent. Leading man and character player of American stage, TV, and films, often in ethnic roles. Raised in Manhattan's Little Italy, he was a journalism major at the University of Missouri but was drawn to acting and later studied with Stella ADLER at the Actors Studio. He made his Broadway debut in 'The Man with the Golden Arm,' in 1955 and his first screen appearance the following year. On TV he starred in the adventure series 'T.H.E. Cat' (1961–63). A versatile player on the screen, he was nominated for an Academy Award as best supporting actor for his portrayal of a seedy detective in *Jagged Edge* (1985).

FILMS INCLUDE: *Somebody Up There Likes Me* 1956; *The Garment Jungle* 1957; *Cop Hater, The Lost Missile* 1958; *Cattle King* 1963; *The Greatest Story Ever Told* (as Joseph) 1965; *The Three Sisters* 1966; *Che!* 1969; *First Love* 1977; *Revenge of the Pink Panther* 1978; *The Ninth Configuration/Twinkle Twinkle Killer Kane* 1980; *S.O.B.* 1981; *An Officer and a Gentleman, The Trail of the Pink Panther* 1982; *Psycho II, Curse of the Pink Panther, Scarface* 1983; *Prizzi's Honor, Jagged Edge* 1985; *Armed and Dangerous, That's Life!* 1986; *Over the Top, Hot Pursuit, The Believers, Gaby—A True Story* 1987; *Big* 1988; *Relentless, Triumph of the Spirit* 1989; *Opportunity Knocks* 1990; *The Marrying Man, Necessary Roughness* 1991; *Gladiator, Innocent Blood* 1992; *Bad Girls, I Love Trouble* 1994; *Coldblooded* 1995; *Lost Highway, Smilla's Sense of Snow, Wide Awake* 1997.

logo. Symbol or trademark identifying a production or distribution company at the beginning of a film, such as MGM's Leo the Lion.

log sheet. A detailed written record of various production activities during filming. The log sheet for camera activity is known as CAMERA REPORT, while the one for recorded sound is often called a "sound report."

Lohmann, Dietrich. Director of photography. Born in Germany. A dominant presence in the early films of Rainer Werner FASSBINDER, he helped the director achieve the claustrophobic, minimalistic style that characterized these productions. He was also instrumental in the works of other filmmakers of the New German Cinema. Lohmann was behind the camera on the monumental miniseries 'War and Remembrance' for American TV.

FILMS INCLUDE: *Liebe ist kälter als der Tod/Love Is Colder Than Death, Katzelmacher* 1969; *Götter der Pest/Gods of the Plague, Warum lauf Herr R Amok?/Why Does Herr R Run Amok?, Der amerikanische Solat/The American Soldier* 1970; *Rio das Mortes, Pioniere in Ingolstadt/Pioneers in Ingolstadt* 1971; *Der Händler der vier Jahrezeiten/Merchant of the Four Seasons, Acht Stunden sin kein Tag/Eight Hours Are Not a Day, Bremer Freiheit/Bremen Freedom* (co-dir., co-sc., co-phot.) 1972; *Wildwechsel/Jail Bait* 1973; *Fontane Effi Briest/Effi Briest* (co-phot.), *Karl May* 1974; *Berlinger, Bomber und Paganini, Das Brot des Bäckers, Der letzte Schrei* 1976; *Hitler—ein Film aus Deutschlan/Hitler—a Film from Germany, Das Schlangenei/The Serpent's Egg* (addnl. phot. only) 1977; *Deutschland im Herbst/Germany in Autumn* (co-phot.), *Taugenichts* 1978; *Der Schneider von Ulm* 1979; *Die Reinheidt des Herzens* 1980; *Strawanzer* 1983; *Forstenbuben* 1985; *Der Joker* 1987; *Zwei Frauen* 1989; *The Lover* 1990.

Lollobrigida, Gina. Actress. Born on July 4, 1927, in Subiaco, Italy. Earthy, buxom beauty of Italian films, glamorized by Hollywood into a standard star. A carpenter's daughter, she studied to become a commercial artist and at first earned a living as a model in illustrated novels, using the name Diana Loris. She participated successfully in several beauty contests before making her screen debut in 1946. By the early 50s she was one of Continental Europe's most popular stars, admired widely as "La Lollo." The admiring French even coined a new colloquial word for curvaceous: *lollobrigidienne.* She was unable, however, to appear in Hollywood films for several years because of a contract dispute with Howard HUGHES. When she finally did, she achieved immediate popularity with American audiences but in the process lost much of her original unadorned sex appeal to the synthetic Hollywood glamour machine. Just the same, for many years her name remained a synonym for beauty and glamour. She retired from the screen in the early 70s to pursue a career as a professional photographer and an executive with fashion and cosmetics firms. She directed a documentary film, *Rittrato di Fidel/Portrait of Fidel Castro* (1975). Although she virtually retired from acting, she was lured back before the cameras in 1984 in the American TV series 'Falcon Crest.'

FILMS INCLUDE: *Aquila Nera, Elisir d'Amore, Lucia di Lammermoor* 1946; *Il Delitto di Giovanni Episcopo, Il Segreto di Don Giovanni, Follie per l'Opera/Mad About Opera* 1947; *I Pagliacci/Love of a Clown* (as Needa) 1948; *Campane A Martello* 1949; *Cuori senza Frontiere/The White Line, Miss Italia/Miss Italy, Vita de Cani, Alina* 1950; *A Tale of Five Cities/A Tale of Five Women* (UK/Fr./It./Ger.), *Achtung! Banditi!, Enrico Caruso/The Young Caruso, La Città si difende, Altri Tempi/Times Gone By* 1951; *Fanfan la Tulipe/Fanfan the Tulip* (Fr./It.), *Les Belles de Nuit/Beauties of the Night* (Fr./It.), *Moglie per una Notte/Wife for a Night, Le Infedeli/The Unfaithful* 1952; *La Provinciale/The Wayward Wife, Il Maestro di Don Giovanni/Crossed Swords* (It./US), *Pane Amore e Fantasia/Bread Love and Dreams* 1953; *Beat the Devil* (UK/It.), *Le Grand Jeu* (Fr./It.), *La Romana/Woman of Rome* (as Adriana), *Pane Amore e Gelosia/Frisky* 1954; *La Donna più Bella del Mondo/Beautiful but Dangerous* (as opera soprano Lina Cavalieri) 1955; *Trapeze* (US), *Notre Dame de Paris/The Hunchback of Notre Dame* (as Esmeralda; Fr./It.) 1956; *Anna di Brooklyn/Fast and Sexy* (It./Fr.) 1958; *La Loi/Where the Hot Wind Blows* (Fr./It.), *Solomon and Sheba* (as the Queen of Sheba; US), *Never So Few* (US) 1959; *Go Naked in the World* (US), *Come September* (US) 1961; *Vénus impériale* (Fr./It.) 1962; *Mare Matto* (It./Fr.) 1963; *Woman of Straw* (UK) 1964; *Le Bambole/The Dolls* (It./Fr.), *Strange Bedfellows* (US) 1965; *Hotel Paradiso* (UK/US) 1966; *Cervantes/The Young Rebel* (Sp./It./Fr.), *La Morte ha Fatto l'Uovo/Plucked* (It./Fr.), *The Private Navy of Sgt. O'Farrell* (US), *Un Bellissimo Novembre/That Splendid November* (It./Fr.) 1968; *Buona Sera Mrs. Campbell* (US) 1969; *Bad Man's River* (Sp.) 1971; *Herzbube/King Queen Knave* (Ger./US) 1972; *Roses rouges et Piments verts/The Lonely Woman* (Fr./It./Sp.) 1975; *Widow's Nest* 1977; *Stelle Emigranti* 1983.

Lom, Herbert. Actor. Born Herbert Charles Angelo Kuchacevich ze Schluderpacheru, on Jan. 9, 1917, in Prague. *ed.* Prague U. A stage and screen actor in his native country from 1936, he went to England in 1939 and received additional training with the Old Vic. He has since appeared in numerous British, American, and Continental films. His piercing eyes and imposing screen personality have been equally effective for suave, dominating romantic leads and evil, menacing character parts. Memorable as Napoleon in *War and Peace* (1956), a role he had played early in his career in *The Young Mr. Pitt* (1942). Late in his career he became closely identified with the comic role of the hapless Inspector Clouseau in the *Pink Panther* movies.

FILMS INCLUDE: *Mein Kampf/My Crimes* 1940; *The Young Mr. Pitt* (as Napoleon) 1942; *The Seventh Veil* 1945; *Appointment with Crime* 1946; *Snowbound, Good Time Girl, Portrait from Life/The Girl in the Painting* 1948; *Night and the City* (US/UK), *The Black Rose* (US/UK), *State Secret/The Great Manhunt, The Golden Salamander, Cage of Gold* 1950; *The Man Who Watched the Trains Go By/The Paris Express* 1952; *The Net/Project M-7* 1953; *The Ladykillers* 1955; *War and Peace* (again as Napoleon; US/It.) 1956; *Fire Down Below* 1957; *I Accuse!, Chase a Crooked Shadow, The Roots of Heaven* (US), *Intent to Kill* 1958; *The Big Fisherman* (as Herod Antipas; US), *Third Man on the Mountain, Passport to Shame/Room 43, North West Frontier/Flame Over India* 1959; *I Aim at the Stars* (US/Ger.), *Spartacus* (US) 1960; *The Frightened City, El Cid* (US/It.), *Mysterious Island* (as Captain Nemo; US/UK) 1961; *The Phantom of the Opera* (title role), *Tiara Tahiti* 1962; *A Shot in the Dark* (US/UK) 1964; *Onkel Toms Hütte/Uncle Tom's Cabin* (as Simon Legree; Ger./It./Yug./Fr.), *Return from the Ashes* (UK/US) 1965; *Our Man in Marrakesh/Bang! Bang! You're Dead!, Gambit* (US) 1966; *Villa Rides* (US) 1968; *Assignment to Kill* (US) 1969; *Das Bildnis des Dorian Gray/Dorian Gray/The Secret of Dorian Gray* (as Lord Henry Wotton; Ger./It./Licht.) 1970; *Vampir/Count Dracula* (Sp.), *Murders in the Rue Morgue* 1971; *Mark of the Devil* 1972; *And Now the Screaming Starts* 1973; *Dark Places, And Then There Were None/Ten Little Indians* 1974; *The Return of the Pink Panther* 1975; *The Pink Panther Strikes Again* 1976; *Revenge of the Pink Panther* (US), *Charleston* 1978; *The Lady Vanishes* 1979; *The Man with Bogart's Face/Sam Marlowe, Private Eye* (US), *Hopscotch* (US) 1980; *The Trail of the Pink Panther* 1982; *Curse of the Pink Panther, The Dead Zone* (US) 1983; *Memed My Hawk* 1984; *King Solomon's Mines* (US) 1985; *Whoops Apocalypse!* 1987; *Going Bananas* (US) 1988; *River of Death* (US), *Ten Little Indians* (US) 1989; *The Masque of the Red Death* (US) 1990; *The Sect* (UK), *The Pope Must Die/The Pope Must Diet* (UK) 1991; *Son of the Pink Panther* (US) 1993.

Lombard, Carole. Actress. *b.* Jane Alice Peters, Oct. 6, 1908, Fort Wayne, Ind. *d.* 1942, in a plane crash. One of Hollywood's most talented and glamorous stars of the 30s, a sophisticated comedienne who infused her screen roles with the wit, charm, and warmth of her personality. Raised in California from the age of six, she played her first screen role at 12 in Allan Dwan's *A Perfect Crime* (1921). After completing junior high school, she returned to films in 1925 as an ingenue under a contract with Fox. Using the screen name of Carol Lombard (it was changed to Carole in 1930), she played standard blonde heroines in several routine films, including two opposite cowboy star Buck Jones, before her contract was terminated by the studio. She then signed with Mack Sennett and in 1927–28 appeared in more than a dozen two-reel knockabout slapstick comedies opposite such comedians as Billy Bevan, Andy Clyde, Chester Conklin, Billy Gilbert, and Mack Swain. Returning to feature films, she again played routine roles in mainly routine productions until she emerged as a top-ranking comedy star, opposite John Barrymore, in Howard Hawks's *Twentieth Century* (1934). It was the first of several hilarious screwball comedies that utilized her special talent to great advantage, followed notably by Gregory La Cava's *My Man Godfrey* (1936), William Wellman's *Nothing Sacred* (1937), and Ernst Lubitsch's *To Be or Not to Be* (1942), her last film.

Lombard was at the peak of her achievement and popularity when she was killed in a plane crash in January 1942 while returning to California from a US Bond–selling tour of the Midwest. Her sudden death stunned millions of fans and left the spirit of her second husband (from 1939), Clark GABLE, crushed for years. (Her first marriage, in 1931, to William POWELL, had ended in divorce in 1933.) President Franklin D. Roosevelt expressed the feeling of many in his condolence telegram to Gable: "She brought great joy to all who knew her and to millions who knew her only as a great artist. She gave unselfishly of time and talent to serve her government in peace and war. She loved her country. She is and always will be a star, one we shall never forget nor cease to be grateful to." Her rewarding relationship with Gable was depicted rather feebly in the 1976 film *Gable and Lombard,* in which she was portrayed by actress Jill Clayburgh, and he by James Brolin.

FEATURE FILMS: *A Perfect Crime* 1921; *Marriage in*

Transit, Hearts and Spurs, Durand of the Badlands 1925; *The Road to Glory* (bit) 1926; *The Divine Sinner, Power, Me Gangster, Show Folks, Ned McCobb's Daughter* 1928; *High Voltage, Big News, The Racketeer* 1929; *The Arizona Kid, Safety in Numbers, Fast and Loose* 1930; *It Pays to Advertise, Man of the World, Ladies' Man, Up Pops the Devil, I Take This Woman* 1931; *No One Man, Sinners in the Sun, Virtue, No More Orchids, No Man of Her Own* 1932; *From Hell to Heaven, Supernatural, The Eagle and the Hawk, Brief Moment, White Woman* 1933; *Bolero, We're Not Dressing, Twentieth Century, Now and Forever, Lady by Choice, The Gay Bride* 1934; *Rumba, Hands Across the Table* 1935; *Love Before Breakfast, The Princess Comes Across, My Man Godfrey* 1936; *Swing High Swing Low, Nothing Sacred, True Confession* 1937; *Fools for Scandal* 1938; *Made for Each Other, In Name Only* 1939; *Vigil in the Night, They Knew What They Wanted* 1940; *Mr. and Mrs. Smith* 1941; *To Be or Not to Be* 1942.

Lomnicki, Tadeusz. Actor. Born in 1925, in Poland. Popular leading man of Polish stage and screen.

FILMS INCLUDE: *Hearts of Steel* 1948; *The Crew* 1952; *Five from Barska Street* 1953; *A Generation* 1954; *Eroica, The Eighth Day of the Week* 1958; *The Sky Is Our Roof* 1959; *Time Past* 1961; *The Dowry* 1963; *The First Day of Freedom* 1964; *Der Arzt stellt fest/The Doctor Says* (Switz./Ger.), *Barrier, Contribution* 1966; *Hands Up!* 1967; *Colonel Wolodyjowski* 1969; *Man of Marble* 1977; *Contract* 1980; *Chronicle of Beloved Events* 1986; *Blind Chance* 1987; *Lava, Dekalog/The Ten Commandments* 1989; *Pension Sonnenschein/Pension Sunshine* (Ger.) 1990.

Loncraine, Richard. Director. Born on Oct. 20, 1946, in Cheltenham, England. He moved into feature films in 1972, following TV experience from 1967, and before long established a reputation for intelligent, imaginative filmmaking.

FILMS: *Radio Wonderful* 1972; *Flame* 1974; *Full Circle/The Haunting of Julia* (UK/Can.) 1976; *Brimstone and Treacle, The Missionary* 1982; *Bellman and True* (also co-sc.) 1988; *The Wedding Gift* 1994; *The Hunted* 1995.

London, Julie. Actress, singer. *b.* Julie Peck, Sept. 26, 1926, in Santa Clara, Calif. *d.* 1992. Sexy, offbeat nightclub and recording blues singer, she effectively played dramatic leads and second leads in many Hollywood films from the late 40s to the early 60s but never became a front-rank star. Occasionally seen in TV series episodes. Her first husband (1945–53) was Jack WEBB. Later married TV actor Bobby Troup, her co-star in the series 'Emergency' (1972–77).

FILMS INCLUDE: *Jungle Woman* 1944; *Nabonga* 1945; *A Night in Paradise* 1946; *The Red House* 1947; *Tap Roots* 1948; *Task Force* 1949; *Return of the Frontiersman* 1950; *The Fat Man* 1951; *The Fighting Chance* 1955; *The Great Man, The Girl Can't Help It* 1956; *Drango* 1957; *A Question of Adultery* (UK), *Saddle the Wind, Voice in the Mirror, Man of the West* 1958; *The Wonderful Country, Night of the Quarter Moon* 1959; *The Third Voice* 1960; *The George Raft Story* 1961; *The Helicopter Spies* 1968.

Lone, John. Actor. Born in 1952 in Hong Kong. Finely chiseled actor of stage and screen. A student of the Chin Chiu Academy of the Peking Opera in Hong Kong, he moved to California, where he studied at the American Academy of Dramatic Art in Pasadena. Made a screen impression as Chinese emperor Pu Yi in *The Last Emperor*. Obie winner for off-Broadway work.

FILMS INCLUDE: *Iceman* 1984; *Year of the Dragon* 1985; *The Last Emperor* (UK/Chin.), *Echoes of Paradise* (Austral.) 1987; *The Moderns* 1988; *Shadow of China* 1991; *M. Butterfly* 1993; *The Shadow* 1994; *The Hunted* 1995.

Long, Audrey. Actress. Born in 1923, in Orlando, Fla. A former model, she played leads and supporting roles in minor films of the 40s and early 50s.

FILMS INCLUDE: *The Male Animal, Yankee Doodle Dandy, Pardon My Sarong* 1942; *A Night of Adventure, Tall in the Saddle* 1944; *A Game of Death, Wanderer of the Wasteland, Pan-Americana* 1945; *Perilous Holiday* 1946; *Born to Kill, Desperate* 1947; *Song of My Heart, Stage Struck, Miraculous Journey, Homicide for Three* 1948; *Duke of Chicago, Air Hostess* 1949; *The Petty Girl* 1950; *Insurance Investigator* 1951; *Indian Uprising* 1952.

Long, Richard. Actor. *b.* Dec. 17, 1927, Chicago. *d.* 1974. He went into films fresh out of high school, making his debut in the role of Claudette Colbert's son in *Tomorrow Is Forever* (1946). He played juvenile supporting roles in a number of other A productions, then matured into leads in second features. In addition to appearing in films, he was featured regularly in such TV series as 'Maverick,' 'Bourbon Street Beat,' '77 Sunset Strip,' 'The Big Valley,' and 'Nanny and the Professor.' Widowed from Suzan Ball in 1955, he married Mara CORDAY in 1957. He died of a heart ailment at 47.

FILMS INCLUDE: *Tomorrow Is Forever, The Stranger, The Dark Mirror* 1946; *The Egg and I* 1947; *Tap Roots* 1948; *Criss Cross, Ma and Pa Kettle* 1949; *Kansas Raiders* (as Frank James) 1950; *Air Cadet* 1951; *Back at the Front* 1952; *All I Desire, The All-American* 1953; *Saskatchewan, Playgirl* 1954; *Cult of the Cobra* 1955; *Fury at Gunsight Pass* 1956; *House on Haunted Hill, Tokyo After Dark* 1959; *Follow the Boys* 1963; *Make Like a Thief* (also co-dir.; Fin./US) 1964.

Long, Shelley. Actress. Born on Aug. 23, 1949, in Fort Wayne, Ind. Bright, expressive, blonde leading lady of American TV and films. Following drama studies at Northwestern University, she got her start in the early 70s as the co-host of 'Sorting It Out,' a magazine show on a local Chicago TV station. She then flaunted her comic talent as a member of Chicago's famed Second City troupe. A pleasant presence in feature films since the early 80s, she had her greatest success on TV, as the brainy, sharp-tongued waitress, Diane, in the long-running (1982–93) series 'Cheers,' a role for which she won an Emmy Award in 1983.

FILMS: *A Small Circle of Friends* 1980; *Caveman* 1981; *Night Shift* 1982; *Losin' It* 1983; *Irreconcilable Differences* 1984; *The Money Pit* 1986; *Outrageous Fortune, Hello Again* 1987; *Troop Beverly Hills* 1989; *Don't Tell Her It's Me* 1990; *Frozen Assets* 1992; *The Brady Bunch Movie* 1995; *A Very Brady Sequel* 1996.

Long, Walter. Actor. *b.* Mar. 5, 1879, Milford, N.H. *d.* 1952. Heavyset character player of the American screen, typically as a snarling, evil-eyed villain. On screen from 1914, he had his start in films of D. W. GRIFFITH. He is memorable for his many confrontations with LAUREL AND HARDY in several of their comedy shorts of the early 30s.

FILMS INCLUDE: *Home Sweet Home, The Escape* 1914; *The Birth of a Nation, Jordan Is a Hard Road, Martyrs of the Alamo* (as Santa Anna) 1915; *Daphne and the Pirate, Intolerance* (as The Musketeer of the Slums in the Modern Story), *Joan the Woman* (as the Executioner) 1916; *The Evil Eye, Hashimura Togo, The Little American, The Woman God Forgot* 1917; *Desert Gold* 1919; *The Sea Wolf* 1920; *The Sheik* 1921; *The Dictator, Blood and Sand* 1922; *The Isle of Lost Ships, The Call of the Wild, The Broken Wing* 1923; *The Lady, Bobbed Hair* 1925; *West of Broadway, Jim the Conqueror* 1926; *The Yankee Clipper, Back to God's Country* 1927; *Gang War* 1928; *The Black Watch* 1929; *Moby Dick* (as Stubb) 1930; *The Maltese Falcon, Pardon Us* 1931; *Any Old Port* (short), *I Am a*

Fugitive from a Chain Gang 1932; *Six of a Kind, Operator 13, Going Bye-Bye* (short), *The Live Ghost* (short), *The Thin Man* 1934; *Naughty Marietta, Frisco Kid, The Whole Town's Talking* 1935; *Pick a Star* 1937; *Union Pacific* 1939; *When the Daltons Rode* 1940; *Wabash Avenue* 1950.

Longden, John. Actor. *b.* Nov. 11, 1900, the West Indies. *d.* 1971. A minister's son and a former mining engineer, he starred in late silent British films and early talkies, often in heroic roles, then switched to character parts. His career was hampered by a drinking problem.

FILMS INCLUDE: *The Ball of Fortune* 1926; *Quinneys, The Flight Commander* 1927; *Blackmail, Atlantic, Juno and the Paycock* 1929; *The Flame of Love, Two Worlds, Children of Chance, Elstree Calling* 1930; *The Skin Game, The Ringer* 1931; *Come Into My Parlor* (dir. only), *Born Lucky* 1932; *Young and Innocent/The Girl Was Innocent, French Leave* 1937; *Q Planes/Clouds Over Europe, Jamaica Inn, The Lion Has Wings* 1939; *Contraband* 1940; *Tower of Terror* 1941; *The Silver Fleet* 1943; *Anna Karenina* 1948; *The Elusive Pimpernel/The Fighting Pimpernel* 1950; *Pool of London, The Magic Box* 1951; *The Ship That Died of Shame* 1955; *An Honorable Murder* 1960; *Lancelot and Guinevere/Sword of Lancelot* 1963; *Frozen Alive* 1964.

long-focus lens. A lens with a focal length greater than that of a normal lens. Its main characteristic is its ability to magnify images.

long shot. A broad view of objects or action of principal interest. The shot requires a wide angle of photography and a scene in depth. The camera is positioned at a distance that allows general recognition of the subject matter at the expense of detail. When used to identify a setting and establish the background for subsequent detail it is known as an ESTABLISHING SHOT. Usually abbreviated in scripts and camera reports as "LS".

Lonsdale, Michel (also **Michael**). Actor. Born in 1931, in Paris. Impressive, versatile character player of numerous French and international films, following experience on the Paris stage. The son of a British Army officer serving in India, and a French mother, he spent much of his childhood in London, but it was in Paris that he developed as an actor under the tutelage of Raymond Rouleau.

FILMS INCLUDE: *C'est arrivé a Aden* 1956; *La Main chaude* 1960; *Adorable Menteuse* 1961; *La Dénonciation/The Immoral Moment, Le Procès/The Trial* 1962; *Behold a Pale Horse* (US), *Les Copains* 1964; *Je vous salue Mafia/Hail! Mafia* 1965; *Les Compagnons de la Marguerite* 1966; *La Mariée était en Noir/The Bride Wore Black, Baisers volés/Stolen Kisses* 1968; *Hibernatus, Détruire dit-elle/Destroy She Said* 1969; *L'Etalon* 1970; *Le Souffle au Coeur/Murmur of the Heart, Les Assassins de l'Ordre, Le Printemps, Jaune le Soleil* 1971; *Il était une fois un Flic* 1972; *The Day of the Jackal* (UK/Fr.), *Glissements progressifs du Plaisir* 1973; *Stavisky, Caravan to Vaccares* (UK/Fr.), *Le Fantôme de la Liberté, Aloise, Les Suspects* 1974; *India Song, Section spéciale/Special Section, Galileo* (as Cardinal Maffeo Barberini, later Pope Urban VIII; UK/US), *The Romantic Englishwoman* (UK), *Le Téléphone rose/The Pink Telephone, Une Folle à tuer* 1975; *Les Oeufs brouilles, Mr. Klein* 1976; *Le Diable dans la Boîte, L'Imprécateur, Die linkshändige Frau/The Left-Handed Woman* (Ger.) 1977; *The Passage,* (US) *Moonraker* (UK) 1979; *Chariots of Fire* 1981; *Le Jeux de la Comtesse Dolingen de Gratz, Douce Enquête sur la Violence, Enigma* (UK/Fr.) 1982; *Erendira* 1983; *Le Juge* 1984; *The Holcroft Covenant* (UK), *L'Eveillé du Pont de l'Alma* 1985; *The Name of the Rose* (W. Ger./It./Fr.) 1986; *Souvenir* (UK) 1989; *Jefferson in Paris* 1995.

loop. 1. A slack length of film between sprocket wheels and camera gate, designed to absorb the tension caused by intermittent movement, thus avoiding the tearing of film as it travels through the camera. 2. A length of film (with sound track) or tape joined head-to-tail to form a continuous belt so that the sound can be repeated endlessly for the purpose of mixing and dubbing.

looping. A dubbing process in which the original sound track recorded during filming is replaced by another, recorded under more favorable conditions.

Loos, Anita. Screenwriter, playwright, novelist. *b.* Apr. 26, 1893, Sisson, Calif. *d.* 1981. She acted briefly on stage with a company managed by her father before turning professional writer while still in her teens. From 1912 to 1916 she wrote numerous screenplays for D. W. GRIFFITH, and her satirical scripts and wisecracking titles helped launch the career of Douglas FAIRBANKS, in a series of films (1916–17) directed by John EMERSON. She married Emerson in 1919. They later collaborated on many screen- and stage plays and on the books *How to Write Photoplays* (1919) and *Breaking Into Movies* (1921). Although primarily a screenwriter, Miss Loos is best known as author of the hilarious 1925 novel *Gentlemen Prefer Blondes,* which she also adapted for the stage and the screen. Her screenplays, for the most part, are lightweight affairs with the accent on clever lines rather than plot and character development. Autobiographies: *A Girl Like I* (1966); *Kiss Hollywood Good-By* (1974); *Cast of Thousands* (1977). Biography: *The Talmadge Girls* (1978).

FILMS INCLUDE (as screenwriter, alone or in collaboration): *The New York Hat* 1912; *The Telephone Girl and the Lady, The Power of the Camera, The Hicksville Epicure, Highbrow Love, A Narrow Escape, The Widow's Kids, The Lady in Black, The Wedding Gown* 1913; *His Awful Vengeance, Gentleman or Thief, A Bunch of Flowers, When a Woman Guides, The Road to Plaindale, The Wall Flower, The Saving Presence, The Fatal Dress Suit, The Girl in the Shack, For Her Father's Sins, The Million-Dollar Bride, A Flurry in Art* 1914; *Mixed Values, Symphony Sal, The Deacon's Whiskers, Pennington's Choice* 1915; *His Picture in the Papers, A Corner in Cotton, Macbeth* (titles only), *Wild Girl of the Sierras, The Little Liar, The Half-Breed, Intolerance* (titles only), *The Social Secretary, Stranded, The Wharf Rat, Manhattan Madness, American Aristocracy, The Matrimaniac, The Americano* 1916; *A Daughter of the Poor, In Again Out Again, Wild and Wooly, Reaching for the Moon* 1917; *Let's Get a Divorce, Hit-the-Trail Holiday, Come on In* 1918; *Getting Mary Married* (co-story, co-prod. only), *Oh You Women!, A Temperamental Wife* (also co-prod.), *The Isle of Conquest, A Virtuous Vamp* (also co-prod.) 1919; *Two Weeks, In Search of a Sinner* (also co-prod.), *The Love Expert, The Perfect Woman, The Branded Woman, Dangerous Business* 1920; *Mama's Affair, Woman's Place* 1921; *Red Hot Romance* (also co-prod.), *Polly of the Follies* 1922; *Dulcy* 1923; *Three Miles Out* 1924; *Learning to Love* 1925; *Stranded* (story only), *Publicity Madness* (story only) 1927; *Gentlemen Prefer Blondes* (co-adapt. from own novel and play) 1928; *The Fall of Eve* (co-story only) 1929; *The Struggle* 1931; *Red-Headed Woman, Blondie of the Follies* (dial. only) 1932; *Hold Your Man, Midnight Mary* (story only), *The Barbarian* 1933; *Social Register* (co-play basis only), *The Girl from Missouri* 1934; *The Biography of a Bachelor Girl* 1935; *Riffraff, San Francisco* 1936; *Mama Steps Out, Saratoga* 1937; *The Women* 1939; *Susan and God* 1940; *Blossoms in the Dust, They Met in Bombay, When Ladies Meet* 1941; *I Married an Angel* 1942; *Gentlemen Prefer Blondes* (remake; co-play basis only) 1953.

Loquasto, Santo. Production and costume designer. Born in 1944, in Wilkes-Barre, Penn. *ed.* Cambridge (King's College), Trained at the Yale Drama School, he began designing sets for repertory companies in the late 60s and for off-Broadway and Broadway productions in the early 70s. He won an Obie Award for the sets and costumes of 'Comedy of Errors' (1976) and Tony Awards for the costumes of 'The Cherry Orchard' (1977) and 'Grand Hotel' (1990). Also an opera and ballet designer, he has been contributing creative, imaginative set and costume designs to films since the late 70s, collaborating most closely with Woody ALLEN. He was nominated for Academy Awards for the costumes of *Zelig* (1983) and the art direction of *Radio Days* (1987).

FILMS: As costume designer—*Sammy Stops the World* (also set dec.) 1978; *Simon* 1980; *Stardust Memories* 1981; *A Midsummer Night's Sex Comedy* 1982; *Zelig* 1983. As production designer—*The Fan, So Fine* 1981; *Falling in Love* 1984; *Desperately Seeking Susan* (also costumes) 1985; *Radio Days, September* 1987; *Bright Lights, Big City, Big, Another Woman* 1988; *New York Stories* ("Oedipus Wrecks" episode), *Crimes and Misdemeanors, She-Devil* 1989; *Alice* 1990; *Shadows and Fog* 1991; *Husbands and Wives* 1992; *Manhattan Murder Mystery* 1993; *Bullets Over Broadway* 1994; *Everyone Says I Love You* 1996.

Lord, Jack. Actor. Born John Joseph Ryan, on Dec. 30, 1928, in New York City, the son of a steamship executive. A seaman in his teens, he later ran a Greenwich Village art school and exhibited his paintings at the Metropolitan and British museums, the Museum of Modern Art, and in various galleries. At the same time, he became interested in acting and has since played lead roles on stage, in films, and on TV. As a writer, he has created several TV shows, and as an actor he has starred in such series as 'Stoney Burke' (1962–63) and 'Hawaii Five-O' (1968–80). He has also directed several TV specials and a number of series episodes.

FILMS INCLUDE: *Project X* 1949; *Cry Murder* 1950; *The Court-Martial of Billy Mitchell* 1955; *The Vagabond King* 1956; *Tip on a Dead Jockey* 1957; *God's Little Acre, Man of the West, The True Story of Lynn Stuart* 1958; *The Hangman* 1959; *Walk Like a Dragon* 1960; *Dr. No* (UK) 1962; *The Ride to the Hangman's Tree* 1967; *The Counterfeit Killer, The Name of the Game Is Kill!* 1968.

Lord, Marjorie. Actress. Born on July 26, 1922, in San Francisco. She began appearing in films at 15, following some experience on the stage, and during the late 30s, 40s, and early 50s played leads in routine films of various studios, getting her best opportunity opposite James Cagney in *Johnny Come Lately* (1943). She fared better later on TV, particularly as Danny Thomas's wife in the series 'Make Room for Daddy,' a role she took over from Jean Hagen in 1957 and played through to the conclusion of the series in 1964. Her first husband was actor John ARCHER. Actress Anne ARCHER is their daughter.

FILMS INCLUDE: *Border Cafe, Forty Naughty Girls, Hideway, On Again—Off Again* 1937; *Escape from Hong Kong, Moonlight in Havana* 1942; *Shantytown, Sherlock Holmes in Washington, Johnny Come Lately, Flesh and Fantasy* 1943; *New Orleans* 1947; *The Argyle Secrets, The Strange Mrs. Crane* 1948; *Masked Raiders* 1949; *Riding High, The Lost Volcano, Chain Gang* 1950; *Rebel City* 1953; *Port of Hell* 1954; *Boy Did I Get a Wrong Number!* 1966.

Lord, Robert. Screenwriter, producer. *b.* May 1, 1902, Chicago. *d.* 1976. *ed.* U. of Chicago; Harvard. In films from the mid-20s, after a stint at *The New Yorker,* he wrote many routine but entertaining original stories and screenplays, mainly for Warner Bros., then produced a number of commercially successful films for that studio during the 30s, sometimes with the nominal screen credit of associate producer under Hal Wallis. He won an Academy Award for the original story of *One Way Passage* (1932). In the late 40s he formed a short-lived partnership with Humphrey Bogart in Santana Productions.

FILMS INCLUDE: As screenwriter—*The Lucky Horseshoe* (story only) 1925; *The Johnstown Flood* 1926; *For Ladies Only, The Swell-Head, A Reno Divorce* 1927; *If I Were Single, My Man, Five and Ten Cent Annie, The Lion and the Mouse, Detectives, Women They Talk About, Beyond the Sierras, Beware of Bachelors* 1928; *Hardboiled Rose, Kid Gloves, No Defense, On with the Show, The Time the Place and the Girl, Gold Diggers of Broadway, So Long Letty, The Sap* 1929; *The Aviator, Hold Everything* 1930; *Fireman Save My Child, The Purchase Price, 20,000 Years in Sing Sing, One Way Passage* (story only) 1932; *The Little Giant, Heroes for Sale* 1933; *He Was Her Man* (story only), *Housewife* (story only), *Dames* 1934; *Bordertown* (story only), *Gold Diggers of 1935* (co-story only), *Page Miss Glory* (also prod.), *Dr. Socrates* 1935; *Colleen* (story only), *The Singing Kid* (story only) 1936; *'Til We Meet Again* (story only) 1940. As producer or associate producer—*Loose Ankles* 1930; *Wonder Bar* 1934; *Oil for the Lamps of China* 1935; *Stage Struck* (also story) 1936; *Black Legion* (also story), *The Prince and the Pauper, Tovarich* 1937; *Brother Rat, The Dawn Patrol, The Amazing Dr. Clitterhouse* 1938; *Dodge City, Confessions of a Nazi Spy, The Private Lives of Elizabeth and Essex* 1939; *The Letter* 1940; *Footsteps in the Dark, Dive Bomber* 1941; *High Wall* 1947; *Knock on Any Door, Tokyo Joe* 1949; *In a Lonely Place* 1950; *Sirocco* 1951.

Loren, Sophia. Actress. Born Sofia Scicolone, on Sept. 20, 1934, in Rome. An illegitimate child, she grew up in a Naples slum in dire wartime poverty. Her mother, a frustrated actress, instilled starring aspirations in the skinny little Sofia (she was nicknamed *Stechetto*—the stick—at the time). When she was 14 she entered the first of several beauty contests in Naples and won the consolation title of "Princess of the Sea." Her mother then took her to Rome, where both appeared as extras in *Quo Vadis* (in 1949; the picture was released in 1951) and other films. She entered the Miss Italy beauty contest and again won a consolation title, "Miss Elegance." She earned a modest livelihood from small cash prizes she won along with the beauty titles and from modeling for illustrated pulp novels. She was not quite 15 when she met Carlo PONTI, the Italian producer, who was a judge on a panel of yet another beauty contest she entered and in which she was an also-ran. He signed her on a contract and began grooming her for a film career. He sent her to drama coaches and put her in films, at first in bit parts as Sofia Lazzaro, then gradually in more important roles under her present name.

By 1954 Miss Loren was an established star and began vying with Gina Lollobrigida for the attention of audiences on both sides of the Atlantic. Tall (5' 8") and statuesque, with facial features that are more sensuous than beautiful and an ample bosom that held special appeal for the American male, she was soon flooded with offers from Hollywood producers. After appearing in several American films shot overseas, she arrived in Hollywood in 1958, preceded by an enormous publicity campaign that heralded her emergence as a new sex goddess. But Hollywood misused its voluptuous new asset, vulgarizing her natural earthiness with artificial glamour treatment. With few exceptions she was sadly miscast in her American films, although she did win the Venice Festival acting award for her performance in *The Black Orchid.*

By 1961, Loren was back in Italy, giving the most memorable performance of her career in De Sica's *La Ciociara/Two Women.* She won Hollywood's Academy Award as well as the Cannes Festival Award and many other international citations for her powerful, tragic portrayal of a mother in war-ravaged

Italy. Her only subsequent exceptional roles were in two De Sica social comedies co-starring Marcello Mastroianni, *Yesterday, Today and Tomorrow* and *Marriage Italian Style.* She won the Moscow Festival acting award for the latter. All her American-sponsored films since 1960 have been made abroad.

Statuesque Loren and pint-sized Ponti, 24 years her senior, were married in 1957, following his Mexican divorce from his estranged wife. But the Italian law did not recognize the divorce and charged them with bigamy. They were forced to have their marriage annulled in 1962, and after four more years of frustration turned in their Italian passports and became citizens of France, where they were finally legally married in 1966. Their baby, Carlo Ponti, Jr., made a brief appearance in Loren's 1970 film *Sunflower.* Special Oscar in 1991 for lifetime achievement. Autobiography: *Sophia—Living and Loving: Her Own Story* (1979).

FILMS: As Sofia Scicolone or Sofia Lazzaro (in extra or bit roles)—*Cuori sul Mare* 1950; *Quo Vadis* (US), *Il Voto, Le Sei Mogli di Barbarlu', Io sono il Capatz, Milano Miliardaria, Anna, Il Mago per Forza* 1951; *Il Sogno di Zorro, E' arrivato l'Accordatore, Era lui si' si'* 1952. As Sophia Loren—*La Favorita, La Tratta delle Bianche/Girls Marked for Danger/The White Slave Trade* 1952; *Afica sotto i Mari/Woman of the Red Sea, Aïda* (title role), *Ci troviamo in Galleria, Carosello Neapolitano/Neapolitan Carousel Tempi Nostri/The Anatomy of Love, La Domenica della Buona Gente* 1953; *Il Paese dei Campanelli, Pellegrini d'Amore, Miseria e Nobilita', Due Notti con Cleopatra/Two Nights with Cleopatra* (dual role, one as Cleopatra), *Atilla, L'Oro di Napoli/Gold of Naples, Un Giorno in Pretura/A Day in Court* 1954; *La Donna del Fiume, Peccato che sia una Canaglia/Too Bad She's Bad, Il Segno di Venere/The Sign of Venus, La Bella Mugnaia/The Miller's Beautiful Wife, Pane Amore E. . . /Scandal in Sorrento* 1955; *La Fortuna di Essere Donna/Lucky to Be a Woman* 1956; *Boy on a Dolphin* (US), *The Pride and the Passion* (US), *Timbuctu/Legend of the Lost* (It./US) 1957; *Desire Under the Elms* (US), *The Key* (UK), *Houseboat* (US) 1958; *The Black Orchid* (US), *That Kind of Woman* (US) 1959; *Heller in Pink Tights* (US), *It Started in Naples* (US), *A Breath of Scandal* (US), *The Millionairess* (UK), *La Ciociara/Two Women* 1960; *El Cid* (US), *Madame Sans-Gëne/Madame* 1961; *Boccaccio '70, Le Couteau dans la Plaie/Five Miles to Midnight* (Fr./It./US), *I Sequestrati di Altona/The Condemned of Altona* 1962; *Ieri Oggi e Domani/Yesterday Today and Tomorrow* 1963; *The Fall of the Roman Empire* (US), *Matrimonio all'Italiana/Marriage Italian Style* 1964; *Operation Crossbow* (UK/It.), *Lady L* (It./Fr./US) 1965; *Judith* (US/Isr.), *Arabesque* (US/UK) 1966; *A Countess from Hong Kong* (UK), *C'era una Volta/More Than a Miracle/Cinderella Italian Style* 1967; *Questi Fantasmi/Ghosts Italian Style* 1968; *I Girasoli/Sunflower* 1969; *La Moglia del Prete/The Priest's Wife* 1970; *La Mortadella/Lady Liberty* 1971; *Man of La Mancha* (as Dulcinea; US) 1972; *Bianco Rosso e. . . /White Sister* 1973; *Il Viaggio/The Voyage* 1974; *Le Testament/The Verdict/Jury of One* (Fr.), *La Puppa del Gangster/Poopsie/Gun Moll* 1975; *The Cassandra Crossing* (US), *Una Giornata Speciale/A Special Day* (It./Can.) 1977; *Angela* (Can.), *Brass Target* (US), *Shimmy Lugano e Tarantelle e Vino* 1978; *Fatto di Sangue/Revenge, Firepower* (UK) 1979; *Sabato Domenica e unedi/Saturday, Sunday, and Monday* 1990; *Ready to Wear* 1994; *Grumpier Old Men* 1995; *Sun* 1997.

Lorentz, Pare. Documentary filmmaker. *b.* Dec. 11, 1905, Clarksburg, W.Va. *d.* 1992. *ed.* Wesleyan Coll. A former journalist and film critic, he was appointed in the early 30s as film advisor to Roosevelt's US Resettlement Administration. In that capacity Lorentz made two films that are considered prime works in the development of the American documentary, *The Plow That Broke the Plains* (1936) and *The River* (1937). The former dealt dramatically and lyrically with the New Deal's efforts to improve the lot of the farmers in the Oklahoma "Dust Bowl." *The River* was a poetic, rhythmically structured, panoramic history of the Mississippi Basin and its ecology showing the effects of soil erosion on the land. Both films were universally acclaimed and shown widely in motion picture theaters despite the opposition of the film industry, which protested against "government-sponsored competition." Lorentz wrote the treatment, but did not direct, for another important American documentary, *The City* (1939).

He organized and headed the US Film Service, through which he made his third highly acclaimed film, *The Fight for Life* (1940), an eloquent probe of the hazards of childbirth among the poor. The unit put out a number of other distinguished documentaries, but it was dissolved when Congress refused to furnish it with further funds. Lorentz produced a number of shorts for RKO in 1941 and for the armed forces during WW II. In 1946 he was appointed chief of the film section of the War Department's Civil Affairs Division, a post he resigned in 1947.

FILMS (as director-writer): *The Plow That Broke the Plains* 1936; *The River* 1937; *The City* (treatment only) 1939; *The Fight for Life* 1940.

Lorre, Peter. Actor. *b.* Laszlo Löwenstein, June 26, 1904, Rosenberg, Hungary. *d.* 1964. Formerly a bank clerk, he received stage training in Vienna and made his debut in Zurich. Despite seven years on stage in Switzerland, Austria, and Germany, and a couple of supporting parts in German films, he was virtually unknown when he was chosen by Fritz Lang to play the central character in his first sound film, *M* (1931). Lorre's portrayal of a psychopathic child murderer is among the most memorable in screen history. His melancholy expression, at once sinister and pathetic, his globular eyes bulging in fear as he is hunted down by both police and the underworld, give the character almost clinical authenticity. The worldwide success of *M* made Lorre internationally famous. He appeared in several other German films, but when the Nazis came to power in 1933 he exiled himself to Paris, London, and finally, in 1935, to Hollywood.

Lorre's first two American films offered him excellent roles. He was a love-crazed surgeon in Karl Freund's *Mad Love,* a remake of *The Hands of Orlac,* and a convincingly anguished Raskolnikov in Josef von Sternberg's *Crime and Punishment.* Later he played the title role of an Oriental detective in the low-budget "Mr. Moto" series, as well as other leads and supporting parts, typically as a mysterious, often quietly menacing, sad-eyed foreigner. Some of his best roles were in a succession of popular Warner Bros. dramas of the 40s (*The Maltese Falcon, Casablanca, The Mask of Dimitrios, Three Strangers, The Verdict,* etc.) in which his small frame provided an apt contrast to the bulk of Sydney GREENSTREET. In 1951, in Germany, Lorre scripted, directed, and starred in a rather remarkable film, *Der Verlorene/The Lost One,* made in a style reminiscent of the expressionism of German films of the early 20s. He then returned to Hollywood, where he resumed playing big and small character parts, memorably as a clown in *The Big Circus.* He died of a heart seizure.

FILMS: In Germany—*Pionier in Inoplastadt* 1928; *Frühlings Erwachen/The Awakening of Spring* 1929; *Die Koffer des Herrn O.F., M, Bomben auf Monte Carlo/Monte Carlo Madness* 1931; *F. P. 1 antwortet nicht, Schuss im Morgengrauen, Fünf von der Jazzband, Der Weisse Dämon* 1932; *Was Frauen träumen, Unsichtbare Gegner* 1933; *Du Haut en Bas* (Fr.), *The*

Man Who Knew Too Much (UK) 1934. In the US—*Mad Love, Crime and Punishment* (as Raskolnikov) 1935; *Secret Agent* (UK) 1936; *Crack-Up, Nancy Steele Is Missing, Think Fast Mr. Moto, Lancer Spy, Thank You Mr. Moto* 1937; *Mr. Moto in Danger Island, Mr. Moto's Gamble, Mr. Moto Takes a Chance, I'll Give a Million, Mysterious Mr. Moto of Devil's Island* 1938; *Mr. Moto's Last Warning, Mr. Moto Takes a Vacation* 1939; *Strange Cargo, I Was an Adventuress, Island of Doomed Men, Stranger on the Third Floor, You'll Find Out* 1940; *The Face Behind the Mask, Mr. District Attorney, They Met in Bombay, The Maltese Falcon* 1941; *All Through the Night, In This Our Life* (cameo), *The Boogie Man Will Get You, Invisible Agent, Casablanca* 1942; *The Constant Nymph, Background to Danger, The Cross of Lorraine* 1943; *Passage to Marseille, The Mask of Dimitrios, Arsenic and Old Lace, The Conspirators, Hollywood Canteen* 1944; *Hotel Berlin, Confidential Agent* 1945; *Three Strangers, Black Angel, The Chase, The Verdict, The Beast with Five Fingers* 1946; *My Favorite Brunette* 1947; *Casbah* 1948; *Rope of Sand* 1949; *Double Confession* (UK), *Quicksand* 1950; *Der Verlorene/The Lost One* (also dir., co-sc.; Ger.) 1951; *Beat the Devil* (UK/It.), *20,000 Leagues Under the Sea* 1954; *Congo Crossing, Meet Me in Las Vegas* (cameo), *Around the World in 80 Days* 1956; *The Buster Keaton Story, Silk Stockings, The Story of Mankind* (as Nero), *The Sad Sack, Hell Ship Mutiny* 1957; *The Big Circus* 1959; *Scent of Mystery* 1960; *Voyage to the Bottom of the Sea* 1961; *Tales of Terror, Five Weeks in a Balloon* 1962; *The Raven, The Comedy of Terrors/The Graveside Story* 1963; *Muscle Beach Party* (cameo), *The Patsy* 1964.

Losey, Joseph. Director. *b.* Jan. 14, 1909, La Crosse, Wis. *d.* 1984. *ed.* Dartmouth; Harvard. The son of a lawyer of Dutch extraction, he abandoned medical studies in favor of a stage career. In 1930 he was playing small parts on the New York stage and at the same time began writing play and book reviews for *The New York Times,* the *Herald Tribune,* and other publications. In 1932 he was the stage manager of the first live show ever produced at New York's Radio City Music Hall and later that year began directing and producing plays out of town. In 1935, during a European trip, he attended several of Eisenstein's film classes in Moscow.

Returning to New York, in 1936, Losey put together the celebrated 'Living Newspaper,' an innovative stage production strongly influenced by Brechtian ideas. In 1938 he made his first contact with film, as supervisor of some 60 documentary shorts for the Rockefeller Foundation. The following year he made his debut as film director with a marionette short for the petroleum industry which was shown at the New York World's Fair. Several other shorts followed. In the early 40s he directed radio dramas for NBC.

Returning from WW II service, Losey realized his most notable stage achievement in 1947, directing the much-praised production of Brecht's *Galileo Galilei,* starring Charles Laughton. In preparing the production, he worked closely with Brecht. As a result of this success, RKO's Dore SCHARY offered Losey the opportunity to direct his first feature film. From the start, Losey's pictures revealed a social concern and a nearly clinical interest in the study of characters under moral and physical duress. He made five Hollywood films at the remarkably efficient rate of three weeks per picture.

Losey was in Italy in 1951 shooting *Stranger on the Prowl,* an American/Italian co-production, when he learned that he had been summoned to testify before the House Un-American Activities Committee after being identified by a witness as a former Communist. Unwilling to interrupt his filming schedule, he returned to Hollywood after the completion of shooting, only to discover that he had been blacklisted by the industry in the interim. Unable to work in America, he settled in England. Even so, out of fear of jeopardizing the American market, he could not be given screen credit for his first two British-made features.

Losey's films of the British period crystallized his style and enhanced his international reputation. They also affirmed his inherent pessimism and continual preoccupation with human frailty and spiritual corruption, to which he now added a persistent interest in the British class system. Losey's reputation reached its peak with *The Servant* (1963), a meticulously crafted, superbly acted, metaphoric character study from a Harold PINTER script, that many consider the director's best achievement. He reached another landmark with *Accident* (1967), another Pinter collaboration remarkable for its stylized precision and multilayered complexity. The film shared the Special Jury Prize at the Cannes Festival. The intellectual cult that was growing around the director's works may have encouraged Losey to the brink of pretension, pomposity, and self-indulgence in his next three films. But he returned to top form with *The Go-Between* (1971), an enchantingly atmospheric period tragedy poignantly rooted in class injustice and a coming-of-age sensibility. Again benefiting from a superior Pinter script, the film won the Palme d'Or at Cannes. In 1976 Losey moved his base of operations to France, where he directed most of his remaining films. The most intriguing of these was *Mr. Klein* (1977), an opaque drama of dual identity involving a Gentile art dealer haunted by the vague presence of a Jewish namesake and alter-ego during the Nazi occupation of Paris. A passionate opera lover, Losey realized a lifelong dream when he directed a spectacular screen version of *Don Giovanni* in 1979. The following year he staged 'Boris Godunov' for the Paris Opera. The director's last few films were disappointing, but could not obliterate a superior body of work that assures him a place among cinema's great. Losey's first wife was writer and fashion designer Elizabeth Hawes; his second, Patricia Losey (née Mohan), collaborated on a couple of his scripts.

FILMS: Shorts—*Pete Roleum and His Cousins* (also prod., sc.) 1939; *A Child Went Forth, Youth Gets a Break* (both also sc.) 1941; *A Gun in His Hand* (for MGM's "Crime Does Not Pay" series) 1945. Features: In the US—*The Boy with Green Hair* 1948; *The Lawless* 1950; *M, The Prowler, The Big Night* (also co-sc.) 1951; *Stranger on the Prowl/Encounter/Imbarco a Mezzanotte* (also prod.; It./US) 1952. In the UK—*The Sleeping Tiger* 1954; *A Man on the Beach* (three-reeler) 1955; *The Intimate Stranger/A Finger of Guilt* 1956; *Time Without Pity* 1957; *The Gypsy and the Gentleman* 1958; *Blind Date/Chance Meeting* 1959; *The Criminal/The Concrete Jungle* 1960; *The Damned/These Are the Damned* 1961; *Eva/Eve* (Fr./It.) 1962; *The Servant* (also co-prod.) 1963; *King and Country* 1964; *Modesty Blaise* 1966; *Accident* 1967; *Secret Ceremony, Boom!* (UK/US) 1968; *Figures in a Landscape* 1970; *The Go-Between* 1971; *L'Assassinio di Trotsky/The Assassination of Trotsky* (It./Fr.) 1972; *A Doll's House* (also prod.) 1973; *Galileo* (also co-sc.; UK/US) 1974; *The Romantic Englishwoman* 1975; *Mr. Klein* (Fr.) 1977; *Les Routes du Sud/The Roads to the South* (also co-sc.; Fr.) 1978; *Don Giovanni* (also co-sc.; Fr./It./Ger.) 1979; *La Truite/The Trout* (also co-sc.; Fr.) 1982; *Steaming* 1985.

lot. An open area adjoining studio property, used for exterior filming and the construction of large sets and other production-related activities.

Louis, Jean. Costume designer. *b.* Oct. 5, 1907, in Paris. *d.* 1997. One of a handful of preeminent costume designers who defined Hollywood glamour. He was head designer at the fashion house of Hattie Carnegie for seven years before being named Chief Designer at Columbia Pictures. In later years, he moved to Universal, and, after that, to freelance work and his own company. His simple, sensuous designs helped to define three of the shapeliest actresses of the studio era, Rita Hayworth, Lana Turner, and Kim Novak. Among his more memorable designs were the young Turner's ubiquitous clinging sweater, the sexy interior decorator's wardrobe for Doris Day in *Pillow Talk*, and the slit strapless gown worn by Hayworth in *Gilda*. He won an Academy Award for costume design for *The Solid Gold Cadillac* and was nominated for ten other films, including *Born Yesterday*.

FILMS INCLUDE: *Strange Affair, Together Again* 1944; *Kiss and Tell, Over 21, Tonight and Every Night, Thousand and One Nights* 1945; *Gilda, Mr. District Attorney, One Way to Love, The Thrill of Brazil, Tomorrow Is Forever, The Jolson Story* 1946; *Down to Earth, Dead Reckoning, Johnny O'Clock* 1947; *The Lady from Shanghai, The Loves of Carmen* 1948; *Johnny Allegro, Jolson Sings Again, Knock on Any Door, Shockproof, Miss Grant Takes Richmond, Tokyo Joe* 1949; *In a Lonely Place, The Walking Hills, We Were Strangers, A Woman of Distinction* 1950; *Born Yesterday* 1951; *The Marrying Kind, Affair in Trinidad, Scandal Sheet* 1952; *The Big Heat, Miss Sadie Thompson, From Here to Eternity, Salome* 1953; *Phffft!, It Should Happen to You, A Star Is Born* 1954; *Picnic, Queen Bee* 1955; *The Eddy Duchin Story, You Can't Run Away from It, The Solid Gold Cadillac, Over-Exposed* 1956; *Jeanne Eagels, The Garment Jungle, The Brothers Rico, The Story of Esther Costello, Pal Joey, 3:10 to Yuma* 1957; *Bell Book and Candle* 1958; *Pillow Talk, The Last Angry Man, Imitation of Life, They Came to Cordura, Suddenly Last Summer* 1959; *Strangers When We Meet, Who Was That Lady* 1960; *Back Street, Judgment at Nuremberg* 1961; *If a Man Answers* 1962; *For Love or Money, The Thrill of It All* 1963; *Send Me No Flowers* 1964; *Mirage, Ship of Fools, Bus Riley's Back in Town* 1965; *Madame X, Gambit* 1966; *Guess Who's Coming to Dinner, Thoroughly Modern Millie* 1967; *P.J., Hell with Heroes* 1968; *House of Cards* 1969; *Waterloo* 1970; *Lost Horizon, Forty Carats* 1973.

Louise, Anita. Actress. *b.* Anita Louise Fremault, Jan. 9, 1915, New York City. *d.* 1970. A stage actress from early childhood, she made her screen debut at age seven, initially billed as Anita Fremault, and developed into a beautiful, angelic leading lady with natural golden hair, blue eyes, and a creamy complexion. In the 30s she was regarded as one of the prettiest and best-dressed stars in films and was voted in one poll as Hollywood's most beautiful actress. She appeared in a variety of films but expressed a preference for period and costume pictures. After retiring from movies, she starred in the 'My Friend Flicka' (1956–57) TV series and appeared in many other TV shows. The widow of producer Buddy ADLER, she married a businessman in 1962 and devoted much of her time to various philanthropic causes.

FILMS INCLUDE: As Anita Fremault—*Down to the Sea in Ships* 1922; *The Sixth Commandment* 1924; *The Music Master* 1927; *Four Devils, A Woman of Affairs* 1928; *The Spirit of Youth, Wonder of Woman* 1929. As Anita Louise—*Square Shoulders, The Marriage Playground* 1929; *The Floradora Girl, Just Like Heaven, The Third Alarm* 1930; *Millie, Everything's Rosie, Heaven on Earth/Mississippi* 1931; *The Phantom of Crestwood* 1932; *Our Betters* 1933; *Cross Streets, Are We Civilized?, I Give My Love, Judge Priest, Madame Du Barry* (as Marie Antoinette), *The Firebird* 1934; *Lady Tubbs, Here's to Romance, A Midsummer Night's Dream* (as Titania) 1935; *The Story of Louis Pasteur, Brides Are Like That, Anthony Adverse* (as Maria Bonnyfeather) 1936; *Green Light, Call It a Day, The Go Getter, That Certain Woman, First Lady, Tovarich* 1937; *My Bill, Marie Antoinette, The Sisters, Going Places* 1938; *The Little Princess, The Gorilla, These Glamour Girls, Main Street Lawyer, Reno* 1939; *Wagons Westward, Glamour for Sale, The Villain Still Pursued Her* 1940; *The Phantom Submarine, Harmon of Michigan* 1941; *Dangerous Blondes* 1943; *Casanova Brown* 1944; *Love Letters, The Fighting Guardsman* 1945; *The Bandit of Sherwood Forest, The Devil's Mask* 1946; *Bulldog Drummond at Bay* 1947; *Retreat Hell!* 1952.

Louise, Tina. Actress. Born Tina Blacker, on Feb. 11, 1934, in New York City. *ed.* Miami U.; Neighborhood Playhouse; Actors Studio. A former model and nightclub singer, she went to Hollywood after her success in the Broadway musical 'Li'l Abner' and has since played leads and second leads in a variety of films. Indelible as The Movie Star Ginger Grant on 'Gilligan's Island,' she was also seen in such TV fare as 'Mannix,' 'Ironside,' 'Kung Fu,' and 'Kojak.' She was married to radio-TV personality Les Crane.

FILMS INCLUDE: *God's Little Acre* 1958; *The Hangman, The Trap* 1959; *L'Assedio di Siracusa/The Siege of Syracuse* (It./Fr.) *Saffo—Venere di Lesbo/The Warrior Empress* (as Sappho; It./Fr.) 1960; *Armored Command* 1961; *For Those Who Think Young* 1964; *The Wrecking Crew, How to Commit Marriage, The Good Guys and the Bad Guys, The Happy Ending* 1969; *The Stepford Wives* 1975; *Mean Dog Blues* 1978; *Canicule/Dog Day* (Fr.) 1984; *Evils of the Night* (release delayed from 1983) 1985; *O.C. and Stiggs* 1987; *Dixie Lanes* 1988; *The Pool, Johnny Suede, Miloha* 1991.

Lourié, Eugène. Art director, director. *b.* 1905, Russia. *d.* 1991. In France from 1921, he was a painter and ballet set designer before becoming one of France's leading art directors in the mid-30s. He is best known for his designs for the films of Jean RENOIR, whom he followed to Hollywood in the early 40s. His ability to combine design with special effects was to serve him well as the director of several science-fiction films in the 50s. He appeared as an actor in *Breathless* (1983).

FILMS INCLUDE: As art director: In France—*Madame Bovary* (co-art dir.) 1934; *Sous les Yeux d'Occident/Razumov, Les Bas-Fonds/The Lower Depths* (co-art dir.) 1936; *L'Alibi, La Grande Illusion/Grand Illusion* 1937; *L'Affaire Lafarge, La Tragédie impériale/Rasputin, Werther* (co-art dir.), *La Bête humaine/The Human Beast* 1938; *La Règle du Jeu/The Rules of the Game* (co-art dir.) 1939; *Sans Lendemain* (co-art dir.) 1940. In the US—*This Land Is Mine* (assoc. prod. only), *Sahara* 1943; *The Southerner, Uncle Harry* 1945; *Diary of a Chambermaid* 1946; *The Long Night, Song of Scheherazade* 1947; *A Woman's Vengeance* 1948; *The River* (co-art dir.) 1951; *Limelight* 1952; *So This Is Paris* 1954; *Confessions of an Opium Eater* (also co-assoc. prod.) 1961; *Shock Corridor* 1963; *Flight from Ashiya* (US/Jap.), *The Naked Kiss* 1964; *Crack in the World* (also special effects dir.) 1965; *Battle of the Bulge* 1966; *Bikini Paradise* 1967; *Custer of the West* (co-art dir.) 1968; *Krakatoa East of Java* (also special effects dir.), *The Royal Hunt of the Sun* 1969; *What's the Matter with Helen?* 1971; *Burnt Offering* 1976; *An Enemy of the People* 1978. As director (complete)—*The Beast from 20,000 Fathoms* 1953; *The Colossus of New York* 1958; *Behemoth—The Sea Monster/The Giant Behemoth* (co-dir. with Douglas Hickox; also sc.; UK) 1959; *Gorgo* (also co-story; UK) 1961.

Love, Bessie. Actress. *b.* Juanita Horton, Sept. 10, 1898, Midland, Tex. *d.* 1986. She entered films in 1915 while still a pupil at a Los Angeles high school. The following year she began showing great promise as a leading lady, notably opposite William S. Hart in *The Aryan* and Douglas Fairbanks in *Reggie Mixes In,* and was featured as the Bride of Cana in the Judean episode of Griffith's *Intolerance.* She was sweet, demure, spirited, and very pretty, but she found top stardom continuously elusive. Her career consisted of occasional peaks and frequent declines. Producers could never make up their minds how to type her. Early in her career she was a sweet-16 heroine; in the early 20s she played serious leading ladies in melodramas. In the late 20s she was seen mostly in light films (she introduced the Charleston to the screen in *The King of Main Street* in 1925).

Of Miss Love's many "comebacks" the most sensational was in 1929 with the switch to sound, when she proved herself to be a highly gifted song-and-dance star in the early talkie musical *The Broadway Melody,* for which performance she was nominated for an Oscar. She was once again very popular but soon after retired from the screen. Also in 1929 she married director William (Bill) Hawks. They divorced in 1935 and she never remarried. In 1931 she appeared at the New York Palace and in 1935 settled in London. She gave many performances in British plays and films, as well as on radio and TV. She also wrote several plays, including 'Homecoming' (1958). Among her late screen appearances was that in *The Loves of Isadora* (1969), in which she played Vanessa Redgrave's mother. In 1972–73 she scored a success in London as Aunt Pittypat in a stage version of 'Gone With the Wind.' She continued appearing sporadically in films through the early 80s.

FILMS INCLUDE: *The Birth of a Nation* (participation as extra unconfirmed) 1915; *The Flying Torpedo, The Aryan, The Good Bad Man, Acquitted, Reggie Mixes In, Stranded, Hell-to-Pay Austin, Intolerance* (as the Bride of Cana in the Judean episode), *A Sister of Six* 1916; *Nina the Flower Girl, A Daughter of the Poor, The Sawdust Ring, Wee Lady Betty, Polly Ann, Cheerful Givers* 1917; *The Great Adventure, How Could You Caroline?, The Little Sister of Everybody, The Dawn of Understanding* 1918; *The Enchanted Barn, The Yankee Princess, The Little Boss, Cupid Forecloses, Carolyn of the Corners* 1919; *Pegeen, Bonnie May* 1920; *Penny of Top Hill Trail, The Swamp, The Sea Lion* 1921; *The Vermilion Pencil, Forget-Me-Not, Bulldog Courage, The Village Blacksmith, Deserted at the Altar* 1922; *Human Wreckage, The Eternal Three, St. Elmo, Slave of Desire, Gentle Julia* 1923; *Torment, Those Who Dance, The Silent Watcher, Sundown, Tongues of Flame* 1924; *The Lost World, Soul-Fire, A Son of His Father, The King on Main Street* 1925; *The Song and Dance Man, Lovey Mary, Young April, Going Crooked* 1926; *Rubber Tires, Dress Parade, A Harp in Hock* 1927; *The Matinee Idol, Sally of the Scandals* (as Sally Rand), *Anybody Here Seen Kelly?* 1928; *The Broadway Melody, The Hollywood Revue, The Idle Rich, The Girl in the Show* 1929; *Chasing Rainbows, Conspiracy, Good News, See America Thirst* 1930; *Morals for Women* 1931; *Atlantic Ferry* (UK) 1941; *Journey Together* (UK) 1945; *The Barefoot Contessa* 1954; *Touch and Go* (UK) 1955; *The Story of Esther Costello* (UK) 1957; *Next to No Time* (UK) 1958; *The Greengage Summer/Loss of Innocence* (UK), *The Roman Spring of Mrs. Stone* (US/UK) 1961; *Children of the Damned* (UK) 1964; *The Wild Affair* (UK) 1965; *Promise Her Anything* (UK) 1966; *Battle Beneath the Earth* (UK/US), *The Loves of Isadora* (UK), *On Her Majesty's Secret Service* (UK) 1969; *Sunday Bloody Sunday* (UK), *Catlow* (UK/Sp.) 1971; *Vampyres* 1975; *The Ritz* 1976; *Gulliver's Travels* (v/o; UK/Bel.) 1977; *L'Amant de Lady Chatterley/Lady Chatterley's Lover* (Fr./UK), *Ragtime, Reds* 1981; *The Hunger* 1983.

Love, Montagu(e). Actor. *b.* 1877, Portsmouth, England. *d.* 1943. Along with Noah BEERY, Sr., he was the silent screen's most notorious villain. A former London newspaper illustrator and stage actor, he came to the US in 1913 and soon after began playing character roles in films. He reached his peak in costume adventures of the late 20s as the cruel opponent of such heroes as Rudolph Valentino and John Barrymore. His villainy was less pronounced in scores of subsequent talkies. In all he appeared in hundreds of films.

FILMS INCLUDE: *Hearts in Exile, A Royal Family* 1915; *A Woman's Way, The Gilded Cage, Bought and Paid For, Friday the 13th, The Challenge* 1916; *The Brand of Satan, Rasputin the Black Monk* (title role), *The Awakening* 1917; *The Cross-Bearer, Vengeance, The Grouch* 1918; *The Hand Invisible, Three Green Eyes, To Him That Hath, A Broadway Saint, Rough Neck, The Steel King* 1919; *The World and His Wife* 1920; *Shams of Society, Forever/Peter Ibbetson* (as Col. Roger Ibbetson), *Love's Redemption* 1921; *The Beauty Shop, The Streets of Paris* 1922; *The Leopardess* 1923; *The Eternal City, Roulette, A Son of the Sahara* (dual role), *Love of Women, Sinners in Heaven* 1924; *Out of the Storm, The Social Highwayman, The Son of the Sheik, Don Juan* 1926; *The Night of Love, The King of Kings, Rose of the Golden West, Jesse James, The Haunted Ship* 1927; *The Devil's Skipper, The Noose, The Wind, The Haunted House* 1928; *The Last Warning, The Synthetic Sin, The Divine Lady, Midstream, Bulldog Drummond, Her Private Life, The Mysterious Island* 1929; *A Notorious Affair, Back Pay, Outward Bound, Kismet, Reno, The Cat Creeps* 1930; *Alexander Hamilton* (as Thomas Jefferson) 1931; *Vanity Fair, Stowaway, The Silver Lining* 1932; *His Double Life, Limehouse Blues* 1934; *Clive of India, The Crusades, The Man Who Broke the Bank at Monte Carlo* 1935; *The Country Doctor, Sutter's Gold, The White Angel, Sing Baby Sing, Lloyds of London* 1936; *One in a Million, The Prince and the Pauper* (as Henry VIII), *Parnell* (as Gladstone), *The Life of Emile Zola, The Prisoner of Zenda* (as Detchard), *A Damsel in Distress, Tovarich* 1937; *The Buccaneer, The Adventures of Robin Hood, Kidnapped, Professor Beware, If I Were King* 1938; *Gunga Din, Juarez, The Man in the Iron Mask, Rulers of the Sea, We Are Not Alone* 1939; *The Lone Wolf Strikes, Dr. Ehrlich's Magic Bullet, Northwest Passage, All This and Heaven Too, The Sea Hawk* (as King Philip II of Spain), *The Mark of Zorro, North West Mounted Police, The Son of Monte Cristo, A Dispatch from Reuters* 1940; *Hudson's Bay, The Devil and Miss Jones* 1941; *The Remarkable Andrew* (as George Washington), *Tennessee Johnson* (as Chief Justice Salmon Chase) 1942; *The Constant Nymph, Holy Matrimony* 1943; *Devotion* (release delayed) 1946.

Lovejoy, Frank. Actor. *b.* Mar. 28, 1914, the Bronx, N.Y. *d.* 1962. A former stage player and radio star, he entered films in the late 40s and subsequently played leads and solid supporting roles in many productions, typically portraying determined, dependable characters.

FILMS INCLUDE: *Black Bart* 1948; *Home of the Brave* 1949; *In a Lonely Place, Three Secrets, Breakthrough, The Sound of Fury* 1950; *I Was a Communist for the FBI, Try and Get Me, Goodbye My Fancy, Force of Arms, I'll See You in My Dreams* 1951; *Retreat Hell!, The Winning Team* 1952; *She's Back on Broadway, The Hitch-Hiker, The System, House of Wax, The Charge at Feather River* 1953; *Beachhead, Men of the Fighting Lady* 1954; *Strategic Air Command, Mad at the World, The Americano, Finger Man, The Crooked Web, Shack Out on 101* 1955; *Julie* 1956; *Three Brave Men* 1957; *Cole Younger—Gunfighter* 1958.

Lovitz, Jon. Actor. Born on July 21, 1957, in Tarzana, Calif. *ed.* U. of Calif., Irvine; Film Actors Workshop. Expressive, off-the-wall comic actor in supporting roles. He started as an improvisational comedian with the Groundlings Sunday Company in Los Angeles. In 1985, he joined the cast of television's 'Saturday Night Live', where he perfected such characters as the Pathological Liar and Annoying Man. His talents have yet to be fully tapped in his film roles.

FILMS INCLUDE: *Last Resort, Ratboy, Jumpin' Jack Flash, Three Amigos!* 1986; *The Brave Little Toaster* (v/o) 1987; *Big, My Stepmother Is an Alien* 1988; *Mr. Destiny* 1990; *An American Tail: Fievel Goes West* (v/o) 1991; *A League of Their Own, Mom and Dad Save the World* 1992; *City Slickers II: The Legend of Curly's Gold, North, Trapped in Paradise* 1994; *The Great White Hype, High School High* 1996; *Liar Liar* 1997.

Low, Warren. Film editor. *b.* Aug. 12, 1905, Pittsburgh. *d.* 1989. He entered films in 1919 as a juvenile player but later gravitated toward lab work. After a four-year stint (1924–28) with the Marines in China and the Philippines, he returned to Hollywood and joined Warner Bros. as an assistant editor in 1930. Turning full editor in 1936, he was responsible for the cutting of many major productions at Warners, and later at Paramount, winning four Oscar nominations in the process.

FILMS INCLUDE: *The White Angel* 1936; *The Great Garrick, The Life of Emile Zola* 1937; *The Amazing Dr. Clitterhouse, Jezebel, The Sisters* 1938; *Juarez, We Are Not Alone* 1939; *All This and Heaven Too, A Dispatch from Reuters, Dr. Ehrlich's Magic Bullet* 1940; *Shining Victory* 1941; *Now Voyager* 1942; *Princess O'Rourke* 1943; *Johnny O'Clock, Desert Fury* 1947; *Sorry, Wrong Number* 1948; *Rope of Sand* 1949; *Dark City, September Affair* 1950; *Peking Express, Sailor Beware* 1951; *Come Back, Little Sheba* 1952; *The Caddy* 1953; *About Mrs. Leslie* 1954; *Artists and Models, The Rose Tattoo* 1955; *The Bad Seed, The Rainmaker* 1956; *Gunfight at the O.K. Corral* 1957; *King Creole* 1958; *Career* 1959; *G.I. Blues* 1960; *Summer and Smoke* 1961; *Wives and Lovers* 1963; *The Sons of Katie Elder, Boeing Boeing* 1965; *Five Card Stud, Will Penny* 1968; *True Grit* 1969; *Willard* 1971.

low-angle shot. A shot taken from a low camera setup with the camera tilted upward. Often used for dramatic impact because it makes people and objects seem tall and overpowering.

low key. The effect of keeping a scene or the tonal range of the subjects in a scene predominantly at the dark end of the gray scale. Low-key lighting utilizes dim illumination and deep shadows to produce a "dense" atmosphere and mysterious, dramatic effects.

Lowe, Edmund. Actor. *b.* Mar. 3, 1890, San Jose, Calif. *d.* 1971. *ed.* Santa Clara U. A judge's son, he taught school briefly before beginning acting with a Los Angeles stock company. Following a stint on Broadway, he entered films in 1917. Typically cast as a suave romantic lead with a waxed mustache, he scored his most memorable screen triumph when he was cast against character as the roughneck Sergeant Quirt in the silent version of *What Price Glory* (1926). Following the success of that film, he was cast in similar raucous roles in a series of adventure films co-starring Victor McLaglen. He subsequently played both drawing-room Romeos and two-fisted heroes in scores of silent and sound films through the late 50s. The second of his three wives was actress Lilyan Tashman.

FILMS INCLUDE: *The Wild Olive* 1915; *The Spreading Dawn* 1917; *The Reason Why, Vive la France!* 1918; *Eyes of Youth* 1919; *The Woman Gives, Madonnas and Men* 1920; *My Lady's Latchkey, The Devil* 1921; *Peacock Alley, Living Lies* 1922; *The White Flower, The Silent Command, In the Palace of the King* 1923; *Nellie the Beautiful Cloak Model, Barbara Frietchie, Honor Among Men* 1924; *Ports of Call, East of Suez, Marriage in Transit, The Kiss Barrier, East Lynne, The Fool* 1925; *Soul Mates, The Palace of Pleasure, Siberia, Black Paradise, What Price Glory* 1926; *Is Zat So?, Publicity Madness, The Wizard* 1927; *Dressed to Kill, Happiness Ahead, Outcast* 1928; *In Old Arizona, Thru Different Eyes, The Cock-Eyed World, This Thing Called Love* 1929; *Born Reckless, The Bad One, Good Intentions, Scotland Yard* (in dual role) 1930; *Men on Call, Don't Bet on Women, Women of All Nations, Transatlantic, The Spider, The Cisco Kid* 1931; *The Misleading Lady, Attorney for the Defense, Guilty as Hell, Chandu the Magician* (title role), *The Devil Is Driving* 1932; *Hot Pepper, I Love That Man, Her Bodyguard, Dinner at Eight* 1933; *Bombay Mail, No More Women, Gift of Gab* 1934; *Best Man Wins, Under Pressure, The Great Hotel Murder, Mr. Dynamite, Black Sheep, King Solomon of Broadway, Grand Exit, The Great Impersonation* (in dual role) 1935; *The Garden Murder Case, Seven Sinners, Mad Holiday* 1936; *Under Cover of Night, Espionage, Murder on Diamond Row* 1937; *Every Day's a Holiday, Secrets of a Nurse* 1938; *Newsboys' Home, The Witness Vanishes* 1939; *Honeymoon Deferred, Wolf of New York, The Crooked Road, I Love You Again, Men Against the Sky* 1940; *Double Date* 1941; *Call Out the Marines* 1942; *Murder in Times Square, Dangerous Blondes* 1943; *The Girl in the Case* 1944; *Dillinger, The Enchanted Forest* 1945; *Good Sam* 1948; *The Wings of Eagles* 1957; *The Last Hurrah* 1958; *Heller in Pink Tights* 1960.

Lowe, Rob. Actor. Born on Mar. 17, 1964, in Charlottesville, Va. Pretty-boy handsome leading man of Hollywood films. Only four when his parents divorced, he moved with his mother and stepfather to Los Angeles, where he began acting at age eight. He had an early start in two after-school specials and in 1979–80 appeared regularly in the series 'A New Kind of Family.' Making his big-screen debut in 1983, he rapidly became established as one of the most popular of the "Brat Pack," the young new male faces that descended on the Hollywood scene in the early 80s. In 1989 he faced a threat to his career when the mother of a teenage girl accused him in a civil law suit in Atlanta of using his celebrity to induce her daughter into performing sex acts that the star videotaped. But Lowe resumed his career successfully in 1990, following a compromise sentence that saw him perform community service for two years. In 1991 he married makeup artist Shirley Birkhoff. His younger brother, Chad Lowe (*b.* Jan. 15, 1968, Dayton, Ohio), is an Emmy-winning TV actor and sometime film actor.

FILMS: *The Outsiders, Class* 1983; *The Hotel New Hampshire, Oxford Blues* 1984; *St. Elmo's Fire* 1985; *Youngblood, About Last Night. . .* 1986; *Square Dance* 1987; *Masquerade, Illegally Yours* 1988; *Stroke of Midnight, Bad Influence* 1990; *Wayne's World, The Finest Hour* 1992; *Tommy Boy* (unbilled) 1995; *Mulholland Falls* (unbilled) 1996; *Contact* 1997.

Lowell, Carey. Actress. Born in 1961, near New York City. *ed.* U. of Colorado; NYU. Tall (nearly six feet), sultry leading lady. A geologist's daughter, she moved around extensively as a child, living for stretches in Europe, the Middle East, and several American states, before the family settled down in Morrison, Colorado. While still in high school, she embarked on a modeling career, reaching the top levels of the profession by her late teens. Movies followed, including a career-boosting role in a James Bond spectacle. In 1989 she married one of her co-stars, Griffin Dunne.

FILMS: *Dangerously Close, Club Paradise* 1986; *Down Twisted/The Treasure of San Lucas* 1987; *License to Kill, Me and Him* 1989; *The Guardian* 1990; *Road to Ruin* 1991.

Lowery, Robert. Actor. *b.* Robert Lowery Hanke, 1914, Kansas City, Mo. *d.* 1971. Originally a band vocalist and stage performer, he was the hero of numerous low-budget action pictures and played supporting parts in many other films. His main claim to nostalgic fame is in the role of Batman in the 1949 serial. His three marriages included that (1951–57) to actress Jean PARKER.

FILMS INCLUDE: *Great Guy* 1936; *Wake Up and Live* 1937; *Alexander's Ragtime Band, Submarine Patrol* 1938; *Young Mr. Lincoln, Hollywood Cavalcade, Drums Along the Mohawk* 1939; *Four Sons, Maryland, The Mark of Zorro* 1940; *Criminal Investigator* 1942; *The Immortal Sergeant, The North Star, Revenge of the Zombies* 1943; *Mystery of the River Boat* (serial), *The Mummy's Ghost* 1944; *Road to Alcatraz, Fashion Model* 1945; *They Made Me a Killer, House of Horrors* 1946; *Danger Street, I Cover the Big Town* 1947; *Heart of Virginia* 1948; *Batman and Robin* (serial; as Batman), *New Adventures of Batman* (serial; as Batman), *The Dalton Gang* 1949; *Border Rangers* 1950; *Jalopy* 1953; *The Rise and Fall of Legs Diamond* 1960; *McLintock* 1963; *Johnny Reno* 1966; *The Ballad of Josie* 1968.

Loy, Myrna. Actress. *b.* Myrna Adele Williams, on Aug. 2, 1905, in Raidersburg, near Helena, Mont. *d.* 1993. The daughter of a cattleman and a former member of the Montana legislature, she grew up in Helena, where she made her first public appearance at 12 as a dancer in a benefit show. When her father died in the 1918 flu epidemic, the family moved to Los Angeles, where she attended high school and occasionally taught dancing. At 18 she joined the chorus line in the prefeature live show at Grauman's Chinese Theater in Hollywood and began making the rounds of studio casting departments. Valentino gave her a screen test, but it was unsuccessful. Soon after, however, she began getting bit parts in films. She was considered for the role of the Madonna in *Ben-Hur,* but it was assigned to Betty Bronson and instead Miss Loy was cast in the part of a hedonist mistress. Before long she was typecast as an exotic vamp, often Oriental, always mysterious. For nearly ten years, in more than 60 films, she rarely stepped out of character.

Although she played increasingly more important parts, often leads, Miss Loy's career seemed doomed to mediocrity, when, in 1934, director W. S. VAN DYKE decided to try her out in a comedy role, opposite William POWELL, in his lighthearted adaptation of Dashiell Hammett's mystery novel *The Thin Man.* The result was sheer delight. The public took immediately to Loy's new image as a bubbly, sophisticated "perfect wife." MGM responded with several sequels featuring Powell and Loy as Nick and Nora Charles and teamed them in several other films. Loy's popularity soared. By 1936 she was Hollywood's number one feminine box-office attraction.

After Pearl Harbor, Miss Loy took a leave of absence from films and except for one wartime picture devoted all her energies to the Red Cross. She later divided her time between films and activity as a US representative with UNESCO. Her most important postwar film was *The Best Years of Our Lives,* in which she played Fredric March's wife. She continued in sizeable roles until the mid-50s, after which she played occasional character parts. She also appeared on TV and on stage and in 1973 made her Broadway debut in a revival of 'The Women.' She became active in the Democratic Party and in 1967 campaigned hard for the presidential nomination of Eugene McCarthy. Tributes to her achievements as an actress and screen personality were many. In 1985, and again in 1987, the Motion Picture Academy paid her homage in New York City gala events. In 1987 a theater was named after her in her hometown of Helena, Montana. In 1988 she was saluted by the John F. Kennedy Center for the Performing Arts. Miss Loy, who never won an Oscar, and had never been nominated for one, received a special honorary Academy Award during the Oscar ceremony of 1991. In that year she donated her private papers to Boston University's 20th Century Archives. Autobiography: *Myrna Loy: Being and Becoming* (1987). Miss Loy was married four times, (1) producer Arthur HORNBLOW, Jr. (1936–42); (2) car-rental heir John Hertz, Jr. (1942–44); (3) producer-screenwriter Gene MARKEY (1946–50); Deputy Assistant Secretary of State (to Dean Acheson) Howland Sergeant (1951–60).

FILMS: *Pretty Ladies* (bit) 1925; *Ben-Hur* (bit), *The Cave Man, The Gilded Highway, Across the Pacific, Why Girls Go Back Home, Don Juan, The Exquisite Sinner, So This Is Paris* 1926; *Finger Prints, Ham and Eggs at the Front, Bitter Apples, The Heart of Maryland, The Jazz Singer, If I Were Single, The Climbers, Simple Sis, A Sailor's Sweetheart, The Girl from Chicago* 1927; *What Price Beauty, Beware of Married Men, Turn Back the Hours, The Crimson City, Pay As You Enter, State Street Sadie, The Midnight Taxi* 1928; *Noah's Ark, Fancy Baggage, The Desert Song, The Black Watch, The Squall, Hardboiled Rose, Evidence, The Show of Shows, The Great Divide* 1929; *Cameo Kirby, Isle of Escape, Under a Texas Moon, Cock o' the Walk, Bride of the Regiment, Last of the Duanes, Renegades, The Jazz Cinderella, The Truth About Youth, The Devil to Pay, Rogue of the Rio Grande* 1930; *Body and Soul, The Naughty Flirt, A Connecticut Yankee* (as Morgan le Fay), *Hush Money, Transatlantic, Rebound, Skyline, Consolation Marriage, Arrowsmith* (as Joyce Lanyon) 1931; *Emma, The Wet Parade, Vanity Fair, The Woman in Room 13, New Morals for Old, Love Me Tonight, Thirteen Women, The Mask of Fu Manchu, The Animal Kingdom* 1932; *Topaze, The Barbarian, When Ladies Meet, Penthouse, Night Flight, The Prizefighter and the Lady* 1933; *Men in White, Manhattan Melodrama, The Thin Man, Stamboul Quest, Evelyn Prentice, Broadway Bill* 1934; *Wings in the Dark, Whipsaw* 1935; *Wife vs. Secretary, Petticoat Fever, The Great Ziegfeld* (as Billie Burke), *To Mary—With Love, Libeled Lady, After the Thin Man* 1936; *Parnell, Double Wedding* 1937; *Man-Proof, Test Pilot, Too Hot to Handle* 1938; *Lucky Night, The Rains Came, Another Thin Man* 1939; *I Love You Again, Third Finger Left Hand* 1940; *Love Crazy, Shadow of the Thin Man* 1941; *The Thin Man Goes Home* 1944; *So Goes My Love, The Best Years of Our Lives* 1946; *The Bachelor and the Bobby-Soxer, The Senator Was Indiscreet* (cameo), *Song of the Thin Man* 1947; *Mr. Blandings Builds His Dream House* 1948; *The Red Pony, That Dangerous Age/If This Be Sin* (UK) 1949; *Cheaper by the Dozen* 1950; *Belles on Their Toes* 1952; *The Ambassador's Daughter* 1956; *Lonelyhearts* 1959; *From the Terrace, Midnight Lace* 1960; *The April Fools* 1969; *Airport 1975* 1974; *The End* (cameo) 1978; *Just Tell Me What You Want* 1980.

Loy, Nanni. Director. Born on Oct. 23, 1925, in Cagliari, Sardinia, Italy. He entered films after a course in documentary production at the Centro Sperimentale di Cinematografia in Rome as an assistant to such directors as ALESSANDRINI, ZAMPA, and GENINA. Piloted two documentaries before his debut as a feature director in 1957. He came into prominence with *The Four Days of Naples* (1962), a film noted for its realistic re-creation of WW II events. His feature film output is sparse, but he has worked frequently for Italian TV and has taught directing at the Centro Sperimentale.

FEATURE FILMS: *Parola di Ladro, Il Marito* (both co-dir. with Gianni Puccini; also co-story, co-sc.) 1957; *Audace Colpo dei Soliti Ignoti/Fiasco in Milan* (also co-sc.) 1959; *Un Giorno da Leoni* (also co-story, co-sc.) 1961; *Le Quattro Giornate di Napoli/The Four Days of Naples* (also co-story, co-sc.) 1962; *Made in Italy* (also co-sc.) 1965; *Il Padre di Famiglia/The Head of the Family* (also co-story, co-sc.) 1967; *L'Inferno del Deserto* (also co-sc.) 1969; *Rosolino Paterno—Soldato/Situation Normal All Fouled Up/Operation Snafu* (also co-sc.) 1970; *Detenuto in attesta di Giudizio/Why* 1971; *Sistemo l'America et torno/Black Is Beautiful* 1973; *La Goduria, Signore e Signori Buonanotte* (co-dir.), *Quelle Strane Occasioni* ("Italian Superman" episode; uncredited) 1976; *Il Caffè è un piacere. . . se non è buono che piacere è?* 1978; *Insieme* 1979 *Caffe Express* 1980; *Scugnizzi* 1989.

LS. Abbreviation for LONG SHOT.

Lualdi, Antonella. Actress. Born Antoinetta De Pascale, on July 6, 1931, in Beirut, Lebanon, to an Italian father and a Greek mother. A talented leading lady of uncommon beauty, she was seen to advantage in numerous Italian and French films of the 50s and 60s. She is married to Franco INTERLENGHI.

FILMS INCLUDE: *Signorinella* 1949; *E più Facile che un Cammello/His Last Twelve Hours* 1950; *Tre Storie proibite/ hree Forbidden Stories, Il Cappotto/The Overcoat, Adorable Créatures/Adorable Creatures* (Fr./It.) 1952; *La Figlia del Regimento* 1953; *Cronache di Poveri Amanti, Casta Diva, Le Rouge et le Noir* (as Mathilde de la Mole; Fr./It.) 1954; *Gli Innamorati/Wild Love, Andrea Chenier* 1955; *Padri e Figli/ Fathers and Sons* 1956; *Méfiez-vous Fillettes/Young Girls Beware* (Fr.) 1957; *Giovani Mariti, Une Vie/End of Desire* 1958; *J'irai cracher sur vos Tombes/I Spit on Your Grave* (Fr.), *La Notte Brava/On Any Street/Bad Girls Don't Cry, A Double Tour/Leda* (Fr./It.) 1959; *Via Margutta/Run with the Devil* 1960; *I Mongoli/The Mongols* 1961; *Il Disordine/Disorder, Arrivano i Titani/My Son the Hero* 1962; *Se Permettete—parliamo di Donne/Let's Talk About Women* 1964; *Bel Ami 2000/How to Seduce a Playboy* (Aus./It./Fr.) 1966; *Vincent François Paul et les autres* (Fr.) 1975; *Non Sparate sui Bambini* 1978; *La Cage aux Folles III ("Elles" se marient)/La Cage aux Folles 3: The Wedding* (Fr./It.) 1985.

Lubin, Arthur. Director. *b.* July 25, 1901, in Los Angeles. *d.* 1995. A graduate of Carnegie Tech, he began in films in the mid-20s as an actor and appeared in such productions as *The Woman on the Jury* (1924), *His People* (1925), *Bardelys the Magnificent* (1926), *Afraid to Love* (1927), *Times Square* (1929), and *Eyes of the Underworld* (1929). He turned to directing in 1934 and subsequently ground out numerous lightweight Hollywood films, mostly for Universal, including many Abbott and Costello comedies, several "Francis, the Talking Mule" episodes, and such high-camp items as *Ali Baba and the 40 Thieves* (1944) and *The Spider Woman Strikes Back* (1946). His films were typically escapist fare, often based on infantile scripts, but he handled them all with a sure-handed, if uninspired, nuts-and-bolts efficiency. His most ambitious and most successful assignment was the 1943 version of *The Phantom of the Opera,* with Claude Rains in the title role. From the late 50s he worked mostly for TV, directing episodes for a number of action series and producing and directing the entire output of the 'Mr. Ed' series.

FILMS: *A Successful Failure* 1934; *Great God Gold, Honeymoon Limited, Two Sinners, Frisco Waterfront* 1935; *The House of a Thousand Candles, Yellowstone* 1936; *Mysterious Crossing, California Straight Ahead, I Cover the War, Idol of the Crowd, Adventure's End* 1937; *Midnight Intruder, Beloved Brat, Prison Break, Secrets of a Nurse* 1938; *Risky Business, Big Town Czar, Mickey the Kid, Call a Messenger* 1939; *The Big Guy, Black Friday, Gangs of Chicago, I'm Nobody's Sweetheart Now, Meet the Wildcat, Who Killed Aunt Maggie?* 1940; *San Francisco Docks, Where Did You Get That Girl?, Buck Privates, In The Navy, Hold That Ghost, Keep 'Em Flying* 1941; *Ride 'Em Cowboy, Eagle Squadron* 1942; *White Savage, The Phantom of the Opera* 1943; *Ali Baba and the 40 Thieves* 1944; *Delightfully Dangerous* 1945; *The Spider Woman Strikes Back, Night in Paradise* 1946; *New Orleans* 1947; *Impact* 1949; *Francis* 1950; *Queen for a Day, Francis Goes to the Races, Rhubarb* 1951; *Francis Goes to West Point, It Grows on Trees* 1952; *South Sea Woman, Francis Covers the Big Town* 1953; *Francis Joins the Wacs* 1954; *Francis in the Navy, Footsteps in the Fog, Lady Godiva* 1955; *Star of India, The First Traveling Saleslady* 1956; *Escapade in Japan* (also prod.) 1957; *Il Ladro di Bagdad/The Thief of Baghdad (It./Fr.)* 1961; *The Incredible Mr. Limpet* 1964; *Hold On!* 1966; *Rain for a Dusty Summer* 1971.

Lubin, Sigmund ("Pop"). Pioneer film executive. *b.* 1851, Breslau, Germany. *d.* 1923. Trained as an optician, he immigrated to the US in the mid-1870s. After an abortive adventure gold prospecting and a stab at a variety of other occupations, he peddled eyeglasses in Philadelphia. His knowledge of optics and interest in photography brought him into the motion picture business in its infancy. As early as 1897 he produced and sold for peep-show exhibition an assortment of short subjects, including a pillow fight between his two daughters. Competing with Edison for the still tiny market, the enterprising Lubin scored a coup by re-creating the 1897 Corbett-Fitzsimmons prizefight using two freight handlers from the Pennsylvania Railroad.

Surviving a patent lawsuit by Edison in 1898, Lubin's company prospered for 20 years, specializing in sensational subjects that brought quick profits at the box office. Its most famous star was Ethel CLAYTON and among its players was future director Frank BORZAGE. The Philadelphia-based company, which used the Liberty Bell as a trademark, produced a number of ambitious, spectacular films in its later years, notably *The Battle of Gettysburg* (1912). The company folded in 1917.

Lubitsch, Ernst. Director. *b.* Jan. 28, 1892, Berlin. *d.* 1947. The son of a prosperous tailor, he was drawn to the stage while participating in plays staged by his high school, which he quit at 16. To satisfy both his own urge to act and his father's desire that he take over the family business, he began leading a double life, working as a bookkeeper at his father's store by day and appearing in cabarets and music halls by night. In 1911 he joined Max REINHARDT's famous Deutsches Theater, where he rapidly advanced from bit parts to character leads. To supplement his income, he took a job in 1912 as an apprentice and general-purpose handyman at Berlin's Bioscope film studios. The following year he began appearing in a series of film comedies, emphasizing ethnic Jewish humor, in which he played a character named Meyer. He became very successful as a comedian and soon began writing and directing his own films.

Gradually, Lubitsch abandoned acting to concentrate on directing and in 1918 he made his mark as a serious director with *Die Augen der Mummie Ma/The Eyes of the Mummy,* a tragic drama starring Pola Negri. That same year he scored an international box-office hit with *Carmen/Gypsy Blood,* also starring Negri. But these early achievements could not compare with his great triumph of 1919, *Die Austernprinzessin/The Oyster Princess,* a sparkling satire caricaturizing American manners. For the first time he demonstrated the subtle humor and the virtuoso visual wit that would in time become known as "the Lubitsch Touch." The style was characterized by a parsimonious compression of ideas and situations into single shots or brief scenes that provided an ironic key to the characters and to the meaning of the entire film. Lubitsch subsequently alternated between escapist comedies and grand-scale historical dramas; he enjoyed great international success with both. His reputation as a grand master of world cinema reached a new peak after the release of his spectacles *Madame Du Barry/Passion* (1919) and *Anna Boleyn/Deception* (1920).

In December of 1921, Lubitsch made his first trip to America, to promote his film *Das Weib des Pharao/The Loves of Pharaoh.* Late the following year he arrived in the US again, this time at the request of Mary Pickford, who wanted him to direct her in *Dorothy Vernon of Haddon Hall.* Upon arrival, he rejected the project and directed her instead in *Rosita* (1923). While deemed a failure from her point of view, it was enthusiastically received by critics. Lubitsch's next American project, *The Marriage Circle* (1924), was a resounding triumph.

Lubitsch grasped the American psychology with an amazing accuracy and focused his satire on two main themes—sex and money. With characteristic laconic wit, he depicted sex as a frivolous pastime, a sophisticated game moneyed people play to occupy their hours of leisure. To be safe, he set his plots against foreign backgrounds—Paris, Vienna, Budapest—or some mythical land, but the implication was clearly American.

Lubitsch's success in Hollywood was astounding. He directed an uninterrupted string of hits surpassing his previous achievement each time. His influence grew with every production, and his sophisticated comedy style was widely imitated by other directors. But none could duplicate Lubitsch at his best—his incisive pictorial detail, his perfect timing, the nuances of gesture and facial expression that enabled his performers to reveal in a single brief shot the psychology of the characters they were playing. His chain of triumphs during the silent period—*Forbidden Paradise, Kiss Me Again, Lady Windermere's Fan, The Student Prince,* etc.—remained unbroken, even during the delicate transition to sound. If anything, witty dialogue and appropriate music and songs gave additional grip to the Lubitsch Touch. *The Love Parade, Monte Carlo,* and *The Smiling Lieutenant* were hailed by critics as masterpieces of the newly emerging musical genre. To everyone's surprise, Lubitsch's next film was a somber offbeat drama, *The Man I Killed* (later retitled *Broken Lullaby*), a fierce antiwar document, but he soon returned to his favorite haunt, the sophisticated comedy.

While most of Lubitsch's silent films had been made for Warner Bros., most of his early sound pictures were for Paramount. In 1935 he was appointed that studio's production manager and subsequently produced his own films and supervised the production of films of other directors. In 1937 he was awarded a special Academy Award for his "25-year contribution to motion pictures." The following year he was made a member of the French Legion of Honor for the same reason. In 1939, Lubitsch scored, at MGM, one of the greatest triumphs of his career with *Ninotchka,* a scintillating political-sexual romp starring Greta Garbo. In 1942 he caused some controversy with his anti-Nazi comedy *To Be or Not to Be.* The following year he signed a producer-director's contract with 20th Century-Fox, but his work was curtailed by failing health. In late 1944 he had to hand over the direction of *A Royal Scandal* to Otto Preminger, although he remained on the project as the nominal producer. Lubitsch had recovered sufficiently to direct *Cluny Brown,* in 1946, but the following year he died of a heart attack, his sixth. His last film, *That Lady in Ermine,* was completed by Otto Preminger and released posthumously in 1948.

FILMS (as director): In Germany—Shorts: *Fräulein Seifenschaum* (also sc., act.) 1914; *Blinde Kuh* (also act.), *Auf Eis geführt* (also act.), *Zucker und Zimt* (co-dir., co-sc., act.) 1915; *Leutnant auf Befehl* (also act.), *Wo ist mein Schatz?* (also act.), *Der Schwarze Moritz* (also act. in black face), *Schuhpalast Pinkus* (also act.), *Der gemischte Frauenchor* (also act.), *Der G.M.B.H. Tenor* (also act.), *Der erste Patient* (also act.) 1916; *Ossis Tagebuch* (also co-sc.), *Der Blusekönig* (also act.), *Wenn vier dasselbe tun* (also co-sc.), *Ein fideles Gefängnis* (also act.), *Der Kraftmeyer* (also act.), *Der letzte Anzug* (also act.) 1917; *Prinz Sami* (also act.), *Der Rodelkavalier* (also act.), *Der Fall Rosentopf* (also act.), *Führmann Henschel, Das Mädel vom Ballet* (also sc.), *Marionetten* 1918; *Meier aus Berlin, Ich möchte kein Mann sein* (also co-sc.), *Schwabenmädle* 1919; *Romeo und Julia im Schnee* (also co-sc.). Features: *Als ich tot war* (also sc., act.) 1916; *Die Augen der Mummie Ma/The Eyes of the Mummy, Carmen/Gypsy Blood* 1918; *Meine Frau die Filmschauspielerin, Die Austernprinzessin/The Oyster Princess* (also co-sc.), *Rausch, Madame Dubarry/Passion, Die Puppe* (also co-sc.) 1919; *Kohlhiesels Töchter* (also co-sc.), *Summurun/One Arabian Night* (also co-adapt., act.), *Anna Boleyn/Deception* 1920; *Die Bergkatze/The Wildcat* (also co-sc.) 1921; *Das Weib der Pharao/The Loves of Pharaoh* 1922; *Die Flamme/Montmartre* 1923. In the US—*Rosita* 1923; *The Marriage Circle, Three Women* (also co-story), *Forbidden Paradise* 1924; *Kiss Me Again, Lady Windermere's Fan* 1925; *So This Is Paris* 1926; *The Student Prince/The Student Prince in Old Heidelberg* 1927; *The Patriot* 1928; *Eternal Love, The Love Parade* 1929; *Paramount on Parade* (co-dir. with ten others), *Monte Carlo* 1930; *The Smiling Lieutenant* (also co-sc.) 1931; *The Man I Killed/Broken Lullaby, One Hour with You, Trouble in Paradise* (also prod.), *If I Had a Million* (one episode; also production supervisor) 1932; *Design for Living* 1933; *The Merry Widow* 1934; *Desire* (prod. only) 1936; *Angel* (also prod.) 1937; *Bluebeard's Eighth Wife* (also prod.) 1938; *Ninotchka* 1939; *The Shop Around the Corner* (also prod.) 1940; *That Uncertain Feeling* (also prod.) 1941; *To Be or Not to Be* (also co-prod., co-story) 1942; *Heaven Can Wait* (also prod.) 1943; *A Royal Scandal* (prod. only) 1945; *Cluny Brown* (also prod.) 1946; *That Lady in Ermine* (also prod.; completed by Otto Preminger) 1948.

Lucas, George. Director. Born on May 14, 1944, in Modesto, Calif., the son of an office equipment retailer. A racing-car enthusiast during his high school days, he gave up competitive driving after a crash that crushed his lungs. He attended Modesto Junior College for two years, then enrolled at the Cinema School of the University of Southern California, where he made several prize-winning films, including the science-fiction short *THX-1138: 4EB/Electronic Labyrinth,* which took the first prize at the 1965 National Student Film Festival. As a result of his success at school, he won a scholarship to observe the production at Warner Bros. of Francis Ford COPPOLA's *Finian's Rainbow* (1968). He became a protégé of Coppola and a production associate on that director's next film, *The Rain People* (1969). He made a two-hour documentary, titled *Filmmaker,* on the making of that film. In 1970 he was one of the many cameramen on the celebrated Rolling Stones documentary *Gimme Shelter,* and in the following year turned out his first feature as a director, *THX 1138,* an expanded version of his prize-winning science-fiction short.

Lucas reversed the impression of technocratic coldness with his next film, *American Graffiti* (1973), a nostalgic, largely autobiographical, warmly charming recreation of West Coast adolescent life in the early 60s, before the trauma of Vietnam. The film, made on a minuscule budget of just over $700,000 and on a back-breaking shooting schedule of just 28 nights, enjoyed great success with both the critics and the public. It was nominated for five Oscars—including best picture, best director, and best screenplay—and went on to earn more than $55 million in North American rentals alone, thus becoming one of the most profitable films in history. Lucas's pay amounted to a mere $20,000.

The film's great success paved the way for the project that was to turn Lucas into one of the biggest moneymakers in Hollywood. A space fantasy that had brewed in the director's mind ever since he became interested in film, *Star Wars* (1977; re-released 1997), materialized after three years of preparation as a movie phenomenon of unprecedented magnitude. Shot on a relatively modest budget on locations in Tunisia and Death Valley, and on 11 sound stages in England, the film boasted some of the most imaginative and complex special effects the screen has ever seen. It was peopled by heroic protagonists, dark villains, and a fascinating assortment of weird creatures, and moved along briskly on the strength of a simple mythological tale of good versus evil. The response at the box office was incredible, with cash registers eventually ringing $194 million in rentals and scores of millions in merchandising income. After being re-released in 1997, the film again shattered records at the box office. Lucas was nominated for Academy Awards as director and screenwriter. The film garnered eight more—including best picture—capturing Oscars for best art direction, best sound, best music score, best costume design, and best editing. The director's wife, Marcia Lucas, shared the award in the latter category.

Star Wars spawned two sequels, *The Empire Strikes Back* (1980; re-released 1997) and *The Return of the Jedi* (1983; re-released 1997), both also huge moneymakers. They were not directed by Lucas, who now was devoting his attention to developing projects for other directors through his growing business empire, whose components included the production company, Lucasfilm, the Northern California filming compound, Skywalker Ranch, and the special effects complex, Industrial Light & Magic. As an executive producer, he was the inspiration and driving force behind Steven Spielberg's adventure blockbuster, *Raiders of the Lost Ark* (1981) and the follow-ups, *Indiana Jones and the Temple of Doom* (1984) and *Indiana Jones and the Last Crusade* (1989), both enormous moneymakers.

Although he lost some of his leverage as the industry entered the 90s, he still looms larger than most on the Hollywood scene. He has also been involved in developing TV films (*The Ewok Adventure*, 1984), TV series ('The Indiana Jones Chronicles'), and multimedia software for educational and entertainment uses, as well as starting production on the long-awaited prequels to the *Star Wars* trilogy.

FEATURE FILMS: *The Rain People* (co-prod. assoc.), *Filmmaker* (doc.; dir. sc.) 1968; *Gimme Shelter* (co-phot.) 1970; *THX 1138* (dir., story, co-sc., edit.) 1971; *American Graffiti* (dir. co-sc.) 1973; *Star Wars* (dir., sc.) 1977; *More American Graffiti* (exec. prod.) 1979; *The Empire Strikes Back* (exec. prod., story, co-sc.), *Kagemusha* (co-exec. prod.; Jap.) 1980; *Raiders of the Lost Ark* (co-exec. prod., co-story) 1981; *Return of the Jedi* (exec. prod. story, co-sc.), *Twice Upon a Time* (exec. prod.) 1983; *Indiana Jones and the Temple of Doom* (co-exec. prod., story) 1984; *Mishima: A Life in Four Chapters* (co-exec. prod.) 1985; *Howard the Duck* (exec. prod.), *Labyrinth* (exec. prod.) 1986; *Powaqqatsi* (co-presenter), *Willow* (exec. prod., story), *Tucker: The Man and His Dream* (exec. prod.), *The Land Before Time* (co-exec. prod.) 1988; *Indiana Jones and the Last Crusade* (co-exec. prod., co-story) 1989; *Hearts of Darkness: A Filmmaker's Apocalypse* (appearance only) 1991; *Radioland Murders* (exec. prod. only) 1994; *Star Wars, The Empire Strikes Back, Return of the Jedi* (all re-released special editions) 1997.

Lucas, Wilfred. Actor, director. *b.* 1871, Ontario, Canada. *d.* 1940. One of the earliest stars of the American silent screen, he entered films in 1907 with Biograph and played a wide range of lead roles in the early films of GRIFFITH, SENNETT, and other leading directors of the day. He moved with Sennett to Keystone in 1912 and the following year directed many shorts for the Comedy King. He later returned to acting and appeared in a great many silent and sound films, both in leads and a variety of character roles.

FILMS INCLUDE: As director—*The Rogues' Gallery, The Horse Thief* 1913; *A Glimpse of Los Angeles* (doc.), *The Desert's Sting* (also act.), *Trey of Hearts* (serial; co-dir., with Henry McRae) 1914; *The Spanish Jade* (also act.) 1915; *Jim Bludso* (co-dir.; also act.), *A Live Sublime* (co-dir.; also co-sc., act.) 1917; *Morgan's Raiders* (co-dir., co-sc.), *The Red Red Heart, The Return of Mary, The Romance of Tarzan* (also co-sc.), *The Testing of Mildred Vane* 1918; *The Girl from Nowhere* (also co-sc. act.) 1919; *The Fighting Breed* (also act., co-story), *The Shadow of Lightning Ridge* (also act., co-story), *The Better Man* (also act.) 1921; *Her Sacrifice* (also act.) 1926. As actor—*The Girls and Daddy, Golden Louis, 1776 or The Hessian Renegades* 1909; *His Trust, The Rocky Road, The Lonedale Operator, Enoch Arden* (title role), *The Primal Call, White Rose of the Wilds, The Rose of Kentucky, Swords and Hearts* 1911; *The Transformation of Mike* (also sc.), *Under Burning Skies, The Girl and Her Trust, Man's Genesis, A Sailor's Heart* (also dir. and sc.), *The Chief's Blanket* (also sc.) 1912; *Cohen's Outing, The Primitive Man* 1913; *The Massacre* 1914; *The Lily and the Rose* 1915; *Acquitted, Wild Girl of the Sierras, Macbeth* (as Macduff), *Hell-to-Pay Austin* 1916; *His Excellency the Governor, Sins of Ambition* 1917; *The Westerners, Soldiers of Fortune, What Every Woman Wants, A Woman of Pleasure* 1919; *The Breaking Point, Through the Back Door, The Beautiful Liar* 1921; *The Barnstormer, The Kentucky Derby, Heroes of the Street* 1922; *Innocence, Jazzmania, The Girl of the Golden West, The Greatest Menace, Trilby* 1923; *The Mask of Lopez, Daughters of Pleasure, Dorothy Vernon of Haddon Hall, The Valley of Hate, Racing for Life* (also story, sc.), *Cornered, The Beautiful Sinner* (story only), *Women First* (story only) 1924; *The Man Without a Country, A Broadway Butterfly, Riders of the Purple Sage, The Snob Buster, The Bad Lands* 1925; *Burnt Fingers, The Nest* 1927; *The Arizona Kid, Those Who Dance, Madam Satan* 1930; *Dishonored, Pardon Us* 1931; *The Tenderfoot* 1932; *I Cover the Waterfront, Fra Diavolo/The Devil's Brother* 1933; *The Count of Monte Cristo* 1934; *Modern Times, Mary of Scotland* 1936; *Criminal Lawyer* 1937; *The Baroness and the Butler* 1938; *Zenobia* 1939; *A Chump at Oxford, Brother Orchid* 1940; *The Sea Wolf* 1941; *It's a Great Feeling* 1949.

Ludwig, Edward. Director. *b.* 1899, Russia. *d.* 1982. He came to the US as a boy and was educated in Canada and New York City. He began in silent films as an actor with Vitagraph and later collaborated on the stories and scripts of several productions. A director from the early 30s, he turned out many routine films, mostly second features, but among these were interspersed a number of productions revealing a flair for neat continuity and a keen visual eye. He worked for several studios in various genres but eventually found his niche in action pictures.

FILMS: *Steady Company* 1932; *They Just Had to Get Married* 1933; *A Woman's Man, Let's Be Ritzy, Friends of Mr. Sweeney* 1934; *The Man Who Reclaimed His Head, Age of Indiscretion, Old Man Rhythm, Three Kids and a Queen* 1935; *Fatal Lady, Adventure in Manhattan* 1936; *Her Husband Lies, The Barrier, The Last Gangster* 1937; *That Certain Age* 1938; *Coast Guard* 1939; *Swiss Family Robinson* 1940; *The Man Who Lost Himself* 1941; *Born to Sing* 1942; *They Came to Blow Up America* 1943; *The Fighting Seabees, Three Is a Family* 1944; *The Fabulous Texan* 1947; *Wake of the Red Witch* 1948; *The Big Wheel* 1949; *Smuggler's Island* 1951; *Caribbean, Big Jim McLain, The Blazing Forest* 1952; *The Vanquished, Sangaree* 1953; *Jivaro* 1954; *Flame of the Islands* 1955; *The Black Scorpion* 1957; *The Gun Hawk* 1963.

Ludwig, William. Screenwriter. Born on May 26, 1912, in New York City. A former lawyer, he wrote the scripts for many "Andy Hardy" episodes as well as other routine screenplays. He shared an Academy Award for the original screenplay of *Interrupted Melody* (1955).

FILMS INCLUDE: *Love Finds Andy Hardy* 1938; *Blackmail* 1939; *Love Crazy* 1941; *Journey for Margaret* 1942; *An American Romance* 1944; *Boys' Ranch* 1946; *Julia Misbehaves, Hills of Home* 1948; *Challenge to Lassie* 1949; *Shadow on the Wall* 1950; *The Great Caruso* 1951; *The Merry Widow* 1952; *The Student Prince* 1954; *Hit the Deck, Interrupted Melody, Oklahoma!* 1955; *Gun Glory* 1957; *Back Street* 1961.

Lugosi, Bela. Actor. *b.* Béla Blasko, Oct. 20, 1882, Lugos, Hungary. *d.* 1956. The son of a baker-turned-banker, he trained for the stage at the Budapest Academy of Theatrical Arts. From 1901 he played lead parts on the Hungarian stage and from 1915 in films, sometimes using the name Arisztid Olt. In 1918, during the collapse of the Hungarian monarchy and the establishment of a communist regime, he was active in politics and organized an actors' union. When the leftists were defeated, in 1919, he fled to Germany, where he appeared in a number of films. In 1921 he emigrated to the US and began playing character parts on the stage and in films. His most notable success was in the title role of the stage presentation of 'Dracula,' which he played for a year (1927) on Broadway and two years on the road. When he repeated the role in Tod Browning's 1931 screen version, introducing himself to film audiences with a heavy, deliberate, inimitable accent, "I—am—Drac—ula. . . ," it was clear that the American screen had found itself a worthy aristocrat of evil.

During the 30s and early 40s, Lugosi shared with Boris KARLOFF the legacy of the silent screen's Lon Chaney. Technically, Lugosi might not have been as good an actor as Karloff, but he had a superior screen personality and as a personification of dark evil had no peer in Hollywood or elsewhere. Unfortunately, he was not choosy about his roles, and in addition to performing in the quality horror films at Universal and other major studios (and his only comic role, in *Ninotchka*) which made him famous, he appeared indiscriminately in scores of infantile films in which he was given the most ludicrous lines.

On the screen, Lugosi portrayed mad scientists and demented megalomaniacs who evoked no pity or compassion in audiences. But his personal life had its pathetic quality. At first under pressure from studio publicity, and later on his own accord, he allowed the vampire image to become part of his real life. He began giving interviews while lying in a coffin, was once seen at a Hollywood premiere accompanied by a gorilla, and in his later films played parodies of himself. Besides, he was almost always involved in money or marital problems. In 1955 he had himself committed to the California State Hospital as a drug addict. He then returned briefly to the screen and even entered his fifth marriage, but in August of 1956 he died. He was buried with his Dracula cape.

FILMS INCLUDE: In Hungary—*Masked Ball, The Royal Life, Leopard* 1917; *Casanova, Lulu* 1918. In Germany—*Sklaven fremdes Willens* 1919; *Der Fluch der Menschheit, Der Januskop/ Janus Faced/Dr. Jekyll and Mr. Hyde, Lederstrump/ Leatherstocking/The Deerslayer/The Last of the Mohicans* 1920; *Der Tanz auf dem Vulkan* 1921. In the US—*The Silent Command* 1923; *The Rejected Woman* 1924; *The Midnight Girl* 1925; *Prisoners, The Thirteenth Chair* 1929; *Such Men Are Dangerous, Renegades* 1930; *Dracula* (title role), *Women of All Nations, The Black Camel* 1931; *Murders in the Rue Morgue, White Zombie, Chandu the Magician, Island of Lost Souls, The Death Kiss* 1932; *The Whispering Shadow* (serial), *International House, Night of Terror* 1933; *The Black Cat, The Return of Chandu* (serial; title role) 1934; *Best Man Wins, The Mysterious Mr. Wong* (title role), *Murder by Television, Mark of the Vampire, The Raven* 1935; *Shadow of Chinatown* (serial), *The Invisible Ray* 1936; *S.O.S. Coast Guard* (serial) 1937; *The Phantom Creeps* (serial), *Son of Frankenstein, The Gorilla, Ninotchka, The Dark Eyes of London/The Human Monster* (UK) 1939; *The Saint's Double Trouble, Black Friday, You'll Find Out, The Devil Bat* 1940; *The Black Cat, The Invisible Ghost, Spooks Run Wild, The Wolf Man* 1941; *Black Dragons, The Ghost of Frankenstein, The Corpse Vanishes, Bowery at Midnight, Night Monster* 1942; *Frankenstein Meets the Wolf Man* (as Frankenstein's Monster), *Ghosts on the Loose, The Return of the Vampire* 1943; *The Voodoo Man, Return of the Ape Man, One Body Too Many* 1944; *Zombies on Broadway, The Body Snatcher* 1945; *Genius at Work* 1946; *Scared to Death* 1947; *Abbott and Costello Meet Frankenstein* (as Dracula) 1948; *Mother Riley Meets the Vampire* (as Dracula; UK), *Bela Lugosi Meets a Brooklyn Gorilla* 1952; *Bride of the Monster, The Black Sleep, Plan 9 from Outer Space* 1956 (released in 1959).

Lukas, Paul. Actor. *b.* Pal Lukàcs, May 26, 1894 (possibly 1887), Budapest. *d.* 1971. The son of an advertising executive, he was invalided out of WW I service in 1915 and made his first screen appearance later that year. He received his stage training at the Hungarian Actors' Academy and made his debut in 1916 on the Budapest stage. He subsequently appeared in many plays and films and before long had achieved a local matinee-idol status. His reputation spread throughout Central Europe and in the 20s he appeared frequently as a guest star in Max REINHARDT productions in Berlin and Vienna. He was brought to the US by Adolph ZUKOR in 1927 and the following year began a long and often impressive career as Hollywood's Continental-in-residence. Initially he was typecast as a smooth, suave seducer, but gradually, as he matured in age and still retained a noticeable Middle European accent, he was cast more and more in outright villainous roles, often of the Nazi type. However, it was in an anti-Nazi role, one of his few sympathetic parts, that he scored his greatest personal triumph on stage and screen. He received superlative notices from critics for that performance on Broadway in Lillian Hellman's 'Watch on the Rhine' (1941) and won the best actor Academy Award as well as the New York Film Critics Award for repeating the role in the 1943 film version. He appeared with distinction in many other pictures, in roles varying in importance and size, before his death of heart failure in Tangier during a search for a retirement home.

FILMS INCLUDE: In Hungary—*Man of the Earth* 1915; *Sphynx* 1917; *Little Fox, Nameless Castle* 1920; *New York Express* 1921. In Germany—*Samson und Dalilah* (as Samson) 1922; *Das unbekannte Morgen* 1923. In the US—*Two Lovers, Three Sinners, Hot News, Loves of an Actress, The Night Watch, The Woman from Moscow, Manhattan Cocktail* 1928; *The Shopworn Angel, The Wolf of Wall Street, Half Way to Heaven* 1929; *Slightly Scarlet, Young Eagles, The Benson Murder Case, Anybody's Woman, The Right to Love* 1930; *Unfaithful, City Streets, The Vice Squad, Women Love Once, The Beloved Bachelor, Strictly Dishonorable* 1931; *No One Man, Tomorrow and Tomorrow, A Passport to Hell, Rockabye* 1932; *Grand Slam, The Kiss Before the Mirror, Sing Sinner Sing, Captured, The Secret of the Blue Room, Little Women* (as Prof. Bhaer), *By Candlelight* 1933; *The Countess of Monte Cristo, Glamour, Affairs of a Gentleman, I Give My Love, The Fountain* 1934; *The Casino Murder Case* (as detective Philo Vance), *Age of Indiscretion, The Three Musketeers* (as Athos), *I Found Stella Parrish* 1935; *Dodsworth* (as Arnold), *Ladies in Love* 1936; *Espionage, Dinner at the Ritz* (UK) 1937; *The Lady Vanishes* (UK) 1938; *A Window in London/Lady in Distress* (UK), *Confessions of a Nazi Spy, Captain Fury* 1939; *The Chinese Bungalow/Chinese Den* (UK), *Strange Cargo, The Ghost Breakers* 1940; *The Monster and the Girl, They Dare Not Love* 1941; *Watch on the Rhine, Hostages* 1943; *Uncertain Glory,*

Address Unknown, Experiment Perilous 1944; *Deadline at Dawn, Temptation* 1946; *Whispering City* 1947; *Berlin Express* 1948; *Kim* (as the Lama) 1950; *20,000 Leagues Under the Sea* (as Prof. Aronnax) 1954; *The Roots of Heaven* 1958; *Scent of Mystery* 1960; *The Four Horsemen of the Apocalypse* 1961; *Tender Is the Night* 1962; *55 Days at Peking, Fun in Acapulco* 1963; *Lord Jim* (as Stein) 1965; *Sol Madrid* 1968.

Luke, Keye. Actor. *b.* June 18, 1904, in Canton, China. *d.* 1991. In the US from early childhood, he was educated at Washington University, in Seattle, and entered the film industry as a commercial artist and poster designer. He later served as a technical advisor on Hollywood films with Chinese themes and in 1934 made his debut as a film actor in *The Painted Veil.* He then appeared in numerous movies, often in minor parts but occasionally in substantial supporting roles, as he did in *The Good Earth* (1937) and *Across the Pacific* (1942). He is perhaps best remembered for his continuing role as Charlie Chan's "Number One Son" in many films of that detective series. He also appeared a number of times in the "Dr. Kildare" film series as Van Johnson's rival for advancement in the hospital hierarchy, and played Kato, the Green Hornet's fighting servant, in two serials in 1940. In the late 50s he appeared successfully on Broadway in the long-running musical 'Flower Drum Song.' He also gave numerous TV performances, most memorably as the ancient Master Po in the 'Kung Fu' series (1972–75). His final screen role was in Woody Allen's *Alice* (1990), 56 years after his screen debut.

FILMS INCLUDE: *The Painted Veil* 1934; *Charlie Chan in Paris, Oil for the Lamps of China, Shanghai, Mad Love* 1935; *King of Burlesque, Charlie Chan at the Opera* 1936; *The Good Earth* 1937; *Mr. Moto's Gamble* 1938; *Disputed Passage, Barricade* 1939; *The Green Hornet, Mr. and Mrs. North, Spy Ship, Invisible Agent, Across the Pacific, Dr. Gillespie's New Assistant, The Falcon's Brother* 1942; *Salute to the Marines* 1943; *Three Men in White, Dragon Seed* 1944; *Secret Agent X-9* (serial), *Tokyo Rose, Between Two Women* 1945; *Dark Delusion* 1947; *Sleep My Love* 1948; *Hell's Half Acre* 1954; *Love Is a Many Splendored Thing* 1955; *The Yangtse Incident* 1957; *Nobody's Perfect* 1968; *The Chairman* 1969; *The Hawaiians* 1970; *Amsterdam Kill* (Hong Kong) 1977; *Just You and Me Kid* 1979; *Gremlins* 1984; *A Fine Mess* 1986; *Dead Heat* 1988; *The Mighty Quinn* 1989; *Gremlins 2: The New Batch, Alice* 1990.

Lulli, Folco. Actor. *b.* 1912, Florence, Italy. *d.* 1970. A robust, solid character actor of countless postwar Italian and Continental films, he was memorable as one of the truck drivers in the Clouzot thriller *Wages of Fear.* His brother, Piero Lulli (*b.* 1923), is also in films.

FILMS INCLUDE: *Il Bandito/The Bandit* 1946; *La Figlia del Capitano, Caccia Tragica/Tragic Hunt, Senza Pietà/Without Pity* 1947; *Fuga in Francia/Flight Into France* 1948; *Nonc'è Pace tra gli Ulivi/Under the Olive Tree* 1950; *Luci del Varietà/ Variety Lights* 1951; *Altri Tempi/Times Gone By, I Figli di Nessuno* 1952; *Le Salaire de la Peur/Wages of Fear* (Fr.), *La Peccatrice dell'Isola/The Island Sinner, Noi Cannibali, Maddalena* 1953; *Carosello Napoletano/Neapolitan Carousel, La Grande Speranza, Orient Express* 1954; *Occhio per Occhio/An Eye for an Eye* 1957; *La Grande Guerra/The Great War* 1959; *La Regina dei Tartari/The Huns* 1960; *I Tartari/The Tartars, Gli Invasori/Erik the Conqueror* 1961; *Lafayette* (Fr./It.) 1962; *I Compagni/The Organizer* 1963; *La Fabuleuse Aventure de Marco Polo/Marco the Magnificent* (Fr./It./Yug./ Eg./Afg.) 1965; *Le Vicompte règle ses Comptes/The Viscount* (Fr./It./Sp.) 1967; *Anche nel West c'era una Volta Dio* 1968.

Lumet, Sidney. Director. Born on June 25, 1924, in Philadelphia. *ed.* Professional Children's School; Columbia. The son of Baruch Lumet and Eugenia Wermus, veteran players of the Yiddish stage, he made his professional debut on radio at age four and stage debut at the Yiddish Art Theatre at five. As a child he appeared in many Broadway plays, including 'Dead End.' He made his only film appearance, at age 15, in *One Third of a Nation* (1939). After returning from WW II service (1942–46) as a radar repairman in India and Burma, he organized an off-Broadway group and became its director. He also directed in summer stock and taught acting in the High School of Professional Arts. In 1950 he joined CBS, where he soon won recognition as a gifted director of TV drama ('You Are There,' 'Omnibus,' 'Best of Broadway,' 'Alcoa Theater,' 'Goodyear Playhouse,' etc.). He was given his first chance to direct a motion picture, *12 Angry Men* (1957), by the film's producer and star, Henry FONDA. Thanks to his TV experience, Lumet was able to complete the tightly structured courtroom drama in 19 days on a budget of merely $343,000. With the help of his cameraman Boris KAUFMAN, Lumet used the space restrictions of the cramped setting to advantage, generating uncommon tension from the claustrophobic confines of the jury room. The film and its director were nominated for Academy Awards. Lumet won the Directors Guild Award and the film was widely praised by critics. Following several lackluster efforts, Lumet received another nod from the Directors Guild for his handling of Eugene O'Neill's *Long Day's Journey Into Night* (1962), on which he applied a masterful mix of static and dynamic camerawork, turning the play into a distinctly cinematic work despite some extended stagy stretches.

Lumet's growing reputation was further enhanced by his intelligent handling of the Cold War thriller, *Fail-Safe* (1964), and his compassionate treatment of a complex psychological theme in *The Pawnbroker* (1965), the profoundly disturbing story of a holocaust survivor's anguished existence in New York's Harlem amidst his haunting memories of the concentration camps. After generating a powerful drama of wretched life in a British military prison, *The Hill* (1965), Lumet entered a middling phase of his now prominent career. It wasn't until 1973's exciting police thriller, *Serpico,* that he enjoyed his next unqualified success. The revival of his career continued with *Dog Day Afternoon* (1975), a realistic, powerful depiction of another true-life crime story, and peaked with *Network* (1976), his greatest commercial triumph. It was a huge moneymaker and earned Academy Award nominations, including best picture and best director. It won four Oscars in the writing and acting categories. Lumet next shared an Academy Award nomination for the screenplay of *Prince of the City* (1981), but his subsequent output in the eighties—with the notable exceptions of *The Verdict* (1982) and *Running on Empty* (1988)—was uneven.

Although critical evaluation of Lumet's work wavered widely from film to film, on the whole the director's body of work has been held in high esteem. Critical opinion has generally viewed him as a sensitive and intelligent director who possesses considerable good taste, the courage to experiment with a variety of techniques and styles, and an uncommon gift for handling actors. The director's first wife was actress Rita GAM; his second (1956–63) socialite Gloria Vanderbilt; his third, Gail Jones (1963–78), Lena Horne's daughter; and fourth (from 1980), Mary Gimbel. The third marriage produced budding screen actress Jenny Lumet.

FILMS: *12 Angry Men* 1957; *Stage Struck* 1958; *That Kind of Woman* 1959; *The Fugitive Kind* 1960; *Vu du Pont/A View from the Bridge* (Fr./It.), *Long Day's Journey Into Night* 1962; *Fail Safe* (also co-exec. prod.) 1964; *The Pawnbroker, The Hill* (UK) 1965; *The Group* 1966; *The Deadly Affair* (also prod.;

UK) 1967; *Bye Bye Braverman* (also prod.), *The Sea Gull* (also prod.; US/UK) 1968; *The Appointment* 1969; *The Last of the Mobile Hotshots* (also prod.), *King: A Film Record. . . Montgomery to Memphis* (compilation doc.; co-dir. with Joseph L. Mankiewicz of connecting sequences only) 1970; *The Anderson Tapes* 1971; *Child's Play* 1972; *The Offence/The Offense* (UK), *Serpico* 1973; *Lovin' Molly, Murder on the Orient Express* (UK/US) 1974; *Dog Day Afternoon* 1975; *Network* 1976; *Equus* 1977; *The Wiz* 1978; *Just Tell Me What You Want* (also co-prod.) 1980; *Prince of the City* (also co-sc.) 1981; *Deathtrap, The Verdict* 1982; *Daniel* (also co-exec. prod.) 1983; *Garbo Talks* 1984; *Power, The Morning After* 1986; *Running on Empty* 1988; *Family Business* 1989; *Q & A* (also sc.) 1990; *A Stranger Among Us* 1992; *Guilty as Sin* 1993; *Night Falls on Manhattan* (also sc.) 1997.

Lumière, Louis. Inventor, pioneer director, and producer. *b.* Oct. 5, 1864, Besançon, France. *d.* 1948. The son of a photographer and manufacturer of photographic products, at 17 he invented a dry-plate process whose worldwide sales had turned the family's Lyons plant into a flourishing business by 1883. The demonstration of Edison's Kinetoscope in Paris in 1894 fired Louis's imagination. The Edison apparatus could record but not project movement. His films were presented peep-show style. Late in 1894, with the aid of his brother Auguste Lumière (*b.* Oct. 19, 1862, Besançon. *d.* 1954), he developed the Cinématographe, a combination camera-projector into which he incorporated the ideas and inventions of such predecessors as Marey, Muybridge, and Edison, plus several of his own, notably an eccentrically driven claw for moving film strip. The invention was patented on February 13, 1895.

On March 22 of that year, the brothers Lumière projected their first film, *La Sortie des Usines Lumière,* showing workers leaving their factory, to members of the Société d'Encouragement pour l'Industrie Nationale. A further demonstration of eight film strips was presented at a photographers' convention in Lyons, on June 10. And on December 28, 1895, a date the French and many other scholars consider the birthday of world cinema, the Lumière brothers projected their films for the first time to a paying public at the Grand Café on the Boulevard des Capucines in Paris.

In addition to *La Sortie des Usines Lumière,* the program consisted of a number of other brief film clips, including *L'Arrivée d'un Train en Gare de la Ciotat,* which thrilled and jolted the audience with a shot of a train roaring toward the camera. Another attraction, the very brief *L'Arroseur Arrosé,* was the first example of cinema farce and the world's first piece of fiction film. However, the typical Lumière films recorded real life and current events; they were the predecessors of the newsreel and documentary traditions.

Lumière directed and shot his first films himself, but he soon turned the job over to a group of skilled photographers. In the summer of 1895 he began dispatching agents to all corners of the earth to sell his Cinématographe, exhibit his films to foreign audiences, and shoot newsworthy footage for his rapidly increasing catalog of short subjects. By 1897 his staff had recorded on film such events as the coronation of Czar Nikolai II in Moscow and the inauguration of President McKinley in Washington. By 1898 the Lumière catalog listed some 1,000 titles, mostly news footage shot all over the world, as well as such dramatizations as *Faust* and *The Life and Passion of Jesus Christ.* Having directed some 60 films and produced about 2,000, Lumière abandoned film production after the Paris Exposition of 1900, during which he exhibited his films on huge screens to large audiences. He thereafter devoted his energies to the invention and manufacture of photographic equipment and processes. Among other inventions he developed was a still projector; a successful color process for still film which he used only experimentally in motion pictures; and a three-dimensional film process that he introduced in his 70s.

Lumière is revered in France and elsewhere as the "father" of the cinema. Certain film scholars see the development of the art of film as proceeding along two distinctive avenues that eventually fused into one: the tradition of reality, originating in the films of Lumière, and the tradition of fantasy, originating in the films of Georges Méliès.

luminaire. A complete lighting unit, including housing, lamp, and stand.

Lumley, Joanna. Actress. Born on Mar. 1, 1946, in Kashmir. Elegant leading lady of British films. A major's daughter and a member of Britain's upper crust, she modeled before entering films in the late 60s. Her TV credits included a co-starring role in 'The New Avengers' series (1976–77). At the height of her popularity she wrote a weekly diary for the *London Times.* Divorced from actor-writer Jeremy Lloyd, she married orchestra conductor Stephen Barlow.

FILMS INCLUDE: *Some Girls Do* 1968; *On Her Majesty's Secret Service* 1969; *Tam Lin/The Devil's Widow, Games That Lovers Play* 1971; *Satanic Rites of Dracula/ Dracula and His Vampire Bride* 1973; *Trail of the Pink Panther* 1982; *Curse of the Pink Panther* 1983; *Shirley Valentine* 1989; *Cold Comfort Farm, A Midwinter's Tale* 1995.

Lund, John. Actor. *b.* Feb. 6, 1913, Rochester, N.Y. *d.* 1992. One of six children of a Norwegian-born glassblower, he dropped out of high school and worked at a variety of manual jobs before joining a New York City advertising agency. A tall, handsome, blue-eyed blond, he was asked by a friend to appear in an industrial show during the 1939 World's Fair. He made his Broadway debut in 1941 in 'As You Like It' and worked frequently on radio as an actor and writer. He wrote the book and lyrics for the Broadway revue 'New Faces of 1943.' After appearing successfully in the play 'The Hasty Heart,' he signed a long-term film contract with Paramount. His best film roles came early in his career in such dramas as *To Each His Own* (1946) and *Night Has a Thousand Eyes* (1948) and such comedies as *A Foreign Affair* and *Miss Tatlock's Millions* (both 1948). Despite his manly good looks, he turned out to be a rather stuffy leading man and ended his film career in the early 60s in minor films and secondary roles.

FILMS: *To Each His Own* 1946; *The Perils of Pauline, Variety Girl* 1947; *A Foreign Affair, Night Has a Thousand Eyes, Miss Tatlock's Millions* 1948; *Bride of Vengeance* (as Alfonso D'Este, Duke of Ferrara and husband of Lucrezia Borgia), *My Friend Irma* 1949; *No Man of Her Own, Duchess of Idaho, My Friend Irma Goes West* 1950; *The Mating Season, Darling How Could You!* 1951; *Steel Town, The Battle at Apache Pass, Bronco Buster, Just Across the Street* 1952; *The Woman They Almost Lynched, Latin Lovers* 1953; *White Feather, Chief Crazy Horse, Five Guns West* 1955; *Battle Stations, High Society, Dakota Incident* 1956; *Affair in Reno* 1957; *The Wackiest Ship in the Army* 1960; *If a Man Answers* 1962.

Lundgren, Dolph. Actor. Born in 1959, in Stockholm. *ed.* Royal Institute of Technology, Sweden; Washington State U.; MIT. Muscle-bound, blond leading man. A former kick-boxing champion, he served as a doorman at a New York disco while studying acting in Manhattan. He was long involved with unpredictable singer-actress Grace Jones, and was among the last few celebrities to be photographed by George Hurrell. He first asserted himself on the screen as Sylvester Stallone's formidable, robot-like, Soviet ring opponent in *Rocky IV* (1985) before disappearing into mainly low-budget action-packers.

FILMS: *A View to a Kill* (bit), *Rocky IV* 1985; *Masters of the Universe* 1987; *The Punisher* 1988; *Red Scorpion* 1989; *I Come in Peace* 1990; *Cover-Up, Showdown in Little Tokyo* 1991; *Universal Soldier* 1992; *Army of One* 1993; *Johnny Mnemonic* 1995.

Lundgren, P. A. Art director. Born in 1911, in Vastra Harg, Sweden. Designer of excellent sets for many Swedish films, especially those of Ingmar BERGMAN.

FILMS INCLUDE: *A Day Shall Dawn* 1944; *It Rains on Our Love* 1946; *Night Is My Future* 1947; *The Devil's Wanton* 1949; *Monika* 1952; *A Lesson in Love* 1954; *Smiles of a Summer Night* 1955; *Song of the Scarlet Flower, The Seventh Seal* 1956; *The Magician* 1958; *The Virgin Spring* 1959; *The Devil's Eye* 1960; *Through a Glass Darkly, Pleasure Garden* 1961; *The Swedish Mistress* 1962; *Winter Light, The Silence* 1963; *491, All These Women* 1964; *My Sister My Love* 1966; *Hagbard and Signe/The Red Mantle, Stimulantia* (co. art-dir.) 1967; *Shame* 1968; *The Passion of Anna* 1969; *The Emigrants* 1971; *The New Land* 1973; *The American Dream* (also co-prod.) 1977.

Lundigan, William. Actor. *b.* June 12, 1914, in Syracuse, N.Y. *d.* 1975. *ed.* Syracuse U. Originally a radio announcer, he entered films in 1937 and played rather bland "nice guy" leads and second leads for various studios through the mid-50s. His prestige was enhanced later in the decade as host of the 'Climax' TV drama series and spokesman for the Chrysler company, which produced the programs. In the 60s he returned to films in occasional roles.

FILMS INCLUDE: *Armored Car* 1937; *Wives Under Suspicion* 1938; *Three Smart Girls Grow Up, Dodge City, They Asked for It, The Forgotten Woman, The Old Maid* 1939; *The Fighting 69th, The Sea Hawk, East of the River, Santa Fe Trail* 1940; *The Case of the Black Parrot, International Squadron* 1941; *The Courtship of Andy Hardy, Sunday Punch* 1942; *Salute to the Marines* 1943; *Dishonored Lady, The Fabulous Dorseys* 1947; *Follow Me Quietly, Pinky* 1949; *Mother Didn't Tell Me, I'll Get By* 1950; *I'd Climb the Highest Mountain, The House on Telegraph Hill, Love Nest, Elopement* 1951; *Down Among the Sheltering Palms, Inferno* 1953; *Riders to the Stars* 1954; *The Underwater City* 1962; *The Way West* 1967; *Where Angels Go Trouble Follows* 1968.

Lunt, Alfred. Actor. *b.* Aug. 19, 1892, Milwaukee. *d.* 1977. He and his wife, Lynn Fontanne (*b.* Dec. 6, 1892, Woodford, England; *d.* 1982), were the most formidable acting team in the history of the American theater, but they appeared in only a handful of films.

FILMS: *Backbone* (Lunt alone, in dual role), *The Ragged Edge* (Lunt alone) 1923; *Second Youth* 1924; *The Man Who Found Himself* (Fontanne alone), *Sally of the Sawdust* (Lunt alone) *Lovers in Quarantine* (Lunt alone) 1925; *The Guardsman* 1931; *Stage Door Canteen* (cameos) 1943.

Lupino, Ida. Actress, director, screenwriter. *b.* Feb. 4, 1918, in London. *d.* 1995. *ed.* RADA. The daughter of celebrated British revue- and film-comedian Stanley Lupino (*b.* May 15, 1893, London; *d.* 1942) and an actress, Connie Emerald, and a descendant of a theatrical family dating back to the 17th century, she made her film debut at 15 under amusing circumstances. During a brief stay in England, American director Allan Dwan was looking for an actress to play a Lolita type in his British film *Her First Affaire.* A casting agent sent girlish-looking actress Connie Emerald for an audition, Dwan thought she was too old for the part but showed interest in the teenage daughter who accompanied Miss Emerald. Ida Lupino got the role.

She appeared in a number of other British films in the same year, 1933, then went to Hollywood on a Paramount contract. Her early Hollywood career was unrewarding, consisting mostly of colorless leads in minor films. However, her roles began improving after her strong performance in *The Light That Failed* (1940). She was signed by Warners and scored in a succession of roles in which she typically portrayed hardened, often vulgar or ambitious women. In 1943 she was named best actress by the New York Film Critics for her role as a domineering sister in *The Hard Way.* But on the whole she considered her Hollywood acting career a failure and once referred to herself as a "poor man's Bette Davis."

An American citizen from 1948, Miss Lupino turned in the early 50s to writing, directing, and producing motion pictures and TV series and movies. She named her company after her mother, Emerald Productions, later restructuring it with her partners into The Filmmakers company. Her first venture as co-producer and co-screenwriter was *Not Wanted* (1949). When the film's director Elmer Cifton was felled by a heart attack three days into shooting, Lupino took over, doing creditably well in transcribing to the screen this sincere story of an unwed mother in search of affection. She did not get screen credit for this unofficial directorial debut. She was less successful with her first "autographed" film as a director, *Never Fear* (1950), about the misery of a dancer stricken by polio. Like *Not Wanted,* it was partly autobiographical, and like the former film it contained some powerful dramatic passages and documentary-like sequences. Lupino had her biggest success, both critical and commercial, with *The Hitch-Hiker* (1953), a harrowing fact-based story of a psychopathic killer. She also drew admiration for *The Bigamist* (also 1953), a compassionate exposition of the fuzzy roots of a dual marital affair. Lupino's creative contribution to American film far exceeded her nominal role as virtually the only woman director working in Hollywood during the 50s. Later in the decade she returned to acting, venturing into directing only once more in 1966. Previously married to actor Lewis HAYWARD (1938–45) and Columbia executive Collyer Young (1948–50), she later wed actor Howard DUFF, who co-starred with her in several films and the TV series 'Mr. Adams and Eve' (1957–58), which was based on the couple's own experiences in Hollywood. They divorced in 1973.

FILMS: As actress—*Her First Affaire* (UK), *Money for Speed* (UK), *High Finance* (UK), *Prince of Arcadia* (UK), *The Ghost Camera* (UK), *I Lived with You* (UK) 1933. In the US—*Search for Beauty, Come on Marines, Ready for Love* 1934; *Paris in Spring, Smart Girl, Peter Ibbetson* 1935; *Anything Goes, One Rainy Afternoon, Yours for the Asking, The Gay Desperado* 1936; *Sea Devils, Let's Get Married, Artists and Models, Fight for Your Lady* 1937; *The Lone Wolf Spy Hunt, The Lady and the Mob, The Adventures of Sherlock Holmes* 1939; *The Light That Failed, They Drive by Night* 1940; *High Sierra, The Sea Wolf, Out of the Fog, Ladies in Retirement* 1941; *Moontide, Life Begins at Eight-Thirty* 1942; *The Hard Way, Forever and a Day, Thank Your Lucky Stars* 1943; *In Our Time, Hollywood Canteen* 1944; *Pillow to Post* 1945; *Devotion* (as Emily Brontë) 1946; *The Man I Love, Deep Valley, Escape Me Never* 1947; *Road House* 1948; *Lust for Gold* 1949; *Woman in Hiding* 1950; *On Dangerous Ground, Beware My Lovely* 1952; *Jennifer* 1953; *Private Hell 36* (also co-sc.) 1954; *Women's Prison, The Big Knife* 1955; *While the City Sleeps, Strange Intruder* 1956; *Backtrack* 1969; *Junior Bonner* 1972; *The Devil's Rain* 1975; *The Food of the Gods* 1976; *My Boys Are Good Boys* 1978; *Deadhead Miles* 1982. As producer—*Not Wanted* (co-prod. co-sc.; also co-dir., uncredited) 1949. As director/co-producer—*Never Fear/The Young Lovers* (also co-sc.), *Outrage* (also co-sc.) 1950; *Hard Fast and Beautiful* 1951; *The Hitch-Hiker* (also co-sc.), *The Bigamist* (also act.) 1953; *The Trouble with Angels* 1966.

Lupu-Pick. See PICK, Lupu.

Lurie, John. Actor, musician. Born in 1952. Wiry, hip American character player and composer of independent films, many by Jim JARMUSCH. As leader of the group the Lounge Lizards, he became a well-known entity of the downtown New York music scene.

FILMS INCLUDE (as actor): *Permanent Vacation* (also mus.), *Underground U.S.A.* 1980; *Subway Riders* (also mus.) 1981; *Variety* (mus. only), *The Loveless* (addnl. music only) 1983, *Paris Texas, Stranger Than Paradise* (also mus.) 1984; *Desperately Seeking Susan* 1985; *Down by Law* (also mus.) 1986; *Slam Dance* (addnl. music only) 1987; *The Last Temptation of Christ, Il Piccolo Diavolo* 1988; *Mystery Train* (also mus.) 1989; *Wild at Heart* 1990; *Till the End of the World/Jusq'au bout du Monde* 1991; *Blue in the Face, Get Shorty* 1995.

Lydon, Jimmy (James). Actor. Born on May 30, 1923, in Harrington Park, N.J. A child actor on Broadway, he entered films as a teenager in 1939 and for the next decade played juvenile leads in a variety of features, including the title role in nine films of the "Henry Aldrich" series. He was popular as a juvenile, but his adult film and TV roles have been secondary. Since the late 50s he has also been active behind the camera, as an associate producer of TV series and occasional features. He has also directed a number of episodes for various TV series.

FILMS INCLUDE: *Back Door to Heaven, Two Thoroughbreds* 1939; *Tom Brown's School Days* (as Tom Brown), *Little Men, Bowery Boy* 1940; *Naval Academy, Henry Aldrich for President* 1941; *Cadets on Parade, Henry Aldrich Editor* 1942; *Aerial Gunner, Henry Aldrich Haunts a House* 1943; *Henry Aldrich Boy Scout, My Best Gal, Henry Aldrich Plays Cupid, When the Lights Go on Again, The Town Went Wild* 1944; *Strange Illusion, Twice Blessed* 1945; *The Affairs of Geraldine* 1946; *Life with Father, Cynthia, Sweet Genevieve* 1947; *The Time of Your Life, Out of the Storm, Joan of Arc* 1948; *Bad Boy, Tucson* 1949; *When Willie Comes Marching Home, Hot Rod* 1950; *Gasoline Alley, The Magnificent Yankee, September Affair, Oh! Susanna* 1951; *Island in the Sky* 1953; *Battle Stations* 1956; *Chain of Evidence* 1957; *The Last Time I Saw Archie* 1961; *Death of a Gunfighter* 1969; *Scandalous John* 1971; *Vigilante Force* 1976.

Lye, Len. Animator. *b.* July 5, 1901, Christchurch, New Zealand. *d.* 1980. *ed.* Wellington Technical Coll.; Canterbury Coll. of Fine Arts. Before going to England in the late 20s, he spent some time in the South Sea Islands, where he became influenced by Polynesian art. He began experimenting with film animation in 1929 in London. In the 30s he was employed by Grierson's GPO Film Unit, working on animation documentaries and publicity films. In 1934 he broke new ground in film animation by inventing a technique for painting directly on film. The abstract short *Colour Box* was the first film in which he utilized this technique, which was later to influence the work of Norman MCLAREN. Lye moved to the US in 1944 and became an American citizen in 1947. In the 40s and early 50s he directed short live-action documentaries but was commercially unsuccessful and in the late 50s left cinema to concentrate on painting and sculpting.

FILMS INCLUDE: *Tusalava* 1929; *Colour Box* 1935; *The Birth of a Robot* (puppet-anim.; co-dir.), *Rainbow Dance* 1936; *Trade Tattoo/In Time with Industry* 1937; *Colour Flight* 1938; *Swinging the Lambeth Walk* 1939; *Musical Poster No. 1, Profile of Britain* (for March of Time) 1940; *Newspaper Train* 1941; *Work Party, Kill or Be Killed* 1942; *Planned Crops* 1943; *Cameramen at War* 1944; *Fox Chase* 1952; *Color Cry, Rhythm* 1953; *Free Radicals* 1957; *Particles in Space* 1966; *Tal Farlow* 1980.

Lynch, David. Director, screenwriter. Born on Jan. 20, 1946, in Missoula, Mont. The son of a research scientist for the Department of Agriculture whose job moved the five-member family around the Northwest, Lynch was raised in Washington and Idaho and finally in Alexandria, Virginia, where he reluctantly attended high school. Intending to become a painter, he trained at art schools in Washington, D.C., and Boston, then entered the job market, getting himself hired and fired from various jobs in rapid succession. He had been already married and the father of a child when he retreated back to school, enrolling at Philadelphia's Pennsylvania Academy of Fine Arts. He lived in a dilapidated home in a crime-ridden neighborhood, an atmosphere that may have nourished the nightmarish vision of his future films. A chance contact with an art patron resulted in a commission for Lynch to make a "moving painting" for the man's living room, consisting of a four-minute film clip the artist entitled *The Alphabet.* Lynch used that clip to get a $5,000 grant from the American Film Institute to make *The Grandmother,* a 35-minute, 16 mm animation-live-action short that told the story of a bed-wetting boy, abused by his parents, who grows a loving grandmother from a seed. The film won several festival awards and helped gain Lynch a fellowship in the AFI's Center for Advanced Film Studies in Beverly Hills in 1970.

It was there in 1971 that he began planning his first feature film, *Eraserhead.* He started shooting in 1972, filming mostly at night and earning a meager income by delivering newspapers. It was a slow, grueling process, during which his funding constantly dried up and his first marriage collapsed. Finally previewed at the 1976 San Francisco Festival and released the following year, *Eraserhead,* a weird, nightmarish, black-and-white movie full of surrealistic, often repulsive imagery, was hardly a hit with critics or ordinary filmgoers when it opened. But it soon found its niche in the midnight movie circuit, and has achieved great popularity as a cult favorite.

Lynch gained mainstream respectability with his very next film, *The Elephant Man* (1980), a moving screen dramatization of the Victorian-period, true case history of a monstrously disfigured young man. The film drew wide critical acclaim and was nominated for eight Oscars, including best picture, best director, and best adapted screenplay. Riding the crest of success, Lynch turned down an offer to direct George Lucas's *Revenge of the Jedi* (later retitled *Return of the Jedi*) and instead took on *Dune* (1984), an excessively elaborate screen adaptation of Frank Herbert's science-fiction saga of the year 10,991. It was a disastrous flop both critically and commercially, despite some incredibly beautiful and nightmarish sequences. The producers re-cut a longer special version for TV airing that was disowned by the director, who removed his name from the credits.

Lynch was back in his element with *Blue Velvet* (1986), a bizarre, erotic mystery replete with obsessive kinky sex and deranged violence that seemed to mirror the director's own and perhaps America's unsavory fantasies. Audiences found the film both repulsive and fascinating, voting with their dollars to make it a box-office smash. Critics were divided but many admired the director's originality, boldness, perverted humor, and fertile imagination.

In 1990, Lynch won the Palme d'Or at Cannes for *Wild at Heart,* a wickedly comic, kinky, fairy tale of outrageous imagination. In that same year, he was helming *Twin Peaks*, a limited television series that was immensely popular for a solid year before burning its viewers out on a steady stream of illogical storylines, heady acting, and creepy sideshow elements. The series, which echoed *Blue Velvet* with its exploration of the dark and often sexual side of small-town Americana, drew worldwide viewership, and was seen in unexpurgated versions by an adoring European and Japanese audience. Long after interest in the series had peaked, Lynch presented a feature film chronicling the events leading up to the action of the series, *Twin Peaks: Fire Walk with Me*, which was an artistic and (at least in America) financial failure, escorting in another down-phase of his tumultuous career.

Lynch's creative urge continues to extend in versatile directions. He is a serious photographer and an exhibited painter of soft, moody, semi-abstract canvases. He also writes lyrics, produces recordings, and draws a syndicated cartoon. He has directed and co-created with composer Angelo Badalementi the experimental theatrical work 'Industrial Symphony No. 1.' Lynch's first marriage, in 1967, to a fellow art student, produced a daughter, Jennifer Lynch (*b.* 1968), who directed her first film, *Boxing Helena,* from her own script in 1992. In 1977 Lynch married Mary Fisk, the sister of his longtime friend, director Jack FISK. They had a son in 1982 but later divorced, leaving Lynch free to become romantically linked with *Blue Velvet* star, Isabella ROSSELLINI.

FILMS (as director-screenwriter): *The Alphabet* (short loop; also phot., anim., edit., song, sound) 1968; *The Grandmother* (short; also prod., phot., anim., edit., sound., act.) 1970; *Eraserhead* (also prod., art dir., edit., lyr., special effects) 1977; *The Elephant Man* (also sound des.) 1980; *Dune* 1985; *Blue Velvet* (also lyr.) 1986; *Weeds* (co-lyr. only) 1987; *Zelly and Me* (act. only) 1988; *Wild at Heart* (also lyr.) 1990; *Twin Peaks: Fire Walk with Me* (also co-exec. prod., act.) 1992; *Crumb* (presenter), *Nadja* (co-prod., act.) 1994; *Lost Highway* 1997.

Lynch, Kelly. Actress. Born in 1959, in Minneapolis. Tall, willowy, leggy, blonde leading lady of Hollywood films of the late 80s and early 90s. A stage performer since childhood, she also studied dance and trained for two summers in a directing workshop at the Guthrie Theater. Skipping college, she moved to New York, where she studied acting with Sanford Meisner and Marilyn Fried and for three years modeled for top fashion agencies and appeared occasionally on TV. Making her feature film debut in 1988, she played her first rewarding role the following year in *Drugstore Cowboy,* as a suburban drug fiend. In portraying the character, she reached back into her own experience, when at age 20 she fractured both thighs in a head-on car collision and narrowly escaped addiction to the painkiller Demerol. She broke ground playing a lesbian in one of Hollywood's first mainstream they-just-happen-to-be-gay romantic comedies *Three of Hearts* (1992).

FILMS: *Bright Lights Big City, Cocktail* 1988; *Road House, Drugstore Cowboy, Warm Summer Rain* 1989; *Desperate Hours* 1990; *Curly Sue* 1991; *Three of Hearts* 1992; *The Beans of Egypt, Maine, Imaginary Crimes* 1994; *White Man's Burden, Virtuosity* 1995; *Heaven's Prisoners* 1996.

Lynde, Paul. Actor. *b.* June 13, 1926, Mt. Vernon, Ohio. *d.* 1982. *ed.* Northwestern. Cynical comic of the American stage, much TV, and some films. He made his Broadway debut in 'New Faces of 1952,' for which he wrote some of the material, and his first film appearance in the screen version of the stage revue two years later. He won plaudits on the nightclub circuit and returned to Broadway and Hollywood in the stage (1960) and screen (1963) versions of *Bye Bye Birdie.* In the early 70s he became popular as the star of his own TV shows, 'The Paul Lynde Show' and 'Temperatures Rising,' and as a regular wisecracking panelist on 'The Hollywood Squares' quiz show.

FILMS: *New Faces* (also co-sc.) 1954; *Son of Flubber, Bye Bye Birdie, Under the Yum Yum Tree* 1963; *For Those Who Think Young, Send Me No Flowers* 1964; *Beach Blanket Bingo* 1965; *The Glass Bottom Boat* 1966; *How Sweet It Is* 1968; *Charlotte's Web* (v/o) 1973; *Journey Back to Oz* (v/o) 1974; *Hugo the Hippo* (v/o) 1976; *The Villain* 1978.

Lyndon, Barré (Alfred Edgar). Screenwriter, playwright, *b.* Aug. 12, 1896, London. *d.* 1972. A former journalist and short-story writer, he began his association with films at 40 when Warner Bros. bought the rights to his first play, 'The Amazing Dr. Clitterhouse,' as a vehicle for Edward G. Robinson shortly after its London premiere in 1936. Two other of his plays, 'They Came by Night' and 'The Man in Half-Moon Street,' were later adapted to the screen. He came to Hollywood in 1941 to write the screenplay from his own magazine serial for Henry Hathaway's *Sundown* and subsequently wrote many other screenplays alone or in collaboration. His most interesting contribution to the film medium came in the mid-40s as the sole screenwriter of two atmospheric, sinister psychological thrillers, *The Lodger* (1944) and *Hangover Square* (1945). Both were directed by John BRAHM and featured Laird CREGAR as a tortured heavy, and both have since become recognized as minor classics of the American screen.

FILMS: *The Amazing Dr. Clitterhouse* (play basis only) 1938; *They Came by Night* (play basis only) 1940; *Sundown* (also story) 1941; *The Lodger, The Man in Half-Moon Street* (play basis only) 1944; *Hangover Square, The House on 92nd Street* (co-sc.) 1945; *Night Has a Thousand Eyes* 1948; *To Please a Lady* (story, co-sc.) 1950; *The Greatest Show on Earth* (co-sc.) 1952; *The War of the Worlds, Man in the Attic* (co-sc., based on *The Lodger*) 1953; *Sign of the Pagan* (co-sc.) 1954; *Conquest of Space* (co-adapt. only) 1955; *Omar Khayyam* (also story) 1956; *The Man Who Could Cheat Death* (play basis only, 'The Man in Half-Moon Street'; UK) 1959; *The Little Shepherd of Kingdom Come* 1961; *Dark Intruder* (also story) 1965.

Lyne, Adrian. Director. Born 1941 in England. Long in the US, he made his reputation with flashy TV commercials, bringing to films a flair for technical brilliance, along with a readiness to work to the taste of the marketplace. His first big moneymaker, *Flashdance* (1983), was a glorified rock video, with glitzy visuals and a riveting music score as its main assets. His next, *9½ Weeks* (1986), promised but barely delivered erotic fireworks. Lyne enjoyed a huge critical and commercial triumph with *Fatal Attraction* (1987), a smoothly told, suspenseful story of psychotic obsession marred only by an incredible ending that was lifted straight out of Henri-Georges Clouzot's *Les Diaboliques.* Originally the film had a quieter ending, more compatible with the rest of its story, but preview audiences indicated a desire for violent retribution, which the director provided. The film was nominated for an Academy Award as best picture and earned Lyne a nomination for best director. After turning down an opportunity to direct *The Bonfire of the Vanities,* Lyne tackled a far more complex task in attempting to capture visually the essence of a nightmare in *Jacob's Ladder* (1990), a film about Vietnam-induced total paranoia. In 1993 he was back in his commercial element with the ostensibly moral blockbuster tale *Indecent Proposal*, about a young couple facing a wealthy tycoon's offer of one million dollars for a night with the wife.

FILMS: *Foxes* 1980; *Flashdance* 1983; *9½ Weeks* 1986; *Fatal Attraction* 1987; *Jacob's Ladder* 1990; *Indecent Proposal* 1993; *Lolita* 1997.

Lynen, Robert. Actor. *b.* May 24, 1921, Paris, to American parents. *d.* 1944. A child star and juvenile lead of French films of the 30s, he is best remembered for the lead role in Julien Duvivier's *Poil de Carotte* (1932). He was executed by the German Gestapo at the age of 23.

FILMS INCLUDE: *Poil de Carotte* 1932; *Le Petit Roi* 1933; *Sans Famille* 1934; *L'Homme du Jour/Man of the Hour,*

La Belle Equipe/They Were Five 1936; *Un Carnet de Bal* 1937; *Mollenard/Hatred, Education de Prince/The Barge-Keeper's Daughter* 1938; *La Vie est Magnifique* 1939.

Lynley, Carol. Actress. Born Carolyn Lee, on Feb. 13, 1942, in New York City. A former teenage model, she started in films in adolescent roles and later developed into an attractive and competent leading lady in motion pictures and television productions. Portrayed Jean Harlow in one of two film biographies of the platinum blonde star which were released concurrently in 1965.

FILMS: *The Light in the Forest* 1958; *Holiday for Lovers, Blue Denim* 1959; *Hound-Dog Man* 1960; *Return to Peyton Place, The Last Sunset* 1961; *The Stripper, Under the Yum Yum Tree, The Cardinal* 1963; *Shock Treatment* 1964; *The Pleasure Seekers, Harlow* (Magna company version, in title role), *Bunny Lake Is Missing* 1965; *The Shuttered Room* (UK) 1967; *Danger Route* (UK) 1968; *The Maltese Bippy, Once You Kiss a Stranger* 1969; *Norwood* 1970; *Beware the Blob!, The Poseidon Adventure* 1972; *The Four Deuces* (Isr./UK) 1975; *Bad Georgia Road* 1977; *The Cat and the Canary* (UK) 1978; *The Shape of Things to Come* (Can.) 1979; *Vigilante/Street Gang* 1983; *Balboa* 1985; *Dark Tower, Blackout* 1988; *Howling VI: The Freaks, Spirits* 1990.

Lynn, Diana. Actress. *b.* Dolores Loehr, Oct. 7, 1926, Los Angeles. *d.* 1971. A musical prodigy, she played the piano professionally at age ten and made her film debut in 1939 as one of a group of students performing classical pieces in the background of *They Shall Have Music,* featuring Jascha Heifetz. She was given some lines of dialogue as well as an opportunity to play Grieg's Piano Concerto in another musical film, *There's Magic in Music/The Hard-Boiled Canary* (1941), and was billed as Dolly Loehr. Her name was changed to Diana Lynn when she signed a long-term Paramount contract that same year. After intensive drama coaching, she made an auspicious acting debut as Ginger Rogers's precocious little roommate in Billy Wilder's comedy *The Major and the Minor* (1942) and subsequently played other irrepressible teenage and young adult roles, most notably in *The Miracle of Morgan's Creek* and *Our Hearts Were Young and Gay* (1944). She was less fortunate with her later assignments as a leading lady, playing a succession of standard ingenue roles in a variety of films at Paramount and elsewhere. In the 50s, with her film career in decline, she began appearing on the stage and became one of the busiest and most successful performers in the emerging medium of television. She died of a stroke at 45 while attempting a comeback in films. She was a daughter-in-law of New York *Post* publisher Dorothy Schiff.

FILMS: *They Shall Have Music* (bit) 1939; *There's Magic in Music/The Hard-Boiled Canary* (bit) 1941; *Star-Spangled Rhythm* (bit), *The Major and the Minor* 1942; *Henry Aldrich Gets Glamour* 1943; *The Miracle of Morgan's Creek, And the Angels Sing, Henry Aldrich Plays Cupid, Our Hearts Were Young and Gay* 1944; *Out of This World, Duffy's Tavern* (cameo) 1945; *Our Hearts Were Growing Up, The Bride Wore Boots* 1946; *Easy Come Easy Go, Variety Girl* (cameo) 1947; *Ruthless, Texas Brooklyn and Heaven, Every Girl Should Be Married* 1948; *My Friend Irma* 1949; *Paid in Full, My Friend Irma Goes West, Rogues of Sherwood Forest, Peggy* 1950; *Bedtime for Bonzo, The People Against O'Hara* 1951; *Meet Me at the Fair, Plunder of the Sun* 1953; *Track of the Cat* 1954; *An Annapolis Story, You're Never Too Young, The Kentuckian* 1955; *Company of Killers/The Protectors* (originally made for TV) 1970.

Lynn, Jeffrey. Actor. Born Ragnar Godfrey Lind, on Feb. 16, 1909, in Auburn, Mass. *ed.* Bates Coll. He taught high school English, speech, and drama before making his acting debut in stock in the early 30s. He was signed by Warner Bros. in 1937 and subsequently appeared in many of the studio's films, in both leads and second leads, typically as a reliable, faithful suitor, boyfriend, or husband. His career tapered off after his return from WW II service as a captain in Army Intelligence, and in the 50s and 60s he was seen more often on the stage and on TV than in feature films. He retired from acting late in the 60s and has since held a variety of managerial jobs to support his seven adopted children.

FILMS INCLUDE: *When Were You Born?, Cowboy from Brooklyn, Four Daughters* 1938; *Yes My Darling Daughter, Daughters Courageous, Espionage Agent, The Roaring Twenties, Four Wives* 1939; *A Child Is Born, The Fighting 69th, It All Came True, All This and Heaven Too, Money and the Woman* 1940; *Four Mothers, Flight from Destiny, Million Dollar Baby, Underground, Law of the Tropics, The Body Disappears* 1941; *Black Bart, For the Love of Mary, Whiplash* 1948; *A Letter to Three Wives, Strange Bargain* 1949; *Captain China* 1950; *Up Front* 1951; *Lost Lagoon* 1958; *Butterfield 8* 1960; *Tony Rome* 1967.

Lynn, Jonathan. Actor, director, screenwriter. Born April 3, 1943. *ed.* Pembroke College. He began his acting career in the 60s as a comedian with England's Cambridge Circus, eventually making his way to the London stage, then on to New York. But it was his directing skills for the award-winning British sitcoms 'Yes, Minister' and 'Yes, Prime Minister' that brought him to international attention. He now works primarily as a director in the US.

FILMS: As actor—*Prudence and the Pill* 1968; *Breaking Glass* 1980; *Into the Night* 1985; *Suspicion* 1987; *Three Men and a Little Lady* 1990; *Greedy* 1994. As director and/or screenwriter—*The Internecine Project* (sc.) 1974; *Clue* (dir., sc.) 1985; *The Policeman's Third Ball* (sc.) 1987; *Nuns on the Run* (dir., sc.) 1990; *The Distinguished Gentleman* (dir. only), *My Cousin Vinny* (dir. only) 1992; *Sgt. Bilko* (dir. only) 1996; *Trial and Error* 1997.

Lyon, Ben. Actor. *b.* Feb. 6, 1901, Atlanta. *d.* 1979. Raised in Baltimore and New York City, he began appearing on the stage at 17 and in films at 18. He starred in numerous Hollywood silents and early talkies, memorably as the hero of Howard Hughes's *Hell's Angels* (1930), in which Lyon piloted his own aircraft and shot some of the airborne scenes. In the late 30s he and his wife since 1930, Bebe DANIELS, left for England, where they became popular in vaudeville and on radio and appeared occasionally in films. A veteran airman, Lyon served with distinction as a combat pilot with the British Royal Air Force during WW II and was released with the rank of lieutenant colonel. In the late 40s he served as an executive talent director for Fox and later headed his own talent agency in London. In 1977 he was awarded the Order of the British Empire by Queen Elizabeth II for his World War II work. After the death of his wife in 1971, he married one of his former screen co-stars, Marion NIXON, and moved back to the US.

FILMS INCLUDE: In the US—*Open Your Eyes* 1919; *The Heart of Maryland* 1921; *Potash and Perlmutter, Flaming Youth* 1923; *Painted People, The White Moth, Wine of Youth, Lily of the Dust, Wages of Virtue* 1924; *So Big, The Necessary Evil, Winds of Chance, The Pace That Thrills, The New Commandment, Bluebeard's Seven Wives* 1925; *The Reckless Lady, The Great Deception, The Prince of Tempters, The Savage* 1926; *The Perfect Sap, The Tender Hour, Dance Magic, For the Love of Mike, High Hat* 1927; *The Air Legion* 1928; *The Quitter, The Flying Marine* 1929; *Lummox, A Soldier's Plaything, Alias French Gertie, What Men Want, Hell's Angels* 1930; *My Past, The Hot Heiress, A Soldier's Plaything, Indiscreet, Night Nurse, Bought, Compromised, Her Majesty Love, Misbehaving Ladies*

1931; *Lady with a Past, Week Ends Only, Hat Check Girl, The Big Timer* 1932; *Girl Missing, I Cover the Waterfront* 1933; *Crimson Romance, The Women in His Life, Lightning Strikes Twice* 1934; *Together We Live* 1935; *Dancing Feet* 1936. In the UK—*Mad About Money/He Loved an Actress* 1938; *I Killed the Count/Who Is Guilty?, Confidential Lady* 1939; *Hi Gang* 1940; *The Dark Tower* 1943; *Life with the Lyons/Family Affair* 1953; *The Lyons in Paris* 1954.

Lyon, Francis D. (Pete). Director, former film editor. Born on July 29, 1905, in Bowbells, N.Dak. He began his film career as an editor and established his reputation in England with several distinguished Rank films. He then returned to Hollywood, where he won an Academy Award for editing *Body and Soul* (1947). His films as director, since 1954, have been mostly routine adventures. He has also helmed many episodes for various TV action series.

FILMS INCLUDE: As editor (partial list)—*Hypnotized* 1932; *Things to Come* (UK), *Rembrandt* (UK) 1936; *Knight Without Armor* (UK) 1937; *Intermezzo: A Love Story* 1939; *The Great Profile* 1940; *Adam Had Four Sons* 1941; *Body and Soul* 1947; *Ruthless* 1948; *He Ran All the Way* 1951; *Red Planet Mars* 1952; *The Diamond Queen* 1953 As director (complete)—*Crazylegs, The Bob Mathias Story* 1954; *Cult of the Cobra* 1955; *The Great Locomotive Chase* 1956; *The Oklahoman, Bailout at 43,000, Gunsight Ridge* 1957; *Cinerama—South Seas Adventure* (co-dir. with four others) 1958; *Escort West* 1959; *Tomboy and the Champ* 1961; *The Young and the Brave* 1963; *Destination Inner Space, Castle of Evil* 1966; *The Destructors, The Money Jungle* 1968; *The Girl Who Knew Too Much* 1969. As producer—*Tiger by the Tail* 1970.

Lyon, Sue. Actress. Born on July 10, 1946, in Davenport, Iowa. She was given a big buildup as an upcoming star, as the screen embodiment of Nabokov's nymphet in Stanley Kubrick's *Lolita,* her very first film. But personal problems hampered her career, and her subsequent film appearances have been sporadic.

FILMS: *Lolita* 1962; *The Night of the Iguana* 1964; *Seven Women* 1966; *The Flim Flam Man, Tony Rome* 1967; *Evel Knievel* 1971; *Tarots* (Sp./Fr.) 1973; *To Love Perhaps to Die* (Sp.) 1975; *Crash, End of the World* 1977; *Towing* 1978; *Alligator* 1980; *Invisible Stranger* 1984.

Lyons, Eddie. See MORAN, Lee.

Lytell, Bert. Actor. *b.* Feb. 24, 1885, New York City. *d.* 1954. Onstage from age three, he developed into one of the most popular leading men of the American silent screen. He starred in many films, often romantic melodramas, light adventures, or action pictures, and portrayed the fictional adventurer "The Lone Wolf" several times. Shortly after the advent of sound he returned to the stage, enjoying success in such Broadway productions as 'The First Legion' (1934), which he also produced, and 'Lady in the Dark' (1941). He directed one film, *Along Came Love* (1936). He served for many years as president of Actors' Equity. His brother, Wilfred Lytell (1892–1954), also appeared in silent films.

FILMS INCLUDE: *The Lone Wolf* (title role) 1917; *The Trail to Yesterday, No Man's Land* (also co-sc.), *Boston Blackie's Little Pal* (as Boston Blackie) 1918; *Faith, Blind Man's Eyes, Blackie's Redemption* (as Boston Blackie), *The Lion's Den, Lombardi Ltd.* 1919; *The Right of Way, Alias Jimmy Valentine* (title role), *The Price of Redemption* 1920; *A Message from Mars, The Man Who, A Trip to Paradise, Ladyfingers, The Idle Rich* 1921; *Sherlock Brown, The Right That Failed, To Have and to Hold, Kick In* 1922; *Rupert of Hentzau* (in dual role as King Rudolf and his impersonator), *The Meanest Man in the World* 1923; *The Eternal City, Born Rich, A Son of the Sahara, Sandra* 1924; *Steele of the Royal Mounted, The Boomerang, Eve's Lover, Never the Twain Shall Meet, Sporting Life, Lady Windermere's Fan* (as Lord Windermere) 1925; *Ship of Souls, The Gilded Butterfly, That Model from Paris, The Lone Wolf Returns* (title role), *Obey the Law* 1926; *The First Night, Alias the Lone Wolf* (title role), *Women's Wares* 1927; *On Trial* 1928; *Brothers, Last of the Lone Wolf* (title role) 1930; *The Single Sin* 1931; *Stage Door Canteen* 1943.

McAlpine, Donald. Director of photography. Born in Australia. A former documentary cameraman with the Commonwealth Film Unit, he began shooting feature films in the early 70s, and through his association with director Bruce BERESFORD soon distinguished himself as one of Australia's leading cinematographers. Late in the decade he drew international acclaim for his striking visuals in such films as *My Brilliant Career* and *Breaker Morant,* paving his way for a successful Hollywood career.

FILMS INCLUDE: In Australia—*The Adventures of Barry Mackenzie* 1972; *Don's Party* 1976; *The Getting of Wisdom* 1977; *Patrick, Money Movers* 1978; *The Odd Angry Shot, My Brilliant Career, The Journalist* 1979; *Breaker Morant, The Earthling, The Club* 1980; *Puberty Blues* 1981; *The Man from Snowy River* 1982. In the US—*Tempest, Don't Cry, It's Only Thunder* 1982; *Blue Skies Again* 1983; *Moscow on the Hudson* 1984; *King David* 1985; *Down and Out in Beverly Hills* 1986; *Predator, Orphans* 1987; *Moving, Moon Over Parador* 1988; *See You in the Morning, Parenthood* 1989; *Stanley and Iris* 1990; *The Hard Way, Career Opportunities* 1991.

McAnally, Ray. Actor. *b.* Raymond McAnally, Mar. 30, 1926, Buncrana, County Donegal, Ireland. *d.* 1989. Versatile character player of stage, TV, and films. He began acting as an amateur at age six, making his professional debut at 16. He later trained at Abbey Theatre and became a member of the company in 1947, eventually appearing in 150 of its plays through 1963. On the screen only sporadically, he gained recognition late in his life, when he powerfully played pivotal roles as a conscience-torn Cardinal in *The Mission* and as a loving, authoritarian father in *My Left Foot.* He was married to actress Ronnie Masterson.

FILMS INCLUDE: *She Didn't Say No!, Sea of Sand/Desert Patrol* 1958; *Shake Hands with the Devil* 1959; *The Naked Edge* 1961; *Billy Budd* 1962; *He Who Rides a Tiger* 1966; *The Looking Glass War* 1970; *Fear Is the Key* 1972; *Cal* 1984; *No Surrender, The Mission* 1986; *The Fourth Protocol, Empire State, The Sicilian* 1987; *White Mischief, Taffin, High Spirits* 1988; *My Left Foot, We're No Angels* 1989.

MacArthur, Charles. Screenwriter, director, playwright. *b.* May 5, 1895, Scranton, Pa. *d.* 1956. Originally a reporter, he collaborated with Ben HECHT on such Broadway hits of the early

30s as 'The Front Page' and 'Twentieth Century' and on many bright, sophisticated screenplays. They also co-directed several films in the mid-30s. In addition, MacArthur wrote screenplays, original screen stories, adaptations, and dialogue, alone or in collaboration with writers other than Hecht. He was married to Helen HAYES and was the stepfather of James MACARTHUR. Hecht paid him an intimate tribute in the 1957 biography *Charlie.*

FILMS: As director-producer-screenwriter-original-story writer, in collaboration with Ben Hecht—*Crime Without Passion* 1934; *Once in a Blue Moon, The Scoundrel* 1935; *Soak the Rich* 1936. As screenwriter, alone or in collaboration with Hecht or others—*The Girl Said No* (dial.), *Billy the Kid* (addnl. dial.), *Way for a Sailor* (co-sc., addnl. dial.), *Paid* (co-sc., dial.) 1930; *The Front Page* (co-play basis only), *The Unholy Garden* (co-story, co-sc., co-dial.), *The Sin of Madelon Claudet* (sc., dial.), *The New Adventures of Get-Rich-Quick Wallingford* (sc., dial.) 1931; *Rasputin and the Empress* (story, sc.) 1932; *Twentieth Century* (co-sc. from own co-play) 1934; *Barbary Coast* (co-story, co-sc.) 1935; *Gunga Din* (co-story), *Wuthering Heights* (co-sc.) 1939; *His Girl Friday* (co-play basis only, 'The Front Page'), *I Take This Woman* (story) 1940; *The Senator Was Indiscreet* (sc.), *Lulu Belle* (co-sc. from own co-play) 1948; *Perfect Strangers* (co-play basis only, 'Ladies and Gentlemen'); *Jumbo* (co-play basis only) 1962; *The Front Page* (co-play basis only) 1974; *Switching Channels* (co-play basis only, 'The Front Page') 1988.

MacArthur, James. Actor. Born on Dec. 8, 1937, in Los Angeles. *ed.* Harvard. The adopted son of Charles MACARTHUR and Helen HAYES, he made his stage debut at eight. He has been in films since 1957 in youthful leads and supporting parts, and is known to TV viewers for his role in the series 'Hawaii Five-O' (1968–79).

FILMS INCLUDE: *The Young Stranger* 1957; *The Light in the Forest* 1958; *Third Man on the Mountain* 1959; *Kidnapped* (as David Balfour), *The Swiss Family Robinson* (as Fritz Robinson) 1960; *The Interns* 1962; *Spencer's Mountain, Cry of Battle* 1963; *The Truth About Spring, The Battle of the Bulge, The Bedford Incident,* 1965; *Ride Beyond Vengeance* 1966; *The Love-Ins* 1967; *Hang 'Em High* 1968; *The Angry Breed* 1969.

McAvoy, May. Actress. *b.* Sept. 18, 1901, New York City. *d.* 1984. A leading star of Hollywood silents; the product of a well-to-do family that owned a livery stable on the Park Avenue block now occupied by the Waldorf-Astoria hotel. Eager to become an actress, she left high school in her third year and began making the rounds of casting offices. A petite brunette with a wide-eyed, innocent, pretty face, she soon found herself modeling and appearing in advertising shorts. In 1916 she began playing extra parts in feature films shot in New York and the following year made her debut as an ingenue in *Hate.* At first she was billed as Mae McAvoy. By 1919 she was playing leading ladies with increasing recognition. After scoring a personal success with *Sentimental Tommy* (1921), an adaptation of a James M. Barrie story, she was signed by Paramount and went to Hollywood, already an established star.

McAvoy soon became quite popular (Carl Sandburg called her "a star-eyed goddess") playing innocent heroines. But in 1923, after refusing Cecil B. De Mille's offer for her to appear scantily dressed in his *Adam's Rib,* her roles decreased in number and importance.

She bought out the remainder of her Paramount contract and began freelancing, commanding high fees for her services. She thus was able to select her vehicles more carefully and did quite well for herself in such films as *The Enchanted Cottage,* opposite Richard Barthelmess, Lubitsch's *Lady Windermere's Fan,* co-starring Ronald Colman, and *Ben-Hur,* as Ramon Novarro's Esther. In 1927 she signed a contract with Warners and after several routine roles was cast as Al Jolson's leading lady in the history-making first talkie *The Jazz Singer.* In 1929 she married a business executive and retired from the screen. She later denied that she had been dropped by Warners because of an alleged lisp, as had been reported at the time. In 1940 she was signed as a contract player by MGM. She remained on the payroll until the mid-50s, but appeared only in unbilled extra and bit parts.

FILMS INCLUDE: *Hate* 1917; *To Hell with the Kaiser!, A Perfect Lady* 1918; *Mrs. Wiggs of the Cabbage Patch, The Way of a Woman* 1919; *Man and His Woman, The House of the Tolling Bell, Forbidden Valley, The Devil's Garden, The Truth About Husbands* 1920; *Sentimental Tommy, A Private Scandal, Everything for Sale, Morals, A Virginia Courtship* 1921; *A Homespun Vamp, The Top of New York, Clarence, Kick In* 1922; *Grumpy, Her Reputation, Only 38* 1923; *West of the Water Tower, The Enchanted Cottage, Three Women, Tarnish* 1924; *The Mad Whirl, Tessie, Lady Windermere's Fan* (as Lady Windermere) 1925; *Ben-Hur* (as Esther), *The Road to Glory, My Old Dutch, The Passionate Quest, The Savage, The Fire Brigade* 1926; *Matinee Ladies, Irish Hearts, Slightly Used, A Reno Divorce, The Jazz Singer* 1927; *If I Were Single, The Little Snob, The Lion and the Mouse, Caught in a Fog, The Terror* 1928; *Stolen Kisses, No Defense* 1929; *Two Girls on Broadway* 1940; *Ringside Maisie* 1941; *Luxury Liner* 1948; *Mystery Street* 1950; *Executive Suite* 1954; *Gun Glory* 1957.

McBride, Jim. Director. Born on Sept. 16, 1941, in New York City. *ed.* NYU. Rooted in Manhattan's underground film scene, he asserted himself in 1967 with *David Holzman's Diary,* a bright black-and-white feature, for which he applied tongue-in-cheek *cinéma vérité* methods in recording a day in the life of a serious filmmaker in the process of recording a day in his own life. Made for only $2,500, the film won the grand prizes at both the Mannheim and Pesaro Film Festivals and went on to become a cult favorite. He continued in the same vein with *My Girl Friend's Wedding* (1969), then tackled semisuccessfully a science-fiction theme in *Glen and Randa* (1971). Unable to sustain a commercially viable career, he drove a cab and taught at NYU to make ends meet before finally surfacing in the 80s as a bankable director of mainstream Hollywood fare. He married costume designer Tracy Tynan.

FILMS: *David Holzman's Diary* (also prod., co-sc., edit.) 1967; *My Girl Friend's Wedding* (also act.) 1969; *Glen and Randa* (also co-sc.) 1971; *Hot Times* (also sc., act.) 1974; *Last Embrace* (act. only) 1979; *Breathless* (also co-sc.) 1983; *The Big Easy* 1987; *Great Balls of Fire* (also co-sc., co-mus.) 1989; *The Wrong Man* 1994.

McCallister, Lon. Actor. Born Herbert Alonzo McCallister, Jr., on Apr. 17, 1923, in Los Angeles. Trained from childhood as a singer, dancer, and actor, he began appearing in films in extra and bit roles at 13 but did not graduate to speaking parts until the early 40s. He gained some popularity in the role of a shy GI named California in *Stage Door Canteen* (1943) and subsequently played juvenile leads in a number of films, typically portraying gentle, boyish young men with a rural background. But his small stature (5' 6") became a handicap when he was chronologically ready for adult leads and he retired from the screen in 1953. After an unsuccessful stab at the stage, he settled for a career in real estate.

FILMS INCLUDE: *Romeo and Juliet* 1936; *Souls at Sea, Stella Dallas* 1937; *The Adventures of Tom Sawyer* 1938; *Babes in Arms, First Love* 1939; *High School* 1940; *Henry Aldrich for President* 1941; *Always in My Heart, Yankee Doodle Dandy,*

Gentleman Jim, Over My Dead Body 1942; *Stage Door Canteen* 1943; *Home in Indiana, Winged Victory* 1944; *The Red House, Thunder in the Valley* 1947; *Scudda-Hoo! Scudda-Hay!* 1948; *The Big Cat, The Story of Sea-biscuit* 1949; *The Boy from Indiana* 1950; *A Yank in Korea* 1951; *Montana Territory* 1952; *Combat Squad* 1953.

McCallum, David. Actor. Born on Sept. 19, 1933, in Glasgow, Scotland. The son of the first violinist of the London Philharmonic (who led that orchestra in the film *Prelude to Fame,* 1950), he played the oboe as a child, but after briefly attending the Royal Academy of Music he switched to the Royal Academy of Dramatic Art and became an actor. He appeared in several British films of the late 50s, then settled in Hollywood. He enjoyed some popularity in the 60s in the role of blond Russian secret agent Ilya Kuryakin, co-hero of the TV series 'The Man From UNCLE' (1964–68) and later in 'The Invisible Man' (1975–76). Several of the episodes from the series have been adapted into feature films in which he has starred. His first wife (1957–67) was Jill IRELAND.

FILMS INCLUDE: In the UK—*The Secret Place, Robbery Under Arms, Violent Playground* 1957; *A Night to Remember* 1958; *The Long and the Short and the Tall/Jungle Fighters, Jungle Street/Jungle Street Girls* 1961; *Billy Budd* 1962. In the US—*Freud* (filmed mainly in England) 1962; *The Great Escape* 1963; *The Greatest Story Ever Told* (as Judas Iscariot) 1965; *The Spy with My Face* (rehashed from 1964 TV episodes), *Around the World Under the Sea* 1966; *Three Bites of the Apple* (also co-music and lyrics, singer of title song) 1967; *Sol Madrid* 1968; *Mosquito Squadron* (UK) 1970; *The Kingfish Caper* (UK) 1976; *Dogs* 1977; *King Solomon's Treasure* (Can.) 1978; *The Watcher in the Woods* (UK) 1981; *Terminal Choice/Deathbed* (Can.) 1985; *The Haunting of Morella, Hear My Song* 1991; *Dirty Weekend* 1993; *Healer* 1994.

McCallum, John. Actor. Born on Mar. 14, 1917, in Brisbane, Australia. Charming leading man and supporting player of British films of the late 40s and early 50s. In 1948 he married Googie WITHERS, with whom he later moved back to Australia, where he directed and produced a number of films.

FILMS INCLUDE: In Australia—*Heritage* 1935; *Joe Came Back* 1936; *A Son Is Born* 1946; *Bush Christmas* (narr.) 1947. In the UK—*The Root of All Evil, The Loves of Joanna Godden, It Always Rains on Sunday* 1947; *The Calendar, Miranda* 1948; *The Woman in Question/Five Angles on Murder* 1950; *Valley of the Eagles, Lady Godiva Rides Again* 1951; *Derby Day/Four Against Fate, Trent's Last Case, The Long Memory* 1952; *Melba, Trouble in the Glen* 1953; *Devil on Horseback* 1954; *Smiley, Port of Escape/Safe Harbor* 1956. In Australia—*Three Is One* 1956; *Nickel Queen* (dir., prod., sc only) 1971.

McCambridge, Mercedes. Actress. Born Carlotta Mercedes Agnes McCambridge, on Mar. 17, 1918, in Joliet, Ill. *ed.* Mundelein Coll. Intense leading lady and character player of the American stage, screen, and broadcasting. She began performing on radio while still a college student and before long became one of the busiest and most respected radio actresses in the country. Orson Welles, who co-starred with her in the 'Ford Theater' series, called her "the world's greatest living radio actress." After several successful appearances on Broadway in the late 40s, she was invited to Hollywood and won an Academy Award as best supporting actress for her very first screen role, in *All the King's Men* (1949). She later appeared only intermittently in films, usually in intense, volatile roles and was nominated again for an Oscar for *Giant* (1956). Her career was interrupted for several years in the 60s during a lengthy bout with alcoholism, which she finally overcame. In 1973 she provided the foul offscreen voice of the Demon for the sound track of the film *The Exorcist.* Her second husband (1950–62) was radio-TV writer and sometime movie director Fletcher Markle (1921–91). Her trouble-ridden life was dealt a tragic blow in 1987, when their son, investment banker John Markle, shot his wife and two daughters, then killed himself. Autobiographies: *The Two of Us* (1960); *A Quality of Mercy* (1981).

FILMS: *All the King's Men* 1949; *Inside Straight, Lightning Strikes Twice, The Scarf* 1951; *Johnny Guitar* 1954; *Giant* 1956; *A Farewell to Arms* 1957; *Touch of Evil* 1958; *Suddenly Last Summer* 1959; *Cimarron* 1960; *Angel Baby* 1961; *Run Home Slow* 1965; *The Counterfeit Killer* 1968; *99 Women* 1969; *The Exorcist* (v/o, uncredited) 1973; *Like a Crow on a June Bug* 1974; *Thieves* 1977; *The Concorde—Airport '79* 1979; *Echoes* 1983.

McCarey, Leo. Director, producer, screenwriter. *b.* Thomas Leo McCarey, Oct. 3, 1898, Los Angeles, of Irish-French descent. *d.* 1969. The son of a leading boxing promoter, he fought in the ring briefly as an amateur and operated an unsuccessful copper mine before completing high school. A graduate of USC's law school, he had just begun practicing his profession when he entered films in 1918 as assistant director to Tod Browning on *The Virgin of Stamboul* (1920). He continued working in films in various capacities until 1923, when he joined Hal ROACH as gag writer and director of Charlie Chase comedy shorts. By 1926 he was vice president and supervisor of comedy production at the Roach studios. He thus supervised and wrote the stories for most of LAUREL AND HARDY's silent shorts and himself directed four of these, which are among the comedy team's best. In 1929, McCarey turned to feature films and soon imposed his own brand of undisciplined, frantic comedy on such comic screen personalities as Eddie Cantor (*The Kid from Spain*), the Marx Brothers (in what is probably one of their two best films, *Duck Soup*), W. C. Fields (*Six of a Kind*), Mae West (*Belle of the Nineties*), and Harold Lloyd (*The Milky Way*). Blending an explosive sense of humor with unabashed sentimentality, McCarey came up with such comedy gems as *Ruggles of Red Gap* and *The Awful Truth* and such maudlin pearls as *Make Way for Tomorrow* and *Going My Way.* Jean Renoir said of him: "Leo McCarey is one of the few directors in Hollywood who understands human beings." He won an Academy Award in 1937 for his direction of *The Awful Truth* and two in 1944 for both directing and writing *Going My Way.* From 1937 he produced practically all his own films and wrote the stories or screenplays for most of them. He also supplied story material for such films as *The Cowboy and the Lady* (1938), *My Favorite Wife* (1940), and *Move Over Darling* (1963). His younger brother, Ray McCarey (*b.* Sept. 6, 1904, Los Angeles; *d.* 1948), was a director of mostly routine low-budget films of the 30s and 40s.

FILMS (as director): Shorts (partial list)—*All Wet* 1924; *Bad Boy, Innocent Husbands* 1925; *Crazy Like a Fox, Dog Shy, Be Your Age* 1926; *We Faw Down* 1928; *Liberty, Wrong Again* 1929. Features (complete)—*Society Secrets* 1921; *The Sophomore, Red Hot Rhythm* (also co-story) 1929; *Wild Company, Let's Go Native, Part Time Wife/The Shepper-Newfounder* (also co-sc.) 1930; *Indiscreet* 1931; *The Kid from Spain* 1932; *Duck Soup* 1933; *Six of a Kind, Belle of the Nineties* 1934; *Ruggles of Red Gap* 1935; *The Milky Way* 1936; *Make Way for Tomorrow* (also prod.), *The Awful Truth* (also prod.) 1937; *Love Affair* (also prod., co-story) 1939; *Once Upon a Honeymoon* (also prod., co-story) 1942; *Going My Way* (also prod., story) 1944; *The Bells of St. Mary's* (also prod., story) 1945; *Good Sam* (also prod., co-story) 1948; *My Son John* (also prod., story, co-sc.) 1952; *An Affair to Remember* (also co-story, co-sc.; remake of *Love Affair*) 1957; *Rally 'Round the Flag Boys!* (also prod., co-sc.) 1958; *Satan Never Sleeps/The Devil Never Sleeps* (also prod., co-sc.; US/UK) 1962.

McCarthy, Andrew. Actor. Born in 1962, in Westfield, N.J. *ed.* NYU. Amiable, boyish member of the Hollywood "Brat Pack" of the 80s, typically in sensitive characterizations. Following training in New York at Circle-in-the-Square, he performed off and on Broadway before and after his screen debut in 1983. At the turn of the decade he matured into romantic leads. He resides in the Greenwich Village section of Manhattan.

FILMS: *Class* 1983; *Heaven Help Us, St. Elmo's Fire* 1985; *Pretty in Pink* 1986; *Mannequin, Waiting for the Moon, Less Than Zero* 1987; *Kansas, Fresh Horses* 1988; *Weekend at Bernie's* 1989; *Jours tranquilles à Clichy/Quiet Days In Clichy* (Fr./It./Ger.), *Dr. M/Club Extinction* (Ger./It./Fr.) 1990; *Year of the Gun* 1991; *Only You* 1992; *The Joy Luck Club, Weekend at Bernie's II* 1993; *Mrs. Parker and the Vicious Circle* 1994; *Dead Man, Mulholland Falls* 1996.

McCarthy, Kevin. Actor. Born on Feb. 15, 1914, in Seattle. The brother of writer Mary McCarthy, he joined a drama club at the University of Minnesota and reached the New York stage in 1938. He appeared in a number of Broadway productions in the 40s, notably 'Death of a Salesman,' in which he impressed in the role of Biff. He later made his film debut in the screen version of that play and subsequently played leads and character roles in a score of Hollywood productions while returning frequently to the stage. Memorable in the lead role in Don Siegel's original version of *Invasion of the Body Snatchers* (1956), he played a significant cameo role in Philip Kaufman's 1978 remake. His numerous television appearances include co-starring roles in the series 'The Survivors' (1969–70) and 'Flamingo Road' (1981–82), and many TV movies.

FILMS INCLUDE: *Death of a Salesman* (as Biff Loman) 1951; *Drive a Crooked Road* 1954; *An Annapolis Story, Stranger on Horseback* 1955; *Nightmare, Invasion of the Body Snatchers* 1956; *The Misfits* 1961; *A Gathering of Eagles, An Affair of the Skin, The Prize* 1963; *The Best Man* 1964; *Mirage* 1965; *A Big Hand for the Little Lady* 1966; *Hotel* 1967; *To Hell with Heroes* 1968; *Ace High* 1969; *Kansas City Bomber* 1972; *Alien Thunder* (Can.) 1974; *El Clan des los Immorales/Order to Kill* (Sp.) 1974; *The Three Sisters* 1977; *Piranha, Invasion of the Body Snatchers* 1978; *Hero at Large, Those Lips Those Eyes* 1980; *The Howling* 1981; *My Tutor, Twilight Zone—The Movie* 1983; *Innerspace, Hostage* 1987; *Dark Tower* 1988; *Fast Food, UHF* 1989; *Eve of Destruction, Love or Money, Sleeping Car, Texas Guns* 1990; *Ghoulies 3: Ghoulies Go to College, Final Approach* 1991; *The Distinguished Gentleman* 1992; *Greedy* 1994; *Just Cause, Steal Big, Steal Little* 1995.

McCartney, Paul. See BEATLES, THE.

McCay, Winsor. Animator. *b.* Sept. 26, 1871, Spring Lake, Mich. *d.* 1934. A graduate of the Ypsilanti Normal School, he began his career as a poster designer, later working as a scenic artist for the Street Dime Museum in Cincinnati. In 1898 he became a cartoonist-reporter for Cincinnatti newspapers and in 1903 began drawing comic strips for the New York *Evening Telegram,* then the *Herald,* achieving success with 'Dreams of a Rarebit Fiend' and 'Little Nemo in Slumberland.' In 1906 McCay began touring the vaudeville circuit with an act that incorporated his cartoons. Around the same time, with the encouragement of film director J. Stuart BLACKTON, he began the laborious task of creating his first animated film cartoon. First shown as part of his vaudeville act in 1911, *Little Nemo* comprised 4,000 separate drawings, all hand-colored. Other animated films followed, culminating in *Gertie the Dinosaur* (1914), a marvelously charming cartoon that continues to delight audiences. McCay's medium-length *The Sinking of the Lusitania* (1918), comprising 25,000 drawings, was long considered cinema's first feature cartoon. But it seems that distinction belongs to an obscure Argentine film, *El Apostol* ('The Apostle'), created by Frederico Valle: completed in 1917, it boasted 50,000 drawings and had a running time of 60 minutes. By the early 20s MacCay had lost interest in film animation and withdrew from the business. His work was soon forgotten. But his pioneering contributions to screen animation were rediscovered in the 60s and he is widely admired today as the American screen's first creative cartoonist.

FILMS INCLUDE: *Little Nemo* 1909; *How a Mosquito Operates/The Story of a Mosquito* 1912; *Gertie the Dinosaur/Gertie the Trained Dinosaur* 1914; *The Sinking of the Lusitania* 1918; *The Centaurs* 1919; *Dreams of a Rarebit Fiend* (series) 1921.

McClure, Doug. Actor. Born on May 11, 1935, in Glendale, Calif. Blond, blue-eyed, rugged but boyish leading man. In films from 1957, it was on TV that he had his best success with such series as 'The Overland Trail' (1960), 'Checkmate' (1960–62), 'The Virginian' (1962–71), and 'Search' (1975–76). The second (1961–63) of his four aborted marriages was to stage and screen actress Barbara Dana (*b.* 1937, New York City) who later married Alan ARKIN.

FILMS INCLUDE: *The Enemy Below* 1957; *Gidget* 1959; *The Unforgiven* 1960; *The Lively Set* 1964; *Shenandoah* 1965; *Beau Geste* 1966; *The King's Pirate* 1967; *Nobody's Perfect* 1968; *Backtrack* 1969; *The Land That Time Forgot* (UK/US) 1974; *What Changed Charley Farthing?* (UK) 1975; *At the Earth's Core* (UK) 1976; *The People That Time Forgot* 1977; *Warlords of Atlantis* 1978; *Humanoids from the Deep* 1980; *The House Where Evil Dwells* 1982; *Cannonball Run II* 1984; *52 Pick-Up* 1986; *Omega Syndrome* 1987; *Dark Before Dawn, Tapeheads* 1988.

McConaughey, Matthew. Actor. Born in 1969, in Texas. *ed.* University of Texas. Handsome, solid leading man of American films. He was "discovered" in a bar in Austin, Texas, by independent filmmaker Richard LINKLATER who eventually cast him in the cult favorite *Dazed and Confused* (1993). Often compared to the young Paul Newman, this down-to-earth actor shot to stardom with his breakthrough role as Drew Barrymore's hunky boyfriend in *Boys on the Side* (1995) and later gave a solid performance in the film adaptation of John Grisham's novel *A Time to Kill.*

FILMS: *The Texas Chainsaw Massacre 2* 1986; *Dazed and Confused, My Boyfriend's Back* 1993; *Angels in the Outfield, Bo* 1994; *Boys on the Side, The Return of the Texas Chainsaw Massacre, Scorpion Spring* 1995; *A Time to Kill, Lone Star, Larger Than Life* 1996; *Contact, Amistad* 1997.

McCord, Ted. Director of photography. *b.* 1898, Sullivan County, Ind. *d.* 1976. McCord entered films as a camera assistant in 1917, beginning his career as a cinematographer in the early 20s. In the sound era, he worked on many routine action pictures through the mid-40s, when he graduated to major productions at Warner Bros. During WW II, as an Army captain, he was among the first Americans to enter Berlin, where he photographed the interior of Hitler's chancellery. He is sometimes billed as T. D. McCord.

FILMS INCLUDE: *Sacred and Profane Love* (co-phot.) 1921; *Flirting with Love, For Sale, So Big* 1924; *The Desert Flower, The Marriage Whirl, Sally, We Moderns* 1925; *Irene* 1926; *The Valley of the Giants* 1927; *The Code of the Scarlet, The Crash, The Phantom City* 1928; *The Wagon Master* 1929; *The Fighting Legion, The Lone Rider, Mountain Justice, Sons of the Saddle* 1930; *Desert Vengeance* 1931; *Carnival Boat, The Big Stampede* 1932; *The Man from Monterey* 1933; *Doomed to Die* 1934; *The Rainmakers* 1935; *Fugitive in the Sky* 1936; *Secret Service of the Air* 1939; *Ladies Must Live* 1940; *The Case of the Black Parrot* 1941; *Wild Bill Hickok Rides, Murder in the Big House* 1942; *Action in the North Atlantic* 1943; *Deep Valley* 1947; *The Treasure of the Sierra Madre, Johnny Belinda, June Bride* 1948; *Flamingo Road* 1949; *The Damned Don't Cry, Young Man with a Horn, The Breaking Point* 1950; *Goodbye My Fancy, Force of Arms, I'll See You in My Dreams* 1951; *Young at Heart* 1954; *East of Eden, I Died a Thousand Times* 1955; *The Helen Morgan Story* 1957; *The Proud Rebel* 1958; *The Hanging Tree* 1959; *The Adventures of Huckleberry Finn* 1960; *Two for the Seesaw* 1962; *The Sound of Music* 1965; *A Fine Madness* 1966.

MacCorkindale, Simon. Actor, producer. Born on Feb. 12, 1952, in Ely, Cambridge, England. Handsome, debonair leading man of British and American stage, TV, and films. He turned to producing in the late 80s, under the banner Amy International. He married actress Susan George.

FILMS INCLUDE: As actor—*Death on the Nile* 1978; *The Riddle of the Sands, Quatermass Conclusion* (orig. for TV) 1979; *Caboblanco* 1980; *The Sword and the Sorcerer* 1982; *Jaws 3-D* 1983; *Sincerely Violet* 1987. As producer—*Stealing Heaven* 1988; *The Summer of White Roses* (also co-sc.) 1989.

McCormack, Patty. Actress. Born on Aug. 21, 1945, in Brooklyn, N.Y. A model at age four and a TV performer at seven, she burst into stardom as the murderous little brat of both the Broadway (1954) and screen (1956) versions of *The Bad Seed.* She went on to play troubled teenagers in routine films of the 60s. On TV she appeared in "Mama" (1953–57) and "The Ropers" (1979–80) and briefly starred in her own series "Peck's Bad Girl" (1959). She also sang with rock bands. In 1988 she returned to movies after a long absence, in a mother's role.

FILMS: *Two Gals and a Guy* 1951; *The Bad Seed* 1956; *All Mine to Give* 1957; *Kathy O'* 1958; *The Adventures of Huckleberry Finn* (as Joanna) 1960; *The Explosive Generation* 1961; *Jacktown* 1962; *Maryjane, The Mini-Skirt Mob, The Young Runaways, Born Wild/The Young Animals* 1968; *Bug* 1975; *Saturday the 14th Strikes Back* 1988.

McCormick, Myron. Actor. *b.* Walter Myron McCormick, Feb. 8, 1907, Albany, Ind. *d.* 1962. A Phi Beta Kappa graduate of Princeton, he persuasively played memorable character parts in many stage plays and, regrettably, only occasional films.

FILMS: *Winterset* 1937; *One Third of a Nation* 1939; *The Fight for Life* 1940; *China Girl* 1943; *Jigsaw, Jolson Sings Again* 1949; *Three for the Show, Not as a Stranger* 1955; *No Time for Sergeants* 1958; *The Man Who Understood Women* 1959; *The Hustler* 1961; *A Public Affair* 1962.

McCowen, Alec. Actor. Born Alexander Duncan McCowen, on May 26, 1925, Tunbridge Wells, England. Distinguished, versatile character player of the British stage and screen. Trained at RADA, he made his debut in repertory in 1942 and his first film appearance a decade later. He has been performing frequently on Broadway and in select distinguished films.

FILMS INCLUDE: *The Cruel Sea* 1953; *The Divided Heart* 1954; *The Deep Blue Sea* 1955; *The Good Companions, The Long Arm/The Third Key* 1956; *Town on Trial, Time Without Pity, The One That Got Away* 1957; *A Night to Remember, The Silent Enemy, The Doctor's Dilemma* 1958; *The Loneliness of the Long Distance Runner* 1962; *In the Cool of the Day* 1963; *The Witches/The Devil's Own* 1966; *The Hawaiians* (US) 1970; *Frenzy, Travels with My Aunt* 1972; *Stevie* 1978; *Hanover Street* 1979; *Never Say Never Again* 1983; *Forever Young* 1984; *The Assam Garden* 1985; *Personal Services, Cry Freedom* 1987; *Henry V* 1989; *The Age of Innocence* 1993.

McCoy, Tim. Actor. *b.* Timothy John Fitzgerald McCoy, Apr. 10, 1891, Saginaw, Mich. *d.* 1978. After studies at Chicago's St. Ignatius College, he settled on a large ranch in Wyoming which bordered on a Sioux Indian reservation and he soon became known as an authority on Indian dialects, customs, and lore. Following WW I military service, from which he was discharged with the rank of lieutenant colonel, he was appointed Indian Agent for his territory. It was in this capacity that he made his first contact with the world of films in 1922, as technical advisor and co-ordinator of Indian extras for James Cruze's *The Covered Wagon* (1923). He is also supposed to have done some trick riding in the film. He later accompanied his Indians on a publicity tour of the US and Europe. Returning home, he resigned his government post to play a key supporting role in the Paramount Western *The Thundering Herd.* In 1925 he was signed by MGM as the star of a series of Westerns and other action pictures, based on episodes in American frontier history.

The films were superior in production values and employed such talented directors as W. S. Van Dyke and such promising actresses as Joan Crawford and Jean Arthur. By the early 30s, when he left MGM, McCoy was one of Hollywood's most popular Western stars. He was the hero of the first sound serial at Universal, *The Indians Are Coming,* then appeared in a string of Westerns for Columbia and independent studios. In 1935 he took to the road with the Ringling Brothers circus and in 1938 started his own ill-fated Wild West show. Returning to films in 1940, he was teamed with Buck Jones and Raymond Hatton in a series of low-budget "Rough Rider" Westerns at Monogram which ended abruptly in 1942 after Jones's tragic death in a fire. Following WW II military service, McCoy retired to his Wyoming ranch, but in 1949 he reappeared in TV and later played a number of cameo roles in films. In 1945 he married Inga Arvad, a well-known Danish-born journalist who passed away in 1973.

FILMS INCLUDE: *The Covered Wagon* (technical advisor and extra co-ordinator only) 1923; *The Thundering Herd* 1925; *War Paint* 1926; *Winners of the Wilderness, California, The Frontiersman, Foreign Devils, Spoilers of the West* 1927; *The Law of the Range, Wyoming, Riders of the Dark, The Adventurer, Beyond the Sierras* 1928; *Morgan's Last Raid, The Overland Telegraph, Sioux Blood, The Desert Rider* 1929; *The Indians Are Coming* (serial) 1930; *The Fighting Fool* 1932; *Man of Action* 1933; *The Westerner* 1935; *Phantom Ranger* 1938; *Texas Marshal* 1941; *West of the Law* 1942; *Around the World in 80 Days* 1956; *Run of the Arrow* 1957; *Requiem for a Gunfighter* 1965.

McCrea, Joel. Actor. *b.* Nov. 5, 1905, South Pasadena, Calif., of Scottish-Irish descent. *d.* 1990. The grandson of a Western stagecoach driver who fought Apaches and the son of a utility executive, he raised and maintained his own horses at an early age. The family moved to Hollywood when he was nine. As a youngster he became fascinated by the filming activity around town and thrilled by the opportunity to hold horses for his cowboy heroes, William S. Hart and Tom Mix. He acquired acting experience at Pomona College and later performed at the Pasadena Community Playhouse. He entered films in 1922 as a wrangler, extra, and stuntman. According to some sources, he doubled for Greta Garbo (!) on horseback in *The Torrent* (1926). He moved into featured roles in 1929 and into leads the following year. During the 30s and early 40s he played a variety of lead roles in a wide range of films, from straight dramas and sophisticated comedies to rugged adventures. His career reached a peak in the early 40s, when he starred in such films as Alfred

Hitchcock's *Foreign Correspondent,* Preston Sturges's *Sullivan's Travels* and *Palm Beach Story,* George Stevens's *The More the Merrier,* and William Wellman's *Reaching for the Sun, The Great Man's Lady,* and *Buffalo Bill.* But from 1946 on he was seen almost exclusively in Westerns. In addition to making many films, he also appeared on TV, on such programs as 'Four Star Playhouse' and the 'Wichita Town' Western series. He invested wisely in livestock and real estate and was among Southern California's wealthiest ranchers. A fervid outdoorsman who believed deeply in the work ethic and virtually never smoked or drank, he was a staunch Republican and was known fondly among his friends as a frugal millionaire. He was married to actress Frances DEE from 1933. The eldest of their three sons, Jody McRae (b. 1934), played young leads in films of the late 50s and the 60s but retired from the screen in 1970 to become a rancher in New Mexico.

FILMS (excluding extra and bit roles): *The Jazz Age, So This Is College, The Single Standard, Dynamite* 1929; *The Silver Horde, Lightnin'* 1930; *Once a Sinner, Kept Husbands, Born to Love, The Common Law, Girls About Town* 1931; *Business and Pleasure, The Lost Squadron, Bird of Paradise, The Most Dangerous Game/Hounds of Zaroff, Rockabye, The Sport Parade* 1932; *The Silver Cord, Bed of Roses, One Man's Journey, Chance at Heaven* 1933; *Gambling Lady, Half a Sinner, The Richest Girl in the World* 1934; *Private Worlds, Our Little Girl, Barbary Coast, Splendor, Woman Wanted* 1935; *These Three, Two in a Crowd, Adventure in Manhattan, Come and Get It, Banjo on My Knee* 1936; *Internes Can't Take Money, Woman Chases Man, Dead End, Wells Fargo* 1937; *Three Blind Mice, Youth Takes a Fling* 1938; *Union Pacific, They Shall Have Music, Espionage Agent* 1939; *He Married His Wife, The Primrose Path, Foreign Correspondent* 1940; *Reaching for the Sun, Sullivan's Travels* 1941; *The Great Man's Lady, The Palm Beach Story* 1942; *The More the Merrier* 1943; *Buffalo Bill, The Great Moment* 1944; *The Unseen* 1945; *The Virginian* 1946; *Ramrod* 1947; *Four Faces West* 1948; *South of St. Louis, Colorado Territory* 1949; *Stars in My Crown, The Outriders, Saddle Tramp* 1950; *Frenchie, The Hollywood Story* (unbilled cameo), *Cattle Drive* 1951; *The San Francisco Story* 1952; *Rough Shoot/Shoot First* (UK), *Lone Hand* 1953; *Border River, Black Horse Canyon* 1954; *Wichita, Stranger on Horseback* 1955; *The First Texan* 1956; *The Oklahoman, Trooper Hook, Gunsight Ridge, The Tall Stranger* 1957; *Cattle Empire, Fort Massacre* 1958; *Gunfight at Dodge City/Guns in the Afternoon* 1959; *Ride the High Country* 1962; *Cry Blood—Apache* 1970; *The Great American Cowboy* (doc.; narrator) 1974; *Mustang Country* 1976; *George Stevens: A Filmmaker's Journey* (doc.) 1985.

McDaniel, Hattie. Actress. *b.* June 10, 1895, Wichita, Kans. *d.* 1952. The daughter of a Baptist preacher and his spiritual-singer wife, she won a drama medal at 15 and began her professional career as a band vocalist. She was the first black woman to sing on American radio and after many performances on such programs as 'Amos 'n' Andy' and the 'Eddie Cantor Show,' starred in 'Beulah,' both on radio and on TV. She appeared in numerous films of the 30s and 40s, typically in the role of a maid, and became closely identified with the screen image of the eternal black mammy. She won an Academy Award as best supporting actress for her performance in *Gone With the Wind* (1939), becoming the first black performer to be so honored.

FILMS INCLUDE: *The Golden West, Blonde Venus* 1932; *I'm No Angel* 1933; *Babbitt, Imitation of Life, Judge Priest* 1934; *The Little Colonel, China Seas, Alice Adams* 1935; *Libeled Lady, Show Boat, Valiant Is the Word for Carrie, Reunion* 1936; *Saratoga, Nothing Sacred* 1937; *The Shopworn Angel, Carefree* 1938; *Gone With the Wind* 1939; *Maryland* 1940; *The Great Lie* 1941; *The Male Animal, In This Our Life* 1942; *Johnny Come Lately* 1943; *Since You Went Away* 1944; *Margie, Never Say Goodbye, Song of the South* 1946; *The Flame* 1947; *Mickey* 1948; *Family Honeymoon* 1949.

McDermott, Dylan. Actor. Born on Oct. 26, 1962, in Waterbury, Conn. Leading man of Hollywood films of the late 80s and early 90s. The son of playwright Eve Ensler, he trained for the stage at New York's Neighborhood Playhouse and appeared on Broadway ('Biloxi Blues') and off Broadway ('Scooncat') before entering films in 1987.

FILMS: *Hamburger Hill* 1987; *The Blue Iguana* 1988; *Twister, Steel Magnolias* 1989; *Hardware* (UK) 1990; *In the Line of Fire* 1993; *The Cowboy Way, Miracle on 34th Street* 1994; *Destiny Turns on the Radio, Home for the Holidays* 1995; *Til There Was You* 1997.

MacDonald, David. Director. *b.* May 9, 1904, Helensburgh, Scotland. *d.* 1983. He ran a Malaya rubber plantation before beginning his film career in Hollywood in 1929 as assistant to C. B. DE MILLE. In 1936 he returned to England as a director, mostly of mystery and adventure yarns. During WW II, as a colonel with the British Army film unit, he produced two celebrated war documentaries, *Desert Victory* (1943) and *Burma Victory* (1945). Most of his postwar films were routine as he gradually switched to TV.

FILMS INCLUDE: *Double Alibi, The Last Curtain, Riding High* 1937; *Dead Men Tell No Tales, This Man Is News* 1938; *This Man in Paris, Spies of the Air* 1939; *Law and Disorder* 1940; *This England* 1941; *The Brothers* 1947; *Good Time Girl, Snowbound* 1948; *Christopher Columbus, The Bad Lord Byron* 1949; *Cairo Road* 1950; *The Adventurers* 1951; *The Lost Hours* 1952; *Devil Girl from Mars* 1954; *Small Hotel* 1957; *The Moonraker* 1958; *Petticoat Pirates* 1961; *The Golden Rabbit* 1962.

McDonald, Francis. Actor. *b.* Aug. 22, 1891, Bowling Green, Ky. *d.* 1968. Romantic leading man, then stock villain and utility character player of hundreds of Hollywood films from 1912. He was considered one of the American screen's most handsome men early in his career. He was once married to Mae BUSCH.

FILMS INCLUDE: *A Bold Impersonation* 1915; *Black Orchids* 1917; *The Gun Woman, I Love You, Real Folks, The Answer, The Ghost Flower, Tony America* 1918; *The Divorce Trap, The Final Close-Up, Prudence on Broadway* 1919; *The Confession, Nomads of the North* 1920; *Puppets of Fate, Hearts and Masks, The Call of the North* 1921; *Monte Cristo* (as Benedetto), *Trooper O'Neill* 1922; *Trilby, Going Up* 1923; *Racing Luck, East of Broadway* 1924; *Northern Code, Satan in Sables, My Lady of Whims* 1925; *The Yankee Señor, Puppets, Battling Butler, The Temptress, The Palace of Pleasure* 1926; *The Wreck, The Notorious Lady* 1927; *A Girl in Every Port, The Legion of the Condemned, The Dragnet* 1928; *Burning Up, Dangerous Paradise, Morocco* 1930; *The Gang Buster* 1931; *The Devil Is Driving* 1932; *Broadway Bad* 1933; *The Trumpet Blows* 1934; *Star of Midnight* 1935; *The Prisoner of Shark Island, The Plainsman, Under Two Flags* 1936; *Wild West Days* (serial) 1937; *If I Were King* 1938; *Union Pacific, The Light That Failed* 1939; *Green Hell, The Sea Hawk, North West Mounted Police* 1940; *The Sea Wolf* 1941; *The Kansan* 1943; *Tangier* 1946; *The Perils of Pauline, Duel in the Sun* 1947; *The Paleface, An Act of Murder* 1948; *Samson and Delilah* 1949; *Rancho Notorious* 1952; *The Ten Commandments* 1956; *The Big Fisherman* 1959.

McDonald, Frank. Director. *b.* Nov. 9, 1899, Baltimore. *d.* 1980. A former railroad man and stage actor-director-writer, he came to Hollywood in 1933 as dialogue director and began directing in 1935. He turned out some 100 B pictures for Warner Bros., Paramount, Republic, and other studios, ranging from light romances and musicals to run-of-the mill mysteries and Westerns, including Gene Autry and Roy Rogers oaters. In addition, he directed numerous episodes for various TV series.

FILMS INCLUDE: *Broadway Hostess* 1935; *The Murder of Dr. Harrigan, Boulder Dam, Treachery Rides the Range, Murder by an Aristocrat, The Big Noise, Love Begins at 20, Isle of Fury* 1936; *Smart Blonde, Midnight Court, Her Husband's Secretary, Fly Away Baby, Dance Charlie Dance, The Adventurous Blonde* 1937; *Over the Wall, Blondes at Work, Reckless Living, Freshman Year, Flirting with Fate* 1938; *They Asked for It, Jeepers Creepers* 1939; *Rancho Grande, Gaucho Serenade, Carolina Moon, Grand Old Opry* 1940; *Country Fair, Flying Blind, Under Fiesta Stars, No Hands on the Clock* 1941; *Mountain Rhythm, Wildcat, Wrecking Crew, The Traitor Within* 1942; *High Explosive, Alaska Highway, Submarine Alert, O My Darling Clementine* 1943; *Timber Queen, Take It Big, One Body Too Many* 1944; *Bells of Rosarita, The Chicago Kid, The Man from Oklahoma, Sunset in El Dorado* 1945; *Song of Arizona, Rainbow Over Texas, My Pal Trigger* 1946; *Hit Parade of 1947, Under Nevada Skies, Bulldog Drummond Strikes Back, When a Girl's Beautiful* 1947; *Mr. Reckless, French Leave, Gun Smugglers* 1948; *The Big Sombrero, Ringside* 1949; *Call of the Klondike* 1950; *Sierra Passage, Texans Never Cry, Father Takes the Air, Northwest Territory* 1951; *Sea Tiger* 1952; *Son of Belle Starr* 1953; *The Big Tip-Off* 1955; *The Purple Gang* 1960; *The Underwater City* 1962; *Gunfight at Comanche Creek* 1963; *Mara of the Wilderness* 1965.

MacDonald, Jeanette. Actress, singer. *b.* June 18, 1901, Philadelphia. *d.* 1965. A Broadway chorus girl in 1920, she rapidly reached stardom in stage musicals and operettas. Richard Dix saw her perform and talked Paramount into giving her a screen test. Ernst Lubitsch saw the test and chose her to star in *The Love Parade* (1929) and then in a couple of other sophisticated screen musicals opposite Maurice Chevalier. With MGM from 1933, she enjoyed increasing popularity as a singing star, especially after teaming up with Nelson EDDY in the most successful singing partnership in musical film history. At the height of their popularity, in the late 30s, the two were known as "America's Sweethearts" and their string of saccharine screen musicals brought millions of American and European customers to the box office.

But wartime audiences were less appreciative and in 1942 MGM terminated Miss MacDonald's contract. She returned to the screen in a cameo and in the late 40s in two mother roles, then retired from films to seek a new career in concert halls and on the stage. Long a subject of ridicule by cynics and stand-up comics, for such corny innocent-age numbers as 'Indian Love Call,' the Eddy-MacDonald musicals have come to enjoy the status of "high camp." Miss MacDonald was married from 1937 to screen actor Gene Raymond. One of her sisters was character actress Marie Blake.

FILMS: *The Love Parade* 1929; *The Vagabond King, Monte Carlo, Let's Go Native, The Lottery Bride, Oh for a Man!* 1930; *Don't Bet on Women, Annabelle's Affairs* 1931; *One Hour with You, Love Me Tonight* 1932; *The Cat and the Fiddle, The Merry Widow* 1934; *Naughty Marietta* 1935; *Rose Marie, San Francisco* 1936; *Maytime, The Firefly* 1937; *The Girl of the Golden West, Sweethearts* 1938; *Broadway Serenade* 1939; *New Moon, Bitter Sweet* 1940; *Smilin' Through* 1941; *I Married an Angel, Cairo* 1942; *Follow the Boys* (cameo, 1944); *Three Daring Daughters* 1948; *The Sun Comes Up* 1949.

MacDonald, J(ohn) Farrell. Actor, director. *b.* June 6, 1875, Waterbury, Conn. *d.* 1952. A veteran of the stage as an actor and a singer, he entered films with IMP in 1911 and for several years played leads in numerous productions, often opposite his wife, who was billed as Mrs. MacDonald. He later worked for other studios and directed a number of films, including *Lonesome Luke—Social Gangster* (1915), one of Harold Lloyd's earliest vehicles. MacDonald gradually moved from leads to supporting roles and by the early 20s had become established as a fine character actor. He figured prominently in many of John Ford's silents and later appeared in several of that director's talkies. In all he appeared in hundreds of films.

FILMS INCLUDE: As director—*Samson, And She Never Knew, The Patchwork Girl of Oz, The Tides of Sorrow* 1914; *Lorna Doone, Lonesome Luke* 1915. As actor—*The Last Egyptian* 1914; *Rags, The Heart of Maryland* 1915; *The Outcasts of Poker Flat, A Fight for Love, Riders of Vengeance, Marked Men* 1919; *Under Sentence, Hitchin' Posts* 1920; *The Freeze Out, Action, Riding with Death* 1921; *Sky High, Manslaughter, The Young Rajah* 1922; *While Paris Sleeps, Quicksands, Drifting, The Age of Desire* 1923; *The Storm Daughter, The Signal Tower, The Iron Horse* 1924; *Lightnin', The Fighting Heart, Thank You* 1925; *The Dixie Merchant, The Shamrock Handicap, Three Bad Men* 1926; *Ankles Preferred, The Cradle Snatchers, Colleen, Paid to Love, Sunrise, East Side West Side* 1927; *The Cohens and the Kellys in Paris, Bringing Up Father* (as Jiggs of "Maggie and Jiggs" cartoon fame), *Abie's Irish Rose, Riley the Cop* 1928; *In Old Arizona, Strong Boy, Masquerade, Four Devils* 1929; *Men Without Women, Song o' My Heart, The Girl of the Golden West, River's End, The Truth About Youth* 1930; *The Easiest Way, The Painted Desert, The Millionaire, The Maltese Falcon, Sporting Blood, The Brat, The Squaw Man* 1931; *Hotel Continental, The Phantom Express* (lead), *The Pride of the Legion/The Big Pay-Off* (lead), *Me and My Gal* 1932; *The Iron Master, Heritage of the Desert, The Working Man, Peg o' My Heart, The Power and the Glory, I Loved a Woman* 1933; *Man of Two Worlds, The Crime Doctor, The Cat's Paw* 1934; *Romance in Manhattan, The Whole Town's Talking, Star of Midnight, Front Page Woman, The Irish in Us* 1935; *Riffraff, Show Boat* 1936; *Slave Ship, Slim, Topper* 1937; *White Banners, Submarine Patrol* 1938; *Zenobia, Susannah of the Mounties* 1939; *Dark Command, Untamed* 1940; *Meet John Doe, The Great Lie* 1941; *Captains of the Clouds* 1942; *The Miracle of Morgan's Creek, The Great Moment* 1944; *A Tree Grows in Brooklyn* 1945; *Smoky, My Darling Clementine* 1946; *Fury at Furnace Creek* 1948; *Whispering Smith, the Beautiful Blonde from Bashful Bend* 1949; *Woman on the Run* 1950; *Mr. Belvedere Rings the Bell, Elopement* 1951.

MacDonald, Joseph P(atrick). Director of photography. *b.* Dec. 15, 1906, Mexico City, to American parents. *d.* 1968. *ed.* USC (mining engineering). An assistant cameraman from the early 20s, he graduated to cinematographer in the early 40s and soon proved himself an excellent craftsman in both black and white and color, achieving equally successful results with interior lighting and outdoor cinematography.

FILMS INCLUDE: *Charlie Chan in Rio* 1941; *Wintertime* 1943; *In the Meantime Darling, The Big Noise* 1944; *Captain Eddie* 1945; *Shock, The Dark Corner, My Darling Clementine* 1946; *Call Northside 777, The Street with No Name, Yellow Sky* 1948; *Down to the Sea in Ships, Pinky* 1949; *Panic in the Streets* 1950; *14 Hours* 1951; *Viva Zapata, What Price Glory, O. Henry's Full House* (co-phot.) 1952; *Niagara, Titanic, Pickup on South Street, How to Marry a Millionaire* 1953; *Hell and High Water, Broken Lance, Woman's World* 1954; *House of Bamboo* 1955; *On the Threshold of Space, Bigger Than Life* 1956; *The True Story of Jesse James, A Hatful of Rain* 1957; *The*

Young Lions, Ten North Frederick, The Fiend Who Walked the West 1958; *Warlock* 1959; *Pepe* 1960; *Walk on the Wild Side, Taras Bulba* 1962; *The List of Adrian Messenger, Kings of the Sun* 1963; *The Carpetbaggers, Rio Conchos* 1964; *Mirage, The Reward* 1965; *Blindfold, Alvarez Kelly, The Sand Pebbles* 1966; *A Guide for the Married Man* 1967; *Mackenna's Gold* 1969.

McDonald, Marie. Actress, singer. *b.* Cora Marie Frye, 1923, Burgin, Ky. *d.* 1965. A former model, showgirl, and band vocalist, she became a movie starlet in the early 40s. Hollywood publicity nicknamed her "The Body," but despite continual mention in gossip columns and involvement in scandals that kept her name in headlines, her career made little headway. She was married seven times (including remarriages) before her sudden death from an overdose of pills.

FILMS INCLUDE: *It Started with Eve* 1941; *Pardon My Sarong, Lucky Jordan* 1942; *Riding High* 1943; *I Love a Soldier, Standing Room Only* 1944; *Guest in the House, It's a Pleasure, Getting Gertie's Garter* 1945; *Living in a Big Way* 1947; *Tell It to the Judge* 1949; *Once a Thief* 1950; *The Geisha Boy* 1958; *Promises! Promises!* 1963.

MacDonald, Richard. Art director. Born in 1919 in Bristol, England. *ed.* Royal College of Art, London. He began his film career in 1954 with a durable collaboration with director Joseph Losey, initially as a "design consultant," then as an art director and production designer. He also designed sets for major films of other directors in England and later in the US.

FILMS INCLUDE: In the UK—*The Sleeping Tiger* 1954; *The Intimate Stranger/Finger of Guilt* 1956; *Time Without Pity* 1957; *The Gypsy and the Gentleman* 1958; *Blind Date/Chance Meeting* 1959; *The Criminal/The Concrete Jungle* 1960; *Eva/Eve* 1962; *The Damned/These Are the Damned, The Servant* 1963; *King and Country* 1964; *Modesty Blaise* 1966; *Far from the Madding Crowd* 1967; *Boom, Secret Ceremony* 1968; *A Severed Head* 1971; *The Assassination of Trotsky* 1972. In the US—*Jesus Christ Superstar, Galileo* (UK/Can.) 1973; *The Day of the Locust, The Romantic Englishwoman* (UK/Fr.) 1975; *Marathon Man* 1976; *Exorcist II: The Heretic* 1977; *. . . And Justice for All, The Rose* 1979; *Something Wicked This Way Comes* 1983; *Crimes of Passion, Electric Dreams, Supergirl* 1984; *Plenty* 1985; *Spacecamp* 1986; *Coming to America* 1988; *The Russia House* 1990; *The Addams Family, The Firm* 1993.

MacDougall, Ranald. Director, screenwriter, producer. *b.* Mar. 10, 1915, Schenectady, N.Y. *d.* 1973. He began as an usher at Radio City Music Hall, then wrote radio plays before turning to screenwriting for Warners in the mid-40s. A former president of Screenwriters Guild, and a director since mid-50s. He was married to actress Nanette Fabray.

FILMS: As screenwriter—*Objective Burma, Mildred Pierce* 1945; *Possessed, The Unsuspected* 1947; *The Decision of Christopher Blake* (also prod.), *June Bride* 1948; *The Hasty Heart, The Breaking Point, Bright Leaf* 1950; *Mr. Belvedere Rings the Bell, I'll Never Forget You* 1951; *The Naked Jungle, Secret of the Incas* 1954; *We're No Angels* 1955; *The Mountain* 1956; *Cleopatra* 1963. As director-writer—*Queen Bee* 1955; *Man on Fire* 1957; *The World the Flesh and the Devil* 1959; *The Subterraneans* (dir. only) 1960; *Go Naked in the World* 1961. As producer—*Jigsaw* 1968; *The Cockeyed Cowboys of Calico County* (also sc.) 1970.

McDonnell, Mary. Actress. Born in 1953, in Wilkes Barre, Pa. High-cheekboned, brunette leading lady of the American stage, TV, and films. Raised in Ithaca, N.Y., she began acting as a student at the State University of New York at Fredonia and gradually acquired a reputation as an intelligent, intuitive performer in regional theater and on Broadway ('The Heidi Chronicles,' among others). In 1984–85 she co-starred with Elliott Gould in the TV series 'E/R.' She made her screen debut in 1984 and made a strong impression in John Sayles's *Matewan* (1987). She won high critical praise and an Academy Award nomination as best supporting actress for her convincing portrayal of a white woman raised since childhood by Sioux Indians in Kevin Costner's *Dances with Wolves* (1990). She is married to actor Randle Mell.

FILMS: *Garbo Talks* 1984; *Matewan* 1987; *Tiger Warsaw* 1988; *Dances with Wolves* 1990; *Grand Canyon* 1991; *Passion Fish, Sneakers* 1992; *Blue Chips* 1994.

McDormand, Frances. Actress. Born in 1958, in Illinois. Serious-minded, versatile character lead of stage and screen. The daughter of a Disciples of Christ preacher who moved his family around the Bible Belt until settling in Pennsylvania when she was eight, she received her stage training at the Yale School of Drama. She appeared in regional theater and eventually on Broadway, where she was nominated for a Tony Award for her performance in a revival of 'A Streetcar Named Desire.' She also co-starred briefly on TV in the police series 'Leg Work.' Making her screen debut in Joel Coen's *Blood Simple* (1984), she later appeared to advantage in the director's *Raising Arizona* (1987). The two became intimate companions and eventually wed. She was nominated for an Academy Award as best supporting actress for *Mississippi Burning* (1989) and took home the best actress Oscar for her offbeat, acclaimed performance as the pregnant Sheriff Marge in *Fargo* (1996), directed by Coen.

FILMS: *Blood Simple* 1984; *Raising Arizona* 1987; *Mississippi Burning* 1988; *Chattahoochee* 1989; *Hidden Agenda* (UK), *Darkman, Miller's Crossing* (uncredited) 1990; *The Butcher's Wife* 1991; *Crazy In Love, Passed Away* 1992; *Short Cuts* 1993; *Beyond Rangoon* 1994; *Fargo, Palookaville, Primal Fear* 1996; *Paradise Road* 1997.

McDowall, Roddy. Actor. Born Roderick Andrew Anthony Jude McDowall, on Sept. 17, 1928, in London. A child actor of British films of the late 30s, he was evacuated to the US during the London Blitz of 1940 and won immense popularity as the child star of such Hollywood films as *How Green Was My Valley* (1941) and *Lassie Come Home* (1942). After a period of maturation on the Broadway stage and on TV in the 50s, he returned to the screen in a broad range of adult roles. He made a not-too-successful debut as a film director with *Tam Lin/The Devil's Widow,* a film starring Ava Gardner, which started to roll in 1968 but wasn't released until 1971. McDowall is a highly respected still photographer with several books to his credit, beginning with *Double Exposure* in 1966, and the owner of one of the best private collections of old motion pictures and movie memorabilia. He has served as the Screen Actors Guild's representative on the National Film Preservation Board.

FILMS INCLUDE: In the UK—*Scruffy, Murder in the Family, Hey! Hey! USA* 1938; *Poison Pen, The Outsider, Dead Man's Shoes, Just William* 1939; *Saloon Bar* 1940; *This England* 1941. In the US—*Man Hunt, How Green Was My Valley* (as Huw), *Confirm or Deny* 1941; *Son of Fury, The Pied Piper, On the Sunny Side* 1942; *My Friend Flicka, Lassie Come Home* 1943; *The White Cliffs of Dover, The Keys of the Kingdom* 1944; *Thunderhead—Son of Flicka, Molly and Me* 1945; *Holiday in Mexico* 1946; *Rocky, Macbeth* (as Malcolm), *Kidnapped* (as David Balfour) 1948; *Tuna Clipper* (also assoc. prod.), *Black Midnight* 1949; *Killer Shark* 1950; *The Steel Fist* 1952; *The Subterraneans, Midnight Lace* 1960; *The Longest Day* 1962; *Cleopatra* (as Octavian) 1963; *Shock Treatment* 1964; *The Greatest Story Ever Told* (as Matthew), *The Loved One, That Darn Cat* 1965; *Inside Daisy Clover, Lord Love a Duck, L'Espion/The Defector* (Fr./Ger.) 1966; *The Adventures of*

Bullwhip Griffin, The Cool Ones, It! (UK) 1967; *Planet of the Apes, 5 Card Stud* 1968; *Hello Down There, Midas Run, Angel Angel Down We Go/Cult of the Damned* 1969; *Tam Lin/The Devil's Widow* (dir. only), *Pretty Maids All in a Row, Escape from the Planet of the Apes, Bedknobs and Broomsticks* 1971; *Conquest of the Planet of the Apes, The Poseidon Adventure, The Life and Times of Judge Roy Bean* 1972; *Battle for the Planet of the Apes, The Legend of Hell House, Arnold* 1973; *Dirty Mary Crazy Larry* 1974; *Funny Lady* 1975; *Mean Johnny Barrows, Embryo* 1976; *Sixth and Main* 1977; *Laserblast, The Cat from Outer Space* 1978; *Circle of Iron, Scavenger Hunt* 1979; *Charlie Chan and the Curse of the Dragon Queen* 1981; *Evil Under the Sun* (UK), *Class of 1984* (Can.) 1982; *Fright Night* 1985; *Dead of Winter, Overboard* (also exec. prod.) 1987; *Doin' Time on Planet Earth* 1988; *The Big Picture* (cameo), *Fright Night: Part 2, Cutting Class* 1989; *Shakma* 1990; *Going Under* 1991; *Double Trouble* 1992; *Last Summer in the Hamptons* 1995; *The Grass Harp, It's My Party* 1996; *Kipling's Second Jungle Book: Mowgli and Balou* 1997.

MacDowell, Andie. Actress. Born Rose Anderson MacDowell, on Apr. 21, 1958, in Gaffney, S.C. Expressive brunette leading lady of films of the late 80s and early 90s. The product of a broken home, she had to take care of an alcoholic mother after her parents divorced when she was six. Dropping out of college in her second year, she pursued a successful career in modeling. After some stage training with Shakespeare and Company and elsewhere, she made her screen debut in *Greystoke: The Legend of Tarzan, Lord of the Apes* (1984), in the role of Jane. Because of her then-pronounced Southern accent, her voice in the film had to be dubbed by Glenn CLOSE. She has since made much progress as an actress, drawing special admiration for her role as the repressed housewife in Steven Soderbergh's *sex, lies, and videotape* (1989). She married former model Paul Qualley in 1986. They moved from New York to a Montana ranch with their two children in 1991.

FILMS: *Greystoke: The Legend of Tarzan, Lord of the Apes* 1984; *St. Elmo's Fire* 1985; *sex, lies, and videotape* 1989; *Green Card* (Austral./Fr.) 1990; *The Object of Beauty, Hudson Hawk* 1991; *The Player* (cameo), *Groundhog Day, Short Cuts* 1993; *Bad Girls, Four Weddings and a Funeral* 1994; *Michael, Multiplicity, Unstrung Heroes* 1996; *The End of Violence* 1997.

McDowell, Claire. Actress. *b.* Nov. 2, 1877, New York City. *d.* 1966. A descendant of a long line of actors and herself a veteran of the stage, she played dramatic leads in D. W. GRIFFITH films between 1910 and 1914. She then retired from the screen to raise a family but returned to films in 1917 in character parts. She specialized in maternal roles and played John Gilbert's mother in *The Big Parade* and Ramon Novarro's in *Ben-Hur*, among many roles.

FILMS INCLUDE: *Love Among the Roses, A Mohawk's Way, Two Little Waifs, Simple Charity* 1910; *His Trust, A Woman Scorned, Swords and Hearts, In the Days of '49, The Primal Call, As in a Looking Glass* 1911; *The Sunbeam, The God Within, Two Daughters of Eve, The Female of the Species, A Cry for Help* 1912; *The Telephone Girl and the Lady, The Wanderer* 1913; *The Massacre, Men and Women* 1914; *As It Happened* 1915; *The Gates of Doom, Fighting Back* 1917; *Follies Girl, Heart o' the Hills* 1919; *The Mark of Zorro, Midsummer Madness, The Woman in the Suitcase* 1920; *Prisoners of Love, What Every Woman Knows, Mother o' Mine, Wealth, Love Never Dies* 1921; *The Gray Dawn, In the Name of the Law, Nice People, Penrod, Quincy Adams Sawyer* 1922; *Human Wreckage, The Westbound Limited, Circus Days, Ashes of Vengeance, Ponjola* 1923; *Black Oxen, Thy Name Is Woman, Secrets* 1924; *The Reckless Sex, Waking Up the Town, The Tower of Lies, The Big Parade* 1925; *Ben-Hur, The Devil's Circus, The Shamrock Handicap, The Unknown Soldier, The Show-Off, The Flaming Forest* 1926; *The Taxi Dancer, Tillie the Toiler, The Shield of Honor, Almost Human* 1927; *The Viking, The Tragedy of Youth* 1928; *Four Devils* 1929; *Redemption, The Big House, Wild Company, Brothers, Mother's Cry* 1930; *An American Tragedy* 1931; *Manhattan Parade, The Strange Love of Molly Louvain, Rebecca of Sunnybrook Farm* 1932; *Wild Boys of the Road* 1933; *High Wide and Handsome* 1937; *Are These Our Parents?* 1944.

McDowell, Malcolm. Actor. Born on June 15, 1943, in Leeds, England. He began his working life serving drinks to customers in his father's pub and later worked at a coffee factory, eventually becoming a regional salesman for the product in Yorkshire. He loathed the job and began attending acting classes, taking months to get rid of his working-class Yorkshire accent. He then joined a repertory theater on the Isle of Wight and a year later the Royal Shakespeare Company, where he spent 18 months carrying a spear. After working briefly as a messenger, he began getting roles on British TV and in 1967 played a small role in *Poor Cow,* his film debut, but his scene was deleted from the final release print. The arrogant, insolent personality he projected on the screen attracted director Lindsay ANDERSON, who chose him for the lead role in the film *If. . .* (1968). These same characteristics made him an ideal choice to play the sneering ogre Alex, the violent Teddy Boy in Stanley Kubrick's *A Clockwork Orange* (1971), a film that demonstrated McDowell's great instinctive talent and established him as one of the leading young stars of the British cinema. McDowell's own experiences as a coffee salesman provided the plot outline for his next film, Lindsay Anderson's *O Lucky Man!* (1973). Divorced (1975–80) from actress-publicist Margot Bennett Dullea (Keir Dullea's ex), he married actress Mary STEENBURGEN in 1980. They divorced in 1990.

FILMS: *Poor Cow* (scene deleted) 1967; *If. . .* 1968; *Figures in a Landscape* 1970; *The Raging Moon/Long Ago Tomorrow, A Clockwork Orange* 1971; *O Lucky Man!* 1973; *Royal Flash* 1975; *Voyage of the Damned, Aces High* 1976; *The Passage, Time After Time* (as H. G. Wells), *Caligula* (title role; It./US) 1979; *Cat People* (US), *Britannia Hospital* 1982; *Blue Thunder* (US), *Cross Creek, Get Crazy* (US) 1983; *The Compleat Beatles Movie* (doc.; narr. only) 1984; *Gulag* 1985; *Sunset* (US) 1988; *Buy and Cell* (US), *The Caller* (release delayed from 1987; US), *Il Maestro* (Fr./Bel.), *Class of 1999* (US), *Jezebel's Kiss* (US), *Schweitzer* (as Albert Schweitzer; US), *Happily Ever After* (v/o), *Maggio Musicale* (It.), *Disturbed* (US), *Moon 44* (Ger.) 1990; *Assassin of the Tsar* (UK/USSR) 1991; *The Player* (cameo) 1992; *Chain of Desire, Bopha!* 1993; *Milk Money, Star Trek: Generations* 1994; *Tank Girl* 1995.

MacFadden, Hamilton. Director, actor. Born on Apr. 26, 1901, in Chelsea, Mass. A graduate of Harvard Law School, he was a stage actor and director before turning to films in the early 30s. He directed many routine entertaining films, then appeared in some low-budget pictures of the late 30s and early 40s.

FILMS (as director): *Oh for a Man!, Harmony at Home, Are You There?, Crazy That Way* 1930; *Their Mad Moment* (co-dir. with Chandler Sprague), *Charlie Chan Carries On, The Black Camel, Riders of the Purple Sage* 1931; *Cheaters at Play, The Fourth Horseman* 1932; *Second Hand Wife, Trick for Trick, The Man Who Dared, Charlie Chan's Greatest Case, As Husbands Go* 1933; *Stand Up and Cheer, She Was a Lady, Hold That Girl* 1934; *Elinor Norton, Fighting Youth* 1935; *Three Legionnaires, It Can't Last Forever, Sea Racketeers, Escape by Night* 1937; *Inside the Law* 1942.

McEnery, Peter. Actor. Born on Feb. 21, 1940, in Walsall, near Birmingham, England. Gentle leading man of British and Continental films of the 60s.

FILMS INCLUDE: *Beat Girl/Wild for Kicks, Tunes of Glory* 1960; *Victim* 1961; *The Moon-Spinners* (US) 1964; *The Fighting Prince of Donegal, La Curée/The Game Is Over* (Fr./It.) 1966; *J'ai tué Rasputin/I Killed Rasputin* (Fr./It.) 1967; *Meglio Vedova/Better a Widow* (It./Fr.), *Negatives* 1968; *The Adventures of Gerard, Entertaining Mr. Sloane* 1970; *Tales That Witness Madness* 1973; *The Cat and the Canary* 1978.

McEveety, Vincent. Director. The son of a film pioneer who served as a production manager at the old Edison studios in New York, he began his own career in 1954 as a second assistant director at the Hal Roach studios. He later directed numerous episodes for TV series, including 'Gunsmoke.' Turning out his first feature in 1968, he worked mainly for Walt DISNEY, specializing in wholesome adventure films. His brother, Bernard McEveety, is also a director. Another brother, Joseph L. McEveety, is a screenwriter.

FILMS: *Firecreek* 1968; *This Savage Land* 1969; *$1,000,000 Duck* 1971; *The Biscuit Eater* 1972; *Charley and the Angel* 1973; *Superdad, The Castaway Cowboy* 1974; *The Strongest Man in the World* 1975; *Gus, Treasure of Matecumbe* 1976; *Herbie Goes to Monte Carlo* 1977; *The Apple Dumpling Gang Rides Again* 1979; *Herbie Goes Bananas, The Watcher in the Woods* (co-dir. of revised vers. only; uncredited) 1980; *Amy* 1981.

McFarland, Spanky. Actor. *b.* George Emmett McFarland, Oct. 2, 1928, in Fort Worth, Tex. *d.* 1993. As a baby he became the chubby little model advertising the products of a Dallas bakery and shortly after his third birthday he was selected to replace Joe Cobb as the fat boy in the "Our Gang" comedy shorts (later reissued on TV as "The Little Rascals"). He soon became the best-known and most popular member of the gang. He appeared in a number of feature films in addition to numerous shorts, but retired from the screen in the mid-40s to tackle a variety of non-acting jobs. He made frequent appearances on TV talk shows to discuss his years as a child star, once coming forward to discredit a man who claimed to be Stymie from the series, when in fact the real Stymie had passed away.

FILMS INCLUDE (short indicated by "s"): *Free Eats* (s), *Spanky* (s) 1932; *Forgotten Babies* (s), *Bedtime Worries* (s), *Day of Reckoning* 1933; *Miss Fane's Baby Is Stolen, For Pete's Sake* (s), *Honkey Donkey* (s), *Kentucky Kernels* 1934; *Teacher's Beau* (s), *O'Shaughnessy's Boy* 1935; *The Trail of the Lonesome Pine, Bored of Education* (s), *General Spanky* 1936; *Rushin' Ballet* (s), *Fishy Tales* (s) 1937; *Aladdin's Lantern* (s), *Practical Jokers* (s) 1938; *Peck's Bad Boy with the Circus, Clown Princes* (s), *Captain Spanky's Show Boat* (s) 1939; *The Big Premiere* (s), *Good Bad Guys* (s) 1940; *Robot Wrecks* (s) 1941; *Going to Press* (s) 1942; *Johnny Doughboy* 1943; *The Woman in the Window* 1944; *Moonrunners* 1975.

McGann, Paul. Actor. Born in 1959, in Liverpool, England. *ed.* RADA. Subtle, intelligent stage and TV performer who made a sparkling screen debut, teaming up with Richard E. Grant, in Bruce Robinson's comedy *Withnail and I* (1987).

FILMS: *Withnail and I, Empire of the Sun* 1987; *The Rainbow, Tree of Hands, Dealers, Drowning in the Shallow End* 1989; *Streets of Yesterday, Paper Mask* 1990; *The Monk, Afraid of the Dark* 1992; *Alien, The Three Musketeers* 1993.

McGann, William. Director. *b.* Apr. 5, 1895, Pittsburgh. *d.* 1977. *ed.* U. of California (Berkeley). He entered films in 1915 as an assistant cameraman and after WW I service returned to films as a director of photography for Douglas Fairbanks, becoming an assistant director in 1923. He began directing in the early 30s and turned out many briskly paced, better-than-average B pictures, mainly for Warner Bros., through the early 40s. He also handled several Spanish-language versions of American films originally directed by others. Several of his early films were made in England.

FILMS (excluding Spanish-language versions): *On the Border* 1930; *I Like Your Nerve* 1931; *Illegal* (UK), *Murder on the Second Floor* (UK), *The Silver Greyhound* (UK), *Little Fella* (UK), *A Voice Said Goodnight* (UK) 1932; *Maybe It's Love, A Night at the Ritz, Man of Iron* 1935; *Freshman Love, Brides Are Like That, Times Square Playboy, Two Against the World, Hot Money, Polo Joe, The Case of the Black Cat* 1936; *Penrod and Sam, Marry the Girl, Alcatraz Island, Sh! The Octopus* 1937; *Penrod and His Twin Brother, When Were You Born?, Girls on Probation* 1938; *Blackwell's Island, Sweepstakes Winner, Everybody's Hobby, Pride of the Blue Grass* 1939; *Wolf of New York, Dr. Christian Meets the Women* 1940; *A Shot in the Dark, The Parson of Panamint, Highway West, We Go Fast* 1941; *In Old California, Tombstone—The Town Too Tough to Die, American Empire* 1942; *Frontier Bad Man* 1943.

McGavin, Darren. Actor. Born on May 7, 1922, in Spokane, Wash. Tough, ready-to-rumble hero and occasional villain of American TV and films. He dropped out of the College of the Pacific after one year to pursue stage training at New York's Neighborhood Playhouse and Actors Studio. While establishing his stage credentials, he began playing small parts in films in 1945. He first attracted notice on the screen a decade later, with memorable roles as a young painter in David Lean's *Summertime/Summer Madness* and especially as the smooth Mephistophelian drug pusher in Otto Preminger's *The Man with the Golden Arm* (both 1955). But his film appearances have been intermittent and he had his best success on TV as the star of such series as 'Crime Photographer' (1951–52), 'Mike Hammer' (1957–59), 'Riverboat' (1968–69), 'The Outsider' (1968–69) and 'Kolchak: The Night Stalker' (1974–75). He portrayed General George Patton on TV's 'Ike' (1979) and appeared in numerous TV movies. Having gained experience as the director of series episodes, he directed and produced in 1973 a first feature, *Happy Mother's Day, Love George,* whose title was later changed to *Run, Stranger, Run.*

FILMS: *A Song to Remember, Counter-Attack Kiss and Tell* 1945; *Fear* 1946; *Queen for a Day* 1951; *Summertime/Summer Madness* (US/UK), *The Man with the Golden Arm, The Court-Martial of Billy Mitchell* 1955; *Beau James, The Delicate Delinquent* 1957; *The Case Against Brooklyn* 1958; *Bullet for a Badman* 1964; *Ride the High Wind* (S. Afr.), *The Great Sioux Massacre* 1965; *Mission Mars* 1968; *Tribes* (orig. made for TV) 1970; *Mrs. Pollifax—Spy* 1971; *Happy Mother's Day Love George/Run Stranger Run* (dir., prod. only) 1973; *The Petty Story* 1974; *No Deposit No Return* 1976; *Airport '77* 1977; *Hot Lead and Cold Feet, Zero to Sixty* 1978; *Hangar 18* 1980; *Firebird 2015 A.D.* 1981; *A Christmas Story* 1983; *The Natural* 1984; *Turk 182!* 1985; *Raw Deal* 1986; *From the Hip* 1987; *Dead Heat* 1988; *Blood And Concrete: A Love Story* 1991; *Billy Madison* 1995; *Small Time* 1996.

McGillis, Kelly. Actress. Born on July 9, 1957, in Newport Beach, Calif. Strapping bright star of American films, typically in roles suggesting an intriguing mix of strength and vulnerability, innocence and sophistication. A doctor's daughter, she remembers herself as an overweight (around 200 pounds) youngster who could rarely get a date. She left high school to attend the Pacific Conservatory of the Performing Arts in Santa Maria, California. In 1979 she enrolled at New York's Juilliard School of Drama, waiting tables to support herself. She made an arresting screen debut in Robert Ellis Miller's *Reuben, Reuben* (1983), then soared to stardom on the strength of her portrayal of a serenely sensual Amish widow in Peter Weir's *Witness* (1985). She was compared by some critics with Grace Kelly, Lauren Bacall, and Ingrid Bergman. Most of her subsequent roles, however, were less rewarding. She scored a personal triumph playing a tough attorney defending a victim of rape (played by Jodie Foster) in *The Accused* (1988). The role echoed her own real-life rape, which the actress discussed publicly in an effort to increase awareness of the issue. Divorced from writer Boyd Black and at one time engaged to actor Barry Tubb, she married yacht broker Fred Tillman in 1989.

FILMS: *Reuben, Reuben* 1983; *Witness* 1985; *Top Gun* 1986; *Made in Heaven, Unsettled Land* (Isr.) 1987; *The House on Carroll Street, The Accused* 1988; *Winter People* 1989; *Cat Chaser* 1990; *Before and After Death, The Babe* 1992; *North* 1994.

MacGinnis, Niall. Actor. Born in 1913 in Ireland. Stocky, professorial character player active since the 1930s. Veteran of London's Old Vic.

FILMS INCLUDE: *Turn of the Tide* 1935; *Edge of the World* 1938; *49th Parallel* 1941; *We Dive at Dawn* 1943; *Henry V* 1945; *No Highway* 1951; *Martin Luther* (as Luther) 1953; *The Battle of the River Plate* 1955; *Curse of the Demon* 1957; *The Nun's Story* 1958; *Billy Budd, A Face in the Rain* 1962; *Becket* 1964; *Island of Terror* 1966; *The Torture Garden* 1967; *Sinful Davey* 1969; *The Mackintosh Man* 1973.

McGinley, John C. Actor. Born August 3, 1959, in New York City. *ed.* New York University. After making his mark on and off Broadway, most notably for his role in 'Requiem for a Heavyweight,' this talented, comedic actor is at his best playing snide, often obnoxious characters. His performance for director Oliver STONE's acclaimed Vietnam epic *Platoon* (1986), and their subsequent working relationship, has provided him with many challenging and varied roles in major Hollywood films.

FILMS: *Platoon, Sweet Liberty* 1986; *Wall Street* 1987; *Shakedown, Talk Radio* 1988; *Born on the Fourth of July, Fat Man and Little Boy, Lost Angels* 1989; *Highlander II: The Quickening, Little Noises, Point Break* 1991; *Article 99, A Moment Clear* 1992; *Hear No Evil, The Last Outlaw, Watch It* 1993; *Car 54, Where Are You?, Mother's Boys, On Deadly Ground, Surviving the Game, Wagons East* 1994; *Assassins, Born To Be Wild, Nixon, Seven* 1995; *Johns, The Last Time I Committed Suicide, Nothing to Lose* 1997.

McGiver, John. Actor. *b.* Nov. 5, 1913, New York City. *d.* 1975. Pudgy character player of American TV and films, mostly in comic roles. A notorious scene stealer, notably as the gracious Tiffany's salesman in *Breakfast at Tiffany's*.

FILMS INCLUDE: *L'Homme à l'Imperméable/The Man in the Raincoat* (Fr.), *Love in the Afternoon* 1957; *The Gazebo* 1960; *Breakfast at Tiffany's, Bachelor in Paradise* 1961; *Mr. Hobbs Takes a Vacation, The Manchurian Candidate* 1962; *My Six Loves, Take Her She's Mine, Who's Minding the Store?* 1963; *Man's Favorite Sport?* 1964; *Marriage on the Rocks* 1965; *Made in Paris, The Glass Bottom Boat* 1966; *Fitzwilly* 1967; *Midnight Cowboy* 1969; *Lawman* 1971; *Arnold* 1973; *Mame* 1974; *The Apple Dumpling Gang* 1975.

McGoohan, Patrick. Actor. Born on Mar. 19, 1928, in Astoria, Queens, N.Y. Assertive leading man of British stage, TV, and films. His screen appearances have been infrequent, partly because of a heavy TV schedule as the star of such series as 'Danger Man,' 'Secret Agent,' 'The Prisoner,' and 'Rafferty.' He won an Emmy for a 1975 guest appearance on 'Columbo.' McGoohan directed some of the episodes of his TV shows and the feature *Catch My Soul* (1974), an adaptation of Shakespeare's 'Othello.'

FILMS INCLUDE: *Passage Home, I Am a Camera* 1955; *Zarak* 1956; *High Tide at Noon, Hell Drivers* 1957; *The Gypsy and the Gentleman, Nor the Moon by Night/Elephant Walk* 1958; *Two Living One Dead* (Sw./UK) 1961; *All Night Long, Life for Ruth/Walk in the Shadow, The Quare Fellow* 1962; *Dr. Syn Alias the Scarecrow* 1963; *The Three Lives of Thomasina* (UK/US) 1964; *Ice Station Zebra* (US) 1968; *The Moonshine War* (US) 1970; *Mary Queen of Scots* (as James Stuart) 1971; *Catch My Soul* (dir. only; US) 1974; *Brass Target* 1978; *Un Genio Due Compari e un Pollo* (It./Fr./Ger.), *Escape from Alcatraz* (US) 1979; *Scanners* (Can.) 1981; *Kings and Desperate Men* (Can.) 1982; *Baby. . . Secret of the Lost Legend* (US) 1985; *Columbo: Agenda for Murder* (TV movie; dir. only) 1990; *Braveheart* 1995.

McGovern, Elizabeth. Actress. Born on July 18, 1961, in Evanston, Ill. Appealing, radiantly fresh-faced leading lady of the American stage and screen. The daughter of a law professor at Northwestern, she moved with her family to Los Angeles when he transferred to UCLA. She began acting in school plays at North Hollywood High, then continued her stage training at the American Conservatory Theatre in San Francisco and the Juilliard School of Dramatic Art in New York. Following a pleasant screen debut in Robert Redford's Oscar-winning *Ordinary People* (1980), she gave a sparkling portrayal of girl-in-a-cage beauty Evelyn Nesbit in Milos Forman's *Ragtime* (1981), a performance for which she earned an Academy Award nomination as best supporting actress. Avoiding a typical movie career, she has continued performing on the stage between film assignments.

FILMS: *Ordinary People* 1980; *Ragtime* 1981; *Lovesick* 1983; *Racing with the Moon, Once Upon a Time in America* 1984; *Native Son* 1986; *The Bedroom Window, Dear America* (doc.; v/o) 1987; *She's Having a Baby* 1988; *Johnny Handsome* 1989; *The Handmaid's Tale, A Shock to the System, Tune in Tomorrow* 1990; *The Favor, I'll Do Anything* 1994; *Wings of the Dove* 1997.

McGowan, J(ohn) P. Director, producer, screenwriter, actor. *b.* February 1880, Terowie, South Australia. *d.* 1952. A veteran of the Australian and American stage, he entered films as an actor with Kalem in 1909 and appeared in such productions as *The Colleen Bawn* (1911) and *From the Manger to the Cross* (1912). He then turned to directing and in that capacity handled many of the films starring his wife, Helen HOLMES, including the hit serials *The Hazards of Helen* (1914–17) and *The Girl and the Game* (1915–16). One of the silent screen's most prolific directors of action pictures, he produced, scripted, and acted in many of his own productions. He also continued performing in films of other directors, including Edward Sutherland's *Mississippi* (1935), Tay Garnett's *Slave Ship* (1937), and John Ford's *Stagecoach* (1939). He directed his last film in 1938.

FILMS INCLUDE (as director): *The Operator at Black Rock* 1914; *The Hazards of Helen* (serial; directed first 48 of 119 episodes; also act.) 1914–15; *The Voice in the Fog, Blackbirds* 1915; *The Girl and the Game* (serial; also co-sc., act.) 1915–16; *The Diamond Runners* (also sc.), *The Manager of the A & B, Whispering Smith* (also act. in title role), *Medicine Bend* (also act.), *Judith of the Cumberlands* 1916; *Lass of the Lumberlands* (serial) 1916–17; *The Lost Express* (serial), *The Railroad Raiders* (serial; also act.) 1917; *Lure of the Circus* (serial) 1918; *The Red Glove* (serial) 1919; *Elmo the Fearless* (serial), *King of the Circus* (serial), *Below the Deadline* 1920; *Do or Die* (serial; also act.), *Tiger True, The Moonshine Menace, Discontented Wives* (also act.), *The Ruse of the Rattler* (also act.) 1921; *Captain Kidd* (serial), *Hills of Missing Men* (also sc., act.), *Reckless Chances* (also act.) 1922; *One Million in Jewels* (also sc., act.), *Stormy Seas* (also act.) 1923; *Baffled, Crossed Trails* (also act.), *The Whipping Boss* (also act.), *Western Vengeance, A Desperate Adventure, Courage* 1924; *Border Intrigue* (also act.), *Outwitted* (also sc., act.), *Barriers of the Law* (also act.), *Duped* (also act.), *The Fighting Sheriff, Blood and Steel, Cold Nerve, Webs of Steel, Peggy of the Secret Service* 1925; *Unseen Enemies, Mistaken Orders, Crossed Signals, The Lost Express, Red Blood* (also act.), *Riding Romance, Peril of the Rail, Fighting Luck* (also prod.) 1926; *Tarzan and the Golden Lion, Red Signals* (also act.), *When a Dog Loves, The Lost Limited* (also act.), *The Outlaw Dog, Aflame in the Sky* 1927; *The Chinatown Mystery* (serial), *Devil's Tower* (also co-sc., act.), *Mystery Valley* (also sc.), *Arizona Days* (also act.), *Silent Trail* (also act.), *West of Santa Fe* (also act.), *Law of the Mounted* (also act.), *Manhattan Cowboy* 1928; *Below the Deadline* (also act.), *Captain Cowboy* (also sc., edit.), *Riders of the Storm* (also sc.), *The Last Roundup* (also prod., act.), *The Fighting Terror* (also prod., act.), *The Man from Nevada* (also prod.), *The Phantom Rider* (also act.), *The Invaders* (also act.), *Code of the West, The Lone Horseman* (also prod., act.), *The Oklahoma Kid* (also prod., act.) 1929; *Covered Wagon Trails* (also act.), *Call of the Desert, Hunted Men, The Man from Nowhere, The Canyon of Missing Men* (also act.), *Near the Rainbow's End, Beyond the Law, Code of Honor, Under Texas Skies, Pioneers of the West* (also prod., sc., act.) 1930; *Riders of the North, The Cyclone Kid* 1931; *The Hurricane Express* (serial; co-dir. with Armand Schaefer), *Human Targets, Mark of the Spur, Tangled Fortunes, The Scarlet Brand* 1932; *When a Man Rides Alone, Deadwood Pass, War of the Range* 1933; *Rough Riding Rhythm* (also act.) 1937; *Where the West Begins, Roaring Six Guns* 1938.

MacGowan, Kenneth. Producer, educator, writer. *b.* Nov. 30, 1888, Winthrop, Mass. *d.* 1963. A graduate of Harvard, he was a drama critic and also a stage producer with Eugene O'Neill's Provincetown Playhouse before going to Hollywood as a story editor for RKO. From 1932 he produced many fine films for RKO, Fox, and other studios, after being nominally credited as an associate producer. He retired from film activity in 1947 to become chairman of the Department of Theater Arts at UCLA. McGowan wrote several books on drama and film, including *Behind the Screen,* a lively history of motion pictures.

FILMS INCLUDE (as producer or associate producer): *The Penguin Pool Murder* 1932; *Topaze, Double Harness, Little Women* 1933; *La Cucaracha* (Academy Award winning short), *Anne of Green Gables* 1934; *Becky Sharp, King of Burlesque, Jalna, The Return of Peter Grimm, Half Angel, Sins of Man* 1935; *Lloyds of London* 1936; *This Is My Affair, Wake Up and Live* 1937; *Four Men and a Prayer, In Old Chicago* 1938; *Young Mr. Lincoln, Stanley and Livingstone, Swanee River* 1939; *Brigham Young, The Return of Frank James, Tin Pan Alley* 1940; *The Great American Broadcast, Man Hunt, Belle Starr* 1941; *Happy Land* 1943; *Lifeboat, Jane Eyre* 1944; *Easy Come Easy Go* 1947.

McGrath, Joseph. Director. Born in 1930, in Scotland. A successful veteran of British TV comedy, he has been directing features intermittently since the late 60s.

FILMS: *Casino Royale* (co-dir.) 1967; *30 Is a Dangerous Age Cynthia* 1968; *The Bliss of Mrs. Blossom* 1969; *Ner ist wer?* (Ger.), *The Magic Christian* 1970; *Digby/Digby, the Biggest Dog in the World* 1974; *The Great McGonagall* 1975; *I'm Not Feeling Myself Tonight* 1976; *Rising Damp* 1980; *Starlets* 1987.

MacGraw, Ali. Actress. Born Alice MacGraw, on Apr. 1, 1938, in Pound Ridge, N.Y. The daughter of artists, she majored in art history at Wellesley College. After graduation, in 1960, she joined *Harper's Bazaar* as an editorial assistant, later becoming a fashion photographer's helper. She gradually moved in front of the camera and by 1967 was a top fashion model, her fresh-scrubbed all-American face decorating the covers of leading women's magazines. She made her film debut in 1968, playing a bit role in *A Lovely Way to Die,* and was catapulted to stardom the following year in the role of Brenda Patimkin, the screen incarnation of the "Jewish-American Princess," in *Goodbye Columbus.* She became established as a leading new personality of the American screen with her next role, as the dying heroine of *Love Story* (1970) but has made only rare film appearances since. In the 1980s, she appeared for a time on the immensely popular series 'Dynasty.' In her autobiography, *Moving Pictures* (1991), Miss MacGraw spoke candidly of her career-stifling problems of alcoholism and an addiction to men. Her second husband (1969–72) was Paramount's then-production chief Bob EVANS and her third (1973–78) actor Steve MCQUEEN. Her son by the former is screen actor Josh Evans (*b.* Jan. 16, 1971, New York City).

FILMS: *A Lovely Way to Die* (bit) 1968; *Goodbye Columbus* 1969; *Love Story* 1970; *The Getaway* 1972; *Convoy* 1978; *Players* 1979; *Just Tell Me What You Want* 1980; *Natural Causes* 1993.

McGraw, Charles. Actor. *b.* May 10, 1914, New York City. *d.* 1980. Tough character actor of Hollywood films, often in heavy roles. Stage and radio background. Later much on TV, including the series 'The Falcon' (1954–55), 'Casablanca' (as Rick; 1955–56), and 'The Smith Family' (1971–72).

FILMS INCLUDE: *The Undying Monster* 1942; *The Moon Is Down, The Mad Ghoul* 1943; *The Impostor* 1944; *The Killers* 1946; *The Long Night* 1947; *Blood on the Moon, Hazard* 1948; *The Black Book/Reign of Terror, Border Incident, The Threat* 1949; *Side Street, Armored Car Robbery* 1950; *Roadblock* (lead), *His Kind of Woman* 1951; *The Narrow Margin* (lead role), *One Minute to Zero* 1952; *Loophole* 1954; *The Bridges at Toko-Ri* 1955; *Away All Boats, Toward the Unknown* 1956; *Slaughter on Tenth Avenue* 1957; *Saddle the Wind, The Defiant Ones* 1958; *The Man in the Net, The Wonderful Country* 1959; *Spartacus, Cimarron* 1960; *The Birds* 1963; *In Cold Blood* 1967; *Hang 'Em High* 1968; *Pendulum, Tell Them Willie Boy Is Here* 1969; *Johnny Got His Gun* 1971; *A Boy and His Dog* 1975; *The Killer Inside Me* 1976; *Twilight's Last Gleaming* 1977.

McGuire, Don. Screenwriter, director, actor. Born Feb. 28, 1919, Chicago. A former journalist and press agent, he entered films in 1945 as an actor. Turned screenwriter in 1950 and was a hit-and-run director in the mid-50s. Much TV activity as writer-director-producer, including the 'Hennessey' TV series. He authored the novels *The Day Television Died, 1600 Flooge Street,* and *The Hell with Walter Cronkite.*

FILMS INCLUDE: As actor—*Pride of the Marines* 1945; *Humoresque* 1946; *Possessed, The Man I Love, Nora Prentiss* 1947; *The Fuller Brush Man, Whiplash* 1948; *The Threat* 1949; *Armed Car Robbery* 1950; *Double Dynamite* 1951; *Fear Strikes Out* 1957. As director-writer—*Johnny Concho* 1956; *The Delicate Delinquent, Hear Me Good* 1957. As screenwriter—*Dial 1119* (story) 1950; *Meet Danny Wilson* 1952; *Walking My Baby Back Home* 1953; *Bad Day at Black Rock* (adapt.), *Three Ring Circus* 1955; *Artists and Models* 1956; *Suppose They Gave a War and Nobody Came* 1970; *Tootsie* (co-story) 1982.

McGuire, Dorothy. Actress. Born on June 14, 1918, in Omaha, Nebr. Gentle, charming leading lady of the American stage and screen. She made her acting debut at 13 at the Omaha Community Playhouse, opposite Henry Fonda, and after many performances in summer stock, came to New York, appeared in a radio soap opera, and made her Broadway debut in 1938 as

Martha Scott's understudy in 'Our Town.' Her big opportunity came three years later as the star of 'Claudia.' David O. Selznick, who acquired the screen rights to the play, brought her out to Hollywood to repeat her stage success in the 1943 film version. She stayed to appear in many other films, notably *A Tree Grows in Brooklyn, The Enchanted Cottage, The Spiral Staircase,* and *Gentleman's Agreement.* She was nominated for an Academy Award as best actress for her performance in the latter. Miss McGuire won wide respect as a mature and intelligent performer who radiates kindness and warmth and projects inner beauty in appealing, unglamorized roles. These qualities later enabled her to make a natural transition from starring roles to character parts without a noticeable change in personal image. Her private life, like her screen character, has been subdued and sheltered from publicity. She returned to the Broadway stage after many years of absence in a revival of 'The Night of the Iguana' in 1976. Although absent from feature films since 1973, she continued playing TV roles well into the 80s. She is the mother of actress Topo Swope by her marriage (from 1943) to famous still photographer John Swope.

FILMS: *Claudia* 1943; *A Tree Grows in Brooklyn* (as Katie Nolan), *The Enchanted Cottage* 1945; *The Spiral Staircase, Claudia and David, Till the End of Time* 1946; *Gentleman's Agreement* 1947; *Mother Didn't Tell Me, Mister 880* 1950; *Callaway Went Thataway, I Want You* 1951; *Invitation* 1952; *Make Haste to Live, Three Coins in the Fountain* 1954; *Trial* 1955; *Friendly Persuasion* 1956; *Old Yeller* 1957; *The Remarkable Mr. Pennypacker, This Earth Is Mine, A Summer Place* 1959; *The Dark at the Top of the Stairs, Swiss Family Robinson* 1960; *Susan Slade* 1961; *Summer Magic* 1963; *The Greatest Story Ever Told* (as the Virgin Mary) 1965; *Flight of the Doves* 1971; *Jonathan Livingston Seagull* (v/o) 1973.

McHugh, Frank. Actor. *b.* Francis Curran McHugh, May 23, 1898, Homestead, Pa. *d.* 1981. Made stage debut at ten with his parents' stock company and in the 20s frequently on Broadway. Appeared in a 1928 short film and in some 150 features since 1930, mainly for Warner Bros., typically in sympathetic character parts. His trademark was a high-pitched, contagious laugh.

FILMS INCLUDE: *The Dawn Patrol, Top Speed* 1930; *The Front Page* 1931; *High Pressure, The Crowd Roars, The Dark Horse, Life Begins, One Way Passage* 1932; *Mystery of the Wax Museum, Grand Slam, Elmer the Great, Lilly Turner, Footlight Parade* 1933; *Fashions of 1934, Return of the Terror* 1934; *Gold Diggers of 1935, The Irish in Us, A Midsummer Night's Dream* (as Quince) 1935; *Freshman Love, Bullets or Ballots, Stage Struck, Three Men on a Horse* 1936; *Ever Since Eve* 1937; *Swing Your Lady, Boy Meets Girl, Four Daughters, Valley of the Giants* 1938; *Dodge City, Dust Be My Destiny, The Roaring Twenties, On Your Toes* 1939; *Virginia City, The Fighting 69th, I Love You Again, City for Conquest* 1940; *Back Street, Manpower* 1941; *All Through the Night, Her Cardboard Lover* 1942; *Going My Way* 1944; *State Fair* 1945; *The Hoodlum Saint* 1946; *Carnegie Hall* 1947; *The Velvet Touch* 1948; *Mighty Joe Young* 1949; *Paid in Full* 1950; *There's No Business Like Show Business* 1954; *The Last Hurrah* 1958; *Career* 1959; *A Tiger Walks* 1964; *Easy Come Easy Go* 1967.

McHugh, Jimmy. Composer, songwriter. *b.* James Francis McHugh, July 10, 1894, Boston. *d.* 1969. While working as an office boy at the Boston Opera House, he acted as an accompanist for rehearsals. Later became a song plugger and eventually an executive for various music-publishing houses. He then began composing songs, including such hits as 'I Can't Give You Anything but Love,' 'I'm in the Mood for Love,' 'On the Sunny Side of the Street,' 'I Love to Whistle,' 'It's a Most Unusual Day,' and 'Singin' the Blues.' His first Broadway success was 'Blackbirds of 1928.' Several other Broadway shows followed. Working mainly with lyricists Dorothy FIELDS and Harold Adamson, he composed many songs for Hollywood films from 1929. He made a guest appearance in *The Helen Morgan Story* (1957), which featured many of his songs.

FILMS INCLUDE: *The Cock-Eyed World* 1929; *Love in the Rough* 1930; *Flying High, Cuban Love Song* 1931; *Dancing Lady, Dinner at Eight* ('Don't Blame Me,' etc.) 1933; *Every Night at Eight* ('I'm in the Mood for Love,' etc.) 1935; *King of Burlesque, Banjo on My Knee, Dimples* 1936; *Top of the Town* ('Where Are You?,' etc.), *Merry-Go-Round of 1938, You're a Sweetheart* 1937; *Mad About Music* ('I Love to Whistle,' etc.), *That Certain Age* 1938; *Down Argentine Way* ('South American Way'), *Buck Benny Rides Again* ('Say It,' etc.) 1940; *Seven Days' Leave* ('Can't Get Out of This Mood,' etc.) 1942; *Higher and Higher* ('A Lovely Way to Spend an Evening,' etc.), *Happy Go Lucky* ('Let's Get Lost,' etc.) 1943; *Four Jills in a Jeep, Something for the Boys* 1944; *Bring On the Girls ('You Moved Right In,' etc.), Nob Hill* 1945; *Doll Face, Do You Love Me?* 1946; *Hit Parade of 1947* 1947; *If You Knew Susie* ('My How the Time Goes By,' etc.), *A Date with Judy* ('It's a Most Unusual Day') 1948; *A Private's Affair* 1959.

McIntire, John. Actor. *b.* June 27, 1907, Spokane, Wash. *d.* 1991. Versatile, commanding character actor, one of Hollywood's best. A lawyer's son, he grew up in Montana, where he learned to raise and ride broncos on the family ranch. After two years at USC, he became a seaman, then entered show business as a radio announcer, gaining national renown as an announcer on 'The March of Time' broadcasts. On the screen from the late 40s, he portrayed a rich gallery of characters, from lawmen and politicians to villains and corrupt officials. His craggy face was also featured frequently on TV in 'Naked City' (1958–59), 'Wagon Train' (1961–65, replacing Ward BOND as the wagonmaster), and 'The Virginian' (1967–68), among others. In 1935 married actress Jeanette NOLAN, a frequent co-player. Their son, actor-singer Tim McIntire (*b.* 1943), died of heart failure in 1986.

FILMS INCLUDE: *Call Northside 777, The Street with No Name, An Act of Murder* 1948; *Down to the Sea in Ships, Scene of the Crime, Top o' the Morning, Johnny Stool Pigeon* 1949; *Ambush, Francis, No Sad Songs for Me, Winchester 73, The Asphalt Jungle, Saddle Tramp* 1950; *Under the Gun* 1951; *Westward the Women, The World in His Arms, Horizons West* 1952; *The Lawless Breed, The Mississippi Gambler, The President's Lady, A Lion Is in the Streets* 1953; *Apache* 1954; *The Far Country, The Scarlet Coat* (as General Robert Howe), *The Kentuckian, The Phenix City Story* 1955; *The Spoilers, Backlash, Away All Boats* 1956; *The Tin Star* 1957; *The Light in the Forest* 1958; *Psycho, Elmer Gantry, Flaming Star* 1960; *Two Rode Together, Summer and Smoke* 1961; *Rough Night in Jericho* 1967; *Herbie Rides Again* 1974; *Rooster Cogburn* 1975; *Honkytonk Man* 1982; *Cloak and Dagger* 1984; *Turner & Hooch* 1989.

Mackaill, Dorothy. Actress. *b.* Mar. 4, 1903, Hull, England. *d.* 1990. A former London showgirl and a Ziegfeld chorine, she played breezy leads in numerous Hollywood silents and early talkies, frequently second-string comedies and light romances. Retiring from the screen in 1938, she moved to Hawaii, where she lived in semiretirement, emerging occasionally for guest roles in the TV series 'Hawaii Five-O.' Her three failed marriages included one (1926–28) to director Lothar MENDES.

FILMS INCLUDE: *A Face at the Window* (UK) 1920; *Bits of Life* 1921; *Isle of Doubt, A Woman's Woman, The Streets of*

New York 1922; *Mighty Lak' a Rose, The Broken Violin, The Fighting Blade, His Children's Children* 1923; *The Next Corner, What Shall I Do?, The Man Who Came Back* 1924; *The Bridge of Sighs, Chickie, One Year to Live, Shore Leave, Joanna* 1925; *The Dancer of Paris, Ranson's Folly, Subway Sadie, Just Another Blonde/The Girl from Coney Island* 1926; *The Lunatic at Large, Convoy, The Crystal Cup, Man Crazy* 1927; *Ladies' Night in a Turkish Bath, Lady Be Good, The Whip, Waterfront, The Barker* 1928; *Children of the Ritz, His Captive Woman, Two Weeks Off, The Love Racket, The Great Divide* 1929; *Strictly Modern, Bright Lights, The Flirting Widow, The Office Wife* 1930; *Once a Sinner, Kept Husbands, The Reckless Hour, Safe in Hell* 1931; *No Man of Her Own, Love Affair* 1932; *The Chief, Curtain at Eight, Picture Brides* 1933; *Cheaters* 1934; *Bulldog Drummond at Bay* (UK) 1937.

McKean, Michael. Actor, screenwriter, musician. Born October 17, 1947, in New York City. *ed.* Carnegie Institute of Technology, Pittsburgh, Pa. Intelligent, wacky comedic actor who rose to fame as the nerd-next-door on television's smash sitcom 'Laverne and Shirley,' and in features as the wigged-out Brit rocker in the cult favorite *This Is Spinal Tap* (1984). He has continued to enjoy a successful career in both mediums. His talent for creating zany characters gained even more exposure from his stint on NBC's 'Saturday Night Live.'

FILMS: *Used Cars* 1980; *Young Doctors In Love* 1982; *This Is Spinal Tap* (also sc., music) 1984; *Clue, D.A.R.Y.L.* 1985; *Jumpin' Jack Flash* 1986; *Double Agent, Light of Day, Planes Trains and Automobiles* 1987; *Short Circuit 2* 1988; *The Big Picture* (also sc., music), *Earth Girls Are Easy* 1989; *Book of Love, Flashback* 1990; *True Identity* 1991; *Man Trouble, Memoirs of an Invisible Man* 1992; *Coneheads* 1993; *Airheads, Radioland Murders* 1994; *The Brady Bunch Movie* 1995.

McKee, Lonette. Actress. Born in 1956 in Detroit, Mich. Elegant, vivacious player of screen and stage. After making an impression in 1976 singing group drama *Sparkle*, she has appeared relatively infrequently on the screen, primarily in supporting roles, which often do not display her musical talents. During the 1980s, she appeared in a number of shows on Broadway, one of them a revival of *Show Boat*, in which she was the first African-American woman to portray the mixed-race Julie.

FILMS INCLUDE: *Sparkle* 1976; *Which Way Is Up?* 1977; *Cuba* 1979; *The Cotton Club* 1984; *Brewster's Millions* 1985; *Round Midnight* 1986; *Gardens of Stone* 1987; *Jungle Fever* 1991; *Malcolm X* 1992.

McKellen, Sir Ian. Actor. Born on May 25, 1939, in Burnley, England. *ed.* Cambridge. One of the contemporary theater's finest classical actors, much admired for his interpretations of Shakespeare. He began performing in college and after graduating in 1961 rapidly established his reputation on the professional stage. He astounded playgoers and later TV viewers with his one-man *tour-de-force* show 'Ian McKellen Acting Shakespeare.' His powerful portrayal of Salieri in the Broadway production of 'Amadeus' earned him a Tony as best actor of 1981. His screen performances have been too sporadic to parallel the impact of his stage career, but they have been memorable. As an openly gay man who has been a leading spokesman for gay rights in Britain, McKellen was publicly criticized when he accepted a knighthood in 1990 after Britain's Clause 28 forbade the government from allocating monies that would in any way "promote" homosexuality. In 1991 he lectured at Oxford as a visiting professor of contemporary theater.

FILMS: *A Touch of Love/Thank You All Very Much, Alfred the Great, The Promise* 1969; *Priest of Love* (as D. H. Lawrence) 1981; *The Keep, Loving Walter/Walter and June* (orig. for TV) 1983; *Plenty* 1985; *Zina* 1986; *Scandal* (as John Profumo) 1989; *The Ballad of Little Jo, Last Action Hero, Six Degrees of Separation* 1993; *I'll Do Anything, The Shadow* 1994; *Cold Comfort Farm, Jack and Sarah, Restoration, Richard III, Thin Ice* 1995.

Mackendrick, Alexander. Director. *b.* 1912, Boston, to Scottish parents on a visit to the US. *d.* 1993. *ed.* School of Art in Glasgow. Started out as a commercial artist and animator of advertising films and entered the British film industry in 1937 as a screenwriter. The following year he began directing shorts and after much documentary production experience during WW II, he turned to directing features. In the late 40s and early 50s he was responsible for several intelligent and highly entertaining Ealing Studio comedies. He shared an Oscar nomination for the screenplay of *The Man in the White Suit* (1951; in US 1952) but is even more fondly remembered for his debut feature, *Whisky Galore/Tight Little Island* (1949), and the hilarious black comedy *The Lady Killers* (1955). Later, he proved himself equally effective with dramatic films, particularly the American-made *Sweet Smell of Success* (1957), a no-holds-barred "exposé" of corruption in the world of press agents and newspaper columnists. Despite a limited output, and several misses, Mackendrick left a bright mark on Anglo-American cinema. He also did some TV work but became relatively inactive as a director after the late 60s, when he was appointed dean of the film department of the California Institute of the Arts. Friends called him Sandy.

FEATURE FILMS: *Whisky Galore/Tight Little Island* (also co-sc.) 1949; *The Man in the White Suit* (also co-sc.) 1951; *Mandy/The Story of Mandy/Crash of Silence* 1952; *The Maggie/High and Dry* (also story) 1954; *The Ladykillers* 1955; *Sweet Smell of Success* (US) 1957; *Sammy Going South/A Boy Ten Feet Tall* 1963; *A High Wind in Jamaica* (US/UK) 1965; *Oh Dad Poor Dad—Mama's Hung You in the Closet and I'm Feelin' So Sad* (addnl. scenes only; US), *Don't Make Waves* (US) 1967.

McKenna, Siobhan. Actress. *b.* May 24, 1923, in Belfast. *d.* 1986. *ed.* National U. of Ireland. On the stage since 1940, she made her name with Dublin's Abbey Theatre before tackling London and Broadway, most memorably in G. B. Shaw's 'Saint Joan.' She became known as the first lady of the Irish theater. Her energetic personality sparked many a stage play but only occasional films. She was the widow of stage-screen actor Dennis O'Dea (1903–78). Her death at 63, of a heart attack following lung-cancer surgery, aborted John Huston's plans to cast her in his last film, *The Dead.*

FILMS: *Hungry Hill* 1946; *Daughter of Darkness* 1948; *The Lost People* 1949; *King of Kings* (as the Virgin Mary; US) 1961; *The Playboy of the Western World* (as Pegeen Mike) 1962; *Of Human Bondage* (as Norah Nesbit) 1964; *Doctor Zhivago* (as Anna Gromeko; US) 1965; *Memed My Hawk* 1984.

McKenna, Virginia. Actress. Born on June 7, 1931, in London. Spunky leading lady of the British stage and screen. A graduate of the Central School of Speech Training and Dramatic Art, she made her stage debut in 1950 and her first film appearance in 1952. Typically seen in appealing, unglamorous roles. Divorced (1954–56) from actor Denholm Elliott, she married Bill Travers in 1957, who was her co-star in *Born Free* (1966) and other films.

FILMS: *The Second Mrs. Tanqueray, Father's Doing Fine* 1952; *The Cruel Sea, The Oracle/The Horse's Mouth* 1953; *Simba, The Ship That Died of Shame* 1955; *A Town Like Alice* 1956; *The Barretts of Wimpole Street, The Smallest Show on Earth* 1957; *Carve Her Name with Pride, Passionate Summer* 1958; *The Wreck of the Mary Deare* (US) 1959; *Two Living—One Dead* (UK/Sw.) 1961; *Born Free* 1966; *Ring of Bright*

Water 1969; *An Elephant Called Slowly, Waterloo* (It./USSR) 1970; *Swallows and Amazons* (UK) 1974; *Christian the Lion* 1976; *Disappearance* (Can.), *Holocaust 2000/The Chosen* (It./UK) 1977; *Blood Link* (It.) 1982.

MacKenzie, John. Director. Born in 1932, in Edinburgh, Scotland. Proficient filmmaker with a track record in TV. After a modest start in features in the early 70s, he impressed strongly with *The Long Good Friday* (1980), a gripping crime drama about a London East Side gang featuring terrific performances by Bob Hoskins and Helen Mirren. He was far less successful with his subsequent output, which comprised TV movies as well as feature films.

FILMS: *One Brief Summer* 1970; *Unman Wittering and Zigo* 1971; *Made* 1972; *A Sense of Freedom* (orig. for TV) 1979; *The Long Good Friday* 1980; *The Honorary Consul/Beyond the Limit* (UK/US) 1983; *The Innocent* 1985; *The Fourth Protocol* 1987; *The Last of the Finest* 1990; *Ruby* 1992; *Car 54 Where Are You?* 1994.

McKern, Leo. Actor. Born Reginald McKern, on Mar. 16, 1920, in Sidney, Australia. Character actor of British stage and screen, usually in strong commanding roles. He shone in the TV mystery series 'Rumpole of the Bailey,' which was a big hit in Britain and later had a successful run in the US on public TV. He won the Australian Film Award and the London Film Critics Award as best actor for his performance in *Traveling North* (1986), as a cantankerous but lovable ex-communist and civil engineer who goes into retirement.

FILMS INCLUDE: *Murder in the Cathedral* 1952; *All for Mary* 1955; *X the Unknown* 1956; *Time Without Pity* 1957; *A Tale of Two Cities* 1958; *The Mouse That Roared, Yesterday's Enemy* 1959; *Scent of Mystery* (US) 1960; *Mr. Topaze/I Like Money, The Day the Earth Caught Fire* 1961; *The Inspector/Lisa* 1962; *Doctor in Distress* 1963; *A Jolly Bad Fellow/They All Died Laughing, Hot Enough for June/Agent 8¾* 1964; *King and Country, The Amorous Adventures of Moll Flanders, Help!* 1965; *A Man for All Seasons* (as Cromwell) 1966; *Assignment K, The Shoes of the Fisherman* (US) 1968; *Ryan's Daughter* 1970; *Rappresaglia/Massacre in Rome* (It./UK) 1973; *The Adventure of Sherlock Holmes' Smarter Brother* (as Prof. Moriarty) 1975; *The Omen* (US) 1976; *Candleshoe* (US) 1978; *Blue Lagoon* (US) 1980; *The French Lieutenant's Woman* 1981; *Ladyhawke* (US), *The Chain* 1985; *Traveling North* (Austral.) 1986.

MacLachlan, Kyle. American actor. Born in 1960. Tall, dark, and coldly handsome leading man of American films. A stage performer in high school and college, he was discovered by David LYNCH in a nationwide search to play the hero in the ill-fated epic *Dune* (1984) and has since gained a cult following for his crisply stylized performances in the director's *Blue Velvet* and 'Twin Peaks'—the TV series (1990) and the movie (1992).

FILMS: *Dune* 1984; *Blue Velvet* 1986; *The Hidden* 1987; *Don't Tell Her It's Me* 1990; *The Doors* (as keyboardist Ray Manzarek) 1991; *Twin Peaks: Fire Walk with Me, Where the Day Takes You* 1992; *The Trial* 1993; *The Flintstones* 1994; *Showgirls* 1995; *Mad Dog Time, The Trigger Effect* 1996; *One Night Stand* 1997.

McLaglen, Andrew V. Director. Born on July 28, 1920, in London. The son of Victor MCLAGLEN, he was raised among movie people, played occasional bits in films of family friends, and gained technical expertise in the production of industrial films. In the early 50s he worked as an assistant director to Budd Boetticher, John Ford, and other directors and turned out his own first feature as a director in 1956. Shortly after, he signed a long-term contract with CBS-TV and directed numerous episodes for such series as 'Have Gun Will Travel,' 'Gunsmoke,' and 'Perry Mason,' in addition to sporadic feature films. He began concentrating on features in the mid-60s, specializing in Westerns that have been noted more for their superficial gloss than for originality. Formerly married to Veda Ann BORG.

FILMS: *Gun the Man Down, The Man in the Vault* 1956; *The Abductors* 1957; *Freckles* 1960; *The Little Shepherd of Kingdom Come* 1961; *McLintock!* 1963; *Shenandoah* 1965; *The Rare Breed* 1966; *Monkeys Go Home!, The Way West* 1967; *The Ballad of Josie, The Devil's Brigade, Bandolero!* 1968; *Hellfighters, The Undefeated* 1969; *Chisum* 1970; *One More Train to Rob, Fools' Parade* (also prod.), *Something Big* (also prod.) 1971; *Cahill—US Marshal* 1973; *Mitchell* 1975; *The Last Hard Men* 1976; *The Wild Geese* 1978; *Sergeant Steiner—das eisene Kreuz 2. teil/Sergeant Steiner 2/Breakthrough* (Ger.) 1979; *North Sea Hijack/Ffolkes* (UK), *The Sea Wolves* (UK) 1980; *Sahara* 1984; *Return to the River Kwai* (UK) 1990; *Eye of the Widow* (Fr.) 1991.

McLaglen, Victor. Actor. *b.* Dec. 10, 1886, Tunbridge Wells, England. *d.* 1959. A character star of some British and innumerable Hollywood silent and sound films, appropriately billed as "The Beloved Brute" after the title of his first American film. The son of a clergyman (later Bishop of Clermont, South Africa), he was a boy soldier during the Boer War, then a prize-fighter in Canada and a vaudeville and circus performer. (He was a "great white hope" to stop famed black boxer Jack Johnson but lost the much-promoted fight in six rounds.) He served as captain with the Irish Fusiliers during WW I and acted for a while as provost marshal of Baghdad. He starred in British films of the early 20s, then went to Hollywood, where he was cast in leads and supporting parts, typically as a big, savage, but soft-hearted man of action. He was a favorite of director John FORD, who used him to advantage in many of his films, often as a tough-soft cavalry sergeant. He won an Academy Award playing the title role of Gypo Nolan in Ford's *The Informer* (1935). McLaglen, five of whose brothers (Arthur, Clifford, Cyril, Kenneth, and Leopold) also were film actors, was the father of director Andrew V. MCLAGLEN.

FILMS INCLUDE: In the UK—*The Call of the Road* 1920; *Carnival* 1921; *The Glorious Adventure* (UK/US) 1922; *In the Blood* 1923. In the US—*The Beloved Brute* 1924; *The Unholy Three, Winds of Chance, The Fighting Heart* 1925; *The Isle of Retribution, Men of Steel, Beau Geste, What Price Glory* 1926; *Loves of Carmen* (as Escamillo) 1927; *A Girl in Every Port, Mother Machree, Hangman's House, The River Pirate* 1928; *Captain Lash, Strong Boy, The Black Watch, The Cock-Eyed World, Hot for Paris* 1929; *On the Level, A Devil with Women* 1930; *Dishonored, Three Rogues, Women of All Nations, Annabelle's Affairs, Wicked* 1931; *The Gay Caballero, Devil's Lottery, Guilty as Hell, Rackety Rax* 1932; *Hot Pepper, Laughing at Life, Dick Turpin* (UK) 1933; *No More Women, The Lost Patrol, Wharf Angel, Murder at the Vanities, The Captain Hates the Sea* 1934; *Under Pressure, The Great Hotel Murder, The Informer* 1935; *Professional Soldier, Klondike Annie, Under Two Flags, The Magnificent Brute* 1936; *Nancy Steele Is Missing, Sea Devils, This Is My Affair, Wee Willie Winkie* 1937; *Battle of Broadway, The Devil's Party, We're Going to Be Rich* (US/UK) 1938; *Pacific Liner, Gunga Din, Let Freedom Ring, Ex-Champ, Captain Fury, Full Confession, Rio, The Big Guy* 1939; *South of Pago-Pago, Diamond Frontier* 1940; *Broadway Limited* 1941; *Call Out the Marines, Powder Town* 1942; *China Girl* 1943; *Tampico, Roger Touhy—Gangster, The Princess and the Pirate* 1944; *Rough Tough and Ready* 1945; *Whistle Stop* 1946; *The Foxes of Harrow* 1947; *Fort Apache* 1948; *She Wore a Yellow Ribbon* 1949; *Rio Grande* 1950; *The Quiet Man* 1952; *Fair Wind to Java* 1953; *Prince Valiant, Trouble in the Glen*

(UK) 1954; *Many Rivers to Cross, City of Shadows, Lady Godiva* 1955; *Around the World in 80 Days* 1956; *The Abductors* 1957; *Sea Fury* (UK) 1958.

MacLaine, Shirley. Actress. Born Shirley MacLean Beaty, on Apr. 24, 1934, in Richmond, Va. Sister of Warren BEATTY. Dancing from the age of two, she made her first public appearance at four. She continued performing with local groups throughout her school days and from age 16 spent her summer vacations in New York in search of dancing jobs. When she graduated from high school she moved to the city and after persistent efforts broke into the chorus line of several Broadway shows, supplementing her income with various modeling assignments. She got her big break in 1954 in a manner befitting a cliché script of a backstage Hollywood musical. She was dancing in the chorus and doubling as Carol Haney's understudy in the Broadway production of 'Pajama Game.' Shortly after opening night Miss Haney broke a leg and Shirley took over. Movie producer Hal WALLIS was in the audience and immediately signed her to a movie contract.

Beginning with Hitchcock's *The Trouble with Harry,* Miss MacLaine proved herself a capable actress in a balanced mixture of dramas and comedies. She was nominated for Academy Awards for *Some Came Running* (1959), *The Apartment* (1960), and *Irma La Douce* (1963). As a result of the latter, she was typecast for a while in the role of a hooker with a heart of gold. Countering her impish, often "kooky" screen image in her personal life, she has campaigned tirelessly for liberal causes and is active in politics. In 1968 she was a Bobby Kennedy–pledged delegate from California at the Democratic convention and in 1972 campaigned with equal zeal for McGovern. She is also a noted globetrotter and maintains eight dwellings in various cities around the world. In 1971–72 she starred in her own TV series 'Shirley's World,' in which she played a world-traveling photo journalist. In 1970 she published a candid memoir, *Don't Fall Off the Mountain,* the first of her many introspective, autobiographical books.

In 1973, Miss MacLaine toured mainland China with a group of women and later recounted her impressions in a book, *You Can Get There from Here,* and in a feature-length, Oscar-nominated documentary, *The Other Half of the Sky: A China Memoir* (released in 1975), which she wrote, produced, and co-directed with Claudia Weill. In 1976 she returned to the stage with a one-woman show, 'A Gypsy in My Soul.' She would dazzle Broadway audiences again in 1984 in 'Shirley MacLaine on Broadway,' a song-and-dance act she had originated in Las Vegas.

As her talent, versatility, and energy belied the advancing years, she carried her screen career strongly into the 90s. She was nominated for yet another Oscar for *The Turning Point* (1977) and won the best actress Academy Award for her performance in *Terms of Endearment* (1983). After several years of absence, she returned to the screen in 1988 to play the title role of an eccentric piano teacher in *Madame Sousatzka,* for which she shared the best actress prize at the Venice Festival.

Apart from her acting, Miss MacLaine is famous for her deep interest in spiritualism and unwavering faith in reincarnation, phenomena she examined in *Out on a Limb* (1983) and other best-selling books. The book provided the basis for a TV miniseries in 1986. It was followed by *Dancing in the Light* (1985), *It's All in the Playing* (1987), and *Going Within* (1989). She also released a mental-fitness videocassette, 'Shirley MacLaine's Inner Workout,' in 1989. She is virtually synonymous with New Age mysticism, and is often the subject of skeptical ribbing. From 1954 to 1982 Miss MacLaine was married to Steve Parker, a producer and packager of Japanese entertainment, who spent most of his time in the Orient, rarely seeing his wife. The marriage produced a daughter, Stephanie Sachiko (*b.* 1956), an actress using the professional name Sachi Parker, who Miss MacLaine believes was her mother in one of several previous lives.

FILMS: *The Trouble with Harry, Artists and Models* 1955; *Around the World in 80 Days* 1956; *The Sheepman, The Matchmaker, Hot Spell* 1958; *Some Came Running, Ask Any Girl, Career* 1959; *Ocean's 11* (cameo), *Can-Can, The Apartment* 1960; *All in a Night's Work, Two Loves* 1961; *The Children's Hour, My Geisha, Two for the Seesaw* 1962; *Irma La Douce* 1963; *What a Way to Go!, The Yellow Rolls-Royce* (UK) 1964; *John Goldfarb Please Come Home* 1965; *Gambit* 1966; *Sept fois Femme/Woman Times Seven* (Fr./It./US) 1967; *The Bliss of Mrs. Blossom* (UK) 1968; *Sweet Charity* 1969; *Two Mules for Sister Sara* 1970; *Desperate Characters* 1974; *The Possession of Joel Delaney* 1972; *The Year of the Woman* (doc.) 1973; *The Other Half of the Sky: A China Memoir* (doc.; sc., prod., co-dir. only) 1975; *The Turning Point* 1977; *Being There* 1979; *A Change of Seasons, Loving Couples* 1980; *Terms of Endearment* 1983; *Cannonball Run II* 1984; *Madame Sousatzka* 1988; *Steel Magnolias* 1989; *Waiting for the Light, Postcards from the Edge* 1990; *Defending Your Life* (as herself) 1991; *Used People* 1992; *Wrestling Ernest Hemingway* 1993; *Guarding Tess* 1994; *The Celluloid Closet* 1995; *Mrs. Winterbourne, The Evening Star* 1996.

MacLane, Barton. Actor. *b.* Dec. 25, 1902, Columbia, S.C. *d.* 1969. *ed.* Wesleyan; AADA. Formerly on the stage, he appeared in some 200 films, mainly at Warner Bros., most often as a heavy, typically portraying a gangster bully or a mean Western outlaw. But he occasionally played good tough guys, sometimes in leads, and co-starred with Glenda Farrell in the "Torchy Blane" film series. He starred as a lawman in the TV series 'The Outlaws.'

FILMS INCLUDE: *The Quarterback* (bit) 1926; *The Cocoanuts* (bit) 1929; *Man of the Forest, Tillie and Gus* 1933; *The Last Round-Up* 1934; *Black Fury, G-Men, Go Into Your Dance, Stranded, Dr. Socrates, Frisco Kid, Man of Iron* (lead) 1935; *Ceiling Zero, The Walking Dead, Bullets or Ballots, Bengal Tiger* (lead) 1936; *Smart Blonde* (lead), *You Only Live Once, The Prince and the Pauper* (as John Canty, the Pauper's father), *Fly Away Baby* (lead), *San Quentin, The Adventurous Blonde* (lead) 1937; *Gold Is Where You Find It, You and Me, Prison Break* (lead), *The Storm, Torchy Gets Her Man* (lead) 1938; *I Was a Convict* (lead), *Big Town Czar* (lead), *Mutiny in the Big House* 1939; *Men Without Souls, Gangs of Chicago, The Secret Seven* (lead) 1940; *High Sierra, Western Union, Come Live with Me, Hit the Road* (lead), *Manpower, Dr. Jekyll and Mr. Hyde, The Maltese Falcon* 1941; *All Through the Night, The Big Street* 1942; *The Mummy's Ghost, The Cry of the Werewolf* 1944; *Tarzan and the Amazons, The Spanish Main* 1945; *San Quentin, Cheyenne* 1947; *The Treasure of the Sierra Madre, Relentless, Silver River* 1948; *Kiss Tomorrow Goodbye, Let's Dance* 1950; *Best of the Badmen* 1951; *Bugles in the Afternoon, The Half-Breed* 1952; *Jack Slade* 1953; *The Glenn Miller Story* 1954; *Hell's Outpost* 1955; *Wetbacks* 1956; *Naked in the Sun* 1957; *The Geisha Boy* 1958; *Pocketful of Miracles* 1961; *Law of the Lawless* 1964; *Town Tamer* 1965; *Arizona Bushwhackers* 1968.

McLaren, Norman. Animator. *b.* Apr. 11, 1914, Stirling, Scotland. *d.* 1987. He began making amateur short films at 19 while attending the Glasgow School of Art and at 21 turned out his first animated film. John GRIERSON saw his work at an amateur film festival and invited him to join his GPO Film Unit in London, in 1936. While there, he worked on live-action documentaries and made his first professional animated film, *Love on the Wing* (1938). In 1939 McLaren emigrated to the US, where he continued making animated films by his favorite method—drawing directly on celluloid. In 1941 he was invited by Grierson to join the newly formed National Film Board, in Ottawa, Canada, and in 1943 he was put in charge of the Board's animation unit. Enjoying complete creative freedom and a generous Canadian government grant, McLaren created numerous cartoons, many of them abstract, by a variety of techniques and in various styles. He gained wide recognition as one of the world's leading animators.

A gifted innovator and a meticulous craftsman, McLaren pioneered in many areas of animation, but his greatest contribution was in developing and perfecting the techniques of drawing directly on film, a cameraless method of animation originated by Len LYE. McLaren also experimented with three-dimensional animation and in the conversion of animated drawings into synthetic sound waves. He won an Oscar for his cartoon *Neighbors* (1952), in which he animated living actors, changing their positions 24 times a second as if they were inanimate objects to achieve robot-like human motion, a process known as pixillation. He also won many other international awards during his illustrious career.

FILMS INCLUDE: *Seven Till Five* 1933; *Camera Makes Whoopee, Color Cocktail* 1935; *Hell Unlimited* 1936; *Book Bargain* 1937; *Love on the Wing* 1938; *Stars and Stripes* 1939; *Dots, Loops, Boogie Doodle* 1940; *V for Victory* 1941; *Dollar Dance* 1943; *Keep Your Mouth Shut* 1944; *A Little Fantasy, Hoppity Pop* 1946; *Fiddle-de-dee* 1947; *Begone Dull Care* 1949; *Neighbors* 1952; *Blinkity Blank* 1954; *Rhythmetic* 1956; *A Chairy Tale* 1957; *Short and Suite* 1959; *Canon* 1964; *Mosaic* 1965; *Pas de Deux* 1968; *Spheres* 1969; *Synchromy* 1971; *Ballet Adagio* 1972; *L'Ecran d'Epingles* (co-dir.) 1973; *Le Movement Image par Image* (series) 1976–78; *Narcissus* 1983.

McLean, Barbara. American film editor. Born in 1909. From the mid-30s through the mid-50s she edited many of 20th Century-Fox's most prestigious productions. She was nominated for seven Academy Awards, winning the Oscar for her work on *Wilson* (1944).

FILMS INCLUDE: *The House of Rothschild, The Affairs of Cellini* 1934; *Clive of India, Les Miserables* 1935; *The Country Doctor, Lloyds of London* 1936; *Seventh Heaven* 1937; *Alexander's Ragtime Band, In Old Chicago, Suez* 1938; *Jesse James, The Rains Came, Stanley and Livingstone* 1939; *Chad Hanna, Down Argentine Way* 1940; *Remember the Day, Tobacco Raod, A Yank in the R.A.F.* 1941; *The Black Swan, The Magnificent Dope* 1942; *The Song of Bernadette* 1943; *Wilson* 1944; *A Bell for Adano* 1945; *Margie* 1946; *Captain from Castille, Nightmare Alley* 1947; *Prince of Foxes* 1949; *Twelve O'Clock High, All About Eve, The Gunfighter* 1950; *David and Bathsheba, People Will Talk* 1951; *O. Henry's Full House, Viva Zapata!* 1952; *The Desert Rats, Niagara, The Robe* 1953; *The Egyptian* 1954; *The Untamed* 1955.

MacLean, Douglas. Actor, producer. *b.* Jan. 14, 1890, Philadelphia. *d.* 1967. A former screen actor, he starred in numerous light silent films, many of which he produced himself. After the advent of sound he abandoned acting, remaining active as a producer and occasional screenwriter till the early 40s. His credits as producer include a couple of W. C. Fields comedies.

FILMS INCLUDE: As actor—*As Ye Sow* 1914; *The Man Who Found Himself* 1915; *Love's Crucible* 1916; *Souls in Pawn* 1917; *The Vamp, The Hun Within, Johanna Enlists, Fuss and Feathers, Mirandy Smiles* 1918; *Captain Kidd Jr., The Homebreaker, Twenty-Three and a Half Hours' Leave* 1919; *Mary's Ankle, Let's Be Fashionable, The Jailbird, The Rookie's Return* 1920; *Chickens, The Home Stretch, Passing Thru* 1921; *The Hottentot* 1922; *The Sunshine Trail, A Man of Action* 1923; *Seven Keys to Baldpate* 1925; *That's My Baby* 1926; *Soft Cushions* 1927; *The Carnation Kid* 1929. As actor-producer—*Going Up* 1923; *The Yankee Consul, Never Say Die* 1924; *Introduce Me* 1925; *Hold That Lion* 1926; *Let It Rain* 1927; *Divorce Made Easy* 1929. As producer—*Laugh and Get Rich* (also sc.), *Cracked Nuts* (also sc.), *Caught Plastered* (also sc.) 1931; *Mama Loves Papa* (also co-story), *Tillie and Gus* 1933; *Six of a Kind* (co-story only), *Ladies Should Listen* 1934; *Mrs. Wiggs of the Cabbage Patch, People Will Talk, Accent on Youth, So Red the Rose* 1935; *Great Guy* 1936; *23½ Hours Leave* (remake) 1937; *New Wine* 1941.

McLeod, Catherine. American actress. *b.* 1921. *d.* 1997. Leading lady of several of Republic's better productions of the late 40s, memorably opposite Philip Dorn in Frank Borzage's *I've Always Loved You* (1946). She later played supporting roles in a number of films of other studios but was busier on TV, in commercials as well as in the daytime soap opera 'Days of Our Lives.'

FILMS INCLUDE: *The Thin Man Goes Home* 1944; *The Harvey Girls, Courage of Lassie, I've Always Loved You* 1946; *That's My Man, The Fabulous Texan* 1947; *Old Los Angeles* 1948; *So Young So Bad* 1950; *My Wife's Best Friend* 1952; *A Blueprint for Murder* 1953; *The Outcast* 1954; *Tammy Tell Me True, The Sergeant Was a Lady* 1963; *Ride the Wild Surf* 1964.

McLeod, Norman Z(enos). Director. *b.* Sept. 20, 1898, Grayling, Mich. *d.* 1964. A clergyman's son, he graduated from the University of Washington with B.S. and M.S. degrees in the natural sciences and during WW I served as a fighter pilot with the Royal Canadian Air Force. He entered films in 1919 as an animator and later gag writer for Al Christie Comedies. His experience as a pilot helped him become William Wellman's assistant director on the famous *Wings* (1927) and script collaborator on Howard Hawks's and Lewis Seiler's *The Air Circus* (1928). He also wrote titles for three other feature films before making his own debut as a director in 1928. With occasional exceptions, McLeod specialized in comedy throughout his career, turning out many entertaining, unpretentious Hollywood films for several studios. His success or failure depended a great deal on the quality of the script material and the talent of the comedians at his disposal. Some of his more successful films starred such comedy greats as the Marx Brothers, W. C. Fields, Danny Kaye, and Bob Hope, most notably Kaye's *The Secret Life of Walter Mitty* (1947) and Hope's *The Paleface* (1948). At the ebb of his career, he worked mainly for TV, directing episodes for 'My Little Margie' and 'Twilight Zone.' In 1962 he suffered a stroke from which he never recovered.

FILMS: *Taking a Chance* 1928; *Along Came Youth* (co-dir. with Lloyd Corrigan) 1930; *Finn and Hattie* (co-dir. with Norman Taurog; also co-sc.), *Monkey Business, Touchdown* 1931; *The Miracle Man, Horse Feathers, If I Had a Million* ("The Forger" episode) 1932; *A Lady's Profession, Mama Loves Papa, Alice in Wonderland* 1933; *Melody in Spring, Many Happy Returns, It's a Gift* 1934; *Redheads on Parade, Here Comes Cookie, Coronado* 1935; *Early to Bed, Pennies from Heaven* 1936; *Mind Your Own Business, Topper* 1937; *Merrily We Live, There Goes My Heart* 1938; *Topper Takes a Trip, Remember?* (also co-story, co-sc.) 1939; *Little Men* 1940; *The Trial of Mary Dugan, Lady Be Good* 1941; *Jackass Mail, Panama Hattie* 1942; *The Powers Girl, Swing Shift Maisie* 1943; *The Kid from Brooklyn* 1946; *The Secret Life of Walter Mitty, Road to Rio* 1947; *Isn't It Romantic?, The Paleface* 1948; *Let's Dance* 1950; *My Favorite Spy* 1951; *Never Wave at a Wac* 1953; *Casanova's Big Night* 1954; *Public Pigeon No. 1* 1957; *Alias Jesse James* 1959.

MacMahon, Aline. Actress. *b.* May 3, 1899, in McKeesport. Pa. *d.* 1991. *ed.* Barnard. The daughter of a broker-turned-magazine-editor, she was raised in New York City and made her stage debut at the Neighborhood Playhouse shortly after graduating from college. In Hollywood from the early 30s, she played soulful, melancholy leads and supporting roles in many films. She was nominated for an Oscar for her supporting role in *Dragon Seed* (1944). Her sad face and eyes were tailor-made for dramas, but she also performed effectively in a number of comic roles. In 1928 she married New York architect Clarence S. Stein, who left her a widow in 1975.

FILMS INCLUDE: *Five Star Final* 1931; *The Heart of New York, The Mouthpiece, Life Begins, One Way Passage, Once in a Lifetime* 1932; *Gold Diggers of 1933, Heroes for Sale, The World Changes* 1933; *Heat Lightning, Side Streets, Big-Hearted Herbert, Babbitt* (as Myra Babbitt) 1934; *I Live My Life, Kind Lady, Ah Wilderness!* (as Lily) 1935; *When You're in Love* 1937; *Back Door to Heaven* 1939; *Out of the Fog* 1941; *The Lady Is Willing* 1942; *Dragon Seed, Guest in the House* 1944; *The Mighty McGurk* 1947; *The Search* 1948; *Roseanna McCoy* 1949; *The Flame and the Arrow* 1950; *The Eddie Cantor Story* 1953; *The Man from Laramie* 1955; *Cimarron* 1960; *The Young Doctors* 1961; *Diamond Head, I Could Go on Singing* (UK), *All the Way Home* 1963.

McMahon, Horace. Actor. *b.* May 17, 1906, South Norwalk, Conn. *d.* 1971. A former newspaper reporter, he began acting in stock while attending the Fordham University Law School. He made his Broadway debut in 1931, arrived in Hollywood in 1937, and was immediately put to work as a character actor. He appeared in numerous films, typically cast as a gangster or a jailbird. After scoring on Broadway in 1949 as Lt. Monoghan in 'Detective Story,' he was retyped by Hollywood as a cop. He also played a police lieutenant in the long-running TV series 'Naked City.' He was married to actress Louise CAMPBELL.

FILMS INCLUDE: *Exclusive* 1937; *King of the Newsboys, Fast Company, Tenth Avenue Kid, Broadway Musketeers* 1938; *I Was a Convict, Big Town Czar, Rose of Washington Square, The Gracie Allen Murder Case, Sabotage* 1939; *Gangs of Chicago, Dr. Kildare's Crisis* 1940; *Come Live with Me, Lady Scarface, Buy Me That Town, Birth of the Blues* 1941; *Jail House Blues* 1942; *Roger Touhy—Gangster* 1944; *Detective Story* 1951; *Man in the Dark* 1953; *Susan Slept Here* 1954; *Blackboard Jungle, My Sister Eileen* 1955; *The Delicate Delinquent* 1957; *Never Steal Anything Small* 1959; *The Swinger* 1966; *The Detective* 1968.

McMillan, Kenneth. Actor. *b.* July 2, 1932, in Brooklyn, N.Y. *d.* 1989. Burly, crude-featured character player of the American stage, TV, and films. A graduate of New York's High School for the Performing Arts, he worked for years at the Gimbels department store in Manhattan, as a salesman, then as a floor manager, while trying in vain to line up acting roles. Finally he quit his job in 1960 to join a touring production of 'Sweet Bird of Youth.' Roles off Broadway and in soap operas followed, before his Broadway debut in 'Borstal Boy' (1970) and his first screen appearance in *Serpico* (1971). Later in the 70s he played Falstaff in a New York Shakespeare Festival production of 'Henry IV, Part I' and became a regular (1977–78) on the TV series 'Rhoda.' But it wasn't until 1981 that he became known as a screen personality, with a brutal portrayal of a bigoted, beer-bellied fire chief in *Ragtime*. His daughter, Allison, is an actress. Another Kenneth McMillan is a British cinematographer who was behind the camera on *Henry V* (1989), among other films.

FILMS: *Serpico* 1971; *The Taking of Pelham One Two Three* 1974; *The Stepford Wives* 1975; *Girlfriends, Bloodbrothers, Oliver's Story* 1978; *Head Over Heels/Chilly Scenes of Winter* 1979; *Little Miss Marker, Hide in Plain Sight, Borderline* 1980; *Eyewitness, True Confessions, Heartbeeps, Ragtime, Whose Life Is It Anyway?* 1981; *Partners, The Killing Hour/The Clairvoyant* 1982; *Blue Skies Again* 1983; *Reckless, The Pope of Greenwich Village, Dune, Protocol* 1984; *Cat's Eye, Runaway Train* 1985; *Armed and Dangerous* 1986; *Malone* 1987; *Three Fugitives* 1989.

McMullen, Ken. Director. Born in 1948, in Manchester, England. Independent, intelligent filmmaker with a penchant for sociopolitical themes, a keen sense of time and place, and a bold, evocative visual style.

FILMS: *Resistance* 1976; *Ghost Dance* (also prod., sc.) 1983; *Being and Doing* (also prod, co-phot.) 1984; *Zina* (also prod., co-sc.) 1986; *Partition* (also sc.) 1988; *1871* (also exec. prod., co-sc.) 1990.

MacMurray, Fred. Actor. *b.* Frederick Martin MacMurray, Aug. 30, 1908 in Kankakee, Ill. *d.* 1991. The son of a concert violinist, he started out as a band saxophonist and vocalist to pay his way through Carroll College in Wisconsin. He traveled with various bands and while performing in California appeared as an extra in a few films of the late 20s. In 1930 he appeared in a Broadway revue with the Californian Collegians and three years later performed with the same group in the Broadway musical 'Roberta.' He was then signed by Paramount on a screen contract and was immediately thrown into a hectic schedule of lead roles in a variety of films. At first he was put indiscriminately into films of all genres, but gradually he found his forte in comedy, of both the sophisticated and farcical kinds. Although he performed convincingly as a heel in occasional dramatic roles, notably in *Double Indemnity* (1944) and *The Apartment* (1960), comedy would remain his bread-and-butter genre for the rest of his prolific film career. Typically playing genial, persistent leading men, he proved himself one of Hollywood's most enduring stars. His fading popularity received a boost in the 60s from the long-running TV series 'My Three Sons' (1960–72) and from a string of successful Disney family-entertainment films in which he played the lead. The nonstop income from films and TV and wise investments combined to make him one of Hollywood's wealthiest citizens. Some say his face provided the model for the comic-strip hero, Captain Marvel. He was married from 1954 until his death in 1991 to actress June HAVER.

FILMS: *Girls Go Wild* (bit), *Glad Rag Doll* (bit), *Tiger Rose* (bit), *Friends of Mr. Sweeney* 1934; *Grand Old Girl, The Gilded Lily, Car 99, Men Without Names, Alice Adams* (as Arthur Russell), *Hands Across the Table, The Bride Comes Home* 1935; *The Trail of the Lonesome Pine, 13 Hours by Air, The Princess Comes Across, The Texas Rangers* 1936; *Champagne Waltz, Maid of Salem, Swing High—Swing Low, Exclusive, True Confession* 1937; *Cocoanut Grove, Sing You Sinners, Men with Wings* 1938; *Cafe Society, Invitation to Happiness, Honeymoon in Bali* 1939; *Remember the Night, Little Old New York, Too Many Husbands, Rangers of Fortune* 1940; *Virginia, One Night in Lisbon, Dive Bomber, New York Town* 1941; *The Lady Is Willing, Take a Letter Darling, The Forest Rangers, Star Spangled Rhythm* 1942; *Flight for Freedom, Above Suspicion, No Time for Love* 1943; *Standing Room Only, And the Angels Sing, Double Indemnity* 1944; *Practically Yours, Where Do We Go from Here?, Murder He Says, Captain Eddie* (as Eddie Rickenbacker) 1945; *Pardon My Past, Smoky* 1946; *Suddenly It's Spring, The Egg and I, Singapore* 1947; *On Our Merry Way/A Miracle Can Happen, The Miracle of the Bells, Don't Trust Your Husband/An Innocent*

Affair 1948; *Family Honeymoon, Father Was a Fullback* 1949; *Borderline, Never a Dull Moment* 1950; *A Millionaire for Christy, Callaway Went Thataway* 1951; *Fair Wind to Java, The Moonlighter* 1953; *The Caine Mutiny* (as Lt. Keefer), *Pushover, Woman's World* 1954; *The Far Horizons* (as Meriwether Lewis of Lewis and Clark expedition), *The Rains of Ranchipur, At Gunpoint* 1955; *There's Always Tomorrow* 1956; *Guns for a Coward, Quantez* 1957; *Day of the Badman* 1958; *Good Day for a Hanging, The Shaggy Dog, Face of a Fugitive, The Oregon Trail* 1959; *The Apartment* 1960; *The Absent-Minded Professor* 1961; *Bon Voyage!* 1962; *Son of Flubber* 1963; *Kisses for My President* 1964; *Follow Me Boys!* 1966; *The Happiest Millionaire* 1967; *Charley and the Angel* 1973; *The Swarm* 1978.

McNally, Stephen. Actor. *b.* Horace McNally, on July 29, 1913, in New York City. *d.* 1994. A former lawyer, he entered films in the early 40s, initially billed under his real name, and gained critical and popular acclaim in 1948 as a detestable heavy in *Johnny Belinda.* He went on to play persuasive leads and supporting parts in many films, at times a hero, more frequently a villain. Much too often wasted on minor pictures. His numerous TV appearances included starring roles in the series 'Target: The Corruptors' (1961–62) and 'W.E.B' (1978).

FILMS INCLUDE: As Horace McNally—*Grand Central Murder, For Me and My Gal, Keeper of the Flame* 1942; *An American Romance, Thirty Seconds Over Tokyo* 1944; *Bewitched* 1945; *The Harvey Girls, Magnificent Doll* 1946. As Stephen McNally—*Johnny Belinda, Rogues' Regiment* 1948; *Criss Cross, City Across the River, The Lady Gambles, Sword in the Desert* 1949; *Woman in Hiding, Winchester 73, No Way Out, Wyoming Mail* 1950; *Air Cadet, Apache Drums, Iron Man, The Lady Pays Off* 1951; *Diplomatic Courier, Duel at Silver Creek, Battle Zone, The Black Castle* 1952; *Split Second, Devil's Canyon, The Stand at Apache River* 1953; *Make Haste to Live, A Bullet Is Waiting* 1954; *Violent Saturday* 1955; *Tribute to a Bad Man* 1956; *Hell's Crossroads* 1957; *The Fiend Who Walked the West, Hell's Five Hours, Johnny Rocco* 1958; *Hell Bent for Leather* 1960; *Requiem for a Gunfighter* 1965; *Panic in the City* 1968; *Once You Kiss a Stranger* 1969; *Black Gunn* 1972.

McNamara, Maggie. Actress. *b.* June 18, 1928, New York City. *d.* 1978. A fashion model while still in her teens, she studied drama and dance for three years before making her Broadway debut in 1951. She later replaced Barbara Bel Geddes in the stage production of 'The Moon Is Blue' and became an instant film star when she repeated that role on the screen in 1953. Despite a reserved evaluation of her performance by the critics, she was nominated for a best actress Academy Award and seemed headed for a successful career in films. She was signed by Fox, but after two other starring roles she disappeared from the screen in the mid-50s, returning only once in 1963 in a supporting part. She was also seen again on Broadway in 1962, in 'Step on a Crack,' then earned her living as a typist. Her marriage to director David SWIFT ended in divorce. Little was heard of her until February of 1978, when she was found dead of an overdose of sleeping pills, a suicide note by her side. The police report said she had a history of mental illness.

FILMS: *The Moon Is Blue* 1953; *Three Coins in the Fountain* 1954; *Prince of Players* 1955; *The Cardinal* 1963.

McNulty, Dorothy. See SINGLETON, Penny.

McNamara, William (Billy). Actor. Born in 1965, in Dallas. Clean-cut, all-American-type young lead of Hollywood films from the late 80s.

FILMS: *The Beat, Stealing Home, Terror at the Opera* 1988; *Dream a Little Dream, Stella* 1989; *Texasville* 1990; *Wildflower* 1991; *Aspen Extreme* 1993; *Chasers, Radio Inside, Surviving the Game* 1994; *Copycat, Girl in the Cadillac, Storybook* 1995.

Macnee, Patrick. Actor. Born on Feb. 6, 1922, in London. *ed.* Eton. Cherubic-faced leading man of British TV and sporadic films. Trained on a scholarship at the Webber Douglas Academy of Dramatic Art, he performed in rep and briefly in London before serving with the Royal Navy from 1942 to 1946. Returning to the stage, he made his first Broadway appearance with the Old Vic in 1954. Although he appeared in many British films from 1943, it was on TV that he became a star, winning popularity as the urbane adventurer Jonathan Steed in the series 'The Avengers' (1960–68) and 'The New Avengers' (1977–78). His first wife was actress Barbara Douglas.

FILMS INCLUDE: *The Life and Death of Colonel Blimp/Colonel Blimp* 1943; *Hamlet* 1948; *The Elusive Pimpernel/The Fighting Pimpernel* 1950; *Scrooge/A Christmas Carol, Flesh and Blood* 1951; *Three Cases of Murder* 1954; *The Battle of the River Plate/Pursuit of the Graf Spee* 1956; *Until They Sail* (US), *Les Girls* (US) 1957; *Incense for the Damned* 1970; *King Solomon's Treasure* (Can./UK) 1977; *The Sea Wolves* 1980; *The Howling* (US), *The Creature Wasn't Nice/Spaceship* (US) 1981; *Young Doctors in Love* (US) 1982; *This Is Spinal Tap* 1984; *A View to a Kill* 1985; *Shadey* 1986; *Lobster Man from Mars* (US), *Masque of the Red Death* (US) 1989; *Chill Factor* (US) 1990; *Eye of the Widow* (Fr.), *Incident at Victoria Falls, Waxwork: Lost in Time* 1991; *Thunder in Paradise* 1993.

McNichol, Kristy. Actress. Born on Sept. 11, 1962, in Los Angeles. Sweet-faced juvenile player, then wholesome ingenue of American TV and films. With the encouragement of her divorced mother, a former actress, she began appearing in commercials at age six and in TV shows at nine. At 12 she became a regular on the TV series 'Apple's Way' (1974–75) and at 15 won her first of two Emmy Awards for her performance in the series 'Family' (1976–80). In 1988 she joined the cast of 'Empty Nest.' In films from the late 70s, she seemed headed for the top in the early 80s, after a winning performance in *Little Darlings* (1980), but a string of poor vehicles later in the decade inhibited her potential for a substantial movie career. After a bout with tabloid exploitation, she announced her retirement from the industry in 1991, citing its toll on her emotional health. Her brother, Jimmy McNichol (*b.* July 2, 1961, Los Angeles), is also a TV and film actor.

FILMS: *Black Sunday* (bit) 1977; *The End, Avalanche* (bit) 1978; *Little Darlings* 1980; *The Night the Lights Went Out in Georgia, Only When I Laugh* 1981; *The Pirate Movie* (Austral.), *White Dog* 1982; *Just the Way You Are* 1984; *Dream Lover* 1986; *You Can't Hurry Love, Two Moon Junction* 1988; *The Forgotten One* 1990.

MacNicol, Peter. Actor. Born on Apr. 10, 1954, Dallas. *ed.* U. of Minnesota. Slightly built leading man of the American stage and screen. He appeared in numerous plays, from Alaska to Broadway, playing much Shakespeare and the classics, but made an uncharacteristic film debut as a valiant sorcerer's apprentice in *Dragonslayer* (1981). He was better suited for his next screen role as Stingo, the Southern writer who finds himself involved in a love triangle when he moves to Brooklyn, in *Sophie's Choice* (1982).

FILMS: *Dragonslayer* 1981; *Sophie's Choice* 1982; *Heat* 1987; *Ghostbusters II, American Blue Note* 1989; *Hard Promises, Housesitter* 1992; *Radioland Murders* 1994; *Dracula: Dead and Loving It* 1995; *Bean* 1997.

Macpherson, Jeannie. Screenwriter, actress. *b.* 1884, Boston. *d.* 1946. Originally a dancer and stage performer, she appeared in many films from 1908, often for D. W. GRIFFITH.

Later she was entrusted with her own unit at Universal, where she directed, wrote, and acted in many two-reel films. A screenwriter exclusively after 1915, she collaborated on the scripts of most of C. B. DE MILLE's silent films.

FILMS INCLUDE: As actress—*Mr. Jones at the Ball* 1908; *Mrs. Jones Entertains, A Corner in Wheat* 1909; *Winning Back His Love* 1910; *Fisher Folks, Enoch Arden* 1911; *The Outlaw Reforms, The Merchant of Venice, Rose of the Rancho, The Ghost Breaker* 1914; *The Girl of the Golden West, Carmen* 1915. As screenwriter—*The Captive* (also act.), *Chimmie Fadden Out West, The Cheat* 1915; *The Golden Chance, The Trail of the Lonesome Pine, The Heart of Nora Flynn, The Love Mask, The Dream Girl, Joan the Woman* 1916; *A Romance of the Redwoods, The Little American, The Woman God Forgot, The Devil-Stone* 1917; *The Whispering Chorus, Old Wives for New, Till I Come Back to You* 1918; *Don't Change Your Husband, For Better for Worse, Male and Female* 1919; *Something to Think About* 1920; *Forbidden Fruit, The Affairs of Anatol* 1921; *Saturday Night, Manslaughter* 1922; *Adam's Rib, The Ten Commandments* 1923; *Triumph* 1924; *The Golden Bed, The Road to Yesterday* 1925; *Red Dice, Young April* 1926; *The King of Kings* 1927; *The Godless Girl, Dynamite* 1929; *Madam Satan* 1930; *Fra Diavolo* 1933; *The Plainsman* (research story material only) 1937; *The Buccaneer* (adapt. only) 1938; *Reap the Wild Wind* (co-adapt. only) 1942; *The Buccaneer* (adapt. basis only) 1958.

McQueen, Butterfly. Actress. Born Thelma McQueen, on Jan. 8, 1911, in Tampa, Fla. The daughter of a stevedore and a domestic, she was only 13 when she joined a theater group in Harlem. She was nicknamed Butterfly after appearing in a production of 'A Midsummer Night's Dream' in which she danced in the Butterfly Ballet. It remained her professional name. She made her Broadway debut in 'Brown Sugar,' in 1937, and two years later played her first and most memorable movie role, that of Prissy, the squeaky-voiced, tearful young slave in *Gone With the Wind* (1939). She appeared in several films of the 40s, nearly always typecast as a sobbing maid. Tiring of the image, she retired from films in 1947 and thereafter worked in various menial jobs in between sporadic theatrical engagements. She returned to the screen in the early 70s in occasional small roles. In 1975, at the age of 64, she received her bachelor's degree in political science from New York's City College. On TV she was a regular on the series 'Beulah' (1950–53) and in 1980 won an Emmy Award for her performance in an ABC after-school special, 'The Seven Wishes of a Rich Kid.'

FILMS: *Gone With the Wind, The Women* 1939; *Affectionately Yours* 1941; *Cabin in the Sky, I Dood It* 1943; *Since You Went Away* 1944; *Flame of the Barbary Coast, Mildred Pierce* 1945; *Duel in the Sun* 1947; *Killer Diller* 1948; *The Phynx* (cameo) 1970; *Amazing Grace* 1974; *The Mosquito Coast* 1986.

McQueen, Steve. Actor. *b.* Terrence Steven McQueen, Mar. 24, 1930, Slater, Mo. *d.* 1980. One of the most popular and highest-paid screen personalities of the 60s and 70s, an appealing combination of a heroic antihero, gregarious loner, and exuberant introvert. Abandoned as a baby by his father, a Navy flyer, he spent part of his childhood at Boys' Republic, a reform school in Chino, Calif., then drifted about as a sailor, lumberjack, oil field worker, carnival barker, and beachcomber. He joined the Marines in 1947, did 41 days in the brig on AWOL charges, and after leaving the service in 1950 returned to itinerant jobs—docker, bartender, salesman, and TV repairman. In 1952 he joined New York's Neighborhood Playhouse and studied acting under Uta Hagen and Herbert Berghof and made his debut as a walk-on in a Second Avenue Yiddish theater, of all places. After gaining experience in stock, and a stint at the Actors Studio, he replaced Ben Gazzara in the Broadway production of 'Hatful of Rain' in 1955 and made his film debut the following year, playing a bit in *Somebody Up There Likes Me.* He got the lead in the science-fiction cult classic, *The Blob,* in 1958, and that same year landed the starring role in the TV series 'Wanted: Dead or Alive.' His popularity as a screen actor ascended gradually in the early 60s and he became an established star after *The Great Escape* (1963), in which he played a supercool POW who attempts an escape in a memorable motorbike chase scene. McQueen, who was a car- and motorcycle-racing enthusiast in real life, performed all the daring stunts himself. He was one of a rare breed of film stars who didn't have to act or do anything in particular to mesmerize a screen audience. He dominated the screen and filled the box-office coffers on the strength of his personality alone. But the flip side of that personality was revealed after the star's sudden death at 50 of a heart attack, in Juarez, Mexico, where he had gone for surgery for chest cancer. In *My Husband, My Friend* (1986), a frank and bitter memoir, McQueen's first wife (1956–71) and mother of his two children, actress Neile Adams (Toffel), depicted him as an insecure, self-destructive man prone to physical cruelty and near-homicidal rage. McQueen's second wife (1973–78) was actress Ali MACGRAW; his third, during the nine final months of his life, was model Barbara Minty. He was nominated for an Academy Award for *The Sand Pebbles* (1966).

FILMS: *Somebody Up There Likes Me* (bit) 1956; *Never Love a Stranger, The Blob* 1958; *The Great St. Louis Bank Robbery, Never So Few* 1959; *The Magnificent Seven* 1960; *The Honeymoon Machine* 1961; *Hell Is for Heroes, The War Lover* 1962; *The Great Escape, Soldier in the Rain, Love with the Proper Stranger* 1963; *Baby the Rain Must Fall, The Cincinnati Kid* 1965; *Nevada Smith, The Sand Pebbles* 1966; *The Thomas Crown Affair, Bullitt* 1968; *The Reivers* 1969; *On Any Sunday* (motorbike-racing doc.), *Le Mans* 1971; *Junior Bonner, The Getaway* 1972; *Papillon* 1973; *The Towering Inferno* 1974; *An Enemy of the People* (as Dr. Stockmann; also exec. prod.) 1977; *Tom Horn, The Hunter* 1980.

McRae, Ellen. See BURSTYN, Ellen.

MacRae, Gordon. Actor, singer. *b.* Mar. 12, 1921, East Orange, N.J. *d.* 1986. Appealing singing star of Hollywood musicals of the 50s. The son of a toolmaker from Scotland who sang on local radio and of a concert pianist, he attended schools in Buffalo and Syracuse, where he played the piano and clarinet and sang in many shows while participating in lacrosse and football. After graduating from the Deerfield Academy, he went to New York City, where he promptly won an amateur singing contest at the 1939–40 World's Fair, paving the way for a two-year stint as a band vocalist. Following WW II service as a navigator with the Air Force, he resumed singing on radio and in 1946 appeared in the Broadway revue 'Three to Make Ready,' a performance that led to his first movie contract. His clean-cut good looks and manly charm soon brought him starring roles, mostly at Warner Bros., both as a singer and as a man of action. He is best remembered in the screen versions of the musicals *Oklahoma!* (1955) and *Carousel* (1956). With the decline of the musical genre, he turned to TV and in 1956 enjoyed brief success as the star of his own show. He later appeared in national tours and in summer stock and performed in nightclubs with his first wife (1941–67), Sheila MacRae (*b.* Sheila Stephens, Sept. 24, 1924, London), who played Alice Kramden on 'The Jackie Gleason Show'. They divorced in 1967. Their daughters, Meredith MacRae (*b.* 1944, Houston) and Heather MacRae, are also TV and movie actresses. Acknowledging late in life that he had been an alcoholic, MacRae made many public appearances for the National Council of Alcoholism, of which he became the honorary chairman in 1983. He died at 64 of cancer of the mouth and jaw, complicated by pneumonia.

FILMS: *The Big Punch* 1948; *Look for the Silver Lining* 1949; *Backfire, The Daughter of Rosie O'Grady, Return of the Frontiersman, Tea for Two, The West Point Story* 1950; *On Moonlight Bay, Starlift* 1951; *About Face* 1952; *By the Light of the Silvery Moon, The Desert Song, Three Sailors and a Girl* 1953; *Oklahoma!* 1955; *Carousel, The Best Things in Life Are Free* 1956; *The Pilot* 1979.

Macready, George. Actor. *b.* Aug. 29, 1899, Providence, R.I. *d.* 1973. *ed.* Brown U. Villain *par excellence* of numerous Hollywood films from the early 40s, following a successful career on the stage. He intended to become a journalist but was talked into an acting career by stage and screen director Richard Boleslawski. He made his Broadway debut in 1926, portraying the Reverend Arthur Dimmesdale in 'The Scarlet Letter' and later appeared in many other stage productions, several times opposite Katharine Cornell. On the screen, he played mostly vicious evildoers; a deep scar on his right cheek, incurred in a car accident, helping to authenticate the aloof, malicious aristocrats he often portrayed. Memorable as Rita Hayworth's ruthless husband in *Gilda* (1946). Offscreen he was known as one of Hollywood's most cultivated citizens. At one time he owned a Los Angeles art gallery in partnership with another notorious film villain, Vincent Price.

FILMS INCLUDE: *The Commandos Strike at Dawn* 1943; *The Story of Dr. Wassell, The Soul of a Monster, The Seventh Cross, The Conspirators* 1944; *A Song to Remember* (as poet-playwright Alfred de Musset), *The Monster and the Ape* (serial), *Counter-Attack, The Fighting Guardsman, My Name Is Julia Ross* 1945; *Gilda, The Bandit of Sherwood Forest, The Return of Monte Cristo* 1946; *Down to Earth, The Swordsman* 1947; *The Big Clock, Coroner Creek, Beyond Glory, The Black Arrow, Gallant Blade* 1948; *Knock on Any Door, Alias Nick Beal, Johnny Allegro, The Doolins of Oklahoma* 1949; *The Nevadan, Fortunes of Captain Blood, Rogues of Sherwood Forest, A Lady Without Passport, The Desert Hawk* 1950; *The Desert Fox, Detective Story* 1951; *Le Gantelet Vert/The Green Glove* (Fr./US) 1952; *Treasure of the Golden Condor, Julius Caesar* (as Marullus), *The Stranger Wore a Gun* 1953; *Vera Cruz* 1954; *A Kiss Before Dying* 1956; *The Abductors, Paths of Glory* 1957; *The Alligator People* 1959; *Two Weeks in Another Town, Taras Bulba* 1962; *Dead Ringer, Seven Days in May, Where Love Has Gone* 1964; *The Human Duplicators, The Great Race* 1965; *Tora! Tora! Tora!* (as Cordell Hull) 1970; *The Return of Count Yorga* 1971.

MacVicar, Martha. See VICKERS, Martha.

McShane, Ian. Actor. Born on Sept. 29, 1942, in Blackburn, England. Dark, brooding leading man and supporting player of British and American films and television. Trained at RADA, he made his stage, screen, and TV debuts all in 1962. His first wife (1965–68) was actress Suzan Farmer.

FILMS INCLUDE: *The Wild and the Willing* 1962; *The Pleasure Girls* 1965; *Sky West and Crooked/Gypsy Girl* 1966; *If It's Tuesday This Must Be Belgium* (US), *The Battle of Britain* 1969; *Freelance, Pussycat Pussycat I Love You* (US) 1970; *Villain, Tam-Lin/The Devil's Widow* 1971; *Sitting Target* 1972; *The Last of Sheila* (US) 1973; *Ransom/The Terrorists, Journey Into Fear* (Can.) 1975; *Behind the Iron Mask/The Fifth Musketeer* (Austral.) 1977; *Yesterday's Hero* 1979; *Cheaper to Keep Her* (US) 1980; *Exposed* (US) 1983; *Torchlight* (US) 1984; *Ordeal by Innocence, Too Scared to Scream* (US; release delayed from 1982) 1985.

McTiernan, John. Director. Born on Jan. 8, 1951, in Albany, N.Y. *ed.* Juilliard; SUNY; AFI. With a background in TV commercials, he brought to features solid technical skills that make his films—typically action-filled adventures—tightly constructed, well paced, and enjoyable to watch. After a weak debut with *Nomads* (1986), he clicked strongly at the box office with *Predator* (1987) and *Die Hard* (1988). He solidified his rapidly growing reputation with *The Hunt for Red October* (1990) before stumbling with *Medicine Man* (1992).

FILMS: *Nomads* (also sc.) 1986; *Predator* 1987; *Die Hard* 1988; *The Hunt for Red October* 1990; *Flight of the Intruder* (exec. prod. only) 1991; *Medicine Man* 1992; *Last Action Hero* 1993; *Die Hard with a Vengeance* 1995.

Maccari, Ruggero. Screenwriter. Born in 1919, in Rome. A former contributor to humor magazines, he entered films in 1950, and soon began collaborating with Ettore SCOLA, together forming a formidable team of comedy screenwriting. Their collaboration continued after Scola turned to directing in the mid-60s. The prolific Maccari also wrote comic and dramatic scripts for other directors, notably Dino RISI.

FILMS INCLUDE: *Vita de Cani* 1950; *Guardie e Ladri/Cops and Robbers* 1951; *Due Notti con Cleopatra/Two Nights with Cleopatra* 1954; *Donatella, Lo Scapolo* 1956; *Mariti in Città* 1957; *Il Marito* 1958; *Il Mattatore/Love and Larceny* 1959; *Adua e le Compagne/Love á la Carte* 1960; *Fantasmi a Roma/Ghosts of Rome* 1961; *Anni ruggenti, La Marcia su Roma/The March on Rome, Il Sorpasso/The Easy Life* 1962; *La Parmigiana, I Mostri/Opiate '67/15 from Rome, La Visita* 1963; *Il Magnico Cornuto/The Magnificent Cuckold* 1963; *Il Gaucho, Se permettete parliamo di Donne/Let's Talk About Women* 1964; *La Congiuntura, Made in Italy* 1965; *L'Archidiavolo/The Devil in Love* 1966; *Le Dolci Signore/Anyone Can Play, Il Padre di Famiglia/Head of the Family, Il Profeta* 1967; *Vedo Nudo* 1969; *La Moglie del Prete/The Priest's Wife* 1970; *Permette? Rocco Papaleo* 1971; *Bianco Rosso e. . .* 1972; *Morrdi e Fuggi, Sono stato lo, Sesso Matto/How Funny Can Sex Be?* 1973; *Profumo di Donna/Scent of a Woman* 1974; *Telefoni bianchi, Brutti sporchi e Cattivi/Down and Dirty* 1976; *I Nuovi Mostri/Viva Italia, Una Giornata particolare/A Special Day* 1977; *Primo Amore/First Love* 1978; *L'Ingorgo—una Storia impossibile/Traffic Jam* 1979; *Passione d'Amore, Nudo di Donna* 1981; *Le Bal* 1983; *Maccheroni/Maccaroni* 1985; *La Famiglia/The Family* 1987.

Macchio, Ralph. Actor. Born on Nov. 4, 1961, in Huntington, Long Island, N.Y. Juvenile lead of TV and Hollywood films of the 80s. Having had his start in commercials, he established himself in the TV series 'Eight Is Enough' (1980–81) and soared to popularity as the star of *The Karate Kid* (1984) and its sequels. He made his Broadway debut in 1986.

FILMS: *Up the Academy* 1980; *The Outsiders* 1983; *The Karate Kid, Teachers* 1984; *Crossroads, The Karate Kid: Part II* 1986; *Distant Thunder* 1988; *The Karate Kid: Part III* 1989; *Too Much Sun* 1990; *My Cousin Vinny* 1992; *Naked in New York* 1994.

Mace, Fred. American actor. *b.* 1872. *d.* 1917. One of the most popular of the early silent screen clowns, this dentist-turned-stage-actor joined Mack SENNETT at Biograph in 1911. He was the hero of many zany one-reel comedies, often portraying a punchy boxer called "One-Round O'Brien," or a fumbling detective. The following year he went with Sennett to Keystone, where his popularity reached its peak. But his career suffered a setback in 1913 when he decided to go it alone, producing and directing as well as starring in his own comedy series. He returned to Keystone in 1915 but never regained his early success.

FILMS INCLUDE: *The Village Hero, A Victim of*

Circumstances, Their First Divorce Case, Abe Gets Even with Father, Caught with the Goods 1911; *Brave and Bold, A Spanish Dilemma, The Brave Hunter, The Leading Man, The Fickle Spaniard, One-Round O'Brien, The Water Nymph, Cohen Collects a Debt, The Ambitious Butler, Mabel's Lovers, A Midnight Elopement, The Drummer's Vacation, Mabel's Adventures, A Family Mixup* 1912; *A Double Wedding, Mabel's Heroes, The Elite Ball, Heinze's Resurrection, A Red Hot Romance, A Doctored Affair, The Sleuth's Last Stand, At Twelve O'Clock, Her New Beau, His Darktown Belle, The Gangster, The Tale of a Black Eye, Algy on the Force, The Foreman of the Jury, The Firebugs* 1913; *Mabel at the Wheel, Without Hope* (feature), *Apollo Fred Becomes a Home Seeker* (also prod.) 1914; *My Valet* (feature), *What Happened to Jones* (feature), *A Janitor's Wife's Temptation, Crooked to the End* 1915; *Love Will Conquer, A Village Vampire, An Oily Scoundrel, Bath Tub Perils, The Fire Chief, Love Comet, His Last Scent* 1916.

Machaty, Gustav. Director. *b.* May 9, 1901, Prague. *d.* 1963. He began his association with the Czech cinema in his early teens as a pianist at motion picture theaters, entered films as an actor at 17, and began directing at 18. After a four-year apprenticeship in Hollywood in the early 20s as an assistant to Griffith and Von Stroheim, he returned to Prague, where he turned out several mature films. The erotic nature of these, notably *Erotikon/Seduction* (1929) and *Extase/Ecstasy* (1933), made him world famous. The latter film introduced the nude beauty of a young unknown actress, Hedy Kiesler, who later became Hollywood's glamorous star Hedy Lamarr. Machaty later directed a number of films in Austria, Italy, the US, and Germany but failed to achieve another commercial success. In Hollywood he did some uncredited work on such films as *The Good Earth, Born Reckless,* and *Madame X* (all 1937).

FILMS: *Teddy Wants to Smoke* (also prod., co-sc., act.) 1919; *The Kreutzer Sonata* (also sc.) 1926; *Schweik as a Civilian* 1927; *Erotikon/Seduction* (also co-prod.) 1929; *From Saturday to Sunday* 1931; *Extase/Ecstasy* (also co-sc.) 1933; *Nocturno* (Aus.) 1934; *Ballerine* (It.) 1936; *The Wrong Way Out* (short; US) 1938; *Within the Law* (US) 1939; *Jealousy* (also co-assoc. prod., co-sc.; US) 1945; *Suchkind 312* (also sc.; Ger.) 1955.

Machin, Alfred. Director, film pioneer. *b.* 1877, Blendecques, France. *d.* 1929. A former still photographer for a French magazine, he was sent to Africa by Pathé in 1907 to shoot newsreel footage of big game hunting. For several years his adventure films, featuring animal "stars," saturated the French screen. From 1910 he utilized aerial cinematography, one of the first to do so. As a representative of Pathé, Machin was among the pioneers of Dutch (from 1911) and Belgian (from 1912) cinema, directing some of the earliest productions of both countries. Back in France, he made WW I's first pacifist film, *Maudite soit la Guerre* (in color) in June of 1914, several months before the war actually broke out. During the war, he co-founded the cinematographic service of the French army. In 1917 he shot the French trenches scenes for D. W. Griffith's *Hearts of the World.* He continued making films until his sudden death in 1929. He wrote the scripts for most of his own films and operated the camera on many.

FILMS INCLUDE: *Chasse à l'Hippopotame sur le Nil Bleu* 1908; *Chasse à la Panthère* 1909; *"Voyage en Afrique"* (series of shorts under various titles) 1910; *Le Cinéma en Afrique, "Babylas"* (humorous series), *La Nuit de Noël* 1911; *Little Moritz Soldat d'Afrique, La Fleur sanglante, L'Or qui brûle, L'Ame des Moulins, The Escape of Hugo Van Groot* (Dutch and English versions), *The Interloper* (Dutch and English versions) 1912; *Un Episode de Waterloo, Le Baiser de l'Empereur, La Ronde infernale, Supreme Sacrifice, Le Diamant noir* 1913; *Napoléon: Du Sacre à Sainte-Hèlène, La Fille de Delft, Maudite soit la Guerre* 1914; *Hearts of the World* (co-phot. French sequences only; US) 1917; *Une Nuit agitée* (co-dir. with Henry Wuhlschleger), *Moi aussi j'accuse* (co-dir.), *Serpentin à engagé Bouboule* 1920; *Pervenche* (co-dir., co-sc.) 1921; *Bûtes... comme les Hommes* (co-dir., co-sc.) 1923; *L'Enigme du Mont Agel, Les Heritiers de l'Oncle James* (both co-dir., co-sc.) 1924; *La Coeur des Gueux* (co-dir., co-sc.) 1925; *La Manoir de la Peur* (co-dir., co-sc.) 1927; *Le Retour* (sc. only) 1928; *De la Jungle a l'Ecran* 1929; *Robinson Junior/Black and White* (released posthumously) 1931.

Mack, Helen. Actress. *b.* Helen McDougall, Nov. 13, 1913, Rock Island, Ill. *d.* 1986. A product of New York's Professional Children's School, she appeared as a child in a number of Broadway plays and East Coast location films. She returned to the screen as an adult in 1931, after a seven-year absence, and played leads and second leads in many Hollywood productions through the mid-40s, typically in weepy, melodramatic roles. Memorable as the female lead in *Son of Kong* (1933) and as the streetwalker Mollie Malloy in Howard Hawks's adaptation of 'The Front Page,' *His Girl Friday* (1941). After retiring from films, she briefly produced a radio show and in the mid-60s co-authored a play, 'The Mating Dance,' under her married name, Helen McAvity.

FILMS INCLUDE: *The Little Red School House* (bit), *Zaza* (bit) 1923; *Grit* (bit), *Pied Piper Malone* (bit) 1924; *The Struggle* 1931; *The Silent Witness, While Paris Sleeps* 1932; *Sweepings, Melody Cruise, Blind Adventure, Christopher Bean, Son of Kong* 1933; *All of Me, Kiss and Make-Up, You Belong to Me, The Lemon Drop Kid, College Rhythm* 1934; *Four Hours to Kill, She, The Return of Peter Grimm* 1935; *The Milky Way* 1936; *The Last Train from Madrid, Fit for a King* 1937; *King of the Newsboys, I Stand Accused, Secrets of a Nurse* 1938; *Gambling Ship, Calling All Marines* 1939; *His Girl Friday, Girls of the Road* 1940; *Power Dive* 1941; *And Now Tomorrow* 1944; *Divorce, Strange Holiday* 1945.

macrocinematography. The filming of small objects by close-up photography but not requiring a microscope. It is usually accomplished with the aid of a macrolens, a lens equipped with a close-up focusing extension.

Macy, William H. Actor. Born March 13, 1950, in Miami, Fla. Stalwart, skilled character and leading man of stage and screen. With a film career that spans more than two decades, this journeyman actor has established himself as a versatile, dependable presence on the screen, specifically for his work in playwright-screenwriter David MAMET's films *Homicide* (1991) and *Oleanna* (1994). His career reached a new peak in 1996, earning an Academy Award nomination for his supporting role in the acclaimed dark comedy *Fargo*.

FILMS: *All Together Now* 1975; *The Late Show* 1977; *Diary of a Young Comic, The Jerk* 1979; *Foolin' Around, Serial, Somewhere in Time* 1980; *My Favorite Year* 1982; *Without a Trace* 1983; *Bad Medicine, Movers and Shakers* 1985; *House of Games, Radio Days* 1987; *Things Change* 1989; *Sibling Rivalry* 1990; *The Doctor, Homicide* 1991; *Me Myself and I, A Private Matter, Shadows and Fog, The Water Engine* 1992; *Benny & Joon, Heart of Justice, Searching for Bobby Fischer, Twenty Bucks* 1993; *Being Human, The Client, Oleanna* 1994; *Mr. Holland's Opus, Murder in the First* 1995; *Down Periscope, Fargo, Ghosts of Mississippi* 1996; *Air Force One, The Last Time I Committed Suicide, Boogie Nights* 1997.

Maddow, Ben. American screenwriter, director. *b.* 1909. *d.* 1992. A graduate of Columbia, he became associated with the American documentary movement in the mid-30s and, in 1936, together with Sidney Meyers, Willard Van Dyke, Irving Lerner, Ralph Steiner, Paul Strand, and Leo Hurwitz, launched "The World Today," a short-lived newsreel that was supposed to become the progressive Left's answer to the conservative "The March of Time." Under the pseudonym of David Wolff, Maddow later collaborated on the script of the documentary *Native Land* (1942). He began writing screenplays for Hollywood features in the late 40s, alone or in collaboration, at times without receiving screen credit. His infrequent contributions as director were outside the mainstream of the commercial cinema, the most notable being his collaboration on the semi-documentary *The Savage Eye* (1960).

FILMS (as screenwriter): *Native Land* (co-sc. under pseudonym of David Wolff) 1942; *Framed* 1947; *Kiss the Blood Off My Hands* (co-adapt.), *The Man from Colorado* (co-sc.) 1948; *Intruder in the Dust* 1949; *The Asphalt Jungle* (co-sc.) 1950; *Shadow in the Sky* 1952; *The Stairs* (also dir.) 1953; *Johnny Guitar* (co-sc., uncredited), *The Naked Jungle* (co-sc., uncredited) 1954; *Men in War* (co-sc., uncredited) 1957; *God's Little Acre* (co-sc., uncredited) 1958; *The Savage Eye* (also co-dir., co-prod. with Joseph Strick and Sidney Meyers), *The Unforgiven* 1960; *Two Loves* 1961; *The Balcony* (also co-prod.), *An Affair of the Skin* (also dir., co-prod.) 1963; *The Way West* (co-sc.) 1967; *The Chairman, The Secret of Santa Vittoria* (co-sc.) 1969; *Storm of Strangers* (also dir.) 1970; *The Mephisto Waltz* 1971.

Madigan, Amy. Actress. Born in 1957, in Chicago. Blonde leading lady and supporting player of American films and TV movies. *ed.* Marquette U. (philosophy). Trained as a pianist at the Chicago Conservatory, she became a rock musician and for ten years toured the country, performing with a band in bars and nightclubs. Following stage training at the Lee Strasberg Institute in Los Angeles, she turned to acting, making her screen debut in the early 80s. She was nominated for an Academy Award as best supporting actress for *Twice in a Lifetime* (1985). In 1983 she married one of her co-stars, Ed HARRIS.

FILMS: *Love Child* 1982; *Love Letters* 1983; *Streets of Fire, Places in the Heart* 1984; *Alamo Bay* (also song), *Twice in a Lifetime* 1985; *Crossroads* (song only) 1986; *Nowhere to Hide* (Can.) 1987; *The Prince of Pennsylvania* 1988; *Field of Dreams, Uncle Buck* 1989; *Female Perversions* 1996.

Madison, Guy. Actor. Born Robert Moseley, on Jan. 19, 1922, in Bakersfield, Calif. A telephone lineman before enlisting in the Navy in 1942, he made his film debut while still in uniform and quickly became a favorite of the bobby-soxer crowd, thanks to his rugged yet boyish all-American good looks. He seemed assured of stardom, but limited acting ability restricted him in the 50s mainly to two-fisted hero roles in action pictures. During that period (1951–58) he also starred in the TV series 'Wild Bill Hickok.' He spent the 60s in Europe, starring in Italian costume adventures and spaghetti Westerns, and low-grade continental action co-productions. His first wife (1949–54) was Gail RUSSELL.

FILMS INCLUDE: In the US—*Since You Went Away* 1944; *Till the End of Time* 1946; *Honeymoon* 1947; *Texas Brooklyn and Heaven* 1948; *Massacre River* 1949; *The Charge at Feather River* 1953; *The Command* 1954; *Five Against the House, The Last Frontier* 1955; *The Beast of Hollow Mountain, On the Threshold of Space, Hilda Crane* 1956; *Bullwhip* 1958; *Jet Over the Atlantic* 1960. In Europe—*La Schiava di Roma* (It.) 1960; *Rosmunda e Alboino/Sword of the Conqueror* (It.) 1961; *Le Prigioniere dell'Isola del Diavolo* (It./Fr.) 1962; *Il Boia di Venezia* (It.) 1963; *Old Shatterhand/Shatterhand* (Ger./It./Fr./Yug.), *Sandokan alla Riscossa* (It.) 1964; *I Misteri della Giungla Nera/The Mystery of Thug Island* (It./Ger.), *Sfida a Rio Bravo/Gunmen of the Rio Grande* (as Wyatt Earp; It./Sp./Fr.) 1965; *7 Winchester per un Massacro/Payment in Blood* (It.) 1967; *This Man Can't Die* (It.) 1970; *Won Ton Ton: The Dog Who Saved Hollywood* 1976; *Where's Willie* 1978.

Madison, Noel. Actor. *b.* Nathaniel Moscovitch, 1898, New York City. *d.* 1975. *ed.* U. of Lausanne (Switzerland); Loudoun House (London). The son of Russian-born actor Maurice Moscovich (1871–1940) and himself a veteran stage performer and director, he played character roles in American and British films of the 30s and early 40s, often as a heavy in crime melodramas.

FILMS INCLUDE: *Sinner's Holiday* 1930; *Little Caesar, The Star Witness* 1931; *The Hatchet Man, Symphony of Six Million, The Last Mile, Me and My Gal* 1932; *Humanity* 1933; *The House of Rothschild* (as Carl Rothschild), *Journal of a Crime, Manhattan Melodrama* 1934; *G-Men, The Morals of Marcus* (UK) 1935; *Champagne Charlie, Missing Girls, Our Relations* 1936; *House of Secrets, Gangway* (UK) 1937; *Sailing Along* (UK), *Crackerjack/Man with 100 Faces* (UK), *Kate Plus Ten/Queen of Crime* (lead; UK), *Climbing High* (UK) 1938; *Charlie Chan in City of Darkness* 1939; *The Great Plane Robbery* 1940; *Footsteps in the Dark* 1941; *Secret Agent of Japan, Bombs Over Burma* (lead) 1942; *The Black Raven, Jitterbugs* 1943; *The Gentleman from Nowhere* 1948.

Madonna. Singer, actress, executive. Born Madonna Louise Veronica Ciccone, on Aug. 16, 1958, in Bay City, Mich. Bold, controversial, self-promoting recording and music-video superstar who has encountered only moderate success in films. Six years old when her mother died of breast cancer, she was raised by a strict father and stepmother and various relatives. As a teenager she took piano and ballet lessons and maintained straight A's in all subjects. After a year at the University of Michigan, she gave up a dance scholarship and headed for New York. She lived hand-to-mouth and trained briefly with the Alvin Ailey dance company while also playing drums and eventually singing with a number of bands. During that lean period, she appeared for no pay in *A Certain Sacrifice* (1979), an "experimental" film of questionable merit over which she would later unsuccessfully sue to have her name removed from the credits. She became involved in the Downtown disco scene, at first as an attention-seeking guest and later as a singer. Her perseverance finally led to a recording contract in 1983 and her first hit album, 'Madonna,' the following year.

She continued her climb to the top of the charts in 1984 with the album 'Like a Virgin,' proving herself a superior manipulator of the emerging medium of music videos. She also became known as one of the most energetic live performers, staging elaborate, provocative extravaganzas around the globe. Growing more flamboyant with every step in her meteoric rise, "The Material Girl" seemed to thrive on controversy, with an exhibitionistic frankness that won her a devoted mass following but was termed sleazy and vulgar by many others. Her fame paved the way to an undistinguished but sold-out Broadway stage debut in David Mamet's Tony-winning 'Speed-the-Plow' in 1988.

Madonna's early screen career was far less spectacular. Following a small though pivotal title role in *Desperately Seeking Susan* (1985) she appeared in several major flops before riding the crest of Warren BEATTY's box-office hit *Dick Tracy* (1990), in which she acted for SAG scale wages. In the film, she sang the Stephen SONDHEIM 1990 Academy Award–winning song, 'Sooner or Later,' one of several songs that she originated in films. She followed *Dick Tracy* with an impressive comedic bit in *A League of Their Own*, but plummeted in *Body of Evidence* (1993), a film featuring sadomasochistic sex scenes that provoked critical guffaws.

Madonna gained further notoriety with her 1992 book *Sex*, an impressionistic collection of erotic photographs and text. In 1991, she founded a production company, Maverick Entertainment, which co-distributed with Miramax one of the most acclaimed films of 1993, *Farewell My Concubine*. A top fundraiser in the fight against AIDS, she was one of the first major stars to embrace the cause, after losing her roommate and best friend to the disease in 1986. In 1985 Madonna married actor Sean PENN. Their stormy relationship ended in 1989. In 1996 she gave birth to her first child, a daughter named Lourdes.

FILMS: *A Certain Sacrifice* 1979; *Vision Quest* (singer in club; co-songs), *Desperately Seeking Susan* (also songs) 1985; *Shanghai Surprise* 1986; *Who's That Girl?* (also co-songs) 1987; *Bloodhounds of Broadway* 1989; *Dick Tracy* 1990; *Truth or Dare/In Bed with Madonna* (doc.; also exec. prod.) 1991; *Shadows and Fog, A League of Their Own* 1992; *Body of Evidence, Dangerous Game* 1993; *Blue in the Face, Four Rooms* 1995; *Evita, Girl 6* 1996.

Madsen, Michael. Actor. Born 1959, in Chicago, Ill. Compelling, intense actor of stage and screen. He got his start at Chicago's famed Steppenwolf Theatre, honing his skills first on the stage and eventually small television roles. After moving to Los Angeles, he began appearing in feature films offering rich, contrasting characterizations, most notably in Quentin TARANTINO's first big success, the indie *Reservoir Dogs* (1992). His sister is actress Virginia MADSEN.

FILMS: *WarGames* 1983; *The Natural, Racing with the Moon* 1984; *The Killing Time* 1987; *Blood Red* 1988; *Kill Me Again* 1989; *The Doors, The End of Innocence, Thelma & Louise* 1991; *Beyond the Law, Reservoir Dogs* 1992; *Dead Connection, Fatal Instinct, Free Willy, Money for Nothing, Trouble Bound* 1993; *The Getaway, Wyatt Earp* 1994; *Free Willy 2: The Adventure Home, Species* 1995; *Mulholland Falls, Winner* 1996; *Donnie Brasco, The Winner* 1997.

Madsen, Virginia. Actress. Born in 1963, in Winnetka, Ill. Glamorous blonde leading lady of Hollywood films of the 80s and early 90s. Raised by an Emmy-winning filmmaker mother, she trained at the drama department of Northwestern University and made her acting debut on public television. On screen from 1983, typically in seductive roles. In 1989 she married Danny Huston, her director in *Mr. North* (1988). Her brother, Michael MADSEN, is also an actor.

FILMS: *Class* 1983; *Electric Dreams, Dune* 1984; *Creator* 1985; *Fire with Fire, Modern Girls* 1986; *Slamdance, Zombie High* 1987; *Mr. North, Hot to Trot* 1988; *Heart of Dixie* 1989; *The Hot Spot* 1990; *Highlander II: The Quickening* 1991; *Becoming Colette, Candyman* 1992; *Money for Nothing* 1993; *Bitter Vengeance* 1994.

Madsen and Schenstrom. Danish actors who preceded Laurel and Hardy as a universally popular skinny/fatty comedy team. Harald Madsen (*b.* Nov. 20, 1890, Silkeborg, Denmark; *d.* 1949), short and fat, became a circus clown at 14. Carl Schenstrom (*b.* Nov. 13, 1881, Copenhagen; *d.* 1942), tall and lean, emigrated as a youth with his family to the US, but returned to Denmark after his father was hit by a Chicago streetcar, and entered films in 1909. They had each appeared separately in sporadic films until 1921, when they were teamed by director Lau Lauritzen (*b.* Mar. 13, 1878, Silkeborg; *d.* 1938) as a comedy duo. Before long they achieved enormous popularity throughout Europe and much of the rest of the world. In Denmark they were known as Fyrtaarnet (literally the Light Tower) and Bigoven (the Trailer), or Fy & Bi for short; in the German-speaking countries as Pat and Patachon; in France as Double-Patte et Patachon; in the UK as Long & Short; and in the US as Ole & Axel. In all they made more than 40 films together before Schenstrom's death in 1942. Their popularity was at its highest in the late 20s, before the advent of sound.

FILMS INCLUDE: *Tyvepak, Film Flirt og Forlovelse* 1921; *Han Hun og Hamlet* 1922; *Darskab Dyd og Driverter* 1923; *Professor Petersens Plejebörn* 1924; *Takt Tone og Tosser, Awei Vagabunden in Prater* (Ger.), *Spritsmuglerne* (Swed.) 1925; *Don Quijote, Likkehjuet* 1926; *Vestervovyov* 1927; *Cocktails* (UK), *Filmens Helte* 1928; *Kys Klap og Kommers, Hallo Afrika Forude Alf's Carpet* (UK) 1929; *Taausend Worte Deutsch* (Ger.) 1930; *Fy og Bi i Kantonnement* 1931; *Han Hun og Hamlet, Lumpenkayliere* (Ger.) 1932; *Med fuld Musik* 1933; *Knox und die lustigen Vagabunden* (Ger.) 1935; *Mädchenräuber* 1936; *Eine Insel wird endeckt/Pat und Patachon im Pardies* (Ger.) 1937; *I de gode gamle Dage* 1940.

Maetzig, Kurt. Director. Born on Jan. 25, 1911, in Berlin. *ed.* U. of Paris. One of the most important figures in postwar East German cinema, he had entered films as an assistant director in 1933. During WW II he engaged in anti-Nazi activity and his first feature film, *Ehe im Schatten/Marriage in the Shadows* (1947), bitterly denounced Hitler's anti-Semitism. He won his country's state award in 1949, 1950, 1954, and 1959.

FILMS INCLUDE: *Ehe im Schatten/Marriage in the Shadows* (also sc.) 1947; *Die Buntkarierten* 1949; *Familie Benthin* (co-dir.) 1950; *Roman einer Ehe* (also co-sc.) 1951; *Ernst Thalmann* (in two parts) 1953–55; *Schlosser und Katen* 1957; *Das Lied der Matrosen* (co-dir.) 1958; *Der Schweigende Stern/First Spaceship on Venus* (also co-sc.; E. Ger./Pol.) 1960; *Septemberliebe* 1961; *Preludio 11* 1964; *Das Madchen auf dem Brett* 1967.

magazine. A camera-mounted film container consisting of two lightproof compartments with a loading capacity of 100 to 1,200 feet. Unexposed film unwinds from a feed roll in one compartment, passes through the camera, where it is exposed, then travels to the take-up compartment, where it rewinds around a core.

Magee, Patrick. Actor. *b.* 1924, Armagh, N. Ireland. *d.* 1982. Intense character player of the British and American stage and screen. 'Krapp's Last Tape' and several other Samuel Beckett plays were written with him in mind. His stage career was highlighted by a forceful performance as the Marquis de Sade in both the London and New York productions of 'Marat/Sade,' a role for which he won Broadway's Tony Award and one he later repeated on the screen. He supported his love for the stage with frequent film appearances, often in horror pictures, typically in sinister roles.

FILMS INCLUDE: *The Criminal* 1960; *Rag Doll* 1961; *A Prize of Arms* 1962; *The Servant, Dementia 13* (US), *The Young Racers* (US) 1963; *The Masque of the Red Death* (US), *Zulu, Seance on a Wet Afternoon* 1964; *The Skull, Die Monster Die!/Monster of Terror* (US/UK) 1965; *The Persecution and Assassination of Jean-Paul Marat. . . /Marat-Sade* (as the Marquis de Sade) 1967; *The Birthday Party* 1968; *Hard Contract* (US) 1969; *Cromwell, You Can't Win 'Em All* 1970; *King Lear* (as the Duke of Cornwall) 1971; *The Fiend, A Clockwork Orange* 1971; *The Trojan Women* (Gr./US), *Young Winston, Asylum* 1972; *And Now the Screaming Starts, The Final Programme/The Last Days of Man on Earth* 1973; *Luther, Demons of the Mind* 1974; *Galileo, Barry Lyndon* 1975; *Telefon* (US) 1977; *Rough Cut* (US/UK), *The Monster Club, Sir Henry at Rawlinson End* 1980; *Chariots of Fire, Il gatto nero/Il gatto di Park Lane* (It.) 1981; *Samuel Beckett: Silence to Silence* (doc.; Ireland) 1982.

Maggi, Luigi. Director, actor. *b.* Dec. 21, 1867. *d.* 1946. A pioneer of early Italian cinema, a former printer and stage actor-director, he made his acting film debut in 1906 and began directing as well in many of his films in 1908. Film historians consider him the first Italian to employ realistic settings in the search for authenticity and artistic veracity in screen adaptations of costume dramas and historical epics.

FILMS INCLUDE (as director): *Gli Ultimi Giorni di Pompei/The Last Days of Pompeii* 1908; *Luigi XI Re di Francia* (also sc., act.), *Spergiura* 1909; *Il Garantiere Rolland* 1910; *Nozze d'Oro* (also act.), *La Gioconda, La Nave* 1911; *Satana* 1912; *Notturno di Chopin, Il Barbiere di Siviglia/The Barber of Seville* (also sc.), *Il Matrimonio di Figaro/The Marriage of Figaro* (also sc.) 1913; *Per un'Ora d'Amore, Il Fornaretto di Venezia* 1914; *Il Mistero dei Bauli neri* (also act.) 1918; *La Danza delle Ore* (also act.), *I Conquistatori* (also act.) 1920; *Teodora* 1927.

Magirama. A triple screen projection process developed in France in 1955 by Abel GANCE and André Debrie. It was demonstrated in Paris in 1956 in a program of shorts.

Magnani, Anna. Actress. *b.* Mar. 7, 1908, Rome. *d.* 1973. Earthy, sensual, passionately forceful star of Italian and international films. The illegitimate child of an Italian mother and an Egyptian father, she was brought up in poverty by her maternal grandmother in a slum district of Rome. After some education at a convent school, she enrolled at Rome's Academy of Dramatic Art and while still there earned her living as a singer of bawdy ballads in seedy nightclubs. She moved on from there to variety shows and in 1926 began performing in dramatic plays in stock. The following year, after returning from an Argentinian tour, she made her screen debut, playing a bit in a silent version of *Scampolo.* She did not return to the screen until 1934, meanwhile acquiring added experience and reputation as a stage actress and singer. In 1936 she married director Goffredo ALESSANDRINI, who considered her unsuitable as a screen actress but nonetheless gave her a supporting role in his film *Cavalleria* (1936). Their marriage was unsuccessful and after a long separation it was annulled in 1950. Magnani's film career remained minor until 1941, when she played the second feminine lead in Vittorio De Sica's *Teresa Venerdì.* In 1942 she gave birth to a son out of wedlock by actor Massimo SERATO. The child would later become a victim of polio and the center of Magnani's devoted attention and care.

After the liberation of Rome, Magnani enjoyed popularity among American servicemen, for whom she sang her bawdy songs in racy revues. Also in 1945, her enormous dramatic talent finally burst forth in *Roma Città aperta/Open City,* Roberto ROSSELLINI's monumental neorealistic salute to displays of human courage in the final days of the Occupation. The film gained her sudden recognition in the US, where in 1946 she was named by the National Board of Review as the best foreign actress of the year. In Italy (and gradually elsewhere) she soon became established as a star, although she lacked the conventional beauty and glamour usually associated with the term. Slightly plump and rather short in stature with a face framed by unkempt raven hair and eyes encircled by deep, dark shadows, she attracted through her seething earthiness and volcanic temperament. Director William Dieterle spoke of her as "the last of the great shameless emotionalists." De Sica called her "Italy's finest actress and one of the most interesting actresses in the world."

In 1955, Magnani climaxed her career with a magnificent performance in Hollywood's screen adaptation of Tennessee Williams's *The Rose Tattoo,* for which she won the best actress Academy Award as well as the New York Critics award. She was nominated for an Oscar again for *Wild Is the Wind* (1957). After that her career slowly declined, although she continued performing admirably in a dozen or so film productions. In her final years she acted mainly on the stage and on Italian TV. She died at 65 after a long bout with a tumor of the pancreas. A huge crowd gathered for her funeral in a final salute that Romans usually reserve for Popes. She was laid to rest in the family mausoleum of Roberto Rossellini, her favorite director and longtime friend. She was the subject of a documentary film, *Io sono Anna Magnani* (1980).

FILMS: *Scampolo* 1927; *La Cieca di Sorrento, Tempo Massimo* 1934; *Cavalleria, Trenta Secondi d'Amore* 1936; *Tarakanova* (Italian-language version of *Tarakanowa/Betrayal;* Fr.) 1938; *Una Lampada alla Finestra* 1940; *Finalmente Soli, La Fuggitiva, Teresa Venerdì/Doctor Beware* 1941; *La Fortuna viene dal Cielo* 1942; *La Vita è Bella, L'Avventura di Annabella, Campo dè Fiori/The Peddler and the Lady, L'Ultima Carrozzella, T'amero sempre* 1943; *Il Fiore sotto gli Occhi* 1944; *Roma Città aperta/Open City, Abbasso la Miseria/Peddlin' in Society* 1945; *Un Uomo ritorna/Revenge, Davanti a lui tremava tutta Roma/Before Him All Rome Trembled/Tosca, Il Bandito/The Bandit, Abbasso la Ricchezza* 1946; *Lo Sconosciuto di San Marino, Quartetto Pazzo, L'Onorevole Angelina/Angelina* (also co-sc.), *Assunta Spina/Scarred* 1947; *L'Amore/Ways of Love* (in two Roberto Rossellini episodes, "La Voce Umana" and "Il Miracolo," only the first of which was included in the subtitled version screened in the US), *Molti Sogni per le Strade/Woman Trouble* 1948; *Vulcano/Volcano* 1950; *Bellissima* 1951; *Camicie rosse/Anita Garibaldi* (as Garibaldi's wife, Anita) 1952; *La Carrozza d'Oro/La Carrosse d'Or/The Golden Coach* (It./Fr.), *Siamo Donne/We the Women* (in Visconti episode; shown in the US as part of another episode film, 1954's *Questa è la Vita/Of Life and Love*) 1953; *The Rose Tattoo* (US) 1955; *Suor Letizia/The Awakening* 1956; *Wild Is the Wind* (US) 1957; *Nella Città l'Inferno/And the Wild Wild Women/Hell in the City* 1958; *The Fugitive Kind* (US), *Risate di Gioia/The Passionate Thief* 1960; *Mamma Roma* 1962; *Le Magot de Joséfa* (Fr.) 1963; *Volles Herz und leere Taschen* (Ger./It.) 1964; *Made in Italy* 1965; *The Secret of Santa Vittoria* (US; filmed in Italy) 1969; *Correva l'Anno di Grazia 1870/1870* (orig. made for TV), *Fellini's Roma* (cameo) 1972.

magnetic film. Perforated film with a magnetic coating, used for sound recording. Since it is of the same dimension as motion picture film, camera and recorder sprockets turn at the same speed, thus keeping picture and sound in perfect synchronization.

magnetic recording. Sound reproduced by magnetic means on tape or film with an iron oxide coating. The recording is usually accomplished in synchronization with motion picture film and later transferred by optical means to photographic film.

magnetic stripes. Bands coated with a ferromagnetic substance running lengthwise along the outer edges of perforated film for the purpose of recording sound.

magnetic tape. A strip of ferromagnetic material with a polyester or Mylar base which is coated with a substance containing iron oxide to make it sensitive to electromagnetic impulses in recording sound for film or picture and sound for television. Professional quarter-inch sound-recording tapes are available in lengths up to 2,400 feet on spools or up to 7,200 feet on cores. During recording, the tape passes through magnetic heads on the tape recorder, producing signals that form an unseen magnetic pattern on the tape. To produce quality sound, high-speed recording is required for professional taping—15 inches per second or at least 7½ inches per second, versus 1⅞ inches per second or 3¾ inches per second in home use. Sprocketed magnetic tape is available in widths of 16 mm and 35 mm for use in synchronization with photographic film. See MAGNETIC FILM.

Magnuson, Ann. Actress. Born in 1956, in Charleston, W.Va. *ed.* Denison U. Appealing leading lady and supporting player of Hollywood films and TV movies. She began her career in 1978 as an intern at New York's Ensemble Studio, then sang in various East Village clubs and with a recording band. On the screen from 1983, initially in bits. Regular on TV sitcom 'Anything But Love.'

FILMS: *The Hunger* 1983; *Perfect Strangers* 1984; *Desperately Seeking Susan, Sleepwalk* (Ger./US) 1985; *Special Effects* 1986; *Making Mr. Right* 1987; *A Night in the Life of Jimmy Reardon, Mondo New York, Tequila Sunrise* 1988; *Checking Out, Heavy Petting* (semidoc.) 1989; *Love at Large* 1990; *Cabin Boy, Clear and Present Danger* 1994; *Before and After* 1996.

magoptical prints. Release prints with both magnetic and optical sound tracks to allow their use in theaters equipped with either system. The separate tracks can also be used for carrying two different language versions on the same print.

Maharis, George. Actor. Born on Sept. 1, 1928, in Astoria, N.Y. Laconic leading man of American television and films. A product of the Actors Studio, he moved to leads in films after successfully starring in TV's 'Route 66' series (1960–63), but having made little impact on the big screen he returned to the tube for 'The Most Deadly Game' (1970–71) and many TV movies.

FILMS: *Exodus* 1960; *Quick Before It Melts* 1964; *Sylvia, The Satan Bug* 1965; *A Covenant with Death, The Happening* 1967; *The Desperados, Land Raiders, El Ultimo Diá de la Guerra/The Last Day of the War* (Sp./It./US) 1969; *The Sword and the Sorcerer* 1982.

Mahin, John Lee. Screenwriter. *b.* 1902, Evanston, Ill. *d.* 1984, of emphysema. A Harvard graduate, he worked for newspapers in Boston and New York and in advertising before being brought out to Hollywood by Ben HECHT. He wrote screenplays, adaptations, and original stories, alone or in collaboration, for many successful films, mainly at MGM, where he was a favorite of director Victor FLEMING. He also doctored many other scripts without screen credits. He was nominated for Academy Awards for *Captains Courageous* (1937) and *Heaven Knows, Mr. Allison* (1957). He was among the founders of the Screen Writers Guild in 1933, but later in the decade helped found and became president of the competing Screen Playwrights, a company union. During the Red Scare of the late 40s and early 50s, he was associated with conservative groups that encouraged the weeding out of purported Communist influences in Hollywood. In 1958 he started the Mahin-Rackin production company with screenwriter Martin RACKIN. At one time he was married to actress Patsy Ruth MILLER.

FILMS: *The Unholy Garden* (uncredited) 1931; *Beast of the City, Scarface, The Wet Parade, Tiger Shark* (uncredited), *Red Dust* 1932; *Eskimo, The Prizefighter and the Lady, Hell Below, Bombshell* 1933; *Treasure Island, Laughing Boy, Chained* 1934; *Naughty Marietta, China Seas* (uncredited), *Riffraff* (uncredited) 1935; *Small Town Girl, Love on the Run, Wife Versus Secretary, The Devil Is a Sissy* 1936; *A Star Is Born* (uncredited), *Captains Courageous, The Last Gangster* 1937; *Test Pilot* (uncredited), *Too Hot to Handle* 1938; *The Wizard of Oz* (uncredited), *Gone With the Wind* (uncredited) 1939; *Foreign Correspondent* (uncredited), *Boom Town* 1940; *Dr. Jekyll and Mr. Hyde, Johnny Eager* 1941; *Woman of the Year* (uncredited), *Tortilla Flat* 1942; *The Adventures of Tartu* 1943; *Adventure* (uncredited) 1945; *The Yearling* (uncredited) 1946; *Down to the Sea in Ships* 1949; *Love That Brute* 1950; *Show Boat, Quo Vadis* 1951; *My Son John* (uncredited) 1952; *Mogambo* (remake of *Red Dust*) 1953; *Elephant Walk* 1954; *Lucy Gallant* 1955; *The Bad Seed* 1956; *Heaven Knows Mr. Allison* 1957; *No Time for Sergeants* 1958; *The Horse Soldiers* 1959; *North to Alaska* 1960; *The Spiral Road* 1962; *Moment to Moment* 1966.

Mahoney, Jock. Actor. *b.* Jacques O'Mahoney, Feb. 7, 1919, Chicago. *d.* 1989. *ed.* U. of Iowa. Tall and athletic, he entered films in 1945 as a stuntman. Within a year he was playing heavies in low-budget Westerns, eventually starring in several films of the genre. He was billed under his real name or as Jack O'Mahoney in his earlier films. In the 50s he starred in two action-packed TV series, 'The Range Rider' (1951–52) and 'Yancy Derringer' (1958–59). After playing the heavy in a 1960 Gordon Scott Tarzan film, he succeeded the latter as the screen's 13th Tarzan. Despite a stroke in 1973 that hindered his career, he continued appearing sporadically in films and on TV into the early 80s. An apparent second stroke resulted in his death at 70. He was the stepfather of actress Sally FIELD through his marriage to actress Margaret Field.

FILMS INCLUDE: *The Fighting Frontiersman* 1946; *South of the Chisholm Trail* 1947; *The Doolins of Oklahoma* 1949; *The Nevadan* 1950; *Overland Pacific* 1954; *Away All Boats, Showdown at Abilene* 1956; *A Time to Love and a Time to Die, Tarzan the Magnificent* 1960; *Tarzan Goes to India* (as Tarzan) 1962; *California, Tarzan's Three Challenges* (as Tarzan) 1963; *The Walls of Hell* 1964; *Runaway Girl* 1966; *The Glory Stompers* 1967; *Bandolero!* 1968; *Tom* 1973; *The Bad Bunch* 1976; *The End* 1978.

Mahoney, John. Actor. Born on June 20, 1940 in Manchester, England. Versatile character player of the American stage and screen. He joined the Stratford Children's Theatre as a boy of ten and stayed with the troupe through age 13. Moving to the US at 19, he joined the Army, then studied and taught English at Quincy College and Western Illinois University. Armed with a master's degree, he freelanced in Chicago as an editor of medical manuscripts and served as an associate editor of a quarterly journal. Drawn back to acting at age 35, he trained for two years at Chicago's St. Nicholas Theatre and made his professional stage debut in 1977 in the world premiere of David Mamet's 'The Water Engine.' He won a Tony Award for his performance on Broadway in John Guare's 'The House of Blue Leaves.' On the screen from the early 80s, often in pivotal supporting roles. Regular on TV sitcom 'Frasier.'

FILMS: *Mission Hill* 1982; *Code of Silence* 1985; *The Manhattan Project, Streets of Gold* 1986; *Tin Men, Suspect, Moonstruck* 1987; *Frantic, Betrayed, Eight Men Out* 1988; *Say Anything* 1989; *Love Hurts, The Russia House* 1990; *Barton Fink* 1991; *Article 99* 1992; *In the Line of Fire* 1993; *Reality Bites, The Hudsucker Proxy* 1994; *The American President* 1995; *Primal Fear, She's the One* 1996.

Maibaum, Richard. Screenwriter, producer. *b.* May 26, 1909, New York City. *d.* 1991. *ed.* NYU; U. of Iowa. He was an established stage actor, producer, and playwright by the time he began writing scripts for Hollywood films in the mid-30s. After WW II service as director of the Army's Combat Film Division, with a final rank of lieutenant colonel, he returned to Hollywood as a producer as well as a screenwriter for Paramount. In the early 50s, for tax reasons, he entered a partnership with producers Irving ALLEN and Albert BROCCOLI to make a number of films in England. Maibaum stayed in London, where he collaborated on many scripts for British TV and films, including most of the James Bond thrillers. His plays included 'The Tree' 'Birthright,' 'Sweet Mystery of Life,' and 'See My Lawyer.' His son, Paul, became a cameraman.

FILMS INCLUDE (as screenwriter, alone or in collaboration): In the US—*We Went to College, Gold Diggers of 1937* (co-play basis only, 'Sweet Mystery of Life') 1936; *They Gave*

Him a Gun, Live Love and Learn 1937; *The Bad Man of Brimstone, Stablemates* 1938; *Coast Guard* 1939; *Twenty-Mule Team* 1940; *I Wanted Wings* 1941; *Ten Gentlemen from West Point* 1942; *See My Lawyer* (co-play basis only) 1945; *O.S.S.* (also prod.) 1946; *The Big Clock* (prod. only), *The Sainted Sisters* (prod. only) 1948; *Bride of Vengeance* (prod. only), *The Great Gatsby* (also prod.), *Song of Surrender* (also prod.) 1949; *Dear Wife* (prod. only), *Captain Carey USA* (prod. only), *No Man of Her Own* (prod. only) 1950. In the UK—*The Red Beret/Paratrooper* 1953; *The Cockleshell Heroes* 1955; *Ransom* (US), *Bigger Than Life* (US), *Zarak* 1956; *No Time to Die/Tank Force* 1958; *Killers of Kilimanjaro* 1959; *The Day They Robbed the Bank of England* (adapt. only) 1960; *Battle of Bloody Beach* (also prod.; US) 1961; *Dr. No* 1962; *From Russia with Love* 1963; *Goldfinger* 1964; *Thunderball* 1965; *Chitty Chitty Bang Bang* (addnl. dial. only) 1968; *On Her Majesty's Secret Service* 1969; *Diamonds Are Forever* 1971; *The Man with the Golden Gun* 1974; *The Spy Who Loved Me* 1977; *For Your Eyes Only* 1981; *Octopussy* 1983; *A View to a Kill* 1985; *The Living Daylights* 1987; *License to Kill* 1989; *Ransom* (co-story) 1996.

Mailer, Norman. Novelist, poet, journalist, filmmaker. Born on Jan. 31, 1923, in Long Branch, N.J. *ed.* Harvard; Sorbonne. The exuberant, multitalented, unpredictable, often garrulous author of *The Naked and the Dead* (1948), *Advertisements for Myself* (1959), *An American Dream* (1965), *The Armies of the Night* (1968), *Marilyn* (a seminal biography of Marilyn Monroe; 1973), *The Executioner's Song* (1979), and *Harlot's Ghost* (1992) among other books, dabbled briefly in filmmaking during the late 60s and early 70s. He directed produced, wrote, and himself appeared in three underground-style feature-length films that impressed some as sincere exercises in personal expression but were dismissed by others as mere "ego trips." Almost two decades later, Mailer took another, more ambitious stab at filmmaking with *Tough Guys Don't Dance* (1987), an offbeat *film noir* starring Ryan O'Neal and Isabella Rossellini. In the interim he made personal appearances in several avant-garde films, portrayed architect Stanford White in Milos Forman's *Ragtime* (1981), and played himself in Jean-Luc Godard's *King Lear* (1987). Mailer's son, Michael, is a film producer and his daughter, Kate, an actress.

FILMS: *The Naked and the Dead* (novel basis) 1958; *An American Dream* (novel basis) 1966; *Wild 90* (dir., prod., co-edit., act.), *Beyond the Law* (dir., co-prod., story outline co-edit., act.), *Will the Real Norman Mailer Please Stand Up?* (as himself) 1968; *Diaries, Notes, and Sketches* (as himself) 1969; *Double Pisces—Scorpio Rising* (appearance) 1970; *Maidstone* (dir., co-prod., sc., co-edit., act.) 1971; *The Year of the Woman* (as himself) 1973; *Diaries, Notes, and Sketches—Lost Lost Lost* (as himself) 1975; *Town Bloody Hall* (as himself) 1979; *Ragtime* (act., as Stanford White) 1981; *Hello Actors Studio* (as himself), *Tough Guys Don't Dance* (dir., sc. from own play, song lyrics), *King Lear* (as himself) 1987.

Main, Marjorie. Actress. *b.* Mary Tomlinson, Feb. 24, 1890, Acton, Ind. *d.* 1975. Salty, crusty character player of numerous Hollywood films; notorious as a devastating scene stealer. A minister's daughter, she joined a local stock company as a youngster, changing her name to save her family embarrassment. She later appeared in vaudeville and on the legitimate stage, making her Broadway debut in 1916. She began playing in films in 1932 and after repeating her stage role in the movie version of *Dead End* (1937), in which she played Humphrey Bogart's mother, she was typecast for a while in dramatic slum mother parts. But it was as a comedienne that she rose to popularity at MGM in the 40s as the frequent screen partner of Wallace BEERY. After her success in the role of a raucous rural lady in *The Egg and I* (1947) she co-starred with Percy KILBRIDE in nine spin-off films, the "Ma and Pa Kettle" series. She retired from the screen in 1957.

FILMS INCLUDE: *A House Divided* 1931; *Hot Saturday* 1932; *Crime Without Passion* 1934; *Dead End, Stella Dallas* 1937; *Boys of the Streets, Penitentiary, King of the Newsboys, Test Pilot, Too Hot to Handle, Three Comrades* 1938; *They Shall Have Music, Angels Wash Their Faces, The Women, Another Thin Man* 1939; *I Take This Woman, Dark Command, Susan and God, Wyoming* 1940; *The Trial of Mary Dugan, A Woman's Face, Barnacle Bill, The Shepherd of the Hills, Honky Tonk* 1941; *The Bugle Sounds, We Were Dancing, Jackass Mail, Tish, Tennessee Johnson* 1942; *Heaven Can Wait, Johnny Come Lately* 1943; *Rationing, Gentle Annie, Meet Me in St. Louis* 1944; *Murder He Says* 1945; *The Harvey Girls, Bad Bascomb, Undercurrent* 1946; *The Egg and I, The Wistful Widow of Wagon Gap* 1947; *Big Jack, Ma and Pa Kettle* (and eight other films in the series through 1957) 1949; *Summer Stock, Mrs. O'Malley and Mr. Malone* 1950; *The Law and the Lady* 1951; *It's a Big Country, The Belle of New York* 1952; *The Long Long Trailer, Rose Marie* 1954; *Friendly Persuasion* 1956; *The Kettles on Old MacDonald's Farm* 1957.

main title. The title announcing the name of a film, usually in larger print than any of the other film credits. See also TITLES.

Mainwaring, Daniel. Screenwriter, novelist. *b.* Feb. 27, 1902, Oakland, Calif. *d.* 1977. The son of a forest ranger, he taught for a year after graduating from Fresno State College, then turned to journalism, becoming a copyboy and reporter on the *San Francisco Chronicle.* He entered films as a publicity writer for Warner Bros. but switched to screenwriting at Paramount in the early 40s. All along, he pursued a parallel career as a mystery novelist, under the pseudonym Geoffrey Homes, a pen name he also used on many of his scripts. His intelligent screenplays, like his novels, provided directors with carefully detailed locales and characterizations. Among his outstanding contributions were the scripts for the realistic corruption drama *Phenix City Story* (1955), and for the gripping science-fiction thriller *Invasion of the Body Snatchers* (1956). His 1946 novel *Hang My Gallows High* provided the basis for *Out of the Past,* a classic *film noir,* the following year, and a weaker remake, *Against All Odds,* in 1983.

FILMS (as screenwriter, alone or in collaboration): *No Hands on the Clock* (novel basis only) 1941; *Secrets of the Underground* 1942; *Crime by Night* (novel basis only, *Forty Whacks*), *Dangerous Passage* 1944; *Scared Stiff, Tokyo Rose* 1945; *Hot Cargo, Swamp Fire, They Made Me a Killer* 1946; *Big Town, Out of the Past* (from his own novel, *Build My Gallows High*) 1947; *Roughshod, The Big Steal* 1949; *The Lawless* (from his own novel, *The Voice of Stephen Wilder*), *The Eagle and the Hawk* 1950; *Roadblock* (story only), *The Tall Target* (story only), *The Last Outpost* 1951; *Bugles in the Afternoon, This Woman Is Dangerous* 1952; *The Hitch-Hiker* (story basis only, uncredited), *Powder River, Those Redheads from Seattle* 1953; *Alaska Seas, Black Horse Canyon, The Desperado, Southwest Passage* 1954; *A Bullet for Joey, An Annapolis Story, The Phenix City Story* 1955; *Invasion of the Body Snatchers, Thunderstorm* 1956; *Baby Face Nelson, East of Kilimanjaro* (story only; UK/It.) 1957; *Cole Younger, Gunfighter, The Gun Runners, Space Master X-7* 1958; *Walk Like a Dragon* 1960; *La Rivolta degli Schiavi* (dial. only for English-language vers. *Revolt of the Slaves;* It.), *Teseo contro il Minotauro* (adapt. only for English-language vers. *The Minotaur;* It.), *Atlantis, the Lost Continent* 1961; *The Woman Who Wouldn't Die/Catacombs* (US/UK), *Convict Stage* 1965; *Against All Odds* (novel basis only, *Hang My Gallows High*) 1983.

Makavejev, Dušan. Director. Born on Oct. 13, 1932, in Belgrade, Yugoslavia. A leading figure of the new Yugoslav cinema, he directed his first amateur short during his sophomore year at Belgrade University, where he majored in psychology, graduating in 1955. He enrolled at the Belgrade Academy of Theater, Radio, Film and Television. Following the exhibition of his graduation short, *Anthony's Broken Mirror,* at the 1957 Amateur Film Festival in Cannes, he began making professional documentaries for the Zagreb film studios and was quite well known in Yugoslav film circles by the time he made his first feature in 1966. The film *Man Is Not a Bird,* revealed Makavejev as an inventive and nonconformist director whose freewheeling style and robust sense of humor provided a fresh departure from the self-conscious films typically produced in his country and elsewhere. Freely intercutting fictional and factual footage, and flashing forward and backward in time, he painted a lusty picture of erotic passion on a drab canvas of antiseptic communist life. He experimented with the language of cinema even more daringly and dealt with sexuality more explicitly in *Love Affair: Or The Case of the Missing Telephone Operator* (1967). Borrowing from Eisenstein, Godard, and Brecht, and adding a large dose of his own spice and verve, he juxtaposed seemingly unrelated images with erotic footage, and resorted to other unorthodox techniques in questioning the very essence of sexuality in the political climate of his society.

Carrying on with his experimentations in montage, Makavejev chose for his next project to rework and add his personal stamp to an existing film. Made in 1940 by an unemployed strongman-acrobat, untrained in filmmaking, the original *Innocence Unprotected* was a charmingly "primitive" film that enjoyed great success locally during WW II as the first "all-talking" Serbian production. Makavejev re-edited the film, removed scenes, added hand-tinting to others, and gave the production new relevance by juxtaposing the whole against his own footage of wartime newsreels and interviews with members of the original cast and crew. Following the 1968 release of the film, he went to the US on a Ford Foundation grant to research the life and works of Wilhelm Reich, the Marxist psychoanalyst who preached sexual enlightenment as a gateway to a better society. With funds from German TV, the director intended to use the material as a basis for a documentary film. But after further research in Europe and extensive shooting in the US, he decided to expand the project into a fictional feature, juxtaposing the factual footage against a dramatic story he shot in Yugoslavia. The resultant film, *WR: Mysteries of the Organism* (1971), uninhibitedly explicit in parts, extolled the virtues of frank sexuality while condemning Stalinist socialism and Western capitalism as spoilers of erotic joy. Under pressure from Moscow, the film was banned in Yugoslavia as politically offensive. Unable to secure film assignments at home, Makavejev went into a long self-exile abroad, making films wherever he found sponsors. Sadly, instead of discovering more creative freedom in the West, he found himself shackled by the meddling of producers and by commercial considerations of the marketplace. None of his foreign-made films matched the originality or verve of his homegrown productions. In the late 80s he resumed his work in Yugoslavia, a much subdued man.

FEATURE FILMS (as director-screenwriter): *Man Is Not a Bird* 1966; *Love Affair: Or The Case of the Missing Switchboard Operator/An Affair of the Heart* 1967; *Innocence Unprotected* 1968; *WR: Mysteries of the Organism* 1971; *Sweet Movie* (Can./Fr./Ger.) 1974; *Montenegro/Pigs and Pearls* (Sw./UK) 1981; *The Coca Cola Kid* (dir. only; Austral.) 1985; *Manifesto* 1988; *Hole in the Soul* (also prod.) 1994.

Makepeace, Chris. Actor. Born on Apr. 22, 1964, in Montreal. Appealing juvenile player, then young leading man of Canadian and American films and TV movies of the 80s.

FILMS: *Meatballs* (Can.) 1979; *My Bodyguard* 1980; *The Last Chase* (Can.) 1981; *A Savage Hunger/The Oasis* 1984; *The Falcon and the Snowman* 1985; *Vamp* 1986; *Captive Hearts* 1987; *Aloha Summer* 1988.

makeup. 1. Cosmetics applied to an actor's face or body to improve or alter their appearance on film. 2. All of the materials, including cosmetics and costumes, worn by an actor in portraying a role. As defined in the first of these two senses, makeup is applied by the makeup artist, whose domain is from the head to the breastbone and the fingers to the elbow. The rest of the body is the province of the BODY MAKEUP ARTIST. Makeup is used to prepare performers for the camera, make them more or less attractive, make them younger or older, simulate scars and bruises, and otherwise suit them to their roles. In the silent era, makeup was often applied by the actors themselves, of whom Lon CHANEY was the most notable practitioner. The WESTMORE family of makeup artists did much to professionalize the trade and develop the standard techniques of the studio era, while Jack PIERCE created horror makeup for numerous monsters. Since the 60s, special effects makeup artists such as William TUTTLE, John Chambers, Dick Smith, Rick BAKER, Tom Savini, Rob Bottin, and Chris WALAS have employed latex appliances and mechanical devices to transform people into creatures and simulate gore. See also SPECIAL EFFECTS.

Makk, Károly. Director. Born in 1925, in Hungary. A leading figure in postwar Hungarian cinema. A graduate of the Budapest Academy of Film Art, he worked as an assistant on Geza von Radvanyi's *Somewhere in Europe* and on other films before making his own debut as a director in 1954. His films show an interest in individuals in distress and a keen observation of social foibles. *The House Under the Rocks* (1958) won first prize at the San Francisco Film Festival. *Love* (1971) shared the Jury Prize at the Cannes Festival.

FEATURE FILMS: *Liliomfi* 1954; *Ward No. 9* 1955; *Tale of the 12 Points* 1956; *The House Under the Rocks* (also co-sc.) 1958; *The 39th Brigade* 1959; *Don't Keep Off the Grass* 1960; *The Fanatics* (also co-sc.) 1961; *The Lost Paradise* 1962; *The Last But One* 1963; *His Majesty's Dates* 1964; *A Clouded Vacation* 1967; *Before God and Man* 1968; *Love* 1971; *Cat's Play* (also co-sc.) 1974; *Behind the Brick Wall* 1979; *Another Way* (also co-sc.) 1982; *Lily in Love* 1985; *The Last Manuscript* (also co-sc.) 1986; *Hungarian Requiem* 1991.

Mala. Actor. *b.* Ray Wise, 1906, near Candle, Alaska. *d.* 1952. The son of an American trader and his Eskimo wife, he made his living as a hunter and fisherman before entering films in 1932. He played starring roles in several Hollywood action productions and exotic supporting roles in many others. Sometimes billed as Ray Mala. He died of a heart attack at 46.

FILMS INCLUDE: *Igloo* 1932; *Eskimo* 1934; *Robinson Crusoe of Clipper Island* (serial), *Last of the Pagans, Jungle Princess* 1936; *Hawk of the Wilderness* (serial), *Call of the Yukon* 1938; *Union Pacific, Mutiny on the Blackhawk, Desperate Trails* 1939; *Zanzibar, Green Hell, North West Mounted Police, Girl from God's Country, The Devil's Pipeline* 1940; *Hold Back the Dawn, Honolulu* 1941; *Girl from Alaska, The Mad Doctor of Market Street, Son of Fury, The Tuttles of Tahiti* 1942; *Red Snow* 1952.

Malaparte, Curzio. Author. *b.* Kurt Eric Suckert, June 9, 1898, Prato, Italy. *d.* 1957. The celebrated author of *Kaputt* and many other works contributed one film to Italian cinema, *Il Cristo Proibito/Forbidden Christ* (1950), which he wrote, directed, and scored. The film was released in the US in 1953 as *Strange Deception.* Just before his death (of cancer) he completed the treatment of another film he had contemplated making, *Il Compagno P.*

Malden, Karl. Actor. Born Malden Sekulovich on Mar. 22, 1913, in Chicago, to Yugoslav-born parents. Bulb-nosed character star of the American stage and screen. Raised in the steel-mill community of Gary, Indiana, he briefly attended Arkansas State Teachers College, then enrolled for three years at Chicago's Goodman Theatre Dramatic School. He made his Broadway debut in 1937 and his first screen appearance in 1940. His career took off after his return from WW II service (1943–45) with the Army Air Force. He became one of Hollywood's more complex character actors, at his best and most disturbing with roles that carry much moral weight or none at all. Won an Academy Award as best supporting actor for *A Streetcar Named Desire* (1951), in which he repeated his 1947 Broadway role of Mitch. Nominated for another Oscar for *On the Waterfront* (1954). He has directed one film, *Time Limit* (1957), and parts of *The Hanging Tree* (1959) during a forced absence of director Delmer Daves. Malden starred in the TV police series 'The Streets of San Francisco' (1972–77) and 'Skag' (1980). He won an Emmy for the TV movie *Fatal Vision* (1984). For years his face popped up frequently on the tube in "Don't Leave Home Without It" commercials for American Express. Married from 1938 to actress Mona Graham, Malden is one of Hollywood's most respected spokesmen. From 1989 to 1993 he was president of the Academy of Motion Picture Arts and Sciences.

FILMS: *They Knew What They Wanted* 1940; *Winged Victory* 1944; *13 Rue Madeleine, Boomerang, Kiss of Death* 1947; *The Gunfighter, Where the Sidewalk Ends* 1950; *Halls of Montezuma, A Streetcar Named Desire* 1951; *The Sellout, Decision Before Dawn, Operation Secret, Diplomatic Courier* 1952; *Ruby Gentry, I Confess, Take the High Ground* 1953; *Phantom of the Rue Morgue, On the Waterfront* 1954; *Baby Doll* 1956; *Time Limit* (dir. only), *Fear Strikes Out, Bombers B-52* 1957; *The Hanging Tree* (also dir. some scenes, uncredited) 1959; *Pollyanna* 1960; *The Great Impostor, Parrish, One-Eyed Jacks* 1961; *All Fall Down, Birdman of Alcatraz, Gypsy, How the West Was Won* 1962; *Come Fly with Me* 1963; *Dead Ringer, Cheyenne Autumn* 1964; *The Cincinnati Kid* 1965; *Nevada Smith, Murderers' Row* 1966; *Hotel, The Adventures of Bullwhip Griffin, Billion Dollar Brain* 1967; *Blue, Hot Millions* 1968; *Patton* (as General Omar Bradley) 1970; *Il Gatto a Nove Code/The Cat o' Nine Tails* (It.), *Wild Rovers* 1971; *Summertime Killer* 1973; *Meteor, Beyond the Poseidon Adventure* 1979; *The Sting II, Twilight Time* 1983; *Billy Galvin* 1986; *Nuts* 1987.

Malick, Terrence (Terry). Director, screenwriter. Born on Nov. 30, 1943, in Ottawa, Ill. The son of an oil-company executive, he was raised in Waco and Austin, Texas, and Bartlesville, Oklahoma. A Harvard graduate and a Rhodes scholar at Oxford, he was a journalist for *Newsweek, Life*, and the *New Yorker* and taught philosophy at MIT before deciding to venture into films. He attended the American Film Institute's Center for Advanced Film Studies, where he directed a graduation short, *Lanton Mills.* In 1971 he reputedly had a hand in the screenplay of Jack Nicholson's *Drive He Said,* but received no credit for his participation. He also worked on a script for *Dirty Harry* but his version was not used in the final product. In 1972 he wrote the script for Stuart Rosenberg's *Pocket Money* and the following year made an auspicious debut as the director-producer-writer of *Badlands,* a haunting and provocative film about a young couple on a senseless murder spree in the Badlands of Dakota and Montana. The film was enthusiastically received by most critics at the 1973 New York Film Festival. Five years elapsed before he released his next film, *Days of Heaven* (1978), another visually stunning evocation of a time gone by and another critical triumph. However, Malick's idiosyncratic approach to the narrative aspect of filmmaking failed to elicit commercially viable audience support. Discouraged by the poor box-office response to the latter film, the reclusive director withdrew from sight. In subsequent years he divided his time between Paris and Texas, occasionally emerging for a lucrative assignment as an uncredited script doctor, and spending the bulk of his time submitting screenplay ideas or mulling over other writers' scripts for a possible comeback.

FILMS: *Drive He Said* (co-sc., uncredited), *Deadhead Miles* (sc.) 1971; *Pocket Money* (sc., act.) 1972; *Badlands* (dir. prod., sc.) 1973; *Gravy Train/The Dion Brothers* (co-sc. under pseudonym David Whitney) 1974; *Days of Heaven* (dir., sc.) 1978.

Malkin, Barry. American film editor. A favorite of Francis COPPOLA, he also worked on major films of other directors of the 80s and early 90s.

FILMS INCLUDE: *Fat Spy* 1966; *Rain People* (as Blackie Malkin) 1969; *Who Is Harry Kellerman. . .* 1971; *Cops and Robbers* 1973; *The Godfather Part II* (co-edit.) 1974; *One Summer Love* 1976; *Last Embrace* 1979; *One-Trick Pony* 1980; *Four Friends* 1981; *Hammett* (co-edit.) 1982; *Rumble Fish* 1983; *The Cotton Club* (co-edit.) 1984; *Peggy Sue Got Married* 1986; *Gardens of Stone* 1987; *Big* 1988; *New York Stories* ("Life Without Zoe" episode) 1989; *The Freshman, The Godfather Part III* (co-edit.) 1990.

Malkovich, John. Actor. Born on Dec. 9, 1953, in Christopher, Ill. Smooth, unconventional, balding leading man of the American stage and screen. Raised in Benton, Illinois, where his grandmother was the publisher of the local newspaper and his father the head of the State Conservation Department, he lost a great deal of weight during his high school years to become a slim ladies' man on the campus of Illinois State University. He began acting in school productions and in 1976, with a group of college friends, he became a founding member of Chicago's Steppenwolf Ensemble. After seven years with the group, he emerged into the New York limelight with an Obie Award–winning performance in the 1983 off-Broadway production of Sam Shepard's 'True West,' which led to the plum role of Biff in the 1984 Broadway revival of Arthur Miller's 'Death of a Salesman' starring Dustin HOFFMAN. He made an equally impressive screen debut in 1984 in Robert Benton's *Places in the Heart,* for which he was nominated for an Academy Award as best supporting actor. A string of strong screen performances culminated in 1988 in his intricate portrayal of an aristocratic seductor in Stephen Frears's *Dangerous Liaisons.* Malkovich, who has periodically returned to the stage as an actor and a director, was married to actress Glenne HEADLY from 1982 to 1990.

FILMS: *Places in the Heart, The Killing Fields* (UK) 1984; *Death of a Salesman* (TV movie in US; theatrically released abroad), *Private Conversations* (doc.), *Eleni* 1985; *Making Mr. Right, The Glass Menagerie, Empire of the Sun* 1987; *Miles from Home, Dangerous Liaisons, The Accidental Tourist* (co-exec. prod. only) 1988; *The Sheltering Sky* 1990; *Queens Logic, The Object of Beauty* (US/UK) 1991; *Shadows and Fog, Jennifer 8, Of Mice and Men* 1992; *Alive, In the Line of Fire, We're Back: A Dinosaur's Story* (v/o) 1993; *Heart of Darkness* 1994; *The Convent* 1995; *Mary Reilly, Mulholland Falls, The Ogre, The Portrait of a Lady* 1996; *Beyond the Clouds, ConAir* 1997.

Malle, Louis. Director. *b.* Oct. 30, 1932, in Thumeries, France, into one of France's wealthiest industrialist families. *d.* 1995. He had an austere Catholic education that culminated in studies at the Jesuit College at Fontainebleau, then enrolled at the Sorbonne, where he majored in political science. From 1951 to 1953 he studied filmmaking at IDHEC and immediately after graduating was picked by Jacques-Yves COUSTEAU to accompany him on a voyage of the *Calypso.* Malle thus co-directed with Cousteau the celebrated underwater documentary *Le Monde de Silence/The Silent World* (1956) and operated the camera on some of the scenes. Malle also directed two shorts and served as Robert Bresson's assistant on *Un Condamné à Mort s'est echappé/A Man Escaped* (1956) before turning out his first solo feature as a director, *Ascenseur pour l'Echafaud/Frantic* (made in 1957 and released early in 1958), a solid psychological thriller noted for Henri Dacaë's darkly atmospheric photography of Paris. The film, which showcased the talent of Jeanne MOREAU, enjoyed considerable success and earned for Malle the coveted Prix Delluc.

Malle's next film, *Les Amants/The Lovers,* also released in 1958, caused much controversy because of what was considered at the time its overly explicit sexuality but proved a big commercial hit, internationally establishing the reputations of both its director and star, again Jeanne Moreau. The lyrical love scenes and fluid tracking shots that distinguished this film at the time of its first showing remain more memorable than its intended comment on the vacuity of the French bourgeoisie. The film won the Special Jury Prize at Venice. Following a change-of-pace production, the frivolous and baffling *Zazie dans le Métro/Zazie* (1960), Malle turned out *Vie privée/A Very Private Affair* (1962), a study of the rise of a film star, starring Brigitte BARDOT in a fictionalized biography of herself.

Once again demonstrating his versatility as a filmmaker and the broad range of his concerns and style, Malle next turned out *Le Feu Follet/The Fire Within* (1963), which many critics consider his most mature and accomplished film. It is a somber, keenly observed, and sensitively told story of the last few days in the life of a suicidal alcoholic in which Malle explores more poignantly than ever before one of the few repetitive themes in the body of his work—isolation and social alienation. Again Malle won the Special Jury Prize at Venice, this time in a tie. Suddenly shifting gears once more, Malle then gave us *Viva Maria* (1965), a fun-filled, visually spectacular bit of nonsense co-starring the two great leading ladies of the French cinema, Bardot and Moreau. Next came *Le Voleur/The Thief of Paris* (1967), a well-executed period crime drama that lovingly re-created turn-of-the-century Paris.

Malle then embarked on a six-month voyage to India, which resulted in a feature-length documentary, *Calcutta* (1969), and a seven-part TV series, *L'Inde fantôme/Phantom India,* broadcast internationally to great acclaim and later also shown in movie theaters. Malle returned to the fictional film with *Le Souffle au Coeur/Murmur of the Heart* (1971), a tenderly and discreetly treated story of adolescence, and *Lacombe Lucien* (1973), a Prix Méliés–winning character study set against the background of the Nazi Occupation. Both films generated their impact from their moving simplicity. Not so *Black Moon* (1975), an eccentric, self-indulgent film inspired by Lewis Carroll's *Alice in Wonderland.* In 1978, Malle released his first American-made film, the controversial, attention-grabbing story of a 12-year-old whore, *Pretty Baby.* The atmospheric, beautifully photographed film made a star of a pubescent Brooke SHIELDS. It is still banned in Canada. Malle continued his North American ventures with the Canadian-French-sponsored *Atlantic City* (1980), a moving, minutely observed character study boasting a superb performance by Burt LANCASTER. The film won several international prizes, including the British Film Academy Award. The director next elicited two delightful performances from two real characters in *My Dinner with Andre* (1981), a remarkably intelligent little film consisting entirely of a dinner conversation between avant-garde theater director Andre Gregory and actor-playwright Wallace SHAWN. Malle closed his American chapter with two disappointing films. His career seemed to be in an irreversible eclipse when he came back triumphantly in 1987 with *Au Revoir les Enfants,* a deeply felt childhood memoir of his traumatic experience at a Catholic boarding school that harbored Jewish children during the Nazi occupation of France. Malle's several international prizes for the film included the Golden Lion at Venice, three Césars (best film, director, and screenplay), the British Film Academy Award for best director, and the European Film Award for best screenplay. His intensely erotic, controlled 1992 film *Damage* offered strong performances from leads Jeremy Irons and Miranda Richardson, but drew only mixed reviews. He was married from 1980 until his death to actress Candice BERGEN.

FEATURE FILMS: *Le Monde du Silence/The Silent World* (doc.; co-dir. with Jacques-Yves Cousteau; also co-phot.) 1956; *Ascenseur pour l'Echafaud/Frantic* (also exec. prod., co-sc.), *Les Amants/The Lovers* (also exec. prod., co-sc.) 1958; *Zazie dans le Métro/Zazie/Zazie in the Underground* (also prod., co-sc.) 1960; *Vie privée/A Very Private Affair* (also co-sc.) 1962; *Le Feu Follet/The Fire Within* (also co-exec. prod., sc.) 1963; *Viva Maria* (also co-prod., so-sc.) 1965; *Le Voleur/The Thief of Paris* (also prod., co-sc.) 1967; *Histories extraordinaires/Spirits of the Dead* ("William Wilson" episode; also sc.) 1968; *Calcutta* (doc.; also prod., sc.), *L'Inde fantôme/Phantom India/L'Inde 68/Louis Malle's India* (six-hour feature presentation of TV doc. series; also prod., sc.) 1969; *Le Souffle au Coeur/Murmur of the Heart* (also prod., sc.) 1971; *Humain trop Humain* (doc.; also prod., sc.) 1972; *Place de la République* (doc.; also prod., co-phot.), *Lacombe Lucien* (also prod., co-sc). 1973; *Black Moon* (also prod., co-sc.) 1975; *Pretty Baby* (also prod., co-story; US) 1978; *Atlantic City* (Can./Fr.) 1981; *My Dinner with Andre* (US) 1981; *Crackers* (US) 1984; *Alamo Bay* (also co-prod.; US), *God's Country* (doc.; orig. for TV; US) 1985; *Au Revoir les Enfants/Goodbye Children* (also co-prod., sc.) 1987; *Milou en Mai/Milou in May/May Fools* (also prod., co-sc.) 1989; *Damage* (US) 1992; *Vanya on 42nd Street* 1994.

Malleson, Miles. Screenwriter, playwright, actor. *b.* William Miles Malleson, May 25, 1888, Croydon, England. *d.* 1969. On the British stage as an actor from 1911 and in films from the early 30s, he also directed many plays and wrote numerous stage plays and screenplays, alone or in collaboration. As an actor in scores of British films, the chubby Malleson typically portrayed jovial characters.

FILMS INCLUDE: As screenwriter—*Perfect Understanding* 1933; *Nell Gwyn* (also act.) 1934; *Peg of Old Drury* 1935; *Rhodes of Africa/Rhodes* (dial. only), *Tudor Rose/Nine Days a Queen* (also act.) 1936; *Victoria the Great* 1937; *Sixty Glorious Years* 1938; *The Thief of Bagdad* (also act., as the Sultan) 1940; *They Flew Alone/Wings and the Woman* (also act.), *The First of the Few/Spitfire* 1942; *The Yellow Canary* 1943. As actor—*The City of Song* 1931; *The Sign of Four* 1932; *Bitter Sweet* 1933; *Knight Without Armor* 1937; *Major Barbara* 1941; *Dead of Night* 1945; *While the Sun Shines* 1947; *Saraband for Dead Lovers/Saraband* 1948; *Kind Hearts and Coronets, The Perfect Woman* 1949; *Stage Fright, Golden Salamander* 1950; *The Man in the White Suit, The Magic Box* 1951; *The Importance of Being Earnest* (as Canon Chasuble), *The Venetian Bird/The Assassin, Folly to Be Wise* 1952; *Trent's Last Case, The Captain's Paradise* 1953; *Geordie/Wee Geordie* 1955; *Private's Progress, Three Men in a Boat* 1956; *Brothers in Law, The Admirable Crichton, The Naked Truth/Your Past Is*

Showing 1957; *Dracula/Horror of Dracula, Gideon's Day/ Gideon of Scotland Yard, The Captain's Table, Bachelor of Hearts* 1958; *The Hound of the Baskervilles, I'm All Right Jack* 1959; *Peeping Tom, The Brides of Dracula* 1960; *The Hellfire Club* 1961; *The Phantom of the Opera* 1962; *Heavens Above!* 1963; *Circus World* (US), *First Men in the Moon, Murder Ahoy* 1964; *You Must Be Joking!* 1965.

Mallory, Boots. Actress. *b.* Patricia Mallory, Oct. 22, 1913, New Orleans. *d.* 1958. A banjo player in a girls' band at age 12 and a vaudeville dancer at 16, she appeared in Broadway musicals before making her screen debut in 1932. In the following few years she played ingenue leads in a number of minor films. Her second husband was producer William Cagney and her third, actor Herbert MARSHALL.

FILMS INCLUDE: *Handle with Care* 1932; *The Wolf Dog* (serial), *Humanity, Hello Sister!, Carnival Lady* 1933; *Sing Sing Nights, Powdersmoke Range* 1935; *Here's Flash Casey* 1938.

Malone, Dorothy. Actress. Born Dorothy Eloise Maloney, on Jan. 30, 1925, in Chicago. The daughter of a telephone company auditor, she modeled as a child and appeared regularly in school plays. At 18 she was spotted by a talent agent while performing in a college play at Southern Methodist University and signed by RKO. She played bits in several of the studio's films, under her real name, and changed her billing to Dorothy Malone when she joined Warners in 1945. Her roles gradually improved, but they consisted mainly of standard pretty girl leads. It wasn't until the mid-50s, more than a decade after her film debut, that she began to emerge as a fine dramatic actress, projecting an erotic blend of strength and vulnerability. She won a supporting actress Oscar in 1956 for her role of a frustrated nymphomaniac in *Written on the Wind.* But like many Oscar winners before her, she found subsequent rewarding roles few and far between. From 1964 to 1969 she starred in the TV series 'Peyton Place.' She had a small part as a murderous lesbian in 1992's *Basic Instinct*. Her first (1959–64) of three husbands was actor Jacques Bergerac.

FILMS: *Gildersleeve on Broadway, The Falcon and the Co-Eds, Higher and Higher* 1943; *Show Business, Seven Days Ashore, Youth Runs Wild, One Mysterious Night* 1944; *Too Young to Know* 1945; *Janie Gets Married, The Big Sleep, Night and Day* 1946; *To the Victor, Two Guys from Texas, One Sunday Afternoon* 1948; *Flaxy Martin, South of St. Louis, Colorado Territory* 1949; *The Nevadan, Convicted, Mrs. O'Malley and Mr. Malone, The Killer That Stalked New York* 1950; *Saddle Legion, The Bushwackers* 1951; *Torpedo Alley, Scared Stiff, Law and Order, Jack Slade* 1953; *Loophole, The Lone Gun, Pushover, Young at Heart, Security Risk, The Fast and the Furious, Private Hell 36* 1954; *Five Guns West, Battle Cry, Tall Man Riding, Sincerely Yours, Artists and Models, At Gunpoint* 1955; *Pillars of the Sky, Tension at Table Rock, Written on the Wind* 1956; *Quantez, Man of a Thousand Faces, Tip on a Dead Jockey* 1957; *The Tarnished Angels, Too Much Too Soon* (as Diana Barrymore) 1958; *Warlock* 1959; *The Last Voyage* 1960; *The Last Sunset* 1961; *Beach Party* 1963; *Fate Is the Hunter* 1964; *Femmine insaziabili/Gli Insaziabili/The Insatiables/ Carnal Circuit* (It./Monaco) 1969; *The Man Who Would Not Die/Target in the Sun, Abduction* 1975; *The November Plan* 1976; *Golden Rendezvous* 1977; *Good Luck Miss Wyckoff, Winter Kills* 1979; *The Day Time Ended* (Sp.) 1980; *The Being* 1983; *Basic Instinct* 1992.

Maltese cross. A mechanism that produces intermittent movement in a motion-picture projector or a camera. Shaped in the form of a Maltese cross, the device is based on the Geneva movement employed in watchmaking. It rotates intermittently when pulled down by the transport mechanism of the projector or camera, bringing each frame into position for exposure.

Maltz, Albert. Screenwriter, playwright, novelist. *b.* Oct. 28, 1908, Brooklyn, N.Y. the son of Jewish immigrants. *d.* 1985. *ed.* Columbia; Yale School of Drama. As a dramatist for the leftist Theatre Union, he wrote several plays, alone or in collaboration, which were presented on the New York stage in the early 30s. He also wrote novels and short stories. In 1941 he settled in Hollywood as a screenwriter. He collaborated on a number of features for Paramount and Warners, including such patriotic WW II films as *Destination Tokyo* (1944) and *Pride of the Marines* (1945). He was nominated for an Oscar for the latter. He also scripted several documentaries, including Academy Award–winner *Moscow Strikes Back* (1942), an American adaptation of the Soviet war propaganda film *The Defeat of the German Armies Near Moscow,* and *The House I Live In* (1944), a documentary on tolerance which won a special Oscar in 1945. In October of 1947, Maltz was one of the HOLLYWOOD TEN who were convicted on charges of contempt of Congress for refusing to testify on their affiliation with the Communist party. He was imprisoned for ten months and blacklisted by the industry after his release from jail. *The Naked City* (1948), Jules Dassin's realistic police drama, was the last film on which Maltz received screen credit until 1970. He lived in Mexico from 1952 to 1962, occasionally collaborating on Hollywood screenplays under pseudonyms. The best known of his several novels was *The Cross and the Arrow* (1944), about the German anti-Nazi resistance movement. Just before his death at 76 of complications from shingles, he defied the effects of a stroke by feverishly completing his last novel, *Bel Canto,* about the French resistance movement.

FILMS INCLUDE: *Afraid to Talk* (co-play basis only, 'Merry-Go-Round') 1932; *Moscow Strikes Back* (doc.; English-language version of Soviet film *The Defeat of the German Armies Near Moscow*), *This Gun for Hire, Casablanca* (uncredited) 1942; *Seeds of Freedom* (doc.) 1943; *Destination Tokyo, The Man in Half Moon Street* (uncredited) 1944; *The House I Live In* (doc.), *Pride of the Marines* 1945; *Cloak and Dagger* 1946; *The Red House* (uncredited) 1947; *The Naked City* 1948; *The Robe* (uncredited) 1953; *Short Cut to Hell* (screenplay basis, unacknowledged, *This Gun for Hire*) 1957; *Two Mules for Sister Sara* 1970; *The Beguiled* (under pseudonym John B. Sherry & Grimes Grice) 1971; *The Possession of Joel Delaney* (under pseudonym Grimes Grice) 1972; *Scalawag* 1973; *Hangup* (under pseudonym John B. Sherry) 1974.

Mamet, David. Playwright, screenwriter, director. Born on Nov. 30, 1947, in Chicago. A graduate of Godard College in Plainfield, Vermont, he remained there through 1973 as artist-in-residence, then returned to Chicago where he founded the St. Nicholas Theatre Company, of which he became the artistic director. He later became associate artistic director of Chicago's Goodman Theatre and a guest lecturer at the University of Chicago, NYU, and the Yale School of Drama. He began writing at the age of 20 when as an actor he started providing fellow performers with dialogue for practice. A produced playwright from 1971, he won Obie Awards for his off-Broadway plays 'Sexual Perversity in Chicago' (1973) and 'American Buffalo' (1976), quickly becoming established as one of America's leading contemporary playwrights. His reputation stretched further in the 80s when he won another Obie for 'Edmond' (1982) and the Pulitzer Prize as well as the New York Drama Critics Circle Award for 'Glengarry Glen Ross' (1984). Earlier in the decade, Mamet had begun gravitating toward the cinema, at first as a screenwriter, then also as a director. He was nominated for an Academy Award for the script of *The Verdict* (1982) and drew superior reviews for his directorial debut, *House of Games* (1987), an intriguing screen drama about the lure of deceit, for which he won the best screenplay prize at Venice. Under his direction, Joe Mantegna and Don Ameche shared best actor honors at Venice for *Things Change* (1988). Notwithstanding his growing involvement with film, Mamet assaulted Hollywood and its ways savagely in his 1988 Tony-winning play, 'Speed-the-Plow.' Formerly married to actress Lindsay CROUSE.

FILMS: *The Postman Always Rings Twice* (sc.) 1981; *The Verdict* (sc.) 1982; *About Last Night. . .* (play basis only, 'Sexual Perversity in Chicago') 1986; *Black Widow* (act.), *The Untouchables* (sc.), *House of Games* (dir., co-story, sc.) 1987; *Things Change* (dir., co-sc.) 1988; *We're No Angels* (sc.) 1989; *Homicide* (dir., sc.) 1991; *Glengarry Glen Ross* (from his play), *Hoffa* (sc., also co-prod.) 1992; *A Life in the Theatre* (sc.), *Rising Sun* (co-sc.) 1993; *Oleanna* (also dir.), *Vanya on 42nd Street* (adapt. sc.) 1994; *American Buffalo* 1996; *The Edge* (sc.) 1997.

Mamoulian, Rouben. Director *b.* Oct. 8, 1898, Tiflis (now Tbilisi), Georgia, Russia, of Armenian descent. *d.* 1987. The son of a bank president, he spent part of his childhood in Paris and later studied criminology at the University of Moscow and trained for the stage at the Moscow Art Theater under Vakhtangov, a disciple of Stanislavsky. In 1918, Mamoulian organized his own drama studio in Tiflis and two years later toured England with the Russian Repertory Theater and remained there to study drama at the University of London. In 1922 he directed his first play in London in the traditional Russian naturalistic style but from then on disavowed realism in favor of a stylized, rhythmic, lyrical impressionism. In 1923 he came to the US and for three years he directed operas and operettas at the George Eastman Theater in Rochester, N.Y. In 1926 he began teaching and producing plays at New York's Theatre Guild and the following year directed on Broadway the Guild's highly successful production of 'Porgy,' the play that would provide the basis for George Gershwin's 1935 opera-musical 'Porgy and Bess,' also under the direction of Mamoulian.

As a result of his growing reputation as an inventive Broadway director, Mamoulian was approached by Paramount to direct the film *Applause* (1929) at the studio's East Coast facilities in Astoria, N.Y. Produced at the dawn of the sound era, *Applause* was amazingly free of the restrictions imposed on other early talkies by primitive recording systems and cameras that were enclosed in soundproof booths. Mamoulian had boldly liberated his camera and allowed it to roam freely, turning a banal sob-story about an aging burlesque queen who sacrifices herself for her daughter into a brilliant exercise in fluid, rhythmic motion.

Mamoulian proved himself equally inventive with his second film, *City Streets* (1931), a gangster story in which he experimented with subjective sound, again achieving striking results with vivid imagery, fluid camera movement, and rhythmic cutting. Mamoulian's third film for Paramount, *Dr. Jekyll and Mr. Hyde* (1932), is considered by many as the best screen adaptation of the Robert Louis Stevenson horror-mystery novella. The film remains famous for its use of the subjective camera, for its marvelous light-and-shadow effects, for its effective on-camera transformation of Fredric March from Dr. Jekyll to Mr. Hyde, for excellent performances by March and Miriam Hopkins, and for its intelligent emphasis on emotion and sexual tension rather than on sheer horror. Mamoulian's inventiveness reached its creative peak with *Love Me Tonight* (1932), a highly original musical screen comedy that he orchestrated skillfully, integrating musical numbers by Rodgers and Hart with a witty, sophisticated script, indulging in stupendous tracking shots and inventive off-camera sound tricks, and even introducing rhyming dialogue.

Mamoulian again demonstrated his skill at directing performers—and especially actresses—with *Song of Songs* (1933), a charming, elegant vehicle for Marlene Dietrich; and *Queen Christina* (1933), a *tour de force* for Greta Garbo.

After extracting another good performance from Samuel Goldwyn's protégée Anna Sten, in *We Live Again* (1934), an adaptation of Tolstoy's *Resurrection,* Mamoulian was invited by MGM to direct Hollywood's first three-color Technicolor feature *Becky Sharp* (1935), from Thackeray's novel *Vanity Fair.* The result was a film distinguished not only for its creative, dramatic use of color but also for its narrative fluidity and fine acting. Some film historians and critics consider *Becky Sharp* Mamoulian's last important screen achievement, but many others disagree and have called for a re-evaluation of the director's underrated works that came later, like the picturesque operettas *The Gay Desperado* (1936) and *High Wide and Handsome* (1937); the elegant Tyrone Power swashbuckler *The Mark of Zorro* (1940); and the pictorially exquisite version of *Blood and Sand* (1941), again starring Power, many images of which were styled after paintings by the likes of Goya, Velasquez, and El Greco. Held in special affection by Mamoulian's admirers are the director's two final films, *Summer Holiday* (1948), an utterly charming musical version of Eugene O'Neill's 'Ah Wilderness!,' and *Silk Stockings* (1957), the vastly underrated poetry-in-motion musical remake of *Ninotchka,* starring Fred Astaire and Cyd Charisse.

Staunchly independent in his ideas of how films should be made, Mamoulian often clashed with the Hollywood studio hierarchy. In 1944 he was removed from the helm of *Laura* and replaced by Otto Preminger. In 1958 he lost the assignment of directing the film version of 'Porgy and Bess,' again to Preminger, and three years later he was fired from the set of *Cleopatra* after completing a ten-minute segment of film.

Throughout his intermittent screen career, Mamoulian continued directing for the theater. Among other plays and musicals he staged were the original Broadway productions of 'A Farewell to Arms' (1930), the previously mentioned 'Porgy and Bess' (1935), 'Oklahoma!' (1943), 'Carousel' (1945), and 'Lost in the Stars' (1949). The film *Never Steal Anything Small* (1959) was based on the play 'The Devil's Hornpipe,' which he wrote in collaboration with Maxwell Anderson. He also collaborated as a writer on the Broadway productions of 'Sadie Thompson' (1944) and 'Arms and the Girl' (1950) and on the adaptation of a number of plays, and authored *Abigayil* (1964), a children's story, and *Hamlet Revised and Interpreted* (1965), a drama textbook.

FILMS: *Applause* 1929; *City Streets* 1931; *Dr. Jekyll and Mr. Hyde* (also prod.), *Love Me Tonight* (also prod.) 1932; *Song of Songs* (also prod.), *Queen Christina* 1933; *We Live Again* 1934; *Becky Sharp* 1935; *The Gay Desperado* 1936; *High Wide and Handsome* 1937; *Golden Boy* 1939; *The Mark of Zorro* 1940; *Blood and Sand* 1941; *Rings on Her Fingers* 1942; *Summer Holiday* 1948; *Silk Stockings* 1957.

Mancini, Henry. Composer, songwriter, arranger. *b.* Apr. 16, 1924, in Cleveland. *d.* 1994. *ed.* Carnegie Tech Music School; Juilliard. Formerly a pianist with dance bands, he joined Universal Pictures as a staff composer in 1951 and before long demonstrated his considerable skills as a music arranger and songwriter with *The Glenn Miller Story* (1954), an effort that earned him the first of many Academy Award nominations. He subsequently composed memorable scores and songs for numerous films. But it was his pulsating theme music for the TV series 'Peter Gunn' (1959), followed by the score for 'Mr. Lucky' (1960), that provided the breakthrough for his tremendous success. He remained a close collaborator of the creator of these series, Blake EDWARDS. Mancini's colorful style integrates well with movie action, and works best with suspenseful or satirical themes. He won Academy Awards for the score of *Breakfast at Tiffany's* (1961) and the song 'Moon River'; the title song of *Days of Wine and Roses* (1962); and the score of *Victor/Victoria* (1982). He has won over 20 Grammy Awards.

FILMS INCLUDE (music scores): *The Glenn Miller Story* (arr., love theme only) 1954; *Six Bridges to Cross* (title song only), *The Benny Goodman Story* (arr., addnl. mus. only) 1956; *Man Afraid* 1957; *Touch of Evil* 1958; *High Time* 1960; *The Great Impostor, Breakfast at Tiffany's, The Second Time Around* (title song only) 1961; *Experiment in Terror, Hatari!* 1962; *Days of Wine and Roses, Charade* 1963; *The Pink Panther, A Shot in the Dark* 1964; *The Great Race* 1965; *Arabesque* 1966; *Two for the Road, Gunn, Wait Until Dark* 1967; *The Party* 1968; *I Girasoli/Sunflower* (It.), *Gaily Gaily* 1969; *The Molly Maguires, The Hawaiians, Darling Lili* 1970; *Sometimes a Great Notion/Never Give an Inch, The Night Visitor* 1971; *Oklahoma Crude, Visions of Eight* 1973; *That's Entertainment* (addnl. mus.), *The White Dawn, The Girl from Petrovka* 1974; *The Return of the Pink Panther, Once Is Not Enough* 1975; *W. C. Fields and Me, Alex and the Gypsy, Silver Streak, The Pink Panther Strikes Again* 1976; *House Calls, Revenge of the Pink Panther, Who Is Killing the Great Chefs of Europe?* 1978; *The Prisoner of Zenda, 10* 1979; *Little Miss Marker, A Change of Seasons* 1980; *Back Roads, S.O.B., Mommie Dearest* 1981; *Victor/Victoria, Trail of the Pink Panther* 1982; *Curse of the Pink Panther, The Man Who Loved Women* 1983; *Harry and Son* 1984; *That's Dancing!, Santa Claus: The Movie* 1985; *The Great Mouse Detective, A Fine Mess, That's Life!* 1986; *Blind Date, The Glass Menagerie* 1987; *Sunset, Heavy Petting* (doc.), *Without a Clue* 1988; *Physical Evidence* 1989; *Ghost Dad* 1990; *Switch* 1991.

Mancuso, Frank. Executive. Born on July 25, 1933, in Buffalo, N.Y. *ed.* SUNY. A former film buyer for a theater chain, he joined Paramount as a local booker in 1962 and gradually rose through the ranks to become the studio's chairman and chief executive officer in 1984, a post he resigned in 1991. His son, Frank Mancuso, Jr. (*b.* Oct. 9, 1958, Buffalo), is a film producer and is now associated with MGM/UA.

Mandel, Babaloo. American screenwriter, usually in collaboration with Lowell GANZ, with whom he shared an Academy Award nomination for *Splash* (1984). He is a father of six.

FILMS: *Night Shift* 1982; *Splash* 1984; *Spies Like Us* 1985; *Gung Ho* 1986; *Vibes* 1988; *Parenthood* 1989; *City Slickers* 1991; *A League of Their Own, Mr. Saturday Night* (also act.) 1992; *Greedy* 1994; *City Slickers II: The Legend of Curly's Gold, Forget Paris* 1995; *Multiplicity* 1996; *Father's Day* 1997.

Mandel, Johnny. Composer. Born John Alfred Mandel, on Nov. 23, 1925, New York City. *ed.* N.Y. Military Academy; Manhattan School of Music; Juilliard. He started out as a trumpeter and trombonist with various bands and orchestras, including those of Jimmy Dorsey, Buddy Rich, and Count Basie. In the late 40s, he emerged as a brilliant arranger of jazz music for Artie Shaw and others, working with increasing frequency in TV. He began composing for films in the late 50s, and won an Academy Award for the song 'The Shadow of Your Smile' in *The Sandpiper* (1965).

FILMS INCLUDE: *You're Never Too Young* (arr. only) 1955; *I Want to Live!* 1958; *The Third Voice* 1960; *The Americanization of Emily* 1964; *The Sandpiper* 1965; *An American Dream, Harper, The Russians Are Coming the Russians Are Coming* 1966; *Point Blank* 1967; *Pretty Poison* 1968; *That Cold Day in August* 1969; *M*A*S*H* 1970; *Journey Through Rosebud* 1972; *The Last Detail, Summer Wishes, Winter Dreams* 1973; *Escape to Witch Mountain* 1975; *The Sailor Who Fell from Grace with the Sea, Freaky Friday* 1976; *Agatha, Being There* 1979; *The Baltimore Bullet, Caddyshack* 1980; *Deathtrap, The Verdict* 1982; *Staying Alive* 1983; *Brenda Starr* 1989.

Mandell, Robert. American director. A graduate of Columbia, he trained at the American Film Institute's Los Angeles facility before turning out his first feature in the early 80s. He scored a success with the inventive action film, *F/X* (1986).

FILMS: *Independence Day* 1983; *F/X, Touch and Go* 1986; *Big Shots* 1987; *Perfect Witness* (cable TV movie) 1989; *The Haunted* 1991; *School Ties* 1992; *The Substitute* 1996.

Mandell, Daniel. Film editor. *b.* 1895, New York City. *d.* 1987. A cutting-room veteran of Hollywood's silent days, he edited many major productions, particularly for Sam GOLDWYN and later for Billy WILDER, winning Academy Awards for *Pride of the Yankees* (1942), *The Best Years of Our Lives* (1946), and *The Apartment* (1960).

FILMS INCLUDE: *The Turmoil* 1924; *Uncle Tom's Cabin* 1927; *Show Boat* 1929; *Holiday* 1930; *The Animal Kingdom* 1932; *Counsellor-at-Law* 1933; *Diamond Jim* 1935; *These Three, Dodsworth* 1936; *You Only Live Once, Dead End* 1937; *Wuthering Heights, The Real Glory* 1939; *The Westerner* 1940; *The Little Foxes, Meet John Doe* 1941; *Pride of the Yankees* 1942; *The North Star, They Got Me Covered* 1943; *Arsenic and Old Lace, The Princess and the Pirate, Up in Arms* 1944; *Wonder Man* 1945; *The Kid from Brooklyn, The Best Years of Our Lives* 1946; *A Song Is Born* 1948; *Roseanna McCoy, My Foolish Heart* 1949; *Edge of Doom* 1950; *I Want You* 1951; *Hans Christian Andersen* 1952; *Guys and Dolls* 1955; *Witness for the Prosecution* 1957; *Porgy and Bess* 1959; *The Apartment* 1960; *One Two Three* 1961; *Irma la Douce* 1963; *Kiss Me Stupid* 1964; *The Fortune Cookie* 1966; *One-Trick Pony* 1980.

Mander, Miles. Actor, director, screenwriter. *b.* Lionel Mander, May 14, 1888, Wolverhampton, England. *d.* 1946. Originally a farmer, then a novelist, playwright, and film exhibitor, he entered British films in 1918, playing an assortment of character parts, often as an unscrupulous type, initially under the pseudonym Luther Miles. Later he also directed several films and wrote a number of screenplays. In 1935 he went to Hollywood, where he played many character parts for Fox, Universal, and other studios until his death of a heart attack at 57.

FILMS INCLUDE (as actor): In the UK—*Once Upon a Time* 1918; *Testimony, The Old Arm Chair* 1920; *The Road to London* 1921; *Half a Truth* 1922; *Lovers in Araby* (also sc.) 1924; *The Pleasure Garden* 1926; *The Fake* 1927; *The Physician, Women of Paris/The Doctor's Women* (Sw.), *The First Born* (also prod., dir., co-sc., from own novel and play) 1928; *The Crooked Billet* 1929; *Balaclava/Jaws of Hell, Loose Ends, Murder* 1930; *The Woman Between* (dir., sc. only), *Fascination* (dir. only) 1931; *The Missing Rembrandt, The Lodger/Phantom Fiend* (co-sc. only) 1932; *Bitter Sweet, Loyalties, The Private Life of Henry VIII, Don Quixote* (as the Duke in English-Language version of Pabst's *Don Quichotte*) 1933; *The Battle, Youthful Folly* (dir. only) 1934; *The Morals of Marcus* (dir., co-sc. only) 1935. In the US—*Here's to Romance, The Three Musketeers* (as King Louis XIII) 1935; *The Flying Doctor* (dir. only; UK), *Lloyds of London* 1936; *Wake Up and Live, Slave Ship* 1937; *Kidnapped* (as Ebenezer Balfour), *Suez* (as Benjamin Disraeli) 1938; *The Three Musketeers* (Ritz Brothers version, as Cardinal Richelieu), *The Little Princess, Wuthering Heights* (as Mr. Lockwood), *The Man in the Iron*

Mask (as Aramis of the Three Musketeers), *Stanley and Livingstone, Tower of London* (as Henry VI) 1939; *Primrose Path, Road to Singapore* 1940; *That Hamilton Woman* 1941; *To Be or Not to Be, This Above All* 1942; *Five Graves to Cairo, The Phantom of the Opera, Guadalcanal Diary, The Return of the Vampire* 1943; *The Scarlet Claw, Pearl of Death, Murder My Sweet/Farewell My Lovely* 1944; *The Picture of Dorian Gray, Confidential Agent* 1945; *Imperfect Lady* 1947.

M and E tracks. Sound tracks carrying music (M) and sound effects (E) but not dialogue. They are used in dubbing and are of particular value in preparing films for international distribution. Since the dialogue is recorded on a separate track, it can be replaced by a foreign language while keeping the original music and sound effects intact.

Manès, Gina. Actress. Born on Apr. 7, 1895, in Paris. Popular femme fatale of French and Continental films of the 20s, she was noted for her strong screen presence. At her best in the leading role of Feyder's *Du sollst nicht Ehe brechen/Thérèse Raquin* (1928). She continued appearing in films through the mid-60s, mostly in character roles. After retiring from the screen, she ran a restaurant and acting school in Morocco.

FILMS INCLUDE: *L'Homme sans Visage* 1919; *L'Auberge rouge, Coeur fidèle* 1923; *Ames d'Artistes* 1925; *Le Train sans Yeux* 1926; *Napoléon* (as Josephine) 1927; *Synd/Sin* (Sw.), *Du sollst nicht Ehe brechen/Thérèse Raquin* (title role; Ger.), *Looping the Loop* (Ger.) 1928; *Nuits de Princes* 1930; *Salto Mortale* (Ger.) 1931; *La Tête d'un Homme* 1933; *Barcarole* (Ger.), *Divine* 1935; *Mayerling* 1936; *Mollenard/Hatred, Nostalgie/The Postmaster's Daughter* 1938; *Marchandes d'Illusions/Nights of Shame* 1954; *La Loi des Rues* 1956; *Rafles sur la Ville* 1958; *Les Amants de Demain* 1959; *Pas de Panique* 1965.

Manfredi, Nino. Actor, occasional director, screenwriter. Born Nino Saturnino, on Mar. 22, 1921, in Castro dei Volsci, Italy. Switching from law studies to drama, he began his acting career on radio and in stage revues and after WW II established his reputation as a solid dramatic player on the legitimate stage. His first work in films was in dubbing voices of other actors, a common practice in the Italian industry. He made his on-screen debut in 1949 and in the next three decades turned in many fine film performances, in both comic and dramatic leading and supporting roles. He took his first stab at directing with an episode in the Italo-German co-production *L'Amore difficile/Erotica/Of Wayward Love* (1962), in which he also starred. He won the "best first film" prize at the Cannes Festival in 1971 for his initial solo effort as a feature director, *Per Grazia Ricevuta*.

FILMS INCLUDE (as actor): *Monastero di Santa Chiara* 1949; *Anema e Core* 1951; *Viva il Cinema!* 1953; *Gli Innamorati, Guardia Guardia scelta Brigadiere e Maresciallo* 1956; *Femmine Tre Volte* 1957; *Camping* (also co-sc.), *Caporale di Giornata, Guardia Ladro e Cameriera, Venezia la Luna e tu* 1958; *Camela è una Bambola, Audace Colpo dei Soliti Ignoti/Fiasco in Milan* 1959; *L'Impiegato, Le Pillole d'Ercole* (also co-sc.), *Crimen/. . . And Suddenly It's Murder!* 1960; *Il Carabiniere a Cavallo, Il Giudizio universale, A Cavallo della Tigre* 1961; *Anni Ruggenti, L'Amore difficile/Erotica/Of Wayward Love* ("The Soldier" episode; also dir., co-sc.), *La Parmigiana* 1962; *Alta Infedeltà/High Infidelity, El Verdugo/La Ballata del Boia/Not on Your Life* (Sp./It.), *Il Gaucho, Controsesso* 1964; *Le Bambole/The Dolls, Questa Volta parliamo di Uomini/Let's Talk About Men, Io Io Io. . . e gli Altri, Made in Italy* 1965; *Thrilling, Adulterio all'Italiana, Operazione San Gennaro/Treasure of San Gennaro* 1966; *Una Rosa per Tutti/A Rose for Everyone/Every Man's Woman* 1967; *Il Padre di Famiglia/The Head of the Family, Italian Secret Service* 1968; *Vedo Nudo* 1969; *Nell'Anno del Signore, Rosolino Paternò—Soldato, Contestazione Generale* 1970; *Per Grazia Ricevuta* (also dir., story, co-sc.), *Trastevere, Roma Bene* 1971; *Girolimoni—Il Mostri di Roma* 1972; *Pane e Cioccolata/Bread and Chocolate* 1973; *C'eravamo tanto Amati/We All Loved Each Other So Much, Attenti al Buffone* 1975; *Brutti Sporchi e Cattivi/Down and Dirty, Signore e Signori—Buonanotte* 1976; *Il Conte di Monte Cristo, Quelle Strane Occasioni, I Nuovi Mostri/Viva Italia!* 1977; *In Nome del Papa Re, La Mazzetta* 1978; *Il Giocattolo* (also co-sc.) 1979; *Café Express* (also co-sc.) 1980; *Nudo di donna* (also dir., co-sc.) 1981; *Spaghetti House* (also co-sc.), *Testa o Croce* (also co-sc.) 1982; *Questo e quello* (also co-sc.) 1983; *Grandi Magazini* 1985; *Il Tenente dei Carbinieri* 1986; *I Picari* 1987; *Alberto Express* (Can./Fr./It.) 1990; *Mima* 1991.

Mangano, Silvana. Actress. *b.* Apr. 21, 1930, Rome *d.* 1989. Leading star of Italian and international films. One of four children of a Sicilian railroad worker and an Englishwoman, she trained as a dancer, did some modeling, and entered Italian films as an extra after winning a beauty contest as Miss Rome. She played minor supporting roles in a couple of postwar films, then gained sudden worldwide popularity as the voluptuous star of Giuseppe De Santis's socio-erotic drama *Riso Amaro/Bitter Rice* (1949). She married the film's producer, Dino DE LAURENTIIS, and subsequently played lead roles in many other films. Although she continued to be assigned to meaty roles, continually improving as an actress, she was soon overshadowed by two other international stars of the Italian screen, Gina Lollobrigida and Sophia Loren. Miss Mangano went into seclusion for several years following the death of her son, Federico, a film producer, in a 1981 plane crash. But she later returned occasionally to the screen. One of her three daughters is producer Raffaella De Laurentiis. Miss Mangano separated from her husband in 1983 and began divorce proceedings in 1988, just a year before her death at 59 of a heart attack and cerebral hemorrhage while recovering from surgery for a tumor between her lungs. She had been suffering from cancer for several years.

FILMS: *Elisir d'Amore/This Wine of Love* 1946; *Il Delitto di Giovanni Episcopo/Flesh Will Surrender* 1947; *Gli Uomini sono Nemici* 1948; *Black Magic/Cagliostro* (US, filmed in Italy), *Riso Amaro/Bitter Rice, Il Lupo della Sila/Lure of the Sila* 1949; *Il Brigante Musolino* 1950; *Anna* 1951; *Mambo, L'Oro di Napoli/Gold of Naples, Ulisse/Ulysses* (in dual role, as Penelope and Circe) 1954; *Uomini e Lupi* 1956; *La Diga sul Pacifico/This Angry Age/The Sea Wall, La Tempesta/Tempest* 1958; *La Grande Guerra/The Great War* 1959; *Jovanka e l'Altri/Five Branded Women, Crimen/. . . And Suddenly It's Murder* 1960; *Il Guidizio Universale, Barabba/Barabbas, Una Vita difficile/A Difficult Life* 1961; *Il Processo di Verona* 1962; *La Mia Signora* 1964; *Il Disco Volante* 1965; *Io Io Io. . . e gli altri* 1966; *Scusi lei e' favorevole o contrario?, Le Streghe/The Witches, Edipo Re/Oedipus Rex* (as Jocasta) 1967; *Capriccio al'Italiana, Teorema* 1968; *Scipione detto anche l'Africano, Morte a Venezia/Death in Venice, Il Decameron/The Decameron* 1971; *Lo Scopone scientifico/The Scientific Cardplayer, D'Amore si muore, Ludwig/Ludwig II* 1972; *Gruppo di Famiglia in un interno/Conversation Piece* 1975; *Dune* (US) 1984; *Oci Ciornie* 1987.

Mankiewicz, Herman J. Screenwriter. *b.* Nov. 7, 1897, New York City, to assimilated German-Jewish immigrants. *d.* 1953. He began his writing career as a reporter for the *New York Tribune* after graduating from Columbia University. Following WW I service in Europe, he remained in Paris as head of the American Red Cross News Service, then moved to Berlin, where he pursued graduate studies at the university while serving for two years as a correspondent for the *Chicago Tribune.* Returning to New York, he joined the editorial staff of *The World,* then became an assistant drama editor at the *New York Times* under George S. Kaufman and the first drama editor of the *New Yorker* magazine. Mankiewicz went to Hollywood in 1926 to write a screen story for Lon Chaney and remained with the studio for several years as a prolific title, dialogue, and script writer, for a while pursuing a parallel career as a drama critic for the *Los Angeles Times.* He later moved over to MGM. Many of his contributions as a producer and writer during the early sound era went uncredited. Among those were *Laughter* (1930), *Monkey Business* (1931), *Horse Feathers, Million Dollar Legs* (both 1932), and *Duck Soup* (1933). He also had an unacknowledged hand in the scripts of several films of the late 30s, including *The Wizard of Oz* (1939). Mankiewicz's supreme achievement was the screenplay for *Citizen Kane* (1941), for which he shared an Academy Award with Orson WELLES. He shared another Oscar nomination for *Pride of the Yankees* (1942). But severe personal problems—enormous gambling debts, a desperate drinking habit, and frequent spats with studio executives—combined to undermine the remainder of his Hollywood career. He was the older brother of director Joseph L. MANKIEWICZ and father of novelist-screenwriter Don M. Mankiewicz (*b.* Jan 22, 1920, Berlin) and syndicated columnist and radio and TV commentator Frank Mankiewicz (*b.* May 16, 1924, New York City), who was press secretary to Robert F. Kennedy and political director of George McGovern's 1972 presidential campaign.

FILMS INCLUDE: *The Road to Mandalay* (co-story), *Stranded in Paris* (co-adapt.) 1926; *Fashions for Women* (co-adapt.), *A Gentleman of Paris* (titles), *The City Gone Wild* (titles), *The Gay Defender* (co-titles) 1927; *Gentlemen Prefer Blondes* (co-titles), *The Last Command* (titles), *A Night of Mystery* (titles), *Abie's Irish Rose* (co-sc.), *The Dragnet* (titles), *The Magnificent Flirt* (titles), *The Mating Call* (titles), *Avalanche* (co-sc.) 1928; *The Dummy* (sc., dial.), *The Canary Murder Case* (titles), *The Man I Love* (story, dial.), *Thunderbolt* (dial.) 1929; *The Vagabond King* (sc., dial.), *Honey* (sc., dial), *Ladies Love Brutes* (co-sc., co-dial.) 1930; *The Royal Family of Broadway* (co-sc.), *Ladies' Man* (sc., dial.) 1931; *Dancers in the Dark* (co-sc.), *Girl Crazy* (co-sc., co-dial.), *The Lost Squadron* 1932; *Dinner at Eight* (co-sc.), *Another Language* (co-sc.) 1933; *Stamboul Quest* (sc.), *The Show-Off* (sc.) 1934; *Escapade* (sc.), *After Office Hours* (sc.) 1935; *My Dear Miss Aldrich* (story, sc.) 1937; *It's a Wonderful World* (co-story) 1939; *Citizen Kane* (co-story, co-sc.), *Rise and Shine* (sc.) 1941; *The Pride of the Yankees* (co-sc.) 1942; *Stand By for Action* (co-sc.) 1943; *Christmas Holiday* (sc.) 1944; *The Enchanted Cottage* (co-sc.), *The Spanish Main* (co-sc.) 1945; *A Woman's Secret* (sc., prod.) 1949; *The Pride of St. Louis* (sc.) 1952.

Mankiewicz, Joseph L(eo). Director, producer, screenwriter. *b.* Feb. 11, 1909, in Wilkes-Barre, Pa. *d.* 1993. *ed.* Columbia. The younger brother of Herman J. MANKIEWICZ, he too began his working career in Berlin as an assistant correspondent for the Chicago *Tribune.* While there, he made his first contact with films as a translator into English of titles for UFA silents headed for distribution in the US and UK. Returning to the US, he joined his brother in Hollywood and began writing titles, dialogue, and screenplays for Paramount films in 1929. In that year he played a reporter in *Woman Trap.* In 1936 he assumed the responsibilities of a producer, initially with Paramount, then with Fox, but a full decade passed before he got his first opportunity to direct. Once given that opportunity, however, as a last-minute replacement for an ailing Ernst Lubitsch on *Dragonwyck* (1946), he proved to be one of Hollywood's most intelligent and literate directors. His early films suffered from dramatic construction that derived its syntax from the theater rather than from the language of cinema, and although his cinematic technique gradually improved, his films on the whole remained overly talkative affairs. But he made up for his pedestrian visual style and rather sluggish pace with intelligent scripts and witty, often sarcastic, dialogue and directed the dialogue admirably, extracting splendid performances from his actors. He won an Oscar as best director and another for best screenplay for his work on *A Letter to Three Wives* (1949). The film was nominated for a best picture Oscar. The next year he again won the best director Academy Award as well as the best screenplay for *All About Eve* (1950). The film was named best picture, also earning an Oscar for George Sanders as best supporting actor and Oscar nominations for Bette Davis, Anne Baxter, and Celeste Holm. Mankiewicz's adaptation of *Julius Caesar* (1953) is considered by many one of the most successful transformations to the screen of a Shakespearean play, but his treatment of *Cleopatra* (1963), the direction of which he took over from Rouben Mamoulian, was a monumental disaster. In 1986 he was honored with the Directors Guild's D. W. Griffith Award for Lifetime Achievement and in the following year he was awarded a Golden Lion for lifetime achievement at the Venice Film Festival. In a special 1991 tribute to Mankiewicz by the Motion Picture Academy, actor Michael Caine called him "the most civilized man I ever met in the cinema." His son is screenwriter-director Tom MANKIEWICZ.

FILMS: As screenwriter (alone or in collaboration)—*The Dummy* (titles only), *Close Harmony* (titles only), *The Studio Murder Mystery* (titles only), *The Man I Love* (titles only), *Thunderbolt* (titles only), *River of Romance* (titles only), *The Mysterious Dr. Fu Manchu* (titles only), *Fast Company* (dial. only), *The Saturday Night Kid* (titles only) 1929; *Slightly Scarlet, Paramount on Parade* (uncredited), *The Social Lion* (adapt., dial. only), *The Sap from Syracuse* (uncredited), *Only Saps Work* 1930; *The Gang Buster* (dial. only), *Finn and Hattie* (dial. only), *June Moon, Skippy, Dude Ranch* (uncredited), *Touchdown* (uncredited), *Sooky* 1931; *This Reckless Age, Sky Bride, Million Dollar Legs, If I Had a Million* 1932; *Diplomaniacs, Emergency Call, Too Much Harmony, Alice in Wonderland* 1933; *Manhattan Melodrama, Our Daily Bread, Forsaking All Others* 1934; *I Live My Life* 1935. As producer—*The Three Godfathers, Fury, The Gorgeous Hussy, Love on the Run* 1936; *The Bride Wore Red, Double Wedding* 1937; *Mannequin, Three Comrades, The Shopworn Angel, The Shining Hour, A Christmas Carol* 1938; *The Adventures of Huckleberry Finn* 1939; *Strange Cargo, The Philadelphia Story* 1940; *The Wild Man of Borneo, The Feminine Touch* 1941; *Woman of the Year, Reunion in France* 1942; *The Keys of the Kingdom* (also co-sc.) 1945. As director—*Dragonwyck* (also sc.), *Somewhere in the Night* (also co-sc.) 1946; *The Late George Apley, The Ghost and Mrs. Muir* 1947; *Escape* 1948; *A Letter to Three Wives* (also sc.), *House of Strangers* 1949; *No Way Out* (also co-sc.), *All About Eve* (also sc.) 1950; *People Will Talk* (also sc.) 1951; *Five Fingers* 1952; *Julius Caesar* (also sc.) 1953; *The Barefoot Contessa* (also exec. prod., sc.) 1954; *Guys and Dolls* (also sc.) 1955; *The Quiet American* (also prod., sc.) 1958; *Suddenly Last Summer* 1959; *Cleopatra* (also co-sc.; US/UK) 1963; *The Honey Pot/It Comes Up Murder* (also co-prod., sc.; US/UK/It.) 1967; *King: A Filmed Record. . . Montgomery to Memphis* (doc.; co-dir. with Sidney Lumet), *There Was a Crooked Man* (also prod.) 1970; *Sleuth* (UK) 1972.

Mankiewicz, Tom. Screenwriter, director. Born on June 1, 1942, in Los Angeles. The son of director-producer-writer Joseph L. MANKIEWICZ and nephew of screenwriter Herman J.

MANKIEWICZ, he was educated at the Exeter Academy and Yale, entered the film industry as a production associate on *The Best Man* (1964), and began writing for the screen in the late 60s. Having gained directorial experience in the TV series 'Hart to Hart,' he made his debut as a feature director in 1987. He has specialized in action-adventure films.

FILMS: *The Best Man* (prod. assoc.) 1964; *The Sweet Ride* (sc.) 1968; *Diamonds Are Forever* (co-sc.) 1971; *Live and Let Die* (sc.) 1973; *The Man with the Golden Gun* (co-sc.) 1974; *Mother, Jugs & Speed* (sc.) 1976; *The Eagle Has Landed* (sc.), *The Cassandra Crossing* (co-sc.) 1977; *Superman* (creative consultant) 1978; *Superman II* (creative cons.) 1980; *Ladyhawke* (co-sc.) 1985; *Hot Pursuit* (co-exec. prod.), *Dragnet* (dir., co-sc.) 1987; *Delirious* (dir.) 1991.

Mankowitz, Wolf. Novelist, playwright, screenwriter. Born on Nov. 7, 1924, in London. *ed.* Downing Coll. (B.A.); Cambridge (M.A.). Formerly a journalist, he has written novels, plays, short stories, and reference works on pottery and porcelain, as well as screenplays for many British films, alone or in collaboration.

FILMS INCLUDE: *Make Me an Offer* (novel and musical play basis, plus addnl. dial.) 1954; *A Kid for Two Farthings* (from own novel), *The Bespoke Overcoat* (short) 1955; *Expresso Bongo* (from own play) 1959; *The Two Faces of Dr. Jekyll, The Millionairess* 1960; *The Long and the Short and the Tall/Jungle Fighters, The Day the Earth Caught Fire* 1961; *Waltz of the Toreadors* 1962; *Where the Spies Are* 1966; *La 25e Heure/The 25th Hour* (Fr./It./Yug.), *Casino Royale* 1967; *Black Beauty, Bloomfield/The Hero* (Isr./UK; also co-prod.) 1971; *Treasure Island* (co-sc. with Orson Welles; UK/Fr./Ger./Sp.) 1972; *The Hireling* 1973; *Almonds and Raisins* (compilation film) 1983.

Mann, Abby. Screenwriter. Born Abraham Goodman, in 1927, in Philadelphia. *ed.* Temple U.; NYU. He made his name on TV as the author of dramas for such distinguished anthology programs as 'Studio One,' 'Alcoa Goodyear Theater,' and 'Playhouse 90.' Two of his early film scripts were based on his own successful TV plays. He won the Academy Award for his screenplay for *Judgment at Nuremberg* (1961) and was nominated for another for *Ship of Fools* (1965). He created the TV series 'Kojak' (1973–78) and shared an Emmy Award as co-executive producer and co-writer of the cable TV movie, *Murderers Among US: The Simon Wiesenthal Story* (1989).

FILMS: *Judgment at Nuremberg* (from own TV play) 1961; *I Sequestrati di Altona/The Condemned of Altona* (It./Fr.) 1962; *A Child Is Waiting* (from own TV play) 1963; *Ship of Fools* 1965; *The Detective* 1968; *Report to the Commissioner* 1975; *War and Love* 1985.

Mann, Anthony. Director. *b.* Emil Anton Bundmann, June 30, 1906, Port Loma, near San Diego. *d.* 1967. The son of philosophy teachers, he showed an early aptitude for acting and began performing as a child in San Diego, then in New York, where the family moved around 1917. He quit high school in 1923, following his father's death, to work a night shift at Westinghouse, while spending his days trying to line up acting assignments. Before long he was playing bits, then increasingly larger roles in off-Broadway and Broadway productions. He began directing for the stage in the early 30s and was still billed under his real name in 1938, the year he left Broadway to join the Selznick company as a casting director, talent scout, and supervisor of screen tests. The following year he moved over to Paramount as an assistant director and worked in that capacity on Preston Sturges's *Sullivan's Travels* (1941), among other films. By now known as Anthony Mann, he began directing low-to-medium-budget films for such studios as RKO and Republic in 1942. His first major production was Universal's *Winchester '73* (1950), a Western starring James Stewart, which had been originally assigned to Fritz Lang. The Western remained Mann's primary and most effective genre, although he tackled other films from time to time, and James Stewart remained his favorite star. Mann brought to his best films—among them *Bend of the River* (1952), *The Naked Spur* (1953), *The Far Country* and *The Man from Laramie* (both 1955), and *Man of the West* (1958)—meticulous craftsmanship, a keen eye for spectacular outdoor cinematography, and an instinctive sense for the visual expression of inner conflict. Mann risked his solid niche as a Western specialist in the early 60s, when he abandoned the genre in favor of huge-budget epic spectacles. But he scored strongly with *El Cid* (1961), a historical saga of 11th-century Spain, and *The Fall of the Roman Empire* (1964), an intelligent eye-filling toga spectacle. He died of a heart attack on location in Berlin during the production of *A Dandy in Aspic*. The film was completed by its star, Laurence HARVEY, and released posthumously in 1968. In 1957 Mann married Spanish actress-singing star Sarita MONTIEL. The marriage, his second of three, was annulled in 1963.

FILMS: *Dr. Broadway, Moonlight in Havana* 1942; *Nobody's Darling* 1943; *My Best Gal, Strangers in the Night* 1944; *The Great Flamarion, Two O'Clock Courage, Sing Your Way Home* 1945; *Strange Impersonation, The Bamboo Blonde* 1946; *Desperate* (also co-story), *Railroaded* 1947; *T-Men, Raw Deal* 1948; *Follow Me Quietly* (co-story only), *Reign of Terror/The Black Book, Border Incident* 1949; *Side Street, Winchester '73, The Furies, Devil's Doorway* 1950; *The Tall Target* 1951; *Bend of the River* 1952; *The Naked Spur, Thunder Bay* 1953; *The Glenn Miller Story* 1954; *The Far Country, Strategic Air Command, The Man from Laramie, The Last Frontier* 1955; *Serenade* 1956; *Men in War, The Tin Star* 1957; *God's Little Acre, Man of the West* 1958; *Cimarron* 1960; *El Cid* (US/It.) 1961; *The Fall of the Roman Empire* 1964; *The Heroes of Telemark* (UK) 1965; *A Dandy in Aspic* (also prod.; Mann died during production; film completed by Laurence Harvey; UK) 1968.

Mann, Daniel. Director. *b.* Daniel Chugerman, Aug. 8, 1912, in Brooklyn, N.Y. *d.* 1991. *ed.* Erasmus Hall, Brooklyn; Professional Children's School. A former musician, actor, and stage and TV director, he brought to the screen a number of worthy dramas, but his theatrical background is much too evident in most of his films. His early pictures, in particular, were stagy and static and lacked visual excitement. He was successful, however, in eliciting strong performances from his players, especially actresses, three of whom—Shirley Booth (in *Come Back, Little Sheba*), Anna Magnani (in *The Rose Tattoo*), and Elizabeth Taylor (in *Butterfield 8*)—won Oscars for their roles in his films. His later pictures, particularly *Our Man Flint* (1966), show greater mastery of film technique but less discrimination in the choice of material. He directed a number of TV movies in the 80s, including the outstanding concentration camp drama, *Playing for Time* (1980).

FILMS: *Come Back Little Sheba* 1952; *About Mrs. Leslie* 1954; *The Rose Tattoo, I'll Cry Tomorrow* 1955; *The Teahouse of the August Moon* 1956; *Hot Spell* 1958; *The Last Angry Man* 1959; *The Mountain Road, Butterfield 8* 1960; *Ada* 1961; *Five Finger Exercise, Who's Got the Action?* 1962; *Who's Been Sleeping in My Bed?* 1963; *Judith, Our Man Flint* 1966; *For Love of Ivy* 1968; *A Dream of Kings* 1969; *Willard* 1971; *The Revengers* 1972; *Interval, Maurie* 1973; *Lost in the Stars* 1974; *Journey Into Fear* (UK) 1975; *Matilda* 1978.

Mann, Delbert. Director. Born on Jan. 30, 1920, in Lawrence, Kans. *ed.* Vanderbilt; Yale School of Drama. A former shoe salesman, WW II bomber pilot, and stage director, he earned a reputation in the early 50s as one of the premier directors of TV drama. He was particularly successful with two Paddy Chayefsky teleplays, 'Marty' and 'The Bachelor Party,' which he later turned into his first two features as film director. He won an Academy Award and the Palme d'Or at the Cannes Festival for the film version of *Marty* (1955), his very first feature. Much like Daniel MANN (no relation), he brought to the screen some worthy subjects, early in his career, which were beautifully acted but lacked cinematic spark. In the 60s he demonstrated a more dynamic film style at the expense of dramatic content by turning to romantic comedies and occasional adventure yarns. From the late 60s through the late 80s, he directed numerous TV movies, including adaptations from classics like *Heidi* (1968), *David Copperfield* (1970), *Jane Eyre* (1971), *The Man Without a Country* (1973), and *All Quiet on the Western Front* (1979).

FILMS: *Marty* 1955; *The Bachelor Party* 1957; *Desire Under the Elms, Separate Tables* 1958; *Middle of the Night* 1959; *The Dark at the Top of the Stairs* 1960; *Lover Come Back, The Outsider* 1961; *That Touch of Mink* 1962; *A Gathering of Eagles* 1963; *Dear Heart* 1964; *Quick Before It Melts* (also co-prod.) 1965; *Mister Buddwing* (also co-prod.) 1966; *Fitzwilly* 1967; *The Pink Jungle* 1968; *Kidnapped* 1971; *Birch Interval* 1976; *Night Crossing* 1982; *Brontë* 1983.

Mann, Hank. Actor. *b.* David W. Lieberman, 1888, New York City. *d.* 1971. A flying trapeze acrobat, he joined Mack Sennett at Keystone in 1912 and soon became a notorious scene stealer in the Keystone Kops comedies. His thick broom mustache and basset-hound face were also seen in several early Chaplin films. In 1917 he moved over to Fox, where he directed and starred in Sunshine Comedies. He also appeared in many talkies. When film roles grew scarce, he became a makeup man and later operated a malt shop in Sierra Madre, Calif.

FILMS INCLUDE: *Algy on the Force, The Waiter's Picnic, Out and In* 1913; *In the Clutches of the Gang, Mabel's Strange Predicament, Caught in a Cabaret, The Alarm, The Knockout, Mabel's Married Life, Tillie's Punctured Romance* 1914; *A Modern Enoch Arden, The Village Blacksmith* (also dir.), *His Bread and Butter, Hearts and Spars* 1916; *The Janitor* 1919; *Mystic Mush* 1920; *Quincy Adams Sayer* 1922; *Don't Marry for Money, Tea—With a Kick, The Wanters* 1923; *Empty Hands, The Man Who Played Square* 1924; *The Sporting Venus* 1925; *The Skyrocket, The Boob, The Flying Horseman* 1926; *The Ladybird, Paid to Love, The Patent Leather Kid, Broadway After Midnight* 1927; *The Garden of Eden, Fazil* 1928; *Spite Marriage, The Donovan Affair* 1929; *The Arizona Kid, Sinner's Holiday* 1930; *City Lights, Annabelle's Affairs* 1931; *The Strange Love of Molly Louvain, Million Dollar Legs* 1932; *Smoky* 1934; *The Devil Is a Woman* 1935; *Modern Times* 1936; *Hollywood Cavalcade* 1939; *The Great Dictator* 1940; *Bullets for O'Hara* 1941; *Bullet Scars, Kings Row, The Man Who Came to Dinner* 1942; *Phantom of the Opera* 1943; *Arsenic and Old Lace, Crime by Night* 1944; *The Perils of Pauline* 1947; *Roseanna McCoy* 1949; *Son of Paleface* 1952; *The Caddy* 1953; *Abbott and Costello Meet the Keystone Cops* 1955; *Man of a Thousand Faces* 1958; *Daddy-O* 1959.

Mann, Michael. Director. Born on Feb. 5, 1943, in Chicago. *ed.* U. of Wisconsin. Trained at the London Film School, he started out in 1965 as a director of commercials and documentaries in England, and among other subjects covered the 1968 student riots in Paris. His short, *Janpuri,* won a Jury Prize at Cannes. Returning to the US in 1972 to direct the documentary *18 Days Down the Line,* he stayed on as a writer of episodes for such TV series as 'Starsky and Hutch,' 'Police Story,' and 'Vegas,' and was executive producer of 'Miami Vice.' He won the DGA Award as best director for his direction of the TV movie, *The Jericho Mile* (1979), then made an auspicious feature debut with *Thief* (1981), a superior drama starring James Caan. *Manhunter* (1986) was a stylish science-fiction treatment of the action-adventure drama, but his greatest success came in 1992, as co-producer, director, and screenwriter of the epic *The Last of the Mohicans* starring Daniel Day-Lewis.

FEATURE FILMS (as director): *Straight Time* (co-sc. only, uncredited) 1978; *Thief* (also exec. prod., sc.) 1981; *The Keep* (also sc.) 1983; *Band of the Hand* (exec. prod. only), *Manhunter* (also sc.) 1986; *The Last of the Mohicans* (co-prod., dir., sc.) 1992; *Heat* (also prod., sc.) 1995.

Mann, Ned. Special-effects man. *b.* 1893, Redkey, Ind. *d.* 1967. Originally a professional auto racer and roller skater, he entered films as an actor in 1920, but his love of gadgets and his mechanical aptitude soon attracted him behind the camera as a trick-photography specialist. He worked in that capacity on a number of Hollywood silents and early talkies, then went to England, where he performed similar services on several notable films of Alexander KORDA.

FILMS INCLUDE: In the US—*The Thief of Bagdad* 1924; *Don Q Son of Zorro* 1925; *The Bat* 1926; *Two Arabian Knights* 1927; *The Bat Whispers* 1930; *The Deluge* 1933. In the UK—*The Scarlet Pimpernel* 1935; *Fire Over England, Rembrandt, Things to Come, The Ghost Goes West, The Man Who Could Work Miracles* 1936; *Thunder in the City, Knight Without Armor, Dark Journey* 1937; *The Divorce of Lady X* 1938; *Beyond Tomorrow* (US) 1940; *Anna Karenina* 1948. In Italy—*Miracolo a Milano/Miracle in Milan* 1950. In the US—*Around the World in 80 Days* 1956.

Mann, Stanley. Screenwriter. Born on Aug. 8, 1928, in Canada. *ed.* McGill (Montreal). In England from the early 50s, he began writing for British TV in 1953 and for features in 1958. After a terrific start on such diverse films as the hilarious comedy *The Mouse That Roared* (1959) and the mature psychological drama *The Mark,* he went to Hollywood, where he shared an Academy Award nomination for the script of *The Collector* (1965). But much of his subsequent output, on either side of the Atlantic, failed to match the high level of his early screenplays.

FILMS INCLUDE: *Another Time Another Place* 1958; *The Mouse That Roared* 1959; *The Mark* 1961; *Woman of Straw* 1964; *Rapture, Up from the Beach, A High Wind in Jamaica, The Collector* 1965; *The Naked Runner* 1967; *The Strange Affair* 1968; *Russian Roulette* 1975; *Sky Riders, Breaking Point* 1976; *Damien—Omen II* 1978; *The Silent Flute/Circle of Iron, Meteor* 1979; *Eye of the Needle* 1981; *Firestarter, Conan the Destroyer* 1984; *Tai-Pan* 1986; *Hanna's War* 1988.

Manners, David. Actor. Born Rauff de Ryther Duan Acklom, on Apr. 30, 1901, in Halifax, Nova Scotia. Leading man of Hollywood films of the 30s, best remembered as the hero of such horror films as *Dracula, The Mummy,* and *The Black Cat.* Studio publicity claimed he was a descendant of William the Conqueror. After retiring from the screen in the mid-30s he appeared occasionally on the stage and wrote several novels.

FILMS: *Journey's End, He Knew Women, Sweet Mama, Kismet* (as the Caliph), *Mother's Cry, The Truth About Youth, The Right to Love* 1930; *Dracula* (as Jonathan Harker), *The Millionaire, The Last Flight, The Miracle Woman, The Ruling Voice* 1931; *The Greeks Had a Word for Them, Lady with a Past, Beauty and the Boss, Man Wanted, Stranger in Town, Crooner, A Bill of Divorcement, They Call It Sin, The Mummy, The Death Kiss* 1932; *From Hell to Heaven, The Warrior's Husband, The Girl in 419, The Devil's in Love, Torch Singer, Roman Scandals* 1933; *The Black Cat, The Great Flirtation, The Moonstone* 1934; *The Perfect Clue, The Mystery of Edwin Drood* (title role),

Jalna (as Eden Whiteoak) 1935; *Hearts in Bondage, A Woman Rebels* 1936.

Manni, Ettore. Actor. *b.* 1927, Rome. *d.* 1979. Handsome leading man, second lead, and supporting player of numerous Italian films and European co-productions.

FILMS INCLUDE: *La Tratta delle Bianche/Girls Marked Danger, I Tre Corsari* 1952; *La Lupa/The She-Wolf, La Nave delle Donne maledette/The Ship of Condemned Women, Cavalleria Rusticana/Fatal Desire* 1953; *Due Notti con Cleopatra/Two Nights with Cleopatra* (as Mark Antony), *Ulisse/Ulysses, Attila* 1954; *Tua per la Vita, Le Amiche/The Girl Friends* 1955; *Marisa la Civetta* 1957; *La Rivolta dei Gladiatori/The Warrior and the Slave* 1958; *Le Legioni di Cleopatra/Legions of the Nile* 1959; *A Porte chiuse* 1960; *La Rivolta degli Schiavi/The Revolt of the Slaves, Il Sepolcro dei Re/Cleopatra's Daughter, le Vergini di Roma/Amazons of Rome, Ercole alla Conquista di Atlantide/Hercules and the Captive Women* (as Androcles) 1961; *The Valiant* (UK/It.), *Lo Sceicco rosso/The Red Sheik* 1962; *Oro per i Cesari/Gold for the Caesars, Roma contro Roma/The War of the Zombies* 1963; *The Battle of the Villa Fiorita* (US/UK) 1965; *Mademoiselle* (Fr./UK), *L'Arcidiavolo/The Devil in Love* 1966; *Un Uomo un Cavallo una Pistola/The Stranger Returns* (It./Ger./US) 1968; *La Battaglia di El Alamein* 1969; *Mazzabubu* 1971; *Karzan il Favoloso Uomo della Jungla* 1973; *Street People* (US/It.), *Divina Creatura/The Divine Nymph* 1976; *Il Nome del Papa Re* 1977; *La Citta' delle Donne/City of Women* 1980.

Manning, Irene. Actress. Born Inez Harvout, on July 17, 1916, in Cincinnati. A former operetta singer, she entered films as Hope Manning, playing leads in low-budget Westerns opposite Gene Autry. She changed her name to Irene when she moved into more respectable lead roles with Warner Bros. In the late 40s she returned to the stage, singing in musicals and operettas and occasionally playing straight dramatic parts.

FILMS INCLUDE: *Two Wise Maids* 1937; *The Big Shot, Yankee Doodle Dandy, Spy Ship* 1942; *The Desert Song* 1943; *Shine On Harvest Moon, The Doughgirls, Hollywood Canteen* 1944; *Escape in the Desert, I Live in Grosvenor Square/A Yank in London* (UK) 1945; *Bonnie Prince Charlie* (UK) 1948.

Manoff, Dinah. Actress. Born on Jan. 25, 1958, New York City. *ed.* CalArts. Spunky leading lady of the American stage, screen, and television. The daughter of playwright Arnold Manoff and actress Lee GRANT, she made her professional acting debut in public television and her first film appearance as a supporting player in the musical *Grease* (1977). She rose to prominence after winning a Tony Award for her performance on Broadway in Neil Simon's 'I Ought to Be in Pictures' (1980), a role she later repeated on the screen. In addition to her features, she also appeared in TV movies and in the series 'Soap' (1978–79) and 'Empty Nest' (from 1989), and television became her mainstay. She divorced French designer Jean-Marc Joubert.

FILMS: *Grease* 1977; *Ordinary People* 1980; *I Ought to Be in Pictures* 1982; *Backfire* 1987; *Child's Play* 1988; *Bloodhounds of Broadway, Staying Together* 1989; *Welcome Home, Roxy Carmichael* 1990.

Mansfield, Jayne. Actress. *b.* Vera Jayne Palmer, Apr. 19, 1933, Bryn Mawr, Pa. *d.* 1967. Bosomy sexpot of Hollywood films of the 50s and 60s. Married at 16 and a mother at 17, she attended drama classes at the University of Texas and later at UCLA, driven by an all-consuming ambition to become a movie star. She entered and won several minor beauty contests, had a few walk-ons on TV, and participated in a publicity drive for a Jane Russell film, *Underwater,* before making her own screen debut as a supporting player in 1955. Her real break came late that year, on the Broadway stage, where, clad in only a Turkish towel, she revealed part of her hidden talent as she rose to answer the telephone in 'Will Success Spoil Rock Hunter?' She later repeated the role—a breathless, dizzy blonde á la Marilyn Monroe—in the 1957 screen version of the play and in most of her other films. But repetition didn't seem to induce improvement no matter how many times she played the same role, and despite the loud publicity that accompanied her every move, her career was in a deep decline by the mid-60s, when she appeared mainly in low-budget European productions, often opposite her second husband (1958–64), muscleman Mickey Hargitay. They were portrayed by Loni Anderson and Arnold SCHWARZENEGGER in the TV movie, *The Jayne Mansfield Story* (1980). Her third husband was director Matt Cimber, who took over as her manager during their brief (1964–66) marriage. She was decapitated in a car accident near New Orleans on her way to a TV engagement. Her daughter is actress Mariska Hargitay.

FILMS INCLUDE: *Pete Kelly's Blues, Illegal* 1955; *Hell on Frisco Bay, Female Jungle, The Girl Can't Help It* 1956; *The Burglar, The Wayward Bus, Will Success Spoil Rock Hunter?, Kiss Them for Me* 1957; *The Sheriff of Fractured Jaw* (UK) 1958; *Gli Amori di Ercole* (It./Fr.), *The Challenge/It Takes a Thief* (UK), *Too Hot to Handle/Playgirl After Dark* (UK) 1960; *The George Raft Story* 1961; *It Happened in Athens* 1962; *Promises! Promises!* 1963; *Panic Button, Einer frisst den anderen/Dog Eat Dog* (Ger./It./US), *L'Amore Primitivo/Primitive Love* (It.) 1964; *The Fat Spy, Las Vegas Hillbillies* 1966; *A Guide for the Married Man* (cameo), *Spree/Las Vegas by Night* (doc.) 1967; *The Wild Wild World of Jayne Mansfield* (compilation film), *Single Room Furnished* 1968.

Mantegna, Joe. Actor. Born on Nov. 13, 1947, in Chicago. *ed.* Morton Junior College. Smooth, soulful leading man of the American stage and screen. Trained at the Goodman School of Drama, he joined Chicago's Organic Theatre Company, with which he twice toured Europe. He then rejoined the Goodman Theatre as an actor and became a protégé of playwright-director David MAMET, starting a long and eventually successful association that culminated in Mantegna's Tony Award–winning performance in Mamet's 1984 Pulitzer Prize–winning play 'Glengarry Glen Ross' on Broadway. On the screen from the late 70s, Mantegna emerged from semiobscurity in 1987 with a magnetic performance as a seductive con man in Mamet's *House of Games.* The following year he shared best actor honors with co-star Don Ameche at the Venice Festival for his role in Mamet's *Things Change.* A devout Chicago Cubs fan, he won an Emmy for co-writing the TV baseball play 'Bleacher Bums,' in which he also starred.

FILMS: *Towing, Who Stole My Wheels?* 1978; *Second Thoughts* 1983; *Compromising Positions* 1985; *The Money Pit, Off Beat, Three Amigos!* 1986; *Critical Condition, House of Games, Weeds, Suspect* 1987; *Things Change* 1988; *Wait Until Spring Bandini* (Bel./Fr./It./US) 1989; *Alice, The Godfather Part III* 1990; *Queens Logic, Homicide, Bugsy* 1991; *Body of Evidence, Family Prayers, Searching for Bobby Fischer* 1993; *Airheads, Baby's Day Out* 1994; *For Better or Worse, Forget Paris* 1995; *Eye for an Eye, Thinner, Up Close and Personal* 1996; *Albino Alligator, Underworld* 1997.

Mara, Adele. Actress. Born Adelaida Delgado, on Apr. 28, 1923, in Highland Park, Mich. Formerly a singer-dancer with Xavier Cugat's orchestra, she played leads and "other woman" parts in scores of low-budget films in the 40s and 50s, including some of Republic's more ambitious releases. She disappeared from the screen in the late 50s, after marrying screenwriter-director Roy HUGGINS, but in the 70s she appeared in several of his TV productions.

FILMS INCLUDE: *Navy Blues* 1941; *Shut My Big Mouth, Alias Boston Blackie, You Were Never Lovelier* 1942; *Reveille with Beverly* 1943; *Atlantic City* 1944; *The Vampire's Ghost, The Tiger Woman, Song of Mexico* 1945; *Traffic in Crime, Night Train to Memphis, The Catman of Paris, I've Always Loved You, The Last Crooked Mile* 1946; *Twilight on the Rio Grande, Web of Danger, Blackmail, Exposed* 1947; *Campus Honeymoon, I Jane Doe, The Gallant Legion, Wake of the Red Witch, Angel in Exile* 1948; *Sands of Iwo Jima, Rock Island Trail, The Avengers, California Passage* 1950; *The Sea Hornet* 1951; *Count the Hours* 1953; *Back from Eternity* 1956; *The Curse of the Faceless Man* 1958; *The Big Circus* 1959.

Marais, Jean. Actor. Born Jean Alfred Villain-Marais, on Dec. 11, 1913, in Cherbourg, France. A physician's son, he was attracted to the stage while still in high school. Turned down by the Paris Conservatory, he worked briefly as a photographer's apprentice, then began playing walk-on parts on the stage. Tall, blond, and athletic, with Nordic good looks, he entered French films in 1933, but a thin voice and limited acting ability restricted him to extra and bit roles for several years. His career received a tremendous lift in the late 30s as a result of a meeting with Jean COCTEAU. The two became close friends and Cocteau guided Marais's career on the stage and eventually also in films. He wrote several plays and screenplays especially for his young protégé and directed his most important films. During the 40s and 50s, Marais was France's most popular leading man. A much improved actor in his more mature years, he was much in demand for lead roles by French directors through the late 60s. He disappeared from the screen in the early 70s but returned for sporadic roles in the 80s. Memoirs: *Mes Quatre Verités* (1957); *Histoire de ma Vie* (1975).

FILMS INCLUDE: *L'Epervier* (also asst. dir.) 1933; *Le Bonheur* 1934; *Le Scandale* 1936; *Le Pavillon brûle* 1941; *L'Eternel Retour/The Eternal Return, Voyage sans Espoir* 1943; *Carmen* (as Don José; release delayed from 1943) 1945; *La Belle et la Bête/Beauty and the Beast* (in triple role, including the Beast and the Prince) 1946; *Les Chouans* 1947; *Ruy Blas* (in dual role, as Ruy Blas and Don Cesari), *L'Aigle à Deux Têtes/Eagle with Two Heads, Les Parents terribles/The Storm Within* 1948; *Aux Yeux du Souvenir/Souvenir, Le Secret de Mayerling/The Secret of Mayerling* (as Crown Prince Rudolph) 1949; *Orphée/Orpheus* (title role), *Le Château de Verre* 1950; *Les Miracles n'ont lieu qu'une Fois* 1951; *Nez de Cuir* 1952; *Julietta, Dortoir des Grandes/Inside a Girls' Dormitory* 1953; *Le Guérisseur, Si Versailles m'était conté/Royal Affairs in Versailles* (as Louis XV) 1954; *Le Comte de Monte-Cristo* (as Edmond Dantès), *Futures Vedettes* 1955; *Eléna et les Hommes/Paris Does Strange Things* 1956; *Typhon sur Nagasaki, Le Notti bianche/White Nights* (It./Fr.), *Amour de Poche/Nude in His Pocket* 1957; *Le Testament d'Orphée/The Testament of Orpheus* (as Orpheus), *Le Captain* 1960; *La Princesse de Clèves, Le Capitain Fracasse* 1961; *Ponzio Pilato* (as Pontius Pilate; It.), *Le Masque de Fer* (as D'Artagnan) 1962; *Patate/Friend of the Family, Fantômas* (in dual role) 1964; *Le Gentleman de Cocody/Man from Cocody* 1965; *Le Saint prend l'affût* (as The Saint) 1966; *Fantômas contre Scotland Yard* 1967; *Le Paria* 1968; *La Provocation* 1970; *Peau d'Ane/Donkey Skin* 1971; *Ombre et Secrets* 1983; *Parking* 1985; *Le Lien de Parenté* 1986

Marceau, Sophie. Actress. Born in 1967, in France. Spirited young leading lady of French films of the 80s and early 90s, typically in roles representing independent, rebellious youth. She soared to popularity in the wake of the enormous commercial success of Pinteau's *La Boum* (1980), her screen debut.

FILMS INCLUDE: *La Boum* 1980; *La Boum 2* 1982; *Fort Saganne, Joyeuses Pâques* 1984; *L'Amour Braque, Police* 1985; *Descente aux Enfers* 1986; *Les Chouans* 1988; *Mes Nuits sont plus belles que vos Jours* 1989; *Pacific Palisades* 1990; *Fanfan* 1993; *La Fille de D'Artagnan/D'Artagnan's Daughter* 1994; *Braveheart* 1995; *Anna Karenina, Beyond the Clouds* 1997.

March, Fredric. Actor. *b.* Ernest Frederick McIntyre Bickel, Aug. 31, 1897, Racine, Wis. *d.* 1975. *ed.* U. of Wisconsin. He resumed his studies after WW I service as an artillery lieutenant and began participating in college dramatics. Planning on a banking career, he went to New York in 1920 and began his apprenticeship at the National City Bank, but while recuperating from an appendicitis attack in a hospital bed he made up his mind to quit the job and seek his future in acting. He made his debut that same year, playing a two-line bit in Belasco's production 'Deburau' in Baltimore. At the same time, he began getting extra assignments in films shooting in New York, including *Paying the Piper* and *The Great Adventure* (both 1921). He played his first Broadway lead in 'The Devil in the Cheese' in 1926. The following year he married actress Florence ELDRIDGE and instead of a honeymoon they went on tour with the Theatre Guild's first traveling repertory company.

March's parody of John Barrymore in the West Coast production of *The Royal Family* resulted in a five-year film contract with Paramount. Starting out as a romantic leading man, March gradually emerged as one of Hollywood's subtlest and most sensitive actors, a performer of considerable range with an intuitive grasp of the specific requirements of screen acting, where the slightest nuance of facial expression can be magnified to great advantage. He played a variety of roles, including comedy and adventure, but was at his best portraying characters in mental anguish. He won his first Academy Award in Rouben Mamoulian's 1932 *Dr. Jekyll and Mr. Hyde,* by far the best of the several screen versions of the Robert Louis Stevenson story, and a second Oscar in 1946 for his portrayal of a returning war veteran in *The Best Years of Our Lives.*

March reserved choice of roles to himself and exercised his option wisely most of the time. Beginning in the late 30s, he returned to the New York stage with great regularity in between film assignments. He achieved perhaps his greatest stage success in 1956, in 'Long Day's Journey Into Night,' for which he won the New York Drama Critics acting award. Florence Eldridge was a frequent partner in his plays but only occasionally co-starred in his films.

FILMS: *The Dummy, The Wild Party, The Studio Murder Mystery, Jealousy, Paris Bound, Footlights and Fools, The Marriage Playground* 1929; *Sarah and Son, Ladies Love Brutes, True to the Navy, Paramount on Parade, Manslaughter, Laughter* 1930; *The Royal Family of Broadway, Honor Among Lovers, The Night Angel, My Sin* 1931; *Dr. Jekyll and Mr. Hyde* (dual title role), *Strangers in Love, Merrily We Go to Hell, Make Me a Star* (cameo), *Smilin' Through* (dual role), *The Sign of the Cross* 1932; *Tonight Is Ours, The Eagle and the Hawk, Design for Living* 1933; *All of Me, Death Takes a Holiday, Good Dame, The Affairs of Cellini* (as Benvenuto Cellini), *The Barretts of Wimpole Street* (as Robert Browning), *We Live Again* (as Prince Nekhludov of Tolstoy's 'Resurrection') 1934; *Les Miserables* (as Jean Valjean), *Anna Karenina* (as Count Vronsky), *The Dark Angel* 1935; *Mary of Scotland* (as the Earl of Bothwell), *The Road to Glory, Anthony Adverse* (title role) 1936; *A Star Is Born, Nothing Sacred* 1937; *The Buccaneer* (as Jean Lafitte), *There Goes My Heart* 1938; *Trade Winds* 1939; *Susan and God, Victory* (as Baron Heyst) 1940; *So Ends Our Night, One Foot in Heaven, Bedtime Story* 1941; *I Married a Witch* 1942; *The Adventures of Mark Twain* (title role), *Tomorrow the World*

1944; *The Best Years of Our Lives* 1946; *Another Part of the Forest* (as Marcus Hubbard), *An Act of Murder/Live Today for Tomorrow* 1948; *Christopher Columbus* (title role; UK) 1949; *Death of a Salesman* (as Willy Loman) 1951; *It's a Big Country* 1952; *Man on a Tightrope* 1953; *Executive Suite* 1954; *The Bridges at Toko-Ri, The Desperate Hours* 1955; *Alexander the Great* (as Philip of Macedonia), *The Man in the Gray Flannel Suit* 1956; *Middle of the Night* 1959; *Inherit the Wind* 1960; *The Young Doctors* 1961; *I Sequestrati di Altona/The Condemned of Altona* (It./Fr.) 1962; *Seven Days in May* 1964; *Hombre* 1967; *Tick Tick Tick* 1970; *The Iceman Cometh* 1973.

Marchal, Arlette. Actress. *b.* 1903, Paris. *d.* 1984. She entered French films in 1923 after winning a beauty contest and played leads and second leads in a variety of productions. In 1926–27 she appeared in a number of Hollywood films, characteristically in peppery, exotic roles, then returned to Europe. After retiring from the screen she ran a fashion establishment.

FILMS INCLUDE: *Sarati le Terrible, La Dame au Ruban de Velours* 1923; *Un Coquin, Die Sklavenkönigin/Moon of Israel* (Ger.) 1924; *Madame Sans-Gêne, L'Image* 1925; *La Châtelaine du Liban* (as Athelstane), *Born to the West* (US), *The Cat's Pajamas* (US), *Diplomacy* (US), *Forlorn River* (US) 1926; *Blonde or Brunette* (US), *Hula* (US), *Wings* (US), *A Gentleman of Paris* (US), *The Spotlight* (US) 1927; *Die Dame mit der Make* (Ger.) 1928; *Figaro* (as Rosine), *La Femme rêvée* 1929; *Don Quichotte, Le Petit Roi* 1933; *Toboggan, La Femme Idéale* 1934; *La Marcia Nuziale* (It.) 1935; *Aux Jardins de Murcie* 1936; *Entente cordiale* (as Queen Alexandra) 1939; *La Loi du Nord* (release delayed from 1939) 1942; *Le Père Serge* 1946; *Sans laisser d'adresse* 1951.

Marchal, Georges. Actor. Born Georges Louis Lucot, on Jan. 10, 1920, in Nancy, France. Tall, handsome, athletic star of French and Italian films. Initially a youthful romantic lead, he later specialized in swashbuckling roles in period costume mini-spectaculars, but he has also starred in a number of fine productions, including several Buñuel films. He was married to Dany Robin.

FILMS INCLUDE: *Fausse Alerte/The French Way* 1940; *Premier Rendez-vous/Her First Affair* 1941; *Lumière d'Eté* 1943; *Vautrin/Vautrin the Thief* 1944; *Les Démons de l'Aube* 1946; *Bethsabée* 1947; *Les Derniers Jours de Pompéi/The Last Days of Pompeii* 1948; *Au Grand Balcon* 1949; *La Soif des Hommes/The Thirst of Men* 1950; *Robinson Crusoe* (title role; It.), *Messalina* (It.) 1951; *Les Amours finissent à l'Aube, Les Trois Mousquetaires/The Three Musketeers* (as D'Artagnan) 1953; *La Castiglione, Teodora—Imperatrice di Bisanzio/Theodora—Slave Empress* (as Emperor Justinian; It.), *Le Vicomte de Bragelonne* (title role) 1954; *Gil Blas* (title role) 1955; *Cela s'appelle l'Aurore, La Mort en ce Jardin/Gina* 1956; *Marchands de Filles/Sellers of Girls/Girl Merchants* 1957; *Filles de Nuit/Girls of the Night, La Rivolta dei Gladiatori/The Warrior and the Slave* (It./Sp.) 1958; *Le Legioni di Cleopatra/Legions of the Nile* (as Mark Antony; It./Fr./Sp.) 1959; *Austerlitz* 1960; *Il Colosso di Rodi/The Colossus of Rhodes* (It./Fr./Sp.) 1961; *Il Colpo Segreto di D'Artagnan/The Secret Mark of D'Artagnan* (It./Fr.) 1962; *Guerre secrète/The Dirty Game* 1965; *Belle de Jour* 1967; *La Voie Lactée/The Milky Way* 1969; *Les Enfants du Placard* 1977; *L'Honneur d'un Capitaine* 1982.

Marchand, Corinne. Actress. Born on Dec. 4, 1937, in Paris. Enigmatic heroine of *Cleo from 5 to 7* (1962). A former photographic model and nightclub singer, she was less effective in several other French films.

FILMS INCLUDE: *Cadet Rousselle* 1954; *Donnez-moi ma Chance* 1957; *Lola* 1961; *Cléo de Cinq à Sept/Cleo from 5 to 7* 1962; *Les Sept Péchés capitaux/Seven Capital Sins* 1963; *L'Heure de la Vérité/The Moment of Truth* 1964; *Les Sultans, Arizona Colt/The Man from Nowhere* 1966; *Passager de la Pluie/Rider on the Rain, Borsalino* 1970; *Travels with My Aunt* (UK), *La Cagna/Liza* (It./Fr.) 1972; *Attention Bandits!/Bandits* 1987.

Marchand, Guy. Actor. Born in 1939, in France. Dominant leading man and character player of French films, often portraying tough guys and heels. Formerly a singer and jazz musician.

FILMS INCLUDE: *Boulevard du Rhum* 1971; *Une Belle Fille comme moi/Such a Gorgeous Kid Like Me* 1972; *Cousin Cousine* 1976; *Tendre Poulet/Dear Inspector/Dear Detective* 1978; *Loulou* 1980; *Plein Sud, Rends-moi la Clé, Garde à Vue/The Inquisitor, Coup de Torchon* 1981; *T'es heureuse? Moi toujours...* (also mus.), *Mortelle randonnée, Cup de Foudre/Entre Nous* 1983; *P'tit Con, La Tête dans le Sac, Stress* 1984; *Hold-Up* 1985; *Conseil de Famille/Family Business, Vaudeville, Je hais les Acteurs/I Hate Actors!* 1986; *La Rumba, Grand Guignol, Chateauroux District, Charlie Dingo, Noyade Interdite* 1987; *Les Maris les femmes les Amants* 1988; *Ripoux Contre Ripoux/My New Partner 2* 1990.

Marchand, Nancy. Actress. Born on June 19, 1928, in Buffalo, N.Y. *ed.* Carnegie Tech. Leading lady, then character player of the American stage, TV, and occasional films. On the professional stage from age 18, she broke through in 1950, when she co-starred in a live TV version of 'Little Women,' and later starred in the original TV version of 'Marty.' She made her Broadway debut in 1951 and in 1960 won an Obie Award for her performance in off Broadway's 'The Balcony' (1960). In films sporadically from 1957, she achieved most of her success on television, winning four Emmy Awards for her role as boss Margaret Pynchon in the series 'Lou Grant' (1977–82). She married actor Paul Sparer.

FILMS: *The Bachelor Party* 1957; *Ladybug Ladybug* 1963; *Me Natalie* 1969; *Tell Me That You Love Me Junie Moon* 1970; *The Hospital* 1971; *The Bostonians* 1984; *From the Hip* 1987; *The Naked Gun* 1988; *Regarding Henry* 1991; *Brain Donors* 1992; *Jefferson in Paris, Sabrina* 1995; *Dear God* 1996.

"The March of Time." A monthly screen-magazine series, launched by Time, Inc., in 1935, which revolutionized existing concepts of film journalism and for 16 years had a great impact on the American and international public. The series was produced by Louis de Rochemont, who drew on the ideas and experience of Roy Larsen's successful radio series of the same title and on the extensive research and reporting resources of *Time* magazine. "The March of Time" programs, usually running between 15 and 25 minutes, fused the styles and techniques of the traditional newsreel with those of the documentary. Some of the segments were criticized for their reliance on re-enactments to dramatize important events, but on the whole the series was highly regarded throughout its run. "The March of Time" style was characterized by dynamic editing, gutsy investigative reporting, and hard-punching, almost arrogant, narration (which was beautifully parodied by Orson Welles in *Citizen Kane*).

Much like the traditional newsreels, the first issues of "The March of Time" consisted of several segments, but gradually the series adopted a one-story-an-issue format, which enabled its editors to probe important stories in depth. As early as its second issue, in 1935, the series took an outspoken stand against fascism in a segment devoted to the rise of Adolf Hitler in Germany. The third issue contained footage that proved quite damaging to the political career of Huey Long. The first single-story issue—*Inside Nazi Germany*—was released in 1938. Occasionally, "The March of Time" dealt with the lighter side of life in a lively and entertaining manner. The series, never a moneymaker, folded in 1951, a victim of television news coverage.

Maretskaya, Vera. Actress. *b.* July 1, 1906, Moscow. *d.* 1978. A popular star of Soviet cinema. Trained at Moscow's Bakhtangova Studio, she made her stage debut in 1924 and her first film appearance the year after. A spunky young woman of sunny disposition, she appeared in many major films, representing honest, hard-working Soviet womanhood.

FILMS INCLUDE: *The Tailor from Torzhok* 1975; *The Green Serpent* 1926; *The House on Trubyana Square, Simple Hearts* 1928; *A Living Corpse* 1929; *The Black Hut* 1933; *Love and Hate* 1935; *A Generation of Conquerors/Revolutionists* 1936; *Paris Commune* 1937; *Member of the Government* 1939; *The Artomonoy Affair* 1940; *She Defends Her Country/No Greater Love* 1943; *The Wedding/Marriage* 1944; *Village Teacher* 1947; *Mother/1905* 1955; *My Little Field* 1956; *Mother and Daughter* 1962; *An Easy Life* 1964.

Marey, Etienne-Jules. Inventor. *b.* Mar. 5, 1830, Beaune, France. *d.* 1904. A physician and physiologist, he took an early interest in the study of animal motion. His research inspired Eadweard MUYBRIDGE to begin his famous experiments in photographically recording the successive phases of animal locomotion. In turn, Marey was strongly influenced by Muybridge's experiments and applied his methods to his own work. In 1882 he went a step further, designing a photographic gun for the purpose of studying the flight of birds. The apparatus, resembling an automatic rifle with a multichamber revolving disc, was capable of shooting 12 pictures per second, not enough to render a complete cycle of motion but a major step toward the development of true motion pictures. In 1887, Marey substituted paper roll film for the glass plates he had previously used in his photographic equipment, and in 1888 he began experimenting with celluloid film. His later experiments included extreme slow motion (as many as 700 frames per second by 1894) and cinemicrography, combining the capabilities of the motion picture camera and the microscope for scientific research.

Margo. Actress. *b.* Marie Marguerita Guadalupe Teresa Estela Bolado Castilla y O'Donnell, May 10, 1917, Mexico City. *d.* 1985. Coached as a child by Eduardo Cansino, Rita Hayworth's father, she began dancing professionally at age nine. Later she appeared with her uncle Xavier CUGAT's band in Mexican nightclubs and accompanied them to New York, where they triumphed introducing the rumba at the Waldorf-Astoria. But it was as a dramatic actress that she became known to Broadway and film audiences from 1934. She danced only in two or three films and was mainly typecast in her other films as a tragic, suffering soul. She was most effective as Claude Rains's murder victim in *Crime Without Passion* (1934), as a slum girl in *Winterset* (1936), in which she repeated her Broadway role, and as the young girl who suddenly ages when she leaves Shangri-la in *Lost Horizon* (1937). Her subsequent film appearances have been sporadic. The Margo listed in the credits of *Taffy and the Jungle Hunter* (1965) is not the actress but an animal performer.

Margo, the actress, became a US citizen in 1942. After retiring from show business she became heavily involved in civic activities. In 1974 she was appointed Commissioner of Social Services for the City of Los Angeles. At the time of her death, she was a member of the Board of the National Council of the National Endowment of the Arts and served as a steering committee member on the President's Committee on the Arts and Humanities. Formerly (1937–40) married to actor Francis LEDERER, she became the wife of actor Eddie ALBERT in 1945. In the 50s they performed as a song-and-dance duo in nightclub revues directed by Herbert Ross. She was the mother of actor Edward ALBERT.

FILMS: *Crime Without Passion* 1934; *Rumba* 1935; *The Robin Hood of Eldorado, Winterset* 1936; *Lost Horizon* 1937; *A Miracle on Main Street* 1940; *The Leopard Man, Behind the Rising Sun, Gangway for Tomorrow* 1943; *The Falcon in Mexico* 1944; *Viva Zapata* 1952; *I'll Cry Tomorrow* 1955; *From Hell to Texas* 1958; *Who's Got the Action?* 1962.

Margheriti, Antonio. Director. Born on Sept. 19, 1930, in Rome. Prolific manufacturer of dumb but often stylish action spectacles. Like several other Italian directors specializing in movies for the masses, he prefers to use an English-sounding pseudonym for presumed added prestige. He bills himself as Anthony B. Dawson on many of his Italian films and international co-productions. Early in his career, he briefly also used the pseudonym Anthony Daisies. He collaborated on many of his scripts and appeared as an actor in several films of other directors.

FILMS INCLUDE: *Space Men/Assignment—Outer Space* 1960; *Il Pineta degli Uomini spenti/Battle of the Worlds* 1961; *Il Crollo di Roma/The Fall of Rome, La Freccia d'Oro/The Golden Arrow* 1962; *L'Arciere delle Mille e Una Notte* 1963; *Danza macabra/Castle of Blood, La Vergine de Norimberga/ Horror Castle, Anthat l'Invincible, Il Pelo nel Mondo/Go Go Go World!/Weird Wicked World* (doc.; co-dir.), *Ursus il Terrore dei Kirghisi* 1964; *Operzione Goldman/Lightning Bolt, I Criminali della Galassia/The Wild Wild Planet, Il Pianeta errante/War Between the Planets* 1966; *Joe l'Implacabile* 1967; *Nude... si muore/The Young the Evil and the Savage, Joko invoca Dio... e muori, Io ti amo* 1968; *E Dio disse a Caino..., L'Inafferrabile/ Invincible Mr. Invisible* 1970; *Nella Stretta Morsa del Ragno/Web of the Spider* 1971; *Finalemente le Mille e Una Notte* 1972; *La Morte negli Occhi del Gatto, Decameron 3* 1973; *Manone il Ladrone, Whisky e Fantasmi, Les Diablesses* (Fr./It./Ger.), *Blood Money* (US/H.K./It./Sp.) 1974; *Take a Hard Ride* (US/It.) 1975; *Con la Rabbia agli Occhi/Death Rage, The Stranger and the Gunfighter* (UK/It.), *The Squeeze/The Rip-Off* (US/It.) 1976; *House of 1,000 Pleasures* 1977; *Killer Fish* (UK/Braz./Fr.) 1978; *The Last Hunter/Hunter of the Apocalypse, Cannibals in the Streets* 1980; *Car Crash* 1981; *Fuga dall'Archipelago maledetto, Cacciatori del Cobra d'Oro/Hunters of the Golden Cobra/ Raiders of the Golden Cobra* 1982; *Yor the Hunter from the Future, Tornado* 1983; *Ark of the Sun God, I Sporavvisuti della Citta' morte, Geheimcode Wilganse/Codename: Wild Geese* (Ger./It.) 1984; *La Leggenda del Rubino malese, Kommando Leopard/Commando Leopard* (Ger./It.) 1985; *L'Isola del Tesoro/Treasure Island* 1987; *The Commander* 1988; *Indio* 1989; *The Revolt* 1991.

Margolin, Janet. Actress. *b.* July 25, 1943, New York City. *d.* 1993. A graduate of New York's High School of the Performing Arts, she made an auspicious Broadway debut at 18 in the role of a mentally disturbed girl in 'Daughter of Silence' (1961), on the strength of which she was chosen for a similar lead role in the film *David and Lisa* (1962). She won the best actress award at the San Francisco film festival for that sensitive portrayal and went on to play tender ingenue roles and leads in other films.

FILMS: *David and Lisa* 1962; *El Ojo de la Cerradura/The Eavesdropper* (Arg.) 1964; *The Greatest Story Ever Told* (as Mary of Bethany), *Bus Riley's Back in Town, Morituri/The Saboteur: Code Name Morituri* 1965; *Nevada Smith* 1966; *Enter Laughing* 1967; *Buona Sera Mrs. Campbell* 1968; *Take the Money and Run* 1969; *Your Three Minutes Are Up* 1973; *Annie Hall* 1977; *Last Embrace* 1979; *Distant Thunder* 1988; *Ghostbusters II* 1989.

Margolin, Stuart. Actor, director. Born on Jan. 31, 1940(?), in Davenport, Iowa. Intent on becoming a writer, he moved to New York in his late teens and had a play of his presented off-off Broadway at 20. In the mid-60s he began playing character roles in TV and films, often portraying shifty, offbeat types. He enjoyed his best success on TV, in support of James GARNER in the series 'The Rockford Files' (1974–80), for which he twice won an Emmy Award. He began directing TV movies in the late 70s and feature films in the late 80s.

FILMS INCLUDE: As actor—*Women of the Prehistoric Planet* 1966; *Don't Just Stand There* 1968; *The Gamblers* 1969; *Kelly's Heroes* 1970; *Limbo/Women in Limbo* 1972; *The Stone Killer* 1973; *Death Wish, The Gambler* 1974; *The Big Bus, Futureworld* 1976; *Days of Heaven* 1978; *A Man a Woman, and a Bank* (co-sc. only; Can.) 1979; *S.O.B.* 1981; *Class* 1983; *Running Hot* 1984; *A Fine Mess* 1986; *Iron Eagle II* 1988; *Bye Bye Blues* (Can.) 1989; *Guilty by Suspicion* 1991. As director—*Paramedics* 1988; *Donna d'Onore* (It.) 1990; *Salt Water Moose* 1995.

Mariano, Luis. Singer, actor. *b.* Mariano Eusebio Gonzalez y Garcia, 1914, Irun, Spain. *d.* 1970. Schmaltzy tenor of French music halls and saccharine films. A popular matinee idol and recording artist throughout Europe in the 50s.

FILMS INCLUDE: *Ramuntcho* 1937; *Le Chant de l'Exilé* 1942; *Histoire de chanter* 1946; *Fandango* 1949; *Andalousie* 1951; *Violettes impériales* 1952; *La Belle de Cadix* 1953; *Napoléon, Der Zarewitsch* (Ger./Fr.) 1954; *Le Chanteur de Mexico* 1956; *Sérénade au Texas* 1958; *Candide* 1960; *Les Pieds dans le Plâtre* 1964.

Máriássy, Félix. Director. *b.* 1919, Hungary. *d.* 1975. In films since 1939, first as an editor, then as an assistant director, he was among the leading creative forces in postwar Hungarian cinema. His heroes were usually simple people, often working women, whom he treated with much compassion. His wife, Judith, wrote most of his screenplays.

FILMS INCLUDE: *Anna Szabo* 1949; *Catherine's Marriage* 1950; *Relatives* 1954; *A Glass of Beer, Springtime in Budapest* 1955; *Smugglers* 1958; *The Sleepless Years* 1959; *Test Trip* 1960; *Every Day Sunday* 1962; *Goliath* 1964; *Figleaf* 1966; *Bondage* 1968.

Marin, Edwin L. Director. *b.* Feb. 21, 1899, Jersey City, N.J. *d.* 1951. *ed.* U. of Pennsylvania. He started in films in 1919 as an assistant cameraman and after working in the industry in several other capacities began directing in the early 30s. He spent much of his career (1934–41) with MGM, proving himself a competent director of medium-budget second features, including some nifty thrillers and bright minor comedies, as well as a solid version of *A Christmas Carol* (1938). He later freelanced with a number of other studios, turning out several effective Randolph SCOTT Westerns and many routine films.

FILMS: *The Death Kiss, A Study in Scarlet, The Avenger, The Sweetheart of Sigma Chi* 1933; *Bombay Mail, The Crosby Case, Affairs of a Gentleman, Paris Interlude* 1934; *The Casino Murder Case, Pursuit* 1935; *The Garden Murder Case, Moonlight Murder, Speed, I'd Give My Life, Sworn Enemy, All American Chump* 1936; *Man of the People, Married Before Breakfast* 1937; *Everybody Sing, Hold That Kiss, The Chaser, Listen Darling, A Christmas Carol* 1938; *Fast and Loose, Society Lawyer, Maisie, Henry Goes to Arizona* 1939; *Florian, Gold Rush Maisie, Hullabaloo* 1940; *Maisie Was a Lady, Ringside Maisie* 1941; *Paris Calling, A Gentleman After Dark, Miss Annie Rooney, Invisible Agent* 1942; *Two Tickets to London* (also prod.) 1943; *Show Business, Tall in the Saddle* 1944; *Johnny Angel* 1945; *Abilene Town, Young Widow, Mr. Ace, Lady Luck, Nocturne* 1946; *Christmas Eve, Intrigue* 1947; *Race Street* 1948; *Canadian Pacific, The Younger Brothers, Fighting Man of the Plains* 1949; *Colt 45, The Cariboo Trail* 1950; *Sugarfoot, Raton Pass, Fort Worth* 1951.

Marin, Richard "Cheech". Actor. Born on July 13, 1946, in Los Angeles. *ed.* California State U. The small, excitable Latino of the CHEECH AND CHONG comedy team of the late 70s and early 80s. Marin and Tommy CHONG first worked together at Vancouver's City Work improvisational troupe. Following their success with several hit records, the duo brought their shenanigans to the screen in 1978 in *Up in Smoke,* a mindless pothead comedy that proved a huge grosser at the box office. They went on to co-star in several progressively poorer, drug-related burlesques before breaking up in 1984. Marin collaborated on all of the scripts. On his own, he played supporting roles in several films. He directed himself in *Born in East L.A.* (1987), an amiable if thin ethnic comedy that he expanded from his own music video parody of a popular Bruce Springsteen song. In 1992 he joined the cast of TV sitcom 'Golden Palace.'

FILMS: *Up in Smoke* (also co-sc.) 1978; *Cheech and Chong's Next Movie* (also co-sc.) 1980; *Cheech and Chong's Nice Dreams* (also co-sc.) 1981; *Things Are Tough All Over* (also co-sc.), *It Came from Hollywood* 1982; *Still Smokin'* (also sc.), *Yellowbeard* 1983; *Cheech and Chong's The Corsican Brothers* (also co-sc.) 1984; *After Hours* 1985; *Born in East L.A.* (also dir., sc., title song lyr.), *Fatal Beauty* (bit) 1987; *Oliver & Company* (v/o) 1988; *Troop Beverly Hills* (cameo), *Ghostbusters II* (cameo), *Rude Awakening* 1989; *Far Out Man* (cameo), *The Shrimp on the Barbie* 1990; *Ferngully* (voice) 1992; *The Lion King* (v/o) 1994; *Desperado, From Dusk Till Dawn* 1995; *Tin Cup* 1996.

Marion, Frances. Screenwriter. *b.* Frances Marion Owens, Nov. 18, 1887, San Francisco. *d.* 1973. A former advertising illustrator, model, and film actress, she began her writing career as a reporter for the San Francisco *Examiner* and during WW I was one of the first female war correspondents to cover actual battles in Europe. Returning to the US in 1915, she began a long and tremendously prolific career as a screenwriter which spanned the silent and early talkie eras. She was among Hollywood's busiest and highest-paid screenwriters and was credited with nearly 150 scenarios, original stories, and adaptations for some of the industry's top directors and stars. Her list of credits is studded with film titles that have since become landmarks in the history of American cinema. She won Academy Awards for the script of *The Big House* (1930) and the original screen story for *The Champ* (1931), both Wallace Beery vehicles. In the early 20s she also directed a number of Marion Davies films. She was the author of *How to Write and Sell Film Stories* (1937) as well as several novels and a volume of memoirs, *Off with Their Heads* (1972). Her third husband (1919–28) was silent film cowboy Fred THOMSON; and her fourth (1930–31) was director George W. HILL.

FILMS INCLUDE (as screenwriter, alone or in collaboration): *Fanchon the Cricket, Little Pal, A Girl of Yesterday* (act. only), *Esmeralda, A Daughter of the Sea* (story only), *Camille* 1915; *The Foundling* (also story), *The Yellow Passport, The Social Highwayman, The Feast of Life* (also story), *The Battle of Hearts* (story only), *La Vie de Bohème, A Woman's Way, Friday the 13th, The Revolt, The Gilded Cage, All Man, On Dangerous Ground* 1916; *The Hungry Heart, A Girl's Folly* (also co-story), *The Web of Desire, Poor Little Rich Girl, Forget-Me-Not* (also story), *Darkest Russia, The Crimson Dove* (also story), *Stolen Paradise* (also story), *The Divorce Game, The Beloved Adventures* (also story), *The Amazons, Rebecca of Sunnybrook Farm, The Little Princess* 1917; *Stella Maris, M'Liss, Johanna Enlists, He Comes Up Smiling, The Temple of Dusk* (also story), *The Goat* (also story) 1918; *Captain Kidd Jr., Anne of Green Gables, A Regular Girl* 1919; *Pollyanna, The Cinema Murder, Humoresque, The Flapper* (also story) 1920; *The Love Light* (also dir., story), *Straight Is the Way, Little Lord Fauntleroy* (act. only) 1921; *Just Around the Corner* (also dir.), *Back Pay, The Primitive Lover, Sonny, The Eternal Flame, East Is West, The Toll of the Sea* (also story) 1922; *The Voice from the Minaret, The Famous Mrs. Fair, The Nth Commandment* (also prod.), *Within the Law, Potash and Perlmutter, The French Doll* 1923; *The Song of Love* (also co-dir. with Chester Franklin), *Abraham Lincoln/The Dramatic Life of Abraham Lincoln* (also story), *Secrets, Cytherea, Sundown, Tarnish* 1924; *A Thief in Paradise, The Lady, His Supreme Moment, Zander the Great, Lightnin', Graustark, The Dark Angel, Lazybones, Simon the Jester* (also prod.), *Thank You, Stella Dallas* 1925; *The First Year, Partners Again, Paris at Midnight* (also prod.), *The Son of the Sheik, The Scarlet Letter, The Winning of Barbara Worth* 1926; *The Red Mill, The Callahans and the Murphys, Madame Pompadour* (UK), *Love* 1927; *Bringing Up Father, The Cossacks, Excess Baggage, The Awakening* (story only), *The Wind, The Masks of the Devil* 1928; *Their Own Desire* 1929; *The Rogue Song, Anna Christie, The Big House* (also story), *Let Us Be Gay, Good News, Min and Bill* 1930; *The Secret Six* (also story), *The Champ* (also story) 1931; *Emma* (story only), *Blondie of the Follies* (also story), *Cynara* 1932; *Secrets* (remake), *Peg o' My Heart, Dinner at Eight, The Prizefighter and the Lady* (story only), *Going Hollywood* (story only) 1933; *Riffraff* (also story) 1936; *Camille, Love from a Stranger, Knight Without Armor* (UK) 1937; *Green Hell* (also story) 1940; *Molly and Me* (story only) 1945; *The Clown* (story only) 1953: *The Champ* (remake; based on her story) 1979.

Maris, Mona. Actress. *b.* Maria Capdevielle, 1903, in Buenos Aires. *d.* 1991. She was convent-educated in France and appeared in several British and German films before embarking in the late 20s upon a Hollywood career that consisted of some leads and many second-lead parts, often as a sultry exotic type. In the 30s she also starred in several Hollywood-made Spanish-language films. Divorced from director Clarence BROWN, she married a Dutch millionaire, retired from films, and became a lifelong resident of Lima, Peru.

FILMS INCLUDE: *The Little People* (UK) 1926; *Die Leibeigenen* (Ger.) 1927; *Rutschbahn/Bondage* (Ger.) *Marquis d'Eon der Spion der Pompadour/The Spy of Madame de Pompadour* (Ger.), *Die Drei Frauen von Urban Hell* (Ger.) 1928; *Romance of the Rio Grande* 1929; *Under a Texas Moon, The Arizona Kid, One Mad Kiss, A Devil with Women* 1930; *The Passionate Plumber, The Man Called Back, Once in a Lifetime* 1932; *The Death Kiss, Secrets, El Precio de un Beso* (Mex.), *La Viuda Romantica, La Melodia prohibida* 1933; *White Heat, Kiss and Make-up, Cuesta Abajo, Tres Amores* 1934; *El Cantante de Napoles* 1935; *Flight from Destiny, Underground, Law of the Tropics, A Date with the Falcon* 1941; *My Gal Sal, Pacific Rendezvous, I Married an Angel, Berlin Correspondent* 1942; *The Desert Hawk* (serial), *Tampico, The Falcon in Mexico* 1944; *Heartbeat* 1946; *The Avengers* 1950; *La Mujer de las Camelias* (Arg.) 1952.

Maritza, Sari. Actress. *b.* Patricia Detering Nathan, Mar. 17, 1910, in Tientsin, China, to a British father, a major, and an Austrian mother. *d.* 1987. She was brought to Hollywood with much fanfare in 1932 in the wake of the international success of her German film, *Bomben auf Monte Carlo/Monte Carlo Madness*. Publicized as another Dietrich, she failed to attract a following among American film fans and retired from the screen within two years.

FILMS INCLUDE: *Bomben auf Monte Carlo/Monte Carlo Madness* (Ger.) 1931; *Forgotten Commandments, Evenings for Sale* 1932; *A Lady's Profession, International House, The Right to Romance* 1933; *Crimson Romance* 1934.

Marken, Jane. Actress. *b.* Jane Krab, Jan. 13, 1895, Paris. *d.* 1976. Talented leading lady and supporting player of the French stage and screen. She played memorable roles in many prominent productions of such directors as Gance, Renoir, Carné, Duvivier, Guitry, and Becker.

FILMS INCLUDE: *Forfaitures* 1915; *La Guerre des Valses* 1933; *La Dame aux Camélias* 1934; *La Garçonne, Un Grand Amour de Beethoven, Une Partie de Campagne/A Day in the Country* 1936; *Paradis perdu, Hotel du Nord* 1938; *Sans Landemain* 1940; *Lumière d'Eté* 1942; *L'Eternel Retour/The Eternal Return* 1943; *Falbalas, Les Enfants du Paradis/Children of Paradise* 1944; *Un Ami viendra ce Soir* 1945; *L'Homme au Chapeau rond/The Eternal Husband, L'Idiot, Petrus, Les Portes de la Nuit* 1946; *Copie conforme/Confessions of a Rogue, Clochemerle/The Scandals of Clochemerle, Dédée d'Anvers/Dedee* 1947; *Une si jolie Petite Plage/Riptide, Le Secret de Mayerling/The Secret of Mayerling* 1948; *La Marie du Port, Manèges/The Cheat* 1949; *Knock/Dr. Knock, Ma Pomme, Caroline Chérie* 1950; *Le Trou Normand/Crazy for Love* 1952; *Mam'zelle Nitouche, Les Compagnons de la Nuit/Companions of the Night* 1953; *Chiens perdus sans Collier, Marie-Antoinette* 1955; *Et Dieu créa la Femme/And God Created Woman* 1956; *Pot-Bouille* 1957; *Maxime, Le Miroir à Deux Faces/The Mirror Has Two Faces* 1958; *La Bonne Soupe/Careless Love, Patate/Friend of the Family* 1964.

Marker, Chris. Director. Born Christian François Bouche-Villeneuve, on July 29, 1921, in Neuilly-sur-Seine, France. An elusive man who shuns interviews and mischievously invents mysterious origins for himself (according to one he was actually born in Outer Mongolia). Little is known about the early life of this talented filmmaker except that he was a Resistance fighter during WW II (according to some sources he was also a parachutist with the US Army) and began his adult life as a writer. He had published a novel, a collection of poems, and many essays and articles and traveled extensively as a journalist before turning to films in the early 50s. His films, mostly medium-length documentaries of varying styles, sometimes in the CINÉMA VÉRITÉ vein, reveal a nondogmatic Marxist political orientation, acute intelligence, and a sincere concern with a wide array of human problems. Marker's only fiction film, *La Jetée* (*The Pier;* made 1962, released 1964), a bleak futuristic poetic-camera vision inventively shot almost entirely as a collage of still photographs, is considered by many his finest achievement. It won the prestigious Prix Jean Vigo. In addition to his work as a director, Marker was involved in numerous projects in various capacities. Among other undertakings, he was an assistant cameraman and still photographer on Costa-Gavras's feature, *L'Aveu/The Confession* (1970), and co-produced Patricio Guzmán's monumental two-part political film, *La Batalla de Chile/The Battle of Chile* (1975–76). In 1967 he formed the film co-operative SLON (Société pour le Lancement des Oeuvres Nouvelles), through which he produced *Loin du Viêtnam/Far from Vietnam* and other politically motivated films. He usually writes and often photographs his own films. He has been called by his admirers "the one true essayist of the French cinema," but others view his didactic and uncompromising films as repetitious and often boring photographed sociopolitical lectures.

FILMS (as director-writer): *Olympia 52* (16 mm short) 1952; *Les Statues meurent aussi* (short; co-dir., co-sc. with Alain Resnais) 1953; *Dimanche à Pekin* (short filmed in China) 1955; *Le Mystère de l'Atelier 15* (short; wrote commentary and collaborated on production in unspecified capacity) 1957; *Lettre de Sibérie/Letter from Siberia* (filmed in Russia) 1958; *Les Astronautes* (short; co-dir. with Walerian Borowczyk), *Description d'un Combat* (short; filmed in Israel) 1960; *Cuba*

Si! (filmed in Cuba) 1961; *Le Joli Mai* 1963; *La Jetée* (short; release delayed from 1962) 1964; *Le Mystère Koumiko/The Koumiko Mystery* (filmed in Japan) 1965; *Si j'avais Quatre Dromadaires* 1966; *Loin du Viêtnam/Far from Vietnam* (prod., edit. only) 1967; *La Sixième Face du Pentagone* (short; with the collaboration of François Reichenbach) 1968; *A bientôt j'espère* (short), *Le Deuxième Procès d'Arthur London* (short), *Journal de Tournage* (short on the making of Costa-Gavras's *The Confession*), *On vous parle de Bresil* (short) 1969; *La Bataille des Dix Millions/Cuba: Battle of the 10,000,000* (filmed in Cuba), *Les Mots ont un Sens, Classe de Luttes* (co-dir.) 1970; *Le Train en marche* (short) 1971; *La Solitude du Chanteur de Fond* 1975; *La Spirale* (co-dir., consultant) 1975; *Le Fond de l'Air est rouge/Quand* 1977; *Quand le Siècle pris Formes* (short) 1978; *Junkopia* (short) 1981; *Sans Soleil* 1982; *2084* (short; co-dir.) 1984; *A.K./A.K.: The Making of Kurosawa's Ran* (Fr./Jap.) 1985; *Mémoire de Simone* 1986; *L'Heritage de la Chouette* 1989; *Prime Time in the Camp* 1994.

Markey, Enid. Actress. *b.* Feb. 22, 1896, Dillon, Colo. *d.* 1981. Petite brunette star of American silents. She entered films around 1913 as a Thomas Ince contract player and made trivial history in 1918 as the screen's first Jane, in *Tarzan of the Apes,* opposite Elmo Lincoln. She starred in Ince's famous *Civilization* (1916) and was William S. HART's leading lady in several films. She disappeared from the screen in the early 20s but returned for character parts in a number of talkies of the 40s and in TV situation comedies of the 60s.

FILMS INCLUDE: *The Battle of Gettysburg* 1914; *The Cup of Life, The Darkening Trail, The Mating, Aloha Oe, The Despoiler, Between Men* 1915; *The Conqueror, The Phantom, Civilization, The Captive God, Jim Grimsby's Boy, The Devil's Double, The Female of the Species* 1916; *Blood Will Tell, The Yankee Way, The Curse of Eve, The Zeppelin's Last Raid* 1917; *Cheating the Public, Tarzan of the Apes, Six Shooter Andy, The Romance of Tarzan* 1918; *Sink or Swim* 1920; *Foolish Mothers* 1923; *Snafu* 1945; *The Naked City* 1948; *Take One False Step* 1949.

Markey, Gene. Screenwriter, producer. *b.* Dec. 11, 1895, Jackson, Mich. *d.* 1980. *ed.* Dartmouth. Wrote many short stories and several novels and plays before entering films in 1928. Contributed stories and screenplays for many light and romantic Hollywood productions of the 30s, alone or in collaboration, and produced a number of films for Fox. Tall, athletic, and handsome, he was a popular man-about-town in Hollywood. His several marriages included those to glamorous film stars Joan BENNETT (1932–37), Hedy LAMARR (1939–40), and Myrna LOY (1946–50). He served as an infantry lieutenant in WW I and as a Navy officer in WW II, retiring as a rear admiral.

FILMS INCLUDE (as screenwriter): *Blinky* (magazine story basis only) 1923; *Range Courage* (from same story) 1927; *Syncopation* (novel basis, *Stepping High,* and addnl. dial.), *The Battle of Paris, Close Harmony* (co-story only), *Lucky in Love, Mother's Boy* 1929; *The Florodora Girl* 1930; *Inspiration, The Great Lover* 1931; *As You Desire Me* 1932; *Baby Face* (story), *Female* (story), *Midnight Mary* 1933; *Fashions of 1934, A Modern Hero, A Lost Lady* 1934; *Let's Live Tonight* 1935; *King of Burlesque, Private Number, Girls' Dormitory* 1936; *Wee Willie Winkie* (assoc. prod. only), *On the Avenue* (also assoc. prod.) 1937; *Suez* (assoc. prod. only) 1938; *The Little Princess* (assoc. prod. only), *Second Fiddle* (prod. only), *The Hound of the Baskervilles* (assoc. prod. only) 1939; *The Blue Bird* (assoc. prod. only), *Lillian Russell* (assoc. prod. only) 1940; *You're the One* (also prod.) 1941; *Moss Rose* (prod. only) 1947; *If This Be Sin* 1950; *Wonder Boy* 1951; *Glory* (story only) 1956.

Markle, Peter. Director. Born on Sept. 24, 1946, in Danville, Penn. A former member of the US national hockey team, he directed documentaries and commercials before first tackling feature films with some skill in the early 80s. He also directed a number of TV movies.

FILMS: *The Personals* (also sc., co-phot.) 1982; *Hot Dog. . . The Movie* 1984; *Youngblood* (also co-story, sc., cam. op.) 1986; *Bat 21* 1988; *Nightbreaker* 1989.

Markopoulos, Gregory. Filmmaker. *b.* Mar. 12, 1928, in Toledo, Ohio. *d.* 1992. *ed.* USC. For many years a leading figure in the American cinema's avant-garde movement. Experimenting with films since boyhood, he achieved prominence in underground circles during the 50s and 60s, drawing censure elsewhere for his preoccupation with phallic symbolism and then-audacious depiction of male homosexuality. He authored *A Quest of Serenity* (1965) and *A Bibliography Containing the Marvelous Distortions of My Films as Reviewed in Books, Programs, Periodicals and Newspapers During 33 Years: 1945–1978* (1978).

FILMS INCLUDE: *De Sang de la Volupté de la Mort* (trilogy) 1947; *The Dead Ones* 1948; *Flowers of Asphalt* 1949; *Swain* 1950; *Arbres aux Champignons* 1951; *Eldora* 1953; *Serenity* 1961; *Twice a Man* 1963; *The Death of Hemingway* 1965; *Galaxie, Through a Lens Brightly, Ming Green* 1966; *Himself as Herself, The Iliac Passion, Bliss, The Divine Damnation, Gammelion* 1967; *Mysteries* 1968; *Index Hans Richter* 1969; *Genius* 1970; *Hagiographia* 1971.

Marks, Richard. Film editor. Born on Nov. 10, 1943, in New York City. Cutting features since the early 70s, he had a hand in the shaping of several prominent contemporary productions.

FILMS INCLUDE: *Little Big Man* (assoc. edit.) 1970; *Bang the Drum Slowly, Serpico* (co-edit.) 1973; *The Godfather Part II* (co-edit.) 1974; *Lies My Father Told Me* (co-edit.; Can.) 1975; *The Last Tycoon* 1975; *Apocalypse Now* 1979; *Pennies from Heaven* 1981; *Max Dugan Returns, Terms of Endearment* 1983; *The Adventures of Buckaroo Banzai* 1984; *St. Elmo's Fire* 1985; *Pretty in Pink* 1986; *Broadcast News* 1987; *Say Anything. . .* 1989; *Dick Tracy* (also co-2nd-unit dir.) 1990.

Marley, John. Actor *b.* 1907, New York City. *d.* 1984, after open-heart surgery. Gritty-voiced character player of the American stage and screen. He dropped out of high school to pursue a career in acting. He was named best actor at the Venice Film Festival for his role as an unhappily married businessman in John Cassavetes' *Faces* (1968) and was nominated for an Academy Award for his portrayal of Ali MacGraw's father in *Love Story* (1970).

FILMS INCLUDE: *Native Land* 1941; *Kiss of Death* 1947; *The Naked City* 1948; *The Mob* 1951; *My Six Convicts* 1952; *The Square Jungle* 1955; *I Want to Live!* 1958; *Pay or Die* 1960; *America America, The Wheeler Dealers* 1963; *Cat Ballou* 1965; *Faces* 1968; *Love Story* 1970; *A Man Called Sledge* (It.) 1971; *Deathdream* (Can.), *Jory, The Godfather* 1972; *Blade* 1973; *Framed* 1975; *W. C. Fields and Me* 1976; *The Car, The Greatest* 1977; *Hooper, It Lives Again, The Private Files of J. Edgar Hoover* 1987; *Tribute* (Can.) 1980; *Mother Lode* 1982; *Threshold* (Can.) 1983.

Marley, J. Peverell. Director of photography. *b.* Aug. 14, 1901, San Jose, Calif. *d.* 1964. He joined Famous Players-Lasky directly out of Hollywood High School and before he reached 22 had collaborated on the cinematography of Cecil B. DE MILLE's *The Ten Commandments* (1923). He was behind the camera on many other sumptuous De Mille silents and during the talkie era worked on many glossy productions for such studios as MGM, Fox, and Warners, demonstrating great technical expertise. In the 30s he married and divorced actress Lina

BASQUETTE and in 1943, while in the uniform of an Army sergeant, he eloped with Linda DARNELL to Las Vegas. They divorced in 1952.

FILMS INCLUDE: *The Ten Commandments* (co-phot.) 1923; *Feet of Clay* 1924; *The Night Club, The Road to Yesterday, The Golden Bed* 1925; *The Volga Boatman, Silence, Three Faces West, Her Man o' War* 1926; *The King of Kings* 1927; *Chicago, Power* 1928; *The Godless Girl, Dynamite, It's a Great Life* 1929; *The Woman Racket* 1930; *Wicked* 1931; *This Day and Age* 1933; *The Mighty Barnum, The House of Rothschild, The Count of Monte Cristo* 1934; *Clive of India, Cardinal Richelieu, The Three Musketeers* 1935; *King of Burlesque, Winterset* 1936; *In Old Chicago, Alexander's Ragtime Band, Suez* 1938; *The Three Musketeers, The Hound of the Baskervilles* 1939; *Hudson's Bay* 1940; *Adam Had Four Sons, Swamp Water, Charley's Aunt* 1941; *Pride of the Marines* 1945; *Night and Day* (co-phot.), *Of Human Bondage* 1946; *Life with Father* 1947; *Whiplash* 1948; *Look for the Silver Lining* 1949; *Kiss Tomorrow Goodbye* 1950; *The Greatest Show on Earth* (co-phot.) 1952; *Phantom of the Rue Morgue* 1954; *The Ten Commandments* (2nd-unit phot.), *Serenade* 1956; *The Spirit of St. Louis* (co-phot.) 1957; *The Left-Handed Gun* 1958; *A Fever in the Blood, The Sins of Rachel Cade* 1961.

Marlowe, Hugh. Actor. *b.* Hugh Herbert Hipple, Jan. 30, 1911, Philadelphia. *d.* 1982. A former radio announcer and stage actor, he entered Hollywood films in the late 30s and played solemn leads, second leads, and eventually character parts, in a variety of motion pictures through the late 60s. His most productive period was during the early 50s, when he was prominently featured in 20th Century-Fox productions. He appeared intermittently on the Broadway stage and frequently on TV, including in the title role of the 'Ellery Queen' series of the 50s and the lead in the daytime soap opera 'Another World' in the 70s. His several marriages included those to actresses Edith Atwater and K. T. Stevens.

FILMS INCLUDE: *It Couldn't Have Happened* 1936; *Married Before Breakfast, Between Two Women* 1937; *Mrs. Parkington, Marriage Is a Private Affair, Meet Me in St. Louis* 1944; *Come to the Stable* 1949; *Twelve O'Clock High, Night and the City, All About Eve* 1950; *Rawhide, Mr. Belvedere Rings the Bell, The Day the Earth Stood Still* 1951; *Bugles in the Afternoon, Wait Till the Sun Shines Nellie, Monkey Business, Way of a Gaucho* 1952; *Casanova's Big Night, Garden of Evil* 1954; *Illegal* 1955; *Earth vs. the Flying Saucers, World Without End* 1956; *The Black Whip* 1957; *Elmer Gantry* 1960; *The Long Rope* 1961; *Birdman of Alcatraz* 1962; *13 Frightened Girls* 1963; *Seven Days in May* 1964; *Castle of Evil* 1966; *The Last Shot You Hear* (UK) 1969.

Marlowe, June. Actress. *b.* Gisela Valaria Goetten, Nov. 6, 1903, St. Cloud, Minn. *d.* 1984. Leading lady of many silent features, including several Rin Tin Tin pictures. She appeared in Laurel and Hardy's first feature, as schoolteacher Miss Crabtree in Our Gang comedies, in Langdon and Chase comedies, and in a number of German and Argentinian films. She retired from the screen after marrying film executive Rodney S. Sprigg.

FILMS INCLUDE: *When a Man's a Man, The Tenth Woman, Find Your Man, A Lost Lady* 1924; *The Man Without a Conscience, Tracked in the Snow Country, The Wife Who Wasn't Wanted, Below the Line, Clash of the Wolves, The Pleasure Buyers* 1925; *The Night Cry, Don Juan, The Old Soak* 1926; *The Fourth Commandment, Alias the Deacon, The Life of Riley, Wild Beauty* 1927; *Their Hour, Free Lips, The Foreign Legion, The Grip of the Yukon, Code of the Air* 1928; *Durch Brandenburger Tor* (Ger.) 1929; *Pardon Us* 1931; *Devil on Deck* 1932; *Riddle Ranch* 1935; *Gente Bien* (Arg.) 1939; *Slave Girl* 1947.

Marly, Florence. Actress, *b.* Hana Smekalova, June 2, 1918, Obrnice, Czechoslovakia. *d.* 1978. Intriguing, Sorbonne-educated leading lady and supporting player of French, Argentinian, Czech, and some American films. Formerly the wife of director Pierre CHENAL. She wrote, produced, and starred in a short, *Spaceboy: A Cosmic Love Affair,* which won an award at Cannes in 1973.

FILMS INCLUDE: In France—*L'Alibi* 1937; *L'Affaire Lafarge, La Maison du Maltais/Sirocco, Café de Paris* 1938; *Dernier Tournant* (Fr.) 1939; *La Piel de Zapa* (Arg.) 1943; *El Fin de la Noche* (Arg.) 1944; *Les Maudits/The Damned* 1947; *Krakatit* (Czech.) 1948. In the US—*Sealed Verdict* 1948; *Tokyo Joe* 1949; *Tokyo File 212* (US/Jap.) 1951; *Gobs and Gals* 1952; *Undersea Girl* 1957; *Queen of Blood/Planet of Blood* 1966; *Games* 1967; *Doctor Death: Seeker of Souls* 1973; *The Astrologer* 1975.

Marmont, Percy. Actor. *b.* Nov. 25, 1883, London. *d.* 1977. On the British stage since 1900, he made his film debut in 1913 during a tour of South Africa. Following his Broadway bow in 1917, he went to Hollywood, where he starred in many silent films, mainly in romantic leads. He returned to England in 1928 and then appeared in many stage productions and played leads and character roles in British talkies, typically portraying refined gentlemen. He was the father of actress Patricia Marmont.

FILMS INCLUDE: In the US—*Rose of the World, The Lie, Turn of the Wheel* 1918; *Three Men and a Girl, The Climbers, The Vengeance of Durand* 1919; *The Branded Woman, Dead Men Tell No Tales* 1920; *What's Your Reputation Worth?, Love's Penalty, Wife Against Wife* 1921; *The First Woman, Married People* 1922; *If Winter Comes, The Midnight Alarm, Broadway Broke, The Light That Failed, The Man Life Passed By* 1923; *The Shooting of Dan McGrew, The Marriage Cheat, The Enemy Sex, The Legend of Hollywood, The Clean Heart, K—The Unknown, Broken Laws, Idle Tongues* 1924; *Daddy's Gone a-Hunting, Just a Woman, The Street of Forgotten Men, Fine Clothes, Lord Jim* (title role), *Infatuation* 1925; *The Miracle of Life, Fascinating Youth, Aloma of the South Seas, Mantrap* 1926; *The Stronger Will, San Francisco Nights* 1928. In the UK—*Yellow Stockings, The Lady of the Lake* 1928; *The Silver King* 1929; *The Squeaker* 1930; *The Loves of Ariane/Ariane, The Written Law* 1931; *The Silver Greyhound, Blind Spot* 1932; *Vanity* 1935; *The Captain's Table* (dir. only), *Secret Agent, Conquest of the Air* 1936; *Les Perles de la Couronne/The Pearls of the Crown* (as Cardinal Wolsey; Fr.), *Young and Innocent/The Girl Was Young* 1937; *Penn of Pennsylvania/Courageous Mr. Penn* 1941; *No Orchids for Miss Blandish* 1948; *Four Sided Triangle* 1953; *Knave of Hearts* 1954; *Footsteps in the Fog* 1955; *Lisbon* (US) 1956; *Hostile Witness* 1968.

Marquand, Christian. Actor, director. Born on Mar. 15, 1927, in Marseilles, France, of Spanish-Arab descent. Virile leading man of many French and a few Italian and Hollywood films. In the 60s he directed two films. His brother, Serge Marquand, is also a screen actor, as is his wife, Tina Marquand (*b.* Maria-Christina Salomons, 1946, Los Angeles), the daughter of Jean-Pierre AUMONT and Maria MONTEZ.

FILMS INCLUDE: As actor—*La Belle et la Bête/Beauty and the Beast* (bit) 1946; *Quai des Orfèvres/Jenny Lamour* (bit) 1947; *Les Mains sales/Dirty Hands* 1951; *Lucrèce Borgia/Sins of the Borgias* 1953; *Senso/The Wanton Contessa* (It.) 1954; *L'Amant de Lady Chatterley/Lady Chatterley's Lover, Impasse des Vertus/Love at Night* 1955; *Et Dieu créa la Femme/And God Created Woman* 1956; *Sait-on jamais?/No Sun in Venice* 1957; *Une Vie/End of Desire* (as Julien de la Mare) 1958; *L'Ile du bout du Monde/Temptation, J'irai cracher sur vos Tombes/I Spit on*

Your Grave 1959; *La Récréation/Playtime* 1961; *Les Parisiennes/Tales of Paris, The Longest Day* (US) 1962; *La Bonne Soupe/Careless Love, Behold a Pale Horse* (US) 1964; *Lord Jim* (US/UK) 1965; *The Flight of the Phoenix* (US) 1966; *Die Hölle von Macao/The Corrupt Ones* (Ger./Fr./It.), *La Route de Corinthe/Who's Got the Black Box?* 1967; *Les Apprentis Sorciers, The Other Side of Midnight* (US) 1977; *La Secte de Marrakech* 1979; *Je vous aime* 1980; *Le Choix des Armes* 1982; *L'Eté prochain/Next Summer* 1985. As director—*Les Grands Chemins/Of Flesh and Blood* (also co-sc.; Fr./It.) 1963; *Candy* (US/Fr./It.) 1968.

Marquand, Richard. Director. *b.* 1938, Cardiff, Wales. *d.* 1987. *ed.* Université d'Aix-Marseilles (France); Cambridge. He began his career as a newscaster in Hong Kong. Back in England, he turned to documentary production and directed some 50 fact films for the BBC. He won an Emmy Award for *The Search for the Nile* (1972) and some acclaim for *Birth of the Beatles* (1979), a dramatization of the early days of the famed rock group. Moving on to features, he was rapidly proving himself a highly skilled director when he suddenly died at 49 of a heart attack, following a stroke.

FEATURE FILMS: *The Legacy* 1979; *Eye of the Needle* 1981; *Return of the Jedi* 1983; *Until September* 1984; *Jagged Edge* 1985; *Hearts of Fire* (also co-prod.) 1987.

married print. British term for a composite print (also known as a "combined print"). A positive film carrying both picture and sound in synchronization. The process of synchronizing the sound and picture on the same film strip is known as "marriage" or "marrying."

Mars, Kenneth. Actor. Born in 1936, in Chicago. Frequently histrionic comedic character player since the 1960s. Memorable as the unreconstructed Nazi author of 'Springtime for Hitler' in *The Producers*. Regular on TV variety series 'The Carol Burnett Show,' among others.

FILMS INCLUDE: *The Producers* 1968; *Butch Cassidy and the Sundance Kid* 1969; *Desperate Characters* 1971; *What's Up Doc?* 1972; *Paper Moon* 1973; *The Parallax View, Young Frankenstein* 1974; *Night Moves* 1975; *The Apple Dumpling Gang Rides Again* 1979; *Full Moon High* 1981; *Yellowbeard* 1983; *Protocol, Prince Jack* 1984; *Fletch* 1985; *Rented Lips, Radio Days* 1987; *For Keeps, Illegally Yours* 1988; *Police Academy 6: City Under Siege* 1989; *The Little Mermaid* (v/o) 1989; *Shadows and Fog* 1992; *Thumbelina* (v/o) 1994; *The Van* 1997.

Marsh, Joan. Actress. Born Nancy Ann Rosher, on July 10, 1913, in Porterville, Calif. The daughter of cameraman Charles ROSHER, she began a stage career as a baby and played child roles in several silent Mary Pickford films on which her father was cinematographer. Initially billed Dorothy Rosher, she returned to films in 1930 as Joan Marsh, a young platinum blonde, and then played leads and supporting roles in many Hollywood productions through the late 50s, usually portraying glamorous types. After her retirement she went into the stationery business.

FILMS INCLUDE: As Dorothy Rosher—*The Mad Maid of the Forest* (short) 1915; *The Little Princess* 1917; *How Could You Jean?, Johanna Enlists, Women's Weapons* 1918; *Captain Kidd Jr., Heart o' the Hills, Daddy Long Legs* 1919; *Suds, Pollyanna* 1920; *Little Lord Fauntleroy* 1921; *Tess of the Storm Country* 1922. As Joan Marsh—*The King of Jazz* (bit), *All Quiet on the Western Front, Little Accident* 1930; *Inspiration, Dance Fools Dance, Three Girls Lost, Shipmates, Politics, Maker of Men* 1931; *The Wet Parade, Bachelor's Affairs, That's My Boy, The Speed Demon* 1932; *Daring Daughters, High Gear, It's Great to Be Alive, Three-Cornered Moon, The Man Who Dared, Rainbow Over Broadway* 1933; *You're Telling Me, Many Happy Returns, We're Rich Again* 1934; *Anna Karenina* 1935; *Dancing Feet, Charlie Chan on Broadway, Life Begins in College, Hot Water* 1937; *The Lady Objects* 1938; *Idiot's Delight, Fast and Loose* 1939; *Road to Zanzibar* 1941; *The Man in the Trunk* 1942; *Follow the Leader* 1944.

Marsh, Mae. Actress. *b.* Mary Wayne Marsh, Nov. 9, 1895, Madrid, N.M. *d.* 1968. Educated in a Hollywood convent, in 1910 she was playing hooky from school to see her older sister, Marguerite, perform in a West Coast Biograph production, when she was noticed by the film's director, D. W. GRIFFITH. During an excursion to California the following winter Griffith invited Mae to appear in his films. In 1912 she went to New York and after a couple of appearances in Kalem films joined Griffith's stock company of players at Biograph. Like Lillian GISH, she made an ideal Griffith heroine, at once youthful and mature, physically frail but spiritually strong. She rapidly became one of the director's favorite actresses, a frequent co-star of Bobby HARRON. As "The Little Sister" she provided some of the most tender and moving moments of *The Birth of a Nation,* memorably in the "homecoming" scene with Henry B. Walthall and in the suicide scene, when she leaps to her death to escape rape.

Miss Marsh surpassed her achievement the following year, with a superior dramatic performance as Robert Harron's grief-stricken wife in the modern episode of *Intolerance.* In 1916 she left Griffith to sign a lucrative contract with Goldwyn. But her roles for this and other studios in the US and Europe rarely did justice to her talent. It wasn't until she returned to a Griffith film, *The White Rose,* in 1923, that she had the opportunity to give another memorably intense dramatic performance. Except for an occasional role, she retired from the screen in 1925 but returned in the early 30s as a character actress and appeared in numerous talkies through the early 60s.

FILMS INCLUDE: *Fighting Blood* 1911; *Home Folks, The Kentucky Girl, The Spirit Awakened, Brutality, Lena and the Geese, Man's Genesis, The Sands of Dee, The New York Hat* 1912; *The Primitive Man, Near to Earth, The Reformers, The Tender-Hearted Boy, Influence of the Unknown, The Wanderer* 1913; *Brute Force, The Battle at Elderbush Gulch, Judith of Bethulia, The Escape, Home Sweet Home, The Avenging Conscience* 1914; *The Birth of a Nation, The Outcast* 1915; *Intolerance, Hoodoo Ann, The Marriage of Molly-O, A Child of the Paris Streets, The Little Liar, The Wild Girl of the Sierras, The Wharf Rat* 1916; *The Cinderella Man, Polly of the Circus, Sunshine Alley* 1917; *The Face in the Dark, All Woman, The Beloved Traitor, The Glorious Adventure* 1918; *The Mother and the Law* (rev. vers. of modern episode in *Intolerance*), *Spotlight Sadie, The Bondage of Barbara* 1919; *The Little 'Fraid Girl* 1920; *Nobody's Kid* 1921; *Till We Meet Again* 1922; *Paddy—The Next Best Thing* (UK), *The White Rose* 1923; *Arabella* (Ger.), *Daddies* 1924; *The Rat* (UK), *Tides of Passion* 1925; *Racing Through* 1928; *Over the Hill* 1931; *Rebecca of Sunnybrook Farm, That's My Boy* 1932; *Alice in Wonderland* 1933; *Little Man What Now?* 1934; *Black Fury* 1935; *Hollywood Boulevard* 1936; *Young People* 1940; *Great Guns* 1941; *Tales of Manhattan* 1942; *Jane Eyre* 1944; *A Tree Grows in Brooklyn* 1945; *Deep Waters* 1948; *Three Godfathers* 1949; *The Gunfighter* 1950; *The Robe* 1953; *Prince of Players* 1955; *While the City Sleeps, Julie* 1956; *Sergeant Rutledge* 1960; *Two Rode Together* 1961; *Donovan's Reef* 1963.

Marsh, Marian. Actress. Born Violet Krauth, on Oct. 17, 1913, in Trinidad. Doll-faced leading lady of Hollywood films of the 30s, which she entered as Marilyn Morgan. She changed her name again the following year when she played her first lead role, as Trilby to John Barrymore's Svengali. She then played leads in mostly routine films until her retirement early in the 40s.

FILMS INCLUDE: *Whoopee* (bit) 1930; *Svengali, Five Star Final, The Mad Genius, The Road to Singapore, Under Eighteen* 1931; *Alias the Doctor, Beauty, Strange Justice, The Sport Parade* 1932; *The Eleventh Commandment, Daring Daughters, Notorious but Nice* 1933; *I Like It That Way, Love at Second Sight* (UK) 1934; *A Girl of the Limberlost, Black Room Mystery, Crime and Punishment* 1935; *Lady of Secrets, The Man Who Lived Twice* 1936; *The Great Gambini, Saturday's Heroes* 1937; *Prison Nurse* 1938; *Missing Daughters* 1939; *Fugitive from a Prison Camp* 1940; *Murder by Invitation* 1941; *House of Errors* 1942.

Marsh, Oliver T. American director of photography. *b.* 1893. *d.* 1941. A lighting cameraman from 1918, he was responsible for the cinematography of several important films of the 30s, mainly at MGM. He shared a special Academy Award for the color cinematography of *Sweethearts* (1938).

FILMS INCLUDE: *All Woman* 1918; *A Virtuous Vamp* 1919; *Dangerous Business* 1920; *Wedding Bells* 1921; *The Masked Bride* 1925; *Kiki* 1926; *The Dove, The Enemy* 1927; *The Divine Woman, Dream of Love, Sadie Thompson* 1928; *Our Modern Maidens, The Single Standard* 1929; *Du Barry, Woman of Passion, Not So Dumb* 1930; *The Phantom of Paris, The Sin of Madelon Claudet* 1931; *Arsene Lupin, Emma, Rain* 1932; *Today We Live* 1933; *The Merry Widow* 1934; *David Copperfield, A Tale of Two Cities* 1935; *After the Thin Man, The Great Ziegfeld, San Francisco* 1936; *The Firefly, Maytime, Rosalie* 1937; *The Girl of the Golden West, Sweethearts* 1938; *Another Thin Man, Broadway Serenade, The Women* 1939; *Bitter Sweet* 1940; *Lady Be Good* 1941.

Marshal, Alan. Actor. *b.* Jan. 20, 1909, Sydney, Australia. *d.* 1961. Dashing romantic leading man and second lead of Hollywood films from the mid-30s. Formerly on the stage, he returned to the theater in the mid-40s, occasionally playing in films in character roles. He died at 52 while appearing onstage with Mae West in 'Sextet.'

FILMS INCLUDE: *The Garden of Allah, After the Thin Man* 1936; *Parnell, Conquest, Night Must Fall* 1937; *Dramatic School, Invisible Enemy, I Met My Love Again* 1938; *Exile Express, The Adventures of Sherlock Holmes, The Hunchback of Notre Dame* 1939; *Married and in Love, Irene, The Howards of Virginia* 1940; *Tom Dick and Harry, Lydia* 1941; *The White Cliffs of Dover, Bride by Mistake* 1944; *The Opposite Sex* 1956; *The House on Haunted Hill, Day of the Outlaw* 1959.

Marshall, Alan. Producer. Born on Aug. 12, 1938, in London. In British films in various capacities since 1952, he became associated in the 70s with director Alan PARKER and served as producer of most of that director's films.

FILMS INCLUDE: *Bugsy Malone* 1976; *Midnight Express* 1978; *Fame* 1980; *Shoot the Moon, Pink Floyd—The Wall* 1982; *Another Country, Birdy* 1984; *Angel Heart* (co-prod.) 1987; *Homeboy* 1988; *Jacob's Ladder* 1990; *Basic Instinct* 1992; *Cliffhanger* 1993; *Showgirls* 1995.

Marshall, Brenda. Actress. Born Ardis Anderson Gaines, on Sept. 29, 1915, on Negros Island, Philippines. Ravishing brunette leading lady of Hollywood films of the 40s, memorably as Errol Flynn's love interest in *The Sea Hawk* (1940). Formerly (1941–70) married to William HOLDEN.

FILMS: *Espionage Agent* 1939; *The Sea Hawk, The Man Who Talked Too Much, Money and the Woman, East of the River, South of Suez* 1940; *Footsteps in the Dark, Singapore Woman, Highway West, The Smiling Ghost* 1941; *You Can't Escape Forever, Captains of the Clouds* 1942; *The Constant Nymph, Paris After Dark, Background to Danger* 1943; *Something for the Boys* 1944; *Strange Impersonation* 1946; *Whispering Smith* 1949; *The Iroquois Trail* 1950.

Marshall, E. G. Actor. Born Everett G. Marshall, on June 18, 1910, in Owatonna, Minn., of Norwegian origin. *ed.* U. of Minnesota. Forceful character actor of the American stage, TV, and films, typically in determined or morally indignant parts. Won two Emmys for his portrayal of a righteous lawyer in the TV series 'The Defenders' (1961–65). Later seen in "The New Doctors" segment (1969–73) of the series 'The Bold Ones.'

FILMS INCLUDE: *The House on 92nd Street* 1945; *13 Rue Madeleine* 1947; *Call Northside 777* 1948; *The Caine Mutiny, Pushover, Broken Lance* 1954; *The Left Hand of God* 1955; *The Mountain* 1956; *Twelve Angry Men, The Bachelor Party* 1957; *The Buccaneer* 1958; *The Journey, Compulsion, Cash McCall* 1959; *Town Without Pity* 1961; *The Chase* 1966; *The Bridge at Remagen* 1969; *Tora! Tora! Tora!* 1970; *The Pursuit of Happiness* 1971; *Independence* (doc. short; narr.) 1976; *Interiors* 1978; *Superman II* 1980; *Creepshow* 1982; *My Chauffeur, Power* 1986; *La Gran Fiesta* (Puerto Rico) 1987; *National Lampoon's Christmas Vacation* 1989; *Due Occhi diabolici/Two Evil Eyes* (It.) 1990; *Consenting Adults* 1992; *Nixon* 1995.

Marshall, Frank. American producer. Born on Sept. 13, 1946, in Los Angeles. The son of TV composer ('The Munsters,' etc.) Jack Marshall. He began his association with film while still attending UCLA, as a protégé of Peter BOGDANOVICH. Following an apprenticeship as a bit actor and crew technician, he assumed the duties of an associate producer on several Bogdanovich films and served as line producer on Orson Welles's unreleased film *The Other Side of the Wind* and Martin Scorsese's *The Last Waltz* (1978), among other productions. In the early 80s, starting with the box-office smash *Raiders of the Lost Ark,* Marshall began a long and hugely profitable association with director Steven SPIELBERG. With producer Kathleen KENNEDY, who became his wife, Marshall entered a partnership with Spielberg, together forming Amblin Entertainment, one of Hollywood's most prosperous production companies. Marshall made a successful debut as a director with the light horror thriller *Arachnophobia* (1990). Another Frank Marshall was a British film director of the late 50s and early 60s.

FILMS INCLUDE: *Targets* (act.) 1968; *The Last Picture Show* (act.) 1971; *Paper Moon* (assoc. prod.) 1973; *Daisy Miller* (assoc. prod.) 1974; *Nickelodeon* (assoc. prod., act.) 1976; *The Driver* (assoc. prod.) 1978; *The Warriors* (exec. prod.) 1979; *Raiders of the Lost Ark* (prod., act.) 1981; *E.T.: The Extra-Terrestrial* (prod. superv.), *Poltergeist* (co-prod.) 1982; *Twilight Zone—The Movie* (exec. prod.) 1983; *Indiana Jones and the Temple of Doom* (co-exec. prod.; co-2nd-unit dir.), *Gremlins* (exec. prod. 1984; *Fandango* (co-exec. prod.), *The Goonies* (co-exec. prod.), *Back to the Future* (co-exec. prod., 2nd-unit dir.), *The Color Purple* (co-prod.), *Young Sherlock Holmes* (co-exec. prod.) 1985; *The Money Pit* (co-prod.), *An American Tail* (co-exec. prod.) 1986; *Innerspace* (co-exec. prod.), *Empire of the Sun* (co-prod., 2nd-unit dir.), *Batteries Not Included* (co-exec. prod.) 1987; *Who Framed Roger Rabbit?* (co-prod.) 1988; *Indiana Jones and the Last Crusade* (co-exec. prod., co-2nd-unit dir.), *Dad* (co-exec. prod.), *Back to the Future Part II* (co-exec. prod.), *Always* (co-prod, 2nd-unit dir.) 1989; *Joe versus the Volcano* (co-exec. prod.), *Back to the Future Part III* (co-exec. prod.), *Gremlins 2: The New Batch* (co-exec prod.), *Arachnophobia* (dir., exec. prod.) 1990; *An American Tale: Fievel Goes West* (co-exec. prod.), *Hook* (co-prod.) 1991; *Noises Off* (prod.), *Swing Kids* (co-exec. prod.), *Alive* (co-exec. prod.) 1992; *Milk Money* 1994; *Congo* (also dir.), *The Indian in the Cupboard* 1995.

Marshall, Garry. Director, producer, screenwriter. Born Garry Marscharelli, on Nov. 13, 1934, in New York City. A graduate of Northwestern University's School of Journalism, he began his working life as a copyboy, then reporter for the New York *Daily News.* At the same time, he pursued parallel careers as a drummer in his own jazz band and a stand-up comedian and writer of comedy material for Joey Bishop, Phil Foster, and others. By the mid-60s he had been contributing regularly to the 'Jack Parr Show' and to such TV sitcoms as 'The Danny Thomas Hour,' 'The Lucy Show,' and 'The Dick Van Dyke Show.' Turning to the production end of the business, he created the comedy series 'Hey Landlord' in 1966, then scored a huge hit in 1970 when he became the executive producer of 'The Odd Couple' series. His string of later TV successes, in partnership with Jerry Belson, included 'Happy Days,' 'Laverne and Shirley,' and 'Mork and Mindy.' He co-wrote the Broadway play 'The Roost' (1980). Marshall began producing and writing features in the late 60s. He turned to directing in the early 80s, scoring an enormous box-office hit at the turn of the decade with *Pretty Woman.* He is the brother of actress-director Penny MARSHALL.

FILMS: As producer-writer—*How Sweet It Is* 1968; *The Grasshopper* 1970. As director—*Young Doctors in Love* (also exec. prod.) 1982; *The Flamingo Kid* (also co-sc.) 1984; *Nothing in Common* 1986; *Overboard* 1987; *Beaches* 1989; *Pretty Woman* 1990; *Frankie and Johnny* 1991; *Exit to Eden* (also prod.) 1994. As actor—*Psych-Out* 1968; *Lost in America* 1985; *Soapdish* 1991; *A League of Their Own* 1992; *Hocus Pocus* 1993; *Dear God* 1996.

Marshall, George. Director. *b.* Dec. 29, 1891, Chicago. *d.* 1975. Among the most prolific and versatile of all major-studio Hollywood directors. A graduate of St. John's Military Academy, he entered the work force early after being expelled from the University of Chicago. In addition to helping out at his father's jewelry shop, he worked for a railroad, sold portraits, played some professional baseball, and served as a cub reporter for a Seattle newspaper, then traveled to Hollywood where he entered films as an extra at Universal in 1912. Later played featured roles, wrote stories and screenplays for comedy shorts, and in 1916 began directing Westerns. Returning from WW I service, he piloted two Ruth Roland serials for Pathé and a number of features for Fox, then began to specialize in comedy and action shorts. He directed scores of these in the 20s in addition to occasional features, and in 1925 was appointed supervising director of the entire Fox shorts output. He performed a similar function for Pathé in 1928–29. He returned to features in 1932 and subsequently directed a wide variety of entertaining films in all genres. He was at his most effective with comedy, in its various manifestations, and among those he handled were such comic talents as Laurel and Hardy, W. C. Fields, Bob Hope, and Martin and Lewis. Marshall's gentle humor was evident even in his noncomic films and was successfully incorporated into many of his enjoyable dramas and action pictures.

FEATURE FILMS: *Love's Lariat* 1916; *The Man from Montana* 1917; *The Adventures of Ruth* (serial) 1919; *Ruth of the Rockies* (serial), *Prairie Trails* 1920; *Why Trust Your Husband?* (also co-story), *Hands Off, A Ridin' Romeo* (also sc.), *After Your Own Heart, The Lady from Longacre, The Jolt* (also co-story) 1921; *Smiles Are Trumps* 1922; *Haunted Valley* (serial), *Don Quickshot of the Rio Grande, Where Is This West?, Men in the Raw* 1923; *A Trip to Chinatown* (prod. superv. only) 1926; *The Gay Retreat* (prod. superv. only) 1927; *Pack Up Your Troubles* (co-dir. with Raymond McCarey), *Their First Mistake* (Laurel & Hardy 2-reeler), *Towed in a Hole* (Laurel & Hardy 2-reeler) 1932; *Ever Since Eve, Wild Gold, She Learned About Sailors, 365 Nights in Hollywood* 1934; *Life Begins at 40, Ten Dollar Raise, In Old Kentucky, Music Is Magic, Show Them No Mercy* 1935; *A Message to Garcia, The Crime of Dr. Forbes, Can This Be Dixie?* (also co-story) 1936; *Nancy Steele Is Missing, Love Under Fire* 1937; *The Goldwyn Follies, Battle of Broadway, Hold That Co-Ed* 1938; *You Can't Cheat an Honest Man, Destry Rides Again* 1939; *The Ghost Breakers, When the Daltons Rode* 1940; *Pot o' Gold, Texas* 1941; *Valley of the Sun, The Forest Rangers, Star Spangled Rhythm* 1942; *True to Life, Riding High* 1943; *And the Angels Sing* 1944; *Murder He Says, Incendiary Blonde, Hold That Blonde* 1945; *The Blue Dahlia, Monsieur Beaucaire* 1946; *The Perils of Pauline, Variety Girl* 1947; *Hazard, Tap Roots* 1948; *My Friend Irma* 1949; *Fancy Pants, Never a Dull Moment* 1950; *A Millionaire for Christy* 1951; *The Savage* 1952; *Off Limits, Scared Stiff, Houdini* 1953; *Money from Home, Red Garters, Duel in the Jungle* 1954; *Destry, The Second Greatest Sex* 1955; *Pillars of the Sky* 1956; *The Guns of Fort Petticoat, Beyond Mombasa, The Sad Sack* 1957; *The Sheepman, Imitation General* 1958; *The Mating Game, It Started with a Kiss* 1959; *The Gazebo* 1960; *Cry for Happy* 1961; *The Happy Thieves, How the West Was Won* ("The Railroad" episode) 1962; *Papa's Delicate Condition* 1963; *L'Intrigo/Dark Purpose* (It./Fr./US), *Advance to the Rear* 1964; *Boy Did I Get a Wrong Number!* 1966; *Eight on the Lam* 1967; *The Wicked Dreams of Paula Schultz* 1968; *Hook Line and Sinker* 1969.

Marshall, Herbert. Actor. *b.* May 23, 1890, London. *d.* 1966. Suave leading man and character star of the British and American stage and films. He began as an apprentice with a London accounting firm and while serving as a business manager for an impresario took an interest in acting. He made his stage debut in Brighton in 1911 and began appearing on the London stage soon after. He lost a leg in WW I action but successfully disguised the handicap during his long stage and screen career. During the 20s he commuted frequently between London and New York and became established as a popular leading man in theaters on both sides of the Atlantic. In 1928 he married actress Edna BEST and they appeared together in many stage productions, soon becoming one of the more popular teams of their time. They divorced in 1940. His four other wives included (1946–58) actress Boots MALLORY. Marshall made his screen debut in England in 1927 but his first important film, *The Letter,* opposite Jeanne Eagels, was made in 1929 in Hollywood. Despite appearances in several early British talkies, he remained primarily a stage actor until 1932, when he began concentrating exclusively on films. He settled in Hollywood, where he perfected his persona as an urbane, mature romantic lead in the 1932 Ernst Lubitsch comedy *Trouble in Paradise.* But advancing age and his reserved manner gradually forced him into character parts (such as the ethical but weak husband of Bette Davis in *The Little Foxes*), which he played ably, relying on a charming personality and a mellifluous voice. In a career that spanned four decades, he appeared opposite many of Hollywood's most glamorous female stars in many memorable films. He died of a heart attack.

FILMS: *Mumsie* (UK) 1927; *Dawn* (UK) 1928; *The Letter* (opposite Jeanne Eagels) 1929; *Murder* (UK) 1930; *The Calendar* (UK), *Michael and Mary* (UK), *Secrets of a Secretary* 1931; *The Faithful Heart* (UK), *Blonde Venus, Trouble in Paradise, Evenings for Sale* 1932; *Clear All Wires* (UK), *The Solitaire Man* (UK), *I Was a Spy* (UK) 1933; *Four Frightened People, Riptide, Outcast Lady, The Painted Veil* 1934; *The Good Fairy, The Flame Within, Accent on Youth, The Dark Angel, If You Could Only Cook* 1935; *The Lady Consents, Till We Meet Again, Forgotten Faces, Girls' Dormitory, A Woman Rebels,*

Make Way for a Lady 1936; *Angel, Breakfast for Two* 1937; *Mad About Music, Always Goodbye, Woman Against Woman* 1938; *Zaza* 1939; *A Bill of Divorcement, Foreign Correspondent, The Letter* (opposite Bette Davis) 1940; *Adventure in Washington, The Little Foxes* (as Horace Giddens), *When Ladies Meet, Kathleen* 1941; *The Moon and Sixpence* (as the narrator/Somerset Maugham), *Forever and a Day, Flight for Freedom, Young Ideas* 1943; *Andy Hardy's Blonde Trouble* 1944; *The Enchanted Cottage, The Unseen* 1945; *Crack-Up, The Razor's Edge* (again as Maugham) 1946; *Duel in the Sun, Ivy* 1947; *High Wall* 1948; *The Secret Garden* 1949; *The Underworld Story* 1950; *Anne of the Indies* 1951; *Captain Blackjack* (US/Sp.) 1952; *Angel Face* 1953; *Riders to the Stars, Gog, The Black Shield of Falworth* 1954; *The Virgin Queen* 1955; *Wicked As They Come* (UK) 1956; *The Weapon* (UK) 1957; *Stage Struck, The Fly* 1958; *College Confidential, Midnight Lace* 1960; *Fever in the Blood*, 1961; *Five Weeks in a Balloon* 1962; *The List of Adrian Messenger, The Caretakers* 1963; *The Third Day* 1965.

Marshall, Penny. Director, actress. Born Penny Marscharelli, on Oct. 15, 1942, in Brooklyn, N.Y. Popular comedienne of American TV and occasional features who turned to film directing in the late 80s. The daughter of an industrial filmmaker and a dance coach, and younger sister of director-producer-writer Garry MARSHALL, she was raised in a show business atmosphere. She dropped out of the University of New Mexico to dance and perform in summer stock. After competing on TV in Ted Mack's 'The Original Amateur Hour,' she appeared in the 1967–68 season of 'The Danny Thomas Hour' and began performing with regularity in various television programs. Her first big break came when she assumed the role of Myrna, Jack Klugman's secretary, in the series 'The Odd Couple' (1971–75). Following more exposure on 'The Bob Newhart Show' (1972–73) and other programs she scored a huge hit as the co-star of the popular 'Laverne & Shirley' (1976–83). She directed some of the episodes of the series, created by her brother, Garry, and produced by her father, Tony. As a feature director since 1986, she had considerable box-office success with *Big* (1988), which was also nominated for Academy Awards for best picture and best actor, but not best director. She struck gold with the 1992 hit *A League of Their Own*. Her second husband (1971–79) was actor-director Rob REINER.

FILMS: As actress—*The Savage Seven, How Sweet It Is!* 1968; *How Come Nobody's on Our Side?* 1975; *1941* 1979; *Movers and Shakers* (cameo) 1985; *The Hard Way* 1991; *Get Shorty* (cameo) 1995. As director—*Jumpin' Jack Flash* 1986; *Big* 1988; *Awakenings* (also co-exec. prod.) 1990; *A League of Their Own* 1992; *Renaissance Man* (also co-prod.) 1994; *The Preacher's Wife* 1996. As executive producer—*Calendar Girl* 1993; *Getting Away with Murder* 1996.

Marshall, Trudy. Actress. Born in 1922, in Brooklyn, N.Y. Leading lady of low-budget films and supporting actress of occasional A pictures, she was formerly a model.

FILMS INCLUDE: *Secret Agent of Japan, Orchestra, Footlight Serenade, Springtime in the Rockies* 1942; *Crash Dive, Heaven Can Wait, The Dancing Masters* 1943; *Ladies of Washington, The Purple Heart, The Sullivans* 1944; *Circumstantial Evidence, The Dolly Sisters* 1945; *Boston Blackie and the Law, Dragonwyck, Sentimental Journey* 1946; *Key Witness, Too Many Winners* 1947; *The Fuller Brush Man, Disaster* 1948; *Barbary Pirate* 1949; *Mark of the Gorilla* 1950; *The President's Lady* 1953; *Full of Life* 1957.

Marshall, Tully. Actor. *b.* William Phillips, Apr. 13, 1864, Nevada City, Calif. *d.* 1943. A graduate of the University of Santa Clara, he appeared in numerous stage plays from 1890 and made his screen debut in 1914. He played occasional leads and hundreds of key character roles in silent and sound Hollywood films.

FILMS INCLUDE: *Paid in Full* 1914; *The Sable Lorcha* 1915; *A Child of the Paris Streets, Oliver Twist* (as Fagin), *Intolerance, Joan the Woman* 1916; *Unconquered, Romance of the Redwoods, Countess Charming, A Modern Musketeer* 1917; *Old Wives for New, M'lss, Bound in Morocco, We Can't Have Everything, Too Many Millions, The Squaw Man* 1918; *Cheating Cheaters, The Grim Game, The Crimson Gardenia, Everywoman* 1919; *Excuse My Dust, Honest Hutch, Double Speed, The Dancin' Fool* 1920; *The Cup of Life, Hail the Woman, Lotus Blossom, Silent Years* 1921; *Penrod, Is Matrimony a Failure?, Any Night, The Village Blacksmith, Deserted at the Altar* 1922; *The Law of the Lawless, The Brass Bottle, The Covered Wagon, Broken Hearts of Broadway, Dangerous Trails, The Hunchback of Notre Dame* (as Louis XI), *Ponjola, Richard the Lion-Hearted* (as the Bishop of Tyre) 1923; *For Sale, The Stranger* (title role), *He Who Gets Slapped* 1924; *Smouldering Fires, The Talker, The Merry Widow, Clothes Make the Pirate* 1925; *The Torrent, Old Loves and New, Twinkletoes* 1926; *Beware of Widows, The Cat and the Canary, The Gorilla* 1927; *Drums of Love, The Trail of '98, Queen Kelly* 1928; *Alias Jimmy Valentine, Conquest, Redskin, The Bridge of San Luis Rey, Thunderbolt, The Mysterious Dr. Fu Manchu, Tiger Rose* 1929; *Mammy, Under a Texas Moon, Common Clay, The Big Trail, Tom Sawyer* (as Muff Potter) 1930; *The Millionaire, The Unholy Garden* 1931; *The Man I Killed/Broken Lullaby, Arsene Lupin, Beast of the City, Grand Hotel, Red Dust, Scarface* 1932; *Night of Terror* 1933; *Black Fury, Diamond Jim, A Tale of Two Cities* 1935; *Souls at Sea* 1937; *A Yank at Oxford* 1938; *Invisible Stripes, Brigham Young, Go West, Chad Hanna* 1940; *Ball of Fire, Moontide, This Gun for Hire* 1942; *Hitler's Madman* 1943.

Marshall, William. Actor, director. Born on Oct. 2, 1917, in Chicago. A vocalist with the Fred Waring Orchestra in 1936, he led his own band the following year and entered films as an actor in 1940. He played leads and second leads in a number of productions at several studios but failed to establish a following and in the early 50s moved into directing, again with limited success. He was formerly married to actresses Michèle MORGAN and Ginger ROGERS. His credits are sometimes confused with those of another William Marshall, a black actor-singer who has been appearing sporadically in films since the early 50s. (See next entry.)

FILMS INCLUDE: As actor—*Flowing Gold, Santa Fe Trail* 1940; *Belle of the Yukon* 1944; *State Fair* 1945; *Murder in the Music Hall, Earl Carroll Sketchbook, That Brennan Girl* 1946; *Calendar Girl, Blackmail* 1947. As director—*Adventures of Captain Fabian* (also prod.) 1951; *The Phantom Planet* 1961.

Marshall, William. Actor. Born on Aug. 19, 1924, in Gary, Ind. *ed.* NYU. Physically impressive, he began playing overpowering blacks in films of the 50s, memorably in his screen debut as the domineering King Dick in *Lydia Bailey* (1952). His film appearances have been sporadic and for the most part confined to supporting roles, but in the early 70s he enjoyed the taste of stardom, portraying a black vampire in *Blacula* (1972) and its sequel, *Scream Blacula Scream* (1973).

FILMS INCLUDE: *Lydia Bailey* 1952; *Demetrius and the Gladiators* 1954; *Something of Value* 1957; *To Trap a Spy* 1966; *The Boston Strangler* (as Attorney General Edward W. Brooke, who later became a US senator) 1968; *Zigzag, Skullduggery* 1970; *Blacula* 1972; *Scream Blacula Scream* 1973; *Abby* 1974; *Twilight's Last Gleaming* 1977; *Curtains* (Can.) 1983.

Martelli, Otello. Director of photography. Born on May

10, 1903, in Rome. In Italian films as an assistant cameraman from age 13, he got his first assignment as a cinematographer at 16, in 1919. He gained an international reputation for his sensitive, intimate work on some key films of the neorealist period of the late 40s, then in the 50s as FELLINI's favorite cameraman.

FILMS INCLUDE: *Oltre la Legge* 1919; *Vecchia Guardia* 1935; *Marcella* 1937; *Kean* 1940; *Don Giovanni* 1942; *Paisà/Paisan* 1946; *Caccia Tragica/Tragic Hunt* 1947; *The Glass Mountain* (UK/It.), *Amore* 1948; *Riso Amaro/Bitter Rice, Stromboli* 1949; *Luci del Varietà/Variety Lights, Anna* 1951; *Roma Ore 11/Rome 11 O'Clock* 1952; *I Vitelloni* 1953; *La Strada* 1954; *Il Bidone* 1955; *Guendalina* 1956; *La Loi/Where the Hot Wind Blows* (Fr./It.) 1959; *La Dolce Vita* 1960; *Boccaccio '70* (Fellini and De Sica episodes) 1962; *I Tre Volti* (co-phot.) 1964; *Menage all'Italiana* 1965.

Martin, Chris-Pin (Christopher). Actor. *b.* Ysabel Ponciana Chris-Pin Martin Piaz, Nov. 19, 1893, Tucson, Ariz. of Mexican parentage. *d.* 1953. Light character player of Hollywood action pictures. Provided comic relief in the Cisco Kid series (as Pancho or Gorditor) and in many other Westerns.

FILMS INCLUDE: *The Rescue* 1929; *Billy the Kid* 1930; *The Squaw Man, The Cisco Kid* 1931; *Girl Crazy, South of Santa Fe* 1932; *Outlaw Justice* 1933; *Four Frightened People* 1934; *Under the Pampas Moon, Bordertown* 1935; *The Gay Desperado* 1936; *The Texans* 1938; *Stagecoach, The Return of The Cisco Kid, Frontier Marshal* 1939; *Lucky Cisco Kid, Down Argentine Way, The Mark of Zorro* 1940; *Weekend in Havana, The Bad Man* 1941; *Undercover Man, Tombstone* 1942; *The Ox-Bow Incident* 1943; *Ali Baba and the 40 Thieves* 1944; *San Antonio* 1945; *The Fugitive* 1947; *Mexican Hayride* 1948; *The Beautiful Blonde from Bashful Bend* 1949; *A Millionaire for Christy* 1951; *Ride the Man Down* 1952.

Martin, Dean. Singer, actor. *b.* Dino Paul Crocetti, on June 7, 1917, in Steubenville, Ohio. *d.* 1996. A former prize-fighter, steel mill laborer, and card shark, he began singing in night spots in his hometown and later around the country. During an Atlantic City engagement in 1946 he met comedian Jerry LEWIS, with whom he formed a partnership. The Martin-Lewis team was soon one of the most phenomenal successes in show-business history. With Martin supplying the crooning and romancing, and Lewis the clowning, the duo enjoyed enormous popularity in live performances, on TV, and in films. When the partnership dissolved ten years and 16 films later, few believed that Martin could make it on his own. But he prospered nicely, at first as a singer, then as an actor and all-around entertainer and star of his own TV variety program, 'The Dean Martin Show' (1965–74). He gave several convincing performances in light and dramatic films, characterized by his typical relaxed manner and devil-may-care charm. As a member of the famed "Rat Pack," he co-starred in the early 60s in several films featuring Frank SINATRA and his gang. In the late 60s he played Matt Helm, a James Bondish adventurer in a series of mediocre spy-film spoofs. He continued touring into the 90s, including celebrated appearances with fellow Rat Packers Sammy DAVIS, Jr., and honorary member Liza MINNELLI. His second of three marriages produced Dean Paul ("Dino") Martin (*b.* Nov. 17, 1951, Santa Monica, Calif.), a rock musician, tennis pro, and a film and TV actor. A captain in the California Air National Guard, Dino was killed in 1987 after his F-4 Phantom jet fighter crashed into a mountain during a routine training mission. Dino was formerly married to actress Olivia HUSSEY.

FILMS: With Jerry Lewis—*My Friend Irma* 1949; *My Friend Irma Goes West* 1950; *At War with the Army, That's My Boy* 1951; *Sailor Beware, Jumping Jacks* 1952; *The Stooge, Scared Stiff, The Caddy* 1953; *Money from Home, Living It Up, Three Ring Circus* 1954; *You're Never Too Young, Artists and Models* 1955; *Pardners, Hollywood or Bust* 1956. Without Lewis—*Ten Thousand Bedrooms* 1957; *The Young Lions* 1958; *Some Came Running, Rio Bravo, Career* 1959; *Who Was That Lady?, Bells Are Ringing, Ocean's Eleven* 1960; *All in a Night's Work, Ada, Canzoni nel Mondo* (compilation film; It.) 1961; *Sergeants 3, Who's Got the Action?* 1962; *Toys in the Attic, Four for Texas, Who's Been Sleeping in My Bed?* 1963; *What a Way to Go!, Robin and the 7 Hoods, Kiss Me Stupid* 1964; *The Sons of Katie Elder, Marriage on the Rocks* 1965; *The Silencers, Texas Across the River, Murderers' Row* 1966; *Rough Night in Jericho, The Ambushers* 1967; *How to Save a Marriage—And Ruin Your Life, Bandolero!, Five Card Stud* 1968; *The Wrecking Crew* 1969; *Airport* 1970; *Something Big* 1971; *Showdown* 1973; *Mr. Ricco* 1975; *The Cannonball Run* 1981; *Cannonball Run II* 1984.

Martin, Mary. Singer, actress. *b.* Dec. 1, 1913, Weatherford, Tex. *d.* 1990, of cancer. One of the major talents of the American musical stage ('South Pacific,' 'Peter Pan,' 'The Sound of Music,' 'I Do, I Do'), she starred in several light films at the early stage of her professional career, later appearing as a guest star in a couple of others. She stretched a stage career into the late 80s, after recovering from severe injuries in a 1982 San Francisco cab crash that also badly hurt former movie star Janet GAYNOR, who would eventually die of complications related to her injuries. Miss Martin's first of two marriages produced actor Larry HAGMAN. Autobiography: *My Heart Belongs* (1976).

FILMS: *Rage of Paris* (bit) 1938; *The Great Victor Herbert* 1939; *Rhythm on the River, Love Thy Neighbor* 1940; *New York Town, Kiss the Boys Goodbye, Birth of the Blues* 1941; *Star Spangled Rhythm* 1942; *True to Life, Happy Go Lucky* 1943; *Night and Day* 1946; *Main Street to Broadway* 1953.

Martin, Millicent. Actress. Born on June 8, 1934, in Romford, England. Attractive performer of British stage, TV, and some films.

FILMS INCLUDE: *Libel* 1959; *The Horsemasters* 1960; *Invasion Quartet* 1961; *Nothing but the Best* 1963; *Those Magnificent Men in Their Flying Machines* 1965; *Alfie, Stop the World I Want to Get Off* 1966.

Martin, Pamela Sue. Actress. Born on Jan. 5, 1953, in Westport, Conn. Sleepy-eyed leading lady of American TV and films. A model and a performer in TV commercials while still attending high school, she began acting on both the small and big screens in the early 70s. She gained some popularity on TV as teenage sleuth Nancy Drew in the series 'The Nancy Drew Mysteries' and 'The Hardy Boys Mysteries' (both 1977–78), a role she played when she was already 24. In 1981–84 she co-starred in the hit TV series 'Dynasty.' Her feature appearances have been sporadic.

FILMS: *To Find a Man, The Poseidon Adventure* 1972; *Our Time/Death of Her Innocence, Buster and Billie* 1974; *The Lady in Red/Guns Sin and Bathtub Gin* 1979; *Torchlight* (also assoc. prod., co-sc.) 1984; *A Cry in the Wild* 1990.

Martin, Ross. Actor *b.* Martin Rosenblatt, on Mar. 22, 1920, Grodek, Poland. *d.* 1981. Versatile character player of American TV and some films. A few days old when his family came to the US, he grew up in New York and graduated from City College, later earning an M.A. in psychometrics at NYU and a law degree from George Washington University. He pursued an acting career all along his educational route, starting out as a stand-up comic and later performing on radio and early TV. He appeared sporadically in films, usually as a detestable heavy. But it was on TV that he won lasting fame, in the constantly changing role of Artemus Gordon, a secret agent of multiple disguises in the series 'The Wild Wild West' (1965–69). He died at

61 after suddenly collapsing in the middle of a tennis game in 100-degree heat.

FILMS: *Conquest of Space* 1955; *The Colossus of New York* 1956; *Geronimo, Experiment in Terror* 1962; *The Ceremony* 1963; *The Man from Button Willow* (v/o), *The Great Race* 1965.

Martin, Steve. Actor, screenwriter, playwright. Born on Aug. 14, 1945, in Waco, Tex. Leading comedy star of American TV and films. The son of a real-estate executive, he was raised in Southern California from age five. In his mid-teens he sold guidebooks and performed magic tricks at Disneyland and at 18 added banjo riffs and comedy routines to his repertoire. He majored in philosophy at California State University at Long Beach, intending to teach, but after a year switched to UCLA, from which he graduated with a degree in theater arts. He landed his first big-time job as a comedy writer for TV's 'The Smothers Brothers Comedy Hour,' for which he earned an Emmy Award in 1969. He went on to perform similar services for Sonny and Cher and other entertainers, and at the same time began appearing with increasing frequency in TV comedy-variety shows. Martin then took to the road as a stand-up comic, eventually scoring great success as a club performer and recording artist. His popularity soared with his frequent appearances as guest or guest host on NBC's 'The Tonight Show' and especially on 'Saturday Night Live,' where he perfected his "Wild and Crazy Guy" routine.

The prematurely gray Martin made his film debut in 1977 and scored his first big hit two years later in *The Jerk.* He quickly emerged as a popular movie performer, bringing to the screen his likeable, self-mocking split personae, forever wavering between vulnerability and overconfidence, between frenzied cheeriness and pathetic heartbreak. He collaborated on the screenplays and participated in the production of several of his films. Martin won the Writers Guild Award for best adapted screenplay and shared the Los Angeles Film Critics Award for *Roxanne* (1987), his modern-day adaptation of *Cyrano de Bergerac.* His switch from comic to romantic lead in light comedies was a complete success, making him a sought-after star into the 90s. Martin achieved status as a playwright with the success of his play 'Picasso at the Lapin Agile,' first produced in Los Angeles then moving to off Broadway. Divorced from actress Victoria TENNANT. Author: *Cruel Shoes* (1979).

FILMS: *The Absent-Minded Waiter* (also sc.) 1977; *Sgt. Pepper's Lonely Hearts Club Band* (also song) 1978; *The Muppet Movie, The Kids Are Alright, The Jerk* (also co-sc.) 1979; *Pennies from Heaven* 1981; *Dead Men Don't Wear Plaid* (also co-sc.) 1982; *The Man with Two Brains* (also co-sc.) 1983; *The Lonely Guy, All of Me* 1984; *Movers and Shakers* (cameo) 1985; *Little Shop of Horrors, Three Amigos!* (also exec. prod., co-sc., song) 1986; *Roxanne* (also sc., exec. prod.), *Planes Trains and Automobiles* 1987; *Dirty Rotten Scoundrels* 1988; *Parenthood* 1989; *My Blue Heaven* 1990; *L.A. Story* (also co-exec. prod., sc.) 1991; *Father of the Bride, Grand Canyon* 1991; *Housesitter, Leap of Faith* 1992; *Mixed Nuts, A Simple Twist of Fate* (also prod., sc.) 1994; *Father of the Bride II* 1995; *Sgt. Bilko* 1996.

Martin, Strother. Actor. *b.* Mar. 26, 1919, Kokomo, Ind. *d.* 1980. *ed.* U. of Michigan. A former National Junior Springboard Diving Champion, he went to Hollywood as a swimming instructor and began playing bit parts in films. He later played character parts in numerous films and TV episodes, mostly as a heavy. In the 60s he came into his own in a succession of offbeat, memorable characterizations.

FILMS INCLUDE: *The Asphalt Jungle* (bit) 1950; *Rhubarb* 1951; *Storm Over Tibet* 1952; *The Magnetic Monster* 1953; *Drum Beat* 1954; *Kiss Me Deadly, The Big Knife* 1955; *Attack!* 1956; *The Horse Soldiers* 1959; *Sanctuary, The Deadly Companions* 1961; *The Man Who Shot Liberty Valance* 1962; *McLintock!* 1963; *Invitation to a Gunfighter* 1964; *The Sons of Katie Elder* 1965; *Harper* 1966; *The Flim Flam Man, Cool Hand Luke* 1967; *The Wild Bunch, True Grit, Butch Cassidy and the Sundance Kid* 1969; *The Ballad of Cable Hogue* 1970; *Red Sky at Morning, Fools' Parade, The Brotherhood of Satan* (lead role), *Hannie Caulder* 1971; *Pocket Money* 1972; *Sssssss* (lead role) 1973; *Rooster Cogburn, Hard Times* 1975; *The Great Scout and Cathouse Thursday* 1976; *Slap Shot* 1977; *The End* 1978; *The Villain, Love and Bullets, The Champ* 1979.

Martin, Tony. Singer, actor. Born Alvin Morris, on Dec. 25, 1912, in San Francisco. *ed.* St. Mary's Coll. A former band saxophonist-vocalist, he played romantic leads in light Hollywood films of the 30s, 40, and 50s and during that period was also popular as a nightclub and recording crooner. He was decorated with a Bronze Star for WW II service sergeant with the USAAF. Formerly married to Alice FAYE, he has been the husband of Cyd CHARISSE since 1948. They frequently appear together in a nightclub act and in 1976 published a book of memoirs, *The Two of Us.*

FILMS: *Follow the Fleet* (bit), *The Farmer in the Dell, Back to Nature, Sing Baby Sing, Pigskin Parade, Banjo on My Knee* 1936; *The Holy Terror, Sing and Be Happy, You Can't Have Everything, Life Begins in College, Ali Baba Goes to Town* 1937; *Sally Irene and Mary, Kentucky Moonshine, Up the River, Thanks for Everything* 1938; *Winner Take All* 1939; *Music in My Heart* 1940; *Ziegfeld Girl, The Big Store* 1941; *Till the Clouds Roll By* 1946; *Casbah* 1948; *Two Tickets to Broadway* 1951; *Easy to Love, Here Come the Girls* 1953; *Deep in My Heart* 1954; *Hit the Deck* 1955; *Quincannon Frontier Scout* 1956; *Let's Be Happy* (UK) 1957.

Martinelli, Elsa. Actress. Born in 1932, in Grosseto, Italy. Attractive brunette leading lady of Italian and international films. The daughter of a low-echelon government employee, she worked as a barmaid and a model before being discovered by Kirk Douglas, who launched her career in *The Indian Fighter* (1955). Her daughter, Cristiana Mancinelli (*b.* 1956), is also a film actress.

FILMS INCLUDE: *The Indian Fighter* (US) 1955; *La Risaia/Rice Girl, Donatella* 1956; *Four Girls in Town* (US), *Manuela/Stowaway Girl* (UK) 1957; *I Battellieri del Volga/Prisoner of the Volga* 1958; *Costa Azzura, Ciao Ciao Bambina, La Notte Brava* 1959; *Un Amore a Roma, Et Mourir de Plaisir/Blood and Roses* (Fr./It.) 1960; *Hatari* (US), *The Pigeon That Took Rome* (US), *Le Procès/The Trial* (Fr./It./Ger.) 1962; *Rampage* (US), *The V.I.P.s* (UK) 1963; *De l'Amour* (Fr./It.), *La Fabuleuse Aventure de Marco Polo/Marco the Magnificent* (Fr./It./Ger.), *La Decima Vittima/The Tenth Victim* 1965; *Maroc 7* (UK) 1966; *Sept fois Femme/Woman Times Seven* (Fr./It./US), *Le plus Vieux Métier du Monde/The Oldest Profession* (Fr./It./Ger.) 1967; *Candy* (US/Fr./It.), *El Millón de Madigan/Madigan's Millions* (Sp./It.), *Maldonne* (Fr./It.), *L'Amica, Les Chemins de Kathmandou* (Fr./It.) 1969; *La Part de Lion* (Fr.), *Una sull'altra/One on Top of the Other* 1971; *L'Araucana Massacro degli Dei* 1972; *Il Garofano Rosso* 1976; *Sono un Fenomeno paranormale* 1986.

Martinson, Leslie H. Director. Born in Boston, of Jewish-Latvian-German origin. *ed.* Boston Conservatory of Music; Boston U. He worked in the advertising department of a newspaper before heading in 1936 to Hollywood, where for 15 years he served as a script clerk on major MGM productions. He quit the studio in 1952 for an opportunity to direct episodes of the 'The Roy Rogers Show' for TV and turned out his first feature for Republic in the following year. He went on to direct hundreds of TV episodes, several TV movies, and a baker's dozen features, mostly modest youth and action fare. His wife, Connie Martinson, hosts a book beat show on public TV.

FILMS: *The Atomic Kid* 1954; *Hot Rod Girl* 1956; *Hot Rod Rumble* 1957; *Lad: A Dog* (co-dir. with Aram Avakian) 1962; *PT-109, Black Gold* 1963; *FBI Code 98, For Those Who Think Young* 1964; *Batman* 1966; *Fathom* 1967; *Mrs. Pollifax—Spy* 1971; *Escape from Angola* 1976; *Cruise Missile* (Ger./Sp./US/Iran) 1978.

Marton, Andrew. Director. *b.* Endre Marton, Jan. 26, 1904, in Budapest. *d.* 1992. Began his film career as a film editor in Vienna in 1922. The following year he accompanied Ernst LUBITSCH to Hollywood, where he edited two of the director's films and made his own debut as a director with a low-budget mystery melodrama, *Two O'Clock in the Morning* (1929). During the late 20s he commuted frequently between the US and Germany, where he became chief editor at the Tobin studios. He directed two German films in the early 30s but left the country with the advent of Nazism in 1933 and worked in Switzerland, Hungary, and England before heading back to Hollywood in 1940. He competently directed a variety of Hollywood productions, mainly for MGM, as well as segments for such TV shows as 'Daktari,' 'Cowboy in Africa,' and 'Sea Hunt.' In addition, he was a second-unit director of action sequences on some major Hollywood spectaculars.

FILMS: As director—*Two O'Clock in the Morning* 1929; *Die Nacht ohne Pause* (co-dir. with Franz Wenzler; Ger.) 1931; *Nordpol-ahoi!* (Ger.) 1933; *Der Dämon der Berge/Demon of the Himalayas* (Switz.) 1934; *Miss President* (Hun.) 1935; *The Secret of Stamboul/The Spy in White* (UK), *Wolf's Clothing* (UK) 1936; *School for Husbands* (UK) 1937; *A Little Bit of Heaven* 1940; *Gentle Annie* 1944; *Gallant Bess* 1946; *King Solomon's Mines* (co-dir. with Compton Bennett) 1950; *The Wild North, Storm Over Tibet, Mask of the Himalayas, The Devil Makes Three* 1952; *Gypsy Colt, Prisoner of War, Men of the Fighting Lady* 1954; *Green Fire* 1955; *Seven Wonders of the World* (co-dir. with four others) 1956; *Underwater Warrior* 1958; *The Longest Day* (co-dir. with three others), *It Happened in Athens* 1962; *The Thin Red Line* 1964; *Crack in the World, Clarence the Cross-Eyed Lion* 1965; *Around the World Under the Sea* (also prod.), *Birds Do It* 1966; *Africa—Texas Style!* (also prod.; US/UK) 1967. As 2nd-unit director (partial list)—*The Red Badge of Courage* 1951; *A Farewell to Arms* 1957; *Ben-Hur* 1959; *55 Days at Peking, Cleopatra* 1963; *The Fall of the Roman Empire* 1964; *Kelly's Heroes, Catch-22* 1970; *Mohammad Messenger of God/The Message* 1977.

Marton, Pierre. See STONE, Peter.

Marvin, Lee. Actor. *b.* Feb. 19, 1924, New York City. *d.* 1987, of a heart attack. The son of an advertising executive and a fashion writer, he turned to acting by sheer accident. Invalided out of WW II service with the Marines, he worked briefly as a plumber's assistant, when he was asked to replace an ailing actor in a bit role in summer stock. He then took up acting at New York's American Theatre Wing, and following a number of appearances off Broadway he landed a part in 1951 in the Broadway production of 'Billy Budd.' He made his screen debut the same year. Tall and rugged, he was typecast throughout the 50s as a brutal heavy, mostly in Westerns and crime melodramas. But in the 60s, following a starring role in the TV series 'M Squad' (1957–60) and a couple of amiable parts in John Wayne pictures, he switched from villain to hero. He became established as a star after winning the best actor Academy Award for his dual role in *Cat Ballou* (1965), a role that also demonstrated his skill at robust comedy. Marvin made headlines in 1979 when, in a landmark legal case that established the California courts' "palimony doctrine," he was sued for half his fortune by a woman he had lived with for six years but never married. Her claim was rejected, but Marvin was ordered to pay her a nominal sum for rehabilitation.

FILMS: *U.S.S. Teakettle/You're in the Navy Now* 1951; *Hong Kong, We're Not Married, Diplomatic Courier, Duel at Silver Creek, Hangman's Knot, Eight Iron Men* 1952; *Seminole, The Glory Brigade, Down Among the Sheltering Palms, The Stranger Wore a Gun, The Big Heat, Gun Fury* 1953; *The Wild One, Gorilla at Large, The Caine Mutiny, The Raid* 1954; *Bad Day at Black Rock, Violent Saturday, Not as a Stranger, A Life in the Balance, Pete Kelly's Blues, I Died a Thousand Times, Shack Out on 101* 1955; *Seven Men from Now, Pillars of the Sky, The Rack, Attack!* 1956; *Raintree County* 1957; *The Missouri Traveler* 1958; *The Comancheros* 1961; *The Man Who Shot Liberty Valance* 1962; *Donovan's Reef* 1963; *The Killers* 1964; *Cat Ballou, Ship of Fools* 1965; *The Professionals* 1966; *The Dirty Dozen, Point Blank, Tonite Let's All Make Love in London/The London Scene* (doc.) 1967; *Sergeant Ryker* (combined from TV episodes made in 1963), *Hell in the Pacific* 1968; *Paint Your Wagon* 1969; *Monte Walsh* 1970; *Pocket Money, Prime Cut* 1972; *Emperor of the North Pole, The Iceman Cometh* 1973; *The Spikes Gang, The Klansmen* 1974; *Shout at the Devil* (UK), *Great Scout and Cathouse Thursday* 1976; *Avalanche Express* 1979; *The Big Red One* 1980; *Death Hunt* 1981; *Gorky Park* 1983; *Canicule/Dog Day* (Fr.) 1984; *The Delta Force* 1986.

Marx Brothers, The. Comedy team. Chico (*b.* Leonard, Mar. 26, 1886; *d.* 1961), Harpo (*b.* Adolph but known as Arthur, Nov. 21, 1888; *d.* 1964), Groucho (*b.* Julius Henry, Oct. 2, 1890; *d.* 1977), and Zeppo (*b.* Herbert, Feb. 25, 1901; *d.* 1979). All were born in New York City, the sons of a dapper but unsuccessful Yorkville Jewish tailor of Alsatian origin. It was their mother, Minna Schoenberg (immortalized in the early 70s in the Broadway musical 'Minnie's Boys'), the daughter of show people and sister of Al Shean of Gallagher and Shean of vaudeville fame, who forged the talents of her children and started them in show business. Chico was given piano lessons (which he passed on to Harpo, since there was enough money only for one); Harpo taught himself to play the harp; and Groucho began his professional career as a boy singer at age 11.

Minnie launched her boys in vaudeville as a musical team that evolved through various combinations, in which a fifth brother, Gummo (*b.* Milton, 1893; *d.* 1977), figured prominently (Gummo left the team before it reached Broadway and was replaced by Zeppo). The brothers started out as "The Three Nightingales" (Groucho, Gummo, and a girl), then "The Four Nightingales" (with Harpo) and "The Six Musical Mascots" (Groucho, Chico, Harpo, Gummo, and Minnie and her sister). It wasn't until they switched to comedy that the Marx Brothers' act began to click. Even then they endured years of hardship on the vaudeville circuit before finally making Broadway in 1924 in the musical comedy 'I'll Say She Is.' They followed this with 'The Cocoanuts' in 1925 and 'Animal Crackers' in 1928. By this time they had developed their inimitable comedy style and the distinctive personal characteristics that were to find their ultimate expression in the brothers' zany, anarchic films of the 30s.

The fast-thinking Groucho, master of the ad lib and the cynical pun, became identified with his crouched walk, incredible mustache (initially painted on), roving, leering eyes, framed by steel-rimmed glasses, and a perennial thick cigar. Harpo, the gifted harpist and inventive pantomimist, never spoke a line, but his actions were louder than words. His cherubic face, topped by a kinky red wig, broke into a smile that combined childlike mischief, idiocy, and utter madness. His broad trousers and oversize coat hid a virtual arsenal of junk. His most celebrated prop was an old-fashioned taxi horn, which he sounded happily in his zaniest moments, especially when chasing a blonde. Chico, wearing an outgrown, modified Tyrolean outfit, interpreted Harpo's visual puns, translating them into his own broken-down English spiced with a heavy Italian accent. He also played the piano with an eccentric virtuosity. Zeppo was never a part of his brothers' shenanigans and played bland romantic roles in the team's Broadway plays and first five films.

Except for a brief appearance by Harpo in the silent film *Too Many Kisses,* the Marx Brothers made their screen debut in 1929 in the film version of 'The Cocoanuts.' It was shot at Paramount's East Coast studios, in Astoria, Long Island City, while the brothers were still playing in the long-running Broadway production of 'Animal Crackers.' They commuted back and forth, shooting the film by day and performing on the stage at night. Despite mediocre direction, contrived romantic plots, and disruptive musical interludes that plagued most of their films, the anarchic, almost surrealist quality of the Marx Brothers' absurd slapstick comedy burst upon the screen with enormous vitality. Unrestrained antics, travesties of logic, and outrageous insults were unleashed in their films with an insane abandon that appealed equally to intellectuals and lowbrows. Character actress Margaret Dumont, although not a regular member of the team, figured prominently in several of the Marx Brothers films; she was the perfect foil for their hilarious schemes.

The Marx Brothers' screen comedy reached a peak of brilliance in their last film for Paramount, *Duck Soup* (1933), briskly directed by Leo McCarey, and their first film for MGM, *A Night at the Opera* (1935), a resounding box-office success directed by Sam Wood under the guidance of Irving Thalberg. Unfortunately, their subsequent vehicles were progressively marred by subplots and limp pace. But even their worst film was so rich in moments of comic brilliance that it was worthwhile. The Marx Brothers made their last appearance as a team in *Love Happy* (1950). All three appeared in Irwin Allen's *The Story of Mankind* (1957) but in unrelated episodes (with Harpo peculiarly cast as Sir Isaac Newton), and they were reunited on TV in a 'General Electric Theater' comedy *The Incredible Jewel Robbery.* Other than that they went their separate ways.

Chico retired early and spent his last years relaxing with cards and friends. Harpo, who after several weeks of shooting was replaced by Alan Young in the title role of the film *Androcles and the Lion* in 1952, made a number of guest appearances on TV and published his memoirs, *Harpo Speaks!,* in 1961. Groucho, the youngest of the three, remained the most active, appearing in occasional films and hosting the TV comedy-quiz show 'You Bet Your Life.' He wrote three uproariously funny autobiographical books—*Groucho and Me* (1959), *Memoirs of a Mangy Lover* (1964), and *The Groucho Letters* (1967). (His son, Arthur, authored *Life with Groucho,* 1952, and *Son of Groucho,* 1972.) He was still ready with a quip and an insult in infrequent guest appearances on TV in the early 70s. But he was senile and frail in the months before his death, precipitating a fight over the custody of his estate. In 1972, at the age of 82, he returned to the New York stage after an absence of 43 years with a one-man show at Carnegie Hall. That same year he was honored with a special award at the Cannes Film Festival.

FILMS (starring Chico, Harpo, and Groucho unless otherwise noted): *Too Many Kisses* (Harpo only) 1925; *The Cocoanuts* (also Zeppo) 1929; *Animal Crackers* (also Zeppo) 1930; *Monkey Business* (also Zeppo) 1931; *Horse Feathers* (also Zeppo) 1932; *Duck Soup* (also Zeppo) 1933; *A Night at the Opera* 1935; *A Day at the Races* 1937; *Room Service* 1938; *At the Circus* 1939; *Go West* 1940; *The Big Store* 1941; *Stage Door Canteen* (Harpo only) 1943; *A Night in Casablanca* 1946; *Copacabana* (Groucho only) 1947; *Love Happy, Mr. Music* (Groucho only) 1950; *Double Dynamite* (Groucho only) 1951; *A Girl in Every Port* (Groucho only) 1952; *Will Success Spoil Rock Hunter?* (Groucho only; cameo), *The Story of Mankind* 1957; *Skidoo* (Groucho only) 1968.

Maselli, Francesco. Director. Born on Dec. 9, 1930, in Rome. Began making amateur films at 14 and entered the Centro Sperimentale di Cinematographia at 16. He assisted directors Luigi Chiarini and Michelangelo Antonioni on several shorts and collaborated on the script of the latter's early features *Cronaca di un Amore/Story of a Love Affair* (1950) and *La Signora senza Camelie/Camille Without Camelias* (1953). He began directing his own professional shorts in 1949 and was heralded a prodigy after having piloted an episode for *Amore in Città/Love in the City* (1953) at the age of 23. He turned out his first solo feature in 1955, then mellowed into mediocrity.

FEATURE FILMS: *Amore in Città/Love in the City* ("Storia di Caterina" episode) 1953; *Gli Sbandati* (also co-story, co-sc.) 1955; *La Donna del Giorno/The Doll That Took the Town* (also co-sc.) 1957; *I Delfini* (also co-story, co-sc.) 1960; *Le Italiane e l'Amore/Latin Lovers* ("Le Adolescenti" episode) 1961; *Gli Indifferenti/Time of Indifference* (also co-sc.) 1964; *Fai in Fretta ad Uccidermi. . . ho Freddo!* (also co-sc.) 1968; *Ruba al Prossimo Tuo/A Fine Pair* (also co-sc.) 1969; *Lettera aperta a un Giornale della Sera* (also story, sc.) 1970; *Il Sospetto* 1975.

Masina, Giulietta. Actress. Born Giulia Anna Masina, on Feb. 22, 1920, in Giorgio di Piano, near Bologna, Italy. *d.* 1994. A schoolteacher's daughter, she began her acting career while a student with a group of university players in Rome. In 1942 she scored a personal success on Italian radio in a play written by fellow student Federico FELLINI. They married the following year and she made her screen debut playing a bit role in Rossellini's *Paisà/Paisan* (1946). Two years later she won the Italian Critics award for best supporting actress for her remarkable portrayal of the role of Marcella in Lattuada's *Without Pity.* She then returned briefly to the stage, but after her late success in *Variety Lights* (Fellini's directorial debut, in collaboration with Lattuada) she turned exclusively to films. She revealed a unique, Chaplinesque talent, capable of moving audiences alternately to laughter and tears as Gelsomina, the simple-hearted, docile, but sensitive gamine in Fellini's *La Strada.*

Miss Masina won the Cannes Festival best actress award for another heart-rending performance, as a naïve prostitute, in Fellini's *Le Notte di Cabiria/The Nights of Cabiria.* Fellini spoke of her as more than an actress, crediting her as the inspiration of both these films and the muse that opened for him new dimensions in his art. But Masina, who had attained the status of a myth by the late 50s, became hampered by the scarcity of roles suitable to her unique talents.

FILMS INCLUDE: *Paisà/Paisan* 1946; *Senza Pietà/Without Pity* 1948; *Luci del Varietà/Variety Lights, Persiane chiuse/Behind Closed Shutters* 1951; *Europa 51/The Greatest Love, Lo Sceicco Bianco/The White Sheik* 1952; *Donne proibite/Angels of Darkness* 1953; *La Strada* 1954; *Il Bidone* 1955; *Le Notti di Cabiria/The Nights of Cabiria/Cabiria* 1956; *Fortunella, Nella Città l'Inferno/And The Wild Wild Women* 1958; *La Grande Vie/Das Kunstseidene Mädchen/La Gran Vita* (Fr./ Ger./It.) 1960; *Landru/Bluebeard* 1972; *Giulietta degli Spiriti/Juliet of the Spirits* 1965; *Non Stuzzicate la Zanzara* 1967; *The Madwoman of Chaillot* (as Gabrielle; UK) 1969;

Frau Holle 1985; *Ginger e Fred/Ginger and Fred* 1986; *Aujourd'Hui Peut-Etre. . . /A Day to Remember* (Fr./It.) 1991.

mask. 1. A device in a camera, projector, or printer designed to limit the effective area of a picture. It usually comes in the form of a plate with a window. 2. A square, flat sheet of metal or opaque screen designed to shield a camera from unwanted reflections during filming. Also known as a FLAG or GOBO.

masking. 1. A process of blocking out any given portion of a photographic image, commonly used in trick photography to produce special effects. 2. A method of obtaining a partial correction of color reproduction.

Maslansky, Paul. Producer. Born on Nov. 23, 1933, in New York City. *ed.* Washington & Lee U.; NYU Law School. A former trumpet player and radio advertising salesman, he studied filmmaking at the Cinémathèque Française in Paris and won an award at Cannes for his graduation documentary, *Letter from Paris.* He began his professional career as an assistant director on *The Counterfeit Traitor* (1962), then served as production manager on several other European-location features. After producing several low-budget horror thrillers, he became involved in the production of larger-scale European and American co-productions, finally striking Hollywood gold with the witless but profitable *Police Academy* series. He directed one film, *Sugar Hill* (1974).

FILMS INCLUDE (as producer or executive producer, alone or in collaboration): *Il Castello dei Morti Vivi/Castle of the Living Dead* (It./Fr.) 1964; *La Sorella di Satana/The She-Beast* (It./Yug.) 1966; *Eyewitness/Sudden Terror* (UK), *La Tenda rosa/The Red Tent* 1970; *Deathline/Raw Meat* (UK) 1973; *Sugar Hill* (dir. only) 1974; *Hard Times* 1975; *The Blue Bird* (USSR/US) 1976; *Damnation Alley* 1977; *Circle of Iron/The Silent Flute* (UK), *Scavenger Hunt, The Villain* 1979; *The Salamander* (US/UK/It.), *Ruckus* 1981; *Love Child* 1982; *Police Academy* (and several sequels) 1984; *Return to Oz* 1985; *Ski Patrol, The Russia House* 1990; *Cop and a Half* 1993.

Mason, James. Actor. *b.* May 15, 1909, Huddersfield, England, the son of a wool merchant. *d.* 1984. After receiving a degree in architecture from Cambridge in 1931, he turned to the stage, reaching the British screen in 1935 as a star of "quota quickies." He became England's leading star and top box-office draw in the mid-40s, following a personal triumph in an otherwise undistinguished film, *The Man in Grey.* This film established the formula for his screen appeal—a romantic villain who brutalized his women and had them beg for more. *The Seventh Veil* (1945), in which he played a sado-romantic Svengali, was a huge international hit. After the critical success of *Odd Man Out* (1947), in which he played one of the best roles of his career, he left for Hollywood, where he lost much of his engaging coarseness but little of his appeal as a cerebral, introspective leading man with sardonic looks, precise acting style, and a distinctive, resonant voice. He appeared rather indiscriminately in numerous films, good, bad, and indifferent, frequently commuting between the US and Europe in quest of assignments. This frenzied schedule was possibly made necessary by the actor's expensive divorce settlement with his first wife (1941–64), Pamela Kellino [Mason] (*b.* Mar. 10, 1922, London). His second (from 1971) was actress Clarissa Kaye. Among the more distinguished performances of his Hollywood career was that of the self-destructive Norman Maine in *A Star is Born.* Autobiography: *Before I Forget* (1981). An American actor by the same name (1890–1959) appeared in numerous silent and sound Hollywood films, mostly Westerns and action pictures, from 1914.

FILMS: In the UK—*Late Extra* 1935; *Twice Branded, Troubled Waters, Prison Breaker, Blind Man's Bluff* 1936; *The Secret of Stamboul, The Mill on the Floss* (as Tom Tulliver), *The High Command, Fire Over England, Catch as Catch Can* 1937; *The Return of the Scarlet Pimpernel* 1938; *I Met a Murderer* (also prod., story) 1939; *This Man Is Dangerous/The Patient Vanishes* 1941; *Hatter's Castle, The Night Has Eyes/Terror House, Alibi, Secret Mission* 1942; *Thunder Rock, The Bells Go Down, The Man in Grey, They Met in the Dark* 1943; *Candlelight in Algeria, Fanny by Gaslight/Man of Evil, Hotel Reserve* 1944; *A Place of One's Own, They Were Sisters, The Seventh Veil* 1945; *The Wicked Lady* 1946; *Odd Man Out, The Upturned Glass* 1947. In the US—*Caught, Madame Bovary* (as Gustave Flaubert), *The Reckless Moment* 1949; *East Side West Side, One Way Street* 1950; *The Desert Fox* (as Field Marshal Rommel), *Pandora and the Flying Dutchman* (UK/US) 1951; *Lady Possessed* (also prod., co-sc.), *Five Fingers, The Prisoner of Zenda* (as Rupert of Hentzau), *Face to Face* ("The Secret Sharer" episode) 1952; *The Story of Three Loves* ("The Jealous Lover" episode), *The Desert Rats* (as Rommel), *Julius Ceasar* (as Brutus), *Botany Bay, The Man Between* (UK), *Charade* (also co-sc.; three-episode film originally made for British TV; UK), *The Telltale Heart* (short) 1953; *The Child* (half-hour featurette; dir. only), *Prince Valiant, A Star Is Born, 20,000 Leagues Under the Sea* (as Captain Nemo) 1954; *Forever Darling, Bigger Than Life* (also prod.) 1956; *Island in the Sun* (UK) 1957; *Cry Terror, The Decks Ran Red* 1958; *North by Northwest, Journey to the Center of the Earth* 1959; *A Touch of Larceny* (UK), *The Trials of Oscar Wilde* (UK) 1960; *The Marriage-Go-Round* 1961; *Hero's Island/The Land We Love* (also co-prod.), *Lolita* (as Humbert Humbert; UK/US), *Escape from Zahrain, Tiara Tahiti* (UK) 1962; *Finchè dura la Tempesta/Beta Som/Torpedo Bay* (It./Fr.) 1963; *The Fall of the Roman Empire, The Pumpkin Eater* (UK) 1964; *Lord Jim* (as Gentleman Brown; UK/US), *Les Pianos mécaniques/The Player Pianos/The Uninhibited* (Fr./Sp./It.), *Genghis Khan* (US/UK/Ger.) 1965; *The Blue Max* (UK), *Georgy Girl* (UK) 1966; *The Deadly Affair* (UK), *Stranger in the House/Cop-Out* (UK) 1967; *Duffy* (UK/US), *The Sea Gull* (as Trigorin; UK/US) 1968; *Mayerling* (as Emperor Franz-Josef; Fr./UK) *The London Nobody Knows* (doc., as narrator-guide), *Age of Consent* (also co-prod.; Austral.) 1969; *Spring and Port Wine* (UK), *De la Part des Copains/Cold Sweat* (Fr./It.) 1970; *Kill! Kill! Kill! Kill!* (Fr./Ger./It./Sp.), *Bad Man's River,* (Sp.) 1971; *Child's Play* 1972; *The Last of Sheila, The Mackintosh Man* (UK), *Frankenstein: The True Story* (originally made for TV) 1973; *The Marseilles Contract/The Destructors* (UK/Fr.), *11 Harrowhouse* (UK), *Trikimia* (UK/Gr.), *Nostro Nero in Casa Nichols* (It.) 1974; *Autobiography of a Princess, The Schoolmistress and the Devil, Inside Out* (UK), *Mandingo, La Polizia interviene—Ordine di Uccidere* (It.) 1975; *Voyage of the Damned* (UK), *People on the Wind* (offscreen narr. only) 1976; *Homage to Chagall* (co-narr. only), *Cross of Iron* (UK/Ger.), *Paura in Città/Hot Stuff* (It.) 1977; *Heaven Can Wait, The Boys from Brazil* 1978; *The Passage* (UK), *Murder by Decree* (as Dr. Watson; UK/Can.), *Bloodline, The Waterbabies* (UK), *North Sea Hijack/ffolkes* (UK) 1979; *Evil Under the Sun* (UK), *The Verdict* 1982; *Alexandre* (Switz.), *Yellowbeard* 1983; *The Shooting Party* 1984; *The Assisi Underground* (It./UK) 1985.

Mason, Marsha. Actress. Born on Apr. 3, 1942, in St. Louis, Mo. *ed.* Webster Coll. Talented brunette leading lady of the American stage and screen. At her most effective portraying anxious, high-strung contemporary women during the 70s and early 80s. A printer's daughter, she began acting in high school. After graduating from college, she came to New York in 1964 to study acting and supported herself as a part-time clerk, waitress, and go-go dancer. Eventually, she began performing in the daytime TV soaper 'Love of Life.' During that lean period she made her screen debut in a cheap 1966 movie. She landed her first off-Broadway role in 1967 and made her Broadway debut in 1970. Moving to California, she began appearing in major films in 1973, winning the first of four Academy Award nominations as best actress for *Cinderella Liberty.* Her other honored performances were for *The Goodbye Girl* (1977), *Chapter Two* (1979), and *Only When I Laugh* (1981), all written by her second husband (1973–83), playwright-screenwriter Neil SIMON. She played a character based on herself in the autobiographical *Chapter Two.* Her first husband (1966–71) was painter-actor Gary Campbell. In the 80s she began directing stage plays.

FILMS: *Hot Rod Hullabaloo* 1966; *Beyond the Law* 1968; *Blume in Love, Cinderella Liberty* 1973; *Audrey Rose, The Goodbye Girl* 1977; *The Cheap Detective* 1978; *Promises in the Dark, Chapter Two* 1979; *Only When I Laugh* 1981; *Max Dugan Returns* 1983; *Heartbreak Ridge* 1986; *Stella* 1990; *Drop Dead Fred* 1991; *I Love Trouble* 1994; *Nick of Time* 1995; *2 Days in the Valley* 1996.

Mason, Sarah Y. See HEERMAN, Victor.

Mason, Shirley. Actress. *b.* Leonie Flugrath, 1901, Brooklyn, N.Y. *d.* 1979. Petite leading lady of numerous Hollywood silents. The sister of screen actresses Edna Flugrath and Viola DANA, she began acting on the stage as a child and entered films as a juvenile lead in 1914. She starred in numerous silent productions, typically in sweet, innocent romantic roles, and retired with the switch to sound. Was married to director Sidney LANFIELD.

FILMS INCLUDE: *Vanity Fair* 1915; *The Tell-Tale Step, The Awakening of Ruth* 1917; *Come On In, Goodbye Bill* 1918; *The Unwritten Code, The Final Close-Up* 1919; *Her Elephant Man, Molly and I, Treasure Island, Love's Harvest, The Little Wanderer, Girl of My Heart* 1920; *Wing Toy, The Lamplighter, The Mother Heart, Lovetime, Ever Since Eve, Queenie, Jackie* 1921; *Little Miss Smiles, The Ragged Heiress, The New Teacher, Youth Must Have Love, Shirley of the Circus* 1922; *Lovebound, The Eleventh Hour, South Sea Love* 1923; *Love Letters, The French Lady, The Great Diamond Mystery, My Husband's Wives* 1924; *Curly Top, The Scarlet Honeymoon, The Talker, Scandal Proof, What Fools Men, Lord Jim* (as Jewel) 1925; *Desert Gold, Sweet Rosie O'Grady, Don Juan's Three Nights, Sin Cargo, Rose of the Tenements* 1926; *Let It Rain, The Wreck, Rich Men's Sons, Stranded, Sally in Our Alley* 1927; *The Wife's Relations, So This Is Love, Runaway Girls* 1928; *Anne Against the World, The Flying Marine, The Show of Shows* 1929.

Massari, Lea. Actress. Born Anna Maria Massatani, in 1933, in Rome. Leading lady of Italian and French films. The daughter of a prosperous engineer, she was educated at a French high school, a Spanish college, and a Swiss school of architecture. She entered films as a protégée and assistant of director Pier Gherardi, but her good looks soon catapulted her in front of the cameras. She brought a cosmopolitan sophistication to her varied screen characterizations, memorably in Antonioni's *L'Avventura* (1960) and Louis Malle's *Murmur of the Heart* (1971).

FILMS INCLUDE: *Proibito* 1954; *I Sogni nel Cassetto* 1957; *Auferstehung/Ressurezione* (Ger./It./Fr.) 1958; *L'Avventura, La Giornata balorda/From a Roman Balcony* 1960; *Il Colosso di Rodi/The Colossus of Rhodes* 1961; *Le Monte-Charge/Paris Pick-up* (Fr./It.), *Le Quattro Giornate di Napoli/The Four Days of Naples, La Città prigioniera/Conquered City* 1962; *L'Insoumis* (Fr.) 1964; *Made in Italy, Le Soldatesse* 1965; *Il Giardino delle Delizie* 1968; *Les Choses de la Vie/The Things of Life* (Fr./It./Switz.) 1970; *Le Souffle au Coeur/Murmur of the Heart* (Fr./It.) 1971; *La Course du Lièvre à Travers les Champs/And Hope to Die* (Fr./US) 1972; *Les Silencieux/Escape to Nowhere* (Fr.), *L'Impossible Objet/Impossible Object* (Fr.) 1973; *La Main à couper* (Fr.) 1974; *Peur sur la Ville/Night Caller* (Fr.) 1975; *L'Ordinateur des Pompes funèbres* (Fr.) 1976; *Violette et François* (Fr.), *Réperages/Faces of Love* (Switz./Fr.), *Antonio Gramsci—i Giorni del Carcere* 1977; *Sale Reveur/Dirty Dreamer* (Fr.) 1978; *Cristo si è fermato a Eboli/Christ Stopped at Eboli* 1979; *La Flambeuse* (Fr.) 1981; *Sarah* (Fr.) 1983; *La Septième Cible* (Fr.) 1984; *Segreti Segreti* 1985; *La Donna spezzata* (also co-sc.) 1988; *Viaggio D'Amore/Journey of Love* 1990.

Massen, Osa. Actress. Born on Jan. 13, 1916, in Copenhagen. Leading lady and second lead of Hollywood films of the 40s.

FILMS INCLUDE: *Honeymoon in Bali* 1939; *Honeymoon for Three, A Woman's Face, You'll Never Get Rich, The Devil Pays Off* 1941; *Iceland* 1942; *Jack London, Background to Danger* 1943; *The Master Race, The Cry of the Werewolf* 1944; *Tokyo Rose* 1945; *Deadline at Dawn, Strange Journey* 1946; *Night Unto Night* 1949; *Rocketship XM* 1950; *Outcasts of the City* 1958.

Massey, Daniel. Actor. Born on Oct. 10, 1933, in London. *ed.* Eton; King's Coll. Son of Raymond MASSEY and brother of actress Anna Massey. Primarily a stage actor, he occasionally appears in British films and was nominated for an Oscar for his portrayal of Noel Coward in *Star!* Formerly (1961–68) married to actress Adrienne CORRI, he wed actress Penelope Wilton in 1976.

FILMS INCLUDE: *In Which We Serve* 1942; *Girls at Sea* 1958; *Girls in Arms/Operation Bullshine, Upstairs and Downstairs* 1959; *The Entertainer* 1960; *The Amorous Adventures of Moll Flanders* 1965; *The Jokers* 1967; *Star!* (as Noel Coward) 1968; *Fragment of Fear* 1970; *Mary Queen of Scots* 1971; *The Vault of Horror* 1973; *The Incredible Sarah* 1976; *Warlords of Atlantis, The Cat and the Canary* 1978; *Bad Timing/Bad Timing: A Sensual Obsession* 1980; *Escape to Victory/Victory* 1981; *Scandal* 1989; *In the Name of the Father* 1993.

Massey, Ilona. Actress, singer. *b.* Ilona Hajmassy, June 16, 1910, Budapest. *d.* 1974. Glamorous blonde star who shone briefly in Hollywood's lesser galaxy following an even briefer operatic and film career in Vienna. Teamed three times with Nelson EDDY in bittersweet musicals. She was active in anti-Communist and Hungarian refugee causes. Her second (1941–42) of four husbands was actor Alan CURTIS.

FILMS: *Knox und die lustigen Vagabunden* (Aus.), *Der Himmel auf Erden* (Aus.) 1935; *Rosalie* 1937; *Balalaika* 1939; *New Wine, International Lady* 1941; *Invisible Agent, Frankenstein Meets the Wolf Man* 1942; *Holiday in Mexico* 1946; *Northwest Outpost* 1947; *The Plunderers* 1948; *Love Happy* 1950; *Jet Over the Atlantic* 1959.

Massey, Raymond. Actor. *b.* Aug. 30, 1896, Toronto. *d.* 1983. Oxford-educated, he began a stage career in London in 1922, making his film debut in 1931. Widely respected as a character star in both British and American films, he became closely identified with the role of Abraham Lincoln, which he played in both the stage and screen versions of *Abe Lincoln in Illinois* and briefly in *How the West Was Won.* More frequently and just as persuasively he played moralists, evildoers, and fanatics. A US citizen since 1944. He was wounded in both World Wars, serving with the Canadian army. In the early 60s he portrayed Dr. Gillespie in the 'Dr. Kildare' TV series (1961–66). His brother, Vincent Massey, was Canada's Governor General. His second (1929–39) of three wives was actress Adrianne Allen (*b.* 1907, Manchester, England), who bore him actors Anna Massey (*b.* Aug. 11, 1937, Sussex) and Daniel MASSEY.

Autobiographies: *When I Was Young* (1976); *A Hundred Lives* (1979).

FILMS: *The Crooked Billet/International Spy* (UK) 1929; *The Speckled Band* (as Sherlock Holmes; UK); *The Face at the Window* (UK), *The Old Dark House* 1932; *The Scarlet Pimpernel* (UK) 1935; *Things to Come* (UK) 1936; *Fire Over England* (UK), *Dreaming Lips* (UK), *Under the Red Robe* (UK), *The Prisoner of Zenda* (as Black Michael), *The Hurricane* 1937; *The Drum/Drums* (UK), *Black Limelight* (UK) 1938; *Abe Lincoln in Illinois* (title role), *Santa Fe Trail* (as abolitionist John Brown) 1940; *49th Parallel/The Invaders* (UK) 1941; *Reap the Wild Wind, Dangerously They Live, Desperate Journey* 1942; *Action in the North Atlantic* 1943; *Arsenic and Old Lace, The Woman in the Window* 1944; *Hotel Berlin, God Is My Co-Pilot* 1945; *A Matter of Life and Death/Stairway to Heaven* (UK) 1946; *Possessed, Mourning Becomes Electra* (as Gen. Ezra Mannon) 1947; *The Fountainhead* (as Gail Wynand), *Roseanna McCoy* 1949; *Chain Lightning, Barricade, Dallas* 1950; *Sugarfoot, David and Bathsheba* (as the prophet Nathan), *Come Fill the Cup* 1951; *Carson City* 1952; *The Desert Song* 1953; *Prince of Players* (as Junius Brutus Booth), *Battle Cry, East of Eden* (as Adam Trask), *Seven Angry Men* (again as John Brown) 1955; *Omar Khayyam* 1957; *The Naked and the Dead* 1958; *The Great Impostor, The Queen's Guards* (UK), *The Fiercest Heart* 1961; *How the West Was Won* (as Abraham Lincoln) 1962; *Mackenna's Gold* 1969.

master positive. A fine-grain print of high quality made from the original negative film and designed to be used in the preparation of duplicate negatives rather than for projection.

master shot. An overall view of a scene; same as an ESTABLISHING SHOT.

Masterson, Mary Stuart. Actress. Born in 1967, in New York City. *ed.* NYU. Engaging, sensitive leading lady of the American screen. The daughter of actor-director Peter MASTERSON and actress Carlin Glynn, she made her film debut at age seven, playing the screen daughter of her actual father in *The Stepford Wives* (1975). After a formal education, stage training by Estelle Parsons, several seasons in summer stock, and a couple of engagements off Broadway, she returned to the screen in the mid-80s as a promising ingenue.

FILMS: *The Stepford Wives* 1975; *Heaven Help Us* 1985; *At Close Range, My Little Girl* 1986; *Some Kind of Wonderful, Gardens of Stone* 1987; *Mr. North* 1988; *Chances Are, Immediate Family* 1989; *Funny About Love* 1990; *Fried Green Tomatoes* 1991; *Married to It, Benny & Joon* 1993; *Bad Girls, Radioland Murders* 1994; *Bed of Roses, Heaven's Prisoners* 1996.

Masterson, Peter. Actor, director, screenwriter. Born Carlos Bee Masterson, Jr., on June 1, 1934, in Houston. *ed.* Rice U. On the New York stage from 1961, he appeared in several Broadway plays and scored a huge commercial success as the co-author and co-director of the Broadway musical 'The Best Little Whorehouse in Texas' (1978), which he would later transcribe to the screen. He appeared as a supporting actor in a number of films of the late 60s and early 70s, and in 1985 made an auspicious debut as a screen director with *The Trip to Bountiful.* Married to actress Carlin Glynn, he is the father of actress Mary Stuart MASTERSON.

FILMS: As actor—*Ambush Bay* 1966; *In the Heat of the Night* 1967; *Counterpoint* 1968; *Von Richthofen and Brown* 1971; *Tomorrow* 1972; *Man on a Swing* 1974; *The Stepford Wives* 1975; *Gardens of Stone* 1987. As screenwriter—*The Best Little Whorehouse in Texas* (co-sc. with Larry L. King from their stage musical) 1982. As director—*The Trip to Bountiful* 1985; *Full Moon in Blue Water* 1988; *Blood Red, Night Game* 1989; *Convicts* 1990.

Mastorakis, Nico. Director, producer, screenwriter. Born on Apr. 28, 1941, in Athens, Greece. A novelist and occasional screenwriter, he began directing modest films, typically in the action-adventure genre, in the early 70s for his own company, Omega productions, in association with British, then American companies.

FILMS INCLUDE (as director-producer-writer): *Death Has Blue Eyes* 1974; *Island of Death* 1975; *The Greek Tycoon* (co-sc. only) 1978; *The Time Traveller/The Next One* 1982; *Blind Date* 1984; *Skyhigh* 1985; *The Zero Boys* 1986; *Double Exposure* (also co-edit.), *The Wind* 1987; *Glitch!, Bloodstone* (prod., co-sc.), *Grandma's House* (prod. only) 1988; *Nightmare at Noon* (filmed in 1987), *Hired to Kill, Ninja Academy, Darkroom* (prod. only) 1990; *In the Cold of the Night* 1991; *At Random* 1992; *Bloodstone* 1997.

Mastrantonio, Mary Elizabeth. Actress. Born on Nov. 17, 1958, in Oak Park, Ill. Appealing, feisty lead of the American stage and screen. The daughter of a first-generation Italian-American bronze foundry operator, she began acting in high school plays. She trained for opera at the University of Illinois at Urbana-Champaign, where she majored in music, performing summers as a singer and dancer at Nashville's Opryland theme park. She dropped out of college after two years to pursue a career in the musical theater and arrived in New York as understudy and vacation replacement for the role of Maria in the Broadway revival of 'West Side Story.' She appeared in several Broadway and off-Broadway productions in the early 80s and in Shakespearean roles in Central Park. She received rave reviews for her portrayal of Viola in the New York Shakespeare Festival production of 'Twelfth Night' in 1989. Making her screen debut in 1983, she made an immediate impression in the role of Al Pacino's sister, Gina, in *Scarface* and went on to garner an Academy Award nomination as best supporting actress for her lead role in *The Color of Money* (1986).

FILMS: *Scarface* 1983; *The Color of Money* 1986; *Slamdance* 1987; *The January Man, The Abyss* 1989; *Fools of Fortune* (UK) 1990; *Class Action, Robin Hood: Prince of Thieves* (as Maid Marian) 1991; *Consenting Adults, White Sands* 1992; *Three Wishes, Two Bits* 1995.

Mastroianni, Marcello. Actor. *b.* Sept. 28, 1923, in Fontana Liri, Italy. *d.* 1996. The son of poor peasants, he worked briefly as a draftsman during WW II, when he was sent by the Germans to a labor camp. He escaped and spent the rest of the war hiding in a Venice attic. After the war he went to Rome, where he worked as a clerk in the accounting department of the British Eagle-Lion Italian office and, in the evenings, began acting with a group of university players. In 1947 he made his screen debut in an Italian version of *Les Misérables* and the following year joined Luchino Visconti's stage stock company. Gradually he built himself a reputation among Italian audiences as a talented and fetching leading man both on the stage and in films. By the mid-50s his reputation was international, and after starring in such films as Visconti's *White Nights,* Fellini's *La Dolce Vita* and *8½*, Antonioni's *La Notte,* and Germi's *Divorce, Italian Style,* he was established as one of the world's leading screen personalities, in a wide range of finely delineated dramatic and comic roles, enjoying universal popularity as a prototype of the modern-day urban European male. He was nominated for *Divorce, Italian Style* (1961), *A Special Day* (1977), and *Dark Eyes* (1987); was named best foreign actor by the British Film Academy for *Divorce, Italian Style* and *Yesterday, Today, and Tomorrow* (1963); and won the best actor prize at Cannes for *The Pizza Triangle* (1970) and *Dark Eyes.* Married since

1950 to Italian actress Flora Carabella, he fathered a daughter in 1972 by actress Catherine DENEUVE.

FILMS INCLUDE: *I Miserabili* 1947; *Vita de Cane, Una Domenica d'Agosto* 1950; *Parigi e sempre Parigi* 1951; *Sensualitá, le Ragazze di Piazza di Spagna/Three Girls from Rome* 1952; *Tempi Nostri/The Anatomy of Love, Cronache di Poveri Amanti, Giorni d'Amore, Casa Ricordi/House of Ricordi* (as Donizetti) 1954; *Peccato che Sia una Canaglia/Too Bad She's Bad, La Bella Mugnaia/The Miller's Beautiful Wife* 1955; *Il Bigamo/The Bigamist, La Fortuna di Essere Donna/Lucky to Be a Woman* 1956; *Padri e Figli/A Tailor's Maid, Il Momento più Bello/The Most Wonderful Moment, Le Notti Bianche/White Nights* 1957; *I Soliti Ignoti/The Big Deal on Madonna Street, Racconti d'Estate/Love on the Riviera* 1958; *La Loi/Il Legge/Where the Hot Wind Blows 1959*; *La Dolce Vita, Il Bell'Antonio, Adua e le Compagne/Love a la Carte* 1960; *La Notte/The Night, Fantasmi a Roma/Ghosts of Rome, L'Assassino/The Lady Killer from Rome, Divorzio all'Italiana/Divorce Italian Style* 1961; *La Vie Privée/A Very Private Affair, Cronaca Familiare/Family Diary* 1962; *Otto e Mezzo/8½, I Compagni/The Organizer, Ieri Oggi Domani/Yesterday Today and Tomorrow* 1963; *Matrimonio all'Italiana/Marriage Italian Style* 1964; *Casanova '70, La Decima Vittima/The Tenth Victim* 1965; *Questi Fantasmi/Ghosts Italian Style, Lo Straniero/The Stranger* 1967; *Gli Amanti/A Place for Lovers* 1968; *I Girasoli/Sunflower* 1969; *Leo the Last* (UK), *Drama della Gelosia/The Pizza Triangle* 1970; *La Moglie del Prete/The Priest's Wife, Scipio il Africano, Permette Rocco Papaleo/Rocco Papaleo, Ça n'arrive qu'aux Autres/It Only Happens to Others* (Fr./It.) 1971; *La Cagna/Liza, Melampo, Che?/What?* 1972; *Rappresaglia/Massacre in Rome, La Grande Bouffe, L'Evénement le plus important depuis que l'Homme a marché sur la Lune/A Slightly Pregnant Man* (Fr.) 1973; *Allonsanfan, Touchez pas la Femme blanche* 1974; *Per le Antiche Scale/Down the Ancient Stairs, C'eravamo tanto Amati/We All Loved Each Other So Much, La Pupa del Gangster/Poopsie/Oopsie Poopsie* 1975; *La Donna della Domenica/The Sunday Woman, Divina Creatura/The Divine Nymph, Salut l'Artiste* (Fr.), *Le Fantasie amorose di Luca Maria nobile Veneto, Signore e Signori Buonanotte* 1976; *Una Giornata Speciale/A Special Day* (It./Can.), *Mogliamante/Wifemistress* 1977; *Doppio Delitto, Bye Bye Monkey, Shimmy Lugano e Tarantelle e Vino, Cosi come Sei/Stay as You Are* 1978; *Fatto di Sangue fra Due Uomini per causa di una Vedova/Revenge/Blood Feud, Giallo Napoetano, L'Ingorgo—una Storia impossibile/Traffic Jam/Bottleneck* 1979; *La Citta' delle Donne/City of Women, Fantasma d'Amore* 1980; *La Pelle/The Skin* (as novelist Curzio Malaparte) 1981; *Oltre la Porta/Beyond the Door, La Nuit de Varennes* 1982; *Storia de Piera, Le Général de l'Armée morte, Gabriela* 1983; *Enrico IV/Henry IV* (title role) 1984; *Maccheroni/Macaroni, Le Due Vite di Mattia Pascal/The Two Lives of Mattia Pascal* (title role), *Ginger e Fred/Ginger and Fred* 1985; *The Beekeeper* (Gr.) 1986; *Intervista* (cameo), *Oci Ciornie/Dark Eyes* 1987; *Miss Arizona* 1988; *Splendor, Che Ora è* 1989; *Tutti stanno benne/Everybody's Fine, Verso Sera/Towards Evening* 1990; *Tchin-Tchin, The Suspended Step of the Stork* (Gr./Fr./Switz./It.) 1991; *A Fine Romance, Used People* (US) 1992; *Ready to Wear* 1994; *According to Pereira, Three Lives and Only One Death* 1996; *Beyond the Clouds* 1997.

Masumura, Yasuzo. Director. Born in 1924, in Tokyo. The holder of a law degree from the University of Tokyo, he entered Japanese films as assistant director in 1948 and in 1953 went to Rome, where he trained at the Centro Sperimentale. He assisted Mizoguchi and Ichikawa before making his own debut as a director in 1957. His films have often dealt with moral corruption in Japanese society or with problems of youth, sometimes in a sensational manner.

FILMS INCLUDE: *Kisses* 1957; *Disobedience* 1958; *The Cast-Off, Across Darkness* 1959; *Afraid to Die, The False Student* 1960; *Love and Life, All for Love, Wife's Confession* 1961; *Stolen Pleasure, Life of a Woman* 1962; *Black Report, Delinquents of Pure Heart* 1963; *Love and Greed, Passion* 1964; *Hoodlum Soldier, The Wife of Seisaku* 1965; *Spider Girl, School for Spies, The Red Angel* 1966; *Two Wives, An Idiot in Love, The Wife of Seishu Hanaoka* 1967; *Evil Trio, The Sex Check, The House of Wooden Blocks, One Day at Summer's End* 1968; *The Blind Beast, Thousand Cranes, Vixen* 1969; *Play It Cool* 1970; *Warehouse/Moju—Blind Beast* 1973; *Double Suicide of Sonezaki* (also co-sc.) 1978.

Masur, Richard. Actor. Born on Nov. 20, 1948, in New York City. *ed.* NYU. Pudgy, pleasant, busy supporting player of Hollywood films since the mid-70s. He directed a short, *Love Struck* (1987), which was nominated for an Academy Award. He is currently the president of the Screen Actors Guild.

FILMS INCLUDE: *Whiffs* 1975; *Bittersweet Love* 1976; *Semi-Tough* 1977; *Who'll Stop the Rain* 1978; *Hanover Street* (UK), *Scavenger Hunt* 1979; *Heaven's Gate* 1980; *I'm Dancing as Fast as I Can, The Thing* 1982; *Timerider, Risky Business, Nightmares, Under Fire* 1983; *The Mean Season, My Science Project* 1985; *Heartburn* 1986; *The Believers, Walker* 1987; *Rent-a-Cop, Shoot to Kill/Deadly Pursuit, License to Drive* 1988; *Far from Home* 1989; *Out of Sight Out of Mind, Vietnam Texas* 1990; *Flashback, Going Under* 1991; *My Girl, Encino Man* 1992; *The Man Without a Face, Six Degrees of Separation* 1993; *My Girl 2, Patriots* 1994; *Forget Paris* 1995.

matching. A stage in the editing process in which the negative is cut and matched with the edited work print.

match line. In animation, an indication on a layout and backgrounds at points where one object crosses another.

Maté, Rudolph (Rudy). Director of photography, director. *b.* Rudolf Matheh, Jan. 21, 1898, Kraków, Poland. *d.* 1964. A graduate of the University of Budapest, he entered Hungarian films in 1919 as an assistant cameraman for Alexander KORDA. Later worked in Vienna and Berlin, where he apprenticed with Karl FREUND and executed second-unit cinematography for Erich POMMER. He shot some of the footage of Carl Dreyer's *Mikaël* (1924), then went to France as the cameraman on Dreyer's *La Passion de Jeanne d'Arc/The Passion of Joan of Arc* (1928) and *Vampyr* (1932). Both films were noted for their creative cinematography and inventive effects. In France he also worked for Fritz LANG and Rene CLAIR and in 1935 he moved on to Hollywood, where he continued his work as a cinematographer for a dozen years, gaining five Academy Award nominations. In 1947 he turned to directing. His work as a director was less distinguished than his achievements as a cinematographer, but his films were usually entertaining, technically effective, and visually appealing. He also directed many episodes for TV's 'Loretta Young Show.' Especially memorable is his suspenseful *film noir* of 1950, *D.O.A.* He died of a heart attack.

FILMS INCLUDE: As director of photography—In Germany: Der Kaufmann von Venedig (co-phot.) 1923; *Mikaël* (addnl. phot.) 1924; *Die Hochstaplerin* 1926. In France: *La Passion de Jeanne d'Arc/The Passion of Joan of Arc* 1928; *Vampyr* 1932; *Liliom* (co-phot.), *Le Dernier Milliardaire* (co-phot.) 1934. In the US: *Metropolitan, Dante's Inferno* 1935; *Come and Get It* (co-phot.), *A Message to Garcia, Our Relations, Dodsworth* 1936; *Stella Dallas, Outcast* 1937; *Blockade, Trade Winds, The Adventures of Marco Polo* 1938; *The Real Glory, Love Affair* 1939; *Foreign Correspondent, My Favorite Wife, Seven Sinners* 1940; *The Flame of New Orleans,*

That Hamilton Woman/Lady Hamilton 1941; *To Be or Not to Be, The Pride of the Yankees* 1942; *They Got Me Covered, Sahara* 1943; *Cover Girl* (co-phot.), *Address Unknown* 1944; *Tonight and Every Night, Over 21* 1945; *Gilda* 1946; *Down to Earth* 1947. As producer—*The Return of October* 1948. As director (complete)—*It Had to Be You* (co-dir. with Don Hartman; also co-phot.) 1947; *The Dark Past* 1949; *No Sad Songs for Me, D.O.A., Union Station* 1950; *Branded, The Prince Who Was a Thief, When Worlds Collide* 1951; *The Green Glove, Paula, Sally and Saint Anne* 1952; *The Mississippi Gambler, Second Chance* 1953; *Forbidden, The Siege at Red River, The Black Shield of Falworth* 1954; *The Violent Men, The Far Horizons* 1955; *Miracle in the Rain, The Rawhide Years, Port Afrique* (UK) 1956; *Three Violent People* 1957; *The Deep Six* 1958; *Serenade einer grossen Liebe/For the First Time* (Ger./US) 1959; *Revak—Lo Schiavo di Cartagine/The Barbarians/Revak the Rebel* (It.), *The Immaculate Road* 1960; *The 300 Spartans* (also co-prod.), *Il Dominatore dei Sette Mari/Seven Seas to Calais* (co-dir. with Primo Zeglio; It.) 1962; *Aliki/Aliki My Love* (also co-prod.; Gr./US) 1963.

Matheson, Richard. Novelist, screenwriter. Born in 1926. A leading creator of science fiction and fantasy, in print and on the screen, he published his first of many short stories in 1950 and his first novel in 1953. His science-fiction novels include *I Am Legend* (1954), *The Shrinking Man* (1956), *Ride the Nightmare* (1959), and *Hell House* (1971), all of which have been adapted to the screen, the second and last by the author. Matheson also wrote a number of original screenplays and screen adaptations, as well as numerous teleplays, including episodes for such series as 'The Twilight Zone,' 'Star Trek,' and 'Night Gallery.'

FILMS: *The Incredible Shrinking Man* (from his novel *The Shrinking Man*) 1957; *The Beat Generation* 1959; *House of Usher* 1960; *Master of the World, The Pit and the Pendulum* 1961; *Night of the Eagle/Burn Witch Burn* (UK), *Tales of Terror* 1962; *The Raven, The Comedy of Terrors/The Graveside Story* 1963; *L'Ultio Uomo della Terra/The Last Man on Earth* (novel basis only, *I Am Legend;* It./US) 1964; *Fanatic/Die! Die My Darling!* (UK) 1965; *The Young Warriors* 1967; *The Devil's Bride* (UK) 1968; *De Sade* 1969; *De la Part de Copains/Cold Sweat* (novel basis only, *Ride the Nightmare;* Fr./It.) 1970; *The Omega Man* (novel basis only, *I Am Legend*) 1971; *The Legend of Hell House* (from his novel *Hell House*) 1973; *Dracula* 1979; *Somewhere in Time* 1980; *The Incredible Shrinking Woman* 1981; *Twilight Zone—The Movie* (3rd & 4th episodes), *Jaws 3-D, Duel* (theatrical release of 1971 teleplay) 1983; *Loose Cannons* 1990.

Matheson, Tim. Actor. Born on Dec. 31, 1947, in Glendale, Calif. *ed.* California State U. Cute child performer, then cute leading man of American TV and films. He began appearing regularly on TV at age 12, reached maturity in such series as 'The Virginian' (1969–70) and 'Bonanza' (1972–73), and as an adult co-starred in 'The Quest' (1976) and 'Tucker's Witch.' On screen sporadically from the late 60s, he played engaging leads in feature films of the late 70s and early 80s. In 1985 he began directing episodes for TV series and music videos and later in the decade acquired the National Lampoon company, becoming its chairman and chief executive officer in 1989.

FILMS: *Divorce American Style* 1967; *Yours Mine and Ours* 1968; *How to Commit Marriage* 1969; *Magnum Force* 1973; *Almost Summer, National Lampoon's Animal House* 1978; *Dreamer, The Apple Dumpling Gang Rides Again, 1941* 1979; *A Little Sex* 1982; *To Be or Not to Be* 1983; *The House of God, Up the Creek, Impulse* 1984; *Fletch* 1985; *Speed Zone, Blind Fury* (also co-prod.; Austral.) 1989; *Solar Crisis* (Jap.) 1990; *Drop Dead Fred* 1991; *Black Sheep, A Very Brady Sequel* 1996.

Mathews, Kerwin. American actor. Born in 1926. Dashing hero of adventure pictures of the late 50s and early 60s. A former teacher, he became briefly popular, thanks to Ray Harryhausen's special effects, after dueling a skeleton in *The Seventh Voyage of Sinbad* (1958) and performing similarly artful stunts in a couple of other action sagas exploiting the Dynamation trick-photography system.

FILMS INCLUDE: *Five Against the House* 1955; *The Garment Jungle* 1957; *Tarawa Beachhead, The Seventh Voyage of Sinbad* (title role) 1958; *The Last Blitzkrieg* 1959; *Man on a String, The Three Worlds of Gulliver* (title role; UK), *Saffo Venere di Lesbo/Sapho/The Warrior Empress* (It./Fr.) 1960; *The Devil at 4 O'Clock* 1961; *Jack the Giant Killer, The Pirates of Blood River* (UK) 1962; *Maniac* (UK), *The Waltz King* (as Johann Strauss, Jr.) 1963; *Banco a Bangkok/Shadow of Evil* (Fr./It.) 1964; *Le Vicomte règle ses Comptes/The Viscount* (Fr./Sp./It./Ger.), *Battle Beneath the Earth* (UK) 1967; *A Boy... a Girl/The Sun Is Up* 1969; *Barquero* 1970; *The Boy Who Cried Werewolf* 1973; *Nightmare in Blood* 1976.

Mathieson, Muir. Conductor, musical director. *b.* Jan. 24, 1911, Stirling, Scotland. *d.* 1975. *ed.* Royal Coll. of Music (London). Musical director and conductor of hundreds of British film scores since the early 30s. He appeared as an actor in the film *The Magic Box* (1951), portraying Sir Arthur Sullivan.

FILMS INCLUDE: *Catherine the Great* 1934; *The Scarlet Pimpernel* 1935; *Things to Come, Rembrandt, The Ghost Goes West* 1936; *Fire Over England, Victoria the Great* 1937; *The Four Feathers* 1939; *The Thief of Bagdad, Gaslight* 1940; *Dangerous Moonlight/Suicide Squadron, Major Barbara* 1941; *In Which We Serve* 1942; *The Way Ahead* 1944; *Henry V, Blithe Spirit, Brief Encounter, The Seventh Veil* 1945; *Caesar and Cleopatra, The Years Between, Brief Encounter, Odd Man Out* 1946; *Hamlet, Oliver Twist* 1948; *Christopher Columbus* 1949; *The Sound Barrier/Breaking Through the Sound Barrier* 1952; *Doctor in the House* 1954; *Richard III* 1956; *Sink the Bismarck, Swiss Family Robinson* 1960; *Waltz of the Toreadors, The L-Shaped Room* 1962; *Becket* 1964; *Lord Jim, Ghengis Khan* 1965; *Shalako* 1968; *My Side of the Mountain* 1969; *You Can't Win 'Em All* 1970.

Mathis, June. Screenwriter. *b.* 1892, Leadville, Colo., into a theatrical family. *d.* 1927. She joined Metro in 1918 after some writing experience for the stage and the following year was appointed chief of the studio's script department. She became influential in Metro's affairs and was instrumental in launching the careers of Rudolph VALENTINO and other important stars of the silent era. In 1923 she was assigned the formidable task of re-editing and reducing Erich von STROHEIM'S *Greed* from 18 reels down to ten. She was deeply involved in the production of the monumental *Ben-Hur* (1926) both as a writer and as an on-location studio representative.

FILMS INCLUDE: *The Upstart, Her Great Price, God's Half Acre, The Sunbeam* 1916; *Blue Jeans, The Barricade, The Call of Her People, The Jury of Fate, Aladdin's Other Lamp, The Voice of Conscience, Red White and Blue Blood* 1917; *The Eyes of Mystery, The Legion of Death, Toys of Fate, Social Quicksands, To Hell with the Kaiser, Eye for Eye* 1918; *The Divorcee, Out of the Fog, Satan Junior, The Island of Intrigue, The Red Lantern, The Microbe, The Man Who Stayed at Home, The Brat* 1919; *The Saphead, The Right of Way, The Willow Tree, Parlor Bedroom and Bath, Polly with a Past, Hearts Are Trumps* 1920; *The Four Horsemen of the Apocalypse, The Conquering Power, A Trip to Paradise, Camille, The Idle Rich* 1921; *Turn to the Right, Kisses, Hate Blood and Sand, The Young Rajah* 1922; *In The Palace of the King, Three Wise Fools,*

The Spanish Dancer, Greed (re-edit., rewrite) 1923; *Sally, The Desert Flower, Classified, We Moderns* 1925; *Ben-Hur, The Greater Glory, Irene* 1926; *The Masked Woman, The Magic Flame* 1927.

Mathis, Samantha. Actress. Born 1970 in New York City. The offspring of an Austrian theatrical family, this appealing young leading lady followed in their footsteps starting off in series television and supporting roles in TV movies. Her feature film debut in *Forbidden Sun* (1989) gave way to a career of solid, enjoyable big screen performances.

FILMS: *Forbidden Sun* 1989; *83 Hours Till Dawn, Extreme Close-up, Pump Up the Volume* 1990; *Ferngully—The Last Rainforest, This Is My Life* 1992; *The Music of Chance, Super Mario Bros., The Thing Called Love* 1993; *Little Women* 1994; *The American President, How To Make an American Quilt, Jack & Sarah* 1995; *Broken Arrow* 1996.

Mathot, Léon. Actor, director. *b.* Mar. 5, 1886, Roubaix, France. *d.* 1968. He entered films as an extra in 1906, became France's leading screen star in the years 1914 to 1923, and later played numerous character parts. He eventually turned director of routine films. At one time he served as vice president of the Cinémathèque Française and as president of the European Union of Film and TV Technicians.

FILMS INCLUDE: As actor—*La Course à la Perruque* 1907; *Le Pont fatal* 1908; *Le Lord Ouvrier* 1915; *Barberousse* (serial), *Le Gaz mortels* (serial) 1916; *Le Droit à la Vie, La Zone de la Mort* 1917; *Monte-Cristo* (serial) 1917–18; *La Course au Flambeau* 1918; *The Empire of Diamonds* (US), *Travail, L'Ami Fritz* 1920; *Blanchette* 1921; *L'Auberge rouge, Coeur fidèle* 1923; *La Diable dans la Ville* 1924; *Le Mirage de Paris* 1925; *Le Puits de Jacob/A Daughter of Israel* 1926; *Yasmina, Rue de la Paix* 1927; *La Maison de la Flèche* 1930; *Deuxième Bureau contre Kommandantur* 1939. As director—*Dans l'Ombre de Harem* (co-dir. with Audré Liabel; also act.) 1928; *L'Appassionata* (co-dir. with Liabel; act.) 1929; *L'Instinct* (also act.) 1930; *Passeport 13444* (also act.) 1931; *Embrassez-moi* 1932; *La Mascotte* 1935; *Les Loups entre eux* 1936; *L'Homme à abattre* 1937; *Le Revolté, Chéri-Bibi* 1938; *Rappel immédiat/Thunder Over Paris* 1939; *L'Honne sans Nom* 1942; *Nuits d'Alerte* 1945; *Le Dernière Chevauchée* 1946; *La Danseuse de Marrakech* 1949; *Mon Gosse de Père* 1952.

Matlin, Marlee. Actress. Born on Aug. 24, 1965, in Morton Grove,, Ill. Deaf before she reached her second birthday, she received special schooling and at age eight performed with the Des Plaines Children's Theatre of the Deaf. She was encouraged to pursue a professional acting career by Henry WINKLER, whom she had met when she was 12 and whose close friend she remains. She later majored in criminal justice at William Rainey Harper College. A pretty brunette, she was selected to play the lead role of a young deaf woman in the screen adaptation of Mark Medoff's play, *Children of a Lesser God,* and walked away with an Academy Award as best actress of 1986 for her astonishing performance. In 1989, she made her speaking debut in the TV film *Bridge to Silence,* and she later appeared in the dramatic series 'Reasonable Doubts.'

FILMS: *Children of a Lesser God* 1986; *Walker* 1987; *The Linguini Incident* 1991; *The Player* 1992; *Hear No Evil* 1993; *It's My Party* 1996.

Matras, Christian. Director of photography. *b.* Dec. 29, 1903, Valence, France. *d.* 1987. One of the most highly regarded lighting cameramen of French films, he began as a newsreel photographer. In the mid-20s he directed several documentaries. As a cameraman, he did remarkable work for RENOIR and Max OPHÜLS and added brilliance to the color costume films of CHRISTIAN-JAQUE.

FILMS INCLUDE: *L'Or des Mers* 1932; *Maternité* 1935; *La Grande Illusion/Grand Illusion* 1937; *Prison sans Barreaux, Entrée des Artistes/The Curtain Rises* 1938; *La Fin du Jour/The End of a Day, Le Dernier Tournant* 1939; *La Duchesse de Langeais* 1942; *La Voyageur sans Bagages* 1943; *Le Bossu* 1944; *Boule de Suif, Seul dans la Nuit* 1945; *L'Idiot/The Idiot* 1946; *Les Jeux sont faits/The Chips Are Down* 1947; *L'Aigle à Deux Têtes/Eagle with Two Heads, D'Hommc à Hommes/Man to Men* 1948; *Singoalla* (Swed./Fr.) 1949; *La Valse de Paris/The Paris Waltz, La Ronde* 1950; *Barbe Bleue* 1951; *Fanfan la Tulipe/Fanfan the Tulip, Violettes impériales, Adorable Créatures/Adorable Creatures* 1952; *Lucrèce Borgia/Sins of the Borgias, Madame de. . . /The Earrings of Madame De* 1953; *Madame du Barry* 1954; *Nana, Lola Montès* 1955; *Oeil pour Oeil/An Eye for an Eye* 1956; *Les Espions* 1957; *Montparnasse 19/Modigliani of Montparnasse, Maxime* 1958; *Les Magiciennes/Double Deception* 1960; *Paris Blues* (US) 1961; *Cartouche, Le Crime ne paie pas/Crime Does Not Pay, Thérèse Desqueyroux/Therese* 1962; *Shéhérazade/Scheherazade* (co-phot.) 1963; *Les Amitiés particulières/This Special Friendship* 1964; *Les Fêtes galantes* 1965; *Sept fois Femme/Woman Times Seven* 1967; *Les Oiseaux vont mourir au Pérou/Birds in Peru* 1968; *La Voie lactée/The Milky Way* 1969; *Le Bal du Comte d'Orgel* 1970; *Varietes* (Sp.) 1971.

matrices. Strips of film carrying relief images as part of a color reproduction process. Each matrix of the set of three absorbs a dye of one of the three primary photographic colors and transfers it to the appropriate areas of the frame as the matrix runs in contact with a release-print-in-the-making.

matte. A masking device of any kind placed in front of a camera or printer lens in order to block out or tone down part of an image. Mattes are extremely useful in SPECIAL EFFECTS because they allow additional elements to be added to a shot. A stationary matte is an actual physical object, made of metal, cardboard, or black tape, that keeps part of the film unexposed so that miniatures or paintings can be added later to expand the scenery. In a GLASS SHOT, the matte is a scenic painting on glass, photographed by the camera, while, in the same take, the actors are photographed through the clear part of the glass. A TRAVELING MATTE consists of footage of a moving image or moving silhouette; it is used with an OPTICAL PRINTER to combine two or more different filmed elements, such as an actor in a studio and a location background. Traveling mattes are most often created through the BLUE SCREEN PROCESS.

matte artist. A special effects artist whose job it is to design and paint false backgrounds for matte shots (known as MATTE PAINTINGS).

matte box. An attachment in front of a camera designed both as a shield against unwanted light and as a holder of filters or mattes during filming. Sometimes called an "effects box," it can be used to bring about a variety of simple special effects, such as matte shots, superimpositions, wipes, and split-screen effects. The matte box can be moved back and forth with the aid of guide rods and can be adjusted both vertically and horizontally.

matte painting. In MATTE effects, a large painting that is photographed separately and composited with other elements. Executed by a MATTE ARTIST, matte paintings may provide background scenery or extensions of a physical set, such as the upper sections of a castle or extra troops for an army.

matte screen. A projection screen treated with a chemical substance (usually magnesium oxide) so that the brightness of images projected upon it is substantially the same at all viewing angles.

matte shot. A camera shot in which two or more different elements are combined through the use of MATTES, masking devices that block the film as it moves through the camera.

Mattes, Eva. Actress. Born in 1954, in Bavaria. A prominent figure in the New German Cinema. The daughter of actress Margret Symo, she performed extensively on the stage before making her screen debut in 1970. She played key roles in films of Werner HERZOG, Percy ADLON, and especially Rainer Werner FASSBINDER, whom she impersonated (!) in Eva Kipplon's biographical film, *A Man Called Eva* (1984).

FILMS INCLUDE: *OK* 1970; *Mathias Kneissel* 1971; *Die bitteren Tränen der Petra von Kant/The Bitter Tears of Petra von Kant* 1972; *Wildwechsel/Jail Bait* 1973; *Fontane Effi Briest/Effi Briest, Supermarket* 1974; *Frauen in New York, Stroszek* 1977; *Im einem Jahr mit 13 Monden/In a Year of 13 Moons* 1978; *David, Woyzeck* 1979; *Deutschland bleiche Mutter/Germany, Pale Mother* 1980; *Celeste* 1981; *Friedliche Tage, Rita Ritter* 1983; *Ein Mann wie Eva/A Man Called Eva* 1984; *Auf immer und ewig* 1986; *Felix* 1987; *Herbstmilch* 1989.

Matthau, Walter. Actor. Born Walter Matuschanskavasky, on Oct. 1, 1920, in New York City. The son of impoverished Jewish-Russian immigrants, he grew up in cold-water tenements of the Lower East Side. When he was 11 years old he got a job selling soft drinks during intermissions in a Second Avenue Yiddish theater and soon found himself playing bit roles on the stage for 50 cents a performance. After graduating from high school, where he excelled in drama and sports, he worked at a variety of menial jobs, including a floor scrubber and cement-bag hauler. Following WW II service as radioman-gunner on Army Air Force bombers, he enrolled in acting classes at the New School's Dramatic Workshop and began acting in summer stock. He soon made it to Broadway, gradually rising from bits to key supporting parts and rapidly gaining recognition as a highly talented and versatile actor. From the mid-50s he shuttled between Broadway and Hollywood, where he began appearing regularly in films, in character parts, typically as a villain. He even directed one low-budget production, *The Gangster,* in 1960. He also often appeared in TV plays and films and starred in the series 'Tallahassee 7000' (1961).

Matthau seemed destined to stay in supporting roles on the stage and in films when, in 1965, he soared to sudden stardom on Broadway in the comedy 'The Odd Couple,' in a role especially written by Neil Simon to accommodate Matthau's personality. Capitalizing on his stage success, he starred in a succession of screen comedies that quickly established him as one of the top box-office attractions in Hollywood, allowing him to reap huge profits from his share in the percentage of several hit movies. He won the supporting actor Academy Award for *The Fortune Cookie* (1966) and was nominated for Oscars as best actor for *Kotch* (1971) and *The Sunshine Boys* (1975). The same slouching posture, awkward walk, unhandsome face, and Lower East Side growl that kept him from becoming a leading man for many years, have proven great assets in his newer role as one of Hollywood's leading comic actors. His second wife (from 1959) is actress-writer Carol Wellington-Smythe Marcus, formerly the wife of novelist William Saroyan. Their son, Charles Matthau (*b.* Dec. 10, 1964, New York City), is a film director.

FILMS: *The Kentuckian, The Indian Fighter* 1955; *Bigger Than Life* 1956; *A Face in the Crowd, Slaughter on Tenth Avenue* 1957; *King Creole, Voice in the Mirror, Onionhead, Ride a Crooked Trail* 1958; *Gangster Story* (also dir.), *Strangers When We Meet* 1960; *Lonely Are the Brave, Who's Got the Action?* 1962; *Island of Love, Charade* 1963; *Ensign Pulver, Fail Safe, Goodbye Charlie* 1964; *Mirage* 1965; *The Fortune Cookie* 1966; *A Guide for the Married Man* 1967; *The Odd Couple, The Secret Life of an American Wife, Candy* 1968; *Hello Dolly!, Cactus Flower* 1969; *A New Leaf, Plaza Suite, Kotch* 1971; *Pete 'n' Tillie* 1972; *Charley Varrick, The Laughing Policeman* 1973; *The Taking of Pelham One Two Three, Earthquake* (cameo as a drunk), *The Front Page* 1974; *The Sunshine Boys* 1975; *The Bad News Bears* 1976; *Casey's Shadow, House Calls, California Suite* 1978; *Little Miss Marker* (also exec. prod.), *Hopscotch* 1980; *First Monday in October, Buddy Buddy* 1981; *I Ought to Be in Pictures* 1982; *The Survivors* 1983; *Movers and Shakers* 1985; *Pirates* (Fr./Tunis) 1986; *The Couch Trip, Il Piccolo Diavolo/The Little Devil* (It.) 1988; *The Incident* 1989; *JFK* 1991; *Dennis the Menace, Grumpy Old Men* 1993; *I.Q.* 1994, *Grumpier Old Men* 1995; *The Grass Harp, I'm Not Rappaport* 1996; *Out to Sea* 1997.

Matthews, Jessie. Actress, dancer, singer. *b.* Mar. 11, 1907, London. *d.* 1981. Popular star of the British light stage and musical films of the 30s. One of 11 children of a poor Soho family, she made her first professional stage appearance at age ten and during her teens was in the chorus line of London musicals and played bit roles in a couple of films. She rose to stardom in musical revues of the late 20s and in the early 30s rode the crest of her popularity to films. Her popularity as a film star spread across the Atlantic and for a decade she remained one of the most beloved screen personalities of the pre–WW II years, despite the mediocrity of many of her film vehicles. Considered one of the most graceful dancers of her time, she was publicized as "The Dancing Divinity." In 1944 she directed a 20-minute wartime short, *Victory Wedding.* Her second (1931–44) of three husbands was actor Sonnie HALE. Autobiography: *Over My Shoulder* (1974).

FILMS: *The Beloved Vagabond* 1923; *Straws in the Wind* 1924; *Out of the Blue* 1931; *There Goes the Bride, The Midshipmaid* 1932; *The Man from Toronto, The Good Companions, Friday the 13th* 1933; *Waltzes from Vienna/Strauss's Great Waltz, Evergreen* 1934; *First a Girl* 1935; *It's Love Again* 1936; *Head Over Heels/Head Over Heels in Love, Gangway* 1937; *Sailing Along* 1938; *Climbing High* 1939; *Forever and a Day* (US) 1943; *Candles at Nine* 1944; *Tom Thumb* 1958; *The Hound of the Baskervilles* 1977; *Never Never Land* 1980.

Mattimore, Van. See ARLEN, Richard.

Mattsson, Arne. Director. Born on Dec. 2, 1919, in Uppsala, Sweden. Prolific director of Swedish films, former assistant to Per Lindberg. He is known abroad mainly for the idyllic *One Summer of Happiness* (1951) and for Hitchcock-style thrillers.

FILMS INCLUDE: *And All These Women* 1944; *Susie* 1945; *Bad Eggs/Incorrigible* 1946; *Father Wanted, A Guest Game* 1947; *Dangerous Spring* 1948; *Woman in White* 1949; *Rolling Sea, One Summer of Happiness* 1951; *The Bread of Love* 1953; *Enchanted Walk, Salka Valka* 1954; *Men of Darkness, The People of Hemso* 1955; *A Little Place of One's Own* 1956; *Spring of Life, No Tomorrow* 1957; *The Phantom Carriage, There Came Two Men, The Lady in Black, Mannequin in Red* 1958; *Rider in Blue* 1959; *When Darkness Falls, Summer and Sinners* 1960; *The Summer Night Is Sweet* 1961; *The Doll, Ticket to Paradise, Lady in White* 1962; *The Yellow Car* 1963; *Blue Boys* 1964; *Two Vikings, Morianna/I the Body* (also co-sc.) 1965; *Nightmare* (also co-sc.), *Woman of Darkness* 1966; *The Murderer* 1967; *Bamse/The Teddy Bear/My Father's Mistress* 1968; *Anne and Eve* 1970; *The Truck* (Sw./Yug.) 1976; *Black Sun* (also sc.) 1978; *The Girl* (also prod.) 1985.

Mature, Victor. Actor. *b.* Jan. 29, 1915, in Louisville, Ky. *d.* 1994. Samson-size star of Hollywood films of the 40s and 50s, billed by studio publicity as a "beautiful hunk of man." The son of a Swiss immigrant scissors grinder, he arrived in

Hollywood penniless and appeared for several years at the Pasadena Playhouse before making his film debut in 1939. He was cast mainly in action roles, using to full advantage all but his facial muscles, which often remained frozen in a toothy grin. However, he never took his own acting ability too seriously and parodied his own screen image in De Sica's *Caccia alla Volpe/After the Fox* (1966). Mature's five marriages all ended in divorce.

FILMS: *The Housekeeper's Daughter* 1939; *One Million B.C., Captain Caution, No No Nanette* 1940; *I Wake Up Screaming, The Shanghai Gesture* 1941; *Song of the Islands, My Gal Sal, Footlight Serenade, Seven Days' Leave* 1942; *My Darling Clementine* (as Doc Holliday) 1946; *Moss Rose, Kiss of Death* 1947; *Fury at Furnace Creek, Cry of the City* 1948; *Easy Living, Red Hot and Blue, Samson and Delilah* (as Samson) 1949; *Wabash Avenue, I'll Get By* (cameo), *Stella* 1950; *Gambling House* 1951; *The Las Vegas Story, Something for the Birds, Million Dollar Mermaid* 1952; *Androcles and the Lion, Affair with a Stranger, The Glory Brigade, The Robe, The Veils of Bagdad* 1953; *Dangerous Mission, Demetrius and the Gladiators, The Egyptian, Betrayed* 1954; *Chief Crazy Horse* (title role), *Violent Saturday, The Last Frontier* 1955; *Safari* (UK), *The Sharkfighters, Zarak* 1956; *Interpol/Pickup Alley* (UK), *The Long Haul* (UK) 1957; *No Time to Die/Tank Force* (UK), *China Doll* 1958; *Escort West, The Bandit of Zhobe* (UK), *The Big Circus, Timbuktu* 1959; *Annibale/Hannibal* (title role; It.) 1960; *I Tartari/The Tartars* (It./Yug.) 1961; *Caccia alla Volpe/After the Fox* (It./US/UK) 1966; *Head* 1968; *Every Little Crook and Nanny* 1972; *Won Ton Ton—The Dog Who Saved Hollywood* (cameo) 1976; *Firepower* 1979; *Samson and Delilah* (TV movie) 1984.

Maura, Carmen. Actress. Born in 1945, in Madrid. Earthy, sensual leading lady of contemporary Spanish cinema. The daughter of an ophthalmologist, she had a strict, upper middle-class, Catholic upbringing. She married at 20 and majored in French at the University of Madrid, intending to become a teacher and translator. When she decided to become an actress, she encountered the strong disapproval of her conservative, Franco-sympathizing parents and lost custody of her son and daughter during a protracted bid for a papal annulment. She began performing in cabarets at 25 and on the legitimate stage somewhat later, gradually rising from bit roles to leads. Her big break came when she was selected to host the popular weekly TV talk show 'Esta Noche' ('Tonight'), which brought her wide national exposure. Although she had been appearing in films since 1970, Maura came into her own as a screen personality in the 80s, when she starred in a string of outrageous comedies by director Pedro ALMODÓVAR that gained her international popularity. She was named best actress at the European Film Awards for *Women on the Verge of a Nervous Breakdown* (1988).

FILMS INCLUDE: *El Hombre oculto* 1970; *La Petición* 1976; *Tigres de Papel* 1977; *Los Ojos vendados, Qué hace una Chica como tú en un Sitio como éste?* 1978; *Gary Cooper que estas en los cieslos/Gary Cooper Who Art in Heaven, La Mano negra, Pepi Luci Bom y otras Chicas del Montón/Pepi Luci, Bom and the Other Girls* 1980; *El Cid cabreador* 1981; *Entre Tinieblas/Dark Habits* 1983; *Qué he hecho yo para merecer ésto/What Have I Done to Deserve This?* 1984; *Extramuros, Sé infiel y no mires con quien* 1985; *Matador, Tata mia* 1986; *La Ley del Deseo/Law of Desire* 1987; *Mujeres al borde de un Ataque de Nervios/Women on the Verge of a Nervous Breakdown, Baton Rouge* 1988; *Ay Carmela!* 1990; *Como ser Mujer y no morir en el intento/How to Be a Woman and Not Die Trying* 1991; *La Reina Anónima, In Heaven as On Earth* 1992; *Sombras en una Batalla, Louis, Enfant Roi* (Fr.) 1993; *How to Be Miserable and Enjoy It* 1994; *Love Kills* 1996.

Maurey, Nicole. Actress. Born in 1925, in Bois-Colombes, France. A leading lady of French and later also American and British films, she trained as a dancer.

FILMS INCLUDE: *Blondine* 1943; *Le Cavalier noir* 1944; *Le Journal d'un Curé de Campagne/Diary of a Country Priest* 1950; *Little Boy Lost* (US), *L'Ennemi public No. 1/The Most Wanted Man, Si Versailles m'était conté/Royal Affair at Versailles, Les Compagnes de la Nuit/Companions of the Night* 1953; *Secret of the Incas* (US), *Napoléon* 1954; *The Constant Husband* (UK) 1955; *The Bold and the Brave* (US), *The Weapon* (UK) 1956; *Me and the Colonel* (US) 1958; *The Scapegoat* (UK), *The House of Seven Hawks* (UK), *The Jayhawkers* (US) 1959; *High Time* (US) 1960; *Don't Bother to Knock/Why Bother to Knock?* (UK) 1961; *Day of the Triffids, The Very Edge* (UK) 1963; *Pleins Feu sur Stanislas* 1965; *Gloria* 1977; *Chanel Solitaire* 1981.

Mauro, Humberto. Director. *b.* Apr. 30, 1897, Volta Grande, Brazil. *d.* 1983. A leading figure in the development of Latin American cinema as an art, he began experimenting with amateur equipment in 1925, turning professional in 1927. Seldom shown overseas, his films are reportedly sensitive, impassioned documents of his society, rarely matched in other South American films. His masterpiece was the richly textured melodrama, *Ganga bruta* (1933). A jack-of-all-trades, he often wrote the scripts, and at times decorated and lighted the scenes, and did the photography for his films, sometimes also acting in them. He turned out some 200 short documentaries in addition to his feature films.

FEATURE FILMS: *Valadiao o Cratera* 1925; *Na Primavera da Vida/In the Springtime of Life* 1926; *Tesouro perdido/Lost Treasure* 1927; *Brasa dormida/Dormant Embers* 1928; *Cataguases* (doc.), *Sangue Mineiro/Blood of Minas* 1929; *Lábios sem Beijos/Lips Without Kisses* 1930; *Ganga bruta/Rough Diamond, A Voz do Carnaval/Voice of the Carnival, Favela dos meus Amores/Favela of My Loves* 1933; *Cidade Mulher/City Woman* 1934; *O Descrobimento do Brasil/The Discovery of Brazil* 1937; *Argila/Clay, O Segrêdo das Asas/The Secret of Wings* 1944; *O Canto da Saudade/Song of Yearning* (medium-length) 1952; *Meus Oito Anos/I Am Eight* (doc. short) 1956; *A Velha a Fiar* (doc. short) 1964.

Maxwell, Lois. Actress. Born Lois Hooker, in 1927, in Canada. She appeared briefly in Hollywood films of the late 40s, then starred in several Italian films, and finally settled in England, where she acted the lead role in minor films. She appeared regularly as Miss Moneypenny in the James Bond film series.

FILMS INCLUDE: In the US—*That Hagen Girl* 1947; *Corridor of Mirrors* (UK), *The Decision of Christopher Blake, The Dark Past* 1948; *The Crime Doctor's Diary, Kazan* 1949. In Italy—*Amori e Veleni/Brief Rapture, Domani e troppo Tardi/Tomorrow Is Too Late* 1950; *The Woman's Angle* (UK) 1952; *Aida* (as Amneris) 1953. In the UK—*Mantrap/Man in Hiding* 1953; *Passport to Treason, The High Terrace, Satellite in the Sky* 1956; *Kill Me Tomorrow, Time Without Pity* 1957; *The Unstoppable Man* 1960; *Lolita, Dr. No* 1962; *Come Fly with Me, The Haunting, From Russia with Love* 1963; *Goldfinger* 1964; *Thunderball* 1965; *OK Connery/Operation Kid Brother* (It.), *You Only Live Twice* 1967; *On Her Majesty's Secret Service* 1969; *The Adventurers* (US) 1970; *Diamonds Are Forever* 1971; *Live and Let Die* 1973; *The Man with the Golden Gun* 1974; *The Spy Who Loved Me* 1977; *Moonraker* 1979; *Mr. Patman* (Can.) 1980; *For Your Eyes Only* 1981; *Octopussy* 1983; *A View to a Kill* 1985.

Maxwell, Marilyn. Actress, singer. *b.* Marvel Marilyn Maxwell, Aug. 3, 1921, Clarinda, Iowa. *d.* 1972. As a child, she traveled with her mother, a piano accompanist for dancer Ruth St. Denis, and made her first stage appearance at age three in a dance number. She later took singing lessons and during her teens became a band vocalist and sang on radio. After dramatic training at the Pasadena Playhouse, she became a contract player for MGM in 1942. She played leads and second leads in many films of that studio and others, both light and dramatic, relying on a voluptuous figure, blonde sex appeal, and some acting ability. She received critical praise for her performance in *Summer Holiday* (1948), a musical version of Eugene O'Neill's 'Ah Wilderness!' She also entertained in top night spots, starred briefly in the TV series 'Bus Stop,' and appeared in a number of stage productions in stock. In 1967 she headlined a burlesque show in which her performance included a stripping act. Her three marriages ended in divorce. The first (1944–46) was to actor John Conte and the third (1954–60) to screenwriter Jerry Davis. She died at 50 of high blood pressure and a pulmonary ailment.

FILMS INCLUDE: *Stand By for Action* 1942; *Presenting Lily Mars, Salute to the Marines, Thousands Cheer* 1943; *Swing Fever, Three Men in White, Lost in a Harem* 1944; *Between Two Women* 1945; *The Show-Off* 1946; *High Barbaree* 1947; *Summer Holiday, Race Street* 1948; *Champion* 1949; *Key to the City, Outside the Wall* 1950; *The Lemon Drop Kid, New Mexico* 1951; *Off Limits, East of Sumatra* 1953; *New York Confidential* 1955; *Forever Darling* 1956; *Rock-a-Bye Baby* 1958; *Critic's Choice* 1963; *The Lively Set* 1964; *Arizona Bushwhackers* 1968; *The Phynx* (cameo) 1970.

Maxwell, Ronald F. Director. Born on Jan. 5, 1947, in Tripoli, Libya. A graduate of the NYU Film School, he directed and produced the PBS 'Theater in America' TV series, as well as several TV movies, before venturing modestly into feature films in the 80s.

FEATURE FILMS: *Little Darlings* 1980; *The Night the Lights Went Out in Georgia* 1981; *Kidco* 1984; *The Killer Angels* (also prod., co-sc.) 1992; *Gettysburg* 1993.

May, Elaine. Actress, director, screenwriter. Born Elaine Berlin, on Apr. 21, 1932, in Philadelphia. As a child she toured in several plays with her father, Yiddish stage actor Jack Berlin. Later, after a teen marriage and a divorce, she studied method acting and worked at a variety of odd jobs, then enrolled at the University of Chicago, where she met another young stage hopeful, Mike NICHOLS. Together they soon formed one of the brightest and most successful satirical teams in the history of American entertainment, culminating their partnership in 1960 with the hit Broadway revue 'An Evening With Mike Nichols and Elaine May.' After they split in 1961, Miss May began writing and directing for the stage and following two film appearances as an actress started writing and directing for the screen as well, specializing in satirical comedy. May shared an Oscar nomination with Warren BEATTY for the screenplay of *Heaven Can Wait* (1978). But her career as a director suffered a setback in the 80s with the expensive failure of her comedy *Ishtar,* which was released in 1987 after long delays. She reappeared on the screen as an actress in *In the Spirit* (1990), written by her daughter, actress Jeannie BERLIN, and made a triumphant return to screenwriting when she reteamed with director Mike Nichols for the comedy hit *The Birdcage* (1996).

FILMS: As actress—*Luv, Enter Laughing* 1967; *California Suite* 1978; *In the Spirit* 1990. As screenwriter—*Such Good Friends* (under pseudonym Esther Dale) 1971; *Heaven Can Wait* (co-sc.) 1978; *Tootsie* (co-sc., uncredited) 1983; *The Birdcage* 1996. As director—*A New Leaf* (also sc., act.) 1971; *The Heartbreak Kid* 1972; *Mikey and Nicky* (also sc.) 1976; *Ishtar* 1987.

May, Joe. Director. *b.* Joseph Mandel, Nov. 7, 1880, Vienna. *d.* 1954. A pioneer of German cinema, he directed some of that country's early serials and numerous feature films, typically melodramas or crime thrillers, many of which starred his wife, Mia May (*b.* Maria Pfleger, June 2, 1884, Vienna). A former businessman and operetta director, he became a film director in 1911 and established his own production company in 1914. He launched the film career of Fritz LANG, who began as a screenwriter on May's films, notably *Mistress of the World* (1920) and *The Indian Tomb* (1921). May's other significant films include *Homecoming* (1928), an engrossing wartime love triangle considered by many his masterpiece, and *Asphalt* (1930), a gloomy, sensitively told "street film." In 1933, after the Nazi takeover, May went via France and England to Hollywood, where he directed a number of routine films. He also contributed screen stories for several productions of the 40s, alone or in collaboration. He spent the last decade of his life running the Blue Danube restaurant in Hollywood.

FILMS INCLUDE: In Germany—*In der Tiefe des Schachts* (also sc.) 1912; *Heimat und Fremde* (also sc.) 1913; *Die Geheimnisvolle Villa* (also prod.), *Die Pagode* (also prod.) 1914; *Der Schuss im Traum* 1915; *Das Gesetz der Mine* (also prod., sc.), *Nebel und Sonne* (also prod.), *Die Sünde der Helga Arndt* (also prod., co-sc.), *Wie Ich Detektiv wurde* (also prod., sc.) 1916; *Hilde Warren und der Tod* (also prod.), *Die Hochzeit im Exentricclub* (also prod.), *Die Silhouette des Teufels* (also prod.), *Der Onyxknopf* (also prod.), *Der Schwarze Chauffeur* (also prod., sc.), *Die Liebe der Hetty Raymond* (also prod.) 1917; *Sein bester Freund* (also prod.), *Opfer* (also prod., sc.), *Ihr grosses Geheimnis* (also prod., sc.), *Veritas vincit* (also prod., co-story) 1918; *Die Gräfin von Monte Christo* (also prod.), *Die wahre Liebe* (also prod., co-sc.) 1919; *Die heilige Simplizia* (also prod.), *Die Herrin der Welt/Mistress of the World* (also prod., co-sc.), *Sodom und Gomorra* (also prod.) 1920; *Das indische Grabmal/The Indian Tomb/Above All Law/Mysteries of India* (also prod.) 1921; *Tragödie der Liebe* (also prod.) 1923; *Der Farmer aus Texas* (also prod., co-sc.) 1925; *Dagfin* (also co-prod., co-sc.) 1926; *Heimkehr/Homecoming* (also prod.) 1928; *Asphalt* (also prod.) 1929; *Ihre Majestät die Liebe* (also prod.), *Und das ist die Hauptsache* 1931. In France—*Paris—Meditérranée/On demande un Compagnon, Le Chemin de Bonheur* 1932; *Voyages des Noces, Tout pour l'Amour, Ein Lied für Dich* (Ger.) 1933. In the US—*Music in the Air* 1934; *Confession* 1937; *Society Smugglers, House of Fear* 1939; *The Invisible Man Returns* (also co-story), *The House of Seven Gables, You're Not So Tough* 1940; *Hit the Road* 1941; *Johnny Doesn't Live Here Any More* 1944. As story writer—*The Invisible Woman* 1941; *The Strange Death of Adolf Hitler* 1943; *Uncertain Glory* 1944; *Buccaneer's Girl* 1950.

Mayer, Carl. Screenwriter. *b.* Nov. 20, 1894, Graz, Austria. *d.* 1944. Orphaned at 16 (his father committed suicide after losing a considerable fortune in gambling), he peddled barometers, sketched portraits, and played bit parts on the provincial stage to support his three younger brothers and himself. In Berlin immediately after WW I, he met a young Czech poet, Hans Janowitz. Together they wrote the script for a film that was to become a classic of German screen expressionism, *The Cabinet of Dr. Caligari.* Mayer subsequently wrote many other screenplays, establishing himself as the single most important author of the "golden age" of the German cinema of the 20s, a key figure in both the Expressionist and *Kammerspiel* movements of the era. His ideas inspired the work of WIENE, RUTTMANN, MURNAU, and other directors. In 1927 he traveled with Murnau to the US, where Mayer wrote the screenplay for the latter's *Sunrise.* In 1930 he returned briefly to Germany, but the following year, after Murnau's death, he emigrated to England, where he worked with Paul Rotha and Gabriel Pascal, among others. He had an uncredited hand in the scripting of such notable British films as *As You Like It* (1936), *Pygmalion* (1938), and *Major Barbara* (1941), as well as Rotha's documentary, *World of Plenty* (1943).

FILMS: *Das Kabinett des Dr. Caligari/The Cabinet of Dr. Caligari* (co-sc.) 1919; *Brandherd, Der Bucklige und die Tänzerin, Der Gang in die Nacht, Genuine, Johannes Goth, Das lachende Grauen* 1920; *Grausige Nächte, Die Hintertreppe/Backstairs, Scherben/Shattered, Schloss Vogelöd/Vogelöd Castle* 1921; *Phantom* (co-sc.), *Tragikomödie, Vanina oder die Galgenhochzeit* 1922; *Erdgeist/Earth Spirit, Der Puppenmacher von Kiang-Ning, Die Strasse/The Street* (idea only), *Sylvester/New Year's Eve* 1923; *Der letzte Mann/The Last Laugh* 1924; *Tartüff/Tartuffe* 1925; *Berlin: die Symphonie einer Grosstadt/Berlin: A Symphony of a Big City* (idea, co-prod. only), *Sunrise* (US) 1927; *The Four Devils* (co-sc.; US) 1929; *Ariane* (co-sc.), *Der Mann der den Mord Beging* (co-sc.) 1931; *Der träumende Mund/Dreaming Lips* (co-sc.) 1932; *Dreaming Lips* (remake; co-sc.; UK) 1937; *Der trämende Mund/Dreaming Lips* (screenplay basis only; Ger.) 1953; *Der letzte Mann* (screenplay basis only) 1955.

Mayer, Edwin Justus. Screenwriter. *b.* Nov. 8, 1896, New York City. *d.* 1960. With only a grade-school education, he became a newspaperman and playwright. He went to Hollywood in the late 20s as a press representative for Samuel Goldwyn, collaborated on titles of several silent films, then on the screenplays of numerous talkies, including a number of entertaining, sophisticated comedies for Paramount.

FILMS INCLUDE (as screenwriter, alone or in collaboration): *Women Love Diamonds* (titles), *The Devil Dancer* (titles), *The Love Mart* (titles) 1927; *The Whip Women* (titles), *The Blue Danube* (co-titles) 1928; *Sal of Singapore* (titles), *The Divine Lady* (co-titles), *The Unholy Night* 1929; *Not So Dumb* (dial.), *Redemption* (dial.), *The Lady of Scandal* (co-dial.), *In Gay Madrid, Romance* 1930; *Never the Twain Shall Meet* 1931; *Merrily We Go to Hell, Wild Girl* 1932; *The Night Is Ours* 1933; *I Am Suzanne, Thirty Day Princess, The Affairs of Cellini* (play basis only, 'The Firebrand'), *Here Is My Heart* 1934; *So Red the Rose, Peter Ibbetson* (addnl. dial.) 1935; *Give Us This Night, Desire, Till We Meet Again* 1936; *The Buccaneer* 1938; *Midnight* (co-story only), *Rio, Exile Express* 1939; *They Met in Bombay* 1941; *To Be or Not to Be* 1942; *A Royal Scandal, Masquerade in Mexico* (remake of *Midnight*) 1945; *The Buccaneer* (remake) 1958; *To Be or Not to Be* (remake; screenplay basis only) 1983.

Mayer, Gerald. Director. Born June 5, 1919, Montreal. *ed.* Stanford U. (journalism). The son of an MGM studio manager, he began as a director of screen tests and short subjects. He directed a number of routine films before moving on to TV, for which he turned out numerous series episodes.

FILMS INCLUDE: *Dial 1119* 1950; *Inside Straight, The Sellout* 1951; *Holiday for Sinners* 1952; *Bright Road* 1953; *The Marauders* 1955; *Diamond Safari* 1958.

Mayer, Louis B. Executive. *b.* Eliezer (Lazar) Mayer, July 4, 1885, Minsk, Russia. *d.* 1957. The son of a laborer, he emigrated with his parents to New York as a child. The family then moved to St. John, in New Brunswick, Canada, where Mayer Sr. became a junk dealer and his wife sold chickens door to door. As soon as he had graduated from elementary school, little Mayer joined his father's business, which by now had become a profitable scrap metal operation. In time young Louis set up his own junk business in Boston, where, in 1904, he married the daughter of a local kosher butcher. In 1907, responding to an ad, he bought a small rundown motion picture theater in Haverhill, Mass., at a bargain price. He renovated the auditorium and announced a policy of top-quality films only. Within several years he had bought a number of additional theaters and before long owned the largest theater chain in New England. By 1914 he had branched out into distribution and the following year he made a huge profit out of distributing Griffith's *The Birth of a Nation* in the New England area.

Mayer next moved into production, with the Alco company (later Metro), which he left in 1917 to form his own production company. He began operations the following year in Los Angeles with one star, Anita Stewart, in a production called *Virtuous Wives*. In 1924, Marcus Loew, already in control of Metro, acquired controlling interests in the Goldwyn company and Louis B. Mayer Pictures and merged the three companies into Metro-Goldwyn-Mayer (MGM). Mayer was appointed vice president and general manager, a position he retained until 1951, when he was ousted in a power struggle with Dore SCHARY, his former aide.

Under Mayer's leadership, MGM had developed in the 30s into the Tiffany of Hollywood studios, with "more stars than there are in the heavens." A ruthless, quick-tempered, paternalistically tyrannical executive, Mayer ruled MGM as one big family, rewarding obedience, punishing insubordination, and regarding opposition as personal betrayal. He made many enemies during his reign but also many admirers of his indefatigable capacity for work and his total devotion to his studio. He wasn't well read and abhorred intellectualism, but he had an uncanny intuitive sense of mass taste and a knack for selecting and handling personnel. Depending on a brilliant production chief, Irving THALBERG (later succeeded by Hunt STROMBERG and Dore SCHARY), and using the best production talent money could buy, Mayer was assured of the consistently slick product for which MGM became famous.

The typical MGM film bore to a large extent Mayer's personal preferences for wholesome escapist entertainment and his moral convictions exalting virtue, patriotism, and family life. A staunch conservative, he was active in politics and for several years was the California state chairman of the Republican party. He was also very active in industry affairs and instrumental in the founding of the Academy of Motion Picture Arts and Sciences in 1927. After being dethroned as MGM's boss in 1951, Mayer acted as advisor to the Cinerama corporation. He spent the last years of his life in a futile attempt to foment rebellion among the stockholders of Loew's, Inc., the parent company of MGM, against the corporation's management. Mayer is a subject of a biography by Bosley Crowther, *Hollywood Rajah* (1960) and another, *Mayer and Thalberg* (1975), by Sam Marx.

Mayes, Wendell. Screenwriter. Born on July 22, 1919, in Hayti, Mo. *ed.* Johns Hopkins; Columbia. A former stage actor, he wrote for television before first tackling features in the late 50s. Equally at ease with serious drama and taut action.

FILMS INCLUDE: *The Spirit of St. Louis, The Way to the Gold, The Enemy Below* 1957; *From Hell to Texas, The Hunters* 1958; *The Hanging Tree, Anatomy of a Murder* 1959; *North to Alaska* 1960; *Advise and Consent* 1962; *In Harm's Way, Von Ryan's Express* 1965; *Hotel* (also prod.) 1967; *The Stalking Moon* 1969; *The Revengers, The Poseidon Adventure* 1972; *Bank Shot, Death Wish* 1974; *Go Tell the Spartans* 1978; *Love and Bullets* 1979; *Monsignor* 1982.

Maynard, Ken. Actor. *b.* July 21, 1895, Vevay, Ind. (according to studio publicity, Mission, Tex.). *d.* 1973. One of Hollywood's most popular cowboy stars. Brother of Kermit MAYNARD. A trick rider with the Buffalo Bill and the Ringling Brothers Wild West shows and later a rodeo champion, he entered films in 1923 and before long developed into a leading cowboy star, widely admired by youngsters for his riding stunts on his equally famous horse, Tarzan. Both man and animal made a smooth transition to sound and Maynard is credited by horse-opera aficionados with introducing song into Westerns, several years ahead of the "first" singing cowboy, Gene AUTRY. But Maynard's popularity waned in the 30s and by the end of the decade he was out of films and back into the rodeo circuit. He returned to the screen briefly in 1943 in very low-budget productions but retired for good two years later except for occasional appearances in rodeos and at state fairs and in rare bits in films. Long an alcoholic, he spent his final years poor and forgotten. After the death of his wife, a former circus aerialist, he lived alone in a trailer and at the time of his death at 77 was found to have been suffering from malnutrition.

FILMS INCLUDE: *The Man Who Won* 1923; *Janice Meredith* (as Paul Revere), *$50,000 Reward* 1924; *The Demon Rider, Fighting Courage, North Star* 1925; *Senor Daredevil, The Unknown Cavalier* 1926; *The Overland Stage, The Land Beyond the Law, The Red Raiders, Gun Gospel* 1927; *The Canyon of Adventure, The Code of the Scarlet, The Glorious Trail, The Phantom City* 1928; *Cheyenne, The Lawless Legion, The Wagon Master* (also exec. prod.), *Senor Americano* (also exec. prod.) 1929; *Parade of the West* (also exec. prod.), *Lucky Larkin* (also exec. prod.), *The Fighting Legion* (also exec. prod.), *Mountain Justice* (also exec. prod.), *Song of the Caballero* (also exec. prod.), *Sons of the Saddle* (also exec. prod.) 1930; *Arizona Terror, Branded Men* 1931; *Hell Fighter, Sunset Trail, Texas Gunfighter* 1932; *King of the Arena, Fargo Express* 1933; *Mystery Mountain* (serial), *In Old Santa Fe* 1934; *Western Courage, Lawless Riders* 1935; *Heroes of the Range* 1936; *Boots of Destiny* 1937; *Phantom Ranger* 1938; *Death Rides the Range* 1940; *Wild Horse Stampede* 1943; *Arizona Whirlwind* 1944; *Blazing Frontier* 1945; *White Stallion* 1947; *Bigfoot* 1970; *Buck and the Preacher* 1972.

Maynard, Kermit (Tex). Actor. *b.* Sept. 20, 1902, Vevay, Indiana. *d.* 1971. *ed.* U. of Indiana. Younger brother of Ken MAYNARD, he went to Hollywood in 1927 as a stuntman and double for Ken and other cowboy stars. By the early 30s he was starring in his own Westerns while continuing stunts in other films. In the 40s he gradually shifted to character parts, typically as a villain.

FILMS INCLUDE: *Prince of the Plains, Ridin' Luck, Wanderer of the West, Wild Born* 1927; *The Drifting Kid* 1928; *The Phantom of the West* (serial) 1931; *Outlaw Justice* 1933; *Sandy of the Mounted* 1934; *Red Blood of Courage, Wilderness Mail* 1935; *Valley of Terror* 1936; *Galloping Dynamite* 1937; *The Great Adventures of Wild Bill Hickok* (serial) 1938; *The Night Riders* 1939; *Billy the Kid* 1941; *The Mysterious Rider* 1943; *Brand of the Devil* 1944; *Jungle Raiders* (serial), *Enemy of the Law* 1945; *Under Arizona Skies* 1946; *Stars Over Texas, The Paleface* 1948; *Lust for Gold, Riders in the Sky* 1949; *The Savage Horde* 1950; *Three Desperate Men, Golden Girl* 1951; *The Farmer Takes a Wife* 1953; *The Oklahoman* 1957; *Once Upon a Horse* 1958; *North to Alaska* 1960.

Mayo, Archie. Director. *b.* Archibald L. Mayo, 1891, New York City. *d.* 1968. He began as a film extra in 1916 after some stage experience. The following year he became gagman and director of comedy shorts. A feature film director from 1926, he turned out a balanced mixture of drama, comedy, and adventure pictures. Some of his numerous films for Warner Bros. in the 30s—notably *Bordertown, The Petrified Forest,* and *Black Legion*—showed an ability to manipulate actors as well as action. His comedies for Fox in the early 40s were often lively but rarely hilarious. Under his direction the Marx Brothers appeared in one of their weaker films, *A Night in Casablanca.*

FILMS: *Money Talks, Unknown Treasures, Christine of the Big Tops* 1926; *Johnny Get Your Hair Cut* (co-dir. with B. Reaves Eason), *Quarantined Rivals, Dearie, Slightly Used, The College Widow* 1927; *Beware of Married Men, The Crimson City, State Street Sadie, On Trial, My Man* 1928; *Sonny Boy, The Sap, Is Everybody Happy? The Sacred Flame* 1929; *Vengeance, Wide Open, Courage, Oh Sailor Behave!, The Doorway to Hell* 1930; *Illicit, Svengali, Bought* 1931; *Under Eighteen, The Expert, Street of Women, Two Against the World, Night After Night* 1932; *The Life of Jimmy Dolan, The Mayor of Hell, Ever in My Heart, Convention City* 1933; *Gambling Lady, The Man with Two Faces, Desirable* 1934; *Bordertown, Go Into Your Dance, The Case of the Lucky Legs* 1935; *The Petrified Forest, I Married a Doctor, Give Me Your Heart* 1936; *Black Legion, Call It a Day, It's Love I'm After* 1937; *The Adventures of Marco Polo, Youth Takes a Fling* 1938; *They Shall Have Music* 1939; *The House Across the Bay, Four Sons* 1940; *The Great American Broadcast, Charley's Aunt, Confirm or Deny* (replaced Fritz Lang) 1941; *Moontide* (replaced Fritz Lang); *Orchestra Wives* 1942; *Crash Dive* 1943; *Sweet and Low Down* 1944; *A Night in Casablanca, Angel on My Shoulder* 1946; *The Beast of Budapest* (prod. only) 1958.

Mayo, Virginia. Actress. Born Virginia Jones, on Nov. 30, 1920, in St. Louis, Mo. Glamorous blonde beauty of Hollywood films of the 40s and 50s, she was once described by the Sultan of Morocco as "tangible proof for the existence of God." A former showgirl, she began her Hollywood career in minor parts, then played leading lady to comedians like Bob Hope and Danny Kaye in Sam Goldwyn color extravaganzas of the 40s. Later she demonstrated some acting ability in straight dramatic parts but continued to be associated by audiences with her voluptuous, slightly cross-eyed presence in Technicolor spectacles. Following the decline of her screen career, she continued performing on the stage well into the 80s. She married actor Michael O'SHEA in 1947 and never remarried after his death in 1973.

FILMS (excluding extra and bit roles): *Jack London* 1943; *Up in Arms, Seven Days Ashore, The Princess and the Pirate* 1944; *Wonder Man* 1945; *The Kid from Brooklyn, The Best Years of Our Lives* 1946; *The Secret Life of Walter Mitty, Out of the Blue* 1947; *Smart Girls Don't Talk, A Song Is Born* 1948; *Flaxy Martin, Colorado Territory, The Girl from Jones Beach, White Heat, Red Light, Always Leave Them Laughing* 1949; *Backfire, The Flame and the Arrow, The West Point Story* 1950; *Along the Great Divide, Captain Horatio Hornblower* (US/UK), *Painting the Clouds with Sunshine, Starlift* 1951; *She's Working Her Way Through College, The Iron Mistress* 1952; *She's Back on Broadway, South Sea Woman, Devil's Canyon* 1953; *King Richard and the Crusades* (US/UK) 1954; *The Silver Chalice, The Pearl of the South Pacific* 1955; *Great Day in the Morning, Congo Crossing, The Proud Ones* 1956; *The Big Land, The Story of Mankind* (as Cleopatra), *The Tall Stranger* 1957; *Fort Dobbs* 1958; *Westbound, Jet Over the Atlantic* 1959; *La Rivolta dei Mercenari/Revolt of the Mercenaries* (It./Sp.) 1962; *Young Fury* 1965; *Castle of Evil* 1966; *Fort Utah* 1967; *Haunted, Won Ton Ton—The Dog Who Saved Hollywood* (cameo) 1976; *French Quarter* 1977; *Evil Spirits* 1991.

Mayron, Melanie. Actress. Born on Oct. 20, 1952, in Philadelphia. Engaging leading lady of the American stage, screen, and television. After training at the American Academy of Dramatic Arts, she toured with 'Godspell,' made her film debut in 1974, and her first New York stage appearance in 1979. Memorable for her glowing performance in Claudia Weill's film, *Girlfriends* (1978), for which she won the best actress prize at the Locarno Festival. She also appeared frequently on

TV, winning an Emmy Award for her 1989 performance in the series 'Thirtysomething.'

FILMS INCLUDE: *Harry and Tonto* 1974; *Gable and Lombard, Car Wash* 1976; *You Light Up My Life* 1977; *The Great Smokey Roadblock/The Last of the Cowboys, Girlfriends* 1978; *Heartbeeps* 1981; *Missing* 1982; *The Boss' Wife* 1986; *Sticky Fingers* (also co-prod., co-sc.) 1988; *Checking Out* 1989; *My Blue Heaven* 1990; *Drop Zone* 1994; *The Baby-Sitter's Club* (dir. only) 1995.

Maysles, Albert and **David.** Documentary filmmakers. Albert born on Nov. 26, 1926; David *b.* Jan. 10, 1932; *d.* 1987. Both born in Brookline, Mass. Both studied psychology, Albert at Syracuse University (B.A.) and Boston University (M.A.), David at Boston University (B.A.). Albert served in the Tank Corps during WW II, then taught for several years at Boston University. In 1955 he made his first documentary, *Psychiatry in Russia,* during a visit to the USSR. David, after service with Army Intelligence, worked as assistant to the producer on two Marilyn Monroe films, *Bus Stop* (1956) and *The Prince and the Showgirl* (1957). The brothers began collaborating in 1957 on the making of documentary films in the *CINÉMA VÉRITÉ* vein (or as they prefer calling it, "Direct Cinema"). Their most successful efforts, *Salesman* (1969) and *Gimme Shelter* (1970), have received wide distribution in motion picture theaters. Both were made in collaboration with Detroit-born filmmaker Charlotte Zwerin. The former film recorded the business routine of four door-to-door Bible salesmen, and the latter was a controversial account of the Rolling Stones 1969 US tour, which climaxed in an on-camera killing during a concert at the Altamont Speedway in California. The Maysles brothers created another controversy with the film *Grey Gardens* (1975), a sympathetic but bizarre depiction of the peculiar lifestyle of an eccentric elderly lady and her daughter, both close relatives of Jacqueline Bouvier Kennedy Onassis. Some critics accused the Maysles of exploiting the grotesque aspects of the women's lives in a sensational tabloid manner, but the filmmakers defended their choice of subject as a reflection of real life and their motive as an honest search for truth. In addition to making their "direct cinema" documentaries, the brothers Maysles turned out numerous industrial and promotional films. Their documentary short, *Christo's Valley Curtain* (1972), was nominated for an Academy Award in 1973. *Vladimir Horowitz: The Last Romantic* (1985) was nominated for an Emmy. Albert, on his own, had worked as a cameraman on a number of documentary productions by other filmmakers in the US and abroad, including *Primary* (1960), *Yanki No!* (1961), the Godard episode in *Paris vu par. . . /Six in Paris* (1965), *Monterey Pop* (1969), and *The Grateful Dead* (1977).

FILMS: *Psychiatry in Russia* (Albert only) 1955; *Youth in Poland* 1957; *Showman* (a portrait of Producer Joseph E. Levine) 1962; *What's Happening: The Beatles in the USA/Yeah Yeah Yeah* 1964; *Meet Marlon Brando* 1965; *With Love from Truman* (a visit with Truman Capote) 1966; *Salesman* (co-dir. with Charlotte Zwerin) 1969; *Gimme Shelter* (co-dir. with Zwerin) 1970; *Christo's Valley Curtain* (co-dir. with Ellen Giffard) 1972; *Grey Gardens* (co-dir. with Ellen Hovde and Muffie Meyer) 1975; *Running Fence* (co-dir. with Zwerin) 1977; *Vladimir Horowitz: The Last Romantic* (orig. for TV) 1985; *Islands* (co-dir. with Zwerin), *Ozawa* (co-dir. with Deborah Dickson and Susan Froemke) 1986; *Horowitz Plays Mozart* (Albert co-dir. with Froemke and Zwerin) 1987; *Jessye Norman Sings Carmen* (Albert co-dir. with Froemke and Zwerin) 1989; *Baroque Diet* 1992.

Mazurki, Mike. Actor. *b.* Mikhail Mazurwski, Dec. 25, 1909, Tarnopol, Austria. *d.* 1990. In the US from age six, he played football for Manhattan College and was a professional heavyweight wrestler before turning to films in the early 40s. His massive build and crude features led to his being typecast as a sharp-knuckled, dull-witted thug. Memorable as the pathetic Moose Malloy in Edward Dmytryk's *Murder My Sweet/Farewell My Lovely* (1945). In a surprise bit of casting he was given the lead role in the kiddie nature-adventure feature *Challenge to Be Free* (1976).

FILMS INCLUDE: *Belle of the Nineties* 1934; *The Shanghai Gesture* 1941; *Behind the Rising Sun* 1943; *Murder My Sweet/Farewell My Lovely, The Spanish Main, Dakota, Dick Tracy* 1945; *Sinbad the Sailor, Nightmare Alley, Unconquered* 1947; *I Walk Alone, Relentless* 1948; *Rope of Sand, Samson and Delilah* 1949; *Night and the City* 1950; *Ten Tall Men, My Favorite Spy* 1951; *The Egyptian* 1954; *Blood Alley, Kismet* 1955; *Comanche* 1956; *The Buccaneer* 1958; *Some Like It Hot* 1959; *Pocketful of Miracles* 1961; *Five Weeks in a Balloon* 1962; *Donovan's Reef, It's a Mad Mad Mad Mad World* 1963; *Cheyenne Autumn* 1964; *Requiem for a Gunfighter* 1965; *Seven Women* 1966; *The Adventures of Bullwhip Griffin* 1967; *The Wild McCullochs* 1975; *Challenge to Be Free* 1976; *One Man Jury* 1978; *The Man with Bogart's Face* 1980; *Doin' Time* 1986; *Amazon Women on the Moon* 1987; *Dick Tracy* 1990.

Mazursky, Paul. Director, producer, screenwriter, actor. Born Irwin Mazursky, on Apr. 25, 1930, in Brooklyn, N.Y., of Russian-Jewish descent. The son of a laborer at a newspaper plant, he took an interest in drama and film at an early age and began acting professionally while still attending Brooklyn College as a literature major. Moving to Manhattan's Greenwich Village, he studied Method acting with Lee STRASBERG and appeared with increasing frequency on the stage and in TV plays, and sporadically also in films. Between assignments he secured a small income as a waiter and drama teacher. In the late 50s he flourished modestly as a stand-up comedian, teaming up with Herb Hartig in the act 'Igor and H.' in top comedy clubs. In 1959 he moved to Los Angeles, where he took film courses at UCLA and performed with the school's repertory company, occasionally also appearing in TV shows. With friend and comedy partner Larry Tucker, he began in 1963 writing regularly for 'The Danny Kaye Show' and other TV programs. After many frustrated efforts to break through into the feature film market, they notched a success with their Oscar-nominated screenplay for *I Love You Alice B. Toklas* (1968), a hippie-era comedy starring Peter SELLERS.

Finally getting his long-desired chance to direct, Mazursky scored a box-office triumph with his very first film, *Bob & Carol & Ted & Alice* (1969), a titillating wife-swapping comedy echoing the emerging sexual freedom of the period. Like several of Mazursky's subsequent films, it lacked subtlety and was marred by a copout ending. Many critics dismissed it as superficial and sophomoric. *Alex in Wonderland* (1970), a semiautobiographical, self-indulgent film about a filmmaker, didn't leave much of an impression on the critics or on the box office. But Mazursky's next two films, *Blume in Love* (1973) and *Harry and Tonto* (1974), were greeted as sincere, appealing, and intelligent productions (Mazursky shared an Academy Award nomination for the latter's screenplay). Not so *Next Stop Greenwich Village* (1976), another semiautobiographical film, based on glimpses of the director's own early career, which many found painfully superficial and replete with immature clichés. In 1978 Mazursky scored his biggest success to date with *An Unmarried Woman,* a compassionate, sharply observed, but in the final analysis characteristically superficial, dramatic satire of contemporary urban mores and lifestyles. The film was nominated for Academy Awards for best picture and best screenplay, and earned its star, Jill CLAYBURGH, an Oscar nomination as best actress. Following *Willie and Phil* (1980), a whimsical romance inspired by Truffaut's *Jules and Jim,* Mazursky haplessly tried to update Shakespeare in *Tempest* (1982). He had better success with *Moscow on the Hudson* (1984), a funny, well-played comedy that runs out of steam halfway through its running length. Two middling comedies, *Down and Out in Beverly Hills* (1986, a remake of Renoir's *Boudu Saved from Drowning*) and *Moon Over Parador* (1988) were followed by *Enemies a Love Story* (1989), the director's best achievement since *An Unmarried Woman* and an Oscar nominee for best screenplay. Like much of Mazursky's best work, this adaptation of an Isaac Bashevis Singer story, was sincere, compassionate, well performed, and intermittently entertaining, but it typically lacked the cohesion and mature sophistication that could have made it great. His subsequent *Scenes from a Mall* was a critical and box-office disappointment.

FILMS: As actor—*Fear and Desire* 1953; *The Blackboard Jungle* 1955; *Deathwatch* 1966; *A Star Is Born* 1976; *A Man a Woman and a Bank* (Can.) 1979; *History of the World Part I* 1981; *Into the Night* 1985; *Punchline* 1988; *Scenes from the Class Struggle in Beverly Hills* 1989; *Man Trouble* 1992; *Love Affair* 1994; *Miami Rhapsody* 1995; *2 Days In the Valley* 1996. As screenwriter—*I Love You Alice B. Toklas* (co-sc., also co-exec. prod.) 1969. As director—*Bob & Carol & Ted & Alice* (also co-sc.) 1969; *Alex in Wonderland* (also co-sc., act.) 1970; *Blume in Love* (also prod., sc., act.) 1973; *Harry and Tonto* (also prod., co-sc.) 1974; *Next Stop Greenwich Village* (also co-prod., sc.) 1976; *An Unmarried Woman* (also co-prod., sc., act.) 1978; *Willie and Phil* (also co-prod., sc., act.) 1980; *Tempest* (also prod., co-sc., act.) 1982; *Moscow on the Hudson* (also prod., co-sc., act.) 1984; *Down and Out in Beverly Hills* (also prod., co-sc., act.) 1986; *Moon Over Parador* (also prod., co-sc., act in bit under pseudonym Carlotta Gerson) 1988; *Enemies a Love Story* (also co-prod. co-sc., act.) 1989; *Taking Care of Business* (exec. prod. only) 1990; *Scenes from a Mall* (also prod., co-sc., act.) 1991; *The Pickle* (also prod., co-sc., act.) 1993; *Faithful* (also act.) 1996.

Mc. See under MAC.

MCA, Inc. See UNIVERSAL.

MCS. Abbreviation for MEDIUM CLOSE SHOT.

meat axe. Studio slang for an adjustable pole that holds small diffusers such as a FLAG or a SCRIM.

Meaney, Colm. Actor. Born 1953 in Dublin, Ireland. *ed.* Dublin Drama School; Abbey Theatre, Dublin. Stocky, compelling character actor of stage, television, and films. After training at the famed Abbey Theatre he joined a traveling theater troupe and toured the US. He eventually ended up in Los Angeles where, with an active film career already underway, he found himself cast in the syndicated spin-off 'Star Trek: Deep Space Nine,' quickly becoming a familiar face to audiences across the nation.

FILMS: *The Dead* 1987; *Come See the Paradise, Dick Tracy, Die Hard 2* 1990; *The Commitments* 1991; *Far and Away, The Last of the Mohicans, Under Siege* 1992; *Into the West, The Snapper* 1993; *The Road to Wellville, The War of the Buttons* 1994; *The Englishman Who Went Up a Hill But Came Down a Mountain* 1995; *The Van* 1997.

mechanical effects. Special effects that are produced by physical means on the set, such as explosions, cave-ins, bullet hits, and animatronic monsters. Also known as physical effects, they are to be distinguished from visual effects, which are achieved through such photographic means as OPTICAL PRINTING, BACK PROJECTION, FRONT PROJECTION, COMPUTER ANIMATION, or digital compositing (see DIGITAL EFFECTS).

Medak, Peter. Director. Born on Dec. 23, 1937, in Budapest. Escaping Hungary following the crushing of the 1956 uprising, he entered the British film industry that same year as a trainee at AB-Pathe. Following a long apprenticeship in the sound, editing, and camera departments, he became an assistant director, then a second-unit director on action pictures. He started directing TV films for Universal in 1963 and theatrical features in 1968. Medak reached the high point of his career early, in 1972, with the release of two highly acclaimed black comedies: the sincerely human *A Day in the Death of Joe Egg* and the robustly irreverent *The Ruling Class* (1972). A California resident since the early 80s, he still works frequently in Europe. Along with his features and several TV movies, both in Britain and the US, he also directed the operas 'Salome' in Minneapolis and 'La Voix humaine' in Paris.

FILMS: A second-unit director—*Kaleidoscope, Funeral in Berlin* 1966; *Fathom* 1967. As director—*Negatives* 1968; *A Day in the Death of Joe Egg, The Ruling Class* 1972; *Ghost in the Noonday Sun* 1974; *The Odd Job* 1978; *The Changeling* (Can.) 1980; *Zorro the Gay Blade* (US) 1981; *The Men's Club* (US) 1986; *The Krays* 1990; *Let Him Have It* 1991; *Beverly Hills Cop III* (act. only), *Pontiac Moon, Romeo is Bleeding* 1994.

Medavoy, Mike. Executive. Born on Jan. 21, 1941, in Shanghai, China. *ed.* UCLA. He was raised in China until 1947, when he moved with his family to Chile, before coming to the US in 1957. He began his motion picture career in the Universal Studios mailroom, worked as a casting director, then became a talent agent, most notably at IFA, where he was vice president in charge of the motion picture department. While at IFA, he had a role in packaging several major hits of the 70s, including *The Sting* and *Jaws*. In 1974, Medavoy joined United Artists as senior vice president for West Coast productions. In 1978, he and four other top executives, dissatisfied with the parent company's policies, left United Artists to found ORION PICTURES, where he was named executive vice president. While overseeing production at United Artists and Orion, he was involved in making seven best picture Oscar winners, from *One Flew Over the Cuckoo's Nest* (1975) to *The Silence of the Lambs* (1991). In 1990, he left Orion to become chairman of TRISTAR PICTURES, a position he resigned in 1994 only to create his own production company, Phoenix Pictures, very soon after.

Medina, Patricia. Actress. Born on July 19, 1919, in Liverpool, England. Striking brunette leading lady of British and Hollywood films; seen often as the heroine of costume action dramas. The former wife (1941–52) of Richard GREENE, she married Joseph COTTEN in 1960.

FILMS INCLUDE: In the UK—*Dinner at the Ritz* 1937; *Simply Terrific* 1938; *Secret Journey* 1939; *The Day Will Dawn/The Avengers* 1942; *Hotel Reserve, Don't Take It to Heart* 1944; *Waltz Time* 1945. In the US—*The Secret Heart* 1946; *Moss Rose, The Foxes of Harrow* 1947; *The Three Musketeers* 1948; *The Fighting O'Flynn* 1949; *Francis, Fortunes of Captain Blood, Abbott and Costello in the Foreign Legion, The Jackpot* 1950; *Valentino, The Lady and the Bandit, The Magic Carpet* 1951; *Lady in the Iron Mask, Desperate Search* 1952; *Siren of Bagdad, Sangaree, Plunder of the Sun, Botany Bay* 1953; *The Black Knight* (UK), *Phantom of the Rue Morgue* 1954; *Il Mantello Rosso/The Red Cloak* (It./Fr.), *Pirates of Tripoli, Mr. Arkadin/Confidential Report* (Sp./Switz.) 1955; *Stranger at My Door, The Beast of Hollow Mountain* 1956; *Battle of the V-1/Missiles from Hell* (UK) 1958; *Count Your Blessings* 1959; *Snow White and the Three Stooges* 1961; *The Killing of Sister George* 1968; *Latitude Zero* (Jap./US) 1969; *Timber Tramp* 1973.

medium close shot (abbreviated **MCS**). A camera setup intermediate between a CLOSE SHOT and a MEDIUM SHOT. The average MCS will cut off the figure of a person at about the knees.

medium long shot (abbreviated **MLS**). A shot utilizing a wider angle than a MEDIUM SHOT but not as wide as a LONG SHOT. The object or action of principal interest is in the middle distance rather than toward the foreground or far in the background.

medium shot (abbreviated **MS**). An intermediate shot between a CLOSE-UP and a LONG SHOT. As with most camera angles, this shot cannot be described with mathematical precision. Generally speaking, it would cover the full figure of a person or a small group of people with a small portion of background showing.

Medoff, Mark. Playwright, screenwriter. Born on Mar. 18, 1940, in Mt. Carmel, Ill. *ed.* U. of Miami (Florida; B.A.); Stanford (M.A.). An associate professor of English at New Mexico State University (Las Cruces) from 1966, he had his first play produced in 1974 and in the following year became the school's dramatist-in-residence, rising to chairman of the drama department in 1978. He shared an Academy Award nomination for the screenplay of *Children of a Lesser God* (1986) which he co-adapted from his Tony Award-winning play.

FILMS: *Good Guys Wear Black* (co-sc.) 1978; *When You Comin' Back Red Ryder?* (from his own play; also act.) 1979; *Children of a Lesser God* (co-sc., from his own play), *Offbeat* 1986; *Clara's Heart* 1988; *Homage* 1996.

Medwin, Michael. Actor, producer. Born in 1923, in London. *ed.* Fischer Institute, Switzerland. Brash character player of numerous postwar British films, often in cheerful cockney roles. He turned successfully to producing in the late 60s, but later returned to acting from time to time.

FILMS INCLUDE: As actor—*Piccadilly Incident* 1946; *An Ideal Husband* 1947; *Anna Karenina* 1948; *The Queen of Spades, Boys in Brown* 1949; *Four in a Jeep* 1950; *Top Secret/Mr. Potts Goes to Moscow* 1952; *Genevieve* 1953; *Above Us the Waves, Doctor at Sea* 1955; *A Hill in Korea/Hell in Korea* 1956; *Carry On Nurse* 1959; *The Longest Day* 1962; *Night Must Fall* 1963; *A Countess from Hong Kong* 1967; *Scrooge* 1970; *The Sea Wolf* 1980; *Never Say Never Again* 1983; *The Jigsaw Man* 1984; *Just Ask for Diamond* 1988. As producer—*Charlie Bubbles* 1967; *If. . .* 1968; *Spring and Port Wine* 1969; *Gumshoe* 1971; *O Lucky Man!* (also act.) 1973; *Law and Disorder* (also cameo; US) 1974; *Memoirs of a Survivor* 1981.

Meehan, John. Screenwriter. *b.* May 8, 1890, Lindsay, Ont., Canada. Deceased. In Hollywood from the late 20s, following a career as an actor, director, and playwright on Broadway. He was nominated for Oscars for the screenplays of *The Divorcee* (1930) and *Boys Town* (1938).

FILMS INCLUDE: *The Lady Lies* 1929; *The Divorcee* 1930; *A Free Soul* 1931; *The Wet Parade, This Modern Age* 1932; *Hell Below* 1933; *The Painted Veil* 1934; *Peter Ibbetson* 1935; *His Brother's Wife* 1936; *Madame X* 1937; *Boys Town* 1938; *Seven Sinners* 1939; *Destination Unknown* 1942; *Kismet* 1944; *The Valley of Decision* 1945; *Three Daring Daughters* 1948.

Meehan, John. Art director. Born on June 13, 1902, in Tehachapi, Calif. *ed.* USC (architecture). Long with Paramount, and later with Columbia, Disney, and Universal, he won Academy Awards for *The Heiress, Sunset Boulevard* (both in collaboration), and *20,000 Leagues Under the Sea.*

FILMS INCLUDE: *Bring on the Girls* 1945; *The Virginian* 1946; *Golden Earrings* 1947; *Sealed Verdict* 1948; *The Heiress* 1949; *Sunset Boulevard* 1950; *The Marrying Kind* 1952; *Salome* 1953; *20,000 Leagues Under the Sea* 1954.

Meek, Donald. Actor. *b.* July 14, 1880, Glasgow, Scotland. *d.* 1946. Slight, bald character actor of scores of Hollywood films whose name aptly describes his timid roles. Also seen in numerous plays, including many Broadway productions.

FILMS INCLUDE: *Six Cylinder Love* 1923; *The Hole in the Wall* 1929; *Murder at the Vanities, The Merry Widow, Mrs. Wiggs of the Cabbage Patch* 1934; *The Whole Town's Talking, Mark of the Vampire, The Informer, Accent on Youth, Top Hat, the Return of Peter Grimm, Barbary Coast, China Seas, Peter Ibbetson, Captain Blood* 1935; *The Toast of New York, Artists and Models, Maid of Salem* 1937; *The Adventures of Tom Sawyer, Little Miss Broadway, You Can't Take It with You* 1938; *Jesse James, Stagecoach, Young Mr. Lincoln, Hollywood Cavalcade, Nick Carter—Master Detective* 1939; *My Little Chickadee, Dr. Ehrlich's Magic Bullet, The Return of Frank James* 1940; *A Woman's Face, Barnacle Bill* 1941; *Babes on Broadway, Tortilla Flat, Keeper of the Flame* 1942; *They Got Me Covered* 1943; *Bathing Beauty* 1944; *State Fair* 1945; *Magic Town* 1947.

Meeker, Ralph. Actor. *b.* Ralph Rathgeber, Nov. 21, 1920, Minneapolis. *d.* 1988, of a heart attack. *ed.* Northwestern. A stage actor from the early 40s, he broke into films after successfully taking over from Marlon Brando the role of Stanley Kowalski in the Broadway presentation of 'A Streetcar Named Desire.' He scored his biggest stage triumph as the star of William Inge's 'Picnic' (1953). On the screen, he played leads and character parts, typically cocky, often with a mean or yellow streak. Memorable as Mike Hammer in Robert Aldrich's *Kiss Me Deadly* (1955).

FILMS: *Teresa, Four in a Jeep* 1951; *Glory Alley, Shadow in the Sky, Somebody Loves Me* 1952; *The Naked Spur, Jeopardy, Code Two* 1953; *Big House USA, Kiss Me Deadly, Desert Sands* 1955; *A Woman's Devotion* 1956; *Run of the Arrow, The Fuzzy Pink Nightgown* 1957; *Paths of Glory* 1958; *Ada, Something Wild* 1961; *Wall of Noise* 1963; *The Dirty Dozen, The St. Valentine's Day Massacre, Gentle Giant* 1967; *The Detective* 1968; *The Devil's Eight* 1969; *Lost Flight, I Walk the Line* 1970; *The Anderson Tapes* 1971; *The Happiness Cage* 1972; *Love Comes Quietly* (Holl./Belg.) 1974; *Brannigan, Johnny Firecloud* 1975; *The Food of the Gods* 1976; *The Alpha Incident* 1977; *Hi-Riders, My Boys Are Good Boys* (also co-prod.) 1978; *Winter Kills* 1979; *Without Warning* 1980.

Meerson, Lazare. Art director. *b.* 1900, Russia. *d.* 1938. He left Russia in the wake of the Bolshevik Revolution and lived for a while in Germany before settling in France in 1924. He revolutionized art design in French films by shunning the existing influences (naturalism, impressionism, expressionism) and introducing a style of "poetic realism" that became dominant in the French cinema of the 30s. His sets, especially the enormous studio-built city streets he constructed for the films of Jacques FEYDER and René CLAIR, have been widely admired for their contribution to the film's humanistic viewpoint and real-life atmosphere. His work influenced a whole generation of art directors both in France and abroad. In 1936 he went to England, where he designed memorable sets of Alexander KORDA productions before his untimely death at 38.

FILMS INCLUDE: In France—*Gribiche, Feu Mathias Pascal* 1925; *Carmen* 1926; *La Proie du Vent, Un Chapeau de Paille d'Italie/An Italian Straw Hat* 1927; *Les Deux Timides* 1928; *Sous les Toits de Paris/Under the Roofs of Paris* 1930; *Le Million, A nous la Liberté, Jean de la Lune* 1931; *Quatorze Juillet, Le Grande Jeu, Ciboulette, Lac aux Dames* 1933; *Amok* 1934; *Pension Mimosas, La Kermesse héroïque* 1935. In the UK—*As You Like It* 1936; *Fire Over England, Knight Without Armor* 1937; *Break the News, The Citadel, The Divorce of Lady X* 1938.

Mehboob (also known as Mehboob Khan). Director. *b.*

Ramjankhan Mehboobkhan, 1907, Bilimora, Gujarat, India. *d.* 1964. At 16 he ran away from his poverty-stricken village to Bombay, where he entered films as an extra in 1923. He slept on railway station benches in the early months of a long but modest acting career, which eventually led nowhere. He was immediately successful, however, when he turned to directing in the early 30s. In 1942 he formed his own company, Mehboob Productions, Ltd. The still-thriving Mehboob Studios, which he founded in 1952, are among the best equipped in all of India. At first he was attracted by social themes, but after the international success of his colorful adventure film *Aan/Savage Princess* (1951), he specialized in entertainment films that enjoyed extensive popularity throughout Asia, Africa, and the Middle East. His best film, *Mother India* (1957), the emotionally loaded remake of his *Woma* (1940), proved so popular that it is rereleased perennially in Indian theaters.

FILMS INCLUDE: *Al Hilal* 1932; *Judgment of Allah* 1935; *Roti/Bread, Watan* 1936; *We Three* 1939; *Aurat/Woman* 1940; *Ali Baba* 1941; *Jadirdar* 1942; *Taqdeer/Fate* 1943; *Amar* 1948; *Aan/Savage Princess* 1952; *Bharat Mata/Mother India* 1957; *A Handful of Grain* 1958; *Son of India* 1960.

Mehrjui, Dariush. Director. Born in 1939, in Teheran. Leading figure in contemporary Iranian cinema. A musician in his teens, he became an avid moviegoer and before long decided to become a filmmaker. After toiling for a year as a hotel manager, he saved enough money to go to the US in 1959 and enroll at UCLA's film program. Disappointed by the level of the courses, he soon switched his major to philosophy. But his passion for the cinema remained unquenched. Returning to Teheran in 1965, he became a journalist and TV scriptwriter, and for a while also taught English, literature, and film aesthetics. He made his film directing debut the following year, with a forgettable James Bond spoof. But in 1970 he astonished the international film community with *Gay/The Cow,* a compelling symbolic drama, about a simple villager and his nearly mystical attachment to his cow. Although it had been funded by the Shah's government, *The Cow* was banned by the Ministry of Culture because of its raw portrayal of impoverished conditions in rural Iran and only released in 1970, a year after its completion, with an added statement that dated the story 50 years back. When the film was still denied an export permit, a friend of the director smuggled out a print to Paris in 1971. Echoing Italian neorealism, this grainy black-and-white, fascinating, "big-little film" brought Mehrjui instant recognition and heralded the belated coming of age of Iranian cinema when it was lauded by the international critics at the Venice Festival. Years later the Ayatollah Ruhollah Khomeini singled it out for praise after seeing it on television.

In 1973 Mehrjui began directing what was to be his most acclaimed film. A vivid portrait of corruption, poverty, misery, and apathy, exposing the horrors of the illicit blood traffic in Teheran, *The Cycle* was co-sponsored by the Ministry of Culture but encountered opposition from the Iranian medical establishment and was banned from release until 1977. It was universally admired abroad. Meanwhile, Mehrjui found himself unable to work in Iran. He sojourned in California for a while, but with the fall of the Shah he returned to Iran, where he directed *The Backyard* (1980). But he soon found working conditions in fundamentalist Iran no less repressive. In 1981 he traveled to Paris and stayed there for several years, during which he made a feature-length semidocumentary for French TV, *Voyage au Pays de Rimbaud* (1983). Feeling homesick, he returned to Teheran in 1985. As dogmatism at the top began to mellow, he resumed his film work and in 1990 enjoyed a local success with *Hanoun/The Desert.*

FEATURE FILMS: *Almast 33/Diamond 33* 1966; *Gay/The Cow* (release delayed from 1969) 1970; *Apahye Hallou/Mr. Naive/Mr. Gullible* (release delayed from 1970) 1971; *Postschi/The Postman/The Mailman* (released delayed from 1970) 1972; *Dayereh Mina/The Cycle* (release delayed from 1974) 1977; *Hayate Poshti/The Backyard/The School We Went To* (held back from release) 1980; *Hanoun/The Desert* 1990; *Sara* (also co-prod., sc.) 1994.

Mehta, Ketan. Director. Born in 1953, in Gujarat, India. After graduating from New Delhi's St. Stephens College, where he majored in economics, he became passionately involved with the theater, gradually gravitating toward radical modes of dramatic expression. At the same time he enrolled at the Film and Television Institute of India, where his diploma film was the half-hour, black-and-white short *The Midday Sun* (1975). After graduating, he made several short documentaries for television. He bolted to the forefront of India's "alternative cinema" with his very first feature, *A Folk Tale* (1980), an exuberant comedy-drama with music about the plight of the untouchables, the lowest level in the Indian caste system. His *Spices* (1987) was widely distributed abroad, including the US, where Mehta was described by some as the Indian counterpart of Spike LEE, because of his audacious style and entertaining treatment of serious subjects. He writes his own screenplays.

FEATURE FILMS: *Bhavni Bhavai/A Folk Tale* 1980; *Holi/Fire Festival* 1984; *Mirch Masala/Spices* 1987; *Hillalal* 1989.

Meighan, Thomas. Actor. *b.* Apr. 9, 1879, Pittsburgh. *d.* 1936. On the stage from his late teens, he achieved some prominence on Broadway at the turn of the century. A leading man of films from 1913, he reached top stardom in 1919 with *The Miracle Man* and *Male and Female.* He remained one of Hollywood's leading screen personalities throughout the 20s, typically playing a mature, dependable, intelligent hero. He continued to play leads in early sound films of the 30s. From 1908 till his death from a bronchial ailment he was married to his Broadway co-star, Frances Ring.

FILMS INCLUDE: *Kindling, The Immigrant, Blackbirds* 1915; *The Sowers, The Trail of the Lonesome Pine, The Storm* 1916; *Sappho, Arms and the Girl, The Land of Promise, The Mysterious Miss Terry* 1917; *Heart of the Wilds, The Forbidden City, M'Liss* 1918; *The Heart of Wetona, The Miracle Man, Male and Female* 1919; *Why Change Your Wife?, Civilian Clothes, Conrad in Quest of His Youth* 1920; *The Easy Road, City of Silent Men, White and Unmarried, A Prince There Was, The Conquest of Canaan* 1921; *Our Leading Citizen, The Bachelor Daddy, Back Home and Broke, Manslaughter* 1922; *The Ne'er-Do-Well, Homeward Bound, Woman-Proof* 1923; *Pied Piper Malone, The Alaskan, The Confidence Man, Tongues of Flame* 1924; *Coming Through, The Man Who Found Himself, Irish Luck* 1925; *The New Klondike, Tin Gods, The Canadian* 1926; *Blind Alleys, We're All Gamblers, The City Gone Wild* 1927; *The Racket, The Mating Call* 1928; *The Argyle Case* 1929; *Young Sinners, Skyline* 1931; *Cheaters at Play, Madison Square Garden* 1932; *Peck's Bad Boy* 1934.

Mekas, Jonas. Filmmaker, theoretician, and spokesman of underground cinema. Born on Dec. 24, 1922, in Semeniskiai, Lithuania. *ed.* Johannes Guttenberg U., Mainz; U. of Tübingen (philosophy and literature). After having spent WW II in a concentration camp, he began studying film during his five years as a displaced person before immigrating to the US in 1950. He has since been actively involved in the activities of the American avant-garde as editor (*Film Culture*), critic (*The Village Voice*), theoretician ("The new cinema is an art of light"), organizer (Film-Makers Cooperative, for the rental of experimental film;

Anthology Film Archives), and "underground" filmmaker. His best-known film is *The Brig,* a screen adaptation of the Living Theater production, shot in one night with a hand-held camera. Although a fictional drama, the film was so realistically photographed that the judges at the 1964 Venice Film Festival voted it the best documentary of 1964. Jonas's brother, Adolfas Mekas (*b.* 1925, Lithuania), is also a prominent avant-garde filmmaker (*Hallelujah the Hills,* 1963; *Windflowers,* 1968). They occasionally work on each other's productions.

FILMS INCLUDE: *Grand Street* 1953; *Silent Journey* 1955; *Guns of the Trees, The Secret Passions of Salvador Dali* 1961; *Film Magazine of the Arts* 1963; *The Brig* 1964; *The Millbrook Report, Hare Krishna* 1966; *Diaries Notes and Sketches* 1969; *Walden* 1970; *Reminiscences of a Journey to Lithuania* 1972; *Lost Lost Lost* 1976; *In Between* 1978; *Paradise Not Yet Lost* 1980; *Notes for Jerome 1981.*

Melato, Mariangela. Actress. Born in 1941, in Milan. *ed.* Milan Theater Academy. Attractive, blonde leading lady of Italian films, following experience on the stage. Skilled at both dramatic and comic roles, she figured prominently in films of Petri, Wertmuller, Monicelli, and other directors.

FILMS INCLUDE: *Per Grazia ricevuta/Between Miracles, La Classe operaia va in Paradiso/The Working Class Goes to Heaven/Lulu the Tool, Il Prete sposato/The Married Priest* 1971; *Mimi metallurgico ferito nell'Onore/The Seduction of Mimi* 1972; *Film d'Amore e d'Anarchia/Love and Anarchy* 1973; *Travolti da un Insolito Destino nell'Azzurro/Swept Away, Nada/The Nada Gang* 1974; *Caro Michele, Todo Modo* 1976; *Il Casotto* 1977; *Il Gatto* 1978; *Dimenticare Venezia/To Forget Venice* 1979; *Flash Gordon* (UK) 1980; *So Fine* (US), *Aiutami a Sognare* 1981; *Bello mio bellezza mia* 1982; *Il Petromane* 1983; *Segreti Segreti* 1984; *Notte d'Estate con Profilo Greco Occhi a Mandorla e Odore di Basilico/Summer Night with Greek Profile Almond Eyes and Scent of Basil* 1986; *Dancers* (US) 1987.

Melcher, Martin. Producer. *b.* Aug. 1, 1915, North Adams, Mass. *d.* 1968. Formerly a talent agent and road manager of the Andrews Sisters, he produced many of the movies of Doris DAY, his wife, and other films for the company they formed jointly in 1952.

FILMS INCLUDE: *Calamity Jane* 1953; *Julie* 1956; *Tunnel of Love* 1958; *Pillow Talk* 1959; *Lover Come Back, That Touch of Mink, Jumbo* 1962; *The Thrill of It All, Move Over Darling* 1963; *Send Me No Flowers* 1964; *Do Not Disturb* 1965; *The Glass Bottom Boat* 1966; *Caprice* 1967; *The Ballad of Josie, Where Were You When the Lights Went Out?, With Six You Get Eggroll* 1968.

Melchior, Ib. Director, screenwriter. Born on Sept. 17, 1917, in Copenhagen. The son of Lauritz MELCHIOR, he began his career as a stage actor and stage manager, after studies at Denmark's Stenhus College. Following WW II service with US military intelligence, he began writing and directing, as well as acting, for American TV. He began his association with motion pictures in the late 50s and has since directed two films and collaborated on the scripts of several others, specializing mainly in juvenile science-fiction fare. He has also directed and written a number of documentaries. In the early 70s he started writing novels. By the end of the 80s he had published nine.

FILMS INCLUDE: *Live Fast Die Young* (co-story, co-sc.), *When Hell Broke Loose* (based on his articles; also tech. adv.) 1958; *The Angry Red Planet* (dir., co-sc.) 1960; *Reptilicus* (co-sc.; US/Den.), *Journey to the Seventh Planet* (co-sc., montage dir.; US/Den.) 1961; *The Case of Patty Smith* (assoc. prod.) 1962; *Robinson Crusoe on Mars* (co-sc.), *The Time Travelers* (dir., co-story, sc.) 1964; *Ambush Bay* (co-sc.) 1966; *Death Race 2000* (story) 1975.

Melchior, Lauritz. Singer, actor. *b.* Mar. 20, 1890, Copenhagen. *d.* 1973. Celebrated Wagnerian tenor who appeared in a number of Hollywood films of the late 40s and early 50s. He began his career as a boy soprano and after performing for several years as a baritone with Copenhagen's Royal Opera, he went to Berlin to study Wagnerian roles and made his debut as a *heldentenor* (heroic tenor) at the Bayreuth Festival of 1924. He first appeared with the Metropolitan Opera in New York in 1926 and before long became one of the world's leading interpreters of Wagnerian roles. A massive, jovial man, he played benevolent roles in a handful of screen musicals but fared only modestly as a film personality. He was the father of Ib MELCHIOR.

FILMS: *Thrill of a Romance* 1945; *Two Sisters from Boston* 1946; *This Time for Keeps* 1947; *Luxury Liner* 1948; *The Stars Are Singing* 1953.

Melford, George. Director, actor. *b.* 1889, Rochester, N.Y. *d.* 1961. *ed.* McGill (Montreal). A former stage actor, he entered films in 1909 as actor, then director, for Kalem. Through the mid-30s he piloted hundreds of shorts and features for Lasky, Paramount, and other studios, then returned to acting in character parts. His films as director during the silent era included many prestigious, high-budget films, but his talkies were routine B productions.

FILMS INCLUDE: As director—*Arizona Bill* (co-dir. with Robert Vignola; also sc.) 1911; *The Struggle* 1913; *The Boer War, The Invisible Power* 1914; *The Fighting Hope, Armstrong's Wife, The Unknown, Stolen Goods, The Marriage of Kitty, The Immigrant, The Puppet Crown, The Woman, Young Romance* 1915; *To Have and to Hold, The Years of the Locust, The Yellow Pawn* 1916; *The Evil Eye, Her Strange Wedding, A School for Husbands, The Cost of Hatred, On the Level, The Call of the East, The Sunset Trail, Nan of Music Mountain, Sandy* 1917; *The Hidden Pearls, Wild Youth, Such a Little Pirate, The Source, The Bravest Way, the Cruise of the Makebelieve* 1918; *Pettigrew's Girl, Men Women and Money, The City of Dim Faces, A Sporting Chance, Everywoman* 1919; *The Sea Wolf, The Round-Up, Behold My Wife* 1920; *The Faith Healer, The Great Impersonation, A Wise Fool, The Sheik* 1921; *Moran of the Lady Letty, Burning Sands, The Woman Who Walked Alone, Ebb Tide* 1922; *You Can't Fool Your Wife, The Light That Failed, Java Head, Salomy Jane* 1923; *Flaming Barriers, The Dawn of a Tomorrow, Big Timber, Tiger Love* 1924; *The Top of the World, Friendly Enemies, Without Mercy, Simon the Jester* 1925; *The Flame of the Yukon, Going Crooked, Rocking Moon, Whispering Smith* 1926; *A Man's Past* 1927; *Lingerie, Sinners in Love, Freedom of the Press* 1928; *The Charlatan, Love in the Desert, Sea Fury, The Woman I Love* 1929; *The Poor Millionaire, La Voluntad del Muerto* (Spanish-language version of *The Cat Creeps*), *Oriente y Occidente* (Spanish-language version of *East Is West*) 1930; *Don Juan Diplomatico* (Spanish-language version of *The Boudoir Diplomat*), *Dracula* (Spanish version only), *The Viking, East of Borneo, Homicide Squad* 1931; *The Boiling Point* 1932; *The Penal Code, Officer 13, Man of Action, The Eleventh Commandment* 1933; *Hired Wife* 1934; *East of Java* 1935; *Jungle Menace* (serial; co-dir. with Harry Fraser) 1937. As actor—*Rulers of the Sea* 1939; *My Little Chickadee* 1940; *Flying Cadets* 1941; *Lone Star Ranger* 1942; *Dixie Dugan* 1943; *The Miracle of Morgan's Creek, Hail the Conquering Hero* 1944; *A Tree Grows in Brooklyn* 1945; *Thunder in the Valley* 1947; *The Robe* 1953; *The Egyptian* 1954; *Prince of Players* 1955; *The Ten Commandments* 1956; *Bluebeard's Ten Honeymoons* 1960.

Méliès, Georges. Director, producer. *b.* Dec. 8, 1861, Paris. *d.* 1938. The son of a wealthy footwear manufacturer, he was expected to enter the family business but showed an early inclination toward the arts and while still at grade school excelled at design, painting, sculpture, and puppetry. After completing his military service as a corporal with the French infantry, he enrolled at the Ecôle des Beaux Arts against the wishes of his father, who made him work at the family plant as a mechanic. In 1884 he went to London, where he continued his art studies, worked for a living in a large store, and became fascinated by the exhibition of stage magic by conjurers. Returning to Paris, he became a conjurer and illusionist himself and at the same time began contributing caricatures to a satirical publication under the pseudonym Geo Smile. Soon after, however, his father retired and Georges and his brother Gaston took over the active management of the family business. But in 1888 an opportunity arose that Georges could not resist. The widow of famed stage performer Robert Houdin put his theater up for sale. Méliès sold his share of the family business to Gaston and purchased the theater. He reopened the Théâtre Robert-Houdin as a stage for his magic and illusion show and soon became famous for his inventive stagecraft and flamboyant showmanship. In time he added a magic lantern presentation to his attractions, realizing the potential value of visual "sorcery" as a means of creating illusion. One can thus imagine his excitement when he witnessed the historic premiere exhibition of the LUMIÉRE brothers' cinématographe at the Grand Café in Paris in December of 1895. Méliès implored the Lumières to sell him their apparatus, but they turned him down.

Undaunted, Méliès, in London, bought a Bioscope projector from Robert W. PAUL and a number of Edison Kinetoscope shorts; and on April 4, 1896, he began showing films regularly as part of his theatrical magic show. Soon after, he had a camera constructed from his own design, based on the Bioscope mechanism, and again set out to London, where he purchased a large quantity of raw Eastman film stock. He was now ready to make his own productions under the banner Star Film. Méliès's early film output was very much an imitation of the Lumière product, a simple, unstaged recording of trivia and everyday events: people playing cards or riding bicycles, a view of the Place de l'Opéra, a train arriving at a terminal. But as soon as he felt comfortable with his new toy, the inventive Méliès began seeking more imaginative ways to exploit the camera other than for the mere recording of reality. He got help accidentally. One day, as he was filming a Paris street scene, the camera jammed. By the time he had it going again, a few seconds had elapsed and naturally the scene changed. When he viewed the developed film, Méliès was amazed by the result, as objects suddenly appeared or disappeared from view or were magically transformed from one to another on the screen. The discovery, soon followed by other findings about the special optical-mechanical characteristics of motion pictures, set the stage for the birth of the trick and fantasy film.

By the end of 1896, Méliès had turned out no fewer than 78 little films, each about 20 meters in length. In 1897 he produced and directed 53 more and converted his theater exclusively to the showing of motion pictures. During that year he built Europe's first film studio at Montreuil and began making films indoors with the aid of artificial lighting. He was now able to shoot "reconstructed" (that is, fake) newsreels as well as real events and to expand his cinematic repertoire to include dramatic adaptations from literature and the stage. The highlight of his 1899 season was a 20-scene presentation of *Cinderella,* and in 1900 his catalog boasted a 12-scene *Jeanne d'Arc* with 500 extras. But it was in the realm of fantasy that he made his most lasting contribution to cinema art. His best-known film, *Le Voyage dans la Lune/A Trip to the Moon* (1902), still amuses and fascinates film audiences with its humor and inventiveness wherever it is shown.

The films of Méliès enjoyed great popularity abroad and were widely distributed and illegally copied in the US. To prevent further infringements of his copyright, he set up an American branch in 1903 under the management of his brother Gaston. In addition to distributing Méliès's French productions, the US branch of Star Film also produced films locally, including a number of Westerns. Gradually, however, the novelty of Méliès's trick films wore off. As the market for his product shrank, the fortune he had amassed evaporated. In 1911 he borrowed heavily from the Pathé brothers, now his distributors, to continue production, and in the following year he turned out one of his most accomplished comedy-fantasy films, *A la Conquête du Pole/The Conquest of the Pole.* It was also one of his last. Several months later he was out of films. He was forced to sell his estate and in 1915 converted his Montreuil studio into a variety theater in which he performed his old magic and illusion tricks. In 1923 he was declared bankrupt and his Théâtre Robert-Houdin was demolished. The following year, he was given a temporary appointment as the manager of a workers' theater in the mine region of the Saar. In 1926, now a dejected and forgotten widower, he chanced upon one of his former stars, Jeanne d'Alcy, who ran a toy concession at the Montparnasse railway station. They married and managed the concession together. A belated re-discovery of his contribution to cinema art began in 1928. In 1931 he was awarded a Legion of Honor medal and in the following year he was given a rent-free apartment, where he spent the remainder of his years.

Méliès's contribution to the development of film art was considerable. Although he made many reality films as well as his numerous fantasy productions, and the Lumière brothers had their fair share of fiction films, certain film historians see the art of cinema developing along two main parallel lines that eventually fused into one: the tradition of reality, originating with Lumière, and the tradition of fiction and fantasy, originating with Méliès. In 1952 director Georges Franju paid a filmic tribute to the grand master of cinema wizardry in the short *Le Grand Méliès.*

FILMS INCLUDE: *Une Partie de Cartes, Séance de Prestidigitation, Un Bon Petit Diable, Les Chevaux du Bois, L'Arroseur, Arrivée d'un Train Gare de Vincennes, Place de l'Opéra, Bateau-Mouche sur la Seine, Une Nuit terrible, Tribulations d'un Concierge, Enfants jouant sur la Plage, Danse serpentine, Cortège du Tsar allant à Versailles, Grandes Manoeuvres, Escamotage d'une Dame chez Robert-Houdin* (first film with stop-motion cinematography), *Le Fakir—Mystère indien, L'Hôtel empoisonné* 1896; *Chicot Dentiste américain, Paulus chantant* (in five parts; first to be shot with artificial light), *Coquin de Printemps, Le Malade imaginaire, L'Hallucination de l'Alchimiste, Le Château hanté, Episode de Guerre* (studio re-creation of Greco-Turkish War), *Exécution d'un Espion, Massacres de Crète, Gugusse et l'Automate, La Cigale et la Fourmi/The Grasshopper and the Ant, Le Cabinet de Méphistophélès, Figaro et l'Auvergnant, Chirurgien américain, Arlequin et Charbonnier, Après le Bal, Vente d'Esclaves au Harem, Faust et Marguerite* 1897; *Carrefour de l'Opéra* (first time-lapse photography), *Magie diabolique, Les Rayons X, Visite de l'Epave du Maine/Battleship Maine, Le Magicien, Illusions fantasmagoriques, Pygmalion et Galathée/Pygmalion and Galathea, Damnation de Faust/The Damnation of Faust, Guillaume Tell et le Clown/William Tell and the Clown, La Lune à un Mètre/L'Homme dans la Lune, La Caverne maudite/The Haunted Cavern* (first double exposure), *Rêve d'Artiste, L'Homme de Têtes/The Man with Four Heads/The Four*

Troublesome Heads (four heads magically replace one another), *Dédoublement cabalistique, Créations spontanées* 1898; *Cléopâtre/Cleopatra, Richesse et Misèrie, Le Spectre, Le Diable au Couvent, La Danse du Feu* (adaptation of *She*), *Le Portrait mystérieux, Le Miroir de Cagliostro, Neptune et Amphitrite, Le Christ marchant sur les Flots, Evocation spirite, L'Affaire Dreyfus/The Dreyfus Case, L'Ile du Diable, Cendrillon/Cinderella, Le Chevalier mystère, Tom Whisky ou l'Illusioniste toqué, Les Miracles du Brahmine* 1899; *Exposition de 1900* (doc. in 16 short scenes), *L'Homme-Orchestre/The One Man Band* (complex exercise in multiple exposure in which Méliès himself appears as seven different persons on the same frame), *Jeanne d'Arc/Joan of Arc* (in 12 scenes with 500 extras), *Les Sept Péchés capitaux/The Seven Deadly Sins, Le Rêve du Radjah/La Forêt enchantée, Le Fou Assassin, Le Livre magique, Spiritisme abracadabrant, L'Illusioniste double et la Tête vivante, Le Rêve de Noël* (in 20 scenes with many special effects, including snow and night effects), *Coppelia, Gens qui pleurent et Gens qui rient, Le Deshabillage impossible, L'Homme aux Cent Trucs, La Maison tranquille, Mésaventures d'un Aéronaute, La Tour maudite, Bouquet d'Illusions* 1900; *Le Petit Chaperon rouge/Little Red Riding Hood* (in 12 scenes), *Chez la Sorcière, Le Temple de la Magie, Le Charlatan, Excelsior!, La Fontaine sacrée/La Vengeance de Bouddah, Barbe-Bleue/Bluebeard, Le Phrénologie burlesque, L'Ecole infernale, Le Rêve du Paria, Le Bataillon élastique, L'Homme à la Tête en Caoutchouc, Le Diable géant/Le Miracle de la Madone, L'Oeuf du Sorcier/L'Oeuf magique prolifique, La Danseuse microscopique* 1901; *Eruption volcanique à la Martinique* (studio re-creation of actual volcanic eruption), *Le Voyage dans la Lune/A Trip to the Moon* (in 30 scenes totaling 845 feet), *La Clownesse Fantôme, Le Sacre d'Edouard VII* (the coronation of King Edward VII re-created in the studio before [!] the event), *Les Trésors de Satan, L'Homme-Mouche* (man turns into a fly), *La Femme volante* (woman is suspended in midair), *L'Equilibre impossible, Le Pochard et l'Inventeur, Le Voyage de Gulliver à Lilliput et chez les Géants/Gulliver's Travels, Les Aventures de Robinson Crusoé/The Adventures of Robinson Crusoe* (in 25 scenes) 1902; *Les Filles du Diable, Le Cake-Walk infernal, Les Mousquetaires de la Reine, La Statue animée, La Flamme merveuilleuse, Le Sorcier, L'Oracle de Delphes, Le Mélomane* (elaborate multi-exposures), *Le Monstre, Le Royaume des Fées* (in 30 scenes), *Le Revenant, Le Tonnerre de Jupiter/Jupiter's Thunderbolts, La Parapluie fantastique, Tom Tight et Dum Dum, La Lanterne magique/The Magic Lantern, Le Rêve du Maître de Ballet, Faust aux Enfers* (in 15 scenes) 1903; *Les Apaches, Au Clair de la Lune/Pierrot malheureux, Le Coffre enchanté, Les Apparitions fugitives, Le Roi du Maquillage, Le Rêve d'Horloger, Les Transmutations imperceptibles, Un Miracle sous l'Inquisition, Benvenuto Cellini/Curieuse Evasion, Damnation du Docteur Faust* (in 20 scenes), *Le Merveilleux Eventail vivant, La Sirène/The Mermaid, Le Barbier de Seville/The Barber of Seville, Les Costumes animés, La Dame Fantôme, Voyage à travers l'Impossible/An Impossible Voyage* (in 40 scenes), *Le Juif errant/The Wandering Jew* 1904; *A President-Elect Roosevelt, Les Cartes vivantes, Le Diable noir, Le Phénix, Le Baquet de Mesmer, Tableau diabolique, Le Miroir de Venise, Une Mésaventure de Shylock, Les Chevaliers du Chloroforme, Le Palais des Mille et Une Nuits/A Thousand and One Nights* (in 30 scenes), *La Tour de Londres/Les Derniers Moments d'Anne de Boleyn, La Légende de Rip van Winkle* 1905; *Le Dirigeable fantastique, Jack le Ramoneur, La Magie à travers les Ages/Magic Through the Ages, Les Incendiaires/L'Histoire d'un Crime* (in 30 scenes), *L'Anarchie chez Guignol, Le Fantôme d'Alger, Les Quatre Cent Farces du Diable/The Merry Frolics of Satan* (in 35 scenes), *L'Alchimiste Parafaragaramus/La Cornue infernale, La Fée Carabosse* 1906; *Le Carton fantastique, La Douche d'Eau bouillante, Vingt Mille Lieues sous les Mers/20,000 Leagues Under the Sea, Le Tunnel sous la Manche/Tunneling the English Channel* (fantasy in 30 scenes in which King Edward VII and the President of France dream jointly of an underwater tunnel between Dover and Calais), *Le Delirium Tremens/La Fin d'un Alcoolique, L'Eclipse de Soleil en Plein Lune, La Marche funèbre de Chopin/Chopin's Funeral March, Hamlet, La Mort de Jules César/The Death of Julius Caesar, Satan en Prison* 1907; *La Cuisine de l'Ogre, La Civilisation à travers les Ages/Civilization Through the Ages, Torches humaines, Le Rêve d'un Fumeur d'Opium, Nuit de Carnaval, La Photographie électrique à distance, La Prophétesse de Thèbes, Mariage de Raison et Mariage d'Amour, L'Avare/The Miser, Le Serpent de la Rue de la Lune, Tartarin de Tarascon, Le Raid Paris–New York en Automobile* (an imaginary car race from Paris to New York), *Au Pays des Jouets/Toyland, Hallucination pharmaceutique, La Poupée vivante, Le Fakir de Singapour* 1908; *Hydrothérapie fantastique, Le Locataire diabolique, Les Illusions fantaisistes, La Gigue merveilleuse* 1909; *Le Papillon fantastique, Si j'etais Roi/If I Were King, L'Homme aux Mille Inventions, Le Secret du Médecin* 1910; *Les Hallucinations du Baron de Münchhausen* 1911; *A la Conquête du Pole/The Conquest of the Pole, Cendrillon/Cinderella* (remake) 1912; *Le Chevalier des Neiges, Le Voyage de la Famille Bourrichon* 1913.

Mellor, William C. American. Director of photography. *b.* 1904. *d.* 1963. He began as a lab assistant at Paramount and after a period of apprenticeship as an assistant cameraman became a full cinematographer in 1934. He worked for Paramount, MGM, and Fox, among other studios, collaborating a number of times with directors William WELLMAN and George STEVENS. He won Academy Awards for the cinematography of *A Place in the Sun* (1951) and *The Diary of Anne Frank* (1959). He died while working on *The Greatest Story Ever Told* and was replaced by Loyal Griggs.

FILMS INCLUDE: *Home on the Range* 1934; *Collegiate* 1935; *Poppy* 1936; *Make Way for Tomorrow* 1937; *Stolen Heaven* 1938; *Hotel Imperial, The Magnificent Fraud* 1939; *Road to Singapore, Typhoon, The Great McGinty* 1940; *Birth of the Blues, Reaching for the Sun* 1941; *The Fleet's In, My Favorite Blonde, Beyond the Blue Horizon, Road to Morocco* 1942; *The Commandos Strike at Dawn, Dixie* 1943; *Abie's Irish Rose* 1946; *Blaze of Noon* 1947; *The Senator Was Indiscreet* 1948; *Love Happy* 1950; *Soldiers Three, A Place in the Sun, Across the Wide Missouri* 1951; *It's a Big Country* (co-phot.), *Westward the Women, Carbine Williams* 1952; *The Naked Spur, The Affairs of Dobie Gillis* 1953; *Bad Day at Black Rock* 1955; *Giant, Johnny Concho, Back from Eternity* 1956; *Love in the Afternoon, Peyton Place* 1957; *The Diary of Anne Frank, Compulsion, The Best of Everything* 1959; *Crack in the Mirror* 1960; *Wild in the Country* 1961; *State Fair* 1962; *The Greatest Story Ever Told* (co-phot.; released posthumously) 1965.

Melnick, Daniel. Producer, executive. Born on Apr. 21, 1934, in New York City. While still a student at NYU, he produced plays for the Children's Theater at Circle on the Square in Greenwich Village. After graduating, he became at 21 the youngest staff producer at CBS-TV, later serving as executive producer of such series as 'East Side West Side' and 'N.Y.P.D.' He moved over to ABC-TV as vice president in charge of programming, then became a partner in David Susskind's Talent Associates. Joining MGM, Melnick served for much of the 70s as the studio's head of production. In 1978 he was named president of Columbia Pictures, but later resigned to become an independent producer.

FILMS INCLUDE (as producer or executive producer, alone or in collaboration): *Straw Dogs* 1971; *That's Entertainment!* 1974; *That's Entertainment, Part 2* 1976; *All That Jazz* 1979; *Altered States, First Family* 1980; *Making Love* 1982; *Unfaithfully Yours, Footloose* 1984; *Quicksilver* 1986; *Roxanne* 1987; *Punchline* 1988; *Mountains of the Moon, Total Recall, Air America* 1990; *L.A. Story* 1991.

Melville, Jean-Pierre. Director. *b.* Jean-Pierre Grumbach, Oct. 20, 1917, Paris. *d.* 1973. An avid filmgoer from childhood, he began making amateur films as a boy with a movie camera he had been given by his father, a wholesale merchant. In 1937 he began compulsory service with the French Army and was still in uniform when WW II broke out. According to some accounts, he was evacuated to England after Dunkirk; according to others, he stayed in Paris for two years as a member of the Resistance, then fled to England, where he joined the Free French and took part in the invasion of Italy and the liberation of Lyon. By the time he could begin to realize his dream of becoming a professional filmmaker he was 30. Unable to gain entry into any of the French studios, he formed his own production company in 1946 and began making films on shoestring budgets, shooting on actual locations with skeleton crews and no stars, at times acting as his own cameraman or art director. His economic methods of independent production served as a model for the directors of the French New Wave, although his style and preoccupations had little in common with that movement. Melville was a precise, methodical director with a predilection for themes of war and crime. The former preoccupation was attributable to his own experiences, and the latter was the probable result of his nostalgic admiration for the Hollywood cinema of the 30s. Melville gained respect for his first feature, *Le Silence de la Mer* (1949), an adaptation of a Resistance novel, which he made and distributed entirely outside the established channels. He achieved prominence with his second, *Les Enfants Terribles* (1950), a superior adaptation of Jean Cocteau's 1929 novel, from a script written by the author and Melville.

Beginning in the early 60s, Melville worked with larger budgets and with name stars like Jean-Paul Belmondo and Alain Delon and showed an increasingly technical mastery of the medium. He appeared as an actor in his own *Deux Hommes dans Manhattan* and in several other French films, including Cocteau's *Orpheus,* Godard's *Breathless,* and Chabrol's *Landru/Bluebeard.* He chose his pseudonym after his favorite novelist, Herman Melville.

FILMS (as director): *Vingt Quatre Heures de la Vie d'un Clown* (short; also sc.) 1946; *Le Silence de la Mer* (also prod., sc., co-edit.) 1949; *Les Enfants Terribles/The Strange Ones* (also prod., co-sc. with Cocteau, art dir.) 1950; *Quand tu lira cette Lettre* 1953; *Bob le Flambeur* (also co-sc., art dir.) 1955; *Deux Hommes dans Manhattan* (also sc., co-phot., act.) 1959; *Léon Morin Prêtre* (also sc.; Fr./It.) 1961; *Le Doulos/Doulos the Finger Man* (also prod., sc.; Fr./It.), *L'Aîné des Ferchaux/Magnet of Doom* (also sc.; Fr./It.) 1962; *Le Deuxième Souffle/Second Breath* (also co-sc.) 1966; *Le Samourai/The Samurai* (also sc.; Fr./It.) 1967; *L'Armée des Ombres/The Shadow Army* (also sc.; Fr./It.) 1969; *Le Cercle rouge* (also sc.; Fr./It.) 1970; *Un Flic/Dirty Money* (also sc.) 1972.

Mendes, Lothar. Director. *b.* May 19, 1894, Berlin. *d.* 1974. A stage actor for Max Reinhardt in Vienna and Berlin, he directed several Austrian and German films before coming to Hollywood in 1926. Supervised many American and several British films before retiring from screen work in the mid-40s. At one time married to actress Dorothy MACKAILL.

FILMS INCLUDE (US and UK films complete): In Austria and Germany—*Der Abenteuer* 1921; *Deportiert* 1922; *SOS—Die Insel der Tränen* 1923; *Liebe macht Blind/Love Makes Us Blind* 1925; *Die drei Kuckucksuhren* 1926. In the US—*The Prince of Tempters* 1926; *Convoy* (completed by and credited to Joseph C. Boyle) 1927; *A Night of Mystery* 1928; *Interference* (dial. scenes dir. by Roy J. Pomeroy), *The Four Feathers* (co-dir. with Merian C. Cooper and Ernest B. Schoedsack), *Illusion, The Marriage Playground, Dangerous Curves* 1929; *Paramount on Parade* (co-dir. with many others) 1930; *Ladies' Man, Personal Maid* (co-dir. with Monta Bell) 1931; *If I Had a Million* (co-dir., uncredited), *Strangers in Love, Payment Deferred* 1932; *Luxury Liner* 1933. In the UK—*Jew Suss/Power* 1934; *The Man Who Could Work Miracles* (UK) 1936; *Moonlight Sonata* (also prod.; UK) 1937. In the US—*International Squadron* 1941; *Flight for Freedom* 1943; *Tampico* 1944; *The Walls Came Tumbling Down* 1946.

Menges, Chris. Director of cinematography, director. Born on Sept. 15, 1940, in Kingston, England. He entered British films at 17 as a cutting-room trainee and before long was making a name for himself as a fearless documentary cameraman in dangerous, faraway locations. He moved into features as a camera operator in the late 60s and as a lighting cameraman in the early 70s. He became established as one of Britain's top cinematographers in the 80s, when he won Academy Awards for two superbly shot productions, *The Killing Fields* (1984) and *The Mission* (1986). He made a successful debut as a director with *A World Apart* (1988), a sensitively told story of South Africa's apartheid as seen through the eyes of a teenage girl.

FILMS INCLUDE: As camera operator—*If. . .* 1968. As director of cinematography—*Kes* 1970; *Black Beauty* 1971; *Gumshoe* 1972; *Black Jack* 1979; *The Empire Strikes Back* (2nd-unit phot.), *Babylon* 1980; *Warlords of the 21st Century* (NZ), *Looks and Smiles* 1981; *Angel* 1982; *Local Hero* 1983; *Winter Flight* (orig. for TV), *Comfort and Joy, The Killing Fields* 1984; *A Sense of Freedom, Marie* (US) 1985; *Singing the Blues in Red/Fatherland, The Mission* 1986; *High Season, Shy People* (US) 1987. As director—*A World Apart* 1988; *Crisscross* 1991; *Second Best* 1994; *Michael Collins* 1996.

Menjou, Adolphe. Actor. *b.* Feb. 18, 1890, Pittsburgh. *d.* 1963. *ed.* Culver Military Acad. (Ind.); Cornell. Trained as an engineer, he briefly managed one of his father's Cleveland restaurants, then went in 1911 to New York, where he tried a variety of odd jobs before accidentally drifting into films in 1914. Following WW I service (1917–19) as a captain in the Ambulance Corps, he briefly served as a production manager for the Van Buren film company in New York, then resumed acting on the screen. After playing supporting roles in several major Hollywood productions, he gained prominence as the suave star of Charlie Chaplin's *A Woman of Paris* (1923). He was thereafter typecast as a dapper, debonair man-of-the-world in countless other films, mostly sophisticated drawing room comedies, at first as a leading man and later as a character actor. He was nominated for a best actor Oscar for his role in *The Front Page* (1931).

Menjou's trademarks were a waxed black mustache and an impeccable wardrobe. For years he was known as Hollywood's and one of the world's best-dressed men, a reputation he worked hard to achieve as part of his star image. A political conservative, he was among the founders in 1944 of the Motion Picture Alliance for the Preservation of American Ideals. He was a "friendly" witness in the 1947 hearings of the House Un-American Activities Committee. The last two of his three marriages were to screen actresses, Kathryn Carver (1928–33) and Verree TEASDALE (from 1934 until his death from chronic hepatitis at 73). Autobiography: *It Took Nine Tailors* (1948).

FILMS INCLUDE: *The Man Behind the Door* 1914; *The*

Price of Happiness, The Crucial Test, The Reward of Patience, Manhattan Madness, The Kiss, Romeo and Juliet 1916; *The Valentine Girl, The Amazons, The Moth* 1917; *Healer, Courage, Through the Back Door, The Three Musketeers* (as Louis XIII), *The Sheik* 1921; *Is Matrimony a Failure?, Pink Gods, The Eternal Flame, Clarence, Singed Wings* 1922; *The World's Applause, Bella Donna, Rupert of Hentzau, A Woman of Paris, The Spanish Dancer* 1923; *The Marriage Circle, Shadows of Paris, Broadway After Dark, The Marriage Cheat, For Sale, Broken Barriers, Sinners in Silk, Open All Night, Forbidden Paradise, The Fast Set* 1924; *The Swan, A Kiss in the Dark, Are Parents People?, Lost—A Wife, The King on Main Street* 1925; *The Grand Duchess and the Waiter, A Social Celebrity, The Sorrows of Satan, The Ace of Cads* 1926; *Blonde or Brunette, Evening Clothes, Service for Ladies, A Gentleman of Paris, Serenade* 1927; *A Night of Mystery, His Tiger Lady, His Private Life* 1928; *Marquis Preferred, Fashions in Love* 1929; *Mon Gosse de Père/The Parisian* (Fr.), *L'Enigmatique Monsieur Parkes* (French-language version of *Slightly Scarlet*), *Morocco* 1930; *New Moon, The Easiest Way, The Front Page, Men Call It Love, The Great Lover, Friends and Lovers* 1931; *Forbidden, Prestige, Bachelor's Affairs, The Night Club Lady, Diamond Cut Diamond/Blame the Woman* (UK), *A Farewell to Arms* (as Rinaldi) 1932; *Morning Glory, Convention City* 1933; *Easy to Love, The Trumpet Blows* (dual role), *Journal of a Crime, Little Miss Marker, The Great Flirtation, The Human Side, The Mighty Barnum* 1934; *Gold Diggers of 1935, Broadway Gondolier* 1935; *The Milky Way, Sing Baby Sing* 1936; *One in a Million, A Star Is Born, Cafe Metropole, 100 Men and a Girl, Stage Door* 1937; *The Goldwyn Follies, Letter of Introduction* 1938; *King of the Turf, Golden Boy* (as Tom Moody), *The Housekeeper's Daughter* 1939; *A Bill of Divorcement, Turnabout* 1940; *Road Show, Father Takes a Wife* 1941; *Roxie Hart, Syncopation, You Were Never Lovelier* 1942; *Hi Diddle Diddle, Sweet Rosie O'Grady* 1943; *Step Lively* 1944; *Heartbeat, The Bachelor's Daughters* 1946; *I'll Be Yours, The Hucksters* 1947; *State of the Union* 1948; *My Dream Is Yours, Dancing in the Dark* 1949; *To Please a Lady* 1950; *The Tall Target, Across the Wide Missouri* 1951; *The Sniper* 1952; *Man on a Tightrope* 1953; *The Ambassador's Daughter* 1956; *Paths of Glory* 1957; *Pollyanna* 1960.

Menken, Alan. Composer. Born in 1950, raised in New Rochelle, N.Y. *ed.* NYU. Leading film composer of 1980s and 1990s. While working at the Lehman Engel Musical Theatre Workshop at BMI, he met future collaborator, lyricist Howard ASHMAN. Together they wrote several off-Broadway scores, including that of 'Little Shop of Horrors.' Their witty, memorable scores for the Disney animated films *The Little Mermaid* and *Beauty and the Beast* played a key role in re-establishing the studio as the maker of sophisticated animated fare and lent high luster to the formerly languishing genre. He won Academy Awards for best song and best score for both films. Following Ashman's death from AIDS while working on the Disney film *Aladdin*, Menken completed the music for that feature with lyricist Tim Rice. It, too, won Academy Awards for best song and best score.

FILMS INCLUDE: *Little Shop of Horrors* 1986; *The Little Mermaid* 1989; *Rocky V* (song) 1990; *Beauty and the Beast* 1991; *Aladdin, Home Alone 2: Lost in New York, Newsies* 1992; *Life with Mikey* 1993; *Pocahontas* 1995; *The Hunchback of Notre Dame* 1996; *Hercules* 1997.

Menzel, Jiři. Director. Born on Feb. 23, 1938, in Prague. A leading figure in the NEW WAVE Czech cinema that blossomed briefly during the "liberal spring" of the late 60s, and still one of his country's foremost filmmakers. The son of a journalist-novelist-playwright-screenwriter, he was raised along with his twin sister in an intellectual atmosphere. An avid reader and drama enthusiast, he enrolled in 1957 at the FAMU film school only after failing to gain entry into the theater department of the Prague Academy of Arts and Music. After completing his diploma film, the medium-length *Mr. Forester Is Dead* (1963), he fulfilled his two-year military service by working on army newsreels. Menzel made an impressive professional debut as the director of "The Death of Mr. Baltasar" episode in the omnibus film, *Pearls of the Deep* (1965). His first solo effort, *Closely Watched Trains* (1966), catapulted the director into the forefront of international cinema. A bittersweet coming-of-age story unfolding against the background of Nazi occupation, the film captivated audiences with its earthy charm and disarming black humor. It won the Grand Prix at the Mannheim Festival and the Academy Award as best foreign film. Menzel applied a similar low-key approach and caring observation of character to *Capricious Summer* (1968), a wryly humorous little film about the frustration of lost youth. Winner of the Grand Prix at Karlovy Vary, the film displayed the by-now familiar Menzel visual style, straightforward and uncomplicated, with little camera movement and much detail within each frame. The Soviet invasion of August 1968 resulted in strict curbs on artistic freedom in Czechoslovakia. Menzel's anti-communist satire, *Larks on a String,* completed in 1969, was banned and held back from distribution until 1990, when it was greeted enthusiastically at the Berlin Film Festival, sharing its top prize, the Golden Bear. In the intervening years, the director stayed behind in Prague and for a while found refuge in the relative safety of the stage. Only after publicly denouncing the errors of the New Wave was he permitted to resume his work in films, under strict supervision. It was not until *Those Wonderful Men in a Crank* (1978), an appealing tribute to the pioneers of Czech cinema, that he recaptured some of his old spirit and touch. He returned to top form with *My Sweet Little Village* (1985), an Oscar nominee for best foreign language film of 1986. Menzel appeared as an actor in several of his own films as well as those of other directors, particularly his early mentor, Vera CHYTILOVÁ. Among the films in which he appeared were *Something Different* (1963), *Everyday Courage/Courage for Every Day* (1964), *Wandering* (1965), *The Apple Game* (1967), *Fandy* (1983), and *Martha and I* (1990). A slight, bespectacled, humorous man, he was called by some the Woody Allen of Czech cinema.

FEATURE FILMS (as director/co-screenwriter): *Pearls of the Deep* ("The Death of Mr. Baltasar" episode; also act.), *Crime at the Girls' School* (title episode) 1965; *Closely Watched Trains* (also act.) 1966; *Capricious Summer* (also act.), *Crime at the Night Club* 1968; *Larks on a String* (also act.; release delayed until 1990) 1969; *Who Seeks a Handful of Gold* (dir. only) 1975; *Seclusion Near a Forest* 1976; *Those Wonderful Men with a Crank/Magicians of the Silver Screen* (also act.) 1978; *Short Cut/Cutting It Short* (also act.) 1980; *The Snowdrop Festival* (dir. only) 1982; *My Sweet Little Village* (dir. only) 1985; *The End of the Good Old Days* 1989; *Martha and I* 1990; *The Beggar's Opera* 1991; *The Life and Extraordinary Adventures of Private Chonkin* 1994.

Menzies, William Cameron. Art director, director, producer. *b.* July 29, 1896, New Haven, Conn. *d.* 1957. One of the most gifted visual masters of the American cinema and one of the most influential in the shaping of his craft as an art. A graduate of Yale, he served with the American Expeditionary Forces in Europe during WW I. After demobilization, he attended New York's Art Student League, then joined the Famous Players as an art director. Bringing to the screen an audacious personal style that became recognizably his, Menzies dominated Hollywood's movie design scene during the golden years of the silent and talkie eras. His enormous prestige helped solidify the position of art directors and set designers in the Hollywood hierarchy. He was among the first of his craft to be billed as a production designer, implying overall responsibility for the look of a film that exceeded the contribution of the conventional art director. He won the very first Academy Award in the "interior decoration" category for the design of both *The Dove* and *Tempest* (1928) and a special Academy plaque "for outstanding achievement in the use of color and the enhancement of dramatic mood in *Gone With the Wind*" (1939). Starting in 1931, Menzies directed a number of acceptable films. But with the notable exception of *Things to Come* (UK, 1936), a stunning visualization of an imaginary world of the future, his output as a director was unremarkable.

FILMS INCLUDE: As art director (alone or in collaboration)—*The Teeth of the Tiger* 1919; *The Deep Purple* 1920; *Serenade* 1921; *Kindred of the Dust* 1922; *Rosita* 1923; *The Thief of Bagdad* 1924; *The Eagle, Cobra* 1925; *The Bat, The Son of the Sheik, Fig Leaves* 1926; *The Beloved Rogue, Two Arabian Knights* 1927; *The Dove, Tempest, Drums of Love, The Garden of Eden, Sadie Thompson* 1928; *Lady of the Pavements, Bulldog Drummond, Taming of the Shrew* 1929; *Raffles, Abraham Lincoln* 1930; *The Adventures of Tom Sawyer* 1938; *Gone With the Wind* 1939; *Our Town, Foreign Correspondent* 1940; *So Ends Our Night, The Devil and Miss Jones* 1941; *For Whom the Bell Tolls* 1943; *Arch of Triumph* 1948. As director (complete)—*The Spider* (co-dir. with Kenneth McKenna), *Always Goodbye* (co-dir. with McKenna; also art dir.) 1931; *Chandu the Magician* (co-dir. with Marcel Varnel) 1932; *I Loved You Wednesday* (co-dir. with Henry King) 1933; *Wharf Angel* (co-dir. with George Somnes) 1934; *Things to Come* (also co-art dir.; UK) 1936; *The Green Cockatoo* (UK) 1937; *Address Unknown* (also prod.) 1944; *Duel in the Sun* (dir. some scenes only, uncredited) 1947; *Drums in the Deep South* (also art dir.), *The Whip Hand* (also art dir.) 1951; *Invaders from Mars* (also art dir.), *The Maze* (also art dir.) 1953. As producer—*The Black Book/Reign of Terror* 1949; *Around the World in 80 Days* (assoc. prod.) 1956.

Mercanton, Louis. Director. *b.* 1879, Switzerland. *d.* 1932. A naturalized Frenchman, he was educated in England and began an acting career on the South African stage in 1904. After managing a theater in London, he turned to film direction in Paris, making his debut with the now-famous Sarah Bernhardt vehicle *Queen Elizabeth.* He later directed several other of her productions and turned out many other films in France and England. His son, Jean Mercanton (*b.* May 17, 1919, Paris; *d.* 1947) appeared from infancy in many of his father's films and also acted in many other French productions. His stepson, Jacques Mercanton (*b.* Jacques Spiri, Nov. 22, 1909, Neuilly-sur-Seine, France), is a veteran director of photography of French films.

FILMS INCLUDE: *Elisabeth Reine d'Angleterre/Queen Elizabeth* (co-dir. with Henri Desfontaines) 1912; *Adrienne Lecouvreur* (co-dir.) 1913; *Jeanne Doré* 1915; *Le Lotus d'Or* 1916; *Mères françaises* (co-dir. with René Hervil) 1917; *Bouclette* (co-dir. with Hervil), *Le Torrent* (co-dir. with Hervil), *Un Roman d'Amour et d'Aventures* (co-dir. with Hervil) 1918; *L'Appel du Sang* 1919; *Miarka la Fille à l'Ours/Miarka the Daughter of the Bear/Gypsy Passion* 1920; *Phroso* 1922; *Les Deux Gosses* 1924; *Monte-Carlo* 1925; *La Petite Bonne du Palace* 1926; *Croquette* 1927; *Vénus* 1929; *La Lettre* (French-language version of 1929's *The Letter* US), *The Nipper* (UK), *La Mystère de la Villa rose* (co-dir. with Hervil) 1930; *These Charming People* (UK), *A Man of Mayfair* (UK), *Marions-nous* 1931; *Il est charmant, Cognasse* 1932.

Mercer, Beryl. Actress. *b.* Aug. 13, 1882, Seville, Spain, to British parents. *d.* 1939. A child actress on the London stage, she went to Hollywood in 1922 and played scores of character roles in films, typically as a long-suffering mother.

FILMS INCLUDE: *Broken Chains* 1922; *The Christian* 1923; *We Americans* 1928; *Mother's Boy, Three Live Ghosts* 1929; *Seven Days Leave, All Quiet on the Western Front, In Gay Madrid, Outward Bound* 1930; *Inspiration, East Lynne, The Public Enemy, The Miracle Woman, Merely Mary Ann* 1931; *Lovers Courageous, Young America, No Greater Love, Lena Rivers, Smilin' Through* 1932; *Cavalcade, Supernatural, Berkeley Square* 1933; *Jane Eyre, Change of Heart, The Little Minister* 1934; *Age of Indiscretion, Magnificent Obsession* 1935; *Night Must Fall* 1937; *The Little Princess, The Hound of the Baskervilles, A Woman Is the Judge* 1939.

Mercer, Johnny. Lyricist, composer. *b.* Nov. 18, 1909, Savannah, Ga. *d.* 1976. A former stage actor and band vocalist, he became one of America's leading lyricists, collaborating with, among others, composers Jerome Kern, Hoagy Carmichael, Harold Arlen, and Henry Mancini. Although he could not read music, he also composed many melodies himself and wrote the entire score for the Broadway musical 'Top Banana.' His numerous popular songs as a lyricist include such hits as 'Laura,' 'That Old Black Magic,' 'Jeepers Creepers,' 'Goody Goody,' and the English lyrics for the French tune 'Autumn Leaves.' He won four Oscars for songs he wrote for the screen: 'On the Atchison, Topeka, and the Santa Fe' from *The Harvey Girls* (1946), 'In the Cool Cool Cool of the Evening' from *Here Comes the Groom* (1951), 'Moon River' from *Breakfast at Tiffany's* (1961), and the title song of *Days of Wine and Roses* (1962). He also appeared in several films.

FILMS INCLUDE (as lyricist): *College Coach* 1933; *Transatlantic Merry-Go-Round* 1934; *Old Man Rhythm* (also act.), *To Beat the Band* (also act.) 1935; *Ready Willing and Able* ('Too Marvellous for Words,' etc.) 1937; *Hollywood Hotel* ('Hooray for Hollywood,' etc.), *Gold Diggers in Paris, Hard to Get* ('You Must Have Been a Beautiful Baby,' etc.), *Going Places* ('Jeepers Creepers,' etc.) 1938; *Naughty but Nice* 1939; *Second Chorus, Blues in the Night* (title song; 'This Time the Dream's on Me,' etc.) 1941; *The Fleet's In* ('Tangerine,' etc.), *You Were Never Lovelier* (title song; 'I'm Old Fashioned,' etc.), *Star Spangled Rhythm* ('That Old Black Magic,' 'Hit the Road to Dreamland,' etc.) 1942; *The Sky's the Limit* ('One for the Road,' etc.) 1943; *Here Come the Waves* ('Accentuate the Positive,' etc.) 1944; *To Have and Have Not* ('How Little We Know'), *Her Highness and the Bellboy* ('Dreams,' lyrics and music) 1945; *The Harvey Girls* ('On the Atchison Topeka and the Santa Fe') 1946; *Here Comes the Groom* ('In the Cool Cool Cool of the Evening') 1951; *Belle of New York* ('Naughty but Nice,' 'Baby Doll,' etc.) 1952; *Dangerous When Wet* 1953; *Top Banana* (lyrics and music), *Seven Brides for Seven Brothers* ('Bless Yore Beautiful Hide,' etc.) 1954; *Daddy Long Legs* (title song, etc.; also music), *I'll Cry Tomorrow* 1955; *Bernadine* (also music) 1957; *Merry Andrew* 1958; *Li'l Abner* 1959; *Breakfast at Tiffany's* ('Moon River') 1961; *Days of Wine and Roses* (title song) 1962; *Charade* (title song) 1963; *The Americanization of Emily* ('Emily'), *The Pink Panther* 1964; *The Great Race* ('The Sweetheart Tree,' etc.) 1965; *Alvarez Kelly* (title song) 1966; *Barefoot in the Park* (title song), *Rosie* (title song) 1967; *Darling Lili* 1970; *Robin Hood* 1973.

Merchant, Ismail. Producer, director. Born on Dec. 25, 1936, in Bombay. *ed.* St. Xavier's Coll., Bombay; NYU. The holder of a master's degree in business administration, he combined his financial know-how and love of film to provide the practical backbone of a career-long partnership with director

James IVORY and screenwriter Ruth Prawer JHABVALA. He produced all of Ivory's films in India, Britain, and the US, and was the guiding hand behind their financing, budgeting, planning, and distribution. He also made occasional excursions into directing. His short, *The Creation of a Woman* (India, 1960), was nominated for an Academy Award. Another short, *Mahatma and the Mad Boy* (1973), and a full-length documentary, *Courtesans of Bombay* (1982), were originally made for TV. In addition to his films as producer for Ivory (for credits, see IVORY, James), he produced *The Deceivers*, *The Perfect Murder* (both 1988), *The Ballad of the Sad Cafe* (1991), and *Feast of July* (1995). He also published a cookbook, *Ismail Merchant's Indian Cuisine* and wrote *Hullaballoo in Old Jaypore: The Making of The Deceivers* (1989).

Merchant, Vivien. Actress. *b.* Ada Thomson, July 22, 1929, Manchester, England. *d.* 1982. Primarily a stage actress (from the age of 14), she met future playwright Harold PINTER when they were appearing together in rep. She married him in 1956 and subsequently played the lead in many of his plays. She also appeared in several British films and often on TV, and was nominated for an Oscar as best supporting actress for her performance in *Alfie* (1966). Following her 1980 divorce from Pinter, she became a chronic alcoholic and died at 53 of cirrhosis of the liver.

FILMS INCLUDE: *Alfie* 1966; *Accident* 1967; *Alfred the Great* 1969; *Under Milk Wood* 1971; *Frenzy* 1972; *The Offence/The Offense, The Homecoming* 1973; *The Maids* 1975.

Mercouri, Melina. Actress. *b.* Maria Amalia Mercouri, Oct. 18, 1923, Athens. *d.* 1994. Exuberant, passionate international screen star and ardent Greek patriot, she was born to a politically prominent family. She pursued a stage career from the age of 17, against the wishes of her father, one-time minister of state and deputy mayor of Athens. She made her screen debut in 1955, in Michael Cacoyannis's *Stella,* and developed into an international star under the guidance of her second husband (from 1966), American expatriate director Jules DASSIN. In 1960 she shared best actress honors (with Jeanne Moreau) at the Cannes Festival for her performance in Dassin's *Never on Sunday* in a memorable role that also brought her a nomination for an Oscar. Long a political activist, she devoted much of her energy in the late 60s and early 70s to campaigning against the ruling colonels' junta of Greece. She was declared an enemy of the state. Her passport was confiscated, her citizenship revoked, and she was forced into exile abroad. She did not return to Greece until 1974, when she was narrowly defeated in her bid for a seat in the Greek parliament. She tried again in November of 1977 and this time won handily, gaining a parliament seat on the Socialist ticket as a representative of the district of Piraeus, the scene of her screen triumph, *Never on Sunday.* In 1981 she became Greece's minister of culture and sciences, a cabinet post she held until 1985, when she was appointed minister of culture, youth and sports. She was later defeated in the election for mayor of Athens. Autobiography: *I Was Born Greek* (1971).

FILMS: *Stella* (Gr.) 1955; *Celui qui doit mourir/He Who Must Die* (Fr./It.) 1957; *The Gypsy and the Gentleman* (UK) 1958; *La Loi/Where the Hot Wind Blows* (Fr./It.) 1959; *Never on Sunday* (Gr.) 1960; *Vive Henri IV—Vive l'Amour* (Fr.), *Il Giudizio Universale* (It.) 1961; *Phaedra* (title role; Gr./US) 1962; *The Victors* (UK/US) 1963; *Topkapi* (US) 1964; *Les Pianos mécaniques/The Uninhibited* (Fr./It./Sp.) 1965; *A Man Could Get Killed* (US), *10:30 P.M. Summer* (US) 1966; *Gaily Gaily* (US) 1969; *La Promesse de l'Aube/Promise at Dawn* (Fr./US) 1970; *Jacqueline Susann's Once Is Not Enough* (US) 1975; *Nasty Habits* (UK) 1976; *A Dream of Passion* (Gr.) 1978.

mercury vapor lamps. Compact high-intensity arc lamps whose light is produced in glass vacuum tubes filled with vaporized mercury. They furnish a cold bluish light and are particularly useful to a cameraman in close-up work.

Meredith, Burgess. Actor. Born George Meredith on Nov. 16, 1908, in Cleveland. *d.* 1997. One of the most gifted and versatile performers of the American stage and screen, he was first a merchant seaman and businessman. He made his stage debut in 1929, scoring a personal triumph in 'Winterset,' in 1935. The following year he went to Hollywood to repeat the role in the screen version and has since been seen in many films either in leads or in key character parts. He directed many stage plays and the films *The Man on the Eiffel Tower* (1949), in which he also acted, and *James Joyce's Women* (1985). He was nominated for Academy Awards as best supporting actor for *The Day of the Locust* (1975) and *Rocky* (1976). He also appeared frequently on TV, memorably as the villainous Penguin in the 'Batman' series, and won an Emmy for his portrayal of lawyer Joseph Welch in 'Tail Gunner Joe' (1977), a docudrama about Senator Joseph McCarthy. His third (1944–49) of four ex-wives was actress Paulette GODDARD. Autobiography: *So Far, So Good: A Memoir* (1994).

FILMS: *Winterset* (as Mio) 1936; *There Goes the Groom* 1937; *Spring Madness* 1938; *Idiot's Delight* 1939; *Of Mice and Men* (as George), *Castle on the Hudson* 1940; *Second Chorus, San Francisco Docks, That Uncertain Feeling, Tom Dick and Harry* 1941; *Street of Chance* 1942; *The Story of G.I. Joe* 1945; *The Diary of a Chambermaid* (also co-prod., sc.), *Magnificent Doll* (as James Madison) 1946; *Mine Own Executioner* (UK) 1947; *On Our Merry Way/A Miracle Can Happen* (also co-prod.) 1948; *The Man on the Eiffel Tower* (also dir.) 1949; *The Gay Adventure* (UK) 1953; *Joe Butterfly* 1957; *Advise and Consent* 1962; *The Cardinal* 1963; *The Kidnappers* 1964; *In Harm's Way* 1965; *Madame X, A Big Hand for the Little Lady, Batman* (as "The Penguin," compiled from TV episodes), *Crazy Quilt* (narr. only) 1966; *Hurry Sundown, Torture Garden* (UK) 1967; *Stay Away Joe, Skidoo* 1968; *Mackenna's Gold, Hard Contract, The Reivers* (narr. only) 1969; *There Was a Crooked Man* 1970; *Such Good Friends, Clay Pigeon* 1971; *A Fan's Notes* (Can.), *The Man* 1972; *Golden Needles* 1974; *The Day of the Locust, 92 in the Shade, The Hindenburg* 1975; *Burnt Offerings, Rocky* 1976; *The Sentinel, Shenanigans/The Great Bank Hoax/The Great Georgia Bank Hoax, Golden Rendezvous* 1977; *Foul Play, The Manitou, A Wedding, Magic* 1978; *Rocky II* 1979; *When Time Ran Out, Final Assignment* (Can.) 1980; *The Last Chase, Clash of the Titans* (UK) *True Confessions* 1981; *Rocky III* 1982; *Twilight Zone—The Movie* 1983; *James Joyce's Women* (dir. only), *Broken Rainbow* (doc.), *Santa Claus: The Movie* 1985; *King Lear* (US/Switz.) 1987; *Full Moon in Blue Water* 1988; *Oddball Hall, State of Grace, Rocky V* 1990; *Night of the Hunter* 1991; *Grumpy Old Men* 1993; *Across the Moon, Camp Nowhere* 1994; *Grumpier Old Men, Tall Tale* 1995.

Meredyth, Bess. Screenwriter. *b.* Helen MacGlashan, 1890, Buffalo, N.Y. *d.* 1969. A petite blonde, she entered films as an extra for D. W. Griffith at Biograph but soon proved more talented as a writer than as an actress. She collaborated on numerous silent and sound scripts.

FILMS INCLUDE: *The Twin Triangle, Spellbound* 1916; *Bringing Home Father, The Little Orphan, Pay Me, Scandal* 1917; *The Grain of Dust, Morgan's Raiders* (also co-dir. with Lucas), *The Romance of Tarzan* 1918; *The Girl from Nowhere* 1919; *The Grim Comedian* 1921; *The Dangerous Age, One Clear Call, Rose o' the Sea, The Woman He Married, The Song of Life* 1922; *Strangers of the Night* 1923; *The Red Lily, Thy Name Is Woman* 1924; *A Slave of Fashion, The Love Hour* 1925;

Ben-Hur, The Sea Beast, Don Juan 1926; *When a Man Loves, The Magic Flame, Rose of the Golden West* 1927; *The Little Shepherd of Kingdom Come, The Yellow Lily, The Mysterious Lady, A Woman of Affairs* 1928; *Wonder of Women* 1929; *Chasing Rainbows, In Gay Madrid, The Sea Bat, Our Blushing Brides, Romance* 1930; *The Prodigal/The Southerner, West of Broadway, Cuban Love Song, Laughing Sinners, The Phantom of Paris* 1931; *Strange Interlude* 1932; *Looking Forward* 1933; *The Affairs of Cellini, The Mighty Barnum* 1934; *Folies Bergere, Metropolitan* 1935; *Half Angel, Under Two Flags, Charlie Chan at the Opera* (story only) 1936; *The Great Hospital Mystery* 1937; *The Mark of Zorro* (co-adapt. only) 1940; *That Night in Rio* 1941; *The Unsuspected* 1947.

Merkel, Una. Actress. *b.* Dec. 10, 1903, Covington, Ky. *d.* 1986. A Lillian Gish look-alike, she began her career as a stand-in for the silent star in such D. W. Griffith films as *Way Down East* (1920) and *The White Rose* (1923), then played the feminine lead in an obscure small-budget production, *The Fifth Horseman* (1924). After several roles on Broadway, she returned to the screen in 1930, playing the key role of Ann Rutledge in Griffith's *Abraham Lincoln.* She played leads in a couple of other films, including the thriller *The Bat Whispers* (1930), then found her niche in comic supporting roles, typically playing a wisecracking friend of the heroine who delivers her biting lines deadpan with a disarming southern drawl. Occasionally she was cast in comic leads, opposite such leading men as Harold Lloyd and Charles Butterworth. Her most productive period was in the 30s, when she appeared in dozens of films, including *Destry Rides Again* (1939), in which she engaged in a memorable saloon brawl with Marlene Dietrich, but she continued appearing in films in a variety of character roles through the late 60s, and gave one of her finest performances as Geraldine Page's mother in the screen version of Tennessee Williams's *Summer and Smoke* (1961). On Broadway she won a Tony Award for her performance in 'The Ponder Heart' (1956) and was one of the stars of the musical 'Take Me Along.' She was almost killed in 1945 when her mother committed suicide by turning on the gas in the New York apartment they shared after the actress's divorce that year from an aircraft executive.

FILMS INCLUDE: *The Fifth Horseman* 1924; *Abraham Lincoln* (as Ann Rutledge), *Eyes of the World, The Bat Whispers* 1930; *Don't Bet on Women, Six-Cylinder Love, The Maltese Falcon, Daddy Long Legs, Wicked, Private Lives* (as Sibyl Chase), *The Secret Witness* 1931; *She Wanted a Millionaire, Red Headed Woman* 1932; *Whistling in the Dark, Clear All Wires, 42nd Street, Reunion in Vienna, Bombshell, Murder in the Private Car* 1933; *The Women in His Life, Bulldog Drummond Strikes Back, The Cat's Paw, The Merry Widow, Evelyn Prentice* 1934; *Biography of a Bachelor Girl, Broadway Melody of 1936, One New York Night, Baby Face Harrington, It's in the Air* 1935; *Riffraff, We Went to College, Born to Dance* 1936; *Don't Tell the Wife, Good Old Soak, Saratoga, True Confession* 1937; *Some Like It Hot, On Borrowed Time, Destry Rides Again* 1939; *Comin' Round the Mountain, The Bank Dick* 1940; *Double Date, Road to Zanzibar, Cracked Nuts* 1941; *The Mad Doctor of Market Street* 1942; *This Is the Army* 1943; *Sweethearts of the USA* 1944; *It's a Joke Son* 1947; *The Bride Goes Wild* 1948; *Kill the Umpire, My Blue Heaven* 1950; *A Millionaire for Christy, Golden Girl* 1951; *With a Song in My Heart, The Merry Widow* 1952; *I Love Melvin* 1953; *The Kentuckian* 1955; *Bundle of Joy* 1956; *The Fuzzy Pink Nightgown* 1957; *The Girl Most Likely* 1958; *The Mating Game* 1959; *The Parent Trap, Summer and Smoke* 1961; *Summer Magic* 1963; *A Tiger Walks* 1964; *Spinout* 1966.

Merman, Ethel. Singer, actress. *b.* Ethel Zimmerman, Jan. 16, 1908, Astoria, Queens, N.Y. *d.* 1984. The first lady of American musical comedy, the owner of a powerful, untrained singing voice and an exuberant stage personality, she left a permanent record of her talents in more than a dozen films. She died in her sleep at 75, ten months after undergoing surgery for the removal of a brain tumor. Her four marriages (and divorces) include a very brief one to Ernest BORGNINE in 1964. Autobiography: *Merman* (1978).

FILMS: *Follow the Leader* 1930; *We're Not Dressing, Kid Millions* 1934; *The Big Broadcast of 1936; Anything Goes, Strike Me Pink* 1936; *Happy Landing, Alexander's Ragtime Band, Straight Place and Show* 1938; *Stage Door Canteen* 1943; *Call Me Madam* 1953; *There's No Business Like Show Business* 1954; *It's a Mad Mad Mad Mad World* 1963; *The Art of Love* 1965; *Journey Back to Oz* (v/o) 1974; *Won Ton Ton—The Dog Who Saved Hollywood* (cameo) 1976; *Airplane!* 1980.

Merrill, Dina. Actress. Born Nedenia Hutton, on Dec. 9, 1925, in New York City. Blonde leading lady of the American stage, screen, and TV, usually cast in cool, aloof roles, in keeping with her aristocratic background. A real-life socialite-heiress (she was the youngest daughter of E. F. Hutton, founder of the Wall Street firm, and Marjorie Merriweather Post of the Post cereal fortune), she dropped out of George Washington University after one year to enroll at the American Academy of Dramatic Arts. After gaining experience in stock and on Broadway and TV, she made her film debut in 1957. In 1966 she married Cliff ROBERTSON. They separated in 1985 and divorced in 1989. In 1988 she launched a film and entertainment development and production company, Pavilion, in partnership with Ted Hartley, a former actor and investment banker. In the following year the partnership acquired RKO Pictures and was renamed RKO Pavilion, with Hartley as chairman and Merrill as creative director. The two married in November of 1989.

FILMS: *Desk Set* 1957; *A Nice Little Bank That Should Be Robbed* 1958; *Don't Give Up the Ship, Operation Petticoat* 1959; *Butterfield 8, The Sundowners* 1960; *The Young Savages* 1961; *The Courtship of Eddie's Father* 1963; *I'll Take Sweden* 1965; *Deliver Us from Evil, The Meal* 1975; *The Greatest* 1977; *A Wedding* 1978; *Just Tell Me What You Want* 1980; *Twisted* 1986; *Caddyshack II* 1988; *True Colors* 1991; *The Player* (cameo) 1992; *Suture* 1993; *Milk and Money* 1996.

Merrill, Gary. Actor. *b.* Aug. 2, 1914, Hartford, Conn. *d.* 1990. *ed.* Bowdoin Coll.; Trinity Coll. Craggy-faced, bushy-browed leading man and character player of the American stage and Hollywood films. Began his stage career in 1937 and made his first film appearance, while in uniform, in *Winged Victory* (1944). In 1949 he signed with 20th Century-Fox and began appearing regularly in films, typically playing determined, often grim and humorless leads and second leads. His many TV roles included that of Dr. Gillespie in 'Young Dr. Kildare' (1972). In 1950 he married Bette DAVIS, opposite whom he played in *All About Eve* that year. They divorced in 1960. Long active in liberal causes, Merrill was deeply involved in the rejuvenation of the Democratic party in Maine and was a driving force behind the election of Edmund Muskie as governor of that state in 1953. He participated in the 1965 civil rights march from Selma to Montgomery. Soon after, disillusioned with the Johnson administration's Vietnam policy, he switched parties and in 1968 made an unsuccessful bid for the Republican nomination for the Maine legislature, as an antiwar, pro-environment primary candidate. Autobiography: *Bette, Rita and the Rest of My Life* (1989).

FILMS INCLUDE: *Winged Victory* 1944; *Slattery's Hurricane* 1949; *Twelve O'Clock High, Where the Sidewalk Ends, All About Eve* 1950; *The Frogmen* 1951; *Decision Before Dawn, Another Man's Poison, Phone Call from a Stranger, Night Without Sleep* 1952; *A Blueprint for Murder* 1953; *Witness to Murder, The Black Dakotas, The Human Jungle* 1954; *Navy Wife* 1956; *The Wonderful Country* 1959; *The Savage Eye* 1960; *The Great Impostor, The Pleasure of His Company, Mysterious Island* (UK/US) 1961; *A Girl Named Tamiko* 1963; *Catacombs/The Woman Who Wouldn't Die* (UK/US) 1965; *Cast a Giant Shadow, Around the World Under the Sea, Destination Inner Space, Ride Beyond Vengeance* 1966; *The Incident, Clambake, The Last Challenge* 1967; *The Power* 1968; *The Secret of the Sacred Forest* 1970; *Huckleberry Finn* (as Pap) 1974; *Thieves* 1977.

Mescall, John. Director of photography. Born on Jan. 10, 1899, in Litchfield, Ill. In Hollywood from the late 1910s, initially as a lab assistant, he became a lighting cameraman in 1920 and was later responsible for the cinematography of many silent and sound films for a number of studios. He worked only intermittently as a cinematographer after the mid-40s, specializing instead as a trick-photography consultant.

FILMS INCLUDE: *It's a Great Life* 1920; *Dangerous Curve Ahead* 1921; *The Glorious Fool* 1922; *Souls for Sale* 1923; *His Hour* 1924; *The Bridge of Sighs, Satan in Sables* 1925; *So This Is Paris, The Social Highwayman, The Love Toy* 1926; *The Student Prince, The Wreck of the Hesperus, Yankee Clipper* 1927; *The Leopard Lady, Captain Swagger* 1928; *Red Hot Rhythm, The Sophomore* 1929; *His First Command* (co-phot.), *Sin Takes a Holiday* 1930; *Almost Married* 1932; *By Candlelight* 1933; *The Black Cat* 1934; *Night Life of the Gods, The Bride of Frankenstein 1935*; *Magnificent Obsession, Show Boat* 1936; *The Road Back* 1937; *Happy Landing, Josette* 1938; *When Tomorrow Comes* 1939; *Kit Carson, South of Pago Pago* 1940; *New Wine* 1941; *Take a Letter Darling* 1942; *Dark Waters* 1944; *Davy Crockett Indian Scout* (co-phot.) 1950; *The Quiet Gun, Not of This Earth* 1957.

Mesguich, Félix. Cameraman. *b.* 1871, Algeria. *b.* 1949. French film historians claim for him the distinction of being the world's first professional cameraman and camera reporter. He worked for LUMIÈRE from 1895, later representing French film interests in Russia and the US.

Messter, Oskar. Inventor, producer, director, film pioneer. *b.* Nov. 22, 1866, Berlin. *d.* 1943. He worked in his father's optical plant, where he developed various motion picture apparatuses and processes. The Germans claim for him the invention of the MALTESE CROSS, which made possible the intermittent movement of film in camera and projector. They also credit him with the close-up shot as early as 1897. Many of the leading actors of the German screen began their career in his films. He produced numerous short films from 1897 and a weekly newsreel from 1914. In 1917 his company was absorbed by UFA.

FILMS INCLUDE (as producer): *Rapunzel* 1897; *Gemütlich beim Kaffee* (also dir.) 1898; *Salome* (also dir.) 1902; *Apachentanz* (also dir.) 1906; *Verkannt* (also dir.) 1910; *Richard Wagner* 1912; *Ungarische Rhapsodie* 1913; *Anna Boleyn/Deception* (co-prod.) 1920; *Tatjana* 1923.

Mészáros, Márta. Director. Born on Sept. 19, 1931, in Budapest. A leading figure in contemporary Hungarian cinema. She received her elementary education in the Soviet Union, where her father, a socialist sculptor, found refuge in 1936 from political persecution at home. She sojourned to Budapest after the Communists gained control of the government in 1946, then returned to Moscow to study at the VGIK film school. She married a Romanian citizen, and after graduating and working briefly at the Budapest newsreel studios, accompanied her husband to Bucharest, where she made several shorts. Returning to Budapest following her 1959 divorce, she continued turning out documentary and educational shorts at an enormous rate on a wide range of subjects. Around 1967, Mészáros was invited to join Group 4, the feature division of Mafilm, the Hungarian state production agency, where she met and later married director Miklós JANCSÓ (they would eventually divorce). Her debut feature, *The Girl* (1968), made in black and white, like her other early films, set the themes, tone, the mood that would characterize her future work. In telling this story of a loveless orphan girl in quest of affection, the director applied assertive but unshowy camerawork, an essentially plotless script, and sparse dialogue to capture the sense of alienation in the midst of a drab, uninviting environment. Concern for the plight of women in a hopelessly oppressive society remained a theme central to the director's work.

A film that best exemplified her themes and style was *Adoption* (1975), about a special relationship that develops between two women, one young, the other nearly middle-aged, that leads the latter to consider adopting a child. It won the Golden Bear at the Berlin Film Festival. *Nine Months* (1976), the story of an unmarried mother who decides to have another baby on her own, away from her reluctant lover, was remarkable for the actual birth on camera by the actress portraying the woman, Lili Monori. *The Two of Them* (1977) again starred Monori, this time in a story of a destructive marriage. With the clearly autobiographical *Diary for My Children* (1984), winner of the Special Jury Prize at Cannes, the director entered the political arena, drawing a vividly personal portrait of state-sanctioned brutality in the Stalinist era. The heroine's father, like the director's, is a Hungarian Communist artist who took his family to Moscow in the 30s and died there, a victim of Stalin's purges. A follow-up, *Diary for My Loved Ones* (1987), tells of the heroine's experiences at the Moscow Film School, while Budapest is fatefully headed for a bloody revolt. *Diary for My Father and Mother* (1990), the concluding part in the autobiographical trilogy, is almost entirely concerned with the events of 1956, integrating newsreel and archive footage with re-enacted material. Together, the three films provide a vivid personal look at Eastern Europe's tragic recent history. Love, motherhood, marriage, children, cultural antagonisms, political conflicts, and social ills—all these and more occupy the concerns and films of one of contemporary cinema's most conscientious voices and one of its truest artists.

FEATURE FILMS: *The Girl* (also sc.) 1968; *Binding Sentiments/Binding Ties* (also sc.) 1969; *Don't Cry, Pretty Girls* 1970; *Riddance/Free Breathing* (also sc.) 1973; *Adoption* (also co-sc.) 1975; *Nine Months* (also co-sc.) 1976; *The Two of Them/Two Women* 1977; *Just Like at Home* 1978; *On the Move* 1979; *Heiresses/The Inheritance* 1980; *Anya and Leanya/Anna/Mother and Daughter* (also co-sc.; Hung./Fr.) 1981; *Silent Cry* (also sc.) 1982; *Land of Mirages* 1983; *Diary for My Children/Intimate Journal* (also sc.) 1984; *Diary for My Loved Ones/Diary for My Loves* (also co-sc.) 1987; *Bye Bye, Red Riding Hood/Little Red Riding Hood, Year 2000* (Hung./Can.) 1989; *Diary for My Father and Mother* (also co-sc.) 1990; *Foetus* 1994.

Metcalf, Laurie. Actress. Born in 1955, in Illinois. Spirited leading lady and supporting player of the American stage, screen, and TV. After graduating from Illinois State University, she joined John MALKOVICH as a member of his newly formed Steppenwolf Theatre Company and won an Obie Award for her performance off Broadway in the group's 'Balm in Gilead.' She brought her versatile talent to the screen in 1985, brightening several films with her offbeat characterizations. In the late 80s she joined the cast of the TV series 'Roseanne,' winning the Emmy for her portrayal of Roseanne's wisecracking sister.

FILMS: *Desperately Seeking Susan* 1985; *Making Mr.*

Right, Candy Mountain (Switz./Can./Fr.) 1987; *Stars and Bars, Miles from Home* 1988; *Uncle Buck* 1989; *Internal Affairs, Pacific Heights* 1990; *JFK* 1991; *Mistress* 1992; *A Dangerous Woman* 1993; *Blink* 1994; *Leaving Las Vegas, Toy Story* (v/o) 1995; *Dear God* 1996.

Metro-Goldwyn-Mayer (MGM). An American film production company established in 1924 as a result of the amalgamation of the Metro Picture Corporation (formed 1915), the Goldwyn Picture Corporation (formed 1917), and Louis B. Mayer Pictures (formed 1918) under the corporate control of Loew's, Inc. Louis B. Mayer was appointed first vice president and head of the studio, and his associate Irving THALBERG vice president in charge of production. As part of a financial empire with powerful banking affiliations and a ready-made market in the form of Marcus Loew's extensive chain of motion picture theaters, MGM grew and prospered rapidly. By the early 30s it was the biggest and richest Hollywood studio, a film factory of unequaled prestige and unprecedented glamour. With generous budgets at their disposal, Mayer and Thalberg could achieve for their product a technical polish that no other studio could consistently match.

During its peak years, in the 30s and early 40s, the MGM roster included many of the most accomplished creative artists, technicians, and stars in the business. Art director Cedric Gibbons became famous for his sumptuous, elegant sets; costume designer Gilbert Adrian created gowns that influenced the fashions of the times; sound engineer Douglas Shearer (brother of Norma) was the most ingenious technician in the business. Cameramen like William Daniels, George Folsey, Karl Freund, Joseph Ruttenberg, and Harold Rosson created brilliant images in high-key lighting which became the studio's trademark. Among the directors who passed through the studio gates were such artists as Von Stroheim, King Vidor, Lang, Lubitsch, Seastrom, and La Cava. But the MGM style was more characteristically represented by the polished craftsmanship of such directors as Clarence Brown, Sidney Franklin, George Cukor, Jack Conway, Victor Fleming, and W. S. Van Dyke.

At the heart of the MGM glamour factory was its grand company of stars. The impressive array included such names as Greta Garbo, Clark Gable, the Barrymores, Jean Harlow, Joan Crawford, Spencer Tracy, Norma Shearer, Robert Taylor, James Stewart, Nelson Eddy, Jeanette MacDonald, Myrna Loy, Mickey Rooney, Judy Garland, William Powell, Greer Garson, Walter Pidgeon, and Elizabeth Taylor, among many, many others. Throughout the 30s and much of the 40s the MGM famous trademark, designed by songwriter-publicist Howard Dietz, a roaring lion (nicknamed Leo) emblazoned with the motto "Ars Gratia Artis," ("Art for art's sake") above the classic mask of the muse of drama represented the highest quality in motion picture entertainment. The accent was on clean, escapist fun. Social themes and controversial subjects were usually avoided or lightened in a manner that was thought to make them palatable to mass public taste.

MGM's history can be divided into several distinct periods. Unquestionably, its most prestigious era was the dozen years of Irving Thalberg's term at the helm. During that time, the company produced such ambitious and distinguished motion pictures as *Greed, The Merry Widow, The Big Parade, Ben-Hur, The Crowd, Broadway Melody, Anna Christie, Grand Hotel, Strange Interlude, Dinner at Eight, Viva Villa, The Thin Man, David Copperfield, Mutiny on the Bounty, Fury, The Great Ziegfeld, Camille, Romeo and Juliet,* and *The Good Earth.* The policy of high-quality production was continued after Thalberg's death in 1936, but the emphasis shifted from the literary to pure, unadulterated entertainment. It was the period of such glittering productions as *Boys Town, The Wizard of Oz, Gone With the Wind* (actually a Selznick production), *Ninotchka, The Philadelphia Story, Mrs. Miniver,* and *Madame Curie,* but it was more characterized by such low-budget, high-profit series as "Andy Hardy," "Dr. Kildare," and "Tarzan." Still, MGM continued its dominance of the Hollywood scene until the end of WW II, turning out between 40 and 50 films a year, usually moneymakers.

The postwar period was marked by changing public tastes, the growing threat of television, and the encroachment of old age on MGM's veteran stars. In addition, there were corporate problems. In 1952, Loew's, Inc. was forced by government antitrust action to divest itself of MGM, which now became a separate corporation with no exclusive links to the Loew's chain of theaters and without the unlimited financial resources of the past. Earlier, Louis B. Mayer had been replaced as head of the studio by his former production chief, Dore Schary.

The literate Schary initiated a series of high-grade, low-budget pictures such as *Intruder in the Dust* and *The Asphalt Jungle.* There were also sumptuous grand-scale productions, like *Quo Vadis* and *Ivanhoe,* occasional high-quality comedies like *Father of the Bride,* and dramas like *The Bad and the Beautiful* and *Julius Caesar.* But the genre that helped MGM maintain its pre-eminence in the late 40s and early 50s was the musical. With a team consisting of producer Arthur Freed, directors Stanley Donen, Vincente Minnelli, and Charles Walters, writers Betty Comden and Adolph Green, and a battery of stars including Fred Astaire, Gene Kelly, Judy Garland, Cyd Charisse, Frank Sinatra, Ann Miller, and many others, the MGM musical had no peer. Gay, spirited, zestful, and staged to perfection, the parade of MGM musicals was most impressive: *The Pirate, Easter Parade, On the Town, Annie Get Your Gun, Show Boat, An American in Paris, Singin' in the Rain,* and *Seven Brides for Seven Brothers,* among many others.

But by the early 60s, Leo the Lion's roar was reduced to a whimper. Along with other major Hollywood studios, MGM was hard hit by the reality of dwindling audiences and wavering production policies. The misses soon outnumbered the hits by a large margin and the balance sheets were increasingly in the red. In 1970 the company was taken over by Kirk Kerkorian of Las Vegas, who installed former CBS production chief James T. Aubrey as president. The new management began an economy drive, ranging from a sharp reduction in personnel and production schedules to the sad end-of-an-era auction in 1970 in which hundreds of thousands of props and costumes from the studio's glorious past were put on the block—from the *Ben-Hur* chariot to Sophia Loren's bloomers from *Lady L.* Oblivious to the value of its own past, MGM sold the props outright to an auctioneer for $1.5 million. The auctioneer, gambling on the public's nostalgia, reaped a profit of $12 million, accepting such bids as $15,000 for Judy Garland's ruby slippers from *The Wizard of Oz.*

In 1973, MGM ceased to distribute its own movies; domestic distribution was licensed to United Artists and foreign distribution to CIC. By the late 70s, MGM was reduced to a marginal force in films, but the company was prospering once more as a result of diversified investments and large profits from its gambling hotels in Las Vegas and Reno.

The descent from glory for MGM continued in the 80s. In 1981 the company acquired United Artists, making UA a wholly owned subsidiary, and two years later renamed itself MGM/UA Entertainment. Disintegration followed. In 1986 Turner Broadcasting System purchased MGM/UA in a complicated cash/stock deal valued at about $1.5 billion and promptly sold the UA portion, along with MGM's film and TV production and distribution business, to Kerkorian's Tracinda Corp. The MGM lot and laboratory facilities were sold to Lorimar-Telepictures (the Metrocolor Laboratories would close down in 1989, after 50 years in the film processing business). Ted Turner retained MGM's priceless heritage, the huge library of unforgettable films that made the studio great, along with MGM-owned pre-1948 Warner Bros. and RKO products—3,300 films in all.

What remained of MGM eventually underwent various permutations, with several changes in corporate structure and constant reshuffling of personnel at the top. In November of 1990, the MGM/UA Communications Corporation was taken over for $1.3 billion by Pathé Communications, a Rome-based conglomerate headed by publishing mogul Giancarlo Parretti, who named the division MGM-Pathé Communications and appointed as its president Israeli-born Yoram GLOBUS, formerly Menahem Golan's partner in Cannon. In April of 1991, under pressure from creditors, Parretti was forced to hand over the parent company's chairmanship to his business partner Cesare De Michelis, a brother of Italy's Foreign Minister. Producer Alan LADD, Jr., replaced Parretti as chairman and chief executive officer of MGM-Pathé. In June of 1991, a failed coup attempt by Parretti and his associates resulted in their dramatic firing and the resignation of De Michelis as top honcho of the parent group.

In May of 1992, the French bank Credit Lyonnais, MGM-Pathé's major creditor, acquired 98.5 percent of the company, closing Parretti out completely and restoring the name Metro-Goldwyn-Mayer Inc. However, MGM's performance at the box office remained as dismal as it had for several years, and in July of 1993 Ladd was replaced as chairman and CEO of MGM by Frank Mancuso, former chairman of Paramount Pictures. Then in 1996, Kerkorian, with Mancuso's assistance, bought back the studio in an effort to revitalize a once thriving Hollywood legend.

Though MGM has never recovered its former luster, its releases since the 60s have included some notable films, including *Dr. Zhivago, Network, Moonstruck, A Fish Called Wanda,* and *Thelma & Louise*.

metteur en scène. French term for "director," or "filmmaker," borrowed from the theatrical lexicon. It has been largely replaced by the modern cinematic term *réalisateur.*

Metter, Alan. American director of amiable light films. He had a box-office smash with *Back to School* (1986).

FILMS: *Girls Just Want to Have Fun* 1985; *Back to School* 1986; *Moving* 1988; *Cold Dog Soup* 1990; *Police Academy VII: Mission to Moscow* 1994.

Metty, Russell. Director of photography. *b.* 1906, Los Angeles. *d.* 1978. Began as a lab assistant and after a period of apprenticeship as an assistant cameraman made his first film as a lighting cameraman in 1935. A creative all-around craftsman, he achieved impressive effects with black-and-white contrasting and twilight and night cinematography in two Orson Welles films, *The Stranger* (1946) and *A Touch of Evil* (1958). He is also known for his mastery of complex crane shots. He won an Academy Award for the color cinematography of *Spartacus* (1960).

FILMS INCLUDE: *West of the Pecos* 1935; *Sylvia Scarlett* 1936; *Bringing Up Baby* 1938; *The Great Man Votes* 1939; *Irene, No No Nanette* 1940; *Forever and a Day* (co-phot.) 1943; *The Master Race* 1944; *The Story of G.I. Joe* 1945; *The Stranger* 1946; *Ivy, A Woman's Vengeance* 1947; *Arch of Triumph, All My Sons, Kiss the Blood Off My Hands* 1948; *We Were Strangers* 1949; *Sierra* 1950; *The World in His Arms, Up Front* 1951; *Seminole* 1952; *Magnificent Obsession* 1954; *Written on the Wind* 1956; *Man of a Thousand Faces* 1957; *A Touch of Evil* 1958; *Imitation of Life, This Earth Is Mine* 1959; *Midnight Lace, Spartacus* 1960; *The Misfits, By Love Possessed* 1961; *That Touch of Mink, Flower Drum Song* 1962; *The Thrill of It All* 1963; *The Art of Love, The War Lord* 1965; *Madame X, The Appaloosa, Texas Across the River* 1966; *Thoroughly Modern Millie* 1967; *Counterpoint, The Secret War of Harry Frigg, Madigan* 1968; *Change of Habit* 1969; *How Do I Love Thee?* 1970; *The Omega Man* 1971; *Ben, Cancel My Reservation* 1972.

Metz, Christian. Theorist. Born on Dec. 12, 1931, in Bézier, France. Pacesetting film semiotician whose ideas and text, *Essais sur la signification au cinema/Film Language: A Semiotics of the Cinema* (two volumes, 1968, 1972), developed the relationship of film scholarship to the existing study of signs. In so doing, he strengthened film studies as a legitimate academic field. He is also the author of *Language and Cinema* (1974) and *The Imaginary Signifier* (1977).

Metzger, Radley. American director-producer. Born in 1930. He began as a third assistant director straight out of college and made a sizable profit in 1966 as the American distributor of the erotic Scandinavian film *I, a Woman.* He has since made his mark as the director-producer of stylish erotic films, which he shoots in Europe in lush colors. He also runs a small publishing company and often lectures in colleges on filmmaking. He uses the pseudonym Henry Paris for his hard-core sex films.

FILMS INCLUDE (as director-producer): *Dark Odyssey/Passionate Sunday* (co-dir., co-prod. with William Kyriakis) 1961; *Dictionary of Sex/Dictionary of Love* (compilation film) 1964; *The Dirty Girls* 1965; *The Alley Cats* 1966; *Carmen Baby* 1967; *Therese and Isabelle* (US/Ger.) 1968; *Camille 2000* 1969; *The Lickerish Quartet* (US/It./Ger.) 1970; *Little Mother* 1972; *Score* 1973; *Naked Came the Stranger, The Private Afternoons of Pamela Mann* 1975; *The Image, The Opening of Misty Beethoven* 1976; *Barbara Broadcast* 1977; *Maraschino Cherry, The Cat and the Canary* (also sc.; UK) 1978; *The Tale of Tiffany Lust* 1981; *The Princess and the Call Girl* 1984.

Metzler, Jim. Actor. Born on June 23, 1955 in Oneonda, N.Y. *ed.* Dartmouth Coll. Handsome, intelligent-looking leading man and supporting player of American films, TV movies, and miniseries.

FILMS: *Four Friends* 1981; *Tex* 1982; *River's Edge* 1987; *Hot to Trot, 976-EVIL* 1988; *Old Gringo* 1989; *Sundown: The Vampire in Retreat, Circuitry Man* 1990; *Delusion, Love Kills* 1991; *One False Move* 1992.

Metzner, Ernö. Art director, director. *b.* Feb. 25, 1892, in Hungary. Deceased. In German films from 1920, following studies at Budapest's Academy of Fine Arts, he contributed impressive sets and visual surroundings to many films of G. W. PABST and other German directors. He also directed several films himself. His main contribution as a director is the abstract *Der Ueberfall,* which influenced the German avant-garde. A Jew, he left Germany with the advent of Nazism in 1933, worked briefly in England and France, then settled in the US.

FILMS INCLUDE (as art director, alone or in collaboration): *Sumurun/One Arabian Night* 1920; *Das Weib des Pharao/The Loves of Pharaoh* 1921; *Salome* (also co-dir. with Ludwig Kozma), *Don Juan* 1922; *Alt Heidelberg/The Student Prince, Fridericus Rex* 1923; *Arabella, Ein Sommernachtstraum* 1924; *Geheimnisse einer Seele/Secrets of a Soul* 1926; *Man steigt nach* (also dir., co-sc.) 1927; *Der Ueber-fall* (also dir., co-sc.) 1928; *Die weisse Hölle von Piz Palü/The White Hell of Pitz Palu, Das Tagebuch einer Verlorenen/Diary of a Lost Girl* 1929; *Westfront 1918/Western Front 1918* 1930;

Kameradschaft/Comradeship 1931; *Die Herrin von Atlantis/L'Atlantide* 1932. In France—*Du Haut en Bas* 1933. In the UK—*Chu Chin Chow* 1934. In the US—*It Happened Tomorrow* 1944.

Meurisse, Paul. Actor. *b.* Dec. 21, 1912, Dunkirk, France. *d.* 1979. A former clerk, he turned to the music hall stage, where his theater career began to blossom thanks to the efforts of his fiancée, singer Edith Piaf. From the early 40s he appeared in numerous French films, playing leads and typically French character parts in both dramatic and wryly humorous roles. Memorable as the male lead in Clouzot's classic thriller, *Les Diaboliques/Diabolique* (1954).

FILMS INCLUDE: *Montmartre sur Seine* 1941; *Mariage d'Amour* 1942; *Macadam/Back Streets of Paris* 1946; *L'Impasse des Deux Anges, Scandale* 1948; *L'Ange rouge/The Red Angel* 1949; *Les Diaboliques/Diabolique* 1954; *La Tête contre les Murs/The Keepers* 1958; *Marie Octobre, Le Déjeuner sur l'Herbe/Picnic on the Grass* 1959; *La Française et l'Amour/Love and the Frenchwoman, La Vérité/The Truth* 1960; *Les Nouveau Aristocrates, Le Monocle noir* 1961; *Du Mouron pour les Petits Oiseaux* 1962; *Méfieiz-vous Mesdames* 1963; *Le Deuxième Souffle/Second Breath* 1966; *L'Armee des Ombres/Army of Shadows* 1969; *Doucement les Basses* 1971; *Le Gitan* 1975.

Mexico. The leading producer of feature films in Latin America today, this country of nearly 90 million people was rather slow in the initial development of its national film industry. As early as 1897, an engineering student, Salvador Toscano Barragan, purchased a Lumière camera, with which he began recording big and small events in the life of his country. (This newsreel footage, compiled over a period of 20 eventful years, was edited in the early 50s by Barragan's daughter into a valuable historical documentary, *The Memoirs of a Mexican*). There were other enterprising filmmakers shooting newsreel and documentary footage early in the century, but fiction films were slow to evolve. The ravages of civil war and competition from Hollywood kept film production in check until the end of WW I. The majority of the films produced during that embryonic period in the history of Mexican films were melodramas of popular appeal in a style imported from Italy.

The first Mexican feature film of any importance was *The Gray Automobile* (1919), based on the true exploits of a criminal gang and directed by Enrique Rosas and Joachim Coss. It was followed by a number of other successful productions dealing with typically Mexican themes and directed by such men as Miguel Contreras Torres and Manuel Ojeda. Following a difficult period of transition to sound, Mexican film production began steadily picking up in quantity and quality.

Inspired by the 1931 visit of Eisenstein to film *Que Viva Mexico* and by such achievements by outsiders as Zinnemann and Strand's *Redes/The Wave* (1935), talented Mexican filmmakers like director Emilio "El Indio" Fernández and cinematographer Gabriel Figueroa put Mexico on the international film map in the 40s with such quality films as *Passion Island* (1941), *Maria Candelaria* (1942), *The Pearl,* and *Enamorada* (both 1946). By the early 1950s, Mexican film production reached a peak of some 150 features annually, many of which gained wide distribution in the Spanish-speaking world. The international reputation of Mexican cinema was boosted by Spanish exile Luis BUÑUEL, who, from 1946 to 1960, made most of his films in Mexico. However, by the mid-60s, the Mexican film industry had declined under economic pressure from American imports and television. Few significant films were made, as producers put their money into low-budget melodramas and exploitation films. The Mexican Academy Awards, the Arieles, which had been presented since 1944, were discontinued from 1958 through 1971 because of disputes within the academy and the poor quality of productions.

By the early 80s, the Mexican film industry was producing more films than at any time since the 50s (upwards of 90 features a year), but the quality of most of these films was as low as it had ever been. The only consolation was the presence of a handful of independent directors, including Arturo Ripstein, Jaime Humberto Hermosillo, Alberto Isaac, and Felipe Cazals, who, raising their own financing and often working in 16 mm, continued to produce works of artistic substance. Mexico's cinematic heritage suffered a further blow when the National Film Library, the largest film archive in Latin America, was destroyed by fire in 1982.

The government took steps to restore the reputation of Mexico's cinema when it created the Mexican Film Institute in 1983, which has co-produced a number of films of artistic quality, including American director John Huston's *Under the Volcano* (1984). However, the domestic and international market for Mexican films continued to shrink, and by 1991, the number of features released had dwindled to 34, its lowest since the 1930s. Even so, the industry's worldwide critical reputation had improved, with acclaim in 1991 for new films by established directors (Hermosillo's *Homework*, Ripstein's *The Woman of the Port*) and by newcomers (Maria Novaro's *Danzon*, Dana Rotberg's *Angel of Fire*). In 1992, Alfonso Arau's *Like Water for Chocolate* crossed borders to become an art-house hit in the US. As the 90s progressed, the state announced its withdrawal from film production, forcing independent directors to search for alternatives.

Other noted Mexican directors of recent years include José Luis Garcia Agraz, Busi Cortes, Juán Antonio de la Riva, Paul Leduc, documentarian Eduardo Maldonado, Sergio Olhovich, and Ariel Zuñiga.

Meyer, Emile. Actor. *b.* 1908, New Orleans. *d.* 1987, of Alzheimer's disease. Beefy character player of Hollywood films; typically in tough roles, often as a ruthless cop or loathsome heavy. He played similar roles in some 200 TV programs.

FILMS INCLUDE: *The People Against O'Hara, The Mob* 1951; *Hurricane Smith* 1952; *Shane* 1953; *Riot in Cell Block 11, The Human Jungle* 1954; *The Blackboard Jungle, The Tall Men, The Girl in the Red Velvet Swing, The Man with the Golden Arm, Man with the Gun* 1955; *The Maverick Queen* 1956; *The Sweet Smell of Success, Baby Face Nelson, Paths of Glory* 1957; *The Lineup, The Fiend Who Walked the West* 1958; *Good Day for a Hanging* 1959; *Young Jesse James, The Threat* 1960; *Taggart* 1964; *Young Dillinger* 1965; *A Time for Killing, Hostile Guns* 1967; *The Outfit* 1973; *Macon County Line* 1974.

Meyer, Nicholas. Director, screenwriter, novelist. Born on Dec. 24, 1945, in New York City. A graduate of the University of Iowa, where he majored in theater and film, he began his career as an associate publicist at Paramount and worked in that capacity on the campaign for *Love Story* (1970). In 1970 he joined Warner Bros. for a two-year stint as a story editor. Turning to writing, he gained fame in 1974 as the author of *The Seven-Per-Cent Solution,* an entertaining best-selling novel in which Sherlock Holmes teams up with Sigmund Freud in solving a mystery. He was nominated for an Academy Award for his 1976 screen adaptation of the book. His other novels included *Target Practice* (1974), *The West End Horror* (1976), *Black Orchid* (co-author, 1977), and *Confessions of a Homing Pigeon* (1981). Meyer made a surprisingly assured debut as a director with *Time After Time* (1979), from his own fanciful screenplay about H. G. Wells using his time machine to pursue Jack the Ripper on the streets of modern-day San Francisco. His harrowing TV movie, *The Day After* (1983), caused much controversy for its grim depiction of the aftermath of a catastrophic nuclear bombing of a Kansas town.

FILMS: *Invasion of the Bee Girls* (sc.) 1973; *The Seven-Per-Cent Solution* (sc., from his own novel) 1976; *Time After Time* (dir., sc.) 1979; *Star Trek II: The Wrath of Khan* (dir.) 1982; *Volunteers* (dir.) 1985; *Star Trek IV: The Voyage Home* (co-sc.) 1986; *Fatal Attraction* (doctored script, uncredited) 1987; *The Deceivers* (dir.) 1988; *Patriots, Company Business* (dir., sc.) 1991; *Star Trek VI: The Undiscovered Country* (dir., co-sc.) 1992; *Sommersby* (co-sc.) 1993.

Meyer, Russ. Director. Born on Mar. 21, 1922, in Oakland, Calif. The son of a policeman and a nurse who married six times, he began making 8 mm amateur films at age 12 and at 15 won second prize in a nationwide Eastman-Kodak contest. During WW II he served as newsreel combat cameraman in the European theater. Back home he turned freelance still photographer and found a ready market in the nudie magazines. He shot six centerfolds for *Playboy* in the magazine's early days, then married one of its Playmates, the namesake of his subsequent film production company, Eve Productions. They have since divorced. He remarried twice.

Meyer began making "skin flicks" in the late 50s and soon became known in the business as "King of the Nudies." His *The Immoral Mr. Teas* (1959) was a landmark of sorts. It was the first soft-core "porno" film to make a large profit, returning more than a million dollars on a $24,000 investment, and it paved the way for other enterprising producers of sexploitation films. Over the next decade, Meyer produced, directed, wrote, and himself photographed some 20 vulgar little films with emphasis on violence and sexual aberrations, with such titles as *Faster, Pussycat! Kill! Kill!* He financed each film himself out of the profits of the last one and before long was a self-made millionaire whose films became synonymous with cartoonishly large-breasted, sexually voracious women in the mold of superstar stripper Kitten Natividad.

For years Meyer was ridiculed by the Hollywood establishment as a schlock operator, but after his tremendous success with a skin flick titled *Vixen* (over $6 million profit on a $76,000 investment), he was welcomed with open arms by profit-hungry 20th Century-Fox. He subsequently directed and produced for Fox two watered down sex-violence films, *Beyond the Valley of the Dolls* (1970) and *The Seven Minutes* (1971). Three of his films were received with curious enthusiasm when they were screened as part of a special "Sex in American Cinema" series at the 16th International Moscow Film Festival in 1989, and the uniquely grungy style of Meyer's films has led to an ongoing re-evaluation of their artistic—albeit underground—merit.

Autobiography: *A Clean Breast: The Life and Loves of Russ Meyer,* 1992.

FILMS INCLUDE: *The Immoral Mr. Teas* 1959; *Eve and the Handyman, Erotica* 1961; *The Immoral West and How It Was Lost* 1962; *Europe in the Raw, Heavenly Bodies* 1963; *Kiss Me Quick!, Lorna, Fanny Hill: Memoirs of a Woman of Pleasure* (US/Ger.) 1964; *Mudhoney, Motor Psycho, Faster Pussycat! Kill! Kill!* 1965; *Mondo Topless* 1966; *Good Morning and Goodbye!, Finders Keepers Lovers Weepers, Vixen* 1968; *Cherry Harry and Raquel* 1969; *Beyond the Valley of the Dolls* 1970; *The Seven Minutes* 1971; *Sweet Suzy/Blacksnake* 1973; *Supervixens* 1975; *Up* 1976; *Beneath the Valley of the Ultravixens* (also act.) 1979; *Amazon Women on the Moon* (act. only) 1987.

Meyers, Sidney. Director, film editor. *b.* 1906, New York City. *d.* 1969. *ed.* CCNY. A former violinist with the Cincinnati Orchestra, he entered the documentary film field in 1936 and acquired much of his experience during WW II as chief film editor for the British Ministry of Information in New York and later for the US Office of War Information. He gained international prominence as the director of the documentary drama *The Quiet One,* which won an International Award at the 1949 Venice Film Festival. He co-directed (with Ben Maddow and Joseph Strick) the offbeat feature film *The Savage Eve,* which won the top award at the Edinburgh Festival of 1959. Meyers directed a number of TV films and edited many more. He was script consultant for *Ulysses* (1967) and edited *Slaves* (1969) and *Tropic of Cancer* (1970), among other films.

FILMS (as director): *White Flood* (co-dir.) 1940; *The History and Romance of Transportation* (co-dir.) 1941; *The Quiet One* (also co-sc., co-edit.) 1949; *The Savage Eye* (co-dir., co-prod., co-sc., co-edit. with Joseph Strick and Ben Maddow) 1959; *The World of Abbott and Costello* (compilation film) 1965.

MGM. See METRO-GOLDWYN-MAYER.

Michael, Gertrude. Actress. *b.* June 1, 1911, Talladega, Ala. *d.* 1965. *ed.* U. of Alabama. A former pianist and stage actress, she played leads, second leads, and finally character parts in numerous films from the early 30s, often as a tough broad. Memorable as the adventurous heroine of *The Notorious Sophie Lang* (1934) and its sequels.

FILMS INCLUDE: *Wayward, Unashamed* 1932; *Ann Vickers, A Bedtime Story, I'm No Angel* 1933; *Bolero, Cleopatra* (as Calpurnia), *Murder at the Vanities, The Notorious Sophie Lang, Menace* 1934; *It Happened in New York, The Last Outpost* 1935; *Woman Trap, Till We Meet Again, Forgotten Faces, The Return of Sophie Lang, Second Wife* 1936; *Sophie Lang Goes West* 1937; *Hidden Power* 1939; *Just Like a Woman* 1940; *Behind Prison Walls* 1943; *Women in Bondage* 1944; *Three's a Crowd* 1945; *Flamingo Road* 1949; *Caged* 1950; *Bugles in the Afternoon* 1952; *Women's Prison* 1955; *Twist All Night* 1962.

Micheaux, Oscar. Director, producer, screenwriter. *b.* 1884, Metropolis, Ill. *d.* 1951. The son of freed slaves, he was raised in poverty, with little formal education. He left home at 17, and after working as a shoeshine boy, laborer, and Pullman porter, settled down as a homesteader on a South Dakota farm. In 1913 he anonymously published a first novel, *The Conquest: The Story of a Negro Pioneer,* a clearly autobiographical account of his success as a farmer, his love affair with a white woman, and his marriage to the daughter of a black minister. He followed it with another, *A Romance of the Darker Races* (1915), and proved himself a skilled entrepreneur when he traveled from town to town selling the books, as well as shares in his own little publishing enterprise, at churches, schools, and other social gatherings. His third book, *The Homesteader* (1917), attracted an offer for the purchase of screen rights by a black film company. When negotiations failed, Micheaux characteristically proceeded to make the film himself, raising cash the same way he had for his books. Released in 1919, the film reportedly returned $5,000 on a $15,000 investment. But Micheaux was in the film business to stay. Over the next three decades he wrote, produced, directed, and edited some 40 feature-length films, most of them now lost. Early on, he would finance his productions by advance cash bookings from theaters specializing in black films, after showing their managers fabricated stills. Most of his films are reputed to have been strictly exploitational, often containing inserts of titillating erotic scenes unrelated to their plots. But some, like *Within Our Gates* (1920), which contained a lynching sequence, or *Birthright* (1939), which dealt with the obstacles facing a black Harvard graduate, showed a concern for the plight of blacks. He avoided, however, addressing problems of the ghetto, focusing instead on the world of the black middle class. One of his few surviving films and possibly his best-known silent, *Body and Soul* (1925), featured Paul ROBESON in his first movie role, portraying a young preacher. Although his productions were technically primitive by mainstream terms, and often disjointed in plot and theme, Micheaux holds a special place in the history of American film as the most prolific and most audacious representative of a dynamic movement of parallel cinema, which for many years thrived modestly and quietly in the shadows of Hollywood.

FILMS INCLUDE: *The Homesteader* 1919; *Within Our Gates* 1920; *The Brute, The Shadow, The Gunsaulus Mystery, The Hypocrite, The Wages of Sin* 1921; *Uncle Jasper's Will, The Dungeon* 1922; *The House Behind the Cedars, Deceit* 1923; *A Son of Satan, Birthright* 1924; *Body and Soul* 1925; *The Conjure Woman, The Devil's Disciple* 1926; *The Spider's Web, The Millionaire, The Girl from Chicago, The Broken Violin* 1927; *Thirty Years Later, When Men Betray* 1928; *A Daughter of the Congo, Easy Street* 1930; *The Exile* (his first talkie) 1931; *The Veiled Aristocrats, Ten Minutes to Live* 1932; *Harlem After Midnight, Lem Hawkins' Confession/The Brand of Cain* 1935; *Swing, Temptation, Underworld* 1936; *God's Stepchildren* 1938; *Birthright* (remake) 1939; *The Notorious Elinor Lee, Lying Lips* 1940; *The Betrayal* 1948.

Michel, Micheline. See PRESLE, Micheline.

Mickey Mouse. Probably the world's most famous, and for many years most popular, cartoon character. Launched by Walt DISNEY in 1928, in the animated short *Plane Crazy,* he was briefly known as Mortimer. Toward the end of that year Mickey was given his characteristic high-pitched voice (provided off-screen by Disney himself) in the experimental sound short *Steamboat Willie.* He was fast gaining the status of a star and by the early 30s was surrounded by a cast of supporting characters, including his girlfriend Minnie, his dog Pluto, and the villain Pegleg Pete. Mickey's character was that of the eternal lovable nice guy, a fact that limited his emotional range and restricted his actions, once he became established as a virtual institution, lest he negatively influence the behavior of his legion of young admirers. This led to Mickey's gradual decline and to the rise in popularity of a rival Disney cartoon character, the tempestuous DONALD DUCK. During the 1930s, however, Mickey's supremacy was uncontested. In 1940 he made his feature film debut in the memorable "Sorcerer's Apprentice" episode in *Fantasia.* He later enjoyed renewed popularity on TV as the main attraction of a daily half-hour kiddie show, 'The Mickey Mouse Club.' In all, Mickey appeared in 118 cartoons through 1953. His popularity spawned a virtual industry of Mickey Mouse toys and games. The Mickey Mouse wristwatch has become a collector's item. Among the celebrities who cherish it is Emperor Hirohito of Japan. In America, the White House was only one setting of nationwide celebrations of Mickey's 50th birthday (officially set at Nov. 18, 1928, the day *Steamboat Willie* opened at the Colony Theater in New York). His 60th birthday was staged in 1988 as a world-wide event, with celebrations held in Moscow and other capitals.

microcinematography. Motion picture photography combining the action of a camera and a microscope for recording the movement of objects too small to be captured by the ordinary camera lens.

microphone boom. A long, movable arm designed to maneuver a microphone into position for sound recording during filming. It is operated by a BOOM MAN.

Middleton, Charles. Actor. *b.* Oct. 3, 1879, Elizabethtown, Ky. *d.* 1949. A carnival and circus performer from his teens, he appeared in vaudeville and stock before entering films in the late 20s. He played character parts, often commanding or villainous, in more than 100 features but is best remembered as Ming the Merciless in the Flash Gordon serials.

FILMS INCLUDE: *The Farmer's Daughter* 1928; *The Bellamy Trial, Welcome Danger* 1929; *Way Out West* 1930; *An American Tragedy* (as Reuben Jephson), *The Miracle Woman, Alexander Hamilton* (as Chief Justice John Jay), *Palmy Days* 1931; *The Hatchet Man, The Strange Love of Molly Louvain, Pack Up Your Troubles* 1932; *This Day and Age, Duck Soup, White Woman* 1933; *David Harum, Murder at the Vanities, Mrs. Wiggs of the Cabbage Patch* 1934; *The Miracle Rider* (serial), *Hop-Along Cassidy* 1935; *Flash Gordon* (serial), *Show Boat* 1936; *Dick Tracy Returns* (serial), *Flash Gordon's Trip to Mars* (serial), *Kentucky* 1938; *Daredevils of the Red Circle* (serial), *Jesse James, The Oklahoma Kid, Captain Fury, The Flying Deuces* 1939; *Flash Gordon Conquers the Universe* (serial), *The Grapes of Wrath, Abe Lincoln in Illinois* (as Tom Lincoln), *Charlie Chan's Murder Cruise, Virginia City* (as Jefferson Davis), *Island of Doomed Men* 1940; *Western Union, Belle Starr* 1941; *Perils of Nyoka* (serial) 1942; *Batman* (serial), *The Black Raven* 1943; *Black Arrow* (serial) 1944; *Who's Guilty?* (serial), *Our Vines Have Tender Grapes* 1945; *The Killers* 1946; *Road to Rio, Jack Armstrong* (serial), *The Pretender* 1947; *The Black Arrow* 1948; *The Last Bandit* 1949.

Middleton, Guy. Actor. *b.* Guy Middleton-Powell, Dec. 14, 1906, Hove, England. *d.* 1973. A former stock exchange broker, he became a light character actor of British films. Typically played a smooth cad.

FILMS INCLUDE: *Jimmy Boy* 1935; *A Woman Alone/Two Who Dared, Fame* 1936; *French Without Tears* 1939; *Dangerous Moonlight/Suicide Squadron* 1940; *The Demi-Paradise/Adventure for Two* 1943; *Champagne Charlie* 1944; *The Rake's Progress* 1945; *The Captive Heart* 1946; *Man About the House* 1947; *No Place for Jennifer* 1949; *The Happiest Days of Your Life* 1950; *The Belles of St. Trinian's* 1954; *Laughter in Paradise* 1951; *The Waltz of the Toreadors* 1962; *Oh! What a Lovely War* 1969; *The Magic Christian* 1970.

Middleton, Robert. Actor. *b.* Samuel G. Messer, May 13, 1911, Cincinnati. *d.* 1977. *ed.* Cincinnati Coll. of Music; U. of Cincinnati; Carnegie Inst. of Technology. Big, brutish character actor, formerly a radio announcer and stage actor.

FILMS INCLUDE: *The Silver Chalice* 1954; *The Big Combo, Trial, The Desperate Hours* 1955; *The Court Jester, The Proud Ones, Friendly Persuasion, Love Me Tender* 1957; *The Tarnished Angels, The Law and Jack Wade* 1958; *Don't Give Up the Ship, Career* 1959; *Hell Bent for Leather* 1960; *The Great Impostor* 1961; *Cattle King* 1963; *For Those Who Think Young* 1964; *A Big Hand for the Little Lady* 1966; *The Cheyenne Social Club, Which Way to the Front?* 1970; *The Harrad Experiment* 1973; *The Lincoln Conspiracy* (as Secretary of War Edwin Stanton) 1977.

midget. A small spotlight utilizing lamps ranging from 50 to 200 watts. It is usually used as a source of FILL LIGHT.

Midler, Bette. Actress, singer. Born on Dec. 1, 1945, in Honolulu, Hawaii. Bawdy, campy, multitalented entertainer of stage, film, TV, nightclubs, and recordings. The daughter of a transplanted New Jersey house painter for the Navy, hers was the only Jewish family in a predominantly Polynesian neighborhood. She dropped out of the University of Hawaii after one year of drama studies, and after working briefly in a pineapple cannery made her show business debut playing a tiny part in the movie *Hawaii* (1966). She then headed for New York, where she struggled to make ends meet as a file clerk and go-go dancer while training at the Herbert Berghof studio. Her first break came when she joined the cast of the Broadway musical 'Fiddler on the Roof' as a chorus girl, gradually moving up to the principal role of Tevye's eldest daughter Tzeitel. But Midler's real springboard to stardom came shortly after, in the winter of 1971, with her exuberant, raunchy comedy-singing act in Manhattan's famous Continental Baths, which attracted an enthusiastic cult following among the city's gay community. Her gay fans remained legendarily loyal throughout her career. Nightclub performances and top-selling records soon followed, and her fame rapidly spread as "The Divine Miss M," after the title of one of her albums. In 1973, she won a Grammy Award as best new artist of the year and a special Tony on Broadway. In 1976 she was named Woman of the Year by Harvard's Hasty Pudding. She triumphed with her 'Clams on the Half Shell' revue and won an Emmy for her 1978 TV special 'Ol' Red Hair Is Back.'

In 1979 Midler took on the movies, and promptly gained an Academy Award nomination for her no-holds-barred performance as a Janis Joplin-esque rock star in *The Rose*. The film's title song, released as a top-selling record, earned her a Grammy as female vocalist of the following year. Following a setback with the properly titled *Jinxed* (1982), she disappeared from features for several years, but re-endowed the screen with her talent and dominant presence later in the 80s in a string of successful Disney/Touchstone productions. As her movie stature escalated, she organized her own production company (All-Girl Productions), daring the public to accept her in a variety of roles, including tearjerkers like *Beaches* (1988), *Stella* (1990)—a maudlin updating of the melodrama *Stella Dallas*—and her most personal project, *For the Boys*, an uneven but energetic romp that found Bette in garish makeup as an aged World War II USO performer. She was again nominated for an Oscar for her performance in the latter.

As her serious film roles dwindled, she returned to the stage in 1993 for the first time in ten years, selling out six weeks at New York's Radio City Music Hall with her 'Experience the Divine' concert. Winning unanimous praise for her return to no-holds-barred live performing, her act featured a send-up of her own film career, in which she proclaimed herself 'Disneyized, Jurassicized'. . . referring to her production deal with Disney.

In 1984 she married Martin Rochus Sebastian von Haselberg, a commodities trader; they have a daughter, Sophie. Author: *A View from a Broad; The Saga of Baby Divine.*

FILMS: *Hawaii* (bit) 1966; *The Rose* 1979; *Divine Madness* (also co-sc., addnl. lyrics) 1980; *Jinxed* 1982; *Down and Out in Beverly Hills, Ruthless People* 1986; *Outrageous Fortune, In the Mood* (addnl. title song lyrics only) 1987; *Big Business, Oliver & Company* (v/o) 1988; *Beaches* (also co-prod., co-songs) 1989; *Stella* 1990; *Scenes from A Mall* 1991; *For the Boys* (also co-prod.) 1992; *Hocus Pocus* 1993; *Get Shorty* (unbilled cameo) 1995; *First Wives Club* 1996; *That Old Feeling* 1997.

Mifune, Toshiro. Actor. Born on Apr. 1, 1920, in Tsingtao, China, to Japanese parents. After WW II service with the Japanese army, he entered films, winning a studio talent contest. His early career was shaped by director Akira KUROSAWA, who first cast him in *Drunken Angel* (1948), made him world famous in *Rashomon* (1950), and later cast him in such films as *Seven Samurai, Throne of Blood,* and *The Lower Depths.* A highly versatile actor with a strong screen presence, he excels in period films and modern themes and in both dramatic and ironic-comic roles. He is by far the best-known Japanese screen personality abroad and has appeared in a number of international productions. He was named best actor at the Venice Festival in 1961 for *Yojimbo* and again in 1965 for *Red Beard.* In 1963 he formed his own production company and directed one film, *The Legacy of the Five Hundred Thousand.* He has also produced several films. He played a pivotal role in the TV miniseries 'Shogun' (1980) a condensed version of which was released as a feature-length video movie.

FILMS INCLUDE: *These Foolish Times* 1946; *Drunken Angel* 1948; *The Silent Duel, Stray Dog* 1949; *Scandal, Rashomon* 1950; *Elegy, The Idiot* 1951; *The Life of Oharu* 1952; *Eagle of the Pacific* 1953; *Seven Samurai* 1954; *I Live in Fear* 1955; *Throne of Blood, The Lower Depths, The Secret Scrolls* 1957; *The Rickshaw Man, The Hidden Fortress* 1958; *Samurai Saga, Saga of the Vagabonds* 1959; *I Bombed Pearl Harbor, The Bad Sleep Well* 1960; *Yojimbo* 1961; *Sanjuro* 1962; *High and Low, The Legacy of the Five Hundred Thousand* (also dir.), *Samurai Pirate, Whirlwind* 1964; *Samurai Assassin* (also prod.), *Red Beard, Judo Saga* 1965; *Grand Prix* (US) 1966; *Rebellion* 1967; *Tunnel to the Sun* (also co-prod.), *Admiral Yamamoto* 1968; *Hell in the Pacific* (US), *Under the Banner of the Samurai/Samurai Banners* (also prod.), *Red Lion* (also prod.) 1969; *Soleil Rouge/Red Sun* (Fr.), *Zato-Ichi Meets Yojimbo* 1971; *Paper Tiger* (UK) 1975; *Midway* (as Admiral Isoroku Yamamoto; US) 1976; *Proof of the Man* 1977; *The Bushido Blade, 1941* (US), *Winter Kills, Onigana/Love and Faith of Ogin* 1979; *Inchon* (S. Korea/US), *The Challenge* (US) 1982; *Jinsei Gekijo* 1983; *Seiha* 1984; *Taketori Monogatari/Princess from the Moon* 1987; *Sen no Rikyu/The Death of a Tea Master* 1989; *Picture Bride* 1995.

Mikhalkov-Konchalovasky, Andrei. See KONCHALOVSKY, ANDREI.

Mikhalkov, Nikita. Director, actor. Born Nikita Sergeyevich Mikhalkov-Konchalovsky, on Oct. 21, 1945, in Moscow. The descendant of famous painters, and the son of a poet (his father was also a playwright, novelist, and screenwriter, and chairman of the Soviet Writers Union), he studied acting at the Stanislavsky Theater Children's Studio, continued his training at the Chuskin School of the Vakhtangov Theater, and performed on the stage and several films (screen debut 1961), usually in romantic leads. He then followed in the footsteps of his older brother, Andrei KONCHALOVSKY, enrolling at VGIK, the state film school in Moscow where, like Andrei, he studied directing under Mikhail ROMM. After submitting his diploma film, *A Quiet Day at the End of the War,* in 1970, he resumed his acting career, delaying his professional debut as a director until 1974. To avoid confusion, the actors divided the hyphenated family name Mikhalkov-Konchalovsky between them, with Nikita billing himself Mikhalkov and Andrei eventually becoming known as Konchalovsky. Mikhalkov first attracted international attention two years later with *A Slave of Love* (1976), a humor-laced bittersweet film about the making of a film in the midst of the 1917 Revolution and the ironic consequences that emerge from the clash between romantic dreams and political reality. Praised in the West for its bright sophistication, the film boasted admirable performances and "Chekhovian" wit, elements that critics were to continue associating with the director's future work. Mikhalkov affirmed his Chekhov connection with his next film, *An Unfinished Piece for Mechanical Piano,* an adaptation of the dramatist's first play, 'Platonov' (written in 1881; published posthumously in 1923, and first produced in 1928), enhanced by material from several of his stories. The film, in which the director also appeared, was enthusiastically received in the USSR and abroad, winning the Grand Prix at the San Sebastian Festival. Among several subsequent literary adaptations was the mammoth two-part *Oblomov.* His Italian-made *Dark Eyes* won the best actor for Marcelllo MASTROIANNI at the 1987 Cannes Film Festival. Mikhalkov reached a peak in his career when he produced, directed, wrote, and starred in the Stalin-era drama *Burnt by the Sun* (1994) earning the Academy Award for best foreign film. Along with his work as a director, Mikhalkov continued to appear as an actor in the films of others, as well as his own.

FILMS: As actor (partial list)—*Meet Me in Moscow* 1964; *The Red and the White* (Hung./USSR) 1967; *A Nest of Gentry* 1969; *The Red Tent* (USSR/It.), *Sport Sport Sport* 1971; *Siberiade* 1978; *Flights of Fancy, Station for Two* 1983; *Cruel Romance* 1984. As director (complete)—*A Quiet Day at the End of the War* (diploma film; also co-sc.) 1970; *At Home Among Strangers/A Stranger Among His Own People* (also co-sc., act.) 1974; *A Slave of Love* 1976 (also act.); *An Unfinished Piece for a Mechanical Piano* (also co-sc., act.) 1977; *Five Evenings* (also co-sc.) 1979; *Oblomov/Several Days in the Life of I. I. Oblomov* (in two parts; also co-sc.; release delayed from 1979) 1980; *Kinfolk/Family Relations* 1982; *Without Witnesses/A Private Conversation* (also co-sc.) 1983; *Oci Ciornie/Dark Eyes* (also co-sc.; It./Fr.) 1987; *Urga* 1991; *Anna* 1993; *Burnt by the Sun* (prod., dir., sc., act.) 1994.

Milchan, Arnon. Producer. Born in 1944, in Israel. An enterprising businessman with a passion for the arts, he started out back home, and later in Europe, as an impresario and stage producer. Among other plays, he produced a version of 'Amadeus' in Paris that starred Roman POLANSKI. In the US from the early 80s, he rapidly claimed a place atop the Hollywood heap. After gaining prestige with such films as *The King of Comedy, Once Upon a Time in America,* and *Brazil,* and scoring huge box-office hits with *War of the Roses* and *Pretty Woman,* he put together a consortium to supply Warner Bros. with 20 films over five years, with a budget totaling $600 million.

FILMS INCLUDE (as producer or exec. producer, alone or in collaboration): *Black Joy* (UK) 1977; *The Medusa Touch* (UK) 1978; *Dizengoff 99* (Isr.) 1979; *The King of Comedy* 1983; *Once Upon a Time in America* 1984; *Brazil, Legend* (UK) 1985; *Man on Fire* (It./Fr.) 1987; *Who's Harry Crumb?, Big Man on Campus/The Hunchback of UCLA, The War of the Roses* 1989; *Q & A, Pretty Woman* 1990; *Switch, Guilty by Suspicion, JFK* 1991; *The Mambo Kings, Memoirs of an Invisible Man, The Power of One, One Hot Summer, Under Siege* 1992; *Sommersby, Falling Down, Made in America* 1993; *Natural Born Killers, Second Best* 1994; *Boys On the Side, Copycat* 1995; *Bogus, The Mirror Has Two Faces, A Time to Kill* 1996; *Murder at 1600, Devil's Advocate, L.A. Confidential* 1997.

Miles, Sir Bernard (Lord Miles). Actor. *b.* Sept. 27, 1907, Uxbridge, England. *d.* 1991. An Oxford graduate, he was a schoolteacher before turning to the stage in 1930 and to British films in 1933. He often played rural characters and simpletons, and was especially memorable in a couple of screen portrayals from the Dickens repertoire. In 1959 he became founder and director of London's Mermaid Theatre. Author of *The British Theatre* (1948). He was created a life peer with the title of baron in 1978.

FILMS INCLUDE: *Channel Crossing* 1933; *The Love Test* 1935; *The Lion Has Wings* 1939; *Pastor Hall* 1940; *Freedom Radio/The Voice in The Night* 1941; *One of Our Aircraft Is Missing, The Day Will Dawn/The Avengers, In Which We Serve, The First of the Few/Spitfire* 1942; *Tawny Pipit* (prod., co-dir. with Charles Saunders, sc.) 1944; *Carnival, Great Expectations* (as Mr. Pip) 1946; *Nicholas Nickleby* (as Newman Noggs), *Fame Is the Spur* 1947; *The Guinea Pig* 1948; *Chance of a Lifetime* (also prod., dir., co-sc.) 1950; *The Magic Box* 1951; *Never Let Me Go* (US/UK) 1953; *The Man Who Knew Too Much* (US), *Moby Dick* (UK/US) 1956; *The Smallest Show on Earth, Saint Joan* 1957; *Tom Thumb* 1958; *Sapphire* 1959; *Heavens Above* 1963; *Run Wild Run Free* 1969.

Miles, Christopher. Director. Born on Apr. 19, 1939, in London. He trained at the French film school IDHEC and began directing shorts in 1960. One of these, *The Six-Sided Triangle* (1963), starred his sister, Sarah MILES. His 1970 feature *The Virgin and the Gypsy,* a literate adaptation of the D. H. Lawrence novella, was well received by the public and critics alike. So was his *Priest of Love* (1981), a screen biography of the author focusing on his troubled final years, marked by a stormy but devoted relationship with his wife and bitter confrontations with censorship. In addition to his features, Miles directed a number of TV movies.

FEATURE FILMS: *Up Jumped a Swagman* 1965; *The Virgin and the Gypsy* 1970; *The Maids, That Lucky Touch* 1975; *Priest of Love* 1981.

Miles, Sarah. Actress. Born on Dec. 31, 1941, in Ingatestone, England. The daughter of a wealthy businessman, she enrolled at 15 at London's Royal Academy of Dramatic Art and made her screen debut in 1962 in the role of a nymphet student who seduces schoolmaster Laurence Olivier in *Term of Trial.* She went on to play seductive roles in other films and developed into one of the most intriguing young leads of the British cinema of the 60s and 70s in such films as *The Servant* (1963), *Ryan's Daughter* (Oscar nomination, 1970), *Lady Caroline Lamb* (1972), and *The Hireling* (1973). In 1967 she married playwright screenwriter-director, Robert BOLT. They divorced in 1976 but remarried in 1988. She is the sister of Christopher MILES.

FILMS: *Term of Trial* 1962; *The Six-Sided Triangle* (short), *The Servant, The Ceremony* 1963; *Those Magnificent Men in Their Flying Machines* 1965; *I Was Happy Here/Time Lost and Time Remembered, Blow-Up* 1966; *Ryan's Daughter* 1970; *Lady Caroline Lamb* 1972; *The Hireling, The Man Who Loved Cat Dancing* (US) 1973; *Pepita Jimenez/Bride to Be* (Sp.) 1975; *The Sailor Who Fell from Grace with the Sea* 1976; *The Big Sleep* 1978; *Priest of Love* 1981; *Venom* 1982; *Ordeal by Innocence, Steaming* 1985; *Loving Walter/Walter and June* (orig. for TV) 1986; *White Mischief, Hope and Glory* 1987.

Miles, Sylvia. Actress. Born on Sept. 9, 1932, in New York City. Offbeat character player and occasional lead of the American stage and Hollywood films, she has been particularly effective in tough-but-vulnerable, eccentric, vulgar floozie roles. Trained at the Actors Studio, she appeared in stock and on TV before registering off Broadway in such productions as 'The Iceman Cometh' and 'The Balcony.' Appearing infrequently in films from 1960, she first gained attention in *Midnight Cowboy* (1969), in a memorable bit part for which she was nominated for a best supporting actress Academy Award. She received a second Oscar nomination for a somewhat larger and equally memorable part in *Farewell My Lovely* (1975). An impulsively energetic, outspoken personality offscreen, she made newspaper headlines in 1973 when she dumped a plate of food on the head of critic John Simon at a busy restaurant in reaction to a bad review of one of her stage appearances.

FILMS INCLUDE: *Murder Inc.* 1960; *Parrish* 1961; *Violent Midnight/Psychomania* 1963; *Terror in the City* 1966; *Midnight Cowboy* 1969; *The Last Movie, Who Killed Mary What's Ername?* 1971; *Heat* 1972; *92 in the Shade, Farewell My Lovely* 1975; *The Great Scout and Cathouse Thursday* 1976; *The Sentinel* 1977; *Shalimar* (India), *Zero to Sixty* 1978; *The Funhouse* 1981; *Evil Under the Sun* (UK) 1982; *Critical Condition, Wall Street* 1987; *Crossing Delancey, Spike of Bensonhurst* 1988; *She-Devil* 1989; *Superstar: The Life and Times of Andy Warhol* (doc.) 1990.

Miles, Vera. Actress. Born Vera Ralston, on Aug. 23, 1929, in Boise City, Okla. She began in films in the early 50s through a beauty contest and a succession of live TV dramas and, after appearing in a number of minor productions, scored as a leading lady of star quality in John Ford's *The Searchers* (1956) and Alfred Hitchcock's *The Wrong Man* (1957). However, with several notable exceptions, she has subsequently been wasted on mostly undistinguished films. She has also appeared in a number of TV movies. Her second husband was screen Tarzan Gordon SCOTT. Her third is Keith LARSEN.

FILMS: *Two Tickets to Broadway* 1951; *For Men Only, The Rose Bowl Story* 1952; *The Charge at Feather River* 1953; *Pride of the Blue Grass* 1954; *Tarzan's Hidden Jungle, Wichita* 1955; *The Searchers, Autumn Leaves, 23 Paces to Baker Street* 1956; *The Wrong Man, Beau James* 1957; *The FBI Story, Web of Evidence, Beyond This Place* (UK) 1959; *Jovanka e le Altre/Five Branded Women* (It./Yug.), *A Touch of Larceny, Psycho* 1960; *Back Street* 1961; *The Man Who Shot Liberty Valance* 1962; *The Hanged Man* (TV movie), *A Tiger Walks, Those Calloways* 1964; *Follow Me Boys!* 1966; *Gentle Giant, The Spirit Is Willing* 1967; *Sergeant Ryker, Kona Coast* 1968; *The Hellfighters, It Takes All Kinds* 1969; *The Wild Country* 1971; *Molly and Lawless John* 1972; *One Little Indian* 1973; *The Castaway Cowboy* 1974; *The Thoroughbreds, Twilight's Last Gleaming* 1977; *Run for the Roses* 1978; *Psycho II, Brainwaves* 1983; *The Initiation* 1984; *Into the Night* 1985.

Milestone, Lewis. Director. *b.* Lev Milstein, Sept. 30, 1895, Kishinev, near Odessa, Russia. *d.* 1980. The son of a prosperous Jewish clothing manufacturer, and older cousin of famous violinist Nathan Milstein, he encountered family opposition to his ambition of becoming an actor. As a precaution, he was sent to Saxony for university studies in engineering. But a year later, in 1913, he quit school, on an impulse, and on his own went to the US. Arriving penniless, he swept floors, operated factory machinery, and worked as a janitor and door-to-door salesman before landing a job as a photographer's assistant. It proved a career turning point. In 1917, when he enlisted in the US Army for WW I service, Milstein was assigned to the photographic unit of the Signal Corps, where he learned much about filmmaking by assisting on shoots and the assembly of combat footage. Following his discharge in 1919, he acquired American citizenship, changing his name in the process to Lewis Milestone, and headed for Hollywood, where he entered films as an assistant cutter. Within a year he was employed as general assistant to Henry King, then moved on to become an assistant director, editor, and story and script collaborator for William A. Seiter and other filmmakers. His screenwriting contributions included *Up and at 'Em* (1922), *The Yankee Consul* (1924), and *The Mad Whirl, Dangerous Innocence, The Teaser,* and *Bobbed Hair* (all 1925).

Milestone was armed with extensive and varied experience when he got his first directing assignment, *Seven Sinners,* from Jack WARNER in 1925. Just two years later he turned out an Academy Award winner (for best comedy direction, a category existing only that year) in the first ever Oscar ceremony for *Two Arabian Knights* (1927). The director surpassed that achievement by far with a superior screen adaptation of Erich Maria Remarque's pacifist novel, *All Quiet on the Western Front* (1930), for Universal. The film, still considered among the screen's most powerful indictments of the futility of war, won Oscars for best picture and best director. It was immediately followed by another success, *The Front Page* (1931), a dynamic, highly entertaining adaptation of the Hecht-MacArthur play that earned Academy Award nominations for best picture and director.

But Milestone's subsequent work was oddly uneven. In the next 30 years he turned out mainly routine, uninspired, if technically polished, productions. There were notable exceptions, like the atmospheric drama of intrigue, *The General Died at Dawn* (1936), the exceptional Steinbeck adaptation, *Of Mice and Men* (1940), and the compassionately humanistic WW II drama, *A Walk in the Sun* (1945). But looking at his career as a whole, the early promise he showed was never fully realized. An excellent craftsman with a fluid camera style and a firm grip on film technique, Milestone proved himself capable of eliciting the most out of good screenplay material. But his complacent attitude toward routine projects rendered too many of his films run-of-the-mill duds. From the mid-50s, he worked for TV, directing episodes for several series. Because of declining health, he retired in 1963. After suffering a series of strokes, he spent the last ten years of his life confined to a wheelchair. Five days before his 85th birthday he died following abdominal surgery, never having regained consciousness. He was married (from 1935) to former screen actress Kendall Lee, who died in 1978.

FILMS: *Seven Sinners* (also co-story, co-sc.) 1925; *The Caveman, The New Klondike* 1926; *Two Arabian Knights* 1927; *The Garden of Eden, The Racket* 1928; *Betrayal, New York Nights* 1929; *Hell's Angels* (co-dir. with Howard Hughes; uncredited), *All Quiet on the Western Front* (also cameo appearance) 1930; *The Front Page* 1931; *Rain* (also prod.) 1932; *Hallelujah I'm a Bum* 1933; *The Captain Hates the Sea* 1934; *Paris in Spring* 1935; *Anything Goes/Tops Is the Limit, The General Died at Dawn* (also act.) 1936; *The Night of Nights* 1939; *Of Mice and Men* (also prod.), *Lucky Partners* 1940; *My Life with Caroline* (also prod.) 1941; *Our Russian Front* (doc.; co-prod., co-dir. with Joris Ivens) 1942; *Edge of Darkness, The North Star/Armored Attack* 1943; *A Guest in the House* (replaced John Brahm; uncredited), *The Purple Heart* 1944; *A Walk in the Sun* (also prod.), *The Strange Love of Martha Ivers* 1946; *Arch of Triumph* (also co-sc.), *No Minor Vices* (also prod.) 1948; *The Red Pony* (also prod.) 1949; *The Halls of Montezuma* 1951; *Kangaroo, Les Miserables* 1952; *Melba* 1953; *They Who Dare* (UK) 1954; *La Vedova/The Widow* (also adapt.; It.) 1955; *King Kelly* (unfinished) 1957; *Pork Chop Hill* 1959; *Ocean's 11* 1960; *Mutiny on the Bounty* 1962; *PT-109* (replaced by Leslie Martinson; uncredited) 1963; *La Guerra Secreta/The Dirty Game* (replaced by Terence Young; uncredited) 1965.

Milhaud, Darius. Composer. *b.* Sept. 4, 1892, Aix-en-Provence, France. *d.* 1974. The eclectic, prolific composer of *La Création du Monde* and hundreds of other musical works also wrote scores for many films. A celebrated member of the Groupe des Six, he first came to the US in 1940 and subsequently commuted across the Atlantic to teach composition at Mills College in Oakland, Calif., and to organize the summer festivals in Aspen, Col.

FILMS INCLUDE: *L'Inhumaine* 1923; *Land Without Bread* 1932; *Madame Bovary* 1934; *The Beloved Vagabond* (UK) 1935; *La Citadelle de Silence* 1937; *La Tragédie Impériale* 1938; *L'Espoir* 1939; *The Private Affairs of Bel Ami* (US) 1947; *Dreams That Money Can Buy* (also personal appearance) 1948; *La Vie commence demain* 1949.

Milian, Tomas (also **Thomas**). Actor. Born Tomás Rodriguez, on Mar. 3, 1937, in Cuba. Raised in the US, he trained at the Actors Studio and appeared in several New York stage productions. Arriving in Italy in the late 60s to participate in the Spoleto Festival, he was discovered by director Mauro BOLOGNINI and stayed on to appear in numerous Italian films, in both leads and character parts, often in neurotic or vicious portrayals.

FILMS INCLUDE: *La Notte brava/On Any Street/Bad Girls Don't Cry* 1959; *Il Bell'Antonio* 1960; *L'Imprevisto* 1961; *Boccaccio '70, Il Disordine/Disorder* 1962; *Gli Indifferenti/*

Time of Indifference 1964; *The Agony and the Ecstasy* (US) 1965; *El Precio de un Hombre/The Bounty Killer/The Ugly Ones* (Sp./It.) 1966; *Django Kid* 1967; *La Resa dei Conti/The Big Gundown, Banditi a Milano/The Violent Four* 1968; *Ruba al prossimo Tuo/A Fine Pair* 1969; *I Cannibali/The Cannibals* 1970; *The Last Movie* (US) 1971; *Cronanca criminale del Far West* 1972; *I Consigliori* 1973; *Folle à tuer* (Fr./It.), *Il Quattro dell'Apocalisse* 1975; *Winter Kills* (US), *La Luna, Roma a Mano armata* 1979; *Milano Odia: La Polizia non puo sparare/Almost Human* 1980; *Monsignor* (US) 1982; *Identificazione di una Donna/Identification of a Woman* 1983; *King David* (US), *Salome* 1985; *Revenge* (US), *Havana* (US) 1990; *Money* (Fr./It./Can.) 1991.

Milius, John. Director, screenwriter. Born on Apr. 11, 1944, in St. Louis. After graduating from Los Angeles City College with a degree in English literature, he wanted to join the Marines but was turned down because of chronic asthma. He then attended the USC film school. While there, he won an award for his animated short, *Marcello, I'm So Bored* (1967), at the National Student Film Festival, paving the way for his hiring by Roger Corman's AIP as assistant to producer Lawrence GORDON. Turning soon after to screenwriting, he prospered in the 70s and after with a string of gutsy, sometimes intelligent, action scripts, sharing an Academy Award nomination with Francis COPPOLA for *Apocalypse Now* (1979). Exhibiting a taste for bloody violence, he made an assertive debut as a director with *Dillinger* in 1973. His subsequent films varied in genre and quality. He also became involved in producing, sometimes in partnership with Steven SPIELBERG. His second wife is actress Celia Kaye.

FILMS: *The Devil's Eight* (co-sc.) 1969; *Evel Knievel* (co-sc.), *Dirty Harry* (co-sc., uncredited) 1971; *Deadhead Miles* (act.), *The Life and Times of Judge Roy Bean* (sc.), *Jeremiah Johnson* (co-sc.) 1972; *Magnum Force* (sc.), *Dillinger* (dir., sc.) 1973; *The Wind and the Lion* (dir., sc.) 1975; *Big Wednesday/Summer of Innocence* (dir., sc.) 1978; *Hardcore* (exec. prod.), *Apocalypse Now* (co-sc.), *1941* (exec. prod., co-story) 1979; *Used Cars* (co-exec. prod.) 1980; *Conan the Barbarian* (dir., co-sc., act. in bit) 1982; *Lone Wolf McQuade* (tech. adv.), *Uncommon Valor* (co-prod.) 1983; *Red Dawn* (dir., co-sc.) 1984; *Extreme Prejudice* (co-story) 1987; *Farewell to the King* (dir., sc.) 1989; *Flight of the Intruder* (dir., co-sc.) 1991; *Clear and Present Danger* (co-sc.) 1994.

Miljan, John. Actor. *b.* Nov. 9, 1892, Lead, S.Dak. *d.* 1960. Suave villain of some 200 silent films and talkies, following a stage career from age 15. He was among Hollywood's leading smooth heavies in the 20s and early 30s.

FILMS INCLUDE: *Love Letters, The Lone Chance* 1924; *The Unchastened Woman, The Phantom of the Opera* 1925; *The Devil's Circus, Devil's Island, The Amateur Gentleman* 1926; *Wolf's Clothing, The Clown, The Yankee Clipper, Old San Francisco, The Satin Woman* 1927; *Glorious Betsy, Lady Be Good, The Terror, Tenderloin* 1928; *Innocents of Paris, The Desert Song, The Unholy Night, Untamed* 1929; *Free and Easy, The Unholy Three, Our Blushing Brides, The Sea Bat, Paid* 1930; *Inspiration, The Secret Six, Politics, Susan Lennox: Her Fall and Rise, Possessed, Hell Divers* 1931; *Emma, Arsene Lupin, The Beast of the City, The Wet Parade, The Kid from Spain, Flesh* 1932; *Whistling in the Dark, The Way to Love* 1933; *Madame Spy, Belle of the Nineties* 1934; *Charlie Chan in Paris, The Ghost Walks* (lead), *Mississippi, Under the Pampas Moon* 1935; *Sutter's Gold* 1936; *The Plainsman* (as General Custer) 1937; *If I Were King* 1938; *The Oklahoma Kid, Juarez* 1939; *Women Without Names, New Moon* 1940; *Bombardier, The Fallen Sparrow* 1943; *The Killers* 1946; *Sinbad the Sailor* 1947; *Samson and Delilah* 1949; *Mrs. Mike* 1950; *M* 1951; *The Pirates of Tripoli* 1955; *The Ten Commandments* 1956; *The Lone Ranger and the Lost City of Gold* 1958.

Milland, Ray. Actor, director. *b.* Reginald Truscott-Jones, Jan. 3, 1907 (per birth certificate; most sources give 1905), Neat, Wales. *d.* 1986. *ed.* U. of Wales. After three years of service as a guardsman with the Royal Household Cavalry in London, he entered British films in 1929. Having adopted the surname of his stepfather, Mullane, he made his screen debut as Spike Milland, but later changed it to Raymond Milland. After several roles, both big and small, he set out for Hollywood in 1930. For several years he played mostly second leads, usually as the hero's friend or rival, but graduated to leads in the mid-30s. Charming and debonair, he played suave, self-assured romantic leading men in many drawing-room comedies and an occasional mystery or adventure. Always an accomplished performer, he drew little attention to his acting until his strong dramatic performance as an alcoholic writer in *The Lost Weekend,* for which he won the 1945 Academy Award. Most of his subsequent roles were less rewarding, but he often proved capable of overcoming minor vehicles with interesting characterizations. Starting in 1955, he directed himself in a number of films with surprising proficiency but less-than-remarkable results. After an absence of several years, he returned to the screen in 1970, playing a character part in *Love Story,* then resumed playing leads in low-budget horror films. He also starred in the TV comedy series 'The Ray Milland Show" (1953–55) and in the drama series 'Markham' (1959–60). A book-loving homebody, Milland kept away from the Hollywood glitter and was rarely mentioned in the gossip columns. He was married to the same woman for 54 years. Autobiography: *Wide-Eyed in Babylon* (1976).

FILMS (as actor): In the UK—*The Playing, The Informer, The Flying Scotsman, The Lady from the Sea/Goodwin Sands* 1929. In the US—*Way for a Sailor, Passion Flower* 1930; *The Bachelor Father, Just a Gigolo, Bought, Ambassador Bill, Blonde Crazy* 1931; *The Man Who Played God, Polly of the Circus, Payment Deferred* 1932; *Orders Is Orders* (UK), *This Is the Life* (UK) 1933; *Bolero, We're Not Dressing, Many Happy Returns, Charlie Chan in London, Menace* 1934; *One Hour Late, The Gilded Lily, Four Hours to Kill, The Glass Key, Alias Mary Dow* 1935; *Next Time We Love, The Return of Sophie Lang, The Big Broadcast of 1937, The Jungle Princess, Three Smart Girls* 1936; *Bulldog Drummond Escapes* (title role), *Wings Over Honolulu, Easy Living, Ebb Tide, Wise Girl* 1937; *Her Jungle Love, Tropic Holiday, Men with Wings, Say It in French* 1938; *French Without Tears* (UK), *Hotel Imperial, Beau Geste* (as John Geste), *Everything Happens at Night* 1939; *Irene, The Doctor Takes a Wife, Untamed, Arise My Love* 1940; *I Wanted Wings, Skylark* 1941; *The Lady Has Plans, Reap the Wild Wind, Are Husbands Necessary?, The Major and the Minor, Star Spangled Rhythm* 1942; *The Crystal Ball, Forever and a Day* 1943; *The Uninvited, Lady in the Dark, Till We Meet Again, Ministry of Fear* 1944; *The Lost Weekend* 1945; *Kitty, The Well Groomed Bride* 1946; *California, The Imperfect Lady, The Trouble with Women, Variety Girl* (cameo), *Golden Earrings* 1947; *The Big Clock, So Evil My Love, Miss Tatlock's Millions* (cameo), *Sealed Verdict* 1948; *Alias Nick Beal, It Happens Every Spring* 1949; *A Woman of Distinction, A Life of Her Own, Copper Canyon* 1950; *Circle of Danger* (UK), *Night Into Morning, Rhubarb, Close to My Heart* 1951; *Bugles in the Afternoon, Something to Live For, The Thief* 1952; *Jamaica Run, Let's Do It Again* 1953; *Dial M for Murder* 1954; *The Girl in the Red Velvet Swing* (as Stanford White), *A Man Alone* (also dir.) 1955; *Lisbon* (also dir., prod.), *Three Brave Men, The River's Edge, High Flight* (UK) 1957; *The Safecracker* (also dir.; UK) 1958; *Premature Burial, Panic in the Year Zero!* (also dir.) 1962; *X—The Man with the X-Ray Eyes* 1963; *The Confession/Quick Let's Get Married* 1965; *Hostile Witness* (also dir.; UK) 1967; *Rose Rosse per il Fuhrer* (It.) 1968; *Company of Killers/The Protectors, Love Story* 1970; *The Big Game* (UK), *Frogs, The Thing with Two Heads, Embassy* 1972; *The House in Nightmare Park/Crazy House* (UK), *Terror in the Wax Museum* 1973; *Gold* (UK) 1974; *Escape to Witch Mountain* 1975; *Aces High* (UK), *The Last Tycoon* 1976; *Slavers* (Ger.), *Oil* (It.), *The Swiss Conspiracy* (UK), *The Uncanny* (UK/Can.) 1977; *La Ragazza in Pigiama giallo/The Girl in the Yellow Pajamas, Blackout* (Can./Fr.), *Oliver's Story* 1978; *Battlestar Gallactica, Game for Vultures* (UK) 1979; *The Attic, Survival Run* 1980; *The Sea Serpent* (Sp.) 1986.

Millar, Stuart. Producer, director. Born in 1929, in New York City. *ed.* Stanford U.; Sorbonne. Gained film experience at the motion picture branch of the State Department and with the Army Signal Corps. In Hollywood since the mid-50s, at first as assistant to William Wyler, he produced several notable films in the 60s and turned to directing early in the 70s. But after only two features he resorted to directing TV movies and occasionally returned to producing.

FILMS INCLUDE: *As producer—The Young Stranger* 1957; *Stage Struck* 1958; *The Young Doctors* 1961; *Bird Man of Alcatraz* (co-prod.) 1962; *I Could Go On Singing* 1963; *The Best Man* 1964; *Paper Lion* 1968; *Little Big Man* 1970; *Shoot the Moon* (co-exec. prod.) 1982. As director—*When the Legends Die* (also prod.) 1972; *Rooster Cogburn* 1975.

Miller, Ann. Actress, dancer. Born Lucille Ann Collier, on Apr. 12, 1919, in Chireno, Tex. A professional dancer from childhood, she broke into films at 17, but for a decade her zestful personality, great legs, and vigorous tap-dancing talents were wasted on mainly minor comedy musicals. By the time she reached the big league of MGM's glossy productions in the late 40s she was 30 and typically cast in comic or bitchy second leads, most memorably in *On the Town* (1949), in which she stole the show with a frenzied cave-woman dance, and *Kiss Me Kate* (1953), in which she appeared in peak form in the role of Bianca. After her film career ended in the mid-50s, she appeared in nightclubs and occasional stage and TV productions. In 1969–70 she inherited the lead role in the musical 'Mame' from Angela Lansbury, and she has toured extensively alongside Mickey ROONEY in the show 'Sugar Babies.' All of her three marriages ended in divorce. Autobiography: *Miller's High Life* (1972).

FILMS: *The Devil on Horseback* 1936; *New Faces of 1937, Stage Door, The Life of the Party* 1937; *Radio City Revels, Having Wonderful Time, You Can't Take It with You, Room Service, Tarnished Angel* 1938; *Too Many Girls, Hit Parade of 1941, Melody Ranch* 1940; *Time Out for Rhythm, Go West Young Lady* 1941; *True to the Army, Priorities on Parade* 1942; *Reveille with Beverly, What's Buzzin' Cousin?* 1943; *Jam Session, Hey Rookie, Carolina Blues* 1944; *Eve Knew Her Apples, Eadie Was a Lady* 1945; *The Thrill of Brazil* 1946; *The Kissing Bandit, Easter Parade* 1948; *On the Town* 1949; *Watch the Birdie* 1950; *Texas Carnival, Two Tickets to Broadway* 1951; *Lovely to Look At* 1952; *Small Town Girl, Kiss Me Kate* (as Bianca) 1953; *Deep in My Heart* 1954; *Hit the Deck* 1955; *The Opposite Sex, The Great American Pastime* 1956; *Won Ton Ton—The Dog Who Saved Hollywood* (cameo) 1976; *That's Entertainment! III* 1994.

Miller, Arthur. Playwright, novelist, essayist. Born on Oct. 17, 1915, in New York City. *ed.* U. of Michigan. One of America's leading dramatists, the Pulitzer Prize–winning author of 'Death of a Salesman' and other successful Broadway plays that have been adapted by others to the screen ('All My Sons,' 'The Crucible,' 'A View from the Bridge'), also wrote the original screenplay for the film *The Misfits* (1961), which starred his second wife (1956–61), Marilyn MONROE. His play 'After the Fall,' which launched the first season of New York's Repertory Theater in 1964, dealt intimately with some of the agonizing aspects of that failed marriage between America's sex symbol and one of its leading intellectuals. In 1978, Miller's adaptation of Henrik Ibsen's play 'An Enemy of the People,' was filmed. He was the subject of Harry Rashy's documentary *Arthur Miller: On Home Ground* (Can., 1979). He returned to screenwriting some 30 years after *The Misfits* with an original script for the Anglo-American co-production *Everybody Wins* (1990). Miller's own adaptation of his play 'The Crucible' made it to the big screen in 1996. His daughter (by his post-Marilyn marriage to photographer Inge Morath) is TV and film actress (*Regarding Henry,* etc.) Rebecca Miller (*b.* 1962, Roxbury, Conn.). Autobiography: *Timebends: A Life* (1987).

Miller, Arthur C. Director of photography. *b.* July 8, 1895, Roslyn, L.I., N.Y. *d.* 1970. One of Hollywood's most accomplished lighting cameramen, an outstanding master of black-and-white cinematography. At 13 he played bit parts in Westerns and doubled as camera assistant. He later became assistant cameraman and laboratory technician for Edwin S. Porter and operating cameraman for Louis Gasnier, for whom he photographed the serial *The Perils of Pauline* (1914). A director of photography from 1918, he worked almost exclusively for eight years with George FITZMAURICE, but his reputation owes most to his work for various 20th Century-Fox directors in the 40s. He won Academy Awards for *How Green Was My Valley* (1941), *The Song of Bernadette* (1943), and *Anna and the King of Siam* (1946). He retired from active work in 1951 after contracting tuberculosis, but soon after became president of A.S.C.

FILMS INCLUDE: *At Bay* 1915; *New York, Arms and the Woman* 1916; *Recoil, The Mark of Cain* 1917; *The Naulahka, A Japanese Nightingale* 1918; *Counterfeit, Common Clay, Avalanche* 1919; *Idols of Clay* 1920; *Experience, Forever/Peter Ibbetson* 1921; *Kick In, Three Live Ghosts, To Have and to Hold* 1922; *Bella Donna, The Cheat, The Eternal City* 1923; *Cytherea, Tarnish* 1924; *A Thief in Paradise, His Supreme Moment* 1925; *For Alimony Only, The Volga Boatman* 1926; *The Angel of Broadway, Vanity* 1927; *The Blue Danube, The Spieler* 1928; *Big News, Strange Cargo* 1929; *The Lady of Scandal* (co-phot.), *the Truth About Youth* 1930; *Bad Company* 1931; *Me and My Gal, Okay America!* 1932; *Sailor's Luck* 1933; *Ever Since Eve, The White Parade* 1934; *The Little Colonel, Black Sheep* 1935; *White Fang, Pigskin Parade, Stowaway* 1936; *Wee Willie Winkie, Heidi* 1937; *The Baroness and the Butler, Rebecca of Sunnybrook Farm, Little Miss Broadway, Submarine Patrol* 1938; *The Little Princess* (co-phot.), *Susannah of the Mounties, The Rains Came* 1939; *The Blue Bird, Johnny Apollo, The Mark of Zorro, Brigham Young* 1940; *Tobacco Road, Man Hunt, How Green Was My Valley* 1941; *This Above All, Iceland* 1942; *The Moon Is Down, The Ox-Bow Incident, The Song of Bernadette* 1943; *The Purple Heart, The Keys of the Kingdom* 1944; *A Royal Scandal* 1945; *Dragonwyck, Anna and the King of Siam, The Razor's Edge* 1946; *Gentleman's Agreement* 1947; *The Walls of Jericho* 1948; *A Letter to Three Wives* 1949; *Whirlpool, The Gunfighter* 1950; *The Prowler* 1951.

Miller, Barry. Actor. Born on Feb. 6, 1958, in Los Angeles. Leading man and supporting player of the American stage, TV, and films, often in ethnic characterizations. On screen from the mid-70s, he first gained notice in the role of Bobby C., John Travolta's friend who jumps to his death off the Verrazano-Narrows Bridge in *Saturday Night Fever* (1977). On the

Broadway stage from 1980 he won a Tony and Drama Desk Awards for his performance in Neil Simon's 'Biloxi Blues' (1985).

FILMS: *Lepke* 1975; *Saturday Night Fever* 1977; *Voices* 1979; *Fame* 1980; *The Chosen* 1981; *The Journey of Natty Gann* 1985; *Peggy Sue Got Married* 1986; *The Last Temptation of Christ* 1988; *Love at Large* 1990; *The Pickle* 1993; *Love Affair* 1994.

Miller, Claude. Director. Born in 1942, in France. A graduate of IDHEC, he was employed in French films from 1965 to 1974 as an assistant director and production supervisor, especially for François TRUFFAUT. He directed three shorts during that period of apprenticeship and in 1976 made an impressive debut as a feature director with *La Meilleure Façon de marcher/The Best Way/The Best Way to Walk,* a sensitively observed story of adolescent sexuality. He again dealt perceptively with troubled adolescence in *L'Effrontée/An Impudent Girl* (1985) and *La Petite Voleuse/The Little Thief* (1988). The latter film was a Truffaut project that Miller took over following the director's sudden death in 1984 and patterned (with wife Annie Miller and frequent script collaborator Luc Béraud) after Truffaut's original treatment, thus acknowledging his former master as the spiritual source of his own thematic heritage.

FILMS: Shorts-*Juliette dans Paris* (1967); *La Question ordinaire* (1969); *Camille et la Comédie catastrophique* (1971). Features—*La Meilleure Façon de marcher/The Best Way/The Best Way to Walk* (also co-sc.) 1976; *Dites-lui que je l'aime/Tell Him I Love Him* (also co-sc.) 1977; *Garde à Vue/The Inquisitor/Under Suspicion* (also co-sc.) 1981; *Mortelle randonnée/Deadly Circuit* 1983; *L'Effrontée/An Impudent Girl* (also co-sc.) 1985; *La Petite Voleuse/The Little Thief* (also co-sc.) 1988.

Miller, Colleen. Actress. Born on Nov. 10, 1932, in Yakima, Wash. Leading lady of mainly minor Hollywood films of the 50s.

FILMS INCLUDE: *The Las Vegas Story* 1952; *Man Crazy* 1953; *Playgirl, Four Guns to the Border* 1954; *The Purple Mask* 1955; *The Rawhide Years* 1956; *The Night Runner, Hot Summer Night* 1957; *Man in the Shadow, Step Down to Terror* 1958; *Gunfight at Comanche Creek* 1963.

Miller, David. Director. *b.* Nov. 28, 1909, in Paterson, N.J. *d.* 1992. He began in 1930 as an editor and later a short-subject director. A feature director since the early 40s, he was a highly competent technician, but with several notable exceptions (*Sudden Fear, Midnight Lace, Lonely Are the Brave*), his films often lacked originality or personal imprint.

FEATURE FILMS: *Billy the Kid* 1941; *Sunday Punch, Flying Tigers* 1942; *Top o' the Morning* 1949; *Love Happy, Our Very Own* 1950; *Saturday's Heroes* 1951; *Sudden Fear* 1952; *The Beautiful Stranger/Twist of Fate* (also story; UK) 1954; *Diane, The Opposite Sex* 1956; *The Story of Esther Costello* 1957; *Happy Anniversary* 1959; *Midnight Lace* 1960; *Back Street* 1961; *Lonely Are the Brave* 1962; *Captain Newman M.D.* 1964; *Hammerhead* (UK) 1968; *Hail Hero!* 1969; *Executive Action* 1973; *Bittersweet Love* 1976.

Miller, Dick (Richard). Actor. Born on Dec. 25, 1928, in New York City. *ed.* CCNY; Columbia; NYU Theater School of Dramatic Arts. Husky, tough-looking supporting player and occasional lead of numerous low-grade Hollywood films. Following underage WW II service, during which he became the Navy's boxing champion, he tried a wide variety of occupations, ranging from semipro football player and commercial artist to radio disc jockey and psychologist at Bellevue and at Queens General Hospital. In 1950 he co-hosted 'Midnight Snack' on CBS's—possibly TV's—first live talk show. He then began performing on the stage, making his screen debut in 1955. He became a fixture in Roger CORMAN films and attracted a cult following after playing the lead character, Walter Paisley, in the director's *A Bucket of Blood* (1959), a role he would reprise in several subsequent cheap horror movies.

FILMS INCLUDE: *Apache Woman* 1955; *It Conquered the World* 1956; *Naked Paradise/Thunder Over Hawaii, Not of This Earth, Carnival Rock, Rock All Night, Sorority Girl, The Undead* 1957; *War of the Satellites* 1958; *A Bucket of Blood* 1959; *The Little Shop of Horrors* 1960; *The Intruder/I Hate Your Guts!* 1961; *The Premature Burial* 1962; *The Terror, X—The Man with the X-Ray Eyes* 1963; *Ski Party* 1965; *A Time for Killing/The Long Ride Home, The Trip, The St. Valentine's Day Massacre, The Dirty Dozen* 1967; *The Wild Racers* 1968; *Which Way to the Front?* (also co-story) 1970; *Executive Action, Student Nurses* 1973; *Candy Stripe Nurses, Big Bad Mama, Truck Turner* 1974; *TNT Jackson* (also co-sc.), *Crazy Mama, White Line Fever, Summer School Teachers, Downtown Strutters* 1975; *Cannonball, Hollywood Boulevard, Moving Violations* 1976; *Mr. Billion, New York New York* 1977; *I Wanna Hold Your Hand, Piranha* 1978; *The Lady in Red, 1941, Rock 'n' Roll High School* 1979; *Used Cars* 1980; *Heartbeeps, The Howling* 1981; *White Dog* 1982; *Get Crazy, Twilight Zone—The Movie, Heart Like a Wheel* 1983; *Gremlins, The Terminator* 1984; *Explorers, After Hours* 1985; *Chopping Mall/Killboots* 1986; *Project X, Innerspace* 1987; *The 'Burbs, Far from Home* 1989; *Gremlins 2: The New Batch* 1990; *Unlawful Entry* 1992; *Matinee* 1993; *Pulp Fiction* 1994; *Tales from the Crypt Presents Demon Knight* 1995.

Miller, (Dr.) George. Director. Born on Mar. 3, 1945, in Chinchilla, near Brisbane, Australia. After graduating in 1970 from the University of New South Wales as a medical doctor, he practiced medicine for a year and a half in a major Sydney hospital. But his life-long passion for the cinema soon interrupted his professional career. While attending a film course offered by the Australian Union of Students at Melbourne University in 1971, he met Byron Kennedy, who became his friend, creative partner, and producer in a joint venture that would eventually become enormously successful. Using Miller's St. Vincent Hospital as a shooting location, they filmed *Violence in the Cinema, Part 1* (1972), a humorous polemical short. They turned out a documentary, *Devil in an Evening Dress* (1973), then became increasingly obsessed with a story idea they developed together about a desolate, violently anarchic futuristic society. They squandered all their savings and raised money wherever they could to come up with a small budget for the production of *Mad Max* (1979). Boasting electrifying action and outstanding cinematic effects, the film became a huge box-office hit on its release in 1979, established Miller as an intuitive, superior technical craftsman, and catapulted American-born Australian actor Mel GIBSON to stardom. A sequel, *Mad Max 2/The Road Warrior* (1981) enjoyed even greater international success, giving Australian cinema a tremendous lift. The Miller-Kennedy partnership ended tragically in 1983 when the producer was killed in a helicopter crash. Miller went on to direct in the US the final episode of *Twiight Zone—The Movie* (1983) and the entertaining sensual fantasy, *The Witches of Eastwick* (1987). He then became involved in several films as a producer. He is not to be confused with another successful Australian director of the same name (see MILLER, George below).

FEATURE FILMS: *Mad Max* (also co-sc.) 1979; *Mad Max 2/The Road Warrior* (also co-sc.) 1981; *Twilight Zone—The Movie* ("Nightmare at 2000 Feet" episode; US) 1983; *Mad Max Beyond Thunderdome* (also co-sc.) 1985; *The Witches of*

Eastwick (US), *The Year My Voice Broke* (co-prod. only) 1987; *Dead Calm* (co-prod. only) 1989; *Flirting* (co-prod. only) 1990; *Lorenzo's Oil* (also co-sc., co-prod.), *Over the Hill* 1992; *Babe* (also co-prod., co-sc.) 1995.

Miller, George. Director. Born George Trumbull Miller, in 1943 in Scotland. He began his working career in 1966 as a production apprentice in Australian television. Progressing through the ranks, he became an assistant cameraman and by 1974 an established director of national TV series. Miller started his association with feature films in 1977 as a still photographer. After serving as an assistant director on Ebsen Storm's *In Search of Anna* (1979) and as a second-unit director and co-associate producer on Ian Barry's *The Chain Reaction* (1980), he made a spectacular debut as a feature director with *The Man from Snowy River* (1982), a sprawling saga, inspired by an epic poem, of the Australian equivalent of the American West. A huge critical and commercial hit at home and abroad, it was described by Miller as his "love letter" to his adoptive land. Hollywood beckoned but after a single, unexciting film, *The Aviator* (1985), Miller returned to Australia, exporting his talent once more in 1990, this time to Germany. Not to be confused with another Australian George MILLER (see above), the director of *Mad Max*.

FEATURE FILMS: *The Man from Snowy River* 1982; *The Aviator* (US) 1985; *Cool Change* 1986; *Les Patterson Saves the World* 1987; *The Neverending Story II: The Next Chapter* (Ger.) 1990; *Frozen Assets* 1992; *Andre* 1994; *Zeus and Roxanne* 1997.

Miller, Jason. Playwright, actor. Born on Apr. 22, 1939, in Long Island City, N.Y. *ed.* Catholic U.; U. of Scranton. He entered a regional playwriting contest while still attending high school and eventually achieved great success as a dramatist with 'That Championship Season,' winner of the Pulitzer Prize, a Tony Award, and the New York Drama Critics Award as best play of 1972. Ten years later he directed his own screen adaptation of the play. Along with his writing, Miller also pursued an acting career, on the stage, in TV, and in films. His son is actor Jason PATRIC.

FILMS INCLUDE (as actor): *The Exorcist* 1973; *The Nickel Ride* 1974; *The Ninth Configuration/Twinkle Twinkle Killer Kane* 1980; *That Championship Season* (dir., sc. only), *Monsignor* 1982; *Toy Soldiers* 1984; *The Exorcist III* 1990; *Rudy* 1993.

Miller, Marilyn. Dancer-singer, actress. *b.* Marilyn Renolds, Sept. 1, 1898, Evansville, Ind. *d.* 1936. Celebrated star of Broadway musicals of the 20s. On stage from age five, she starred in only three early sound films. She was portrayed by June Haver in the film biography *Look for the Silver Lining* (1949) and earlier by Judy Garland in *Till The Clouds Roll By* (1946). Miss Miller was a former (1922–27) wife of actor Jack PICKFORD, her second of three husbands. She died of poisoning at 37.

FILMS: *Sally, Sunny* 1930; *Her Majesty Love* 1931.

Miller, Max. Actor. *b.* Thomas Sargent, 1895, London. *d.* 1963. A popular British music hall comedian, he was nicknamed "The Cheeky Chappie." In show business from age eight, he starred in some films of the 30s and played cameos in others.

FILMS INCLUDE: *The Good Companions, Channel Crossing, Friday the 13th* 1933; *Princess Charming* 1934; *Things Are Looking Up* 1935; *Don't Get Me Wrong* 1937; *Everything Happens to Me* 1938; *The Good Old Days* 1939; *Asking for Trouble* 1943.

Miller, Patsy Ruth. Actress. Born Patricia Ruth Miller, on June 22, 1905, in St. Louis, Mo. Convent-educated. A leading lady of Hollywood silents and early talkies, she entered films at 16, supporting Valentino and Nazimova in the 1921 version of *Camille.* She later played competent leads in many silent films, most memorably as Esmeralda to Lon Chaney's *Hunchback of Notre Dame* (1923) but never became a top-flight star. She appeared in some minor early talkies but did not survive the advent of sound and retired in 1931. She then turned to writing radio scripts and short stories, and is also the author of a novel, *The Flanagan Girl* (1939), and the book for a Broadway musical about Tchaikovsky, 'Music in My Heart.' Married and divorced director Tay GARNETT, then, screenwriter John Lee MAHIN.

FILMS INCLUDE: *Camille, The Sheik* 1921; *Omar the Tentmaker, Remembrance, Fortune's Mask* 1922; *The Girl I Loved, The Hunchback of Notre Dame, The Drivin' Fool* 1923; *My Man, The Yankee Consul, Daughters of Today, Fools in the Dark, The Breath of Scandal* 1924; *Red Hot Tires, Rose of the World, Hogan's Alley, Lorraine of the Lions* 1925; *Oh What a Nurse!, Hell-Bent for Heaven, Why Girls Go Back Home, So This Is Paris, Private Izzy Murphy, Broken Hearts of Hollywood, King of the Turf* 1926; *Wolf's Clothing, The First Auto, Painting the Town, Shanghaied, What Every Girl Should Know* 1927; *We Americans, Hot Heels, Marriage by Contract, Tragedy of Youth, Beautiful but Dumb* 1928; *The Fall of Eve, Twin Beds, The Hottentot, The Sap, So Long Letty* 1929; *The Aviator, Wide Open, Last of the Lone Wolf* 1930; *Lonely Wives, Night Beat* 1931; *Quebec* 1951.

Miller, Penelope Ann. Actress. Born on Jan. 13, 1964, in Santa Monica, Calif. Pleasant, empathetic leading lady of American films and TV. The daughter of actor-filmmaker Mark Miller and journalist Bea Miller, she dropped out of Menlo College after one year and moved to Manhattan, where she waited tables while training with Herbert Berghof. After several commercials and appearances in daytime soaps, she landed the ingenue part of Daisy in the Broadway production of 'Biloxi Blues,' a role she would later reprise in the play's 1988 screen version. She has since co-starred with several of Hollywood's leading actors—Robert DeNiro, Al Pacino, Arnold Schwarzenegger—but has not seen success with a star vehicle of her own.

FILMS: *Adventures in Babysitting* 1987; *Biloxi Blues, Big Top Pee-Wee, Miles from Home* 1988; *Dead-Bang* 1989; *The Freshman, Downtown, Awakenings, Kindergarten Cop* 1990; *Other People's Money* 1991; *Year of the Comet, The Gun in Betty Lou's Handbag, Chaplin* 1992; *Carlito's Way* 1993; *The Shadow* 1994; *The Relic* 1997.

Miller, Rebecca. See MILLER, Arthur.

Miller, Robert Ellis. American director. Born on July 13, 1932, in New York City. A stage actor from boyhood, he directed and produced for Broadway and TV before switching to feature films in the late 60s. His output has been respectable but unspectacular.

FILMS: *Any Wednesday* 1966; *Sweet November, The Heart Is a Lonely Hunter* 1968; *The Buttercup Chain* (UK) 1970; *The Girl from Petrovka* 1974; *The Baltimore Bullet* 1980; *Reuben Reuben* 1983; *Hawks* (UK) 1988; *Bed and Breakfast, Brenda Starr, Triangle* 1992.

Miller, Ron. Producer. Born Ronald W. Miller, on Apr. 17, 1933, in Los Angeles. *ed.* USC. A former football player with the Los Angeles Rams, he joined Walt Disney in 1957 as second assistant director and before long became associate producer of the company's TV fare. During the 60s and 70s he produced or co-produced many of the Disney feature films. He was named Disney's president and chief executive officer in 1980 but resigned in 1984.

FILMS INCLUDE: *Bon Voyage* 1962; *Son of Flubber* 1963; *The Lively Set* 1964; *That Darn Cat* 1965; *Monkeys Go*

Home! 1967; *The Boatniks* 1970; *The Wild Country* 1971; *Freaky Friday* 1976; *Herbie Goes to Monte Carlo, Pete's Dragon, Candleshoe* 1967; *The Cat from Outer Space, Return from Witch Mountain* 1978; *The Black Hole* 1979; *The Watcher in the Woods, The Last Flight of Noah's Ark, Herbie Goes Bananas* 1980; *Condorman* (exec. prod.) 1981; *Tex* (exec. prod.), *Iron* (exec. prod.) 1982; *Never Cry Wolf* (exec. prod.) 1983.

Miller, Seton I. Screenwriter, producer. *b.* May 3, 1902, Chahalis, Wash. *d.* 1974. *ed.* Yale. He went to Hollywood in 1926 as a technical advisor and actor in MGM's *Brown of Harvard* and remained as a screenwriter for Fox, Warners, Paramount, and other studios. In the late 20s and early 30s he contributed solid scripts, alone or in collaboration, to Howard Hawks films. He worked with a variety of directors, including Keighley, Curtiz, King, and Fritz Lang. He shared an Academy Award with Sidney Buchman for the script of Alexander Hall's comedy-fantasy *Here Comes Mr. Jordan* (1941). In the 40s he produced a number of films, including Lang's *The Ministry of Fear* (1944).

FILMS INCLUDE: *Paid to Love* 1927; *A Girl in Every Port, Fazil, The Air Circus* 1928; *The Dawn Patrol* 1930; *The Criminal Code* 1931; *Scarface, The Crowd Roars, If I Had a Million* 1932; *The Eagle and the Hawk* (co-adapt. only) 1933; *It Happened in New York, G-Men* 1935; *Bullets or Ballots* 1936; *Kid Galahad* 1937; *The Adventures of Robin Hood, Penitentiary, Valley of the Giants, Dawn Patrol* 1938; *Castle on the Hudson, The Sea Hawk* 1939; *Hear Comes Mr. Jordan* 1941; *The Black Swan, My Gal Sal* 1942; *The Ministry of Fear* (also prod.) 1944; *Two Years Before the Mast* (also co-prod.) 1946; *California* (prod. only), *Calcutta* (also prod.), *Singapore* 1947; *Fighter Squadron* (also prod.) 1948; *Convicted* 1950; *The Mississippi Gambler* 1953; *The Shanghai Story* 1954; *Istanbul* 1957; *The Last Mile* 1959; *Confessions of an Opium Eater* (uncredited) 1962; *Pete's Dragon* (co-story only) 1977.

Miller, Winston. Screenwriter. Born on June 22, 1910, in St. Louis. *ed.* Princeton. He wrote scripts, alone and in collaboration, for numerous Hollywood films of the 40s and 50s, mainly crime melodramas and Westerns, notably John Ford's *My Darling Clementine* (1946).

FILMS INCLUDE: *Gone With the Wind* (co-sc., uncredited) 1939; *Carolina Moon* 1940; *Man from Cheyenne* 1942; *Good Morning, Judge* 1943; *Home in Indiana* 1944; *My Darling Clementine, They Made Me a Killer* 1946; *Danger Street* 1947; *Fury at Furnace Creek, Station West, Relentless* 1948; *Rocky Mountain, Tripoli* 1950; *Hong Kong, The Last Outpost* 1951; *Carson City* 1952; *The Vanquished* 1953; *The Bounty Hunter, The Boy from Oklahoma* 1954; *The Far Horizons, Lucy Gallant, Run for Cover* 1955; *April Love* 1957; *Mardi Gras* 1958; *Hound-Dog Man* 1959.

Millican, James. Actor, *b.* 1910, Palisades, N.Y. *d.* 1955. *ed.* USC. Utility character actor, in numerous action films, either as a heavy or a tough good guy.

FILMS INCLUDE: *The Sign of the Cross* 1932; *Mills of the Gods* 1935; *The Remarkable Andrew* 1942; *So Proudly We Hail* 1943; *The Story of Dr. Wassell* 1944; *Tokyo Rose* 1945; *Hazard, The Man from Colorado, Command Decision* 1948; *The Dalton Gang, Fighting Man of the Plains* 1949; *Winchester 73, Mister 880* 1950; *Al Jennings of Oklahoma, 14 Hours, I Was a Communist for the FBI* 1951; *Springfield Rifle* 1952; *Bugles in the Afternoon, Jubilee Trail* 1954; *Strategic Air Command, Chief Crazy Horse, The Man from Laramie* 1955; *Red Sundown* 1956.

Milligan, Spike. Actor. Born Terence Alan Milligan, on Apr. 16, 1918, in Ahmaddnagar, India. Zany comedy star of the British stage, radio, TV, and films. The son of a British military man, he was raised in India, Burma, and Ceylon, arriving in England in 1933. He started his career three years later as a singer and trumpeter, later also playing the guitar. His big break came on radio in the 50s in a show called 'Crazy People,' which eventually became the legendary off-the-wall 'Goon Show.' He wrote much of his own comedy material for that show as well as for his many TV vehicles, which included 'Idiots Weekly,' 'A Show Called Fred,' 'Milligan's Wake,' and 'Curry and Chips.' In addition to his radio and TV scripts, he also co-wrote the play 'The Bed-Sitting Room,' wrote several comic novels, including 'Adolf Hilter—My Part in His Downfall,' and penned books of nonsense and verse. His screen career, which started in 1951, never matched his success on radio and TV.

FILMS INCLUDE: *Let's Go Crazy* 1951; *Down Among the Z-Men* 1952; *The Case of the Mukkinese Battlehorn* (short) 1956; *The Running, Jumping, and Standing Still Film* (short), *Watch Your Stern, Suspect* 1960; *Invasion Quartet* 1961; *Postman's Knock* 1962; *The Bed-Sitting Room* (also co-play basis) 1969; *The Magic Christian* 1970; *The Magnificent Seven Deadly Sins* 1971; *Rentadick, The Adventures of Barry McKenzie, Adolf Hitler—My Part in His Downfall* (also novel basis), *Alice's Adventures in Wonderland* 1972; *Digby the Biggest Dog in the World* 1973; *The Three Musketeers, The Great McGonagall* 1974; *Man About the House* 1976; *The Hound of the Baskeryvilles, The Last Remake of Beau Geste* 1977; *The Prisoner of Zenda* 1978; *Monty Python's Life of Brian* 1979; *History of the World, Part I* 1981; *Yellowbeard* 1983.

Mills, Hayley. Actress. Born on Apr. 18, 1946, in London. The daughter of John Mills and novelist-playwright Mary Hayley Bell, and the younger sister of Juliet Mills, she made an auspicious screen debut at 13, portraying a frightened little witness in one of her father's vehicles, *Tiger Bay* (1959). She won critical kudos and an acting award at the Berlin Film Festival for her effort and was signed by Walt Disney to a five-year contract. She immediately emerged as a captivating child star and won a special Oscar for her performance in *Pollyanna* (1960). She went on to play sweetly innocent children and adolescents in several other Disney productions before suddenly shattering her Pollyanna screen image with a nude scene in the British comedy *The Family Way* (1967) and with a well-publicized love affair with producer-director Roy Boulting, 33 years her senior. They were married in 1971 and, after having a son, divorced in 1976. She has another son by actor Leigh Lawson.

FILMS INCLUDE: *Tiger Bay* 1959; *Pollyanna* 1960; *The Parent Trap, Whistle Down the Wind, In Search of The Castaways* 1962; *Summer Magic, The Chalk Garden* 1963; *The Moon-Spinners, The Truth About Spring* 1964; *That Darn Cat, Sky West and Crooked/The Gypsy Girl* 1965; *The Daydreamer* (voice of Little Mermaid), *The Trouble with Angels* 1966; *The Family Way, Africa—Texas Style! Pretty Polly/A Matter of Innocence* 1967; *Twisted Nerve* 1968; *Take a Girl Like You* 1970; *Forbush and the Penguins/Cry of the Penguins* 1971; *Endless Night* 1972; *Deadly Strangers* 1974; *What Changed Charley Farthing?, The Diamond Hunters/The Kingfisher Caper* 1975; *Appointment with Death* 1988; *After Midnight* 1989; *A Troll in Central Park* 1994.

Mills, Sir John. Actor. Born Feb. 22, 1908, North Elmham, England. The son of a teacher, he worked as a clerk before making his professional debut as a song-and-dance chorus boy in a London revue in 1929. He moved on to the legitimate stage the following year and into films in 1932. Gradually landing more substantial roles, he developed into one of Britain's leading screen personalities during the WW II years, typically portraying stiff-upper-lip, low-key heroes. Although unprepossessing in stature, he remained a popular star through the early 50s, when he gradually switched into character parts. He won an Academy Award as best supporting actor for his portrayal of a village idiot in *Ryan's Daughter* (1970). Mills directed and produced one film, *Sky West and Crooked/Gypsy Girl* (1966). Divorced (1931–40) from actress Aileen Raymond, and married from 1941 to novelist-playwright Mary Hayley Bell, he is the father of actresses Hayley MILLS and Juliet MILLS. His son, Jonathan Mills (*b.* Dec. 3, 1949, London), became an assistant director. John Mills was knighted in 1977. Autobiography: *Up in the Clouds, Gentlemen Please* (1981).

FILMS: *The Midshipmaid* 1932; *Britannia of Billingsgate, The Ghost Camera* 1933; *River Wolves, A Political Party, Those Were the Days, The Lash, Blind Justice, Doctor's Orders* 1934; *Royal Cavalcade, Forever England/Born for Glory, Charing Cross Road* 1935; *First Offense, Tudor Rose/Nine Days a Queen* 1936; *OHMS/You're in the Army Now, The Green Cockatoo* 1937; *Goodbye Mr. Chips* (Peter Colley as a young man) 1939; *Old Bill and Son, Cottage to Let, The Black Sheep of Whitehall* 1941; *The Young Mr. Pitt, The Big Blockade, In Which We Serve* 1942; *We Dive at Dawn* 1943; *This Happy Breed, Waterloo Road* 1944; *The Way to the Stars/Johnny in the Clouds* 1945; *Great Expectations* (as Mr. Pip) 1946; *So Well Remembered, The October Man* 1947; *Scott of the Antarctic* (title role) 1948; *The History of Mr. Polly* (also prod.), *The Rocking Horse Winner* (also prod.) 1949; *Morning Departure/Operation Disaster* 1950; *Mr. Denning Drives North* 1951; *The Gentle Gunman, The Long Memory* 1952; *Hobson's Choice* 1954; *The Colditz Story, The End of the Affair, Above Us the Waves, Escapable* 1955; *War and Peace* (US/It.), *It's Great to Be Young, The Baby and the Battleship, Around the World in 80 Days* (cameo) 1956; *Town on Trial, Vicious Circle/The Circle* 1957; *Dunkirk, Ice Cold in Alex, I Was Monty's Double* 1958; *Tiger Bay* 1959; *Summer of the 17th Doll, Tunes of Glory, Swiss Family Robinson* (US/UK) 1960; *The Singer Not the Song* 1961; *Flame in the Streets, The Valiant, Tiara Tahiti* 1962; *The Chalk Garden* 1963; *The Truth About Spring* 1964; *Operation Crossbow, Sky West and Crooked/The Gypsy Girl* (dir., prod. only), *King Rat* (US) 1965; *The Wrong Box* 1966; *The Family Way, Africa—Texas Style!* (US/UK), *Chuka* (US) 1967; *Lady Hamilton—zwischen Smach und Liebe/Emma Hamilton/Lady Hamilton* (Ger./It./Fr.) 1968; *Oh! What a Lovely War, Run Wild Run Free, La Morte non ha Sesso/A Black Veil for Lisa* (It./Ger.) 1969; *Adam's Woman* (Austral.), *Ryan's Daughter* 1970; *Dulcima* 1971; *Young Winston* (as Gen. Kitchener), *Lady Caroline Lamb* 1972; *Oklahoma Crude* (US) 1973; *The Human Factor* 1975; *Trial by Combat/Dirty Knight's Work* 1976; *The Devil's Advocate* 1977; *The Big Sleep, The 39 Steps* 1978; *Zulu Dawn, Quatermass/The Quatermass Conclusion* 1979; *Gandhi* 1982; *Sahara* (US) 1984; *When the Wind Blows* (v/o) 1986; *Who's That Girl?* (US) 1987; *Hamlet* 1996; *Bean* 1997.

Mills, Juliet. Actress. born on Nov. 21, 1941, in London. The daughter of novelist-playwright Mary Hayley Bell and actor John MILLS, and sister of Hayley MILLS, she made her screen "debut" as an 11-week-old baby in *In Which We Serve* (1942), a film co-directed by her godfather, Noël COWARD. She appeared infrequently in films, at first as a child and later in romantic leads, and became best known for her work on the stage, mostly in London and occasionally on Broadway. Formerly married to American songwriter Russ Alquist, Jr., she spent much of her time in the US. She starred in the TV series 'Nanny and the Professor' (1970–71) and played leads in other American TV productions, including an Emmy-winning performance in the drama 'QB VII' (1975). She married heartthrob Maxwell Caulfield (*b.* Nov. 23, 1959, Glasgow).

FILMS: *In Which We Serve* 1942; *So Well Remembered, The October Man* 1947; *The History of Mr. Polly* 1949; *No My Darling Daughter!* 1961; *Twice Round the Daffodils* 1962; *Nurse on Wheels* 1963; *Carry On Jack/Carry on Venus* 1964; *The Rare Breed* (US) 1966; *Oh! What a Lovely War* 1969; *Les Galets d'Etrata* (Fr.), *Les Portes de Feu* (Fr.), *Avanti!* (US) 1972; *Riata, Jonathan Livingston Seagull* (v/o; US) 1973; *Chi sei?/Beyond the Door* 1975; *El Segundo Poder* (Sp.), *Barnaby and Me* (US) 1977.

Milner, Victor. Director of photography. *b.* Dec. 15, 1893, New York City. *d.* 1972. In films from age 15, first as a lab assistant, then projectionist, then newsreel cameraman, he became a cinematographer in 1913. He was behind the camera on scores of silent and sound films for various studios but spent most of his career with Paramount, where he worked on several notable Lubitsch early talkies, and later supplied glossy images for several sumptuous C. B. De Mille productions. He won an Academy Award for the cinematography of the 1934 *Cleopatra* and garnered seven more Oscar nominations. Early in his career he was also billed as Victor Miller.

FILMS INCLUDE: *Hiawatha* 1913; *The House of a Thousand Candles* 1915; *The Velvet Hand, The Cabaret Girl* 1918; *A Fugitive from Matrimony* 1919; *The White Dove, Haunting Shadows* 1920; *Live Wires* 1921; *Human Hearts* (co-phot.), *The Kentucky Derby* 1922; *The Love Letter* 1923; *Thy Name Is Woman, The Red Lily* 1924; *East of Suez, The Spaniard, The Wanderer* 1925; *Kid Boots, The Cat's Pajamas* 1926; *Children of Divorce, The Way of All Flesh* 1927; *The Street of Sin* (co-phot.), *Loves of an Actress, The Woman from Moscow, Sins of the Fathers* 1928; *The Wolf of Wall Street, The Marriage Playground, The Love Parade* 1929; *The Texan, Paramount on Parade* (co-phot.), *Monte Carlo* 1930; *Man of the World, Kick In, I Take This Woman* 1931; *Broken Lullaby/The Man I Killed, One Hour with You, Love Me Tonight, Trouble in Paradise* 1932; *Song of Songs, Design for Living* 1933; *All of Me, Cleopatra* 1934; *The Gilded Lily, So Red the Rose, The Crusades* 1935; *Give Us This Night, Till We Meet Again, The General Died at Dawn* 1936; *The Plainsman* (co-phot.), *High Wide and Handsome, Artists and Models* 1937; *The Buccaneer* 1938; *Union Pacific, The Great Victor Herbert* 1939; *Seventeen, North West Mounted Police* (co-phot.) 1940; *The Lady Eve, The Monster and the Girl* 1941; *Reap the Wild Wind* (co-phot.), *The Palm Beach Story* 1942; *Hostages* 1943; *The Story of Dr. Wassell* (co-phot.), *The Great Moment, The Princess and the Pirate* 1944; *Wonder Man* 1945; *The Strange Love of Martha Ivers* 1946; *You Were Meant for Me, Unfaithfully Yours* 1948; *The Furies* 1950; *September Affair, My Favorite Spy* 1951; *Carrie* 1952; *Jeopardy* 1953.

Milo, Sandra. Actress. Born Sandra Marini, in 1935, in Milan. Vivacious leading lady of Italian and French films of the 50s and 60s.

FILMS INCLUDE: *Lo Scapolo* 1955; *Eléna et les Hommes/Paris Does Strange Things* (Fr.), *Les Aventures d'Arsène Lupin* (Fr.) 1956; *Le Miroir a Deux Faces/The Mirror Has Two Faces* (Fr.) 1958; *La Jument verte/The Green Mare* (Fr.), *Il Generale della Rovere/General Della Rovere* 1959; *Classe tous Risques/The Big Risk* (Fr./It.), *Adua e la Campagne/Love à la Carte* 1960; *Fantasmi a Roma/Ghosts of Rome, Vanina Vanini* 1961; *Otto e Mezzo/8½* 1962; *Le Voci bianche/White Voices, La Visita/The Visit* 1963; *Un Monsieur de Compagnie/Male Companion* (Fr.) 1964; *Giulietta degli Spiriti/Juliet of the Spirits, L'Ombrellone/Weekend Italian Style* 1965; *Come imparai ad amare le Donne/How I Got and Loved the Women* 1967; *Bang Bang Kid* 1968.

Milton, Robert. Director. *b.* Robert Davidor, on Jan. 24,

1890, in Dinaburgh, Russia. Directed early Hollywood talkies, following extensive stage experience in New York as a playwright, director, producer, and actor, then returned to Broadway. He collaborated on the story and screenplay of *The Land of Hope* (1921).

FILMS: *The Dummy, Charming Sinners* 1929; *Behind the Makeup, Outward Bound, Sin Takes a Holiday* 1930; *Devotion, The Bargain, Husband's Holiday* 1931; *Westward Passage* 1932; *Bella Donna* (UK) 1934.

Mimieux, Yvette. Actress. Born on Jan. 8, 1942, in Los Angeles. Attractive, blonde leading lady of American films, stage, and TV. A versatile personality, she has dabbled in art, poetry, music, and the dance and presides over a broad range of business investments. She married director Stanley DONEN in 1972.

FILMS INCLUDE: *The Time Machine, Platinum High School/Trouble at 16, Where the Boys Are* 1960; *Light in the Piazza, The Four Horsemen of the Apocalypse, The Wonderful World of the Brothers Grimm, Diamond Head* 1962; *Toys in the Attic* 1963; *Joy in the Morning, The Reward* 1965; *The Caper of the Golden Bulls, Monkeys Go Home!* 1967; *Dark of the Sun, Three in the Attic* 1968; *The Delta Factor* 1970; *The Picasso Summer* 1971; *Sky-jacked* 1972; *The Neptune Factor* 1973; *Journey Into Fear* (UK) 1975; *Jackson County Jail* 1976; *The Black Hole* 1979; *Mystique/Circle of Power/Brainwash/The Naked Weekend* 1983.

Mineo, Sal. Actor. *b.* Salvatore Mineo, Jan. 10, 1939, the Bronx, N.Y. *d.* 1976, a homicide victim. Sad-eyed juvenile, then young lead of the US stage, films, and TV. Dismissed from a parochial school at eight as a troublemaker, he began attending a dancing class and two years later he was cast as a child in the Broadway production of 'The Rose Tattoo.' In 1952 he took over the part of Yul Brynner's son in 'The King and I.' He made his first film appearance in 1955 and subsequently appeared in many screen productions, typically portraying troubled youths. He was nominated twice for Oscars in the supporting capacity, for *Rebel Without a Cause* (1955) and *Exodus* (1960). He also appeared in several TV productions and directed a play, 'Fortune and Men's Eyes,' on the West Coast and on Broadway. He was stabbed to death as he returned to his Hollywood home from a rehearsal for another play.

FILMS: *Six Bridges to Cross, The Private War of Major Benson, Rebel Without a Cause* 1955; *Rock Pretty Baby, Crime in the Streets, Somebody Up There Likes Me, Giant* 1956; *Dino, The Young Don't Cry* 1957; *Tonka* 1958; *A Private's Affair, The Gene Krupa Story* (title role) 1959; *Exodus* 1960; *Escape from Zahrain, The Longest Day* 1962; *Cheyenne Autumn* 1964; *The Greatest Story Ever Told, Who Killed Teddy Bear?* 1965; *80 Steps to Jonah, Krakatoa East of Java* 1969; *Escape from the Planet of the Apes* 1971.

Miner, Steve. Director. Born Stephen C. Miner, on June 18, 1951, in Chicago. He entered films as a production assistant in 1970 and later operated his own editing service in New York through which he directed, produced, and edited industrial, educational, and sports films. He ventured into features as a producer in 1978 and as a director in 1981.

FILMS INCLUDE (as director): *Friday the 13th, Part 2* (also prod.) 1981; *Friday the 13th, Part 3* 1982; *House, Soul Man* 1986; *Warlock* (also prod.) 1989; *Wild Hearts Can't Be Broken* 1991; *My Father the Hero* 1994; *Big Bully* 1996.

Minghella, Anthony. Director, screenwriter, playwright. Born January 6, 1954, in Isle of Wight, England. *ed.* University of Hull. Recognized by the London Theatre Critics with the best play award for 'Made in Bangkok' (1986), this gifted wordsmith added to his skills the ability to write and direct for television and films. At one time aligned with the late producer-puppeteer Jim HENSON, Minghella's talent for helming more romantic fare became evident with his first feature *Truly, Madly, Deeply* (1991) and lead the way to his acclaimed, sweeping love story *The English Patient* (1996), which earned nine Academy Awards including best director and best adapted screenplay for Minghella's adaptation of Michael Ondaatje's novel.

FILMS: *Truly, Madly, Deeply* (dir., sc.; UK) 1991; *Mr. Wonderful* (dir., sc.) 1993; *The English Patient* (dir., sc.) 1996.

miniature. A greatly reduced model of an object or a scene too complex or too expensive to build or stage life size for the cameras. Thus, a great sea battle can be set up in a studio tank using miniature battleships, miniature buildings may be burned down or otherwise demolished at low cost, and miniature spaceships can be photographed in motion and matted against starry backdrops. The design, construction, and photography of miniatures require careful planning and execution to achieve the semblance of reality. This is especially true when the miniatures include people or creatures (see PUPPETS).

minibrute. A compact, high-intensity lighting unit designed chiefly to supplement daylight on outdoor locations. Housing a special 650-watt lamp, it is also used as a source of FILL LIGHT for color work in the studio.

minilite. A compact, high-intensity lighting unit equipped with four-leaf barn doors and a reflector. Accommodating a 650-watt lamp, it is used mainly for FILL LIGHTING.

minimount. A compact stabilized camera mount designed for shooting from moving helicopters, planes, cars, and boats.

Minnelli, Liza. Actress, singer. Born on Mar. 12, 1946, in Los Angeles. The daughter of Judy GARLAND and Vincente MINNELLI, she was practically born in a trunk. She was barely two and a half when she appeared in one of her mother's films, *In the Good Old Summertime*. At seven she danced on the stage of New York's Palace Theater while Judy sang 'Swanee.' She also learned about filmmaking firsthand from frequent visits on the sets where her father was directing. Her celebrated parents divorced when she was five, and she attended a score or so of different schools while living in various places with one parent or the other. At 16 she even attended the Sorbonne in Paris but dropped out after several months.

Liza began carving out a show business career on her own in New York, making a modest debut in the third lead in a 1963 off-Broadway revival of 'Best Foot Forward.' Two years later, at 19, she became Broadway's youngest best actress Tony Award winner, for her title part in 'Flora, the Red Menace.' In between, she sang and danced with her mother at the London Palladium. Recordings and TV appearances followed, as well as a tour of nightclubs which soon established her as one of the most electrifying cabaret performers in the nation. Her appearance, her mannerisms, the urgency of her delivery, the vibrato of her voice are reminiscent of her mother's style, but her personality has a magnetism all its own.

Since making her film debut in 1968, Liza has emerged as a capable actress and sometimes mercurial screen personality. She was nominated for an Oscar for *The Sterile Cuckoo* (1969) and won the best actress Academy Award for an electrifying performance in Bob Fosse's *Cabaret* (1972). In the same year she won an Emmy for her TV special 'Liza with a Z' and in the following year a Special Tony for her 'Liza at the Winter Garden' stage show. In 1978 she won another Tony, as best lead actress in a musical, for her part in 'The Act.' Although her screen career, with the exception of *Arthur* (1981), lay fallow in the 80s, Minnelli continued a frantic schedule on the stage and in TV, in nightclubs, and in recording studios. The pace, combined with the emotional strain of personal problems—including heartbreak romances with Peter SELLERS, Martin SCORSESE, and Desi Arnaz, Jr. and later a number of miscarriages—led to alcohol abuse and eventual treatment in 1984–86 at the Betty Ford Center. In 1987 she hosted a PBS documentary tribute to her father, 'Minnelli on Minnelli: Liza Remembers Vincente.' In 1988 she made a successful national tour with Frank SINATRA. In 1991 she triumphed in New York and on the road with 'Liza Minnelli: Stepping Out at Radio City.' She has been married and divorced three times: to the late gay Australian singer Peter Allen (1967–72), director Jack Hailey, Jr. (1974–79), and sculptor and stage producer Mark Gero (1979–1991).

FILMS: *In the Good Old Summertime* (bit as child) 1949; *Charlie Bubbles* (UK) 1967; *The Sterile Cuckoo* 1969; *Tell Me That You Love Me Junie Moon* 1970; *Cabaret* 1972; *Journey Back to Oz* (v/o), *That's Entertainment* (on-camera co-narr.) 1974; *Lucky Lady* 1975; *Silent Movie* (unbilled cameo), *A Matter of Time* (US/It.) 1976; *New York New York* 1977; *Arthur* 1981; *The King of Comedy* (cameo) 1983; *The Muppets Take Manhattan* (cameo) 1984; *That's Dancin'!* (co-narr.) 1985; *Rent-a-Cop, Arthur 2: On the Rocks* 1988; *Stepping Out* 1991.

Minnelli, Vincente. Director. *b.* Feb. 28, 1903, Chicago, into a family of touring entertainers. *d.* 1986. He began performing at the age of three with the Minnelli Brothers Dramatic Tent Show but "retired" five years later, when the show folded, to take up the normal life of a student. During his summer vacations he worked for a billboard painter and before long began showing a talent for drawing. He left school at 16, and after a stint as an apprentice at a photographic studio, he joined Chicago's Balaban and Katz motion picture theater chain as an assistant stage manager and costume designer for its live prefeature program. Shortly after, he transferred to New York's Paramount Theater as set and costume designer. In 1932 he created the décor and costumes for the operetta 'Du Barry' at the request of its star, Grace Moore, and the following year he was appointed art director of New York's Radio City Music Hall.

Turning director in 1935, he staged such successful Broadway musicals as 'At Home Abroad,' 'The Show Is On,' 'Ziegfeld Follies,' and 'Very Warm for May,' before being invited to Hollywood by MGM producer Arthur FREED in 1940. For two years he was given intensive training in film technique and was gradually eased into directing, first staging isolated musical numbers for Judy GARLAND in Busby BERKELEY'S *Strike Up the Band* (1940) and *Babes on Broadway* (1942). This apprenticeship, coupled with his stage experience and flair for design, combined to make Minnelli a highly successful film director right from the start. Within just several years he was firmly established as an outstanding director of film musicals of sweeping scope and lavish visual style, some of which have become classics of the genre. Two of these, *Meet Me in St. Louis* and *The Pirate,* as well as a drama, *The Clock,* starred Judy Garland, who became his first wife in 1945. The following year, their daughter, Liza MINNELLI, was born. They divorced in 1951.

Minnelli's musicals are noted for their judicious use of color and the successful integration of musical numbers with a film's narrative theme. They include some of the finest productions in the history of the genre, most notably *An American in Paris* (1951), winner of a best picture Academy Award, *The Band Wagon* (1953), and *Gigi* (1958), winner of both best picture and best director Oscars. But although Minnelli remains most closely identified with the screen musical, he worked extensively in other genres. In fact, most of his films were nonmusicals. He directed some fine comedies, like *Father of the Bride* (1950), and dramas like *The Bad and the Beautiful* (1952), as well as an exquisitely etched screen biography of Vincent van Gogh, *Lust for Life* (1956). Minnelli's reputation declined somewhat in the 60s, when the quality of his films was inconsistent, but he remains one of the dominant artists in the history of the American screen. He authored a book of memoirs: *I Remember It Well* (1974).

FILMS: *Cabin in the Sky, I Dood It* 1943; *Meet Me in St. Louis* 1944; *The Clock, Yolanda and the Thief* 1945; *Ziegfeld Follies, Undercurrent Till the Clouds Roll By* (three Judy Garland numbers only) 1946; *The Pirate* 1948; *Madame Bovary* 1949; *Father of the Bride* 1950; *Father's Little Dividend, An American in Paris* 1951; *The Bad and the Beautiful* 1952; *The Story of Three Loves* ("Mademoiselle" episode), *The Band Wagon* 1953; *The Long Long Trailer, Brigadoon* 1954; *The Cobweb, Kismet* 1955; *Lust for Life, Tea and Sympathy* 1956; *Designing Woman, The Seventh Sin* (co-dir. with Ronald Neame; uncredited) 1957; *Gigi, The Reluctant Debutante* 1958; *Some Came Running* 1959; *Home from the Hill, Bells Are Ringing* 1960; *The Four Horsemen of the Apocalypse, Two Weeks in Another Town* 1962; *The Courtship of Eddie's Father* 1963; *Goodbye Charlie* 1964; *The Sandpiper* 1965; *On a Clear Day You Can See Forever* 1970; *A Matter of Time* (US/It.) 1976.

Minter, Mary Miles. Actress. *b.* Juliet Reilly, Apr. 1, 1902, Shreveport, La. *d.* 1984. On stage from age six, she was billed as "Little Juliet Shelby" and within several years became one of the most popular child stars of the American theater, notably in 'The Littlest Rebel.' Driven by an ambitious mother, she reached films at age ten. Both as a child performer and later as a childlike romantic lead in the Mary Pickford tradition, she was one of Hollywood's leading stars. But her career suffered a fatal blow with the unsolved murder of her sometime director and reputed lover William Desmond TAYLOR in 1922. Although the mystery was never officially solved, amateur sleuths over the years speculated about the identity of the killer. The cast of suspects included Mabel Normand, who at the time was also having an affair with the director. Miss Minter unsuccessfully sued CBS and producer Rod Serling after the latter portrayed her as one of three suspects in the killing. In 1967 director King VIDOR, haunted by the events that affected the lives of people he had known during his early days in Hollywood, conducted his own thorough investigation of the murder as possible material for a future film project. He concluded that Taylor was murdered by Charlotte Shelby, Miss Minter's greedy and vicious stage mother. Not yet 20 when her career ended, the former star moved briefly to New York, then spent the remainder of her years in obscure but wealthy retirement in Santa Monica, living off successful real-estate investments. She made the local news in 1981 when she was found beaten, gagged, and left for dead on her kitchen floor following a robbery at her home. She died at 82 of heart failure following a stroke. At her request, her cremated ashes were scattered at sea.

FILMS INCLUDE: As Juliet Shelby—*The Nurse* 1912. As Mary Miles Minter—*The Fairy and the Waif, Always in the Way, Barbara Frietchie* 1915; *Dimples, Lovely Mary, Faith* 1916; *The Gentle Intruder, Her Country's Call* 1917; *Beauty and the Rogue, The Eyes of Julia Deep* 1918; *The Amazing Imposter, Anne of Green Gables* 1919; *Judy of Rogue's Harbor, Nurse Marjorie, Jenny Be Good, A Cumberland Romance* 1920; *All Souls' Eve, Moonlight and Honeysuckle* 1921; *Tillie, South of Suva, The Cowboy and the Lady* 1922; *Drums of Fate, The Trail of the Lonesome Pine* 1923.

Miou-Miou. Actress. Born Sylvette Herry, on Feb. 22, 1950, in Paris. Sensual leading lady of French films. As a child, she helped her greengrocer mother haul fruits and vegetables to the Les Halles market and as a teenager she worked as an apprentice in an upholstery shop. She entered show business in 1968, teaming up with COLUCHE and Patrick DEWAERE at the

Café de la Gare coffee-theater. In films from the early 70s, she first gained celebrity in Bertrand Blier's cult film *Les Valseuses/Going Places* (1974) and in the following years developed into a fine performer and one of the French screen's most arresting female personalities. Memorable in Diane Kurys's *Coup de Foudre/Entre Nous* (1983).

FILMS INCLUDE: *La Cavale* 1971; *Themroc* 1972; *Les Aventures de Rabbi Jacob/The Mad Adventures of Rabbi Jacob* 1973; *Les Valseuses/Going Places, La Grande Trouille/Tendre Dracula* 1974; *Pas de Problème, D'Amour et d'Eau fraîche* 1975; *Marcia Trionfale* (It./Fr.), *F comme Fairbanks, On aura tout vu, Jonas qui aura Vingt Cinq Ans en l'An 2000/Jonah Who Will Be 25 in the Year 2000* 1976; *Dites-lui que je l'aime/Tell Him I Love Him* 1977; *Les Routes du Sud* 1978; *Au revoir à Lundi/Bye—See You Monday, L'Ingorgo—una Storia impossibile/Traffic Jam/Bottleneck* (It./Fr./Sp./Ger.), *La Dérobade* 1979; *La Femme Flic* 1980; *La Guele du Loup* 1981; *Joséphа, Guy de Maupassant* 1982; *Coup de Foudre/Entre Nous, Attention—Une Femme peut en cacher une autre!/My Other Husband* 1983; *Canicule/Dog Day, Le Vol du Sphinx/The Flight of the Phoenix* 1984; *Blanche et Marie* 1985; *Tenue du Soirée/Ménage/Evening Dress* 1986; *La Lectrice/The Reader, Les Portes tournantes/Revolving Doors* 1988; *Milou en Mai/Milou in May/May Fools* 1989; *Germinal, Tango* 1993; *Montparnasse Pondichery* 1994.

Miramax Films. Independent distribution and production company. Founded in 1979 by New Yorkers Bob and Harvey Weinstein, it became one of the most successful INDEPENDENTS in the business, maintaining profitability when other "indies" of the 70s and 80s had folded. The company gained a reputation for spotting bankable art films, both foreign and American, and building large US audiences for them. From 1988 to 1991, films released by Miramax received foreign-language Oscars four times in a row (*Pelle the Conqueror, Cinema Paradiso, Journey of Hope*, and *Mediterraneo*). The company's 1989 release, *sex, lies, and videotape*, set a box-office record for specialty films, a record later broken by Miramax's *The Crying Game* (1992). In 1989, Miramax branched into producing films with a co-production, *Scandal*. Since then, Miramax has co-produced as well as distributed such films as *Enchanted April, Map of the Human Heart*, and *Into the West*. Other Miramax distribution successes include Errol Morris's documentary *The Thin Blue Line*, Alfonso Arau's *Like Water for Chocolate*, Jim Sheridan's *My Left Foot*, and Chen Kaige's *Farewell My Concubine*. In 1993, Miramax was acquired as an autonomous subsidiary by the Walt DISNEY COMPANY.

Miranda, Carmen. Singer, dancer, actress. *b.* Maria do Carmo Miranda da Cunha, Feb. 9, 1909, Marco de Canavezes, near Lisbon, Portugal. *d.* 1955. Dynamic, flamboyant, temperamental entertainer who enlivened Hollywood films of the 40s with her staccato singing and frantic dancing. As a child she moved with her parents to Rio de Janeiro, where her father ran a prosperous wholesale fruit business and where she was convent-educated. She began singing on local radio and before long became a popular recording star. She appeared in several Brazilian films before being imported to Broadway by the Shuberts in 1939. Following her success in the musical 'Streets of Paris' and a now-legendary engagement at the Waldorf-Astoria, she was signed by Fox on a film contract. Billed as the "Brazilian Bombshell," she added exotic spice to more than a dozen Hollywood musical films, typically performing in extravagant costumes and high headgear, usually adorned by an assortment of tropical fruit. She died suddenly of a heart attack, at 46, shortly after a demanding number on a segment of the Jimmy Durante TV show. Her body was flown to Brazil, where her death was cause for national mourning. The Carmen Miranda Museum in Rio is a popular tourist attraction, containing many of the entertainer's flamboyant dresses and headgear as well as odd memorabilia, including a key to the islands of Kauai and Hawaii, a written tribute from the Air Force Association, and a standard contract with the William Morris Agency.

FILMS: In Brazil—*A Voz do Carnaval* 1933; *Alo Alo Brasil, Estudantes* 1935; *Alo Alo Carnaval* 1936; *Banana da Terra* 1939. In the US—*Down Argentine Way* 1940; *That Night in Rio, Week-End in Havana* 1941; *Springtime in the Rockies* 1942; *The Gang's All Here* 1943; *Four Jills in a Jeep, Greenwich Village, Something for the Boys* 1944; *Doll Face, If I'm Lucky* 1946; *Copacabana* 1947; *A Date with Judy* 1948; *Nancy Goes to Rio* 1950; *Scared Stiff* 1953.

Miranda, Isa. Actress. *b.* Inèes Isabella Sampietro, July 5, 1909, Milan. *d.* 1982. Leading lady of international films. A former clerk and model, she trained for the stage at the Milan Academy and was appearing as an extra and bit player in Italian films when she was selected by Max OPHÜLS to play the lead in *La Signora di Tutti* (1934). She subsequently starred in many Italian, as well as some German, French, British, and American films, and received the best actress award at the Cannes Festival for her performance in *Au-delà des Grilles/The Walls of Malapaga* (1949). She also appeared in many stage and TV productions in Italy and elsewhere and was a respected poet, novelist, and painter. She was married to film producer Alfredo Guarini.

FILMS INCLUDE: *Tenebre* 1933; *La Signora di Tutti, Come le Foglie/Like the Leaves* 1934; *Du bist mein Glück* (Ger.), *Passaporto Rosso, Il Fu Mattia Pascal/L'Homme de nulle part/The Late Mathias Pascal/The Man from Nowhere* 1936; *Scipione l'Africano/Scipio Africanus, Una Donna fra Due Mondi/Between Two Worlds, Le Menzogne di Nina Petrovna/The Lie of Nina Petrovna* (Fr.) 1937; *Hotel Imperial* (US) 1939; *Adventure in Diamonds* (US) 1940; *Malombra* 1942; *Zazà* 1943; *Lo Sbaglio di essere Vivo/My Widow and I* 1945; *Au-delà des Grilles/Le Mura di Malapaga/The Walls of Malapaga* (Fr./It.) 1948; *La Ronde* (Fr.) 1950; *Les sept Péchés capitaux/The Seven Deadly Sins* (Fr./It.) 1952; *Siamo Donne/We the Women, Avant le Deluge* 1953; *Rasputin* 1954; *Summer Madness/Summertime* (UK/US) 1955; *Il Tesoro di Rommel* 1956; *Une Manche et la Belle/What Price Murder* (Fr.) 1957; *La Noia/The Empty Canvas* 1963; *The Yellow Rolls-Royce* (UK) 1964; *The Shoes of the Fisherman* (UK/It.) 1968; *Das Bildnis des Dorian Gray/Dorian Gray* (Ger./It./Liecht.), *Un'Estate con Sentimento* 1970; *Il Portiere di Notte/The Night Porter* (It./UK), *Le Faro da Padre/Bambina* 1974.

Mirisch, Walter. Producer, executive. Born on Nov. 8, 1921, in New York City. *ed.* CCNY; U. of Wisconsin, Harvard Graduate School of Business Administration. He started in films at 17 as a management trainee with a motion picture theater chain and worked his way up the administrative ladder during his college years. Following WW II service, he joined Monogram as producer of low-budget films and in 1951 he was appointed executive producer of the company's subsidiary Allied Artists. In 1957 he founded with his brother Marvin Mirisch (*b.* Mar. 19, 1918, NYC) and half brother Harold (*b.* May 4, 1907, NYC; *d.* 1968.) an independent production company, Mirisch Company, Inc., of which Walter became vice president in charge of production. (Harold was named president and Marvin vice president and director.) The company soon gained a reputation for its quality of production and for its policy of allowing creative freedom to independent producers and directors whose pictures it financed. *In the Heat of the Night* won the Academy Award as best picture of 1967. Walter became president of the Academy of Motion Picture Arts and Sciences in 1973, a post he held through 1977. He was presented with the Irving Thalberg Memorial Award during the Oscar ceremony of 1978. The Mirisch Corporation continued in business into the 90s, with Marvin as chairman and CEO and Walter as president.

FILMS INCLUDE: *Fall Guy* 1947; *Bomba the Jungle Boy* 1949; *Flight to Mars* 1951; *Hiawatha* 1952; *The Maze* (exec. prod.) 1953; *An Annapolis Story, The Warriors* 1955; *The Oklahoman* 1957; *Man of the West* 1958; *The Magnificent Seven* 1960; *West Side Story* (exec. prod.), *By Love Possessed* 1961; *Two for the Seesaw* 1962; *Toys in the Attic* 1963; *Hawaii* 1966; *In the Heat of the Night, Fitzwilly* 1967; *Some Kind of a Nut* 1969; *The Hawaiians* 1970; *The Organization* 1971; *Scorpio* 1973; *The Spikes Gang, Mr. Majestyk* 1974; *Midway* 1976; *Gray Lady Down, Same Time Next Year* 1978; *The Prisoner of Zenda, Dracula* 1979; *Romantic Comedy* 1983.

Miró, Pilar. Director. Born in 1940, in Madrid. She studied law and journalism at the University of Madrid before enrolling in Spain's Official School of Cinematography as a scriptwriting major. She began her career in 1960 as a program assistant in Spanish television. In 1963, at the age of 23, she became Spain's first woman TV director. Making her feature debut in 1976 with the controversial feminist drama, *La Petición,* she soon attained an international reputation for the quality and originality of her work. Her second film, the fact-based political outcry, *El Crimen de Cuenca,* was hailed at the Berlin Festival but was banned at home and its director brought to military trial. Her third, *Gary Cooper Who Art in Heaven,* was an obviously autobiographical film about a young TV director frustrated by her encounters with male machismo. Miró took leave of filmmaking from 1983 to 1985, when she served as director of the Film Division of Spain's Ministry of Culture. After directing one more film in 1986, she was appointed general director of Spanish TV (RTVE), but later resigned, protesting the industry's attitude toward women.

FILMS: *La Petición/The Demand/The Engagement Party* 1976; *El Crimen de Cuenca/The Cuenca Crime* 1979; *Gary Cooper que estas en los Cielos/Gary Cooper Who Art in Heaven* 1980; *Hablamos esta Noche/Let's Talk Tonight* 1982; *Werther* 1986.

Mirren, Helen. Actress. Born Ilyena Mirnoff, on July 26, 1945, in Leigh-on-Sea, Essex, England. Intelligently expressive leading lady of British (and American) stage and screen. The granddaughter of a White Russian émigré nobleman and daughter of a driving-license tester, she attended a teacher's college to please her family but pursued her real love, acting, during weekends and vacations at the National Youth Theatre. Rave reviews for her portrayal of Cleopatra in 'Antony and Cleopatra' at the Old Vic in 1965 led to her joining the Royal Shakespeare Company in 1967, the year she also made her film debut. While continuing to impress theatergoers in London and New York with her energy and talent, she exhibited her considerable physical attributes in some of her early screen appearances, specializing in erotic, raunchy roles, in such films as *Savage Messiah* and *Caligula.* But in the 80s her screen repertoire greatly improved and included several memorable performances. She gained greater recognition for her television role in 'Prime Suspect' in the 90s.

FILMS: *Herostratus* 1967; *A Midsummer Night's Dream* 1968; *Age of Consent* (Austral.) 1969; *Savage Messiah* 1972; *O Lucky Man!* 1973; *Hamlet* 1976; *SOS Titanic, Caligula* (It./US) 1979; *Hussy, The Long Good Friday, The Fiendish Plot of Dr. Fu Manchu* (US) 1980; *Excalibur* (as Morgana; Ire./US) 1981; *Cal, 2010* (US) 1984; *White Nights* (US) 1985; *Heavenly Pursuits/The Gospel According to Vic, The Mosquito Coast* (US) 1986; *Pascali's Island* 1988; *When the Whales Came, The Cook the Thief His Wife and Her Lover* 1989; *Bethune: The Making of a Hero* (Can./China/Fr.), *The Comfort of Strangers* (It./US) 1990; *Where Angels Fear to Tread* 1991; *The Madness of King George* 1994; *Losing Chase, Some Mother's Son* 1996.

mirror shutter. A camera shutter with reflecting mirrors enabling a cameraman to view the identical image he is filming, thus freeing him from adjustments for PARALLAX.

mise-en-scène. French term—literally, the placing of a scene—for the act of staging or directing a play or a film. Derived from the terminology of the theater, the term has acquired in recent years an additional meaning in its application to the cinema. André BAZIN, and subsequently other theoreticians and critics, have used it to describe a style of film directing basically distinct from that known as MONTAGE. Whereas montage derives its meaning from the relationship between one frame to the next through editing, *mise-en-scène* emphasizes the content of the individual frame. Its proponents see montage as disruptive to the psychological unity of man with his environment and cite such films as Orson Welles's *Citizen Kane* with its deep-focus camera compositions (by Gregg Toland) and the films of Murnau and Ophüls as examples to support their argument. The schism between *mise-en-scène* and montage is deeper in theory than in practice; most filmmakers employ both in directing their films.

Misraki, Paul. French composer. Born Paul Misrachi, on Jan. 28, 1908, in Istanbul. Prolific writer of songs and film scores, somewhat influenced by his Middle Eastern origin.

FILMS INCLUDE: *Minuit Place Pigalle* 1934; *Retour à l'Aube* 1938; *Battements de Coeur* 1939; *Manon* 1949; *Nous irons à Paris* 1950; *Knock/Dr. Knock, Atoll K/Utopia* 1951; *La Minute de Vérité/The Moment of Truth* 1952; *Les Orgueilleux/The Proud and the Beautiful* 1953; *Mr. Arkadin/Confidential Report* 1955; *La Mort en ce Jardin/Gina/Death in the Garden, Et Dieu créa la Femme/And God Created Woman* 1956; *Montparnasse 19/Modigliani of Montparnasse* 1958; *A Double Tour/Leda, Les Cousins/The Cousins* 1959; *La Fièvre mont á El Pao/Los Ambiciosos/Fever Mounts at El Pao/Republic of Sin* (also co-sc.; Fr./Mex.), *Les Bonnes Femmes* 1960; *Alphaville* 1965; *Un Meurtre est un Meurtre/A Murder Is a Murder* 1972; *La Bulle* 1976; *Un Si joli Village* 1979; *Aujourd'Hui Peut-Etre. . . /A Day to Remember* 1991.

Mitchell, Cameron. Actor. *b.* Cameron Mizell, on Nov. 18, 1918, in Dallastown, Pa., a minister's son. *d.* 1994. He performed on Broadway and served as a bombardier in WW II before making his film debut in 1945. Gaining stature as a result of his portrayal of Happy in both the stage and screen versions of *Death of a Salesman,* he later played intense leads and character roles in many other films and starred in the TV series 'The Beachcomber' (1960–61), 'The High Chaparral' (1967–71), and 'Swiss Family Robinson' (1975–76). His career was marred in its latter phases by indiscriminate appearances in too many bottom-grade, low-budget films.

FILMS INCLUDE: *What Next Corporal Hargrove?, They Were Expendable* 1945; *High Barbaree, Cass Timberlane* 1947; *Homecoming* 1948; *Command Decision* 1949; *Death of a Salesman* (as Happy) 1951; *Okinawa, Outcasts of Poker Flat, The Sellout, Les Miserables* 1952; *Man on a Tightrope, Powder River, How to Marry a Millionaire* 1953; *Hell and High Water, Gorilla at Large, Garden of Evil, Desiree* (as Joseph Bonaparte) 1954; *Strange Lady in Town, Love Me or Leave Me, House of Bamboo, The Tall Men* 1955; *Carousel* (as Jigger) 1956; *Monkey on My Back, No Down Payment* 1957; *All Mine to Give* 1959; *The Unstoppable Man* (UK) 1960; *L'Ultimo dei Vichinghi/Last of the Vikings* (as Harald; It./Fr.), *Gli Invasori/Erik the Conqueror* (It./Fr.) 1961; *Dulcinea* (Sp.) 1962; *Giulio Cesare il Conquistatore delle Gallie/Caesar the Conqueror* (as Julius Caesar; It.), *Il Duca Nero/The Black Duke* (as Cesare Borgia; It.) 1963; *Sei Donne per l'Assassino/Blood and Black Lace* (It./Fr./Ger.) 1964; *Minnesota Clay* (It./Sp./Fr.) 1965; *Das Geheimnis der Todesinsel/Island of the Doomed* (Ger./Sp.), *Hombre* 1967; *Nightmare in Wax* 1969; *Rebel Rousers* 1970; *Buck and the Preacher, Slaughter* 1972; *The Midnight Man, The Klansmen* 1974; *The Taste of the Savage* 1975; *Slavers* (Ger.), *Viva Knievel!, Haunts/The Veil* 1977; *The Swarm, Texas Detour, The Toolbox Murders* 1978; *Supersonic Man* (Sp.) 1979; *Silent Scream, Without Warning* 1980; *Texas Lightning, Screamers* 1981; *Kill Squad, Raw Force, My Favorite Year* 1982; *Killpoint* 1984; *Night Train to Terror* 1985; *Low Blow, The Tomb* 1986; *The Messenger, The Offspring/From a Whisper to a Scream* 1987; *Space Mutiny* 1988; *Cult People, No Justice, Easy Kill* 1989; *Crossing the Line* 1990; *Terror in Beverly Hills* 1991.

Mitchell, Grant. Actor. *b.* June 17, 1874, Columbus, Ohio. *d.* 1957. The son of a general and a graduate of Yale and the Harvard Law School, he turned to the stage in 1902, to films in 1931. He typically played meek and respectable character parts, in scores of films.

FILMS INCLUDE: *Radio-Mania* 1923; *Man to Man* 1930; *Three on a Match* 1932; *Dinner at Eight* 1933; *A Midsummer Night's Dream, Seven Keys to Baldpate* 1935; *The Devil Is a Sissy* 1936; *The Life of Emile Zola, The Last Gangster* 1937; *Juarez, Mr. Smith Goes to Washington* 1939; *The Grapes of Wrath, Edison the Man* 1940; *Tobacco Road, Nothing but the Truth, The Great Lie, The Man Who Came to Dinner* 1941; *My Sister Eileen* 1942; *Arsenic and Old Lace, Laura* 1944; *Conflict, Leave Her to Heaven* 1945; *It Happened on Fifth Avenue, Honeymoon* 1947; *Who Killed Doc Robbin?* 1948.

Mitchell, Millard. Actor. *b.* 1900, Havana, to American parents. *d.* 1953. Proficient character actor with stage background, often in tough-talking roles.

FILMS INCLUDE: *Secrets of a Secretary* 1931; *Dynamite Delaney* 1938; *Mr. and Mrs. Smith* 1940; *Grand Central Murder* 1942; *A Double Life, Kiss of Death* 1947; *A Foreign Affair* 1948; *Twelve O'Clock High, Thieves' Highway* 1949; *The Gunfighter, Winchester 73, Mister 880, Convicted* 1950; *My Six Convicts, Singin' in the Rain* 1952; *The Naked Spur* 1953.

Mitchell, Thomas. Actor. *b.* July 11, 1892, Elizabeth, N.J. *d.* 1962. One of the most accomplished character actors of the American stage and screen, a performer of dazzling range. He began as a reporter with the Elizabeth *Daily Journal* and he later wrote a number of plays, some of which were successfully produced on the stage and adapted to films. 'Little Accident,' which he wrote in collaboration with Floyd Dell, was adapted to the screen in 1930 and 1939, and again in 1944 as *Casanova Brown.* In 1934 he collaborated on the screenplay of *All of Me.* Except for a single appearance in a silent film of the 20s, he remained a stage actor until the mid-30s, when he turned almost exclusively to the screen. He won an Academy Award as best supporting actor for his memorable portrayal of the tipsy Doc Boone in John Ford's *Stagecoach.* That same year he appeared as Scarlett O'Hara's father in *Gone With the Wind* and played another memorable role in *Only Angels Have Wings.*

FILMS: *Six-Cylinder Love* 1923; *Craig's Wife, Adventure in Manhattan, Theodora Goes Wild* 1936; *When You're in Love, Man of the People, Lost Horizon (as Henry Barnard), I Promise to Pay, Make Way for Tomorrow, The Hurricane* 1937; *Love Honor and Behave* 1938; *Trade Winds, Stage Coach, Only Angels Have Wings, Mr. Smith Goes to Washington, Gone With the Wind* (as Gerald O'Hara), *The Hunchback of Notre Dame* 1939; *Swiss Family Robinson, Three Cheers for the Irish, Our Town* (as Dr. Gibbs), *The Long Voyage Home, Angels Over Broadway* 1940; *Flight from Destiny, Out of the Fog* 1941; *Joan of Paris, Song of the Islands, Moontide, This Above All* (as Monty Montague), *Tales of Manhattan, The Black Swan* 1942; *The Immortal Sergeant, The Outlaw* (as Pat Garrett), *Bataan, Flesh and Fantasy* 1943; *The Sullivans, Buffalo Bill, Wilson, Dark Waters, The Keys of the Kingdom* 1944; *Within These Walls, Captain Eddie* 1945; *Adventure, Three Wise Fools, The Dark Mirror, It's a Wonderful Life* 1946; *High Barbaree, The Romance of Rosy Ridge* 1947; *Silver River* 1948; *Alias Nick Beal, The Big Wheel* 1949; *Journey Into Light* 1951; *High Noon* 1952; *Secret of the Incas* 1954; *Destry* 1955; *While the City Sleeps* 1956; *Handle with Care* 1958; *By Love Possessed, Pocketful of Miracles* 1961.

Mitchell, Yvonne. Actress. *b.* Yvonne Joseph, 1925, London. *d.* 1979. On the British stage from age 14, she rose to prominence with the Old Vic in the late 40s and early 50s, playing a gamut of leads ranging from Ophelia in 'Hamlet' to Eliza Doolittle in 'Pygmalion.' She remained one of Britain's most prominent stage performers, but her film roles, though memorable, were infrequent. She won the British Film Academy (BFA) Award for her performance in *The Divided Heart* (1954) and a Berlin Festival Award for *Woman in a Dressing Gown* (1957). She was a respected playwright and novelist and wrote an autobiography, *Actress* (1957).

FILMS: *Queen of Spades* 1949; *Children of Chance* 1951; *Turn the Key Softly* 1953; *The Divided Heart* 1954; *Escapade* 1955; *Yield to the Night/Blonde Sinner* 1956; *Woman in a Dressing Gown* 1957; *Passionate Summer* 1958; *Tiger Bay, Sapphire* 1959; *Conspiracy of Hearts, The Trials of Oscar Wilde* 1960; *Johnny Nobody* 1961; *The Main Attraction* 1963; *Genghis Khan* 1965; *The Corpse/Crucible of Horror* 1970; *The Great Waltz* 1972; *Demons of the Mind* 1974; *Widow's Nest* (US/Sp.) 1977.

Mitchum, Robert. Actor. *b.* Aug. 6, 1917, in Bridgeport, Conn. *d.* 1997. Left fatherless in early infancy, he led an uprooted childhood and a rather adventurous youth, including an arrest for vagrancy at 16, for which he was sentenced for seven days on a Georgia chain gang. Before he discovered an urge to act, he wandered about the country working at a colorful variety of odd jobs—as an engine wiper on a freighter, a nightclub bouncer, a promoter for a California astrologer, for example. After his marriage to a high school sweetheart in 1940, and the birth of a son, he decided to settle down and began working for Lockheed Aircraft as a drop hammer operator. In 1942 he joined the Long Beach Theater Guild and was soon spending much of his free time rehearsing and acting in its productions. The following year he made a modest entry into films as the heavy in a succession of "Hopalong Cassidy" Westerns. He also played supporting roles in an assortment of war films, comedies, and dramas. In all, he appeared in no fewer than 18 movies during 1943.

The film that brought Mitchum out of anonymity and started him on the road to stardom was *The Story of G.I. Joe* (1945), for which he was nominated for a best supporting actor Oscar. Shortly after completing his vivid portrayal of Lt. Walker in that film, he was drafted and spent the next eight months in training as a private. Resuming his screen career as a star in 1946, he gained rapid popularity as a rugged, nonchalant leading man. His career survived a serious test in 1948–49, when he was arrested for the possession of marijuana and served 50 days of a jail term. Despite the then-shocking transgression and his persistent reputation as Hollywood's Bad Boy, Mitchum thrived as a leading star for the next four decades. His film portrait gallery ranged from loner heroes to unscrupulous villains. The I-don't-care attitude that characterizes his screen personality is very much part of the real Mitchum. During the 80s, with his screen career slowly declining, the actor enjoyed great success as the star of three prestigious TV miniseries, 'The Winds of War' (1983), 'North and South' (1985), and 'War and Remembrance' (1988). His two sons, James and Christopher, have also been appearing in films, Jim Mitchum (*b.* May 8, 1941) since the late 50s and Chris Mitchum (*b.* Oct. 16, 1943) since the early 70s.

FILMS: *Hoppy Serves a Writ, The Leather Burners, Border Patrol, Follow the Band, Colt Comrades, The Human Comedy, We've Never Been Licked, Beyond the Last Frontier, Bar 20, Doughboys in Ireland, Corvette K-225, Aerial Gunner, Lone Star Trail, False Colors, The Dancing Masters, Riders of the Deadline, Cry Havoc, Gung Ho!* 1943; *Johnny Doesn't Live Here Any More, When Strangers Marry, The Girl Rush, Thirty Seconds Over Tokyo, Nevada* 1944; *West of the Pecos, The Story of G.I. Joe* 1945; *Till the End of Time, Undercurrent, The Locket* 1946; *Pursued, Crossfire, Desire Me, Out of the Past* 1947; *Rachel and the Stranger, Blood on the Moon* 1948; *The Red Pony, The Big Steal, Holiday Affair* 1949; *Where Danger Lives* 1950; *My Forbidden Past, His Kind of Woman, The Racket* 1951; *Macao, One Minute to Zero, The Lusty Men* 1952; *Second Chance, Angel Face, White Witch Doctor* 1953; *She Couldn't Say No, River of No Return, Track of the Cat* 1954; *Not as a Stranger, The Night of the Hunter, Man with the Gun* 1955; *Foreign Intrigue, Bandido* 1956; *Heaven Knows Mr. Allison, Fire Down Below, The Enemy Below* 1957; *Thunder Road, The Hunters* 1958; *The Angry Hills, The Wonderful Country* 1959; *Home from the Hill, The Sundowners, The Night Fighters, The Grass Is Greener* 1960; *The Last Time I Saw Archie* 1961; *Cape Fear, The Longest Day, Two for the Seesaw* 1962; *The List of Adrian Messenger, Rampage* 1963; *Man in the Middle, What a Way to Go!* 1964; *Mister Moses* 1965; *The Way West, El Dorado* 1967; *Villa Rides, Anzio, 5 Card Stud, Secret Ceremony* 1968; *Young Billy Young, The Good Guys and the Bad Guys* 1969; *Ryan's Daughter* 1970; *Going Home* 1971; *The Wrath of God* 1972; *The Friends of Eddie Coyle* 1973; *The Yakuza, Farewell My Lovely* (as private eye Philip Marlowe) 1975; *Midway* (as Admiral William Halsey), *The Last Tycoon* (as Pat Brady) 1976; *The Amsterdam Kill* (Hong Kong) 1977; *Matilda, The Big Sleep* (again as Philip Marlowe; UK) 1978; *Sergeant Steiner/Breakthrough* (Ger.) 1979; *Agency* (Can.) 1981; *That Championship Season* 1982; *The Ambassador, Maria's Lovers* 1985; *Mr. North, Scrooged* 1988; *Cape Fear* (remake) 1991; *Tombstone* 1993; *Backfire* 1994; *Dead Man* 1996.

Mitra, Subatra. Director of photography. Born in 1931, in India. One of the leading cinematographers of the Indian cinema. A former still photographer, he began his film career with Satyajit RAY as the cinematographer of the famed Apu Trilogy. Later worked for other directors, including James IVORY.

FILMS INCLUDE: *Pather Panchali* 1955; *Aparajito* 1956; *The Philosopher's Stone* 1957; *The Music Room, The World of Apu* 1958; *Devi/The Goddess* 1960; *Kanchenjungha* 1962; *Mahanagar/The Big City* 1963; *Gharbar/The Householder, Charulata/The Lonely Wife* 1964; *Shakespeare Wallah* 1965; *Nayak/The Hero* 1966; *The Arch* (China) 1967; *The Guru* 1969; *Bombay Talkie* 1970.

Mitry, Jean. Film theoretician, critic, historian, and filmmaker. *b.* Jean-René-Pierre Goetgheluck Le Rouge Tillard des Acres de Presfontaines, Nov. 7, 1907, Soissons, France. *d.* 1988. A film enthusiast since his early teens, he was Marcel L'Herbier's assistant in 1924. The following year he co-founded France's first film society and in 1936 was among the founders of the Cinémathèque Française. In 1929 he began directing experimental shorts, mostly exercises in visual rhythm. His only excursion into fiction film, the feature length *Enigme aux Folies-Bergère* (1959, starring Bela Darvi), was a disastrous failure. Mitry's work as a filmmaker was quite marginal, but he became probably the most profound and highly respected film theoretician and historian in France. He wrote numerous articles and essays on the cinema, as well as a number of books, the best known of which is the two-volume *Esthétique et Psychologie du Cinéma* (Paris, 1963), considered by some critics the most important scholarly work in the literature of film. The author of critical works on Sergei Eisenstein, John Ford, Charlie Chaplin, and René Clair, Mitry compiled the exhaustive (but not always accurate) *Filmographie universelle,* a 30-volume index of French and international filmographies and motion picture credits. He taught film at IDHEC, the University of Montreal, and the University of Paris, often using in his lectures his self-made text-films to illustrate the language of cinema for students.

FILM SHORTS INCLUDE: *Paris Cinéma* (co-dir. with Pierre Chenal) 1929; *Pacific 231* 1949; *Le Paquebot Libérté* 1950; *Images pour Debussy* 1951; *Symphonie mécanique* 1955; *Le Miracle des Ailes* 1956; *Chopin* 1957; *Enigme aux Folies-Bergère* (feature) 1959; *Rencontres* 1960; *La Machine et l'Homme* 1962.

mix. The process by which separate sound tracks (dialogue, music, and sound effects) are combined on a single sound track for eventual use in the composite print. Also called DUBBING, the process is carried out by technicians called MIXERS at a mixing console or dubbing panel equipped with many control knobs and push buttons for balancing the various sound elements. There are usually three people in the crew: the dialogue mixer, who generally serves as the head mixer; the music mixer; and the sound effects mixer. The term "mix" is sometimes also used interchangeably with DISSOLVE.

Mix, Tom. Actor. *b.* Thomas Mix, Jan. 6, 1880, Mix Run, Pa. *d.* 1940. Legendary cowboy star of Hollywood silents and early talkies. According to studio publicity, he was the son of a cavalry officer and educated at the Virginia Military Institute. But a biography carefully documented by a close relative of Mix reveals that his father was actually a poor lumberman, that Tom dropped out of school after completing the fourth grade, and that although he actually served in the US Artillery as a career sergeant, he never saw action in battle and was officially listed as a deserter in 1902. A skilled rider from childhood, he did serve briefly as a Texas Ranger and in 1906 he joined the famous Miller Brothers 101 Ranch Wild West Show, winning the national riding and rodeo championship in 1909.

Mix was appearing with another Wild West show later that year when he was hired by the Selig Polyscope company to round up cattle for the film *Ranch Life in the Great Southwest* (released 1910) and eventually was given a supporting role in the film. He remained with Selig as a supporting player and before long had been launched as a Western star. Between 1911 and 1917 he appeared in well over 100 one- and two-reelers, many of which he also produced or directed. Initially quickies with emphasis on folksy humor, Mix's Selig films gradually improved in quality, increased in length, and accelerated in pace. In time they were filled with action and daredevil stunts and were very popular with youngsters. Mix rarely used doubles for his stunts and suffered frequent injuries during production.

When the Selig company went out of business in 1917, Mix joined Fox, where he rapidly became the silent screen's most popular cowboy star. Mix's action-packed features were carefully packaged, with great attention to detail and locale. Handled by top directors and photographed by a highly talented cameraman, Dan B. Clark, Mix's Fox films provided exciting escapist entertainment, in a marked departure from the slow, authentic style established by William S. Hart and imitated by other cowboy stars of the period. Although Mix directed only a few of his 60-plus Fox pictures, he was very much in charge of his own vehicles and had much to do with establishing the successful formula that set the pattern for all Western films to follow. In 1928, Mix left Fox to join F.B.O., for which he made his last silent films. After a three-year tour with the Ringling Bros. Circus, accompanied by his famous horse Tony, Mix returned to the screen in 1932 for a number of sound Westerns at Universal, then retired in 1934. 'The Tom Mix Show,' a radio series exploiting the star's popularity, had a 17-year run, from 1933 until 1950, ten years after his death in an automobile crash.

FILMS INCLUDE: *On the Little Big Horn or Custer's Last Stand* 1909; *The Long Trail, The Range Riders* 1910; *Back to the Primitive, An Arizona Wooing* 1911; *The Law and the Outlaw, An Apache's Gratitude, The Escape of Jim Dolan* (also sc.) 1913; *Chip of the Flying "U," Cactus Jake—Heartbreaker* (also dir.), *In the Days of the Thundering Herd, The Moving Picture Cowboy* (also dir., sc.), *The Ranger's Romance* (also dir., sc.) 1914; *The Range Girl and the Cowboy* (also dir., sc.), *A Child of the Prairie* (also dir., sc.), *Cactus Jim's Shop Girl, Pals in Blue, On the Eagle Trail* (also dir.) 1915; *The Taming of Grouchy Bill, Local Color, Twisted Trails* 1916; *The Heart of Texas Ryan* 1917; *Western Blood, Six-Shooter Andy, Ace High* 1918; *The Wilderness Trail, Fighting for Gold, Fame and Fortune* 1919; *The Feud, The Daredevil, The Cyclone, The Terror, The Untamed, Rough Riding Romance* 1920; *The Road Demon, The Queen of Sheba* (supervised chariot race only), *A Ridin' Romeo, Trailin'* 1921; *Chasing the Moon, Do and Dare, Just Tony, Catch My Smoke, Arabia/Tom Mix in Arabia* 1922; *Lone Star Ranger, Eyes of the Forest, Romance Land, North of Hudson Bay* 1923; *The Heart Buster, The Trouble Shooter, Teeth* 1924; *Dick Turpin* (title role), *Riders of the Purple Sage, The Rainbow Trail, The Lucky Horseshoe, The Everlasting Whisper, The Best Bad Man* 1925; *The Yankee Señor, My Own Pal, Tony Runs Wild, Hard Boiled* 1926; *The Last Trail, The Circus Ace, The Arizona Wildcat, Silver Valley, The Broncho Twister* 1927; *Hello Cheyenne, Painted Post, Son of the Golden West, King Cowboy, A Horseman of the Plains* 1928; *The Big Diamond Robbery, The Drifter, Outlawed* 1929; *Destry Rides Again, My Pal the King, Rider of Death Valley* 1932; *Terror Trail, Rustler's Roundup* 1933; *The Miracle Rider* (serial) 1935.

mixer. A sound technician who blends and balances individual sounds into a single track. See MIX.

Miyagawa, Kazuo. Director of photography. Born on Feb. 25, 1908, in Kyoto, Japan. One of Japan's most brilliant cinematographers, a master of camera tracking, an art he demonstrated beautifully in Kurosawa's *Rashomon* (1950) and in scores of other productions, including several films of Ichikawa, Inagaki, and Mizoguchi. In 1981 he was honored with a special tribute and retrospective screenings by the American Academy of Motion Picture Arts and Sciences.

FILMS INCLUDE: *Ochiyogasa* 1935; *Matchless Sword* 1937; *A Great Power Rising* 1938; *Mazo* 1939; *Miyamoto Musashi* 1940; *The Life of Matsu the Untamed* 1943; *The Last Abdication* 1945; *Soshi Gekijo* 1947; *Children Hand in Hand* 1948; *Ghost Train* 1949; *Rashomon* 1950; *Brilliant Murder, Miss Oyu, A Tale of Genji* 1951; *Sisters of Nishijin* 1952; *A Thousand Cranes, Ugetsu Monogatari/Ugetsu, Desires, Gion Music/A Geisha* 1953; *Sansho Dayu/The Bailiff/Sansho the Bailiff, The Woman in the Rumor, A Tale from Chikamatsu* 1954; *New Tales of the Taira Clan* 1955; *Street of Shame* 1956; *Conflagration* 1958; *The Key/Odd Obsession, Floating Weeds* 1959; *Bonchi* 1960; *Yojimbo* 1961; *The Sin* 1962; *The Bamboo Doll* 1963; *Money Talks* 1964; *Tokyo Olympiad* (co-superv.) 1965; *Spider Girl* 1966; *The Devil's Temple, The Magoichi Saga* 1969; *Zatoichi Meets Yojimbo* 1970; *The Ballad of Orin/Orin, a Blind Woman, Melody in Gray/Banished* 1978; *Kagemusha* (co-phot.) 1980; *MacArthur's Children* 1984; *Yari no Gonza/Gonza the Spearman* 1985; *Die Tanzerin/The Dancer* (co-phot.; Ger./Jap.) 1990.

Mizoguchi, Kenji. Director. *b.* May 16, 1898, Tokyo. *d.* 1956. The son of a carpenter, he grew up in dire poverty and as a child witnessed the sale of his older sister into the life of a geisha, an event that was to have a profound influence on his work in films. At age 13 he quit school to work in a hospital and at 17, after his mother's death, he left home to live with his geisha sister. Drawn to the graphic arts since childhood, he now enrolled at an art school specializing in Western-style painting. At 19 he went to work for a newspaper as an advertising designer. In his spare time he wrote poetry and organized a stage group that performed in the open air. At 20 he entered Japanese cinema as an actor and was soon moved to the position of assistant director. He made his debut as director in 1922.

In a career that spanned 34 years, Mizoguchi made more than 80 films, many of which rank among the finest in Japanese cinema. Two of these, *The Life of Oharu* (1952) and *Ugetsu Monogatari/Ugetsu* (1953), are acknowledged masterpieces of world cinema. Mizoguchi approached his films with the eye of a painter and the soul of a poet. Shunning frequent camera setups and disruptive close-ups, he developed a visual style rich in beauty and physical and psychological detail. He emphasized the internal design of his images, creating aesthetically pleasing compositions, then explored them lovingly and at length with gentle camera movements. He thus created a realistic and unified universe, concrete in mood and atmosphere, in which he proceeded to explore the psychological interplay of his characters. His main theme was the social condition of the Japanese woman and her role in a society polarized between traditional and modernizing forces. His interest in and profound understanding of female psychology are consistent features of his films.

A fragile man afflicted with crippling rheumatism from childhood, Mizoguchi died of leukemia at 58.

FILMS: *Resurrection of Love, Hometown/Native Land* (also sc.), *Dreams of Youth* (also sc.), *City of Desire* (also sc.), *Failure's Song Is Sad* (also sc.), *813: The Adventures of Arsene Lupin, Foggy Harbor* (based on O'Neill's *Anna Christie), Blood and Soul* (also sc.), *The Night* (also sc.), *In the Ruins, The Song of the Mountain Pass* (also sc.) 1923; *The Sad Idiot* (also story), *The Queen of Modern Times, Women Are Strong, This Dusty World, Turkeys in a Row, A Chronicle of May Rain, No Money No Fight, A Woman of Pleasure* (also story), *Death at Dawn* 1924; *Queen of the Circus, Out of College* (also sc.), *The White Lily Laments, The Earth Smiles, Shining in the Red Sunset, The Song of Home, Ningen/The Human Being, Street Sketches* 1925; *General Nogi and Kuma-san, The Copper Coin King* (also sc.), *A Paper Doll's Whisper of Spring, My Fault—New Version, The Passion of a Woman Teacher, The Boy of the Sea, Money* (also story) 1926; *The Imperial Grace, The Cuckoo/Bird of Mercy* 1927; *A Man's Life* (also sc.), *My Loving Daughter* (also co-sc.) 1928; *Nihombashi/Nihon Bridge* (also sc.), *Tokyo March, The Morning Sun Shines* (co-dir.), *Metropolitan Symphony* 1929; *Home Town, Mistress of a Foreigner* 1930; *And Yet They Go On* 1931; *The Man of the Moment, The Dawn of Manchuria and Mongolia* 1932; *Taki no shiraito/The Water Magician/White Threads of the Waterfall, Gion Festival* (also sc.), *The Jimpu Group* (also sc.) 1933; *The Mountain Pass of Love and Hate, The Downfall of Osen/Osen of the Paper Cranes* 1934; *Oyuki the Virgin/Oyuki the Madonna* (based on de Maupassant's *Boule de Suif), Poppy* 1935; *Osaka Elegy* (also story), *Sisters of the Gion* (also story) 1936; *The Straits of Love and Hate* 1937; *Ah, My Home Town, The Song of the Camp* 1938; *The Story of the Last Chrysanthemum/The Story of the Late Chrysanthemums* 1939; *The Woman of Osaka* (also story) 1940; *The Life of an Actor* 1941; *The Loyal 47 Ronin* (in two parts) 1941–42; *Three Generations of Danjuro, Musashi Miyamoto/The Swordsman* 1944; *The Famous Sword Bijomary/The Noted Sword, Victory Song* (co-dir.) 1945; *The Victory of Women, Utamarro and His Five Women* 1946; *The Love of Sumako the Actress* 1947; *Women of the Night* 1948; *My Love Has Been Burning/My Life Burns* 1949; *A Picture of Madame Yuki* 1950; *Miss Oyu, Lady Musashino* 1951; *The Life of Oharu* 1952; *Ugetsu Monogatary/ Ugetsu/Tales of the Pale and Silvery Moon After the Rain, Gion Festival Music/Gion Music/A Geisha* 1953; *Sansho Dayu/ Sansho the Bailiff/The Bailiff, The Woman in the Rumor, Chikamatsu Monogatari/A Story from Chikamatsu/The Crucified Lovers* 1954; *Yokihi/Yang Kwei-Fei/The Princess Yang Kwei-fei/The Empress Yang Kwi-Fei, The Taira Clan/New Tales of the Taira Clan* 1955; *Street of Shame/Red Light District* 1956.

Mizrahi, Moshe (also **Misrahi**). Director. Born in 1931, in Egypt. In 1946, at age 15, he emigrated to Israel (then still Palestine), where he settled in a kibbutz and served in the Israeli Defense Forces during the 1948–49 War of Independence. In 1958 he moved to France, where he entered the film industry as an assistant director. He went back to Israel for location shooting for his first feature film as a director, *Le Cliente de la Morte Saison* (1969), a Franco-Italian co-production, and later returned there periodically for film projects. He enjoyed his best success in France with two sensitively handled sentimental Simone Signoret vehicles, *Madame Rosa* (1977) and *I Sent a Letter to My Love* (1980). The former won an Oscar as best foreign film. For TV he directed the French-Italian-Canadian miniseries 'A Man of Influence' (1990). He usually writes or collaborates on the screenplays of his own films and has also penned film criticism.

FILMS: *Le Client de la Morte Saison* 1969; *Stances á Sophie/Sophie's Way* 1970; *I Love You Rosa* (Isr.) 1973; *The House on Chelouche Street* (Isr.) 1974; *Daughters! Daughters!* (Isr.) 1975; *Rachel's Man* (Isr.) 1976; *La Vie devant soi/Madame Rosa* 1977; *Chère inconnu/I Sent a Letter to My Love* 1980; *La Vie continue* 1981; *Une Jeunesse* 1983; *The Children's War/War and Love* (Isr./US) 1985; *Every Time We Say Goodbye* (Isr.) 1986; *Mangeclous* 1988.

MLS. Abbreviation for MEDIUM LONG SHOT.

Mnouchkine, Alexandre. French producer of Russian descent. Born in 1908. His career spanned more than 50 years of Gallic cinema and included some notable films by Decoin, Cocteau, Christian-Jaque, Duvivier, de Broca, Lelouch, Resnais, and other front-rank directors. He capped his career in 1989 with *The French Revolution,* a $50 million international co-production, the most expensive motion picture ever undertaken in Europe.

FILMS INCLUDE: *Alerte en Méditerrané* 1938; *Non Coupable, L'Aigle á Deux Têtes/The Eagle with Two Heads* 1947; *Les Parents terribles/The Storm Within* 1948; *Fanfan la Tulipe* 1951; *Lucrèce Borgia/Sins of the Borgias* 1952; *Le Retour de Don Camillo/The Return of Don Camillo* 1953; *Madame du Barry* 1954; *Si tous les Gares du Monde/If All the Guys in the World, Til l'Espiège/Til Eulenspiegel* 1956; *Une Parisienne* 1957; *Babette s'en va-t-en Guerre/Babette Goes to War, Rue des Prairies/Rue de Paris* 1959; *L'Amant de Cinq Jours/Five-Day Lover, La Loi c'est la Loi/Where the Hot Wind Blows* 1960; *Cartouche* 1961; *L'Homme de Rio/That Man from Rio* 1963; *Les Tribulations d'un Chinois en Chine/Up to His Ears* 1965; *Vivre pour vivre/Live for Life* 1967; *Les Gauloises bleus* 1968; *Le Voyou/The Crook* 1970; *L'Aventure c'est l'Aventure/Money Money Money* 1972; *L'Emmerdeur/A Pain in the A. . . .* 1973; *Stavisky* 1974; *Un autre Homme une autre Chance/Another Man Another Chance, Tendre Poulet/Dear Detective/Dear Inspector* 1977; *Le Cavaleur/Practice Makes Perfect* 1979; *Garde à Vue/The Inquisitor/Under Suspicion* 1981; *La Balance* 1982; *The Name of the Rose* (Ger./ It./Fr.) 1986; *Spirale* 1987; *Nuovo Cinema Paradiso/Cinema Paradiso* (co-assoc. prod.; It./Fr.) 1988; *La Revolution Française/The French Revolution* 1989.

Mockridge, Cyril J. Composer, music director. *b.* Aug. 6, 1896, London. *d.* 1979. *ed.* Royal Academy of Music (London). Scored and arranged music for numerous Hollywood films from the early 30s, mainly for Fox. Later also composed for TV. He produced the film *Mother Didn't Tell Me* (1950).

FILMS INCLUDE: *Judge Priest* 1934; *The Little Colonel* 1935; *Poor Little Rich Girl* 1936; *Stanley and Livingstone, The Hound of the Baskervilles* 1939; *Johnny Apollo* 1940; *I Wake Up Screaming* 1942; *Happy Land, The Ox-Bow Incident* 1943; *The Sullivans* 1945; *Claudia and David, The Dark Corner, Cluny Brown, My Darling Clementine* 1946; *Miracle on 34th Street, Nightmare Alley* 1947; *Walls of Jericho, Road House* 1948; *I Was a Male War Bride* 1949; *Cheaper by the Dozen* 1950; *How to Marry a Millionaire* 1953; *River of No Return* 1954; *Bus Stop* 1956; *Flaming Star* 1960; *All Hands on Deck* 1961; *The Man Who Shot Liberty Valance* 1962; *Donovan's Reef* 1963.

mock-up. A full-scale model of a prop or part of a large prop constructed on a set for the purpose of simulating a real object. Typical mock-ups are building façades and portions of cars and other vehicles. See also MODEL.

Mocky, Jean-Pierre. Actor, director. Born Jean Mokijewski, on July 6, 1929, in Nice, France, to parents of Polish origin. In French and some Italian films as an actor since the mid-40s, he became a director in the late 50s. His most successful film in this capacity was his first, *Les Dragueurs.* His directing style is rather casual and his scripts often display a fierce brand of black humor. A prolific worker, he gained a reputation as an undisciplined and completely unpredictable film-maker. He is his own producer and screenwriter, and usually edits or co-edits his own films.

FILMS INCLUDE: As actor—*L'Affaire du Collier de la Reine* 1945; *Vive la Liberté!* 1946; *Orphée/Orpheus* 1950; *I Vinti* (It.) 1952; *Le Comte de Monte-Cristo* 1953; *Gli Sbandati* (It.) 1955; *La Tête contre les Murs* 1959. As director/screen-writer and often editor (complete)—*Les Dragueurs/The Chasers* 1959; *Un Couple* 1960; *Snobs* 1961; *Les Vierges* 1962; *Un Drôle de Paroissien/Thank Heaven for Small Favors* 1963; *La Grande Frousse* 1964; *La Bourse et la Vie* 1965; *Les Compagnons de la Marguerite* 1967; *La Grande Lessive* 1968; *L'Etalon, Solo* (also act.) 1969; *L'Albatross* (also act.), *Pavane pour un Crétin defunt* 1971; *Chut!* 1972; *L'Ombre d'une Chance* (also act.) 1973; *Un Linceul n'a pas de Poches* (also act.) 1974; *L'Ibis rouge* 1975; *Le Roi des Bricoleurs* 1977; *Le Temoin* 1978; *Le Piège à Cons* (also act.) 1979; *Litan* (also act.), *Y'a-t-il un Français dans la Salle?* 1982; *A Mort l'Arbitre!* 1984; *La Pactole* 1985; *La Machine à découdre* (also act.) 1986; *Le Miracule, Agent Trouble* (also act.) 1987; *Les Saisons du Plaisir/The Seasons of Pleasure* 1988; *Ville à Vendre/City for Sale* 1991; *Le ari de Léon* 1993.

model. 1. A scale replica, usually in miniature, used in filming to represent real objects. The design and photography of models is an essential part of special effects and is used widely in trick photography and in the simulation of such difficult-to-stage realities as battle scenes, explosions, space travel, and natural disasters. See also MINIATURE, MOCK-UP. 2. A person filling in for a performer in close-up shots requiring only part of the performer's body—a hand squeezing a gun's trigger, a foot kicking a ball, for example.

modeling light. Illumination designed to emphasize the texture and contour of a subject. Also called "counter key," it is aimed at the subject from a direction opposite that of the KEY LIGHT.

model sheet. In animation, specification drawings concerning the proportions of cartoon characters, used as a guide for in-betweeners and assistant animators. See also IN-BETWEENS.

Modine, Matthew. Actor. Born on Mar. 22, 1959, in Loma Linda, Calif. Versatile, idiosyncratic leading man of Hollywood films of the 80s and 90s. The youngest of seven children, he was raised partly in Utah, where his father managed drive-in theaters. At 18 he moved to New York to study acting with Stella ADLER and eventually got his professional start doing TV commercials and appearing in a soap opera. In 1983, the year of his film debut, he shared with thc ensemble of Robert Altman's *Streamers* the best male acting prize at the Venice Festival. In the following year he gave an astounding performance in the difficult role of a schizophrenic Vietnam mental casualty in Alan Parker's allegorical *Birdy.* Other offbeat leading roles followed, notably the wisecracking marine recruit in *Full Metal Jacket* and the addled FBI agent in *Married to the Mob*.

FILMS: *Baby It's You, Private School, Streamers* 1983; *The Hotel New Hampshire, Birdy, Mrs. Soffel* 1984; *Vision Quest* 1985; *Full Metal Jacket, Orphans* 1987; *Married to the Mob, La Partita/The Gamble/The Match* (It.) 1988; *Gross Anatomy* 1989; *Memphis Belle* (UK/US), *Pacific Heights* 1990; *Wind* 1992; *Equinox, Last Action Hero, Short Cuts* 1993; *The Browning Version* 1994; *Bye Bye Love, Cutthroat Island, Fluke* 1995.

Modot, Gaston. Actor. *b.* Dec. 30, 1887, Paris. *d.* 1970. A former Montmartre painter, a friend of Picasso and Modigliani (the latter painted Modot's portrait in 1918), he turned to acting in films in 1908. His career spanned more than five decades of French cinema, during which he appeared in many landmark productions. He directed a highly regarded medium-length film, *La Torture par l'Espérance* (1928), and collaborated on the script of several films, including Louis Daquin's *Nous les Gosses/Portrait of Innocence* (1941).

FILMS INCLUDE: *Onèesime* (series) 1910–14; *Cent Dollars mort ou vif* 1912; *Le Collier vivant* 1913; *Mater Dolorosa, La Zone de la Mort, Monte-Cristo* 1917; *La Fête espagnole* 1919; *Mathias Sandorff* 1920; *Fièvre, La Terre du Diable* 1921; *Les Mystères de Paris* 1922; *Le Miracle des Loups/The Miracle of the Wolves* 1924; *Carmen* 1926; *La Merveilleuse Vie de Jeanne d'Arc* 1928; *Monte-Cristo* (remake), *Das Schiff der verlorenen Menschen/The Ship of Lost Souls* (Ger./Fr.), *Shéhérazade/Secrets of the Orient* (Fr./Ger.) 1929; *Sous les Toits de Paris/Under the Roofs of Paris, L'Age d'Or* 1930; *L'Opera de Quat'sous* (as Peachum in French-language version of Pabst's *Die Dreigroschenoper/The Threepenny Opera/The Beggar's Opera*) 1931; *Fantômas* 1932; *Quatorze Juillet/July 14th* 1933; *Crainquebille* 1934; *La Bandera/Escape from Yesterday, Lucrèce Borgia* 1935; *Pépé le Moko, Mademoiselle Docteur, La Grande Illusion/Grand Illusion* 1937; *La Marseillaise, Le Joueur d'Echecs/The Devil Is an Empress* 1938; *La Règle du Jeu/The Rules of the Game, La Fin du Jour/The End of a Day* 1939; *Dernier Atout* 1942; *Les Enfants du Paradis/Children of Paradise* 1945; *Antoine et Antoinette/Antoine and Antoinette, Le Silence est d'Or* 1947; *Le Point du Jour, L'Ecole buissonnière/Passion for Life* 1949; *La Beauté du Diable/Beauty and the Devil* 1950; *Casque d'Or* 1952; *French Cancan/Only the French Can* 1955; *Cela s'appelle l'Aurore, Eléna et les Hommes/Paris Does Strange Things* 1956; *Les Amants/The Lovers* 1958; *Les Menteurs/The Liars* 1961; *Le Diable et les Dix Commandments/The Devil and the Ten Commandments* 1962.

Moffat, Donald. Actor, director. Born December 26, 1930, in Plymouth, England. *ed.* Royal Academy of Dramatic Arts, London. A sterling, stalwart character actor, for many years a favorite of West End theatergoers beginning with his performance in 'Macbeth.' He has since become a familiar face to international audiences through numerous television and film roles.

FILMS: *Rachel Rachel* 1968; *R.P.M.* 1970; *The Devil and Miss Sarah* 1971; *The Great Northfield Minnesota Raid* 1972; *Showdown* 1973; *Earthquake, The Terminal Man* 1974; *The Land of No Return* 1978; *Promises in the Dark, Winter Kills* 1979; *On the Nickel, Popeye* 1980; *The White Lions* 1981; *The Thing* 1982; *The Right Stuff, Wagner* 1983; *Licence To Kill* 1984; *Alamo Bay* 1985; *The Best of Times, Monster in the Closet* 1986; *Desperado* 1987; *The Bourne Identity, Far North, The Unbearable Lightness of Being* 1988; *Cross Fire, Music Box* 1989; *The Bonfire of the Vanities* 1990; *Class Action, Regarding Henry* 1991; *HouseSitter* 1992; *Clear and Present Danger, Trapped in Paradise* 1994; *The Evening Star* 1996.

Moguy, Léonide. Director. *b.* Léonide Moguilevsky, July 14, 1899, St. Petersburg, Russia. *d.* 1976. *ed.* U. of Odessa (law). In Russian films in technical capacities since 1918, he became director of the newsreel department at the studio in Kiev in 1923. In 1928 he was a laboratory chief in Moscow and the following year he emigrated to France, where he became a director in the mid-30s. During WW II he sought refuge in the US and directed a number of Hollywood films. He later resumed his activity in Europe, winning a number of awards for his French and Italian films, which usually concerned social problems. In the 60s and early 70s he headed the film department of the International Red Cross.

FILMS INCLUDE: In France—*Le Mioche/Forty Little Mothers* 1936; *Prison sans Barreaux/Prison Without Bars, Conflit/The Affair Lafont* 1938; *Le Déserteur/Je t'attendrai/Three Hours* 1939; *L'Empreinte du Dieu/Two Women* 1940. In the US—*Paris After Dark* 1943; *Action in Arabia* 1944; *Whistle Stop* 1946. In France—*Bethsabée* 1947. In Italy—*Domani è troppo tardi/Tomorrow Is Too Late* 1950; *Domani è un altro Giorno* 1951. In France—*Les Enfants de l'Amour* 1953; *Le Long des Trottoirs/Diary of a Bad Girl* 1956; *Donnez-moi ma Chance* 1957; *Les Hommes veulent vivre/Gli Uomini Vogliono Vivere* (Fr./It.) 1962.

Mohr, Gerald. Actor. *b.* June 11, 1914, New York City. *d.* 1968. A veteran of the stage and radio, he played suave leads in low-budget crime and action Hollywood films of the 40s and 50s, including the title role in several sequels of 'The Lone Wolf' series. He also played supporting roles in higher-budget productions through the late 60s as well as on TV. He was the voice of both 'The Lone Wolf' and private-eye Philip Marlowe during his radio career.

FILMS INCLUDE: *Charlie Chan at Treasure Island* 1939; *The Sea Hawk* 1940; *Jungle Girl* (serial), *The Monster and the Girl* 1941; *The Lady Has Plans, Woman of the Year* 1942; *The Desert Song, Lady of Burlesque, Murder in Times Square* 1943; *Gilda, The Notorious Lone Wolf, The Catman of Paris* 1946; *The Lone Wolf in Mexico, The Lone Wolf in London* 1947; *The Emperor Waltz, Two Guys from Texas* 1948; *The Blonde Bandit* 1949; *Sirocco, Ten Tall Men, Detective Story* 1951; *The Sniper, The Ring, Duel at Silver Creek* 1952; *Invasion USA, The Eddie Cantor Story* 1953; *Money from Home* 1954; *Guns Girls and*

Gangsters 1959; *This Rebel Breed, Angry Red Planet* 1960; *Funny Girl* 1968.

Mohr, Hal. Director of photography. *b.* Aug. 2, 1894, San Francisco. *d.* 1974. A cinematography enthusiast as a high school teenager, he built his own camera and after some experimentation dropped out of school to earn a living selling photographed news clips to newsreel companies. He later managed Sol Lesser's newsreel company and worked in various capacities in the film industry before becoming a director of photography in 1918. An accomplished craftsman and a highly skilled technician, he contributed many innovations to the art of cinematography. In 1929 he introduced complex crane shots into Paul Fejos's *Broadway,* and he was among the first cameramen to employ dolly and boom shots liberally. He won an Academy Award for the cinematography of *A Midsummer Night's Dream* (1935) and shared another Oscar for *The Phantom of the Opera* (1943). He directed the film *When Love Is Young* (1937). At one time married to actress Evelyn VENABLE. From the mid-50s worked mainly for TV.

FILMS INCLUDE: *Restitution* (co-phot.) 1918; *The Golden Trail* (co-phot.), *Deceiver* (co-phot.) 1920; *The Unfoldment* (co-phot.) 1922; *Vanity's Price* 1924; *The Monster, Little Annie Rooney* (co-phot.), *Playing with Souls* 1925; *The Marriage Clause, Sparrows* (co-phot.) 1926; *The Third Degree, A Million Bid, The Heart of Maryland, The Jazz Singer, Old San Francisco* 1927; *The Wedding March* (co-phot.) 1928; *The Last Warning, Noah's Ark* (co-phot.), *Broadway* 1929; *Captain of the Guard* (co-phot.), *The King of Jazz* (co-phot.), *The Cat Creeps* (co-phot.), *Outward Bound* 1930; *The Front Page* (co-phot.), *Devotion* 1931; *A Woman Commands, Tess of the Storm Country* 1932; *State Fair, The Warrior's Husband* 1933; *Change of Heart, Carolina, David Harum, Servants' Entrance* 1934; *A Midsummer Night's Dream, Captain Blood* 1935; *Bullets or Ballots, The Green Pastures, The Walking Dead* 1936; *When Love Is Young* (also dir.) 1937; *I Met My Love Again* 1938; *Destry Rides Again* 1939; *When the Daltons Rode* 1940; *Cheers for Miss Bishop* 1941; *The Phantom of the Opera* (co-phot.), *Watch on the Rhine* 1943; *The Climax, San Diego I Love You* 1944; *Salome—Where She Danced* (co-phot.) 1945; *Night in Paradise* (co-phot.), *Because of Him* 1946; *Song of Scheherazade* (co-phot.), *The Lost Moment* 1947; *Another Part of the Forest, An Act of Murder/Live Today for Tomorrow* 1948; *Johnny Holiday, Woman on the Run* 1950; *The Big Night* 1951; *Rancho Notorious* 1952; *The Four Poster, Member of the Wedding* 1953; *The Wild One* 1954; *The Boss* 1956; *Baby Face Nelson* 1957; *The Lineup* 1958; *The Last Voyage* 1960; *Underworld USA* 1961; *The Man from the Diners' Club* 1963; *The Bamboo Saucer* 1968; *Topaz* (phot. consultant only) 1969.

Mokae, Zakes. Actor. Born on Aug. 5, 1935, in Johannesburg. Trained at London's RADA, he became one of South Africa's leading black performers on the stage and later also in films. His strong portrayal of Father Kani in *Cry Freedom* (1987) led to his relocation to America in the late 80s.

FILMS INCLUDE: *The Comedians* 1967; *The Island* 1980; *Roar* 1981; *Cry Freedom* 1987; *The Serpent and the Rainbow* 1988; *A Dry White Season, Gross Anatomy, Dad* 1989; *A Rage in Harlem* 1991; *The Doctor, Body Parts* 1992; *Dust Devil* (Fr./UK) 1993; *Outbreak, Vampire in Brooklyn, Waterworld* 1995.

Molander, Gustaf (Gustav). Director, screenwriter. *b.* Nov. 18, 1888, Helsinki (then Helsingfors), Finland, a Swedish national. *d.* 1973. The son of the director of the Finnish branch of the Swedish National Theater, he joined his father's company as an actor in 1909, following training at the DSRDT in Stockholm (he would return to the school in the early 20s as a teacher, with Greta Garbo as one of his students). Rapidly becoming established as a fine actor on the Finnish, then Swedish stage, Molander gravitated in 1916 toward the burgeoning Swedish film industry as a screenwriter for SJÖSTRÖM, STILLER, and other leading directors of the period, and in 1920 turned out his own first film as a director. His career spanned nearly the entire cycle of Swedish cinema, from the "golden age" through the period of decline (following the departure to Hollywood of both Sjöström and Stiller) and into the great revival that began in the late 40s. His *One Night* (1931), a beautifully shot drama of love and death, is considered a masterpiece of the early sound era. Often writing his own scripts, he directed numerous silent and sound films, gaining a reputation abroad with the romantic drama *Intermezzo* (1936), a film that led to the international career of its star, Ingrid BERGMAN. Another of his protégées who made it to Hollywood was Signe HASSO. His first wife (1910–18) was Karin MOLANDER. He was the older brother of Olof MOLANDER.

FILMS INCLUDE: As screenwriter (alone or in collaboration)—*Miller's Document* 1916; *Terje Vigen, Thomas Graal's Best Film* 1917; *Thomas Graal's First Child, Song of the Scarlet Flower* 1918; *Sir Arne's Treasure* 1919; *Gunnar Hede's Saga, Pirates on Lake Malär* 1923. As director—*King of Boda* (also sc.) 1920; *Thomas Graal's Ward* (also sc.), *The Amateur Film* 1922; *33,333* (also sc.) 1924; *Constable Paulus's Easter Bomb* (also sc.), *The Ingmar Inheritance* (also co-sc.) 1925; *To the Orient* (also co-sc.), *She's the Only One* 1926; *His English Wife/Discord, Sealed Lips* 1927; *Women of Paris/The Doctor's Women, Sin* 1928; *Triumph of the Heart* 1929; *Charlotte Löwensköld, Frida's Songs* 1930; *One Night* 1931; *Black Roses, Love and Deficit, We Go Through the Kitchen* (also co-sc.) 1932; *Dear Relatives* (also co-sc.) 1933; *A Quiet Affair, My Aunt's Millions, Bachelor Father* 1934; *Swedenhielms, Under False Colors* 1935; *The Honeymoon Trip, On the Sunny Side, Intermezzo* (also co-sc.), *The Family Secret* 1936; *Sara Learns Manners* 1937; *Dollar* (also co-sc.), *A Woman's Face, One Single Night* 1938; *Variety Is the Spice of Life, Emilie Högguist* (also co-sc.) 1939; *One but a Lion* 1940; *Bright Prospects* (also co-sc.), *Tonight or Never, The Fight Goes On* (also co-sc.) 1941; *Jacob's Ladder, Ride Tonight!* (also co-sc.) 1942; *Darling, I Surrender, Ordet/The Word* (also co-sc.), *There Burned a Flame* 1943; *The Invisible Wall, The Emperor of Portugal* (also co-sc.) 1944; *Mandragora* (also co-sc.) 1945; *It's My Model/Affairs of a Model* 1946; *Woman Without a Face* (also co-sc.) 1947; *Life Begins Now, Eva* (also co-sc.) 1948; *Love Will Conquer* (also co-sc.) 1949; *The Quartet That Split Up* (also co-sc.) 1950; *Fiancée for Hire, Divorced* 1951; *Defiance, Love* (also co-sc.) 1952; *Unmarried* (also co-sc.) 1953; *Sir Arne's Treasure* (also co-sc.) 1954; *The Unicorn* (also co-sc.) 1955; *The Song of the Scarlet Flower* 1956; *Stimulantia* ("The Necklace" episode; also co-sc.) 1967.

Molander, Karin. Actress. Born Karin Edwertz, on May 20, 1890, in Vardinge, Sweden. Vivacious star of early Swedish silents, heroine of many SJÖSTRÖM and STILLER films. She was married (1910–18) to Gustaf MOLANDER and (1922–65) to Lars HANSON.

FILMS INCLUDE: *Half-Breed* 1913, *The Red Tower, Hearts That Meet* 1914; *Madame de Thebes* 1915; *The Avenger, Love and Journalism* 1916; *Thomas Graal's Best Film, A Girl from the Marsh Croft* 1917; *Thomas Graal's First Child* 1918; *The Bomb* 1919; *Erotikon* 1920; *Gabrielle* 1954.

Molander, Olof. Swedish director, screenwriter, actor. *b.* Oct. 18, 1892, Helsinki, Finland. *d.* 1966. Younger brother of Gustaf MOLANDER, he turned to the stage, working in films only intermittently. He specialized in Strindberg productions and for a while headed Stockholm's Royal Dramatic Theatre. His films were typically somber but well handled and superbly acted, with well-defined characterizations.

FILMS (as director): *The Lady of the Camellias* 1925; *Married Life* 1926; *Only a Dancing Girl* (also sc.) 1927; *General von Dobeln* (also co-sc.) 1942; *Women in Prison, I Killed* 1943; *Appassionata* (also sc.) 1944; *Between Us Thieves* (also co-sc.) 1945; *Johansson and Vestman* 1946.

Molina, Alfred. Actor. Born in 1954, in London. *ed.* Guildhall School of Music and Drama. Solid character player of British stage, TV, and films. A first-generation Englishman (his father is Spanish, his mother Italian), he started out as a street-corner stand-up comic, augmenting tips with odd jobs and welfare checks. After many months of struggle, he joined the Royal Shakespeare Company in 1977 and made his screen debut in 1981, playing a small role in *Raiders of the Lost Ark.* Memorable for standout performances as a Russian sailor in Chris Bernard's *Letter to Brezhney* (1985) and as Kenneth Halliwell, the lover-murderer of 60s playwright Joe Orton, in Stephen Frears's *Prick Up Your Ears* (1987).

FILMS: *Raiders of the Lost Ark* (US) 1981; *Meantime* (orig. for TV) 1983; *Number One, Ladyhawke* (US), *Letter to Brezhney* 1985; *Prick Up Your Ears* 1987; *Manifesto* (Yug./US) 1988; *Drowning in the Shallow End* 1989; *Not Without My Daughter* (US), *American Friends* 1991; *Enchanted April* 1992; *The Trial* 1993; *Maverick, White Fang 2: Myth of the White Wolf* 1994; *Species* 1995; *Before and After, Dead Man, The Perez Family, When Pigs Fly* 1996; *Anna Karenina* 1997.

Molina, Angela. Actress. Born in 1953, in Madrid, the daughter of a flamenco dancer. Sensual leading lady of Spanish films and European co-productions. Memorable in Buñuel's last film, *That Obscure Object of Desire,* and several films by Gutierrez ARAGON.

FILMS INCLUDE: *Las Largas Vacaciones del 36* 1975; *Camada negra* 1976; *A un Dio desconocido/To an Unknown God, Cet Obscure Object du Désir/That Obscure Object of Desire* (Fr./Sp.) 1977; *Ogro* (It./Sp.), *Buono Notirie* (It./Sp.) 1978; *L'Ingorgo—una Storia impossible/Traffic Jam* (It./Fr./Sp./Ger.), *La Sabina/The Sabina* 1979; *Gli Occhie la Bocca/The Eyes the Mouth* (It./Fr.), *Demonios en el Jardin/Demons in the Garden* 1982; *Fuego eterno* 1984; *Un Complicato Intrigo di Donne vicoli e delliti/Camorra* (It.) 1985; *Lola, Streets of Gold* (US), *La Mitad del Cielo/Half of Heaven* 1986; *Fuegos, Laura* 1987; *Volvevo i pantaloni/I Wanted Pants* (Ital.), *Sandino* (Sp./Chile), *Rio Negro* (Venez./Fr.) 1990.

Molinaro, Édouard. Director. Born on May 13, 1928, in Bordeaux, France. Intelligent, versatile director who, unlike his New Wave contemporaries, has chosen the route of commercially popular cinema with emphasis on slickness. He directed amateur films, industrial shorts, and documentaries before turning to features in the late 50s. He scored an enormous international box-office hit with *La Cage aux Folles* (1978), an uproarious comedy of gay life, which he handled with unbridled zest mitigated by good taste and clever discretion. It was nominated for an Academy Award as best foreign film. He directed one Hollywood production in 1984.

FILMS: *Le Dos au Mur/Back to the Wall, Un Témoin dans la Ville* 1958; *Des Femmes disparaissent/The Road to Shame* 1959; *Une Fille pour l'Eté/A Mistress for the Summer* (also co-sc.) 1960; *La Mort de Belle/The Passion of Slow Fire* 1961; *Les Sept Péchés capitaux/Seven Capital Sins* ("Envy" episode), *Les Ennemis, Arsène Lupin Contre Arsène Lupin* (also co-sc.) 1962; *Une Ravissante Idiote/A Ravishing Idiot* (also co-sc.), *La Chasse à l'Homme/Male Hunt* 1964; *Quand passent les faisans/Les Escrocs* 1965; *Peau d'Espion/To Commit a Murder* (also co-sc.) 1967; *Oscar* (also co-sc.) 1968; *Hibernatus, Mon Oncle Benjamin* 1969; *La Libertéen Croupe* (also co-sc.) 1970; *Les Aveux les plus doux* 1971; *La Mandarine* 1972; *Allez-vous perdre ailleurs, L'Emmerdeur/A Pain in the A. . . , Le Gang des Otages/The Hostages* 1973; *L'Ironie du Sort* 1974; *Le Téléphone rose/The Pink Telephone* 1975; *Dracula Père et Fils* (also co-sc.) 1976; *L'Homme pressé/Man in a Hurry* 1977; *La Cage aux Folles* (also co-sc.) 1978; *Cause toujours tu m'intéresses* 1979; *Les Séducteurs/Sunday Lovers* (French episode), *La Cage au Folles II* 1980; *Pour Cent Briques t'as plus rien* (also co-sc.) 1982; *Just the Way You Are* (US) 1984; *Palace, L'Amour en Douce* (also co-adapt.) 1985; *Enchanté, A gauche en sortant de l'Acenseur* 1988; *Le Souper* 1993.

Monicelli, Mario. Director. Born on May 15, 1915, in Viareggio (Tuscany), Italy. *ed.* U. of Pisa; U. of Milan (literature and philosophy). The son of a noted journalist, he began as a film critic and amateur filmmaker. His 16 mm, feature-length *I Ragazzi della Via Paal,* based on Molnar's *The Boys of Paul Street*, won an amateur prize at Venice in 1935. He then worked as an assistant director and screenwriter before becoming a director in the late 40s. From 1949 to 1953 he collaborated with STENO (Stefano Vanzina) on eight minor comic films starring Totò, which in time have been re-appraised as important building blocks in the development of a unique bittersweet comedy, Italian-style, that successfully blended genuine social pathos with laughs. Working alone since 1953, he scored an international triumph with *I Soliti Ignoti/Big Deal on Madonna Street* (1958), a delightfully funny satire about a gang of fumbling would-be robbers. His other major achievement is *La Grande Guerra/The Great War* (1959), a biting satire on World War I, which won an award at the Venice Festival. His *I Compagni/The Organizer* is an incisive study of Italian labor unions. Monicelli, who collaborated on most of his own scripts, also contributed to the screenplays of other important directors. These included *Il Documento* (Camerini, 1939), *I Bambini ci guardano/The Children Are Watching Us* (De Sica, 1943), *Aquila nera* (Freda, 1946), *I Miserabili/Les Miserables* (Freda, 1947), *Gioventù perduta/Lost Youth* (Germi, 1947), *In Nome de la Legge/Mafia* (Germi, 1949), *Riso Amaro/Bitter Rice* (De Santis, 1949), *Il Brigante Musolino* (Camerini, 1950), and *A Cavallo della Tigre* (Comencini, 1961). His numerous awards include the best direction prize at Berlin for *Fathers and Sons/The Tailor's Maid* (1957), the Golden Lion at Venice for *The Great War* (1959), the best direction prize at Berlin for *Caro Michele* (1976), and the best direction prize at Berlin for *The Marquess of Grillo* (1982).

FILMS (as director and usually also co-screenwriter): In collaboration with Steno—*Al Diavolo la Celebrità* 1949; *Totò cerca Casa, Vita da Cani, E arrivato il Cavaliere* 1950; *Guardie e Ladri/Cops and Robbers* 1951; *Totò e i Re di Roma* 1952; *Totò e le Donne, Le Infedeli* 1953. Alone—*Proibito* 1954; *Totò e Carolina, Un Eroe dei Nostri Tempi* 1955; *Donatella* 1956; *Padri e Figli/Fathers and Sons/The Tailor's Maid, Il Medico e lo Stregone* 1957; *I Soliti Ignoti/Big Deal on Madonna Street* 1958; *La Grande Guerra/The Great War* 1959; *Risate di Gioia/The Passionate Thief* 1960; *Boccaccio '70* ("Renzo e Luciana" episode) 1962; *I Compagni/The Organizer* 1963; *Alta Infedeltà/High Infidelity* ("Modern People" episode) 1964; *Casanova '70, L'Armata Brancaleone* 1965; *Le Fate/The Queens* ("Queen Armenia" episode) 1966; *La Ragazza con la Pistola/Girl with a Gun, Capriccio all'Italiana* ("La Bambinaia" episode) 1968; *To'è Morta la Nonna* 1969; *Le Coppie* ("Il Frigorifero" episode), *Brancaleone alle Crociate* 1970; *La Mortadella/Lady Liberty* 1971; *Vogliamo di Colonnelli* 1973; *Romanzo Popolare, Amici miei/My Friends* (took over from Germi) 1975; *Caro Michele, Signore e Signori—*

Buonanotte (one episode), *La Goduria* (one episode) 1976; *Un Borghese Piccolo Piccolo, I Nuovi Mostri/The New Monsters/Viva Italia!* (co-dir. with Nino Risi and Ettore Scola) 1977; *Viaggio con Anita/Travels with Anita/Lovers and Liars* 1979; *Temporale Rosy/Hurricane Rosy* 1980; *Camera d'Albergo* 1981; *Il Marquese del Grillo/The Marquess of Grillo, Amici mie—Ato II/Amici miei II* 1982; *Bertolodo Bertoldini e Cacasenno* 1984; *Le Due Vite di Mattia Pascal/The Two Lives of Mathias Pascal* (condensed feature version of longer TV presentation) 1985; *Speriamo che sia Femmina/Let's Hope It's a Girl* 1986; *I Picari/The Rogues* 1987; *Il Male oscuro/The Obscure Illness* 1990.

monitor. A system for checking the quality of a picture or sound while shooting or recording is in process.

monochrome. A single color. The term is usually used to describe black and white but can also apply to the gradations of a single color or hue.

Monogram. An American film production company established in 1930 as an outgrowth of Rayart Productions (formed 1924) by W. Ray Johnston. The company specialized in the production of low-budget films, mostly Westerns, serials, and other action pictures, competing with Republic for leadership in that field. In possession of one of the best ranch locations of any studio, Monogram occasionally turned out some exciting Westerns among its many routine productions. On its roster of cowboy stars of the 30s were Bill Cody, Bob Steele, Rex Bell, Tom Keene, Tim McCoy, and Tex Ritter. John Wayne made a dozen or so Westerns at Monogram during the mid-30s. In the 40s the company gradually improved the quality of its product. In 1946 it formed a wholly owned subsidiary, Allied Artists Productions, to handle its higher-budget films, while continuing to produce B pictures under the banner of Monogram. In 1953 the corporate name was changed from Monogram Pictures Corporation to Allied Artists Pictures Corporation. Film buffs remember Monogram for such low-budget series as the "Bowery Boys" and "Charlie Chan" and a mixed bag of crime melodramas and horror films. Jean-Luc Godard dedicated his first feature film, *Á Bout de Souffle/Breathless,* to Monogram.

monopack. An integral tripack color film with three layers of emulsion, each sensitive to one of the photographic color primaries.

monopole. An adjustable hanger from which studio lights are suspended.

Monroe, Marilyn. Actress. *b.* Norma Jean Mortenson, June 1, 1926, Los Angeles. *d.* 1962. Legendary star of Hollywood films of the 50s. Her mother, Gladys Pearl Baker (née Monroe), was a negative cutter at Columbia and RKO with a history of mental disturbance and suicide in her family. Only when she was 16 and applying for a marriage license did Norma Jean discover that she was illegitimate and that the name entered in her birth certificate as her father's was that of Edward Mortenson, an itinerant baker, who was killed in a motorcycle accident when she was three.

For most of Norma Jean's childhood, her mother was confined in mental institutions. From the age of five, the little girl lived in a succession of foster homes, in which she was subjected to neglect, humiliation, and once even to rape. At nine she was placed in an orphanage and at 11 she went to live with a friend of her mother's. At 16 she quit high school and sought escape from her loveless childhood in a marriage to Jim Dougherty, a 21-year-old aircraft plant worker. A year later she attempted suicide, but it was a halfhearted try. In 1944, when her husband was sent overseas as a merchant marine, she began working as a paint sprayer in a defense plant. It was there that she was discovered by an Army photographer, who asked her to pose for morale-boosting photographs. Her pinups won some popularity among GIs: the Seventh Division Medical Corps voted her the girl they would most like to examine. Soon other photographers began taking notice and one of them introduced her to a modeling agency, where her brown hair was bleached and shortened. By now (1946) she was divorced and looking ahead to a bright career as a model. She was sent to a charm school and her photos soon began appearing on the covers of male magazines and attracting attention in Hollywood. Howard Hughes offered her a screen test, but he was beaten to the punch by 20th Century-Fox, which signed Marilyn to a year's contract in August 1946, at $125 a week. Her name was changed to Marilyn Monroe and she was given the usual starlet buildup—cheesecake photos, mention in gossip columns, poses with celebrities, and acting, singing, and dancing lessons. Everything but actual roles in films.

When she finally made her debut in a bit part in *Scudda-Hoo! Scudda-Hay!* (1948), Marilyn's few close shots were dropped on the cutting-room floor. She played a bit in another film before being dropped by Fox. Undaunted, she continued taking acting classes and in March of 1948 she was signed by Columbia for a lead part in the low-budget musical *Ladies of the Chorus.* But Columbia, too, allowed her option to expire and she found herself again out of work. It was during this period of unemployment that she posed for her famous nude calendar photo. She was paid $50 for her services. The calendar company realized a profit of $750,000 on the million copies it sold.

After a six-month absence, Marilyn returned to the screen in a succession of small roles, typically cast as a dumb platinum blonde. In 1950 she was again signed by Fox and gradually her parts grew in size and importance. Marilyn's rise was now rapid. By the time she married baseball hero Joe DiMaggio, in January of 1954, she was Fox's biggest box-office attraction and Hollywood's newest sex goddess. Her wiggle, her pout, her husky voice, were becoming the object of women's imitation and men's dreams. She exuded breathless sensuality that was at once erotic and wholesome, invitingly real and appealingly funny.

While working on *The Seven Year Itch,* the film with the famous shot of her standing over a subway grating with her skirt blowing up to her face, Marilyn divorced DiMaggio, nine months after their marriage. After completing the film, in a gesture of defiance against Fox and her stereotyped roles, she went to New York, where she announced to the press the formation of Marilyn Monroe Productions, with herself as president, in partnership with photographer Milton Greene. She told reporters she was eager to play serious parts, citing as an example the role of Grushenka in *The Brothers Karamazov.* She ignored the mocking and snickering reactions to her statements and began attending acting classes at the Actors Studio, under the personal tutelage of Lee and Paula Strasberg. She mingled with New York's intellectual crowd and became particularly attached to playwright Arthur MILLER.

In December of 1955, Marilyn was lured back into the Fox fold with a contract that was lucrative and gave her approval over her films' directors. She surprised critics with her subtle performance in her first film under the new contract, *Bus Stop.* Director Joshua Logan commented: "She has the makings of a great comedienne." In June of 1956, Marilyn married Arthur Miller, after converting to Judaism, an Owl and Pussycat match if ever there was one. They left together for England, where Marilyn starred in *The Prince and the Showgirl,* opposite Sir Laurence Olivier, who also directed. The film fizzled critically and commercially, but her next, back in Hollywood, *Some Like It Hot,* was a smash hit.

Marilyn's last film was *The Misfits* (1961), the script of which was written especially for her by Miller. By sad coincidence, it was also the last film of Clark Gable, who died shortly after its completion. The production was beset by difficulties and went far over its budget, largely because of Marilyn's frequent illnesses and spells of depression. At one point she collapsed on the set from an overdose of sleeping pills and was rushed to a hospital. As her tensions grew, her dosage of sleeping pills increased and she began mixing them with alcoholic drinks. She was now seeing her psychiatrist daily and suffering from total physical exhaustion. On January 21, 1961, a week before the opening of *The Misfits,* she divorced Miller. A month after the premiere she entered a hospital for intensive psychiatric care.

Seemingly recovered in the summer of 1962, Marilyn began working in Fox's production *Something's Got to Give.* But her habitual tardiness and frequent absences, tolerated in the past, were so damaging to the progress of production that she was fired from the set. A month later, on the morning of August 5, 1962, her housekeeper found Marilyn Monroe's body nude and lifeless on her bed. An empty bottle of sedatives was found nearby. The coroner's verdict called her death the result of an overdose of barbiturates and a possible suicide. For years after she passed away, stories kept spreading about Monroe's intimate relations with President John F. Kennedy and his brother, Bobby, and speculation abounded about the "real" cause of her death, with many writers and amateur sleuths suspecting foul play and suggesting a political conspiracy to keep her quiet. By 1990 no fewer than 15 postmortem biographies of the star appeared in print and more were announced for publication. Her autobiography, *My Story,* was published in 1974. Documentary, compilation, and dramatized films and TV movies about the star's life and career have also been periodically released. A bewildered superstar in her lifetime, in her death Marilyn Monroe basked in the aura of a myth.

FILMS: *Scudda-Hoo! Scudda-Hay!* (bit), *Dangerous Years* (bit), *Ladies of the Chorus* 1948; *Love Happy, A Ticket to Tomahawk, The Asphalt Jungle, All About Eve, Right Cross, The Fireball* 1950; *Hometown Story, As Young As You Feel, Love Nest, Let's Make It Legal* 1951; *Clash by Night, We're Not Married, Don't Bother to Knock, Monkey Business, O. Henry's Full House* 1952; *Niagara, Gentlemen Prefer Blondes, How to Marry a Millionaire* 1953; *River of No Return, There's No Business Like Show Business* 1954; *The Seven Year Itch* 1955; *Bus Stop* 1956; *The Prince and the Showgirl* 1957; *Some Like It Hot* 1959; *Let's Make Love* 1960; *The Misfits* 1961.

montage. A term derived from the French word for hoisting, setting up, mounting, or assembling—hence, staging in theater usage and editing in film terminology. In the US, the term has been used in a sense akin to that of "photomontage" in still photography—that is, the combining of several images on one frame by superimposition. As applied to motion pictures, this came to specifically describe a sequence made up of a quick succession of brief shots blending and dissolving into one another, created to compress action and convey the passage of time. The technique, typically featuring linked images of such items as calendar pages, newspaper headlines, place names, and train wheels, was particularly popular in Hollywood films of the 30s.

The term *montage* as it is generally understood today is associated with the work and theory of Sergei EISENSTEIN, in which it came to represent the rhetorical arrangement of shots in juxtaposition so that the clash between two adjoining images suggests a third, independent entity and creates a whole new meaning. Eisenstein's ideas of montage were inspired by the editing techniques of D. W. GRIFFITH and the laboratory experiments of Lev KULESHOV. Eisenstein saw montage as a means of eliciting emotional responses from the audience. He identified five types, or levels, of montage: metric, rhythmic, tonal, overtonal, and intellectual, the latter capable of expressing abstract ideas visually.

Montagu, Ivor. Filmmaker, writer. *b.* Apr. 23, 1904, London. *d.* 1984. *ed.* Royal College of Science, London (B.A.); Cambridge (M.A.). The son of a titled banker, he enjoyed a privileged youth that enabled him to indulge early on in two lifelong passions—the cinema and leftist politics. In 1925 he co-founded with Sidney Bernstein London's Film Society, the world's first film club dedicated to the presentation of noncommercial films of artistic merit. In the following years, Montagu became involved in the British film industry in such capacities as importer, exhibitor, film editor, title writer, producer, and director of shorts. He was the first film critic of *The Observer* and *New Statesman and Nation.* His political commitment to the Left led him to translate, from the Russian, Pudovkin's *Film Technique* and Eisenstein's lectures on *Film Form.* A longtime friend and correspondent of Eisenstein's, Montagu was his companion and associate during the Soviet director's trip to Berlin, Paris, and London (1929–30) and his ill-fated Hollywood sojourn in 1930. Montagu later published a book-length account of the trip, *With Eisenstein in Hollywood* (first published in East Germany in 1968). In the mid-30s, Montagu collaborated on several Alfred Hitchcock films. He was associate producer on *The Man Who Knew Too Much* (1934) and *The 39 Steps* (1935) and co-producer of *The Secret Agent* (1936). In 1938 he went to Spain to make propaganda films for the Republicans during the Civil War and, after returning to England, made a compilation film on the conflict, *Peace and Plenty* (1939). During WW II he made films for the British Ministry of Information and later joined the Ealing studios, where, among other assignments, he collaborated on the script of the celebrated feature *Scott of the Antarctic* (1948). From the late 50s he was active in British TV. He was awarded the Lenin Peace Prize in 1959. In 1964 he published *Film World,* a guide to film appreciation. Autobiography: *The Youngest Son* (1970).

Montalban, Ricardo. Actor. Born on Nov. 25, 1920, in Mexico City. Partly educated in the US. He played bit roles in several Broadway productions before making his film debut in his native land in the early 40s. He was recruited by MGM in 1947 and was used as a "Latin lover" type in a number of the studio's films. He tried to break away from the image with nonromantic dramatic roles at MGM and later elsewhere and eventually was given an opportunity to demonstrate a wider acting range on TV. He has appeared in numerous TV dramas, including many segments of 'The Loretta Young Show,' starring his sister-in-law, Loretta YOUNG. He also appeared in a number of Broadway plays and in the early 70s toured the US with Agnes MOOREHEAD and Paul HENREID in a dramatic reading from G. B. Shaw's 'Don Juan in Hell,' playing the title role. Late in his career, he enjoyed great popularity on TV as the star of the series 'Fantasy Island' (1978–84) and as a regular on 'Dynasty II: The Colbys' (1985–87). He won an Emmy for the TV movie *How the West Was Won, Part II* (1978). The actor's older brother, Carlos Montalban (1905–91) appeared in American films occasionally, but was best known for his portrayal of "El Exigente" ("The Demanding One") in a long-running string of TV coffee commercials. Autobiography: *Reflections: A Life in Two Worlds* (1980).

FILMS INCLUDE: In Mexico—*El Verdugo de Sevilla* 1942; *Santa, La Fuga* 1943; *La Hora de la Verdad* 1944. In the US—*Fiesta* 1947; *On an Island with You, The Kissing Bandit* 1948; *Neptune's Daughter, Border Incident, Battleground* 1949;

Mystery Street, Right Cross, Two Weeks with Love 1950; *Across the Wide Missouri, Mark of the Renegade* 1951; *My Man and I* 1952; *Sombrero, Latin Lovers* 1953; *The Saracen Blade* 1954; *A Life in the Balance* 1955; *Three for Jamie Dawn* 1956; *Sayonara* 1957; *Let No Man Write My Epitaph* 1960; *Love Is a Ball* 1963; *Cheyenne Autumn* 1964; *The Money Trap, Madame X, The Singing Nun* 1966; *Sol Madrid, Blue* 1968; *Sweet Charity* 1969; *La Spina Dorsale del Diavolo/The Deserter* (Sp.), *Escape from the Planet of the Apes* 1971; *Conquest of the Planet of the Apes* 1972; *The Train Robbers* 1973; *Joe Panther* 1976; *Star Trek: The Wrath of Khan* 1982; *Cannonball Run II* 1984; *The Naked Gun: From the Files of Police Squad* 1988.

Montaldo, Giuliano. Director. Born on Feb. 22, 1930, in Genoa, Italy. A former actor, he appeared in such films as *Achtung Banditi!* (1951), *Cronache dei Povery Amanti/ Chronicle of Poor Lovers* (1954), and *La Donna del Giorno* (1957), before moving behind the camera as an assistant director and occasional screenwriter. Making his directing debut in 1961, he soon gained some renown for his stylish handling of crime films and political thrillers, like *Grand Slam* (1968) and *Sacco and Vanzetti* (1971). He was the second-unit director on Gillo Pontecorvo's famous *The Battle of Algiers* (1966) and in 1982 directed for Italian TV the celebrated miniseries 'Marco Polo.'

FILMS (as director): *Tiro al Picione* 1961; *Extraconiugale* ("La Moglie svedese" episode), *Una Bella Grinta* (also co-sc.) 1965; *Adogni Costo/Grand Slam* 1967; *Gli Intoccabili/Machine Gun McCain* (also co-sc.), *Gott mit uns* (also co-sc.) 1969; *Sacco e Vanzetti/Sacco and Vanzetti* (also co-story, co-sc.) 1971; *Giordano Bruno* (also co-sc.) 1973; *L'Agnese va a morire* (also co-sc.) 1976; *Circuito chiuso* (also co-sc.), *Il Giocattolo* (also co-sc.) 1978; *Gli occhiali d'oro/The Gold-Rimmed Glasses* 1987; *Tempo di Uccidere/The Short Cut* (also co-sc.) 1989.

Montand, Yves. Actor, singer. *b.* Ivo Livi, Oct. 13, 1921, in Monsummano Alto, Italy. *d.* 1991. His peasant anti-Fascist family fled Italy when Mussolini came to power and he was raised in Marseilles, France, in conditions of poverty. He quit school at 11 and worked in various capacities—busboy, apprentice barber, bartender, and factory laborer among them—before making his singing debut at a local club at 18. He worked his way up to the top Paris music halls and while singing at the Moulin Rouge met Edith Piaf, who took an interest in his career and guided him to stardom as one of France's leading chansonniers. It was she, too, who gave him his first film role in one of her rare screen vehicles, *Etoile sans Lumière/Star Without Light* (1946). He remained primarily known, however, as a singing star until 1953, when he came to the fore with a convincing performance as a dramatic actor in Clouzot's thriller *La Salaire de la Peur/Wages of Fear.* He subsequently starred in many French and European films, and following a triumphant one-man show on Broadway in 1959 he also appeared, not too comfortably, in a number of Hollywood productions. His international reputation was enhanced by solid performances in several Costa-Gavras political thrillers of the late 60s and early 70s. Montand's wife (from 1951 till her death in 1985), actress Simone SIGNORET, co-starred in several of these and other of his films. He remained married to her even through widely rumored affairs, including a candid liaison with Marilyn MONROE while they filmed *Let's Make Love* (1960). Just when it seemed to be slowly fading, his screen career was buttressed in the mid-80s by commanding performances in Claude Berri's twin films *Jean de Florette* and *Manon of the Spring* (both 1986). In 1988 he was honored in a special gala event by the Film Society of Lincoln Center. That year, at age 67, he became a father for the first time by his 28-year-old assistant and girlfriend Carole Amiel. Montand was held in such high regard by his countrymen that in the late 80s he was being seriously considered for the presidency of France. At his death, the national mourning was unprecedented.

FEATURE FILMS: *Etoile sans Lumière/Star Without Light, Les Portes de la Nuit/Gates of the Night* 1946; *L'Idole* 1948; *Souvenirs perdus/Lost Property* 1950; *Paris chante toujours, Parigi e' sempre Parigi* (It.) 1951; *Le Salaire de la Peur/The Wages of Fear, Tempi Nostri* 1953; *Napoléon, Les Héros sont fatigués/Heroes and Sinners* 1955; *Marguerite de la Nuit* (as Mephistopheles) 1956; *Uomini e Lupi* (It.), *Les Sorcières de Salem/The Witches of Salem/The Crucible* 1957; *La Grande Strada Azzura* (It.), *Premier Mai/Le Père et l'Enfant* 1958; *La Loi/Where the Hot Wind Blows* 1959; *Let's Make Love* (US) 1960; *Sanctuary* (US), *Aimez-vous Brahms?/Goodbye Again* (Fr./US) 1961; *My Geisha* (US) 1962; *Compartiment tueurs/The Sleeping Car Murder* 1965; *La Guerre est finie, Paris brûle-t-il?/Is Paris Burning?* (US/Fr.), *Grand Prix* (US) 1966; *Vivre pour vivre/Live for Life* 1967; *Mister Freedom, Le Diable par la Queue/The Devil by the Tail, Un Soir. . . un Train, Z* 1969; *L'Aveu/The Confession, On a Clear Day You Can See Forever* (US) 1970; *Le Cercle rouge, La Folie des Grandeurs/Delusions of Grandeur* 1971; *Tout va Bien, Cesar et Rosalie* 1972; *Etat de Siège/State of Siege* 1973; *Le Hasard et la Violence* 1974; *Le Sauvage/The Savage/Lovers Like Us, Vincent François Paul et les autres/Vincent François Paul and the Others* 1975; *Police Python 357, Le Grand Escogriffe* 1976; *La Menace* 1977; *Les Routes du Sud/The Roads to the South* 1978; *Clair de Femme/Womanlight, I. . . comme Icare* 1979; *Le Choix des Armes/Choice of Arms* 1981; *Tout Feu tout Flamme/All Fired Up* 1982; *Garçon!* 1983; *Jean de Florette, Manon des Sources/Manon of the Spring* 1986; *Trois Places pour le 26* 1988; *Netchaiev est de retour* 1991.

Montez, Maria. Actress. *b.* Maria Africa Vidal de Santo Silas, June 6, 1918, Barahona, Dominican Republic, the daughter of the Spanish consul to that province. *d.* 1951. Exotic beauty of Arabian Nights–style Hollywood adventures of the 40s, she had tried stage acting in Europe before becoming a New York model. In 1941 she started her screen career playing bit parts in Universal films. Pathetically unskilled at acting (or singing or dancing for that matter), she nevertheless became immensely popular in a string of glossy-cheap but highly profitable color adventure yarns, often co-starring fellow camel riders Jon Hall, Sabu, or Turhan Bey. In her heyday she was known affectionately as "The Queen of Technicolor." When her career began sinking in the sand dunes, partly because of a weight problem, she went to Europe with her second husband (from 1943), Jean-Pierre AUMONT, and appeared in a number of French and Italian action pictures. Long after her premature death from a heart attack while taking a bath, she remains the object of an extensive fan cult brought on by nostalgia and a thirst for high camp. Her (and Aumont's) daughter, Tina Marquand (*b.* Maria-Christina Salomons, Feb. 14, 1946, Los Angeles), is an actress in French and international films.

FILMS: *The Invisible Woman* 1940; *Lucky Devils, The Boss of Bullion City, That Night in Rio, Raiders of the Desert, Moonlight in Hawaii, South of Tahiti* 1941; *Bombay Clipper, The Mystery of Marie Roget, Arabian Nights* (as Scheherazade) 1942; *White Savage* 1943; *Ali Baba and the Forty Thieves, Follow the Boys, Cobra Woman, Gypsy Wildcat, Bowery to Broadway* 1944; *Sudan* 1945; *Tangier* 1946; *The Exile, Pirates of Monterey* 1947; *Siren of Atlantis* (as Antinea), *Portrait d'un Assassin* (Fr.) 1949; *Hans le Marin/The Wicked City* (Fr.), *Il Ladro di Venezia/The Thief of Venice* (It.) 1950; *Amore e Sangue/City of Violence/Sensuality* (It./Ger.), *La Vendetta del Corsaro/The Pirate's Revenge* (It.) 1951.

Montgomery, Douglass. Actor. *b.* Robert Douglass Montgomery, Oct. 29, 1907, Brantford, Ontario, Canada. *d.* 1966. Leading man of Hollywood films of the 30s, mostly second features, at first known as Kent Douglass. In the 40s he appeared in several British films.

FILMS INCLUDE: As Kent Douglass—*Paid* 1930; *Daybreak, Five and Ten, Waterloo Bridge, A House Divided* 1931. As Douglass Montgomery—*Little Women* 1933; *Eight Girls in a Boat, Little Man What Now?, Music in the Air* 1934; *The Mystery of Edwin Drood, Lady Tubbs, Harmony Lane* 1935; *Counsel for Crime* 1937; *The Cat and the Canary* 1939; *The Way to the Stars/Johnny in the Clouds* (UK) 1945; *Woman to Woman* (UK) 1946; *Forbidden* (UK) 1948.

Montgomery, George. Actor. Born George Montgomery Letz, on Aug. 29, 1916, in Brady, Mont. Ruggedly handsome leading man of numerous Hollywood Westerns and action pictures. One of 14 children of an immigrant Russian farmer, he attended the University of Montana for two years, majoring in interior decorating and excelling in collegiate heavyweight boxing. He began appearing in low-budget Republic action films as an extra, stuntman, and bit player in 1935, using his real name, George Letz. It wasn't until the early 40s, however, that he graduated to leading roles at Fox as George Montgomery. He became popular for a while, thanks to his masculine good looks and publicity surrounding his successive engagements to such Hollywood stars as Ginger Rogers and Hedy Lamarr and his 1943 marriage to Dinah SHORE, which ended in divorce in 1963. His career was interrupted by WW II service, after which he was seen for the most part in minor action productions from Columbia and other studios. In the late 50s he starred in the TV series 'Cimarron City' (1958–59) and in the early 60s he branched out briefly into directing-producing-writing of low-budget adventure films, which he shot for economy reasons in the Philippines.

FILMS INCLUDE: As George Letz—*The Singing Vagabond* 1935; *Conquest* 1937; *The Lone Ranger* (serial), *Billy the Kid Returns* 1938; *Wall Street Cowboy* 1939. As George Montgomery—*The Cisco Kid and the Lady, Star Dust, Young People* 1940; *The Cowboy and the Blonde, Accent on Love, Riders of the Purple Sage, Cadet Girl* 1941; *Roxie Hart, Ten Gentlemen from West Point, Orchestra Wives* 1942; *China Girl, Coney Island, Bomber's Moon* 1943; *Three Little Girls in Blue* 1946; *The Brasher Doubloon* (as private eye Philip Marlowe) 1947; *Lulu Belle, The Girl from Manhattan, Belle Starr's Daughter* 1948; *Dakota Lil, Davy Crockett—Indian Scout* (title role), *The Iroquois Trail* 1950; *The Sword of Monte Cristo, The Texas Rangers* 1951; *Indian Uprising, Cripple Creek* 1952; *The Pathfinder, Fort Ti, Gun Belt* 1953; *The Battle of Rogue River, The Lone Gun* 1954; *Masterson of Kansas, Robber's Roost* 1955; *Huk!* 1956; *Last of the Badmen, Street of Sinners, Pawnee* 1957; *The Man from God's Country, Black Patch* 1958; *Watusi* 1959; *The Steel Claw* (also dir., prod., co-sc.) 1961; *Samar* (also dir., prod., co-sc.) 1962; *From Hell to Borneo* (also dir., prod., sc.), *Guerrillas in Pink Lace* (also dir., prod., sc.) 1964; *Battle of the Bulge* 1965; *Bomb at 10:10* (Yug.), *Hallucination Generation* 1966; *Hostile Guns* 1967; *Warkill* 1968; *Devil's Harvest* 1971; *The Daredevil* 1972.

Montgomery, Peggy. Actress. Born in 1907, in Rock Island, Ill. A silent film star, confused for many years with the actress who was the former BABY PEGGY. Little is known about this Peggy Montgomery other than the films she appeared in from 1924 to 1929. It is speculated that a difficult transition from silent films to talkies, as well as marriage, may have prompted her disappearance from the screen after 1929. See also BABY PEGGY.

FILMS: *Rainbow Rangers* 1924; *The Dangerous Dub, Fighting Courage, The Hollywood Reporter, Looking for Trouble, Prisoners of the Storm, The Speed Demon* 1926; *The Desert of the Lost, Sensation Seekers, The Sonora Kid* 1927; *Arizona Days, Saddle Mates, Silent Trail* 1928; *Fighters of the Saddle* 1929.

Montgomery, Robert. Actor, director. *b.* Henry Montgomery, Jr., May 21, 1904, Beacon, N.Y. *d.* 1981. The son of a rubber company president, he was educated at exclusive private schools but was forced to work as a railroad mechanic and oil tanker deckhand after his father's death left the family penniless in 1920. He then moved to New York, hoping to become a writer, but after repeated rejections of his short stories he was persuaded by a friend to try acting and made his stage debut in 1924. By the late 20s he was an established Broadway performer and in 1929 joined many other stage actors in the mass migration into films that followed the advent of sound. As an MGM contract player, he was typecast for years as a happy-go-lucky, debonair leading man, opposite such glittering stars as Norma Shearer, Greta Garbo, Joan Crawford, and Myrna Loy; but now and then—once as "punishment" for defying studio management—he was allowed to alter the image and turned out sterling performances as a psychotic in such films as *The Big House* (1930) and *Night Must Fall* (1937). He was nominated for Academy Awards as best actor for the latter as well as for *Here Comes Mr. Jordan* (1941). In 1935 he was elected to the first of four terms as president of SAG (Screen Actors Guild). In that capacity, he gained much publicity in 1939 when he helped expose labor racketeering in the film industry. In 1941 he was commissioned a lieutenant in the US Naval Reserve and after serving briefly as assistant naval attaché at the embassy in London, he was assigned to set up a naval operations room in the White House. He later commanded a PT boat in the Pacific and was an operations officer aboard a destroyer during the D-Day invasion of France. By that time a lieutenant commander, he was awarded the Bronze Star and was later decorated as a Chevalier of the French Legion of Honor.

After his discharge from the service, Montgomery returned to Hollywood, this time as director as well as actor. At first he filled in for John Ford during the latter's illness on the set of *They Were Expendable* (1945); then, receiving his first director's screen credit, he turned out an unusual, controversial production, *Lady in the Lake* (1947), a Raymond Chandler mystery thriller told in the first person through tricky subjective camera angles. He went on to direct and star in several other films with variable success before retiring from the screen and turning his attention to TV, the stage, and politics.

From 1950 through 1957 Montgomery produced, directed, hosted, and occasionally starred in 'Robert Montgomery Presents,' a highly regarded weekly drama anthology series on TV. In 1955 he won a Tony as best director on Broadway for the play 'The Desperate Hours.' He later formed Cagney-Montgomery Productions with James Cagney to produce *The Gallant Hours* (1960), his final effort as a film director.

Back in 1947, Montgomery, as a political activist with a conservative outlook, headed the Hollywood Republican Committee to elect Thomas E. Dewey president. That same year he testified as a "friendly witness" in the first round of the House Un-American Activities Committee, denouncing communist infiltration into Hollywood. After helping Eisenhower's 1952 campaign, he was appointed a special consultant to the president on TV and public communications.

Also in the 60s, Montgomery served as a communications consultant to John D. Rockefeller III and a director of R. H. Macy, the Milwaukee Telephone Company, and Lincoln Center for the Performing Arts. In 1969–70 he was president of Lincoln Center's Repertory Theater. His daughter, Elizabeth Montgomery (*b.* Apr. 15, 1933, Los Angeles; *d.* 1994), beloved as the well-meaning witch Samantha in the TV series 'Bewitched,' also starred in many made-for-television movies as well as the features *Who's Been Sleeping in My Bed?* (1963) opposite Dean MARTIN and *Johnny Cool* (also 1963).

FILMS: As actor—*The Single Standard* (bit), *So This Is College, Three Live Ghosts, Untamed, Their Own Desire* 1929; *Free and Easy, The Divorcee, The Big House, Sins of the Children, Our Blushing Brides, Love in the Rough, War Nurse* 1930; *Inspiration, The Easiest Way, Strangers May Kiss, Shipmates, The Man in Possession, Private Lives* (as Elyot Chase) 1931; *Lovers Courageous, But the Flesh Is Weak, Letty Lynton, Blondie of the Follies, Faithless* 1932; *Hell Below, When Ladies Meet, Made on Broadway, Another Language, Night Flight* 1933; *Fugitive Lovers, The Mystery of Mr. X, Riptide, Hide-Out, Forsaking All Others* 1934; *Biography of a Bachelor Girl, Vanessa: Her Love Story, No More Ladies* 1935; *Petticoat Fever, Trouble for Two, Piccadilly Jim* 1936; *The Last of Mrs. Cheyney, Night Must Fall, Ever Since Eve, Live Love and Learn* 1937; *The First 100 Years, Yellow Jack, Three Loves Has Nancy* 1938; *Fast and Loose* 1939; *The Earl of Chicago, Busman's Honeymoon/Haunted Honeymoon* (as fictional detective Lord Peter Wimsey; UK) 1940; *Mr. and Mrs. Smith, Rage in Heaven, Here Comes Mr. Jordan, Unfinished Business* 1941; *They Were Expendable* (also part dir., uncredited) 1945; *The Saxon Charm, June Bride* 1948. As director-actor—*Lady in the Lake, Ride the Pink Horse* 1947; *Once More My Darling* 1949; *Your Witness/Eye Witness* (UK) 1950; *The Gallant Hours* (dir., prod., unbilled cameo appearance) 1960.

Montiel, Sarita (Sara). Singer, actress. Born Maria Antonia Abad, in 1928, in Campo de Criptana, Spain. Popular singer and movie star of the Spanish-speaking world, she also appeared in several Hollywood films. Once married to director Anthony MANN.

FILMS INCLUDE: *Te quiero para mi* 1944; *Bambu* 1945; *Por el Gran Premio* 1946; *Don Quijote de la Mancha/Don Quixote* (as Antonia), *Confidencia, Vidas confusas* 1947; *Locura de Amor/The Mad Queen* 1948; *El Capitan Veneno* 1950; *El Fuerte, Emigrantes* 1952; *That Man from Tangier* (US) 1953; *Vera Cruz* (US) 1954; *Serenade* (US) 1956; *Run of the Arrow* (US) 1957; *La Violetera* 1958; *Carmen de la Ronda/The Devil Made a Woman/A Girl Against Napoleon* 1959; *Mi Ultimo Tango* 1960; *Pecado de Amor* 1961; *La Bella Lola* 1962; *Samba* 1963; *Varieties* 1971.

Montuori, Carlo. Director of photography. *b.* Aug. 3, 1885, Casacalenda, Italy. Deceased. Dean of Italian motion picture cameramen, with a career that spanned the history of Italian cinema from its beginnings, through neorealism, and into the early 60s. Most important work: *The Bicycle Thief* (1948). His son, Mario Montuori (*b.* 1920, Rome), is also a director of photography of Italian films.

FILMS INCLUDE: *La Fuga degli Amanti* 1914; *I Borgia* 1918; *Dante* 1921; *Ben-Hur* (2nd unit) 1926; *Nerone* 1930; *Resurrection* 1931; *Darò un Milione* 1936; *Don Pasquale* 1940; *Umanità, Vivere in Pace/To Live in Peace* 1946; *Il Passatore/A Bullet for Stefano* 1947; *Anni difficili/Difficult Years, Ladri di Biciclette/The Bicycle Thief* 1948; *Cuori senza Frontiere/The White Line* 1950; *Altri Tempi/Times Gone By* (co-phot.), *La Città si difende* 1951; *La Nemica* 1952; *L'Oro di Napoli/Gold of Naples, Pane Amore e Gelosia/Frisky* 1954; *Il Segno di Venere/The Sign of Venus* 1955; *Il Tetto/The Roof* 1955; *Le Bambole/The Dolls* (Comencini episode) 1965.

Monty Python. Collective name for a comedy group headed by six zany British performer-writers who scored great success in the 60s and 70s on BBC-TV with the inventive, literate, and bawdy series 'Monty Python's Flying Circus.' The series became a hit on American public television and inspired several off-the-wall feature films, including a parody of Arthurian romances, *Monty Python and the Holy Grail* (1974), and a parody of the life of Christ, *The Life of Brian* (1979). The core ensemble comprised Graham CHAPMAN, John CLEESE, Terry GILLIAM (the sole American), Eric IDLE, Terry JONES, and Michael PALIN. Though Chapman is deceased and the group no longer performs as Monty Python, the surviving members have gone on to individual success as directors, screenwriters, and actors, often appearing in each other's projects.

FILMS: *And Now for Something Completely Different* 1972; *Monty Python and the Holy Grail* 1974; *The Life of Brian* 1979; *Monty Python Live at the Hollywood Bowl* 1982; *Monty Python's The Meaning of Life* 1983.

mood music. Prerecorded music written in various moods and styles to provide appropriate backgrounds for a given film or sequence. Usually acquired from a music library, such music is cataloged under appropriate headings—cheerful, sad, romantic, etc. This type of "canned" music is sometimes used for background in features with very low budgets and more commonly in documentaries, industrial films, travelogs, and other nonfeature productions that cannot afford an original score.

Moody, Ron. Actor, singer. Born Ronald Moodnick, on Jan. 8, 1924, in London. Sad-faced character comedian of British stage, TV, and films. He played Fagin in both the stage and screen versions of *Oliver!*

FILMS INCLUDE: *Davy* 1957; *Follow a Star* 1959; *Make Mine Mink* 1960; *A Pair of Briefs* 1962; *The Mouse on the Moon* 1963; *Murder Most Foul* 1964; *Oliver!* (as Fagin) 1968; *David Copperfield* (as Uriah Heep; US/UK), *The Twelve Chairs* (US) 1970; *Flight of the Doves* (US) 1971; *Legend of the Werewolf* 1974; *Dogpound Shuffle* 1977; *The Spaceman and King Arthur/Unidentified Flying Oddball* 1979; *Wrong Is Right* (US) 1982; *Where Is Parsifal?* 1984.

Moore, Clayton. Actor. Born on Sept. 14, 1908, in Chicago. A former circus aerialist and male model, he entered films in 1938, performing stunts and playing bits until 1942, when he began playing lead roles. He starred in many serials and low-budget action pictures and played villains in some others, and is best known as the Lone Ranger in the long-running TV series (1949–52 and again 1954–57) and its two-feature offspring. Years after his 1959 retirement from the screen, Moore continued appearing in commercials and promotional events, donning the costume and mask of his celluloid alter ego. He attracted wide sympathy in 1980, when the owners of the Lone Ranger copyright, planning a feature film with a younger actor, obtained a court order denying Moore the right to wear the outfit in public. Fan outcry later helped the actor regain that right.

FILMS INCLUDE: *Dick Tracy Returns* (serial) 1938; *Sergeant Madden* 1939; *Kit Carson, The Son of Monte Cristo* 1940; *International Lady* 1941; *Perils of Nyoka* (serial), *Black Dragons* 1942; *The Crimson Ghost* (serial) 1946; *Jesse James Rides Again* (serial), *Along the Oregon Trail* 1947; *Adventures of Frank and Jesse James* (serial) 1948; *The Ghost of Zorro* (serial), *Frontier Investigator, Masked Raiders* 1949; *Bandits of El Dorado* 1951; *Son of Geronimo* (serial) 1952; *Jungle Drums of Africa* 1953; *The Black Dakotas* 1954; *The Lone Ranger* 1956; *The Lone Ranger and the Lost City of Gold* 1958; *The Ghost of Zorro* 1959.

Moore, Cleo. Actress. *b.* Oct. 31, 1928, Baton Rouge, La.

d. 1973. Brassy leading lady of Hollywood films of the 50s, habitual heroine of shrill Hugo HAAS melodramas. After retiring from the screen, she ran unsuccessfully for governor of Louisiana.

FILMS: *Congo Bill* (serial) 1948; *Dynamite Pass, This Side of the Law, Rio Grande Patrol, Hunt the Man Down* 1950; *Gambling House* 1951; *On Dangerous Ground, The Pace That Thrills, Strange Fascination* 1952; *The Neighbor's Wife, One Girl's Confession* 1953; *Bait, The Other Woman* 1954; *Women's Prison, Hold Back Tomorrow* 1955; *Over-Exposed* 1956; *Hit and Run* 1957.

Moore, Colleen. Actress. *b.* Kathleen Morrison, Aug. 19, 1900, Port Huron, Mich. *d.* 1988. Popular star of Hollywood silents and early talkies who at the height of her career personified the independent "flapper" of the Roaring Twenties and strongly influenced the hairstyle and fashions of the period. The daughter of an irrigation engineer, she was convent-educated and later studied piano at the Detroit Conservatory. According to her autobiography, *Silent Star* (1968), she was taken into films as repayment by D. W. Griffith to her uncle, Walter Howey (editor of the Chicago *Examiner,* who was immortalized by Hecht-MacArthur in *The Front Page*), for helping Griffith clear *The Birth of a Nation* and *Intolerance* through the censors. Contrary to many sources, she never appeared in *Intolerance,* not even as an extra, having arrived in Hollywood in 1917, the year following the picture's release. She began her screen career modestly, as a leading lady in B pictures and Westerns, several times opposite Tom Mix, but in the 20s she gained sudden popularity as a star as an exuberant flapper, portraying bobbed-haired, light-hearted jazz-age heroines in many films for First National. Her first (1923–30) of four husbands, John McCormick, was production head of that company, a subsidiary of Warner Bros. Her next two husbands were stockbrokers and she herself successfully invested her earnings from films (she was among Hollywood's highest-paid stars) in the stock market. In 1983, aged 83, she married a building contractor who survived her. She authored, in addition to her autobiography, a book on investments, *How Women Can Make Money in the Stock Market,* and a book about a prized collection of miniatures, *Colleen Moore's Doll House.*

FEATURE FILMS: *The Bad Boy, An Old Fashioned Young Man, Hands Up!, The Savage* 1917; *A Hoosier Romance, Little Orphan Annie* 1918; *The Busher, The Wilderness Trail, The Man in the Moonlight, The Egg Crate Wallop, Common Property* 1919; *The Cyclone, When Dawn Came, The Devil's Claim, So Long Letty, Dinty* 1920; *The Sky Pilot, The Lotus Eater, His Nibs* 1921; *Come On Over, The Wall Flower, Affinities, Forsaking All Others, Broken Chains, The Ninety and Nine* 1922; *Look Your Best, The Nth Commandment, Slippy McGee, Broken Hearts of Broadway, The Huntress, April Showers, Flaming Youth* 1923; *Through the Dark, Painted People, The Perfect Flapper, Flirting with Love* 1924; *So Big, Sally, The Desert Flower, We Moderns* 1925; *Irene, Ella Cinders, It Must Be Love, Twinkletoes* 1926; *Orchids and Ermine, Naughty but Nice* 1927; *Her Wild Oat, Happiness Ahead, Lilac Time, Oh Kay!* 1928; *Synthetic Sin, Why Be Good?, Smiling Irish Eyes, Footlights and Fools* 1929; *The Power and the Glory* 1933; *Social Register, Success at Any Price, The Scarlet Letter* 1934.

Moore, Constance. Actress, singer. Born on Jan. 18, 1919, in Sioux City, Iowa. A band vocalist and radio singer, she entered films after starring on Broadway in 'By Jupiter' (1942). She played leads and second leads in many productions of the late 30s and 40s, mostly second features, returning to the screen once in the 50s and once in the 60s. She co-starred with Robert Young in the short-lived TV series 'Window on Main Street' (1961–62).

FILMS INCLUDE: *Prescription for Romance* 1937; *The Crime of Dr. Hallet, Prison Break, The Missing Guest, Swing That Cheer* 1938; *Buck Rogers* (serial), *You Can't Cheat an Honest Man, Mutiny on the Blackhawk, Hawaiian Nights, Charlie McCarthy—Detective* 1939; *Framed, La Conga Nights, Argentine Nights* 1940; *Las Vegas Nights, I Wanted Wings, Buy Me That Town* 1941; *Take a Letter Darling* 1942; *Show Business, Atlantic City* 1944; *Earl Carroll Vanities, Delightfully Dangerous, Mexicana* 1945; *In Old Sacramento, Earl Carroll Sketchbook* 1946; *Hit Parade of 1947* 1947; *The 13th Letter* 1951; *Spree* 1967.

Moore, Demi. Actress. Born Demi Guynes, on Nov. 1, 1963, in Roswell, N.M. Spunky, independent-minded leading lady of Hollywood films of the 80s and 90s. The daughter of a novice newspaperman-advertising man who moved the family around in pursuit of jobs, she kept changing schools and friends until finally settling down in West Hollywood with her mother and brother, following the divorce of her parents. At 16, she quit school and left home, determined to become a "movie star." She posed nude on the cover of *Oui* magazine and stumbled into a teenage marriage with a rock musician named Freddy Moore before landing a part in the soap opera 'General Hospital.' Movie roles followed, starting in 1981. But success remained elusive for a number of years, during which she indulged in drugs, got divorced, became engaged to actor Emilio ESTEVEZ, and appeared in inconsequential movies as just another promising face in Hollywood's "Brat Pack" gallery. In 1987 she married actor Bruce WILLIS and three years later she soared to top stardom in the wake of the success of the hit romantic fantasy *Ghost.* Taking charge of the future course of her now-sizzling career, she formed her own production company, Rufglen. Moore received much publicity in 1991 after she was featured nude in the eighth month of her pregnancy on a cover of *Vanity Fair*, a gambit she later repeated after giving birth to show off her regained figure. After a number of major flops in 1991, Moore continued to secure her position as one of Hollywood's favorite and most bankable leading ladies in such box-office hits as *A Few Good Men* and *Indecent Proposal*. She has three children with Willis.

FILMS: *Choices* 1981; *Young Doctors in Love, Parasite* 1982; *Blame It on Rio, No Small Affair* 1984; *St. Elmo's Fire* 1985; *About Last Night. . ., One Crazy Summer, Wisdom* 1986; *The Seventh Sign* 1988; *We're No Angels* 1989; *Ghost* 1990; *Nothing But Trouble, The Butcher's Wife, Mortal Thoughts* (also co-prod.) 1991; *A Few Good Men* 1992; *Indecent Proposal* 1993; *Disclosure* 1994; *Now and Then* (also co-prod.), *The Scarlet Letter* 1995; *The Hunchback of Notre Dame* (v/o), *The Juror, Striptease, Beavis and Butt-head Do America* (unbilled cameo) 1996; *G.I. Jane* (also co-prod.) 1997.

Moore, Dickie. Actor. Born on Sept. 5, 1925, in Los Angeles. Popular child star of the 30s. He was an infant just beyond his first birthday when he made his screen debut playing John Barrymore as a baby in *The Beloved Rogue* (1927). He later appeared in scores of features as well as many "Our Gang" comedy shorts, remaining one of Hollywood's best-liked boy actors for about a decade. He fared less successfully in adolescent and juvenile roles in the 40s, although he received much publicity when he gave Shirley Temple her first screen kiss in *Miss Annie Rooney* (1942). He later played a number of adult roles before retiring from the screen in the early 50s for a career in publicity. He also produces industrial shows.

FILMS INCLUDE: *The Beloved Rogue* 1927; *Object—Alimony* 1928; *Son of the Gods, Passion Flower* 1930; *Aloha,*

Seed, The Star Witness, The Squaw Man, Husband's Holiday 1931; *Manhattan Parade, Union Depot, The Expert, Disorderly Conduct, So Big, No Greater Love, Winner Take All, Million Dollar Legs, Blonde Venus, Deception, The Devil Is Driving* 1932; *Obey the Law, Gabriel Over the White House, Oliver Twist* (title role), *Cradle Song, A Man's Castle* 1933; *Gallant Lady, This Side of Heaven, In Love with Life, Upper World, The Human Side* 1934; *Little Men, The World Accuses, Peter Ibbetson, So Red the Rose* (as Middleton Bedford) 1935; *The Story of Louis Pasteur, The Little Red School House, Timothy's Quest, Star for a Night* 1936; *The Life of Emile Zola, The Bride Wore Red* 1937; *My Bill, The Gladiator, The Arkansas Traveler* 1938; *Hidden Power, The Under-Pup* 1939; *The Blue Bird, A Dispatch from Reuters* 1940; *Sergeant York* 1941; *Adventures of Martin Eden, Miss Annie Rooney* 1942; *Heaven Can Wait, Happy Land, Jive Junction, The Song of Bernadette* (bit) 1943; *The Eve of St. Mark, Youth Runs Wild* 1944; *Out of the Past* 1947; *16 Fathoms Deep* 1948; *Bad Boy* 1949; *Cody of the Pony Express* (serial), *Killer Shark* 1950; *Eight Iron Men* 1952; *The Member of the Wedding* 1953.

Moore, Dudley. Actor, musician, composer. Born on Apr. 19, 1935, in Dagenham, Essex, England. *ed.* Guildhall School of Music; Oxford. Diminutive (5' 2"), implausible romantic screen star of impish, teddy-bear appeal. A railway electrician's son, he was a musical prodigy who attended Oxford (1954–58) on an organ scholarship. He became involved in school dramatics and teamed up with Cambridge undergraduates Jonathan Miller, Peter Cook, and Alan Bennett to form the popular student satirical revue 'Beyond the Fringe.' At the same time he was making a name as a jazz pianist, performing with his trio in fashionable nightclubs, and releasing some bawdy recordings. After gaining national exposure as the star of his own TV shows, he began appearing in British film, for some of which he also composed songs or scores. He was propelled to movie stardom in 1979 on the strength of his disarming performance as a frantic mid-lifer who lusts after Bo DEREK in Blake Edwards's Hollywood's hit film *10.* Thereafter, he stayed in America. His popularity was enhanced by Steve Gordon's *Arthur* (1981), but later gradually diminished because of poorly selected screen vehicles. Moore's passion for beautiful women extended beyond his movie roles. He has had a number of wives, including British actress Suzy KENDALL, American actress Tuesday WELD, former Miss America Susan Anton, and model Brogan Lane.

FILMS (as actor): In the UK—*The Wrong Box* 1966; *Bedazzled* (also co-story, mus.) 1967; *30 Is a Dangerous Age Cynthia* (also co-sc., mus.), *Inadmissible Evidence* (mus., singing only) 1968; *Monte Carlo or Bust/Those Daring Young Men in Their Jaunty Jalopies, Staircase* (mus. only; US), *The Bed Sitting Room* 1969; *Alice's Adventures in Wonderland* (as the Dormouse) 1972; *The Hound of the Baskervilles* (as both Dr. Watson and Sherlock Holmes's mother; also co-sc., mus.) 1977. In the US—*Foul Play* (also mus.) 1978; *10* 1979; *Wholly Moses* 1980; *Arthur* 1981; *Six Weeks* (also mus.) 1982; *Lovesick, Romantic Comedy* 1983; *Unfaithfully Yours, Best Defense, Micki and Maude* 1984; *Santa Claus: The Movie* 1985; *Koneko Monogatari* (Jap.) 1986; *Like Father Like Son* 1987; *Arthur 2: On the Rocks* (also exec. prod.) 1988; *The Adventures of Milo and Otis* (narr.) 1989; *Crazy People* 1990; *Blame it on the Bellboy* 1992; *The Pickle* 1993.

Moore, Grace. Singer, actress. *b.* Mary Willie Grace Moore, Dec. 5, 1901, Slabtown (Cocke Co.), Tenn. *d.* 1947. Vivacious blonde lyrical soprano of Broadway musicals, then the Metropolitan Opera, she starred in two MGM films of the early 30s but was fired when she put on too much weight. She was then hired by Columbia and starred in a string of successful productions, which helped to popularize opera on the screen. She was nominated for a best actress Academy Award for her performance in *One Night of Love* (1934). She was killed in a plane crash over Copenhagen during a European concert tour. She had written an autobiography, *You're Only Human Once* (1944). Kathryn Grayson portrayed her in the film biography *So This Is Love* (1953).

FILMS: *A Lady's Morals* 1930; *New Moon* 1931; *One Night of Love* 1934; *Love Me Forever* 1935; *The King Steps Out* 1936; *When You're in Love, I'll Take Romance* 1937; *Louise* (Fr.) 1939.

Moore, Ida. Actress. *b.* 1883, Altoona, Kans. *d.* 1964. Character player of the American stage and Hollywood films. She played kindly mothers or sweet little old ladies in numerous films of the 40s and 50s.

FILMS INCLUDE: *The Merry Widow, Thank You* 1925; *The Uninvited, Once Upon a Time* 1944; *Easy to Look At* 1945; *The Dark Mirror, From This Day Forward, To Each His Own* 1946; *Easy Come Easy Go, The Egg and I* 1947; *Good Sam, Johnny Belinda* 1948; *Ma and Pa Kettle, Roseanna McCoy, Rope of Sand* 1949; *Backfire, Mr. Music, Fancy Pants, Harvey* 1950; *The Lemon Drop Kid, Show Boat* 1951; *Scandal Sheet* 1952; *Scandal at Scourie* 1953; *The Country Girl* 1954; *Desk Set* 1957; *Rock-a-Bye Baby* 1958.

Moore, Juanita. Actress. Born in 1922. Warm, intelligent African-American actress often seen in wise, beleaguered character roles. Received Academy Award nomination as self-sacrificing mother and housekeeper in *Imitation of Life*. Also active in TV from the 1950s–1970s.

FILMS INCLUDE: *Lydia Bailey, Affair in Trinidad* 1952; *Witness to Murder* 1954; *Women's Prison* 1955; *Ransom, The Girl Can't Help It* 1956; *A Band of Angels, Green Eyed Blonde* 1957; *Imitation of Life* 1959; *Tammy Tell Me True, A Raisin in the Sun* 1961; *Walk on the Wild Side* 1962; *Papa's Delicate Condition* 1963; *The Singing Nun* 1966; *Rosie, Up Tight* 1968; *The Skin Game* 1971; *Fox Style* 1973; *Thomasine and Bushrod, Abby* 1974; *Two Moon Junction* 1988.

Moore, Julianne. Actress. Born Julie Smith, ca. 1961. *ed.* School of Fine Arts, Boston. Striking, lovely actress of stage and screen who gained attention for her work on and off Broadway, particularly in plays by Caryl Churchill. Moving on to daytime television and earning an Emmy for her role on 'As the World Turns' in 1988, she made the transition to several major feature film roles for such notable directors as Robert ALTMAN, the late Louis MALLE, and the lead in independent filmmaker Todd HAYNES's *Safe* (1995).

FILMS: *Tales from the Darkside: The Movie* 1990; *The Gun in Betty Lou's Handbag, The Hand That Rocks the Cradle* 1992; *Benny & Joon, Body of Evidence, The Fugitive, Short Cuts* 1993; *Vanya On 42nd Street* 1994; *Assassins, Nine Months, Roommates, Safe* 1995; *Surviving Picasso* 1996; *Boogie Nights, The Lost World, The Myth of Fingerprints* 1997.

Moore, Kieron. Actor. Born Kieron O'Hanrahan, in 1925, in Skibbereen, Ireland. Husky, stern leading man of many British and several Hollywood films. On the stage since 1942. In the late 70s he directed and narrated two documentary films about the struggle for survival in the Third World.

FILMS INCLUDE: *The Voice Within* 1945; *A Man About the House, Mine Own Executioner* 1947; *Anna Karenina* (as Count Vronsky) 1948; *Saints and Sinners* 1949; *The Naked Heart/Maria Chapdelaine* (UK/Fr.) 1950; *David and Bathsheba* (as Uriah the Hittite; US), *Ten Tall Men* (US) 1951; *The Green Scarf* 1954; *Satellite in the Sky* 1956; *The Key* 1958; *The Angry Hills, Darby O'Gill and the Little People* (US) 1959; *The League of Gentlemen, The Day They Robbed the Bank of England* 1960; *Doctor Blood's Coffin* 1961; *I Thank a Fool, The*

300 Spartans (US) 1962; *Hide and Seek, The Thin Red Line* (US) 1964; *Crack in the World* (US) 1965; *Arabesque* (US/UK) 1966; *Run Like a Thief* (US/Sp.), *Bikini Paradise* (US) 1967; *Custer of the West* (US) 1968; *The Progress of Peoples* (dir., narr. only) 1975; *The Parched Land* (dir., narr. only) 1979; *The Zoo Gang* 1985.

Moore, Marjorie. See REYNOLDS, Marjorie.

Moore, Mary Tyler. Actress. Born on Dec. 29, 1936, in Brooklyn, N.Y. Sparkling TV comedienne who made only occasional excursions into features. Trained as a dancer, she was first seen by television audiences singing and dancing atop appliances in Hotpoint commercials. Following appearances in several series, she hit the big time as the co-star of 'The Dick Van Dyke Show' (1961–66), through which she earned great popularity and two Emmy Awards. She then went on to reach the peak of her success with 'The Mary Tyler Moore Show' (1970–77), gaining three more Emmys and a special award (in 1974) as Series Actress of the Year. Following several indifferent roles in films, she was nominated for an Academy Award for her strong characterization in Robert Redford's *Ordinary People* (1980), the story of a family coming to grips with the accidental death of a young son. Ironically, Moore lost her own 24-year-old son to suicide that same year. The eventful 1980 also brought her a Special Tony Award for her performance on Broadway in 'Whose Life Is It Anyway?' In 1984 she entered the Betty Ford Center for treatment of a 'social drinking' habit that was worsening her diabetic condition. She was victorious at the 1992 Emmys for her supporting role as an amoral dealer of children. Moore's second husband (1962–81) was NBC-TV executive Grant Tinker. In 1983 she married Dr. Robert Levine, 15 years her junior.

FILMS: *X-15* 1961; *Thoroughly Modern Millie* 1967; *Don't Just Stand There!, What's So Bad About Feeling Good?* 1968; *Change of Habit* 1969; *Ordinary People* 1980; *Six Weeks* 1982; *Just Between Friends* 1986; *Flirting with Disaster* 1996; *Keys to Tulsa* 1997.

Moore, Matt. Actor. *b.* Jan. 8, 1888, County Meath, Ireland. *d.* 1960. In the US from age ten, he followed his older brothers, Owen and Tom MOORE, into films in 1913 and in the following two decades starred in numerous Hollywood silents and early talkies as a romantic lead and a two-fisted hero. By the early 30s he had graduated into character roles and he continued playing supporting parts in many films into the late 50s.

FILMS INCLUDE: *Traffic in Souls* 1913; *Pawns of Destiny, A Singular Cynic* 1914; *20,000 Leagues Under the Sea* 1916; *The Pride of the Clan* 1917; *Heart of the Wilds* 1918; *The Unpardonable Sin, Sahara, A Regular Girl* 1919; *Don't Ever Marry, Hairpins, Love Madness, Whispers* 1920; *The Passionate Pilgrim, Straight Is the Way, The Miracle of Manhattan, A Man's Home* 1921; *Back Pay, Sisters, The Storm, The Jilt* 1922; *Drifting, Strangers of the Night, White Tiger* 1923; *No More Women, The Breaking Point, Fools in the Dark, The Wise Virgin, The Narrow Street* 1924; *A Lost Lady, The Way of a Girl, How Baxter Butted In, Grounds for Divorce, The Unholy Three, His Majesty Bunker Bean* 1925; *Three Weeks in Paris, His Jazz Bride, The Cave Man, The First Year, Early to Wed, The Mystery Club, Diplomacy, Summer Bachelors* 1926; *Tiller the Toiler, Married Alive* 1927; *Beware of Blondes, Dry Martini, Phyllis of the Follies* 1928; *Coquette, Side Street* 1929; *Call of the West, The Squealer* 1930; *The Front Page, Penrod and Sam, Consolation Marriage* 1931; *Cock of the Air, Rain* 1932; *Deluge* 1934; *Anything Goes* 1936; *Range War* 1939; *My Life with Caroline* 1941; *Wilson* 1944; *The Hoodlum Saint* 1946; *Good Sam* 1948; *That Forsyte Woman* 1949; *The Big Hangover* 1950; *Invitation, Plymouth Adventure* 1952; *Seven Brides for Seven Brothers* 1954; *The Birds and the Bees* 1956; *An Affair to Remember* 1957.

Moore, Michael. Director, writer. Born ca. 1954 in Davison, Mich. *ed.* Univ. of Mich. Iconoclastic filmmaker. After writing for alternative periodicals *The Michigan Voice* and *Mother Jones*, he became a filmmaker, chronicling the decline of the American auto industry through the rise and fall of one GM town, Flint, Michigan, in the documentary *Roger & Me*. Mixing wry distance, pathos, and black humor, he traced the town's move from optimism in the 1950s to desolation and hopelessness in the 1980s, as 40,000 GM jobs were lost. He revisited the town in the later short, *Pets or Meat: The Return to Flint*.

FILMS INCLUDE: *Roger & Me* 1989; *Canadian Bacon* 1995.

Moore, Owen. Actor. *b.* Dec. 12, 1886, County Meath, Ireland. *d.* 1939. Star of American silents and early talkies, the brother of Matt and Tom MOORE. He entered films with Biograph in 1908 and appeared in many of D. W. Griffith's early productions. He was Mary PICKFORD's regular leading man in the early stages of her career and married her secretly in early 1911. They divorced in 1919 and he later married screen actress Kathryn Perry.

FILMS INCLUDE: *The Valet's Wife* 1908; *A Burglar's Mistake, Two Memories, The Honor of Thieves, In Old Kentucky, The Salvation Army Lass, The Lonely Villa, Pippa Passes, Resurrection, The Cricket on the Hearth, The Violin Maker of Cremona* 1909; *All on Account of the Milk, The Dancing Girl of Butte, The Call to Arms, Their First Misunderstanding* 1910; *The Courting of Mary, The Aggressor, Flo's Discipline* 1911; *In Swift Waters, After All, The Angel of the Studio* 1912; *The Appeal, Caprice* 1913; *The Battle of the Sexes, The Escape, Aftermath, Home Sweet Home, Cinderella* 1914; *Mabel Lost and Won, The Little Teacher, Mistress Nell, Nearly a Lady, Jordan Is a Hard Road* 1915; *Little Meena's Romance, Under Cover, A Coney Island Princess, The Kiss, Betty of Graystone* 1916; *A Girl Like That, The Little Boy Scout* 1917; *The Crimson Gardenia* 1919; *Piccadilly Jim* 1920; *The Chicken in the Case, A Divorce of Convenience* 1921 *Love Is an Awful Thing, Reported Missing, Oh Mabel Behave* 1922; *The Silent Partner, Modern Matrimony, Her Temporary Husband, Thundergate* 1923; *Torment, East of Broadway* 1924; *The Parasite, Code of the West, Go Straight, Camille of the Barbary Coast* 1925; *Married?, The Skyrocket, The Black Bird, Money Talks, The Road to Mandalay, False Pride* 1926; *The Red Mill, The Taxi Dancer, Tea for Three, Women Love Diamonds, Becky* 1927; *The Actress, Husbands for Rent* 1928; *Stolen Love, High Voltage, Side Street* 1929; *Outside the Law, What a Widow!, Extravagance* 1930; *Hush Money* 1931; *As You Desire Me* 1932; *She Done Him Wrong* 1933; *A Star Is Born* 1937.

Moore, Robert. Director. *b.* Aug. 17, 1927, Detroit. *d.* 1984. He directed two sparkling mystery spoofs and one screen adaptation of an autobiographical Neil Simon play before his untimely death at 57.

FEATURE FILMS: *Murder by Death* 1976; *The Cheap Detective* 1978; *Chapter Two* 1980.

Moore, Roger. Actor. Born on Oct. 14, 1927, in London. Tall, handsome, suave leading man of British and American TV and films. A London bobby's son, he studied painting at an art school and drama at the Royal Academy of Dramatic Art, and in 1945 began playing small roles on the London stage and in British films. Following postwar military service as a lieutenant with an entertainment unit in Germany, he resumed his stage and screen career, and in the early 50s traveled to the US, where he began appearing on the stage, in TV, and in films. He gained popularity as the star of such TV series as 'Ivanhoe' (1957–58), 'The Alaskans' (1959–60), 'Maverick' (1960–61), 'The Saint' (1967–69), and 'The Persuaders' (1971–72), but remained a relatively minor big-screen personality until the early 70s, when he inherited the role of James Bond from Sean Connery. Audiences initially resented the switch but gradually accepted Moore's less virile and abrasive but lighter and smoother interpretation of the heroic agent 007. The success of the spy films propelled him at a relatively mature age to the status of a highly paid, bankable star. He made his last appearance as 007 in 1985's *A View to A Kill*, after which the role went, briefly, to Timothy Dalton. He shuttles between homes in London, Beverly Hills, Gstaad, and the South of France. In 1991 he was named a Special Representative of UNICEF, the UN children's organization on whose behalf he had been active for a number of years. Divorced from singer Dorothy Squires, his second wife (1953–69), he married in 1969 former Italian starlet Luisa Mattioli. Another Roger Moore played supporting roles in Hollywood films from the late 30s through the early 50s.

FILMS: In the UK—*Perfect Strangers/Vacation from Marriage, Caesar and Cleopatra* 1945; *Gaiety George/ Showtime, Piccadily Incident* 1946; *Paper Orchid, Trottie True/Gay Lady* 1949. In the US—*The Last Time I Saw Paris* 1954; *Interrupted Melody, The King's Thief* 1955; *Diane, The Miracle* 1959; *The Sins of Rachel Cade, Gold of the Seven Saints* 1961. In Italy—*Il Ratto delle Sabine/Rape of the Sabines/ Romulus and the Sabines* (as Romulus), *Un Branco di Vigliacchi/No Man's Land* 1962. In the UK—*Crossplot* (also prod.) 1969; *The Man Who Haunted Himself* 1970; *Live and Let Die* (as James Bond) 1973; *Gold, The Man with the Golden Gun* (as Bond) 1974; *That Lucky Touch* 1975; *Shout at the Devil, Gli Esecutori/Street People/The Sicilian Cross* (It./US) 1976; *The Spy Who Loved Me* (as Bond) 1977; *The Wild Geese* 1978; *Escape to Athena, Moonraker* (as Bond), *North Sea Hijack/ffolkes/Assault Force* 1979; *The Sea Wolves, Les Seducteurs/Sunday Lovers* (Fr./It.) 1980; *The Cannonball Run* (US), *For Yours Eyes Only* (as Bond) 1981; *Octopussy* (as Bond), *Curse of the Pink Panther* (cameo) 1983; *The Naked Face* 1984; *A View to a Kill* (as Bond) 1985; *The Magic Snowman* (v/o) 1987; *Bullseye!* 1989; *Fire, Ice and Dynamite* 1991; *The Quest* 1996.

Moore, Ted. Director of photography. Born in 1914, in South Africa. In England from 1930, he served during WW II as an RAF pilot and later with the RAF's Film Unit. He flew many combat missions and was decorated for bravery. After the war he entered the British film industry and worked as camera operator on such productions as *Outcast of the Islands* (1951), *The African Queen* (1951), and *Genevieve* (1953). A lighting cameraman from the mid-50s, in the 60s he developed into one of Britain's most accomplished color and wide-screen cinematographers and was assigned to most of the expensively mounted James Bond productions. He won an Academy Award for the cinematography of *A Man for All Seasons* (1966).

FILMS INCLUDE: *A Prize of Gold* 1955; *The Gamma People, The Cockleshell Heroes* (co-phot.), *Safari, Zarak* (co-phot.) 1956; *Interpol/Pickup Alley* 1957; *The Bandit of Zhobe, The Killers of Kilimanjaro* 1959; *The Trials of Oscar Wilde* 1960; *Johnny Nobody, The Hellions* 1961; *Dr. No* 1962; *From Russia with Love* 1963; *Goldfinger* 1964; *The Amorous Adventures of Moll Flanders, Thunderball* 1965; *A Man for All Seasons* 1966; *The Last Safari* 1967; *Shalako, The Prime of Miss Jean Brodie* 1968; *Country Dance/Brotherly Love* 1970; *Diamonds Are Forever* 1971; *Live and Let Die, The Golden Voyage of Sinbad* 1973; *The Man with the Golden Gun* 1974; *Sinbad and the Eye of the Tiger* (US), *Orca* (US) 1977; *Clash of the Titans, Priest of Love* 1981.

Moore, Terry. Actress. Born Helen Koford, on Jan. 7, 1929, in Los Angeles. Busty Hollywood "sexpot," on the screen from age 11 following a career as a child model. She used the screen names of Helen Koford, Judy Ford, and Jan Ford before settling on Terry Moore in 1948. She was nominated for an Oscar in the supporting category for *Come Back, Little Sheba* (1952) but generally got less press coverage for her film roles than for her romantic escapades, which included four official marriages, three official divorces, one legal separation, and many publicized dates, from Howard HUGHES to Henry Kissinger. In 1983 she won a long-fought legal battle when a court recognized her as Hughes's widow. According to her deposition, she had secretly married the mystery billionaire on his yacht in 1949 and bore him a stillborn baby girl in 1952. They never divorced.

FILMS INCLUDE: *Maryland, The Howards of Virginia* 1940; *My Gal Sal* 1942; *Since You Went Away, Gaslight* 1944; *Son of Lassie* 1945; *The Devil on Wheels* 1947; *The Return of October, Mighty Joe Young* 1949; *The Great Rupert, Gambling House* 1950; *The Barefoot Mailman* 1951; *Come Back, Little Sheba* 1952; *Man on a Tightrope, Beneath the 12-Mile Reef, King of the Khyber Rifles* 1953; *Daddy Long Legs* 1955; *Between Heaven and Hell* 1956; *Bernadine, Peyton Place* 1957; *A Private's Affair* 1959; *Platinum High School* 1960; *Town Tamer, Black Spurs* 1965; *Waco* 1966; *A Man Called Dagger* 1968; *The Daredevil* 1972; *Double Exposure* 1982; *Hellhole* 1985; *Beverly Hills Brats* (also co-prod., co-story) 1989.

Moore, Tom. Actor. *b.* 1885, County Meath, Ireland. *d.* 1955. Star of Hollywood silents and early talkies. He entered films in 1912, and like his younger brothers, Matt and Owen MOORE, enjoyed a long and successful career on the American screen, typically in virile romantic roles. He retired from films in the mid-30s, returning a decade later in minor supporting parts. His several marriages included those to actresses Alice JOYCE (1914–20), who co-starred in many of his early films, and Renée ADORÉE (1921–24). In 1931 he married actress Eleanor Merry. His daughter, Alice Moore (1916–60), appeared in a number of films.

FILMS INCLUDE: *A Daughter's Sacrifice, A Race with Time* 1912; *The American Princess, The Adventure of an Heiress, The Artist's Sacrifice, The Heart of an Actress, The Shadow, The Hunchback, An Unseen Terror* 1913; *The Dance of Death, Nina of the Theater, The Brand, The Vampire's Trail, The Mystery of the Sleeping Death, Barefoot Boy* 1914; *The Adventure at Briarcliff* 1915; *Who's Guilty?* (serial), *Dollars and the Woman* 1916; *The Primrose Ring, The Jaguar's Claws, The Cinderella Man* 1917; *Brown of Harvard, Go West, Young Man, The Floor Below, The Kingdom of Youth, Thirty a Week* 1918; *A Man and His Money, One of the Finest, The City of Comrades, Heartsease, Lord and Lady Algy, Toby's Bow* 1919; *The Gay Lord Quex, Duds, Stop Thief!, The Great Accident* 1920; *Hold Your Horses, Made in Heaven, Beating the Game* 1921; *Mr. Barnes of New York, Over the Border, The Cowboy and the Lady, Pawned* 1922; *Marriage Morals, Rouged Lips, Big Brother* 1923; *Manhandled, One Night in Rome, Dangerous Money* 1924; *On Thin Ice, Adventure, Pretty Ladies, The Trouble with Wives* 1925; *A Kiss for Cinderella, The Song and Dance Man, Good and Naughty, The Clinging Vine, Syncopating Sue* 1926; *Cabaret, The Love Thrill, The Wise Wife* 1927; *The Siren, Has Anybody Here Seen Kelly?, His Last Haul* 1928; *The Yellowback, Side Street* 1929; *The Woman Racket, The Costello Case* 1930; *The Last Parade* 1931; *The Cannonball Express* 1932; *Mr. Broadway* 1933; *Bombay Mail* 1934; *Trouble for Two, Reunion* 1936; *Behind Green Lights* 1946; *Moss Rose, Forever Amber* 1947; *The Fighting O'Flynn* 1949; *The Redhead and the Cowboy* 1950.

Moore, Victor. Actor. *b.* Feb. 24, 1876, Hammonton, N.J. *d.* 1962. Endearing comedian of vaudeville, the legitimate stage, and films. On screen, with frequent returns to the stage, from 1915. Short and pudgy, he typically portrayed bumbling, helpless little men.

FILMS INCLUDE: *Snobs, Chimmie Fadden, Chimmie Fadden Out West* 1915; *The Clown, The Race* 1916; *The Man Who Found Himself* 1925; *Heads Up, Dangerous Dan McGrew* 1930; *Romance in the Rain, Gift of Gab* 1934; *Gold Diggers of 1937, Swing Time* 1936; *We're on the Jury, Make Way for Tomorrow, Meet the Missus, The Life of the Party* 1937; *Radio City Revels, This Marriage Business* 1938; *Louisiana Purchase* 1941; *Star Spangled Rhythm* 1942; *True to Life, The Heat's On, Riding High* 1943; *Carolina Blues* 1944; *It's in the Bag, Duffy's Tavern* 1945; *Ziegfeld Follies* 1946; *It Happened on Fifth Avenue* 1947; *On Our Merry Way/A Miracle Can Happen* 1948; *A Kiss in the Dark* 1949; *We're Not Married* 1952; *The Seven Year Itch* 1955.

Moorehead, Agnes. Actress. *b.* Dec. 6, 1906, Clinton, Mass. *d.* 1974. *ed.* U. of Wisconsin (M.A.); Bradley U. (Ph.D. in literature); AADA. The daughter of a Presbyterian minister, she first appeared on the stage at the age of three and made her professional debut at 11 in the ballet and the chorus of the St. Louis Opera. In her teens she sang regularly on local radio. After graduating from college, she taught speech and drama in high schools and spent her vacations appearing in stock. In 1928 she began playing small parts on Broadway but soon after turned to radio, appearing in the "March of Time," "Cavalcade of America," and starring in a soap opera series. Between 1933 and 1936 she toured in vaudeville with Phil Baker. Things began happening to her career in 1940 when she joined Orson Welles's Mercury Theater Company. Welles cast her in the small but memorable role of Kane's mother in his first film, *Citizen Kane* (1941). The following year she won the New York Film Critics best actress award and was nominated for the best supporting actress Oscar for her portrayal of a spinster in Welles's *The Magnificent Ambersons* (1942).

It was the first of her five Academy Award nominations. Miss Moorehead subsequently appeared in numerous films, typically portraying possessive, neurotic, puritanical characters but also playing a wide range of other roles from somber to humorous, with equal subtlety and skill. In the 40s, too, she gave a memorable performance in the oft-rebroadcast radio play 'Sorry, Wrong Number.' In the early 50s she toured the US and Europe with Charles Boyer, Charles Laughton, and Sir Cedric Hardwicke in readings of Shaw's 'Don Juan in Hell.' In 1954 she began touring with her one-woman show, *The Fabulous Redhead,* which she later played intermittently in some 200 cities throughout the world. She appeared on a number of television programs, lastly as Endora, the witch, in the series 'Bewitched' (1964–72). Both her former husbands were actors, John Griffith Lee (1930–52) and Robert Gist (1953–58). She died of lung cancer.

FILMS: *Citizen Kane* 1941; *The Magnificent Ambersons, The Big Street* 1942; *Journey into Fear, The Youngest Profession, Government Girl* 1943; *Jane Eyre* (as Mrs. Reed), *Since You Went Away, Dragon Seed, The Seventh Cross, Mrs. Parkington, Tomorrow the World* 1944; *Keep Your Powder Dry, Our Vines Have Tender Grapes, Her Highness and the Bellboy* 1945; *Dark Passage, The Lost Moment* 1947; *The Woman in White, Summer Holiday, Johnny Belinda, Station West* 1948; *The Stratton Story, The Great Sinner, Without Honor* 1949; *Caged* 1950; *Fourteen Hours, Show Boat* (as Parthy Hawks), *The Blue Veil, The Adventures of Captain Fabian* 1951; *Captain Black Jack, The Blazing Forest* 1952; *The Story of Three Loves, Scandal at Scourie, Those Redheads from Seattle, Main Street to Broadway* 1953; *Magnificent Obsession* (as Nancy Ashford) 1954; *Untamed, The Left Hand of God* 1955; *All That Heaven Allows, Meet Me in Las Vegas, The Conqueror, The Swan, The Revolt of Mamie Stover, Pardners, The Opposite Sex* 1956; *The True Story of Jesse James, Jeanne Eagels, The Story of Mankind* (as Queen Elizabeth I), *Raintree County* 1957; *Night of the Quarter Moon, Tempest, The Bat* 1959; *Pollyanna* 1960; *Twenty Plus Two, Bachelor in Paradise* 1961; *Jessica, How the West Was Won* 1962; *Who's Minding the Store?* 1963; *Hush Hush. . . Sweet Charlotte* 1965; *The Singing Nun* 1966; *What's the Matter with Helen?* 1971; *Dear Dead Delilah* (title role) 1972; *Charlotte's Web* (v/o) 1973.

Mora, Philippe. Director. Born in 1949, in Paris. Raised in Melbourne, Australia, he began making 9 mm amateur films at age nine. He was active in the Film Society of Melbourne's La Trobe University, which he attended for one year as an art student. He went to London to exhibit his paintings and while there he made his professional debut as a film director in 1969. He turned out several notable documentaries and compilation films, among them *Swastika* (1973), which for the first time incorporated color footage of Hitler, shot by Eva Braun. Mora used no narration to illuminate events, letting the pictures speak for themselves, a technique he also used in *Brother, Can You Spare a Dime?* (1975), a chronicle of the Depression that he compiled in Canada and the US. He then returned to Australia, where he made his first story film, *Mad Dog Morgan* (1976), a violent account of a legendary 19th-century Australian outlaw, with American Dennis Hopper in the title role. The success of the film opened the gates for Mora's entry into the international feature arena, an opportunity which he is yet to put to full advantage.

FILMS: *Trouble in Molopolis* (doc.; UK) 1969; *The Double-Headed Eagle* (doc.; UK) 1972; *Swastika* (doc.; UK) 1974; *Brother Can You Spare a Dime?* (doc.; Can./US) 1975; *Mad Dog Morgan/Mad Dog* (also sc.; Austral.) 1976; *The Times They're a-Changin'* (unreleased doc.; UK) 1978; *The Beast Within* (US) 1982; *The Return of Captain Invincible/Legend in Leotards* (Austral./US) 1983; *A Breed Apart* (US) 1984; *Howling II. . . Your Sister Is a Werewolf* (US/UK) 1985; *Death of a Soldier* (Austral.) 1986; *Howling III/Howling III: The Marsupials* (also sc.; Austral.) 1987; *Communion* (also co-prod.; US) 1989; *Art Deco Detective* 1994.

Morahan, Christopher. Director. Born on July 9, 1929, in London. A prolific stage and TV director, he ventured only periodically into feature films. He shared an Emmy as co-director of the celebrated TV miniseries 'The Jewel in the Crown' (1983).

FEATURE FILMS: *Diamonds for Breakfast* 1968; *All Neat in Black Stockings* 1969; *In the Secret State* 1985; *Clockwise* 1986; *Paper Mask* 1990.

Morales, Esai. Actor. Born in 1963, in Brooklyn, N.Y., of Hispanic descent. Raised as a ward of the state and as a foster child, he showed early talent and attended New York's famous High School of the Performing Arts. He made his New York stage debut at 17 and three years later made a strong first impression in the film *Bad Boys.* His screen career was boosted by a superior portrayal of Richie Valens's troubled brother in *La Bamba* (1987).

FILMS: *Bad Boys* 1983; *Rainy Day Friends* 1986; *La Bamba, The Principal* 1987; *Bloodhounds of Broadway* 1989; *In the Army Now, Rapa Nui* 1994; *Mi Familia/My Family* 1995; *The Disappearance of Garcia Lorca* 1997.

Moran, Lee. Actor. *b.* June 23, 1888, Chicago. *d.* 1961. In films from 1909, he enjoyed great popularity after teaming in 1915 with Eddie Lyons (*b.* 1886, Beardstown, Ill.; deceased) in a highly successful string of two-reel comedies under the "Star" banner. After the partnership broke up in 1920, Moran turned to character parts in feature films. Lyons went on to produce, direct, and star in many comedy shorts for the Arrow company.

FILMS INCLUDE: *Almost an Actress* 1913; *All Aboard, Little Egypt Malone, Mrs. Plumb's Pudding, Some Fixer, Almost a Knockout, Wanted—A Leading Lady, When the Mummy Cried for Help, Love and a Savage, Some Chaperone* 1915; *War Bridegrooms, Ducks Out of Water, Bolsheviks, Robinson Trousseau* 1917; *La La Lucille* 1920; *A Shocking Night* 1921; *Daring Youth, Gambling Wives, The Fast Worker* 1924; *Fifth Avenue Models, After Business Hours, Where Was I?, Tessie, My Lady of Whims* 1925; *The Little Irish Girl, Her Big Night, Syncopating Sue, Take It from Me* 1926; *Wolf's Clothing, Fast and Furious, Spring Fever, The Irresistible Lover* 1927; *A Woman Against the World, Thanks for the Buggy Ride, The Actress, The Racket, Ladies of the Night Club, Show Girl, Outcast* 1928; *Children of the Ritz, No Defense, The Glad Rag Doll, On with the Show, The Madonna of Avenue A, Gold Diggers of Broadway, Hearts in Exile, The Show of Shows, Dance Hall* 1929; *The Aviator, Mammy, Hide-Out, Pardon My Gun, Sweet Mama, Golden Dawn, A Soldier's Plaything* 1930; *Stowaway, Uptown New York, The Death Kiss* 1932; *Grand Slam, Racetrack, High Gear, Goldie Gets Along* 1933; *The Circus Clown* 1934; *Circumstantial Evidence* 1935; *The Calling of Dan Matthews* 1936.

Moran, Lois. Actress. *b.* Lois Darlington Dowling, Mar. 1, 1908, Pittsburgh. *d.* 1990. Leading lady of Hollywood silents and early talkies. Brought to France as an infant by her mother, a physician's widow, she danced (1922–24) with the Paris National Opera and appeared in French films before making an auspicious Hollywood debut in the role of Laurel in Sam Goldwyn's *Stella Dallas* (1925). But most of her subsequent roles were routine. After retiring from the screen in 1931, she starred in several stage musicals, scoring a success on Broadway in 'Of Thee I Sing.' But in 1935 she gave up acting to marry an assistant secretary of commerce (and later Pan Am executive) Clarence M. Young. In the 50s she taught drama and dance at Stanford University and returned briefly to acting as Preston Foster's co-star in the TV series 'Waterfront' (1953–56). F. Scott Fitzgerald is said to have based the character of Rosemary on her in his novel *Tender Is the Night.*

FILMS: In France—*La Galerie des Monstres* 1924; *Feu Mathias Pascal/The Late Mathias Pascal/The Living Dead Man* 1925. In the US—*Stella Dallas* 1925; *Just Suppose, The Reckless Lady, The Road to Mandalay, Padlocked, The Prince of Tempters, God Gave Me Twenty Cents* 1926; *The Music Master, The Whirlwind of Youth, The Irresistible Lover, Publicity Madness* 1927; *Sharp Shooters, Love Hungry, Don't Marry, The River Pirate, Blindfold* 1928; *True Heaven, Making the Grade, Joy Street, Behind That Curtain, Words and Music, A Song of Kentucky* 1929; *Mammy, Not Damaged, The Dancers* 1930; *Under Suspicion, Transatlantic, The Spider, Men in Her Life, West of Broadway* 1931.

Moran, Peggy. Actress. Born on Oct. 23, 1918, in Clinton, Iowa. Attractive brunette leading lady of Hollywood B pictures of the late 30s and early 40s, mainly at Universal. Retired from the screen after her 1942 marriage to director Henry KOSTER.

FILMS INCLUDE: *Boy Meets Girl, Girls' School* 1938; *Little Accident, The Big Guy, Ninotchka* 1939; *Oh Johnny—How You Can Love, West of Carson City, Alias the Deacon, Hot Steel, The Mummy's Hand, Spring Parade, Argentine Nights, Slightly Tempted, Trail of the Vigilantes, One Night in the Tropics* 1940; *Horror Island, Double Date, Flying Cadets* 1941; *Treat 'Em Rough, Drums of the Congo, Seven Sweethearts* 1942; *King of the Cowboys* 1943.

Moran, Polly. Actress. *b.* Pauline Theresa Moran, June 28, 1884, Chicago. *d.* 1952. Raucous, buck-toothed comic star and character comedienne of numerous silents and talkies. A veteran of vaudeville, she began her screen career with Mack SENNETT and appeared in numerous shorts through early 1918, when she returned to the stage. But she was back in films by the early 20s, this time in features. She enjoyed a surge of popularity early in the sound era, in a successful series of comedies co-starring Marie DRESSLER.

FILMS INCLUDE: Shorts—*The Janitor* 1913; *Ambrose's Little Hatchet, Their Social Splash, Those College Girls, Her Painted Hero, The Hunt* 1915; *Love Will Conquer, The Village Blacksmith, By Stork Delivery, His Wild Oats, Vampire Ambrose, Safety First Ambrose* 1916; *Her Fame and Shame, His Naughty Thought, Cactus Nell, She Needed a Doctor, His Uncle Dudley, Roping Her Romeo, The Pullman Bride* 1917; *Sheriff Nell's Tussle, Saucy Madeline, The Battle Royal, Two Tough Tenderfeet, She Loved Him Plenty* 1918. Features—*Skirts, The Affairs of Anatol* 1921; *Luck* 1923; *The Callahans and the Murphys, The Thirteenth Hour, Buttons, The Enemy, London After Midnight* 1927; *The Divine Woman, Bringing Up Father, Rose-Marie, Telling the World, While the City Sleeps, Show People* 1928; *China Bound, The Hollywood Revue, Honeymoon, Speedway, The Unholy Night, So This Is College, Hot for Paris* 1929; *Chasing Rainbows, The Girl Said No, Caught Short, Way Out West, Remote Control, Way for a Sailor, Paid* 1930; *Reducing, It's a Wise Child, Politics, Guilty Hands* 1931; *The Passionate Plumber, Prosperity* 1932; *Alice in Wonderland* (as the Dodo Bird) 1933; *Hollywood Party, Down to Their Last Yacht* 1934; *Two Wise Maids* 1937; *Ladies in Distress* 1938; *Ambush* 1939; *Tom Brown's School Days* 1940; *Adam's Rib* 1949; *The Yellow Cab Man* 1950.

Moranis, Rick. Actor. Born on Apr. 18, 1954, in Toronto. Small-framed, nerdy-looking, comic character lead of TV and films. While still at high school, he worked part time as a radio engineer. After graduating, he hosted his own comedy show on radio and later performed in Toronto nightclubs, cabarets, and TV. His career developed rapidly in the early 80s after he joined the Second City ensemble (SCTV) on Canadian television, for which he created, with Dave Thomas, the popular off-the-wall characters, the McKenzie Brothers. Moranis and Thomas introduced themselves to filmgoers in *Strange Brew* (1983), which they also co-wrote and co-directed. Moranis went on to appear in many films, typically in goofy, ne'er-do-well roles.

FILMS: *Strange Brew* (also co-dir., co-sc.) 1983; *Streets of Fire, Ghostbusters, The Wild Life* 1984; *Brewster's Millions, Head Office* 1985; *Club Paradise, Little Shop of Horrors* 1986; *Spaceballs* 1987; *Ghostbusters II, Honey I Shrunk the Kids, Parenthood* 1989; *My Blue Heaven* 1990; *L.A. Story* 1991; *Honey I Blew Up the Kid* 1992; *The Flintstones, Little Giants* 1994; *Big Bully* 1996.

Moravia, Alberto. Novelist, screenwriter. *b.* Alberto Picherele, Nov. 28, 1907, Rome. *d.* 1990. The celebrated Italian author of many novels, short stories, and essays collaborated on a good number of screenplays, in addition to the films adapted to the screen by others from his novels and short stories. The son of a prosperous Jewish architect-painter from Venice and an Austro-Hungarian countess, he contracted crippling tuberculosis at age eight and spent much of his childhood bedridden, educated by private tutors, and reading voraciously in several languages. Spending his youth in solitude, he never attended school and never played with other children. At 16 he entered a sanitarium in the Alps, and there began his first novel, *Gli Indifferenti/The Time of Indifference,* which was published in 1929. His many novels explored alienation and social traumas, often featuring obsessive human sexuality. Having been earlier condemned by the Fascists, his books were declared immoral by the Vatican in 1952 and placed on the forbidden list. Most have been translated into English and other languages. Many consider him the greatest Italian novelist of his generation.

FILMS INCLUDE: *Ultimo Incontro* (co-sc.), *Sensualità* (co-sc.) 1951; *Tempi Nostri* (co-sc.), *La Provinciale/The Wayward Wife* (co-sc. from own novel) 1952; *Villa Borghese* (co-sc.) 1953; *La Donna del Fiume* (co-sc.) 1954; *La Romana/The Woman of Rome* (co-sc. from own novel) 1955; *Racconti Romani/Roman Tales* (co-sc. from own stories) 1956; *Racconti d'Estate/Love on the Riviera/Summer Tales* (story, co-sc., act.) 1958; *La Ciociara/Two Women* (novel basis only), *I Delfini/The Dauphins* (co-story, so-sc.), *La Giornata Balorda/From a Roman Balcony* (co-sc. from own stories) 1960; *Una Domenica d'Estate* (co-story, co-sc.) 1961; *Agostino* (co-sc. from own novel) 1962; *Le Mepris/Contempt* (novel basis only), *La Noia/The Empty Canvas* (novel basis only), *Ieri Oggi Domani/Yesterday Today and Tomorrow* (co-story, co-sc.) 1963; *Gli Indifferenti/Time of Indifference* (novel basis only), *Le Ore Nude* (co-sc. from own novel) 1964; *Comizi d'Amore* (co-sc., personal appearance; doc.) 1965; *L'Occhio Selvaggio/The Wild Eye* (co-sc.) 1967; *La Donna Invisible/The Invisible Woman* (story basis only) 1969; *Il Conformista/The Conformist* (novel basis only), *L'Amore coniugale* (novel basis only) 1970; *Desideria/La Vita interiore* (novel basis only) 1980; *L'Attenzione/The Lie* (novel basis only) 1985; *Me and Him* (novel basis only; Ger.) 1988.

More, Kenneth. Actor. *b.* Sept. 20, 1914, Gerrard's Cross, England. *d.* 1982. Pleasant, likable leading man of the British stage and screen. Worked briefly as an engineer's apprentice and fur trapper in Canada before beginning his acting career in the mid-30s with bit roles in plays and films. His career began taking shape after he returned from WW II service as a Navy lieutenant. He became a popular star in the 50s, following his lead roles in two highly successful screen comedies, *Genevieve* (1953) and *Doctor in the House* (1954). He received the BFA (British Film Academy) Award as Britain's best actor for his performance in the latter film. In 1955 he was awarded the best actor prize at Venice for his dramatic performance in *The Deep Blue Sea.* He continued playing comic and dramatic roles with equal ease and conviction and remained popular through the early 60s, when his film career declined and he devoted more of his time to the stage and TV. Memorable in the BBC TV series 'The Forsyte Saga.' He died of Parkinson's Disease. Memoirs: *Happy Go Lucky* (1959); *Kindly Leave the Stage* (1965); *More or Less* (1978).

FILMS INCLUDE: *Look Up and Laugh* 1935; *Windmill Revels* 1938; *Scott of the Antarctic* 1948; *Now Barabbas* 1949; *Chance of a Lifetime, The Clouded Yellow* 1950; *No Highway/No Highway in the Sky, The Galloping Major, Appointment with Venus/Island Rescue* 1951; *Brandy for the Parson, The Yellow Balloon* 1952; *Never Let Me Go, Genevieve, Our Girl Friday/The Adventures of Sadie* 1953; *Doctor in the House, Raising a Riot* 1954; *The Deep Blue Sea* 1955; *Reach for the Sky* 1956; *The Admirable Crichton/Paradise Lagoon* (title role) 1957; *A Night to Remember, Next to No Time, The Sheriff of Fractured Jaw, The 39 Steps* 1958; *North West Frontier/Flame Over India* 1959; *Sink the Bismark!, Man in the Moon* 1960; *The Greengage Summer/Loss of Innocence* 1961; *The Longest Day, Some People* 1962; *The Comedy Man* 1963; *The Mercenaries/Dark of the Sun* 1968; *Fräulein Doktor* (It./Yug.), *Oh! What a Lovely War* (as Kaiser Wilhelm II), *The Battle of Britain* 1969; *Scrooge* (as the Ghost of Christmas Present) 1970; *The Slipper and the Rose* 1976; *Viaje al Centro de la Tierra/Journey to the Center of the Earth* (Sp.) 1977; *Leopard in the Snow* 1978; *The Spaceman and King Arthur/Unidentified Flying Oddball* 1979.

Moreau, Jeanne. Actress. Born on Jan. 23, 1928, in Paris. A graduate of the Paris Conservatory of Dramatic Art, she made both her stage and screen debuts in 1948. But while her theatrical career was gaining momentum almost from the start, with the Comédie-Française and later with the Théâtre National Populaire, she remained a rather obscure screen actress for ten years. It was Louis MALLE, then a fledgling director, who launched her into stardom and international recognition with *Ascenseur pour l'Echafaud/Frantic* in 1957 and *Les Amants/The Lovers* in 1958. She has since become a widely respected star of French and international films, an incarnation of French femininity, an intelligent, subtle, intuitive actress, projecting both worldly sophistication and earthy sensuality, both strength and vulnerability, in a wide range of roles, from Antonioni's *La Notte* and Trauffaut's *Jules and Jim* to Welles's *Falstaff/Chimes at Midnight* and Fraker's *Monte Walsh.* In the 70s she graduated gracefully into character roles, memorably in *Les Valseuses/Going Places* (1974), still sustaining the aura of mysterious sensuality and eternal femininity. Moreau, who was married briefly in the late 40s to director Jean-Louis Richard, confesses to being "a passionate woman who falls in love very easily." In 1976 she made her debut as a director with *La Lumière,* a film of ambiguous charm, for which she also wrote the script and in which she also starred. She married director William FRIEDKIN in 1977 but they divorced in 1980.

FILMS: *Dernier Amour* 1948; *Meurtres/Three Sinners, Pigalle—Saint-Germain-des-Prés* 1950; *L'Homme de ma Vie, Il est Minuit Docteur Schweitzer* 1952; *Secrets d'Alcove/Il Letto/The Bed, Dortoir des Grandes/Inside a Girls' Dormitory, Julietta* 1953; *Touchez pas au Grisbi/Grisbi, La Reine Margot, Les Intrigantes* 1954; *Les Hommes en Blanc/The Doctors, M'sieur la Caille, Gas-Oil* 1955; *Le Salaire du Péché, Jusq'au Dernier* 1956; *Echec au Porteur, L'Etrange M. Stève, Trois Jours à vivre, Les Louves/Demoniaque* 1957; *Ascenseur pour l'Echafaud/Frantic, Le Dos au Mur/Back to the Wall, Les Amants/The Lovers* 1958; *Les Liaisons dangereuses* 1959; *Moderato Cantabile, Jovanka e le Altre/Five Branded Women* (It./Yug.) 1960; *Le Dialogue des Carmélites, La Notte* (It./Fr.), *Une Femme est une Femme/A Woman Is a Woman, Jules et Jim/Jules and Jim* 1961; *Le Baie des Anges/Bay of the Angels, Eva, Le Procès/The Trial* (as Fräulein Burstner) 1962; *Le Feu Follet/The Fire Within, The Victors* (UK/US) 1963; *Le Journal d'une Femme de Chambre/Diary of a Chambermaid, Le Train/The Train* (Fr./It./US), *Peau de Banane/Banana Peel, The Yellow Rolls-Royce* (UK) 1964; *Mata Hari—Agent H-21* (title role), *Viva Maria* 1965; *Falstaff/Chimes at Midnight* (as Doll Tearsheet; Sp./Switz.), *Mademoiselle* (Fr./UK) 1966; *The Sailor from Gibraltar* (UK), *Le plus vieux Métier du Monde/The Oldest Profession* 1967; *La Mariée etait à Noir/The Bride Wore Black, Histoire immortelle/The Immortal Story, Great Catherine* (as Catherine the Great; UK) 1968; *Le Corps de Diane, Le Petit Théâtre de Jean Renoir* (orig. for TV) 1969; *Monte Walsh* (US), *Alex in Wonderland* (cameo; US), *Comptes à Rebours* 1970; *L'Humeur vagabonde, Chère Louise, Nathalie Granger* 1972; *Joanna Francesca* (Braz.) 1973; *Je t'aime* (Can.), *Les Valseuses/Going Places, La Race des Seigneurs, Le Jardin qui bascule* 1974; *Hu-Man, Souvenirs d'en France/French Provincial* 1975; *Lumière* (also dir., sc.), *Mr. Klein, The Last Tycoon* (US) 1976; *L'Adolescente/The Adolescent* (dir., co-sc. only) 1979; *Au-dela de cette Limite votre Ticket n'est plus valable/Your ticket is no longer valid* (Can./Fr.) 1980; *Plein Sud/Heat of Desire* 1981; *Mille Milliards de Dollars, Querelle,*

La Truite/The Trout 1982; *Der Bauer von Babylon/The Wizard of Babylon* (doc.) 1983; *Le Paltoquet, Sauve-toi Lola* 1986; *Le Miraculé* 1987; *La Nuit d'Océan* 1988; *Nikita/La Femme Nikita, Alberto Express* (Can./Fr./It.) 1990; *La Femme fardée, Anna Karamazoya* (USSR/Fr.), *The Suspended Step of the Stork* (Gr./Fr./Switz./It.) 1991; *Until the End of the World, Map of the Human Heart, The Old Lady Who Wades in the Sea* 1992; *The Summer House* 1993; *Beyond the Clouds, I Love You I Love You Not, The Proprietor* 1996.

Moreland, Mantan. Actor. *b.* Sept. 3, 1901, Monroe, La. *d.* 1973. Character comedian of well over 100 Hollywood films of the 40s, often stereotyped as a scared, wide-eyed black manservant. He played Charlie Chan's chauffeur in many of the series. A runaway at 12, he toured in a nightclub and stage act before entering films in the late 30s.

FILMS INCLUDE: *Shall We Dance* 1937; *Spirit of Youth* 1938; *One Dark Night* 1939; *The Man Who Wouldn't Talk, Star Dust* 1940; *King of the Zombies, Dressed to Kill, Ellery Queen's Murder Mystery, Sign of the Wolf* 1941; *The Palm Beach Story, The Strange Case of Dr. R, Eyes in the Night, Tarzan's New York Adventure* 1942; *Cabin in the Sky, Revenge of the Zombies* 1943; *Mystery of the River Boat* (serial), *Charlie Chan in the Secret Service, The Chinese Cat* 1944; *The Scarlet Clue, The Spider* 1945; *Mantan Runs for Mayor, Dark Alibi* 1946; *The Chinese Ring* 1947; *The Feathered Serpent* 1948; *Sky Dragon* 1949; *Rockin' the Blues* 1956; *Enter Laughing* 1967; *Watermelon Man* 1970; *The Young Nurses* 1973.

Morell, André. Actor. *b.* André Mesritz, Aug. 20, 1909, London. *d.* 1978. Cerebral, introspective character player of the British stage and films. He began his stage career as an amateur in 1930, made his professional debut in 1934, and his first London appearance in 1936. He joined the Old Vic company in 1938 and in that first year appeared in his first film. His stage and screen career began taking shape in the late 40s, after his return from WW II service as a major with the Royal Welsh Fusiliers. He played leads in a number of horror films and occasionally appeared in American productions. In 1973–74 he served as president of British Actors Equity. He was married to Joan GREENWOOD from 1960.

FILMS INCLUDE: *Thirteen Men and a Gun* 1938; *Ten Days in Paris/Missing Ten Days* 1939; *No Place for Jennifer* 1949; *Stage Fright, Madeleine, Trio, Seven Days to Noon, So Long at the Fair, The Clouded Yellow* 1950; *High Treason* 1951; *The Tall Headlines/The Frightened Bride* 1952; *His Majesty O'Keefe* (US/UK), *The Black Knight* 1954; *Three Cases of Murder, Summer Madness/Summertime* (UK/US) 1955; *The Man Who Never Was* 1956; *The Bridge on the River Kwai* 1957; *Paris Holiday* (US), *The Camp on Blood Island* 1958; *The Hound of the Baskervilles* (as Dr. Watson), *Behemoth the Sea Monster/The Giant Behemoth, Ben-Hur* (US) 1959; *Cone of Silence/Trouble in the Sky* 1960; *Mysterious Island, The Shadow of the Cat* 1961; *Woman of Straw, The Moon-Spinners* (US/UK) 1964; *She* 1965; *Judith* (US/Isr.), *The Plague of the Zombies, The Wrong Box* 1966; *The Mummy's Shroud* 1967; *The Vengeance of She, The Mercenaries/Dark of the Sun* 1968; *Julius Caesar* (as Cicero) 1970; *10 Rillington Place* 1971; *Pope Joan* (as Emperor Louis) 1972; *Barry Lyndon* 1975; *The Slipper and the Rose, The Message* 1976; *The First Great Train Robbery/The Great Train Robbery* 1979.

Moreno, Antonio. Actor. *b.* Antonio Garride Monteagudo, Sept. 26, 1886, Madrid. *d.* 1967. Dapper Latin lover of numerous Hollywood silents following some stage experience. He began his career in 1912, under D. W. Griffith, and was quite popular during the 20s, when he played leads opposite such female stars as Gloria Swanson, Pola Negri, Bebe Daniels, Marion Davies, and Greta Garbo. Although he first arrived in the US as a boy of 14, he retained a foreign accent noticeable enough to limit his career in talkies, and after the advent of sound he was seen mainly in character roles. In all, he appeared in hundreds of films.

FILMS INCLUDE: *Voice of the Million, Two Daughters of Eve, The Musketeers of Pig Alley* 1912; *By Man's Law, The House of Discord* 1913; *His Father's House, Strongheart, The Song of the Ghetto, John Rance—Gentleman, Memories in Men's Souls, The Hidden Letters, Politics and the Press, The Loan Shark King, The Peacemaker, Under False Colors, In the Latin Quarter, Sunshine and Shadows* 1914; *The Quality of Mercy, The Island of Regeneration, On Her Wedding Night, Anselo Lee, The Dust of Egypt, The Gypsy Trail* 1915; *Kennedy Square, The Supreme Temptation, The Tarantula, Rose of the South* 1916; *The Magnificent Meddler, Aladdin from Broadway* 1917; *The House of Hate* (serial), *The Iron Test* (serial), *The Naulahka, The First Law* 1918; *Perils of Thunder Mountain* (serial) 1919; *The Invisible Hand* (serial), *The Veiled Mystery* (serial) 1920; *The Secret of the Hills, A Guilty Conscience* 1921; *My American Wife, Lost and Found, The Trail of the Lonesome Pine, The Exciters, The Spanish Dancer* 1923; *Flaming Barriers, Bluff, Tiger Love, The Story Without a Name, The Border Legion* 1924; *Learning to Love, One Year to Live, Her Husband's Secret* 1925; *Mare Nostrum, Beverly of Graustark, The Temptress, The Flaming Forest, Love's Blindness* 1926; *Venus of Venice, It, Madame Pompadour* (UK) 1927; *Come to My House, The Whip Woman, The Midnight Taxi, The Air Legion, Adoration, Nameless men* 1928; *Synthetic Sin, Careers, Romance of the Rio Grande* 1929; *Rough Romance, One Mad Kiss* 1930; *The Bohemian Girl* 1936; *Rose of the Rio Grande* 1938; *Seven Sinners* 1940; *Valley of the Sun* 1942; *The Spanish Main* 1945; *Notorious* 1946; *Captain from Castile* 1947; *Lust for Gold* 1949; *Crisis, Dallas* 1950; *Mark of the Renegade* 1951; *Thunder Bay, Wings of the Hawk* 1953; *Creature from the Black Lagoon* 1954; *The Searchers* 1956.

Moreno, Rita. Actress, dancer, singer. Born Rosita Dolores Alverio, on Dec. 11, 1931, in Humacao, Puerto Rico. A dancer from childhood, she reached Broadway at 13, Hollywood at 14, at first using the name Rosita Moreno. She won a 1961 Academy Award as best supporting actress for *West Side Story.* A tempestuous, dynamic performer, she is the first, and so far the only woman to win an Oscar, a Tony (for 'The Ritz,' 1975), an Emmy (she won two, for appearances in 'The Muppet Show,' 1977, and 'The Rockford Files,' 1978), and a Grammy (for the music from 'The Electric Company,' 1972). In 1982–83 she co-starred in the TV series '9 to 5.'

FILMS INCLUDE: *A Medal for Benny* 1945; *So Young So Bad, The Toast of New Orleans, Pagan Love Song* 1950; *Singin' in the Rain, The Ring* 1952; *Latin Lovers, Fort Vengeance* 1953; *Jivaro, The Yellow Tomahawk, Garden of Evil* 1954; *Untamed, Seven Cities of Gold* 1955; *The Lieutenant Wore Skirts, The King and I, The Vagabond King* 1956; *The Deerslayer* 1957; *This Rebel Breed* 1960; *West Side Story, Summer and Smoke* 1961; *Cry of Battle* 1963; *The Night of the Following Day, Popi, Marlowe* 1969; *Carnal Knowledge* 1971; *The Ritz* 1976; *The Boss' Son* 1978; *Happy Birthday Gemini* 1980; *The Four Seasons* 1981; *Life in the Food Chain* 1991; *I Like It Like That* 1994; *Bogus* 1996.

More O'Ferrall, George. Director. *b.* 1906, England. *d.* 1982. In British films as assistant director from the early 30s, he directed several neat dramas and thrillers in the early 50s, then turned to TV.

FILMS: *Angels One Five, The Holly and the Ivy* 1952; *The Heart of the Matter* 1953; *The Green Scarf* 1954; *Three Cases of Murder* (co-dir.), *The Woman for Joe* 1955; *The March Hare* 1956.

Moretti, Nanni. Director, screenwriter, actor. Born on Aug. 19, 1953, in Brunico, Bolzano, Italy. Bright, offbeat, maverick, all-around artist of contemporary Italian cinema who writes his own scripts and usually appears in his own films. A self-declared communist, he resorts to intriguing cinematic means to explore his social and political ideas. He won the Special Jury Prize (Silver Bear) at the Berlin Film Festival for *The Mass Is Ended* (1986), in which he also played the lead role of a priest. In *Palombella rossa* ["Red Lob"] (1989), he uses a water polo match as a microcosm of the embattled post-glasnost Italian Communist party.

FILMS (as director-screenwriter-actor): *Io sono un Autarchico* (also prod.) 1976; *Ecce Bombo* 1978; *Sogni d'Oro* 1981; *Bianca* 1983; *La Messa e finita/The Mass Is Ended* 1986; *Palombella rossa* (also co-sc.) 1989; *Il Portaborse/The Factotum* (co-prod., act. only) 1991; *Dear Mary* 1993.

Morgan, Dennis. Actor, singer. Born Stanley Morner, on Dec. 30, 1910, in Prentice, Wis. A former radio announcer, stock player, and small-time opera singer, he made his film debut in the mid-30s, using his real name or the pseudonym Richard Stanley. In 1939 he became Dennis Morgan and soon after moved into lead roles, playing for the most part pleasant heroes of Warner Bros. musical comedies and occasional Westerns and dramas. Jack CARSON was often cast as his sidekick. In 1959 he starred in the TV series '21 Beacon Street.'

FILMS INCLUDE: As Stanley Morner—*Suzy, The Great Ziegfeld* 1936; *Navy Blue and Gold* 1937. As Richard Stanley—*Men with Wings, King of Alcatraz* 1938; As Dennis Morgan—*Waterfront, The Return of Dr. X* 1939; *The Fighting 69th, Three Cheers for the Irish, Flight Angels, River's End, Kitty Foyle* 1940; *Affectionately Yours, Bad Men of Missouri* 1941; *Captains of the Clouds, In This Our Life, Wings for the Eagle* 1942; *The Hard Way, Thank Your Lucky Stars, The Desert Song* 1943; *The Very Thought of You, Shine On Harvest Moon* 1944; *God Is My Co-Pilot, Christmas in Connecticut* 1945; *One More Tomorrow, Two Guys from Milwaukee, The Time the Place and the Girl* 1946; *Cheyenne, My Wild Irish Rose* 1947; *To the Victor, Two Guys from Texas, One Sunday Afternoon* 1948; *It's a Great Feeling, The Lady Takes a Sailor* 1949; *Perfect Strangers, Pretty Baby* 1950; *Painting the Clouds with Sunshine* 1951; *This Woman Is Dangerous, Cattle Town* 1952; *The Nebraskan* 1953; *The Gun That Won the West, Pearl of the South Pacific* 1955; *Uranium Boom* 1956; *Rogue's Gallery* 1968; *Won Ton Ton—The Dog Who Saved Hollywood* (cameo) 1976.

Morgan, Frank. Actor. *b.* Francis Phillip Wupperman, June 1, 1890, New York City. *d.* 1949. One of 11 children of a prosperous manufacturer of bitters for cocktails, he worked at various odd jobs before following in the footsteps of his older brother, actor Ralph MORGAN, making his Broadway debut in 1914. Two years later he began playing leads in Vitagraph films produced in the New York area. For a decade he worked intermittently in films while pursuing his stage career, but in the early 30s he settled in Hollywood permanently and before long became a fixture in MGM films, specializing in amiable, befuddled, absentminded, often roguish middle-aged types, occasionally in character leads but mostly in key supporting parts. He appeared in dozens of films but is probably best remembered for the title role in *The Wizard of Oz* (1939).

FILMS INCLUDE: *The Suspect* 1916; *A Modern Cinderella, The Girl Philippa, A Child of the Wild, Baby Mine, Raffles the Amateur Cracksman* 1917; *The Knife* 1918; *The Golden Shower* 1919; *Manhandled, Born Rich* 1924; *The Man Who Found Himself, The Crowded Hour, Scarlet Saint* 1925; *Love's Greatest Mistake* 1927; *Dangerous Nan McGrew, Queen High, Laughter, Fast and Loose* 1930; *Secrets of the French Police, The Half-Naked Truth* 1932; *The Billion Dollar Scandal, Luxury Liner, Hallelujah I'm a Bum, Reunion in Vienna, The Kiss Before the Mirror, The Nuisance, When Ladies Meet, Best of Enemies, Broadway to Hollywood, Bombshell* 1933; *The Cat and the Fiddle, Sisters Under the Skin, The Affairs of Cellini* (as the Duke of Florence), *A Lost Lady, There's Always Tomorrow* 1934; *The Good Fairy, Enchanted April, Naughty Marietta, Escapade, I Live My Life, The Perfect Gentleman* 1935; *The Great Ziegfeld, Trouble for Two, Dancing Pirate, Piccadilly Jim, Dimples* 1936; *The Last of Mrs. Cheyney, The Emperor's Candlesticks, Saratoga, Beg Borrow or Steal, Rosalie* 1937; *Paradise for Three, Port of Seven Seas, The Crowd Roars, Sweethearts* 1938; *Broadway Serenade, The Wizard of Oz* (title role), *Balalaika, Henry Goes Arizona* 1939; *The Shop Around the Corner, The Ghost Comes Home, Broadway Melody of 1940, The Mortal Storm, Boom Town, Hullabaloo* 1940; *Wild Man of Borneo, Washington Melodrama, Honky Tonk* 1941; *The Vanishing Virginian, Tortilla Flat, White Cargo* 1942; *A Stranger in Town, The Human Comedy* (as Willy Grogan), *Thousands Cheer* 1943; *The White Cliffs of Dover, Casanova Brown* 1944; *Yolanda and the Thief* 1945; *Courage of Lassie, The Cockeyed Miracle, Lady Luck* 1946; *Green Dolphin Street, Summer Holiday, The Three Musketeers* (as Louis XIII) 1948; *The Stratton Story, The Great Sinner, Any Number Can Play* 1949; *Key to the City* 1950.

Morgan, Harry (Henry). Actor. Born Harry Bratsburg, Apr. 10, 1915, in Detroit. *ed.* U. of Chicago. Character actor of stage, TV, and films. Early in his career he was known as Henry Morgan, but he later changed his name to avoid confusion with the cynical radio and TV (and occasional film) comedian of that name (*b.* Mar. 31, 1915, New York City). On the big screen, he convincingly portrayed a wide variety of characters, from treacherous weasels to best friends. On TV he had the distinction of playing major parts in no fewer than ten regular series, perhaps more than anyone else. Among these were 'December Bride' (1954–59), 'Pete and Gladys' (1960–62), 'The Richard Boone Show' (1963–64), 'Kentucky Jones' (1964–65), 'Dragnet' (1967–70), 'Hec Ramsey' (1972–74), 'M*A*S*H' (1975–83; Emmy 1980), and 'AfterMASH' (1983–84). He portrayed Harry S. Truman in the TV drama 'Backstairs at the White House' (1979). His son, Chris Morgan, is a TV producer.

FILMS INCLUDE: *To the Shores of Tripoli* 1942; *Crash Dive, Ox-Bow Incident, Happy Land* 1943; *Wing and a Prayer* 1944; *A Bell for Adano, State Fair* 1945; *Dragonwyck, From This Day Forward* 1946; *The Gangster* 1947; *All My Sons, The Big Clock* 1948; *Yellow Sky, Madame Bovary* (as Hippolyte) 1949; *Dark City* 1950; *The Well, The Blue Veil* 1951; *Bend of the River, My Six Convicts, High Noon, What Price Glory* 1952; *Thunder Bay, Torch Song* 1953; *The Glenn Miller Story* 1954; *Not as a Stranger* 1955; *The Teahouse of the August Moon* 1956; *Inherit the Wind* 1960; *How the West Was Won* 1962; *Frankie and Johnny* 1966; *The Flim-Flam Man* 1967; *Support Your Local Sheriff, Viva Max* 1969; *The Barefoot Executive, Support Your Local Gunfighter, Scandalous John* 1971; *Snowball Express* 1972; *Charley and the Angel* 1973; *The Apple Dumpling Gang* 1975; *The Shootist* 1976; *The Cat from Outer Space* 1978; *The Apple Dumpling Gang Rides Again* 1979; *Dragnet* 1987.

Morgan, Helen. Actress, singer. *b.* Helen Riggins, Aug. 2, 1900, Danville, Ill. *d.* 1941. Broadway and nightclub star of the 20s and 30s, the original "torch singer." A farmer's daughter, she worked as a biscuit packer, shop girl, and manicurist before starting on her road to fame in a small Chicago cabaret. She appeared in only a handful of films early in the sound era, typically portraying fallen women as she had done on the stage, most memorably as the pathetic Kitty Darling in Rouben Mamoulian's *Applause* (her debut film, made and first shown in 1929 but not released until 1930) and as the tragic Julie in James Whale's *Show Boat* (1936), in which she repeated her triumphant Broadway role. She had also appeared in the part-talking 1929 film version of that musical. The manager of several speakeasies during the Prohibition era, she fell into a heavy drinking habit and her career was eventually shattered by alcoholism. She died at 41 of cirrhosis of the liver. Ann Blyth portrayed her in the film biography *The Helen Morgan Story* (1957).

FILMS: *Show Boat* (as Julie), *Glorifying the American Girl* 1929; *Applause* 1929–30; *Roadhouse Nights* 1930; *You Belong to Me, Marie Galante* 1934; *Sweet Music, Go Into Your Dance* 1935; *Show Boat* (remake; again as Julie), *Frankie and Johnnie* 1936.

Morgan, Henry. See MORGAN, Harry.

Morgan, Marilyn. See MARSH, Marian.

Morgan, Michèle. Actress. Born Simone Roussel, on Feb. 29, 1920, in Neuilly-sur-Seine, France. Leading personality of French and international films since the mid-30s; a classic beauty—delicate, feminine, worldly, and remote, with unforgettably big, expressive eyes. She studied drama under René Simon, entered films at 15, and quickly advanced from bits to lead roles. She soon became the most popular screen actress in France. During WW II she made several films in Hollywood, but most of her American directors failed to utilize her unique personality. She won the best actress award at Cannes for her performance in Jean Delannoy's *La Symphonie pastorale* (1946). She was named Chevalier of the Legion of Honor in 1969. Her first husband (1942–49) was American actor William MARSHALL. Their son, Mike Marshall (*b.* 1944, Hollywood), has also done some screen acting. She is the widow of French actor Henri VIDAL, to whom she was married from 1950 until his sudden death in 1959. Autobiography: *Avec ses Yeux/With Those Eyes* (1977).

FILMS INCLUDE: *Mademoiselle Mozart* (bit) 1935; *Le Mioche/Forty Little Mothers* 1936; *Gribouille/Heart of Paris* 1937; *Orage, Quai des Brumes/Port of Shadows* 1938; *Les Musiciens du Ciel* 1940; *Remorques/Stormy Waters* 1941; *La Loi du Nord* (release delayed from 1939), *Joan of Paris* (US) 1942; *Untel Père et Fils/The Heart of a Nation* (release delayed from 1940; world premiere in the US), *Two Tickets to London* (US), *Higher and Higher* (US) 1943; *Passage to Marseille* (US) 1944; *The Chase* (US), *La Symphonie pastorale* 1946; *The Fallen Idol* (UK), *Fabiola* (It.) 1948; *Aux Yeux du Souvenir/Souvenir* 1949; *La Belle que voilà, The Naked Heart/Maria Chapdelaine* (UK/Fr.; filmed in Canada), *Le Château de Verre* 1950; *L'Etrange Madame X* 1951; *La Minute de Vérité/The Moment of Truth* 1952; *Destinées/Daughters of Destiny* (as Joan of Arc in Delannoy's episode), *Les Orgueilleux/The Proud and the Beautiful* 1953; *Obsession* 1954; *Napoléon* (as Josephine), *Oasis, Les Grandes Manoeuvres/The Grand Maneuver* 1955; *Marguerite de la Nuit, Marie-Antoinette* (title role) 1956; *Retour de Manivelle/There's Always a Price Tag, The Vintage* (US) 1957; *Le Miroir à Deux Faces/The Mirror Has Two Faces, Maxime, Racconti d'Estate/Love on the Riviera* (It./Fr.) 1958; *Menschen im Hotel/Grand Hotel* (Ger./Fr.) 1959; *Les Scélérats* 1960; *Le Puits aux Trois Vérités/Three Faces of Sin* 1961; *Le Crime ne paie pas/Crime Does Not Pay* 1962; *Landru/Bluebeard* 1963; *Constance aux Enfers/Web of Fear* 1964; *Lost Command* (US) 1966; *Benjamin* 1968; *Le Chat et la Souris/Cat and Mouse* 1975; *Robert et Robert* (cameo) 1978; *Un Homme et une Femme: Vingt Ans déjà/A Man and a Woman: 20 Years Later* (cameo) 1986; *Tutti stanno benne/Everybody's Fine* (It./Fr.) 1990.

Morgan, Ralph. Actor. *b.* Raphael Kuhner Wupperman, July 6, 1882, New York City. *d.* 1956. Veteran character of the American stage and screen; brother of Frank MORGAN and father of actress Claudia Morgan. A graduate of Columbia, he abandoned a law career for show business. He appeared in scores of films, occasionally in character leads, often in supporting roles, typically as a dominating figure, often a villain.

FILMS INCLUDE: *Penny Philanthropist* (lead) 1923; *The Man Who Found Himself* 1925; *Honor Among Lovers* 1931; *Charlie Chan's Chance, Devil's Lottery, Strange Interlude* (as Charlie Marsden) 1932; *Rasputin and the Empress* (as Czar Nicholas II), *Humanity* (lead), *Trick for Trick* (lead), *The Power and the Glory, Shanghai Madness, Doctor Bull, The Kennel Murder Case, The Mad Game* 1933; *Orient Express, Stand Up and Cheer, No Greater Glory, The Last Gentleman, A Girl of the Limberlost* (lead) 1934; *Little Men* (lead), *Star of Midnight* 1935; *Magnificent Obsession, Human Cargo, Speed, Little Miss Nobody* 1936; *Exclusive, The Life of Emile Zola, The Outer Gate* (lead), *Wells Fargo* 1937; *Mannequin, Shadows Over Shanghai, Out West with the Hardys* 1938; *Fast and Loose, Man of Conquest* (as Stephen Fuller Austin) 1939; *Geronimo, Forty Little Mothers* 1940; *Dick Tracy vs. Crime Inc.* (serial), *The Mad Doctor* 1941; *Gang Busters* (serial) 1942; *Hitler's Madman, Jack London* 1943; *The Impostor, Weird Woman* 1944; *The Monster and the Ape* (serial), *This Love of Ours* 1945; *Black Market Babies* (lead) 1946; *Song of the Thin Man* 1947; *Sleep My Love* 1948; *Blue Grass of Kentucky* 1950; *Gold Fever* 1953.

Morgan, Terence. Actor. Born on Dec. 8, 1921, in London. *ed.* RADA. Handsome leading man of British stage, screen, and TV. He starred in the TV series 'The Adventures of Sir Francis Drake' (1962).

FILMS INCLUDE: *Hamlet* (as Laertes) 1948; *Captain Horatio Hornblower* (US/UK), *Trio* 1951; *Mandy/The Story of Mandy/Crash of Silence, It Started in Paradise, Street Corner/Both Sides of the Law* 1952; *Turn the Key Softly, Always a Bride* 1953; *Svengali, Dance Little Lady* 1954; *They Can't Hang Me* 1955; *The Scamp* 1957; *Tread Softly Stranger* 1958; *The Shakedown* 1959; *The Curse of the Mummy's Tomb* 1964; *The Penthouse* 1967; *Hide and Seek* 1972; *Yesterday's Warriors* 1979.

Mori, Masayuki. Actor. *b.* Jan. 13, 1911, Tokyo. *d.* 1973, of cancer. *ed.* Kyoto U. In Japanese films since 1942 following stage experience, he is best known to Western audiences for his intelligent interpretation of the role of the taunted husband in *Rashomon* (1950) and that of the enchanted potter in *Ugetsu Monogatari/Ugetsu* (1953).

FILMS INCLUDE: *A Mother's Card* 1942; *Sanshiro Sugata/Judo Saga Part II, The Men Who Tread on the Tiger's Tail* 1945; *Those Who Make Tomorrow* 1946; *Apostasy* 1948; *A Fool's Love* 1949; *Rashomon* 1950; *Stolen Love, The Idiot* (title role) 1951; *Ugetsu Monogatari/Ugetsu* 1953; *The Heart* 1954; *Floating Clouds, Yang Kwei Fei* 1955; *Elegy of the North* 1957; *Night Drum/The Adulteress* 1958; *The Setting Sun* 1959; *When a Woman Ascends the Stairs, This Greedy Old Skin, The Bad Sleep Well* 1960; *Challenge to Live, Design for Dying, Love Old and New* 1961; *Bushido, Alone on the Pacific/My Enemy the Sea* 1963; *Homecoming* 1964; *Admiral Yamamoto, Sun Above Death Below* 1968; *Through Days and Months, Gateway to Glory* 1969; *Zaitochi* 1970; *Ken to Hana* 1972.

Moriarty, Cathy. Actress. Born on Nov. 29, 1960, in Bronx, N.Y. Statuesque supporting player. She was nominated for an Academy Award for her performance as the second wife of Jake La Motta (Robert De Niro) in *Raging Bull*. She has displayed a spirited comedic bent in her subsequent films. She also runs a pizza parlor in California.

FILMS INCLUDE: *Raging Bull* 1980; *Neighbors* 1981; *White of the Eye* (Brit.) 1987; *Kindergarten Cop* 1990; *Soapdish, The Mambo Kings* 1991; *The Gun in Betty Lou's Handbag* 1992; *Matinee* 1993; *Pontiac Moon* 1994; *Casper, Forget Paris* 1995; *Foxfire* 1996; *A Brother's Kiss, Cop Land* 1997.

Moriarty, Michael. Actor. Born on Apr. 5, 1941, in Detroit. *ed.* Dartmouth. Multitalented leading player of the American stage, TV, and films. Trained for the stage at the London Academy of Music and Dramatic Arts, he joined the New York Shakespeare Festival in 1963 and later appeared in a wide range of roles from the classic and modern repertoire in various cities and on Broadway. In 1974 he won a Tony Award for his performance in the Broadway production of 'Find Your Way Home' and an Emmy Award for his supporting role as the gentleman caller in a TV production of 'The Glass Menagerie,' starring Katharine Hepburn. He was also voted best TV supporting actor of that year, regardless of category. He won another Emmy in 1978 for his performance as a Nazi in 'Holocaust.' His film roles have been few but impressive, particularly that of the pitcher Henry Wiggen in *Bang the Drum Slowly*. He has written a play, 'Flight to the Fatherland,' and composed music. A gifted jazz pianist, he has played the piano professionally in night spots and in 1976 released a piano recording.

FILMS: *My Old Man's Place* 1971; *Hickey and Boggs* 1972; *Bang the Drum Slowly, The Last Detail* 1973; *Shoot It: Black—Shoot It: Blue* 1974; *Report to the Commissioner* 1975; *Who'll Stop the Rain?* 1978; *Blood Link* (It.), *Q/The Winged Serpent* 1982; *Pale Rider, The Stuff* 1985; *Troll* 1986; *The Hanoi Hilton, Return to Salem's Lot, It's Alive III: Island of the Alive* 1987; *Dark Tower* 1988; *The Secret of the Ice Cave* 1989; *Full Fathom Five* 1990; *Courage Under Fire, Shiloh* 1996.

Morison, Patricia. Actress. Born Eileen Patricia Augusta Fraser Morison, on Mar. 19, 1914, in New York City. The daughter of a playwright-actor and a theatrical agent, she trained at the Art Students League and the Neighborhood Playhouse, studied dancing under Martha Graham, and worked as a dress designer at a Fifth Avenue shop before making her Broadway debut in 1933. A dark-haired, blue-eyed beauty with talent to spare, she was signed by Paramount in 1938, but her Hollywood career with that and other studios in the following decade was marred by many unrewarding roles, either leads in low-budget melodramas and thrillers or supporting roles in some major films, sometimes as a villainess. She retired from films in 1948 and that year scored a personal triumph on Broadway in 'Kiss Me Kate.' She returned to the screen only once, in 1960, playing George Sand in the Liszt biofilm *Song Without End*, and has since confined her activity to stage musicals and occasional TV.

FILMS INCLUDE: *Persons in Hiding, The Magnificent Fraud* 1939; *Untamed, Rangers of Fortune* 1940; *Romance of the Rio Grande, The Roundup, One Night in Lisbon* 1941; *Beyond the Blue Horizon, Night in New Orleans, Are Husbands Necessary?* 1942; *Silver Skates, Hitler's Madman, The Fallen Sparrow, Calling Dr. Death, The Song of Bernadette* (as Empress Eugenia) 1943; *Where Are Your Children?* 1944; *Without Love, Lady on a Train* 1945; *Dressed to Kill, Danger Woman* 1946; *Tarzan and the Huntress, Queen of the Amazons, Song of the Thin Man* 1947; *Sofia, The Prince of Thieves* 1948; *Song Without End* (as George Sand) 1960; *Won Ton Ton—The Dog Who Saved Hollywood* (cameo) 1976.

Morita, Pat. Actor. Born Noriyuki Morita, on June 28, 1930, in Isleton, Calif. Robust character player of films and TV. Along with his parents and other Japanese-Americans, he was interned as a youngster during WW II. He began his show business career as a nightclub comic and an actor in TV commercials, and later appeared regularly on TV in such series as 'Sanford and Son,' 'M*A*S*H,' and 'Happy Days.' In films from the late 60s, he gained popularity in the 80s in the role of Ralph Macchio's fatherly martial-arts mentor in *The Karate Kid* (Academy Award nomination, 1984) and its sequels.

FILMS: *Thoroughly Modern Millie* 1967; *The Shakiest Gun in the West* 1968; *Every Little Crook and Nanny, Cancel My Reservation, Where Does It Hurt?* 1972; *Midway* 1976; *When Time Ran Out* 1980; *Full Moon High* 1981; *Jimmy the Kid, Savannah Smiles* 1982; *Slapstick of Another Kind, The Karate Kid, Night Patrol, The Karate Kid Part II, Captive Hearts* (also co-sc.) 1987; *The Karate Kid Part III* 1989; *Collision Course* 1990; *Do or Die, Lena's Holiday* 1991; *Honeymoon in Vegas* 1992; *Even Cowgirls Get the Blues, The Next Karate Kid* 1994.

Morlay, Gaby. *b.* Blanche Fumoleau, June 8, 1897, Biska, Algeria, to French parents. *d.* 1964. Radiant star of French silents and talkies. Enormously popular, especially among female audiences, for her touching performances in melodramas, memorably *The Blue Veil* (1942). Her career suffered a setback after the liberation of France because of her marriage to a minister in the Vichy cabinet. She soon resumed acting, but in lesser films and in diminishing roles.

FILMS INCLUDE: *La Sandale rouge* 1913; *Au Paradis des Enfants, Le Chevalier de Gaby* 1916; *Les Epaves de l'Amour* 1917; *L'Agonie des Aigles* 1921; *Faubourg Montmartre* 1922; *Les Nouveaux Messieurs* 1929; *Accusée—levez-vous* 1930; *Après l'Amour* 1931; *Faubourg Montmartre* (remake) 1932; *Mélo* (French version of Czinner's *Die träumende Mund*) 1933; *Le Maître de Forges, Le Scandale* 1934; *Le Bonheur* 1935; *Samson, Le Roi/The King* 1936; *Le Messager, Nuit de Feu/The Living Corpse* 1937; *Les Nuits blanches de Saint-Pétersbourg/The Kreutzer Sonata, Giuseppe Verdi/The Life of Giuseppe Verdi* (It./Fr.), *Quadrille* 1938; *Entente cordiale* (as Queen Victoria), *Derrière la Façade/32 Rue de Montmartre* 1939; *L'Arlésienne, Le Destin fabuleux de Désirée Clary/Mlle. Desiree* (as Napoleon's Desiree), *Le Voile bleu/The Blue Veil* 1942; *L'Enfant de l'Amour* 1944; *Lunegarde, Un Revenant/A Lover's Return, Mensonges* 1946; *Les Amants du Pont Saint-Jean* 1947; *Gigi* 1949; *Millionaires d'un Jour/A Simple Case of Money, Prima Communione/Father's Dilemma* (It.) 1950; *Anna* (It.) 1951; *Le Plaisir/House of Pleasure* 1952; *L'Amour d'une Femme, Papa Maman la Bonne et Moi/Mama Papa the Maid and I, Si Versailles m'était conté/Royal Affairs in Versailles* 1954; *Mitsou, Crime et Châtiment/Crime and Punishment* 1956; *Fortunat* 1960; *Monsieur* 1964.

Morley, Karen. Actress. Born Mabel Linton, on Dec. 12, 1905, in Ottumwa, Iowa. *ed.* U. of California. Unconventional leading lady of Hollywood films of the 30s, following some stage experience with the Pasadena Community Players. She left the screen in 1940 to go on the stage but later returned occasionally in secondary roles. Her career ended abruptly in the early 50s after she invoked the Fifth Amendment when queried about her alleged membership in the Communist party before the House Un-American Activities Committee. In 1954 she ran unsuccessfully for the office of New York State's lieutenant governor on the American Labor Party ticket. At one time (1932–43) married to director Charles VIDOR, she later married actor Lloyd GOUGH.

FILMS INCLUDE: *Inspiration, Daybreak, Never the Twain Shall Meet, Politics, The Sin of Madelon Claudet, The Cuban Love Song, Mata Hari* 1931; *Arsene Lupin, Scarface, Man About Town, The Washington Masquerade, The Phantom of Crestwood, The Mask of Fu Manchu, Flesh* 1932; *Gabriel Over the White House, Dinner at Eight* 1933; *The Crime Doctor, Straight Is the Way; Our Daily Bread, Wednesday's Child* 1934; *Black Fury, $10 Raise, The Littlest Rebel* 1935; *Devil's Squadron, Beloved Enemy* 1936; *Outcast, The Girl from Scotland Yard, The Last Train from Madrid, On Such a Night* 1937; *Kentucky* 1938; *Pride and Prejudice* (as Charlotte Lucas) 1940; *Jealousy* 1945; *The Unknown* 1946; *Framed, The 13th Hour* 1947; *Samson and Delilah* 1949; *M* 1951; *Born to the Saddle* 1953.

Morley, Robert. Actor, playwright. *b.* 1908, Semley, England. *d.* 1992. Rotund, triple-chinned, delightful character player of the British and American stage and screen, at his best in jovial or pompous comedy roles. He was educated at Wellington College and in Germany, France, and Italy, preparing for a diplomatic career, but eventually decided on acting and trained for the stage at the Royal Academy of Dramatic Art. He made his London stage debut in 1929 and in 1938 first appeared on Broadway, repeating his London success in the title role in 'Oscar Wilde.' That same year he made a memorable film debut in Hollywood, playing the feeble-minded Louis XVI opposite Norma Shearer in *Marie Antoinette,* a role that earned him an Academy Award nomination. He subsequently played excellent supporting roles in many British and some American films. He has written several plays, including (in collaboration with Noel Langley) the successful 'Edward My Son,' which was adapted to the screen in 1949, and was for years a witty, erudite guest on American TV talk shows. Autobiography: *Robert Morley, Responsible Gentleman* (1966).

FILMS INCLUDE: *Marie Antoinette* (as Louis XVI; US) 1938; *Major Barbara* (as Andrew Undershaft) 1941; *The Young Mr. Pitt* (as British Statesman Charles James Fox), *The Foreman Went to France/Somewhere in France* 1942; *I Live in Grosvenor Square/A Yank in London* 1945; *The Small Back Room* 1949; *Outcast of the Islands* (as Almayer), *The African Queen* (US/UK) 1951; *Curtain Up* (lead) 1952; *Melba* (as Oscar Hammerstein; US), *The Story of Gilbert and Sullivan/Gilbert and Sullivan* (as W. S. Gilbert), *The Final Test* (lead) 1953; *Beat the Devil* (UK/It.), *Beau Brummel* (as King George III; US/UK) 1954; *The Adventures of Quentin Durward/Quentin Durward* (as Louis XI) 1955; *Around the World in 80 Days* (US) 1956; *Law and Disorder* 1958; *The Journey* (US), *The Doctor's Dilemma, Libel, The Battle of the Sexes* 1959; *Oscar Wilde* (title role), *Giuseppe venduto dai Fratelli/The Story of Joseph and His Brethren* (as Potiphar; It.) 1960; *The Road to Hong Kong* (US/UK) 1962; *Nine Hours to Rama* (US/UK), *Murder at the Gallop, The Old Dark House* (US/UK), *Take Her—She's Mine* (US) 1963; *Topkapi* (US), *Of Human Bondage, Hot Enough for June/Agent 8¾* 1964; *Those Magnificent Men in Their Flying Machines, A Study in Terror* (as Mycroft Holmes, Sherlock's brother; UK/Ger.), *Life at the Top, Genghis Khan* (US/UK/Ger.), *The Loved One* (US) 1965; *The Alphabet Murders, Hotel Paradiso* (US/UK), *Tendre Voyou/Tender Scoundrel* (Fr./It.), *Way. . . Way Out* (US) 1966; *Sept fois Femme/Woman Times Seven* (Fr./It./US), *The Trygon Factor* 1967; *Hot Millions* 1968; *Sinful Davey* 1969; *Cromwell* (as the Earl of Manchester), *Song of Norway* (US) 1970; *When Eight Bells Toll* 1971; *Theatre of Blood* 1973; *The Blue Bird* (as Father Time; US/USSR) 1976; *Who Is Killing The Great Chefs of Europe?* (US/Ger.) 1978; *The Human Factor* 1979; *One Heavenly Dog* (US), *Loophole* 1980; *The Great Muppet Caper* 1981; *High Road to China* 1983; *Second Time Lucky* (Austral./NZ) 1984; *The Wind* (US), *The Trouble with Spies* (release delayed from 1984), *Little Dorrit* (as Decimus Barnacle) 1987; *Istanbul: Keep Your Eyes Open* (Sw.) 1990.

Morley, Ruth. Costume designer. *b.* 1926, Vienna. *d.* 1991. She came to the US as a WW II refugee and in the early 50s began a notable career as a designer of costumes for Broadway plays and City Center operas. She also designed for TV and in the late 50s began working in films. She was nominated for an Academy Award for one of her early productions, *The Miracle Worker* (1962). Her thrown-together outfits for Diane Keaton in *Annie Hall* (1977) sparked a fashion trend. Her daughters, Melissa Hacker and Emily Hacker, are filmmakers.

FILMS INCLUDE: *Never Love a Stranger* 1958; *The Young Doctors, The Hustler* 1961; *The Connection, The Miracle Worker* 1962; *Lilith* 1964; *A Thousand Clowns* 1965; *The Brotherhood* 1968; *Diary of a Mad Housewife* 1970; *To Find a Man, The Hot Rock* 1972; *The Front, Taxi Driver* 1976; *Annie Hall* 1977; *The Brinks Job* 1978; *Kramer vs. Kramer* 1979; *Little Miss Marker* 1980; *The Chosen* 1981; *One from the Heart, Hammett, Tootsie* 1982; *The Money Pit* 1986; *Hello Again* 1987; *The Dream Team, Parenthood* 1989; *Ghost* 1990.

Morner, Stanley. See MORGAN, Dennis.

Moroder, Giorgio. Composer. Born on Apr. 26, 1940, in Ortisei, Italy. A synthesizer specialist, he composed and orchestrated scores and songs for several hit records and, from the late 70s, motion pictures as well. He won an Academy Award for the pulsating score of *Midnight Express* (1978), his first film, another for the song, 'Flashdance—What a Feeling,' in *Flashdance* (1983), and a third for the song, 'Take My Breath Away,' in *Top Gun* (1986). Moroder wrote the score for the reconstructed 1984 version of Fritz Lang's 1926 classic *Metropolis.*

FILMS INCLUDE: *Midnight Express* 1978; *Foxes, American Gigolo* 1980; *Cat People* 1982; *D.C. Cab, Scarface* 1983; *Metropolis* (revised sound version), *Electric Dreams, The Neverending Story* (Ger.) 1984; *Top Gun* (song only) 1986; *Over the Top, Beverly Hills Cop II* (songs only) 1987; *Mamba* (also assoc. prod.) 1988; *Let It Ride* 1989; *The Neverending Story II: The Next Chapter* (songs only; Ger.) 1990; *Cyberden* 1993.

morphing. A special effects technique in which COMPUTER ANIMATION is used to transform one digitally stored image into another. The computer uses a grid of control points on the start and end images to determine what points are analogous (the top of the head, the base of the feet, etc.), then calculates a series of intermediate steps to convert one into the other. Developed at INDUSTRIAL LIGHT & MAGIC, the technique was first introduced in the film *Willow* (1988) and exploited fully in *Terminator 2: Judgment Day* (1991), in which the android villain changes shape at will. The technique has since become a staple of fantasy features, music videos, and commercials.

Morricone, Ennio. Composer. Born on Oct. 11, 1928, in Rome. A graduate of Rome's Santa Cecilia Conservatory, he began composing regularly for Italian films in the early 60s and has since also worked on numerous international productions. He is among the most prolific and most versatile composers currently working in films. His long list of credits—more than 350 by the start of the 90s—includes melodic scores for intimate dramas, light farces, spaghetti Westerns, mystery thrillers, and spectacular epics. Among his most impressive offerings was the tense, pulsating score for *The Untouchables*; his best known may be the witty, epic score to *The Good, the Bad, and the Ugly.* Possibly to avoid seeming to be cornering the market, the ultra-prolific (and yet continually inventive) Morricone sometimes hides in credits behind the pseudonyms Leo Nichols or Nicola Piovani.

FILMS INCLUDE: *Il Federale/The Fascist* 1961; *La Voglia Matta/Crazy Desire* 1962; *Il Successo, Le Monachine/The Little Nuns* 1963; *Per un Pugno di Dollari/A Fistful of Dollars, Prima della Revoluzione/Before the*

Revolution 1964; *I Pugni in Tasca/Fist in His Pocket, Uccelacci e Uccellini/The Hawks and the Sparrows, Il Buono il Brutto il Cattivo/The Good the Bad and the Ugly, La Battaglia di Algeri/The Battle of Algiers, El Greco, Un Fiume di Dollari/The Hills Run Red* 1966; *Le Streghe/The Witches, La Cina e Vicina/China Is Near, Ad ogni Costo/Grand Slam, Da Uomo a Uomo/Death Rides a Horse, Matchless, Arabella* 1967; *Dalle Ardenne all'Inferno/Dirty Heroes, La Bataille de San Sebastian/Guns for San Sebastian* (Fr./It./US/Mex.), *Teorema, Diabolik/Danger: Diabolik, Grazie Zia/Come Play with Me, C'era una Volta il West/Once Upon a Time in the West, Un Tranquillo Posto di Campagna/A Quiet Place in the Country, Un Bellissimo Novembre/That Splendid November* 1968; *Il Mercenario/The Mercenary, Fräulein Doktor, La Monaca di Monza/The Lady of Monza, Le Clan des Siciliens/The Sicilian Clan* (Fr.), *Quemada!/Burn!* 1969; *Two Mules for Sister Sara* (US/Mex.), *Indagine su un Cittadino al di Spora di ogni Sospetto/Investigation of a Citizen Above Suspicion, L'Uccello dalle Piume di Cristallo/The Bird with the Crystal Plumage, Metello* 1970; *Krasnaya Palatka/The Red Tent* (USSR/It.), *Maddalena, Le Casse* (Fr.), *Sans Mobile apparent/Without Apparent Motive, La Classe Operaia va in Paradiso/Lulu the Tool* 1971; *Giù la Testa/Duck You Sucker!, Bluebeard* (Hung.), *L'Attentat/The French Conspiracy* (Fr./It.), *Un Uomo di rispetare/Hearts and Minds* 1972; *Le Serpent/The Serpent* (Fr.), *Rappresaglia/Massacre in Rome* 1973; *Le Trio infernal* (Fr.), *Le Secret* (Fr.), *Mussolini: Ultimo Atto, Fatti di Gente Perbene/La Grande Bourgeoise* 1974; *The Devil Is a Woman* (UK/It.), *Peur sur la Ville/Night Caller* (Fr.), *Der Richter und sein Henker/The End of the Game* (Ger./It.), *Salo o le Centoventi Giornate di Sodoma/Salo—120 Days of Sodom* 1975; *Moses* (UK/It.), *La Donna della Domenica/The Sunday Woman, Marcia trionfale/Victory March, Eredita' Ferramonti/The Inheritance, Divina Creatura/The Divine Nymph, Novecento/1900, Il Desierto dei Tartari/The Desert of the Tartars* 1976; *Exorcist II: The Heretic* (US), *Orca* (US) 1977; *Days of Heaven* (US), *La Cage aux Folles* (Fr./It.), *Cosi come sei/Stay As You Are* 1978; *Viaggio con Anita/Travels with Anita/Lovers and Liars, Il Prato/The Meadow* 1979; *Salto nel Vuoto/Leap Into Void, Il Ladrone/The Thief, The Island* (US) 1980; *So Fine* (US), *La Tragedia di un Uomo ridicolo/The Tragedy of a Ridiculous Man* 1981; *Il Marchese del Grillo/The Marquess of Grillo, Butterfly* (US), *The Thing* (US), *White Dog* (US), *La Notte di San Lorenzo/The Night of the Shooting Stars, Gli Occhi la Bocca/The Eyes the Mouth, La Vela incantata/The Magic Screen* 1982; *Once Upon a Time in America* (US), *Kaos* 1984; *Ginger e Fred/Ginger and Fred, Red Sonja* (US) 1985; *The Mission* (UK), *La Messa e' finita/The Mass Is Ended* 1986; *Mosca Addio, Intervista, Gli Occhiali d'Oro, Good Morning Babilonia/Good Morning Babylon, The Untouchables* (US) 1987; *Frantic* (US), *A Time of Destiny* (US), *Manifesto* (Yug./US) 1988; *Casualties of War* (US), *Tempo di Uccidere/The Short Cut, Fat Man and Little Boy* (US), *Nuovo Cinema Paradiso/Cinema Paradiso* 1989; *Il Male oscuro, Il Sole anche di Notte, Dimenticare Palermo/To Forget Palermo, Tutti stanno benne/Everybody's Fine, The Big Man* (UK), *State of Grace* (US), *Hamlet* (UK) 1990; *Hors la Vie* (Fr./It./Bel.), *Money* (Fr./It./Can.) 1991; *Love Affair, The Night and the Moment, Wolf* 1994; *Disclosure* 1995.

Morris, Anita. Actress. *b.* 1943, Durham, N.C. *d.* 1995. Shapely, sultry, redheaded, mature nymph of the American stage and screen, typically in funny, bawdy temptress roles. First seen on Broadway in a small part in 'Jesus Christ Superstar,' she was the standout performer in the 1982 musical 'Nine' (based on Fellini's *8½*), in which she displayed a keen sense of comedy, along with earthy, uninhibited sexuality, qualities that also served her well on the screen in the 80s.

FILMS INCLUDE: *The Broad Coalition* 1972; *The Happy Hooker* 1975; *The Hotel New Hampshire* 1984; *Maria's Lovers* 1985; *Absolute Beginners, Blue City, Ruthless People* 1986; *Aria* (UK) 1987; *18 Again!* 1988; *Bloodhounds of Broadway* 1989; *Martians Go Home* 1990; *Radioland Murders* 1994.

Morris, Chester. Actor. *b.* John Chester Brooks Morris, Feb. 16, 1901, New York City. *d.* 1970. The son of a well-known Broadway actor and actress, he appeared in silents as a child, then went on the stage in his teens and was a seasoned player by the time he made his adult film debut in *Alibi* (1929), a performance that earned him an Academy Award nomination. Somewhat resembling the Dick Tracy cartoon character, jutting jaw, hooked nose, and all, he typically played a determined, two-fisted hero. He portrayed Boston Blackie in 13 of the series' action films. He died of an overdose of barbiturates shortly after completing a comeback appearance in *The Great White Hope* (1970).

FILMS INCLUDE: *An Amateur Orphan* 1917; *The Beloved Traitor* 1918; *Loyal Lives* 1923; *The Road to Yesterday* 1925; *Alibi, Fast Life, Woman Trap* 1929; *The Case of Sergeant Grischa* (title role), *Playing Around, The Divorcee, The Big House, The Bat Whispers* 1930; *Corsair* 1931; *Cock of the Air, The Miracle Man, Sinners in the Sun, Red Headed Woman* 1932; *Blondie Johnson, Infernal Machine, Tomorrow at Seven, King for a Night* 1933; *Let's Talk It Over, The Gay Bride* 1934; *Society Doctor, Princess O'Hara, Public Hero No. 1* 1935; *The Three Godfathers, Moonlight Murder, Frankie and Johnnie, Counterfeit, They Met in a Taxi* 1936; *Devil's Playground, I Promise to Pay, Flight from Glory* 1937; *Law of the Underworld, Sky Giant, Smashing the Rackets* 1938; *Pacific Liner, Blind Alley, Five Came Back, Thunder Afloat* 1939; *Wagons Westward, Girl from God's Country* 1940; *Meet Boston Blackie, No Hands on the Clock* 1941; *Canal Zone, Alias Boston Blackie, I Live on Danger* 1942; *Aerial Gunner, Tornado, The Chance of a Lifetime* 1943; *Gambler's Choice, Secret Command, One Mysterious Night, Double Exposure* 1944; *Rough Tough and Ready, One Way to Love* 1945; *A Close Call for Boston Blackie, The Phantom Thief* 1946; *Blind Spot* 1947; *Boston Blackie's Chinese Venture* 1949; *Unchained* 1955; *The She-Creature* 1956; *The Great White Hope* 1970.

Morris, Errol. Filmmaker. Born in 1948, in Hewlett, Long Island, N.Y. Orphaned from his father, a doctor, when he was two, he was raised by his mother, a Juilliard graduate who taught music in a public school. He studied the cello at the Putney School in Vermont but gave up on music when he enrolled at the University of Wisconsin as a history major. Graduating in 1969, he drifted about for a couple of years, earning a bare living as a cable TV salesman and a term-paper writer. After briefly attending the graduate school at Princeton, he transferred in 1972 to the University at California at Berkeley as a Ph.D. candidate, eventually leaving the school with a master's degree in philosophy. While there, he became involved in the activities of the Pacific Film Archives, a local cinematheque, and was determined to become a filmmaker. With $120,000, subsidized by his own family and a wealthy classmate, he shot in the spring and summer of 1977 an extraordinary documentary he later titled *Gates of Heaven,* about two pet cemeteries—one failing, the other successful—and the people who run them. To achieve his objective of discovering people the way they are and not simply appear to be, he used an immobile fixed-lens camera that stayed on his subjects and kept them talking until they began revealing the true nature of their personalities. He used that technique effectively again in making *Vernon, Florida* (1981), a profile of a small Southern town that exposed the eccentric side of seemingly ordinary people. Several years went by before Morris could raise the funds for another film. What followed proved to be his greatest achievement, *The Thin Blue Line* (1988), a stunning feature-length documentary, budgeted at $1 million, in which the director set out to prove on camera the innocence of a hitchhiker convicted of the 1976 murder of a Dallas policeman. The presentation was so convincing that shortly after the film premiered the case was reopened and the accused man exonerated. The film's success prompted offers for Morris to direct large-budget Hollywood productions. In 1990 he agreed to make *A Brief History of Time*.

FILMS: *Gates of Heaven* 1978; *Vernon, Florida* 1981; *The Thin Blue Line* 1988; *The Dark Wind, Eat Cheap, Out of Control* 1997.

Morris, Howard. Actor, director. Born on Sept. 4, 1919, in New York City. *ed.* NYU. A veteran of the stage, he was active in TV in the 50s as a TV comedian-writer with Sid Caesar's 'Your Show of Shows.' He appeared in several films of the early 60s, then turned to directing, scoring a hit with his first feature, the highly amusing comedy *Who's Minding the Mint?* (1967). He achieved weaker results with two subsequent comedy efforts, then returned to TV work.

FILMS: As actor—*Boys' Night Out* 1962; *40 Pounds of Trouble, The Nutty Professor* 1963; *Fluffy* 1965; *Way... Way Out* 1966; *Ten from Your Show of Shows* (compilation film of old TV clips) 1973. As director—*Who's Minding the Mint?* 1967; *With Six You Get Egg Roll* 1968; *Don't Drink the Water* (also act.) 1969; *Goin' Coconuts* 1978.

Morris, John. Composer. Born on Oct. 18, 1926, in Elizabeth, N.J. *ed.* Juilliard; U. of Washington; New School for Social Research. Prolific scorer, arranger, and conductor for the American stage, TV, and films. His motion picture scores include nearly all of Mel Brooks's productions. He was nominated for Oscars for *Blazing Saddles* and *The Elephant Man*.

FILMS INCLUDE: *The Producers* 1967; *The Italian Job* (UK) 1969; *The Twelve Chairs* 1970; *Blazing Saddles, The Bank Shot, Young Frankenstein* 1974; *The Adventures of Sherlock Holmes' Smarter Brother* 1975; *Silent Movie* 1976; *High Anxiety* 1977; *The In-Laws* 1979; *The Elephant Man* (UK) 1980; *History of the World: Part I* 1981; *Table for Five, Yellowbeard, To Be or Not to Be* 1983; *The Woman in Red, Johnny Dangerously* 1984; *Haunted Honeymoon* 1986; *Spaceballs, Dirty Dancing, Ironweed* 1987; *Stella* 1990; *Life Stinks* 1991.

Morris, Oswald ("Ossie"). Director of photography. Born on Nov. 22, 1915, in Ruislip, England. An early interest in films led him to work as a projectionist during school vacations. At 16 he dropped out of school to enter the film industry as an unpaid apprentice and later as a clapper boy. He became an assistant cameraman in 1935 and in 1938 began working as a camera operator on "quota quickies." After WW II service as an RAF bomber pilot, he resumed working as an operator, on such films as *Green for Danger* (1946), *Captain Boycott* (1947), and *Oliver Twist* (1948), before graduating to lighting cameraman. He soon established himself as one of Britain's leading cinematographers, widely respected throughout the industry on both sides of the Atlantic. He worked on several of John HUSTON's films, achieving extraordinary color effects with light-scattering filters and smoke-filled sets in *Moulin Rouge* (1952) and unusual color and monochrome mixtures in *Moby Dick* (1956). He won an Academy Award for the cinematography of *Fiddler on the Roof* (1961).

FILMS INCLUDE: *Golden Salamander* 1950; *Circle of Danger* 1951; *The Card/The Promoter, Moulin Rouge* 1952; *Stazione Termini/Indiscretion of an American Wife* 1953; *Beat the Devil, Knave of Hearts/Monsieur Ripois/Lovers Happy Lovers, Beau Brummell* 1954; *The Man Who Never Was, Moby Dick* 1956; *Heaven Knows Mr. Allison, A Farewell to Arms* 1957; *The Key, The Roots of Heaven* 1958; *Look Back in Anger, Our Man in Havana* 1959; *The Entertainer* 1960; *The Guns of Navarone* 1961; *Satan Never Sleeps, Lolita, Term of Trial* 1962; *Come Fly with Me, The Ceremony* 1963; *Of Human Bondage, The Pumpkin Eater* 1964; *Mister Moses, The Hill* 1965; *The Spy Who Came in from the Cold, Life at the Top, Stop the World—I Want to Get Off* 1966; *The Taming of the Shrew* 1967; *Reflections in a Golden Eye, Oliver!* 1968; *Goodbye Mr. Chips* 1969; *Scrooge* 1970; *Fiddler on the Roof* 1971; *Lady Caroline Lamb, Sleuth* 1972; *The Mackintosh Man* 1973; *The Odessa File* 1974; *The Man Who Would Be King* 1975; *The Seven-Per-Cent Solution* 1976; *Equus* 1977; *The Wiz* 1978; *Just Tell Me What You Want* 1980; *The Great Muppet Caper* 1981; *The Dark Crystal* 1982.

Morris, Wayne. Actor. *b.* Bert de Wayne Morris, Feb. 17, 1914, Los Angeles. *d.* 1959. *ed.* Pasadena Playhouse. Blond all-American type of hero of numerous Hollywood action pictures. His budding career was interrupted by WW II, during which he served with valor as a Navy aviator. He was credited with shooting down seven Japanese aircraft in aerial dogfights and with sinking an enemy gunboat and two destroyers. He was awarded four Distinguished Flying Crosses and two Air Medals and was discharged as a lieutenant commander. He returned to films and appeared in many productions, mostly low-budget action programmers, but never regained his prewar popularity. He died of a heart attack at 45 while watching aerial maneuvers aboard an aircraft carrier.

FILMS INCLUDE: *China Clipper* 1936; *Kid Galahad, Submarine D-1* 1937; *The Kid Comes Back, Love Honor and Behave, Men Are Such Fools, Valley of the Giants, Brother Rat* 1938; *The Kid from Kokomo, The Return of Dr. X* 1939; *Double Alibi, Flight Angels, Ladies Must Live, The Quarterback* 1940; *I Wanted Wings, Bad Men of Missouri, The Smiling Ghost* 1941; *Deep Valley, The Voice of the Turtle* 1947; *The Time of Your Life, The Big Punch* 1948; *John Loves Mary, A Kiss in the Dark, The Younger Brothers, The House Across the Street, Task Force* 1949; *Johnny One-Eye, The Tougher They Come* 1950; *Stage to Tucson, Sierra Passage, The Big Gusher* 1951; *Desert Pursuit, Arctic Flight* 1952; *Star of Texas, The Marksman, The Fighting Lawman* 1953; *Riding Shotgun, The Desperado, The Master Plan* (UK), *Port of Hell* 1954; *The Green Buddha* (UK), *Lonesome Trail* 1955; *The Crooked Sky* (UK), *Paths of Glory, Plunder Road* 1957; *Buffalo Gun* (released delayed from 1958) 1961.

Morris, William. See WILLIAM MORRIS AGENCY.

Morrison, Duke. See WAYNE, John.

Morrissey, Paul. Director. Born in 1939, in New York City. *ed.* Fordham. A former insurance clerk and social worker, he began making short underground films early in the 60s, then joined Andy Warhol's "factory" as a production assistant and occasional cameraman. He gradually took over the directorial reins of Warhol's films, bringing to the productions a semblance of orderly structure and more conventional film techniques and making them more palatable to the tastes of general audiences. In the 70s he directed two campy French-Italian horror films and a poor British version of a Sherlock Holmes thriller, then returned to the US to continue an essentially mediocre screen career. His shot-in-Vienna *Beethoven's Nephew* (1985) sought to expose the lunatic side of the composer's personality. Morrissey made personal appearances in several films by others.

FILMS INCLUDE: *Taylor Mead Dances* (short) 1963; *Civilization and Its Discontents* (medium-length) 1964; *Flesh* (also sc., phot.), *Lonesome Cowboys* (exec. prod., phot., edit. only) 1968; *Blue Movie/Fuck* (exec. prod. only) 1969; *Trash* (also sc., phot.) 1970; *Heat* 1972; *L'Amour* (co-dir., co-sc. with Andy Warhol; also exec. prod.) 1973; *Andy Warhol's Frankenstein/Flesh for Frankenstein* (also sc.), *Andy Warhol's Dracula/Blood for Dracula* (also sc.) 1974; *The Hound of the Baskervilles* (also co-sc.; UK) 1977; *Madame Wang's* 1981; *Forty-Deuce* 1982; *Mixed Blood* (also sc.) 1984; *Le Neveu de Beethoven/Beethoven's Nephew* (also co-sc.; Fr./Ger./Aus.) 1985; *Spike of Bensonhurst* (also story, co-sc.) 1988.

Morrow, Jeff. Actor. *b.* Jan. 13, 1913, New York City. *d.* 1993. *ed.* Pratt Institute. A former commercial artist and stage actor, he played leads and supporting parts in films of the 50s and early 60s. He also starred for two years on radio's 'Dick Tracy' and in the TV series 'Union Pacific' (1958–59) and 'Temperatures Rising' (1973–74).

FILMS INCLUDE: *The Robe, Flight to Tangier* 1953; *The Siege at Red River, Tanganyika* 1954; *Captain Lightfoot, Sign of the Pagan, This Island Earth* 1955; *World in My Corner, The Creature Walks Among Us, The First Texan, Pardners* 1956; *The Giant Claw, Kronos* 1957; *The Story of Ruth* 1960; *Harbor Lights* 1963; *Il Giovane normale* (It.) 1969; *Octaman* 1971; *Legacy of Blood* 1973.

Morrow, Vic. Actor. *b.* Feb. 14, 1932, Bronx, N.Y. *d.* 1982. *ed.* Florida Southern Coll. Vicious heavy of occasional films, he starred for several years (1962–67) in the 'Combat' TV series. After having directed several off-Broadway plays, he tackled film directing with a couple of shorts and the feature *Deathwatch* (1966), which he also co-produced and co-adapted from the Genet play. However, after directing one more feature, he returned to acting. He was killed tragically, along with two Vietnamese children, when a low-hovering helicopter accidentally set off special-effects explosives and crashed down on the actors during the filming of the final sequence for the John Landis episode of *Twilight Zone—The Movie.*

FILMS INCLUDE: As actor—*The Blackboard Jungle* 1955; *Tribute to a Bad Man* 1956; *Men in War* 1957; *God's Little Acre, King Creole, Hell's Five Hours* 1958; *Cimarron* 1960; *Portrait of a Mobster* (lead, as "Dutch" Schultz), *Posse from Hell* 1961; *How to Make It/Target Harry* 1969; *Dirty Mary Crazy Larry* 1974; *Babysitter* (It./Fr./Ger.) 1975; *The Bad News Bears, Treasure of Matecumbe* 1976; *Funeral for an Assassin* 1977; *Message from Space* (Jap.) 1978; *The Evictors* 1979; *Humanoids from the Deep* 1980; *L'Ultimo Squalo/The Great White* (It.) 1981; *1990-The Bronx Warriors/The Bronx Warriors* (It.) 1982; *Twilight Zone—The Movie* 1983. As director—*Last Year at Malibu* (short) 1962; *Deathwatch* (also co-prod., co-sc.) 1966; *Sledge/A Man Called Sledge* (It.) 1970.

Morse, David. Actor. *b.* October 11, 1953, in Beverly, Mass. After working with Boston Repertory Theatre, this youthful, resourceful actor made his way to New York, working off Broadway as well as bus-and-truck theater companies. Eventually he landed a role on the long-running television series 'St. Elswhere,' for which he garnered critical acclaim. He branched out into feature films and has since established himself as a gutsy, capable actor with a reputation for delivering solid, believable performances.

FILMS: *Inside Moves* 1980; *Max Dugan Returns, Desperate Hours* 1990; *The Indian Runner* 1991; *The Good Son* 1993; *The Getaway* 1994; *The Crossing Guard, Twelve Monkeys* 1995; *The Long Kiss Goodnight, Extreme Measures* 1996; *Contact, George B.* 1997.

Morse, Helen. Actress. Born in 1948, in Melbourne, Australia. *ed.* National Institute of Dramatic Art. Leading lady of several key Australian films of the 70s. Also memorable in the internationally syndicated TV miniseries 'A Town Like Alice' (1981).

FILMS INCLUDE: *Adam's Woman* 1969; *Stone, Petersen/Jock Petersen* 1974; *Picnic at Hanging Rock* 1975; *Caddie* 1976; *Agatha* (UK) 1979; *Far East* 1982; *Out of Time* (NZ) 1984.

Morse, Robert. Actor. Born on May 18, 1931, in Newton, Mass. Mischievous comedian of stage and films. He scored a big hit in Broadway's 'How to Succeed in Business Without Really Trying' (Tony Award, 1962), a role he repeated on the screen. He won another Tony in 1990 for his portrayal of Truman Capote in the play 'Tru.'

FILMS: *The Proud and the Profane* 1956; *The Matchmaker* 1958; *The Cardinal* 1963; *Honeymoon Hotel* 1964; *Quick Before It Melts, The Loved One* 1965; *How to Succeed in Business Without Really Trying, Oh Dad Poor Dad. . . , A Guide for the Married Man* 1967; *Where Were You When the Lights Went Out?* 1968; *The Boatniks* 1970; *Hunk* 1987; *The Emperor's New Clothes* 1989.

mortars. Steel containers for explosives used in simulating explosions during filming.

Mortensen, Viggo. Actor. Born 1958 in New York City. Offbeat, darkly handsome film actor whose eye-catching performances have kept him working steadily from the mid-80s, most notably for then first-time director Sean Penn's offering *The Indian Runner* (1991) and again, re-teaming with Penn as actor, this time under the direction of Brian De Palma in *Carlito's Way* (1993).

FILMS: *Witness* 1985; *Salvation* 1987; *Fresh Horses, Prison* 1988; *Let's Get Lost* 1989; *Leatherface: Texas Chainsaw Massacre III, The Reflecting Skin* (UK), *Young Guns II* 1990; *The Indian Runner* 1991; *Boiling Point, Carlito's Way, Deception* 1993; *Floundering* 1994; *Crimson Tide, The Prophecy* 1995; *Albino Alligator, G.I. Jane* 1997.

M.O.S. Script abbreviation calling for a silent shot or scene accompanied by neither dialogue nor sound effects. It is said to have originated with a German-speaking Hollywood director who habitually referred to such shots as "mit out sound." At first used jokingly by cinema crews, the abbreviation stuck in film terminology. A shot of a scene without sound is sometimes also called a "wild picture," a term borrowed from its counterpart, "wild sound," the recording of sound without an accompanying picture.

Mosjoukine, Ivan. See MOZHUKHIN, Ivan.

Moskvin, Andrei. Director of photography. *b.* Feb. 14, 1901, St. Petersburg, Russia. *d.* 1961. One of the most gifted cameramen of Soviet cinema. A co-founder of FEX (Factory of the Eccentric Actor), he worked on many of the films of KOZINTSEV and TRAUBERG and was responsible for the magnificent interior shots in Eisenstein's *Ivan the Terrible,* Part I, and the entire photography of Part II.

FILMS INCLUDE: *The Devil's Wheel, The Cloak, Katka's Reinette Apples* 1926; *The Club of the Big Deed* 1927; *The New Babylon* (co-phot.) 1929; *Alone* 1931; *The Youth of Maxim* 1935; *The Return of Maxim* 1937; *The Vyborg Side* (co-phot.) 1939; *Ivan the Terrible Part I* (co-phot.) 1944; *Ivan the Terrible Part II* 1946; *Pirogov* (co-phot.) 1947; *Bielinsky* 1953; *Don Quixote* (co-phot.) 1957; *Stories About Lenin* (b/w photography only) 1958; *The Lady with the Dog* (co-phot.) 1960.

Moss, Arnold. Actor. *b.* Jan. 28, 1910, Brooklyn, N.Y. *d.* 1989. A Phi Beta Kappa graduate of New York's City College (Latin and Greek), he received a master's degree in Old French from Columbia University, and in the early 60s returned to school for a Ph.D. in theater from NYU. Trained at Eva Le Gallienne's Civic Repertory Theatre, he was essentially a stage actor, excelling in classical roles and at one point headed his own repertory company, the Shakespeare Festival Players, with which he toured the country when not appearing on Broadway or broadcasting for the New York Philharmonic Orchestra. He also taught drama at several universities. On the screen, the gaunt Moss typically played sly, evil character parts.

FILMS: *Temptation* 1946; *The Loves of Carmen* 1948; *Reign of Terror/The Black Book, Border Incident* 1949; *Kim* 1950; *Quebec, Mask of the Avenger, My Favorite Spy* 1951; *Viva Zapata!* 1952; *Salome* 1953; *Casanova's Big Night, Bengal Brigade* 1954; *Jump Into Hell, Hell's Island* 1955; *The 27th Day* 1957; *The Fool Killer* 1965; *Gambit* 1966; *Caper of the Golden Bulls* 1967.

Mostel, Zero. Actor. *b.* Samuel Joel Mostel, Feb. 28, 1915, Brooklyn, N.Y., a rabbi's son. *d.* 1977. Exuberant performer of the American stage and screen, a man of titanic dimensions and talent. After graduating from CCNY as an art and English major and briefly attending NYU for a master's degree, he worked during the Depression as a factory laborer, longshoreman, and miner and filled other itinerant jobs, then lectured on art and began painting for a living. He began his professional career as an entertainer in 1942, as a stand-up comic in nightclubs, and within months was performing on radio and in vaudeville. He made his Hollywood debut the following year, playing a dual comic role in *Du Barry Was a Lady.*

After WW II service, Mostel resumed his stage and screen career. He played character roles in a number of films, memorably as a menacing heavy in *Panic in the Streets* (1950) and *The Enforcer* (1951), when his career was suddenly shattered by blacklisting. Although he denied before the House Un-American Activities Committee past or present membership in the Communist party, he could find no work as an actor for several years. He returned to his first love, painting, and eked out a living from his art before returning to the Broadway stage in 1958. In the early 60s he scored three successive personal triumphs on the stage, winning Tony Awards for his performances in 'Rhinoceros' (1961), 'A Funny Thing Happened on the Way to the Forum' (1963), and 'Fiddler on the Roof' (1964). His portrayal of Tevye in the latter musical play remains one of the most memorable characterizations of any Broadway season. Now a heralded star, he resumed his film career in 1966, after a 15-year absence from the screen. In *The Front,* his last film role, before his death of a cardiac arrest, he convincingly portrayed an actor who like himself was victimized by the Hollywood blacklist. Zero's second wife (from 1944) was former Radio City Rockette and actress Katherine Harkin (Kate Mostel, 1918–86). Their son, Josh Mostel (*b.* Dec. 21, 1946, New York City), is a heavy-set character player of stage, TV, and films.

FILMS: *Du Barry Was a Lady* (dual role) 1943; *Panic in the Streets* 1950; *The Enforcer, Sirocco, The Guy Who Came Back, Mr. Belvedere Rings the Bell* 1951; *The Model and the Marriage Broker* 1952; *A Funny Thing Happened on the Way to the Forum* 1966; *The Producers* 1967; *Great Catherine* (UK) 1968; *The Great Bank Robbery* 1969; *The Angel Levine* 1970; *The Hot Rock* 1972; *Marco* (as Kublai Khan), *Once Upon a Scoundrel* 1973; *Rhinoceros* 1974; *Foreplay* (dual role), *Journey Into Fear* (UK) 1975; *The Front* 1976; *Watership Down* (v/o) 1978; *Best Boy* (doc.) 1979.

motion control. In special effects, a computerized system that allows a camera and a model to move together along a predetermined path. The motions are precisely programmed and can be repeated as often as needed, making it easier to add other elements to the shot. Motion control systems are used for such purposes as photographing spaceship movements. The miniature spaceship is mounted on a support that allows it limited movement from side to side; the camera is mounted on a crane that allows it to swoop toward the miniature. To create a fleet of spaceships out of a single miniature, the miniature is photographed several times, each time with a slightly different program of movement; the separate elements are then combined and set against a starry background through TRAVELING MATTE techniques. Motion control technology is also used in modern ANIMATION STANDS, allowing precise movement of the camera above or beside the animation artwork. The first sophisticated computerized motion control system was the DYKSTRAFLEX, invented by John DYKSTRA for the movie *Star Wars* (1977).

Motion Picture Association of America. See MPAA.

Motion Picture Patents Company. A powerful trust founded in 1908 by a group of pioneer film producers and distributors representing the companies Edison, Vitagraph, Biograph, Kalem, Lubin, Selig, Essanay, Pathé Exchange, Méliès, and Gaumont. These companies pooled all their patents claims and formally assigned them to Edison. They then proclaimed that no one was entitled to produce, distribute, or exhibit films in the United States unless so licensed by their corporation. They also set a system of fees and royalties to be paid for the use of cameras, projectors, or any other motion picture equipment covered by their patents. The Patents Company, soon to become known as the "Edison Trust," established the General Film Company in 1910 to distribute the films of its member companies only to licensed theaters. Through this concern the Patents Company launched a campaign of pressure and intimidation, at the end of which they bought out or drove out of business all but one of the large exchanges in the country. The sole survivor was headstrong William Fox, who filed a suit against General in the Federal courts which eventually led to the dissolution of the Patents Company as a trust operating in restraint of trade. In another acquisition spree the Patents Company had also taken over control of most of the large motion picture theaters in the country. Its biggest headache was the enforcement of its regulations on a growing number of independent producers. Mavericks like Carl Laemmle engaged in clandestine production, seeking refuge from the long reach of the New York-based Patents Company in California and Europe. Jeremiah J. Kennedy of Biograph, the Patent Company's staunchest executive, organized a vast espionage network to track down rebel producers and conducted frequent raids on their businesses. But there was too much money to be made in the film business for his disciplinary schemes to succeed.

As a result of Fox's court suits, the government started dissolution hearings against the Patents Company in 1913. The case dragged on until 1917, when the company was ordered to "discontinue unlawful acts." By that time both the Patents Company and its subsidiary General Film were no longer much of a factor in the film business. Of all the production companies that comprised the Patents group, only Vitagraph survived past WW I.

motor. Early motion picture camera motors were mechanical, driven by spring action and wound by a handle. Professional motion picture cameras are now driven by electrical motors designed to provide a constant rate of operation with minimum effort. Synchronized picture and sound work requires a synchronous or an interlock type of motor. Motors of the latter kind are usually provided with a soundproof covering to make them completely noiseless and maintain a speed that is accurately controlled. Variable speed motors, which are noisier, are used for shooting without sound. Their speed can be regulated at from four to 50 or more frames per second.

Mouloudji, Marcel (also known simply as **Mouloudji).** Actor, singer. Born on Sept. 16, 1922, in Paris. In French films from age 14, he played many adolescent leads, then troubled juveniles and perplexed young men. Memorable in André Cayatte's *Justice est faite/Justice Is Done* and *Nous sommes tous des Assassins/We Are All Murderers.* He has enjoyed a successful career as a popular singer and a published novelist in addition to his film work.

FILMS INCLUDE: *Jenny, La Guerre des Gosses/Generals Without Buttons, Ménilmontant* 1936; *Claudine à l'Ecole/ Claudine* 1937; *Les Disparus de Saint-Agil/Boys' School* 1938; *L'Enfer des Anges* 1939; *Les Inconnus dans la Maison/ Strangers in the House* 1942; *Adieu Léonard* 1943; *Boule de Suif/Angel and Sinner* 1945; *Le Bataillon du Ciel/They Are Not Angels, Les Jeux sont faits/The Chips Are Down* 1947; *Bagarres/The Wench* 1948; *La Maternelle, Les Eaux troubles* 1949; *La Souricière, Justice est faite/Justice Is Done* 1950; *Nous sommes tous des Assassins/We Are All Murderers* 1952; *Secrets d'Alcove/Il Letto/The Bed* 1954; *Rafles sur la Ville/Sinners of Paris* 1958; *La Planque* 1961.

mountain films. A film genre started in the early 20s and virtually monopolized through the early 30s by Dr. Arnold FANCK of Germany. The films exalted the beauties of nature and derived their dramatic content from the struggle of dedicated climbers to conquer the mountaintops. Early films in the series, like *Marvels of Ski* (1921), were documentary in concept, but the emphasis increasingly shifted to human drama and emotional conflict against a mountain setting. The films and their hero-worship psychological connotations were extremely popular with the German public (and with audiences abroad) and inspired a cult of mountain climbing among German youth in the years immediately preceding the rise of Hitler. Director Leni RIEFENSTAHL started her film career in Fanck's mountain films and later directed several mountain films of her own, as did another Fanck graduate, Luis TRENKER. Among the best known films of the genre were *Peak of Fate* (1924), *Peaks of Destiny* (1926), *Struggle for the Matterhorn* (1927), *The White Hell of Pitz Palü* (1929), *Avalanche* (1930), *The White Ecstasy/The White Frenzy* and *The Doomed Battalion* (both 1931), and *The Blue Light* (1932).

Moussinac, Léon. Critic, novelist, essayist, educator. *b.* Jan. 19, 1890, Migennes, France. *d.* 1964. A noted writer and journalist, he contributed film criticism to important French publications and published several books of film theory, aesthetics, and history. He was director of studies at the Film Institute of the University of Paris, director general of IDHEC, and administrator of the Cinémathèque Française. Among his books are *Naissance du Cinéma* (1925), *Cinéma Expression sociale, Panoramique du Cinéma* (1926); *Le Cinéma soviétique* (1928); *L'Age ingrat du Cinéma* (1946); *Sergei Eisenstein* (1963).

Movietone. Trademark for a sound-on-film process developed in the late 20s for the Fox film company by Theodore W. Case, Earl I. Sponable, and the staff of General Electric. Unlike Warner's Vitaphone sound system used in the history-making first talkie, *The Jazz Singer,* which relied on synchronized discs to produce its sound, Movietone was the first sound system to employ sound directly on film much as it is still done today. See SOUND.

Shorts utilizing the Movietone sound system were produced by Fox from the early months of 1927. In October of that year the studio launched its now-famous Fox Movietone newsreel at New York's Roxy Theater. Several weeks earlier Fox had released F. W. Murnau's feature *Sunrise* with music, but no dialogue, directly on film. During 1928 a number of part talkies were made by Fox, and other major studios were converting to the system. The success of Fox's all-talking *In Old Arizona* (released in January of 1929) resulted in the immediate abandonment of Warner's Vitaphone and other sound-on-disc systems in favor of the much more efficient and reliable sound-on-film systems.

moving shot. See TRAVELING SHOT; DOLLY SHOT.

Moviola. A motor-driven editing device with a small viewing screen that shows film running at sound or slower speed. Originally (and still) a trademark item, it has become a generic term for various editing machines of this type. The Moviola can be stopped or started on individual frames to enable an editor to examine scenes closely and to mark them for sound synchronization or optical effects. The machine reproduces sound as well as picture and can be operated by a foot pedal for speed regulation and instant stopping and starting. Once an essential piece of equipment in a professional editing room, the vertical Moviola has been largely replaced by bulkier but more efficient, and easier-to-operate flatbed editing tables or by VIDEO EDITING SYSTEMS.

Mowbray, Alan. Actor. *b.* Aug. 18, 1893, London. *d.* 1969. In the US from 1923, he appeared in many stage plays before going to Hollywood, where he became a busy character actor. He appeared in nearly 200 films, generally portraying an assortment of pompous or eccentric Britishers, from butlers to diplomats, but sometimes also distinguished "foreign" personalities. Mowbray wrote and directed a Broadway play and starred in his own TV series, 'Colonel Humphrey Flack' (1953–54 and again in 1958). He was married to actress Lorayne Carpenter. Their daughter, Patricia, was married to character actor Douglas Dumbrille.

FILMS INCLUDE: *God's Gift to Women, Alexander Hamilton* (as George Washington), *The Honor of the Family* 1931; *The World and the Flesh, The Man from Yesterday, Sherlock Holmes* 1932; *Peg o' My Heart, A Study in Scarlet* (as Inspector Lestrade), *Voltaire, Berkeley Square, The World Changes, Roman Scandals* 1933; *The House of Rothschild* (as Metternich), *Little Man What Now?, The Girl from Missouri, One More River, Charlie Chan in London* 1934; *Night Life of the Gods* (lead), *Becky Sharp* (as Captain Rawdon Crawley), *The Gay Deception* 1935; *Rose Marie, Give Us This Night, Desire, Mary of Scotland, My Man Godfrey* 1936; *On the Avenue, The King and the Chorus Girl, Topper, Music for Madame* 1937; *Hollywood Hotel, Merrily We Live, There Goes My Heart* 1938; *Never Say Die* 1939; *Music in My Heart, Curtain Call* (lead), *The Boys from Syracuse* 1940; *The Hamilton Woman* (as Sir William Hamilton), *That Uncertain Feeling, I Wake Up Screaming* 1941; *We Were Dancing, A Yank at Eton, The Devil with Hitler* (as "The Devil") 1942; *Holy Matrimony, His Butler's Sister* 1943; *Where Do We Go from Here?* (again as George Washington), *Men in Her Diary* 1945; *Terror by Night, My Darling Clementine* 1946; *Lured* 1947; *Captain from Castile* 1948; *Abbott and Costello Meet the Killer Boris Karloff* 1949; *Wagonmaster, The Jackpot* 1950; *Blackbeard the Pirate* 1952; *Androcles and the Lion* 1953; *The King's Thief* 1955; *The Man Who Knew Too Much, The King and I* 1956; *A Majority of One* 1962.

Moxey, John. Director. Born in 1920, in Burlingham, England. Essentially a TV producer-director, he also directed a number of British feature thrillers in the 60s. He then moved to Hollywood where, billed as John Llewelyn Moxey, he directed dozens of TV movies.

FILMS: *City of the Dead/Horror Hotel, Foxhole in Cairo* 1960; *Death Trap, The £20,000 Kiss* 1962; *Ricochet* 1963; *Downfall, Face of a Stranger* 1964; *Strangler's Web* 1965; *Circus of Fear/Psycho-Circus The Tormentor* 1967.

Mozhukhin, Ivan (also known as **Mosjoukine** in France; **Mosjukine** in the US; and **Moskine** in Germany). Actor. *b.* Sept. 26, 1889, Penza, Russia. *d.* 1939. The son of prosperous landowners, he quit his law studies in Moscow in 1910 to join a Kiev traveling troupe, with which he toured the Russian provinces. In 1911 he returned to Moscow, where he rapidly acquired a reputation as both a stage and a screen actor. Tall and handsome, with a powerful screen presence, by 1914 he was the most popular romantic lead and character star of Russian films of the Czarist era. In the wake of the Bolshevik Revolution, in 1919 he escaped from Russia to Turkey with a group of directors and actors which included his frequent co-star Nathalia Lissenko, whom he married and later divorced. The group, headed by director Yakov PROTAZANOV, shot a film record of their hazardous journey which they titled *L'Angoissante Aventure (Agonizing Adventure).* The film was completed in Paris, where Mozhukhin now settled, changing the spelling of his name to Mosjoukine. Entering French films, he gained immediate popularity as an exotic and mysterious leading man. Except for occasional excursions to Germany and a single Hollywood film (*Surrender,* 1927), he confined his activity to France, where he held the status of a superstar for the duration of the silent era. The arrival of sound dealt a heavy blow to his career and his roles diminished in number and importance. He died poor and forgotten in a Neuilly clinic.

FILMS INCLUDE: In Russia—*The Kreutzer Sonata, A Life for the Czar, The Defense of Sevastopol* 1911; *Man: A Modern Drama, The Brothers, A Peasant's Fate, Workers' Quarters, War and Peace, The Living Corpse, Mirele Efros* 1912; *The Sorrows of Sara, The Troika, A Terrible Revenge, Christmas Eve* (as the Devil), *Drunkenness and Its Consequences* 1913; *Jealousy, Woman of Tomorrow, Children of the City, Life in Death, Chrysanthemums, Sleeping Beauty, Silent Witnesses* 1914; *Ruslan and Ludmila, Natasha Rostova, Resurrection, The Deluge, The Suicide Club, Nikolai Stavrogin, Diary of a Madman, The Seagull* 1915; *Blind Passion, Queen of the Screen, The Queen of Spades, Woman with a Dagger, Danse Macabre* (also sc.), *Sin* (also sc.) 1916; *Public Prosecutor* (also sc.), *Father and Son, A Daughter of Israel, Andrei Kozhukhov, Blood Need Not Be Spilled, Cursed Millions, Satan Triumphant* 1917; *Father Sergius* 1918; *The Queen's Secret* 1919. In France—*L'Angoissante Aventure* (also co-sc.) 1919; *La Nuit du 11 Septembre* 1920; *L'Enfant du Carnaval* 1921; *Tempêtes, La Maison du Mystère* (serial) 1922; *Le Brasier ardent* (also co-dir. with Alexander Volkov, sc.) 1923; *Kean/Edmund Kean—Prince Among Lovers, Le Lion des Mogols* (also sc.) 1924; *Feu Mathias Pascal/The Late Mathias Pascal/The Living Dead Man* 1925; *Michel Strogoff/Michael Strogoff* 1926; *Casanova/The Loves of Casanova, Surrender* (US) 1927; *Der Präsident* (Ger.), *Der geheime Kurier/Le Rouge et le Noir* (Ger.) 1928; *Manolescu* (Ger.) 1929; *Der weisse Teufel/The White Devil* (Ger.) 1930; *Le Sergent X* 1931; *La Mille et Deuxième Nuit* 1932; *Les Amours de Casanova* (remake) 1933; *L'Enfant du Carnaval* (remake) 1934; *Nitchevo* 1936.

MPAA (Motion Picture Association of America). A trade association, formed in 1922 as Motion Picture Producers and Distributors of America (MPPDA) by the major Hollywood studios to co-ordinate industry policies and practices and to represent the industry in its dealings with the public and official and private organizations. MPPDA was originally created in the wake of widely publicized scandals concerning the private lives of Hollywood personalities and of growing demands by various groups to institute some sort of censorship on films. Under the leadership of Will H. HAYS, a former US Postmaster General, the MPPDA created the Motion Picture Production Code, a strict self-regulatory censorship charter popularly known as "The Hays Code," which for years to come governed the shape and content of Hollywood films.

In the mid-40s the organization changed its name to the present Motion Picture Association of America, and Eric Johnston replaced Hays at the helm. But the production code remained unchanged until 1966, when it was replaced by a much mitigated self-censorship system involving ratings. This was done at the initiative of the present MPAA president, Jack Valenti, because of court rulings regarding obscenity and increasing social permissiveness. The international arm of the organization, MPEAA (Motion Picture Export Association of America), was formed in 1945 to promote the elimination of trade barriers, negotiate agreements with other nations, and protect American copyrights. See also PRODUCTION CODE, RATING.

MS. Abbreviation for MEDIUM SHOT.

Mueller-Stahl, Armin. Actor. Born on Dec. 17, 1930, in Tilsit, East Prussia (later Sovtesk, Russian USSR). Leading man and character player of the German stage and films. A violin prodigy, he studied music at the Berlin Conservatory but later switched to drama school. He began performing on the East Berlin stage in the early 50s and soon became established as a romantic matinee idol. Prominent in East German films since the late 50s, he won the GDR State Prize in 1973. But in 1976, after joining other notable artists in protesting the stifling policies of the regime, he was blacklisted and in 1980 he crossed to the West, where he made a strong impression in two Fassbinder films. He has since made his presence felt in international productions, memorably as Jessica Lange's war-criminal father in Costa-Gavras's American film, *Music Box* (1989), as the Jewish grandfather in Barry Levinson's *Avalon* (1990), and as the domineering father of pianist David Helfgott in *Shine* (1996) for which he earned a supporting actor Oscar nomination.

FILMS INCLUDE: *Heimliche Ehen* 1956; *Fünf Patronenhülsen* 1960; *Königskinder* 1962; *Nakt unter Wölfen/Naked Among the Wolves* 1963; *Preludio 11* 1964; *Ein Lord am Alexander-Platz* 1967; *Der Dritte, Januskopf* 1972; *Der sieben Affären der Donna Juanita* 1973; *Jakob der Lügner/Jacob the Liar* 1975; *Die Flucht* 1977; *Lola* 1981; *Die Sehnsucht der Veronika Voss/Veronika Voss* 1982; *Glut, L'Homme blesse* (Fr.), *Eine Liebe in Deutschland/Love in Germany* 1983; *Trauma, Bittere Ernte/Angry Harvest* 1984; *Vergesst Mozart/Forget Mozart, Der Angriff der Gegenwart auf die übrige Zeit/The Blind Director, Colonel Redl* (as Archduke Franz Ferdinand) 1985; *Momo der Fall Franza* 1986; *Der Joker/Lethal Obsession* 1967; *Midnight Cop, Der Gorilla* 1988; *Das Spinnennetz, Music Box* (US) 1989; *Avalon* (US) 1990; *Bronsteins Kinder, Kafka, Night on Earth* 1991; *The Power of One, Utz* (Ger./It./UK) 1992; *The House of the Spirits* 1993; *The Last Good Time, Holy Matrimony* 1994; *A Pyromaniac's Love Story* 1995; *Conversation with the Beast* (also dir.), *Shine* 1996; *The Game, The Peacemaker* 1997.

Muir, Jean. Actress. Born Jean Muir Fullarton, on Feb. 13, 1911, in New York City. On the Broadway stage from 1930, she headed for Hollywood and a Warners contract following a personal triumph in the play 'Saint Wench' (1933). She soon proved herself an attractive screen personality, a tall, pretty blonde who could emote and project sincerity and warmth effectively and believably. But her talent was all too often wasted on mediocre films and in the late 30s she returned to the stage, appearing only intermittently in films through 1943. Her career suffered a severe blow in 1950 when she was "exposed" as a Communist sympathizer by the infamous Red Channels newsletter and immediately removed from the cast of 'The Aldrich Family' TV series, in which she was to appear as the mother. The blacklisting caused her emotional problems and led to a lengthy bout with alcoholism. But she survived the crisis and by the early 60s was back on Broadway and on TV. In 1968 she moved from

Westchester County, N.Y., to Columbia, Mo., where she taught drama at Stephens College.

FILMS: *The World Changes, Son of a Sailor* 1933; *Bedside, As the Earth Turns, A Modern Hero, Dr. Monica, Desirable, Gentlemen Are Born, Female* 1934; *The White Cockatoo, Oil for the Lamps of China, Orchids for You, A Midsummer Night's Dream, Stars Over Broadway* 1935; *White Fang, Fugitive in the Sky* 1936; *Once a Doctor, Her Husband's Secretary, Draegerman Courage, The Outcasts of Poker Flat, White Bondage, Dance Charlie Dance* 1937; *And One Was Beautiful, The Lone Wolf Meets a Lady* 1940; *The Constant Nymph* 1943.

Mulcahy, Russell. Director. Born in 1953, in Melbourne, Australia. His background in music videos has been evident in his few less-than-refined feature films.

FILMS: *Derek and Clive Get the Horn* (recording of comedy act by Dudley Moore and Peter Cook; UK) 1980; *Razorback* (Austral.) 1984; *Highlander* (UK/US) 1986; *Highlander II—The Quickening* (UK/US) 1991; *The Real McCoy* 1993; *The Shadow* 1996.

Mulhall, Jack. Actor. *b.* John Joseph Francis Mulhall, on Oct. 7, 1887, Wappingers Falls, N.Y. *d.* 1979. Prolific leading man of Hollywood silents and early talkies. Began his show business career as a boy singer with a traveling show, then toured in stock and vaudeville. While in New York as an art student, he began appearing in films at the Edison and the American Biograph studios. In 1914 he set out for Los Angeles, where he soon developed into a popular leading man in the fledgling Hollywood industry. He starred in numerous films, opposite some of the top female stars of the silent era. He had no trouble making the transition to sound and, despite his advancing age, continued playing lead roles in early talkies, mostly routine programmers and serials. By the mid-30s he was reduced to supporting parts, but he continued in films through the late 50s. In all, he appeared in hundreds of productions playing both light and dramatic roles, in a career that spanned more than four decades.

FILMS INCLUDE: *The House of Discord* 1913; *The Rejuvenation of Aunt Mary* 1914; *Tides of Retribution* 1915; *Wanted—A Home, The Price of Silence* 1916; *Love Aflame, The Terror, The Hero of the Hour, The Midnight Man, Sirens of the Sea* 1917; *The Grand Passion, Madame Spy, Wild Youth* 1918; *Whom the Gods May Destroy, Fools and Their Money, The Spite Bride, The Merry-Go-Round* 1919; *Should a Woman Tell?, All of a Sudden Peggy, The Hope, You Never Can Tell* 1920; *The Off-Shore Pirate, Two Weeks with Pay, Molly O'* 1921; *Turn to the Right, Broad Daylight, Dusk to Dawn, Flesh and Blood, The Forgotten Law, Midnight, Heroes of the Street* 1922; *Within the Law, The Call of the Wild, Dulcy, The Bad Man, The Drums of Jeopardy* 1923; *The Goldfish, T.N.T./The Naked Truth, The Breath of Scandal* 1924; *The Folly of Vanity, She Wolves, The Mad Whirl, Classified, We Moderns, Joanna* 1925; *Silence, Subway Sadie, The Dixie Merchant, The Far Cry, Just Another Blonde/The Girl from Coney Island* 1926; *See You in Jail, Orchids and Ermine, The Poor Nut, Man Crazy* 1927; *Ladies' Night in a Turkish Bath, Lady Be Good, Waterfront* 1928; *Naughty Baby, Children of the Ritz, Two Weeks Off, Twin Beds, Dark Streets* 1929; *In the Next Room, Murder Will Out, The Golden Calf, Showgirl in Hollywood, The Fall Guy, Road to Paradise* 1930; *Reaching for the Moon, Lover Come Back, Murder at Dawn* 1931; *Passport to Paradise, Night Beat, Lovebound* 1932; *The Three Musketeers* (serial) 1933; *Cleopatra, It's a Gift, Burn 'Em Up Barnes* (serial and feature versions), *The Old-Fashioned Way* 1934; *Mississippi, People Will Talk, Sweet Adeline, The Big Broadcast of 1936* 1935; *The Clutching Hand* (serial), *The Preview Murder Mystery, Hollywood Boulevard* 1936; *100 Men and a Girl* 1937; *You and Me, The Storm* 1938; *Buck Rogers* (serial), *First Love* 1939; *Strike Up the Band, Black Friday, The Son of Monte Cristo* 1940; *Adventures of Captain Marvel* (serial), *Cheers for Miss Bishop, The Invisible Ghost* 1941; *The Glass Key, Sin Town* 1942; *The Ape Man* 1943; *Lady in the Dark* 1944; *The Phantom of 42nd Street* 1945; *Monsieur Beaucaire* 1946; *Sky Liner* 1949; *Up in Smoke* 1957; *The Atomic Submarine* 1960.

Mull, Martin. Actor. Born on Aug. 18, 1943, in Chicago. Seemingly square, unexpectedly hip TV comedian who played offbeat character roles in films of the 80s and early 90s. Trained as a painter at the Rhode Island School of Design, he started his professional career as a humorist, creating parody recordings for Warner Bros. and other companies. After appearing regularly in 1976–77 on the 'Mary Hartman, Mary Hartman' series, he became popular as a mock talk show host on TV's 'Fernwood 2-Night' (1977–78) and in 1984 starred briefly in his own series 'Domestic Life.' He was one of the creative forces behind 'Roseanne' in the late 80s and through the first half of the 90s, and had a recurring role on that show as Roseanne's gay boss, Leon. On the screen from 1978.

FILMS INCLUDE: *FM* 1978; *My Bodyguard, Serial* 1980; *Take This Job and Shove It* 1981; *Mr. Mom* 1983; *Bad Manners* 1984; *Clue* 1985; *The Boss' Wife* 1986; *O.C. and Stiggs, Home Is Where the Heart Is* 1987; *Rented Lips* (also exec. prod., sc.) 1988; *Cutting Class* 1989; *Think Big, Ski Patrol, Far Out Man* 1990; *The Player* (cameo), *Ted and Venus* 1992; *The Day My Parents Ran Away, Mrs. Doubtfire* 1993; *Mr. Write* 1994; *Edie and Pen* 1996.

Müller, Renate. Actress. *b.* 1907, Munich. *d.* 1937, a suicide. Popular blonde star of German films of the 30s. The daughter of a prominent newspaper editor, she trained for the stage under the tutelage of Max Reinhardt.

FILMS INCLUDE: *Peter der Matrose* 1929; *Liebe in Ring, Liebling der Götter/Der grosse Tenor/Darling of the Gods, Das Flötenkonzert von Sanssouci* 1930; *Sunshine Susie* (UK), *Die Blumenfrau von Lindenau, Liebeslied, Die Privatsekretärin* (and UK version, *Office Girl*) 1931; *Mädchen zum Heiraten* (and UK version *Marry Me*) 1932; *Walzerkrieg/War of the Waltzes/Waltz Time in Vienna, Viktor und Viktoria, Saison in Kairo* 1933; *Die englische Heirat* 1934; *Lisolette von der Pfalz/The Private Life of Louis XIV, Liebesleute* 1935; *Eskapade/For Her Country's Sake* 1936; *Togger* 1937.

Müller, Robby. Director of photography. Born on Apr. 4, 1940, in the Netherlands. A graduate of the Dutch Film School, he began his career as an assistant cameraman in his own country, then moved to Germany where he established an international reputation in the 70s as the favorite cinematographer of Wim Wenders. He later collaborated with other prominent directors in Europe and the US.

FILMS INCLUDE: *Summer in the City* 1970; *Die Angst des Tormanns beim elfmeter/The Goalie's Anxiety at the Penalty Kick* 1971; *Der Schalahtrote Buchstabe/The Scarlet Letter* 1972; *Alice in den Stäten/Alice in the Cities* 1974; *Falsche Beweung/Wrong Movement* 1975; *Im Lauf der Zeit/Kings of the Road* 1976; *Der Amerikanische Freund/The American Friend, Die linkshändige Frau/The Left-Handed Woman* 1977; *Saint Jack* (US) 1979; *Honeysuckle Rose* (US) 1980; *They All Laughed* (US) 1981; *Un Dimanche de Flic* (Fr.) 1983; *Tricheurs* (also act.; Fr./Ger./Port.), *Repo Man* (US), *Body Rock* (US), *Paris Texas* (US) 1984; *To Live and Die in L.A.* (US) 1985; *Down by Law* (US) 1986; *The Believers, Barfly* 1987; *Il Piccolo Diavolo/The Little Devil* (It.) 1988; *Mystery Train* (US) 1989;

Korczak (Pol.) 1990; *Jusq'au bout du Monde/Till the End of the World* (Fr) 1991; *Breaking the Wave, Dead Man* 1997.

Mulligan, Richard. Actor. Born on Nov. 13, 1932, The Bronx, N.Y. Rangy character player of stage and screen who found stardom on TV. Planned to become a priest, then playwright, before becoming a performer. In films sporadically from the early 60s, he landed his own series, 'The Hero' (1966–67) and reached the peak of his success in the popular comedy series 'Soap' (1977–81). He won an Emmy in 1980 for the latter and another in 1989 for his performance in 'Empty Nest.' His second of three aborted marriages was to actress Joan HACKETT.

FILMS INCLUDE: *Love with the Proper Stranger* 1963; *One Potato Two Potato* 1964; *The Group* 1966; *The Undefeated* 1969; *Little Big Man* 1970; *From the Mixed-Up Files of Mrs. Basil E. Frankweiler/The Hideaways* 1973; *Visit to a Chief's Son* 1974; *The Big Bus* 1976; *Scavenger Hunt* 1979; *S.O.B.* 1981; *Trail of the Pink Panther* 1982; *Meatballs Part II, Teachers, Micki and Maude* 1984; *The Heavenly Kid* 1985; *A Fine Mess* 1986; *Oliver & Company* (v/o) 1988.

Mulligan, Robert. Director. Born on Aug. 23, 1925, in the Bronx, N.Y. The son of a New York City policeman, he intended to become a priest, but his theological studies were interrupted by WW II service as a radio operator with the Marines. Returning to civilian life, he worked as a copyboy at *The New York Times,* studied radio communications at Fordham, then joined CBS as a messenger. He quickly advanced in the ranks and during the 50s gained recognition as one of the leading directors of quality TV drama. In 1957 he piloted his first feature, *Fear Strikes Out,* an intimate and disturbing account of baseball star Jimmy Piersall's bout with mental illness. On this and most of his other films of the 60s, Mulligan teamed up with producer Alan J. PAKULA. Mulligan was nominated for an Academy Award as best director for *To Kill a Mockingbird* (1962), a film that was also nominated for the best picture Oscar and fetched awards for best actor (Gregory PECK), best adapted screenplay, and best art direction. Mulligan's work has fluctuated between slickly entertaining films, with no apparent personal imprint or point of view, and intimate dramas characterized by discreet handling and careful attention to characterization. He has been married since 1952 to former actress Jane Lee Sutherland.

FILMS: *Fear Strikes Out* 1957; *The Rat Race* 1960; *The Great Impostor, Come September* 1961; *The Spiral Road, To Kill a Mockingbird* 1962; *Love with the Proper Stranger* 1963; *Baby the Rain Must Fall* 1965; *Inside Daisy Clover* 1966; *Up the Down Staircase* 1967; *The Stalking Moon* 1969; *The Pursuit of Happiness, Summer of '42* 1971; *The Other* (also prod.) 1972; *The Nickel Ride* (also prod.) 1974; *Bloodbrothers/A Father's Love, Same Time Next Year* (also co-prod.) 1979; *Kiss Me Goodbye* (also co-prod.) 1982; *Clara's Heart* 1988; *The Man in the Moon* 1991.

Mulroney, Dermot. Actor. Born on Oct. 31, 1963, in Alexandria, Va. *ed.* Northwestern U. Quirky, dark-haired actor frequently seen in offbeat dramas.

FILMS INCLUDE: *Sunset, Young Guns* 1988; *Staying Together* 1989; *Survival Quest, Longtime Companion* 1990; *Samantha, Career Opportunities, Bright Angel* 1991; *Where the Day Takes You* 1992; *Point of No Return, The Thing Called Love* 1993; *Angels in the Outfield, Bad Girls, Silent Tongue* 1994; *Copycat, How To Make an American Quilt* 1995; *Kansas City, The Trigger Effect* 1996.

multibroad. A variable-focus lighting unit, adjustable by the turning of a knob.

multicam. The use of two or more cameras simultaneously to shoot a scene from more than one angle. Scenes must be carefully planned and cameras placed so that one camera does not appear in the viewing field of another during filming.

multihead printer. A printing machine capable of making two or more copies of a film simultaneously.

multilayer film. Film with three layers of emulsion, each sensitive to one of the primary photographic colors—red, green, and blue. The film also has several interlayers and an antihalation layer (see HALATION).

multiplane. In animation, a method for achieving a sense of deep perspective by placing a number of glass layers between the camera lens and the animation board.

multiple-image shot. A split-screen effect in which the same image is repeated a number of times in the same film frame. The effect is achieved optically, by matting each section of the frame separately and finally combining all the exposed images into one printed frame. A cruder variation of the multiple-image shot can be made more easily but less effectively with the aid of a special lens that produces repetitions of the same image in one simple take.

multiple runs. In animation and special effects, different actions photographed on the same length of film by rewinding to the starting point and reshooting.

multiplex. A theater with multiple screening rooms, allowing it to show several films at one time. This capacity minimizes risk and increases potential profits, since a hit on one screen can compensate for a flop on another. Beginning in the 70s, multiplex theaters have proliferated in the US and abroad, sometimes not without a struggle from fans of old movie palaces that were segmented into small screening rooms. New theaters in the US are now usually built as multiplexes, often in cavernous buildings or inside shopping malls.

multiscreen. A system of film presentation employing several screens (usually three) and a similar number of interlocked projectors. A multiscreen system, CINEORAMA, was presented as early as 1900. Abel GANCE used a triptych effect in his *Napoléon* in the late 20s. Technically improved multiscreen presentations were demonstrated in world's fairs of the 60s. See also CINERAMA.

Mulvey, Laura. Filmmaker, critic. Since the 1970s, she has collaborated with critic and theorist Peter WOLLEN on a number of articles about the effects of gender on filmmaking and the film experience, as well as on several avant-garde films that provide an alternative psychosocial approach, including *Riddles of the Sphinx* (1977) and *Penthesilea* (1974). Author of the highly influential 1975 essay, "Visual Pleasure and Narrative Cinema," which analyzes the long prevailing convention of the "male gaze" in the narrative fiction film in order to pave the way for "a new language of desire." It is included in a collection of her essays, *Visual and Other Pleasures*, in 1989, and has been reprinted widely. She has also written *Citizen Kane*, a critical monograph.

Mundin, Herbert. Actor. *b.* Aug. 21, 1898, Lancashire, England. *d.* 1939. Short, plump character actor of many Hollywood films of the 30s until his death. He came to the US following stage and screen experience in England. His career was cut short by a fatal car crash.

FILMS INCLUDE: *Enter the Queen* (UK) 1930; *The Silent Witness, Love Me Tonight, Chandu the Magician, Sherlock Holmes* 1932; *Cavalcade, Pleasure Cruise, Adorable, Shanghai Madness, Hoopla* 1933; *Orient Express, Bottoms Up, Ever Since Eve, Call It Luck* (lead) 1934; *David Copperfield* (as Barkis), *Mutiny on the Bounty* 1935; *A Message to Garcia, Under Two Flags, Tarzan Escapes* 1936; *Another Dawn, Angel* 1937; *The Adventures of Robin Hood, Lord Jeff* 1938; *Society Lawyer* 1939.

Muni, Paul. Actor. *b.* Muni Weisenfreund, Sept. 22, 1895, Lemberg, Austria (later Lwow, Poland; now Lvov, USSR). *d.* 1967. The son of an itinerant actor and actress, he appeared on the stage with his parents from early childhood. When he was seven, the family emigrated to the US, settled on New York's Lower East Side, and continued its theatrical activity on the Yiddish stage. In 1918, Muni joined the then-thriving Yiddish Art Theater company, with which he toured the US and Europe. He was 31 when he made his English-language stage debut in the 1926 Broadway production of 'We Americans.' By 1929 he was sufficiently established on Broadway to be signed by Fox. He was nominated for an Oscar for his very first role, in *The Valiant.* But, unhappy with his second film, *Seven Faces,* in which he played seven different roles, Muni returned to Broadway, where he scored a notable success in 1931 in 'Counsellor-at-Law.' Returning to the screen, he reaped two successive personal triumphs with *Scarface* and *I Am a Fugitive from a Chain Gang.* He was again nominated for an Oscar for the latter.

Muni was next signed to a long-term contract by Warners and rapidly established himself as the studio's most distinguished thespian. An extremely conscientious actor, he insisted on choice of roles and took meticulous care with the makeup required for authenticity in his portrayals. After completing a cycle of social dramas he scored his biggest success with a string of portrayals of famous people in the Warners biofilms of the 30s. He won an Academy Award for *The Story of Louis Pasteur,* the New York Film Critics Award for *The Life of Emile Zola,* and wide esteem for *Juarez.* But disagreements with studio management over subsequent roles led to the termination of his contract by mutual consent. From the early 40s he alternated between stage and screen. His film roles were few and far between, but each was still anticipated with some excitement by the critics and the public. He scored a hit on Broadway in 1955 with 'Inherit the Wind' and played his last role in either medium in the film *The Last Angry Man* (1959). Deteriorating health and advancing blindness kept him virtually inactive until his death of a heart ailment.

FILMS: *The Valiant, Seven Faces* (in seven roles, including impersonations of Napoleon, Schubert, and Don Juan) 1929; *Scarface/Scarface: The Shame of the Nation* (character loosely based on Al Capone), *I Am a Fugitive from a Chain Gang* 1932; *The World Changes* 1933; *Hi Nellie!* 1934; *Bordertown, Black Fury, Dr. Socrates* 1935; *The Story of Louis Pasteur* (title role) 1936; *The Good Earth* (as Wang Lung), *The Woman I Love, The Life of Emile Zola* (title role) 1937; *Juarez* (title role), *We Are Not Alone* 1939; *Hudson's Bay* (as French explorer Pierre Radisson) 1941; *The Commandos Strike at Dawn, Stage Door Canteen* (cameo) 1943; *A Song to Remember* (as composer Joseph Elsner, Chopin's teacher), *Counter-Attack* 1945; *Angel on My Shoulder* 1946; *Imbarco a Mezzanotte/Stranger on the Prowl/Encounter* (It.) 1952; *The Last Angry Man* 1959.

Munk, Andrzej. Director. *b.* Oct. 16, 1921, Kraków, Poland. *d.* 1961. Graduating from high school just before the outbreak of WW II, he spent the Occupation years in Warsaw as a freedom fighter of the Polish underground. After the war, he studied architecture, then law and economics, but soon abandoned the university to enroll at the film school in Lodz, graduating in 1950 as both director and cameraman. Following a series of distinguished documentaries, in which he experimented with the exclusive use of natural sounds, he turned to feature films in 1956. An intelligent and iconoclastic director, he used bittersweet irony to comment on various aspects of Polish life, cynically probing such "sacred cows" of the regime as the merits of military heroism and the wisdom of the bureaucracy. Along with Andrzej Wajda, Munk held a key position in the New Wave of Polish cinema. He died in an automobile crash in the midst of shooting *Passenger.* The film was completed by friends and released in 1963.

FILMS: Documentaries—*Art of Youth* (graduation film; also sc.) 1949; *It Began in Spain* (compilation film) 1950; *Science Closer to Life* (also co-phot.), *Direction: Nowa Huta* 1951; *The Tale of Ursus, Diaries of the Peasants* (also sc.) 1952; *A Railwayman's Word* (also sc.) 1953; *The Stars Must Shine* (co-dir., also sc.) 1954; *Sunday Morning* (also sc.), *Men of the Blue Cross* (also sc.) 1955; *A Walk in the Old City of Warsaw* (also sc.) 1959. Features—*Man on the Track* (also co-sc.) 1956; *Eroica* 1958; *Bad Luck* 1960; *The Passenger* (also co-sc.) 1963.

Munro, Janet. Actress. *b.* 1934, Blackpool, England, of Scottish descent. *d.* 1972. Leading lady of UK and US films, including several Disney productions, following stage experience. Her career was hampered by an alcohol problem. Formerly married to actors Tony Wright (1956–61) and Ian HENDRY (1963–71), she died freakishly at 38 as a result of choking while she was drinking tea.

FILMS INCLUDE: *Small Hotel* 1957; *The Trollenberg Terror/The Crawling Eye* 1958; *Darby O'Gill and the Little People, Tommy the Toreador, Third Man on the Mountain* 1959; *Swiss Family Robinson* 1960; *The Day the Earth Caught Fire* 1961; *Life for Ruth/Walk in the Shadow* 1962; *Bitter Harvest* 1963; *Hide and Seek, A Jolly Bad Fellow/They All Died Laughing* 1963; *Daylight Robbery* 1964; *Sebastian* 1967; *Cry Wolf* (bit) 1968.

Munshin, Jules. Actor. *b.* 1915, New York City. *d.* 1970. A tall, sad-eyed comedian, he clowned, danced, and sang his way from Catskill resorts and vaudeville into Broadway stardom in the 1946 musical 'Call Me Mister.' He subsequently enlivened several MGM musicals of the late 40s, memorably *On the Town* as one of three sailors (the others were Gene Kelly and Frank Sinatra) on a New York romp. After returning to the stage he appeared occasionally in films. He died of a heart attack at 54.

FILMS: *Easter Parade* 1948; *Take Me Out to the Ball Game, That Midnight Kiss, On the Town* 1949; *Nous irons à Monte Carlo/Monte Carlo Baby* (Fr.) 1951; *Ten Thousand Bedrooms, Silk Stockings* 1957; *Wild and Wonderful* 1964; *Monkeys Go Home!* 1967.

Munson, Ona. Actress. *b.* June 16, 1906, Portland, Ore. *d.* 1955. A vaudeville performer at 16, she starred in Broadway musicals and intermittently played dramatic leads and supporting roles in Hollywood films, typically as a straying woman. She is best remembered as the scandalous Belle Watling in *Gone With the Wind* (1939). She died at 49 of an overdose of sleeping pills, leaving a suicide note behind. Her first of three husbands was actor-director Edward ("Eddie") BUZZELL.

FILMS: *Going Wild, The Hot Heiress, Broad Minded, Five Star Final* 1931; *His Exciting Night, Dramatic School* 1938; *Scandal Sheet, Legion of Lost Flyers, The Big Guy, Gone With the Wind* (as Belle Watling) 1939; *Wagons Westward* 1940; *Lady from Louisiana, Wild Geese Calling* 1941; *The Shanghai Gesture, Drums of the Congo* 1942; *Idaho* 1943; *The Cheaters, Dakota* 1945; *The Red House* 1947.

mural. Any large photograph or painting used as a background on a film set.

Murat, Jean. Actor. *b.* July 13, 1888, Périgueux, France. *d.* 1968. A former journalist and WW I correspondent, he entered films in his mid-30s and played young leading men well into his 40s. He was among the principal male leads of French films between the two world wars. At one time married to actress ANNABELLA.

FILMS INCLUDE: *La Sirène de Pierre* 1922; *Les Yeux de l'Ame* 1923; *La Galerie des Monstres* 1924; *Le Stigmate* 1925; *Carmen, La Proie du Vent* 1926; *Valencia* (Ger.), *Duel* 1927; *Escaped from Hell* (USSR/Ger.), *La Grande Epreuve/The Legion of Honor/The Soul of France, L'Eau du Nil* 1928; *Vénus, La Divine Croisière* 1929; *La Nuit est à nous* 1930; *Barcarolle d'Amour* 1931; *Paris-Mediterranée* 1932; *L'Homme à l'Hispano* 1933; *La Châtelaine du Liban* 1934; *L'Equipage/ Flight Into Darkness, Deuxième Bureau/Second Bureau, La Kermesse héroïque/Carnival in Flanders* 1935; *Les Mutinés de l'Elseneur, La Guerre des Gosses/Generals Without Buttons* 1936; *Troïka sur la Piste blanche, L'Homme à abattre, Aloha* 1937; *J'étais une Aventurière* 1938; *Le Capitaine Benoit* 1939; *Les Hommes sans Peur* 1941; *L'Eternel Retour/The Eternal Return* 1943; *Bethsabée* 1947; *Bagarres/The Wench* 1948; *On the Riviera* (US), *Rich Young and Pretty* (US) 1951; *La Nuit est à nous* (remake), *Alerte au Sud* 1953; *Huis clos/No Exit* 1954; *L'Amant de Lady Chatterley/Lady Chatterley's Lover* 1955; *Les Misérables, Les Grandes Familles/The Possessors* 1958; *Résurrection* 1959; *It Happened in Athens* (US) 1962; *Le Pont des Soupirs* 1964.

Murch, Walter. Sound designer, film editor. Born in New York City. *ed.* USC (film). A specialist in a field ignored by movie fans and neglected by film scholars, he was responsible for the special aural quality of several notable productions of Francis Ford COPPOLA and other directors. He was nominated for an Oscar for the unique sound track of *The Conversation* (1974), a film about eavesdropping, and won the Academy Award for the sound of *Apocalypse Now* (1979). In addition, he has excelled in the more conventionally recognized area of film editing, and was nominated for his work in that capacity for *Julia* (1977). Murch was far less successful in his single excursion into directing, *Return to Oz* (1985), an inept, purported sequel to *The Wizard of Oz.* However, over a decade later, Murch received two more Oscars, this time for editing and achievement in sound for Anthony MINGHELLA's sweeping epic *The English Patient* (1996).

FILMS INCLUDE: As sound specialist—*The Rain People* 1969; *Gimme Shelter* 1970; *THX 1138* (also co-sc.) 1971; *American Graffiti* 1973; *The Conversation* (also co-edit.) 1974; *The Godfather Part II* 1974; *Apocalypse Now* 1979. As director—*Return to Oz* (also co-sc.) 1985. As editor—*Julia* 1977; *The Unbearable Lightness of Being* 1988; *Ghost, The Godfather Part III* 1990; *Romeo Is Bleeding* 1994; *The English Patient* 1996.

Muren, Dennis. American special effects artist. Born ca. 1950. Fascinated by film trickery from childhood, he began experimenting with a cheap 8 mm camera at age ten and read voraciously on the subject. In 1968, his freshman year as a business major in college, he produced and directed *Equinox,* a feature-length science-fiction film, with $8,000 he borrowed from friends. Producer Jack E. Harris bought the rights to the 16 mm film, had it partly reshot with additional scenes by director-writer Jack Woods, and released it in 1970 with Muren's special effects footage intact. For the remainder of his college days Muren supported himself by working on TV commercials. After graduating, he tried unsuccessfully to raise money for film production. The turning point in his career came when he joined George Lucas's then-fledgling special-effects shop, INDUSTRIAL LIGHT & MAGIC (ILM), as a stop-motion and miniature photography specialist, fields in which he has few rivals. He shared Academy Awards for the visual effects of *The Empire Strikes Back* (1980), *E.T.* (1982), *Return of the Jedi* (1983), *Indiana Jones and the Temple of Doom* (1984), *Innerspace* (1987), *The Abyss* (1989), and *Terminator 2: Judgment Day* (1991), and has supervised the production of effects for several other megabuck films notable for their flamboyant technique. As senior effects supervisor at ILM, he has presided over the development of COMPUTER ANIMATION as a major special effects technique in such films as *Jurassic Park* (1993).

FILMS INCLUDE: *Equinox* (also co-dir. uncredited, assoc. prod.) 1970; *Star Wars, Close Encounters of the Third Kind* 1977; *The Empire Strikes Back* 1980; *Dragonslayer* 1981; *E.T.—The Extraterrestrial* 1982; *Return of the Jedi* 1983; *Indiana Jones and the Temple of Doom* 1984 *Young Sherlock Holmes* 1985; *Innerspace, Empire of the Sun* 1987; *Willow* 1988; *Ghostbusters II, The Abyss* 1989; *Terminator 2: Judgment Day* 1991; *Jurassic Park* 1993; *Dragonworld* 1994; *Casper, Jumanji* 1995.

Murfin, Jane. Playwright, screenwriter. *b.* 1893, Quincy, Mich. *d.* 1955. She wrote a number of successful stage plays, sometimes in collaboration with Jane Cowl, several of which were later adapted into films. In Hollywood from the late 1910s, she also wrote numerous stories and screenplays directly for the screen, alone or in collaboration, mainly romantic comedies and dramas for RKO and MGM, producing or directing a few of her own films. She was at one time (1932–44) married to Donald CRISP.

FILMS INCLUDE (as screenwriter alone or in collaboration): *Daybreak* (co-play basis only) 1918; *Marie Ltd., A Temperamental Wife* (co-play basis only, 'Information Please'), *The Right to Life* (story only) 1919; *The Amateur Wife* 1920; *The Silent Call* 1921; *Brawn of the North* (co-story, co-prod.) 1922; *The Love Master* (co-story, co-prod.), *Flapper Wives* (also co-prod., co-dir.) 1924; *White Fang, A Slave of Fashion* 1925; *The Savage, Meet the Prince* 1926; *Notorious Lady, The Prince of Headwaiters* 1927; *Lilac Time* (co-play basis only) 1928; *Half Marriage, Street Girl, Dance Hall* 1929; *Seven Keys to Baldpate, The Pay Off, Leathernecking* 1930; *Too Many Crooks, Friends and Lovers* 1931; *What Price Hollywood, Rockabye, Smilin' Through* (co-play basis only), *Young Bride* 1932; *Our Betters, The Silver Cord, Double Harness, Ann Vickers, After Tonight* (also story) 1933; *The Crime Doctor, Spitfire, This Man Is Mine, The Fountain, The Little Minister* 1934; *Romance in Manhattan, Roberta, Alice Adams* 1935; *Come and Get It* 1936; *That Girl from Paris* (story adapt. only), *I'll Take Romance* 1937; *The Shining Hour* 1938; *Stand Up and Fight, The Women* 1939; *Pride and Prejudice* 1940; *Andy Hardy's Private Secretary, Smilin' Through* (co-play basis only) 1941; *Flight for Freedom* 1943; *Dragon Seed* 1944.

Murnau, F. W. Director. *b.* Friedrich Wilhelm Plumpe, Dec. 28, 1888, Bielefeld, Germany. *d.* 1931. The son of a textile merchant of Swedish descent, he was drawn to drama as a child and often played make-believe theater with his siblings and friends. After studies of art and literature history at the University of Heidelberg, he went to Berlin, where he became a pupil of, then actor and assistant director to, Max REINHARDT. During WW I he served as a combat pilot. Straying off course in a heavy fog on one flight, he landed in Switzerland. He spent the rest of the war there, directing a play and compiling propaganda footage for the German embassy in Berne. Returning to Germany, he began his career as film director in 1919. Most of the films he made before 1921 have been lost.

It was with *Nosferatu—Eine Symphonie des Grauens/ Nosferatu the Vampire* (1922) that Murnau made his initial impact on world cinema. Adapted from Bram Stoker's *Dracula,* it was distinguished from the other Caligari-inspired macabre films of German expressionism in that it was shot on real locations rather than on stylized studio sets and derived its horror and sense of mystery from setting its sinister story in familiar surroundings among everyday people and events.

Murnau's next masterpiece, *Der letzte Mann/The Last Laugh* (1924), established his reputation as one of the world's most prominent directors. Among the finest achievements of the silent cinema, *The Last Laugh* was so expressive in visual terms that it completely did away with the customary film titles without sacrificing the clarity of its plot or the significance of its action. Its creative use of freewheeling camera movement (by Karl FREUND) was a virtual milestone in the history of films, the beginning of a tradition of *MISE-EN-SCÈNE* that was to be further explored by such masters of the cinema as Orson Welles, Max Ophüls, and Kenji Mizoguchi. It was on the strength of *The Last Laugh* that Murnau was invited to Hollywood by Fox, early in 1927.

His first American film, *Sunrise,* subtitled *A Story of Two Humans,* has been called "the last high peak of German silent cinema." Hailed by critics of the French *Cahiers du Cinéma* as the greatest film of all time, *Sunrise* echoes the concern for spatial and dramatic integrity and the inherently pessimistic outlook and sense of doom that characterized Murnau's German films. Made from a script by Murnau's longtime German collaborator Carl MAYER and backed by the financial resources of a large American studio, the film merged the traditions of UFA and Hollywood into a work of great lyrical beauty that survives the artificial ending imposed on it by the industry's then yet-unwritten moral code.

Murnau made two additional films for Fox, then entered a partnership with celebrated documentary director Robert FLAHERTY. Their first and last realized joint project was *Tabu,* a film shot on location in the South Seas. When the two strongly individualistic directors could not agree on an approach and a style, Murnau bought out Flaherty's share in the picture and completed it himself. What might have started as an expressive semidocumentary affair, balancing the divergent personalities and styles of both directors, ended up a characteristic Murnau film despite its exotic trimmings. It is the inner world of the islanders, the psychic conflicts of its proponents, that the film is concerned with, rather than their physical surroundings. The film was a big commercial success. But a week before it premiered, on March 11, 1931, en route from Los Angeles to Monterey, Murnau was tragically killed in an automobile crash. He was only 42, and one can but speculate about the direction his brilliant career might have taken in American films, which had just learned to talk.

FILMS: *Der Knabe in Blau/Der Todessmaragd* 1919; *Satanas, Sehnsucht/Bajazzo, Der Bucklige und die Tänzerin, Der Januskopf/Schrecken/Janus-Faced* (based on R. L. Stevenson's *Dr. Jekyll and Mr. Hyde*), *Abend. . . Nacht. . . Morgen, Der Gang in die Nacht* 1920; *Schloss Vogelöd/Haunted Castle* 1921; *Marizza—gennant die Schmugglermadonna, Nosferatu—Eine Symphonie des Grauens/Nosferatu the Vampire* (based on 'Dracula'), *Der brennende Acker/Burning Soil, Phantom* 1922; *Die Austreibung/Driven from Home* 1923; *Die Finanzen des Grossherzogs/The Grand Duke's Finances, Der letzte Mann/The Last Laugh* 1924; *Tartüff/Tartuffe, Faust* 1926; *Sunrise/Sunrise: A Story of Two Humans* (US) 1927; *Four Devils* (N.Y. premiere; released the following year; US) 1928; *City Girl/Our Daily Bread* (US), *Die zwölfte Stunde—Eine Nacht des Grauens* (a revised sound version of 1922's *Nosferatu—Eine Symphonie des Grauens/Nosferatu the Vampire)* 1930; *Tabu* (co-dir., co-sc. with Robert Flaherty; US) 1931.

Murphy, Audie. Actor. *b.* June 20, 1924, near Kingston, Tex. *d.* 1971. Born to a poverty-stricken family of cotton sharecroppers, he rose to fame as WW II's most decorated GI, the recipient of 24 decorations, including the Congressional Medal of Honor. Boyishly handsome, he began a film career in the late 40s that consisted for the most part of skinny, baby-faced hero leads in low-budget Westerns. He played himself in the screen biography *To Hell and Back* (1955), based on his 1949 book, which depicted his battlefront heroics and his rise from anonymous private to national-hero lieutenant. His film career and business affairs suffered setbacks in the late 60s. In 1968 he was declared bankrupt and in 1970 he was cleared of a charge of attempted murder after beating up a man in a barroom brawl. He was killed, along with five others, in a small plane crash on a business trip he had hoped would put him back on his feet. His first wife (1949–50) was Wanda HENDRIX.

FILMS: *Texas Brooklyn and Heaven, Beyond Glory* 1948; *Bad Boy* 1949; *The Kid from Texas* (as Billy the Kid), *Sierra, Kansas Raiders* (as Jesse James) 1950; *The Red Badge of Courage* 1951; *The Cimarron Kid, Duel at Silver Creek* 1952; *Gunsmoke, Column South, Tumbleweed* 1953; *Ride Clear of Diablo, Drums Across the River* 1954; *Destry, To Hell and Back* (as himself) 1955; *World in My Corner, Walk the Proud Land* 1956; *The Guns of Fort Petticoat, Joe Butterfly, Night Passage* 1957; *The Quiet American, Ride a Crooked Trail, The Gun Runners* 1958; *No Name on the Bullet, The Wild and the Innocent, Cast a Long Shadow* 1959; *Hell Bent for Leather, The Unforgiven, Seven Ways from Sundown* 1960; *The Battle at Bloody Beach, Posse from Hell* 1961; *Six Black Horses* 1962; *Showdown* 1963; *War Is Hell* (narr. only), *The Quick Gun, Bullet for a Badman, Apache Rifles, Gunfight at Comanche Creek* 1964; *Arizona Raiders* 1965; *Gunpoint, Trunk to Cairo* (Isr./Ger.) *The Texican* 1966; *40 Guns to Apache Pass* 1967; *A Time for Dying* (again as Jesse James; also prod.) 1971.

Murphy, Dudley. Director, producer, screenwriter. Born on July 10, 1897, in Winchester, Mass. *ed.* MIT. The son of a Harvard professor, he was a journalist and assistant drama editor before turning to films in the early 20s, beginning with a string of one-reelers. In 1924 he went to France, where he produced and helped direct Fernand Léger's experimental classic *Ballet mécanique.* On returning to the US he wrote a number of screenplays and directed feature films. In the 40s he moved his operations to Mexico.

FILMS (as director): *High Speed Lee* (also sc.) 1923; *Alex the Great* (also sc.), *Stocks and Blondes* (also story, sc.) 1928; *Confessions of a Co-Ed* (co-dir. with David Burton) 1931; *The Sport Parade* 1932; *The Emperor Jones* 1933; *The Night Is Young* 1935; *Don't Gamble with Love* 1936; *One Third of a Nation, Main Street Lawyer* 1939; *Yolanda* (co-dir. with Manuel Reachi; Mex.) 1942; *Alma del Bronce* (also sc.; Mex.) 1944.

Murphy, Eddie. Actor. Born on Apr. 3, 1961, in Brooklyn (Bushwick section), N.Y. Enormously successful black comedy star of American films, TV, concert tours, and recordings. Orphaned from his policeman father when he was eight, he was raised in the relative comfort of suburban Hempstead, Long Island, by his mother and a stepfather. At 15, while still attending Roosevelt High School, he performed comedy routines in youth centers and local bars. After graduating, he worked the comedy-club circuit and at 19 joined the cast of NBC TV's comedy program 'Saturday Night Live.' Impersonating such characters as a streetwise Gumby; Velvet Jones, the pimp; Tyrone Green, the illiterate poet-convict; the canny Mr. Robinson, a Mr. Rogers takeoff; and Buckwheat of 'Our Gang' fame, he soon attained great popularity. Murphy proved to be a charismatic big-screen personality as well when teamed with Nick NOLTE for his film debut in *48 Hrs.* (1982). He went on to become one of Hollywood's top money-making stars, enriching himself as well as the studios in the process before a major slump that plagued him in the early 90s. He has also attracted a huge following with his recordings and live concert tours whose racially charged comedy text is mile-a-minute and generously sprinkled with four-letter words. His first stab at directing, *Harlem Nights* (1989), proved disastrous. However, commercial and critical success were waiting for Murphy with the release of his remake of *The Nutty Professor* (1996). He wed in 1993.

FILMS: *48 Hrs.* 1982; *Trading Places* 1983; *Best Defense, Beverly Hills Cop* 1984; *The Golden Child* 1986; *Hollywood Shuffle* (cameo), *Beverly Hills Cop II* (also co-story), *Eddie Murphy Raw* (concert film; also sc., co-exec. prod.) 1987; *Coming to America* 1988; *Harlem Nights* (also dir., sc., exec. prod.) 1989; *Another 48 Hrs.* 1990; *Boomerang, The Distinguished Gentleman* 1992; *Beverly Hills Cop III* 1994; *Vampire In Brooklyn* (also co-prod.) 1995; *The Nutty Professor* (also co-exec. prod.) 1996; *Metro* 1997.

Murphy, Fred. American director of photography. A lighting cameraman from the late 70s, he started out with low-budget films for independent directors like Martha COOLIDGE and Claudia WEILL. In the late 80s and early 90s he distinguished himself with superior work on a number of major productions.

FILMS INCLUDE: *Not a Pretty Picture* 1976; *Girlfriends* 1978; *Heartland* 1979; *Tell Me a Riddle* 1980; *Der Stand der Dinge/The State of Things* (co-phot.; Ger./US) *Q/The Winged Serpent* 1982; *Touched* 1983; *Key Exchange* 1985; *Hoosiers, The Trip to Bountiful* 1986; *Best Seller, The Dead* 1987; *Five Corners, Fresh Horses, Full Moon in Blue Water* 1988; *Night Game, Enemies a Love Story* 1989; *Funny About Love* 1990; *Scenes from a Mall* 1991; *Murder in the First* 1995.

Murphy, Geoff. Director. Born in 1938, in New Zealand. Leading figure in the 1980s revival of New Zealand cinema. He gained national renown in the 60s and early 70s with a traveling multimedia road show featuring actor Bruno Lawrence. Murphy's fame spread internationally in the 80s, when he directed some of his country's best films, several of them starring Lawrence. His reputation as one of New Zealand's top filmmakers led to his first Hollywood assignment in 1990.

FILMS: *Wildman* (also sc.) 1976; *Goodbye Pork Pie* (also co-prod., sc.) 1980; *Utu* (also co-prod., sc.) 1983; *The Quiet Earth* (also prod., sc.) 1985; *Never Say Die* (also co-prod., sc., act.) 1988; *Young Guns II* (US) 1990; *Freejack* (US) 1992.

Murphy, George. Actor, dancer, politician. *b.* July 4, 1902, in New Haven, Conn. *d.* 1992. The son of a noted track coach who prepared the US team for the 1912 Olympics, he ran away from home at 15 after his father's death to join the Navy but later returned, completed his high school education, and enrolled at Yale. He dropped out of college in his junior year and after trying several itinerant occupations, among them toolmaking and coal loading, began dancing for a living in restaurants, cocktail lounges, and nightclubs. His show business career picked up momentum after he formed a duo act with his girlfriend, and later wife, Julie Johnson (*née* Juliette Henkel). By 1927 they had reached Broadway, where, after a string of successes together, Murphy became established on his own as a hoofer and light actor. In Hollywood from the mid-30s, he tap-danced and smiled his way through numerous screen musicals and light romances but gradually moved into rather bland straight dramatic roles. A former Democrat, Murphy joined the Republican party in 1939 and became active in politics and industry affairs. During the mid-40s he served two terms as President of the Screen Actors Guild. In 1947 he was among the founders of the Hollywood Republican Committee and in the following years became identified with the party's conservative wing. In 1950 he was awarded a special honorary Oscar "for services in interpreting the film industry to the country at large." Retiring from the screen in 1952, he became a public relations spokesman for MGM and later performed similar duties for Desilu and Technicolor. Meanwhile, he continued his political activity and in 1953–54 served as chairman of the Republican National Convention. In 1964 he was elected US senator from California, defeating Democratic candidate Pierre Salinger, but hampered by a throat operation for cancer which left his voice a whisper, he lost his bid for a second term. Autobiography: *Say—Didn't You Use to Be George Murphy?* (1970).

FILMS: *Kid Millions, Jealousy* 1934; *I'll Love You Always, After the Dance, The Public Menace* 1935; *Woman Trap* 1936; *Top of the Town, Women Men Marry, London by Night, Broadway Melody of 1938, You're a Sweetheart* 1937; *Little Miss Broadway, Letter of Introduction, Hold That Co Ed* 1938; *Risky Business* 1939; *Broadway Melody of 1940, Two Girls on Broadway, Public Deb No. 1, Little Nellie Kelly* 1940; *A Girl a Guy and a Gob, Tom Dick and Harry, Ringside Maisie, Rise and Shine* 1941; *The Mayor of 44th Street, For Me and My Gal, The Navy Comes Through, The Powers Girl, Bataan, This Is the Army* 1943; *Broadway Rhythm, Show Business, Step Lively* 1944; *Having Wonderful Crime* 1945; *Up Goes Maisie* 1946; *The Arnelo Affair, Cynthia* 1947; *Tenth Avenue Angel, Big City* 1948; *Border Incident, Battleground* 1949; *No Questions Asked* 1951; *It's a Big Country, Walk East on Beacon, Talk About a Stranger* 1952.

Murphy, Mary. Actress. Born on Jan. 26, 1931, in Washington, D.C. Leading lady of Hollywood films of the 50s. Perhaps most memorable for her lead role opposite Marlon BRANDO in the motorbike classic, *The Wild One* (1954). Later in occasional character roles. At one time married to Dale ROBERTSON.

FILMS INCLUDE: *The Lemon Drop Kid* 1949; *When Worlds Collide* 1951; *Carrie* 1952; *Off Limits, Main Street to Broadway* 1953; *The Wild One, Beachhead, Make Haste to Live, The Mad Magician, Sitting Bull* 1954; *Hell's Island, The Desperate Hours, The Intimate Stranger/A Finger of Guilt* (UK), *A Man Alone* 1955; *The Maverick Queen* 1956; *Live Fast Die Young* 1958; *Crime and Punishment USA* 1959; *The Electronic Monster* (UK) 1960; *Forty Pounds of Trouble* 1963; *Harlow* 1965; *Junior Bonner* 1972.

Murphy, Michael. Actor. Born on May 5, 1938, in Los Angeles. *ed.* U. of Arizona. Versatile character player of the American screen. A former English and drama teacher in the L.A. high school system, he played supporting roles in many films since the late 60s, perhaps most memorably as Jill Clayburgh's unfaithful husband in Paul Mazurskys's *An Unmarried Woman* (1978). He figured prominently in several Robert Altman productions, starting with *Countdown* (1968).

FILMS INCLUDE: *Double Trouble* 1967; *Countdown* 1968; *That Cold Day in the Park, The Arrangement* 1969; *M*A*S*H, Count Yorga Vampire, Brewster McCloud* 1970; *McCabe and Mrs. Miller* 1971; *What's Up Doc?* 1972; *Phase IV* 1974; *Nashville* 1975; *The Front* 1976; *The Class of Miss MacMichael* (UK/US), *An Unmarried Woman* 1978; *Manhattan* 1979; *Dead Kids/Strange Behavior* (NZ) 1981; *The Year of Living Dangerously* (Austral.) 1982; *Cloak and Dagger* 1984; *Salvador, Mesmerized* (UK/Austral./NZ) 1986; *Shocker* 1989; *Folks, Batman Returns* 1992; *Clean Slate* 1994; *Bad Company* 1995; *Kansas City* 1996.

Murphy, Ralph. Director. *b.* 1895, Rockville, Conn. *d.* 1967. A former stage actor and director, he entered films in the late 20s as dialogue director and screenwriter. Soon after, he became director, turning out medium- to low-budget films through the mid-50s.

FILMS INCLUDE: *The Tip-Off* (dial. dir.) *The Big Shot* 1931; *Panama Flo, 70,000 Witnesses* 1932; *Strictly Personal,*

Song of the Eagle, Golden Harvest, Girl Without a Room 1933; *She Made Her Bed, Private Scandal, The Great Flirtation, Menace, The Notorious Sophie Lang* 1934; *McFadden's Flats, Men Without Names, Collegiate* 1935; *Florida Special, The Man I Marry* 1936; *Top of the Town, Night Club Scandal* 1937; *Our Neighbors the Carters, I Want a Divorce* 1940; *You're The One, Las Vegas Nights, Pacific Blackout* 1941; *Mrs. Wiggs of the Cabbage Patch* 1942; *Night Plane from Chungking* 1943; *The Man in Half Moon Street, Rainbow Island, The Town Went Wild* 1944; *The Spirit of West Point* 1947; *Mickey* 1948; *Red Stallion in the Rockies* 1949; *Stage to Tucson, Never Trust a Gambler, The Lady and the Bandit* 1951; *Captain Pirate, Lady in the Iron Mask* 1952; *Mystery of the Black Jungles* 1955.

Murphy, Richard. Screenwriter, director. *b.* May 8, 1912, in Boston. *d.* 1993. *ed.* Williams Coll. A former *Literary Digest* editor, he wrote the screenplays for a number of prominent Hollywood films, twice also trying his hand at directing. He later turned to TV, creating the series 'The Felony Squad.'

FILMS INCLUDE (as screenwriter): *Back in the Saddle* 1941; *I Live on Danger, X Marks the Spot* 1942; *Boomerang* 1947; *Deep Waters, Cry of the City* 1948; *Slattery's Hurricane* 1949; *Panic in the Streets* 1950; *Les Miserables* 1952; *The Desert Rats* 1953; *Broken Lance* 1954; *Three Stripes in the Sun* (also dir.) 1955; *Compulsion, The Last Angry Man* 1959; *The Wackiest Ship in the Army* (also dir.) 1960; *The Kidnapping of the President* (Can.) 1980.

Murray, Bill. Actor. Born on Sept. 21, 1950, in Wilmette, Ill., a Chicago suburb. Hip, cynical, irascible comedy star of American films and television. The fifth of nine children of a lumber salesman, he dropped out of the Jesuit-run Regis College in Denver after one year and shortly after was put on probation, following an arrest at Chicago's O'Hare Airport for possession of marijuana. After a series of manual jobs, including hauling concrete blocks and baking pizzas, he followed his older brother Brian (now known as Brian Doyle Murray) into Chicago's comedy improvisation troupe, Second City. In 1975 he joined such other future comedy stars as John Belushi, Dan Aykroyd, and Gilda Radner in 'The National Lampoon Radio Show' and later in the New York cabaret revue 'The National Lampoon Show.' In 1977 he joined the zany, talent-rich cast of NBC-TV's 'Saturday Night Live,' where his rapid rise in popularity soon led to a highly rewarding film career. Murray's only foray into serious drama, the lead role of soul-searching Larry Darrel in the 1984 remake of Maugham's *The Razor's Edge,* was poorly received, as was his first stab at directing, *Quick Change* (1990). He was roundly praised for his humane performance in the romantic comedy *Groundhog Day* (1993).

FILMS: *Shame of the Jungle* (v/o in American re-recorded version of French-Belgian 1975 animated feature *La Honte de la Jungle), Meatballs, Mr. Mike's Mondo Video* 1979; *Where the Buffalo Roam, Caddyshack, Coming Attractions/Loose Shoes* 1980; *Stripes* 1981; *Tootsie* 1982; *Ghostbusters, Nothing Lasts Forever, The Razor's Edge* (also co-sc.) 1984; *Little Shop of Horrors, Scrooged* 1986; *Ghostbusters II* 1989; *Quick Change* (also co-dir., co-prod.) 1990; *What About Bob?* 1991; *Mad Dog and Glory* 1992; *Groundhog Day* 1993; *Ed Wood* 1994; *Larger Than Life, Space Jam* (unbilled) 1996.

Murray, Charlie (Charles). Actor. *b.* June 22, 1872, Laurel, Ind. *d.* 1941. A circus performer from childhood, he later appeared in vaudeville and repertory. He formed the Murray and Mack stage comedy team with Ollie Mack (Oliver Trumbull), which became one of the most successful in the country. In 1911 he joined Biograph, switching in 1915 to Keystone, where he became one of the most popular comics in the Sennett roster, often appearing as a character named Hogan. His popularity reached a peak in the 20s and early 30s when he played Kelly in the successful 'The Cohens and Kellys' feature series, and starred in many other comic productions. Often teamed with George SIDNEY or Polly Morgan.

FILMS INCLUDE: *A Disappointed Mama* 1912; *All Hail to the King, Almost a Wild Man* 1913; *The Passing of Izzy, Fatal Flirtation, Mabel's Married Life, The Masquerader, Tillie's Punctured Romance* 1914; *Hogan's Wild Oats, A Game Old Knight, Her Painted Hero, The Great Vacuum Robbery* 1915; *A Love Riot, Fido's Fate, The Girl Guardian* 1916; *Her Fame and Shame, A Bedroom Blunder, That Night* 1917; *Watch Your Neighbor, His Wife's Friend* 1918; *Puppy Love, Yankee Doodle in Berlin* 1919; *By Golly* (also dir.), *Gee Whiz, Love Honor and Behave, Married Life* 1920; *A Small Town Idol, Home Talent* 1921; *The Crossroads of New York* 1922; *Luck, Bright Lights of Broadway* 1923; *Painted People, Lilies of the Field, Empty Hearts, Sundown* 1924; *Percy, The Wizard of Oz* (title role), *White Fang, Classified* 1925; *Mike, The Reckless Lady, The Cohens and Kellys* (as Patrick Kelly), *Irene, The Boob, Sweet Daddies, Subway Sadie, Paradise* 1926; *McFadden's Flats* (as Dan McFadden), *Lost at the Front, The Poor Nut, The Life of Riley* (as Riley), *The Gorilla* 1927; *The Cohens and Kellys in Paris, Flying Romeos, Vamping Venus* (dual lead role), *The Head Man, Do Your Duty* 1928; *Clancy in Wall Street* (as Clancy), *The Cohens and Kellys in Scotland, Around the Corner, Caught Cheating* 1930; *The Cohens and Kellys in Africa* 1931; *The Cohens and Kellys in Hollywood, Hypnotized* 1932; *The Cohens and Kellys in Trouble* 1933; *Dangerous Waters* 1936; *Breaking the Ice, Road to Reno* 1938.

Murray, Don. Actor. Born on July 31, 1929, in Hollywood, Calif. Tall, rangy, boyish-looking leading man of the American stage and screen. The son of a stage manager-dance director and a former Ziegfeld Girl, he trained for the stage at the American Academy of Dramatic Arts and after performing in stock made his Broadway debut in 'The Rose Tattoo' in 1951. His stage career was interrupted the following year because of his refusal as a conscientious objector to serve in the Korean War. He worked instead with refugees before returning to Broadway in 1955 in 'The Skin of Our Teeth.' He was seen by Joshua Logan, who gave him his first, and best-remembered, screen role, as the gauche cowboy who romances Marilyn Monroe in *Bus Stop* (1956). He was Oscar-nominated for his performance in the film. On the set he met actress Hope LANGE, whom he married that same year and divorced in 1961. Apart from such notable exceptions as *The Bachelor Party* (1957) and *The Hoodlum Priest* (1961), Murray's subsequent screen roles have been largely unrewarding. One of Hollywood's most principled citizens, he has often turned down films that haven't agreed with his political or social beliefs and helped sponsor others that did. In 1968–69 he starred in the TV Western series 'The Outcasts.' In 1970 he directed his first film, *The Cross and the Switchblade,* a biographical drama about a country priest who comes to New York to aid a gang of teenagers. He later directed another biographical drama about a priest, *Damien* (1977), who works with lepers and becomes a leper himself. It was never released. Murray later co-starred in the TV series, 'Knots Landing' (1979–81), and appeared sporadically in films of the 80s.

FILMS: *Bus Stop* 1956; *The Bachelor Party, A Hatful of Rain* 1957; *From Hell to Texas* 1958; *These Thousand Hills, Shake Hands with the Devil* 1959; *One Foot in Hell* 1960; *The Hoodlum Priest* (also co-prod., co-sc. under pseudonym of Don Deer) 1961; *Advise and Consent, Escape from East Berlin/Tunnel 28* (US/Ger.) 1962; *One Man's Way* (as Rev. Norman Vincent Peale) 1964; *Baby the Rain Must Fall* 1965;

Kid Rodelo (US/Sp.), *The Plainsman* (as Wild Bill Hickok) 1966; *Sweet Love Bitter/It Won't Rub Off Baby!/Black Love—White Love, The Viking Queen* (UK) 1967; *Childish Things/Tale of the Cock* (also prod., sc.; filmed in 1966; delayed release) 1969; *The Cross and the Switchblade* (dir., co-sc. only) 1970; *Happy Birthday Wanda June* 1971; *Conquest of the Planet of the Apes* 1972; *The Sex Symbol* (doc. on Marilyn Monroe) 1974; *Deadly Hero* 1976; *Damien/Damien's Island* (dir., sc. only; unreleased) 1977; *Charlie Chan and the Curse of the Dragon Queen* (cameo), *Endless Love* 1981; *I am the Cheese* 1983; *Peggy Sue Got Married, Radioactive Dreams, Scorpion/The Summons* 1986; *Made in Heaven* 1987; *Ghosts Can't Do It* 1990.

Murray, James. Actor. *b.* Feb. 9, 1901, the Bronx, N.Y. *d.* 1936. After appearing in a Yale University three-reeler, he went to Hollywood, hoping to start a film career, but appeared in only routine productions until King VIDOR cast him as the hero of *The Crowd.* He starred in a succession of other films but soon experienced a decline, caused primarily by chronic alcoholism. His early death resulted from a jump or fall into the Hudson River. Murray's tragic life provided the basis for a script by Vidor which the director was hoping to turn into a film in 1979. The project never materialized.

FILMS INCLUDE: *The Pilgrims* (3-reeler made at Yale) 1923; *In Old Kentucky, The Lovelorn* 1927; *The Crowd, Rose-Marie, The Big City* 1928; *The Little Wildcat, The Shakedown, Thunder, Shanghai Lady* 1929; *The Rampant Age, Bright Lights, Hide-Out* 1930; *Kick In, In Line of Duty* 1931; *Bachelor Mother, The Reckoning* 1932; *Air Hostess, Frisco Jenny, High Gear, Central Airport, Heroes for Sale, Baby Face* 1933; *$20 a Week, Skull and Crown* 1935.

Murray, Ken. Actor. *b.* Kenneth Doncourt, July 14, 1903, New York City. *d.* 1988. The son of a famous vaudevillian, he drew on his own experience in vaudeville to produce a highly successful revue 'Ken Murray's Blackouts,' which ran from 1942 to 1949. Primarily a stage performer, he also made sporadic film appearances from the late 20s. An amateur cameraman, he recorded candid 16 mm personal episodes in the lives of Hollywood stars which were later shown on television. He produced and starred in *Bill and Coo* (1947), a feature length fantasy about birds which won a special Academy Award "for a novel and entertaining use of the medium of motion pictures." He starred on early TV as the host of his own variety program, 'The Ken Murray Show' (1950–53) and was later a regular on 'The Judy Garland Show' (1964). Author of *Life on a Pogo Stick* (1960), an autobiography, and *The Golden Days of San Simeon* (1971).

FILMS: *Half Marriage* 1929; *Leathernecking* 1930; *Ladies of the Jury, Crooner* 1932; *Disgraced, From Headquarters* 1933; *You're a Sweetheart* 1937; *Swing Sister Swing* 1938; *A Night at Earl Carroll's* 1940; *Swing It Soldier* 1941; *Juke Box Jenny* 1942; *Bill and Coo* (also prod.) 1947; *The Marshal's Daughter* 1953; *The Man Who Shot Liberty Valance* 1962; *Son of Flubber* 1963; *Follow Me Boys!* 1966; *The Power* 1968; *Won Ton Ton—The Dog Who Saved Hollywood* (cameo) 1976.

Murray, Mae. Actress. *b.* Marie Adrienne Koening, May 10, 1885, Portsmouth, Va. *d.* 1965. The daughter of Austrian and Belgian immigrants, she began dancing in childhood and in 1906 reached Broadway as Vernon Castle's partner in 'About Town.' She subsequently starred in several editions of the 'Ziegfeld Follies.' In 1916 she made her screen debut in *To Have and to Hold,* opposite Wallace Reid. Despite her limited acting skills, she went on to become an important star of the silent screen, thanks to a beautiful face (she was once billed "The Girl with the Bee-Stung Lips"), a vibrant personality, and a dancer's graceful posture. She usually played glamorous blondes and she counted among her screen partners such idols as Rudolph Valentino and John Gilbert. Some of her better films were directed by her third husband (1918–25), Robert Z. LEONARD, but her best screen performance came in *The Merry Widow,* under the iron-handed direction of Erich von Stroheim.

Mae's career began to falter in 1926 after her fourth marriage, to Prince David Modivani, who took control of her affairs. At his insistence she walked out of her MGM contract and subsequently had difficulty in obtaining roles. She appeared in a couple of early talkies, then faded into obscurity. Occasionally her name would pop up in the papers, mostly in sad circumstances—the loss of custody of her son after divorcing the prince in 1933 and her declaration of bankruptcy, for example. Once one of Hollywood's highest-paid stars, she was completely forgotten by 1959, when her autobiography, *The Self-Enchanted,* was published. Her obscurity was sadly reflected in the book's limited sales.

FILMS INCLUDE: *To Have and to Hold, Sweet Kitty Bellairs, The Dream Girl, The Big Sister, The Plow Girl* 1916; *A Mormon Maid, The Primrose Ring, Princess Virtue* 1917; *Face Value* (also co-story), *The Bride's Awakening, Her Body in Bond, Modern Love* (also co-story) 1918; *What Am I Bid?, The Delicious Little Devil, The Big Little Person, The A.B.C. of Love* 1919; *On with the Dance, The Right to Love, Idols of Clay* 1920; *The Gilded Lily, Peacock Alley* 1921; *Fascination, Broadway Rose* 1922; *Jazzmania, The French Doll, Fashion Row* (dual role) 1923; *Mademoiselle Midnight, Circe the Enchantress* 1924; *The Merry Widow, The Masked Bride* 1925; *Valencia* 1926; *Altars of Desire* 1927; *Show People* (cameo) 1928; *Peacock Alley* 1930; *Bachelor Apartment, High Stakes* 1931.

Murray, Stephen. Actor. *b.* Sept. 6, 1912, Partney, England. *d.* 1983. Leading character actor of British stage, TV, and films. On London stage from 1933, he played leads as well as supporting roles in films since the late 30s.

FILMS INCLUDE: *Pygmalion* 1939; *The Prime Minister* (as Gladstone) 1941; *Next of Kin* 1942; *Undercover* 1943; *Master of Bankdam* 1947; *London Belongs to Me/Dulcimer Street* 1948; *Silent Dust, For Them That Trespass, Now Barabbas* 1949; *The Magnet, Alice in Wonderland* (as Lewis Carroll) 1950; *24 Hours of a Woman's Life* 1952; *Four Sided Triangle* 1953; *The End of the Affair* 1955; *Guilty* 1956; *A Tale of Two Cities* (as Dr. Manette) 1958; *The Nun's Story* 1959; *Master Spy* 1963.

Musante, Tony. Actor. Born on June 30, 1936, in Bridgeport, Conn. *ed.* Oberlin Coll. A former schoolteacher, he appeared in stock and in off-Broadway productions before making his film debut in 1965. He played tough character roles in a number of Hollywood films, then went to Italy, where he was elevated to hero leads in a number of films of the late 60s and early 70s. He starred in the TV series 'Toma' (1973–74), a precursor of 'Baretta.'

FILMS INCLUDE: *Once a Thief* (US/Fr.) 1965; *The Incident* 1967; *The Detective* 1968; *Il Mercenario/The Mercenary* (It./Sp.), *Metti una Sera a Cena/One Night at Dinner* (It.) 1969; *L'Uccello dalle Piume di Cristallo/The Bird with the Crystal Plumage* (It./Ger.) 1970; *Anonimo Veneziano/The Anonymous Venetian* (It.), *The Last Run, The Grissom Gang* 1971; *Eutanasia di un Amore* (It.) 1978; *The Pope of Greenwich Village* 1984; *Collector's Item* (It.) 1989.

Muse, Clarence. Actor. *b.* Oct. 7, 1889, Baltimore. *d.* 1979. The holder of a law degree from Dickerson University in Pennsylvania, he sang and acted in concert, on radio, and in vaudeville. He worked in the South with various black legitimate stage troupes and later joined the Lincoln Players in New York. He was among the founders of the Lafayette Players of Harlem. Entering films in the late 20s, he appeared in numerous Hollywood productions, often playing submissive Uncle Toms but occasionally portraying intelligent, dignified blacks. He also collaborated on a couple of scripts and composed many spirituals and other songs. In 1973 he was among those honored in the first Black Filmmakers Hall of Fame.

FILMS INCLUDE: *Hearts in Dixie* 1929; *Guilty?, A Royal Romance, Rain or Shine* 1930; *The Last Parade, Dirigible, Huckleberry Finn* (as Jim) 1931; *The Wet Parade, Attorney for the Defense, Night World, Winner Take All, White Zombie, Hell's Highway, Cabin in the Cotton, Washington Merry-Go-Round* 1932; *Flying Down to Rio, From Hell to Heaven* 1933; *Massacre, Black Moon, The Personality Kid, The Count of Monte Cristo, Broadway Bill* 1934; *O'Shaughnessy's Boy, Harmony Lane, So Red the Rose* 1935; *Show Boat, Follow Your Heart, Daniel Boone* 1936; *Spirit of Youth, The Toy Wife* 1938; *Way Down South* (also co-story, co-sc., co-songs) 1939; *Broken Strings* (lead; also sc.), *Zanzibar, Maryland, Sporting Blood* 1940; *The Flame of New Orleans, The Invisible Ghost* 1941; *Tales of Manhattan, The Black Swan* 1942; *Shadow of a Doubt, Heaven Can Wait, Watch on the Rhine, Flesh and Fantasy* 1943; *Jam Session* 1944; *Night and Day* 1946; *Two Smart People* 1947; *An Act of Murder* 1948; *Riding High* 1950; *My Forbidden Past, Apache Drums* 1951; *Jamaica Run* 1953; *Porgy and Bess* 1959; *Buck and the Preacher* 1972; *The World's Greatest Athlete* 1973; *Car Wash* 1976; *The Black Stallion* 1979.

Museum of Modern Art Department of Film. Film archives established in 1935 as part of the cultural activities of New York's Museum of Modern Art (founded in 1929). The collection contains more than 12,000 films and videos, 4 million stills, hundreds of shooting scripts, diverse memorabilia, and numerous books and periodicals on cinema. Daily screenings of rare and important films are given in the museum's two auditoriums. A Film Study Center offers research facilities for students and scholars. A leading force in film preservation and restoration, the department publishes monographs on significant directors and puts out various other publications relating to film. The collection was started by Iris Barry. The department's chief curator is Mary Lea Bandy.

music, film. See SCORE.

music library. See LIBRARY.

music mixer. A sound man responsible for controlling, balancing, and blending film scores.

music track. A sound track containing the musical score of a film, as distinguished from the tracks for dialogue and sound effects. All tracks are eventually blended into a single sound track in the process of the MIX.

Musidora. Actress. *b.* Jeanne Roques, on Feb. 23, 1889, in Paris. *d.* 1957. Star of Feuillade's silent serials and the first "vamp" of French films. A bright, cultured woman, she directed and wrote scripts for many of her own films, several in Spain, where she lived for much of the early 20s. Directed a number of her films and wrote the screenplays for many others. After retiring from the screen she became a journalist and wrote many articles on cinema, as well as two novels, a play, and a poetry collection. She was later associated with the Cinémathèque Française. She borrowed her single, exotic professional name from the heroine of Théophile Gautier's novel *Fortunio*.

FILMS INCLUDE: *Les Misères de l'Aiguille* 1913; *La Tangomanie/La Ville de Madame Tango, Le Calvaire* 1914; *Les Leçons de la Guerre, La Petite Réfugiée, Bout de Zan et l'Espion, Noces d'Argent, Triple Entente, Le Grand Souffle, Une Page de Gloire* 1915; *Les Vampires* (serial) 1915–16; *Le Pied qui étreint* (serial), *Le Poéte et sa Folle Amante, Cambrioleur, Fille d'Eve* 1916; *Judex* (serial), *Le Maillot noir* (also dir., sc.), *Mon Oncle, Les Chacals* 1917; *La Vagabonda* (also co-sc.; It.) 1918; *Mam'zelle Chiffon* 1919; *La Famme cachée* (also co-dir., sc.; release delayed from 1918), *Vicenta* (also dir., sc.) 1920; *Pour Don Carlos/La Capitana Algeria* (also co-dir., sc.; Sp.), *La Geole* 1921; *Una Aventura de Musidora en España* (also dir, sc.; Sp.), *Sol y Sombra* (also co-dir., sc.; Sp.) 1922; *La Tierra de los Toros* (also dir., sc.; Sp.) 1924; *Le Berceau de Dieu* (also dir.), *Les Ombres du Passé* 1926; *La Magique Image* (compilation feature of old film clips) 1951.

Mustin, Burt. Actor. *b.* 1884. *d.* 1977. Often comedic character player who debuted in films when he was 67. Regular on TV sitcoms 'Phyllis' and 'All in the Family'; in the latter, he was part of an elderly couple living in sin.

FILMS INCLUDE: *Detective Story* 1951; *The Lusty Men* 1953; *The Desperate Hours* 1955; *The Big Country* 1957; *Huckleberry Finn* 1961; *The Thrill of It All* 1963; *Cat Ballou* 1965; *Speedway* 1968; *Hail Hero* 1970; *The Skin Game* 1971.

Musuraca, Nicholas (Nick). American director of photography. *b.* 1895. He began his association with films in 1918 as J. Stuart Blackton's chauffeur and later performed a variety of duties at Vitagraph before becoming a cinematographer in the early 20s. He worked behind the camera on numerous silent and early sound Westerns and low-budget action pictures before developing in the late 30s into one of RKO's prime cameramen. He remained with that studio through 1954, when he began freelancing. Later worked mainly for TV.

FILMS INCLUDE: *On the Banks of the Wabash* 1923; *Hell Bent for Heaven, The Passionate Quest* 1926; *The Sonora Kid* 1927; *South Sea Love, Terror, Phantom of the Range* 1928; *The Cuckoos* 1930; *Cracked Nuts* 1931; *Cross Fire* 1933; *Long Lost Father* 1934; *Old Man Rhythm* 1935; *Saturday's Heroes, Quick Money* 1937; *Crashing Hollywood, Blind Alibi* 1938; *Golden Boy* 1939; *A Bill of Divorcement, Swiss Family Robinson, Tom Brown's Schooldays, The Stranger on the Third Floor* 1940; *Little Men* 1941; *Cat People* 1942; *Forever and a Day* (co-phot.), *The Fallen Sparrow, The Seventh Victim* 1943; *Curse of the Cat People* 1944; *Back to Bataan, The Spiral Staircase* 1945; *Bedlam, The Locket* 1946; *Out of the Past* 1947; *I Remember Mama, Blood on the Moon* 1948; *Born to Be Bad, The Woman on Pier 13/I Married a Communist* 1950; *Clash by Night* 1952; *The Hitch-Hiker, Split Second, The Blue Gardenia* 1953; *Susan Slept Here* 1954; *The Story of Mankind* 1957; *Too Much Too Soon* (co-phot.) 1958.

mute. A British term for a print or negative carrying a picture but no sound track.

Muti, Ornella. Actress. Born Francesca Rivelli, in 1955, in Rome. Exquisite leading lady of Italian and international films. She modeled for illustrated novels before starting her screen career at 15. Directors Monicelli and Risi were largely responsible for her rise to stardom in the 70s, but it was Marco FERRERI who later best utilized her tantalizing sexuality, memorably in *The Last Woman* (1976) and *Tales of Ordinary Madness* (1981). She also figured strikingly in Volker Schlöndorff's *Swann in Love* (1984), among other films.

FILMS INCLUDE: *La Moglie più bella* 1970; *Un Solo Grande Amore* 1972; *Paolo il Caldo/The Sensual Sicilian* 1973; *Tutti Figli di Mamma Santissima/Italian Graffiti, Romanzo popolare/Come Home and Meet My Wife, Appassionata* 1974; *Léonor* (Fr./It.) 1975; *L'Ultima Donna/The Last Woman, Come un Rosa al Naso/Virginity* 1976; *La Stanza del Vescovo/The Bishop's Bedroom, Ritrato di un Borghese in Nero/Nest of Vipers, I Nuovi Mostri/Viva Italia!* 1977; *Eutanasia di un Amore, Primo Amore* 1978; *Giallo Napoletano, La Vita é bella/Freedom to Love* 1979; *Flash Gordon* (UK/US) 1980; *Inamorato Pazzo, Nessuno é perfetto, Storie di Ordinaria Follia/Tales of Ordinary Madness* 1981; *La Ragazzza di Trieste, Love and Money (US)* 1982; *Bonnie e Clyde all'Italiana/Bonnie and Clyde, Italian Style* 1983; *Un Amour de Swann/Swann in Love* (Fr./Ger.), *Il Futuro e Donna* 1984; *Tutta colpa del Paradiso, Grandi Magazzini* 1985; *Stregati* 1986; *Cronaca di una Morte annunciata/Chronicle of a Death Foretold* 1987; *Il Frullo del Passero* 1988; *Wait Until Spring Bandini* (Bel./Fr./It./US) 1989; *Il Vaggio Di Capitan Fracassa* 1990; *Oscar* (US), *Stasera a Casa di Alice* 1991; *Once Upon a Crime* 1992; *El Amante Bilingüe* 1993; *Just For Laughs* 1996.

Mutoscope. A viewing machine, manufactured by the American Mutoscope Company, beginning in 1895, which created the illusion of movement by employing the "flicker book" principle. The apparatus contained a series of continuous photographs arranged on a horizontal axis. When a customer dropped a coin into a slot, he was able to operate a hand crank, leafing rapidly through the pictures to create the illusion of movement. Mutoscope Parlors sprang up all over America in the late 1890s. For many years the machines remained in operation in peep show galleries and some are still around in the older establishments.

Mutual Film Corporation. An American releasing and distribution company formed in 1912 by Harry E. Aitken and others. Its many subsidiary production units included Keystone, the maker of the famous KEYSTONE comedies. Mutual's greatest claim to fame was the employment of Charlie CHAPLIN, who in 1916 made some of his most brilliant comedies for the company. Through various corporate transmutations, Mutual was eventually absorbed by Film Booking Offices of America (FBO), which in turn evolved into RKO.

Muybridge, Eadweard James. Photographer, inventor. *b.* Edward James Muggeridge, Apr. 4, 1830, Kingston-on-Thames, England. *d.* 1904. In the US from youth. In 1872 under the sponsorship of Governor Leland Stanford of California, he began in Sacramento a series of photographic studies of animal locomotion. These studies, inspired by the animal-motion research of Etienne-Jules MAREY of France, were an essential step towards the development of motion pictures as we know them today. Muybridge arranged 24 still cameras in a row along a track. By attaching the shutter mechanism of each camera to a long trip wire and stretching the wires across the track so that a galloping horse would trigger each shutter as he went past the cameras, the inventor was able to obtain a photographic record of successive phases in the horse's motion. He later used more sophisticated shutter-release methods in his movement studies of other animals, including humans. From 1880 he traveled extensively in the US and abroad, lecturing and projecting his serial pictures by means of a device he called the Zoopraxiscope, a machine based on the principles of PLATEAU's Phenakistiscope.

Strictly speaking, Muybridge's serial photos were not motion pictures, but his experiments provided the essential link between still photography and the movies. His experiments strongly influenced such innovators as Professor Marey and Thomas Alva EDISON and stimulated their subsequent discoveries, and his Zoopraxiscope with its rotating disc was definitely a forerunner of today's motion picture projector. In 1887, in Philadelphia, Muybridge published an 11-volume summary of his experiments: *Animal Locomotion: An Electro-photographic Investigation of Consecutive Phases of Animal Movements,* accompanied by thousands of photos. A complete collection of his photographic plates is preserved at London's South Kensington Museum.

Myers, Carmel. Actress. *b.* Apr. 4, 1899, San Francisco, the daughter of a rabbi. *d.* 1980. She entered films in 1916 as a protégée of D. W. Griffith at Triangle. She starred in many silent and several early sound Hollywood productions for Universal and other studios, opposite such leading men as Rudolph Valentino, Douglas Fairbanks, John Barrymore, and John Gilbert, frequently portraying a "vamp" type. One of her more famous roles was that of Iras in *Ben-Hur* (1926). She retired from the screen in the early 30s but returned occasionally in character parts. In 1951–52 she hosted an early TV talk program, 'The Carmel Myers Show.'

FILMS INCLUDE: *Intolerance* (bit), *Mr. Matrimaniac* 1916; *A Love Sublime, A Daughter of the Poor, Might and the Man, Sirens of the Sea, The Lash of Power* 1917; *The Marriage Lie, The Wine Girl, A Broadway Scandal, Society Sensation, All Night, My Unmarried Wife* 1918; *The Little White Savage, Who Will Marry Me?* 1919; *The Gilded Dream, Beautifully Trimmed* 1920; *The Mad Marriage, The Dangerous Moment, Cheated Love, The Kiss, Daughter of the Law* 1921; *The Love Gambler* 1922; *The Famous Mrs. Fair, The Last Hour, Dancer of the Nile, The Love Pirate, Slave of Desire, Reno* 1923; *Beau Brummel, Broadway After Dark, Babbitt, Poisoned Paradise* 1924; *Ben-Hur, The Devil's Circus, Tell It to the Marines, The Gay Deceiver* 1926; *The Understanding Heart, The Demi-Bride, Sorrell and Son, The Girl from Rio* 1927; *A Certain Young Man, Prowlers of the Sea, Four Walls, Dream of Love* 1928; *The Ghost Talks, Careers, The Careless Age, Broadway Scandals* 1929; *The Ship from Shanghai, A Lady Surrenders* 1930; *Svengali, The Mad Genius, Pleasure, The Lion and the Lamb, Chinatown After Dark* 1931; *Nice Women* 1932; *The Countess of Monte Cristo* 1934; *Lady for a Night* 1942; *Whistle Stop* 1946; *Won Ton Ton—The Dog Who Saved Hollywood* (cameo) 1976.

Myers, Harry. Actor. *b.* 1882, New Haven, Conn. *d.* 1938. Leading man of Hollywood silents and early talkies. Memorable as the eccentric drunken millionaire who alternately befriends and rejects Charlie Chaplin in *City Lights* (1931). Early in his career he also directed a number of films, sometimes being billed Harry C. Myers or Henry Myers.

FILMS INCLUDE: *Jonesy* (series) 1908; *Her Two Sons* 1911; *Art and Honor, When the Earth Trembled* 1913; *The Accusation* (also dir.) 1914; *Baby* (also dir.), *The Artist and the Vengeful One* (also dir.), *The Earl of Pawtucket* (also dir., sc.), *The Man of Shame* (also dir., sc., des.) 1915; *Housekeeping* 1916; *The Face in the Dark, Conquered Hearts* 1918; *Sky Eye, La La Lucille, Forty-Five Minutes from Broadway, Peaceful Valley* 1920; *Why Trust Your Husband?, A Connecticut Yankee at King Arthur's Court* (title role), *Nobody's Fool, R.S.V.P.* 1921; *Handle with Care, Turn to the Right, Kisses, The Top o' the Morning, The Beautiful and Damned* 1922; *Brass, Main Street, The Brass Bottle, The Printer's Devil, The Bad Man, The Common Law, Stephen Steps Out* 1923; *The Marriage Circle, Daddies, Behold This Woman, Tarnish, Reckless Romance* 1924; *She Wolves, Zander the Great, Grounds for Divorce* 1925; *The Beautiful Cheat, Monte Carlo, The Nut-Cracker, Up in Mabel's Room, Exit Smiling* 1926; *The First Night, Getting Gertie's Garter, The Bachelor's Baby* 1927; *The Dove, The Street of Illusion, Dream of Love* 1928; *Montmartre Rose, Wonder of Women* 1929; *City Lights* 1931; *Strange Adventure* 1932; *Mary Stevens, M.D.* 1933; *We Live Again* 1934; *Mississippi* 1935; *The Milky Way, San Francisco, Hollywood Boulevard* 1936; *Vogues of 1938* 1937.

Myers, Stanley. Composer. Born in 1939, in London. Entering the industry in the mid-60s, he wrote effective scores for dozens of British as well as American films and European co-productions.

FILMS INCLUDE: *Kaleidoscope* 1966; *Ulysses* (US/UK)

1967; *No Way to Treat a Lady* (US), *Otley* 1968; *The Night of the Following Day* (US) 1969; *Tropic of Cancer* (US) 1970; *A Severed Head, The Raging Moon/Long Ago Tomorrow* 1971; *Strohfeuer/A Free Woman/Summer Lightning* (Ger.), *Herzbube/King, Queen, Knave* (Ger./US), *Zee & Co./X Y & Zee* 1972; *Conduct Unbecoming* 1975; *Der Fangschuss/Coup de Grace* (Ger./US) 1976; *The Greek Tycoon* (US), *The Deer Hunter* (US) 1978; *A Portrait of the Artist as a Young Man* (UK/US) 1979; *The Watcher in the Woods* (US) 1980; *L'Amant de Lady Chatterley/Lady Chatterley's Lover* (Fr./UK) 1981; *Moonlighting* 1982; *The Honorary Consul/Beyond the Limit* (UK/US), *Eureka* 1983; *Blind Date* (US), *Success Is the Best Revenge* 1984; *Insignificance, Dreamchild, The Lightship* (US) 1985; *The Second Victory* 1986; *Castaway, Prick Up Your Ears, Wish You Were Here, Sammy and Rosie Get Laid* 1987; *Taffin* (co-mus.), *Stars and Bars* (US), *Track 29, The Boost* (US) 1988; *Paperhouse* (co-mus.), *Torrents of Spring* (It./Fr./UK), *Scenes from the Class Struggle in Beverly Hills* (US) 1989; *The Witches* (UK/US), *Rosencrantz and Guildenstern Are Dead, Torrents of Spring* 1990; *Heading Home, Voyager* (Ger./Fr.) 1991; *Cold Heaven* 1992.

mylar. A material used as a base for the ferromagnetic coating of magnetic tape and as an adhesive in dry splicing of film.

N

Nader, George. Actor. Born on Oct. 9, 1921, in Pasadena, Calif. *ed.* Occidental Coll.; Pasadena Playhouse. Rugged leading man of Hollywood films and much TV, mainly seen in action and adventure pictures. He was a dependable male lead in Universal films of the 50s but slipped into low-budget European co-productions in the 60s, achieving some popularity in Germany in the recurring role of FBI agent Jerry Cotton in a number of cheap thrillers. On US TV he played the title role in the series 'Adventures of Ellery Queen' (1958–59) and later starred in 'Man and the Challenge' (1959–60) and 'Shannon' (1961–62). He wrote a novel, *Chrome.* He produced and directed one film, *Walk by the Sea,* in 1963.

FILMS INCLUDE: *Rustlers on Horseback* 1950; *The Prowler, Take Care of My Little Girl* 1951; *Phone Call from a Stranger, Monsoon* 1952; *Sins of Jezebel* (as Jehu) 1953; *Carnival Story, Four Guns to the Border* 1954; *Six Bridges to Cross, Lady Godiva, The Second Greatest Sex* 1955; *Away All Boats, The Unguarded Moment* 1956; *Four Girls in Town, Man Afraid, Joe Butterfly* 1957; *The Female Animal, Nowhere to Go* (UK), *Flood Tide* 1958; *Il Colpo segreto di d'Artagnan/The Secret Mark of d'Artagnan* (title role; It.) 1962; *Walk by the Sea* (prod., dir.) 1963; *The Human Duplicators* 1965; *Sumuru/The Million Eyes of Su-Muru* (UK), *Das Haus der tausend Freuden/House of 1,000 Dolls* (Ger.) 1967; *Der Tod im roten Jaguar* 1968; *Todeschüsse am Broadway* 1969; *Beyond Atlantis* 1973.

Nagel, Anne. Actress. *b.* Ann Dolan, Sept. 30, 1912, Boston. *d.* 1966. The daughter of a Technicolor expert, she was the heroine of many B pictures of the 30s and 40s and played second leads in many others. Memorable as Madame Gorgeous in W. C. Fields's *Never Give a Sucker an Even Break* (1941) and in several horror films and serials. She was married to Ross ALEXANDER from 1933 till his death in 1937. She died of cancer.

FILMS INCLUDE: *I Loved You Wednesday* 1933; *Stand Up and Cheer* 1934; *Hot Money, China Clipper, Here Comes Carter* 1936; *Three Legionnaires, Hoosier Schoolboy, Guns of the Pecos, The Case of the Stuttering Bishop, Escape by Night* 1937; *Mystery House, Gang Bullets* 1938; *Legion of Lost Flyers, Should a Girl Marry?* 1939; *Black Friday, The Green Hornet* (serial), *My Little Chickadee, Diamond Frontier, Argentine Nights* 1940; *Man-Made Monster, Don Winslow of the Navy* (serial), *The Invisible Woman, Never Give a Sucker an Even Break* 1941; *The Secret Code* (serial), *Nazi Spy Ring, The Mad Doctor of Market Street* 1942; *Women in Bondage* 1944; *Murder in the Music Hall* 1946; *The Hucksters, The Spirit of West Point* 1947; *One Touch of Venus, Every Girl Should Be Married* 1948; *Prejudice, The Stratton Story* 1949.

Nagel, Conrad. Actor. *b.* Mar. 16, 1896, Keokuk, Iowa. *d.* 1970. Matinee idol of the American stage and romantic star of scores of Hollywood films in the 20s and 30s. Later in character roles. A co-founder and former president of the Academy of Motion Picture Arts and Sciences, he was involved in the creation of the Academy Awards and until his death was president of Associated Actors and Artists of America (AAAA). In 1947 he received a special Academy Award for his work on the Motion Picture Relief Fund. He directed one film, *Love Takes Flight,* in 1937. On early TV he hosted the drama anthology series 'The Silver Theater' (1949–50) and emceed the quiz show 'Celebrity Time' (1949–52).

FILMS INCLUDE: *The Lion and the Mouse, Little Women* 1919; *The Fighting Chance, Midsummer Madness* 1920; *The Last Romance, Sacred and Profane Love, What Every Woman Knows, Fool's Paradise* 1921; *Nice People, Saturday Night, The Ordeal, Singed Wings, Hate* 1922; *Lawful Larceny, Grumpy, Rendezvous, Bella Donna* 1923; *Name the Man, The Rejected Woman, Sinners in Silk, Three Weeks, The Snob, Tess of the d'Urbervilles* (as Angel Clare), *So This Is Marriage, Married Flirts* 1924; *Pretty Ladies, Cheaper to Marry, Sun-Up, the Only Thing, Lights of Old Broadway* 1925; *Memory Lane, The Waning Sex, Tin Hats, Dance Madness, The Exquisite Sinner* 1926; *Quality Street, Heaven on Earth, London After Midnight, The Girl from Chicago* 1927; *The Mysterious Lady, Glorious Betsy* (as Jérôme Bonaparte), *If I Were Single, Tenderloin, Caught in the Fog, State Street Sadie, Red Wine* 1928; *The Redeeming Sin, The Idle Rich, Kid Gloves, Dynamite, The Kiss, The Thirteenth Chair, The Sacred Flame* 1929; *The Ship from Shanghai, Redemption, The Divorcée, Second Wife, One Romantic Night, DuBarry—Woman of Passion, Today, Numbered Men, A Lady Surrenders, Free Love* 1930; *East Lynne, The Right of Way, Bad Sister, Son of India, Pagan Lady, The Reckless Hour, Hell Divers* 1931; *The Man Called Back, Divorce in the Family, Kongo, Fast Life* 1932; *Ann Vickers, The Constant Woman* 1933; *Dangerous Corner* 1934; *Death Flies East* 1935; *Wedding Present, Yellow Cargo* 1936; *Love Takes Flight* (dir. only), *Navy Spy, The Gold Racket* 1937; *Juarez and Maximilian/The Mad Empress* (as Maximilian; Mex.) 1939; *One Million B.C., I Want a Divorce* 1940; *The Adventures of Rusty*

1945; *The Vicious Circle, Stage Struck* 1948; *All That Heaven Allows* 1956; *Hidden Fear* 1957; *Stranger in My Arms, The Man Who Understood Women* 1959.

Nagy, Käthe von. Actress. Born Kate Nagy, on Apr. 4, 1909, in Subotica, near Budapest. Popular, lively star of light European films of the 30s. On Hungarian stage before making film debut in Germany in 1927. In 1935, after divorcing German director Constantin J. David and marrying a Frenchman, she moved to Paris and appeared mostly in French films, working under the name of Kate de Nagy.

FILMS INCLUDE: *Das brennende Schiff, Männer von vor der Ehe* 1927; *Die Königin seines Herzens* 1928; *Rotaie* (It.), *Der Weg durch die Nacht, Unschuld* 1929; *Der Andere* 1930; *Ihre Majestät Liebe, Meine Frau die Hochstaplerin, Ronny* 1931; *Ich bei Tag und Du bei Nacht, Das Schöne Abenteuer, Der Sieger* 1932; *Liebe Tod und Teufel, Princess Turandot* 1934; *Die Pompadour, La Route impériale* (Fr.) 1935; *Ave Maria, Cargaison blanche* (Fr.) 1936; *La Bataille silencieuse* (Fr.) 1937; *Unsere Kleine Frau/Our Little Wife, Nuit des Princes* (Fr.) 1938; *Renate im Quartett* 1939; *Malhia la Métisse* (Fr.) 1942; *Die Försterchristel* 1952.

Nair, Mira. Director. Born in 1957, in Bhubaneswar, India. The daughter of a civil servant, she did some amateur acting while studying sociology at Delhi University. She came to the US on a scholarship to Harvard. A course there in documentary filmmaking motivated her to try her hand at directing. With New York City as her home base, she made four nonfiction films in India, all concerned with the country's changing culture. One of these, *India Cabaret* (1985), which explored the double standard male audiences in Bombay apply to female strippers, won the best documentary prize at the American Film Festival. She scored an international triumph with her first fictional feature, *Salaam Bombay* (1987), a powerfully distressing drama of a country boy's misadventures in city streets swarming with hustlers, prostitutes, and drug addicts. The film, effectively featuring actual street people rather than professional actors, won the Camera d'Or (Golden Camera) prize for first feature, as well as the Prix de Publique as the audience's favorite, at the Cannes Film Festival, and was nominated for an Academy Award as best foreign film. Miss Nair next filmed *Mississippi Masala* (1991), a saga of an Indian family expelled by Uganda's Idi Amin, whose members discover in America's South that racial bias has no boundaries.

FILMS: *Jama Masjid Street Journal* (doc.) 1979; *So Far from India* (doc.) 1982; *India Cabaret* (doc.) 1985; *Children of a Desired Sex* (doc.) 1986; *Salaam Bombay!* (also prod., co-story) 1987; *Mississippi Masala* (also prod., co-story, co-sc.) 1991; *The Perez Family* 1995; *Kamasutra* 1996.

Naish, J. Carrol. Actor. *b.* Joseph Patrick Carrol Naish, Jan. 21, 1897, New York City. *d.* 1973. A descendant of a long line of Irish peers, and a great-great-grandson of a Lord Chancellor of Ireland, he grew up in the tough Yorkville-Harlem area of turn-of-the-century New York and at 16 dropped out of school to enlist in the Navy. During WW I he saw action in Europe with the aviation section of the Army Signal Corps. After his discharge, he roamed about Europe, performing various odd jobs and acquiring a working knowledge of several languages. He returned to the US aboard a tramp steamer that dropped him off on the West Coast. He appeared in Hollywood as an extra and stuntman in a few films, then headed for Broadway in 1926 as an understudy with the road company of 'The Shanghai Gesture.' He later had parts in a couple of Broadway productions and returned to Hollywood in 1930 as a featured player. He soon became established as a reliable and versatile character actor who specialized in the portrayal of foreigners, particularly Italians and other Latins. A master of dialect, he also portrayed Chinese, Japanese, Jewish, Arab, and Indian characters but because of his swarthy complexion never played an Irishman. He appeared in some 200 films, playing amiable types and villains with equal conviction, and was nominated twice for an Academy Award, for *Sahara* (1943) and *A Medal for Benny* (1945). He also starred in the radio comedy series 'Life With Luigi.' A TV version of the series was seen briefly in 1952–53. Naish also starred in the TV series 'The New Adventures of Charlie Chan' (1956–57) and played Chief Hawkeye in the series 'Guestward Ho!' (1960–61).

FILMS INCLUDE: *What Price Glory* (extra) 1926; *Good Intentions, Scotland Yard* 1930; *Gun Smoke, Homicide Squad* 1931; *The Hatchet Man, The Beast of the City, Tiger Shark, The Kid from Spain, Cabin in the Cotton* 1932; *Mystery Squadron* (serial), *Infernal Machine, The Mad Game* 1933; *Return of the Terror, British Agent* 1934; *The Lives of a Bengal Lancer, Black Fury, Front Page Woman, Captain Blood* 1935; *The Robin Hood at El Dorado, Ramona, Anthony Adverse, The Charge of the Light Brigade* 1936; *Think Fast Mr. Moto, Bulldog Drummond Comes Back* 1937; *Her Jungle Love, King of Alcatraz, Illegal Traffic* 1938; *King of Chinatown, Hotel Imperial, Beau Geste, Island of Lost Men* 1939; *Typhoon, Down Argentine Way* 1940; *That Night in Rio, Blood and Sand, Birth of the Blues, The Corsican Brothers* 1941; *Dr. Broadway, The Pied Piper, Tales of Manhattan* 1942; *Batman* (serial), *Behind the Rising Sun, Sahara, Gung Ho!, Calling Dr. Death* 1943; *Voice in the Wind, The Monster Maker, The Whistler, Jungle Woman, Dragon Seed, Enter Arsene Lupin* 1944; *House of Frankenstein, A Medal for Benny, The Southerner* 1945; *The Beast with Five Fingers, Humoresque* 1946; *The Fugitive* 1947; *Joan of Arc, The Kissing Bandit* 1948; *That Midnight Kiss* 1949; *Black Hand, Annie Get Your Gun* (as Sitting Bull), *The Toast of New Orleans, Rio Grande* (as General Sheridan) 1950; *Mark of the Renegade, Across the Wide Missouri* 1951; *Class by Night* 1952; *Beneath the 12-Mile Reef* 1953; *Sitting Bull* (title role) 1954; *New York Confidential, Hit the Deck, Violent Saturday, The Last Command* 1955; *Rebel in Town* 1956; *The Young Don't Cry* 1957; *Force of Impulse* 1961; *The Hanged Man* 1964; *Dracula vs. Frankenstein/Blood of Frankenstein/They're Coming to Get You* (as Frankenstein) 1971.

Naismith, Laurence. Actor. *b.* Lawrence Johnson, Dec. 14, 1908, in Ditton, England. *d.* 1992. Solid character player of the British and American screen. A former merchant marine, he joined the Bristol Repertory Company in 1930. He entered films in the late 40s, following extended WW II service with the Royal Artillery. Typically played congenial roles.

FILMS INCLUDE: *Trouble in the Air* 1948; *The Happiest Days of Your Life* 1950; *High Treason* 1951; *The Beggar's Opera, Mogambo* (US) 1953; *The Black Knight* 1954; *Richard III* 1955; *The Man Who Never Was, Lust for Life* (US) 1956; *Seven Days from Now/Abandon Ship!, The Barretts of Wimpole Street, Boy on a Dolphin* (US) 1957; *Naked Earth, A Night to Remember, La Tempesta/Tempest,* (It./Fr.), *I Accuse* 1958; *Solomon and Sheba* (US) 1959; *Sink the Bismarck!, The Trials of Oscar Wilde, The World of Suzie Wong* (US/UK) 1960; *Greyfriars Bobby* (US/UK), *The Singer Not the Song* 1961; *The 300 Spartans* (US) 1962; *Jason and the Argonauts, Cleopatra* (US/UK) 1963; *The Three Lives of Thomasina* (US/UK) 1964; *Sky West and Crooked, Gypsy Girl, Deadlier Than the Male* 1966; *Camelot* (US), *Fitzwilly* (US), *The Long Duel* 1967; *The Bushbaby, Scrooge* 1970; *The Amazing Mr. Blunden, Young Winston* (as Lord Salisbury) 1972.

Najimy, Kathy. Actress. Energetic, talented comedic character player who made a lasting impression as sister Mary

Patrick in *Sister Act* (1992). A stage-trained actress before entering films, she had a long run off Broadway with the politically charged 'The Kathy and Mo Show,' opposite Mo Gaffney.

FILMS INCLUDE: *The Fisher King, The Hard Way, Soapdish* 1991; *Sister Act, This Is My Life* 1992; *Hocus Pocus, Sister Act II: Back in the Habit* 1993; *It's Pat* 1994; *Jeffrey* 1995; *Nevada* 1997.

Nakadai, Tatsuya. Actor. Born in 1930, in Tokyo. A former shop clerk, he was discovered by director Masaki KOBAYASHI, who gave him his start in films in 1953 and the opportunity to become an internationally famous star in the role of Kaji the Idealist in the trilogy *The Human Condition* (1959–61). During the 60s he often portrayed villainous warriors in period sagas, crossing swords in several films with heroic Toshiro MIFUNE, memorably in Akira Kurosawa's *Yojimbo* (1961). More recently he gave an unforgettable performance as a warlord modeled after King Lear in Kurosawa's *Ran* (1985).

FILMS INCLUDE: *Room with Thick Walls* 1953; *Black River* 1957; *Enjo/Conflagration/Flame of Torment, The Naked Sun* 1958; *Ningen no Joken/The Human Condition I/No Greater Love, Odd Obsession/The Key, Ningen no Joken II/The Human Condition II/Road to Eternity* 1959; *When a Woman Ascends the Stairs, Daughters Wife and a Mother* 1960; *Ningen noo Joken III/The Human Condition III/A Soldier's Prayer, Yojimbo, The Bitter Spirit/Immortal Love* 1961; *Sanjuro, The Inheritance, Harakiri* 1962; *A Woman's Life, High and Low* 1963; *Kwaidan* 1964; *Ghost Story/Illusion of Blood* 1965; *The Sword of Doom, The Face of Another* 1966; *Kojiro, Rebellion* 1967; *Kill* 1968; *Goyokin, Battle of the Japan Sea, Portrait of Hell* 1969; *The Scandalous Adventures of Buraikan, The Ambitious* 1970; *The Wolves* 1972; *Kagemusha* 1980; *Onimasa* 1982; *Ran* 1985; *Hachi-Ko* 1988; *Return to the River Kwai* 1989.

Naldi, Nita. Actress. *b.* Anita Donna Dooley, Apr. 1, 1899, New York City. *d.* 1961. Torrid, tempestuous leading lady of Hollywood silents of the 20s, following some success with the 'Ziegfeld Follies.' Her most famous role was that of the temptress opposite Valentino in *Blood and Sand* (1922). She retired from the screen with the arrival of sound but was later seen occasionally on the New York stage and on TV.

FILMS INCLUDE: *Dr. Jekyll and Mr. Hyde, The Common Sin/For Your Daughter's Sake, Life* 1920; *Experience, A Divorce of Convenience, The Last Door* 1921; *Blood and Sand, Anna Ascends* 1922; *Glimpses of the Moon, You Can't Fool Your Wife, Lawful Larceny, The Ten Commandments* 1923; *Don't Call It Love, The Breaking Point, A Sainted Devil* 1924; *The Lady Who Lied, The Marriage Whirl, Clothes Make the Pirate, Cobra* 1925; *The Miracle of Life, The Unfair Sex* 1926; *What Price Beauty* 1928.

Nannuzzi, Armando. Director of photography. Born in 1925, in Rome. A lighting cameraman since the late 50s, he captured memorable images for Bolognini, Lattuada, Scola, Visconti, Zeffirelli, and many other contemporary Italian directors.

FILMS INCLUDE: *La Donna del Giorno/The Doll That Took the Town* 1957; *Giovani Mariti/Young Husbands* 1958; *La Notte brava/On Any Street/Bad Girls Don't Cry* 1959; *Il Bell'Antonio, Adua e le Compagne/Love a la Carte* 1960; *Boccaccio '70* (Monicelli episode), *Mafioso* 1962; *Der Besuch/The Visit* (Ger./It./Fr./US), *Il Magnifico Cornuto/The Magnificent Cuckold* 1964; *Vaghe Stelle dell'Orsa/Sandra* 1965; *L'Ombrellone/Weekend, Italian Style* 1966; *Il Padre di Famiglia/The Head of the Family* 1968; *Porcile/Pig Pen/Pigsty, La Caduta degli Dei/Götterdämmerung/The Damned* 1969; *Waterloo* (It./USSR) 1970; *Per Grazia ricevuta/Between Miracles* 1971; *Ludwig* 1973; *Il mio Nome e Nessuno/My Name Is Nobody* 1974; *Oltro Bene e il Male/Beyond Good and Evil* 1977; *Ritrato di Borghese in nero/Nest of Vipers* 1979; *La Cage aux Folles II* 1980; *La Nuit de Varennes* 1982; *Nana* 1983; *Pianoforte* 1984; *Silver Bullet* (US) 1985; *Maximum Overdrive* (US) 1986; *Gli occhiali d'oro* 1987; *La Bohème* 1988; *Buon Natale Buon Anno/Merry Christmas, Happy New Year, L'Avaro/The Miser, Frankenstein Unbound* (co-phot.) 1990.

Napier, Alan. Actor. *b.* Alan Napier-Clavering, Jan. 7, 1903, Birmingham, England. *d.* 1988. *ed.* Birmingham U. Tall (6' 5"), distinguished character player of Hollywood films. A cousin of Neville Chamberlain, Britain's prime minister from 1937 to 1940, he performed on the British stage and screen before coming to Hollywood in 1939. He played suave roles in numerous films, but is possibly best remembered for his role as Alfred Pennyworth, Batman's trusted servant in the campy TV series of 1966–68.

FILMS INCLUDE: In the UK—*Caste* 1930; *In a Monastery Garden* 1932; *Loyalties* 1933; *Four Just Men/The Secret Four* 1939. In the US—*We Are Not Alone* 1939; *The Invisible Man Returns, The House of the Seven Gables* 1940; *Confirm or Deny* 1941; *A Yank at Eton, Random Harvest, Cat People* 1942; *Lassie Come Home, The Song of Bernadette* 1943; *Ministry of Fear, The Uninvited, The Hairy Ape, 30 Seconds Over Tokyo* 1944; *Hangover Square, Isle of the Dead* 1945; *House of Horrors, Three Strangers* 1946; *Sinbad the Sailor, Fiesta, Ivy, Unconquered, Forever Amber* 1947; *Joan of Arc* (as the Earl of Warwick), *Macbeth, Johnny Belinda* 1948; *Criss Cross, The Red Danube, Tarzan's Magic Fountain* 1949; *Double Crossbones* 1950; *The Great Caruso, Across the Wide Missouri, The Blue Veil* 1951; *Big Jim McLain* 1952; *Young Bess, Julius Caesar* (as Cicero) 1953; *Desiree* 1954; *Moonfleet* 1955; *The Court Jester* 1956; *Until They Sail* 1957; *Journey to the Center of the Earth* 1959; *The Premature Burial, Tender Is the Night* 1962; *Marnie, My Fair Lady* 1964; *The Loved One, Signpost to Murder* 1965; *Batman* 1966.

Napier, Charles. American actor. Tough-looking character player of Hollywood films. After a dubious start as a leading man in cheap melodramas and several X-rated Russ Meyer movies, he settled in the 70s on a modest career as a sturdy supporting actor, often in brawny, knavish roles. His parts improved steadily in the 80s, especially after his effective portrayal of Murdock, Sylvester Stallone's ruthless nemesis, in *Rambo* (1985). In 1987 he stepped up to a lead role in *The Night Stalker.*

FILMS INCLUDE: *The Hanging of Jake Ellis/The Calico Queen, Cherry Harry & Raquel/Three Ways to Love* 1969; *Beyond the Valley of the Dolls, Moonfire* 1970; *The Seven Minutes* 1971; *Supervixens* 1975; *Citizens Band/Handle with Care* 1977; *Last Embrace* 1979; *The Blues Brothers, Melvin and Howard* 1980; *Wacko, In Search of a Golden Sky* 1983; *Swing Shift* 1984; *Rambo: First Blood Part II* 1985; *Something Wild* 1986; *The Night Stalker, Instant Justice* (Gibraltar), *Deep Space* 1987; *Married to the Mob* 1988; *Hit List, One Man Force* 1989; *Ernest Goes to Jail, Miami Blues, Future Zone, The Grifters* 1990; *The Silence of the Lambs, Soldier's Fortune* 1991; *Indio 2: The Revolt, Center of the Web* 1992; *National Lampoon's Loaded Weapon I, Philadelphia* 1993; *Skeeter* 1994; *Jury Duty* 1995; *Steel* 1997.

Nares, Owen. Actor. *b.* Owen B. Ramsay, Aug. 11, 1888, Maiden Erleigh, England. *d.* 1943. Matinee idol of London stage and star of numerous British silent films. Later in character roles.

FILMS INCLUDE: *His Choice* 1913; *Dandy Donovan* 1914; *Milestones* 1916; *Flames* 1917; *The Man Who Won* 1918; *The Last Rose of Summer, All the Winners* 1920; *The Faithful Heart* 1922; *This Marriage Business* 1927; *Loose Ends, The Middle Watch* 1930; *Sunshine Susie* 1931; *Aren't We All, The*

Impassive Footman/Woman in Chains, There Goes the Bride 1932; *The Private Life of Don Juan* 1934; *Royal Cavalcade* 1935; *The Show Goes On* 1937; *The Loves of Madame DuBarry* (as Louis XV) 1938; *The Prime Minister* (as Lord Derby) 1941.

Narizzano, Silvio. Director. Born on Feb. 8, 1927, in Montreal. *ed.* Bishop's U. (Quebec). A stage actor-director and later an award-winning director of TV plays in Canada, Britain, and the US, he turned to British feature films in the 60s and scored with the critics and at the box office with *Georgy Girl* (1966), a comedy-drama about the London swinging scene. He was less successful with his other efforts.

FILMS: *Under Ten Flags* (co-dir.) 1960; *Fanatic/Die! Die! My Darling!* 1965; *Georgy Girl* 1966; *Blue* (US) 1968; *Loot* 1971; *Senza Ragione/Redneck* (It./UK) 1973; *The Sky Is Falling* 1976; *Why Shoot the Teacher* (Can.) 1977; *The Class of Miss MacMichael* 1978; *Choices* (Can.) 1981.

narrow-gauge film. Film narrower than the standard professional 35 mm width, most commonly 16 mm, 9.5 mm, 8 mm, Super 8, and Single 8. Narrow-gauge films of various widths have existed since the turn of the century for amateur use. More recently, especially since the advent of TV, the 16 mm gauge has become widely used in professional film production. Although lacking the quality of standard motion picture film, narrow-gauge film is cheaper to buy and process and can be used with lighter and less-expensive equipment and accessories than can 35 mm film.

Naruse, Mikio. Director. *b.* Aug. 20, 1905, Tokyo. *d.* 1969. The son of a destitute embroiderer, he was raised in dire poverty and could only attend a two-year technical school in lieu of an academic secondary education. At 15, following his father's death, he was forced to enter the job market, accidentally finding employment as a prop man at the Shochiku film company's Kamata studios. He toiled there for a decade in a variety of low-level, low-paying positions, including assistant to several directors, before getting his first chance to direct in 1930. His early films, many from his own screenplays, were typically a blend of slapstick and melodrama. In the 50s, he evolved, reaching his creative peak as a serious, uncompromisingly honest director of frequently pessimistic films that echoed memories of his unhappy youth. They typically dealt with everyday lives of common people and paid special attention to the status of women in Japanese society. His first wife (1937–44) was actress Sachiko Chiba, one of his early stars.

FILMS INCLUDE: *Mr. and Mrs. Swordsplay, Pure Love* 1930; *Flunky! Work Hard!* (also sc.) 1931; *Motheaten Spring* 1932; *Apart from You* (also sc.), *Everynight Dreams* (also idea) 1933; *Three Sisters with Maiden Hearts* (also sc.), *Wife! Be Like a Rose!* (also sc.), *The Girl in the Rumor* (also sc.) 1935; *A Woman's Sorrows* (also co-sc.) 1937; *The Whole Family Works* (also sc.) 1939; *Traveling Actors* (also sc.) 1940; *Shanghai Moon* 1941; *Mother Never Dies* 1942; *The Song Lantern* 1943; *The Way of Drama* 1944; *Until Victory* 1945; *Both You and I* (also sc.) 1946; *Spring Awakens* (also co-sc.) 1947; *Conduct Report on Prof. Ishinaka, White Beast* 1950; *Ginzza Cosmetics, Dancing Girl, Repast* 1951; *Mother, Lightning* 1952; *Husband and Wife, Wife, Older Brother, Younger Sister* 1953; *Sound of the Mountain, Late Chrysanthemums* 1954; *Floating Clouds* 1955; *Sudden Rain, A Wife's Heart, Flowing* 1956; *Untamed* 1957; *Anzukko* (also co-sc.), *Herringbone Clouds/Summer Clouds* 1958; *When a Woman Ascends the Stairs, Daughters Wife and a Mother, Evening Stream* 1960; *The Other Woman* 1961; *A Woman's Place/The Wiser Age, Lonely Lane/A Wanderer's Notebook* 1962; *Yearning* 1964; *The Stranger Within a Woman/The Thin Line, Hit and Run/Moment of Terror* 1966; *Scattered Clouds/Two in the Shadow* 1967.

Nat, Marie-José. Actress. Born on Apr. 20, 1940, in Bonifacio, Corsica. Talented, distinguished leading lady of the French stage, TV, and films. She went to Paris in 1955 as the winner of a photo contest and, following a brief career as a high-fashion model, made her screen debut in 1956. In 1961 she married Michel DRACH, the director of several of her films. She won the best actress prize at Cannes for his *Les Violons du Bal* (1974).

FILMS INCLUDE: *Crime et Châtiment/Crime and Punishment* 1956; *Arènes joyeuse* 1957; *Rue des Prairies/Rue de Paris* 1959; *La Française et l'Amour/Love and the Frenchwoman* (René Clair's "Marriage" episode), *La Vérité/The Truth* 1960; *La Menace, Amélie ou le Temps d'aimer* 1961; *L'Education sentimentale, Les Sept Péchés capitaux/Seven Capital Sins* 1962; *La Vie conjugale/Anatomy of a Marriage, Les Belles Conduites* 1964; *Le Journal d'une Femme en Blanc/A Woman in White* 1965; *Safari Diamant* 1966; *La Paria* 1969; *Elise ou la Vraie Vie* 1970; *Embassy* 1972; *Les Violons du Bal, Dis-moi que tu m'aime* 1974; *Le Passé simple* 1977; *La Disubbidienza* (It./Fr.), *Anya es Leanya/Une Mère une Fille/Anna* (Hung./Fr.) 1981; *Litan* 1982; *Rio Negro* (Venez./Fr.) 1990.

Natanson, Jacques. Novelist, playwright, screenwriter. Born on May 15, 1901, Asnières, France. Collaborated on screenplays, adaptations, and dialogue of many French films, notably for Max Ophüls.

FILMS INCLUDE: *L'Ordonnance, Paprika* 1933; *Les Nuits moscovites, Volga en Flammes* 1934; *Les Yeux noirs/Dark Eyes* 1935; *Michel Strogoff, Taras Bulba, Mademoiselle Docteur* 1936; *Forfaiture* 1937; *De Mayerling à Sarajevo/Mayerling to Sarajevo* 1939; *La Ronde* 1950; *Le Plaisir/House of Pleasure* 1952; *La Rage au Corps/Devil in the Flesh* 1953; *Lola Montès* 1955.

National Association of Theatre Owners. See NATO.

National Board of Review. A nonprofit organization founded in New York in 1909 as the National Board of Censorship by a volunteer group of film-oriented citizens for the purpose of previewing and evaluating films before their release to the public. The liberally bent group was originally created in direct response to a threat by New York officially to close down motion picture theaters in the city, and in the hope that its reviewing activities would help avert government censorship.

Enjoying the full support of the film industry, the Board, the nation's first voluntary censorship body, functioned in its semi-official capacity until 1921, when New York State passed a film-licensing law. Robbed of its function as a censor (a much too liberal one in the opinion of its detractors), the Board changed its name to the National Board of Review of Films and continued its existence but as a powerless group devoted to the support of high-quality motion pictures through the classification and evaluation of films and the dissemination of information about them. Of the Board's several past publications only the monthly *Films in Review* is still being published.

The Board is America's oldest motion picture award-giving organization, dating back to 1917 when it instituted the Exceptional Photoplay Committee Awards. In 1930 the Board began selecting a list of ten best films, a format that changed over the years to include Oscar-style citations in various categories, now known as the D. W. Griffith Awards.

National Catholic Office for Motion Pictures. See LEGION OF DECENCY.

National Film Board. See CANADA, DOCUMENTARY.

National Film Preservation Act. A 1988 Congressional Act which authorizes the Librarian of Congress to select up to 25 American films each year that are "culturally, historically, or esthetically significant" for inclusion in a National Film Registry. The Act, adopted as a compromise measure in response to the outcry against colorization and other tampering with film classics, requires that notice must be served when selected films are colored or otherwise substantially altered. A 13-member National Film Preservation Board—representing motion picture organizations, professional guilds, critics, and academicians—first met in January of 1989. After much deliberation it submitted in September the initial list of America's cinematic treasures (to be eligible a film must be at least ten years old). They are, in alphabetical order: William Wyler's *The Best Years of Our Lives* (1946), Michael Curtiz's *Casablanca* (1943), Orson Welles's *Citizen Kane* (1941), King Vidor's *The Crowd* (1928), Staney Kubrick's *Dr. Strangelove* (1964), Buster Keaton's *The General* (1927), Victor Fleming's *Gone With the Wind* (1939), John Ford's *The Grapes of Wrath* (1940), Fred Zinnemann's *High Noon* (1952), D. W. Griffith's *Intolerance* (1916), Gordon Parks's *The Learning Tree* (1969), John Huston's *The Maltese Falcon* (1941), Frank Capra's *Mr. Smith Goes to Washington* (1939), Charlie Chaplin's *Modern Times* (1936), Robert Flaherty's *Nanook of the North* (1922), Elia Kazan's *On the Waterfront* (1954), John Ford's *The Searchers* (1956), Gene Kelly and Stanley Donen's *Singin' in the Rain* (1952), Walt Disney's *Snow White and the Seven Dwarfs* (1937), Billy Wilder's *Some Like It Hot* (1959), George Lucas's *Star Wars* (1977), F. W. Murnau's *Sunrise* (1927), Billy Wilder's *Sunset Boulevard* (1950), Alfred Hitchcock's *Vertigo* (1958), and Victor Fleming's *The Wizard of Oz* (1939).

National Film Registry. See NATIONAL FILM PRESERVATION ACT.

NATO. In motion picture industry parlance, *not* the North Atlantic Treaty Organization but the National Association of Theatre Owners, Inc., a nationwide organization representing interests of exhibitors. Founded in 1965, it is headquartered in New York with branches in nearly every state.

Natwick, Grim. Animator. *b.* Myron Natwick, Aug. 16, 1890, Wisconsin. *d.* 1990. Trained at art schools in Chicago, New York, and Vienna, he began his career as an illustrator of magazine and sheet music covers. Through contact with a former schoolmate, animator-turned-director Gregory LA CAVA, he entered the animation field in 1921 with the Hearst Film Service. He quickly learned the craft, earning the nickname "Grim" for his solemn persistence and determined work habits. He kept it as a professional name while working on such cartoon series as 'Happy Hooligan' and 'Jerry on the Job' before the company folded in the late 20s. It was when he joined animators Dave and Max FLEISCHER that Natwick earned his place in animation history as the creator of BETTY BOOP, the vampy, voluptuous cartoon character that has remained popular to this day. The following year he joined Ub IWERKS as animator and studio supervisor and in 1935 went to work for Disney, where he was one of the principal animators of *Snow White and the Seven Dwarfs* (1937). His later work included *Gulliver's Travels* (1939) for Fleischer, *Raggedy Ann and Raggedy Andy* (1977) for Richard Williams, and numerous cartoon shorts for TV and theatrical release. His 100th birthday, just two months before his death, was celebrated by 400 fellow animators.

Natwick, Mildred. Actress. *b.* June 19, 1908, in Baltimore. *d.* 1994. *ed.* Bryn Mawr. Gifted character player of the American stage and screen. She began appearing in amateur productions in Baltimore directly out of college and made her professional debut on Broadway in 1932. Even as a youngster she was assigned character roles, usually playing women older than herself, and before long she became established as one of the most reliable supporting players of the New York stage. She appeared in films off and on from 1940, at her best with eccentric characterizations. She was nominated for an Oscar as best supporting actress for *Barefoot in the Park* (1967). On TV, she co-starred with Helen HAYES in the mystery series 'The Snoop Sisters' (1973–74).

FILMS: *The Long Voyage Home* 1940; *The Enchanted Cottage, Yolanda and the Thief* 1945; *The Late George Apley* (as Amelia) 1947; *A Woman's Vengeance, The Kissing Bandit* 1948; *Three Godfathers, She Wore a Yellow Ribbon* 1949; *Cheaper by the Dozen* 1950; *The Quiet Man, Against All Flags* 1952; *The Trouble with Harry* 1955; *The Court Jester, Teenage Rebel* 1956; *Tammy and the Bachelor* 1957; *Barefoot in the Park* 1967; *If It's Tuesday This Must Be Belgium, The Maltese Bippy, Trilogy* 1969; *Daisy Miller* (as Mrs. Costello) 1974; *At Long Last Love* 1975; *Kiss Me Goodbye* 1982; *Dangerous Liaisons* 1988.

Naughton, David. Actor. Born on Feb. 13, 1951, in Hartford, Conn. *ed.* U. of Pennsylvania. Leading man of the American stage, TV, and films. Trained at London's Academy of Music and Dramatic Arts, he made his first professional appearance as a singer-dancer in a series of Dr. Pepper soft drink TV commercials. He co-starred in the short-lived TV series 'Makin' It' (1979) before making his big-screen debut in 1980. He is the younger brother of award-winning stage and TV star James Naughton (*b.* Dec. 6, 1945, Middletown, Conn.), who played supporting roles in several films, notably *The Paper Chase* (1973) and *The Glass Menagerie* (1987).

FILMS: *Midnight Madness* 1980; *Separate Ways, An American Werewolf in London* 1981; *Hot Dog. . . The Movie, Not for Publication* 1984; *Separate Vacations* (Can.), *The Boy in Blue* (Can.) 1986; *Kidnapped* 1987; *Ti presento un'Amica/Private Affairs* (It.) 1988; *The Sleeping Car, Overexposed, Steel & Lace* 1990; *Wild Cactus* 1992.

Naumov, Vladimir. Soviet director. Born in 1927. All his films have been made in collaboration with Alexander Alov, with whom he graduated from Moscow's Cinema Institute in 1951. For a complete list of credits see ALOV, Alexander.

Nava, Gregory. Director. Born on Apr. 10, 1949, in San Diego, Calif. A graduate of the film program at UCLA, he made a strong first impression with *The Confessions of Amans* (1976), a minimally budgeted ($20,000), barely distributed medieval love story, shot in Spain with costumes left over from *El Cid,* which won the best first feature prize at the Chicago Film Festival. He received a much larger audience and broader-based critical admiration for another independently financed film, *El Norte* (1984), a compassionate, deeply moving saga of the harrowing experiences of a brother and sister on their flight from a terror-ridden village in Guatemala through the corrupt migrant routes of Mexico into a frighteningly unknown future in Southern California. Beautifully shot with documentary-like authenticity, the film was Oscar-nominated for best screenplay. The director fared far less well with his first studio-sponsored film, *Time of Destiny* (1988), a fairly conventional soap-operatic melodrama. Nava's wife, Anna Thomas (*b.* July 12, 1948, Stuttgart, Germany), has collaborated on all of his films as a producer, co-screenwriter, or both. He, in turn, functioned as associate producer and cameraman on his wife's made-in-Scotland supernatural thriller, *The Haunting of M.*

FILMS: *The Confessions of Amans* (also prod., co-sc., phot., edit.) 1976; *The Haunting of M* (assoc. prod., phot. only) 1979; *The End of August* (co-sc. only) 1982; *El Norte/The North* (also co-sc., addnl. phot.) 1984; *A Time of Destiny* (also co-sc.) 1988; *Mi Familia/My Family* 1995; *Selena* 1997.

Nazarro, Ray. Director. *b.* Sept. 25, 1902, Boston. *d.* 1986. Long with Columbia, he directed many of the studio's low-budget Westerns and action pictures in the 40s and 50s. Later worked in European films and in American TV.

FILMS INCLUDE: *Outlaws of the Rockies, Song of the Prairie* 1945; *Cowboy Blues, The Desert Horseman, Galloping Thunder, Roaring Rangers, Two-Fisted Stranger* 1946; *The Lone Hand Texan, Terror Trail, West of Dodge City, Last Days of Boot Hill* 1947; *Phantom Valley, Six-Gun Law* 1948; *Laramie, Bandits of El Dorado, Frontier Outpost, Quick on the Trigger* 1949; *The Palomino, Texas Dynamo, The Tougher They Come* 1950; *Al Jennings of Oklahoma, Flame of Stamboul, China Corsair, Cyclone Fury* 1951; *Indian Uprising, Montana Territory, Cripple Creek* 1952; *Gun Belt, The Bandits of Corsica, Kansas Pacific* 1953; *The Lone Gun, The Black Dakotas, South Passage* 1954; *Top Gun* 1955; *The White Squaw* 1956; *The Phantom Stagecoach, The Hired Gun, The Domino Kid* 1957; *Apache Territory* 1958; *Einer frisst den anderen/Dog Eat Dog* (Ger./It.) 1964; *Arrivederci Cowboy* (It.) 1967.

Nazimova, Alla. Actress. *b.* June 4, 1879, in Yalta, Crimea, Russia. *d.* 1945. Legendary star of the Russian and American stage and of many silent Hollywood films. She studied music at the St. Petersburg Conservatory and at Odessa and was an accomplished violinist by the time she began studying acting with Stanislavsky in Moscow. In 1905 she emigrated to the US and quickly established herself as a leading interpreter of Ibsen on the Broadway stage. She began appearing in films in 1916. Her screen vehicles, several of them produced by herself and some directed by her husband, Charles Bryant, were often bizarre, haunting, and boldly conceived, and her acting in them was highly stylized. Her public image was remote and beguiling. She retired from the screen in 1925 to return to the stage but reappeared in character parts in several films of the early 40s. She was also known simply as Nazimova.

Her 1912 marriage to Bryant was never officially recognized, because her first husband (from 1904), Russian actor Paul Orleneff, refused to divorce her. She continued to live with Bryant as a common-law wife until their separation in 1925.

FILMS: *War Brides* 1916; *Revelation, Toys of Fate, Eye for Eye* (also exec. prod.) 1918; *Out of the Fog, The Red Lantern* (also prod.), *The Brat* (also exec. prod., co-sc.) 1919; *Stronger Than Death* (also exec. prod.), *The Heart of a Child* (also prod.), *Billions* (also prod., titles, art dir., co-edit.), *Madame Peacock* (also sc.) 1920; *Camille* (title role; also prod.) 1921; *A Doll's House* (as Nora; also prod.) 1922; *Salome* (title role; also prod.) 1923; *Madonna of the Streets* 1924; *The Redeeming Sin, My Son* 1925; *Escape* 1940; *Blood and Sand* 1941; *In Our Time, The Bridge of San Luis Rey* (as the Marquesa), *Since You Went Away* 1944.

Nazzari, Amedeo. Actor. *b.* Salvatore Amedeo Buffa, Dec. 10, 1907, Cagliari, Sardinia, Italy. *d.* 1979. Robust leading man of numerous Italian films from the mid-30s, following a busy stage career. Playing a variety of roles, in films ranging from neorealism to costume melodramas, he remained a popular star in Italy for four decades, even as he gradually eased into character parts.

FILMS INCLUDE: *Ginevra degli Almieri* 1935; *Cavalleria* 1936; *Luciano Serra—Pilota* 1938; *Montevergine/La Grande Luce/The Great Light* 1939; *Il Cavaliere senza Nome* 1940; *Caravaggio, La Cena della Beffe, Scampolo* 1941; *Fedora, Bengasi* 1942; *L'Invasore* 1943; *I Dieci Comandamenti/The Ten Commandments* 1945; *Un Giorno nella Vita, Il Cavaliere del Sogno/Donizetti/The Life of Donizetti* (title role), *Il Bandito/The Bandit* 1946; *La Figlia del Capitano* 1947; *Il Lupo della Sila/Lure of the Sila, Il Brigante Musolino, Tormento, Amori e Veleni/Brief Rapture, Donne e Briganti/Of Love and Bandits* 1950; *I Figli di nessuno, Lebbra bianca/Brief Rapture, Altri Tempi/Times Gone By, Ultimo Incontro, Sensualità* 1951; *Nous sommes tous des Assassins/We Are All Murderers* (Fr./It.), *Processo alla Città, Fiammata* 1952; *Un Marito per Anna Zaccheo/A Husband for Anna* 1953; *Proibito* 1954; *Angelo bianco* 1955; *Le Notti di Cabiria/Cabiria/Nights of Cabiria* 1956; *Anna di Brooklyn/Fast and Sexy, La Maja Desnuda/The Naked Maja* 1958; *Carmen de la Ronda/The Devil Made a Woman* (Sp.), *Il Mondo dei Miracoli, Labyrinth* 1959; *Antinea—l'Amante della Città Sepolta/L'Atlantide/Journey Beneath the Desert, I Due Nemici/The Best of Enemies* 1961; *Nefertite—Regina del Nilo/Queen of the Nile, La Leggenda di Fra Diavolo* 1962; *Le Monachine/The Little Nuns* 1963; *Il Gaucho* 1964; *The Poppy is Also a Flower* (UN/US) 1966; *Le Clan des Siciliens/The Sicilian Clan* (Fr.) 1969; *Joe Valachi—I Segretti di Cosa Nostra/The Valachi Papers* 1972; *A Matter of Time* (US/It.) 1976.

NC-17. See RATING.

Neagle, Dame Anna. Actress. *b.* Marjorie Robertson, Oct. 20, 1904, Forest Gate, London. *d.* 1986. A professional dancer at 14, then a budding heroine of West End musicals, she was discovered and developed into England's leading screen star by her producer, director, and later (from 1943 till his death in 1977) husband, Herbert WILCOX. Specializing first in musical comedies, then in historical portrayals, and finally in frothy romances, she sustained her popularity with British audiences for nearly two decades and for seven straight years in the 40s was voted the United Kingdom's best-loved star. She appeared in several Hollywood productions during WW II. Also in many stage plays and musicals, she made the *Guinness Book of World Records* as one of "the most durable leading actors" for her 2,062 straight performances in 'Charlie Girl' between 1965 and 1971. Created a Dame of the British Empire in 1969. Autobiographies: *It's Been Fun* (1949); *There's Always Tomorrow* (1974).

FILMS: *Should a Doctor Tell?* 1930; *The Chinese Bungalow* 1931; *Goodnight Vienna/Magic Night* 1932; *The Flag Lieutenant, The Little Damozel, Bitter Sweet* 1933; *The Queen's Affair, Nell Gwyn* (title role) 1934; *Peg of Old Drury* 1935; *Limelight, The Three Maxims* 1936; *London Melody/Girl in the Street, Victoria the Great* (as Queen Victoria) 1937; *Sixty Glorious Years* (again as Queen Victoria) 1938; *Nurse Edith Cavell* (title role; US) 1939; *Irene* (US), *No No Nanette* (US) 1940; *Sunny* (US) 1941; *They Flew Alone/Wings and the Woman* (as flyer Amy Johnson) 1942; *Forever and a Day* (US), *The Yellow Canary* 1943; *I Live in Grosvenor Square/A Yank in London* 1945; *Piccadilly Incident* 1946; *The Courtneys of Curzon Street/The Courtney Affair/Kathy's Love Affair* 1947; *Spring in Park Lane* 1948; *Maytime in Mayfair, Elizabeth of Ladymead* 1949; *Odette* 1950; *The Lady with the Lamp* (as Florence Nightingale) 1951; *Derby Day* 1952; *Lilacs in the Spring/Let's Make Up* 1954; *King's Rhapsody* 1955; *My Teenage Daughter* 1956; *These Dangerous Years* (prod. only), *No Time for Tears* 1957; *Wonderful Things* (prod. only), *The Man Who Wouldn't Talk* 1958; *The Heart of a Man* (prod. only), *The Lady Is a Square* 1959.

Neal, Patricia. Actress. Born on Jan. 20, 1926, in Packard, Ky., the daughter of a coal company bookkeeper. Accomplished leading actress of the American stage and screen. She studied drama at Northwestern University and worked as a model before making her Broadway debut in 'The Voice of the Turtle' in 1946. Her success in 'Another Part of the Forest' led to a film career that started in 1949 with *John Loves Mary.* She made a strong impression that same year in *The Fountainhead,* opposite Gary Cooper, and for the next few years performed competently in mainly routine productions of Warner Bros. and other studios. She and Cooper became entangled in a well-publicized romance, at the end of which she suffered a nervous breakdown. In 1953 she married British writer Roald Dahl and for several years was absent from the screen. She returned in excellent form in 1957, in *A Face in the Crowd,* and from then on seemed to become more selective about her film roles. In 1963 she won an Academy Award for her performance in *Hud.* Two years later, during her fifth pregnancy, she suffered a series of massive strokes that damaged her nervous system and left her confined to a wheelchair in a state of semiparalysis with severely impaired speech. But she fought back courageously and made a remarkable recovery, returning to screen work in 1968 in *The Subject Was Roses,* with a performance that brought her another Oscar nomination. President Johnson presented her that year with the Heart of the Year Award. Her courage carried her through other personal tragedies. One of her five children, a boy, was hit by a cab as a baby and survived eight brain operations, and another, a girl, died at 13 of measles. Neal's bravery and her husband's devotion were the subject of a 1981 TV movie, *The Patricia Neal Story,* in which they were portrayed by Glenda JACKSON and Dirk BOGARDE. In 1983, however, the couple endured a much-publicized divorce, following Neal's discovery that Dahl had been having an affair with one of her best friends. She left their home in England and moved to New York, where she resumed her working career. Autobiography: *As I Am* (1988).

FILMS: *John Loves Mary, The Fountainhead, It's a Great Feeling* (cameo) 1949; *The Hasty Heart* (US/UK), *Bright Leaf, Three Secrets, The Breaking Point* 1950; *Operation Pacific, Raton Pass, The Day the Earth Stood Still, Weekend with Father* 1951; *Diplomatic Courier, Something for the Birds, Washington Story* 1952; *La tua Donna* (It.), *Stranger from Venus/Immediate Disaster* (UK) 1954; *A Face in the Crowd* 1957; *Breakfast at Tiffany's* 1961; *Hud* 1963; *Psyche 59* (UK) 1964; *In Harm's Way* 1965; *The Subject Was Roses* 1968; *The Road Builder/The Night Digger* (UK) 1971; *Baxter* (UK) 1972; *Hay que matar a B/B Must Die* (Sp.), *Happy Mother's Day—Love, George/Run Stranger Run* 1973; *Nido de Vidudas/Widow's Nest* (Sp.) 1977; *The Passage* (UK) 1979; *Ghost Story* 1981; *An Unremarkable Life* 1989.

Neal, Tom. Actor. *b.* Jan. 28, 1914, Evanston, Ill. *d.* 1972. Leading man and supporting player of numerous Hollywood B pictures whose own life was probably more dramatic than any role he played on the screen. A banker's son, he went to Northwestern University, where he excelled in sports, particularly boxing. After a season in summer stock he made his Broadway debut in 1935, but after three successive failures, he left the stage for Harvard University, where he received a law degree in 1938. That same year he left for Hollywood and began his screen career in minor MGM productions. In the 40s and early 50s he appeared in dozens of films for various studios, mainly bottom-of-the-bill action pictures, typically playing tough guys. But his busy and largely undistinguished film career suddenly collapsed in the wake of a 1951 love-triangle brawl in which he battered and smashed the nose of actor Franchot TONE over the affections of actress Barbara PAYTON. Tone landed in the hospital and married Miss Payton, but a few months later they were divorced and she returned to Neal. As a result of the notoriety, no Hollywood studio would employ Neal and he became a gardener in Palm Springs. He eventually established a landscaping business, but it failed and he went into bankruptcy. In 1965 he was charged with murdering his third wife, Gail Evatt. Claiming his gun went off accidentally during a family struggle, he succeeded in reducing the charge to involuntary manslaughter and spent the next six years in jail. In August of 1972, eight months after his release, he was found dead in his North Hollywood home from congestive heart failure.

FILMS INCLUDE: *Out West with the Hardys* 1938; *Four Girls in White, Another Thin Man, Within the Law, 6,000 Enemies* 1939; *Sky Murder* 1940; *Jungle Girl* (serial) 1941; *The Miracle Kid, Flying Tigers, China Girl, Ten Gentlemen from West Point, Bowery at Midnight* 1942; *Air Force, Klondike Kate, Behind the Rising Sun* 1943; *Two-Man Submarine, The Racket Man, The Unwritten Code, Thoroughbreds* 1944; *Crime Inc., First Yank Into Tokyo, Detour, Club Havana* 1945; *Blonde Alibi, My Dog Shep* 1946; *The Hat-Box Mystery, The Case of the Baby-Sitter* 1947; *Beyond Glory* 1948; *Bruce Gentry* (serial), *Amazon Quest* 1949; *Radar Secret Service* 1950; *Danger Zone* 1951; *The Great Jesse James Raid* 1953.

Neame, Ronald. Director, former director of photography, producer. Born on Apr. 23, 1911, in London. *ed.* University College School; Hurstpierpoint College. The son of a photographer—sometime-film-director (Elwin Neame) and British screen actress Ivy Close, he began his film career as an assistant cameraman on Hitchcock's *Blackmail* (1929). As director of photography from the mid-30s and producer and director since the mid-40s, he made a notable contribution to British films. Although his product as a director has been on the whole uneven, several of his films of the 50s offered solid entertainment. Among his later films, *The Prime of Miss Jean Brodie* (1969), is a standout. One of Britain's surer craftsmen, he lists a number of slick Hollywood productions among his credits. He has occasionally worked in the US.

FILMS INCLUDE: As director of photography—*Drake of England* 1934; *Pygmalion* 1938; *Major Barbara* 1939; *In Which We Serve* 1942; *Blithe Spirit* 1945. As producer—*Brief Encounter* (co-prod.) 1945; *Great Expectations* (co-prod., co-sc.) 1946; *Oliver Twist* 1948; *The Passionate Friends* 1949; *The Magic Box* 1951. As director (complete)—*Take My Life* 1947; *The Golden Salamander* (also co-sc.) 1950; *The Card/The Promoter* (also prod.) 1952; *The Million Pound Note/Man with a Million* 1953; *The Man Who Never Was* 1956; *The Seventh Sin* 1957; *Windom's Way* 1958; *The Horse's Mouth* 1959; *Tunes of Glory* 1960; *Escape from Zahrain* (also prod.; US) 1962; *I Could Go On Singing* 1963; *The Chalk Garden* 1964; *Mister Moses* (US) 1965; *A Man Could Get Killed* (co-dir. with Cliff Owen; US), *Gambit* (US) 1966; *Prudence and the Pill* (co-dir. with Fielder Cook), *The Prime of Miss Jean Brodie* 1969; *Scrooge* 1970; *The Poseidon Adventure* (US) 1972; *The Odessa File* 1974; *Meteor* (US) 1979; *Hopscotch* (US) 1980; *First Monday in October* (US) 1981; *Foreign Body* 1986.

Nebenzal, Seymour. Producer. *b.* Seymour Nebenzahl, July 22, 1899, New York City. *d.* 1961. Active in Berlin in the 20s and early 30s, he was responsible for several notable productions of Pabst and Lang. After the Nazi takeover he continued his activity in Paris and at the outbreak of WW II returned to the US. He was the father of screenwriter-producer Harold Nebenzal.

FILMS INCLUDE: In Germany—*Abenteuer einer Nacht* (co-prod.) 1923; *Der Buchse der Pandora/Pandora's Box, Menschen am Sonntag/People on Sunday* 1929; *Westfron 1918/Comrades of 1918* 1930; *Die Dreigroschenoper/The Threepenny Opera, Ariane, M, Kameradschaft/Comradeship* 1931; *Die Herrin von Atlantis/The Mistress of Atlantis* 1932; *Das Testament des Dr. Mabuse/The Testament of Dr. Mabuse* 1933. In France—*Mayerling* 1936; *Werther* 1937; *Tarakanowa/Betrayal* 1938; *Les Otages/The Mayor's Dilemma* 1939. In the US—*We Who Are Young* 1940; *Hitler's Madman* 1943; *Summer Storm* 1944; *Whistle Stop, The Chase* 1946; *Heaven Only Knows* 1947; *Siren of Atlantis* 1948; *M* 1951. In Germany—*Biz zu Ende aller Tage/The Girl from Hong Kong* 1961.

Needham, Hal. Director. Born on Mar. 6, 1931, in

Memphis, Tenn. A US Army paratrooper during the Korean War, he became a stuntman in the mid-50s and a bit actor, stunts coordinator, and second-unit action director in the 60s. He worked in any or a combination of these capacities in such films as *McLintock!* (1963), *Beau Geste* (1966), *The War Wagon* (1967), *The Ballad of Josie* (1968), *The Bridge at Remagen* (1969), *Little Big Man* (1970), *One More Train to Rob* (1971), *The French Connection II* (1975), *Nickelodeon* (1976), *Semi-Tough* (1977), and *Foul Play* (1978), among many others. He then turned to directing, specializing in witless, boisterous action fare, often starring Burt REYNOLDS.

FILMS (as director): *Smokey and the Bandit* (also co-story) 1977; *Hooper* 1978; *The Villain* 1979; *Smokey and the Bandit, Part II* 1980; *The Cannonball Run* 1981; *Megaforce* (also co-sc.) 1982; *Stroker Ace* (also co-sc.) 1983; *Cannonball Run II* (also co-sc., act.) 1984; *Rad* 1986; *Body Slam* 1987.

Neeson, Liam. Actor. Born in 1952, in Ballymena, Northern Ireland. Tall (6' 4"), handsome, serious leading man and character player of the Irish stage and British and American films. The product of a staunchly Catholic family, he drove a brewery truck and indulged in amateur boxing before stumbling into acting by responding in 1976 to an advertisement by the Lyric Players' Theatre in Belfast for a tall player in a bit part. He stayed with the company for two years, then joined Dublin's famed Abbey Theatre. He was discovered there by director John BOORMAN who cast him as Sir Gawain in the film *Excalibur* (1981). Neeson has since played wide-ranging leads and supporting roles to growing acclaim in a variety of British and Hollywood films. For his earnest, winning portrayal of Oskar Schindler in Steven SPIELBERG's powerful holocaust drama *Schindler's List* (1993), Neeson received an Academy Award nomination as best actor. He is married to actress Natasha RICHARDSON.

FILMS: *Excalibur* (as Sir Gawain) 1981; *Krull* 1983; *The Bounty* 1984; *The Innocent, Lamb, The Mission, Duet for One* 1986; *A Prayer for the Dying, Suspect* 1987; *Satisfaction, The Dead Pool, The Good Mother, High Spirits* 1988; *Next of Kin* 1989; *Darkman, The Big Man* 1990; *Crossing the Line, Shining Through, Under Suspicion* 1991; *Ethan Frome, Ruby Cairo, Schindler's List* 1993; *Nell* 1994; *Rob Roy* 1995; *Before and After, Michael Collins* 1996.

Neff, Hildegard. See KNEF, Hildegard.

negative. Exposed and processed film containing images whose colors and tonal values are the exact opposite of those of the original subject matter. Colors and tones will revert to their original values in the process of positive printing. The term is also used to describe the raw film stock before exposure and the raw stock in the camera after exposure but before processing.

negative cutter. The person who cuts negative film to match the WORK PRINT in the process of preparing an ANSWER PRINT.

negative cutting. The process of matching negatives frame by frame with a WORK PRINT, using EDGE NUMBERS as a guide, so that the negative may be correctly spliced for subsequent printing.

Negri, Pola. Actress. *b.* Barbara Apolonia Chalupiec, Dec. 31, 1894, Janowa, Poland. *d.* 1987. Glamorous, tempestuous star of the silent screen. Her early life is shrouded in calculated mystery and unintended confusion, with her own and studio versions of dates and events conflicting with those established by other sources. According to her own account, in her 1970 autobiography *Memoirs of a Star,* she was born in 1899, in Lipno, Poland, the daughter of an impoverished noblewoman and a Slovak immigrant tin master who was arrested for revolutionary activity and never returned. Others say her mother was a poor commoner and her father a Gypsy violinist who simply disappeared. Here the different versions converge. Moving to a Warsaw slum with her mother, who was forced to work as a cook, she trained at the Imperial Ballet School and made her debut with the Imperial Ballet as a cygnet in 'Swan Lake,' later dancing the lead in a Fokine production of 'Coppelia.' A bout with tuberculosis ended her dancing career, but she soon recovered enough to attend Warsaw's Imperial Academy of Dramatic Arts. Making her dramatic stage debut in 1913 and her first film appearance the following year, Negri quickly became established as one of Poland's leading stars. In 1917 she went to Berlin at the invitation of Max REINHARDT to appear on the stage in 'Sumurun' and remained there for five years to gain international fame as the star of several important German films by Ernst LUBITSCH and other directors.

Hollywood responded with a shower of contract offers. Starting the American phase of her career with Paramount in 1923, the exotic, passionate, mysterious Negri became enormously popular. Although few of her US films were of lasting value, most were successful at the box office. The star's romantic exploits off-screen helped keep the public intrigued, as did her long-running feud with rival Gloria SWANSON. Having divorced Polish Count Eugene Dambski just before arriving at the movie capital, Negri made headlines with her stormy relationship with Charlie CHAPLIN, to whom she was briefly engaged. Of even greater benefit to her image as a sex siren was her widely publicized love affair with movie idol Rudolf VALENTINO. The start of her decline coincided with his untimely death in 1926. The American public soon tired of her flamboyant histrionics and offbeat screen personae. The advent of sound proved another handicap.

In 1929 Negri returned to Europe, accompanied by her husband (since 1927) Prince Serge Modivani, formerly of Russian Georgia (his brother David wed actress Mae MURRAY). They divorced in 1931, after she had accused him of mismanaging her investments during the stock market crash. She had starred successfully in several German films of the mid-30s when Joseph Goebbels ordered her barred from the national industry because of suspicions that she was part Jewish. But Adolf Hitler, who confessed he was so fond of her film *Mazurka* (1935), a tearjerker about mother love, that he watched it at least once weekly, overruled his propaganda minister, prolonging her German stay till the outbreak of WW II. News stories that linked her romantically to Hitler were retracted after she successfully sued a French magazine that initiated the rumor. A resident of the French Riviera when the Germans invaded France, Negri returned to the US in 1941 and ten years later became an American citizen. Apart from two isolated screen appearances, she lived in comfortable seclusion in New York, then California, and eventually San Antonio, Texas, where she died of pneumonia, after refusing for two years to undergo treatment for a brain tumor.

FILMS: *Slaves of Passion* 1914; *Beast, The Black Book* 1915; *His Last Exploit, Zona, Students, Arabella* 1916. In Germany—*Zügelloses Blut, Die toten Augen* 1917; *Der gelbe Schein/The Yellow Ticket, Mania, Die Augen der Mumie Ma/The Eyes of the Mummy, Carmen/Gypsy Blood* (title role) 1918; *Das Karusell des Lebens, Madame Dubarry/Passion* (title role), *Comptesse Doddy* 1919; *Geschlossene Kette, Das Marthyrium, Sumurun/One Arabian Night* 1920; *Marchesa d'Armiani, Vendetta, Arme Violetta/The Red Peacock* (as Camille), *Medea* (unrealized Lubitsch project), *Die Bergkatze/The Mountain Cat, Sappho/Mad Love* 1921; *Die Dame im Glashaus, Die Flamme/Montmartre* 1922. In the US (complete)—*Bella Donna, The Cheat, Hollywood* (cameo), *The Spanish Dancer*

1923; *Shadows of Paris, Men, Lily of the Dust, Forbidden Paradise* (as Catherine the Great) 1924; *East of Suez, The Charmer, Flower of Night, A Woman of the World* 1925; *The Crown of Lies, Good and Naughty* 1926; *Hotel Imperial, Barbed Wire, The Woman on Trial* 1927; *Three Sinners, The Secret Hour, Loves of an Actress* (as famed French actress Rachel), *The Woman from Moscow* 1928. In the UK—*The Woman He Scorned* 1930. In the US—*A Woman Commands* 1932. In France—*Fanatisme* 1932. In Germany—*Mazurka* 1935; *Moskau-Shanghai* 1936; *Madame Bovary* 1937; *Tango Notturno, Die fromme Lüge, Die Nacht der Entscheidung* 1938. In the US—*Hi Diddle Diddle* 1943; *The Moon-Spinners* (US/UK) 1964.

Negroni, Baldassare. Director. *b.* Jan. 21, 1877, Rome. *d.* 1948. A count by title and an attorney by profession, he entered Italian films as a pastime, first as a cameraman, then as a director. He directed many melodramas and pseudohistorical films, often starring his wife, HESPERIA (Olga Mambelli). After 1937 he worked as a production supervisor.

FILMS INCLUDE: *La Gloria, Idillio Tragico* 1912; *L'Ultima Carta, Storia di un Pierrot* 1913; *L'Ereditiera, L'Ostacolo* 1914; *La Signora delle Camelie* 1915; *La Morsa, La Principessa di Bagdad* 1916; *La Donna abandonata* 1917; *Madame Flirt* 1918; *Vertigine* 1919; *Bimbi lontani* 1920; *Madame Sans-Gêne* 1921; *Il Figlio di Madame Sans-Gêne/The Little Corporal* 1922; *Beatrice Cenci, Gli Ultimi Zar* 1926; *Giuditta e Oloferne* 1929; *Due Cuori felici* 1932; *L'Ambasciatore* 1936.

Negulesco, Jean. Director. *b.* Feb. 26, 1900, Craiova, Rumania. *d.* 1993. Formerly a painter and a Parisian stage decorator, he came to New York in 1927 to exhibit his works and remained. He made his entry into films in the early 30s as an assistant producer, then second-unit director (*A Farewell to Arms, Captain Blood*) and associate director (*Kiss and Make Up, Crash Donovan*). Later in the decade he collaborated on several screenplays and original stories for such minor films as *Expensive Husbands, Fight for Your Lady* (both 1937), *Beloved Brat, Swiss Miss* (both 1938), and *Rio* (1939). He also directed an experimental film, *Three and a Day,* featuring Mischa AUER, and some 50 Warner Bros. two-reel shorts in the 'Melodie Masters' and other series between 1940 and 1944. He was given a crack at a first feature in 1941, but was removed from the helm of *Singapore Woman* in mid-production, nonetheless retaining sole screen credit as the film's director. Negulesco fared much better with his next feature, *The Mask of Dimitrios* (1944), an offbeat atmospheric thriller boasting a terrific performance by Peter LORRE. He went on to direct several hard-hitting, black-and-white melodramas for Warners, notably *Humoresque* (1946), culminating his work there with *Johnny Belinda* (1948), an effective drama about a raped deaf-mute that earned an Academy Award as best actress for Jane WYMAN and garnered seven other Oscar nominations, including best picture and best director. Moving on to 20th Century-Fox, Negulesco briefly sustained his creative momentum with *Road House* (1948) and *Three Came Home* (1950). But in the 50s, color, CinemaScope, and overly generous budgets, while enchancing the visual brilliance of his work, combined to corrupt his style and deprive his films of depth and sincerity. He scored well at the box office with the lavishly entertaining *How to Marry a Millionaire* (1953) and *Three Coins in the Fountain* (1954). But on the whole, the latter phase of his career was marked by hollow mediocrity. At a 1984 nine-day New York retrospective coinciding with his 84th birthday, he was hailed "The Prince of Melodrama," in memory of his earlier work. Later that year he completed on autobiography, *Things I Did and Things I Think I Did.*

FEATURE FILMS: *Singapore Woman* 1941; *The Mask of Dimitrios, The Conspirators* 1944; *Three Strangers, Nobody Lives Forever, Humoresque* 1946; *Deep Valley* 1947; *Johnny Belinda, Road House* 1948; *Brittania Mews/The Forbidden Street* (UK/US) 1949; *Under My Skin, Three Came Home, The Mudlark* 1950; *Take Care of My Little Girl* 1951; *Phone Call from a Stranger, Lydia Bailey, Lure of the Wilderness, O. Henry's Full House* ("The Last Leaf" episode) 1952; *Titanic, How to Marry a Millionaire, Scandal at Scourie* 1953; *Three Coins in the Fountain, Woman's World* 1954; *Daddy Long Legs, The Rains of Ranchipur* 1955; *Boy on a Dolphin* 1957; *The Gift of Love, A Certain Smile* 1958; *Count Your Blessings, The Best of Everything* 1959; *Jessica* (also prod.) 1962; *The Pleasure Seekers* 1964; *The Heroes/The Invincible Six* (Iran/US) 1969; *Hello-Goodbye* 1970.

Neilan, Marshall (Mickey). Director, actor. *b.* Apr. 11, 1891, San Bernardino, Calif. *d.* 1958. Having lost his father, a civil engineer, at a very young age, he dropped out of school at 11 to help his mother as a messenger, office boy, and blacksmith's apprentice. On occasion he also played boys' parts with various California stock companies. As a teenager he returned to school for short spells, only to re-enter the job market or appear on the stage in bit parts. He entered the film world in 1911 as D. W. Griffith's chauffeur at Biograph and was advised by the director to try film acting. Tall, handsome, and smooth-mannered, he signed with the Kalem studios in Santa Monica and soon rose from bits to leads opposite Ruth Roland and other early stars at Kalem. In 1912 he joined the American Film Company (Flying A), where he frequently worked under the direction of Allan DWAN. Occasionally he would also write screenplays or direct some scenes in the pictures in which he starred. He appeared in dozens of films, mainly one- and two-reel comedies for American, Rex, and Biograph, then returned to Kalem, where he began directing in 1914 and for a while had charge of the studio's overall operations. The following year he joined the Selig company, where he starred in several productions opposite Mary PICKFORD. Then, just as he was becoming established as a romantic leading man, he gave up acting to concentrate on a career as director. After several shorts for Selig, he piloted his first feature in 1916. He supervised Pickford in several of her most successful films and other popular silent stars, including Blanche SWEET, whom he married and later divorced. Still in his 20s, Neilan became one of the busiest and highest paid of Hollywood's directors, a "boy wonder" whose services were constantly in demand for lavish silent productions. But a growing reputation as a playboy and rascal who was often late or absent from the set began to damage his career during the mid-20s. His work became increasingly erratic as he spent more and more of his time drinking and romancing some of Hollywood's most glamorous stars. Although his assignments declined in importance, he continued directing on and off through 1937, when he made his last film. After that he was able to find occasional employment on the fringes of the film industry but could not hold on to a job because of his drinking problem. In 1957, a year before his death of cancer, he played a character role as a senator in Elia Kazan's film *A Face in the Crowd.*

FILMS INCLUDE: As actor—*How Jim Proposed, The Reward of Valor, The Stranger at Coyote, The Wanderer* 1912; *The Animal, The Harvest of Flame* (also co-dir., uncredited), *The Wall of Money* (also sc.), *Two Men of the Desert, The Wedding Gown, The House of Discord* 1913; *The Sentimental Sister, Classmates, The Billionaire, Men and Women* 1914; *The Commanding Officer, May Blossoms, The Country Boy, Little Pal* (also co-sc.), *Rags, A Girl of Yesterday, Madame Butterfly* (as Pinkerton) 1915; *Mice and Men, The Crisis* 1916; *Broadway*

Gold 1923; *A Face in the Crowd* 1957. As director (features complete)—*The American Princess* (also sc.) 1913; *Ham the Piano Mover* (also sc.), *Ham the Lineman* (also sc.) 1914; *The Cycle of Fate* (also sc.), *The Prince Chap, The Country God Forgot* (also sc.) 1916; *Those Without Sin, The Bottle Imp, The Tides of Barnegat, The Girl at Home, The Silent Partner, Freckles, The Jaguar's Claws, Rebecca of Sunnybrook Farm, The Little Princess* 1917; *Stella Maris, Amarilly of Clothesline Alley, M'Liss, Hit-the-Trail Holliday, Heart of the Wilds, Out of a Clear Sky* 1918; *Three Men and a Girl, Daddy Long Legs* (also act.), *The Unpardonable Sin, Her Kingdom of Dreams* 1919; *In Old Kentucky, The River's End, Don't Ever Marry* (co-dir. with Victor Heerman), *Go and Get It, Dinty* 1920; *Bob Hampton of Placer* (also prod.), *Bits of Life* (also prod., co-story), *The Lotus Eater* (also prod.) 1921; *Penrod* (also prod.), *Fools First* (also prod.), *Minnie* (co-dir. with Frank Urson; also prod., sc.), *The Stranger's Banquet* (also prod., co-sc.) 1922; *The Eternal Three* (co-dir. with Urson; also story), *The Rendezvous* 1923; *Dorothy Vernon of Haddon Hall, Tess of the D'Urbervilles* 1924; *The Sporting Venus, The Great Love* (also story) 1925; *Mike* (also story), *The Skyrocket, Wild Oats Lane* (also prod.), *Diplomacy, Everybody's Acting* (also story) 1926; *Venus of Venice, Her Wild Oat* 1927; *Three-Ring Marriage, Take Me Home, Taxi 13, His Last Haul* 1928; *Black Waters* (UK), *The Awful Truth, Tanned Legs, The Vagabond Lover* 1929; *Hell's Angels* (co-story only), *Sweethearts on Parade* 1930; *Chloe, Social Register, The Lemon Drop Kid, This Is the Life* 1935; *Sing While You're Able, Thanks for Listening, Swing It Professor* 1937.

Neill, Roy William. Director. *b.* Roland de Gostrie, 1886, aboard ship off Ireland. *d.* 1946. A stage actor from childhood, he served as a war correspondent in China in 1912. In 1915 he went to work for Thomas H. Ince and the following year began directing feature films. A competent and budget-minded director, he turned out scores of better-than-average silent and sound films in a variety of genres for three decades. His talkies were mainly B pictures, typically smooth mysteries and action films. He worked in England in the late 30s, directing Max MILLER comedies among other films. Returning to the US at the outbreak of WW II, he produced and directed a string of Sherlock Holmes mysteries for Universal.

FEATURE FILMS: *The Girl Glory, The Mother Instinct, They're Off, The Price Mark, Love Letters* 1917; *Flare-up Sal, Love Me, Free and Equal, Tyrant Fear, The Mating of Marcella, The Kaiser's Shadow/The Triple Cross, Green Eyes, Vive la France!* 1918; *Puppy Love, Charge It to Me, Trixie from Broadway, The Career of Katherine Bush, The Bandbox* 1919; *The Inner Voice, The Woman Gives, Yes or No, Good References, Dangerous Business* 1920; *Something Different, The Idol of the North, The Conquest of Canaan, The Iron Trail* 1921; *What's Wrong with the Women?* 1922; *Radio-Mania, Toilers of the Sea* (also prod.) 1923; *By Divine Right/The Way Men Love, Vanity's Price, Broken Laws* 1924; *The Kiss Barrier, Marriage in Transit, Greater Than a Crown, Percy* 1925; *The City, Black Paradise, The Cowboy and the Countess, The Fighting Buckaroo, A Man Four-Square* 1926; *Marriage, The Arizona Wildcat* 1927; *San Francisco Nights, Lady Raffles, The Olympic Hero/The All American* (also story, sc.), *The Viking* 1928; *Behind Closed Doors, Wall Street* 1929; *The Melody Man, Cock o' the Walk* (co-dir. with Walter Lang), *Just Like Heaven* 1930; *The Avenger, The Good Bad Girl, Fifty Fathoms Deep* 1931; *The Menace, That's My Boy* 1932; *The Circus Queen Murder, As the Devil Commands, Above the Clouds* 1933; *Fury of the Jungle, The Ninth Guest, Whirlpool, Black Moon, Blind Date, I'll Fix It, Jealousy* 1934; *Mills of the Gods, Eight Bells, The Back Room* 1935; *The Lone Wolf Returns* 1936; *Dr. Syn* (UK) 1937; *Thank Evans, The Viper, Simply Terrific, Everything Happens to Me, Many Thanks Mr. Atkins* (all UK) 1938; *The Good Old Days, Murder Will Out* (also co-sc.), *Hoots Man* (also co-sc.; all UK) 1939; *Madame Spy* 1942; *Eyes of the Underworld, Sherlock Holmes and the Secret Weapon, Frankenstein Meets the Wolf Man, Rhythm of the Islands, Sherlock Holmes in Washington* (also prod.), *Sherlock Holmes Faces Death* (also prod.) 1943; *Spider Woman/Sherlock Holmes and the Spider Woman* (also prod.), *The Scarlet Claw* (also prod.), *Pearl of Death* (also prod.), *Gypsy Wildcat* (also prod.) 1944; *The House of Fear* (also prod.), *The Woman in Green* (also prod.), *Pursuit to Algiers* (also prod.) 1945; *Terror by Night* (also prod.), *Dressed to Kill* (also prod.), *Black Angel* (also co-prod.) 1946.

Neill, Sam. Actor. Born Nigel Neill, in 1947, in Ireland. *ed.* U. of Canterbury. Darkly handsome leading man of international films. Raised in New Zealand, he performed locally on the stage and in three films before establishing star status in Australia with *My Brilliant Career* (1979).

FILMS: *Landfall* (NZ), *Ashes* (NZ) 1975; *Sleeping Dogs* (NZ) 1977; *My Brilliant Career* (Austral.), *The Journalist* (Austral.), *Just Out of Reach* (Austral.) 1979; *Attack Force Z* (Austral./Taiwan) 1900; *The Final Conflict* (US), *Possession* (Fr./Ger.) 1981; *Enigma* (Fr./UK) 1983; *The Country Girls* (UK), *Le Sang des Autres/The Blood of Others* (Fr./Can.) 1984; *Robbery Under Arms* (Austral.), *Plenty* (US/UK) 1985; *For Love Alone, The Umbrella Woman/The Good Wife* (Austral.) 1986; *Evil Angels/A Cry in the Dark* (Austral.) 1988; *Dead Calm* (Austral.), *La Revolution Française/The French Revolution* (as Lafayette; Fr./Ger./It./Can.) 1989; *The Hunt for Red October* (US), *Death in Brunswick* (Austral.) 1990; *Jusqu'au bout du Monde/Till the End of the World* (Fr.) 1991; *Memoirs of an Invisible Man* (US), *Hostage* 1992; *Jurassic Park, The Piano* 1993; *The Jungle Book, Rainbow Warrior, Sirens* 1994; *The Country Life, In the Mouth of Madness, Restoration* 1995; *Children of the Revolution* 1996; *Event Horizon* 1997.

Neilson, James. American director. *b.* 1910. *d.* 1979. A former still photographer and TV producer, he turned to directing films in the late 50s and for several years found a home at the Disney studios.

FILMS: *Night Passage* 1957; *The Country Husband* 1958; *Moon Pilot, Bon Voyage!* 1962; *Dr. Syn* (UK), *Summer Magic* 1963; *The Moon-Spinners* (US/UK) 1964; *The Adventures of Bullwhip Griffin, Gentle Giant* 1967; *Where Angels Go Trouble Follows!* 1968; *The First Time, Flareup* 1969.

Nelligan, Kate. Actress. Born on Mar. 16, 1951, London, Ont., Canada. Talented, appealing stage star who has also appeared sporadically in films. She discovered the theater during her studies at the University of Toronto and at the end of her sophomore year transferred to the Central School of Speech and Drama in London, England. After graduating, she performed for a year with the Bristol Old Vic Company, then made her London stage debut in 1974. She has since starred in many West End and Broadway productions and was nominated for Tony Awards three times. Now a US resident, she married pianist-arranger Robert Reale in 1989.

FILMS: *The Romantic Englishwoman* (UK/Fr.) 1975; *Licking Hitler* (UK) 1977; *Dracula* (US) 1979; *Mr. Patman* (Can.) 1980; *Eye of the Needle* (US) 1981; *Without a Trace* (US) 1983; *The Mystery of Henry Moore* (doc.; Can.) 1984; *Eleni* (US) 1985; *Il Giorno prima* (It.) 1987; *White Room* (Can.) 1990; *Frankie and Johnny, The Prince of Tides* (both US) 1991; *Shadows and Fog* 1992; *Wolf* 1994; *How To Make an American Quilt* 1995; *Up Close and Personal* 1996; *Margaret's Museum* 1997.

Nelson, Barry. Actor. Born Robert Haakon Nielsen, on Apr. 16, 1920, in Oakland, Calif., of Scandinavian descent. *ed.* U. of California (Berkeley). Entered films in 1941 directly out of college and played pleasant leads and supporting roles in a variety of MGM productions. He enjoyed only moderate success as a screen personality but later fared much better as a stage actor, as the star of several hit Broadway plays, including 'The Rat Race,' 'The Moon Is Blue,' 'Mary Mary,' and 'Cactus Flower.' He also starred in the TV series 'The Hunter' (1952–54) and 'My Favorite Husband' (1953–55).

FILMS INCLUDE: *Shadow of the Thin Man, Johnny Eager* 1941; *Stand By for Action, Dr. Kildare's Victory, Rio Rita, A Yank on the Burma Road, Eyes in the Night* 1942; *The Human Comedy, Bataan* 1943; *A Guy Named Joe, Winged Victory* 1944; *The Beginning or the End, Undercover Maisie* 1947; *Tenth Avenue Angel* 1948; *The Man with My Face* 1951; *The First Traveling Saleslady* 1956; *Mary Mary* 1963; *Airport* 1970; *Pete 'n' Tillie* 1972; *The Shining* 1980; *Island Claws/Night of the Claw* 1981.

Nelson, Craig T. Actor. Born on Apr. 4, 1946, in Spokane, Wash. *ed.* U. of Arizona. Husky leading man and supporting player of American films and TV. After a slow start as a comedy writer and performer in Los Angeles, at one point partnering with Barry LEVINSON, he retreated with his family to a wilderness cabin near Mount Shasta, California. Returning to show business after a four-year absence, he began appearing in films in the late 70s, at first in bits and small supporting roles, then in leads, starting with *Poltergeist* (1982), and major character parts. He has also played frequent guest roles on television, and starred in two series, 'Call to Glory' and 'Coach.'

FILMS: *. . . And Justice for All* 1979; *The Formula, Where the Buffalo Roam, Private Benjamin, Stir Crazy* 1980; *Poltergeist* 1982; *Man Woman and Child, All the Right Moves, The Osterman Weekend, Silkwood* 1983; *The Killing Fields* (UK) 1984; *Poltergeist II: The Other Side* 1986; *Red Riding Hood* (US/Isr.), *Rachel River* 1987; *Action Jackson, Me and Him* (Ger./US) 1988; *Troop Beverly Hills, Turner & Hooch* 1989; *Ghosts of Mississippi, I'm Not Rappaport* 1996; *The Devil's Advocate* 1997.

Nelson, Gary. American director of several proficient features and numerous TV movies. He was nominated for an Emmy for directing the miniseries 'Washington: Behind Closed Doors' (1977).

FEATURE FILMS: *Molly and Lawless John* 1972; *Santee* 1973; *Freaky Friday* 1977; *The Black Hole* 1979; *Jimmy the Kid* 1983; *Alan Quatermain and the Lost City of Gold* 1987.

Nelson, Gene. Dancer, actor, director. *b.* Gene Berg, on Mar. 24, 1920, in Seattle. *d.* 1996. Formerly a skater with Sonja Henie's ice show, he played song-and-dance leads and second leads in Hollywood musicals of the 50s. After attempting a number of straight dramatic parts he turned to directing light, if loud, films. He has also directed numerous episodes for various TV series.

FILMS INCLUDE: As actor—*I Wonder Who's Kissing Her Now* 1947; *Apartment for Peggy* 1948; *The Daughter of Rosie O'Grady, Tea for Two, The West Point Story* 1950; *Lullaby of Broadway, Painting the Clouds with Sunshine* 1951; *She's Working Her Way Through College* 1952; *She's Back on Broadway, Three Sailors and a Girl* 1953; *So This Is Paris, Crime Wave* 1954; *Oklahoma!* 1955; *The Atomic Man* (UK), *The Way Out* (UK) 1956; *20,000 Eyes, The Purple Hills* 1961; *Thunder Island* 1963; *S.O.B.* 1981. As director (complete)—*Hand of Death* 1962; *Hootenanny Hoot* 1963; *Kissin' Cousins, Your Cheatin' Heart* 1964; *Harum Scarum* 1965; *The Cool Ones* 1967.

Nelson, Judd. Actor. Born on Nov. 28, 1959, in Portland, Me. Youthful leading man of the American screen. One of the Hollywood Brat Pack that emerged on the scene in the 80s. He began acting in high school productions and during vacations in summer stock. After graduating from Haverford College with a degree in philosophy, he headed for New York, where he trained for two years with Stella ADLER before making his screen debut in 1984. In 1989 he was cast against type in the role of a deranged serial killer in *Relentless.*

FILMS: *Making the Grade* 1984; *Fandango, The Breakfast Club, St. Elmo's Fire* 1985; *Blue City, The Transformers* (v/o) 1986; *From the Hip, Dear America* (doc.; v/o) 1987; *Relentless* 1989; *Far Out Man* (as himself) 1990; *New Jack City* 1991; *The Dark Backward* 1991; *Primary Motive* 1992; *Caroline at Midnight* 1993; *Airheads, Every Breath* (also sc.), *Hail Caesar* 1994; *Steel* 1997.

Nelson, Lori. Actress. Born Dixie Kay Nelson, on Aug. 15, 1933, in Santa Fe, N.M. A former child actress and model, she played leads in Hollywood films of the 50s and co-starred in the TV series 'How to Marry a Millionaire' (1957–58). She later ran a cosmetics company. At one time married to choir leader Johnny Mann.

FILMS INCLUDE: *Bend of the River, Ma and Pa Kettle at the Fair, Francis Goes to West Point* 1952; *The All-American, All I Desire, Walking My Baby Back Home* 1953; *Destry* 1954; *Underwater!, Revenge of the Creature, I Died a Thousand Times* 1955; *Mohawk, Pardners, Hot Rod Girl* 1956; *Untamed Youth* 1957.

Nelson, Ozzie. Actor, bandleader. *b.* Oswald George Nelson, Mar. 20, 1907, Jersey City, N.J. *d.* 1975. An all-around athlete at Rutgers, where he received his B.A. and law degrees, he formed a dance band upon graduation which enjoyed popularity in the early 30s. In 1935 he married his vocalist, Harriet HILLIARD (*b.* 1914, Des Moines; *d.* Oct. 2, 1994), and as a team they gained popularity in the late 30s and early 40s on the radio shows of comedians Joe Penner and Red Skelton. The Nelsons' success led to the creation of their own radio show in 1944, 'The Adventures of Ozzie and Harriet,' which became one of American broadcasting's all-time long-running hits, eight years on radio and 14 more (1952–66) on television. The series featured Ozzie and Harriet's sons, Ricky Nelson (*b.* Eric Nelson, May 8, 1940, Teaneck, N.J.; *d.* 1985, in plane crash) and David Nelson (*b.* Oct. 24, 1936, New York City), both of whom also appeared in a number of films. Ricky was a popular rock singer in the 60s, and David became a TV producer and director who also directed three feature films in the early 80s. Ozzie Nelson himself appeared only intermittently in films. He directed and produced many of the Ozzie and Harriet series' episodes as well as a film starring Ricky, *Love and Kisses* (1965). In 1973, Ozzie and Harriet returned to TV in the series 'Ozzie's Girls.' He died two years later following surgery for cancer of the liver. Autobiography: *Ozzie* (1973).

FILMS: *The Letter* (with his orchestra) 1940; *Sweetheart of the Campus* 1941; *The Big Street, Strictly in the Groove* 1942; *Honeymoon Lodge* 1943; *Hi Good Lookin', Take It Big* 1944; *People Are Funny* 1946; *Here Come the Nelsons* 1952; *Love and Kisses* (dir., prod., sc. only) 1965; *The Impossible Years* 1968.

Nelson, Ralph. Director. *b.* Aug. 12, 1916, Long Island City, N.Y. *d.* 1987. A stage actor from the age of 17, following a troubled youth and a criminal record as a juvenile delinquent, he appeared in a number of Broadway productions and in the 40s wrote and directed several plays. After WW II service as a flight instructor with the Army Air Force, he began acting, directing, and producing for television and during the 50s turned out numerous TV dramas, according to some estimates as many as

1,000 between 1948 and 1960. He is widely credited with playing a major role in bringing innovation and consistent quality to live dramatic programming in the early days of television. After winning an Emmy for directing Rod Serling's teleplay 'Requiem for a Heavyweight,' he made his big-screen debut in 1962 with a feature version of the same drama. In his subsequent films he tackled both serious and light themes sensibly but not always convincingly. He had his best success with *Lilies of the Field* (1963), a film he also produced, which gained a best actor Oscar for Sidney POITIER and was nominated for several other Academy Awards, including best picture. He played minor roles in several of his own films. At one time (1938–39) married to Celeste HOLM.

FILMS: *Requiem for a Heavyweight* 1962; *Lilies of the Field* (also prod., act.), *Soldier in the Rain* 1963; *Fate Is the Hunter, Father Goose* 1964; *Once a Thief* (also co-exec. prod.) 1965; *Duel at Diablo* (also co-prod.) 1966; *Counterpoint* (also act.), *Charly* (also prod., act.) 1968; *. . . Tick. . . Tick. . . Tick. . .* (also co-prod.), *Soldier Blue* (also act.) 1970; *Flight of the Doves* (also prod., co-sc.; UK) 1971; *The Wrath of God* (also sc.) 1972; *The Wilby Conspiracy* (UK) 1975; *Embryo* 1976; *A Hero Ain't Nothin' but a Sandwich* 1977.

Nelson, Willie. Singer, composer, actor. Born on Apr. 30, 1933, in Abbott, Tex. Scruffy country music entertainer who played leads and supporting roles in several films. A former salesman, he entered show business as a radio announcer and host of country-music shows on local stations. While a bass player with a band, he began writing songs in the 60s (Patsy Cline's signature 'Crazy' among others) and performing with increasing popularity in the 70s. In the late 80s, he had highly public run-ins with the IRS and went bankrupt, but continued performing and helping to organize benefits for farmers and their families (Farm Aid). He has five children from three marriages. Autobiography: *Willie* (1988).

FILMS: *The Electric Horseman* 1979; *Honeysuckle Rose* (also mus.) 1980; *Thief* 1981; *Barbarosa* 1982; *Songwriter* 1984; *Red Headed Stranger* (also co-prod., mus.) 1986; *Walking After Midnight* (doc.) 1988; *Welcome Home* (singing of title song only) 1989.

Nêmec, Jan. Director. Born on July 2, 1936, in Prague. A graduate of the Prague film school, he won a prize at a film students' festival in Amsterdam for his graduation film, the 1960 short *A Loaf of Bread* (also known as *A Bite to Eat* or *The Morsel*). This early work contains some of the elements that were later to characterize his feature films, mainly a concern with the inner mind of characters and a fascination with the psychology of oppression. During his military service he directed another short, the documentary *The Memory of Our Day* (1963), which revealed another of his preoccupations, human memory. All these elements were present in Nêmec's first feature, *Diamonds of the Night* (1964), an examination of the mental anguish, memories, and hallucinations of two young men who escape from a Nazi transport train. His next solo feature, *A Report on the Party and the Guests* (1966), was a Kafkaesque, claustrophobic study of tyranny in a family context. He collaborated on the scripts of this and his next film, *Martyrs of Love* (also 1966), with Ester Krumbachova, to whom he was briefly married at the time. He later married Marta Kubisova, a popular singer whose performances were banned after the Soviet invasion of 1968. Nêmec's own career suffered badly after the invasion, and the last film he made in Czechoslovakia was *Oratorio for Prague* (1968), a documentary recording that grim event. After years of inactivity, he was allowed to leave for France in 1974, and the following year he directed a French/German coproduction in Munich. Failing to consummate any further projects, Nêmec moved to the United States, but here too he couldn't get his career re-started, and apart from a "special consultant" credit on Philip Kaufman's *The Unbearable Lightness of Being* (1988), had no film assignments at all.

FEATURE FILMS: *Diamonds of the Night* (also co-sc.) 1964; *Pearls of the Deep* (one episode; also sc.) 1965; *A Report on the Party and the Guests* (also co-sc., act.), *Martyrs of Love* (also co-sc.) 1966; *Oratorio for Prague* (doc.) 1968; *Le Décolleté dans le Dos* (Fr./Ger.) 1975; *The Unbearable Lightness of Being* (special consultant only; US) 1988.

neorealism. A term first used in 1942–43 by Italian critics Antonio Pietrangeli and Umberto Barbaro to describe a movement in the Italian cinema that began with Luchino Visconti's *Ossessione* (1942). *Ossessione* was a free adaptation of James Cain's *The Postman Always Rings Twice* that shifted the story to an Italian setting. It was filmed on actual locations, achieving a visual authenticity that contrasted sharply with the artificial aura imposed on Italian films of the period by the Fascist regime.

Actually, neorealism was not a wholly new trend, as the term might suggest, but a revival of a veristic style that characterized certain Italian films of the mid-1910s and later some films made in France, the USSR, and elsewhere. Japanese critics used a variation of the term to describe the ultra-realistic films of Yasajiro Shimazu in the 20s and 30s. But it wasn't until the 40s, in Italy, that the style emerged as a conscious, full-fledged movement. Several films in the neorealistic mold were made in the wake of *Ossessione,* among them Vittorio De Sica's *I Bambini ci guardano/The Children Are Watching Us* (1943). However, because of the war none of them was seen abroad, and it remained for Roberto Rossellini's *Roma Città aperta/Open City* (1945) to herald neorealism internationally. Other neorealist films quickly followed, including Rossellini's *Paisà/Paisan* (1946) and *Germania Anno Zero/Germany Year Zero* (1947); De Sica's *Sciuscia/Shoeshine* (1946) and *Ladri di Biciclette/The Bicycle Thief* (1948); Aldo Vergano's *Il Sole sorge ancora/Outcry* (1947); Alberto Lattuada's *Senza Pietà/Without Pity* (1948); and Pietro Germi's *In Nome della Legge/Mafia* (1949) and *Il Camino della Speranza/The Path of Hope* (1950). Giuseppe De Santis's *Riso amaro/Bitter Rice* (1949), which brought sensuality, melodrama, and star glamour (Silvana Mangano) to the rice fields of the Po Valley, represented a commercial exploitation of the neorealist idea and the beginning of the end of the movement that had brought the Italian cinema artistic vitality and social significance in the 40s, particularly in the early postwar years. Neorealism was gradually phased out of the Italian cinema in the early 50s, as economic conditions improved and film producers succumbed to the growing public demand for escapist entertainment. But the influence of the neorealist style has lasted far beyond the demise of the movement and is evident today in the films of many nations. See also ITALY.

Nero, Franco. Actor. Born Francesco Spartanero, in 1941, in Palermo, Italy. Handsome leading man of Italian and international films. Acknowledged father of Carlos, the 1969-born son of Vanessa Redgrave, his co-star in his best-known film, *Camelot.*

FILMS INCLUDE: *La Celestina P.R.* 1965; *I Criminali della Galassia/Wild Wild Planet, Gli Uomini del Passo Pesante/The Tramplers, Tecnica di un Omicidio/The Hired Killer, Tempo di Massacro/The Brute and the Beast, La Bibbia/The Bible. . . In the Beginning* (as Abel; US/It.) 1966; *Camelot* (as Lancelot; US) 1967; *Il Mercenario/The Mercenary, Un Tranquillo Posto di Campagna/A Quiet Place in the Country* 1968; *Il Giorno della Civetta/Mafia, Un Detective/Detective Belli* 1969; *Tristana* (Sp./Fr./It.), *The Virgin and the Gypsy* (UK), *Dropout, The Battle of Neretva* (Yug./It./Fr.) 1970;

Compañeros (Sp./It.) 1971; *Pope Joan* (UK), *Il Monaco, La Vacanza* 1972; *Delitto Matteoti, Los Amigos/Deaf Smith and Johnny Ears* (Sp./It.) 1973; *Mussolini: Ultimo Atto/The Last Four Days, Corruzione al Palazzo di Giustizia* 1974; *Il Cipollaro/Cipola Colt/Cry Onion, Perche si uccide un Magistrato, Les Magiciens* (Fr./It.), *Scandalo/Submission, Marcia trionfale/Victory March, I Quatro dell'Apocalisse* 1975; *Gente di Rispetto, Koema* 1976; *Django—Il Grande Ritorno* 1977; *Force 10 from Navarone* (UK) 1978; *Un Dramma borghese* 1979; *The Man with Bogart's Face/Sam Marlowe, Private Eye* (US), *Il Giorno del Cobra/Day of the Cobra* 1980; *Enter the Ninja* (US), *The Salamander* (UK/It./US) 1981; *Kamikaze '89* (Ger.), *Querelle* (Fr.), *Red Bells/Mexico in Flames* (USSR) 1982; *Wagner* (UK/Hung./Aus.) 1983; *The Girl* (Swed.) 1985; *Sweet Country* (Greece/Pan.), *Garibaldi* 1986; *Il Giovane Toscanini/The Young Toscanini* 1988; *Die Hard 2* (US) 1990; *Amelia Loves O'Neill* (Chile/Fr./Switz.) 1991; *Di Ceria dell'Untore/The Plague Sower* 1992; *Jonathan of the Bears* 1994.

Nesbitt, Cathleen. Actress. *b.* Nov. 24, 1888, Cheshire, England. *d.* 1982. A veteran character player of the British and American stage, she appeared in hundreds of theater productions since 1910, but in relatively few films. In addition she performed in such TV series as 'The Farmer's Daughter' and 'Upstairs Downstairs.' Autobiography: *A Little Love and Good Companions* (1973).

FILMS INCLUDE: In the UK—*The Frightened Lady/Criminal at Large* 1932; *The Passing of the Third Floor Back* 1935; *The Beloved Vagabond* 1936; *Gaslight/Angel Street* 1940; *Fanny by Gaslight/Man of Evil* 1944; *The Agitator* 1945; *Jassy, Nicholas Nickleby* 1947; *Madness of the Heart* 1949; *So Long at the Fair* 1950. In the US—*Three Coins in the Fountain, Black Widow, Desiree* (as Mme. Bonaparte) 1954; *An Affair to Remember* 1957; *Separate Tables* 1958; *The Parent Trap* 1961; *Promise Her Anything* (UK) 1966; *The Trygon Factor* (UK) 1967; *Staircase* 1969; *Villain* (UK) 1971; *French Connection II* 1975; *Family Plot* 1976; *Full Circle* (UK/Can.), *Julia* 1977.

Netherlands, The. A leader among European countries in the quality production of documentary films, this constitutional monarchy of more than 15 million inhabitants did not possess a viable feature-film industry until very recently. A rudimentary industry had arisen in Holland at the turn of the century, but its achievements were nullified by a long maritime blockade during WW I (in which the country was a neutral) which prevented the exportation of Dutch films. By the time the war ended, a film industry no longer existed. In the absence of local production, the screens were dominated by American and German films and it soon became evident that with rare exceptions (such as *The Black Tulip*, in 1921) Dutch-made feature films could not recover their cost at the box office.

Young Dutch filmmakers had little choice but to gravitate toward the production of documentary films. Notable among them was Joris IVENS, whose brilliant documentary shorts marked the beginning of a tradition of excellence for which the Netherlands remains famous to this day. The tradition has been kept alive, with the help of government grants, by such documentarians as Bert HAANSTRA, Herman van der Horst, Johan van der Keuken, Hans Heljnen, Karen Junger, Niek Koppen, and Tom Verheul.

Limited feature production began gaining some momentum in the mid-70s, relying on aid from both the government and private investment. Since then, the industry has garnered international acclaim out of proportion to its modest output. The industry's greatest success story, director Paul VERHOEVEN, gained worldwide notice for such films as *Soldier of Orange* (1977), *Spetters* (1980), and *The Fourth Man* (1983), before coming to Hollywood to practice his blend of sex, violence, suspense, and social commentary in larger scale in such blockbusters as *Robocop* (1987), *Total Recall* (1990), and *Basic Instinct* (1992). Director George Sluizer also came to the US to remake his respected 1988 French-Dutch production *The Vanishing* (though the 1993 result was considered a pale imitation of the original). Dutch actors who have become internationally known include Jeroen KRABBÉ, Rutger HAUER, Derek de Lint, Renée Soutendjik, and Johanna ter Steege. Dutch cinematographers such as Jan DE BONT and Theo van der Sande are also widely respected.

The Dutch film industry continues to be small, with few films making a profit and Dutch audiences overwhelmingly preferring Hollywood fare. However, the Dutch Film Days, which showcases Dutch cinema and annually presents the Golden Calf awards, is the most popular media event in the Netherlands. In addition to the filmmakers named above, acclaimed Dutch directors include Ate de Jong, Frans Wiesz, Jos Stelling, Ben Verbong, Orlow Seunke, Ruud van Hemert, Dick Maas, Paul Ruven, Rudolf van den Berg, Pieter Verhoeff, and Alex van Warmerdam (whose 1986 *Abel* was picked by many Dutch critics as the best Dutch film of the 80s).

Nettleton, Lois. Actress. Born on Aug. 6, 1929, in Oak Park, Ill. leading lady of Hollywood films of the 60s and early 70s. Later seen in character roles. Trained at Chicago's Goodman Theatre and at New York's Actors Studio, she also performed on the stage and on TV, winning Emmy Awards in 1977 and 1983.

FILMS INCLUDE: *Period of Adjustment* 1962; *Come Fly with Me* 1963; *Mail Order Bride* 1964; *Valley of Mystery* 1967; *The Bamboo Saucer* 1968; *The Good Guys and the Bad Guys* 1969; *Dirty Dingus McGee* 1970; *The Honkers* 1972; *The Man in the Glass Booth* 1975; *Echoes of a Summer* 1976; *Deadly Blessings* 1981; *Butterfly, The Best Little Whorehouse in Texas* 1982; *Raven Dance* 1994.

Neufeld, Mace. Producer. Born on July 13, 1928, in New York, N.Y. *ed.* Yale. Producer of film action dramas and comedies since the 1970s. A photographer at the start of his career, he became a production assistant at the Dumont TV network, and later a songwriter for top performers including Sammy Davis, Jr. From 1951, he worked as an independent producer and personal manager for TV. In 1976, he struck gold with the theatrical hit *The Omen*. In the 80s he worked in partnership with Marvin Davis; beginning in 1989, he and Robert Rehme formed a partnership that produced a successful series of adaptations of Tom Clancy techno-thrillers.

FILMS INCLUDE: *The Omen* 1976; *Damien—Omen II* 1978; *The Frisco Kid* 1979; *The Funhouse* 1981; *The Aviator, Transylvania 6-5000* 1985; *No Way Out* 1987; *The Hunt for Red October* 1990; *Flight of the Intruder, Necessary Roughness* 1991; *Patriot Games* 1992; *Beverly Hills Cop III, Clear and Present Danger* 1994; *The Saint* 1997.

Neumann, Kurt. Director. *b.* Apr. 5, 1906, Nuremberg, Germany, *d.* 1958. He directed comedy shorts and foreign versions of Hollywood films before becoming a feature director early in the 30s. With few exceptions, turned out routine low- to medium-budget entertainment fare, often with an accent on action or fantasy. He also produced and wrote the screenplays for some of his films.

FILMS: *Fast Companions, Information Kid, My Pal the King* 1932; *The Big Cage, The Secret of the Blue Room, King for a Night* 1933; *Let's Talk It Over, Half a Sinner, Wake Up and Dream* 1934; *Alias Mary Dow, The Affair of Susan* 1935; *Let's Sing Again, Rainbow on the River* 1936; *Espionage, Make a Wish, Hold 'Em Navy* 1937; *Wide Open Faces, Touchdown*

Army 1938; *Ambush, Unmarried, Island of Lost Men, All Women Have Secrets* 1939; *Ellery Queen—Master Detective, A Night at Earl Carroll's* 1940; *Brooklyn Orchid, About Face, The McGuerins from Brooklyn* 1942; *Fall In, Taxi Mister, Yanks Ahoy!, The Unknown Guest, The Return of the Vampire* (co-dir. with Lew Landers) 1943; *Tarzan and the Amazons* (also assoc. prod.) 1945; *Tarzan and the Leopard Woman* (also assoc. prod.) 1946; *Tarzan and the Huntress* (also assoc. prod.) 1947; *The Dude Goes West* 1948; *Bad Men of Tombstone, Bad Boy* 1949; *The Kid from Texas, Rocketship X-M* (also prod., sc.) 1950; *Cattle Drive, Reunion in Reno* 1951; *Son of Ali Baba, The Ring, Hiawatha* 1952; *Tarzan and the She-Devil* 1953; *Carnival Story* (also co-sc.) 1954; *They Were So Young* (also prod., co-sc.) 1955; *Mohawk, The Desperadoes Are in Town* (also prod., co-sc.) 1956; *Kronos* (also prod.), *The She-Devil* (also prod., co-sc.), *The Deerslayer* (also prod., co-sc.) 1957; *The Fly* (also prod.), *Circus of Love* (also co-sc.; Ger.), *Machete* (also prod., co-sc.) 1958; *Watusi, Counterplot* (also prod.) 1959.

neutral-density filter. A filter for a camera lens, used for reducing exposure and contrast without altering color values.

Neuwirth, Bebe. Actress, dancer. Born in Newark, N.J. *ed.* Juilliard. Lithe, expressive supporting player of stage and screen. The daughter of a mathematician and an artist, she established herself in Broadway musicals in the 1980s, including 'A Chorus Line'; and she won Tonys for her performances in 'Sweet Charity' and 'Chicago.' She won two Emmys as Lilith Sternin-Crane on TV sitcom 'Cheers'. Married theater director Paul Dorman.

FILMS INCLUDE: *Say Anything* 1989; *Green Card, Penny Ante* 1990; *Bugsy* 1991; *Malice* 1993; *Jumanji* 1995; *All Dogs Go to Heaven* (v/o), *The Associate, Pinocchio* 1996.

Newborn, Ira. Composer. Born on Dec. 26, 1949, in New York City. A former bandleader, he performed on TV on the 'Manhattan Transfer' variety show in the mid-70s. He scored many Hollywood films of the 80s and early 90s, mostly comedies and youth-oriented light fare.

FILMS INCLUDE: *The Blues Brothers* 1980; *All Night Long* 1981; *Sixteen Candles* 1984; *Into the Night, Weird Science* 1985; *Wise Guys, Ferris Bueller's Day Off* 1986; *Dragnet, Amazon Women on the Moon, Planes Trains and Automobiles* 1987; *Caddyshack II, The Naked Gun* 1988; *Uncle Buck* 1989; *Short Time, My Blue Heaven* 1990; *The Naked Gun 2½: The Smell of Fear* 1991; *The Naked Gun 33⅓: The Final Insult* 1994; *The Jerky Boys, Mallrats* 1995.

Newell, Mike. Director. Born in 1942, in England. He directed for the stage and for British TV before moving on to feature films. His best-regarded film, in a decidedly mixed lot, is *Dance with a Stranger* (1985) a gripping account of the self-destructive life of Ruth Ellis, who in 1955 became the last woman ever executed in Britain. His *Enchanted April* (1992) was another acclaimed effort, and a huge success in America as a British import.

FILMS: *The Awakening* (US) 1988; *Bad Blood* (NZ) 1983; *Dance with a Stranger* 1985; *The Good Father* 1986; *Amazing Grace and Chuck* (US) 1987; *Soursweet* 1988; *Enchanted April* (UK) 1992; *Into the West* 1993; *Four Weddings and a Funeral* 1994; *An Awfully Big Adventure* 1995; *Donnie Brasco* 1997.

Newfield, Sam. Director. *b.* Samuel Neufeld, Dec. 6, 1899, New York City. *d.* 1964. Associated with motion pictures from 1919, he directed many comedy shorts before turning feature director early in the 30s. His enormously prolific output consisted of hundreds of routine low-budget action pictures, nearly all produced by poverty-row studios, like Tower, Ambassador, Puritan, and PRC. He frequently used pseudonyms—Sherman Scott and Peter Stewart, for example—to avoid an embarrassing avalanche of screen credits to his own name.

FILMS INCLUDE: *Reform Girl, Important Witness* 1933; *Marrying Widows, Beggar's Holiday* 1934; *Northern Frontier, Racing Luck* 1935; *Federal Agent, Burning Gold, The Lion's Den, Ghost Patrol, The Traitor* 1936; *The Gambling Terror, Trail of Vengeance, Guns in the Dark, Doomed at Sundown, Boothill Brigade, The Colorado Kid* 1937; *Paroled—to Die, The Feud Maker, Code of the Rangers, Desert Patrol, The Phantom Ranger, The Terror of Tiny Town* 1938; *The Invisible Killer, Goose Step/Beasts of Berlin* 1939; *Secrets of a Model, I Take This Oath, Hold That Woman!, Marked Man, Billy the Kid in Texas* 1940; *The Lone Rider Rides On, The Texas Marshal, Billy the Kid Wanted, The Lone Rider Fights Back* 1941; *The Mad Monster, Jungle Siren* 1942; *Queen of Broadway, Dead Men Walk, Law and Order, The Black Raven, Tiger Fangs* 1943; *Nabonga, The Monster Maker, Valley of Vengeance, The Contender, Swing Hostess, I Accuse My Parents* 1944; *The Lady Confesses, Gangster's Den, Stagecoach Outlaws, Apology for Murder* 1945; *Murder Is My Business, Larceny in Her Heart, Queen of Burlesque, Blonde for a Day, Gas House Kids* 1946; *Three on a Ticket, Adventure Island* 1947; *Money Madness, The Counterfeiters, Lady at Midnight, The Strange Mrs. Crane* 1948; *State Department—File 649* 1949; *Radar Secret Service, Western Pacific Agent, Motor Patrol, Hi-Jacked* 1950; *Three Desperate Men, Fingerprints Don't Lie, Mask of the Dragon, Skipalong Rosenbloom, The Lost Continent, Leave It to the Marines, Sky High* 1951; *Outlaw Women* (co-dir. with Ron Ormond), *Lady in the Fog/Scotland Yard Inspector* (UK), *The Gambler and the Lady* (UK) 1952; *Thunder Over Sangoland* 1955; *Frontier Gambler, The Three Outlaws* 1956; *Flaming Frontier* (also prod.), *Wolf Dog* 1958.

Newley, Anthony. Actor, composer, singer, stage director. Born on Sept. 24, 1931, in London. Gifted, versatile entertainer of British stage and screen with a knack for comedy. Began as a child star in the mid-40s. Co-authored, co-composed (with Leslie Bricusse), and directed 'Stop the World—I Want to Get Off' for the London stage and later for Broadway. He appeared in both but not in the film version. He tackled film directing for the first time in the late 60s. He was the second husband (1963–70) of Joan COLLINS.

FILMS INCLUDE (as actor): *Adventures of Dusty Bates, Vice Versa, The Little Ballerina* 1947; *The Guinea Pig, Oliver Twist* (as the Artful Dodger) 1948; *Highly Dangerous* 1950; *Those People Next Door* 1952; *The Cockleshell Heroes, Above Us the Waves* 1955; *Port Afrique, X the Unknown, The Good Companions* 1956; *How to Marry a Rich Uncle, Fire Down Below, High Flight* 1957; *The Man Inside, No Time to Die* (1958); *Idle on Parade, Killers of Kilimanjaro* 1959; *The Small World of Sammy Lee* 1963; *Goldfinger* (co-title song only) 1964; *Doctor Dolittle* (US) 1967; *Sweet November* (US) 1968; *Can Hieronymus Merkin Ever Forget Mercy Humppe and Find True Happiness?* (also dir., prod., co-sc., co-songs) 1969; *Willy Wonka and the Chocolate Factory* (music only; US), *Summertree* (dir. only; US) 1971; *Vampira* (title song only), *Mr. Quilp* (also mus., lyrics) 1975; *It Seemed Like a Good Idea at the Time* 1976; *Sammy Stops the World* (co-story, co-mus., co-lyrics only) 1979; *The Garbage Pail Kids Movie* (US) 1987.

New Line Cinema Corporation. Independent New York–based distribution and production company. Founded in 1967 by chairman and CEO Robert Shaye, it became one of the movie industry's most flourishing independents. Specializing in low-budget and offbeat films for young audiences, it developed big commercial franchises with the two series that began with *A Nightmare on Elm Street* (1984) and *Teenage Mutant Ninja Turtles* (1990). In 1991, the company formed a new division, Fine Line Features, oriented to an adult, upscale audience. New

Line and Fine Line became known for such critically acclaimed films as *An Angel at My Table* (1990), *My Own Private Idaho* (1992), *Glengarry Glen Ross* (1992), *Menace II Society* (1993), and Robert Altman's *The Player* (1992) and *Short Cuts* (1993). New Line is also involved in home video distribution and television production. One of the few independents to emerge successfully from the boom and bust of the 80s and early 90s, it became a subsidiary of Turner Broadcasting System in 1993.

Newman, Alfred. Composer, conductor, music director. *b.* Mar. 17, 1901, New Haven, Conn. *d.* 1970. One of Hollywood's most prolific, versatile, and inspired film scorers. A concert pianist at age seven, he was a conductor of symphony orchestras and Broadway musicals before going to Hollywood in 1930. He was associated with some 200 films, mostly for 20th Century-Fox, winning nine Academy Awards, indicated AA below. He was the father of screen composer David NEWMAN. Three of his brothers (he was one of nine siblings) were also associated with the industry: Robert V. Newman (1903–82) was a studio executive; Lionel NEWMAN was in charge of music at Fox and supervised and orchestrated more than 250 films, sharing an Oscar for *Hello Dolly!* (1969); and Marc Newman (*d.* 1980) was an agent. Another brother, Irving Newman, was the personal physician of many Hollywood personalities and father of singer-composer Randy NEWMAN.

FILMS INCLUDE: *Whoopee* 1930; *Arrowsmith* 1931; *The Bowery, Roman Scandals* 1933; *Nana, Moulin Rouge, Our Daily Bread, The House of Rothschild* 1934; *Cardinal Richelieu, Les Miserables, Call of the Wild, Broadway Melody of 1936, Barbary Coast* 1935; *Dodsworth, Modern Times* (mus. dir. only), *Ramona* 1936; *The Hurricane, Stella Dallas, You Only Live Once, Dead End* 1937; *Alexander's Ragtime Band* (AA) 1938; *Wuthering Heights, Young Mr. Lincoln, Drums Along the Mohawk, The Rains Came, Gunga Din* 1939; *Tin Pan Alley* (AA), *The Grapes of Wrath, Lillian Russell, Foreign Correspondent* 1940; *Man Hunt, Tobacco Road, How Green Was My Valley* 1941; *Son of Fury, The Black Swan* 1942; *The Song of Bernadette* (AA), *Claudia* 1943; *A Tree Grows in Brooklyn* 1945; *Dragonwyck, The Razor's Edge* 1946; *Mother Wore Tights* (AA), *Gentleman's Agreement* 1947; *The Yellow Sky, The Snake Pit, A Letter to Three Wives* 1948; *Pinky, Twelve O'Clock High* 1949; *The Gunfighter, All About Eve* 1950; *With a Song in My Heart* (AA) 1952; *Call Me Madam* (AA), *How to Marry a Millionaire, The Robe* 1953; *The Egyptian* 1954; *Love Is a Many Splendored Thing* (AA), *The Seven Year Itch* 1955; *The King and I* (AA), *Bus Stop* (co-comp.), *Anastasia* 1956; *A Certain Smile* 1958; *The Diary of Anne Frank* 1959; *State Fair, The Counterfeit Traitor, How the West Was Won* 1962; *The Greatest Story Ever Told* 1965; *Nevada Smith* 1966; *Camelot* (AA; adapt. only) 1967; *Firecreek* 1968; *Airport* 1970.

Newman, David. Composer, conductor. Born in 1954, in Los Angeles. *ed.* USC. The son of noted Hollywood composer Alfred NEWMAN, he scored and orchestrated many films of the late 80s and early 90s, often quirky and offbeat. In 1987 he became the music director of Robert Redford's Sundance Institute, heading a program designed to encourage young talent and to preserve and reconstruct old film music for performance by symphonic orchestras.

FILMS INCLUDE: *Critters* 1986; *Malone, The Brave Little Toaster, Throw Momma from the Train* 1987; *Heathers, Disorganized Crime, Little Monsters, Gross Anatomy, The War of the Roses* 1989; *Madhouse, Fire Birds, Duck Tales: The Movie—Treasure of the Lost Lamp, The Freshman, Mr. Destiny* 1990; *The Marrying Man, Don't Tell Mom the Babysitter's Dead, Bill & Ted's Bogus Journey* 1991; *Undercover Blues* 1993; *The Air Up There, The Flintstones, I Love Trouble* 1994; *Boys On the Side, Operation Dumbo Drop, Tommy Boy* 1995; *Jingle All the Way* 1996.

Newman, David. Screenwriter. Born on Feb. 4, 1937, in New York City. ed. U. of Michigan. A former magazine writer and an editor at *Esquire,* he formed a screenwriting team with Robert BENTON that lasted through several plays and screenplays. They wielded an enormous impact with their first film collaboration, *Bonnie and Clyde* (Academy Award nomination 1967), and went on to write several other successful scripts before parting company in the late 70s when Benton turned to directing. Newman has since collaborated (with diminishing success) with others, including his wife, cookbook author and food columnist Leslie Newman.

FILMS: *Bonnie and Clyde* 1967; *There Was a Crooked Man* 1970; *What's Up Doc?, Bad Company, Oh! Calcutta!* 1972; *Superman* 1978; *Superman II* 1980; *Jinxed, Still of the Night* (co-story only) 1982; *Superman III* 1983; *Sheena* 1984; *Santa Claus: The Movie* 1985; *The Running Man* (uncredited contribution) 1987; *Moonwalker* 1988.

Newman, Joseph M. Director. Born on Aug. 7, 1909, in Logan, Utah. He began in films at age 16 as an MGM office boy, later working his way up to script clerk, assistant director, and director of short subjects. A director of feature films since the early 40s, he sometimes managed to treat routine action themes astutely and sensibly. During WW II he turned out many Signal Corps films, serving with the rank of major.

FEATURE FILMS: *Northwest Rangers* 1942; *Diary of a Sergeant* (feature-length doc.) 1945; *Jungle Patrol* 1948; *The Great Dan Patch, Abandoned* 1949; *711 Ocean Drive* 1950; *Lucky Nick Cain/I'll Get You for This, The Guy Who Came Back, Love Nest* 1951; *Red Skies of Montana/Smoke Jumpers, Pony Soldier, The Outcasts of Poker Flat* 1952; *Dangerous Crossing* 1953; *The Human Jungle* 1954; *This Island Earth, Kiss of Fire* 1955; *Flight to Hong Kong* (also prod., co-sc.), *Death in Small Doses* 1957; *Fort Massacre* 1958; *The Gunfight at Dodge City, The Big Circus, Tarzan the Ape Man* 1959; *King of the Roaring Twenties: The Story of Arnold Rothstein, A Thunder of Drums, Twenty Plus Two, The George Raft Story* 1961.

Newman, Lionel. Composer, arranger. *b.* 1916, in Los Angeles, Calif. *d.* 1989. Music director at 20th Century-Fox who supervised and orchestrated scores for more than 250 films. After a stint as piano accompanist to Mae West, he joined the studio as a rehearsal pianist in 1943. In his 40 years there he worked on over 250 films, from musicals to *film noir* to comedy. He won an Academy Award for *Hello, Dolly!*.

FILMS INCLUDE: *Cry of the City* (mus. dir.), *Road House, Give My Regards to Broadway* (mus. dir.), *Green Grass of Wyoming* (mus. dir.), *The Street with No Name* (mus. dir.), *You Were Meant for Me* (mus. dir.) 1948; *Father Was a Fullback* (mus. dir.) 1949; *Cheaper By the Dozen* (mus. dir.), *The Jackpot, Halls of Montezuma, I'll Get By* (mus. dir.), *Where the Sidewalk Ends* (mus. dir.), *Wabash Avenue* (mus. dir.) 1950; *Follow the Sun* (mus. dir.), *Fixed Bayonets* (mus. dir.), *The Frogmen* (mus. dir.), *The Guy Who Came Back* (mus. dir.), *U.S.S. Tea Kettle, Meet Me After the Show* (mus. dir.), *I Can Get It For You Wholesale* (mus. dir.), *I'd Climb the Highest Mountain* (mus. dir.) 1951; *Don't Bother to Knock* (mus. dir.), *Diplomatic Courier* (mus. dir.), *Bloodhounds of Broadway* (mus. dir.) 1952; *The Silver Whip* (mus. dir.), *Powder River* (mus. dir.), *Pickup on South Street* (mus. dir.), *Niagara* (mus. dir., song), *Man in the Attic* (mus. dir.) *The Kid in the Attic, City of Bad Men, Gentlemen Prefer Blondes* (mus. dir.) 1953; *Three Young Texans* (mus. dir.), *The Gambler from Natchez, Garden of Evil* (song), *There's No Business Like Show Business* (mus. dir.), *Rocket*

Man, The Siege at Red River, Princess of the Nile, River of No Return (song) 1954; *The Killer is Loose, How to Be Very, Very Popular* (mus. dir) 1955; *The Girl Can't Help It* (mus. dir.), *The Proud Ones, The Last Wagon, Teenage Rebel* (song), *A Kiss Before Dying* (also song), *Love Me Tender* 1956; *Bernardine, Sing Boy Sing, The Way to the Gold, Kiss Them for Me* (also song) 1957; *The Bravados, In Love and War* (cond.), *The Gift of Love* (cond.), *The Long Hot Summer* (cond.), *In Love and War* (cond.), *Mardi Gras* (cond., mus. sup.), *Rally Round the Flag Boys!* (cond.), *A Nice Little Bank That Should Be Robbed, The Remarkable Mr. Pennypacker* (cond.), *Ten North Frederick* (cond.), *The Sound and the Fury* (cond.), *Villa!* (song), *The Young Lions* (cond.) 1958; *Compulsion, Woman Obsessed* (cond.), *Holiday for Lovers* (cond.), *Hound Dog Man* (cond.), *Journey to the Center of the Earth* (cond.), *A Private's Affair* (cond.), *Say One for Me* (mus. sup.; cond.), *Warlock* 1959, *Let's Make Love* (mus. dir.), *Flaming Star* (mus. dir.), *North to Alaska* 1960; *Cleopatra, Move Over Darling* 1963; *The Pleasure Seekers* 1964; *Do Not Disturb* 1965; *The Sand Pebbles* (cond.), *I Deal in Danger* (mus. sup.) 1966; *Doctor Dolittle, The St. Valentine's Day Massacre* (cond.) 1967; *The Boston Strangler* 1968; *Hello Dolly!* (mus. dir., adapt.) 1969; *Myra Breckinridge, The Great White Hope* 1970; *The Salzburg Connection* (mus. sup.) 1972; *The Blue Bird* 1976; *Alien* (mus. dir.), *Breaking Away* (mus. dir.) 1979; *The Final Conflict* (mus. dir.) 1981; *Cross Creek* (mus. cond.), *Unfaithfully Yours* (mus. sup.) 1983.

Newman, Nanette. Actress. Born in 1934, in Northampton, England. Attractive leading lady of British films; a performer since childhood. Married from 1954 to writer-producer-director Bryan FORBES, she is the author of cookbooks and children's stories.

FILMS INCLUDE: *Here We Come Gathering* 1945; *Personal Affair* 1953; *The League of Gentlemen* 1960; *The L-Shaped Room* 1962; *The Wrong Arm of the Law* 1963; *Of Human Bondage* (as Sally Athelney), *Seance on a Wet Afternoon* 1964; *The Wrong Box* 1966; *The Whisperers* 1967; *Deadfall* 1968; *The Madwoman of Chaillot, Captain Nemo and the Underwater City* 1969; *The Raging Tide/Long Ago Tomorrow* 1971; *The Stepford Wives* (US), *Man at the Top* 1975; *International Velvet* 1978; *Restless Natives* (cameo) 1985.

Newman, Paul. Actor, director, producer. Born on Jan. 26, 1925, in Cleveland. Enduring superstar of Hollywood films. The son of the Jewish owner of a sporting goods store and a Catholic mother of Hungarian descent, he served during WW II in the Pacific as a radioman with the Navy Air Corps, then entered Kenyon College, in Ohio, to study economics but discovered drama instead. He appeared briefly in stock, then enrolled for graduate studies at the Yale Drama School and attended New York's Actors Studio. The success of his first Broadway appearance, 'Picnic' (1953), led to a film contract with Warner Bros. and a first screen role in a weak epic, *The Silver Chalice* (1955). Despite the handicap of this nearly disastrous film debut, Newman's career picked up rapidly. He gave convincing portrayals of boxer Rocky Graziano in Robert Wise's *Somebody Up There Likes Me* (1956) and of Billy the Kid in Arthur Penn's *The Left-Handed Gun* (1958), won the Cannes Festival award as best actor for his performance in Martin Ritt's *The Long Hot Summer,* and received an Oscar nomination for *Cat on a Hot Tin Roof,* all in the same year. A winning combination of an athletic physique, classic handsome features, expressive blue eyes, an intelligent grasp of roles, and a captivating sense of humor established Newman in the 60s as a favorite star among filmgoers and critics alike. He has had the good fortune, or discriminating judgment, to appear in a high percentage of superior films. He was nominated for Academy Awards for his performances in *The Hustler* (1961), *Hud* (1963), *Cool Hand Luke* (1967), *Absence of Malice* (1981), and *The Verdict* (1982), and after many near-misses won the Oscar for *The Color of Money* (1986).

In 1968, Newman made an impressive debut as a filmmaker, directing his second wife, Joanne WOODWARD, in *Rachel, Rachel,* a drama about loneliness, an Oscar nominee for best picture. He has since taken other occasional stabs at directing and has produced a number of films, sometimes under the banner of First Artists, a production company he owns in partnership with Sidney Poitier, Barbra Streisand, and others. Newman and Miss Woodward, whom he met in 1953 and married in 1958, are among the acting profession's most visible political activists. They have campaigned for a wide range of liberal causes and for a number of political candidates. In 1978 Newman was appointed by President Jimmy Carter as a US delegate to the UN Conference on Nuclear Disarmament. The Newmans have also been deeply committed to many charities and social causes, among them the antidrug Scott Newman Foundation, which they founded following the 1978 death of Newman's son from his first marriage (to actress Jackie Witte, 1949–57). The foundation and other charities are partly financed by a line of food products Newman successfully launched in the 80s. Trim and sprightly, defying the advancing years, Newman is actively engaged in athletics and is an avid car racer.

FILMS (as actor): *The Silver Chalice* 1955; *Somebody Up There Likes Me* (as boxer Rocky Graziano), *The Rack* 1956; *The Helen Morgan Story, Until They Sail* 1957; *The Long Hot Summer, The Left-Handed Gun* (as Billy the Kid), *Cat on a Hot Tin Roof, Rally 'Round the Flag Boys!* 1958; *The Young Philadelphians* 1959; *From the Terrace, Exodus* 1960; *The Hustler, Paris Blues* 1961; *Sweet Bird of Youth, Hemingway's Adventures of a Young Man* 1962; *Hud, A New Kind of Love, The Prize* 1963; *What a Way to Go!, The Outrage* 1964; *Lady L* (US/Fr./It.) 1965; *Harper, Torn Curtain* 1966; *Hombre, Cool Hand Luke* 1967; *The Secret War of Harry Frigg, Rachel Rachel* (dir., prod. only) 1968; *Winning* (also co-exec. prod.), *Butch Cassidy and the Sundance Kid* (as Cassidy; also co-exec. prod.) 1969; *King* (doc.; co-narrator), *WUSA* (also co-prod.) 1970; *They Might Be Giants* (co-prod. only), *Sometimes a Great Notion/Never Give an Inch* (also dir., co-exec. prod.) 1971; *Pocket Money* (also co-exec. prod.), *The Effect of Gamma Rays on Man-in-the-Moon Marigolds* (dir., prod. only), *The Life and Times of Judge Roy Bean* (title role; also co-exec. prod.) 1972; *The Mackintosh Man* (UK), *The Sting* 1973; *The Towering Inferno* 1974; *The Drowning Pool* (also co-exec. prod.) 1975; *Silent Movie* (unbilled cameo), *Buffalo Bill and the Indians. . . or Sitting Bull's History Lesson* (as Buffalo Bill) 1976; *Slap Shot* 1977; *Quintet* 1979; *When Time Ran Out* 1980; *Fort Apache the Bronx, Absence of Malice* 1981; *The Verdict* 1982; *Harry and Son* (also dir., co-prod., co-story, co-sc.) 1984; *The Color of Money* 1986; *The Glass Menagerie* (dir. only) 1987; *Fat Man and Little Boy* (as Gen. Leslie R. Groves, overseer of the Manhattan Project); *Blaze* (as Governor of Louisiana Earl Long) 1989; *Mr. & Mrs. Bridge* 1990; *The Hudsucker Proxy, Nobody's Fool* 1994.

Newman, Randy. Composer. Born in Nov. 28, 1943 in Los Angeles, Calif. *ed.* UCLA. Thoughtful, wry songwriter for films since the 1970s. Nephew of composers Lionel and Alfred NEWMAN, he established himself as a thinking-person's songwriter and performer before becoming known as a film composer in the 1980s. Crested Billboard charts with anti-prejudice song *Short People.* He has been nominated eight times for an Academy Award for his memorable film scores, music, and lyrics.

FILMS INCLUDE (as composer): *Performance* (mus. dir.) 1970; *Cold Turkey, The Pursuit of Happiness* 1971; *Ragtime* 1981; *The Natural* 1984; *April Fool's Day, Three Amigos!, Huey Long* (doc., co-mus.) 1986; *Parenthood* 1989; *Avalon, Awakenings* 1990; *Maverick, The Paper* 1994; *How To Make an American Quilt, Toy Story, Unstrung Heroes* 1995; *Michael* 1996.

Newmar, Julie. Actress. Born Julia Charlene Newmeyer, on Aug. 16, 1935, in Los Angeles. Tall, voluptuous star of Broadway, TV ('The Living Doll' series, Catwoman on 'Batman'), and some Hollywood films.

FILMS: *Seven Brides for Seven Brothers* 1954; *Li'l Abner, The Rookie* 1959; *The Marriage-Go-Round* 1960; *For Love or Money* 1963; *Mackenna's Gold, The Maltese Bippy* 1969; *Up Your Teddy Bear* 1970; *Hysterical* 1983; *Evils of the Night* 1986; *Body Beat/Dance Academy* (It.) 1988; *Nudity Required* 1990; *Ghosts Can't Do It* 1991; *To Wong Foo Thanks for Everything Julie Newmar* (cameo as herself) 1995.

Newmeyer, Fred C. Director. *b.* Aug. 9, 1888, Central City, Col. *d.* 1937(?). A former professional baseball player, he entered films in 1913 as an extra with Universal. He later worked at other studios as a prop man and after several years as an assistant director began making his own films in the early 20s. He directed several of the most successful silent comedies of Harold Lloyd, often in collaboration with Sam Taylor (Newmeyer usually directed the action, Taylor the comedy gags), and later handled such stars as Richard Dix, Reginald Denny, and W. C. Fields. His career declined after the advent of sound.

FILMS: *Now or Never* (three-reeler; co-dir. with Sam Taylor), *I Do* (two-reeler; co-dir. with Taylor), *Among Those Present* (three-reeler; co-dir. with Taylor), *Never Weaken* (three-reeler; co-dir. with Taylor), *A Sailor-Made Man* 1921; *Grandma's Boy, Doctor Jack* 1922; *Safety Last* (co-dir. with Taylor), *Why Worry?* (co-dir. with Taylor) 1923; *Girl Shy* (co-dir. with Taylor), *Hot Water* (co-dir. with Taylor) 1924; *The Freshman* (co-dir. with Taylor), *Seven Keys to Baldpate, The Perfect Clown* 1925; *The Savage, The Quarterback* 1926; *The Lunatic at Large, The Potters, Too Many Crooks, On Your Toes* 1927; *That's My Daddy, Warming Up, The Night Bird* 1928; *It Can Be Done, The Rainbow Man, Sailor's Holiday* 1929; *The Grand Parade, Queen High, Fast and Loose* (with dial. dir. Bertram Harrison) 1930; *Subway Express* 1931; *Discarded Lovers, They Never Came Back, The Fighting Gentleman, The Gambling Sex* 1932; *Easy Millions* 1933; *The Big Race, The Moth* 1934; *No Ransom, Secrets of Chinatown* 1935; *General Spanky* (co-dir. with Gordon Douglas) 1936.

newsreel. A film journal of current events. The beginning of ciné-journalism coincides with the birth of cinema. The earliest films made anywhere were usually photographed records of real life. The world's very first newsreel footage was probably LUMIÈRE's *La Sortie des Usines Lumière* (shot in August 1894), which merely showed workers leaving a factory. Within months motion picture cameras everywhere were similarly capturing glimpses of life or even turning to really newsworthy events. In the summer of 1895, Lumière began dispatching agents to the four corners of the earth. Their role was dual: to show Lumière's films to audiences everywhere and to record interesting events with their cameras as they traveled. In the following years they recorded such events as the coronation of Czar Nikolai II in Moscow and the inauguration of President McKinley in the United States.

Lumière soon faced competition from Charles PATHÉ and Léon GAUMONT of France, the BIOGRAPH and VITAGRAPH companies in the US, Robert PAUL and Birt ACRES in England, and Oskar Meester in Germany, among others. Competition became so fierce that enterprising filmmakers began reconstructing or otherwise faking major events when they were not able to get actual footage. In Kiev, a Lumière cameraman, noticing the interest of the Jewish community in the Dreyfus case, spliced unrelated footage of a French military parade and anchored warships and presented it to packed houses as the trial and exile of Dreyfus. In the US, in 1897, Sigmund "Pop" LUBIN hired two husky railroad men to re-enact the Corbett-Fitzsimmons prizefight, using a newspaper blow-by-blow account as a script. The most blatant fakes were made during the Spanish-American War of 1898 when one filmmaker, Edward H. Amet, reconstructed the entire naval battle of the Bay of Santiago in a bathtub with miniature boats.

Charles Pathé began releasing a regular newsreel series in 1907 and launched a weekly newsreel in the modern format (several unrelated news stories strung together) in 1910. It was presented as Pathé-Journal in France and as Pathé Gazette in its British and American versions. In the years that followed, regular newsreels proliferated throughout the world. The newsreel came of age during WW I, when combat cinematographers captured vivid scenes of the battlegrounds in their filmed reports. In the years after the war the newsreel grew in scope and by the late 20s news-gathering facilities had been established throughout the world by Pathé, Fox Movietone, Metrotone, International Newsreel, and other companies. The advent of sound and the development of the single-system sound camera gave newsreels an additional dimension. Events could be not only seen but also heard, and dynamic offscreen narration replaced cluttered title cards. But, in general, newsreels between the World Wars were flimsy in content and often dull, consisting largely of routine footage describing official ceremonies, military parades, and the like.

Beginning in 1935 a new concept in screen journalism, combining elements of the traditional newsreel with those of the documentary, was offered by THE MARCH OF TIME and other screen-magazine-format series that followed it. The political and military events of WW II helped lift the newsreels of many nations out of their routine doldrums, but the advent of television in the years immediately following the war—in particular, the medium's ability to record current events "live," or as they happened, on its news programs—soon deprived the newsreel of its primary appeal. As a result, motion picture theaters gradually dropped newsreels from their programs and by the late 50s they had completely disappeared from American screens.

Newton, Robert. Actor. *b.* June 1, 1905, Shaftesbury, England. *d.* 1956. Imposing character star of British and some American films who stole many a scene with his thundering voice and a wild look in his rolling eyes. He was especially adept at portraying cunning villains, yet ranked among the leading box-office attractions in Britain in the late 40s and early 50s. Memorable as Bill Sikes in *Oliver Twist* (1948) and as Long John Silver in *Treasure Island* (1950) and *Long John Silver* (1955), as well as in the short-lived TV series 'Long John Silver.'

FILMS: *Reunion* 1932; *Dark Journey, Fire Over England, Farewell Again/Troopship, The Squeaker/Murder on Diamond Row, The Green Cockatoo, I Claudius* (unfinished) 1937; *Vessel of Wrath/The Beachcomber, Yellow Sands* 1938; *Dead Men Are Dangerous, Jamaica Inn, Poison Pen, Hell's Cargo* 1939; *Bulldog Sees It Through, 21 Days/21 Days Together* (release delayed from 1937), *Gaslight/Angel Street, Busman's Honeymoon/Haunted Honeymoon, Channel Incident* (short) 1940; *Major Barbara* (as Bill Walker), *Hatter's Castle* 1941; *They Flew Alone/Wings and the Woman* (as aviator Jim Mollison) 1942; *This Happy Breed, Henry V* (as Pistol) 1944; *Night Boat to Dublin* 1946; *Odd Man Out, Temptation Harbor*

1947; *Snowbound, Oliver Twist* (as Bill Sikes), *Kiss the Blood Off My Hands* (US) 1948; *Obsession/The Hidden Room* 1949; *Treasure Island* (as Long John Silver; US/UK), *Waterfront* 1950; *Soldiers Three* (US), *Tom Brown's School Days* (as Dr. Arnold) 1951; *Les Miserables* (as Javert; US), *Blackbeard the Pirate* (title role; US) 1952; *Androcles and the Lion* (US), *The Desert Rats* (US) 1953; *The High and the Mighty* (US), *The Beachcomber* 1954; *Long John Silver* (title role; Austral.) 1955; *Around the World in 80 Days* (US) 1956.

Newton-John, Olivia. Actress, singer. Born on Sept. 26, 1948, in Cambridge, England. The granddaughter of German-born British Nobel Prize laureate (1954) physicist Max Born, she moved at age five to Australia, where her Welsh-born university professor father relocated to become the headmaster of Melbourne's University College. At 15 she won a trip to England in a talent contest and soon became a phenomenally successful pop singer on the international scene, with a string of hit records and Grammy Awards. She had at least one Top 10 hit every year for over a dozen years and has come to epitomize the pop culture of the 70s. A spunky, youthful blonde beauty, she was 30 years old when she played a high school senior in the blockbuster movie version of the musical *Grease* (1978). Despite the film's success, her screen career was short-lived, although she continued recording and performing on TV. She made headlines in 1983 when she was stalked by a mass murderer and found refuge in Australia until his arrest by the FBI. Later that year she launched Koala Blue, a chain of US clothing stores featuring Australian merchandise. The stores went belly-up in the early 90s, and just as she was about to embark on a musical comeback, she was stricken with breast cancer. She fought the cancer successfully, but has yet to plunge back into her career. In 1984 she married actor Matt Lattanzi, 11 years her junior.

FILMS: *Tomorrow* (UK) 1970; *Grease* 1978; *Xanadu* 1980; *Two of a Kind* 1983; *It's My Party* 1996.

newton rings. Distorted rings, often colored, appearing on film as a result of light reflection between two smooth surfaces during filming.

New Wave. See NOUVELLE VAGUE; FRANCE.

New World Pictures. Independent production and distribution company. Founded in 1970 by low-budget film impresario Roger CORMAN and his brother Gene Corman, New World became the largest "indie" in the US, launching the careers of such directors as Peter Bogdanovich and Jonathan Kaplan and distributing such prestigious foreign films as *Cries and Whispers* (1973), *Amarcord* (1974), and *Dersu Uzala* (1978). The company was equally famed for its action-exploitation films, including *Big Bad Mama* (1974) and *Eat My Dust!* (1976). In 1983, Corman sold New World to a trio of investors, Harry E. Sloan, Lawrence E. Kuppin, and Larry A. Thompson. Despite some successes (including *Angel*, 1984), the company fared poorly and did not long survive Corman's departure.

New York Film Festival. See FILM FESTIVAL.

New Zealand. With a population of under four million, this Pacific island-chain nation southeast of Australia did not develop a viable feature-film industry until the late 1970s. That industry has remained small, sometimes producing fewer than five or ten features a year, but the quality of its output has been high. With state aid through the New Zealand Film Commission (founded in 1978), a number of directors have gained international reputations. In 1981, their efforts were further supported by the building of the National Film Unit, a $10 million film production complex near Wellington.

Roger DONALDSON was the first New Zealand director to gain international acclaim with *Sleeping Dogs* (1977), a politically charged thriller that became the first New Zealand film to open in the US. His subsequent work included the domestic box-office hit *Smash Palace* (1981). Geoff MURPHY, a former rock band member who built the country's first film crane, became known internationally with *Wildman* (1976), the comedy-adventure *Goodbye Pork Pie* (1980), and the colonial epic *Utu* (1983), the first New Zealand feature chosen for the main competition at Cannes. Vincent Ward crafted the medieval time-travel fantasy *The Navigator* (1988), while Sam Pillsbury (*The Scarecrow*, 1981) and Peter Jackson (*Braindead*, 1991) directed unusual horror tales. Working mainly in Australia, New Zealand-born director Jane CAMPION gained acclaim for such films as an *An Angel at My Table* (1990) and *The Piano*, which won the Palme d'Or at Cannes in 1993. Other New Zealand directors of note include John Laing, Derek Morton, Alison Maclean, and Ian Mune. Sam NEILL, an Irish-born actor raised in New Zealand, has become an international film star.

In the late 80s and early 90s, the nascent New Zealand film industry was battered by the pressures of a recessionary economy and international competition. However, the industry survived, and New Zealand cinema-goers welcomed the country's first multiplex, the Downtown 6 in Palmerston North, in 1991.

Ney, Richard. Actor. Born in 1918, in New York City. Leading man and supporting player of sporadic films since the early 40s, at one time (1943–47) married to Greer GARSON, whose son he had played in *Mrs. Miniver* (1942). Now a financier and business consultant, he is the author of the best-selling books *The Wall Street Jungle, The Wall Street Gang,* and *Making It in the Market.*

FILMS INCLUDE: *Mrs. Miniver, The War Against Mrs. Hadley* 1942; *The Late George Apley* (as John Apley), *Ivy* 1947; *Joan of Arc* (as Charles de Bourbon) 1948; *The Fan, The Lovable Cheat, The Secret of St. Ives* 1949; *Miss Italia/Miss Italy* (It.) 1950; *Babes in Bagdad* 1952; *Midnight Lace* 1960; *The Premature Burial* 1962.

n.g. "No good," usually in reference to a bad take that can't be used and therefore must be re-shot.

Ngor, Haing S. Actor. *b.* 1950 in Cambodia. *d.* 1996. Trained as a doctor in Cambodia, he was captured and tortured for years by the Khmer Rouge following their takeover of the country. He escaped to Thailand and finally settled in the US, where he worked various jobs and came to be cast in *The Killing Fields*. He won an Academy Award for his performance and remained somewhat active in film as well as TV until his sudden death in 1996. His autobiography is *A Cambodian Odyssey*.

FILMS INCLUDE: *The Killing Fields* 1984; *The Iron Triangle* 1989; *Ambition* 1991; *Heaven and Earth, My Life* 1993.

Niblo, Fred. Director, actor. *b.* Federico Nobile, Jan. 6, 1874, York, Nebr. *d.* 1948. He began as a vaudeville entertainer, touring with George M. Cohan's troupe and later appearing in Cohan's Broadway shows. His first wife, Josephine, was Cohan's sister. Their son, Fred Niblo, Jr. (*b.* Jan. 23, 1903, N.Y.C.; *d.* 1973), was a screenwriter of Hollywood action films. An experienced stage producer-director, Fred Sr. joined the INCE outfit in Hollywood in 1917 and, after appearing in a couple of productions as an actor, directed a dozen films starring his second wife, Enid BENNETT. He gained stature in the 20s as the director of Douglas Fairbanks and Rudolph Valentino costume spectacles like *The Mark of Zorro, The Three Musketeers,* and *Blood and Sand,* and was assigned the formidable task of directing the monumental production of the silent *Ben-Hur.* Later in the decade he was entrusted with Garbo and Talmadge vehicles, but his career faded after sound. After trying unsuccessfully to make a comeback as a director in England, he appeared as an actor in several Hollywood talkies, including *Free and Easy* (1930), *Ellery Queen—Master Detective* (1940), and *Life with Henry* (1941). He co-wrote the screenplay for *Four Jills in a Jeep* (1944).

FILMS (as director): *The Marriage Ring, When Do We Eat?, Fuss and Feathers* 1918; *Happy Though Married, The Haunted Bedroom, The Law of Men, Partners Three, The Virtuous Thief, Stepping Out, What Every Woman Learns* 1919; *The Woman in the Suitcase, Dangerous Hours, Sex, The False Road, Hairpins, Her Husband's Friend, The Mark of Zorro, Silk Hosiery* 1920; *Mother o' Mine, Greater Than Love, The Three Musketeers* 1921; *The Woman He Married, Rose o' the Sea, Blood and Sand* 1922; *The Famous Mrs. Fair, Strangers of the Night* (also co-prod.) 1923; *Thy Name Is Woman, The Red Lily* (also story) 1924; *Ben-Hur, The Temptress* 1926; *Camille* (also prod.), *The Devil Dancer* (also prod.) 1927; *The Enemy* (also prod.), *Two Lovers* (also prod.), *The Mysterious Lady, Dream of Love* 1928; *Redemption* (also prod.), *Way Out West* 1930; *Donovan's Kid, The Big Gamble* 1931; *Two White Arms* (UK), *Diamond Cut Diamond* (co-dir. with Maurice Elvey; UK), *Blame the Woman* 1932.

Nicaud, Philippe. Actor. Born on June 27, 1926, in Paris. Romantic lead, then supporting player, of the French stage, films, and TV.

FILMS INCLUDE: *Les Amoureux sont seuls au Monde/Monelle* 1948; *Aux Yeux du Souvenir/Souvenir* 1949; *Maya, Meurtres/Three Sinners, Miquette et sa Mère/Miquette, Ballerina/Dream Ballerina* 1950; *Les Amants de Bras-Mort* 1951; *Fantasie d'un Jour, La Môme Pigalle/The Maiden* 1955; *Miss Catastrophe* 1956; *Le Dos au Mur/Back to the Wall, En Légitime Défense, La Prima Notte/Noces vénitiennes* (It./Fr.) 1958; *Voulez-vous danser avec moi?/Come Dance with Me!* 1959; *Le Gigolo* 1960; *L'Inconnue de Hong Kong, Que personne ne sorte* 1963; *Il Magnifico Cornuto/The Magnificent Cuckold* (It./Fr.) 1964; *La Dame dans l'Auto avec des Lunettes et un Fusil/The Lady in the Car with Glasses and a Gun* (Fr./US) 1970; *L'Ile mysterieuse/The Mysterious Island of Captain Nemo* 1973; *Comme une Femme/Self-Made Woman* 1980; *Chanel Solitaire* 1981; *Le Corbillard de Jules* 1982; *La Cage aux Folles III ("Elles" se marient)/La Cage aux Folles 3: The Wedding* (co-sc. only) 1985; *Johann Strauss—Der König ohne Krone* (as composer Jacques Offenbach; Aus./Ger./Fr.) 1986.

Nicholas, Fayard. Born in 1917. **Nicholas, Harold.** Born in 1924. Energetic, distinctive American dancers of the 1930s and 1940s, who performed together as the Nicholas Brothers. Born to a show business family whose band performed in black vaudeville clubs, the self-taught dancers made their debut in 1931 on "The Horn and Hardart Kiddie Hour." A multi-year stint at New York's Cotton Club followed, as well as appearances in Broadway musicals, including 'Babes in Arms.' They entered films in 1932 and by the 1940s were renowned for their jumps, back flips, and splits, most notably in *Stormy Weather*. In the 1960s, they appeared on TV; in the 1980s, Harold appeared on Broadway in 'The Tap Dance Kid' and 'Sophisticated Ladies.' Harold is divorced from actress Dorothy DANDRIDGE.

FILMS INCLUDE: *Pie Pie Blackbird* 1932; *Stoopnocracy* (Harold only) 1933; *Kid Millions* 1934; *Black Network: An All Colored Vaudeville Show, The Big Broadcast of 1936* 1936; *Calling All Stars* 1937; *Tin Pan Alley, The Great American Broadcast, Down Argentine Way* 1941; *Sun Valley Serenade* 1942; *Orchestra Wives, Stormy Weather* 1943; *Take It Or Leave It, Carolina Blues* (Harold only) 1944; *The Pirate* 1948; *The Liberation of L. B. Jones* (Harold only) 1970; *That's Entertainment, Uptown Saturday Night* (Harold only) 1974; *That's Dancing* 1985; *Tap* (Harold only) 1989.

Nichols, Barbara. Actress. *b.* Barbara Nickerauer, Dec. 30, 1929, Jamaica, Queens, N.Y. *d.* 1976. A former stripper, chorus girl, and model, she appeared onstage and in TV before making her film debut in the mid-50s. She typically played or caricatured blonde broads, floozies, and gun molls, often with humor and a touch of pathos. She died of a liver disease at 47.

FILMS: *River of No Return* 1954; *Manfish, Miracle in the Rain, Beyond a Reasonable Doubt, The King and Four Queens, The Wild Party* 1956; *Sweet Smell of Success, The Pajama Game, Pal Joey* 1957; *Ten North Frederick, The Naked and the Dead* 1958; *Woman Obsessed, That Kind of Woman* 1959; *Who Was That Lady?, Where the Boys Are* 1960; *The George Raft Story* 1961; *House of Women, The Scarface Mob* 1962; *Looking for Love, The Disorderly Orderly* 1964; *Dear Heart, The Human Duplicators, The Loved One* 1965; *The Swinger* 1966; *The Power* 1968; *Charley and the Angel* 1973; *Won Ton Ton—The Dog Who Saved Hollywood* 1975.

Nichols, Dudley. Screenwriter, director. *b.* Apr. 6, 1895, Wapakoneta, Ohio. *d.* 1960. One of Hollywood's most highly regarded screenwriters of the 30s and 40s, particularly for his collaborations with director John FORD. A former New York *World* reporter, he settled in Hollywood in 1929 and collaborated with such directors as Hawks, Renoir, Clair, Cukor, and Fritz Lang. He also directed three intelligent films in which the emphasis was on the spoken word rather than the moving image. He won an Academy Award for the screenplay of *The Informer* (1935) and received Oscar nominations for *The Long Voyage Home* (1940), *Air Force* (1943), and *The Tin Star* (1957).

FILMS INCLUDE: As screenwriter—*Men Without Women, Born Reckless, A Devil with Women* 1930; *Seas Beneath, Hush Money, Skyline* 1931; *This Sporting Age* 1932; *Pilgrimage* (dial. only), *Robbers' Roost* 1933; *Hold That Girl, The Lost Patrol, Judge Priest* 1934; *The Informer, The Arizonian, The Crusades, Steamboat Round the Bend, The Three Musketeers* 1935; *Mary of Scotland* 1936; *The Plough and the Stars, The Toast of New York, The Hurricane* 1937; *Carefree* (co-story), *Bringing Up Baby* 1938; *The 400 Million* (doc.), *Stagecoach* 1939; *The Long Voyage Home* 1940; *Man Hunt, Swamp Water* 1941; *This Land Is Mine* (also co-prod.), *Air Force, For Whom the Bell Tolls, Government Girl* (also dir., prod.) 1943; *It Happened Tomorrow* 1944; *And Then There Were None, The Bells of St. Mary's, Scarlet Street* 1945; *Sister Kenny* (also dir., prod.) 1946; *Mourning Becomes Electra* (also dir., co-prod.), *The Fugitive* 1947; *Pinky* 1949; *Rawhide* 1951; *The Big Sky* 1952; *Prince Valiant* 1954; *Run for the Sun* 1956; *The Tin Star* 1957; *The Hangman* 1959; *Heller in Pink Tights* 1960; *Stagecoach* (based on his 1939 script) 1966.

Nichols, Leo. See MORRICONE, Ennio.

Nichols, Mike. Director. Born Michael Igor Peschkowsky, on Nov. 6, 1931, in Berlin. He arrived in the US with his family at age seven as an emigré from Nazi Germany. When he was 12 his doctor-father, a Russian-born Jew, died, leaving the family financially hard pressed. However, a bright student and aggressive, Nichols was able to continue his education thanks to a succession of scholarships and a variety of odd jobs. While at the University of Chicago, he made his living as a night janitor, post office clerk, hotel desk clerk, and delivery truck driver, among other things. It was at the university that he first felt the urge to perform. He went to New York and studied acting with Lee Strasberg but was unable to land any roles. Returning to Chicago, he joined with Elaine MAY, Alan ARKIN, Barbara HARRIS, and Paul Sills to form an improvisational group that performed at the Compass, a restaurant-cabaret.

Nichols and May then took to the road and by 1957 were nationally acclaimed for the spontaneity and wit of their improvised social satire. They scored a tremendous success on Broadway in 1960 with 'An Evening with Mike Nichols and Elaine May,' then broke up in 1961 after the show closed. The following year Nichols played the lead in a May play that closed after several performances in Philadelphia. In 1963 he made his debut as a Broadway director, scoring a hit with 'Barefoot in the Park.' He has since been known as a man with the Midas touch. Every play he subsequently directed ('Luv,' 'The Odd Couple,' etc.) was a critical and popular smash.

In the mid-60s, Nichols began directing films with equal success, applying the same formula that characterized his work onstage—crisp timing, an eye for detail, and a special knack for working with actors. He made the most of his first opportunity, creating a crackling screen version of Edward Albee's play *Who's Afraid of Virginia Woolf?* (1966), with Richard BURTON and Elizabeth TAYLOR in top form, supplying a barrage of foul-mouthed fireworks. The film broke many taboos of the Hollywood morality code and was a big financial as well as critical success. It was nominated for best picture, best director, and all four acting Oscars, earning the Academy Awards for best actress (Taylor), best supporting actress (Sandy DENNIS), cinematography, art direction, and costumes. Nichols won the best director award for his next film, *The Graduate* (1967), a landmark production that catapulted Dustin HOFFMAN to instant stardom and has endured as a symbol of youthful alienation and a desire for change.

Nichols's subsequent films were of lesser magnitude, with two or three even considered outright failures, but all were marked by intelligence, wit, and professional proficiency, though lacking a personal style. He went on to garner two more best director Academy Award nominations, for *Silkwood* (1983), a strong drama of nuclear radiation perils in the workplace, and *Working Girl* (1988), a cute comedy of an ambitious secretary's improbable rise to the top of the corporate ladder. Nichols, who never lived in Hollywood and kept his residence in New York, continued all along to direct for the stage and won a sixth Tony Award in 1984 for 'The Real Thing.' In 1988 he married TV news personality Diane Sawyer, his fourth wife.

FILMS: *Who's Afraid of Virginia Woolf?* 1966; *The Graduate* 1967; *Catch-22* 1970; *Carnal Knowledge* (also prod.) 1971; *The Day of the Dolphin* 1973; *The Fortune* (also co-prod.) 1975; *Gilda Live* (filmed Gilda Radner stage performance) 1980; *Silkwood* (also co-prod.) 1983; *The Longshot* (exec. prod. only), *Heartburn* (also co-prod.) 1986; *Biloxi Blues, Working Girl* 1988; *Postcards from the Edge* (also co-prod.) 1990; *Regarding Henry* (also co-prod.) 1991; *The Remains of the Day* (co-prod. only) 1993; *Wolf* 1994; *The Birdcage* 1996; *The Designated Mourner* (act. only) 1997.

Nicholson, Jack. Actor, director, screenwriter. Born on Apr. 22, 1937, in Neptune, N.J. A veteran of numerous Hollywood B pictures whose versatile talent was finally recognized in the 70s after many years of relative anonymity. Raised by his mother, the owner of a beauty parlor, after his father, an alcoholic, deserted the family, he chanced on films at the age of 17 during a trip to California to visit a sister. He started out as an office boy at MGM's cartoon department and after training as an actor with a group called the Players Ring Theater began performing on the stage and in TV soap operas. He made his first film appearance in 1958, playing the lead in a Roger Corman cheapie, *The Cry Baby Killer,* and subsequently appeared in other quickie horror, motorcycle, and action films by Corman and other directors operating on the fringes of the industry's mainstream. Collaborating with another Corman protégé, Monte Hellman, he soon began producing and writing some of these films. For reasons of economy, several of their films were made in the Philippines. After years of frustration and disappointments, Nicholson got his big break when he was called in to replace Rip Torn in *Easy Rider* (1969). He made the most of the small role of a dropout lawyer and for his effort received the first of several Oscar nominations.

In the ensuing years, Nicholson emerged as one of the American screen's most intriguing personalities, a multifaceted, versatile performer, capable not only of interpreting a wide range of roles but also of changing his appearance from film to film. He turned in an exceptional, complex performance in Bob Rafelson's *Five Easy Pieces* (Oscar nomination, 1970), then went on to display his enigmatic personality and uncommon acting skill in such disparate films as Mike Nichols's *Carnal Knowledge* (1971), Hal Ashby's *The Last Detail* (Oscar nomination, 1973), Roman Polanski's *Chinatown* (Oscar nomination, 1974), and Michelangelo Antonioni's *The Passenger* (1975). The one common link among most of his roles has been the characterization of the eternal outsider, the sardonic drifter who bucks the system. After two successive also-ran positions in the Academy Awards race, he won the best actor Oscar for his performance in Milos Forman's *One Flew Over the Cuckoo's Nest* (1975), in which he once again played an outsider, a free-spirited individualist whose arrival at a hospital's mental ward catalyzes the patients' lives.

Nicholson went on to register memorable performances in many other films, gaining additional best actor Academy Award nominations for *Reds* (1981), *Prizzi's Honor* (1985), and *Ironweed* (1987), a best supporting actor nomination for *A Few Good Men* (1992), and a best supporting actor award for *Terms of Endearment* (1983). Equally outstanding recent roles that went unrewarded included those of a delightfully lecherous devil in *The Witches of Eastwick* (1987) and a demented Joker in *Batman* (1989).

Nicholson directed several films, starting in 1971, with modest distinction. In 1990 he directed and acted in *The Two Jakes,* a long-delayed and badly received sequel to Roman Polanski's *Chinatown.* The actor-director, whose only marriage (1962–67), to actress Sandra Knight, came early in his career, was for many years the steady companion of actress Anjelica HUSTON. He is the father of two children.

FILMS (as actor): *The Cry Baby Killer* 1958; *Too Soon to Love, The Wild Ride, Studs Lonigan* 1960; *The Little Shop of Horrors* 1961; *The Broken Land* 1962; *The Raven, The Terror* (also dir. some scenes, uncredited), *Thunder Island* (co-story, co-sc. only) 1963; *Ensign Pulver, Back Door to Hell* 1964; *The Shooting* (also co-prod.), *Ride the Whirlwind* (also story, sc., co-prod.), *Flight to Fury* (also sc.) 1966; *The St. Valentine's Day Massacre* (bit), *Hell's Angels on Wheels, The Trip* (story, sc. only) 1967; *Psych-Out, Head* (co-story, co-sc., co-prod. only) 1968; *Easy Rider* 1969; *Rebel Rousers* (filmed in 1967), *On a Clear Day You Can See Forever, Five Easy Pieces* 1970; *Drive He Said* (dir., co-sc., co-prod. only), *Carnal Knowledge, A Safe Place* 1971; *The King of Marvin Gardens* 1972; *The Last Detail* 1973; *Chinatown* 1974; *Tommy* (UK), *Professione: Reporter/The Passenger* (It.), *The Fortune, One Flew Over the Cuckoo's Nest* 1975; *The Missouri Breaks, The Last Tycoon* 1976; *Goin' South* (also dir.) 1978; *The Shining* 1980; *The Postman Always Rings Twice, Reds* (as Eugene O'Neill) 1981; *The Border* 1982; *Terms of Endearment* 1983; *Prizzi's Honor* 1985; *Heartburn* 1986; *The Witches of Eastwick, Broadcast News* (cameo), *Ironweed* 1987; *Batman* 1989; *The Two Jakes* (also dir.) 1990; *Man Trouble, A Few Good Men, Hoffa* 1992; *Wolf* 1994; *The Crossing Guard* 1995; *The Evening Star, Mars Attacks!* 1996; *Blood and Wine* 1997.

nickelodeon. A makeshift motion picture theater, often a converted store, which proliferated all over the US during the first decade of the century. Nickelodeons were so called because they charged a nickel (five cents) for admission. They were particularly popular in working-class areas of the major cities. Several of Hollywood's biggest moguls began as operators of highly profitable nickelodeons.

Nicol, Alex. Actor, sometime director. Born on Jan. 20, 1919, in Ossining, N.Y. Trained at the Fagin School of Dramatic Arts and the Actors Studio, he made his stage debut in 1938 and his first screen appearance in 1950. He has played leads as well as supporting roles in numerous Hollywood films and some European co-productions, mainly of the action variety. He has also directed several low-budget films and TV dramas.

FILMS INCLUDE (as actor): *The Sleeping City* 1950; *Tomahawk, Target Unknown, Air Cadet* 1951; *Meet Danny Wilson, Red Ball Express, Because of You* 1952; *The Redhead from Wyoming, Lone Hand, Champ for a Day* 1953; *About Mrs. Leslie, Dawn at Socorro* 1954; *Strategic Air Command, The Man from Laramie, Sincerely Yours* 1955; *Great Day in the Morning* 1956; *The Screaming Skull* (also dir.) 1958; *Jovanka e le Altre/Five Branded Women* (It./Yug.), *Via Margutta/Run with the Devil* (It./Fr.), *Tutti a Casa/Everybody Go Home!* (It./Fr.), *Sotto Dieci Bandiere/Under Ten Flags* (It./US); *Look in Any Window, Then There Were Three* (also dir., prod.), *A Matter of Who* (UK) 1961; *Tierra Brutal/The Savage Guns* (Sp./US) 1962; *Los Pistoleros de Casa Grande/Gunfighters of Casa Grande* (Sp./US) 1964; *Bloody Mama, Homer* 1970; *Point of Terror* (dir. only) 1973; *Woman in the Rain, A*P*E** 1976.

Nielsen, Asta. Actress. *b.* Sept. 11, 1883, Copenhagen. *d.* 1972. Legendary superstar of the European silent cinema. The daughter of a washerwoman, she attended the children's school of Copenhagen's Royal Theater, making her stage debut at 18. She was an established stage personality by the time she began appearing in Danish films in 1910 as a discovery of director August BLOM. Her career was guided from the start by director Urban GAD, who became her husband and directed some 30 of her films through WW I, when they divorced. In 1911 they both went to Germany, where Nielsen soon became a leading star. She was considered one of the most enchanting women of her day, a pallid beauty with blazing dark eyes, and was widely admired as a trendsetter in fashions. Her acting style was remarkably restrained in comparison with that of other screen personalities of the period and she attempted a wide range of roles, including the title (!) role in a 1920 production of *Hamlet* which she herself produced, with Sven(d) Gade as the director. She was at her grandest as a tragic heroine and her dozens of German films included such classic roles as Strindberg's *Fräulein Julie/Miss Julie* (1922) and Ibsen's *Hedda Gabler* (1924). One of her last roles was a character part as a murderess in G. W. Pabst's *Die freudlose Gasse/Street of Sorrow* (1925), a film starring Greta Garbo and in which Marlene Dietrich appeared as an unbilled extra. The end of Nielsen's film career coincided with the advent of sound. For several years she pursued a stage career in Germany, returning to the screen once in 1932 for her only sound film appearance. The following year, when Hitler came to power, she returned to Denmark, although Goebbels reportedly offered her a film studio of her own. She retired from acting at the outbreak of WW II and later received a life pension from the Danish government. In 1970, two years before her death at 89, she married for the fifth time, a Copenhagen art dealer 18 years her junior. She wrote a book of memoirs, *Die Tiende Muse* (*The Silent Muse,* 1945).

FILMS INCLUDE: In Denmark—*Afgrunden/The Abyss, Ved Faenslets Port* 1910; *Livets Störme, Belletdanserinden, Den Sorte Dröm* 1911. In Germany—*Der fremde Vogel, Der schwarze Traum, Die Sünden der Väter* 1911; *Zigeunerblut, Die arme Jenny, Das Mädchen ohne Vaterland, Der Totentanz* 1912; *Engelein, Die Filmprimadonna, Die Suffragetten, Der Tod in Sevilla* 1913; *Elena Fontana, Die ewige Nacht, Das Feuer, Die Tochter der Landstrasse, Weisse Rosen, Zapatas Bande* 1914; *Das Liebes-ABC* 1916; *Das Eskimo-Baby, Die Rose der Wildnis* 1917; *Der Fackelträger* 1918; *Das Ende vom Lied, Rausch/ Intoxication* 1919; *Der Idiot/The Idiot, Der Reigen, Hamlet* (title role; also prod.), *Die Spielerin* 1920; *Die geliebte Roswolskys, Irrende Seelen, Die Spionin* (as Mata Hari) 1921; *Die Buchse der Pandora/Pandora's Box, Fräulein Julie/Miss Julie, Vanina Vanini/Vanina* 1922; *Erdgeist, I.N.R.I./Crown of Thorns* 1923; *Die Frau im Feuer, Hedda Gabler, Lebende Buddhas* 1924; *Die freudlose Gasse/Street of Sorrow/The Joyless Street, Atheleten, Die Gesunkenen/The Sunken* 1925; *Dirnentragödie/Tragedy of the Street/Women Without Men, Gehetze Frauen, Kleinstadtsünden/ Small Town Sinners, Laster der Menschheit* 1927; *Unmögliche Liebe* 1932.

Nielsen, Leslie. Actor. Born on Feb. 11, 1922, in Regina, Sask., Canada. Tall, rugged leading man, then character player of American films and television. A Mountie's son, he served with the Royal Canadian Air Force during WW II before starting a career as a radio announcer and disc jockey. On a scholarship to New York's Neighborhood Playhouse, he studied acting with Sanford Meisner and dance with Martha Graham, then performed onstage and in early TV before making his film debut in the mid-50s. He played a wide mixture of leads and supporting roles, some blandly pleasant, some sneaky or menacing, but had his best success late in his career when he found his niche in broad comedy in such films as *Airplane!* and *Naked Gun.* His numerous TV appearances included starring roles in such series as 'The New Breed' (1961–62) 'Peyton Place' (1965), 'The Protectors' (1969–70), 'Bracken's World,' 'Police Squad' (1982), 'Shaping Up' (1984), as well as many TV movies.

FILMS INCLUDE: *Ransom, Forbidden Planet, The Vagabond King, The Opposite Sex* 1956; *Hot Summer Night, Tammy and the Bachelor* 1957; *The Sheepman* 1958; *Night Train to Paris* (UK), *Harlow* (Carroll Baker version), *Dark Intruder* 1965; *Beau Geste, The Plainsman* (as Custer) 1966; *The Reluctant Astronaut, Gunfight in Abilene, Rosie* 1967; *Counterpoint, Dayton's Devils* 1968; *How to Commit Marriage, Change of Mind* 1969; *The Resurrection of Zachary Wheeler* 1971; *The Poseidon Adventure* 1972; *Project: Kill* 1976; *Amsterdam Kill* (Hong Kong), *Viva Knievel, Day of the Animals* 1977; *City on Fire* (Can.) 1979; *Airplane!, Prom Night* 1980; *The Creature Wasn't Nice* 1981; *Wrong Is Right, Creepshow* 1982; *The Patriot, Soul Man* 1986; *Nightstick, Nuts, Home Is Where the Heart Is* 1987; *The Naked Gun: From the Files of Police Squad* 1988; *Repossessed* 1990; *The Naked Gun 2½: The Smell of Fear* 1991; *All I Want for Christmas* 1992; *The Naked Gun 33⅓: The Final Insult* (also co-exec. prod.) 1994; *Dracula: Dead and Loving It* 1995; *Spy Hard* 1996.

Niépce, Joseph-Nicéphore. Inventor. *b.* Mar. 7, 1765, Chalon-sur-Saône, France. *d.* 1833. An amateur scientist, he is credited with the invention of photography in a camera, rather than by cruder means of exposing chemicals to light. As early as 1816 he photographed images with a camera equipped with a lens. After his death his inventions were perfected and exploited commercially by his partner Louis DAGUERRE; his cousin, Abel Niépce de Saint-Victor; and his son, Isidore Niépce.

Nigh, Jane. Actress. Born Bonnie Lenora Nigh, on Feb. 25, 1926, in Hollywood, Calif. Wholesome leading lady of Hollywood B pictures of the late 40s and early 50s. A former defense plant worker, she also played supporting parts in several major productions. She co-starred in the TV series 'Big Town' (1952–53).

FILMS INCLUDE: *Something for the Boys, Laura* 1944; *State Fair* 1945; *Dragonwyck* 1946; *Unconquered* 1947; *Sitting Pretty, Give My Regards to Broadway, Cry of the City* 1948; *Red Hot and Blue, Fighting Man of the Plains* 1949; *Blue Grass of Kentucky, Captain Carey U.S.A., Border Treasure, Rio Grande Patrol* 1950; *Blue Blood, Disc Jockey* 1951; *Fort Osage, Rodeo* 1952; *Hold That Hypnotist* 1957.

Nigh, William. Director. *b.* Oct. 12, 1881, Berlin, Wis. *d.* 1955. In films from 1911, initially as an actor, he began his directing career with Mack SENNETT comedy shorts, then ventured into features in 1915. He appeared in many of his early films, often in the lead. During a career spanning three and a half decades, he directed numerous films, both silents and talkies, in a wide variety of genres, ranging from romantic comedies and melodramas to mysteries and action pictures. He was quite highly regarded during the silent era, but most of his sound films were in the low-budget category.

FILMS INCLUDE: *Salomy Jane* (credit disputed; also act.) 1914; *Mignon, A Royal Family* (also act.), *Emmy of Stork's Nest, A Yellow Streak* (also sc.) 1915; *Her Debt of Honor* (also sc., act.), *The Kiss of Hate, His Great Triumph/Notorious Gallagher* (also sc., act.), *The Child of Destiny* (also co-sc.), *Life's Shadows* (also sc., act.) 1916; *The Blue Streak* (also sc., act.), *The Slave* (also sc.), *Wife Number Two* (also sc.), *Thou Shalt Not Steal* 1917; *My Four Years in Germany* (also edit., act.) 1918; *The Fighting Roosevelts, Beware* (also act.) 1919; *Democracy* (also act.) 1920; *Skinning Skinners, Why Girls Leave Home* (also sc.), *School Days* (also sc.), *The Soul of Man* 1921; *Notoriety* (also sc.), *Your Best Friend* (also sc.) 1922; *Marriage Morals* (also sc.) 1923; *Born Rich* (also sc.) 1924; *Fear-Bound* (also sc.) 1925; *Casey of the Coast Guard* (serial), *The Little Giant* (also adapt.), *The Fire Brigade* 1926; *Mr. Wu, The Nest* 1927; *Across to Singapore, Four Walls, The Law of the Range* 1928; *Desert Nights, Thunder* 1929; *Fighting Through, Lord Byron of Broadway, Today* 1930; *The Single Sin, The Sea Ghost* (also sc.) 1931; *The Night Rider* 1932; *The House of Mystery, Mystery Liner, Monte Carlo Nights* 1934; *The Mysterious Mr. Wong, Dizzy Dames, She Gets Her Man, His Night Out* 1935; *Don't Get Personal, Crash Donovan, North of Nome* 1936; *The 13th Man, Atlantic Flight, The Hoosier Schoolboy* 1937; *Boy of the Streets, Female Fugitive, Rose of the Rio Grande, I Am a Criminal, Gangster's Boy, Mr. Wong—Detective* 1938; *Streets of New York, Mr. Wong in Chinatown, Mutiny in the Big House* 1939; *The Fatal Hour, Doomed to Die, The Ape, The Underdog* 1940; *Secret Evidence, The Kid from Kansas, No Greater Sin, Mob Town* 1941; *Mr. Wise Guy, The Strange Case of Dr. Rx, The Lady from Chunking, City of Silent Men, Black Dragons* 1942; *The Ghost and the Guest, Corregidor* 1943; *Where Are Your Children?, Are These Our Parents?, Trocadero* 1944; *Allotment Wives, Divorce* 1945; *Partners in Time, Beauty and the Bandit, The Gay Cavalier* 1946; *Stage Struck* 1948.

night effect. See DAY-FOR-NIGHT CINEMATOGRAPHY.

Nilsson, Anna Q. Actress. *b.* Anna Querentia Nilsson, Mar. 30, 1890, Ystad, Sweden. *d.* 1974. The first notable Hollywood import from Sweden, she entered American films in 1911, following some experience as a model. She starred in scores of silent films for Kalem and later other studios before a riding accident and the advent of the talkies combined to end her career abruptly in the late 20s. Later she returned to the screen occasionally in character roles or cameos. She appeared briefly as herself in *Sunset Boulevard* (1950). Nilsson was married for a few months in 1916 to screen actor Guy Coombs. Her only other marriage (1923–25) was to a shoe manufacturer.

FILMS INCLUDE: *Molly Pitcher* 1911, *War's Havoc, Under a Flag of Truce, The Siege of Petersburg, The Soldier Brothers of Suzanna* 1912; *The Battle of Bloody Ford, Prisoners of War, Shenandoah, The Breath of Scandal, Uncle Tom's Cabin, Retribution* 1913; *The Ex-Convict, The Man in the Vault, Wolfe—Or the Conquest of Quebec* 1914; *The Haunting Fear, Regeneration, Barbara Fritchie* 1915; *The Scarlet Road, Who's Guilty?* (series), *The Supreme Sacrifice* 1916; *Infidelity, The Moral Code, The Inevitable, Seven Keys to Baldpate, Over There* 1917; *The Trail to Yesterday, The Heart of the Sunset, No Man's Land, In Judgment Of, The Vanity Pool* 1918; *Auction of Souls, Cheating Cheaters, Venus in the East, Soldiers of Fortune, The Love Burglar, Her Kingdom of Dreams* 1919; *The Luck of the Irish, The Thirteenth Commandment, The Toll Gate, One Hour Before Dawn, The Fighting Chance, In the Heart of a Fool, The Brute Master* 1920; *Without Limit, The Oath, The Lotus Eater, What Women Will Do, Why Girls Leave Home* 1921; *Three Live Ghosts, The Man from Home, Pink Gods* 1922; *The Rustle of Silk, The Isle of Lost Ships, Hearts Aflame, Adam's Rib, The Spoilers, Ponjola, Innocence* 1923; *Painted People, Flowing Gold, Between Friends, Broadway After Dark, The Side Show of Life, Vanity's Price, Inez from Hollywood* 1924; *If I Marry Again, The Top of the World, The Talker, The Splendid Road, One Way Street, Winds of Chance* 1925; *The Greater Glory, Midnight Lovers, Miss Nobody, Too Much Money, Her Second Chance* 1926; *Easy Pickings, Lonesome Ladies, Babe Comes Home* (opposite Babe Ruth), *The Masked Woman, Sorrell and Son, The Thirteenth Juror* 1927; *Blockade, The Whip* 1928; *The World Changes* 1933; *The Little Minister* 1934; *School for Girls* 1935; *Paradise for Three* 1938; *The Trial of Mary Dugan* 1941; *They Died with Their Boots On, Crossroads, The Great Man's Lady* 1942; *Cry Havoc* 1943; *The Valley of Decision* 1945; *The Secret Heart* 1946; *The Farmer's Daughter, Cynthia, It Had to Be You* 1947; *Fighting Father Dunne, The Boy with Green Hair* 1948; *In the Good Old Summertime, Adam's Rib* 1949; *Malaya, The Big Hangover, Sunset Boulevard* 1950; *Show Boat, The Law and the Lady, An American in Paris* 1951; *Seven Brides for Seven Brothers* 1954.

Nilsson, Leopoldo Torre. See TORRE NILSSON, Leopoldo.

Nilsson, Rob. Director, screenwriter. Born in 1939, in the US, of Norwegian descent. After graduating from Harvard as an English major, he joined the Peace Corps, wrote poetry, and painted before turning to filmmaking in the mid-70s. Operating within a left-wing filmmakers' collective, he directed three documentaries about farmers, out of which grew his first feature film, the remarkable *Northern Lights* (co-directed with John Hanson, 1979). A stunning recreation of the struggle for survival of American Norwegian farmers in pre–WW I North Dakota, the low-budget, independently made production won the Camera d'Or Prize at the Cannes Festival for best first film. Despite the prestigious success, Nilsson had a great deal of trouble raising money to finance further projects. Necessity prompted him to experiment with a novel approach to filmmaking he called "Direct Action." He had actor friends improvise lines and action from a general outline and camera, and sound operators similarly improvised as they followed the cast around in an unpredictable fashion. The action was shot and edited inexpensively on videotape, and after considerable trimming transferred to film. The two films he made using this method, *Signal 7* (about cabbies) and *Heat and Sunlight* (about a photographer's love angst), were inevitably anarchic and uneven but acceptably worthy, and best of all they had each cost less than $150,000 to make. The latter won the Grand Prize at the 1988 United States Film Festival in Park City, Utah. Nilsson was less successful with his more conventional mainstream film, *On the Edge*.

FILMS (as director-screenwriter): *Northern Lights* (co-dir., co-prod., co-sc., co-edit. with John Hanson) 1979; *On the Edge* (also co-prod., co-story), *Signal 7* 1986; *Heat and Sunlight* (also act.) 1987.

Nimoy, Leonard. Actor, director. Born on Mar. 26, 1931, in Boston into a middle-class Jewish home. *ed.* Boston Coll.; Antioch Coll. Trained at the Pasadena Playhouse, he played supporting roles in several movies and TV series before gaining wide popularity in the late 60s in the co-starring role of Mr. Spock, the pointy-eared half-human, half-Vulcan science officer of the USS *Enterprise,* in the TV series 'Star Trek' (1966–69). He later repeated the role in several blockbuster motion picture spin-offs of the series, two of which he also directed. Nimoy directed several other films, including the smash hit *Three Men and a Baby* (1987). He is also remembered for the role of Paris, the master of disguises, in the TV series 'Mission Impossible' (1969–71) and as host of the pseudo-documentary series 'In Search Of. . . ' (1976–82). He enjoyed success on Broadway in 'Equus' in 1977 and later impressed in 'Vincent,' a one-man show in which he impersonated the painter Van Gogh. A versatile artist, he published several collections of his poetry—including *You and I* (1973), *I Think of You* (1974), and *We Are all Children Searching for Love* (1977)—and an autobiography, *I Am Not Spock* (1975), as well as recording now-collectible cover versions of popular 60s tunes.

FILMS: (as actor) *Queen for a Day, Rhubarb* 1951; *Kid Monk Baroni, Zombies of the Stratosphere* (serial, re-released in 1958 in a feature version, *Satan's Satellites*), *Francis Goes to West Point* 1952; *Old Overland Trail* 1953; *The Brain Eaters* 1958; *The Balcony* 1963; *Deathwatch* (also co-prod.) 1966; *Valley of Mystery* 1967; *Catlow* 1971; *Invasion of the Body Snatchers* 1978; *Star Trek—The Motion Picture* 1979; *Star Trek II: The Wrath of Khan* 1982; *Star Trek III: The Search for Spock* (also dir.) 1984; *The Transformers* (v/o), *Star Trek IV: The Voyage Home* (also dir., co-story) 1986; *Three Men and a Baby* (dir. only) 1987; *The Good Mother* (dir. only) 1988; *Star Trek V: The Final Frontier* 1989; *Funny About Love* (dir. only) 1990; *Star Trek VI: The Undiscovered Country* (also exec. prod., co-sc.) 1991; *The Pagemaster* (v/o) 1994.

9.5 mm film. An early narrow-gauge film for amateur cinematography having 40 frames per foot and a single perforation between frames. Introduced in France in 1922, it enjoyed great popularity in Europe but was eventually replaced by 8 MM FILM.

Nissen, Greta. Actress. *b.* Grethe Ruzt-Nissen, Jan. 30, 1906, Oslo. *d.* 1988. Blue-eyed, blonde leading lady of Hollywood silents and early talkies. She began as a ballerina and later acted briefly on the stage and ended her screen career in the mid-30s in low-budget British films.

FILMS INCLUDE: *Lost—A Wife, In the Name of Love, The Wanderer, The King on Main Street* 1925; *The Love Thief, The Lady of the Harem, The Popular Sin, The Lucky Lady* 1926; *Blonde or Brunette, Blind Alleys* 1927; *Fazil, The Butter and Egg Man* 1928; *Women of All Nations, Transatlantic, Ambassador Bill, Good Sport* 1931; *The Silent Witness, Rackety Rax, The Unwritten Law* 1932; *The Circus Queen Murder, Melody Cruise, Best of Enemies, On Secret Service/Spy 77* (UK) 1933; *Red Wagon* (UK) 1934; *Honors Easy* (UK) 1935.

nitrate. The shortened name for "cellulose nitrate base," the material used in the manufacture of most 35 mm film until 1950. Highly flammable and quick to deteriorate, it required precautionary measures in storage and handling. It has gradually been replaced by various types of safety film with an acetate base. At the same time, a mammoth effort has been under way all over the world to transfer old nitrate-base negatives and prints to safety stock.

Nitzsche, Jack. Composer. Born in 1937, in Chicago. One of contemporary Hollywood's leading scorers of motion picture music.

FILMS INCLUDE: *The T.A.M.I. Show* (concert film) 1964; *Village of the Giants* 1965; *Performance* (UK) 1970; *Greaser's Palace* 1972; *One Flew Over the Cuckoo's Nest* 1975; *Heroes* 1977; *Hardcore, When You Comin' Back Red Ryder?* 1979; *Cruising* 1980; *Cutter and Bone/Cutter's Way* 1981; *Personal Best, An Officer and a Gentleman* 1982; *Without a Trace* 1983; *The Razor's Edge, Starman* 1984; *The Jewel of the Nile* 1985; *9½ Weeks* (co-mus.), *Stand by Me, Streets of Gold* (co-mus.) 1986; *The Seventh Sign* 1988; *Next of Kin* 1989; *Revenge, The Hot Spot, Mermaids* 1990; *The Indian Runner* 1991; *Blue Sky* 1994; *The Crossing Guard* 1995.

Niven, David. Actor. *b.* James David Graham Niven, Mar. 1, 1909, Kirriemuir, Scotland. *d.* 1983. Durable star of Hollywood and British films, a longtime screen incarnation of urbane wit and dapper charm. A descendant of two generations of professional soldiers (his father was killed at the Dardanelles), he attended the Sandhurst military school and served with the Highland Light Infantry in Malta before becoming a world drifter. His travels finally took him to Los Angeles, where he entered films as an extra in 1934. He rapidly developed into a reliable leading man and second lead, initially using his clipped diction and charming manner to cover up his lack of acting experience and steadily gaining confidence and ability in his new craft. At the outbreak of WW II he was among the first Hollywood stars to join the war effort, entering the British army as a lieutenant with the commandos. He was discharged as a colonel. He was given leave to appear in two British war propaganda films and later commuted frequently between Hollywood and London, appearing in a great number of both American and British productions. Typically seen in urbane comedy roles, he proved himself on several occasions an accomplished dramatic actor and won both an Oscar and the New York Critics best actor award for his dramatic performance in *Separate Tables* (1958). In 1952 he was a co-founder of the prosperous Four Star TV production company. He starred in the TV drama anthologies 'Four Star Playhouse' (1952–56) and 'Alcoa Theatre' (1957–58), hosted 'The David Niven Show' (1959), and co-starred in the adventure comedy series 'The Rogues' (1964–65). Niven wrote two novels, *Round and Rugged Rocks* (1951; in US *Once Over Lightly*) and *Go Slowly, Come Back Quickly* (1981), and two witty autobiographical volumes, *The Moon Is a Balloon* (1971) and *Bring on the Empty Horses* (1975), both republished in 1985 under one cover, titled *Niven.* His son, David Niven, Jr. (*b.* Dec. 15, 1942, London), is a film and TV production executive.

FILMS: *Mutiny on the Bounty* (extra), *Barbary Coast, Without Regret, A Feather in Her Hat, Splendor* 1935; *Rose Marie, Palm Springs, Thank You Jeeves, Dodsworth* (as Major Clyde Locket), *The Charge of the Light Brigade, Beloved Enemy* 1936; *We Have Our Moments, The Prisoner of Zenda* (as Fritz von Tarlenheim), *Dinner at the Ritz* 1937; *Bluebeard's Eighth Wife, Four Men and a Prayer, Three Blind Mice, Dawn Patrol* 1938; *Wuthering Heights* (as Edgar), *Bachelor Mother, The Real Glory, Eternally Yours* 1939; *Raffles* 1940; *The First of the Few/Spitfire* (UK) 1942; *The Way Ahead* (UK) 1944; *A Matter of Life and Death/Stairway to Heaven* (UK), *Magnificent Doll* (as Aaron Burr) 1946; *The Perfect Marriage, The Other Love, The Bishop's Wife* 1947; *Bonnie Prince Charlie* (as Prince Charles Edward Stuart; UK), *Enchantment* 1948; *A Kiss in the Dark* 1949; *The Elusive Pimpernel/The Fighting Pimpernel* (UK), *A Kiss for Corliss, The Toast of New Orleans* 1950; *Soldiers Three, Happy Go Lovely* (UK), *Appointment with Venus/Island Rescue* (UK) 1951; *The Lady Says No* 1952; *The*

Moon Is Blue 1953; *The Love Lottery* (UK), *Happy Ever After/Tonight's the Night* (UK) 1954; *Carrington V.C./Court Martial* (UK), *The King's Thief* 1955; *The Birds and the Bees, Around the World in 80 Days* (as Phileas Fogg) 1956; *Oh Men! Oh Women!, The Little Hut, My Man Godfrey, The Silken Affair* (UK) 1957; *Bonjour Tristesse* (UK), *Separate Tables* 1958; *Ask Any Girl, Happy Anniversary* 1959; *Please Don't Eat the Daisies* 1960; *The Guns of Navarone* (UK/US), *I Due Nemici/The Best of Enemies* (It./UK) 1961; *The Road to Hong Kong* (US/UK), *Guns of Darkness* (UK), *La Città Prigioniera/Conquered City* (It.) 1962; *55 Days at Peking* 1963; *The Pink Panther, Bedtime Story* 1964; *Lady L* (Fr./It./US) 1965; *Where the Spies Are* (UK) 1966; *Casino Royale* (UK), *Eye of the Devil* (UK) 1967; *Prudence and the Pill* (UK), *The Impossible Years* 1968; *The Extraordinary Seaman, Before Winter Comes* (UK), *Le Cerveau/The Brain* (Fr./It.) 1969; *The Statue* 1971; *Herzbube/King Queen Knave* (Ger.) 1972; *Vampira/Old Dracula* (as Dracula; UK) 1974; *Paper Tiger* (UK) 1975; *No Deposit—No Return, Murder by Death* 1976; *Candleshoe, Death on the Nile* 1978; *Escape to Athena* (UK), *A Nightingale Sang in Berkeley Square* (UK) 1979; *Rough Cut* (UK), *The Sea Wolves* (UK/US) 1980; *The Trail of the Pink Panther, Ménage à Trois/Better Late Than Never* (UK) 1982; *Curse of the Pink Panther* 1983.

Nixon, Cynthia. Actress. *b.* April 6, 1966, in New York City. Gifted, comedic supporting player of television and film from the early 80s.

FILMS INCLUDE: *Little Darlings* 1980; *Prince of the City* 1981; *I Am the Cheese* 1983; *Amadeus* 1984; *The Manhattan Project* 1986; *Let It Ride* 1989; *Face of a Stranger* 1991; *Addams Family Values, The Pelican Brief* 1993; *Baby's Day Out* 1994; *Marvin's Room* 1996.

Nixon, Marian (also **Marion**). Actress. *b.* Oct. 20, 1904, Superior, Wis. *d.* 1983. A former vaudeville chorine, she entered films in 1922 and after appearing in comedy shorts became a leading lady to such Western stars as Buck Jones and Tom Mix. The range of her roles gradually broadened and she played a variety of fetching leads during the late silent and early sound eras. She typically portrayed sweet, demure young women, much in the style of Janet Gaynor, although many of Nixon's films were second rate. She retired from the screen in 1936 to marry director William SEITER, her third husband. Widowed in 1964, she married actor Ben LYON in 1972.

FILMS INCLUDE: *Rosita, Big Dan, Cupid's Fireman* 1923; *Vagabond Trail, The Circus Cowboy, The Last of the Duanes, Just Off Broadway* 1924; *Sporting Life, Riders of the Purple Sage, I'll Show You the Town, The Hurricane Kid, Where Was I?* 1925; *Hands Up!, Rolling Home, Devil's Island, Spangles* 1926; *Heroes of the Night, The Auctioneer, Out All Night* 1927; *The Chinese Parrot, The Fourflusher, How to Handle Women, Out of the Ruins, Red Lips, Jazz Mad* 1928; *Geraldine, The Rainbow Man, Man Woman and Wife, In the Headlines, Say It with Songs, Young Nowheres, General Crack, Silks and Saddles* 1928; *Courage, The Pay-Off, College Lovers, Scarlet Pages, Ex-Flame, The Lash/Adios* 1930; *Sweepstakes, A Private Scandal* 1931; *Charlie Chan's Chance, After Tomorrow, Amateur Daddy, Winner Take All, Rebecca of Sunnybrook Farm, Madison Square Garden, Too Busy to Work* 1932; *Face in the Sky, Pilgrimage, Best of Enemies, Doctor Bull, Chance at Heaven* 1933; *Strictly Dynamite, We're Rich Again, Embarrassing Moments* 1934; *Sweepstakes Annie* 1935; *Tango, The Dragnet, Captain Calamity* 1936.

Nixon, Marni. Singer. Born Marni McEathron, on Feb. 22, 1929, in Altadena, Calif. A former child actress and soloist with the Roger Wagner Chorale, she excelled in both opera and pop singing and had a lucrative career as a recording and performance star. She appeared in only one film, in the small part of a nun in *The Sound of Music* (1965) but made a lasting contribution to the Hollywood musical as a "ghost" singer, lending her soprano voice for lip-synching by famous stars. Among others, she provided a singing voice for Margaret O'BRIEN in *Big City* (1948), for Deborah KERR in *The King and I* (1956), for Natalie WOOD in *West Side Story* (1961), and for Audrey HEPBURN in *My Fair Lady* (1964). Nixon's first husband (1950–69) was composer Ernest GOLD.

Nöel, Magali. Actress. Born Magali Guiffrai, in 1932, in Smyrna, Turkey. Leading lady and later character player of French and Italian films from the early 50s. She played interesting roles in a number of Fellini productions, notably *Amarcord* (1973), in which she represented the memory of the director's adolescent sexual fantasies.

FILMS INCLUDE: *Demain nous divorçons* 1951; *Seul dans Paris* 1952; *Du Rififi chez les Hommes/Rififi, Razzia sur la Chnouf/Razzia, Les Grandes Manoeuvres/The Grand Maneuver* 1955; *Eléna et les Hommes/Paris Does Strange Things, Les Possédées/Passionate Summer* 1956; *Assassins et Voleurs* 1957; *La Piège/No Escape* 1958; *L'Ile du Bout du Monde/Temptation, Des Femmes diaparaissent/The Road to Shame* 1959; *La Dolce Vita* (It./Fr.) 1960; *Le Secret de d'Artagnan/The Secret Mark of D'Artagnan* 1962; *Totò e Cleopatra* (It./Fr.) 1963; *La Traite des Balances/Frustrations* 1965; *Z, Fellini Satyricon* (It./Fr.) 1969; *Tropic of Cancer* (US), *The Man Who Had Power Over Women* (UK) 1970; *Il Prete sposato/The Married Priest* (It./Fr.) 1971; *Amarcord* (It./Fr.) 1973; *Il Tempo degli Assassini* (It./Fr.); *Les Rendez-vous d'Anna* 1978; *Le Chemin perdu* 1980; *Qu'est qui fait courir David?* 1982; *La Mort de Mario Ricci/The Death of Mario Ricci* 1983; *Vertiges* 1985; *Exit-Exil* 1986; *Pentimento* 1990.

Noël-Noël. Actor, screenwriter. *b.* Lucien Noël, Aug. 9, 1897, Paris. *d.* 1989. A leading comic and character actor of French films, he is best known for his characterization of the befuddled soldier Ademaï in films of the 30s and petit bourgeois types in the 40s and 50s. A former bank clerk, cartoonist for leftist publications, and satirical songwriter, he also wrote many of his own screenplays and directed one film, *La Vie chantée* (1951).

FILMS INCLUDE: *Ménages modernes* 1931; *Mon Coeur balance, Papa sans le savoir, Mistigri* 1932; *Vive la Compagnie* 1933; *Ademaï Aviateur* (also sc.) 1934; *Pierrot mon Ami, Le Centenaire* (also sc.) 1935; *Les Aventures de Moutonnet* (also sc.) 1936; *Mannequins, L'Innocent/Bouquets from Nicholas* (also sc.) 1938; *Le Plancher des Vaches* (also sc.) 1939; *Le Femme que j'ai le plus aimée* 1942; *Ademaï Bandit d'Honneur* 1944; *La Cage aux Rossignols/A Cage of Nightingales* (also co-sc.) 1945; *Le Père tranquille/Mr. Orchid* (also sc.) 1946; *Les Casse-Pieds/The Spice of Life* (also sc.) 1950; *La Vie chantée* (also dir., sc.) 1951; *Les Sept Péchés capitaux/The Seven Deadly Sins* (Carlo Rim's episode) 1952; *Les Carnets du Major Thompson/The French They Are a Funny Race* 1955; *Les Truands* 1956; *A Pied à Cheval et un Spoutnik/A Dog a Mouse and a Sputnik* 1958; *Les Vieux de la Vieille* 1960; *Jessica* (US/Fr./It.) 1962; *La Sentinelle endormie* (also sc.) 1966.

Noiret, Philippe. Actor. Born on Oct. 1, 1930, in Lille, France. Gifted, admirably versatile, amazingly prolific leading man and character player of the Paris stage, French films, and international co-productions. Trained by Roger Blin at the Centre Dramatique de l'Ouest, he entertained in nightclubs before developing in the 50s into a solid stage performer, equally adept at dramatic and light roles. He began playing small roles in films in the late 40s but it was in the 60s that he attained high stature, especially after winning the Venice Festival Prize as best actor for his portrayal of a dull husband in Franju's *Thérèse Desqueyroux* (1962). His many other memorable roles, spanning an astonishing range, included a transvestite artist in Malle's *Zazie dans le Métro* (1960), a loveable lazy farmer in Robert's *Alexandre le bienheureux* (1968), a César-winning performance in Enrico's *Le Vieux Fusil* (1975), a ruthlessly cruel judge in Tavernier's *Le Juge et l'Assassin* (1976), and more recently the beloved projectionist in Tornatore's *Cinema Paradiso* (1988). Since 1962 he has been married to actress Monique Chaumette.

FILMS INCLUDE: *Gigi* (bit) 1948; *Olivia* (bit) 1950; *La Pointe courte* 1956; *Zazie dans le Mètro/Zazie* 1960; *Le Crime ne paie pas/Crime Does Not Pay, Tout l'Or du Monde, Les Amours célèbres, Thérèse Desqueyroux/Therese* 1962; *La Porteuse de Pain, Cyrano et d'Artagnan* (as Louis XIII) 1963; *Monsieur, Les Copains* 1964; *Lady L* (US/Fr./It.) 1965; *La Vie de Château/A Matter of Resistance, Tendre Voyou/Tender Scoundrel* 1966; *La Nuit des Généraux/The Night of the Generals* (Fr./UK), *Sept fois Femme/Woman Times Seven* (Fr./It./US), *L'Une et l'autre* 1967; *Alexandre le bienheureux/Very Happy Alexander* 1968; *Mister Freedom, The Assassination Bureau* (UK), *Justine* (US), *Topaz* (US) 1969; *Les Caprices de Marie/Give Her the Moon* 1970; *Murphy's War* (UK) 1971; *La Mandarine, L'Attentat/The French Conspiracy* 1972; *Le Serpent/The Serpent, La Grande Bouffe* 1973; *Touchez pas la Femme blanche, Le Secret/The Secret, L'Horloger de Saint-Paul/The Clockmaker* 1974; *Que la Fête commence!/Let Joy Reign Supreme, Le Vieux Fusil/The Old Gun, Amici miei/My Friends* (It.) 1975; *Monsieur Albert, Une Femme à sa Fenêtre/A Woman at Her Window, Le Juge et l'Assassin/The Judge and the Assassin, Le Désert des Tartares* 1976; *Un Taxi mauve/The Purple Taxi, Tendre Poulet/Dear Detective/Dear Inspector* 1977; *La Barricade du Point du Jour, Coup de Foudre, Who Is Killing the Great Chefs of Europe?* (US/Ger.), *Le Temoin* 1978; *Due Pezzi di Pane* (It./Fr.), *La Mort en irect/Deathwatch* 1979; *Pile ou Face/Heads or Tails, Une semaine de Vacances/A Week's Vacation* 1980; *The Fratelli/Three Brothers* (It./Fr.), *Coup de Torchon/Clean Slate* 1981; *L'Etoile du Nord* 1982; *L'African/The African* 1983; *Fort Saganne, Les Ripoux/My New Partner/Le Cop* 1984; *L'Eté prochain/Next Summer, Le Quatrième Pouvoir* 1985; *Autour de Minuit/Round Midnight* (US/Fr.) 1986; *Masques, La Famiglia/The Family* (It./Fr.), *Gli occhiali d'oro* (It./Fr./Yug.), *Noyade interdite* 1987; *Nuovo Cinema Paradiso/Cinema Paradiso* (It./Fr.), *Il Frullo del Passero* (It./Fr.) 1988; *La Vie et rien d'autre/Life and Nothing But* 1989; *Ripoux Contre Ripoux/My New Partner 2, Dimenticare Palermo/To Forget Palermo* (It./Fr.), *Faux et Usage de Faux/Forgery and the Use of Forgeries* 1990; *Uranus* (Fr.) 1991; *I Don't Kiss, The Two of Us* 1992; *Tango* 1993; *Grosse Fatigue/Dead Tired, The Daughter of Artagnan, Il Postino/The Postman* 1994; *Sun* 1997.

noise. Any undesired sound or disturbance in recording that is audible in reproduction.

Nolan, Doris. Actress. Born on July 14, 1916, in New York City. Leading lady of a few Hollywood films of the late 30s and early 40s, following brief modeling and stage experience. She retired after marrying Alexander KNOX but returned to the screen in a small role in 1975.

FILMS: *The Man I Marry* 1936; *Top of the Town, As Good As Married* 1937; *Holiday* 1938; *One Hour to Live* 1939; *Irene, Moon Over Burma* 1940; *Follies Girl* 1943; *The Romantic Englishwoman* (UK) 1975.

Nolan, Jeanette. Actress. Born on Dec. 30, 1911, in Los Angeles, Calif. Character actress of radio, TV ('The Virginian'), stage, and films. Memorable as Lady Macbeth in Orson Welles's *Macbeth.* The widow of John MCINTIRE, she was the mother of actor Tim McIntire, who died of heart failure in 1986 at age 42.

FILMS INCLUDE: *Macbeth* (as Lady Macbeth), *Words and Music* 1948; *Abandoned* 1949; *No Sad Songs for Me, Saddle Tramp* 1950; *The Secret of Convict Lake* 1951; *The Happy Time, Hangman's Knot* 1952; *The Big Heat* 1953; *Tribute to a Bad Man, The Seventh Cavalry* 1956; *April Love, Guns of Fort Petticoat* 1957; *The Deep Six* 1958; *The Rabbit Trap* 1959; *The Great Impostor, Two Rode Together* 1961; *The Man Who Shot Liberty Valance* 1962; *Twilight of Honor* 1963; *My Blood Runs Cold* 1965; *Chamber of Horrors* 1966; *The Reluctant Astronaut* 1967; *Did You Hear the One About the Traveling Saleslady?* 1968; *The Winds of Autumn* 1976; *The Rescuers* 1977; *Avalanche* 1978; *True Confessions* 1981; *Cloak and Dagger* 1984.

Nolan, Lloyd. Actor. *b.* Aug. 11, 1902, San Francisco. *d.* 1985. *ed.* Stanford U. A stage actor since 1927, he played leads in numerous low-budget action pictures of the 30s and early 40s, typically as a breezy detective or reporter. Occasionally he played the male lead in serious dramas, but was best known for his solid support roles, particularly in Elia Kazan's *A Tree Grows in Brooklyn* (1943). Won belated recognition in the 50s as a fine actor for his original portrayal of Captain Queeg in both the stage (New York Drama Critics Award, 1954) and TV (Emmy Award, 1955) versions of 'The Caine Mutiny Court-Martial.' He starred in the TV series 'Martin Kane, Private Eye' (1951–52), 'Special Agent 7' (1958–59), and 'Julia' (1968–71). The father of an autistic child, he was chairman of the annual Autistic Children's Telethon.

FILMS INCLUDE: *Stolen Harmony, G-Men, Atlantic Adventure, One-Way Ticket* 1935; *You May Be Next, Big Brown Eyes, The Texas Rangers* 1936; *King of Gamblers, Exclusive, Ebb Tide, Wells Fargo* 1937; *Every Day's a Holiday, Tip-Off Girls, Hunted Men, Prison Farm, King of Alcatraz* 1938; *St. Louis Blues, Ambush, Undercover Doctor, The Magnificent Fraud* 1939; *The Man Who Wouldn't Talk, Johnny Apollo, Gangs of Chicago, The Man I Married, Pier 13, Michael Shayne Private Detective* (title role) 1940; *Behind the News, Sleepers West, Mr. Dynamite, Dressed to Kill, Buy Me That Town, Blues in the Night* 1941; *The Man Who Wouldn't Die, Apache Trail, It Happened in Flatbush, Just Off Broadway, Manila Calling, Time to Kill* 1942; *Bataan, Guadalcanal Diary* 1943; *A Tree Grows in Brooklyn, Circumstantial Evidence, Captain Eddie, The House on 92nd Street* 1945; *Somewhere in The Night* 1946; *Lady in the Lake, Two Smart People, Wild Harvest* 1947; *Green Grass of Wyoming, The Street with No Name* 1948; *Bad Boy, The Sun Comes Up, Easy Living* 1949; *The Lemon Drop Kid* 1951; *Island in the Sky* 1953; *The Last Hunt, Toward the Unknown* 1956; *Seven Waves Away/Abandon Ship!* (UK), *A Hatful of Rain, Peyton Place* 1957; *Portrait in Black, Girl of the Night* 1960; *Susan Slade* 1961; *The Girl Hunters* 1963; *Circus World* 1964; *Never Too Late* 1965; *An American Dream* 1966; *The Double Man* (UK) 1967; *Sergeant Ryker, Ice Station Zebra* 1968; *Airport* 1970; *Earthquake* 1974; *The Private Files of J. Edgar Hoover* 1977; *My Boys Are Good Boys* 1978; *Prince Jack* 1984; *Hannah and Her Sisters* 1986.

Nolte, Nick. Actor. Born on Feb. 8, 1934, in Omaha, Nebr. Brawny (6' 1", 210 pounds), rugged, blond, raspy-voiced leading man of the American screen. The son of an Iowa State football player, he excelled in high school in baseball, basketball, wrestling, track, and football. He got into Arizona State on a football scholarship, but did not get passing grades. Over the next few years he played but barely studied at four other schools—including Eastern Arizona Junior College, Phoenix

City College, and Pasadena City College—before finding himself out of options as a jock. After briefly holding a job as a Los Angeles ironworker, he discovered the theater and for the next 14 years roamed the country with various regional companies and at New York's Cafe La Mama. Although he settled down considerably during his travels, marrying his first of three wives and catching up on his education by attending classes at various universities, the still-rebellious Nolte was arrested for counterfeiting draft cards and was given five years probation. But things improved dramatically for Nolte after he returned to California in 1973. He began appearing in films and TV shows, and in 1976 achieved a breakthrough as the co-star of the miniseries 'Rich Man Poor Man.' Movie stardom quickly followed. By the early 80s he was among Hollywood's most popular leading men, a tough guy with soul and a natural acting ability. Best known for action films such as *48 Hrs* (1983), he won recognition as a bankable dramatic star with his deep, sympathetic performance in Barbra Streisand's adaptation of Pat Conroy's novel *The Prince of Tides* (1991), earning an Academy Award nomination as best actor.

FILMS: *Return to Macon County* 1975; *The Deep* 1977; *Who'll Stop the Rain?* 1978; *North Dallas Forty* 1979; *Heart Beat* 1980; *Cannery Row, 48 Hrs* 1982; *Under Fire* 1983; *Teachers* 1984; *Grace Quigley* 1985; *Down and Out in Beverly Hills* 1986; *Extreme Prejudice, Weeds* 1987; *Three Fugitives, New York Stories* ("Life Lessons" episode), *Farewell to the King* 1989; *Everybody Wins* (UK/US), *Q & A, Another 48 Hrs* 1990; *Cape Fear, The Prince of Tides* 1991; *The Player* (cameo), *Lorenzo's Oil* 1992; *Blue Chips, I'll Do Anything, I Love Trouble* 1994; *Jefferson in Paris* 1995; *Mother Night, Mulholland Falls, Nightwatch* 1996; *U-Turn* 1997.

nontheatrical. A film designated for limited distribution among specialized audiences, such as schools and social groups, or directly for TV or videocassette distribution, but not for general release to motion picture theaters.

Noonan, Tommy. Actor. *b.* Thomas Noon, Apr. 29, 1921, Bellingham, Wash. *d.* 1968. Exuberant, bespectacled comic character player of Hollywood films. The half brother of actor John IRELAND, he started performing in his teens and had been a successful comedy writer and nightclub entertainer by the time he began appearing in films regularly in the mid-40s. He produced three of his films in the 60s, also directing one of them.

FILMS INCLUDE: *Boys Town* (bit) 1938; *George White's Scandals, Dick Tracy* 1945; *The Truth About Murder* 1946; *The Big Fix* 1947; *Open Secret* 1948; *I Shot Jesse James, The Set-Up, Adam's Rib* 1949; *The Return of Jesse James* 1950; *The Model and the Marriage Broker, Starlift, FBI Girl* 1951; *Gentlemen Prefer Blondes* 1953; *A Star Is Born* 1954; *Violent Saturday, How to Be Very Very Popular* 1955; *The Ambassador's Daughter, Bundle of Joy* 1956; *The Girl Most Likely* 1958; *The Rookie* (also prod., co-sc.) 1960; *Swingin' Along* 1962; *Promises! Promises!* (also co-prod., co-sc.) 1963; *Three Nuts in Search of a Bolt* (also dir., co-prod., co-sc.) 1964; *Cottonpickin' Chicken-pickers* 1967.

Norden, Christine. Actress. *b.* Mary Lydia Thornton, 1924, England. *d.* 1988. Busty leading lady of British films of the late 40s and early 50s. A former singer and dancer, she was a "discovery" of Sir Alexander KORDA. She played brassy *femmes fatales* in a handful of films, briefly reigning as Britain's first postwar sex symbol before the advent of Diana DORS. During the height of her popularity she inspired the mock hymn 'Onward Christine's Shoulders.' A complex mathematical formula was named after her by her fifth (and last) husband, a scientist.

FILMS: *Night Beat, Mine Own Executioner* 1947; *Idol of Paris, A Yank Comes Back, An Ideal Husband* 1948; *Saints and Sinners, The Interrupted Journey* 1949; *The Black Widow* 1950; *A Case for P.C. 49* 1951; *Reluctant Heroes* 1952; *Little Shop of Horrors* (US) 1986.

Nordisk. A Danish production company established in 1906 which, prior to WW I, dominated the world market with its immense output of unpretentious, often sensational, entertainment films. Known in America as the Great Northern Film Company, Nordisk boasted such internationally popular stars as Asta Nielsen, Valdemar Psilander, and Olaf Fonss. Among its world-famous directors were Viggo Larsen, August Blom, Urban Gad, Holger Madsen, Robert Dinesen, and Benjamin Christensen. The company's Copenhagen studio was among the best equipped in the world during the early days of cinema. Nordisk is still in business, the oldest film production company in the world in continuous existence. See also DENMARK.

Noris, Assia. Born Anastasia von Gerzfeld, on Feb. 26, 1912, in Petrograd (later Leningrad), Russia, to a German officer and his Ukrainian wife. She starred in many Italian films of the 30s and early 40s. Her second husband, Mario CAMERINI, directed many of these films, in which she often co-starred with Vittorio DE SICA. There was no room for her in the postwar neorealistic films and she emigrated to Egypt with her third husband, a British military officer.

FILMS INCLUDE: *Tre Uomini in Frak* 1932; *La Signorina dell'Autobus, Giallo* 1933; *Quei Due* 1934; *Darò un Milione* 1935; *Una Donna fra Due Mondi/Between Two Worlds, Il Signor Max* 1937; *Grandi Magazzini, Dora Nelson* 1939; *Una Romantica Avventura* 1940; *Un Colpo di Pistola* 1941; *Una Storia d'Amore* 1942; *Le Capitaine Fracasse* (Fr.) 1943; *I Dieci Comandamenti/The Ten Commandments, Che Distinta Famiglia!* 1945; *Amina* (Egypt) 1949; *La Celestina* 1964.

Norman, Leslie. Producer, director. Born in 1911, in London. In British films from age 16, he was an editor before turning producer and director.

FILMS INCLUDE: As editor—*The Man from Chicago* 1930; *Mimi* 1935; *The Overlanders* 1946; *Nicholas Nickleby* 1947. As producer—*Eureka Stockade/Massacre Hill* (also edit.) 1948; *Where No Vultures Fly* (also sc.) 1951; *Mandy/The Story of Mandy/A Crash of Silence* 1952; *The Cruel Sea* 1953. As director (complete)—*Dangerous to Live* (co-dir.) 1939; *The Night My Number Came Up* 1955; *X the Unknown* 1956; *The Shiralee* 1957; *Dunkirk* 1958; *Summer of the Seventeenth Doll/Season of Passion* (Austral./UK) 1959; *The Long and the Short and the Tall/Jungle Fighters, Spare the Rod* 1961; *Mix Me a Person* 1962; *The Lost Continent* (replaced by Michael Carreras after start of production; uncredited) 1968.

Normand, Mabel. Actress. *b.* Nov. 16, 1894, Boston. *d.* 1930. The daughter of an itinerant vaudeville pianist and a working mother, she was pretty much on her own from early childhood. In 1908 the family moved to New York, where 13-year-old Mabel began modeling for artists and photographers. She was barely 16 when she went to work for Biograph, then located on East 14th Street in New York. She left Biograph briefly to join Vitagraph but returned late in 1911 and became an important star of the company, working mostly under the direction of Mack SENNETT. In 1912, when Sennett left Biograph to form Keystone, she joined him and remained with him for many years. Sennett was deeply enamored of his radiant and talented star, whom he once described as being "as beautiful as a spring morning." They were on the verge of marrying several times, but their wedding plans were put off time and again and never materialized.

Mabel was a brilliant comedienne, perhaps the most talented comic star of the silent screen. She starred in numerous

Sennett shorts, some of which she also directed or co-directed, notably several of CHAPLIN'S early films. The six-reel *Tillie's Punctured Romance* (1914), in which she co-starred with Chaplin, was a tremendous success and she began pressing for more roles in feature films. In 1916, Sennett and his backers, Bauman and Kessel, set up the Mabel Normand Feature Film Company just for that purpose. In *Mickey,* the first feature produced by the new company, she proved she could handle a more complex role than the standard Sennett slapstick by giving a warm and moving performance combining pathos with whimsical comedy as a country tomboy and her adventures in city society. For some reason, the film was shelved by Sennett until 1918. When it was finally released it proved to be a big hit, but by that time the disgruntled Mabel had signed a five-year contract to make features at Goldwyn.

Separated from Sennett for the first time in seven years, the impulsive and restless Mabel was soon caught up in the Hollywood social whirl. Her wild all-night parties became the talk of the town and rumors began circulating that she was addicted to drugs. In 1922 her career was dealt a heavy blow by the mysterious murder of director William Desmond TAYLOR, with whom she was romantically linked. Since she was one of the last persons to see him alive, her name was dragged into the case, and although she was proved innocent beyond doubt, her image was permanently tarnished by the lurid press coverage of the case.

Just as Mabel seemed to be recovering from the effects of this scandal, her chauffeur was found standing over the body of Cortland S. Dines, a Hollywood millionaire. The pistol in his hand was said to have belonged to Mabel. The double scandal shattered her completely. She continued making films, but the effect of her personal tragedy was clearly visible on the screen, and her popularity rapidly waned. In 1923 she made her last feature, then returned to two-reelers in several Hal Roach comedies. Desperately clinging to a semblance of a normal life, she married Lew CODY, who had played the villain in *Mickey.* She died of a combination of pneumonia and tuberculosis. She was portrayed by Bernadette Peters in the 1974 Broadway musical 'Mack and Mabel.'

FILMS INCLUDE: *Over the Garden Wall* 1910; *Picciola, Betty Becomes a Maid, Subduing of Mrs. Nag, The Squaw's Love, The Diving Girl, Her Awakening* 1911; *The Eternal Mother, The Mender of Nets, The Fatal Chocolate, Tomboy Bessie* (also co-dir.), *Oh Those Eyes!, Cohen Collects a Debt, The Water Nymph, The Flirting Husband, Mabel's Adventures, Mabel's Stratagem* 1912; *The Mistaken Masher, Mabel's Heroes, A Red Hot Romance, Her New Beau, Mabel's Awful Mistake, The Speed Queen, For Love of Mabel, Mabel's Dramatic Career, The Gypsy Queen, Cohen Saves the Flag, The Gusher* 1913; *In the Clutches of the Gang, Mabel's Stormy Love Affair, Won in a Closet* (also dir.), *Mabel's Strange Predicament, Mabel at the Wheel* (also co-dir. with Sennett), *Caught in a Cabaret* (also co-dir. with Chaplin), *Mabel's Nerve* (also dir.), *The Fatal Mallet, Her Friend the Bandit* (also co-dir. with Chaplin), *Mabel's Busy Day* (also co-dir. with Chaplin), *Mabel's Married Life* (also co-dir. with Chaplin), *Mabel's New Job* (also dir.), *Gentlemen of Nerve, Tillie's Punctured Romance* 1914; *Mabel's and Fatty's Wash Day* (also co-dir. with Eddie Dillon), *Mabel's and Fatty's Simple Life* (also co-dir. with Dillon), *The Little Band of Gold, Fatty and Mabel Viewing the World's Fair at San Francisco* (also co-dir. with Roscoe "Fatty" Arbuckle), *The Little Teacher, My Valet, Stolen Magic* 1915; *Fatty and Mabel Adrift, My Valet, Bright Lights* 1916; *Dodging a Million, The Floor Below, Joan of Plattsburg, The Venus Model, Back to the Woods, Mickey, Peck's Bad Girl, A Perfect 36* 1918; *Sis Hopkins, The Pest, When Doctors Disagree, Upstairs, Jinx* 1919; *Pinto, The Slim Princess, What Happened to Rosa* 1920; *Molly O* 1921; *Oh Mabel Behave* 1922; *Suzanna, The Extra Girl* 1923; *One Hour Married, Raggedy Rose* 1926; *Should Men Walk Home?* 1927.

Norris, Alexander M. See NOSSECK, Max.

Norris, Chuck. Actor. Born Carlos Ray Norris, in 1939, in Ryan, Okla., of Irish and Cherokee Indian descent. He became an avid martial arts devotee during his service with the Air Force in Korea in the early 60s. After his discharge, he pursued karate professionally, reigning as the world's middleweight champion from 1968 to 1974. His karate school in Los Angeles attracted a number of celebrity pupils, paving the way to a movie career that started modestly in the late 60s and reached its peak in the 80s, when he starred as Vietnam vet Col. James Braddock in the action-packed *Missing in Action* (1984) and its sequels. Several of his films were directed by his brother, former stuntman Aaron Norris.

FILMS: *The Wrecking Crew* 1968; *The Student Teachers, Return of the Dragon* (HK) 1973; *Breaker Breaker* 1976; *Good Guys Wear Black* 1978; *Game of Death, A Force of One* 1979; *The Octagon* 1980; *An Eye for an Eye, Slaughter in San Francisco* (HK) 1981; *Silent Rage, Forced Vengeance* 1982; *Lone Wolf McQuade* 1983; *Missing in Action* 1984; *Missing in Action 2—The Beginning, Code of Silence, Invasion U.S.A.* 1985; *The Delta Force, Born American, Firewalker* 1986; *Braddock: Missing in Action III* (also co-sc.), *Hero and the Terror* 1988; *Delta Force 2: The Colombian Connection* 1990; *The Hitman* 1991; *Sidekicks* 1992; *Hellbound* 1994; *Top Dog* 1995.

Norris, Edward. Actor. Born in 1910, in Philadelphia. A former reporter and stage actor, he played some leads but mostly supporting roles in many Hollywood films of the 30s, 40s, and early 50s. At one time (1936–39) married to Ann SHERIDAN.

FILMS INCLUDE: *Queen Christina* 1933; *Murder in the Fleet, Show Them No Mercy* 1935; *The Magnificent Brute* 1936; *They Won't Forget* 1937; *Boys Town* 1938; *Tail Spin! On Trial, Gorilla, Frontier Marshal, The Escape* 1939; *Dr. Ehrlich's Magic Bullet, The Lady in Question* 1940; *Here Comes Happiness, Angels with Broken Wings* 1941; *The Lady Has Plans, The Man with Two Lives, The Mystery of Marie Roget* 1942; *You Can't Beat the Law* 1943; *Men on Her Mind, End of the Road* 1944; *Night Club Girl* 1945; *The Truth About Murder, Decoy* 1946; *Trapped by Boston Blackie* 1948; *Forgotten Women* 1949; *Surrender, Killer Shark* 1950; *Highway 301* 1951; *Murder Without Tears* 1953; *The Kentuckian* 1955.

Norris, Patricia. Costume designer. One of contemporary Hollywood's leading wardrobe fashioners. Equally creative at modern and period styles. In the late 80s she began designing sets as well as costumes.

FILMS INCLUDE: *The Good Guys and the Bad Guys* 1969; *The Candidate* 1972; *Zandy's Bride* 1974; *Smile, The Sunshine Boys* 1975; *Silent Movie, The Missouri Breaks* 1976; *California Suite, Days of Heaven, Capricorn One* 1978; *Heart Beat* 1979; *The Elephant Man* 1980; *Four Friends, History of the World, Part I* 1981; *Frances, Victor/Victoria* 1982; *Scarface, The Star Chamber* 1983; *Johnny Dangerously, Micki and Maude, 2010, Racing with the Moon* 1984; *The Best of Times, A Fine Mess* (also prod. des.), *Blue Velvet* (also prod. des.) 1986; *Black Widow* 1987; *Little Nikita* 1988; *Tap* (also prod. des.) 1989; *Wild at Heart* 1990.

North, Alex. Composer. *b.* Dec. 4, 1910, Chester, Pa. *d.* 1991. *ed.* Curtis Institute; Juilliard School of Music; Moscow Conservatory. Also trained by Ernst Toch and Aaron Copeland, he began his career as a composer for fact films, writing the music for some 50 documentary shorts between 1937 and 1950. During the same period he also composed for the New York stage ('Life and Death of an American' 1939; 'Of V We Sing' 1942; 'Death of a Salesman' 1949, etc.), wrote ballet music for Martha Graham, Agnes de Mille, and Anna Sokolow, and composed orchestral pieces, including 'Revue for Clarinet and Orchestra' for Benny Goodman and his first of three symphonies. North began scoring feature films in the early 50s and rapidly established himself as one of Hollywood's most imaginative and versatile composers, his music ranging from intimate chamber works to full-blown symphonic orchestrations. He was nominated for 15 Academy Awards but did not win one until 1986 (during the ceremony for 1985), when the Motion Picture Academy presented him with an honorary life-achievement Oscar "in recognition of his brilliant artistry in the creation of memorable music for a host of distinguished motion pictures."

FILMS INCLUDE: *The 13th Letter, A Streetcar Named Desire, Death of a Salesman* 1951; *Viva Zapata!, Les Miserables, The Member of the Wedding* 1952; *Desiree* 1954; *Unchained, Daddy Long Legs, The Man with the Gun, I'll Cry Tomorrow, The Rose Tattoo* 1955; *The Bad Seed, The Rainmaker* 1956; *The Long Hot Summer* 1958; *The Sound and the Fury, The Wonderful Country* 1959; *Spartacus* 1960; *Sanctuary, The Misfits* 1961; *The Children's Hour, All Fall Down* 1962; *Cleopatra* 1963; *Cheyenne Autumn* 1964; *The Agony and the Ecstasy* 1965; *Who's Afraid of Virginia Woolf?* 1966; *The Shoes of the Fisherman* 1968; *Hard Contract, A Dream of Kings* 1969; *Willard* 1971; *Pocket Money* 1972; *Lost in the Stars* (mus. dir.), *Shanks* 1974; *Bite the Bullet* 1975; *The Passover Plot* 1976; *Wise Blood* 1979; *Carny* 1980; *Dragonslayer* 1981; *Under the Volcano* 1984; *Prizzi's Honor* 1985; *The Dead, Good Morning Vietnam* 1987; *The Penitent* 1988; *Ghost* (song only) 1990; *Le Dernier Papillon/The Last Butterfly* (Fr./Czech.) 1991.

North, Edmund H. Screenwriter. *b.* Mar. 12, 1911, New York City. *d.* 1990. He spent much of his childhood on the road, trouping with his parents, vaudeville, burlesque, and Ziegfeld Follies players Bobby North and Stella Maury (as Robert Norton, his father later produced many Hollywood B pictures of the 30s and 40s). At the Culver Military Academy of Indiana, he and friend Joshua LOGAN wrote their first plays. He later attended Stanford University but dropped out after two years to write in Paris. He began writing for the screen in the mid-30s, but came into prominence only in the 50s, following five years of WW II military service as a major with the Army Signal Corps, for which he made many training and educational films. He shared the Academy Award with Francis Ford COPPOLA for the story and screenplay of *Patton* (1970).

FILMS INCLUDE: *One Night of Love* 1934; *I Dream Too Much, All the King's Horses* 1935; *Murder on a Bridle Path, Bunker Bean* 1936; *I'm Still Alive* 1940; *Dishonored Lady* 1947; *Flamingo Road* (dial. only), *Colorado Territory* 1949; *Young Men with a Horn, In a Lonely Place* 1950; *Only the Valiant, The Day the Earth Stood Still* 1951; *The Outcasts of Poker Flat* 1952; *Destry, The Far Horizons* 1955; *The Proud Ones* 1956; *Cowboy* 1958; *Sink the Bismarck!* (UK) 1960; *The Fiercest Heart* 1961; *H.M.S. Defiant/Damn the Defiant!* (UK) 1962; *Patton* 1970; *Meteor* 1979.

North, Sheree. Actress. Born Dawn Bethel, on Jan. 17, 1933, in Hollywood, Calif. A professional dancer at age ten, a bride at 15 and a mother at 16, she modeled and danced in clubs and for under-the-counter film loops before making her feature film debut, an unbilled bit, in *Excuse My Dust* (1951). She first attracted attention in 1953 with a wild dance number in the Broadway musical 'Hazel Flagg' and returned to Hollywood the following year to repeat the role in the screen adaptation of the play, the Martin-Lewis comedy vehicle *Living It Up.* In 1954 she was signed by Fox and groomed by the studio as a platinum-blonde sexpot and a potential substitute for their often-reluctant star, Marilyn Monroe. After a big publicity buildup, Miss North starred in several light Fox productions, proving herself a talented comedienne as well as a bouncy dancer and later also a passable dramatic actress. But by 1958 she had been replaced as the studio's resident "dumb blonde" by the likes of Jayne Mansfield and Mamie Van Doren. She disappeared from the screen for nearly a decade, during which she performed in stock, on the road, and on TV. She returned to films in the late 60s, mainly in character roles.

FILMS: *Excuse My Dust* (bit) 1951; *Here Come the Girls* (bit) 1953; *Living It Up* 1954; *How to Be Very Very Popular* 1955; *The Lieutenant Wore Skirts, The Best Things in Life Are Free* 1956; *The Way to the Gold, No Down Payment* 1957; *In Love and War, Mardi Gras* 1958; *Destination Inner Space* 1966; *Madigan* 1968; *The Trouble with Girls, The Gypsy Moths* 1969; *Lawman, The Organization* 1971; *Charley Varrick* 1973; *The Outfit* 1974; *Breakout* 1975; *Survival* (release delayed from 1969), *The Shootist* 1976; *Telefon* 1977; *Rabbit Test* (cameo) 1978; *Only Once in a Lifetime* 1979; *Maniac Cop* 1988; *Cold Dog Soup* 1990; *Defenseless* 1991.

Norton, Edward. Actor. Born in 1970, in Columbia, Md. *ed.* Yale University. This versatile young actor, whose father is a noted lawyer, his mother a high school teacher, is the oldest of three children. At the age of five, he was captivated by a performance of 'Cinderella,' and later Sir Ian McKellan's 'Acting Shakespeare.' This propelled him to a career off Broadway in playwright Edward Albee's 'Fragments.' After months of searching for the right actor without luck, the producers of *Primal Fear* (1996) came upon this young stage actor and cast him in the pivotal role of a boy battling dual personalities, resulting in a supporting actor Academy Award nomination for Norton and launching a career of great promise.

FILMS: *Everyone Says I Love You, The People vs. Larry Flynt, Primal Fear* 1996.

Norton, Jack. Actor. *b.* Mortimer J. Naughton, 1889, Brooklyn, N.Y. *d.* 1958. Character actor and bit player typecast as an amiable drunk in well over 100 Hollywood films of the 30s and 40s, following long vaudeville career. In real life he never took a drink. A favorite nostalgia subject among trivia fans.

FILMS INCLUDE: *Cockeyed Cavaliers* 1934; *Bordertown, Stolen Harmony* 1935; *Marked Woman A Day at the Races* 1937; *Thanks for the Memory* 1938; *The Farmer's Daughter, The Bank Dick* 1940; *Road Show, Louisiana Purchase* 1941; *The Spoilers, The Palm Beach Story, The Fleet's In* 1942; *Taxi Mister* 1943; *Hail the Conquering Hero, The Big Noise* 1944; *Flame of Barbary Coast, Wonder Man, Her Highness and the Bellboy, Strange Confession, Man Alive* 1945; *Blue Skies, Bringing Up Father, The Kid from Brooklyn* 1946; *Mad Wednesday* 1947; *Variety Time* 1948.

Norway. Unlike its neighbors Sweden and Denmark, this Scandinavian country of about four million has only recently developed a feature-film industry of international stature. Ironically, the Norwegian capital of Kristiania (now Oslo) was the site of the first cinema screening in Scandinavia, held on Apr. 6, 1896. Film production was slow to develop, but exhibition of foreign films took hold quickly. The first permanent movie theater was built in the capital in 1904, and in 1913 Norway established a unique system of municipal cinemas that persists to this day. The system is one in which municipalities independently license and control theaters which, though often not profitable, serve as a network of community cultural centers.

Norway's first feature film is considered to be *The Perils of a Fisherman* (1907), produced by Hugo Hermansen and shot by Julius Jaenzon. But film production was negligible until the municipal cinemas founded Norsk Film A/S, which opened its studio in 1935. Norsk Film enjoyed some commercial success in the 30s with directors such as Tancred Ibsen (*Fant*, 1937), and survived takeover by the Nazis during Hitler's occupation of Norway in WW II. After the war, the central government became more involved in film production; by the 70s, it had taken control of Norsk Film, while the municipal cinemas had established a Norwegian Cinema and Film Foundation to promote a national cinema. Government support (which continues to this day) proved vital in bringing to the screen several films that won international acclaim in the 70s, including Anja Breien's improvisational, feminist *Wives* (1974), Laila Mikkelsen's *Us* (1975), Vibeke Likkeberg's *The Revelation* (1976), and Lasse Glomm's *The Second Shift* (1977). Norway also gained fame for its children's films, long an important genre in Scandinavia.

The prevailing style of social realism was challenged in the 80s by such controversial films as Roar Skolman's surrealistic, subjective *Junior Heads* (1981). Oddvar Einarson also showed himself an experimentalist with his first feature *X* (1986), which won a Silver Lion at Venice. Other gifted Norwegian directors include Svend Wam and Petter Venner (who collaborated on *Julia-Julia—The Story of a Downfall*, 1981), Ola Solum (*Orion's Belt*, 1985), Nils Gaup (*Pathfinder*, 1988), and Martin Asphaug (*A Handful of Time*, 1989).

Nosseck, Max. Director. *b.* Sept. 19, 1902, Nakel, Poland. *d.* 1972. *ed.* U. of Berlin; art school in Vienna. A former stage actor, he directed films in various European countries before settling in the US in the late 30s. In Hollywood he directed mostly second features, some with skill. He returned to Europe in the late 50s and settled in Germany. He also worked under the name Alexander M. Norris.

FILMS INCLUDE: In Austria—*Um die Welt ohne Geld* (also act.) 1927. In Germany—*Der Tanz ins Gluck* 1930; *Der Schlemiel* 1931; *Einmal möcht' ich keine Sorgen haben* 1932; In Portugal—*Gado Bravo* 1933. In Spain—*Alegre Voy!, Una Semana de Felicidad/One Week of Happiness, Ponderoso Caballero* 1934. In France—*Le Roi des Champs Elysées* (starring Buster Keaton) 1934. In the US (complete)—*Overture to Glory* (in Yiddish), *Girls Under 21* 1940; *Gambling Daughters* 1941; *Dillinger, The Brighton Strangler* (also co-sc.) 1945; *Black Beauty* 1946; *The Return of Rin Tin Tin* 1947; *Kill or Be Killed* 1950; *The Hoodlum, Korea Patrol* 1951; *Body Beautiful* 1953; *Der Hauptmann und sein Held* (Ger.) 1955; *Singing in the Dark* 1956; *The Garden of Eden* (also co-sc.) 1957. In Germany—*Gesch-minkte Jugend* 1960.

notch. A cue mark made by the film editor or a lab technician at the edge of a strip of film to indicate a change or correction in the printing density.

Nouvelle Vague. Literally, "New Wave." Term designated by the Paris press to describe a group of French filmmakers who turned out their first feature films in a burst of creative energy between 1958 and 1960. Unlike Italian NEOREALISM, it was not a cohesive movement aesthetically or stylistically but a conglomeration of talent brought together by economic, social, and historic circumstance. The movement had its roots in the critical writings of young film enthusiasts who in the early 50s served their theoretical apprenticeship under the guidance of André BAZIN, the co-founder with Jacques DONIOL-VALCROZE of the influential magazine CAHIERS DU CINÉMA. Leading members of the group included Claude CHABROL, François TRUFFAUT, Jean-Luc GODARD, Eric ROHMER, and Jacques RIVETTE. In their writings they developed an AUTEUR THEORY, inspired by the CAMÉRA-STYLO manifesto of Alexander ASTRUC. This led to a rejection of "papa's cinema," the old-fashioned, worn-out format of smooth but impersonal filmmaking, and conversely to the endorsement of a free, more personal style of filming, independent of the restrictions of established industry practices. On the practical side, the movement gained encouragement from such semi-independent ventures as Jean-Pierre MELVILLE'S *Le Silence de la Mer* (1949), Astruc's *Le Rideau carmoisi/The Crimson Curtain* (1953), and Agnès VARDA'S *La Pointe courte* (1954).

The breakthrough of the *Nouvelle Vague* into the mainstream of the French cinema was partly facilitated by the great commercial success of the film *Et Dieu Créa la Femme/And God Created Woman* (1956), made by a young, then unknown, director, Roger VADIM. The film was in no way revolutionary, and its box-office success stemmed mainly from its erotic content and the candid sexuality of its star, Brigitte BARDOT. But it convinced producers of the commercial viability of young filmmakers with a fresh point of view on the current young generation. With the stranglehold of the established producers thus broken, the floodgates opened for the rapid surge of the New Wave. Louis MALLE established his credentials with *Ascenseur pour l'Echafaud/Frantic* and *Les Amants/The Lovers* (both 1958). Chabrol was the first of the inner *Cahiers* circle to break through, with *Le Beau Serge* (1958), which he partly sponsored himself with money inherited from his wife. Truffaut followed with *Les 400 Coups/The 400 Blows* (1959), Rohmer with *Le Signe de Lion/The Sign of Leo* (1959), Godard with *Á Bout de Souffle/Breathless* (1960), and Rivette with *Paris nous appartient* (1960). The movement peaked in 1962, when the *Cahiers* devoted an entire issue to the Nouvelle Vague, but soon after, its impact began to wither. Each of its leading directors, except the increasingly militant Godard, went on to a successful individual career within the established commercial industry. By the end of the 60s second and third waves had emerged, in a rather feeble reaction to complacency within the cinema establishment. Little changed in the 70s, by which time the force of the Nouvelle Vague had completely dissolved both as an impetus for new ideas and as a reviving force at the box office. See also FRANCE.

Novak, Eva. Actress. *b.* 1899, St. Louis, Mo. *d.* 1988. Shapely leading lady of American silents. The younger sister of silent star Jane NOVAK, she began her career as a Mack Sennett Bathing Beauty, making her feature debut in 1919. She seemed equally at home in society melodramas and outdoor adventures, performing her own stunts in Westerns and action pictures, often opposite Tom MIX. Like her sister's, her career ended with the advent of sound, but she returned to the screen in the late 40s in character parts.

FILMS INCLUDE: *The Speed Maniac, The Feud* 1919; *Silk Husbands and Calico Wives, The Daredevil, Desert Love, Up in Mary's Attic, The Testing Block* 1920; *The Torrent, O'Malley of the Mounted, Society Secrets, The Smart Sex, The Rough Diamond, Trailin'* 1921; *Sky High, Chasing the Moon, The Man from Hell's River, The Man Who Saw Tomorrow* 1922; *Temptation, Boston Blackie, The Man Life Passed By* 1923; *The Battling Fool, Racing for Life, The Beautiful Sinner, Laughing at Danger, The Triflers* 1924; *The Fearless Lover, Sally* 1925; *Irene, No Man's Gold, 30 Below Zero* 1926; *Red Signals* 1927; *The Medicine Man, Phantom of the Desert* 1930; *The Bells of St. Mary's* 1945; *Blackmail* 1947; *Four Faces West, I Jane Doe* 1948; *Hellfire, Sunset Boulevard* 1950; *Tall Man Riding* 1955; *Sergeant Rutledge* 1960; *The Man Who Shot Liberty Valance* 1962; *Wild Seed* 1965.

Novak, Jane. Actress. *b.* 1896, St. Louis. Mo. *d.* 1990.

Pretty, blonde leading lady of American silents. Discovered at age 16, when a director saw her photo on the dressing table of her aunt, Vitagraph early star Anne Schafer. She began appearing in films in 1913. For the next 15 years she starred in some 100 shorts and features, opposite such leading men as William S. Hart, Harold Lloyd, Hobart Bosworth, Charles Ray, Edmund Lowe, Richard Dix, and Buck Jones. She was engaged to Hart at one point in the 20s, after divorcing her first husband, actor Frank Newburg. She remained popular until the advent of sound, after which she played small supporting roles in sporadic films. She amassed a fortune at the height of her career, after entering a business partnership with director Chester Bennett, which included film production and labs, an auto dealership, and real estate ventures. She owned large chunks of the San Fernando Valley, but she lost her entire fortune in the 1929 stock market crash. Her sister, Eva NOVAK, was also a silent movie star.

FILMS INCLUDE: *The Sign of Angels* 1913; *The Kiss, A Little Madonna, Hunger Knows No Law* 1914; *Into the Light, The Scarlet Sin, A Little Brother of the Rich* 1915; *The Target, The Iron Hand* 1916; *The Eyes of the World, The Innocent Sinner, The Spirit of '76* 1917; *The Tiger Man, Selfish Yates, The Claws of the Hun, A Nine O'Clock Town, The Temple of Dusk, String Beans* 1918; *Treat 'Em Rough, The Money Corral, Man's Desire, Wagon Tracks The Wolf* 1919; *Behind the Door, The Great Accident, The River's End, Isobel or the Trail's End* 1920; *Roads of Destiny, The Other Woman, Kazan* 1921; *The Rosary, Belle of Alaska, Colleen of the Pines, Thelma* 1922; *Divorce, Jealous Husbands, The Man Life Passed By* 1923; *The Lullaby, The Man Without a Heart, The Prude's Fall* (UK) 1924; *The Blackguard* (UK/Ger.), *The Danger Signal, The Substitute Wife, Lazybones* 1925; *Lost at Sea* 1926; *Closed Gates, What Price Love* 1927; *Free Lips* 1928; *Redskin* 1929; *Hollywood Boulevard* 1936; *Ghost Town* 1937; *The Yanks Are Coming* 1942; *Desert Fury* 1947; *The File on Thelma Jordan, Paid in Full* 1950; *The Boss* 1956.

Novak, Kim. Actress. Born Marilyn Pauline Novak, on Feb. 13, 1933, in Chicago. Blonde star of Hollywood films whose somewhat bland blend of standoffish coolness and earthy sensuality combined to mold her into a properly cryptic sex symbol of the 50s and early 60s. The daughter of a railroad worker of Slavic descent, she ran an elevator, worked as a salesgirl at a five-and-ten-cent store, and toured the country as "Miss Deepfreeze," demonstrating refrigerators, before stumbling into films in 1954, playing a bit in a Jane Russell vehicle, *The French Line*. That same year she was signed by Columbia and groomed to stardom by studio chief Harry COHN as a hopeful replacement for the rebellious Rita Hayworth as a box-office magnet. Despite her lack of experience as an actress and her evident discomfort in front of the camera, she quickly developed into a popular star, thanks to an appealing combination of her classical beauty and earthy, lush sensuality, or as director Richard Quine put it, "the proverbial quality of the lady in the parlor and the whore in the bedroom." By 1956 she was America's number one box-office attraction, but her popularity faded by the early 60s despite her increasing dramatic skills. During her heyday as a star, Miss Novak's name appeared frequently in the newspapers romantically linked to such celebrities as Frank Sinatra, Cary Grant, and Aly Khan. She made the headlines in 1958 when an expensive sports car given to her by the playboy son of Dominican dictator Rafael Trujillo became a subject of discussion in the US Congress. She was briefly (1965–66) married to English actor Richard JOHNSON, her co-star in *The Amorous Adventures of Moll Flanders* (1965). In 1976 she married a veterinarian and several years later retired from the screen to devote herself to breeding horses and raising llamas in Oregon and Carmel, California. She returned to film acting in the late 80s, in the process of a sobering attempt to sum up her career for an autobiography.

FILMS: *The French Line* (bit), *Pushover, Phffft* 1954; *Son of Sinbad* (bit), *Five Against the House, The Man with the Golden Arm* 1955; *Picnic, The Eddy Duchin Story* 1956; *Jeanne Eagels* (title role), *Pal Joey* 1957; *Vertigo, Bell Book and Candle* 1958; *Middle of the Night* 1959; *Strangers When We Meet, Pepe* 1960; *Boys' Night Out, The Notorious Landlady* 1962; *Of Human Bondage* (as Mildred Rogers), *Kiss Me Stupid* 1964; *The Amorous Adventures of Moll Flanders* (title role; UK) 1965; *The Legend of Lylah Clare* 1968; *The Great Bank Robbery* 1969; *Tales that Witness Madness* (UK) 1973; *The White Buffalo* 1977; *Schöner Giigolo—armer Gigolo/Just a Gigolo* (Ger.) 1979; *The Mirror Crack'd* (UK) 1980; *Es hat mir sehr gefreut* (Ger.) 1987; *The Children* (UK/Ger.) 1990; *Liebestraum* 1991.

Novarro, Ramon. Actor. *b.* Ramon Samaniegos, Feb. 6, 1899, Durango, Mexico. *d.* 1968. Romantic idol of Hollywood silents of the 20s. In Los Angeles from 1914, he was a singing waiter and vaudeville performer before breaking into films as an extra in 1917. It wasn't until 1922 that he became a star, launched by studio publicity as a "Latin lover." Overshadowed by Valentino in that role, he soon sought a broader range and a less exotic image. His most famous part was the title role in the monumental production of *Ben-Hur.* Still, he never approached the popularity of Valentino or the reigning romantic lead of the era, John Gilbert. He continued playing romantic leads into the early 30s, however, but gradually faded out, except for bits and character parts now and then. He occasionally directed the Spanish versions of films in which he starred. Reportedly gay, he never married and lived alone in a Hollywood Hills home. On October 31, 1968, his nude body was found, beaten to death by young hustlers.

FILMS INCLUDE: *The Hostage, The Little American, Joan the Woman* (bits) 1917; *The Goat* (bit) 1918; *A Small Town Idol* 1921; *Mr. Barnes of New York, The Prisoner of Zenda* (as Rupert of Hentzau), *Trifling Women* 1922; *Where the Pavement Ends, Scaramouche* 1923; *The Arab, Thy Name Is Woman, The Red Lily* 1924; *The Midshipman, A Lover's Oath* 1925; *Ben-Hur* (title role) 1926; *Lovers?, The Road to Romance, The Student Prince* 1927; *Across to Singapore, A Certain Young Man, Forbidden Hours* 1928; *The Flying Fleet, The Pagan* 1929; *Devil-May-Care, In Gay Madrid, Call of the Flesh* (and Spanish and French versions, *La Sevillana* and *Le Chanteur de seville/The Singer of Seville,* both of which he also directed) 1930; *Daybreak, Son of India, Mata Hari* 1931; *Huddle, Son-Daughter* 1932; *The Barbarian* 1933; *The Cat and the Fiddle, Laughing Boy, The Night Is Young* 1934; *Contra la Corriente* (prod., dir., sc. only; Mex.) 1936; *The Sheik Steps Out* 1937; *A Desperate Adventure* 1938; *La Comédie du Bonheur* (Fr.) 1940; *La Virgen que forjó una Patria* (Mex.) 1942; *We Were Strangers, The Big Steal* 1949; *The Outriders, Crisis* 1950; *Heller in Pink Tights* 1960.

Novelli, Amleto. Actor. *b.* Oct. 18, 1881, Bologna, Italy. *d.* 1924. Leading star of early Italian silent films, he was the hero of numerous historical spectacles, playing opposite the great "divas" of the contemporary Italian screen.

FILMS INCLUDE: *Il Conte Ugolino* 1909; *Quo Vadis, Gerusalemme liberata* 1912; *Cajus Julius Caesar, Marcantonio e Cleopatra* 1913; *Ivan the Terrible* 1914; *Christus* 1916; *Fabiola* 1917; *Beatrice* 1919; *Amore rosso, La Morte civile* 1920; *Marco Visconti* 1922; *Il Corsaro* 1924.

Novello, Ivor. Actor, playwright, screenwriter, composer. *b.* David Ivor Novello Davies, Jan. 15, 1893, Cardiff, Wales. *d.* 1951. A matinee idol of the British stage, he starred in many

British and some Continental and Hollywood films, typically as a romantic or adventurous lead. He produced numerous stage plays and authored a number of dramas and romantic musicals, several of which were turned into films. Occasionally he also wrote directly for the screen.

FILMS INCLUDE (as actor): *L'Appel du Sang* (Fr.), *Miarka la Fille a l'Ours/Miarka the Daughter of the Bear* (Fr.) 1920; *Carnival* 1921; *The Bohemian Girl* 1922; *The White Rose* (US), *Bonnie Prince Charlie, The Man Without Desire* 1923; *The Rat* (also co-play basis) 1925; *The Lodger/The Case of Jonathan Drew* 1926; *Downhill* (also co-play basis), *The Vortex* 1927; *The Constant Nymph, The South Sea Bubble* 1928; *The Return of the Rat* 1929; *Once a Lady* (US) 1931; *But the Flesh Is Weak* (sc. only from his own play, 'The Truth Game'; US), *The Lodger/The Phantom Fiend* (remake) 1932; *Sleeping Car, I Lived with You* (also sc. from own play) 1933; *Autumn Crocus* 1934; *The Rat* (remake; co-play basis only) 1937; *Free and Easy* (play basis only, 'The Truth Game'; US) 1941; *The Dancing Years* (play basis only) 1950.

Nowicki, Jan. Actor. Born on Nov. 5, 1939, in Kanal, Poland. Versatile leading man and character player of Polish and East European films. A graduate of the Kraków School of Theater and Film. Early in his career, in the late 60s, he was known as the Polish James Dean, for his handsome features and the angry young man roles he played. Later he figured prominently in several Hungarian films of Márta MÉSZÁROS.

FILMS INCLUDE: *Ashes* 1965; *Barrier* 1966; *Colonel Wolodyjowski* 1968; *Family Life* 1970; *The Third Part of the Night* 1971; *Anatomy of Love, The Klepsydra* 1972; *Story in Scarlet* 1973; *Hour After Hour* 1974; *Nine Months* (Hung.), *Red Thorns* 1976; *The Two of Them/Two Women* (Hung.) 1977; *Just Like at Home* (Hung.), *The Spiral, Moloch/Golem* 1978; *On the Move* (Hung.) 1979; *Heiresses/The Inheritance* (Hung.) 1980; *Anya and Leanya/Anna/Mother and Daughter* (Hung.) 1981; *Diary for My Children/Intimate Journal* (Hung.) 1984; *Diary for My Loved Ones/Diary for My Loves* (Hung.) 1987; *Lava* 1989; *Stowaways* (Hung.), *Diary for My Father and Mother* (Hung.) 1990.

Noyce, Phillip. Director. Born on Apr. 29, 1950, in Griffith, NSW, Australia. The son of a country lawyer, he moved with his family to Sydney when he was 12. As a teenager he began experimenting with an 8 mm camera. He turned the hobby into a passion after viewing a program of American underground films, when he realized one didn't need much of a budget to capture exciting images on film. With tiny donations by friends, he made his first short, *Better to Reign in Hell,* in 1968. He then enrolled as a law student at Sydney University but after a year switched over to the arts. Throughout his studies he continued making short films with equipment owned by the university's film society. He also became the manager of a filmmakers co-operative and worked briefly as an assistant on professional productions. In 1972 he was one of the first dozen students at the Australian Film and Television School, where he made two fiction shorts, *Caravan Park* and *That's Showbiz,* and a 50-minute documentary, *Castor and Pollux.* The latter won the Rouben Mamoulian Award at the 1974 Sydney Film Festival and represented the school at the Grenoble (France) Festival. The success of his first professional film, *God Knows Why, But It Works* (1975), a dramatized documentary about the work of a Greek-born doctor among the Aborigines, paved the way for Noyce's first feature, *Backroads* (1977), a powerful drama about race relations. He followed this immensely impressive though low-budgeted film with *Newsfront* (1978), a heartfelt valentine to newsreel filmmakers before the advent of television. After a couple of lesser dramas, Noyce returned strongly with the suspenseful thriller *Dead Calm* (1989). That film won him an invitation from Hollywood, where he has since made such big-budget films as *Patriot Games* (1992).

FEATURE FILMS: *Backroads* (also prod, addnl. sc.) 1977; *Newsfront* (also sc.) 1978; *Heatwave* (also co-sc.) 1982; *Shadows of the Peacock/Echoes of Paradise* 1987; *Dead Calm, Blind Fury* 1989; *Patriot Games* (US) 1992; *Sliver* (US) 1993; *Clear and Present Danger* 1994; *The Saint* 1997.

Nugent, Elliott. Director, actor, playwright, screenwriter. *b.* Sept. 20, 1899, Dover, Ohio. *d.* 1980. *ed.* Ohio State U. Onstage from early childhood, he appeared with his parents and sister in vaudeville and made his Broadway debut in 'Dulcy' (1921). Before long, he became established as a popular stage actor and successful playwright, often collaborating with his father, John Charles Nugent (1868–1947), who had authored more than 100 plays as well as several screenplays. Elliott's greatest success as a playwright, 'The Male Animal,' came in 1940, in collaboration with college chum James Thurber. Nugent also starred in the play and later adapted it to the screen.

Nugent made his first screen appearance in 1925 but did not act regularly in films until 1929. He played leads and second leads in a number of early Hollywood talkies, sometimes opposite his wife, Norma Lee, before becoming a film director in 1932. Working at Paramount and other studios, he specialized in comedy and light romances and effectively handled a number of screen vehicles of such stars as Harold Lloyd, Bob Hope, and Danny Kaye. However, he was less successful with his occasional ventures into drama. His film career collapsed in the early 50s, when he began suffering from the effects of alcoholism and mental problems. But he continued producing and directing for the Broadway stage for several years before retiring altogether in 1957. He later authored a novel, *Of Cheat and Charmer* (1962), and an autobiography, *Events Leading Up to the Comedy* (1965).

FILMS: As actor—*Headlines* 1925; *The Poor Nut* (co-play basis only) 1927; *Wise Girls* (also co-dial. dir., co-sc.; from own co-play, 'Kempy'), *So This Is College, Navy Blues* (co-dial. only) 1929; *Not So Dumb, Sins of the Children/The Richest Man in the World* (also co-dial.; from own co-play, 'Father's Day'), *The Single Standard* (bit), *The Unholy Three* (also co-sc.), *For the Love o' Lil, Romance* 1930; *Virtuous Husband, The Last Flight, Local Boy Makes Good* (co-play basis only, 'The Poor Nut') 1931; *Stage Door Canteen* 1943. As director—*The Mouthpiece* (co-dir. with James Flood), *Life Begins* (co-dir. with Flood) 1932; *Whistling in the Dark* (also sc.), *Three-Cornered Moon, If I Were Free* 1933; *Two Alone, Strictly Dynamite, She Loves Me Not* 1934; *Enter Madame, Love in Bloom, College Scandal, Splendor* 1935; *And So They Were Married, Wives Never Know* 1936; *It's All Yours* 1937; *Professor Beware, Give Me a Sailor* 1938; *Never Say Die, The Cat and the Canary* 1939; *Nothing but the Truth* 1941; *The Male Animal* (also co-play basis) 1942; *The Crystal Ball* 1943; *Up in Arms* 1944; *My Favorite Brunette, Welcome Stranger* 1947; *My Girl Tisa* 1948; *Mr. Belvedere Goes to College, The Great Gatsby* 1949; *The Skipper Surprised His Wife* 1950; *My Outlaw Brother* (also act.) 1951; *Just for You* 1952.

Nugent, Frank S. Screenwriter, film critic. *b.* May 27, 1908, New York City. *d.* 1965. A Columbia journalism graduate, he joined *The New York Times* as a reporter in 1929 and began writing film reviews for the newspaper in 1934. In Hollywood from 1940, he doctored other writers' scripts until turning screenwriter toward the end of the decade. At his best with Western themes, he collaborated on a number of important films of John FORD. In the late 50s Nugent was president of the Screen Writers Guild.

FILMS: *Fort Apache* 1948; *Three Godfathers, She Wore a Yellow Ribbon, Tulsa* 1949; *Wagonmaster, Two Flags West* 1950; *The Quiet Man* 1952; *Angel Face, The Red Beret/Paratrooper* (UK) 1953; *Trouble in the Glen* (UK), *They Rode West* 1954; *Mister Roberts, The Tall Men* 1955; *The Searchers* 1956; *The Rising of the Moon* 1957; *Gunman's Walk, The Last Hurrah* 1958; *Two Rode Together* 1961; *Donovan's Reef* 1963; *Incident at Phantom Hill* 1966.

number board. See SLATE.

numbering machine. A device for printing EDGE NUMBERS on a strip of film at regular intervals.

Nureyev, Rudolf. Dancer, actor. *b.* Mar. 17, 1938, in Irkutsk, USSR. *d.* 1993. *ed.* Leningrad Ballet School. Once one of the world's greatest contemporary ballet dancers. A star of the Kirov Ballet, he defected to the West in 1961, during a performance tour in Paris. He starred in a handful of films, but his acting proved excessive, limiting his effectiveness in nondancing roles. Based mainly in Paris, he performed internationally and in 1982 became a citizen of Austria. In 1989 he starred (and sang) in the US in a stage revival of the musical 'The King and I.' He died prematurely of AIDS.

FILMS: *Le Corsaire* (short; USSR) 1958; *An Evening with the Royal Ballet* (UK) 1963; *Romeo and Juliet* (UK) 1966; *Swan Lake* (also choreog.; US/Ger.) 1967; *The Invincible Six* (choreog. only; US/Iran) 1970; *The Sleeping Beauty* 1971(?); *I Am a Dancer* (doc.; UK) 1972; *Don Quixote* (also co-dir., choreog.; Austral.) 1973; *Valentino* (title role; UK) 1977; *Exposed* (US) 1983.

Nuyen, France. Actress. Born France Nguyen Vannga, on July 31, 1939, in Marseilles, France. Eurasian (French-Chinese) leading lady of several Hollywood films and star of Broadway's 'The World of Suzie Wong' (1958). In the 80s, she was a regular on TV's 'St. Elsewhere.'

FILMS: *South Pacific, In Love and War* 1958; *The Last Time I Saw Archie* 1961; *Satan Never Sleeps* 1962; *Diamond Head, A Girl Named Tamiko* 1963; *The Man in the Middle* 1964; *Dimension 5* 1966; *One More Train to Rob* 1971; *Battle for the Planet of the Apes* 1973; *China Cry* 1990; *The Joy Luck Club* 1993; *Passion to Kill* 1994.

Nuytte, Bruno. Director of photography, director. Born on Aug. 28, 1945, in Paris. A leading cinematographer of the new French cinema. Raised comfortably but unhappily by a doctor father and pharmacist mother, he was encouraged by his Flemish grandfather to take up painting. After studying art at the Académie Colarossi in Paris, he tried to enroll at the prestigious IDHEC film school in Paris but flunked the entrance exam and attended instead the Belgian film school, INSA. A lighting cameraman since the early 70s, he got his first big break in Bertrand Blier's *Going Places* (1974). On the set of *Barocco* (1976) he became romantically involved with the film's star, Isabelle ADJANI, who remained his companion for a number of years and bore him a son, Barnabé. He won the first of several César Awards for this film, the Cannes best cinematography prize for *L'Invitation au Voyage* (1982), and the British Film Academy Award for Claude Berri's *Jean de Florette* (1986). In 1988 he made an auspicious debut as a director with *Camille Claudel,* a riveting biography of the French sculptress (played by Adjani) and her obsessive relationship with Auguste Rodin. The film swept the César Awards, winning five, including best director, and was nominated for an Oscar as best foreign language picture.

FILMS INCLUDE (as cinematographer): *Le Chien* 1970; *Tristan et Iseult* 1973; *Les Valseuses/Going Places* 1974; *India Song, Souvenirs d'en France/French Provincial* 1975; *La Meilleure Facon de marcher/The Best Way to Walk, Barocco* 1976; *Le Camion* 1977; *La Tortue sur le Dos/Like a Turtle on Its Back* 1978; *Les Soeurs Brontë/The Bronte Sisters, French Postcards* (Ger./Fr.) 1979; *Brubaker* (US) 1980; *Possession* (Fr./W. Ger.), *Garde à Vue/The Inquisitor/Under Suspicion, Hotel Des Amériques* 1981; *L'Invitation au Voyage* 1982; *La Vie est un Roman/Life Is a Bed of Roses, Tchao Pantin* 1983; *Fort Saganne, La Pirate* 1984; *Détective* 1985; *Double Messieurs* (co-sc. only), *Jean de Florette, Manon des Sources/Manon of the Spring* 1986; *Camille Claudel* (dir., co-sc. only) 1988.

Nyby, Christian. Director. Born on Sept. 9, 1913, in Los Angeles. A former film editor with Warner Bros., he directed only a handful of films. One of these—*The Thing* (1951)—stands out as a classic of the science-fiction genre, suggesting perhaps the stronger than usual personal involvement of its producer, Howard HAWKS, in the directing process. Nyby's son, Christian Nyby II (*b.* June 1, 1941, Glendale, Calif.), is a prolific director of TV movies and series episodes.

FILMS INCLUDE: As editor—*Destination Tokyo, Hollywood Canteen, To Have and Have Not* 1944; *The Big Sleep, Cloak and Dagger* 1946; *Pursued, Cheyenne* 1947; *Red River* 1948; *Southside 1-1000* 1950; *The Big Sky* 1952. As director (complete)—*The Thing (From Another World)* 1951; *Hell on Devil's Island* 1957; *Young Fury, Operation CIA* 1965; *First to Fight* 1967.

Nykvist, Sven. Director of photography. Born on Dec. 3, 1922, in Moheda, Sweden. The son of missionaries who spent most of their time in Africa, he was raised by relatives and rarely saw his parents until he was 13. Despite a strict upbringing and an enforced limitation on his one childhood passion, film-going, he entered Swedish cinema as an assistant cameraman at 19, in 1941, and graduated to cinematographer in 1945. He rose to prominence in the 60s as Ingmar BERGMAN's regular cameraman, succeeding Gunnar FISCHER. An intimate friend, as well as collaborator, of Bergman, he has shared with the director great passion for light and successfully integrated lighting, composition, and camera movement with the psychological mood of Bergman's films. He won an Oscar for the cinematography of Bergman's *Cries and Whispers* (1972) and another for the director's *Fanny and Alexander* (1983). One of cinema's most accomplished lighting cameramen, he has also worked for other European and American directors, increasingly shunning technical gloss and tricky setups in favor of expressive simplicity. Widely acclaimed as one of cinema's greatest living cinematographers, he was honored with a best artistic contribution prize at Cannes for his work on Tarkovsky's *The Sacrifice* (1986). He was nominated for a third Oscar for his remarkable photography on Philip Kaufman's *The Unbearable Lightness of Being* (1988). He has also directed several documentaries and three features, one in collaboration, *Gorilla* (1956), and two solo, *The Vine Bridge* (1965) and *The Ox* (1991). His son, Carl-Gustaf Nykvist, made an impressive debut as a director in 1989 with *Women on the Roof.*

FILMS INCLUDE: *13 Chairs* 1945; *Spring at Sjösala* 1949; *Under The Southern Cross* (doc. on Albert Schweitzer; also co-dir., co-sc. with Olof Bergström), *When Lilacs Blossom* 1952; *Barabbas* (co-phot.), *The Naked Night* (co-phot.) 1953; *Salka Valka, Karin Mansdotter, Storm Over Tjurö* 1954; *Gorilla* (also co-dir. with Lars Henrik Ottoson), *Children of the Night, Girl in a Dressing Gown* 1956; *A Dreamer's Walk* 1957; *Lady in Black* 1958; *The Virgin Spring, The Judge, A Matter of Morals* (Sw./US) 1960; *Through a Glass Darkly* 1961; *Winter Light, The Silence* 1963; *All These Women, To Love, Loving Couples* 1964; *The Vine Bridge* (also dir.) 1965; *Persona* 1966; *Hour of the Wolf, Shame* 1968; *The Ritual, The Passion of Anna* 1969; *Erste Liebe/First Love* (Switz./Ger.) 1970; *The Touch* (Sw./US),

The Last Run (US), *One Day in the Life of Ivan Denisovich* (UK/Nor.) 1971; *Cries and Whispers, Siddhartha* (Ind./US) 1972; *Scenes from a Marriage* 1973; *The Dove* (US), *A Free Woman, The Magic Flute* 1974; *Black Moon* (Fr.), *Ransom/The Terrorists* (UK) 1975; *Face to Face, Le Locataire/The Tenant* (Fr.) 1976; *The Serpent's Egg* (Ger./US) 1977; *One Plus One* (also co-dir.), *Herbstsonate/Autumn Sonata* (Ger./Nor./UK), *Pretty Baby* (US), *King of the Gypsies* (US) 1978; *Hurricane* (US), *Starting Over* (US) 1979; *Aus dem Leben der Marionetten/From the Life of the Marionettes* (Ger.), *Willie and Phil* (US) 1980; *The Postman Always Rings Twice* (US) 1981; *Cannery Row* 1982; *Fanny and Alexander, Star 80* (US), *La Tragédie de Carmen* (Fr.) 1983; *Un Amour de Swann/Swann in Love, After the Rehearsal* 1984; *Agnes of God* (US) 1985; Dream Lover (US), *The Sacrifice* (Sw./Fr.) 1986; *The Unbearable Lightness of Being* (US), *Another Woman* (US) 1988; *New York Stories* ("Oedipus Wrecks" episode), *Crimes and Misdemeanors* 1989; *Buster's Bedroom* (Ger./Can./Port.) 1991; *The Ox* (dir., co-sc. only; Sw.), *Chaplin* (US) 1992; *Sleepless in Seattle, What's Eating Gilbert Grape?* 1993; *Mixed Nuts, Only You, With Honors* 1994; *Something to Talk About* 1995.

O

Oakie, Jack. Actor. *b.* Lewis Delaney Offield, Nov. 12, 1903, Sedalia, Mo. *d.* 1978. A popular portly comic with vaudeville and Broadway experience who borrowed his stage name from the state of Oklahoma, where he was raised from age five. His family later moved to New York, where Oakie attended a business school and found work as a telephone clerk in a Wall Street brokerage house. Showing comic talent in a company annual benefit show, he was persuaded to turn to acting professionally and made his stage debut in 1922, in the chorus of George M. Cohan's 'Little Nellie Kelly.' Entering films in 1928, Oakie appeared in scores of screen productions, in both leads and supporting roles, typically portraying a slow-witted, happy-go-lucky buffoon. During the 30s he was often featured in comedies and musicals with college campus backgrounds, although he looked too old and too dumb to be believable as a *bona fide* student. During that period, he perfected the traditional comic double take into a triple-take effect. He played his most memorable role in Chaplin's *The Great Dictator* (1940) as Benzini Napaloni, dictator of Bacteria, a takeoff on Mussolini. He was nominated for an Oscar in the supporting category for that portrayal. During the 40s he played mainly supporting roles, mostly in comic relief, on rare occasions dramatic, and after 1950 appeared only sporadically in films and on TV. His widow was actress Victoria Horne.

FILMS INCLUDE: *Finders Keepers* (bit), *Road House, The Fleet's In* 1928; *The Dummy, Chinatown Nights, The Wild Party, Close Harmony, The Man I Love, Street Girl, Hard to Get, Fast Company, Sweetie* 1929; *Hit the Deck, The Social Lion, The Sap from Syracuse, Let's Go Native, Sea Legs* 1930; *The Gang Buster, June Moon, Dude Ranch, Touchdown* 1931; *Dancers in the Dark, Million Dollar Legs, Madison Square Garden, Once in a Lifetime, If I Had a Million, Uptown New York* 1932; *Sailor Be Good, From Hell to Heaven, The Eagle and the Hawk, College Humor, Too Much Harmony, Sitting Pretty, Alice in Wonderland* (as Tweedledum) 1933; *Looking for Trouble, Murder at the Vanities, Shoot the Works, College Rhythm* 1934; *The Call of the Wild, The Big Broadcast of 1936* 1935; *King of Burlesque, Collegiate, Colleen, Florida Special, The Texas Rangers* 1936; *That Girl from Paris, Champagne Waltz, Super-Sleuth, The Toast of New York, Hitting a New High* 1937; *Radio City Revels, The Affairs of Annabel, Thanks for Everything* 1938; *Young People, The Great Dictator, Tin Pan Alley, Little Men* 1940; *The Great American Broadcast, Navy Blues, Rise and Shine* 1941; *Song of the Islands, Iceland* 1942; *Hello Frisco Hello, Wintertime* 1943; *It Happened Tomorrow, The Merry Monahans, Sweet and Low Down, Bowery to Broadway* 1944; *That's the Spirit* 1945; *She Wrote the Book* 1946; *When My Baby Smiles at Me* 1948; *Thieves' Highway* 1949; *Last of the Buccaneers* 1950; *Tomahawk* 1951; *Around the World in 80 Days* (cameo) 1956; *The Wonderful Country* 1959; *The Rat Race* 1960; *Lover Come Back* 1962.

Oakland, Simon. Actor. *b.* 1922, New York City. *d.* 1983. Burly, versatile character actor of stage, TV, and films. He was formerly a violinist.

FILMS INCLUDE: *The Brothers Karamazov, I Want to Live!* 1958; *The Rise and Fall of Legs Diamond, Psycho, Murder Inc.* 1960; *West Side Story* 1961; *Hemingway's Adventures of a Young Man, Follow That Dream* 1962; *Wall of Noise* 1963; *The Raiders* 1964; *The Satan Bug* 1965; *The Plainsman* (as Black Kettle), *The Sand Pebbles* 1966; *Tony Rome* 1967; *Bullitt* 1968; *On a Clear Day You Can See Forever* 1970; *The Hunting Party* (UK), *Scandalous John* 1971; *Chato's Land* 1972; *Emperor of the North Pole/Emperor of the North, Happy Mother's Day—Love George/Run Stranger Run* 1972.

oater. Slang for a Western movie. Synonyms: horse opera, sagebrusher.

Oates, Warren. Actor. *b.* July 5, 1928, Depoy, Ky. *d.* 1982. *ed.* U. of Louisville, where he got his first taste of acting in a campus play. In 1954 he headed for New York, hoping for a career on stage or in TV. Instead, he found himself checking coats at the "21" club, washing dishes, and testing gags for 'Beat the Clock.' He finally broke into live TV dramas and when these became scarce he headed for Hollywood, where he became a stock villain in numerous TV and motion picture Westerns. Steadily gaining recognition as a superb character actor, by the early 70s he had developed into a dominant screen personality in both offbeat unglamorous leads and key supporting roles. His sudden death of a heart attack at 53 robbed the American screen of one of its more interesting characters.

FILMS INCLUDE: *Up Periscope!, Yellowstone Kelly* 1959; *The Rise and Fall of Legs Diamond* 1960; *Ride the High Country* 1962; *Mail Order Bride* 1964; *Major Dundee* 1965; *Return of the Seven* 1966; *Welcome to Hard Times, In the Heat of the Night* 1967; *The Split* 1968; *Smith!, The Wild Bunch* 1969; *Barquero, There Was a Crooked Man* 1970; *Two-Lane Blacktop, The Hired Hand* 1971; *Chandler* 1972; *Tom Sawyer, Kid Blue, The Thief Who Came to Dinner, Dillinger* (title role) 1973; *Badlands, The White Dawn, Bring Me the Head of Alfredo Garcia, Cockfighter* 1974; *Race with the Devil, 92 in the Shade* 1975; *Dixie Dynamite, Drum* 1976; *Sleeping Dogs* (New

Zealand) 1977; *China 9 Liberty 37/Clayton and Catherine, The Brink's Job* 1978; *1941* 1979; *Stripes* 1981; *The Border* 1982; *Tough Enough, Blue Thunder* 1983.

O'Bannon, Dan. Screenwriter, director. Born in 1946, in St. Louis, Mo. A science-fiction specialist, he wrote a number of imaginative scripts, alone and in collaboration. He made an unremarkable debut as a director in 1985 with *The Return of the Living Dead,* a spoof of George Romero's zombie films.

FILMS (as screenwriter): *Dark Star* (also des., edit., sp. eff.) 1974; *Alien* 1979; *Dead and Buried, Heavy Metal* (co-story only) 1981; *Blue Thunder* 1983; *Lifeforce, The Return of the Living Dead* (also dir.) 1985; *Invaders from Mars* 1986; *Total Recall* 1990; *The Resurrected* 1991; *Toys* 1992.

Oberhausen Manifesto. See GERMANY.

Oberon, Merle. Actress. *b.* Estelle Merle O'Brien Thompson, Feb. 19, 1911, Tasmania (or, according to a 1985 biography, Bombay, to a British railway engineer and a Ceylonese mother). *d.* 1979. Beautiful, dark-haired leading lady of British and Hollywood films. Raised and educated in India from age seven, she arrived in London at 17 and began her career as a café hostess, under the name Queenie O'Brien. She entered British films as an extra in 1930 and played bits in a number of productions as Estelle Thompson before being discovered and groomed to stardom by Alexander KORDA, whom she married in 1939 and divorced in 1945. She graduated to leads by 1932, and in 1935, when Korda sold a share of her contract to Sam Goldwyn, she began commuting between London studios and Hollywood, rapidly establishing herself as a prominent leading lady on both sides of the Atlantic. She was nominated for an Academy Award for her performance in *The Dark Angel* (1935). She wasn't a very exciting personality or a particularly good actress, but her regal beauty adorned many important productions and proved a durable asset through the late 60s. Her near-fatal injury in a 1937 car crash caused the abandonment in midproduction of the ambitious spectacle *I Claudius,* in which she co-starred with Charles Laughton under the direction of Josef von Sternberg. Her second husband (1945–49) was cinematographer Lucien BALLARD. In 1957 she married a wealthy Italian industrialist, with whom she resided in Mexico until her divorce in 1973. That same year she returned to the screen after a long absence in *Interval,* a film she also produced and co-edited. She later married for the fourth time, to her co-star in that film, Robert Wolders, a man many years her junior, who ironically had played in *Interval* the role of a younger man who falls in love with the aging Oberon. Both were familiar members of the international jet set. She died of a stroke at 68, leaving a million dollars of her estate to the Motion Picture Country House and Hospital, where a rose garden now bears her name.

FILMS: In the UK—*The Three Passions* (bit) 1929; *A Warm Corner* (bit), *Alf's Button* (bit) 1930; *Never Trouble Trouble* (bit), *Fascination* (bit) 1931; *Service for Ladies/Reserved for Ladies* (bit), *For the Love of Mike* (bit), *Ebb Tide* (bit), *Aren't We All?* (bit), *Wedding Rehearsal, Men of Tomorrow* 1932; *The Private Life of Henry VIII* (as Anne Boleyn) 1933; *The Battle/Hara-Kiri/Thunder in the East, The Broken Melody, The Private Life of Don Juan* 1934; *The Scarlet Pimpernel* 1935. In the US—*Folies-Bergère, The Dark Angel* 1935; *These Three, Beloved Enemy* 1936; *I Claudius* (as Messalina; unfinished; UK), *Over the Moon* (UK) 1937; *The Divorce of Lady X* (UK), *The Cowboy and the Lady* 1938; *Wuthering Heights* (as Cathy Linton), *The Lion Has Wings* (UK) 1939; *'Til We Meet Again* 1940; *That Uncertain Feeling, Affectionately Yours, Lydia* 1941; *Forever and a Day, Stage Door Canteen, First Comes Courage* 1943; *The Lodger, Dark Waters* 1944; *A Song to Remember* (as George Sand), *This Love of Ours* 1945; *Night in Paradise, Temptation* 1946; *Night Song* 1947; *Berlin Express* 1948; *Pardon My French* (a French-language version, *Dans la Vie tout s'arrange*) 1951; *24 Hours of a Woman's Life/Affair in Monte Carlo* (UK) 1952; *Todo es Posible en Granada* (Sp.), *Desiree* (as Empress Josephine), *Deep in My Heart* (as lyricist Dorothy Donnelly) 1954; *The Price of Fear* 1956; *Of Love and Desire* 1963; *The Oscar* 1966; *Hotel* 1967; *Interval* (also prod., co-edit.) 1973.

object animation. A form of animation in which three-dimensional objects (puppets, fragments, etc.) are photographed one frame at a time, and moved slightly between frames to create the illusion of continuous motion. The technique is better known as STOP MOTION.

Oboler, Arch. Director, producer, screenwriter. *b.* Dec. 7. 1909, Chicago. *d.* 1987. *ed.* U. of Chicago. Long-time producer-writer of radio plays, notably the terrifying drama anthology series 'Lights Out,' he turned out a number of gimmicky, supernaturally flavored motion pictures, including the first 3-D production, *Bwana Devil* (1952). He also wrote a Broadway play, 'Night of the Auk' (1956), contributed screenplays for *Escape* (1940) and *Gangway for Tomorrow* (1943), and wrote the original story for King Vidor's *On Our Merry Way/A Miracle Can Happen* (1948). At the ebb of his career he wrote and directed a 3-D X-rated porno film, *The Stewardesses* (1969), under the assumed name Alf Silliman, Jr.

FILMS (as director): *Bewitched* (also story, sc.), *Strange Holiday* (also sc.) 1945; *The Arnelo Affair* (also sc.) 1947; *Five* (also prod., sc.) 1951; *Bwana Devil* (also prod., sc.; in 3-D) 1952; *The Twonky* (also prod., sc.) 1953; *1 + 1: Exploring the Kinsey Reports* (also prod., sc., from own play; US/Can.) 1961; *The Bubble/Fantastic Invasion of Planet Earth* (also prod., sc.; in Tri-Optiscope, or "Space-Vision") 1966; *The Stewardesses* (dir., sc. under pseudonym of Alf Silliman, Jr.) 1969; *Domo Arigato* (doc.; also prod.) 1972.

O'Brian, Hugh. Actor. Born Hugh J. Krampe, on Apr. 19, 1925, in Rochester, N.Y. *ed.* U. of Cincinnati. Virile leading man of American stage, TV, and films; popular for several years as the TV incarnation of Sheriff Wyatt Earp. Raised in Chicago, he enlisted in the Marines at 18 and became one of the youngest drill instructors in the history of the corps. After WW II he began his acting career in California repertory, often using the stage name of Jaffer Gray. He made his screen debut in 1950 and played leads and supporting roles, mainly in action pictures. But it was on TV that he became a popular star, playing the lead in 'The Life and Legend of Wyatt Earp,' which ran for six seasons (1955–61) and later had syndicated reruns. He invested his earnings in a number of successful business enterprises and became known for his charitable activity for various causes.

FILMS INCLUDE: *Never Fear, The Return of Jesse James, Rocketship XM* 1950; *Vengeance Valley, Little Big Horn* 1951; *Red Ball Express, Sally and Saint Anne, Meet Me at the Fair, Battle at Apache Pass, The Lawless Breed, Seminole, Back to God's Country, The Raiders* 1952; *The Man from the Alamo* 1953; *Saskatchewan, Broken Lance, There's No Business Like Show Business* 1954; *White Feather* 1955; *The Brass Legend* 1956; *The Fiend Who Walked the West* 1958; *Come Fly with Me* 1963; *Love Has Many Faces, In Harm's Way* 1965; *Ten Little Indians* (UK), *Ambush Bay* 1966; *Africa—Texas Style!* (US/UK) 1967; *Strategy of Terror* (originally presented on TV in 1965 as 'In Darkness Waiting') 1969; *Killer Force* (UK) 1975; *The Shootist* 1976; *The Game of Death* 1976; *Doin' Time on Planet Earth, Twins* 1988.

O'Brien, Dave (Tex). Actor. *b.* David Barclay, May 31, 1912, Big Springs, Tex. *d.* 1969. A former song-and-dance man, he played small roles in Hollywood films of the 30s before turning stuntman, then second lead and star of serials and action pictures. Throughout the 40s he was the hapless hero of the *Pete Smith Specialty* MGM comedy shorts. In the 60s he wrote comedy material for Red Skelton and directed TV programs.

FILMS INCLUDE: *Devil and the Deep, Rasputin and the Empress* 1932; *Footlight Parade, 42nd Street, Jennie Gerhardt* 1933; *The Little Colonel, Welcome Home* 1935; *The Black Coin* (serial) 1936; *Frontier Scout* 1938; *Mutiny in the Big House* 1939; *East Side Kids, The Ghost Creeps, Devil Bat* 1940; *The Spider Returns* (serial), *Flying Wild* 1941; *Captain Midnight* (serial; title role), *King of the Stallions* 1942; *Border Buckaroos, Trail of Terror, The Rangers Take Over* 1943; *Gunsmoke Mesa, Outlaw Roundup, Pinto Bandit, Spook Town, Boss of Rawhide, Dead or Alive, Tahiti Nights* 1944; *Marked for Murder, The Man Who Walked Alone, The Phantom of 42nd Street, Flaming Bullets* 1945; *Kiss Me Kate* 1953; *The Desperadoes Are in Town* 1956.

O'Brien, Edmond. Actor. *b.* Sept. 10, 1915, New York City. *d.* 1985 of Alzheimer's disease. As a boy of ten, he performed amateur magic tricks that he learned from Harry Houdini, a neighbor. In amateur dramatics from his late teens, he dropped out of Fordham University after one year to take advantage of a scholarship to the Neighborhood Playhouse School of the Theatre and supported himself as a bank clerk while struggling to obtain stage roles. After a season in summer stock, he began playing small roles on Broadway and in 1937 joined Orson Welles's Mercury Players, performing both on radio programs and in stage productions. He began appearing in films in 1938 and for a while played a mixture of leads and supporting roles, memorably as a dying man in search of his killer in *D.O.A.* (1950). But his stocky build, pudgy features, and heavy jowls soon marked him for character roles. Somewhat of a ham, but always interesting to watch, he played many screen roles with distinction and won an Academy Award as best supporting actor for his portrayal of a sweaty press agent in *The Barefoot Contessa* (1954). He was nominated for another Oscar for *Seven Days in May* (1964). He has also appeared frequently on TV and in the early 60s starred in the series 'Johnny Midnight' (1960), 'Sam Benedict' (1962–63), and 'The Long Hot Summer' (1965). He directed several TV episodes as well as two feature films, *Shield for Murder* (1954), in collaboration with Howard W. Koch, and *Mantrap* (1961). His first wife (1941–42) was actress Nancy KELLY; his second (1948–67) was Olga San Juan (*b.* Mar. 16, 1927, Brooklyn, N.Y.), the "Puerto Rican Pepper Pot" who enlivened some musicals of the 40s with her fiery Latin temperament. Their daughter, Maria O'Brien (*b.* 1950), is a TV and film actress.

FILMS INCLUDE: *Prison Break* 1938; *The Hunchback of Notre Dame* (as Pierre Gringoire) 1939; *Parachute Battalion* 1941; *Obliging Young Lady, Powder Town* 1942; *The Amazing Mrs. Holliday* 1943; *Winged Victory* 1944; *The Killers* 1946; *The Web* 1947; *A Double Life, Another Part of the Forest* (as Ben Hubbard), *For the Love of Mary, An Act of Murder/Live Today for Tomorrow, Fighter Squadron* 1948; *White Heat* 1949; *Backfire, D.O.A., 711 Ocean Drive, Between Midnight and Dawn, The Admiral Was a Lady* 1950; *The Redhead and the Cowboy, Two of a Kind, Warpath, Silver City* 1951; *The Denver and the Rio Grande, The Turning Point* 1952; *Man in the Dark, The Hitch-Hiker, Julius Caesar* (as Casca), *The Bigamist* 1953; *Shield for Murder* (also co-dir. with Howard W. Koch), *The Shanghai Story, The Barefoot Contessa* 1954; *Pete Kelly's Blues* 1955; *D-Day the Sixth of June, A Cry in the Night, 1984* (as Winston Smith; UK), *The Rack, The Girl Can't Help It* 1956; *The Big Land* 1957; *The World Was His Jury, Sing Boy Sing* 1958; *L'Ambitieuse/The Climbers* (Fr.), *Up Periscope* 1959; *The Last Voyage, The Third Voice* 1960; *The Great Impostor, Man-Trap* (dir., co-prod. only) 1961; *Moon Pilot, The Man Who Shot Liberty Valance, Birdman of Alcatraz, The Longest Day* 1962; *Seven Days in May, Rio Conchos* 1964; *Sylvia, Synanon* 1965; *Fantastic Voyage* 1966; *Le Vicomte règle ses Comptes/The Viscount* (in English-language version only; Fr./It./Sp.), *Peau d'Espion/To Commit a Murder* (Fr./It./Ger.) 1967; *The Wild Bunch* 1969; *They Only Kill Their Masters* 1972; *A Proposito Lucky Luciano/Re: Lucky Luciano* (It.), *99 44/100% Dead* 1974.

O'Brien, Eugene Actor. *b.* Nov. 14, 1882, Boulder, Colo. *d.* 1966. Romantic leading man of the American stage and silent Hollywood films, often opposite Norma Talmadge. He had abandoned medical practice for an acting career.

FILMS INCLUDE: *Moonstone* 1915; *Poor Little Peppina, Return of Eve, Scarlet Woman* 1916; *Poppy, Rebecca of Sunnybrook Farm, The Moth* 1917; *A Romance of the Underworld, By Right of Purchase, Under the Greenwood Tree, The Safety Curtain, De Luxe Annie* 1918; *Fires of Faith, Come Out of the Kitchen, The Perfect Lover, Broken Melody* 1919; *Wonderful Chance* (dual role), *A Fool and His Money, The Figurehead, Broadway and Home* 1920; *Worlds Apart, Gilded Lies, The Last Door, Is Life Worth Living?, Clay Dollars* 1921; *Chivalrous Charlie, The Prophet's Paradise, Channing of the Northwest, John Smith* 1922; *The Voice from the Minaret* 1923; *Secrets, The Only Woman* 1924; *Frivolous Sal/Flaming Love, Dangerous Innocence, Siege, Graustark, Souls for Sables, Simon the Jester* 1925; *Flames, Fine Manners* 1926; *The Romantic Age* 1927; *Faithless Lover* 1928.

O'Brien, George. Actor. *b.* Apr. 19, 1900, San Francisco, the son of that city's chief of police. *d.* 1985. Muscular star of Hollywood silents and talkies. An all-around athlete in Santa Clara College and heavyweight boxing champion of the Pacific Fleet during WW I, he entered films in 1922 as an assistant cameraman but soon became a stuntman and bit player. A virtual unknown when selected by John Ford to star in *The Iron Horse* (1924), he was a popular leading man by the time he starred in Murnau's *Sunrise* (1927). Studio publicity nicknamed him "The Chest" because of his rugged physique. In the 30s he became strictly a Western star, a leading cowboy on the Fox, then RKO lots. Re-enlisted in the Navy in WW II, he saw extensive action in the Pacific, receiving numerous decorations. He also participated in filmmaking capacities in the Korean War and Vietnam conflict. Married at one time (1933–48) to Marguerite CHURCHILL.

FILMS INCLUDE: *White Hands* 1922; *The Ne'er-Do-Well, Woman-Proof* 1923; *Shadows of Paris, The Man Who Came Back, The Iron Horse, The Roughneck* 1924; *The Dancers, The Fighting Heart, Havoc* 1925; *The Blue Eagle, Three Bad Men, Fig Leaves, Silver Treasure* 1926; *Paid to Love, Sunrise, East Side West Side, Is Zat So?* 1927; *Sharp Shooters, Honor Bound, Blindfold* 1928; *True Heaven, Noah's Ark* (as Japheth), *Salute, Masked Emotions* 1929; *The Lone Star Ranger, Rough Romance, Last of the Duanes* 1930; *Fair Warning, Seas Beneath, A Holy Terror, Riders of the Purple Sage* 1931; *The Gay Caballero, Mystery Ranch* 1932; *Robber's Roost, Life in the Raw* 1933; *Frontier Marshal, Ever Since Eve* 1934; *When a Man's a Man, Hard Rock Harrigan, The Cowboy Millionaire* 1935; *O'Malley of the Mounted, Daniel Boone* 1936; *Hollywood Cowboy* 1937; *Painted Desert, Gun Law* 1938; *The Arizona Legion, The Fighting Gringo* 1939; *Bullet Code* 1940; *My Wild Irish Rose* 1947; *Fort Apache* 1948; *She Wore a Yellow Ribbon* 1949; *Gold Raiders* 1951; *Cheyenne Autumn* 1964.

O'Brien, Margaret. Actress. Born Angela Maxine O'Brien, on Jan. 15, 1937, in Los Angeles. Charming, natural child star of MGM films of the 40s; considered by many the best little thespian ever to adorn the screen. Modeling from the age of three, she made her screen debut at four in *Babes on Broadway* as a child auditioning for a show with the line, "Don't send my brother to the chair. Don't let him burn." She later figured prominently in a variety of productions, both dramas and musicals, notably as the younger sister Tootie in *Meet Me in St. Louis*. In 1944 she received a special Academy Award as "Outstanding Child Actress" of her day. But like most other child stars, she failed in her bid to graduate into adolescent roles and in 1951 she retired from the screen. She later unsuccessfully tried a comeback as an ingenue and subsequently appeared in only a handful of scattered films. She remained active on TV and on the dinner-theater circuit. In 1979 she began a stint as a civilian aide for Southern California to Secretary of the Army Clifford Alexander.

FILMS: *Babes on Broadway* 1941; *Journey for Margaret* 1942; *Dr. Gillespie's Criminal Case, Thousands Cheer, Madame Curie* 1943; *Lost Angel, Jane Eyre, The Canterville Ghost, Meet Me in St. Louis, Music for Millions* 1944; *Our Vines Have Tender Grapes* 1945; *Bad Bascomb, Three Wise Fools* 1946; *The Unfinished Dance, Tenth Avenue Angel* 1947; *Big City* 1948; *Little Women, The Secret Garden* 1949; *Her First Romance* 1951; *Glory* 1956; *Heller in Pink Tights* 1960; *Diabolic Wedding* (Peru) 1971; *Annabelle Lee* (Peru) 1972; *Amy* 1981.

O'Brien, Pat. Actor. *b.* William Joseph Patrick O'Brien, Nov. 11, 1899, Milwaukee. *d.* 1983. Hollywood's Irishman-in-residence, he played hard-boiled types in scores of films of the 30s and 40s. He was a childhood friend of Spencer TRACY, and the two future actors attended a military school together and joined the Navy together during WW I. After the war, they both went to a drama school in New York. O'Brien began his stage career as a song-and-dance man and in the late 20s played dramatic roles on Broadway. He had the lead in an isolated Western film in 1921 but did not begin appearing regularly in films until the advent of sound. During the 30s he represented the forces of good in many of the Warner Bros. social-justice and gangster films, typically in the garb of a cop or a priest, often in conflict with James Cagney. His many memorable parts included the title role in *Knute Rockne—All American* (1940), in which he portrayed the famed Notre Dame coach who exhorted his team to "go out and win one for the Gipper" (played by Ronald Reagan). He continued playing lead roles and supporting parts at a hectic pace through the 40s and at a much slower rate in the 50s, mainly in character parts. For years he was a favorite TV guest on St. Patrick's Day. He was married to actress Eloise Taylor from 1931 till his death of a heart attack at 81. Autobiography: *The Wind at My Back* (1964).

FILMS INCLUDE: *Shadows of the West* 1921; *Fury of the Wild* 1929; *Honor Among Lovers, The Front Page, Personal Maid, Consolation Marriage* 1931; *The Final Edition, Hell's House, American Madness, Hollywood Speaks, Virtue, Air Mail* 1932; *Laughter in Hell, Destination Unknown, The World Gone Mad, Bureau of Missing Persons, Bombshell* 1933; *Gambling Lady, 20 Million Sweethearts, Here Comes the Navy, The Personality Kid, Flirtation Walk, I Sell Anything* 1934; *Devil Dogs of the Air, In Caliente, Oil for the Lamps of China, The Irish in Us, Page Miss Glory, Stars Over Broadway* 1935; *Ceiling Zero, I Married a Doctor, Public Enemy's Wife, China Clipper* 1936; *The Great O'Malley, Slim, San Quentin, Submarine D-1* 1937; *Women Are Like That, Cowboy from Brooklyn, Boy Meets Girl, Garden of the Moon, Angels with Dirty Faces* 1938; *Off the Record, Indianapolis Speedway, The Night of Nights* 1939; *The Fighting 69th, Castle on the Hudson, 'Til We Meet Again, Torrid Zone, Knute Rockne—All American* (title role) 1940; *Escape to Glory/Submarine Zone, Two Yanks in Trinidad, Broadway, Flight Lieutenant* 1942; *Bombardier, The Iron Major, His Butler's Sister* 1943; *Secret Command, Marine Raiders* 1944; *Having Wonderful Crime, Man Alive* 1945; *Perilous Holiday, Crack-up* 1946; *Riff-raff* 1947; *Fighting Father Dunne, The Boy with Green Hair* 1948; *A Dangerous Profession* 1949; *Johnny One-Eye, The Fireball* 1950; *The People Against O'Hara, Criminal Lawyer* 1951; *Okinawa* 1952; *Ring of Fear* 1954; *Kill Me Tomorrow* 1957; *The Last Hurrah* 1958; *Some Like It Hot* 1959; *Town Tamer* 1965; *The Phynx* (cameo) 1970; *The End* 1978; *Ragtime* 1981.

O'Brien, Virginia. Actress, singer. Born on Apr. 8, 1921, in Los Angeles. Deadpan singing comedienne of MGM musicals and other light films of the 40s. The daughter of the captain of detectives of the Los Angeles police and on her mother's side a niece of film director Lloyd Bacon, she appeared briefly on the stage before making her film debut in 1940. She enlivened some 15 films with her sphinx-like song delivery, often opposite comedian Red SKELTON, and was dubbed "Miss Red Hot Frozen Face" by fan magazines. Her gimmick wore thin, however, after several years, and she retired from films in 1947, returning to the screen only once more, in 1955. Her first husband was actor Kirk ALYN.

FILMS: *Hullabaloo, Sky Murder* 1940; *The Big Store, Ringside Maisie, Lady Be Good* 1941; *Ship Ahoy, Panama Hattie* 1942; *Du Barry Was a Lady, Thousands Cheer* 1943; *Two Girls and a Sailor, Meet the People* 1944; *The Harvey Girls, Ziegfeld Follies, The Show-Off, Till the Clouds Roll By* 1946; *Merton of the Movies* 1947; *Francis in the Navy* 1955.

O'Brien, Willis H. Special-effects artist. *b.* 1886, Oakland, Calif. *d.* 1962. A former newspaper cartoonist (the San Francisco *Daily News*) and commercial sculptor (San Francisco World's Fair, 1913), he began experimenting with special effects in short trick films in 1914. From the mid-20s he contributed some of the most amazing special effects ever to be seen on the American screen, pioneering the technique of STOP MOTION animation to create the illusion of living dinosaurs and other giant creatures. His effects for *King Kong* (1933) are still considered by many to be the best example of stop-motion photography. He received an Academy Award for the special effects of *Mighty Joe Young* (1949). His assistant on that film, Ray HARRYHAUSEN, went on to become a prominent stop-motion animator in his own right.

FILMS INCLUDE: *The Dinosaur and The Missing Link* (short) 1914; *The Ghost of Slumber Mountain* (short) 1918; *The Lost World* 1925; *King Kong, Son of Kong* 1933; *The Last Days of Pompeii* 1935; *The Dancing Pirate* 1936; *Mighty Joe Young* 1949; *The Beast of Hollow Mountain* (story only), *The Animal World* 1956; *The Black Scorpion* 1957; *The Giant Behemoth* 1959; *The Lost World* (remake) 1960; *It's a Mad Mad Mad Mad World* 1963.

O'Connell, Arthur. Actor. *b.* Mar. 29, 1908, New York City. *d.* 1981. A veteran of vaudeville and the legitimate stage, he played character parts in numerous Hollywood films from the late 30s, usually a sincere, folksy type. Also active on TV. He was nominated for Oscars for memorable performances in *Picnic* (1956) and *Anatomy of a Murder* (1959).

FILMS INCLUDE: *Murder in Soho/Murder in the Night* (UK), *Freshman Year* 1939; *Dr. Kildare Goes Home* 1940; *Citizen Kane* 1941; *Canal Zone* 1942; *It Happened Tomorrow* 1944; *One Touch of Venus, State of the Union, Naked City, Force of Evil* 1948; *The Whistle at Eaton Falls* 1951; *Picnic, The Man in the Gray Flannel Suit, The Proud Ones, Bus Stop, The Solid Gold Cadillac* 1956; *Operation Mad Ball, April Love* 1957; *Voice in the Mirror, Man of the West* 1958; *Gidget, Anatomy of a Murder, Operation Petticoat* 1959; *Cimarron* 1960; *The Great Impostor, Misty, Pocketful of Miracles* 1961; *Follow That Dream* 1962; *The Seven Faces of Dr. Lao, Kissin' Cousins* 1964; *Nightmare in the Sun, The Great Race, The Third Day* 1965; *The Silencers, Fantastic Voyage* 1966; *A Covenant with Death, The Reluctant Astronaut* 1967; *The Power* 1968; *Suppose They Gave a War and Nobody Came* 1970; *The Last Valley* (UK) 1971; *Ben, They Only Kill Their Masters, The Poseidon Adventure* 1972; *Wicked Wicked* 1973; *Huckleberry Finn* 1974; *The Hiding Place* 1975.

O'Connolly, Jim. Director. Born in 1924, in England. He made several standard potboilers in the 60s and early 70s, with the exception of *The Little Ones* (1965), an unusual thriller about child runaways, and *The Valley of Gwangi* (1969), a film memorable for its special effects by Ray HARRYHAUSEN. He collaborated on his own scripts and several screenplays by other directors, occasionally also producing.

FILMS (as director): *The Hi-Jackers, Smokescreen* 1964; *The Little Ones* 1965; *Berserk* 1967; *Crooks and Coronets/Sophie's Place, The Valley of Gwangi* 1969; *Beyond the Fog/Horror on Snape Island/Tower of Evil* 1972; *Mistress Pamela* 1974.

O'Connor, Carroll. Actor. Born on Aug. 2, 1922, the Bronx, N.Y. *ed.* University College, Dublin; U. of Montana. After four years as a merchant marine, he made his stage debut in Ireland with Dublin's Gate Theatre, and his first Broadway appearance in 1958. During the 60s he played supporting roles in many films and TV productions. After years of relative obscurity, he gained "instant" fame and wealth as Archie Bunker, the narrow-minded, bigoted, but still lovable hero of the hit TV series 'All in the Family' (1971–79) and its follow-up 'Archie Bunker's Place' (1979–83), winning Emmy Awards in 1972, 1977, 1978, and 1979. In the 80s he returned to Broadway for a couple of plays, one of which he also directed. Despite heart bypass surgery in 1989, he continued an energetic schedule, which included the TV series 'In the Heat of the Night.'

FILMS: *A Fever in the Blood, Parrish, By Love Possessed* 1961; *Belle Sommers, Lad: A Dog, Lonely Are the Brave* 1962; *Cleopatra* 1963; *In Harm's Way* 1965; *What Did You Do in the War Daddy?, Hawaii, Not with My Wife You Don't!* 1966; *Warning Shot, Point Blank, Waterhole #3* 1967; *The Devil's Brigade, For Love of Ivy* 1968; *Death of a Gunfighter, Marlowe* 1969; *Kelly's Heroes* 1970; *Doctors' Wives* 1971; *Law and Disorder* 1974.

O'Connor, Donald. Actor. Born on Aug. 28, 1925, in Chicago. Breezy, sprightly, eternally youthful song-and-dance comedian of Hollywood films. The son of circus performers turned vaudevillians, he joined the family act as an infant and was 11 years old when he made his film debut, performing a specialty routine with two of his brothers in *Melody for Two* (1937). He was signed by Paramount in 1938 and played adolescent roles in several films, including Huckleberry Finn in *Tom Sawyer—Detective* (1938) and Beau as a child in *Beau Geste* (1939). He then returned to vaudeville for a couple of years, reappearing on the screen in 1942 for a long string of low-budget Universal musical films in which he played the juvenile lead, often opposite another exuberant youngster, Peggy Ryan, or such youthful starlets as Gloria Jean, Ann Blyth, and Susanna Foster. In the early 50s his sagging career received a healthy lift from a talking mule, thanks to the inane but popular comedy series "Francis." During the 50s he also co-starred in several major musical films, notably *Singin' in the Rain* (1952), and in 1953 won an Emmy for 'The Colgate Comedy Hour,' of which he was a rotating host in 1951–54. In 1954–55 he starred in 'The Donald O'Connor Texaco Show.' In 1957 he portrayed screen comedian Buster Keaton in the pallid film biography *The Buster Keaton Story.* He subsequently appeared in only a handful of sporadic films and instead concentrated on composing music for the concert hall. In 1956 he conducted the Los Angeles Philharmonic in the premiere performance of his first symphony, *Reflections d'un Comique.* An album of his music was later recorded in Europe by the Brussels Symphony Orchestra.

FILMS: *Melody for Two* 1937; *Sing You Sinners, Sons of the Legion, Men with Wings, Tom Sawyer—Detective* (as Huck Finn) 1938; *Unmarried, Night Work, Boy Trouble, Million Dollar Legs, Beau Geste, Death of a Champion, On Your Toes* 1939; *What's Cookin', Private Buckaroo, Give Out Sisters, Get Hep to Love* 1942; *When Johnny Comes Marching Home, It Comes Up Love, Strictly in the Groove, Mister Big, Top Man* 1943; *Chip off the Old Block, Follow the Boys, This Is the Life, Bowery to Broadway, The Merry Monahans* 1944; *Patrick the Great* 1945; *Something in the Wind* 1947; *Are You with It?, Feudin' Fussin' and A-Fightin'* 1948; *Yes Sir That's My Baby* 1949; *Francis, Curtain Call at Cactus Creek, The Milkman* 1950; *Double Crossbones, Francis Goes to the Races* 1951; *Singin' in the Rain, Francis Goes to West Point* 1952; *Call Me Madam, I Love Melvin, Francis Covers the Big Town, Walkin' My Baby Back Home* 1953; *Francis Joins the Wacs, There's No Business Like Show Business* 1954; *Francis in the Navy* 1955; *Anything Goes* 1956; *The Buster Keaton Story* (title role) 1957; *Cry for Happy, Le Meraviglie di Aladino/Les Mille et Une Nuits/The Wonders of Aladdin* (as Aladdin; It./Fr.) 1961; *That Funny Feeling* 1965; *That's Entertainment* (on-screen co-narrator) 1974; *Ragtime* 1981; *Pandemonium* 1982; *A Time to Remember* (doc.) 1990; *Toys* 1992; *That's Entertainment! III* 1994; *Out to Sea* 1997.

O'Connor, Glynnis. Actress. Born on Nov. 19, 1955, in New York City. *ed.* State U. of New York, at Purchase. Petite ingenue and leading lady of American films of the 70s and early 80s. The daughter of producer Daniel O'Connor and actress Lenka Peterson, she also performed on stage and in TV, including the series 'Sons and Daughters' (1974).

FILMS: *Jeremy* 1973; *Baby Blue Marine, Ode to Billy Joe* 1976; *Kid Vengeance* 1977; *California Dreaming* 1979; *Those Lips Those Eyes* 1980; *Melanie* (Can.), *Night Crossing* 1982; *Johnny Dangerously* 1984.

O'Connor, Kevin J. Actor. Born in 1964 in Illinois. *ed.* DePaul U. Trained at Chicago's Goodman Theatre School of Drama, he played young leads and supporting roles in Hollywood films of the late 80 and early 90s. Not to be confused with Kevin O'Connor (*b.* May 7, 1938, Honolulu), a New York–based stage actor who also appeared in occasional films.

FILMS: *Peggy Sue Got Married, Once More Saturday Night* 1986; *Candy Mountain* (Can./Switz./Fr.) 1987; *The Moderns* (as Hemingway) 1988; *Signs of Life, Steel Magnolias* 1989; *Love at Large* 1990; *F/X2* 1991; *Hero* 1992; *Equinox* 1993; *Color of Night, No Escape* 1994; *Canadian Bacon, Lord of Illusions, Virtuosity* 1995.

O'Connor, Pat. Director. Born 1943 in Ardmore, Ireland. A restless Catholic high school graduate, he went to London to broaden his horizons, earning his keep there as a ditch digger and wine bottle corker. After a stint as a lab technician at Oxford University, he crossed the Atlantic and enrolled at UCLA as a liberal arts undergraduate. From there, he headed northeast to study filmmaking at Toronto's Ryerson Polytechnical Institute. Returning to Ireland, he directed numerous documentaries and dramas for Irish television, winning a British Academy Award for 'A Ballroom of Romance' (1981). His work on fact films about the strife in Northern Ireland prepared him well for his first feature, *Cal* (1984), a no-punches-pulled, excellently played drama set against that background. It gained a best actress prize for Helen MIRREN at Cannes. O'Connor received another critical nod for *A Month in the Country* (1987), but his American-made *Stars and Bars* (1988) and *The January Man* (1989) represented serious setbacks in a seemingly promising career.

FEATURE FILMS: *Cal* (Ire./UK) 1984; *A Month in the Country* (UK) 1987; *Stars and Bars* (US) 1988; *The January Man* (US) 1989; *Fools of Fortune* (UK) 1990; *Circle of Friends* 1995; *Inventing the Abbotts* 1997.

O'Connor, Una. Actress. *b.* Agnes Teresa McGlade, Oct. 23, 1880, Belfast. *d.* 1959. Birdlike character actress of numerous Hollywood films of the 30s and 40s. She started her career at Dublin's Abbey Theatre and later appeared on the London and New York stage. She appeared in a wide variety of films, typically portraying Irish or English maids, spinsters, or gossips, or a combination of all three. She perfected an ear-piercing shriek, which she used most effectively in a couple of horror films.

FILMS INCLUDE: *Dark Red Roses* (UK) 1929; *Murder* (UK) 1930; *Cavalcade, Pleasure Cruise, The Invisible Man* 1933; *Orient Express, Stingaree, Chained, The Barretts of Wimpole Street* 1934; *David Copperfield* (as Mrs. Gummidge), *Bride of Frankenstein, The Informer* 1935; *Little Lord Fauntleroy, Rose Marie, Suzy, Lloyds of London* 1936; *The Plough and the Stars* (as Mrs. Gogan), *The Adventures of Robin Hood* 1938; *We Are Not Alone* 1939; *Lillian Russell, The Sea Hawk* 1940; *Strawberry Blonde, How Green Was My Valley* 1941; *Always in My Heart, My Favorite Spy, Random Harvest* 1942; *This Land Is Mine, Holy Matrimony* 1943; *The Canterville Ghost* 1944; *The Bells of St. Mary's* 1945; *Cluny Brown, Of Human Bondage, The Return of Monte Cristo* 1946; *Ivy* 1947; *Adventures of Don Juan* 1948; *Witness for the Prosecution* 1958.

O'Day, Dawn. See SHIRLEY, Anne.

Odets, Clifford. Playwright, screenwriter, director. *b.* July 18, 1906, Philadelphia. *d.* 1963. A stage actor from the mid-20s, he became one of America's leading dramatists in the 30s with a succession of plays produced under the aegis of the famous Group Theatre. In the mid-30s he went to Hollywood, where he wrote a number of screenplays and doctored many others. He later also directed two solid screen dramas, *None but the Lonely Heart* (1944) and *The Story on Page One* (1959). His first wife (1937–40) was actress Luise RAINER.

FILMS (as screenwriter): *The General Died at Dawn* 1936; *Golden Boy* (play basis only) 1939; *Black Sea Fighters* (English commentary for Soviet doc.) 1943; *None but the Lonely Heart* (also dir.) 1944; *Deadline at Dawn* 1946; *Humoresque* 1947; *Clash by Night* (play basis only) 1952; *The Country Girl* (play basis only) 1954; *The Big Knife* (play basis only) 1955; *Sweet Smell of Success* 1957; *The Story on Page One* (also dir.) 1959; *Wild in the Country* 1961.

O'Donnell, Cathy. Actress. *b.* Ann Steely, July 6, 1923, Siluria, Ala. *d.* 1970. Fragile young leading lady of Hollywood films of the late 40s and 50s. Most memorable in her first screen role, as the sweetheart of WW II amputee Harold Russell in *The Best Years of Our Lives* (1946). She died at 46 of a cerebral hemorrhage.

FILMS: *The Best Years of Our Lives* 1946; *Bury Me Dead* 1947; *The Amazing Mr. X/The Spiritualist* 1948; *They Live by Night* 1949; *Side Street, The Miniver Story* 1950; *Never Trust a Gambler, Detective Story* 1951; *The Woman's Angle* (UK) 1952; *Eight O'Clock Walk* (UK), *L'Amante di Paride/Loves of Three Queens/The Face That Launched a Thousand Ships* (It./Fr.) 1954; *Mad at the World, The Man from Laramie* 1955; *The Deerslayer, The Story of Mankind* 1957; *My World Dies Screaming* 1958; *Ben-Hur* (as Tirzah) 1959.

O'Donnell, Chris. Actor. Born Christopher Eugene O'Donnell, June 26, 1970, in Chicago, Ill. *ed.* Loyola Academy, Chicago; Boston College; University of California, Los Angeles. After his feature film debut as Jessica LANGE's oldest son in *Men Don't Leave* (1990), this innocent-looking, clean-cut young leading man has gone on to become one of the most popular young stars of the 90s. His high-profile performance as "the boy wonder" in the tremendously successful *Batman Forever* (1995) and its sequel *Batman and Robin* (1997) have given him box-office clout and an opportunity to shine in a variety of roles in major Hollywood films.

FILMS: *Men Don't Leave* 1990; *Fried Green Tomatoes* 1991; *Scent of a Woman, School Ties* 1992; *The Three Musketeers* 1993; *Blue Sky* 1994; *Batman Forever, Circle of Friends, Mad Love* 1995; *The Chamber, In Love and War* 1996; *Batman and Robin* 1997.

O'Donnell, Rosie. Actress, comedian. Born 1962 in Commack, N.Y. *ed.* Dickinson College; Boston University. Effusive, endearing comic-turned-actress whose film career took off after appearing in the touching ensemble piece *A League of Their Own* (1993). Between film roles and after a side trip to Broadway in the revival of 'Grease,' she has since become the host of her own very successful syndicated talk show.

FILMS: *A League of Their Own, Another Stakeout, Sleepless In Seattle* 1993; *Car 54 Where Are You?, Exit To Eden, The Flintstones, I'll Do Anything* 1994; *Now and Then* 1995; *Beautiful Girls, Harriet the Spy* 1996; *Wide Awake* 1997.

Odorama. See AROMA-RAMA.

O'Driscoll, Martha. Actress. Born on Mar. 4, 1922, in Tulsa, Okla. Hollywood juvenile player of the late 30s and leading lady in the 40s.

FILMS INCLUDE: *Collegiate* 1935; *Champagne Waltz* 1937; *Mad About Music* 1938; *The Secret of Dr. Kildare, Judge Hardy and Son* 1939; *Laddie, Forty Little Mothers, Li'l Abner* 1940; *The Lady Eve, Pacific Blackout* 1941; *Reap the Wild Wind, My Heart Belongs to Daddy* 1942; *The Fallen Sparrow, Crazy House* 1943; *Follow the Boys, Ghost Catchers* 1944; *Here Come the Co-Eds, Her Lucky Night, The Daltons Ride Again, House of Dracula* 1945; *Blonde Alibi, Down Missouri Way, Criminal Court* 1946; *Carnegie Hall* 1947.

O'Ferrall, George More. See MORE O'FERRALL, George.

off camera. Not within the field of view of a shot, such as an actor who does not appear in a shot but whose presence is felt by implication.

off mike. Directed away from a microphone and therefore lacking in clarity. It refers to sound that is normally unusable but is sometimes deliberately recorded to suggest distance, cavernous space, etc.

off register. Showing a rocking effect on the screen as a result of camera vibration. Often done deliberately to simulate the aftereffects of explosions, volcanic eruptions, etc.

off scene. Refers to a sound whose source is not visible on the screen. Abbreviated as "OS."

Ogier, Bulle. Actress. Born in 1939, in Boulogne-sur-Seine, France. Gifted blonde leading lady of the Paris stage and French films. A pioneer of the café-theater movement, she began appearing on the screen in the late 60s and before long proved herself a capable interpreter of difficult roles in films of such unconventional directors as Rivette, Duras, Tanner, Schmid, and Schroeder. She was memorable as the compassionate dominatrix who caters lovingly to a masochistic clientele in the latter's *Maîtresse* (1976). Her daughter, Pascale Ogier (1960–84), was a rising star who died tragically at 24, shortly after winning the best actress award at Cannes for Eric Rohmer's *Les Nuits de la Pleine Lune/Full Moon in Paris* (1984).

FILMS INCLUDE: *L'Amour fou* 1968; *Pauline s'en va, Pierre et Paul, Piège* 1969; *Les Stances à Sophie/Sophie's Ways* 1970; *La Salamndre/The Salamander, Rendez-vous à Bray* 1971; *La Vallée/The Valley, La Charme discret de la Bourgeoisie/The Discreet Charm of the Bourgeoisie* 1972; *Le Gang des Otages/The Hostages, Io e lui* (It.), *Projection privée* 1973; *Céline et Julie vont en Bateau/Celine and Julie Go Boating, La Paloma* 1974; *Mariage/Marriage, Un Divorce Heureux, Maîtresse/Mistress* 1975; *Jamais plus toujours, Duelle, Serail des Journées entières dans les Arbres/Days in the Trees* 1976; *Le Navire Night, La Mémoire courte* (Bel./Fr.), *Die dritte Generation/The Third Generation* (Ger.) 1979; *Agatha et les Lectures limitées* 1981; *Le Pont du Nord* (also co-sc.) 1982; *La Derelitta* 1983; *Tricheurs* 1984; *O Meu Caso/Mon cas* (Port./Fr.) 1986; *Das weite Land* (Ger.) 1987; *Candy Mountain* (Can./Switz./Fr.) 1987; *La Bande des Quatre* 1989; *North* 1991; *Personne ne M'Aime/No One Loves Me, Regarde les Hommes Tomber* 1994; *Irma Vep* 1996.

O'Hara, Catherine. Actress, comedienne, writer. Born on March 4, 1954, in Toronto, Canada. Dry, energetic comedic lead of screen, TV, and stage. After performing as part of the Second City improvisational troupe in Toronto in the early 1970s, she co-founded SCTV in 1976. She made her film debut in 1980 and has remained active in Hollywood comedies, including the massively successful *Home Alone* entries, in which she portrayed the mother. Awarded Emmy for TV writing.

FILMS INCLUDE: *Nothing Personal* (US/Can.) 1980; *Rock & Rule* (v/o) 1983; *After Hours* 1985; *Heartburn* 1986; *Beetlejuice* 1987; *Dick Tracy, Little Vegas, Betsy's Wedding, Home Alone* 1990; *Home Alone 2: Lost in New York, There Goes the Neighborhood* 1992; *Tim Burton's The Nightmare Before Christmas* (v/o) 1993; *The Paper, A Simple Twist of Fate, Wyatt Earp* 1994; *Tall Tale* 1995; *The Last of the High Kings* 1996.

O'Hara, Gerry. Director. Born in 1924, in Boston, Lincolnshire, England. He entered British films at 17 as production assistant on documentaries and became assistant director on features in 1945. He graduated to director in the early 60s and has since turned out many episodes for TV series ('The Avengers,' 'Man in a Suitcase,' etc.) and a number of routine feature films. Several of his features have been of the sexploitational type.

FILMS: *That Kind of Girl/Models Inc., A Game for Three Losers* 1963; *The Pleasure Girls* (also sc.) 1965; *Maroc 7* 1966; *Amsterdam Affair* 1968; *Fidelia* 1970; *All the Right Noises* (also sc.) 1971; *The Brute* 1976; *Leopard in the Snow* (Can./UK) 1978; *The Bitch* (also sc.) 1979; *Fanny Hill* 1983; *Strictly for Cash* 1984; *Ten Little Indians* (co-sc. only) 1989.

O'Hara, John. Novelist, screenwriter. *b.* Jan. 31, 1905, Pottsville, Pa. *d.* 1970. The prolific chronicler of America's upper middle class was a film critic (for the N.Y. *Morning Telegraph*) early in his career and collaborated on a number of original screenplays. Many of his novels (*Pal Joey, From the Terrace, Butterfield 8, A Rage to Live,* etc.) were adapted for the screen by others.

FILMS (as screenwriter): *He Married His Wife* (co-sc.), *I Was an Adventuress* (co-sc.) 1940; *Moontide* 1942; *On Our Merry Way* (story) 1948; *The Best Things in Life Are Free* (story) 1956.

O'Hara, Maureen. Actress. Born Maureen FitzSimons, on Aug. 17, 1920, in Millwall, near Dublin, Ireland. Beautiful, fiery redhead who starred in many Hollywood productions of the 40s and 50s. Trained at Dublin's Abbey School, she performed on radio as a child and was playing ingenue roles with the Abbey Players before making her film debut in London in 1938. The following year she was signed on a contract by the partnership of Erich Pommer and Charles Laughton and left with the latter for Hollywood, where she began her starring career playing Esmeralda to his Quasimodo in *The Hunchback of Notre Dame.* Her career received an important lift from the lead female role of Angharad in John FORD's *How Green Was My Valley* (1941), the first of several roles she would play over the years in the director's films. She appeared in many productions of RKO, Fox, and other studios, looking particularly splendid in technicolor, perhaps most memorably as Mary Kate Danaher, the Irish wife and sparring partner of John WAYNE in *The Quiet Man.* O'Hara's first husband (1939–41) was director George Hanley Brown; her second (1941–52) was director Will Price. In 1968 she married Brigadier General (retired) Charles Blair, the first pilot to fly solo over the Arctic Ocean and the North Pole. He was killed in a plane crash in 1978. In 1991 she was coaxed out of retirement on the island of St. Croix to return to the screen after an absence of two decades.

FILMS: *Kicking the Moon Around/The Playboy/Millionaire Merry-Go-Round* (bit; UK) 1938; *My Irish Molly/Little Miss Molly* (UK), *Jamaica Inn* (UK), *The Hunchback of Notre Dame* (as Esmeralda) 1939; *A Bill of Divorcement, Dance Girl Dance* 1940; *They Met in Argentina, How Green Was My Valley* (as Angharad Morgan) 1941; *To the Shores of Tripoli, Ten Gentlemen from West Point, The Black Swan* 1942; *The Immortal Sergeant, This Land Is Mine, The Fallen Sparrow* 1943; *Buffalo Bill* 1944; *The Spanish Main* 1945; *Sentimental Journey, Do You Love Me?* 1946; *Sinbad the Sailor, The Homestretch, Miracle on 34th Street, The Foxes of Harrow* 1947; *Sitting Pretty* 1948; *The Forbidden Street/Britannia Mews* (US/UK), *A Woman's Secret, Father Was a Fullback, Bagdad* 1949; *Comanche Territory, Tripoli, Rio Grande* 1950; *Flame of Araby* 1951; *At Sword's Point, Kangaroo, The Quiet Man, Against All Flags* 1952; *The Redhead from Wyoming* 1953; *War Arrow, Malaga/Fire Over Africa* (UK/US) 1954; *The Long Gray Line, The Magnificent Matador, Lady Godiva* (title role) 1955; *Lisbon, Everything but the Truth* 1956; *The Wings of Eagles* 1957; *Our Man in Havana* (UK) 1959; *The Parent Trap, The Deadly Companions/Trigger Happy* 1961; *Mr. Hobbs Takes a Vacation* 1962; *Spencer's Mountain, McLintock!* 1963; *The Battle of the Villa Fiorita* (US/UK) 1965; *The Rare Breed* 1966; *How Do I Love Thee?* 1970; *Big Jake* 1971; *Only the Lonely* 1991.

O'Herlihy, Dan. Actor. Born on May 1, 1919, in Wexford, Ireland. *ed.* National U. of Ireland (architecture). Offbeat leading man and supporting player of British, then American and Continental films. Memorable in Buñuel's *The Adventures of Robinson Crusoe* (1952), for which he was nominated for an Academy Award as best actor. Tall and distinguished looking, he first turned to the stage as a set designer but soon after began acting with Dublin's Abbey Players and on Irish radio. In addition to many films, he made numerous appearances on TV. His brother, Michael O'Herlihy (*b.* Apr. 1, 1928, Dublin), is a prolific director of American TV movies and series who in the late 60s directed such Disney features as *The Fighting Prince of Donegal, The One and Only Genuine, Original Family Band,* and *Smith!*

FILMS INCLUDE: In the UK—*Hungry Hill* 1946; *Odd Man Out* 1947. In the US—*Kidnapped, Macbeth* (as Macduff) 1948; *The Desert Fox, Soldiers Three, The Blue Veil* 1951; *Actors and Sin, The Adventures of Robinson Crusoe* (title role; Mex.), *At Sword's Point* (as musketeer Aramis), *Invasion USA, Operation Secret* 1952; *The Black Shield of Falworth* (as Prince Hal), *Bengal Brigade* 1954; *The Purple Mask, The Virgin Queen* 1955; *Home Before Dark* 1958; *Imitation of Life, City After Midnight* 1959; *The Night Fighters, One Foot in Hell* 1960;

King of the Roaring 20s 1961; *The Cabinet of Dr. Caligari* (title role) 1962; *Fail Safe* 1964; *The Big Cube, 100 Rifles* 1969; *Waterloo* (as Marshal Ney; It./USSR); *The Carey Treatment* 1972; *The Tamarind Seed* (UK) 1974; *MacArthur* (as Franklin D. Roosevelt) 1977; *Halloween III: Season of the Witch* 1982; *The Last Starfighter* 1984; *The Whoopee Boys* 1986; *The Dead* 1987; *RoboCop 2* 1990.

Okada, Eiji. Born on June 13, 1920, in Chiba Prefecture, Japan. *ed.* Keio U. Leading man of Japanese stage and screen, best known to Western audiences for his starring roles in the French *Hiroshima mon Amour* (1959) and Hollywood's *The Ugly American* (1963).

FILMS INCLUDE: *Until the Day We Meet Again* 1950; *Mother* 1952; *The Tower of Lilies, Hiroshima* 1953; *Forsaken* 1954; *Christ in Bronze* 1955; *A Story of Pure Love* 1957; *Fearless Opposition* 1958; *Hiroshima mon Amour* (Fr.) 1959; *The Pirates* 1960; *The Ugly American* (US), *She and He* 1963; *Woman in the Dunes, The Assassin, The Scent of Incense* 1964; *The Scarlet Camellia, Judo Saga, Samurai Spy* 1965; *The Face of Another* 1966; *Rebellion of Japan, The X from Outer Space, Portrait of Chieko* 1967; *Tattooed Temptress, Tunnel to the Sun, Stormy Era* 1968; *Bullet Wound, Vixen* 1969; *Zatoichi's Conspiracy* 1973; *Love and Faith of Ogin* 1982; *Antarctica* 1983; *The Death of a Tea Master* 1989.

O'Keefe, Dennis. Actor. *b.* Edward Vance Flanagan, Mar. 29, 1908, Fort Madison, Iowa. *d.* 1968. Tall, rugged leading man of numerous Hollywood films of the 30s and 40s. On the vaudeville stage from infancy with his parents' act. At age 16 he wrote scripts for "Our Gang" comedies and later briefly attended USC before returning to vaudeville. He entered films in the early 30s as an extra and bit player and appeared in scores of films under the name Bud Flanagan. He changed his name to Dennis O'Keefe after joining MGM as a contract player in 1937, subsequently playing tough but genial leads for various studios, most frequently in lightly flavored action-oriented productions. Late in his career he directed a couple of films and wrote a number of mystery stories. In 1958 he starred in a short-lived TV series, 'The Dennis O'Keefe Show.' He died at 60 of cancer of the lung. His widow is actress Steffi Duna.

FILMS INCLUDE: As Bud Flanagan—*Reaching for the Moon, Cimarron* 1931; *I Am a Fugitive from a Chain Gang* 1932; *Gold Diggers of 1933, I'm No Angel, Duck Soup* 1933; *Wonder Bar* 1934; *Anna Karenina* 1935; *Mr. Deeds Goes to Town, 13 Hours by Air, The Plainsman* 1936; *Captains Courageous, Saratoga* 1937. As Dennis O'Keefe—*The Bad Man of Brimstone, Hold That Kiss, The Chaser, Vacation from Love* 1938; *Unexpected Father, Burn 'Em Up O'Connor* 1939; *La Conga Nights, Girl from Havana, Arise My Love* 1940; *Mr. District Attorney, Lady Scarface, Topper Returns, Weekend for Three* 1941; *The Affairs of Jimmy Valentine* 1942; *Hangmen Also Die, Tahiti Honey, The Leopard Man, Hi Diddle Diddle* 1943; *The Fighting Seabees, Up in Mabel's Room, The Story of Dr. Wassell, Abroad with Two Yanks* 1944; *Brewster's Millions, The Affairs of Susan, Getting Gertie's Garter, Doll Face* 1945; *Mr. District Attorney* (2nd version), *Dishonored Lady* 1947; *T-Men, Raw Deal, Siren of Atlantis, Walk a Crooked Mile* 1948; *The Great Dan Patch, Abandoned* 1949; *The Eagle and the Hawk, Woman on the Run, The Company She Keeps* 1950; *Follow the Sun, Passage West* 1951; *Everything I Have Is Yours, One Big Affair* 1952; *The Lady Wants Mink* 1953; *The Diamond Wizard* (also dir.; UK), *Drums of Tahiti* 1954; *Angela* (also dir.), *Las Vegas Shakedown, Chicago Syndicate* 1955; *Inside Detroit* 1956; *Dragoon Wells Massacre* 1957; *All Hands on Deck* 1961; *The Naked Flame* (Can.) 1965.

O'Keefe, Michael. Actor. Born on Apr. 24, 1955, in Larchmont, N.Y. (or Paulland, N.J.). *ed.* NYU. Wholesome, athletic leading man of the American screen. Trained at the AADA, he has performed on Broadway and on TV as well as in films. He was a co-founder of New York's Colonnades Theatre Lab.

FILMS: *Gray Lady Down* 1978; *The Great Santini/The Ace* 1979; *Caddy Shack* 1980; *Split Image* 1982; *Nate and Hayes* 1983; *Finders Keepers* 1984; *The Slugger's Wife* 1985; *The Whoopee Boys* 1986; *Ironweed* 1987; *Fear, Out of the Rain* 1990; *Me & Veronica* 1992; *Kangaroo Court, Nina Takes a Lover* 1994; *Three Wishes* 1995; *Edie and Pen, Ghosts of Mississippi* 1996.

Okey, Jack. American art director. In Hollywood from the early 20s, he designed bold and inventive sets for many films over four decades, including several extravagantly spectacular musicals of Busby BERKELEY, a number of *film noir* classics, and Frank Capra's evergreen fantasy *It's a Wonderful Life.* An accomplished architect, he designed and supervised the construction of Alexander Korda's elaborate Denham Studios near London in 1934–35. He resumed his work in Hollywood in the early 40s.

FILMS INCLUDE: *Without Benefit of Clergy* 1921; *Outlaws of the Sea* 1923; *Torment, The White Moth* 1924; *Old Loves and New* 1926; *Showgirl in Hollywood, The Dawn Patrol* 1930; *Five Star Final, The Last Flight* 1931; *I Am a Fugitive from a Chain Gang, Tiger Shark* 1932; *Female, The Kennel Murder Case, 42nd Street, Footlight Parade, The World Changes* 1933; *Fashions of 1934, Flirtation Walk, Wonder Bar* 1934; *Bordertown* 1935; *Jungle Book* (set dec. only) 1942; *Johnny Come Lately* 1943; *Experiment Perilous, None But the Lonely Heart* 1944; *The Spiral Staircase, Crack-Up, It's a Wonderful Life, Till the End of Time* 1946; *Out of the Past* 1947; *Rachel and the Stranger* 1948; *The Set-Up* 1949; *The Racket* 1951; *The Narrow Margin* 1952; *Split Second* 1953; *Run for the Arrow* 1957; *The Young Land* 1959.

Okhlopkov, Nikolai. Director, actor. *b.* May 6, 1900, Irkutsk, Russia. *d.* 1967. Trained by Vsevolod Meyerhold, he joined the Soviet Odessa Studio as a director in 1927 and soon gained acclaim as a comedy specialist. He earned the warm approval of the Communist party bureaucracy for his second film, *The Sold Appetite* (1928), which ridiculed capitalism. But he was harshly attacked when his third, *The Way of the Enthusiasts* (1930), applied similar satirical means to depict conflicts between Soviet workers and peasants. The film was promptly banned. Vowing never to direct again, Okhlopkov turned to the stage and in the early 30s became the director of Moscow's Realist Theater. He returned intermittently to the screen as an actor.

FILMS INCLUDE: As director (complete)—*Mitya* (also act.) 1927; *The Sold Appetite* 1928; *The Way of the Enthusiasts* (also sc.) 1930. As actor—*Death Bay, Traitor* 1926; *Men and Jobs* 1932; *Lenin in October* 1937; *Alexander Nevsky* 1938; *Lenin in 1918* 1939; *Kutuzov/1812* 1944; *Story of a Real Man* 1948; *Far from Moscow* 1950.

Oland, Warner. Actor. *b.* Werner Ohlund, Oct. 3, 1880, Umea, Sweden. *d.* 1938. In the US from age ten, he began his career in the theater as an actor, set designer, and Strindberg translator, switching to films in 1912. He played numerous character parts, often as a heavy, and was soon typecast as an Asian. He starred in the title role of many "Charlie Chan" episodes from 1931 till his death. His wife, Edith Shearn (1870–1968), was also a stage and screen actress.

FILMS INCLUDE: *The Life of John Bunyan: Pilgrim's Progress* (dual role as Bunyan/Christian) 1912; *Sin, Destruction* 1915; *The Serpent, The Fool's Revenge, The Reapers, The Eternal Sappho, The Eternal Question* 1916; *Patria* (serial), *The*

Fatal Ring (serial), *The Cigarette Girl* 1917; *Convict 993, The Naulahka, The Yellow Ticket* 1918; *Mandarin's Gold, The Avalanche, The Twin Pawns* 1919; *The Third Eye* (serial), *The Phantom Foe* (serial) 1920; *The Yellow Arm, Hurricane Hutch* (both serials) 1921; *East Is West, The Pride of Palomar* 1922; *The Fighting American, So This Is Marriage, Curly Top* 1924; *Riders of the Purple Sage, Flower of Night, Don Q Son of Zorro* 1925; *Infatuation, Mystery Club, Don Juan, The Marriage Clause, Twinkletoes* 1926; *The Jazz Singer, A Million Bid, Old San Francisco, Goodtime Charley* 1927; *Wheel of Chance, The Scarlet Lady* 1928; *Chinatown Nights, The Mysterious Dr. Fu Manchu* (title role), *The Studio Murder Case, The Mighty* 1929; *The Vagabond King, Dangerous Paradise, The Return of Dr. Fu Manchu* (title role) 1930; *The Black Camel* (as Charlie Chan), *Dishonored, Charlie Chan Carries On* (title role), *Daughter of the Dragon* 1931; *Shanghai Express, A Passport to Hell* 1932; *Charlie Chan's Greatest Case* (title role) 1933; *Bulldog Drummond Strikes Back, Mandalay, The Painted Veil* 1934; *Shanghai, Werewolf of London* 1935; *Charlie Chan at the Circus* (title role) 1936; *Charlie Chan at the Opera* (title role), *Charlie Chan at the Olympics* (title role) 1937; *Charlie Chan at Monte Carlo* (title role) 1938.

Olbrychski, Daniel. Actor. Born on Feb 27, 1945, in Lowicz, Poland. *ed.* Warsaw School of Drama. Fair-haired, athletic leading man and supporting player of Polish and international films. On screen from age 19, he rapidly became established in films by Wajda and other directors as one of his country's most popular players. Worldwide recognition followed, as did roles in films of several other nations. His characterizations ranged widely from angelic heroes to crafty villains.

FILMS INCLUDE: *Wounded in the Forest* 1964; *Ashes* 1965; *The Boxer* 1966; *Jovita* 1967; *Everything for Sale, The Leap* 1968; *Colonel Wolodyjowski, Hunting Flies, The Structure of Crystals* 1969; *The Birch Wood, Agnus Dei* (Hung.), *Landscape After the Battle* 1970; *La Pacifista/The Pacifist* (It./Fr./Ger.), *Salt of This Black Earth, Family Life, Liberation* 1971; *The Wedding* 1972; *Roma rivuole Cesare* (It.) 1973; *The Deluge* 1974; *Land of Promise/Promised Land* 1975; *Screen Test* 1977; *The Girls from Wilko* (Pol./Fr.), *Die Blechtrommel/The Tin Drum* (Ger.) 1979; *Kung Fu* 1980; *Les Uns et les autres/Bolero* (Fr.) 1981; *La Derelitta* (Fr./It.) 1983; *Eine Liebe in Deutschland/Love in Germany* (Ger.), *La Diagonale du Fou/Dangerous Moves* (Fr.) 1984; *Rosa Luxemburg* (Ger.) 1986; *Mosca Addio* (It.) 1987; *The Unbearable Lightness of Being* (US), *La Boutique de l'Orfèvre/The Jeweller's Shop* (Fr./It./Can.) 1988; *Dekalog/The Ten Commandments* (Pol.), *The Last Bet* (Gr.), *L'Orchestre rouge* (Fr./It.) 1989; *Le Silence d'ailleurs/The Silence of Elsewhere* (Fr.) 1990.

Olcott, Sidney. Director. *b.* John Sidney Alcott, Sept. 20, 1873, Toronto. *d.* 1949. Energetic, prolific director of Hollywood silents. A former newspaper boy and a New York stage performer, he entered films in 1904 as an actor with Mutoscope and shortly after became general manager at Biograph. As Kalem's first director (from 1907), he got the company involved in a losing court case over the author's copyright to his one-reel version of *Ben-Hur* (shot at Manhattan Beach). He was the first Hollywood director to shoot regularly on location, going to Ireland for a number of films and to Palestine for *From the Manger to the Cross* (made during Easter of 1912; released in January 1913). He is also recognized as a pioneer director of Westerns and documentary films. During his Middle East trip of 1912, he shot several vivid fact films about Egypt and the region. In the early phase of his career (through 1915), Olcott wrote many of his own screenplays (most were written by his business partner and favorite female star, Gene Gauntier) and often played leading roles in his own films. Around 1914 he married actress Valentine Grant, who starred in several of his productions. In 1915 he joined Famous Players and directed several films starring Mary Pickford. His influence on early American cinema was considerable.

FILMS INCLUDE (as director): *The Sleigh Bells, Ben-Hur* (co-dir. with Frank Oakes), *The Wooing of Miles Standish* 1907; *The Scarlet Letter* 1908; *A Florida Feud, Escape from Andersonville, The Factory Girl, The Tomboy, The Conspirators, The Man and the Girl, Dora, The Governor's Daughter, The Geisha Who Saved Japan, The Law of the Mountains* 1909; *The Feud, The Miser's Child, The Indian Scout's Vengeance, The Love Romance of the Girl Spy, The Bravest Girl in the South, A Priest of the Wilderness, The Lad from Old Ireland, The Stranger* 1910; *In Old Florida, To the Aid of Stonewall Jackson, When the Dead Return, The Fiddler's Requiem, The Colleen Bawn, Arrah-Na-Poque* 1911; *His Mother, The Vagabonds, The Fighting Dervishes of the Desert, Captured by Bedouins, Tragedy of the Desert, A Day in Jerusalem* (doc.), *From Jerusalem to the Dead Sea* (doc.), *Palestine* (doc.), *Egypt the Mysterious* (doc.), *Prisoner of the Harem, Along the River Nile* (doc.), *The Kerry Gow, Ireland the Oppressed, The Shaughraun* 1912; *From the Manger to the Cross, The Wives of Jamestown, Lady Peggy's Escape, A Daughter of the Confederacy* (co-dir. with George Melford), *The Mystery of Pine Creek Camp, In the Power of a Hypnotist* (co-dir. with Thomas Hayes Hunter), *The Vampire* (co-dir. with Hunter), *The Perils of the Sea* (co-dir. with Melford), *In the Clutches of the Ku Klux Klan, The Octoroon* 1913; *When Men Would Kill, A Passover Miracle, Come Back to Erin, A Mother of Men, Tricking the Government* 1914; *The Moth and the Flame, All for Old Ireland, Bold Emmett—Ireland's Martyr, The Irish in America, Seven Sisters, Nan o' the Backwoods, The Ghost of the Twisted Oaks, The Taint, Madame Butterfly* 1915; *My Lady Incog./My Lady Incognito, Poor Little Peppina, Diplomacy, The Innocent Lie, The Smugglers, The Daughter of MacGregor/Jean o' the Heather* 1916; *The Belgian* 1918; *Marriage for Convenience* 1919; *Scratch My Back* 1920; *The Right Way/The Gray Brother/Making Good/Within Prison Walls, Pardon My French, God's Country and the Law* 1921; *Timothy's Quest* 1922; *The Green Goddess, Little Old New York* 1923; *The Humming Bird, Monsieur Beaucaire, The Only Woman* 1924; *Salome of the Tenements, The Charmer, Not So Long Ago, The Best People* 1925; *Ranson's Folly, The Amateur Gentleman, The White Black Sheep* 1926; *The Claw* 1927.

Oldman, Gary. Actor. Born on Mar. 21, 1958, in New Cross, South London, England. Enormously talented stage and screen performer. Shattered at age seven when his father, a welder, left home and never returned, he had a dismal childhood in a dreary working-class neighborhood and at a brutal boys' school. He was relieved of the boredom of a sales clerk's job at a local sporting goods job by training for a stage career with the Greenwich Young People's Theatre. His success there led to a scholarship to the Rose Buford College of Speech and Drama and eventually to an increasingly appreciated career on the London stage and British and American films. He gave extraordinarily complex portrayals of punk rock star Sid Vicious in *Sid and Nancy* (1986) and of doomed gay playwright Joe Orton in *Prick Up Your Ears* (1987). He brought a romantic creepiness to the role of Count Dracula in *Bram Stoker's Dracula* (1992). In addition to features, he also appeared in several TV movies. He is divorced from actresses Lesley Manville and Uma THURMAN.

FILMS: *Remembrance* 1981; *Meantime* (TV movie released theatrically in the US) 1983; *Sid and Nancy* (as punk rock star Sid Vicious) 1986; *Prick Up Your Ears* (as playwright Joe Orton) 1987; *Track 29* (US), *We Think the World of You* 1988; *Criminal Law* (US), *Chattahoochee* (US) 1989; *State of Grace* (US), *Rosencrantz and Guildenstern are Dead* (as Rosencrantz) 1990; *Heading Home, JFK* (as Lee Harvey Oswald) 1991; *Bram Stoker's Dracula* (title role) 1992; *True Romance* 1993; *Immortal Beloved, The Professional, Romeo is Bleeding, Thumbelina* (v/o) 1994; *Murder in the First, The Scarlet Letter* 1995; *Basquiat* 1996; *Air Force One, Fifth Element* 1997.

old-timer. Film trade term for a flexible pole that holds small FLAGS or SCRIMS.

Olin, Lena. Actress. Born in 1955, in Stockholm. Striking leading lady of the Swedish stage and international films. The daughter of actors, she showed no early interest in drama and after graduating from high school worked briefly as a hospital aide and substitute teacher. It was Ingmar BERGMAN, a friend of the family, who encouraged her to enroll at drama school. She was the only graduate accepted that year to the Royal Dramatic Theater in Stockholm, where she rapidly became a rising star. Since the late 70s she has appeared in Swedish films, and in the late 80s energized several American productions with her radiant sensuality. After being ideally cast as a mysterious, sexually independent woman in Phillip Kaufman's *The Unbearable Lightness of Being* (1988), she was nominated for an Academy Award as best supporting actress for her portrayal of a sultry, two-timing married woman in Paul Mazursky's *Enemies, a Love Story* (1989). She has a son, August (after Strindberg), by actor Orjan Ramberg. Her father, Stig Olin (*b.* 1920, Stockholm), was a leading man of Swedish films of the 40s and early 50s, including several early Bergman works. He directed a number of light films of the 50s and later became a radio executive.

FILMS INCLUDE: *Face to Face* (bit) 1976; *The Adventures of Picasso* 1978; *Love* 1980; *Fanny and Alexander* 1983; *After the Rehearsal* 1984; *Flucht in den Norden* (Ger./Fin.) 1985; *A Matter of Life and Death* 1986; *Friends* 1987; *The Unbearable Lightness of Being* (US) 1988; *Enemies, a Love Story* (US), *S/V Gladjen* 1989; *Havana* (US) 1990; *Mr. Jones* (US) 1993; *Romeo is Bleeding* 1994; *Night and the Moment* 1996; *Night Falls on Manhattan* 1997.

Oliveira, Manuel de. Director. Born on Dec. 12, 1908, in Oporto, Portugal. The son of a prominent industrialist, he became involved in the family business at a young age. He also indulged in athletics and competed successfully in intercontinental car races. He also showed an early interest in cinema and in 1928 appeared as an actor in the film *Fátima Milagrosa.* After several aborted attempts, he wrote, produced, directed, and edited his first film, *Hard Labor on the River Douro* (1931), a documentary short, depicting abysmal working conditions in his own hometown. During the next decade, he experimented with filmmaking sporadically and appeared as an actor in Portugal's first talkie feature, Continelli Telmo's *Song of Lisbon* (1933). In 1942 he directed his first feature, the children's film *Aniki-Bóbó,* notable for its use of non-actors and on-location realism. Finding local critics and the public unreceptive, he turned to farming and other business pursuits. It wasn't until 1956 that he returned to filmmaking with *The Painter and the City,* a 45-minute poetic color documentary about the painter Antonio Cruz and the impact of the city of Oporto on his art. Still working largely alone, often operating his own camera, Oliveira began receiving wider notice outside of Portugal in the mid-60s, after winning the Grand Prix at the Siena Film Festival for his two-hour lyrical documentary *The Passion of Jesus* (1964). But the mature, most accomplished phase of his career did not start until the early 70s, when he was well into his 60s. Leaning increasingly toward romantic fiction, he described this phase as the "stage of the bourgeoisie," in contrast to his earlier "stage of the people." Ostensibly comprising a cycle of stories about frustrated love, his films of the 70s are admired by critics for their aesthetic poesy and modernist complexity. Oliveira's harvest of the 80s consisted of both fact and fiction films, bringing to a culmination the wide-ranging creative career of a man who won belated recognition as one of Europe's leading filmmakers.

FILMS: *Douro Faina fluvial/Hard Labor on the River Douro* (short doc.; also sc., edit.) 1931; *Estatuas de Lisboa/The Statues of Lisbon* (short doc.; also prod., edit.) 1932; *Já se fabricam Automíveis em Portugal* (short doc.; also pro., sc., edit.) 1938; *Miramar Praia de Rosas* (short doc.; also prod., sc., edit.) 1939; *Famalcao* (short doc.; also prod., sc., edit.) 1940; *Aniki-Bóbó* (also sc.) *O Pintor e a Cidade/The Painter and the City* (medium-length doc.; also prod., sc., phot., edit.) 1956; *O Pao/Bread* (medium-length doc.; also sc., phot., edit.) 1959; *O Coraçao/The Heart* (short; also sc.) 1960; *Acto da Primavera/The Passion of Jesus* (feature-length doc.; also prod., sc., phot., edit.) 1963; *A Caça/The Hunt* (short; also sc., phot., edit.) 1964; *As Pinturas do meu Irmao Julio/My Brother Julio's Paintings* (short doc.; also prod., phot., edit.) 1965; *O Passado e o Presente/Past and Present* (also co-prod., edit.) 1972; *Benilde ou a Virgem Mae/Benilde: Virgin and Mother* (also edit.) 1975; *Amor de Perdiçao/Doomed Love/Ill-Fated Love* (also sc.) 1978; *Francisca* 1981; *Memorias e Confissoes/ Memories and Confessions* (doc.; to be released only after director's death) 1982; *Lisboa Cultural/Cultural Lisbon* (doc.; orig. for TV) 1983; *Nice á propos de Jean Vigo* (doc. orig. for French TV) 1984; *O Sapato de Setim/Le Soulier de Satin/The Satin Slipper* (also sc.; Port./Fr.) 1985; *O Meu Caso/Mon Cas* (also sc., co-edit.; Port./Fr.) 1985; *A Bandeira Nacional/The National Flag* (short doc.; *Os Canibais/The Cannibals* (Port./Fr./It./ Switz./Ger.) 1988; *Nao ou a va Gloria de Mandar/No or the Vain Glory of Command* (also sc., co-edit.; Port./Fr./Sp.) 1990; *The Divine Comedy* 1991; *Days of Despair* 1992; *Vale Abreao* 1993; *Blind Man's Bluff* 1994.

Oliver, Edna May. Actress. *b.* Edna May Nutter, Nov. 9, 1883, Malden, Mass. *d.* 1942. Eccentric, horse-faced character actress of the American stage and Hollywood silents and talkies. She usually played droll or sarcastic spinsters, memorably as Aunt March in *Little Women* (1933), Aunt Betsey Trotwood in *David Copperfield* (1935), Miss Pross in *A Tale of Two Cities* (1935), the nurse in *Romeo and Juliet* (1936), and the Widow McKlennar in *Drums Along the Mohawk* (1939). She was nominated for an Oscar in the supporting category for her portrayal of the latter. She also played leads in a number of low-budget comedies and mysteries.

FILMS INCLUDE: *Wife in Name Only, Three O'Clock in the Morning* 1923; *Icebound, Manhattan* 1924; *The Lucky Devil, Lovers in Quarantine* 1925; *The American Venus, Let's Get Married* 1926; *The Saturday Night Kid* 1929; *Cimarron, Laugh and Get Rich, Cracked Nuts, Newly Rich, Fanny Foley Herself* 1931; *Ladies of the Jury, The Penguin Pool Murder, The Conquerors* 1932; *It's Great to Be Alive, Ann Vickers, Only Yesterday, Little Women* (as Aunt March), *Alice in Wonderland* (as the Red Queen) 1933; *The Poor Rich, Murder on the Blackboard, We're Rich Again, The Last Gentleman* 1934; *David Copperfield* (as Betsey Trotwood), *Murder on a Honeymoon, No More Ladies, A Tale of Two Cities* (as Miss Pross) 1935; *Romeo and Juliet* (as the Nurse) 1936; *Parnell, Rosalie* 1937; *Paradise for Three, Little Miss Broadway* 1938; *The Story of Vernon and Irene Castle, Second Fiddle, Nurse Edith Cavell, Drums Along the Mohawk* (as the Widow McKlennar) 1939; *Pride and Prejudice* (as Lady Catherine de Bourgh) 1940; *Lydia* 1941.

Oliver, Susan. Actress. *b.* Charlotte Gercke, Feb. 13, 1937, New York City. *d.* 1990, of cancer. Blonde leading lady of American films and TV. The daughter of a newspaperman and an astrologer, she attended the Tokyo International College while her father was stationed in Japan as an official of the US Information Agency. On returning to the US, she enrolled at Swarthmore College, then received professional training at the Neighborhood Playhouse School of Theater. On screen from 1957, she also performed on the stage and was seen frequently on TV, including the 'Peyton Place' series and the original pilot (1966) for 'Star Trek.' In the 70s she participated in the American Film Institute's workshop program for women and later wrote, produced, and directed a short film, *Cowboy-San!*; a 50-minute video, *The Spy Who Came to America*; as well as episodes for the series 'M*A*S*H' and 'Trapper John, M.D.' An accomplished aviator, she survived a crash of a Piper Cub in 1966 to win the Powder Puff Derby air race in 1970 and earn Pilot of the Year honors. In her 1983 memoir *Odyssey,* she described her heroic attempt to become the first woman to fly a single-engine plane solo from New York to Moscow. She made it as far as Denmark but was denied permission to enter Soviet air space.

FILMS INCLUDE: *The Green-Eyed Blonde* 1957; *The Gene Krupa Story* 1959; *Butterfield 8* 1960; *The Caretakers* 1963; *Looking for Love, The Disorderly Orderly* 1964; *Your Cheatin' Heart* 1965; *The Love-Ins* 1967; *A Man Called Gannon, Change of Mind, The Monitors* 1969; *Company of Killers* 1970; *Ginger in the Morning* 1973; *Nido de Viudas/Widow's Nest* (Sp.) 1977; *Murder by Decree* (UK) 1979; *Hardly Working* 1981.

Olivera, Hector. Director. Born in 1931, in Olivos, Argentina. A prominent figure in Argentine and Latin American cinema. He entered films at age 16 as an assistant director and later freelanced as a production supervisor. In 1956 he founded with director Fernando Ayala a production company, Aries, that survived as a successful enterprise into the 90s. A director since the late 60s, Olivera became internationally admired for his earthy, robustly humorous approach to social issues. But he also handled dramatic literary adaptations and historical epics. He won the Special Jury Prize and shared the International Critics Prize at the Berlin Film Festival for *A Funny, Dirty Little War* (1984), a viciously funny political satire. He was far less successful with several US-Argentine co-productions. Olivera usually collaborates on his scripts. He produced most of his own films as well as a number of notable works by other directors.

FILMS (as director): *Psexoanalisis* 1967; *Las Venganzas de Beto Sánchez* 1972; *La Patagonia rebelde/Revolt in Patagonia* 1974; *El Muerto* 1975; *La Nona* 1978; *Los Viernes de la Eternidad* 1981; *Buenos Aires Rock 82* (doc.) 1983; *No Habrá más Penas ni Olvido/A Funny Dirty Little War* 1984; *Wizards of the Lost Kingdom* (US/Arg.), *Barbarian Queen* (US/Arg.) 1985; *Cocaine Wars* (US/Arg.), *Night of the Pencils* 1986; *Two to Tango* (US/Arg.) 1989; *Midnight Black* (US/Arg.), *The Gospel According to Marcus* (Sp./Arg.) 1990; *The Maria Soledad Case* 1993; *A Shadow You Soon Will Be* 1994.

Olivier, Sir Laurence (Lord Olivier). Actor, director, producer. *b.* May 22, 1907, Dorking, Surrey, England. *d.* 1989. A brilliant performer of the British and American stage and screen, hailed as perhaps the greatest classical player and Shakespearean interpreter of his time. The son of a strict Anglican clergyman of Huguenot ancestry who curiously encouraged him to take up acting, he made his debut as a schoolboy of nine, playing Brutus in an abbreviated version of 'Julius Caesar' at London's All Saints Choir School. His mature performance astonished Dame Sybil Thorndike, who was in the audience. At 14, as a pupil at Oxford's St. Edward's School, he played a convincing Katharina(!) in a boy's performance of *The Taming of the Shrew* at the Shakespeare Festival Theatre at Stratford-on-Avon. He then joined the Birmingham Repertory (1926–28) and made his first appearance on Broadway in 1929. His British screen debut was in 1930 and his Hollywood debut the following year. But his early career both onstage and onscreen was fraught with fiascos and disappointments.

Within just a few years, through a succession of memorable Shakespearean roles onstage and several romantic portrayals in Hollywood films, Olivier emerged as one of the most exciting and versatile actors in the English-speaking world. Through such heartthrob roles as Heathcliff in *Wuthering Heights,* de Winter in *Rebecca,* Dr. Darcy in *Pride and Prejudice,* and Lord Nelson in *That Hamilton Woman*, he was establishing himself in the banner years 1939–40 as a glamorous Hollywood star, when WW II broke out. In 1939 he volunteered for the Royal Air Force but was turned down. Undaunted, he piled up 200 flight hours on his own and in 1941 joined the Fleet Air Arm of the Royal Navy. He was released twice to make propaganda films and in 1944 he was discharged from service and appointed co-director (with Ralph Richardson) of the Old Vic Theatre. While supervising the restoration of the distinguished theatrical institution to its prewar glory, Olivier began his first film as director, *Henry V.* It was an astounding critical success and won for him a special Academy Award (foreign films were then not competing) for his triple triumph as the director, producer, and star of the film. His second film, *Hamlet,* won the best picture and best actor (Olivier) Academy Awards as well as a number of other Oscars. He was afterwards nominated for Oscars nine times. In the 1979 Academy Award ceremony (for 1978) he was awarded a special Oscar.

He directed himself in only two more films in the next two decades, an excellently played adaptation of Shakespeare's *Richard III* and the rather stodgy *The Prince and the Showgirl,* in which he co-starred with Marilyn Monroe. However, he continued appearing in occasional films and in numerous plays, demonstrating his virtuosity in a wide range of roles, from Shakespeare, Sophocles, and Chekhov, to John Osborne's *The Entertainer* and the Runyon-Swerling-Burrows musical 'Guys and Dolls' (as Nathan Detroit).

In 1963 he became the director of England's National Theatre Company. The following year, Olivier, famous for his boldness as an actor, was uncharacteristically overcome by a severe case of stage fright. "It pursued me for five years and became a monster of a nightmare," he later recalled. Although he eventually conquered his fear, he played his final role onstage in 1974, a year in which he became stricken with dermatomyositis, a crippling muscle disease. Although he was plagued by other persistent illnesses, including leg thrombosis and prostate cancer, he continued appearing in films and TV, in roles large and small, with amazing frequency. Knighted in 1947, Olivier was made a peer of the realm with the title baron in 1970. In 1971 he took his seat in the House of Lords. But he was possibly more flattered by the adulation of his professional peers who in 1975 named the London theater's equivalents of Broadway's Tonys, the Olivier Awards. In 1983 he was honored for his lifetime achievements by the Film Society of Lincoln Center.

Although he shunned publicity, Olivier's private life was the subject of much public speculation. He had been married since 1930 to stage and screen actress Jill ESMOND when he fell in love with the also-married Vivien LEIGH on the set of their 1937 film *Fire Over England.* Amidst much nasty gossip, Esmond was granted a divorce in 1940, on the grounds of adultery. Several months later Olivier married Leigh. Their tempestuous marriage lasted 20 years, surviving frequent conflicts and Leigh's bouts with depression and eventually mental illness. In 1960, Leigh, naming actress Joan PLOWRIGHT as a co-respondent, obtained a divorce on the grounds of adultery. The following year Olivier married Plowright, to whom he remained married until his death. He wrote an autobiography, *Confessions of an Actor* (1982), and the books *Five Seasons of the Old Vic Theatre Company* (in collaboration, 1950) and *On Acting* (1986), in which he described in detail how he created some of his finest roles.

FEATURE FILMS (as actor): *Too Many Crooks, The Temporary Widow* (English-language version of the German *Hokuspokus/Hocuspocus*) 1930; *Potiphar's Wife/Her Strange Desire, The Yellow Ticket/The Yellow Passport* (US), *Friends and Lovers* (US) 1931; *Westward Passage* (US) 1932; *Perfect Understanding, No Funny Business* 1933; *Moscow Nights/I Stand Condemned* 1935; *As You Like It* (as Orlando), *Conquest of the Air* (semidoc.; release delayed) 1936; *Fire Over England* 1937; *The Divorce of Lady X* 1938; *Q Planes/Clouds Over Europe, Wuthering Heights* (as Heathcliff; US) 1939; *21 Days/21 Days Together* (release delayed from 1937), *Rebecca* (as Maxim de Winter; US), *Pride and Prejudice* (as Dr. Fitzwilliam Darcy; US) 1940; *That Hamilton Woman/Lady Hamilton* (as Lord Nelson; US), *49th Parallel/The Invaders* 1941; *The Demi-Paradise/Adventure for Two* 1943; *Henry V* (title role; also dir., prod., co-sc.) 1944; *Hamlet* (title role; also dir., prod.) 1948; *The Magic Box* (cameo) 1951; *Carrie* (US) 1952; *The Begger's Opera* (as McHeath; also co-prod.), *A Queen Is Crowned* (doc.; v/o) 1953; *Richard III* (title role; also dir., prod.) 1955; *The Prince and the Showgirl* (also dir., prod.) 1957; *The Devil's Disciple* (as General Burgoyne; US/UK) 1959; *The Entertainer, Spartacus* (US) 1960; *The Power and the Glory* (TV movie shown theatrically in the UK) 1961; *Term of Trial* 1962; *Uncle Vanya* (as Dr. Astrov; filmed stage production of the Chichester Festival Theatre) 1963; *Bunny Lake Is Missing, Othello* (title role; filmed stage production of the National Theatre of Great Britain) 1965; *Khartoum* (as The Mahdi) 1966; *Romeo and Juliet* (narrator only; UK/It.), *The Shoes of the Fisherman* (US) 1968; *Oh! What a Lovely War* (as Field Marshal Sir John French), *The Dance of Death* (filmed theater), *Battle of Britain* (as Air Chief Marshal Sir Hugh Dowding) 1969; *David Copperfield* (bit; as Mr. Creakle; orig. made for US TV), *The Three Sisters* (as Dr. Ivan Chebutikin; also dir.) 1970; *Nicholas and Alexandra* (as Count Witte) 1971; *Sleuth, Lady Caroline Lamb* (as the Duke of Wellington) 1972; *The Rehearsal* (semidoc.; unreleased) 1974; *Love Among the Ruins* (TV movie; US) 1975; *Marathon Man* (US), *The Seven-Percent Solution* (as Prof. Moriarty), *Cat on a Hot Tin Roof* (as Big Daddy; TV movie) 1976; *Jesus of Nazareth* (bit as Nicodemus; TV movie; UK/It.), *A Bridge Too Far, Come Back Little Sheba* (as Doc Delaney; TV movie) 1977; *The Betsy* (US), *The Boys from Brazil* (US) 1978; *A Little Romance* (US/Fr.), *Dracula* (as Prof. Van Helsing; US) 1979; *The Jazz Singer* 1980; *Clash of the Titans* (as Zeus), *Inchon* (as Gen. MacArthur; Korea/US) 1981; *Wagner* (orig. miniseries; UK/Hung./Aus.) 1983; *The Last Days of Pompeii* (TV movie; US/UK/It.), *The Jigsaw Man, The Bounty* 1984; *Wild Geese II* 1985; *Directed by William Wyler* (doc.), *A Talent for Murder* (TV movie) 1986; *War Requiem* 1988.

Olmi, Ermanno. Director. Born on July 24, 1931, in Bergamo, Italy. His parents were peasants who settled in the city and became factory workers. After his father's death during WW II, both he and his mother took jobs in the Edison-Volta electric plant. Beginning as a clerk, Ermanno soon became involved in the theatrical and cinematic activities organized and sponsored by the company, and before long he was assigned to the electrical industry's cinematographic section as the producer and director of documentary films. Between 1952 and 1959 he made some 40 short documentaries, including *Mannon: Finestra 2, Tre Fili fino a Milano, Venezia Città Moderna,* and *Il Pensionato.* In 1959 he turned to feature-length films, beginning with the semidocumentary *Il Tempo si è fermato/Time Stood Still.* It was with his second feature, *Il Posto/The Job/The Sound of Trumpets* (1961), that Olmi began attracting international attention. Made on a tight schedule, for a mere $15,000, it told with disarming tenderness and humor a simple, partly autobiographical story of the travails of a young clerk in the process of reconciling his hopes and dreams with the disheartening realities of his post in a large, impersonal company. Olmi brought a similar ironic compassion to his next film, *I Fidanzati/The Fiancés* (1963), a keenly observed tale of a long-engaged couple whose relationship survives transformations of time and space. Although he later worked with larger budgets and broader themes, Olmi remained rooted in the regional heritage of his Lombardian hometown of Bergamo. Thematically and stylistically, he acknowledged a debt to the postwar neorealists, particularly Vittorio DE SICA. Like them, he prefers unadorned camera techniques and the employment of nonprofessional actors. He shares their concern for the human dignity of ordinary people, but has expressed it in less obvious, more ambiguous terms. After years of relative obscurity, Olmi emerged into the limelight of long-deserved recognition with *L'Albero deqli Zoccoli/The Tree of Wooden Clogs,* winner of the Palme d'Or, as well as the Ecumenical Prize, at the 1978 Cannes Film Festival. He later shared the Silver Lion for *Lunga Vita alla Signora/Long Live the Lady!* (1987) and won the Golden Lion for *La Legenda del Santo Bevitore/Legend of the Holy Drinker* (1988) at Venice. Olmi always writes his own scripts and often shoots and edits his own films.

FEATURE FILMS: *Il Tempo si è fermato/Time Stood Still* (also sc.) 1959; *Il Posto/The Sound of Trumpets/The Job* (also sc.) 1961; *I Fidanzati/The Fiancés* (also prod., sc.) 1963; *E venne un Uomo/And There Came a Man/A Man Called John* (also co-sc.) 1965; *Un certo Giorno/One Fine Day* (also sc., edit.) 1968; *I Recuperanti/The Scavengers* (also co-sc., phot., originally for Italian TV) 1969; *Durante l'Estate/During the Summer* (also co-sc., phot., edit.; originally for TV) 1971; *La Circostanza/The Circumstance* (also prod., sc., phot., edit; originally for TV) 1974; *L'Albero degli Zoccoli/The Tree of Wooden Clogs* (also sc., phot., edit.) 1978; *Camminacammina/Cammina Cammina* (also sc., phot., edit., des.) 1983; *Milano '83/Milan '83* (doc.; also sc., phot., edit.) 1984; *Lunga Vita alla Signora/Long Live the Lady!* (also sc., co-phot., edit.) 1987; *La Legenda del Santo Bevitore/Legend of the Holy Drinker* (also sc., edit.) 1988; *Legend of the Old Wood* 1993; *Genesis: The Creation and the Flood* 1994.

Olmos, Edward James. Actor. Born on Feb. 24, 1947, in Los Angeles. Rugged, moustachioed, Hispanic leading man of the American stage, films, and television. The son of a Mexican-born welder, he grew up in the rough Boyles Heights barrio and managed to escape the neighborhood's snare of drugs and violence and the pain of his parents' divorce by becoming involved in semipro baseball and music. The rock band he formed, Eddie James and the Pacific Ocean, helped pay for his education at East Los Angeles College and later at California State University. Following drama training at the Lee Strasberg Institute, he began playing small parts in such TV series as 'Kojak' and 'Hawaii Five-O' and eventually major roles in films. His big break came in 1978, when he won the Los

Angeles Drama Critics Circle Award and was later nominated for a Broadway Tony for his performance in the musical play 'Zoot Suit' (1978). He was nominated for an Oscar for his convincing portrayal of a tough but inspiring high school mathematics teacher in *Stand and Deliver* (1988). Television audiences know him best for his co-starring role as Lt. Martin Castillo (Emmy Award 1985) in the popular crime series 'Miami Vice' (1984–89). Olmos is also well known as a dedicated volunteer for many social causes and for his personal war on drugs and gang violence in the Latino neighborhoods which led to an impressive directorial debut, *American Me* (1992). He is married to actress Lorraine Bracco.

FILMS: *Aloha Bobby and Rose* (bit) 1975; *Alambrista!* 1977; *Virus* (Jap.) 1980; *Wolfen, Zoot Suit* 1981; *Blade Runner* 1982; *The Ballad of Gregorio Cortez* (also assoc. prod., co-mus.) 1983; *Saving Grace* 7 1986; *Stand and Deliver* 1988; *Triumph of the Spirit* 1989; *Maria's Story* 1990; *A Talent for the Game* 1991; *American Me* (also dir., co-prod.) 1992; *A Mission to Juan, Mi Familia/My Family* 1994; *Caught* 1996; *Selena, The Disappearance of Garcia Lorca* 1997.

Olmstead (also billed as **Olmsted), Gertrude.** Actress. *b.* 1897, Chicago. *d.* 1975. A beauty contest winner, she signed a Hollywood contract in 1920 and, after playing a number of supporting roles, starred in many silents of the 20s, retiring shortly after the advent of sound. She was married to director Robert Z. Leonard.

FILMS INCLUDE: *The Big Adventure, The Fighting Lover, The Fox* 1921; *Robinson Crusoe* (serial), *The Scrapper, The Loaded Door* 1922; *Trilby, Cameo Kirby* 1923; *Ladies to Board, George Washington Jr., Babbitt* (as Eunice Littlefield), *Empty Hands, Lovers' Lane* 1924; *The Monster, California Straight Ahead, Time the Comedian, Cobra* 1925; *Sweet Adeline, The Torrent, Monte Carlo, The Boob, Puppets* 1926; *The Cheerful Fraud, Mr. Wu, The Callahans and the Murphys, Becky, Buttons* 1927; *The Cheer Leader, Sporting Goods, Bringing Up Father, Midnight Life, Hit the Show, The Passion Song* 1928; *The Lone Wolf's Daughter, Sonny Boy, The Time the Place and the Girl, The Show of Shows* 1929.

Olsen, Moroni. Actor. *b.* Nov. 22, 1889, Ogden, Utah. *d.* 1954. Tall, bulky character player of the American stage and screen. Appeared in numerous Hollywood films from the mid-30s through the mid-50s, playing imposing friendly types and men of prominence as well as villains or other corrupt persons.

FILMS INCLUDE: *The Three Musketeers* (as Porthos), *Annie Oakley* (as Buffalo Bill), *Seven Keys to Baldpate* 1935; *Yellow Dust, Mary of Scotland* (as John Knox) 1936; *The Plough and the Stars* (as General Connolly) 1937; *Gold Is Where You Find It, Kidnapped, Submarine Patrol, Kentucky* 1938; *The Three Musketeers* (Ritz Brothers version), *Rose of Washington Square, Susannah of the Mounties, Dust Be My Destiny, Barricade, Invisible Stripes* 1939; *Brigham Young, Santa Fe Trail* (as Robert E. Lee) 1940; *Dive Bomber, One Foot in Heaven* 1941; *Dangerously They Live, My Favorite Spy, Nazi Agent, The Glass Key* 1942; *Air Force, Reunion in France, Mission to Moscow, The Song of Bernadette* 1943; *Ali Baba and the Forty Thieves, Buffalo Bill, Cobra Woman* 1944; *Pride of the Marines, Mildred Pierce* 1945; *Night in Paradise, Notorious* 1946; *The Beginning or the End, Possessed, Life with Father, The Long Night* 1947; *Call Northside 777* 1948; *Command Decision, The Fountainhead, Samson and Delilah* 1949; *Father of the Bride* 1950; *Lone Star* (as Sam Houston), *Washington Story* 1952; *So This Is Love* 1953; *The Long Long Trailer, The Sign of the Pagan* 1954.

Olsen, Ole. Actor. *b.* John Sigvard Olsen, Nov. 6, 1892, Wabash, Ind. *d.* 1963. Vaudeville comedian who starred in a number of films with stage partner Chic Johnson. For a complete list of their films together, see Johnson, Chic. Another Ole Olsen (*b.* 1863) was a pioneer of the Danish film industry, as co-founder of Nordisk, an internationally important hub of film-making before WW I.

Olson, James. Actor. Born on Oct. 8, 1930, in Evanston, Ill. *ed.* Northwestern U. Slender stage-trained character player. In addition to performances in modern and Shakespearean plays in New York, he has appeared in a smattering of screen and TV dramas since the 1950s.

FILMS INCLUDE: *The Sharkfighters* 1956; *The Strange One* 1957; *Rachel Rachel* 1967; *The Andromeda Strain, Moon Zero Two* 1970; *Wild Rovers* 1971; *The Groundstar Conspiracy* 1972; *The Mafu Cage* 1978; *Ragtime, Amityville II: The Possession* 1982; *Commando* 1985; *Rachel River* 1987.

Olson, Nancy. Actress. Born on July 14, 1928, in Milwaukee, a physician's daughter. *ed.* UCLA. Fresh-faced, engaging leading lady of Hollywood films of the early 50s. She participated in college dramatics before being signed by Paramount for her film debut in 1949. The following year she was nominated for an Oscar for her performance in the ingenue role in *Sunset Boulevard.* In this and several other movies she was teamed with William Holden. She retired from films in 1955 but returned to the screen in 1960 for occasional character roles. In 1984 she co-starred in the TV series 'Paper Dolls.' The third (1950–57) of eight wives of songwriter Alan Jay Lerner, she later married Alan Livingston, then president of Capitol Records.

FILMS: *Canadian Pacific* 1949; *Sunset Boulevard, Union Station, Mr. Music* 1950; *Force of Arms, Submarine Command* 1951; *Big Jim McLain* 1952; *Donovan's Brain, So Big* 1953; *The Boy from Oklahoma* 1954; *Battle Cry* 1955; *Pollyanna* 1960; *The Absent-Minded Professor* 1961; *Son of Flubber* 1963; *Smith!* 1969; *Snowball Express* 1972; *Airport 1975* 1974; *Making Love* 1982.

O'Malley, Pat. Actor. *b.* Patrick H. O'Malley, Jr., Sept. 3, 1891, Forest City, Pa. *d.* 1966. Leading man of Hollywood silents, mainly romantic melodramas, who later played character roles in many talkies. He entered films with the Edison company in 1907. His name is often confused with actors John P. O'Malley (*b.* 1916, Australia; *d.* 1959), who appeared in several Hollywood films of the 50s, and J. Pat O'Malley (*b.* 1901, England; *d.* 1985), who played character roles in Hollywood films from the late 50s.

FILMS INCLUDE: *The Papered Door* 1911; *On Dangerous Paths, Gladiola* 1915; *The Law of the North, The Tell-Tale Step, The Love That Lives, The Adopted Son* 1917; *Hit-the-Trail Holliday, She Hired a Husband* 1918; *The Red Glove* (serial), *False Evidence, The Heart of Humanity* 1919; *The Blooming Angel, Sherry, Go and Get It, The Breath of the Gods, Dinty* 1920; *The Breaking Point, Bob Hampton of Placer, False Kisses* 1921; *The Game Chicken, My Wild Irish Rose, Brothers Under the Skin* 1922; *Brass, The Last Hour, Wandering Daughters, Souls in Bondage, The Virginian, The Eternal Struggle* 1923; *Happiness, The Fighting American, Bread, Fools' Highway, The Mine with the Iron Door, Worldly Goods, The Beauty Prize* 1924; *Proud Flesh, The Teaser, The White Desert, Let Women Alone, Tomorrow's Love* 1925; *The Midnight Sun, My Old Dutch, Spangles, Watch Your Wife* 1926; *Cheaters, Perch of the Devil, Pleasure Before Business, The Rose of Kildare, The Slaver, Woman's Law, A Bowery Cinderella* 1927; *The House of Scandal* 1928; *Alibi, The Man I Love* 1929; *The Fall Guy* 1930; *Sky Spider* 1931; *American Madness* 1932; *Frisco Jenny, Mystery of the Wax Museum, I Love That Man* 1933; *Crime Doctor* 1934; *Behind the Evidence, The Man on the*

Flying Trapeze, The Perfect Clue 1935; *Hollywood Boulevard* 1936; *Frontier Marshal, The Night of Nights* 1939; *Captain Caution, A Little Bit of Heaven* 1940; *Meet Boston Blackie* 1941; *Paris Calling, Over My Dead Body* 1942; *Lassie Come Home* 1943; *Adventures of Mark Twain* 1944; *Mule Train* 1950; *The Kid from Broken Gun* 1951; *Invasion of the Body Snatchers* 1956.

omnidirectional microphone. A microphone capable of picking up sound from any direction.

Ondra, Anny. Actress. *b.* Anna Sophie Ondrakowa, May 15, 1903, Tarnow, Poland. *d.* 1987. Pretty blonde star of Czech, Austrian, German, and British films. A former dancer, she was at her best in cute comedy roles. But she also played straight dramatic parts, memorably in Hitchcock's early talkie, *Blackmail* (1929), for which her thickly accented voice was dubbed. She frequently worked under the guidance of director-husband Karel LAMAÇ, whom she divorced in 1933 to marry boxer Max Schmeling.

FILMS INCLUDE: In Czechoslovakia—*Woman with Small Feet* 1919; *Song of Gold, Dratenicek* 1920; *Gilly in Prague* 1921. In Austria and Germany—*Zigeunerliebe* 1922; *Der Mann ohne Herz* 1923; *Ich liebe Dich* 1925; *Der erste Kuss* 1928. In the UK—*God's Clay* 1928; *Blackmail, Glorious Youth, The Manxman* 1929. In Germany—*Das Mädel aus USA, Die grosse Sehnsucht, Eine Freundin so goldig wie Du* 1930; *Mamsell Nitouche, Die Fledermaus* 1931; *Baby, Kiki, Eine Nacht im Paradies* 1932; *Die Tochter des Regiments* 1933; *Klein Dorrit, Polenblut* (Ger./Czech.) 1934; *Knock-Out, Der Junge Graf* 1935; *Ein Mädel vom Ballett, Donogoo Tonka* 1936; *Der unwiderst Ehliche/The Irresistible Man* 1937; *Narren im Schnee* 1938; *Der Gasmann* 1941; *Himmel wir erben ein Schloss* 1943; *Schön muss man sein* 1951; *Zürcher Velobung* 1957.

Ondricek, Miroslav. Director of photography. Born in 1933, in then Czechoslovakia. A graduate of the Barrandov training school, he began his career at the Documentary Film Studios. Moving into features in the early 60s, he became closely associated with director Milos FORMAN, for whom he did outstanding work on several notable Czech "new wave" films. He also served Lindsay ANDERSON well in three excursions to England. After the 1968 Soviet crush of the "Prague Spring," he joined Forman in the US, where he collaborated with several directors, winning Academy Award nominations for the brilliant cinematography of Forman's *Ragtime* (1981) and *Amadeus* (1984).

FILMS INCLUDE: In Czechoslovakia—*Audition/Talent Competition* (medium-length) 1963; *Loves of a Blonde, Intimate Lighting* 1965; *Martyrs of Love* 1966; *The Fireman's Ball* 1967. In the UK—*The White Bus* (medium-length) 1967; *If. . .* 1968. In the US—*Taking Off* 1971; *Slaughterhouse-Five* 1972; *O Lucky Man!* (UK) 1973; *The Divine Emma* (Czech.), *The Black Sun* (Czech.), *Hair* 1979; *Ragtime* 1981; *The World According to Garp* 1982; *Silkwood* 1983; *Amadeus* 1984; *Heaven Help Us* 1985; *F/X* 1986; *Distant Harmony* (doc.), *Big Shots* 1987; *Funny Farm* 1988; *Valmont* (Fr./UK) 1989; *Awakenings* 1990; *A League of Their Own* 1992; *The Preacher's Wife* 1996.

O'Neal, Patrick. Actor. *b.* Sept. 26, 1927, in Ocala, Fla. *d.* 1994. *ed.* U. of Florida; Actors Studio; Neighborhood Playhouse. American stage, TV, and film lead and supporting player, often in unsympathetic parts. Directed training shorts during his WW II service with the Air Force.

FILMS INCLUDE: *The Mad Magician, The Black Shield of Falworth* 1954; *From the Terrace* 1960; *A Matter of Morals* 1961; *The Cardinal* 1963; *In Harm's Way, King Rat* 1965; *A Fine Madness, Alvarez Kelly, Chamber of Horrors* 1966; *Where Were You When the Lights Went Out?, The Secret Life of an American Wife* 1968; *Assignment to Kill, Stiletto, Castle Keep* 1969; *The Kremlin Letter, El Condor* 1970; *Corky* 1972; *The Way We Were* 1973; *Silent Night—Bloody Night* 1974; *The Stepford Wives* 1975; *Independence* (Bicentennial short; as George Washington) 1976; *The Stuff* 1985; *Like Father Like Son* 1987; *New York Stories* 1989; *Q & A, Alice* 1990; *For the Boys* 1992.

O'Neal, Ron. Actor. Born on Sept 1, 1937, in Utica, N.Y. The son of a jazz-musician-turned-factory-worker, he grew up in Cleveland's black ghetto. After attending Ohio State University for one semester, he joined Cleveland's Karamu House, an interracial troupe of players, and stayed with that company for nine years (1957–66), appearing in some 40 stage productions. In 1967 he came to New York, taught acting in Harlem, and began performing in summer stock and off Broadway. His big break came in 1970 when he joined Joseph Papp's Public Theatre and starred in 'No Place To Be Somebody,' reaping rave reviews and winning the Obie, the Drama Desk, and other awards. He became an instant movie star in 1972 as Priest, the cool pusher-hero of the action-packed film *Superfly.* He made his debut as a film director the following year with a sequel, *Superfly TNT,* again starring himself. His success was brief, however, and by the end of the decade he was mainly playing supporting roles. He co-starred in the TV series 'Bring 'Em Back Alive' (1982–83) and 'The Equalizer' (1986–89).

FILMS: *Move* 1970; *The Organization* 1971; *Superfly* 1972; *Superfly TNT* (also dir., co-story) 1973; *The Master Gunfighter* 1975; *Brothers* 1977; *When a Stranger Calls, A Force of One* 1979; *The Final Countdown* 1980; *St. Helens* 1981; *Red Dawn* 1984; *Mercenary Fighters, Hero and the Terror* 1988; *Up Against the Wall* (also dir.) 1991.

O'Neal, Ryan. Actor. Born Patrick Ryan O'Neal, on Apr. 20, 1941, in Los Angeles. The son of screenwriter and sometime novelist Charles O'Neal and actress Patricia Callaghan O'Neal, he lived through an aimless, nomadic adolescence on the beaches of California and in several foreign countries. A former lifeguard and amateur boxer (he competed in the 1956 and 1957 Los Angeles Golden Gloves championships), he once spent 51 days in jail for assault and battery during a New Year's Eve party. When he was 17 he joined his parents in Munich, Germany, where they were working on a TV series. It was there that he got his first taste of show business, as a stuntman in a TV series, 'Tales of the Vikings.' Returning to the US, he played occasional roles in various TV shows and was a regular on the Western series 'Empire' (1962–63). He got his first big break in the long-running (1964–69) 'Peyton Place' series, in which he co-starred in more than 500 episodes.

Blond, handsome, and boyish, he was selected from among more than 300 candidates who auditioned for the male lead in Erich Segal's *Love Story,* a role that got him an Oscar nomination and established him as a promising young Hollywood star. The promise was fulfilled for much of the 70s but O'Neal's popularity faded somewhat in the 80s. The actor, whose brother, Kevin O'Neal, is also a film and TV performer, is the father of actress Tatum O'NEAL and troubled actor Griffin O'Neal (*b.* Oct. 28, 1964, Los Angeles) from his first marriage (1963–67) to actress Joanna Moore. His second marriage (in 1967) to actress Lee TAYLOR-YOUNG also ended in divorce. His long-term relationship with actress-model Farrah FAWCETT, with whom he has a son, Redmond Fawcett, ended in 1997.

FILMS: *The Big Bounce* 1969; *The Games, Love Story* 1970; *Wild Rovers* 1971; *What's Up Doc?* 1972; *The Thief Who Came to Dinner, Paper Moon* 1973; *Barry Lyndon* (title role) 1975; *Nickelodeon* 1976; *A Bridge Too Far* (UK) 1977; *The*

Driver, Oliver's Story 1978; *The Main Event* 1979; *Green Ice* (UK), *So Fine* 1981; *Partners* 1982; *Irreconcilable Differences* 1984; *Fever Pitch* 1985; *Tough Guys Don't Dance* 1987; *Chances Are* 1989; *Faithful* 1996.

O'Neal, Tatum. Actress. Born on Nov. 5, 1963, in Los Angeles. Child star of Hollywood films of the 70s; the daughter of Ryan O'NEAL and actress Joanna Moore. She won an Oscar as best supporting actress for her memorable portrayal of a nine-year-old tough-talking, cigarette-smoking con artist in her first movie, *Paper Moon* (1973). She is the youngest person ever to win that award. Returning to the screen after a three-year absence, she received $350,000 and 9 percent of the net profit for playing the role of a fearless Little League pitcher in *The Bad News Bears* (1976), thus becoming the highest-paid child in the history of the movies. She appeared only sporadically as a young adult in films of the 80s and early 90s. She made her New York stage debut in 1992's 'A Terrible Beauty.' In 1986 she married vitriolic tennis star John McEnroe, but their marriage later ended in divorce.

FILMS: *Paper Moon* 1973; *The Bad News Bears, Nickelodeon* 1976; *International Velvet* 1978; *Little Darlings, Circle of Two* (Can.) 1980; *Prisoners* (NZ) 1984; *Certain Fury* 1985; *Little Noises* 1991; *Basquiat* 1996.

O'Neil, Barbara. Actress. *b.* July 10, 1909, St. Louis, Mo. *d.* 1980. Capable, good-looking leading lady, second lead, and character player of stage and screen. The product of a socially prominent New England family, she began appearing on Broadway in 1930 and in Hollywood films in 1937. Memorable as Scarlett O'Hara's mother in *Gone With the Wind* (1939) and for her Oscar-nominated performance as best supporting actress in *All This and Heaven Too* (1940). She was briefly married to playwright-director Joshua LOGAN.

FILMS INCLUDE: *Stella Dallas* 1937; *The Toy Wife, I Am the Law* 1938; *The Sun Never Sets, When Tomorrow Comes, Tower of London* (as Queen Elizabeth), *Gone With the Wind* (as Ellen O'Hara) 1939; *All This and Heaven Too* 1940; *Shining Victory* 1941; *The Secret Beyond the Door, I Remember Mama* 1948; *Whirlpool* 1950; *Angel Face* 1953; *Flame of the Islands* 1956; *The Nun's Story* 1959.

O'Neil (also billed **O'Neill), Sally.** Actress. *b.* Virginia Louise Concepta Noonan, Oct. 23, 1908, Bayonne, N.J. *d.* 1968. Pert, petite leading lady of late silent and early sound Hollywood films. One of 11 children of a judge, and sister of actress Molly O'Day, she was convent-educated and made her screen debut at 17 and played Pickford-like urchin roles in a number of entertaining productions. She was quite popular for several years, but her career faded by the mid-30s.

FILMS INCLUDE: *Don't, Sally Irene and Mary* 1925; *Mike, The Auction Block, Battling Butler* 1926; *Slide Kelly Slide, Frisco Sally Levy, the Callahans and the Murphys, Becky, The Lovelorn* 1927; *Bachelor's Paradise, The Mad Hour, The Battle of the Sexes* 1928; *Broadway Fever, The Girl on the Barge, Hardboiled, On with the Show, the Sophomore, Jazz Heaven, Broadway Scandals* 1929; *Girl of the Port, Hold Everything, Sisters, Kathleen Mavourneen* (title role) 1930; *Salvation Nell, Murder by the Clock, The Brat* 1931; *Ladies Must Love* 1933; *Sixteen Fathoms Deep* 1934; *Kathleen Mavourneen/Kathleen* (title role; Ire./UK) 1937.

O'Neill, Henry. Actor. *b.* Aug. 10, 1891, Orange, N.J. *d.* 1961. Versatile character actor of some 200 Hollywood films, mainly for Warners and MGM, after solid stage experience. Usually played kind, patrician roles.

FILMS INCLUDE: *I Loved a Woman, The World Changes, The Kennel Murder Case, Lady Killer* 1933; *Massacre, Fashions of 1934, Wonder Bar, Midnight, The Key, Madame Du Barry, Flirtation Walk* 1934; *The Man Who Reclaimed His Head, Bordertown, Black Fury, Oil for the Lamps of China, Special Agent, Dr. Socrates* 1935; *The Story of Louis Pasteur* (as bacteriologist Emile Roux), *The Walking Dead, Bullets or Ballots, The White Angel, Anthony Adverse* (as Father Xavier) 1936; *Green Light, Marked Woman, The Life of Emile Zola* (as Colonel Picquart), *Wells Fargo* (as Henry Wells) 1937; *Jezebel, White Banners, The Amazing Dr. Clitterhouse, Brother Rat* 1938; *Dodge City* (as Col. Dodge), *Juarez, Confessions of a Nazi Spy* 1939; *Dr. Ehrlich's Magic Bullet, They Drive by Night, Santa Fe Trail* 1940; *Men of Boys Town, Billy the Kid, Blossoms in the Dust, Whistling in the Dark, Honky Tonk, Shadow of the Thin Man* 1941; *Johnny Eager, Tortilla Flat, White Cargo* 1942; *The Human Comedy, Stand By for Action, Air Raid Wardens, Girl Crazy, A Guy Named Joe* 1943; *The Heavenly Body, Lost Angel* 1944; *Anchors Aweigh* 1945; *The Green Years, The Virginian* 1946; *The Beginning or the End* 1947; *Alias Nick Beal, The Reckless Moment* 1949; *No Man of Her Own, The Flying Missile* 1950; *The People Against O'Hara* 1951; *Untamed* 1955; *The Wings of Eagles* 1957.

O'Neill, Jennifer. Actress. Born on Feb. 20, 1947, in Rio de Janeiro, to American parents, on a visit with her grandfather, who was president of the Bank of Rio de Janeiro. She was raised in Detroit, New Rochelle, N.Y., and Wilton, Conn., and attended Dalton School in Manhattan and later the Professional Children's School there. An excellent rider, she won scores of trophies in horse show competition in her teens. A leggy, fresh-faced brunette of warm and natural beauty, she began modeling at 15 and within a year or two was one of the top models in the business, appearing on the covers of national magazines and in TV commercials for beauty products. She made her film debut in 1968, playing a bit in *For Love of Ivy.* In 1970 she played the feminine lead in Howard Hawks's *Rio Lobo* and the following year became established as a star with *Summer of '42.* In the late 70s she was in several Italian productions. With her movie career declining in the 80s, she became increasingly involved in TV work. She starred in the short-lived series "Cover-Up," on the set of which her handsome male lead, Jon-Erik Hexum, accidentally killed himself with a prop gun.

FILMS: *For Love of Ivy* (bit) 1968; *Futz* (bit) 1969; *Rio Lobo* 1970; *Summer of '42, Such Good Friends* 1971; *Glass Houses, The Carey Treatment* 1972; *Ice Lady* 1973; *The Reincarnation of Peter Proud, Whiffs, Gente di Rispetto/Flower in His Mouth* (It.) 1975; *L'Innocento/The Innocent* (It.) 1976; *Sette Note in Nero/The Psychic* (It.) 1977; *Caravans* (US/Iran) 1978; *A Force of One* 1979; *Cloud Dancer* (release delayed from 1978), *Steel* 1980; *Scanners* (Can.) 1981; *Committed, I Love N.Y.* 1988; *Love is Like That* 1991; *Invasion of Privacy, The Gentle People* 1992.

one-light print. A print made with a single light setting without the process of GRADING. Used as a work print but unsuitable for release.

one-two-threes. Animator's indication on an exposure sheet regarding the number of exposures for each drawing. The indication is usually made in writing on the exposure sheet, a printed form containing instructions for the photography of each and every frame. The number of exposures desired for a drawing is entered into columns on the sheet which are headed "ones," "twos," and "threes" respectively, hence the term "one-two-threes." Also called "ones, twos, threes."

Ontkean, Michael. Actor. Born on Jan. 24, 1946, in Vancouver, Canada. Appealing leading man and supporting player of American TV and films. The son of actors (Leonard Ontkean and Muriel Cooper), he began acting at age four with his father's repertory company. Later he was a child actor with the Stratford Shakespeare Festival and Canadian TV and semi-documentary films. He attended the University of New Hampshire for two years on a hockey scholarship. His skills in the sport helped him years later to land a lead role in *Slap Shot* (1977) opposite Paul Newman. His US TV work includes co-starring roles in 'The Rookies' (1972–74) and David Lynch's cult series 'Twin Peaks' (1989).

FILMS INCLUDE: *The Peace Killers* 1971; *Pickup on 101, Necromancy* 1972; *Hot Summer Week* (Can.) 1973; *Slap Shot* 1977; *Voices* 1979; *Willie and Phil* 1980; *Making Love* 1982; *Le Sang des autres/The Blood of Others* (Fr./Can.), *Just the Way You Are* 1984; *The Allnighter, Maid to Order* 1987; *Clara's Heart* 1988; *Bye Bye Blues* (Can.), *Cold Front* (Can.), *Street Justice* 1989; *Postcards from the Edge* 1990; *Swann* 1996.

opaque. Impenetrable by light. The relative density of film in terms of light that can be transmitted through it is indicated by its opacity.

opaquing. In animation, the process of filling in the tones and colors on a CEL. The artists who specialize in this are known as "opaquers." They color a drawing in accordance with a color chart prepared by the animator.

Opatoshu, David. Actor. Born on Jan. 30, 1918, in New York City. Versatile character actor of American stage and occasional films, seen in both kindly and evil roles. Began his career as a teenager in the Yiddish theater.

FILMS INCLUDE: *The Light Ahead* (in Yiddish) 1939; *The Naked City* 1948; *Thieves' Highway* 1949; *Molly* 1951; *L'Ennemi public No. 1/The Most Wanted Man* (Fr./It.) 1953; *Crowded Paradise* 1956; *The Brothers Karamazov* 1958; *Exodus, Cimarron* 1960; *I Due Nemici/The Best of Enemies* (It./UK) 1961; *Guns of Darkness* (UK) 1962; *Sands of Beersheba* (Isr./US) 1965; *Torn Curtain, Tarzan and the Valley of Gold, L'Espion/The Defector* (Fr./Ger.) 1966; *Enter Laughing* 1967; *The Fixer* 1968; *Death of a Gunfighter* 1969; *Romance of a Horsethief* 1971; *Who'll Stop the Rain?* 1978; *Americathon* 1979; *Beyond Evil* 1980; *Forced Vengeance* 1982; *Almonds and Raisins* (compilation doc. on history of Yiddish cinema) 1985.

opening up. Increasing the aperture of a lens.

operator. See CAMERA OPERATOR.

Ophüls, Marcel. Director. Born Marcel Oppenheimer, on Nov. 1, 1927, in Frankfurt-am-Main, Germany. The only son of director Max OPHÜLS and actress Hilde Wall, he moved with his parents to Paris after Hitler's rise to power, in 1933, and became a French citizen in 1938. During his father's American exile of the 40s, Marcel attended Hollywood High. In 1946 he served with a theatrical unit of the US occupation forces in Japan. After his demobilization, he attended Occidental College, then the University of California at Berkeley. In 1950, after acquiring American citizenship, he returned with his family to France. Following philosophy studies at the Sorbonne, he began his film career as an assistant to Julien DUVIVIER, Anatole LITVAK, and his own father. He made a short film on the life and works of Matisse in 1960 and, thanks to his friendship with François Truffaut, he was assigned to direct the West German episode of *L'Amour à Vingt Ans/Love at Twenty* (1962). On his first venture as a solo director, he turned out an entertaining, commercially viable film, *Peau de Banane/Banana Peel* (1964), starring Jeanne Moreau and Jean-Paul Belmondo, but the failure of his next feature, an Eddie Constantine action quickie, signified a temporary reversal in his budding career.

After a period of unemployment, Ophüls found work on French television, for which he produced brief filmed news reports and a three-and-a-half-hour documentary investigation of Munich in 1938. This led to an ambitious undertaking that was to occupy Ophüls for three full years. With German-Swiss backing, he made *Le Chagrin et la Pitié/The Sorrow and the Pity*, a scathing examination of the conduct of the French people under the German Occupation. French television refused to show the film, but it was exhibited in theaters all over France with great success, amid much controversy. The film revealed Ophüls as a brilliant documentarian and superb interviewer, with a remarkable capacity to handle complex intellectual issues over long stretches of film without for a moment boring his audience, and the ability to inject personal statements in the flow of the film without jeopardizing its objectivity.

Although he had always preferred making entertainment films for the commercial market, Ophüls was now entrapped by his own success into years of work as a documentarian. After turning out a sensitive documentary about the conflict in Northern Ireland, *A Sense of Loss* (1972), he started a monumental project that was to consume many years of work and enmesh him in a painful battle with his British-German backers. He began shooting *The Memory of Justice* in 1973, setting out to draw a comparison between Nazi atrocities and the conduct of French troops in Algeria and US G.I.s in Vietnam. After shooting and compiling 90 hours of film and cutting the material down to a little under five hours, Ophüls found himself in deep disagreement with his backers over the shape and style of the final product. Among other points of conflict was the refusal of Ophüls, who is an American citizen, to "enliven" the film by drawing facile comparisons between Nazi Germany and the US military machine in ways he could not substantiate through his research. Charges and countercharges followed. The producers assigned the final editing to another director, and Ophüls conducted, in New York, private screenings of his original version, which was smuggled out of London by a loyal assistant. Heartbroken over the incident and nearly broke financially, Ophüls vowed never to make another documentary film. To make ends meet, he went into teaching and lectured on film at Princeton and the University of California at Santa Barbara. In 1975 he became a staff producer of documentaries at CBS News and two years later he joined ABC-TV's '20/20' as a contributing producer. In 1979 he returned to Paris, where he made the Oscar-winning documentary *Hotel Terminus: Klaus Barbie—His Life and Times* (1988).

FILMS: *Matisse ou le Talent du Bonheur* (short doc.; also sc.) 1960; *L'Amour à Vingt Ans/Love at Twenty* ("West Germany" episode; also sc.; Fr./It./Jap./Pol./Ger.) 1962; *Peau de Banane/Banana Peel* (also co-sc.; Fr./It.) 1964; *Feu à Volonte* (Fr./It.) 1965; *Till Eulenspiegel* (co-dir. co-sc. uncredited for Ger. TV) 1966; *Munich ou la Paix pour Cent Ans* (TV doc.; also sc.; Fr.) 1967; *Clavigo* (TV movie; Fr.), *The Harvest of My Lai* (TV doc.; also sc.; Fr.), *Le Chagrin et la Pitié/The Sorrow and the Pity* (doc.; also co-sc.; Fr./Switz./Ger.), *America Revisited* (TV doc.; also sc.; Fr.), *Zwei ganze Tage* (TV movie; Ger.) 1971; *A Sense of Loss* (doc.; also sc.; US/Switz.) 1972; *The Memory of Justice* (doc.; also sc.; UK/Ger.) 1976; *Kortner Gescichte* (TV doc.; also sc.; Ger.) 1980; *Yorktown: Le Sens d'un Bataille* (TV doc.; also sc.; Fr.) 1982; *Hotel Terminus: Klaus Barbie—His Life and Times* 1988; *November Days: Voices and Choices* (TV doc.) 1990; *The Troubles We've Seen* 1994.

Ophüls (Opuls in the US), **Max.** Director. *b.* Max Oppenheimer, May 6, 1902, Saarbrucken, Germany. *d.* 1957. The son of a conservative German-Jewish family in the garment business, he changed his name to avoid embarrassing his parents when he became a stage actor at the age of 17 after a brief stint in journalism. In 1923 he began directing plays. By 1926 he was famous enough to be invited to direct at Vienna's Burgtheater. There he met and married Hilde Wall, a well-known actress. Their only child is director Marcel OPHÜLS.

By the time the senior Ophüls entered German films in 1930 he had directed some 200 stage plays in Germany and Austria, including one he wrote himself, 'Fips and Stips.' Originally employed by UFA as dialogue director for Anatole Litvak, he was asked to direct a 40-minute featurette. It was successful and he decided that his future was in films, although he continued directing plays until 1932.

The following year, immediately after the Reichstag fire, Ophüls saw the writing on the wall and took his family out of Germany to France. For the next six years he directed films there and in Holland and Italy. He was also offered a two-year contract by the Soviet Union but stipulated he would sign only if he liked the country. He went to Russia for two months, did not like it, and returned to France, where he became a naturalized citizen in 1938.

In 1940, after the fall of France, Ophüls went to Switzerland, where he directed a play and an unfinished screen version of Molière's *L'Ecole des Femmes.* The US was the next stop in his nomadic travels. He arrived in Hollywood in 1941. Five years and several abortive projects later, he was assigned by Howard Hughes to direct what was to be his first American film, *Vendetta.* But after a few days of shooting he was dismissed from the set.

In the next three years Ophüls, billed in the US as Opuls, directed four Hollywood films: *The Exile,* a Douglas Fairbanks, Jr., costume adventure yarn; *Letter from an Unknown Woman,* the most romantic, elegant, European, and best of his American films; and *Caught* and *The Reckless Moment,* both tense suspense melodramas starring James Mason. His reputation as one of the great directors of cinema stems not from the content of his films, which was often rather flimsy, but from their form. Ophüls was a virtuoso of the directing style that emphasized the MISE-EN-SCÈNE. His camera was incredibly fluid, constantly moving in an intoxicating array of tracking shots, crane shots, tilts, and pans, and sensuously caressing the luxurious baroque texture of the timeless world in which his romantic characters moved. These ingredients, which marked Ophüls's personal style, are present in most of his works but found ultimate expression in his last four films, all made in France in the early 50s—*La Ronde, Le Plaisir, Madame de. . . ,* and *Lola Montès.* Ironically, it was for the screenplays, not the inspired direction, of the first two of these that he shared Oscar nominations.

In 1956 Ophüls went to Hamburg, Germany, to direct a Beaumarchais play on the stage. The play opened successfully in January of 1957. Two months later he died of a rheumatic heart condition in a Hamburg clinic. He had been scheduled to direct the film *Montparnasse 19/Modigliani of Montparnasse* (1958). After his death the direction was assigned to Jacques Becker, who dedicated the film to the memory of Ophüls. Another admirer, Jacques DEMY, dedicated his film *Lola* (1961) to the memory of the director who remains one of the most revered figures in the annals of cinema.

FILMS: In Germany—*Das schon lieber Lebertran* (medium length; also co-adapt.) 1930; *Die verliebte Firma, Die verkaufte Braut/The Bartered Bride* 1932; *Die lachende Erben* (release delayed from 1931), *Liebelei* 1933. In France—*Une Histoire d'Amour* (French-language version of *Liebelei*) 1933; *On a volé un Homme* 1934. In Italy—*La Signora di Tutti* (also co-sc.) 1934. In France—*Divine* (also co-adapt.) 1935. In Holland—*Komedie om Geld* (also co-sc.) 1936. In France—*Ave Maria* (short), *La Valse brillante* (short), *La Tendre Ennemie/The Tender Enemy* (also co-sc.) 1936; *Yoshiwara (also co-sc.)* 1937; *Werther/Le Roman de Werther* (also co-adapt.) 1938; *Sans Lendemain, De Mayerling à Sarajevo/Mayerling to Sarajevo, L'Ecole des Femmes* (unfinished) 1940. In the US—*Vendetta* (removed after several days of shooting; uncredited; film's release delayed for several years) 1946; *The Exile* 1947; *Letter from an Unknown Woman* 1948; *Caught, The Reckless Moment* 1949. In France—*La Ronde* (also co-sc.) 1950; *Le Plaisir/House of Pleasure* (also co-sc.) 1952; *Madame de. . . /The Earrings of Madame De* (also co-sc.; Fr./It.) 1953; *Lola Montès/The Sins of Lola Montes/Lola Montez* (also co-sc.; Fr./Ger.) 1955.

optical composite. A special effects shot in which two or more separate images have been combined through the use of an OPTICAL PRINTER.

optical print. See ANSWER PRINT.

optical printer. A device combining the features of both a camera and a projector, capable of re-photographing previously processed film, reducing or enlarging portions of the picture information, and adding a variety of visual effects. The projector and camera mechanisms work in synchronization, and, in modern versions, are computer-controlled. The projector is pointed at the camera lens and focused on the film stock in the camera; as each frame is projected, it is re-exposed on the camera film. If the projected film depicts a moving miniature of a spaceship, and the film in the camera depicts a starry background with a moving blank hole exactly corresponding to the spaceship, the result will be a film of a spaceship moving against the stars. (The two complementary elements are created in advance through a TRAVELING MATTE process.) The process of re-photographing film images by this method is known as "optical printing" or "projection printing."

Most optical printers incorporate two or more projectors, to allow a greater number of images to be combined. The projectors may be positioned at different angles to the camera, with beam splitters (partially silvered mirrors or prisms) used to direct the projected images toward the camera lens. An "aerial image printer," the type of optical printer now most widely in use, is one in which a projected image from one film is focused onto a second strip of film that has a complementary image; a camera focuses on the combined images and re-photographs them.

opticals. Optical effects, a general term for any effects made using an OPTICAL PRINTER. They include composite shots and such transitional effects as the FADE, the DISSOLVE, and the WIPE.

optical sound track. A sound track produced on photographic film by photographic means. Modulations are electrically converted from light impulses to audible sound during projection. It is to be distinguished from a DIGITAL SOUND TRACK, made by converting sound into binary digital information.

optical system. An arrangement of lenses in a camera, projector, or printer.

Opuls, Max. See OPHÜLS, Max.

Orbach, Jerry. Actor. Born on Oct. 20, 1935, in the Bronx, N.Y. *ed.* U. of Illinois; Northwestern U. Star of the musical stage who emerged in the 80s as a capable, versatile character player in films. The son of an ex-vaudevillian restaurant manager, he was raised in Waukegan, Illinois. After graduating from college, he headed for New York, where he trained with Herbert Berghof and Lee Strasberg while pounding the pavements for roles. He got his first job in 1955 as an understudy in 'The Threepenny Opera.' He worked his way up to the lead role and in 1960 headed the original cast of the long-running off-Broadway musical 'The Fantasticks.' He later starred in 'Carnival' (1961), 'Promises Promises' (1968), 'Chicago' (1975) and '42nd Street' (1980), among other Broadway musicals. Onscreen intermittently from the late 50s, he suddenly emerged in the 80s as a viable movie personality.

FILMS INCLUDE: *Cop Hater* 1958; *Mad Dog Coll* 1961; *John Goldfarb, Please Come Home* 1964; *The Gang That Couldn't Shoot Straight* 1971; *A Fan's Notes* (Can.) 1972; *Foreplay* 1975; *The Sentinel* 1977; *Prince of the City* 1981; *Brewster's Millions* 1985; *The Imagemaker, F/X* 1986; *Dirty Dancing, Someone to Watch Over Me* 1987; *Crimes and Misdemeanors, Last Exit to Brooklyn* (Ger.) 1989; *Dead Women In Lingerie* 1990 *Delusion, Toy Soldiers, Out for Justice* 1991; *The Cemetery Club, Delirious, Beauty and the Beast* (v/o), *Mr. Saturday Night, Straight Talk, Universal Soldier* 1992; *A Gnome Named Gnorm* 1994.

original. 1. The original negative or reversal positive exposed in the camera during filming. It is of a higher quality than subsequent "generations," or reprints. 2. In films, script material written directly for the screen, rather than an adaptation from a printed or staged work.

Orion Pictures Corporation. American motion picture financing, production, and distribution company. It was founded in 1978 by five former top executives at UNITED ARTISTS who had disagreed with the policies of the parent company, Transamerica: Robert S. Benjamin, William Bernstein, Arthur Krim, Mike MEDAVOY, and Eric Pleskow. Named for the five-star constellation Orion, the company was headed by Krim and initially had close ties to Warner Bros. In 1982, Orion merged with Filmways Inc., a film, television, and publishing company.

Orion enjoyed several successes through the 80s, including the films of Woody ALLEN, who had worked with Orion's founders when they were at United Artists and moved with them to the new company after 1980 (a relationship that ended in 1992). Orion's hits included *10* (1979), *Arthur* (1981), *Amadeus* (1984), *Platoon* (1986), and *Robocop* (1987), along with the TV series 'Cagney and Lacey.' With a record that included several best picture Oscars and the founding of an art film division called Orion Classics, Orion was widely considered a new major studio, but its financial position by the early 90s was worse than many people suspected. Despite box-office successes like *Dances with Wolves* (1990) and *The Silence of the Lambs* (1991), both of which won best picture Oscars, Orion was reeling under the pressures of expensive flops and over-expansion.

In December of 1991, Orion filed for chapter 11 bankruptcy. While a reorganization plan was worked out (made effective November 5, 1992), the company was forced to postpone the release of several completed films. Chastened but resilient, it returned to the theatrical marketplace in late 1993 with *Robocop 3*. In July of 1993, the company formed a motion picture production partnership with Metromedia Company, while continuing its other operations independently.

Orlova, Lyubov. Actress. *b.* Jan. 29, 1902, Russia. *d.* 1975. *ed.* Moscow Conservatory; Moscow School of Musical Theater. The first popular "star" of Soviet cinema, blond heroine of the light musical films of Grigori ALEXANDROV, who later became her husband.

FILMS INCLUDE: *Petersburg Night, Jolly Fellows/Jazz Comedy/Moscow Laughs* 1934; *The Circus* 1936; *Volga-Volga* 1938; *Bright Road* 1940; *The Artamanov Affair* 1941; *Spring* 1947; *Meeting on the Elbe* 1949; *Moussorgsky* 1950; *Glinka/Man of Music* 1952; *Russian Memory* 1960.

Ormond, Julia. Actress. Born January 4, 1965, in England. *ed.* West Surrey College of Art and Design; Webber Douglas Academy of Dramatic Art. Captivating, accomplished actress of the British stage, television, and eventually American films. Hollywood took notice of her dramatic performances for PBS's 'Masterpiece Theatre' and quickly cast her opposite Brad Pitt in Edward Zwick's *Legends of the Fall* (1995) and the title role in the re-make of the classic film *Sabrina* (1996).

FILMS: *The Baby of Macon* 1993; *Captives, Nostradamus* 1994; *First Knight, Legends of the Fall, Sabrina* 1995; *Smilla's Sense of Snow* 1997.

Ornitz, Arthur J. Director of photography. *b.* Nov. 28, 1916, New York City. *d.* 1985. *ed.* UCLA. The son of screenwriter Samuel Ornitz, he began his career in documentaries, graduating to features in the late 50s. Based mainly in New York, he captured well the sights and dynamics of the city for a number of major directors. He also worked with notable independent filmmakers like Joris Ivens and Shirley Clarke. He occasionally directed for television.

FILMS INCLUDE: *Power and the Land* (doc.; co-phot.) 1940; *The Goddess* 1958; *The Pusher* 1960; *The Young Doctors* 1961; *The Connection, Requiem for a Heavyweight* 1962; *Act One, The World of Henry Orient* 1964; *A Thousand Clowns* 1965; *A Midsummer Night's Dream* (ballet film) 1966; *The Tiger Makes Out* 1967; *Charly* 1968; *Me Natalie* 1969; *The Boys in the Band, House of Dark Shadows* 1970; *The Anderson Tapes, Minnie and Moskowitz* 1971; *The Possession of Joel Delaney* 1972; *Serpico, Sweet Suzy/Blacksnake* 1973; *Death Wish, Law and Disorder* 1974; *Next Stop Greenwich Village* 1976; *Thieves* 1977; *Oliver's Story, An Unmarried Woman* 1978; *Tattoo, The Chosen* 1981; *Hanky Panky* 1982.

Orry-Kelly. Costume designer. *b.* John Kelley, Dec. 31, 1897, Kiama, near Sydney, Australia. *d.* 1964. One of Hollywood's most prolific and most celebrated gown fashioners. Trained as an artist, he came to New York hoping to become an actor but wound up designing titles for Fox silent films. After becoming established as a designer of scenery and costumes for Schubert revues and several editions of 'George White's Scandals' on Broadway, he headed in the early 30s to Hollywood, where he rapidly became a top costume designer for Warner Bros., a favorite of Bette Davis and other stars. From the late 40s he also worked for Universal, RKO, MGM, and other studios. In all, he was involved in hundreds of films. He won Academy Awards for *An American in Paris* (in collaboration, 1951), *Les Girls* (1957), and *Some Like It Hot* (1959), and was nominated for another Oscar for *Gypsy* (1962).

FILMS INCLUDE: *Maybe It's Love* 1930; *I Am a Fugitive from a Chain Gang, One Way Passage, Cabin in the Cotton, Tiger Shark, Three on a Match* 1932; *20,000 Years in Sing Sing, 42nd Street, Gold Diggers of 1933, Voltaire, Female, Ex-Lady* 1933; *Wonder Bar, Dames, Fashions of 1934, Flirtation Walk* 1934; *Ceiling Zero, Oil for the Lamps of China, G-Men, Bordertown, Dangerous* 1935; *The Petrified Forest* 1936; *Marked Woman, Another Dawn, Confession, Kid Galahad* 1937; *Jezebel, The Sisters* 1938; *Dark Victory, Juarez, The Oklahoma Kid, The Private Lives of Elizabeth and Essex, On Your Toes, The Old Maid* 1939; *All This and Heaven Too, The Letter, The Sea Hawk* 1940; *The Great Lie, The Little Foxes, The Maltese Falcon, The Strawberry Blonde, They Died with Their Boots On* 1941; *In This Our Life, The Man Who Came to Dinner, Now Voyager, Kings Row, Casablanca* 1942; *Old Acquaintance, Watch on the Rhine, Mission to Moscow* 1943; *Mr. Skeffington, Arsenic and Old Lace* 1944; *The Dolly Sisters, The Corn Is Green* 1945; *A Stolen Life* 1946; *Mother Wore Tights* 1947; *One Touch of Venus* 1948; *Take One False Step* 1949; *South Sea Sinner* 1950; *An American in Paris* 1951; *Pat and Mike, The Star* 1952; *I Confess* 1953; *Oklahoma!* 1955; *Les Girls* 1957; *Auntie Mame, Too Much Too Soon* 1958; *Some Like It Hot* 1959; *A Majority of One* 1961; *Five Finger Exercise, Four Horsemen of the Apocalypse* 1962; *Sweet Bird of Youth, Gypsy* 1963; *Sunday in New York, Irma la Douce* 1963.

Ortega, Kenny. Choreographer, director. Born Palo Alto, Calif. *ed.* Canada Coll. A dancer in his youth, he studied under scholarships to dance academies and appeared in regional theater, including a production of 'Hair.' Years later he turned to dance choreography, and got his first big break choreographing a Cher TV special. He began to choreograph for film as an assistant on *The Rose* and then on his own in similar youth-oriented Hollywood fare, most notably *Dirty Dancing*. Began directing in 1992. Active as concert and video choreographer.

FILMS INCLUDE: *Xanadu* 1980, *One from the Heart* 1982; *St. Elmo's Fire* 1985; *Pretty in Pink, Ferris Bueller's Day Off* 1986; *And God Created Woman* (act. only), *Dirty Dancing* 1987; *Salsa* (also assoc. pr.) 1988; *Shag* 1989; *Newsies* (also dir.) 1992; *Hocus Pocus* (also dir.) 1993; *To Wong Foo Thanks for Everything Julie Newmar* 1995.

Orth, Frank. Actor. *b.* Feb. 21, 1880, Philadelphia. *d.* 1962. A veteran of vaudeville and the legitimate stage, he entered films in 1929 and for the next three years co-starred with his wife, Ann Codee (1890–1961), in a series of comedy shorts in which they repeated many of their vaudeville routines. He began appearing in features in 1935 and in the following 18 years played character roles and bits in numerous productions, typically portraying an Irishman, often a bartender or a cop. He was seen in many Fox musicals of the 40s as well as in several episodes of MGM's "Dr. Kildare" series.

FILMS INCLUDE: *Welcome Stranger* 1935; *Hot Money* 1936; *Footloose Heiress* 1937; *Fast and Furious* 1939; *His Girl Friday, Dr. Kildare's Strange Case* 1940; *Strawberry Blonde, I Wake Up Screaming* 1941; *Dr. Kildare's Victory, To the Shores of Tripoli, My Gal Sal, The Magnificent Dope, Footlight Serenade, Orchestra Wives, Tales of Manhattan, Springtime in the Rockies* 1942; *Hello Frisco Hello, The Ox-Bow Incident, Coney Island, Sweet Rosie O'Grady* 1943; *Buffalo Bill, Greenwich Village* 1944; *The Dolly Sisters, The Lost Weekend* 1945; *Doll Face, The Strange Love of Martha Ivers* 1946; *Mother Wore Tights, It Had to Be You* 1947; *Fury at Furnace Creek* 1948; *Cheaper by the Dozen, Father of the Bride* 1950; *Houdini, Here Come the Girls* 1953.

Osborn, Paul. Playwright, screenwriter. *b.* Sept. 4, 1901, Evansville, Ind. *d.* 1988. A graduate of the University of Michigan, he taught English there for a while, then studied playwriting at Yale. Many of his plays—several of them dramatizations of novels—were produced on Broadway from 1928 and a few were adapted to film by others, including *Should Ladies Behave?* (1933), *On Borrowed Time* (1939), and *The World of Suzie Wong* (1960). In addition, he wrote screenplays alone or in collaboration.

FILMS (as screenwriter): *The Young in Heart* 1938; *Cry Havoc, Madame Curie* 1943; *The Yearling* 1947; *Homecoming* 1948; *Portrait of Jennie* 1949; *Invitation* 1952; *East of Eden* 1955; *Sayonara* 1957; *South Pacific* 1958; *Wild River* 1960.

Osborne, John. Playwright, screenwriter. Born on Dec. 12, 1929, in London. The son of a barkeeper-commercial artist and a barmaid, he wrote for trade journals and acted on the stage before gaining sudden fame with his play 'Look Back in Anger,' which heralded the advent of a generation of "angry young men" in English literature. He collaborated on the adaptation of three of his own plays to the screen and won an Academy Award for writing the script of Henry Fielding's *Tom Jones* (1963). He has also appeared in a couple of films as an actor. His second of five marriages was to actress Mary URE. The third was to novelist and film critic Penelope Gilliatt.

FILMS: *Look Back in Anger* (addnl. dial. only, from own play) 1959; *The Entertainer* (co-sc., from own play) 1960; *Tom Jones* (sc.) 1963; *Inadmissible Evidence* (sc., from own play) 1968; *Erste Liebe/First Love* (act. only; Switz./Ger.) 1970; *Get Carter* (act. only) 1971; *Luther* (play basis only) 1974; *The Entertainer* (play basis only; remake) 1975; *Tomorrow Never Comes* (act. only) 1978; *Flash Gordon* 1980.

Osborne, Vivienne. Actress. *b.* Dec. 10, 1896, Des Moines, Iowa. *d.* 1961. On stage as a dancer from the age of five, she made her screen debut in 1920, but her main film career came in the 30s, following a long succession of leads on Broadway. In films she played both leads and "vampy" second leads, typically as the "other woman."

FILMS INCLUDE: *In Walked Mary, Over the Hill to the Poor House* 1920; *The Right Way/The Gray Brother/Making Good/Within Prison Walls, Mother Eternal* 1921; *The Good Provider* 1922; *The Beloved Bachelor, Husband's Holiday* 1931; *Two Kinds of Women, The Famous Ferguson Case, Two Seconds, Week-End Marriage, The Dark Horse, Life Begins* 1932; *Luxury Liner, Sailor Be Good, Supernatural, Tomorrow at Seven, The Devil's in Love. The Phantom Broadcast* 1933; *No More Ladies* 1935; *Follow Your Heart, Wives Never Know* 1936; *Sinner Take All, Champagne Waltz* 1937; *Primrose Path, Captain Caution* 1940; *Dragonwyck* 1946.

Oscar. The statuette awarded to winners in the various categories of the ACADEMY AWARDS. Designed by art director Cedric Gibbons and executed by sculptor George Stanley, the 13½-inch-tall figurine (a man holding a sword and standing on a reel of film) is made of metal and plated with gold. The statuette was nameless until 1931, when, according to Hollywood legend, Margaret Herrick, a secretary who later became executive director of the Academy, looked at the figurine and exclaimed, "Why, he reminds me of my uncle Oscar [Pierce]." A columnist overheard her remark, printed it, and before long the name had stuck. In time it came to replace the term "Academy Award" in popular usage.

Oscarsson, Per. Actor. Born in 1927, in Stockholm. Tall, lean, introspective leading man and supporting player of the Swedish stage and screen. He won a Cannes Festival acting award for *Hunger.* He also directed the films *Elton Lundin* (1973) and *Sverige at Svenskarana* (1900). His son, Roman Oscarsson, is also a stage and screen actor.

FILMS INCLUDE: *The Street* 1949; *Meeting Life* 1951; *Defiance* 1952; *Barabbas* 1953; *Karin Mansdotter* 1954; *Wild Birds* 1955; *The Summer Night Is Sweet* 1961; *The Doll* 1962; *Adam and Eve* 1963; *My Sister My Love, Here's Your Life, Hunger* 1966; *Doctor Glas* (Den.) 1967; *A Dandy in Aspic* (UK) 1968; *The Last Valley* (UK), *The Night Visitor* (UK) 1971; *Honeycomb* (UK/Sp.), *The New Land* 1972; *The Blockhouse* (UK) 1974; *Dream City* (Ger.) 1976; *Dagny* (Pol./Nor.), *Victor Frankenstein, The Assignment, The Brothers Lionheart* 1977; *Secrets* (release delayed from 1971; US) *The Adventures of Picasso* 1978; *Montenegro* (UK/Swed.) 1981.

O'Shea, Michael. Actor. *b.* Mar. 17, 1906, Hartford, Conn. *d.* 1973. Easygoing leading man of Hollywood films of the 40s and 50s. First in vaudeville, from 1923, then on the legitimate stage, he played amiable leads in a variety of films but never developed into a popular star. In 1954–56 he starred in the TV series 'It's a Great Life.' He died of a heart attack, leaving as a widow Virginia MAYO, his wife since 1947.

FILMS INCLUDE: *Lady of Burlesque, Jack London* (title role) 1943; *The Eve of St. Mark, Man from Frisco, Something for the Boys* 1944; *Circumstantial Evidence, It's a Pleasure* 1945; *Mr. District Attorney, Violence, Last of the Redmen* (as Hawkeye) 1947; *Smart Woman, Parole Inc.* 1948; *The Big Wheel, The Threat* 1949; *Captain China, The Underworld Story* 1950; *Fixed Bayonets* 1951; *The Model and the Marriage Broker, Bloodhounds of Broadway* 1952; *It Should Happen to You* 1954.

O'Shea, Milo. Actor. Born on June 2, 1925, in Dublin,

Ireland. Character player discovered by films in the late 60s, after a lengthy stage career with Dublin's Abbey Players. Impressive as Leopold Bloom in the screen adaptation of Joyce's *Ulysses.*

FILMS INCLUDE: *Talk of a Million/You Can't Beat the Irish* 1951; *Carry On Cabby* 1963; *Never Put It in Writing* 1964; *Ulysses* (as Leopold Bloom) 1967; *Romeo and Juliet* (as Friar Lawrence), *Barbarella* 1968; *The Adding Machine* 1969; *The Angel Levine, Paddy* 1970; *Sacco and Vanzetti* (It.), *Loot* 1971; *Theatre of Blood, The Hebrew Lesson* 1973; *Digby—The Biggest Dog in the World, Percy's Progress/It's Not the Size That Counts* 1974; *Arabian Adventure, The Pilot* 1979; *The Verdict* 1982; *The Purple Rose of Cairo* 1985; *The Dream Team* 1989; *Opportunity Knocks* 1990; *Only the Lonely* 1991; *The Playboys* 1992.

Oshima, Nagisa. Director. Born on Mar. 31, 1932, in Kyoto, Japan. A leading figure in the New Wave that began sweeping Japanese cinema in the late 50s. The son of an intellectual government official of Samurai ancestry, who died when Nagisa was six, he was raised by a working mother, enlivening his modest circumstances by playing baseball and reading voraciously. As a high school student, he began writing prose and poetry. After graduating, he took up law and political science at the University of Kyoto, where he soon became a leading force behind the students' militant movement. He entered the film industry in 1954 as an assistant director at Shochiku's Ofuna studios. While learning his craft, he began publishing articles critical of the Japanese film establishment and in 1956 started his own film magazine, *Eiga Hihyo.* He directed his first film in 1959. From the start he established himself as an iconoclastic filmmaker, an angry and outspoken critic of traditional values of Japanese society and a radical spokesman for Japan's younger generation, relentless in the pursuit of what he considered truth. His films often dealt with problems of the young, especially as they reflect disillusionment with old values. The plots were frequently based on true events but were developed to a point between realism and fantasy, typically emphasizing violence and sex. After the financial debacle of his deeply personal film, *Night and Fog in Japan* (1960), in which he summarized his bitterness over the destructive effect by radical leftist elements on the student movement, Oshima left Shochiku. For the next five years he freelanced, experimenting with different styles and forms of expression and broadening his themes. In 1965 he formed an independent production company, Sozosha ("Creation"), in partnership with his wife, actress Akiko Koyama, who also became an important member in his evolving stock company of regular performers. Gradually he began attracting international attention with films like *Death by Hanging* (1968), in which he exposed the cruel bias against Japan's Korean minority, and *Boy* (1969), in which explored the fantasy world of a child who is morally corrupted by his parents. Oshima dissolved his company in 1973. Two years later he founded Oshima productions and set out on a new course, involving larger-budget international co-productions. In 1976 his Japanese-French film *Ai No Corrida/L'Empire des Sens/In the Realm of the Senses,* an explicit depiction of sexual obsession in the form of a marathon fornication session from the picture's passionate beginning to its violent end, was banned by US Customs as obscene on the eve of its showing at the New York Film Festival. It was removed from the program but was later cleared for exhibition and hailed by many as an erotic masterpiece. In Japan, Oshima was prosecuted for obscenity but the charges against him were eventually dropped. Entirely different in theme, tone, and style was Oshima's Japanese-British co-production *Merry Christmas, Mr. Lawrence* (1983), a compelling, mostly English-spoken psychological drama pitting the hearts and minds of East versus West in a WW II Japanese POW camp. Oshima published several collections of essays dealing with film theory and analysis. In 1980 he was elected president of Japan's directors guild.

FILMS: *A Town of Love and Hope* (also sc.) 1959; *Naked Youth/Cruel Story of Youth* (also sc.), *The Sun's Burial* (also co-sc.), *Night and Fog in Japan* (also co-sc.) 1960; *The Catch* 1961; *The Revolutionary/The Christian Rebel* (also sc.) 1962; *A Child's First Adventure* (also co-sc.), *I'm Here Bellett* (also sc.) 1964; *The Pleasures of the Flesh* (also sc.), *The Diary of Yunbogi* (doc. short; also prod., sc., phot.), *Violence at Noon/Daytime Assailant* 1966; *Band of Ninja* (also co-prod., co-sc.), *A Treatise on Japanese Bawdy Songs/Sing a Song of Sex* (also co-prod., co-sc.), *Japanese Summer: Double Suicide* (also co-prod., co-sc.) 1967; *Death by Hanging* (also co-sc., off-screen narrator), *Three Resurrected Drunkards/A Sinner in Paradise* (also co-sc.), *Diary of a Shinjuku Thief* (also co-sc.) 1968; *Boy* 1969; *He Died After the War/The Man Who Left His Will on Film* (also co-sc.) 1970; *The Ceremony* (also co-sc.) 1971; *Dear Summer Sister* (also co-sc.) 1972; *In the Realm of the Senses/Empire of the Senses* (also sc.; Jap./Fr.) 1976; *Empire of Passion/Phantom Love* (also co-prod., sc.; Jap./Fr.) 1978; *Merry Christmas Mr. Lawrence* (also co-sc.; UK/Jap./NZ) 1983; *Max Mon Amour* (also co-sc.; Fr.) 1986; *Hollywood Zen* 1992.

O'Steen, Sam. American film editor, director. Born on Mar. 6, 1923. He entered films as an assistant editor in 1956, graduating to full editor by the mid-60s. Rapidly becoming established as a creative cutter, he was associated with many major productions for Mike Nichols, Roman Polanski, and others, gaining Academy Award nominations for *Who's Afraid of Virginia Woolf?* (1966), *Chinatown* (1974), and *Silkwood* (1983). He has directed a number of TV movies since 1973 as well as a single feature, *Sparkle* (1976), a slickly made if unremarkable film about the rise of a black singing group.

FILMS INCLUDE (as editor): *Robin and the Seven Hoods, Youngblood Hawke* 1964; *None But the Brave* 1965; *Who's Afraid of Virginia Woolf?* 1966; *Cool Hand Luke, The Graduate* 1967; *Rosemary's Baby* 1968; *The Sterile Cuckoo* 1969; *Catch-22* 1970; *Carnal Knowledge* 1971; *Portnoy's Complaint* 1972; *The Day of the Dolphin* 1973; *Chinatown* 1974; *Sparkle* (dir. only) 1976; *Straight Time* 1978; *Hurricane* 1979; *Amityville II: The Possession* 1982; *Silkwood* 1983; *Heartburn* 1986; *Nadine* 1987; *Frantic, Biloxi Blues, Working Girl* 1988; *A Dry White Season* 1989; *Postcards from the Edge* 1990; *Regarding Henry* 1991; *Wolf* 1994; *Night Falls on Manhattan* 1997.

Ostriche, Muriel. Actress. *b.* 1896, New York City. *d.* 1989. Popular star of early silents. She entered films late in 1911 and by 1913 placed second to Alice Joyce in a popularity poll by a leading fan magazine. At the height of her career, from 1915 to 1920, she was known as the Moxie Girl for the frequent use of her face in advertising and on promotional merchandise by a popular soft drink of that name. She retired in 1921 to raise a family.

FILMS INCLUDE: *A Tale of the Wilderness, A Blot in the 'Scutcheon* 1912; *Lobster Salad and Milk* 1913; *The Strike, A Telephone Strategy* 1914; *Mortmain, The Daughter of the Sea/The Fisher Girl* 1915; *A Circus Romance, Kennedy Square, Sally in Our Alley, The Men She Married* 1916; *Moral Courage, Youth, The Good for Nothing, The Volunteer* 1917; *The Way Out, What Love Forgives, The Purple Lily, Leap to Fame, Journey's End, Tinsel, Merely Players, The Road to France* 1918; *The Bluffer, The Moral Deadline, The Hand Invisible* 1919; *The Sacred Flame* 1920; *The Shadow* 1921.

O'Sullivan, Maureen. Actress. Born on May 17, 1911, in Boyle, County Roscommon, Ireland. Delicately pretty ingenue of the Hollywood films of the 30s and early 40s; best remembered in the role of the scantily clad Jane, Johnny Weissmuller's mate, in several MGM Tarzan jungle adventures. Educated at a convent near London and at a finishing school in Paris, she was discovered at Dublin's International Horse Show, in 1930, by American director Frank BORZAGE and arrived in Hollywood that same year on a contract with Fox. After several films she transferred to MGM, where she was assigned primarily second leads in some of the studio's major films and lead roles in many of its secondary productions. She retired from the screen in 1942 to raise her growing family from her 1936 marriage to writer-director John FARROW (their union eventually produced seven children, including actresses Mia FARROW and Tisa Farrow), but later returned to films occasionally. She also hosted a syndicated TV series, 'Irish Heritage,' in the 50s and was briefly a member of the team of the 'Today' show. In the 60s she appeared in several Broadway productions, including 'Never Too Late,' in a role she later repeated in the film version. A widow since 1963, she married a real-estate contractor in 1983.

FILMS: *Song o' My Heart, So This Is London, Just Imagine, The Princess and the Plumber* 1930; *A Connecticut Yankee* (as Alisande), *Skyline, The Big Shot* 1931; *Tarzan the Ape Man* (as Jane), *The Silver Lining, Fast Companions, Skyscraper Souls, Information Kid, Strange Interlude* (as Madeline Arnold), *Okay America, Payment Deferred* 1932; *Robbers' Roost, The Cohens and Kellys in Trouble, Tugboat Annie, Stage Mother* 1933; *Tarzan and His Mate* (as Jane), *The Thin Man, Hide-Out, The Barretts of Wimpole Street* (as Henrietta Barrett) 1934; *David Copperfield* (as Dora), *West Point of the Air, Cardinal Richelieu, The Flame Within, Woman Wanted, Anna Karenina* (as Kitty), *The Bishop Misbehaves* 1935; *The Voice of Bugle Ann, The Devil Doll, Tarzan Escapes* (as Jane) 1936; *A Day at the Races, The Emperor's Candlesticks, Between Two Women, My Dear Miss Aldrich* 1937; *A Yank at Oxford, Hold That Kiss, Port of Seven Seas, The Crowd Roars, Spring Madness* 1938; *Let Us Live, Tarzan Finds a Son* (as Jane) 1939; *Sporting Blood, Pride and Prejudice* (as Jane Bennet) 1940; *Maisie Was a Lady, Tarzan's Secret Treasure* (as Jane) 1941; *Tarzan's New York Adventure* (as Jane) 1942; *The Big Clock* 1948; *Where Danger Lives* 1950; *Bonzo Goes to College* 1952; *All I Desire, Mission Over Korea* 1953; *Duffy of San Quentin, The Steel Cage* 1954; *The Tall T* 1957; *Wild Heritage* 1958; *Never Too Late* 1965; *The Phynx* (cameo) 1970; *Too Scared to Scream* (release delayed from 1982) 1985; *Hannah and Her Sisters, Peggy Sue Got Married* 1986; *Stranded* 1987.

Oswald, Gerd. Director. *b.* June 9, 1916, Berlin. *d.* 1989. Son of producer-director Richard OSWALD and actress Käte Waldeck, he was a child actor and production apprentice in Europe before accompanying his celebrated father to the US in 1938. Here he progressed the hard way from assistant director with Monogram and other studios through production manager and associate producer with Fox, to independent director in the mid-50s. He treated low-budget B pictures with flair and personal flavor. He also directed many episodes for TV series, like 'Perry Mason,' 'Outer Limits,' 'Bonanza,' 'Star Trek,' and 'Twilight Zone.' His son, Richard, became an assistant director.

FILMS: *A Kiss Before Dying, The Brass Legend* 1956; *Crime of Passion, Fury at Showdown, Valerie* 1957; *Paris Holiday, Screaming Mimi* 1958; *Am Tag als der Regen Kam/The Day the Rains Came* (Ger.) 1959; *Die Schachnovelle/Brainwashed/The Royal Game* (also co-sc.; Ger.) 1960; *The Longest Day* (one sequence only) 1962; *Tempestà su Ceylon/The Scarlet Eye* (It./Fr.) 1963; *Agent for H.A.R.M.* 1966; *80 Steps to Jonah* 1969; *Bunny O'Hare* 1971; *Bis zur bitteren Neige/To the Bitter End* (Aus./Ger.) 1975.

Oswald, Richard. Director, producer. *b.* Richard Ornstein, Nov. 5, 1880, Vienna. *d.* 1963. Father of director Gerd OSWALD. Prolific director of innumerable German and a handful of British, French, and American films. A former stage actor and director, he began piloting films in 1914, establishing his own company in 1916. Thereafter, he directed and produced a great many commercially successful films, discovering along the way such film personalities as William Dieterle, Conrad Veidt, and Lya de Putti. After the Nazi takeover, he sought refuge briefly in Britain and France and eventually settled in the US.

FILMS INCLUDE (as director-producer): *Das eisener Kreuz* 1914; *Hoffmanns Erzählungen/Tales of Hoffmann* (also co-sc.), *Seine letzte Maske, Zirkusblut* 1916; *Das Bildnis des Dorian Gray/The Picture of Dorian Gray, Des Goldes Fluch, Die Rache der Toten* (also sc.), *Die Seeschlacht, Die Sintflut* 1917; *Dida Ibsens Geschichte, Es werde Licht* (also co-sc.), *Der lebende Leichnam/The Living Dead/The Living Corpse, Das Tagebuch einer Verlorenen* 1918; *Anders als die anderen, Lache Bajazzo, Das Laster* (also sc.), *Prostitution* (in two parts, also co-sc.), *Die Reise um die Erde in 80 Tagen/Around the World in 80 Days, Die Schwarze Katze, Sündige Eltern* (also co-sc.), *Unheimliche Geschichten* (also sc.), *Der Tod des Andern* 1919; *Algol, Antisemiten, Das Geheimnis von London, Der grosse Krach, Kurfürstendamm, Die letzte Menschen, Manolescus Memoiren, Der Reigen* (also sc.), *Nachtgestalten, Der Selbstmörderklub/The Suicide Club, Die Spielerin, Die Tragödie eines Kindes* 1920; *Das Leben des Menschen, Macbeth, Engelchen* 1921; *Lady Hamilton, Lukrezia Borgia* (also sc.) 1922; *Carlos und Elisabeth* (also sc.), *Lumpen und Seide* 1924; *Halbseide* (also sc.) 1925; *Als Ich wiederkam, Eine tolle Nacht* (also sc.) 1926; *Feme, Funkzauber, Gehetzte Frauen* 1927: *Die Rothausgasse, Villa Falconieri* 1928; *Ehe in Not, Frühlings Erwachen/The Awakening of Spring, Die Herrin und ihr Knecht, Der Hund von Baskerville/The Hound of the Baskervilles* (dir. only) 1929; *Alraune* (dir. only), *Dreyfuss, Wien—Du Stadt der Lieder/Vienna City of Song* 1930; *1914: Die letzten Tage vor dem Welt-brand/1914: The Last Days Before the War, Arm wie eine Kirchenmaus, Der Hauptmann von Köpenick/The Captain of Koepenick* (dir. only), *Viktoria und ihr Husar* (dir. only), *Schuberts Frühlingstraum* 1931; *Unheimliche Geschichten* (dir. only), *Gräfin Mariza* (dir. only) 1932; *Ein Lied geht um die Welt/The Joseph Schmidt Story* 1933 (and British version, *My Song Goes Round the World*) 1934; *Tempête sur l'Asie* (dir. only; Fr.) 1938; *The Captain of Koepenick* (dir. only; US) 1941; *Isle of Missing Men* (dir. only; US) 1942; *The Loveable Cheat* (dir. only; US) 1949.

Oswalda, Ossi. Actress. *b.* Oswalda Stäglich, 1897, Berlin. *d.* 1948. Germany's most popular film star of the mid-20s. A former model and chorus dancer, she was discovered and developed by Ernst LUBITSCH, who cast her in such films as *The Oyster Princess* and *The Doll* (both 1919). She retired shortly after the coming of sound.

FILMS INCLUDE: *Nacht des Grauens, Schupalast Pinkus, Der Gmb-H Tenor* 1916; *Ossis Tagebuch, Wenn Vier dasselbe machen, Ein fideles Gefängnis* 1917; *Prinz Sami, Der Rodelkavalier, Der Fall Rosentopf, Das Mädel vom Ballet* 1918; *Meier aus Berlin, Meine Frau die Filmschauspielerin, Schwabenmädle, Die Austerprinzessin/The Oyster Princess, Die Puppe/The Doll* 1919; *Der blinde Passagier, Das Mädel mit der Maske* 1922; *Colibri* (also prod.) 1924; *Blitzzug der Liebe/Express Train of Love, Das Mädchen mit Protektion* 1925; *Die Kleine vom Varieté, Ein tolle Nacht* 1926; *Wochenendbraut, Eddy Polo mit Pferd und Lasso, Das Haus ohne Männer, Ossi hat die Hosen an* 1928; *Der keusche Joseph* 1930; *Der Stern von Valencia* 1933.

O'Toole, Annette. Actress. Born on Apr. 1, 1953, in Houston, Tex. *ed.* UCLA. Red-haired, freckle-faced leading lady of American TV and films. A former dancer.

FILMS: *Smile* 1975; *One on One* 1977; *King of the Gypsies* 1978; *Foolin' Around* 1980; *Cat People, 48 Hrs.* 1982; *Superman III* 1983; *Cross My Heart* 1987 *Love at Large* 1990; *Andre* (v/o), *Imaginary Crimes* 1994.

O'Toole, Peter. Actor. Born on Aug. 2, 1932, in Connemara, Ireland. *ed.* RADA. He grew up in Leeds, England, where his father made his living as a racetrack bookmaker. At 14, Peter quit school and began working for the Yorkshire *Evening Post* as messenger and copy boy, eventually graduating to cub reporter. At 17 he made his stage debut as an amateur at the Leeds Civic Theatre. Following two years of service with the Royal Navy as signalman and decoder, he began his professional acting career in 1955 with the Bristol Old Vic company, with which he stayed until 1958. He was first seen on the screen in 1960, in secondary roles, and in 1962 soared to international fame with his rich and enigmatic performance in the title role of *Lawrence of Arabia,* for which he received an Oscar nomination. After *Becket* (1964) and *Lord Jim* (1965) he was comfortably entrenched as a top movie star. Blond and blue-eyed, with a virile physique and sensitive face, he was among the leading box-office attractions in the late 60s and early 70s. His dark-humored performance as the messianic aristocrat in *The Ruling Class* (1972) has acquired cult status.

A serious drinking problem, leading to major stomach surgery, caused a decline in O'Toole's career in the 70s and, in 1979, to the destruction of his 20-year marriage to Welsh actress Sian PHILLIPS. His two actress daughters from that marriage, Kate and Pat, took care of him during a long period of recovery. In 1983 he fathered the son of California model Karen Brown. O'Toole bounced back in the 80s with a succession of flamboyant character roles, beginning with the villainous movie director in *The Stunt Man* (1980), a role perfectly suited to his persona as a golden-tongued megalomaniac. In addition to his nomination for *Lawrence of Arabia*, he has earned best actor Academy Award nominations (though no awards) for six other films: *Becket*, *The Lion in Winter*, *Goodbye Mr. Chips*, *The Ruling Class*, *The Stunt Man*, and *My Favorite Year*.

FILMS: *Ombre bianche/Les Dents du Diable/The Savage Innocents* (It./Fr./UK), *The Day They Robbed the Bank of England, Kidnapped* 1960; *Lawrence of Arabia* (as T. E. Lawrence) 1962; *Becket* (as Henry II; UK/US) 1964; *Lord Jim* (title role; UK/US), *What's New Pussycat?* (US/Fr.), *The Sandpiper* (v/o; US) 1965; *La Bibbia/The Bible* (as the Three Angels; It./US), *How to Steal a Million* (US) 1966; *La Nuit des Généraux/The Night of the Generals* (Fr./UK), *Casino Royale* 1967; *The Lion in Winter* (again as Henry II), *Great Catherine* 1968; *Goodbye Mr. Chips* (title role; UK/US) 1969; *Country Dance/Brotherly Love* 1970; *Murphy's War, Under Milk Wood* 1971; *The Ruling Class, Man of La Mancha* (as Don Quixote/Miguel de Cervantes/Alonso Quijana; US) 1972; *Rosebud* (US), *Man Friday* (as Robinson Crusoe) 1975; *Foxtrot/Other Side of Paradise* 1976; *Power Play* (Can./UK) 1978; *Zulu Dawn, Caligula* (It./US) 1979; *The Stunt Man* (US) 1980; *My Favorite Year* (US) 1982; *Supergirl* 1984; *Creator* (US) 1985; *Club Paradise* 1986; *The Last Emperor* (UK/It./China) 1987; *High Spirits* 1988; *In Una Notte di chiaro di Luna/On a Moonlit Night/Crystal or Ash Fire or Wind, As Long as It's Love* 1989; *Buried Alive, Wings of Fame* (Hol.), *The Rainbow Thief, The Nutcracker Prince* (v/o; Can.) 1990; *King Ralph* (US), *Isabelle Eberhardt* (Fr./Austral.) 1991; *Worlds Apart* (UK), *Rebecca's Daughters* (UK), *The Seventh Coin* 1992.

Otowa, Nobuko. See SHINDO, Kaneto.

Ottinger, Ulrike. Filmmaker. Born in 1942, in Konstanz, Germany. An experimental avant-gardist, she studied and practiced art in Paris in the 60s before moving into filmmaking with no formal training in the early 70s. Focusing on social and cultural themes from a feminist and at times lesbian viewpoint, she tends to subjugate traditional narrative devices in her films to exaggeration and parody, through visual metaphors which she achieves by the innovative manipulation of images and sound tracks. She produces, writes, edits, and operates the camera on all of her films.

FILMS: *Lackoon und Soehene/Laccoon and Sons* 1973; *Die Betoenung der blauen Matrosen/The Bewitchment of Drunken Sailors* 1975; *Madame X—Eine absolute Herrscherin/Madame X—An Absolute Ruler* 1977; *Bildnis einer Trinkerin—alais jamais retour/Portrait of a Female Alcoholic—Ticket of No Return* 1979; *Freak Orlando: Kleines Welttheater in fünf Episoden/Freak Orlando: Small World Theater in Five Episodes* 1981; *Dorian Gray im Spiegel der Boulevardpresse/Dorian Gray in the Mirror of the Popular Press* 1984; *China—Die Künste—Der Alltaq/China—The Arts—Everyday Life* (doc.) 1985; *Johanna d'Arc of Mongolia* 1988; *Countdown* (doc.) 1991.

Ouedraogo, Idrissa. African director, screenwriter. Born in 1952 in Banfora, Burkina Faso. After studying at the African Institute of Cinematography in Ouagadougou and in Kiev and Paris, he received international notice with his first feature film, *Yam Daabo* (1987), which was presented at Cannes. His next film, *Yaaba* (1989), about the relationship between two rural children and an old woman shunned as a witch, received even more praise. His third film, *Tilaï* (1990), won the special jury prize at Cannes, confirming his reputation as a major figure in African cinema.

FILMS INCLUDE: (as director-screenwriter): *Yam Daabo* 1987; *Yaaba* 1989; *Tilaï* 1990; *Karim na Sala* 1991; *Samba Traoré* 1993; *Le Cri de Couer* 1994.

"**Our Gang.**" A long-running (1922–44) series of comedy shorts featuring a frisky band of children in an amusing variety of mischievous situations. The series was launched by Hal Roach in 1922 as an offshoot of the success of the "Sunshine Sammy" comedies (1921–22) starring Ernie Morrison, a fetching black child actor. The juvenile cast for the "Our Gang" series was assembled at the end of a talent hunt that emphasized physical types rather than acting experience. Original members of the Gang included chubby and good-natured Joe Cobb; the sweet and pretty Mary Kornman (the daughter of Harold Lloyd's still cameraman), who provided the "love" interest (she was later replaced by Jean Darling); freckle-faced and mischievous Mickey Daniels; black and resourceful Allen Clayton Hoskins; wholesome-looking Jackie David (Harold Lloyd's little brother-in-law); Jackie Condon, and Pete, a phlegmatic dog with an unlikely black circle around his right eye. The inventive antics of the gang and the spontaneous performances of the little actors made the series very popular with audiences and kept it alive through the transition to sound.

Naturally, the cast changed from time to time as the children grew into adolescence. In 1929, in a major shuffle, the new faces included Jackie Cooper, who stayed briefly with the series before rising to stardom; Norman "Chubby" Chaney, who replaced Joe Cobb; Bobby "Wheezer" Hutchins; and Matthew "Stymie" Beard. Future child stars Dickie Moore and Scotty Beckett joined the cast in the early 30s, as did Spanky McFarland, who took over the role of the chubby leader of the gang in 1932. Other important additions in the early 30s were the freckle-faced Carl "Alfalfa" Switzer and the pretty Darla Hood.

Among the directors of the series were Robert McGowan, Anthony Mack, Gus Meins, Gordon Douglas, George Sidney,

Edward Cahn, and Cy Endfield. One "Our Gang" short, *Bored of Education,* won an Academy Award in 1936. That same year the Gang's only feature film, *General Spanky,* was released. In 1938, Roach sold the rights to the series to MGM, which continued producing "Our Gang" shorts until 1944. In 1955 nearly 100 of the Roach shorts were released for TV but as "The Little Rascals" because the rights to the title "Our Gang" belonged to MGM. The films were still running successfully on syndicated TV in the 70s.

Oury, Gérard. Actor, director. Born Max-Gérard Houry Tannenbaum, on Apr. 29, 1919, in Paris. *ed.* National Conservatory of Dramatic Art. A former member of the Comédie-Française, he turned to film acting in the mid-40s and began directing in the late 50s. A facile filmmaker of light fare, he turned out many commercially successful productions, mainly thrillers and comedies featuring such stars as Bourvil, De Funès, and Belmondo. His daughter, Danièle Thompson, collaborated on several of his screenplays, as well as some by other directors.

FILMS INCLUDE: As actor—*Antoine et Antoinette/Antoine and Antoinette* 1947; *Le Secret de Mayerling/The Secret of Mayerling* 1949; *La Belle que voila, Sans laisser d'Adresse* 1950; *La Nuit est mon Royaume/The Night Is My Kingdom* 1951; *Sea Devils* (UK/US), *The Sword and the Rose* (as the Dauphin; UK/US), *The Heart of the Matter* (UK) 1953; *Father Brown/The Detective* (UK) 1954; *Les héros sont fatigués/Heroes and Sinners* 1955; *La Meuilleure Part* 1956; *Mefiez-vous Fillettes/Young Girls Beware* 1957; *Le Dos au Mur/Back to the Wall, Le Septième Ciel, Le Miroir a Deux Faces/The Mirror Has Two Faces* (also co-sc.) 1958; *The Journey* (US) 1959; *The Prize* (US) 1963. As director—*La Main chaude* (also co-sc., act.) 1960; *La Menace* 1961; *Le Crime ne paie pas/Crime Does Not Pay* (also co-sc.) 1962; *Le Corniaud/The Sucker* (also story, co-sc.) 1965; *La Grande Vadrouille/Don't Look Now* (also sc.; Fr./UK) 1966; *Le Cerveau/The Brain* (also co-sc.) 1969; *La Folie des Grandeurs/Delusions of Grandeur* (also co-sc.) 1971; *Les Aventures de Rabbi Jacob/The Mad Adventures of Rabbi Jacob* (also co-sc.) 1973; *La Carapate* (also co-sc., act.) 1978; *Le Coup de Parapluie* (also co-sc.) 1980; *L'As des As/Ace of Aces* 1982; *La Vengeance du Serpent à Plumes* (also co-sc.) 1984; *Levy et Goliath* (also co-sc.) 1987; *Vanille fraise* (also co-sc.) 1989; *Le Grippe Sou* 1992; *La Soif de l'Or* 1993.

Ouspenskaya, Maria. Actress. *b.* July 29, 1876, Tula, Russia. *d.* 1949. Tiny but forceful character actress of Hollywood films of the late 30s and 40s with beady eyes and thick Slavic accent. She came to the US in 1923 with the Moscow Art Theater and stayed. She played on Broadway and ran a New York acting school before going to Hollywood in 1936. She was nominated for Oscars for *Dodsworth* (1936) and *Love Affair* (1939), but is probably best remembered as the cryptic gypsy fortuneteller Maleva in *The Wolf Man* 1941. She died tragically in a fire that destroyed her Los Angeles apartment.

FILMS: In Russia—*The Cricket on the Hearth* 1915; *Worthless* 1916; *Dr. Torpokov* 1917; *Buried Alive* 1918; *Khveska/Hospital Guard* 1923; *Tanka—Traktirshista Protiv Otsa* 1929. In the US—*Dodsworth* (as the Baroness von Obersdorf) 1936; *Conquest* 1937; *Love Affair, The Rains Came, Judge Hardy and Son* 1939; *Dr. Ehrlich's Magic Bullet, Waterloo Bridge, The Mortal Storm, The Man I Married, Dance Girl Dance, Beyond Tomorrow* 1940; *The Wolf Man* 1941; *The Shanghai Gesture, Kings Row* (as Madame Von Eln), *The Mystery of Marie Roget* 1942; *Frankenstein Meets the Wolf Man* 1943; *Destiny* 1944; *Tarzan and the Amazons* 1945; *I've Always Loved You* 1946; *Wyoming* 1947; *A Kiss in the Dark* 1949.

outline. Synopsis of a film story and a brief description of the intended approach prepared by a screenwriter prior to the writing of a detailed TREATMENT.

out of sync. A term used to describe a section of film in which the sound track is not exactly synchronized with the action. The error is particularly noticeable with lip movements.

out-takes. Takes that are rejected and not used in the final version of a film. See also TRIMS.

overdeveloped. Referring to negative film developed in excess of the required time or bathed in solutions of higher temperatures than required. In either case, the film becomes extremely contrasty.

overexposure. Unsatisfactory reproduction of tonal values resulting from prolonged exposure, the use of too large an aperture setting, or the use of film too sensitive for the available illumination. Overexposed prints appear unusually light and lacking in detail.

overhead clusters. Suspended lighting units providing soft illumination.

overhead strips. Suspended lighting units producing illumination over a broad area.

overlap. 1. The extension of action, dialogue, music, or sound effects from one scene into the next to allow smooth transition and uninterrupted continuity. 2. The overlapping of two ends of film for splicing. 3. Extra length of a shot allowed for superimposition in the preparation of a DISSOLVE, a FADE, or a WIPE.

Overman, Lynne. Actor. *b.* Sept. 19, 1887, Naryville, Mo. *d.* 1943. Dependable light character player of Paramount films of the 30s and early 40s. A former jockey, then vaudeville and stock performer, he often played cynical but friendly characters.

FILMS INCLUDE: *Midnight, Little Miss Marker, The Great Flirtation, Broadway Bill* 1934; *Enter Madame, Rumba, Men Without Names, Paris in Spring, Two for Tonight* 1935; *Collegiate, Poppy, The Jungle Princess* 1936; *Nobody's Baby* (lead), *Partners in Crime, Night Club Scandal, True Confession* 1937; *The Big Broadcast of 1938, Her Jungle Love, Spawn of the North, Men with Wings* 1938; *Persons in Hiding* (lead), *Union Pacific, Death of a Champion* (lead) 1939; *Typhoon, Edison the Man, Safari, North West Mounted Police* 1940; *The Hard-Boiled Canary/There's Magic in Music, Caught in the Draft, Aloma of the South Seas, New York Town* 1941; *Roxie Hart, Reap the Wild Wind, The Forest Rangers* 1942; *Dixie* 1943; *The Desert Song* 1944.

overshoot. See UNDERSHOOT.

Ovitz, Michael. Talent agent and executive. Born on Dec. 14, 1946, in Encino, Calif. *ed.* UCLA. The son of a liquor wholesaler, he attended law school for a short time before turning to agenting. He got his start in 1968 with the William Morris Agency, which he left in 1975 to co-found Creative Artists Agency. As chairman, he built it into the mightiest agency in Hollywood, representing the most bankable movie stars, directors, and other talent. Able to get almost anything his clients want, he has often been at or near the top of the list of Hollywood's most-powerful people. His activities have included putting together movie packages, negotiating transitions for studio heads, and consulting on studio takeovers, notably the 1992 purchase of MGM by Credit Lyonnais.

In a move that shocked many in the industry, Ovitz left the chairmanship of CAA behind to accept a lucrative offer from Michael EISNER to become his number two man at DISNEY. But in a little over a year, the two parted ways with Ovitz walking away with close to $90 million in compensation and the freedom to pursue other career options.

Owen, Cliff. Director. Born on Apr. 22, 1919, in London. In British films as assistant director from 1937, he began directing TV episodes ('Third Man' series, etc.) in the 50s and feature films in the 60s.

FILMS: *Offbeat* 1961; *Prize of Arms* 1962; *The Wrong Arm of the Law* 1963; *A Man Could Get Killed* (co-dir. with Ronald Neame; US), *That Riviera Touch* 1966; *The Magnificent Two/What Happened at Campo Grande?* 1967; *The Vengeance of She* 1968; *Steptoe and Son* 1972; *Ooh... You Are Awful, No Sex Please—We're British* 1973; *The Adventures of Tom Jones/The Bawdy Adventures of Tom Jones, Get Charlie Tully* 1976.

Owen, Reginald. Actor. *b.* Aug. 5, 1887, Wheathampstead, England. *d.* 1972. A graduate of Tree's Academy of Dramatic Art, he made his professional acting debut on the London stage in 1905 and his first Broadway appearance in 1924. He went to Hollywood at the advent of the talkies and over a span of four decades appeared in dozens of major films, playing a wide range of memorable character parts as well as occasional leads.

FILMS INCLUDE: In the UK—*Henry VIII* (as Cromwell) 1911; *Sally in Our Alley* 1916; *The Grass Orphan* 1922. In the US—*The Letter* 1929; *Platinum Blonde* 1931; *A Woman Commands, Lovers Courageous, Sherlock Holmes* (as Dr. Watson) 1932; *A Study in Scarlet* (as Sherlock Holmes), *Voltaire* (as Louis XV), *Queen Christina* 1933; *Fashions of 1934, Nana* (as Bordenave), *Mandalay, The House of Rothschild, Stingaree, Where Sinners Meet, Of Human Bondage* (as Mr. Athelney), *Madame Du Barry* (again as Louis XV), *Music in the Air, Here Is My Heart* 1934; *The Good Fairy, Escapade, The Call of the Wild, Anna Karenina, A Tale of Two Cities* (as Mr. Stryver) 1935; *Rose Marie, Petticoat Fever, The Great Ziegfeld, Trouble for Two, Adventure in Manhattan, Love on the Run* 1936; *The Bride Wore Red, Conquest* (as Talleyrand) 1937; *Kidnapped* (as Captain Hoseason), *A Christmas Carol* (as Scrooge) 1938; *Fast and Loose, Hotel Imperial, The Real Glory, Remember?* 1939; *The Earl of Chicago, Florian* (as Emperor Franz Josef) 1940; *A Woman's Face, They Met in Bombay, Charley's Aunt, Lady Be Good, Tarzan's Secret Treasure* 1941; *Woman of the Year, We Were Dancing, Mrs. Miniver, I Married an Angel, Cairo, Random Harvest* 1942; *Reunion in France, Above Suspicion, Madame Curie* 1943; *The Canterville Ghost, National Velvet* 1944; *The Valley of Decision* 1945; *Kitty, Cluny Brown, The Diary of a Chambermaid, Monsieur Beaucaire* (again as Louis XV) 1946; *Green Dolphin Street* 1947; *The Pirate, Julia Misbehaves, The Three Musketeers* (as De Treville) 1948; *Challenge to Lassie* 1949; *The Miniver Story, Kim* 1950; *The Great Diamond Robbery* 1953; *Red Garters* 1954; *Darby's Rangers* 1958; *Five Weeks in a Balloon* 1962; *The Thrill of It All* 1963; *Mary Poppins* 1964; *Rosie* 1967.

Owen, Seena. Actress, screenwriter. *b.* Signe Auen, 1894, Spokane, Wash. *d.* 1966. Strikingly beautiful leading lady of Hollywood silents, primarily in melodramatic roles. Initially billed under her real name, Signe Auen. Memorable as Attarea, the Princess Beloved, in D. W. Griffith's *Intolerance* (1916) and as Queen Regina in Erich von Stroheim's *Queen Kelly* (1928). After retiring from the screen she turned to writing and collaborated on screenplays and original stories for a number of films in the 30s and 40s. At one time (1916–24) she was married to actor George WALSH.

FILMS INCLUDE: As actress—*Out of the Air* 1914; *The Craven, An Old-Fashioned Girl, The Fox Woman, Bred in the Bone, A Yankee from the West, The Lamb, The Penitents* 1915; *Martha's Vindication, Intolerance* 1916; *A Woman's Awakening, Madame Bo-Peep* 1917; *Branding Broadway* 1918; *The Sheriff's Son, A Man and His Money, The Life Line, City of Comrades, Victory* 1919; *The Price of Redemption, The Gift Supreme, House of Toys* 1920; *The Woman God Changed, Lavender and Old Lace, The Cheater Reformed* 1921; *Back Pay, Sisters, At the Crossroads, The Face in the Fog* 1922; *The Go-Getter, Unseeing Eyes* 1923; *For Woman's Favor, I Am the Man* 1924; *Faint Perfume, The Hunted Woman* 1925; *The Flame of the Yukon, Shipwrecked* 1926; *The Rush Hour, The Blue Danube, Man-Made Woman, His Last Haul, Sinners in Love, Queen Kelly* 1928; *The Marriage Playground* 1929. As screenwriter—*The Lemon Drop Kid* (co-sc.) 1934; *Rumba* (co-story), *McFadden's Flats* (co-sc.) 1935; *This Way Please* (co-sc.), *Thrill of a Lifetime* (co-story, co-sc.) 1937; *Aloma of the South Seas* (co-story, co-sc.) 1941; *The Great Man's Lady* (co-story) 1942; *Rainbow Island* (story) 1944; *Carnegie Hall* (story) 1947.

Owens, Patricia. Actress. Born in 1925, in Canada. Leading lady of mainly routine UK and US films of the 50s and 60s.

FILMS INCLUDE: In the UK—*Miss London Ltd.* 1943; *While the Sun Shines* 1947; *The Happiest Days of Your Life* 1950; *The Good Die Young* 1954; *Island in the Sun* 1957. In the US—*Sayonara, No Down Payment* 1957; *The Law and Jake Wade, The Fly, The Gun Runners* 1958; *These Thousand Hills, Five Gates to Hell* 1959; *Hell to Eternity* 1960; *Seven Women from Hell, X-15* 1961; *Walk a Tightrope* 1964; *Black Spurs* 1965; *The Destructors* 1968.

Oz, Frank. Puppeteer-performer, director. Born Frank Oznowicz, on May 25, 1944, in Hereford, England. He came into prominence as a principal contributor to public TV's 'Sesame Street' and 'The Muppet Show,' for which he created, manipulated, and provided the voice for such characters as Miss Piggy, Fozzie Bear, Animal, Sam the Eagle, and the Swedish Chef from 1976 through 1981, winning three Emmy Awards. He also performed in the subsequent muppet features and made personal appearances in several live-action films. He made his directing debut with the fantasy tale *The Dark Crystal* (1982) in collaboration with his mentor, Jim HENSON, and has since done quite well on his own.

FILMS: *The Muppet Movie* (puppet-performer, creative consultant) 1979; *The Empire Strikes Back* (puppet-performer, as Yoda), *The Blues Brothers* (act.) 1980; *The Great Muppet Caper* (co-prod., puppet-performer), *An American Werewolf in London* (act.) 1981; *The Dark Crystal* (co-dir. with Jim Henson, puppet-performer) 1982; *Trading Places* (act.), *Return of the Jedi* (puppet-performer, as Yoda) 1983; *The Muppets Take Manhattan* (dir., co-sc., puppet-performer) 1984; *Sesame Street Presents: Follow That Bird* (puppet-performer), *Spies Like Us* (act.) 1985; *Labyrinth* (act.), *Little Shop of Horrors* (dir.) 1986; *Dirty Rotten Scoundrels* (dir.) 1988; *What About Bob?* (dir.) 1991; *HouseSitter* (dir.) 1992; *The Indian in the Cupboard* 1995; *Muppet Treasure Island* 1996; *In and Out* 1997.

Ozep, Fedor. Director. *b.* Fyodor Otsep, Feb. 9, 1895, Moscow. *d.* 1949. He entered Russian films as a screenwriter in 1916 while still a student at the University of Moscow and adapted Pushkin's *Queen of Spades* for the Protazanov film. He subsequently wrote a number of other screenplays and directed several Soviet films. In 1928 he went to Germany to direct a Soviet/German co-production of Tolstoy's *The Living Corpse* with Pudovkin playing the lead. He did not return to Russia with the rest of the crew but continued his film work in Germany. When the Nazis came to power, he went to France, where he directed a number of films. As a displaced person, he was put into an internment camp by the French at the outbreak of WW II. Freed after the fall of Paris, he went to Morocco, and from there to Canada and the US.

FILMS INCLUDE (as director): In Russia—*The Queen of Spades* (sc. only) 1916; *Polikushka* (sc. only) 1919; *Aelita* (co-sc. only) 1924; *Miss Mend* (co-dir. with Boris Barnet; also co-sc.) 1926; *Earth in Chains/The Yellow Pass/The Yellow Ticket* (also sc.) 1928. In Germany—*Der lebende Leichnam/The Living Corpse* (USSR/Ger.) 1929; *Der Mörder Dimitri Karamasoff/ Karamazov/The Brothers Karamazov* 1931. In France—*Mirages de Paris* 1933; *Amok* 1934; *La Dame de Pique/The Queen of Spades* 1937; *Tarakanowa/Betrayal, Gibraltar/It Happened in Gibraltar* 1938. In Canada—*Le Père Chopin/The Music Master* 1943. In the US—*Three Russian Girls* (co-dir. with Henry Kesler) 1944. In Canada—*La Fortresse/Whispering City* 1948.

Ozu, Yasujiro. Director. *b.* Dec. 12, 1903, Tokyo. *d.* 1963. At age ten he was sent by his father, a fertilizer merchant, to a remote school at the family's ancestral hometown. He was raised by his devoted, pampering mother and until he was 20 rarely saw his stern father. Some critics would later find traces of this unusual childhood in many of Ozu's films. He was an undisciplined youth, with little patience for formal schooling but a growing passion for Hollywood movies. After finishing middle school, he worked for a year as an assistant teacher at a village school. Back in Tokyo at 20, he landed, through an uncle's connections, a dream-come-true job as an assistant cameraman at the Shochiku film company. Despite a one-year hiatus for compulsory military service, he made rapid headway and by the end of 1926 had become an assistant director. A year later, he made his first film. Ozu's early work was raw and unfocused, and reputedly influenced by his long exposure to Hollywood films. But gradually he developed his own disciplined style and thematic concerns. By the early 30s he was among Japans's most popular and most highly regarded directors. In 1945 he was interned for six months in a British POW camp.

Before his death of cancer at 60 he had made 54 films, all remarkably consistent in their milieu, theme, and style. His films almost invariably deal with the lives and domestic problems of the Japanese middle-class family. His style is exquisite in its simplicity. Technically, it is characterized by stationary-camera shots usually taken from a low angle, about three feet above the ground, which corresponds with the eye-level of a Japanese adult crouching on a cushion, a position customarily taken by his tradition-bound characters. For this reason, his sets were constructed with ceilings long before Welles and *Citizen Kane.* He seldom varied his camera angle and almost never resorted to such devices as fades, dissolves, pans, or tracking shots. He also ignored the traditional rule of consistent camera direction through 180-degree space for the purpose of matching action on the screen for greater clarity of the narrative. Ozu shot his scenes in a circular 360-degree space, achieving dramatic visual effect, often at the expense of narrative logic. Yet despite this laconic use of some of the basic "phrases" and punctuation marks in the language of the cinema, and the resultant static long scenes, he turned out films of great beauty and magnetic power. In Japan, where he was considered the most Japanese of all the national directors, his films won frequent awards. Since the mid-50s his work has been increasingly appreciated in the Western world as well.

FILMS: *Sword of Penitence* (also idea, from George Fitzmaurice's US film *Kick-In*) 1927; *Dreams of Youth* (also sc.), *Wife Lost, Pumpkin* (also story), *A Couple on the Move, Body Beautiful* (also co-sc.) 1928; *Treasure Mountain* (also story), *Days of Youth* (also co-sc.), *Fighting Friends, I Graduated but. . . , The Life of an Office Worker, A Straightforward Boy* 1929; *Introduction to Marriage, Walk Cheerfully, I Flunked but. . . ,* (also story), *That Night's Wife, The Revengeful Spirit of Eros, Lost Luck/Luck Touched My Legs, Young Miss* 1930; *The Lady and the Beard/The Lady and Her Favorites, Beauty's Sorrows, Tokyo Chorus* (also co-sc.) 1931; *Spring Comes with the Ladies* (also story under pseudonym James Maki), *I Was Born but. . .* (also story as Maki), *Where Are the Dreams of Youth?, Until the Day We Meet Again* 1932; *Woman of Tokyo* (also story under pseudonym Ernst Schwartz), *Dragnet Girl/Women on the Firing Line* (also story as Maki), *Passing Fancy* (also story as Maki) 1933; *A Mother Should Be Loved, A Story of Floating Weeds* 1934; *An Innocent Maid/The Young Virgin, Tokyo Is a Nice Place* (also sc.; unfinished), *An Inn in Tokyo* 1935; *College Is a Nice Place* (also story as Maki), *The Only Son* (also story as Maki) 1936; *What Did the Lady Forget?* (also co-sc. as Maki) 1937; *The Toda Brothers and Sisters* (also co-sc.) 1941; *There Was a Father* (also co-sc.) 1942; *The Record of a Tenement Gentleman* (also co-sc.) 1947; *A Hen in the Wind* (also co-sc.) 1948; *Late Spring* (also co-sc.) 1949; *The Munekata Sisters* (also co-sc.) 1950; *Early Summer* (also co-sc.) 1951; *The Flavor of Green Tea Over Rice/Tea and Rice* (also co-sc.) 1952; *Tokyo Story* (also co-sc.) 1953; *Early Spring* (also co-sc.) 1956; *Tokyo Twilight* (also co-sc.) 1957; *Equinox Flower* (also co-sc.) 1958; *Ohayo/Good Morning* (also co-sc.), *Floating Weeds* (also co-sc.) 1959; *Late Autumn* (also co-sc.) 1960; *Early Autumn/The End of Summer/Last of Summer* (also co-sc.) 1961; *An Autumn Afternoon* (also co-sc.) 1962.

P

P.A. Abbreviation for: 1. "production assistant," an apprentice on a film crew assigned to a variety of duties and chores; 2. "public address system," sometimes used by a director in addressing a large group of extras.

Pabst, G. W. Director. *b.* Georg Wilhelm Pabst, Aug. 27, 1885, Raudnitz, Bohemia, to Viennese parents. *d.* 1967. The son of a railroad official, he was raised in Vienna, where he went to technical school to become an engineer. But he found himself strongly drawn to the arts, and after two years of study at Vienna's Academy of Decorative Arts, he went to Switzerland in 1906 and began a career as a stage actor. After gaining experience touring with various companies through Central Europe, he sailed to New York with a troupe of German-language players. Except for a brief return trip to Vienna in 1912, he remained in the US until 1914, acting and directing German-language plays in New York (at the Irving Place Theater) and in various other cities. He was passing through France on his way back to Austria when WW I broke out.

Detained by the French for the duration of the war, Pabst took advantage of his command of French to stage a number of plays. Returning to Vienna, he resumed his career as director at an experimental theater. In 1921 he turned down an offer to become the director of the famous Burgtheater and instead went to Berlin to enter films as an actor, assistant director, and screenwriter for Carl FROELICH. A film director from 1923, Pabst soon moved away from expressionism and became a prime mover in a trend toward pessimistic realism in German cinema, noted for a keen interest in human psychology.

In *Die freudlose Gasse/The Street of Sorrow* (1925), starring Werner Krauss, Asta Nielsen, and Greta Garbo (with Marlene Dietrich as an extra), Pabst took a bitter view of the moral disintegration and economic misery stemming from inflationary woes in the aftermath of WW I. In *Geheimnisse einer Seele/Secrets of a Soul* (1926) he dramatized psychoanalytical theory with the help of two of Freud's assistants. The film is famous for its dream sequences, expressed in multilayered superimpositions, which were executed in the camera through rewinding and multiple exposures. After returning to stark social realism in *Die Liebe der Jeanne Ney/The Love of Jeanne Ney,* Pabst unleashed the forces of Freudian sexuality in *Die Büchse der Pandora/Pandora's Box* and *Das Tagebuch einer Verlorenen/The Diary of a Lost Girl,* in both of which he untapped undreamed-of erotic depths in Hollywood actress Louise Brooks.

Pabst's early sound films are among the most important achievements in his career. His first talkie, *Westfront 1918/Comrades of 1918,* is among the most sincere and unrelenting antiwar films in the history of cinema. His *Die Dreigroschenoper/The Threepenny Opera* was a fine adaptation of the Brecht-Weill musical play, although Brecht was unhappy about some of the changes and sued the production company. The film was made in two versions, German and French. It fared much better in France than it did in Germany, where its release was held up because of the legal controversy.

In 1931, Pabst stirred up political controversy with his call for solidarity of workers of all nations in the German/French coproduction *Kameradschaft/La Tragédie de la Mine.* The message was symbolized by a mine disaster on the French-German border during which German mine workers overcome their chauvinistic inclinations and come to the rescue of trapped French comrades over the objections of their employers. Pabst seemed committed to a leftist political view, an impression that was strengthened by his absence from Germany from the day the Nazis took over. Late that year (1933), after completing two French films, he went to Hollywood, where he directed one film, *A Modern Hero* (1934). But he failed in his attempts to get other assignments and, disillusioned, resumed his career in France. Just before WW II broke out in 1939 he announced his intention of emigrating to the US and becoming an American citizen. Then, inexplicably, he crossed the Swiss border into Austria and spent the entire war in Germany, where he made two films for the Nazi regime. Curiously, his first project after the war was *The Trial,* a denunciation of anti-Semitism, for which he won the best director prize at the 1948 Venice Film Festival. Several of his subsequent films probed the phenomenon of Nazi Germany. He retired in 1956 after a mild stroke.

FILMS: *Der Schatz/The Treasure* (also sc.) 1923; *Gräfin Donelli* 1924; *Die freudlose Gasse/The Street of Sorrow/Joyless Street* 1925; *Geheimnisse einer Seele/Secrets of a Soul, Man spielt nicht mit der Liebe/Don't Play with Love* 1926; *Die Liebe der Jeanne Ney/The Love of Jeanne Ney* 1927; *Abwege/ Begierde/ Crisis* 1928; *Die Büchse der Pandora/Pandora's Box, Die weisse Hölle vom Piz Palü/The White Hell of Pitz Palu* (co-dir. with Arnold Fanck), *Das Tagebuch einer Verlorenen/The Diary of a Lost Girl* (also prod.) 1929; *Westfront 1918/Comrades of 1918, Skandal um Eva* 1930; *Die Dreigroschenoper/The Threepenny Opera/The Beggar's Opera* (Ger./US; also French-language version, *L'Opéra de Quat'sous), Kameradschaft/La Tragédie de la Mine* (German- and French-language versions; Ger./Fr.) 1931; *Die Herrin von Atlantis/L'Atlantide* (German- and French-language versions) 1932; *Don Quichotte/Don Quixote* (Fr.), *Du Haut en Bas* (Fr.) 1933; *A Modern Hero* (US) 1934; *Mademoiselle Docteur/ Salonique Nid d'Espions/Street of Shadows* (Fr.) 1937; *Le Drame de Shanghai/The Shanghai Drama* (Fr.) 1938; *Jeunes Filles en Détresse* (Fr.) 1939; *Komödianten* (also co-sc.) 1941; *Paracelsus* 1943; *Der Fall Molander* (confiscated by Russians; release delayed) 1945; *Der Prozess/In Name der Menschlichkeit/ The Trial* (Aus.) 1948; *Geheimnisvolle Tiefen* (also co-prod.; Aus.) 1949; *La Voce del Silenzio/The Voice of Silence* (also co-sc.; It.) 1952; *Cose da Pazzi* (It.) 1953; *Das Bekenntnis der Ina Kahr/The Confession of Ina Kahr* 1954; *Der letzte Akt/The Last Ten Days, Es geschah am 20. Juli/The Jackboot Mutiny* 1955; *Rosen für Bettina/Ballerina, Durch die Wälder durch die Auen* (also co-sc.) 1956.

Pacino, Al. Actor. Born Alfredo Pacino, on Apr. 25, 1940, in New York City, of Sicilian descent. Intense, brooding, compactly built antiheroic star of Hollywood films of the 70s. Raised in the South Bronx by his mother and grandparents from age two, after his father, a mason, left the family, he showed little interest in academic studies, but his enthusiasm for acting led to his acceptance by Manhattan's High School of Performing Arts. He dropped out of school at 17 and spent several years drifting from job to job, working in such menial occupations as those of delivery boy, usher, porter, and apartment-building superintendent, all the while maintaining a desire for a career on the stage. He finally saved up enough money to attend Herbert Berghof's acting school, where he was tutored by Charles LAUGHTON, and began playing small roles in off-off-Broadway productions. In 1966 he was admitted to Lee Strasberg's Actors Studio and two years later he won an Obie Award for his performance in the role of a drunken psychotic in the off-Broadway play 'The Indian Wants the Bronx.' In 1969 he won the coveted Tony for playing a drug addict in 'Does a Tiger Wear a Necktie?' on Broadway and made his screen debut, playing a small role in *Me Natalie.* On the strength of his performance as a junkie in *The Panic in Needle Park* (1971), he was selected for the complex key role of Michael Corleone, Don Vito's designated heir, in Francis Ford Coppola's *The Godfather* (1972), for which he was nominated for a best supporting actor Academy Award. It became the pivotal role in Paramount's *The Godfather Part II* (1974), for which he gained an Oscar nomination as best actor. Pacino also scored personal triumphs with (and received additional Academy Award nominations for) *Serpico* (1973), *Dog Day Afternoon* (1975), *. . . And Justice for All* (1979), *Dick Tracy* (1990), and *Glengarry Glen Ross* (1992). He finally won the elusive Oscar for his performance in *Scent of a Woman* (1992). Despite his success in films, he remains committed to his first love, the stage, and in 1977 he returned to Broadway in 'The Basic Training of Pavlo Hummel,' for which he won his second Tony.

FILMS: *Me Natalie* 1969; *The Panic in Needle Park* 1971; *The Godfather* 1972; *Scarecrow, Serpico* 1973; *The Godfather Part II* 1974; *Dog Day Afternoon* 1975; *Bobby Deerfield* 1977; *. . . And Justice for All* 1979; *Cruising* 1980; 1982–84 he was co-artistic director (with Ellen BURSTYN) of the Actors Studio; *Author! Author!* 1982; *Scarface* 1983; *Revolution* 1986; *Sea of Love* 1989; *The Local Stigmatic* (shot in 1986; unreleased), *Dick Tracy* (as Big Boy Caprice), *The Godfather Part III* 1990; *Frankie and Johnny* 1991; *Glengarry Glen Ross, Scent of a Woman* 1992; *Carlito's Way* 1993; *Heat, Two Bits* 1995; *City Hall, Looking for Richard* 1996; *The Devil's Advocate, Donnie Brasco* 1997.

Pacula, Joanna. Actress. Born in 1959, in Tomszowau Belski, Poland. A model and stage and screen star in her native country, she was stranded in Paris in 1981 when martial law was declared back home. She headed for the US, where she enjoyed success as a cover girl and played leads in mostly secondary movies, gaining exposure in 1992's controversial but little-seen erotic melodrama *Husbands and Lovers*.

FILMS INCLUDE: *Gorky Park* 1983; *Not Quite Jerusalem/ Not Quite Paradise* (UK) 1985; *Death Before Dishonor* 1987; *The Kiss* 1988; *Sweet Lies* (release delayed from 1987; Fr./US)), *Options* 1989; *Marked For Death* 1990; *Silence of the Hams, Tombstone* 1994; *In Praise of Older Women* 1997.

Padovani, Lea. Actress. Born in 1920, in Montalto di Castto, Italy. Leading lady and supporting player of Italian films and European co-productions.

FILMS INCLUDE: *L'Innocente Casimiro* 1945; *Il Sole sorge ancora/Outcry, Vanità* 1946; *Il Diavolo bianco* 1947; *Give Us This Day* (UK) 1949; *Tre Passi a Nord/Three Steps North* 1950; *Roma Ore 11/Rome 11 O'Clock, Totò e le Donne, Don Lorenzo* 1952; *Donne proibite/Angels of Darkness, Tempi Nostri/The Anatomy of Love, Amori di Mezzo Secolo, Gran Varietà* 1953; *La Contessa di Castiglione, Il Seduttore* 1954; *Dossier noir* (Fr./It.), *Pane Amore e. . . /Scandal in Sorrento* 1955; *Oeil pour Oeil/An Eye for an Eye* (Fr./It.) 1957; *Montparnasse 19/Modigliani of Montparnasse* (Fr./It.) 1958; *La Maja desnuda/The Naked Maja* 1959; *La Princesse de Clèves* (Fr./It.) 1960; *The Reluctant Saint* (US/It.), *Germinal* (Fr./It.) 1962; *La Noia/The Empty Canvas* 1963; *Amore all'Italiana* 1966; *Candy* (US/Fr./It.) 1968; *Ciao Gulliver* 1971.

Pagano, Bartolomeo. Actor. *b.* 1878, Sant'Illario, Italy. *d.* 1947. The screen's first strongman. The star of Pastrone's landmark *Cabiria* (1914) and numerous other action epics, he enjoyed worldwide popularity several years before the advent of Hollywood's Tarzan. A former Genoa longshoreman, he was also known as Maciste, after the powerful character he created in *Cabiria* and repeated in many heroic silents.

FILMS INCLUDE: *Cabiria* 1914; *Maciste* 1915; *Maciste Alpino* 1916; *Maciste contro Maciste* 1917; *Il Viaggio di Maciste* 1918; *Maciste innamorato* 1919; *Maciste e il Nipote d'America* 1921; *Maciste Imperatore* 1924; *Maciste all'Inferno, Il Gigante delle Dolomiti* 1926; *Gli Ultimi Zar, Giuditta e Oloferne* 1928.

Page, Anthony. Director. Born on Sept. 21, 1935, in Bangalore, India, to British parents. He began directing stage plays while still a student at Oxford and later at New York's Neighborhood Playhouse School of Theatre. In 1964–65, he served as artistic director of the Royal Court and directed a number of successful stage productions in London and on Broadway. Branching out into films in the late 60s, he turned out several intelligent if unremarkable features. More recently, working mainly in Hollywood, he has specialized in TV movies.

FEATURE FILMS: *Inadmissable Evidence* 1968; *Alpha Beta* 1973; *I Never Promised You a Rose Garden* (US) 1977; *The Lady Vanishes* 1979; *Absolution* (release delayed from 1978) 1981; *Forbidden* (cable TV in US; theatrical abroad; US/UK/Ger.) 1985.

Page, Don. See ALVARADO, Don.

Page, Gale. Actress. *b.* Sally Perkins Rutter, July 23, 1913, Spokane, Wash. *d.* 1983. Wholesome leading lady and second lead of some Warner Bros. films of the late 30s and early 40s. She was the fourth wheel to the three LANE sisters in *Four Daughters* (1938) and its sequels. Earlier she was a vocalist with the Ted Weems band and an actress on radio.

FILMS INCLUDE: *Crime School, The Amazing Dr. Clitterhouse, Four Daughters* 1938; *You Can't Get Away with Murder, Daughters Courageous, Naughty but Nice, Indianapolis Speedway, Four Wives* 1939; *A Child Is Born, They Drive by Night, Knute Rockne—All American* 1940; *Four Mothers* 1941; *The Time of Your Life* 1948; *Anna Lucasta* 1949; *About Mrs. Leslie* 1954.

Page, Genevieve. Actress. Born Geneviève Bronjean, on Dec. 13, 1930, in Paris. Leading lady and supporting player of the Paris stage and French and international films.

FILMS INCLUDE: *Ce Siècle a Cinquante Ans* 1949; *Fanfan la Tulipe, Plaisirs de Paris* 1952; *Nuits andalouses* 1953; *Cherchez la Femme* 1955; *Foreign Intrigue* (US), *The Silken Affair* (UK), *Michael Strogoff* (Yug.) 1956; *Un Amour de Poche/Nude in His Pocket* 1957; *Song Without End* (US) 1960; *El Cid* (US/It.) 1961; *Le Jour et l'Heure/The Day and the Hour* 1963; *Youngblood Hawke* (US) 1964; *Trois Chambres à Manhattan* 1965; *Grand Prix* (US) 1966; *Tendre Voyou/Tender Scoundrel* 1966; *Belle de Jour* 1967; *Decline and Fall. . . of a Bird Watcher* (UK), *Mayerling* (UK/Fr.) 1968; *The Private Life of Sherlock Holmes* (US/UK) 1970; *La Cavale, Brother Carl* (Sw.) 1971; *L'Embryon* 1974; *Buffet froid* 1979; *Beyond Therapy* (US) 1987; *Mortelle randonné* 1983; *Aria* (UK) 1987; *Les Bois noirs* 1989; *L'Inconnu dans la Maison/Stranger in the House* 1992.

Page, Geraldine. Actress. *b.* Nov. 22, 1924, Kirksville, Mo. *d.* 1987. A superb performer of the American stage, films, and TV; an intuitive, unpretentious, unconventional, at times eccentric star, who for years was a leading exponent of "Method" acting. A physician's daughter, she began acting in stock at 17 and broke through in 1952 with a memorable off-Broadway performance in 'Summer and Smoke.' She later enjoyed other personal triumphs on the stage and screen, but her appearances in either medium were relatively infrequent and she was known to turn down work that did not meet her taste or mood. She received the New York Drama Critics award for her stage performances in Tennessee Williams's 'Summer and Smoke' (1952) and 'Sweet Bird of Youth' (1959) and won the Emmy Award for her roles in the teleplays 'A Christmas Memory' (1967) and 'The Thanksgiving Visitor' (1969). She was nominated for Academy Awards as best actress for *Summer and Smoke* (1961), *Sweet Bird of Youth* (1962), and *Interiors* (1978) and as best supporting actress for *Hondo* (1953), *You're a Big Boy Now* (1967), *Pete 'n' Tillie* (1972), and *The Pope of Greenwich Village* (1984), finally winning the best actress Oscar for *A Trip to Bountiful* (1985). Divorced (1954–57) from violinist Alexander Schneider, she married actor Rip TORN in 1963. She was heavily involved in stage and screen work when she died of a heart attack during the Broadway revival of Noel Coward's 'Blithe Spirit,' in which she played a leading role.

FILMS: *Out of the Night* 1947; *Taxi, Hondo* 1953; *Summer and Smoke* 1961; *Sweet Bird of Youth* 1962; *Toys in the Attic* 1963; *Dear Heart* 1965; *The Three Sisters* (videotape recording of Actors Studio performance) 1966; *Monday's Child* (filmed theater), *You're a Big Boy Now, The Happiest Millionaire* 1967; *What Ever Happened to Aunt Alice?, Trilogy* ("A Christmas Memory" episode; orig. shown on TV in 1966) 1969; *The Beguiled* 1971; *J. W. Coop, Pete 'n' Tillie* 1972; *Happy as the Grass Was Green/Hazel's People* 1973; *The Day of the Locust* 1975; *Nasty Habits* (UK) 1976; *The Rescuers* (v/o), *The Three Sisters* 1977; *Interiors* 1978; *Harry's War, Honky Tonk Freeway* 1981; *I'm Dancing as Fast as I Can* 1982; *The Pope of Greenwich Village* 1984; *The Bride, Flanagan, White Nights, The Trip to Bountiful* 1985; *My Little Girl, Native Son* 1986.

Page, Louis. Director of photography. Born on Mar. 16, 1905, in Lyons, France. Formerly a painter, he entered French films in 1930 as assistant to Cocteau on *Blood of a Poet.* In the late 30s and early 40s he contributed harshly realistic photography to several films of artistic merit. Later he worked on many Jean Gabin vehicles as well as routine commercial productions.

FILMS INCLUDE: *Jeunes Filles de Paris* 1937; *Espoir* 1939; *L'Arlèsienne, Lumière d'Eté* 1942; *Le Ciel est à vous* 1943; *Sortilèges* 1944; *Le Pays sans Etoile* 1945; *Macadam, Un Revenant/A Lover's Return* 1946; *La Vie en Rose* 1947; *Audeld des Grilles* 1948; *Histoires extraordinaires* 1949; *Maltre après Dieu* 1950; *La Lumière d'en Face* 1955; *En effeuillant la Marguerite/Please Mr. Balzac, La Mariée est trop Belle/The Bride Is Much Too Beautiful* 1956; *Le Désordre et la Nuit/Night Affair, Maigret tend un Piège/Inspector Maigret* 1958; *Les Grandes Familles/The Possessors, Archimède le Clochard/The Magnificent Tramp* 1959; *Le Président* 1960; *Un Singe en Hiver/A Monkey in Winter* 1962; *Mélodie en Sous-Sol/Any Number Can Win* 1963; *La Grosse Caisse* 1965.

Page, Marco. See KURNITZ, Harry.

Paget, Alfred. American actor. *b.* 1880(?). *d.* 1925. Leading man and character star of early silents. Memorable as Belshazzar in the Babylonian episode of *Intolerance* (1916), he also figured prominently in other D. W. Griffith films of the period.

FILMS INCLUDE: *A Romance of the Western Hills, The Call to Arms, The Masher, The Banker's Daughters* 1910; *The Two Paths, Enoch Arden, Conscience, Out from the Shadow* 1911; *The Goddess of Sagebrush Gulch, The Lesser Evil, The Inner Circle, A Temporary Truce* 1912; *Oil and Water, Just Gold, The Primitive Man* 1913; *The Massacre, The Battle at Elderbush Gulch* 1914; *The Lamb, Enoch Arden* (remake; title role), *Martyrs of the Alamo* (as Jim Bowie) 1915; *Intolerance* (as Belshazzar), *The Old Folks at Home* 1916; *Nina the Flower Girl, Big Timber, Aladdin and the Wonderful Lamp* 1917; *Cupid's Roundups* 1918; *When a Girl Loves* 1919.

Paget, Debra. Actress. Born Debralee Griffin, on Aug. 19, 1933, in Denver, Colo. Sultry-innocent leading lady of Hollywood films of the 50s, often cast in exotic parts, sometimes as an Indian squaw, mainly at Fox. Her first marriage, in 1958, to actor-singer David Street, ended in annulment within four months. She married director Budd BOETTICHER in 1960, but they separated 22 days later and divorced the following year. Her third marriage, to a Chinese-American oilman, a nephew of Mme. Chiang Kai-Shek, lasted from 1964 to 1971.

FILMS INCLUDE: *Cry of the City* 1948; *House of Strangers* 1949; *Broken Arrow* 1950; *14 Hours, Bird of Paradise, Anne of the Indies* 1951; *Belles on Their Toes, Les Miserables* (as Cosette), *Stars and Stripes Forever* 1952; *Prince Valiant, Demetrius and the Gladiators, Princess of the Nile* 1954; *White Feather, Seven Angry Men* 1955; *The Ten Commandments, The Last Hunt, Love Me Tender* 1956; *Omar Khayyam, The River's Edge* 1957; *From the Earth to the Moon* 1958; *Der Tiger von Eschnapur/Das Indische Grabmal/Journey to the Lost City* (Ger./Fr./It.) 1959; *Why Must I Die?* 1960; *Il Sepolcro die Re/Cleopatra's Daughter* (It./Fr.), *Most Dangerous Man Alive* 1961; *Tales of Terror* 1962; *The Haunted Palace* 1963.

Pagliero, Marcello (Marcel). Director, screenwriter, actor. *b.* Jan. 15, 1907, London, to an Italian father and French mother. *d.* 1980. In Italy from age seven, he graduated from law school, then turned to journalism as an art and literary critic. He entered Italian films in the late 30s, initially dubbing voices for English-speaking films. He began collaborating on screenplays in 1941 and turned out his first film as a director two years later. But it was as an actor that he first became known internationally, playing the key role of Manfredi in Roberto Rossellini's *Roma Città aperta/Open City* (1945). The following year he contributed one of the stories for and collaborated on the screenplay of Rossellini's *Paisà/Paisan.* In 1947 he moved to France, where he continued his activities as both director and actor, returning occasionally to work in Italy. After 1960 he did not make any feature films but appeared in several as an actor and directed a number of productions for French TV.

FILMS: As director (complete): In Italy—*07 Taxi* (also sc.) 1943; *Desiderio/Woman* (co-dir. with Roberto Rossellini; also co-sc.), *Roma Città libera* 1946. In France—*Un Homme marche dans la Ville* 1950; *La Rose Rouge, Les Amants de Bras-Mort* 1951; *La P. . . respectueuse/The Respectful Prostitute* (co-dir. with Charles Brabant) 1952; *Destinées/Daughters of Destiny* ("Due Donne" episode) 1953; *Vestire gli Ignudi* (It.), *Vergine Moderna* (also act.; It.) 1954; *Chéri-Bibi* 1955; *L'Odyssée de Capitaine Steve/La Vallée du Paradis* (filmed in Australia) 1956; *Vingt mille Lieues sur la Terre* (doc.; also sc.; Fr./USSR) 1960. As actor (partial list)—*Roma Città aperta/Open City* 1945; *Paisà/Paisan* (also co-story, co-sc.) 1946; *L'Altra* 1947. In France—*Les Jeux sont faits/The Chips Are Down* 1947; *Dedée d'Anvers/Dedee* 1948; *Tourbillon* 1952; *Seven Thunders* (UK) 1957; *Le Bel Age* 1958; *Les Mauvais Coups/Naked Autumn* 1961; *Tom Ombre est la mienne/Your Shadow Is Mine* 1962; *Je vous salue Mafia/Hail! Mafia* 1965; *Les Gauloises bleues* 1966.

Pagnol, Marcel. Playwright, screenwriter, director, producer. *b.* Feb. 28, 1895, Aubagne, France. *d.* 1974. Following in his father's footsteps, he started out as an English teacher in the Marseilles region. He spent much of his spare time writing plays (his first at age 15), which were produced by local groups. In 1922 he was assigned to a school in Paris. To his amazement he found the Paris theaters as responsive to his work as the provincial ones had been and he soon abandoned teaching in favor of full-time playwriting. Gaining great prominence as a playwright in the late 20s with 'Topaze' and 'Marius,' he decided to enter the new world of sound films. He established his own studio, releasing through Gaumont.

Pagnol's attitude toward the cinema has been governed by his love of the theater. Films, he has maintained, are nothing more than a means of giving stage plays a wider circulation and recording them for posterity. If there had been such a thing as an art of film, it died with the advent of sound. True to his theory, Pagnol made films that were essentially photographed theater. But it was theater at its best, filled with the authentic flavor of Southern France. The French cinema also owes to his films the discovery of such great acting talents as RAIMU and FERNANDEL. In addition to directing films from his own plays and screenplays, Pagnol wrote the script and dialogue for a number of screen adaptations of his plays which were directed by others, including Alexander Korda's *Marius* (1930), Marc Allégret's *Fanny* (1932), Louis Gasnier's *Topaze* (1932), James Whale's *Port of Seven Seas* (from 'Fanny,' 1938), Peter Sellers' *Mr. Topaze/I Love Money* (1961), and Joshua Logan's *Fanny* (also 1961). Audiences rediscovered Pagnol's work in the 80s through such films as Claude Berri's *Jean de Florette* and *Manon des Sources/Manon of the Spring* (both 1986) and Yves Robert's *La Gloire de mon Pères/My Father's Glory* (1990). Pagnol directed two remake versions of *Topaze* in 1936 and 1951. His wife, the former Jacqueline Bouvier (*b.* 1926, Paris), starred as Jacqueline Pagnol in several of his films. Earlier, he married and divorced actresses Orane Demazis and Josette DAY.

FILMS (as director): *Direct au Coeur* (co-dir. with Roger Lion; also prod., sc., dial., from own play), *Le Gendre de Monsieur Poirier* (also prod., dial.), *Léopold le Bien-Aimé* (also prod., dial.) 1933; *Jofroi/Ways of Love,* (also prod., sc., dial.), *Angèle* (also prod., sc.), *Le Voyage de Monsieur Perrichon* (also prod.), *L'Article 330* (also prod., dial.) 1934; *Merlusse* (also prod.), *Cigalon* (also prod., dial.) 1935; *César* (also prod., sc., from own play), *Topaze* (remake; dir., sc. only) 1936; *Regain/Harvest* (also prod., sc., dial.) 1937; *Le Schpountz/Heartbeat* (also prod., sc.), *La Femme du Boulanger/The Baker's Wife* (also prod., sc., dial.) 1938; *La Fille du Puisatier/The Well-Digger's Daughter* (also prod., sc., dial.) 1941; *La Belle Meunière* (also prod., sc.) 1948; *Topaze* (2nd remake; also prod., sc.) 1951; *Manon des Sources* (also prod., sc.) 1952; *Les Lettres de mon Moulin/Letters from My Windmill* (also sc.) 1954; *Le Curé de Cucugnan* (also prod., sc.; for TV) 1967.

Paige, Janis. Actress. Born Donna Mae Tjaden, on Sept. 16, 1922, in Tacoma, Wash. Peppery second lead of Warner Bros. films of the 40s. Trained as an opera singer, she was discovered for films while working as a waitress-singer at the Hollywood Canteen. A vivacious redhead, she enlivened many Warner Bros. light films of the 40s, typically playing the zestful friend of the heroine, often opposite second-lead Jack CARSON. After leaving the studio in 1949, she briefly teamed up with Carson in a nightclub act, then appeared at New York's Copacabana, on the stage, and on TV. She reached the high point of her career in 1954 as co-star of the Broadway musical 'Pajama Game.' She later starred in her own short-lived TV series 'It's Always Jan' (1955–56) and returned occasionally to the big screen, usually in supporting roles. She appeared in several TV movies in the 80s, as well as in the series 'Trapper John, M.D.' (1985–86). Her third husband (from 1962 till his death in 1976) was the late Oscar-winning (for the song "Zip-a-Dee-Doo-Dah") composer Ray Gilbert.

FILMS: *Bathing Beauty* (bit), *Hollywood Canteen* 1944; *Her Kind of Man, Of Human Bondage, Two Guys from Milwaukee, The Time the Place and the Girl* 1946; *Love and Learn, Cheyenne, Always Together* 1947; *Winter Meeting, Wallflower, Romance on the High Seas, One Sunday Afternoon* 1948; *The Younger Brothers, The House Across the Street* 1949; *This Side of the Law* 1950; *Mr. Universe, Fugitive Lady, Two Gals and a Guy* 1951; *Silk Stockings* 1957; *Please Don't Eat the Daisies* 1960; *Bachelor in Paradise* 1961; *Follow the Boys, The Caretakers* 1963; *Welcome to Hard Times* 1967.

Paige, Mabel. Actress. *b.* 1880, New York City. *d.* 1954. On the stage from age four, she appeared in a dozen or so silent comedy shorts in 1915–16, often opposite her husband, one Charles Ritchie, and sometimes alongside a young Oliver Hardy. But she is known primarily for her many matronly character parts in Hollywood films of the 40s, mainly at Paramount and Columbia. At her best in humorous, sharp-tongued, sarcastic roles, she gave a memorable dramatic performance playing the lead in Republic's melodrama *Someone to Remember* (1943).

FILMS INCLUDE: *Mixed Flats* (short) 1915; *Lucky Jordan* 1942; *The Crystal Ball, Happy Go Lucky, Someone to Remember, True to Life* 1943; *Out of This World, Murder He Says, Dangerous Partners* 1945; *Behind Green Lights, Nocturne* 1946; *Johnny O'Clock* 1947; *If You Knew Susie, The Mating of Millie, Johnny Belinda, Hollow Triumph/The Scar* 1948; *Roseanna McCoy* 1949; *Edge of Doom* 1950; *The Sniper* 1952; *Houdini* 1953.

Paige, Robert. Actor. *b.* John Arthur Paige, Dec. 2, 1910, Indianapolis. *d.* 1987. Leading man of B films and minor musicals of the 40s, mostly for Universal. He dropped out of West Point to pursue a career as a radio singer and announcer and began appearing in film shorts in 1931 as David Carlyle. He made his feature debut in 1935 and gradually rose from bits to romantic leads, switching to the screen name of Robert Paige in 1938, when he joined Columbia as a contract player. He moved to Paramount the following year and to Universal in 1941. From the early 50s he appeared mostly on TV as an actor and quiz-show host and, later, as a Los Angeles area newscaster. He later became an executive with a public relations firm in Hollywood.

FILMS INCLUDE: As David Carlyle—*Annapolis Farewell* 1935; *Cain and Mabel* 1936; *Smart Blonde* 1937. As Robert Paige—*Who Killed Gail Preston?, The Main Event, Highway Patrol* 1938; *Flying G-Men* (serial), *Homicide Bureau* 1939; *Parole Fixer, Women Without Names, Golden Gloves* 1940; *The Monster and the Girl, San Antonio Rose, Hellzapoppin* 1941; *Almost Married, Pardon My Sarong, Get Hep to Love* 1942; *Cowboy in Manhattan, Frontier Bad Man, Fired Wife, Son of Dracula* 1943; *Her Primitive Man, Can't Help Singing* 1944; *Shady Lady* 1945; *Tangier* 1946; *The Red Stallion* 1947; *The Flame* 1948; *The Green Promise* (also co-prod.) 1949; *Abbott and Costello Go to Mars, Split Second* 1953; *The Big Payoff* 1958; *Marriage-Go-Round* 1960; *Bye Bye Birdie* 1963.

Pakula, Alan J. Producer, director. Born on Apr. 7, 1928, in the Bronx, N.Y., of Polish-Jewish parents. The son of a printing and advertising businessman, he began writing and acting in plays as a high school student. After graduating from the Yale Drama School, he entered films in 1949 as an assistant at the Warner Bros. cartoon department. In 1950 he joined MGM as an apprentice and the following year went to work for Paramount as a production assistant. In 1957 he produced his first film, *Fear Strikes Out,* and in the early 60s formed his own production company in partnership with that film's director, Robert MULLIGAN. They scored a success with their first production, *To Kill a Mockingbird* (1962), an Oscar nominee for best picture, and went on to collaborate on five more films with Pakula producing and Mulligan directing. Pakula made his own debut as director in 1969 with *The Sterile Cuckoo,* an earnest and sensitive, if at times plodding, look at a grotesque love relationship. He forged ahead with his next film as a director, *Klute,* a sexy thriller with psychological overtones which enjoyed success with both the critics and the public. Pakula soared to the fore as one of Hollywood's most sought-after directors following the great box-office success of *All the President's Men* (1976), for which he was nominated for an Oscar as best director. Working mainly out of New York City, Pakula subsequently meandered through several unremarkable productions before regaining stature with the critics with an excellently played screen adaptation of William Styron's *Sophie's Choice* (1982). The film earned a best actress Academy Award for Meryl Streep and an Oscar nomination for Pakula's screenplay. He scored a popular success with *Presumed Innocent* (1990). Having married and divorced (1963–69) actress Hope LANGE, Pakula wed writer Hannah Cohn Boorstin in 1973.

FILMS: As producer—*Fear Strikes Out* 1957; *To Kill a Mockingbird* 1962; *Love with the Proper Stranger* 1963; *Baby the Rain Must Fall, Inside Daisy Clover* 1965; *Up the Down Staircase* 1967; *The Stalking Moon* 1969. As director—*The Sterile Cuckoo* (also prod.) 1969; *Klute* (also prod.) 1971; *Love and Pain and the Whole Damn Thing* (also prod.; UK/US) 1973; *The Parallax View* (also prod.) 1974; *All the President's Men* 1976; *Comes a Horseman* 1978; *Starting Over* (also co-prod.) 1979; *Rollover* 1981; *Sophie's Choice* (also co-prod., sc.) 1982; *Dream Lover* (also co-prod.) 1986; *Orphans* (also co-prod.) 1987; *See You in the Morning* (also co-prod, sc.) 1989; *Presumed Innocent* (also co-sc.) 1990; *Consenting Adults* (also prod.) 1992; *The Pelican Brief* (also co-prod., sc.) 1993; *The Devil's Own* 1997.

Pal, George. Producer, director, special effects expert. *b.* Feb. 1, 1908, Cegled, Hungary. *d.* 1980. An architecture major at the Budapest Academy of Arts, he began his film career in Budapest, then designed sets for UFA in Berlin and went to Holland, where he directed puppet shorts for the Philips company. In Hollywood since 1940, he produced the Puppetoons puppet-cartoon series for Paramount, utilizing a new technique, for which he received a special Academy Award in 1943. He turned to feature films early in the 50s as producer, then became a producer-director. He won five Oscars (designated AA below) for special effects. Pal and his work were the subject of the film *The Fantasy Film World of George Pal* (1986). His animated short subjects of the 30s and 40s were compiled into a collage by Arnold Liebovit in *The Puppetoon Movie* (1987).

FEATURE FILMS: As producer-special-effects man: *The Great Rupert, Destination Moon* (AA) 1950; *When Worlds Collide* (AA) 1951; *War of the Worlds* (AA), *Houdini* 1953; *The Naked Jungle* 1954; *The Conquest of Space* 1955; *The Power* 1968; *Doc Savage—The Man of Bronze* (also co-sc.) 1975. As producer-director-special-effects man—*Tom Thumb* (AA) 1958; *The Time Machine* (AA) 1960; *Atlantis the Lost Continent* 1961; *The Wonderful World of the Brothers Grimm* (co-dir. with Henry Levin) 1962; *The Seven Faces of Dr. Lao* 1964.

Palance, Jack. Actor. Born Walter Jack Palahnuik, on Feb. 18, 1919, in Lattimer, Pa. *ed.* U. of North Carolina; Stanford U. The son of a coal miner, he worked briefly in the mines before turning to school athletics and professional boxing. The crash of a bomber that he was piloting during WW II resulted in severe burns and plastic surgery, which gave his features the gaunt, taut-skinned look familiar to filmgoers since 1950. Arriving in Hollywood after several years on the stage, he made a memorable debut as a gangster carrying the bubonic plague in Elia Kazan's *Panic in the Streets.* He was cast at first almost exclusively as a sinister heavy but revealed an anguished, soulful side of his personality in some of his later films. He was nominated for an Oscar as best supporting player for *Sudden Fear* (1952) and *Shane* (1953). Since the late 50s he has appeared in many foreign films, especially in Italy. He starred in the TV series 'The Greatest Show on Earth' (1963–64) and 'Bronk' (1975–76) and hosted 'Ripley's Believe It or Not' (1982–86). He also appeared in a number of teleplays, winning an Emmy Award for 'Requiem for a Heavyweight' (1956), and several TV movies, notably a version of *Dracula* (1973), in which he gave a touchingly pathetic portrayal of the title role. His big-screen comeback in *City Slickers* (1991) earned him an Oscar as best supporting actor, and his outrageous appearance on the Oscars telecast—during which he did one-handed push-ups—was memorable. A lover of the American West, Palance runs a 150-cattle ranch—Land of Big Acorn—in California's Tehachapi Mountains. He is the father of actress Holly Palance (*b.* Aug. 5, 1950, Los Angeles) and actor Cody Palance (*b.* 1956) from his only marriage (1949–68) to actress Virginia Baker.

FILMS INCLUDE: *Panic in the Streets, Halls of Montezuma* 1950; *Sudden Fear* 1952; *Shane, Second Chance, Arrowhead, Flight to Tangier, Man in the Attic* 1953; *Sign of the Pagan* (as Attila the Hun) 1954; *The Silver Chalice* (as Simon Magus), *Kiss of Fire, The Big Knife, I Died a Thousand Times* 1955; *Attack!* 1956; *The Lonely Man, House of Numbers, Flor de Mayo/Beyond All Limits* (Mex.) 1957; *The Man Inside* (UK) 1958; *Ten Seconds to Hell* (UK/US) 1959; *Austerlitz* (Fr./It.) 1960; *I Mongoli/The Mongols* (It./Fr.), *Barabba/Barabbas* (It.), *Alboino e Rosmunda/Sword of the Conqueror* (It.), *Il Giudizio Universale* (It.) 1961; *La Guerra continua/Warriors 5* (It./Fr.) 1962; *Le Mépris/Contempt* (Fr./It.) 1963; *Les Tueurs de San Francisco/Once a Thief* (Fr./US) 1965; *The Professionals* 1966; *Torture Garden* (UK), *Kill a Dragon* 1967; *Las Vegas 500 Millones/They Came to Rob Las Vegas* (Sp./It./Fr./Ger.) 1968; *Il Mercenario/The Mercenary* (It./Sp.), *The Desperados, Che!* (as Fidel Castro) 1969; *The McMasters, Monte Walsh* 1970; *The Horsemen* 1971; *Chato's Land* 1972; *Oklahoma Crude* 1973; *Craze* (UK) 1974; *The Four Deuces, Africa Express* (It.), *L'Infirmiera/The Sensuous Nurse* 1975; *The Great Adventure* (It./Sp.), *God's Gun* (It.), *Eva nera* (It.), *Safari Express* (It.) 1976; *I Padroni della Città/Mister Scarface* (It.), *Welcome to Blood City* (UK/Can.), *Jim Buck/Portrait of a Hitman* 1977; *One Man Jury* 1978; *The Shape of Things to Come* (Can.), *Dead on Arrival, Cocaine Cowboys* 1979; *Angels Brigade/Seven from Heaven, Without Warning, Hawk the Slayer* (UK) 1980; *Alone in the Dark* 1982; *Gor, Out of Rosenheim/Bagdad Cafe* (Ger.), *Young Guns* 1988; *Batman, Tango and Cash* 1989; *Solar Crisis* (Jap.) 1990; *City Slickers* 1991; *Tombstone* 1993; *Cops and Robbersons, City Slickers 2: The Legend of Curly's Gold, The Swan Princess* (v/o) 1994.

Palcy, Euzhan. Director. Born in 1957, in Martinique. A TV director-writer in her native country, she moved in her early 20s to Paris, where she studied French literature at the Sorbonne and film at the Vaugirard School. After some experience as a film editor and director of shorts, she took advantage of a French government grant to make an auspicious debut as a feature director with *Sugar Cane Alley* (1983), a beautifully shot, deeply felt Third World drama which sensitively portrayed the growing pains and joys of a bright 12-year-old boy in a poverty-stricken Martinique plantation of the colonial 30s. The film won a Silver Lion at Venice for best first feature, as well as best actress prize for Darling Legitimus, who played the orphan boy's grandmother. Palcy was far less successful with her American-sponsored film, *A Dry White Season* (1989), a contrived story set against the background of South African apartheid.

FEATURE FILMS (as director): *Rue Cases Nègres/Sugar Cane Alley* (also sc.; Fr./Mart.) 1983; *A Dry White Season* (also co-sc.; US) 1989; *Simeon* (also co-sc.) 1993.

Palin, Michael. Actor, screenwriter. Born on May 5, 1943, in Sheffield, England. A graduate of Oxford, where he majored in history, he made his London stage debut in 1964 in a satirical production of that university's Experimental Theatre Club. After establishing himself as a comedy writer-performer with such British TV programs as 'Do Not Adjust Your Set' (1977–79) and 'Complete and Utter History of Britain' (1969), he joined the cast of Monty Python's Flying Circus and later took part in many of the troupe's features. He also appeared in other films, memorably as a hapless clergyman in *The Missionary* (1982) and as a stuttering bumbler in *A Fish Called Wanda* (1988), a role that earned him the British Film Academy Award as best supporting actor.

FILMS INCLUDE (as actor): *And Now for Something Completely Different* (also co-sc.), *Monty Python and the Holy Grail* (also co-sc.) 1975; *Jabberwocky* 1976; *Monty Python's Life of Brian* (also co-sc.) 1979; *Time Bandits* (also co-sc.) 1981; *The Secret Policeman's Other Ball* (also co-sc.), *The Missionary* (also co-prod., sc.) 1982; *Monty Python's The Meaning of Life* (also co-sc.) 1983; *A Private Function* 1984; *Brazil* 1985; *Consuming Passions* (co-play basis only, 'Secrets'), *A Fish Called Wanda* 1988; *American Friends* (UK) 1991; *Fierce Creatures* 1997.

Pallette, Eugene. Actor. *b.* July 8, 1889, Winfield, Kans. *d.* 1954. Trim leading man of early Hollywood silents and later a rotund, frog-voiced, often jovial character actor of numerous talkies—hundreds of pictures in all. Entered films in 1910 after six years on the stage and by 1913 was playing leading roles. But WW I service interrupted his career and after 1920 he was seen exclusively in supporting parts.

FILMS INCLUDE: *The Tattooed Arm, When Jim Returned, Broken Nose Bailey* 1913; *The Horse Wrangler, The Peach Brand, The Burden, On the Border, The Sheriff's Prisoner, The Beat of the Year* 1914; *After Twenty Years, The Birth of a Nation, The Emerald Brooch, The Spell of the Poppy, The Isle of Content, The Scarlet Lady, The Penalty* 1915; *Intolerance* (as Prosper Latour in French episode), *Going Straight* 1916; *The World Apart, The Heir of the Ages, The Ghost House, A Man's Man* 1917; *His Robe of Honor, Madam Who* 1918; *The Amateur Adventuress, Fair and Warmer* 1919; *Terror Island, Alias Jimmy Valentine, Parlor Bedroom and Bath* 1920; *Fine Feathers, The Three Musketeers* (as Aramis) 1921; *Two Kinds of Women* 1922; *To the Last Man, North of Hudson Bay* 1923; *Wandering Husbands, The Wolf Man* 1924; *The Light of the Western Stars, Without Mercy* 1925; *Whispering Smith, Mantrap* 1926; *Moulders of Men, Chicago* 1927; *Lights of New York, His Private Life* 1928; *The Dummy, The Canary Murder Case, The Studio Murder Case, The Love Parade, The Virginian* 1929; *Slightly Scarlet, The Border Legion, The Sea God, The Santa Fe Trail, Playboy of Paris* 1930; *Fighting Caravans, It Pays to Advertise, Huckleberry Finn, Girls About Town* 1931; *Shanghai Express, Strangers of the Evening, The Half-Naked Truth* 1932; *Hell Below, The Kennel Murder Case, Shanghai Madness* 1933; *The Dragon Murder Case, Caravan* 1934; *Bordertown, Steamboat Round the Bend, The Ghost Goes West* (UK) 1935; *The Golden Arrow, My Man Godfrey, Stowaway* 1936; *Topper, 100 Men and a Girl* 1937; *The Adventures of Robin Hood* (as Friar Tuck) 1938; *Mr. Smith Goes to Washington, First Love* 1939; *Young Tom Edison, The Mark of Zorro* 1940; *The Lady Eve, The Bride Came C.O.D., World Premiere, Appointment for Love* 1941; *The Male Animal, The Big Street, Tales of Manhattan* 1942; *It Ain't Hay, Heaven Can Wait, The Gang's All Here* 1943; *Pin Up Girl, Step Lively, Lake Placid Serenade* 1944; *The Cheaters* 1945; *Suspense* 1946.

Palmer, Ernest G. American director of photography. *b.* 1885. *d.* 1978. One of the American screen's most prolific and most durable cinematographers, he began his career in films in the early 1910s. He worked on numerous productions for various studios, including several Frank Borzage films of the late 20s. During that period and in the 30s and 40s he was behind the camera mainly for Fox, where he shared an Academy Award with Ray Rennahan for the cinematography of Rouben Mamoulian's *Blood and Sand* (1941). He was also nominated for several other Oscars. In the 50s he worked mainly in England. He was among the founding members of the A.S.C.

FILMS INCLUDE: *The Prisoner of Zenda, Ivanhoe* (co-phot.) 1913; *Mother* 1917; *Hypocrites* 1918; *The Miracle Man* 1919; *Prisoners of Love* 1921; *The Song of Life* 1922; *The Wanters* 1923; *Flames of Desire* 1924; *The Dancers* (co-phot.), *Wings of Youth, Wages for Wives* 1925; *The Palace of Pleasure, Yellow Fingers* (co-phot.), *Early to Wed, Marriage License?* 1926; *Seventh Heaven,* 1927; *Street Angel* (co-phot.), *Four Devils* (co-phot.) 1928; *The River, Sunny Side Up* (co-phot.) 1929; *City Girl* 1930; *A Connecticut Yankee, Delicious* 1931; *Down to Earth* 1932; *Cavalcade, Pleasure Cruise, Berkeley Square, Hoopla* 1933; *Stand Up and Cheer, Caravan* (co-phot.), *Music in the Air* 1934; *Way Down East* 1935; *Under Two Flags, Banjo on My Knee* 1936; *Slave Ship, Second Honeymoon, Ali Baba Goes to Town* 1937; *Four Men and a Prayer, Three Blind Mice, Kentucky* 1938; *Wife Husband and Friend, News Is Made at Night, Hollywood Cavalcade* (co-phot.) 1939; *The Great Profile, Chad Hanna* (co-phot.) 1940; *Tall Dark and Handsome, Blood and Sand* (co-phot.), *Week-End in Havana, Belle Starr* 1941; *Song of the Islands, My Gal Sal, Springtime in the Rockies* 1942; *Coney Island, Sweet Rosie O'Grady* 1943; *Pin Up Girl, Something for the Boys* 1944; *Diamond Horseshoe, The Dolly Sisters* 1945; *Centennial Summer* 1946; *I Wonder Who's Kissing Her Now* 1947; *Scudda-Hoo! Scudda-Hay!* 1948; *Broken Arrow* 1950; *It's a Grand Life* (UK) 1953; *The Heart Within* (UK) 1957; *Woman-eater/Woman Eater* (UK) 1958; *Hidden Homicide* (UK) 1959; *Zoo Baby* (UK) 1960.

Palmer, Lilli. Actress. *b.* Lillie Marie Peiser, May 24, 1914, Posen, Germany. *d.* 1986. Elegant, worldly, gentle, intelligent star of international films. The daughter of a surgeon and an Austrian actress, she made her stage debut in Berlin in 1932. After the Nazi takeover she went to Paris, where she appeared in an operetta staged in the Moulin Rouge. She made her screen debut in London in 1935 and for the next decade appeared in many British films and plays. In 1945 she came to the US with her first (1943–57) husband, Rex HARRISON. She starred in Hollywood movies and Broadway plays before returning to Europe in 1954 and later played leads and supporting parts in film productions of several nations. Her second husband (from 1957) was actor Carlos THOMPSON.

Author: *Change Lobsters and Dance* (autobiography, 1975); *The Red Raven* (novel, 1978).

FILMS INCLUDE: In the UK—*Crime Unlimited* 1935; *Secret Agent* 1936; *The Great Barrier/Silent Barriers, Sunset in Vienna/Suicide Legion, Command Performance* 1937; *Crackerjack/Man with 100 Faces* 1938; *A Girl Must Live* 1939; *The Door with Seven Locks* 1940; *Thunder Rock* 1942; *The Gentle Sex* 1943; *English Without Tears/Her Man Gilbey* 1944; *The Rake's Progress/Notorious Gentleman* 1945; *Beware of Pity* 1946. In the US—*Cloak and Dagger* 1946; *Body and Soul* 1947; *My Girl Tisa, No Minor Vices* 1948. In Europe—*Hans le Marin* (Fr.) 1950; *The Long Dark Hall* (UK) 1951; *The Four Poster* (US) 1952; *Main Street to Broadway* (cameo; US) 1953; *Feuerwerk* (Ger.) 1954; *Teufel in Seide/Devil in Silk* (Ger.), *Anastasia—Die letzte Zarentochter/Is Anna Anderson Anastasia?* (title role; Ger.) 1956; *Wie ein Sturmwind/Tempestuous Love* (Ger.) 1957; *Montparnasse 19/Modigliani of Montparnasse* (Fr./It.), *Der gläserne Turn/The Glass Tower* (Ger.), *Mädchen in Uniform* (Ger.) 1958; *But Not for Me* (US) 1959; *Conspiracy of Hearts* (UK) 1960; *The Pleasure of His Company* (US), *Leviathan* (Fr.), *Le Rendezvous de Minuit* (Fr.) 1961; *The Counterfeit Traitor* (US), *Adorable Julia* (Fr./Aus.), *L'Amore Difficile/Of Wayward Love* (It./Ger.) 1962; *Finchè dura la Tempesta/Torpedo Bay (It./Fr.), Das grosse Liebesspiel/And So to Bed* (Aus./Ger.), *Miracle of the Wild Stallions* (US) 1963; *Le Grain de Sable* (Fr.) 1964; *Operation Crossbow* (UK/It.), *The Amorous Adventures of Moll Flanders* (UK) 1965; *Jack of Diamonds* (cameo; US/Ger.) 1967; *Sebastian* (UK), *Nobody Runs Forever/The High Commissioner* (UK/US), *Oedipus the King* (as Jocasta; UK) 1968; *De Sade* (US/Ger.), *Hard Contract* (US) 1969; *La Residencia/The House That Screamed* (Sp.) 1970; *Murders in the Rue Morgue* (US/Sp.) 1971; *Lotte in Weimar* (E. Ger.) 1975; *The Boys from Brazil* (US) 1978; *The Holcroft Covenant* (UK) 1985.

Palminteri, Chazz. Actor, playwright, screenwriter. Born Calogero Lorenzo Palminteri, May 16, 1951, in the Bronx, NY. Tall, winning actor most known for his tough wise-guy roles in *A Bronx Tale* (1993), which he adapted for the screen from his own play, as well as his comedic star turn in Woody ALLEN's 1994 offering *Bullets Over Broadway,* for which he was Oscar nominated as best supporting actor. He got his start writing and acting in off-Broadway productions and has since established himself as an actor able to play most any role with great energy and style.

FILMS: *Home Free All* 1983; *The Last Dragon* 1985; *Oscar* 1991; *Innocent Blood, Night and the City, There Goes the*

Neighborhood 1992; *A Bronx Tale* (also sc.) 1993; *Bullets Over Broadway* 1994; *Jade, The Perez Family, The Usual Suspects* 1995; *Diabolique, Faithful* (also sc.), *Mulholland Falls* 1996.

Paltrow, Gwyneth. Actress. Born September 28, 1972, in Los Angeles. *ed.* University of California, Santa Barbara. Luminous, accomplished performer of the American stage and screen. The daughter of actress Blythe DANNER and producer-director Bruce Paltrow, this young leading lady got her start at the Williamstown Theatre in Massachusetts and has quickly become one of the most sought-after actresses working in Hollywood. Behind her dignified appearance, Paltrow has demonstrated a fresh, free-spiritedness, making her performances, notably the title role in *Emma* (1996), memorable.

FILMS: *Hook, Shout* 1991; *Cruel Doubt* 1992; *Flesh and Bone, Malice* 1993; *Mrs. Parker and the Vicious Circle* 1994; *Jefferson in Paris, Moonlight and Valentino, Seven, The Walking Dead* 1995; *The Pallbearer, Emma* 1996; *Great Expectations, Hard Eight* 1997.

Pampanini, Silvana. Actress. Born on Sept. 25, 1925, in Rome. Trained as a concert singer, she entered Italian films in 1947 after winning the Miss Italy beauty title. A voluptuous brunette, she reigned briefly in the early 50s as the "sex goddess" of the Italian screen.

FILMS INCLUDE: *L'Apocalisse, Il Segreto di Don Giovanni/When Love Calls* 1947; *Antonio di Padova/Anthony of Padua, La Forza del Destino* 1949; *Gli Amanti dell'Infinito, La Bisarca* 1950; *Una Bruna indiavolata, OK Nerone/OK Nero* (as Poppea) 1951; *La Donna che inventò l'Amore, Processo alla Città, La Presidentessa/Mademoiselle Gobette, Canzoni di Mezzo Secolo/Half a Century of Song, Viva il Cinema!* 1952; *La Peccatrice dell'Isola/The Island Sinner, Koenigsmark, Un Marito per Anna Zaccheo, Canzoni Canzoni Cazoni/Cavalcade of Song, Noi Cannibali, Il Matrimonio, Amori di Mezzo Secolo* 1953; *Orient Express, Un Giorno in Pretura/A Day in Court, La Schiava del Peccato, La torre del Piacere/La Tour de Nesle* 1954; *La Bella di Roma, Racconti romani, Napoleon* 1955; *Sed de Amor* (Mex.) 1958; *Il Terrore dei Mari/Guns of the Black Witch* 1961; *Il Gaucho* 1964; *Mazzabubu* 1971.

pan. A camera movement on a horizontal plane from one part of a scene to another. A contraction of "panorama" or "panoramic," the term is sometimes used to describe any pivotal movement of the camera. See also TILT.

Pan, Hermes. Dance director. *b.* Hermes Panagiotopolous, 1905 (possibly 1910), Nashville, Tenn. *d.* 1990. Choreographed many of Hollywood's most successful musical films, notably those of Fred Astaire and of Betty Grable, winning an Academy Award for *A Damsel in Distress* (1937). Bearing an uncanny facial and physical resemblance to Astaire, Pan became known as the dancer's alter ego. They worked closely on 17 films and several TV specials, with Pan occasionally doubling for Astaire in long shots. Pan won an Emmy in 1959 for 'An Evening with Fred Astaire.' In 1980 Pan was presented with a National Film Award for achievement in cinema and in 1986 he received a special award from the Joffrey Ballet.

FILMS INCLUDE: *Flying Down to Rio* 1933; *The Gay Divorcee* 1934; *Roberta, Top Hat* 1935; *Follow the Fleet, Swing Time* 1936; *Shall We Dance, A Damsel in Distress* 1937; *Carefree* 1938; *Second Chorus, That Night in Rio, Moon Over Miami* (also dancer), *Sun Valley Serenade, Week-End in Havana, Rise and Shine* 1941; *Song of the Islands, My Gal Sal* (also dancer), *Footlight Serenade, Springtime in the Rockies* 1942; *Coney Island, Sweet Rosie O'Grady* (also dancer) 1943; *Pin Up Girl* (also dancer), *Irish Eyes Are Smiling* 1944; *Diamond Horseshoe* 1945; *Blue Skies* 1946; *I Wonder Who's Kissing Her Now* 1947; *That Lady in Ermine* 1948; *The Barkleys of Broadway* 1949; *Let's Dance, A Life of Her Own* (act. only), *Three Little Words* 1950; *Texas Carnival* 1951; *Lovely to Look At* 1952; *Kiss Me Kate* 1953; *The Student Prince* 1954; *Hit the Deck* 1955; *Meet Me in Las Vegas* 1956; *Silk Stockings, Pal Joey* (also dancer) 1957; *Porgy and Bess* 1959; *Can-Can* 1960; *Flower Drum Song* 1961; *Cleopatra* 1963; *The Pink Panther, My Fair Lady* 1964; *Finian's Rainbow* 1968; *Darling Lili* 1970; *Lost Horizon* 1973.

Panama, Norman. Screenwriter, producer, director. Born on Apr. 21, 1914, in Chicago. *ed.* U. of Chicago. Longtime collaborator of Melvin FRANK, first as screenwriter, then also as producer and director.

FILMS: As screenwriter—See FRANK, Melvin. As director—In collaboration with Melvin Frank (both sharing director, producer, and screenwriter credit): *The Reformer and the Redhead* 1950; *Strictly Dishonorable, Callaway Went Thataway* 1951; *Above and Beyond* 1953; *Knock on Wood* 1954; *The Court Jester, That Certain Feeling* 1956. Directing alone—*The Trap* (also co-prod., co-sc.) 1959; *The Road to Hong Kong* (also co-sc.; US/UK) 1962; *Not with My Wife You Don't!* (also prod., co-story, co-sc.) 1966; *How to Commit Marriage, The Maltese Bippy* 1969; *I Will I Will. . . for Now* (also co-sc.) 1976.

pan-and-tilt head. A fitting on a camera tripod which makes it possible for the camera to move horizontally (PAN) or vertically (TILT) during filming.

Panavision. Trade name for a group of wide-screen processes. The basic system involves the use of 35 mm film and an ANAMORPHIC LENS. Super Panavision, also known as Panavision 70, utilizes 65 mm film without distortion. It was first used in the filming of *Ben-Hur* (1959). Ultra Panavision utilizes 65 mm film and an anamorphic lens.

panchromatic. A photographic emulsion on black-and-white film which is sensitive to all colors in the visible spectrum.

panchromatic master positive. A 35 mm black-and-white print made from a color negative for the purpose of making a black-and-white duplicate negative.

Panfilov, Gleb. Director. Born on Dec. 21, 1934, in Magnitogorsk, Ural Mountains, then the USSR. After graduating in 1957 from the Ural Polytechnical Institute with a degree in chemical engineering, he worked briefly as a factory supervisor but soon got distracted by his growing fascination with the cinema. In 1959 he wrote, directed, and photographed a documentary film, *Join Our Ranks.* Encouraged by the response, he began a correspondence course at VGIK, the state film school, and in 1962–63 wrote and directed three shorts for the Sverdlosk Film Studios, *Mila Melivizinova, Killed at War,* and *The Case of Kurt Clausewitz.* In 1963 he headed for Moscow, where he enrolled at VGIK as a directing student of Yuli RAIZMAN. With his very first feature, *No Ford in the Fire/No Crossing Under Fire* (1968), Panfilov asserted himself as a creative film artist with a voice of his own and the courage to exert it. Like his subsequent films, it subtly examined aspects of life and art in Soviet society. Like them, it generated dramatic tension through character exploration and limited camera movement. And like them, it starred his wife, Inna Churikova. The film won the Grand Prix and best actress prize at the 1969 Locarno Festival. Panfilov's rapidly rising reputation was enhanced by *Nachalo* (1970), known in the West as *The Debut, The Beginning,* or *A Girl from the Factory,* and *Proshu Slova* (1975), variously translated as *I Wish to Speak* or *May I Have the Floor,* the third in an undeclared trilogy of films centering on a woman as the protagonist. In his next film, *Tema/The Theme,* completed in 1980, a woman is the catalyst but a male character takes center stage as the flawed protagonist, a victim of his own weakness within a bureaucratic system that promotes artistic mediocrity and discourages independent expression. A censored version of the film was shown at the 1981 Moscow Festival. It was then shelved, resurfacing briefly at the 1983 Moscow Film Festival, but not officially cleared for release until 1986. It went on to win the Golden Bear, as well as the International Critics Prize at the 1987 Berlin Film Festival. In the intervening years, Panfilov played it safe by making film adaptations of literary works. He scored a success with *Vassa* (1983), adapted from a Gorky play. After a long hiatus, Panfilov resurfaced in 1990 with a new version of Gorky's *Mother.* He writes his own scripts, alone or in collaboration.

FEATURE FILMS (as director-screenwriter): *Vognu Broda net/No Ford in the Fire/No Crossing Under Fire* (also co-sc.) 1968; *Nachalo/The Debut/The Beginning/A Girl from the Factory* 1970; *Proshu Slova/I Wish to Speak/May I Have the Floor?* 1975; *Tema/The Theme* (release delayed to 1986) 1980; *Valentina* 1981; *Vassa* 1983; *Mat'/Mother* (USSR/It.) 1990.

Pangborn, Franklin. Actor. *b.* Jan. 23, 1893, Newark, N.J. *d.* 1958. For many years a dramatic actor on the stage (Messala in *Ben-Hur,* etc.), he is more familiar to cinema audiences in pathetic-comic character roles, typically as a harassed, flustered hotel clerk or store manager. Seen in scores of films, mostly in the 30s and 40s.

FILMS INCLUDE: *Exit Smiling* 1926; *Getting Gertie's Garter, The Night Bride, The Cradle Snatchers, The Rejuvenation of Aunt Mary* 1927; *A Blonde for a Night, My Friend from India, On Trial* 1928; *Lady of the Pavements, The Sap* 1929; *Not So Dumb, A Lady Surrenders* 1930; *International House, Only Yesterday, Design for Living, Flying Down to Rio* 1933; *Cockeyed Cavaliers, College Rhythm* 1934; *Mr. Deeds Goes to Town, My Man Godfrey* 1936; *A Star Is Born, Easy Living, It Happened in Hollywood, Stage Door* 1937; *Mad About Music, Bluebeard's Eighth Wife, Rebecca of Sunnybrook Farm, Joy of Living, Vivacious Lady, Four's a Crowd, Carefree, Just Around the Corner,* 1938; *Topper Takes a Trip, Broadway Serenade, Fifth Avenue Girl* 1939; *Spring Parade, Christmas in July, The Bank Dick* 1940; *The Flame of New Orleans, Never Give a Sucker an Even Break, Sullivan's Travels* 1941; *Now Voyager, The Palm Beach Story* 1942; *Holy Matrimony, Crazy House* 1943; *Hail the Conquering Hero, The Great Moment* 1944; *The Horn Blows at Midnight* 1945; *Two Guys from Milwaukee* 1946; *Addio Mimi/Her Wonderful Lie* (It.), *Mad Wednesday* 1947; *My Dream Is Yours* 1949; *Oh Men! Oh Women!, The Story of Mankind* 1957.

pan glass. A brownish yellow or bluish green filter, typically dangling from a cord around a director's or a cameraman's neck, used for evaluating tone values in a scene about to be shot. Looking through it one can have an approximation of the tonal appearance of the photographed image.

panning gear. In animation, the mechanism that moves a camera or an animation board carrying a panoramic background horizontally or vertically. Each movement receives one exposure.

Panzer, Paul. Actor. *b.* Paul Wolfgang Panzerbeiter, 1872, Wurzburg, Germany, *d.* 1958. A romantic lead of early American silents, he made his mark as a villain in the role of Pearl White's crafty guardian in the 1914 serial *The Perils of Pauline* and subsequently played other screen heavies.

FILMS INCLUDE: *Stolen by Gypsies* 1904; *Romeo and Juliette* (as Romeo), *Antony and Cleopatra* (as Antony), *The Merchant of Venice* 1908; *Sunshine in Poverty Row, The New Magdalen, The Maid of Niagara* 1910; *The Life of Buffalo Bill* (also dir.) 1911; *The Arrowmaker's Daughter* 1912; *The Governor's Double* (dual role), *The Cheapest Way* 1913; *The Perils of Pauline* (serial), *The Last Volunteer* 1914; *The Spender* 1915; *Autumn, The Iron Claw* (serial) 1916; *The Woman the Germans Shot* 1918; *The Mystery Mind* (serial) 1920; *The Bootleggers* 1922; *Unseeing Eyes, Enemies of Women* 1923; *Son of the Sahara, Wages of Virtue* 1924; *The Fool, Thunder Mountain, The Ancient Mariner* (title role) 1925; *Siberia, The Johnstown Flood* 1926; *Sally in Our Alley, The Girl from Chicago* 1927; *Glorious Betsy, George Washington Cohen* 1928; *The Black Book* (serial), *Redskin, Hawk of the Hills* 1929; *Der Tanz geht weiter* (German-language version of *Those Who Dance*) 1930; *The Montana Kid* 1931; *A Bedtime Story* 1933; *Bolero* 1934; *Beasts of Berlin* 1939; *Hotel Berlin, Mildred Pierce* 1945; *A Stolen Life* 1946; *The Perils of Pauline* 1947; *A Kiss in the Dark* 1949.

Papas, Irene. Actress. Born Irene Lelekou, on Mar. 9, 1926, in Chiliomodion, Greece. A striking woman and superb tragedienne in the classic Greek tradition, she started her career in her teens as a singer-dancer in variety shows. In films since the early 50s, she has played leading parts and pivotal supporting roles in many international productions and has appeared frequently on the American stage and screen.

FILMS INCLUDE: *Lost Angels* (Gr.) 1950; *Necropolitia/Dead City* (Gr.) 1951; *Le Infedeli* (It.), *Dramma nella Casbah/The Man from Cairo* (It./US) 1953; *Theodora Imperatrice di Bisanzio/Theodora Slave Empress* (It.), *Attila* (It.) 1954; *Tribute to a Bad Man* (US) 1956; *Antigone* (title role; Gr.) 1960; *The Guns of Navarone* (UK/US) 1961; *Electra* (title role; Gr.) 1962; *The Moon-Spinners* (UK/US), *Zorba the Greek* (Gr./US) 1964; *Mas alla de las Montanas/The Desperate Ones* (Sp./US), *A ciascuno il suo/We Still Kill the Old Way* (It.) 1967; *The Brotherhood* (US) 1968; *Z* (Fr./Alg.), *Anne of the Thousand Days* (as Queen Catherine of Aragon; UK/US), *A Dream of Kings* (US) 1969; *The Trojan Women* (as Helen of Troy; Gr./US), *Roma Bene* (It./Fr.) 1971; *Le Faro da Padre/Bambina* (It.) 1974; *Moses* (as Zipporah; UK/It.), *The Message/Mohammad Messenger of God* (UK) 1976; *Iphigenia* (as Clytemnestra; Gr.) 1977; *Bloodline* (US), *Cristo si e fermato a Eboli* (It./Fr.) 1979; *Lion of the Desert* (Libya/UK) 1980; *Erendira* (Pan./Fr.) 1983; *Into the Night* (US), *The Assissi Underground* (It./UK) 1985; *Sweet Country* (Pan./Gr.) 1986; *High Season* (UK), *Cronica de una Muerte anunciada/Chronicle of a Death Foretold* (It./Fr.) 1987; *Island* (Austral.) 1989; *Drums of Fire* (UK), *Banquet* (US) 1991; *Zoe* (UK) 1992; *Up Down and Sideways* 1993.

Papatakis, Nico. Director. Born on July 18, 1918, in Addis Ababa, Ethiopia, of Greek parents. In Paris from an early age, he ran a prosperous Left Bank night spot before making a stunning debut as a film director in 1963 with *Les Abysses.* Ostensibly a dramatization of a true story about two housemaids who in a state of hysteria suddenly turned on their masters in a bloodbath of murder (the same event that provided the plot for Jean Genêt's play *The Maids*), the film contained subtle references to sensitive areas in French social and political life, including the war in Algeria. It caused near riots during its original release and its presentation at the 1963 Cannes Festival. Despite the excellence of the production, Papatakis was unable to get another directing assignment in France. He made only three other films, in the span of the next 23 years. He was formerly married to actress Anouk AIMÉE.

FILMS: *Les Abysses* (Fr.) 1963; *Les Pâtres du Désordre/Thanos and Despina/The Shepherds of Confusion* (also sc.; Fr./Gr.) 1968; *Gloria Mundi* (also sc.) 1975; *I Photographia/The Photograph* (also sc.) 1986.

Paquin, Anna. Actress. Born 1982 in Wellington, NZ. Engaging, knowing-beyond-her-years young actress who attained major attention early on for her riveting portrayal of the articulate, emotionally complicated daughter in Jane CAMPION's *The Piano* (1993) for which she earned the best supporting actress Academy Award. One of the youngest performers to have received the honor, she has gone on to prove herself a strong, capable actress.

FILMS: *The Piano* 1993; *Fly Away Home, Jane Eyre* 1996.

Paradjanov (also Paradzhanov), Sergei. Director. *b.* Sarkis Paradjanian (or Paradjanian), Mar. 18, 1924, Tiflis (Tbilisi), Georgia, USSR, of Armenian descent. *d.* 1990. A multifaceted artist—painter, musician, and filmmaker—he attended the Kiev Conservatory of Music for three years (1942–45), intending to become a singer, then switched over to VGIK, the Moscow film institute, where he studied directing under Igor SAVCHENKO and Lev KULESHOV. From the start, with his 1951 graduation short *Moldavian Fairy Tale,* he demonstrated his great love for folk poetry, which would become the cornerstone of his film career. Assigned to the Kiev studios in the Ukraine, he turned out films notable for their lyrical inspiration and great esthetic beauty. At first conceding grudgingly to the official taste for social realism, Paradjanov unchained himself of all restrictions with *Shadows of Our Forgotten Ancestors* (1964), an exquisitely rich film which wove, through stunning imagery, a regionally flavored, brooding tale of love and betrayal in a 19th-century Carpathian village. The film enjoyed great success on the international festival circuit, winning the Grand Prix at Mar del Plata and the British Academy Award for best foreign production. But it infuriated Soviet authorities with its "decadent" formalism and political symbolism. In disfavor and out of work, Paradjanov made matters worse for himself by vocally supporting political dissidents. After being arrested and later released on charges of Ukrainian nationalism, he was exiled to the Amo Bek-Nazarov studios in Armenia, where his scripts and project proposals were repeatedly rejected. The only exception was *Sayat Nova/The Color of Pomegranates,* a film ballad of sumptuous beauty about the troubled life of a rebellious 18th-century Armenian poet-minstrel. The film was shot in 1969 but was promptly banned and only given a half-hearted release, in a heavily censored form, several years later. Thereafter, Paradjanov became the victim of constant harassment by the authorities. He was barred from films and arrested numerous times on trumped-up charges, ranging from homosexuality and spreading veneral diseases to fraud, black marketeering, and "incitement to suicide." He was convicted in 1974 and sentenced to five years of hard labor. A rising wave of international protest finally led to his release in 1978. Paradjanov returned to Tiflis, where he stayed with relatives, barely surviving by selling old possessions. He was denied an exit visa or access to foreigners, and in 1982 was jailed briefly on unspecified charges. The advent of Gorbachev's glasnost enabled Paradjanov to resume his career as a feature director in 1985, but five years later he died of lung cancer at age 66 before realizing a projected autobiographical film, *Confession.* His prison memories served as a basis for the film *Swan Lake—The Zone* (1990), directed by his brilliant cameraman Yuri Illienko. Paradjanov wrote his own screenplays, alone or in collaboration.

FILMS: *Moldavian Fairy Tale* (diploma short) 1951; *Andriesh* (co-dir. with Y. Bzelian) 1954; *The First Lad* 1958; *Ukrainian Rhapsody* 1961; *The Stone Flower* 1963; *Dumka/The Ballad* 1964; *Shadows of Our Forgotten Ancestors* 1965; *Sayat Nova/The Color of Pomegranates/Red Pomegranate* (release delayed to 1972) 1969; *Return to Life* (short) 1978; *The Legend of the Suram Fortress* (co-dir. with Dodo Abashidze) 1985; *Arabesques on Themes from Pirsomani* (doc.) 1986; *Ashik Kerib* 1988; *Swan Lake—The Zone* (story basis only) 1990.

parallax. The apparent displacement between an area observed through a camera viewfinder and the area actually being photographed. The phenomenon is a source of annoyance to cameramen when shooting close-ups with a camera equipped with a separate viewfinder lens rather than with a through-the-lens viewing system. Adjustments in the position of the camera must be made to allow for the displacement.

parallel. An elevated platform on wheels designed to raise a camera and its crew above ground for taking high-angle shots. It can also support overhead lights.

parallel action. A narrative technique utilizing alternate shots of separate actions to suggest they are taking place simultaneously—for example, shots of Indians attacking settlers alternating with shots of the cavalry coming to the rescue. The technique is basic to motion picture editing and is used both for creating suspense and for condensing the passage of time in the construction of a sequence.

parallelism. In motion picture theory, the term has been used to describe a parallel relationship between an image and its corresponding sound track—for instance, a shot of a person speaking accompanied by a sound track of his synchronized recorded voice. The visual and aural elements support or repeat each other. The opposite situation, when images do not parallel the accompanying sound track, has been termed COUNTERPOINT.

Paramount. An American motion picture production and distribution company. For many years one of Hollywood's major studios, Paramount traces its history back to 1912, when Adolph ZUKOR, a furrier, founded the Famous Players Film Company with the profits he had made as the American distributor of the French film *Queen Elizabeth,* starring Sarah Bernhardt. The company's greatest asset was Mary PICKFORD, already a popular star and well on her way to becoming "America's Sweetheart." In 1914, Zukor entrusted the distribution of his films to a newly formed company, Paramount Pictures Corporation, which had been founded that year by W. W. Hodkinson, a veteran of the General Film Company and the spearhead of "Edison's Trust." Paramount also took over the distribution of the films of the Jesse L. LASKY Feature Play Company, which had been formed in 1913 by vaudeville musician Lasky, glove salesman Samuel Goldfish (later Sam GOLDWYN), and aspiring playwright Cecil B. DE MILLE. They enjoyed an immediate success with their first venture, *The Squaw Man,* released early in 1914, the first feature-length film ever made in Hollywood.

In 1916, Zukor's Famous Players and Lasky's company merged to form the Famous Players-Lasky Corporation. Zukor was named president and Lasky vice president in charge of production. In the following year 12 other production companies merged with Famous Players-Lasky. In another merger, the company acquired a distribution arm by absorbing Artcraft and Paramount Pictures Corporation. In 1919 the company started a theater acquisition program that within a decade put it in control of hundreds of motion picture theaters throughout the US. In 1927 the corporate name was changed to Paramount Famous Lasky Corporation and in 1930 to Paramount Publix Corporation.

The company rapidly developed into a major studio. During the silent era it employed such stars as Gloria Swanson, Mary Miles Minter, Pola Negri, Mae Murray, Marguerite Clark, Clara Bow, Rudolph Valentino, Wallace Reid, Douglas Fairbanks, and John Barrymore. In one year, 1923, it produced two of the biggest moneymakers in the history of film, James Cruze's *The Covered Wagon* and De Mille's *The Ten Commandments.* B. P. SCHULBERG, who took over as head of production in 1925, discovered and developed such new stars as Gary Cooper, Claudette Colbert, Fredric March, and George

Raft. From Germany, he brought over Emil Jannings and Marlene Dietrich. By the early 30s he had under contract such distinguished directors as Josef von Sternberg, Ernst Lubitsch, and Rouben Mamoulian, and such talented art directors as Hans Dreier and Ernst Fegte.

Despite the company's continued prestige, the consistent high quality of its films, and frequent box-office hits, Paramount had a reputation for financial instability. The company's financial position became particularly precarious during the transition to sound. The crisis resulted in the ousting of both Lasky and Schulberg in the midst of a major executive shuffle. In 1933, Paramount Publix was declared bankrupt by a New York Federal District Court, but it was re-organized in 1935 as Paramount Pictures, Inc. The company was soon back on its feet, thanks to the profits from a string of entertaining light films starring, among others, Mae West, W. C. Fields, Bing Crosby, Bob Hope, Dorothy Lamour, Fred MacMurray, Ray Milland, Gary Cooper, Claudette Colbert, and Jean Arthur.

The return of De Mille to the Paramount fold after a period of self-exile also proved beneficial, as did the work of Mitchell Leisen, an excellent and much underrated director of lightweight fare. In the 40s, Paramount's roster of directors was buttressed by the addition of Preston Sturges, a master of sophisticated comedy, and the versatile, highly talented Billy Wilder, and his collaborator Charles Brackett. New stars on the payroll included Alan Ladd, Veronica Lake, and Paulette Goddard. In 1947 producer Hal Wallis joined Paramount and counterbalanced the company's emphasis on light escapist entertainment with a series of melodramas starring new discoveries like Burt Lancaster, Lizabeth Scott, and Kirk Douglas. Paramount's biggest hit of the decade was Leo McCarey's *Going My Way* (1944), the winner of numerous Academy Awards.

In 1949, along with other major Hollywood companies, Paramount was forced by government action to divest itself of its large chain of theaters. Despite this blow and the growing competition from television, the company enjoyed relative prosperity thanks to the enormous popularity of its new comedy team, Martin and Lewis, the solid profits of De Mille's remake of *The Ten Commandments,* and such high-quality films as William Wyler's *The Heiress* and *Detective Story,* George Stevens's *Shane,* Billy Wilder's *Stalag 17* and *Sabrina,* and Alfred Hitchcock's *Rear Window, Vertigo,* and *Psycho.* In 1954, Paramount introduced VistaVision, its own wide-screen answer to the threat of TV and Fox's CinemaScope.

In 1966, Paramount became a subsidiary of Gulf & Western Industries. In the 60s and early 70s Paramount suffered symptoms similar to those afflicting all other major Hollywood studios. Production dropped sharply and quality varied greatly from one film to the next. With Robert EVANS at the helm as head of production, the studio enjoyed the fruits of such box-office hits as *Love Story* (1970), *The Godfather* (1972), and *The Godfather Part II* (1974), but incurred losses on many other films. The ebb and flow continued after Evans's departure in 1975 and the installment of Barry DILLER as chief executive. After a brief period of decline, Paramount bounced back to economic health and in 1978 set a new industry record for domestic film rentals, $290 million, mainly from the box-office receipts of *Grease, Saturday Night Fever,* and *Heaven Can Wait.*

In 1983, Martin S. Davis became the chairman and CEO of the parent company, Gulf & Western. In 1984, Diller was replaced as studio boss by Frank MANCUSO, a Paramount executive who had risen through the ranks. Paramount continued to play a dominant role in the film business throughout the 80s and into the 90s, thanks in part to the financial strength of its conglomerate parent company. Paramount films of this period included *Raiders of the Lost Ark* (1981) and its sequels, *Star Trek* (1979) and its sequels, *Beverly Hills Cop* (1984), *Crocodile Dundee* (1986), *Top Gun* (1986), *Fatal Attraction* (1987), *Ghost* (1990), *The Hunt for Red October* (1990), *The Addams Family* (1991), and *Wayne's World* (1992).

In 1989 Gulf & Western changed its name to Paramount Communications. Davis continued to serve as chairman and CEO of the parent organization, with Stanley Jaffe named president and COO in 1991. In 1991, Frank Mancuso was ousted as chairman of the movie division, Paramount Pictures, and replaced by Brandon Tartikoff, a former NBC executive, who was in turn replaced by Sherry Lansing 15 months later.

In 1993, the media company Viacom made a friendly multibillion-dollar offer to buy Paramount Communications, but its move was countered by a hostile bid from the home shopping concern QVC Network, headed by former Paramount studio boss Diller, a longtime foe of Davis. In the drawn-out, high-profile struggle that ensued, Viacom gained control in 1994, keeping Lansing on as head of production.

Paré, Michael. Actor. Born on Oct. 9, 1959, in Brooklyn, N.Y. Ruggedly handsome leading man of American TV and films. A graduate of the Culinary Institute of America in Hyde Park, N.Y., he was a chef and a model before starting his acting career in the TV series 'The Greatest American Hero' (1981–83). He made a successful feature debut as an actor and singer in *Eddie and the Cruisers* (1983), but appeared mainly in low-budget productions in the US and abroad.

FILMS: *Eddie and the Cruisers, Undercover* (Austral.) 1983; *Streets of Fire, The Philadelphia Experiment* 1984; *Space Rage* 1985; *Instant Justice* (Gibraltar), *The Women's Club* 1987; *World Gone Wild* 1988; *Eddie and the Cruisers II: Eddie Lives* (Can.) 1989; *The Closer, Il Sole Buio* (It.), *Moon 44* (Ger.) 1990; *Into the Sun, The Last Hour, Killing Streets* 1991; *First Light, Into the Sun* 1992; *Warriors* (Can./Isr.) 1994; *Raging Angels, Village of the Damned* 1995; *Bad Moon* 1996.

Paris, Henry. See METZGER, Radley.

Paris, Jerry. Actor, director. *b.* July 25, 1925, San Francisco. *d.* 1986, of brain tumor. *ed.* Actors Studio. Tall character actor of many films and TV episodes, he played Dick Van Dyke's neighbor on TV for five years before he took over as director of the Van Dyke series in 1966. Encouraged by an Emmy Award, he went on to direct other TV shows, then turned to feature films and TV movies. He directed many episodes of the popular TV series 'Happy Days.'

FILMS INCLUDE: As actor—*Outrage, Cyrano de Bergerac, The Flying Missile* 1950; *Call Me Mister* 1951; *Sabre Jet* 1953; *The Wild One, The Caine Mutiny* 1954; *Marty, The View from Pompey's Head, Good Morning Miss Dove* 1955; *D-Day the Sixth of June* 1956; *Zero Hour* 1957; *The Lady Takes a Flyer, Sing Boy Sing, The Naked and the Dead* 1958; *The Great Imposter* 1961. As associate producer—*The Caretakers* (also co-story). As director (complete)—*Don't Raise the Bridge—Lower the River, Never a Dull Moment, How Sweet It Is!* 1968; *Viva Max!* 1969; *The Grasshopper* 1970; *Star Spangled Girl* 1971; *Leo and Loree* (also act.) 1980; *Police Academy Two: Their First Assignment* 1985; *Police Academy Three: Back in Training* 1986.

Parke, Harry. See PARKYAKARKUS.

Parker, Alan. Director. Born on Feb. 14, 1944, in Islington, London, England. He entered advertising as an office boy, directly out of high school. Moving from one agency to another in a span of several years, he eventually became a copywriter. An association with would-be producer David PUTTNAM, then an advertising executive, led in 1966 to Parker's first film assignment, a screenplay for the feature *Melody,* which wasn't released until 1971. In the interim, Parker began directing TV commercials. With another advertising colleague, Alan MARSHALL, who would become his career-long producer, Parker launched in 1970 a thriving commercial production house, one of Britain's most prestigious. Turning to fiction films, Parker directed two shorts, *Footsteps* and *Our Cissy* (both 1973) and the BBC-TV featurette *No Hard Feelings* and full-length teleplay 'The Evacuees' (1975). Their success led to his first feature film, *Bugsy Malone* (1976), a coy musical spoof of prohibition-era gangster movies in which all characters were played by children. With his next feature, *Midnight Express* (1978), Parker established himself as a front-rank director. A powerful, if manipulative, semifactual drama of the brutal treatment of a young American jailed in Turkey for drug smuggling, the riveting film was tightly constructed and well paced, with authentic touches that gave a believable aura to a far-fetched script. Parker and the picture were nominated for Oscars. The screenplay, by Oliver Stone, won the Academy Award.

Parker's next film, *Fame* (1980), was entirely different in mood and style. Made for Hollywood, it was a fictionalized, emotionally charged but finally upbeat musical account of the varied lives of students at Manhattan's High School for the Performing Arts. It was a huge box-office hit, spawning a successful TV series. Once again changing pace, Parker next filmed *Shoot the Moon,* a sincerely observed drama about the breakup of a marriage. Returning to England, he risked his growing reputation on *Pink Floyd—The Wall* (1982), a strikingly original, if self-indulgent, metaphorical visual rendition of a best-selling rock album. Even more daringly unique was *Birdy* (1985), an adaptation of William Wharton's allegorical novel about an emotionally scarred Vietnam vet who hallucinates about flying. It won the Special Grand Prize at the Cannes Film Festival. Many critics clobbered *Angel Heart* (1987), especially for its far-fetched script. But like much of Parker's work, it is a hauntingly mesmerizing film whose imagery lingers in memory long after viewing. Parker was nominated for a second Academy Award as best director for *Mississippi Burning* (1988), a vivid recreation of the civil rights struggle of the 60s. It was a hit, both critically and commercially. Continuing his diversified film interests, Parker directed *The Commitments* (1991), a rousing look at the rise of an Irish band. The film was an international success and spawned a hit sound track consisting of cover versions of classic soul tracks. Another of his films with a hit sound track was the long-awaited screen adaptation of the Andrew Lloyd Weber smash musical *Evita* (1996), a film most Hollywood insiders thought would never get made.

Parker wrote the children's books *Puddles in the Rain* (1977) and *Hares in the Gate* (1983) and the chronicle *A Filmmaker's Diary* (1984). In 1985 he directed for British TV the documentary *A Turnip Head's Guide to the British Cinema*.

FEATURE FILMS: *Bugsy Malone* (also sc.) 1976; *Midnight Express* 1978; *Fame* (US) 1980; *Shoot the Moon* (US) 1981; *Pink Floyd—The Wall* 1982; *Birdy* (US) 1985; *Angel Heart* (also sc.) 1987; *Mississippi Burning* (US) 1988; *Come See the Paradise* (US) 1990; *The Commitments* (also cameo) 1991; *The Road to Wellville* (also co-prod., sc.) 1994; *Evita* 1996.

Parker, Albert. Director. *b.* 1889, Brooklyn, N.Y. *d.* 1974. The son of the American representative of a British company, he traveled frequently to England as a child. At 17 he worked briefly for his father, then at Macy's, before pursuing an acting career on the stage. He entered films in 1916 as a supporting player in two Douglas Fairbanks vehicles, *American Aristocracy* (1916) and *In Again—Out Again* (1917). Moving behind the camera, he directed Fairbanks and such stars as Gloria Swanson, Norma Talmadge, Clara Kimball Young, and John Barrymore in a string of successful silents. He is best known as the director of *Sherlock Holmes* (1922), with Barrymore in the title role, and *The Black Pirate* (1926), a spectacular Fairbanks swashbuckler that made cinematic history as the first film made in two-color Technicolor. Parker's directing career faded with the advent of sound. After serving as dialogue director on one talkie, he became a talent scout for Fox. In 1936 he moved to England, where he directed two routine thrillers before becoming a talent agent, representing James Mason and other top British stars. After his 1946 divorce from American actress Margaret Greene, his wife from 1911, Parker married British actress Margaret Johnston.

FILMS: *Her Excellency the Governor, The Food Gamblers, The Man Hater, For Valor* 1917; *The Other Woman, From Two to Six, Annexing Bill, Waifs, Sifting Sands, Secret Code, Arizona* 1918; *The Knickerbocker Buckaroo* (also co-sc.), *Eyes of Youth* (also sc.) 1919; *The Branded Woman* 1920; *Love's Redemption* 1921; *Sherlock Holmes* 1922; *Second Youth, The Rejected Woman* 1924; *The Black Pirate* 1926; *The Love of Sunya* 1927; *Follow the Leader* (dial. dir. only) 1930; *Murder in the Family, Second Thoughts/The Crime of Peter Frame* 1938.

Parker, Cecil. Actor. *b.* Cecil Schwabe, Sept. 3, 1897, Hastings, England. *d.* 1971. Stiff-upper-lipped character player of the British stage and screen. He took an interest in acting after his return from WW I military service, making his professional debut in 1922. He first appeared on the London stage in 1925 and in films in 1929. On the screen, he usually played men of position and influence, sometimes in the lead.

FILMS INCLUDE: *The Woman in White* 1929; *A Cuckoo in the Nest* 1933; *The Silver Spoon* 1934; *The Man Who Changed His Mind/The Man Who Lived Again* 1936; *Storm in a Teacup* 1937; *The Lady Vanishes, The Citadel, Housemaster* 1938; *The Stars Look Down* 1939; *Dangerous Moonlight/Suicide Squadron, Ships with Wings* 1941; *Caesar and Cleopatra* (as Britannus) 1945; *The Magic Bow, Hungry Hill* 1946; *Captain Boycott* (title role), *The Woman in the Hall* 1947; *Quartet* (lead in "The Colonel's Lady" episode), *The Weaker Sex* (lead) 1948; *Under Capricorn* (UK/US), *The Chiltern Hundreds/The Amazing Mr. Beecham* (lead), *Dear Mr. Prohack* (lead) 1949; *Tony Draws a Horse* (lead) 1950; *The Man in the White Suit, The Magic Box* 1951; *I Believe in You* (lead) 1952; *Father Brown/The Detective* 1954; *The Ladykillers, The Constant Husband* 1955; *The Court Jester* (US), *23 Paces to Baker Street* (US), *It's Great to Be Young* 1956; *The Admirable Crichton* (as Lord Loam) 1957; *Indiscreet* (US/UK), *A Tale of Two Cities* (as Jarvis Lorry), *I Was Monty's Double* 1958; *The Wreck of the Mary Deare* (US) 1959; *A French Mistress* (lead), *The Swiss Family Robinson* (US/UK), *The Pure Hell of St. Trinian's* 1960; *The Amorous Prawn/The Playgirl and the War Minister* (lead) 1962; *Heavens Above!* 1963; *Guns at Batasi* 1964; *The Amorous Adventures of Moll Flanders, A Study in Terror, Lady L* (US/Fr./It.) 1965; *Circus of Fear/Psycho-Circus* 1967; *Oh! What a Lovely War* 1969.

Parker, Claire. See ALEXEIFF, Alexandre.

Parker, Dorothy. Poet, satirist, short-story writer, screenwriter. *b.* Dorothy Rothschild, Aug. 22, 1893, West End, N.J. *d.* 1967. A celebrated wit of American literary circles, she collaborated on a number of screenplays.

FILMS INCLUDE (as screenwriter in collaboration): *Here is My Heart* (uncredited) 1934; *One Hour Late, The Big Broadcast of 1936* (co-songs only), *Paris in Spring* (co-songs only), *Hands Across the Table* (co-song only), *Mary Burns Fugitive* (co-song only) 1935; *The Moon's Our Home* (co-addnl. dial. only), *Suzy, Three Married Men, Lady Be Careful* 1936; *A*

Star Is Born, Woman Chases Man 1937; *Sweethearts* 1938; *Trade Winds* 1939; *The Little Foxes* (co-addnl. dial. only), *Weekend for Three* 1941; *Saboteur* 1942; *Smash-Up* (co-story only) 1947; *The Fan* 1949; *A Star Is Born* (remake based on her collaboration on the script of the original version in 1937) 1954.

Parker, Eleanor. Actress. Born on June 26, 1922, in Cedarville, Ohio. Ravishing redheaded leading lady of Hollywood films of the 40s and 50s. She was put under contract by Warner Bros. following some experience on the Cleveland stage, in stock, and with the Pasadena Playhouse. She played increasingly important roles in the studio's films of the 40s and reached her career peak in the 50s with MGM. Talented as well as beautiful, she played an assortment of leads, ranging from shrewish vixens to long-suffering wives, but her performances were sometimes marred by a tendency to overact. She was nominated for Oscars as best actress for *Caged* (1950), *Detective Story* (1951), and *Interrupted Melody* (1955). Four-times married, Parker is the mother of four.

FILMS: *They Died with Their Boots On* (bit) 1941; *Busses Roar* 1942; *Mission to Moscow, The Mysterious Doctor* 1943; *Between Two Worlds, Crime by Night, The Last Ride, The Very Thought of You, Hollywood Canteen* 1944; *Pride of the Marines* 1945; *Of Human Bondage* (as Mildred Rogers), *Never Say Goodbye* 1946; *Escape Me Never, Always Together* (cameo) 1947; *The Voice of the Turtle, The Woman in White* (in dual role) 1948; *It's a Great Feeling* (cameo) 1949; *Chain Lightning, Caged, Three Secrets* 1950; *Valentino, A Millionaire for Christy, Detective Story* 1951; *Scaramouche* 1952; *Above and Beyond, Escape from Fort Bravo* 1953; *The Naked Jungle, Valley of the Kings* 1954; *Many Rivers to Cross, Interrupted Melody* (as opera singer Marjorie Lawrence), *The Man with the Golden Arm* 1955; *The King and Four Queens* 1956; *Lizzie, The Seventh Sin* 1957; *A Hole in the Head* 1959; *Home from the Hill* 1960; *Return to Peyton Place* 1961; *Madison Avenue* 1962; *Panic Button* 1964; *The Sound of Music* 1965; *The Oscar, An American Dream* 1966; *Warning Shot, The Tiger and the Pussycat* 1967; *Eye of the Cat* 1969; *Sunburn* 1979.

Parker, Fess. Actor. Born on Aug. 16, 1925, in Fort Worth, Tex. *ed.* U. of Texas; USC. Rugged, wholesome leading man of Hollywood action films; a former college athlete. Best known for TV and screen incarnation of pioneer heroes Davy Crockett (on TV 1954–55) and Daniel Boone (1964–70). He also starred in the TV series 'Mr. Smith Goes to Washington' (1962–63). Retiring from acting in the mid-70s, he went into business and real estate.

FILMS INCLUDE: *Untamed Frontier, Springfield Rifle* 1952; *The Kid from Left Field, Island in the Sky* 1953; *Them* 1954; *Battle Cry, Davy Crockett—King of the Wild Frontier* (title role) 1955; *Davy Crockett and the River Pirates* (title role), *The Great Locomotive Chase* 1956; *Westward Ho the Wagons* 1957; *Old Yeller, The Light in the Forest* 1958; *The Hangman, The Jayhawkers* 1959; *Hell Is for Heroes* 1962; *Smoky* 1966.

Parker, Jean. Actress. Born Luise Stephanie Zelinska, on Aug. 11, 1912, in Butte, Mont. Pleasantly pretty leading lady of Hollywood films of the 30s and early 40s. She started her career at 20 with MGM and for several years played mainly ingenues in distress. Her career declined after she left the studio in the late 30s and she appeared mostly in B productions until her retirement in 1944. She was seen in several stage productions, on Broadway and in stock, before returning to the screen for occasional supporting roles in the early 50s. Her fourth husband (1951–57) was actor Robert LOWERY.

FILMS INCLUDE: *Divorce in the Family* 1932; *The Secret of Madame Blanche, Gabriel Over the White House, What Price Innocence?, Made on Broadway, Storm at Daybreak, Lady for a Day, Little Women* (as Beth) 1933; *Two Alone, You Can't Buy Everything, Lazy River, Operator 13, Caravan, Limehouse Blues, A Wicked Woman* 1934; *Sequoia, Princess O'Hara, Murder in the Fleet, The Ghost Goes West* (UK) 1935; *The Texas Rangers* 1936; *Life Begins with Love, The Barrier* 1937; *Penitentiary, The Arkansas Traveler* 1938; *Romance of the Redwoods, Zenobia, Parents on Trial, The Flying Deuces* 1939; *Knights of the Range, Beyond Tomorrow* 1940; *Roar of the Press, Power Dive, No Hands on the Clock* 1941; *Torpedo Boat, I Live on Danger* 1942; *High Explosive, Deerslayer* 1943; *Lady in the Death House, Detective Kitty O'Day, Dead Man's Eyes, Bluebeard, One Body Too Many* 1944; *Adventures of Kitty O'Day* 1945; *The Gunfighter* 1950; *Those Redheads from Seattle* 1953; *Black Tuesday, A Lawless Street* 1955; *The Parson and the Outlaw* 1957; *Apache Uprising* 1966; *Stigma* 1972.

Parker, Mary-Louise. Actress. Born in 1964. Wide-eyed player of screen, often in quiet roles. Established presence as mistreated wife turned café owner in *Fried Green Tomatoes*.

FILMS INCLUDE: *Signs of Life* 1989; *Longtime Companion* 1990; *Grand Canyon* 1991; *Fried Green Tomatoes* 1992; *Mr. Wonderful* 1993; *Bullets Over Broadway, The Client, Naked in New York* 1994; *Boys On the Side, Reckless* 1995; *The Portrait of a Lady* 1996.

Parker, Sarah Jessica. Born on March 25, 1965, in Nelsonville, Ohio. Spirited, saucy lead of screen, stage, and TV. A professional performer since her youth, she danced with the Cincinnati Ballet and the American Ballet Theatre and played the title role in *Annie* for two years on Broadway before her film debut. Always memorable, especially as the girlfriend-as-gambling-payoff in *Honeymoon in Vegas*. Also appeared in several TV series in the 1980s. Married to actor Matthew BRODERICK.

FILMS INCLUDE: *Rich Kids* 1979; *Somewhere Tomorrow* 1983; *Footloose* 1984; *Girls Just Want to Have Fun* 1985; *Flight of the Navigator* 1986; *L.A. Story* 1991; *Honeymoon in Vegas* 1992; *Hocus Pocus, Striking Distance* 1993; *Ed Wood* 1994; *Miami Rhapsody* 1995; *Extreme Measures, First Wives Club, If Lucy Fell, Mars Attacks!, The Substance of Fire* 1996; *Til There Was You* 1997.

Parker, Suzy. Actress. Born Cecilia Parker, on Oct. 28, 1933, in San Antonio, Tex. A top high-fashion model of the 50s, she brought her tall figure and prominent cheekbones to the screen late in that decade but failed to click as a film star, despite two good opportunities as a leading lady to Cary Grant and Gary Cooper. She is married to actor Bradford DILLMAN.

FILMS: *Funny Face, Kiss Them for Me* 1957; *Ten North Frederick* 1958; *The Best of Everything* 1959; *Circle of Deception* 1961; *The Interns* 1962; *Flight from Ashiya* 1964; *Chamber of Horrors* 1966.

Parker, Willard. Actor. Born Worster Van Eps, on Feb. 5, 1912, in New York City. Tall, wavy-haired leading man and second lead of Hollywood action films. Former tennis pro. He also starred in the TV series 'Tales of the Texas Rangers' (1958–59). Married since 1951 to actress Virginia Field.

FILMS INCLUDE: *That Certain Woman* 1937; *A Slight Case of Murder* 1938; *What a Woman!* 1943; *The Fighting Guardsman* 1945; *Renegades* 1946; *The Mating of Millie, The Wreck of the Hesperus, Relentless, You Gotta Stay Happy* 1948; *Slightly French, Bodyhold* 1949; *Hunt the Man Down, David Harding—Counterspy, Emergency Wedding* 1950; *My True Story, Apache Drums* 1951; *Sangaree, Kiss Me Kate, The Great Jesse James Raid* 1953; *The Naked Gun* 1956; *Lone Texan* 1959; *Walk Tall, The High-Powered Rifle, Young Jesse James* (as Cole Younger) 1960; *Air Patrol* 1962; *The Earth Dies Screaming* (UK) 1964; *Waco* 1966.

Parkins, Barbara. Actress. Born on May 22, 1942, in

Vancouver, B.C., Canada. Slim brunette leading lady of Hollywood and international films. She co-starred in the TV series 'Peyton Place' (1964–69).

FILMS INCLUDE: *20,000 Eyes* 1961; *Valley of the Dolls* 1967; *The Kremlin Letter* 1970; *The Mephisto Waltz, La Maison sous les Arbres/The Deadly Trap* (Fr.), *Puppet on a Chain* (UK) 1971; *Christina* (UK) 1974; *Shout at the Devil* (UK) 1976; *The Disappearance* (UK) 1977; *The Magician of Lublin* (Isr./Ger.) 1979; *Bear Island* (UK/Can.) 1980.

Parks, Gordon. Director, author, composer, photographer. Born on Nov. 30, 1912, in Fort Scott, Kans. *ed.* Kansas State. Hollywood's first black director of major films. The youngest of 15 children in a poor farm family, he was in turn a busboy in Chicago, a piano player in a Minnesota bordello, a Harlem dope runner, and a professional basketball player before settling on a 20-year stint (1948–68) as a *Life* magazine photographer-reporter. While in Paris he wrote two autobiographical books, one of which served as a basis for his first feature, *The Learning Tree* (1969). The film, a mild memoir of growing up black in Kansas, was among the first 25 productions designated "culturally, historically, or esthetically significant" for inclusion in the National Film Registry of the Library of Congress. Earlier he had directed three shorts. He scored a huge commercial hit with his second feature, *Shaft.* Parks has written several volumes of poetry and fiction and has composed music for the concert hall as well as for films. His son, Gordon Parks, Jr., who directed the films *Superfly* (1972), *Thomasine and Bushrod* and *Three the Hard Way* (both 1974), and *Aaron Loves Angela* (1975) was killed in 1979, at the age of 44, in a small-plane crash near Nairobi, Kenya, while scouting locations for a film.

FILMS (as director): *The Learning Tree* (also prod., sc., music) 1969; *Shaft* 1971; *Shaft's Big Score* 1972; *The Super Cops* 1974; *Leadbelly* 1976; *Solomon Northup's Odyssey* (TV movie) 1985.

Parks, Larry. *b.* Samuel Lawrence Klausman Parks, Dec. 13, 1914, Olathe, Kans. *d.* 1975. *ed.* U. of Illinois. A former Carnegie Hall usher and bit stage player, he began in the early 40s what seemed to be a terminal career as a small-time Hollywood actor but shot to sudden fame in 1946 impersonating Al Jolson in *The Jolson Story,* then in its sequel, *Jolson Sings Again* (1949). His career plummeted just as suddenly in the early 50s after he admitted to his past membership in the Communist party before the House Un-American Activities Committee. He was never officially blacklisted, but Columbia terminated his contract and other studios shunned his services. He returned to the screen only twice in character roles, and appeared infrequently on the stage and on TV with his wife (from 1944), Betty GARRETT.

FILMS INCLUDE: *Mystery Ship, You Belong to Me* 1941; *Canal Zone, Atlantic Convoy, You Were Never Lovelier, The Boogie Man Will Get You* 1942; *Power of the Press, Reveille with Beverly, Deerslayer* 1943; *The Black Parachute, Hey Rookie!, She's a Sweetheart* 1944; *Sergeant Mike, Counter-Attack* 1945; *Renegades, The Jolson Story* (as Al Jolson) 1946; *Down to Earth, The Swordsman* 1947; *The Gallant Blade* 1948; *Jolson Sings Again* 1949; *Emergency Wedding* 1950; *Love Is Better Than Ever* 1952; *Tiger by the Tail/Cross-Up* (UK) 1955; *Freud* 1962.

Parks, Michael. Actor. Born on Apr. 4, 1938, in Corona, Calif. Darkly handsome leading man of American TV and films. A truck driver's son, he spent much of his early youth wandering aimlessly, supporting himself with odd jobs, before he discovered acting. Sinewy and curly-haired, he was cast as Adam in one of his early films, John Huston's *The Bible* (1966), and later impersonated Bobby Kennedy in *The Private Files of J. Edgar Hoover* (1977). His numerous TV appearances included the title role in the adventure series 'Then Came Bronson' (1969–70).

FILMS: *Wild Seed, Bus Riley's Back in Town* 1965; *La Bibbia/The Bible, The Idol* 1966; *The Happening* 1967; *The Last Hard Men* 1976; *Sidewinder One, The Private Files of J. Edgar Hoover* (as Robert F. Kennedy) 1977; *Love and the Midnight Auto Supply* 1978; *Sergeant Steiner/Breakthrough* (Ger.) 1978; *The Evictors, North Sea Hijack/ffolkes* (UK) 1979; *Hard Country* 1981; *Savannah Smiles* 1983; *Club Life/King of the City, The Return of Josey Wales* 1986; *Arizona Heat* 1988; *Caged Fury* (also co-assoc. prod.) 1990; *The Hitman* 1991; *Deathwish V* 1994; *From Dusk Till Dawn* 1996; *That Darn Cat* 1997.

Parkyakarkus. Entertainer. *b.* Harry Einstein, 1904, Boston. *d.* 1958. A popular comic on the Eddie Cantor radio show in the 1930s, he appeared in scattered films in the 30s and 40s. Also known as Harry Parke. Father of actor/director Albert BROOKS.

FILMS INCLUDE: *Strike Me Pink* 1936; *New Faces of 1937, The Life of the Party* 1937; *She's Got Everything* 1938; *Glamour Boy* 1941; *The Yanks Are Coming* 1942; *Sweethearts of the USA* 1944; *Earl Carroll's Vanities, Out of This World* 1945.

Parlo, Dita. Actress. *b.* Grethe Gerda Kornstadt (or Kornwald), Sept. 4, 1906, Stettin, Germany. *d.* 1971. Delicate romantic star of the 30s. A product of the UFA acting school, she entered German films in 1928 and quickly became a popular star. In 1931 she went to Hollywood but failed to make the grade and two years later returned to Europe, where she began the third, perhaps the most rewarding phase of her career, in French films. But shortly after the outbreak of WW II, she was arrested as an alien by French authorities and deported to Germany.

FILMS INCLUDE: In Germany—*Die Dame mit der Maske/The Lady with the Mask, Geheimnisse des Orients/Secrets of the Orient, Heimkehr/Homecoming, Ungarische Rhapsodie/Hungarian Rhapsody* 1928; *Manolescu, Melodie des Herzens/Melody of the Heart* 1929. In the US—*The Hollywood Revue of 1929 (German-language version), Menschen hinter Gittern* (German-language version of *The Big House*) 1930; *Kismet* (German-language version), *Honor of the Family* 1931; *Mr. Broadway* 1933. In France—*Rapt/The Mystic Mountain* (Fr./Switz.), *L'Atalante* 1934; *Mademoiselle Docteur/Street of Shadows* (title role), *L'Affaire du Courrier de Lyon/The Courier of Lyons, La Grande Illusion/Grand Illusion* 1937; *Ultimatum, Paix sur le Rhin* 1938; *L'Inconnue de Monte-Carlo* 1939; *Justice est faite/Justice Is Done* 1950; *Quand le Soleil montera* 1956; *La Dame de Pique* 1965.

Parrish, Helen. Actress. *b.* Mar. 12, 1922, Columbus, Ga. *d.* 1959. The daughter of actress Laura Parrish and younger sister of director-to-be Robert PARRISH, she entered films at age five, playing Babe Ruth's daughter in a silent production. She later appeared in "Our Gang" comedy shorts and played child roles in many features of the early 30s, graduating to leads and second leads, mainly in routine B pictures, by the early 40s. She died of cancer at 37. Her first husband (1942–54) was screenwriter Charles LANG; her second, TV producer John Guedel.

FILMS INCLUDE: *Babe Comes Home* 1927; *Words and Music* 1929; *His First Command, The Big Trail* 1930; *Cimarron, X Marks the Spot* 1931; *When a Feller Needs a Friend* 1932; *There's Always Tomorrow* 1934; *A Dog of Flanders* 1935; *Make Way for a Lady* 1936; *Mad About Music, Little Tough Guy* 1938; *Three Smart Girls Grow Up, Winter Carnival, First Love* 1939; *I'm Nobody's Sweetheart Now, You'll Find Out* 1940; *Where Did You Get That Girl?, Six Lessons from*

Madam La Zonga, Too Many Blondes 1941; *In Old California, They All Kissed the Bride, X Marks the Spot* (remake) 1942; *The Mystery of the 13th Guest* 1943; *They Live in Fear* 1944; *Trouble Makers* 1948; *The Wolf Hunters* 1949.

Parrish, Robert. Director, film editor, actor. Born on Jan. 4, 1916, in Columbus, Ga. Like his younger sister, Helen PARRISH, he entered films as a child actor in the late 20s. He appeared in several John Ford films, among other productions, rejoined Ford's team as a bit player at age 17, and became assistant editor and then sound editor. He stayed with Lt. Comdr. Ford through the WW II years and edited the latter's renowned war documentaries. He also co-directed, with Garson Kanin, the documentary *German Manpower* (1943). Returning to Hollywood as a full editor, he cut a number of distinguished features, sharing an Academy Award with Francis Lyon for his work on *Body and Soul* (1947). He began directing in the early 50s and, despite limited budgets, was able to demonstrate a high level of technical proficiency, benefiting from his long experience in the cutting room. However, after a promising start, highlighted by such films as *Cry Danger* (1951), *The Purple Plain* (UK, 1954), and *The Wonderful Country* (1959), his output has been erratic. In the late 60s and early 70s he worked mainly in Europe. In 1983, after nearly a decade away from film production, he co-directed with a close friend, Frenchman Bertrand TAVERNIER, *Mississippi Blues,* a documentary record about their two-month journey along Route 61, echoing memories of the civil rights struggle of the 60s. Memoirs: *Growing Up in Hollywood* (1976); *Hollywood Doesn't Live Here Anymore.*

FILMS INCLUDE: As actor—*Mother Machree, Four Sons* 1928; *The Iron Mask* 1929; *Men Without Women, All Quiet on the Western Front, Up the River, The Right to Love* 1930; *City Lights* 1931; *Dr. Bull* 1933; *Judge Priest* 1934; *The Whole Town's Talking, The Informer* 1935; *The Prisoner of Shark Island* 1935. As assistant editor—*Mary of Scotland* 1936. As sound editor—*Young Mr. Lincoln, Drums Along the Mohawk* 1939; *The Grapes of Wrath, The Long Voyage Home* 1940; *Tobacco Road* 1941. As film editor (complete)—*The Battle of Midway* (doc. short) 1942; *December 7th* (doc. short) 1943; *Body and Soul* (co-edit.) 1947; *A Double Life, No Minor Vices* 1948; *All the King's Men* (co-edit.), *Caught* 1949; *Of Men and Music* (concert feature; co-edit.) 1950. As director (complete)—*Cry Danger, The Mob* 1951; *The San Francisco Story, Assignment—Paris, My Pal Gus* 1952; *Rough Shoot/Shoot First* (UK) 1953; *The Purple Plain* (UK) 1954; *Lucy Gallant* 1955; *Fire Down Below* 1957; *Saddle the Wind* 1958; *The Wonderful Country* 1959; *In the French Style/A la francaise* (also co-prod.; US/Fr.) 1963; *Up from the Beach* 1965; *Casino Royale* (co-dir. with several others; UK), *The Bobo* (UK) 1967; *Duffy* (UK/US) 1968; *Doppelgänger/Journey to the Far Side of the Sun* (UK) 1969; *A Town Called Bastard/A Town Called Hell* (UK/Sp.) 1971; *The Marseille Contract/The Destructors* (UK/Fr.) 1974; *Pays d'Octobre/Mississippi Blues* (doc.; co-dir. with Bertand Tavernier; Fr.) 1983.

Parrott, Charles. See CHASE, Charlie.

Parry, Gordon. Director. *b.* July 24, 1908, Aintree, England. *d.* 1981. In British films since 1929, first as actor, then as assistant director, associate producer, etc. He was second-unit director on *In Which We Serve* (1942) and began directing in the mid-40s. He was the father of stage and screen actress Natasha Parry (*b.* 1930), who was the wife of director Peter BROOK and mother of actress Irina Brook.

FILMS: *Bond Street, Third Time Lucky* 1948; *Now Barabbas, Golden Arrow* 1949; *Midnight Episode* 1950; *Tom Brown's School Days* 1951; *Women of Twilight* 1952; *Innocents in Paris* 1953; *Front Page Story, Fast and Loose* 1954; *A Yank in Ermine* 1955; *Sailor Beware/Panic in the Parlor* 1956; *The Surgeon's Knife* 1957; *Tread Softly Stranger* 1958; *The Navy Lark, Friends and Neighbors* 1959.

Parsons, Estelle. Actress. Born on Nov. 20, 1927, in Lynn, Mass. *ed.* Connecticut Coll. for Women; Boston U. Law School. She was involved in local politics before entering show business as a production assistant, later to become a writer and feature producer, on TV's 'Today' show. In the late 50s she began appearing in satirical revues and stage productions, in stock, on Broadway, and off Broadway, and in the 60s became a superb addition to the roster of Hollywood's character personalities. She won an Academy Award as best supporting actress for her marvelous portrayal of the neurotic Blanche Barrow in *Bonnie and Clyde* (1967) and was nominated for another for her work in *Rachel Rachel* (1968). She has since etched a number of other memorable characterizations on the stage, screen, and TV, including a vivid portrait of Bess Truman in the miniseries 'Backstairs at the White House' (1979). In 1983 she starred in the feminist one-woman show 'Adulto Orgasmo Escapes from the Zoo.' For years she has also taught acting. She was a series regular on the TV sitcom "Roseanne."

FILMS: *Ladybug Ladybug* 1963; *Bonnie and Clyde* 1967; *Rachel Rachel* 1968; *Don't Drink the Water* 1969; *Watermelon Man, I Walk the Line, I Never Sang for My Father* 1970; *Two People* 1973; *For Pete's Sake* 1974; *Foreplay* 1975; *The Lemon Sisters* 1989; *Dick Tracy* (as Mrs. Trueheart) 1990; *Boys On the Side* 1995; *Looking for Richard* 1996; *That Darn Cat* 1997.

Parsons, Louella. Columnist. *b.* Louella Oettinger, Aug. 6, 1893, Freeport, Ill. *d.* 1972. Highly influential gossip writer in Hollywood's heyday, syndicated in Hearst newspapers. As famous for her malapropisms as for her frequent scoops, she wrote two volumes of memoirs, *The Gay Illiterate* (1944) and *Tell It to Louella* (1961). She also appeared in several films, including *Hollywood Hotel* (1937), *Without Reservations* (1946), and *Starlift* (1951). Her daughter, Harriet Parsons (*b.* 1911, Burlington, Iowa), produced a number of films and wrote the screenplays for others.

Parton, Dolly. Singer, songwriter, actress. Born on Jan. 19, 1946, in Locust Ridge, near Sevierville, Tenn., of Dutch, Irish, and Cherokee Indian descent. Voluptuous, enormously busty, blonde-wigged country music star who also ventured successfully into films. The fourth of 12 children of a dirt farmer and a preacher's daughter, she brightened the shabby circumstances of her childhood by singing and playing gospel music. By the time she was 11 she was performing on radio in Knoxville. Directly out of high school, she took off for Nashville, where she began her career as a country singer. In 1967 she joined Porter Wagoner's Wagon Masters band, with which she performed for the next seven years at the Grand Ole Opry, in tours, and in recording sessions. On her own from 1974, she rapidly gained popularity as a singer and prolific songwriter and by the end of the 70s she had become a media celebrity on TV specials and talk shows. In the 80s she emerged as a capable screen actress, with an appealing personality and energy to spare. She was nominated for an Academy Award for the music and lyrics of *9 to 5* (1980), her debut film. She commands her own $100 million entertainment empire, Dolly Parton Enterprises, to which she added in 1986 the theme park Dollywood, a tourist attraction near Pigeon Forge, Tennessee.

FILMS: *9 to 5* (also title song) 1980; *The Best Little Whorehouse in Texas* (also addnl. songs) 1982; *Rhinestone* (also mus., songs) 1984; *Steel Magnolias* 1989; *Straight Talk* 1991.

Pascal, Gabriel. Producer, director. *b.* June 4, 1894, Arad, Transylvania. *d.* 1954. A stage actor in Vienna, he began producing and directing films in various European capitals. In

England from the mid-30s, he was entrusted by Bernard Shaw with the filming of the Shavian plays. The financial fiasco of his extravagant spectacle *Caesar and Cleopatra* (1945) virtually ended Pascal's career.

FILMS INCLUDE (as producer): In Germany—*Friedricke, Unheimliche Geschichten/The Living Dead* 1932. In the UK—*Reasonable Doubt* 1936; *Pygmalion* 1938; *Major Barbara* (also dir.) 1941; *Caesar and Cleopatra* (also dir.) 1945. In the US—*Androcles and the Lion* 1953.

Pasinetti, Francesco. Film critic and historian, director, and screenwriter. *b.* June 1, 1911, Venice. *d.* 1949. He wrote extensively on the art of cinema in leading Italian periodicals and is also the author of a film lexicon (1948) and several books on the history, technique, and aesthetics of film. He taught the principles of film theory at Rome's Centro Sperimentale and directed a feature length semidocumentary, *Il Canale degli Angeli* (1934), and several shorts about Venice and other subjects. He also wrote a number of screenplays. A Pasinetti Prize, commemorating his name, was for many years awarded annually at the Venice Film Festival.

Pasolini, Pier Paolo. Director, screenwriter, novelist, poet, essayist, journalist, film critic, and theorist. *b.* Mar 5, 1922, Bologna, Italy. *d.* 1975, a homicide victim. The son of an army officer, he was a published poet at 19 while a student at the University of Bologna, and was an established novelist and essayist by the time he entered Italian films in 1954, as a screenwriter on Mario Soldati's *La Donna del Fiume.* He later collaborated on the scripts of such films as Fellini's *Le Notti di Cabiria/The Nights of Cabiria/Cabiria* (1956) and Mauro Bolognini's *La Notte Brava* (1959) and *Il Bell'Antonio* (1960) before turning director in 1961. He created an immediate impact with his first film, *Accattone!,* which was based on one of his own novels, *Una Vita Violenta (A Violent Life),* a grim depiction of the sordid existence of a pimp in a squalid section of Rome in which Pasolini had lived in the 40s. His next film, *Mama Roma* (1962), dealt with a Roman prostitute (Anna Magnani) aspiring to a middle-class life. These films, like Pasolini's novels of the 50s, reveal a compassion for the proletariat of the slums motivated by a paradoxical combination of influences: a commitment to Marxism of the extreme left, on the one hand, and a deeply felt, mystical religiosity, on the other.

Pasolini's unorthodox religious views led to his arrest in 1962 on charges that he had insulted the church in his "La Ricotta" episode in the film *Rogopag,* in which he parodized Hollywood-style Biblical epics. He then proceeded to formulate his own idea of a religious film, presenting the story of the gospel in a radically new style in his *Il Vangelo Secondo Matteo/The Gospel According to St. Matthew* (1964). For the themes of his subsequent films, Pasolini reached into such divergent sources as classic Greek drama, medieval literature, Arabian tales, and the contemporary political and social scene. Although he kept returning to literary sources of the past, such as *Oedipus Rex* (1967), *The Decameron* (1971), *The Canterbury Tales* (1972), and *The Arabian Nights* (1974), he seemed most successful and convincing with themes of the contemporary scene like *Teorema* (1968) and the modern story in *Porcile/Pigsty/Pig Pen* (1969), through which he was able to vent his social and political concerns more directly, albeit metaphorically.

Pasolini clashed frequently with the Italian authorities and the church over the content of his films, which frequently included generous doses of sex, violence, and anti-establishmentarian "blasphemy." Both *The Canterbury Tales* and *Salo—The 120 Days of Sodom* (1975) were declared obscene by the courts and their release in Italy was delayed for months. In November of 1975 Pasolini met his death in circumstances that were not far removed from the squalid world of *Accattone!* and some of his other films. He was bludgeoned to death by a 17-year-old youth who claimed Pasolini had made homosexual advances toward him.

Although inconsistent and erratic in the quality of his film work, Pasolini was certainly among the most intriguing and controversial of contemporary directors, a complex artist constantly juggling the conflicting forces that influenced his art, in a brave attempt to reconcile his allegiances to Marx, Freud, and Jesus Christ.

FILMS (as director-screenwriter): *Accattone!* (from his own 1959 novel, *Una Vita Violenta*) 1961; *Mama Roma, Rogopag* ("La Ricotta" episode) 1962; *La Rabbia* (1st episode, withdrawn after one showing and never released) 1963; *Sopraluoghi in Palestina* (an hour-long documentary, reporting on discussions between Pasolini and Father Rossi in Israel, filmed during preparations for *The Gospel According to St. Matthew;* see below), *Il Vangelo Secondo Matteo/The Gospel According to St. Matthew* 1964; *Comizi d'Amore* (feature-length doc.) 1965; *Uccellacci e Uccellini/The Hawks and the Sparrows* 1966; *Le Streghe/The Witches* ("The Earth As Seen from the Moon" episode), *Edipo Re/Oedipus Rex* 1967; *Capriccio all'Italiana* ("Che Cosa sono le Nuvole" episode), *Appunti per un Film Indiano* (short), *Teorema* (from his own novel) 1968; *Amore e Rabbia/Vangelo 70/Love and Anger* ("La Sequenza del Fiore di Carta" episode), *Porcile/Pigsty/Pig Pen* (in two parts) 1969; *Medea* 1970; *Il Decamerone/The Decameron* (also act., as Giotto) 1971; *I Racconti di Canterbury/The Canterbury Tales* (also act.) 1972; *Il Fiore delle Mille e Una Notte/A Thousand and One Nights/The Arabian Nights* 1974; *Salò o le Centoventi Giornate di Sodoma/Salo—The 120 Days of Sodom* 1975; *Orestiade Africano, La Ricotta* 1976.

Passer, Ivan. Director, screenwriter. Born on July 10, 1933, in Prague. Raised comfortably in early childhood by wealthy, artistically inclined parents (his mother was a noted poster painter, his grandmother a screenwriter of Czech silents), he soon suffered the consequences of his background, first under the Nazis as a Jew, then under the Communist regime as the son of capitalists. After being kicked out of high school, he became a bricklayer and toolmaker, but a bout with hepatitis forced him to abandon manual labor for an office job as a clerk. After two years on the road with a circus band, he enrolled at FAMU, the film school of Prague's music and arts academy. Although he never graduated, he made the necessary contacts and in the early 60s served as an assistant to several directors, notably Milos FORMAN, who remained a lifelong friend. After collaborating on the screenplays of several Forman films, Passer directed the medium-length *A Boring Afternoon* (1965). At first intended as an episode in the omnibus film *Pearls of the Deep,* it was released separately to a chorus of acclaim, winning prizes at the Locarno and Mannheim festivals. Passer immediately followed it with his first, and to many still his most accomplished feature, *Intimate Lighting* (1965). A gentle, beautifully played, lyrically told account of a reunion between two musicians, the film demonstrated its director's enchantment with life's simpler pleasures, his delight with nature, and his keen interest in the psychological observation of character. It won the Cannes Youth Prize and a Special Award from the American National Society of Film Critics. It turned out to be Passer's last Czech production. After the Soviet invasion of Prague, he slipped out of the country early in 1969 and, following brief stays in Paris and London, headed for New York. After a short period of adjustment, working as a longshoreman while learning English, he made his first American film in 1971. Highlighted by the amusing *Law and Disorder* (1974) and the intriguing *Cutter and Bone/Cutter's Way* (1981), Passer's American work is yet to find a cohesive course or consistent level.

FILMS: As screenwriter: *Audition/Talent Competition* 1963; *Black Peter/Peter and Pavla* (also asst. dir.) 1964; *Loves of a Blonde* (also asst. dir.) 1965; *The Fireman's Ball* 1967. As director: In Czechoslovakia—*A Boring Afternoon* (also co-sc.; medium-length), *Intimate Lighting* (also co-sc.) 1965. In the US—*Born to Win/Born to Lose/Addict* 1971; *Law and Disorder* (also co-sc.) 1974; *Crime and Passion/An Ace Up My Sleeve* 1976; *Silver Bears* 1978; *Cutter and Bone/Cutter's Way* 1981; *Creator* 1985; *Haunted Summer* 1988.

passing shot. A shot in which a subject moves past a stationary camera or one in which the subject remains stationary while the camera moves past him.

Pasternak, Joe (Joseph). Producer. *b.* Sept. 19, 1901, Szilagy-Somlyo, Transylvania, Hungary. *d.* 1991. In the US from his late teens, he served as busboy, then waiter at the Paramount studios before making his film entry as second assistant director in 1923. Three years later he joined Universal and after directing the two-reel El Brendel comedy *Help Yourself,* was appointed manager of the company's operations in Berlin. In 1935, after producing a succession of hit musical films in Europe, he returned to Hollywood with director Henry KOSTER and soon after saved Universal from financial disaster with a string of highly successful Deanna Durbin musicals. He is also credited with saving the career of Marlene Dietrich, which was faltering in the late 30s before she joined Universal, where under the guidance of Pasternak, she was given a new, tempestuous look, reviving her popularity. In the 40s he moved to MGM, where he continued feeding the public with light, happy entertainment. He helped popularize classical music on the screen and told his life story in the ghostwritten autobiography *Easy the Hard Way* (1956). Parkinson's disease forced his retirement in the late 60s.

FILMS INCLUDE: In Europe—*Das Schweigen im Walde* (Ger.) 1929; *Zwei Menschen* (Ger.), *Die Grosse Sehnsucht* (Ger.) 1930; *Fräulein Paprika* (Aus.) 1932; *Skandal in Budapest* (Ger./Hung.), *Csibi* (Aus.) 1933; *Frühlingsparade* (Aus.) 1934; *Kleine Mutter* (Aus./Hung.), *Katharine* (Aus.) 1935. In the US—*Three Smart Girls* 1936; *100 Men and a Girl* 1937; *Mad About Music, That Certain Age* 1938; *Three Smart Girls Grow Up, The Under-Pup, First Love, Destry Rides Again* 1939; *It's a Date, Spring Parade, A Little Bit of Heaven, Seven Sinners* 1940; *Nice Girl?, The Flame of New Orleans, It Started with Eve* 1941; *Seven Sweethearts* 1942; *Presenting Lily Mars, Thousands Cheer* 1943; *Song of Russia, Two Girls and a Sailor* 1944; *Music for Millions, Thrill of a Romance, Anchors Aweigh* 1945; *Two Sisters from Boston, Holiday in Mexico, No Leave No Love* 1946; *The Unfinished Dance, This Time for Keeps* 1947; *Three Daring Daughters, Big City, On an Island with You, A Date with Judy, Luxury Liner, The Kissing Bandit* 1948; *In the Good Old Summertime, That Midnight Kiss* 1949; *Nancy Goes to Rio, Duchess of Idaho, Summer Stock, The Toast of New Orleans* 1950; *The Great Caruso, Rich Young and Pretty* 1951; *Skirts Ahoy!, The Merry Widow, Because You're Mine* 1952; *Small Town Girl, Latin Lovers, Easy to Love* 1953; *The Flame and the Flesh, The Student Prince, Athena* 1954; *Hit the Deck, Love Me or Leave Me* 1955; *Meet Me in Las Vegas, The Opposite Sex* 1956; *Ten Thousand Bedrooms, This Could Be the Night* 1957; *Party Girl* 1958; *Ask Any Girl* 1959; *Please Don't Eat the Daisies, Where the Boys Are* 1960; *The Horizontal Lieutenant, Jumbo* 1962; *The Courtship of Eddie's Father, A Ticklish Affair* 1963; *Girl Happy* 1965; *Made in Paris, Spinout* 1966; *The Sweet Ride* 1968.

Pastrone, Giovanni. Director, producer. *b.* Sept. 11, 1883, Montechiaro d'Asti, Italy. *d.* 1959. A leading figure in the formative years of Italian cinema, he began in 1905 as an administrator and technical pioneer, then (1908) began producing and directing. His monumental *Cabiria* (1914) is a landmark in the history of films. He often used the pseudonym Piero Fosco.

FILMS INCLUDE (as director): *Giordano Bruno* 1908; *La Maschera di Ferro* 1909; *La Caduta di Troia/The Fall of Troy, Manon Lescaut, lucia de Lammermoor, Agnese Visconti* 1910; *Padre* 1912; *Cabiria* 1914; *Masciste, Il Fuoco* 1915; *Tigre Reale* 1916; *Hedda Gabler* 1919; *Povere Bimbe* 1923.

patch panel. A board containing plugs, jacks, and sockets to provide connections for a studio's electrical equipment.

Paterson, Bill. Actor. Born in 1945 in Scotland. *ed.* Royal Scottish Academy of Music and Drama. Stage-trained character actor. After helping to found the Glasgow Citizens Theatre and the 7:84 Company (referring to the percentage of property owners in Britain and the amount of property they own), he began to appear in films in the 70s.

FILMS INCLUDE: *The Odd Job* 1978; *The Ploughman's Lunch* 1983; *Comfort and Joy, The Killing Fields, A Private Function* 1984; *Defence of the Realm* 1985; *The Adventures of Baron Munchausen, Just Ask for Diamond* 1988; *The Return of the Musketeers* (UK/Fr./Sp.) 1989; *Truly Madly Deeply, The Witches* 1990; *The Object of Beauty* 1991.

Paterson, Neil. Novelist, screenwriter. Born James Edmund Paterson, on Dec. 31, 1915, in Scotland. *ed.* Edinburgh U. A winner of the Atlantic Award of Literature in 1946, a TV executive, and a former governor of the British Film Institute, he wrote a number of screenplays for British movies, receiving an Academy Award for the script of *Room at the Top* (1959). His novel *Man on a Tightrope* provided the basis for the 1953 film by that title.

FILMS INCLUDE: *The Little Kidnappers* 1953; *High Tide at Noon* 1957; *Room at the Top* 1959; *The Spiral Road* 1962.

Pathé, Charles. Industrialist, film pioneer. *b.* Dec. 25, 1863, Chevry-Cossigny, France. *d.* 1957. He was the son of a pork butcher and a cook and joined the labor force at age 12. After five years of military service, he went to Argentina hoping to make a fortune but returned to France empty-handed in 1891. He tried several occupations without success and then, in 1894, he finally hit the jackpot when he bought an Edison phonograph and began exhibiting it at fairs all over France. Business was good and within several months he was an established importer and merchant of phonographs. By 1896 he had extended his business interests to include the sale of motion picture projectors and even directed a number of simple films in imitation of Lumière. The same year, with his brothers Émile, Jacques, and Théophile, he founded the Pathé Frères company.

The sale of phonographs constituted the major source of Pathé Frères' profits until 1901. In that year Charles left the phonograph end of the business in Émile's charge (Jacques and Théophile had by then left the company) and began devoting his energies to film production, with the aid of director-producer Ferdinand ZECCA. In 1902, Pathé built a studio in Vincennes and began turning out short films assembly-line style, at the rate of one or two a day. The following year he began forming foreign branches, at first in London, then in Moscow and New York. Before long Pathé branches were popping up in such other faraway places as Kiev, Budapest, Calcutta, and Singapore. By 1908, the Pathé company was an international empire, selling twice as many films in the United States as all American companies combined. It was by far the world's largest movie producer.

Expanding rapidly, Pathé went into the manufacturing of raw film and motion picture equipment and virtually monopolized the business by building studios, laboratories, and motion picture theaters. The company developed a color process, Pathé-Color, and launched the world's first weekly newsreel, "Pathé-Journal," made in France as well as in other countries, including the US. With WW I shutting down some of his operations in France and causing chaotic conditions in others, Pathé came to the US at the end of 1914 and centered his efforts on solidifying the position of his American branch, the Pathé Exchange.

When Pathé returned home in 1917, he found conditions profoundly changed. Production costs had soared and the local market was saturated with foreign films, mostly American. Foreign markets, on the other hand, especially the American market, were turning French exports down. In desperation he ordered his filmmakers to produce films geared specifically to the American taste, but he could not stop the trend. In 1918 he began the long and agonizing process of divesting his empire of its various branches and affiliates. Merrill, Lynch & Company acquired a controlling interest in the Pathé company in 1923; the interest was sold to Blair and Company in 1926.

In 1929 Charles Pathé sold his last interest in the business and retired to the Riviera. The remnants of the Pathé company as a producer and distributor were sold to RKO in 1931, though the company survived as a film-financing entity and laboratory facility. In the 90s, the name "Pathé" became prominent again during a brief period when the entertainment company Pathé Communications Corporation owned MGM/UA, renaming it MGM-Pathé.

Patinkin, Mandy. Actor, singer. Born Mandel Patinkin, on Nov. 30, 1947, in Chicago. *ed.* U. of Kansas; Juilliard School of Drama. Imposing character lead of the American stage and screen. He performed in regional theater before coming to New York, where he appeared frequently in Shakespeare Festival productions and made his Broadway debut in 'Shadow Bow' (1977). He rose to prominence with his Tony Award–winning portrayal of Che Guevara in the musical 'Evita' (1980) and later starred in Stephen Sondheim's musical 'Sunday in the Park with George' (1984), the one-man show 'Mandy Patinkin on Broadway: Dress Casually' (1989), and the acclaimed AIDS piece 'Falsettos' (1992). He has played a wide range of supporting roles for the screen, but has yet to establish himself as a star. In 1980 he married actress Kathryn Grody.

FILMS: *The Big Fix* 1978; *French Postcards, The Last Embrace* 1979; *Night of the Juggler* 1980; *Ragtime* 1981; *Daniel, Yentl* 1983; *Maxie* 1985; *The Princess Bride* 1987; *The House on Carroll Street, Alien Nation* 1988; *Dick Tracy, Impromptu* (as Alfred de Musset) 1990; *True Colors* 1991; *The Doctor* 1992; *The Music of Chance* 1993; *Life with Mikey* (cameo), *Squanto: A Warrior's Tale* 1994.

Patric, Jason. Actor. Born in 1966, in Queens, New York. The son of actor and Pulitzer Prize–winning playwright Jason MILLER and the grandson of the late Jackie GLEASON, this talented young leading man is adept at creating complex characters. Often taking his time choosing film roles, he was suddenly sought after in Hollywood with his performance in the teen thriller *The Lost Boys* (1987), then reached critical success with an earnest portrayal of an undercover cop falling into drugs while pursuing a bust in *Rush* (1991).

FILMS: *Solarbabies* 1986; *The Lost Boys* 1987; *The Beast* 1988; *After Dark, My Sweet, Roger Corman's Frankenstein Unbound* 1990; *Denial, Rush* 1991; *Geronimo: An American Legend* 1993; *The Journey of August King, Sleepers* 1996; *Incognito, Speed 2: Cruise Control* 1997.

Patrick, Gail. Actress. *b.* Margaret LaVelle Fitzpatrick, June 20, 1911, Birmingham, Ala. *d.* 1980. Elegant and feminine but often aloof and cynical brunette of Hollywood films of the 30s and 40s. A graduate of Howard College, she stayed at her alma mater for a while as a dean of women students and briefly attended the University of Alabama's law school. She arrived in Hollywood in 1932 as a finalist in a Paramount-sponsored "Panther Woman" contest. She lost but stayed on as a contract player and subsequently appeared in numerous films, playing both leads and second leads and being particularly effective in cold, often nasty "other woman" roles. She retired from films in the late 40s, after her third marriage, to Thomas Cornwall Jackson, Erle Stanley Gardner's literary agent. In 1956 she and her husband initiated the highly successful 'Perry Mason' TV series, of which she became the executive producer. They divorced in 1969. She died of leukemia.

FILMS INCLUDE: *If I Had a Million* 1932; *Murders in the Zoo, The Phantom Broadcast, Cradle Song* 1933; *Death Takes a Holiday, Murder at the Vanities, Wagon Wheels* 1934; *Rumba, Mississippi, No More Ladies, Doubting Thomas* 1935; *The Lone Wolf Returns, The Preview Murder Mystery, My Man Godfrey, Murder with Pictures, White Hunter* 1936; *Her Husband Lies, Artists and Models, Stage Door* 1937; *Mad About Music, Wives Under Suspicion, King of Alcatraz* 1938; *Disbarred, Man of Conquest, Grand Jury's Secrets, Reno* 1939; *My Favorite Wife, The Doctor Takes a Wife* 1940; *Love Crazy, Kathleen* 1941; *We Were Dancing, Tales of Manhattan, Quiet Please—Murder* 1942; *Hit Parade of 1943* 1943; *Women in Bondage, Up in Mabel's Room* 1944; *Brewster's Millions, Twice Blessed* 1945; *The Madonna's Secret, Claudia and David* 1946; *King of the Wild Horses* 1947; *Inside Story* 1948.

Patrick, John (Jack). Playwright, screenwriter. Born John Patrick Goggan, on May 17, 1905, in Louisville, Ky. *ed.* Harvard; Columbia. The author of 'The Teahouse of the August Moon,' he also wrote numerous Hollywood screenplays from the mid-30s through the late 60s.

FILMS INCLUDE: *Educating Father, 36 Hours to Live, 15 Maiden Lane* 1936; *Time Out for Romance, Born Reckless, One Mile from Heaven* 1937; *International Settlement, Battle of Broadway, Mr. Moto Takes a Chance, Five of a Kind, Up the River* 1938; *The Strange Love of Martha Ivers* (story only) 1946; *Framed* (story only) 1947; *Enchantment* 1948; *The Hasty Heart* (play basis only) 1949; *The President's Lady* 1953; *Three Coins in the Fountain* 1954; *Love Is a Many Splendored Thing* 1955; *The Teahouse of the August Moon* (from his play), *High Society* 1956; *Les Girls* 1957; *Some Came Running* 1958; *The World of Suzie Wong* 1961; *Gigot* 1962; *The Main Attraction* (also prod.) 1963; *The Shoes of the Fisherman* 1968.

Patrick, Lee. Actress. *b.* Nov. 22, 1906, New York City. *d.* 1982. On Broadway from age 13, she later became a fixture in Hollywood films, playing some leads and numerous character parts, typically as a hardened blonde. Memorable as Humphrey Bogart's gal Friday in *The Maltese Falcon* (1941) and as Cosmo Topper's ditzy wife in the TV series 'Topper' (1953–55). Also seen in TV series such as 'Mr. Adams and Eve.' After a long absence, she returned to the big screen in 1975.

FILMS INCLUDE: *Strange Cargo* 1929; *Border Cafe, Music for Madame* 1937; *Law of the Underworld, Crashing Hollywood, The Sisters* 1938; *Fisherman's Wharf* 1939; *Invisible Stripes, Saturday's Children, City for Conquest* 1940; *Footsteps in the Dark, The Nurse's Secret, The Maltese Falcon* 1941; *Dangerously They Live, In This Our Life, Now Voyager, A Night to Remember* 1942; *Jitterbugs* 1943; *Mrs. Parkington* 1944; *Mildred Pierce* 1945; *Mother Wore Tights* 1947; *Inner Sanctum, The Snake Pit* 1948; *The Doolins of Oklahoma* 1949; *Caged, The Lawless* 1950; *There's No Business Like Show Business* 1954; *Vertigo, Auntie Mame* 1958; *Pillow Talk* 1959; *Visit to a Small Planet* 1960; *Summer and Smoke, Goodbye*

Again 1961; *Wives and Lovers* 1963; *The Seven Faces of Dr. Lao, The New Interns* 1964; *The Black Bird* 1975.

Patrick, Nigel. Actor, occasional director. *b.* Nigel Dennis Wemyss, May 2, 1913, London. *d.* 1981. Leading man and character player of the British stage and screen with a penchant for playing cynics. The son of an actor and actress, he made his stage debut in 1932 and his first film appearance in 1939. His film career took shape after his return from WW II service as a lieutenant colonel in the infantry. He directed a number of plays and two films. He was married to actress Beatrice Campbell (*b.* 1923; *d.* 1980) from 1951.

FILMS INCLUDE (as actor): *Mrs. Pym of Scotland Yard* 1939; *Noose, Spring in Park Lane* 1948; *Silent Dust, Jack of Diamonds* (also sc.), *The Perfect Woman* 1949; *Morning Departure/Operation Disaster, Trio* ("Mr. Know-All" episode) 1950; *The Browning Version, Pandora and the Flying Dutchman* (UK/US), *Encore* ("The Ant and the Grasshopper" episode), *Young Wives' Tale* 1951; *Who Goes There?/The Passionate Sentry, The Sound Barrier/Breaking Through the Sound Barrier, Meet Me Tonight/Tonight at 8:30* ("Ways and Means" episode) 1952; *The Pickwick Papers* (as Mr. Jingle) 1953; *A Prize of Gold* (UK/US) 1955; *How to Marry a Rich Uncle* (also dir.), *Raintree County* (US), *Count Five and Die* 1957; *The Man Inside* 1958; *Sapphire* 1959; *The League of Gentlemen, The Trials of Oscar Wilde* (as Sir Edward Clarke) 1960; *Johnny Nobody* (also dir.) 1961; *The Informers/Underworld Informers* 1963; *Battle of Britain, The Virgin Soldiers* 1969; *The Executioner* 1970; *Tales from the Crypt* 1971; *The Great Waltz* (as Johann Strauss, Sr.; US) 1972; *The Mackintosh Man* 1973.

Patsy Awards. The Oscars of the animal world, presented each year (since 1951) by the American Humane Association, in co-ordination with major Hollywood studios, to the "best performing" animals in films (from 1958 also in TV). The name Patsy was coined from the initials for Picture Animal Top Star of the Year. The winner of the first ceremony was Francis the mule. Subsequent winners have included an assortment of dogs and cats and an occasional horse, tiger, or dolphin. The 1969 winner was a raccoon.

Patterson, Elizabeth. Actress. *b.* Mary Elizabeth Patterson, Nov. 22, 1874, Savannah, Tenn. *d.* 1966. Veteran character actress of American stage and screen, often in devoted mother or crochety old lady roles. Memorable for her lead role in *Tobacco Road* (1941).

FILMS INCLUDE: *The Boy Friend, The Return of Peter Grimm* 1926; *Words and Music, South Sea Rose* 1929; *The Lone Star Ranger, The Cat Creeps* 1930; *Tarnished Lady, The Smiling Lieutenant, Daddy Long Legs* 1931; *So Big, Love Me Tonight, Life Begins, A Bill of Divorcement, No Man of Her Own* 1932; *Hold Your Man, Dinner at Eight, Doctor Bull* 1933; *Hide-Out* 1934; *So Red the Rose* 1935; *Small Town Girl, Go West Young Man/Old Hutch* 1936; *High Wide and Handsome* 1937; *Bluebeard's Eighth Wife, Sing You Sinners* 1938; *The Story of Alexander Graham Bell, Our Leading Citizen, The Cat and the Canary* 1939; *Remember the Night, Earthbound* 1940; *Tobacco Road, Belle Starr* 1941; *Her Cardboard Lover, My Sister Eileen, I Married a Witch* 1942; *The Sky's the Limit* 1943; *Hail the Conquering Hero, Together Again* 1944; *Lady on a Train* 1945; *Colonel Effingham's Raid, I've Always Loved You* 1946; *Welcome Stranger* 1947; *Miss Tatlock's Millions* 1948; *Little Women, Intruder in the Dust* 1949; *Bright Leaf* 1950; *Washington Story* 1952; *Las Vegas Shakedown* 1955; *Pal Joey* 1957; *The Oregon Trail* 1959; *Tall Story* 1960.

Patton, Will. Actor. Born on June 14, 1954, in Charleston, S.C. *ed.* North Carolina School of the Arts. Spindly stage-trained supporting player, frequently in villainous roles. After a stint on TV soap operas and a series of celebrated performances off Broadway, including two Obie Awards, one for Sam Shepard's 'Fool for Love,' he established himself in film. Known for his role as a shifty government aide in *No Way Out*.

FILMS INCLUDE: *Silkwood* 1983; *After Hours, Desperately Seeking Susan* 1985; *Belizaire the Cajun* 1986; *No Way Out* 1987; *Stars and Bars* 1988; *Signs of Life, Everybody Wins, A Shock to the System* 1990; *The Rapture* 1991; *Cold Heaven, In the Soup* 1992; *The Client, The Puppet Masters, Romeo Is Bleeding* 1993; *Tollbooth* 1994; *Copycat* 1995.

Paul, Robert William. Inventor, pioneer producer and director. *b.* Oct. 3, 1869, Highbury, England. *d.* 1943. An engineer by training, he settled in London in 1891 as a scientific-instrument maker. In 1894 he received an order to duplicate the Edison Kinetoscope, which was not patented in Great Britain. Collaborating with Birt ACRES, he modified the Edison apparatus and successfully built a camera of his own, with which he and Acres began recording various events in 1895. The following year Acres and Paul parted ways. On his own, Paul designed and patented the Theatregraph projector, which he later renamed the Animatographe. In 1897 he built an open-air set, where he produced (and sometimes directed) shorts, specializing in trick subjects. One of his films of that year, *The Twins' Tea Party*, contains an early example of a close-up. He continued experimenting with trick effects, slow motion, and animation at England's first indoor studio, which he constructed in 1899. In 1910 he liquidated his motion picture interests and returned to instrument making.

FILMS INCLUDE (mostly as producer, some as director): *The Derby* 1895; *The Soldier's Courtship, The Terrible Railway Accident* 1896; *The Twins' Tea Party, The Last Days of Pompeii* 1897; *The Deserter, Glasgow Fire Engine, London Express* 1898; *Army Life* 1900; *The Haunted Curiosity Shop* 1901; *A Chess Dispute, Voyage to the Arctic* 1903; *A Collier's Life* 1904; *The Motorist, The Dancer's Dream* 1906; *Biblical Scenes* 1908; *The Butterfly* 1910.

Paul, Taffy. See POWERS, Stephanie.

Pavan, Marisa. Actress. Born Marisa Pierangeli, on June 19, 1932, in Cagliari, Sardinia. Gentle leading lady of Hollywood films of the 50s. Nominated for an Oscar as best supporting actress for *The Rose Tattoo* (1955). Sister of Pier ANGELI and wife of Jean-Pierre AUMONT.

FILMS INCLUDE: *What Price Glory* 1952; *Down Three Dark Streets, Drum Beat* 1954; *The Rose Tattoo* 1955; *Diane, The Man in the Gray Flannel Suit* 1956; *The Midnight Story* 1957; *John Paul Jones, Solomon and Sheba* (as Abishag) 1959; *L'Evénement le plus important depuis que l'Homme a marché sur la Lune/A Slightly Pregnant Man* (Fr.) 1973.

Pavlow, Muriel. Actress. Born on June 27, 1921, in England. Attractive, petite leading lady of British stage and films. Married to Derek FARR.

FILMS INCLUDE: *Romance in Flanders* 1937; *Quiet Wedding* 1940; *Night Boat to Dublin* 1945; *The Shop at Sly Corner* 1946; *It Started in Paradise* 1952; *The Net/Project M-7, Malta Story, Doctor in the House* 1953; *Conflict of Wings/Fuss Over Feathers* 1954; *Simon and Laura* 1955; *Reach for the Sky* 1956; *Doctor at Large* 1957; *Rooney* 1958; *Whirlpool* 1959; *Murder She Said* 1961.

Paxinou, Katina. Actress. *b.* Katina Constantopoulos, 1900, Piraeus, Greece. *d.* 1973. Formidable tragedienne and character player of the international stage and screen. She graduated a Gold Medalist from the Geneva Conservatoire and started out as an opera singer. She switched to acting in 1929 and shortly after joined the Greek National Theater. When WW II broke out, she was performing in London and, unable to return to Greece, came to the United States, making her Broadway debut in 'Hedda Gabler' in 1942. The following year, she gained international fame and an Oscar as best supporting actress for her powerful portrayal of Pilar in Hollywood's *For Whom the Bell Tolls.* She appeared in several other Hollywood productions but later returned to Athens, where she and her husband, Alexis Minotis (1900–90), established the Royal Theater of Athens, which became one of the most celebrated in Europe. She also appeared sporadically in European films.

FILMS INCLUDE: *For Whom the Bell Tolls* (as Pilar), *Hostages* 1943; *Confidential Agent* 1945; *Mourning Becomes Electra* (as Christine Mannon), *Uncle Silas/The Inheritance* (as Mme. de Rougierre; UK) 1947; *Prince of Foxes* 1949; *Mr. Arkadin/Confidential Report* (Sp./Fr.) 1955; *The Miracle* 1959; *Rocco e i suoi Fratelli/Rocco and His Brothers* (It./Fr.) 1960; *Tante Zita/Zita* (Fr.) 1968; *Un Eté sauvage* (Fr.) 1972.

Paxton, Bill. Actor. Born 1955 in Fort Worth, Tex. Quirky supporting player, usually in action-oriented films. After getting his start in the business as a set dresser for the low-budget *Big Bad Mama*, he made his film debut shortly thereafter and has remained active ever since. Praised for performance in *noir*-like crime drama *One False Move* (1992), he has gone on to become one of the most sought-after stars in Hollywood with his roles in *True Lies* (1994), *Apollo 13* (1995), and the box-office blockbuster *Twister* (1996). For a time, he was often confused with fellow actor Bill PULLMAN.

FILMS INCLUDE: *Stripes* 1981; *Mortuary, Taking Tiger Mountain* (also prod. des.; US/Wales) 1983; *The Lords of Discipline* 1983; *Streets of Fire, Impulse* 1984; *Aliens* 1986; *Near Dark* 1987; *Next of Kin* 1989; *The Last of the Finest, Navy SEALS, Predator 2* 1990; *One False Move, Trespass, The Vagrant* 1992; *True Lies* 1994; *Apollo 13* 1995; *The Evening Star, The Last Supper, Twister* 1996; *Traveller* (also co-prod. 1997).

Paxton, John. Screenwriter. *b.* May 21, 1911, Kansas City, Mo. *d.* 1985. *ed.* U. of Missouri. A former journalist and publicist, he wrote a number of hard-hitting Hollywood screenplays.

FILMS INCLUDE: *Murder My Sweet/Farewell My Lovely* 1944; *Cornered, Crack-Up* 1946; *Crossfire, So Well Remembered* 1947; *Rope of Sand* (addnl. dial. only) 1949; *Of Men and Music, 14 Hours* 1951; *The Wild One* 1954; *A Prize of Gold* (UK/US), *The Cobweb* 1955; *How to Murder a Rich Uncle* (also prod.; UK), *Interpol/Pickup Alley* (UK) 1957; *On the Beach* 1959; *Kotch* 1971.

Paymer, David. Actor. Born in Long Island, N.Y. *ed.* Univ. of Mich. Amiable, soft-faced actor, often in comedic roles. Son of a pianist/musical director and a travel agent, he is known for his Academy Award–nominated performance as the long-suffering brother in *Mr. Saturday Night*. Regular on TV series 'Diff'rent Strokes' and 'Cagney and Lacey.'

FILMS INCLUDE: *The In-Laws* 1979; *Airplane II: The Sequel* 1982; *Irreconcilable Differences* 1984; *Perfect* 1985; *The Creeps, Howard the Duck* 1986; *No Way Out* 1987; *Crazy People* 1990; *City Slickers* 1991; *Mr. Saturday Night* 1992; *Heart and Souls* 1993; *City Slickers 2: The Legend of Curly's Gold, Quiz Show* 1994; *The American President, Nixon* 1995; *City Hall, Unforgettable* 1996.

Payne, John. Actor. *b.* May 23, 1912, Roanoke, Va. *d.* 1989. *ed.* Roanoke Coll.; Columbia (drama); Juilliard (voice). Masculine leading man of Hollywood films, popular in the early 40s as the star of Fox musicals, often opposite Alice FAYE or Betty GRABLE. The son of a gentleman farmer and an opera soprano, he started out as a vocalist and acted briefly in stock before arriving in Hollywood in 1935. In the 50s he adjusted to the hardening of his boyish facial features by switching to Westerns and action pictures, appearing in medium-budget productions of various studios through 1957, when he retired from the screen to star in his own TV series 'The Restless Gun.' He returned to films briefly in the late 60s. In 1973 he reunited with Alice Faye in a nostalgic revival of the stage musical 'Good News.' A shrewd investor in real estate, he owned many parcels of land in Southern California and a ranch near Billings, Montana. His first two of three marriages were to actresses Anne SHIRLEY and Gloria DEHAVEN.

FILMS INCLUDE: *Dodsworth* 1936; *Fair Warning* 1937; *College Swing, Garden of the Moon* 1938; *Wings of the Navy, Kid Nightingale* 1939; *Star Dust, Maryland, The Great Profile, Tin Pan Alley* 1940; *The Great American Broadcast, Sun Valley Serenade, Week-End in Havana, Remember the Day* 1941; *To the Shores of Tripoli, Footlight Serenade, Iceland, Springtime in the Rockies* 1942; *Hello Frisco Hello* 1943; *The Dolly Sisters* 1945; *Sentimental Journey, The Razor's Edge* 1946; *Wake Up and Dream, Miracle on 34th Street* 1947; *Larceny, The Saxon Charm* 1948; *El Paso, The Crooked Way, Captain China* 1949; *The Eagle and the Hawk, Tripoli* 1950; *Passage West, Crosswinds* 1951; *Caribbean, Kansas City Confidential* 1952; *Raiders of the Seven Seas, The Vanquished, 99 River Street* 1953; *Rails Into Laramie, Silver Lode* 1954; *Santa Fe Passage, Hell's Island, The Road to Denver, Tennessee's Partner* 1955; *The Boss* (also prod., co-sc.), *Slightly Scarlet, Hold Back the Night* 1956; *Hidden Fear* 1957; *They Ran for Their Lives* (also dir.) 1968; *The Savage Wild* (doc. drama) 1970.

Payton, Barbara. Actress. *b.* Nov. 16, 1927, Cloquet, Minn. *d.* 1967. Leading lady of Hollywood films of the early 50s. Better known for her sexy looks than for her acting prowess, she gained much publicity in 1951 when actors Franchot TONE and Tom NEAL engaged in a fierce brawl for the right to date her. Tone landed in a hospital with a fractured cheekbone, broken nose, and brain concussion and eventually married Miss Payton, but the union lasted only a month and she returned to Neal.

FILMS INCLUDE: *Trapped* 1949; *Dallas, Kiss Tomorrow Goodbye* 1950; *Only the Valiant, Drums in the Deep South, Bride of the Gorilla* 1951; *Four-Sided Triangle* (UK), *Run for the Hills, Bad Blonde, The Great Jesse James Raid* 1953; *Murder Is My Beat* 1955.

Pearce, Alice. Actress. *b.* Oct. 16, 1913, New York City. *d.* 1966. Homely, delightful character comedienne of stage and screen musicals. Unforgettable as chronic sneezer Lucy Schmeeler in *On the Town.* On TV she hosted her own show in 1949 and was a regular, as the befuddled neighbor Gladys, in the series 'Bewitched' (1964–66), a role that earned her an Emmy Award. She died of cancer.

FILMS: *On the Town* 1949; *The Belle of New York* 1952; *How to Be Very Very Popular* 1955; *The Opposite Sex* 1956; *Lad: A Dog* 1962; *My Six Loves, Tammy and the Doctor, The Thrill of It All* 1963; *Dear Heart, the Disorderly Orderly, Kiss Me Stupid* 1964; *Dear Brigitte, Bus Riley's Back in Town* 1965; *The Glass Bottom Boat* 1966.

Pearce, Richard. Director. Born in 1944, in San Diego, Calif. *ed.* Yale (English literature); New School for Social Research (M.A. in political economics). He entered films as a socially conscious cameraman, working in that capacity on such notable documentaries as *America Is Hard to See* (1969), *Woodstock* (1970), *Marjoe* (1972), and *Hearts and Minds* (1974). In 1970 he directed in Chile the award-winning documentary *Campamento,* which he also wrote and photographed. Following a successful shift to the mainstream with several TV movies of the late 70s, he made an impressive debut as a theatrical feature director with *Heartland* (1979), in which he beautifully recreated the rigorous lifestyle of the harsh frontier of the Rockies circa 1910. Pearce further manifested his compassion for the human condition in *Threshold* (1981–83), an understated drama about the first artificial heart transplant, and *Country* (1984), in which he took an empathetic look at the plight of the American farmer. He fared less well in his incursion into sensual melodrama, *No Mercy* (1986), and completely missed the mark with his send-up of televangelists, with Steve Martin starring in *Leap of Faith* (1992). He was nominated for an Emmy for his direction of the TV movie *The Final Days* (1989).

FEATURE FILMS: *Heartland* 1979; *Threshold* (Can.; release delayed from 1981) 1983; *Country* 1984; *No Mercy* 1986; *The Long Walk Home* 1990; *Leap of Faith* 1992; *A Family Thing* 1996.

Pearson, George. Director. *b.* 1875. London. *d.* 1973. An Oxford-educated schoolmaster, he entered British films in 1912 as director of educational films but the following year turned to entertainment features and soon became recognized as one of Britain's leading silent film directors. He formed his own company and produced and wrote many of his own films. A technical innovator and a passionate storyteller, he guided the British film industry in its formative years and was instrumental in popularizing British films in the US. His sound output, however, is mostly routine, consisting mainly of "quota quickies." In all, he turned out more than 100 pictures. Autobiography: *Flashback* (1957).

FILMS INCLUDE: *The Fool, Sentence of Death* 1913; *The Live Wire, A Study in Scarlet* 1914; *John Halifax Gentleman, Ultus the Man from the Dead* (serial) 1915; *Sally Bishop* 1916; *The Better 'Ole* 1918; *Nothing Else Matters* 1920; *Squibs* 1921; *Love Life and Laughter* 1923; *Reveille* 1924; *Satan's Sister* 1925; *The Little People, Blinkeyes* 1926; *Love's Option* 1928; *Auld Lang Syne* 1929; *East Lynne on the Western Front* 1931; *The Third String* 1932; *A Shot in the Dark* 1933; *Four Masked Men* 1934; *Gentleman's Agreement, Checkmate* 1935; *Murder by Rope* 1936; *The Fatal Hour* 1937; *Land of Water* (doc.) 1940; *British Youth* (doc.) 1941.

Peck, Gregory. Actor. Born Eldred Gregory Peck, on Apr. 5, 1916, in La Jolla, Calif. Leading star of Hollywood films whose tall, dark, and handsome figure has projected for three decades of filmgoers moral and physical strength, intelligence, virtue, and sincerity. A graduate of San Diego State College, he was a premed student at the University of California at Berkeley when he became interested in an acting career. He enrolled at New York's Neighborhood Playhouse and made an impressive Broadway debut in Emlyn Williams's 'The Morning Star' in 1942. He appeared in another play before heading for Hollywood, where he became quickly established as a leading star in the absence of many of the veteran personalities in the waning years of WW II. He himself was barred from military service by a spine injury he had incurred in a college rowing match. He has since remained a popular film hero, a likable, dependable leading man whose forthright personality has dominated the screen in a variety of genres—dramas, romantic comedies, adventures, military sagas, and Westerns. After several Oscar nominations (for *The Keys of the Kingdom, The Yearling, Gentleman's Agreement,* and *Twelve O'Clock High*), he won the best actor Academy Award for his performance as the steadfastly ethical Atticus Finch in *To Kill a Mockingbird* (1962).

Among Hollywood's leading citizens, Peck has been active in many charitable, liberal political, and film industry causes. In 1965 he became a member of the National Council on Arts and the following year was elected chairman of the American Cancer Society. From 1967 to 1969 he served as chairman of the board of trustees of the American Film Institute and from 1967 to 1970 as president of the Academy of Motion Picture Arts and Sciences. He is the recipient of the Medal of Freedom Award and the Academy's Jean Hersholt Humanitarian Award. He was honored in Life Achievement salutes by the American Film Institute in 1989, by New York's Museum of Modern Art in 1990, and by both the John F. Kennedy Center and the Film Society of Lincoln Center in 1991. Peck's two marriages produced five children, the oldest of whom committed suicide in 1975. The two youngest, Tony (Anthony) Peck (*b.* 1956) and Cecilia (*b.* 1958) are film actors. Autobiography: *An Actor's Life* (1978).

FILMS: *Days of Glory* 1944; *The Keys of the Kingdom, The Valley of Decision, Spellbound* 1945; *The Yearling* (as Penny Baxter) 1946; *The Macomber Affair, Duel in the Sun, Gentleman's Agreement* 1947; *The Paradine Case, Yellow Sky* 1948; *The Great Sinner* 1949; *Twelve O'Clock High, The Gunfighter* 1950; *Only the Valiant, David and Bathsheba* (as King David), *Captain Horatio Hornblower* (title role; US/UK) 1951; *The Snows of Kilimanjaro, The World in His Arms* 1952; *Roman Holiday* 1953; *Night People, The Million Pound Note/Man with a Million* (UK), *The Purple Plain* (UK) 1954; *The Man in the Gray Flannel Suit, Moby Dick* (as Ahab; UK) 1956; *Designing Woman* 1957; *The Bravados, The Big Country* (also co-prod.) 1958; *Pork Chop Hill, Beloved Infidel* (as F. Scott Fitzgerald), *On the Beach* 1959; *The Guns of Navarone* (UK/US) 1961; *To Kill a Mockingbird, Cape Fear, How the West Was Won* 1962; *Captain Newman M.D., Behold a Pale Horse* 1964; *Mirage* 1965; *Arabesque* (US/UK) 1966; *The Stalking Moon, Mackenna's Gold, The Chairman/The Most Dangerous Man in the World* (US/UK), *Marooned* 1969; *I Walk the Line* 1970; *Shoot-Out* 1971; *The Trial of the Catonsville Nine* (prod. only) 1972; *Billy Two Hats, The Dove* (prod. only) 1974; *The Omen* 1976; *MacArthur* (as Gen. Douglas MacArthur) 1977; *The Boys from Brazil* 1978; *The Sea Wolves* 1980; *Directed by William Wyler* (doc.) 1986; *Amazing Grace and Chuck* 1987; *Old Gringo* 1989; *Other People's Money, Cape Fear* 1991.

Peckinpah, Sam. Director, screenwriter. *b.* David Samuel Peckinpah, Feb. 21, 1925, Fresno, Calif. *d.* 1984, of a heart attack. A descendant of pioneer Western settlers, he was the son of a cowboy-lawyer and grandson of a Congressman and Superior Court judge. An undisciplined, macho boy, he played football at Fresno high school but constantly sought additional outlets for his violent temper and gained a reputation as a boozer and brawler. On the advice of family friends, he spent his senior year at the San Rafael Military School. In 1943 he joined the Marines. Returning from service in China, he enrolled in 1947 at Fresno State College, where he met and married Marie Selland, a drama student who got him interested in the theater. After obtaining a master's degree in drama from USC, he worked in the theater as director and actor, then joined a local TV station as stagehand. In the mid-50s he became dialogue director and assistant to Don SIEGEL and began writing screenplays for TV ('Gunsmoke,' etc.) and films. He also created and directed segments of TV's 'The Rifleman,' 'The Westerner,' etc. He became a feature film director early in the 60s and almost immediately gained a reputation as an uncompromising filmmaker with a strong personal vision. His second feature, *Ride the High Country* (1962), was a glorious visual love poem to the American West and its passing legacy, one of the best of the genre, as was *The Wild Bunch* (1969), despite its massive bloody violence. His preoccupation with the omnipresence of violence and the ambivalence of morality made for complex characters, never sure of their identity or their moral standing. But there was nothing ambiguous about Peckinpah's own view of man as an ignoble beast, though many questioned his insistence that the gratuitous gore in his films was in truth an expression of the director's quest for a better world.

FILMS: As screenwriter—*Invasion of the Body Snatchers* (rewrite and bit role only) 1956; *The Glory Guys* 1966; *Villa Rides!* 1968. As director—*The Deadly Companions Trigger Happy* 1961; *Ride the High Country* (also co-sc., uncredited) 1962; *Major Dundee* (also co-sc.) 1965; *The Wild Bunch* (also co-sc.) 1969; *The Ballad of Cable Hogue* 1970; *Straw Dogs* (also co-sc.; UK) 1971; *Junior Bonner, The Getaway* 1972; *Pat Garrett and Billy the Kid* 1973; *Bring Me the Head of Alfredo Garcia* (also co-sc.) 1974; *The Killer Elite* 1975; *Cross of Iron* (UK/Ger.) 1977; *Convoy* 1978; *The Osterman Weekend* 1983.

Peerce, Larry. Director. Born 1935 in the Bronx, N.Y. The son of tenor Jan Peerce, he made an auspicious entry into films in 1964 with *One Potato Two Potato,* a sensitively told drama of interracial courtship and marriage. But his subsequent work has been often erratic.

FILMS: *One Potato Two Potato* 1964; *The Big T.N.T. Show* (recorded review) 1966; *The Incident* 1967; *Goodbye Columbus* 1969; *The Sporting Club* 1971; *A Separate Peace* 1972; *Ash Wednesday* 1973; *The Other Side of the Mountain* 1975; *Two-Minute Warning* 1976; *The Other Side of the Mountain—Part 2* 1978; *The Bell Jar* 1979; *Why Would I Lie?* 1980; *Love Child* 1982; *Hard to Hold* 1984; *Wired* 1989.

Pelissier, Anthony. Director. *b.* 1912, London. *d.* 1988. Son of Fay COMPTON. He directed a number of British films, but most of his activity was confined to the stage.

FILMS: *The History of Mr. Polly* (also sc.), *The Rocking Horse Winner* (also sc.) 1949; *Encore* (co-dir.), *Night Without Stars* 1951; *Meet Me Tonight/Tonight at 8:30* 1952; *Personal Affair, Meet Mr. Lucifer* 1953.

Pellegrin, Raymond. Actor. Born Raymond Pellegrini, on Jan. 1, 1925, in Nice, France, of Italian descent. Leading man and character player of French films, often in cerebral, intense, or introspective roles. Married to actress Gisele Pascal (*b.* Gisèle Tallone, 1923, Cannes), a vivacious screen personality formerly engaged to Prince Rainier of Monaco. Also active on the Paris stage and in French TV.

FILMS INCLUDE: *Naïs* 1945; *La Femme en Rouge* 1946; *Un Flic* 1947; *Topaze* 1951; *Trois Femmes, Nous sommes tous des Assassins/We Are All Murderers, Le Fruit défendu/ Forbidden Fruit* 1952; *Manon des Sources, Les Compagnes de la Nuit/Companions of the Night, La Rage au Corps/Tempest in the Flesh* 1953; *Le Grand Jeu/Flesh and the Woman, Les Intrigantes, Napoléon* (title role), *La Romana/Woman of Rome* (It.), *Marchandes d'Illusion/Nights of Shame, Le Feu dans la Peau/Fire Under Her Skin* 1954; *Les Hommes en Blanc/The Doctors, Chantage* 1955; *La Lumière d'en face/The Light Across the Street, La Loi des Rues* 1956; *Amère Victoire/Bitter Victory* 1957; *Vu du Pont/A View from the Bridge* (Fr./It.) 1962; *La Bonne Soupe/Careless Love, Behold a Pale Horse* (US) 1964; *Furia à Bahia pour OSS 117/OSS 117—Mission for a Killer* 1965; *Le Deuxième Souffle/Second Breath* 1966; *Le Sant de L'Ange* 1971; *Un Officier de Police sans Importance* 1973; *Scandalo/Submission* (It.), *L'Uomo della Strada fa Giustizia* (It.) 1975; *Quand la Ville s'eveille* 1976; *Zerschussene Träume/L'Appât* (Aus./Ger./Fr.) 1976; *Colpo grosso degli Uomini squalo* (It.) 1977; *Tre Scimmie d'oro* (It.) 1978; *Le Rose et le Blanc* 1980; *Les Uns et les Autres/Bolero* 1981; *Louisiane* 1984.

Peña, Elizabeth. Actress. Born on Sept. 23, 1961, in Elizabeth, N.J. Sultry, mercurial leading lady and supporting player of the American stage, screen, and TV. Raised in Cuba, she began performing as a child. In 1969 she moved with her parents to Manhattan where her father established himself as an actor, director, and writer, and her mother eventually became the administrator of the Latin American Theatre Ensemble. She made her movie debut directly after graduating from the High School for the Performing Arts.

FILMS: *El Super* 1979; *Times Square* 1980; *They All Laughed* 1981; *Crossover Dreams* 1985; *Down and Out in Beverly Hills* 1986; *La Bamba, *batteries not included* 1987; *Vibes* 1988; *Blue Steel, Jacob's Ladder* 1990; *The Waterdance* 1992; *Across the Moon* 1994; *Fair Game, Free Willy 2: The Adventure Home* 1995; *Lone Star* 1996.

Pendleton, Austin. Actor. Born on Mar. 27, 1940, in Warren, Ohio. *ed.* Yale U. Lean character actor of stage and screen, he is also an accomplished stage director.

FILMS INCLUDE: *Skidoo* 1968; *Catch-22* 1970; *Every Little Crook and Nanny, What's Up Doc?* 1972; *The Thief Who Came to Dinner* 1973; *The Front Page* 1974; *The Great Smokey Roadblock* 1988; *Starting Over* 1979; *The Muppet Movie* (UK) 1979; *Simon, First Family* 1980; *My Man Adam* 1985; *Off Beat, Short Circuit* 1986; *Hello Again* 1987; *Mr. & Mrs. Bridge* 1990; *The Ballad of the Sad Café* 1991; *My Cousin Vinny, Rain Without Thunder* 1992; *Mr. Nanny, My Boyfriend's Back, Searching for Bobby Fischer* 1993; *Forrest Gump, Greedy, Guarding Tess* 1994; *Dangerous Minds, Home for the Holidays* 1995; *The Proprietor, Sgt. Bilko, Two Much* 1996; *Trial and Error* 1997.

Pendleton, Nat. Actor. *b.* Aug. 8, 1895, Davenport, Iowa. *d.* 1967. A former Olympic, then professional, wrestler, he entered the theater in bit roles requiring mat experience and gradually broadened the range of his characterizations. In some 150 films from the late silent era, he typically played a well-meaning clod or the slow-grasping butt of the antics of such comics as the Marx Brothers and Abbott and Costello. Portrayed the dumb ambulance driver in many "Dr. Kildare" films.

FILMS INCLUDE: *The Hoosier Schoolmaster* 1924; *Let's Get Married* 1926; *The Laughing Lady* 1929; *The Big Pond, Last of the Duanes, Liliom, The Sea Wolf* 1930; *Seas Beneath, The Spirit of Notre Dame, Blonde Crazy, Manhattan Parade* 1931; *Taxi, Horse Feathers, The Sign of the Cross, Deception* (also story) 1932; *Whistling in the Dark, Lady for a Day, Penthouse, I'm No Angel, College Coach* 1933; *Lazy River, Manhattan Melodrama, The Thin Man, The Defense Rests, The Cat's Paw, Death on the Diamond, The Gay Bride* 1934; *Reckless, Murder in the Fleet, It's in the Air* 1935; *The Garden Murder Case, The Great Ziegfeld, Trapped by Television, Sworn Enemy* 1936; *Under Cover of Night, Gangway* (UK), *Life Begins in College* 1937; *Swing Your Lady, Arsene Lupin Returns, The Shopworn Angel, The Crowd Roars, Young Dr. Kildare* 1938; *It's a Wonderful World, On Borrowed Time, At the Circus, Another Thin Man* 1939; *Northwest Passage, Dr. Kildare's Strange Case* 1940; *Flight Command, Buck Privates, Top Sergeant Mulligan* (lead role) 1941; *Jail House Blues, Calling Dr. Gillespie* 1942; *Swing Fever* 1944; *Buck Privates Come Home* 1947; *Death Valley* 1949.

Penn, Arthur. Director. Born on Sept. 27, 1922, in Philadelphia, of Russian-Jewish descent. Although trained in watchmaking, his father's trade, he was drawn to the theater while still in high school. He formed a small dramatic group at Fort Jackson, S.C., where he was stationed during part of his WW II service with the Infantry. He later joined Joshua Logan's stage company as an actor and continued his education at Black Mountain College in Asheville, N.C., and the universities of Perugia and Florence in Italy. He also attended the Actors Studio Los Angeles branch and studied acting with Michael Chekhov. In 1951 he joined NBC-TV as a floor manager on the 'Colgate

Comedy Hour.' Within two years he had begun writing TV dramas and directing plays for the 'Philco Playhouse' and later for 'Playhouse 90.' Penn's career came to an important junction in 1958. During that year he directed 'Two for the Seesaw,' the first of several successful plays he would stage on Broadway, and he turned out his first film, *The Left-Handed Gun,* an offbeat view of Billy the Kid emphasizing psychology and character study. He flourished as a theater director with such Broadway hits as 'The Miracle Worker' (1959), 'Toys in the Attic' (1960), and 'All the Way Home' (1960). He finally returned to films in 1962 with a beautifully acted screen version of *The Miracle Worker,* which won the best actress Academy Award for Anne Bancroft and the best supporting actress Oscar for Patty Duke. In 1963, Penn was assigned to direct the American-French-Italian co-production *The Train,* but he was removed from the helm after several days of filming and replaced by John Frankenheimer.

After directing a successful Broadway production of 'Golden Boy' with Sammy Davis, Jr., in the title role, in 1964, Penn suffered another setback as a film director with *Mickey One* (1965), a vastly underrated study of paranoia that did poorly at the box office but increased interest in Penn's work among serious critics. *The Chase* (1966), starring Marlon Brando as an honest sheriff betrayed by a corrupt town, met with a mixture of raves and boos. But Penn's next film, *Bonnie and Clyde* (1967), was an unqualified hit, both with the public and the critics. The film's success finally focused attention on Penn's special gifts as a director and on themes recurrent in the entire body of his previous work. Bonnie and Clyde, the famous outlaws of the Depression era, like the central characters in Penn's other films, are outsiders alienated by a society indifferent, even hostile, to their needs and desires. Many see his films of the 60s as the most "relevant" screen work of that tumultuous decade. The superlative performances of Warren Beatty as Clyde and Faye Dunaway as Bonnie once again demonstrated Penn's ability to extract inspired performances from actors. Technically, too, the film was electrifying, and its climactic slow-motion brutal death scene later found many imitators among American and foreign filmmakers.

After *Alice's Restaurant* (1969), a whimsical, satirical, but at the end melancholy view of life among the flower children of the hippie movement, in which he dealt directly with the current scene without the customary past-present allegory characteristic of his other films, Penn returned to the past and to the American West in *Little Big Man* (1970), a complex, offbeat, epic-size view of the clash between pioneer and Indian, climaxing with Custer's last stand at Little Big Horn. The film treated the Indian side of the story with restrained compassion, without patronization or sentimental pitying.

As if to confirm his reputation as a spokesman for the traumatic 60s, it was five years before Penn turned out his next feature film, *Night Moves* (1975), a stark and perceptive modern thriller about a Los Angeles private eye that boasts an excellent performance from Gene Hackman. Penn then returned to the past and the great American outdoors with *The Missouri Breaks* (1976), extracting powerful performances from Marlon Brando and Jack Nicholson. Penn, who was nominated for Academy Awards as best director for *The Miracle Worker* (1962), *Bonnie and Clyde* (1967), and *Alice's Restaurant* (1969), occupied a high position in the Hollywood pantheon through the 60s and early 70s. His subsequent output, decidedly more erratic, nudged his reputation into a decline. He has been married since 1955 to Peggy Maurer, an actress who later became a family therapist. Their son, Matthew, is an actor.

FILMS: *The Left-Handed Gun* 1958; *The Miracle Worker* 1962; *Mickey One* (also prod.) 1965; *The Chase* 1966; *Bonnie and Clyde* 1967; *Alice's Restaurant* (also co-sc.) 1969; *Little Big Man* 1970; *Visions of Eight* (Olympics doc.; "The Highest" episode) 1973; *Night Moves* 1975; *The Missouri Breaks* 1976; *Four Friends* (also co-prod.) 1981; *Target* 1985; *Dead of Winter* 1987; *Penn and Teller Get Killed* (also prod.) 1989; *Inside* 1997.

Penn, Christopher (Chris). Actor. Born in 1964, in Los Angeles. Likable, heavy-set supporting-lead player of American films. Early in his career, he often played the role of the dumb, athletic type with a heart of gold, specifically as Kevin BACON's sidekick in *Footloose* (1983). He later graduated to more serious roles such as his turns in *Reservoir Dogs* (1992) and *True Romance* (1993), proving his ability to create intriguing, fast-paced, often wise-cracking characters. He is the brother of actor-director Sean PENN.

FILMS: *All the Right Moves, Rumble Fish* 1983; *Footloose, The Wild Life* 1984; *Pale Rider* 1985; *At Close Range* 1986; *Made in U.S.A.* 1987; *Best of the Best* 1989; *Futurekick, Leather Jackets, Mobsters* 1991; *Resevoir Dogs* 1992; *Beethoven's 2nd, Best of the Best 2, Josh and S.A.M., The Music of Chance, The Pickle, Short Cuts, True Romance* 1993; *Imaginary Crimes* 1994; *To Wong Foo Thanks for Everything Julie Newmar, Under the Hula Moon* 1995; *Mulholland Falls* 1996.

Penn, Sean. Actor, director. Born on Aug. 17, 1960, in Burbank, Calif. Intense, gifted performer whose accomplishments as a movie player were often overshadowed by his reputation as a spoiled brat and his penchant for violent outbursts offscreen. The son of TV and film director Leo Penn and actress Eileen Ryan, he skipped college and joined the Group Repertory Theatre of Los Angeles as an apprentice directly after graduating from Santa Monica High School. He made his professional debut in 1979 as a guest performer in an episode of the TV series 'Barnaby Jones' and his first film appearance in 1981, in *Taps.* From the start he struck audiences as different, an actor with a natural gift and estimable range whose intense personality shone through even in mediocre vehicles. But Penn's reputation as Hollywood's bad boy continued to plague his career, especially after his 1985 marriage to flamboyant singer-actress MADONNA. The constant press attention surrounding the star marriage led him to fits of temper and public brawling. In 1987 he served a six-month jail term for assault. After the stormy on-again off-again marriage ended in divorce in 1989, Penn married actress Robin WRIGHT and seemed to have gained peace of mind. In 1991, while prematurely announcing his retirement from screen acting, he made his debut as a film director-writer with *The Indian Runner,* a raw and rambling drama about two brothers of conflicting outlooks and temperaments. His next turn as director and screenwriter (*The Crossing Guard,* 1995) was again met with lukewarm enthusiasm, but Penn again proved his talent as an intensely sensitive, uniquely gifted actor with his gritty, no-holds-barred performance as a man on death row in Tim ROBBINS's provocative *Dead Man Walking,* receiving an Academy Award nomination as best actor. Penn's brother, Christopher PENN, is also a film actor.

FILMS: As actor—*Taps* 1981; *Fast Times at Ridgemont High* 1982; *Bad Boys* 1983; *Crackers, Racing with the Moon* 1984; *The Falcon and the Snowman* 1985; *At Close Range, Shanghai Surprise* 1986; *Dear America* (doc.; v/o) 1987; *Colors, Judgment in Berlin* 1988; *Casualties of War, We're No Angels* 1989; *State of Grace* 1990; *Carlito's Way, The Last Party* (doc.) 1993; *Dead Man Walking* 1995. As director—*The Indian Runner* (also sc.) 1991; *The Crossing Guard* (also sc.) 1995; *The Game, She's So Lovely, U-Turn* 1997.

Pennebaker, D(onn) A(lan). Filmmaker. Born on July 15, 1925, in Evanston, Ill. *ed.* Yale; MIT. After two years of service with the Navy, he worked as an engineer in New York for six months, then started his own firm, Electronics Engineering, which manufactured the first computerized airline reservation system. Seeking a more creative outlet, he quit the business after five years and began writing advertising copy, painting, and eventually making experimental and documentary films. In 1959 he entered into a co-operative venture, called Filmmakers, with other cinéasts of the *cinéma vérité* school (Richard Leacock, Shirley Clarke, Willard Van Dyke, and Albert Maysles) to share equipment and work on joint projects. Most of Pennebaker's films, many of which have been released theatrically or on TV, are joint projects in which several filmmakers shared the physical work and the creative responsibility. More recently, his regular directing collaborator is his wife, Chris Hegedus, with son Frazer Pennebaker serving as producer and business manager.

FILMS INCLUDE (as director, alone or in collaboration): *Daybreak Express* (release delayed to 1958) 1953; *Suez* (prod., edit. only) 1956; *Gypsy, Loop Films for Brussels World's Fair* 1958; *Opening in Moscow, Skyscraper* (co-phot. only) 1959; *Primary, Balloon* 1960; *Mooney vs. Fowle, Blackie* 1961; *Susan Starr, Jane* 1962; *Eddie, Crisis, Mr. Pearson* 1963; *Lambert & Co.* 1964; *Elizabeth and Mary* 1965; *Casals at 88* 1966; *Don't Look Back* 1967; *Beyond the Law* (co-phot. only) 1968; *Monterey Pop* 1969; *Maidstone* (co-phot. only), *One P.M., Sweet Toronto/Keep On Rockin'* 1971; *Town Bloody Hall* (release delayed to 1979) 1972; *Bowie/Ziggy Stardust and the Spiders from Mars* 1973; *Jingle Bells, Company* 1978; *The Energy War* 1979; *Baltimore* 1980; *Elliott Carter, DeLorean* 1981; *Rockaby* 1983; *Dance Black America* 1985; *Jimi Plays Monterey* 1986; *Depeche Mode 101* 1989; *Suzanne Vega: Open Hand, Jerry Lee Lewis: The Story of Rock 'n Roll* 1990; *Chuck Berry, Little Richard* 1991; *Branford Marsalis* 1992; *The War Room* (editor, cinematographer) 1994.

Peploe, Clare. Screenwriter, director. Came into prominence as co-screenwriter with husband Bernardo BERTOLUCCI for *Zabriskie Point*. Sister of screenwriter Mark PEPLOE.

FILMS INCLUDE: *Zabriskie Point* (co-sc.) 1970; *La Luna/Luna* 1979; *High Season* (co-sc.; also dir.) 1987; *Rough Magic* (dir., co-sc.) 1997.

Peploe, Mark. Screenwriter, director. Has collaborated with Italian directors Bernardo BERTOLUCCI, and Michaelangelo ANTONIONI. Brother and sometime collaborator of Clare PEPLOE.

FILMS INCLUDE: *The Pied Piper* 1972; *The Passenger, The Babysitter* 1975; *The Last Emperor* 1987; *High Season* (co-sc.) 1988; *The Sheltering Sky* 1990; *Afraid of the Dark* (also dir.) 1991.

Peppard, George. Actor. *b.* Oct. 1, 1928, in Detroit. *d.* 1994. *ed.* Purdue; Carnegie Tech. Leading man of the American stage, TV, and films. The son of a building contractor and a former light-opera singer, he started out in radio and in stock and after training at New York's Actors Studio began appearing in TV dramas and on Broadway. He made his film debut in 1957 and seemed headed for top screen stardom after playing the male lead opposite Audrey Hepburn in *Breakfast at Tiffany's*. But few of his subsequent film roles have been interesting enough to support more than a routine leading man's career, with an accent on a tough-hero image. Peppard took a modest stab at directing with *Five Days from Home* (1978). He enjoyed some success on TV as star of the series 'Banacek' (1972–74), 'Doctors' Hospital' (1975–76), and 'The A-Team' (1983–87). The second (1966–72) of his four marriages was to actress Elizabeth ASHLEY.

FILMS: *The Strange One* 1957; *Pork Chop Hill* 1959; *Home from the Hill, The Subterraneans* 1960; *Breakfast at Tiffany's* 1961; *How the West Was Won* 1962; *The Victors* (UK/US) 1963; *The Carpetbaggers* 1964; *Operation Crossbow* (UK/It.), *The Third Day* 1965; *The Blue Max* (UK) 1966; *Tobruk, Rough Night in Jericho* 1967; *P.J., What's So Bad About Feeling Good?* 1968; *House of Cards, Pendulum* 1969; *The Executioner* (UK), *Cannon for Cordoba* 1970; *One More Train to Rob* 1971; *The Groundstar Conspiracy* (Can.) 1972; *Newman's Law* 1974; *Damnation Alley* 1977; *Five Days from Home* (also dir., prod.) 1978; *Da Dunkerque alla Vittoria/From Hell to Victory* (It./Fr.) 1979; *Battle Beyond the Stars* 1980; *Race to the Yankee Zephyr/Treasure of the Yankee Zephyr* (Austral.) 1981; *Target Eagle* (Sp./Mex.), *Au-dela de cette Limite votre Ticket n'est plus valable/Your ticket Is No Longer Valid* (Can./Fr.) 1982; *Zwei Frauen/Silence Like Glass* (Ger.) 1989; *Night of the Fox* 1990; *The Tigress* 1992.

Percy, Eileen. Actress. *b.* Aug. 1, 1899, Belfast. *d.* 1973. Raised in Brooklyn, she began appearing in Broadway plays as a child of 11. Later a model and a Ziegfeld Girl, she made an auspicious start in films in 1917 as Douglas Fairbanks's leading lady in four successive hit productions but later settled into a modest career as a minor star mainly in minor films. After retiring from the screen in the early 30s she wrote a society column for the Los Angeles *Examiner.* In 1936 she married her second husband, songwriter Harry Ruby. In the film biography of Ruby and lyricist Burt Kalmar, *Three Little Words* (1950), she was portrayed by Arlene Dahl.

FILMS INCLUDE: *Wild and Woolly, Down to Earth, The Man from Painted Post, Reaching for the Moon* 1917; *The Empty Cab* 1918; *Brass Buttons, In Mizzoura, Where the West Begins, Beloved Cheater* 1919; *The Third Eye* (serial), *Her Honor the Mayor, Beware of the Bride, The Man Who Dared* 1920; *Why Trust Your Husband?, The Blushing Bride, Hicksville to Broadway, Little Miss Hawkshaw, Maid of the West, The Tomboy* 1921; *Elope If You Must, Western Speed, The Fast Mail, The Flirt* 1922; *The Prisoner, Within the Law, Children of Jazz, East Side West Side, The Fourth Musketeer, Let's Go* 1923; *Missing Daughters, Tongues of Flame* 1924; *Under the Rouge, Souls for Sables, Fine Clothes, The Unchastened Woman, The Shadow on the Wall, Cobra* 1925; *The Phantom Bullet, Race Wild, Lovely Mary, That Model from Paris* 1926; *Backstage, Burnt Fingers, Twelve Miles Out, Spring Fever* 1927; *Telling the World* 1928; *The Broadway Hoofer* 1929; *Wicked* 1931; *The Cohens and Kellys in Hollywood* 1932.

Pereira, Hal. Production designer. *b.* 1905, Chicago, Ill. *d.* 1983. *ed.* Univ. of Ill. Top designer who shared in the creation of some of the most representative worlds in Hollywood films of the studio era. Originally a stage designer in Chicago, he landed in California in 1942, where he joined Paramount as a unit art director. In 1947 he was moved to an executive position at the studio's headquarters. From 1950 to 1968, he was the supervising art director of the entire Paramount output. He shared an Academy Award for *The Rose Tattoo* and was nominated for over 20 other films. After working on over 150 films, he retired to become a design consultant to the architectural firm of his brother, William L. Pereira. Although his credits span epics (*The Ten Commandments*), swashbucklers (*The Buccaneer*), and Westerns (*The Sons of Katie Elder*), he was particularly adept at modern urban fare, evoking the chic charm and excitement of cities like the Rome of *Roman Holiday*, the Paris of *Funny Face*, and the New York of *Rear Window* and *Breakfast at Tiffany's*.

FILMS INCLUDE (most in collaboration): *Double Indemnity, Ministry of Fear* 1944; *Ace in the Hole/The Big Carnival, Detective Story, When Worlds Collide* 1951; *The Greatest Show on Earth, Carrie* 1952; *War of the Worlds, Shane,*

Stalag 17, Roman Holiday 1953; *The Country Girl, Rear Window, Red Garters, Sabrina, White Christmas* 1954; *Strategic Air Command, The Desperate Hours, Artists and Models, The Rose Tattoo, The Scarlet Hour, To Catch a Thief, The Trouble with Harry, We're No Angels* 1955; *The Man Who Knew Too Much, The Proud and the Profane, The Ten Commandments* 1956; *Gunfight at the O.K. Corral, Desire Under the Elms, Funny Face* 1957; *As Young As We Are, The Black Orchid, The Buccaneer, The Colossus of New York, The Geisha Boy, Hot Spell, Houseboat, King Creole, Maracaibo, The Matchmaker, The Party Crashers, Rock-a-Bye Baby, The Space Children, St. Louis Blues, Teacher's Pet, Vertigo, The Young Captives* 1958; *Alias Jesse James, But Not For Me, Career, Don't Give Up the Ship, The Five Pennies, The Jayhawkers, L'il Abner, The Trap* 1959; *It Started in Naples, Visit to a Small Planet* 1960; *Blue Hawaii, Pocketful of Miracles, Breakfast at Tiffany's, One-Eyed Jacks, Summer and Smoke* 1961; *The Man Who Shot Liberty Valance, Hatari!, The Pigeon That Took Rome* 1962; *Come Blow Your Horn, Hud, Love with the Proper Stranger* 1963; *Billie, The Family Jewels, Red Line 7000, The Slender Thread, The Sons of Katie Elder, The Spy Who Came in from the Cold* 1965; *Apache Uprising, Assault on a Queen, The Last of the Secret Agents, Nevada Smith, The Oscar* 1966; *Barefoot in the Park, The Busy Body, El Dorado* 1967; *Will Penny, Arizona Bushwhackers, The Odd Couple, Project X* 1968.

Pereira dos Santos, Nelson. Director. Born on Oct. 26, 1928, in Sao Paolo, Brazil. A tailor's son, he studied law and practiced journalism but his true love was cinema. After graduating from law school, he traveled to Paris, where he enrolled at the IDHEC film school. Returning to Brazil, he made two shorts in Sao Paolo, then moved to Rio de Janeiro, where he entered the industry as an assistant director. His first feature as a director, *Rio 40 Degrees* (1955), contained many of the elements that would characterize his work and propel him to a leadership position in *Cinema Novo,* Brazil's vibrant New Cinema movement of the 60s and 70s. Echoing the movement's ideal to create a popular national cinema rooted in the ethnic culture, free of foreign influence, the film was shot on city streets and featured real people. It dealt realistically but entertainingly with typical problems, stressing the gulf between rich and poor in Brazilian society. *Barren Lives* (1963) is considered by many to be Pereira dos Santos's masterpiece. An early landmark production of *Cinema Novo,* it was a faithful, powerful adaptation of a novel that has been compared to *The Grapes of Wrath* in its vivid depiction of the plight of drought-ridden migrants and their struggle to survive. The director's best-known film abroad is perhaps *How Tasty Was My Little Frenchman* (1971), a robust, lusty, often humorous allegorical mini-epic about a 16th-century French adventurer captured by Indians in the Brazilian jungle who believes he is fully assimilated in the tribe but is instead eaten by his captors as part of a ritual celebration. Hailed by colleagues as "the conscience of *Cinema Novo,*" Pereira dos Santos has certainly been its heart, ears, and eyes.

FEATURE FILMS (as director-screenwriter): *Rio Quarenta Graus/Rio 40 Degrees/Rio 100 Degrees F* (also prod.) 1955; *Rio Zona Norte* 1957; *Mandacaru Vermelho* (also co-prod., act.) 1961; *Cinco Vezes Favela* ("Pedeiro de Sao Diego" episode), *O Boca de Ouro/The Golden Mouth* 1962; *Vidas Secas/Barren Lives* 1963; *El Justiciero* 1967; *Fome de Amor/Hunger for Love/Desperate for Love* 1968; *Azyllo mouito Louco/The Craziest Asylum* 1970; *Como era gostoso o meu Fraces/How Tasty Was My Little Frenchman* (also co-prod.) 1971; *Quem e Beta?/Who Is Beta?* 1973; *O Amuleto de Oqum/The Amulet of Oqum* 1974; *Tenda dos Milagres/Tent of Miracles* 1977; *Estrada da Vida/The Highway of Life* 1980; *Memorias do Carcere/Memories of Prison* 1984; *Jubiaba* 1986; *Castro Alves* 1987.

Perelman, S(idney) J(oseph). Humorist. *b.* Feb. 1, 1904, Brooklyn, N.Y. *d.* 1979. *ed.* Brown U. One of the leading funnymen of American letters, he was invited to Hollywood in the early 30s to collaborate as a gag and screenwriter on two Marx Brothers films, following the success of his first humorous book, *Dawn Ginsbergh's Revenge* (1929). Later during his varied literary career he collaborated on occasional film stories and screenplays, sometimes with his wife Laura, a sister of Nathanael West.

FILMS INCLUDE: *Monkey Business* 1931; *Horse Feathers* 1932; *Sitting Pretty* 1933; *Paris Interlude* (co-play basis only) 1934; *The Big Broadcast of 1936* (treatment only) 1935; *Early to Bed, Florida Special* 1936; *Ambush, Boy Trouble* 1939; *The Golden Fleecing* 1940; *Larceny Inc.* (co-play basis, 'The Night Before Christmas') 1942; *One Touch of Venus* (play basis only) 1948; *Around the World in 80 Days* 1956.

Perez, Rosie. Born ca. 1968. *ed.* Grover Cleveland H.S., Los Angeles Community Coll. (marine biology). Flamboyantly sexy screen lead of Puerto Rican descent. One of ten children, she was raised in Brooklyn, N.Y., and had a troubled childhood. When she was 12, she was removed from school and placed in a group home for slitting a woman's neck. Eventually she completed high school and entered college, where she pursued her desire to become a marine biologist. She turned to show business when she was spotted dancing at a club by a 'Soul Train' scout and was put on the show. At dance clubs she also met Spike LEE, who cast her as the foul-mouthed teenaged mother in *Do the Right Thing*. She was nominated for an Academy Award as best supporting actress for her dramatic turn in *Fearless* (1993) as a mother who survives but loses her child in a plane crash. She is also an accomplished choreographer/dancer.

FILMS INCLUDE: *Do the Right Thing* 1989; *Night on Earth, White Men Can't Jump* 1992; *Fearless, Untamed Heart* 1993; *It Could Happen to You* 1994; *Somebody to Love* 1996; *A Brother's Kiss* 1997.

perforations. The regularly spaced holes punched at the edge of motion picture film throughout its length. They are designed to be engaged by the teeth of sprockets and pins in the mechanisms of cameras, projectors, and other film machinery to allow accurate travel and precise registration of film during the operation of motion picture equipment. Perforations on positive film are usually of stronger design than those on negative film so that they can withstand the strain of repeated projection.

Perier, Etienne. Director. Born in 1931, in Brussels. Competent filmmaker of Belgian and international films. He usually collaborates on his own screenplays.

FILMS: *Bobosse* (Bel.) 1959; *Meurtre en 45 Tours/Murder at 45 R.P.M.* (Bel.) 1960; *Bridge to the Sun* (US/Fr.) 1961; *Lo Spadacino di Siena/Le Mercenaire/Swordsman of Siena* (It/.Fr.) 1962; *Di-moi qui tueur* (Bel.) 1965; *Des Garçons et des Filles* (Fr.) 1968; *El Rublo de los Caras/The Day the Hot Line Got Hot* (Sp./Fr.) 1969; *When Eight Bells Toll* (UK), *Zeppelin* (UK) 1971; *Un Meurtre est un Meurtre/A Murder Is a Murder. . . Is a Murder* (Fr.) 1972; *La Main a couper* (Fr./It.) 1974; *Un si jolie Village/The Investigation* (Fr.), *La Part du Feu* (Fr.) 1978; *Venezia Rosso Sangue/Venice Blood Red* (It./Fr.) 1989.

Périer, François. Actor. Born François Pillu, on Nov. 10, 1919, in Paris. Leading man and solid character actor of French stage and films. Playing bit parts from 1938, he rose to eminence after WW II.

FILMS INCLUDE: *La Chaleur du Sein, Hôtel du Nord* 1938; *La Fin du Jour/End of a Day* 1939; *Premier Bal* 1941; *Lettres d'Amour* 1942; *Sylvie et le Fantôme/Sylvie and the*

Phantom, Un Revenant/A Lover's Return 1946; *Le Silence est d'Or/Man About Town, La Vie en Rose* 1947; *Retour à la Vie* 1948; *Jean de la Lune* 1949; *Orphée/Orpheus* 1950; *Villa Borghese/It Happened in the Park* (It./Fr.), *Cadet Rousselle, Secrets d'Alcove/The Bed* 1954; *Gervaise, Le Notti di Cabiria/ Nights of Cabiria* (It./Fr.) 1956; *Les Louves/ Demoniaque* 1957; *Le Testament d'Orphée/Testament of Orpheus, La Corde raide/Lovers on a Tightrope, La Française et l'Amour/Love and the Frenchwoman* 1960; *L'Amant de Cinq Jours/The Five Day Lover* 1961; *I Compagni/The Organizer* (It./Fr.), *Dragées au Poivre/Sweet and Sour, La Visita* (It.) 1963; *Le Samourai/The Godson, Un Homme de trop/Shock Troops* 1967; *Z* 1969; *Les Caprices de Marie/Give Her the Moon, Juste avant la Nuit/Just Before Nightfall* 1971; *Le Cercle rouge* 1970; *L'Attentat/The French Conspiracy* 1973; *Antoine et Sebastian, Stavisky* 1974; *Docteur François Gailland* 1975; *Police Python 357* 1976; *Baxter Vera Baxter* 1977; *La Raison d'Etat* 1978; *Le Bar du Téléphone* 1980; *Le Battant* 1983; *Soigne ta Droite* 1987; *Lacenaire* 1990; *La Pagaille* 1991.

Peries, Lester James. Director. Born on Apr. 5, 1919, in Colombo, Ceylon (now Sri Lanka). The son of a Roman Catholic doctor, he was pressured by his parents to study for the priesthood, but dropped out of college after one year to pursue a variety of secular interests, among them the writing of movie reviews and of stage and radio plays. He began making short films during a six-year stay in England (1946–52). On returning home, he joined the Government Film Unit as an assistant director. He quit the post in 1955 to make his debut as an independent feature director with *Rekava/The Line of Destiny* (1956). Unlike the studio-bound, Indian-dominated Sinhalese films of the day, he shot *Rekava* on location, in a remote jungle village, cast it with real people, and infused it with real feeling. During the 60s, Peries became established as his country's premier filmmaker, a serious artist and sincere humanist with a true compassion for the celluloid characters he so carefully draws. Some have compared him to Renoir or Ozu. He is married to director-editor Sumitra Gunawardana.

FEATURE FILMS: *Rekava/The Line of Destiny/The Line of Life* (also prod., sc.) 1956; *Sandesaya/The Message* (also co-sc.) 1960; *Gamperaliya/Changes in the Village* 1964; *Devolak Athara/Between Two Worlds* (also co-sc.) 1966; *Ran Salu/The Yellow Robe* 1967; *Golu Hadwatha/Silence of the Heart* 1968; *Akkaa Paha/Five Acres of Land* 1969; *Nidhanya/The Treasure* 1970; *Desa Nisa/The Eyes* 1972; *The God King* 1973; *Madol Duwa/Enchanted Island* 1976; *Ahasin Polawatha/White Flowers for the Dead* 1978; *Veera Puran Appu/Rebellion* 1979; *Baddegsms/Village in the Jungle* 1980; *Kaliyugaya/The Time of Kali* 1982; *Yuganthayo/End of an Era* 1983.

Périnal, Georges. Director of photography. *b.* 1897, Paris. *d.* 1965. One of the world's most distinguished lighting cameramen, he contributed much to early sound cinema in Europe. In French films from 1913, he began gaining recognition in the mid-20s when he collaborated on the shorts of Jean GRÉMILLON, then solidified his reputation in the early 30s with the films of René CLAIR. In 1933 he was lured away to London by Alexander KORDA. He subsequently photographed many prestigious British films, winning an Academy Award for the rich color photography of *The Thief of Bagdad* (1940).

FILMS INCLUDE: In France—*Chartres* 1923; *La Bière* 1924; *L'Auvergne* 1925; *Gratuites* 1927; *La Tour* (co-phot.), *Les Nouveaux Messieurs* (co-phot.) 1928; *Gardiens de Phare* 1929; *Le Sang d'un Poète/Blood of a Poet, Jean de la Lune, Sous les Toits de Paris/Under the Roofs of Paris* 1930; *Le Million, A nous la Liberté* 1931; *Quatorze Juillet/July 14th* 1932. In the UK—*The Private Life of Henry VIII* 1933; *The Private Life of Don Juan, Catherine the Great* 1934; *Sanders of the River/Bozambo* 1935; *Things to Come, Rembrandt* 1936; *I Claudius* (unfinished) 1937; *The Drum/Drums* 1938; *The Four Feathers* 1939; *The Thief of Bagdad* 1940; *The First of the Few/Spitfire* 1942; *The Life and Death of Colonel Blimp* 1943; *Perfect Strangers/Vacation from Marriage* 1945; *Nicholas Nickleby* 1946; *An Ideal Husband, The Fallen Idol* 1948; *The Mudlark* 1950; *No Highway/No Highway in the Sky* 1951; *Three Cases of Murder, L'Amant de Lady Chatterley* (Fr.) 1955; *A King in New York, Saint Joan* 1957; *Bonjour Tristesse, Tom Thumb* 1958; *Once More with Feeling* (US), *Oscar Wilde* 1960.

Perkins, Anthony. Actor. *b.* Apr. 4, 1932, in New York City. *d.* 1992. *ed.* Rollins Coll.; Columbia. The son of stage and screen actor Osgood Perkins (1892–1937), he began acting in summer stock at 15 and made his film debut at 21, playing Jean Simmons's boyfriend in *The Actress* (1953). He later appeared on Broadway and in TV dramas before returning to the screen in 1956, in *Friendly Persuasion,* in a role that brought him an Oscar nomination as best supporting actor. The following year, he excelled in the impersonation of the emotionally scarred baseball star Jimmy Piersall in *Fear Strikes Out.* For a while he specialized in the portrayal of awkward, gawky, anxious, often neurotic adolescents, a period in his career that culminated in his most memorable performance, in the role of Norman Bates, the psychopathic, grotesque motel keeper in Hitchcock's *Psycho* (1960). The film's success catapulted him into international prominence and in the 60s he appeared in several European productions, only a couple of which have been advantageous to his career. Late in the decade he returned to the US and played convincingly an assortment of roles in a variety of Hollywood films but was never able to duplicate his success in *Psycho.* In the 80s he starred in two sequels to the Hitchcock classic, the second marking his debut as a director in 1986. In 1973 he married photographer Berinthia Berenson, the sister of actress Marisa Berenson and granddaughter of the famed Elsa Schiaparelli. He died of AIDS in 1992.

FILMS: *The Actress* 1953; *Friendly Persuasion* 1956; *Fear Strikes Out* (as baseball player Jimmy Piersall), *The Lonely Man, The Tin Star* 1957; *Desire Under the Elms* (as Eben Cabot), *La Diga sul Pacifico/This Angry Age/The Sea Wall* (It./Fr.), *The Matchmaker* 1958; *Green Mansions* (as Abel), *On the Beach* 1959; *Tall Story, Psycho* 1960; *Aimez-vous Brahms?/Goodbye Again* (Fr./US) 1961; *Phaedra* (Gr./US), *Le Procès/Der Prozess/The Trial* (as Joseph K.; Fr./Ger./It.), *Le Couteau dans la Plaie/Five Miles to Midnight* (Fr./It./US) 1962; *Le Glaive et la Balance/Two Are Guilty* (Fr./It.) 1963; *Une Ravissante Idiote/A Ravishing Idiot* (Fr./It.) 1964; *The Fool Killer* 1965; *Paris brûle-t-il?/Is Paris Burning?* (Fr./US) 1966; *Le Scandale/The Champagne Murders* (Fr.) 1967; *Pretty Poison* 1968; *Catch-22, WUSA* 1970; *Quelqu'un derrière la Porte/Someone Behind the Door* (Fr.) 1971; *La Décade prodigieuse/Ten Days' Wonder* (Fr./It.), *Play It As It Lays, The Life and Times of Judge Roy Bean* 1972; *The Last of Sheila* (also co-sc.) 1973; *Lovin' Molly, Murder on the Orient Express* (UK/US) 1974; *Mahogany* 1975; *Remember My Name* 1978; *The Black Hole, Twice a Woman* (Hol.), *Winter Kills, North Sea Hijack/ffolkes* (UK) 1979; *Double Negative* (Can.) 1980; *Psycho II* 1983; *Crimes of Passion* 1984; *Psycho III* (also dir.) 1986; *Destroyer/Shadow of Death, Lucky Stiff* (dir. only) 1988; *Edge of Sanity* 1989; *Naked Target* 1991.

Perkins, Elizabeth. Actress. Born on Nov. 18, 1960, in Queens, N.Y. Engaging leading lady of the American stage and screen. She was raised in Vermont by her divorced mother, a social worker, and stepfather, a gentleman farmer. After graduating from high school, she moved to Chicago, where she lived with her father, a writer and businessman, and attended the Goodman School of Drama. She began her career in 1984 with the national touring company of 'Brighton Beach Memoirs' and later performed on Broadway and in Shakespeare in the Park productions, making her film debut in 1986. In 1985 she married stage actor-director Terry Kinney.

FILMS: *About Last Night. . .* 1986; *From the Hip* 1987; *Big, Sweet Hearts Dance* 1988; *Love at Large, Enid Is Sleeping, Avalon* 1990; *He Said She Said* 1991; *The Doctor* 1992; *The Flintstones, Miracle on 34th Street* 1994; *Moonlight and Valentino* 1995.

Perkins, Millie. Actress. Born on May 12, 1938, in Passaic, N.J. Fragile ingenue of a handful of Hollywood films. The daughter of a sea captain, she was a successful junior model and cover girl when she was chosen by Fox over numerous other candidates to play the title role in the film version of *The Diary of Anne Frank* (1959). Despite a big promotion drive, she failed to become established as a film personality. Her first husband (1960–64) was actor Dean STOCKWELL and her second screenwriter-director Robert Thom.

FILMS: *The Diary of Anne Frank* 1959; *Wild in the Country* 1961; *Ensign Pulver* 1964; *Wild in the Streets* 1968; *Cockfighter* 1974; *Lady Cocoa* 1975; *The Witch Who Came from the Sea* 1976; *Table for Five* 1983; *At Close Range, Jake Speed* 1986; *Slamdance, Wall Street* 1987; *Two Moon Junction* 1988; *Pistol: The Birth of a Legend, Sharkskin* 1991.

Perón, Eva. Political leader, former actress. *b.* Maria Eva Duarte, May 7, 1919, Los Toldos, Argentina. *d.* 1952. The illegitimate child of a farm laborer, she was raised in a small pampas village near Buenos Aires and at 15 ran away from home to seek fame and fortune in the big city. She became a moderately successful radio performer, known as "Señorita Radio." In the early 40s she played leads in a number of films, under the name Eva Duarte, but retired from the screen in 1945, after secretly marrying Juan Perón (1895–1974), who became president of Argentina the following year. She became very influential in the affairs of the state and won great popularity—she was known affectionately as Evita (Little Eva)—among Argentina's poor through charitable acts, dispensation of gifts, strong ties with the labor movement, and a magnetic personal appeal. She was suddenly stricken with cancer at the age of 29 but continued her political activity for several years, until her death at 33. Her body was embalmed but disappeared mysteriously after Perón was overthrown in 1955. It was recovered just as mysteriously when Perón returned to power in 1973. He died the following year and was buried by her side. She was the subject of the Andrew Lloyd Weber hit Broadway musical 'Evita' (1979), starring Patti Lupone; the 1981 TV movie, *Evita Peron,* in which she was portrayed by Faye DUNAWAY; and finally, after many failed attempts by directors and actors, as well as uneasiness on the part of studios, brought to the silver screen in 1996, in Alan PARKER'S adaptation of the Weber musical *Evita,* with MADONNA in the title role.

FILMS INCLUDE: *La Carga de los Valientes* 1940; *El mas Infeliz del Pueblo* 1941; *Una Novia en Apuros* 1942; *La Cabalgata del Circo, La Prodiga* 1945.

Perreau, Gigi. Actress. Born Ghislaine Elizabeth Marie Thérèse Perreau-Saussine, on Feb. 6, 1941, in Los Angeles, to French fugitives from Nazi-occupied Paris. Appealing child star of Hollywood films of the 40s and early 50s. Despite her personal charm and proven acting ability, she failed in her bid for a career in films as a young adult. Her sister Janine and her brother Gerald also appeared in films, the latter mainly under the pseudonym Peter Miles.

FILMS INCLUDE: *Madame Curie* 1943; *Mr. Skeffington* 1944; *Yolanda and the Thief* 1945; *Song of Love, Green Dolphin Street* 1947; *Enchantment, Family Honeymoon, Roseanna McCoy* 1949; *My Foolish Heart, Shadow on the Wall, Never a Dull Moment, For Heaven's Sake* 1950; *Reunion in Reno, Weekend with Father* 1951; *Has Anybody Seen My Gal?, Bonzo Goes to College* 1952; *The Man in the Gray Flannel Suit* 1956; *Wild Heritage* 1958; *Girls Town* 1959; *Look in Any Window, Tammy Tell Me True* 1961; *Journey to the Center of Time, Hell on Wheels* 1967.

Perret, Léonce. Director, producer, screenwriter, actor. *b.* May 13, 1880, Niort, France. *d.* 1935. Originally a stage actor, he began his screen career in 1907 as a dramatic player in a series of French films manufactured in Berlin by Gaumont. He later also appeared in several of the films of Louis Feuillade. He began directing in 1908 and by the time of his death had made some 200 shorts and features of all genres. Between 1910 and 1912 he directed himself in a series of comic shorts, "Léonce," but later tended more toward melodrama and during WW I turned out a number of highly chauvinistic propaganda films. He came to the US in 1916 and worked in Hollywood for several years, directing for Pathé, then returned to France, where he directed intermittently through the mid-30s. He wrote some of his own scripts and produced some of his own films. He died while preparing a remake of *Keonigsmark.* The film was later made by Maurice Tourneur from Perret's script.

FILMS INCLUDE (as director): In France—*Le Voile des Nymphes, Le Petit Soldat, Noël d'Artistes* 1908; *Pauvres Gosses, André Chénier, Daphné* 1909; *Molière, Mimosa* 1910; *L'Ame de Violon, L'Amour et l'Argent, Le Chrysanthème rouge* 1911; *La Dette d'Honneur, Main de Fer* 1912; *L'Enfant de Paris, Molière* (remake), *L'Ange de la Maison, Par l'Amour* 1913; *L'Heure de Rêve* 1914; *La Voix de la Patrie, Les Mystères de l'Ombre, Le Roi de la Montagne, Mort au Champ d'Honneur, Le Dernier Amour, Les Héros de l'Yser, Françaises veillez, Aimer pleurer mourir, France et Angleterre Forever* 1915; *La Fiancée du Diable, L'Imprévu, La Belle aux Cheveux d'Or* 1916. In the US—*The Silent Master, The Mad Lover* 1917; *Lest We Forget, Accidental Honeymoon, Lafayette We Come!, The Million Dollar Dollies* 1918; *Unknown Love, The Thirteenth Chair, The Twin Pawns, The A.B.C. of Love* 1919; *Lifting Shadows, A Modern Salome, The Empire of Diamonds* 1920; *The Money Maniac* 1921. In France—*L'Ecuyère* 1922; *Koenigsmark* 1923; *Après l'Amour* 1924; *Madame Sans-Gêne* (US; starring Gloria Swanson) 1925; *La Femme nue* 1926; *Morgane la Sirène/Morgane the Enchantress, La Danseuse Orchidée* 1928; *La Possession* 1929; *Quand nous etions Deux* 1930; *Après l'Amour* (remake) 1931; *Il était une fois* 1933; *Sapho* 1934; *Les Précieuses ridicules* 1935.

Perrin, Jacques. Actor, producer. Born Jacques Simonet, on July 13, 1941, in Paris. The son of a Comédie-Française director, he trained for the stage at the Paris Conservatory and made his screen debut in 1957. Darkly handsome, he asserted himself in the 60s as a solid leading man of intercontinental productions. In 1966 he won a dual best actor prize at Venice for his performances in Italy's *Half a Man* and Spain's *The Search.* He later pursued a parallel career as a producer, counting among his credits Costa-Gavras's Oscar-nominated *Z* (1969) and Annaud's Oscar winner *Black and White in Color* (1976).

FILMS INCLUDE (as actor): *La Peau de l'Ours* 1957; *Les Tricheurs/The Cheaters* 1958; *La Verité, La Ragaza con la Valigia/Girl with a Suitcase* (It./Fr.) 1960; *Cronaca familiare/Family Diary* (It.) 1962; *La Corruzione/The Corruption* (It.) 1963; *La 317e Section* 1964; *Compartiments Tueurs/The Sleeping Car Murder* 1965; *Un Uomo a Meta/Half a Man* (It.), *La Busca/The Search* (Sp.) 1966; *Les Demoiselles de Rochefort/*

The Young Girls of Rochefort, Un Homme de trop/Shock Troops 1967; *Z* (also co-prod.; Alg./Fr.) 1969; *Historia de una Soledad/Goya* (Sp.) 1970; *Peau d'Ane/Donkey Skin, La Guerre d'Algerie* 1972; *La Spirale* (also prod.) 1974; *Section speciale/Special Section* 1975; *La Victorie en chantant/Black and White in Color* (co-prod. only), *Il Deserto dei Tartari/The Desert of the Tartars* (It./Fr./Iran) 1976; *Le Crabe-Tambour* 1977; *L'Adoption* (also co-prod.) 1978; *L'Honneur d'un Capitaine* 1982; *Le Juge, L'Année des Méduses/The Year of the Jellyfish, Paroles et Musique/Love Songs* (Can./Fr.) 1984; *Parole de Flic* 1985; *Nuovo Cinema Paradiso/Cinema Paradiso* (It./Fr.), *Le Peuple Singe* (doc.; prod. only), Vanille Fraise 1989; *Fuga Dal Paradiso/Escape from Paradise* (It./Fr./Ger.) 1990; *Hors la Vie* (prod. only; Fr./It./Bel.) 1991.

Perrine, Valerie. Actress. Born on Sept. 3, 1944, in Galveston, Tex. Tall, sexy, uninhibited leading lady of Hollywood films of the 70s. The daughter of a career military officer and a former showgirl, she grew up as an army brat and spent part of her childhood in Japan and other overseas posts. She briefly attended the universities of Arizona and Nevada, intending to become a psychologist but soon quit her studies to become a Las Vegas topless showgirl. After an interim period of soul searching, experimentation with drugs, and a hippie hand-to-mouth existence in Europe, she settled in Hollywood, living for a while on unemployment compensation and welfare. She finally broke into films in 1972, playing the role of Montana Wildhack, an outer space sex siren in George Roy Hill's *Slaughterhouse Five.* Other screen roles quickly followed. She was nominated for an Academy Award as best actress for her convincing performance as Honey, Lenny Bruce's stripper-junkie wife, in *Lenny* (1974).

FILMS: *Slaughterhouse Five* 1972; *The Last American Hero* 1973; *Lenny* 1974; *W.C. Fields and Me* 1976; *Mr. Billion/The Windfall* 1977; *Superman* 1978; *The Magician of Lublin* (Isr./Ger.), *The Electric Horseman* 1979; *Can't Stop the Music* 1980; *Agency* (Can.), *Superman II* 1981; *The Border* 1982; *Water* (UK) 1985; *Maid to Order* 1987; *Bright Angel* 1990; *Boiling Point* 1993.

Perry, Frank. Director. *b.* Aug. 21, 1930, in New York City. *d.* 1995. *ed.* U. of Miami. He began his association with the theater as a teenager, parking cars for customers of the Westport Country Playhouse in Connecticut. After a period of apprenticeship he worked in the theater as a stage manager and eventually producer. Back from military service during the Korean War, he entered films as a production assistant and later co-produced and moderated a TV documentary series, 'Playwright at Work.' Having studied directing with Lee STRASBERG, he made an auspicious debut as a film director in 1962 with *David and Lisa,* a sensitively observed, independently made study of two mentally disturbed teenagers, for which he was nominated for an Oscar. Perry's subsequent films have varied in quality but despite flaws were all marked by his sincerity and serious exploration of human relationships. Working mainly out of New York, Perry is among a few American directors who have shunned the glamour of Hollywood and its commercial rewards in the name of personal and professional integrity. His late wife, Eleanor Perry (1916–81), wrote the scripts for his films until their professional and legal separation in 1970. They divorced in the following year. He later married journalist-novelist Barbara Goldsmith. In 1977 he made his debut as a Broadway director with Paul Zindel's 'Ladies of the Alamo.' In 1991 and 1992 he shot an autobiographical documentary, *On the Bridge.*

FILMS: *David and Lisa* (also co-exec. prod.) 1962; *Ladybug Ladybug* (also prod.) 1963; *The Swimmer* (also co-prod.; one scene directed by Sydney Pollack) 1968; *Last Summer, Trilogy* (also prod.; two of three episodes originally made for TV) 1969; *Diary of a Mad Housewife* (also prod.) 1970; *Doc* (also prod.) 1971; *Play It As It Lays* (also prod.) 1972; *Man on a Swing* 1974; *Rancho Deluxe* 1975; *Mommie Dearest* (also co-sc.) 1981; *Monsignor* 1982; *Compromising Positions* (also prod.) 1985; *Hello Again* (also prod.) 1987; *On the Bridge* (doc.; also prod., sc., act.) 1992.

persistence of vision. The phenomenon, basic to motion pictures, of the retention of an image on the eye's retina, so that a picture remains briefly visible after its actual disappearance. It is this phenomenon that permits the illusion of movement in the viewing of motion pictures, since a succession of still pictures projected on a screen at a sufficient speed will provide the human eye with enough successive stimuli so that it will accept them as continuous motion.

Persoff, Nehemiah. Actor. Born on Aug. 14, 1920, in Jerusalem, Israel. A former electrician and signal maintenance man on New York's subway, he was trained for the stage by Stella Adler and the Actors Studio. He made his stage debut in 1940 off Broadway and his first screen appearance in 1948. Played many character parts in films and on TV, usually as a heavy.

FILMS INCLUDE: *The Naked City* 1948; *On the Waterfront* 1954; *The Harder They Fall, The Wild Party* 1956; *The Wrong Man, Men in War* 1957; *La Diga sul Pacifico/This Angry Age* (It.), *The Badlanders* 1958; *Never Steal Anything Small, Green Mansions, Al Capone, Some Like It Hot* 1959; *The Comancheros* 1961; *The Hook* 1963; *A Global Affair, Fate Is the Hunter* 1964; *The Greatest Story Ever Told* 1965; *The Power, The Money Jungle, Panic in the City* 1968; *Il Giorno della Civetta/Mafia* (It./Fr.) 1969; *The People Next Door* 1970; *Mrs. Pollifax—Spy, Red Sky at Morning* 1971; *Psychic Killer* 1975; *Voyage of the Damned* (UK) 1976. *Yentl* 1983; *An American Tail* (v/o) 1986; *The Last Temptation of Christ* 1988; *An American Tail: Fievel Goes West* (v/o) 1991.

Persson, Jörgen. Director of photography. Born in 1936, in Helsingborg, Sweden. A graduate of the Swedish Film Institute's school, he gained international praise for the lyrical impressionistic cinematography of *Elvira Madigan* (1967). He remains one of Europe's most creative lighting cameramen.

FILMS INCLUDE: *Elvira Madigan* 1967; *Adalen 31* 1969; *Joe Hill* 1971; *The Simple-Minded Murderer* 1984; *My Life as a Dog* 1985; *Pelle the Conqueror* 1987; *Blackjack* 1990.

Pertwee, Michael. Playwright, screenwriter. *b.* Apr. 24, 1916, London. *d.* 1991. The son of actor-playwright-screenwriter Roland Pertwee, he began writing for the screen in the late 30s. He wrote screenplays, alone or in collaboration, for many British and some American films, proving his best with satirical comedy. His brother, Jon Pertwee (*b.* July 7, 1919, London), is a comic actor of the British stage and screen.

FILMS INCLUDE: *Crackerjack/Man with 100 Faces* 1938; *A Girl Must Live* (co-adapt. only) 1939; *They Came by Night* 1940; *2,000 Women* 1943; *Against the Wind* (adapt. only) 1948; *Silent Dust* (from own co-play, 'The Paragon'), *Interrupted Journey* 1949; *Laughter in Paradise* 1951; *Curtain Up, Top Secret/Mr. Potts Goes to Moscow* 1952; *Happy Ever After/Tonight's the Night* 1954; *Now and Forever* 1956; *The Naked Truth/Your Past Is Showing* 1957; *Too Many Crooks* 1959; *Make Mine Mink* 1960; *In the Doghouse* 1961; *The Mouse on the Moon, Ladies Who Do* 1963; *Strange Bedfellows* (US) 1965; *A Funny Thing Happened on the Way to the Forum* (US), *Finders Keepers* 1966; *Salt and Pepper* (US/UK) 1968; *One More Time* (US/UK) 1970; *Digby—The Biggest Dog in the World* 1974; *Don't Just Lie There Say Something* 1976.

Pesci, Joe. Actor. Born on Feb. 9, 1943, in Newark, N.J.

Brash, diminutive character player with a penchant for portraying tough gangsters. The son of a blue-collar worker, he began performing on the stage at age five and at ten was a regular on the TV variety show 'Startime Kids.' In his early 20s he began singing in nightclubs and cutting a few records under the pseudonym Joe Ritchie. Later he played guitar with the Joey Dee and the Starliters band, then teamed up with Frank Vincent in a vaudeville-style nightclub comedy act. After appearing in the low-budget film *The Death Collector* (1975), which was shot in New Jersey, he went to Hollywood, hoping for a movie career. Instead, he worked there as a barber, postal clerk, and grocer's helper before returning deflated to the East Coast. He was ready to give up on acting, when he was invited to audition for the role of Jake La Motta's brother in *Raging Bull* (1980), which eventually earned him an Oscar nomination as best supporting actor. He won the Academy Award for his pivotal role in another Martin Scorsese film, *Goodfellas* (1990). He displayed his ability to play a comedic lead in *My Cousin Vinny*, the sleeper comedy hit of 1992.

FILMS: *Hey Let's Twist* (bit) 1961; *Death Collector/ Family Enforcer* 1975; *Raging Bull* 1980; *I'm Dancing as Fast as I Can* 1981; *Dear Mr. Wonderful* (Ger.) 1982; *Eureka* (UK), *Easy Money* 1983; *Tutti Dentro* (It.), *Once Upon a Time in America* 1984; *Man on Fire* (It./Fr.) 1987; *Moonwalker* (also co-prod.) 1988; *Lethal Weapon 2* 1989; *Backtrack, Betsy's Wedding, Goodfellas, Home Alone* 1990; *Catchfire, The Super, JFK* 1991; *My Cousin Vinny, Tuti Dentro* (It.), *Lethal Weapon 3, Home Alone 2* 1992; *Jimmy Hollywood, With Honors* 1994; *Casino* 1995; *8 Heads in a Duffle Bag, Gone Fishing* 1997.

Peters, Bernadette. Actress. Born Bernadette Lazzara, on Feb. 28, 1944, in Ozone Park, N.Y. *ed.* Quintano School for Young Professionals. Bubbly, naughtily comic, leading lady of the American stage, nightclubs, TV, and films. The daughter of a first-generation Italian-American who drove a bread truck, she made her professional debut at age five on TV's 'Horn and Hardart Children's Hour.' She made her first legitimate stage appearance in a New York revival of 'The Most Happy Fella' in 1955 and later toured with the road company of 'Gypsy.' By the late 60s she was starring in Broadway musicals, scoring a personal triumph in off-Broadway's 'Dames at Sea' (1968), for which she won her first Drama Desk Award. She won another, as well as a Tony, for Andrew Lloyd Weber's 'Song and Dance' (1985) and continued to make stage appearances well into the 90s. In 1975–76 she co-starred in the TV series 'All's Fair.' Her vivacious appeal and comic talent have not been well showcased in many of the movies she has made since 1973.

FILMS: *Ace Eli and Rodger of the Skies* 1973; *The Longest Yard* 1974; *W. C. Fields and Me, Vigilante Force, Silent Movie* 1976; *The Jerk* 1979; *Tulips* (Can.), *Heartbeeps, Pennies from Heaven* 1981; *Annie* 1982; *Slaves of New York, Pink Cadillac* 1989; *Alice* 1990; *Impromptu* (as Marie D'Agoult; US/Fr.) 1992.

Peters, Brock. Actor, singer. Born Brock Fisher, on July 2, 1927, in New York City. *ed.* U. of Chicago; CCNY. Deep-voiced, intense player of the American stage, nightclubs, TV, and films. A performer since his teens, he appeared in only two isolated films in the 50s but in the 60s and early 70s established himself as one of the American screen's leading black actors, typically personifying hardened brutes but also covering a broad range of other roles. He co-produced *Five on the Black Hand Side* (1973).

FILMS INCLUDE: *Carmen Jones* 1954; *Porgy and Bess* 1959; *The L-Shaped Room* (UK), *To Kill a Mockingbird* 1962; *Heavens Above* (UK) 1963; *Major Dundee, The Pawnbroker* 1965; *The Incident* 1967; *P. J., The Daring Game* 1968; *The McMasters* 1970; *Black Girl* 1972; *Soylent Green, Slaughter's Big Ripoff* 1973; *Lost in the Stars* 1974; *Framed* 1975; *Two-Minute Warning* 1976; *Star Trek IV: The Voyage Home* 1986; *Alligator 2: The Mutation* 1990; *Star Trek VI: The Undiscovered Country* 1991; *The Importance of Being Earnest* 1992.

Peters, House. Actor. *b.* 1879, Bristol, England. *d.* 1967. Handsome hero of early American silents. Imported from the stage by Adolph Zukor's Famous Players in 1913, he played leads in many productions of various studios. He retired at the advent of the talkies, returning to the screen only once, for a guest appearance in a Gene Autry vehicle, *The Old West* (1952). His son, House Peters, Jr. (*b.* Jan. 12, 1916, New Rochelle, N.Y.), has played character roles, mostly heavy, in numerous Westerns, action pictures, serials, and TV programs.

FILMS INCLUDE: *In the Bishop's Carriage, An Hour Before Dawn, Port of Doom, Lea Kleschna, A Lady of Quality* 1913; *The Pride of Jennico, The Brute, Salomy Jane, Mrs. Wiggs of the Cabbage Patch* 1914; *The Girl of the Golden West, Mignon, The Warrens of Virginia, The Unafraid, The Captive, Stolen Goods, The Winged Idol, The Great Divide, Between Men* 1915; *The Hand of Peril, The Closed Road, The Velvet Paw* 1916; *As Men Love, The Highway of Hope, The Heir of the Ages* 1917; *Thunderbolt of Fate, The Forfeit, You Never Know Your Luck* 1919; *The Leopard Woman, The Great Redeemer, Isobel* 1920; *Lying Lips, The Invisible Power, The Man from Lost River* 1921; *The Storm, Human Hearts, Rich Men's Wives* 1922; *Lost and Found, Held to Answer, Don't Marry for Money* 1923; *The Tornado* 1924; *Head Winds, Raffles the Amateur Cracksman, The Storm Breaker, Counsel for the Defense* 1925; *The Combat, Prisoners of the Storm* 1926; *Rose-Marie* 1928; *The Old West* 1952.

Peters, Jean. Actress. Born Elizabeth Jean Peters, on Oct. 15, 1926, in Canton, Ohio. *ed.* U. of Michigan; Ohio State. Pretty brunette leading lady of Hollywood films of the late 40s and early 50s. She won a trip to Hollywood in 1946 as a prize for winning the Miss Ohio State popularity contest and made her screen debut the following year as Tyrone Power's leading lady in *Captain from Castile.* She starred in many other Fox productions before retiring from the screen in 1955. In 1957 she secretly married mystery millionaire Howard HUGHES. They spent much of their married life separately as Hughes retreated into reclusion and were divorced in 1971. Shortly thereafter, Miss Peters married film executive Stanley Hough. She resumed her acting career on TV, in 1973.

FILMS: *Captain from Castile* 1947; *Deep Waters* 1948; *It Happens Every Spring* 1949; *Love That Brute* 1950; *Take Care of My Little Girl, As Young As You Feel, Anne of the Indies* 1951; *Viva Zapata!, Wait Till the Sun Shines Nellie, Lure of the Wilderness, O. Henry's Full House* 1952; *Niagara, Pickup on South Street, A Blueprint for Murder, Vickie* 1953; *Three Coins in the Fountain, Apache, Broken Lance* 1954; *A Man Called Peter* 1955.

Peters, Jon. Producer, executive. Born in 1947, in Van Nuys, Calif. After the death of his father, a Cherokee Indian cook, he proved too unruly for his mother, a hairdresser of Neapolitan descent. He did time in reform school and dropped out of school after the seventh grade. At 12 he went on his own to New York, where he cut hair in a beauty shop and at 14 he returned to California with a 15-year-old wife. With borrowed money he established the elegant Jon Peters Salon on Rodeo Drive and before long presided over a multimillion-dollar empire of beauty shops and cosmetic products. The character portrayed by Warren Beatty in *Shampoo* (1975) was supposedly patterned after Peters. Having divorced his first wife, he married actress Lesley Ann WARREN in 1967 and took charge of her career. His interest in show business increased after Barbra STREISAND hired him to cut her hair for the film *For Pete's Sake* (1974). Their professional relationship became personal and after divorcing Miss Warren in 1975, Peters became Streisand's lover, personal manager, and film and record producer. Following the box-office success of his first production, *A Star Is Born* (1976), he devoted his energies entirely to film, producing *The Eyes of Laura Mars* (1978), *The Main Event* (1979), and *Die Laughing* and *Caddyshack* a year later. That same year, he teamed up with Peter GUBER to form one of the most successful partnerships in recent Hollywood history, a success-studded collaboration that eventually led to their co-chairmanship of Columbia Pictures. In 1991, Peters quit his executive post to pursue independent production, leaving Guber as sole chairman. For details and credits of the collaboration, see GUBER, Peter.

Peters, Susan. Actress. *b.* Suzanne Carnahan, July 3, 1921, Spokane, Wash. *d.* 1952. Young leading lady of Hollywood films of the 40s, initially billed under her real name, Suzanne Carnahan. She was nominated for an Oscar for her supporting performance in *Random Harvest* (1942). In 1944 she suffered a severe spinal injury in a hunting accident, tried a comeback in a wheelchair, but finally retired and soon after died. At one time (1943–48) married to Richard QUINE.

FILMS INCLUDE: *Santa Fe Trail, Susan and God* 1940; *Strawberry Blonde, Meet John Doe* 1941; *The Big Shot, Tish, Random Harvest, Dr. Gillespie's New Assistant, Andy Hardy's Double Life* 1942; *Assignment in Brittany, Young Ideas* 1943; *Song of Russia* 1944; *Keep Your Powder Dry* 1945; *The Sign of the Ram* 1948.

Petersen, William (L.). Actor. Born 1953 in Evanston, Ill. *ed.* Idaho State University. Slender, dynamic leading and supporting actor of the American stage, television, and films. With years of theatrical experience behind him on the stages of Chicago, he made his mark in feature films as the almost-moral cop in William Friedkin's intense, high-voltage actioner *To Live and Die in L.A.* (1985).

FILMS: *To Live and Die in L.A.* 1985; *Manhunter* 1986; *Amazing Grace and Chuck, Long Gone* 1987; *Cousins* 1989; *Young Guns II* 1990; *Hard Promises* (also prod.) 1991; *Passes Away* 1992; *Fear* 1995.

Petersen, Wolfgang. Director. Born on Mar. 14, 1941, in Emden, Germany. He began his career at 19 as an assistant director at Hamburg's Ernst Deutsh Theater. At 20 he directed his first stage production. Following training at the Berlin Film and Television Academy, he directed a prize-winning, six-part thriller series, 'Scenes of the Crime,' for German TV. Turning to feature films in 1973, he won the German National Film Prize as best new director for *Einer von uns beiden* ('One of Us Two'). Petersen first attracted international attention with *The Consequence* (1977), in which he dealt sincerely and delicately with male homosexuality. He then gained worldwide admiration for *Das Boot/The Boat* (1981), a meticulously crafted, dramatically intense odyssey of a German submarine on a WW II mission. He was nominated for Oscars for both the film's direction and screenplay. In an abrupt change of style and pace, he next directed *The Neverending Story* (1984), a charming children's fantasy and his first English-language film. Hollywood productions followed. After a number of moderate successes, he established himself strongly in Hollywood with the droll, well-paced Clint Eastwood thriller *In the Line of Fire*.

FILMS (as director-screenwriter): *Einer von uns beiden* 1973; *Vier gegen die Blank, Reifezeugnis* 1976; *Planubung, Die Konsequenz/The Consequence* 1977; *Schwarz und weiss wie Tage und Nachte/Black and White Like Day and Night* 1978; *Das Boot/The Boat* 1981; *The Neverending Story* 1984; *Enemy Mine* (dir. only; US) 1985; *Shattered* (US/Ger.) 1991; *In the Line of Fire* 1993; *Outbreak* (also co-prod.) 1995; *Air Force One* (also co-prod.), *Red Corner* (Exec. Prod. only) 1997.

Petri, Elio. Director. *b.* Jan. 29, 1929, Rome. *d.* 1982. A graduate of Rome University, where he majored in literature, he first became involved with films as a critic for the Communist daily *L'Unita.* He directed a number of documentaries and collaborated on many scripts for films of De Santis and other directors before making his own debut as a feature director in 1961. Petri's films have been noted for their modish style and their concern with the direction of modern society. His *Investigation of a Citizen Above Suspicion,* a Kafkaesque thriller about a Fascist police chief who kills his mistress and challenges the authorities with tantalizing clues, won an Oscar as the best foreign film for 1970. *Lulu the Tool* won the Grand Prize at Cannes in 1972. During the 60s and 70s he was among the most politically challenging figures in world cinema.

FILMS (as director and co-screenwriter): *L'Assassino/The Lady Killer of Rome* 1961; *I Giorni Contati* 1962; *Il Maestro di Vigevano* 1963; *Alta Infedeltà/High Infidelity* ("Sin in the Afternoon" episode) 1964; *La Decima Vittima/The Tenth Victim* 1965; *A Ciascuno il suo/We Still Kill the Old Way* 1967; *Un Tranquillo Posto di Campagna/A Quiet Place in the Country* 1968; *Indagine su un Cittadino al di sopra di Ogni Sospetto/Investigation of a Citizen Above Suspicion* 1970; *La Classe Operaia va in Paradiso/Lulu the Tool/The Working Class Goes to Heaven* 1971; *La Proprietà non è piu un Furto* 1973; *Todo Modo* 1976; *Le Mani sporche* (for TV) 1978; *Le Buone Notizie* 1979.

Petrie, Daniel. Director. Born on Nov. 26, 1920, in Glace Bay, Nova Scotia, Canada. *ed.* St. Francis Xavier (B.A. communications); Columbia (M.A.); Northwestern U. (postgraduate). In the US from 1945, following WW II service with the Canadian Army, he began his career as a Broadway actor. As a TV director from 1950, he handled many episodes for such TV series as 'The Defenders,' 'East Side West Side,' 'Marcus Welby, M.D.,' 'Medical Center,' and 'MacMillan and Wife.' He also directed numerous TV dramas, including the Emmy Award–winning 'Eleanor and Franklin' (1976) and 'Eleanor and Franklin: The White House Years' (1977). A feature director from 1960, he scored a critical success with his second film, *A Raisin in the Sun* (1961), a superb screen adaptation of Lorraine Hansberry's play about a Chicago black family. With the exception of *Fort Apache, The Bronx* (1981), a strong drama about police action in a crime-ridden New York neighborhood, much of Petrie's subsequent work has been routine. He won a Canadian Genie Award for the screenplay of his autobiographical film, *The Bay Boy* (1984). He has also directed for the stage. His two sons (he also has twin daughters) are also in film, Daniel Petrie, Jr., a screenwriter-producer (nominated for an Oscar for the script of *Beverly Hills Cop,* and Donald Petrie, a director (*Mystic Pizza, Opportunity Knocks).*

FILMS: *The Bramble Bush* 1960; *A Raisin in the Sun* 1961; *The Main Attraction, Stolen Hours* 1963; *The Idol* (UK), *The Spy with a Cold Nose* (UK) 1966; *The Neptune Factor* 1973; *Buster and Billie* 1974; *Lifeguard* 1976; *The Betsy* 1978; *Resurrection* 1980; *Fort Apache The Bronx* 1981; *Six Pack* 1982; *The Bay Boy* (also sc.; Can./Fr.) 1984; *Square Dance* (also prod.) 1986; *Rocket Gibraltar, Cocoon: The Return* 1988; *Toy Soldiers* (also co-sc.) 1991; *In the Army Now, Lassie* 1994.

Petrov, Vladimir. Director. *b.* 1896, St. Petersburg, Russia. *d.* 1966. Studied drama in London and directed for the Russian stage before entering Soviet films as an assistant in 1925. A director from 1929, he is best known for his two opulent two-part films, *Peter the First* and *Battle of Stalingrad.* His films have been criticized for their overly careful composition and theatrical movement but praised for their rich imagery.

FILMS: *Golden Honey* (co-dir.), *Dzhoi and His Friends* (co-dir., co-sc.) 1928; *Address by Lenin* 1929; *Fritz Bauer* (also sc.), *Children of the New Day, The Cold Feast* (also co-sc.) 1930; *The Fugitive* (also co-sc.), *The Carpenter* (also sc.) 1932; *Thunderstorm* (also sc.) 1934; *Peter the First* (also co-sc.) 1937; *The Conquests of Peter the Great* (Pt. II of *Peter the First;* also co-sc.) 1939; *Chapayev Is with Us* 1941; *The Elusive Jan* (co-dir.) 1943; *Kutuzov/1812, Jubilee* (also sc.) 1944; *Guilty Though Innocent* (also sc.) 1945; *The First Front* (Pt. I of *Battle of Stalingrad*) 1949; *The Victors and the Vanquished* (Pt. II of *Battle of Stalingrad*) 1950; *Sporting Honor* 1951; *Revizor/The Inspector General* (also sc.) 1952; *300 Years Ago* 1956; *The Duel* (also sc.) 1957; *Parvi Urok/The Old Lady* (Bulg./USSR), *On the Eve* 1959; *The Russian Forest* 1963.

Petrova, Olga. Actress. *b.* Muriel Harding, 1886, England. *d.* 1977. Vamp star of Hollywood silents, billed by studio publicity as a Russian noblewoman born in Warsaw, Poland. A former vaudeville headliner and Broadway lead, she was Metro's first big star, typically in *femme fatale* roles. Produced and scripted several of her own films. Retiring from the screen in 1918, she returned to the stage and authored three of the plays in which she starred. Autobiography: *Butter with My Bread* (1942).

FILMS INCLUDE: *The Tigress* 1914; *The Vampire, The Heart of a Painted Woman, My Madonna* 1915; *The Scarlet Woman, Extravagance, The Soul Market, The Eternal Question, Black Butterfly* 1916; *Daughters of Destiny, The Undying Flame, Exile, The Law of the Land, The Soul of a Magdalene, The Silence Sellers, More Truth Than Poetry* 1917; *The Life Mask, Tempered Steel, The Light Within, Panther Woman* 1918.

Petrović, Aleksander. Director. Born in 1929, in Yugoslavia. Leading figure of the Yugoslav cinema of the 60s. Began as film critic and documentary director. Won first prize at Karlovy Vary for *Three* and shared the Cannes Festival Grand Prize in 1967 for *I Even Met Some Happy Gypsies.* Both films were nominated for Oscars the same year.

FILMS INCLUDE: *Where Love Has Gone/Two* 1961; *The Days* 1963; *Three* 1965; *I Even Met Some Happy Gypsies* 1967; *It Rains in My Village* 1969; *Il Maestro e Margherita/The Master and Margarita* (It./Yug.) 1972; *Gruppenbild mit Dame* (Ger./Fr.) 1977; *The Most Glorious War* 1989.

Pettet, Joanna. Actress. Born on Nov. 16, 1944, in London. Raised in Canada and trained for the stage at New York City's Neighborhood Playhouse, she has played leads in a handful of American and international films.

FILMS: *The Group* (US) 1966; *La Nuit des Généraux/The Night of the Generals* (Fr./UK), *Casino Royale* (UK), *Robbery* (UK) 1967; *Blue* (US) 1968; *The Best House in London* (UK) 1969; *Welcome to Arrow Beach/Tender Flesh* (US) 1974; *The Evil* (US) 1978; *Double Exposure* (US) 1982; *Sweet Country* (Gr./Pan.) 1986; *Terror in Paradise* (US/Philip.) 1990.

Petty, Lori. Actress. Born in 1964, in Chattanooga, Tenn. With a dynamic on-screen personality, this actress's career in features started off with a small role in *Cadillac Man* (1990) and quickly progressed to its early peak with a leading role in the well-received Penny MARSHALL hit *A League of Their Own* (1992).

FILMS: *Cadillac Man* 1990; *Point Break* 1991; *A League of Their Own* 1992; *Free Willy, Poetic Justice* 1993; *In the Army Now* 1994; *The Glass Shield, Tank Girl* 1995.

Pevney, Joseph. Director. Born in 1920, in New York City. *ed.* NYU. A vaudeville song-and-dance man at age 13, he later became a nightclub entertainer and Broadway actor. In Hollywood as actor from the mid-40s, he appeared in such films as *Nocturne* (1946), *Body and Soul* (1947), *Street with No Name* (1948), and *Thieves' Highway* (1949) before turning director early in the 50s. Directed with certain flair many simpleminded Universal action and adventure pictures along with some more ambitious productions. Also much TV. He was married to the late Mitzi GREEN.

FILMS: *Shakedown, Undercover Girl* 1950; *Air Cadet, Iron Man, The Lady from Texas, The Strange Door* 1951; *Meet Danny Wilson, Flesh and Fury, Just Across the Street, Because of You* 1952; *Desert Legion, It Happens Every Thursday, Back to God's Country* 1953; *Yankee Pasha, Playgirl* 1954; *Three Ring Circus, Six Bridges to Cross, Foxfire, Female on the Beach* 1955; *Away All Boats, Congo Crossing* 1956; *Istanbul, Tammy and the Bachelor, The Midnight Story, Man of a Thousand Faces* 1957; *Twilight for the Gods, Torpedo Run* 1958; *Cash McCall, The Plunderers* (also prod.), *The Crowded Sky* 1960; *Portrait of a Mobster* 1961; *The Night of the Grizzly* 1966; *Prisoners of the Sea* 1985.

Pfeiffer, Michelle. Actress. Born on Apr. 29, 1957, in Santa Ana, Calif. Alluring, melancholy, blonde leading lady of Hollywood films. The daughter of an air-conditioning contractor, she worked as an optometrist's assistant and supermarket checkout clerk, among other jobs during and following her studies at Fountain Valley High School, Golden West Junior College, and Whitley College, where she trained to become a court reporter. After winning the Miss Orange County beauty contest (she later lost in the Miss L.A. competition), she began appearing in TV commercials, then moved to Los Angeles for acting classes. Following a one-line bit in an episode of the series 'Fantasy Island,' she landed a regular part as a bimbo named Bombshell in TV's 'Delta House' (1979). Making her film debut in the following year, she gradually toiled her way through unrewarding roles until 1987, when she emerged as an appealing, capable actress in *The Witches of Eastwick.* With Oscar nominations for *Dangerous Liaisons* (as best supporting actress, 1988), *The Fabulous Baker Boys* (as best actress, 1989), and *Love Field* (as best actress, 1992), she rapidly ranked among Hollywood's leading stars and most respected actresses. Her fiendishly appealing turn as Catwoman in the 1992 film *Batman Returns* displayed her talents for dark humor, while her subtle performance the next year in *The Age of Innocence* revealed further capacities for understatement. In 1993 she became an adoptive single mother. Formerly (1982–88) married to actor Peter Horton, she married TV producer David Kelley in 1993.

FILMS: *Falling in Love Again, The Hollywood Knights* 1980; *Charlie Chan and the Curse of the Dragon Queen* 1981; *Grease 2* 1982; *Scarface* 1983; *Into the Night, Ladyhawke* 1985; *Sweet Liberty* 1986; *The Witches of Eastwick, Amazon Women on the Moon* 1987; *Married to the Mob, Tequila Sunrise, Dangerous Liaisons* 1988; *The Fabulous Baker Boys* 1989; *The Russia House* 1990; *Frankie and Johnny* 1991; *Batman Returns* (as Catwoman), *Love Field* 1992; *The Age of Innocence* 1993; *Wolf* 1994; *Dangerous Minds* 1995; *One Fine Day* (also co-exec. prod.), *To Gillian on Her 37th Birthday, Up Close and Personal* 1996; *A Thousand Acres* 1997.

PG. See RATING.

Phalke, D. G. Director. *b.* Dhundiraj Govind Phalke, Apr. 30, 1870, Trymbakeshwar, India. *d.* 1944. A leading pioneer of Indian cinema. Formerly a painter, engraver, printer, and still photographer, he made his first film, a short, in 1911. The following year he built a studio in Bombay, where he shot India's first feature, *Rajah Harishandra* (1913). He directed well over 100 films, many dealing with Indian mythology.

FILMS INCLUDE: *Growth of a Pea Plant* (short) 1911;

Rajah Harishandra 1913; *The Legend of Mohini* 1914; *The Life of Krishna* 1918; *Kaliya Maradan* 1919; *Sati Manahanda* 1923; *Bridge Over the Ocean* 1927; *Setu Bandahan* 1932; *Gangavataran* 1937.

Phenakisticope (also known as **Phenakistiscope** or **Fantascope).** A device constructed in 1832 by Joseph PLATEAU which produced an illusion of motion by placing a rotating disc with drawings in front of a mirror. It was similar in concept to William George Horner's Zoötrope (or Zoetrope) and other persistence-of-vision mechanisms that preceded and led to the birth of motion pictures.

Philbin, Mary. Actress. *b.* July 16, 1903 in Chicago. *d.* 1993. A former beauty queen who became a star of Hollywood silents. Best known as the heroine of Lon Chaney's *The Phantom of the Opera.* Retired at the advent of sound.

FILMS INCLUDE: *The Blazing Trail, Danger Ahead, False Kisses* 1921; *Human Hearts* 1922; *Penrod and Sam, Merry-Go-Round, The Age of Desire, Where Is This West?, The Temple of Venus* 1923; *Fools' Highway, The Gaiety Girl, The Rose of Paris* 1924; *Fifth Avenue Models, The Phantom of the Opera, Stella Maris* 1925; *The Man Who Laughs, Surrender* 1927; *Drums of Love, Love Me and the World Is Mine* 1928; *Girl Overboard, The Last Performance, After the Fog, The Shannons of Broadway* 1929.

Philipe, Gérard. Actor. *b.* Dec. 4, 1922, Cannes, France. *d.* 1959. France's leading romantic star of the postwar years, a handsome, sensitive, soulful hero of many films and stage plays. The son of a hotel manager, he was intended for a medical career but chose acting instead and began playing small roles on the stage and in films in the early 40s. He was catapulted to stardom and international fame on the strength of his touching performance in the role of an awkward adolescent in love with a married woman (Micheline Presle) in Claude Autant-Lara's *Le Diable au Corps/Devil in the Flesh* (1946). Over the next few years he matured into an elegant, confident leading man, a unique stage and screen personality whose physical handsomeness and glowing spirit combined to make him France's most popular star of his generation and one of the most admired in the history of French theater and film. He became ill during the production of Buñuel's *La Fièvre monte à El Pao/Republic of Sin* and died of a heart attack before his 37th birthday. His image adorned a commemorative French postage stamp in a 1961 issue honoring the French theater.

FILMS: *Les Petites du Quai aux Fleurs* 1944; *La Boîte aux Rêves* 1945; *Le Pays sans Etoiles, L'Idiot/The Idiot* (as Mishkin), *Le Diable au Corps/Devil in the Flesh* 1946; *La Chartreuse de Parme* (Fr./It.) 1948; *Une si Jolie Petite Plage/Riptide, Tous les Chemins mènent à Rome* 1949; *La Beauté du Diable/Beauty and the Devil* (as Faust), *La Ronde, Souvenirs perdus* 1950; *Juliette ou la Clé des Songes* 1951; *Fanfan la Tulipe/Fanfan the Tulip* (title role), *Les Sept Péchés capitaux/The Seven Deadly Sins, Avec André Gide* (doc.), *Les Belles de Nuit/Beauties of the Night* 1952; *Les Orgueilleux/The Proud and the Beautiful* (Fr./Mex.) 1953; *Si Versailles m'était conté/Royal Affairs in Versailles* (as D'Artagnan), *Monsieur Ripois/Knave of Hearts/Lovers Happy Lovers* (UK/Fr.), *Villa Borghese/It Happened in the Park* (It./Fr.), *Le Rouge et le Noir* (as Julien Sorel) 1954; *Les Grandes Manoeuvres/The Grand Maneuver* 1955; *La Meilleure Part, Si Paris nous était conté, Les Aventures de Till l'Espiègle/Bold Adventure* (also dir., co-sc.) 1956; *Pot-Bouille* 1957; *Montparnasse 19/Modigliani of Montparnasse* (as Modigliani), *La Vie à Deux, Le Joueur* 1958; *Les Liaisons dangereuses* 1959; *La Fièvre monte à El Pao/Los Ambiciosos/Republic of Sin* (Mex./Fr.) 1960.

Phillips, Julia and Michael. A husband-wife team of producers, now divorced, who enjoyed a string of movie triumphs in the 70s. Julia (*b.* Julia Miller, Apr. 7, 1944, New York City), a graduate of Mt. Holyoke College, was an editorial assistant with several magazines before entering films as a story editor for Paramount, later rising to head of production for Mirisch and creative executive for First Artists. Michael (*b.* June 29, 1943, Brooklyn, N.Y.) was educated at Dartmouth and at the NYU Law School, becoming a practicing attorney and securities analyst. In 1970 they formed Bill/Phillips Productions with Tony BILL and proceeded to produce three of the decade's most prestigious productions: *The Sting* (1973), winner of the Academy Award for best picture (first Oscar in that category ever won by a woman producer); *Taxi Driver* (1976), winner of the Palme d'Or at Cannes; and *Close Encounters of the Third Kind* (1977), a mammoth box-office hit. But their meteoric rise proved ephemeral, partly because of Julia's growing addiction to drugs. Although she recovered after treatment, she found herself a social and professional pariah in Tinseltown. She wreaked her revenge on Hollywood in 1991 with a vicious best-selling exposé, *You'll Never Eat Lunch in This Town Again.*

FILMS: Julia and Michael—*Steelyard Blues* (with Tony Bill), *The Sting* (with Bill) 1973; *The Big Bus, Taxi Driver* 1976; *Close Encounters of the Third Kind* 1977. Julia only—*The Beat* 1988. Michael only—*Heartbeeps* 1981; *Cannery Row* 1982; *The Flamingo Kid* 1984; *Don't Tell Mom the Babysitter's Dead* 1991; *Mom and Dad Save the World* 1992.

Phillips, Lou Diamond. Actor. Born on Feb. 17, 1962, in the Philippines, of Filipino, Cherokee Indian, Scottish-Irish, Hawaiian, and Hispanic descent. Charismatic young lead of Hollywood films, often in ethnic roles. Raised in Arlington, Tex., he supplemented his drama studies at the University of Texas with training in film technique by Adam Roarke. Following appearances in regional theater and sporadic TV roles, he began a film career that gained a strong boost from his portrayal of the late singing star Richie Valens in *La Bamba* (1987). He married the film's assistant director, Julie Cypher. Having had a hand in a couple of scripts, he announced in 1991 his plans to become a director.

FILMS: *Angel Alley* (unreleased), *Interface* (unreleased) 1984; *Harley* (unreleased) 1986; *Trespasses* (also co-sc.; release delayed from 1983), *La Bamba* (as singer Richie Valens) 1987; *Stand and Deliver, Young Guns, Dakota* (also assoc. prod.) 1988; *Disorganized Crime, Renegades* 1989; *The First Power, A Show of Force, Young Guns II* 1990; *Ambition* (also sc.), *The Dark Wind, Cocaine Fever* 1991; *Shadow of the Wolf* 1992; *The Dark Wind, Sioux City* (also dir.) 1994; *Courage Under Fire* 1996.

Phillips, Sian. Actress. Born in 1934 in Bettws, Carmarthenshire, Wales. *ed.* RADA, London. Stately actress of British stage and screen. She made her London stage debut in 1957 in the title role of 'Hedda Gabler' and subsequently appeared in many plays, including 'The Taming of the Shrew' (as Katherine). Known best to TV audiences for her incarnation of the stunningly evil empress Livia in the PBS miniseries 'I, Claudius.' Over the years her screen appearances have been limited. Married (1959–79) to Peter O'TOOLE; their two children are Kate and Pat. In 1979 she married actor Robin Sachs.

FILMS INCLUDE: *Becket* 1964; *Young Cassidy* 1965; *Laughter in the Dark, Goodbye Mr. Chips* 1969; *Murphy's War* 1971; *Under Milk Wood* 1973; *Nijinsky* 1980; *Clash of the Titans* 1981; *Dune* (US) 1984; *The Doctor and the Devils* 1985; *Valmont* (Fr.) 1989; *The Age of Innocence* 1993.

Phoenix, River. Actor. *b.* Aug. 23, 1970, in Madras, Ore. *d.* 1993. Expressive blond, blue-eyed, young lead of Hollywood films. His parents were nature-loving, spiritually inclined hippies (father John, a former carpenter; mother Arlyn, a divorced Jewish secretary from the Bronx) who met in California in 1968 and subsisted for a while as itinerant fruit pickers. They joined a cultish sect called Children of God and when River was two, moved as missionaries to South America, where John served as "Archbishop of Venezuela and the Caribbean Islands." Five years later, disillusioned and broke, they moved back to the US and eventually settled in Los Angeles, changing the family name to Phoenix to symbolize their hope to rise from the ashes of the past. They also determined that the future of their children—River, Rainbow, Summer, Leaf, and Liberty—was in the movies. River proved the most successful. By the time he was ten he was singing, playing the guitar, and acting professionally on TV. He made his feature debut in 1985 and rapidly established himself as one of Hollywood's brightest young talents, performing with his own rock band as well as in a handful of films. In 1988, he was nominated for an Academy Award as best supporting actor for his role in Sidney Lumet's *Running on Empty*. He went on to deliver an outstanding performance as Mike, a narcoleptic gay street hustler, in Gus Van Sant's *My Own Private Idaho* (1991). In 1993 Phoenix collapsed and died under mysterious circumstances outside the Viper Room, a Los Angeles club owned by actor Johnny Depp. He was at one time romantically involved with actress Martha PLIMPTON.

FILMS: *Explorers* 1985; *Stand by Me, The Mosquito Coast* 1986; *A Night in the Life of Jimmy Reardon, Little Nikita, Running on Empty* 1988; *Indiana Jones and the Last Crusade* (as Young Indiana) 1989; *I Love You to Death* 1990; *Dogfight, My Own Private Idaho* 1991; *Sneakers* 1992; *The Thing Called Love* 1993; *Silent Tongue* 1994.

photoelectric cell (P.E.C.). A device capable of converting light rays into electric current. When light strikes the photocell of an exposure meter, it activates the exposure pointer; similarly, in sound projectors, when light directed at the film's sound track falls on the cell, it produces current variations that are subsequently converted into audible sounds.

photoflood. An incandescent tungsten lamp in which high intensity is obtained by overloading the voltage at the cost of shortening the life of the bulb.

photogenic. Having the ability to look well in a photograph. A term used to describe a performer's face that registers well on film and, in a broader sense, any object or arrangement of objects forming an attractive subject for photography.

photometer. A precision exposure meter, used for accurate measurement of brightness.

photoplay. Early term for a motion picture, coined in 1910 in a contest sponsored by the Essanay film company. The term served as the title for the popular fan magazine *Photoplay*, published from 1911 to 1980.

Pialat, Maurice. Director. Born on Aug. 21, 1925, in Puy-de-Dome, France. In Paris from age three, he attended L'Ecôle des Arts Décoratifs and L'Ecôle des Beaux Arts and for several years eked out a living as a painter, supplementing his income through various odd jobs and occasional acting. In 1958 he took an interest in filmmaking and directed several shorts, one of which, *L'Amour existe,* won a prize at the Venice Festival. After a decade of professional work for French television, he made his debut as a feature director with *L'Enfance nue/Naked Childhood/Me,* a simple, charming, touching, partly autobiographical story about adolescence that was shot in the *CINÉMA VÉRITÉ* style with a cast of nonprofessionals. It was warmly received at the 1968 New York Film Festival and won the Prix Jean Vigo in 1969. The same stark honesty that characterized that film also typified Pialat's next production, *Nous ne vieillirons pas ensemble/We Won't Grow Old Together/Break-Up* (1972), a lamentful account of the breakup of a long romantic relationship, which was based on the director's own unhappy experience. In these and several of his subsequent films, Pialat leaned toward topics of everyday life, focusing on their troubles, conflicts, and harsh realities. He won the best film César and the Prix Louis Delluc for *A Nos Amours* (1983), a family drama centering on the promiscuity of a teenaged daughter, and the Palme d'Or at the 1967 Cannes Festival for *Sous le Soleil de Satan,* an exploration of the inner life of a rural priest. He writes his own scripts, alone or in collaboration, and sometimes appears as an actor in his own films.

FEATURE FILMS (as director-writer): *L'Enfance nue/Naked Childhood/Me* 1968; *Nous ne vieillirons pas ensemble/We Won't Grow Old Together/Break-Up* 1972; *La Gueule ouverte* (also prod.) 1974; *Passe ton Bac d'abord/Graduate First* 1979; *Loulou* 1980; *A Nos Amours* (also act.) 1983; *Police* 1985; *Sous le Soleil de Satan/Under Satan's Sun/Under the Sun of Satan* (also act.) 1987; *Van Gogh* 1991; *Le Garcu* 1996.

Piccoli, Michel. Actor. Born Jacques Daniel Michel Piccoli, on Dec. 27, 1925, in Paris, of Italian parentage. Bald leading man and character player of the French stage, TV, and films. On the screen from the late 40s, he played many secondary roles before emerging in leads in the 60s. His elegant, intelligent, often sardonic portrayals have brought him many plum roles and international acclaim. Memorable in Godard's *Contempt* and Buñuel's *Belle de Jour.* Versatile and prolific, Piccoli played substantial roles in more than 100 films. He won the best actor prize at the 1980 Cannes Festival for *Leap Into Void* and shared the award in 1982 at Berlin for *A Strange Affair.* His second (1966–77) of three marriages was to actress-singer Juliet GRECO. Co-author: *Dialogues égoïstes* (1976).

FILMS INCLUDE: *Sortilèges/The Bellman* 1945; *Le Point du Jour* 1949; *Sans laisser d'Adresse* 1950; *Destinées/Daughters of Destiny* 1953; *French Cancan/Only the French Can, Les Mauvaises Rencontres* 1955; *La Mort en ce Jardin/Gina* (Fr./Mex.), *Les Sorcières de Salem/Witches of Salem* 1956; *Nathalie/The Foxiest Girl in Paris* 1957; *Rafles sur la Ville/Sinners of Paris* 1958; *Le Doulos/Doulos—The Finger Man, Le Jour et l'Heure/The Day and the Hour, Le Mépris/Contempt* 1963; *Le Journal d'une Femme de Chambre/Dairy of a Chambermaid* 1964; *De l'Amour, Masquerade* (UK), *Lady L* (Fr./It./US), *Le Coup de Grâce, Compartiments Tueurs/The Sleeping Car Murder* 1965; *Paris brûle-t-il?/Is Paris Burning?* (US/Fr.), *La Curée/The Game Is Over, La Guerre est finie* (Fr./Sw.), *Les Créatures* (Fr./Sw.) 1966; *Un Homme de trop/Shock Troops, Les Demoiselles de Rochefort/The Young Girls of Rochefort, Belle de Jour* 1967; *Benjamin, Danger: Diabolik, La Chamade, La Prisonnière, Dillinger è Morto/Dillinger Is Dead* (It.) 1968; *La Voie lactée/The Milky Way, Topaz* (US), *L'Invitata* (It.) 1969; *Les Choses de la Vie/The Things of Life, L'Invasion* 1970; *La Poudre d'Escampette/Touch and Go* 1971; *La Décade prodigieuse/Ten Days' Wonder, Le Charme discret de la Bourgeoisie/The Discreet Charm of the Bourgeoisie, La Cagna/Liza* (It./Fr.) 1972; *Themroc* (also co-prod.), *Les Noces rouges/Wedding in Blood, La Grande Bouffe, L'Attentat/The French Conspiracy* 1973; *Le Trio infernal, La Fantôme de la Liberté* 1974; *Vincent François Paul et les autres/Vincent Francois Paul and the Others* 1975; *La Dernière Femme/The Last Woman, F comme Fairbanks, Mado, Todo Modo* (It.) 1976; *René la Canne, L'Imprécateur Des Enfants pâtés/Spoiled Children* 1977; *La Part du Feu, L'Etat sauvage/The Savage State, La Petite Fille en Velours bleu, Le Sucre* 1978; *Giallo Napoletano* (It.), *Le Divorcement, Le Mors aux Dents* 1979; *Salto nel Vuoto/Leap Into Void* (It./Fr.), *Atlantic City* (Can./Fr.) 1980; *Une Etrange Affaire/A Strange Affair*

1981; *Espion lève-toi, La Passante de Sans-Souci/La Passante, La Nuit de Varennes* (It./Fr.) *Passion, Oltre la Porta/Beyond the Door* (It.), *Gli Occhi la Bocca/The Eyes the Mouth* (It./Fr.), *Une Chambre en Ville* 1982; *La Prix du Danger, Le Général de l'Armée morte* 1983; *Viva la Vie, La Diagonale du Fou/Dangerous Moves, Success Is the Best Revenge* (UK) 1984; *Péril en la Demeure/Peril/Death in a French Garden, Partir revenir, Adieu Bonaparte* 1985; *Le Paltoquet, Mauvais Sang/Bad Blood/The Night Is Young, La Puritaine* 1986; *La Rumba, L'Homme voilé, Maladie d'Amour, Das weite Land* (Ger.) 1987; *Y'a Bon les Blancs* (It./Fr.), *Blanc de Chine* 1988; *Milou en Mai/Milou in May/May Fools* (Fr./It.), *Le Peuple Singe* (doc.; narrator), *La Révolution Française/The French Revolution* (cameo) 1989; *Martha und Ich* (Ger./Fr.) 1990; *La Belle Noiseuse* 1991; *The Children Thief, Archipelago* 1992; *La Cavale des Fous, Le Souper, Ruptures* 1993; *Toy Nights* 1995; *Tykho Moon* 1997.

Picerni, Paul. Actor. Born on Dec. 1, 1922, in New York City. *ed.* Loyola U. (Los Angeles). Second lead and character player of Hollywood films and TV ('The Untouchables,' etc.).

FILMS INCLUDE: *Breakthrough* 1950; *Operation Pacific, The Tanks Are Coming, Force of Arms* 1951; *Mara Maru, Operation Secret* 1952; *House of Wax, The System* 1953; *To Hell and Back* 1955; *Miracle in the Rain* 1956; *Omar Khayyam* 1957; *Marjorie Morningstar* 1958; *The Young Philadelphians* 1959; *Strangers When We Meet* 1960; *The Scarface Mob* 1962; *The Scalphunters* 1968; *Che!* 1969; *Airport* 1970; *Kotch* 1971.

Pichel, Irving. Director. *b.* June 25, 1891, Pittsburgh. *d.* 1954. After graduating from Harvard, he tried a variety of jobs, finally becoming a stage actor. He then joined MGM's script department in 1927 but soon gravitated to screen acting and throughout the 30s played important character roles in films of various studios. At the same time, he took on directing assignments and by 1940 had phased out his acting career to concentrate exclusively on directing. His early work included collaboration on a well-made adventure thriller, *The Most Dangerous Game* (also known as *The Hounds of Zaroff,* 1932) and the fantasy yarn *She* (1935), but most of his films of the 30s were low-budget Republic productions. In the 40s he worked with bigger budgets for Fox, then Paramount, RKO, and Universal, establishing a reputation as a competent but rather impersonal director, with credits in a variety of genres—comedy, drama, action, and science fiction—and a marked preference for tearjerkers.

FILMS INCLUDE: As actor—*The Right to Love* 1930; *Murder by the Clock, An American Tragedy* (as Orville Mason), *The Cheat,* 1931; *The Miracle Man, Forgotten Commandments, Westward Passage, The Painted Woman, Madame Butterfly* (as Yomadori) 1932; *King of the Jungle, The Woman Accused, Oliver Twist* (as Fagin), *The Story of Temple Drake, I'm No Angel* 1933; *Return of the Terror, Cleopatra* (as Apollodorus), *British Agent* (as Joseph Stalin) 1934; *Special Agent* 1935; *The House of a Thousand Candles, Dracula's Daughter* 1936; *High Wide and Handsome* 1937; *Jezebel, Topper Takes a Trip* 1938; *Juarez, Rio* 1939. As director (complete)—*The Most Dangerous Game* (co-dir. with Ernest B. Schoedsack) 1932; *Before Dawn* 1933; *She* (co-dir. with Lansing C. Holden) 1935; *The Gentleman from Louisiana, Beware of Ladies* 1936; *Larceny on the Air, The Sheik Steps Out, The Duke Comes Back* 1937; *Earthbound, The Man I Married* 1940; *Hudson's Bay, Dance Hall, Swamp Water* (prod. only), *The Great Commandment* (made in 1939; release delayed) 1941; *Secret Agent of Japan, The Pied Piper, Life Begins at Eight-Thirty* 1942; *The Moon Is Down* (also act.), *Happy Land* 1943; *And Now Tomorrow* 1944; *A Medal for Benny* 1945; *Colonel Effingham's Raid, Tomorrow Is Forever, OSS, The Bride Wore Boots, Temptation* 1946; *They Won't Believe Me, Something in the Wind* 1947; *Miracle of the Bells, Mr. Peabody and the Mermaid* 1948; *Without Honor* 1949; *The Great Rupert, Quicksand, Destination Moon* 1950; *Santa Fe* (also sc., act.) 1951; *Martin Luther* (also act.) 1953; *Day of Triumph* 1954.

Pick, Lupu (often hyphenated: **Lupu-Pick**). Director, actor. *b.* Jan. 2, 1886, Iasi (Jassy), Rumania. *d.* 1931, of poisoning. Formerly a stage actor in Bucharest, Hamburg, and Berlin, he entered German films as an actor in 1915 and began directing in 1918. In the early 20s he rose to prominence as the most eloquent representative of the *Kammerspiel* (literally: chamber play) in German films, a style of expressionist naturalism characterized by sparse decor, a minimum of characters, and rigorous unity of time, place, and action. He made his most important films—*Shattered* and *New Year's Eve*—in collaboration with screenwriter Carl MAYER, who virtually dominated the Kammerspiel genre as Pick had the expressionist movement that preceded it. He was scheduled to direct *The Last Laugh* from Mayer's script, but he and Mayer quarreled and the assignment went to Murnau. After the parting with Mayer, the quality of Pick's films deteriorated noticeably.

FILMS INCLUDE: As actor—*Die Pagode, Der Schlemihl* 1915; *Hoffmans Erzählungen/Tales of Hoffman, Nacht des Grauens, Homunuculus* 1916; *Es werde Licht/Let There Be Light* 1918; *Fliehende Schatten* (also co-sc.) 1922; *Spione/The Spy* 1928. As director—*Die Liebe des Van Royk* 1918; *Die tolle Heirat von Lalo, Der Herr Uber Leben und Tod, Marionetten der Leidenschaft, Grauen, Oliver Twist, Tötet nicht mehr* 1920; *Grausige Nächte, Scherben/Shattered* 1921; *Zum Paradies der Damen* 1922; *Sylvester/New Year's Eve, Weltspiegel* 1923; *Das Haus der Lüge* 1925; *Das Panzergewölbe/Armored Vault* (also co-sc.) 1926; *Eine Nacht in London/A Night in London* (also prod.; Ger./UK) 1928; *Napoleon auf St. Helena* 1929; *Gassenhauer* 1931.

Pickens, Slim. Actor. *b.* Louis Bert Lindley, Jr., June 29, 1919, Kingsberg, Calif. *d.* 1983. Wiry, hoarse, capable character player of numerous Hollywood Westerns. He appeared in rodeos from the age of 12 and was one of the top clowns on the rodeo circuit before entering films in 1950. Although he was most closely associated with Western films, he is perhaps best remembered as the madly chauvinistic bomber pilot who rides a nuclear bomb bronco-style all the way down to its target on Soviet soil in Stanley Kubrick's political black comedy *Dr. Strangelove.*

FILMS INCLUDE: *Rocky Mountain* 1950; *Colorado Sundown, The Story of Will Rogers* 1952; *Old Overland Trail* 1953; *The Outcast, The Boy from Oklahoma* 1954; *Santa Fe Passage, The Last Command* 1955; *The Great Locomotive Chase* 1956; *Gunsight Ridge* 1957; *The Sheepman* 1958; *Escort West* 1959; *One-Eyed Jacks* 1961; *Savage Sam* 1963; *Dr. Strangelove* 1964; *Major Dundee, In Harm's Way* 1965; *Stagecoach* 1966; *The Flim-Flam Man, Rough Night in Jericho* 1967; *Will Penny, Never a Dull Moment* 1968; *80 Stops to Jonah* 1969; *The Ballad of Cable Hogue* 1970; *The Deserter* 1971; *The Cowboys, The Honkers, The Getaway* 1972; *Pat Garrett and Billy the Kid* 1973; *Blazing Saddles* 1974; *The Apple Dumpling Gang, White Line Fever, Rancho Deluxe, The Legend of Earl Durand* 1975; *Hawmps* 1976; *Mr. Billion, The White Buffalo* 1977; *The Swarm* 1978; *Beyond the Poseidon Adventure, 1941* 1979; *Tom Horn, Honeysuckle Rose* 1980; *The Howling* 1981; *Pink Motel* 1983.

Pickford, Jack. Actor. *b.* Jack Smith, Aug. 18, 1896, Toronto. *d.* 1933. The brother of Mary PICKFORD, he followed in his older sister's footsteps as a child actor on the stage and as a juvenile, then as a romantic lead in films. Mary got him into

Biograph in 1910. When she signed her famous million-dollar deal with First National in 1917, one of her stipulations was a lucrative contract for her brother. He became a star in his own right and later also co-directed a couple of films. Jack, who had a playboy's reputation, was married to movie star Olive THOMAS from 1917 till her tragic death in 1920. He later married and divorced actresses Marilyn MILLER (1922–27) and Mary Mulhern (1930–32).

FILMS INCLUDE: *The Kid, White Roses, A Plain Song, Two Little Waifs—A Modern Fairy Tale* 1910; *For Her Brother's Sake* 1911; *The Inner Circle, The Would-Be Shriner, A Dash Through the Clouds, Musketeers of Pig Alley, Heredity* 1912; *The Unwelcome Guest, The Sneak* 1913; *The Gangsters, The Massacre, The Mysterious Shot, The Eagle's Mate, Home Sweet Home, Wildflower* 1914; *A Girl of Yesterday, The Commanding Officer, The Pretty Sister of Jose* 1915; *Poor Little Peppina, Seventeen* 1916; *Great Expectations* (as Pip), *The Dummy, Freckles, The Varmint, Tom Sawyer* (title role), *The Ghost House, Jack and Jill* 1917; *The Spirit of '17, Huck and Tom* (as Tom Sawyer), *Sandy, Mile-a-Minute Kendall, His Majesty Bunker Bean* 1918; *Bill Apperson's Boy* 1919; *The Little Shepherd of Kingdom Come, Just Out of College* 1920; *Through the Back Door* (co-dir. only, with Alfred E. Green), *Little Lord Fauntleroy* (co-dir. only, with Green) 1921; *Garrison's Finish* (also prod.) 1923; *The Hill Billy* (also prod.) 1924; *Waking Up the Town, My Son, The Goose Woman* 1925; *The Bat, Brown of Harvard, Exit Smiling* 1926; *Gang War* 1928.

Pickford, Mary. Actress. *b.* Gladys Smith, Apr. 8, 1893, Toronto. *d.* 1979. When she was five, her father, a laborer, was killed in a job-related accident and she found herself prematurely burdened with the dual role of mother's helper to sister Lottie, three, and brother Jack, two, and breadwinner. Billed as "Baby Gladys," she toured with various road companies, and within several years had gained enough experience and confidence to feel she was ready for Broadway. At 14 she stormed into David Belasco's office and charmed him into giving her a starring role in his play 'The Warrens of Virginia.' It was he who rechristened her Mary Pickford. In 1909, at 16, she used a similar combination of childlike charm and feminine wile to win over D. W. GRIFFITH at Biograph and begin a unique film career that made her the most popular star in screen history.

Like all other Biograph personalities, she was not identified by name, because it was feared that publicity might cause stars to demand higher wages; but she had a trademark, a head of golden curls, and once played a character identified in the film's continuity titles as "Little Mary." Within several months she proved to be so popular that exhibitors were advertising her as "The Girl with the Golden Hair" or simply "Little Mary." When she was lured away from Biograph in 1910 by Carl LAEMMLE's IMP, that company proudly pronounced in its ads: "Little Mary is an Imp now."

An astute businesswoman, Miss Pickford moved from company to company, driving a hard bargain for higher wages and greater control over her vehicles. She started at $40 a week at Biograph in 1909. In 1910 she was earning $175 a week at IMP; in 1911, $275 at Majestic. She then returned briefly to Biograph, and in 1912 she went to work for Adolph ZUKOR's Famous Players Company at $500 a week. Her salary was doubled periodically, and in mid-1916 she signed an astounding contract with Zukor calling for $10,000 weekly and a $300,000 bonus, plus the formation of an affiliate, The Mary Pickford Company, a studio devoted exclusively to the making of her films, and also a share in the profits of the studio. But even that proved not enough. In the following year she signed with First National for $350,000 a picture.

Mary Pickford's appeal was international. A born charmer with a radiant, dimpled, child-woman beauty and a spirited and spontaneous screen personality, she captivated audiences' emotions with a natural ease. For many years she remained the nation's biggest box-office draw. During her long career she played a variety of parts, but was best loved and remembered in her typical role as a sweet, innocent, lovable little girl, for which she was dubbed "America's Sweetheart" (she was known as "The World's Sweetheart" abroad). From time to time she tried to rebel against her standardized screen portrayals but found herself giving in to public pressure and returning to sweet-innocent-little-thing roles. As late as 1920, at the age of 27, she played a girl of 12 in *Pollyanna,* and similar parts in other films.

From an early point in her career, Miss Pickford exercised veto power over her films and was given a choice of script, director, and co-stars. As a result, her vehicles usually boasted high production values and most were immensely profitable. In 1919 she entered a partnership with three other formidable luminaries of the business—Charlie CHAPLIN, D. W. Griffith, and Douglas FAIRBANKS—to form the United Artists Corporation. The following year she married Fairbanks, her second husband (she had married the first, actor Owen MOORE, in 1911 and divorced him after he became an incurable alcoholic). The marriage to Fairbanks, although not a happy one, had the public aura of a dream come true. To starstruck millions, the couple represented Hollywood royalty at its loftiest and their legendary home, Pickfair (a combination of their last names), a fairy tale castle.

In 1928, in a daring rebellious rage, she had her famous blond curls shorn and acquired the then-contemporary shingled hairstyle. In 1929 she made her first talkie, *Coquette,* wearing her new hairstyle and playing a modern swinger role. She won an Academy Award for her performance, but the film and her new personality did not click with audiences. Her next vehicle, a much-publicized screen adaptation of Shakespeare's 'The Taming of the Shrew' (famous for the credit line "additional dialogue by Sam Taylor"), co-starring Fairbanks, was a catastrophe that virtually ended her career. After appearing in two other disheartening failures, she retired from the screen in 1933. In the mid-30s she made frequent broadcasts on network radio and published several books, including her memoirs, *Sunshine and Shadow* (1955). Having divorced Fairbanks in 1936 she married former co-star Charles "Buddy" ROGERS in 1937. In 1953 she and Chaplin, the sole survivors of the partnership, sold United Artists. Miss Pickford, who in the early 30s bought out many of her early silent films with the intention of having them burned at her death, had a change of heart and in 1970 donated 50 of more than 130 of her Biograph-period films to the American Film Institute. She received a special Academy Award in 1975, in recognition of her contribution to the American film. Mary's younger sister, Lottie Pickford (*b.* Lottie Smith, 1895, Toronto; *d.* 1936), and her brother Jack PICKFORD, also had careers in films.

FILMS INCLUDE: *The Violin Maker of Cremona, The Lonely Villa, Her First Biscuits, Two Memories, The Way of Man, Sweet and Twenty, 1776 or The Hessian Renegades, The Gibson Goddess, The Slave, Getting Even, In Old Kentucky, The Little Darling, His Wife's Visitor, The Little Teacher* (also co-sc.), *The Restoration, To Save Her Soul* 1909; *The Englishman and the Girl, As It Is in Life, An Affair of Hearts, Ramona, The Kid, A Rich Revenge, In the Season of Buds, May and December* (also sc.), *A Son's Return, The Call to Arms, A Child's Impulse, Love Among the Roses, What the Daisy Said, The Indian Runner's Romance, Wilful Peggy, The Sorrows of the Unfaithful, The Arcadian Maid, The Masher, The Awakening, A Lucky*

Toothache, Simple Charity, The Song of the Wildwood Flute, Sunshine Sue, Their First Misunderstanding, A Plain Song, A Summer Tragedy, White Roses 1910; *The Italian Barber, All on Account of the Milk, The Dream, Maid or Man, The Woman from Mellon's, Artful Kate, When the Cat's Away, A Manly Man, Her Darkest Hour, In Old Madrid, The Fisher-Maid, A Decree of Destiny, Three Sisters, For Her Brother's Sake, Science, In the Sultan's Garden, The Aggressor, Behind the Stockade, The Courting of Mary, Little Red Riding Hood* 1911; *The Mender of Nets, Fate's Interception, Won by a Fish, The Old Actor, A Lodging for the Night, A Beast at Bay, Home Folks, Lena and the Geese* (also sc.), *The Narrow Road, A Pueblo Legend, With the Enemy's Help, The Inner Circle, So Near Yet So Far, The One She Loved, Friends, The Informer, My Baby, The New York Hat* 1912; *The Unwelcome Guest, In a Bishop's Carriage, Caprice* 1913; *A Good Little Devil, Hearts Adrift* (also sc.), *Tess of the Storm Country, The Eagle's Mate, Such a Little Queen, Behind the Scenes, Cinderella* (title role) 1914; *Mistress Nell* (as Nell Gwyn), *Fanchon the Cricket, The Dawn of a Tomorrow, Little Pal, Rags, A Girl of Yesterday* (also sc.), *Esmeralda, Madame Butterfly* 1915; *Poor Little Peppina, The Foundling, The Eternal Grind, Hulda from Holland, Less Than the Dust* (also exec. prod.) 1916; *The Pride of the Clan, The Poor Little Rich Girl* (also exec. prod.), *A Romance of the Redwoods* (also exec. prod.), *The Little American* (also exec. prod.), *Rebecca of Sunnybrook Farm* (also exec. prod.), *The Little Princess* (also exec. prod.) 1917; *Stella Maris* (also exec. prod.), *Amarilly of Clothes-Line Alley* (also exec. prod.), *M'Liss* (also exec. prod.), *How Could You Jean?* (also exec. prod.), *Johanna Enlists* (also exec. prod.) 1918; *Captain Kidd Jr.* (also exec. prod.), *Daddy Long Legs* (also prod.), *The Hoodlum* (also exec. prod.), *Heart o' the Hills* (also exec. prod.) 1919; *Pollyanna* (also exec. prod.), *Suds* (also exec. prod.) 1920; *The Love Light* (also prod.), *Little Lord Fauntleroy* (dual role; also prod.), *Through the Back Door* (also prod.) 1921; *Tess of the Storm Country* (remake; also prod.) 1922; *Rosita* (also prod.) 1923; *Dorothy Vernon of Haddon Hall* (also prod.) 1924; *Little Annie Rooney* (also prod.) 1925; *Sparrows* (also prod.) 1926; *My Best Girl* (also prod.), *The Gaucho* 1927; *Coquette, The Taming of the Shrew* (as Katharina) 1929; *Kiki* 1931; *Secrets* 1933; *The Desperado* (prod. only) 1936.

pickups. Shots filmed after the completion of the regular shooting schedule, usually in an effort to cover up gaps in continuity which are discovered in the cutting room.

picture duplicate negative. See DUPE NEGATIVE.

picture negative. Negative developed in the lab from film exposed in the camera.

picture print. Processed film carrying a positive image. Also called a "silent print."

picture release negative. Picture negative from which release prints are made.

Pidgeon, Walter. Actor. *b.* Sept. 23, 1897, East St. John, New Brunswick, Canada. *d.* 1984. *ed.* U. of New Brunswick; New England Conservatory of Music (Boston). Durable star of Hollywood films since late in the silent era, typically in sober, intelligent leads. After recovering from a WW I injury in France that kept him hospitalized for 17 months, he worked briefly as a bank runner in Boston, then moved to New York in pursuit of an acting career. Entering films after a very brief stage exposure, he first played supporting parts and inconsequential leading roles. Early musical talkies made use of his baritone singing voice. He reached his peak in the 40s when he appeared in Lang's *Man Hunt* and Ford's *How Green Was My Valley* and enjoyed a measure of popularity in a string of eight MGM films of the 40s co-starring Greer GARSON. He was nominated for Academy Awards as best actor for two of these, *Mrs. Miniver* (1942) and *Madame Curie* (1943). In the 50s he gradually shifted to character roles, which he played with the same dignity and urbane charm that typified his work as a leading man. During that decade he served for five years as president of the Screen Actors Guild. In 1956 Pidgeon returned to Broadway in 'The Happiest Millionaire' and in 1959 he starred in the musical 'Take Me Along.'

FILMS: *Mannequin, The Outsider, Old Loves and New, Miss Nobody, Marriage License?* 1926; *The Heart of Salome, The Girl from Rio, The Gorilla, The Thirteenth Juror* 1927; *The Gateway of the Moon, Woman Wise, Turn Back the Hours, Clothes Make the Woman, Melody of Love* 1928; *The Voice Within, Her Private Life, A Most Immoral Lady* 1929; *Showgirl in Hollywood* (unbilled cameo), *Bride of the Regiment, Sweet Kitty Bellairs, Viennese Nights* 1930; *Kiss Me Again, Going Wild, The Gorilla* (remake), *The Hot Heiress* 1931; *Rockabye* 1932; *The Kiss Before the Mirror* 1933; *Journal of a Crime* 1934; *Big Brown Eyes, Fatal Lady* 1936; *She's Dangerous, Girl Overboard, As Good As Married, Saratoga, My Dear Miss Aldrich, A Girl with Ideas* 1937; *Man-Proof, The Girl of the Golden West, The Shopworn Angel, Too Hot to Handle, Listen Darling* 1938; *Society Lawyer, 6,000 Enemies, Stronger Than Desire, Nick Carter—Master Detective* (title role) 1939; *The House Across the Bay, It's a Date, Dark Command, Phantom Raiders* (again as Nick Carter), *Sky Murder* (again as Nick Carter) 1940; *Flight Command, Man Hunt, Blossoms in the Dust, How Green Was My Valley* (as Mr. Gruffydd), *Design for Scandal* 1941; *Mrs. Miniver, White Cargo* 1942; *The Youngest Profession, Madame Curie* (as Pierre Curie) 1943; *Mrs. Parkington* 1944; *Weekend at the Waldorf* 1945; *Holiday in Mexico, The Secret Heart* 1946; *Cass Timberlane* (unbilled cameo), *If Winter Comes* (as Mark Sabre), *Julia Misbehaves* 1948; *Command Decision, The Red Danube, That Forsyte Woman/The Forsyte Saga* (as Young Jolyon Forsyte) 1949; *The Miniver Story* 1950; *Soldiers Three, The Unknown Man, Calling Bulldog Drummond* (title role) 1951; *The Sellout, Million Dollar Mermaid, The Bad and the Beautiful* 1952; *Scandal at Scourie, Dream Wife* 1953; *Executive Suite, Men of the Fighting Lady, The Last Time I Saw Paris, Deep in My Heart* (as impresario J. J. Shubert) 1954; *Hit the Deck* 1955; *Forbidden Planet, These Wilder Years, The Rack* 1956; *Voyage to the Bottom of the Sea* 1961; *Advise and Consent, Big Red* 1962; *I Due Colonnelli/Two Colonels* (It.), *Il Giorno piu Corto* (It.) 1963; *Warning Shot* 1967; *Funny Girl* (as Florenz Ziegfeld) 1968; *Rascal* 1969; *Skyjacked* 1972; *The Neptune Factor, Harry in Your Pocket* 1973; *Won Ton Ton—the Dog Who Saved Hollywood* (cameo), *Two-Minute Warning* 1976; *Sextette* 1978.

Pierce, Jack P. Makeup artist. *b.* 1889, New York City. *d.* 1968. Inventive creator of such horror-film figures as Frankenstein's Monster, the Mummy, Dracula, and the Wolf Man. A former stage actor, film stuntman, character actor, assistant director, and cameraman, he was appointed head of the makeup department at Universal in 1936, a position he held for more than a decade.

FILMS INCLUDE: *Frankenstein* 1931; *White Zombie, The Old Dark House, The Mummy* 1932; *The Invisible Man* 1933; *The Black Cat* 1934; *The Bride of Frankenstein, Werewolf of London, The Raven* 1935; *The Invisible Ray* 1936; *The Road Back* 1937; *Son of Frankenstein* 1939; *The Wolf Man* 1941; *The Mummy's Tomb, The Ghost of Frankenstein* 1942; *Phantom of the Opera, Frankenstein Meets the Wolf Man* 1943; *The Climax, The Mummy's Ghost* 1944; *House of Frankenstein, House of Dracula* 1945; *The Killers, Magnificent Doll* 1946; *Joan of Arc, Abbott and Costello Meet Frankenstein* 1948; *Reign of Terror/The Black Book* 1949; *The Curse of Frankenstein* (UK)

1957; *Beyond the Time Barrier* 1960; *The Devil's Hand* 1961; *The Creation of the Humanoids, Beauty and the Beast* 1962.

Pierson, Frank. Screenwriter, director. Born on May 12, 1925, in Chappaqua, N.Y. *ed.* Harvard. A former correspondent for *Time* and *Life* magazines, he began his show business career as a story editor on the TV series 'Have Gun Will Travel,' later serving as the show's producer-writer. Turning to screenwriting in the mid-60s, he shared Academy Award nominations for his first two contributions, *Cat Ballou* (1965) and *Cool Hand Luke* (1967). He won the Oscar for *Dog Day Afternoon* (1975). He was only moderately successful in his occasional efforts as a director.

FILMS (as screenwriter, alone or in collaboration): *Cat Ballou* 1965; *Cool Hand Luke, The Happening* 1967; *The Looking Glass War* (also dir., UK) 1970; *The Anderson Tapes* 1971; *Dog Day Afternoon* 1975; *A Star Is Born* (also dir.) 1976; *King of the Gypsies* (also dir.) 1978; *In Country* 1989; *Presumed Innocent* 1990.

Pillsbury, Sarah. Producer. Born in New York. *ed.* Yale. After beginning as a solo producer of documentaries, she joined with Midge Sanford in 1980 to produce a number of successful independent feature films. Nominated for Academy Award for documentary *The California Reich*.

FILMS INCLUDE: *The California Reich* (doc.) 1976; *Desperately Seeking Susan* 1985; *River's Edge* 1987; *Eight Men Out* 1988; *Immediate Family* 1989; *Love Field* 1992; *How To Make an American Quilt* 1995.

pilot pins. Precision pins in the film gate of a camera which engage film perforations while each frame is being exposed and withdraw when the film moves on. Also called "register pins."

Pinchot, Bronson. Actor. Born on May 20, 1959, in New York, N.Y. *ed.* Yale. Baby-faced, offbeat comedic player of screen and TV. After a childhood in California, he studied drama at Yale and gained film notice in 1984 as indistinguishably accented art gallery worker in *Beverly Hills Cop*. Also played humorously accented lead in TV sitcom 'Perfect Strangers.'

FILMS INCLUDE: *Risky Business* 1983; *The Flamingo Kid, Beverly Hills Cop* 1984; *Hot Resort, After Hours* 1985; *Second Sight* 1989; *Blame It on the Bellboy* 1991; *True Romance* 1993; *Beverly Hills Cop III* 1994; *Courage Under Fire, First Wives Club, It's My Party* 1996.

pincushion distortion. Distortion resulting from a defective lens which causes square images on film to appear curved inward in the shape of a pincushion.

Pine, William H. See THOMAS, William C.

Pinelli, Tullio. Screenwriter, playwright. Born on June 24, 1908, in Turin, Italy. A former attorney. He has collaborated on the screenplays of many Italian films since the mid-40s, including most of FELLINI's through the mid-60s and again the 80s. He shared the Oscars for *La Dolce Vita* and *8½*. In the late 60s and early 70s he often worked with Pietro GERMI. He has also written for the stage.

FILMS INCLUDE: *Senza Pietà/Without Pity* 1947; *Il Mulino del Po/The Mill on the Po, In Nome della Legge/In the Name of the Law* 1949; *Il Cammino della Speranza/The Path of Hope* 1950; *Luci del Varietà/Variety Lights, La Città si difende* 1951; *Lo Sceicco bianco/The White Sheik* 1952; *Amore in Città/Love in the City, I Vitelloni* 1953; *La Strada, Sinfonia d'Amore* 1954; *Il Bidone/The Swindle* 1955; *Le Notti di Cabiria/Cabiria/The Nights of Cabiria* 1956; *Fortunella* 1957; *La Dolce Vita, A due e le Compagne/Love a la Carte* 1960; *Boccaccio '70* (Fellini episode) 1962; *La Steppa/The Steppe, Otto e Mezzo/8½* 1963; *Le Bambole* (Comencini episode), *Giulietta degli Spiriti/Juliet of the Spirits* 1965; *L'Immorale/The Climax* 1967; *Galileo, Serafino* 1968; *Alfredo Alfredo* 1973; *Per le Antiche Scale/Down the Ancient Stairs, Amici miei/My Friends* 1975; *Viaggio con Anita/Travels with Anita/Lovers and Liars* 1979; *Speriamo che sia Femmina/Let's Hope It's a Girl, Ginger e Fred/Ginger and Fred* 1985; *La Voce della Luna/The Voice of the Moon* 1990.

Pinter, Harold. Playwright, screenwriter. Born on Oct. 10, 1930, in London. A leading British dramatist whose cryptic, laconic plays have characteristically featured a mysterious symbolic menace and the breakdown of communication between people. The son of a Jewish tailor of Portuguese birth, he attended London's Royal Academy of Dramatic Art and started out as an actor, under the pseudonym David Baron. A contributor of poetry and prose to magazines since his teens, he wrote his first play in 1957 and rose to prominence in 1960 with 'The Caretaker,' which he later adapted to the screen. Several of his plays were originally written for British radio or TV. He has contributed intelligent scripts to a number of outstanding films, drawing Oscar nominations for *The French Lieutenant's Woman* (1981) and *Betrayal* (1983). He has directed a number of stage plays and the American Film Theatre production of *Butley* (1974). Formerly (1956–80) married to actress Vivien MERCHANT. In 1977 he published a screenplay based on Proust's *A la Recherche du Temps perdu.* It remains unproduced.

FILMS (as screenwriter): *The Servant* (also act.), *The Caretaker/The Guest* (from own play) 1963; *The Pumpkin Eater* 1964; *The Quiller Memorandum* (UK/US) 1966; *Accident* (also act.) 1967; *The Birthday Party* (from own play) 1968; *The Go-Between* 1971; *The Homecoming* (from own play) 1973; *Butley* (dir. only) 1974; *The Last Tycoon* (US) 1976; *The French Lieutenant's Woman* 1981; *Betrayal* (from own play) 1983; *Turtle Diary* (also act.) 1985; *Reunion* (Fr./Ger./US) 1989; *The Handmaid's Tale, The Comfort of Strangers* 1990; *The Trial* 1993.

Pintoff, Ernest. Director, animator. Born on Dec. 15, 1931, in Watertown, Conn. *ed.* Syracuse U. Raised in New York City, he started out as a jazz trumpeter and later taught painting and design at Michigan State University. In 1956 he joined UPA as an animator and two years later set up his own animation studio. A highly original comic cartoonist, he turned out many entertaining animation shorts for theatrical presentation and for television, as well as TV commercials. In 1965 he directed, wrote, and co-produced his first live-action feature, *Harvey Middleman—Fireman.* He was associate producer of the Italian film *Questi Fantasmi/Ghosts Italian Style* (1967) and wrote the dialogue for the English-language version of that production.

FILMS INCLUDE: Animated shorts—*The Wounded Bird, Aquarium, The Martians Come Back, Blues Pattern* 1956; *Flebus, The Haunted Night* 1957; *The Violinist* 1960; *The Interview, The Shoes* (live action) 1961; *The Old Man and the Flower* 1962; *The Critic* 1963. Live-action features—*Harvey Middleman—Fireman* (dir., sc., co-prod.) 1965; *Who Killed Mary What's'ername?* (dir.) 1971; *Dynamite Chicken* (feature doc., dir.) 1972; *Blade* (exec. prod., co-sc. only) 1973; *Jaguar Lives* 1979; *Lunch Wagon/Lunch Wagon Girls/Come 'n' Get It* 1980; *St. Helens* 1981.

Pinza, Ezio. Singer, actor. *b.* Fortunato Pinza, May 8, 1892, Rome. *d.* 1957. The celebrated basso of Milan's La Scala, New York's Metropolitan Opera, and Broadway's musical stage ('South Pacific' and 'Fanny'), he also starred in a number of Hollywood films.

FILMS: *Carnegie Hall* 1947; *Mr. Imperium, Strictly Dishonorable* 1951; *Tonight We Sing* 1953.

Pirosh, Robert. Screenwriter, director. *b.* Apr. 1, 1910, in Baltimore, Md. *d.* 1990. After studies at the Sorbonne and the

University of Berlin, he turned to advertising. In Hollywood as screenwriter from the mid-30s, he directed occasional films in the 50s. He won an Academy Award for the script of *Battleground* and produced and wrote segments for many TV shows.

FILMS INCLUDE: As screenwriter—*The Winning Ticket* 1935; *A Day at the Races* 1937; *I Married a Witch* 1942; *Up in Arms* (also assoc. prod.) 1944; *Battleground* 1949; *Hell Is for Heroes* 1962; *A Gathering of Eagles* 1963; *What's So Bad About Feeling Good?* 1968. As director-screenwriter (complete)—*Go for Broke* 1951; *Washington Story* 1952; *Valley of the Kings* 1954; *The Girl Rush* 1955; *Spring Reunion* 1957.

Pisier, Marie-France. Actress. Born on May 10, 1944, in Dalat, Indochina (Vietnam). The daughter of a French government official, she grew up in Indochina and later in New Caledonia before her family settled in Paris, when she was 12. A petite, pretty brunette, she began appearing in French films at 17 and continued acting sporadically during her studies at the University of Paris, from which she graduated with degrees in law and political science. For several years, in the late 60s and early 70s, she appeared mainly in offbeat films of young, unestablished directors, gaining no wide public recognition. But in 1975 she achieved sudden popularity in Paris as winner of the César—the French equivalent of the Oscar—for her performance in the film *Cousin Cousine.* The unexpected success of that film in the US led to a Hollywood screen test and to the lead role in *The Other Side of Midnight* (1977). Having contributed to the screenplays of Jacques Rivette's *Celine and Julie Go Boating* (1974) and François Truffaut's *Love on the Run* (1979), she made her debut as a director with *Le Bal Du Governeur/The Governer's Party* (1990), fashioning the screenplay from her own best-selling novel.

FILMS INCLUDE: *Qui ose nous accuser?* 1961; *L'Amour à Vingt Ans/Love at Twenty* (Truffaut's episode) 1962; *La Mort d'un Tueur* 1963; *Les Yeux cernés* 1964; *Trans-Europ Express* 1967; *Baisers volés/Stolen Kisses* 1968; *Paulina s'en va* 1969; *Le Journal d'un Suicidé* 1971; *Céline et Julie vont en Bateau/Celine and Julie Go Boating* (also co-sc.) 1974; *Cousin Cousine, Souvenirs d'en France/French Provincial* 1975; *Serail, Barocco, Le Corps de mon Ennemi* 1976; *Les Apprentis Sorciers, The Other Side of Midnight* (US) 1977; *L'Amour en fuite/Love on the Run* (also co-sc.), *Le Soeurs Brontë/The Brontë Sisters* (as Charlotte Brontë), *French Postcards* (Ger./Fr.) 1979; *La Banquière* 1980; *Chanel Solitaire* (as fashion designer Gabrielle "Coco" Chanel; UK/Fr.) 1981; *L'As des As, Der Zauberberg/The Magic Mountain* 1982; *Le Prix du Danger/The Prize of Peril, L'Ami de Vincent, Der stille Ozean/The Silent Ocean* 1983; *Les Nanas, Parking* 1985; *L'Inconnu de Vienne* 1986; *L'Oeuvre au Noir* 1988; *Le Bal Du Governeur/The Governer's Party* (dir., sc. only, from her own novel) 1990; *Blue Note* 1991; *Pourquoi Maman Est dans Mon Lit?, Tous les Jours Dimanche* 1994.

pitch. Pertaining to motion picture film, the distance between two successive film perforations.

Pitt, Brad. Actor. Born in 1963, in Shawnee, Okla. *ed.* Univ. of Missouri at Columbia (journalism). Studied acting with Roy London. Wiry, seductive screen lead, often in offbeat dramas. He made a strong impression as the slit-eyed drifter in *Thelma and Louise* (1991) and has gone on to become one of the biggest stars in Hollywood. For his critically acclaimed performance in director Terry GILLIAM's *Twelve Monkeys* (1995), he earned a supporting actor Academy Award nomination.

FILMS: *The Dark Side of the Sun* 1988; *Cutting Class, Happy Together* 1989; *Across the Tracks, Thelma and Louise, The Favor, Johnny Suede* 1991; *Cool World, A River Runs Through It* 1992; *Kalifornia, True Romance* 1993; *The Favor, Legends of the Fall* 1994; *Seven, Twelve Monkeys* 1995; *Sleepers* 1996; *The Devil's Own, Seven Years in Tibet* 1997.

Pitts, ZaSu. Actress. *b.* Jan. 3, 1898, Parsons, Kans. *d.* 1963. Raised in California, she began her film career at 19 as a supporting player in two successive Mary Pickford vehicles. She played leads as well as supporting roles in many other Hollywood silents, both comedies and dramas, gaining prominence as the dramatic lead in Erich von Stroheim's *Greed* (1924). She also played key supporting dramatic roles in such films as von Stroheim's *The Wedding March* and Ludwig Berger's *Sins of the Fathers* (1928). But after the advent of sound she veered almost exclusively toward comedy, leaving her mark as a scatterbrained character comedienne on numerous light productions. She supported Thelma TODD in a long series of two-reel comedies, starred in a number of light features, often opposite Slim SUMMERVILLE, and enlivened many others in a supporting capacity with her zany presence and "oh me, oh my!" bewilderment. In the 50s she co-starred in the TV series 'Oh! Susanna,' which later became 'The Gale Storm Show.' Her unusual first name was derived from combining the names of two of her father's sisters, Eliza and Susan. Her death of cancer robbed the American screen of one of its most delightful personalities.

FILMS INCLUDE: *The Little Princess, Rebecca of Sunnybrook Farm, A Modern Musketeer* 1917; *A Society Sensation* 1918; *Better Times, The Other Half, Poor Relations* 1919; *Bright Skies* 1920; *Patsy* 1921; *Is Matrimony a Failure?, For the Defense* 1922; *Poor Men's Wives, Three Wise Fools, Tea—With a Kick* 1923; *Daughters of Today, Triumph, The Goldfish, Changing Husbands, The Legend of Hollywood, The Fast Set, Greed* 1924; *The Great Divide, A Woman's Faith, Pretty Ladies, Thunder Mountain, Lazybones, Wages for Wives* 1925; *Mannequin, Monte Carlo, Early to Wed, Sunny Side Up, Her Big Night* 1926; *Casey at the Bat* 1927; *Wife Savers, Buck Privates, The Wedding March, Sins of the Fathers* 1928; *The Dummy, Twin Beds, Oh Yeah!, Paris, This Thing Called Love* 1929; *No No Nanette, Honey, All Quiet on the Western Front* (in original silent version only; replaced by Beryl Mercer in released sound version), *The Devil's Holiday, Monte Carlo, The Lottery Bride, River's End* 1930; *Finn and Hattie, Bad Sister, Beyond Victory, Seed, The Guardsman* 1931; *The Unexpected Father, Broken Lullaby/The Man I Killed, Strangers of the Evening, Make Me a Star, Back Street, Blondie of the Follies, Once in a Lifetime* 1932; *They Just Had to Get Married, Out All Night, Professional Sweetheart, Her First Mate, Meet the Baron, Love Honor and Oh Baby!, Mr. Skitch* 1933; *The Meanest Gal in Town, Love Birds, Sing and Like It, Private Scandal, Dames, Their Big Moment, Mrs. Wiggs of the Cabbage Patch, The Gay Bride* 1934; *Ruggles of Red Gap* 1935; *13 Hours by Air, The Plot Thickens* 1936; *Forty Naughty Girls, 52nd Street* 1937; *Nurse Edith Cavell, Eternally Yours* 1939; *It All Came True, No No Nanette* (remake) 1940; *Broadway Limited, Miss Polly* 1941; *Meet the Mob/So's Your Aunt Emma, Tish* 1942; *Let's Face It* 1943; *The Perfect Marriage, Life with Father* 1947; *Francis* 1950; *The Denver and the Rio Grande* 1952; *This Could Be the Night* 1957; *Teenage Millionaire* 1961; *The Thrill of It All, It's a Mad Mad Mad Mad World* 1963.

Place, Mary Kay. Actress. Born on Sept. 23, 1947, in Tulsa, Okla. *ed.* Univ. of Tulsa. Amicable comedic supporting player of screen and TV. An assistant to Tim Conway and Norman Lear, she also worked as a scriptwriter for top 1970s sitcoms 'The Mary Tyler Moore Show,' 'M*A*S*H*,' 'Maude,' and 'Phyllis' before her film debut in *Bound for Glory.* Best known for performance as would-be single mother in *The Big*

Chill. Awarded Emmy (best supporting actress, Comedy Series) for 'Mary Hartman, Mary Hartman.'

FILMS INCLUDE: *Bound for Glory* 1976; *New York New York* 1977; *More American Graffiti, Starting Over* 1979; *Private Benjamin* 1980; *Modern Problems* 1981; *Waltz Across Texas* 1982; *The Big Chill, Terms of Endearment* (v/o) 1983; *Explorers, Smooth Talk* 1985; *A New Life* 1988; *Bright Angel* 1991; *Captain Ron, Samantha* 1992; *Citizen Ruth, Manny & Lo* 1996; *Eye of God* 1997.

Planck, Robert H. American director of photography. *b.* 1894. *d.* 1963. Following a period of apprenticeship, he became a lighting cameraman in 1929. During the 1930s he demonstrated his skill with black-and-white cinematography for Fox and other studios and in the 40s and early 50s was behind the camera on many glossy MGM productions, either monochrome or color. After retiring from films in 1957 he worked for several years on the TV series 'My Three Sons.'

FILMS INCLUDE: *Three Live Ghosts* 1929; *Be Yourself* (co-phot.), *The Bat Whispers* (65 mm version only) 1930; *Reaching for the Moon* (co-phot.) 1931; *It's Great to Be Alive* 1933; *Our Daily Bread, Frontier Marshal, Jane Eyre* 1934; *The Last of the Mohicans, We Who Are About to Die* 1936; *Thin Ice* (co-phot.), *Life Begins in College* 1937; *Always Goodbye* 1938; *The Man in the Iron Mask* 1939; *Escape, Strange Cargo, Susan and God* 1940; *A Woman's Face, When Ladies Meet* 1941; *We Were Dancing, Her Cardboard Lover* (co-phot.) 1942; *Above Suspicion* 1943; *The Heavenly Body, The Canterville Ghost* 1944; *Anchors Aweigh* (co-phot.), *Weekend at the Waldorf* 1945; *Love Laughs at Andy Hardy* 1946; *It Happened in Brooklyn, Cass Timberlane* 1947; *The Three Musketeers, Luxury Liner* 1948; *Little Women* (co-phot.), *Madame Bovary* 1949; *Summer Stock* 1950; *Texas Carnival, Royal Wedding* 1951; *The Belle of New York* 1952; *Lili, Torch Song* 1953; *Rhapsody* 1954; *Moonfleet, The King's Thief* 1955; *Diane, Gaby* 1956; *Jeanne Eagels, The Girl Most Likely* 1957.

Planer, Franz (also known in the US as **Frank F. Planer**). Director of photography. *b.* Mar. 29, 1894, Karlsbad (now Karlovy Vary), Czechoslovakia. *d.* 1963. A former portrait photographer, he entered German films in 1919. In Hollywood from 1937, using the name Frank F. Planer. He did his best work under the direction of Max OPHÜLS, for whom he executed the fluid camera movement on *Letter to an Unknown Woman* (1948).

FILMS INCLUDE: In Germany—*Der Ochsenkrieg* 1919; *Das schwarze Gesicht* 1922; *Die Finanzen der Grossherzogs* (co-phot.) 1924; *Finale der Liebe* 1925; *Only a Dancer* (Sw.) 1927; *Alraune/Unholy Love, Wolga-Wolga* 1928; *Die Drei von der Tankstelle* 1930; *L'Aiglon* (Fr.), *Nie wieder Liebe* 1931; *Die Gräfin von Monte Cristo, Der schwarze Husar* 1932; *Liebelei, Leise flehen maine Lieder/Unfinished Symphony* (Ger./Aus.) 1933; *Maskerade/Masquerade in Vienna* (Aus.), *Les Nuits moscovites/Moscow Nights* (Fr.) 1934; *The Dictator/The Love Affair of the Dictator/Loves of a Dictator* (UK), *Casta Diva* (It.), *The Divine Spark* (UK) 1935; *The Beloved Vagabond* (UK), *Tarass Boulba* (Fr.), *Im Sonnenschein/Opernring/Thank You Madame* (Aus.) 1936; *Premiere, Capriolen* 1937. In the US—*Holiday* 1938; *Glamour for Sale* 1940; *The Face Behind the Mask, Our Wife* 1941; *The Adventures of Martin Eden, Flight Lieutenant* 1942; *Appointment in Berlin, Destroyer* 1943; *Once Upon a Time, Carolina Blues* 1944; *The Chase* 1946; *The Exile* 1947; *Letter from an Unknown Woman, One Touch of Venus* 1948; *Criss Cross, Champion* 1949; *Three Husbands, Cyrano de Bergerac, Vendetta* 1950; *The Blue Veil, The Scarf, Death of a Salesman* 1951; *Roman Holiday* (co-phot.), *The 5,000 Fingers of Dr. T* 1953; *Bad for Each Other, 20,000 Leagues Under the Sea, The Caine Mutiny* 1954; *Not as a Stranger, The Left Hand of God* 1955; *The Mountain* 1956; *The Pride and the Passion* 1957; *Stage Struck, The Big Country* 1958; *The Nun's Story* 1959; *The Unforgiven* 1960; *King of Kings* (co-phot.), *Breakfast at Tiffany's* 1961; *The Children's Hour* 1962.

Plateau, Joseph. Inventor. *b.* Oct. 14, 1801, Brussels. *d.* 1883. An anatomy professor at the University of Ghent, he investigated the principle of PERSISTENCE OF VISION and its effect upon simulated movement. Although he became blind in 1843, his research was carried on by others, and in 1883 he was responsible for the invention of the PHENAKISTICOPE (also known as Phenakistiscope or Fantascope), a primitive apparatus producing an apparently moving picture from a series of drawings. He may thus be considered the inventor of animation.

platen. In animation, a flat sheet of glass used to hold CELS in the correct position over backgrounds during filming.

Platt, Louise. Actress. Born on Aug. 3, 1915, in Stamford, Conn. Leading lady of Hollywood films of the late 30s and early 40s, memorably John Ford's *Stagecoach* (1939). The daughter of a high-ranking Navy officer, she was educated in New York, Manila, and Hong Kong and appeared in several Broadway productions before entering films in 1938. She retired in 1942 and returned briefly to the stage.

FILMS: *I Met My Love Again, Spawn of the North* 1938; *Stagecoach, Tell No Tales* 1939; *Forgotten Girls, Captain Caution* 1940; *Street of Chance* 1942.

Platt, Oliver. American actor. Dark-haired character actor, usually playing garrulous urban or suburban types. Made impression as merrily amoral lawyer in *Indecent Proposal*.

FILMS INCLUDE: *Crusoe, Married to the Mob, Working Girl* 1988; *Flatliners, Postcards from the Edge* 1990; *Beethoven, Diggstown* 1992; *Benny & Joon, Indecent Proposal, The Temp, The Three Musketeers* 1993; *Funny Bones, Tall Tale* 1995; *Executive Decision, A Time to Kill* 1996.

Platt, Polly. American production designer, screenwriter, producer. She began her film career as a collaborator with her then husband (1962–70), director Peter BOGDANOVICH. Making her name mainly as a production designer (she was nominated for an Oscar for *Terms of Endearment,* 1983), she also engaged in screenwriting and in 1987 became a producer.

FILMS INCLUDE: As production designer—*Targets* (also co-story) 1968; *The Last Picture Show* 1971; *What's Up Doc?* 1972; *Paper Moon, The Thief Who Came to Dinner* 1973; *The Bad News Bears, A Star Is Born* 1976; *Young Doctors in Love* 1982; *The Man with Two Brains, Terms of Endearment* 1983; *The Witches of Eastwick* 1987. As screenwriter—*Pretty Baby* 1978; *Good Luck Miss Wyckoff* 1979. As producer or executive producer—*Broadcast News* 1987; *Say Anything* (also act.), *The War of the Roses* 1989; *I'll Do Anything* (co-prod. only) 1994; *Bottle Rocket* (co-prod. only) 1996.

playback. 1. The immediate reproduction of a recording for monitoring purposes. 2. The replay of prerecorded music through loudspeakers onstage while filming musical numbers. The music, recorded under controlled acoustical conditions, is played back while the singers and dancers go through their performances. The live action is filmed without sound and is subsequently synchronized with the prerecorded track.

Pleasence, Donald. Actor. *b.* Oct. 5, 1919, in Worksop, England. *d.* 1995. Dominant character player of the London and New York stage and of British and international films, he made his stage debut in 1939. Three years later joined the RAF and later was a prisoner of war. He began appearing in films in the mid-50s and before long established himself as an effective character actor, at his most convincing as an evil villain with a fixed gaze in his unblinking blue eyes. Prolific and not too discriminating in his choice of roles, he appeared in the 80s in countless low-budget films—often horror and occult quickies—performing in no fewer than 17 in 1987–89 alone. His daughter, Angela Pleasence, is an actress.

FILMS INCLUDE: *The Beachcomber* 1954; *1984* 1956; *Manuela/Stowaway Girl* 1957; *A Tale of Two Cities* 1958; *Look Back in Anger* 1959; *The Big Day, Flesh and the Fiends/Mania, Suspect/The Risk, Circus of Horrors, Sons and Lovers* 1960; *Les Mains d'Orlac/The Hands of Orlac* (Fr./UK), *No Love for Johnnie* 1961; *The Inspector/Lisa* 1962; *Dr. Crippen* (title role), *The Great Escape* (US), *The Caretaker/The Guest* 1963; *Maniac* 1964; *The Greatest Story Ever Told* (as the Devil; US), *The Hallelujah Trail* (US) 1965; *Cul-de-Sac, Fantastic Voyage* (US) 1966; *La Nuit des Généraux/The Night of the Generals* (Fr./UK), *Eye of the Devil, Matchless* (It.), *You Only Live Twice* 1967; *Will Penny* (US) 1968; *Mr. Freedom* (Fr.), *The Madwoman of Chaillot* 1969; *Soldier Blue* (US) 1970; *THX 1138* (US), *Kidnapped, Outback* 1971; *The Jerusalem File, Innocent Bystanders, The Pied Piper* 1972; *Henry VIII and His Six Wives* (as Thomas Cromwell), *Wedding in White, Raw Meat, Tales That Witness Murder* 1973; *The Mutations, The Black Windmill* 1974; *From Beyond the Grave, Escape to Witch Mountain* (US), *Hearts of the West* (US), *Journey Into Fear* 1975; *The Count of Monte Cristo, I Don't Want to Be Born/Devil Within Her, Dirty Knights' Work, The Passover Plot* (as Pontius Pilate; US/Isr.), *The Last Tycoon* (US), *The Eagle Has Landed* (as Heinrich Himmler) 1976; *Oh God* (US), *Telefon* (US) 1977; *Les Liens de Sang/Blood Relatives* (Fr./Can.), *Tomorrow Never Comes* (UK/Can.), *L'Ordre et la Securité du Monde* (Fr.), *Sgt. Pepper's Lonely Hearts Club Band* (US), *Meteor* (US), *Power Play* (Can./UK), *Halloween* 1978; *L'Homme en Colère/The Angry Man* (Fr./Can.), *Jaguar Lives* (US), *Good Luck Miss Wyckoff* (US), *Dracula* (US) 1979; *The Monster Club* 1980; *Escape from New York* (as US President; US), *Halloween II* (US), *Race to the Yankee Zephyr/Treasure of the Yankee Zephyr* (NZ/UK) 1981; *Alone in the Dark* (US) 1982; *The Devonsville Terror, El tesoro de la Amazona/The Treasure of the Amazon* (Mex./US) 1983; *A Breed Apart* (US), *Where Is Parsifal?* 1984; *The Ambassador* (US), *Phenomena/Creepers* (It.) 1985; *Pompeii/Warrior Queen* (It.), *Sotto il vestito niente/Nothing Underneath* (It.) 1986; *Nosferatu a Venezia* (It.), *Prince of Darkness* (US), *Ground Zero* (Austral.) 1987; *Halloween 4: The Return of Michael Myers, Hanna's War, Phantom of Death* (It.) 1988; *River of Death, Ten Little Indians, Halloween 5: The Revenge of Michael Myers* (US) 1989; *Buried Alive, The House of Usher* 1990; *Miliardi/Billions* (It.), *American Tiger* (It.) 1991; *Shadows and Fog* (US) 1992; *The Advocate* 1994; *Halloween: The Curse of Michael Myers* 1995.

Pleshette, Suzanne. Actress. Born on Jan. 31, 1937, in New York City. *ed.* Finch Coll.; Syracuse U. Talented, attractive leading lady of American stage, TV, and films. The only child of ballerina Geraldine Rivers (née Kaplan) and stage manager (later TV production executive) Eugene Pleshette, she attended Manhattan's High School for the Performing Arts and later trained at the Neighborhood Playhouse before starting her career on the New York stage. On the screen from the late 50s, she also enjoyed some success on TV, most memorably as the sensible wife in the long-running 'Bob Newhart Show' (1972–78). Divorced in 1964 from actor Troy DONAHUE after only nine months of marriage, she married Texas oilman Thomas Joseph Gallagher III in 1968.

FILMS: *The Geisha Boy* 1958; *Rome Adventure* 1962; *40 Pounds of Trouble, The Birds, Wall of Noise* 1963; *A Distant Trumpet, Fate Is the Hunter, Youngblood Hawke* 1964; *A Rage to Live* 1965; *The Ugly Dachshund, Nevada Smith, Mister Buddwing* 1966; *The Adventures of Bullwhip Griffin* 1967; *Blackbeard's Ghost, The Power* 1968; *If It's Tuesday This Must Be Belgium, How to Make It* 1969; *Suppose They Gave a War and Nobody Came* 1970; *Support Your Local Gunfighter* 1971; *The Shaggy D.A.* 1976; *Hot Stuff* 1979; *Oh God! Book II* 1980.

Plimpton, Martha. Actress. Born in 1970, in New York City. Attractive young lead of Hollywood films. The daughter of actors Shelley Plimpton and Keith CARRADINE, who never married and separated before her birth, she was raised by her mother on Manhattan's Upper West Side. At age eight she joined a film-acting workshop and at 11 appeared in her first movie and in a series of controversial commercials for Calvin Klein jeans. Playing her first substantial role at 14, she virtually grew up on the screen, developing from a precocious teenager to a self-assured, if underused leading lady. She has been romantically linked with actors Christian SLATER and the late River PHOENIX.

FILMS: *Rollover* (bit) 1981; *The River Rat* 1984; *The Goonies* 1985; *The Mosquito Coast* 1986; *Shy People* 1987; *Stars and Bars, Running on Empty, Another Woman* 1988; *Zwei Frauen* (Ger.), *Parenthood* 1989; *Stanley and Iris, Silence Like Glass* 1990; *Inside Monkey Zetterland, Samantha* 1992; *Josh & S.A.M.* 1993; *Beans of Egypt Maine, Mrs. Parker and the Vicious Circle, My Life's in Turnaround* 1994; *Last Summer in the Hamptons* 1995; *Beautiful Girls, I'm Not Rappaport, I Shot Andy Warhol* 1996; *Eye of God* 1997.

Plowright, Joan. Actress. Born on Oct. 28, 1929, in Brig, England. A celebrated stage performer with sparse but impressive film credits. Trained at the Old Vic Theatre School, she made her stage debut in repertory in 1951, her first London appearance in 1954, and her screen debut in 1956. Memorable in *The Entertainer* (1960), in which she co-starred with her soon-to-be second husband, Laurence OLIVIER (1961 till his death in 1989), *Three Sisters* (also with Olivier), *Equus* (1977), and a string of prominent character roles of the 80s and 90s.

FILMS: *Moby Dick* 1956; *Time Without Pity* 1957; *The Entertainer* 1960; *Uncle Vanya* (as Sonya) 1963; *Three Sisters* (as Masha) 1970; *Equus* 1977; *Britannia Hospital, Brimstone and Treacle* 1982; *Wagner* 1983; *Revolution* 1985; *Drowning by Numbers, The Dressmaker* 1988; *I Love You to Death, Avalon* 1990; *Enchanted April* (UK) 1992; *Last Action Hero, Dennis the Menace, The Summer House* 1993; *Widow's Peak* 1994; *Hotel Sorrento, A Pyromaniac's Love Story* 1995; *101 Dalmations, Jane Eyre, Mr. Wrong, Surviving Picasso* 1996.

Plummer, Amanda. Actress. Born on Mar. 23, 1957, in New York City. Idiosyncratic leading lady of the American stage and screen. The daughter of actors Christopher PLUMMER and Tammy GRIMES, she won the Tony Award as well as a Drama Desk Award for her portrayal of the title role in Broadway's 'Agnes of God' (1982). Her screen roles have as yet been less substantive than those on the stage.

FILMS: *Cattle Annie and Little Britches* 1981; *The World According to Garp* 1982; *Daniel* 1983; *The Hotel New Hampshire* 1984; *Static* (UK) 1986; *Made in Heaven* 1987; *Prisoners of Inertia* 1989; *Joe Versus the Volcano* 1990; *The Fisher King* 1991; *Freejack* 1992; *Needful Things, So I Married an Axe Murderer* 1993; *Nostradamus, Pulp Fiction* 1994; *Drunk, The Prophecy* 1995; *Freeway, Hercules* (v/o), *A Simple Wish* 1997.

Plummer, Christopher. Actor. Born Arthur Christopher Orme Plummer, on Dec. 13, 1927, in Toronto. Highly rated performer of stage, TV, and films on both sides of the Atlantic. On the Canadian stage from 1950; Broadway since 1954. He scored a triumph in the three-hour British TV production of 'Hamlet.' On the screen, he played a wide range of leads and supporting roles at an accelerated pace that reached an overly prolific stage in the late 80s. His first wife (1956–60) was actress Tammy GRIMES with whom he has a daughter, actress Amanda PLUMMER. His third (from 1970) is actress Elaine Taylor.

FILMS: *Stage Struck, Wind Across the Everglades* 1958; *The Fall of the Roman Empire* 1964; *The Sound of Music* (as the Baron von Trapp) 1965; *Inside Daisy Clover, Triple Cross* (Fr./UK) 1966; *La Nuit des Généraux/The Night of the Generals* (as Field Marshal Rommel; Fr./UK) 1967; *Oedipus the King* (title role; UK), *The High Commissioner/Nobody Runs Forever* (US/UK) 1968; *The Royal Hunt of the Sun* (as Emperor Atahualpa of Peru; US/UK), *Battle of Britain* (UK), *Lock Up Your Daughters* (UK) 1969; *Waterloo* (as the Duke of Wellington; It./USSR) 1970; *The Pyx* (Can.) 1973; *The Return of the Pink Panther* (UK), *Conduct Unbecoming* (UK), *The Man Who Would Be King* (as Rudyard Kipling; UK) 1975; *Aces High* (UK), *Assassination at Sarajevo/The Day That Shook the World* (Yug./Czech.) 1976; *The Assignment* (Sw.), *The Disappearance* (Can.) 1977; *Murder by Decree* (as Sherlock Holmes; UK/Can.), *International Velvet* (UK), *The Silent Partner* (Can.) 1978; *Starcrash, Hanover Street* (UK), *Riel* (Can.), *Arthur Miller on Home Ground* (doc.) 1979; *Highpoint* (Can.), *Somewhere in Time* 1980; *Eyewitness, Being Different* (narr. only) 1981; *The Amateur* 1982; *Dreamscape* 1984; *Lili in Love/Friz and Lili* (Hung.), *Ordeal by Innocence* (UK) 1985; *The Boy in Blue* (Can.), *An American Tail* (v/o), *The Boss' Wife* 1986; *Nosferatu a Venezia/Vampires in Venice, L'Homme qui plantait les Arbres* (Can.), *Dragnet, I Love N.Y.* 1987; *Souvenir* (UK), *Light Years, Shadow Dancing* 1988; *Mindfield* (Can.), *Kingsgate* 1989; *Where the Heart Is, Red Blooded American Girl* (Can.) 1990; *Firehead, Rock-a-Doodle* (v/o), *Money* (Fr./It./Can.) 1991; *Liar's Edge* (US), *Impolite* (US) 1992; *Wolf* 1994; *12 Monkeys, Dolores Claiborne* 1995.

Plunkett, Walter. Costume designer. *b.* June 5, 1902, Oakland, Calif. *d.* 1982. A former vaudeville and stock actor, he created the wardrobes for many prestigious Hollywood films as well as for many Broadway shows and Metropolitan Opera productions. His greatest claim to fame was his design of the elaborate costumes for *Gone With the Wind* (1939). He shared an Academy Award with Orry-Kelly and Irene Sharaff for the costumes of *An American in Paris* (1951).

FILMS INCLUDE: *Hard Boiled Haggerty* 1927; *Love in the Desert* 1929; *Morning Glory, Little Women, Flying Down to Rio* 1933; *The Gay Divorcee, Of Human Bondage, The Little Minister* 1934; *The Informer, Alice Adams, The Three Musketeers* 1935; *Mary of Scotland* 1936; *Nothing Sacred, Quality Street* 1937; *Stagecoach, The Story of Vernon and Irene Castle, Gone With the Wind* 1939; *Captain Caution* 1940; *Lydia, Sundown* 1941; *Along Came Jones* 1945; *Duel in the Sun* 1946; *Green Dolphin Street, Song of Love* 1947; *Summer Holiday, The Three Musketeers* 1948; *Adam's Rib, Little Women, Madame Bovary, That Forsyte Woman* 1949; *Father of the Bride, King Solomon's Mines, The Miniver Story* 1950; *Showboat, An American in Paris* 1951; *Plymouth Adventure, The Prisoner of Zenda, Singin' in the Rain* 1952; *The Actress, Kiss Me Kate* 1953; *Seven Brides for Seven Brothers, Valley of the Kings* 1954; *Moonfleet* 1955; *Lust for Life* 1956; *Raintree County* 1957; *The Brothers Karamazov* 1958; *Pollyanna, Bells Are Ringing* 1960; *Pocketful of Miracles* 1961; *The Four Horsemen of the Apocalypse, Two Weeks in Another Town, How the West Was Won* 1962; *Marriage on the Rocks* 1965; *Seven Women* 1966.

Podestà, Rossanna. Actress. Born Carla Podestà on June 20, 1934, in Tripoli, Libya, to Italian-Argentine parents. Leading lady of Italian and international films. A striking beauty, she received worldwide publicity in the mid-50s when she was chosen to star in the costly international spectacle *Helen of Troy.* She subsequently appeared in a couple of Hollywood films but failed to click in the US.

FILMS INCLUDE: *Domani è un Altro Giorno* 1949; *Guardie e Ladri/Cops and Robbers* 1951; *La Voce del Silenzio, I Sette Nani alla Viscossa/The Seven Dwarfs to the Rescue* (as Snow White) 1952; *La Red/The Net* (Mex.) 1953; *Ulisse/Ulysses* (as Penelope/Circe) 1954; *Helen of Troy* (title role; US/It.), *Santiago* (US) 1956; *Raw Wind in Eden* (US) 1958; *L'Ile du Bout du Monde/Temptation* (Fr.) 1959; *La Furia dei Barbari/Fury of the Pagans* 1960; *Sodom and Gomorrah* (US/Fr./It.) 1961; *Solo contro Roma/Alone Against Rome, La Freccia d'Oro/The Golden Arrow* 1962; *La Vergine di Norimberga/Horror Castle* 1964; *Sette Uomini d'Oro/Seven Golden Men* 1965; *Homo Eroticus/Man of the Year, Il Prete Sposato/The Married Priest* 1971; *L'Uccello Migratore* 1972; *Paolo il Caldo/The Sensuous Sicilian/The Sensual Man* 1973; *Il Padre* 1975; *Il Letto in Piazza* 1976; *Sotto Choc* 1978; *Sette Ragazze pericolose* 1979; *Sunday Lovers* (UK/It./Fr./US) 1980; *Ercole/Hercules* 1983; *Segretti Segretti* 1985.

Poe, James. Screenwriter. *b.* Oct. 4, 1921, Dobbs Ferry, N.Y. *d.* 1980. *ed.* St. John's Coll. (Minneapolis, Minn.). One of Hollywood's most literate screenwriters, he did screen adaptations of the works of some of America's leading writers and also wrote, sometimes in collaboration, a number of solid original stories and screenplays. Formerly with "The March of Time." He shared an Academy Award for the script of *Around the World in 80 Days* (1956).

FILMS: *Close-Up* (story only) 1948; *Without Honor* 1949; *Scandal Sheet, Paula* 1952; *A Slight Case of Larceny* (story only) 1953; *The Big Knife* 1955; *Attack!, Around the World in 80 Days* 1956; *Hot Spell, Cat on a Hot Tin Roof* 1958; *Last Train from Gun Hill* 1959; *Sanctuary, Summer and Smoke* 1961; *Toys in the Attic, Lilies of the Field* 1963; *The Bedford Incident* 1965; *Riot, They Shoot Horses Don't They?* 1969.

point-of-view (POV) shot. A shot filmed at such a camera angle that an object or an action appears to be seen from a particular actor's viewpoint. This is usually accomplished by placing the camera alongside the player (or at a spot he would have occupied if he were present on the set) from whose viewpoint the scene is shot. Other players look at the point designated as the player's position (or at the player, if he is present) but not into the lens.

Poitier, Sidney. Actor, director. Born on Feb. 20, 1924, in Miami, Fla., to poor tomato growers from Cat Island in the Bahamas. The American screen's first prominent black star. Raised in the Bahamas, he dropped out of school at 13 and worked at a variety of menial jobs and served in the Army before joining the American Negro Theater and making his Broadway debut in the 1946 all-black production of 'Lysistrata.' In films beginning in 1950, he rapidly became Hollywood's number one black actor and by the 60s he was established as a popular screen star with charismatic personal appeal and the ability to tackle an ever-widening range of roles. He was nominated for a best actor Oscar for his role in *The Defiant Ones* (1958) and won the Academy Award in the same category for *Lilies of the Field* (1963). His success helped pave the way for the entry of other black stars into the mainstream of the American commercial cinema. Poitier reached a peak of popularity with magnetic performances in three superior films of 1967, *In the Heat of the Night, To Sir with Love,* and *Guess Who's Coming to Dinner.* With his acting career slipping in the early 70s, he turned to directing, at first his own films, then those starring others. He was 64 years old by the time he made a mini-comeback as a leading man in 1988 after a decade-long absence from the screen. In 1991 he portrayed Supreme Court Justice Thurgood Marshall in the TV movie *Separate but Equal.* In 1992 he became the first black recipient of the American Film institute's Life Achievement Award. Poitier has been married to actress Joanna Shimkus (*b.* Oct. 30, 1943, Halifax, N.S., Canada), his second, since 1976. Autobiography: *The Life* (1980).

FILMS (as actor): *From Whence Cometh Help* (US Army doc.) 1949; *No Way Out* 1950; *Cry the Beloved Country, Red Ball Express* 1952; *Go Man Go!* 1954; *The Blackboard Jungle* 1955; *Goodbye My Lady* 1956; *Edge of the City, Something of Value, Band of Angels* 1957; *The Mark of the Hawk, The Defiant Ones* 1958; *Porgy and Bess* (as Porgy) 1959; *All the Young Men, Virgin Island* 1960; *A Raisin in the Sun, Paris Blues* 1961; *Pressure Point* 1962; *Lilies of the Field* 1963; *The Long Ships* (UK/Yug.) 1964; *The Greatest Story Ever Told* (as Simon of Cyrene), *The Bedford Incident* (UK/US), *A Patch of Blue, The Slender Thread* 1965; *Duel at Diablo* 1966; *In the Heat of the Night, To Sir with Love* (UK), *Guess Who's Coming to Dinner* 1967; *For Love of Ivy* (also story) 1968; *The Lost Man* 1969; *King* (doc.), *They Call Me Mr. Tibbs* 1970; *Brother John, The Organization* 1971; *Buck and the Preacher* (also dir.) 1972; *A Warm December* (also dir.) 1973; *Uptown Saturday Night* (also dir.) 1974; *Let's Do It Again* (also dir.), *The Wilby Conspiracy* (UK) 1975; *A Piece of the Action* (also dir.) 1977; *Stir Crazy* (dir. only) 1980; *Hanky Panky* (dir. only) 1982; *Fast Forward* (dir. only) 1985; *Shoot to Kill/Deadly Pursuit, Little Nikita* 1988; *Ghost Dad* (dir. only) 1990; *Sneakers* 1992; *The Jackal* 1997.

Poland. Film production began early but proceeded slowly in this culturally rich but then economically poor and politically subjugated East European country. A young engineer, Kazimierz Proszynski, designed a camera he called a "pleographe" with which he began making short fiction films in 1902. However, regular production did not begin until 1908. It started picking up steam after 1910, mostly because of the popularity of a newly discovered star, Apollonia Chalupiec, later to gain fame and fortune in Hollywood as Pola NEGRI. Most production took place on the streets and on interior locations and it wasn't until 1920, two years after Poland regained its independence, that the first studio was built, in Warsaw. Still, Polish cinema remained technically poor and creatively uninspired through the rest of the silent era. The most important directors of the period were Aleksander HERTZ, who guided the career of the very popular actress Jadwiga Smosarska; Richard Ordynski, who adapted literary classics to the screen; and Wiktor Bieganski, who was the first Polish director to seek a specifically cinematic style. Also prominent was cameraman Ryczard (Richard) BOLESLAWSKI, who later became famous as a Hollywood director.

While the transition to sound presented technical, production, distribution, and exhibition difficulties, the Polish film industry had stabilized by the mid-30s. The theoretical ideas of START (Society of the Devotees of Artistic Film), an avant-garde student group formed in 1929 and urging the production of "socially useful" films, were influential in the development of Polish cinema in the 30s and even more so in the postwar years. Among the members of the group were directors Wanda JAKUBOWSKA, Jerzy Bossak, and Aleksander (or Alexander) FORD. Ford, a key figure in Polish cinema whose work was to provide the vital link between the past and the present in the postwar years, made two of the most important Polish films of the 30s, *Legion of the Streets* (1932) and *People of the Vistula* (1937). Also successful were two films of Josef Lejtes, *The Young Forest* (1934) and *The Day of the Great Adventure* (1936).

The devastation of WW II virtually eradicated the Polish cinema's past and in 1945 forced the newly nationalized industry to rebuild from scratch. The few films produced in the immediate postwar years typically dealt with the Nazi occupation, the horrors of the ghetto, and the heroics of the Resistance. The two most impressive of these were Jakubowska's *The Last Stop* and Ford's *Border Street* (both 1948). The early 50s saw a decline in the quality of Polish films, resulting from official pressure on filmmakers to follow the dogmas of Socialist Realism promoted by Poland's Communist leadership. The only exceptions were Ford's *Young Chopin* (1952) and *Five from Barska Street* (1953).

But the mid-50s saw a resurgence of creativity and the emergence of a new generation of filmmakers whose vitality and originality raised Polish cinema to international prominence. Their films were characterized by an introspective re-examination of social and political myths past and present, focusing on individual psychology, as well as by an adventurous variety of approaches and styles. Prominent among the directors of this new school of Polish cinema were Andrzej WAJDA, whose famous trilogy (*A Generation,* 1954; *Kanal,* 1957; and *Ashes and Diamonds,* 1958) probed the psychology of the wartime and postwar years; Andrzej MUNK, who applied sharp irony to the exploration of similar themes in *Man on the Track* (1956) and *Eroica* (1957); and Jerzy KAWALEROWICZ, who is best known for his 1961 mystic suspense drama *Mother Joan of the Angels.*

Much of the fervor of the new Polish cinema began to dissipate in the early 60s, but two outstanding young directors emerged during this period: Roman POLANSKI, whose shorts and first feature, *Knife in the Water* (1962), were universally acclaimed, and Jerzy SKOLIMOWSKI, whose *Walkover* (1965) and *Barrier* (1966) daringly challenged the social structure of present-day Poland. Skolimowski did some of his work abroad, and Polanski, working abroad since the mid-60s, can no longer be considered a Polish director.

The Polish cinema suffered a severe blow in the late 60s in the wake of the 1968 student demonstrations and the subsequent purges and political turmoil. Many leading figures in the industry were replaced or demoted. Aleksander Ford emigrated to Israel, and other Jewish directors and film executives became victims of an anti-Semitic outburst that followed the disturbances.

Despite these traumatic events, widespread resistance to totalitarian rule contributed to the development of a "cinema of moral anxiety," focusing on the isolation of honorable individuals in a corrupt society. Veteran filmmakers such as Wajda and Skolimowski and newer ones such as Krzysztof ZANUSSI (*Family Life, Behind the Wall*, 1971), Krzysztof KIESLOWSKI (*Camera Buff*, 1979), and Janusz Kijowski challenged state censorship to prepare the ground for the democratization movement that reached its peak with the Solidarity labor strikes of 1980–81. Polish cinema became recognized internationally as a vehicle of democratic resistance, leading to the award of the 1981 Palme d'Or at Cannes to Wajda's *Man of Iron*, an account of the Gdansk strike of 1980.

The Polish government also recognized the power of the national cinema. When martial law was declared on Dec. 13, 1981, all 2,000 Polish movie theaters were closed down as part of the ban on popular assemblies. When the theaters re-opened, films were subject to heavy censorship, and audiences responded with a sharp decline in attendance and an outright boycott of the cinemas on the 13th of each month. Though the Solidarity labor union was outlawed, and many film directors and personnel moved abroad, the Polish Filmmakers Union managed to survive and keep its integrity. A handful of filmmakers, including Kawalerowicz (*Austeria*, 1983) and Tadeusz Konwicki (*The Issa Valley*, 1983), continued to create films of artistic merit.

By the late 80s, the Communist government of Poland had collapsed, but Polish cinema faced a new set of obstacles, economic rather than political. Film production was privatized and subsidies from the government shrank. However, by 1992, state assistance had stabilized and film production had rebounded, with over 20 features released annually, including new films by Wajda, Zanussi, Kijowski, and Kieslowski. Other recent directors of note include Marcia Ziebidski, Janusz Zaorski, and Andrzej Zulawski.

Polanski, Roman. Director. Born on Aug. 18, 1933, in Paris, to Polish-Jewish parents who returned to Kraków when he was three. His childhood was terrifying. When he was eight his parents were taken to a Nazi concentration camp, where his mother died. He escaped from the Kraków ghetto just before it was liquidated and wandered about the Polish countryside seeking refuge with a succession of Catholic families. He witnessed many horrors along the way and was himself the victim of a sadistic game played by several German soldiers: They used him for target practice and delighted at his desperate scampering to duck their bullets. These terrible memories of his formative years no doubt have contributed to the preoccupation with obsession and fear which has characterized his films.

Toward the end of the war, Polanski returned to Kraków, where he sold newspapers on the streets and developed a growing passion for the cinema, which expressed itself in the addictive habit of seeing at least one movie every day. When he was 12 he was reunited with his father, who sent him to a technical school to receive his first formal education. At the same time he began acting in kiddie-hour radio shows. When he was 14 he became a stage actor and he remained in the theater for six years. He was turned down by the state's acting school but was accepted as a student at the famous Polish Film School at Lodz. During his five years (1954–59) at the school, he appeared as an actor in a number of Polish films and directed several documentary shorts. One of these, *Two Men and a Wardrobe,* a 15-minute semisurrealistic exercise, won five international awards, including third prize at the Brussels World's Fair international competition of experimental films.

After graduating from the school, Polanski spent two years in Paris, where he made a short, *The Fat and the Lean,* a study of a master-slave relationship in which he played one of the two parts, the lean servant. Returning to Poland, he made the award-winning short *Mammals* and his first feature film, *Knife in the Water,* a mature, subtle psychological triangle drama that catapulted the young director into international prominence. It won the critics' prize at the Venice Film Festival and was nominated for an Academy Award as best foreign language film. Polanski subsequently returned to Paris for a three-year stay, then went on to London and Hollywood. From the mid-60s, all his films have been made in English and have been characterized by technical virtuosity, a deep sense of alienation, explicit violence, and a personal fascination with various aspects of horror and aberrations of the human mind, especially as expressed by the behavior symptoms of sexuality. He won the Silver Bear at the 1965 Berlin Film Festival for his first British production, *Repulsion,* and the Golden Bear at the same event in the following year for *Cul-de-Sac.*

In addition to the mental scars of his tortured childhood, Polanski acknowledges the influences on his work of Beckett, Ionesco, Pinter, Kafka, and Buñuel. Atmosphere is the most important element of his films and the core around which he builds his plots and develops his characters. Like Hitchcock, he considers actors as simple pawns in the game of filmmaking and reportedly subjects them to much abuse on the set, especially the actresses. Yet in *Repulsion* he succeeded in tapping the till-then unsuspected acting talent of Catherine Deneuve and in *Rosemary's Baby* extracted the finest performance of Mia Farrow's career. Although his reputation in America was tarnished by the release of a mutilated version of his horror-parody *Dance of the Vampires/The Fearless Vampire Killers,* his American-made *Rosemary's Baby* was a critical and commercial triumph that earned him an Academy Award nomination for best screenplay and assured him virtual *carte blanche* with Hollywood producers.

Polanski was considering several promising new projects when yet another blow was dealt him. In August of 1969, while he was in London working on a script, his wife (since 1968), actress Sharon Tate, eight months pregnant, and several of their close friends were viciously murdered by a frenzied band of youths, the so-called Manson family. After a period of inactivity, the resilient Polanski resumed filmmaking in 1971 with an ultraviolent screen adaptation of Shakespeare's 'Macbeth' which contained a number of bloodbath scenes painfully reminiscent of the Tate massacre.

Following the Tate tragedy, Polanski abandoned his Hollywood residence, returned to Europe, and eventually obtained French citizenship. He came back to the US periodically to work and visit friends, and it was here that he enjoyed his greatest commercial and critical success since *Rosemary's Baby* with *Chinatown* (1974), a stylish political mystery starring Jack Nicholson and featuring Polanski himself in a character role. He cast himself as the star of his next project, *Le Locataire/The Tenant* (1976), a film replete with autobiographical coincidences and Kafkaesque obsessions, which he shot in a neighborhood of Paris where he spent some of his leaner days. Polanski was back on a Hollywood sojourn when, in March of 1977, he again made the newspaper headlines in a capacity not related to his work. He was arrested by Los Angeles police and brought to court on charges of drugging and raping a 13-year-old model and aspiring actress at the home of Jack Nicholson while presumably taking pictures of her for the French edition of *Vogue.* At the time, he was about to start production on a Columbia picture, *The First Deadly Sin,* but after his arraignment he was assigned by Dino De Laurentiis to a quick start on another film, *Hurricane,* to be shot for Paramount in Tahiti. At first, Polanski denied the rape charge, then entered a partial guilty plea. Free on bail, he was allowed to leave the country to complete *Hurricane.* He never returned and was declared by the court a fugitive from justice. As it turned out, Polanski's next film was *Tess* (1979), an English-language, French-British adaptation of Thomas Hardy's novel *Tess of the D'Urbervilles. Hurricane* was reassigned to director Jan Troell. It bombed. *Tess,* on the other hand, was a glorious success, a beautifully shot, elegantly told, sumptuously produced romantic epic that proved a hit with the critics and the public alike. It earned Polanski a César and a second Oscar nomination as best director (his first was for *Chinatown*). Remaining in Paris, Polanski experienced a rare flop with *Pirates* (1986), which he then followed with the moderately successful American-sponsored thriller *Frantic* (1988). In 1989 he married the film's French star, 22-year-old Emmanuelle Seigner. Autobiography: *Roman* (1984).

FILMS (as director): Shorts—*The Bicycle* (unfinished) 1955; *Breaking Up the Dance* (also sc.), *Two Men and a Wardrobe* (also sc., act.), *The Lamp* (also sc.), *When Angels Fall* (also sc., act.) 1959; *Le Gros et le Maigre/The Fat and the Lean* (also co-sc., act.; Fr.) 1960; *Mammals* (also co-sc., act.) 1962. Features—*Knife in the Water/The Young Lover/The Long Sunday* (also co-sc.) 1962; *Les plus Belles Escroqueries du Monde/The Beautiful Swindlers* ("Amsterdam" episode; also co-sc.; Fr./It./Jap./Holl.) 1964; *Repulsion* (also co-sc., act. in bit; UK) 1965; *Cul-de-Sac* (also co-sc.) 1966; *Dance of the Vampires/The Fearless Vampire Killers or Pardon Me but Your Teeth Are in My Neck* (also co-sc., act.; UK/US) 1967; *Rosemary's Baby* (also sc.; US) 1968; *Macbeth* (also co-sc.; UK/US) 1971; *Che?/What?* (also co-sc., act.; It./Fr.) 1973; *Chinatown* (also act.; US) 1974; *Le Locataire/The Tenant* (also co-sc., act.; Fr.) 1976; *Tess* (also co-sc.; Fr./UK) 1980; *Pirates* (also co-sc.; Fr./Tunis) 1986; *Frantic* (also co-sc.; US) 1988; *Back in the USSR* (act. only) 1991; *Bitter Moon, Death and the Maiden, Grosse Fatigue* (act. only), *A Pure Formality* (act. only) 1994.

Polaroid filter. A filter designed to cut down glare and unwanted reflections. Also called "pola screen."

pola screen. See POLAROID FILTER.

polecat. A device for supporting studio lamps.

Polglase, Van Nest. Art director. *b.* Aug. 25, 1898, Brooklyn, N.Y. *d.* 1968. One of the most influential production designers of the American cinema. Trained as an architect at New York's Beaux Arts, he spent a year in Cuba helping on the design of the presidential palace in Havana, then entered films in 1919 as an art director for Famous Players-Lasky, later working for Paramount and MGM. In 1932 he was appointed supervising art director of the entire RKO product, a position he lost ten years later because of a drinking problem. He later worked for Columbia and other studios.

FILMS INCLUDE: *A Kiss in the Dark, Stage Struck* 1925; *Untamed* 1929; *Little Women, King Kong, Flying Down to Rio* 1933; *The Lost Patrol, Of Human Bondage, The Little Minister* 1934; *Roberta, Alice Adams, She, Top Hat, The Informer, The Last Days of Pompeii, The Three Musketeers, Annie Oakley, Seven Keys to Baldpate* 1935; *Follow the Fleet, Mary of Scotland, Winterset* 1936; *The Toast of New York, The Plough and the Stars, Shall We Dance?, Stage Door* 1937; *Carefree, Room Service* 1938; *Gunga Din, The Hunchback of Notre Dame* 1939; *Kitty Foyle* 1940; *Citizen Kane* 1941; *Suspicion* 1942; *The Fallen Sparrow* 1943; *Together Again* 1944; *A Song to Remember* 1945; *Gilda* 1946; *The Crooked Way* 1949; *Passion* 1954; *Tennessee's Partner* 1955; *Slightly Scarlet* 1956; *The River's Edge* 1957.

Polito, Sol. Director of photography. *b.* Salvatore (later Salvador) Polito, 1892, Palermo, Italy. *d.* 1960. In the US from an early age, he was educated in New York and first entered films as a publicity still photographer. He was a lab and camera assistant before graduating to lighting cameraman in 1917. For the next three decades he worked on scores of films for various studios, but his reputation rests mainly on his fine black-and-white cinematography for Warner Bros. in the 30s and 40s, when he frequently worked with such directors as Michael CURTIZ and Mervyn LEROY.

FILMS INCLUDE: *Rip Van Winkle* 1914; *The Butterfly, The Cotton King* 1915; *Fruits of Desire* 1916; *The Runaway* 1917; *Ruling Passions* 1918; *Soldiers of Fortune* 1919; *Alias Jimmy Valentine* 1920; *The Roof Tree* 1921; *Trimmed* 1922; *The Girl of the Golden West* (co-phot.), *Mighty Lak' a Rose, The Bad Man* 1923; *A Cafe in Cairo, The Flaming Forties, The Siren of Seville, Why Men Leave Home* 1924; *Soft Shoes, The Bad Lands* (co-phot.) 1925; *Satan Town* 1926; *The Overland Stage* 1927; *The Border Patrol, The Haunted House, The Shepherd of the Hills, Show Girl* 1928; *The House of Horror* (co-phot.), *The Isle of Lost Ships, Paris, Seven Footprints to Satan, The Man and the Moment, Scarlet Seas, Broadway Babies* 1929; *The Girl of the Golden West* (remake), *No No Nanette, Madonna of the Streets, Numbered Men* 1930; *Five Star Final, The Ruling Voice* 1931; *Three on a Match, I Am a Fugitive from a Chain Gang* 1932; *Gold Diggers of 1933, 42nd Street* 1933; *Wonder Bar* 1934; *G-Men, In Caliente* (co-phot.) 1935; *The Petrified Forest, The Charge of the Light Brigade* 1936; *The Prince and the Pauper* 1937; *Valley of the Giants* (co-phot.), *The Adventures of Robin Hood* (co-phot.) 1938; *Confessions of a Nazi Spy, The Private Lives of Elizabeth and Essex, Dodge City* 1939; *Virginia City, City for Conquest* (co-phot.), *The Sea Hawk, Santa Fe Trail* 1940; *Sergeant York* (co-phot.), *The Sea Wolf* 1941; *Captains of the Clouds, Now Voyager* 1942; *Old Acquaintance* 1943; *Arsenic and Old Lace, The Adventures of Mark Twain* 1944; *The Corn Is Green, Rhapsody in Blue* 1945; *Cloak and Dagger, A Stolen Life* (co-phot.) 1946; *The Long Night, The Voice of the Turtle* 1947; *Sorry Wrong Number* 1948; *Anna Lucasta* 1949.

Pollack, Sydney. Director, producer, actor. Born July 1, 1934, Lafayette, Ind. The son of first-generation Russian-Jewish Americans, he was raised in South Bend, where he graduated from high school in 1952, then went to New York and enrolled at the Neighborhood Playhouse School of the Theatre, training under Sanford Meisner. Following a two-year hitch in the Army in 1957–58, he returned to the Playhouse as an acting instructor and began performing in TV plays. A role in a John Frankenheimer TV play led to an assignment for Pollack as dialogue coach on the director's feature *The Young Savages* (1961), an experience which kindled his interest in directing. Pollack directed several teleplays and scores of episodes for such TV series as 'The Defenders,' 'The Fugitive,' 'Naked City,' 'Dr. Kildare,' and 'Ben Casey' before making his debut as a feature director in 1965 with *The Slender Thread,* a competent if unremarkable drama. He turned out several other credible but routine productions before asserting himself as a major director with *They Shoot Horses, Don't They?* (1969). A powerful downbeat drama that used a Depression-era dance marathon as a microcosm of society's ills, it earned Pollack an Oscar nomination for best director and won an Academy Award for best actor for Gig YOUNG. Scoring another triumph with *The Way We Were* (1973), an era-captivating, touching love story told against the background of political activism, Pollack enhanced his reputation as an effective if conventional filmmaker with a special knack for eliciting great performances from his actors. He was nominated again for best director for the hilarious comedy *Tootsie* (1982), which also received a best picture nomination, and finally won the Academy Awards in both categories for the exquisitely shot *Out of Africa* (1985). In recent years Pollack became increasingly involved in producing.

FILMS: As actor—*War Hunt* 1962; *Hello Actors Studio* 1987; *Death Becomes Her, Husbands and Wives, The Player* 1992. As director—*The Slender Thread* 1965; *This Property Is Condemned* 1966; *The Swimmer* (one sequence only), *The Scalp-hunters* 1968; *Castle Keep, They Shoot Horses Don't They?* 1969; *Jeremiah Johnson* 1972; *The Way We Were* 1973; *The Yakuza* (also prod.), *Three Days of the Condor* 1975; *Bobby Deerfield* (also prod.) 1977; *The Electric Horseman* 1979; *Absence of Malice* (also prod.) 1981; *Tootsie* (also prod., act.) 1982; *Out of Africa* (also prod.) 1985; *Havana* (also prod.) 1990; *The Firm* 1993; *Sabrina* (also prod.) 1995. As producer or executive producer (alone or in collaboration)—*Honeysuckle Rose* 1980; *Songwriter, Sanford Meisner—The Theater's Best Kept Secret* (doc.) 1984; *Bright Lights Big City* 1988; *The Fabulous Baker Boys, Major League* 1989; *Presumed Innocent, White Palace* 1990; *Dead Again* 1991; *Leaving Normal* 1992; *Flesh and Bone, Searching for Bobby Fischer* 1993; *Sense and Sensibility* 1995.

Pollak, Kevin. Actor, writer. Born October 30, 1958, in San Francisco, Calif. After getting his start as a stand-up comic on the club circuit, this likable, engaging supporting actor rose to success with his ability to impersonate the famous which led to roles in television movies and sitcoms. His film career received a boost with his intelligent, dignified performance opposite Tom CRUISE in *A Few Good Men* (1992) as well as his role in the ensemble piece *The Usual Suspects* (1995).

FILMS: *Million Dollar Mystery* 1987; *Willow* 1988; *Avalon* 1990; *L.A. Story, Ricochet* 1991; *A Few Good Men* 1992; *Grumpy Old Men, Indian Summer, The Opposite Sex (And How to Live with Them), Wayne's World 2* 1993; *Clean Slate, Reality Bites* 1994; *Canadian Bacon, Casino, Grumpier Old Men, Miami Rhapsody, The Usual Suspects* 1995; *That Thing You Do, Nowhere Man, House Arrest* 1996; *Truth or Consequences, N.M.* 1997.

Pollard, Harry A. Director, actor. *b.* Jan. 23, 1883, Republic, Kans. *d.* 1934. A former stage actor, he joined the Selig company in 1912 and starred in many of its pictures. The following year he also doubled as director and eventually gave up acting entirely for directing. His wife, Margarita Fischer, starred in many of his films.

FILMS INCLUDE: As actor—*On the Shore* 1912; *Uncle Tom's Cabin* 1913. As director—*The Peacock Feather Fan* (also act.), *Motherhood* 1914; *The Quest* (also act.), *The Girl from His Town, Infatuation* (also act.), *The Miracle of Life* 1915; *The Dragon, The Pearl of Paradise* (also sc., act.) 1916; *The Devil's Assistant, The Girl Who Couldn't Grow Up* 1917; *The Danger Game* 1918; *The Invisible Ray* (serial) 1920; *Trimmed, The Loaded Door, Confidence* 1922; *Trifling with Honor* 1923; *Sporting Youth, The Reckless Age, K—The Unknown* 1924; *Oh Doctor!, I'll Show You the Town, California Straight Ahead* 1925; *The Cohens and Kellys, Poker Faces* 1926; *Uncle Tom's Cabin* (remake) 1927; *Show Boat, Tonight at Twelve* 1929; *Undertow* 1930; *Shipmates, The Prodigal* 1931; *When a Feller Needs a Friend, Fast Life* 1932.

Pollard, Harry ("Snub"). Actor. *b.* Harold Frazer, 1886, Melbourne, Australia. *d.* 1962. Slapstick comic of numerous one- and two-reel silent comedies, he came to the US with an Australian light opera company and joined Hal ROACH in 1915. For the next four years he supported Harold LLOYD in scores of one-reel comedies, then in 1919, was given his own one-reel comedy series directed by Charles PARROTT. A little man with a drooping moustache, he typically played henpecked husbands and other vulnerable characters. In 1922 he graduated to starring in two-reelers. In 1926 he left Roach to form his own company, but he could not sustain his earlier popularity and soon disappeared from the screen. He returned in the early 30s, playing occasional bit parts in feature films. His sister, comedienne Daphne Pollard (1892–1978), also appeared in many silents and talkies.

FILMS INCLUDE: Shorts—*Great While It Lasted, Lonesome Luke—Gangster* 1915; *Luke Laughs Last* 1916; *Bliss, Rainbow Island, The Flirt* 1917; *The Lamb, The Big Idea* 1918; *Captain Kidd's Kids, From Hand to Mouth, His Royal Slyness, Start Something, All at Sea, It's a Hard Life, How Dry I Am, Looking for Trouble, Tough Luck* 1919; *Red Hot Hottentots, The Dippy Dentist, All Lit Up, Getting His Goat, Flat Broke, Don't Weaken, Trotting Through Turkey, Grab the Ghost, Any Old Port, Live and Learn, A London Bobby, Money to Burn, Insulting the Sultan* 1920; *The Morning After, His Best Girl, Fellow Romans, Big Game, Blue Sunday, The High Rollers, Law and Order, Hocus-Pocus, The Hustler* 1921; *Stage Struck, Down and Out, Pardon Me, Days of Old, In the Movies, Punch the Clock, The Dumb Bell, Bed of Roses, The Stone Age, Hook Line and Sinker, Nearly Rich* 1922; *A Tough Winter, California or Bust, The Courtship of Miles Sandwich, Jack Frost, The Mystery Man, It's a Gift* 1923; *The Big Idea, Why Marry?* 1924; *Are Husbands Human?* 1925; *The Doughboy* (also prod.), *The Yokel* (also prod.) 1926; *The Bum's Rush* (also prod.) 1927. Features—*Ex-Flame* 1930; *East Lynne* 1931; *The Purchase Price* 1932; *Stingaree, Cockeyed Cavaliers* 1934; *The Gentleman from Louisiana* 1936; *Arizona Days* 1937; *Frontier Town* 1938; *Casanova Brown* 1944; *Kitty, The Kid from Brooklyn* 1945; *Magic Town, Miracle on 34th Street, The Perils of Pauline* 1947; *Family Honeymoon, Johnny Belinda* 1948; *The Crooked Way* 1949; *Carrie, Limelight* 1952; *Pete Kelly's Blues* 1955; *Man of a Thousand Faces* 1957; *Who Was That Lady?* 1960; *One-Eyed Jacks, Pocketful of Miracles* 1961.

Pollard, Michael J. Actor. Born Michael J. Pollack, on May 30, 1939, in Pacific, N.J. Impish character actor of the American stage and screen in offbeat parts, he gained popularity following his portrayal of C. W. Moss, the goofy junior partner in *Bonnie and Clyde* (1967), for which he was nominated for a best supporting actor Oscar. He moved briefly into lead roles, then reverted to supporting parts of diminishing importance, mostly in low-budget productions.

FILMS INCLUDE: *Hemingway's Adventures of a Young Man* 1962; *The Stripper, Summer Magic* 1963; *The Russians Are Coming the Russians Are Coming, The Wild Angels* 1966; *Caprice, Enter Laughing, Bonnie and Clyde* 1967; *Jigsaw* 1968; *Hannibal Brooks* 1969; *Little Fauss and Big Halsy* 1970; *Les Petroleuses/The Legend of Frenchy King* (Fr.) 1971; *Dirty Little Billy* 1972; *Sunday in the Country* 1975; *Between the Lines* 1977; *Melvin and Howard* 1980; *Heated Vengeance* 1985; *The American Way/Riders of the Storm* (UK), *The Patriot, America* (release delayed from 1982) 1986; *Roxanne, American Gothic* (UK) 1987; *Scrooged* 1988; *Fast Food, Night Visitor/Never Cry Devil, Next of Kin, Tango and Cash* 1989; *Dick Tracy, Enid Is Sleeping, I Come in Peace, The Arrival* 1990; *The Art of Dying, Motorama* 1991; *Split Second* 1992; *Arizona Dream* 1993; *Skeeter* 1994.

Pollock, George. Director. Born in 1907, in Leicester, England. In British films in various capacities since 1933, he began directing in the mid-50s, and is best known for the "Miss Marple" comedy-mystery cycle in the 60s.

FILMS: *Stranger in Town* 1957; *Rooney, Sally's Irish Rogue/The Poacher's Daughter* (Ire.) 1958; *A Broth of a Boy* (Ire.), *Don't Panic Chaps!* 1959; *And the Same to You* 1960; *Murder She Said* 1961; *Village of Daughters, Kill or Cure* 1962; *Murder at the Gallop* 1963; *Murder Most Foul, Murder Ahoy* 1964; *Ten Little Indians* 1966.

Polo, Eddie. Actor. *b.* Edward A. Polo, 1875, Los Angeles. *d.* 1961. Legendary hero of silent serials and action pictures. A former circus acrobat, he entered films in 1913 as a stuntman but quickly became a popular Universal star billed as the "Hercules of the Screen." His exploits on and off the screen were given much publicity. In 1915 he became the first man to jump by parachute from the Eiffel Tower, and he later set a record for parachuting from a plane. In the mid-20s, after quitting Universal and failing to realize a profit from his own company, he tried his fortune in German films. His career ended with the coming of sound, but he returned to the screen in the early 40s in rare bit roles.

FILMS INCLUDE: *The Broken Coin* (serial), *The Yellow Streak* 1915; *The Adventures of Peg o' the Ring* (serial), *Liberty—A Daughter of the USA* (serial), *Heritage of Hate* 1916; *The Gray Ghost* (serial), *Money Madness, A Kentucky Cinderella* 1917; *Bull's-Eye* (serial), *The Lure of the Circus* (serial) 1918; *Cyclone Smith Plays Trumps, Cyclone Smith's Comeback* (and other action shorts in the *Cyclone Smith* series) 1919; *The Vanishing Dagger* (serial), *King of the Circus* (serial) 1920; *The Secret Four* (serial), *Do or Die* (serial), *The White*

Horseman (serial) 1921; *Captain Kidd* (serial), *With Stanley in Africa* (serial) 1922; *The Knock on the Door, Dangerous Hour, Prepared to Die* 1923; *Cowboy Love* (Ger.) 1929; *Son of Roaring Dan* 1940; *The Wolf Man* 1941; *Between Us Girls* 1942; *Hers to Hold* 1943.

Polonsky, Abraham. Director, screenwriter, novelist. Born on Dec. 5, 1910, in New York City. *ed.* CCNY; Columbia Law School. The son of Russian-Jewish immigrants, he was strongly influenced by the passionate socialist ideals of his intellectual pharmacist father. He practiced law, taught at New York's City College, wrote essays, radio scripts, and several novels, and signed a screenwriter's contract with Paramount before leaving for Europe to serve with the OSS during WW II. Returning to Hollywood after the war, he was assigned to write the screenplay for Mitchell Leisen's *Golden Earrings,* but Paramount decided to have his script revised. Although he shared screen credit with two other writers, none of his original work survived in the released film, which failed badly both with the critics and with the public. Upon leaving Paramount, Polonsky fared much better with his next screenplay, for Robert Rossen's *Body and Soul* (Academy Award nomination, 1947). He closely followed the actual production of the film and to his surprise was encouraged by the producer, Bob Robertson, and the star, John Garfield, to accept the direction of their next project. Polonsky's first directorial effort, *Force of Evil* (1948), a darkly intense crime melodrama, notable for its compact action and a stylized rhythmic language that approached poetry, was largely ignored by American critics or dismissed as a routine gangster drama, but it was highly praised in such respected British film publications as *Sight and Sound* and *Sequence.* In retrospect, it has been evaluated by Andrew Sarris as "one of the great films of the modern American cinema." Nearly a quarter of a century was to elapse before Polonsky would be given the chance to direct his second film, *Tell Them Willie Boy Is Here* (1970).

After completing *Force of Evil,* Polonsky went to Europe to write a novel and acquire the screen rights for Thomas Mann's short story *Mario and the Magician.* Returning to Hollywood, in 1950, he concluded a deal to direct his next project for 20th Century-Fox. But in April of 1951 he was subpoenaed to appear before the House Un-American Activities Committee, and after refusing to affirm or deny membership in the Communist party, he was blacklisted by the industry. Curiously, he did better financially under the blacklist than before, writing TV scripts ('You Are There,' etc.) and doctoring motion picture screenplays. But it wasn't until 1968 that he could use his own name in credits, starting with screenwriter for *Madigan.* The following year he briefly resumed his career as a director. *Tell Them Willie Boy Is Here* (1970) was a polished Western morality tale in the guise of a chase story, which involved a reluctant sheriff and the doomed Indian he must hunt down and kill. It was well received. Barely seen and generally scorned by those who did was Polonsky's next and last film, *Romance of a Horsethief* (1971). Set in Poland at the turn of the century, this amiable but stagnant production provided a sad coda to a career whose promise was squelched by ugly politics.

FILMS: As screenwriter—*Golden Earrings* (co-sc.), *Body and Soul* 1947; *I Can Get It for You Wholesale* 1951; *Madigan* 1968; *Avalanche Express* 1979; *Body and Soul* (1947 screenplay basis only) 1981; *Monsignor* (co-sc.) 1982. As director-screenwriter—*Force of Evil* 1948; *Tell Them Willie Boy Is Here* 1970; *Romance of a Horsethief* 1971.

Polyvision. A triple-screen projection system developed by director Abel GANCE, who first used it in 1927 in his monumental film *Napoléon.*

Pommer, Erich. Producer. *b.* July 20, 1889, Hildesheim, Germany. *d.* 1966, in Hollywood. An employee of Gaumont in Paris from the age of 18, he later became the company's director of operations in Central Europe. In 1915, after recovering from serious WW I battle injuries, he founded Decla (Deutsche Eclair), a film production company that later merged with Bioscop to form Decla-Bioscop and was absorbed by UFA in 1923. A shrewd impresario with a keen eye for quality properties and promising talent, Pommer produced many of the most successful German films of the 20s and early 30s. The percentage of the artistic and commercial hits among his German—and later French, British, and American—films was nothing short of amazing. Until 1933, except for a brief stint in Hollywood (1926–27), he made all his films in Germany. But after the advent of the Nazis, the Jewish Pommer began a long exile that took him to Paris (1933), Hollywood (1934), London (where he founded Mayflower Pictures with Charles LAUGHTON in 1937), and again to Hollywood (1940). In 1946 he returned to Germany, in US Army uniform, to oversee the restoration of the shattered German film industry. He remained in Germany to produce a number of films, then returned to Hollywood in 1956.

FILMS INCLUDE: *Das Kabinett des Dr. Caligari/The Cabinet of Dr. Caligari, Halbblut* 1919; *Die Spinnen/The Spiders* (in two parts) 1919–20; *Das indische Grabmal/The Indian Tomb* (in two parts) 1920–21; *Der müde Tod/Between Worlds/Destiny* 1921; *Dr. Mabuse der Spieler/Dr. Mabuse the Gambler, Phantom, Der brennende Acker/Burning Soil* 1922; *Die Nibelungen* (in two parts), *Der letzte Mann/The Last Laugh, Mikaël* 1924; *Tartüff, Variété/Variety* 1925; *Metropolis, Faust* 1926; *Hotel Imperial* (US), *Barbed Wire* (US) 1927; *Spione/Spies, Heimkehr/Homecoming* 1928; *Asphalt* 1929; *Liebeswalzer, Der blaue Engel/The Blue Angel* 1930; *Bomben auf Monte Carlo/Monte Carlo Madness, Der Kongress tanzt/The Congress Dances, Stürme der Leidenschaft* 1931; *Ein blonder Traum/A Blonde Dream* 1932; *On a volé un Homme* (Fr.) 1933; *Liliom* (Fr.), *Music in the Air* (US) 1934; *Farewell Again/Troopship* (UK), *Fire Over England* (UK) 1937; *Vessel of Wrath/The Beachcomber* (also dir.; UK), *St. Martin's Lane/Sidewalks of London* (UK) 1938; *Jamaica Inn* (UK) 1939; *Dance Girl Dance* (US), *They Knew What They Wanted* (US) 1940; *Illusion in Moll* 1952; *Kinder Mutter und ein General* 1955.

Pons, Lily. Opera singer, actress. *b.* Alice Josephine Pons, Apr. 12, 1898, Draguignan, near Cannes, France. *d.* 1976. Celebrated coloratura soprano of the Metropolitan Opera who starred in several Hollywood films. The daughter of a French engineer and a mother of Italian descent, she started her musical training as a pianist and was an accomplished keyboard artist when she suddenly switched to singing toward the end of WW I. During that period of transition she also played ingenue roles on the Paris stage. She made her singing debut in Alsace in 1928 and was relatively unknown when she made her bow at the Met in *Lucia di Lammermoor* in 1931. But she soon became one of the most popular stars in the history of the New York company, appearing in 280 performances during the next 30 years. She retired in 1962 but gave an impressive one-night recital at Lincoln Center's Philharmonic Hall in 1972. During the 30s she played starring roles in three mediocre film productions as RKO's answer to Columbia's Grace Moore. Miss Pons's fourth film appearance was as one of several concert artists whose performances provided the backbone of the nearly plotless *Carnegie Hall* (1947). From 1938 to 1958 she was married to conductor Andre Kostelanetz. She died of cancer of the pancreas. A town in Maryland had been named Lilypons in her honor.

FILMS: *I Dream Too Much* 1935; *That Girl from Paris, Hitting a New High* 1937; *Carnegie Hall* 1947.

Pontecorvo, Gillo. Director. Born Gilberto Pontecorvo, on Nov. 19, 1919, in Pisa, Italy. One of ten children of a wealthy Jewish industrialist, and younger brother of world-famous scientist Bruno Pontecorvo, he received a degree in chemistry before turning to journalism and becoming a correspondent in Paris for various leftist Italian publications. In 1941 he joined the Communist Party and returned to Italy, where he helped organize a network of anti-Fascist partisans and became a leader of the Garibaldi Brigade, using the *nom de querre* Barnaba. He was among the commanders of the Milan Resistance from 1943 until the capitulation of Italy to the Allies. After WW II, he entered films as an assistant to Yves Allégret, Mario Monicelli, and other directors, and turned out his first of several documentary shorts in 1953. In 1956 he contributed an episode to the Joris Ivens-Alberto Cavalcanti women's rights film *Die Windrose,* which was produced in East Germany. The following year he made his first solo feature as director and in 1966 created his most important film, *La Battaglia di Algeri/The Battle of Algiers,* a remarkably realistic re-creation of the Algerian rebellion against the French, which achieved authentic effects through newsreel-like graininess of images and the employment of nonactors. The film, which was subsidized by the Algerian government, was awarded the Golden Lion prize at the Venice Festival. His next film, *Quemada!/Burn!* (1969), an Italian/French co-production starring Marlon Brando, dealt less successfully with a similar theme—the self-destructive nature of colonialism.

FEATURE FILMS: *Die Windrose* ("Giovanna" episode; E. Ger.) 1956; *La Grande Strada Azzurra/La Lunga Strada Azzurra/The Long Blue Road* (also co-sc.) 1957; *Kapò* (also co-sc.) 1960; *La Battaglia di Algeri/The Battle of Algiers* (also co-story, co-music) 1966; *Quemada!/Burn!* (also co-story) 1969; *Ogro/Operasion Ogro/The Tunnel* (also co-sc.) 1979; *The Stupids* (act. only) 1996.

Ponti, Carlo. Producer. Born on Dec. 11, 1910, in Magenta, Milan, Italy. The holder of a law degree, he began producing Italian films early in the 40s, overseeing the production of such directors as Comencini, Lattuada, and Zampa. In 1950 he began a fortuitous partnership with Dino DE LAURENTIIS which resulted in some of Italy's most important productions of the period. In 1957 the partnership was dissolved and Ponti extended his activity as producer or co-producer to France, England, and Hollywood. That same year he married Sophia LOREN in Mexico, a marriage not recognized by Italian authorities, who contested his previous divorce. In 1964 he obtained French citizenship, a move that finally enabled him to legalize his marital status, but continued working in Italy as well as France, England, and the United States. In 1979 he was sentenced in absentia by an Italian court to a four-year jail term and fined $25 million for smuggling currency and art abroad, but as a French citizen he was immune from extradition to his native land.

FILMS INCLUDE: *Piccolo Mondo Antico/Old-Fashioned World* 1940; *Giacomo l'Idealista* 1942; *Un Americano in Vacanza* 1945; *Vivere in Pace/To Live in Peace* 1946; *I Miserabili, Gioventù perduta/Lost Youth, Senza Pietà/Without Pity* 1947; *Il Mulino del Po/The Mill on the Po* 1949; *Vita di Cani, Il Brigante Musolino* 1950; *Sensualità, Europa '51, Anna* 1951; *Mambo, La Strada* 1954; *Ulisse/Ulysses, La Donna del Fiume, La Bella Mugnaia/The Miller's Beautiful Wife* 1955; *Guerra e Pace/War and Peace* (US/It.) 1956; *Guendalina* 1957; *The Black Orchid* (US), *That Kind of Woman* (US) 1959; *Heller in Pink Tights* (US), *La Ciociara/Two Women* 1960; *Lola, Une Femme est une Femme/A Woman Is a Woman* 1961; *Cléo de 5 à 7/Cleo from 5 to 7, Boccaccio '70* 1962; *I Sequestari di Altona/The Condemned of Altona, Landru/Bluebeard, Le Mépris/Contempt, La Noia/The Empty Canvas, Ieri Oggi e Domani/Yesterday Today and Tomorrow, Les Carabinieres* 1963; *Matrimonio all'Italiana/Marriage Italian Style* 1964; *Operation Crossbow* (UK/It.), *Doctor Zhivago* (US), *La Decima Vittima/The 10th Victim, Lady L* (US/It./Fr.), 1965; *Blow-Up* (UK/It.) 1966; *C'era una Volta/More Than a Miracle, Questi Fantasmi/Ghosts Italian Style* 1967; *Gli Amanti/A Place for Lovers* 1968; *I Girasoli/Sunflower* 1969; *Zabriskie Point* (US) 1970; *La Móglie del Prete/The Priest's Wife, La Mortadella/Lady Liberty* 1971; *Che?/What?, Massacre in Rome* 1972; *Bianco Rosso e. . . /White Sister* 1973; *Torso, Andy Warhol's Frankenstein, Andy Warhol's Dracula* 1974; *The Passenger, Babysitter* 1975; *L'Infermiera, Mercati Generale, Brutti Sporchi e Cattivi/Down and Dirty* 1976; *The Cassandra Crossing* (UK/It./Ger.), *Una Giornata particolare/A Special Day* 1977; *Saturday Sunday and Monday* (co-exec. prod.) 1990; *Oscar* (US) 1991.

Popeye the Sailor. Gruff, tattooed, ham-fisted cartoon character who rivaled Mickey Mouse for popularity among child audiences in the 30s and 40s. Produced from 1933 for Paramount by Max Fleischer, who had borrowed the character from a newspaper comic strip, the plots of the Popeye animated cartoons were mostly variations on the same basic situation: Popeye's violent encounters with the brutish, oversized Bluto. Their bone of contention was often Olive Oyl, Popeye's skinny, squeaky-voiced girlfriend. In the typical story, Bluto would abuse Olive Oyl and bully Popeye, who had come to her rescue. At a chosen climactic moment, Popeye would reach for a can of spinach, take a couple of swallows, and suddenly become an invincible strongman, inflicting heavy punishment on Bluto. The old Popeye cartoons, as well as many installments drawn later, are perennials of kiddie TV.

porno films. See SEXPLOITATION FILMS.

Porten, Henny. Actress. *b.* Apr. 7, 1888, Magdeburg, Germany. *d.* 1960. Germany's first screen superstar, she was discovered by Oskar Messter and sometimes directed by her father, former opera singer Franz Porten, or her first husband, Kurt Stark. She formed her own production company around 1914, and her career carried over into the sound era, but she barely worked during the Nazi period, her second husband being a Jew.

FILMS INCLUDE: *Apachentanz* 1906; *Lohengrin* 1907; *Wiegenlied, Desdemona* 1908; *Andreas Hofer* 1909; *Die Blinde, Zwei Frauen* 1911; *Maskierte Liebe, Eva* 1912; *Die grosse Sünderin, Ungarische Rhapsodie* 1913; *Adoptivkind* (also prod.), *Alexandra* 1914; *Gelöste Ketten* (also prod.) 1915; *Das wandernde Licht* 1916; *Das goldene Kalb* (also prod.) 1917; *Die Schuld* (also prod.), *Die blaue Laterne* 1918; *Rose Bernd* (also prod.), *Die lebende Tote* (also co-prod.) 1919; *Anna Boleyn/Deception* 1920; *Die Hintertreppe/Backstairs* 1921; *Frauenopfer* (also prod.), *Mona Lisa* (also prod.) 1922; *I.N.R.I./Crown of Thorns, Das alte Gesetz/The Ancient Law, Inge Larsen* (also prod.) 1923; *Mutter und Kind* 1924; *Tragödie* (also prod.), *Rosen aus dem Süden* (also prod.) 1925; *Die Flamme lügen* (also prod.) 1926; *Die grosse Pause* (also prod.), *Violanta* (also prod.) 1927; *Liebe und Diebe* (also prod.), *Lotte* (also prod.), *Zuflucht/Refuge* (also prod.) 1928; *Mutter Liebe/Mother Love* (also prod.) 1929; *Skandal um Eva/Scandal About Eva, Kohlhiesels Töchter/Gretel and Liesel* 1930; *Luise—Königin von Preussen* 1931; *Mutter und Kind* (remake) 1933; *Krach im Hinterhaus/Trouble Back Stairs* 1935; *Der Optimist* 1938; *Komödianten* 1941; *Symphonie des Lebens* 1942; *Familie Buchholz* 1944; *Carola Lamberti/Woman of the Circus* 1954; *Die Schatze des Teufels* 1955.

Porter, Cole. Composer, lyricist. *b.* June 9, 1892, Peru, Ind. *d.* 1964. Celebrated songwriter and *bon vivant.* Composed his first song at age 11. An heir to a fortune, he went to Yale University and Harvard Law School, then, during a period of personal crisis, joined the French Foreign Legion in 1916. Two years later he had his first Broadway hit. In 1937 he suffered a riding accident that resulted in multiple operations and finally the amputation of a leg in 1958. Through years of agonizing pain he had continued to travel, entertain lavishly, and compose for Broadway and Hollywood his popular songs, famous for their witty, risqué lyrics. Most of his hit Broadway musicals, which he composed over a period of 40 years, were transferred to film with similar success. He was portrayed by Cary Grant in the film biography *Night and Day* (1946).

FILMS INCLUDE: *The Battle of Paris* 1929; *Fifty Million Frenchmen* 1931; *The Gay Divorcee* 1934; *Anything Goes, Born to Dance* 1936; *Rosalie* 1937; *Broadway Melody* 1940; *You'll Never Get Rich* 1941; *Panama Hattie* 1942; *Something to Shout About, Du Barry Was a Lady, Let's Face It* 1943; *Night and Day* 1946; *the Pirate* 1948; *Kiss Me Kate* 1953; *Anything Goes* (remake) 1956; *High Society, Silk Stockings, Les Girls* 1957; *Can-Can* 1959.

Porter, Edwin S(tanton). Director, film pioneer. *b.* Apr. 21, 1869, Connellsville, Pa. *d.* 1941. The most prominent innovator in American cinema during the embryonic years of the industry. A merchant's son, he quit school at 14 and worked successively as a railway newsboy, sign painter, plumber, telegrapher, theater cashier, tailor, stagehand for a traveling comic-opera company, and machinist. Then, while serving in the Navy, from 1893 to 1896, he assisted in the development of the Fiske electric gunnery range finder. Returning to civilian life, he worked for Raff & Gammon, the company that marketed the Edison Vitascope. As part of his job, he helped set up the historic first screening of projected motion pictures at New York's Koster & Bial's Music Hall, on April 23, 1896. After spending a summer at Thomas Edison's Menlo Park Laboratories in West Orange, N.J., Porter and two partners traveled through the West Indies and South America, exhibiting Edison films and trying to sell a primitive projector, the Projectoscope, to a resistant market. Returning to New York, Porter worked as a projectionist for various establishments and in 1898 developed an improved projector, the Beadnell, which provided a brighter, steadier picture, and began manufacturing projectors and cameras with a wealthy partner. But the business was ruined by a fire in 1900 and never rebuilt.

Even while pursuing these business interests, however, Porter had begun in 1899 to photograph news events and other brief film clips, which he sold on a freelance basis to the Edison company and other clients. After the 1900 fire that destroyed his manufacturing plant, Porter became an Edison employee, at first working in the mechanical department, designing and building cameras, and then shortly afterward as a combination director-cameraman. Before long he was put in charge of all production at Edison's skylight studio on East 21st St. in New York. For the next few years he personally directed and photographed much of the Edison film output. Porter's early films were typically crude one-idea, one-situation affairs. Most were shot from a static camera position, but some employed trick photography and primitive special effects, including double exposures, matte shots, stop-motion photography, and even split screens. His work between 1899 and 1902 was probably influenced by the trick films of Georges MÉLIÈS.

Early in 1903, Porter turned out the first of several films that proved important milestones in the development of American cinema. *The Life of an American Fireman,* while still crude, was perhaps for the first time in American films a motion picture created in the cutting room, a legitimate if at times confusing attempt to edit material into a cohesive narrative. The material consisted of a mixture of original footage that Porter himself had shot and some library stock of fire-fighting scenes he found around the studio. The film remains famous as the first known example of intercutting in American cinema. It also contains a close-up, an early use of that cinematic device. During the same year, Porter directed an ambitious early literary screen adaptation, an elaborate version of *Uncle Tom's Cabin,* consisting of a prologue and 14 scenes. But he remains known chiefly for another film he directed that year, *The Great Train Robbery,* a 12-minute action film to which, for years, film historians and critics attributed a whole array of motion picture firsts. Although some of these claims have since proved erroneous, *The Great Train Robbery* remains one of the most important milestones in screen history. The film was conceived, executed, and marketed on an "epic" scale for its time. It was nearly 12 minutes long, boasted a cast of 40, contained a logical, semiscripted narrative, and moved along briskly toward its final climax. Although it contained no new cinematic effects, it utilized existing ones to best advantage and ended amusingly with the now-famous close-up of a bandit firing a pistol at the audience. It advanced the cause of the story-film dramatically, and although by no means the screen's first Western, it certainly set the direction and the tone of this classically American film genre for many years to come. The film's success was phenomenal and it remained the most famous and profitable film until D. W. Griffith's *The Birth of a Nation* (1915). Incidentally, it was Porter who gave Griffith his first film job, hiring him as an actor for *Rescued from an Eagle's Nest* (1907).

Porter remained with the Edison company through 1909, directing numerous films in a variety of genres and supervising the production of many others. He often wrote his own scripts and usually operated his own camera and executed his own editing. His films of the period include several social-justice dramas, notably *The Ex-Convict* (1904) and *The Kleptomaniac* (1905), but these turned out rather awkward despite the moral sincerity of the director. *The Dream of a Rarebit Fiend* (1906), a virtuoso trick film in the Méliès mold, and *The Teddy Bears* (1907), a primitive stop-motion animation film, were more typical of Porter's best product. He was interested more in the mechanical aspects of film and in creating special effects than in developing themes or directing actors, and later in his career he would collaborate with other directors to free himself for the mere technical aspects of his work. He seemed always to be tinkering with pieces of equipment, even while directing, and in 1908, while still with Edison, he began developing a new projecting apparatus that he later developed with a fellow inventor into a well-known product, the Simplex projector.

In November of 1909, Porter left Edison and with a partner established an independent production company, Defender Pictures. Within a year he had organized the Rex Film Company with a group of businessmen, but in 1912 sold his interest in Rex and joined Adolph ZUKOR in the creation of Famous Players in Famous Plays, the forerunner of Paramount. Porter was appointed the director general and treasurer of Famous Players and in addition to personally directing many of the company's most prestigious films, he supervised the production of its entire output. The films Porter made for Famous Players were mainly feature length adaptations from literature and the stage, starring some of the important stage names of the day. They were directed by Porter in a straightforward manner that suggested little of the innovator and pathfinder he had been early in his film career.

Porter's position at Famous Players was reduced from

director general to technical director during a long absence from the studio for the location shooting in Rome of one of his most successful films, *The Eternal City* (1915). He directed only a few films after this, spending much of his time on experimentation with sound, color cinematography, wide-screen projection, and a crude 3-D process. Late in 1915, he sold his share of Famous Players for $800,000 and invested much of the money in the Precision Machine Corporation, the manufacturer of the Simplex projector, and thus became its president. He continued experimenting with various film techniques while trying to develop new motion picture equipment. His business prospered, but he lost most of his fortune in the 1929 stock market crash. He spent his final years in forgotten anonymity, experimenting with motion picture devices in a small machine shop. His death at 72 was hardly noted by the industry or widely reported in the press.

FILMS INCLUDE (as director and frequently also writer, cameraman, and editor): Shorts—*The America's Cup Race* 1899; *Why Mrs. Jones Got a Divorce, Animated Luncheon, An Artist's Dream, The Mystic Swing, Ching Lin Foo Outdone, Faust and Marguerite, The Clown and the Alchemist, A Wringing Good Joke, The Enchanted Drawing* 1900; *Terrible Teddy the Grizzly King, Love in a Hammock, A Day at the Circus, What Demoralized the Barber Shop, The Finish of Bridget McKeen, Happy Hooligan Surprised, Martyred Presidents, Love by the Light of the Moon, Circular Panorama of the Electric Tower, Panorama of the Esplanade by Night, The Mysterious Café* 1901; *Uncle Josh at the Moving Picture Show, Charleston Chain Gang, Burlesque Suicide, Rock of Ages, Jack and the Beanstalk* 1902; *The Life of an American Fireman, The Still Alarm, Arabian Jewish Dance, Razzle Dazzle, Seashore Frolics, Scenes in an Orphans' Asylum, The Gay Shoe Clerk, The Baby Review, The Animated Poster, The Office Boy's Revenge, Uncle Tom's Cabin, The Great Train Robbery* 1903; *The Ex-Convict, Cohen's Advertising Scheme, European Rest Cure, Parsifal* 1904; *The Kleptomaniac, Stolen by Gypsies, How Jones Lost His Roll, The Little Train Robbery, The White Caps, Seven Ages, The Life of an American Policeman* 1905; *The Dream of a Rarebit Fiend, The Life of a Cowboy, Three American Beauties, Kathleen Mavourneen* 1906; *Daniel Boone, Lost in the Alps, The Midnight Ride of Paul Revere, Laughing Gas, Rescued from an Eagle's Nest, The Teddy Bears* 1907; *Nero and the Burning of Rome, The Painter's Revenge, The Merry Widow Waltz Craze, The Gentleman Burglar, Honesty Is the Best Policy, Love Will Find a Way, Skinny's Finish, The Face on the Barroom Floor, The Boston Tea Party, Romance of a War Nurse, A Voice from the Dead, Saved by Love, She, Lord Feathertop, The Angel Child, Miss Sherlock Holmes, An Unexpected Santa Claus* 1908; *The Adventures of an Old Flirt, A Midnight Supper, Love Is Blind, A Cry from the Wilderness, Hard to Beat, On the Western Frontier, Fuss and Feathers, Pony Express* 1909; *All on Account of a Laundry Mark, Russia—The Land of Oppression, Too Many Girls, Almost A Hero, The Toymaker the Doll and the Devil* 1910; *By the Light of the Moon, On the Brink, The White Red Man, Sherlock Holmes Jr., Lost Illusions* 1911; *A Sane Asylum, Eyes That See Not, The Final Pardon, Taming Mrs. Shrew* 1912; *His Neighbor's Wife* 1913. Features (complete)—*The Prisoner of Zenda* (co-dir. with Hugh Ford), *In the Bishop's Carriage* (co-dir. with J. Searle Dawley), *The Count of Monte Cristo* (co-dir. with Joseph Golden) 1913; *Hearts Adrift, A Good Little Devil* (co-dir. with Dawley), *Tess of the Storm Country, The Spitfire* (co-dir. with Frederick Thomson), *Such a Little Queen* (co-dir. with Ford), *The Crucible* (co-dir. with Ford) 1914; *The Eternal City* (co-dir. with Ford), *The Morals of Marcus* (co-dir. with Ford), *Niobe* (co-dir. with Ford), *When We Were 21* (co-dir. with Ford), *Jim the Penman, Zaza* (co-dir. with Ford), *The White Pearl* (co-dir. with Ford), *Sold* (co-dir. with Ford), *Bella Donna* (co-dir. with Ford), *The Prince and the Pauper* (co-dir. with Ford) 1915; *Lydia Gilmore* (co-dir. with Ford) 1916.

Portman, Eric. Actor. *b.* July 13, 1903, Yorkshire, England. *d.* 1969. Distinguished character actor of British stage since 1924 and screen since 1934. He played leads early in his film career, typically as a haughty, cynical aristocrat, then reverted to character parts, often villainous.

FILMS INCLUDE: *The Girl from Maxim's* 1933; *Abdul the Damned, Hyde Park Corner* 1935; *Hearts of Humanity, The Cardinal* 1936; *The Prince and the Pauper* (US), *Moonlight Sonata* 1937; *49th Parallel/The Invaders* 1941; *One of Our Aircraft Is Missing, Squadron Leader X, Uncensored* 1942; *We Dive at Dawn, Millions Like Us* 1943; *A Canterbury Tale* 1944; *Great Day* 1945; *Wanted for Murder, Men of Two Worlds/Kisenga—Man of Africa* 1946; *Dear Murderer, The Mark of Cain* 1947; *Corridor of Mirrors, Daybreak, The Blind Goddess* 1948; *The Spider and the Fly* 1949; *Cairo Road* 1950; *The Magic Box, His Excellency* 1951; *South of Algiers/The Golden Mask* 1952; *The Colditz Story* 1954; *The Deep Blue Sea* 1955; *The Good Companions* 1957; *The Naked Edge* 1961; *Freud* (US) 1962; *The Man Who Finally Died* 1963; *The Bedford Incident* 1965; *The Spy with a Cold Nose* 1966; *The Whisperers* 1967; *Deadfall* 1968; *Assignment to Kill* (US) 1969.

Portman, Natalie. Actress. Born June 9, 1981, in Jerusalem, Israel. Remarkable in her ability to express deep emotions at an early age, this stunning young ingenue of the American stage and films made an auspicious debut in the violent, controversial Luc BESSON thriller *The Professional* (1994). Her screen presence has been compared to that of a young Audrey HEPBURN with the ability to convincingly convey an endearing vulnerability and undeniable charm evident in her performance as the lovestruck little-girl-next-door in *Beautiful Girls* (1996).

FILMS: *The Professional* (Fr./US) 1994; *Beautiful Girls, Everyone Says I Love You, Mars Attacks!* 1996; *Ice Storm* 1997.

Posey, Parker. Actress. Born November 8, 1968, in Baltimore, Md. *ed.* State University of New York, Purchase. With an offbeat sense of style and on-screen presence, this fine comedic actress developed a career in features via the independent film circuit, notably with director Richard LINKLATER's critical and cult favorite *Dazed and Confused* (1993) as well as her turn in the wacky comedy *Party Girl* (1995).

FILMS: *Coneheads, Dazed and Confused, Dead Connection, Joey Breaker* 1993; *Amateur, Mixed Nuts, Sleep with Me* 1994; *The Doom Generation, Flirt, Kicking and Screaming, Party Girl* 1995; *Drunks* 1996; *Clockwatchers, The Daytrippers, House of Yes, Suburbia, Waiting for Guffman* 1997.

positive. A print made from a negative.

Post, Ted. Director. Born on Mar. 31, 1918, in Brooklyn, N.Y. Technically proficient director of many stage plays, television shows, TV movies, and occasional feature films.

FEATURE FILMS: *The Peacemaker* 1956; *The Legend of Tom Dooley* 1959; *Hang 'Em High* 1968; *Beneath the Planet of the Apes* 1970; *The Baby, The Harrad Experiment, Magnum Force* 1973; *Whiffs* 1975; *Good Guys Wear Black, Go Tell the Spartans* 1978; *Nightkill* (Ger.) 1980.

Postlethwaite, Pete. Actor. Born in 1948. This British actor got his start on the stage in England at the Manchester Royal Exchange as well as theater troupes in Bristol and Liverpool. After years of solid work in British films and television, his feature film career in the US was launched with a driven, passionate performance in the acclaimed Irish/US film *In the Name of the Father* (1993), earning a supporting actor Academy Award nomination.

FILMS: *The Duellists* (UK) 1977; *A Private Function* (UK) 1985; *Distant Voices Still Lives* (UK), *The Dressmaker* (UK), *To Kill a Priest* (Fr./US) 1988; *Hamlet* (US) 1990; *Alien 3* (US), *The Last of the Mohicans* (US), *Split Second* (UK/US), *Waterland* (UK) 1992; *Anchoress* (US), *In the Name of the Father* (Ire./US) 1993; *The Usual Suspects* (US) 1995; *Dragonheart* (US), *James and the Giant Peach* (v/o; US) 1996; *Brassed Off, The Lost World, Amistad* 1997.

postsynchronization. The recording of sound in synchronization with a picture after filming has been completed. Similar to the PLAYBACK technique of prerecorded music, postsynchronization is intended to provide a film with a quality sound track when original recording cannot be made under the proper acoustical conditions. It is also used to substitute one performer's voice for another or in dubbing from one language to another or to correct errors in the original recording. Usually, a GUIDE TRACK is recorded with the picture. LOOPS made from the guide track are then played back to the performers as they watch the corresponding picture on a screen. They can thus rehearse dialogue and other sounds until they can match lines to the photographed lip movements. Specialized technicians similarly match sound effects to the picture. Traditionally, most Italian films are postsynchronized.

Potter, Dennis. Screenwriter. *b.* May 17, 1935, in Forest of Dean, England. *d.* 1994. *ed.* Oxford. Gifted, often controversial author of stage plays, teleplays, and film scripts. He made a brilliant first impression on the screen with *Pennies from Heaven* (1981), an imaginative Oscar-nominated adaptation of his own TV miniseries, in which bright period pop songs offered an ironic contrast to a drab story of the Depression. A victim of crippling attacks of psoriatic arthritis that force him into periodic seclusion, Potter tended to incorporate themes of confinement into his stories. He made his debut as a director in 1990.

FILMS: *Pennies from Heaven* 1981; *Brimstone and Treacle* 1982; *Gorky Park* 1983; *Dreamchild* (also co-exec. prod.) 1985; *Track 29* 1988; *Blackeyes* (also dir.) 1990.

Potter, H. C. ("Hank"). Director. *b.* Henry Codman Potter, Nov. 13, 1904, New York City. *d.* 1977. *ed.* Yale Drama School. A versatile stage and screen director, he worked with a variety of genres but proved to be at his best with comedy material, notably in the zany, free-for-all *Hellzapoppin* (1941). He enjoyed great success with his Broadway production of 'A Bell for Adano' (1944).

FILMS: *Beloved Enemy* 1936; *Wings Over Honolulu* 1937; *Romance in the Dark, The Cowboy and the Lady, The Shopworn Angel* 1938; *The Story of Vernon and Irene Castle, Blackmail* 1939; *Congo Maisie* 1940; *Second Chorus, Hellzapoppin* 1941; *Victory Through Air Power* (doc.), *Mr. Lucky* 1943; *The Farmer's Daughter, A Likely Story* 1947; *Mr. Blandings Builds His Dream House, The Time of Your Life, You Gotta Stay Happy* 1948; *The Miniver Story* 1950; *Three for the Show* 1955; *Top Secret Affair* 1957.

Potts, Annie. Actress. Born on Oct. 28, 1957, in Nashville, Tenn. *ed.* Stephens Coll., Mo. Spunky, light leading lady and supporting player of Hollywood films. On the amateur stage from age 12, she later performed in summer stock and in such TV series as 'Goodtime Girls,' 'Designing Women,' and 'Love and War' of the 80s and 90s. In features since the late 70s.

FILMS: *Corvette Summer, King of the Gypsies* 1978; *Heartaches* (Can.) 1981; *Ghostbusters, Crimes of Passion* 1984; *Pretty in Pink, Jumpin' Jack Flash* 1986; *Pass the Ammo* 1988; *Who's Harry Crumb?, Ghostbusters II* 1989; *Texasville* 1990; *Breaking the Rules* 1992; *Toy Story* (v/o) 1995.

Poverty Row. Name given in the 1920s to the section of Hollywood around Sunset Boulevard and Gower Street where fly-by-night producers tried to make movies on the cheap. The shabby buildings housed a tiny maze of offices, often ornamented with exposed wires and pipes. Its most famous success story was COLUMBIA PICTURES, which had its start here before becoming a major studio. In the studio era, the term "Poverty Row" came to refer not to a geographical location but to any production by minor companies such as Grand National, Mascot, and P.R.C. (Producers Releasing Corporation).

Powell, Dick. Actor, director, producer. *b.* Richard E. Powell, Nov. 14, 1904, Mountain View, Ark. *d.* 1963. Cherubic crooner of Warner Bros. musicals of the 30s, often opposite Ruby KEELER, he made a surprising transition to dramatic roles, becoming particularly adept at portraying tough heroes of private-eye thrillers. A former band vocalist and instrumentalist and occasional MC, he made his film debut in 1932. After a decade of choirboy-type leads, he hit the tough-guy stride in the mid-40s. In the early 50s he entered yet another phase of his colorful career, making his bow as producer-director of several unremarkable films and as president of the prosperous Four Star TV production company. Like many of the cast (John Wayne, Susan Hayward, etc.) and crew of one of his productions, *The Conqueror* (1956), which was filmed in Utah near an atomic test site, Powell died of cancer. His second wife (1936–45) was Joan BLONDELL; his widow (married in 1945) is June ALLYSON. He was impersonated on the screen by his son, Dick Powell, Jr, in John Schlesinger's *The Day of the Locust* (1975).

FILMS: As actor—*Blessed Event, Too Busy to Work* 1932; *The King's Vacation, 42nd Street, Gold Diggers of 1933, Footlight Parade, College Coach, Convention City* 1933; *Wonder Bar, Dames, Twenty Million Sweethearts, Happiness Ahead, Flirtation Walk* 1934; *Gold Diggers of 1935, Page Miss Glory, Broadway Gondolier, Shipmates Forever, Thanks a Million, A Midsummer Night's Dream* 1935; *Colleen, Hearts Divided, Stage Struck, Gold Diggers of 1937* 1936; *On the Avenue, The Singing Marine, Varsity Show, Hollywood Hotel* 1937; *Cowboy from Brooklyn, Hard to Get, Going Places* 1938; *Naughty but Nice* 1939; *Christmas in July, I Want a Divorce* 1940; *In the Navy, Model Wife* 1941; *Star Spangled Rhythm, Happy Go Lucky, True to Life, Riding High* 1943; *Meet the People, It Happened Tomorrow* 1944; *Murder My Sweet, Cornered* 1945; *Johnny O'Clock* 1947; *To the Ends of the Earth, Station West, Pitfall, Rogue's Regiment* 1948; *Mrs. Mike* 1949; *The Reformer and the Redhead, Right Cross* 1950; *The Tall Target, Cry Danger, You Never Can Tell* 1951; *The Bad and the Beautiful* 1952; *Susan Slept Here* 1954. As director-producer—*Split Second* 1952; *The Conqueror, You Can't Run Away from It* 1956; *The Enemy Below* 1957; *The Hunters* 1958.

Powell, Eleanor. Dancer, actress. *b.* Nov. 21, 1910, Springfield, Mass. *d.* 1982. Tap-dancing star of MGM musicals of the late 30s and early 40s. She began dancing at 11, reached Broadway at 17, and landed in films in 1935 acknowledged as the world's best tap dancer. Leggy, shapely, and exuberant, she danced her way through a dozen film productions, but by the mid-40s her popularity declined along with the fading public interest in the art of tap dancing. She retired from the screen shortly after marrying actor Glenn FORD in 1943 and her only subsequent film appearance was a guest spot in *Duchess of Idaho* (1950). After their 1959 divorce, she made a brief but highly successful comeback in Las Vegas and New York nightclubs, then returned to charity and church work, activities that occupied much of her time during many years of professional retirement.

FILMS: *George White's Scandals, Broadway Melody of 1936* 1935; *Born to Dance* 1936; *Broadway Melody of 1938, Rosalie* 1937; *Honolulu* 1939; *Broadway Melody of 1940* 1940;

Lady Be Good 1941; *Ship Ahoy* 1942; *Thousands Cheer, I Dood It* 1943; *Sensations of 1945* 1944; *Duchess of Idaho* 1950.

Powell, Jane. Singer, actress. Born Suzanne Burce, on Apr. 1, 1929, in Portland, Ore. Teenage singing star, then young leading lady of MGM musicals and light romances. On radio since childhood, she entered films at 15, soon gaining popularity for her engaging personality and rich and wide-ranging coloratura soprano voice. A vivacious blue-eyed blonde, she typically played sugary blossoming maidens experiencing innocent first romances, periodically interrupting the familiar plot with a song. Her career reached a peak in 1954 with the feminine lead in the musical *Seven Brides for Seven Brothers* but declined soon afterward as she was unable to shake off her eternal adolescent image even as she neared 30. Failing to secure suitable roles, she retired from the screen in 1958 and has since appeared on TV, in stock, and in nightclubs. In 1973 she replaced Debbie Reynolds as the star of the Broadway revival of 'Irene.' In 1978 she married writer-producer David Parlour, her fourth husband. They divorced in 1981. In 1988 she married her fifth, former child star Dickie MOORE, now a business executive. Autobiography: *The Girl Next Door. . . And How She Grew* (1988).

FILMS: *Song of the Open Road* 1944; *Delightfully Dangerous* 1945; *Holiday in Mexico* 1946; *Three Daring Daughters, A Date with Judy, Luxury Liner* 1948; *Nancy Goes to Rio, Two Weeks with Love* 1950; *Royal Wedding, Rich Young and Pretty* 1951; *Small Town Girl, Three Sailors and a Girl* 1953; *Seven Brides for Seven Brothers, Athena, Deep in My Heart* 1954; *Hit the Deck* 1955; *The Girl Most Likely* 1957; *The Female Animal, Enchanted Island* 1958; *Marie* (cameo as singer at rally) 1985.

Powell, Michael. Director, producer, screenwriter. *b.* Sept. 30, 1905, Bekesbourne, near Canterbury, England. *d.* 1990. *ed.* King's School, Canterbury; Dulwich Coll. The son of a hop grower, he showed an early interest in making films but started his working life in 1922 as a bank clerk. In 1925, during a visit to his long-separated father, now a hotelier on the French Riviera, he made the acquaintance of American artist and would-be director Harry LACHMAN and through him secured an apprentice's position on Rex INGRAM's film *Mare Nostrum.* Powell stayed on with Ingram, working as a grip on *The Magician* (1926) and as an actor, providing comic relief in *The Garden of Allah* (1927). He then returned to England as a protegé of Lachman and worked at the Elstree studios on varied assignments, including still photography on Hitchcock's *Champagne* (1928) and an uncredited collaboration on the script of *Blackmail* (1929). After contributing credited screenplays for *Caste* (1930) and *77 Park Lane* (1931), Powell began his career as a director with a string of medium-length "QUOTA QUICKIES." Over the next five years, he turned out some two dozen unremarkable features and featurettes, growing increasingly proficient and self-assured.

Powell's first substantial film was *The Edge of the World* (1937), a drama notable for its semidocumentary authenticity. The production's success led to a contract offer from Alexander KORDA and to the start of a long and fertile collaboration with another Korda recruit, Emeric PRESSBURGER. Beginning with *The Spy in Black* (1939), an espionage thriller that enjoyed box-office success in the US as *U-Boat 29,* Powell rapidly asserted himself as one of Britain's foremost filmmakers. During WW II he directed several highly regarded propaganda-oriented films, most notably *One of Our Aircraft Is Missing* (1941) and *49th Parallel* (1942). But his most glorious achievement of the period was the enchanting Arabian Nights fantasy *The Thief of Bagdad* (1940), which he co-directed with Ludwig BERGER.

In 1942 Powell and Pressburger established their own production company, The Archers, and set out to write, produce, and direct an extraordinary succession of remarkable films, noted for their vivid imagery and exceptional beauty. Among the most striking of these were *The Life and Death of Colonel Blimp* (1943), an affectionate, witty look at the loves and long military career of a British officer; *A Matter of Life and Death/Stairway to Heaven* (1946), a whimsical celestial fantasy about Anglo-American relations; and *Black Narcissus* (1947), a visually stunning, dramatically riveting tale of Anglican nuns enduring physical and emotional hardships in attempting to set up a mission in a remote Himalayan outpost. Their best-known production was perhaps *The Red Shoes* (1948), still acclaimed as the quintessential ballet film against which others are measured. *The Tales of Hoffman* (1951), a fabulously eccentric filmic rendition of the Jacques Offenbach fantasy operetta, was another triumphant example of artistic fusion—inventive, bizarre, and thoroughly cinematic.

Following several lesser collaborations, Powell and Pressburger dissolved The Archers and parted amicably in 1956. On his own, Powell put his very career at risk with *Peeping Tom* (1960), a blood-and-gore thriller about a pornographically inclined psychopathic slasher who records on a movie camera the dying moments of his female victims. The film opened to a chorus of critical loathing, but was later reassessed by many as a complex film-within-film essay on voyeurism and the psychology of motion-picture viewing. Some called the film Powell's masterpiece. The director's career never recovered from the ordeal. In 1980 he was appointed senior director in residence at Francis Coppola's Zoetrope Studio in Los Angeles. In 1984, a year after the death of his first wife, Powell married Thelma Schoonmaker, a film editor who won an Academy Award for Martin Scorsese's *Raging Bull* and worked on several of his other films. One of his two sons, Kevin Powell, is an Australian-based filmmaker. Michael Powell wrote a suspense novel, *A Waiting Game* (1975), and an autobiography, *A Life in Movies* (1986).

FILMS: As director—*Two Crowded Hours, My Friend the King, Rynox, The Rasp, The Star Reporter* (also addnl. phot.) 1931; *Hotel Splendide, C.O.D., His Lordship, Born Lucky* 1932; *The Fire Raisers* (also co-sc.) 1933; *The Night of the Party/The Murder Party, Red Ensign/Strike!* (also co-sc.), *Something Always Happens, The Girl in the Crowd* 1934; *Lazybones, The Love Test, The Phantom Light, The Price of a Song, Someday* 1935; *Her Last Affairs, The Brown Wallet, Crown vs. Stevens, The Man Behind the Mask* 1936; *The Edge of the World* (also sc.) 1937; *The Spy in Black/U-Boat 29, The Lion Has Wings* (co-dir. with Brian Desmond Hurst and Adrian Brunel) 1939; *Contraband* (also co-sc.), *The Thief of Bagdad* (co-dir. with Ludwig Berger) 1940; *An Airman's Letter to His Mother* (short; also phot.), *49th Parallel/The Invaders* (also prod.) 1941; *One of Our Aircraft Is Missing* (also co-prod., co-sc.) 1942.; *The Silver Fleet* (co-prod. only) 1943. As director-producer-writer in collaboration with Emeric Pressburger—*The Life and Death of Colonel Blimp/Colonel Blimp, The Volunteer* (medium-length) 1943; *A Canterbury Tale* 1944; *I Know Where I'm Going* 1945; *A Matter of Life and Death/Stairway to Heaven* 1946; *Black Narcissus, The End of the River* (co-prod. only) 1947; *The Red Shoes* 1948; *The Small Back Room/Hour of Glory* 1949; *Gone to Earth/The Wild Heart* (co-dir., co-sc. only), *The Elusive Pimpernel/The Fighting Pimpernel* (co-dir., co-sc. only) 1950; *The Tales of Hoffman* 1951; *The Sorcerer's Apprentice* (short; dir. alone), *Oh Rosalinda!/Fledermaus '55* 1955; *The Battle of the River Plate/Pursuit of the Graf Spee* 1956; *111 Met by Moonlight/Night Ambush* 1957. As director-producer—*Luna de Miel/Honeymoon* (also co-sc.; Sp./UK) 1959; *Peeping Tom*

1960; *The Queen's Guards* 1961; *Bluebeard's Castle* (dir. only) 1964; *They're a Weird Mob* (Austral./UK) 1966; *Sebastian* (co-prod. only) 1968; *Age of Consent* (Austral.) 1969; *The Boy Who Turned Yellow* (dir. only) 1972; *Pavlova/A Woman for All Time* (co-supervisor only) 1983.

Powell, Robert. Actor. Born on June 1, 1944, in Salford, England. *ed.* Manchester U. Soulfully magnetic leading man of British TV and films. He made his screen debut in 1967, following brief stage experience in rep. His career was boosted by a lead in the TV series 'Doomwatch' and reached its peak with the title roles in Ken Russell's feature *Mahler* (1974) and Franco Zeffirelli's miniseries 'Jesus of Nazareth' (1978). He was named best actor at the 1982 Venice Festival for Krzysztof Zanussi's *Imperative*.

FILMS INCLUDE: *Robbery, Far from the Madding Crowd* 1967; *Joanna* 1968; *The Italian Job* 1969; *Secrets* 1971; *Running Scared, Asylum/House of Crazies, The Asphyx/Horror of Death* 1972; *Mahler* (as composer Gustav Mahler) 1974; *Tommy* 1975; *Oltre il Bene e il Male/Beyond Good and Evil* (It./Fr./Ger.) 1977; *The 39 Steps* 1978; *Harlequin/Dark Forces* (Austral.), *Jane Austen in Manhattan* (US) 1980; *The Survivor* (Austral.) 1981; *Imperativ/Imperative* (Ger.) 1982; *The Jigsaw Man* 1984; *D'Annunio and I Down There in the Jungle* 1987; *Romeo-Juliet* (v/o; Belg.) 1990; *Once on Chunuk Bair* 1991; *The Mystery of Edwin Drood* 1993.

Powell, William. Actor. *b.* July 29, 1892, Pittsburgh. *d.* 1984. *ed.* AADA. Smooth villain of Hollywood silents and suave, sophisticated, impeccably dressed, pleasantly cynical leading man of sound romantic comedies and amusing detective stories. Intended for a legal career by his accountant father, he dropped out of the University of Kansas after several weeks to pursue his love of drama in New York. On Broadway from 1912, he began his screen career a decade later, making his debut in support of John Barrymore in *Sherlock Holmes* (1922). In his early films he typically played suave nasties. His good-guy image began taking shape with the transition to sound with a string of light mysteries in which he portrayed the S. S. Van Dine sleuth Philo Vance and reached a peak with *The Thin Man,* based on a Dashiell Hammett mystery novel. The latter was made as a low-budget project but turned into a resounding box-office success and gained for Powell a nomination for an Academy Award. The casting of Powell and Myrna LOY as Nick and Nora Charles proved a boost to the careers of both, and they went on to co-star in several sequels and in other films. The Thin Man of the title was actually a mysterious stranger and not the hero, but somehow it was attached to Powell and became part of his screen identity. Other landmark films in his career were the title roles in *The Great Ziegfeld, My Man Godfrey,* and *Life with Father.* He was nominated for Oscars for the last two. Powell's first wife (1915–31) was actress Eileen Wilson. He was briefly (1931–33) married to Carole LOMBARD and was engaged to Jean HARLOW at the time of her death in 1937. From 1940 till his death at 92 he was married to actress Diana ("Mousie") Lewis.

FILMS: *Sherlock Holmes, When Knighthood Was in Flower* (as King Francis I), *Outcast* 1922; *The Bright Shawl, Under the Red Robe* (as the Duke of Orleans) 1923; *Dangerous Money, Romola* (as Tito Melema) 1924; *Too Many Kisses, Faint Perfume, My Lady's Lips, The Beautiful City* 1925; *White Mice, Sea Horses, Desert Gold, The Runaway, Aloma of the South Seas, Beau Geste, Tin Gods, The Great Gatsby* (as George Wilson) 1926; *New York, Love's Greatest Mistake, Senorita, Special Delivery, Time to Love, Paid to Love, Nevada, She's a Sheik* 1927; *The Last Command, Beau Sabreur, Feel My Pulse, Partners in Crime, The Dragnet, The Vanishing Pioneer, Forgotten Faces, Interference* 1928; *The Canary Murder Case* (as private eye Philo Vance), *The Four Feathers, Charming Sinners, The Greene Murder Case* (again as Philo Vance), *Pointed Heels* 1929; *Behind the Make-Up, Street of Chance, The Benson Murder Case* (again as Philo Vance), *Paramount on Parade, Shadow of the Law, For the Defense* 1930; *Man of the World, Ladies' Man, The Road to Singapore* 1931; *High Pressure, Jewel Robbery, One Way Passage, Lawyer Man* 1932; *Private Detective 62, Double Harness, The Kennel Murder Case* (again as Philo Vance), *Fashions of 1934, Manhattan Melodrama, The Key, The Thin Man* (as private eye Nick Charles), *Evelyn Prentice* 1934; *Star of Midnight, Reckless, Escapade, Rendezvous* 1935; *The Great Ziegfeld* (as Florenz Ziegfeld), *The Ex-Mrs. Bradford, My Man Godfrey, Libeled Lady, After the Thin Man* (again as Nick Charles) 1936; *The Last of Mrs. Cheyney, The Emperor's Candlesticks, Double Wedding* 1937; *The Baroness and the Butler* 1938; *Another Thin Man* (again as Nick Charles) 1939; *I Love You Again* (dual role) 1940; *Love Crazy, Shadow of the Thin Man* (again as Nick Charles) 1941; *Crossroads* 1942; *The Youngest Profession* (cameo) 1943; *The Heavenly Body* 1944; *The Thin Man Goes Home* (again as Nick Charles) 1945; *Ziegfeld Follies* (again as Florenz Ziegfeld), *The Hoodlum Saint* 1946; *Life with Father* (as Clarence Day), *Song of the Thin Man* (again as Nick Charles) 1947; *The Senator Was Indiscreet, Mr. Peabody and the Mermaid* 1948; *Take One False Step, Dancing in the Dark* 1949; *It's a Big Country, The Treasure of Lost Canyon* 1952; *The Girl Who Had Everything, How to Marry a Millionaire* 1953; *Mister Roberts* (as Doc) 1955.

Power, Tyrone (Sr.). Actor. *b.* Frederick Tyrone Power, May 2, 1869, London. *d.* 1931. Grandson of famed Irish stage actor Tyrone Power (1797–1841) and father of screen star Tyrone POWER (Jr.). He was sent by his family to Florida at the age of 17 to learn the citrus fruit business but soon found himself attracted to the theater and for a few years toured with repertory companies. He gradually gained recognition and by the turn of the century was a popular matinee idol on Broadway. In 1914 he made his first of many intermittent appearances in silent films, starting out in leads but gradually switching to character roles, often villainous. His famous booming voice was heard only once in a talkie, *The Big Trail* (1930), in which he played a secondary role.

FILMS INCLUDE: *Aristocracy* 1914; *A Texas Steer* 1915; *John Needham's Double, Where Are My Children?* 1916; *The Planter, Lorelei of the Sea* 1917; *The Great Shadow* 1920; *Dream Street, The Black Panther's Cub, Footfalls* 1921; *Bright Lights of Broadway, The Day of Faith, The Daring Years, Fury, The Truth About Wives* 1923; *The Lone Wolf, Janice Meredith* (as Lord Cornwallis), *The Story Without a Name, Greater Than Marriage, Damaged Hearts* 1924; *Where Was I?, The Wanderer, A Regular Fellow* 1925; *Red Kimono, Bride of the Storm, Hands Across the Border, Out of the Storm, The Test of Donald Norton* 1926; *The Big Trail* 1930.

Power, Tyrone. Actor. *b.* Tyrone Edmund Power, Jr., May 5, 1913, Cincinnati. *d.* 1958. Romantic lead of Hollywood films and one of Hollywood's most popular stars in the late 30s and early 40s. The son of matinee idol Tyrone POWER (Sr.), he went on the stage in his teens and played bit parts in films and plays of the early 30s. Banking on extreme good looks, a pleasantly sincere personality, and some acting ability, he broke through as a 20th Century-Fox star in 1937. He was a major box-office asset of that company until WW II service interrupted his career. After demobilization, he attempted serious acting with occasional success, notably in *Nightmare Alley.* But his popularity was on the wane and he frequently sought solace in the theater ('The Dark Is Light Enough,' 'John Brown's Body,' etc.). He died of a heart attack in Madrid while filming *Solomon and Sheba.* His three wives included ANNABELLA (1939–48) and Linda CHRISTIAN (1949–55). His daughter, Romina Power (*b.* Oct. 1951), and son, Tyrone Power, Jr. [or IV] (*b.* Jan. 22, 1959), have appeared in films.

FILMS: *Tom Brown of Culver* 1932; *Flirtation Walk* 1934; *Girls' Dormitory, Ladies in Love* 1936; *Lloyds of London, Love Is News, Cafe Metropole, Thin Ice, Second Honeymoon* 1937; *In Old Chicago, Alexander's Ragtime Band, Marie Antoinette, Suez* (as Ferdinand De Lesseps) 1938; *Jesse James* (title role), *Rose of Washington Square, Second Fiddle, The Rains Came, Day-Time Wife* 1939; *Johnny Apollo, Brigham Young—Frontiersman, The Mark of Zorro* (as Zorro) 1940; *Blood and Sand* (as Juan), *A Yank in the R.A.F.* 1941; *Son of Fury, This Above All* (as Clive Briggs), *The Black Swan* 1942; *Crash Dive* 1943; *The Razor's Edge* (as Larry Darrell) 1946; *Nightmare Alley, Captain from Castile* 1947; *The Luck of the Irish, That Wonderful Urge* 1948; *Prince of Foxes* 1949; *The Black Rose, An American Guerilla in the Philippines* 1950; *Rawhide/Desperate Siege, The House in the Square/I'll Never Forget You* (UK/US) 1951; *Diplomatic Courier, Pony Soldier* 1952; *The Mississippi Gambler* 1953; *King of the Khyber Rifles* 1954; *The Long Gray Line, Untamed* 1955; *The Eddie Duchin Story* (title role) 1956; *Seven Waves Away/Abandon Ship!* (UK), *The Rising of the Moon* (in prologue; Ire.), *The Sun Also Rises* (as Jake Barnes) 1957; *Witness for the Prosecution* 1958.

Powers, Mala. Actress. Born Mary Ellen Powers, on Dec. 29, 1931, in San Francisco. *ed.* UCLA. Leading lady of Hollywood films with stage and radio experience. In show business since childhood.

FILMS INCLUDE: *Tough As They Come* 1942; *Edge of Doom, Outrage, Cyrano de Bergerac* (as Roxane) 1950; *Rose of Cimarron* 1952; *City Beneath the Sea, City That Never Sleeps* 1953; *Yellow Mountain* 1954; *Rage at Dawn, Bengazi* 1955; *Tammy and the Bachelor, Storm Rider, Man on the Prowl* 1957; *The Colossus of New York* 1958; *Fear No More, Flight of the Lost Balloon* 1961; *Daddy's Gone A-Hunting* 1969; *Seis Pasajes al Inferno/Six Tickets to Hell* (Arg.) 1975.

Powers, Richard. See DURYEA, George.

Powers, Stefanie. Actress. Born Stefania Federkiewicz, on Nov. 2, 1942, in Hollywood, Calif. Attractive, athletic, brunette leading lady of routine Hollywood films of the 60s and 70s and numerous TV appearances, including the series 'The Girl from U.N.C.L.E.' (1966–67) and 'Hart to Hart' (1979–84; revived in 1993). A graduate of Hollywood High, she broke into movies in the early 60s as a Columbia starlet, at first using the name Taffy Paul. After her 1974 divorce from actor Gary LOCKWOOD, her husband from 1966, she became the constant companion of actor William HOLDEN. Following his death in 1981, she carried on with the William Holden Wildlife Foundation, dedicated to the creation of a big-game preserve and study center in Kenya.

FILMS INCLUDE: *Tammy Tell Me True* 1961; *Experiment in Terror, The Interns, If a Man Answers* 1962; *Palm Springs Weekend, McLintock!* 1963; *The New Interns* 1964; *Love Has Many Faces, Fanatic/Die! Die! My Darling!* (UK), *The Young Sinner* 1965; *Stagecoach* 1966; *Warning Shot* 1967; *The Boatniks* 1970; *The Magnificent Seven Ride!, Crescendo* 1972; *Herbie Rides Again* 1974; *Gone with the West* 1975; *Escape to Athena* (UK) 1979; *Invisible Strangler* 1984.

Praxinoscope. A device for viewing serial pictures. It was developed by Emile REYNAUD in 1876 for his "Théâtre Optique" ("Optical Theater"). It was a much improved version of Plateau's PHENAKISTICOPE and Horner's Zoötrope (or Zoetrope), producing a relatively smooth illusion of motion.

Préjean, Albert. Actor. *b.* Oct. 27, 1894, Paris. *d.* 1979. A former nightclub singer-acrobat and WW I ace, he entered French films in the early 20s and soon rose to popularity as the typical-Parisian hero of René CLAIR's films. After the early 30s he appeared mostly in routine commercial films.

FILMS INCLUDE: *Les Trois Mousquetaires/The Three Musketeers* 1921; *Le Miracle des Loups/Miracle of the Wolves, Paris qui dort* 1924; *Le Fantôme du Moulin Rouge, Le Voyage imaginaire* 1925; *Un Chapeau de Paille d'Italie/The Italian Straw Hat/The Horse Ate the Hat* 1927; *L'Aventure de Luna Park* (also dir.), *Les Nouveaux Messieurs* 1929; *Sous les Toits de Paris/Under the Roofs of Paris, Le Chant du Marin* 1930; *L'Opéra de Quat' Sous/The Threepenny Opera* (French-language version of Pabst's *Die Dreigroschenoper;* as Mack the Knife) 1931; *Théodore et Cie, Un Fils d'Amérique* 1932; *Paquebot Tenacity, Volga en Flammes, La Crise est finie* 1934; *L'Or dans la Rue, Quelle Drôle de Gosse!* 1935; *Un Mauvais Garçon, Jenny* 1936; *L'Alibi* 1937; *Hollenard/Hatred, La Rue sans Joie* 1938; *Métropolitain* 1938; *Dédé de Montmartre* 1939; *L'Or du Cristobal* 1940; *Caprices* 1942; *Au Bonheur des Dames/Shop-Girls of Paris* 1943; *L'Homme de la Nuit* 1946; *Les Frères Bouquinquant* 1947; *L'Idole* 1948; *Les Nouveaux Maîtres* 1949; *Le Désir et l'Amour* 1951; *Les Amants du Tage/Lovers' Net* 1955; *De la Poudre et des Balles* 1961.

Prelle, Micheline. See PRESLE, Micheline.

Preminger, Otto. Director, producer. *b.* Dec. 5, 1905, Vienna. *d.* 1986. The son of a successful lawyer who was once the attorney general of the Austro-Hungarian Empire, he studied law but was more strongly attracted by the theater. By the time he received his doctor of law degree from the University of Vienna in 1926, he had had two years of experience as actor and assistant of Max Reinhardt. He then began producing and directing and before long was put in charge of Reinhardt's Theatre der Josefstadt in Vienna. He also directed one German-language film, *Die Grosse Liebe* (1931). In 1935 he came to the US to direct 'Libel,' a courtroom drama that he had presented successfully in Vienna. He then went from Broadway to Hollywood to work for 20th Century-Fox and spent some eight months on the sets and in the cutting rooms studying the work of various directors before being assigned to the direction of a couple of B pictures. He was fired after an argument with Darryl ZANUCK, just a week or so after beginning his third project, the big-budget *Kidnapped,* a film he had reluctantly agreed to direct. The film, completed and credited to Alfred Werker, ended up a considerable flop. Virtually blacklisted in Hollywood, Preminger returned to Broadway and scored a hit with Clare Boothe Luce's play 'Margin for Error,' in which he had cast himself in the role of a Nazi villain.

Although he was Jewish, the shaven-headed Preminger looked so convincingly Prussian that he was immediately rushed to Hollywood to play a Nazi in the Fox film *The Pied Piper.* He was then offered the Nazi role in the screen version of 'Margin for Error' but refused to do the part unless he could also direct. With Zanuck away on war service, he got his wish and when the film was completed he was assigned to several other projects. Back from the war, Zanuck was outraged at this development but permitted Preminger to complete his last project, *Laura,* as producer only. Rouben Mamoulian was assigned to direct, but the rushes were disappointing and Zanuck reluctantly agreed to let Preminger direct. *Laura* was a tremendous commercial and critical success and is still regarded by many as its director's masterpiece. It earned him his first Academy Award nomination as best director. (He would be nominated again two decades later for *The Cardinal.*) Having become a US citizen in 1943, Preminger remained with Fox, for which he piloted, with varying success, a couple of Lubitsch-inspired comedies, a number of murky, sometimes offbeat melodramas, and an expensive flop, *Forever Amber.* In the early 50s he turned independent producer.

Preminger's first independent production, *The Moon Is Blue* (1953), caused a storm of controversy as the first Hollywood film to employ such unmentionable words as "virgin" and "pregnant" in its dialogue track. It was released without the Production Code Seal of Approval and became a landmark of sorts in the history of Hollywood censorship. Preminger again stirred up controversy with *The Man with the Golden Arm,* Hollywood's first excursion into the world of the drug addict. He scored a qualified hit with the all-black *Carmen Jones,* an unqualified miss with the all-black *Porgy and Bess,* a critical and commercial disaster with his screen version of Shaw's *Saint Joan,* and a big commercial and critical hit with *Anatomy of a Murder* (1959).

In the 60s, Preminger made a comfortable transition to the wide-screen format, which seemed to agree with his preference for long takes and camera movement over cutting and reaction shots. Although no consistent theme is discernible in his pictures, there are some basic ingredients that are common to most, such as the objective camera viewpoint and a fascination with the duality and ambiguity of character. Preminger has been aptly called (by Andrew Sarris) a director with the personality of a producer. Cost-conscious in the extreme, he consistently lived within the limitations of his budgets and managed to stay afloat much longer than his more artistically ambitious but economically reckless colleagues in independent production.

In Hollywood circles Preminger was famous for his tempestuous personality. Among actors, who were often victimized by his ego-wilting temper tantrums on the set, he was known as "Otto the Terrible." But he was also known for his courageous independence and the risks he took in offering jobs to blacklisted talent. An outspoken man who seemed to enjoy coming across as outrageous in his frequent appearances on TV talk shows, Preminger entertained few pretensions about his films and seemed equally unimpressed with either the vitriol or praise of film critics. In 1971, shortly after the death of Gypsy Rose Lee, the thrice-married Preminger revealed to the press that he was the father of the stripper's 26-year-old son, casting director Erik Kirkland. He adopted Kirkland, who changed his name to Eric Lee Preminger and worked for his father's company as associate producer and screenwriter. Otto's brother, Hollywood agent Ingo Preminger, made his debut as a producer with *M*A*S*H* in 1970. Memoirs: *Preminger: An Autobiography* (1977).

FILMS (as director): *Die Grosse Liebe* (Aus./Ger.) 1931; *Under Your Spell* 1936; *Danger—Love at Work* 1937; *The Pied Piper* (act. only) 1942; *Margin for Error* (also act.), *They Got Me Covered* (act. only) 1943; *In the Meantime Darling, Laura* (also prod.) 1944; *A Royal Scandal, Fallen Angel* (also prod.) 1945; *Centennial Summer* (also prod.) 1946; *Forever Amber, Daisy Kenyon* (also prod.) 1947; *That Lady in Ermine* (begun by and credited to Lubitsch) 1948; *The Fan* (also prod.) 1949; *Whirlpool, Where the Sidewalk Ends* (both also prod.) 1950; *The Thirteenth Letter* (also prod.) 1951; *Angel Face, The Moon Is Blue* (both also prod.), *Stalag 17* (act. only) 1953; *River of No Return, Carmen Jones* (also prod.) 1954; *The Man with the Golden Arm* (also prod.), *The Court-Martial of Billy Mitchell* 1955; *Saint Joan* (also prod.) 1957; *Bonjour Tristesse* (also prod.) 1958; *Porgy and Bess, Anatomy of a Murder* (also prod.) 1959; *Exodus* (also prod.) 1960; *Advise and Consent* (also prod.) 1962; *The Cardinal* (also prod.) 1963; *In Harm's Way, Bunny Lake Is Missing* (both also prod.) 1965; *Hurry Sundown* (also prod.) 1967; *Skidoo!* (also prod.) 1968; *Tell Me That You Love Me Junie Moon* (also prod.) 1970; *Such Good Friends* (also prod.) 1971; *Rosebud* (also prod.) 1975; *The Human Factor* (also prod.) 1980.

premix. The process of combining several sound tracks into a composite track as a preliminary step toward the eventual mixing of this composite track with additional sound tracks. The technique is used as a means of simplifying an unusually complex mixing assignment involving a large number of tracks. For instance, the music and sound-effects tracks may be combined in the premix stage into a single track, which would subsequently be mixed with the dialogue tracks in the final mix.

Prentiss, Paula. Actress. Born Paula Ragusa, on Mar. 4, 1939, in San Antonio, Tex. *ed.* Northwestern. Leading lady of Hollywood films, adept at urbane-screwball comedy roles. Married since 1961 to Richard BENJAMIN, her co-star on TV's 'He and She' (1967–68).

FILMS: *Where the Boys Are* 1960; *The Honeymoon Machine, Bachelor in Paradise* 1961; *The Horizontal Lieutenant* 1962; *Follow the Boys* 1963; *Man's Favorite Sport?, The World of Henry Orient, Looking for Love* 1964; *In Harm's Way, What's New Pussycat?* 1965; *Catch-22, Move* 1970; *Born to Win* 1971; *Last of the Red Hot Lovers* 1972; *The Parallax View, Crazy Joe* 1974; *The Stepford Wives* 1975; *The Black Marble* 1980; *Saturday the 14th, Buddy Buddy* 1981; *Mrs. Winterbourne* (unbilled cameo) 1996.

prequel. A film sequel set in a time period prior to that of the previous film. Examples include *Another Part of the Forest* (1947), which tells of events that took place before those in *The Little Foxes* (1941), and *Butch and Sundance: The Early Days* (1979), a prequel to *Butch Cassidy and the Sundance Kid* (1969).

prerecording. The recording of sound tracks prior to filming, a procedure usually followed in animation.

prescoring. The preparation of a music score for a scene or an entire film before the scene or the film is shot. It is a reversal of the standard procedure, in which the music score is composed, orchestrated, or borrowed from a music library after the completion of filming.

Presle (Prelle in the US), **Micheline.** Actress. Born Micheline Chassagne, on Aug. 22, 1922, in Paris. Convent-educated. Sophisticated, coquettish leading lady of French and some international films, she made her screen debut at 16 as Micheline Michel, was put immediately into leading roles, and reached a peak of success in the late 40s, when she co-starred with Gérard Philipe in *Devil in the Flesh* in the role of an older woman in love with a younger man. Hollywood hoped to cash in on her international popularity and she was assigned leads in several American films, as Micheline Prelle, but her brief American stint was only moderately successful and she resumed her career in Europe in the early 50s. Formerly married to American actor William Marshall.

FILMS INCLUDE: *Je chante* 1938; *Jeunes Filles en Détresse* 1939; *Paradis perdu/Four Flights to Love* 1940; *Histoire de Rire/Foolish Husbands* 1941; *La Comédie du Bonheur, La Nuit fantastique* 1942; *La Belle Aventure/Twilight, Félicie Nanteuil, Falbalas/Paris Frills, Boule de Suif/Angel and Sinner* 1945; *Le Diable au Corps/Devil in the Flesh, Les Jeux sont faits/The Chips Are Down* 1947; *Les Derniers Jours de Pompéi/Sins of Pompeii* 1948; *Under My Skin* (US), *An American Guerilla in the Philippines* (US) 1950; *Adventures of Captain Fabian* (US) 1951; *La Dame aux Camélias* (as Camille) 1953; *L'Amour d'une Femme, Si Versailles m'était conté/Royal Affairs in Versailles, Villa Borghese/It Happened in the Park, Casa Ricordi/House of Ricordi* 1954; *Napoléon* 1955; *Beatrice Cenci* 1956; *Les Louves/Demoiaque* 1957; *Blind Date/Chance*

Meeting (UK) 1959; *Une Fille pour l'Eté/Mistress for the Summer* 1960; *L'Amant de Cinq Jours/The Five Day Lover, Les Grandes Personnes/Time Out for Love, L'Assassino/The Lady Killer of Rome* 1961; *If a Man Answers* (US), *Les Sept Péchés capitaux/Seven Capital Sins, Le Diable et les Dix Commandements/The Devil and the 10 Commandments, Vénus Impériale* 1962; *The Prize* (US) 1963; *La Chasse à l'Homme/Male Hunt* 1964; *La Religieuse/The Nun, Je vous salue Mafia/Hail! Mafia* 1965; *Le Roi de Coeur/King of Hearts* 1966; *Le Bal du Comte d'Orgel, Peau d'Ane/Donkey Skin* 1970; *Les Petroleuses/The Legend of Frenchy King* 1971; *L'Evénement le plus important depuis que l'Homme a marché sur la Lune/A Slightly Pregnant Man, L'Oiseau Rare* 1973; *Eulallie quitte les Champs* 1974; *Mord pas on t'aime, Nea* 1976; *Le Diable dans la Boîte/Your Turn My Turn* 1978; *Certains Nouvelles, Démons de Midi* 1979; *Tout dépend des Files* 1980; *Le Sang des Autres/The Blood of Others, Les Fausses Confidences* 1984; *Beau Temps mais orageux en fin de Journée/Good Weather But Stormy Late This Afternoon, Le Chien* (release delayed from 1984) 1986; *Alouette je te plumerai* 1988; *I Want to Go Home* 1989; *La Fête des Pères, Après Aprés-Demain* 1990; *Fanfan, Je M'Appelle Victor* 1993; *Pas Trés Catholique* 1994; *Les Miserables* 1995; *Diary of a Seducer* 1997.

Presley, Elvis. Singer, actor. *b.* Jan. 8, 1935, Tupelo, Miss. *d.* 1977. Bumping-grinding rock 'n' roll idol of the 50s whose influence on American pop music and lifestyle was considerable. The survivor of identical twins, he moved with his family to Memphis, Tennessee, when he was 13. He was an usher at a movie theater and a truck driver before beginning one of the most phenomenal careers in the history of show business. After touring locally as "The Hillbilly Cat" and recording a number of singles for a regional label, he was signed by RCA in 1955 and became an instant hit on the airwaves and in concert halls. By the time of his death he had sold some 600 million singles and albums, probably more than any other artist. When he sang on the stage, his pelvic gyrations (for which he was nicknamed "Elvis the Pelvis") caused mass hysteria among teenage audiences and moral concern among parents and religious leaders. So great was the fear for the "threatened sexual standards" of the young generation that during Presley's TV appearances, cameramen were ordered to cut him off at the waist.

Presley's film career began in 1956. He starred in 33 movies, none of which was highly thought of by critics or the discriminating public. But the films, tailor-made vehicles for his personality and talent, fared extremely well at the box office, grossing more than $150 million for their producers. Presley's singing career declined somewhat in the 60s with the advent of the Beatles and the influx of other new talent from the British Isles. He made only rare personal appearances, but his movies and recordings continued doing well. In the early 70s he resumed his concert and nightclub work with amazing success, winning the adulation of young audiences as well as of their parents, who had remained his ardent fans. In 1972 the city of Memphis, Tenn., his home for many years, renamed one of its major arteries Presley Boulevard.

While Presley's popularity was booming anew, his health was deteriorating. He gained considerable weight, the result of a steady diet of junk food—especially his favorite soft drinks, jelly doughnuts, and banana splits. After his sudden death of a heart attack at 42, close associates revealed he had been heavily dependent on a whole array of stimulant and depressant pills. Years after his death he remains the object of vast adulation, with thousands of fans flocking to his Memphis shrine, Graceland, many holding on to wild theories that he is still alive. By 1990 more than 60 biographies of Presley were in print. His former wife (1967–73), Priscilla PRESLEY, performs periodically in TV and films.

FILMS: *Love Me Tender* 1956; *Loving You, Jailhouse Rock* 1957; *King Creole* 1958; *G.I. Blues, Flaming Star* 1960; *Wild in the Country, Blue Hawaii* 1961; *Follow That Dream, Kid Galahad, Girls! Girls! Girls!* 1962; *It Happened at the World's Fair, Fun in Acapulco* 1963; *Kissin' Cousins, Viva Las Vegas, Roustabout* 1964; *Girl Happy, Tickle Me, Harum Scarum* 1965; *Frankie and Johnny, Paradise Hawaiian Style, Spinout* 1966; *Easy Come Easy Go, Double Trouble, Clambake* 1967; *Stay Away Joe, Speedway, Live a Little Love a Little* 1968; *Charro!, The Trouble with Girls, Change of Habit* 1969; *Elvis—That's the Way It Is* (doc.) 1970; *Elvis on Tour* (doc.) 1972.

Presley, Priscilla [Beaulieu]. Actress. Born on May 24, 1945, in Brooklyn, N.Y. Attractive light actress best featured as a comedic foil in the *Naked Gun* films. A child of an Air Force officer, she was a teenager in West Germany in 1959 when she was introduced to Army recruit Elvis PRESLEY, to whom she was married in 1967 following a courtly eight-year romance. In the final years of their tempestuous marriage, she studied acting and karate. After his death, she became a businesswoman and actress in films and TV ('Dallas'). She was one of the executive producers of the TV movie *Elvis and Me* (1988), based on her memoir.

FILMS INCLUDE: *The Naked Gun: From the Files of Police Squad!* 1988; *The Adventures of Ford Fairlane* 1990; *The Naked Gun 2½: The Smell of Fear* 1991; *The Naked Gun 33⅓: The Final Insult* 1994.

Pressburger, Emeric. Director, producer, screenwriter. *b.* Imre Pressburger, Dec. 5, 1902, Mikolc, Hungary. *d.* 1988. An amateur violinist as a boy, he also showed prodigious mathematical skills. He studied civil engineering at the Universities of Prague and Stuttgart, but was forced to quit and look for work after the death of his father. He became a journalist, then a screenwriter for German films. Among other productions, he collaborated on early works for Robert SIODMAK and Max OPHÜLS. After the Nazi takeover of 1933 he left for France, where he collaborated on three screenplays before moving on to England with a stateless passport in 1935. In 1938 he was recruited by Alexander KORDA and assigned to write the script for *The Spy in Black* for director Michael POWELL. Other collaborations followed and in 1942 Powell and Pressburger established their own production company, The Archers, through which they wrote, produced, and directed some of Britain's most prestigious productions of the 40s and early 50s. Their partnership dissolved in 1956. Pressburger used the pseudonym Richard Imrie on his last two films. For further detail, see POWELL, Michael.

FILMS: As screenwriter (alone or in collaboration): In Germany—*Abschied/Farewell/Adieu, Dann schon lieber Lebertran* (medium-length 1930; *Das Ekel, Der kleine Seitensprung, Ronny* 1931; *Das schöne Abenteuer, Sehnsucht* (Ger./Aus.) 1932; . . . *Und es leuchtet die Puszta* (Ger./Hung.) 1933. In France: *Une Femme au volant* 1933; *Monsieur Sans-Gêne* (script later provided basis for 1936 US film *One Rainy Afternoon*), *La Vie Parisienne* 1935. In the UK—*The Challenge* 1938; *The Spy in Black/U-Boat 29* 1939; *Contraband* 1940; *49th Parallel/The Invaders* 1941; *One of Our Aircraft Is Missing* 1942; *The Silver Fleet* (co-prod. only). As director-producer-writer in collaboration with Michael Powell—*The Life and Death of Colonel Blimp/Colonel Blimp, The Volunteer* (medium-length) 1943; *A Canterbury Tale* 1944; *I Know Where I'm Going* 1945; *A Matter of Life and Death/Stairway to Heaven* 1945; *Black Narcissus, The End of the River* (co-prod. only) 1947; *The Red Shoes* 1948; *The Small Back Room/Hour of*

Glory 1949; *Gone to Earth/The Wild Heart* (co-dir., co-sc. only), *The Elusive Pimpernel/The Fighting Pimpernel* (co-dir., co-sc. only) 1950; *The Tales of Hoffman* 1951; *Twice Upon a Time* (dir., prod., sc. alone) 1953; *Oh Rosalinda!/Fledermaus '55* 1955; *The Battle of the River Plate/Pursuit of the Graf Spee* 1956; *Ill Met by Moonlight/Night Ambush* (co-exec. prod. only), *Miracle in Soho* (prod., sc. only) 1957; *Behold a Pale Horse* (novel basis only, *Killing a Mouse on Sunday*) 1964; *Operazione Crossbow/Operation Crossbow* (co-sc. only, as Richard Imrie; It./UK) 1965; *They're a Weird Mob* (sc. only, as Richard Imrie) 1966; *The Boy Who Turned Yellow* (sc. only) 1972.

Pressman, Edward R. Producer. Born 1946 in New York City. After graduating from Stanford he attended the London School of Economics, then stayed in England to start his film career. Returning to the US, he produced or served as an executive producer on many American films. His track record indicates a frequent interest in original ideas and a courage to undertake risky ventures and take a chance on unproven talent. He had a hand in several notable international co-productions. In 1988 he was honored with a retrospective at the Museum of Modern Art.

FILMS INCLUDE (as producer or executive producer, alone or in collaboration): *Out of It* 1969; *The Revolutionary* (UK) 1970; *Dealing* 1972; *Sisters, Badlands* 1973; *Phantom of the Paradise* 1974; *Eine Reise ins Licht/Despair* (Ger.) 1977; *Paradise Alley* 1978; *Old Boyfriends* 1979; *Heart Beat* 1980; *The Hand, Das Boot* (Ger.) 1981; *Conan the Barbarian* 1982; *The Pirates of Penzance* 1983; *Plenty* 1985; *Crimewave* (also act.), *True Stories, Half Moon Street* 1986; *Good Morning Babilonia/Good Morning Babylon* (It./Fr./US), *Masters of the Universe, Walker, Wall Street* 1987; *Cherry 2000, Talk Radio* 1988 *Blue Steel, Waiting for the Light, Martians Go Home, To Sleep with Anger, Reversal of Fortune* 1990; *Homicide, Year of the Gun, Iron Maze* 1991; *Storyville, The Bad Lieutenant, Hoffa* 1992; *The Crow* 1994; *Judge Dredd* 1995; *City Hall, The Island of Dr. Moreau* 1996; *The Winter Guest* 1997.

Pressman, Michael. Director. Born on July 1, 1950, in New York City, into a show business family. He began as an actor, performing in productions of his school, the California Institute of Arts. In addition to several features, he directed a good number of TV movies.

FEATURE FILMS: *The Great Texas Dynamite Chase* 1976; *The Bad News Bears in Breaking Training* 1977; *Boulevard Nights* 1979; *Those Lips Those Eyes* 1980; *Some Kind of a Hero* 1982; *Doctor Detroit* 1983; *Teenage Mutant Ninja Turtles II: The Secret of the Ooze* 1991; *To Gillian on her 37th Birthday* 1996.

pressure plate. A plate behind the aperture of a camera (and projectors, printers, etc.) which holds the film firmly and accurately in the focal plane during exposure. The plate incorporates rollers to minimize frictional contact with the film. In animation, a pressure plate (also known as a "pressure pad" or "pressure glass") is a sheet of glass in a wood or metal frame which is hinged to the animation board. Its function is to keep cels and background evenly flat during photography.

Preston, Robert. Actor. *b.* Robert Preston Meservey, June 8, 1918, Newton Highlands, Mass. *d.* 1987. Sturdy, capable, dynamic leading man of the American stage and screen. He was raised in Hollywood, where his father played for a local minor league baseball team. He dropped out of school at 16 to become an actor, joined a small Shakespearean group, then trained at the Pasadena Community Playhouse and performed in dozens of the theater's productions. Signed by Paramount in 1938, he endured some 20 years of relative anonymity, during which he played leads in routine B pictures and second leads in major productions. It was on the stage that he finally got his opportunity to shine, displaying enormous charm and vibrancy as a breezy, fast-talking confidence man in the Broadway musical 'The Music Man' (1957), for which he won his first Tony Award. He won another for 'I Do! I Do!' (1966) and in 1974 portrayed Mack Sennett in the Broadway musical 'Mack and Mabel.' Preston's stage success paid dividends on the screen, too, in the film version of *The Music Man* (1962) and in such fine dramas as *The Dark at the Top of the Stairs* (1960) and *All the Way Home* (1965). He enjoyed great success as a facile supporting player in films of the 80s, earning an Academy Award nomination for his amusing portrayal of a transvestite nightclub performer in *Victor/Victoria* (1982). He was married from 1946 to actress Catherine Craig (née Kay Feltus).

FILMS: *King of Alcatraz, Illegal Traffic* 1938; *Disbarred, Union Pacific, Beau Geste* 1939; *Typhoon, North West Mounted Police, Moon Over Burma* 1940; *The Lady from Cheyenne, Parachute Battalion, New York Town, Pacific Blackout, The Night of January 16th* 1941; *Reap the Wild Wind, This Gun for Hire, Wake Island, Star Spangled Rhythm* (cameo) 1942; *Night Plane from Chungking* 1943; *Variety Girl* (cameo), *The Macomber Affair, Wild Harvest* 1947; *Big City, Blood on the Moon* 1948; *Whispering Smith, Tulsa, The Lady Gambles* 1949; *The Sundowners* 1950; *My Outlaw Brother, When I Grow Up, Best of the Badmen, Cloudburst* (UK) 1951; *Face to Face* 1952; *The Last Frontier* 1956; *The Dark at the Top of the Stairs* 1960; *The Music Man, How the West Was Won* 1962; *Island of Love, All the Way Home* 1963; *Junior Bonner, Child's Play* 1972; *Mame* 1974; *Semi-Tough* 1977; *S.O.B.* 1981; *Victor/Victoria* 1982; *The Last Starfighter* 1984.

Prévert, Jacques. Screenwriter, poet. *b.* Feb. 4, 1900, Neuilly-sur-Seine, France. *d.* 1977. Affiliated with the surrealist movement in the late 20s, he began writing poetry in 1930 and screenplays in 1932. From the mid-30s to the mid-40s he ranked as France's most important film writer, exerting considerable influence on the "poetic realism" school in general and on the films of RENOIR and CARNÉ in particular. His poems were immensely popular among French youth of the post–WW II generation. His many lyrics for pop songs included the world-famous 'Les Feuilles mortes' ('Autumn Leaves'), first heard in the film *Les Portes de la Nuit/Gates of the Night* (1946). He was nominated for an Oscar for his screenplay for *Children of Paradise* (1945; US release 1946). Three of Prévert's screenplays—*L'Affaire est dans le Sac* (1932), *Adieu Léonard* (1943), and *Voyage-Surprise* (1947)—were skillfully directed by his younger brother, Pierre Prévert (*b.* May 26, 1906, Paris; *d.* 1988).

FILMS INCLUDE (screenplays alone or in collaboration): *L'Affaire est dans le Sac* (also act.) 1932; *Ciboulette* (also act.) 1933; *L'Hôtel du Libre-Echange* (also act.) 1934; *Un Oiseau rare* 1935; *Le Crime de Monsieur Lange/The Crime of Monsieur Lange, Jenny* 1936; *The Mysterious Mr. Davis/My Partner Mr. Davis* (UK), *Drôle de Drame/Bizarre Bizarre* 1937; *Quai des Brumes/Port of Shadows, Ernest le Rebelle* 1938; *Le Jour se lève/Daybreak* 1939; *Remorques/Stormy Waters, Le Soleil a toujours Raison* (also co-songs) 1941; *Les Visiteurs du Soir/The Devil's Envoys* 1942; *Lumière d'Eté, Adieu Léonard* (also co-song) 1943; *Les Enfants du Paradis/Children of Paradise, Sortilèges/The Bellman* 1945; *Les Portes de la Nuit/Gates of the Night* (based on his own co-ballet 'Le Rendez-vous'; also co-songs, including lyrics for the famous 'Les Feuilles mortes'/'Autumn Leaves') 1946; *Voyage-Surprise* 1947; *Les Amants de Vérone/The Lovers of Verona* 1949; *Souvenirs perdus* 1950; *La Bergère et le Ramoneur* (also co-songs) 1953; *Notre-Dame de Paris/The Hunchback of Notre Dame* 1956; *Les Amours célèbres* 1961.

preview. The advance showing of a film before its official release, either to an invited group (the press, industry brass, etc.), or to a paying audience in a preselected "test" theater in an attempt to gauge public reaction to the film. See also SNEAK PREVIEW.

Previn, André. Composer, conductor, arranger, musical director, pianist. Born André Prewin, on Apr. 6, 1929, in Berlin, of Russian-Jewish descent. A piano prodigy, he was accepted into Berlin's High School of music at age six, but in 1938 was forced to leave with his family for France, where he continued his studies at the Paris Conservatory. The following year, the family migrated to the US, settling in Los Angeles, where the father's cousin, Charles Previn (*b.* 1888, Brooklyn; *d.* 1973), was a musical director at Universal Studios. Becoming a US citizen in 1943, he began working for MGM as an orchestrator even before graduating from high school. Later he conducted and scored numerous films for various studios, winning several Academy Awards (designated "AA" below). In the early 60s he began conducting major symphony orchestras in the US and abroad and in 1968 he became the principal conductor of the London Symphony Orchestra, later assuming a similar role with the Pittsburgh Symphony and London's Royal Philharmonic. In addition to films scores, he also wrote a symphony and other concert-hall works and composed such Broadway musicals as 'Coco' (1969) and 'The Good Companions' (1974). In 1970 he divorced his second wife (of four) to marry actress Mia FARROW after she had given birth to twin boys. They later had another natural son and adopted four Vietnamese orphans before divorcing in 1979.

FILMS INCLUDE (as composer or arranger): *The Sun Comes Up* 1948; *Scene of the Crime, Challenge to Lassie* 1949; *Three Little Words* 1951; *Bad Day at Black Rock* 1954; *It's Always Fair Weather* 1955; *Designing Woman* 1957; *Gigi* (AA) 1958; *Porgy and Bess* (AA) 1959; *Elmer Gantry* 1960; *One Two Three* 1961; *Long Day's Journey Into Night* 1962; *Irma La Douce* (AA) 1963; *My Fair Lady* (supervisor-conductor only; AA), *Kiss Me Stupid* 1964; *Inside Daisy Clover* 1965; *The Fortune Cookie, The Swinger* (title song only) 1966; *Thoroughly Modern Millie* (musical numbers only), *Valley of the Dolls* (songs only) 1967; *Paint Your Wagon* (addnl. songs only) 1969; *Mrs. Pollifax—Spy* (dance music and theme only) 1971; *Rollerball* 1975; *One-Trick Pony* 1980.

Prevost, Marie. Actress. *b.* Mary Bickford Dunn, Nov. 8, 1898, Sarnia, Ontario, Canada. *d.* 1937. Popular star of Hollywood silents and early talkies. Educated at a Montreal convent and a Los Angeles high school, she was employed briefly as a stenographer with a legal firm before starting her film career in 1916 as a Mack Sennett Bathing Beauty. Within months she was promoted to leading lady, remaining with Sennett through 1921, when she joined Universal. She soon emerged as a leading star, specializing in romantic comedy roles. She reached the peak of her career in three Ernst LUBITSCH features, *The Marriage Circle, Three Women* (both 1924), and *Kiss Me Again* (1925). In 1926 she moved over to the PDC company, for which she starred in a string of bedroom farces. Her second husband (1924–27) was screen star Kenneth HARLAN. She made a successful transition to talkies, but a worsening weight problem hampered and finally ended her career in the mid-30s. In a desperate attempt to resurrect that career, she went on a crash diet and eventually stopped eating altogether. On January 23, 1937, at the age of 38, she was found dead at her home in a state of extreme malnutrition. Her sister, Marjorie Prevost, also played in some films, including *The Old Swimmin' Hole* (1921), an appearance wrongly attributed by many sources to Marie.

FILMS INCLUDE: *Unto Those Who Sin* 1916; *Her Nature Dance, Secrets of a Beauty Parlor* 1917; *Sleuths, The Village Chestnut* 1918; *East Lynne with Variations, When Love Is Blind, Yankee Doodle in Berlin* 1919; *Down on the Farm, Love Honor and Behave* 1920; *A Small Town Idol, Moonlight Follies, Nobody's Fool, A Parisian Scandal* 1921; *Don't Get Personal, The Dangerous Little Demon, Kissed, Her Night of Nights, The Married Flapper, The Beautiful and the Damned, Heroes of the Street* 1922; *Brass, Red Lights, The Wanters* 1923; *The Marriage Circle, Daughters of Pleasure, How to Educate a Wife, Being Respectable, Cornered, Tarnished, Three Women, The Lover of Camille, The Dark Swan* 1924; *Recompense, Kiss Me Again, Bobbed Hair, Seven Sinners* 1925; *His Jazz Bride, The Caveman, Other Women's Husbands, Up in Mabel's Room, Almost a Lady, For Wives Only, Man Bait* 1926; *Getting Gertie's Garter, The Night Bride, The Girl in the Pullman* 1927; *The Rush Hour, On to Reno, A Blonde for a Night, The Racket, The Sideshow* 1928; *The Godless Girl, The Flying Fool, Divorce Made Easy* 1929; *Party Girl, Ladies of Leisure, Sweethearts on Parade, War Nurse, Paid* 1930; *Sporting Blood, Reckless Living, The Sin of Madelon Claudet, Hell Divers* 1931; *Three Wise Girls, Slightly Married* 1932; *Parole Girl, Only Yesterday* 1933; *Hands Across the Table* 1935; *Tango, 13 Hours by Air* 1936; *Ten Laps to Go* 1938.

Price, Dennis. Actor. *b.* Dennistoun Franklyn John Rose-Price, June 23, 1915, Twyford, England. *d.* 1973. Elegant, cultivated leading man and character player of the British stage and screen, typically in sardonic, urbane roles. The son of a general, he was educated at Oxford and made his stage debut with a stock company in 1937. Later that year he joined John Gielgud's company in London's West End. He began his screen career in 1944, shortly after being invalided out of the British army in WW II action, and subsequently appeared in scores of films, memorably as the devilishly scheming heir who kills off his family in *Kind Hearts and Coronets* (1949).

FILMS INCLUDE: *A Canterbury Tale* 1944; *A Place of One's Own* 1945; *Caravan, The Magic Bow, Hungry Hill* 1946; *Dear Murderer, Jassy, Holiday Camp, Master of Bankdam, The White Unicorn/Bad Sister* 1947; *Good Time Girl, Easy Money, Snowbound* 1948; *The Bad Lord Byron* (title role), *Kind Hearts and Coronets, The Lost People* 1949; *The Dancing Years, Murder Without Crime, The Adventurers* 1950; *The Magic Box, Lady Godiva Rides Again, The House in the Square/I'll Never Forget You* (UK/US) 1951; *The Intruder* 1953; *Oh Rosalinda* 1955; *Private's Progress, Charley Moon* 1956; *The Naked Truth/Your Past Is Showing* 1957; *I'm All Right Jack* 1959; *School for Scoundrels, Oscar Wilde, The Millionairess, Tunes of Glory, The Pure Hell of St. Trinian's* 1960; *No Love for Johnnie, Victim* 1961; *The Wrong Arm of the Law, The V.I.P.s, Tamahine* 1963; *A Jolly Bad Bellow/They All Died Laughing, Murder Most Foul* 1964; *High Wind in Jamaica* (US/UK) 1965; *Ten Little Indians* 1966; *Rocket to the Moon/Those Fantastic Flying Fools* 1967; *Venus in Furs* 1969; *Horror of Frankenstein* 1971; *Pulp* 1972; *Theatre of Blood* 1973.

Price, Richard. Screenwriter, actor, novelist. Born on Oct. 12, 1949, in New York, N.Y. *ed.* Cornell U.; Columbia U. (M.F.A., writing); Stanford U. While establishing himself as a writer of taut, evocative urban novels, he began a second career as a screenwriter. His first original screenplay, *The Color of Money*, was nominated for an Academy Award. Among his novels are *Bloodbrothers, The Wanderers, Ladies' Man*, and *Clockers*.

FILMS INCLUDE (as screenwriter): *Bloodbrothers* (from novel) 1978; *The Wanderers* (from novel, also act.) 1979; *The Color of Money* (also act.) 1986; *New York Stories* ("Life

Lessons" segment, also act.) 1989; *Sea of Love* 1989; *Night and the City* (also act.) 1992; *Mad Dog and Glory* (also co-pr., act.) 1993; *Kiss of Death* (also cameo), *The Paper* (act. only) 1994; *Clockers* (from novel) 1995; *Ransom* (also cameo) 1996.

Price, Vincent. *b.* May 27, 1911, in St. Louis, Mo. *d.* 1993. Cultivated character star of the American stage, films, radio, and TV. The son of a well-to-do candy manufacturer, he had a privileged youth and an early introduction to the fine arts, including a grand tour of Europe's art museums as a gift upon graduation from high school. After receiving his bachelor's degree in art history and English from Yale, he tried unsuccessfully to crack the New York stage, then went to England, where he obtained his master's degree in fine arts at the University of London and made his stage debut playing a small part in 'Chicago,' starring John Gielgud, in 1935. That same year he was cast in the lead part of Prince Albert in the West End production of 'Victoria Regina'; then starred in the same play on Broadway opposite Helen Hayes. He was an established stage star by the time he began his film career with Universal in 1938. On the screen Price initially played some romantic leads but soon proved himself better suited for character roles, at his best as a treacherous or effete villain. His mellifluous voice served him well in the numerous horror films in which he starred from the 50s, notably *House of Wax* (1953), *The Fly* (1958), and Roger Corman's Poe cycle of the 60s. A noted art collector and connoisseur, Price often lectured on art and for several years served as art-buying consultant of the Sears Roebuck company. He authored or edited a number of art books as well as several volumes on his other great love, the culinary arts. His books include *I Like What I Know* (autobiography; 1959), *The Book of Joe* (1962), *Drawings of Delacroix* (1962), *The Michelangelo Bible* (1965), *A Treasury of Great Recipes* (1965), *National Treasury of Cooking* (1967), *Looking Around* (1969), *The Come Into the Kitchen Cook Book* (1969), and *The Vincent Price Treasury of American Art* (1972). His cookbooks were written in collaboration with his second wife (1949–73), fashion designer Mary (Grant) Price; his first (1938–48) was actress Edith Barrett. He was married to actress Coral BROWNE from 1974 till her death in 1991.

FILMS: *Service de Luxe* 1938; *The Private Lives of Elizabeth and Essex* (as Sir Walter Raleigh), *Tower of London* (as the Duke of Clarence) 1939; *The Invisible Man Returns* (title role), *Green Hell, The House of the Seven Gables* (as Clifford Pyncheon), *Brigham Young—Frontiersman* (as Joseph Smith, founder of the Mormon religion) 1940; *Hudson's Bay* (as King Charles II) 1941; *The Song of Bernadette* (as Dutour) 1943; *The Eve of St. Mark, Wilson* (as Secretary of the Treasury William Gibbs McAdoo), *Laura* 1944; *The Keys of the Kingdom, A Royal Scandal* (as the Marquis de Fleury), *Leave Her to Heaven* 1945; *Shock, Dragonwyck* 1946; *The Web, Moss Rose, The Long Night* 1947; *Up in Central Park, Abbott and Costello Meet Frankenstein* (v/o, as the Invisible Man), *The Three Musketeers* (as Cardinal Richelieu), *Rogues' Regiment* 1948; *The Bribe, Bagdad* 1949; *Champagne for Caesar, The Baron of Arizona, Curtain Call at Cactus Creek* 1950; *His Kind of Woman, Adventures of Captain Fabian* 1951; *The Las Vegas Story, Pictura* (feature-length art documentary compiled from several segments; on-camera narrator only) 1952; *House of Wax* 1953; *Dangerous Mission, Casanova's Big Night* (cameo, as Casanova), *The Mad Magician* 1954; *Son of Sinbad/Nights in a Harem* (as Omar Khayyam) 1955; *Serenade, While the City Sleeps, The Vagabond King* (narrator only), *The Ten Commandments* 1956; *The Story of Mankind* (as the Devil) 1957; *The Fly* 1958; *House on Haunted Hill, The Big Circus, The Bat, Return of the Fly, The Tingler* 1959; *The House of Usher* (as Roderick Usher) 1960; *The Pit and the Pendulum, Master of the World, Naked Terror* (doc.; narrator only) 1961; *Nefertite—Regina del Nilo/Queen of the Nile* (It.), *Gordon il Pirato Nero/Rage of the Buccaneers* (It.), *Tales of Terror, Convicts 4, Confessions of an Opium Eater, Tower of London* (as Richard of Gloucester) 1962; *The Raven, Diary of a Madman, Beach Party, Twice Told Tales, The Comedy of Terrors/The Graveside Story, I Tabù/Taboos of the World* (doc.; narrator only; It.) 1963; *The Haunted Palace, L'Ultimo Uomo della Terra/The Last Man on Earth* (It./US), *The Masque of the Red Death* (US/UK), *The Tomb of Ligeia* (UK) 1964; *War-Gods of the Deep/City Under the Sea* (US/UK), *Dr. Goldfoot and the Bikini Machine* 1965; *Dr. Goldfoot and the Girl Bombs* (US/It.) 1966; *Das Haus der tausend Freuden/House of 1000 Dolls* (Ger./Sp.), *The Jackals* (never released) 1967; *Witchfinder General/The Conqueror Worm* (UK), *Histoires extraordinaires/Spirits of the Dead* (narrator only of English-language version; Fr./It.) 1968; *More Dead Than Alive, The Oblong Box* (US/UK), *The Trouble with Girls* 1969; *Scream and Scream Again* (UK), *Cry of the Banshee* (UK) 1970; *The Abominable Dr. Phibes* (UK) 1971; *Dr. Phibes Rises Again* (UK) 1972; *Theatre of Blood* (UK) 1973; *Madhouse* (UK), *The Devil's Triangle* (doc.; narrator only), *Percy's Progress/It's Not the Size That Counts* (UK) 1974; *Journey Into Fear* (Can.) 1975; *The Butterfly Ball* (doc.; narr.) 1976; *Days of Fury* (doc.; narr.) 1978; *Scavenger Hunt* (cameo) 1979; *The Monster Club* (UK) 1980; *House of the Long Shadows* (UK) 1983; *Bloodbath at the House of Death* (UK) 1984; *The Great Mouse Detective* (v/o) 1986; *The Offspring/From a Whisper to a Scream, The Whales of August* 1987; *Dead Heat* 1988; *Edward Scissorhands, Backtrack/Catchfire* 1990.

primary colors. The three basic colors in the spectrum that in mixture yield other colors. In art they have traditionally been red, yellow, and blue, but in color cinematography they are red-orange, green, and blue-violet.

Prince, The artist formerly known as. Singer, songwriter, actor, director. Born Prince Rogers Nelson, on June 7, 1958, in Minneapolis, Minn. Versatile, innovative musician/performer who successfully fused in his work elements of rock, jazz, soul, gospel, funk, and hip-hop, and shrouded his stage persona in ambisexual exotica. The son of a black jazz musician father and a mother of Mediterranean descent who divorced when he was seven, he turned to music in his teens and taught himself to play some 20 instruments. He released his first album in 1978 and went on to a spectacular career in concerts and on the recording charts. Expanding into movies in 1984, he won an Academy Award for best original song score for *Purple Rain,* in which he also made his acting debut in the seemingly autobiographical role of a black young man struggling to break through with a daring brand of futuristic rock music. His soundtrack album for the movie sold 13.5 million copies worldwide. Since then, his record sales have steadily decreased, but he has remained one of pop's most influential and respected voices. He has virtually disappeared from filmmaking.

FILMS: *Purple Rain* (act., songs, song scores) 1984; *Under the Cherry Moon* (dir., act., mus., songs) 1986; *Sign o' the Times* (concert film; dir., act., mus., songs) 1987; *Batman* (songs) 1989; *Graffiti Bridge* (dir., sc., mus., songs, act.) 1990.

Prince, William. Actor. *b.* Jan. 26, 1913, in Nichols, N.Y. *d.* 1996. *ed.* Cornell. A stage actor since 1937, he also played leads and supporting parts in occasional Hollywood films. In the 60s he appeared regularly in TV soap operas.

FILMS INCLUDE: *Destination Tokyo, The Very Thought of You* 1944; *Objective Burma, Pillow to Post* 1945; *Cinderella Jones* 1946; *Dead Reckoning, Carnegie Hall* 1947; *Lust for Gold* 1949; *Cyrano de Bergerac* (as Christian) 1950; *The Vagabond King, Secret of Treasure Mountain* 1956; *Macabre*

1958; *Sacco e Vanzetti/Sacco and Vanzetti* (It.) 1971; *The Heartbreak Kid* 1972; *Blade* 1973; *The Stepford Wives* 1975; *Family Plot, Network* 1976; *The Gauntlet* 1977; *The Cat from Outer Space* 1978; *The Promise* 1979; *Bronco Billy* 1980; *Love and Money, The Soldier* 1982; *Movers and Shakers, Spies Like Us* 1985; *Nuts* 1987; *Vice Versa* 1988; *Second Sight, Spontaneous Combustion* 1989; *The Taking of Beverly Hills* 1991; *The Paper* 1996.

Pringle, Aileen. Actress. *b.* Aileen Bisbee, July 23, 1895, San Francisco. *d.* 1989. Leading lady of Hollywood silents and early talkies. As a young socialite she was educated in Europe and made her acting debut on the London stage in 1915. Returning to the US, she later appeared on Broadway and made her screen debut in 1919 as Aileen Savage. She starred in many films of the 20s, typically as an exotic siren, most successfully in two productions based on scripts by Elinor Glyn that were considered daring at the time for their sexual frankness and heralded the "It" Girl idea—*Three Weeks* and *His Hour* (both 1924). Pringle continued playing leads after the switch to sound, but most of her talkie vehicles were undistinguished. Her roles gradually diminished and she retired in 1939 but played bits in several films of the early 40s. Her first husband (1912–33) was Sir Charles MacKenzie Pringle, governor of the Bahamas and later lieutenant-governor of Jamaica. Her second and last (1944–47) was novelist James Cain.

FILMS INCLUDE: *Redhead* 1919; *Stolen Moments, Earthbound* 1920; *Oath-Bound* 1922; *My American Wife, The Christian, In the Palace of the King, Souls for Sale* 1923; *Name the Man, Three Weeks, True As Steel, His Hour, Wife of the Centaur* 1924; *A Thief in Paradise, A Kiss in the Dark, Wildfire, One Year to Live, The Mystic* 1925; *Soul Mates, The Wilderness Woman, The Great Deception, Tin Gods* 1926; *Adam and Evil, Tea for Three, Body and Soul* 1927; *Wickedness Preferred, Beau Broadway, Dream of Love, The Baby Cyclone* 1928; *A Single Man, Night Parade, Wall Street* 1929; *Puttin' on the Ritz, Soldiers and Women, Prince of Diamonds* 1930; *Subway Express, Murder at Midnight, The Age of Consent, Convicted* 1931; *By Appointment Only* 1933; *Love Past Thirty, Jane Eyre* 1934; *Sons of Steel* 1935; *The Unguarded Hour, Piccadilly Jim* 1936; *The Last of Mrs. Cheyney, Nothing Sacred* 1937; *The Night of Nights* 1939; *They Died with Their Boots On* 1942; *Since You Went Away, Laura* 1944.

print. A positive copy made from an original or dupe negative.

printer. A machine that reproduces images from one film onto another. The four basic types of printer are (1) the contact printer, in which the raw stock is held in intimate contact with the image-bearing film; (2) the optical printer, in which a lens system copies the original image; (3) the continuous printer, in which the raw stock and the image-bearing film are in continuous movement during exposure; and (4) the step printer, in which both films move intermittently and are stationary at the moment of exposure of each frame.

printer light. The variable-setting, light-intensity control on a PRINTER which may be adjusted in processing to compensate for differences in negative density resulting from inconsistent exposure during shooting.

printing. The laboratory process of exposing raw stock by using the image of another film as the light modulator. Through printing, one may produce a positive print from negative film; negative film from positive film; and when using a reversal process, positives from positives or negatives from negatives.

"Print it!" A director's exclamation indicating that he is satisfied with a take and wants it sent to the laboratory for processing.

Prinz, LeRoy. Dance director. *b.* July 14, 1895, St. Joseph, Mo. *d.* 1983. A former member of the Foreign Legion and an aviator, he began his show business career as a choreographer for Max REINHARDT, the Folies Bergère, and other European companies. In Hollywood since the early 30s, he choreographed the dance numbers for numerous films. He directed two features and a short subject, *A Boy and His Dog* (1946), for which he won an Academy Award, and also produced and directed many industrial and instructional films.

FILMS INCLUDE (as dance director): *Innocents of Paris* 1929; *Madame Satan* 1930; *The Sign of the Cross* 1932; *Too Much Harmony* 1933; *Bolero, Cleopatra* 1934; *Rumba, The Big Broadcast of 1936, The Crusades* 1935; *Show Boat* 1936; *High Wide and Handsome* 1937; *Road to Singapore* 1940; *All American Co-Ed* (also prod., dir.), *Fiesta* (also prod., dir.), *Road to Zanzibar* 1941; *Yankee Doodle Dandy, Thank Your Lucky Stars, This Is the Army* 1943; *The Desert Song, Hollywood Canteen* 1944; *Rhapsody in Blue* 1945; *Night and Day* 1946; *April Showers* 1948; *Tea for Two* 1950; *April in Paris, The Jazz Singer* 1953; *The Ten Commandments* 1956; *The Helen Morgan Story* 1957; *South Pacific* 1958.

process body. A simulation car, train, or any other vehicle with removable sides and front to allow interior photography, usually in conjunction with a PROCESS SHOT.

processing. The combined term for the various photochemical procedures involved in the course of developing and printing film. In the first stage, film exposed during shooting is guided over rollers into a chemical developing solution. It is then washed and carried along to a fixing bath, washed again, and finally dried. The developed negative is then ready for PRINTING. In the 90s, digital film processing, performed on a computer, began to be introduced for certain shots requiring special effects compositing, removal of stunt wires, or other alteration of filmed elements.

process shot. A shot taken against a moving or still background consisting of previously filmed footage which is projected through a transparent screen behind the current action being filmed, a technique known as BACK PROJECTION or "rear projection." A routine example is the commonly seen shot of actors in a car moving through city traffic. The actors sit in a mock car in the studio while rear-projected footage of city streets is glimpsed through the window behind them.

Prochnow, Jurgen. Actor. Born in 1941, in Berlin. Tall, sinewy leading man and character player of the German stage and screen and later also Hollywood films. Memorable as the submarine captain in *Das Boot/The Boat* (1981).

FILMS INCLUDE: *Zoff* 1971; *Zartlchkeit der Wolfe* 1973; *Die Verrhohung des Franz Blum* 1974; *Die verlorene Ehre der Katharina Blum/The Lost Honor of Katharina Blum* 1975; *Die Consequenz/The Consequence* 1977; *Einer von uns beiden* 1978; *Unter Verschluss* 1979; *Das Boot/The Boat* 1981; *Krien und Frieden/War and Peace* (doc.), *The Keep* (US) 1983; *Dune* (US) 1984; *Forbidden* (TV movie in US; theatrically released in Europe; US/UK/Ger.), *Der Bülle und das Mädchen* 1985; *Killing Cars* 1986; *Terminus* (Fr./Ger./Hung.), *Beverly Hills Cop II* (US), *Devil's Paradise* 1987; *The Seventh Sign* (US) 1988; *A Dry White Season* (US) 1989; *The Fourth War* (US), *The Man Inside* (Fr./US) 1990; *Robin Hood* (scaled down to cable) 1991; *Body of Evidence* 1993; *Judge Dredd* 1995; *The English Patient* 1996; *Air Force One* 1997.

producer. The person exercising overall control over the production of a motion picture and holding ultimate responsibility for its success or failure. Ideally, a producer should be a combination of shrewd businessman, tough taskmaster, prudent cost accountant, flexible diplomat, and creative visionary. But producers vary widely in personality, in the extent of their authority, and in the degree of their involvement in the various phases of production. Typically, however, their job begins long before the start of production and does not end until long after the film is "in the can." Their involvement begins where all films begin, with an idea or the acquisition of a promising PROPERTY.

Whether he himself has chosen the idea or the property or was assigned one by a studio's executive producer, his responsibility is the same: to guide the development of the property into a successful motion picture. He may be assigned a screenwriter or choose one or several from the studio roster or from the free-lance market or, if he happens to be one of the rarer breed of producer-writers (Nunnally Johnson, for example), assign himself to the project. If the screenwriter is someone else, the producer discusses the outlines of the story with him (there may be more than one), and together they work out a TREATMENT, which is submitted to the studio heads or financial backers for approval. Given the go-ahead, the writer now begins the task of writing the screenplay. Normally he would submit portions of the screenplay to the producer, several pages at a time. They would hold frequent conferences, which might or might not result in re-writing.

Meanwhile, the producer proceeds with the selection of a director. Again, the director may be assigned to the project by studio management. Preferably, he would be selected by the producer, whose decision is usually influenced by the director's proven skill with the specific type of film at hand (action, drama, comedy, etc.). The producer who can also direct or the director who also produces (Hitchcock, Preminger, Hawks, etc.) is at a great advantage: he can maintain the fullest possible control over his films. When there is a separate producer and director, they confer on the various creative and technical aspects, from the general approach to the theme to such specifics as the desirability and extent of location shooting and the choice of film stock and technical crew. The uppermost factor in the producer's mind is the limitations of his budget, whether these are set by the studio or by himself if he is an independent producer. His goal is to achieve maximum quality at a minimum price tag. This budgetary concern governs his position regarding such important decisions as the selection of cast (stars, feature players, the number of extras), studio versus location shooting, the elaborateness of sets and costumes, and the duration of filming.

Once the actual shooting begins, the prudent producer removes himself from the set to allow the director freedom of action. But he must not let control leave his grasp. He keeps abreast of the daily progress in production and ascertains that the director and the crew are functioning smoothly in adherence to the timetable and within the boundaries of the budget. He must be available at all times as a troubleshooter, in case of personality or labor conflicts on the set, or if some unforeseeable technical problems arise during shooting. Once shooting is completed, the creative producer becomes involved in the postproduction phase of filmmaking. His functions would normally include supervision of the editing, scoring, sound effects, mixing, optical effects, titles, and all other steps that must be taken before a film is ready for release.

When all is done and the film is "IN THE CAN," the producer may take his film on a trial run—a SNEAK PREVIEW, as it is known in the business—and, depending on initial reaction, he may call for additional cutting and tightening of the film or even for the re-shooting of sequences. He remains with the film through the exploitation stage, co-ordinating the distribution and participating in the planning and execution of the publicity campaign for the initial theatrical release, the home video release, and eventual re-runs in theaters and on TV.

In the past, the majority of Hollywood producers were salaried studio employees who more often than not were assigned their projects, their budgets, their casts, and their crews. They were accountable, for every major decision, to an executive producer or the studio's vice president in charge of production. The truly creative producers (like Val Lewton with the RKO horror cycle of the 40s or Arthur Freed with the MGM musicals of the 40s and 50s) left a personal imprint on their productions which was often more distinct than that of the directors themselves.

A rarity in the traditional Hollywood studio setup was the independent producer of the stature of a Samuel Goldwyn, who put up his own money and exercised complete financial and creative control over his productions. Midway between the independent producer and the studio-salaried producer was the producer who set up his own independent unit, within the framework of a major studio, an arrangement that did not always work very well, as exemplified by the Stanley Kramer–Columbia Pictures arrangement of the early 50s.

Since the disintegration of the traditional studio structure in the 50s and 60s, independent production has become commonplace. Today's typical producer is not a salaried studio employee but an active partner of a studio or a distributor or whoever else might have raised the money to finance his picture. He is a packager who invests in the acquisition of a property, persuades a director and stars to commit themselves to his project, then offers the entire package to a financial sponsor in return for a cut in the profits.

production breakdown. See BREAKDOWN.

Production Code. A self-regulatory code of ethics created in 1930 by the Motion Picture Producers and Distributors of America (MPPDA), under Will H. HAYS, and put into strict effect on July 1, 1934, with Joseph I. Breen as director of the Code Administration. The code set forth general standards of "good taste" and specific do's and don't's concerning what could and could not be shown in American movies. Among the general principles of the code was the requirement that "no picture shall be produced which will lower the standards of those who see it. Hence the sympathy of the audience should never be thrown to the side of crime, wrongdoing, evil or sin."

The specific regulations included the following typical examples: "Revenge in modern times shall not be justified"; "Methods of crime shall not be explicitly presented"; "Illegal drug traffic must never be presented"; "The sanctity of the institution of marriage and the home shall be upheld. Pictures shall not infer that low forms of sex relationships are the accepted or common thing"; "Scenes of passion should not be introduced when not essential to the plot"; "Excessive and lustful kissing, lustful embracing, suggestive postures and gestures, are not to be shown"; "Seduction or rape should be never more than suggested. . . . They are never the proper subject for comedy"; "Sex perversion or any inference to it is forbidden"; "Miscegenation (sex relationships between the white and black races) is forbidden"; "Sex hygiene and venereal diseases are not subjects for motion pictures"; "Children's sex organs are never to be exposed"; "Pointed profanity (this includes the words God, Lord, Jesus, Christ—unless used reverently—Hell, S.O.B., damn, Gawd), or other profane or vulgar expressions, however used, is forbidden"; "Indecent or undue exposure is forbidden"; "Ministers of religion. . . should not be used as comic characters or as villains."

As compared with its strict language regarding the treatment of sex, the code was lenient on the presentation of violence, requiring only that "actual hangings or electrocutions. . . brutality and possibly gruesomeness. . . be treated within the careful limits of good taste." In any case, the Production Code, modified only slightly over the years, had a profound and far-reaching effect on American cinema. Its seal of approval was denied any film that did not meet its morality standards, a risk few producers dared take. Only occasionally would the effectiveness of the Production Code Seal be tested by such producers as Howard Hughes (*The Outlaw*) and Otto Preminger (*The Moon Is Blue*). But the pressure of social change, Supreme Court decisions concerning obscenity, and civil liberties groups, brought a sweeping revision in the code in 1966. The new code still paid tribute to virtue and condemned sin but suggested restraint in treating sexual themes on the screen, rather than forbidding them outright, and corrected the balance by forbidding explicit detail of violence and brutality. In 1968 a RATING system was put into effect, classifying films according to their suitability for viewing by the young.

production designer. See ART DIRECTOR.

production manager. See UNIT PRODUCTION MANAGER.

production track. The sound recorded during the actual filming of a scene. Consisting mainly of dialogue, it is also called the DIALOGUE TRACK.

programmer. In motion picture trade jargon, a run-of-the-mill film, usually a B picture of limited commercial appeal deserving only routine exploitation.

projection booth. A compartment in a movie theater from which the picture is projected onto the screen.

projectionist. The person who operates a motion picture projector.

projection printer. See OPTICAL PRINTER.

projection sync. The spacing between a picture and its corresponding sound track in a composite print, made necessary by the stagger between the picture gate and the sound head in a sound PROJECTOR. Since film is driven through the picture gate by intermittent movement and through the sound head by continuous movement, the picture gate and the sound head must be separated from each other at some distance. This spacing must be accounted for when a sound track is printed on the same film that carries the picture. In 35 mm film, the sound track is set 20 frames ahead of the picture; in 16 mm, 26 frames.

projector. An apparatus for throwing images on a screen. When a succession of such images is projected at a rapid enough rate, the illusion of motion pictures is created because of a physical phenomenon known as PERSISTENCE OF VISION. That rate is 24 f.p.s. (frames per second) for sound films and 16 f.p.s. for silent films. During projection, the film is transported from a feed reel to a take-up reel over a number of sprocket wheels that engage the film's perforations. As each frame approaches the projector's aperture—known as the "picture GATE"—it is guided into precise position by pins or claws whose stop-and-go intermittent movement causes each frame to remain momentarily still at the aperture while it is being illuminated by a light beam. As soon as the individual frame has been projected, a shutter closes and prevents the light from spilling through the gate until the next frame is moved into position for projection.

In sound projection, the film must also travel on through a sound head, which is positioned forward of the corresponding picture gate by the length of 20 frames in 35 mm and 26 frames in 16 mm equipment. The movement of the film through the sound head is continuous rather than intermittent. At the sound head, a narrow light beam from an exciter lamp is focused on the passing sound-track area of the film. The variable patterns on the track determine the amount of light that is allowed to fall on a photoelectric cell. The resultant electric impulses pass through an amplifier, where they are converted into sound waves, which are transmitted as audible sound through the theater's loudspeakers.

The standard 35 mm projector in motion picture theaters is equipped with an arc lamp of up to 11,000 watts of illumination. The level of illumination required to produce a bright picture is determined largely by the size of the screen. The reel capacity of the standard theater projector is 2,000 feet of film, allowing approximately 20 minutes of continuous projection (this is known as a double reel; the unit of measurement is usually a single reel of 1,000 feet running approximately ten minutes). To avoid the necessity of stopping the show to rethread the projector every 20 minutes, at least two projectors are used in most motion picture theaters. While one projector is operating, the other is at a standby position, threaded and ready for use. A series of cue marks on successive frames toward the end of the reel alert the projectionist, who immediately proceeds to execute a change-over from one machine to another. While the second machine is in operation, he rewinds the film on the first, replaces it, and threads the new reel for the next changeover. Changeovers in modern equipment are now made automatically or semiautomatically. Fully automated projection booths, some with a capacity of four and a half hours of continuous programming, came increasingly into use in American theaters in the late 70s, virtually eliminating the need for full-time projection personnel.

Prokofiev, Sergei. Composer. *b.* Apr. 11, 1891, Sontzovka, Russia. *d.* 1953. A leading figure in 20th-century symphonic music, he contributed several scores to Soviet cinema. His collaboration with Eisenstein (*Alexander Nevsky, Ivan the Terrible*) was most notable for the creative counterpoint the two men achieved between the visual image and the accompanying musical score.

FILMS: *Lieutenant Kije* 1934; *Queen of Spades* 1936; *Alexander Nevsky* 1938; *Kotovsky, Lermontov* 1943; *Ivan the Terrible* (Pt. I, II) 1944, 1946; *Romeo and Juliet* (from his ballet music) 1955; *Cinderella* (from his ballet music) 1961; *Romeo and Juliet* (from his ballet music; UK) 1966.

Promio, A. French cameraman. *b.* 1870(?). *d.* 1927. Chief cameraman of Louis LUMIÈRE, he is credited by some with the first TRAVELING SHOT, photographed from a moving gondola in Venice in 1896.

property. 1. See PROPS. 2. A novel, play, short story, or any other written work bought or optioned by a motion picture studio with the intention of adapting it to the screen.

prop man. Short for "property man." The person responsible for the availability, maintenance, and placement of all props on a set. In the studio vernacular, he is often simply called "props."

props. 1. An abbreviated term for properties: furnishings, fixtures, decorations, or any other movable items that are seen or used on a motion picture (or stage) set but that are not structurally parts of the set. A property department or supply house manufactures, stores, and catalogs an enormous variety of props, from standard pistols to huge, mechanized, custom-made contraptions of great complexity. 2. An abbreviated term for "prop man."

Prosky, Robert. Actor. Born on Dec. 13, 1930, in Philadelphia, Pa. *ed.* Temple Univ. Dependable character actor of screen and TV. After winning a TV talent contest, he studied under scholarship at New York's American Theatre Wing and acted for over 20 years with Arena Stage in Washington, D.C., and later on Broadway, where he earned two Tony nominations. He made his film debut in 1981.

FILMS INCLUDE: *Thief* 1981; *Hanky Panky, Monsignor* 1982; *Christine, The Lords of Discipline, The Keep* 1983; *The Natural* 1984; *Big Shots, Outrageous Fortune, Broadcast News* 1987; *Things Change, The Great Outdoors* 1988; *Loose*

Cannons, Funny About Love, Green Card, Gremlins 2: The New Batch 1990; *Far and Away, Hoffa* 1992; *Last Action Hero, Mrs. Doubtfire* 1993; *Miracle on 34th Street* 1994; *Dead Man Walking, The Scarlet Letter* 1995; *The Chamber* 1996.

Protazanov, Yakov. Director. *b.* Feb. 4, 1881, Moscow. *d.* 1945. A prolific, energetic, sure-handed filmmaker, he began his career in 1905 as an actor, then directed more than 40 Russian films between 1909 and 1917. Many of these were grand-scale historical panoramas and literary adaptations, often starring Ivan MOZHUKHIN. Protazanov continued his activity in Soviet films during and after the October Revolution with the exception of the early 20s, which he spent working in France. His *Aelita* (1924) is the Soviet cinema's first science-fiction film. Other career landmarks included *Keys to Happiness* (1913), *War and Peace* (1915), *The Queen of Spades* (1916), *Father Serqius* (1919), *The Forty-First* (1927), and his last film, *Nasreddin in Bukhara* (1943). He often collaborated on his films' scripts.

FILMS INCLUDE: *The Fountain of Bakhchisrai, The Death of Ivan the Terrible* 1909; *A Night in May* 1910; *The Prisoner's Song* (1911); *Anfisa, Departure of a Grand Old Man* 1912; *Keys to Happiness* (co-dir.), *The Shattered Vase, How Fine How Fresh the Roses Were, Honoring the Russian Flag, A Chopin Nocturne* 1913; *Love, Dance of the Vampire, The Devil, Guardian of Virtue* 1914; *War and Peace* (co-dir.), *Plebeian, Nikolai Stavrogin* 1915; *Sin* (co-dir.), *The Queen of Spades, House of Death, Woman with a Dagger* 1916; *Public Prosecutor, Damned Millions, Andrei Kozhukhov, Satan Triumphant* 1917; *Father Sergius, Parasites of Life* 1918; *The Queen's Secret, The Black Horde* 1919; *Member of Parliament* 1920; *Justice d'Abord* (Fr.) 1921; *Le Sens de la Mort* (Fr.) 1922; *L'Ombre du Péché* (Fr.), *Pour une Nuit d'Amour* (Fr.) 1923; *Aelita* 1924; *Broken Chains/His Call* 1925; *The Case of the Three Million/Three Thieves* 1926; *The Man from the Restaurant, The Forty-First* 1927; *The White Eagle/The Lash of the Czar* 1928; *Ranks and People/An Hour with Chekhov* 1929; *Holiday of St. Jorgen* 1930; *Three Thieves* 1930; *Tommy/ Siberian Patrol* 1931; *Marionettes* 1934; *Without Dowry* 1937; *Salavat Yulayev* 1941; *Nasreddin in Bukhara/Adventures in Bokhara* 1943.

Prouty, Jed. Actor. *b.* Apr. 6, 1879, Boston. *d.* 1956. Light character actor of numerous silent and sound Hollywood films. He began acting on the stage in his teens and is remembered as the bespectacled father in the "Jones Family" comedies of the late 30s.

FILMS INCLUDE: *The Great Adventure, Room and Board, The Conquest of Canaan* 1921; *Kick In* 1922; *Souls for Sale, The Girl of the Golden West, The Gold Diggers* 1923; *The Coast of Folly, The Knockout, The Unguarded Hour* 1925; *Miss Nobody, Don Juan's Three Nights, Everybody's Acting* 1926; *Orchids and Ermine, No Place To Go* 1927; *The Siren, Domestic Meddlers* 1928; *Sonny Boy, The Broadway Melody, Fall of Eve* 1929; *The Floradora Girl, The Devil's Holiday* 1930; *Strangers May Kiss* 1931; *Business and Pleasure* 1932; *Jimmy and Sally* 1933; *Music in the Air* 1934; *George White's Scandals, Black Sheep, Navy Wife* 1935; *Educating Father, Back to Nature, The Texas Rangers* 1936; *Off to the Races, Big Business, 100 Men and a Girl, Life Begins in College, Hot Water* 1937; *A Trip to Paris, Love on a Budget, Safety in Numbers* 1938; *Exile Express, Too Busy to Work, Hollywood Cavalcade* 1939; *Young As You Feel* 1940; *Roar of the Press* 1941; *Mug Town* 1943; *Guilty Bystander* 1950.

Provine, Dorothy. Actress, singer-dancer. Born on Jan. 20, 1937, in Deadwood, S. Dak. Capable, attractive leading lady. She had more rewarding parts on TV as co-star of the series 'The Alaskans' (1959–60) and especially 'The Roaring Twenties' (1960–62). She retired from the screen after her 1969 marriage to cinematographer Robert DAY.

FILMS INCLUDE: *Live Fast Die Young, The Bonnie Parker Story* (title role) 1958; *The 30-Foot Bride of Candy Rock* 1959; *Wall of Noise, It's a Mad Mad Mad Mad World* 1963; *Good Neighbor Sam* 1964; *The Great Race, That Darn Cat* 1965; *One Spy Too Many, Se tutte le Donne del Mondo/Kiss the Girls and Make Them Die* (It./US), *Who's Minding the Mint?* 1967; *Never a Dull Moment* 1968.

Prowse, Juliet. Dancer, actress. *b.* Sept. 25, 1936, in Bombay. *d.* 1996. Brought up in South Africa. Long-limbed leading lady of stage, TV, and films. In addition to several features, she starred in her own TV series, 'Mona McCluskey' (1965–66). In 1989 she narrowly escaped death when she was mauled by a leopard during rehearsals for the CBS-TV special 'Circus of the Stars.'

FILMS INCLUDE: *Gentlemen Marry Brunettes* 1955; *Can-Can, G.I. Blues* 1960; *The Fiercest Heart, The Right Approach, The Second Time Around* 1961; *Who Killed Teddy Bear?, Dingaka* 1965; *Run for Your Wife* 1966; *Spree* 1967.

Pryce, Jonathan. Actor. Born on June 1, 1947, in North Wales. Versatile, offbeat, enormously talented performer of the British and American stage and screen. He studied art before winning a scholarship to RADA. After graduating in 1972, he joined the Liverpool Everyman Theatre. In 1975 he enjoyed great success in Nottingham and London in 'Comedians,' later winning a Tony Award for repeating the role on Broadway. He appeared to advantage in several unusual films, most notably Terry GILLIAM's *Brazil* (1985). Pryce was at the center of a controversy in 1990 when Actors Equity objected to having Pryce, a non-Asian, play a Eurasian pimp in the Broadway production of 'Miss Saigon,' a role he had played in London. The union backed down after the producer threatened to cancel the show.

FILMS: *Voyage of the Damned* 1976; *Breaking Glass, Loophole* 1980; *Praying Mantis* 1982; *Something Wicked This Way Comes* (US), *The Ploughman's Lunch* 1983; *Brazil, The Doctor and the Devils* 1985; *Haunted Honeymoon* (US), *Jumpin' Jack Flash* (US) 1986; *Hotel London, Man on Fire* (It./Fr.) 1987; *Consuming Passions* 1988; *Adventures of Baron Munchausen, The Rachel Papers* 1989; *Glengarry Glen Ross* (US) 1992; *The Age of Innocence* (US) 1993; *A Business Affair, Deadly Advice, Great Moments in Aviation History, Shopping* 1994; *Carrington* 1995; *Evita* 1996.

Pryor, Richard. Actor, director, screenwriter. Born on Dec. 1, 1940, in Peoria, Ill. Sharp, brash comedy star of American nightclubs, TV, and films. Raised in seedy poverty amidst sleazy pool halls and whorehouses, he dropped out of school at 14 and after working at various menial jobs spent two years with the Army in Germany. He started his career as a stand-up comic in provincial clubs and achieved national fame on TV's 'Ed Sullivan Show' and the 'Tonight Show.' His earthy, profane humor and his amusing characterizations of street-wise blacks—pimps, junkies, and winos—soon earned him great popularity. He made his screen debut in 1968 and played his first important role as Diana Ross's piano man in *Lady Sings the Blues* in 1972. That same year he released his first comedy album, 'That Nigger Is Crazy,' and in 1974 he won an Emmy for best writing, for a Lily Tomlin TV special. He collaborated on the screenplay of Mel Brooks's comedy classic *Blazing Saddles* (1974) and in the late 70s enjoyed growing popularity in films, especially after teaming up with Gene WILDER in *Silver Streak* (1976). In 1980, while preparing to freebase cocaine, Pryor accidentally set himself on fire and received third-degree burns over half his body. After recovering, he mellowed considerably, toning down his incendiary public image as well as his personal life. He was later stricken with multiple sclerosis and was the subject of an outpouring of public and celebrity support. Pryor's third of five aborted marriages was to actress Jennifer Lee. In 1989 he was ordered by a court to pay child support for the two-year-old son of actress Geraldine Mason.

FILMS: *The Busy Body* 1968; *Wild in the Streets* 1969; *The Phynx* 1970; *You've Got to Walk It Like You Talk It or You'll Lose That Beat* 1971; *Dynamite Chicken, Lady Sings the Blues* 1972; *Wattstax, The Mack Hit! Some Call It Loving* 1973; *Blazing Saddles* (co-sc. only), *Uptown Saturday Night* 1974; *Adios Amigo, The Bingo Long Traveling All-Stars and Motor Kings, Car Wash, Silver Streak* 1976; *Greased Lightning, Which Way Is Up?* 1977; *Blue Collar, The Wiz, California Suite* 1978; *Richard Pryor Live in Concert, The Muppet Movie* 1979; *Wholly Moses!, In God We Trust, Stir Crazy* 1980; *Bustin' Loose* (also co-prod., story) 1981; *Richard Pryor Live on the Sunset Strip* (also prod., sc.), *Some Kind of a Hero, The Toy* 1982; *Superman III, Richard Pryor Here and Now* (also dir., sc.) 1983; *Brewster's Millions* 1985; *Jo Jo Dancer Your Life Is Calling* (also dir., prod., co-sc.) 1986; *Critical Condition* 1987; *Moving* 1988; *See No Evil Hear No Evil, Harlem Nights* 1989; *Look Who's Talking Two* (v/o) 1990; *Another You* 1991.

Pryor, Roger. Actor. *b.* Aug. 27, 1901, New York City. *d.* 1974. The son of Arthur Pryor, a well-known bandleader and musician, he made his stage debut in stock at 18 and, after performing with several repertory companies, went to Broadway in 1925. During the 30s and early 40s he played leads in many low-budget films, typically crime melodramas. He fared better in the 40s on radio as a producer, narrator, and host of a number of prestigious network programs and as a trombone player and leader of his own dance band. He retired from show business in 1947 to become an advertising executive. His second wife (1936–42) was Ann SOTHERN.

FILMS INCLUDE: *Moonlight and Pretzels* 1933; *I Like It That Way, Romance in the Rain, Belle of the Nineties, Wake Up and Dream, Lady by Choice* 1934; *Dinky, The Girl Friend, The Case of the Missing Man* 1935; *The Return of Jimmy Valentine, Ticket to Paradise, Missing Girls, Sitting on the Moon* 1936; *The Man They Could Not Hang* 1939; *Fugitive from Justice, The Man with Nine Lives, Glamour for Sale* 1940; *She Couldn't Say No, South of Panama, Bullets for O'Hara, Gambling Daughters, The Officer and the Lady* 1941; *Meet the Mob* 1942; *Thoroughbreds* 1944; *The Kid Sister, Scared Stiff* 1945.

Pszoniak, Wojciech. Actor. Born on May 2, 1942, in Lvov, Poland. One of Eastern and Central Europe's most prominent contemporary stage and screen performers, famous for his portrayal of complex, ambivalent characters. On the stage from the mid-60s, he made his screen debut in 1970 and achieved distinction in the films of Andrzej WAJDA, notably *The Promised Land* (1975) and *Danton* (as Robespierre, 1982).

FILMS INCLUDE: *Angel Face* 1970; *The Devil, Pilatus und Andere/Pilate and Others* (Ger.), *The Wedding* 1972; *The Nest, Condemned* 1974; *The Promised Land* 1975; *The Shadow Line* 1976; *Recollection, The Gorgonow Affair* 1977; *The Golem, Die Blechtrommel/The Tin Drum* (Ger.), *Aria for Athletes* 1979; *Olimpiada 40* 1980; *The Window, A Quiet Place, Austeria, Daimler-Benz Limousine* 1981; *Danton* (as Robespierre; Fr./Pol.), *The Art of Acting* 1982; *La Diagonale du Fou/Dangerous Moves* (Fr.) 1984; *Bitterre Ernte/Angry Harvest* 1985; *Je hais les Acteurs/I Hate Actors!* (Fr.) 1986; *Venezia Rosso Sanque/Venice Blood Red* (as Vivaldi; It./Fr.) 1989; *Korczak* 1990; *Gawin* (Fr.) 1991; *Mad Dog Time* 1996.

Ptushko, Alexander. Director. *b.* Apr. 6, 1900, Lugansk, the Ukraine. *d.* 1973. *ed.* Plekhanov Institute of Economics. Imaginative and technically gifted creator of filmed fairy tales and children's fiction. He entered Soviet films in 1927 as animator of short puppet films and in 1935 he executed the special effects on Dovzhenko's *Aerograd* and directed *The New Gulliver,* the world's first feature length puppet film. During WW II he worked mostly on special effects, then turned to directing live-action feature films. His *Stone Flower* (1946) was internationally popular and won the Cannes Festival award as best color film. *Sadko* (1953) won a Silver Lion at Venice.

FILMS INCLUDE: *The New Gulliver* 1935; *The Golden Key* 1939; *The Stone Flower* 1946; *Three Encounters* (co-dir. with Yutkevich and Pudovkin) 1948; *Sadko* 1953; *Ilya Murometz* 1956; *The Sword and the Dragon* 1959; *Crimson Sails* 1961; *Tales of Lost Time* 1964; *The Tale of Czar Saltan* 1966.

publicist. In the film industry, a person engaged in the promotion and publicity aspects of a motion picture studio: preparing press releases, planting items in newspapers, tipping off columnists, securing publicity stills, arranging press conferences and special premieres, and generally seeking the greatest exposure for his company's films and stars. The chief publicist of a studio is known as a "publicity director."

publicity still. A still photograph taken before, during, or after the shooting of a film for the purpose of advertising, publicity, and display in motion picture theaters.

Pudovkin, Vsevolod I. Director. *b.* Feb. 6, 1893, Penza, Russia. *d.* 1953. The son of a commercial traveler of peasant stock, he settled with his family in Moscow, where he studied physics and chemistry at the university. His studies were interrupted by the outbreak of WW I, in which he saw action with the artillery. In February of 1915 he was wounded in battle and taken prisoner but managed to escape from a German POW camp early in 1918. Back in Moscow, he returned to chemistry but was drawn by the magic of cinema after seeing Griffith's *Intolerance.* In 1920 he enrolled at Moscow's State Institute of Cinematography, he mixed his film studies with active duties as actor, screenwriter, decorator, and assistant director to the school's co-principals, Ivan Perestiani and Vladimir Gardin. In 1922 he joined KULESHOV's "experimental laboratory" and soon distinguished himself as the teacher's most brilliant pupil and assistant. In 1925 he began working on his first assignment as director, the scientific documentary *Mechanics of the Brain,* which was not released until November of 1926, a full year after the release of his two-reel comedy *Chess Fever* and a month after the premiere of his great masterpiece, *Mother.*

With *Mother* and his two subsequent silent films, *The End of St. Petersburg* and *Storm Over Asia/Heir to Genghis Khan,* Pudovkin took his place alongside EISENSTEIN and DOVZHENKO at the summit of Soviet cinema and in the forefront of world cinema. Like Eisenstein's, Pudovkin's basic creative tool was montage. But where Eisenstein juxtaposed separate shots to achieve conflict and collision, Pudovkin used them as building blocks; while the masses were Einstein's collective heroes, Pudovkin's heroes were individuals, sometimes idealized figures, who personified the masses. By emphasizing narrative and characterization, Pudovkin was able to involve his audiences emotionally while driving home the same revolutionary message that Eisenstein approached intellectually.

During the filming of *Mother,* Pudovkin began writing his theoretical pamphlets, which were eventually published as *Film Technique* and *Film Acting* (English translations by Ivor Montagu). Pudovkin's ideas are not the most original or profound, but his observations are keen and clearly explained, and his enthusiasm is contagious. For Pudovkin, separate shots are like separate words, which gain their full meaning in the context of a sentence. A film is not simply "shot" but constructed from a series of images. Filming is not merely a matter of recording events from a neutral perspective but a process of selection of the proper plastic material—what is to be photographed and what excluded, from what angle it should be shot, and at what balance of light and shadow. These and all other considerations involved in the shooting of a scene determine the specific representation of the events taking place before the camera. The difference between an actual event and the manner in which it is portrayed on the screen is what makes cinema an art form.

Pudovkin, who acknowledges Griffith as his master, devotes much of *Film Technique* to the art of editing, which he divides into three categories: (1) The basic process of linking together long, medium, and close-up shots from various angles; (2) the more complex form of cutting parallel action to heighten tension, a form he attributes to Griffith; and (3) "relational cutting," under which he groups various editing devices for achieving special impact. Several of Pudovkin's theoretic ideas were severely tested with the advent of sound. In 1928 he joined Eisenstein and ALEXANDROV in a manifesto advocating audiovisual counterpoint as a basic technique in sound films. Of his sound films, only *Deserter* and *Suvorov* lived up to Pudovkin's reputation. Much of his later work was hampered by the limitations imposed on Soviet film directors by party officials.

In 1935, Pudovkin was injured in an auto accident in which his screenwriter, Nathan Zarkhi, was killed. After a long period of convalescence, Pudovkin returned to filmmaking, in 1938. He was awarded the Stalin Prize in 1941 for *Suvorov* and in 1947 for the 1946 *Admiral Nakhimov.* In 1953 he was decorated with the Order of Lenin.

FILMS: Miscellaneous functions—*In the Days of Struggle* (act.) 1920; *Sickle and Hammer* (asst. dir., act.) 1921; *Locksmith and Chancellor* (co-sc.) 1923; *The Extraordinary Adventures of Mr. West in the Land of the Bolsheviks* (co-sc., asst. dir., art dir., act.) 1924; *The Death Ray* (sc., asst. dir., art dir., act.), *Little Bricks* (act.) 1925; *The Living Corpse* (act., co-edit; Ger./USSR), *The Gay Canary* (act.), *The New Babylon* (cameo) 1929; *Ivan the Terrible* (act.) 1944. As director—*Hunger—Hunger—Hunger* (co-dir., co-sc., act.) 1921; *Chess Fever* (co-dir.) 1925; *Mother/Mother 1905, Mechanics of the Brain* (also sc.) 1926; *The End of St. Petersburg* (also act.) 1927; *Storm Over Asia/The Heir to Genghis Khan* 1928; *A Simple Case/Life Is Beautiful* 1932; *Deserter* 1933; *Victory/Mother and Sons* (co-dir. with Mikhail Doller) 1938; *Minin and Pozharsky* (co-dir. with Doller) 1939; *Twenty Years of Cinema* (compilation film; co-dir. with Esther Shub) 1940; *Suvorov/General Suvorov* (co-dir. with Doller), *Feast at Zhirmunka* (for "Fighting Film Album," a propaganda compilation of newsreels and combat documentaries; co-dir.) 1941; *The Murderers Are Coming* (co-dir., co-sc.) 1942; *In the Name of the Fatherland* (co-dir. with Dimitri Vasiliev) 1943; *Admiral Nakhimov* (also act.) 1946; *Three Encounters* (co-dir. with Sergei Yutkevich and Alexander Ptushko) 1948; *Zhukovsky* (co-dir. with Vasiliev) 1951; *Vasili's Return/The Return of Vasili Bortnikov* 1953.

Puenzo, Luis. Director. Born in 1945(?) in Argentina. Bold filmmaker who achieved international acclaim with his second feature, *The Official Story* (1985), a powerful indictment of the brutality of his country's recent military dictatorship. The low-budget production ($300,000) won an Oscar as the year's best foreign language film, the first Argentine feature to receive an Academy Award. Puenzo was also nominated for best screenplay. Following the relative failure of his American film *Old Gringo* (1989), he returned to Argentina to direct a $14-million internationally sponsored screen adaptation of Albert Camus's *The Plague.*

FEATURE FILMS: *Light of My Shoes* (also prod., sc.) 1973; *La Historia oficial/The Official Story/The Official Version* (also co-sc.) 1985; *Old Gringo* (also co-sc.; US) 1989; *The Plague* (US/Fr./Arg.) 1992.

Puglia, Frank. Actor. *b.* 1892, Sicily. *d.* 1975. Versatile character actor of the American stage, Hollywood films, and TV, he typically portrayed foreigners, sometimes villainous. In Italian opera from age 13. In the US from 1907.

FILMS INCLUDE: *Orphans of the Storm* 1922; *Isn't Life Wonderful?, Romola* 1924; *The Beautiful City* 1925; *The Man Who Laughs* 1927; *Viva Villa!, Men in White* 1934; *Bordertown* 1935; *Garden of Allah* 1936; *When You're in Love, Bulldog Drummond's Revenge* 1937; *Spawn of the North* 1938; *In Old Caliente, Maisie* 1939; *Down Argentine Way, The Mark of Zorro* 1940; *That Night in Rio, Billy the Kid* 1941; *Jungle Book, Now Voyager* 1942; *Casablanca, Action in the North Atlantic, Mission to Moscow, The Phantom of the Opera, For Whom the Bell Tolls* 1943; *Ali Baba and the 40 Thieves* 1944; *Blood on the Sun, A Song to Remember* 1945; *Brute Force, Fiesta, Road to Rio* 1947; *Joan of Arc* 1948; *Bagdad* 1949; *The Black Hand, The Desert Hawk* 1950; *The Caddy* 1953; *The Burning Hills* 1956; *Duel at Apache Wells* 1957; *Cry Tough* 1959; *Girls! Girls! Girls!* 1962; *The Sword of Ali Baba* 1965.

Pullman, Bill. Actor. Born in 1954 in Delphi, N.Y. *ed.* SUNY, U. Mass. Slender, stage-trained supporting actor comfortable in broad comedy and high Hollywood drama.

FILMS INCLUDE: *Ruthless People* 1986; *Spaceballs* 1987; *The Serpent and the Rainbow, Rocket Gibraltar, The Accidental Tourist* 1988; *Cold Feet* 1989; *Sibling Rivalry* 1990; *Bright Angel, Libestraum* 1991; *A League of Their Own, Singles, Newsies* 1992; *Sleepless in Seattle, Malice* 1993; *The Favor, The Last Seduction, Wyatt Earp* 1994; *Casper, Mr. Wrong, While You Were Sleeping* 1995; *Independence Day* 1996; *Lost Highway, The End of Violence* 1997.

Pulver, Liselotte (Lilo). Actress. Born on Oct. 11, 1929, in Berne, Switzerland. Leading lady of German films and European co-productions. Trained for the stage at Berne, she was appearing at a Zurich theater when she was discovered by Leopold LINDTBERG.

FILMS INCLUDE: *Swiss Tour/Four Days' Leave* (Switz./US) 1949; *Föhn* 1950; *Heidelberger Romanze* 1951; *Klettermaxe* 1952; *Ich und Du* 1953; *Uli der Knecht* (Switz.), *Der letzte Sommer* 1954; *Hanussen* 1955; *Les Aventures d'Arsène Lupin* (Fr.) 1956; *Bekenntnisse des Hochstaplers Felix Krull/The Confessions of Felix Krull* 1957; *Das Wirtshaus im Spessart/The Spessart Inn, A Time to Love and a Time to Die* (US), *Le Joueur* (Fr.) 1958; *Helden/Arms and the Man, Buddenbrooks* (as Antonie Buddenbrook) 1959; *Das Glas Wasser/A Glass of Water* (as Queen Anne) 1960; *One Two Three* (US) 1961; *Maléfices/Where the Truth Lies* (Fr.), *Lafayette* (as Marie Antoinette; Fr./It.) 1962; *Monsieur* (Fr./It./Ger.), *A Global Affair* (US) 1964; *La Religieuse/The Nun* (Fr.) 1965; *L'Ombrellone/Weekend Italian Style* (It./Fr./Sp.), *Hokuspokus* 1966; *Pistol Jenny* 1969; *Brot und Steine* (Switz.) 1979.

pup. A small focused light source, usually of 500-watt intensity.

puppets. Dolls with movable limbs that are used in "creature" special effects and in the making of three-dimensional animated films. A puppet typically begins its existence as a sketch in a designer's workshop, then is made into a clay model. Once approved by the producer and director, the model serves as the basis for a working puppet, usually consisting of a flexible armature to which sculpted skin, hair, or clothes are added.

A variety of methods can be used to animate puppets. The oldest method, perfected by *King Kong* creator Willis H. O'BRIEN, is STOP MOTION animation, in which puppets are photographed one frame at a time. Between exposures, the arms, legs, and mouths of the puppets are moved by technicians, creating an illusion of continuous motion. In the modern technique of GO-MOTION, preprogrammed, computer-controlled rods are used to animate the creatures while the camera shutter is open. Classical puppeteering techniques of rods, hands, and marionettes are also sometimes used in film. Actors may be inside a costume that includes puppeteered facial features or appendages.

Animatronic puppets are animated by internal mechanisms, whether cable-actuated, radio-controlled, or computer-controlled. Some are animatronic suits, with a person hidden inside. Large, massive, animatronic puppets are actuated by hydraulic systems. Animatronic puppets may be able to perform motion as broad as the swipe of a tail and as detailed as the furrowing of a brow. Their movements are sometimes governed by Waldos, duplicate puppets or suits with telemetry systems connected to the actual puppet. When a technician physically moves an element of the Waldo, the corresponding part of the actual puppet moves in response. The sequence of motions can be captured by a computer and played back precisely in successive takes.

Most big-budget films with complex puppet effects, such as *E.T., Aliens,* and *Jurassic Park*, use not one but several of the above techniques to create their magic. A single creature may be filmed using several different puppets—a man in a suit in one shot, a rod-controlled paw in another, a full-size animatronic head and neck in another, a stop-motion miniature in another. COMPUTER-GENERATED images of the creatures may supplement the work of the puppeteers. When done well, all the techniques blend seamlessly, giving the audience no clue as to how a given shot was done.

Purcell, Dick. Actor. *b.* Aug. 6, 1908, Greenwich, Conn. *d.* 1944. *ed.* Fordham. He entered films in 1935, following some stage experience, and subsequently appeared in numerous productions, mostly B features, typically in two-fisted heroic roles but often as a second lead or even a villain. He died of a heart attack at 36.

FILMS INCLUDE: *Doorway to Hell* (bit) 1930; *Ceiling Zero* 1935; *Bullets or Ballots, The Case of the Velvet Claws, King of Hockey* 1936; *Men in Exile, Slim, Alcatraz Island, Navy Blues, Missing Witness* 1937; *The Daredevil Drivers, Over the Wall, Mystery House, Valley of the Giants, Broadway Musketeers, Air Devils, Nancy Drew—Detective* 1938; *Blackwell's Island, Streets of New York* 1939; *New Moon, Arise My Love, The Bank Dick* 1940; *Flight Command, No Hands on the Clock* 1941; *In Old California, Phantom Killer* 1942; *Aerial Gunner, The Mystery of the 13th Guest* 1943; *Captain America* (serial) 1944.

Purdom, Edmund. Actor. Born on Dec. 19, 1924, in Welwyn Garden City, near London. Dashingly handsome leading man of Hollywood films and international co-productions. The son of a drama critic, he made his stage debut in British repertory in 1945 and in December of 1951 appeared on Broadway with Laurence Olivier's company in 'Caesar and Cleopatra' and 'Anthony and Cleopatra.' His dark good looks and resonant voice attracted Hollywood's attention and for several years he starred in sumptuous costume productions of MGM and Fox. But his Hollywood career was short-lived and by the late 50s he was appearing in minor Continental action spectacles. His third wife (1962–63) was actress Linda CHRISTIAN.

FILMS INCLUDE: *Titanic, Julius Caesar* (as Strato) 1953; *The Student Prince* (title role), *The Egyptian, Athena* 1954; *The Prodigal* (title role), *The King's Thief* 1955; *Strange Intruder* 1956; *Agguato a Tangieri/Trapped in Tangiers* (It./Sp.) 1957; *Erode il Grande/Herod the Great* (It./Fr.) 1958; *I Cosacchi/The Cossacks* (It./Fr.) 1959; *Moment of Danger/Malaga* (UK), *Les Nuits de Raspoutine/The Night They Killed Rasputin* (as Rasputin; Fr./It.), *La Furia dei Barbari/Fury of the Pagans* (It.) 1960; *Solimano il Conquistatore/Suleiman the Conqueror* (as Ibrahim Pasha; It.), *L'Ultimo dei Vichinghi/Last of the Vikings* (It./Fr.) 1961; *L'Ammutinamento/White Slave Ship* (It./Fr.), *Lafayette* (as Silas Deane; Fr./It.), *Nefertite—Regina del Nilo/Queen of the Nile* (It.) 1962; *The Comedy Man* (UK) 1963; *The Beauty Jungle/Contest Girl* (UK), *The Yellow Rolls-Royce* (UK) 1964; *L'Uomo che ride/The Man Who Laughs* (It.) 1965; *House of Freaks* (It.) 1973; *Perche?!* (It.), *Povero Cristo* (It.), *Night Child* (UK/It.) 1975; *Il Padrone della Città/Mr. Scarface* 1976; *Safari Cannibal* 1981; *Pieces* (Sp./PR) 1982; *Ator the Fighting Eagle* 1983; *Don't Open Till Christmas* (also dir.; UK), *After the Fall of New York* (It./Fr.) 1984; *Funny Boy* 1987.

Purviance, Edna. Actress. *b.* 1894, Lovelock, Paradise Valley, Nev. *d.* 1958. Charlie CHAPLIN's leading lady in many of his silent films. A San Francisco secretary, she was picked by Chaplin in 1915 to replace Mabel Normand. Purviance starred in nearly all his films through 1923, when their relationship became strained. Chaplin chose another leading lady for *The Gold Rush* and, as producer, refused to release *A Woman of the Sea/The Sea Gull,* in which Purviance starred under the direction of Josef von Sternberg. But he kept her under contract and continued paying her a salary. Many years later she was seen briefly as an extra in two of Chaplin's sound films.

FILMS: *A Night Out, The Champion, In the Park, A Jitney Elopement, The Tramp, By the Sea, Work, A Woman, The Bank, Shanghaied, A Night in the Show* 1915; *Burlesque on Carmen, Police, Triple Trouble, The Floorwalker, The Fireman, The Vagabond, The Count, The Pawnshop, Behind the Screen, The Rink* 1916; *Easy Street, The Cure, The Immigrant, The Adventurer* 1917; *A Dog's Life, The Bond, Shoulder Arms* 1918; *Sunnyside, A Day's Pleasure* 1919; *The Kid, The Idle Class* 1921; *Pay Day* 1922; *The Pilgrim, A Woman of Paris* 1923; *L'Education de Prince* (Fr.), *A Woman of the Sea/The Sea Gull* 1926; *Monsieur Verdoux* (extra) 1947; *Limelight* (extra) 1952.

Puttnam, Sir David. Producer, executive. Born on Feb. 25, 1941, in London. A newspaper photographer's son, he dropped out of school at 16 to join an advertising company as a messenger boy. By the time he reached 20 he was handling his own accounts, later starting his own agency to represent Richard Avedon and other successful photographers. He entered movies in the late 60s, initially producing small-budget, trendy films with modest success. After co-producing two of Ken Russell's eccentric screen biographies, Puttnam broke through the box-office barrier as executive producer of Alan Parker's *Bugsy Malone* (1976). He scored an even greater hit as co-producer of Parker's *Midnight Express* (1978), a film nominated for a best picture Oscar. He won the best picture Academy Award for *Chariots of Fire* (1981) and went on to produce other Oscar-nominated British films such as *The Killing Fields* (1984) and *The Mission* (1986). His growing reputation as a judge of talent (directors Ridley Scott, Hugh Hudson, and Adrian Lyne made their first films for him) and strict enforcer of tight budgets and schedules led in August of 1986 to Puttnam's appointment as chairman and chief executive officer of Columbia Pictures, then a division of Coca Cola. He hoped and promised to deliver quality pictures at reasonable cost, while revamping the studio's inflated salary structure and holding down the increasingly outrageous fees for directors and stars. But Puttnam's candor and no-nonsense style were no match for the entrenched, wasteful practices of the Hollywood system. After 13 months of effort, Puttnam resigned in disgust. He returned to London, where in September of 1988 he announced a $50-million joint Anglo-American-Japanese venture to produce several films for distribution by Warner Bros. In 1989, he was appointed chairman of ITEL International TV Distribution.

FILMS INCLUDE (as producer or executive producer, alone or in collaboration): *Melody/S.W.A.L.K.* 1971; *The Pied Piper* 1972; *Swastika* (doc.) 1973; *That'll Be the Day, Mahler, The Final Programme/The Last Days of Man on Earth* 1974; *Stardust, Brother Can You Spare a Dime?* (doc.), *James Dean—The First American Teenager* (doc.), *Lisztomania* 1975; *Bugsy Malone* 1976; *The Duellists* 1977; *Midnight Express* 1978; *Foxes* 1980; *Chariots of Fire* 1981; *Local Hero, Experience Preferred But Not Essential* 1983; *Secrets, P'tang Yang Kipperbang/Kipperbang, The Killing Fields, Cal, Those Glory Glory Days, Forever Young* (UK) 1984; *The Frog Prince/French Lesson* (UK) 1985; *Defense of the Realm/Defense of the Realm, Winter Flight, Mr. Love, The Mission* 1986; *Memphis Belle* (UK) 1990; *Meeting Venus* (UK) 1991; *Being Human, War of the Buttons* 1994.

Pyriev, Ivan. Director. *b.* 1901, Kamen, Russia. *d.* 1968. Following military service in WW I and the Civil War, he studied directing at Moscow's Dramatic Arts Institute and in 1923 started his career as a stage actor for Sergei EISENSTEIN. He entered films in 1925 as an assistant director and made his directing debut in 1929. He gained recognition in the USSR and abroad, at first for well-executed comedies and musical films, then for dramas as well, notably several Dostoevski adaptations. He won the Stalin Prize in 1944 for his optimistic WW II propagandistic romance *At Six P.M. After the War.*

FILMS: *Strange Woman/The Other Woman* 1929; *The Functionary* 1930; *Conveyor of Death/Assembly Line of Death* (also co-sc.) 1933; *The Party Card* 1936; *The Rich Bride/Country Bride* 1938; *Tractor Drivers* 1939; *The Loved One* 1940; *Swineherd and Shepherd/They Met in Moscow* 1941; *Secretary of the District Committee/We Will Come Back* 1942; *At 6 P.M. After the War/Six P.M.* 1944; *Tales of the Siberian Land/Song of Siberia/Symphony of Life* (also co-sc.) 1947; *Cossacks of the Kuban* 1949; *We Are All for Peace/Friendship Triumphs/World Festival of Song and Dance* (co-dir. with Jores Ivens; USSR/E. Ger.) 1952; *Test of Fidelity* (also co-sc.) 1954; *The Idiot* (also sc.) 1958; *A Summer to Remember* 1959; *White Nights* (also sc.) 1960; *Our Mutual Friend* (also co-sc.) 1961; *Light of a Distant Star* 1965; *The Brothers Karamazov* (also sc.) 1968.

Q

Quaid, Dennis. Actor, singer, songwriter. Born on April 9, 1954, in Houston, Tex. *ed.* Univ. of Houston. Amiably rakish lead of screen and stage. Son of an electrician, he followed brother Randy QUAID into acting. After gaining attention as the confused teenage cyclist in *Breaking Away* and the sweet-talking detective in *The Big Easy*, he has been cast in a variety of roles that showcase his easy physicality and ability to convey unplanned self-reflection. A musician with the rock band The Electrics, he has portrayed musicians in several films and has composed songs for a number of his films. Formerly married to actress P. J. Soles; now married to Meg RYAN, whom he met on the set of *Innerspace*. They have a son, Jack.

FILMS INCLUDE: *Crazy Mama* 1975; *9/30/55* 1977; *Our Winning Season, Seniors* 1978; *Breaking Away* 1979; *The Long Riders, G.O.R.P* 1980; *All Night Long, The Night the Lights Went Out in Georgia* (also songs), *Caveman* 1981; *Tough Enough* 1982; *The Right Stuff, Jaws 3-D* 1983; *Dreamscape* 1984; *Enemy Mine* 1985; *The Big Easy* (also songs) 1986; *Innerspace, Suspect* 1987; *Everybody's All-American, D.O.A.* 1988; *Great Balls of Fire* 1989; *Come See the Paradise, Postcards from the Edge* 1990; *Wilder Napalm, Undercover Blues, Flesh and Bone* 1993; *Wyatt Earp* 1994; *Hideaway* (co-prod. only), *Something to Talk About* 1995; *Dragonheart* 1996; *Going West in America, Switch Back* 1997.

Quaid, Randy. Actor. Born on Oct. 1, 1950, in Houston, Tex. *ed.* Univ. of Houston. Burly actor effective in both affable and menacing character roles. While still in college, he was cast by director Peter BOGDANOVICH in his *Targets* and *The Last Picture Show*, in which he portrayed a drab would-be suitor of Cybill Shepherd. He has remained active throughout the next two decades, bringing subtlety to often exaggerated roles. Noted for performance as the young Lyndon Johnson in TV drama 'LBJ: The Early Years.' Regular, 'Saturday Night Live' (1985–86), 'Davis Rules.' Brother of Dennis QUAID.

FILMS INCLUDE: *Targets* 1968; *The Last Picture Show* 1971; *What's Up Doc?* 1972; *Paper Moon, Lolly-Madonna XXX, The Last Detail* 1973; *The Apprenticeship of Duddy Kravitz* (Can.) 1974; *Breakout* 1975; *The Missouri Breaks, Bound for Glory* 1976; *The Choirboys* 1977; *Midnight Express* (UK) 1978; *Foxes, The Long Riders* 1980; *Heartbeeps* 1981; *National Lampoon's Vacation* 1983; *The Wild Life* 1984; *The Slugger's Wife, Fool for Love* 1985; *The Wraith, Sweet Country* 1986; *Dear America* (doc.; v/o), *No Man's Land* 1987; *Moving, Caddyshack II* 1988; *Parents, Bloodhounds of Broadway, Cold Dog Soup, Out Cold, National Lampoon's Christmas Vacation* 1989; *Martians Go Home!, Days of Thunder, Quick Change, Texasville* 1990; *Freaked* 1993; *Curse of the Starving Class, Major League II, The Paper* 1994; *Bye Bye Love* 1995; *Independence Day, Kingpin, Last Dance* 1996; *The Flood, Vegas Vacation, Woman Undone* 1997.

Qualen, John. Actor. *b.* John Oleson, on Dec. 8, 1899, in Vancouver, B.C., of Norwegian descent. *d.* 1987. *ed.* Northwestern U. Began acting in tent shows and stock productions, to the dismay of his father, a minister, and made his Broadway debut in 'Street Scene,' in 1929. He went to Hollywood two years later to repeat his role in the screen version of the play and subsequently appeared in more than 100 films, portraying a variety of character roles, often as a well-meaning patsy and occasionally with a Norwegian accent. He played the father of the Dionne Quintuplets in several films that featured the little celebrities in the late 30s. He appeared on countless TV programs.

FILMS INCLUDE: *Street Scene, Arrowsmith* 1931; *Counsellor-at-Law* 1933; *Our Daily Bread* 1934; *Black Fury, The Farmer Takes a Wife, The Three Musketeers* (as Planchet) 1935; *The Country Doctor, Meet Nero Wolfe, The Road to Glory, Reunion* 1936; *Seventh Heaven* (as the Sewer Rat), *Nothing Sacred* 1937; *Joy of Living, Five of a Kind* 1938; *Stand Up and*

Fight, Four Wives 1939; *His Girl Friday, The Grapes of Wrath* (as Muley Graves), *The Long Voyage Home, Knute Rockne—All American, Angels Over Broadway* 1940; *Out of the Fog, The Shepherd of the Hills, All That Money Can Buy* 1941; *Jungle Book, Larceny Inc., Tortilla Flat, Arabian Nights* (as Aladdin) 1942; *Casablanca* 1943; *The Impostor, Dark Waters, An American Romance* 1944; *Roughly Speaking, River Gang, Captain Kidd* 1945; *Adventure* 1946; *Song of Scheherazade, The Fugitive* 1947; *My Girl Tisa, Hollow Triumph/The Scar* 1948; *The Big Steal* 1949; *The Jackpot, The Flying Missile* 1950; *Goodbye My Fancy* 1951; *Hans Christian Andersen* 1952; *The Student Prince, The High and the Mighty* 1954; *The Searchers* 1956; *The Big Land* 1957; *Anatomy of a Murder* 1959; *North to Alaska* 1960; *Two Rode Together* 1961; *The Man Who Shot Liberty Valance* 1962; *The Prize* 1963; *The Seven Faces of Dr. Lao, Cheyenne Autumn* 1964; *The Sons of Katie Elder, A Patch of Blue* 1965; *A Big Hand for the Little Lady* 1966; *Firecreek* 1968; *Hail Hero!* 1969; *Frasier the Sensuous Lion* 1973.

Quaranta, Lydia (*b.* 1891, Turin, Italy; *d.* 1928) and **Letizia** (*b.* Dec. 30, 1892, Turin). Sister stars of the Italian silent screen. Lydia was the heroine of the monumental *Cabiria* (1914) and starred in many other film spectaculars through 1925. Letizia specialized in comedies and adventure films, often directed by her husband, Carlo Campogalliani. She continued to play, in occasional character parts, in films of the 50s. Letizia's twin sister, Isabella Quaranta, was also in films.

FILMS INCLUDE: Lydia—*I Cavalieri della Morte, Dopo la Battaglia* 1910; *Padre* 1912; *Addio Giovinezza!* 1913; *Cabiria* 1914; *Le Memorie del Diavolo, Il Romanzo di un Atleta* 1915; *Nel Votice del Peccato* 1916; *Gioiello sinistro* 1917; *Notte di Nozze* 1918; *Fiamma* 1919; *I Tre Sentimentali* 1920; *Una Donna passo* 1922; *La Taverna verde* 1924; *Voglio tradire mio Marito* 1925. Letizia—*Idillio campagnolo* 1909; *Addio Giovinezza!, Nerone e Agrippina* 1913; *I Mariti allegri, L'Eterno Romanzo* 1914; *L'Isola tenebrosa* 1916; *L'Ombra che parla* 1918; *La Casa della Paura, Masciste contro la Morte, La Nave dei Morti* 1919; *Tempesta in un Cranio, La Signora delle Miniere* 1920; *La Mujer de Medianoche* (Braz.) 1924; *La Lanterna del Diavolo* 1931; *Musica proibita* 1943; *La Gondola del Diavolo* 1947; *L'Orfana del Ghetto* 1955.

Quayle, Sir Anthony. Actor. *b.* Sept. 7, 1913, in Ainsdale, England. *d.* 1989. *ed.* Rugby; RADA. Authoritative, forceful character lead of the British, and occasionally American, stage and screen. He made his stage debut in 1931 and joined the Old Vic company the following year, making his Broadway bow in 1936. He began directing as well as acting in plays after WW II and from 1948 through 1956 he managed the Shakespeare Memorial Theatre Company of Stratford-on-Avon. His several New York appearances include memorable performances in 'Galileo' (title role) and 'Sleuth.' In 1971 he starred in the short-lived mystery TV series 'The Strange Report.' Despite his heavy theatrical schedule, Quayle appeared in many films from the late 40s, sometimes in the lead but mainly in a supporting capacity. His roles included Colonel Brighton in *Lawrence of Arabia* (1962) and Cardinal Wolsey in *Anne of the Thousand Days* (1969); for the latter performance he was nominated for a best supporting actor Academy Award. He also appeared in TV productions, including the miniseries 'QB VII' (1974). During his six-year WW II service with the Royal Artillery (demobilized a major) he authored two novels, *Eight Hours from England* and *On Such a Night.* He was knighted in 1985.

FILMS INCLUDE: *Hamlet* (as Marcellus), *Saraband for Dead Lovers/Saraband* 1948; *Oh Rosalinda/Fledermaus '55* 1955; *The Battle of the River Plate/Pursuit of the Graf Spee* 1956; *The Wrong Man* (US), *Woman in a Dressing Gown* 1957; *The Man Who Wouldn't Talk, Ice Cold in Alex/Desert Attack* 1958; *Serious Charge/Immoral Charge/A Touch of Hell, Tarzan's Greatest Adventure* 1959; *The Challenge/It Takes a Thief* 1960; *The Guns of Navarone* (UK/US) 1961; *H.M.S. Defiant/Damn the Defiant, Lawrence of Arabia* 1962; *The Fall of the Roman Empire* (US), *East of Sudan* 1964; *Operation Crossbow* (UK/It.), *A Study in Terror* (UK/Ger.) 1965; *The Poppy Is Also a Flower* (UN/US) 1966; *Before Winter Comes, Mackenna's Gold* (US), *Anne of the Thousand Days* (as Cardinal Wolsey) 1969; *Everything You Always Wanted to Know About Sex but Were Afraid to Ask* (US) 1972; *A Bequest to the Nation/The Nelson Affair* (as Lord Minto) 1973; *The Tamarind Seed* 1974; *Moses* (as Aaron; UK/It.), *The Eagle Has Landed* 1976; *Holocaust 2000* (It./UK) 1977; *Sherlock Holmes: Murder by Decree* (UK/Can.) 1979; *The Endless Game* (UK) 1989.

Quedens, Eunice. See ARDEN, Eve.

"queer" cinema. See GAY AND LESBIAN CINEMA.

Queneau, Raymond. Poet, novelist. *b.* Feb. 21, 1903, Le Havre, France. *d.* 1976. *ed.* U. of Paris. A leading figure in French letters, active in the surrealist movement of the 20s and later a highly regarded editor of the Pléiade encyclopedia, he also was involved on and off with films. He directed a short, *Le Lendemain* (1950), wrote scripts and dialogue for a number of films, appeared as an actor in Jean-Pierre Mocky's *Un Couple* (1960), and portrayed Clemenceau in Chabrol's *Landru/Bluebeard* (1962). His novel *Zazie dans le Metro* provided the basis for a delightful film by Louis Malle. His novel *Dimanche de la Vie* was adapted to film in 1967.

FILMS INCLUDE: (as screenwriter or dialogue writer, in collaboration): *Monsieur Ripois/Knave of Hearts* 1954; *La Mort en ce Jardin/Gina/Death in the Garden* 1956; *Amère Victoire/Bitter Victory* 1957; *Un Couple (also act.)* 1960; *Landru/Bluebeard* (act. only, as Clemenceau) 1963.

Quilici, Folco. Documentary filmmaker. Born on Apr. 9, 1930, in Ferrara, Italy. Although trained as a lawyer, he attended a two-year course at the Centro Sperimentale di Cinematografia and later joined expeditions to Africa, South America, and Oceania, which he covered in magazine articles, books, and short and feature-length documentaries. The most successful of the latter were *The Lost Continent* (1954) and *The Last Paradise* (1955), both award winners at international film festivals.

FILMS INCLUDE: *Pinne e Arpioni* (short) 1952; *Troffei d'Africa* (short), *Brazza* (short), *Storia di un Elefante* (short), *Sesto Continento/The Lost Continent/The Sixth Continent/Blue Continent* 1954; *Paul Gauguin* (short), *L'Ultimo Paradiso/The Last Paradise* 1957; *Dagli Appennini alla Ande* 1958; *Ti-Koyo e il suo Pescecane/Tiko and the Shark* 1962; *Le Schiave esistono ancora/Slave Trade in the World Today* (co-dir., with Roberto Malenotti) 1963; *Oceano* 1971; *Orca* (dir. of underwater scenes) 1977.

Quillan, Eddie. Actor. *b.* Mar. 31, 1907, in Philadelphia. *d.* 1990. Light leading man and supporting player of Hollywood films with prominent eyeballs, youthful energy, and a knack for the comic double take. On the vaudeville stage with a family act from the age of seven, he entered films in 1926 and appeared in a number of Mack Sennett two-reelers before making his feature film debut in 1928. He played a mixture of light leads and supporting roles in many Hollywood productions and later also on TV.

FILMS INCLUDE: Shorts—*A Love Sundae, Her Actor Friend* 1926; *The Plumber's Daughters, College Kiddo, The Bullfighter, Love in a Police Station* 1927. Features—*Show Folks* 1928; *Geraldine, Noisy Neighbors, The Godless Girl, The Sophomore* 1929; *Big Money, Night Work* 1930; *Sweepstakes,*

The Tip-Off 1931; *The Big Shot, Girl Crazy* 1932; *Strictly Personal, Broadway to Hollywood* 1933; *Hollywood Party* 1934; *Mutiny on the Bounty* (as Ellison) 1935; *London by Night, Big City* 1937; *Made for Each Other, Young Mr. Lincoln* 1939; *The Grapes of Wrath* (as Connie Rivers), *Margie* 1940; *The Flame of New Orleans* 1941; *Kid Glove Killer* 1942; *Melody Parade* 1943; *Mystery of the River Boat* (serial), *The Impostor, This Is the Life* 1944; *Jungle Queen* (serial), *Song of the Sarong* 1945; *Sensation Hunters* 1946; *Sideshow* 1950; *Brigadoon* 1954; *Promises! Promises!, Move Over Darling* 1963; *The Bounty Killer* 1965; *The Ghost and Mr. Chicken* 1966; *Angel in My Pocket* 1969; *How to Frame a Figg* 1971; *The Strongest Man in the World* (bit) 1975.

Quimby, Fred. American short-subject producer. *b.* 1886. *d.* 1965. A former motion picture theater owner and Pathé executive, he organized MGM's short-feature department, which he headed from 1926 until his retirement in 1956. Developed a number of popular cartoon series, including "Tom and Jerry," and received eight Academy Awards for animated films made under his supervision.

Quine, Richard. Director, former actor. *b.* Nov. 12, 1920, in Detroit. *d.* 1989. An actor's son, he began performing in vaudeville and on radio as a child singer-dancer-actor, making his screen debut at 12. He played supporting parts in films through the 40s, then turned director. His films were often lively and handled intelligently but were rarely original. From 1943 to 1948 he was married to the late Susan PETERS.

FILMS INCLUDE: As actor—*The World Changes, Counselor-at-Law* 1933; *Jane Eyre, Dames, Little Men* 1934; *A Dog of Flanders, Dinky* 1935; *Babes on Broadway* 1941; *My Sister Eileen, For Me and My Gal, Dr. Gillespie's New Assistant* 1942; *We've Never Been Licked* (lead) 1943; *The Cockeyed Miracle* 1946; *Words and Music, Command Decision* 1948; *No Sad Songs for Me, The Flying Missile* 1950. As director (complete)—*Leather Gloves* (co-dir., co-prod. with William Asher) 1948; *Sunny Side of the Street, Purple Heart Diary* 1951; *Sound Off* (also co-sc.), *Rainbow 'Round My Shoulder* (also co-sc.) 1952; *All Ashore, Siren of Bagdad, Cruisin' Down the River* (also co-sc.) 1953; *Drive a Crooked Road* (also co-sc.), *Pushover* 1954; *So This Is Paris, My Sister Eileen* (also co-sc.) 1955; *The Solid Gold Cadillac* 1956; *Full of Life, Operation Mad Ball* 1957; *Bell Book and Candle* 1958; *It Happened to Jane* (also prod.) 1956; *Strangers When We Meet* (also co-prod.), *The World of Suzie Wong* 1960; *The Notorious Landlady* 1962; *Paris When It Sizzles* (also co-prod.), *Sex and the Single Girl* 1964; *How to Murder Your Wife, Synanon* (also prod.) 1965; *Oh Dad Poor Dad Mama's Hung You in the Closet and I'm Feelin' So Sad, Hotel* 1967; *A Talent for Loving* 1969; *The Moonshine War* 1970; *"W"* 1974; *The Prisoner of Zenda* 1978.

Quinlan, Kathleen. Actress. Born on November 19, 1954, in Pasadena, Calif. Stage-trained actress on screen and TV, active since the 1970s. Best known for performance as young schizophrenic in then-graphic 1977 *I Never Promised You a Rose Garden*. Nominated for a supporting actress Academy Award for her performance as Marilyn Lovell in *Apollo 13* (1995).

FILMS INCLUDE: *American Graffiti* 1973; *Lifeguard* 1976; *Airport '77, I Never Promised You a Rose Garden* 1977; *The Promise, The Runner Stumbles* 1979; *Sunday Lovers* (US/UK/Fr./It.) 1981; *Hanky Panky* 1982; *Twilight Zone—The Movie, Independence Day, The Last Winter* (Isr.) 1983; *Warning Sign* 1985; *Wild Thing, Man Outside* 1987; *Sunset, Clara's Heart* 1988; *The Doors* 1991; *Trial By Jury* 1994; *Apollo 13, Perfect Alibi* 1995; *Breakdown, Event Horizon, Zeus and Roxanne* 1997.

Quinn, Aidan. Actor. Born on March 8, 1959, in Chicago, Ill. Lanky lead of screen and television. After spending part of his childhood in Belfast, he returned to Chicago, where he worked as a roofer and became involved in the city's theater. He established himself in the offbeat comedy *Desperately Seeking Susan*, and has since become known not only for his dreamy blue-eyed gaze and languid countenance but for his demonstrated ability to play a range of roles. Noted for performance in one of the first dramas about AIDS, *An Early Frost*.

FILMS INCLUDE: *Reckless* 1984; *Desperately Seeking Susan* 1985; *The Mission* 1986; *Stakeout* 1987; *Crusoe* 1988; *The Handmaid's Tale, The Lemon Sisters* 1989; *Avalon* 1990; *At Play in the Fields of the Lord* 1991; *The Playboys* 1992; *Benny & Joon* 1993; *Blink, Legends of the Fall, Mary Shelley's Frankenstein* 1994; *The Stars Fell on Henrietta* 1995; *Michael Collins* 1996; *Commandments* 1997.

Quinn, Anthony. Actor. Born on Apr. 21, 1915, in Chihuahua, Mexico, of Irish-Mexican parentage. In the US from childhood, he entered films in 1936 after brief stage experience. The following year he married Cecil B. De Mille's adopted daughter, Katherine (divorced 1965), but his father-in-law did nothing to advance his career and Quinn continued playing bit and supporting parts through the 40s, usually as a foreign heavy or ferocious Indian. His career picked up dramatically in the 50s following a sabbatical on Broadway, where he appeared as Stanley Kowalski in 'A Streetcar Named Desire.' He has won two Academy Awards for best supporting actor (*Viva Zapata,* 1952, and *Lust for Life,* 1956) and began playing leading parts in films that emphasized his earthiness and brute masculinity. Several of these were filmed in Europe, notably Fellini's *La Strada,* in which Quinn was memorable as Zampano. In 1958 he attempted a switch to directing, but his *Buccaneer* was a resounding failure. His acting career reached a new peak in the 60s with such films as *Requiem for a Heavyweight* and *Zorba the Greek.* He has appeared in some 100 films, at times coming up with truly remarkable performances but too often indulging in hammed-up variations on his favorite role: himself as a mystic life force. He disappeared from the silver screen throughout much of the 80s, but returned with character roles in several films, most notably Spike Lee's *Jungle Fever* (1991). In the early 1970s he starred in the TV series 'The Man and the City.' The father of actors Francesco, Valentina, and Danielle Quinn, he renewed his reputation for masculinity by again becoming a father, this time of an illegitimate child, when in his late 70s. Autobiography: *The Original Sin* (1972).

FILMS: *Parole!, Sworn Enemy, Night Waitress* 1936; *The Plainsman, Swing High Swing Low, Waikiki Wedding, The Last Train from Madrid, Partners in Crime, Daughter of Shanghai* 1937; *The Buccaneer, Dangerous to Know, Tip-Off Girls, Hunted Men, Bulldog Drummond in Africa, King of Alcatraz* 1938; *King of Chinatown, Union Pacific, Island of Lost Men, Television Spy* 1939; *Emergency Squad, Road to Singapore, Parole Fixer, The Ghost Breakers, City for Conquest, Texas Rangers Ride Again* 1940; *Blood and Sand, Knockout, Thieves Fall Out, Bullets for O'Hara, They Died with Their Boots On* (as Chief Crazy Horse), *The Perfect Snob* 1941; *Larceny Inc., Road to Morocco, The Black Swan* 1942; *The Ox-Bow Incident, Guadalcanal Diary* 1943; *Buffalo Bill, Roger Touhy—Gangster, Ladies of Washington, Irish Eyes Are Smiling* 1944; *China Sky, Where Do We Go from Here?, Back to Bataan* 1945; *California, Sinbad the Sailor, The Imperfect Lady, Black Gold, Tycoon* 1947; *The Brave Bulls, Mask of the Avenger* 1951; *Viva Zapata!* (as Eufemio Zapata), *The Brigand, The World in His Arms, Against All Flags* 1952; *City Beneath the Sea, Seminole* (as Chief Osceola), *Ride Vaquero, East of Sumatra, Blowing Wild*

1953; *Ulisse/Ulysses* (as Antinous; It.), *Cavalleria Rusticana/Fatal Desire* (as Alfio; It.), *Donne Proibite/Angels of Darkness* (It.), *Attila* (title role; It./Fr.), *La Strada* (It.), *The Long Wait* 1954; *The Magnificent Matador, The Naked Street, Seven Cities of Gold* 1955; *Lust for Life* (as Paul Gauguin), *Man from Del Rio, The Wild Party, Notre Dame de Paris/The Hunchback of Notre Dame* (as Quasimodo; Fr.) 1956; *The River's Edge, The Ride Back, Wild Is the Wind* 1957; *Hot Spell, The Buccaneer* (dir. only), *The Black Orchid* 1958; *Warlock, Last Train from Gun Hill* 1959; *Heller in Pink Tights, Ombre Bianche/Les Dents du Diable/The Savage Innocents* (It./Fr./UK), *Portrait in Black* 1960; *The Guns of Navarone* (UK/US), *Barabba/Barabbas* (title role; It.) 1961; *Requiem for a Heavyweight, Lawrence of Arabia* (UK) 1962; *Behold a Pale Horse, Der Besuch/The Visit* (Ger./Fr./It./US), *Zorba the Greek* (title role; Gr./US) 1964; *A High Wind in Jamaica* (UK/US), *La Fabuleuse Aventure de Marco Polo/Marco the Magnificent* (as Kublai Khan; Fr./It./Eg./Afgan.) 1965; *Lost Command* 1966; *La 25e Heure/The 25th Hour* (Fr./It./Yug.), *The Happening, L'Avventuriero/The Rover* 1967; *La Bataille de San Sebastian/Guns for San Sebastian* (Fr./It./US/Mex.), *The Shoes of the Fisherman, The Magus* (UK) 1968; *The Secret of Santa Vittoria, A Dream of Kings* 1969; *A Walk in the Spring Rain, R.P.M., Flap* 1970; *The City* (initially a TV pilot) 1971; *Across 110th Street* 1972; *Los Amigos/Deaf Smith and Johnny Ears* (Sp./It.), *The Don Is Dead* 1973; *The Marseille Contract/The Destructors* (UK) 1974; *Eredità Ferramonti/The Inheritance* (It.), *Bluff/High Rollers* (It.), *The Message/Mohammad Messenger of God* (UK), *Tigers Don't Cry* (S. Afr.) 1976; *The Greek Tycoon* (as a thinly disguised Aristotle Onassis), *The Children of Sanchez* (US/Mex.) 1978; *Caravans, The Passage, Omar Mukhtar—Lion of the Desert* 1979; *Revenge, Ghosts Can't Do It* 1990; *A Star for Two, Only the Lonely, Jungle Fever, Mobsters* 1991; *Last Action Hero* 1993; *A Walk in the Clouds* 1995; *Somebody To Love, Seven Servants* 1996.

Quirk, Billy (William). An American actor. *b.* 1881. *d.* 1926. Very popular, debonair star of early comedies of the American silent screen. In films from 1909, he started out as Mary Pickford's co-star in a series of early D. W. Griffith films. He reached a peak of popularity around 1915 as the co-star of Constance TALMADGE, but following a sudden decline in his acting career and a brief unhappy stab at directing, he suffered a breakdown and, in 1920, attempted suicide. He subsequently returned to films in minor supporting roles.

FILMS INCLUDE: *A Sound Sleeper, Sweet and Twenty, They Would Elope, His Wife's Visitor, The Little Darling, 1776 or The Hessian Renegades, The Gibson Goddess, The Test* 1909; *The Woman from Mellon's, A Rich Revenge, An Affair of Hearts, Muggsy's First Sweetheart, Muggsy Becomes a Hero* 1910; *Parson Sue, Hubby Does the Washing, Algie the Minor, The Animated Bathtub, Fra Diavolo, The Blood Stain* 1912; *Billy Fools Dad, Billy's Troubles* 1913; *The Arrival of Josie, In Bridal Attire, Father's Timepiece, The Egyptian Mummy* 1914; *Billy's Wager, The Green Cat, The Young Man Who Figgered, A Study in Tramps, Master of His House, The Boarding House Feud, The Vanishing Vault, Spades Are Trump, Bertie's Strategem* 1915; *The Old Maid's Baby* (dir. only), *Sawdust Doll* (dir. only), *The Devil's Trail* (dir. only) 1919; *At the Stage Door* 1921; *My Old Kentucky Home* 1922; *The Glimpses of the Moon, Success, Salomy Jane, Broadway Broke* 1923; *The Dixie Handicap* 1925.

"quota quickies." A rash of low-budget, low-quality films produced in Britain in the late 20s through the 30s in order to meet the requirements of the 1927 Cinematograph Act. This act of Parliament stipulated that a certain percentage (about 30 percent) of motion pictures shown on local screens must be made in the United Kingdom. Although the intent of the act was to encourage British film production, the consequences hindered rather than advanced the development of quality British cinema.

R

R. See RATING.

Rabal, Francisco. Actor. Born Francisco Valera, on Mar. 8, 1925, in Aguilas, Spain. Discovered by a director while working as an electrician on a studio set, he developed into one of the leading personalities of Spanish films and international co-productions. Memorable in several Buñuel films, notably in the title role in *Nazarin* (1959). In 1984 he shared the best actor prize at Cannes for *The Holy Innocents.*

FILMS INCLUDE: *La Prodiga* 1945; *Luna de Sangre* 1952; *El Beso de Judas* 1954; *El Canto del Gallo* 1955; *La Grande Strada azzurra* (It.), *Gerusalemme liberata/The Mighty Crusades* (as Tankred; It.) 1957; *Nazarin* (Mex.), *Sonatas* 1959; *La Mano en la Trampa/The Hand in the Trap* (Arg./Sp.), *Viridiana* (Sp./Mex.) 1961; *Fra Diavolo, Mathias Sandorf, L'Eclisse/Eclipse* (It./Fr.) 1962; *Le Gros Coup* (Fr.), *Maria Rosa* 1964; *España insolita, La Religieuse/The Nun* (Fr.) 1965; *Le Streghe/The Witches* (It./Fr.), *Belle de Jour* (Fr./It.) 1967; *El Che Guevara* (title role; It.), *Cervantes/The Young Rebel* (Sp./Fr./It.) 1968; *Ann and Eve* (Sw.) 1970; *Pianeta Venera* (It.) 1972; *Corruzione al Palazzo di Giustizia/Counselor at Crime* (It.) 1974; *The Devil Is a Woman* (UK/It.) 1975; *Las Largas Vacaciones del '36, Le Desert des Tartares* (Fr./It./Iran) 1976; *Sorcerer* (US) 1977; *Corleone* (It.), *Coi come sei/Come As You Are* (It./Sp.) 1978; *Incubo sulla Città contaminata/City of the Walking Dead/Nightmare City* (It.) 1980; *El Tesoro de las Cuatro Coronas/Treasure of the Four Crowns* 1982; *La Colmena, Epiloqo* 1983; *Un Delitto* (It.), *Los Santos Inocentes/The Holy Innocents, Los Zancos* 1984; *Padre Nuestro* (Sp.), *Marbella* 1985; *Un Complicato Intriqo di Donne Vicoli e Delitti/Camorra* (It.) 1986; *La storia/History* (It./Fr./Sp.), *Divinas Palabras* 1987; *A Time of Destiny* (US) 1988; *Manuel* (Can.) 1989; *Atame!/Tie Me Up! Tie Me Down!* 1990; *La Blanca Paloma/The White Dove* 1991; *Airbag* 1997.

Rabe, David. Playwright, screenwriter. Born on Mar. 10, 1940, in Dubuque, Iowa. *ed.* Loras Coll. A former bellhop, parking-lot attendant, and teacher, he began writing feature articles for the *New Haven Register* in 1969. He won an Obie Award for his first off-Broadway play, 'The Basic Training of Pavlo Hummel' (1971) and a Tony for his first Broadway play, 'Sticks and Bones' (1972). After his 1979 marriage to film actress Jill CLAYBURGH he turned to screenwriting.

FILMS: *I'm Dancing as Fast as I Can* (also exec. prod.)

1982; *Streamers* (from his own play) 1983; *Casualties of War* 1989; *State of Grace* (co-sc.) 1990; *The Firm* (co-sc.) 1993.

Rabier, Jean. Director of photography. Born on Apr. 21, 1927, in Paris. Favorite lighting cameraman of several New Wave directors in the 60s. A former industrial artist, he started out as a camera operator in 1948 and during the 50s worked on many shorts as operator or co-cinematographer. He was Henri DECAË's camera operator on Claude CHABROL's early films (*Le Beau Serge,* 1958; *Les Cousins,* 1959, etc.), then became Chabrol's regular cinematographer and worked for other directors of the French New Wave, like Agnès Varda and Jacques Demy. Rabier is a highly creative cameramen whose exquisite color cinematography established the tone of many of Chabrol's better films.

FILMS INCLUDE: *Les Godelureaux* 1960; *Les Sept Péchés capitaux/Seven Capital Sins* ("Avarice" episode), *L'Oeil du Malin/The Third Lover, Cléo de 5 à 7/Cleo from 5 to 7* 1962, *Ophélia, Landru/Bluebeard, La Baie des Anges/Bay of the Angels* 1963; *Les Parapluies de Cherbourg/The Umbrellas of Cherbourg. Peau de Banane/Banana Peel* 1964; *Le Bonheur* (co-phot.) 1965; *La Ligne de Démarcation* 1966; *Le Scandale/ The Champagne Murders, La Petite Vertu, La Route de Corinthe/Who's Got the Black Box?* 1967; *Les Biches* 1968; *La Femme Infidèle, Que la Bête meure/This Man Must Die* 1969; *Le Boucher, La Rupture* 1970; *Juste avant la Nuit/Just Before Nightfall* 1971; *Docteur Popoul, La Décade prodigieuse/Ten Days' Wonder* 1972; *Les Noces rouges/Wedding in Blood* 1973; *Nada* 1974; *Une Partie de Plaisir/A Piece of Pleasure* 1975; *Folies Bourgeoises* 1976; *Alice ou la Dernière Fugue/Alice or the Last Escapade* 1977; *Les Liens de Sang* (Fr./Can.), *Violette Nozière/Violette* 1978; *Le Cheval d'Orqeuil/Horse of Pride* 1980; *Le Fantômes du Chapelier/The Hatter's Ghost* 1982; *Poulet au Vinaigre/Cop au Vin* (UK) 1985 *Inspecteur Lavardin* 1986; *Masques, Le Cri du Hibou* 1987; *En Toute Innocence, Une Affaire de Femmes* 1988; *Jours tranquilles à Clichy/Quiet Days in Clichy, Dr. M/Club Extinction* (Ger./It./Fr.) 1990; *Madame Bovary* 1991.

race movies. Features with all-black casts made specifically for African-American audiences. The first African-American movies appeared in the silent era, filmed by independent black directors such as Emmett J. Scott, George and Noble Johnson, and Oscar Micheaux, partly in response to the offensive portrayal of blacks in D. W. Griffith's *The Birth of a Nation* (1915). In time, dozens of film companies in numerous cities became involved in producing low-budget films for African-American audiences in segregated theaters. Some of the companies were black-owned, some white-owned; many of the producers, directors, and distributors were also white. While most race movies were low in quality, confining themselves to imitations of Hollywood genres (Westerns, melodramas, musicals, etc.), the films did provide black actors the chance to play something other than the servant roles usually offered by Hollywood, and gave black audiences the chance to see African-Americans portrayed onscreen as heroes and professionals. Financing and distribution problems, along with the growing demands of African-Americans for equality, brought the era of race movies to a close by the end of the 1940s.

rack. 1. A framelike stand for hanging strips of film over a bin in the cutting room. 2. A device for winding film during processing. 3. The act of threading film in a viewing or projection apparatus. 4. The act of aligning a frame with the picture gate of a projector or an editing machine.

Rackin, Martin. Screenwriter, producer, production executive. *b.* July 31, 1918, New York City. *d.* 1976. A former newspaper reporter and feature writer, and later a publicity man and speech writer, he entered films in the early 40s as a screenwriter and began producing in the mid-50s. He was head of production at Paramount from 1960 to 1964, then set up a production company. He died at 58 of an apparent heart attack in London during a business trip.

FILMS INCLUDE: As screenwriter (alone or in collaboration)—*Buy Me That Town* (co-story only) 1941; *Air Raid Wardens, Bombardier* (co-story only) 1943; *Marine Raiders* (co-story only) 1944; *Riff-Raff* 1947; *Fighting Father Dunne, Race Street* 1948; *A Dangerous Profession* 1949; *Three Secrets* 1950; *The Enforcer, Distant Drums* 1951; *Sailor Beware, Loan Shark* 1952; *The Clown, The Stooge* 1953; *Long John Silver* 1955; *Hell on Frisco Bay* 1956; *The Big Land* 1957; *North to Alaska* 1960. As producer—*Santiago* (also co-sc. from own novel) 1956; *Top Secret Affair, The Helen Morgan Story* (co-prod.) 1957; *Darby's Rangers, The Deep Six* 1958; *The Horse Soldiers* (co-prod., co-sc.) 1959; *Stagecoach* 1966; *Rough Night in Jericho* 1967; *Two Mules for Sister Sara* (co-prod.) 1970; *The Revengers* 1972.

rackover. A provision on some high-quality motion picture cameras for shifting the entire film mechanism to one side so that a viewfinder may be brought into position behind the lens for parallax-free viewing. Viewing and filming at the same time cannot be accomplished by this method, and the lens must be racked back before shooting begins.

RADA. Commonly used abbreviation for Britain's Royal Academy of Dramatic Art, a famous London drama school founded in 1904 by Sir Herbert Beerbohm Tree. Many of Britain's finest stage and screen actors have received their training at RADA.

Rademakers, Fons. Director. Born on Sept. 5, 1920, in Roosendael, Holland. Leading Dutch director. A graduate of Amsterdam's Academy of Dramatic Art, he was a stage actor and director before gaining film experience as an assistant to Jean Renoir, Vittorio De Sica, and Charles Crichton. He made his debut as a film director in 1958 and soon gained recognition as one of his country's top filmmakers. His films reveal an interest in human conflict and an insight into psychology. He won the best foreign language film Academy Award for *The Assault* (1986). His wife, Lili Rademakers, is also a filmmaker.

FILMS: *Village on the River/Dotir in the Village* 1958; *The Joyous Eve* 1960; *The Knife* 1961; *The Spitting Image/Like Two Drops of Water* 1963; *The Dance of the Heron* 1966; *Mira* 1971; *Because of the Cats* 1973; *Max Havelaar* 1976; *Mysteries* 1978; *My Friend/The Judge's Friend* 1979; *The Assault* (also prod.) 1986; *Diary of an Old Man* 1987; *The Rose Garden* (Ger./US) 1989.

Radford, Basil. Actor. *b.* June 25, 1897, Chester, England. *d.* 1952. Character comedian of the British stage (from 1922) and films, he was memorable in Hitchcock's *The Lady Vanishes* (1938), in which he and Naunton Wayne played a pair of unshakeable Englishmen on a trip abroad. The two later appeared as a team in several other films. Radford played another memorable role, as a pompous British commander in *Whisky Galore/Tight Little Island* (1949). He died of a heart attack.

FILMS INCLUDE: *Barnum Was Right* (US) 1929; *There Goes the Bride* 1932; *Broken Blossoms* 1936; *Jump for Glory/When Thief Meets Thief, Young and Innocent* 1937; *Convict 99, The Lady Vanishes, Climbing High* 1938; *Night Train to Munich/Night Train, The Girl in the News* 1940; *Flying Fortress, Next of Kin* 1942; *Dear Octopus/The Randolph Family, Millions Like Us* 1943; *The Way to the Stars/Johnny in the Clouds, Dead of Night* 1945; *A Girl in a Million, The Captive Heart* 1946; *The Winslow Boy, Quartet* 1948; *Passport to Pimlico, Whisky Galore/Tight Little Island* 1949; *Chance of a Lifetime* 1950; *The Galloping Major, White Corridors* 1951.

Radford, Michael. Director. Born on Nov. 14, 1950, in New Delhi, to British parents. Initially a documentary filmmaker, he turned to features with middling success until 1995 when Miramax released the poetic charmer *Il Postino/The Postman.* Radford's film was nominated for five Academy Awards including best picture, director, screenplay, and a win for original music score.

FILMS: *Van Morrison in Ireland* (doc.) 1981; *Another Time Another Place* (also sc.) 1983; *1984* (also sc.) 1984; *White Mischief* (also co-sc.) 1987; *Il Postino/The Postman* (also co-sc.; Fr./UK) 1995.

Radner, Gilda. Actress. *b.* June 28, 1946, Detroit. *d.* 1989. Bright, popular comedienne of the American stage, TV, and several films. The product of an upper-middle-class Jewish family, she was drawn to comedy from childhood. After graduating from the University of Michigan as an education major, she headed for Toronto, where she started her career with the Second City improvisation group. With another member, John BELUSHI, she later starred in 'The National Lampoon Radio Hour' and 'The National Lampoon Show.' In 1975 she became an original cast member of TV's 'Saturday Night Live,' soon gaining popularity with her parodies of newscasters: Ba Ba Wawa, Emily Litella, and Rosanne Rosanna-Dana. In 1979 she starred on Broadway in 'Gilda Live,' a show that became a film the following year. Radner's first husband (1980–82) was rock guitarist G. E. Smith. Her second, from 1984 till her death of ovarian cancer at 42, was actor Gene WILDER. Memoir: *It's Always Something* (1989).

FILMS: *The Last Detail* (bit) 1973; *Mr. Mike's Mondo Video* 1979; *Gilda Live* (also co-sc.), *First Family* 1980; *Hanky Panky, It Came from Hollywood* 1982; *The Woman in Red* 1984; *Movers and Shakers* 1985; *Haunted Honeymoon* 1986.

Radnitz, Robert B. Producer. Born in 1925, in Great Neck, Long Island, N.Y. *ed.* U. of Virginia. A former college instructor, he wrote scripts for RKO shorts and produced for the Broadway stage before turning to film producing in the early 60s. He has specialized in family films, several of which are noted for their sincerity and child appeal. *Sounder* (1972) was nominated for four Oscars, including best picture. In 1973 Radnitz was hailed for his work by a joint resolution of Congress.

FILMS: *A Dog of Flanders* 1960; *Misty* 1961; *Island of the Blue Dolphins* 1964; *. . . And Now Miguel* 1966; *My Side of the Mountain* 1969; *The Little Ark, Sounder* 1972; *Where the Lilies Bloom* 1974; *Birch Interval, Sounder II* 1976; *A Hero Ain't Nothin' But a Sandwich* 1977; *Cross Creek* 1983.

Radvànyi, Geza von. Director. *b.* Dec. 17, 1907, Kaschau, Hungary. *d.* 1986. Active in various European countries, he is known internationally for only one important film, *It Happened in Europe* (Hung., 1947), inspired by the aftermath of WW II. Most of his other films are routine and tend to be saccharine.

FILMS INCLUDE: *Inferno giallo* (It.) 1942; *Valahol Europaban/Irgendwo in Europa/It Happened in Europe/ Somewhere in Europe* (Hung./Ger.) 1947; *Donne senza Nome/ Women Without Names* (It.) 1949; *L'Etrange Désir de Monsieur Bard* (Fr.) 1953; *Ingrid—Die Geschichte eines Fotomodells* (Ger.), *Mädchen ohne Grenzen* (Ger.) 1955; *Das Schloss in Tirol* (Ger.), *Das Arzt von Stalingrad* (Ger.), *Mädchen in Uniform* (Ger.), *Douze Heures d'Horloge* (Fr.) 1958; *Ein Engel auf Erden/Angel on Earth* (Ger./Fr.) 1959; *Das Riesenrad* (Ger.) 1961; *Onkel Toms Hütte/Uncle Tom's Cabin* (Ger./Fr./It./Yug.) 1965; *Wiener Kongress* (Ger.) 1966; *Circus Maximus* 1980.

Rafelson, Bob. Director. Born on Feb. 21, 1933, in New York City, into a middle-class, Upper West Side, intellectual Jewish family (one of his uncles was playwright-screenwriter Samson RAPHAELSON). He entered TV as a writer, adapting many stage productions for 'The Play of the Week.' He later turned to producing and directing and made his debut as a motion picture director with an inventive rock film, *Head* (1968), featuring the Monkees, a group Rafelson had originally assembled and created for a TV show. He asserted himself as a bright new talent two years later with *Five Easy Pieces,* an original and incisive study of alienation and self-searching, for which he won the best director award from the New York Film Critics. Critics were more divided over but generally pleased with Rafelson's *The King of Marvin Gardens* (1972) and *Stay Hungry* (1976) but were decidedly unimpressed by the director's 1980s incursions into the *film noir* genre, *The Postman Always Rings Twice* (1981) and *Black Widow* (1987). Rafelson is known as an intense, emotionally charged filmmaker. He was fired from the set of *Brubaker* (1980). In the 80s and 90s he has continued to appear in and make films, with middling success.

FILMS: *Head* (also co-prod., co-sc. with Jack Nicholson) 1968; *Five Easy Pieces* (also co-prod., co-story) 1970; *The King of Marvin Gardens* (also prod., co-sc.) 1972; *Stay Hungry* (also co-prod., co-sc.) 1976; *Brubaker* (part-dir., uncredited) 1980; *The Postman Always Rings Twice* (also co-prod.) 1981; *Always* (act. only) 1985; *Black Widow* 1987; *Mountains of the Moon* (also co-sc.) 1990; *Man Trouble* 1992; *Erotic Tales* (co-dir.), *Wed* (sc.) 1994; *Blood and Wine* 1997.

Rafferty, Chips. Actor. *b.* John Goffage, 1909, Australia. *d.* 1971. Australia's best-known screen personality. In films from the late 30s, first as a tall (6' 6") and lanky leading man, later as a character actor. He often played roles that symbolized the rugged free spirit of the indomitable "Aussie." He also appeared in some UK and US films. He died of a heart attack on a Sydney street.

FILMS INCLUDE: *Ants in His Pants* 1938; *Dan Rudd M.P.* 1939; *Forty Thousand Horsemen* 1940; *The Rats of Tobruk, Bush Christmas* (UK/Austral.), *The Overlanders* (UK/ Austral.) 1946; *Eureka Stockade/Massacre Hill* (UK/Austral.) 1948; *Bitter Springs* 1951; *Kangaroo* (US) 1952; *The Desert Rats* (US) 1953; *King of the Coral Sea* 1954; *Walk Into Hell, Smiley* 1957; *The Sundowners* (US), *The Wackiest Ship in the Army* (US) 1960; *Mutiny on the Bounty* (US) 1962; *Double Trouble* (US) 1967; *Kona Coast* (US) 1968; *Skullduggery* (US) 1970; *Outback* 1971.

Rafferty, Frances. Actress. Born on June 26, 1922, in Sioux City, Iowa. *ed.* UCLA. Leading lady and second lead of MGM films of the 40s, mainly in standard ingenue roles. Her screen career rapidly deteriorated after 1947, when she began freelancing with various small studios. In 1954–59 she was a regular on the TV series 'December Bride,' in the role of Spring Byington's daughter. Later seen in 'Pete and Gladys' (1961–62).

FILMS INCLUDE: *Fingers at the Window, The War Against Mrs. Hadley, Seven Sweethearts* 1942; *Thousands Cheer, Girl Crazy* 1943; *Dragon Seed* (as Orchid), *Barbary Coast Gent, Mrs. Parkington* 1944; *The Hidden Eye, Abbott and Costello in Hollywood* 1945; *Bad Bascomb* 1946; *Adventures of Don Coyote, Lost Honeymoon, Curley* 1947; *Money Madness, Lady at Midnight* 1948; *An Old Fashioned Girl* 1949; *Rodeo* 1952; *Shanghai Story* 1954; *Wings of Chance* 1961.

Raffill, Stewart. Director. Born in 1942, in Kettering, England. A graduate of England's Morton Morrel Agricultural College, where he studied animal husbandry, he came to the US in 1961 and shortly after began his Hollywood career as an animal trainer. He also stunted for screen Tarzans Mike Henry and Ron Ely. Before long, he assembled some 50 wild animals for rental by studios and began shooting nature films and doing second-unit directing for Disney and others. He has been directing features since the early 70s.

FILMS: *The Tender Warrior* (also sc.) 1971; *Napoleon and Samantha* (sc. only) 1972; *The Adventures of the Wilderness Family* 1975; *Across the Great Divide* 1976; *The Sea Gypsies* (also sc.) 1978; *High Risk* (also sc.) 1981; *The Ice Pirates* (also co-sc.) 1983; *The Philadelphia Experiment* 1984; *Mac and Me* (also co-sc.) 1988; *Mannequin 2: On the Move* 1990.

Raffin, Deborah. Actress. Born on Mar. 13, 1953, in Los Angeles. *ed.* Valley Coll. Tall, striking, wholesome leading lady of American TV and films. The daughter of screen actress Trudy MARSHALL, she began studying drama at 15 but started professionally as a fashion model. With her husband, producer Michael Viner, she heads Dove Audio, the world's second largest publisher of books on tape, and Dove Films, a production company.

FILMS: *Forty Carats* 1973; *The Dove* 1974; *Once Is Not Enough* 1975; *Gold Told Me To/Demon* 1976; *The Sentinel, Assault on Paradise/Maniac/Ransom* 1977; *Touched by Love* 1980; *Dance of the Dwarfs/Jungle Heat* 1983; *Death Wish 3, Claudia* 1985; *Scanners II: The New Order* (Can.) 1991; *Morning Glory* (also co-prod.) 1993.

Raft, George. Actor. *b.* George Ranft, Sept. 26, 1895, New York City. *d.* 1980. Sleek tough guy of Hollywood gangster films, memorable as the coin-flipping Guido Rinaldo in *Scarface* (1932). Raised in New York's notorious Hell's Kitchen area by parents of German and Italian origin whose home he left at 13, he was a prizefighter, then a ballroom dancer before moving up to nightclubs and Broadway. By his own account, he kept close ties with top gang racketeers during his early struggles. Arriving in Hollywood in the late 20s, he was heralded as a second Valentino but soon became typecast as a gangster, occasionally falling back on his reputation as the world's fastest Charleston dancer to star in films with a dance theme. Raft enjoyed considerable income and reputation by the mid-40s, when he began experiencing a reversal in his career, triggered by a poor choice of roles. In the early 50s he tried to revive his reputation in European films but to no avail. His TV series 'I Am the Law' (1952–53) resulted in severe personal financial loss and in 1959 his Havana gambling casino was closed down by the new Castro regime without compensation. To make things worse, he was hounded by the US Government for back taxes and in the mid-60s was refused entry into Britain, where he managed a posh London gambling club, because of alleged underworld associations. A glamorized version of his life story was told in the film *The George Raft Story,* starring Ray Danton.

FILMS: *Queen of the Night Clubs* 1929; *Quick Millions, Hush Money, Palmy Days* 1931; *Taxi!, Dancers in the Dark, Scarface, Night World, Love Is a Racket, Madame Racketeer, Night After Night, If I Had a Million, Under-Cover Man* 1932; *Pick Up, Midnight Club, The Bowery* 1933; *All of Me, Bolero, The Trumpet Blows* (dual role), *Limehouse Blues* 1934; *Rumba, Stolen Harmony, The Glass Key, Every Night at Eight, She Couldn't Take It* 1935; *It Had to Happen, Yours for the Asking* 1936; *Souls at Sea* 1937; *You and Me, Spawn of the North* 1938; *The Lady's from Kentucky, Each Dawn I Die, I Stole a Million, Invisible Stripes* 1939; *The House Across the Bay, They Drive by Night* 1940; *Manpower* 1941; *Broadway* 1942; *Stage Door Canteen* (cameo), *Background to Danger* 1943; *Follow the Boys, Nob Hill, Johnny Angel* 1945; *Whistle Stop, Mr. Ace, Nocturne* 1946; *Christmas Eve, Intrigue* 1947; *Race Street* 1948; *Outpost in Morocco, Johnny Allegro, A Dangerous Profession, Red Light* 1949; *Nous irons à Paris* (Fr.) 1950; *Lucky Nick Cain/I'll Get You for This* (US/UK) 1951; *Loan Shark* 1952; *I'll Get You, Dramma nella Casbah/The Man from Cairo* (It./US) 1953; *Rogue Cop, Black Widow* 1954; *A Bullet for Joey* 1955; *Around the World in 80 Days* (cameo) 1956; *Some Like It Hot, Jet Over the Atlantic* 1959; *Ocean's Eleven* (cameo) 1960; *The Ladies' Man* (cameo); *Two Guys Abroad* (unreleased) 1962; *For Those Who Think Young* (cameo), *The Patsy* (cameo) 1964; *Du Rififi a Paname/The Upper Hand* (Fr./It./Ger.) 1966; *Casino Royale* (cameo; UK) 1967; *Five Golden Dragons* (cameo; UK), *Skidoo* (cameo), *El Millòn de Madigan/Madigan's Millions* (cameo; Sp./It.) 1968; *Deadhead Miles* (release delayed) 1971; *Hammersmith Is Out* 1972; *Sextette* (cameo) 1978; *The Man with Bogart's Face/Sam Marlowe Private Eye* 1980.

rails. Bars or scaffolds high above a movie set on which lamps are mounted for overhead illumination.

Raimi, Sam. American director, producer, actor. Born in 1960, in Detroit. A movie fanatic from childhood, he spent much of his time and money at Michigan State University making super-8 mm films. With the help of his brother, Ivan, and friend, Robert Tapert, he turned out a 30-minute preview version of a horror film he was hoping to produce, and presented it to potential investors. With the $500,000 he raised, Raimi formed a production company, Renaissance Motion Pictures, with producer Tapert and actor Bruce Campbell, and directed his first feature, *The Evil Dead* (1983). The stylish but gory film was the talk of the 1983 Cannes Festival, and has come to be considered by some critics a horror classic. Other chic, ghoulish films followed, to the delight of cult followers.

FILMS: As director and/or producer—*The Evil Dead* (also sc., co-exec. prod.) 1983; *Crimewave/Broken Hearts and Noses* (also co-sc.) 1985; *Evil Dead 2: Dead by Dawn* (also co-sc.) 1987; *Darkman* (also story, co-sc.) 1990; *Lunatics: A Love Story* (co-prod. only) 1992; *Army of Darkness* (also co-sc.), *Hard Target* (ex-prod.), *Indian Summer* 1993; *The Hudsucker Proxy* (co-sc., also act.), *Timecop* (prod.) 1994; *The Quick and the Dead* 1995. As actor—*Spies Like Us* 1985; *Maniac Cop* 1988; *Miller's Crossing* 1990; *The Flintstones* 1994.

Raimu. Actor. *b.* Jules Auguste César Muraire, Dec. 17, 1883, Toulon, France. *d.* 1946. Character star of the French stage (from 1899) and screen; unforgettable in his portrayals for Marcel PAGNOL. Orson Welles has called him "the greatest actor who ever lived." He started out as a music hall extra, gained popularity in café concerts, and solidified his reputation in the late 20s on the Paris stage.

FILMS: *L'Homme nu* 1912; *L'Agence Cacaouette* 1914; *Le Blanc et le Noir, Mam'zelle Nitouche, Marius* (as Pagnol's César) 1931; *La Petite Chocolatière, Fanny* (again as César), *Les Gaîtés de l'Escadron* 1932; *Théodore et Cie, Charlemagne* 1933; *Ces Messieurs de la Santé, Tartarin de Tarascon* (title role), *J'ai une Idée* 1934; *Minuit Place Pigalle, Faisons un Rêve, L'Ecole des Cocottes, Gaspard de Besse/Dawn Over France* 1935; *Le Secret de Polichinelle, Le Roi/The King, Les Jumeaux de Brighton* (in three roles), *César* (title role) 1936; *Vous n'avez rien à declarer?, Les Perles de la Couronne/The Pearls of the Crown* (cameo), *La Chaste Suzanne, Les Rois du Sport, Le Fauteuil 47, Gribouille/Heart of Paris, Un Carnet de Bal* 1937; *Les Héros de la Marne/Heroes of the Marne, L'Etrange Monsieur Victor, Les Nouveaux Riches, La Femme du Boulanger/The Baker's Wife* 1938; *Noix de Coco, Monsieur Brotonneau, Dernière Jeunesse/Last Desire, L'Homme qui cherche la Vérité/The Man Who Seeks the Truth* 1939; *La Fille du Puisatier/The Well-Digger's Daughter, Le Duel, Parade en Sept Nuits* 1941; *Les Inconnus dans la Maison/Strangers in the House, L'Arlésienne, Monsieur la Souris/Midnight in Paris, Le Bienfaiteur, Les Petits Riens* 1942; *Untel Père et Fils/The Heart of a Nation* (release delayed from 1939), *Le Colonel Chabert* (title role) 1943; *Les Gueux au Paradis/Hoboes in Paradise, L'Homme au Chapeau rond/The Eternal Husband* 1946.

Raine, Norman Reilly. Screenwriter. *b.* June 23, 1895, Wilkes-Barre, Pa. *d.* 1971. He began his professional career at 19 as a reporter in Buffalo, N.Y., and after WW I service as an officer with the Canadian Expeditionary Force, he became an assistant editor of Canada's *MacLean's* magazine. He later wrote numerous short stories for *The Saturday Evening Post* and other leading magazines, notably the "Tugboat Annie" serialization, which was adapted to the screen in 1933 and in 1940. His play 'Hangman's Whip' was adapted to the screen as *White Woman* in 1933, and his novel *Sea of Lost Ships* was made into a film in 1953. In Hollywood from the mid-30s, he wrote many screenplays for Warner Bros. and other studios, mostly in collaboration. He shared an Academy Award for the script of *The Life of Emile Zola* (1937).

FILMS INCLUDE: *God's Country and the Woman, Mountain Justice, The Life of Emile Zola, The Perfect Specimen* 1937; *The Adventures of Robin Hood, Men Are Such Fools* 1938; *Each Dawn I Die, The Private Lives of Elizabeth and Essex* 1939; *The Fighting 69th* 1940; *Captains of the Clouds, Eagle Squadron* 1942; *We've Never Been Licked* 1943; *Ladies Courageous* 1944; *Nob Hill, A Bell for Adano, Captain Kidd* 1945; *M* 1951; *Woman of the North Country* 1952.

rain effects. Rain can be easily simulated on a set through the use of hoses, perforated pipes, and sprinkler systems. Among the most common rain-making devices are the "rain standard," a sprinkler mounted on a movable tripod some 20 or 30 feet above the players or a limited area of action, and the "rain cluster," a whole system of sprinklers, suspended from cables, which is designed to provide rain over large areas. To increase the realistic effect of rain, puddles may be set up before shooting and glossy materials applied to ground and wall surfaces. Rain may also be optically added to a scene by superimposing stock footage rain on a "dry" scene. In this case, clothing worn by actors are presoaked to make the simulation more believable.

Rainer, Luise. Actress. Born on Jan. 12, 1910, in Vienna. On Austrian and German stage from childhood, she trained with Max Reinhardt and appeared in several minor Austro-German films before arriving in Hollywood in the mid-30s, heralded as another Garbo. Here she established a dramatic rise-and-fall record, winning two successive Academy Awards—for moving, weepy roles in *The Great Ziegfeld* (1936) and *The Good Earth* (1937)—and seeing her career evaporate, all within three years. The blame for her premature retirement is placed by some on a poor choice of roles by her studio, MGM, and by others on bad advice from her husband at the time (1937–40), Clifford ODETS. She now lives in London with her second husband, a publisher.

FILMS: In Austria and Germany—*Ja der Himmel uber Wien* 1930; *Sehnsucht 202* 1932; *Heute kommt's drauf an* 1933. In the US—*Escapade* 1935; *The Great Ziegfeld* 1936; *The Good Earth* (as O-Lan), *The Emperor's Candlesticks, Big City* 1937; *The Toy Wife, The Great Waltz, Dramatic School* 1938; *Hostages* 1943.

Rainer, Yvonne. Filmmaker, dancer, choreographer. Born in 1934, in San Francisco. She moved to New York in 1957 to study acting, but was soon drawn to modern dance and in the 60s emerged as an innovative dancer and choreographer with the Judson Dance Theater, which she co-founded in 1962. She pioneered the minimalist style, which advocated limited movement and a limited emotive idiom, in effect divesting dance of convention and artifice. In her search for new means of expression, she began experimenting with the incorporation of other media into her choreography, including short films. Gradually, in the late 60s, she was drawn to filmmaking for its own sake, and in 1972 turned out her first feature-length production. Like her dance, Rainer's films have typically been collages of reality and fiction, thought-provoking blends of visuals and sounds that shun the conventions of narrative cinema and invite audiences to participate Brechtian-style in exercises of the mind in response to major political, sociologial, and psychological issues. In 1990 she was a recipient of a MacArthur Foundation "genius" award.

FILMS: Shorts—*Volleyball/Foot Film* 1967; *Hand Movie, Rhode Island Red, Trio Film* 1968; *Line* 1969. Feature-length—*Lives of Performers* 1972; *Film About a Woman Who. . .* 1974; *Kristina Talking Pictures* 1976; *Journeys from Berlin/1971* 1980; *The Man Who Envied Women* 1985; *Privilege* 1990; *Murder and Murder* (dir., sc., act.) 1996.

Raines, Ella. Actress. *b.* Ella Wallace Raubes, Aug. 6, 1921, Snoqualmie Falls, Wash. *d.* 1988, of cancer. *ed.* U. of Washington. Attractive leading lady of Hollywood films of the 40s who looked her mysterious best in thrillers. An engineer's daughter, she broke into films in 1943 as the sole contract star of a new production company, B-H Productions, established that year by actor Charles Boyer and director Howard Hawks. She was later signed by Universal, for which she played her most memorable role in the thriller *Phantom Lady* (1944). But few of her subsequent parts were rewarding and she ended her career in the early 50s in cheap Republic productions.

FILMS: *Corvette K-225, Cry Havoc* 1943; *Phantom Lady, Hail the Conquering Hero, Tall in the Saddle, Enter Arsene Lupin* 1944; *The Suspect, The Strange Affair of Uncle Harry* 1945; *The Runaround, White Tie and Tails* 1946; *Time Out of Mind, The Web, Brute Force* 1947; *The Senator Was Indiscreet* 1948; *The Walking Hills, Impact, A Dangerous Profession* 1949; *Singing Guns, The Second Face* 1950; *The Fighting Coast Guard* 1951; *Ride the Man Down* 1952; *Man in the Road* (UK) 1956.

Rainger, Ralph. Composer. *b.* Ralph Reichenthal, Oct. 7, 1901, New York City. *d.* 1942. A former lawyer, he wrote the music for many film songs of the 30s and early 40s, usually in collaboration with Leo ROBIN. They won an Academy Award for the song "Thanks for the Memory" from the film *The Big Broadcast of 1938.*

FILMS INCLUDE: *Be Yourself* 1930; *Blonde Venus, A Farewell to Arms, The Big Broadcast* 1932; *International House, Song of Songs, A Bedtime Story, She Done Him Wrong* 1933; *Bolero, Kiss and Make UP, Little Miss Marker, The Trumpet Blows, Here Is My Heart* ("June in January," etc.) 1934; *Rumba, Ruggles of Red Gap, The Devil Is a Woman, The Big Broadcast of 1936* 1935; *Palm Springs* 1936; *Blossoms on Broadway, Waikiki Wedding* ("Blue Hawaii," etc.), *Swing High Swing Low* 1937; *The Big Broadcast of 1938, Artists and Models Abroad* 1938; *Paris Honeymoon, Gulliver's Travels* 1939; *Rise and Shine, Moon Over Miami* 1941; *Footlight Serenade, My Gal Sal, Tales of Manhattan* 1942; *Coney Island, Riding High* 1943.

Rains, Claude. Actor. *b.* William Claude Rains, Nov. 10, 1889, London. *d.* 1967. A suave character actor of superbly controlled sardonic manner, he was charming even when playing villains, which he was called upon to do frequently on the screen. On the London stage from age 11, he first toured the US in 1914 appeared in an isolated British silent film in 1920, and became a leading player of the Theatre Guild in 1926. He was a middle-aged man by the time he got regularly into films in 1933. A slight, unhandsome man, he was sought out by Hollywood thanks to his stage reputation as an actor with an expressive face, but ironically that face was kept in bandages or entirely unseen in his motion picture talkie debut, the title role in *The Invisible Man.* Subsequently, however, Rains's face, as well as his distinctive voice and manner, enhanced a long string of films at Warners and other studios in which he played with subtlety a wide range of character leads and supporting roles. He was nominated for Oscars for *Mr. Smith Goes to Washington* (1939), *Casablanca* (1943), *Mr. Skeffington* (1944), and *Notorious* (1946), but never won an Academy Award. He was particularly effective in a number of appearances opposite Bette DAVIS. The first (1913–20) of his six marriages was to actress Isabel JEANS.

FILMS: *Build Thy House* (UK) 1920; *The Invisible Man* (title role) 1933; *Crime Without Passion* 1934; *The Man Who Reclaimed His Head, The Mystery of Edwin Drood* (as John Jasper), *The Clairvoyant* (UK), *The Last Outpost* 1935; *Hearts Divided* (as Napoleon), *Anthony Adverse* (as Don Luis) 1936; *Stolen Holiday, The Prince and the Pauper, They Won't Forget* 1937; *Gold Is Where You Find It, The Adventures of Robin Hood* (as Prince John), *White Banners, Four Daughters* 1938; *They Made Me a Criminal, Juarez* (as Napoleon III), *Daughters Courageous, Mr. Smith Goes to Washington, Four Wives* 1939; *Saturday's Children, The Sea Hawk, The Lady with Red Hair* (as playwright David Belasco) 1940; *Four Mothers, Here Comes Mr. Jordan* (title role), *The Wolf Man* 1941; *Kings Row* (as Dr. Tower), *Moontide, Now Voyager* 1942; *Casablanca, Forever and a Day, The Phantom of the Opera* (title role) 1943; *Passage to Marseille, Mr. Skeffington* 1944; *Strange Holiday, This Love of Ours, Caesar and Cleopatra* (as Julius Caesar; UK) 1945; *Notorious, Deception, Angel on My Shoulder* 1946; *The Unsuspected* 1947; *The Passionate Friends/One Woman's Story* (UK), *Rope of Sand, Song of Surrender* 1949; *The White Tower, Where Danger Lives* 1950; *Sealed Cargo* 1951; *The Man Who Watched the Trains Go By/The Paris Express* (UK) 1953; *Lisbon* 1956; *This Earth Is Mine* 1959; *The Lost World* 1960; *The Pied Piper of Hamelin* (originally presented on TV in 1957), *Il Pianeta degli Uomini Spenti/Battle of the Worlds* (It.) 1961; *Lawrence of Arabia* (UK) 1962; *Twilight of Honor* 1963; *The Greatest Story Ever Told* (as Herod the Great) 1965.

Raizman (also **Raisman**), **Yuli.** Director. Born on Dec. 15, 1903, in Moscow. The Soviet cinema's most enduring major filmmaker. Following literature studies at Moscow University, he entered films in 1924 as a literary consultant with the Mezharbpom. The following year he played a small role in Pudovkin's *Chess Fever* and was assigned as an assistant to directors Konstantin Eggert and Yakov Protazanov before making his own directing debut in 1927 with a little known studio, Gosvoyenkino (State Military Films). He first drew attention with his second film, *Forced Labor* (1928), a grim account of the brutal treatment of political prisoners in a Czarist-era penal camp. Moving on to the Vostok studios, Raizman scored another success with *The Earth Thirsts* (1930), a semidocumentary depicting the efforts of Komsomol youths to bring modern irrigation to a remote village. Re-released the following year with a sound track of effects and music, it was officially registered as the Soviet Union's first sound film. Raizman's popularity rose in the 30s, after he joined Mosfilm, the giant Moscow studio, on the strength of films like *Aviators* (1935), a rousing celebration of flying set in a pilot training school. He drew international acclaim for *The Last Night* (1937), a delicately drawn story of young love amidst the brewing Revolution of 1917. Raizman reached a peak of success in the 40s with such WW II films as *Mashenka* (1942) and *Moscow Sky* (1944). His postwar output was on the whole less remarkable, though it was intermittently highlighted by such films as *The Communist* (1958), which glorified the sacrifice of a party hero, and *If This Be Love* (1961), a bitter study of young love doomed by social hypocrisy. Raizman's remarkably long career extended into the 80s, when he enjoyed renewed appreciation with *A Private Life* (1982), a sincere, melancholy study of a workaholic coming to grips with early retirement. The resilient Raizman continued not only directing but also supervising the entire product of a busy unit of Mosfilm well into his 80s.

FILMS: *The Circle/The Ring/Duty and Love* (co-dir. with A. Gavronsky) 1927; *Forced Labor/Penal Servitude* 1928; *The Earth Thirsts* 1930; *The Story About Omar Khaptsoko* (short) 1932; *Aviators/Flyers/Pilots/Men on Wings* 1935; *The Last Night* (also co-sc.) 1937; *Virgin Soil Upturned* 1940; *Mashenka* 1942; *About the Truce with Finland* (doc.; also co-sc.), *Moscow Sky* 1944; *Berlin/The Fall of Berlin* (doc.; also co-sc.) 1945; *The Train Goes East* 1948; *Rainis* 1949; *Cavalier of the Golden Star/Dream of a Cossack* 1951; *A Lesson in Life/Conflict* 1955; *The Communist* 1958; *If This Be Love* (also co-sc.) 1961; *Your Contemporary* 1967; *A Courtesy Call* 1973; *A Strange Woman* (also co-sc.) 1977; *Private Life* 1982; *A Tale of Wishes* 1984.

Rakoff, Alvin. Director. Born in 1937, in Toronto. *ed.* U. of Toronto. A former journalist, he settled in England, where he began directing films in the late 50s. His features have been, for the most part, routine. He had greater success with his numerous TV productions, winning Emmy Awards for 'Call Me Daddy' (1968) and 'A Voyage Around My Father' (1982). He served as president of Britain's Directors Guild.

FEATURE FILMS: *Passport to Shame/Room 43, The Treasure of San Teresa/Hot Money Girl* 1959; *On Friday at 11* (Ger./UK) 1961; *World in My Pocket* (Ger./Fr./It.) 1962; *The Comedy Man* 1964; *Crossplot* 1969; *Hoffman, Say Hello to Yesterday* 1971; *King Solomon's Treasure* (Can.) 1978; *City on Fire* (Can.) 1979; *Death Ship* (Can.) 1980; *Dirty Tricks* (Can.) 1981.

Raksin, David. Composer. Born on Aug. 4, 1912, in Philadelphia. *ed.* U. of Pennsylvania. He studied under Arnold Schoenberg and composed orchestral and chamber works as well as music for ballet, stage, TV, and films. He arranged Chaplin's music for *Modern Times* (1936) and is perhaps best known as the composer of the theme song from *Laura* (1944).

FILMS INCLUDE: *Dancing Pirate* 1936; *52nd Street* 1937; *Suez* 1938; *Hollywood Cavalcade, Stanley and Livingstone* 1939; *The Magnificent Dope* 1942; *Laura* 1944; *Fallen Angel* 1945; *The Secret Life of Walter Mitty, Daisy Kenyon, Forever Amber* 1947; *Force of Evil* 1948; *Whirlpool* 1949; *Across the Wide Missouri* 1951; *Carrie, The Bad and the Beautiful* 1952; *Suddenly* 1954; *Jubal* 1956; *Separate Tables* 1958; *Al Capone* 1959; *Too Late Blues, Two Weeks in Another Town* 1962; *Invitation to a Gunfighter* 1964; *Sylvia* 1965; *A Big Hand for the Little Lady* 1966; *Will Penny* 1968; *What's the Matter with Helen?* 1971; *Glass Houses* 1972.

Ralph, Jessie. Actress. *b.* Jessie Ralph Chambers, Nov. 5, 1864, Gloucester, Mass. *d.* 1944. Character actress with long Broadway experience, typically in kindly if sometimes tyrannical mother, grandmother, governess, or maid roles. She retired in 1941 following a leg amputation.

FILMS INCLUDE: *The Galloper, Mary's Lamb* 1915; *New York* 1916; *Such a Little Queen* 1921; *Child of Manhattan, Elmer the Great, Cocktail Hour* 1933; *Nana* (as Zoe), *Murder at the Vanities, The Affairs of Cellini, One Night of Love, We Live Again, Evelyn Prentice* 1934; *David Copperfield* (as Nurse Peggotty), *Vanessa: Her Love Story, Les Miserables, Mark of the Vampire, Jalna* (as Grandma Whiteoak), *I Live My Life, Metropolitan, Captain Blood* 1935; *Little Lord Fauntleroy, The Unguarded Hour, San Francisco, Walking on Air, After the Thin Man* 1936; *Camille* (as Nanine), *The Good Earth, The Last of Mrs. Cheyney, Double Wedding* 1937; *Love Is a Headache, Port of Seven Seas* 1938; *St. Louis Blues, Café Society, Drums Along the Mohawk* 1939; *The Blue Bird, The Bank Dick* 1940; *They Met in Bombay* 1941.

Ralston, Esther. Actress. *b.* Sept. 17, 1902, Bar Harbor, Me. *d.* 1994. Beautiful blonde heroine of Hollywood silents and early talkies, publicized as "The American Venus" after the title of one of her films. In vaudeville with her parents' act from the age of two, she made her screen debut at 14 and after several small roles became one of the silent screen's highest-paid stars. She usually played wholesome roles. After retiring from films in 1941, she performed in radio soap operas, worked in a department store, and held executive positions with a talent agency, then an upstate New York electric company.

FILMS INCLUDE: *Phantom Fortunes* 1916; *Huckleberry Finn* 1920; *Crossing Trails* 1921; *Pals of the West, Remembrance, Oliver Twist* (as Rose Maylie) 1922; *Railroaded, Blinky, The Wild Party, Pure Grit* 1923; *The Marriage Circle, The Heart Buster* 1924; *Peter Pan* (as Mrs. Darling), *The Goose Hangs High, The Little French Girl, Beggar on Horseback, The Lucky Devil, The Trouble with Wives, The Best People, A Kiss for Cinderella* (as the Fairy Godmother), *Womanhandled* 1925; *The American Venus, The Blind Goddess, The Quarterback, Old Ironsides* 1926; *Fashions for Women, Children of Divorce, Ten Modern Commandments, Figures Don't Lie, The Spotlight* 1927; *Love and Learn, Something Always Happens, Half a Bride, The Sawdust Paradise* 1928; *The Case of Lena Smith, Betrayal, The Wheel of Life, The Mighty* 1929; *Lonely Wives, The Prodigal* 1931; *Rome Express* (UK) 1932; *After the Ball* (UK), *Black Beauty, To the Last Man* 1933; *Sadie McKee, Romance in the Rain, The Marines Are Coming* 1934; *Strange Wives, Mr. Dynamite, Ladies Crave Excitement* 1935; *Hollywood Boulevard, Reunion* 1936; *As Good as Married, Shadows of the Orient* 1937; *Letter of Introduction* 1938; *Tin Pan Alley* 1940; *San Francisco Docks* 1941.

Ralston, Jobyna. Actress *b.* Nov. 24, 1902, South Pittsburgh, Tenn. *d.* 1967. A former chorus girl, she entered films in 1921 and starred in Harold LLOYD comedies and other silent films of the 20s. At one time (1927–45) was married to Richard ARLEN.

FILMS INCLUDE: *The Call of Home, The Three Must-Get-Theres* 1922; *Why Worry?* 1923; *Girl Shy, Hot Water* 1924; *The Freshman* 1925; *For Heaven's Sake, Sweet Daddies, Gigolo* 1926; *The Kid Brother, Special Delivery, Lightning, Pretty Clothes, A Racing Romeo, Wings* 1927; *The Night Flyer, The Count of Ten, Black Butterflies, The Big Hop, The Power of the Press, The Toilers* 1928; *The College Coquette* 1929; *Rough Waters* 1930; *Sheer Luck* 1931.

Ralston, Ken. Special effects expert. Born in 1955. A movie fanatic from early childhood, he began experimenting with camera tricks as a boy and won a Kodak prize for one of his 8 mm films. He began his professional career in commercials and in 1976 joined Industrial Light and Magic as a camera assistant on *Star Wars.* His expertise and technical intuition soon elevated him to a key position on the team as a specialist in stop-motion animation. In 1983 he shared the Special Achievement Academy Award for the special effects of *Return of the Jedi.* He won additional Oscars for *Cocoon* (1985) and for the special visual effects of the groundbreaking animation/live action spectacle *Who Framed Roger Rabbit?* (1988).

FILMS INCLUDE: *Star Trek II: The Wrath of Khan* 1982; *Return of the Jedi* 1983; *Star Trek III: The Search for Spock* 1984; *Back to the Future, Cocoon* 1985; *Star Trek IV: The Voyage Home* 1986; *Who Framed Roger Rabbit?* 1988; *Back to the Future Part II* 1989; *Back to the Future Part III* 1990; *Forrest Gump* 1994; *American President*, *Jumanji* 1995; *Phenomenon* 1996; *Contact* 1997.

Ralston, Vera Hruba. Actress. Born Vera Helena Hruba, on July 12, 1919, in Prague, Czechoslovakia. Runner-up to Sonja Henie in the 1936 Olympic Games ice-skating event, she sustained the "also ran" image in her ensuing Hollywood career. She starred in many of the more ambitious films turned out by poverty-row studio Republic in the 40s and 50s, first as Vera Hruba, then as Vera Hruba Ralston, and finally as Vera Ralston. In 1952 she married Republic's chief executive, Herbert YATES, who had taken charge of her career from the start and contrary to the usual studio policy spent lavishly on her productions.

FILMS: As Vera Hruba—*Ice-Capades* 1941; *Ice-Capades Revue* 1942. As Vera Hruba Ralston—*The Lady and the Monster, Storm Over Lisbon, Lake Placid Serenade* 1944; *Dakota* 1945; *Murder in the Music Hall* 1946. As Vera Ralston—*The Plainsman and the Lady* 1946; *Wyoming, The Flame* 1947; *I Jane Doe, Angel of the Amazon* 1948; *The Fighting Kentuckian* 1949; *Surrender* 1950; *Belle le Grand, The Wild Blue Yonder* 1951; *Hoodlum Empire* 1952; *A Perilous Journey, Fair Wind to Java* 1953; *Jubilee Trail* 1954; *Timberjack* 1955; *Accused of Murder* 1956; *Spoilers of the Forest* 1957; *Gunfire at Indian Gap, The Notorious Mr. Monks, The Man Who Died Twice* 1958.

Ramaldi, Carlo. Special effects artist. Italian creator of puppet and costume effects in Italian and American fantasy and horror films. He shared three Oscars for his creatures in *King Kong, Alien,* and *E.T.*

FILMS INCLUDE: *Deep Red* (It.), *King Kong* 1976; *Alien, Nightwing* 1979; *The Hand* 1981; *E.T. The Extra-Terrestrial* 1982; *King Kong Lives* 1986; *Primal Rage* (It.) 1990.

Rambeau, Marjorie. Actress. *b.* July 15, 1889, San Francisco. *d.* 1970. Character star of Hollywood films after extensive work on the stage from age 12. In the 1910s and 20s, when she starred on Broadway, she was noted for her beauty and grace. She also appeared in several silent films, but by the time she made Hollywood her home in the 30s, she was a middle-aged woman pegged for character roles, typically as blowsy aging harlots and fallen women. She played some leads but appeared mainly in supporting roles, some of them memorable. She was nominated for Oscars as best supporting actress for *The Primrose Path* (1940) and *Torch Song* (1953). Her first of three husbands was actor-playwright-screenwriter Willard Mack.

FILMS INCLUDE: *The Greater Woman, Motherhood, The Debt, The Mirror, The Dazzling Miss Davison, Mary Moreland* 1917; *The Common Cause* 1918; *The Fortune Teller* 1920; *Syncopating Sue* 1926; *Her Man, Min and Bill* 1930; *Inspiration, The Easiest Way, Strangers May Kiss, The Secret Six, Laughing Sinners, Son of India, Silence, Leftover Ladies, Hell Divers* 1931; *Strictly Personal, The Warrior's Husband, A Man's Castle* 1933; *Palooka, A Modern Hero, Grand Canary* 1934; *Under Pressure, Dizzy Dames* 1935; *First Lady* 1937; *Merrily We Live* 1938; *The Rains Came* 1939; *Primrose Path, Twenty-Mule Team, East of the River, Tugboat Annie Sails Again* (title role) 1940; *Tobacco Road* (as Bessie Lester) 1941; *Broadway* 1942; *In Old Oklahoma* 1943; *Oh! What a Night!* 1944; *Salome—Where She Danced* 1945; *The Walls of Jericho* 1948; *Any Number Can Play, Abandoned/Abandoned Woman* 1949; *Torch Song* 1953; *Bad for Each Other, Forever Female* 1954; *A Man Called Peter, The View from Pompey's Head* 1955; *Slander, Man of a Thousand Faces* 1957.

Ramis, Harold. Screenwriter, director, producer, actor. Born on Nov. 21, 1944, in Chicago. *ed.* Washington U., St. Louis (education). A former mental-ward orderly and jokes editor for *Playboy,* he started his show business career as a writer-performer for the Second City improvisation comedy troupe. Moving to New York City, he teamed up with Bill Murray, John Belushi, and Gilda Radner in the 'National Lampoon Show' on the stage and in 1977–78 co-starred in 'Second City TV.' Movies followed, usually rambunctious, lowbrow comedies with box-office appeal, to which he contributed in various capacities, mainly as a screenwriter, sometimes as director or producer, and often as a manic performer.

FILMS: *National Lampoon's Animal House* (co-sc.) 1978; *Meatballs* (co-sc.) 1979; *Caddyshack* (dir., co-sc.) 1980; *Stripes* (co-sc., act.), *Heavy Metal* (v/o) 1981; *National Lampoon's Vacation* (dir., co-sc.) 1983; *Ghostbusters* (co-sc., act.) 1984; *Back to School* (co-exec. prod., co-sc.), *Club Paradise* (dir., co-sc.), *Armed and Dangerous* (exec. prod., co-sc.) 1986; *Baby Boom* (act.) 1987; *Caddyshack II* (co-sc.), *Stealing Home* (act.) 1988; *Ghostbusters II* (co-sc., act.) 1989; *Rover Dangerfield* (co-story; uncredited) 1991; *Groundhog Day* (dir.) 1993; *Airheads* (act. only), *Love Affair* (act. only) 1994; *Stuart Saves His Family* 1995; *Multiplicity* (dir., co-sc., co-prod.) 1996.

Rambova, Natasha. See VALENTINO, Rudolph.

Rampling, Charlotte. Actress. Born on Feb. 5, 1945, in Sturmer, England. Provocative, sensual leading lady of British and international films. The daughter of a British colonel who became a NATO commander, she was educated at Jeanne d'Arc Academie pour Jeunes Filles in Versailles and at the exclusive St. Hilda's school in Bushey, England. Tall and slinky, she was a model before entering films in 1965. She first attracted serious attention in Visconti's *The Damned* (1969) and was advantageously cast in Cavani's *The Night Porter* (1974). In 1983 she married Jean-Michel Jarre, millionaire composer of synthesizer music.

FILMS: *The Knack... and How to Get It, Rotten to the Core* 1965; *Georgy Girl* 1966; *The Long Duel* 1967; *Sequestro di Persona* (It.) 1968; *La Caduta degli Dei/Götterdammerung/The Damned* (It./Ger.), *Target: Harry/How to Make It* (US), *Three* (US/Fr.) 1969; *Addio Fratello Crudele/'Tis Pity She's a Whore* (It.), *The Ski Bum* 1971; *Corky/Looking Good* (US) 1972; *Henry VIII and His Six Wives* (as Anne Boleyn), *Asylum, Giordano Bruno* (It.) 1973; *Zardoz, Il Portiere di Notte/The Night Porter* (It.), *Caravan to Vacares* (UK/Fr.), *La Chair de l'Orchidée* (Fr.) 1974; *Farewell My Lovely, Yupi-Du* (It.) 1975; *Foxtrot/The Other Side of Paradise* (Mex./Switz.) 1976; *Un Taxi mauve/The Purple Taxi* (Fr./It./Ire.), *Orca* (US) 1977; *Stardust Memories* (US) 1980; *The Verdict* (US) 1982; *Viva la Vie* (Fr.) 1984; *Tristesse et Beauté* (Fr.), *On ne meurt que deux fois/He Died with His Eyes Open* (Fr.) 1985; *Max Mon Amour* (Fr.) 1986; *Angel Heart* (US), *Mascara/Makeup for Murder* (Bel./Hol./Fr.) 1987; *D.O.A.* (US), *Rebus* (It.) 1988; *Paris by Night, Helmut Newton: Frames from the Edge* (doc.) 1989; *Hammers Over the Anvil* 1993; *Time Is Money* 1994; *Anna Oz* 1996; *Wings of a Dove* 1997.

Rand, Sally. Fan dancer, actress. *b.* Helen Gould Beck, 1903, Hickory County, Mo. *d.* 1979. The daughter of a mailman, she left home at 13 to work as a cigarette girl in a Kansas City nightclub and after similar jobs elsewhere arrived in Hollywood in the mid-20s. She played leads and supporting roles in a score of films, mostly routine, but was forced out of Hollywood with the coming of sound. She tried unsuccessfully to capitalize on her modest past but could find work only as a chorus girl in a Chicago World's Fair extravaganza in 1933. However, she was catapulted to fame when she was arrested for giving an "obscene performance" in the show and within months became a highly paid national celebrity. Over the years she acquired the reputation of being the greatest fan dancer of them all. In the late 70s, well into her own 70s, she was still doing her fan dance to appreciative audiences in nightclubs coast to coast.

FILMS INCLUDE: *The Texas Bearcat, The Road to Yesterday* 1925; *Bachelor Brides, Gigolo, Man Bait* 1926; *The Night of Love, Getting Gertie's Garter, The King of Kings, His Dog, Galloping Fury, Heroes in Blue* 1927; *Crashing Through, A Girl in Every Port, Black Feather, Golf Widows* 1928; *Bolero* 1934.

Randall, Addison ("Jack"). See LIVINGSTON, Robert (Bob).

Randall, Tony. Actor. Born Leonard Rosenberg, on Feb. 26, 1920, in Tulsa, Okla. *ed.* Northwestern. Intelligent, urbane comedian of American stage, radio, TV, and films whose screen manner often suggests the happy melancholy of a big corporation junior executive. The son of an art dealer, he came to New York at 19, and after training under Sanford Meisner made his stage debut in 'The Circle of Chalk' (1941). Following WW II service with the US Army (1942–46), he performed on radio and early television. He began appearing in movies in 1957, but it was on TV that he really shined, most memorably as the fastidious Felix Unger in the hit series 'The Odd Couple' (1970–75), for which he won an Emmy Award. His other series include 'One Man's Family' (1950–52), 'Mr. Peepers' (1952–55), 'The Tony Randall Show' (1976–78), and 'Love, Sidney' (1981–83). He is also a witty, erudite guest on TV talk shows and game panels. In 1991 he realized a long-held dream by creating and heading the National Actors Theatre, a repertory company.

FILMS: *Oh Men! Oh Women!, Will Success Spoil Rock Hunter?, No Down Payment* 1957; *The Mating Game, Pillow Talk* 1959; *The Adventures of Huckleberry Finn* (as The King), *Let's Make Love* 1960; *Lover Come Back* 1961; *Boys' Night Out* 1962; *Island of Love* 1963; *The Brass Bottle, Robin and the 7 Hoods* (cameo), *The Seven Faces of Dr. Lao* (multiple roles), *Send Me No Flowers* 1964; *Fluffy* 1965; *The Alphabet Murders* (as Detective Hercule Poirot; UK), *Our Man in Marrakesh/Bang! Bang! You're Dead!* (UK) 1966; *Hello Down There* 1969; *Everything You Always Wanted to Know About Sex but Were Afraid to Ask* 1972; *Scavenger Hunt* 1979; *Foolin' Around* 1980; *The King of Comedy* 1983; *My Little Pony* (v/o) 1986; *That's Adequate* (narrator), *It Had to Be You* 1989; *Gremlins 2: The New Batch* (v/o) 1990; *Fatal Instinct* 1993.

Randell, Ron. Actor. Born on Oct. 8, 1918, in Sydney, Australia. On the Australian radio and stage from age 14, he later played some leads and numerous supporting roles in US, UK, and Continental films. He has also appeared on Broadway and on the London stage and on both American and British TV.

FILMS INCLUDE: In Australia—*Smithy/Pacific Adventure* 1946. In the US—*Bulldog Drummond at Bay* (title role), *It Had to Be You* 1947; *The Sign of the Ram, The Mating of Millie, The Loves of Carmen* 1948; *The Lone Wolf and His Lady* (as the Lone Wolf) 1949; *Tyrant of the Sea* 1950; *Lorna Doone* (as Tom Faggus) 1951; *The Brigand* 1952; *The Mississippi Gambler, Kiss Me Kate* (as Cole Porter) 1953; *I Am a Camera* (UK) 1955; *Beyond Mombasa* (UK) 1956; *The Story of Esther Costello* (UK), *The Girl in Black Stockings* 1957; *Most Dangerous Man Alive, King of Kings* 1961; *The Longest Day* 1962; *Follow the Boys, Oro per i Cesari/Gold for the Caesars* (It./Fr.) 1963; *Pampa Salvaje/Savage Pampas* (Arg./Sp./US) 1966; *The Seven Minutes* 1971; *Exposed* 1983.

Randolph, Lillian. Actress. *b.* 1915. *d.* 1980. Younger sister of actress Amanda Randolph, she appeared in films for five decades. Often cast as a sensible but outspoken maid, notably the Bailey family housekeeper in *It's a Wonderful Life* and the maid Birdie in the TV and radio series 'The Great Gildersleeve.'

FILMS INCLUDE: *Life Goes On* 1938; *Am I Guilty?, Mr. Smith Goes Ghost, Little Men* 1940; *West Point Widow, Gentleman from Dixie* 1941; *The Mexican Spitfire Sees a Ghost, The Great Gildersleeve* 1942; *Gildersleeve on Broadway, Gildersleeve's Bad Day* 1943; *Gildersleeve's Ghost* 1944; *It's a Wonderful Life* 1946; *The Bachelor and the Bobby-Soxer* 1947;

Dear Brat, That's My Boy 1951; *Hush Hush Sweet Charlotte* 1964; *The Great White Hope* 1970; *How to Seduce a Woman* 1974; *Once is Not Enough, Rafferty and the Gold Dust Twins* 1975; *Magic* 1978; *The Onion Field* 1979.

Rank, Lord J(oseph) Arthur. Film magnate. *b.* Dec. 22, 1888, Hull, England. *d.* 1972. Heir to a flour and milling fortune, he entered films modestly in 1933 as the promoter of religious (Methodist) productions and within several years virtually monopolized the British film industry. He began building his celluloid empire in 1935 by systematically acquiring control over every phase of the business—production, processing, distribution, and exhibition. By the mid-40s his companies owned more than half of the British studios and more than 1,000 theaters. He thus was largely responsible for both the achievements and the failures of British cinema during a quarter of a century. "King Arthur," as he came to be called, also extended his activities overseas to Canada and the US. The Rank Organisation, of which he was chairman until 1969, then president, has diversified in recent years into many fields, including bowling alleys and xerography. He was created a baron in 1957, in recognition of his achievements. American filmgoers associate Rank's name with the exotic trademark that preceded his company's films—a bare-chested strongman (ex-boxer "Bombardier" Wells) striking a huge gong.

Ransohoff, Martin. Producer. Born in 1927, in New Orleans. *ed.* Colgate. He started his career in 1949, in advertising. In 1952 he formed Filmways, a major TV production company through which he produced such hit series as 'Mister Ed' (1961–66), 'The Beverly Hillbillies' (1962–71), 'Petticoat Junction' (1963–70), and 'The Addams Family' (1964–66). He also produced many features through Filmways before resigning in 1972 to become an independent producer.

FILMS INCLUDE: *Boys' Night Out* 1962; *The Wheeler Dealers* 1963; *The Americanization of Emily, Topkapi* 1964; *The Sandpiper* (also orig. story), *The Loved One* (exec. prod.), *The Cincinnati Kid* 1965; *Don't Make Waves, Eye of the Devil* 1967; *Ice Station Zebra* 1968; *Hamlet* (co-exec. prod.), *Castle Keep* 1969; *Catch-22* (co-prod.), *The Moonshine War* 1970; *10 Rillington Place* (co-prod.; UK), *Blind Terror/See No Evil* (co-prod.; UK) 1971; *Fuzz* (exec. prod.) 1972; *The White Dawn* 1974; *Silver Streak* (co-exec. prod.) 1976; *Nightwing, The Wanderers* 1979; *A Change of Seasons* 1980; *American Pop* 1981; *Hanky Panky* 1982; *Class* 1983; *Jagged Edge* 1985; *The Big Town* 1987; *Switching Channels* 1988; *Physical Evidence, Welcome Home* 1989; *Guilty as Sin* 1993; *Turbulence* 1997.

Rapaport, Michael. Actor. Born March 18, 1970, in New York. With a background in stand-up comedy, this bright, appealing young character actor appeared in several television series before landing feature film roles. His distinctive New York tough-guy accent has kept him primarily typecast in the obvious roles but his talent for creating believable, emotionally charged characters has allowed him to shine in a variety of similar roles. Especially memorable as the struggling actor caught up in a drug deal gone wrong in the Quentin TARANTINO scripted *True Romance* (1993).

FILMS: *Zebrahead* 1992; *Money For Nothing, Poetic Justice, Point of No Return, True Romance* 1993; *The Scout* 1994; *The Basketball Diaries, Higher Learning, Kiss of Death, Mighty Aphrodite* 1995; *Beautiful Girls, The Pallbearer* 1996; *A Brother's Kisses, Cop Land, Kicked in the Head, Metro* 1997.

Rapf, Harry. Producer, executive. *b.* Oct. 16, 1882, New York City. *d.* 1949. Raised in Denver, Colorado, he began staging amateur shows there while still in high school. He started his professional career in a minstrel show with Gus Edwards. After several years in New York vaudeville, he entered films around 1915, producing independently. In 1919 he went to work for the Selznick company and in 1921 joined Warner Bros., for whom he discovered Rin Tin Tin and produced the popular dog's profitable movies. In 1924 he joined the newly merged MGM where he became one of the studio's top triumvirate, sharing production responsibility with Irving THALBERG under Louis B. MAYER. While Thalberg produced MGM's prestige films, Rapf was assigned the "program pictures," the run-of-the-mill movie output, personally producing some of these films. He was credited with discovering Joan Crawford and other major stars, as well as important directors and writers who started their careers under his guidance. A heart attack curtailed his activities in the late 30s. For a while he headed MGM's shorts department and late in his career teamed with Dore SCHARY in managing the studio's experimental B unit. His sons Matthew and Maurice were also involved in the industry, the former as a film and TV producer-writer, the latter as a screenwriter whose career was cut short by blacklisting.

FILMS INCLUDE: *The Argyle Case, The Mad Lover* 1917; *Wanted For Murder* 1918; *Blind Youth* 1920; *The Greatest Love, School Days* 1921; *Heroes of the Street, Rags to Riches* 1922; *Brass, Lucretia Lombard, Where the North Begins* 1923; *Broadway After Dark, So This Is Marriage* 1924; *The Broadway Melody, The Hollywood Revue of 1929* 1929; *Min and Bill* 1930; *The Sin of Madelon Claudet, The Champ* 1931; *Christopher Bean, Tugboat Annie* 1933; *Hollywood Party, The Night Is Young* 1934; *The Murder Man* 1935; *Piccadilly Jim, Mad Holiday, Old Hutch* 1936; *Espionage, Live Love and Learn, They Gave Him a Gun, Bad Man of Brimstone* 1937; *Everybody Sing, Stablemates, The Girl Downstairs* 1938; *Let Freedom Ring, The Ice Follies of 1939* 1939; *Forty Little Mothers* 1940; *Gallant Bess* 1946; *Scene of the Crime* 1949.

Raphael, Frederic. Novelist, screenwriter. Born on Aug. 14, 1931, in Chicago. A graduate of Cambridge, he has been working in England. He won an Academy Award for the screenplay of *Darling* (1965) and an Oscar nomination for *Two for the Road* (1967). He wrote many novels, biographies, essays, and teleplays.

FILMS INCLUDE: *Bachelor of Hearts* (co-sc.) 1958; *Nothing but the Best* 1964; *Darling* (also co-story) 1965; *Two for the Road, Far from the Madding Crowd* 1967; *Guilt* 1970; *A Severed Head* 1971; *Daisy Miller* (US) 1974; *Carmela* 1975; *Richard's Things* (from his own novel) 1980; *The King's Whore* (co-sc.; Fr./It.) 1990.

Raphaelson, Samson. Playwright, screenwriter. *b.* Mar. 30, 1896, New York City. *d.* 1983. *ed.* U. of Illinois. A former advertising man and journalist, he wrote many effervescent screenplays, alone or in collaboration, beginning in the early 30s, notably for the films of Ernst LUBITSCH.

FILMS INCLUDE: *The Jazz Singer* (play basis only) 1927; *The Smiling Lieutenant* (co-sc.), *The Magnificent Lie* 1931; *One Hour with You, Broken Lullaby/The Man I Killed* (co-sc.), *Trouble in Paradise* 1932; *Caravan, The Merry Widow* (co-sc.), *Servants' Entrance* 1934; *Accent on Youth* (play basis only) 1935; *The Last of Mrs. Cheyney* (co-sc.), *Angel* 1937; *The Shop Around the Corner* 1940; *Suspicion* (co-sc.), *Skylark* (play basis only) 1941; *Heaven Can Wait* 1943; *The Harvey Girls* (co-sc.), *The Perfect Marriage* (play basis only) 1946; *Green Dolphin Street, That Lady in Ermine* 1948; *In the Good Old Summertime* 1949; *Mr. Music* (play basis only) 1950; *The Jazz Singer* (remake; play basis only), *Main Street to Broadway* 1953; *Hilda Crane* (play basis only) 1956; *But Not for Me* (based on his play 'Accent on Youth') 1959; *The Jazz Singer* (play basis only) 1980.

Rappeneau, Jean-Paul. Director, screenwriter. Born in 1932, in France. He entered films as an assistant director, later directing a number of shorts. As a screenwriter from the late 50s, he collaborated with Louis MALLE and shared an Oscar nomination for Philippe de Broca's *That Man from Rio* (1964). He made an auspicious debut as a director with *La Vie de Château,* for which he won the Prix Delluc in 1965. His subsequent output, however, was sparse and not universally admired until 1990, when he turned out a sumptuous, definitive screen adaptation of *Cyrano de Bergerac,* starring Gérard DEPARDIEU.

FILMS: As screenwriter—*Signé Arsène Lupin* 1958; *Zazie dans le Métro/Zazie, La Française et l'Amour/Love and the Frenchwoman* 1960; *La Vie privée/A Very Private Affair, Le Combat dans l'Ile* 1962; *L'Homme de Rio/That Man from Rio* 1964; *La Fabuleuse Aventure de Marco Polo/Marco the Magnificent* 1965. As director-screenwriter—*La Vie de Château/A Matter of Resistance* 1965; *Les Mariées de l'An II* 1970; *Le Sauvage/The Savage* 1975; *Tout Feu Tout Flamme* 1982; *Cyrano de Bergerac* 1990.

Rapper, Irving. Director. Born in 1898, in London. In the US from age eight, he joined the Washington Square Players as a stage director while studying at New York University. He later appeared and directed on Broadway and arrived in Hollywood in the mid-30s as an assistant director and a dialogue coach. He worked in these capacities on such Warner films as *The Story of Louis Pasteur* (1935), *The Life of Emile Zola* (1937), *Four Daughters* (1938), *Juarez* (1939), and *Dr. Ehrlich's Magic Bullet* (1940) before making his debut as a full director in 1941. Although his film work tends to betray his theatrical background and is often stagy and talky, he was occasionally able to overcome this limitation with a flair for developing dramatic plots and directing actors. His *Now, Voyager* (1942) is a superior soap opera, grandly spun and beautifully played by Bette Davis and Claude Rains. Some of his early work is equally interesting, but the bulk of his product since the late 40s, when he left the Warners fold, has been uninspired.

FILMS: *Shining Victory, One Foot in Heaven* 1941; *The Gay Sisters, Now Voyager* 1942; *The Adventures of Mark Twain* 1944; *The Corn Is Green, Rhapsody in Blue* 1945; *Deception* 1946; *The Voice of the Turtle* 1947; *Anna Lucasta* 1949; *The Glass Menagerie* 1950; *Another Man's Poison* (UK) 1952; *Bad For Each Other, Forever Female* 1954; *Strange Intruder, The Brave One* 1956; *Marjorie Morningstar* 1958; *The Miracle* 1959; *Giuseppe venduto dai Fratelli/The Story of Joseph and His Brethren* (English version only; Italian version directed by Luciano Ricci; It.) 1960; *Ponzio Pilato/Pontius Pilate* (It./Fr.) 1962; *The Christine Jorgensen Story* 1970; *Born Again* 1978.

Rasp, Fritz. Actor. *b.* Heinrich Rasp, May 13, 1891, Bayreuth, Germany. *d.* 1976. Prominent character actor of German films, specializing in obnoxious and lecherous types. A member of Max Reinhardt's theater in Berlin, he entered the movies in 1915 and after a succession of minor roles rose to prominence in the 20s as a key character player in films of Fritz LANG and other directors of the German silent screen. He remained in films through the mid-60s.

FILMS INCLUDE: *Schupalast Pinkus* 1916; *Jugend* 1922; *Der Mensch am Wege, Schatten/Warning Shadows* 1923; *Arabella, Komödianten* 1924; *Ein Sommernachtstraum/A Midsummer Night's Dream, Die Puppe von Lunapark* 1925; *Das Haus der Lüge* 1926; *Metropolis, Der letzte Walzer/The Last Waltz, Die Liebe der Jeanne Ney/The Love of Jeanne Ney* 1927; *Schinderhannes/The Prince of Rogues, Der geheimnisvolle Spiegel/The Mystic Mirror, Spione/Spies* 1928; *Der Hund von Baskerville/The Hound of the Baskervilles, Die Frau im Mond/By Rocket to the Moon/Girl in the Moon, Tagebuch einer Verlorenen/The Diary of a Lost Girl, Frühlings Erwachen/The Awakening of Spring* 1929; *Die grosse Sehnsucht, Dreyfus* 1930; *Der Mörder Dimitri Karamasoff/Karamazof/The Brothers Karamazov* (as Smerdyakov), *Die Dreigroschenoper/The Threepenny Opera/The Beggar's Opera* (as Peachum), *Emil und die Detektive/Emil and the Detectives* 1931; *Der Hexer* 1932; *Der Judas von Tirol* 1933; *Grenzfeuer, Charleys Tante/Charley's Aunt, Lockvogel* 1934; *Frau im Strom* 1939; *Leidenschaft/Passion* 1940; *Paracelsus* 1943; *Irgendwo in Berlin/Somewhere in Berlin* 1946; *Haus des Lebens* 1952; *Magic Fire* (US) 1956; *Der rote Kreis/The Red Circle, Die Bande des Schreckens/The Terrible People* 1960; *Die seltsame Gräfin/The Strange Countess* 1961; *Der Zinker/The Squeaker* 1963; *Dr. Med. Hiob Praetorius* 1965; *Lina Braake* 1976.

Rasumny, Mikhail. Actor. *b.* 1890, Odessa, Russia. *d.* 1956. A cantor's son, he made his stage debut at 14. He arrived in the US in 1935 with the Moscow Art Theatre and appeared and directed on Broadway. In Hollywood from 1940, he played many character parts, usually as a Slav or some other foreigner.

FILMS INCLUDE: *Comrade X* 1940; *Hold Back the Dawn* 1941; *The Shanghai Gesture, Wake Island, This Gun for Hire, Road to Morocco* 1942; *For Whom the Bell Tolls* (as Rafael), *Hostages* 1943; *And the Angels Sing* 1944; *A Royal Scandal, The Unseen, A Medal for Benny, Masquerade in Mexico* 1945; *Heartbeat, Anna and the King of Siam* 1946; *Her Husband's Affairs* 1947; *The Kissing Bandit, Saigon* 1948; *Anything Can Happen* 1952; *Tonight We Sing* 1953; *Hot Blood* 1956.

Rathbone, Basil. Actor. *b.* Philip St. John Basil Rathbone, June 13, 1892, Johannesburg, South Africa, to British parents. *d.* 1967. The American screen's finest villain and most memorable Sherlock Holmes. Educated in England, he made his stage debut there in 1911. He played many classical roles, including much Shakespeare, on both sides of the Atlantic. On the screen from the early 20s, often in romantic leads, he rose to prominence after the coming of sound, when his distinctive voice complemented his polished manner. Gaunt, saturnine, and cerebral, he made an ideal archenemy for many of Hollywood's leading heroes, crossing swords and exchanging innuendos with such stars as Errol Flynn and Tyrone Power. The same qualities made him a convincing, cunning, and aloof Sherlock Holmes in 14 films of the 40s. He was nominated for Academy Awards as best supporting actor for *Romeo and Juliet* (1936) and *If I Were King* (1938). His second wife, Ouida Bergere (1886–1974), was a supporting actress of Hollywood films of the 20s who also collaborated on a number of screenplays.

FILMS: In the UK—*Innocent, The Fruitful Vine* 1921; *The Loves of Mary Queen of Scots* (bit), *The School for Scandal* (as Joseph Surface) 1923. In the US—*Trouping with Ellen* 1924; *The Masked Bride* 1925; *The Great Deception* 1926; *The Last of Mrs. Cheyney* 1929; *The Bishop Murder Case* (as detective Philo Vance), *A Notorious Affair, The Lady of Scandal, This Mad World, The Flirting Widow, A Lady Surrenders, Sin Takes a Holiday* 1930; *A Woman Commands* 1932; *One Precious Year* (UK), *After the Ball* (UK), *Loyalties* (as Ferdinand de Levis; UK) 1933; *David Copperfield* (as Mr. Murdstone), *Anna Karenina* (as Karenin), *The Last Days of Pompeii* (as Pontius Pilate), *A Feather in Her Hat, A Tale of Two Cities* (as the Marquis St. Evremonde), *Captain Blood, Kind Lady* 1935; *Private Number, Romeo and Juliet* (as Tybalt), *The Garden of Allah* 1936; *Confession, Love from a Stranger, Make a Wish, Tovarich* 1937; *The Adventures of Marco Polo, The Adventures of Robin Hood* (as the evil Sir Guy of Gisbourne), *If I Were King* (as Louis XI), *Dawn Patrol* 1938; *Son of Frankenstein* (as the Baron von Frankenstein), *The Hound of the Baskervilles* (as Sherlock Holmes), *The Sun Never Sets, The Adventures of Sherlock Holmes* (title role), *Rio, Tower of London* (as Richard

III) 1939; *Rhythm on the River, The Mark of Zorro* 1940; *The Mad Doctor, The Black Cat, International Lady* 1941; *Paris Calling, Fingers at the Window, Crossroads, Sherlock Holmes and the Voice of Terror* (title role) 1942; *Sherlock Holmes and the Secret Weapon* (title role), *Sherlock Holmes in Washington* (title role), *Above Suspicion, Sherlock Holmes Faces Death* (title role), *Crazy House* (unbilled cameo) 1943; *Spider Woman* (as Sherlock Holmes), *The Scarlet Claw* (as Sherlock Holmes), *Bathing Beauty, Pearl of Death* (as Sherlock Holmes), *Frenchman's Creek* 1944; *The House of Fear* (as Sherlock Holmes), *The Woman in Green* (as Sherlock Holmes), *Pursuit to Algiers* (as Sherlock Holmes) 1945; *Terror by Night* (as Sherlock Holmes), *Heartbeat, Dressed to Kill* (as Sherlock Holmes) 1946; *Ichabod and Mr. Toad* (narrator only of "Mr. Toad" episode) 1949; *Casanova's Big Night* 1954; *We're No Angels* 1955; *The Court Jester, The Black Sleep* 1956; *The Last Hurrah* 1958; *Ponzio Pilato/Pontius Pilate* (as Caiaphas; It./Fr.), *The Magic Sword, Tales of Terror, Two Before Zero/Russian Roulette* (doc.; on-screen co-narrator) 1962; *The Comedy of Terrors/The Graveside Story* 1963; *Queen of Blood/Planet of Blood, The Ghost in the Invisible Bikini* 1966; *Voyage to a Prehistoric Planet, Autopsia de un Fantasma/Autopsy of a Ghost* (Mex.), *Hillbillys in a Haunted House* 1967.

rating. A system of classifying motion pictures according to certain predetermined categories. A rating system has existed in the United Kingdom for many years as an essential part of the British censorship philosophy, whose aim has always been to protect the young rather than to dictate taste to adults. Many countries have followed the British example, but there was no similar system in the United States until 1968, when rating classifications were incorporated into the self-regulatory PRODUCTION CODE. American ratings originally consisted of four categories: G (general audiences; all ages admitted), PG (at first M. GP.; all ages admitted but parental guidance is suggested), R (restricted; youngsters under 17 admitted only if accompanied by parent or adult guardian), and X (no one under 17 admitted; the age limit may vary upward). The guidelines remained unchanged until 1984, when a fifth category, PG–13, was added, following a campaign headed by Steven SPIELBERG, to address concerns of parents of preteen children who might have been frightened by the director's wholesome but scary films *Indiana Jones and the Temple of Doom* or *Gremlins.* Another change came in 1990, after a staggering ten mainstream films were slapped with an X rating, which over the years became synonymous in the public mind with sleazy porno movies. Among these were Peter Greenaway's *The Cook, the Thief, His Wife, and Her Lover* and Pedro Almodóvar's *Tie Me Up! Tie Me Down!.* When the X rating was attached to Philip Kaufman's *Henry & June,* the director and his powerful studio, Universal, aided by civil liberties advocate and law professor Alan M. Dershowitz, blitzed the system and forced the quick adoption of a sixth category, NC–17 (no children under 17), for nonpornographic films containing sexual material deemed unsuitable for viewing by non-adults. The ratings are issued by the Code and Rating Administration of the Motion Picture Association of America.

In the United Kingdom, ratings are determined by the British Board of Film Censors. Until July 1, 1970, the categories were U (universal admission), A (youngsters under 16 admitted only with adult), and X (youngsters under 16 not admitted). The new categories are U (universal), A (parental discretion suggested), AA (youngsters under 14 not admitted), and X (youngsters under 18 not admitted). The age limit for X-rated films varies from country to country. It is probably the lowest in Sweden, where youngsters over 15 are considered adults by the censors.

ratio. See ASPECT RATIO; SHOOTING RATIO.

Ratoff, Gregory. Director, actor. *b.* Apr. 20, 1897, in St. Petersburg, Russia. *d.* 1960. *ed.* U. of St. Petersburg (law, then drama). He served with the Czar's army and appeared with the Moscow Art Theatre before coming to the US. He appeared in New York with the Yiddish Players and produced, directed, and acted on Broadway before making his Hollywood debut as actor in the early 30s. He was often typecast as a foreigner with a thick accent, sometimes as an eccentric director or producer. By the mid-30s he had begun really directing films. In addition to his many routine pictures, there are several that are memorable, including *Intermezzo—A Love Story* (1939), Ingrid Bergman's first Hollywood film, and an exciting swashbuckling adventure, *The Corsican Brothers* (1941).

FILMS INCLUDE: As actor—*Symphony of Six Million, What Price Hollywood, Skyscraper Souls, Once in a Lifetime, Secrets of the French Police* 1932; *Professional Sweetheart, I'm No Angel, Broadway Thru a Keyhole, Sitting Pretty* 1933; *George White's Scandals* 1934; *Remember Last Night?* 1935; *King of Burlesque, Under Two Flags, The Road to Glory, Sing Baby Sing* 1936; *Seventh Heaven, Top of the Town, Cafe Metropole* (also story) 1937; *Sally Irene and Mary, Gateway* 1938; *The Great Profile* 1940; *All About Eve* 1950; *O. Henry's Full House* 1952; *The Sun Also Rises* 1957; *Once More with Feeling, Exodus* 1960; *The Big Gamble* 1961. As screenwriter—*The Great Flirtation* (story only) 1934; *You Can't Have Everything* (story only) 1937. As director (complete)—*Sins of Man* (co-dir. with Otto Brower) 1936; *Lancer Spy* 1937; *Wife Husband and Friend, Rose of Washington Square, Hotel for Women, Intermezzo—A Love Story, Day-Time Wife, Barricade* 1939; *I Was an Adventuress, Public Deb No. 1* 1940; *Adam Had Four Sons, The Men in Her Life* (also prod.), *The Corsican Brothers* 1941; *Two Yanks in Trinidad, Footlight Serenade* 1942; *Something to Shout About* (also prod.), *The Heat's On* 1943; *Song of Russia, Irish Eyes Are Smiling* 1944; *Where Do We Go from Here?, Paris Underground* 1945; *Do You Love Me?* 1946; *Carnival in Costa Rica, Moss Rose* 1947; *Black Magic* (also prod.), *That Dangerous Age/If This Be Sin* (also prod.; UK) 1949; *My Daughter Joy/Operation X* (also prod.; UK) 1950; *Taxi* 1953; *Abdullah's Harem* (also prod., act.; Egypt) 1956; *Oscar Wilde* (UK) 1960.

Rattigan, Sir Terence. Playwright, screenwriter. *b.* June 10, 1911, London. *d.* 1977. A diplomat's son and an Oxford scholar in modern history, he began writing successful plays in the mid-30s. He served as an air gunner in WW II. Not only have films been adapted from his plays, but he also wrote many original screenplays, alone or in collaboration. He was knighted in 1971.

FILMS INCLUDE: *French Without Tears* (play basis only) 1939; *Quiet Wedding* 1940; *The Day Will Dawn/The Avengers* 1942; *The Way to the Stars/Johnny in the Clouds, Journey Together* (doc.) 1945; *English Without Tears/Her Man Gilbey* 1946; *While the Sun Shines* (from his own play), *Brighton Rock/Young Scarface* 1947; *Bond Street, The Winslow Boy* (from his own play) 1948; *The Browning Version* (from his own play) 1951; *The Sound Barrier/Breaking Through the Sound Barrier* (also story) 1952; *The Final Test* (also story) 1953; *The Man Who Loved Redheads* (also story), *The Deep Blue Sea* (from his own play) 1955; *The Prince and the Showgirl* (from his own play 'The Sleeping Prince') 1957; *Separate Tables* (from his own play; US) 1958; *The V.I.P.s* (also story) 1963; *The Yellow Rolls-Royce* (also story) 1964; *Goodbye Mr. Chips* (UK/US) 1969; *A Bequest to the Nation/The Nelson Affair* (from his play) 1973.

Ravetch, Irving. Screenwriter. Born on Nov. 14, 1920, in

Newark, N.J. In films since the late 40s, he often worked in collaboration with his wife, Harriet Frank, Jr. Two of their scripts, *Hud* (1963) and *Norma Rae* (1979), were nominated for Academy Awards.

FILMS INCLUDE: *Living in a Big Way* 1947; *The Outriders* 1950; *Vengeance Valley* 1951; *Lone Hand* (story only) 1953; *Run for Cover* (story only), *Ten Wanted Men* 1955; *The Long Hot Summer* 1958; *The Sound and the Fury* 1959; *Home from the Hill* 1960; *Hud* (also co-prod.) 1963; *Hombre* (also co-prod.) 1967; *The Reivers* (also prod.), *House of Cards* (under pseudonym James P. Bonner) 1969; *The Cowboys* 1972; *Conrack, The Spikes Gang* 1974; *Norma Rae* 1979; *Murphy's Romance* 1985; *Stanley & Iris* 1990.

Rawlins, John. Director. Born on June 9, 1902, in Long Beach, Calif. He started in films in the 20s as a stuntman and actor in action pictures and serials. In the early 30s he wrote gags for screen comedies and became a film editor for Columbia. A director since the late 30s, mostly of B action pictures, including a couple of Universal desert adventures starring Maria Montez.

FILMS: *State Police, Young Fugitives, The Missing Guest, Air Devils* 1938; *The Green Hornet Strikes Again* (serial; co-dir. with Ford Beebe), *Junior G-Men* (serial; co-dir. with Beebe), *The Leather Pushers* 1940; *Sea Raiders* (serial; co-dir. with Beebe), *Six Lessons from Madame La Zonga, A Dangerous Game, Mr. Dynamite, Mutiny in the Arctic, Men of the Timberland, Raiders of the Desert* 1941; *Overland Mail* (serial; co-dir. with Beebe), *Bombay Clipper, Unseen Enemy, Mississippi Gambler, Half Way to Shanghai, Sherlock Holmes and the Voice of Terror, The Great Impersonation, Arabian Nights* 1942; *We've Never Been Licked* 1943; *Ladies Courageous* 1944; *Sudan* 1945; *Strange Conquest, Her Adventurous Night* 1946; *Dick Tracy's Dilemma, Dick Tracy Meets Gruesome* 1947; *The Arizona Ranger, Michael O'Halloran* 1948; *Massacre River* 1949; *Boy from Indiana, Rogue River* 1950; *Fort Defiance* 1951; *Shark River* 1953; *Lost Lagoon* 1958.

Rawlinson, Herbert. Actor. *b.* 1885, Brighton, England. *d.* 1953. Popular star of Hollywood silents. A former vaudeville and legitimate stage actor, he entered American films in 1911 and subsequently played leads in scores of silent productions, often romantic dramas and crime thrillers. A middle-aged man by the advent of sound, he switched to character roles, playing a variety of supporting parts, often as a distinguished gentleman, through the early 50s, when he died of lung cancer.

FILMS INCLUDE: *The Novice* 1911; *The Ace of Spades, The Coming of Columbus, The God of Gold, Monte Cristo/The Count of Monte Cristo* 1912; *The Old Clerk, The Sea-Wolf* 1913; *The Spy, Martin Eden, Damon and Pythias* (as Pythias) 1914; *The Black Box* (serial) 1915; *The Eagle's Wing* 1916; *Come Through, Flirting with Death* 1917; *The Flash of Fate* (also prod.), *Smashing Through, Back to the Woods, The Turn of the Wheel, Kiss or Kill* 1918; *Good Gracious Annabelle, A House Divided* 1919; *Passers-By, Man and His Woman* 1920; *Playthings of Destiny, Charge It, Wealth, The Conflict, The Millionaire, Cheated Hearts* 1921; *The Scrapper, The Man Under Cover, Don't Shoot, Confidence, Another Man's Shoes, One Wonderful Night* 1922; *The Prisoner, Fools and Riches, The Victor* 1923; *Stolen Secrets, The Dancing Cheat, High Speed* 1924; *The Adventurous Sex, Every Man's Wife, The Man in Blue, The Unnamed Woman, The Great Jewel Robbery* 1925; *The Millionaire Policeman, Men of the Night, The Belle of Broadway* 1926; *Burning Gold, The Bugle Call, Wages of Conscience* 1927; *Moonlight and Pretzels* 1933; *Men Without Names, Show Them No Mercy* 1935; *Bullets or Ballots, Hollywood Boulevard* 1936; *That Certain Woman* 1937; *Secrets of an Actress, Marie Antoinette* 1938; *Dark Victory* 1939; *Swiss Family Robinson, Seven Sinners* 1940; *I Wanted Wings* 1941; *Lady Gangster* 1942; *Old Acquaintance* 1943; *Shake Hands with Murder* 1944; *Joan of Arc* 1948; *Brimstone* 1949; *Gene Autry and the Mounties* 1951; *Jail Bait* 1954.

raw stock. Film that has not been exposed.

Ray, Aldo. Actor. *b.* Aldo DaRe, Sept. 25, 1926, Pen Argyl, Pa. *d.* 1991. *ed.* U. of California. Husky, bull-necked, foghorn-voiced leading man of Hollywood and some European films. He served as a Navy frogman in WW II, then served briefly as constable of Crockett, Calif., a town in which he had been raised from the age of two. His best screen roles came in the 50s, when he represented the American redneck, in and out of uniform. His career declined in the 60s and reached a nadir in the late 70s, when he appeared in the hardcore porno Western *Sweet Savage* (1979), although he did not participate in any nude or sex scenes. He continued performing in films and on TV but in progressively lesser roles and poorer vehicles. In 1986 he was expelled from SAG, the Screen Actors Guild, for working in non-union productions. He died at 64 of complications from throat cancer and pneumonia. One of his three marriages (1954–56) was to actress Jeff DONNELL. One of his three children, Eric DaRe, is an actor.

FILMS INCLUDE: *Saturday's Hero* 1951; *The Marrying Kind, Pat and Mike* 1952; *Let's Do It Again, Miss Sadie Thompson* 1953; *We're No Angels, Battle Cry, Three Stripes in the Sun* 1955; *Nightfall* 1956; *Men in War* 1957; *God's Little Acre, The Naked and the Dead* 1958; *The Day They Robbed the Bank of England* (UK) 1960; *Johnny Nobody* (UK) 1961; *Nightmare in the Sun, Sylvia* 1965; *What Did You Do in the War Daddy?, Dead Heat on a Merry-Go-Round* 1966; *Riot on Sunset Strip, Welcome to Hard Times, The Violent Ones* 1967; *The Power, The Green Berets* 1968; *Angel Unchained* 1970; *La Course du Lièvre à travers les Champs/And Hope to Die* (Fr./US) 1972; *Tom* 1973; *The Centerfold Girls* 1974; *Inside Out* (UK), *Seven Alone, The Man Who Would Not Die, Gone with the West, Psychic Killer,* 1975; *The Bad Bunch* 1976; *Haunts/The Veil* 1977; *Sky Dove* 1978; *Sweet Savage, The Glove* 1979; *Human Experiments, Freeze Bomb/Death Dimension* (release delayed from 1978) 1980; *Don't Go Near the Park* 1981; *The Secret of Nimh* (v/o), *Bonoffice* 1982; *The Executioner Part II, Frankenstein's Great Aunt Tillie* 1984; *Biohazard, Prison Ship 2005/Star Slammer, Evils of the Night, Flesh and Bullets* 1985; *Terror on Alcatraz* 1986; *Hollywood Cop, The Sicilian* 1987; *Blood Red* 1988; *Swift Justice* 1989; *The Shooters, Shock 'Em Dead* 1990.

Ray, Charles. Actor. *b.* Mar. 15, 1891, Jacksonville, Ill. *d.* 1943. Popular star of Hollywood silents, typically cast as an innocent country boy who overcomes an assortment of odds and his own clumsiness to win the heroine at the end of each picture. Brought to films from the stage by Thomas INCE, he reached a peak of success around 1920. His popularity soon waned, however, with the growing sophistication of cinema audiences, who lost interest in rural Americana with the onrush of the Roaring 20s. He suffered a grave financial loss in an attempt to establish his own production company, for which he directed his own films in the early 20s, and was no more successful in trying to switch to city-slicker roles. He continued appearing in occasional films until shortly before his death.

FILMS INCLUDE: *The Favorite Son, A Slave's Devotion, Witch of Salem, The Lost Dispatch* 1913; *The Path of Genius, City of Darkness, The Rightful Heir* 1914; *The Coward, The Cup of Life, The Lure of Woman, The Painted Soul, The Forbidden Adventure,* 1915; *Peggy, Home, Honor Thy Name, Plain Jane,*

The Deserter 1916; *The Pinch Hitter, The Weaker Sex, Sudden Jim, The Clodhopper* 1917; *The Claws of the Hun, A Nine O'Clock Town, The Law of the North, String Beans* 1918; *The Girl Dodger, The Sheriff's Son, Greased Lightning, The Busher, Bill Henry, Red Hot Dollars* 1919; *Alarm Clock Andy, Homer Come Home, Village Sleuth, Peaceful Valley, An Old-Fashioned Boy, Forty-Five Minutes from Broadway* (also prod.) 1920; *The Old Swimmin' Hole* (also prod.), *A Midnight Bell* (also dir., prod.), *Two Minutes to Go* (also dir., prod.), *Scrap Iron* (also dir., prod.), *R.S.V.P.* (also dir., prod.) 1921; *Alias Julius Caesar* (also dir., prod.), *The Barnstormer* (also dir., prod.), *The Deuce of Spades* (also dir., prod.), *Gas Oil and Water* (also dir., prod.), *Smudge* (also dir., prod.), *A Tailor Made Man* (also prod., sc.) 1922; *The Girl I Loved* (also prod.), *Ponjola, The Courtship of Miles Standish* (also prod.) 1923; *Dynamite Smith* 1924; *Percy, Bright Lights* 1925; *The Auction Block, Paris, Sweet Adeline, The Fire Brigade* 1926; *Nobody's Widow, Getting Gertie's Garter, Vanity* 1927; *The Count of Ten, The Garden of Eden* 1928; *Ladies Should Listen, School for Girls* 1934; *Welcome Home* 1935; *Hollywood Boulevard* 1936; *A Little Bit of Heaven* 1940; *Tennessee Johnson* 1942.

Ray, Fred Olen. Director. Born on Sept. 10, 1954, in Wellston, Ohio. *ed.* Brown U. (engineering). Prolific maker of bottom-budget horror and fantasy thrillers. The son of a NASA electronics engineer, he was raised in Florida, where he began his working career as an engineer for an Orlando radio station. A horror-film buff from childhood, he used his mother's credit line, with his own motorbike as part collateral, to raise the $15,000 needed for his first film, *The Alien Dead* (made 1978, released 1981), Buster Crabbe's last movie. Moving to California, he supported himself for several years as a makeup-effects artist before hitting his stride as a director-producer of cheap, profitable, quickie 'B' pictures.

FILMS INCLUDE: *The Alien Dead/It Fell from the Sky* 1981; *Scalps* 1984; *Bicharard, The Tomb, Star Slammer/Prison Ship 2005* 1985; *Armed Response* 1986; *Cyclone, Commando Squad* 1987; *Hollywood Chainsaw Hookers, The Phantom Empire* 1988; *Deep Space, Beverly Hills Vamp, Warlords, Alienator* 1989; *Terminal Force, Mob Boss, Spirits* 1990; *Bad Girls from Mars, Inner Sanctum, Little Devils, Angel Eyes* 1991; *Haunting Fear, Wizards of the Demon Sword* 1992.

Ray, Man. Painter, photographer, avant-garde filmmaker. *b.* Emmanuel Rudnitsky, Aug. 27, 1890, Philadelphia. *d.* 1976. A founder of the New York Dada movement and later a convert to surrealism, he extended his plastic arts search to motion pictures while in Paris in the 20s. He experimented with a process that bypassed the camera and reproduced outlines of moving objects by placing them directly on negative film and exposing them to light. He wrote an autobiography, *Self Portrait* (1963).

FILMS INCLUDE: *Le Retour à la Raison* 1923; *Emak Bakia* 1927; *L'Etoile de Mer* 1928; *Les Mystères du Château du Dé/The Mystery of the Chateau of the Dice* 1929; *Dreams That Money Can Buy* (co-sc.) 1944–46.

Ray, Nicholas. Director. *b.* Raymond Nicholas Kienzle, Aug. 7, 1911, Galesville, Wis. *d.* 1979. Darling of the *auteur* theory cultists. A dynamic, socially conscious director with a keen visual sense and a gift for attaining fluid motion on the screen. The son of a builder of Norwegian descent, he was raised in La Crosse and after attending the Universities of Chicago and Wisconsin for one year each, studied architecture under Frank Lloyd Wright. At the same time, he became increasingly involved with the theater as an actor, and occasionally director, with touring groups. In 1932 he moved to New York, where he became associated with the left-wing theater, appearing in some of the earliest plays staged by Elia KAZAN. He then joined John HOUSEMAN's Phoenix Theatre company in New York and during WW II wrote and directed radio propaganda programs for the Office of War Information under Houseman's supervision. After assisting on several films, among them Kazan's *A Tree Grows in Brooklyn* (1945), directing a Broadway play, and working briefly for TV, he made his debut as a feature film director under the aegis of Houseman with an RKO screen adaptation of Edward Anderson's novel *Thieves by Night.* Projecting themes and style elements that would characterize some of Ray's future work, *They Live by Night* dealt sensitively and compassionately with the doomed love of emotionally scarred young fugitives from justice (Farley Granger and Cathy O'Donnell). Other key Ray films are *In a Lonely Place* (1950), a gripping drama about a screenwriter (Humphrey Bogart) and his weird relationship with a Hollywood starlet (Gloria Grahame) as he is trying to clear himself from suspicion of murder; *Johnny Guitar* (1954), a fascinating, most unusual, kinkily Freudian Western starring Joan Crawford, Sterling Hayden, and Mercedes McCambridge; and, of course, *Rebel Without a Cause* (1955), the quintessential youth-alienation movie starring James Dean. Ray was nominated for an Academy Award for the latter film's story. Ray's training as an architect is evident in his films not only in terms of the general visual flair but more specifically through the effect of locale and environment on the relationships and lives of his characters. His heroes are frequently anguished social rebels who consume themselves in the quest for love or in fast and furious living. Technically, his work is characterized by tense and restless camera movement that matches the turbulence of the action on the screen. Although he was inactive as a Hollywood feature director after 1963, Ray's cult worship continued to grow among film lovers. But the adulation hardly compensated Ray for his vanishing career. In the decade that followed his last film, *55 Days at Peking* (1963), he saw project after project fail to materialize or be aborted halfway through. He began lecturing on the college circuit and in 1971 joined the faculty of New York State University at Binghamton as professor of cinema studies at Harpur College. Under his supervision, the students turned out a joint project, *You Can't Go Home Again,* which was greeted by jeers at the 1973 Cannes Festival. The only other work by Ray that reached the screen was an episode in a 13-part Dutch soft-core porno movie, *Dreams of 13* (1974). In 1977 Ray played a prominent featured role in Wim Wenders's German-French film *The American Friend* and in 1979 he appeared in a bit in Milos Forman's *Hair.* Ray's relationship with Wenders led to a collaboration between the two directors on a bizarre, mesmerizing film, half-real, half-imagined, documenting the final days of Ray as he was visibly withering away, dying of cancer. Entitled *Lightning Over Waters/Nick's Film*, it both appalled and intrigued filmgoers when it was released posthumously in 1980. Ray's four marriages included actress Gloria GRAHAME (1948–52) who, in 1961, would marry his son from a previous marriage (her own stepson) Anthony Ray, an actor-turned-producer who in the 70s produced several of Paul Mazursky's films.

FILMS: *They Live by Night/The Twisted Road* (also adapt.) 1948–49; *A Woman's Secret, Knock on Any Door* 1949; *In a Lonely Place, Born to Be Bad* 1950; *Flying Leathernecks* 1951; *On Dangerous Ground, The Lusty Men* 1952; *Johnny Guitar* (also assoc. prod.) 1954; *Run for Cover, Rebel Without a Cause* (also story) 1955; *Hot Blood, Bigger Than Life* 1956; *The True Story of Jesse James, Amère Victoire/Bitter Victory* (also co-sc.; Fr.) 1957; *Wind Across the Everglades, Party Girl* 1958; *Ombre bianche/Les Dents du Diable/The Savage Innocents* (also sc.; It./Fr./UK) 1960; *King of Kings* 1961; *55 Days at Peking* (also act.) 1963; *You Can't Go Home Again* (made over a period of several years with students at New York State U.) 1973–76;

Dreams of 13 ("The Janitor" episode; Hol.) 1974; *Lightning Over Water/Nick's Film* (co-dir. with Wim Wenders; also act.) 1980.

Ray, Satyajit. Director. *b.* May 2, 1921, in Calcutta, into a family prominent in Indian arts and letters. *d.* 1992. After graduating with honors from the University of Calcutta, where he majored in economics with a minor in physics, he attended Shantiniketan, a university run by an old friend of his family, the Hindu poet Rabindranath Tagore, where he studied painting and art history. In 1942 he returned to Calcutta and the following year joined a British-run advertising firm as an art director. He also began illustrating books, one of which, *Pather Panchali,* left a deep impression on him. He became fascinated with the idea of filming this autobiographical novel dealing with Bengali village life but could not decide on the proper approach. The decision came in 1950 when on a business trip to London he saw De Sica's *The Bicycle Thief,* which was shot on location with nonprofessional players. Returning to India, Ray tried unsuccessfully to raise money for his project. Nonetheless, he and a group of amateur friends began shooting the film on weekends and holidays with the moral encouragement of Jean Renoir, who was then shooting *The River* in India.

Ray spent his entire salary, sold all his possessions, and pawned his wife's jewels to keep the project going. He was about to abandon the film, after a year and a half of work, when the Bengal government stepped in and sponsored the completion of the project. *Pather Panchali* (1955) made an enormous impact at the 1956 Cannes Film Festival. It introduced Indian cinema to the West as cataclysmically as *Rashomon* had done for Japanese films. A human document of timeless simplicity and exquisite beauty, *Pather Panchali* stunned the critics and won a special jury prize at the festival.

Encouraged by the reception given *Pather Panchali,* Ray went on to make two sequels, *Aparajito* (1956) and *The World of Apu* (1959), comprising the 'Apu Trilogy,' one of the most brilliant film series in screen history. Ray maintained a high artistic level in most of his subsequent films but found it impossible to match the authenticity, sincerity, beauty, and magic of the trilogy. At the same time, Ray's later output boasts a bolder, more complex style and a sharper, more pointed voice. Above all, he sustained throughout his career the humanist values that have made his films universally appealing. Many of Ray's films were awarded prizes at international film festivals. He won the Silver Bear for best direction at the Berlin Film Festival two years in succession, in 1964 for *Mahanagar/The Big City* and in 1965 for *Charulata/The Lonely Wife.* In 1966 the festival awarded him an honorable mention for *The Nayak/The Hero* and for the body of his work. He wrote all of his own scripts and from the early 60s also composed the music for his films. He was also heavily involved in the costume design of his productions. Virtually all his films were made in the Bengali language but in 1977 he issued his first non-Bengali production, *The Chess Players,* which was released in Hindi and English versions. Ray was slowed down in the 80s by several heart attacks. One of these forced him to hand over the completion of *The Home and the World* (1984) to his son, director Sandip Ray. Satyajit Ray stayed away from filming for four years. He returned to work under a doctor's supervision, restricting his activity to a studio setting. The result was an uncharacteristically static and stagy screen adaptation of Ibsen's *An Enemy of the People* (1989), set in West Bengal. Ray seemed to return to fuller activity and in 1992 turned out *The Visitor*, one of his best films in years. It became his swan song, and he died shortly after receiving an Honorary Academy Award in 1992.

FILMS: As director-screenwriter—*Pather Panchali/Father Panchali* 1955; *Aparajito/The Unvanquished* 1956; *Parash Pather/The Philosopher's Stone* 1957; *Jalsaghar/The Music Room* 1958; *Apu Sansar/The World of Apu* 1959; *Devi/The Goddess* 1960. As director-screenwriter-composer—*Rabindranath Tagore* (doc.), *Teen Kanya/Two Daughters* 1961; *Kanchanjungha, Abhijan/The Expedition* 1962; *Mahanagar/The Big City* 1963; *Charulata/The Lonely Wife* 1964; *Kapurush-o-Mahapurush/The Coward and the Saint/The Coward and the Holy Man* 1965; *Nayak/The Hero* 1966; *Chiriakhana/The Zoo* 1967; *Goopy Gyne Bagha Byne/The Adventures of Goopy and Bagha* 1969; *Aranyer din Ratri/Days and Nights in the Forest, Two* (short) 1970; *Pratiwandi/The Adversary/Siddharta and the City* 1971; *Simbaddha/Company Limited, Sikkim* (doc.) 1972; *Ashanti Sanket/Distant Thunder* 1973; *The Inner Eye* (doc. short), *Sonar Kella/The Golden Fortress* 1974; *Jana Aranya/The Middleman, Bala* (doc.) 1976; *Shatranj ke Khilari/The Chess Players* 1977; *Joi Baba Felunath/The Elephant God* 1978; *Hirok Rajar Deshe/The Kingdom of Diamonds* 1980; *Pikoo's Day* (short for French TV), *Sadghati/Deliverance* 1981; *Ghare-Baire/The Home and the World* 1984; *Ganashatru/An Enemy of the People* (also co-edit.) 1989; *Goopy Bagha Phire Elo/The Return of Goopy and Bhaga* (sc., mus., lyr. only for film directed by son Sandip Ray), *Shakha Prosakha/Branches of the Tree/Family Reunion* (Ind./Fr.) 1990; *Agantuk/The Visitor* 1992; *Broken Journey* (sc. only) 1994.

Raye, Martha. Actress. *b.* Margaret Teresa Yvonne O'Reed, on Aug. 27, 1916. *d.* 1994. Born in the charity ward of a hospital in Butte, Mont., where her touring vaudeville parents had found themselves stranded. By the time she was three she had joined the family act and at 13 she was a specialty singer with a band. She was a 19-year-old veteran of the stage and nightclubs when she broke into films in 1935. A zestful, boisterous comedienne with a huge elastic mouth and forceful lungs, she enlivened many a light film with her zany antics. Most of her roles were in minor Hollywood productions. The notable exception was in Chaplin's *Monsieur Verdoux* (1947), in which she was highly entertaining as an indestructible intended murder victim. After that, she made only rare film appearances but continued performing energetically in nightclubs and burlesque shows and on TV, where she hosted 'The Martha Raye Show' (1955–56). In 1967 she replaced Ginger Rogers in 'Hello Dolly' on Broadway and in 1972 took over a lead in the revival of 'No No Nanette.' Most of all, she is known for her morale-boosting excursions into the battlefronts of WW II, the Korean War, and Vietnam War. She received presidential praise and a special 1969 Academy Award for entertaining troops in the latter war. The first two of her marital unions were to movie makeup expert Bud (Hamilton) Westmore (for four months in 1937) and composer-conductor David Rose (1938–40). Most of Raye's estate was the result of her years endorsing a denture toothpaste in a series of TV commercials. Also on TV, she played supporting roles in 'McMillan and Wife' (1976–77) and 'Alice' (1982–84).

FEATURE FILMS: *Rhythm on the Range, Hideaway Girl, The Big Broadcast of 1937, College Holiday* 1936; *Waikiki Wedding, Mountain Music, Artists and Models, Double or Nothing* 1937; *The Big Broadcast of 1938, Give Me a Sailor, College Swing, Tropic Holiday* 1938; *Never Say Die, $1,000 a Touchdown* 1939; *The Farmer's Daughter, The Boys from Syracuse* 1940; *Navy Blues, Keep 'Em Flying, Hellzapoppin* 1941; *Four Jills in a Jeep, Pin Up Girl* 1944; *Monsieur Verdoux* 1947; *Jumbo* 1962; *The Phynx* (cameo), *Pufnstuf* (v/o) 1970; *The Concorde—Airport '79* 1979.

Raymond, Gene. Actor. Born Raymond Guion, on Aug. 13, 1908, in New York City. Handsome blond leading man of romantic Hollywood second features of the 30s. On the stage from age five, he attended New York's Professional Children's School and made his Broadway debut in 1920. He went into films in the early 30s, changing his name from Guion to Raymond. He enjoyed only modest popularity and was best known among film fans as the husband (from 1937 till her death in 1965) of Jeanette MacDonald. Raymond produced and directed one unsuccessful film, *Million Dollar Weekend,* in 1948, has written a TV play, and composed a number of songs for his wife's concert tours. Although still seen occasionally in character parts on TV, he devotes most of his time to business investments.

FILMS INCLUDE: *Personal Maid, Ladies of the Big House* 1931; *Forgotten Commandments, The Night of June 13th, Red Dust, If I Had a Million* 1932; *Zoo in Budapest, Ex-Lady, Ann Carver's Profession, Brief Moment, The House on 56th Street, Flying Down to Rio* 1933; *I Am Suzanne, Coming-Out Party, Sadie McKee, Transatlantic Merry-Go-Round* 1934; *Behold My Wife, The Woman in Red, Hooray for Love, Seven Keys to Baldpate* 1935; *Love on a Bet, The Bride Walks Out, Walking on Air* 1936; *That Girl from Paris, The Life of the Party, She's Got Everything* 1937; *Stolen Heaven* 1938; *Cross Country Romance* 1940; *Mr. and Mrs. Smith, Smilin' Through* 1941; *The Locket* 1946; *Assigned to Danger, Million Dollar Weekend* (also dir., prod.), *Sofia* 1948; *Hit the Deck* 1955; *Plunder Road* 1957; *The Best Man, I'd Rather Be Rich* 1964; *Five Bloody Graves* (v/o, as Death) 1969.

Raymond, Paula. Actress. Born Paula Ramona Wright, in 1923, in San Francisco. A Hollywood leading lady, mostly in second features, she was formerly a model and stage actress.

FILMS INCLUDE: *Rusty Leads the Way* 1948; *Devil's Doorway, Duchess of Idaho, Crisis, Grounds for Marriage* 1950; *The Tall Target, The Sellout* 1951; *The Bandits of Corsica, The Beast from 20,000 Fathoms* 1953; *King Richard and the Crusaders, The Human Jungle* 1954; *The Gun That Won the West* 1955; *Flight That Disappeared* 1961; *Hand of Death* 1962; *The Spy with My Face* 1966; *Blood of Dracula's Castle, Five Bloody Graves* 1969.

Rea, Stephen. Actor. Born 1946 in Belfast, Ireland. One of four children in a working-class Protestant family, he has acted in both English and Irish films and stage productions. Made his film debut in *Angel*, also first film of Neil Jordan; his performance as a tormented Irish Republican Army gunman in Jordan's *The Crying Game* (1992) established his quiet, complex screen presence, earning an Academy Award nomination as best actor. He appeared on Broadway in 'Someone Who'll Watch Over Me.' Married to former Irish Republican Army member Dolours Price.

FILMS INCLUDE: *Angel/Danny Boy* 1982; *The Company of Wolves* 1984; *Life is Sweet* 1991; *The Crying Game* 1992; *Bad Behaviour* 1993; *Angie, Interview with the Vampire, Princess Caraboo, Ready to Wear* 1994; *The Last of the High Kings, Michael Collins* 1996; *Trojan Eddie* 1997.

reaction shot. A close shot of a person (or persons) reacting to something that is said or done off scene or in a previous shot. A reaction shot may be used as a standard continuity device, such as cutting from one player speaking to another who is reacting to his words, or as a cutaway device, such as cutting from the main action in a boxing ring to the reaction of a spectator in the audience, then returning to the main action.

reader. An employee of a studio's scenario department whose job it is to read, synopsize, and sometimes pass judgment on literary and dramatic properties considered as possible source materials for the production of a motion picture.

Reagan, Ronald. Actor, politician, former US president. Born on Feb. 6, 1911, in Tampico, Ill. A graduate of Eureka College (economics and sociology), he started out as a sportscaster for a Des Moines, Iowa, radio station and for a while announced the baseball games of the Chicago Cubs. He went to Hollywood in the mid-30s, and after signing with Warner Bros. in 1937 he played square romantic leads in some 50 films, mainly routine B productions. Among a few highlights in an otherwise rather pedestrian screen career were his sensitive performances in Sam Wood's *Kings Row* (1942) and in Vincent Sherman's *The Hasty Heart* (1950). Reagan was also memorable as the dying halfback George Gipp in the football classic *Knute Rockne—All American* (1940), famous for the quote, "win just one for the Gipper"—although his detractors rather like to associate him with the role of a chimpanzee-raising professor in the schlock movie *Bedtime for Bonzo* (1951). In the 50s he freelanced among several studios with meager success, but his declining career was revived by TV. After hosting 'The Orchid Award' variety show (1953–54), he hosted and frequently starred in the 'General Electric Theater' drama anthology program (1954–62), then hosted the Western series 'Death Valley Days' (1965–66).

Reagan, who served as a captain with the USAAF during WW II and was assigned mainly to the production of training films, became involved in industry affairs after returning to civilian life. He served as president of the Screen Actors Guild from 1947 till 1952, and again in 1959, and was gradually drawn into political activity. For many years he was known as a staunch liberal but turned full circle in 1962, becoming a champion of conservatism. A dedicated Goldwater supporter in the 1964 presidential campaign, he managed to survive the debacle of his mentor and in 1966 emerged as the conservative Republican governor of California, a state that had been run by liberals for years. During his eight-year term as governor of California, Reagan became an influential force in the Republican party and in the 1976 primaries narrowly lost to Gerald Ford the GOP's candidacy for the US presidency. Elected President of the United States in November of 1980, Reagan served two controversial terms, during which he used charismatic geniality and a disarming gift of gab to maintain a lofty level of popularity, despite strong opposition from liberals and intellectuals who abhorred his staunchly conservative views. In 1981 he was the target of an assassination attempt by John W. Hinkley, who claimed he shot the President to impress actress Jodie Foster. Sharing the White House with Reagan was his second wife (from 1952), former actress Nancy Davis, who, as Nancy Reagan, proved a devoted accomplice but occasionally a source of embarrassment to the President. His first wife (1940–48) was actress Jane Wyman. Autobiography; *Where's the Rest of Me?* (1965).

FILMS: *Love Is on the Air, Submarine D-1* (bit deleted from final print) 1937; *Sergeant Murphy, Swing Your Lady, Hollywood Hotel, Accidents Will Happen, Cowboy from Brooklyn, Boy Meets Girl, Girls on Probation, Brother Rat, Going Places* 1938; *Secret Service of the Air, Dark Victory, Code of the Secret Service, Naughty but Nice, Hell's Kitchen, Angels Wash Their Faces, Smashing the Money Ring* 1939; *Brother Rat and a Baby, An Angel from Texas, Murder in the Air, Knute Rockne—All American, Tugboat Annie Sails Again, Santa Fe Trail* 1940; *The Bad Man, Million Dollar Baby, Nine Lives Are Not Enough, International Squadron* 1941; *Kings Row, Juke Girl, Desperate Journey* 1942; *This Is the Army* 1943; *Stallion Road, That Hagen Girl, The Voice of the Turtle* 1947; *John Loves Mary, Night Unto Night, The Girl from Jones Beach, It's a Great Feeling* (cameo) 1949; *The Hasty Heart, Louisa* 1950; *Storm Warning, Bedtime for Bonzo, The Last Outpost* 1951;

Hong Kong, The Winning Team, She's Working Her Way Through College 1952; *Tropic Zone, Law and Order* 1953; *Prisoner of War, Cattle Queen of Montana* 1954; *Tennessee's Partner* 1955; *Hellcats of the Navy* 1957; *The Killers* 1964.

rear projection. See BACK PROJECTION; PROCESS SHOT.

Reason, Rex. Actor. Born on Nov. 20, 1928, in Berlin. *ed.* Pasadena Playhouse. A leading man of Hollywood second features of the 50s, he is also known as Bart Roberts. He co-starred in the TV series 'Man Without a Gun' (1957–59) and 'The Roaring Twenties' (1960–62).

FILMS INCLUDE: *Storm Over Tibet* 1952; *Salome* 1953; *Yankee Pasha, This Island Earth, Smoke Signal, Kiss of Fire* 1955; *Raw Edge, The Creature Walks Among Us* 1956; *A Band of Angels, Under Fire, Badlands of Montana* 1957; *The Rawhide Trail, Thundering Jets* 1958; *The Sad Horse, Miracle of the Hills* 1959.

recordist. A technician in charge of sound recording on a motion picture set. Also known as "recording supervisor." He is responsible for the correct placement and positioning of microphones on the set and for the quality, clarity, and level of the sound recorded during production. A "recording supervisor," also known as a "mixer," is responsible on the other hand for the postproduction mixing of the various tracks into one final composite track.

Redford, Robert. Actor, director, producer. Born Charles Robert Redford, Jr., on Aug. 18, 1937, in Santa Monica, Calif. Highly popular Hollywood star. An accountant's son, he attended the University of Colorado on a baseball scholarship but dropped out in 1957 and traveled through Europe in pursuit of an early ambition to become a painter. Returning to the US, he enrolled as an art student at Brooklyn's Pratt Institute and at the same time began training as an actor at the American Academy of Dramatic Arts. He made his Broadway debut in 1959, playing a minor supporting role in 'Tall Story.' His stage parts gradually increased in importance and culminated in 1963 in the starring role in the Broadway romantic comedy hit 'Barefoot in the Park.' During the early 60s he also appeared on TV, in segments of such shows as 'Playhouse 90,' 'Twilight Zone,' and 'Alfred Hitchcock Presents.' After an isolated screen role in 1962, he began appearing regularly in films in 1965, initially playing standard pleasant leads in routine films. He was catapulted to the top in 1969 as a result of the great commercial success of *Butch Cassidy and the Sundance Kid,* in which he proved an excellent match in the Kid role to Paul NEWMAN's Butch. The two stars were teamed again, even more successfully, in the 1973 blockbuster *The Sting,* for which Redford was nominated for an Oscar. By then the blue-eyed, blond Redford had surpassed Newman in the box-office popularity rankings, thanks to appealing performances in such films as *Downhill Racer* (1969), *The Candidate* (1972), *Jeremiah Johnson* (1972), and *The Way We Were* (1973). By 1974 he was America's number one crowd pleaser, popular among female audiences for his manly, open-faced handsomeness and among males for his convincing portrayals of square-jawed, sky-eyed, loner heroes. Before long, he established his own production company, Wildwood Enterprises, through which he became instrumental in bringing to the screen *All the President's Men* (1976), the story of the Watergate investigation, in which he portrayed *Washington Post* reporter Bob Woodward. He scored a success with his first attempt at directing, winning an Academy Award as best director for *Ordinary People* (1980). He continued to impress with his directorial talent in *The Milagro Beanfield War* (1988); the well-regarded documentary of a Native American demonized by the FBI, *Incident at Oglala* (1992); and, in the same year, with the film adaptation of the best-selling novel *A River Runs Through It.* Though he has always been extremely selective in his acting roles, he has grown even more cautious since the 80s, with some disappointing (*Havana*) and some commercially successful (*Indecent Proposal*) results.

Offscreen, Redford is known as a dedicated outdoorsman and a versatile, daring athlete who indulges abundantly in many sports, from tennis and horse riding to skiing, motor racing, and air gliding. A dedicated conservationist, he maintains a home in Manhattan and offices in Hollywood, but spends much of his time in Utah, where he owns vast stretches of wild land, encompassing a ranch, a quarter-horse training farm, and the famous Sundance Ski Resort. In nearby Park City in 1980, Redford founded the SUNDANCE INSTITUTE, a workshop and training ground for young filmmakers, and the site of the United States Film Festival.

FILMS: *War Hunt* 1962; *Situation Hopeless—But Not Serious* 1965; *Inside Daisy Clover, The Chase, This Property Is Condemned* 1966; *Barefoot in the Park* 1967; *Butch Cassidy and the Sundance Kid* (as the Sundance Kid), *Downhill Racer* (also exec. prod.) 1969; *Tell Them Willie Boy Is Here, Little Fauss and Big Halsy* 1970; *The Hot Rock, The Candidate* (also co-exec. prod.), *Jeremiah Johnson* 1972; *The Way We Were, The Sting* 1973; *The Great Gatsby* (title role) 1974; *The Great Waldo Pepper, Three Days of the Condor* 1975; *All the President's Men* (as *Washington Post* reporter Bob Woodward; also exec. prod.) 1976; *A Bridge Too Far* (UK) 1977; *The Electric Horseman* 1979; *Brubaker, Ordinary People* (dir. only) 1980; *The Natural* 1984; *Out of Africa* 1985; *Legal Eagles* 1986; *Promised Land* (co-exec. prod. only), *The Milagro Beanfield War* (dir., co-prod. only), *Some Girls* (exec. prod. only) 1988; *Havana* 1990; *The Dark Wind* (co-exec. prod. only) 1991; *Incident at Oglala* (documentary; prod., narr.), *A River Runs Through It* (dir. only), *Sneakers* 1992; *Indecent Proposal* 1993; *Quiz Show* (dir., prod. only) 1994; *She's the One* (co-prod. only), *Up Close and Personal* 1996.

Redgrave, Lynn. Actress. Born on Mar. 8, 1943, in London. Tall (5' 10"), brash, endearing player of the British and American stage, TV, and films. The daughter of Sir Michael and sister of Corin and Vanessa REDGRAVE, she attended London's Central School of Music and Drama and made her stage debut in 1962 and her first film appearance the following year. She emerged a star from the film *Georgy Girl* (1966), in which she gave a touching and marvelously funny portrayal of a plump ugly duckling, a role for which she was nominated for an Oscar and won the New York Film Critics best actress award in a tie with Elizabeth Taylor (for *Who's Afraid of Virginia Woolf?*). She has subsequently played leads in both British and American films and on the London and the New York stage. Permanently settling in the US in 1974, she appeared frequently on TV talk and game shows and co-hosted NBC's syndicated talk show 'Not for Women Only.' She later co-starred in the TV series 'House Calls' (1979–81), 'Teachers Only' (1982–83), and 'Chicken Soup' (1989–90), in the latter opposite comedian Jackie Mason. Having shed dozens of pounds in the 1980s, a svelte Redgrave became a spokeswoman for a weight-loss program in TV commercials. Although they disagree politically, she and her sister Vanessa Redgrave co-starred in a London production of Chekhov's 'The Three Sisters' in 1990 and in 1991 appeared together in a TV remake of the film *What Ever Happened to Baby Jane?* She also appeared on Broadway in a one-woman show, *Shakespeare for My Father*. Married since 1967 to actor-producer-director John Clark and mother of three. Author of *This Is Living: An Inspirational Guide to Freedom* (1988).

FILMS: *Tom Jones* 1963; *Girl with Green Eyes* 1964;

Georgy Girl 1966; *The Deadly Affair, Smashing Time* 1967; *The Virgin Soldiers* 1969; *The Last of the Mobile Hotshots* (US) 1970; *Los Guerilleros/Killer from Yuma* (Sp./It.), *Viva la Muerte—tua!/Don't Turn the Other Cheek!* (It./Ger./Sp.), *Every Little Crook and Nanny* (US), *Everything You Always Wanted to Know About Sex but Were Afraid to Ask* (US) 1972; *The National Health* 1973; *The Happy Hooker* (as madam Xaviera Hollander; US) 1975; *The Big Bus* (US) 1976; *Sunday Lovers* (Fr./It./UK); *Morgan Stewart's Coming Home* (US) 1987; *Getting It Right* (US/UK), *Midnight* (US) 1989; *Shine* 1996.

Redgrave, Sir Michael. Actor. *b.* Mar. 20, 1908, Bristol, England. *d.* 1985. *ed.* Cambridge. Eminent leading man and character star of the British stage and screen, the son of British actor Roy Redgrave (1872–1922), who appeared in Australian silent movies. A former journalist and schoolmaster, he made his stage debut in 1934 and before long became one of England's most distinguished and versatile players. Specializing in cerebral roles, he appeared in numerous films from 1936, reaching the peak of his screen career in the late 40s and early 50s, when he appeared in such films as *The Captive Heart, The Browning Version,* and *The Importance of Being Earnest.* He was nominated for an Oscar for his performance in *Mourning Becomes Electra* (1947) and won the best actor prize at the Cannes Festival for *The Browning Version* (1951). Redgrave produced and directed many plays and wrote for the stage 'The Seventh Man' and 'Circus Boy' (both 1935), as well as 'The Aspern Papers' (1959), an adaptation of the Henry James novella. He was also the author of *The Actor's Ways and Means* (1955), the novel *The Mountebank's Tale* (1959), and the autobiographies *Mask or Face: Reflections in the Actor's Mirror* (1958) and *In My Mind's Eye* (1983). He was knighted in 1959. His marriage (from 1935 until his death of Parkinson's disease) to actress Rachel Kempson (*b.* May 28, 1910, Dartmouth, England) produced actor Corin Redgrave (*b.* July 16, 1939, London) and stage and screen stars Vanessa and Lynn REDGRAVE.

FILMS: *The Secret Agent* (bit) 1936; *The Lady Vanishes* 1938; *Climbing High, A Stolen Life, A Window in London/Lady in Distress, The Stars Look Down* (as David Fenwick) 1939; *Kipps/The Remarkable Mr. Kipps* (title role), *Atlantic Ferry/Sons of the Sea, Jeannie* 1941; *The Big Blockade, Thunder Rock* 1942; *The Way to the Stars/Johnny in the Clouds, Dead of Night* 1945; *The Years Between, The Captive Heart* 1946; *The Man Within/The Smugglers, Fame Is the Spur, Mourning Becomes Electra* (as Orin Mannon; US) 1947; *The Secret Beyond the Door* (US) 1948; *The Browning Version, The Magic Box* 1951; *The Importance of Being Earnest* (as Ernest Worthing) 1952; *The Green Scarf, The Sea Shall Not Have Them* 1954; *Mr. Arkadin/Confidential Report* (Sp./Fr./Switz.), *The Night My Number Came Up, The Dam Busters, Oh Rosalinda!/Fledermaus '55* 1955; *1984* 1956; *Time Without Pity, The Happy Road* (US/Fr.) 1957; *The Quiet American* (US), *Law and Disorder, Behind the Mask* 1958; *Shake Hands with the Devil* (Ire./US), *The Wreck of the Mary Deare* (US) 1959; *No My Darling Daughter!, The Innocents* (UK/US) 1961; *The Loneliness of the Long Distance Runner* 1962; *Uncle Vanya* 1963; *Young Cassidy* (as W. B. Yeats; UK/US), *The Hill, The Heroes of Telemark* 1965; *La 25e Heure/The 25th Hour* (Fr./It./Yug.) 1967; *Assignment K* 1968; *Oh! What a Lovely War* (as Gen. Sir Henry Wilson), *Battle of Britain, Goodbye Mr. Chips* (US/UK) 1969; *David Copperfield* (as Dan Peggotty; orig. made for US TV), *Connecting Rooms, Goodbye Gemini* 1970; *The Go-Between, Nicholas and Alexandra* 1971.

Redgrave, Vanessa. Actress. Born on Jan. 30, 1937, in London. Radiant star of the London stage and British and international films. The daughter of Sir Michael and sister of Lynn and Corin REDGRAVE, she trained at London's Central School of Music and Drama and made her stage debut in 1957 and her first screen appearance the following year, playing the on-screen daughter of her real celebrated father in a minor film, *Behind the Mask.* She began gaining a reputation as a superior actress during her stint with Britain's Royal Shakespeare Company in the early 60s, but it wasn't until 1966 that she returned to the screen. Despite mostly mediocre vehicles, she soon became one of the more popular film performers of the late 60s and early 70s, a delicate yet sensuous beauty whose personality fills the screen as well as the theatrical stage. She won the best actress prize at Cannes for *Morgan!* (1966) and was nominated for best actress Academy Awards for *Morgan!, Isadora* (1968), *Mary, Queen of Scots* (1971), and *The Bostonians* (1984), winning the Oscar as best supporting actress for *Julia* (1977). She was named best supporting actress by the New York Critics for *Prick Up Your Ears* (1987).

An independent, determined woman, she broke away from a strict, bourgeois upbringing to become a vocal champion of left-wing causes. She was arrested during a Ban-the-Bomb demonstration, led anti–Vietnam War marches on the US embassy, expressed sympathy for the IRA, and loudly supported Yasser Arafat's PLO. She was repeatedly frustrated in her bids for a seat in the British Parliament as a candidate of the Workers' Revolutionary Party, which called for the destruction of capitalism and abolition of the British monarchy. She was reprimanded for making a political statement during the 1978 Oscar ceremony and encountered protests from Jewish groups in the US when she portrayed a concentration camp survivor in the TV movie *Playing for Time* (1980), for which she won an Emmy. In 1984 she sued the Boston Symphony Orchestra following the cancellation of her performance as a narrator of 'Oedipus Rex.' Redgrave's 1962 marriage to director Tony RICHARDSON produced actresses Natasha RICHARDSON and Joely Richardson. In 1967 she divorced him on the grounds of adultery, naming Jeanne MOREAU as co-respondent. In 1969 she bore a son to actor Franco NERO, who had played Lancelot to her Guinevere in *Camelot.*

FILMS: *Behind the Mask* 1958; *Morgan—A Suitable Case for Treatment/Morgan!, A Man for All Seasons* (cameo, as Anne Boleyn), *Blow-Up* (It./UK) 1966; *The Sailor from Gibraltar, Red and Blue, Camelot* (as Guinevere; US) 1967; *Tonight Let's All Make Love in London* (doc.), *The Charge of the Light Brigade, Isadora/The Loves of Isadora* (as Isadora Duncan), *The Sea Gull* (as Nina; US/UK), *Un Tranquillo Posto di Campagna/A Quiet Place in the Country* (It./Fr.) 1968; *Oh! What a Lovely War* 1969; *Dropout* (It.) 1970; *La Vacanza* (It.), *The Trojan Women* (as Andromache; US/UK/Gr.), *The Devils* (UK/US), *Mary Queen of Scots* (title role) 1971; *Murder on the Orient Express* 1974; *Out of Season* 1975; *The Seven-Per-Cent Solution* 1976; *Yanks* 1979; *Bear Island* 1980; *Wagner* (as Cosima Wagner) 1983; *The Bostonians* (US) 1984; *Steaming, Wetherby* 1985; *Prick Up Your Ears, Comrades* 1987; *Consuming Passions* 1988; *Diceria dell'Untore* (It.), *Romeo-Juliet* (v/o; Belg.) 1990; *The Ballad of the Sad Cafe* (US/UK) 1991; *The Children* (UK), *Howards End* (UK) 1992; *The House of the Spirits* 1993; *Little Odessa, Mother's Boys* 1994; *A Month by the Lake* 1995; *Looking for Richard, Mission: Impossible* 1996; *Smilla's Sense of Snow* 1997.

reduction print. A motion picture print made from an original of a wider gauge. For example, a 16 mm copy that has been reduced from a 35 mm film, or an 8 mm copy made from either a 16 mm or a 35 mm original. The process of reduction printing is the opposite of BLOW-UP.

Reed, Sir Carol. Director. *b.* Dec. 30, 1906, London. *d.*

1976. He was intended to become a farmer and after graduating from King's School at Canterbury was sent by his family to the US for on-the-job training at a large chicken farm. But his love of the theater prevailed and after six months he returned home to begin a career as an actor. He made his London debut in 1924 with Sybil Thorndyke's troupe and after a long succession of mainly minor roles he began working for Edgar Wallace in 1927 as an advisor on the adaptation of the writer's mystery novels to the stage and as an actor and stage manager in the resulting productions. Turning to films in the early 30s, he began as a dialogue director and assistant to producer-director Basil DEAN and graduated to director in 1935. His early features were mainly modest-budget ventures for local consumption, but his reputation grew steadily thanks to such films as *Bank Holiday/Three on a Week-End* (1938), *The Stars Look Down* (1939), *Night Train to Munich/Night Train* (1940), *Kipps/The Remarkable Mr. Kipps* (1941), and *The Young Mr. Pitt* (1942). During WW II he was assigned to the British army's film unit, for which he directed a propaganda short, *A Letter from Home* (1941), and a training short for new recruits, *The New Lot* (1942). As a result of the success of the latter film, he was commissioned to direct a feature-length documentary along a similar theme, *The Way Ahead* (1944). It remains one of the most memorable nonfiction films of the war years. In 1945 he co-directed, with Garson Kanin, *The True Glory,* an Oscar-winning compilation documentary recording the progress of the war in Europe from D day to VE day.

Reed's reputation reached its peak in the late 40s and early 50s, when he directed five of his finest films: *Odd Man Out* (1947), a meticulously conceived and richly executed chase melodrama about the final hours in the life of an Irish revolutionary; *The Fallen Idol* (1948), a keenly observed and intelligently told drama of the adult world as seen through the eyes of a child; *The Third Man* (1949), his best-known film, a fascinating thriller set against the seedy background of postwar Vienna; *Outcast of the Islands* (1952), a fine adaptation of the Joseph Conrad story about moral corruption in the South Seas; and *The Man Between* (1953), a flawed but intriguing drama set in postwar Berlin. The second and third of these films, based on material by Graham Greene, were particularly successful, receiving unanimous critical praise. Reed's best work was characterized by a keen sense of locale and atmosphere, a sharp eye for small but revealing details, a sympathetic treatment of characters, skillful plot development, and a civilized, warm, but restrained tone. From the mid-50s, Reed's reputation went into a steady decline, as his films, some made for Hollywood studios, grew larger in scope and budget, obliterating his gifts for detail and atmosphere and magnifying dramatic and technical flaws. In 1962 he began directing *Mutiny on the Bounty* but was soon replaced by Lewis Milestone. In 1968, however, he won an Academy Award as best director for the musical *Oliver!* The film won a best picture Oscar as well. Reed's first wife (1943–47) was actress Diana WYNYARD. In 1948 he married actress Penelope DUDLEY WARD.

FILMS: *It Happened in Paris* (co-dir. with Robert Wyler), *Midshipman Easy/Men of the Sea* 1935; *Laburnum Grove* 1936; *Talk of the Devil* (also story), *Who's Your Lady Friend?* 1937; *Bank Holiday/Three on a Week-End, No Parking* (story only), *Penny Paradise* 1938; *Climbing High, A Girl Must Live, The Stars Look Down* 1939; *Night Train to Munich/Night Train* 1940; *The Girl in the News, Kipps/The Remarkable Mr. Kipps, A Letter from Home* (doc. short) 1941; *The New Lot* (doc. short), *The Young Mr. Pitt* 1942; *The Way Ahead* (doc.) 1944; *The True Glory* (doc.; co-dir. with Garson Kanin) 1945; *Odd Man Out* (also prod.) 1947; *The Fallen Idol* (also prod.) 1948; *The Third Man* (also prod.) 1949; *Outcast of the Islands* (also prod.) 1951; *The Man Between* (also prod.) 1953; *A Kid for Two Farthings* (also prod.) 1955; *Trapeze* (US) 1956; *The Key* 1958; *Our Man in Havana* (also prod.) 1959; *Mutiny on the Bounty* (replaced by Lewis Milestone, who received sole credit; US) 1962; *The Running Man* (also prod.) 1963; *The Agony and the Ecstasy* (also prod.; US) 1965; *Oliver!* 1968; *Flap* (US) 1970; *Follow Me* 1972.

Reed, Donna. Actress. *b.* Donna Belle Mullenger, Jan. 27, 1921, Denison, Iowa. *d.* 1986. Wholesome leading lady of Hollywood films of the 40s and 50s. Raised on a farm, she was chosen beauty queen of her hometown high school and later elected Campus Queen at Los Angeles City College, where she participated in school dramatics. She was signed by MGM in 1941 and for several years played small roles in minor films, at first under the name Donna Adams, before maturing into a leading lady in the mid-40s. In 1951 she moved over to Columbia, where her second husband, Tony Owen, a former journalist and talent agent, worked as an executive assistant to Harry Cohn. Here, as at MGM, she continued playing sincere, wholesome types, perhaps most memorably in Frank Capra's Christmas perennial *It's a Wonderful Life* (1946). The one exception to her typecasting was the role of Alma, the prostitute in *From Here to Eternity* (1953), for which she received an Academy Award as best supporting actress. Despite the Oscar, her career declined for lack of rewarding roles and she retired from the screen in 1958 to star on TV in her own long-running series 'The Donna Reed Show' (1958–66). In 1984 she emerged from semiretirement to join the cast of TV's popular soap 'Dallas,' as a replacement for Barbara Bel Geddes, in the role of Ellie. When Bel Geddes reclaimed the role in 1985, Miss Reed sued the show's producers for breach of contract and accepted $1 million as settlement. Several months later she died at 64 of pancreatic cancer.

FILMS: *The Get-Away, Shadow of the Thin Man* 1941; *Babes on Broadway, The Bugle Sounds, The Courtship of Andy Hardy, Mokey, Calling Dr. Gillespie, Apache Trail, Eyes in the Night* 1942; *The Human Comedy* (as Bess Macauley), *Dr. Gillespie's Criminal Case, Thousands Cheer, The Man from Down Under* 1943; *See Here Private Hargrove, Mrs. Parkington* 1944; *The Picture of Dorian Gray* (as Gladys Hallward), *Gentle Annie, They Were Expendable* 1945; *Faithful in My Fashion, It's a Wonderful Life* 1946; *Green Dolphin Street* 1947; *Beyond Glory* 1948; *Chicago Deadline* 1949; *Saturday's Hero* 1951; *Scandal Sheet, Hangman's Knot* 1952; *Trouble Along the Way, Raiders of the Seven Seas, From Here to Eternity* (as Alma), *The Caddy, Gun Fury* 1953; *Three Hours to Kill, The Last Time I Saw Paris, They Rode West* 1954; *The Far Horizons* 1955; *Ransom!, The Benny Goodman Story, Backlash, Beyond Mombasa* (UK) 1956; *The Whole Truth* 1958; *Pepe* (cameo) 1960; *Yellow-Headed Summer* (unreleased) 1974.

Reed, Luther. Director, screenwriter. *b.* July 14, 1888, Berlin, Wis. *d.* 1961. A graduate of Columbia University, he started out as a journalist and was at one time music and theater critic for the New York *Herald.* He entered films in 1916 as a screenwriter for Lasky and after WW I service in France wrote scripts for Metro, Thomas Ince, and William Randolph Hearst's Cosmopolitan Pictures, for the last of which he scripted several of Marion Davies' films. He joined Paramount as a screenwriter in 1925 and within several months switched to directing. He directed a number of successful silents and early talkies, but his career faltered shortly after the advent of sound.

FILMS INCLUDE: As screenwriter—*Let's Be Fashionable* 1920; *Beau Revel, Enchantment, Get-Rich-Quick Wallingford, The Lure of Youth* (also story) 1921; *Beauty's*

Worth, The Young Diana, When Knighthood Was in Flower 1922; *Adam and Eva, Little Old New York* 1923; *The Great White Way, Yolanda* 1924; *Lovers in Quarantine* (co-sc.), *Woman-handled* 1925; *Let's Get Married* (adapt.), *Kid Boots* (co-sc.) 1926; *The Sweetheart of Sigma Chi* (co-sc.) 1933. As director (complete)—*The Ace of Cads* 1926; *New York, Evening Clothes, The World at Her Feet, Shanghai Bound, Honeymoon Hate* 1927; *The Sawdust Paradise* 1928; *Rio Rita* (also sc.) 1929; *Hit the Deck* (also adapt.), *Dixiana* (also adapt.) 1930; *Convention Girl* 1935.

Reed, Oliver. Actor. Born on Feb. 13, 1938, in Wimbledon, London, England. Burly, powerfully built leading man of British and international films. A nephew of film director Sir Carol REED, he dropped out of school and ran away from home at 17, supporting himself as a Soho nightclub bouncer, a boxer, and a cab driver, among other things. After military service with the Medical Corps, he began playing extra and bit parts in British films and in 1961 landed his first lead, the title role in a cheap Hammer horror production, *The Curse of the Werewolf.* For a while he specialized in sullen, scowling, often vicious roles, but he gradually emerged as a versatile actor and leading screen personality with strong masculine appeal through such films as *Oliver!* (1968), *Women in Love* (1969), *The Devils* (1971), and *The Three Musketeers* (1974). However, a continuing weight problem, coupled with a legendary thirst for alcohol, soon diminished his career and by the 80s he had reverted to playing brooding, often mean characters, mainly in low-budget productions. He was married briefly to actress Kate Byrne.

FILMS INCLUDE: *Value for Money* 1955; *The Captain's Table* 1958; *The Angry Silence, The League of Gentlemen* 1960; *No Love for Johnnie, The Rebel/Call Me Genius, Sword of Sherwood Forest, The Curse of the Werewolf* (title role) 1961; *The Pirate of Blood River, Captain Clegg/Night Creatures* 1962; *The Damned/These Are the Damned, Paranoiac, The Scarlet Blade/The Crimson Blade* 1963; *The System/The Girl-Getters* 1964; *The Party's Over, The Brigand of Kandahar* 1965; *The Trap* (Can./UK) 1966; *The Shuttered Room, The Jokers, I'll Never Forget What's 'Is Name* 1967; *Oliver!* (as Bill Sikes) 1968; *The Assassination Bureau, Hannibal Brooks, Women in Love* 1969; *La Dame dans l'Auto avec des Lunettes et un Fusil/The Lady in the Car with Glasses and a Gun* (Fr./US), *Take a Girl Like You* 1970; *The Hunting Party* (Sp.), *The Devils* 1971; *Zero Population Growth/Z.P.G., Sitting Target* 1972; *Triple Echo* 1973; *The Three Musketeers* (as Athos) 1974; *The Four Musketeers* (again as Athos), *Royal Flash* (as Bismarck), *Tommy, Ten Little Indians, Blood in the Streets* (It./Fr./Ger.) 1975; *The Sellout, Burnt Offerings* 1976; *The Prince and the Pauper/Crossed Swords* (as Miles Hendon), *Maniac, The Sell Out* 1977; *Tomorrow Never Comes* (UK/Can.), *The Big Sleep* 1978; *The Class of Miss MacMichael* 1978; *The Brood* (Can.) 1979; *Dr. Heckyll and Mr. Hype* (US) 1980; *Lion of the Desert* (Libya/UK), *Condorman* 1981; *Venom* 1982; *Spasm* (Can.; release delayed from 1981), *The Sting II* (US), *Two of a Kind* (US) 1983; *Captive/Heroine* (UK/Fr.), *Castaway* 1986; *Wheels of Terror/The Misfit Brigade* (UK/US) 1987; *Gor* (US), *Skeleton Coast* 1988; *Rage to Kill* (US), *Adventures of Baron Munchausen, Return of the Musketeers* (as Athos; UK/Sp./Fr.) 1989; *Panama Sugar* (It.), *The House of Usher* (US) 1990; *The Pit and the Pendulum* (US), *Hired to Kill* (US) 1991; *Severed Ties* (US) 1992; *Blue in the Face, Funny Bones* 1995.

Reed, Pamela. Actress. Born on Apr. 2, 1949, in Tacoma, Wash. Perky, athletically built, leading lady of the American stage, TV, and films. Raised in Silver Spring, Maryland, she ran a day-care center and worked on the Trans-Alaska pipeline before earning her B.A. in drama from the University of Washington. She was in her late 20s by the time she began performing professionally on TV and on the New York stage. Making her screen debut in 1980, she displayed talent and versatility in a wide range of second leads and supporting roles but remained relatively obscure until she co-starred with Arnold Schwarzenegger in the box-office hit *Kindergarten Cop* (1990). She is married to Sandy Smolar, who directed her in *Rachel River* (1987).

FILMS: *The Long Riders* (as Belle Starr), *Melvin and Howard* 1980; *Eyewitness* 1981; *Young Doctors in Love* 1982; *The Right Stuff* 1983; *The Goodbye People* 1984; *The Best of Times, The Clan of the Cave Bear* 1986; *Rachel River* 1987; *Chattahoochee* 1989; *Cadillac Man, Kindergarten Cop* 1990; *Prime Target* 1991; *Passed Away, Bob Roberts* 1992; *Junior* 1994; *Bean* 1997.

Reed, Philip. Actor. Born in 1908, in New York City. *ed.* Cornell. Darkly handsome leading man and second lead of mainly routine Hollywood films, following experience in vaudeville and on the legitimate stage. On the screen he sometimes played self-centered characters with a mean streak.

FILMS INCLUDE: *It's a Deal* 1930; *Female, The House on 56th Street* 1933; *Fashions of 1934, Jimmy the Gent, Journal of a Crime, Glamour, Affairs of a Gentleman, British Agent* 1934; *Sweet Music, The Case of the Curious Bride, The Girl from 10th Avenue, Accent on Youth* 1935; *Klondike Annie, The Last of the Mohicans* (as Uncas) 1936; *Madam X* 1937; *Merrily We Live* 1938; *Aloma of the South Seas, Weekend for Three* 1941; *A Gentleman After Dark* 1942; *Old Acquaintance* 1943; *Hot Cargo, Her Sister's Secret* 1946; *Song of Scheherazade, I Cover Big Town, Song of the Thin Man, Pirates of Monterey* 1947; *Bodyguard, Unknown Island* 1948; *Daughter of the West, Manhandled* 1949; *Davy Crockett—Indian Scout, Tripoli, Bandit Queen* 1950; *Take Me to Town* 1953; *The Girl in the Red Velvet Swing* (as publisher Robert Collier) 1955; *The Tattered Dress* 1957; *Harum Scarum* 1965.

reel. A metal or plastic spool on which motion picture film is wound. The capacity of a single reel has been so standardized over the years that the reel has come to be used in the trade as an approximate unit of measurement for the length of film. The standard 35 mm reel has a capacity of 1,000 feet of film, but in practice holds a little more than 900 feet of film in length, providing approximately ten minutes of running time in projection. The standard 16 mm reel has a capacity of 400 feet but usually holds some 360 feet of film, also providing for a running time of ten minutes. Although much larger reels are now often used, the basic unit remains the standard ten-minute reel. Thus, a 35 mm reel with a capacity of 2,000 feet is known as a "double reel." See also FEED REEL; TAKE-UP REEL.

Reeve, Christopher. Actor. Born on Sept. 25, 1952, in New York City. *ed.* Cornell; Juilliard. Handsome leading man of the American stage and screen. The son of a writer/English professor and his journalist wife, who divorced when he was four, he began his acting career in summer stock and while still attending college appeared in the TV soap 'Love of Life.' He made his Broadway debut in 'A Matter of Gravity' (1976), playing Katharine Hepburn's grandson, but was virtually unknown in 1978, when he was chosen out of 200 candidates to become the screen's incarnation of the mighty cartoon character, Superman. He charmed audiences with his deft handling of the dual personality of the comic-book hero. He has since divided his time between the stage and the movies, as well as occasional television appearances, including the role of Vronsky in the TV movie *Anna Karenina* (1985).

An avid horseman, Reeve was thrown from his horse in a jumping competition in May 1995, sustaining a near-fatal injury that rendered him paralyzed from the neck down. Now confined to a wheelchair, he continues to recover, making appearances for charity and special events and earning the respect and admiration of millions as he strives to rehabilitate. His appearance at the 1996 Academy Awards invoked a standing ovation from his peers inspired by his persistence and courage. He continues to work and has directed the TV movie "In the Gloaming."

FILMS: *Gray Lady Down, Superman* (title role) 1978; *Superman II, Somewhere in Time* 1980; *Deathtrap, Monsignor* 1982; *Superman III* 1983; *The Bostonians* 1984; *The Aviator* 1985; *Street Smart, Superman IV: The Quest for Peace* (also co-story) 1987; *Switching Channels* 1988; *Noises Off* 1992; *Morning Glory, The Remains of the Day* 1993; *Speechless* 1994; *Village of the Damned* 1995.

Reeves, George. Actor. *b.* George Besselo, Apr. 6, 1914, Woodstock, Iowa. *d.* 1959, a suicide. A supporting player and minor lead of Hollywood films of the 40s, he gained stardom on TV in the 50s as the incarnation of the cartoon-character Superman. Reeves, a former Golden Gloves boxer, became so closely identified with his role in 'The Adventures of Superman' (1951–57) that after the series ended he had trouble landing other acting parts. Despairing, he shot himself in the head.

FILMS INCLUDE: *Gone With the Wind* (as Brent Tarleton) 1939; *'Til We Meet Again, Torrid Zone, Ladies Must Live, Argentine Nights, Always a Bride* 1940; *Strawberry Blonde, Blood and Sand, Lydia, Man at Large* 1941; *So Proudly We Hail, Border Patrol, Bar 20* 1943; *Winged Victory* 1944; *The Sainted Sisters, Jungle Goddess, Jungle Jim* 1948; *Samson and Delilah, Adventures of Sir Galahad* (serial), *Thunder in the Pines, The Great Lover* 1949; *The Good Humor Man* 1950; *Superman and the Mole Men* 1951; *Bugles in the Afternoon, Rancho Notorious* 1952; *The Blue Gardenia, From Here to Eternity* 1953; *Forever Female* 1954; *Westward Ho the Wagons* 1957.

Reeves, Keanu. Actor. Born in 1965, in Beirut, Lebanon, to an English mother and a father of Chinese-Hawaiian descent. Almond-eyed, strapping young lead of Hollywood films from the late 80s. Raised in Australia and in New York before moving to Canada, he attended Toronto's High School for the Performing Arts and received further acting training at Second City. Following a summer of apprenticeship at the Hedgerow Theatre in Pennsylvania, he made his professional debut in a local Toronto TV show. On the screen he often portrayed problematic or goofy youngsters, most effectively in *Bill and Ted's Excellent Adventure* (1989), which established him as a popular teen attraction. Rather than continue as window dressing, Reeves undertook a provocative role in Gus Van Sant's moody picture of gay street hustlers, *My Own Private Idaho* (1991), opposite his real-life friend River PHOENIX. Their presence in the film played a large part in the film's financing. He continued to move away from his teen image in such films as *Bram Stoker's Dracula* (1992), *Much Ado About Nothing* (1993), and the box-office champ *Speed* (1994).

FILMS: *The Prodigal* (Can.) 1984; *Flying* (Can.) 1985; *Youngblood* 1986; *River's Edge* 1987; *The Night Before, Permanent Record, The Prince of Pennsylvania, Dangerous Liaisons* 1988; *Bill and Ted's Excellent Adventure, Parenthood* 1989; *I Love You to Death, Tune in Tomorrow* 1990; *Point Break, Bill & Ted's Bogus Journey, My Own Private Idaho* 1991; *Bram Stoker's Dracula* 1992; *Much Ado About Nothing* 1993; *Even Cowgirls Get the Blues, Little Buddha, Speed* 1994; *Johnny Mnemonic, A Walk in the Clouds* 1995; *Feeling Minnesota* 1996; *Devil's Advocate* 1997.

Reeves, Michael. Director. *b.* 1944, London. *d.* 1969. *ed.* Radley Coll. Entering films at 18, he served in various support capacities in Hollywood, London, and Rome before making his directing debut at 20. Specializing in horror, he created a fine example of the genre in *Witchfinder General/The Conqueror Worm* (1968) and seemed on his way to a promising career. It proved to be his last film. Shortly after its release, he died of a drug overdose. He was 24.

FILMS: *Il Castello dei Morti Vivi/Castle of the Living Dead* (took over from credited director Herbert Wise [Luciano Ricci]; It.) 1964; *The Revenge of the Blood Beast/The She Beast* (UK/It./Yug.) 1966; *The Sorcerers* (also co-sc.; UK) 1967; *Witchfinder General/The Conqueror Worm* (also co-sc.; UK) 1968.

Reeves, Steve. Actor, muscleman. Born on Jan. 21, 1926, in Glasgow, Mont. A former Mr. America, Mr. World, Mr. Universe, and bit player, he gained fame and fortune in Italy as the star of numerous costume spectaculars in which he portrayed Hercules and other mythological heroes.

FILMS INCLUDE: In the US—*Athena* 1954. In Italy—*Le Fatiche di Ercole/Hercules* 1957; *Ercole e la Regina di Lidia/Hercules Unchained, Agi Murad—Il Diavolo bianco/The White Warrior, Gli Ultimi Giorni di Pompeii/The Last Days of Pompeii, La Battaglia di Maratona/The Giant of Marathon, Il Terrore dei Barbari/Goliath and the Barbarians* 1959; *Morgan il Pirata/Morgan the Pirate* 1960; *Il Ladro di Bagdad/The Thief of Bagdad, La Guerra di Troia/The Trojan Horse, Romolo e Remo/Duel of the Titans* 1961; *Il Figlio di Spartacus/The Slave, La Leggenda di Enea/The Avenger* 1962; *Sandokan/Sandokan the Great* 1964; *Vivo per la tua Morte/A Long Ride from Hell* 1968.

reflector. A panel covered with light-reflecting material, usually a metallic surface, to control, boost, or direct light to where it is most needed. The degree of reflection varies with the nature of the surface material. As a rule, the lighter-toned and shinier it is, the harsher the light it will reflect. Flat reflectors tend to spread available light over relatively large areas, while curved reflectors concentrate light rays and direct them to smaller areas. Reflectors are incorporated into studio and projector lamps to prevent the spillage of light from the back of the lamps. In exterior shooting of motion pictures, reflectors are used to direct sunlight on actors, objects, or shaded areas of a scene.

reflex camera. A camera equipped with an optical system allowing viewfinding through the lens while filming is in progress. The image is reflected to the viewfinder by a rotating shutter whose blades are silvered. It reaches the operator's eye intermittently during the split-second intervals when the shutter is closed. Some reflex optical systems employ a mirror as the reflecting agent instead of the shutter blades. The great advantage of through-the-lens viewing in reflex cameras is that the operator can see the scene exactly as it is registered on the film. The system eliminates the problem of PARALLAX and the time-consuming adjustments that have to be made to compensate for possible errors when shooting at close range. Also, when changing lenses there is no need to change viewfinders, as is the case with many nonreflex cameras.

Reggiani, Serge. Actor. Born on May 2, 1922, in Regio Emilia, Italy. Intense, sincere-looking, slightly built leading man and supporting player of French and some international films, often in tragic roles. In France from the age of four, he was a blue-collar worker before beginning his stage and screen career in the late 30s. He was striking in Carné's *Gates of the Night* (1946), Clouzot's *Manon* (1949), Ophüls's *La Ronde* (1950), and most of all in Becker's *Casque d'Or* (1952). In the 60s he turned to singing, with considerable success.

FILMS INCLUDE: *Le Voyageur de la Toussaint, Le Carrefour des Enfants perdus/Children of Chaos* 1943;

François Villon (title role) 1945; *Etoile sans Lumière/Star Without Light, Les Portes de la Nuit/Gates of the Night* 1946; *Les Dessous des Cartes* 1948; *Manon* (as Léon Lescaut), *Les Amants de Vérone/The Lovers of Verona, Retour à la Vie, Au Royaume des Cieux/The Sinners* 1949; *La Ronde* 1950; *Casque d'Or, Camicie Rosse/Anita Garibaldi* (It.), *Secret People* (UK) 1952; *Un Acte d'Amour/Act of Love* (US/Fr.) 1954; *Napoléon* 1955; *Les Salauds vont en Enfer* 1956; *Les Misérables* (as Enjolas) 1958; *Marie Octobre* 1959; *Tutti a Casa/Everybody Go Home!* (It./Fr.) 1960; *Paris Blues* (US) 1961; *La Guerra continua/Warriors 5* (It./Fr.) 1962; *Le Doulos/Doulos—The Finger Man, Il Gattopardo/The Leopard* (It./Fr.) 1963; *La 25e Heure/The 25th Hour, Les Aventuriers/The Last Adventure* (Fr./It.) 1967; *Il Giorno della Civetta/Mafia* (It./Fr.) 1968; *L'Armée des Ombres/Army of Shadows* 1969; *Touchez pas la Femme blanche* 1974; *Le Chat et la Souris/Cat and Mouse, Vincent François Paul et les autres/Vincent Francois Paul and the Others* (Fr.) 1975; *Le Bon et les Méchants/The Good and the Bad* (Fr.) 1976; *Une Fille cousue de Fil blanc, Violette et François* 1977; *L'Empreinte des Géants, Fantastica* (Fr./Can.), *La Terrazza/The Terrace* (It./Fr.) 1980; *Mauvais Sang/Bad Blood/The Night Is Young, O Melisskosmos/The Beekeeper* (Gr.) 1986; *Ne reveillez pas un Flic qui dort* 1988; *Il y a des Jours. . . et des Lunes, Plein Fer, I Hired a Contract Killer* (Fin./Sw.) 1990.

Reggio, Godfrey. Director. Born in New Orleans. *ed.* College of Santa Fe, N.M. A former member of a Catholic Brothers Teaching Order, he was disrobed in 1968 because of ideological insubordination and became involved in the production of TV programs dealing with social issues. In 1974 he conceived the idea for a nonnarrative film that expressed the concerns and hopes of modern man for his environment. He took nine years to complete and present *Koyaanisqatsi* (1983), a fascinating collage of images and sounds, accompanied by a mesmerizing score by Philip Glass. He borrowed the film's title from the Hopi Indian word for "life out of balance." Five years later he directed the second segment of his intended trilogy *Powaqqatsi,* which was similar in style but less impressive than his debut film.

FILMS: *Koyaanisqatsi* (also prod., co-sc.) 1983; *Powaqqatsi* (also co-prod., co-sc.) 1988.

register pins. See PILOT PINS.

registration. The exact positioning of a frame of film in the picture gate of a camera, projector, or printer so that it is held steady while being exposed. When frames are accurately positioned they are said to be "in register." In animation, registration is the act of aligning drawings, cels, and background materials to ensure that they are correctly positioned in relation to one another during exposure. "Register holes" are punched in the drawing paper and cels and the materials are held in place by "register pegs."

Reichenbach, François. Documentary director. Born on July 3, 1922, in Paris. A reporter with a camera, a keen observant eye, and a distinct point of view, he has been directing short and feature-length documentary films in the *CINÉMA VÉRITÉ* style since the mid-50s, after several years as an amateur filmmaker. Before that, he wrote songs for Edith Piaf and other French entertainers and was an art consultant for American buyers in Europe. He entered films with the encouragement of producer Pierre BRAUNBERGER. One of his main sources of inspiration has been the United States, through which he has traveled extensively, and he has observed some of the more bizarre aspects of American life in several of his films. Reichenbach has operated his own camera on most of his shorts and several of his features. He won a Cannes Festival Award for *L'Amerique insolite* (1960) and an Oscar for *Arthur Rubinstein: L'Amour de la Vie/Arthur Rubinstein: Love of Life* (1970). He has also directed extensively for French TV and worked as co-cameraman on Chris Marker's *La Sixième Face du Pentagone* (1968) and Herbert von Karajan's *Carmen* (1967).

FILMS INCLUDE: Shorts—*New York Ballade, Visages de Paris, Impressions de New York* 1955; *Houston Texas, Le Grand Sud* 1956; *Au Pays de Porgy and Bess, Les Marines, Carnaval à la Nouvelle Orléans* 1957; *Retour à New York, L'Amerique Lunaire, Le Paris des Mannequins* 1962; *Artifices, Illuminations* 1963; *Anges Gardiens* 1964; *East African Safari* 1965; *Aurura* 1966; *Impressions de Paris* 1967. Features—*L'Amérique insolite* 1960; *Un Coeur gros comme ça/The Winner* 1961; *Les Amoureux du "France"* (co-dir. with Pierre Grimblat) 1963; *Treize Jours en France/Grenoble* (co-dir. with Claude Lelouche) 1968; *Mexico Mexico* 1969; *Arthur Rubinstein: L'Amour de la Vie/Arthur Rubinstein: Love of Life* (co-dir. with Gerard Patris), *L'Indiscrete* 1970; *La Caravane d'Amour/Medicine Ball Caravan, Yehudi Menuhin—Chemin de la Lumière/Yehudi Menuhin—Road of Light* (co-dir. with Bernard Gavoty) 1971; *La Raison du plus Fou* (co-dir.) 1973; *F for Fake* (addnl. footage and act. only), *Don't You Hear the Dogs Bark?* (Mex.) 1975; *Sex O'Clock USA, Another Way to Love* 1976; *Pele* 1977; *Houston Texas* 1980; *Le Japon de François Reichenbach/François Reichenbach's Japan* 1983.

Reicher, Frank. Director, actor. *b.* Franz Reichert, Dec. 2, 1875, Munich, Germany. *d.* 1965. In the US from 1899, he acted and directed on the American stage before entering films as a director in 1915. He directed many silent productions—mainly melodramas—for Paramount, Metro, and other studios but returned to the stage in 1921. He came back to Hollywood as an actor in 1926 and became one of the screen's busiest character players, appearing in some 200 films through the early 50s, often in authoritative roles.

FILMS INCLUDE: As director—*The Clue* (co-dir.), *The Secret Orchard, The Case of Becky, The Chorus Lady, The Secret Sin, Mr. Grew of Monte Carlo* 1915; *Pudd'nhead Wilson, For the Defense, The Love Mask, Alien Souls, The Dupe, Public Opinion, The Victory of Conscience, Witchcraft* (also prod.), *The Storm* 1916; *The Black Wolf, Castles for Two, Sacrifice, Unconquered, The Eternal Mother, An American Widow* 1917; *The Claim, Treasure of the Sea, The Only Road, The Sea Waif, The Prodigal Wife* 1918; *Suspense, The American Way, The Black Circle* 1919; *Empty Arms, The Scarlet Dragon* 1920; *Idle Hands, Behind Masks, Out of the Depths, Wise Husbands* 1921; *Paris Bound* (dial. dir., dial. writer), *Big News* (dial dir., dial. writer), *Mister Antonio* (co-dir. with James Flood; also act.) 1929; *The Grand Parade* (dial. dir.) 1930. As actor—*Beau Sabreur, Four Sons, The Blue Danube, The Masks of the Devil, Napoleon's Barber* (title role in this John Ford short), *Sins of the Fathers* 1928; *Strange Cargo* 1929; *Beyond Victory, Suicide Fleet, Mata Hari* 1931; *A Woman Commands, Scarlet Dawn* 1932; *Topaze, King Kong, Son of Kong* 1933; *Hi Nellie!, Journal of a Crime, No Greater Glory, Return of the Terror* 1934; *Star of Midnight, Rendezvous* 1935; *Magnificent Obsession, The Invisible Ray, The Story of Louis Pasteur, The Country Doctor, Under Two Flags, Anthony Adverse, Girls' Dormitory* 1936; *Stolen Holiday, The Road Back, The Emperor's Candlesticks, Stage Door, Lancer Spy* 1937; *City Streets, Suez* 1938; *Juarez, The Magnificent Fraud* 1939; *Typhoon, The Man I Married, The Lady in Question* 1940; *Shining Victory, Underground* 1941; *To Be or Not to Be, Nazi Agent, Night Monster* 1942; *Mission to Moscow, The Song of Bernadette* 1943; *Address Unknown, The Mummy's Ghost* 1944; *Hotel Berlin* 1945; *The Secret Life of Walter Mitty* 1947; *Samson and Delilah* 1949; *Kiss Tomorrow Goodbye* 1950; *The Lady and the Bandit* 1951.

Reid, Beryl. Actress. *b.* June 17, 1920, in Hereford, England. *d.* 1996. Comedienne of British revues and stage since 1936, she turned in some memorable character performances in UK and US films of the late 60s. She appeared on Broadway in 'The Killing of Sister George' (1966), later repeating her role in the film.

FILMS INCLUDE: *The Belles of St. Trinian's* 1954; *Two Way Stretch* 1960; *The Dock Brief/Trial and Error* 1962; *Inspector Clouseau, The Killing of Sister George* (US), *Star!* (US) 1968; *The Assassination Bureau* 1969; *Entertaining Mr. Sloane* 1970; *The Beast in the Cellar* 1971; *Dr. Phibes Rises Again* 1972; *The Death Wheelers* 1973; *Joseph Andrews* 1977; *Carry On Emmanuelle* 1978; *Yellowbeard* 1983; *The Doctor and the Devils* 1985.

Reid, Carl Benton. Actor. *b.* 1893, Lansing, Mich. *d.* 1973. Versatile character actor with solid stage experience from the early 20s. Memorable as Oscar Hubbard in both the Broadway and Hollywood versions of *The Little Foxes.* He was a regular in the TV series 'Burke's Law.'

FILMS INCLUDE: *The Little Foxes* (as Oscar Hubbard) 1941; *Tennessee Johnson* 1942; *The North Star/Armored Attack* 1943; *In a Lonely Place, The Killer That Stalked New York* 1950; *The Great Caruso, Lorna Doone* (as Sir Ensor Doone) 1951; *Boots Malone, Carbine Williams, The Story of Will Rogers* 1952; *Escape from Fort Bravo* 1953; *Broken Lance, The Egyptian* 1954; *The Left Hand of God, The Spoilers* 1955; *A Day of Fury, The First Texan* (as Andrew Jackson), *The Last Wagon* 1956; *Battle Hymn, Time Limit* 1957; *The Trap* 1959; *The Bramble Bush, The Gallant Hours* 1960; *Pressure Point* 1962; *The Ugly American* 1963; *Madame X* 1966.

Reid, Dorothy. See DAVENPORT, Dorothy.

Reid, James Hallek (Hal). See REID, Wallace.

Reid, Virginia. See CARVER, Lynne.

Reid, Wallace. Actor, director, screenwriter. *b.* William Wallace Reid, Apr. 15, 1891, St. Louis, Mo. *d.* 1923. Tall, handsome star of silent films whose career ended tragically as a result of drug addiction. The son of stage and screen actor-director James Halek ["Hal"] Reid (1860–1920), he first went on the stage at age four in his parents' act. He was kept away from the theater during his studies at a Pennsylvania prep school, where he developed talents as a musician, a painter, and an athlete. Returning to the stage as a young adult, he made his film debut in 1910 with the Selig company in Chicago, for which his father was working as a screenwriter. He next went over to Vitagraph, where he occasionally played character parts, sometimes doubling as cameraman and player of mood music for the stars on the set. But he quickly developed into a busy leading man, starring in countless two-, three-, and four-reelers, many of which he also directed, for such companies as American, Reliance, and Universal. Several of these early films were directed by his father.

In 1913 he married Dorothy DAVENPORT, his co-star in many films. After playing a small but memorable role as a fighting blacksmith in Griffith's *The Birth of a Nation,* he became a leading star on the Paramount lot. In 1919, while his popularity was at a peak, he suffered head injuries in a train crash on the way to a location and was given frequent doses of morphine to ease his pain. He became addicted to the drug and aggravated the condition by turning to heavy drinking. He continued appearing in films, but toward the end of 1922 he was placed in a sanitarium, where he died in agony shortly afterward at 32.

FILMS INCLUDE (as actor): *The Phoenix* 1910; *The Leading Lady, The Reporter* 1911; *Chumps, Indian Romeo and Juliet, The Telephone Girl, The Seventh Son, The Illumination, Brothers, The Victoria Cross, The Hieroglyphic, Kaintuck* (also sc.), *Before the White Man Came* (also sc.), *A Man's Duty, The Secret Service Man, His Only Son, The Indian Raiders, Every Inch a Man, The Tribal Law* 1912; *Love and the Law* (also dir.), *A Rose of Old Mexico* (also co-dir. with Allan Dwan), *The Ways of Fate* (also dir.), *When Jim Returned* (also dir., sc.), *The Tattooed Arm* (also dir., sc.), *The Deerslayer, Youth and Jealousy, The Kiss* (also dir.), *Her Innocent Marriage* (also co-dir. with Dwan), *His Mother's Son, The Modern Snare* (also dir.), *Via Cabaret* (also dir.), *Hearts and Horses* (also co-dir. with Dwan), *In Love and War, Women and War* (also sc.), *Dead Man's Shoes* (also dir., sc.), *Pride of Lonesome* (also dir.), *The Foreign Spy* (also dir.), *Mental Suicide* (also sc.), *The Animal, The Harvest of Flame* (also dir., sc.), *The Mystery of the Yellow Aster Mine* (also dir.), *The Gratitude of Wanda* (also dir.), *The Heart of a Cracksman* (also co-dir. with Willis Lobards, sc.), *Cross Purposes* (also co-dir. with Lobards), *Fires of Fate* (also co-dir. with Lobards, sc.), *Retribution* (also co-dir. with Lobards), *The Lightning Bolt* (also dir., sc.), *A Hopi Legend* (also dir., sc.) 1913; *The Intruder* (also dir.), *The Wheel of Life* (also dir.), *Fires of Conscience* (also dir.), *The Greater Devotion* (also dir.), *A Flash in the Dark* (also dir.), *Breed o' the Mountains* (also dir.), *Regeneration* (also dir.), *The Voice of Viola* (also dir.), *The Heart of the Hills* (also dir., co-sc.), *The Way of a Woman* (also dir.), *The Mountaineer* (also dir., sc.), *Cupid Incognito* (also dir., sc.), *A Gypsy Romance* (also dir.), *The Fruit of Evil* (also dir., sc.), *The Test* (also dir.), *Women and Roses* (also dir., co-sc.), *The Skeleton* (also dir.), *The Quack* (also dir.), *The Siren* (also dir.), *The Man Within* (also dir.), *Passing of the Beast* (also dir.), *Children of Fate/Love's Western Flight* (also dir.), *The Den of Thieves* (also dir.), *Arms and the Gringo, A City Beautiful, Moonshine Molly, Sierra Jim's Reformation, Her Awakening, The Niggard, The Odalisque, Another Chance, At Dawn* 1914; *The Craven, Three Brothers, The Birth of a Nation, The Lost House, Enoch Arden, A Yankee from the West, The Chorus Lady, Old Heidelberg, Carmen* (as Don José), *The Golden Chance* 1915; *To Have and to Hold, The Love Mask, Maria Rosa, The Selfish Woman, Intolerance* 1916; *Joan the Woman, The Golden Fetter, The Prison Without Walls, The World Apart, The Squaw Man's Son, The Woman God Forgot, Nan of Music Mountain, The Devil Stone* 1917; *The Things We Love, The House of Silence, Believe Me Xantippe, The Firefly of France, Less Than Kin, The Source, Too Many Millions* 1918; *The Dub, Alias Mike Moran, The Roaring Road, You're Fired, The Love Burglar, Valley of the Giants, The Lottery Man, Hawthorne of the USA* 1919; *Double Speed, Excuse My Dust, The Dancin' Fool, What's Your Hurry?, Always Audacious* 1920; *The Charm School, The Love Special, Too Much Speed, The Affairs of Anatol, The Hell Diggers, Forever/Peter Ibbetson* (title role), *Don't Tell Everything* 1921; *Rent Free, The World's Champion, Across the Continent, The Dictator, Nice People, The Ghost Breaker, Clarence, Thirty Days* 1922.

Reiner, Carl. Comic actor, writer, producer, director. Born on Mar. 20, 1922, in the Bronx, N.Y. In his late teens he enrolled in the WPA Dramatic Workshop and during WW II became part of Major Maurice Evans's GI troupe in the South Pacific. Returning to civilian life, he appeared in stage productions with various road companies and on Broadway, then gained popularity as second banana to Sid Caesar in the early TV comedy program 'Your Show of Shows' (1950–54). The tall, balding, affable Reiner later created the successful 'Dick Van Dyke Show' series (1961–66). In the span of a decade (1956–67) he won eight Emmy Awards as a performer, producer, and writer. With Mel BROOKS impersonating the legendary "2,000-year-old man," Reiner co-created and co-starred in one of the most successful comedy records of all time. He wrote a funny, semiautobiographical novel, *Enter Laughing* (1958), which was later adapted into a play (1963) and a film (1967). On the screen as an actor from the late 50s, he ventured into directing in the late 60s. His off-the-wall *Where's Poppa?* (1970) has enjoyed a lasting cult following. He scored box-office hits with several Steve Martin comedies of the early 80s, and attempted a farcical spoof of *Basic Instinct* and its ilk with 1993's *Fatal Instinct*. Reiner's wife, Estelle, began a late-blooming career as a nightclub singer in 1984. They are the parents of Lucas and Rob REINER, both directors.

FILMS: As actor—*Happy Anniversary* 1959; *The Gazebo* 1960; *Gidget Goes Hawaiian* 1961; *The Thrill of It All* (also co-story, sc.), *It's a Mad Mad Mad Mad World* 1963; *The Art of Love* (also sc.) 1965; *Alice of Wonderland in Paris* (v/o), *Don't Worry—We'll Think of a Title* (cameo), *The Russians Are Coming! The Russians Are Coming!* 1966; *A Guide for the Married Man* (cameo) 1967; *Generation* 1969; *Ten from Your Show of Shows* (compilation film of old TV clips) 1973; *The End* 1978; *The Spirit of '76* (prod.) 1990; *Fatal Instinct* 1993; *Bullets Over Broadway, Mixed Nuts* 1994; *Bye Bye Love* 1995. As director—*Enter Laughing* (also co-prod., co-sc.) 1967; *The Comic* (also co-prod., co-sc., act.) 1969; *Where's Poppa?* 1970; *Oh God* (also act.) 1977; *The Jerk* (also act.) 1979; *Dead Man Don't Wear Plaid* (also co-sc.) 1982; *The Man with Two Brains* (also co-sc.) 1983; *All of Me* 1984; *Summer Rental* 1985; *Summer School* (also act.) 1987; *Bert Rigby, You're a Fool* (also sc.) 1989; *Sibling Rivalry* 1990; *North* (co-sc. only) 1994; *That Old Feeling* 1997.

Reiner, Rob. Actor, director. Born on Mar. 6, 1945, in New York City. The son of actor-director Carl REINER, he grew up in a show business atmosphere, often commuting between homes in Manhattan and Beverly Hills. After attending UCLA he began performing in regional theaters and with improvisation troupes. He played occasional small comic roles in various TV series and made his big-screen debut in his father's *Enter Laughing* (1967). He also wrote material for 'The Smothers Brothers Comedy Hour' and other TV shows. His big break came in 1971 when he was cast as Mike "Meathead" Stivic, the exasperated son-in-law, in the long-running (through 1978) TV comedy hit series 'All in the Family,' for which he won Emmy Awards in 1974 and 1978. In 1978 he created and briefly starred in his own comedy series, 'Free Country.' Reiner made a successful debut as a film director with *This Is Spinal Tap* (1984), a bright spoof of rock documentaries. He has since proven to be a capable director of both comedy and drama while sustaining his acting career on TV and in films. He established himself as a director of serious commercial works with the coming-of-age film *Stand By Me* (1986), and solidified his position with the romantic comedy *When Harry Met Sally. . .* (1989). He won the Golden Antenna prize at the Avoriaz Fantasy Film Festival for *The Princess Bride* (1988). His military drama *A Few Good Men* (1992) was nominated for several Oscars, including one for best film. He shares control over a production company, Castle Rock Entertainment. His first wife (1971–79) was actress-director Penny MARSHALL, with whom he appeared occasionally in the TV sitcom 'The Odd Couple.'

FILMS: As actor—*Enter Laughing* 1967; *Halls of Anger, Where's Poppa?* 1970; *Summertree* 1971; *How Come Nobody's on Our Side?* 1975; *Fire Sale* 1977; *Throw Momma from the Train* 1987; *Postcards from the Edge, The Spirit of '76* 1990; *Regarding Henry* 1991; *Sleepless in Seattle* 1993; *Bullets Over Broadway* 1994; *Bye Bye Love* 1995; *Mad Dog Time* 1996. As director—*This Is Spinal Tap* (also co-sc., co-songs, act.) 1984; *The Sure Thing* 1985; *Stand by Me* 1986; *The Princess Bride* (also co-prod.) 1987; *When Harry Met Sally* (also co-prod.) 1989; *Misery* (also co-prod.) 1990; *A Few Good Men* 1992; *North* 1994; *The American President* 1995; *Ghosts of Mississippi* 1996.

Reinhardt, Gottfried. Screenwriter, producer, director. *b.* 1911, in Berlin. *d.* 1994. The son of Max REINHARDT, he was a stage actor before coming to the US as personal assistant to director Ernst LUBITSCH and later as an assistant to producer Walter WANGER. A screenwriter from the mid-30s, he turned producer in the 40s and director in the 50s.

FILMS INCLUDE: As screenwriter—*I Live My Life* 1935; *The Great Waltz* 1938; *Bridal Suite* 1939. As producer—*Comrade X* 1940; *Rage in Heaven, Two-Faced Woman* 1941; *Command Decision* 1948; *The Great Sinner* 1949; *The Red Badge of Courage* 1951; *Young Man with Ideas* 1952. As director—*Invitation* 1952; *The Story of Three Loves* ("The Jealous Lover" and "Equilibrium" episodes) 1953; *Betrayed* 1954; *Vor Sonnenuntergang* (Ger.) 1956; *Menschen im Hotel* (Ger./Fr.), *Abschied der Götter/Rebel Flight to Cuba* (Ger.) 1959; *Town Without Pity* (also prod.; US/Switz./Ger.) 1960; *Elf Jahre und ein Tag* (also prod., co-sc.; Ger.) 1963; *Situation Hopeless—But Not Serious* (also prod.) 1965.

Reinhardt, Max. Director. *b.* Maximilian Goldman, Sept. 8, 1873, Baden, near Vienna, Austria. *d.* 1943. Germany's most important stage producer and director during the first third of the 20th century, he indirectly exerted enormous influence on the course of German and international cinema. All the important directors (except Fritz LANG) and actors of the "golden age" of German films in the 20s and early 30s, many of whom later worked in the US and elsewhere, trained and developed under him. The list includes such directors as Murnau, Leni, Lubitsch, Wegener, Dieterle, and Preminger. Among the actors were such stars as Veidt, Jannings, Bergner, Rainer, Dietrich, and Schildkraut. Above all, he was instrumental in the emergence of the expressionistic style, which dominated the German theater and cinema of the period. He owned and operated a chain of theaters in Germany and Austria, including the famed Deutsches Theater in Berlin. His direct film activity was limited to several early German silents and to the American *A Midsummer Night's Dream* (1935), which he co-directed with William Dieterle. When the Nazis came to power in Germany, Reinhardt lost all his theaters and after a tour of Europe as guest director of various companies, he spent the rest of his years in the United States, where he produced and directed a number of stage productions and founded an acting school and theater workshop in Hollywood.

FILMS: *Sumurun* 1908; *Das Mirakel* 1912; *Insel der Seligen* 1913; *Venezianische Nacht* 1914; *A Midsummer Night's Dream* (co-dir. with William Dieterle; US) 1935.

Reinhold, Judge. Actor. Born Edward Ernest Reinhold, 1956, in Wilmington, Del. *ed.* Mary Washington Coll.; North Carolina School of the Arts. Tall, lean, gawky young lead and supporting player of Hollywood films. He performed in regional theaters, including Burt REYNOLDS's Dinner Theater in Florida, before gaining national exposure on TV. On the screen from the late 70s, he played mostly genial, light characters in a varied assortment of films.

FILMS: *Running Scared* 1979; *Stripes* 1981; *Pandemonium/Thursday the 12th/Saturday the 14th, Fast Times at Ridgemont High* 1982; *The Lords of Discipline* 1983; *Gremlins, Roadhouse 66, Beverly Hills Cop* 1984; *Head Office* 1985; *Off Beat, Ruthless People* 1986; *Beverly Hills Cop II* 1987; *A Soldier's Tale* (NZ/US), *Vice Versa* 1988; *Rosalie Goes Shopping* (Ger.) 1989; *Daddy's Dyin'. . . Who's Got the Will?*

1990; *Zandalee* 1991; *Enid is Sleeping, Near Misses* 1992; *Beverly Hills Cop III* 1993; *The Santa Clause* 1994.

Reiniger, Lotte. Animator. *b.* June 2, 1899, Berlin. *d.* 1981. Cinema's leading practitioner of silhouette animation. While still a student at Max Reinhardt's theater school in Berlin in 1916, she designed silhouettes for intertitles in a Paul Wegener film. She later created a special technique of silhouette animation, which she utilized in many shorts and feature-length films, most notably *The Adventures of Prince Achmed* (1926), the world's first full-length animation film and an international success. In 1935 she moved to England and remained there for the duration of WW II. She returned there permanently in 1950 and later became a British citizen. In the late 70s she worked for the National Film Board of Canada. She often collaborated with Carl Koch, her husband from 1921 who, until his death in 1963, produced and photographed her films. She wrote *Shadow Theatres and Shadow Films* (1970), among several other books.

FILMS INCLUDE (shorts, unless otherwise noted): In Germany—*Rüberahis Hochzeit* (feature; intertitles only) 1916; *Der Rattenfänger von Hamelin/The Pied Piper of Hamelin* (feature; intertitles only) 1918; *Das Ornament des verliebten Herzens, Der fliegende Koffer, Aschenputtel/Cinderella, Der Stern von Bethlehem* 1922; *Die Abenteuer des Prinzen Achmed/The Adventures of Prince Achmed* (feature) 1926; *Doktor Dolittle und seine Tiere/The Adventures of Dr. Dolittle* (composed of three shorts) 1928; *Zehn Minuten Mozart, Die Jagd nach dem Glück* (feature; silhouette sequences only) 1930; *Harlekin* 1931; *Sissi* 1932; *Carmen* 1933; *Das gestohlene Herz/The Stolen Heart* 1934; *Papagono, Galathea, Das kleine Schornsteinfeger/The Little Chimney Sweep* 1935. In the UK—*The King's Breakfast* 1936; *Le Marseillaise* (feature; animation sequence only; Fr.) 1938; *Mary's Birthday* 1951; *Aladdin, The Magic Horse, Snow White and Rose Red* 1953; *The Three Wishes, The Grasshopper and the Ant, The Frog Prince, The Gallant Little Tailor, The Sleeping Beauty* 1954; *Hansel and Gretel, Thumbelina, Jack and the Beanstalk/Jack the Giant Killer* 1955; *The Star of Bethlehem* 1956; *La Belle Hélène* 1957; *The Seraglio* 1958; *The Pied Piper of Hamelin* 1960; *The Frog Prince* 1961; *Cinderella* 1963; *The Lost Son* 1974; *Aucassin et Nicolette* 1976; *The Rose and Ring* 1979.

Reis, Irving. Director. *b.* May 7, 1906, New York City. *d.* 1953. *ed.* Columbia. The founder and director of CBS Radio's Columbia Workshop, which flourished in the mid-30s, he wrote, produced, and directed many radio dramas and gave Orson Welles his first radio job. Reis began in films in 1938 as a screenwriter for Paramount and turned out his first film as director for RKO in 1940. His early output consisted of routine B productions, but after returning from WW II service he directed a number of quality films.

FILMS: *One Crowded Night, I'm Still Alive* 1940; *Footlight Fever, The Gay Falcon, Weekend for Three, A Date with the Falcon* 1941; *The Falcon Takes Over, The Big Street* 1942; *Crack-Up* 1946; *The Bachelor and the Bobby-Soxer* 1947; *All My Sons, Enchantment* 1948; *Roseanna McCoy, Dancing in the Dark* 1949; *Three Husbands* 1950; *Of Men and Music* (concert feature; co-dir. with Alex Hammid), *New Mexico* 1951; *The Four Poster* 1952.

Reisch, Walter. Screenwriter, occasional director. *b.* May 23, 1903, Vienna. *d.* 1983. He entered films in his late teens as an assistant to Alexander KORDA and later contributed screenplays for numerous Austrian and German productions, alone or in collaboration. Leaving Germany at the advent of the Nazis, he returned to Austria, then worked briefly in England before moving on to Hollywood in 1938. He shared an Academy Award for the script of *Titanic* (1953).

FILMS INCLUDE (as screenwriter, alone or in collaboration): In Austria—*Miss Hobbs* 1921; *Der Fluch, Ein Walzer von Strauss, Pratermizzi* (also co-dir. with several others) 1927. In Germany—*Der Bettelstudent, Die indiskrete Frau* 1927; *Dragonerliebchen* 1928; *Der schwarze Domino, Die Nacht gehört uns, Dich hab'ich geliebt/Because I Loved You* 1929; *Brand in der Oper/Barcarole, Das Flötenkonzert von Sanssouci, Hokuspokus/Hocuspocus, Ein Tango Für Dich* 1930; *Die lustigen Weiber von Wien, Der Raub der Mona Lisa/The Theft of the Mona Lisa* 1931; *Ein blonder Traum/A Blonde Dream, F.P.1 antwortet nicht/F.P.1, Die Gräfin von Monte Christo,* 1932; *Ich und die Kaiserin/Heart Song, Saison in Kairo* 1933. In Austria—*Leise flehen meine Lieder/Unfinished Symphony* (story only) 1933; *Maskerade/Masquerade in Vienna* 1934; *Episode* (also dir.) 1935. In the UK—*Men Are Not Gods* (story, dir.) 1936. In the US—*Gateway* (story only), *The Great Waltz* 1938; *Ninotchka* 1939; *My Love Came Back* (story only), *Comrade X* (story only) 1940; *That Hamilton Woman, That Uncertain Feeling* 1941; *Somewhere I'll Find You, Seven Sweethearts* 1942; *The Heavenly Body, Gaslight* 1944; *Song of Scheherazade* (also dir.) 1947; *The Countess of Monte Cristo* (story only) 1948; *The Fan* 1949; *The Mating Season* 1951; *The Model and the Marriage Broker* 1952; *Niagara, Titanic* 1953; *Die Mücke* (also dir.; Ger.) 1954; *Der Cornet* (also dir.; Ger.), *The Girl in the Red Velvet Swing* 1955; *Teenage Rebel* 1956; *Stopover Tokyo* 1957; *The Remarkable Mr. Pennypacker, Journey to the Center of the Earth* 1959.

Reisner (also known as **Riesner**), **Charles F. (Chuck).** Director, actor, screenwriter. *b.* Mar. 14, 1887, Minneapolis. *d.* 1962. A former semipro prizefighter and a vaudeville and musical stage star, he entered films during WW II as a comedian and screenwriter, working for Keystone, Vitagraph, and other studios. He was associate director on Charlie Chaplin's *A Dog's Life* (1918), *The Kid* (1921), *The Pilgrim* (1923), and *The Gold Rush* (1925), playing nasty villains in the first three. He also appeared as an actor in a number of other features of the 20s. A director from the mid-20s, he specialized in comedy, working with such talent as Syd(ney) Chaplin, Buster Keaton, W. C. Fields, the Marx Brothers, Marie Dressler, and Abbott and Costello. He directed at various studios but mainly at MGM. Working with ever-diminishing budgets, he retired from feature films in 1950 and switched over to TV. His son, Dean Riesner (Reisner), has been involved sporadically in films as an actor and screenwriter. He directed the film *Bill and Coo* (1948).

FILMS (as director): *The Man on the Box* (also act.) 1925; *Oh What a Nurse!, The Better 'Ole* 1926; *What Every Girl Should Know, The Missing Link* (also story), *The Fortune Hunter* 1927; *Steamboat Bill Jr., Fools for Luck, Brotherly Love* 1928; *Noisy Neighbors, China Bound, The Hollywood Revue of 1929* 1929; *Chasing Rainbows/The Road Show, Caught Short, Love in the Rough* 1930; *Reducing, Stepping Out, Politics, Flying High* 1931; *Divorce in the Family* 1932; *The Chief* 1933; *You Can't Buy Everything, The Show-Off, Student Tour* 1934; *The Winning Ticket* (also co-prod.), *It's in the Air* 1935; *Everybody Dance* (also act.; UK) 1936; *Murder Goes to College, Sophie Lang Goes West, Manhattan Merry-Go-Round* 1937; *Winter Carnival* 1939; *The Big Store* 1941; *This Time for Keeps* 1942; *Harrigan's Kid* 1943; *Meet the People, Lost in a Harem* 1944; *The Cobra Strikes, In This Corner* 1948; *The Traveling Saleswoman* 1950.

Reisz, Karel. Director. Born on July 21, 1926, in Ostrava, Czechoslovakia. The son of a Jewish lawyer, he was whisked out to England at age 12, just before the Nazi invasion. His parents stayed behind and perished in a concentration camp. After graduating from a Quaker school in Reading, he served as a fighter pilot in the Czech squadron of the RAF during the waning years of WW II, then studied chemistry at Cambridge. After teaching grammar school for two years, he became a freelance writer and in the early 50s began contributing film criticism to *Sequence,* a magazine associated with the Film Society of Oxford University and dedicated to the exploration of the aesthetic and moral aspects of film. In 1952 he co-edited with Lindsay ANDERSON the final issue of that highly respected publication, which influenced the ideas of Britain's FREE CINEMA. In 1953, Reisz wrote *The Technique of Film Editing* for the British Film Academy, which is not a technical textbook, as its title might suggest, but an intelligent study of the aesthetic function of editing in filmmaking with numerous examples from actual films. The book, which has become a classic teaching tool, was revised and enlarged in 1968 in collaboration with Gavin Millar.

In the mid-50s, Reisz became a leading figure in Britain's Free Cinema movement, along with Lindsay Anderson and Tony RICHARDSON. He co-directed with the latter the short *Momma Don't Allow* (1955) and by himself piloted a celebrated 52-minute documentary about a London youth club, *We Are the Lambeth Boys* (1959), which was sponsored by the Ford Motor Company. During that period he also directed a number of advertising films for Ford and in 1960 turned out his first feature film, *Saturday Night and Sunday Morning,* an incisive, uninhibited view of Britain's working class, which enjoyed critical as well as commercial success. He has since directed only a handful of features, selecting his projects carefully but not always successfully. One of his better efforts was *Morgan: A Suitable Case for Treatment/Morgan!* (1966), a refreshingly offbeat exercise in black humor mixed with touches of pathos. Reisz has also occasionally produced. He was co-producer of Lindsay Anderson's documentary *Every Day Except Christmas* and solo producer on Anderson's feature *This Sporting Life* (1963). In 1974 he directed in the US *The Gambler,* an incisive study of the psychology of human frailty. A standout among his later films was *The French Lieutenant's Woman* (1981), a flawed but persuasively passionate screen adaptation of the John Fowles romantic period novel. He has also directed for British TV and in recent years has made many TV commercials. His second wife was actress Betsy BLAIR.

FILMS: *Momma Don't Allow* (short; co-dir. with Tony Richardson; also co-sc.) 1955; *We Are the Lambeth Boys* (medium-length doc.) 1959; *Saturday Night and Sunday Morning* 1960; *Night Must Fall* (also co-prod.) 1964; *Morgan: A Suitable Case for Treatment/Morgan!* 1966; *Isadora/The Loves of Isadora* 1968; *The Gambler* (US) 1974; *Who'll Stop the Rain?* (US) 1978; *The French Lieutenant's Woman* 1981; *Sweet Dreams* 1985; *Everybody Wins* 1990.

Reitherman, Wolfgang ("Woolie"). American animator, director, producer. *b.* 1909. *d.* 1985. Joining Walt Disney as an animator in 1933, he worked on many of the studio's shorts and feature-length classics. Gradually, he moved on to directing segments of animated features and in the early 60s he became a solo director. After Disney's death in 1966, Reitherman became the producer of the studio's entire animated feature output. He won an Academy Award for the short *Winnie the Pooh and the Blustery Day* (1968). Retired from 1981, he was killed in a car crash.

FILMS INCLUDE: *Snow White and the Seven Dwarfs* (co-anim.) 1937; *Pinocchio* (seq. dir.), *Fantasia* (anim. superv. "The Rite of Spring" segment) 1940; *The Reluctant Dragon* (co-anim.), *Dumbo* (co-anim. dir.) 1941; *Saludos Amigos* (co-anim.) 1943; *Fun and Fancy Free* (co-anim. dir.) 1947; *Ichabod and Mr. Toad* (co-anim. dir.) 1949; *The Truth About Mother Goose* (featurette; co-dir.) 1957; *Cinderella* (co-anim. dir.) 1950; *Alice in Wonderland* (co-anim. dir.) 1951; *Peter Pan* (co-anim. dir.) 1953; *Lady and the Tramp* (co-anim. dir.) 1955; *Sleeping Beauty* (seq. dir.) 1959; *101 Dalmatians* (co-dir.) 1961; *The Sword in the Stone* (dir.) 1963; *Winnie the Pooh and the Honey Tree* (short; dir.) 1966; *The Jungle Book* (dir.) 1967; *Winnie the Pooh and the Blustery Day* (short; dir.) 1968; *The Aristocats* (dir., co-prod.) 1970; *Robin Hood* (dir., prod.) 1973; *The Rescuers* (co-dir., prod.) 1977; *The Fox and the Hound* (co-prod.) 1981.

Reitman, Ivan. Director. Born on Oct. 27, 1946, in Komarmo, Czechoslovakia. In Canada from age four, with his Holocaust-surviving refugee parents, he graduated from McMaster University in Hamilton, Ontario, as a music major, then attended the National Film Board's Summer Institute at that school. As a student, he directed three shorts, one of which, *Orientation* (1968), received theatrical distribution throughout Canada. He began directing and producing professionally in the early 70s, demonstrating from the start a keen instinct for commercially viable, if not always tasteful, material. He was fined $300 and sentenced to a year's probation for *Columbus of Sex* (1970), a film based on the Victorian novel *My Secret Life.* After scoring big box-office hits as the co-producer of *National Lampoon's Animal House* (1978) and director of *Meatballs* (1979), he launched a financially spectacular Hollywood career, which was capped by the whimsical blockbuster *Ghostbusters* (1984). Other rowdy and highly profitable comedies followed. His production company is Northern Lights Entertainment. He is married to actress Geneviève Robert (née Deloir).

FEATURE FILMS: *Columbus of Sex/My Secret Life* (prod., mus.) 1970; *Foxy Lady* (dir., prod., edit., mus.) 1971; *Cannibal Girls* (dir., prod.) 1973; *Shivers/They Came from Within* (prod.) 1976; *Death Weekend/The House by the Lake* (prod.), *Rabid* (co-exec. prod.) 1977; *National Lampoon's Animal House* (co-prod.) 1978; *Meatballs* (dir.) 1979; *Stripes* (dir., co-prod.), *Heavy Metal* (prod.) 1981; *Spacehunter: Adventures in the Forbidden Zone* (exec. prod.) 1983; *Ghostbusters* (dir., prod.) 1984; *Legal Eagles* (dir., prod., co-story) 1986; *Big Shots* (exec. prod.) 1987; *Casual Sex?* (exec. prod.), *Feds* (exec. prod.), *Twins* (dir., prod.) 1988; *Ghostbusters II* (dir., prod.) 1989; *Kindergarten Cop* (dir., co-prod.) 1990; *Stop! Or My Mom Will Shoot* (prod.), *Beethoven* (exec. prod.) 1992; *Dave* (dir., pr.), *Beethoven's 2nd* (exec. prod.) 1993; *Junior* 1994; *Space Jam* 1996; *Commandments* (prod.), *Father's Day* (dir., co-prod.).

Reitz, Edgar. Director. Born on Nov. 1, 1932, in Moorbach, Germany. A watchmaker's son, he grew up with a divided interest in science and the arts. Midway through engineering college, he switched over to the University of Munich, where he studied literature, drama, and art history. Staying in Munich after graduation, he assisted local filmmakers in various capacities before turning out his first film in 1958. In the following decade he directed numerous short documentaries, industrials, and inventive experimental films, several of which won top prizes at international festivals. With Alexander KLUGE and 24 other young filmmakers he signed in 1962 the famous Oberhausen Manifesto, which called for the abolition of Germany's stagnant "papa's cinema" and the infusion of young blood and new ideas into the national motion picture industry. During the same year, Reitz, Kluge, and several of the others established a film school, the Institut für Filmgestaltung, at the Academy for Advanced Design in Ulm, where Reitz taught film technique and served as the director until 1968. All the while he continued directing shorts and in 1966 served as co-cinematographer on Kluge's breakthrough film *Abschied von Gestern/Yesterday Girl.* The following year Reitz directed his own first feature, *Mahlzeiten/Mealtimes,* a film rich in ironic double entendre that won the prize for best first feature at the 1967 Venice Festival. Several features later, Reitz directed what could be the most ambitious film of all time, and is certainly the longest. He devoted more than five years to write, shoot, and edit *Heimat/Homeland/Made in Germany* (1984), a 15-hour and 24-minute memory-based saga of a German family and its joys and tribulations from the end of WW I to the dawn of the 80s. Some critics faulted the film's undisciplined structure and questioned the moral fortitude of its view of German society during the Nazi era. But many hailed *Heimat* as a masterpiece, one of the most significant achievements of contemporary cinema.

FEATURE FILMS: *Mahlzeiten/Mealtimes/Lust for Love, Fussnoten* ("footnote" elaborations on *Mahlreiten*) 1967; *Uxmal* (unreleased) 1968; *Cadillac* 1969; *Geschichten vom Kübelkind* (co-dir.) 1970; *Kino II* (experimental), *Das goldene Ding/The Golden Fleece* (co-dir.) 1971; *Die Reise nach Wien* 1973; *In Gefahr und gröster Not bringt der Mittelweg den Tod/The Middle of the Road Is a Very Dead End* (co-dir.) 1974; *Stunde Null/Zero Hour* 1976; *Deutschland im Herbst/Germany in Autumn* (co-dir.), *Der Schneider von Ulm/The Tailor from Ulm* 1978; *Heimat/Homeland* (Made in Germany) 1984.

release. In film industry terms, the official launching of a motion picture into general distribution. Most American films have specific release dates that may or may not coincide with the actual date of a film's premiere. Some films are officially released months after they have been shown to a limited audience. But, generally, release dates precede or coincide with exhibition dates. European films do not usually have an official release date, a fact that tends to breed confusion in dating them accurately. Some film historians date the films according to the year in which the principal shooting took place, others by the actual premiere dates. The result is often a profusion of dates for any given film in the various sources available to a film historian.

release negative. A complete negative from which release prints are made.

release print. A composite print, complete with picture and sound, and ready for distribution to motion picture theaters.

Relph, Michael. Producer, screenwriter, occasional director. Born in 1915, in England. The son of stage and screen actor George Relph (1888–1960), he began his film career in 1932 as an assistant art director at Gaumont-British. In the early 40s he graduated to set designer and art director at Ealing and in those capacities worked on such films as *Champagne Charlie* (1944), *Dead of Night* (1945), and *Nicholas Nickleby* (1947), all for director Alberto CAVALCANTI. He then became associate producer to Michael Balcon and finally a producer, often in association with Basil DEARDEN. He also directed and scripted a number of films, several in collaboration with Dearden.

FILMS INCLUDE: As associate producer—*The Captive Heart* 1946; *Frieda* 1947; *Saraband for Dead Lovers/Saraband* 1948; *Kind Hearts and Coronets* 1949; *The Blue Lamp* 1950. As director—*I Believe in You* (co-dir. with Basil Dearden; also co-prod., co-sc.), *The Gentle Gunman* (co-dir. with Dearden; also co-prod.) 1952; *The Square Ring* (co-dir. with Dearden; also co-prod.) 1953; *Out of the Clouds* (co-dir. with Dearden; also co-prod., co-sc.), *The Ship That Died of Shame* (co-dir. with Dearden; also co-prod., co-sc.) 1955; *Davy* 1957; *Rockets Galore/Mad Little Island* 1958; *Desert Mice* (also co-prod.) 1959. As producer—*The Smallest Show on Earth* 1957; *Violent Playground* 1958; *Sapphire* 1959; *The League of Gentlemen, Man in the Moon* (also co-sc.) 1960; *The Secret Partner, Victim* 1961; *All Night Long, Life for Ruth/Walk in the Shadow* 1962; *The Mind Benders* 1963; *Woman of Straw* (also co-sc.) 1964; *Masquerade* (also co-sc.) 1965; *The Assassination Bureau* (also sc.) 1969; *The Man Who Haunted Himself* (also co-sc.) 1970; *An Unsuitable Job for a Woman* 1982; *Heavenly Pursuits/The Gospel According to Vic* 1986.

remake. A newer version of a motion picture that had been filmed before. For example, Lewis Milestone's *Mutiny on the Bounty* (1962), starring Marlon Brando, is a remake of Frank Lloyd's *Mutiny on the Bounty* (1935), which starred Clark Gable.

Rembrandt lighting. Hollywood term for dramatic lighting with pronounced shadows, somewhat reminiscent of the tone of Rembrandt's paintings. Many cameramen and directors claim to have introduced this type of lighting to motion pictures, but the phrase "Rembrandt lighting" is attributed to Cecil B. De Mille. He supposedly responded to a telegraphed complaint about the clarity of actors' faces in one of his films by explaining he was employing Rembrandt lighting.

Remick, Lee. Actress. *b.* Dec. 14, 1935, Quincy, Mass. *d.* 1991. *ed.* Barnard Coll. Talented, attractive leading lady of Hollywood films. A former dancer, she gained dramatic experience on the stage and TV before making her film debut in the role of a sexy drum majorette in *A Face in the Crowd* (1957). She attracted attention in a bigger role as the flirtatious wife of Tony Franciosa in *The Long Hot Summer* (1958), asserted herself in *Anatomy of a Murder* (1959) as an alleged rape victim, and won a nomination for an Academy Award for her strong performance as the pitiable alcoholic wife of Jack Lemmon in *Days of Wine and Roses* (1962). In addition to many subsequent leads in films, often in sensual roles, she continued performing successfully on the stage and on TV. Following her 1968 divorce from TV director-producer William Colleran, her husband from 1957, she married British director William Rory "Kip" Gowens in 1970 and moved temporarily to England, where she starred in a number of films. With her feature career at a virtual standstill in the 80s, she frequently appeared in miniseries and TV movies. In 1988 she formed a partnership in a production company with James GARNER and Peter Duchow. Shortly after, she was diagnosed with cancer, of which she died at 55.

FILMS: *A Face in the Crowd* 1957; *The Long Hot Summer* 1958; *These Thousand Hills, Anatomy of a Murder* 1959; *Wild River* 1960; *Sanctuary* 1961; *Experiment in Terror, Days of Wine and Roses* 1962; *The Running Man, The Wheeler Dealers* 1963; *Baby the Rain Must Fall, The Hallelujah Trail* 1965; *No Way to Treat a Lady, The Detective* 1968; *Hard Contract* 1969; *A Severed Head* (UK), *Loot* (UK), *Sometimes a Great Notion/Never Give an Inch* 1971; *A Delicate Balance* 1973; *Hennessy* (UK) 1975; *The Hunted* (UK), *The Omen* 1976; *Telefon* 1977; *The Medusa Touch* (UK) 1978; *The Europeans* (UK) 1979; *Tribute* (Can.), *The Competition* 1980; *Emma's War* (Austral.) 1985; *The Vision* (UK) 1987.

Renaldo, Duncan. Actor. *b.* Apr. 23, 1904, Spain. *d.* 1980. Leading man and supporting player of Hollywood films. A foundling, he never knew his parents and was never able to ascertain his date and place of birth. He was raised and educated in various European countries and arrived in the US in the early 20s as a stoker on a Brazilian coal ship. After despairing of his plans of earning a living as a portrait painter, he found his way into films as a producer of shorts and after failing in that enterprise signed up as an actor with MGM in 1928. The official studio biography gave his place of birth as Camden, N.J., but capitalized on his Hispanic looks to type him as a Latin lover in a few late silents and early talkies. Renaldo's career suffered a setback in 1932 when he was briefly imprisoned after running afoul of immigration authorities on a charge of illegal entry. But he soon returned to the screen and played leads and supporting roles in minor films of various studios, mainly Republic. By the early 40s he had found his niche in Westerns as one of the Three Mesquiteers and in the middle of the decade he became the star of his own Western series, playing the role he is best known for, that of the screen's fourth Cisco Kid. The series was quite popular and in the early 50s became a TV staple, with Renaldo still in the lead.

FILMS INCLUDE: *Clothes Make the Woman, The Naughty Duchess* 1928; *The Bridge of San Luis Rey, Pals of the Prairie* 1929; *Trader Horn* 1931; *Trapped in Tia Juana* 1932; *Public Stenographer* 1933; *Moonlight Murder* 1936; *Jungle Menace* (serial), *Zorro Rides Again* (serial) 1937; *Rose of the Rio Grande, Spawn of the North* 1938; *The Lone Ranger Rides Again* (serial), *Zaza, Cowboys from Texas, The Kansas Terrors* 1939; *Heroes of the Saddle, Pioneers of the West, Covered Wagon Days* 1940; *Outlaws of the Desert, Down Mexico Way* 1941; *King of the Mounties* (serial) 1942; *Secret Service in Darkest Africa* (serial), *For Whom the Bell Tolls* 1943; *The Tiger Woman* (serial), *The Fighting Seabees* 1944; *The Cisco Kid Returns* 1945; *Jungle Flight* 1947; *Sword of the Avenger* 1948; *The Gay Amigo, The Daring Caballero, Satan's Cradle, We Were Strangers* 1949; *The Capture* 1950; *Zorro Rides Again* 1959.

Renaud, Madeleine. Actress. Born on Feb. 21, 1903, in Paris. Veteran star of French stage and screen, wife of Jean-Louis Barrault (from 1940) and co-director of the famous Renaud-Barrault Paris stage company since 1947. Her film roles are few but select.

FILMS INCLUDE: *Vent Debout* 1922; *La Terre qui meurt* 1926; *Jean de la Lune* 1931; *La Belle Marinière, La Couturière de Lunéville, Mistigri* 1932; *La Maternelle* 1933; *Maria Chapdelaine/The Naked Heart* 1934; *Hélène* 1936; *L'Etrange M. Victor* 1938; *Remorques/Stormy Waters* 1941; *Lumière d'Eté* 1943; *Le Ciel est à Vous/The Woman Who Dared* 1944; *Le Plaisir* 1952; *Le Dialogue des Carmélites* 1960; *The Longest Day* 1962; *Le Diable par la Queue/The Devil by the Tail* 1969; *L'Humeur vagabonde* 1971; *La Mandarine* 1972; *Des Journées entières dans les Arbres* 1976; *La Lumière du Lac* 1988.

Rennahan, Ray(mond). Director of photography. *b.* May 1, 1896, Las Vegas, N.M. *d.* 1980. A Hollywood cameraman from 1917, he pioneered in color cinematography as early as 1921 and in the early 30s shot some of the earliest productions using Technicolor's new three-color system, including the ground-breaking short *La Cucaracha* (1934). In addition to being sole director of photography on many films, he worked on a number of important productions as color specialist and shared Academy Awards for the cinematography of *Gone With the Wind* (1939) and *Blood and Sand* (1941). After retiring from films in the late 50s he worked extensively for TV.

FILMS INCLUDE: *Blood Test, The Ten Commandments* (color prologue only) 1923; *Gold Diggers of Broadway* (co-phot.) 1929; *The Vagabond King* (co-phot.), *Whoopee!* (co-phot.), *The King of Jazz* (co-phot.) 1930; *Doctor X* (co-phot.) 1932; *Mystery of the Wax Museum* 1933; *Becky Sharp* 1935; *Wings of the Morning* 1937; *Her Jungle Love* 1938; *Drums Along the Mohawk, Gone With the Wind* (co-phot.) 1939; *Maryland* (co-phot.), *Chad Hanna* (co-phot.), *Down Argentine Way* (co-phot.) 1940; *Blood and Sand* (co-phot.), *That Night in Rio* (co-phot.), *Belle Starr* (co-phot.) 1941; *For Whom the Bell Tolls* 1943; *Lady in the Dark, Up in Arms* 1944; *Incendiary Blonde. A Thousand and One Nights* 1945; *California, Duel in the Sun* (co-phot.), *The Perils of Pauline, Unconquered* 1947; *The Paleface, Whispering Smith* 1948; *Streets of Laredo, A Connecticut Yankee in King Arthur's Court* 1949; *The Great Missouri Raid, Warpath, Silver City* 1951; *Flaming Feather, The Denver and Rio Grande, Hurricane Smith* 1952; *Arrowhead, Pony Express* 1953; *A Lawless Street* 1955; *The Seventh Cavalry* 1956; *The Halliday Brand, The Guns of Fort Petticoat* 1957; *Terror in a Texas Town* 1958.

Rennie, Michael. Actor. *b.* Aug. 25, 1909, in Bradford, England. *d.* 1971. *ed.* Cambridge. Tall, gaunt leading man of UK and US films. A former salesman, he entered British films as an extra in the mid-30s. He developed into a Hollywood star in the 50s and gained popularity as the hero of the TV series 'The Third Man.'

FILMS INCLUDE: In the UK—*Secret Agent* 1936; *Bank Holiday/Three on a Weekend, The Divorce of Lady X* 1938; *Dangerous Moonlight/Suicide Squadron, Ships with Wings, Pimpernel Smith/Mister V, Tower of Terror* 1941; *The Big Blockade* 1942; *The Wicked Lady, Caesar and Cleopatra* 1945; *White Cradle Inn* 1947; *The Golden Madonna* 1949; *Trio* ("Sanitorium" episode), *The Black Rose* (as Edward I; UK/US) 1950; *The House in the Square/I'll Never Forget You* (UK/US) 1951. In the US—*The Thirteenth Letter, The Day the Earth Stood Still* 1951; *Phone Call from a Stranger, Five Fingers, Les Miserables* (as Jean Valjean) 1952; *Single-handed/Sailor of the King* (UK), *The Robe* (as the apostle Peter), *Dangerous Crossing, King of the Khyber Rifles* 1953; *Mambo* (It.), *Princess of the Nile, Demetrius and the Gladiators* (again as Peter), *Desiree* (as Bernadotte) 1954; *Soldier of Fortune, Seven Cities of Gold, The Rains of Ranchipur* 1955; *Teenage Rebel* 1956; *Island in the Sun* (UK), *Omar Khayyam* 1957; *Battle of the V-1* (UK) 1958; *Third Man on the Mountain* (UK) 1959; *The Lost World* 1960; *Mary Mary* 1963; *Ride Beyond Vengeance, Cyborg 2087* 1966; *Hotel* 1967; *The Power, The Devil's Brigade, Nude. . . si Muore/The Young the Evil and the Savage* (It.) 1968; *Subterfuge* (US/UK) 1969.

Renoir, Claude. Director of photography. *b.* Dec. 4, 1914, in Paris. *d.* 1993. The son of Pierre Renoir, he began his career under the direction of his uncle, Jean Renoir, after a period of apprenticeship with Christian Matras and Boris Kauffman. His color photography, with its sensual effects, was particularly impressive. He is not to be confused with his uncle Claude Renoir (*b.* Aug. 4, 1901, Paris), brother of Jean and Pierre Renoir and producer or production manager on several of Jean's films.

FILMS INCLUDE: *Toni* (co-phot.) 1935; *La Vie est á nous* (co-phot.), *Une Partie de Campagne/A Day in the Country* (co-phot.) 1936; *La Grande Illusion/Grand Illusion* (co-phot.) 1937; *La Bête humaine/The Human Beast* (co-phot.) 1938; *Opéra-Musette* (also co-dir. with Réné Lefèvre) 1942; *Jéricho, Le Père tranquille* 1946; *Monsieur Vincent* 1947; *Rendez-vous de Juillet* 1949; *The River* (filmed in India) 1951; *La Carrozza d'Oro/The Golden Coach* (It./Fr.) 1952; *Eléna et les Hommes/Paris Does Strange Things, Le Mystère Picasso/The Picasso Mystery* (doc.), *Crime et Châtiment/Crime and Punishment* 1956; *Les Sorcières de Salem/The Witches of Salem* 1957; *Une Vie/End of Desire, Les Tricheurs/The Cheaters* 1958; *Et mourir de Plaisir/Blood and Roses, Terrain vague* 1960; *Lafayette, Les Amants de Teruel/The Lovers of Teruel* 1962; *Cleopatra* (2nd-unit phot. only; US/UK) 1963; *Circus World* (2nd-unit phot. only; US) 1964; *La Curée/The Game Is Over* 1966; *Barbarella* 1968; *The Madwoman of Chaillot* (co-phot.; UK) 1969; *The Adventurers* (US), *La Dame dans l'Auto avec des Lunettes et un Fusil/The Lady in the Car with Glasses and a Gun* (Fr./US) 1970; *The Horseman* (US), *Le Casse/The Burglars* 1971; *Le Serpent/The Serpent, L'Impossible Objet/Impossible Object* 1973; *Paul and Michelle* (UK) 1974; *French Connection II* (US) 1975; *Docteur Françoise Gailland/No Time for Breakfast, Calmos/Femmes Fatales, Une Femme fidèle, L'Aile et la Cuisse* 1976; *The Spy Who Loved Me* (UK), *L'Animal* 1977; *La Zizanie, Attention! Les*

Enfants regardent/Attention, The Kids Are Watching 1978; *Le Toubib* 1979.

Renoir, Jean. Director. *b.* Sept. 15, 1894, in Paris. *d.* 1979. The second son of impressionist painter Auguste Renoir, younger brother of actor-to-be Pierre RENOIR and uncle of cinematographer Claude RENOIR, he was raised in a household that emphasized creative expression over intellectual pursuit, a robust, lively home open to a constant flow of artists and other family friends. He divided his childhood between the family's house in Paris and a country estate in the south of France, thus enjoying the benefits of both the cultural life of the city—the galleries, the theater, the coffeehouse entertainment—and the sense of freedom and beauty he learned to associate with nature and later evoked so beautifully in his films.

After completing his studies in philosophy and mathematics, Renoir joined the cavalry in 1913. By the time WW I broke out the following year he had attained the rank of sergeant, but before he could see any action he was hospitalized as a result of a kick by a horse. He quit the cavalry and in 1915 left for the front as a second lieutenant with the Alpine Infantry. Before long he was injured again, this time by a bullet in a thighbone, and nearly lost his leg when the wound became infected with gangrene. The injury left him with a permanent slight limp. After a long convalescence, much of which he spent watching and developing a passion for movies, he saw further WW I action as a pilot and was again injured, in a landing mishap, before finally being discharged with the rank of full lieutenant.

Returning home, Jean tended the increasingly frail Auguste Renoir, now crippled with arthritis, and fell in love with his father's beautiful redheaded model Andrée Heuchling (later famous as actress Catherine HESSLING). Auguste Renoir died on Dec. 3, 1919. Several weeks later, on January 24, 1920, Jean Renoir married Miss Heuchling. For several years he dedicated himself to making pottery, but he became increasingly impassioned with the cinema, and with the money he inherited from his father he was able to set up his own independent production company, mainly for the purpose of launching the screen career of his beautiful wife. The first film he financed, *Une Vie sans Joie/Catherine,* was directed in 1924 by actor Albert Dieudonné from a script by Renoir. Renoir participated in the shooting as a supporting actor with the intention of learning all he could about filmmaking.

Armed with bits of technical knowledge he had picked up on the set, the artistic instinct he had inherited from his father, and the influence of films he had seen, especially von Stroheim's *Foolish Wives* (1922), which he had viewed several times, Renoir set out to direct his first film, *La Fille de l'Eau.* The film, starring Catherine Hessling, was shot during the summer of 1924 and first shown in April of 1925. The plot was melodramatic and insignificant, and the camera technique awkward, but the production already contained some of the elements that would later become hallmarks of Renoir's work—a marvelous sense of visual realism, a deep love of nature, and the capacity to express the physical environment poetically.

While visual aspects provided the main attraction of Renoir's first film, the emphasis in his next, an adaptation of Zola's *Nana* (1926), was on acting, especially the stylized performance of Catherine Hessling in the title role. It was an ambitious large-scale production with expensive sets by Claude Autant-Lara and a record-breaking budget of one million francs. Although the film was fairly well received by critics, its resounding failure at the box office nearly ruined Renoir financially. He had to borrow money to make *Charleston/Sur un Air de Charleston/Charleston-Parade* (1927), a humorous erotic dance fantasy that scandalized some viewers with its provocative sexuality and the orgiastic gyrations of Miss Hessling in an all but nude state.

Renoir next accepted a commercial directing assignment, *Marquitta* (1927), simply as a means of earning some money, then appeared as an actor opposite Miss Hessling in Alberto Cavalcanti's *La P'tite Lili* (1927) before returning to independent production with *La Petite Marchande d'Allumettes/The Little Match Girl* (co-directed with Jean Tedesco; 1928), an adaptation of the Hans Christian Andersen fairy tale which stood apart from the rest of Renoir's silent work in its nonrealism and the use of expressionistic technical effects favored by French avant-garde filmmakers of the period. *Tire-au-Flanc* (1928), a boisterous, largely improvised comedy of army life, which might have been influenced by the silent comedies of Charlie Chaplin, represented the first collaboration between Renoir and Michel SIMON, the actor who would figure prominently in Renoir's early sound films. Two commissioned commercial works, *Le Tournoi/Le Tournoi dans la Cité* (1928) and *Le Bled* (1929), closed Renoir's silent period, which despite some remarkable achievements must be considered as no more than a term of apprenticeship leading to the director's great films of the sound era.

The transition to sound also represented a transitional stage in the relationship of Renoir and Catherine Hessling, whose presence had dominated his silent films. Not too long after they co-starred in two films made by other directors, Cavalcanti's *Le Petit Chaperon rouge/Little Red Riding Hood* (Miss Hessling in the title role, Renoir as the Wolf) and Rochus Gliese's German-made *Die Jagd nach dem Glück/La Chasse à la Fortune,* Renoir and Miss Hessling separated. The new woman in Renoir's life became Marguerite Mathieu, a film editor who worked on all but one of the director's films of the 30s and later edited most of Jacques Becker's productions. Although she never married Renoir, she took and kept his name and remained known throughout her career as Marguerite Renoir. She was but one of a creative entourage of collaborators and colleagues who habitually surrounded and inspired Renoir during the preparation and execution of his films, much like the circle of friends that had constantly surrounded his painter father when he was alive. Renoir loved working collectively and readily accepted suggestions from any of the performers or crew, frequently improvising scenes as the shooting went along, thus achieving in his films a sense of spontaneity that few directors could equal.

Sound did not represent a stumbling block in Renoir's progress the way it did for many other directors who had their roots in the silent film. On the contrary, he was looking forward to incorporating sound and dialogue as an added dimension to his productions. The problem Renoir had to overcome at this juncture of his career was the poor showing of his recent films at the box office. To continue working in the industry, he first had to prove that he was a commercially viable director. He did this successfully with his first talkie, *On purge Bébé* (1931), a quickie domestic drama that was completed in a few weeks on a tight schedule and tiny budget and brought the producers considerable profits. The commercial success of the film enabled Renoir to assert certain creative control over the production of his next film, *La Chienne* (1931), the first of his great talkies of the 30s. It was a powerfully realistic allegorical drama that painted a vivid picture of Montmartre life, depicting the social milieu in which the characters moved as an inexorable force that seals their fate, a theme to which Renoir would return in several of his films. The result was a critical success but a humiliating commercial failure.

Following an engrossing and properly mysterious adaptation of a Georges Simenon novel, *La Nuit du Carrefour* (1932), featuring Pierre Renoir in the role of Inspector Maigret, Jean Renoir again availed himself of the services of actor Michel Simon, the incomparable protagonist of *La Chienne,* for *Boudu sauvé des Eaux/Boudu Saved from Drowning* (1932). In *Boudu* as in *La Chienne,* Simon plays with admirable abandon a character who symbolizes the anarchic spirit of liberty in rebellion against the restrictive hypocrisy of middle-class values. In both films, the fluid, uninhibited performance by Simon gained an additional dimension of freedom through Renoir's use of deep-focus photography, which allowed the director to follow his performers without separating them from each other or from their environment. Depth-of-field cinematography remained a significant characteristic feature of the Renoir *mise-en-scène,* a typically artless, unspectacular style of directing in which camera technique was made to serve the dramatic requirements of Renoir's humanistic themes and his multileveled exploration of human relationships.

Critical opinion was widely divided on his decorative adaptation of Flaubert's *Madame Bovary* (1934). *Toni* (1935), now generally recognized as a masterpiece, was generally misunderstood and unappreciated at the time of its initial release. Shot on location against real backgrounds with a cast of mostly nonprofessionals, *Toni* foreshadowed the Italian postwar neorealist movement in its method of production and theme of social concern. Social consciousness became the hallmark of Renoir's films of the late 30s. *Le Crime de M. Lange/The Crime of Monsieur Lange* (1936), made by Renoir in collaboration with members of the radical left-wing French theater ensemble Groupe Octobre, was an impassioned plea for collectivism and working-class solidarity and against the evils of capitalism. But Renoir transcended the rather crude political polemics with an inspired production that, despite some technical flaws, contained some of the director's most inventive use of camera movement.

Although he was not a party member, Renoir agreed to produce and direct a propaganda film for the Communist party, *La Vie est à nous/The People of France* (1936), because of his sympathies for the working class. Its exhibition to the general public in France was restricted by the censors until 1969, but it was shown theatrically in 1937 in the US, where it was criticized for the blunt repetitious insistence of its ideological diatribe but praised for the magnificence of some of its scenes. *Une Partie de Campagne/A Day in the Country* (shot in 1936 but not released until 1946) provided a lyrical, pastoral, romantic interlude in a period otherwise characterized by Renoir's social commitment. *Les Bas-Fonds/The Lower Depths* (1936) was a fascinating adaptation of a Gorki play in which, according to the playwright himself, "nothing happens. . . . The whole thing is atmosphere. . . nothing but atmosphere."

Then came *La Grande Illusion/Grand Illusion* (1937), Renoir's first great international success, a perfectly constructed, marvelously restrained film that derives its dramatic force not from its ostensible antiwar theme nor the heroism of its prisoner-of-war protagonists, but from the subtle examination of personal relationships and, above all, from the intriguing juxtaposition of national loyalties and universal class affinities. Renoir's next film, *La Marseillaise* (1938), initially commissioned and financed by France's Popular government, was a panoramic chronicle of the French Revolution oddly devoid of drama or historic bias in its quest of documentary-like authenticity.

Renoir's international reputation was enhanced by *La Bête humaine/The Human Beast* (1938), a tragedy of the railroads adapted from a Zola novel. The film remains memorable for the beauty and power of its imagery, especially the rhythmic cutting of its opening and closing sequences, and for the excellence of the acting of Jean Gabin and Simone Simon as characters whose tragic actions are predetermined by heredity and destiny. However, *La Règle du Jeu/The Rules of the Game* (1939), now generally accepted as Renoir's masterpiece, was one of his greatest commercial failures at the time of its initial release. It was Renoir's most personal film, an abrupt move away from naturalism toward a more poetic, more classical style of expression. The result was a film generally misunderstood by the critics and the public, a profound, subtle, utterly pessimistic, though often seemingly comic, view of the social code and of the viability of such values as truth, love, and friendship in those vulnerable moments that unmask the absurdity of the games people play. *The Rules of the Game* was so great a commercial disaster that it was almost immediately withdrawn from circulation. Renoir was forced to cut the film drastically, mostly affecting the central role of Octave, which he played himself, but to no avail. The film remained a box-office dud when it was re-released in mutilated form after WW II, and it wasn't until the later 50s, when it was restored to its original length, that it was finally received with the wide accolade it deserves. In 1962 it was chosen by an international poll of critics as the third greatest film ever made.

In the summer of 1939, Renoir went to Rome as part of a cultural exchange to promote Franco-Italian relations. He taught at the Centro Sperimentale di Cinematografia and with Luchino Visconti and Carl Koch wrote the script for *La Tosca,* which Renoir was supposed to direct. When WW II broke out in September, Renoir returned to Paris, where he was attached to the French army's Film Service. He was sent back to Rome in the spring of 1940 to begin filming *La Tosca.* He had directed the first sequence when production was interrupted by Italy's entry into the war in June. Renoir immediately returned to France, and the film was eventually directed by Koch.

In the autumn of 1940 Renoir traveled to Lisbon and from there, in February of 1941, to the US, in response to a letter by Robert Flaherty. He brought with him Dido Freire, his script girl on *The Rules of the Game* and Alberto Cavalcanti's niece. They married in 1944, although Renoir's divorce from Catherine Hessling was not recognized in Europe, making him technically a bigamist. Renoir became an American citizen (though he retained his French citizenship as well) and settled in Hollywood, where he resumed his interrupted film career on a contract with 20th Century-Fox.

Renoir's American period was marked by difficulty in adapting to a new, unfamiliar environment. Although he found the studios receptive and co-operative, he had trouble adjusting his improviser's temperament to the exacting requirements of a commercially oriented production machine, and, for that matter, to working in isolation without the moral and psychological support of the circle of close associates that had surrounded him in France. Renoir's first American film, *Swamp Water* (1941), an atmospheric folksy tale shot on location in the Georgia swamps, failed to ignite much enthusiasm among American critics and was panned by their French colleagues when it reached Europe after the war. As with so many other Renoir films, critical opinion of *Swamp Water* was in later years more favorable.

Departing from Fox, Renoir next considered a Deanna Durbin film at Universal, among other unrealized projects, and finally made *This Land Is Mine* (1943), an anti-Nazi propaganda film starring Charles Laughton and Maureen O'Hara for RKO. Although it was quite effective as a wartime patriotic drama about the French Resistance movement, the film was much maligned by the critics in France when it was belatedly screened there after the war. Renoir then made a two-reel propaganda documentary, *Salute to France,* and a number of training shorts for the US Army, before embarking on his next feature production for an independent company, *The Southerner* (1945), generally acknowledged as his best American film. It is a sincere and forthright drama, told in a realistic, leisurely paced style, of a determined sharecropper and his struggle for survival against the cruelties of both nature and his fellow man. *The Diary of a Chambermaid* (1946), in a marked contrast to the near-documentary flavor of *The Southerner* and the realism of his films of the 30s, was largely theatrical in conception and treatment, artificially re-creating French period atmosphere in a Hollywood studio. Renoir's last film of the American period, *The Woman on the Beach* (1947), was a suspenseful melodrama of passion and emotional intensity more reminiscent of the US films of Fritz Lang.

Nature as a life force and a source of eternal beauty, and especially the flow of bodies of water, had figured prominently in Renoir's work ever since his first film, *La Fille de l'Eau.* This lifelong fascination reached its supreme expression in his *The River* (1951), which he directed in India under conditions of total creative freedom. It is a dazzlingly beautiful production, his first in color, photographed by his nephew, Claude Renoir, a film as rich in its poetic metaphor as it is in its panoramic loveliness.

Returning to Europe, Renoir first stopped in Italy, where he directed *La Carrozza d'Oro/Le Carrosse d'Or/The Golden Coach* (1953), a free adaptation of Prosper Mérimée's *Le Carrosse du Saint-Sacrement.* Starring Anna Magnani, the film commented on theater and life in a two-dimensional style more akin to the stage than to the properties of the cinema, emphasizing lush décor and beautiful composition over camera movement and cinematic pace. It was a commercial failure and generally a critical setback as well.

Renoir staged a production of 'Julius Caesar' at the arena in Arles, his first contribution to the theater, before returning to the Paris film studios after an absence of 15 years to make *French Cancan/Only the French Can* (1955), a spirited, sentimental tribute to Paris of the Belle Epoque that recalled in its gaiety and vivid colors the impressionist paintings of the director's father. Although it was less original and less profound than *The Golden Coach, French Cancan* was a success at the box office both in France and abroad, helping to restore Renoir's credibility as a box-office draw. Renoir returned to the theater in 1955 as the director of his own play, 'Orvet,' before turning out his next film, *Eléna et les Hommes/Paris Does Strange Things* (1956), a romantic comedy starring Ingrid Bergman. Some critics admired it, but most, especially the Americans, found it baffling and generally one of Renoir's weaker efforts. *Le Déjeuner sur l'Herbe/Picnic on the Grass* (1959) had the visual quality of an impressionist painting and an appealing sensual flavor but an inconsequential plot and tentative structure. *Le Testament du Dr. Cordelier* (1961), a modernized free adaptation of Robert Louis Stevenson's *Dr. Jekyll and Mr. Hyde,* utilized five cameras and other TV production techniques. It has never been shown commercially in the US. Renoir then returned to the prisoner-of-war world of *Grand Illusion* with *Le Caporal épinglé/The Elusive Corporal* (1962), a bittersweet ode to freedom.

A long hiatus then followed in Renoir's film work, during which he wrote two books, a biographical study of his father, *Renoir/Renoir My Father* (1962) and a novel, *Les Cahiers du Capitaine Georges* (1966). In 1968 he directed himself directing a stage actress in a 27-minute short, *La Direction d'Acteur par Jean Renoir.* In 1969 he played himself in an American film, James Frawley's *The Christian Licorice Store,* which was released in 1971. In the summer of 1969 he directed his final film, *Le Petit Théâtre of Jean Renoir,* a charming and witty three-episode production originally made for French TV. It wasn't released until 1971. In 1974, Renoir published an autobiography, *Ma Vie et mes Films/My Life and My Films.* In the Academy Award ceremony for that year (held in 1975) he won an honorary Oscar for his cumulative work. In 1977, following a public tribute in Hollywood by the Academy of Motion Picture Arts and Sciences, Renoir was inducted as an officer of the French Legion of Honor at a ceremony held at the home of the French consul in Los Angeles. Many of Renoir's collaborators and performers who had appeared in his films flew in from France to attend the event. It was a belated and rather modest official tribute to the man whose name had become synonymous with greatness in French and international cinema.

FILMS (as director): In France—*La Fille de l'Eau* (also prod., art dir.) 1925; *Nana* (also prod., edit.) 1926; *Charleston/Sur un Air de Charleston/Charleston-Parade* (three-reeler; also prod.), *Marquitta* 1927; *La Petite Marchande d'Allumettes/The Little Match Girl* (co-dir. with Jean Tedesco; also co-prod., sc.), *Tire-au-Flanc* (also co-sc.), *Le Tournoi/Le Tournoi dans la Cité* (also adapt.) 1928; *Le Bled* (also adapt.) 1929; *On purge Bébé* (also sc.), *La Chienne* (also co-exec. prod., co-sc., co-edit.) 1931; *La Nuit de Carrefour* (also sc.), *Boudu sauvé des Eaux/Boudu Saved from Drowning* (also co-sc.) 1932; *Chotard et Compagnie* (also co-sc.) 1933; *Madame Bovary* (also sc.) 1934; *Toni/Les Amours de Toni* (also co-sc.) 1935; *Le Crime de M. Lange/The Crime of Monsieur Lange* (also co-sc.), *La Vie est à nous/The People of France, Une Partie de Campagne/A Day in the Country* (also sc., act.; release delayed until 1946; shown in the US in 1950 as part of the episode film *Ways of Love), Les Bas-Fonds/The Lower Depths* (also co-sc.) 1936; *La Grande Illusion/Grand Illusion* (also co-sc.) 1937; *La Marseillaise* (also sc.), *La Bête humaine/The Human Beast* (also sc., act.) 1938; *La Règle du Jeu/The Rules of the Game* (also co-sc., act.) 1939. In Italy—*La Tosca* (dir. one sequence only, comprising five shots; also co-sc.; It./Fr.) 1940. In the US—*Swamp Water* 1941; *This Land Is Mine* (also co-prod., co-sc.) 1943; *Salute to France* (WW II propaganda two-reeler; co-dir., co-sc.) 1944; *The Southerner* (also sc.) 1945; *The Diary of a Chambermaid* (also co-sc.) 1946; *The Woman on the Beach* (also co-sc.) 1947. In India—*The River* (also co-sc.; Ind./US) 1951. In Italy—*La Carrozza d'Oro/Le Carrosse d'Or/The Golden Coach* (also co-sc.; It./Fr.) 1953. In France—*French Cancan/Only the French Can* (also sc.) 1955; *Eléna et les Hommes/Paris Does Strange Things* (also co-adapt., sc.) 1956; *Le Déjeuner sur l'Herbe/Picnic on the Grass* (also exec. prod., sc.) 1959; *Le Testament du Dr. Cordelier* (also co-exec. prod., sc.; orig. made for French TV) 1961; *Le Caporal épinglé/The Elusive Corporal* (also co-sc., dial.) 1962; *La Direction d'Acteur par Jean Renoir* (three-reeler) 1968; *Le Petit Théâtre de Jean Renoir* (also prod., sc., on-camera narr.) 1971.

Renoir, Pierre. Actor. *b.* Mar. 21, 1885, Paris. *d.* 1952. Imposing character player of French stage and screen; son of painter Auguste Renoir, brother of Jean Renoir, father of Claude Renoir.

FILMS INCLUDE: *La Digue* 1911; *La Robe rouge* 1912; *La Nuit du Carrefour* (as Inspector Maigret) 1932; *L'Agonie des Aigles* 1933; *Madame Bovary* (as Charles Bovary) 1934; *Veille d'Armes/Sacrifice d'Honneur, La Route impériale, La Bandera/Escape from Yesterday* 1935; *Sous les Yeux d'Occident/Razumov* 1936; *La Citadelle du Silence/The Citadel of Silence* 1937; *La Marseillaise* (as Louis XVI), *Les Nuits blanches de Saint Pétersbourg/The Kreutzer Sonata, Mollenard/ Hatred, La Maison du Maltais/Sirocco, Le Patriote/The Mad Emperor* 1938; *Pièges/Personal Column* 1939; *Histoire de Rire/Foolish Husbands* 1941; *Dernier Atout* 1942; *Le Voyageur sans Bagages*

1943; *Les Enfants du Paradis/Children of Paradise, Peloton d'Exécution/Resistance* 1945; *Le Jugement du Dieu* 1949; *Knock/Dr. Knock* 1951.

rentals. Moneys paid by exhibitors (movie theaters) to a film's distributors in return for the right to show the film. Depending on the licensing agreement, the rental fee may be a percentage of the BOX OFFICE earnings or a flat fee. A film's GROSS RECEIPTS are usually calculated in terms of total rentals.

Republic. A motion picture production company formed in 1935 as the result of the merger of four minor studios. The man who initiated the merger and became the company's president, Herbert J. Yates, entered the industry in 1915 by acquiring a film laboratory. He turned Republic into a highly profitable factory, producing B pictures, mostly Westerns, assembly-line fashion. The typical Republic B product was technically highly polished for its budget and strong on action, but its plots were often hackneyed, lacking in originality. Among Republic's top screen personalities were John Carroll and Vera Hruba Ralston, president Yates's wife. Among its Western stars were Bob Steele, Johnny Mack Brown, John Wayne, Gene Autry, and Roy Rogers. Occasionally Republic undertook the production of a major picture, usually under the direction of John Ford or Raoul Walsh. But the great majority of the films were profitable quickies. During the 50s, when B pictures were gradually eliminated from the program at motion picture theaters, Republic abandoned film production for TV fare.

rerecording. The process of transferring sound from one film to another. The term is also used as a synonym for "mixing." See MIX.

Resnais, Alain. Director. Born on June 3, 1922, in Vannes, France. A pharmacist's son, he made his first amateur 8 mm film at 14, but not until he reached his mid 20s did filmmaking become his profession. In the interim, he studied acting for the stage and took directing courses at the IDHEC, the French cinema school. He was drafted in 1945 and served with a unit entertaining Allied Occupation troops in Germany and Austria. Demobilized the following year, he began making 16 mm shorts and medium-length films, mostly silent documentaries but occasionally also dramatic films. Some of his early product was shown on French TV. He also worked during that formative period as cameraman and editor on films of other directors. Resnais's career as a professional director really started in 1948 with the release of his first 35 mm short, *Van Gogh,* which was also his first commissioned work. His reputation as a filmmaker grew with every successive short and reached a peak with *Night and Fog,* a disturbing excursion into the world of the Nazi concentration camps, in which he first revealed his preoccupation with the theme of memory and the rudiments of a future visual style that emphasized probing camera tracking.

The theme acquired deeper meaning and the style took a more complex form in Resnais's first feature film, *Hiroshima mon Amour* (1959). Taking a philosophical cue from Bergson and a literary one from Proust, Resnais departed from conventional concepts of narrative time, fusing past, present, and future into one and introducing complex flashback techniques to reconcile reality with memory. In his second feature, *Last Year at Marienbad,* Resnais's exercise in the manipulation of multidirectional time results in a film that is completely plotless (in the conventional sense) and highly ambiguous. The narrative structure is the subjective recreation of the past as it appears in the memory of the protagonist. The film won the grand prize at the 1961 Venice Festival.

Following *Muriel* (1963), another complex exercise in the audiovisual exploration of memory, Resnais turned out *La Guerre est finie* (1966), a far more accessible film with a near-linear plot about the inner conflicts of an anti-Franco revolutionary. It won the Prix Delluc and several festival prizes and enjoyed a successful commercial run in many countries. The failure of *Je t'aime je t'aime* (1968) handicapped Resnais's viability for several years and prompted him to make *Stavisky* (1974), a stylish screen biography of a French crook that represented the director's most conventionally narrative film to date. *Providence* (1977), Resnais's first English-language film, reflected on the creative process in scrutinizing the inner mind of a cancer-ridden writer (John Gielgud) as he agonizes over his next novel. The film, deemed bizarre and muddled by some, brilliantly original by others, was poorly received in the US but won seven César awards in France and much acclaim around Europe. Resnais's next three films—*Mon Oncle d'Amérique* (1980), *La Vie est un Roman/Life Is a Bed of Roses* (1983), and *L'Amour á Mort/Love Unto Death* (1984)—all scripted by Jean Gruault, formed an undeclared trilogy summarizing some of the director's philosophical, esthetic, and ethical concerns, encompassing themes ranging from love to theology.

An impeccable formalist, Resnais is probably the single most important director to emerge from the ranks of the French *Nouvelle Vague.* Although he has relied on collaboration with writers in all his films, he is considered an *auteur* by critics subscribing to the theory, because of his consistent adherence to distinctive themes and the highly personal technique he has developed to meet the special problems presented by the exploration of these themes.

FILMS: Shorts (35 mm only)—*Van Gogh* (also edit.) 1948; *Guernica* (co-dir. with Robert Hessens; also edit.) 1950; *Gauguin* (also edit.) 1951; *Les Statues meurent aussi* (co-dir., co-sc. with Chris Marker; also edit.) 1953; *Nuit et Brouillard/Night and Fog, Toute la Mémoire du Monde* (also edit.) 1956; *Le Mystère de l'Atelier 15* (co-dir. with André Heinrich) 1957; *Le Chant du Styrène* (also edit.) 1958. Features—*Hiroshima mon Amour* 1959; *L'Année dernière à Marienbad/Last Year at Marienbad* (Fr./It.) 1961; *Muriel ou le Temps d'un Retour/Muriel* (Fr./It.) 1963; *La Guerre est finie/The War Is Over* (Fr./Sw.) 1966; *Loin du Viêtnam/Far from Vietnam* (film essay; one episode) 1967; *Je t'aime je t'aime* (also co-adapt., co-dial.) 1968; *Stavisky/L'Empire d'Alexandre* (Fr./It.) 1974; *Providence* (Fr./Switz.) 1977; *Mon Oncle d'Amérique* 1980; *La Vie est un Roman/Life Is a Bed of Roses* 1983; *L'Amour A Mort/Love Unto Death* 1984; *Mélo* (also sc.) 1986; *I Want to Go Home* 1989; *Smoking/No Smoking* 1993.

resolution. Also called "resolving power." The relative capacity of a lens or of photographic materials to reproduce an image in fine detail.

retake. The re-shooting of a scene previously filmed but not satisfactorily.

Rettig, Tommy. Child actor. Born on Dec. 10, 1941, in Jackson Heights, N.Y. Child star of American stage, radio, TV, and films, he started his career at age six, touring with Mary Martin in 'Annie Get Your Gun,' and made his screen debut at nine. During the early 50s he appeared in 17 films, most memorably as a boy with a vivid imagination in *The 5,000 Fingers of Dr. T.* (1953), and gained wide popularity in the 'Lassie' TV series as Jeff, Lassie's first master, from 1954 to 1958. Failing in his bid for adult roles, he retired with his wife to a California farm, where he was arrested in 1972 for growing marijuana. He was sentenced to two years probation. In 1975 he was arrested on charges of smuggling cocaine and sentenced to five years in federal prison. The charges were dropped after an appeal, as was another drug-related indictment in 1980. When last heard from, Rettig was employed as a computer programmer and drug-addiction counselor.

FILMS INCLUDE: *Panic in the Streets, The Jackpot, Two Weeks with Love, For Heaven's Sake* 1950; *Elopement, Weekend with Father* 1951; *Paula* 1952; *The Lady Wants Mink, The 5,000 Fingers of Dr. T, So Big* 1953; *River of No Return, The Raid, The Egyptian* 1954; *The Cobweb, At Gunpoint* 1955; *The Last Wagon* 1956.

Reubens, Paul. See HERMAN, Pee-Wee.

revamping. The act of altering an existing set and adapting its flats and props for use in another sequence in the same film or in another production.

Revere, Anne. Actress. *b.* June 25, 1903, New York City, a stockbroker's daughter. *d.* 1990. *ed.* Wellesley Coll. Excellent character player of the American stage and screen. Trained for the stage at the American Laboratory Theatre, she appeared in stock before making her Broadway debut in 1931. She made an isolated film appearance in 1934, repeating her stage role in *Double Door,* and in 1940 moved to Hollywood to begin a decade-long career in films that culminated in 1945 in an Academy Award as best supporting actress for her performance as Elizabeth Taylor's mother in *National Velvet.* She was also nominated for Oscars for *The Song of Bernadette* (1943) and *Gentleman's Agreement* (1947). She was at the peak of her career in 1951 when she was blacklisted by the industry for taking the Fifth Amendment before the House Un-American Activities Committee. Unable to obtain any roles in films or on TV, she was out of work for several years but in 1958 returned to Broadway and two years later won a Tony Award for her performance in 'Toys in the Attic.' It wasn't until 1970 that she returned to the screen, making a brief appearance in Preminger's *Tell Me That You Love Me, Junie Moon,* and not until 1976 that she could be seen again in a substantial film role, in *Birch Interval.* She was married for 49 years to stage director Samuel Roser.

FILMS: *Double Door* 1934; *One Crowded Night, The Howards of Virginia* 1940; *The Devil Commands, Men of Boys Town, The Flame of New Orleans, Remember the Day* 1941; *Meet the Stewarts, The Falcon Takes Over, Are Husbands Necessary?, The Gay Sisters, Star Spangled Rhythm* 1942; *The Meanest Man in the World, Shantytown, Old Acquaintance, The Song of Bernadette* 1943; *Standing Room Only, Rainbow Island* 1944; *National Velvet, The Keys of the Kingdom, Sunday Dinner for a Soldier, The Thin Man Goes Home, Don Juan Quilligan, Fallen Angel* 1945; *Dragonwyck* 1946; *The Shocking Miss Pilgrim, Carnival in Costa Rica, Forever Amber, Gentleman's Agreement* 1947; *Secret Beyond the Door, Scudda-Hoo! Scudda-Hay!, Deep Waters* 1948; *You're My Everything* 1949; *The Great Missouri Raid, A Place in the Sun* 1951; *Tell Me That You Love Me Junie Moon, Macho Callahan* 1970; *Birch Interval* 1976.

reversal film. A type of film stock that after exposure and processing becomes a direct positive print without first going through a negative stage. Additional *reversal prints* are made from the *reversal original.*

reverse action. Also called "reverse motion." A trick effect achieved by running film backward in the camera or during optical printing. When projected, actions in the scene appear in reverse sequence. For example, a diver may be made to rise from the water and defy the law of gravitation by returning to the diving board. There are many legitimate applications to the reverse-action trick. A crash may be staged without risking lives by beginning shooting from the point of impact and having the cars drive backward. The action is filmed in reverse and when the scene is projected the sense of collision will appear very realistic. A familiar example of reverse action is the Hertz TV commercial in which a man is seen floating down from the sky into the driver's seat. He is actually being pulled up, a much simpler procedure, and the action is reversed.

reverse angle shot. A shot taken from an angle opposite the one from which the preceding shot has been taken. The reverse angle technique is frequently employed in dialogue scenes to provide the editor with alternate facial shots of the actors speaking.

reverse scene. A scene that has been flipped during printing so that the resultant image is reversed as if reflected by a mirror; the right side of the image becomes left and vice versa. Care must be taken that no lettering appears in such a scene, for letters, numbers, and other familiar symbols would read backward.

Revier, Dorothy. Born Doris Velegra, on Apr. 18, 1904, in San Francisco. Leading lady of Hollywood silents and early talkies, typically in blonde-vamp roles. A musician's daughter, she started as a cabaret dancer and made her screen debut in 1922 in *The Broadway Madonna,* a film directed by her first husband, Harry J. Revier (*b.* Mar. 16, 1889, Philadelphia; deceased), who specialized in action pictures. She played desirable women and femmes fatales in numerous minor melodramas, including Milady de Winter in Allan Dwan's *The Iron Mask* (1929), but her roles declined in the early 30s and she ended her career in Buck Jones Westerns.

FILMS INCLUDE: *The Broadway Madonna* 1922; *The Wild Party* 1923; *Marry in Haste, The Martyr Sex, The Other Kind of Love, The Virgin, Call of the Mate, The Rose of Paris, Man from God's Country* 1924; *Dangerous Pleasure, Just a Woman, The Danger Signal, An Enemy of Men, Sealed Lips, The Fate of a Flirt, When Husbands Flirt* 1925; *Poker Faces, The False Alarm, When the Wife's Away* 1926; *Wandering Girls, The Price of Honor, Poor Girls, The Clown, The Drop Kick, The Warning, The Tigress, The Siren* 1927; *The Red Dance, Beware of Blondes, Sinner's Parade, Submarine* 1928; *The Iron Mask, The Quitter, The Donovan Affair, Father and Son, The Dance of Life, The Mighty* 1929; *Murder on the Roof, Vengeance, Call of the West, The Squealer, The Way of All Men, The Bad Man* 1930; *The Avenger, The Black Camel, Anybody's Blonde, The Last Ride* 1931; *Sally of the Subway, Arm of the Law, Night World, Widow in Scarlet* 1932; *The Thrill Hunter, Above the Clouds, By Candlelight* 1933; *The Fighting Ranger, Unknown Blonde* 1934; *Circumstantial Evidence, The Eagle's Brood* 1935; *The Cowboy and the Kid* 1936.

Revill, Clive. Actor. Born on Apr. 18, 1930, in Wellington, New Zealand. *ed.* Victoria U. (Wellington). A character actor of British stage, TV, and films, he also played on Broadway (Fagin in 'Oliver!'; 'Irma La Douce,' etc.) and in Hollywood. He is at his best in comic roles.

FILMS INCLUDE: *Reach for the Sky* 1956; *The Headless Ghost* 1959; *Bunny Lake Is Missing* 1965; *Modesty Blaise, A Fine Madness, Kaleidoscope* 1966; *Fathom, The Double Man* 1967; *The Shoes of the Fisherman* (US), *Nobody Runs Forever/The High Commissioner* (UK/US) 1968; *The Assassination Bureau* 1969; *A Severed Head, The Private Life of Sherlock Holmes* (UK/US), *The Buttercup Chain* 1970; *Boulevard du Rhum/Rum Runner* (Fr.) 1971; *Avanti!* (US) 1972; *The Legend of Hell House* 1973; *The Black Windmill* (UK/US), *The Little Prince* 1974; *Galileo* (UK/US), *One of Our Dinosaurs Is Missing* (UK/US) 1975; *Matilda* 1978; *The Empire Strikes Back* (voice of Emperor; US) 1980; *Zorro the Gay Blade* (US) 1981; *The Transformers* (v/o) 1986; *Rumplestiltskin* 1987; *Mack the Knife* (US) 1989; *Let Him Have It* 1991.

Reville, Alma. Screenwriter. *b.* 1900, England. *d.* 1982. In British films from the early 20s, starting out as an editor's assistant, she worked as a script girl on Alfred HITCHCOCK's first film as director, *The Pleasure Garden,* in 1925, and the following year, after working as his assistant on *The Lodger,* she married the director. She subsequently collaborated on the scripts of many of his films and occasionally on the films of other directors.

FILMS INCLUDE: *The Ring* 1927; *Juno and the Paycock, Murder* 1930; *The Skin Game* 1931; *Rich and Strange* 1932; *Waltzes from Vienna* 1933; *The Passing of the Third Floor Bank, The 39 Steps* 1935; *Secret Agent, Sabotage* 1936; *Young and Innocent/The Girl Was Young* 1937; *The Lady Vanishes* 1938; *Jamaica Inn* 1939; *Suspicion* (US) 1941; *Shadow of a Doubt* (US) 1943; *It's in the Bag* (US), *The Paradine Case* (US) 1948; *Stage Fright* 1950.

rewind. A geared device for rewinding film in the cutting room or projection booth. Rewinds usually come in pairs, one for a feed reel and the other for a take-up reel. Most conventional rewinds are cranked by hand, but some are driven by electric motors.

rewinding. The act of re-threading film back onto the original reel.

Rey, Fernando. Actor. *b.* Fernando Casado Arambillet Vega, on Sept. 20, 1915, in La Coruna, Spain. *d.* 1994. *ed.* U. of Madrid (School of Architecture). Impressive, usually bearded character player of international films, typically in suave, dominant roles. He fought in the Spanish Civil War before turning to stage and screen acting, at first as an extra and bit player. Over the span of more than five decades he appeared in scores of productions, most memorably in several Buñuel and Bardem films and as the elusive criminal mastermind in *The French Connection* (1971) and its sequel. He was named best actor at the 1977 Cannes Film Festival for *Elisa Vida mia.*

FILMS INCLUDE: *Los Cuatro Robinsones* (Sp.) 1940; *Tierra sedienta* (Sp.) 1945; *Don Quijote de la Mancha/Don Quixote* (as Samson Carrasco; Sp.) 1947; *Locura de Amor/The Mad Queen* (as King Philip I, The Handsome; Sp.) 1948; *Mare Nostrum* (It.) 1950; *Esa Pareja feliz/That Happy Pair* (Sp.) 1951; *Bienvenido Mr. Marshall/Welcome Mr. Marshall* (Sp.) 1952; *Cómicos* (Sp.) 1953; *Marcelino Pan y Vino/Marcelino* (Sp./It.) 1955; *Don Juan/Pantaloons* (Fr./Sp.) 1956; *La Venganza/Vengeance* (Sp./It.) 1958; *Gli Ultimi Giorni di Pompei/The Last Days of Pompeii* (as the High Priest; It./Sp.), *Sonatas* (Sp.) 1959; *La Rivolta degli Schiavi/The Revolt of the Slaves* (It./Sp./Ger.), *Viridiana* (Mex./Sp.) 1961; *Tierra brutal/Savage Guns* (Sp./US), *El Cara del Terror/Face of Terror* (Sp.) 1962; *El Valle de las Espadas/The Castilian* (as Ramiro I, King of Leon), *The Running Man* (UK), *The Ceremony* (US/Sp.) 1963; *Echappement libre/Backfire* (Fr./It./Sp.) 1964; *Campanados a Medianoche/Falstaff/Chimes at Midnight* (as Worcester; Sp./Switz.), *El Greco* (as King Philip II; It./Fr.), *Return of the Seven* (US/Sp.) 1966; *Le Vicomte règle ses Comptes/The Viscount* (Fr./It./Sp.) 1967; *Cervantes/The Young Rebel* (again as Philip II; Sp./Fr./It.), *Une Histoire immortelle/The Immortal Story* (Fr.), *Villa Rides* (US) 1968; *Guns of the Magnificent Seven* (US) 1969; *The Adventurers* (US), *Tristana* (Fr./It./Sp.), *Land Raiders* (US) 1970; *A Town Called Bastard/A Town Called Hell* (UK/Sp.), *The Light at the Edge of the World* (US/Sp./Liechtenstein), *The French Connection* (US) 1971; *La Charme discret de la Bourgeoisie/The Discreet Charm of the Bourgeoisie* (Fr.), *Antony and Cleopatra* (as Lepidus; UK) 1972; *Bianco Rosso e . . . /White Sister* (It.) 1973; *Tarots* (Sp./Fr.), *La Femme aux Bottes rouges/The Woman with Red Boots* (Fr.), *Fatti di Gente Perbene/La Grande Bourgeoise* (It./Fr.), *Corruzione al Palazzo di Giustizia* (It.) 1974; *French Connection II* (US), *Il Contesto* (It.) 1975; *Pasqualino Sette Belleze/Seven Beauties* (It.), *Cadaveri Eccellenti/Illustrious Corpses* (It.), *Le Désert des Tartares/Il Deserto dei Tartari* (Fr./It./Iran), *A Matter of Time* (US/It.), *Voyage of the Damned* (UK) 1976; *El Segundo Poder* (Sp.), *Elisa Vida mia Elisa My Love* (Sp.), *The Assignment* (Sw.), *Cet Obscur Objet du Désir/That Obscure Object of Desire* (Fr.) 1977; *Le Dernier amant romantique/The Last Romantic Lover* (Fr.) 1978; *Quintet* (US), *L'Ingorgo—una Storia impossibile/Traffic Jam/Bottleneck* (It./Fr./Sp./Ger.) 1979; *Caboblanco* (US) 1981; *Monsignor* (US) 1982; *Bearn o la Sala de Munecas* (Sp.) 1983; *The Hit* (UK) 1984; *Padre Nuestro* (Sp.), *Rustler's Rhapsody* (US) 1985; *Saving Grace* (US) 1986; *Hotel du Paradis* (UK/Fr.) 1987; *Diario de Invierno, El Bosque encantado* (Sp.), *Moon Over Parador* (US) 1988; *Naked Tango* (US) 1990; *1492* (US), *After the Dream, Di Ceria dell'Untore/The Plague Sower* 1992; *El Cianuro Solo o con Leche?* 1993; *Al Otro Lado del Tunel* 1994.

Reynaud, Emile. Inventor, animation pioneer. *b.* Dec. 8, 1844, Montreuil, near Paris. *d.* 1918. The son of a medal engraver, he grew up in poverty and at age 13 began working as an apprentice mechanic and later as assistant to a photographer. After his father's death he went to live with a wealthy physician uncle and was able to educate himself through access to a vast library. He obtained a teaching position in physics and began a series of inventions that were to present animation to audiences before the invention of cinema proper. In 1876 he introduced his Praxinoscope, a device for presenting a series of drawings on a moving strip with the aid of mirrors set at an angle. Two years later he patented an improved version that made it possible to project images on a screen for a theater audience. In 1888 he began painting his images directly on strips of perforated celluloid, approximately the width of the now-standard 35 mm. From 1892 to 1900 these films were shown to huge audiences at the Paris Musée Grévin as an attraction called "Théâtre Optique." But soon the invention of cinema proper made Reynaud's inventions obsolete. In 1910, dejected and penniless, he threw his apparatus and most of his films into the Seine. Eight years later he died in abject poverty at an institution.

FILMS INCLUDE: Praxinoscope items—*L'Aquarium* 1878; *Un Bon Bock* 1891. Film clips—*Clown et ses Chiens, Pauvre Pierrot* 1892; *Rêve au coin du Feu* 1894; *William Tell, La Premier Cigare* 1896.

Reynolds, Ben (Benjamin F.). American director of photography. In Hollywood from the early silent days, he worked in various capacities at Universal before becoming a lighting cameraman in 1917. He worked on John FORD's first films and later for Erich von Stroheim and other directors at Universal, MGM, Famous Players, Warners, Paramount, and other studios.

FILMS INCLUDE: *The Scrapper, The Soul Herder, The Secret Man* 1917; *The Scarlet Drop, Hell Bent, A Woman's Fool* 1918; *Blind Husbands,* 1919; *The Devil's Passkey* 1920; *False Kisses* 1921; *Foolish Wives* (co-phot.), *The Long Chance, Shattered Dreams* 1922; *Merry-Go-Round* (co-phot.), *The Ghost Patrol, The Prisoner* 1923; *Butterfly, The Signal Tower, Greed* (co-phot.) 1924; *The Merry Widow* (co-phot.), *A Slave of Fashion* 1925; *The Devil's Circus, Tin Hats, The Waning Sex* 1926; *Silk Stockings, The 13th Juror* 1927; *Queen Kelly* (co-phot.), *The Wedding March* (co-phot.), *The Way of the Strong* 1928; *Kid Gloves, Sonny Boy* 1929; *Vengeance* 1930; *To the Last Man, Tillie and Gus, The Thundering Herd* 1933; *Come On Marines!, The Witching Hour, The Old-Fashioned Way* 1934; *McFadden's Flats, Men Without Names, It's a Great Life* 1935.

Reynolds, Burt. Actor. Born on Feb. 11, 1936, in Waycross, Ga. Virile leading man of Hollywood films of the 60s and 70s. Raised in Palm Beach, Fla., where his father, a former cowboy, was the town's police chief, he ran away from home at 14 but later returned and won a football scholarship to Florida

State University. He became an All-Star Southern Conference halfback, but a knee injury and a car accident aborted his athletic career and he switched to college dramatics. He dropped out of school in 1955 and headed to New York, hoping for a stage career, but all he could land were occasional bits on TV, and he supplemented his meager income by washing dishes at Schrafft's and bouncing drunks at Roseland. Two years later he appeared in a New York City Center revival of 'Mister Roberts,' then signed a TV contract with Universal and appeared in such TV series as 'Riverboat' (1959–60), 'Gunsmoke' (1962–65), 'Hawk' (1966), and 'Dan August' (1970–71), often portraying Indian half-breeds (in real life his mother is of Italian origin and his paternal grandmother is a full-blooded Cherokee). He began appearing in films in the early 60s, initially as a stuntman, but it wasn't until the early 70s that he became a popular star, thanks to great spots on TV talk shows, in which he proved himself a glib and humorous participant with a knack for devastating put-downs. In 1972, his career received an important lift from his role in John Boorman's backwoods drama *Deliverance*, but Reynolds's performance lost out in hoopla to his appearance on the pages of the April issue of *Cosmopolitan* magazine, in which he was featured as the first nude male centerfold. He has since starred in many films, typically in tough "macho" roles, establishing himself as a leading TV and screen personality popular with female audiences as a sex symbol and with males for his nonchalant toughness. He was consistently among Hollywood's top money-making stars for a long stretch in the 70s and early 80s. In 1976 he directed his first of several films, *Gator.* In 1979 he established the Burt Reynolds Dinner Theatre in Florida, to which he later devoted more and more of his time as his screen career ebbed. In 1991 he won an Emmy for his starring role in the TV comedy series 'Evening Shade.' Formerly (1963–66) married to the 'Laugh-In' "Sock-it-to-me" girl, Judy Carne, he has been romantically linked to Dinah Shore, 19 years his senior, as well as Chris Evert and Sally Field. In 1988 he married TV actress Loni Anderson, and for years they appeared a strong match. That match ended in 1993, when the two embarked on one of the ugliest Hollywood divorce proceedings of the decade.

FILMS: *Angel Baby, Armored Command* 1961; *Operation CIA* 1965; *Navajo Joe* 1967; *Sam Whiskey, 100 Rifles, Impasse, Shark!* 1969; *Skullduggery* 1970; *Fuzz, Deliverance, Everything You Always Wanted to Know about Sex but Were Afraid to Ask* 1972; *Shamus, The Man Who Loved Cat Dancing, White Lightning* 1973; *The Longest Yard* 1974; *W. W. and the Dixie Dancekings, At Long Last Love, Lucky Lady, Hustle* 1975; *Silent Movie* (unbilled cameo), *Gator* (also dir.), *Nickelodeon* 1976; *Smokey and the Bandit, Semi-Tough* 1977; *The End* (also dir.), *Hooper* 1978; *Starting Over* 1979; *Smokey and the Bandit II, Rough Cut* (UK) 1980; *The Cannonball Run, Paternity, Sharkey's Machine* (also dir.) 1981; *The Best Little Whorehouse in Texas, Best Friends* 1982; *Stroker Ace, Smokey and the Bandit Part 3, The Man Who Loved Women* 1983; *Cannonball Run II, City Heat* 1984; *Stick* (also dir.) 1985; *Uphill All the Way* (cameo) 1986; *Heat, Malone* 1987; *Rent-a-Cop, Switching Channels* 1988; *Physical Evidence, Breaking In, All Dogs Go to Heaven* (v/o) 1989; *Modern Love* 1990; *The Player* (cameo), *Cop-and-a-Half* 1992; *Citizen Ruth, Mad Dog Time, Striptease* 1996; *Bean, Boogie Nights, Meet Wally Sparks* 1997.

Reynolds, Debbie. Actress. Born Mary Frances Reynolds, on Apr. 1, 1932, in El Paso, Tex. Bouncy, wholesome, girl-next-door type of Hollywood star of the 50s and 60s. She entered films with Warners in 1948 after winning the Miss Burbank beauty contest and two years later moved to MGM, where she quickly gained popularity in musicals and other light films with her exuberance and innocent charm. In 1955 she married another popular performer, singer Eddie Fisher, a union that was described as "perfect" by fan magazines. But in 1959 Fisher left Miss Reynolds to marry a friend of the family, Elizabeth TAYLOR, a turn of events that elicited a wave of fan sympathy for the "wronged woman" and brought her popularity to a peak. The following year she married the wealthy owner of a chain of shoe stores and continued her successful career in films as well as on TV. In the early 70s, as her film career ebbed, she starred on Broadway in a hit revival of 'Irene,' then in an extravagant revue, 'The Debbie Reynolds Show.' Miss Reynolds then endured a troubling period when her husband's business failed and she became responsible for $2 million of his debts. They divorced in 1975. In 1984 she married a real-estate developer. In 1985 she recorded the first of two aerobic exercise videotapes and in 1988 published an autobiography, *Debbie: My Life.* Her collection of vintage Hollywood costumes and memorabilia is renowned, and in 1993 she launched a Las Vegas club, where she performs and gives tours of her collection. The mother (by her first marriage) of actress Carrie FISHER; a son, Todd Fisher, is a TV director.

FILMS: *June Bride* 1948; *The Daughter of Rosie O'Grady, Three Little Words* (as boop-boop-a-doop singer Helen Kane), *Two Weeks with Love* 1950; *Mr. Imperium* 1951; *Singin' in the Rain, Skirts Ahoy!* (cameo) 1952; *I Love Melvin, The Affairs of Dobie Gillis* 1953; *Give a Girl a Break, Susan Slept Here, Athena* 1954; *Hit the Deck, The Tender Trap* 1955; *The Catered Affair, Meet Me in Las Vegas* (cameo), *Bundle of Joy* 1956; *Tammy and the Bachelor* 1957; *This Happy Feeling* 1958; *The Mating Game, Say One for Me, It Started with a Kiss* 1959; *The Gazebo, The Rat Race, Pepe* (cameo) 1960; *The Pleasure of His Company, The Second Time Around* 1961; *How the West Was Won* 1962; *My Six Loves, Mary Mary* 1963; *The Unsinkable Molly Brown, Goodbye Charlie* 1964; *The Singing Nun* 1966; *Divorce American Style* 1967; *How Sweet It Is* 1968; *What's the Matter with Helen?* 1971; *Charlotte's Web* (v/o; as Charlotte) 1973; *That's Entertainment* (on-screen co-narr.) 1974; *Heaven and Earth* 1993; *That's Entertainment! III* 1994; *Mother* 1996; *In and Out, Wedding Bell Blues* 1997.

Reynolds, Kevin. Director, screenwriter. Born 1949 in Waco, Tex. *ed.* Baylor University; USC, Los Angeles. After entering professional life as an attorney, Reynolds decided to enroll in film school at USC. His abilities eventually led to a working relationship with actor-director Kevin COSTNER and the two later collaborated on the box-office champ *Robin Hood: Prince of Thieves* (1991). They later re-teamed for the notoriously over-budget actioner *Waterworld* (1995), but the relationship suffered in the process, with Reynolds leaving the project in postproduction, citing artistic differences as the reason for his departure. The film went on to do major box office overseas with a respectable performance domestically.

FILMS: *Red Dawn* (sc.) 1984; *Fandango* (sc.) 1985; *The Beast* (dir.) 1988; *Robin Hood: Prince of Thieves* (dir.) 1991; *Into the West* (act. only) 1993; *Rapa Nui* (dir., sc.) 1994; *Waterworld* (dir.) 1995; *187* (dir.) 1997.

Reynolds, Marjorie. Actress. *b.* Marjorie Goodspeed, on Aug. 12, 1921, in Buhl, Idaho. *d.* 1997. A performer since early childhood, she was seen briefly in a number of silent films, then reappeared in Hollywood in the early 30s as Marjorie Moore, dancer-actress. Changing her name to Reynolds in 1937, she played leads in minor action films. However, she had more success in the early 40s, when she changed from brunette to blonde and starred in several big Paramount productions opposite such leading men as Bing Crosby (in *Holiday Inn*) and Ray Milland (in Fritz Lang's *Ministry of Fear*). But within several years she was back into minor action films. She regained her popularity in the 50s as William Bendix's TV wife in the long-running series 'The Life of Riley' (1953–58). She was married to film editor Jon M. Haffen, who died in 1985.

FILMS INCLUDE: *Scaramouche* 1923; *Revelation* 1924; *Wine Women and Song* 1933; *Collegiate* 1935; *Murder in Greenwich Village* 1937; *The Overland Express, Black Bandit, Six-Shootin' Sheriff* 1938; *Mystery Plane, Streets of New York, The Phantom Stage, Racketeers of the Range, Mr. Wong in Chinatown, Sky Patrol* 1939; *Enemy Agent, Doomed to Die, The Fatal Hour, Midnight Limited* 1940; *Robin Hood of the Pecos, Secret Evidence, The Great Swindle* 1941; *Holiday Inn* 1942; *Dixie* 1943; *Up in Mabel's Room, Ministry of Fear, Three Is a Family* 1944; *Duffy's Tavern, Bring on the Girls* 1945; *Monsieur Beaucaire, The Time of Their Lives* 1946; *Heaven Only Knows* 1947; *Bad Men of Tombstone, That Midnight Kiss* 1949; *The Great Jewel Robber, Customs Agent* 1950; *His Kind of Woman* 1951; *Models Inc.* 1952; *Mobs Inc* 1955; *Juke Box Rhythm* 1959; *The Silent Witness* 1962.

Rhames, Ving. Actor. Born 1961 in New York City. *ed.* Juilliard, New York. Striking, powerful performer of the American stage and screen. After graduating from Juilliard, he went on to make his mark on and off Broadway, then on to daytime television. His solid work paved the way for his debut in *Casualties of War* (1989) and a series of memorable, often comedic turns, in many successful films, specifically *Pulp Fiction* (1994).

FILMS: *Casualties of War* 1989; *Jacob's Ladder, The Long Walk Home* 1990; *Flight of the Intruder, Homicide, The People Under the Stairs* 1991; *Stop! Or My Mom Will Shoot* 1992; *Bound By Honor, Dave, The Saint of Fort Washington* 1993; *Drop Squad, Pulp Fiction* 1994; *Kiss of Death* 1995; *Mission: Impossible* 1996; *ConAir, Dangerous Ground, Rosewood* 1997.

Rhodes, Erik. Actor. *b.* Ernest Sharpe, 1906, El Reno (or Oklahoma City), Okla. *d.* 1990. Character comedian of Hollywood films of the 30s, following radio and Broadway experience. He specialized in suave Continental gigolo or effete types, memorably in two Astaire-Rogers musicals, *The Gay Divorcee* (1934) and *Top Hat* (1935). He returned to the stage in the 40s, after serving with an intelligence unit of the Army Air Force during WW II. In the early days of TV he was featured with Gloria Swanson in the variety show 'Wonder Boy.'

FILMS INCLUDE: *The Gay Divorcee* 1934; *Charlie Chan in Paris, A Night at the Ritz, Nitwits, Old Man Rhythm, Top Hat* 1935; *Two in the Dark, Chatterbox, Special Investigator, One Rainy Afternoon, Second Wife* 1936; *Criminal Lawyer, Woman Chases Man, Music for Madame, Fight for Your Lady, Beg Borrow or Steal* 1937; *Meet the Girls, Mysterious Mr. Moto, Say It in French, Dramatic School* 1938; *On Your Toes* 1939.

Rhys-Davies, John. Actor. Born in 1944 in Salisbury, Wiltshire, England. *ed.* Univ. of East Anglia; RADA. Burly supporting actor of stage and screen. Raised in Wales and East Africa, he was employed as a teacher before becoming a full-time actor. A prolific performer of Shakespeare, he is best known to screen audiences for his humorous performances in two Steven Spielberg Indiana Jones vehicles.

FILMS INCLUDE: *The Black Windmill* 1974; *Sphinx* 1980; *Raiders of the Lost Ark* 1981; *Victor/Victoria, Sword of the Valiant* (UK) 1982; *Best Revenge, Sahara, In the Shadow of Kilimanjaro* 1984; *King Solomon's Mines* 1985; *Firewalker* 1986; *The Living Daylights* 1986; *Predator* 1987; *Il Giovane Toscanini, Waxwork* 1988; *Indiana Jones and the Last Crusade, Rising Storm* 1989; *Tusks* (also sc.) 1990; *The Lost World* 1993; *The Return to the Lost World* 1994; *The Great White Hype* 1996.

Ricci, Christina. Actress. Born 1980 in Santa Monica, Calif. Winning, sweet-faced young film actress who made her film debut as Cher's daughter in *Mermaids* (1990). She has since been cast in several major Hollywood films, notably as Wednesday in the successful film versions of the popular television series 'The Addams Family.'

FILMS: *Mermaids* 1990; *The Addams Family, The Hard Way* 1991; *The Cemetery Club* 1992; *Addams Family Values* 1993; *Casper, Gold Diggers: The Secret of Bear Mountain, Now and Then* 1995; *The Ice Storm, That Darn Cat* 1997.

Rice, Florence. Actress. *b.* Feb. 14, 1907, in Cleveland. *d.* 1974. Leading lady of numerous Hollywood second features of the 30s and early 40s, mainly at MGM, often as Robert Young's sweet and wholesome girlfriend. The daughter of famous sportscaster and columnist Grantland Rice, she appeared in a couple of Broadway productions before her film debut in 1934. Her second of three husbands was actor Robert Wilcox. She died of lung cancer.

FILMS INCLUDE: *Fugitive Lady* 1934; *Best Man Wins, Under Pressure, Carnival, Escape from Devil's Island* 1935; *Panic on the Air, Pride of the Marines, The Blackmailer, Sworn Enemy, The Longest Night* 1936; *Under Cover of Night, Man of the People, Riding on Air, Married Before Breakfast, Double Wedding, Beg Borrow or Steal, Navy Blue and Gold* 1937; *Paradise for Three, Fast Company, Vacation from Love, Sweethearts* 1938; *Stand Up and Fight, Four Girls in White, The Kid from Texas, Miracles for Sale, At the Circus* 1939; *Broadway Melody of 1940, Girl in 313, Phantom Raiders, The Secret Seven, Cherokee Strip* 1940; *Mr. District Attorney, Doctors Don't Tell, Father Takes a Wife, Blonde from Singapore* 1941; *Tramp Tramp Tramp, Boss of Big Town* 1942; *The Ghost and the Guest* 1943.

Rice, Joan. Actress. Born on Feb. 3, 1930, in Derby, England. Leading lady of British films of the 50s. Later in infrequent character roles.

FILMS INCLUDE: *Blackmailed* 1950; *The Story of Robin Hood* (as Maid Marian), *Curtain Up, The Gift Horse/Glory at Sea* 1952; *A Day to Remember* 1953; *His Majesty O'Keefe* (US/UK), *The Crowded Day* 1954; *Women Without Men* 1956; *The Long Knife* 1958; *Operation Bullshine* 1959; *Payroll* 1961; *The Horror of Frankenstein* 1970.

Rice, John C. See Irwin, May.

Rich, David Lowell. Director. Born on Aug. 31, 1920, in New York City. Starting out in live television drama in 1950, he moved into features in the late 50s. His films, technically polished, have been otherwise undistinguished. Most of his prolific recent output consists of TV movies. One of these, *The Defection of Simas Kudrika* (1978), earned him an Emmy Award.

FILMS: *No Time to Be Young* 1957; *Senior Prom* 1958; *Hey Boy! Hey Girl!, Have Rocket Will Travel* 1959; *Madame X, The Plainsman* 1966; *Rosie!* 1967; *Three Guns for Texas* (film comprising three episodes from TV's 'Laredo' series made by three directors; one of these episodes, "Yahoo," was originally directed for TV by Rich in 1965), *A Lovely Way to Die* 1968; *Eye of the Cat* 1969; *That Man, The Concorde—Airport '79* 1979; *Chu Chu and the Philly Flash* 1981.

Rich, Irene. Actress. *b.* Irene Luther, Oct. 13, 1891, Buffalo, N.Y. *d.* 1988. Leading lady of Hollywood silents. A twice-married real estate agent before breaking into films in 1918 as an extra in Mary Pickford's *Stella Maris,* she starred in scores of women-oriented screen melodramas of the 20s, usually in mature, woman-of-the-world roles. By the advent of sound she had graduated into maternal parts and was teamed up with Will Rogers as his nagging wife in several films of the early 30s. She retired from the screen in 1932 to become a highly popular radio star with the long-running program series 'Dear John.' During the mid-30s she also appeared in several Broadway shows, including 'Seven Keys to Baldpate,' opposite George M. Cohan. She returned to films in 1938, playing mothers and other character roles in a variety of productions.

FILMS INCLUDE: *Stella Maris* (bit), *The Girl in His House* 1918; *Castles in the Air, The Lone Star Ranger* 1919; *Water Water Everywhere, The Strange Boarder, Jes' Call Me Jim, Stop Thief* 1920; *A Tale of Two Worlds, A Voice in the Dark, Boys Will Be Boys, The Invisible Power, Desperate Trails, The Poverty of Riches* 1921; *The Call of Home, The Trap, A Fool There Was, Brawn of the North* 1922; *Dangerous Trails, Brass, Yesterday's Wife, Rosita, Defying Destiny, Lucretia Lombard, Boy of Mine* 1923; *Beau Brummel, Cytherea, Captain January, A Woman Who Sinned, Behold This Woman, A Lost Lady* 1924; *My Wife and I, Eve's Lover, The Wife Who Wasn't Wanted, Compromise, The Pleasure Buyers, Lady Windermere's Fan* 1925; *The Honeymoon Express, My Official Wife* 1926; *Don't Tell the Wife, The Climbers, Dearie, The Desired Woman, The Silver Slave* 1927; *Beware of Married Men, Women They Talk About, The Perfect Crime, Craig's Wife* 1928; *Ned McCobb's Daughter, Shanghai Rose, The Exalted Flapper, They Had to See Paris* 1929; *So This Is London, On Your Back* 1930; *Beau Ideal, Father's Son, Strangers May Kiss, Five and Ten, The Mad Parade, Wicked, The Champ* 1931; *Down to Earth, Her Mad Night, Manhattan Tower* 1932; *That Certain Age* 1938; *The Mortal Storm, The Lady in Question* 1940; *Keeping Company* 1941; *Angel and the Badman, New Orleans* 1947; *Fort Apache, Joan of Arc* 1948.

Rich, John. Director. Born on July 6, 1925, in Rockaway Beach, N.Y. *ed.* U. of Michigan. A veteran TV director and producer, he ventured briefly into feature films in the mid-60s, after winning an Emmy Award for 'The Dick Van Dyke Show.' He turned out a number of glossy though unexciting entertainment films, then returned to television and won two Emmy Awards in succession for directing and producing segments of 'All in the Family.'

FILMS: *Wives and Lovers* 1963; *The New Interns, Roustabout* 1964; *Boeing Boeing* 1965; *Easy Come Easy Go* 1967.

Richard, Cliff. Singer, actor. Born Harold Webb, on Oct. 14, 1940, in India. The "British Elvis," a recording star and teen idol, later a respected rock-and-roller; occasionally in films.

FILMS: *Serious Charge/Immoral Charge/A Touch of Hell* 1959; *Expresso Bongo* 1960; *The Young Ones/Wonderful to Be Young* 1961; *Summer Holiday* 1963; *Wonderful Life/Swingers' Paradise* 1964; *Finders Keepers* 1966; *Two a Penny* 1968; *Take Me High/Hot Property* 1973.

Richard, Pierre. Actor, director. Born Pierre Defays, in 1934, in France. Amiable light leading man of French films. A product of the Paris Music Hall, he became extremely popular as a screen personality after playing the title role in *The Tall Blond Man with One Black Shoe* (1972). He successfully directed several of his own films. Many of his comic vehicles have been widely exhibited in the US and some have spawned Hollywood remakes.

FILMS INCLUDE (as actor): *Heures chaudes/Hot Hours* 1959; *Trois Hommes sur un Cheval, Un Idiot à Paris* 1967; *Alexandre le Bienheureux/Very Happy Alexander* 1968; *Le Distrait/The Daydreamer* (also dir., co-sc.) 1970; *Les Malheurs d'Alfred* (also dir.) 1971; *Le Grand Blond avec une Chaussure noire/The Tall Blond Man with One Black Shoe* 1972; *Je ne sais rien mais je dirai tout* (also dir., co-sc.) 1973; *La Moutarde me monte au Nez/Lucky Pierre, Le Retour du Grand Blond/The Return of the Tall Blond Man with One Black Shoe* 1974; *La Course à l'Echalote/The Wild Goose Chase* 1975; *On aura tout vu/The Bottom Line* 1976; *Le Jouet/The Toy* 1977; *Je suis Timide mais je me soigne/Too Shy to Try* (also dir., co-sc.), *La Carapte* 1978; *C'est pas moi c'est lui!* (also co-dir., co-sc.), *Le Coup du Parapluie* 1980; *La Chèvre* 1981; *Les Compères* 1983; *Le Jumeau* (also co-prod.) 1984; *Les Fugitifs* 1986; *La Gauce en sortant de L'Ascenseur, Mangeclous* 1988; *Bienvenue à Bord!. . .* 1990; *Chef in Love* 1997.

Richards, Addison. Actor. *b.* 1887, Zanesville, Ohio. *d.* 1964. Solid character player of some 200 Hollywood films. A graduate of Washington State College at Pullman, he joined the Pasadena Community Playhouse in 1931 and entered films two years later. Tall and imposing, he often played judges, prosecuting attorneys, military commanders, and other men of authority, mainly for Warners and MGM.

FILMS INCLUDE: *Riot Squad* 1933; *British Agent, Our Daily Bread, The St. Louis Kid* 1934; *Home on the Range, G-Men, Front Page Woman, The Crusades, Frisco Kid, Ceiling Zero* 1935; *Colleen, Sutter's Gold, China Clipper, Anthony Adverse* 1936; *Black Legion, Alcatraz Island* 1937; *Boys Town, Valley of the Giants* 1938; *Andy Hardy Gets Spring Fever, Espionage Agent, Thunder Afloat, Nick Carter—Master Detective* 1939; *Geronimo, My Little Chickadee, Northwest Passage, Edison the Man* 1940; *Flight Command, Arizona, Strawberry Blonde, I Wanted Wings, Men of Boys Town, The Great Lie, Badlands of Dakota* (as General Custer), *Texas* 1941; *My Favorite Blonde, Friendly Enemies, The Pride of the Yankees, A-Haunting We Will Go, Flying Tigers* 1942; *Air Force, A Guy Named Joe* 1943; *The Sullivans, The Fighting Seabees, Since You Went Away* 1944; *The Mummy's Curse, Bewitched, Spellbound, Leave Her to Heaven* 1945; *Anna and the King of Siam, Angel on My Shoulder* 1946; *Call Northside 777* 1948; *Davy Crockett—Indian Scout* 1950; *Illegal* 1955; *Walk the Proud Land* 1956; *The Oregon Train* 1959; *Saintly Sinners* 1962; *For Those Who Think Young* 1964.

Richards, Ann. Actress. Born Shirley Ann Richards, on Dec. 20, 1918, in Sydney, Australia, to an American father and New Zealander mother. An ingenue and leading lady in Australian films of the late 30s, she arrived in Hollywood after the outbreak of WW II and played leads and second leads in films of MGM and other studios. Despite proven talent, she found good roles elusive and retired from the screen in the early 50s. She has since appeared occasionally on the stage and has published two volumes of her poetry, *The Grieving Senses* (1971), and *Odyssey for Edmond* (1991) and a verse play, 'Helen of Troy,' in which she has performed. She has also lectured extensively on subjects ranging from Hollywood to Tibet.

FILMS INCLUDE: In Australia—*It Isn't Done* 1937; *Tall Timber* 1938; *Dad and Dave Come to Town, Lovers and Luggers* 1939; *Come Up Smiling* 1940. In the US (complete)—*Random Harvest, Dr. Gillespie's New Assistant* 1942; *Three Hearts for Julia* 1943; *An American Romance* 1944; *Love Letters* 1945; *Badman's Territory, The Searching Wind* 1946; *Lost Honeymoon, Love from a Stranger* 1947; *Sorry Wrong Number* 1948; *Breakdown* 1952; *Ann Richards in the USSR* (doc.) 1982; *Don't Call Me Girlie* (Austral.) 1984.

Richards, Beah. Actress. Born in Vicksburg, Miss. *ed.* Dillard Univ. Controlled veteran stage actress who has had some success on film and TV. After apprenticing in the theater for three years in San Diego, she came to New York, where she established herself on and off Broadway, notably in 'The Amen Corner.' Active in film since the 1960s, she was nominated for an Academy Award as the wise mother of Sidney Poitier in *Guess Who's Coming to Dinner*.

FILMS INCLUDE: *Take a Giant Step* 1959; *The Miracle*

Worker 1962; *Gone are the Days* 1963; *Hurry Sundown, In the Heat of the Night, Guess Who's Coming to Dinner* 1967; *The Great White Hope* 1970; *The Biscuit Eater* 1972; *Mahogany* 1976; *Inside Out* 1986; *Drugstore Cowboy* 1989; *Homer and Eddie* 1990.

Richards, Dick. Director. Born Richard M. Richards, in 1936, in New York City. Trained and employed by the US Army as a photojournalist, he later worked as a photographer for *Life, Look, Time, Esquire,* and other magazines, winning numerous awards for news and commercial still photography before turning to films in the early 70s. The most interesting of his scattered output is *Farewell, My Lovely* (1975), a taut, brooding, well-crafted third screen version of the Raymond Chandler novel. He co-produced the popular *Tootsie* (1982) with director Sydney Pollack.

FILMS: *The Culpepper Cattle Company* (also story) 1972; *Rafferty and the Gold Dust Twins, Farewell My Lovely* 1975; *March or Die* (also co-prod., co-story; UK) 1977; *Death Valley* 1981; *Tootsie* (co-prod. only) 1982; *Man Woman and Child* 1983; *Heat* 1987.

Richards, Stephen. See STEVENS, Mark.

Richardson, Miranda. Actress. Born in 1958, in Lancashire, England. Gifted, versatile leading lady of stage, TV, and films. The younger of two daughters of a clothing-store marketing executive, she trained for two years at the Bristol Old Vic Theatre School before starting her career with a provincial theater in Manchester. Following a couple of years of touring in repertory, she settled in London, where she rapidly became established as an intriguing new performer, mainly in TV dramas. She made an astonishing screen debut in 1985 with her superlative portrayal of murderous ex-prostitute Ruth Ellis, the last woman to be hanged in Britain, in Mike Newell's film *Dance with a Stranger.* That performance later prompted Steven Spielberg to assign her the female lead in his epic *Empire of the Sun* (1987). She gained further mainstream celebrity with 1992's *Damage* and *The Crying Game*, and 1994's *Tom and Viv*, all of which led to several nominations for international awards, including a supporting actress Oscar nomination for *Damage* and a best actress nomination for *Tom and Viv.*

FILMS: *Dance with a Stranger, The Innocent* 1985; *Underworld, The Death of the Heart* 1986; *Eat the Rich* (cameo), *Empire of the Sun* (US) 1987; *El Sueno del Mono Loco/The Mad Monkey* (Sp./Fr.) 1989; *The Fool* 1990; *The Bachelor, Enchanted April* 1991; *Damage* (UK), *The Crying Game* (UK) 1992; *Century* (UK), *Tom and Viv* 1994; *The Evening Star, Kansas City, Night and the Moment, Swann* 1996; *The Designated Mourner, The Saint* 1997.

Richardson, Natasha. Actress. Born on May 11, 1963, in London. Talented leading lady of stage, screen, and TV. The older daughter of actress Vanessa REDGRAVE and director Tony RICHARDSON, she trained at the Central School of Speech and Drama and performed at the Leeds Playhouse before graduating to lead roles in 'A Midsummer Night's Dream' and 'Hamlet' (as Ophelia) with London's Old Vic. In 1985 she co-starred with her mother and aunt Lynn Redgrave in a much-acclaimed production of Chekhov's 'The Three Sisters.' The following year she won the London Theatre Critics' Most Promising Newcomer award. She has shown equal promise in films since her screen debut in 1984. In 1993, she starred in the PBS remake of 'Suddenly, Last Summer' and portrayed the title role in 'Anna Christie' on Broadway. Her younger sister, Joely Richardson (*b.* Jan. 9, 1965, London), is also a stage and screen actress. She is married to actor Liam NEESON.

FILMS: *Every Picture Tells a Story* 1984; *Gothic* 1986; *A Month in the Country* 1987; *Patty Hearst* (title role; US) 1988; *Fat Man and Little Boy* (US) 1989; *The Handmaid's Tale* (US) 1990; *The Favour, The Watch and The Very Big Fish* (Fr./UK), *The Comfort of Strangers* (UK), *King Ralph* (US) 1991; *Past Midnight* (US) 1992; *Nell, Widow's Peak* 1994.

Richardson, Sir Ralph. Actor. *b.* Dec. 19, 1902, Cheltenham, England. *d.* 1983. Eminent character player of the British stage and screen. He worked briefly as an office boy with an insurance company before beginning his acting career in 1920, and rose to prominence with the Old Vic in the 30s and 40s. His film career, which started in 1933, has been secondary to his stage work, and only a few of his screen roles did full justice to his talent. Among these were Karenin in *Anna Karenina,* the manservant in *The Fallen Idol* (both 1948), Dr. Sloper in *The Heiress* (1949), and Buckingham in *Richard III* (1955). He typically played well-bred, unassuming intellectual characters. He appeared frequently on the Broadway stage and occasionally in Hollywood films and was nominated for Oscars for *The Heiress* (1949) and for *Greystoke: The Legend of Tarzan, Lord of the Apes* (1984), his penultimate film role. He directed himself in one film, *Home at Seven/Murder on Monday* (1952). Richardson was knighted in 1947. Widower of actress Muriel Hewitt, his marriage to actress Meriel Forbes-Robertson lasted from 1945 till his death at 80.

FILMS: *The Ghoul, Friday the 13th* 1933; *The Return of Bulldog Drummond, Java Head, The King of Paris* 1934; *Bulldog Jack/Alias Bulldog Drummond* 1935; *Things to Come, The Man Who Could Work Miracles* 1936; *Thunder in the City* 1937; *South Riding, The Divorce of Lady X, The Citadel* (as Denny) 1938; *Q Planes/Clouds Over Europe, Four Feathers, The Lion Has Wings, On the Night of the Fire/The Fugitive* 1939; *The Day Will Dawn/The Avengers, The Silver Fleet* 1942; *The Volunteer* (doc.) 1943; *School for Secrets/Secret Flight* 1946; *Anna Karenina* (as Karenin), *The Fallen Idol* 1948; *The Heiress* (as Dr. Austin Sloper in this adaptation of Henry James's *Washington Square;* US) 1949; *Outcast of the Islands* 1951; *Home at Seven/Murder on Monday* (also dir.), *The Sound Barrier/Breaking Through the Sound Barrier, The Holly and the Ivy* 1952; *Richard III* (as Buckingham) 1955; *Smiley* 1956; *The Passionate Stranger/A Novel Affair* 1957; *Our Man in Havana* 1959; *Oscar Wilde* (as Sir Edward Carson), *Exodus* (US) 1960; *The 300 Spartans* (as Themistocles; US), *Long Day's Journey Into Night* (as James Tyrone; US) 1962; *Woman of Straw* 1964; *Doctor Zhivago* (as Alexander Gromeko; US) 1965; *Falstaff/Chimes at Midnight* (narrator only; Sp./Switz.), *Khartoum* (as Prime Minister Gladstone), *The Wrong Box* 1966; *Midas Run* (US), *Oh! What a Lovely War* (as Sir Edward Grey), *The Bed Sitting Room, Battle of Britain* 1969; *The Looking Glass War, David Copperfield* (as Micawber) 1970; *Eagle in a Cage, Who Slew Auntie Roo?* 1971; *Tales from the Crypt, Alice's Adventures in Wonderland* (as the Caterpillar), *Lady Caroline Lamb* (as King George IV) 1972; *A Doll's House* (as Dr. Rank), *O Lucky Man!* (in dual role) 1973; *Rollerball* (US) 1975; *Watership Down* (v/o) 1978; *Time Bandits, Dragonslayer* (US/UK) 1981; *Wagner* 1983; *Greystoke: The Legend of Tarzan Lord of the Apes, Give My Regards to Broad Street* 1984.

Richardson, Robert. American director of photography. Oliver STONE's favorite lighting cameraman, he invigorated that director's films with documentary-like cinematography. He was nominated for Oscars for *Platoon* (1986) and *Born on the Fourth of July* (1989).

FILMS INCLUDE: *Salvador, Platoon* 1986; *Wall Street, Dudes* 1987; *Eight Men Out, Talk Radio* 1988; *Born on the Fourth of July* 1989; *The Doors, JFK* 1991.

Richardson, Tony. Director. *b.* Cecil Antonio Richardson, June 5, 1928, Shipley, England. *d.* 1991, of a neurological infection brought on by AIDS. A pharmacist's son, he spent his formative years without parental coddling, when his secondary school was moved to the country in WW II. The experience led him to "hate all authority," as he later recalled. A graduate of Oxford, where he presided over the university's Dramatic Society, he began his professional career in the early 50s as a theater director and as a producer for BBC-TV. In the middle of the decade he became associated with Britain's Free Cinema movement, through which he directed and wrote a short, *Momma Don't Allow* (1955), in collaboration with Karel REISZ. During this period he also contributed articles on film to the magazine *Sight and Sound.* In 1956 he scored a notable success at London's Royal Court Theatre with 'Look Back in Anger,' the first of many plays he would direct for the English Stage Company, which he co-founded with George Devine. This play also marked the beginning of a productive collaboration with playwright John OSBORNE and set the tone for the "Angry Young Men" movement that blossomed briefly among British intellectuals. In 1958 he formed Woodfall, a film production company, with Osborne and the following year directed the screen version of *Look Back in Anger,* his first feature film. He reached a peak of prestige in the early 60s, when he turned out such films as the sordidly lyrical, intimate drama *A Taste of Honey* (1961), the intriguing, technically inventive *The Loneliness of the Long Distance Runner* (1962), and the lusty, visually dazzling *Tom Jones* (1963), for which he won an Oscar. However, with the notable exception of *The Charge of the Light Brigade* (1968), a nonheroic but robust view of the famous 1854 battle at Balaclava, Richardson's later pictures were mainly lackluster. He produced several of his own films as well as Karel Reisz's *Saturday Night and Sunday Morning* (1960). He was executive producer on Desmond Davis's *Girl with Green Eyes* (1964). Formerly (1962–67) married to actress Vanessa REDGRAVE (she divorced him on the grounds of adultery, naming Jeanne MOREAU as co-respondent), he is the father of actresses Joely Richardson and Natasha RICHARDSON.

FILMS: *Momma Don't Allow* (short; co-dir. with Karel Reisz; also co-sc.) 1955; *Look Back in Anger* 1959; *The Entertainer* 1960; *Sanctuary* (US), *A Taste of Honey* (also prod., co-sc.) 1961; *The Loneliness of the Long Distance Runner* (also prod.) 1962; *Tom Jones* (also prod.) 1963; *The Loved One* (US) 1965; *Mademoiselle* (Fr./UK) 1966; *The Sailor from Gibraltar* (also co-sc.) 1967; *Red and Blue* (short), *The Charge of the Light Brigade* 1968; *Laughter in the Dark/La Chambre obscure* (UK/Fr.), *Hamlet* 1969; *Ned Kelly* (also co-sc.) 1970; *A Delicate Balance* (US), *Dead Cert* 1973; *Joseph Andrews* (also adapt.) 1977; *The Border* (US) 1982; *The Hotel New Hampshire* (also sc.; US) 1984; *Blue Sky* (completed 1991, released posthumously; US) 1994.

Richler, Mordecai. Novelist, essayist, screenwriter. Born on Jan. 27, 1931, in Montreal. *ed.* Sir George Williams U. A leading Canadian author, he contributed screenplays, alone or in collaboration, to British and American, as well as Canadian films. He was nominated for an Oscar for the script of *The Apprenticeship of Duddy Kravitz* (1974), which was based on his 1959 novel about a hustling Jewish teenager trying to make it in Montreal. A similar milieu provided the background for *Joshua Then and Now* (1985), which he adapted from his 1980 novel.

FILMS: *No Love for Johnnie* (co-sc.; UK) 1961; *Tiara Tahiti* (addnl. dial.; UK) *Young and Willing* (co-sc.; UK) 1962; *Life at the Top* (sc.; UK) 1965; *The Apprenticeship of Duddy Kravitz* (sc., from own novel; Can.) 1974; *Fun with Dick and Jane* (co-sc.; US) 1977; *Jacob Two-Two Meets the Hooded Fang* (sc., from own book; Can.) 1978; *Joshua Then and Now* (sc., from own novel; Can.) 1985.

Richmond, Kane. Actor. *b.* Fred W. Bowditch, Dec. 23, 1906, Minneapolis. *d.* 1973. *ed.* U. of Minnesota. Square-jawed hero of low-budget Hollywood action films and serials. A regional film booker and theater manager, he was on a business trip to Hollywood when a Universal executive asked him to test for the lead in the "Leather Pusher" two-reel action series. He got the part and went on to appear in many other films through the late 40s. He later became involved in the ladies' fashion business. He was married to one of his co-stars, Marion Burns.

FILMS INCLUDE: *Leather Pusher* 1930; *Politics* 1931; *Huddle* 1932; *Devil Tiger* 1934; *The Lost City* (serial and feature versions), *The Adventures of Rex and Rinty* (serial) 1935; *Private Number* 1936; *The Devil Diamond, Nancy Steele Is Missing, Tough to Handle* 1937; *Mars Attacks the World* 1938; *Tail Spin, The Return of the Cisco Kid, Charlie Chan in Reno, The Escape* 1939; *Murder Over New York* 1940; *Play Girl, Great Guns, Double Cross* 1941; *Spy Smasher* (serial) 1942; *Action in the North Atlantic* 1943; *Haunted Harbor* (serial), *Ladies Courageous, Roger Touhy—Gangster* 1944; *Brenda Starr—Reporter* (serial), *Jungle Raiders* (serial), *Black Market Babies, The Tiger Woman* 1945; *The Shadow Returns, Passkey to Danger, Don't Gamble with Strangers, Behind the Mask, The Missing Lady, Traffic in Crime* 1946; *Brick Bradford* (serial), *Black Gold* 1947; *Stage Struck* 1948.

Richter, Hans. Painter, avant-garde filmmaker, film theorist. *b.* 1888, Berlin. *d.* 1976. A former apprentice carpenter, he studied art in Berlin and Weimar. Invalided from active WW I duty in 1916, he became involved in the activities of the Dada movement in Switzerland, then in Germany. Along with Walter RUTTMANN and Viking EGGELING, he pioneered avant-garde film making in the early 20s. He and Eggeling shared an apartment, working together on sequential scroll paintings approximating animation. Richter later experimented alone with abstract animation and eventually was recognized as Germany's most important exponent of surrealism. In 1929 he participated in the international Congress of Independent Film, during which he shot a short subject in collaboration with EISENSTEIN and others. In 1933, when the Nazis took over Germany, he began wandering through Europe and finally emigrated to the US in 1941.

Shortly after his arrival Richter was appointed director of the Institute of Film Techniques at New York's City College, a post he held for more than a decade. Among his American-made films was the famous *Dreams That Money Can Buy,* a feature-length color film based on scenarios by artists Alexander Calder, Marcel Duchamps, Max Ernst, Fernand Léger, and Man Ray. It was a prize winner at the 1947 Venice Film Festival. Another experimental feature, *8 x 8,* had, among others, Jean Cocteau as a contributor. In 1952 Richter returned to Europe and settled in Switzerland. He wrote several books and many important articles about film and art theory and his struggles as an artist.

FILMS INCLUDE: *Rhythmus 21* 1921; *Rhythmus 23* 1923; *Rhythmus 25* 1925; *Filmstudie 25/Film Study* 1926; *Inflation* 1927; *Vormittagsspuk/Ghosts Before Breakfast* (also act., along with composers Paul Hindemith and Darius Milhaud) 1928; *Rennsymphonie/Race Symphony, Everyday* (shot in London, with Eisenstein playing a bobby) 1929; *Neues Leben/New Life* (Switz.) 1930; *Europa Radio* (Holl.) 1931; *Hallo Everybody* 1933; *Eine kleine Welt im dunkelem/A Small World in the Dark, Hans in Glück* (both Switz.) 1938; *The Movies Take a Holiday* (compilation films; US) 1944; *Dreams That Money Can Buy* (US) 1946; *Forty Years of Experiment* (in two parts, 1951, 1961; excerpts from his experimental films); *Dadascope I, II* 1956–57; *Passionate Pastime, 8 x 8* 1957; *From Dada to Surrealism* 1961; *Alexander Calder: From the Circus to the Moon* 1963.

Richter, W. D. Screenwriter, director. Born on Dec. 7, 1945, in New Britain, Conn. *ed.* Dartmouth; USC Graduate Film School. Writing for the screen since the early 70s, he shared an Academy Award nomination for *Brubaker* (1980). In 1984 he took a first crack at directing with *The Adventures of Buckaroo Banzai Across the Eighth Dimension,* an off-the-wall, pop-culture film that became a cult favorite.

FILMS (as screenwriter): *Slither* 1972; *Peeper* 1975; *Nickelodeon* 1976; *Invasion of the Body Snatchers* 1978; *Dracula* 1979; *Brubaker* 1980; *All Night Long, Hard Feelings* 1981; *The Adventures of Buckaroo Banzai Across the Eighth Dimension* (dir., prod. only) 1984; *Big Trouble in Little China* (adapt.) 1986; *Hang Tough* 1990; *Late for Dinner* (dir., prod. only) 1991; *Needful Things* 1993; *Home for the Holidays* 1995.

Rickman, Alan. Actor. Born 1946 in Hammersmith, London, England. *ed.* Royal College of Art, London; Royal Academy of Dramatic Arts, London. Understated, yet powerful and debonair actor who distinguished himself on the stages of London's West End and as a member of the Royal Shakespeare Company. He earned international acclaim in the drama 'Les Liaisons Dangereuses' (1987), and then ventured out to Hollywood where he was primarily cast as the villain, most notably in *Die Hard* (1988). His versatility, however, has enabled him to break out of that mold with a romantic turn in director Ang LEE's *Sense and Sensibility* (1996).

FILMS: *Die Hard* 1988; *The January Man* 1989; *Quigley Down Under* 1990; *Close My Eyes, Closet Land, Robin Hood: Prince of Thieves, Truly Madly Deeply* 1991; *Bob Roberts* 1992; *An Awfully Big Adventure, Sense and Sensibility* 1995; *Michael Collins* 1996; *The Winter Guest* (dir. only) 1997.

Ridgely, John. Actor. *b.* John Huntington Rea, Sept. 6, 1909, Chicago. *d.* 1968. *ed.* Stanford U. Dependable, likable character player of scores of Hollywood films, mainly at Warners. He usually played supporting roles, often as the hero's or heroine's friend, but he had one memorable starring role in Howard Hawks's famed war film *Air Force* (1943).

FILMS INCLUDE: *Submarine D-1* 1937; *The Invisible Menace, White Banners* 1938; *King of the Underworld, They Made Me a Criminal, Wings of the Navy, Indianapolis Speedway* 1939; *Torrid Zone, Brother Orchid, They Drive by Night* 1940; *Strange Alibi, The Wagons Roll at Night, International Squadron* 1941; *The Man Who Came to Dinner, The Big Shot* 1942; *Air Force, Northern Pursuit* 1943; *Destination Tokyo, The Doughgirls, Arsenic and Old Lace* 1944; *God Is My Co-Pilot, Pride of the Marines* 1945; *My Reputation, The Big Sleep* 1946; *The Man I Love, Nora Prentiss, Possessed, Cheyenne, Cry Wolf, High Wall* 1947; *The Iron Curtain, Luxury Liner, Sealed Verdict* 1948; *Command Decision, Task Force, Border Incident* 1949; *Edge of Doom, Saddle Tramp,* 1950; *The Last Outpost, A Place in the Sun, The Blue Veil* 1951; *The Greatest Show on Earth, The Outcasts of Poker Flat* 1952; *Off Limits* 1953.

Ridges, Stanley. Actor. *b.* 1892, Southampton, England. *d.* 1951. Solid character player of many Hollywood films, both major and minor, typically in commanding, pivotal supporting roles.

FILMS INCLUDE: *Success* 1923; *Crime Without Passion* 1934; *The Scoundrel* 1935; *Winterset* (as Shadow) 1936; *Sinner Take All* 1937; *Yellow Jack, If I were King, The Mad Miss Manton* 1938; *Let Us Live, Union Pacific, Each Dawn I Die, Espionage Agent, Dust Be My Destiny, Nick Carter—Master Detective* 1939; *Black Friday* 1940; *The Sea Wolf* (as Johnson), *Sergeant York, They Died with Their Boots On* 1941; *To Be or Not to Be, The Lady Is Willing, The Big Shot* 1942; *Air Force, Tarzan Triumphs, This Is the Army* 1943; *The Story of Dr. Wassell, Wilson* (as Admiral Grayson), *The Master Race* 1944; *The Suspect, Captain Eddie* 1945; *Canyon Passage, Mr. Ace* 1946; *Possessed* 1947; *An Act of Murder* 1948; *Streets of Laredo, Task Force* 1949; *The File on Thelma Jordon, No Way Out* 1950; *The Groom Wore Spurs* 1951.

Riefenstahl, Leni. Director, actress. Born Helene Bertha Amalie Riefenstahl on Aug. 22, 1902, in Berlin, the daughter of a wealthy businessman. A former dancer (ballet and modern) and painter, she entered German films in the mid-20s as the attractive, athletic blonde star of Arnold Fanck's MOUNTAIN FILMS. On the set she learned the fundamentals of film technique and in 1931 she made her first film, *The Blue Light,* which she produced, directed, edited, and co-wrote with Béla Balázs and in which she also starred. She released it through her own production company, Leni Riefenstahl Studio-Film. When the Nazis came to power, she won Hitler's favor and was entrusted with the filming of the Nuremberg Party Convention in 1934. She used 30 cameras, equipped with a variety of mounts and lenses, and 120 assistants to accomplish the feat. The result was a remarkable documentary, *Triumph of the Will,* the most powerful propaganda film ever made. She followed it with the equally impressive masterpiece of rhythmic editing, *Olympia,* ostensibly a filmic record of the 1936 Berlin Olympic Games but in essence an idealized hymn to the human body and the glory of physical might. She deployed 45 cameras—some sunk in the ground or underwater, others floated by balloons—to shoot the event from every possible angle, then meticulously and brilliantly edited 200 hours of film down to four hours of some of the most dazzling footage ever brought to the screen. *Olympia* won the Mussolini Cup, the top prize, at the 1938 Venice Film Festival. The following year, Riefenstahl covered the German invasion of Poland as a photojournalist and in 1940 began filming *Tiefland,* a nonmusical screen version of the Eugen d'Albert opera. For one of the sequences she used gypsy inmates of a concentration camp. She completed the film in 1944 but the allied victory delayed its release.

After WW II Riefenstahl was imprisoned, first by the Americans, then by the French, for taking an active part in the Nazi propaganda machine and spent nearly four years in various prisons and detention camps. Her vehement denials that she had been Hitler's mistress or devoted admirer were skeptically dismissed. In 1952, after a West German denazification court formally cleared her of charges of Nazi collaboration, which included her witnessing of a massacre of Polish civilians by German troops in 1939, she was able to work again. In 1954 she finally released *Tiefland,* but her repeated efforts to resurrect her career were unsuccessful. She later returned to Africa as a still photographer and subsequently worked in that capacity for various magazines and newspapers, also publishing several books. In 1974 she was honored at the Telluride Film Festival in Colorado and endured a chorus of boos from protesting Holocaust survivors. She wrote a controversial autobiography, *Leni Riefenstahl: A Memoir* (1993), in which she claimed that political ignorance, not sympathy toward the Nazis, lay behind her wartime activities.

FILMS: As actress—*Der heilige Berg/Peaks of Destiny* 1926; *Der grosse Sprung/The Big Leap* 1927; *Die weisse Hölle vom Piz Palü/The White Hell of Pitz Palü, Das Schicksal dere von Habsburg* 1929; *Stürme über dem Mont Blanc/Storms on Mont Blanc/Avalanche* 1930; *Der weisse Rausch/The White Ecstasy/The White Destiny/The Ski Chase* 1931; *SOS Eisberg/SOS Iceberg* 1933. As director—*Das blaue Licht/The Blue Light* (also prod., story, act.) 1932; *Sieg des Glaubens* 1933; *Triumph des Willens/Triumph of the Will, Tag der Freiheit—Unsere Wehrmacht* 1935; *Olympische Spiele/Olympiad/Olympia* (in two parts: *Fest der Völker/Festival of the*

Nations and Fest der Schönheit/Festival of Beauty (also sc.) 1938; *Tiefland* (also prod., sc., phot., act.) 1954.

Riegert, Peter. Actor. Born on Apr. 11, 1947, in New York City. *ed.* U. of Buffalo (English). Pleasant, mild-mannered leading man of stage, TV, and films. He was an English teacher, social worker, and campaign aide to Congresswoman Bella Abzug before starting his acting career off-off Broadway in the early 70s. He later performed with the improvisational comedy group War Babies and made his Broadway debut in the musical 'Dance With Me' (1975). In films since the late 70s, memorably as the oil company rep in *Local Hero* (1983), and as the romantic pickle vendor in *Crossing Delancey* (1988).

FILMS: *National Lampoon's Animal House* 1978; *Head Over Heels/Chilly Scenes of Winter, Americathon* 1979; *National Lampoon Goes to the Movies* 1981; *Local Hero* (UK), *Le Grand Carnaval* (Fr.) 1983; *City Girl* 1984; *Un Homme amoureun/A Man in Love* (Fr./It.), *The Stranger* (Arg./US)) 1987; *Crossing Delancey* 1988; *That's Adequate* 1989; *A Shock to the System, Beyond the Ocean* (It.) 1990; *The Object of Beauty* (US/UK), *Oscar, The Runestone* 1991; *Passed Away* 1992; *The Mask* 1994; *Infinity* 1996.

Riesner, Charles F. See REISNER, Charles F.

rifle mike. A long, narrow directional microphone that can be aimed like a rifle at an isolated sound source.

rifle spot. A cylindrically shaped studio spot lamp which produces a narrow long-range beam of light.

Rigg, Dame Diana. Actress. Born on July 20, 1938, in Doncaster, England. *ed.* RADA. Attractive leading lady who established her reputation in Shakespeare but gained international fame and popularity as the karate-skilled secret agent Emma Peel in TV's action series 'The Avengers' (1965–67 in UK, 1966–68 in US). She later briefly starred in her own TV show, 'Diana' (1973–74).

FILMS: *A Midsummer Night's Dream* (as Helena), *The Assassination Bureau* 1968; *On Her Majesty's Secret Service* 1969; *Julius Caesar* (as Portia) 1970; *The Hospital* (US) 1971; *Theatre of Blood* 1973; *A Little Night Music* (Aus./Ger./US) 1977; *The Great Muppet Caper* 1981; *Evil Under the Sun* 1982; *Snow White* 1989; *A Good Man in Africa* 1994.

riggers. Stage hands who work on the construction of scaffolding (also known as "rigs" or "rails") on a motion picture set.

rigging. 1. The placing of studio lights on a motion picture set at approximate positions in advance of shooting. 2. See CATWALK.

Rilla, Wolf. Director. Born in 1920, in Germany. The son of German actor Walter Rilla (1895–1980), he moved with his family to England in his teens, shortly after the advent of Hitler. He began directing British TV programs and mostly routine films in the early 50s. His single important achievement was *Village of the Damned* (1960), an eerie chiller he skillfully adapted from a John Wyndham novel about weird children taking over a small town. He wrote several books, including *The A–Z of Making Movies* (1970) and *The Writer and the Screen.* Semiretired, he lives in France.

FILMS INCLUDE: *Marilyn, Noose for a Lady* 1953; *End of the Road* 1954; *The Blue Peter* 1955; *Pacific Destiny* 1956; *The Scamp* 1957; *Bachelor of Hearts* 1958; *Witness in the Dark* 1959; *Die zornigen jungen Männer* (Ger.), *Village of the Damned* (also co-sc.), *Piccadilly Third Stop* 1960; *Cairo* (US/UK), *The World Ten Times Over/Pussycat Alley* (also sc.) 1963; *Pax* 1968; *Rosie/Naughty Wives* 1975; *Training Salesmen* (doc.) 1980.

rim light. A light placed behind a subject to produce a halo effect.

Ringwald, Molly. Actress. Born on Feb. 14, 1968, in Sacramento, Calif. Sweet-faced teen star who emerged in the mid-80s, under the guidance of director John HUGHES, as the foremost female member of the Hollywood Brat Pack. The daughter of blind jazz musician Bob Ringwald, she began performing at age four with his Great Pacific Jazz Band and at six recorded an album, 'Molly Sings.' On the legitimate stage from age five, she appeared in plays and TV shows like the 'New Mickey Mouse Club' and the series 'The Facts of Life' (1979–80). In films since 1982, she soon enjoyed a meteoric rise that peaked in 1986, when she made the cover of *Time* magazine. Her box-office appeal receded later in the decade, as she struggled to make the transition to adult roles.

FILMS: *P.K. and the Kid* (release delayed to 1987), *Tempest* 1982; *Spacehunter: Adventures in the Forbidden Zone* 1983; *Sixteen Candles* 1984; *The Breakfast Club* 1985; *Pretty in Pink* 1986; *The Pick-Up Artist, King Lear* (as modern-day Cordelia; US/Switz.) 1987; *For Keeps, Fresh Horses* 1988; *Betsy's Wedding, Strike It Rich* 1990; *Face the Music* 1992; *Tous les Jours Dimanche* (Fr.) 1994; *Malicious* 1995.

Rin Tin Tin. Animal star. *b.* 1916, Germany. *d.* 1932, Hollywood. Handsome German shepherd found in a German trench during WW I by one Captain Lee Duncan, who brought him back to Los Angeles and trained him for a film career. A popular hero of numerous silent features and serials of the 20s, for several years the dog provided Warner Bros. with its main source of revenue. Accordingly, he was given top billing, ahead of his human fellow stars. The scripts for the films—typically mixing drama, comedy, and adventure—were frequently written by Darryl F. ZANUCK. The canine star made a smooth transition to sound, barking vigorously through several early talkies before his death. A successor, Rin Tin Tin, Jr., carried on the heroics through the mid-30s. A fictionalized, satirical biography of Rin Tin Tin, *Won Ton Ton—The Dog Who Saved Hollywood,* was released in 1976. The title role was played by a canine named Augustus von Shumacher.

FILMS INCLUDE: *The Man from Hell's River* 1922; *Where the North Begins* 1923; *Find Your Man* 1924; *Clash of the Wolves* 1925; *The Night Cry, When London Sleeps* 1926; *Dog of the Regiment, Jaws of Steel* 1927; *Rinty of the Desert* 1928; *The Million Dollar Collar, Frozen River, Tiger Rose, The Show of Shows* 1929; *The Lone Defender* (serial), *Rough Waters* 1930; *Lightning Warrior* (serial) 1931.

Ripley, Arthur. Screenwriter, director. *b.* 1895, New York City. *d.* 1961. He began in films at 14 as an apprentice at Kalem and worked his way up to cutter. At 17 he joined Vitagraph as chief cutter and then worked as director of photography at Universal, Fox, and Metro. In 1920 he began directing a version of *Alias Jimmy Valentine* but was replaced by Edward Mortimer, who received sole credit for the completed film. He later became a gag writer for Mack Sennett and by the early 20s was a full-fledged screenwriter. His best material was written late in the silent era, when he contributed stories and screenplays for comedian Harry LANGDON, sometimes in collaboration with Frank CAPRA. He directed a handful of films in spurts from 1938. The best of these was *Voice in the Wind* (1944), a strangely haunting drama about a pianist seeking refuge from Nazi oppression, which Ripley also produced for his own company.

FILMS INCLUDE: As director of photography—*A Celebrated Case* 1914; *Should a Mother Tell?, The Wonderful Adventure* 1915; *The Green-Eyed Monster* (co-phot.) 1916. As screenwriter—*The Third Generation* (co-sc.) 1920; *Life's Darn Funny* (co-sc.) 1921; *A Lady of Quality* 1924; *The Strong Man* (story) 1926; *His First Flame* (co-sc.), *Long Pants* (story), *Three's a Crowd* (story) 1927; *The Chaser* (story), *Heart Trouble* (story) 1928; *Barnum Was Right* (co-sc.) 1929; *Hide-*

Out (co-story, co-sc.), *Captain of the Guard* 1930; *Hypnotized* (story) 1933; *Waterfront* 1939. As director (complete)—*I Met My Love Again* (co-dir. with Joshua Logan) 1938; *Prisoner of Japan* 1942; *Voice in the Wind* (also prod.) 1944; *The Chase* 1946; *Thunder Road* 1958.

riser. A small platform used on a set to, among other things, elevate a prop or an actor who is not as tall as his leading lady.

Risi, Dino. Director, screenwriter. Born on Dec. 23, 1917, in Milan. A doctor's son and himself a former practicing psychiatrist, he showed his initial interest in cinema as a film critic and screenwriter and in the early 40s worked briefly as an assistant director to Mario Soldati and Albert Lattuada. Detained in Switzerland during the late WW II years, he attended film courses given there by Jacques Feyder and upon his return to Italy began directing short documentaries. In the early 50s he gave up his psychiatric practice for good and became a feature director. His specialty is the Neapolitan-style bittersweet humor, casting a cynical, winking eye on unwholesome aspects of life in contemporary Italian society, the rich as well as the poor. An enormously prolific director, he has collaborated on the stories and screenplays of most of his own films, whose robust buffoonery often thinly veils serious social satire. Risi's brother, Nelo Risi (*b.* 1920), was also a film director, who in the early 70s turned to TV. His son, Marco Risi (*b.* June 4, 1951, Milan), is an up-and-coming director. Another son, Claudio Risi, is also in films.

FEATURE FILMS (as director and co-screenwriter): *Vacanze col Gangster* 1952; *Il Viale della Speranza, Amore in Città/Love in the City* ("Paradiso per Quattro Ore" episode) 1953; *Il Segno di Venere/The Sign of Venus, Pane Amore e . . . /Scandal in Sorrento* 1955; *Poveri ma Belli/Poor but Beautiful* 1956; *La Nonna Sabella, Bella ma Povere/Beautiful but Poor* 1957; *Venezia la Luna e Tu* 1958; *Poveri Milionari, Il Vedovo* 1959; *Il Mattatore/Love and Larceny, Un Amore a Roma/L'Inassouvie, A Porte chiuse/Behind Closed Doors* 1960; *Una Vita difficile/A Difficult Life* 1961; *La Marcia su Roma/The March on Rome, Il Sorpasso/The Easy Life,* 1962; *Il Successo* (co-dir., uncredited, with Mauro Morassi), *I Mostri/Opiate '67/15 from Rome, Il Giovedì* 1963; *Il Gaucho* 1964; *Le Bambole/The Dolls* ("La Telefonata" episode), *I Complessi* ("Una Giornata decisiva" episode) 1965; *L'Ombrellone/Weekend Italian Style/Weekend Wives, I Nostri Mariti* ("Il Marito di Attila"/"Nei Secoli fedele" episode), *Operazione San Gennaro/Treasure of San Gennaro* 1966; *Il Tigre/The Tiger and the Pussycat* (It./US), *Il Profeta/The Prophet* 1967; *Straziami ma di Baci Saziami* 1968; *Vedo Nudo, Il Giovane Normale* 1969; *La Moglie del Prete/The Priest's Wife* 1970; *Noi Donne siamo fatte così* 1971; *In Nome del Popolo Italiano* 1972; *Mordi e Fuggi, Sesso Matto/How Funny Can Sex Be?* 1973; *Profumo di Donna/Scent of a Woman* 1974; *Telefoni bianchi/The Career of a Chambermaid* 1975; *Anima persa/Lost Soul/The Forbidden Room* 1976; *La Stanza del Vescovo/The Bishop's Room, I Nuovi Mostri/The New Monsters/Viva Italia* (co-dir. with Mario Monicelli and Ettore Scola) 1977; *Primo Amore/First Love* 1978; *Caro Papà* 1979; *Sono Photogenico, I Seduttori della Domenica/Sunday Lovers* ("Roma" episode; Fr./It./UK) 1980; *Fantasma d'Amore/Ghost of Love* 1981; *Sesso e Volentieri/Sex and Violence* 1982; *Le Bon Roi Dagobert* (Fr./It.) 1984; *Scemo di Guerra/Madman at War* 1985; *Il Commissario lo Gatto, Teresa* 1987; *Tolgo il Disturbo, Come un Bambino* 1990.

Riskin, Robert. Screenwriter, playwright. *b.* 1897, New York City. *d.* 1955. A leading Hollywood scenarist, noted for his association with Frank CAPRA on a succession of compassionate social comedies in the 30s. A writer of original scripts at age 17, Riskin wrote a number of stage plays in the 20s before going on the Columbia payroll in 1931. He won an Academy Award (1934) for *It Happened One Night.* In 1942 he married Fay WRAY.

FILMS INCLUDE: *Illicit* (co-play basis only), *Miracle Woman* (play basis only), *Platinum Blonde* (dial. only), *Men in Her Life* 1931; *American Madness, Night Club Lady, Virtue* 1932; *Ann Carver's Profession* (adapt. from his story), *Lady for a Day* (adapt.) 1933; *It Happened One Night, Broadway Bill* 1934; *Carnival, The Whole Town's Talking* 1935; *Mr. Deeds Goes to Town* 1936; *When You're in Love* (also dir.), *Lost Horizon* 1937; *You Can't Take It with You* 1938; *The Real Glory, They Shall Have Music* (both assoc. prod. only) 1939; *Meet John Doe* 1941; *The Thin Man Goes Home* (also prod.) 1944; *Magic Town* (also prod.) 1947; *Mister 880, Riding High* 1950; *Here Comes the Groom* (story), *Half Angel* 1951; *You Can't Run Away from It* (based on his script for *It Happened One Night*) 1956; *Pocketful of Miracles* (based on *Lady for a Day*) 1961.

Ritchie, Michael. Director. Born on Nov. 28, 1938, in Waukesha, Wis. He received his high school education in Berkeley, where the family moved after his father, a psychology professor, joined the faculty of the University of California. While studying history and literature at Harvard, he began directing school plays. His success with the 1959 premiere production of Arthur Kopit's 'Oh Dad, Poor Dad, Mama's Hung You in the Closet and I'm Feelin' So Sad' led, after his graduation, to a TV job as an assistant director on the 'Omnibus' series. He later became an associate producer and eventually a director on the 'Profiles in Courage' series. After helming segments for such other TV series as 'Man From U.N.C.L.E.,' 'Dr. Kildare,' and 'Felony Squad,' and a two-hour pilot for 'The Outsider' series, he turned out his first feature film, *Downhill Racer,* in 1969. An unflattering portrait of an Olympic skier (Robert Redford), the film boasted daring skiing footage, much of it authentically photographed *cinéma-vérite* style with handheld cameras. Ritchie displayed similar attention to authenticity and detail in his subsequent films, proving himself a superior technician with humor and occasional wit who can advance plot and action with facility and verve. A good storyteller, he has been handicapped by scarcity of stories worth telling.

FILMS: *Downhill Racer* 1969; *Prime Cut, The Candidate* 1972; *Smile* (also prod.) 1975; *The Bad News Bears* 1976; *Semi-Tough* 1977; *The Bad News Bears Go to Japan* (prod. only) 1978; *An Almost Perfect Affair* (also co-story) 1979; *The Island, Divine Madness* (concert film; also prod.) 1980; *The Survivors* 1983; *Fletch* 1985; *Wildcats, The Golden Child* 1986; *The Couch Trip* 1988; *Fletch Lives* 1989; *Diggstown* 1992; *Cops and Robbersons, The Scout* 1994; *A Simple Wish* 1997.

Ritt, Martin. Director. *b.* Mar. 2, 1914, New York City. *d.* 1990. The son of Jewish immigrants, he was raised on Manhattan's Lower East Side, graduated from the DeWitt Clinton High School in the Bronx, and went on to Elon College in North Carolina with an athletic scholarship, where he excelled in football and boxing. He then enrolled as a law student at St. John's University but got sidetracked by a growing passion for drama after befriending Elia KAZAN. Ritt joined Kazan in New York's Group Theater and began a brief career as an actor, appearing in 'Golden Boy' (1937) and other socially conscious Depression-era plays. During his WW II service with the Army Air Force, he appeared in both the stage (1943) and screen (1944) versions of 'Winged Victory' and made his directing debut with an all-GI production of 'Yellow Jack.' After the war he returned to the theater as a director, staging his first Broadway play in 1946. He then turned to the newly emerging TV medium, for which he directed some 150 live dramas and acted in some 100 more between 1948 and 1951. His career then came to a sudden standstill when he was blacklisted for his past Communist affiliation. For six years he made ends meet by performing and directing occasionally for the stage and teaching at the Actors Studio, where his students included such future stars as Paul Newman, Joanne Woodward, Lee Remick, and Rod Steiger.

It was producer David Susskind who resurrected Ritt's career by offering him in 1956 the opportunity to direct his first film. Released early in 1957, *Edge of the City,* adapted from Arthur Alan Arthur's TV play *A Man Is Ten Feet Tall,* was an auspicious debut, a powerfully realistic waterfront drama with racial overtones. The film was prototypical of the best of Ritt's screen work: a sincere concern over social issues and a skill to elicit strong performances from his actors. Although his subsequent films varied in quality, he developed and sustained a reputation as a "thinking" director of serious, worthwhile fare. Of his three films adapted from Faulkner novels or stories, only *The Long Hot Summer* (1958) did justice to the author's sensibility, though it was marred by a studio-imposed happy ending. Notable Ritt films of the 60s included *Paris Blues* (1961), with its memorable jazz score, and *Hud* (1963), a superlative drama of alienated youth in the modern West. It earned Ritt an Academy Award nomination for best director and fetched Oscars for actress Patricia Neal, supporting actor Melvyn Douglas, and cinematographer James Wong Howe. Also much admired were *The Spy Who Came in from the Cold* (1965), considered the best of several realistic spy yarns that flooded the screen at the time, and to a lesser degree *Hombre* (1967), an offbeat Western starring Paul Newman. Standouts among Ritt's films of the 70s were *Sounder* (1972), which offered a compassionate look at the lives of black sharecroppers during the Depression; *The Front* (1976), which viewed Hollywood's blacklisting from a comic perspective; and *Norma Rae* (1979), which earned an Oscar as well as a Cannes Festival best actress award for Sally Field in the role of a textile worker who gradually matures into a champion of the union cause. None of Ritt's films of the 80s were as memorable. In addition to his role in *Winged Victory* (1944), Ritt appeared as an actor in *Der Richter und sein Henker/End of the Game* (Ger., 1975) and *The Slugger's Wife* (1985). He made personal appearances in the documentaries *Hollywood on Trial* (1986) and *50 Years of Action* (1986). In 1985 he was named the first Distinguished Director in Residence at UCLA's College of Fine Arts.

FILMS: *Edge of the City, No Down Payment* 1957; *The Long Hot Summer* 1958; *The Black Orchid, The Sound and the Fury* 1959; *Jovanka e l'Altri/Five Branded Women* (It./Yug.) 1960; *Paris Blues* 1961; *Hemingway's Adventures of a Young Man* 1962; *Hud* (also co-prod.) 1963; *The Outrage* (also exec. prod.) 1964; *The Spy Who Came in from the Cold* (also prod.; UK) 1965; *Hombre* (also co-prod.) 1967; *The Brotherhood* (also exec. prod.) 1968; *The Molly Maguires* (also co-prod.), *The Great White Hope* (also co-exec. prod.) 1970; *Sounder, Pete 'n' Tillie* 1972; *Conrack* (also co-prod.) 1974; *The Front* (also prod.) 1976; *Casey's Shadow* 1978; *Norma Rae* (also co-prod.) 1979; *Back Roads* 1981; *Cross Creek* 1983; *Murphy's Romance* (also co-exec. prod.) 1985; *Nuts* 1987; *Stanley & Iris* 1990.

Ritter, John. Actor. Born on Sept. 17, 1948, in Burbank, Calif. Amiable, light leading man of American TV and films. The son of Western singing star Tex RITTER and actress Dorothy Fay, he majored in psychology at USC but halfway through became involved in school dramatics and after graduation began performing on the stage. He made his film debut in 1971 but his career developed primarily in TV. Following guest roles in several series and a semiregular stint as the Rev. Fordwick on 'The Waltons' (1972–74), he gained popularity (and an Emmy in 1984) as co-star of the TV comedy series 'Three's Company' (1977–84), in the role of Jack Tripper, a young man who feigns homosexuality so that he can share an affordable apartment with two females. He reprised the role in the spin-off series 'Three's a Crowd' (1984–85) and in 1988 starred in 'Hooperman.' His busy TV schedule curtailed his movie career. He married actress Nancy Morgan.

FILMS: *The Barefoot Executive, Scandalous John* 1971; *The Other* 1972; *The Stone Killer* 1973; *Nickelodeon* 1976; *Breakfast in Bed* 1978; *Americathon* 1979; *Hero at Large, Wholly Moses* 1980; *They All Laughed* 1981; *Real Men* 1987; *Skin Deep* 1989; *Problem Child* 1990; *Problem Child 2* 1991; *Noises Off, Stay Tuned* 1992; *North* 1994; *Sling Blade* 1996; *Nowhere* 1997.

Ritter, Tex. Actor, singer. *b.* Woodward Maurice Ritter, Jan. 12, 1905, near Murvaul, Tex. *d.* 1974. Cowboy star, Grand Ole Opry headliner, recording artist, and folk hero, and the only entertainer to be elected to both the Cowboy Hall of Fame and the Country Music Hall of Fame. He became interested in cowboy ballads and Southwest folklore while studying political science at the University of Texas, and dropped out of Northwestern University's law school to begin a folksinging career on radio and the stage. In 1930 he landed his first part on Broadway and in 1936 made his debut in films. His popularity with moviegoers was instantaneous, rivaling that of Gene Autry, as the screen's top singing cowboy, and at the peak of his career, in the early 40s, he was often labeled "America's Most Beloved Cowboy." Later in the decade, with his film popularity on the ebb, Ritter took to the road with his horse, White Flash, starring in coast-to-coast live shows. At the same time he continued his lucrative recording career, most notably with the title song of *High Noon,* which he recorded for the film. In 1970 he made an unsuccessful bid for the Republican nomination for US Senator from Tennessee. He was married to actress Dorothy Fay. Their son is actor John RITTER, in films since 1971 and the star of TV's popular 'Three's Company.'

FILMS INCLUDE: *Song of the Gringo* 1936; *Trouble in Texas, Sing Cowboy Sing, Mystery of the Hooded Horsemen* 1937; *Frontier Town, Starlight Over Texas, Where the Buffalo Roam* 1938; *Song of the Buckaroo, Sundown on the Prairie* 1939; *The Cowboy from Sundown, Rainbow Over the Range* 1940; *King of Dodge City, Roaring Frontiers* 1941; *Deep in the Heart of Texas, The Old Chisholm Trail* 1942; *Frontier Badmen, Arizona Trail* 1943; *Marshall of Gunsmoke, Dead or Alive* 1944; *Enemy of the Law, Frontier Bullets* 1945; *Holiday Rhythm* (cameo) 1950; *Apache Ambush* (cameo) 1955; *The Girl from Tobacco Row* 1966; *What Am I Bid?* (cameo) 1967.

Ritter, Thelma. Actress. *b.* Feb. 14, 1905, Brooklyn, N.Y. *d.* 1969. Excellent character actress of Hollywood films, typically in cynical, wisecracking, disarmingly outspoken roles. She entered films in the late 40s after many unrewarding years on the stage and was nominated for an Academy Award six times within a span of just 12 years (nomination marked "AAN" below).

FILMS: *Miracle on 34th Street* 1947; *Call Northside 777* 1948; *A Letter to Three Wives, City Across the River, Father Was a Fullback* 1949; *Perfect Strangers, All About Eve* (AAN), *I'll Get By* 1950; *The Mating Season* (AAN), *As Young As You Feel, The Model and the Marriage Broker* 1951; *With a Song in My Heart* (AAN) 1952; *Titanic, The Farmer Takes a Wife, Pickup on South Street* (AAN) 1953; *Rear Window* 1954; *Daddy Long Legs, Lucy Gallant* 1955; *The Proud and the Profane* 1956; *A Hole in the Head, Pillow Talk* (AAN) 1959; *The Misfits, The Second Time Around* 1961; *Birdman of Alcatraz* (AAN), *How the West Was Won* 1962; *For Love or Money, A New Kind of*

Love, Move Over Darling 1963; *Boeing Boeing* 1965; *The Incident* 1967; *What's So Bad About Feeling Good?* 1968.

Ritz Brothers, The. Zany comic trio whose clowning, dancing, and singing enlivened light Hollywood films of the late 30s and early 40s. The sons of Max Joachim, a haberdasher from Austria, they were all born in Newark, N.J.: Al on Aug. 27, 1901 (*d.* 1965), Jim on Oct. 5, 1903 (*d.* 1985), and Harry on May 22, 1906 (*d.* 1986). They were raised in Brooklyn, N.Y., where they attended high school and entertained early dreams of a career in show business. Al, who won an amateur contest as a child, was the first to enter vaudeville, as a dancer. The others followed as they graduated from high school, but pursued separate careers until 1925, when they first appeared as a team in Coney Island, with a fourth brother, George, acting as their manager. Before long, they became a top attraction in vaudeville, in nightclubs, and on the musical stage, and appeared regularly in the various editions of 'Earl Carroll's Vanities.' In 1934 they made their first film, the Al Christie short *Hotel Anchovy* (Al had appeared as an extra in a 1918 silent feature, *The Avenging Trail*). They were then signed by Fox and for four years provided many entertaining moments with their comic antics and musical routines in some of the studio's lesser musical films. They lacked the anarchic abandon and the comic brilliance of the Marx Brothers but in their own way proved a successful team and for a while were quite popular with the public, if not with most critics. They ended their association with Fox in 1939 and, after making four low-budget Universal features, retired from the screen in 1943. They continued appearing, however, in nightclubs, and later occasionally on TV. A successful comeback in major night spots ended abruptly with Al's death in 1965. Harry and Jim made cameo appearances in *Blazing Stewardesses* (1975) and *Won Ton Ton* (1976). Harry alone appeared in *Silent Movie* (1976).

FEATURE FILMS: *The Avenging Trail* (Al only, in bit) 1918; *Sing Baby Sing* 1936; *One in a Million, On the Avenue, You Can't Have Everything, Life Begins in College* 1937; *The Goldwyn Follies, Kentucky Moonshine, Straight Place and Show* 1938; *The Three Musketeers, The Gorilla, Pack Up Your Troubles* 1939; *Argentine Nights* 1940; *Behind the Eight Ball* 1942; *Hi' Ya Chum, Never a Dull Moment* 1943; *Blazing Stewardesses* (Harry and Jim only) 1975; *Won Ton Ton—The Dog Who Saved Hollywood* (Harry and Jim only), *Silent Movie* (Harry only) 1976.

Riva, Emmanuelle. Actress. Born on Feb. 24, 1927, in Chénimenil (Vosges), France. A former dressmaker, she went on the Paris stage in 1954. Four years later she made a memorable screen debut in Alain Resnais's *Hiroshima mon Amour.* Other important film roles followed.

FILMS INCLUDE: *Hiroshima mon Amour* 1958; *Le Huitième Jour/The Eighth Day* 1959; *Recours en Grâce, Kapo* (It./Fr./Yug.), *Adua e le Compagne/Love à la Carte* (It.) 1960; *Climats, Léon Morin—Prêtre* 1961; *Thérèse Desqueyroux/Thérèse* (title role) 1962; *Le Ore dell'Amore/The Hours of Love* (It.), *Le Gros Coup* 1963; *Le Coup de Grâce, Thomas L'Imposteur/Thomas the Imposter* 1965; *Les Fruits amers* 1966; *Les Risques du Métier* 1967; *L'Homme de Désir, La Modification* 1970; *Les Portes de Feu* 1972; *Le Diable au Coeur* 1976; *Gli Occhi la Bocca/The Eyes The Mouth* (It./Fr.) 1982; *Un Homme à Mataille* 1983; *Liberté la Nuit* 1984; *Funny Boy* 1987; *Niezwykla Balthazara Kobera/Les Tribulations de Balthasar Kober* (Pol/Fr.) 1988; *Pour Sacha* 1991; *Blue* 1993.

Rivette, Jacques. Director. Born on Mar. 1, 1928, in Rouen, France. Controversial filmmaker of the French New Wave whose few, unorthodox films have baffled or bored some critics and fascinated others. A former staff critic of *Cahiers du Cinéma,* he began as an assistant to Renoir and Becker, was a cameraman on 16 mm shorts of Truffaut and Rohmer, and himself directed several shorts before turning out his first feature-length film, *Paris nous appartient/Paris Belongs to Us,* in 1960. With the exception of *La Religieuse/The Nun* (1965), an adaptation from a novel by Diderot which conformed with such commercial film conventions as plot and continuity, and the complex but accessible *Celine and Julie Go Boating* (1974), Rivette's films have typically shunned the traditions of cinema. *L'Amour Fou* (1968), for example, was over four hours long and mixed 35 and 16 mm footage with little regard for technical quality. *Out One,* originally made in 1971 but never released, was nearly 13 hours long. An abridged version, *Out One: Specter* (1973), ran over four hours. Much of what goes on before the camera is left to intuition, to actors' improvisation, or simply to chance, and the film medium itself seems at certain moments to become Rivette's message. Rivette, who was served as editor-in-chief of *Cahiers du Cinéma* from 1963 to 1965, is the only New Wave director, with the possible exception of Jean-Luc Godard, who remained tenaciously faithful to the movement's stated principles, an uncompromising filmmaker with an unwavering personal vision. He was awarded a Special Mention and the International Critics Prize at the 1989 Berlin Film Festival for *La Bande des Quatre.*

FILMS: (as director and co-screenwriter) *Aux Quatre Coins* (short), *Le Quadrille* (short) 1950; *Le Divertissement* (short) 1952; *Le Coup du Berger* (short) 1956; *Paris nous appartient/Paris Belongs to Us/Paris Is Ours* (also act.) 1961; *La Religieuse/Suzanne Simonin La Religieuse de Denis Diderot/The Nun* (release delayed), *Jean Renoir le Patron/Jean Renoir—The Boss* (TV doc.) 1967; *L'Amour fou* 1968; *Out One: Noli me tangere* (for TV; never released) 1971; *Out One: Spectre/Out One Out Two, Céline et Julie vont en Bateau/Celine and Julie Go Boating* 1974; *Duelle/Twilight* 1976; *Noroft/Northwest* 1977; *Merry-Go-Round* (release delayed to 1983) 1978; *Paris s'en va* (unreleased) 1980; *Le Pont du Nord/North Bridge* 1982; *L'Amour par Terre/Love on the Ground* 1984; *Hurlevent/Wuthering Heights* 1985; *La Bande des Quatre/The Gang of Four* 1989; *La Belle Noiseuse* 1991; *Jeanne le Pucelle* 1994; *Up/Down/Fragile* 1997.

RKO. A motion picture production company with a highly complex corporate history. Its beginnings can be traced back to a single Milwaukee nickelodeon that opened its doors in 1909. Through a series of expansions and mergers the business became the nucleus of the Mutual Film Corporation, a major production and distribution concern before the end of WW I. The company underwent a succession of additional mergers, acquisitions, and other corporate transformations until, in 1928, it emerged as Radio-Keith-Orpheum, or RKO, a wide-ranging enterprise with production, distribution, and exhibition arms. In 1933 the parent company went into receivership but its subsidiaries, including the RKO Pictures Corporation, were not affected and production proceeded as normal. However, the financial position of the company remained shaky and despite a good number of distinguished productions, it never shared the relative stability of Hollywood's major studios.

Among its prestigious films in the 30s and early 40s were the Astaire-Rogers musicals, a cycle of high-quality horror pictures, comedies starring Katharine Hepburn and Cary Grant, and such individual productions as Hitchcock's *Suspicion* and Welles's *Citizen Kane.* In 1948, after mystery multimillionaire Howard Hughes acquired a controlling interest in RKO, a period of confusion ensued during which many key employees left the company and production dwindled to a trickle. In the early 50s, a group of stockholders brought suit against Hughes for his handling of the company's affairs. The litigation was settled out of court when Hughes purchased all the outstanding shares of RKO at double the market price. The following year he sold the entire assets of the company to a subsidiary of General Tire at a considerable profit. The corporate name was changed to RKO General and the company abandoned the motion picture field in favor of broadcasting and cable TV. The RKO Hollywood studios had been acquired by Desilu in 1953.

Surviving as a corporation, RKO resumed limited feature production in the 80s. In 1989 majority control of the company was acquired by Pavilion Communications, a production and development outfit co-owned by Dina MERRILL. In the 1980s, the rights to some of the RKO film library were acquired by media mogul Ted TURNER.

Roach, Hal. Producer, director, screenwriter. *b.* Jan. 14, 1892, in Elmira, N.Y. *d.* 1992. He drifted into films as a bit player in 1912, following a colorful variety of odd occupations ranging from mule skinning to Alaska gold prospecting. He began his film career at Universal as a stuntman, extra, and minor actor in Westerns and action pictures. At the studio he met another bit player, Harold LLOYD, whom he thought had potential as a comedy star. They kept in touch after they both left Universal, and when Roach inherited $3,000 and formed his own company, early in 1915, he hired Lloyd to play a character called Willie Work in a proposed series of comedy shorts. But Roach found no market for his product and when his money ran out he went to work for Essanay as a director, while Lloyd tried his luck at Mack Sennett's Keystone. Within several months, however, Roach found a sponsor and a distributor in Pathé, formed the Rolin Film Company (named for the first letters of Roach's and his partner Dan Linthicum's names), and recalled Lloyd from Keystone. Lloyd's screen character was changed from Willie Work to Lonesome Luke and his comedy series was titled "Phun-Philms." Roach himself directed many of the films in the series and gradually turned Lloyd from a Chaplin imitator into a comedy star in his own right.

In contrast to that of his rival, Mack Sennett, the Roach comedy formula emphasized story and structure over visual gags. Consequently, his product proved much more acceptable to an increasingly sophisticated cinema audience in the 20s and 30s. While Sennett declined, Roach prospered. By the early 20s, he was devoting less and less of his time to directing and more and more to the organization of his growing company and the supervision of its increasing output. His stable of talent rapidly expanded to include such comedy stars as Harry "Snub" Pollard, Will Rogers, Charlie Chase, Edgar Kennedy, and the inimitable Laurel and Hardy. He entrusted their direction to such gifted men as Fred Newmeyer, Sam Taylor, Fred Guiol, and the incomparable Leo McCarey. However, Roach continued to direct from time to time and participated in the scripting and gag-writing of many of his films.

Blessed with an extraordinary sense of taste trends, Roach diversified his product in the 20s to include feature films, dramas as well as comedies, Westerns, and action pictures. He then began a process of weeding out his least profitable series and by the late 20s was concentrating on developing his three major attractions—Laurel and Hardy, Charlie Chase, and the "Our Gang" comedies, which were swiftly becoming very popular. He managed to accomplish a relatively smooth transition to sound and in the early 30s he introduced to the market a variety of new comedy shorts, including "The Boy Friends," the "All-Star Comedies," the "Hal Roach Musicals," and the famous Thelma Todd-ZaSu Pitts comedy series. His vast product was released and distributed by MGM, and he won Oscars for two of his shorts, *The Music Box* (1932) and *Bored of Education* (1936). By the mid-30s Roach realized that two-reel shorts were being edged out of the market by the increasing popularity of second features on a double-feature bill, so he gradually shifted to feature production. In 1938 he sold the rights to Our Gang to MGM and set up a distribution arrangement with United Artists for his feature films.

Working in close collaboration with his son, Hal Roach, Jr. (*b.* 1921, Los Angeles; *d.* 1972), Roach enjoyed renewed prosperity with his features, many of which enjoyed commercial success. He also directed some of these, including *One Million B.C.*, which he originally assigned to D. W. Griffith. The most important film he produced during this period was *Of Mice and Men.* During WW II Colonel Hal Roach produced propaganda and training films for the Army and the Air Force. After returning to Hollywood, he switched from motion pictures to television production. Alternating between success and failure in the new medium, the Roach company folded in the late 50s. Its studio was physically demolished in 1963 and the site turned into an automobile showroom. In the late 60s Roach came out of retirement to produce the successful compilation film, *The Crazy World of Laurel and Hardy.* He was a robust 92 when he received an Honorary Academy Award during the 1984 Oscar ceremonies. He was still up and about on his 100th birthday in January of 1992, actively promoting the colorized version of the Laurel and Hardy classic *Way Out West* and traveling coast to coast and between London and Paris to attend numerous salutes to his century of achievements. He died later that year.

FILMS INCLUDE: As producer-director—*Just Nuts, Lonesome Luke* 1915; *Lonesome Luke's Movie Muddle* 1916; *Lonesome Luke on Tin Can Alley, All Aboard, The Flirt* 1917; *Fireman Save My Child, Pipe the Whiskers* 1918; *Bumping into Broadway, Captain Kidd's Kids, From Hand to Mouth, His Royal Slyness* 1919; *Haunted Spooks, An Eastern Westerner, High and Dizzy, Get Out and Get Under, Number Please* 1920. As producer—*Now or Never, Among Those Present, I Do, Never Weaken, A Sailor-Made Man* (also co-story) 1921; *White Wings, Grandma's Boy* (also co-story), *Doctor Jack* (also co-story), *Our Gang, Young Sherlocks* 1922; *Safety Last* (also co-story), *Why Worry?, The Call of the Wild, Uncensored Movies* 1923; *All Wet, The Battling Orioles* (also story), *The King of Wild Horses* (also story), *Jubilo Jr., The White Sheik* (also dir., sc.), *A Truthful Liar* 1924; *Bad Boy, Innocent Husbands, Black Cyclone* (also story) 1925; *The Devil Horse* (also story), *45 Minutes from Hollywood, Mighty Like a Moose* 1926; *Slipping Wives, No Man's Law, The Second Hundred Years, Putting Pants on Philip, The Battle of the Century* (also story) 1927; *Leave 'Em Laughing* (also story), *You're Darn Tootin', Two Tars, Early to Bed* 1928; *Liberty, Big Business, Double Whoopee, Perfect Day* (also co-story) 1929; *Men of the North* (also dir.), *Brats* (also co-story), *Hog Wild, The Laurel-Hardy Murder Case, Another Fine Mess* 1930; *Be Big, Pardon Us, Our Wife* 1931; *Helpmates, The Music Box, On the Loose, Pack Up Your Troubles, Their First Mistake, Towed in a Hole* 1932; *Fra Diavolo/The Devil's Brother* (also co-dir. with Charles Rogers), *Busy Bodies, Sons of the Desert* 1933; *Babes in Toyland* 1934; *Tit for Tat, Bonnie Scotland* 1935; *The Bohemian Girl, General Spanky, Bored of Education, Our Relations* 1936; *Nobody's Baby, Way Out West, Topper* 1937; *Merrily We Live* (exec. prod.), *Swiss Miss, Block-Heads, There Goes My Heart* 1938; *Captain Fury* (also dir.), *The Housekeeper's Daughter* (also dir.), *Of Mice and Men, Topper Takes a Trip, Zenobia* 1939; *One Million B.C.* (also co-dir. with Hal Roach, Jr.), *Turnabout* (also dir.), *A Chump at Oxford, Saps at Sea* 1940; *Road Show* (also dir.), *Topper Returns, Broadway Limited, Tanks a Million* 1941; *The Devil with Hitler* (co-prod.) 1944; *One Million Years B.C.* (remake; assoc. prod.; UK) 1966; *The Crazy World of Laurel and Hardy* (compilation film) 1967.

road show. In motion picture industry terms, a special release of a film for exhibition at a prestigious theater, usually on a reserved-seat basis and at a hiked admission price.

Robards, Jason. Actor. *b.* Dec. 31, 1892, Hillsdale, Mich. *d.* 1963. *ed.* AADA. A prominent actor of the American stage, he also appeared in more than 100 Hollywood films. He played starring roles in many silents, typically as an innocent rural hero, graduating to character roles after the advent of sound, often as a villain. He was the father of Jason ROBARDS, Jr.

FILMS INCLUDE: *The Gilded Lily, The Land of Hope* 1921; *Stella Maris* 1925; *Footloose Widows, The Cohens and Kellys, The Third Degree* 1926; *Hills of Kentucky, White Flannels, Irish Hearts, The Heart of Maryland, Jaws of Steel, Polly of the Movies, Wild Geese, Streets of Shanghai, Casey Jones* 1927; *On Trial* 1928; *Some Mother's Boy, Trial Marriage, The Gamblers, Paris, The Isle of Lost Ships* 1929; *Peacock Alley, The Last Dance, Abraham Lincoln* (as William Herndon, Lincoln's law partner), *Sisters, Lightnin', The Jazz Cinderella* 1930; *Charlie Chan Carries On, Subway Express, Salvation Nell* 1931; *Docks of San Francisco* 1932; *Corruption, Devil's Mate, Dance Hall Hostess* 1933; *Burn 'Em Up Barnes* (serial), *Broadway Bill, All of Me, The President Vanishes* 1934; *Ladies Crave Excitement, The Crusades* 1935; *The White Legion* 1936; *Damaged Lives* 1937; *Juarez and Maximilian/The Mad Empress* (as Juarez; Mex.) 1939; *The Master Race* 1944; *A Game of Death* 1945; *The Falcon's Alibi, Bedlam* 1946; *Riff-Raff, Seven Keys to Baldpate* 1947; *Mr. Blandings Builds His Dream House* 1948; *Impact* 1949; *The Second Woman* 1951; *Wild in the Country* 1961.

Robards, Jason, Jr. Actor. Born on July 22, 1922, in Chicago. The son of Jason ROBARDS, he served seven years in the Navy, was in the Pearl Harbor attack, and received the Navy Cross before coming to New York in search of a stage career. Settling in Greenwich Village, he drove a cab and taught school in between minor stage engagements and roles in radio soap operas and live TV dramas. After years of obscurity, he gained sudden recognition in the Circle in the Square production of O'Neill's 'The Iceman Cometh,' in 1956. The following year he won a New York Drama Critics Award for 'Long Day's Journey into Night' and has since remained a Broadway favorite. His concurrent TV and film career has been equally rewarding. Robards is especially effective in soul-searching roles. He won two successive Oscars as best supporting actor, for his work in *All the President's Men* (1976, as Washington *Post* editor Ben Bradlee) and *Julia* (1977, as novelist Dashiell Hammett) and was nominated for another for his portrayal of Howard Hughes in *Melvin and Howard* (1980). Robards's first marriage (1948–58) to actress Eleanor Pitman produced three children, including actor Jason III (*b.* 1948); his third (1961–69), to movie star Lauren BACALL, produced actor Sam Robards (*b.* Dec. 16, 1961). He has two more children from his fourth marriage (from 1970) to actress Lois O'Connor. Some time after his father's death, he dropped Jr. from his name, and has since been billed as Jason Robards.

FILMS: *The Journey* 1959; *By Love Possessed* 1961; *Tender Is The Night* (as Dick Diver), *Long Day's Journey Into Night* (as Jamie Tyrone) 1962; *Act One* (as George S. Kaufman) 1963; *A Thousand Clowns* 1965; *A Big Hand for the Little Lady, Any Wednesday* 1966; *Divorce American Style, The St. Valentine's Day Massacre* (as Al Capone), *Hour of the Gun* (as Doc Holliday) 1967; *The Night They Raided Minsky's, C'era una Volta/Once Upon a Time in the West* (It./US), *Isadora/The Loves of Isadora* (UK) 1968; *Rosolino Paterno—Soldato/Situation Normal All Fouled Up/Operation Snafu* (It.), *Julius Caesar* (as Brutus; UK), *The Ballad of Cable Hogue, Tora! Tora! Tora!* (US/Jap.), *Fools* 1970; *Johnny Got His Gun, Jud, Murders in the Rue Morgue* 1971; *The War Between Men and Women* 1972; *Tod eines Fremden/Death of a Stranger* (Isr./Ger.), *Pat Garrett and Billy the Kid* (as Governor Lew Wallace of New Mexico, who authored *Ben-Hur*) 1973; *Mr. Sycamore* 1975; *A Boy and His Dog, All the President's Men* (as Ben Bradlee, managing editor of the Washington *Post*) 1976; *Julia* (as author Dashiell Hammett) 1977; *Comes a Horseman* 1978; *Hurricane* 1979; *Raise the Titanic!, Melvin and Howard* (as Howard Hughes) 1980; *Caboblanco, The Legend of the Lone Ranger* (as President Grant) 1980; *Burden of Dreams* (doc.) 1982; *Max Dugan Returns, Something Wicked This Way Comes* 1983; *Square Dance* 1987; *Bright Lights Big City, The Good Mother* 1988; *Dream a Little Dream, Reunion/L'Ami retrouvé* (Ger./Fr./UK), *Parenthood, Black Rainbow* (UK/US) 1989; *Quick Change* 1990; *Storyville* 1992; *The Adventures of Huck Finn, Philadelphia, The Trial* (UK) 1993; *Crimson Tide* (unbilled cameo), *Little Big League, The Paper* 1994; *A Thousand Acres* 1997.

Robbe-Grillet, Alain. Novelist, director, screenwriter. Born on Aug. 18, 1922, in Brest, France. Trained as an agricultural engineer, he turned to writing and became a leading figure in the *Nouveau Roman* school of French letters. His literary style is a reflection of his thesis (he calls it *chosisme*) that the physical world is the only true reality and that the only way to approach concepts, including memory, is through physical objects and not through consciousness. He made his first attempt to translate his literary style to the screen with his script for Alain Resnais's *Last Year at Marienbad,* a film replete with Bergsonian and Proustian idioms. Encouraged by the results, he turned to directing his own films. Like his books, Robbe-Grillet's films are structurally unconventional and thematically irreverent. Several contained violently erotic images that some audiences have found offensive and disturbing. In 1989 he taught film and literature for a semester at NYU. During that period, a retrospective of his films was shown in Manhattan.

FILMS: As screenwriter—*L'Année dernière à Marienbad/Last Year at Marienbad* 1961. As director-screenwriter—*L'Immortelle* 1963; *Trans-Europe Express* (also act.) 1967; *L'Homme qui ment/The Man Who Lies* (Fr./Czech.) 1968; *L'Eden et après/Eden and Afterwards* (Fr./Czech./Tunis.) 1971; *N a pris les Dés/N Took the Dice* (release delayed) 1972; *Glissements progressifs du Plaisir/Progressive Slidings Into Pleasure* 1974; *Giocare col Fuoco/Le Jeu avec le Feu/Playing with Fire* (It./Fr.) 1975; *La Belle Captive/The Beautiful Prisoner* 1983; *Taxandria* (sc. only; Ger.) 1990; *The Blue Villa, Un Bruit Qui Rend Fou* 1994.

Robbins, Jerome. Choreographer, director. Born Jerome Rabinowitz, on Oct. 11, 1918, in Weehawken, N.J. A former dancer, he has created many inventive, exhilarating ballets and musical numbers for the stage and directed a growing list of successful Broadway plays. For films, he choreographed *The King and I* (1956) and choreographed and co-directed *West Side Story* (1961), sharing an Academy Award with Robert Wise for directing the latter. His 1944 ballet *Fancy Free* inspired 'On the Town' (1949) and his choreography for Broadway's 'Gypsy' was adapted for the 1963 film version. More recently, his choreography for the stage musical 'Fiddler on the Roof' provided the basis for the dance numbers in the 1971 film. In 1972 he became joint ballet master of the New York City Ballet. A musical celebrating his past contributions, 'Jerome Robbins' Broadway,' opened in New York in 1989.

Robbins, Matthew. American director, screenwriter. A graduate of the US film school, he wrote several successful screenplays in collaboration with Hal Barwood, before becoming a director in the late 70s.

FILMS: *The Sugarland Express* (co-sc.) 1974; *The Bingo Long Traveling All-Stars & Motor Kings* (co-sc.) 1976; *MacArthur* (co-sc.) 1977; *Corvette Summer* (dir., co-sc.) 1978; *Dragonslayer* (dir., co-sc.) 1981; *The Legend of Billie Jean* (dir.), *Warning Sign* (co-sc.) 1985; *Batteries Not Included* (dir., co-sc.) 1987; *Bingo* (dir.) 1991.

Robbins, Tim. Actor. Born on Oct. 16, 1958, in West Covina, Calif. Tall (6' 4"), offbeat character lead of the American stage and screen. The son of Greenwich Village folk singer Gill Robbins, he joined a New York experimental theater at age 12 and continued performing on the stage while attending high school. Midway through drama studies at the State University of New York at Plattsburgh, he transferred to the UCLA theater program. He was among the founders in 1981 of L.A.'s The Actors Gang, of which he later became the artistic director. He scored a success as co-writer and director of that company's play, 'Carnage.' On the screen since 1984, he has displayed talent and versatility in a wide range of roles, memorably in *Bull Durham* (1988) and in Robert ALTMAN'S *The Player* (1992); together, the two made him a star. Later in 1992 he debuted as a director with *Bob Roberts,* a mock documentary about a right-wing businessman/folk singer who becomes a national hero and runs for the Senate. His talent as a director was fully realized with the release of *Dead Man Walking* (1995), a gutsy, riveting look into the life of a convicted killer on death row through the eyes of a nun, earning Robbins an Oscar nomination as best director. He lives with longtime companion actress Susan SARANDON and their family.

FILMS: *Toy Soldiers, No Small Affair* 1984; *Fraternity Vacation, The Sure Thing* 1985; *Top Gun, Howard the Duck* 1986; *Five Corners, Bull Durham, Tapeheads* (also co-songs) 1988; *Miss Firecracker, Erik the Viking* (title role; UK/Sw.) 1989; *Cadillac Man, Jacob's Ladder* 1990; *The Player, Bob Roberts* (also dir., sc.) 1992; *Short Cuts* 1993; *The Hudsucker Proxy, I.Q., Ready to Wear, The Shawshank Redemption* 1994; *Dead Man Walking* (dir. only) 1995; *Nothing to Lose* 1997.

Robert, Yves. Actor, director. Born on June 19, 1920, in Saumur, France. He tried a wide variety of occupations before deciding on an acting career, making his stage debut in 1942 and his first screen appearance in 1949. Before long he was established as a popular light leading man and supporting player, typically in bright, pleasant roles. In 1951 he directed his first film, a short, and in 1954 his first feature. In the following years he pursued dual careers as both an actor and a director. In 1956 he married actress Danièle DELORME. Together they formed the La Gueville production company, scoring a critical and commercial hit with the company's first film, *La Guerre des Boutons/War of the Buttons* (1962), which Robert also directed and co-scripted. He has since produced and directed a number of other box-office hits. His 1990 pair of films, *My Father's Glory* and *My Mother's Castle,* both adapted from Marcel Pagnol's memoirs, shared first-place honors in audience voting at the 1991 Seattle Film Festival.

FILMS INCLUDE: As actor—*Les Dieux du Dimanche* 1949; *Trois Télégrammes* 1950; *La Rose rouge, Juliette ou la Clé des Songes* 1951; *Suivez cet Homme* 1953; *Virgile* 1954; *Futures Vedettes, Les Grandes Manoeuvres/The Grand Maneuver, Les Mauvaises Rencontres* 1955; *Les Truands* 1956; *Folies Bergère* 1957; *Les Femmes sont marrantes* 1958; *La Jument verte/The Green Mare* 1959; *La Française et l'Amour/Love and the Frenchwoman* 1960; *La Morte de Belle/The Passion of Slow Fire* 1961; *Cléo de 5 à 7/Cleo from 5 to 7* 1962; *Le Pistonné/The Man with Connections, Le Voyou/The Crook* 1970; *Le Cinéma de Papa* 1971; *Le Viager, Chère Louise, Absences répétées* 1972; *La Raison du plus Fou* 1973; *Section speciale/Special Section* 1975; *Le Juge et l'Assassin/The Judge and the Assassin* 1976; *Il sont Grands ces Petits* 1979; *Un Mauvais Fils* 1980; *Vive la Sociale* 1983; *Billy-Ze-Kick* 1985; *Le Debutant* 1986; *Cher Frangin, Le Crime D'Antoine* 1989. As director (complete)—*Les Bonnes Manières* (short) 1951; *Les Hommes ne pensent qu'à ca* 1954; *Ni vu ni connu* (also co-sc.) 1958; *Signé Arsène Lupin* (also co-adapt., act.) 1959; *La Famille Fenouillard* (also co-sc.) 1961; *La Guerre des Boutons/War of the Buttons* (also co-prod., co-sc.) 1962; *Bébert et l'Omnibus* (also co-prod.) 1963; *Les Copains* (also co-prod.) 1964; *Monnaie de Singe* (also co-prod., co-sc.) 1965; *Alexandre le Bienheureux/Very Happy Alexander/Alexander* (also co-prod., co-sc. from his own story) 1968; *Clérambard* (also co-prod., co-sc.) 1969; *Le Grand Blond avec une Chaussure noire/The Tall Blond Man with One Black Shoe* (also co-prod., co-sc., act. in bit) 1972; *Salue l'Artiste* (also co-prod., co-sc.) 1973; *Le Retour du Grand Blond/The Return of the Tall Blond Man with One Black Shoe* (also co-prod., co-sc.) 1974; *Un Eléphant ça trompe énormément/Pardon mon Affaire* (also co-prod., co-sc.) 1976; *Nous irons tous au Paradis* (also co-prod., co-story, co-sc.) 1977; *Courage Fuyons* (also co-prod., co-sc.) 1979; *Le Jumeau* (also co-prod., co-sc.) 1984; *La Gloire de mon Père/My Father's Glory* (also co-sc.), *Le Château de ma Mère/My Mother's Castle* (also co-sc.) 1990; *Le Bal des Casse-Pieds* 1992; *Montparnasse Pondichery* 1994.

Roberti, Lyda. Actress, singer. *b.* May 20, 1906, Warsaw. *d.* 1938. Platinum-blonde leading lady of light Hollywood films of the 30s. The daughter of a circus clown, she accompanied her father on his global tours, appearing as a trapeze artist from early childhood. Upon arriving in the US, she appeared in vaudeville and on Broadway before making her screen debut in 1932. At her best in exuberant, uninhibited, man-chasing comedy roles. She died suddenly of a heart attack after appearing in only 11 feature films and several shorts.

FEATURE FILMS: *Dancers in the Dark, Million Dollar Legs, The Kid from Spain* 1932; *Three-Cornered Moon, Torch Singer* 1933; *College Rhythm* 1934; *George White's 1935 Scandals, The Big Broadcast of 1936* 1935; *Nobody's Baby, Pick a Star* 1937; *Wide Open Faces* 1938.

Roberts, Bart. See REASON, Rex.

Roberts, Eric. Actor. Born on Apr. 18, 1956, in Biloxi, Miss. Intense, gifted leading man of the American stage and screen. The son of Walter Roberts, a drama teacher who founded the Actors and Writers Workshop in Atlanta, he began performing on the stage at age five. At 17 he went to London for two years of training at the Royal Academy of Dramatic Art, then continued his studies at the American Academy before resuming his stage career as a young adult. On the screen since the late 70s, he suffered an early setback because of a car crash, but soon established himself as a talented actor, capable of a wide emotional range. He starred on Broadway in 1989's 'Burn This,' and was nominated for an Oscar as best supporting actor for *Runaway Train* (1985). His younger sister is actress Julia ROBERTS.

FILMS INCLUDE: *King of the Gypsies* 1978; *Raggedy Man* 1981; *Star 80* 1983; *The Pope of Greenwich Village* 1984; *The Coca Cola Kid* (Austral.), *Runaway Train* 1985; *Nobody's Fool* 1986; *Dear America: Letters Home from Vietnam* (doc.; co-narrator) 1987; *Options, Rude Awakening, Blood Red, Best of the Best* 1989; *The Ambulance* 1990; *Lonely Hearts* 1991; *Final Analysis* 1992; *Best of the Best 2, By the Sword* 1993; *Baby Fever, The Specialist* 1994; *Heaven's Prisoners, It's My Party* 1996; *American Strays* 1997.

Roberts, Julia. Actress. Born on Oct. 28, 1967, in Smyrna, Ga. Tall, willowy star of Hollywood films. The younger sister of Eric ROBERTS, she began acting in her teens, at her parents' theater workshop in Atlanta. A soft, all-American beauty, her film career took off meteorically within a year of her 1988 screen debut. She was nominated for Academy Awards as best supporting actress for her role as Sally Fields's troubled diabetic daughter in *Steel Magnolias* (1989) and as best actress for *Pretty Woman* (1990), in which she was perfectly cast as a kooky hooker with a strong business sensibility. Much newsprint has been devoted to her romantic escapades, including the last-minute cancellation of her 1991 wedding to actor Kiefer SUTHERLAND and her subsequent affair with actor Jason PATRIC. During this period, and while she was filming Steven SPIELBERG's *Hook*, Roberts shunned the press. She left the business for a year, then resurfaced with a starring role in *The Pelican Brief* (1993) and a new, candid outlook toward interviews. Her surprise 1993 marriage to high-haired rocker Lyle Lovett came after a brief courtship, but ended amicably shortly thereafter.

FILMS: *Satisfaction, Mystic Pizza* 1988; *Blood Red, Steel Magnolias* 1989; *Pretty Woman, Flatliners* 1990; *Sleeping with the Enemy, Dying Young, Hook* (as Tinkerbell) 1991; *The Player* (cameo) 1992; *The Pelican Brief* 1993; *I Love Trouble, Ready to Wear* 1994; *Something to Talk About* 1995; *Everyone Says I Love You, Mary Reilly, Michael Collins* 1996; *Conspiracy Theory, My Best Friend's Wedding* 1997.

Roberts, Lynn(e). Actress. *b.* Nov. 22, 1919, in El Paso, Tex. *d.* 1978. Heroine of numerous Hollywood B pictures and serials. She entered films in 1937 as Mary Hart but, failing to make much headway, changed her name to Lynn Roberts the following year. In 1943 she slightly altered her first name to Lynne. However, despite the new name and a good measure of talent and charm she never hurdled the barrier to big-time stardom and retired from the screen in 1953.

FILMS INCLUDE: As Mary Hart—*Dangerous Holiday, Love Is on the Air* 1937. As Lynn Roberts—*Call the Mesquiteers, The Lone Ranger* (serial), *Dick Tracy Returns* (serial), *The Stadium Murders, Billy the Kid Returns* 1938; *The Mysterious Miss X, Rough Riders' Round-Up* 1939; *Hi-Yo Silver!, Star Dust, Street of Memories, Romance of the Rio Grande* 1940; *Ride on Vaquero, Last of the Duanes, The Bride Wore Crutches, Moon Over Miami* 1941; *The Man in the Trunk, Dr. Renault's Secret, Quiet Please Murder* 1942. As Lynne Roberts—*The Ghost That Walks Alone* 1944; *Behind City Lights, The Chicago Kid, The Big Bonanza, Girls of the Big House, The Phantom Speaks* 1945; *The Magnificent Rogue, Sioux City Sue* 1946; *Winter Wonderland* 1947; *Madonna of the Desert, Secret Service Investigator, Eyes of Texas* 1948; *Trouble Preferred* 1949; *The Blazing Sun, The Great Plane Robbery* 1950; *Because of You* 1952; *Port Sinister* 1953.

Roberts, Rachel. Actress. *b.* Sept. 20, 1927, Llanelly, Wales. *d.* 1980. *ed.* U. of Wales; RADA. The daughter of a Baptist clergyman, she began her professional career in 1951. She developed primarily as a stage actress, but also made some notable appearances in British films, especially as the widow in *This Sporting Life* (1963), for which she was nominated for an Oscar as best supporting actress. She was subsequently often typecast in similar roles as a blowsy, sensual housewife. In the mid-70s she became a resident of Los Angeles and was regularly featured as the feisty but lovable housekeeper, Mrs. McClellan, on CBS-TV's 'The Tony Randall Show' (1976–78). Her first husband (1955–61) was actor Alan Dobie (*b.* 1932); her second (1962–71) actor Rex HARRISON. Her death at 53 of barbiturate poisoning was ruled a suicide.

FILMS INCLUDE: *Valley of Song/Men Are Children Twice* 1953; *The Weak and the Wicked* 1954; *The Good Companions* 1957; *Our Man in Havana* 1959; *Saturday Night and Sunday Morning* 1960; *This Sporting Life* 1963; *La Puce à l'Oreille/A Flea in Her Ear* (Fr./US) 1968; *The Reckoning* 1969; *Doctors' Wives* (US), *The Wild Rovers* (US) 1971; *The Belstone Fox/Free Spirit, Oh Lucky Man!* (triple role), *Alpha Beta* 1973; *Murder on the Orient Express* 1974; *Picnic at Hanging Rock* (Austral.) 1976; *Foul Play* (US) 1978; *Yanks, When a Stranger Calls* (US) 1979; *Charlie Chan and the Curse of the Dragon Queen* (US) 1981.

Roberts, Stephen R. Director. *b.* Nov. 23, 1895, Summersville, W. Va. *d.* 1936. A WW I pilot, he performed stunt aerobatics in country fairs after discharge from the service. When an accident ended his flying career, he entered films as a stuntman and double. He became a director of comedy shorts early in the 20s and a feature director early in the 30s. His films are insignificant but entertaining and mainly in the lower-budget category.

FILMS: *Sky Bride, Lady and Gent, The Night of June 13th, If I Had a Million* (one episode) 1932; *The Story of Temple Drake, One Sunday Afternoon* 1933; *The Trumpet Blows, Romance in Manhattan* 1934; *Star of Midnight, The Man Who Broke the Bank at Monte Carlo* 1935; *The Lady Consents, The Ex-Mrs. Bradford* 1936.

Roberts, Tanya. Actress. Born Leigh Roberts, on Oct. 15, 1955, in the Bronx, N.Y. Shapely, light-haired, blue-eyed sexpot of mostly low-budget Hollywood films. A former model, she began appearing in films in the mid-70s and became one of the three 'Charlie's Angels' in the TV series' final season (1980–81). Her scantily clad figure amply compensated for her limited acting range in such inane action pictures as *Beastmaster* (1982) and *Sheena* (1984) and the James Bond thriller *A View to a Kill* (1985). In the 90s, she turned to making 'classy' erotica.

FILMS INCLUDE: *Forced Entry* 1975; *The Yum-Yum Girls* 1976; *Fingers* 1978; *Tourist Trap, California Dreaming* 1979; *The Beastmaster* 1982; *Sheena* 1984; *A View to a Kill* (UK) 1985; *Body Slam* 1987; *Purgatory* 1988; *Inner Sanctum* 1991; *Almost Pregnant* 1992.

Roberts, Theodore. Actor. *b.* Oct. 2, 1861, San Francisco. *d.* 1928. Impressive character actor of Hollywood silents, usually in the role of a patriarch, king, or dominant heavy. A veteran of the stage, he was held in high esteem by the young film industry and was often referred to as the "grand duke of Hollywood." He was a regular member of the Cecil B. De Mille team from its inception, appearing in 23 of the director's films, notably as Moses in the original *The Ten Commandments* (1923).

FILMS INCLUDE: *Uncle Tom* (as Simon Legree) 1910; *Arizona* 1913; *The Call of the North, Where the Trail Divides, The Man from Home, Ready Money, The Ghost Breaker, The Circus Man* 1914; *After Five, The Girl of the Golden West, The Captive, Stolen Goods, The Arab* 1915; *Temptation, The Trail of the Lonesome Pine, Pudd'n Head Wilson, The Storm, The Dream Girl, Joan the Woman* (as Bishop Peter Cauchon) 1916; *The American Consul, The Cost of Hatred, The Little Princess* 1917; *M'Liss, We Can't Have Everything, The Source, Such a Little Pirate, Arizona* (remake), *The Squaw Man* 1918; *Don't Change Your Husband, The Roaring Road, Fires of Fate, The Woman Thou Gavest Me, You're Fired!, Secret Service, Hawthorne of the USA, Male and Female, Everywoman* 1919; *Double Speed, Excuse My Dust, Something to Think About* 1920; *Forbidden Fruit, The Love Special, The Affairs of Anatol, Miss Lulu Bett, Hail the Woman* 1921; *Saturday Night, Across the Continent, Our Leading Citizen, The Old Homestead, The Man Who Saw Tomorrow* 1922; *Grumpy, Prodigal Daughters, Racing Hearts, Stephen Steps Out, To the Ladies, The Ten Commandments* (as Moses) 1923; *Locked Doors, Forty Winks* 1925; *The Cat's Pajamas* 1926; *The Masks of the Devil* 1928; *Noisy Neighbors, Ned McCobb's Daughter* 1929.

Roberts, Tony. Actor. Born David Anthony Roberts, on Oct. 22, 1939, in New York City. Tall, curly-haired, pleasant leading man and supporting player of the American stage, TV, and films. The son of radio and TV announcer Ken Roberts, and a cousin of Everett SLOANE, he studied drama at Northwestern University. After a slow professional start, which included a regular featured role in the daytime soap opera 'Edge of Night' from 1965 to 1967, he gradually established himself in the 70s on Broadway and in films. His screen career was helped by several pivotal parts in Woody ALLEN films.

FILMS INCLUDE: *The Beach Girls and the Monster* 1965; *$1,000,000 Duck, Star Spangled Girl* 1971; *Play It Again Sam* 1972; *Serpico* 1973; *The Taking of Pelham 123* 1974; *Le Sauvage/The Savage* (Fr.) 1975; *Annie Hall* 1977; *Just Tell Me What You Want, Stardust Memories* 1980; *A Midsummer Night's Sex Comedy* 1982; *Amityville 3-D* 1983; *Key Exchange* 1985; *Hannah and Her Sisters* (cameo) 1986; *Radio Days* 1987; *18 Again!* 1988; *Popcorn, Switch* 1991.

Robertson, Cliff. Actor. Born Clifford Parker Robertson III, on Sept. 9, 1925, in La Jolla, Calif. The son of wealthy landowners, he was adopted at age two and raised by his maternal grandmother, following the divorce of his parents. An enterprising, independent youth, he trapped lobsters for extra money and at 13 scrubbed airplanes in exchange for flying lessons. After briefly attending Antioch College as a journalism major, he played small roles in a couple of Hollywood films, then served a two-and-a-half-year stint as a merchant marine. He arrived in New York in 1947, in pursuit of an acting career. He tailed subjects for a private detective, parked cars at the Stork Club, and performed with a Catskills troupe to pay for tuition at the Actors Studio. After a long struggle, he began performing on TV in the early 50s, and finally made it to Broadway in 1953. On the screen from the mid-50s, Robertson enjoyed increased popularity after he was picked by President John F. Kennedy to portray him as a young WW II Navy lieutenant in the filmed memoir *PT-109* (1963). In 1966 he won an Emmy for the TV drama 'The Game.' But his movie roles continued to be generally unremarkable until 1968, when he gave an Academy Award–winning performance as a mental retardee in *Charly*. He made an impressive debut as a director with *J. W. Coop* (1972). Known as a nonconformist, Robertson often feuded with the Hollywood hierarchy. He was a central figure in the 1977 David Begelman scandal, an embezzlement scheme that was discovered after Robertson complained that the Columbia executive had forged his signature on a $10,000 studio check. Although Hollywood got rid of Begelman, the studios resented Robertson's whistleblowing and for several years the actor found work elusive. In 1983–84 he starred in the TV series 'Falcon Crest.' His second wife (1966–89) was actress Dina MERRILL.

FILMS: *We've Never Been Licked, Corvette K-225* 1943; *Picnic* 1955; *Autumn Leaves* 1956; *The Girl Most Likely* 1957; *The Naked and the Dead* 1958; *Gidget, Battle of the Coral Sea* 1959; *As the Sea Rages* 1960; *All in a Night's Work, Underworld USA, The Big Show* 1961; *The Interns* 1962; *My Six Loves, PT-109* (as John F. Kennedy) 1963; *Sunday in New York, The Best Man, 633 Squadron* 1964; *Love Has Many Faces, Masquerade, Up from the Beach* 1965; *The Honey Pot* 1967; *The Devil's Brigade, Charly* 1968; *Too Late the Hero* 1970; *J. W. Coop* (also dir., prod., sc.), *The Great Northfield Minnesota Raid* 1972; *Ace Eli and Rodger of the Skies* 1973; *Man on a Swing* 1974; *Out of Season* (UK), *Three Days of the Condor* 1975; *Shoot* (Can.), *Midway, Obsession* 1976; *Fraternity Row* 1977; *Dominique* (UK) 1978; *The Pilot* (also dir., co-sc.) 1979; *Class, Brainstorm, Star 80* 1983; *Shaker Run* (NZ) 1985; *Malone* 1987; *Wild Hearts Can't Be Broken* 1991; *Wind* 1992; *Renaissance Man* 1994; *Escape from L.A.*. 1996.

Robertson, Dale. Actor. Born Dayle Robertson, on July 14, 1923, in Harrah, Okla. *ed.* Oklahoma Military Coll. Tall, rugged leading man of Westerns and occasionally films of other genres. Formerly a prizefighter, he has done much TV, including the series 'Tales of Wells Fargo' (1957–62) and 'The Iron Horse' (1966–68). He also hosted the series 'Death Valley Days' (1968–72) and played the title role in the TV movies *Melvin Purvis—G-Man/The Legend of Machine Gun Kelly* (1974), also starring in its sequel, *The Kansas City Massacre* (1975). He appeared as a guest on 'Dynasty' and other TV shows in the early 80s. At one time married to actress Mary MURPHY.

FILMS INCLUDE: *Johnny Belinda* (bit), *The Boy with Green Hair* (bit) 1948; *Flamingo Road, The Girl from Jones Beach, Fighting Man of the Plains* (as Jesse James) 1949; *Two Flags West* 1950; *Call Me Mister, Take Care of My Little Girl, Golden Girl* 1951; *Return of the Texan, The Outcasts of Poker Flat, Lydia Bailey, O. Henry's Full House* 1952; *The Farmer Takes a Wife, Devil's Canyon, The Silver Whip, City of Bad Men* 1953; *The Gambler from Natchez, Sitting Bull* 1954; *Son of Sinbad* 1955; *A Day of Fury, Dakota Incident* 1956; *Hell Canyon Outlaws* 1957; *Anna di Brooklyn/Fast and Sexy* (It./Fr.) 1958; *Law of the Lawless, Blood on the Arrow* 1964; *The Man from Button Willow* (animated cartoon; prod. and intro. only), *Coast of Skeletons* (UK) 1965; *One-Eyed Soldiers* (US/UK/Yug.) 1967.

Robertson, John S. Director. *b.* June 14, 1878, in London, Ont., Canada. *d.* 1964. A forgotten director who carried much prestige in the silent days, when he was known as Hollywood's most liked filmmaker. He was highly acclaimed for his sincerity and restrained craftsmanship by film historians. A former stage actor, he entered films in 1915 as an actor for Vitagraph but soon after switched to directing. His best-known film is the John Barrymore version of *Dr. Jekyll and Mr. Hyde* (1920), but he directed many other major productions featuring stars such as Mary Pickford and Greta Garbo.

FILMS: *Intrique, The Money Mill, Baby Mine* (co-dir. with Hugo Ballin), *The Bottom of the Well* 1917; *The Menace, The Better Half, The Girl of Today* (also co-sc.), *The Make-Believe Wife, Little Miss Hoover* 1918; *Here Comes the Bride, The Test of Honor, Let's Elope, Come Out of the Kitchen, The Misleading Widow, Sadie Love, Erstwhile Susan* 1919; *Dr. Jekyll and Mr. Hyde, Away Goes Prudence, A Dark Lantern, 39 East* 1920; *The Magic Cup, Sentimental Tommy, Footlights* 1921; *Love's Boomerang, The Spanish Jade, Tess of the Storm Country* 1922; *The Bright Shawl, The Fighting Blade, Twenty-One* 1923; *The Enchanted Cottage, Classmates* 1924; *New Toys, Soul Fire, Shore Leave* 1925; *Annie Laurie, Captain Salvation, The Road to Romance* 1927; *The Single Standard, Shanghai Lady* 1929; *Night Ride, Captain of the Guard* (co-dir. with Paul Fejos), *Madonna of the Streets* 1930; *Beyond Victory, The Phantom of Paris* 1931; *Little Orphan Annie* 1932; *One Man's Journey* 1933; *The Crime Doctor, His Greatest Gamble, Wednesday's Child* 1934; *Captain Hurricane, Grand Old Girl, Our Little Girl* 1935.

Robertson-Justice, James. Actor. *b.* James Norval Harald Robertson-Justice, June 15, 1905, Wigtown, Scotland. *d.* 1975. *ed.* Marlborough Coll. (Eng.); Bonn U. (Ger.). Imposing supporting player whose luxuriant beard and booming voice enhanced the cast of many UK and US films from the mid-40s. Perhaps best remembered as Sir Lancelot Spratt, the irascible senior surgeon in the British comedy *Doctor in the House* (1954) and its several sequels. The holder of a Ph.D. degree and formerly a journalist and a naturalist, he became an expert in falconry and trained Prince Charles in that ancient hunting art. He held the honorary post of rector of the University of Edinburgh. Early in his career he was billed simply as James Robertson.

FILMS INCLUDE: *Champagne Charlie, Fiddlers Three* 1944; *Appointment with Crime* 1946; *Hungry Hill, Scott of the Antarctic, Against the Wind* 1948; *Christopher Columbus* (as explorer Martin Pinzón), *Whisky Galore/Tight Little Island* 1949; *The Black Rose* (UK/US) 1950; *David and Bathsheba* (as Abishai; US), *Captain Horatio Hornblower* (US/UK), *Pool of London* 1951; *The Lady Says No* (US), *The Story of Robin Hood* (as Little John), *Les Miserables* (US), *The Voice of Merrill/Murder Will Out* 1952; *The Sword and the Rose* (as Henry VIII; US/UK), *Rob Roy the Highland Rogue/Rob Roy* (UK/US) 1953; *Doctor in the House* 1954; *Land of the Pharaohs* (US), *Doctor at Sea, Storm Over the Nile, Above Us the Waves* 1955; *Moby Dick* (UK/US), *Checkpoint* 1956; *Doctor at Large* 1957; *Orders to Kill* 1958; *Upstairs and Downstairs* 1959; *A French Mistress, Foxhole in Cairo* 1960; *Raising the Wind/Roommates, The Guns of Navarone* (UK/US), *Murder She Said, Very Important Person/A Coming-Out Party* 1961; *Guns of Darkness, Crooks Anonymous* 1962; *Dr. Crippen, Doctor in Distress* 1963; *Up from the Beach* (US), *The Face of Fu Manchu* 1965; *A Coeur joie/Two Weeks in September* 1967; *Chitty Chitty Bang Bang, Mayerling* (as Edward, Prince of Wales; UK/Fr.) 1968; *Doctor in Trouble* 1970.

Robeson, Paul. Actor, singer. *b.* Apr. 9, 1898, Princeton, N.J. *d.* 1976. The son of a Presbyterian minister who had escaped from slavery in his youth and of a schoolteacher mother, he won a scholarship to Rutgers and graduated as a four-letter man and the holder of a Phi Beta Kappa key. He played some pro football while attending Columbia University's law school. During the same period he was also persuaded to take part in an amateur stage production at the Harlem YMCA. His success was so great that after being admitted to the New York bar he chose not to practice law but to respond to Eugene O'Neill's personal request that he star in his plays 'All God's Chillun Got Wings' and 'The Emperor Jones.' The critical reaction was enthusiastic. Robeson, who also began giving singing recitals and starring in films, won rapid recognition as one of the most accomplished performers of his day. His fame spread across Europe, where he began spending much of his time in stage performances and concerts. In 1934 he made his first of several trips to the Soviet Union and subsequently became increasingly enchanted with leftist ideology as a possible answer to discrimination against blacks in the US.

In the early 40s Robeson enjoyed a triumphant Broadway run and long national tour with 'Othello.' But his political views made him a progressively controversial figure as the Cold War intensified. In 1946 he denied under oath that he had ever been a member of the Communist Party but refused to do so in a subsequent probe; as a result his passport was revoked by the State Department in 1950. It wasn't until 1958 that he was able to leave the country and to officially receive the Stalin Peace Prize, which he had been awarded in 1952. Despite his bitterness he refused to renounce his American citizenship and symbolized black consciousness and pride to many in the African-American community. He resumed touring Europe successfully until the early 60s, when he was taken ill and returned to the US. He was living in almost total seclusion and in poor health in Harlem at the time of his death at 77. He was the subject of a documentary, *Paul Robeson: Portrait of an Artist* (1979).

FILMS: *Body and Soul* 1925; *The Emperor Jones* (as Brutus Jones) 1933; *Sanders of the River/Bosambo* (UK) 1935; *Song of Freedom* (UK), *Show Boat* (as Joe) 1936; *Big Fella* (UK), *King Solomon's Mines* (as Umpoba; UK), *Jericho/Dark Sands* (UK) 1937; *Proud Valley* (UK) 1940; *Native Land* (narrator), *Tales of Manhattan* 1942; *Das Lied der Ströme/Song of the Rivers* (doc.; singing v/o; E. Ger.) 1954.

Robin, Dany. Actress. Born on Apr. 14, 1927, in Clamart, France. Pretty, elegant leading lady of French films and international co-productions who started her career as a ballerina with the Paris Opera. Formerly married to actor Georges MARCHAL, she is the wife of British producer Michael Sullivan.

FILMS INCLUDE: *Lunegarde, Les Portes de la Nuit/Gates of the Night* 1946; *L'Eventail/Naughty Martine, Le Silence est d'Or/Man About Town* 1947; *Les Amoureux sont seuls au Monde/Monelle* 1948; *La Passagère* 1949; *La Soif des Hommes/The Thirst of Men* 1950; *Deux Sous de Violettes, Une Histoire d'Amour* 1951; *La Fête à Henriette/Holiday for Henrietta* 1952; *Les Amants de Minuit, Julietta, Tempi Nostri/The Anatomy of Love* (It./Fr.) 1953; *Un Acte d'Amour/Act of Love* (Fr./US) 1954; *Escale à Orly, Frou-Frou* (It./Fr.), *Napoléon* (as Désirée Clary) 1955; *Paris Coquin/Maid in Paris* 1956; *Mimi Pinson* 1958; *Les Dragueurs/The Chasers* 1959; *La Française et l'Amour/Love and the Frenchwoman* 1960; *Les Amours célèbres* 1961; *Waltz of the Toreadors* (UK), *Les Parisiennes/Tales of Paris* 1962; *Follow the Boys* (US) 1963; *The Best House in London* (UK), *Topaz* (US) 1969.

Robin, Leo. Lyricist. *b.* Apr. 6, 1895, Pittsburgh. *d.* 1984. A former actor and newspaperman, he wrote many popular songs for Hollywood films, often in collaboration with composer Ralph RAINGER. He won an Academy Award for the lyrics of 'Thanks for the Memory,' from the film *The Big Broadcast of 1938.*

FILMS INCLUDE: *Innocents of Paris* ('Louise,' etc.), *Close Harmony, Syncopation, The Man I Love* 1929; *Hit the Deck, Paramount on Parade, Morocco, Playboy of Paris, The Vagabond King, Monte Carlo* ('Beyond the Blue Horizon,' etc.) 1930; *Blonde Venus, The Big Broadcast* 1932; *She Done Him Wrong, International House* 1933; *Kiss and Make Up, Little Miss Marker* 1934; *The Devil Is a Woman* 1935; *Anything Goes, Desire* 1936; *Champagne Waltz, Artists and Models, Waikiki Wedding* ('Blue Hawaii,' etc.) 1937; *The Big Broadcast of 1938* 1938; *Gulliver's Travels* 1939; *Moon Over Miami, Rise and Shine* 1941; *Footlight Serenade, My Gal Sal, Tales of Manhattan* 1942; *Coney Island, The Gang's All Here, Wintertime, Riding High* 1943; *Greenwich Village* 1944; *Wonder Man* 1945; *The Time the Place and the Girl* 1946; *Something in the Wind* ('I Love a Mystery,' etc.) 1947; *Casbah* ('For Every Man There's a Woman,' etc.), *That Lady in Ermine* 1948; *Two Tickets to Broadway* 1951; *Just for You* 1952; *Gentlemen Prefer Blondes* 1953; *Hit the Deck, My Sister Eileen* 1955.

Robinson, Arthur. Director. *b.* June 25, 1888, Chicago, to German-Jewish parents. *d.* 1935. A graduate of the University of Munich's medical school, he was a practicing physician for several years before making his stage debut as an actor in Switzerland. He later appeared on the German stage and entered films in 1914 as script editor and screenwriter, turning out his first film as director in 1916. Seven years later he created his best-known film, *Schatten/Warning Shadows,* a powerful psychological drama subtitled "A Nocturnal Hallucination," which is widely accepted as a classic of the expressionist period of German cinema. With the exception of *Manon Lescaut* (1926), most of his other films were routine although commercially successful. In 1929 he directed an early version of O'Flaherty's *The Informer* in England and in the early 30s he piloted German and French versions of MGM films in Hollywood. He then returned to Europe, where he died.

FILMS INCLUDE: *Nächte des Grauens* 1916; *Schatten/Warning Shadows* (also co-sc.), *Zwischen Abend und Morgen* (also sc.) 1923; *Pietro der Korsar/Peter the Pirate* (also sc.) 1924; *Manon Lescaut* (also sc.) 1926; *Der Letzte Walzer/The Last Waltz* (also co-sc.) 1927; *Looping the Loop* (also co-sc.) 1928; *The Informer* (UK) 1929; *Mordprozess Mary Dugan* (German version of *The Trial of Mary Dugan;* US) 1931; *Eines Prinzen Junge Liebe* 1933; *Fürst Woronzeff* 1934; *Monsieur le Marquis* (Fr.), *Mach' mich glücklich, Der Student von Prag* 1935.

Robinson, Bill ("Bojangles"). Dancer, actor. *b.* Luther Robinson, May 25, 1878, Richmond, Va. *d.* 1949. Black dancing star of vaudeville, the musical stage, and films. The originator of the stair tap routine, he was considered one of the world's foremost tap dancers. A school dropout at seven, he began dancing professionally at eight, earning the nickname "Bojangles" for his happy-go-lucky manner. He is best remembered for his film appearances with Shirley TEMPLE in *The Little Colonel, The Littlest Rebel,* and *Rebecca of Sunnybrook Farm.* In a joint 1989 resolution, Congress designated his birth date as National Tap Dancing Day.

FILMS: *Dixiana* 1930; *Harlem Is Heaven* 1932; *The Little Colonel, Hooray for Love, In Old Kentucky, The Big Broadcast of 1936, The Littlest Rebel* 1935; *Dimples* (chor. only) 1936; *Hot from Harlem, One Mile from Heaven* 1937; *Rebecca of Sunnybrook Farm, The Road Demon, Just Around the Corner, Up the River* 1938; *Stormy Weather* (lead) 1943.

Robinson, Bruce. Director, screenwriter, actor. Born in 1946, in Broadstairs, Kent, England. Trained at London's School of Speech and Drama, he made his screen acting debut as Benvolio in Franco Zeffirelli's *Romeo and Juliet* (1968). After portraying the dashing Lt. Pinson, the object of Isabelle Adjani's obsession, in François Truffaut's *The Story of Adele H* (1975), he quit acting to devote himself to the writing of novels and screenplays. After several tries and misses he scored a success with his screenplay for *The Killing Fields* (1984), for which he was nominated for an Oscar and won the British Film Academy Award. He then turned to directing, drawing kudos for the charming wit in *Withnail & I* (1987) and the robust, irreverent humor of *How to Get Ahead in Advertising* (1989).

FILMS INCLUDE: As actor—*Romeo and Juliet* (as Benvolio) 1968; *The Music Lovers, Private Road, Tam Lin/The Devil's Widow* (US) 1972; *L'Histoire d'Adele H./The Story of Adele H.* (Fr.) 1975; *Beyond and Back* (US) 1978; *Harry's War* (US) 1981. As screenwriter (complete)—*The Killing Fields* 1984; *Fat Man and Little Boy* (US), *Ghost Dad* (co-sc.) 1990; *Jennifer 8* 1992. As director-screenwriter (complete)—*Withnail and I* 1987; *How to Get Ahead in Advertising* 1989.

Robinson, Casey. Screenwriter. *b.* Kenneth C. Robinson, Oct. 17, 1903, Logan, Utah. *d.* 1979. *ed.* Cornell. He began in films in 1927 as a title writer after studying at Cornell. He wrote many prominent screenplays from the early 30s to the late 50s, alone or in collaboration. He also directed a number of short subjects and produced several features. He was at one time married to Russian ballerina Tamara Toumanova.

FILMS INCLUDE: *The Private Life of Helen of Troy* (titles only) 1927; *Bare Knees, Hawk's Nest* (both titles only) 1928; *Times Square* (titles only) 1929; *The Squealer* 1930; *Last Parade* (story only) 1931; *Is My Face Red?* 1932; *I Love That Man* (dial. only) 1933; *Here Comes the Groom* 1934; *McFadden's Flats, I Found Stella Parrish, Captain Blood* 1935; *Hearts Divided, Stolen Holiday* 1936; *Call It a Day, Tovarich, It's Love I'm After* 1937; *Four's a Crowd* 1938; *Dark Victory, The Old Maid* 1939; *All This and Heaven Too* 1940; *One Foot in Heaven* 1941; *Kings Row, Now Voyager* 1942; *This Is the Army* 1943; *Passage to Marseille, Days of Glory* (also prod.) 1944; *The Corn Is Green, Saratoga Trunk* 1945; *The Macomber Affair* (also co-prod.) 1947; *Under My Skin* (also prod.), *Two Flags West* (also prod.) 1950; *Diplomatic Courier* (also prod.), *The Snows of Kilimanjaro* 1952; *A Bullet Is Waiting, The Egyptian* 1954; *While the City Sleeps* 1956; *This Earth Is Mine* (also prod.) 1959; *Il Figlio di Capitano Blood/The Son of Captain Blood* (It./Sp./US) 1962.

Robinson, Edward G. Actor. *b.* Emmanuel Goldenberg, Dec. 12, 1893, Bucharest. *d.* 1973. Forceful, authoritative character star of Hollywood films, memorable for his tough impersonation of gangster boss Rico Bandello in *Little Caesar* (1931) and many other characterizations of underworld types in Warners' crime cycle of the 30s. In the US from age ten, he grew up on New York's Lower East Side and gave up plans to become a rabbi or a lawyer in favor of acting during studies at City College, where he was elected to the Elizabethan Society. He won a scholarship to the American Academy of Dramatic Arts and, changing his name to Edward G. (for Goldenberg) Robinson, began appearing in stock in 1913. He made it to Broadway in 1915 and over the next 15 years appeared with increasing recognition in a wide variety of plays, including 'The Kibitzer' (1929), a three-act comedy that he also wrote with Jo Swerling. He made an isolated film appearance during the silent era, playing a supporting role in *The Bright Shawl* (1923), but it was only after the advent of sound that he began to be seen regularly in movies. After his great success with *Little Caesar* (1931), a performance that became a prototype for screen gangster portrayals, Robinson was typecast for several years in similar roles, but he gradually broadened his range and proved himself a highly skilled actor in a great variety of parts. He gave memorable performances in two screen biographies *Dr. Ehrlich's Magic Bullet* (1940), the story of the German scientist who developed a cure for venereal disease, and *A Dispatch from Reuters* (also 1940), the chronicle of the man who pioneered the telegraphic news agency. Some of his best portrayals were in psychological dramas of the 40s, notably *Flesh and Fantasy* (1943), *Double Indemnity* (1944), *The Woman in the Window* (1944), and *Scarlet Street* (1945).

Robinson's personal life was beset by problems in the 50s. Despite a well-known record of activity for patriotic causes during and after WW II, his name was linked by Red Channels with Communist-front organizations. He was called to testify before the House Un-American Activities Committee but was cleared of all suspicion. In 1956 he was forced to sell his famous art collection, one of the world's largest privately owned, as part of his divorce settlement with his wife of 29 years, actress Gladys Lloyd. During this period he was also troubled by the maladjustments of his only son, who got into frequent frictions with the law and attempted suicide several times. Despite the personal setbacks, Robinson continued his busy acting career, on television as well as in films. In 1956 he returned to Broadway after a long absence, scoring a success in the role of an elderly widower who marries a young bride in Paddy Chayefsky's 'Middle of the Night.' His film appearances during the 60s were mainly in the supporting capacity. In the Academy Award ceremonies that took place shortly after his death of cancer in 1973, Robinson was awarded a special Oscar in recognition of his achievements in films, in a magnificent career that spanned five decades of cinema. His life provided the basis for the 1979 play *Manny,* by Raymond Serra, who also played the title role. Autobiography: *All My Yesterdays* (1973).

FILMS: *The Bright Shawl* 1923; *The Hole in the Wall* 1929; *Night Ride, A Lady to Love, Outside the Law, East Is West, The Widow of Chicago* 1930; *Little Caesar, Smart Money, Five Star Final* 1931; *The Hatchet Man, Two Seconds, Tiger Shark, Silver Dollar* 1932; *The Little Giant, I Loved a Woman* 1933;

Dark Hazard, The Man with Two Faces 1934; *The Whole Town's Talking* (dual roles), *Barbary Coast* 1935; *Bullets or Ballots* 1936; *Thunder in the City* (UK), *Kid Galahad, The Last Gangster* 1937; *A Slight Case of Murder, The Amazing Dr. Clitterhouse, I Am the Law* 1938; *Confessions of a Nazi Spy, Blackmail* 1939; *Dr. Ehrlich's Magic Bullet* (as Dr. Paul Ehrlich), *Brother Orchid, A Dispatch from Reuters* (as Julius Reuter) 1940; *The Sea Wolf* (as Wolf Larsen), *Manpower, Unholy Partners* 1941; *Larceny Inc., Tales of Manhattan* 1942; *Destroyer, Flesh and Fantasy* 1943; *Tampico, Mr. Winkle Goes to War, Double Indemnity, The Woman in the Window* 1944; *Journey Together* (RAF propaganda film; UK), *Our Vines Have Tender Grapes, Scarlet Street* 1945; *The Stranger* 1946; *The Red House* 1947; *All My Sons, Key Largo, Night Has a Thousand Eyes* 1948; *House of Strangers, It's a Great Feeling* (cameo) 1949; *My Daughter Joy/Operation X* (UK) 1950; *Actors and Sin* 1952; *Vice Squad, Big Leaguer, The Glass Web* 1953; *Black Tuesday* 1954; *The Violent Men, Tight Spot, A Bullet for Joey, Illegal* 1955; *Hell on Frisco Bay, Nightmare, The Ten Commandments* (as Dathan) 1956; *A Hole in the Head* 1959; *Seven Thieves, Pepe* (cameo) 1960; *My Geisha, Two Weeks in Another Town* 1962; *Sammy Going South/A Boy Ten Feet Tall* (UK), *The Prize* 1963; *Good Neighbor Sam, Robin and the 7 Hoods* (cameo), *The Outrage, Cheyenne Autumn* 1964; *The Cincinnati Kid* 1965; *La Blonde de Pékin/Peking Blonde* (Fr./It./Ger.), *Ad Ogni Costo/Grand Slam* (It./Sp./Ger.), *Uno Scacco Tutto Matto/Mad Checkmate/It's Your Move* (It.), *Operazione San Pietro/Operation St. Peter's* (It.) 1967; *The Biggest Bundle of Them All* (US/It.), *Never a Dull Moment* 1968; *Mackenna's Gold* 1969; *Song of Norway* 1970; *Soylent Green, Neither by Day or Night* (Isr.) 1973.

Robinson, Madeleine. Actress. Born Madeleine Svoboda, on Nov. 5, 1916, in Paris, of Czech origin. Highly esteemed leading lady and later character actress of French theater and films, usually in intense roles. She has won several acting awards.

FILMS INCLUDE: *Soldats sans Uniformes* 1934; *Le Mioche/Forty Little Mothers* 1936; *Nuits de Feu/The Living Corpse* 1937; *L'Innocent/Bouquets from Nicholas, Tempête sur l'Asie* 1938; *Lumière d'Eté, Douce/Love Story* 1943; *Sortilèges/The Bellman* 1945; *Les Frères Bouquinquant* 1947; *La Grande Maguet* 1948; *Une si Jolie Petite Plage/Riptide, Entre Onze Heures et Minuit/Between Eleven and Midnight* 1949; *Dieu a besoin des Hommes/God Needs Men* 1950; *Le Garçon sauvage/Savage Triangle* 1951; *L'Affaire Maurizius* 1954; *Les Possédées/Passionate Summer* 1956; *Les Louves/Demoniaque* 1957; *Péché de Jeunesse/Sins of Youth* 1958; *A Double Tour/Leda* 1959; *Léviathan* 1961; *Le Diable et le Dix Commandements/The Devil and the Ten Commandments, Le Procès/The Trial* (as Frau Grubach) 1962; *Un Mondo nuovo/Un Monde nouveau/A Young World* (It./Fr.) 1966; *Le Coeur fou* 1970; *Le Petit Matin* 1971; *On peut le dire sans facher* 1977; *L'Amant de Poche, Une Histoire Simple* 1978; *7 Dias de Enero* (Sp.) 1979; *J'ai épousé une Ombre/I Married a Shadow* 1983; *Hors-La-Loi* 1985; *Camille Claudel* 1988.

Robinson, Phil Alden. American director, screenwriter. A graduate of Union College in Schenectady, N.Y., he had his first script produced in 1984 and made a pleasing debut as a director in 1987 with *In the Mood* (UK title *The Woo Woo Kid*), a comedy based on a true story about a 15-year-old California boy whose penchant for affairs with older women made headlines in 1944. Robinson was nominated for an Academy Award for the screenplay of his next directorial effort, the enchanting baseball fantasy *Field of Dreams* (1989).

FILMS: As screenwriter—*Rhinestone* (also lyr.), *All of Me* (also assoc. prod.) 1984; *Relentless* (under pseudonym Jack T. D. Robinson) 1989. As director-screenwriter—*In the Mood/The Woo Woo Kid* (also lyr.) 1987, *Field of Dreams* 1989; *Sneakers* 1992.

Robson, Dame Flora. Actress. *b.* Mar. 28, 1902, South Shields, Durham, England. *d.* 1984. Superb character player of the British stage and screen. Graduating from the Royal Academy of Dramatic Art as a Bronze Medallist, she made her stage debut in 1921 and later figured prominently in many productions of both the classic and modern repertoire on London's West End and occasionally on Broadway. On the screen since the early 30s, she played memorable roles in numerous British films and a handful of Hollywood productions, dominating many a scene with her powerful portrayals. She was nominated for an Oscar for her performance in *Saratoga Trunk* (1946). In recognition of her professional achievement, she was created Dame of the British Empire in 1960.

FILMS: *A Gentleman of Paris, Dance Pretty Lady* 1931; *One Precious Year* 1933; *Catherine the Great* (as Empress Elizabeth) 1934; *Fire Over England* (as Queen Elizabeth), *Farewell Again/Troopship, I Claudius* (unfinished; as Livia, the Empress Dowager) 1937; *Wuthering Heights* (as Ellen Dean; US), *Poison Pen, The Lion Has Wings, We Are Not Alone* (US), *Invisible Stripes* (US) 1939; *The Sea Hawk* (again as Queen Elizabeth; US) 1940; *Bahama Passage* (US) 1942; *2,000 Women* 1944; *Great Day, Caesar and Cleopatra* (as Ftatoteeta) 1945; *Saratoga Trunk* (US), *The Years Between* 1946; *Black Narcissus, Frieda, Holiday Camp* 1947; *Good Time Girl, Saraband for Dead Lovers/Saraband* 1948; *The Tall Headlines/The Frightened Bride* 1952; *Malta Story* 1953; *Giulietta e Romeo/Romeo and Juliet* (as the Nurse; It./UK) 1954; *High Tide at Noon, No Time for Tears* 1957; *The Gypsy and the Gentleman, Innocent Sinners* 1958; *55 Days at Peking* (as the Dowager Empress Tzu Hsi; US), *Murder at the Gallop* 1963; *Guns at Batasi* 1964; *Young Cassidy* (UK/US), *Those Magnificent Men in Their Flying Machines* 1965; *Seven Women* (US) 1966; *The Shuttered Room, Eye of the Devil, Cry in the Wind* (Gr./UK) 1967; *Fragment of Fear* 1970; *The Beast in the Cellar* 1971; *La Grande Scrofa nera* (It.), *Alice's Adventures in Wonderland* (as the Queen of Hearts) 1972; *Dominique* 1978; *Clash of the Titans* 1981.

Robson, Mark. Director. *b.* Dec. 4, 1913, in Montreal. *d.* 1978. *ed.* UCLA (political science and economics); Pacific Coast U. (law). Entered films in 1932 as a property boy at Fox and later worked as an assistant at the studio's art department. He joined RKO in 1935 and worked for that studio in various capacities, eventually becoming an editor. He collaborated with Robert Wise on the editing of Orson Welles's *Citizen Kane* (1941) but did not receive screen credit for his work. With Wise again, he co-edited Welles's *The Magnificent Ambersons* (1942) and was solo editor on *Journey Into Fear* (1942–43). After cutting *Cat People* (1942) for Val LEWTON, he was entrusted with the direction of five of the producer's horror thrillers. He later worked for various producers and studios in a variety of genres and styles, demonstrating technical proficiency and directorial skill but no particular personal taste or point of view. Among his more successful productions in the post-Lewton period were the boxing dramas *Champion* (1949) and *The Harder They Fall* (1956) and the racial drama *Home of the Brave* (1949). Among his commercial hits were *Peyton Place* (1957) and *Earthquake* (1974).

Beginning in the late 50s, Robson produced several of his own films. In 1971 he formed a production corporation, The Filmmakers Group, with Robert Wise and Bernard Donnenfeld. In 1974 they formed a partnership, the Tripar Group, in place of the corporation. In June of 1978 Robson collapsed of a heart attack while completing the film *Avalanche Express* on location in northern Italy. He died ten days later in a London hospital.

FILMS: *The Seventh Victim, The Ghost Ship* 1943; *Youth Runs Wild* 1944; *Isle of the Dead* 1945; *Bedlam* (also co-sc.) 1946; *Champion, Home of the Brave, Roughshod, My Foolish Heart* 1949; *Edge of Doom* 1950; *Bright Victory, I Want You* 1951; *Return to Paradise* 1953; *Hell Below Zero* (also co-story; UK), *Phffft* 1954; *The Bridges at Toko-Ri, A Prize of Gold* (UK), *Trial* 1955; *The Harder They Fall* 1956; *The Little Hut* (also co-prod.), *Peyton Place* 1957; *The Inn of the Sixth Happiness* (UK) 1958; *From the Terrace* (also prod.) 1960; *The Inspector/Lisa* (prod. only; UK/US) 1962; *Nine Hours to Rama* (also prod.; UK/US), *The Prize* 1963; *Von Ryan's Express* (also exec. prod.) 1965; *Lost Command* (also prod.) 1966; *Valley of the Dolls* (also co-exec. prod.) 1967; *Daddy's Gone A-Hunting* (also prod.) 1969; *Happy Birthday Wanda June* 1971; *Limbo* 1972; *Earthquake* (also prod.) 1974; *Avalanche Express* (also prod.) 1979.

Robson, May. Actress. *b.* Mary Jeanette Robison, Apr. 19, 1858, Melbourne, Australia. *d.* 1942. In the US from her late teens, she stumbled on acting as a means of livelihood when she was left a widow with three children in 1884. She appeared in numerous stage productions on the road and on Broadway, in both leads and supporting roles, and by the turn of the century had developed into a highly respected character player. She made occasional appearances in silent films, sometimes billed as Mrs. Stuart Robson, but her main screen career took place in the 30s, when she played a long string of character roles in a variety of major Hollywood productions. She typically portrayed a crusty or domineering society matron but is best remembered for her striking portrayal of Damon Runyon's Apple Annie in Frank Capra's *Lady for a Day* (1933), for which she was nominated for an Oscar as best actress.

FILMS INCLUDE: *The Trail of the Lonesome Pine* 1914; *How Molly Malone Made Good* 1915; *A Night Out* 1916; *The Prodigal Wife* 1918; *A Broadway Saint, The Lost Battalion* 1919; *Paradise* 1926; *The King of Kings, The Rejuvenation of Aunt Mary* (title role), *The Angel of Broadway, A Harp in Hawk, Chicago* 1927; *The Blue Danube* 1928; *Mother's Millions* (title role) 1931; *Letty Lynton, Red-Headed Woman, Strange Interlude, If I Had a Million, Little Orphan Annie* 1932; *The White Sister, Reunion in Vienna, Dinner at Eight, Lady for a Day* (as Apple Annie), *Dancing Lady, Alice in Wonderland* (as the Queen of Hearts) 1933; *You Can't Buy Everything* (lead), *Straight Is the Way, Lady by Choice* (lead) 1934; *Grand Old Girl* (lead), *Vanessa: Her Love Story, Reckless, Anna Karenina* 1935; *Wife vs. Secretary, Rainbow on the River* 1936; *A Star Is Born* 1937; *The Adventures of Tom Sawyer* (as Aunt Polly), *Bringing Up Baby, The Texans, Four Daughters* 1938; *They Made Me a Criminal, Daughters Courageous, Nurse Edith Cavell, Four Wives* 1939; *Granny Get Your Gun* (title role), *Irene* 1940; *Four Mothers, Playmates* 1941; *Joan of Paris* 1942.

Roc, Patricia. Actress. Born Felicia Riese, on June 7, 1918, in London. Lovely blonde leading lady of British films of the 40s and 50s, following brief stage exposure. She also appeared in two Hollywood productions.

FILMS INCLUDE: *The Rebel Son/Taras Bulba, The Gaunt Stranger/The Phantom Strikes* 1938; *A Window in London/ Lady in Distress* 1939; *Three Silent Men* 1940; *Let the People Sing* 1941; *Millions Like Us* 1943; *2,000 Women, Love Story/A Lady Surrenders, Madonna of the Seven Moons* 1944; *The Wicked Lady, Johnny Frenchman* 1945; *Canyon Passage* (US) 1946; *The Brothers, So Well Remembered, Jassy, Holiday Camp* 1947; *One Night with You* 1948; *The Perfect Woman* 1949; *The Man on the Eiffel Tower* (US), *Blackjack/Captain Blackjack* (Fr./UK/Sp.) 1950; *Circle of Danger* 1951; *Something Money Can't Buy* 1952; *La Vedova X/The Widow* (It.) 1955; *The Hypnotist/Scotland Yard Dragnet* 1957; *Bluebeard's Ten Honeymoons* 1960.

Rocha, Glauber. Director. *b.* Mar. 14, 1938, Vitoria da Conquista, Bahia, Brazil. *d.* 1981. A leading figure in Cinema Nôvo (New Cinema) movement. Addicted to film in his teens, he helped organize cine-clubs and began experimenting with a movie camera. Later, as a young journalist, he specialized in film critique. In 1957 he founded his own production company, Lemanaja-Filmes. Although enrolled at a law school two years later, he never became a practicing attorney. Instead, he got more deeply involved in filmmaking and the writing of essays, urging a new direction for Brazilian cinema that would have at its core "the esthetics of hunger and violence." In 1961 he took over the direction of *Barravento* midway through production, after rewriting the script. Initially banned in Brazil, the neorealist feature about the exploitation of black Bahia fishermen made a strong impression at international film festivals in 1962. More characteristic of Rocha's own style and themes was his next feature *Black God, White Devil* (1964), which gave a lyrical though violent expression to the uniquely intricate cultural-mystical-ritualistic-political Brazilian experience. In Rocha's much-acclaimed masterpiece *Antonio das Mortes* (1969), a ruthless bounty hunter, a catalyst in the story, becomes the title hero of the film. The operatic-scale spectacle, Rocha's first film in color, shared the best director prize at the Cannes Film Festival. The film's success brought sharp criticism of Rocha from the rightist political establishment. Angry over the banning of the film and threatened by imprisonment, he shuttered his production company and went into self-exile, shooting in Africa, then working in Italy, France, and Spain. He returned to Brazil in 1976, when the political climate improved. Disappointed over the reception of his *The Age of the Earth* (1980), he went into a second self-exile in Europe, in search of new projects. He was preparing for a production of *The Empire of Napoleon,* an epic that was to star Orson Welles in the title role, when he was felled by a lung infection and flown back to Brazil, where he died at 43. Rocha left behind only a handful of features, but was mourned as the new Brazilian cinema's guiding spirit, an outspoken rebel with a cause who used a movie camera and creative intuition to express his ideas about changing the tormented course of his country's social and political experience. In addition to numerous essays and articles on cinema, the best known of which was *Una Estetica de Fame* (*The Aesthetics of Violence*), he wrote several books on cinema, among them *Revisao critica do Cinema Brasiliero* (1963), *Revoluco do Cinema Nôvo* (1981), and *O Seculo do Cinema* (1983). He also published a novel, *Riverao Sussuarana* (1981).

FILMS: *Um Dia na Rampa* (short; co-dir.) 1957; *O Pâtio* (short), *A Cruz na Praça* (short) 1958; *Barravento/The Turning Wind/The Storm* (also co-sc.) 1962; *Deus e o Diabo na Terra do Sol/Black God White Devil* (also co-prod., sc., art dir., lyr.) 1964; *Amazonas Amazonas* (doc. short; also sc.), *Maranhâo '66* (doc. short; also sc.) 1966; *Terra em transe/Land Entranced/ Anguished Land* (also sc.) 1967; *O Cancer* (also sc.; release delayed to '74) 1968; *Antonio das Mortes/O Draqâo da Maldade contra o Santo Guerreiro* (also co-prod., sc., art dir.) 1969; *Der Leone have Sept Cabecas/The Lion Has Seven Heads* (also co-sc., co-edit.; shot in Africa) 1970; *Cabezas cortadas/Severed Heads* (also sc.; shot in Africa) 1971; *Historia do Brasil* (doc.; co-dir.) 1974; *Claro!* (also sc.) 1975; *Di* (doc. short) 1978; *Jorjamado no Cinema* (doc. short) 1979; *A Idade da Terra/The Age of the Earth* (also prod., sc.) 1980.

Rochefort, Jean. Actor. Born on Apr. 29, 1930, in Paris. Leading man, second lead, and character player of the French stage, TV, and films. He was trained at the Paris Conservatory, a classmate of Jean-Paul Belmondo, and after military service began his performing career at a Left Bank cabaret. He has played a broad range of roles in numerous screen productions since the late 50s. He won a César Award for his work in *Le Crabe-Tambour* (1977).

FILMS INCLUDE: *Une Balle dans le Canon* 1958; *Capitaine Fracasse* 1961; *Cartouche* 1962; *Symphonie pour un Massacre/Symphony for a Massacre, La Porteuse du Pain* 1963; *Angélique Marquise des Anges* 1964; *Les Tribulations d'un Chinois en Chine/Up to His Ears* 1965; *A Coeur Joie/Two Weeks in September* 1967; *Pour un Amour lointain* 1968; *Le Diable par la Queue/The Devil by the Tail* 1969; *Le Temps de Mourir* 1970; *L'Oeuf, Le Feu de la Chandeleur, Le Grand Blond avec une Chaussure noire/The Tall Blond Man with One Black Shoe* 1972; *L'Héritier/The Inheritor, Le Complot, Salut l'Artiste!* 1973; *L'Horloger de Saint-Paul/The Clockmaker, Le Fantôme de la Liberté, Le Retour du Grand Blond/The Return of the Tall Blond with One Black Shoe* 1974; *Que la Fête commence!/Let Joy Reign Supreme, Les Innocents aux Mains sales/Dirty Hands, Un Divorce heureux* 1975; *Calmos/Femmes fatales, Un Eléphant ça trompe énormément/Pardon mon Affaire* 1976; *Le Diable dans la Boîte, Le Crabe-Tambour/The Crab Drum, Nous irons tous au Paradis* 1977; *Who Is Killing the Great Chefs of Europe?* (US/Ger.) 1978; *Le Cavaleur/Practice Makes Perfect, French Postcards* (Ger./Fr.) 1979; *Chere Inconnu/I Sent a Letter to My Love* 1980; *Il faut tuer Birgitt Haas/Birgitt Haas Must Be Killed* 1981; *L'Ami de Vincent* 1983; *Frankenstein 90* (title role) 1984; *David, Thomas et les Autres* (Fr./Hung.) 1985; *La Galette du Roi* 1986; *Le Moustachu, Tandem* 1987; *I Miei Primi Quarant'Anni/My First Forty Years* (It.) 1988; *Le Mari de la Coiffeuse/The Hairdresser's Husband, Le Château de ma Mère* 1990; *Tango, Tombes du Ciel, Wild Target, La Prossima Volta il Fuoco* 1993; *Tom Est Tout Seul* 1994; *Ridicule* 1996.

Roddam, Franc. Director. Born Francis George Roddam, on Apr. 29, 1946, Stockton, England. *ed.* London Film School. Following a brief career as an advertising copywriter, he joined the BBC in 1970 as a filmmaker and won several awards for shorts and series he directed. He made an auspicious debut as a feature director with *Quadrophenia* (1979), a street-gang drama, inspired and energized by a rock album by The Who. After making the most of a routine script in Hollywood's military school drama *The Lords of Discipline* (1983), he returned to England for *The Bride* (1985), a half-baked updated remake of the 1935 horror classic *The Bride of Frankenstein.*

FILMS: *Quadrophenia* (also co-sc.) 1979; *The Lords of Discipline* (US) 1983; *The Bride* 1985; *Aria* ("Tristan und Isolde" segment; also sc.) 1987; *War Party* (also co-exec. prod.; US) 1989; *K2* (UK/US/Jap.) 1991.

Rodgers, Richard. Composer. *b.* June 28, 1902, New York City. *d.* 1979. *ed.* Columbia; Juilliard. America's most successful creator of show music for both stage and films, at first in collaboration with lyricist Lorenz HART and from 1943 with Oscar HAMMERSTEIN II. His first song was produced on the stage when he was 17 and his first Broadway musical when he was 18. He also produced many of his own musicals and after Hammerstein's death wrote some of his own lyrics. He made a personal appearance in the film *Main Street to Broadway* (1953). The film *Words and Music* told the story of his association with Hart, with Tom Drake as Rodgers and Mickey Rooney as Hart.

FILMS INCLUDE: *Spring Is Here, Heads Up* 1930; *A Connecticut Yankee* 1931; *Love Me Tonight* ('Isn't It Romantic?,' 'Mimi,' etc.) 1932; *Dancing Lady, Hallelujah I'm a Bum* ('You Are Too Beautiful,' etc.) 1933; *Manhattan Melodrama* 1934; *Mississippi* ('Easy to Remember,' etc.) 1935; *Fools for Scandal* 1938; *On Your Toes, Babes in Arms* ('Where or When') 1939; *The Boys from Syracuse, Too Many Girls* 1940; *I Married an Angel* 1942; *Higher and Higher* 1944; *State Fair* ('It Might As Well Be Spring,' Academy Award) 1945; *Words and Music* 1948; *Main Street to Broadway* (also appeared) 1953; *Victory at Sea* (doc.) 1954; *Oklahoma!* 1955; *Carousel, The King and I* 1956; *Pal Joey* 1957; *South Pacific* 1958; *Flower Drum Song* 1961; *Jumbo* 1962; *The Sound of Music* 1965; *The Swinger* 1966.

Rodriguez, Richard. Director, screenwriter. Born 1969 in San Antonio, Tex. *ed.* University of Texas, Austin. At the ripe old age of 13, Rodriguez began making home movies. He continued on through adolescence, borrowing equipment and using family members as performers, honing his skills as a filmmaker. After graduating from college, he raised $7,000 and shot his first feature, *El Mariachi* (1992). Astounded by the quality of the film considering its budget, Hollywood embraced the upstart filmmaker and he entered into a contract with Columbia Pictures where he continues to produce primarily violent, action films similar to those of his contemporary Quentin TARANTINO.

FILMS: *El Mariachi* (co-prod., dir., sc., ed., cinem.) 1992; *Desperado* (prod., dir., sc.), *Four Rooms* (dir., sc., ed.) 1995; *From Dusk Till Dawn* (ex-prod., dir., ed.) 1996.

Roeg, Nicolas. Director, former director of photography. Born on Dec. 15, 1928, London. Following military service as a projectionist, he entered the film industry in 1947 as an office boy and editing apprentice at a small studio. In 1950 he moved over to MGM's London studios, where he gradually worked his way up from clapper boy to cinematographer by 1959. During the 60s he was the lighting cameraman on several distinguished British films and in addition worked as a second-unit cameraman on *Lawrence of Arabia* (1962) and other sumptuous spectacles. He also collaborated on a couple of routine scripts. He handled the camera himself on his first two outings as a director. Roeg's first film as a director was *Performance* (1970), a complex collaborative effort (with Donald Cammell) that juggled reality and fantasy in a visually exhilarating exploration of hedonism, perversity, and decadence. Splendid cinematography was also the hallmark of his first solo feature, *Walkabout* (1971), filmed in the wilds of Australia, whose enigmatic script was dominated by fascinating imagery. Roeg's rejection of traditional narrative was expressed more emphatically in *Don't Look Now* (1973), a visually dazzling exercise in story fragmentation (it was adapted from a straightforward supernatural suspense novel by Daphne Du Maurier), in which past, present, and future are intercut to evoke an impressionistic psychological reality. A similar approach characterized *The Man Who Fell from Earth* (1976) and *Bad Timing* (1980), technically striking, visually stunning productions whose originality and invention unabashedly neared the point of pretension. As he later demonstrated with *Insignificance* (1985), winner of the Technical Excellence award at Cannes, and the entertaining *The Witches* (1989), Roeg is perfectly comfortable with more traditional storytelling. But it is as the virtuoso explorer of unconventional narrative forms that he made a lasting contribution to contemporary cinema.

FILMS: As director of photography—*The Great Van Robbery* 1959; *Jazz Boat* 1960; *Information Received* 1961; *Lawrence of Arabia* (2nd-unit phot.) 1962; *Just for Fun, Dr. Crippen, The Caretaker/The Guest* 1963; *Nothing But the Best, The Masque of the Red Death* (US/UK), *The System/The Girl Getters* 1964; *Everyday's a Holiday/Seaside Swingers, Victim*

Five/Code 7 Victim 5! 1965; *Judith* (2nd-unit phot.; US/Isr.), *A Funny Thing Happened on the Way to the Forum* (US), *Fahrenheit 451* 1966; *Casino Royale* (some scenes only), *Far from the Madding Crowd* 1967; *Petulia* (UK/US). As screenwriter—*A Prize of Arms* 1961; *Death Drums Along the River/Sanders* 1963. As director—*Performance* (co-dir. with Donald Cammell; also phot.) 1970; *Walkabout* (also phot.) 1971; *Don't Look Now* (UK/Fr./It.) 1973; *The Man Who Fell to Earth* 1976; *Bad Timing/Bad Timing: A Sensual Obsession* 1980; *Eureka* 1983; *Insignificance* 1985; *Castaway* 1986; *Aria* ("Un Ballo in Maschera" segment; also sc.) 1987; *Track 29* 1988; *The Witches* (UK/US), *Without You I'm Nothing* (exec. prod. only), *Sweet Bird of Youth* (TV movie starring Elizabeth Taylor and Mark Harmon) 1990; *Cold Heaven* 1992; *Two Deaths* 1996.

Roemer, Michael. Director. Born on Jan. 1, 1928, in Berlin. In the US since 1945, after spending the WW II years in England, he directed his first film while attending Harvard. The film, *A Touch of the Times* (1947–49), a comedy-fantasy about kite flying, is possibly America's first college-made feature length production. After eight years as production manager, assistant director, and editor with Louis De Rochemont, he directed many educational shorts and co-directed (with his partner Bob Young) a never-released documentary feature, *Cortile Cascino,* about a Sicilian slum. His first fiction feature, *Nothing but a Man* (1964), was one of the first American films to present black life with sincerity and credibility. It won two awards at the 1965 Venice Film Festival and was acclaimed by French New Wave critics. *The Plot Against Harry,* his insightful little film about an aging racketeer, shelved since 1969, delighted critics when it was finally released 20 years later. He teaches at Yale.

FILMS: *A Touch of the Times* 1949; *Cortile Cascino/The Inferno* (doc.; co-dir. with Robert M. Young) 1962; *Nothing But a Man* (co-dir. with Young; also sc.) 1964; *Faces of Israel* (doc.) 1967; *Dying* (doc.) 1976; *Pilgrim Farewell* (also sc.) 1980; *Haunted* (TV movie; also sc.) 1984; *The Plot Against Harry* (also prod., sc.; release delayed from 1969) 1989.

Rogell, Albert S. Director. *b.* Aug. 1, 1901. *d.* 1987. He entered films in his teens as assistant cameraman, soon after advancing to cameraman and assistant director. By the early 20s he was directing low-budget action films, including Art Acord and Ken Maynard Westerns. He directed many second features of all genres until the 50s, when he turned to TV production.

FILMS INCLUDE (talkies complete): *The Danger Point* (tech. dir. only) 1922; *The Greatest Menace* 1923; *The Mask of Lopez, The Silent Stranger, The Dangerous Coward* 1924; *Easy Money, Super Speed, The Snob Buster, Youth's Gamble, The Knockout Kid, The Circus Cyclone* (also story) 1925; *Men of the Night, Senor Daredevil, The Man of the West* 1926; *The Overland Stage, The Western Whirlwind* (also story), *The Sunset Derby, Men of Daring, The Devil's Saddle, The Red Raiders* 1927; *The Shepherd of the Hills, The Glorious Trail, The Phantom City* 1928; *Cheyenne, The Lone Wolf's Daughter, The California Mail, The Flying Marine, Painted Faces* 1929; *Mamba* 1930; *Aloha, Sweepstakes, The Tip Off, Suicide Fleet* 1931; *Carnival Boat, The Rider of Death Valley* 1932; *Air Hostess, Below the Sea/Hell's Cargo, The Wrecker* (also story), *East of Fifth Avenue, Fog* 1933; *No More Women, The Hell Cat, Among the Missing, Name the Woman, Fugitive Lady* 1934; *Unknown Woman, Air Hawks, Atlantic Adventure, Escape from Devil's Island* 1935; *You May Be Next, Roaming Lady, Grand Jury* 1936; *Murder in Greenwich Village* 1937; *Start Cheering, The Lone Wolf in Paris, City Streets, The Last Warning* 1938; *For Love or Money, Hawaiian Nights, Laugh It Off* 1939; *Private Affairs, I Can't Give You Anything but Love Baby, Argentine Nights, Li'l Abner* 1940; *The Black Cat, Tight Shoes, Public Enemies* 1941; *Jail House Blues, Sleepytime Gal, Butch Minds the Baby, True to the Army, Priorities on Parade, Youth on Parade* 1942; *Hit Parade of 1943, In Old Oklahoma* 1943; *Love Honor and Goodbye* (also story) 1945; *Earl Carroll's Sketchbook* 1946; *The Magnificent Rogue, Heaven Only Knows* 1947; *Northwest Stampede* (also prod.) 1948; *Song of India* (also prod.) 1949; *The Admiral Was a Lady* 1950; *Before I Wake/Shadow of Fear* (UK) 1954.

Rogers, Charles ("Buddy"). Actor. Born on Aug. 13, 1904, in Olathe, Kans. *ed.* University of Kansas. Pleasant leading man of light Hollywood films. In 1937 married Mary PICKFORD, his leading lady in *My Best Girl* and 11 years his senior.

FILMS INCLUDE: *Fascinating Youth, So's Your Old Man* 1926; *My Best Girl, Get Your Man, Wings* 1927; *Abie's Irish Rose, Varsity, Someone to Love, Red Lips* 1928; *Close Harmony, Illusion, River of Romance, Half-Way to Heaven* 1929; *Heads Up, Paramount on Parade, Safety in Numbers, Follow Thru, Young Eagles, Along Came Youth* 1930; *The Lawyer's Secret, The Road to Reno* 1931; *This Reckless Age* 1932; *Best of Enemies, Take a Chance* 1933; *Dance Band, Old Man Rhythm* 1935; *Once in a Million* 1936; *This Way Please* 1937; *Let's Make a Night of It* 1938; *Golden Hoofs, Mexican Spitfire's Baby, Sing for Your Supper* 1941; *Mexican Spitfire at Sea* 1942; *An Innocent Affair/Don't Trust Your Husband* 1948; *The Parson and the Outlaw* 1957.

Rogers, Ginger. Actress, dancer. *b.* Virginia Katherine McMath, on July 16, 1911, in Independence, Mo. *d.* 1995. Lively, versatile, durable star of Hollywood films of the 30s, 40s, and 50s. Groomed from early childhood by her divorced mother for a show-business career, she took dancing and singing lessons and at five appeared in a few commercials produced in Kansas City for regional consumption. At six she went to Hollywood, then to New York with her mother, who became a screenwriter for Fox, and was offered a film contract as a child actress, but her mother decided Ginger was not yet ready for a career. She finally made her professional debut at 14, filling in for a week as a dancer with Eddie Foy's vaudeville troupe at Fort Worth, Tex., where her mother was now working as a reporter and drama critic. The following year, Ginger won a Charleston contest and began singing and dancing on the vaudeville circuit, at first with her own act, then briefly in 1928 with her first husband (1928–31), Jack Pepper, as the duo Ginger and Pepper, then again in a solo act with the Eddie Lowry band in Chicago and the Paul Ash orchestra in New York. During that period she appeared in several shorts, including the three-reeler *Campus Sweethearts,* opposite Rudy Vallee.

The turning point in Miss Rogers's career came late in 1929, when she was selected for the second female lead in the Kalmar and Ruby Broadway musical 'Top Speed.' During the run of that show and her next Broadway musical, George Gershwin's 'Girl Crazy' (1930–31), she began her film career, playing leads and second leads in minor Paramount features that were shot at the studio's East Coast facilities in Astoria, Queens. In 1931 she went to Hollywood on a contract with Pathé, and after appearing in several of the studio's B films, typically playing wisecracking blondes, freelanced with various companies, finally settling at RKO. It was here that she soon emerged a popular star as Fred Astaire's dancing partner in a string of diverting romantic screen musicals. The duo's elegant, graceful, flawlessly fluid dance numbers provided film audiences of the 30s with many moments of aesthetic delight. The Astaire-Rogers partnership was among the most magical the screen has ever known and their films— ten in all—still thrill audiences on their frequent revivals on TV.

During the 40s, Miss Rogers proved her versatility with competent, likable performances in both light and dramatic roles. She won a best actress Oscar for her dramatic performance in *Kitty Foyle* (1940) and demonstrated her light touch with such popular comedies as *Tom, Dick and Harry* (1941) and *The Major and the Minor* (1942). She continued straddling both comedy and drama in films of the 50s, increasingly in mature roles, devoting more and more of her time to the stage. In 1965 she enjoyed a successful comeback on Broadway when she took over the lead role in the musical 'Hello Dolly!' from Carol Channing, and in 1969 scored a personal hit as the star of the London production of 'Mame.' Her second husband (1934–41) was actor Lew AYRES, her fourth (1953–57) actor Jacques Bergerac, and fifth (1961–62) actor-director-producer William MARSHALL.

FILMS: *Young Man of Manhattan, Queen High, The Sap from Syracuse, Follow the Leader* 1930; *Honor Among Lovers, The Tip Off, Suicide Fleet* 1931; *Carnival Boat, The Tenderfoot, The Thirteenth Guest, Hat Check Girl, You Said a Mouthful* 1932; *42nd Street, Broadway Bad, Gold Diggers of 1933, Professional Sweetheart, A Shriek in the Night, Don't Bet on Love, Sitting Pretty, Flying Down to Rio, Chance at Heaven* 1933; *Rafter Romance, Finishing School, 20 Million Sweethearts, Change of Heart, Upper World, The Gay Divorcee, Romance in Manhattan* 1934; *Roberta, Star of Midnight, Top Hat, In Person* 1935; *Follow the Fleet, Swing Time* 1936; *Shall We Dance, Stage Door* 1937; *Having Wonderful Time, Vivacious Lady, Carefree* 1938; *The Story of Vernon and Irene Castle* (as dancer-actress Irene Castle), *Bachelor Mother, Fifth Avenue Girl* 1939; *Primrose Path, Lucky Partners, Kitty Foyle* 1940; *Tom Dick and Harry* 1941; *Roxie Hart, Tales of Manhattan, The Major and the Minor, Once Upon a Honeymoon* 1942; *Tender Comrade* 1943; *Lady in the Dark, I'll Be Seeing You* 1944; *Weekend at the Waldorf* 1945; *Heartbeat, Magnificent Doll* (as Dolly Madison) 1946; *It Had to Be You* 1947; *The Barkleys of Broadway* 1949; *Perfect Strangers, Storm Warning* 1950; *The Groom Wore Spurs* 1951; *We're Not Married, Monkey Business, Dreamboat* 1952; *Forever Female* 1953; *Black Widow, Beautiful Stranger/Twist of Fate* (UK) 1954; *Tight Spot* 1955; *The First Traveling Saleslady, Teenage Rebel* 1956; *Oh Men! Oh Women!* 1957; *The Confession/Seven Different Ways/Quick Let's Get Married* (release delayed to 1971) 1964; *Harlow* (as Jean Harlow's mother in Carol Lynley version) 1965.

Rogers, Jean. Actress. *b.* Eleanor Lovegren, Mar. 25, 1916, Belmont, Mass. *d.* 1991. A beauty contest winner, she played leading ladies in many Hollywood B features of the 30s and 40s but is best remembered as the heroine of several serials, including two Flash Gordon adventures.

FILMS INCLUDE: *Eight Girls in a Boat* 1934; *The Great Air Mystery* (serial), *Manhattan Moon* 1935; *Flash Gordon* (serial), *Ace Drummond* (serial), *The Adventures of Frank Merriwell* (serial), *My Man Godfrey, Conflict, Mysterious Crossing* 1936; *Night Key, Reported Missing* 1937; *Flash Gordon's Trip to Mars* (serial), *Time Out for Murder, Always in Trouble, While New York Sleeps* 1938; *Inside Story, Hotel for Women, Stop Look and Love* 1939; *Heaven with a Barbed Wire Fence, The Man Who Wouldn't Talk, Viva Cisco Kid, Charlie Chan in Panama, Brigham Young—Frontiersman, Yesterday's Heroes* 1940; *Let's Make Music, Design for Scandal* 1941; *Dr. Kildare's Victory, Sunday Punch, Pacific Rendezvous* 1942; *A Stranger in Town, Whistling in Brooklyn* 1943; *Rough Tough and Ready* 1945; *Gay Blades, Hot Cargo* 1946; *Backlash* 1947; *Speed to Spare* 1948; *The Second Woman* 1951.

Rogers, Mimi. Actress. Born on Jan. 27, 1956, in Coral Gables, Fla. Attractive leading lady of Hollywood films. Making her movie debut in 1983, she gained popularity in the TV series 'The Rousters' (1983–84) and 'Paper Dolls' (1984) before returning to the big screen with impressive performances in *Gung Ho* (1986) and *Someone to Watch Over Me* (1987). From 1987 to 1990 she was married to actor Tom CRUISE.

FILMS: *Blue Skies Again* 1983; *Gung Ho* 1986; *Street Smart, Someone to Watch Over Me* 1987; *The Mighty Quinn, Hider in the House* 1989; *Dimenticare Palermo/The Palermo Connection* (It./Fr.), *Desperate Hours* 1990; *The Doors* (cameo), *The Rapture* 1991; *The Player* (cameo), *White Sands* 1992; *Monkey Trouble* 1994; *The Mirror Has Two Faces, Trees Lounge* 1996.

Rogers, Roy. Actor, singer. Born Leonard Slye, on Nov. 5, 1911, in Cincinnati. Along with Gene Autry, Hollywood's most popular singing cowboy. After arriving in California in 1929 as a migratory fruit picker, he began his show business career by forming a singing duo with a cousin. Later he changed his name to Dick Weston and formed a singing group, The Sons of the Pioneers, with which he appeared on Los Angeles radio (and later in films). He broke into films in bit roles in 1935, sometimes in support of Gene Autry, whom he was to succeed as "King of the Cowboys" by 1942. Rogers starred in scores of lively Westerns through the early 50s, often teamed with sidekick Gabby HAYES and heroine Dale EVANS, his second wife (from 1947). His regular horse, Trigger, was billed as "the smartest horse in the movies." With the decline of the B Western, he moved his act to television, starring in 'The Roy Rogers Show' (1951–57) and later co-hosting the variety program 'The Roy Rogers and Dale Evans Show' (1962). A shrewd businessman, Rogers formed a chain of enterprises in the 50s, including his own TV production company, and is also involved in the manufacturing and distribution of a variety of Western products, real estate, cattle, thoroughbred horses, a rodeo show, and a chain of restaurants. His personal wealth is estimated at close to $100 million. In 1975 he returned to the screen after a long absence.

FILMS INCLUDE: *Tumbling Tumbleweeds* 1935; *The Big Show* 1936; *Under Western Stars, Billy the Kid Returns* 1938; *The Arizona Kid, Days of Jesse James* 1939; *Dark Command, The Border Legion* 1940; *Robin Hood of the Pecos, Red River Valley* 1941; *Sons of the Pioneers, Romance on the Range* 1942; *King of the Cowboys, Song of Texas* 1943; *The Cowboy and the Senorita, The Yellow Rose of Texas, Lake Placid Serenade* 1944; *Utah, Don't Fence Me In* 1945; *My Pal Trigger, Song of Arizona, Helldorado* 1946; *Apache Rose, Springtime in the Sierras* 1947; *Eyes of Texas, Melody Time* 1948; *Grand Canyon Trail* 1949; *North of the Great Divide* 1950; *Heart of the Rockies* 1951; *Son of Paleface* 1952; *Alias Jesse James* (cameo) 1959; *Mackintosh and T.J.* 1975.

Rogers, Will. Actor, wit, folk hero. *b.* William Penn Adair Rogers, Nov. 4, 1879, Colagah, Indian Territory (now Oklahoma). *d.* 1935, in an air crash with aviator Wiley Post. Immensely popular entertainer and homespun philosopher, roving ambassador of rural Americana and spokesman of common folk everywhere. An expert rider and rope twirler from boyhood, he made his public bow in a Johannesburg, South Africa, Wild West show during the Boer War. Back in the US, he continued demonstrating his skills in fairs and vaudeville, eventually adding bits of topical humor to his act. In 1912 he got into musical comedy and in 1917 he starred with the Ziegfeld Follies. The movies tried to capitalize on his popularity and he starred in many features and shorts from 1918, but there was little he could contribute to silent cinema and he lost much of his own money when he tried to produce and direct his own films.

The situation changed with the advent of sound, when

Rogers rapidly became a top box-office attraction. His popularity spread to other media, notably radio and the press, in which his political commentary carried much weight. He declined a nomination for the governorship of Oklahoma, served as mayor of Beverly Hills, and was instrumental in the election of FDR as president in 1932. A tribute to his achievements was paid in the 1952 film biography *The Story of Will Rogers.* His son, actor-entertainer (and later newspaper publisher and congressman) Will Rogers, Jr. (*b.* Oct. 20, 1911, NYC), played the title role in this film and impersonated his celebrated father twice more, in the pictures *Look for the Silver Lining* (1949) and *The Eddie Cantor Story* (1953). Keith Carradine and Mac Davis portrayed the legendary Will senior in the Tony-winning biographical Broadway musical 'The Will Rogers Follies.'

FILMS: *Laughing Bill Hyde* 1918; *Almost a Husband* (also titles), *Jubilo* 1919; *Water Water Everywhere, The Strange Boarder, Jes' Call Me Jim, Cupid the Cowpuncher, Guile of Women* 1920; *Boys Will Be Boys, An Unwilling Hero, Doubling for Romeo* (also co-outline, titles), *A Poor Relation* 1921; *One Glorious Day, The Headless Horseman* (also co-titles), *The Ropin' Fool* (short; also prod., sc., titles), *Fruits of Fate* (short; also prod., titles) 1922; *One Day in 365* (unreleased short, possibly home movie; also prod., sc., titles) 1922; *Hustling Hank* (short), *Hollywood* (cameo), *Jus' Passing Through* (short), *Uncensored Movies* (short) 1923; *Two Wagons Both Covered* (short parody on *The Covered Wagon;* also sc.), *The Cake Eater* (short), *The Cowboy Sheik* (short; also titles), *Big Moments from Little Pictures* (short), *High Brow Stuff* (short), *Going to Congress* (short; also sc., titles), *Don't Just Park There* (short), *Jubilo Jr.* ("Our Gang" short), *Our Congressman* (short; also titles), *A Truthful Liar* (short), *Gee Whiz Genevieve* (short) 1924; *Will Rogers, Our Unofficial Ambassador Abroad* (series of 12 one-reel European travelogues; also sc.), *Tip Toes, A Texas Steer* 1927; *They Had to See Paris, Happy Days* 1929; *So This Is London, Lightnin'* 1930; *A Connecticut Yankee, Young As You Feel, Ambassador Bill* 1931; *Business and Pleasure, Down to Earth, Too Busy to Work* 1932; *State Fair, Doctor Bull, Mr. Skitch* 1933; *David Harum, Handy Andy, Judge Priest* 1934; *The County Chairman, Life Begins at 40, Doubting Thomas, Steamboat 'Round the Bend, In Old Kentucky* 1935.

Rogosin, Lionel. Documentary producer-director. Born in 1924, in New York City. The son of a Russian Jewish immigrant who became a wealthy industrialist, he studied chemistry at Yale and served in the Navy as an engineer during WW II before joining his father's business as head of the textile division. Troubled by the sight of the skid row scene near his Greenwich Village home, and motivated by a creative urge, he used his own money to produce and direct *On the Bowery* (1956), an hour-long documentary that was nominated for an Oscar and won the top prize in its category at the Venice Film Festival as well as the British Film Academy Award for best documentary. Rogosin confirmed his position as a leading voice of social consciousness in the film community with *Come Back Africa* (1960), a dramatized documentary about the horrific plight of a dislocated Zulu family in Johannesburg. He shot the film in South Africa, partly with a concealed camera, and smuggled much of the footage out of the country to avoid scrutiny by the authorities. Although dramatically flawed, the film contained explosively revealing footage and was hailed as politically and socially significant. When he found no exhibiting outlet for the film, Rogosin leased and renovated an old Greenwich Village theater, renamed it the Bleecker Street Cinema, and premiered his film there. Until he sold it in 1974, the theater represented a popular outlet for quality "alternative" films. Regaining his course as a social critic, Rogosin assailed the horrors of war in *Good Times, Wonderful Times* (1966), exposed racial outrage in *Black Roots* (1970) and *Black Fantasy* (1972), and explored the nature of the Middle East conflict in *Arab Israeli Dialogue* (1974). None of his subsequent projects materialized.

FILMS: *On the Bowery* 1956; *Come Back Africa* 1960; *Oysters Are in Season* (short) 1963; *How Do You Like Them Bananas?* (short), *Good Times Wonderful Times* 1966; *Black Roots* 1970; *Black Fantasy* 1972; *Woodcutters of the Deep South* 1973; *Arab-Israeli Dialogue* 1974.

Rohmer, Eric. Director. Born Jean-Marie Maurice Scherer, on Apr. 4, 1920, in Nancy, France. Literate, articulate, searching filmmaker who emerged in the late 60s as France's most stimulating "new" director. For eight years before entering the world of film in 1950, he taught literature at a provincial high school. A director of shorts since the early 50s, he received more attention during that period for his astute film criticism in important French publications. In 1950 he founded with GODARD and RIVETTE the short-lived *La Gazette du Cinéma.* In 1957 he became editor in chief of the influential New Wave periodical *Cahiers du Cinéma,* a post he held until 1963, when he quit amid a right-left controversy. The following year he entered French television, for which he made a number of varied documentaries. His first feature film, *Les Petits Filles Modèles,* made in 1952, was never completed; his second, *The Sign of Leo,* released three years after its making, failed to arouse much interest.

It was in the 60s, with his cycle of *six contes moraux,* and especially after the international success of *Ma Nuit chez Maud/My Night at Maud's,* that Rohmer finally won recognition. The cycle comprises one short, *La Boulangère de Monceau* (1962), a 60-minute featurette, *La Carrière de Suzanne* (1963), and four feature-length films, *La Collectionneuse* (1967), *Ma Nuit chez Maud* (1969), *Le Genou de Claire/Claire's Knee* (1970), and *L'Amour l'après-midi/Chloe in the Afternoon* (1972). They are all variations on a similar theme and have a common structure: intimate verbal exchanges between characters whose intellectual inflexibility is challenged by a tempting new set of physical circumstances, with ensuing inconsistencies between words spoken by the characters and their actions. After taking a breather from the intimacy of the "Six Moral Tales" with two literary adaptations—*The Marguise of O. . .* (1976), from the novella by Kleist, and *Perceva le Gallois* (1978), from the 12th-century manuscript by Chrétien de Troyes—Rohmer began a new cycle of films with *The Aviator's Wife* (1980). Rohmer called the cycle *comédies et proverbs.* Like the *contes moreaux,* the films in the new cycle centered on words, thoughts, and emotions rather than on plot and action. But while in the former Rohmer focused on the inner world of individual characters, in the latter series he expanded his scope to encompass groups of characters or an entire social milieu. With *Conte de Printemps/A Tale of Springtime* (1990), Rohmer inaugurated yet another new cycle of morality parables, "Tales of Four Season." One of the most intelligent and original thinkers of the contemporary cinema, Rohmer is also an accomplished filmmaker. Using uncomplicated, economical, but fluid camera techniques, he succeeds in capturing on film not only the evocative imagery of locales but also the inner worlds of his characters and the psychological atmosphere that grows from their encounters. An intensely private, reclusive person, Rohmer rarely discusses his creative process. His films grow out of careful, patient observation that often involves the recording of everyday conversations with people who interest him as potential protagonists, especially young women whose inner world he has long explored. Technically, he is a minimalist who maximizes the effect of the modest means he allows himself in the process of making films. His many awards include the Prix Max Ophüls for *My Night at Maud's* (1970); a Prix Louis Delluc and Prix Méliès as well as the top prize at San Sebastian for *Claire's Knee* (1971); the Special Jury Prize at Cannes for *The Marquise of O. . .* (1976); and the Silver Bear as best director and a share of the International Critics Prize at Berlin for *Pauline at the Beach* (1983). He has written the screenplays for all his films. He is the co-author with Claude CHABROL of *Hitchcock* (1957), a notable critical study of the work of the cinema's master of suspense.

FILMS INCLUDE (as director-writer): *Journal d'un Scélérat* (short) 1950; *Présentation ou Charlotte et son Steak* (short) 1951; *Les Petites Filles Modèles* (co-dir.; unfinished) 1952; *Bérénice* (short; also act.) 1954; *La Sonate à Kreutzer/The Kreutzer Sonata* (medium-length; also act.) 1956; *Véronique et son Cancre* (short) 1958; *Le Signe du Lion/The Sign of Leo* 1959; *La Boulangère de Monceau* (short) 1962; *La Carrière de Suzanne* (medium-length) 1963; *Nadja à Paris* (short) 1964; *Paris vu par. . ./Six in Paris* ("Place de l'Etoile" episode) 1965; *Une Etudiante d'Aujour'hui* (short), *La Collectionneuse* 1967; *Fermière a Montfauçon* (short) 1968; *Ma Nuit chez Maud/My Night at Maud's* 1969; *Le Genou de Claire/Claire's Knee* 1970; *L'Amour l'après-midi/Chloe in the Afternoon* 1972; *Die Marquise von O/La Marquise d'O/The Marquise of O. . .* (Ger./Fr.) 1976; *Perceval le Gallois/Perceval* 1978; *La Femme de l'Aviateur/The Aviator's Wife* 1980; *Le Beau Mariage/The Perfect Marriage* 1982; *Pauline à la Plage/Pauline at the Beach* 1983; *Les Nuits de la Pleine Lune/Full Moon in Paris* 1984; *Le Rayon vert/The Green Ray/Summer* 1986; *Quatre Aventures de Reinette et Mirabelle/Four Adventures of Reinette and Mirabelle, L'Amie de mon Amie/Boyfriends and Girlfriends/My Girlfriend's Boyfriend* 1987; *Les Pyramides bleues/Paris Calling* (artistic advisor only; Fr./Mex.) 1988; *Conte de Printemps/A Tale of Springtime* 1990; *Conte d'hiver/A Tale of Winter* 1992; *L'Arbre, Le Maire et La Médiathèque* 1993; *Rendezvous in Paris* 1996.

Röhrig, Walter. Art director. *b.* 1897, in Germany. d. 1945. Important figure in the German expressionist movement, at first as stage decorator and after WW I as designer of film sets. He collaborated on the design of many prominent silent films, often in collaboration with Robert HERLTH. From the mid-30s he worked on routine entertainment films.

FILMS INCLUDE (mostly in collaboration): *Das Kabinett des Dr. Caligari/The Cabinet of Dr. Caligari, Die Pest von Florenz* 1919; *Der Golem/The Golem, Das lachende Grauen, Das Geheimnis von Bombay, Der Idiot/The Idiot* 1920; *Der Müde Tod/Destiny, Satansketten* 1921; *Fräulein Julie/Miss Julie* 1922; *Komödie des Herzens, Der letzte Mann/The Last Laugh* 1924; *Zur Chronik von Grieshuus, Tartüff/Tartuffe* 1925; *Faust* 1926; *Luther* 1927; *Looping the Loop* 1928; *Die wunderbare Luge der Nina Petrowna/The Wonderful Lie of Nina Petrovna* 1929; *Hokuspokus/Hocuspocus* 1930; *Der Kongress tanzt/The Congress Dances* 1931; *Die Gräfin von Monte Cristo* 1932; *Walzerkrieg/Waltz Time in Vienna* 1933; *Prinzessin Tournadot* 1934; *Barcarole, Amphytrion* 1935; *Hans im Glück* 1936; *Capriccio* 1938; *Heimkehr* 1941; *Rembrandt* 1942.

Roizman, Owen. Director of photography. Born on Sept. 22, 1936, in Brooklyn, N.Y. *ed.* Gettysburgh Coll. The son of a Fox Movietone News cameraman, he shot TV commercials before entering features in the early 70s. He quickly became established as one of Hollywood's most dependable and inventive cinematographers, with four Oscar nominations to his credit. He took a leave of absence from feature films for much of the 80s to run his own commercials production house.

FILMS INCLUDE: *The French Connection* 1971; *Play It Again Sam, The Heartbreak Kid* 1972; *The Exorcist* 1973; *The Taking of Pelham One Two Three* 1974; *The Stepford Wives, Three Days of the Condor* 1975; *The Return of the Man Called Horse, Network* 1976; *Straight Time, Sgt. Pepper's Lonely Hearts Club Band* 1978; *The Electric Horseman* 1979; *The Black Marble* 1980; *True Confessions, Absence of Malice, Taps* 1981; *Tootsie* 1982; *Vision Quest* 1985; *I Love You to Death, Havana* 1990; *The Addams Family, Grand Canyon* 1991; *Wyatt Earp* (also act.) 1994.

Roland, Gilbert. Actor. *b.* Luis Antonio Damaso de Alonso, on Dec. 11, 1905, in Juarez (or Chihuahua), Mexico. *d.* 1994. Durable Latin lover of the silent and sound screen. The son of a Spanish bullfighter, he trained for the ring but chose a career in films after his family moved to the US. He made his movie debut as an extra at age 13 and began playing dashing leading men in the mid-20s, notably as Armand in the silent version of *Camille,* opposite Norma Talmadge. He later appeared in numerous films, in both leads and supporting roles. His first wife was Constance BENNETT.

FILMS INCLUDE: *The Plastic Age* 1925; *The Campus Flirt, The Blonde Saint* 1926; *Camille* (as Armand), *Rose of the Golden West, The Love Mart* 1927; *The Dove, The Woman Disputed* 1928; *New York Nights* 1929; *Men of the North* 1930; *Monsieur Le Fox* 1931; *The Passionate Plumber, The Woman in Room 13, Life Begins, No Living Witness, Call Her Savage* 1932; *She Done Him Wrong, Our Betters, Gigolettes of Paris, After Tonight* 1933; *Elinor Norton* 1934; *Mystery Woman* 1935; *The Last Train from Madrid, Thunder Trail* 1937; *Gateway* 1938; *La Vida Bohemia/La Bohème* (US film in Spanish; as Rodolfo), *Juarez* 1939; *The Sea Hawk* 1940; *Isle of Missing Men* 1942; *The Desert Hawk* (serial) 1944; *Captain Kidd* 1945; *The Gay Cavalier, Beauty and the Bandit, South of Monterey* 1946; *King of the Bandits, Robin Hood of Monterey* 1947; *We Were Strangers* 1949; *Malaya, The Torch, Crisis, The Furies* 1950; *Ten Tall Men, The Bullfighter and the Lady, Mark of the Renegade* 1951; *My Six Convicts, Glory Alley, The Miracle of Our Lady of Fatima, Apache War Smoke, The Bad and the Beautiful* 1952; *Thunder Bay, Beneath the 12-Mile Reef* 1953; *The French Line* 1954; *Underwater!, The Racers, That Lady* 1955; *Bandido* 1956; *Three Violent People, The Midnight Story* 1957; *The Big Circus* 1959; *Guns of the Timberland* 1960; *Samar* 1962; *Cheyenne Autumn* 1964; *The Reward* 1965; *Vado. . . l'Amazzo e Torno/Any Gun Can Play* (It.) 1968; *The Christian Licorice Store* 1971; *Johnny Hamlet* (It.) 1972; *Deliver Us from Evil* 1975; *Islands in the Stream* 1977; *Caboblanco* 1981; *Barbarosa* 1982.

Roland, Ruth. Actress. *b.* Aug. 26, 1892, San Francisco. *d.* 1937. Queen of Hollywood silent serials. A former child stage star, billed as "Baby Ruth," she entered films in 1911, making her debut in Kalem Western comedies. In 1915 she began her spectacular career as a serial heroine, rivaling Pearl WHITE in popularity and athletic prowess. She also starred in some feature films.

FILMS INCLUDE: *A Chance Shot, Arizona Bill* 1911; *Hypnotic Nell, Ranch Girl on a Rampage, The Hoodoo Hat, The Beauty Parlor of Stone Gulch* 1912; *Absent-minded Abe, While Father Telephoned* 1913; *And the Villain Still Pursued Her, Hoodooed on His Wedding Day, Ham the Lineman, Ham and the Villain Factory, Ham the Piano Mover* 1914; *Who Pays?* (serial), *The Apartment House Mystery, Comrade John* 1915; *The Red Circle* (serial) 1915–16; *The Sultana* 1916; *The Devil's Bait, The Fringe of Society, The Neglected Wife* (serial) 1917; *Hands Up!* (serial) 1918; *The Tiger's Trail* (serial), *The Adventures of Ruth* (serial), *Love and the Law* 1919; *Ruth of the Rockies* (serial), *What Would You Do?* 1920; *The Avenging Arrow* (serial)

1921; *The Timber Queen* (serial), *White Eagle* (serial) 1922; *Haunted Valley* (serial), *Ruth of the Range* (serial) 1923; *Where the Worst Begins, Dollar Down* 1925; *The Masked Woman* 1927; *Reno* 1930; *From Nine to Nine* (Can.) 1936.

Rolfe, Guy. Actor. Born on Dec. 27, 1911, in London, England. Gaunt leading man and supporting player of British and some American films. On the stage since 1936, following a brief boxing career.

FILMS INCLUDE: *Knight Without Armour* (bit) 1936; *The Drum/Drums* (bit) 1938; *Hungry Hill* 1946; *Odd Man Out, Nicholas Nickleby, Uncle Silas/The Inheritance* (as Sepulchre Hawkes) 1947; *Easy Money, Broken Journey, Saraband for Dead Lovers/Saraband, Portrait from Life/The Girl in the Painting* 1948; *The Spider and the Fly* 1949; *Prelude to Fame, The Reluctant Widow* 1950; *Ivanhoe* (as Prince John; UK/US) 1952; *Young Bess* (as Ned Seymour; US), *The Veils of Bagdad* (US) 1953; *King of the Khyber Rifles* (US), *Dance Little Lady* 1954; *It's Never Too Late* 1956; *Girls at Sea* 1958; *Yesterday's Enemy, The Stranglers of Bombay* 1959; *Snow White and the Three Stooges* (US), *King of Kings* (as Caiphas; US), *Mr. Sardonicus* (US) 1961; *Taras Bulba* (US) 1962; *The Fall of the Roman Empire* (US) 1964; *The Alphabet Murders* 1966; *Land Raiders* (US) 1970; *Nicholas and Alexandra* 1971; *And Now the Screaming Starts* 1973; *Bloodline* 1979; *The Bride* 1985; *Dolls* (US) 1987.

roll. Any length of film wound on a core.

"Roll 'em!" (or: **"Roll it!"**). The cue given to the camera operator (usually by the assistant director) to start the camera motor running for a take. It is usually followed by the command "Action!," given by the director once the camera is up to speed.

rolling title. Also called "creeping title," "crawl title," or "running title." Film credits that roll up from the bottom of the screen and disappear at the top.

Rollins, Howard, Jr. Actor. *b.* Oct. 17, 1950, in Baltimore. *d.* 1996. *ed.* Towson State Coll. Tall, impressive leading man of the American stage, TV, and films. He was nominated for an Academy Award as best supporting actor for his dominant role as a defiant black young man in Milos Forman's *Ragtime* (1981). Also memorable in Norman Jewison's *A Soldier's Story* (1984) and in the TV series 'In the Heat of the Night.'

FILMS: *The House of God* 1979; *Ragtime* 1981; *A Soldier's Story* 1984; *Dear America* (doc.; co-narrator only) 1987; *On the Block* 1989; *Drunks* 1997.

Rollins, Jack. See JOFFE, Charles H.

Roman, Ruth. Actress. Born on Dec. 22, 1924, in Boston. *ed.* Bishop Lee Dramatic School. Leading lady of Hollywood films since the mid-40s, following stage experience. She typically plays a determined, strong-willed character, and also has several short stories to her credit. She is a survivor of the sinking of the Andrea Doria cruise liner.

FILMS INCLUDE: *Stage Door Canteen* 1943; *Since You Went Away* 1944; *The Jungle Queen* (serial) 1945; *Good Sam, Belle Starr's Daughter* 1948; *Champion, The Window, Beyond the Forest, Always Leave Them Laughing* 1949; *Barricade, Colt .45, Three Secrets, Dallas* 1950; *Lightning Strikes Twice, Strangers on a Train, Tomorrow Is Another Day* 1951; *Invitation, Mara Maru, Young Man with Ideas* 1952; *Blowing Wild* 1953; *Tanganyika, Down Three Dark Streets, The Shanghai Story* 1954; *The Far Country* 1955; *The Bottom of the Bottle, Joe Macbeth, Rebel in Town* 1956; *Five Steps to Danger* 1957; *Bitter Victory* 1958; *Look in Any Window* 1961; *Love Has Many Faces* 1965; *The Baby, The Killing Kind* 1973; *A Knife for the Ladies, Dead of Night* 1974; *Impulse* 1975; *Day of the Animals* 1977; *Echoes* 1983.

Romance, Viviane. Actress. Born Pauline Ortmans, on July 4, 1912, in Roubaix, France. Popular star of French films, often in sensual "vamp" and coquette roles. Elected Miss Paris in 1930, she entered films as an extra the following year and was at the peak of her career from the mid-30s to the mid-40s. In the early 50s she tried unsuccessfully to double as her own producer.

FILMS INCLUDE: *La Chienne* (bit) 1931; *Ciboulette* (bit) 1933; *Liliom* (bit) 1934; *Les Yeux noirs/Dark Eyes, La Bandera* 1935; *La Belle Equipe/They Were Five* 1936; *L'Ange du Foyer, Mademoiselle Docteur/Street of Shadows, Naples au Baiser de Feu/The Kiss of Fire* 1937; *Le Puritain, Prison de Femmes/Marked Girls, L'Etrange Monsieur Victor, Le Joueur, La Maison du Maltais/Sirocco, Gibraltar/It Happened in Gibraltar* 1938; *L'Esclave blanche/The Pasha's Wives, La Tradition de Minuit* 1939; *Angelica* 1940; *La Vénus aveugle, Une Femme dans la Nuit* 1941; *Cartacalha, Feu Sacré* 1942; *Carmen* (title role; release delayed from 1943), *La Boîte aux Rêves* 1945; *Panique/Panic, L'Affaire du Collier de la Reine/The Queen's Necklace* 1946; *La Colère des Dieux, La Carrefour des Passions* 1947; *Maya* (also prod.) 1950; *Passion* (also prod.) 1951; *Au Coeur de la Casbah* 1952; *La Chair et le Diable/Flesh and Desire* (also prod.) 1953; *Gueule d'Ange/Pleasures and Vices, L'Affaire des Poisons* 1955; *Pitié pour les Vamps* (also prod.) 1956; *Mélodie en Sous-Sol/Any Number Can Win* 1963; *Nada* 1973.

Romberg, Sigmund. Composer. *b.* July 29, 1887, in Szegedin, Hungary. *d.* 1951. He wrote many light operettas, some of which have been adapted to the screen, and also composed several scores directly for films. José Ferrer portrayed him in the 1954 film biography *Deep in My Heart.*

FILMS INCLUDE: *The Desert Song* 1929, 1944, 1953; *Viennese Nights* 1930; *New Moon* 1931, 1940; *The Night Is Young* 1935; *Maytime* 1937; *The Girl of the Golden West* 1938; *Balalaika, Broadway Serenade, Let Freedom Ring* 1939; *Up in Central Park* 1948; *The Student Prince* 1954.

Rome, Stewart. Actor. *b.* Septimus Wernham Ryott, Jan. 30, 1886, Newbury, England. *d.* 1965. Leading man of scores of British silents and later a character actor in sound films.

FILMS INCLUDE: *A Throw of the Dice* (short) 1913; *Brothers, Terror of the Air* 1914; *Barnaby Rudge, The Battle, The White Hope* 1915; *Face to Face, Annie Laurie* 1916; *The Cobweb, The American Heiress, The Eternal Triangle* 1917; *A Great Coup* 1919; *The Romance of a Movie Star* 1920; *The Imperfect Lover* 1921; *The Prodigal Son* 1923; *The Desert Sheik* (US), *The Eleventh Commandment* 1924; *The Silver Treasure* (US), *Thou Fool* 1926; *Zero* 1928; *Dark Red Roses* 1929; *The Last Hour* 1930; *Betrayal, Reunion* 1931; *Temptation* 1935; *Men of Yesterday* 1936; *Wings of the Morning, The Squeaker/Murder on Diamond Row, Dinner at the Ritz* 1937; *One of Our Aircraft Is Missing* 1942; *The Magic Bow* 1946; *The White Unicorn/Bad Sister* 1947; *Woman Hater* 1948; *Let's Have a Murder* 1950.

Romero, Cesar. Actor. *b.* Feb. 15, 1907, New York City, of Cuban parentage. *d.* 1994. Tall, dark "Latin lover" of Hollywood films of the 30s, 40s, and 50s, mainly with Fox, later in suave character parts. Formerly a ballroom, nightclub, and musical stage dancer and briefly a Broadway actor, he portrayed the Cisco Kid in several installments of the light adventure screen series. A confirmed bachelor, he never married. He was seen on TV as the Joker in 'The Batman' series of the late 60s and as Peter Stavros in 'Falcon Crest' of the late 80s.

FILMS INCLUDE: *The Shadow Laughs* 1933; *The Thin Man, British Agent* 1934; *Clive of India, The Good Fairy, Cardinal Richelieu, Hold 'Em Yale, The Devil Is a Woman, Diamond Jim, Metropolitan, Rendezvous, Show Them No Mercy* 1935; *Love Before Breakfast, Public Enemy's Wife, 15 Maiden Lane* 1936; *Wee Willie Winkie, Dangerously Yours* 1937; *Happy*

Landing, Always Goodbye, My Lucky Star, Five of a Kind 1938; *Wife Husband and Friend, The Little Princess, The Return of the Cisco Kid* (not in title role), *Frontier Marshal* (as Doc Holliday), *Charlie Chan at Treasure Island, The Cisco Kid and the Lady* (first as the Cisco Kid) 1939; *He Married His Wife, Viva Cisco Kid* (title role), *Lucky Cisco Kid* (title role), *The Gay Caballero* (as the Cisco Kid), *Romance of the Rio Grande* (as the Cisco Kid) 1940; *Tall Dark and Handsome, Ride on Vaquero* (as the Cisco Kid), *The Great American Broadcast, Dance Hall, Weekend in Havana* 1941; *A Gentleman at Heart, Orchestra Wives, Tales of Manhattan, Springtime in the Rockies* 1942; *Coney Island, Wintertime* 1943; *Carnival in Costa Rica* 1947; *Captain from Castile* (as Cortez), *Deep Waters, That Lady in Ermine, Julia Misbehaves* 1948; *The Beautiful Blonde from Bashful Bend* 1949; *Love That Brute, Once a Thief* 1950; *Happy Go Lovely* (UK), *Lost Continent, FBI Girl* 1951; *Lady in the Fog/Scotland Yard Inspector* (UK), *The Jungle* 1952; *Street of Shadows/The Shadow Man* (UK) 1953; *Vera Cruz* 1954; *The Americano, The Racers* 1955; *The Leather Saint, Around the World in 80 Days* 1956; *The Story of Mankind* 1957; *Villa!* 1958; *Ocean's Eleven* 1960; *Seven Women from Hell* 1961; *El Valle de las Espadas/The Castilian* (Sp./US), *We Shall Return, Donovan's Reef* 1963; *A House Is Not a Home* 1964; *Sergeant Deadhead, Marriage on the Rocks* 1965; *Batman* 1966; *Hot Millions, Skidoo, El Millòn de Madigan/Madigan's Millions* (Sp./It.) 1968; *Midas Run, How to Make It, Latitude Zero* (Jap./US), *Crooks and Coronets/Sophie's Place* (UK/US) 1969; *The Computer Wore Tennis Shoes* 1970; *Now You See Him Now You Don't, The Proud and the Damned* 1972; *The Spectre of Edgar Allan Poe* 1973; *The Strongest Man in the World* 1975 *Monster* 1975; *Lust in the Dust* 1985; *Mortuary Academy* 1988; *Simple Justice* 1989.

Romero, George A. Director. Born on Feb. 4, 1939, The Bronx, N.Y. A film enthusiast from childhood, he began experimenting with an 8 mm camera at 14. After graduating from the Carnegie-Mellon Institute, where he had studied art, design, and drama, he formed the Pittsburgh-based Latent Image company, through which he produced and directed industrial films and TV commercials. Romero's first feature, *Night of the Living Dead* (1968), remains a landmark of the modern horror film, a gory, creepy, spine-chilling zombie movie that gained a huge cult following. Two sequels ensued: the equally gripping *Dawn of the Dead* (1979) and the disappointing *Day of the Dead* (1985). Both were enhanced by a sprinkling of social satire and by the craftsmanship of makeup artist Tom Savini, who was also instrumental in the success of Romero's *Martin* (1978). Although Romero's work has been uneven and at its best erratic, the influence of his blood-and-gore approach to horror can be detected in the films of such directors as Brian De Palma, John Carpenter, David Cronenberg, and Wes Craven.

FEATURE FILMS: *Night of the Living Dead* (also story, phot., edit.) 1968; *There's Always Vanilla/The Affair* (also phot., edit.) 1972; *The Crazies/Code Name: Trixie* (also sc., edit.), *Hungry Wives* (also sc., phot., edit.) 1983; *Martin* (also sc., edit.) 1978; *Dawn of the Dead* (also sc., edit., act.) 1979; *Knightriders* (also sc., co-edit.) 1981; *Creepshow* (also co-edit.) 1982; *Day of the Dead* (also sc.) 1985; *Flight of the Spruce Goose* (act. only) 1986; *Creepshow 2* (sc. only) 1987; *Monkey Shines* (also sc.) 1988; *Due Occhi diabolici/Two Evil Eyes* ("The Truth About the Valdemar Case" episode; also sc.; It.), *Tales from the Darkside: The Movie* ("Cat From Hell" episode; sc. only), *Night of The Living Dead* (co-exec. prod., sc. only) 1990; *The Silence of The Lambs* (act. only) 1991; *The Dark Half* (also sc., exec. prod.) 1993.

Romm, Mikhail. Director. Born Jan. 24, 1901, Zaigrayevo, near Irkutsk, Siberia, Russia. The son of an exiled Jewish doctor, he attended high school locally, then went to Moscow, where he studied sculpture, and later also literature and drama, at the Academy of Fine Arts. His studies were interrupted by a three-year stint with the Red Army during the civil war. He was in his late 20s by the time he entered films as a screenwriter and assistant director and a ripe 33 when he made his directing debut in 1934. His first film, *Pyshka,* was an adaptation of *Boule de Suif,* the Guy de Maupassant story that would later provide the basis for John Ford's *Stagecoach.* French critic Georges Sadoul considered it the best screen adaptation ever made of a Maupassant work. Romm's next film, *The Thirteen* (1937), was a Central Asian imitation of Ford's *The Lost Patrol.* It was well received and much liked by Stalin, who requested that Romm be assigned a major film to commemorate the 20th anniversary of the October Revolution. The result was *Lenin in October* (1937), the great success of which prompted a sequel, *Lenin in 1918* (1939). Apart from *Girl No. 217* (1944), a harshly realistic depiction of the harrowing experience of a young Russian woman deported by the Nazis to Germany, Romm's subsequent output consisted largely of mediocre party-line productions. He reclaimed his reputation as a creative artist in the early 60s with *Nine Days of One Year* (1962), a gripping drama about a scientist's divided loyalties to work and family, and the monumental compilation documentary *Ordinary Fascism* (1964). Romm, who was also a professor at Moscow's Cinema Institute, was awarded the Order of Lenin and five Stalin Prizes during his career.

FILMS: *Pyshka/Boule de Suif* (also sc.) 1934; *The Thirteen* (also co-sc.), *Lenin in October* 1937; *Lenin in 1918* 1939; *Dream* (also co-sc.) 1943; *Girl No. 217* (also co-sc.) 1944; *The Russian Question* (also sc.), *Vladimir Ilyîch Lenin/Lenin* 1948; *Secret Mission* 1950; *Admiral Ushakov, Attack from the Sea/The Ships Storm the Bastions* (Part II of *Admiral Ushakov*) 1953; *Murder on Dante Street* (also co-sc.) 1956; *Nine Days of One Year* (also co-sc.) 1962; *Ordinary Fascism/Triumph Over Violence* (feature doc.; also co-sc., narrator) 1964; *Lost Letters* (short), *A Night of Thought* 1966.

Ronet, Maurice. Actor. *b.* Apr. 13, 1927, Nice, France. *d.* 1983. Intelligent, elegant leading man of French and international films. A second-generation actor (both his parents were on the stage), he studied drama at the Paris Conservatoire and performed in the theater for two years before making his film debut in 1949. He went on to appear in scores of films in France and elsewhere, performing a broad range of lead roles. He took a tentative first stab at directing in 1964 with *Le Voleur de Tibidabo,* in which he also starred, but did not attempt to direct another film until 1978.

FILMS INCLUDE: *Rendez-vous de Juillet* 1949; *Un Grand Patron/The Perfectionist* 1951; *Les Sept Péchés capitaux/The Seven Deadly Sins, La Jeune Folle/Desperate Decision* 1952; *Horizons sans Fin, Lucrèce Borgia/Sins of the Borgias* 1953; *Le Guérisseur, Casa Ricordi/House of Ricordi* (as Vincenzo Bellini; It./Fr.), *Châteaux en Espagne, Casta Diva* (It./Fr.) 1954; *Gueule d'Ange/Pleasures and Vices, Les Aristocrates* 1955; *La Sorcière* 1956; *Celui qui doit mourir/He Who Must Die* 1957; *Ascenseur pour l'Echafaud/Frantic, Carve Her Name with Pride* (UK) 1958; *Carmen de la Ronda/The Devil Made a Woman* (as Don Jose; Sp.) 1959; *Plein Soleil/Purple Noon* 1960; *Les Grandes Personnes/Time Out for Love, Le Rendez-vous de Minuit* 1961; *La Dénonciation/The Immoral Moment* 1962; *Le Meurtrier/Enough Rope, Le Feu follet/The Fire Within, The Victors* (UK/US) 1963; *Le Voleur de Tibidabo* (also dir.), *La Ronde/Circle of Love* 1964; *Lost Command* (US) 1966; *Le Scandale/The Champagne Murders, La Route de Corinthe/*

Who's Got the Black Box? 1967; *Les Oiseaux vont mourir au Pérou/Birds in Peru, How Sweet It Is!* (US) 1968; *Le Femme infidèle, La Piscine/The Swimming Pool* 1969; *Qui?/The Sensuous Assassin* 1970; *Raphaël ou le débauché, La Maison sous les Arbres/The Deadly Trap* 1971; *L'Ile des Dragons* (short; dir. only), *Sans Sommation, La Chambre rouge, La Seduzione* (It./Fr.), *Don Juan '73* 1973; *The Marseille Contract/The Destructors* (UK/Fr.) 1974; *Jackpot* (UK) 1975; *Nuit d'Or* 1976; *Madame Claude, Emmenez-moi au Ritz, Mort d'un Pourri* 1977; *Bartleby* (also dir.) 1978; *Bloodline* (US) 1979; *Sphinx* (US), *Beau Père* 1981; *La Balance* 1982.

Rooker, Michael. Actor. Born in 1955, in Jasper, Alabama. Intense, tough-looking character player whose icy blue eyes spelled menace in Hollywood films of the late 80s. A truckdriver's son, he was 13 when his parents divorced and he moved with his mother and five sisters to Chicago, where they subsisted on welfare in a crime-ridden neighborhood. He caught the acting bug while attending a local community college, then studied drama on a scholarship at Chicago's Goodman School of Drama. Entering films in 1986, he specialized in the portrayal of vicious, deranged brutes and drew wide acclaim for the title role in *Henry: Portrait of a Serial Killer* (1990).

FILMS: *Rent-a-Cop, Eight Men Out, Mississippi Burning* 1988; *Sea of Love, Music Box* 1989; *Henry: Portrait of a Serial Killer* (title role; filmed in 1986), *Days of Thunder* 1990; *JFK* 1991; *The Dark Half, Cliffhanger* 1993; *The Hard Truth, Suspicious, Tombstone* 1994; *Mallrats* 1995; *The Trigger Effect* 1996.

Room, Abram (also **Avram; Alexander**). Director. *b.* 1894, Vilnius, Lithuania, of Jewish descent. *d.* 1976. He became involved in amateur dramatics in his late teens, but later studied psychiatry and neurology and during the civil war served as a doctor with the Red Army. He then went to Moscow, where he worked as a journalist and joined Meyerhold's Theater of the Revolution as an actor and director. After training under Lev Kuleshov at the State Film School, he began directing for the screen in 1924, and three years later enjoyed great success with *Bed and Sofa,* a psychologically perceptive satire on the consequences of Moscow's housing shortage, which is considered a classic of the silent Soviet cinema. Room's talkies are far less notable.

FILMS INCLUDE: *The Pursuit of Moonshine/The Moon-Shiners/The Vodka Chase* 1924; *Death Bay, Traitor* 1926; *Bed and Sofa/Third Meshchanskaya* (also co-sc.), *The Jew on the Land* 1927; *Bumps/Hard Life/Ruts/Pits* 1928; *Plan of Great Works/The Five Year Plan* (doc.; USSR's first sound film), *The Ghost That Will Not Return* 1930; *Criminals* 1933; *A Stern Young Man* 1936; *Squadron No. 5,* 1939; *Wind from the East* 1941; *Invasion* 1945; *In the Mountains of Yugoslavia* 1946; *Court of Honor* 1949; *School for Scandal* (filmed stage production) 1952; *Silver Dust* (filmed stage production) 1953; *The Heart Beats Again* 1956; *The Garnet Bracelet* (also co-sc.) 1965; *Yakov Bogomolov* 1970; *Belated Flowers* (also sc.) 1972; *The Untimely Man* 1973.

room tone. The acoustic modulations characteristic of the enclosed environment in which sound film is shot. Every enclosure has its own background noise that goes unnoticed by the casual listener. After filming dialogue or an interview, the sound man must record this background "presence" for a BUZZ TRACK, asking all persons present to refrain from talking or making pronounced noises. The room tone is later matched during editing with the dialogue track to cover all pauses in conversation. Complete silence between snatches of dialogue produces an unnatural and annoying effect.

Rooney, Mickey. Actor. Born Joe Yule, Jr., on Sept. 23, 1920, in Brooklyn, N.Y. Pint-sized (5' 3"), dynamic, versatile performer of the American screen. The son of vaudevillians, he made his first stage appearance at 15 months and before long became an indispensable part of the family act, singing, dancing, mimicking, and telling jokes. He made his film debut at six, playing a midget in the short *Not to Be Trusted* (1926) and in the following year appeared in the silent feature *Orchids and Ermine* (1927). Between 1927 and 1933 he starred in some 50 two-reel comedies in the "Mickey McGuire" series, in which he portrayed a then-popular comic-strip character, a brash, gruff kid with adult-size misadventures. He legally adopted the name of the character, Mickey McGuire. He became Mickey Rooney in 1932 when he began playing small roles in features of Universal and other studios. In 1934 he was signed by MGM and the following year, on loan to Warner Bros., he accomplished one of the most remarkable acting feats by an adolescent on the screen, playing a memorable Puck in Max Reinhardt and William Dieterle's *A Midsummer Night's Dream.* Another turning point in his career occurred in 1937, when he was cast in the role of Andy Hardy, a cocky, wisecracking small-town judge's son, in *A Family Affair,* a modest B programmer that spawned a series of 15 highly popular Andy Hardy films, sentimental comedies that exalted the virtues of domestic tranquility and the simple life.

Rooney's popularity climbed steadily, thanks to the Hardy series, a memorable performance in *Boys Town* (1938), and several hectic musicals in which he co-starred with Judy GARLAND. In 1938 he shared a special Academy Award with Deanna Durbin for "significant contribution in bringing to the screen the spirit and personification of youth, and as a juvenile player setting a high standard of ability and achievement." By 1939 he was America's most popular star, taking over from Shirley Temple the top spot at the box office. Rooney's popularity reached a peak in the early 40s with such films as *The Human Comedy* (1943) and *National Velvet* (1944), but the momentum was interrupted by WW II service, after which his career went into a sharp decline. In 1948 he terminated his MGM ties and later formed his own production company. He promptly went broke and was forced into an assortment of roles in quickie films to pay off his debts. But he gradually recovered, starring on TV in 'The Mickey Rooney Show' (1954–55) and proving himself a fine character actor in such films as *The Bold and the Brave* (1956) and *Baby Face Nelson* (1957). Despite constant reversals in his financial and personal affairs, he kept bouncing back with uncommon determination and boundless energy. In 1962 he filed for bankruptcy, revealing he had nothing left of $12 million in career earnings. Much of the money had been consumed by alimony payments. The diminutive star, with a predilection for tall, well-endowed mates, has been married eight times. His first wife (1942–43) was actress Ava GARDNER and his third (1949–51) Martha VICKERS. The 1970s found him plump and balding but as active as ever, performing in films, on TV ('Mickey' comedy series in 1964–65, etc.), and in nightclubs, and involved in a wide assortment of business ventures. In 1978 he announced his retirement from acting but few took him seriously. In the following year he made a sensational Broadway debut in the musical 'Sugar Babies.' He was nominated for an Academy Award as best supporting actor for *The Black Stallion* (1979), and in 1982 he won an Emmy Award for his portrayal of a retarded old man in the TV movie *Bill.* He continued to tour with 'Sugar Babies,' and later joined the cast of Broadway's 'The Will Rogers Follies' (1993). Autobiographies: *i.e.* (1965); *Life Is Too Short* (1991).

FEATURE FILMS: *Orchids and Ermine* 1927; *Information Kid, Sin's Pay Day, The Beast of the City, High Speed, My*

Pal the King 1932; *The Big Cage, The Life of Jimmy Dolan, Broadway to Hollywood, The Big Chance, The World Changes, The Chief* 1933; *The Lost Jungle* (serial), *Beloved, I Like It That Way, Love Birds, Manhattan Melodrama* (playing Clark Gable as a boy), *Half a Sinner, Chained, Hide-Out, Blind Date, Upper World, Death on a Diamond* 1934; *The County Chairman, The Healer, Reckless, A Midsummer Night's Dream* (as Puck), *Ah Wilderness!* 1935; *Riffraff, Little Lord Fauntleroy, The Devil Is a Sissy, Down the Stretch* 1936; *A Family Affair* (first as Andy Hardy), *Captains Courageous* (as Dan Troop), *Slave Ship, The Hoosier Schoolboy, Live Love and Learn, Thoroughbreds Don't Cry, You're Only Young Once* (as Andy Hardy) 1937; *Love Is a Headache, Judge Hardy's Children* (as Andy Hardy), *Hold That Kiss, Lord Jeff, Love Finds Andy Hardy* (title role), *Boys Town, Stablemates, Out West with the Hardys* (as Andy Hardy) 1938; *The Adventures of Huckleberry Finn* (title role), *The Hardys Ride High* (as Andy Hardy), *Andy Hardy Gets Spring Fever* (title role), *Babes in Arms, Judge Hardy and Son* (as Andy Hardy) 1939; *Young Tom Edison* (title role), *Andy Hardy Meets Debutante* (as Andy Hardy), *Strike Up the Band* 1940; *Andy Hardy's Private Secretary* (as Andy Hardy), *Men of Boys Town, Life Begins for Andy Hardy* (title role) 1941; *Babes on Broadway, The Courtship of Andy Hardy* (title role), *A Yank at Eton, Andy Hardy's Double Life* (title role) 1942; *The Human Comedy* (as Homer Macauley), *Thousands Cheer, Girl Crazy* 1943; *Andy Hardy's Blonde Trouble* (title role), *National Velvet* 1944; *Love Laughs at Andy Hardy* (title role), *Killer McCoy* 1947; *Summer Holiday, Words and Music* (as lyricist Lorenz Hart) 1948; *The Big Wheel* 1949; *Quicksand, The Fireball, He's a Cockeyed Wonder* 1950; *My True Story* (dir. only), *My Outlaw Brother, The Strip* 1951; *Sound Off* 1952; *All Ashore, Off Limits, A Slight Case of Larceny* 1953; *Drive a Crooked Road, The Atomic Kid* 1954; *The Bridges at Toko-Ri, The Twinkle in God's Eye* 1955; *The Bold and the Brave, Francis in the Haunted House, Magnificent Roughnecks* 1956; *Operation Mad Ball, Baby Face Nelson* (title role) 1957; *Andy Hardy Comes Home* (title role), *A Nice Little Bank That Should Be Robbed* 1958; *The Last Mile, The Big Operator* 1959; *Platinum High School, The Private Lives of Adam and Eve* (also co-dir. with Albert Zugsmith) 1960; *King of the Roaring 20s, Breakfast at Tiffany's* 1961; *Requiem for a Heavyweight* 1962; *It's a Mad Mad Mad Mad World* 1963; *The Secret Invasion* 1964; *How to Stuff a Wild Bikini, 24 Hours to Kill* (UK) 1965; *Ambush Bay, L'Arcidiavolo* (It.) 1966; *Skidoo* 1968; *The Extraordinary Seaman, 80 Steps to Jonah, The Comic* 1969; *The Cockeyed Cowboys of Calico County, Hollywood Blue* (doc.) 1970; *B.J. Presents* 1971; *Richard, Pulp* 1972; *That's Entertainment* (on-screen co-narr.), *Journey Back to Oz* (v/o), *Ace of Hearts* 1974; *Bon Baisers de Hong Kong* (Fr.), *Rachel's Man* (UK/Isr.) 1975; *Find the Lady* (Can./UK) 1976; *The Domino Principle, Pete's Dragon* 1977; *The Magic of Lassie* 1978; *An Arabian Adventure* (UK), *The Black Stallion* 1979; *The Fox and the Hound* (v/o), *L'Empereur du Pérou/The Emperor of Posey of the Pacific* (Fr.) 1981; *The Care Bears Movie* (v/o; Can.) 1985; *Lightning—The White Stallion* 1986; *Erik the Viking* (UK/Sw.) 1989; *My Heroes Have Always Been Cowboys, Silent Night Deadly Night 5: The Toymaker* 1991; *The Legend of Wolf Mountain, Little Nemo* (v/o) 1992.

Roos, Fred. Producer. Born on May 23, 1934, in Santa Monica, Calif. *ed.* UCLA. He directed documentaries for the Armed Forces Network and worked in Hollywood as a talent agent, story editor, and casting director. As a producer, he is closely associated with Francis Ford COPPOLA.

FILMS INCLUDE (as producer or executive producer, alone or in collaboration): *Back Door to Hell* 1964; *Flight to Fury* 1966; *Drive He Said* (assoc. prod.) 1971; *The Conversation, The Godfather Part II* 1974; *The Black Stallion, Apocalypse Now* 1979; *One from the Heart, The Escape Artist, Hammett* 1982; *The Outsiders, Rumble Fish* 1983; *The Cotton Club* 1984; *Gardens of Stone, Barfly* 1987; *Tucker: The Man and His Dream* 1988; *New York Stories* 1989; *Wait Until Spring Bandini* (Bel./Fr./It./US), *The Godfather Part III* 1990; *Hearts of Darkness: A Filmmaker's Apocalypse* (doc.) 1991; *The Secret Garden* 1993.

Roos, Jorgen. Documentary filmmaker. Born on Aug. 4, 1922, in Killeleje, Denmark. Denmark's leading documentary director and one of the most prominent in postwar Europe. He began with amateur experimental shorts early in the 40s, becoming a professional late in the decade after a period of apprenticeship with Carl DREYER. His many international awards included a Silver Bear at the Berlin Film Festival for *Knud* (1966).

FILMS INCLUDE: *The Flight* (co-dir. with Albert Mertz) 1942; *Thief of Hearts* (co-dir. with Mertz) 1943; *Opus I, Reflexfilm* 1948; *Jean Cocteau* 1949; *Hamlet's Castle* (script by Carl Dreyer) 1951; *Slum* 1952; *The Newborn, Guilty Though Innocent* 1953; *Murals* 1954; *My Life Story* 1955; *Johannes Larsen* 1957; *Magic of the Diamond* (Belg.), *The Six Days* 1958; *Pure Air* 1959; *A City Called Copenhagen, Danish Design* 1960; *Hamburg* 1961; *Oslo* 1963; *Carl Th. Dreyer, Knud* 1966; *17 Minutes of Greenland* 1967; *Ultima Thule* 1968; *Andersens Hemmelighed* 1971; *The Pyramids* 1974; *Monarchy and Democracy* 1977; *Greenland* 1980; *Knud Rasmussen's Expedition* 1982; *Little Circus* 1984; *Den levende Virkelighed* 1989.

Rosay, Françoise. Actress. *b.* Françoise Bandy de Nalèche, Apr. 19, 1891, Paris. *d.* 1974. Commanding character actress of the French and international stage and screen. A graduate of the Conservatoire National de Déclamation in Paris, she made her stage debut in 1908, initially pursuing an operatic career. She later appeared in many plays, but after her marriage to director Jacques FEYDER in 1917 she temporarily retired from the theater and later became primarily a screen actress. Her remarkable film career spanned six decades, during which she gave memorable characterizations in some 100 productions, British, American, Italian, and German as well as French. She authored a volume of memoirs, *Le Cinéma notre Métier* (1956).

FILMS INCLUDE: *Falstaff* 1913; *Crainquebille* 1923; Gribiche 1926; *Les Deux Timides* 1928; *Le Procès de Mary Dugan* (French-language version of *The Trial of Mary Dugan;* US), *The One Woman Idea* (US) 1929; *Si l'Empereur savait ça!* (French-language version of *His Glorious Night;* US), *Le Petit Café* (French-language version of *Playboy of Paris;* US) 1930; *Jenny Lind* (French-language version of *A Lady's Morals;* US), *The Magnificent Lie* (US), *La Chance* 1931; *Le Rosier de Madame Husson/He* 1932; *L'Abbé Constantin, Remous/Whirlpool* 1933; *Le Grand Jeu* 1934; *Pension Mimosas, Maternité, La Kermesse héroïque/Carnival in Flanders* (and in German-language version, *Die klugen Frauen*) 1935; *Jenny* 1936; *Un Carnet de Bal, Drôle de Drame/Bizarre Bizarre* 1937; *Paix sur le Rhin, Ramuntcho, Le Joueur d'Echecs/The Devil Is an Empress* (as Catherine the Great), *Les Gens du Voyage* (and in German-language version, *Fahrendes Volk*) 1938; *Die Hochzeitstreise* (Ger.) 1939; *Elles étaient Douze Femmes* 1940; *Une Femme disparaît/Portrait of a Woman* (in four roles; Switz./Fr.) 1942; *Half-Way House* (UK) 1944; *Johnny Frenchman* (UK) 1945; *Macadam/Back Streets of Paris* 1946; *Saraband for Dead Lovers/Saraband* (as Sophia, Electress of Hanover; UK), *Quartet* (UK) 1948; *The Naked Heart/Maria Chapdelaine* (UK/Fr.; filmed in Canada), *Donne senza*

Nomme/Women Without Names (It.) 1950; *September Affair* (US), *The Thirteenth Letter* (US), *L'Auberge rouge/The Red Inn* 1951; *Les Sept Péchés capitaux/The Seven Deadly Sins* 1952; *That Lady* (UK), *La Reine Margot* 1954; *The Seventh Sin* (US), *Interlude* (US) 1957; *Me and the Colonel* (US), *Le Joueur* 1958; *The Sound and the Fury* (US), *Du Rififi chez les Femmes/Riff Raff Girls* 1959; *The Full Treatment/Stop Me Before I Kill!* (UK), *Frau Cheney's Ende* (Ger./Switz.), *Le Cave se rebiffe/The Counterfeiters of Paris* 1961; *The Longest Day* (US) 1962; *Up from the Beach* (US) 1965; *La 25e Heure/The 25th Hour* 1967; *Faut pas prendre les Enfants du Bon Dieu pour des Canards sauvages/Operation Leontine* 1968; *Un Merveilleux Parfum d'Oseille* 1969; *Der Fussgänger/The Pedestrian* (Ger.) 1974.

Rose, Helen. Costume designer. *b.* Feb. 2, 1904, Chicago. *d.* 1985. *ed.* Chicago Academy of Fine Arts. One of Hollywood's most accomplished wardrobe fashioners. Working from age 15, she designed for nightclubs and the Ice Follies for many years before entering films in the early 40s, briefly with 20th Century-Fox, then for three decades with MGM. She was nominated for Academy Awards ten times and won Oscars for *The Bad and the Beautiful* (1952) and *I'll Cry Tomorrow* (1955). Her fame as the designer of Grace Kelly's wedding gown in 1956 helped her establish a thriving fashion business when she retired from films in the late 60s.

FILMS INCLUDE: *Hello Frisco Hello, Stormy Weather* 1943; *Ziegfeld Follies* 1945; *The Harvey Girls* 1946; *Till the Clouds Roll By, Good News* 1947; *Homecoming* 1948; *Act of Violence, West On the Town, Take Me Out to the Ball Game* 1949; *Father of the Bride, Annie Get Your Gun, Three Little Words, Summer Stock, The Toast of New Orleans* 1950; *The Great Caruso* 1951; *The Belle of New York, The Merry Widow, The Bad and the Beautiful* 1952; *The Story of Three Loves, Dream Wife, Mogambo* 1953; *Executive Suite, Rhapsody, Rose Marie* 1954; *The Glass Slipper, I'll Cry Tomorrow, Interrupted Melody, Love Me or Leave Me, The Tender Trap* 1955; *High Society, The Power and the Prize, The Opposite Sex, The Swan, Tea and Sympathy* 1956; *Designing Woman, Silk Stockings* 1957; *Cat on a Hot Tin Roof* 1958; *The Gazebo* 1959; *Butterfield 8* 1960; *The Courtship of Eddie's Father* 1963; *Goodbye Charlie* 1964; *Mister Buddwing* 1966; *How Sweet It Is* 1968.

Rose, Jack. Screenwriter, producer. Born on Nov. 4, 1911, in Warsaw. *ed.* Ohio U. A former comedy writer for Bob Hope's radio show, he wrote screenplays for many light Hollywood films, often in collaboration with Melville SHAVELSON. He shared an Oscar nomination with Melvin Frank for *A Touch of Class* (1973).

FILMS INCLUDE (as screenwriter): *Road to Rio, Ladies' Man, My Favorite Brunette* 1947; *The Paleface* (gags only) 1948; *The Great Lover, Sorrowful Jones, It's a Great Feeling, Always Leave Them Laughing* 1949; *The Daughter of Rosie O'Grady, Riding High* 1950; *On Moonlight Bay* 1951; *Room for One More, I'll See You in My Dreams* 1952; *April in Paris, Trouble Along the Way* 1953; *Living It Up* 1954; *The Seven Little Foys* (also prod.) 1955; *Beau James* (also prod.) 1957; *Houseboat* (also prod.) 1958; *The Five Pennies* (also prod.) 1959; *It Started in Naples* (also prod.) 1960; *On the Double* (also prod.) 1961; *Who's Got the Action?* (also prod.) 1962; *Papa's Delicate Condition* (also prod.), *Who's Been Sleeping in My Bed?* (also prod.) 1963; *The Incredible Mr. Limpet* (also prod.) 1964; *A Touch of Class* 1973; *The Duchess and the Dirtwater Fox* 1976; *Lost and Found* 1979; *The Great Muppet Caper* 1981.

Rose, William. Screenwriter. *b.* 1918, Jefferson City, Mo. *d.* 1987. He entered British films in 1947 and wrote several memorable comedy scripts. Repatriated to the US in the late 50s, he continued his activity in Hollywood. He won an Academy Award for *Guess Who's Coming to Dinner.*

FILMS INCLUDE: *Once a Jolly Swagman* 1948; *The Gift Horse/Glory at Sea* 1951; *Genevieve* 1953; *The Maggie* 1954; *Touch and Go, The Lady Killers* 1955; *The Smallest Show on Earth* 1957; *It's a Mad Mad Mad Mad World* 1963; *The Russians Are Coming! The Russians Are Coming!* 1966; *The Flim-Flam Man, Guess Who's Coming to Dinner* 1967; *The Secret of Santa Vittoria* 1969.

Rosen, Phil (Philip E.). Director. *b.* May 8, 1888, Marienburg, Russia. *d.* 1951. In the US from an early age, he joined the Edison company as a cameraman in 1912 and was soon entrusted with the cinematography of some of Theda Bara's most lavish vehicles. In 1920 he launched a prolific career as a director. During the silent period, he directed several major productions, including the much-acclaimed *Abraham Lincoln/The Dramatic Life of Abraham Lincoln* (1924), but most of his sound-era assignments were routine low-budget thrillers and action pictures.

FILMS INCLUDE: *The Road to Divorce, The Path She Chose, Are All Men Alike?* 1920; *Extravagance, The Lure of Youth* 1921; *The World's Champion, The Young Rajah, Across the Continent, The Bonded Woman* 1922; *Abraham Lincoln/The Dramatic Life of Abraham Lincoln, Being Respectable, This Woman* 1924; *The Bridge of Sighs, The Heart of a Siren, The White Monkey* 1925; *The Adorable Deceiver, The Exquisite Sinner, Rose of the Tenements, A Woman's Heart* 1926; *The Cancelled Debt, Closed Gates, The Cruel Truth, Stolen Pleasures, Heaven on Earth, Pretty Clothes, Salvation Jane, Stranded, The Woman Who Did Not Care* 1927; *Burning Up Broadway, The Apache, Modern Mothers, Undressed* 1928; *The Peacock Fan, The Faker, The Phantom in the House* 1929; *Extravagance* (remake), *Lotus Lady, The Rampant Age, Second Honeymoon* 1930; *Arizona Terror, Range Law, Branded Men* 1931; *A Man's Land, Klondike, The Vanishing Frontier, Lena Rivers, The Gay Buckaroo* 1932; *The Sphinx, The Phantom Broadcast, Hold the Press, Black Beauty, Devil's Mate, Picture Brides, Shadows of Sing Sing* 1933; *Beggars in Ermine, Cheaters, Take the Stand, Dangerous Corner, Woman in the Dark, Little Men* 1934; *Death Flies East, Born to Gamble* 1935; *The Calling of Dan Matthews, Missing Girls, The President's Mystery, Bridge of Sighs, Easy Money, Ellis Island, Tango* 1936; *Roaring Timber, Two Wise Maids, Youth on Parole* 1937; *The Marines Are Here* 1938; *Ex-Champ, Missing Evidence* 1939; *Double Alibi, The Crooked Road, Forgotten Girls, The Phantom of Chinatown, Queen of the Yukon* 1940; *Murder by Invitation, Gangs Incorporated, The Deadly Game, I Killed That Man, Spooks Run Wild* 1941; *Road to Happiness, The Mystery of Marie Roget* 1942; *Wings Over the Pacific, Prison Mutiny* 1943; *Charlie Chan in the Secret Service, Return of the Ape Man, The Chinese Cat, Black Magic, Call of the Jungle* 1944; *The Jade Mask, Captain Tugboat Annie, The Scarlet Clue, The Red Dragon* 1945; *The Shadow, The Strange Mr. Gregory, Step by Step* 1946; *The Secret of St. Ives* 1949.

Rosenberg, Aaron. Producer. *b.* Aug. 26, 1912, New York City. *d.* 1979. A former USC All-American football star, he entered films in the mid-30s as assistant director. After WW II service as a naval officer, he returned to Hollywood as associate producer, becoming a full producer for Universal late in the 40s. Later with MGM and Fox, he also produced for TV.

FILMS INCLUDE: *Larceny* 1948; *Johnny Stool Pigeon* 1949; *Winchester '73* 1950; *The Iron Man* 1951; *Bend of the River, The World in His Arms, Red Ball Express* 1952; *Gunsmoke, Thunder Bay, The Man from the Alamo* 1953; *The Glen Miller Story, Saskatchewan* 1954; *The Far Country, Man Without a Star,*

The Shrike, To Hell and Back 1955; *The Benny Goodman Story, Walk the Proud Land, Four Girls in Town* 1956; *Joe Butterfly, Night Passage* 1957; *The Badlanders* 1958; *Never Steal Anything Small* 1959; *Go Naked in the World* 1961; *Mutiny on the Bounty* 1962; *Move Over Darling* 1963; *Shock Treatment* 1964; *The Reward* 1965; *Tony Rome, Caprice* 1967; *The Detective, Lady in Cement* 1968; *The Boy Who Cried Werewolf* 1973.

Rosenberg, Philip. Art director/production designer. Born on Jan. 15, 1935, in Brooklyn, N.Y. A graduate of Brooklyn College, he studied stage design at the Yale School of Drama and began his career in the theater. In films from 1970, he specialized in New York–based productions, for Sidney Lumet and other leading directors. He shared an Oscar with Tony Walton for the design of *All That Jazz* (1979).

FILMS INCLUDE: *The Owl and the Pussycat* 1970; *The Anderson Tapes* 1971; *The Possession of Joel Delaney, Child's Play* 1972; *The Gambler* 1974; *Next Stop Greenwich Village, Network* 1976; *The Sentinel* 1977; *The Wiz* 1978; *All That Jazz* 1979; *Eyewitness* 1981; *Lovesick, Daniel* 1983; *Garbo Talks* 1984; *The Manhattan Project* 1986; *Moonstruck* 1987; *Running on Empty* 1988; *The January Man, Family Business* 1989; *Q & A* 1990; *Other People's Money* 1991; *Close to Eden* 1992.

Rosenberg, Stuart. Director. Born on Aug. 11, 1927, in Brooklyn, N.Y. A graduate of NYU, where he majored in Irish literature, he remained at the university for a spell as an instructor and in the late 50s began a prolific career as a director of hundreds of episodes for TV series like 'The Untouchables,' 'Naked City,' 'The Defenders,' and 'Run for Your Life.' He began his first feature film, *Murder Inc.* (1960), in 1959, but production was interrupted by an actors' strike and the film was completed by Burt Balaban. Rosenberg's reputation soared with his third feature, *Cool Hand Luke,* a crisply directed and superbly acted prison drama starring Paul Newman and George Kennedy, who won a supporting actor Oscar for his performance. Rosenberg's standing as a director slipped considerably in the following years after a succession of mediocre films but his reputation revived intermittently with such fine efforts as *Voyage of the Damned* (1976) and *The Pope of Greenwich Village* (1984).

FILMS: *Murder Inc.* (co-dir. with Burt Balaban) 1960; *Question 7* (US/Ger.) 1961; *Cool Hand Luke* 1967; *The Counterfeit Killer* (expanded by director Josef Leytes from 'The Faceless Man,' a TV drama directed by Rosenberg in 1966) 1968; *The April Fools* 1969; *Move* (also co-exec. prod.), *WUSA* (also co-exec. prod.) 1970; *Pocket Money* 1972; *The Laughing Policeman* (also prod.) 1973; *The Drowning Pool* 1975; *Voyage of the Damned* (UK) 1976; *Love and Bullets, The Amityville Horror* 1979; *Brubaker* 1980; *The Pope of Greenwich Village* 1984; *Let's Get Harry* (under pseudonym "Alan Smithee") 1986; *My Heroes Have Always Been Cowboys* 1991.

Rosenbloom, "Slapsie" Maxie. Prizefighter, actor. *b.* Max Rosenbloom, 1903, New York City. *d.* 1976. Runyonesque character comedian of Hollywood films after a brilliant career in the ring, he typically portrayed punch-drunk characters. He began boxing at age 12, after getting out of reform school, under the aegis of George Raft. After winning the New York State heavyweight amateur title, he turned professional and held the light-heavyweight world championship for four years in the early 30s. It was Damon Runyon, then a sportswriter, who nicknamed him "Slapsie Maxie," for his unorthodox slapping style in the ring. He spent his last years in a hospital bed, suffering from the cumulative effect of blows he had received during his boxing days.

FILMS INCLUDE: *Mr. Broadway* 1933; *Muss 'Em Up, Kelly the Second* 1936; *Nothing Sacred* 1937; *The Kid Comes Back, Mr. Moto's Gamble, Gangs of New York, The Amazing Dr. Clitterhouse, Submarine Patrol* 1938; *Women in the Wind, The Kid from Kokomo, Each Dawn I Die, 20,000 Men a Year* 1939; *Passport to Alcatraz* 1940; *Ringside Maisie, Louisiana Purchase* 1941; *To the Shores of Tripoli, The Boogie Man Will Get You* 1942; *Swing Fever, Irish Eyes Are Smiling* 1944; *Men in Her Diary* 1945; *Hazard* 1948; *Skipalong Rosenbloom, Mr. Universe* 1951; *Abbott and Costello Meet the Keystone Kops* 1955; *Hollywood or Bust* 1956; *The Beat Generation* 1959; *Don't Worry We'll Think of a Title* 1966.

Rosenblum, Ralph. Film editor. Born on Oct. 13, 1925, in Brooklyn, N.Y. Denied a college education because of his father's illness, he worked as a shipping clerk at a garment factory and as a messenger at the Office of War Information, where he eventually apprenticed under Sidney Meyers in the cutting room of the documentary unit. After the war, he was an assistant editor on Robert J. Flaherty's last film, *Louisiana Story* (1948), then worked in television as an editor, before branching into features in the late 50s. Based in Manhattan, he distinguished himself in the 60s and 70s as a creative cutter of East Coast productions, notably for Sidney Lumet and Woody Allen. He won the British Film Academy Award for *Annie Hall* (1977). Later he directed TV movies and a feature, *Stiffs* (1986), and provided consulting services on several films of the 80s. He is the co-author of an illuminating memoir, *When the Shooting Stops. . . The Cutting Begins: A Film Editor's Story* (1979).

FILMS INCLUDE: *Country Music Holiday* 1958; *Pretty Boy Floyd, Murder Inc.* 1960; *Long Day's Journey Into Night* 1962; *Gone Are the Days/Purlie Victorious* 1963; *Fail Safe* 1964; *The Pawnbroker, The Fool Killer, A Thousand Clowns* 1965; *The Group* 1966; *The Producers* 1967; *The Night They Raided Minsky's* 1968; *Goodbye Columbus, Take the Money and Run, Don't Drink the Water, Trilogy* 1969; *Something for Everyone* 1970; *Bad Company* 1972; *Sleeper* 1973; *Love and Death* 1975; *Annie Hall* 1976; *Interiors, Shenanigans/The Great Bank Hoax* (also co-prod.) 1978; *Stuck on You* (co-edit.) 1983; *Stiffs* (dir. only) 1986; *Forever Lulu* (edit. consultant only) 1987.

Rosenman, Leonard. Composer. Born on Sept. 7, 1924, in Brooklyn, N.Y. A former painter, he turned to music after WW II service with the Air Force and studied theory and composition under Arnold Schoenberg. He began composing for the screen in the mid-50s. His compositions include choral and chamber pieces and a one-act opera. He won successive Academy Awards for the adapted scores of *Barry Lyndon* (1975) and *Bound for Glory* (1976).

FILMS INCLUDE: *East of Eden, Rebel Without a Cause, The Cobweb* 1955; *Edge of the City* 1956; *The Bramble Bush* 1959; *The Rise and Fall of Legs Diamond, The Savage Eye* 1960; *Convicts 4, Hell Is for Heroes, The Chapman Report* 1962; *Fantastic Voyage* 1966; *Countdown* 1968; *Hellfighters* 1969; *A Man Called Horse, Beneath the Planet of the Apes* 1970; *Battle for the Planet of the Apes* 1973; *Barry Lyndon, Race with the Devil* 1975; *Birch Interval* 1976; *The Car, 9/30/55* 1977; *An Enemy of the People, The Lord of the Rings* 1978; *Prophecy, Promises in the Dark* 1979; *Hide in Plain Sight, The Jazz Singer* 1980; *Making Love* 1981; *Criss Cross, Miss Lonely Hearts* 1983; *Sylvia* (NZ) 1985; *Star Trek IV: The Voyage Home* 1986; *Robocop 2* 1990; *Ambition* 1991.

Rosenthal, Laurence. Composer. Born on Nov. 4, 1926, in Detroit. After international music studies and a five-year stint as composer for the US Air Force, he began writing motion picture scores early in the mid-50s. He has also composed a ballet and chamber and orchestral works as well as music for Broadway and TV productions.

FILMS INCLUDE: *Yellowneck* 1955; *Naked in the Sun* 1957; *A Raisin in the Sun* 1961; *The Miracle Worker, Requiem for a Heavyweight* 1962; *Becket* 1964; *Hotel Paradiso* 1966; *The Comedians* 1967; *A Gunfight* 1971; *Man of La Mancha* (adapt. from stage production, conduct. only) 1972; *The Wild Party, Rooster Cogburn* 1975; *The Island of Dr. Moreau* 1977; *Who'll Stop the Rain, Brass Target* 1978; *Meeting with Remarkable Men* (UK), *Meteor* 1979; *Clash of the Titans* (UK) 1981; *Heart Like a Wheel, Easy Money* 1983; *Blackout* 1988.

Roshal, Grigori (also **Gregory**). Director. Born on Oct. 2, 1899, in Nivosibkov, Ukraine. A former member of the Moscow Jewish Habimah theater group (now Israel's national theater), he turned to films in 1925 and in the following four decades turned out many Soviet films of various genres. Some of his early productions were "message" films, but most of his later work was nonpolitical. His generally entertaining films include adaptations from literary sources and several musical biographies. He collaborated on the scripts of many of his own films, sometimes with his wife, Vera Stroyeva, and occasionally on scripts for other directors, notably Alexander Ptushko's *A New Gulliver* (1935).

FILMS: *Gospoda Skotininy/The Skotinins* (also co-sc.) 1927; *His Excellency/Seeds of Freedom* (also co-sc.), *The Salamander* (USSR/Ger.) 1928; *Two Women* (also co-sc.) 1930; *David Gorelick/A Jew at War* (also co-sc.) 1931; *Petersburg Nights* (co-dir.; co-sc. with Vera Stroyeva) 1934; *Dawn in Paris/ Paris Commune* (also co-sc.) 1937; *The Oppenheim Family* 1939; *In Search of Happiness* (co-dir.; co-sc. with Stroyeva) 1940; *The Artamanov Affair* 1941; *Giants of the Steppes* 1942; *Song of Abaya* (co-dir. with E. Aron) 1946; *Academician Ivan Pavlov/Ivan Pavlov* 1949; *Mussorgsky* (also co-sc.) 1950; *Rimsky-Korsakov* (also co-sc.) 1953; *Aleko* (co-dir. with Sergei Sidelov; also co-sc.) 1954; *Voltinitsa/Salt of the Sea/Flames on the Volga* 1956; *Sisters* (first in trilogy based on Alexei Tolstoy's *Ordeal*) 1957; *1918* (second in trilogy) 1958; *Gray Dawn* (last in trilogy) 1959; *Judgment of the Mad* (also sc.) 1962; *The Flight of Mr. McKinley* 1965; *They Are Neighbors* 1968.

Rosher, Charles. Director of photography. *b.* 1885, England. *d.* 1974. In the US from 1908, he was among Hollywood's earliest film pioneers, setting up shop there in 1911. He contributed many technical innovations during the industry's formative years, including the use of stand-ins for stars and dummies in dangerous action scenes, and was responsible for the then-incredible special effect by which Mary Pickford, in a dual role, kissed herself in *Little Lord Fauntleroy* (1921). He was behind the lens on many of Pickford's most successful silent productions. He was among the founders of the ASC in 1918 and was its first vice president. During a career that spanned more than four decades, he worked on many distinguished productions at MGM and other studios, sharing an Academy Award for the cinematography of *Sunrise* (1927) and another Oscar for *The Yearling* (1946). He was the father of actress Joan MARSH and cinematographer Charles Rosher, Jr.

FILMS INCLUDE: *Early Days in the West* 1912; *With General Pancho Villa in Mexico* 1913; *The Oath of a Viking* 1914; *Blackbirds* 1915; *The Dumb Girl of Portici, The Sowers, The Clown, Anton the Terrible* 1916; *Hashimura Togo, The Primrose Ring, The Secret Game* 1917; *One More American, Honor of His House, Johanna Enlists, Too Many Millions* 1918; *The Dub, Captain Kidd Jr., Daddy Long Legs* (co-phot.), *The Hoodlum, Heart o' the Hills* 1919; *Pollyanna, Suds* 1920; *The Love Light, Through the Back Door, Little Lord Fauntleroy* 1921; *Smilin' Through* (co-phot.), *Tess of the Storm Country* 1922; *Rosita, Tiger Rose* 1923; *Dorothy Vernon of Haddon Hall* 1924; *Little Annie Rooney* (co-phot.) 1925; *Sparrows* (co-phot.) 1926; *Sunrise* (co-phot.), *My Best Girl* 1927; *Tempest* 1928; *Atlantic* (UK) 1929; *La Route est Belle* (Fr.), *Two Worlds* (UK), *Paid* 1930; *Dance Fools Dance, Laughing Sinners, This Modern Age* 1931; *What Price Hollywood, Rockabye* 1932; *Our Betters, The Silver Cord, Bed of Roses* 1933; *Moulin Rouge, The Affairs of Cellini, What Every Woman Knows, Outcast Lady* 1934; *After Office Hours, The Call of the Wild, Broadway Melody of 1936* 1935; *Little Lord Fauntleroy, Small Town Girl* 1936; *The Woman I Love, The Perfect Specimen* 1937; *Hollywood Hotel* (co-phot.), *White Banners* 1938; *Espionage Agent* 1939; *My Love Came Back* 1940; *Four Mothers, One Foot in Heaven* 1941; *Stand By for Action* 1942; *Assignment in Brittany* 1943; *Kismet* 1944; *Yolanda and the Thief* 1945; *Ziegfeld Follies* (co-phot.), *The Yearling* (co-phot.) 1946; *Fiesta, Song of the Thin Man* 1947; *On an Island with You, Words and Music* (co-phot.) 1948; *Neptune's Daughter, The Red Danube* 1949; *East Side West Side, Annie Get Your Gun* 1950; *Show Boat* 1951; *Scaramouche* 1952; *The Story of Three Loves* (co-phot.), *Young Bess, Kiss Me Kate* 1953; *Jupiter's Darling* (co-phot.) 1955.

Rosenthal, Rick. Director. Born on June 15, 1949, in New York City. He began his filmmaking career with a New Hampshire TV station, then moved to Los Angeles, where he studied at the American Film Institute's school and made the student film *Moonface* (1973). Becoming a feature director in the early 80s, he impressed with his second film, *Bad Boys* (1983), an effective, moving drama of juvenile delinquency starring Sean Penn; but the rest of his output has been merely routine.

FILMS: *Halloween II* 1981; *Bad Boys* 1983; *American Dreamer* 1984; *Russkies* 1987; *Distant Thunder* 1988.

Rosi, Francesco. Director. Born on Nov. 15, 1922, in Naples, Italy. A former law student, book illustrator, and radio reporter and performer, he entered Italian films in the late 40s as assistant to Visconti, later also working under Emmer, Monicelli, and Antonioni, as an assistant and screenwriter. He made his directorial debut early in the 50s, completing a film for Goffredo Alessandrini, and won a Special Jury Prize at the 1958 Venice Festival for his first solo film, *La Sfida/The Challenge*. He emerged as a major talent in the early 60s with *Salvatore Giuliano* (1962), a masterly reconstruction of a police inquiry into the life and death of a legendary Sicilian bandit, for which Rosi was named best director at the Berlin Film Festival, and *Hands Over the City* (1963), a powerful probe of corruption in Naples, winner of the Golden Lion at Venice. Other outstanding efforts followed in a similar neodocumentary style, notably *The Mattei Affair* (1972), another relentless investigation of political corruption, which shared the Golden Palm at Cannes, *Illustrious Corpses* (1975), *Three Brothers* (1981), and an exhilarating rendition of *Carmen* (1984). The last two of these earned the director the David di Donatello Awards. Rosi is an aggressive, uncompromising social crusader, a journalist with a camera, working in the traditions of postwar Italian neorealism. His world is usually that of the economically poor and politically corrupt Italian south, and he depicts it with blunt, unadorned directness. He has collaborated on the scripts of all of his own films.

FILMS: *Camicie rosse/Anita Garibaldi* (completed for Goffredo Alessandrini) 1952; *Kean* (technical dir. to Vittorio Gassman, co-sc. only) 1956; *La Sfida/The Challenge* (also story, co-sc.) 1958; *I Magliari* (also co-story, co-sc.) 1959; *Salvatore Giuliano* (also co-story, co-sc.) 1962; *Le Mani sulla Città/Hands Over the City* (also co-story, co-sc.) 1963; *Il Momento della Verità/The Moment of Truth* (also story, sc., co-prod.; It./Sp.) 1965; *C'era una Volta/More Than a Miracle* (also co-story, co-sc.; It./Fr.) 1967; *Uomini Contro* (also co-sc.; It./Yug.) 1970; *Il Caso Mattei/The Mattei Affair* (also co-story, co-sc.) 1972; *A*

Proposito Lucky Luciano/Re: Lucky Luciano (also co-sc.) 1973; *Il Contesto* 1975; *Cadaveri Eccelenti/Illustrious Corpses* (also co-sc.; It./Fr.) 1976; *Cristo si è fermato a Eboli/Christ Stopped at Eboli* (also co-sc.) 1979; *Tre Fratelli/Three Brothers* (also co-sc.) 1981; *Carmen/Bizet's Carmen* (also co-sc.) 1984; *Cronica di una Morte anunciada/Chronicle of a Death Foretold* (also co-sc.) 1987; *Dimenticare Palermo/To Forget Palermo* 1990; *The Truce* 1997.

Rosmer, Milton. Actor, director. *b.* Arthur Milton Lunt, Nov. 4, 1881, Southport, England. *d.* 1971. Leading man of British silent films, later in character parts. The son of an actor, he made his stage debut as a child. He directed a number of films in the 30s without abandoning acting.

FILMS INCLUDE: As actor—*The Mystery of a Hansom Cab* 1915; *The Man Without a Soul/I Believe, Lady Windermere's Fan* 1916; *Little Women* 1917; *The Chinese Puzzle* 1919; *Wuthering Heights* 1920; *The Will* 1921; *The Passionate Friends* 1922; *Shadow of Egypt* 1924; *High Treason* 1929; *The W Plan* 1930; *Grand Prix* 1934; *The Phantom Light* 1935; *South Riding* 1938; *Goodbye Mr. Chips, The Lion Has Wings, The Stars Look Down* 1939; *Hatter's Castle* 1941; *Frieda, Fame Is the Spur, Daybreak* 1947; *The Small Back Room* 1948. As director—*Balaclava/Jaws of Hell* (co-dir. with Maurice Elvey) 1930; *Dreyfus/The Dreyfus Case* (co-dir. with F. W. Krämer), *The Perfect Lady* 1931; *After the Ball* (co-dir.) 1932; *Channel Crossing* 1933; *The Guv'nor/Mister Hobo, Maria Marten/Murder in the Old Red Barn, Emil and the Detectives/Emil* 1935; *The Great Barrier/Silent Barriers* 1937; *The Challenge* 1938.

Ross, Frank. Producer. *b.* Aug. 12, 1904, Boston. *d.* 1990. A graduate of Princeton, he was in the construction business before entering films in 1929 as an actor. Turning producer in the late 30s, he shared an Academy Award with Mervyn LeRoy for *The House I Live In* (1945), a short on the subject of intolerance. He produced the first-ever Cinemascope film, the Oscar-nominated *The Robe* (1953) and in his only outing as a screenwriter shared an Academy Award nomination for *The More the Merrier* (1943). Several of his productions starred his first wife (1932–49), actress Jean ARTHUR, and his second (1950–60), actress Joan CAULFIELD.

FILMS INCLUDE: *Of Mice and Men* (assoc. prod.) 1939; *The Devil and Miss Jones* 1941; *The More the Merrier* (co-sc. only), *The Lady Takes a Chance* 1943; *The Flame and the Arrow* 1950; *The Robe* 1953; *Demetrius and the Gladiators* 1954; *The Rains of Ranchipur* 1955; *Kings Go Forth* 1958; *One Man's Way* 1964; *Mister Moses* 1965; *Walk Don't Run* (co-script basis only), *The More the Merrier* 1966; *Where It's At* 1969; *Maurie* (co-prod.) 1973.

Ross, Herbert. Director, choreographer. Born on May 13, 1927, in New York City. A former actor and dancer, he choreographed many Broadway and Hollywood musical productions in the 50s and 60s and became resident choreographer at the American Ballet Theatre. Among the films he choreographed are *Carmen Jones* (1954), *The Young Ones* (1961), *Summer Holiday* (UK, 1963), *Inside Daisy Clover* (1966), *Doctor Dolittle* (1967), and *Funny Girl* (1968). He also directed a number of Broadway musicals, including 'House of Flowers' (1954), 'Finian's Rainbow' (1960), 'I Can Get It for You Wholesale' (1962), and 'Kelly' (1965), and in 1969 turned out his first film as director, the musical version of *Goodbye Mr. Chips.* He subsequently competently directed other lavish entertainment films. His output, often comprising adaptations from the stage, ranged from Woody Allen and Neil Simon comedies to fine dramas and films centering on the dance. His *Turning Point* (1977) was nominated for Academy Awards for best picture and best director. Several of his films were co-produced by his late wife, ballet dancer Nora Kaye, who died in 1987. In 1988 he married fashion executive Lee Bouvier Radziwill, the sister of Jackie Kennedy Onassis.

FILMS (as director): *Goodbye Mr. Chips* 1969; *The Owl and the Pussycat* 1970; *T. R. Baskin* 1971; *Play It Again Sam* 1972; *The Last of Sheila* (also prod.) 1973; *Funny Lady, The Sunshine Boys* 1975; *The Seven-Per-Cent Solution* (also prod.; UK) 1976; *The Turning Point* (also co-prod.), *The Goodbye Girl* 1977; *California Suite* 1978; *Nijinsky* (UK) 1980; *Pennies from Heaven* (also co-prod.) 1981; *I Ought to Be in Pictures* (also co-prod.) 1982; *Max Dugan Returns* (also co-prod.) 1983; *Footloose, Protocol* 1984; *The Secret of My Success* (also prod.), *Dancers* 1987; *Steel Magnolias* 1989; *My Blue Heaven* (also co-prod.) 1990; *True Colors* (also co-prod.), *Soapdish* (exec. prod. only) 1991; *Cloak and Diaper* (exec. prod. only) 1992; *Undercover Blues* 1993; *Boys on the Side* 1995.

Ross, Katharine. Actress. Born on Jan. 29, 1942, in Los Angeles. *ed.* Santa Rosa Coll. One of Hollywood's brightest new faces in the 60s, she had gained acting experience with the San Francisco Workshop and on various television shows before making her motion picture debut in 1965. She was nominated for an Oscar for her performance in *The Graduate* (1967) and seemed on her way to a brilliant career after *Butch Cassidy and the Sundance Kid* (1969). But poor role selection inhibited her early promise. In the late 80s she co-starred in the TV series 'Dynasty II: The Colbys.' In 1984 she married actor Sam ELLIOTT, her fifth.

FILMS: *Shenandoah* 1965; *The Singing Nun, Mr. Buddwing* 1966; *Games, The Graduate* 1967; *Hellfighters, Butch Cassidy and the Sundance Kid* 1969; *Tell Them Willie Boy Is Here, Fools* 1970; *Get to Know Your Rabbit, They Only Kill Their Masters* 1972; *Le Hasard et la Violence* (Fr.) 1974; *The Stepford Wives* 1975; *Voyage of the Damned* (UK) 1976; *The Betsy, The Swarm* 1978; *The Legacy* 1979; *The Final Countdown* 1980; *Wrong Is Right* 1982; *Red-Headed Stranger* 1986; *A Row of Crows* 1991.

Ross, Leonard Q. See ROSTEN, Leo.

Ross, Shirley. Actress, singer. *b.* Bernice Gaunt, Jan. 7, 1909, Omaha, Nebr. *d.* 1975. A former band vocalist, she starred in light Hollywood films of the 30s and early 40s, several times pairing with Bob Hope.

FILMS INCLUDE: *Bombshell* (bit) 1933; *Manhattan Melodrama* (bit), *The Merry Widow* (bit) 1934; *Age of Indiscretion* 1935; *Devil's Squadron, San Francisco, The Big Broadcast of 1937, Hideaway Girl* 1936; *Waikiki Wedding, Blossoms on Broadway* 1937; *The Big Broadcast of 1938, Prison Farm, Thanks for the Memory* 1938; *Paris Honeymoon, Cafe Society, Some Like It Hot, Unexpected Father* 1939; *Sailors on Leave* 1941; *A Song for Miss Julie* 1945.

Ross, Steven J. See WARNER BROS.

Rossellini, Isabella. Actress. Born on June 18, 1952, in Rome. Sensitive, sensual, delicately beautiful leading lady of American and international films. The daughter of director Roberto ROSSELLINI and actress Ingrid BERGMAN, she moved at 19 to New York, where she attended Finch College and the New School for Social Research. She later taught Italian at the New School, worked as a translator for the Italian News Bureau, and for three years served as a New York correspondent for Italian TV. She made her screen debut in 1976, playing a walk-on as a nurse in a film co-starring her mother. Her first lead was in the Taviani brothers' Italian film *The Meadow* (1979). But it was as a highly paid TV and magazine model for a cosmetics company that she first attracted wide admiration. Her movie career was boosted in the mid-80s by her enigmatic role in David Lynch's controversial *Blue Velvet* (1986), and she has often chosen demanding, intriguing roles in direct contrast to her image of graceful perfection as a model. From 1979 to 1983 she was married to director Martin SCORSESE.

FILMS: *A Matter of Time/Nina* (US/It.) 1976; *Il Prato/The Meadow* (It.) 1979; *Il Pap'Occhio* (It.) 1981; *White Nights* 1985; *Blue Velvet* 1986; *Red Riding Hood* (US/Isr.), *Tough Guys Don't Dance, Siesta* 1987; *Zelly and Me* 1988; *Cousins* 1989; *Wild at Heart, Dames Galantes/Galant Ladies* (Fr./It./Can.) 1990; *Death Becomes Her* 1992; *Fearless, The Innocent, The Pickle* 1993; *Immortal Beloved, Wyatt Earp* 1994; *Big Night, The Funeral* 1996.

Rossellini, Roberto. Director. *b.* May 8, 1906, Rome. *d.* 1977. An architect's son, he had an early interest in everything mechanical and invented a number of ingenious devices in his youth. He also developed an early passion for cinema and spent many hours of his childhood in the darkness of a Roman motion picture theater designed by his father. Much later in his life Rossellini was to combine his two passions by inventing a variety of camera, lens, and lighting devices that he used successfully in the production of his own films.

Rossellini began his film career as an amateur, making short subjects in a room he turned into a studio in the family villa near Rome. The second of these, *Prelude à l'après-Midi d'un Faune* (1938), was banned by the Italian censors as indecent. At the same time, the Fascist regime was trying to attract young talent from well-to-do families to the national film industry. Rossellini was recruited to collaborate on the script of *Luciano Serra Pilota* (1938), a propaganda film directed by Alessandrini and supervised by Vittorio Mussolini, the Duce's son. After several more collaborations, Rossellini was assigned to direct a documentary about a hospital ship. He began shooting it as a fact film, but in midproduction the project developed into a feature-length dramatic film, which he entitled *La Nava bianca* (1941). Before the Allied invasion of Italy, he directed two more Fascist-commissioned films and in 1943 began shooting *Desiderio,* a modest precursor of the neorealist style, which he dropped in midproduction. The film was completed by another director in 1946.

In the early postwar years, Rossellini burst upon the international scene as a leading figure in the neorealism movement that suddenly made Italian films the rage among intellectual audiences the world over. Rossellini's WW II–theme trilogy set the tone for the Italian movement. Its three units were landmarks in postwar European cinema. *Open City/Roma Città aperta* (1945) inaugurated the neorealist style and stunned American audiences with its raw, newsreel-like depiction of war-ravaged Europe. Based partly on true events, it told of the hunting down, capture, and torture of a Communist resistance leader and his friends by the Gestapo. The film was shot on the streets and in the apartment buildings of Rome and included such naturalistic touches as shots of toilets and babies sitting on their potties. The film's power derived not merely from its authentic settings but from the successful integration of locations and characters in advancing its drama. The film also boasted two superlative performances, by Anna Magnani and Aldo Fabrizi, but most of its performers were nonprofessionals.

Rossellini's second postwar film, *Paisà/Paisan* (1946), consisted of six separate episodes, each dealing with another aspect of interaction between liberated Italians and liberating Americans. *Germany Year Zero/Germania Anno Zero* (1947) was a somber study of the corrupting influence of Nazi ideology on the mind of a young Berlin boy who poisons his sickly father and finally kills himself. Rossellini moved away from the neorealist movement with *L'Amore/Woman/Ways of Love* (1948), a two-part film that he presented as a homage to the art of its star, Anna Magnani.

The early 50s became designated as the "Bergman period" in Rossellini's career. Swedish-born Ingrid BERGMAN, then at the height of her success as a Hollywood star, wrote a fan letter to Rossellini in which she expressed her admiration for his films and offered to work for him "for the sheer pleasure of the experience." They met, fell in love, and married in 1950 amid a clamor of public indignation. The fact that both left their former spouses to enter their union and lived as lovers in the interim period both scandalized and titillated the public and led to an unofficial boycott of their films in America and other countries. Rossellini was denounced by a US senator and labeled a "scoundrel" by India's Prime Minister Nehru. The Rossellini-Bergman union produced a son and twin girls but proved disastrous to both their careers. None of their films was much of a commercial or critical success, although in more recent years Rossellini's Bergman films have been favorably re-evaluated by many critics. The tastemakers of *Cahiers du Cinéma* have listed *Voyage en Italie/Strangers* as one of the great films of all time, but the best known of the Rossellini-Bergman collaborations remains their first, *Stromboli* (1949), a critical and commercial disaster at the time of its release in 1949.

In 1957, Rossellini again scandalized the puritan public with his affair with Indian screenwriter Somali Das Gupta, whose pregnancy led to his separation and divorce from Miss Bergman. The following year audiences at the Moscow Film Festival booed and walked out of the showing of Rossellini's documentary feature *India.* The film failed badly elsewhere as well, although many serious critics termed it brilliant.

It wasn't until 1959 that Rossellini regained his erstwhile prestige, with *General Della Rovere,* a dramatization of a true WW II story about an opportunist who impersonates a general and winds up a hero despite himself. The role was superbly played by Vittorio De Sica. In the 60s, Rossellini directed a number of feature-length films for Italian TV, one of which, *The Rise of Louis XIV* (1966), enjoyed a successful run in international art theaters. Only three of his films after 1962 were made for initial theatrical release. Rossellini also directed for the stage and the opera and he supervised a number of films directed by others. He collaborated on most of his own screenplays. He gave courses on filmmaking at Yale and at Houston's Rice University. His brother, Renzo Rossellini (*b.* 1908, Rome; *d.* 1982), was a composer and music critic who scored many Italian films, including most of Roberto's. Roberto Rossellini was the father of actress Isabella ROSSELLINI.

FILMS (as director): *Daphne* (short) 1936; *Prelude à l'après-Midi d'un Faune* (short), *Luciano Serra Pilota* (assoc. dir., co-sc. only) 1938; *Fantasia Sottomarina* (short), *Il Tacchino Prepotente* (short), *La Vispa Teresa* (short) 1939; *Il Ruscello di Ripasottile* (short), *La Nave Bianca* (also co-sc.) 1941; *Una Pilota Ritorna* (also co-sc.) 1942; *L'Uomo della Croce* (also co-sc.), *L'Invasore* (co-sc., superv. only), *Desiderio* (co-dir. with Marcello Pagliero, co-sc.) 1943; *Roma Città aperta/Open City* (also co-sc.) 1945; *Paisà/Paisan* (also prod., co-story, co-sc.) 1946; *Germania Anno Zero/Germany Year Zero* (also story, co-sc.) 1947; *L'Amore/Woman/Ways of Love* (comprising two episodes: "Una Voce Umana," adapted by Rossellini from a one-act play by Cocteau; and "Il Miracolo," which Rossellini co-scripted from a story by Fellini), *La Macchina Ammazzacattivi* (also co-sc.) 1948; *Stromboli—Terra di Dio/Stromboli* (for his own production company; also story, co-sc.) 1949; *Francesco—Giullare di Dio/Flowers of St. Francis* (also co-sc.) 1950; *Les Sept Péchés capitaux/The Seven Deadly Sins* ("Envy" episode; also story, co-sc.), *Europa '51/The*

Greatest Love (also story, co-sc.) 1952; *Dov'è la Libertè?* (also story), *Viaggio in Italia/Strangers/The Lonely Woman* (also co-sc.), *Siamo Donne* (Ingrid Bergman episode) 1953; *Amori di Mezzo Secolo* ("Napoli '43" episode; also sc.), *Giovanna d'Arco al Rogo/Joan of Arc at the Stake* (also sc.), *Die Angst/La Paura/Fear* (Ger./It.), *Orient Express* (superv. only) 1954; *L'India visita da Rossellini* (ten-episode documentary for Italian TV; also prod.), *India* (also story, co-sc.) 1958; *Il Generale della Rovere/General Della Rovere* (also co-sc.) 1959; *Era Notte a Roma* (also co-sc.) *Viva l'Italia* (also co-sc.) 1960; *Vanina Vanini/The Betrayer* (also co-sc.), *Torino Nei Centi'anni* (45-min. TV doc.) 1961; *Benito Mussolini/Blood on the Balcony* (doc.; prod., superv. only), *Anima Nera* (also sc.), *Rogopag* ("Illibatezza" episode; also sc.) 1962; *Les Carabiniers* (co-sc. only) 1963; *L'Eta del Ferro* (five one-hr. doc. segments for TV; superv., sc. only) 1964; *La Prise de Pouvoir par Louis XIV/The Rise of Louis XIV* (originally made for French TV) 1966; *Idea di un'Isola* (doc.; originally made for US TV; also prod.), *La Lotta dell'Uomo per la sua Sopravvivenza* (12 one-hour semidoc. episodes for Italian TV; prod., sc., superv. only) 1967; *Atti degli Apostoli* (five feature-length episodes for Italian TV; also co-prod., co-sc.) 1968; *Socrate/Socrates* (originally made for TV; also co-prod., co-sc.) 1970; *Agostino di Ippona* 1972; *Blaise Pascal* (originally made for TV), *Anno Uno* 1975; *Il Messia/The Messiah* (also co-sc.) 1978.

Rossen, Robert. Director, screenwriter, producer. *b.* Robert Rosen, Mar. 16, 1908, New York City. *d.* 1966. *ed.* NYU. The son of Russian-Jewish immigrants, he was raised in the poverty and violence of the Lower East Side. He boxed professionally for a brief while but gradually oriented himself toward the stage as a director and a playwright in stock, off Broadway, and finally on Broadway. He met with only mild success and after seeing his play 'The Body Beautiful' close on Broadway after only four performances, he went to Hollywood in 1936 as a contract screenwriter for Warners. A social idealist, he gravitated toward membership in the Hollywood cell of the Communist Party, a move that was to have grave consequences on his life and career in later years. His political concerns were also reflected in his scripts, which often dealt with social problems and the threat of tyranny. But in 1944 he became deeply disillusioned with the Party. He took a year's sabbatical in New York for reflection, in 1945, then returned to Hollywood and severed all ties with the Communist Party.

He took another important step in the late 40s by becoming a director and an independent producer. But like many of his characters, his past soon caught up with him. In 1947 he was subpoenaed to testify before the House Un-American Activities Committee, but the hearings were suspended after the conviction of the Hollywood Ten, and Rossen was able to continue his work. During the interval between the 1947 and 1951 hearings, Rossen made a reputation for himself as a gutsy, hard-hitting director of such solid dramas as *Johnny O'Clock, Body and Soul,* and *All the King's Men.* The latter, a sturdy drama of political corruption, won the best picture Academy Award for 1949. In the 1951 round of hearings by the House Un-American Activities Committee, Rossen was identified as a Communist by several witnesses. In his own testimony, he denied present membership in the Party but refused to testify about past membership and to identify other Hollywood personalities as past members. He was promptly blacklisted by the industry.

After two years of inactivity and soul-searching, Rossen wrote to the Committee, requesting a special hearing, during which he admitted his past association with the Communist Party and named more than 50 colleagues. He was able to work again but never returned to Hollywood, choosing instead to work in other locations. He withdrew within himself and was described by friends as a tortured person. In the early 60s, he regained some of his lost prestige in the eyes of the critics with *The Hustler.* But his last film, *Lilith,* was a critical and commercial failure in America. He died before learning that the film was included in the cumulative list of ten best films published annually by the widely respected French magazine *Cahiers du Cinéma.*

FILMS: As screenwriter—*Marked Woman* (co-story, co-sc.), *They Won't Forget* (co-sc.) 1937; *Racket Busters* (co-story, co-sc.) 1938; *Dust Be My Destiny, The Roaring Twenties* (co-sc.) 1939; *A Child Is Born* 1940; *The Sea Wolf, Out of the Fog* (co-sc.), *Blues in the Night* 1941; *Edge of Darkness* 1943; *A Walk in the Sun, The Strange Love of Martha Ivers* 1946; *Desert Fury* 1947; *The Treasure of Sierra Madre* (co-sc., uncredited) 1948. As producer—*The Undercover Man* 1949. As director—*Johnny O'Clock* (also sc.), *Body and Soul* 1947; *All the King's Men* (also prod., sc.) 1949; *The Brave Bulls* (also prod.) 1951; *Mambo* (also co-sc.; It.) 1955; *Alexander the Great* (also prod., sc.) 1956; *Island in the Sun* 1957; *They Came to Cordura* (also co-sc.) 1959; *The Hustler* (also prod. co-sc.), *Lilith* (also prod., co-sc.) 1964.

Rossi Drago, Eleonora. Actress. Born Palmira Omiccioli, on Sept. 23, 1925, Quinto, near Genoa, Italy, to an Italian father and a Spanish mother. Sensual leading lady of Italian and international films, she was formerly a salesgirl.

FILMS INCLUDE: *I Pirati di Capri* 1949; *Persianc chiuse* 1950; *Verginita, Tre Storie proibite/Three Forbidden Stories* 1951; *La Tratta delle Bianche, Sensualita* 1952; *I Sette dell'Orsa Maggiore/Hell Raiders of the Deep, La Fiammata, L'Esclave, Destinees/Daughters of Destiny* 1953; *L'Affaire Maurizius, Napoléon* 1954; *Le Amiche/The Girl Friends* 1955; *Suor Letizia/The Awakening, Donne Sole* 1956; *Kean* 1957; *Un Maledetto Imbroglio/The Facts of Murder, Estate Violenta/Violent Summer* 1959; *David e Golia/David and Goliath, Sotte Dieci Bandiere/Under Ten Flags* 1960; *Rosamunda e Alboino/Sword of the Conqueror, Caccia all'Uomo* 1961; *L'Amour à Vingt Ans/Love at Twenty* 1962; *Hipnosis/Hypnosis* (Sp./It./Ger.) 1963; *L'Idea fissa/Love and Marriage, Se permettete. . . parliamo di Donne/Let's Talk About Women* 1964; *Onkel Toms Hütte/Uncle Tom's Cabin* (as Mrs. St. Clare; Ger./It./Fr./Yug.) 1965; *La Bibbia/The Bible. . . In the Beginning* (as Lot's Wife; US/It.) 1966; *Camille 2000* (US) 1969; *Das Bildnis des Dorian Gray/Dorian Gray* (Ger./It.) 1970.

Rossif, Frédéric. Director. *b.* Aug. 14, 1922, Cetinje, Montenegro, Yugoslavia. *d.* 1990, of a heart attack. After WW II service with the French Foreign Legion, he worked for several years as a draftsman for Renault and Citroën and briefly as a bouncer for a Left Bank nightclub. He began his association with films as an employee of the Cinémathèque Française and in the 50s directed occasional programs for French TV. Specializing in compilation films, he began turning out shorts in 1958 and feature-length documentaries in 1961. Several of his films won international prizes. The best known among them is *Mourir à Madrid/To Die in Madrid* (1963), a moving compilation film on the Spanish Civil War which enjoyed worldwide commercial distribution and was nominated for an Academy Award. Some of the footage was used in the opening sequence of Fred Zinnemann's *Behold a Pale Horse* (1964).

FEATURE FILMS: *Le Temps du Ghetto/The Witnesses* (also co-sc.) 1961; *Mourir à Madrid/To Die in Madrid, Les Animaux/The Animals* (also sc.) 1963; *La Révolution d'Octobre/The October Revolution* 1967; *Un Mur à Jerusalem/A Wall in Jerusalem* (co-dir. with Albert Knobler) 1968; *Pourquoi l'Amérique* 1969; *Aussi loin que l'Amour* (also co-sc.) 1971; *La Fête sauvage* 1976; *Pablo Picasso, Brel* 1982;

Sauvage et Beau 1984; *Le Coeur Musicien* (also co-sc.) 1987; *Tatie Danielle* (act., only) 1990.

Rosson, Hal (Harold). Director of photography. *b.* 1895, New York City. *d.* 1988. One of Hollywood's most celebrated cinematographers. The younger brother of: Arthur Rosson (*b.* Aug. 24, 1889, London; *d.* 1960), a prolific director of silent films who in the 30s and 40s served as an associate director and 2nd-unit director on many Cecil B. De Mille productions; silent screen director Richard Rosson (*b.* 1894, New York City; *d.* 1953) whose career extended briefly into talkies; and silent screen star Helen(e) Rosson. He entered films as a bit player with Vitagraph in 1908. He moved to Los Angeles in 1913 and after training in various capacities became a camera operator in 1915 and a lighting cameraman the following year. He was behind the camera of scores of silents and talkies, including many major productions, mainly at MGM, and was a favorite cinematographer of such directors as Josef Von Sternberg, Howard Hawks, Alan Dwan, Cecil B. De Mille, Victor Fleming, King Vidor, and George Cukor. He shared a Special Academy Award for his pioneering Technicolor work on *The Garden of Allah* (1936). He was the last (1933–35) husband of movie star Jean HARLOW, his second of three wives, who accused him of "mental cruelty" for reading in bed.

FILMS INCLUDE: *David Harum* (cam. op.) 1915; *The Honorable Friend, Oliver Twist* 1916; *Panthea* (co-phot.), *The American Consul* 1917; *The Cinema Murder, Heliotrope* 1920; *Buried Treasure* 1921; *For the Defense* 1922; *Dark Secrets, The Glimpses of the Moon, Quicksands* (co-phot.), *Zaza* 1923; *Manhattan, Manhandled, A Society Scandal* 1924; *The Street of Forgotten Men, Infatuation, A Man Must Live* 1925; *Man Bait, Up in Mabel's Room* (co-phot.) 1926; *A Gentleman of Paris, Jim the Conqueror, Service for Ladies* 1927; *Gentlemen Prefer Blondes, The Docks of New York, The Dragnet, Three Week-Ends* 1928; *Abie's Irish Rose, The Far Call, The Case of Lena Smith, Frozen Justice, South Sea Rose, Trent's Last Case* 1929; *Madame Satan, Passion Flower* 1930; *The Prodigal, The Squaw Man, Son of India, Sporting Blood, The Cuban Love Song* 1931; *Tarzan the Ape Man* (co-phot.), *Red-Headed Woman, Red Dust* 1932; *The Barbarian, Penthouse* (co-phot.), *Bombshell* (co-phot.) 1933; *This Side of Heaven, The Cat and the Fiddle, Treasure Island* (co-phot.) 1934; *The Scarlet Pimpernel* (UK), *The Ghost Goes West* (UK) 1935; *As You Like It* (UK), *The Devil Is a Sissy, The Garden of Allah* 1936; *They Gave Him a Gun, Captains Courageous, The Emperor's Candlesticks* 1937; *A Yank at Oxford, Too Hot to Handle* 1938; *The Wizard of Oz* 1939; *I Take This Woman, Edison the Man, Boom Town* 1940; *Flight Command, The Penalty, Men of Boys Town, Honky Tonk* 1941; *Johnny Eager, Somewhere I'll Find You, Tennessee Johnson* 1942; *Thirty Seconds Over Tokyo* (co-phot.), *An American Romance* 1943; *No Leave No Love* (co-phot.) 1946; *Duel in the Sun* (co-phot.), *The Hucksters* 1947; *Homecoming* 1948; *Command Decision, The Stratton Story, On the Town* 1949; *Key to the City, The Asphalt Jungle* 1950; *The Red Badge of Courage* 1951; *The Lone Star, Singin' in the Rain* 1952; *The Story of Three Loves* (co-phot.), *The Actress* 1953; *Mambo* (It.), *Ulisse/Ulysses* (co-phot.; It.) 1954; *Pete Kelly's Blues* 1955; *The Bad Seed, Toward the Unknown* 1956; *The Enemy Below* 1957; *No Time for Sergeants* 1958; *El Dorado* 1967.

Rosten, Leo. Author, screenwriter. Born on Apr. 11, 1908, in Lodz, Poland. *ed.* U. of Chicago (Ph.D.); London School of Economics. A well-known novelist (*Captain Newman, M.D.*, etc.) and nonfiction writer (*The Washington Correspondents, Hollywood: The Movie Colony, The Joys of Yiddish*, etc.), he has also written a number of screenplays alone or in collaboration, sometimes using the pseudonym Leonard Q. Ross.

FILMS INCLUDE: *All Through the Night* (co-story only) 1942; *They Got Me Covered* (co-story only) 1943; *The Conspirators* 1944; *The Dark Corner* (story only) 1946; *Lured* 1947; *Sleep My Love* (from own novel), *The Velvet Touch* 1948; *Where Danger Lives* (story only) 1950; *Double Dynamite* (story only) 1951; *Walk East on Beacon* 1952; *Mister Cory* (story only) 1957; *Captain Newman M.D.* (novel basis only) 1964.

rostrum. 1. A small platform on collapsible legs on which a camera or lighting unit may be mounted. 2. In animation a rostrum is a rigid support for the camera and the animation board, holding them both in a desired position relative to each other during photography. In rostrum photography the camera is positioned above the horizontal animation board and it can be made to slide up and down in relation to the animation board to alter the field of view and produce zoom effects, but it remains rigid horizontally.

Rota, Nino. Composer. *b.* Dec. 31, 1911, Milan, Italy. *d.* 1979. A child prodigy, he composed an oratorio at the age of 11 and later studied at Rome's Santa Cecilia Academy and at Philadelphia's Curtis Institute. He later gained international recognition as a contemporary composer of distinction. He wrote four symphonies, eight operas, several concertos, ballet scores, and many other orchestral works in addition to numerous scores for the Italian stage and screen. His film scores were noted for their appealing simplicity and were usually melodic and memorable. He won an Oscar for the music of *The Godfather, Part II* (1974), but his most notable film work was for Federico FELLINI, a director-composer collaboration that lasted for a quarter of a century. Rota also composed for Visconti, among other directors. He was for 37 years director of the Bari Conservatory. His music was used posthumously in several films of the 80s.

FILMS INCLUDE: *Treno Popolare* 1933; *Zaza* 1943; *Vivere in Pace/To Live in Peace* 1946; *Sotto il Sole di Roma, Senza Pietà/Without Pity, In Nome della Legge, The Glass Mountain* (UK) 1948; *Obsession* (UK) 1949; *Napoli Milionaria, E Primavera, Vita da Cani* 1950; *Anna* 1951; *Lo Sceicco bianco/The White Sheik, Due Soldi di Speranza* 1952; *I Vitelloni* 1953; *La Strada, Mambo* 1954; *Il Bidone, Amici per la Pelle/Friends for Life, La Bella di Roma* 1955; *War and Peace* (US/It.), *Le Notti di Cabiria/Cabiria/Nights of Cabiria* 1956; *Le Notti bianche/White Nights* 1957; *La Grande Guerra/The Great War* 1959; *La Dolce Vita, Plein Soleil/Purple Noon, Rocco e i suoi Fratelli/Rocco and His Brothers* 1960; *Le Due Nemici/The Best of Enemies* (It./UK) 1961; *Boccaccio '70* (Fellini and Visconti episodes), *I Sequestrati di Altona/The Condemned of Altona, The Reluctant Saint* (US/It.) 1962; *Il Gattopardo/The Leopard, Otto e Mezzo/8½* 1963; *Giulietta degli Spiriti/Juliet of the Spirits* 1965; *The Taming of the Shrew* (US/It.) 1967; *Histoires extraordinaires/Spirits of the Dead* (Fellini episode; Fr./It.), *Romeo and Juliet* (UK/It.) 1968; *Fellini Satyricon* 1969; *I Clowns/The Clowns, Waterloo* (It./USSR) 1970; *The Godfather* (US), *Roma/Fellini's Roma* 1972; *Film d'Amore e d'Anarchia/Love and Anarchy, Amarcord* 1973; *The Abdication* (UK), *The Godfather Part II* (US) 1974; *Caro Michele, Casanova/Fellini's Casanova* 1976; *Death on the Nile* (UK) 1978; *Prova d'Orchestra/Orchestra Rehearsal, Hurricane* (US) 1979. Posthumously: *Hold-Up* (excerpts from *La Strada*) 1984; *I Soliti Ignoti Vent'Anni Dopo/Big Deal on Madonna Street (20 Years After)* 1986; *Intervista* 1987; *The Godfather Part III* 1990.

Roth, Ann. Costume designer. Born on Oct. 30, 1931, in Hanover, Penn. *ed.* Carnegie Tech. Leading costumer for Broadway plays (from the late 50s) and Hollywood films (from the mid-60s). A farmer's daughter, she worked briefly as a scenic painter for the Pittsburgh Opera before switching to costumes, at first as an assistant to Irene Sharaff. She received an Academy Award for her costume designs for *The English Patient* (1996).

FILMS INCLUDE: *The World of Henry Orient* 1964; *A Fine Madness* 1966; *Up the Down Staircase, Sweet November* 1967; *Pretty Poison* 1968; *Midnight Cowboy* 1969; *The Owl and the Pussycat* 1970; *Klute, They Might Be Giants* 1972; *The Day of the Locust* 1975; *Murder by Death* 1976; *The Goodbye Girl* 1977; *California Suite, Coming Home* 1978; *Hair* 1979; *The Island, Dressed to Kill, Nine to Five* 1980; *Honky Tonk Freeway, Only When I Laugh* 1981; *The World According to Garp* 1982; *The Man Who Loved Women, Silkwood* 1983; *Places in the Heart* 1984; *Sweet Dreams, Jagged Edge* 1985; *Heartburn, The Morning After* 1986; *The Unbearable Lightness of Being, Biloxi Blues, Working Girl* 1988; *Her Alibi, Family Business* 1989; *Q & A, Postcards from the Edge, Pacific Heights, The Bonfire of the Vanities* 1990; *Regarding Henry* 1991; *Consenting Adults* 1992; *Dave* 1993; *Guarding Tess* 1994; *Just Cause* 1995; *The English Patient* 1996.

Roth, Eric. Screenwriter. *ed.* Columbia University, New York City; UCLA. After receiving the Samuel Goldwyn Writing Award at UCLA, he began his film career writing documentaries and at the same time sold a script for a television movie which led to his first feature *The Nickel Ride* (1975). For a number of years thereafter, he had alternating success re-writing others' screenplays yet establishing himself as a reliable professional. But it was his adaptation of the Winston Groom novel *Forrest Gump* (1994) and its subsequent success that propelled him to prominence and the Academy Award for best adapted screenplay.

FILMS: *The Nickel Ride* 1975; *The Concorde—Airport '79* 1979; *Suspect* 1987; *Memories of Me* 1988; *Mr. Jones* 1993; *Forrest Gump* 1994.

Roth, Joe. Director, producer, executive. Born on June 13, 1948, in New York City. A graduate of Boston University, majoring in communications, he began his career in San Francisco as a production assistant on commercials and feature films. At about the same time, he operated the lights for the improvisational group Pitchel Players, with whom he moved to Los Angeles as the show's producer. For a scant budget of $25,000 he produced the group's film *Tunnelvision* (1976), a crude parody of future TV programming, which went on to earn $17 million at the box office. He showed a similar Midas touch with some other films he subsequently produced and in 1986 branched out intermittently into directing. In 1987 he co-founded with Jim Robinson the independent production company Morgan Creek, whose commercial successes included *Young Guns*. In 1989 he was appointed chairman of Fox Film Corporation, the newly formed theatrical production unit of 20th Century-Fox. In 1992, before the bad news hit about his box-office disappointments *Toys* and *Hoffa*, he left Fox to eventually become chairman of Walt Disney Pictures.

FILMS INCLUDE: *Tunnelvision* (prod.) 1976; *Cracking Up* (exec. prod.) 1977; *Our Winning Season* (prod.) 1978; *Americathon* (prod.) 1979; *The Final Terror* 1981; *Ladies and Gentlemen... The Fabulous Stains* (prod.) 1982; *The Stone Boy* (co-prod.), *Bachelor Party* (exec. prod.) 1984; *Moving Violations* (co-prod.) 1985; *Where the River Runs Black, Streets of Gold* (dir., co-prod.), *Off Beat* (co-prod.) 1986; *Revenge of the Nerds II: Nerds in Paradise* (dir., exec prod.) 1987; *Young Guns* (co-prod.), *Dead Ringers* (prod.) 1988; *Skin Deep* (co-exec. prod.), *Renegades* (co-exec. prod.), *Enemies, A Love Story* (co-exec. prod.) 1989; *Coup De Ville* (dir.), *Young Guns II* (co-exec. prod.), *The Exorcist III* (co-exec. prod.), *Pacific Heights* (co-exec. prod.) 1990; *Toys, Hoffa* 1992; *The Three Musketeers* 1993; *Angels in the Outfield* (prod.) 1994; *Houseguest* (prod.), *While You Were Sleeping* (ex-prod.) 1995.

Roth, Lillian. Actress, singer. *b.* Lillian Rutstein, Dec. 13, 1910, Boston. *d.* 1980. Star of stage and screen whose career was wrecked by alcoholism and eight divorces. In show business from age six, she appeared in films, plays, and revues, billed as "Broadway's youngest star." Her career reached a peak in the late 20s and early 30s, when she starred on the stage in 'Earl Carroll's Vanities' and Ziegfeld's 'Midnight Frolics' as well as in a string of successful Hollywood films. By the late 30s she had disappeared from sight. She was still all but forgotten in 1953 when she told her tragic story to millions of Americans on TV's 'This Is Your Life.' The following year her autobiography, *I'll Cry Tomorrow,* became an international best-seller. The 1955 film version, starring Susan Hayward, was equally successful. As a result of the publicity she was able to make a modest comeback in nightclubs, on the stage, and on TV. In 1977 she returned to the screen for the first time after an absence of 44 years.

FILMS INCLUDE (sound features complete): *Pershing's Crusaders* 1918; *Illusion, The Love Parade* 1929; *The Vagabond King, Animal Crackers, Sea Legs, Paramount on Parade, Madame Satan, Honey* 1930; *Take a Chance, Ladies They Talk About* 1933; *Communion* 1977.

Roth, Tim. Actor. Born in 1962, in London. Dynamic, blond, boyish young lead of British and international films. He studied sculpture before turning to the stage, then TV and films. He rapidly lived up to his early promise, receiving critical kudos for his roles in *Reservoir Dogs* (1992), *Pulp Fiction* (1994), and an Oscar-nominated turn as Cunningham in *Rob Roy* (1995).

FILMS INCLUDE: *Meantime* (orig. for TV) 1983; *The Hit* 1984; *Return to Waterloo* 1985; *A World Apart, Le Complot/To Kill A Priest* (Fr.) 1988; *The Cook the Thief His Wife and Her Lover* (Hol./Fr.) 1989; *Vincent and Theo* (as Vincent van Gogh; UK/Fr.), *Farend* (Fr.), *Rosencrantz and Guildenstern Are Dead* (as Guildenstern) 1990; *Backsliding* (Austral./UK), *Jumpin' at the Boneyard* 1991; *Reservoir Dogs* 1992; *Bodies Rest and Motion* 1993; *Little Odessa, Pulp Fiction* 1994; *Captives, Four Rooms, Rob Roy* 1995; *Everyone Says I Love You* 1996; *Gridlock'd, Hoodlum, No Way Home* 1997.

Rotha, Paul. Director, producer, film historian. *b.* Paul Thompson, June 3, 1907, London. *d.* 1984. A leading figure in the British documentary movement. The son of a doctor/medical archivist, he studied at London's Slade School of Fine Arts and began his career as a painter, book illustrator, and stage designer. He won the International Theater Design Award at the 1925 Paris Exhibition and in 1927 he became art critic for *The Connoisseur.* He made his initial contact with films in 1928 as a prop man, then as an assistant designer to Alfred Hitchcock, but was fired later that year after he published a scathing article on the stagnant state of British cinema. In 1930 he published *The Film Till Now,* a critical historical survey of world cinema that remained a standard source for film students for many years. Although it was updated periodically, many of the book's views and ideas now seem outdated and its critical judgments are deemed lacking in perception or depth. His subsequent books included *Celluloid* (1931), *Documentary Film* (1935), *Movie Parade* (1936), *Rotha on the Film* (1958), *The Innocent Eye: A Biography of Robert Flaherty* (1963), and *Documentary Diary* (1973).

In 1931 Rotha joined John Grierson's documentary unit at the Empire Marketing Board but he left after only six months to pursue his own projects as a producer-director of documentaries, several of them notable for their innovative style and sincere social consciousness. He won Gold Medals at Venice (1934), Brussels (1935), and Leipzig (1962), and British Academy Awards in 1947 and 1952. His *The World Is Rich* (1947) was nominated for an Oscar. From 1953 to 1955 he served as head of the documentary unit at BBC television. Rotha was far less successful, however, with his three sporadic excursions into feature films. His third wife was Irish actress Constance Smith.

FILMS (as director-screenwriter): *Contact, The Rising Tide/Great Cargoes* 1933; *Shipyard* 1934; *The Face of Britain, Death on the Road* 1935; *The Future's in the Air, Cover to Cover, The Way to the Sea, Peace of Britain* 1936; *Statue, Today We Live, Here Is the Land* 1937; *New Worlds for Old, Roads Across Britain* (co-dir. with Sidney Cole) 1939; *The Fourth Estate* (not shown until '64); *Mr. Borland Thins Again* 1940; *World of Plenty* 1943; *Soviet Village* 1944; *Land of Promise, Total War in Britain* 1945; *A City Speaks* 1946; *The World Is Rich* 1947; *No Resting Place* (fiction feature) 1951; *World Without End* (co-dir. with Basil Wright) 1953; *Hope for the Hungry, The Waiting People* 1954; *No Other Way, The Wealth of Waters, The Virus Story* 1955; *Cat and Mouse* (fiction feature) 1958; *Cradle of Genius* 1959; *Das Leben von Adolf Hitler/The Life of Adolf Hitler* (Ger./UK) 1961; *De Overval/The Silent Raid* (fiction feature; Hol.) 1962.

Rothman, Stephanie. Director, writer. Born on Nov. 9, 1936, in Paterson, N.J. *ed.* Univ. of Calif. (sociology); USC. Director and writer of several of the trademark films from the B-studio factories of Roger CORMAN.

FILMS INCLUDE (as director and co-sc.): *It's a Bikini World, Blood Bath* (co-dir.) 1966; *The Student Nurses* 1970; *The Velvet Vampire* 1971; *Group Marriage* 1972; *Terminal Island, Beyond Atlantis* (co-sc. only) 1973; *The Working Girls* (sc.) 1974.

rotoscope. An ANIMATION technique in which film frames are blown up and traced individually onto animation cels. The technique can be used to transform live-action figures into animated ones, but is also used to enhance live-action scenes with animated special effects. For example, rotoscoping was used to produce the glowing light sabers in the *Star Wars* films. Live-action footage was shot of actors wielding stick swords; the stick swords were rotoscoped onto animation cels, painted in brilliant colors, then optically combined with the original footage.

Rotunno, Giuseppe. Director of photography. Born on Mar. 19, 1923, in Rome. He began in Italian films at 17 as a still photographer and, after a period of apprenticeship as camera assistant, worked as camera operator on several productions, including Visconti's *Senso* (1954), before graduating to lighting cameraman. He has since gained a reputation as a leading cinematographer of Italian and international films, noted for the special warm quality of his color photography as well as for his earlier work in black and white. In the 70s he began a close working relationship with Fellini and in the 80s and early 90s he worked frequently in Hollywood. He was nominated for an Academy Award for the cinematography of *All That Jazz* (1979).

FILMS INCLUDE: *Pane Amore e . . . /Scandal in Sorrento* 1955; *Tosca* 1956; *Le Notti bianche* 1957; *Anna di Brooklyn/Fast and Sexy, La Maja Desnuda/The Naked Maja* 1958; *La Grande Guerra/The Great War, On the Beach* (US) 1959; *Rocco e i suoi Fratelli/Rocco and His Brothers* 1960; *I Due Nemici/The Best of Enemies* 1961; *Boccaccio '70* (Visconti episode), *Cronaca familiare/Family Diary* 1962; *Il Gattopardo/The Leopard, I Compagni/The Organizer, Ieri Oggi e Domani/Yesterday Today and Tomorrow* 1963; *La Bibbia/The Bible. . . In the Beginning* (US/It.) 1966; *Le Streghe/The Witches, Lo Straniero/The Stranger* 1967; *Lo Sbarco di Anzio/Anzio, Candy* (US/Fr./It.) 1968; *The Secret of Santa Vittoria* (US), *Fellini Satyricon, I Girasoli/Sunflower* 1969; *Carnal Knowledge* (US) 1971; *Roma/Fellini's Roma, Man of La Mancha* (US/It.) 1972; *Film d'Amore e d'Anarchia/Love and Anarchy, Amarcord* 1973; *Tutto a Posto e Niente in Ordine/All Screwed Up* 1974; *Casanova/Fellini's Casanova* 1976; *Sturmtruppen* 1977; *The End of the World in Our Usual Bed in a Night Full of Rain* (US) 1978; *All That Jazz* (US), *Prova d'Orchestra/Orchestra Rehearsal* 1979; *Popeye* (US) 1980; *La Città delle Donne/City of Women, Rollover* (US) 1981; *Five Days One Summer* (UK/US) 1982; *E la Nave va/And the Ship Sails On* 1983; *Desiderio* 1984; *Red Sonja* (US), *Orfeo/Orpheus* (Fr./It./Can.) 1985; *Hotel Colonial* (It./US) 1986; *Julia and Julia* (It.) 1977; *Rent-a-Cop* (US), *Haunted Summer* (US) 1988; *Adventures of Baron Munchausen* (UK) 1989; *Regarding Henry* (US), *The Bachelor* (US) 1991; *Once Upon a Crime* (US) 1992; *Wolf* 1994; *Sabrina* 1995; *The Night and the Moment* 1996.

Rouch, Jean. Director, documentary filmmaker. Born on May 31, 1917, in Paris, the son of a naval officer who later became director of the oceanographic museum in Monaco. The holder of a Ph.D. in literature and a civil engineering degree, he began using a motion picture camera as a tool of documentation in ethnographic research in Africa. Gradually he switched to filmmaking for its own sake, turning out short and full-length documentaries and semidocumentaries in the *CINÉMA VÉRITÉ* method. Most of his films were shot in 16 mm and many have interracial relations as their central theme. Several of his films won prizes at major international festivals. *Chronique d'un Eté/Chronicle of a Summer* (1961), celebrating Paris, shared the International Critics Prize at Cannes. Rouch has served as secretary general of the International Committee of Ethnographic and Sociological Film, as director of research at the National Center of Scientific Research, and as president of the Cinémathèque Française.

FILMS INCLUDE: Shorts—*Au Pays des Mages noirs* (co-dir., sc., phot.) 1947; *Hombroi* (also sc.), *Les Magiciens noirs* (co-dir., prod., phot.), *La Circoncision* (also prod., phot.) 1949; *Bataille sur le Grand Fleuve* (also phot.), *Les Hommes qui font la Pluie* (also phot.), *Les Gens du Mil* (also phot.) 1951; *Les Maîtres fous* (also phot., narr.) 1955; *Moro Naba* (also phot.) 1957; *Hampi* (also sc.) 1960; *Abidjan—Port de la Pêche* (also sc.), *Urbanisme Africain* (also sc.), *Pêcheurs du Niger* (also sc.) 1962; *Les Cocotiers* 1963; *Les Veuves de Quinze Ans* 1964; *Le Signe* (co-dir., sc.) 1969. Feature-length films (complete)—*Les Fils de l'Eau* (compiled from several shorts) 1955; *Moi un Noir* (also sc., co-phot.) 1958; *La Pyramide humaine* (also sc., co-phot.) 1959; *Chronique d'un Eté/Chronicle of a Summer* (co-dir., co-sc. with Edgar Morin; also on-camera interviewer) 1961; *La Punition* 1963; *La Fleur de l'Age ou Les Adolescentes/The Adolescents/That Tender Age* ("Marie-France and Veronica" episode; also sc.; Can./Fr./It./Jap.) 1964; *Paris vu par. . . /Six in Paris* ("Gare du Nord" episode; also sc.), *La Chasse au Lion a l'Arc/The Lion Hunters* (also sc., phot., narr.) 1965; *La Goumbe des Jeunes Noceurs* (also phot.) 1966; *Jaguar* (also phot.) 1967; *Petit à Petit* (also story, phot.) 1970; *Chantons sous l'Occupation* (co-phot. only), *Babatu* (also phot.) 1976; *Cocorico Monsieur Poulet* (also co-story, co-sc.; filmed in Nigeria) 1977; *Le Vieil Anaï* (co-dir., phot.) 1980; *Ambara Dama* (co-dir.) 1982; *Dionysos* (also sc., phot.) 1984; *Bac ou Mariage* 1988; *Cantate pour Deux Généraux* (also sc., phot.) 1990.

rough cut. The stage in editing between ASSEMBLY and FINE CUT in which the entire film is put into a coherent sequence with scenes spliced in approximate order and length.

Rouleau, Raymond. Actor, director. *b.* June 4, 1904, Brussels. *d.* 1981. A prominent actor and director of the Belgian, then the Paris stage, he also appeared in many French films from the late 20s, in both leads and supporting roles. His infrequent incursions into film directing were effective but, with the notable exception of *Les Sorcières de Salem/Witches of Salem* (1957), unremarkable.

FILMS INCLUDE: As actor—*L'Argent* 1929; *La Femme nue* 1932; *Incognito* 1933; *Volga en Flammes* 1934; *Les Beaux Jours* 1935; *L'Affaire Lafarge, Le Drame de Shanghai/The Shanghai Drama, Conflit/The Affair Lafont* 1938; *L'Esclave blanche* 1939; *L'Assassinat du Père Noël/Who Killed Santa Claus?, Premier Bal* 1941; *Dernier Atout* 1942; *L'Honorable Catherine/The Honorable Catherine* 1943; *Flabalas/Paris Frills* 1945; *Une Grande Fille toute simple/Just a Big Simple Girl* 1948; *Mission à Tanger* 1949; *Méfiez-vous des Blondes* 1950; *Massacre en Dentelles* 1952; *Les Intrigantes* 1954; *Le Fric* 1959; *Deux Heures à tuer* 1965. As director (complete)—*Suzanne* (co-dir. with Leo Joannon; also act.) 1932; *Une Vie perdue* (also act.) 1933; *Rose* 1936; *Trois-Six-Neuf* (also act.), *Le Messager* 1937; *Le Couple idéal* (co-dir. with Bernard Roland, act.) 1946; *Les Sorcières de Salem/Witches of Salem* (also act.) 1957; *Les Amants de Teruel/The Lovers of Teruel* (also sc.) 1962.

Roundtree, Richard. Actor. Born on Sept. 7, 1937, in New Rochelle, N.Y. The son of a chauffeur and a housekeeper, he went to Southern Illinois University on a football scholarship and began participating in college dramatics. Dropping out of school in his sophomore year, he worked for a while as a janitor and a men's clothing salesman, then enjoyed some success as a male model. In 1967 he joined the Negro Ensemble Company and appeared in several of its productions. He made his screen debut, a bit, in 1970 and became an instant star the following year as the hip hero of the action film *Shaft.* He has since played the role in two sequels and in a TV series of the same title (1973–74) and starred in a number of other films. He gradually retreated into supporting roles. By the late 80s he was performing indiscriminately in numerous low-budget productions.

FILMS INCLUDE: *What Do You Say to a Naked Lady* (bit) 1970; *Shaft* 1971; *Shaft's Big Score!, Embassy* 1972; *Charley-One-Eye, Shaft in Africa* 1973; *Earthquake* 1974; *Diamonds* (Isr./US/Switz.), *Man Friday* (as Robinson Crusoe's Friday; UK) 1975; *Game for Vultures* (UK) 1978; *Escape to Athens* (UK) 1979; *An Eye for an Eye* 1981; *Inchon* (Korea/US), *Q* 1982; *The Big Score, Young Warriors* 1983; *Killpoint, City Heat* 1984; *Opposing Force, Maniac Cop* 1986; *Jocks* 1987; *Party Line* 1988 *Night Visitor/Never Cry Devil, The Banker, Crack House* 1989; *Bad Jim* 1990; *A Time to Die, Bloodfist III: Forced to Fight* 1991; *Lost Memories* 1992; *Amityville: A New Generation, Body of Influence* 1993; *Seven* 1995; *Once Upon a Time. . . When We Were Colored, Theodore Rex* 1996; *George of the Jungle, Steel* 1997.

Rouquier, Georges. Director. *b.* June 23, 1909, Lunel-Viel, France. *d.* 1989. A former linotype operator, he made an amateur film at age 20 and began turning out documentary films regularly in the early 40s. In 1946 he wrote and directed his masterpiece, *Farrebique,* a feature-length documentary giving a poetic account of a French farm family's life through the four seasons. The film parallels events in the family's life with those in the course of the surrounding nature, reaching a lyrical climax with striking time-lapse photography of the coming of spring. The film won awards at Cannes, Venice, and other festivals. Rouquier was not very successful with two subsequent fiction feature films and in the 60s turned mostly to television work. In 1983 Rouquier returned to the farming region depicted in *Farrebique* to shoot a sequel, *Biquefarre,* winner of the Special Jury Prize at that year's Venice Film Festival.

FILMS (documentary shorts unless otherwise noted): *Vendanges* (also prod., sc., phot.) 1929; *Le Tonnelier* (also sc.) 1942; *Le Charron* (also sc.), *L'Économie de Métaux, La Part de l'Enfant* 1943; *Farrebique* (feature doc.; also sc.) 1946; *Pasteur* (co-dir.) 1947; *Le Chaudronnier* 1949; *Le Sel de la Terre* 1950; *Les Galeries de Malgovert* 1952; *Le Lycée sur la Colline, Un Jour comme les autres* 1953; *Sang et Lumière* (fiction feature) 1954; *Lourdes et ses Miracles* (comprising three shorts), *Arthur Honegger* 1955; *S.O.S. Noronha* (fiction feature) 1957; *La Bête noire, Une Belle Peur* 1958; *Le Bouclier* 1960; *Sire le Roy n'a plus rien dit* (Fr./Can.) 1964; *Jeff* (act. only) 1968; Z (act. only) 1969; *Biquefarre* 1983.

Rourke, Mickey. Actor. Born Philip André Rourke, Jr., in 1950, in Schenectady, N.Y. Charismatic, rebellious, softly tough leading man of Hollywood films. The son of a country-club caretaker, he was seven when his parents divorced and he reluctantly moved with his mother and siblings to Miami, where he grew up in the poor, primarily black section of Liberty City. He showed promise as a baseball player and later as an amateur boxer but, lacking discipline, quit both and spent much of his youth just "hanging out" and getting into trouble. He was saved from delinquency by the acting bug he caught at a junior college. With $400 he borrowed from a sister he flew to New York, where he studied with acting coach Sandra Seacat, supporting himself as a parking lot attendant, massage-parlor night manager, a Good Humor man, a pretzel vendor, and other odd jobs. He was cast in a few off-off-Broadway productions but often quit during rehearsals because of disagreements with directors. He showed similar contempt for the Actors Studio, which he attended briefly. Things changed rapidly for Rourke when he headed to Los Angeles, where he began getting small parts in films in 1979. Before long he attracted notice as the earringed arsonist in *Body Heat* (1981) and as Boogie, the soft-talking beautician in *Diner* (1982). Leading roles soon followed in such films as *The Pope of Greenwich Village* (1984), *9½ Weeks* (1986), *Angel Heart,* and *Barfly* (both 1987), in which Rourke emerged as a rough-edged antihero, at times reminiscent of his childhood idol John Garfield. Several of his films have boasted graphic sexual content, notably *9½ Weeks* and *Wild Orchid.* While his appeal at the US box office has been only moderate, Rourke is admired enormously in France. In 1991 he won his first professional boxing bout in Florida using the pseudonym Marielito.

FILMS: *1941* 1979; *Fade to Black, Heaven's Gate* 1980; *Body Heat* 1981; *Diner* 1982; *Eureka* (UK), *Rumble Fish* 1983; *The Pope of Greenwich Village* 1984; *Year of the Dragon* 1985; *9½ Weeks* 1986; *Angel Heart, A Prayer for the Dying* (UK), *Barfly* 1987; *Homeboy* (also story) 1988; *Francesco* (It.), *Johnny Handsome, Wild Orchid* 1989; *Desperate Hours* 1990; *Harley Davidson & the Marlboro Man* 1991; *White Sands* 1992; *F.T.W., Last Ride* 1994; *Double Team* 1997.

Rouse, Russell. Director, screenwriter. *b.* Apr. 3, 1913, New York City. *d.* 1987. The son of film pioneer Edwin Russell, he began his film career in Paramount's prop department, later becoming a screenwriter. A director of offbeat films from the early 50s, he usually collaborated on his own scripts with producer Clarence GREENE. His early work is the more interesting, as represented by *The Well* (1951), a stark study in mob psychology, and the courageous though mostly unsuccessful experiment of omitting all dialogue from *The Thief* (1952). As a screenwriter, he shared an Academy Award nomination for *The Well* and shared the Oscar for the original story of *Pillow Talk* (1959).

FILMS: As co-screenwriter—*Nothing But Trouble, The Town Went Wild* 1945; *The Great Plane Robbery, D.O.A.* 1950; *Pillow Talk* (co-story only) 1959; *Color Me Dead* (remake of *D.O.A.;* Austral./US) 1969. As director/co-screenwriter—*The Well* (co-dir., co-sc. with Leo Popkin) 1951; *The Thief* 1952; *Wicked Woman* 1954; *New York Confidential* 1955; *The Fastest*

Gun Alive 1956; *House of Numbers* 1957; *Thunder in the Sun* 1959; *A House Is Not a Home* 1964; *The Oscar* 1966; *The Caper of the Golden Bulls* 1967.

Rousselot, Philippe. Director of photography. Born in 1945, in Meurthe-et-Moselle, France. A highly regarded cinematographer of contemporary French and international films. A former camera assistant to Nestor ALMENDROS on *My Night at Maud's* (1969) and other Eric Rohmer films, he asserted himself in the 80s as one of France's most gifted lighting cameramen, winning César awards for *Diva* (1981) and *Thérèse* (1986). Late in the decade he expanded his services abroad, including Hollywood. He was nominated for Oscars for the British *Hope and Glory* (1987) and the American *Henry and June* (1990).

FILMS INCLUDE: *Absences répétées* 1972; *Paradiso, Diablo Menth/Peppermint Soda* 1977; *La Drolesse* 1979; *Cocktail Molotov, La Provinciale/The Girl from Lorraine* 1980; *Diva* 1981; *Guy de Maupassant* 1982; *La Lune dans le Caniveau/The Moon in the Gutter* 1983; *Les Voleurs dans la Nuit/Thieves After Dark, Nemo/Dream One* (Fr./UK) 1984; *The Emerald Forest* (UK), *Night Magic* (Can./Fr.) 1985; *Thérèse* 1986; *Hope and Glory* (UK) 1987; *L'Ours/The Bear, Dangerous Liaisons* (US) 1988; *Trop Belle pour toi!/Too Beautiful for You, We're No Angels* (US) 1989; *Henry and June* (US) 1990; *The Miracle* (UK), *Merci La Vie* 1991; *Sommersby* (US) 1993; *Interview with the Vampire, Queen Margot* 1994; *Mary Reilly, The People vs. Larry Flynt* 1996.

Rowland, Roy. Director. Born on Dec. 31, 1910, in New York City. After law studies at USC, he entered films in the early 30s as script clerk, soon after becoming assistant director. In the late 30s he began directing shorts, including Benchley's "How To" series, "Pete Smith Specialities," and "Crime Doesn't Pay." His career as feature director, since the early 40s, has been seesawing from good to mediocre, with technical proficiency as the only constant ingredient. His son, Steve Rowland, is an actor.

FEATURE FILMS: *A Stranger in Town, Lost Angel* 1943; *Our Vines Have Tender Grapes* 1945; *Boys' Ranch* 1946; *The Romance of Rosy Ridge, Killer McCoy* 1947; *Tenth Avenue Angel* 1948; *Scene of the Crime* 1949; *The Outriders, Two Weeks with Love* 1950; *Excuse My Dust* 1951; *Bugles in the Afternoon* 1952; *The 5,000 Fingers of Dr. T., Affair with a Stranger, The Moonlighter* 1953; *Rogue Cop, Witness to Murder* 1954; *Many Rivers to Cross, Hit the Deck* 1955; *Slander, These Wilder Years, Meet Me in Las Vegas* 1956; *Gun Glory* 1957; *The Seven Hills of Rome* (US/It.) 1958; *The Girl Hunters* (also co-sc., UK) 1963; *The Gunfighters of Casa Grande* (US/Sp.) 1964; *Sie nannten ihn Gringo* (Ger./It.) 1966; *Surcouf—l'Eroe dei Sette Mari/The Sea Pirate* (sources conflict on director's identity; It./Fr./Sp.) 1967; *Land Raiders* (assoc. prod. only) 1970.

Rowlands, Gena. Actress. Born Virginia Rowlands, on June 19, 1934, in Cambria, Wis. *ed.* U. of Wisconsin; AADA. Cool, tough, blonde leading lady of the American stage, TV, and films. She made Broadway in 1952 as an understudy for the lead in 'The Seven Year Itch' and later took over the role. After playing the Broadway lead in 'Middle of the Night' (1956–57) she went out to Hollywood, making her screen debut in 1958. She appeared in several of the films of her husband (from 1958 till his death in 1989), actor-director John CASSAVETES and was nominated for Academy Awards as best actress for her performance in his *A Woman Under the Influence* (1974) and *Gloria* (1980). She was named best actress at the 1978 Berlin Film Festival for *Opening Night* and won an Emmy for her portrayal of the First Lady in the TV movie *The Betty Ford Story* (1987).

FILMS: *The High Cost of Loving* 1958; *Lonely Are the Brave, The Spiral Road* 1962; *A Child Is Waiting* 1963; *Tony Rome* 1967; *Faces* 1968; *Gli Intoccabili/Machine Gun McCain* (It.) 1969; *Minnie and Moskowitz* 1971; *A Woman Under the Influence* 1974; *Two-Minute Warning* 1976; *Opening Night, The Brink's Job* 1978; *Gloria* 1980; *Tempest* 1982; *"I'm Almost Not Crazy . . ." John Cassavetes: The Man and His Work* (doc.), *Love Streams* 1984; *Light of Day* 1987; *Another Woman* 1988; *Once Around, Night on Earth, Ted and Venus* 1991; *Parallel Lives* 1994; *The Neon Bible, Something to Talk About* 1995; *Unhook the Stars* 1996; *She's So Lovely* 1997.

Roy, Bimal. Director, producer. *b.* July 12, 1909, Dacca, Bengal. *d.* 1966. A leading figure of postwar Indian cinema, he started out in the early 30s as an assistant cameraman, soon graduating to director of photography. He began directing in 1942 but gained international recognition only after his 1953 *Do Bigha Zamin/Two Acres of Land* (also known as *Calcutta Cruel City*), a film hailed by European critics as "the Indian *The Bicycle Thief.*" In 1952 he established his own production company.

FILMS INCLUDE: *Udahir Pathe* 1943; *Humrahi* 1945; *Pehla Admi* 1948; *Mantra Mugdh* 1949; *Do Bigha Zamin/Two Acres of Land/Calcutta Cruel City* (also prod.) 1953; *Nakurai* (also prod.), *Biraj Bahu* 1954; *Amanat* (co-dir., prod.), *Gautama the Buddha* (co-dir., prod.) 1955; *Devdas* (also prod.) 1956; *Madhumati* (also prod.), *Yahudi* 1958; *Sujata* 1959; *Parakh* 1960; *Kabuliwala* (also prod.) 1961; *Prem Patra* (also prod.) 1962; *Bandini* 1963.

Rozsa, Miklos. Composer. Born on Apr. 18, 1907, in Budapest. Educated in Leipzig, Paris, and London. A violin player at age five, he wrote a ballet in his 20s and later composed many chamber and symphonic works. He began scoring films in England in the late 30s for fellow Hungarian Alexander KORDA. In Hollywood since the early 40s, he wrote full-bodied scores for many major films. His music was much in demand for psychological dramas of the 40s and later also for historical epics. He won Academy Awards for *Spellbound* (1945), *A Double Life* (1947), and *Ben-Hur* (1959) out of 16 nominations.

FILMS INCLUDE: In the UK—*Knight Without Armour* 1937; *The Divorce of Lady X* 1938; *The Spy in Black/U-Boat 29, The Four Feathers* 1939; *The Thief of Bagdad* 1940. In the US—*That Hamilton Woman/Lady Hamilton, Lydia, Sundown* 1941; *Jungle Book* 1942; *Five Graves to Cairo, Sahara, Woman of the Town, So Proudly We Hail* 1943; *Dark Waters, Double Indemnity* 1944; *A Song to Remember* (adapt.), *Blood on the Sun, Lady on a Train, The Lost Weekend, Spellbound* 1945; *The Killers, The Strange Love of Martha Ivers* 1946; *Song of Scheherazade* (adapt.), *Brute Force, Desert Fury, The Red House, A Double Life, Secret Beyond the Door* 1947; *The Naked City, Command Decision, Kiss the Blood Off My Hands* 1948; *Madame Bovary, Criss Cross, East Side West Side, Adam's Rib* 1949; *The Asphalt Jungle, Crisis* 1950; *Quo Vadis* 1951; *Ivanhoe, Plymouth Adventure* 1952; *Julius Caesar, The Story of Three Loves, Young Bess* 1953; *Knights of the Round Table* 1954; *Bhowani Junction, Lust for Life* 1956; *Something of Value* 1957; *The World the Flesh and the Devil, Ben-Hur* 1959; *El Cid, King of Kings, Sodoma e Gomorra/Sodom and Gomorrah* (It./Fr./US) 1961; *The V.I.P.s* (UK) 1963; *The Power, The Green Berets* 1968; *The Private Life of Sherlock Holmes* (also cameo as ballet conductor; UK/US) 1970; *The Golden Voyage of Sinbad* 1973; *Providence* (Fr.) 1977; *Fedora* (Ger./Fr.) 1978; *Last Embrace, Time After Time* 1979; *Eye of the Needle* (UK/US) 1981; *Dead Men Don't Wear Plaid* 1982.

Rub, Christian. Actor. *b.* Apr. 13, 1887, Austria. *d.* 1956. Character player of Hollywood films, often as an eccentric foreign type. His screen personality and voice were used by Disney to create the Gepetto character for the animated *Pinocchio* (1940).

FILMS INCLUDE: *The Trial of Vivienne Ware, The Man from Yesterday* 1932; *Humanity* 1933; *Man of Two Worlds, No Greater Glory, Little Man What Now?, The Fountain, Music in the Air* 1934; *Oil for the Lamps of China, Metropolitan, Peter Ibbetson* 1935; *Next Time We Love, Mr. Deeds Go to Town, Dracula's Daughter, Sins of Man, Suzy* 1936; *Cafe Metropole, 100 Men and a Girl, Heidi, Tovarich* 1937; *Mad About Music, Professor Beware, You Can't Take It with You, The Great Waltz* 1938; *Never Say Die, Everything Happens at Night* 1939; *The Swiss Family Robinson, Earthbound, Four Sons* 1940; *Dangerously They Live, Berlin Correspondent, Tales of Manhattan* 1942; *The Adventures of Mark Twain* 1944; *Strange Confession* 1945; *Fall Guy* 1947; *Something for the Birds* 1952.

Ruben, J. Walter. Director, producer, screenwriter. *b.* Aug. 14, 1899, New York City. *d.* 1942. *ed.* Columbia. A stage actor in his late teens, he later wrote publicity and vaudeville material. He entered films in 1924 as a distributor for MGM and began writing screenplays in 1927 and directing in 1931. He piloted mainly second features, mostly for RKO and MGM, through the late 30s, when he turned producer. Both as a director and a producer he was responsible for many Wallace BEERY vehicles.

FILMS INCLUDE: As screenwriter (alone or in collaboration)—*The Last Outlaw, The Gay Retreat* 1927; *Under the Tonto Rim, Fools for Luck, The Fleet's In, Avalanche* 1928; *Jazz Heaven, Dance Hall, The Marriage Playground* 1929; *Lovin' the Ladies, Shooting Straight* 1930. As director (complete)—*The Public Defender, Secret Service* 1931; *Roadhouse Murder* (also co-sc.), *The Phantom of Crestwood* (also co-sc.) 1932; *No Other Woman, The Great Jasper, No Marriage Ties, Ace of Aces* 1933; *Man of Two Worlds, Success at Any Price, Where Sinners Meet* 1934; *Public Hero No. 1* (also co-sc.), *Java Head* 1935; *Riffraff, Trouble for Two, Old Hutch* 1936; *Good Old Soak* 1937, *The Bad Man of Brimstone* (also story) 1938. As producer—*Sergeant Madden, Maisie, Thunder Afloat* 1939; *Twenty-Mule Team* 1940; *Flight Command, The Bad Man, The Get Away* (also story) 1941; *The Bugle Sounds, Her Cardboard Lover, Tennessee Johnson* 1942; *Assignment in Brittany* 1943.

Ruben, Joseph. Director. Born in 1951, in Briarcliff, N.Y. *ed.* U. of Michigan (theater and film); Brandeis U. Following a fitful start in the late 70s with a string of low-budget trifles, he made a first bid for respectability in 1984 with the imaginative fantasy *Dreamscape.* He had further successes with the thrillers *The Stepfather* (1987) and *True Believer* (1989), and in 1991 scored a box-office hit with *Sleeping with the Enemy.*

FILMS: *The Sister-in-Law* (also co-prod., sc.) 1975; *The Pom Pom Girls* (also prod., sc.) 1976; *Joyride* (also co-sc.) 1977; *Our Winning Season* 1978; *Gorp* 1980; *Dreamscape* (also co-sc.) 1984; *The Stepfather* 1987; *True Believer* 1989; *Sleeping with the Enemy* 1991; *The Good Son* 1993; *Money Train* 1995.

Rubens, Alma. Actress. *b.* Alma Smith, 1897, San Francisco. *d.* 1931. Beautiful star of silent Hollywood films with musical comedy experience. A heroin addict, she died in misery of pneumonia before reaching her 34th birthday. Her first husband (for less than a month, in 1918) was actor Franklyn FARNUM; her second (1923–25) director-producer-author-physician Daniel Carson Goodman; and third and last (from 1926) actor Ricardo CORTEZ. Early in her career she was also billed as Alma Reuben or Reubens.

FILMS INCLUDE: *The Half-Breed, Reggie Mixes In, Intolerance* 1916; *Truthful Tulliver, The Americano, The Firefly of Tough Luck* 1917; *I Love You, The Answer, The Love Brokers, Madame Sphinx, The Painted Lily, The Ghost Flower* 1918; *Restless Souls, Diane of the Green Van* 1919; *Humoresque, Thoughtless Women, The World and His Wife* 1920; *Find the Woman, The Valley of Silent Men* 1922; *Enemies of Women, Under the Red Robe* 1923; *Gerald Cranston's Lady, Is Love Everything?, The Rejected Woman, Cytherea, Week End Husbands, The Price She Paid* 1924; *The Dancers, East Lynne, She Wolves, The Winding Stair, A Woman's Faith, Fine Clothes* 1925; *The Gilded Butterfly, Siberia, Marriage License?* 1926; *The Heart of Salome* 1927; *The Masks of the Devil* 1928; *Show Boat, She Goes to War* 1929.

Rudin, Scott. Producer and executive. Born on July 14, 1958, in New York, N.Y. Successful independent producer of the 1980s and 1990s. After stints on Broadway as a production director and casting assistant, he became the executive vice president for production at 20th Century-Fox and in 1986 its president. In 1987 he resigned, becoming the producer of high-quality commercially successful fare.

FILMS INCLUDE: *The Addams Family, Little Man Tate* 1991; *Sister Act* 1992; *The Firm* 1993; *Clueless, I.Q.* 1994; *Sabrina* 1995; *Marvin's Room, Ransom* (co-prod.), *Up Close and Personal* 1996.

Rudolph, Alan. Director. Born on Dec. 18, 1943, in Los Angeles. The son of veteran movie actor Oscar Rudolf who later became a film (*Twist Around the Clock,* etc.) and TV director, he appeared as a child in his father's first feature *The Rocket Man* (1954). In the early 60s he dropped out of UCLA, where he had studied accounting, to enter the industry as a general helper at various studio departments. In 1969 he enrolled at the Directors Guild's training program for assistant directors. While honing his skills, he made a few shorts and two obscure features, then started his true professional career as an assistant to Robert ALTMAN on *The Long Goodbye* (1973), *California Split* (1974), and *Nashville* (1975). Rudolph collaborated with Altman on the screenplay of *Buffalo Bill and the Indians, or Sitting Bull's History Lesson* (1976), then set out to carve a distinguished path of his own, starting with *Welcome to L.A.* (1977) and continuing with such fine films as *Remember My Name* (1979) and *Choose Me* (1984). He crowned his achievements of the 80s with *The Moderns* (1988), a loving evocative recreation (shot in Montreal!) of bohemian Paris of the 20s and its colony of American expatriates. Like his mentor Altman, Rudolph functions well with tight budgets. Also like Altman, he prefers working with a regular company of actors, a repertory troupe that often includes Keith Carradine, Geneviève Bujold, and Geraldine Chaplin.

FILMS: *Premonition* (also sc.) 1972; *Barn of the Naked Dead/Terror Circus* (also sc.) 1973; *Buffalo Bill and the Indians, or Sitting Bull's History Lesson* (co-sc. only) 1976; *Welcome to L.A.* (also sc.) 1977; *Remember My Name* (also sc.) 1979; *Roadie* (also co-story) 1980; *Endangered Species* (also co-sc.) 1982; *Return Engagement* (doc.) 1983; *Choose Me* (also sc.), *Songwriter* 1984; *Trouble in Mind* (also sc.) 1985; *Made in Heaven* 1987; *The Moderns* (also co-sc.) 1988; *Love at Large* (also sc.) 1990; *Mortal Thoughts* 1991; *The Player* (act. only—cameo) 1992; *Equinox* (also sc.) 1993; *Mrs. Parker and the Vicious Circle* 1994; *Evita* 1996.

Ruehl, Mercedes. Actress. Born in 1954 in Queens, N.Y. *ed.* College of New Rochelle. Lanky, expressive lead of stage and screen. Raised in suburban Silver Spring, Md., she followed years of training in regional theater (and a near-abandonment of acting for a job with the Baltimore Gas and Electric Company) with an array of widely praised performances on Broadway. She was awarded an Obie for *The Marriage of Bette and Boo* and a Tony for *Lost in Yonkers*. Making her film debut in the 1980s, she has often been featured in New York-based roles, through them demonstrating the poignancy and outrageousness of modern urban life. She won an Academy Award for her performance in *The Fisher King*.

FILMS INCLUDE: *The Warriors* 1979; *Heartburn* 1986; *84 Charing Cross Road* (UK), *Leader of the Band, Radio Days, The Secret of My Success* 1987; *Big, Married to the Mob* 1988; *Crazy People* 1990; *Another You, The Fisher King* 1991; *Lost in Yonkers, Last Action Hero* 1993; *For Roseanna* 1997.

Ruggles, Charles. Actor. *b.* Feb. 8, 1886, Los Angeles. *d.* 1970. Genial, disarming character comedian of American stage and screen, typically as a timid, mischievously wistful man, often the henpecked screen husband of Mary BOLAND. He appeared in many stage plays and close to 100 films, most memorably in *Charley's Aunt* (1930), *Ruggles of Red Gap* (1935), and *Bringing Up Baby* (1938), and in several Lubitsch productions of the early 30s. He was the brother of Wesley RUGGLES.

FILMS INCLUDE: *Peer Gynt* (as the Button Moulder) 1915; *The Heart Raider* 1923; *Gentlemen of the Press, The Lady Lies, The Battle of Paris* 1929; *Roadhouse Nights, Young Man of Manhattan, Queen High, Her Wedding Night, Charley's Aunt* (as Lord Babberly) 1930; *Honor Among Lovers, The Smiling Lieutenant, The Girl Habit, Husband's Holiday* 1931; *This Reckless Age, One Hour with You, This Is the Night, Love Me Tonight, The Night of June 13th, Trouble in Paradise, Evenings for Sale, If I Had a Million, Madame Butterfly* 1932; *Murders in the Zoo, Melody Cruise, Mama Loves Papa, Goodbye Love, Girl Without a Room, Alice of Wonderland* (as the March Hare) 1933; *Six of a Kind, Melody in Spring, Friends of Mr. Sweeney, The Pursuit of Happiness* 1934; *Ruggles of Red Gap* (as Egbert Floud), *People Will Talk, No More Ladies* 1935; *Anything Goes, Hearts Divided, Early to Bed, Wives Never Know* 1936; *Mind Your Own Business, Turn Off the Moon, Exclusive* 1937; *Bringing Up Baby, Service de Luxe* 1938; *Boy Trouble, Invitation to Happiness, Night Work, Balalaika* 1939; *The Farmer's Daughter, Maryland, No Time for Comedy, The Invisible Woman* 1940; *Honeymoon for Three, Model Wife, The Parson of Panamint* 1941; *Friendly Enemies* 1942; *The Dough-girls, Our Hearts Were Young and Gay, Three is a Family* 1944; *Incendiary Blonde* 1945; *A Stolen Life* 1946; *The Perfect Marriage, It Happened on Fifth Avenue, Ramrod* 1947; *Give My Regards to Broadway* 1948; *Look for the Silver Lining* 1949; *All in a Night's Work, The Pleasure of His Company, The Parent Trap* 1961; *Son of Flubber, Papa's Delicate Condition* 1963; *I'd Rather Be Rich* 1964; *The Ugly Dachshund, Follow Me Boys!* 1966.

Ruggles, Wesley. Director. *b.* June 11, 1889, Los Angeles. *d.* 1972. Brother of Charles RUGGLES. He was an actor in stock when he entered films in 1914 as a Keystone Cop and supporting comedy player, appearing in, among other films, Chaplin shorts such as *The Bank, Shanghaied* (both 1915), *Police, Carmen* (both 1916), and *Triple Trouble* (1918). A director from 1918 to 1946, he had an uneven career, enjoying his best period in the late 20s (*Silk Stockings*) and in the early 30s (*Cimarron* and *I'm No Angel*). He was the first (1931–37) of seven husbands of actress Arline JUDGE.

FEATURE FILMS (as director): *For France* 1917; *The Blind Adventure* 1918; *The Winchester Woman* 1919; *Piccadilly Jim, Sooner or Later, The Desperate Hero, The Leopard Woman, Love* 1920; *The Greater Claim, Uncharted Seas, Over the Wire* 1921; *Wild Honey, If I Were Queen* 1922; *Slippery McGee, Mr. Billings Spends His Dime, The Remittance Woman, The Heart Raider* 1923; *The Age Of Innocence* 1924; *The Plastic Age, Broadway Lady* 1925; *The Kick-off, A Man Of Quality* 1926; *Beware of Widows, Silk Stockings* 1927; *The Fourflusher, Finders Keepers* 1928; *Street Girl, Scandal, Condemned, Girl Overboard* 1929; *Honey, The Sea Bat* 1930; *Cimarron, Are These Our Children?* (also co-sc.) 1931; *Roar of the Dragon, No Man of Her Own* 1932; *The Monkey's Paw, College Humor, I'm No Angel* 1933; *Bolero, Shoot the Works* 1934; *The Gilded Lily, Accent on Youth, The Bride Comes Home* (also prod.) 1935; *Valiant Is the Word for Carrie* (also prod.) 1936; *I Met Him in Paris* (also prod.), *True Confession* 1937; *Sing You Sinners* (also prod.) 1938; *Invitation To Happiness* (also prod.) 1939; *Too Many Husbands* (also prod.), *Arizona* (also prod.), *You Belong to Me* (also prod.) 1941; *Somewhere I'll Find You* 1942; *Slightly Dangerous* 1943; *See Here Private Hargrove* 1944; *London Town/My Heart Goes Crazy* (also prod., story; UK) 1946.

Rühmann, Heinz. Actor, sometime director and producer. Born on Mar. 6, 1912, in Essen, Germany. Diminutive character star of some 100 German films; particularly adept at comedy. Also active on the stage.

FILMS INCLUDE (as actor): *Das Deutsche Mutterherz* 1926; *Die Drei Von Der Tankstelle* 1930; *Bomben Auf Monte Carlo/Bombardment of Monte Carlo/Monte Carlo Madness, Der Mann Der Seinen Mörder Sucht, Man Braucht Kein Geld/You Don't Need Any Money* 1931; *Lachende Erben* 1933; *Die Finanzen Die Grossherzogs/The Grand Duke's Finances, Ein Walzer Für Dich* 1934; *Der Mann Der Sherlock Holmes Wär* 1937; *Lauter Lügen* (dir. only) 1938; *Lauter Liebe* (dir. only) 1940; *Sophienlund* (dir. only) 1943; *Der Engel Mit Dem Saitenspiel* (dir. only) 1944; *Die Kupferne Hochzeit* (dir. only) 1948; *Briefträger Müller* (also co-dir.) 1953; *Charleys Tante/Charley's Aunt, Der Hauptmann Von Köpenick/The Captain from Koepenick* 1956; *Es Geschah Am Hellichten Tage/It Happened in Broad Daylight* 1958; *Der Brave Soldat Schwejk/The Good Soldier Schweik, Der Jugendrichter/The Judge and the Sinner* 1960; *Ship of Fools* (US) 1965; *Das Chinesische Wunder, Gesundenes Fressen* 1977.

Ruiz, Raúl. Director. Born on July 25, 1941, in Puerto Montt, Chile. The son of a ship's captain, he studied law and theology at the University of Chile, then used a Rockefeller Foundation grant to devote several carefree years to the prolific writing of scores of stage plays. Following rudimentary film studies in Santa Fe, Argentina, he became involved as a technician and writer in the production of Chilean and Mexican TV programs. With money borrowed from family and friends he directed his first feature in 1968. The film, *Tres Tristes Tigres* ("Three Sad Tigers") won the Grand Prix at the Locarno Festival, immediately establishing Ruiz as one of his country's top filmmakers. Inventive as well as conscientious, Ruiz became an ingenious observer of his country's tumultuous political and social scene. After the fall of the leftist Allende regime, he went into exile in Europe, residing mainly in France but working all over the continent, making features and TV movies at a prolific pace. His bold narrative style and innovative use of lighting and camera techniques earned him the admiration of the Paris avant-garde. *The Golden Boat* (1990), shot in New York City in black and white with a 16 mm camera, is his first film in English. In addition to the writing of his own scripts he has collaborated on screenplays of films directed by his wife, Valeria Sarmiento, among them *Notre Mariage* (1985) and *Amelia Lopes O'Neill* (1991). He appeared as an actor in *Palombella Rossa* (1989).

FEATURE FILMS (as director-screenwriter): *Tres Tristes Tigres* 1968; *Que Hacer?* (co-dir.) 1970; *La Colonia Penal, Nadje Dijo Nada* 1971; *La Exproprioacion* 1972; *El Realismo Socialista, Palomilla Brava, Palomita Blanca* (co-dir.; unfinished) 1973; *Diálogo de Exilados* 1974; *Mensch Verstreut und Verkehrt* (Ger.) 1975; *La Vocation Suspendue* (Fr.) 1977; *L'Hypothèse du Tableau Volé/Hypothesis of the Stolen Painting* (Fr.) 1978; *De Grands Evéements et des Gens Ordinaires* (Fr.) 1979; *Le Borgne* (Fr.), *The Territory* (Port./US) 1981; *On Top of the Whale* (Hol.) 1982; *Les Trois Couronnes du Matelot/Three Crowns of the Sailor* (Fr.) 1983; *Bérénice, La Ville des Pirates* (Fr./Port.) 1984; *L'Eveillé du Pont de l'Alma* (Fr.), *Les Destins de*

Mancel 1985; *Régime Sans Pain* (Fr.), *Rihard Iii, L'Ile au Trésor/Treasure Island* (Fr./US), *Mammame* (also des.; Chile/Fr.) 1986; *Mémoire des Apparences/La Vie Est un Songe/Life Is a Dream* (Fr.), *La Chouette Aveugle* (Fr./Switz.) 1987; *The Golden Boat* (B & W, 16 mm; US) 1990; *The Dark Night of the Inquisitor* 1994; *Three Lives and Only One Death* 1996.

Rule, Janice. Actress. Born on Aug. 15, 1931, in Norwood, Ohio. Leading lady of the American stage, TV, and films; formerly a nightclub dancer. Long married (1961–79) to Ben GAZZARA, she began a new career as a psychoanalyst in the mid-70s but continued appearing occasionally in films.

FILMS: *Goodbye My Fancy, Starlift* 1951; *Holiday for Sinners* 1952; *Rogue's March* 1953; *A Woman's Devotion* 1956; *Gun for a Coward* 1957; *Bell Book and Candle* 1958; *The Subterraneans* 1960; *Invitation to a Gunfighter* 1964; *The Chase, Alvarez Kelly* 1966; *Welcome to Hard Times, The Ambushers* 1967; *The Swimmer* 1968; *Doctors' Wives, Gumshoe* (UK) 1971; *Kid Blue* 1973; *Three Women* 1977; *Missing* 1982; *American Flyers* 1985; *Rainy Day Friends* 1986.

Ruman(n), Sig (Siegfried). Actor. *b.* Siegfried Albon Rumann, 1884, Hamburg, Germany. *d.* 1967. Character player of more than 100 Hollywood films after stage experience in Germany and on Broadway. In the US from 1924, he began his screen career in 1929 as Siegfried Rumann but later simplified his professional name to Sig Ruman. He typically played excited *dummkopfs* and caricatures of Prussian pomposity. Memorable as one of a trio of flustered Soviet emissaries in *Ninotchka* (1939).

FILMS INCLUDE: *The Royal Box* 1929; *The World Moves On, Marie Galante* 1934; *Under Pressure, The Wedding Night, The Farmer Takes a Wife, A Night at the Opera* 1935; *The Princess Comes Across* 1936; *On the Avenue, Maytime, Seventh Heaven, A Day at the Races, The Great Hospital Mystery, Love Under Fire, Thin Ice, Lancer Spy, Heidi, Nothing Sacred* 1937; *The Saint in New York, Suez, The Great Waltz* 1938; *Honolulu, Never Say Die, Confession of a Nazi Spy, Only Angels Have Wings, Ninotchka, Remember?* 1939; *Dr. Ehrlich's Magic Bullet, Four Sons, Bitter Sweet, Comrade X* 1940; *Victory* (as Wilhelm Schomberg), *So Ends Our Night, The Wagons Roll at Night, Shining Victory, Love Crazy, World Premiere* 1941; *To Be or Not to Be, Crossroads, Berlin Correspondent, Desperate Journey* 1942; *China Girl, Tarzan Triumphs, They Came to Blow Up America, The Song of Bernadette* 1943; *The Hitler Gang* (as General von Hindenburg), *It Happened Tomorrow* 1944; *House of Frankenstein, A Royal Scandal, The Dolly Sisters* 1945; *Night and Day, A Night in Casablanca* 1946; *Mother Wore Tights* 1947; *The Emperor Waltz* 1948; *Border Incident* 1949; *On the Riviera* 1951; *The World in His Arms, Stalag 17, Houdini* 1953; *The Glenn Miller Story, Living It Up, White Christmas* 1954; *Many Rivers to Cross* 1955; *The Wings of Eagles* 1957; *The Errand Boy* 1961; *Robin and the 7 Hoods* 1964; *The Fortune Cookie* 1966.

runners. Overhead scaffolding high above a motion picture set from which studio lamps, accessories, and background materials may be hung.

running lines. Rehearsing dialogue.

running shot. A traveling shot in which the moving camera keeps up with the pace of a moving person or object.

running speed. The rate at which film runs through a motion picture camera or projector. See F.P.S. (frames per second).

running time. The length of time it takes to run a motion picture through a projector at standard speed.

run-through. The film set equivalent to a dress rehearsal. Actors speak their lines and go through their actions. Camera movements may also be rehearsed, but no actual shooting takes place.

Rush, Barbara. Actress. Born on Jan. 4, 1927, in Denver. *ed.* U. of California; Pasadena Playhouse. Pretty brunette leading lady of Hollywood films with stage experience from age ten. Also much on TV. Her career reached a peak in the late 50s but has since declined. Her first husband (1950–55) was Jeffrey HUNTER.

FILMS INCLUDE: *Molly, The First Legion, Flaming Feather, When Worlds Collide* 1951; *It Came from Outer Space* 1953; *Magnificent Obsession, The Black Shield of Falworth* 1954; *Captain Lightfoot, Kiss of Fire* 1955; *World in My Corner, Bigger Than Life* 1956; *No Down Payment* 1957; *The Young Lions* 1958; *The Young Philadelphians* 1959; *The Bramble Bush, Strangers When We Meet* 1960; *Come Blow Your Horn* 1963; *Robin and the 7 Hoods* 1964; *Hombre* 1967; *Strategy of Terror* 1969; *The Man* 1972; *Superdad* 1974; *Can't Stop the Music* 1980; *Summer Lovers* 1982.

Rush, Richard. Director. Born in 1930, in New York City. Independent, budget-bound filmmaker who emerged in 1980 from the relative obscurity of cheap motorcycle movies and brutal Westerns with the outstanding drama/black comedy *The Stunt Man.* The project had taken him nine years to get off the ground and two more to move from the shelf to the screen. But it earned Rush Academy Award nominations for best director and best screenplay. It was his last directorial effort.

FILMS (as director): *Too Soon to Love* (also prod., sc.) 1960; *Of Love and Desire* (also co-sc.) 1963; *The Fickle Finger of Fate, Thunder Alley, Hells Angels on Wheels* 1967; *A Man Called Dagger, Psych-Out, The Savage Seven* 1968; *Getting Straight* (also prod.) 1970; *Freebie and the Bean* (also prod.) 1974; *The Stunt Man* (also prod., adapt.; release delayed from 1978) 1980; *Air America* (co-sc. only) 1990; *Color of Night* 1994.

rushes. See DAILIES.

Russell, Gail. Actress. *b.* Sept. 21, 1924, Chicago. *d.* 1961. Intriguingly lovely leading lady of Hollywood films of the 40s. She entered films with Paramount directly out of Santa Monica High School with no previous acting experience, and after much coaching and grooming starred in many of the studio's films and in several productions of other companies. A dark-haired, blue-eyed beauty, she is best remembered for her roles in three supernatural tales, *The Uninvited* (1944), *The Unseen* (1945), and *Night Has a Thousand Eyes* (1948). An insecure introvert, she suffered throughout her career from stage fright, and her inability to cope with the pressures of film work finally drove her to alcoholism. After several well-publicized arrests for drunken driving in the early 50s and a romantic scandal involving John Wayne, she found film assignments elusive. In 1954 she divorced Guy MADISON, whom she had married in 1949. In August of 1961 she was found dead in her apartment, surrounded by empty liquor bottles. She was only 36.

FILMS: *Henry Aldrich Gets Glamour* 1943; *Lady in the Dark, The Uninvited, Our Hearts Were Young and Gay* 1944; *Salty O'Rourke, The Unseen, Duffy's Tavern* 1945; *Our Hearts Were Growing Up, The Bachelor's Daughters* 1946; *Calcutta, Angel and the Badman, Variety Girl* 1947; *Night Has a Thousand Eyes, Moonrise, Wake of the Red Witch* 1948; *Song of India, El Paso, The Great Dan Patch, Captain China* 1949; *The Lawless* 1950; *Air Cadet* 1951; *Seven Men from Now* 1956; *The Tattered Dress* 1957; *No Place to Land* 1958; *The Silent Call* 1961.

Russell, Harold. World War II veteran. Born in 1914, in Sydney, Nova Scotia, Canada. Raised in Boston. A paratroop sergeant in WW II, he lost both hands in a hand-grenade explosion. He appeared in an Army documentary, *The Diary of a*

Sergeant, depicting the rehabilitation of an amputee. Later he was chosen by William Wyler to play a key role in *The Best Years of Our Lives* and won the 1946 best supporting actor Academy Award for his natural performance as an amputee struggling to adjust to civilian life, as well as a second, special Academy Award "for bringing hope and courage to his fellow veterans." He is the only actor ever to win two Oscars for the same role. In 1949 he published his autobiography, *Victory in My Hands.* Later a business executive, in 1964 he was appointed by President Johnson as chairman of the President's Committee on Hiring the Handicapped. He returned to the screen in 1980 in *Inside Moves*. In 1992, Russell became the only Oscar recipient to sell his award, in order to raise money for his wife's medical expenses.

Russell, Jane. Actress. Born Ernestine Jane Geraldine Russell, on June 21, 1921, in Bemidji, Minn. Voluptuous star of Hollywood films, TV, and nightclubs whose cleavage provided the most crucial issue in the controversy surrounding the public showing of Howard Hughes's *The Outlaw* in the 40s. The daughter of a former actress, she worked as a chiropodist's receptionist, modeled for a photographer, and studied acting at Max REINHARDT's Theatrical Workshop and with Maria Ouspenskaya before her 38-inch bustline came to the attention of Hughes, who was conducting a nationwide chest hunt for the film's leading female role. The film, mild and innocuous in today's terms, was completed and briefly shown in 1941, released briefly in 1943, but not officially released until January 1950. Meanwhile, it resulted in much vulgar publicity for its star, who was once introduced by Bob Hope as "the two and only Miss Russell." She survived the image, however, and subsequently proved she had other, less obvious talents, playing with proficiency an assortment of roles, typically as a cynical, experienced dame. In 1971 she replaced Elaine Stritch as the star of the Broadway musical 'Company.' In the mid-70s she was appearing in TV commercials promoting brassieres. Her first husband (1943–68) was football star Bob Waterfield. Her second, actor Roger Barrett, died less than three months after their 1968 wedding. She lives in Sedona, Arizona with her third husband, a real-estate agent. Autobiography: *My Path and Detours* (1985).

FILMS: *The Outlaw* 1943; *Young Widow* 1946; *The Paleface* 1948; *His Kind of Woman, Double Dynamite* 1951; *The Las Vegas Story, Macao, Montana Belle, Son of Paleface, Road to Bali* (cameo) 1952; *Gentlemen Prefer Blondes* 1953; *The French Line* 1954; *Underwater!, Foxfire, The Tall Men, Gentlemen Marry Brunettes* 1955; *Hot Blood, The Revolt of Mamie Stover* 1956; *The Fuzzy Pink Nightgown* 1957; *Fate Is the Hunter* 1964; *Johnny Reno, Waco* 1966; *The Born Losers* 1967; *Darker Than Amber* 1970.

Russell, John. Actor. *b.* Jan. 3, 1921, Los Angeles. *d.* 1991. *ed.* UCLA. Tall, darkly handsome leading man, second lead, and smooth heavy of American films and television. He entered films in 1937 as a juvenile player. Following WW II service with the Marines, during which he received a battlefield commission as a second-lieutenant for valor at Guadalcanal, he returned to the screen as a young adult. Usually in tough, humorless roles, he also starred in the TV series 'Soldiers of Fortune' (1955–56) and 'The Lawman' (1958–62), and in the kiddie daytime action show 'Jason of Star Command' (1979–81).

FILMS INCLUDE: *The Frame-Up, The Duke Comes Back* 1937; *Always Goodbye* 1938; *Jesse James, Sabotage, Mr. Smith Goes to Washington* 1939; *The Blue Bird, The Man I Married* 1940; *A Bell for Adano* 1945; *Somewhere in the Night* 1946; *Forever Amber* 1947; *Sitting Pretty, Yellow Sky* 1948; *Slattery's Hurricane, The Story of Molly X, Undertow* 1949; *Saddle Tramp* 1950; *The Barefoot Mailman* 1951; *Hoodlum Empire* 1952; *The Sun Shines Bright, Fair Wind to Java* 1953; *Jubilee Trail* 1954; *The Last Command* 1955; *Untamed Youth* 1957; *Fort Massacre* 1958; *Rio Bravo, Yellowstone Kelly* 1959; *Apache Uprising* 1966; *Fort Utah, Hostile Guns* 1967; *Buckskin* 1968; *Cannon for Cordoba* (as General Pershing) 1970; *Adonde muere el Viento/Smoke in the Wind* (Arg.) 1975; *Seis Pasajes al Infierno/Six Tickets to Hell* (Arg.) 1976; *Honkytonk Man* 1982; *Pale Rider* 1985; *Under the Gun* 1989.

Russell, Ken. Director. Born on July 3, 1927, in Southampton, England. Flamboyant, controversial director of British TV and films. A graduate of the Nautical College at Pangbourne, he joined the British merchant navy in 1945 and served with the RAF from 1946 to 1949. In 1950, shunning the family shoe business, he joined the Ny Norsk Ballet as a dancer and the following year the Garrick Players as an actor. After some training in photography at the Southampton Technical College, he became a freelance still photographer, contributing to *Picture Post* and other illustrated magazines. In the late 50s he made several amateur short films, among them *Amelia and the Angel* (1957), *Peep Show* (1958), and *Lourdes* (1958), the quality of which paved his way to freelance assignments with BBC-TV as producer and director of programs dealing with the arts. After turning out several TV shows about contemporary artists, he delighted, stunned, and upset BBC viewers with a series of fictionalized biographies of such famous composers as Elgar, Prokofiev, Debussy, Bartók, Delius, and Richard Strauss and the dancer Isadora Duncan. These TV films have been noted for their originality, imagination, extravagance, attention to period detail, mixture of fact and fantasy, an interest in character psychology, rich imagery, and bold self-indulgence—elements that have also characterized Russell's theatrical films. Russell, who made his first feature film in 1963, burst upon the international scene in 1969 with his lavish and self-indulgent screen adaptation of D. H. Lawrence's *Women in Love,* which earned him an Academy Award nomination as best director. He has since remained a controversial figure in British cinema. He has been compared with Orson WELLES in his reputation for flamboyance, unpredictability, and excesses. Following the commercial success of *Women in Love,* he was able to convince backers to sponsor his sensational biography of Tchaikovksy, *The Music Lovers* (1971), by describing it as a "love story between a homosexual and a nymphomaniac." He fanned even more controversy with *The Devils* (1971), his visually exciting if overblown screen version of Aldous Huxley's *The Devils of Loudun.* The film was released in a trimmed-down version under pressure from British censors. He was still courting controversy in 1991 with the release of *Whore*, a highly unglamorous film about prostitutes. Russell's films are often coarse, symbol-ridden, pretentious, and confusing, but also often exciting and filled with a creative energy that sustains interest.

FEATURE FILMS: *French Dressing* 1963; *Billion Dollar Brain* 1967; *Women in Love* 1969; *The Music Lovers* (also prod.), *The Devils* (also sc., co-prod.), *The Boy Friend* (also sc., prod.) 1971; *Savage Messiah* (also prod.) 1972; *Mahler* (also sc.) 1974; *Tommy* (also sc., co-prod.), *Lisztomania* (also sc.) 1975; *Valentino* (also co-sc.) 1977; *Altered States* (US) 1980; *Crimes of Passion* (US) 1984; *Gothic, Aria* ("Turandot" segment; also sc.) 1987; *Salome's Last Dance* (also co-sc., act.), *The Lair of the White Worm* (also prod., sc.) 1988; *The Rainbow* (also prod., co-sc.) 1989; *The Russia House* (act. only) 1990; *Whore* (also co-sc.) 1991.

Russell, Kurt. Actor. Born on Mar. 17, 1951, in Springfield, Mass. Clean-cut juvenile player, then husky, square-jawed leading man of Hollywood films. The son of Bing Russell, a baseball player-turned-actor (deputy sheriff in 'Bonanza'), he began performing in films and TV before his tenth birthday. He got his big break at 12, playing the title role in the series 'The Travels of Jaimie McPheeters' (1963–64), and subsequently gained popularity portraying all-American boys in many Disney shows and movies. Following a prolonged timeout for a career in professional baseball, which ended in injury, Russell returned to acting with an Emmy-nominated portrayal of Elvis Presley in the TV movie *Elvis* (1979). Back in features in 1980, he made a bid for stardom the following year in John Carpenter's *Escape from New York* and for recognition as a serious actor in *Silkwood* (1983). Formerly married to actress Season HUBLEY, he shares a home in Aspen, Colorado, with Goldie HAWN and their family.

FILMS: *The Absent-Minded Professor* (bit) 1961; *It Happened at the World's Fair* 1963; *Follow Me Boys!* 1966; *The One and Only Genuine Original Family Band, The Horse in the Gray Flannel Suit* 1968; *The Computer Wore Tennis Shoes* 1969; *The Barefoot Executive, Fools' Parade* 1971; *Now You See Him Now You Don't* 1972; *Charley and the Angel* 1973; *Superdad* 1974; *The Strongest Man in the World* 1975; *Used Cars* 1980; *The Fox and the Hound* (v/o), *Escape from New York* 1981; *The Thing* 1982; *Silkwood* 1983; *Swing Shift* 1984; *The Mean Season* 1985; *The Best of Times, Big Trouble in Little China* 1986; *Overboard* 1987; *Tequila Sunrise* 1988; *Winter People, Tango & Cash* 1989; *Backdraft* 1991; *Unlawful Entry, Captain Ron* 1992; *Tombstone* 1993; *Stargate* 1994; *Escape from L.A.* (also co-prod.), *Executive Decision* 1996; *Breakdown* 1997.

Russell, Rosalind. Actress. *b.* June 4, 1908, Waterbury, Conn. *d.* 1976. *ed.* Marymount Coll.; American Academy of Dramatic Arts. Stylish, versatile Hollywood star with a penchant for sophisticated comedy. The daughter of a lawyer and a fashion editor, she went on the stage in the late 20s and made her film debut in 1934. At first she played many dramatic parts but in the early 40s found her niche in bright comedies, in which she was often typecast as a well-tailored, efficient career girl trading sarcastic witticisms with her men. Later in the decade she returned to dramas and her career went on a decline. She bounced back in the late 50s with *Auntie Mame,* repeating her earlier triumph on the stage, for which she received her fourth Oscar nomination. She was nominated for best actress Academy Awards for *My Sister Eileen* (1942), *Sister Kenny* (1946), *Mourning Becomes Electra* (1947), and *Auntie Mame* (1958). In 1972 she received a special Oscar, the Jean Hersholt Humanitarian Award, for her charity work. From the 60s she was seen mostly in character parts. She was married to producer Frederick Brisson.

FILMS: *Evelyn Prentice, The President Vanishes, Forsaking All Others* 1934; *The Night Is Young, West Point of the Air, The Casino Murder Case, Reckless, China Seas, Rendezvous* 1935; *It Had to Happen, Under Two Flags, Trouble for Two, Craig's Wife* 1936; *Night Must Fall, Live Love and Learn* 1937; *Man-Proof, Four's a Crowd, The Citadel* (UK/US) 1938; *Fast and Loose, The Women* 1939; *His Girl Friday, Hired Wife, No Time for Comedy* 1940; *This Thing Called Love, They Met in Bombay, The Feminine Touch, Design for Scandal* 1941; *Take a Letter Darling, My Sister Eileen* 1942; *Flight for Freedom, What a Woman* 1943; *Roughly Speaking, She Wouldn't Say Yes* 1945; *Sister Kenny* 1946; *The Guilt of Janet Ames, Mourning Becomes Electra* (as Lavinia Mannon) 1947; *The Velvet Touch* 1948; *Tell It to the Judge* 1949; *A Woman of Distinction* 1950; *Never Wave at a Wac* 1953; *The Girl Rush* 1955; *Picnic* 1956; *Auntie Mame* 1958; *A Majority of One, Five Finger Exercise, Gypsy* 1962; *The Trouble with Angels* 1966; *Oh Dad Poor Dad Mama's Hung You in the Closet and I'm Feeling So Sad, Rosie* 1967; *Where Angels Go Trouble Follows* 1968; *Mrs. Pollifax—Spy* 1971.

Russell, Theresa. Actress. Born Theresa Paup, on Mar. 30, 1957, in San Diego, Calif. Intriguing leading lady of the American and British screen. A model from age 12, she trained at Lee Strasberg's Theatre Institute in Hollywood before entering films at 19. Memorable in Bob Rafelson's *Black Widow* (1987) and Nicolas Roeg's *Insignificance*. In 1982 she married Roeg, thirty years her senior.

FILMS: *The Last Tycoon* 1976; *Straight Time* 1978; *Bad Timing/Bad Timing: A Sensual Obsession* 1982; *Eureka* 1983; *The Razor's Edge* 1984; *Insignificance* 1985; *Black Widow, Aria* 1987; *Track 29* 1988; *Physical Evidence* 1989; *Impulse* 1990; *Whore, Kafka, Cold Heaven* 1991; *Being Human* (narr.) 1994; *The Spy Within* 1995; *Gentlemen Don't Eat Poets* 1997.

Russell, William. Actor. *b.* William Lerche, Apr. 12, 1884, the Bronx, N.Y. *d.* 1929. *ed.* Fordham. Dashing leading man of the American silent screen. A semiprofessional athlete, he divided his time between boxing bouts and acting appearances in vaudeville and on the legitimate stage before entering films in 1912. He starred in numerous silent productions, often in roles requiring physical prowess, including Westerns. He was married to actress Helen Ferguson.

FILMS INCLUDE: *The Merchant of Venice, Undine, Lucile, The Star of Bethlehem* 1912; *Cymbeline, Robin Hood* 1913; *The Straight Road, The Cricket on the Hearth* 1914; *The Diamond from the Sky* (serial), *The Garden of Lies* 1915; *The Pride of a Man, The Sea Master* 1917; *Midnight Trail* 1918; *Brass Buttons* 1919; *The Valley of Tomorrow, The Man Who Dared* 1920; *Bare Knuckles, Children of the Night, The Lady from Longacre, Desert Blossoms* 1921; *Money to Burn, The Men of Zanzibar, A Self-Made Man, The Crusader, The Great Night* 1922; *Boston Blackie* (title role), *Man's Size, Times Have Changed, Anna Christie* (as Matt Burke) 1923; *The Beloved Brute* 1924; *On Thin Ice, The Way of a Girl, Before Midnight, Big Pal* (also prod.) 1925; *The Still Alarm, The Blue Eagle, Wings of the Storm* 1926; *The Desired Woman, The Girl from Chicago, Brass Knuckles* 1927; *Woman Wise, The Escape, Danger Patrol, State Street Sadie, The Midnight Taxi, The Head of the Family* 1928; *Girls Gone Wild* 1929.

Russia. See SOVIET UNION.

Russo, Rene. Actress. *b.* ca. 1954 in Los Angeles. This stunning beauty began as a model–cover girl who turned her attentions to acting with a few stints on television which led to her feature debut in *Major League* (1989). She has since proven herself a capable, compelling actress effective in sensitive dramas as well as romantic comedies such as *Tin Cup* (1996).

FILMS: *Major League* 1989; *Mr. Destiny* 1990; *One Good Cop* 1991; *Freejack, Lethal Weapon 3* 1992; *In the Line of Fire* 1993; *Get Shorty, Outbreak* 1995; *Ransom, Tin Cup* 1996; *Buddy* 1997.

Rutherford, Ann. Actress. Born on Nov. 2, 1917, in Toronto. Pert brunette of Hollywood films of the 30s and 40s. The daughter of former Metropolitan Opera tenor John Guilberty (Rutherford), and an actress mother, she was raised in California, where she made her stage debut at the age of five. She appeared in many plays and on radio before being signed by Mascot/Republic in 1934 as a leading lady of low-budget Westerns, opposite heroes such as Gene Autry and John Wayne. In 1937 she moved over to MGM, where she soon gained popularity in the role of Polly Benedict, Mickey ROONEY's ever-faithful girlfriend in the "ANDY HARDY" series. In addition to appearing in 12 Hardy films, she played leads and supporting roles in many other MGM pictures through the early 40s, when she began freelancing, to the detriment of her career. She retired from the screen in 1950 but returned in 1972 in a secondary role. Her second husband was producer William Dozier.

FILMS INCLUDE: *The Fighting Marines* (serial), *Waterfront Lady, Melody Trail, The Singing Vagabond* 1935; *The Lawless Nineties, The Harvester, Comin' Round the Mountain, Down Under the Sea, The Oregon Trail* 1936; *The Devil Is Driving, Public Cowboy No. 1, The Bride Wore Red, Espionage, You're Only Young Once* 1937; *Of Human Hearts, Judge Hardy's Children, Love Finds Andy Hardy, Dramatic School, A Christmas Carol* (as the Ghost of Christmas Past) 1938; *Four Girls in White, Andy Hardy Gets Spring Fever, These Glamour Girls, Dancing Co-Ed, Gone With the Wind* (as Carreen O'Hara) 1939; *The Ghost Comes Home, Andy Hardy Meets Debutante, Pride and Prejudice* (as Lydia Bennet), *Wyoming* 1940; *Andy Hardy's Private Secretary, Washington Melodrama, Life Begins for Andy Hardy, Whistling in the Dark, Badlands of Dakota* 1941; *This Time for Keeps, The Courtship of Andy Hardy, Orchestra Wives, Whistling in Dixie* 1942; *Happy Land, Whistling in Brooklyn* 1943; *Bermuda Mystery* 1944; *Two O'Clock Courage, Bedside Manner* 1945; *The Madonna's Secret, Murder in the Music Hall, Inside Job* 1946; *The Secret Life of Walter Mitty* 1947; *Adventures of Don Juan* 1948; *Operation Haylift* 1950; *They Only Kill Their Masters* 1972; *Won Ton Ton—The Dog Who Saved Hollywood* 1976.

Rutherford, Dame Margaret. Actress. *b.* May 11, 1892, London. *d.* 1972. Delightfully eccentric character actress of the British stage and screen. Formerly a teacher of speech and piano, she studied drama at the Old Vic and made her stage debut in 1925 and her first London appearance in 1933. In films from the mid-30s, she gave many memorable performances, unforgettably as the bicycle-riding medium in *Blithe Spirit* (1945) and as the inquisitive Miss Marple in four Agatha Christie mystery films of the 60s. She won an Oscar as best supporting actress for her performance in *The V.I.P.s* (1963). She was created Dame of the British Empire in 1967. Her husband, Stringer Davis, often appeared in her films. One of their four adopted children, writer Gordon Langley Hall, having undergone a sex-change operation in 1968, wrote a biography of the actress in 1983, signing it Dawn Langley Hall. Autobiography: *Margaret Rutherford* (1972).

FILMS: *Dusty Ermine/Hideout in the Alps, Talk of the Devil* 1936; *Beauty and the Barge, Catch as Catch Can* 1937; *Quiet Wedding* 1940; *The Yellow Canary, The Demi-Paradise/Adventure for Two* 1943; *English Without Tears/Her Man Gilbey* 1944; *Blithe Spirit* 1945; *Meet Me at Dawn* 1946; *While the Sun Shines* 1947; *Miranda* 1948; *Passport to Pimlico* 1949; *The Happiest Days of Your Life, Her Favorite Husband/The Taming of Dorothy* 1950; *The Magic Box* (cameo) 1951; *Curtain Up, Castle in the Air, Miss Robin Hood, The Importance of Being Earnest* (as Miss Prism) 1952; *Innocents in Paris, Trouble in Store* 1953; *The Runaway Bus, Mad About Men, Aunt Clara* 1954; *An Alligator Named Daisy* 1955; *The Smallest Show on Earth, Just My Luck* 1957; *I'm All Right Jack* 1959; *On the Double* (US), *Murder She Said* 1961; *The V.I.P.s, Murder at the Gallop, The Mouse on the Moon* 1963; *Murder Ahoy, Murder Most Foul* 1964; *The Alphabet Murders* (cameo), *Campanadas a Medianoche/Falstaff/Chimes at Midnight* (Sp./Switz.) 1966; *A Countess from Hong Kong, The Wacky World of Mother Goose* (v/o; US) 1967; *Arabella* (It.) 1968.

Ruttenberg, Joseph. Director of photography. *b.* July 4, 1889, St. Petersburg, Russia. *d.* 1983. In the US from early childhood, he began as a newsboy on a Boston newspaper and later became a reporter and news photographer. After gaining motion picture experience as a newsreel cameraman and producer, he joined Fox in 1915. He served as cinematographer on many silent features, but it was not until the late 30s that he became established as one of Hollywood's leading cameramen. Working mainly for MGM, he won Academy Awards for the cinematography of *The Great Waltz* (1938), *Mrs. Miniver* (1942), *Somebody Up There Likes Me* (1956), and *Gigi* (1958).

FILMS INCLUDE: *Thou Shalt Not Steal* 1917; *The Debt of Honor* 1918; *The Fallen Idol* 1919; *The Thief, The Shark* 1920; *A Virgin Paradise* 1921; *Silver Wings* (co-phot.) 1922; *If Winter Comes* 1923; *The Fool* 1923; *Summer Bachelors* 1926; *The Struggle* 1931; *The People's Enemy* 1935; *Three Godfathers, Fury, Piccadilly Jim* 1936; *A Day at the Races, Big City* 1937; *The Great Waltz, Three Comrades, The Shopworn Angel, Spring Madness* 1938; *On Borrowed Time, The Women* (co-phot.), *Balalaika* (co-phot.) 1939; *Waterloo Bridge, The Philadelphia Story, Comrade X* 1940; *Two-Faced Woman, Dr. Jekyll and Mr. Hyde* 1941; *Woman of the Year, Mrs. Miniver, Random Harvest* 1942; *Presenting Lily Mars, Madame Curie* 1943; *Mrs. Parkington, Gaslight* 1944; *The Valley of Decision* 1945; *Adventure* 1946; *Desire Me* 1947; *B.F.'s Daughter* 1948; *The Bribe, That Forsyte Woman* 1949; *The Miniver Story* 1950; *The Great Caruso* 1951; *The Prisoner of Zenda* 1952; *Julius Caesar* 1953; *Brigadoon, The Last Time I Saw Paris* 1954; *The Prodigal, Kismet* 1955; *Somebody Up There Likes Me, The Swan* 1956; *Gigi, The Reluctant Debutante* 1958; *Green Mansions* 1959; *Butterfield 8* (co-phot.) 1960; *Who's Got the Action?* 1962; *A Global Affair* 1964; *Harlow* 1965; *The Oscar* 1966; *Speedway* 1968.

Ruttmann, Walter. Director. *b.* Dec. 28, 1887, Frankfurt, Germany. *d.* 1941. An architect and painter, he turned to abstract films after completing his WW I service as a lieutenant on the eastern front. As a disciple of Viking EGGELING he experimented with geometric forms in motion in the early 20s. But it was in the field of the documentary, later in the decade, that he was to have a lasting influence on world cinema. His *Berlin—Symphony of a Great City* is a classic of rhythmic montage. Evidently inspired by VERTOV and his Kino-Eye principles, but not by his style, the film captures the pulse and the tempo of the German capital from dawn to midnight through ingenious cutting to a musical beat. It set the pattern for many subsequent CITY SYMPHONIES throughout the world. His *World Melody* similarly influenced future documentary filmmaking. In the late 30s he lent his talents to the Nazi propaganda machine. He served as advisor to Leni RIEFENSTAHL on the editing of *Olympia* (1938), and in 1940 he recorded on film the German occupation of France. The following year he was mortally wounded while covering the eastern front for a newsreel.

FILMS: *Die tönnende Welle* (experimental sound film without images, just tones; not shown until 1928) 1921; *Opus I, Die Sieger, Opus II, Das verlorene Paradies, Kantorowitz, Gesolei* 1923; *Der Falkentraum* (dream sequence in Fritz Lang's *Die Nibelungen*), *Opus III* 1924; *Opus IV* 1925; *Hoppla wir leben* (film insert for stage production; co-dir.), *Berlin—Die Symphonie einer Grosstadt/Berlin—Symphony of a Great City* 1927; *Deutscher Rundfunk* 1928; *Wochende/Weekend, Melodie der Welt* (doc. feature) 1929; *In der Nacht, Feind im Blut* (both made in Switzerland) 1931; *Acciaio/Arbeit macht Frei/Steel* (feature made in Italy) 1933; *Altgermanische Baurenkultur, Metall des Himmels* 1934; *Stadt der Verheissung, Kleiner Film einer grossen Stadt: Düsseldorf, Stuttgart: Grosstadt zwischen Wald und Reben, Volkfest Kannstadt* 1935; *Schiff in Not* 1936; *Mannesmann* 1937; *Hamburg: Weltstrasse See, Im Zeichen des Vertrauens, Im Dienste der Menschlichkeit, Henkel—Ein deutsches Werk in sein-*

er Arbeit 1938; *Die deutsche Waffenschmiede, Deutsche Panzer, Aberglaube* 1940; *Volkkrankheit Krebs/Jeder Achte* 1941.

Ryan, Frank. Director. *b.* Oct. 18, 1907, Urbana, Ohio. *d.* 1947. A former magazine cartoonist and humorist, he directed a number of light Hollywood films of the 40s, including a couple of Deanna Durbin vehicles. He also collaborated on several scripts.

FILMS (as director): *Call Out the Marines* (co-dir., co-sc. with William Hamilton) 1942; *Hers to Hold* 1943; *Can't Help Singing* (also co-sc.) 1944; *Patrick the Great* 1945; *So Goes My Love* 1946.

Ryan, Kathleen. Actress. *b.* 1922, Ireland. *d.* 1985. Dark-haired leading lady of British films of the late 40s and 50s, usually in rather gloomy roles. Memorable in her screen debut, in Carol Reed's *Odd Man Out* (1947).

FILMS: *Odd Man Out, Captain Boycott* 1947; *Esther Waters* 1948; *Christopher Columbus, Give Us This Day/Salt to the Devil* 1949; *Prelude to Fame* 1950; *Try and Get Me* (US) 1951; *Laxdale Hall/Scotch on the Rocks, The Yellow Balloon* 1952; *Captain Lightfoot* (US) 1955; *Jacqueline* 1956; *Sail Into Danger* 1957.

Ryan, Meg. Actress. Born on Nov. 19, 1961, Fairfield, Conn. Winsome blonde leading lady of Hollywood films of the 80s and 90s. The daughter of an actress-turned-casting agent, she began her own acting career directly out of high school, playing Candice Bergen's daughter in *Rich and Famous* (1980). Later, while taking night classes in journalism at NYU, she performed in commercials and gained a measure of popularity among soap-opera fans with her two-year stint in the daytime serial 'As the World Turns.' Secondary parts in films followed, including a small but pivotal role in *Top Gun* (1986). *When Harry Met Sally. . .* (1989), in which she demonstrated her ability to fake an orgasm to great comic effect, made her a star. She continued to appear as a reliable romantic lead and reached even greater success with the romantic comedy *Sleepless in Seattle* (1993). In 1991 she married actor Dennis QUAID, with whom she has starred in a handful of films.

FILMS: *Rich and Famous* 1981; *Amityville 3-D/Amityville: The Demon* 1983; *Top Gun, Armed and Dangerous* 1986; *Innerspace* 1987; *Promised Land, D.O.A., The Presidio* 1988; *When Harry Met Sally. . .* 1989; *Joe Versus the Volcano* 1990; *The Doors* 1991; *Prelude to a Kiss* 1992; *Sleepless in Seattle, Flesh and Bone* 1993; *I.Q., When a Man Loves a Woman* 1994; *French Kiss* (also co-prod.), *Restoration* 1995; *Courage Under Fire* 1996; *Addicted to Love* 1997.

Ryan, Peggy. Actress. Born Margaret O'Rene Ryan, on Aug. 28, 1924, in Long Beach, Calif. Lively young comedienne, singer, and dancer of light Hollywood films of the 40s, often teamed with Donald O'CONNOR, in minor Universal musicals. She began as a child performer in vaudeville and entered films at 13. After retirement early in the 50s she ran a dancing school. A resident of Hawaii, she appeared in some segments of the TV series 'Hawaii Five-O' in the role of Jack Lord's secretary.

FILMS INCLUDE: *Top of the Town* 1937; *The Flying Irishman* 1939; *The Grapes of Wrath* 1940; *What's Cookin', Miss Annie Rooney, Private Buckaroo, Give Out Sisters, Get Hep to Love* 1942; *When Johnny Comes Marching Home, Mister Big, Top Man* 1943; *Chip Off the Old Block, Follow the Boys, This Is the Life, The Merry Monahans, Babes on Swing Street, Bowery to Broadway* 1944; *Here Come the Co-Eds, Patrick the Great, That's the Spirit, On Stage Everybody, Men in Her Diary* 1945; *Shamrock Hill* 1949; *There's a Girl in My Heart* 1950; *All Ashore* 1953.

Ryan, Robert. Actor. *b.* Nov. 11, 1909, Chicago. *d.* 1973. Capable, versatile leading man and character star of Hollywood films. The son of a construction firm executive, he studied at Chicago's Loyola Academy, then at Dartmouth, where he excelled in sports and for four years held the college's heavyweight boxing championship. After graduating, he worked at a variety of odd jobs, including as a ranch hand, ship stoker, male model, salesman, and debt collector, then trained for the stage at the Max Reinhardt Theatrical Workshop in Hollywood. He made his stage debut in 1939 and in the following year began playing small roles in Paramount films. In 1941–42 he appeared on Broadway in 'Clash by Night,' then returned to Hollywood with an RKO contract. His career began taking shape after his return from WW II service with the Marines.

Ryan played some of his best roles in the late 40s and early 50s, notably as Joan Bennett's illicit lover in Jean Renoir's suspenseful triangle drama *The Woman on the Beach* (1947), as the anti-Semitic murderer in Edward Dmytryk's *Crossfire* (1947), as the nemesis who menaces Van Heflin in Fred Zinnemann's *Act of Violence* (1949), as the paranoid millionaire husband of Barbara Bel Geddes in Max Ophüls's *Caught* (1949), as a washed-up boxer in Robert Wise's powerful ring drama *The Set-Up* (1949), and, repeating his stage role, as the cynical lover in Fritz Lang's *Clash by Night* (1952). He later freelanced, appearing indiscriminately in a great number of films of variable quality, but still managed to come up with excellent performances, either as hero or villain, in such films as *About Mrs. Leslie* (1954), *Bad Day at Black Rock* (1955), *God's Little Acre* (1958), *Billy Budd* (1962), and *The Wild Bunch* (1969). He also appeared successfully in occasional stage productions, including the American Shakespeare Festival 1960 production of 'Antony and Cleopatra,' in which he played Antony to Katharine Hepburn's Cleopatra, the 1968 Broadway revival of 'The Front Page,' and the 1971 off-Broadway revival of 'Long Day's Journey into Night.'

Ryan was a modest, low-keyed man in his private life and a committed activist for such liberal groups as SANE and the American Civil Liberties Union. He was also active in education, was among the founders of the UCLA Theatre Group, and founded a nonsectarian private school in California's San Fernando Valley. He died of cancer.

FILMS: *The Crooked Road, The Ghost Breakers, Queen of the Mob, Golden Gloves, Texas Rangers Ride Again, North West Mounted Police* 1940; *The Feminine Touch* 1941; *Bombardier, The Sky's the Limit, Behind the Rising Sun, The Iron Major, Gangway for Tomorrow* 1943; *Tender Comrade, Marine Raiders* 1944; *Trail Street, The Woman on the Beach, Crossfire* 1947; *Berlin Express, Return of the Badmen, The Boy with Green Hair* 1948; *Act of Violence, Caught, The Set-Up, I Married a Communist/The Woman on Pier 13* 1949; *The Secret Fury, Born to Be Bad* 1950; *Best of the Bad Men, Flying Leathernecks, The Racket* 1951; *On Dangerous Ground, Clash by Night, Beware My Lovely, Horizons West* 1952; *City Beneath the Sea, The Naked Spur, Inferno* 1953; *Alaska Seas, About Mrs. Leslie, Her Twelve Men* 1954; *Bad Day at Black Rock, Escape to Burma, House of Bamboo, The Tall Men* 1955; *The Proud Ones, Back from Eternity* 1956; *Men in War* 1957; *God's Little Acre* 1958; *Lonelyhearts, Day of the Outlaw, Odds Against Tomorrow* 1959; *Ice Palace* 1960; *The Canadians* (US/Can./UK), *King of Kings* (as John the Baptist) 1961; *Billy Budd, The Longest Day* 1962; *The Crooked Road* (UK/Yug.), *Battle of the Bulge, Guerre secrète/The Dirty Game* (Fr./It./Ger.) 1965; *The Professionals* 1966; *The Busy Body, The Dirty Dozen, Hour of the Gun* 1967; *Custer of the West, Escondido/Un Minuto per Pregare un Instante per Morire/A Minute to Pray a Second to Die/Dead or Alive* (It./US), *Lo Sbarco di Anzio/Anzio* (It.) 1968; *The Wild Bunch, Captain Nemo and the Underwater*

City (title role; UK) 1969; *The Love Machine, Lawman* 1971; *La Course du Lievre à Travers les Champs/And Hope to Die* (Fr./US) 1972; *Lolly-Madonna XXX, The Iceman Cometh, Executive Action* 1973; *The Outfit* 1974.

Ryan, Sheila. Actress. *b.* Katherine Elizabeth McLaughlin, June 8, 1921, Topeka, Kans. *d.* 1975. Leading lady of numerous routine Hollywood B pictures of the 40s and 50s. A graduate of Hollywood High School, she began her acting career in 1938, performing in closed-circuit experimental TV, and made her screen debut in 1940. She died of a lung ailment. She was married to Gene Autry's comic sidekick Pat Buttram.

FILMS INCLUDE: *The Gay Caballero* 1940; *Dead Men Tell, Dressed to Kill, Great Guns* 1941; *Pardon My Stripes, Lone Star Ranger, A-Hunting We Will Go* 1942; *The Gang's All Here* 1943; *Song of Texas, Something for the Boys* 1944; *The Caribbean Mystery, Getting Gertie's Garter* 1945; *Deadline for Murder, Slightly Scandalous* 1946; *The Lone Wolf in Mexico, The Big Fix, Heartaches, Railroaded, Philo Vance's Secret Mission* 1947; *Caged Fury* 1948; *Ringside* 1949; *Mule Train, Western Pacific Agent* 1950; *Fingerprints Don't Lie, Mask of the Dragon, Gold Raiders, Jungle Manhunt* 1951; *On Top of Old Smoky* 1953; *Street of Darkness* 1958.

Rydell, Mark. Director, producer, actor. Born on Mar. 23, 1934, in New York City. *ed.* Juilliard School of Music. He trained for the stage at New York's Neighborhood Playhouse and later became a member of the Actors Studio. He appeared in several Broadway productions of the 50s, moonlighting as a jazz pianist during lulls in his schedule, and for six years played a lead role in the TV soap opera 'As the World Turns.' In 1956 he played a featured role in the film *Crime in the Streets* but did not return to the screen as an actor until 1973, when he appeared in Robert Altman's *The Long Goodbye.* In the interim, he went to Hollywood as a TV director and turned out many episodes for such series as 'Ben Casey,' 'I Spy,' and 'Gunsmoke.' He made an impressive debut as a feature director with *The Fox* (1968), an intimate erotic drama from a novella by D. H. Lawrence which he filmed in Canada. He later directed several entertaining features in a variety of genres and styles, achieving a critical and commercial success with *Cinderella Liberty* (1973). He was nominated for an Academy Award as best director for *On Golden Pond* (1981), a film that was also Oscar-nominated as best picture. He formed a production company, Sanford, with director Sidney Pollack.

FILMS: As actor—*Crime in the Streets* 1956; *The Long Goodbye* 1973; *Punchline* 1988; *Havana* 1990. As director—*The Fox* 1968; *The Reivers* 1969; *The Cowboys* (also prod.) 1972; *Cinderella Liberty* (also prod.) 1973; *Harry and Walter Go to New York* 1976; *The Rose* 1978; *On Golden Pond* 1981; *The River* 1984; *The Man in the Moon* (prod. only), *For the Boys* (also exec. prod.) 1991; *Intersection* (also co-prod.) 1994.

Ryder, Winona. Actress. Born Winona Laura Horowitz, in October, 1971, near Winona, Minn. Petite, intense, brunette young lead of Hollywood films, particularly adept at personifying the ambiguity of sophisticated innocence. The daughter of the archivist to LSD guru Timothy Leary, she moved with her family to Northern California at age four and spent part of her childhood in San Francisco and in a nearby hippie agricultural commune. At 11 she began training at San Francisco's prestigious American Conservatory Theatre. On the screen from age 15, she rapidly became one of the most sought-after young movie personalities. Overworked to near exhaustion, she abandoned the plum role of Michael Corleone's daughter in *The Godfather Part III.* She continued her screen successes with well-received roles in *Bram Stoker's Dracula* in 1992 and *The Age of Innocence* in 1993. In 1990 Ryder was engaged to but did not marry actor-musician Johnny DEPP.

FILMS: *Lucas* 1986; *Square Dance* 1987; *Beetlejuice, 1969* 1988; *Heathers, Great Balls of Fire* 1989; *Welcome Home Roxy Carmichael, Edward Scissorhands, Mermaids* 1990; *Night on Earth* 1991; *Bram Stoker's Dracula* 1992; *The Age of Innocence* 1993; *The House of the Spirits, Little Women, Reality Bites* 1994; *Boys, How To Make an American Quilt* 1995; *The Crucible* 1996.

Ryskind, Morrie. Playwright, screenwriter. *b.* Oct. 20, 1895, Brooklyn, N.Y. *d.* 1985. *ed.* Columbia. A collaborator with George S. KAUFMAN on a number of successful Broadway musical comedies, he also contributed entertaining screenplays for more than a dozen Hollywood films, alone or in collaboration, notably a number of zany MARX BROTHERS vehicles. He shared a Pulitzer Prize for the stage musical 'Of Thee I Sing' (1931–32), which he wrote with Kaufman and Ira Gershwin. It was the first "best play" Pulitzer ever awarded to a musical. He shared Academy Award nominations for the scripts of *My Man Godfrey* (1936) and *Stage Door* (1937). Ryskind was blacklisted in 1947 for leftist associations but over the years gravitated toward the conservative wing of the Republican party. He served as one of the original editors of *The National Review,* and was said to be a member of the John Birch Society.

FILMS INCLUDE: *The Cocoanuts* 1929; *Animal Crackers* 1930; *Palmy Days* 1931; *A Night at the Opera, Anything Goes, Ceiling Zero* 1935; *My Man Godfrey* 1936; *Stage Door* 1937; *Room Service* 1938; *Man About Town* 1939; *Louisiana Purchase* (play basis only), *Penny Serenade* 1941; *Claudia* 1943; *Where Do We Go from Here?* 1945; *Heartbeat* (adapt. only) 1946; *My Man Godfrey* ('36 screenplay basis only) 1957.

S

Sabu. Actor. *b.* Sabu Dastagir, Jan. 27, 1924, Karapur, Mysore, India. *d.* 1963. A former stable boy at the court of an Indian maharajah, he was discovered by Robert Flaherty, who cast him in the title role of the film *Elephant Boy* (1937). He played exotic boys in several other British films, then went to Hollywood, where he played similar parts in a succession of popular Eastern adventure films at Universal, often co-starring Jon HALL and Maria MONTEZ. When the vogue for Arabian Nights yarns faded in the late 40s, he sought unsuccessfully to salvage his career in Continental films. He died of a heart attack at 39.

FILMS: In the UK—*Elephant Boy* 1937; *The Drum/Drums* 1938; *The Thief of Bagdad* 1940. In the US—*Jungle Book, Arabian Nights* 1942; *White Savage* 1943; *Cobra Woman* 1944; *Tangier* 1946; *Black Narcissus* (UK), *The End of the River* (UK) 1947; *Man-Eater of Kumaon* 1948; *Song of India* 1949; *Savage*

Drums 1951; *Buongiorno Elefante/Hello Elephant* (It.) 1952; *Il Tesoro del Bengala/Jungle Hell* (It.) 1953; *Jaguar* 1956; *Sabu and the Magic Ring* 1958; *Herrin der Welt/Il Mistero dei Tre Continenti* (Ger./It.) 1960; *Rampage* 1963; *A Tiger Walks* 1964.

Sadoul, Georges. Film critic, historian, theorist. *b.* Feb. 4, 1904, Nancy, France. *d.* 1967. After law studies, he became active in the surrealist movement in the late 20s, but in the early 30s converted to Marxism and participated in the Congress of Revolutionary Writers in Kharkov, USSR. Shortly thereafter he began writing regularly on cinema and in the 40s launched a weekly film-review column in *Les Lettres Françaises,* which he continued until his death. In 1945 he became general secretary of the Fédération Française de Ciné-Clubs and for the next decade remained one of the most influential film critics and tastemakers in France. His published works include numerous essays and several important books on film, the most ambitious of which is the six-volume *Histoire Générale de Cinéma.* Among other works is a twin set of film dictionaries, *Dictionnaire des Cinéastes* and *Dictionnaire des Films,* which were published in an English translation by the University of California as *Dictionary of Film Makers* and *Dictionary of Films.* He also wrote a definitive index to the works of Georges Méliès, historic surveys of French and Hungarian cinema, and a biography of Charlie Chaplin. His theoretical and critical works were noticeably influenced by his Marxist bias. In 1956 he received a doctorate in art history from Moscow University. He taught film theory at IDHEC and at the French Institute of Filmology.

safety film. Film whose base (usually cellulose or acetate) is noncombustible and has a slow burning rate. It was available to amateur filmmakers since before WW I, but because of its inferior quality and high cost it failed to gain acceptance among professional producers, who continued to use the highly flammable nitrate-base film for many years. Only as the quality of safety film improved did the motion picture industry move to accept it. By the early 50s nitrate-base film had been completely replaced. Also, most old movies in studio vaults have been transferred to safety film stock.

SAG (Screen Actors Guild). A union in which some 75,000 motion picture performers are organized. It was established in 1933 and is affiliated with the Associated Actors and Artists of America (AAAA) and the American Federation of Labor (AFL).

Sagal, Boris. Director. *b.* Oct. 18, 1923, Dnepropetrovsk, Russia. *d.* 1981. *ed.* UCLA; Harvard Law School; Yale Drama School. Encouraged by success in television, he ventured into feature films early in the 60s with modest results. In the early 70s he switched from features to TV movies. He was nominated for Emmy Awards for the TV movie *A Case of Rape* (1974) and for the miniseries 'Rich Man, Poor Man' (1975) and 'Masada' (1981). He was killed in a filming accident in Portland, Oregon, leaving a widow, his wife from 1977, actress-dancer Marge CHAMPION.

FILMS: *Dime with a Halo, Twilight of Honor* 1963; *Girl Happy* 1965; *Made in Paris* 1966; *The 1,000 Plane Raid* 1969; *Mosquito Squadron* 1970; *The Omega Man* 1971; *Angela* (Can.) 1978.

Sagan, Françoise. Novelist, screenwriter. Born Françoise Quoirez, on June 21, 1935, in Carjat (Cajarc), France. An internationally famous novelist at 19, she has collaborated on the screenplays of several films. In addition, others have adapted her novels or plays to the screen. She also played a cameo role in Jean Cocteau's *Le Testament d'Orphée/The Testament of Orpheus* (1960). In 1977 she directed a first film, *Les Fougères bleues.*

FILMS INCLUDE: Based on her novels/plays—*Bonjour Tristesse* (UK/US), *A Certain Smile* (US) 1958; *Aimez-vous Brahms?/Goodbye Again* (Fr./US) 1961; *Chateau en Suède/Nutty Naughty Chateau* 1963. As screenwriter—*La Récréation/Playtime* (original story only) 1961; *Landru/Bluebeard* (co-sc. with Claude Chabrol) 1963; *La Chamade* (co-sc., co-dial. from own play) 1968; *Le Bal du Comte d'Orgel* (dial. only) 1970; *Les Fougères bleues* (also dir.) 1977; *La Femme Fardee* (story basis only) 1990.

Sagan, Leontine. Director. *b.* Leontine Schlesinger, 1889, Vienna. *d.* 1974. Primarily a woman of the theater, she was trained by Max REINHARDT and became prominent as a stage actress and director in Germany and Austria. In 1931 she scored an international success with her first film, *Mädchen in Uniform,* a study of emotional pressures in an authoritarian girls' school, which created an uproar because of its frank handling of a lesbian theme. The following year she went to England, where she directed a film for Alexander Korda, then returned to stage work in England and South Africa. She was instrumental in the development of the South African theater during WW II and was a co-founder of the National Theatre in Johannesburg.

FILMS: *Mädchen in Uniform* (Ger.) 1931; *Men of Tomorrow* (UK) 1932.

Sägebrecht, Marianne. Actress. Born in 1945, in Starnberg, Bavaria, Germany. Hefty, Kewpie doll-like character player of the German stage and screen. At 15 she moved to Munich, where she became a driving force in cabaret revues and the underground theater. Her fame spread abroad through pivotal roles in such Percy Adlon films as *Sugarbaby* (1985) and *Bagdad Cafe* (1987), which was later fashioned into a US television series. She has since appeared in some Hollywood productions.

FILMS INCLUDE: *Irrsee* 1984; *Zuckerbaby/Sugarbaby* 1985; *Out of Rosenheim/Bagdad Cafe* (Ger./US) 1987; *Moon Over Parador* (US) 1988; *Rosalie Goes Shopping* (Ger./US), *The War of the Roses* (US) 1989; *Martha und Ich/Martha and I* 1990; *La Vida Lactea/The Milky Way* 1992; *Dust Devil: The Final Cut* (Fr./UK) *Erotique* (Ger./US) 1993; *Mona Must Die* (US) 1994; *The Ogre* 1996; *Sun* 1997.

sagebrusher. Slang for a Western movie, usually a routine low-budget production. Also known as a "horse opera" or "oater."

Saint, Eva Marie. Actress. Born on July 4, 1924, in Newark, N.J. *ed.* Bowling Green State U. Sensitive, fragile leading lady of Hollywood films. She began her acting career in radio and TV dramas and in 1953 scored a success on Broadway in 'The Trip to Bountiful,' for which she received the Drama Critics Award. She made her film debut the following year, winning an Oscar as best supporting actress for her delicate portrayal of Marlon Brando's girlfriend in *On the Waterfront*; she was also notable as the cool spy in *North by Northwest.* But her subsequent film appearances have been infrequent and few of her roles have proved either suited to or worthy of her unique personality and talent. She returned to the New York stage in 1983 after a decade's absence and later co-starred in the TV series 'Moonlighting.' She is married to stage and TV producer-director Jeffrey Hayden.

FILMS: *On the Waterfront* 1954; *That Certain Feeling* 1956; *A Hatful of Rain, Raintree County* 1957; *North by Northwest* 1959; *Exodus* 1960; *All Fall Down* 1962; *36 Hours* 1964; *The Sandpiper* 1965; *The Russians Are Coming the Russians Are Coming, Grand Prix* 1966; *The Stalking Moon* 1969; *Loving* 1970; *Cancel My Reservation* 1972; *Nothing in Common* 1986.

St. Clair, Malcolm (Mal). Director. *b.* May 17, 1897, Los Angeles. *d.* 1952. A former newspaper cartoonist, he joined

Mack Sennett in 1915 as a bit player and gag writer. He began directing comedy shorts for Sennett in 1919. Freelancing from 1921, he directed two Buster Keaton comedies, then turned to feature films in 1923. After a modest start with a couple of Rin Tin Tin action pictures, he scored an impressive success with *Are Parents People?* (1925) and subsequently was engaged to direct other sophisticated social comedies. At the height of his success in the mid-20s, he rivaled Lubitsch in the esteem of film critics. In the late 20s the quality of his films declined abruptly and inexplicably and his talkies were for the most part routine programmers. He directed several Laurel and Hardy features that were among the least funny of the duo's comedies.

FILMS: Shorts—*Rip & Stitch Tailors* (co-dir. with William H. Watson), *The Little Widow* (co-dir. with Bert Roach), *No Mother to Guide Him* (co-dir. with Erle C. Kenton) 1919; *Don't Weaken, Young Man's Fancy, He Loved Like He Lied* 1920; *The Night Before, Wedding Bells Out of Tune, Sweetheart Days, Call a Cop, The Goat* (co-dir., co-sc. with Buster Keaton) 1921; *Bright Eyes, The Blacksmith* (co-dir., co-sc. with Keaton), *Rice and Old Shoes, Christmas, Entertaining the Boss, Keep 'Em Home, Their First Vacation, Twin Husbands* 1922; *Fighting Blood* (12 one-reel episodes) 1923; *The Telephone Girl* (12 two-reel episodes) 1924. Features—*George Washington Jr., Find Your Man, The Lighthouse by the Sea* 1924; *On Thin Ice, After Business Hours, Are Parents People?, The Trouble with Wives, A Woman of the World* 1925; *The Grand Duchess and the Waiter, A Social Celebrity, Good and Naughty, The Show-Off, The Popular Sin* 1926; *Knockout Reilly, Breakfast at Sunrise* 1927; *Gentlemen Prefer Blondes, Sporting Goods, Beau Broadway* (also story), *The Fleet's In* 1928; *The Canary Murder Case, Side Street* (also story, co-sc.), *Night Parade* 1929; *Montana Moon, Dangerous Nan McGrew, Remote Control* (co-dir. with Nick Grinde), *The Boudoir Diplomat* 1930; *Goldie Gets Along, Olsen's Big Moment* 1933; *Crack-Up, Time Out for Romance, She Had to Eat, Born Reckless, Dangerously Yours* 1937; *A Trip to Paris, Safety in Numbers, Down on the Farm, Everybody's Baby* 1938; *The Jones Family in Hollywood, The Jones Family in Quick Millions, Hollywood Cavalcade* (one sequence only) 1939; *Young As You Feel, Meet the Missus* 1940; *The Beautiful Bachelor* 1941; *The Man in the Trunk, Over My Dead Body* 1942; *Two Weeks to Live, Jitterbugs, The Dancing Masters* 1943; *Swing Out the Blues, The Big Noise* 1944; *The Bullfighters* 1945; *Arthur Takes Over, Fighting Back* 1948.

Saint-Cyr, Renée. Actress. Born Marie-Louise Vittore, on Nov. 16, 1907, in Beausoleil, France. A leading star of French films of the 30s, she later played character parts. From the 50s occasionally also a producer. She has written a memoir, *Les Temps de Vivre.* She is the mother of film director Georges LAUTNER, in many of whose films she appeared in the 70s and early 80s.

FILMS INCLUDE: *Les Deux Orphelines, Toto* 1933; *Arlette et ses Papas, Le Dernier Milliardaire* 1934; *L'Ecole des Cocottes, La Valse royale* (Ger./Fr.) 1935; *La Valse éternelle* (Fr./Czech.), *Paris, Les Loups entre eux* 1936; *Les Perles de la Couronne/The Pearls of the Crown* 1937; *Prisons de Femmes/Marked Girls, The Strange Boarders* (UK) 1938; *Nuit de Décembre* 1939; *Rose Scarlatte* (It.) 1940; *La Symphonie fantastique* 1942; *Madame et le Mort, Marie-Martine, Retour de Flamme, Pierre et Jean* 1943; *Paméla* 1945; *Le Beau Voyage* 1947; *Fusillé à l'Aube/Secret Document—Vienna* (also prod.) 1950; *Capitaine Ardant* (also co-prod.) 1951; *Le Chevalier de la Nuit* (also co-prod.) 1954; *Si Paris nous etait conte* (as the Empress Eugenie) 1955; *Lafayette* 1961; *Fleur d'Epine* 1967; *On aura tout vu* 1976; *Ils sont fous ces Sorciers* 1978; *Le "Cowboy"* 1985.

St. Jacques, Raymond. Actor. *b.* James Arthur Johnson, Mar. 1, 1930, Hartford, Conn. *d.* 1990, of cancer. *ed.* Yale. He majored in psychology, intending to become a social worker, but was sidetracked by the theater. After touring with various productions, including Shakespeare, he moved to New York, where he worked as a dishwasher, houseboy, male model, and a Bloomingdale's salesman until he landed a role in an off-Broadway production in 1954. He studied at the Actors Studio and began getting meatier and more frequent roles on the stage ('The Blacks,' etc.) and on TV. He became established as one of the premier black performers of the American screen of the 60s and 70s. In 1973 he directed his first film, *Book of Numbers.* Tall (6' 3"), imposing, deep-voiced, and dignified, he helped break color barriers for blacks in television and films.

FILMS: *Black Like Me* 1964; *The Pawnbroker, Mister Moses* 1965; *Mister Buddwing* 1966; *The Comedians* 1967; *Madigan, The Green Berets, If He Hollers Let Him Go!, Uptight* 1968; *Change of Mind* 1969; *Cotton Comes to Harlem* 1970; *Cool Breeze, The Final Comedown, Come Back Charleston Blue* 1972; *Book of Numbers* (also dir., prod.) 1973; *Lost in the Stars* 1974; *Blast* 1976; *The Private Files of J. Edgar Hoover* (as Dr. Martin Luther King, Jr.) 1977; *Eyes of Laura Mars, Born Again* 1978; *Cuba Crossing* 1980; *The Evil That Men Do* 1984; *The Wild Pair* 1987; *They Live* 1988; *Glory* (as abolitionist Frederick Douglass) 1989; *Voodoo Dawn* 1990.

Saint James, Susan. Born Susan Miller, on Aug. 14, 1946, Los Angeles. *ed.* Connecticut Coll. for Women. A former model, she has appeared in a number of Hollywood films but is best known from her starring roles in the TV series 'The Name of the Game' (1968–71, Emmy 1969), 'McMillan and Wife' (1971–76), and 'Kate and Allie' (1984–87).

FILMS: *P.J., Where Angels Go. . . Trouble Follows!, What's So Bad About Feeling Good?, Jigsaw* 1968; *Outlaw Blues* 1977; *Love at First Bite* 1979; *How to Beat the High Cost of Living* 1980; *Carbon Copy* 1981; *Don't Cry It's Only Thunder* 1982.

St. John, Al ("Fuzzy"). Actor. *b.* Sept. 10, 1893, Santa Ana, Calif. *d.* 1963. A nephew of Roscoe ("Fatty") ARBUCKLE, he began his show business career as a boy trick bicyclist in a local theater. In 1913 he joined Sennett's Keystone comedies, where he played second banana to his uncle, Chaplin, and other top comics. He typically portrayed a country hick, wearing plaid shirts, oversize pants held up by suspenders, and a skull cap. When Arbuckle left Sennett in 1916, St. John followed him and continued supporting him in many of his independent comedies. He later starred in his own comedy shorts at Paramount and Fox, many of which he directed and wrote himself in the early 20s. In 1924 he moved to Educational and at the same time began playing character parts in feature films. Early in the sound era, St. John reunited with Arbuckle in a brief series of Vitaphone shorts at Warners. In the 30s, St. John began a new phase of his career as a grizzly sidekick of various cowboy stars in countless low-budget Westerns. One of the characters he played frequently was called "Fuzzy Q. Jones," hence his nickname. He retired from the screen in 1950. In all he appeared in many hundreds of films.

FILMS INCLUDE: *Algy on the Force, The Gangsters, The Waiters' Picnic* 1913; *Mabel's Strange Predicament, The Alarm, The Knockout, The Sky Pirate, Mabel's New Job, The Rounders, Tillie's Punctured Romance* 1914; *Dirty Work in a Laundry, Mabel's Willful Way, Our Dare Devil Chief, A Village Scandal, Fickle Fatty's Fall* 1915; *Fatty and Mabel Adrift, He Did and He Didn't, Bright Lights, His Wife's Mistake, The Other Man* 1916; *Butcher Boy, A Country Hero, A Reckless Romeo* 1917; *Moonshine, The Bellboy* 1918; *Speed* (also dir., sc.) 1920; *The Slicker* (also dir.), *Fast and Furious* 1921; *The City Chap* (also dir.), *The Village Sheik* (also dir.) 1922; *Young and Dumb* (also dir.), *The Salesman* (also dir.) 1923; *Stupid but Brave* (also dir., sc.), *Love Mania* (also dir., sc.), *The Garden of Weeds* 1924; *Curses* 1925; *Pink Elephants* 1926; *American Beauty, Casey Jones* 1927; *Hello Cheyenne, Painted Post* 1928; *She Goes to War, The Dance of Life* 1929; *Hell Harbor, The Land of Missing Men* 1930; *The Painted Desert* 1931; *Fame Street* 1932; *The Wanderer of the Wasteland* 1935; *The Outcasts of Poker Flat, Saturday's Heroes* 1937; *Call of the Yukon* 1938; *Billy the Kid's Fighting Pals* 1940; *Fuzzy Settles Down* 1944; *Frontier Revenge* 1948; *Outlaw Country* 1949.

St. John, Jill. Actress. Born Jill Oppenheim, on Aug. 19, 1940, in Los Angeles. *ed.* UCLA. Vivacious leading lady of Hollywood films of the 60s. Began her acting career on radio at age six. A well-built redhead, she is typically cast as an empty-headed broad, but in reality she boasts a colorful personality and a very high IQ. She dated several prominent men, including Henry Kissinger. Her four marriages included singer Jack Jones (1967–69) and actor Robert WAGNER (from 1990).

FILMS INCLUDE: *Thunder in the East* (bit) 1953; *Summer Love* 1958; *Holiday for Lovers* 1959; *The Lost World* 1960; *The Roman Spring of Mrs. Stone* 1961; *Tender Is the Night* 1962; *Come Blow Your Horn, Who's Minding the Store?, Who's Been Sleeping in My Bed?* 1963; *Honeymoon Hotel* 1964; *The Liquidator* (UK), *The Oscar* 1966; *Tony Rome, Banning* 1967; *Diamonds Are Forever* (UK) 1971; *Sitting Target* (UK) 1972; *The Concrete Jungle* 1982; *The Act* 1984; *The Player* (cameo) 1992.

Sakall, S. Z. ("Cuddles"). Actor. *b.* Eugene Gero Szakall, Feb. 2, 1884, Budapest. *d.* 1955. Character comedian of Central European stage and screen (as Szöke Szakall) and, from 1940, Hollywood films. Fractured English, flabby jowls, and an excitable personality were his stock-in-trade in a long list of endearing portrayals. He enjoyed great popularity in early German talkies, especially musicals and comedies, but was forced to leave Germany after the advent of the Nazis, and for several years appeared in Hungarian and Austrian films. He arrived in Hollywood after the outbreak of WW II and quickly became one of the American screen's most beloved light supporting players, appearing mainly in musicals, often as a bewildered impresario.

FILMS INCLUDE: In Hungary—*Suszterherceg* 1916. In Germany—*Zwei Herzen im 3/4 Takt/Two Hearts in Waltz Time, Susanne macht Ordnung, Komm mit mir zum Rendezvous/Rendez-Vous* 1930; *Der Hampelmann, Ihre Majestät die Liebe, Walzerparadies, Der unbekannte Gast* 1931; *Melodie der Liebe, Eine Stadt steht Kopf, Kaiserwalzer, Gräfin Mariza* 1932; *Eine Frau wie Du* 1933. In Hungary—*Skandal in Budapest/Romance in Budapest* (Hung./Ger.) 1933; *Anything for the Woman* 1934; *Keep Smiling* 1935. In Austria—*Das Tagebuch der Geliebten/Marie Bashkirtseff/The Affairs of Maupassant* (Aus./It.) 1935. In the US—*It's a Date, Spring Parade* 1940; *That Night in Rio, The Devil and Miss Jones* 1941; *Ball of Fire, Yankee Doodle Dandy, Broadway, Seven Sweethearts* 1942; *Casablanca, Wintertime, The Human Comedy, Thank Your Lucky Stars* 1943; *Shine On Harvest Moon* 1944; *Wonder Man, Christmas in Connecticut, The Dolly Sisters, San Antonio* 1945; *Two Guys from Milwaukee, Never Say Goodbye, The Time the Place and the Girl* 1946; *Cynthia* 1947; *April Showers, Romance on the High Seas* 1948; *My Dream Is Yours, In the Good Old Summertime, It's a Great Feeling, Oh You Beautiful Doll* 1949; *Montana, The Daughter of Rosie O'Grady, Tea for Two* 1950; *Lullaby of Broadway, Painting the Clouds with Sunshine* 1951; *It's a Big Country* 1952; *Small Town Girl* 1953; *The Student Prince* 1954.

Saks, Gene. Director. Born on Nov. 8, 1921, in New York City. *ed.* Cornell. A former actor, he trained at the Dramatic Workshop of the New School for Social Research and in the late 40s became active off Broadway, forming a co-operative troupe at the Cherry Lane Theatre. He later joined the Actors Studio and appeared on Broadway in both classic and modern plays, as well as in TV dramas. He began directing for Broadway in 1963 and four years later extended his activity to Hollywood. His films have generally been screen adaptations of successful stage comedies and musicals. He won Tony Awards for his direction of *I Love My Wife, Brighton Beach Memoirs,* and *Biloxi Blues*. He is divorced from actress Beatrice Arthur.

FILMS: As actor—*A Thousand Clowns* 1965; *The Prisoner of Second Avenue* 1975; *The One and Only* 1978; *Lovesick* 1983; *The Goodbye People* 1984; *Funny* (doc.) 1989; *I.Q., Nobody's Fool* 1994. As director—*Barefoot in the Park* 1967; *The Odd Couple* 1968; *Cactus Flower* 1969; *Last of the Red Hot Lovers* 1972; *Mame* 1974; *Brighton Beach Memoirs* 1986; *Tchin-Tchin* (It.) 1991; *A Fine Romance* (It./US) 1992.

Salce, Luciano. Director. *b.* Sept. 25, 1922, Rome. *d.* 1989. A graduate of the Accademia Nazionale d'Arte Drammatica in Rome, he began directing stage plays in 1947. He spent the early 50s in Brazil, where he served as artistic director of the Teatro Brasiliero de Comédia, produced a number of plays, and appeared as an actor in such local films as *Angela* (1952), *Uma Pulga na Balanca,* and *Floradas na Serra* (both 1953). Returning to Italy, he directed for the stage, radio, and TV before becoming a feature film director in 1960. A competent technician, he worked in a variety of genres, with varying results. From the early 60s he acted in several of his own films as well as in films of other directors.

FILMS: *Le Pillole di Ercole* 1960; *Il Federale/The Fascist* (also co-sc., act.) 1961; *La Voglia Matta/Crazy Desire* (also co-sc., act.), *La Cuccagna/The Land of Plenty* (also co-sc., act.) 1962; *Le Ore dell'Amore/The Hours of Love* (also co-sc., act.), *Le Monachine/The Little Nuns* 1963; *Alta Infedeltà/High Infidelity* ("The Victim" episode; It./Fr.) 1964; *Oggi Domani e Dopodomani/Kiss the Other Sheik* ("The Blonde Wife" episode; also co-story, co-sc., act.), *Slalom* (It./Fr./Eg.) 1965; *El Greco* (also co-sc.; It./Fr.), *Le Fate/The Queens* ("Queen Sabina" episode; also co-sc.; It./Fr.) 1966; *Ti ho Sposato per Allegria/I Married You for Fun* (also co-sc.) 1967; *La Pecora Nera* (also co-sc.), *Colpo di Stato* (also co-sc.) 1969; *Il Prof. Dott. Guido Tersilli primario della Clinica Villa Celeste Convenzionata con le Mutue* 1970; *Basta Guardarla* (also co-sc., act.), *Il Provinciale* 1971; *Il Sindicalista* 1972; *Io e lui* 1973; *Alla mis cara Mamanel Giorno del su compleanno* 1974; *Tragico Fantorri/Fantorri, L'Anatra all'Arancia/Duck in Orange Sauce* 1975; *Il Secondo Tragico Fantorri* 1976; *La Presidentessa, Il Bel Paese* 1977; *Dove vai in Vacanza?* (one episode) 1978; *Professor Kranz Tedesco di Germania* (It./Braz.) 1979; *Riavanti. . . marschi* 1980; *Vieni avanti Cretino* 1982; *Vediamoci chiaro* 1984; *Quelli del Casco* 1988.

Sale, Richard. Director, screenwriter. *b.* Dec. 17, 1911, in New York City. *d.* 1993. *ed.* Washington and Lee. Prolific short-story writer and novelist, he directed and wrote routine light films from the mid-40s, with one notable exception—the tightly directed, tense drama *Seven Waves Away/Abandon Ship!* (1957), which he made in England. At one time married to Anita Loos.

FILMS INCLUDE: As director (complete)—*Spoilers of the North* 1947; *Campus Honeymoon* (also co-sc.) 1948; *A Ticket to Tomahawk* (also co-story, co-so.), *I'll Get By* (also co-sc.) 1950; *Meet Me After the Show* (also co-sc.), *Half Angel, Let's Make It Legal* 1951; *My Wife's Best Friend* 1952; *The Girl*

Next Door 1953; *Fire Over Africa* 1954; *Gentlemen Marry Brunettes* (also co-prod., co-sc.) 1955; *Seven Waves Away/Abandon Ship!* (also sc.; UK) 1957. As screenwriter only—*Strange Cargo* (novel basis only) 1940; *Rendezvous with Annie* 1946; *Northwest Outpost* 1947; *The Dude Goes West* 1948; *Mother Is a Freshman, Mr. Belvedere Goes to College* 1949; *When Willie Comes Marching Home* 1950; *Let's Do It Again* 1951; *Suddenly!, The French Line, Woman's World* 1954; *Around the World in 80 Days* (co-sc.) 1956; *Torpedo Run* 1958; *The Oscar* (novel basis only) 1966; *The White Buffalo* (from his own novel) 1977; *Assassination* 1987.

Salkind, Alexander. Producer. *b.* ca. 1915, in Gdansk, Poland (at times Danzig, Germany), of Russian-Jewish descent. *d.* 1997. He was raised in Berlin, where his father, Michael (later Miguel) produced films, and later accompanied his father to Cuba for production ventures and remained in Latin America. Returning to Europe in the late 50s, he produced a number of high-budget, multinational spectaculars, often in collaboration with his son, Ilya (*b.* 1948, Mexico City).

FILMS INCLUDE: *Austerlitz/The Battle of Austerlitz* 1960; *The Trial* 1962; *Ballad in Blue/Blues for Lovers* 1965; *Cervantes/Young Rebel* 1967; *The Light at the Edge of the World* 1971; *Kill!/Kill Kill Kill, Bluebeard* 1972; *The Three Musketeers* 1974; *The Four Musketeers* 1975; *The Prince and the Pauper/Crossed Swords* 1977; *Superman* 1978; *Superman II* 1981; *Superman III* 1983; *Supergirl* 1984; *Santa Claus: The Movie* 1985.

Salkow, Sidney. Director. Born on June 16, 1909, in New York City. *ed.* CCNY; Columbia; Harvard Law School. He directed several Broadway plays in the early 30s before arriving in Hollywood as a screenwriter in 1936. Within months he switched to film directing and for the next three decades turned out numerous second features, mainly of the action variety. His most ambitious and rewarding effort was *The Adventures of Martin Eden* (1942), from the Jack London seafaring tale. Most of his other films have been routine entertainment fare.

FILMS: *Four Days' Wonder, Girl Overboard, Behind the Mike* 1937; *That's My Story, The Night Hawk, Storm Over Bengal* 1938; *Fighting Thoroughbreds, Woman Doctor, Street of Missing Men, Zero Hour, She Married a Cop, Flight at Midnight* 1939; *Cafe Hostess/Street of Missing Women, The Lone Wolf Strikes, The Lone Wolf Meets a Lady, Girl from God's Country* 1940; *The Lone Wolf Keeps a Date* (also sc.), *The Lone Wolf Takes a Chance* (also sc.), *Time Out for Rhythm, Tillie the Toiler* 1941; *The Adventures of Martin Eden, Flight Lieutenant* 1942; *City Without Men, The Boy from Stalingrad* 1943; *Faithful in My Fashion* 1946; *Millie's Daughter, Bulldog Drummond at Bay* 1947; *Sword of the Avenger* (also prod.) 1948; *La Strada Buia/Fugitive Lady* (co-dir. with Marino Girolami; It.), *La Rivale dell'Imperatrice* (co-dir. with Jacopo Comin; It.) 1949; *Shadow of the Eagle* (UK) 1950; *Scarlet Angel, The Golden Hawk, The Pathfinder* 1952; *Prince of Pirates, Jack McCall—Desperado, Raiders of the Seven Seas* (also prod., sc.) 1953; *Sitting Bull* (also co-sc.) 1954; *Robber's Roost* (also co-sc.), *Las Vegas Shakedown, Toughest Man Alive* 1955; *Gun Brothers, The Long Rifle and the Tomahawk* (co-dir. with Sam Newfield) 1956; *The Iron Sheriff, Gun Duel in Durango, Chicago Confidential* 1957; *The Big Night* 1960; *Twice Told Tales* 1963; *The Quick Gun, The Last Man on Earth, Blood on the Arrow* 1964; *The Great Sioux Massacre* 1965; *The Murder Game* 1966.

Salmi, Albert. Actor. *b.* Mar. 11, 1928, Coney Island, Brooklyn, N.Y. *d.* 1990. Beefy character player of the American stage, screen, and TV. He took up acting after WW II service, receiving his training at the Dramatic Workshop of the American Theater Wing and at the Actors Studio. He appeared in live TV drama and numerous off-Broadway productions and in 1955 scored a personal triumph on Broadway in 'Bus Stop.' He appeared in many films intermittently from the late 60s, but it was TV that kept him busiest. Once (1956–63) married to actress Peggy Ann GARNER, Salmi was found dead next to the body of his estranged wife, Roberta, in Spokane, Wash., in April of 1990. A police investigation suggested the actor had shot his wife, then himself, in an apparent murder-suicide.

FILMS INCLUDE: *The Brothers Karamazov* (as Smerdyakov), *The Bravados* 1958; *The Unforgiven, Wild River* 1960; *The Outrage* 1964; *The Flim-Flam Man, Hour of the Gun, The Ambushers* 1967; *Three Guns for Texas* 1968; *Lawman, Something Big* 1971; *The Legend of Earl Durand, Truckin'* 1975; *Black Oak Conspiracy, Moonshine County Express, Viva Knievel, Empire of the Ants* 1977; *The Sweet Creek County War* 1979; *Brubaker, Caddyshack* 1980; *Dragonslayer* 1981; *Love Child* 1982; *The Guns and the Fury* 1983; *Hard to Hold* 1984; *Born American* 1986; *Breaking In* 1989.

Salomon, Mikael. Director of cinematography. Born in 1945 in Copenhagen, Denmark. A prominent cinematographer in Denmark, he established himself in the US with several impressive spectacles.

FILMS INCLUDE: *Fantasterne* 1967; *Mig og min lillebror og Boelle* 1970; *Et doegn med Ilse, Welcome to the Club, Hvorfor goer de det, Mine Soestres Hoern, Naar de Club* 1971; *Motorvejdpaa Sengekanten, Rektor paa sengekanten, Z.P.G.* (addnl. phot. only) 1972; *The Hottest Show in Town* 1974; *Hjerter er Trumf, Kun Sandheden, Violer er bla/Violets Are Blue* 1975; *Stroemer* 1976; *Elvis! Elvis!, Pas paa ryggen professor* 1977; *Slaegten/The Heritage* 1979; *The Flying Devils* 1985; *Barndommens gade, The Wolf at the Door* 1986; *Peter von Scholten, Time Out* (aerial phot.) 1977; *Stealing Heaven, Torch Song Trilogy, Zelly and Me* 1988; *The Abyss* (also underwater lighting superv.), *Always* 1989; *Arachnophobia* (also Gyrosphere oper.) 1990; *Backdraft* 1991; *Far and Away* 1992.

Salt, Waldo. Screenwriter. *b.* Oct. 18, 1914, Chicago. *d.* 1987. *ed.* Stanford U. A former college drama and music instructor, he began writing scripts for Hollywood films in the late 30s but was blacklisted in 1951 after refusing to testify on Communist affiliations before the House Un-American Activities Committee. It wasn't until the early 60s that he was able to resume his film work. Working alone or in collaboration, he added a number of important films to his screen credits. He won an Academy Award for the screenplay of *Midnight Cowboy* (1969) and shared another for *Coming Home* (1978). He was also Oscar-nominated for *Serpico* (1973). His daughter, Jennifer Salt (*b.* Sept. 4, 1944, Los Angeles), played appealing leads in several Hollywood films of the late 60s and early 70s.

FILMS: *The Shopworn Angel* 1938; *The Wild Man of Borneo* 1941; *Tonight We Raid Calais* 1943; *Mr. Winkle Goes to War* 1944; *Rachel and the Stranger* 1948; *The Flame and the Arrow* 1950; *M* (addnl. dial. only) 1951; *Taras Bulba* 1962; *Flight from Ashiya, Wild and Wonderful* 1964; *Midnight Cowboy* 1969; *The Gang That Couldn't Shoot Straight* 1971; *Serpico* 1973; *The Day of the Locust* 1975; *Coming Home* 1978.

Salter, Hans J. Composer, music director. *b.* Jan. 14, 1896, in Vienna. *d.* 1994. A graduate of the Academy of Music of Vienna, he was music director at that city's Volksoper and later at the State Opera in Berlin. He entered films as composer-conductor for UFA in 1929. In the US from 1937, he scored or orchestrated some 150 films for Universal in the following three decades, earning four Academy Award nominations.

FILMS INCLUDE: *Young Fugitive* 1938; *Big Guy* 1939; *Black Friday, Enemy Agent, First Love, Seven Sinners, Spring Parade* 1940; *The Black Cat, The Wolf Man, Hold That Ghost,*

It Started with Eve 1941; *Pittsburgh, The Spoilers* 1942; *The Amazing Mrs. Holiday, His Butler's Sister, Son of Dracula* 1943; *House of Frankenstein, The Merry Monahans, Christmas Holiday* 1944; *Scarlet Street, This Love of Ours* 1945; *Magnificent Doll* 1946; *The Web* 1947; *The Sign of the Ram* 1948; *The Reckless Moment* 1949; *Tomahawk* 1951; *Bend of the River* 1952; *The 5,000 Fingers of Dr. T* 1953; *The Creature from the Black Lagoon, The Far Country, Sign of the Pagan* 1954; *The Far Horizons, Man Without a Star* 1955; *Autumn Leaves* 1956; *The Incredible Shrinking Man, The Tall Stranger* 1957; *Come September* 1961; *If a Man Answers* 1962; *Showdown* 1963; *Bedtime Story* 1964; *Beau Geste* 1966.

Saltzman, Harry. Producer. *b.* Oct. 27, 1915, in St. John, Canada. *d.* 1994. In the US from infancy, he entered the film field in the mid-40s and struck it rich in Britain in the 60s with the James Bond series, which he co-produced through 1974 with his partner Albert R. BROCCOLI through their Eon Productions company. The partnership dissolved in the mid-70s, with Broccoli retaining the rights to the lucrative Bond series.

FILMS INCLUDE (as producer or co-producer): *The Iron Petticoat* 1956; *Look Back in Anger* 1959; *The Entertainer* (exec. prod.), *Saturday Night and Sunday Morning* (exec. prod.) 1960; *Dr. No* 1962; *From Russia with Love* 1963; *Goldfinger* 1964; *The Ipcress File, Thunderball* 1965; *Funeral in Berlin* 1966; *You Only Live Twice, Billion Dollar Brain* 1967; *Play Dirty* 1968; *The Battle of Britain, On Her Majesty's Secret Service* 1969; *Diamonds Are Forever* 1971; *Live and Let Die* 1973; *The Man with the Golden Gun* 1974; *Nijinsky* (exec. prod.) 1980.

Salvatori, Renato. Actor. *b.* Mar. 20, 1933, Porte dei Marmi, Italy. *d.* 1987. Ruggedly handsome leading man and supporting player of Italian films and international co-productions. The son of a Carrara marble laborer, he banked on a sincere expression and robust physique in portraying earthy, often gruff, working-class characters. Memorable as the ambitious boxer brother in Visconti's *Rocco and His Brothers* (1960) and as the domineering husband in De Sica's *Brief Vacation* (1973). In 1962 he married actress Annie GIRARDOT.

FILMS INCLUDE: *Le Ragazze di Piazza di Spagna/Three Girls from Rome* 1952; *Poveri ma Belli/Poor but Beautiful* 1956; *Marisa la Civetta, Mariti in Città* 1957; *I Soliti Ignoti/Big Deal on Madonna Street, Nella Città l'Inferno/. . . And the Wild Wild Women/Hell in the City* 1958; *Audace Colpo dei Soliti Ignoti/Fiasco in Milan* 1959; *Era Notte a Roma, Rocco e i suoi Fratelli/Rocco and His Brothers, La Ciociara/Two Women* 1960; *Smog, Il Disordine/Disorder* (It./Fr.) 1962; *Le Glaive et la Balance/Two Are Guilty* (Fr./It.), *Les Grands Chemins/Of Flesh and Blood* (Fr./It.), *I Compagni/The Organizer* (It./Fr./Yug.) 1963; *Tre Notti d'Amore/Three Nights of Love* 1964; *Bel Ami 2000/100 Ragazze per un Playboy/How to Seduce a Playboy* (Aus./It./Fr.) 1966; *Z* (Fr./Alg.), *Quemada!/Burn!* (It./Fr.) 1969; *The Light at the Edge of the World* (US), *Le Casse/The Burglars* (Fr.) 1971; *Etat de Siège/State of Siege* (Fr.), *Una Breva Vacanza/A Brief Vacation* 1973; *Flic Story* (Fr.), *Le Gitan* (Fr.) 1975; *La Dernière Femme* (Fr./It.), *Todo Modo* 1976; *Armaguedon, Le Soupçon* (Fr./It.) 1977; *Ernesto* 1978; *La Luna* 1979; *La Tragedia di un Uomo ridiolo/The Tragedy of a Ridiculous Man* 1981.

Samoilova (or **Samoylova), Tatyana.** Actress. Born on May 4, 1934, in Leningrad. The daughter of a distinguished stage actor, she took up ballet as a child and on leaving school was trained in drama at the Vakhtangov Theatre in Moscow. She then joined the Mayakovsky Theater. She began appearing in films in the mid-50s and gained international fame as the heroine of *The Cranes Are Flying* (1957). Her father, Evgeny (or Yevgeni) Samoilov (or Samoylov), is primarily a stage actor, but he has played heroic roles in occasional Soviet films, most notably the lead in Alexander Dovzhenko's *Shchors/Shors* (1939).

FILMS INCLUDE: *The Mexican* 1956; *The Cranes Are Flying* 1957; *The Letter That Was Never Sent* 1960; *Alba Regia* (Hung.) 1962; *Italiani Brava Gente/Italiano Brava Gente* (It./USSR) 1964; *Anna Karenina* (title role) 1967; *No Return* 1974.

sample print. A composite print submitted by the lab for final approval before release prints are made.

Samsonov, Samson. Director. Born Samson Edelstein, in 1921, in Novozybkov, Russia. A former stage actor and director, he trained at the Moscow Film School under Sergei GERASIMOV. His first film, *The Grasshopper,* was internationally acclaimed as an excellent screen adaptation of Chekhov and was awarded a Silver Prize at the 1955 Venice Festival. However, his later work drew far less attention, although *The Optimistic Tragedy* (1963) won a special prize at Cannes. He was appointed executive producer at the Mosfilm studios. His wife, Margaret Volodina, appeared in several of his films.

FILMS: *The Grasshopper, Behind the Shop Window* 1955; *Miles of Fire* 1957; *As Old as the Century* 1960; *The Optimistic Tragedy* 1963; *The Three Sisters* 1964; *The Arena* 1968.

Sanda, Dominique. Actress. Born Dominique Varaigne, in 1948, in Paris. Beautiful, talented leading lady of French and international films. Married at 15 and divorced at 17, she was a successful fashion model before making her auspicious screen debut in Robert Bresson's *Une Femme douce* (1969). She has since starred in films of such directors as Bernardo Bertolucci, Vittorio De Sica, John Frankenheimer, John Huston, Luchino Visconti, and Mauro Bolognini. She shared the best actress award at Cannes for *Eredità Ferramonti* (1976) and shares a child with actor Christian MARQUAND.

FILMS INCLUDE: *Une Femme douce* 1969; *Erste Liebe/First Love* (Switz./Ger.), *Il Conformista/The Conformist* (It./Fr.) 1970; *Il Giardino dei Finzi-Contini/The Garden of the Finzi-Continis* (It./Ger.), *Sans Mobile Apparent/Without Apparent Motive* 1971; *L'Impossible Objet/Impossible Object, The Mackintosh Man* (UK) 1973; *Steppenwolf* (UK/It./Ger.) 1974; *Gruppo di Famiglia in un Interno/Conversation Piece* (It./Fr.) 1975; *Novecento/1900* (It.), *Eredità Ferramonti/The Inheritance* (It.) 1976; *Oltre il Bene e il Male* (It./Fr./Ger.), *Damnation Alley* (US) 1977; *Remember My Name* (US), *Utopia* 1978; *Le Voyage en Douce* 1980; *Caboblanco* (US) 1981; *Une Chambre en Ville/A Room in Town* 1982; *Le Matelot 512* 1984; *Corps et biens* 1986; *Les Mendiants* 1988; *Guerreros y Cautivas/Warriors and Captives* (Arg./Fr./Switz.) 1989; *Yo la peor de todas/I The Worst of Them All* (Arg.) 1990; *Der Grun Heinrich/Green Henry* (Sw.), *Nobody's Children* 1994.

Sanders, Denis. Director. *b.* Jan. 21, 1925, New York City. *d.* 1987. *ed.* Yale; UCLA. With brother Terry Sanders (*b.* Dec. 30, 1931, N.Y.C.) as producer, co-writer, and cameraman, he directed a two-reel short to fulfill a film course requirement at UCLA. The film, *A Time Out of War* (1954), based on a Civil War incident, went on to win an Academy Award and first prizes at the Venice and Edinburgh Festivals. Venturing into features, the brothers collaborated on the screenplay of Raoul Walsh's *The Naked and the Dead* (1958), then split responsibilities on several films, Denis directing and Terry producing. The National Board of Review listed their *War Hunt,* a Korean War story, among the Ten Best Films of 1962. But their other features fizzled and they soon parted, retreating separately into documentaries and TV. Denis won a second Oscar for the documentary short *Czechoslovakia 1968* (1969).

FEATURE FILMS: *Crime and Punishment USA* 1959; *War Hunt* 1962; *One Man's Way, Shock Treatment* 1964; *Elvis—That's the Way It Is* (feature-length doc. on Presley) 1970; *Soul to Soul* (feature-length doc. on soul and gospel singers' tour of Ghana) 1971; *Invasion of the Bee Girls* 1973.

Sanders, George. Actor *b.* July 3, 1906, St. Petersburg, Russia, to British parents. *d.* 1972. The family returned to England during the Russian Revolution, and George, after studies at Brighton College and Manchester Technical College, went into the textile, then the tobacco business. He made his stage debut early in the 30s and by the middle of the decade was acting in British films. In 1936 he went to Hollywood, where he soon became an important star, playing both leading men and suave cads. During WW II he often played Nazis but also starred as the hero of "The Saint" and "The Falcon" adventure series. Eventually he managed to terminate his Falcon period by turning the role over to his brother, Tom CONWAY. Sanders played his first meaty part as the cynical hero of *The Moon and Sixpence* and reached another career landmark eight years later as the venomous drama critic in *All About Eve,* a role for which he won an Academy Award as best supporting actor.

In the 60s he appeared mostly in European films. He was married four times. His second wife (1949–57) was Zsa Zsa GABOR; his third (1958–67), Benita HUME; and fourth (briefly in 1970) Zsa Zsa's sister, Magda Gabor. Autobiography: *Memoirs of a Professional Cad* (1960).

FILMS: In the UK—*Find the Lady, Strange Cargo, The Man Who Could Work Miracles, Dishonour Bright* 1936. In the US—*Lloyds of London, Love Is News, Slave Ship, The Lady Escapes, Lancer Spy* 1937; *International Settlement, Four Men and a Prayer* 1938; *Mr. Moto's Last Warning, The Saint Strikes Back* (title role), *Confessions of a Nazi Spy, The Saint in London* (title role), *The Outsider* (UK), *So This Is London* (UK), *Nurse Edith Cavell, Allegheny Uprising* 1939; *Green Hell, The Saint's Double Trouble* (dual title role), *Rebecca* (as Jack Favell), *The House of the Seven Gables* (as Jaffrey Pyncheon), *The Saint Takes Over* (title role), *Foreign Correspondent, Bitter Sweet, The Son of Monte Cristo* 1940; *The Saint in Palm Springs* (title role), *Rage in Heaven, Man Hunt, The Gay Falcon* (title role), *Sundown, A Date with the Falcon* (title role) 1941; *Son of Fury, The Falcon Takes Over* (title role), *Her Cardboard Lover, Tales of Manhattan, The Falcon's Brother* (last as the Falcon), *The Moon and Sixpence* (as Charles Strickland, modeled after Paul Gauguin), *The Black Swan* 1942; *Quiet Please—Murder, They Came to Blow Up America, This Land Is Mine, Appointment in Berlin, Paris After Dark* 1943; *The Lodger, Action in Arabia, Summer Storm* 1944; *Hangover Square, The Picture of Dorian Gray* (as Lord Henry Wotton), *The Strange Affair of Uncle Harry* 1945; *A Scandal in Paris* (as François Eugene Vidocq, the Paris chief of detectives who turned to crime), *The Strange Woman* 1946; *The Private Affairs of Bel Ami* (title role), *The Ghost and Mrs. Muir, Lured, Forever Amber* (as King Charles II) 1947; *The Fan* (as Lord Darlington), *Samson and Delilah* 1949; *Black Jack/Captain Blackjack* (UK/Fr./Sp.), *All About Eve* 1950; *I Can Get It for You Wholesale, The Light Touch* 1951; *Ivanhoe* (as Sir Brian de Bois-Guillbert; UK/US), *Assignment—Paris* 1952; *Call Me Madam, Viaggio in Italia/The Lonely Woman* (It.) 1953; *Witness to Murder, King Richard and the Crusaders* (as Richard I; US/UK) 1954; *Jupiter's Darling* (as Fabius Maximus), *Moonfleet, The Scarlet Coat, The King's Thief* (again as Charles II) 1955; *Never Say Goodbye, While the City Sleeps, That Certain Feeling, Death of a Scoundrel* 1956; *The Seventh Sin* 1957; *The Whole Truth* (UK), *From the Earth to the Moon* 1958; *That Kind of Woman, A Touch of Larceny* (UK), *Solomon and Sheba* (as Adonijah) 1959; *Bluebeard's Ten Honeymoons* (as Landru; UK), *The Last Voyage, Cone of Silence/Trouble in the Sky* (UK), *Village of the Damned* (UK) 1960; *Cinque Ore in Contanti/Five Golden Hours* (It./UK), *The Rebel/Call Me Genius* (UK) 1961; *Operation Snatch* (UK), *In Search of the Castaways* (UK/US) 1962; *Cairo* (US/UK), *Ecco/Mondo di Notte* (on-screen narrator; It.) 1963; *L'Intigo/Dark Purpose* (It./Fr./US), *The Cracksman* (UK), *A Shot in the Dark* (US/UK), *The Golden Head* (Hun.) 1964; *The Amorous Adventures of Moll Flanders* (UK) 1965; *Trunk to Cairo* (Isr./Ger.), *The Quiller Memorandum* (UK/US) 1966; *Warning Shot, Good Times, The Jungle Book* (v/o) 1967; *Rey di Africa/One Step to Hell* (Sp./It./US) 1968; *The Candy Man, The Best House in London* (UK), *The Body Stealers* (UK/US) 1969; *The Kremlin Letter* 1970; *Psychomania/The Death Wheelers* 1972.

Sanders-Brahms, Helma. Director, screenwriter. Born Helma Sanders, on Nov. 20, 1940, in Emden, Germany. A prominent figure in the New German Cinema. Raised by a fiercely independent mother, a descendant of composer Johannes Brahms, while her father was fighting the war, she showed an early interest in theater and film. After two years of acting training in Hanover, she determined that her future was in directing and enrolled at Cologne University for four years of drama and literature studies. She supported herself as a factory worker, sales clerk, and nurse's aide, work experience that she would later reach back to in the context of her films. After graduating, she worked for a year as a teacher, then joined a Cologne TV station as an announcer and interviewer on cultural programs. It was in German television that Sanders-Brahms began her career as a director in 1970, at first with shorts and documentaries, then with network-sponsored features. Before long she began producing her own films and gained increasing recognition at home and abroad, while winning prizes at international festivals. Though not formally affiliated with any group, Sanders-Brahms (she added her mother's maiden name to avoid confusion with another New German Cinema woman director, Helke Sander [*b.* 1937]) echoes in her films the concerns of the radical left. Among other themes, her films have dealt with urban alienation, technological dehumanization, and feminist issues. In *Shirin's Wedding* (1976) and other films she empathized with the plight of Germany's Turkish migrant workers and in her best known work, *Germany, Pale Mother* (1980), she reached back to memories of her own childhood to explore mother-daughter relations against the harrowing background of WW II and its aftermath. She writes all of her own scripts and has herself produced several of her films.

FEATURE FILMS (as director-screenwriter): *Gewalt/Violence* 1971; *Der Angestellte/The Employee* 1972; *Die letzten Tage von Gomorrah/The Last Days of Gomorrah, Erdbeben in Chile/Earthquake in Chile* 1974; *Unter dem Pflaster ist der Strand/The Sand Under the Pavement* 1975; *Shirins Hochzeit/Shirin's Wedding* 1976; *Heinrich* 1977; *Deutschland bleiche Mutter/Germany Pale Mother* 1980; *Die Berührte/No Mercy No Future/No Exit No Panic* 1981; *Flügel und Fesseln/L'Avenir d'Emilie/The Future of Emily* (Ger./Fr.) 1984; *Laputa* 1986; *Felix* 1987; *Geteilte Liebe/Divided Love* 1988.

Sandrelli, Stefanià. Actress. Born in 1946, in Viareggio, Italy. Sexy leading lady of Italian films and international co-productions since the early 60s. A former dancer and beauty-contest winner, she proved to be an instinctive actress with a natural capacity to project both innocence and sensuality. She played some of her best roles in films of Germi, Monicelli, Bertolucci, and Scola.

FILMS INCLUDE: *Gioventu di Notte, Il Federale/The Fascist, Divorzio all'Italiana/Divorce—Italian Style* 1961; *Les Vièrges* (Fr./It.), *La Bella di Lodi* 1962; *Seddotta e Abbandonata/*

Seduced and Abandoned, La Chance et l'Amour (Fr./It.) 1964; *Tendre Voyou/Tender Scoundrel* (Fr./It.) 1966; *L'Immorale/The Climax/Too Much for One Man* 1967; *Partner* 1968; *Il Conformista/The Conformist* 1970; *La Tarantola del Ventro Nero/The Black Belly of the Tarantula* 1972; *Alfredo Alfredo* 1973; *Delitto d'Amore* 1974; *C'Eravamo tanto Amati/We All Loved Each Other So Much* 1975; *Police Python 357* (Fr.), *Novecento/1900, Le Voyage de Noces* (Fr.) 1976; *Donna in Guerra, Quelle Strane Occasioni, Tra Moglie e Marito* 1977; *Io sono mia, Dove vai in Vacanza?* 1978; *L'Ingorgo—una Storia impossibile/Traffic Jam/Bottleneck* 1979; *La Terrazza/The Terrace* 1980; *La Disubbidienza* 1981; *Bello mio bellezza mia* 1982; *La Chiave/The Key* 1983; *Vacanza di Natale, Una Donna allo Specchio/Woman in the Mirror, Magic Moments* 1984; *Segretti Segretti/Secrets Secrets, L'Attenzione* (It) 1985; *Speriamo che sia Femmina/Let's Hope It's a Girl* 1936; *Gli occhiali d'oro, La Famiglia/The Family, Noyade Interdite* (Fr./It.) 1987; *Il Piccolo Diavolo/The Little Devil* 1988; *Lo Zio indegno/The Sleazy Uncle* 1989; *Il Male oscuro/The Obscure Illness, Evelina e i suoi figli/Evelina and Her Sons, L'Africana/The Woman from Africa* 1990; *Per Amore, Solo per Amore, Of Love and Shadows* 1994; *The Nymph* 1996; *Nirvana* 1997.

Sandrich, Mark. Director. *b.* Aug. 26, 1900, New York City. *d.* 1945. A graduate of Columbia, he entered films in 1922 as a prop man and, after working his way up through several studio departments, began directing comedy shorts in 1927, including Lupino Lane two-reelers. He made his debut as a feature director the following year, but his promotion coincided with the technically complex arrival of sound, and after completing only two productions he was returned to shorts. When one of these, *So This Is Harris,* won an Oscar in the 1932–33 ceremony, he was once again entrusted with features. Following several routine productions, he hit his stride with several memorable Astaire-Rogers musicals. He produced all his films from 1940 on. He died during the production of *Blue Skies* (1946), which was completed by and credited to Stuart Heisler.

FILMS: *Runaway Girls* 1928; *The Talk of Hollywood* (also story) 1929; *Melody Cruise* (also co-sc.), *Aggie Appleby—Maker of Men* 1933; *Hips Hips Hooray, Cockeyed Cavaliers, The Gay Divorcee* 1934; *Top Hat* 1935; *Follow the Fleet, A Woman Rebels* 1936; *Shall We Dance?* 1937; *Carefree* 1938; *Man About Town* 1939; *Buck Benny Rides Again* (also prod.), *Love Thy Neighbor* (also prod.) 1940; *Skylark* (also prod.) 1941; *Holiday Inn* (also prod.) 1942; *So Proudly We Hail* (also prod.) 1943; *Here Come the Waves* (also prod.), *I Love a Soldier* (also prod.) 1944.

Sands, Julian. Actor. Born in 1953, in Yorkshire, England. Tall, blond leading man of British and international films. A graduate of London's Central School of Speech and Drama, he formed a small punk troupe that performed at schools and youth clubs. On the screen from the early 80s, he played his first substantial role in *A Room with a View* (1986).

FILMS: *Privates on Parade* (bit) 1982; *Oxford Blues, The Killing Fields* 1984; *After Darkness, The Doctor and the Devils* 1985; *A Room with a View, Gothic* (as poet Percy Bysshe Shelley) 1986; *Siesta* (US) 1987; *Vibes* (US), *Wherever You Are* (Ger./Pol./It./Fr./Hol.) 1988; *Manika: Une Vie plus tard/Manika Manika* (Fr.), *Warlock* (US), *Tennessee Nights* (US) 1989; *Il Sole anche di Notte/The Sun Also Shines at Night* (It./Fr./Ger.), *Arachnophobia* (US), *Impromptu* (as composer Franz Liszt; US/Fr.) 1990; *Cattiva/Wicked* (It.), *Grand Isle* (US), *Naked Lunch* (Can./UK) 1991; *Husbands and Lovers* (US), *Wicked* (US) 1992; *Boxing Helena, Warlock 2* (US) 1993; *The Browning Version* 1994; *Leaving Las Vegas* 1995; *End of Summer, Nirvana, One Night Stand* 1997.

Sands, Tommy. Singer, actor. Born on Aug. 27, 1937, in Chicago. Popular rock 'n' roll singer-guitarist. He was on TV from age 11 and in films from the late 50s. His career was interrupted in the late 60s by a series of breakdowns and a serious liver ailment. A resident of Hawaii, he appeared in the early 70s in a number of episodes of the TV series 'Hawaii Five-O.'

FILMS: *Sing Boy Sing, Mardi Gras* 1958; *Love in a Goldfish Bowl, Babes in Toyland* 1961; *The Longest Day* 1962; *Ensign Pulver* 1964; *None but the Brave* 1965; *The Violent Ones* 1967.

Sangster, Jimmy. Screenwriter, producer, director. Born on Dec. 2, 1924, in England. He entered British films in the mid-40s as a production manager, switching to screenwriting in the late 50s. Mostly alone, sometimes in collaboration, he has written the scripts for numerous Hammer horror pictures. He began producing some of these in the early 60s and directing in the early 70s. He has also written extensively for British and American TV.

FILMS INCLUDE (as screenwriter): *The Curse of Frankenstein* 1957; *Dracula/Horror of Dracula, The Trollenberg Terror/The Crawling Eye, Intent to Kill* 1958; *The Mummy, Jack the Ripper* 1959; *The Brides of Dracula, The Criminal/The Concrete Jungle* (story only), *The Siege of Sidney Street* 1960; *A Taste of Fear/Scream of Fear* (also prod.) 1961; *Terra Bruta/The Savage Guns* (prod. only; US/Sp.) 1962; *Maniac* (also prod.), *Paranoiac* 1963; *Nightmare* (also prod.) 1964; *Hysteria* (also prod.), *The Nanny* (also prod.) 1965; *Deadlier Than the Male* 1966; *The Anniversary* (also prod.) 1968; *The Horror of Frankenstein* (also prod., dir.) 1970; *Lust for a Vampire* (dir. only), *Who Slew Auntie Roo?* 1971; *Fear in the Night* (also prod., dir.), *Crescendo* 1972; *The Monstrous Defect* 1975; *The Legacy* 1979; *Phobia* (Can.) 1980; *The Devil and Max Devlin* (co-story only) 1981.

San Giacomo, Laura. Actress. Born in 1962, in New Jersey. A graduate of the drama program at Carnegie-Mellon, she performed on the stage before making her auspicious screen debut in the role of the uninhibited Cynthia in Steven Soderberg's *sex, lies and videotape* (1989). She was at one time signed to the lead in a film on the life of Mexican artist/icon Frida Kahlo, but the project was scrapped over protests about San Giacomo's non-Mexican heritage.

FILMS: *sex lies and videotape* 1989; *Pretty Woman, Quigley Down Under, Vital Signs* 1990; *Once Around, Under Suspicion* 1991; *Where the Day Takes You* 1992; *Stuart Saves His Family* 1995.

San Juan, Olga. See O'BRIEN, Edmond.

Sanjinés, Jorge. Director. Born on July 31, 1936, in La Paz, Bolivia. Militant leftist filmmaker who consciously and skillfully harnessed the language of cinema to draw attention to the plight of his country's exploited peasantry, mostly of Indian descent. A product of a comfortable upper middle-class home, he supported himself as a laborer while studying philosophy at the University of San Andres in La Paz. While continuing his studies at the University of Chile in 1959, he decided to try film as a tool for social change and enrolled as a student at the Chilean Film Institute. Returning to Bolivia the following year, he formed a film collective, for which he began directing documentary shorts. The success of one of these, *Revolución* (1962), at international festivals led Sanjinés to his first feature, *Ukamau* (1966), a bleak, realistic tale of rape and vengeance, performed by native peasants. The black-and-white film, Bolivia's first full-length fiction film, went on to win awards at Cannes and Locarno. But at home it embarrassed many who complained it presented Bolivia's society as primitive. The government ordered all the prints destroyed and abolished the

Bolivian Cinematographic Institute, an organization Sanjinés had headed since 1964. Undaunted, Sanjinés proceeded to direct his best-known film, *Yawar Malku/Blood of the Condor* (1969), a piercing outcry against the sterilization of unsuspecting peasant women as part of a deceitful, American-guided, birth-control program. Initially banned by Bolivian censors, the film caused a furor when it was finally released following fervent street demonstrations. An ensuing investigation eventually led to reforms and the expulsion of the Peace Corps. It established Sanjinés as one of the world's leading practitioners of militant cinema.

FEATURE FILMS: *Ukamau* 1966; *Yawar Malku/Blood of the Condor* 1969; *El Coraje del Pueblo/The Courage of the People/The Night of San Juan* 1971; *Jatun Aua/El Enemigo principal/The Main Enemy* 1974; *Llucsi Caimanta/Fuera de aqui!* 1977; *Las Banderas del amanecer/The Flags of Dawn* 1984; *La Nación clandestina/The Secret Nation* 1989.

Sanson, Yvonne. Actress. Born in 1926, in Saloniki, Greece. Leading lady and later character player of Italian films, since the mid-40s. She enjoyed a worldwide reputation in the early 50s, when she starred in several notable productions, but for the most part she was seen in routine melodramas.

FILMS INCLUDE: *Aquila Nera* 1946; *Il Delitto di Giovanni Episcopo/Flesh Will Surrender* 1947; *La Grande Aurora* 1948; *Nerone e Messalina* 1949; *L'Imperatore di Capri* 1950; *Il Figlio di Nessuno, Tormento* 1951; *Il Cappotto/The Overcoat, Nous sommes tous des Assassins/We Are All Murderers* (Fr.) 1952; *Noi Peccatori, Les Trois Mousquetaires* (as Milady; Fr.) 1953; *Star of India* (UK/US) 1954; *L'Angelo bianco, La Bella Mugnaia/The Miller's Beautiful Wife* 1955; *Il Campanile d'Oro* 1956; *La Diga sul Pacifico/This Angry Age/The Sea Wall, We Have Only One Life* (Gr.), *L'Ultima Violenza* 1958; *Anima Nera* 1961; *The Biggest Bundle of Them All* (US/It.) 1967; *Il Conformista/The Conformist* 1970; *Un Apprezzato Professionista di Sicuro Avvenire* 1972.

Santell, Alfred. Director. *b.* Sept. 14, 1895, San Francisco. *d.* 1981. He began writing short stories while training as an architect in Los Angeles, and shortly after entered films with the Lubin company as comedy writer, set decorator, and occasionally, actor. In 1915, at the age of 20, he began directing comedy shorts for Kalem, then for World, Mack Sennett, and other companies, and made his debut as a feature director in 1920. He subsequently directed dozens of silent and sound films of all genres, many of them routine but some exceptionally fine, notably an inspired screen adaptation of Maxwell Anderson's *Winterset* (1936) and an effective film version of Eugene O'Neill's *The Hairy Ape* (1944).

FILMS (features complete): *My Valet* (short) 1915; *Beloved Rogues* (also sc.), *Out of the Bag* (short) 1917; *Home James* (short), *Vamping the Vamp* (short) 1918; *It Might Happen to You* (also sc.) 1920; *Wildcat Jordan* 1922; *Lights Out* 1923; *Fools in the Dark, Empty Hearts, The Man Who Played Square* 1924; *The Marriage Whirl, Parisian Nights, Classified* 1925; *Bluebeard's Seven Wives, The Dancer of Paris, Sweet Daddies, Subway Sadie, Just Another Blonde* 1926; *Orchids and Ermine, The Patent Leather Kid, The Gorilla* 1927; *The Little Shepherd of Kingdom Come, Wheel of Chance, Show Girl* 1928; *This Is Heaven, Twin Beds, Romance of the Rio Grande* 1929; *The Arizona Kid, The Sea Wolf* 1930; *Body and Soul, Daddy Long Legs, Sob Sister* 1931; *Polly of the Circus, Rebecca of Sunnybrook Farm, Tess of the Storm Country* 1932; *Bondage, The Right to Romance* 1933; *The Life of Vergie Winters* 1934; *People Will Talk, A Feather in Her Hat* 1935; *Winterset* 1936; *Internes Can't Take Money, Breakfast for Two* 1937; *Cocoanut Grove, Having Wonderful Time, The Arkansas Traveler* 1938; *Our Leading Citizen* 1939; *Aloma of the South Seas* 1941; *Beyond the Blue Horizon* 1942; *Jack London* 1943; *The Hairy Ape* 1944; *Mexicana* (also prod.) 1945; *That Brennan Girl* (also prod.) 1946.

Santley, Joseph. Director. *b.* Joseph Mansfield, Jan. 10, 1889, Salt Lake City. *d.* 1971. The stepson of a veteran stage actor, Eugene Santley, he began his theatrical career at the age of three and a half and attained Broadway stardom at nine, when he was billed as "America's Greatest Boy Actor." As a child he also appeared in a number of silent films and as a young adult he starred in stage musical comedies, often opposite his wife, English-born actress Ivy Sawyer. Arriving in Hollywood as a director during the transition to sound, he successfully coped with the antics of the Marx Brothers in their first film, *The Cocoanuts* (1929), which he co-directed with Robert Florey. He later directed many early talkie shorts, starring Eddie Cantor, Rudy Vallee, and Miss Sawyer, and numerous low-budget light features, at times quite entertaining but seldom better than routine. He retired from films in 1950 and was among the first Hollywood directors to turn to TV, for which he produced and directed many variety shows.

FEATURE FILMS: *The Cocoanuts* (co-dir. with Robert Florey) 1929; *Swing High* (also co-story) 1930; *The Loudspeaker, Young and Beautiful* (also co-story) 1934; *Million Dollar Baby* (also story, co-sc.), *Harmony Lane* (also co-sc.), *Waterfront Lady* 1935; *Dancing Feet, Laughing Irish Eyes, Her Master's Voice, The Harvester, We Went to College, Walking on Air, The Smartest Girl in Town* 1936; *Meet the Missus, There Goes the Groom* 1937; *She's Got Everything, Blonde Cheat, Always in Trouble, Swing Sister Swing* 1938; *Spirit of Culver, The Family Next Door, Two Bright Boys* 1939; *Music in My Heart, Melody and Moonlight, Melody Ranch, Behind the News* 1940; *Dancing on a Dime, Sis Hopkins, Rookies on Parade, Puddin'head, Ice-Capades, Down Mexico Way* 1941; *A Tragedy at Midnight, Yokel Boy, Remember Pearl Harbor, Joan of Ozark, Call of the Canyon* 1942; *Chatterbox, Shantytown, Thumbs Up, Sleepy Lagoon, Here Comes Elmer* 1943; *Rosie the Riveter, Jamboree, Goodnight Sweetheart, Three Little Sisters, Brazil* 1944; *Earl Carroll Vanities, Hitchhike to Happiness* 1945; *Shadow of a Woman* 1946; *Make Believe Ballroom* 1949; *When You're Smiling* 1950.

Santschi, Tom. Actor. *b.* Oct. 14, 1878, Kokomo, Ind. *d.* 1931. Rugged star of Hollywood silents. After entering films in 1909, he appeared in scores of productions, playing both brutish heroes and ruthless villains, mainly in melodramas and action pictures. He directed several of his own vehicles in the mid-1910s.

FILMS INCLUDE: *Heart of Race Trout, On the Border, Up San Juan Hill, Faust* 1909; *Across the Plains, Davy Crockett, Mazeppa* 1910; *Kit Carson's Wooing, The Heart of John Barlow* 1911; *A Waif of the Sea, The Coming of Columbus, Monte Cristo/The Count of Monte Cristo, Kings of the Forest, The Indelible Stain, The God of Gold* 1912; *The Three Wise Men, Alas! Poor Yorick!, Alone in the Jungle, The Wild Ride, When May Weds December, Thor—Lord of the Jungles* 1913; *The Adventures of Kathlyn* (serial), *The Spoilers, How They Stopped the Run on the Bank, The Test, The Abyss, Caryl of the Mountains* (also dir.) 1914; *The Heart of Paro* (also dir.), *The Octopus* (also dir., sc.), *His Fighting Blood* (also dir.), *The Blood Seedling* (also dir.), *A Sultana of the Desert* (also dir.) 1915; *The Country That God Forgot, The Crisis, The Garden of Allah* 1916; *The City of Purple Dreams, The Still Alarm, The Hell Cat, Code of the Yukon, Little Orphan Annie* 1918; *Shadows, The Stronger Vow, The Love That Dares* 1919; *The Cradle of Courage, The North Wind's Malice* 1920; *Two Kinds of Women,*

Found Guilty 1922; *Brass Commandments, Thundering Dawn* 1923; *The Storm Daughter, The Plunderer, Little Robinson Crusoe, Life's Greatest Game, The Street of Tears* 1924; *The Night Ship, The Pride of the Force, The Primrose Path* 1925; *My Own Pal, Siberia, The Hidden Way, Three Bad Men, The Third Degree* 1926; *Jim the Conqueror, When a Man Loves, Eyes of the Totem, Tracked by the Police, The Haunted Ship, The Land of the Lawless* 1927; *Vultures of the Sea* (serial), *Law and the Man, Honor Bound, Into No Man's Land, Isle of Lost Men* 1928; *In Old Arizona, The Wagon Master, The Shannons of Broadway* 1929; *Paradise Island, The Utah Kid, River's End* 1930; *The Last Ride* 1931.

Sara, Mia. Actress. Born in 1968, in Brooklyn, N.Y. Sweet-faced, innocent-looking young lead of Hollywood films of the late 80s and early 90s, following experience in commercials and in the daytime soap opera 'All My Children.' She portrayed Merle Oberon in the biographical TV movie *Queenie* (1987).

FILMS INCLUDE: *Legend* (UK) 1985; *Ferris Bueller's Day Off* 1986; *Long Lost Friend/Apprentice to Murder* (Can./Nor.) 1988; *Shadows in the Storm, Any Man's Death* 1990; *A Climate for Killing, A Row of Crows* 1991; *By the Sword, A Stranger Among Us* 1992; *Timecop* 1994; *The Pompatus in Us, Black Day/Blue Night* 1996.

Sarafian, Richard C. Director, actor. Born on Apr. 28, 1925, in New York City, of Armenian descent. A veteran of TV, he began directing feature films in the early 60s. Despite low budgets, he turned out a number of uncommon films. At his best with outdoor themes. In the 80s, he branched out into acting. He appeared in the TV series 'Foley Square' (1985–86) and in several features, including *Bugsy* (1991).

FILMS: *Terror at Black Falls* (also prod., sc.) 1962; *Andy* (also prod., sc.) 1965; *Run Wild Run Free* (UK) 1969; *Fragment of Fear* (UK) 1970; *Man in the Wilderness* (UK), *Vanishing Point* 1971; *Lolly Madonna XXX, The Man Who Loved Cat Dancing* 1973; *The Next Man* (also act. in bit) 1976; *Sunburn* 1979; *The Bear* 1984; *Eye of the Tiger* 1986; *Solar Crisis* (Jap./US) 1990; *The Crossing Guard* (act. only), *Don Juan DeMarco* (act. only) 1995.

Sarandon, Chris. Actor. Born on July 24, 1942, in Beckley, W.Va. Husky, sensual player of the American stage and screen. A graduate of the University of West Virginia, he began his career touring with Catholic University's National Players in a repertoire of Shakespeare and Molière, then performed with an improvisational troupe in Washington, D.C. before heading on to Broadway and films. He was nominated for an Oscar as Best Supporting Actor for his first screen role as Al PACINO's gay lover in *Dog Day Afternoon* (1975). Formerly (1967–79) married to actress Susan SARANDON.

FILMS: *Dog Day Afternoon* 1975; *Lipstick* 1976; *The Sentinel* 1977; *Cuba* 1979; *The Osterman Weekend* 1983; *Protocol* 1984; *Fright Night* 1985; *The Princess Bride* 1987; *Child's Play* 1988; *Slaves of New York, Forced March* 1989; *Collision Course, Whispers* (Can.) 1990; *The Resurrected* 1991; *The Nightmare Before Christmas* (v/o) 1993; *Edie and Pen* 1994; *Just Cause* 1995; *Tales from the Crypt: Bordello of Blood* 1996.

Sarandon, Susan. Actress. Born Susan Abigail Tomalin, on Oct. 4, 1946, in New York City. Expressive, sad-eyed leading lady of the American screen. The eldest of nine children in a Catholic family, she grew up in Metuchen, New Jersey. While studying English at Catholic University, she met aspiring actor Chris SARANDON and soon switched her major to drama. They married in 1967 (divorced in 1979) and later moved to New York, where she promptly landed her first movie role in *Joe* (1970) while accompanying her husband to an audition. She became a cult favorite after appearing in the midnight movie *The Rocky Horror Picture Show* (1975) and gained affirmation of her rising status as a capable actress with an Oscar nomination for *Atlantic City* (1980) and a prize at Venice for *Tempest* (1982). After further nominations for *Thelma & Louise* (1991), *Lorenzo's Oil* (1992), and *The Client* (1994), Sarandon won the elusive Oscar for best actress in 1996 for her soulful portrayal of Sister Helen Prejean in *Dead Man Walking*. She has established herself as one of the American screen's most dependable and versatile leading ladies. Known offscreen for her outspoken independence and liberal activism, she has a daughter with Italian director-screenwriter Franco Amurri and two sons with actor Tim ROBBINS, with whom she resides.

FILMS: *Joe* 1970; *La Mortadella/Lady Liberty* (It.) 1971; *Lovin' Molly, The Front Page* 1974; *The Great Waldo Pepper, The Rocky Horror Picture Show* (UK) 1975; *Dragonfly/One Summer Love* 1976; *The Other Side of Midnight* 1977; *Checkered Flag or Crash, Pretty Baby, Last of the Cowboys/The Great Smokey Roadblock* (also co-prod.), *King of the Gypsies* 1978; *Something Short of Paradise* 1979; *Loving Couples, Atlantic City* (Can./Fr.) 1980; *Tempest* 1982; *The Hunger* 1983; *In Our Hands* (doc.), *The Buddy System* 1984; *Compromising Positions* 1985; *The Witches of Eastwick* 1987; *Bull Durham, Sweet Hearts Dance* 1988; *The January Man, A Dry White Season* 1989; *Through the Wire* (narr. only), *White Palace* 1990; *Thelma & Louise* 1991; *The Player* (cameo) 1992, *Bob Roberts, Light Sleeper, Lorenzo's Oil* 1992; *The Client, Little Women* 1994; *The Celluloid Closet, Dead Man Walking, Safe Passage* 1995; *James and the Giant Peach* (v/o) 1996.

Sarde, Philippe. Composer. Born on June 21, 1945, in Neuilly-sur-Seine, Paris. A graduate of the Paris Conservatory, he began scoring films in the late 60s and rapidly developed into France's most prolific screen composer. He contributed music of astonishing wide range, at an amazing rate, to the diverse films of many directors, winning an Oscar nomination for *Tess* (1979) and several César awards. His brother, Alain Sarde, is one of France's leading producers.

FILMS INCLUDE: *Les Choses de la Vie/The Things of Life* 1970; *Le Chat/The Cat, La Veuve Couderc/The Widow Couderc* 1971; *La Cagna/Liza, César et Rosalie, La Droit d'aimer/The Right to Love* 1972; *La Grande Bouffe* 1973; *L'Horloger de Saint-Paul/The Clockmaker, Lancelot du Lac/Lancelot of the Lake* 1974; *Souvenirs d'en France/French Provincial, Vincent François Paul et les autres* 1975; *La Dernière Femme/The Last Woman, Le Locataire/The Tenant, Mado, Le Juge et l'Assassin/The Judge and the Assassin, Barocco* 1975; *Les Enfants gâtés/Spoiled Children, Un Taxi mauve/The Purple Taxi, Le Crabe Tambour* 1977; *Une Histoire simple/A Simple Story* 1978; *Tess* 1979; *Chère Inconnu/I Sent a Letter to My Love* 1980; *Beau Père, Storie di Orinaria Follia/Tales of Ordinary Madness* (It./Fr.), *Le Choix des Armes/Choice of Arms, Ghost Story* (US), *Coup de Torchon/Clean Slate, La Guerre du Feu/Quest for Fire* 1981; *L'Etoile du Nord/The North Star* 1982; *Lovesick* (US), *J'ai épousé une Ombre/I Married a Shadow, Garcon!* 1983; *Fort Saganne, Un Dimanche à la Campagne/Sunday in the Country, La Pirate* 1984; *Hors-La-Loi, Rendez-vous, Joshua Then and Now* (Can.), *Harem* 1985; *Pirates, I Love You, Le Lieu du Crime/Scene of the Crime, The Manhattan Project* (US), *L'Etat de Grace, La Puritaine* 1986; *Quelques Jours avec moi/A Few Days with Me, L'Ours/The Bear* 1988; *Reunion, Lost Angels* (US), *The Music Box* (US) 1989; *Eve of Destruction* (US), *La Baule-Les Pins, Lord of the Flies* (US), *Faux et Usage de Faux/Forgery and the Use of Forgeries, Le Petit Criminel/The*

Little Gangster 1990; *La Tribu/The Tribe, Pour Sacha/For Sacha, J'embrasse pas* 1991; *My Favorite Season* 1993; *La fille D'Artagnon, Uncovered* 1994; *Nelly and Mr. Arnaud* 1996.

Sargent, Alvin. American screenwriter. Entered films in the mid-60s after extensive experience as a writer for TV. He has written a number of intelligent scripts, winning Academy Awards for *Julia* (1977) and *Ordinary People* (1980), following an Oscar nomination for *Paper Moon* (1973).

FILMS: *Gambit* 1966; *The Stalking Moon* 1968; *The Sterile Cuckoo* 1969; *I Walk the Line* 1970; *The Effect of Gamma Rays on Man-in-the-Moon Marigolds* 1972; *Love and Pain. . . and the Whole Damn Thing* (UK), *Paper Moon* 1973; *Bobby Deerfield, Julia* 1977; *Straight Time* 1978; *Ordinary People* 1980; *Nuts* 1987; *Dominick and Eugene* 1988; *White Palace* 1990; *What About Bob?* (co-story only), *Other People's Money* 1991; *Hero* 1992; *Bogus* 1996.

Sargent, Joseph. Director. Born Giuseppe Danielle Sorgente, on July 25, 1925, in Jersey City, N.J. *ed.* New School for Social Research (drama). A competent craftsman, he gained much experience in TV, where he directed episodes for 'The Man from U.N.C.L.E.' and other series. His feature films have been technically glossy and generally well paced. At his best with thrillers. In addition to his handful of features, he directed numerous TV movies, winning two Emmys out of several nominations.

FILMS: *One Spy Too Many* (compiled from 'The Man from U.N.C.L.E.' TV episodes) 1966; *The Hell with Heroes* 1968; *The Forbin Project/Colossus—The Forbin Project, Tribes* (originally made for TV) 1970; *The Man* 1972; *White Lightning* 1973; *The Taking of Pelham 123* 1974; *MacArthur* 1977; *Goldengirl* 1979; *Coast to Coast* 1980; *Nightmares* 1983; *Jaws the Revenge* (also prod.) 1987.

Saroyan, William. Novelist, playwright, short-story writer. *b.* Aug. 31, 1908, Fresno, Calif., of Armenian parentage. *d.* 1981. This noted author's one major contribution to the screen was the original story for MGM's sentimental drama of wartime America, *The Human Comedy* (1943), for which he won an Academy Award. He later adapted the script material to a novel, which was also published in 1943. *The Time of Your Life* (1948), based on his 1939 Broadway production of the same name, is the only film adapted from any of his many plays, novels, and stories, which usually are loose in structure, form, and plot. In 1942 he directed a documentary film, *The Good Job.*

Sarrazin, Michael. Actor. Born Jacques Michel André Sarrazin, on May 22, 1940, in Quebec City, Canada. Appealing leading man of Hollywood films with boyish features suggesting innocence. He prepared for the stage at New York's Actors Studio and made his screen debut in National Film Board of Canada documentaries, later getting into feature films via American TV.

FILMS: *Gunfight in Abilene, The Flim-Flam Man* 1967; *Journey to Shiloh, The Sweet Ride* 1968; *They Shoot Horses Don't They?, Eye of the Cat, A Man Called Gannon* 1969; *In Search of Gregory* 1970; *The Pursuit of Happiness, Sometimes a Great Notion/Never Give an Inch, Believe in Me* 1971; *The Groundstar Conspiracy* (Can.) 1972; *Harry in Your Pocket* 1973; *For Pete's Sake* 1974; *The Reincarnation of Peter Proud* 1975; *The Lives and Times of Scaramouche* (title role; It./Yug.), *The Gumball Rally* 1976; *A Night Full of Rain* 1977; *Caravans* 1978; *Double Negative* (Can.) 1979; *The Seduction, Fighting Back/Death Vengeance* 1982; *Joshua Then and Now* (Can.) 1985; *Captive Hearts, Mascara* (Bel./Hol./Fr.), *Keeping Track* (Can.) 1987; *Malarek* (Can.) 1989; *The Phone Call* (Can./Fr.) 1990; *Lena's Holiday* 1991.

Sarris, Andrew. Critic, theorist. Born on October 31, 1928, in Brooklyn, N.Y. *ed.* Columbia Coll. Highly influential public arbiter of film theory. While a critic for the *Village Voice* (1960–89), he introduced to the American audience the AUTEUR THEORY of film analysis. The theory was even more widely popularized in his 1968 book, *The American Cinema: Directors and Directions 1929–1968*, in which he used the theory to evaluate and categorize American directors. Author of *The John Ford Movie Mystery*, among others. Professor of Film at Columbia University.

Sartain, Gailard. Actor, comedian. Born September 18, 1946, in Tulsa, Okla. *ed.* University of Tulsa. Plump, sturdy veteran character actor of television and film. He got his start on local television in Oklahoma and from there has carved a long and successful acting career playing primarily simple, good ole' boy roles. Quite memorable as the corrupt sheriff in *Mississippi Burning* (1988). His film credits span almost twenty years of impressive, solid performances.

FILMS INCLUDE: *The Buddy Holly Story* 1978; *The Hollywood Knights, Roadie* 1980; *Hard Country* 1981; *Endangered Species* 1982; *The Outsiders* 1983; *Uphill All the Way* 1985; *The Big Easy, Ernest Goes To Camp, Leader of the Band, Made in Heaven* 1987; *Ernest Saves Christmas, Mississippi Burning, The Moderns* 1988; *Blaze* 1989; *Ernest Goes to Jail, The Grifters, Love at Large* 1990; *Fried Green Tomatoes, Guilty By Suspicion, Sharkskin* 1991; *Stop! Or My Mom Will Shoot* 1992; *Equinox, The Real McCoy* 1993; *Clean Slate, Getting Even with Dad, Speechless* 1994; *Open Season* 1996.

Sartre, Jean-Paul. Philosopher, novelist, playwright, screenwriter. *b.* June 21, 1905, Paris. *d.* 1980. The diminutive leader of France's postwar intellectual community and standard-bearer of the existentialist movement wrote a couple of screenplays in addition to those of his works that have been adapted by others to the screen. He was featured as himself in Nicole Vedres's film *La Vie Commence demain/Life Begins Tomorrow* (1949), a dramatization of a philosophical symposium. He is the subject of a three-hour documentary by Alexandre Astruc, *Sartre par lui-même* (1976).

FILMS INCLUDE: *Les Jeux sont faits/The Chips Are Down* (sc., co-dial.) 1947; *Les Mains sales/Dirty Hands* (play basis only) 1951; *La P . . . respectueuse/The Respectful Prostitute* (co-addnl. dial., to own play) 1952; *Les Orgueilleux/T he Proud and the Beautiful* (story) 1953; *Huis Clos/No Exit* (play basis only) 1954; *Les Sorcières de Salem/Witches of Salem* (sc. from Arthur Miller's play 'The Crucible') 1957; *I Sequestrati di Altona/The Condemned of Altona* (inspired by his play 'Les Séquestrés d'Altona'; It./Fr.), *Huis Clos/No Exit* (play basis only; Arg./US) 1962; *Le Mur* (novel basis only) 1967.

saturation. In color cinematography, the degree of color intensity in a photographed image. The more vivid the color, the higher the saturation.

Saul, Oscar. Screenwriter. Born on Dec. 26, 1912, in Brooklyn, N.Y. *ed.* Brooklyn Coll. A former radio writer and occasionally a playwright and novelist. He began writing for the screen in the 40s. He has since contributed screenplays, alone or in collaboration, for both major and minor productions of various studios.

FILMS INCLUDE: *Once Upon a Time* 1944; *The Dark Past* (co-adapt. only), *Road House* (story) 1948; *Woman in Hiding* 1949; *A Streetcar Named Desire* (adapt. only), *The Secret of Convict Lake, Thunder on the Hill* 1951; *Affair in Trinidad* 1952; *Let's Do It Again* (prod. only) 1953; *The Joker Is Wild, The Helen Morgan Story* 1957; *The Second Time Around* 1961; *Major Dundee* 1965; *The Silencers* 1966; *Man and Boy* 1972; *Los Amigos/Deaf Smith and Johnny Ears* 1973.

Saulnier, Jacques. Art director. Born on Sept. 8, 1928, in Paris. Favorite set designer of the new French cinema and international films, praised for his spare but effective sets. A graduate of IDHEC, he entered films in 1948 as assistant to Alexander TRAUNER and came into his own a decade later, at first in collaboration with Bernard EVEIN.

FILMS INCLUDE (alone or in collaboration): *Les Amants/The Lovers, Les Cousins/The Cousins* 1958; *A Double Tour/Leda, Les Jeux de l'Amour/The Games of Love* 1959; *Le Farceur/The Joker, La Morte-Saison des Amours/The Season for Love, L'Année dernière à Marienbad/Last Year at Marienbad* 1961; *Vu du Pont/A View from the Bridge* 1962; *Landru/Bluebeard, Muriel* 1963; *La Bonne Soupe* 1964; *La Fabuleuse Aventure de Marco Polo/Marco the Magnificent, What's New Pussycat?* (US/Fr.) 1965; *La Vie de Château, Mademoiselle* (UK/Fr.), *La Guerre est finie* 1966; *Le Voleur/The Thief of Paris* 1967; *Tante Zita/Zita, La Prisonnière* 1968; *Le Clan des Siciliens/The Sicilian Clan* 1969; *Le Chat, Le Casse/The Burglars* 1971; *Le Serpent/The Serpent* 1973; *French Connection II* (US) 1975; *Providence* 1977; *Mon Oncle d'Amérique* 1980; *Chanel Solitaire* 1981; *La Vie est un Roman/Life Is a Bed of Roses* 1983; *Un Amour de Swann/Swann in Love, L'Amour á Mort/Love Unto Death, Le Jumeau* 1984; *Mélo* 1986; *La Couleur du Vent* 1988; *I Want To Go Home* 1989; *L'Autrichienne* 1990.

Saunders, John Monk. Author, screenwriter, *b.* Nov. 22, 1897, Hinckley, Minn. *d.* 1940. *ed.* U. of Washington; Oxford. A former journalist (N.Y. *Tribune,* L.A. *Times*) and second lieutenant in the Army Air Corps, he wrote many short stories and some screenplays, often on the subject of aviation. He co-directed Alexander Korda's semidocumentary tribute to flight, *Conquest of the Air* (1936), which starred Laurence Olivier. At one time (1928–39) he was married to Fay WRAY.

FILMS: *Too Many Kisses* (story) 1925; *Wings* (story) 1927; *Legion of the Condemned* (co-sc.), *The Docks of New York* (story) 1928; *She Goes to War* (dial., titles) 1929; *The Finger Points* (co-sc.), *The Dawn Patrol* (story) 1930; *The Last Flight* (story) 1932; *The Eagle and the Hawk* (story), *Ace of Aces* (story) 1933; *Devil Dogs of the Air* (story), *West Point of the Air* (story), *I Found Stella Parrish* (story) 1935; *Conquest of the Air* (co-dir., story; UK) 1936; *Star of the Circus/Hidden Menace* (co-sc.; UK), *Dawn Patrol* (story) 1938.

Saura, Carlos. Director. Born on Jan. 4, 1932, in Huesca, Spain, the son of an attorney and his pianist wife. A professional still photographer from age 18, he enrolled at Madrid's Instituto de Investigaciones y Experiencias Cinematografistas (later Escuela Oficial de Cinematografo) in 1953. While there, he directed an amateur short, then a graduation short. He stayed at the school as a teacher through 1963. He next directed a medium-length documentary, then turned out his first feature, *Los Golfos,* with limited means and a cast made up largely of nonprofessionals. A stark drama about juvenile delinquents who hope to break their cycle of poverty by becoming bullfighters, the technically flawed film was shown at the Cannes Festival of 1960 but was poorly received and did not qualify for commercial release until 1962. It was with his third feature, *La Caza/The Hunt* (1966), that Saura first grabbed the world's attention. Ostensibly a psychological thriller about a hunting party gone awry, the film, like several other early Saura productions, served as an allegorical critique of the moral disintegration of Spanish society under Franco. It went on to win the Silver Bear for Best Direction at the Berlin Festival. The strict censorship imposed by the Franco regime caused Saura and other liberal-minded filmmakers of his generation to camouflage controversial themes behind a net of hints, allusions, symbols, and parables. Saura's international reputation grew with every film. Among other prizes, he won another Silver Bear for Best Direction at Berlin for *Peppermint frappé* (1968), a revealing exploration of sexuality in a repressive society; the Jury Prize at Cannes for *La Prima Angelica* (1974), a poignant recollection of the Spanish Civil War; the Special Jury Prize at Berlin for *Cría Cuervos* (1976), a fascinating, ambiguously haunting memoir of mayhem, perhaps real, probably symbolic; the Golden Bear at Berlin for *Deprisa, deprisa* (1981), a fiercely realistic exposé of the street life of poor youths; and the British Film Academy's best foreign language film award for his exhilarating music and dance celebration, *Carmen* (1983). *Carmen* was the second of an unannounced musical trilogy, which had started with *Bodas de Sangre/Blood Wedding* (1981) and concluded with a brilliantly colorful rendition of De Falla's *El Amor brujo* (1986). The most "Spanish" of Spain's directors, Saura has been his country's leading filmmaker for more than two decades. Several of his films of the 70s starred his longtime companion Geraldine CHAPLIN. He wrote all of his own screenplays, alone or in collaboration.

FILMS (as director-screenwriter): *Antonio Saura* (student film about his brother, an abstract expressionist painter) 1955; *La Tarde del Domingo* (graduation short) 1957; *Cuenca* (medium-length doc.) 1958; *Los Golfos/The Hooligans/The Urchins/The Urchins* (also act.) 1960; *Llanto por un Bandido/Lament for a Bandit* 1964; *La Caza/The Hunt* 1966; *Peppermint frappé* 1967; *Stress es Tres Tres* 1968; *La Madriquera/The Honeycomb* 1969; *El Jardin de las Delicias/The Garden of Delights* 1970; *Ana y los Lobos/Anna and the Wolves* 1973; *La Prima Angélica/Cousin Angelica* 1974; *Cría Cuervos/Raise Ravens/Cria!* 1976; *Elisa Vida mía/Elisa My Love* 1977; *Los Ojos vendados/Blindfold* 1978; *Mama cumple Cien Años/Mama Turns 100* 1979; *Deprisa deprisa/ Hurry Hurry/Fast Fast* 1980; *Dulces Horas/Sweet Hours, Bodas de Sangre/Blood Wedding* 1981; *Antonieta* (Fr./Mex.) 1982; *Carmen* (also co-chor.) 1983; *Los Zancos/The Stilts* 1984; *El Amor brujo/Love the Magician* (also co-chor.) 1986; *El Dorado* 1988; *La Noche oscura/The Dark Night* (Sp./Fr.) 1989; *Ay Carmela!* (Sp./It.) 1990; *Sevillanas* 1992; *Dispara* (also co-sc.), *Marathon* 1993; *Taxi* 1996; *Flamenco* 1997.

Sautet, Claude. Director. Born on Feb. 23, 1924, in Montrouge, a suburb of Paris, a businessman's son. *ed.* Ecole des Arts decoratifs. A former social worker and music critic, he graduated from IDHEC in the late 40s and after a period of apprenticeship produced and wrote for French TV. He directed his first film, a short, in 1951, but it was as a screenwriter and script doctor that he first made himself known in feature films. Among other productions, he collaborated on the scripts of Franju's *Les Yeux sans Visage/The Horror Chamber of Dr. Faustus* (1960), Deray's *Symphonie pour un Massacre/Symphony for a Massacre* (1963), Marcel Ophüls's *Peau de Banane/Banana Peel* (1964), Rappeneau's *La Vie de Château* (1965), and Deray's *Borsalino* (1970). His early feature films as a director were well-paced gangster thrillers. But starting with his Prix Delluc winner *Les Choses de la Vie/The Things of Life* (1970), he became best known for his discreet, perceptive, and sensitive character studies of the French bourgeoisie, especially the middle-aged. Sautet's style is direct and unflashy. Although he is an accomplished craftsman, he seems less interested in flaunting camera technique than in advancing his simple plots and exploring the psychology of his ordinary characters and their social environment. His *A Simple Story* (1978) was nominated for an Oscar as best foreign language film. Sautet writes his own scripts, mostly in collaboration.

FILMS: *Nous n'irons plus au Bois* (short) 1951; *Bonjour Sourire* 1955; *Classe tous Risques/The Big Risk* (also co-sc.) 1960; *L'Arme à Gauche/Guns for the Dictator* (also sc.) 1965; *Les Choses de la Vie/The Things of Life* (also co-sc.) 1970; *Max et les Ferrailleurs* (also co-sc.) 1971; Cèsar et Rosalie/Cesar and Rosalie (also co-sc.) 1972; *Vincent François Paul... et les autres/Vincent François Paul and the Others* (also co-sc.) 1975; *Mado* (also co-sc.) 1976; *Une Histoire simple/A Simple Story* (also co-sc.) 1978; *Un Mauvais Fils/A Bad Son* (also co-sc.) 1980; *Garçon* (also co-sc.) 1983; *Quelques Jours avec moi/A Few Days with Me* (also co-sc.), *Mon Ami le Traitre* (co-sc. only) 1988; *A Heart in Winter* 1993; *Nelly and Monsieur Armaud* 1996.

Savage, Ann. Actress. Born Bernie Lyon, on Feb. 19, 1921, in Columbia, S.C. Leading lady of low-budget Hollywood films of the 40s and early 50s.

FILMS INCLUDE: *Two Senoritas from Chicago, What a Woman!, Passport to Suez, After Midnight with Boston Blackie, Klondike Kate* 1943; *Two-Man Submarine, Ever Since Venus, The Unwritten Code* 1944; *Detour, Midnight Manhunt, Apology for Murder, Scared Stiff* 1945; *The Dark Horse, The Last Crooked Mile, Renegade Girl* 1946; *Jungle Flight* 1947; *Satan's Cradle* 1949; *Pygmy Island* 1950; *Pier 23* 1951; *The Woman They Almost Lynched* 1953; *Fire with Fire* 1986.

Savage, Fred. Actor. Born on July 9, 1976, in Highland Park, Ill. Juvenile lead of American TV and films. He was still in kindergarten when he began appearing in commercials and not yet ten when he made his screen debut. He gained popularity as the star of the TV series 'The Wonder Years.' His sister, Kala, and brother, Ben, are also actors.

FILMS: *The Boy Who Could Fly* 1986; *The Princess Bride* 1987; *Vice Versa* 1988; *Little Monsters, The Wizard* 1989.

Savage, John. Actor. Born on Aug. 25, 1949, in Old Bethpage, Long Island, N.Y. *ed.* AADA. Wholesome, fair-haired leading man of the American stage and screen. He reached a career peak in the late 70s, when he was cast to advantage in such films as *The Deer Hunter* (1978), *Hair, The Onion Field* (both 1979), and *Inside Moves* (1980).

FILMS INCLUDE: *Love Is a Carousel* 1970; *Bad Company* 1972; *Steelyard Blues, The Killing Kind* 1973; *The Sister-in-Law* 1975; *The Deer Hunter* 1978; *Hair, The Onion Field* 1979; *Inside Moves* 1980; *Cattle Annie and Little Britches* 1981; *The Amateur* (Can.) 1982; *Brady's Escape* (US/Hung.) 1984; *Maria's Lovers* 1985; *Salvador, Hotel Colonial* (It./US) 1986; *Beauty and the Beast* (as the Beast) 1987; *Caribe* (Can.), *The Beat* 1988; *Do the Right Thing, Hunting* (Austral.) 1989; *Any Man's Death, Point of View* (release delayed from 1988; Isr.), *The Godfather Part III* 1990; *Primary Motive* 1992; *Killing Obsession* 1994; *Carnoasaur II, The Crossing Guard* 1995; *American Strays, White Squall* 1996.

Saval, Dany. Actress. Born Danielle-Nadine-Suzanne Salle, on Jan. 5, 1940, in Paris. Pert leading lady of French films; formerly a dancer. Ex-wife of composer Maurice JARRE.

FILMS INCLUDE: *Les Tricheurs/The Cheaters, Le Miroir a Deux Faces/The Mirror Has Two Faces* 1958; *Nathalie Agent secret* 1959; *Pleins Feux sur l'Assassin* 1960; *Les Parisiennes/Tales of Paris, Les Sept Péchés capitaux/Seven Capital Sins, Moon Pilot* (US), *Le Diable et les Dix Commandments/The Devil and the Ten Commandments, Du Mouron pour les Petits Oiseaux* 1962; *Strip-Tease/Sweet Skin* 1963; *Constance aux Enfers/Web of Fear* 1964; *Boeing Boeing* (US) 1965; *L'Animal* 1977; *La Vie parisienne* 1978; *Ciao les Mecs* 1979.

Savalas, Telly. Actor. *b.* Aristotle Savalas, Jan. 21, 1924, Garden City, N.Y., of Greek extraction. *d.* 1994. A graduate of Columbia, he started his adult life as a GI in WW II, was injured in action and decorated with a Purple Heart. After the war, he joined the Information Services of the State Department, then went to work for ABC News, where he rose to senior director of news and special events, winning a Peabody Award for his 'Your Voice of America' series. He was in his late 30s when he began a second career as an actor, at first on TV, then also in feature films. Bald and stocky, he typically portrayed loathsome villains in numerous films of the 60s. He was nominated for an Oscar as best supporting actor for *Birdman of Alcatraz* (1962). He directed himself in *Beyond Reason* (1977). Cast against type, he gained international popularity as the hero star of the hit TV police series 'Kojak' (1973–78). The character was revived in 1989 for a string of TV movies. His brother, George ("Demosthenes") Savalas (*b.* Dec. 5, 1928, the Bronx, N.Y.; *d.* 1985), provided comic relief for the series and also appeared in a number of feature films.

FILMS INCLUDE: *Mad Dog Call, The Young Savages* 1961; *Cape Fear, Birdman of Alcatraz, The Interns* 1962; *The Man from the Diners' Club, Love Is a Ball, Johnny Cool* 1963; *The New Interns* 1964; *The Greatest Story Ever Told* (as Pontius Pilate), *Genghis Khan, Battle of the Bulge, The Slender Thread* 1965; *Beau Geste* 1966; *The Dirty Dozen* 1967; *The Scalphunters, Sol Madrid* 1968; *Buona Sera Mrs. Campbell, The Assassination Bureau* (UK), *Mackenna's Gold, Crooks and Coronets/Sophie's Place* (US/UK), *On Her Majesty's Secret Service* (UK) 1969; *Kelly's Heroes, The Land Raiders, Città Violenta/The Family* (It./Fr.) 1970; *A Town Called Bastard/A Town Called Hell* (UK/Sp.), *Pretty Maids All in a Row, Clay Pigeon* 1971; *La Banda J. & S.—Cronaca Criminale del West/Sonny and Jed* (It./Sp.), *Una Ragione per Vivere e una per Morire/A Reason to Live a Reason to Die* (It.), *I Familiari delle Vittime non saranno avertiti/Crime Boss, Pancho Villa* (Sp./Mex.) 1972; *Redneck* (It./Sp.) 1973; *Panico en el Transiberiano/Horror Express* (Sp./UK) 1974; *Killer Force* (UK), *Inside Out* (UK), *House of Exorcism* (It.) 1975; *Beyond Reason* (also dir.) 1977; *Capricorn One* 1978; *Beyond the Poseidon Adventure, The Muppet Movie, Escape to Athena* (UK) 1979; *Cannonball Run II* 1984; *Gobots: Battle of the Rocklords* (v/o) 1986; *Les Predateurs de la Nuit/Faceless* (Fr.) 1988.

Saville, Philip. Director. Born 1930 in England. Primarily known for his TV work, he turned out a number of features of some charm but rather sluggish pace.

FILMS: *Stop the World—I Want to Get Off* 1966; *Oedipus the King* 1968; *The Best House in London* 1969; *Secrets* 1971; *Those Glory Glory Days* 1983; *Shadey* 1986; *The Fruit Machine/Wonderland* 1988; *Fellow Traveller* (UK/US) 1990.

Saville, Victor. Director, producer. *b.* Sept. 15, 1897, Birmingham, Eng. *d.* 1979. He entered British films as a salesman in 1916, after being wounded in WW I action with the London Irish Rifles. He later became involved in filmmaking as a production manager and in 1920 joined Gaumont-British as a screenwriter. He directed his first film in 1927 and during the 30s directed or produced some of Britain's finest films of the period. He then went to Hollywood, where the films he directed for MGM and other studios seemed less inspired than his British output. He had better success in America as a producer. In 1960 he returned to England, where he formed an independent production company but ended his long and fruitful career after producing but a single feature film.

FILMS: As director—In the UK: *Conquest of Oil* (doc.) 1921; *The Arcadians* (also prod., sc.), *A Woman in Pawn/A Woman in the Night* (co-dir. with Edwin Greenwood; also prod.), *The Glad Eye/Fanny Hawthorn* (co-dir. with Maurice Elvey; also prod., sc.) 1927; *Tesha* (also prod., story, sc.) 1928; *Kitty* (also prod.), *Woman to Woman* (also co-prod.), *Me and the Boys* (short; also prod.) 1929; *The W Plan* (also prod., sc.), *A Warm Corner* (also prod., sc.) 1930; *The Sport of Kings* (also prod., sc.), *The Calendar* (co-dir. with T. Hayes Hunter), *Sunshine Susie/Office Girl, Michael and Mary* 1931; *Hindle*

Wakes (also sc.), *The Faithful Heart, Love on Wheels* 1932; *The Good Companions, I Was a Spy, Friday the 13th* 1933; *Evensong, Evergreen, The Iron Duke* 1934; *The Dictator/The Love Affair of the Dictator/Loves of a Dictator, Me and Marlborough, First a Girl* 1935; *It's Love Again* 1936; *Dark Journey* (also prod.), *Storm in a Teacup* (co-dir. with Ian Dalrymple; also prod.), *Action for Slander* (co-dir. with Tim Whelan; also prod.) 1937; *South Riding* (also prod.) 1938. In the US—*Forever and a Day* (co-dir., co-prod.) 1943; *Tonight and Every Night* (also prod.) 1945; *The Green Years* 1946; *Green Dolphin Street, If Winter Comes* 1947; *Conspirator* (US/UK) 1949; *Kim* 1950; *Calling Bulldog Drummond* (US/UK) 1951; *24 Hours of a Woman's Life/Affair in Monte Carlo* (UK) 1952; *The Long Wait* 1954; *The Silver Chalice* 1955. As producer—In the UK: *Hindle Wakes* (also sc.), *Roses of Picardy, A Sister to Assist 'Er, Flight Commander* 1927; *The Citadel* (UK/US) 1938; *Goodbye Mr. Chips* (UK/US) 1939. In the US—*The Earl of Chicago, The Mortal Storm, Bitter Sweet* 1940; *A Woman's Face, Dr. Jekyll and Mr. Hyde* (co-prod.), *The Chocolate Soldier, Smilin' Through* 1941; *White Cargo* 1942; *Keeper of the Flame, Above Suspicion* 1943; *I the Jury* 1953; *The Greengage Summer/Loss of Innocence* (UK) 1961.

Savoca, Nancy. Director, screenwriter, actress. Born in 1960, in the Bronx, N.Y., to immigrants from Sicily and Argentina. A graduate of the NYU film program, she spent several years raising a tiny budget of $750,000 for her first film, *True Love,* from a script she had written in 1982 with her husband and producer Richard Guay. The film, an atmospheric, minutely detailed recreation of an Italian-American courtship and wedding, won the Grand Prize at the United States Film Festival. She could not attend the ceremony in Utah because she was giving birth to her second child in the Bronx. Made for the considerably heftier but still modest budget of $8 million, Savoca's next film, *Dogfight* (1991), about a day in the life of a marine on his last night before heading out to Vietnam, also enjoyed critical esteem.

FILMS: As actress—*Married to the Mob, Something Wild* 1986. As director—*Bad Timing: A Sensual Obsession* (sc. only; UK) 1980; *Renata* (also sc.) 1982; *True Love* (also co-sc.) 1989; *Dogfight* 1991; *Household Saints* (also sc.) 1993.

Saxon, John. Actor. Born Carmen Orrico, on Aug. 5, 1935, in Brooklyn, N.Y. Dark, handsome leading man of Hollywood films. He was a male model and studied acting with Stella Adler before making his screen debut in the mid-50s. He was popular for a while with the teenage crowd but by the early 60s was appearing mainly in minor productions in the US and abroad. He directed himself in *Death House* (1988). Saxon, who co-starred in the TV series 'The Doctors' (1969–72), has also been seen in many TV movies, miniseries, and series episodes, and has occasionally appeared on the stage.

FILMS INCLUDE: *Running Wild* 1955; *The Unguarded Moment* 1956; *The Restless Years, The Reluctant Debutante, This Happy Feeling, Summer Love* 1958; *The Big Fisherman, Cry Tough* 1959; *Portrait in Black, The Unforgiven, The Plunderers* 1960; *Posse from Hell* 1961; *Mr. Hobbes Takes a Vacation, War Hunt* 1962; *La Ragazza che sapeva troppo/The Evil Eve* (It.), *The Cardinal* 1963; *Sette contro la Morte/The Cavern* (It./Ger.), *The Ravagers* 1965; *The Appaloosa, Queen of Blood, The Night Caller/Blood Beast from Outer Space* (UK) 1966; *For Singles Only* 1968; *Death of a Gunfighter* 1969; *Company of Killers* 1970; *Joe Kidd* 1972; *Enter the Dragon* 1973; *Black Christmas* (Can.) 1974; *Family Killer* (It.), *Mitchell, Tony Saitta/Tough Tony* 1975; *Napoli Violenta* (It.) 1976; *Strange Shadows in an Empty Room* (It.), *Moonshine County Express, E specialiste del 44* (It./Aus.), *The Swiss Conspiracy* 1977; *The Bees, Shalimar/Deadly Thief* (Ind.), *The Glove* 1978; *Fast Company* (Can.), *The Electric Horseman* 1979; *Beyond Evil, Battle Beyond the Stars, Apocalypse Domani/Hunter of the Apocalypse/The Last Hunter/Savage Apocalypse/Cannibals in the Streets* (It.) 1980; *Blood Beach* 1981; *Wrong Is Right, Tenebrae/Unsane* (It.) 1982; *The Big Score* 1983; *A Nightmare on Elm Street* 1984; *Fever Pitch* 1985; *Atomic Cyborg/Hands of Steel* (It.) 1986; *A Nightmare on Elm Street 3: Dream Warriors* 1987; *Death House* (also dir.), *Criminal Act, Aftershock* 1988; *My Mom's a Werewolf* 1989; *Blood Salvage, Blackmail, Payoff* 1991; *Beverly Hills Cop III, Wes Craven's New Nightmare* 1994; *From Dusk Till Dawn* 1996.

Sayles, John. Director, screenwriter, novelist, actor. Born on Sept. 28, 1950, in Schenectady, N.Y., the son of schoolteachers. A multifaceted, fiercely independent creative artist whose work has spanned a broad spectrum of the contemporary American cultural scene. After graduating from Williams College with a degree in psychology, he supported himself with a variety of odd jobs, ranging from nursing-home attendant to meat packer in a sausage factory, while writing short stories and attempting to place them. The first story he sold, to *Atlantic Monthly,* earned him an O. Henry Award. Another served as the basis for his first novel, *Pride of the Bimbos* (1975), about baseball players in drag. His second novel, *Union Dues* (1977), was nominated for both the National Book and National Book Critics Circle Awards. He then began writing screenplays for Roger CORMAN and in 1980 made an auspicious debut as a director with *Return of the Secaucus Seven,* a low-budget ($60,000), highly regarded precursor to *The Big Chill.* He was nominated for an Academy Award for the film's script. Sayles continued writing "quickie" screenplays for others and used the proceeds, as well as money from a MacArthur "genius" grant he won in 1983, to finance his own films, through which he expressed his social and political concerns. He explored marriage and lesbianism in *Lianna* (1982), race relations in *The Brother from Another Planet* (1984), and labor unions in *Matewan* (1987). *Eight Men Out* (1988) superbly recreated the 1919 Chicago "Black Sox" World Series scandal and in *City of Hope* (1991) he powerfully decried corruption in American politics. Sayles also created several TV programs, including the series 'Shannon's Deal' (1989–91) and three hit music videos for Bruce Springsteen, including 'Born in the U.S.A.' Author of *Thinking in Pictures* (1987), about the making of *Matewan,* and several novels, including *Los Gusanos,* about exiled Cubans. He played pivotal roles in several of his own films and acted in those of other directors. Sayles shares a home in Hoboken, N.J., and a farm in upstate New York, with longtime companion Maggie Renri, an actress and producer on several of his films.

FILMS: *Piranha* (sc.) 1978; *The Lady in Red* (sc.) 1979; *Battle Beyond the Stars* (sc.) 1980; *Return of the Secaucus Seven* (dir., sc., edit., act.), *Alligator* 1980; *The Howling* (co-sc., act.) 1981; *The Challenge* (co-sc.) 1982; *Lianna* (dir., sc., edit., act.), *Baby It's You* (dir., sc.) 1983; *The Brother from Another Planet* (dir., sc., edit., act.) 1984; *Enormous Changes at the Last Minute* (co-sc.) 1985; *The Clan of the Cave Bear* (sc.), *Hard Choices,* (act.), *Something Wild* (act.) 1986; *Wild Thing* (co-story, sc.), *Matewan* (dir., sc., act.) 1987; *Eight Men Out* (dir., sc., act.) 1988; *Breaking In* (sc.), *Untama Giru* (act., Jap.) 1989; *Little Vegas* (act.) 1990; *City of Hope* (dir., sc., edit., act.) 1991; *Malcolm X* (act. only), *Passion Fish* (sc., ed.), *Straight Talk* (act.) 1992; *Matinee* (act. only) 1993; *My Life's in Turnaround* (act. only), *The Secret of Roan Inish* (dir., ed.) 1994; *Lone Star* 1996.

Scacchi, Greta. Actress. Born on Feb. 18, 1960, in Milan. Radiant, sensual leading lady of the international screen. Following the divorce of her parents, an Italian art dealer and his British ex-dancer wife, she was raised by her mother in England, then Australia, where she briefly attended the University of Western Australia and began her career on the stage in Perth. Returning to England, she performed for three years with the Bristol Old Vic Theatre and appeared on British TV before her big screen debut in the early 80s. She appeared in films of several nations before settling in Hollywood in 1990.

FILMS: *Das zweite Gesicht* (Ger.) 1982; *Heat and Dust* (UK) 1983; *The Coca Cola Kid* (Austral.), *Burke and Wills* (Austral.) 1985; *Defence of the Realm* (UK) 1986; *White Mischief* (UK.), *Good Morning Babilonia/Good Morning Babylon* (It./Fr./US), *Un Homme amoureaux/A Man in Love* (Fr./It.) 1987; *Paura e Amore/Fear and Love/Three Sisters* (It./Fr./W Ger.), *La Donna della Luna* (It.) 1988; *Presumed Innocent* (US) 1990; *Fires Within* (US), *Shattered* (US) 1991; *The Player* (US), *Turtle Beach* 1992; *The Browning Version* 1994; *Jefferson in Paris* 1995; *Emma* 1996.

Scala, Gia. Actress. *b.* Giovanna Sgoglio, Mar. 3, 1934, Liverpool, England, to an Irish mother and an Italian father. *d.* 1972. Raised in Rome from age three, she came to the US in 1951 and after drama studies with Stella Adler in New York, began appearing on TV and in films. A tall and lissome brunette with green eyes, she played standard leads in American and British films of the late 50s and early 60s. She became an American citizen in 1956. Her career was hampered by a drinking problem that led to several arrests on charges of intoxication. She died at 38 from an accidental overdose of drugs and alcohol.

FILMS INCLUDE: *All That Heaven Allows, The Price of Fear* 1956; *Four Girls in Town, The Big Boodle, The Garment Jungle, Tip on a Dead Jockey, Don't Go Near the Water* 1957; *Ride a Crooked Trail, The Tunnel of Love, The Two-Headed Spy* (UK) 1958; *The Angry Hills* (UK), *Battle of the Coral Sea* 1959; *I Aim at the Stars* (US/Ger.) 1960; *The Guns of Navarone* (UK/US) 1961; *Operation Delilah* (US/Sp.) 1966.

Scarwid, Diana. Actress. Born on Aug. 27, 1955, in Savannah, Ga. Pleasant, blonde leading lady and supporting player of the American stage, TV, and films. After training briefly at the University of Georgia (Athens) Theatre Workshop, she headed for New York, where she continued her studies at the AADA and at Pace University. She began her career with the National Shakespeare Conservatory in Woodstock, N.Y., and performed in regional theater before moving to Hollywood in 1976. She was nominated for an Academy Award as best supporting actress for *Inside Moves* (1980).

FILMS: *Pretty Baby* 1978; *Honeysuckle Rose, Inside Moves* 1980; *Mommie Dearest* (as Christina Crawford, adult) 1981; *Strange Invaders, Rumble Fish, Silkwood* 1983; *The Ladies Club, Psycho III, Extremities* 1986; *Heat* 1987; *Brenda Starr* 1992; *The Cure, Gold Diggers: Secret of Bear Mountain* 1995; *The Neon Bible* 1996.

scenario. Old-fashioned term for SCREENPLAY.

scene. In the strictest sense, a section of a motion picture which is unified as to time and place. It is made up from a series of shots of varying angles and is usually filmed in one session. As a unit of film language, the scene is larger than a SHOT and smaller than SEQUENCE. The term "scene" is also often used broadly and loosely to describe any distinct unit of a film, such as a TAKE, a shot, or a sequence.

scenery. The parts of a motion picture set that represent or simulate a locale.

scenic artist. An employee of a studio's art department whose job it is to paint backings, murals, and other illustrations that are part of the SCENERY on a film set.

Schaefer, George. Director. *b.* on Dec. 16, 1920, in Wallingford, Conn. *d.* 1997. *ed.* Lafayette Coll.; Yale Drama School. Following extensive experience as a Broadway and TV director and producer ('Macbeth,' '1960,' etc.), he turned to feature films late in the 60s, but before long returned to TV, where the excellence of his product brought him eight Emmy Awards. In 1986 he joined the faculty of UCLA as chairman of theater, film, and TV studies.

FILMS: *Macbeth* (expanded feature version of a TV production) 1963; *Pendulum, Generation* 1969; *Doctors' Wives* 1971; *Once Upon a Scoundrel* (US/Mex.) 1974; *An Enemy of the People* (also prod.) 1978.

Schaffner, Franklin J. Director. *b.* May 30, 1920, Tokyo. *d.* 1989, of cancer. The son of Protestant American missionaries, he was raised in Japan till age five, when his father's death forced the family back to the US. He grew up in Lancaster, Pennsylvania, and graduated from Franklin & Marshall College where he majored in government and English. He took up law at Columbia University, but his studies there were interrupted by WW II service as a lieutenant with the Navy Amphibious Forces in North Africa and Europe and with the Office of Strategic Services (OSS) in India, Burma, and China. Returning to civilian life, he joined "The March of Time" as an assistant director, then joined CBS-TV's news and public affairs department, soon graduating to director of such programs as Edward R. Murrow's 'Person to Person.' Switching to the drama department, he directed many noteworthy programs for such distinguished dramatic series as 'Studio One,' 'Playhouse 90,' 'Kaiser Aluminum Hour,' and 'Dupont Show of the Week.' Among the many plays he directed for TV were such memorable productions as 'Twelve Angry Men' and 'The Caine Mutiny Court-Martial.' He won Emmy Awards for his TV work in 1954, 1955, and 1962 and a special Emmy for his documentary 'Tour of the White House,' which featured Jacqueline Kennedy. In 1960 he directed the successful Broadway production of 'Advise and Consent' and in 1963 turned out his first feature film, *The Stripper,* an adaptation of the William Inge play 'A Loss of Roses,' starring Joanne Woodward as an aging stripper who falls in love with a younger man. He won a prize at the Karlovy Vary festival for his next film, *The Best Man* (1964), a political drama scripted by Gore Vidal from his own stage play. In these, as in his subsequent films, Schaffner proved himself a proficient craftsman who is capable of handling large-scale productions as well as intimate dramas. He won the best director Academy Award for *Patton* (1970), a film that reaped seven other Oscars, including best picture. He scored another triumph with *Papillon* (1973), eliciting a great performance from Dustin Hoffman, but ended his career on a downslide.

FILMS: *The Stripper* 1963; *The Best Man* 1964; *The War Lord* 1965; *The Double Man* (UK) 1967; *Planet of the Apes* 1968; *Patton* 1970; *Nicholas and Alexandra* (UK) 1971; *Papillon* (also co-prod.) 1973; *Islands in the Stream* 1977; *The Boys from Brazil* 1978; *Sphinx* 1981; *Yes Giorgio* 1982; *Lionheart* 1987; *Welcome Home* 1989.

Schary, Dore. Producer, screenwriter, playwright, director. *b.* Aug. 31, 1905, Newark, N.J. *d.* 1980. He began his career as an actor in stock, making his Broadway debut in 1930 in support of Spencer Tracy in 'The Last Mile.' He also dabbled briefly in journalism and was hired to write newspaper publicity for Admiral Richard E. Byrd. Failing to make much headway as a playwright in the early 30s, he set out for Hollywood and a career as a screenwriter. He worked for several studios before hitting his stride with MGM, where he shared an Academy

Award for the original story of *Boys Town* (1938). In 1941 he was appointed executive producer of MGM's B productions, but he resigned his post in 1943 as a result of a rift with his employers over a project, joining David O. Selznick's independent company as a producer. In 1947 he moved over to RKO as executive vice president in charge of production, but the following year he clashed with the company's new boss, Howard Hughes, and returned to MGM as chief of production.

His eight-year tenure at the helm of MGM was marked by a two-pronged policy that resulted in glittering entertainment films on one hand and serious "message" pictures on the other. The clash of personalities and viewpoints between Schary and veteran MGM boss Louis B. Mayer led to the latter's ouster from the company in 1951. When Schary himself was fired from his post in 1956, he returned to New York, where he wrote and produced the play 'Sunrise at Campobello,' which won five Tony Awards. He also formed his own film production company and continued working in both media as a writer, producer, and occasional director. He directed a number of successful plays but only one film, *Act One* (1963). A staunch liberal who attempted to resist Hollywood's blacklist during the McCarthy era, Schary was actively involved in a variety of civil liberties causes. Among the public offices he held were those of the national chairman of B'Nai B'rith's Anti-Defamation League and of the New York City Commissioner of Cultural Affairs. In addition to writing or producing many films himself (some are listed below), he was responsible for the creation of hundreds of other pictures in his capacity as chief of production. Author: *Case History of a Movie* (1950), *For Special Occasions* (1962), *Storm in the West* (with Sinclair Lewis, 1963).

FILMS INCLUDE: As screenwriter—*Fury of the Jungle, He Couldn't Take it* 1933; *Murder in the Clouds* 1934; *Chinatown Squad, Silk Hat Kid, Mississippi, The Raven* 1935; *Outcast, Big City* 1937; *Boys Town* 1938; *Young Tom Edison, Edison the Man* (co-story only) 1940; *It's a Big Country* 1952. As producer—*I'll Be Seeing You* 1945; *The Spiral Staircase, Till the End of Time* 1946; *Crossfire* (exec. prod.), *The Farmer's Daughter, The Bachelor and the Bobby-Soxer* 1947; *The Boy with Green Hair* (exec. prod.), *Mr. Blandings Builds His Dream House* (exec. prod.) 1948; *Battleground* 1949; *The Next Voice You Hear* 1950; *Plymouth Adventure* 1952; *Take the High Ground* 1953; *Bad Day at Black Rock* 1955; *The Swan* 1956; *Designing Woman* 1957; *Lonelyhearts* (also sc.) 1959; *Sunrise at Campobello* (also sc. from own play) 1960; *Act One* (also dir., sc.) 1963.

Schatzberg, Jerry. Director. Born on June 26, 1927, in New York City. *ed.* U. of Miami. A former fashion photographer and director of TV commercials, he made a shaky debut as a feature director with *Puzzle of a Downward Child* in 1970, but made a powerful impact the following year with *The Panic in Needle Park,* a harrowing depiction of the New York drug scene featuring Al Pacino in his first starring role. Strong performances by Pacino and Gene Hackman boosted Schatzberg's next film, *Scarecrow,* which shared the Palme d'Or at the 1973 Cannes Festival. European critics adored his *Reunion* (1989), a French-German-British co-production about the rise of nazism in 1930s Germany.

FILMS: *Puzzle of a Downfall Child* (also co-story) 1970; *The Panic in Needle Park* 1971; *Scarecrow* 1973; *Sweet Revenge/Dandy the All American Girl* (also prod.) 1976; *The Seduction of Joe Tynan* 1979; *Honeysuckle Rose* 1980; *Misunderstood, No Small Affair* 1984; *Street Smart* 1987; *Reunion/L'Ami retrouvé* (Fr./Ger./UK) 1989.

Schayer, Richard. Screenwriter. *b.* Dec. 13, 1882, Washington, D.C. Deceased. *ed.* Georgetown U. The son of an Army career officer, he was drawn to acting and after training at New York's American Academy of Dramatic Arts he appeared with various stock companies for four years. He then switched to journalism and worked as a reporter for New York, Chicago, and Washington dailies. He entered films as a screenwriter after returning from WW I service and soon proved himself one of the most prolific men in the business. He wrote scores of screenplays for silent and sound Hollywood films of all genres, many of them run-of-the-mill action pictures, and reached a peak of productivity with MGM in the late 20s and early 30s, when he wrote a number of hilarious scripts for Buster KEATON comedies, as well as several worthy dramatic screenplays.

FILMS INCLUDE: *The Killer, The Spenders, The Lure of Egypt, Beach of Dreams, Black Roses* 1921; *The Gray Dawn* 1922; *The Victor, The Thrill Chaser* 1923; *The Dangerous Flirt, Silk Stocking Sal* 1924; *The Hurricane Kid, The Man in Blue* 1925; *Tell It to the Marines, The Unknown Soldier, The Terror* 1926; *On Ze Boulevard* 1927; *Circus Rookies, The Actress, Across to Singapore, The Cameraman* 1928; *The Flying Fleet, Spite Marriage, Where East Is East, Wild Orchids, Hallelujah* (treatment only), *Devil-May-Care* (adapt. only) 1929; *Free and Easy, Children of Pleasure, Doughboys, Men of the North* 1930; *Just a Gigolo, Trader Horn, Private Lives* (co-sc.) 1931; *The Mummy* (co-story only) 1932; *The Winning Ticket* 1935; *Dangerous Waters, The Devil Is a Sissy* 1936; *The Black Arrow* 1948; *Kim* (co-sc.) 1950; *The Texas Rangers, Lorna Doone* 1951; *Gun Belt* 1953; *Gun Fight* 1961; *Lancelot and Guinevere/Sword of Lancelot* (UK) 1963; *Arizona Raiders* (co-story only) 1965.

Scheider, Roy. Actor. Born on Nov. 10, 1932, in Orange, N.J., of German-Irish descent. *ed.* Rutgers; Franklin and Marshall Coll. Dynamic, sinewy leading man and character actor of the American stage and screen. Trained in college dramatics, he made his professional stage debut in 1961, playing Mercutio in the New York Shakespeare Festival production of 'Romeo and Juliet.' He spent several years in repertory, playing mainly classic roles, and in the mid-60s made his first film appearance. By the mid-70s he had developed into a versatile and intriguing leading man and character player in both American and French films. His career received added impetus in 1975 from a star billing in the box-office blockbuster *Jaws.* He gave an engrossing portrayal of director-choreographer Bob Fosse in the latter's autobiographical film *All That Jazz* (1979). Scheider was nominated for an Academy Award as best actor for that performance and as best supporting actor for his role in *The French Connection* (1971). His usually tough screen characterizations have benefited from a broken nose, à la Belmondo, that he sustained in Golden Gloves boxing preliminaries during his high school days. He starred on TV in the science fiction series 'SeaQuest DSV.'

FILMS INCLUDE: *The Curse of the Living Corpse* 1964; *Stiletto* 1969; *Loving, Puzzle of a Downfall Child* 1970; *Klute, The French Connection* 1971; *The Outside Man* (Fr.) 1972; *L'Attentat/The French Conspiracy* (Fr.), *The Seven Ups* 1973; *Sheila Levine Is Dead and Living in New York, Jaws* 1975; *Marathon Man* 1976; *Sorcerer* 1977; *Jaws 2* 1978; *The Last Embrace, All That Jazz* 1979; *Still of the Night* 1982; *Blue Thunder* 1983; *In Our Hands* (doc.), *2010* 1984; *Mishima* (narrator only) 1985; *The Men's Club, 52 Pick-Up* 1986; *Cohen & Tate, Listen to Me, Night Game* 1989; *The Fourth War, The Russia House* 1990; *Naked Lunch* (Can./UK) 1991; *Romeo Is Bleeding* 1994; *The Myth of Fingerprints* 1997.

Schell, Maria. Actress. Born Margarete Schell, on Jan. 5, 1926, in Vienna. Intense, soulful leading lady of international films. The daughter of a Swiss poet-playwright and an Austrian actress, and the older sister of actor-director Maximilian

SCHELL, she made her screen debut in Switzerland at age 16, under the name of Gritli Schell. Gradually gaining prominence, she reached the peak of her career in the 50s, when she won the 1954 Cannes Festival award as best actress for her performance in Helmut Käutner's *Die letzte Brücke/The Last Bridge* and the 1956 Venice Festival prize for René Clément's *Gervaise.* She also gave memorable, touching performances in Luchino Visconti's *Le Notti bianche/White Nights* (1957) and Alexandre Astruc's *Une Vie/End of Desire* (1958). Her career declined sharply in the 60s as the public's appetite for weepy, suffering women roles decreased along with gains in female independence. She retired from the screen in 1963 but returned in 1968, gradually retreating into character roles.

FILMS INCLUDE: *Steibruch* (Switz.) 1942; *Der Engel mit der Posaune* (Aus./Ger.) 1948; *Angel with the Trumpet* (UK version of preceding film), *Die letzte Nacht* (Ger.) 1949; *Es Kommt ein Tag* (Ger.) 1950; *Dr. Holl/Angelika* (Ger.), *The Magic Box* (UK) 1951; *So Little Time* (UK) 1952; *Tagebuch einer Verliebten* (Ger.), *Der träumende Mund/Dreaming Lips* (Ger.), *The Heart of the Matter* (UK) 1953; *Die letzte Brücke/The Last Bridge* (Ger./Yug.), *Napoléon* (as Marie-Louise of Austria; Fr.), *Die Ratten/The Rats* (Ger.) 1955; *Gervaise* (title role; Fr.), *Liebe* (Ger.) 1956; *Rose Bernd/The Sins of Rose Bernd* (Ger.); *Le Notti bianche/White Nights* (as Natalia; It./Fr.) 1957; *Une Vie/End of Desire* (as Jeanne Dandieu; Fr./It.), *The Brothers Karamazov* (as Grushenka; US) 1958; *Raubfischer in Hellas/As the Sea Rages* (Ger./Yug.), *The Hanging Tree* (US) 1959; *Cimarron* (US) 1960; *The Mark* (UK) 1961; *Ich bin auch nur eine Frau/Only a Woman* (Ger.) 1962; *L'Assassin connaît la Musique* (Fr.) 1963; *Le Diable par la Queue/The Devil by the Tail* (Fr./It.), *99 Mujeres/99 Women* (Sp./It./Ger./UK) 1969; *Night of the Blood Monster* (Sp./Ger./UK) 1971; *The Odessa File* (UK) 1974; *Folies Bourgeoises* (Fr.), *Voyage of the Damned* (UK), *So oder so ist das Leben* (also co-prod.; Ger.) 1976; *Schöner Gigolo—armer Gigolo/Just a Gigolo* (Ger.), *Superman* (US) 1978; *La Passante du Sans-Souci/La Passante* 1982; *1919* (UK) 1985.

Schell, Maximilian. Actor, director, producer, screenwriter. Born on Dec. 8, 1930, in Vienna. Dark, handsome leading man of international films who began a second career as a producer and director in the late 60s. The younger brother of Maria SCHELL (siblings Karl and Edith are also actors), he was raised mainly in Switzerland, to which the family had fled after the Anschluss of 1938, and was educated at the universities of Zurich, Basel, and Munich. He began appearing professionally on the stage in 1952 and made his film debut three years later. After appearing on Broadway in the play 'Interlock,' he played his initial role in a Hollywood film as a German officer in *The Young Lions* (1958). Three years later he won an Oscar as best actor for his performance as an enigmatic defense attorney in *Judgment at Nuremberg.* But the award did little to advance his career and he was cast mainly in minor films of various nations, in both leads and supporting roles. Unhappy with the direction his career was taking, he plunged into production in 1968 with *Das Schloss,* a screen version of Franz Kafka's *The Castle,* in which he also starred. He made his debut as director in 1970 with *Erste Liebe/First Love,* a lavish adaptation of a Turgenev romantic story. *Der Füssganger/The Pedestrian* (1974), a drama about responsibility for war crimes notable for its subtle detail, which he produced, directed, wrote, and starred in, was nominated for an Oscar as best foreign film. In 1984, he wrote and organized a fascinating documentary on *Judgment at Nuremburg* co-star Marlene DIETRICH, using cryptic audio-only interviews with the recalcitrant icon and recreating her Paris apartment on a sound stage in order to capture her personal life. It was nominated for an Academy Award as best documentary. Schell still appears as an actor in films of other directors and was nominated for Academy Awards for his performances in *The Man in the Glass Booth* (1975) and *Julia* (1977). In addition to continuing his work in films, Schell has been active as director, writer, and actor on the Continental stage.

FILMS INCLUDE: As actor—*Kinder Mütter und ein General* (Ger.) 1955; *Der 20. Juli* (Ger.), *Reifende Jugend* (Ger.), *Ein Herz kehrt heim* (Ger.) 1956; *The Young Lions* (US) 1958; *Hamlet* (title role; orig. made for TV; Ger.) 1960; *Judgment at Nuremberg* (US) 1961; *Five Finger Exercise* (US), *The Reluctant Saint* (US/It.) 1962; *I Sequestrati di Altona/The Condemned of Altona* (It./Fr.) 1963; *Topkapi* (US) 1964; *Return from the Ashes* (US/UK) 1965; *The Deadly Affair* (UK), *Mas allá de las Montañas/The Desperate Ones/Beyond the Mountains* (Sp./US) 1967; *Counterpoint* (US), *Das Schloss/The Castle* (as K.; also prod.; Ger./Switz.) 1968; *Krakatoa East of Java* (US) 1969; *Trotta* (co-sc. only; Ger.) 1971; *Paulina 1880* (Fr.), *Pope Joan* (UK) 1972; *The Odessa File* (UK) 1974; *The Man in the Glass Booth* (US) 1975; *Einsichten eines Clowns* (co-prod. only; Ger.), *St. Ives* (US), *Assassination in Sarajevo/The Day That Shook the World* (Yug./Czech.) 1976; *A Bridge Too Far* (UK), *Cross of Iron* (UK/Ger.), *Julia* (US) 1977; *Amo non amo/I Love You I Love You Not/Together* (It.), *Players* (US), *Avalanche Express* (US), *The Black Hole* (US) 1979; *The Chosen* (US) 1981; *Les Iles* (Fr.) 1983; *Morgen in Alabama* (Ger.) 1984; *The Assisi Underground* (It./UK/Isr.) 1985; *The Rose Garden* (Ger./US) 1989; *Labyrinth* (Ger.), *The Freshman* (US) 1990; *Tales from the Vienna Woods* (also prod., co-sc.; Ger./Aus.) 1979; *Marlene* (doc.; also sc., interviewer; Ger.) 1984; *An American Place* (Ger./US) 1990; *A Far Off Place* 1993; *Little Odessa* 1994. As director—*Erste Liebe/First Love* (also co-prod., co-sc., act.; Switz./Ger.) 1970; *Der Füssganger/The Pedestrian* (also prod., dir., sc., act.; Ger.) 1974; *Der Richter und Sein Henker/End of the Game* (also co-prod., co-sc., Ger./It.) 1975; *Geschichten aus dem Wienerwald* 1979.

Schenck, Aubrey. Producer. Born on Aug. 26, 1908, in Brooklyn, N.Y. *ed.* Cornell. A lawyer, he entered the film business in 1936 as an attorney to a theater chain. He switched to production in the mid-40s and has since produced many low- and medium-budget films.

FILMS INCLUDE: *Shock* 1946; *T-Men* 1947; *Mickey* 1948; *Port of New York, Undercover Girl* 1950; *Target Unknown, The Fat Man* 1951; *Shield for Murder* 1954; *Big House USA* 1955; *Untamed Youth* 1957; *Frankenstein 1970* 1958; *Up Periscope* 1959; *Wild Harvest* 1961; *Robinson Crusoe on Mars* 1964; *Ambush Bay* (exec. prod.) 1966; *Kill a Dragon* (exec. prod.) 1967; *More Dead Than Alive, Impasse* (both exec. prod.) 1969; *Barquero* (exec. prod.) 1970; *Daughters of Satan* 1972.

Schenck, Joseph M. Executive, producer. *b.* Dec. 25, 1876, Rybinsk, Russia. *d.* 1961. In the US from his mid-teens (1892), he started as an errand boy and eventually worked his way up to ownership of a couple of New York City drugstores with his brother, Nicholas Schenck (*b.* Nov. 15, 1880, Rybinsk; *d.* 1969), as partner. In 1908 the brothers opened an amusement park at Fort George in upstate New York and in 1912 acquired the Palisades Amusement Park in Fort Lee, N.J. It was in that venture that they became business associates of Marcus Loew, the chief executive of a rapidly expanding chain of motion picture theaters. Both brothers became top executives with the Loew organization, which eventually became the parent company of MGM. But while Nicholas remained with Loew, and would go on to become the company's president in 1927 and chairman of the board in 1955, Joseph left in 1917 to become an independent producer. He signed Roscoe ("Fatty") Arbuckle for a comedy series distributed by Paramount, and his leading star was his own wife, Norma TALMADGE, whom he married in 1917 but later divorced. He also produced the films of her sisters, Constance and Natalie Talmadge, and most importantly all the silent films of Natalie's husband, Buster KEATON, as well as some of the later films of D. W. GRIFFITH.

In 1924, Schenck was elected chairman of the board of United Artists, and in 1933 he founded 20th Century with Darryl Zanuck and became the company's president. When the company merged with Fox in 1935 he became chairman of the board of 20th Century-Fox. He resigned his position in 1941 after being sentenced to a year in jail on charges involving income tax irregularities and union payoffs. He served four months of the sentence, than returned to the company in an executive producer's capacity. In 1952 he won a special Academy Award "for long and distinguished service to the motion picture industry." The following year he co-founded the Magna corporation with Michael Todd to exploit the Todd-AO wide-screen system.

FILMS INCLUDE (as producer): *Panthea, Butcher Boy* (short), *Poppy, The Moth* 1917; *By Right of Purchase, The Forbidden City* 1918; *The Heart of Wetons, The New Moon, The Way of a Woman, The Isle of Conquest, A Virtuous Vamp* 1919; *A Daughter of Two Worlds, The Branded Woman* 1920; *The Passion Flower, The Sign on the Door, Wedding Bells, Woman's Place, Love's Redemption* 1921; *Polly of the Follies, The Primitive Lover, The Eternal Flame, East Is West* 1922; *Within the Law, Ashes of Vengeance, Three Ages, The Song of Love* 1923; *The Goldfish, Secrets, Sherlock Jr., The Navigator, Her Night of Romance* 1924; *The Lady, Seven Chances, Graustark, Her Sister from Paris, Go West* 1925; *Kiki, Battling Butler, The Duchess of Buffalo* 1926; *The General, Venus of Venice, Camille, College, Sorrell and Son* 1927; *Steamboat Bill Jr., The Dove, The Woman Disputed, The Battle of the Sexes* 1928; *Lady of the Pavements, Alibi, Eternal Love, New York Nights* 1929; *Be Yourself!, One Romantic Night, Abraham Lincoln, Du Barry—Woman of Passion, The Bat Whispers* 1930.

Schenck, Nicholas M. See SCHENCK, Joseph M.

Schenstrom, Carl. See MADSEN AND SCHENSTROM.

Schepisi, Fred. Director. Born Frederici Alan Schepisi, on Dec. 26, 1939, in Melbourne. The son of a used car dealer, he attended a Roman Catholic boarding school. Showing little aptitude for academics or enthusiasm for the priesthood, he lasted only two years at a seminary, dropping out at 15. After briefly working as a mechanic on his father's lot, he entered advertising as a messenger boy in 1955. He moved gradually up the agency ladder, and before long began writing copy and directing TV commercials. He also wrote and directed documentaries, one of which, *People Make Papers,* won a Golden Reel at the Australian Film Institute Awards. In 1966 he formed his own production company, The Film House, that soon acquired a reputation for the technical excellence of its documentaries and commercials. All the while, however, Schepisi was eager to move into features. He got his first opportunity with 'The Priest' episode of the omnibus film *Libido* (1973). His first solo feature, *The Devil's Playground* (1976), was a sensitive, loosely autobiographical exploration of pubescent sexuality at a Catholic boarding school. It was showered with Australian Film Awards, including best film, best direction, and best screenplay. Schepisi gained an international reputation with *The Chant of Jimmie Blacksmith* (1978), a powerful examination of the exasperating world of a half-breed aborigine. The film's success opened for Schepisi the gates to Hollywood and a prosperous career.

FEATURE FILMS: In Australia—*Libido* ("The Priest" episode) 1973; *The Devil's Playground* (also prod., sc.) 1976; *The Chant of Jimmie Blacksmith* (also prod., sc.) 1978. In the US—*Barbarosa* 1982; *Iceman* 1984; *Plenty* 1985; *Roxanne* 1987; *Evil Angels/A Cry in the Dark* (also co-sc.; Austral.) 1988; *The Russia House* (also co-prod.) 1990; *Mr. Baseball* (US), *Six Degrees of Separation* 1993; *I.Q.* 1994; *Fierce Creatures* (co-dir.) 1997.

Schertzinger, Victor. Director, musician. *b.* Apr. 8, 1880, Mahanoy City, Pa. *d.* 1941. *ed.* Brown U.; U. of Brussels. A concert violinist, he toured Europe for several years before returning to the US to conduct musical-comedy orchestras. He made his entry into films as composer of the accompanying score for Thomas Ince's *Civilization* (1916) and other silent pictures, then turned director of many commercially successful silent and sound films. He wrote songs or scores for many of his own musical films. He spent his last years with Paramount, for which he directed a couple of the popular Hope-Crosby-Lamour "Road" pictures.

FILMS (as director): *The Clodhopper, The Millionaire Vagrant, The Pinch Hitter, Sudden Jim, The Son of His Father* 1917; *His Mother's Boy, The Hired Man, The Family Skeleton, Playing the Game, His Own Home Town, The Claws of the Hun, A Nine O' Clock Town, String Beans* 1918; *The Homebreaker, Hard Boiled, The Lady of Red Butte, Other Men's Wives, The Sheriff's Son, Quicksand, Upstairs, The Peace of Roaring River, When Doctors Disagree, The Jinx* 1919; *Pinto, The Blooming Angel, The Slim Princess* 1920; *Made in Heaven, The Concert, What Happened to Rosa?, Beating the Game* 1921; *Mr. Barnes of New York, Head Over Heels, The Bootlegger's Daughter, The Kingdom Within, Scandalous Tongues* 1922; *The Lonely Road, The Scarlet Lily, Refuge, Dollar Devils, The Man Next Door, Long Live the King, The Man Life Passed By, Chastity* 1923; *A Boy of Flanders, Bread* 1924; *Frivolous Sal, Man and Maid, The Wheel, Thunder Mountain, The Golden Strain* 1925; *Siberia, The Lily, The Return of Peter Grimm* 1926; *Stage Madness, The Heart of Salome, The Secret Studio* 1927; *The Showdown, Forgotten Faces, Manhattan Cocktail* 1928; *Redskin, Fashions in Love* (also co-songs), *The Wheel of Life* (also song), *Nothing but the Truth, Betrayal* (co-story only), *The Love Parade* (co-songs only), *The Laughing Lady* 1929; *Paramount on Parade* (co-dir.), *Safety in Numbers, Heads Up* (also song), *The Climax* (song only) 1930; *The Woman Between, Friends and Lovers* 1931; *Strange Justice, Uptown New York* 1932; *Cocktail Hour, The Constant Woman/Auction in Souls, My Woman* (also song) 1933; *Beloved* (also theme song), *One Night of Love* (also theme song) 1934; *Let's Live Tonight* (also songs), *Love Me Forever* (also story, theme song) 1935; *The Music Goes 'Round* (also songs), *Follow Your Heart* (songs only) 1936; *Something to Sing About* (also story, music) 1937; *The Mikado* (UK) 1939; *Road to Singapore* (also co-songs), *Rhythm on the River* 1940; *Road to Zanzibar, Kiss the Boys Goodbye* (also co-songs), *Birth of the Blues* 1941; *The Fleet's In* (also co-songs) 1942.

Schiaffino, Rosanna. Actress. Born in 1939, in Genoa. Leading lady of Italian and international films, usually in sensual roles.

FILMS INCLUDE: *Totó Lascia o Raddoppia?* 1956; *La Sfida* 1958; *La Notte Brava* 1959; *Le Bal des Espions* (Fr./It.) 1960; *Teseo contro il Minotauro/The Minotaur* (in dual role, as Ariadne/Phaedra), *I Briganti Italiani, Le Miracle des Loups/Blood on His Sword* (Fr./It.) 1961; *La Fayette/Lafayette* (Fr./It.), *Le Crime ne paie pas/Crime Does Not Pay* (Fr./It.), *Two Weeks in Another Town* (US) 1962; *The Victors* (UK/US) 1963; *The Long Ships* (UK/Yug.) 1964; *Sette contro la Morte/The Cavern* (It./Ger.), *La Mandragola* 1965; *El Greco* (It./Fr.), *La Strega in Amore/The Witch, Drop Dead Darling!/Arrivederci Baby!* (UK)

1966; *L'Avventuriero/The Rover, Encrucijada para una Monja/A Nun at the Crossroads* (Sp./It.) 1967; *Simon Bolivar* (It./Sp.) 1969; *Seven Times a Day* (Can./Isr.), *Travestere* 1971; *The Man Called Noon* (UK), *Gli Eroi/The Heroes* 1973; *La Trastienda* (Sp.), *Cagliostro* 1976.

Schiffman, Suzanne. Screenwriter, director. Born in 1929, in Paris. *ed.* Sorbonne. She entered French films as a continuity clerk for Jean-Luc Godard and François Truffaut and gradually developed into the latter's trusted associate, serving as his assistant director and script collaborator. Following her mentor's death, she ventured successfully into directing. Nathalie Baye portrayed her in Truffaut's autobiographic film *Day for Night* (1974), a film for which Schiffman shared an Oscar nomination for best screenplay. She also collaborated on the scripts of other directors, notably Jacques Rivette.

FILMS (as co-screenwriter): *Out 1: Noli me Tangère* 1971; *La Nuit américaine/Day for Night* 1973; *Out 1: Spectre* 1974; *L'Histoire d'Adèle H./The Story of Adele H.* 1975; *L'Argent de Poche/Small Change* 1976; *L'Homme qui aimait les Femmes/The Man Who Loved Women* 1977; *L'Amour en fuite/Love on the Run* 1979; *Le Dernier Métro/The Last Metro* 1980; *La Femme d'à coté/The Woman Next Door* 1981; *Le Pont du Nord* 1982; *Merry Go Round* (release delayed from 1979), *Vivement Dimanche!/Confidentially Yours* 1983; *L'Amour par Terre/Love on the Ground* 1984; *Hurlevent/Wuthering Heights* 1985; *La Moine et la Sorcière/Sorceress* (also dir.; Fr./US) 1987; *Femme de Papier/Front Woman* (also dir.), *Corpos perdidos/Corps perdus* (Arg./Fr.) 1989.

Schifrin, Lalo (Boris). Composer. Born on June 21, 1932, in Buenos Aires. A child prodigy, he first studied music under his father, a concertmaster of the Teatro colón. In 1950 he went to Paris, where he studied classical music and jazz and represented Argentina in the 1955 International Jazz Festival. Returning to Argentina, he formed his own jazz band and in 1958 went to New York as an arranger for Xavier Cugat and later (1960–62) became pianist-composer with the Dizzy Gillespie band. In 1964 he settled in Hollywood, where he soon gained prominence as a fertile composer of movie and TV music. One of his more memorable scores was the scintillating theme for the TV series 'Mission Impossible.' Schifrin also wrote for the concert hall, becoming known for his experiments in bringing the jazz idiom to religious music. His oratorio, 'The Rise and Fall of the Third Reich' (1967), incorporated an actual recording of a Hitler speech and other startling realistic effects.

FILMS INCLUDE: In Argentina—*El Jefe* 1957. In France—*Les Félins/Joy House* 1964. In the US—*Rhino* 1964; *The Cincinnati Kid* 1965; *Blindfold* 1966; *The President's Analyst, Cool Hand Luke* 1967; *The Fox, The Brotherhood, Bullitt* 1968; *Che!* 1969; *Kelly's Heroes* 1970; *The Beguiled, Pretty Maids All in a Row, THX-1138* 1971; *Dirty Harry, Prime Cut* 1972; *Charlie Varrick, Enter the Dragon, Magnum Force* 1973; *The Four Musketeers* (UK) 1975; *Sky Riders, Voyage of the Damned* (UK) 1976; *The Eagle Has Landed* (UK), *Telefon* 1977; *Return from Witch Mountain* 1978; *The Amityville Horror* 1979; *Serial, Brubaker, The Competition* 1980; *Caveman, Buddy Buddy* 1981; *The Sting II* (adapt.), *Sudden Impact, The Osterman Weekend* 1983; *Tank* 1984; *The Mean Season* 1985; *The Ladies Club* 1986; *The Fourth Protocol* (UK) 1987; *The Dead Pool, Berlin Blues* (Sp.), *Little Sweetheart* 1988; *Return from the River Kwai* (UK) 1989; *Naked Tango* 1990; *FX2: The Deadly Art of Illusion* 1991; *Mission: Impossible* 1996; *Money Talks* 1997.

Schildkraut, Joseph. Actor. *b.* Mar. 22, 1895, Vienna. *d.* 1964. The son of Rudolph Schildkraut (1862–1930), a celebrated star of Max REINHARDT's Berlin stage company (and later Broadway and German and American films), he trained for the stage under his father's rival, Albert Basserman. In 1910 he accompanied his father on the latter's US tour and enrolled at the American Academy of Dramatic Arts. Returning to Germany in 1913, he joined Reinhardt's stage company, and he soon became a star. In 1920 he settled in the US and within a year was a leading matinee idol on Broadway ('Liliom' opposite Le Gallienne, 1921, etc.). His parallel screen career saw him transform from a suave leading man in films of the 20s and early 30s to a smooth character actor, often villainous. Alternating between films and the stage, he was absent from the screen for a decade before repeating his stage success in *The Diary of Anne Frank.* He won an Academy Award for portraying Dreyfus in *The Life of Emile Zola* (1937) and wrote an autobiography, *My Father and I* (1959).

FILMS: In Germany—*The Wandering Jew* 1908; *Schlemiel* 1915; *The Life of Theodore Herzl* 1918. In Austria—*Der Roman der Komtesse Orth* 1920. In the US—*Orphans of the Storm* 1922; *The Song of Love* 1924; *The Road to Yesterday* 1925; *Shipwrecked, Meet the Prince, Young April* 1926; *The King of Kings* (as Judas), *The Heart Thief, His Dog, The Forbidden Woman* 1927; *The Blue Danube, Tenth Avenue* 1928; *Show Boat* (as Gaylord Ravenal), *The Mississippi Gambler* 1929; *Night Ride, Cock o' the Walk, Die Sehnsucht jeder Frau* (German-language version of *A Lady to Love*) 1930; *Carnival* (UK) 1931; *The Blue Danube* (UK) 1932; *Viva Villa!, Sisters Under the Skin, Cleopatra* (as King Herod) 1934; *The Crusades* (as Conrad of Montferrat) 1935; *The Garden of Allah* 1936; *Slave Ship, Souls at Sea, The Life of Emile Zola* (as Capt. Alfred Dreyfus), *Lancer Spy* 1937; *Lady Behave!, The Baroness and the Butler, Marie Antoinette* (as the Duke d'Orleans), *Suez* 1938; *Idiot's Delight, The Three Musketeers* (as Louis XIII), *Mr. Moto Takes a Vacation, The Man in the Iron Mask* (as Fouquet), *Lady of the Tropics, The Rains Came, Pack Up Your Troubles* 1939; *The Shop Around the Corner, Phantom Raiders, Rangers of Fortune, Meet the Wildcat* 1940; *The Parson of Panamint* 1941; *Flame of the Barbary Coast, The Cheaters* 1945; *Monsieur Beaucaire, The Plainsman and the Lady* 1946; *Northwest Outpost* 1947; *Old Los Angeles, The Gallant Legion* 1948; *The Diary of Anne Frank* (as Otto Frank) 1959; *King of the Roaring 20s* 1961; *The Greatest Story Ever Told* (as Nicodemus) 1965.

Schildkraut, Rudolph (also **Rudolf**). Actor. *b.* 1862, Constantinople (now Istanbul). *d.* 1930. A famous star of Max Reinhardt's Berlin stage company and later Broadway, he also appeared in both German and American films, usually in character leads. Father of Joseph SCHILDKRAUT.

FILMS: In Germany—*Dämon und Mensch, Lache Bajazzo, Ivan Koschula* 1914; *Schlemiel* 1915; *Der Fluck* 1920. In the US—*His People/Proud Heart* 1925; *Pals in Paradise, Young April* 1926; *The King of Kings* (as Caiphas), *The Country Doctor, A Harp in Hawk, The Main Event, Turkish Delight* 1927; *A Ship Comes In* 1928; *Christina* 1929.

Schilling, Gus. Actor. *b.* August E. Schilling, June 20, 1908, New York City. *d.* 1957. A veteran comedian of burlesque and stage musicals, he entered films early in the 40s through his association with Orson Welles in the Mercury Players' stage and radio plays. He usually played jittery types.

FILMS INCLUDE: *Mexican Spitfire Out West* 1940; *Citizen Kane, Ice-Capades, It Started with Eve, Appointment for Love* 1941; *The Magnificent Ambersons, Broadway, You Were Never Lovelier* 1942; *Chatterbox, Hers to Hold* 1943; *It's a Pleasure, A Thousand and One Nights* 1945; *Calendar Girl* 1947; *The Lady from Shanghai, Macbeth* 1948; *Our Very Own* 1950; *On Dangerous Ground* 1952; *Run for Cover* 1955; *Bigger Than Life* 1956.

Schlesinger, John. Director. Born on Feb. 16, 1926, in London, the son of a Jewish pediatrician. He began his association with "show business" during his WW II service, entertaining troops with a magic act. Returning to civilian life, he began acting in student plays at Oxford University. In the 50s he played character parts in many plays and in a number of films, including *Oh Rosalinda!, Brothers-in-Law,* and *The Battle of the River Plate.* Having made several amateur films, he joined BBC-TV in 1957 as a director. He piloted a monthly documentary series and several episodes of the Churchill series *The Valiant Years.* In 1961 he won first prize at the Venice Film Festival for his 45-minute documentary *Terminus,* in which he captured the daily drama of London's Waterloo Station. The success of the film made it possible for him to switch to feature films.

Schlesinger's documentary background and his experience as an actor were evident in his very first feature, *A Kind of Loving* (1962), a keenly observed account of a dreary working-class marriage in England's industrial north. Notable for its precise realism and excellent performances, it won the Golden Bear at the Berlin Film Festival. Equally admired for its background detail and acting was the director's *Billy Liar* (1963), a sad-funny look at the fantasy life of an ambitious undertaker's clerk. It proved instrumental in the careers of its leading players, Tom Courtenay and Julie Christie. The latter soared to stardom in the director's next film, *Darling* (1965), for which she won the best actress Oscar for her role as an opportunistic model. The film won a slew of other awards, including best direction by the New York Film Critics and Oscar nominations for best picture and best director. It was later included in many lists as one of the best films of the 60s.

It was in Hollywood, with his first American film, that Schlesinger reached the peak of his success. A shattering story of hope, despair, and friendship, *Midnight Cowboy* (1969) brought into powerful focus the director's career-long interest in complex relationships and the individual search for security and happiness. The film won Academy Awards for best picture and best director, among many other prizes. On a more modest scale, Schlesinger scored critical successes with *Sunday Bloody Sunday* (1971), a mature drama centering on a bisexual triangle; *The Day of the Locust* (1975), a solid adaptation of Nathanael West's novel about Hollywood in the 30s; and a commercial bonanza with the Nazi-hunt thriller *Marathon Man* (1976). Many liked Schlesinger's recreation of England's WW II home-front atmosphere in *Yanks* (1979). Only *Madame Sousatzka* (1988) stands out among his films of the 80s.

FEATURE FILMS: *Terminus* (medium-length doc.) 1961; *A Kind of Loving* 1962; *Billy Liar* 1963; *Darling* (also co-story) 1965; *Far from the Madding Crowd* 1967; *Midnight Cowboy* (US) 1969; *Sunday Bloody Sunday* 1971; *Visions of Eight* (doc. on Munich Olympics; "The Longest" episode) 1973; *The Day of the Locust* (US) 1975; *Marathon Man* (US) 1976; *Yanks* 1979; *Honky Tonk Freeway* (U) 1981; *Privileged* (consulting dir. only) 1982; *The Falcon and the Snowman* (also co-prod.; US) 1985; *The Believers* (also co-prod.; US) 1987; *Madame Sousatzka* (US) 1988; *Pacific Heights* (US) 1990; *The Innocent* (US) 1993; *Eye for an Eye* 1995; *Cold Comfort Farm* 1996.

Schlöndorff, Volker. Director. Born on Mar. 31, 1939, in Wiesbaden, Germany. A physician's son, he moved with his family in 1956 to Paris, where he completed his secondary education, then studied political science and economics at the Sorbonne and directing at IDHEC, the famous film school. He began his professional career in 1960 as an assistant to directors Louis Malle, Alain Resnais, and Jean-Pierre Melville. On his own he made a short, *Wen Kümmert's* (1960), and TV documentaries about the conflicts in Algeria and Vietnam. Returning to Germany in the mid-60s, Schlöndorff established himself at the forefront of the talent-poor national cinema with his very first feature, *Young Torless* (1966). Ostensibly a psychological study of the moral complacency of an arrogant young man who witnesses cruelties at a boarding school in turn-of-the-century Germany, the film represented a not-too-subtle indictment of the complicity of German people in the face of Nazi atrocities. The technically accomplished production shared the International Critics Prize at that year's Cannes Festival. It represented the first success of the emerging New German Cinema.

Unlike other young filmmakers who followed—Fassbinder, Herzog, Wenders, Straub—Schlöndorff typically shunned experimentation and stylistic adventure. Although he shared their political radicalism, he differed in his approach, applying high-polish, Hollywood-style technique and traditional storytelling to make his films easily accessible to mass audiences. A fine example is *The Tin Drum* (1979), a highly literate, technically brilliant adaptation of the Günther Grass allegorical novel about a child who stopped growing once the Nazis came to power. The sprawling production won the Oscar for best foreign language film and shared the Palme d'Or at Cannes with *Apocalypse Now.* Many of the director's other films were also adaptations from literary works. Schlöndorff's fluency in several languages enabled him to work occasionally abroad, including the US, where he directed a much-liked TV movie version of *Death of a Salesman* (1985) and the less successful futuristic feminist fantasy *The Handmaid's Tale* (1990). Schlöndorff has been married since 1969 to Margarethe von TROTTA, who after years of collaborating with her husband as a screenwriter and actress, emerged as a highly esteemed director on her own.

FEATURE FILMS: *Der junge Törless/Young Torless* (also sc.) 1966; *Mord und Totschlag/A Degree of Murder* (also co-sc.) 1967; *Michael Kohlhass—Der Rebell* (also co-sc.) 1969; *Baal* (orig. for TV; also sc.) 1970; *Der plötzliche Reichtum der armen Leute von Kombach/The Sudden Wealth of the Poor People of Kombach* (also prod., co-sc.) 1971; *Die Moral der Ruth Halbfass* (also co-sc.) 1971; *Strohfeuer/A Free Woman/Summer Lightning* (also co-sc.) 1972; *Uberachtung in Tirol* (for TV; also co-sc.), *Georginas Gründe* (for TV; also co-sc.) 1974; *Die verlorene Ehre der Katharina Blum/The Lost Honor of Katherina Blum* (co-dir., co-sc. with Margarethe von Trotta) 1975; *Der Fangschuss/Coup de Grace* (Ger./Fr.) 1976; *Nur rum Spass nur um Spiel: Kaleidoskop Valeska Gert* (doc.; also prod., sc.) 1977; *Deutschland im Herbst/Germany in Autumn* (one episode) 1978; *Die Blechtrommel/The Tin Drum* (also co-sc.) 1979; *Der Kandidat* (doc.; also co-sc.), *Die Fälschung/Circle of Deceit* (also co-sc.; Ger./Fr.) 1981; *Kreig und Frieden/War and Peace* (doc.; co-dir.) 1983; *Un Amour de Swann/Swann in Love* (also adapt.; Fr./Ger.) 1984; *Death of a Salesman* (TV movie in US; theatrically released abroad; US) 1985; *A Gathering of Old Men* (TV movie; US/Ger.), *Vermischte Nachrichten/Odds and Ends* (co-dir.) 1987; *The Handmaid's Tale* (US/Ger.) 1990; *Passagier Faber/Voyager* (also co-sc.; Ger./Fr.) 1991; *The Ogre* 1996.

Schnee, Charles. Screenwriter, producer. *b.* Aug. 6, 1916, Bridgeport, Conn. *d.* 1963. *ed.* Yale (B.A.); Yale Law School. He quit law practice for a writing career in films in the mid-40s and won an Oscar for the script of *The Bad and the Beautiful* (1952). In the mid-50s he dropped screenwriting to become a producer and production executive but later returned to writing.

FILMS INCLUDE: As screenwriter—*From This Day Forward* 1946; *I Walk Alone* 1947; *Red River* 1948; *Scene of the Crime, They Live by Night* 1949; *Paid in Full, The Next Voice You Hear, The Furies, Right Cross* 1950; *Bannerline, Westward the Women* 1951; *When in Rome, The Bad and the Beautiful* 1952; *Butterfield 8, The Crowded Sky* 1960; *By Love Possessed* (under pseudonym John Dennis) 1961; *Two Weeks in Another Town* 1962. As producer—*Torch Song* (exec. prod.) 1953; *The Prodigal, Trial* 1955; *Somebody Up There Likes Me* 1956; *The Wings of Eagles, House of Numbers, Until They Sail* 1957.

Schneer, Charles H. Producer. Born on May 5, 1920, in Norfolk, Va. *ed.* Columbia. He specialized in science-fiction and trick films, later diversifying into other genres. Since the early 60s he has operated mostly from England.

FILMS INCLUDE: *It Came from Beneath the Sea* 1955; *Earth vs. the Flying Saucers* 1956; *Twenty Million Miles to Earth* 1957; *The 7th Voyage of Sinbad* 1958; *The Three Worlds of Gulliver* (US/UK/Sp.), *I Aim at the Stars* (US/Ger.) 1960; *Mysterious Island* (US/UK) 1961; *Jason and the Argonauts* (UK) 1963; *First Men in the Moon* (UK) 1964; *Half a Sixpence* (co-prod.; UK/US) 1967; *The Valley of the Gwangi* 1969; *The Executioner* (UK), *Land Raiders* 1970; *The Golden Voyage of Sinbad* (co-prod.; UK) 1973; *Sinbad and the Eye of the Tiger* (co-prod.) 1977; *Clash of the Titans* (UK) 1981.

Schneider, Magda. Actress. Born on May 7, 1908, in Augsburg, Bavaria. Highly popular star of numerous German and Austrian films of the 30s. Trained as a singer and a dancer, she began her career in operetta, entering films in 1931. She specialized in light romantic leads, memorably in Max Ophüls's *Liebelei* (1933). The mother of actress Romy SCHNEIDER, she supported Romy on the screen in several films of the 50s.

FILMS INCLUDE: *Zwei in einem Auto* (German-language version of the French *Paris-Máditerranée*), *Das Lied einer Nacht* (and English-language version, *Tell Me Tonight/Be Mine Tonight*), *Sehnsucht 202, Marion das gehört sich nicht* 1932; *Glückliche Reise, Liebelei* 1933; *Fräulein Liselott, Geschichten aus dem Wienerwald* (Aus.), *Ich kenn' Dich und ich liebe Dich* 1934; *Vergissmeinnicht, Winternachtstraum, Eva* (Aus.), *Die lustigen Weiber* 1935; *Die Puppenfee* (Aus.), *Rendezvous in Wien* (Aus.) 1936; *Wiener Prater/Der Weg des Herzens* (Aus.), *Musik für Dich* (Aus.), *Ihr Leibhusar* (Aus./Hung.) 1937; *Die Frau am Scheidewege* (Ger./Hung.), *Frühlingsluft* 1938; *Das Recht auf Liebe* 1939; *Mädchen im Vorzimmer* 1940; *Liebeskomödie* 1942; *Die heimlichen Bräute* 1944; *Die Sterne lügen nicht* 1950; *Wenn der weisse Flieder wieder blüht* 1953; *Mädchenjahre einer Königin/The Story of Vickie* 1954; *Sissi* (Aus.), *Die Deutschmeister* (Aus.) 1955; *Sissi—Die junge Kaiserin* (Aus.) 1956; *Von allen geliebt, Robinson soll nicht sterben/The Girl and the Legend* 1957; *Sissi—Schicksalsjahre einer Kaiserin* (Aus.), *Das Dreimäderlhaus/The House of the Three Girls* (Aus.) 1958; *Die Halbzarte* (Aus.) 1959; *Morgen beginnt das Leben* (Aus.) 1961.

Schneider, Maria. Actress. Born on Mar. 27, 1952, in Paris. The daughter of actor Daniel GÉLIN and a Rumanian-born Parisian bookstore keeper, she made her stage debut at 15 without the benefit of formal training. She began playing secondary parts in films in 1971 and in the following year was selected by Bernardo BERTOLUCCI from among 100 candidates for the plum starring role opposite Marlon Brando in the commercially successful and highly controversial film *Last Tango in Paris*. Along with Bertolucci and Brando, she was indicted by an Italian court on charges of obscenity for participating in the making of the erotic production. She has since starred opposite Jack Nicholson in Antonioni's *The Passenger* (1975) and many lesser films.

FILMS INCLUDE: *Madly/The Love Mates, La Vieille Fille, Helle* 1971; *Ultimo Tango a Parigi/Last Tango in Paris* (It.) 1972; *Reigen/Merry-Go-Round* (Ger.) 1974; *Professione: Reporter/The Passenger* (It.), *Babysitter* (It./Fr./Ger.) 1975; *Caligula* (It.), *Donna in Guerra* (It./Sp.) 1977; *Io sono mia* (It./Ger./Sp.) 1978; *A Woman Like Eve* (Hol.), *La Dérobade* 1979; *Haine, Mama Dracula* (Bel./Fr.) 1980; *Cercasi Gesù* (It./Fr.) 1982; *Balles perdues* 1983; *Résidence surveillée* 1987; *L'Art De Survivre/Bunker Palace Hotel* 1989; *Ecrans de Sable/Sand Screens* 1991; *Les Nuits Fauves/Savage Nights* 1993.

Schneider, Romy. Actress. *b.* Rosemarie Albach-Retty, Sept. 23, 1938, Vienna. *d.* 1982. The daughter of stage and screen actor Wolf Albach-Retty (*b.* 1908, Vienna) and popular film star of the 30s Magda SCHNEIDER. She became a star in her teens as the heroine of the saccharine "Sissi" series about the Austro-Hungarian royal family, a series very popular in the German-speaking world in the 50s and released in the US in 1962 as a combined feature entitled *Forever My Love.* Romy's career took on an adult shape and international dimensions in the 60s thanks to VISCONTI, who directed her in an episode of *Boccaccio '70* and later in a stage play, and to Orson WELLES, who used her intriguingly in *The Trial* (both 1962). She was one of the busiest, most intriguing leading ladies of the international screen when she died of a heart attack at 43.

FILMS INCLUDE: *Wenn der weisse Flieder wieder blüht* 1953; *Feuerwerk, Mädchenjahre einer Konigin/The Story of Vickie* (as young Queen Victoria) 1954; *Der letzte Mann* 1955; *Sissi* (as Princess Elizabeth of Austria), *Kitty und die grosse Welt* 1956; *Sissi—Die junge Kaiserin* (as Empress Elizabeth of Austria), *Robinson soll nicht sterben/The Girl and the Legend, Monpti* 1957; *Sissi—Schicksalsjahre einer Kaiserin* (again as Empress Elizabeth), *Scampolo, Mädchen in Uniform* 1958; *Christine* (Fr.), *Ein Engel auf Erden/Angel on Earth* (Fr./Ger.) 1959; *Katia/Magnificent Sinner* (Fr.) 1960; *Boccaccio '70* (It./Fr.), *Le Procès/Der Prozess/The Trial* (as Leni; Fr./Ger./It.) 1962; *The Victors* (UK/US), *The Cardinal* (US) 1963; *Good Neighbor Sam* (US) 1964; *What's New Pussycat?* (US/Fr.) 1965; *10:30 P.M. Summer* (US/Sp.), *Triple Cross* (Fr./UK) 1966; *Otley* (UK) 1968; *La Piscine/The Swimming Pool* (Fr./It.) 1969; *My Lover My Son* (US/UK), *Qui?/The Sensuous Assassin, Les Choses de la Vie/The Things of Life* (Fr./It./Switz.) 1970; *Bloomfield/The Hero* (Isr./UK) 1971; *César et Rosalie* (Fr.), *L'Assassinat de Trotsky/The Assassination of Trotsky* (Fr./It./UK) 1972; *Ludwig* (again as Empress Elizabeth; It./Ger.), *Le Train* 1973; *Le Trio infernal* (Fr.), *Un Amour de Pluie/Loving in the Rain* (Fr.), *Le Mouton enragé/Love At the Top/The French Way* (Fr.) 1974; *L'Important c'est d'aimer/The Most Important Thing: Love* (Fr.), *Les Innocents aux Mains sales/Dirty Hands* (Fr.), *Le Vieux Fusil/The Old Gun* (Fr.) 1975; *Une Femme à sa Fenêtre/A Woman at Her Window* (Fr./It./Ger.), *Mado* (Fr.) 1976; *Gruppenbild mit Dame/Group Portrait with Lady* (Ger./Fr.) 1977; *Une Histoire simple/A Simple Story* (Fr.) 1978; *Bloodline* (US) 1979; *Clair de Femme/Womanglow* (Fr./It./Ger.) 1979; *La Mort en direct/Deathwatch* (Fr./Ger.), *La Banguière* (Fr.) 1980; *Fantasma d'Amore/Ghost of Love* (It./Fr./Ger.), *Garde à Vue/Under Suspicion* 1981; *La Passante du Sans-Souci/La Passante* (Fr./Ger.) 1982.

Schoedsack, Ernest B(eaumont). Director. *b.* June 8, 1893, Council Bluffs, Iowa. *d.* 1979. He worked on a San Francisco road-repair gang before entering films as cameraman for Mack Sennett at Keystone in 1914. During WW I he was a combat cameraman for the Signal Corps and after the armistice continued as a newsreel cameraman. In 1920 he met Merian C. COOPER in Poland. They embarked on several joint projects and co-directed two successful documentaries in the Near and Far East, followed by feature films with exotic or mysterious backgrounds, among them the excellent, atmospheric thriller *The Most Dangerous Game/The Hounds of Zaroff* (1932), which both of them produced and Schoedsack co-directed with Irving Pichel. Their most famous collaboration was on *King Kong,* a classic in the fantasy-horror field. Schoedsack's wife, screenwriter Ruth Rose, collaborated on the script. The association of the two men thereafter remained that of producer (Cooper) and director (Schoedsack) and ended in the late 30s. For fuller career details, see COOPER, Merian C.

FEATURE FILMS: *Grass* (doc.; co-dir., co-prod., co-sc., co-phot. with Merian C. Cooper and Marguerite Harrison) 1926; *Chang* (doc.; co-dir., co-prod. with Cooper) 1927; *The Four Feathers* (co-dir., co-prod. with Cooper and Lothar Mendes) 1929; *Range* (doc.; also prod.) 1931; *The Most Dangerous Game/The Hounds of Zaroff* (co-dir. with Irving Pichel; co-prod.) 1932; King Kong (co-dir., co-prod. with Cooper), *Son of Kong, Blind Adventure* 1933; *Long Lost Father* 1934; *The Last Days of Pompeii* 1935; *Trouble in Morocco, Outlaws of the Orient* 1937; *Dr. Cyclops* 1940; *Mighty Joe Young* 1949; *This Is Cinerama* (prologue only) 1952.

Schoonmaker, Thelma. American film editor. Born in 1945. A schoolmate of Martin Scorsese at NYU, she later collaborated on several of the director's films, winning an Academy Award for the editing of *Raging Bull* (1980). She was nominated for Academy Awards for Michael Wadleigh's feature documentary *Woodstock* (1970) and Scorese's *Goodfellas* (1990). She was married to British director Michael POWELL from 1984 until his death in 1990.

FILMS: *Passages from Finnegans Wake* (co-edit.) 1967; *The Virgin President* (co-edit.), *Who's That Knocking at My Door?* 1968; *Woodstock* 1970; *Raging Bull* 1980; *The King of Comedy* 1983; *After Hours* 1985; *The Color of Money* 1986; *The Last Temptation of Christ* 1988; *New York Stories* ("Life Lessons" episode) 1989; *Goodfellas* 1990; *Cape Fear* 1991; *Age of Innocence* 1993; *Casino* 1995.

Schorm, Evald. Director. *b.* Dec. 15, 1931, Prague. *d.* 1988. Raised in a Bohemian village, he attended an agricultural school and began his working life as a construction worker and tractor driver. He first became involved in the arts during his military service, when he became a member of the Czech army's opera company. In 1957 he enrolled at Prague's FAMU film school, later joining the school's faculty as a teacher. He began his filmmaking career as a documentary director. It wasn't until 1964 that he directed his first feature, *Everyday Courage.* A searing critique of the betrayal of ideals by opportunistic party apparatchniks, the film was suppressed from export by the Novotny government but garnered several prizes when it reached international festivals in 1966. Schorm's compassionate treatment of humanistic themes in this and subsequent films earned him the appellation "the conscience of the Czech New Wave." The 1968 Russian invasion that ended the "Prague spring" and forced Czech filmmakers into inactivity or exile silenced the courageous voice of Schorm, who converted his talent to directing stage and opera productions at home and abroad. He also handled occasional TV shows and *Laterna Magica* segments and appeared as an actor in a number of features. Swept back into action by the liberalization of the political climate in the late 80s, Schorm reunited the stars of *Everyday Courage* in a nostalgic comeback production, *Killing with Kindness.* He died of a heart attack shortly after completing the film, which opened two months later at the 1989 Berlin Festival.

FEATURE FILMS: *Everyday Courage/Courage for Every Day* (also co-sc.) 1964; *Pearls of the Deep* ("House of Joy" episode; also co-sc.) 1965; *The Return of the Prodigal Son* (also story, sc.) 1966; *Saddled with Five Girls* (also co-sc.) 1967; *Revenge* (one episode; also sc.), *Prague Nights* ("Slipper of Bread" episode; also sc.), *The End of a Priest* (also co-sc.) 1968; *The Seventh Day the Eighth Night* (also co-sc.) 1969; *Dogs and People* 1970; *Killing with Kindness* 1989.

Schrader, Paul. Screenwriter, director. Born on July 22, 1946, in Grand Rapids, Mich. The son of strict Calvinists of Dutch-German descent, he did not see a single movie until he was 18. He made up for this when he moved West, away from his parents' influence, ostensibly to study divinity at Calvin College seminary, by gobbling up films at a phenomenal rate. A summer film course at New York's Columbia University helped convince him to choose movies as a career. After graduating at Calvin in 1968, he enrolled at UCLA's graduate film program. Before long he became a film critic for the Los Angeles *Free Press* and editor of the magazine *Cinema.* He also published a volume of serious film critique for the University of California Press, *Transcendental Style: Ozu, Bresson, Dreyer.* He also tried screenwriting but endured a period of personal depression, accented by heavy drinking, before selling his first script (written in collaboration with Robert Towne) for Sydney Pollack's *The Yakuza* (1975). Schrader reached back to the pits of his own bleak experience during the darkest moments of despair for the inspiration for his best screenplay, *Taxi Driver.* The script, which Schrader had written during two frenzied weeks while convalescing in a hospital, would be turned by director Martin SCORSESE into a harrowing portrait of violent madness and urban alienation. Self-revelation continued to be a hallmark of Schrader's work when he turned to directing in 1978. Moral ambivalence, traceable to his background, is much in evidence in his early films in which sex, sleaze, and violence are viewed dispassionately in a mixture of disgust and fascination. The director indicated he had modeled George C. Scott 's character as a Calvinist father searching for his runaway porno-movie actress daughter in *Hardcore* (1979) after his own father. While his *Cat People* was a disappointing remake of the Jacques Tourneur/Val Lewton 1942 horror classic, Schrader's *Mishima: A Life in Four Chapters* (1985) was an ambitious attempt to bring into focus the life and works of the controversial Japanese novelist who committed ritualistic suicide in 1970. The stylized film won the best artistic contribution prize at the Cannes Festival. Schrader, who married actress Mary Beth HURT (his second) in 1983, continues writing screenplays for others (especially Martin Scorsese) as well as for most of his own films, sometimes in collaboration with his brother, screenwriter-director (*Naked Tango*) Leonard Schrader.

FILMS: *The Yakuza* (co-sc.) 1975; *Taxi Driver* (sc.), *Obsession* (sc.) 1976; *Rolling Thunder* (co-sc.), *Close Encounters of the Third Kind* (co-sc. early version; uncredited) 1977; *Blue Collar* (dir., sc.) 1978; *Hardcore* (dir., sc.), *Old Boyfriends* (exec. prod., co-sc.) 1979; *American Gigolo* (dir., sc.), *Raging Bull* (co-sc.) 1980; *Cat People* (dir.) 1982; *Mishima: A Life in Four Chapters* (dir., co-sc.) 1985; *The Mosquito Coast* (sc.) 1986; *Light of Day* (dir., sc.) 1987; *The Last Temptation of Christ* (sc.), *Patty Hearst* (dir.) 1988; *The Comfort of Strangers* (dir.) 1990; *Light Sleeper* (dir., sc.) 1992; *City Hall* (co-sc.), *Touch* (dir., sc.) 1996.

Schreck, Max. Actor. *b.* 1879, Berlin. *d.* 1936. Character player of German stage and screen, he is best remembered for the role of the vampire, the screen's first Dracula, in Murnau's *Nosferatu* (1922). On the stage, he was notably associated with Max REINHARDT's Berlin company, the Berlin Staatstheater, and the Kammerspiele of Munich.

FILMS INCLUDE: *Am Narrenseil* 1921; *Nosferatu—Eine Symphonie des Grauens/Nosferatu the Vampire* (title role) 1922; *Die Strasse/The Street, Die Finanzen des Grossherzogs/The Grand Duke's Finances* 1923; *Krieg im Frieden* 1925; *Luther, Ramper—der Tiermensch/The Strange Case of Captain Ramper, Am Rande der Welt/At the Edge of the World* 1927; *Rasputins*

Liebesabenteuer/Rasputin: The Holy Devil 1928; *Ludwig II* 1929; *Das Land des Lächelns* 1930; *Der Tunnel, Roman einer Nacht* 1933; *Donogoo Tonka* 1936.

Schroeder, Barbet. Producer, director. Born on Aug. 26, 1941, in Teheran. The son of a German geologist, he was raised in Iran and Argentina before settling down in France. Graduating from the Sorbonne in Paris with a degree in philosophy, he became a film critic for the *Cahiers du Cinéma* and *L'Air de Paris,* then an impresario for jazz concerts and a photo journalist. In 1963 he served as Jean-Luc Godard's assistant on *Les Carabiniers* and played the role of a car salesman in the film. The following year he formed his own production company, Les Films du Losange, and began producing the films of Eric Rohmer as well as some by other directors. He himself turned to directing in 1969. He first drew international attention with *Idi Amin Dada* (1974), a revealing documentary about the Ugandan strongman. His *Maîtresse* (1976) was an intriguing exposé of deviant sexuality; *Koko the Talking Gorilla* was an entertaining fact film about a San Francisco Zoo ape who reached an astonishing near-human level in his capacity to communicate with people in sign language. Schroeder achieved success with his first American film, *Barfly* (1987), an effective adaptation of the autobiographical novel by the eccentric boozer Charles Bukowski. The director was nominated for an Academy Award for *Reversal of Fortune* (1990), an incisive screen treatment of the Alan Dershowitz book about the Claus von Bulow case. In 1992, he scored an unexpected international commercial hit with the paranoid thriller *Single White Female*. Schroeder has appeared in several films as an actor.

FILMS INCLUDE: As producer—*Paris vu par. . . /Six in Paris* 1965; *La Collectioneuse* 1966; *Ma Nuit chez Maud/My Night at Maud's* (co-prod.) 1969; *Le Genou de Claire/Claire's Knee* 1970; *Celine et Julie vont en Bateau/Celine and Julie Go Boating* (also act.) 1973; *Perceval le Gallois* 1978; *Le Pont du Nord* (co-prod.) 1982; *Mauvaise Conduite* (co-prod.) 1984. As director (complete)—*More* (also story, co-sc.) 1969; *Sing-Sing* (medium-length doc. filmed in New Guinea) 1971; *La Valée/The Valley* (also story, co-sc.) 1972; *Général Idi Amin Dada/Idi Amin Dada* (doc.; also sc.) 1974; *Maîtresse* (also co-sc.) 1976; *Koko le Gorille qui parle/Koko the Talking Gorilla* (doc.; also sc.) 1978; *Tricheurs* (also co-sc.) 1984; *The Charles Bukowski Tapes* (doc.) 1985; *Barfly* (also co-prod.; US) 1987; *Reversal of Fortune* (US) 1990; *Single White Female* (US) 1992; *Queen Margot* (act. only) 1994; *Kiss of Death* 1995; *Before and After* (also prod.), *Extreme Measures*, *Mars Attacks!* (act. only) 1996.

Schroeter, Werner. Director. Born on Apr. 7, 1945, in Georgenthal, Thurinigia, Germany. Innovative, flamboyant, controversial figure of the New German Cinema. A former journalist, he began making 9 mm shorts in 1967 and in the following few years directed extensively for German TV. Moving into features, he soon established a reputation for artistic originality and intellectual arrogance through visually striking, highly stylized, emotionally charged films that appealed to a select circle of the educated elite but outraged and alienated general audiences. Salvation through passionate love and artistic expression is a recurrent theme in Schroeter's films, whose protagonists are usually outsiders, often homosexuals, eccentrics, and foreigners. Music, particularly opera, plays an important part in the director's films, whose sound track is often manipulated to clash provocatively with the visuals. His *Palermo or Wolfsburg* shared the Golden Bear at the 1980 Berlin Film Festival.

FEATURE FILMS: *Eika Katappa, Nicaragua* 1969; *Der Bomberpilot* 1970; *Salome, Macbeth* (for TV) 1971; *Der Tod der Maria Malibran/The Death of Maria Malibrun* 1972; *Willow Springs* 1973; *Der schwarze Engel/The Black Angel* 1974; *Johanes Traum* 1975; *Neapolitanische Geschwister/Il Regno di Napoli/Reign of Naples/Kingdom of Naples* 1978; *Palermo oder Wolfsburg/Palermo or Wolfsberg, Weisse Reise/White Journey, Die Generalprobe/La Répetition générale/The Dress Rehearsal* 1980; *Der Tag der Idicten/Day of the Idiots, Das Liebesonril/Lovers' Council* 1982; *Der lachende Stern/The Smiling Star* 1983; *Zum beispiel Argentinien/De l'Argenine* (doc.), *Der Rosenköniq/The Rose King* 1985; *Malina* 1991.

Schüfftan, Eugen (changed to **Eugene Shuftan** in the US). Director of photography. *b.* July 21, 1893, Breslau (Wroclaw), Germany. *d.* 1977. Outstanding, inventive lighting cameraman of German, French, British, and American films. A former painter, sculptor, designer, and architect, he began in German films in the early 20s as a photographic effects specialist and invented the SCHÜFFTAN PROCESS. He was behind the camera on several important German productions before emigrating to France in 1933 in the wake of the Nazi takeover. There he lent his exquisite imagery to the poetic realism of Marcel Carné and other directors. In 1940 he emigrated to the US, where he became a naturalized citizen in 1947. In the 50s and 60s he worked internationally, winning an Academy Award for the photography of *The Hustler* (1961). In 1975 he received the Billy Bitzer Award for "outstanding contribution to the motion picture industry."

FILMS INCLUDE: In Germany—*Königin Luise/Queen Louise* 1927; *Menschen am Sonntag/People on Sunday* (doc.) 1929; *Abschied* 1930; *Das Ekel* (co-phot.; also co-dir. with Franz Wenzler) 1931; *Die Herrin von Atlantis/L'Atlantide* (co-phot.) 1932; *Der Läufer von Marathon* 1933. In France—*Du Haut en Bas* 1934; *La Tendre Ennemie, Le Scandale* 1936; *Drôle de Drame/Bizarre Bizarre, Mademoiselle Docteur* 1937; *Le Drame de Shanghai/The Shanghai Drama* (co-phot.), *Quai des Brumes/Port of Shadows* 1938; *Sans Landemain, Les Musiciens du Ciel* 1939; *L'Emigrante* 1940. In the US—*It Happened Tomorrow* (tech. dir. only) 1944; *The Dark Mirror* (tech. superv. only) 1946; *Women in the Night* 1948. In France—*Le Traqué/Gunman in the Streets* 1950; *La P. . . respectueuse/The Respectable Prostitute, Le Rideau carmoisi/The Crimson Curtain* 1952; *Marianne de ma Jeunesse* 1954; *Ulisse/Ulysses* (special phot. only; It./US) 1955; *La Tête contre les Murs* 1958; *The Bloody Brood* (Can.) 1959; *Les Yeux sans Visage/The Horror Chamber of Dr. Faustus, Un Couple* 1960. In the US—*The Hustler, Something Wild* 1961; *Captain Sinbad* (co-phot.) 1963; *Lilith* 1964. In France—*Trois Chambres à Manhattan* 1965. In Germany/Switzerland—*Der Arzt stellt fest/Angeklagt nach Paragraph 218/The Doctor Says* 1966.

Schüfftan process. An optical trick shot named after its inventor, Eugen Schüfftan. The process makes possible the combination into one shot of miniature representations of scenery in the background and actual action in the foreground. This is done by scraping off a predetermined portion of the silver surface on a mirror and placing the mirror at a 45-degree angle to the axis of the camera lens. The actual action taking place before the camera is shot through the now-clear portion of the mirror while the miniature sets are reflected through the untouched remainder of the mirror, thus creating the illusion that action is truly unfolding against a real background. Schüfftan used this composite effect successfully in Fritz Lang's *Metropolis* (1927) but it has since been superseded by the simpler and more effective MATTE process.

Schulberg, B(enjamin) P(ercival). Producer, executive. *b.* Jan. 19, 1892, Bridgeport, Conn. *d.* 1957. *ed.* CCNY. Father of Budd SCHULBERG. A former reporter with New York's *Evening Mail* and an editor of a film trade publication, he entered films in 1911 as screenwriter and publicity director for

Rex Films. The following year he joined Adolph Zukor's newly formed Famous Players and helped launch the publicity drive for *Queen Elizabeth.* Later, as an independent producer, he discovered Clara Bow and made her famous as the "It" Girl. In 1925 he joined Paramount as producer with the nominal title of associate producer and in 1928 became general manager of the company's West Coast production. In 1932 he became an independent producer again, then worked as a staff producer for several Hollywood companies but was unable to obtain work after WW II.

FILMS INCLUDE: *Stranger Than Fiction* 1921; *The Infidel, Rich Men's Wives, Shadows, The Woman Conquers* 1922; *The Hero, Refuge, The Lonely Road, The Scarlet Lily, The Broken Wing, The Virginian, April Showers, Maytime, Chastity* 1923; *Poisoned Paradise, The Breath of Scandal, White Man, The Triflers* 1924; *Capital Punishment* (also story), *The Boomerang, The Parasite, Parisian Love, My Lady's Lips, Free to Love, The Plastic Age* 1925; *Mantrap, You'd Be Surprised, The Eagle of the Sea, Kid Boots, We're in the Navy Now, Man of the Forest, Old Ironsides* 1926; *It, Special Delivery, The Rough Riders, Man Power, Senorita, Ritzy, Rough House Rosie, Rolled Stockings, Afraid to Love, Tell It to Sweeney, Hula, Fireman Save My Child, The Woman on Trial, Get Your Man* 1927; *The Last Command, Red Hair, The Street of Sin, Abie's Irish Rose* 1928; *Illusion* 1929; *Jenny Gerhardt, Three-Cornered Moon* 1933; *30-Day Princess, Good Dame, Little Miss Marker, Kiss and Make Up* 1934; *Behold My Wife, Crime and Punishment* 1935; *Lady of Secrets, Counterfeit* 1936; *Her Husband Lies, The Great Gambini, She's No Lady* 1937; *He Stayed for Breakfast* 1940; *Bedtime Story* 1941; *Flight Lieutenant* 1942.

Schulberg, Budd. Novelist, screenwriter. Born on Mar. 27, 1914, in New York City. *ed.* Dartmouth. The son of B. P. SCHULBERG, he grew up in Hollywood surrounded by motion picture people and went to work for Paramount at age 17 as a publicist and at 19 as a screenwriter. He was fired in 1939 after a disastrous collaboration with an ailing Scott Fitzgerald on *Winter Carnival.* In 1941 he shocked Hollywood with his best-selling novel about film industry people, *What Makes Sammy Run?* He spent the WW II years with John Ford's documentary film unit. In 1951 he testified before the House Un-American Activities Committee about his brief association with the Communist party in the 30s and named several of his Hollywood colleagues as fellow travelers. A boxing aficionado, he frequently covered championship matches in the press. He wrote the biography, *Loser and Still Champion: Muhammed Ali* (1981), and the autobiography, *Moving Pictures: Memories of a Hollywood Prince.* He was married to actresses Virginia Ray (1936–42), Virginia Anderson (1943–64), and Geraldine BROOKE (1964–77).

FILMS INCLUDE: *A Star Is Born* (addnl. dial. only) 1937; *Little Orphan Annie* 1938; *Winter Carnival* 1939; *Weekend for Three* (story only) 1941; *City Without Men* 1943; *On the Waterfront* (also story) 1954; *The Harder They Fall* (novel basis only) 1956; *A Face in the Crowd* (from own story) 1957; *Wind Across the Everglades* 1958; *Joe Louis: For All Times* (doc.; also prod.) 1985.

Schulman, Arnold. Screenwriter. Born on Aug. 11, 1925, in Philadelphia. *ed.* U. of North Carolina. A former stage actor, long associated with the American Theatre Wing and the Actors Studio, he wrote several plays (notably 'A Hole in the Head,' 1957) and many teleplays, as well as scripts for features. He was nominated for Academy Awards for his screenplays for *Love with the Proper Stranger* (1964) and *Goodbye, Columbus* (1969). He fared poorly in two ventures as a producer.

FILMS: *Wild Is the Wind* 1957; *A Hole in the Head* (from his own play) 1959; *Cimarron* 1960; *Love with the Proper Stranger* 1964; *The Night They Raided Minsky's* 1968; *Goodbye Columbus* 1969; *To Find a Man* 1971; *Funny Lady* 1975; *Won Ton Ton—the Dog Who Saved Hollywood* (also co-prod.) 1976; *Players* (also exec. prod.) 1979; *A Chorus Line* 1985; *Tucker: The Man and His Dream* 1988.

Schultz, Carl. Director. Born on Sept. 19, 1939, in Budapest, Hungary. Raised in Australia, he started his career in television, but soon moved on to feature films and scored an international triumph with *Careful, He Might Hear You* (1983), a superbly crafted, exceptionally powerful drama of a battle for child custody.

FEATURE FILMS: *Blue Fin* 1978; *Goodbye Paradise* 1982; *Careful He Might Hear You* 1983; *Bullseye, Traveling North* 1986; *The Seventh Sign* (US) 1988.

Schultz, Michael. Director. Born on Nov. 10, 1938, in Milwaukee. *ed.* U. of Wisconsin; Marquette. He directed his first play at Princeton in 1966, then joined the Negro Ensemble Company and directed several of its stage productions of the late 60s, graduating to Broadway in 1969. Having enjoyed some success with a 1971 TV production, 'To Be Young, Gifted, and Black,' he turned to films in the mid-70s and has since directed a number of entertaining pictures.

FILMS: *Together for Days* 1973; *Honeybaby Honeybaby* 1974; *Cooley High* 1975; *Car Wash* 1976; *Greased Lightning, Which Way Is Up?* 1977; *Sgt. Pepper's Lonely Hearts Club Band* 1978; *Scavenger Hunt* 1979; *Carbon Copy* 1981; *The Last Dragon/Berry Gordy's The Last Dragon, Krush Groove* 1985; *Disorderlies* (also co-prod.) 1987; *Livin' Large* 1992.

Schumacher, Joel. Director. Born in 1939, in New York City. While attending Parson's School of Design, he began his working career as a display artist for the fashionable Henri Bendel department store. He later operated his own boutique, then joined Revlon as a designer of clothing and packaging. Entering films in the early 70s as a costume designer, he branched out several years later into screenwriting, then into directing. His usually slick output was conventionally proficient, and consisted for the most part of diverting youth-oriented fare until the early 90s, when he attempted to grapple with more adult themes.

FILMS: As costume designer—*Play It as It Lays* 1972; *The Last of Sheila, Blume in Love, Sleeper* 1973; *The Prisoner of Second Avenue* 1975; *Interiors* 1978. As screenwriter—*Sparkle, Car Wash* 1976; *The Wiz* 1978. As director—*The Incredible Shrinking Woman* 1981; *D. C. Cab* (also sc.) 1983; *St. Elmo's Fire* (also co-sc.) 1985; *The Lost Boys* 1987; *Cousins* 1989; *Flatliners* 1990; *Dying Young* 1991; *Falling Down* 1993; *The Client* 1994; *Batman Forever* 1995; *A Time to Kill* 1996; *Batman and Robin* 1997.

Schünzel, Reinhold. Director, actor. *b.* Nov. 7, 1886, Hamburg, Germany. *d.* 1954. A former businessman and journalist, he turned stage and film actor during WW I, appearing mostly in character parts. From 1919 he directed numerous German films while continuing his career as actor. Many of these were internationally popular, notably *Viktor und Viktoria* (1933), the source of Blake Edwards's 1982 comedy hit *Victor/Victoria.* In 1938 he went to Hollywood, where he directed a number of films with little success, then settled on an acting career. He returned to Germany shortly before his death.

FILMS: As director: In Germany—*Maria Magdalena* (also act.) 1919; *Der Graf von Cagliostro* (also exec. prod., act.), *Katherina die Grosse* (also co-sc.), *Marquis d'Or* (also prod., act.) 1920; *Mädchen aus der Ackerstrasse* (also act.), *Der Roman eines Dienstmädchens* (also act.) 1921; *Don Juan und die drei Marien/Die drei Marien und der Herr von Marana* (also act.; Ger./Aus.), *Das Geld auf der Strasse/Bertrüger des Volkes* (also act.), *Der Pantoffelheld* (also act.; Aus.) 1922; *Alles für Geld/Fortune's Fool* (also act.) 1923; *Windstärke 9/Die Geschichte einer reichen Erbin* 1924; *Die Frau fur 24 Stunden* (also co-sc.) 1925; *Hallo Caesar!* (also prod., co-sc., act.), *In der Heimat da gibt's ein Wiedersehn!* (co-dir. with Leo Mittler; also prod., act.) 1926; *Gustav Mond... Du gehst so stille* (also prod., act.), *Ueb' immer Treu und Redlichkeit* (also prod., co-sc., act.) 1927; *Adam und Eva* (also prod., co-sc., act.), *Don Juan in der Mädchenschule* (also prod., act.) 1928; *Kolonne X* (also prod., act.), *Peter der Matrose* (also prod., act.), *Phantome des Glücks/Der Mann in Fesseln* (also sc.) 1929; *Liebe im Ring* 1930; *Der kleine Seitensprung* (also co-sc.), *Ronny* (German- and French-language versions; also co-sc.) 1931; *Das Schone Abenteuer* (also co-sc.; and French-language version *La Belle Aventure*), *Wie sag ich's meinem Mann* 1932; *Viktor und Viktoria* (also sc.; and French-language version, *Georges et Georgette*), *Saison in Kairo* 1933; *Die Töchter Ihrer Exzellenz* (and French-language version, *La Jeune Fille d'une Nuit*), *Die englische Heirat* 1934; *Amphitryon/Aus den Wolken kommt das Glück* (also sc.; and French-language version, *Les Dieux s'amusent*) 1935; *Das Mädchen Irene* (also co-sc.), *Donogoo Tonka* (also sc.) 1936; *Land der Liebe* (also co-sc.) 1937. In the US—*Rich Man Poor Girl* 1938; *Ice Follies of 1939, Balalaika* 1939; *New Wine* 1941. As actor (partial list): In Germany—*Die Stricknadeln* 1916; *Es werde Licht* (Pt. 4), *Das Tagebuch einer Verlorenen/The Diary of a Lost Girl* 1918; *Das Karussell des Lebens/The Last Payment, Madame Dubarry/Passion, Prostitution, Die Reise um die Welt in 80 Tagen* 1919; *Weltbrand* 1920; *Lady Hamilton* 1922; *Neuland* 1924; *Der Hahn im Korb* (also co-sc.) 1925; *Der Himmel auf Erden* (also prod., co-sc.) 1927; *Die Dreigroschenoper/The Threepenny Opera/The Beggar's Opera* (as Tiger Brown), *Ihre Hoheit befielt, 1914: Die letzten Tage vor dem Weltbrand/1914: The Last Days Before the War* (as Czar Nicholas II of Russia) 1931. In the US—*Hangmen Also Die, First Comes Courage* 1943; *The Hitler Gang* (as General Ludendorff), *The Man in Half Moon Street* 1944; *Dragonwyck, Notorious, The Plainsman and the Lady* 1946; *Golden Earrings* 1947; *Berlin Express, The Vicious Circle* 1948; *Washington Story* 1952; *Eine Liebesgeschichte* (Ger.) 1954.

Schuster, Harold. Director. *b.* Aug. 1, 1902, Cherokee, Iowa. *d.* 1986. A former actor and assistant cameraman, he made a name for himself as editor, cutting such films as *Sunrise* (1927), *A Zoo in Budapest* (1933), and *The Farmer Takes a Wife* (1935). After a promising beginning as a director, he turned out mostly routine films until the 50s, when he switched to TV work.

FILMS: *Wings of the Morning, Dinner at the Ritz* 1937; *Swing That Cheer, Exposed* 1938; *One Hour to Live* 1939; *Framed, Zanzibar, Ma! He's Making Eyes at Me, South to Karanga, Diamond Frontier* 1940; *A Very Young Lady, Small Town Deb, A Modern Monte Cristo* 1941; *On the Sunny Side, The Postman Did Not Ring, Girl Trouble* 1942; *My Friend Flicka* 1943; *Marine Raiders* 1944; *Breakfast in Hollywood* 1946; *The Tender Years* 1947; *So Dear to My Heart* 1948; *Kid Monk Baroni* 1952; *Jack Slade* 1953; *Loophole, Security Risk, Port of Hell* 1954; *Finger Man, The Return of Jack Slade, Tarzan's Hidden Jungle* 1955; *Dragoon Wells Massacre, The Courage of Black Beauty, Portland Expose* 1957.

Schwartz, Arthur. Composer, sometime producer. *b.* Nov. 25, 1900, Brooklyn, N.Y. *d.* 1984. *ed.* NYU; Columbia. A former schoolteacher and lawyer, he began composing for Broadway in the late 20s, often collaborating with Howard DIETZ. After 1930 he also scored and wrote songs for films.

FILMS INCLUDE: As composer—*Follow the Leader* 1930; *That Girl from Paris* 1937; *Navy Blues* 1941; *Cairo* 1942; *Thank Your Lucky Stars* 1943; *The Time the Place and the Girl* 1946; *Excuse My Dust* 1951; *Dangerous When Wet, The Band Wagon, Torch Song* 1953; *You're Never Too Young* 1955; *I Could Go On Singing* 1963. As producer—*Cover Girl* 1944; *Night and Day* 1946.

Schwartz, Maurice. Actor. *b.* June 18, 1890, in Sedikov, Russia. *d.* 1960. In the US from age 12, he was founder, director, and star of the Yiddish Art Theatre in New York, occasionally also appearing on Broadway. He also starred in many American-made Yiddish films and played character parts in several Hollywood productions.

FILMS INCLUDE: *Broken Hearts* (also dir.) 1926; *The Unfortunate Bride* 1930; *Uncle Moses* 1932; *The Man Behind the Mask* (UK) 1936; *Tevya* (title role; also dir.) 1939; *Mission to Moscow* 1943; *Bird of Paradise* 1951; *Salome* (as Ezra), *Slaves of Babylon* (as Nebuchadnezzar) 1953.

Schwarzenegger, Arnold. Actor. Born on July 30, 1947, in Graz, Austria. *ed.* U. of Wisconsin (business and economics). Musclebound star of the American screen. At 15 he rebelled against the wishes of his father, a stern police chief, and chose bodybuilding over a career as a professional soccer player. After winning the Junior Mr. Europe title, he arrived in the US in 1968, billed as 'The Austrian Oak,' and went on to claim the Mr. World, Mr. Universe (five times), and Mr. Olympia (seven times) titles before retiring undefeated in 1980. He invested his winning purses and revenues from his mail-order company in real estate and became a millionaire while still in his 20s. Although he began appearing in films (as Arnold Strong) in 1970, it wasn't until he played himself in George Butler's documentary *Pumping Iron* (1977) that Schwarzenegger first drew wide attention. His screen career took off after his fortuitous casting in the mythical epic *Conan the Barbarian* (1982) and its sequel *Conan the Destroyer* (1984), both huge box-office hits. *The Terminator* (1984), a science-fiction saga, catapulted him to superstardom. Curiously, Schwarzenegger's limited acting range, his deadpan expression, and thick-accented delivery of American slang phrases proved assets rather than liabilities in his rise to top popularity, providing his toughest characterizations with a touch of humorous ease. Schwarzenegger, whose Cinderella rise from humble beginnings to one of Hollywood's top money-making stars embodies the realization of the American dream, became a naturalized US citizen in 1983. In 1986, the staunchly Republican Schwarzenegger married glamorous TV journalist Maria Shriver, a niece of John F. Kennedy. In 1990 he was appointed by George Bush as chairman of the President's Council of Physical Fitness and Sports. In 1992 he made his debut as a feature-length movie director with a cable TV remake of 1945's *Christmas in Connecticut*.

FILMS: As Arnold Strong—*Hercules in New York* (title role) 1970; *The Long Goodbye* 1973. As Arnold Schwarzenegger —*Stay Hungry* 1976; *Pumping Iron* (doc.; as himself) 1977; *The Villain* 1979; *Conan the Barbarian* 1982; *Conan the Destroyer, The Terminator* 1984; *Commando, Red Sonja* 1985; *Raw Deal* 1986; *Predator, The Running Man* 1987; *Red Heat, Twins* 1988; *Total Recall, Kindergarten Cop* 1990; *Terminator 2: Judgment Day* 1991; *The Last Action Hero* 1993; *Junior, True Lies* 1994; *Eraser, Jingle All the Way* 1996; *Batman and Robin* 1997.

Schygulla, Hanna. Actress. Born on Dec. 25, 1943, in Katowice, Poland (then German-occupied Kattowitz). Provocative leading lady of the German stage and screen and international productions. Raised in Germany, she studied languages and literature at Munich University, intending to become a teacher, but instead became involved with Munich's avant-garde Action Theater. It was there that she met director Rainer Werner FASSBINDER, who would become her mentor. She figured prominently in many of his plays and in about half of his 40 films, as well as in numerous productions by other directors, portraying a diverse range of fascinating characters. Somewhat chunkily built and not particularly beautiful by today's standards, she nonetheless became one of Europe's most sought-after leading ladies, thanks to her intriguing personality and expressive sensuality. She won the best actress prize at the 1979 Berlin Film Festival for *The Marriage of Maria Braun.*

FILMS INCLUDE: *Der Bräutiqam die Komödiantin und der Zuhälter/The Bridegroom the Comedienne and the Pimp* (short) 1968; *Liebe ist kalter als der Tod/Love Is Colder Than Death* 1969; *Katzelmacher* 1969; *Götter der Pest/Gods of the Plague, Warum läuft Herr R amok?/Why Does Herr R Run Amok?, Baal* 1970; *Rio das Mortes, Pioniere in Ingolstadt/Pioneers in Ingolstadt, Whity, Warnung vor einer heiligen Nutte/Beware of the Holy Whore* 1971; *Der Händler der vier Jahrzeiten/The Merchant of Four Seasons, Die bitteren Tränen der Petra von Kant/The Bitter Tears of Petra von Kant, Wildnechsel/Jail Bait* 1973; *Fontane Effi Briest/Effi Briest* 1974; *Falsche Bewequnq/Wrong Move, Ansichten eines Clowns* 1975; *Die Heimkehr des alten Herrn* 1977; *Die Ehe der Maria Braun/The Marriage of Maria Braun, Die dritte Generation/The Third Generation, Berlin Alexanderplatz* 1979; *Lili Marleen, Die Fälschung/Circle of Deceit* 1981; *La Nuit de Varennes* (It./Fr.), *Passion* (Fr./Switz.), *La Storia di Piera* (It./Fr.), *Antonieta* (Fr./Mex.), *Heller Wahn/Sheer Madness/A Labor of Love/Friends and Husbands* 1982; *Ein Liebe in Deutschland/A Love in Germany, Il Futuro e Donna/The Future Is Woman* (It./Fr./Ger.) 1984; *The Delta Force* (US) 1986; *Forever Lulu* (US) 1987; *Miss Arizona* (It./Hung.), *El Verano de la Señora Forbes* (Mex./Sp.) 1988; *Abraham's Gold, Aventure de Catherine C.* (Fr.) 1990; *Dead Again* (US) 1991; *Au Petits Bonheurs* 1994; *Word* 1996.

Sciorra, Annabella. Actress. Born 1964 in Connecticut. Young, versatile, brunette leading lady of American films of the late 80s and early 90s. Raised in New York City, she began training for the stage at 13 at the HB Studio and later studied at the American Academy of Dramatic Arts. She made her greatest impression as an Italian-American woman who has a relationship with an African-American man in Spike LEE's *Jungle Fever* (1991).

FILMS: *True Love* 1989; *Internal Affairs, Reversal of Fortune, Cadillac Man* 1990; *The Hard Way, Jungle Fever, The Hand That Rocks the Cradle* 1991; *Whispers in the Dark* 1992; *Mr. Wonderful, The Night We Never Met, Romeo is Bleeding* 1993; *The Addiction, The Cure* 1995; *The Funeral* 1996; *Cop Land, The Innocent Sleep, Underworld* 1997.

Scofield, Paul. Actor. Born David Paul Scofield, on Jan. 21, 1922, in Hurstpierpoint, England. Distinguished, introspective star of the British stage (from the age of 14), he has appeared in only a handful of British and American films. He won an Academy Award for his portrayal of Sir Thomas More in *A Man for All Seasons,* a repeat of his stage success.

FILMS: *That Lady* (as King Philip II of Spain) 1954; *Carve Her Name with Pride* 1958; *Le Train/The Train* (Fr./It./US) 1964; *A Man for All Seasons* (as Sir Thomas More) 1966; *Tell Me Lies* (cameo) 1968; *King Lear* (title role), *Bartleby* 1971; *Scorpio* (US), *A Delicate Balance* (US) 1973; *1919* 1985; *Henry V* (as French King), *When the Whales Came* 1989; *Hamlet* (as the Ghost) 1990; *Utz* 1992; *Quiz Show* 1994; *The Crucible* 1996.

Scola, Ettore. Director, screenwriter. Born on May 10, 1931, in Trevico, Italy. Following law studies at the University of Rome, he began his working career as a writer for humor magazines. Entering the film industry as a screenwriter in 1953, he contributed bright material to films of Dino Risi and other directors, often in collaboration with Ruggero MACCARI. As a director from 1964, he started with traditional Italian-style comedies but increasingly his films took on a serious edge, revealing a maturing social concern and a growing search for a meaningful dramatic context. His *We All Loved Each Other So Much* (1974), dedicated to Vittorio De Sica, wistfully captured the essence of 30 years of postwar Italian cinema through the graceful observation of the divergent but intertwined lives of three friends, veterans of the Resistance. Scola won the best direction prize at Cannes for *Brutti, sporchi e Cattivi/Down and Dirty* (1976), a vivid portrait of misery. His *A Special Day* (1977)—a politically based allegorical depiction of a brief liaison between a jaded housewife (Sophia Loren) and a homosexual radio journalist (Marcello Mastroianni) under the gathering clouds of WW II—was nominated for an Oscar as best foreign language film. Perhaps his most ambitious film was *La Nuit de Varennes* (1982), a masterful, fanciful, visually striking, idea-rich costume epic of the French Revolution. History, politics, and people, and the effect they have on one another, continue to be a core theme in the films of Scola, one of the most highly regarded figures in European cinema today.

FILMS INCLUDE: As screenwriter—*Due Notti con Cleopatra/Two Nights with Cleopatra, Una Parigina a Roma* 1954; *Lo Scapolo* 1955; *Nata di Marzo* 1958; *Il Mattatore/Love and Larceny, Adua e le Compagne/Love à la Carte, Fantasmi a Roma/Ghosts of Rome* 1960; *Il Sorpasso/The Easy Life, L'Amore difficile/Of Wayward Love* 1962; *Il Successo, I Mostri/Opiate '67, La Visita* 1963; *Alta Infedeltà/High Infidelity, Il Gaucho, Il Magnifico Cornuto/The Magnificent Cuckold* 1964; *Made in Italy* 1965; *Follie d'Estate* 1966; *Le Dolci Signore/Anyone Can Play* 1967; *Noi Donne siamo fatte cosi* 1971; *Cuori nella Tormenta* 1984. As director-screenwriter (complete)—*Se permettete parliamo di Donne/Let's Talk About Women* 1964; *La Congiuntura* 1965; *Thrilling* ("Il Vittimista" episode), *L'Arcidiavolo/Il Diavolo innamorato/The Devil in Love* 1966; *Riusciranno i nostri Eroi a trovare l'Amico misteriosamente scomparso in Africa?* 1968; *Il Commissario Pepe* 1969; *Dramma della Gelosia—Tutti i particolari in Cronaca/The Pizza Triangle/A Drama of Jealousy (and Other Things)* 1970; *Permette? Rocco Papaleo/Rocco Papaleo* 1971; *La Più Bella Serata della mia Vita* 1972; *Trevico-Torino: Viaqqio nel Fiat-Nam, Festival dell'Unità* (doc.) 1973; *C'eravamo tanto amati/We All Loved Each Other So Much, Confronto Partecipazione Unità* (doc.) 1975; *Brutti sporchi e cattivi/Ugli Dirty and Mean/Down and Dirty, Silenzio e Complicità* (doc.; co-dir.), *Signore e Signori Buonanotte!* (one episode) 1976; *Una Giornata particolare/A Special Day, I Nuovi Mostri/The New Monsters/Viva Italia!* (one episode) 1977; *La Terrazza/The Terrace* 1980; *Passione d'Amore* 1981; *La Nuit de Varennes/That Night In Varennes* 1982; *Le Bal* 1983; *Maccheroni/Macaroni* 1985; *La Famiglia/The Family* 1987; *Splendor, Che Ore è/What Time Is It?* 1989; *Il Vaqqio Di Capitan Fracassa/Captain Fracassa's Journey* 1990; *Mario, Maria & Mario* 1994.

scoop. A wide-angle floodlighting unit. So named because of its resemblance to a grocer's scoop.

score. A musical composition written as an accompaniment to a motion picture or another dramatic presentation. Even before films acquired a voice, producers recognized the potential power of music to change the mood of a scene and enhance the emotional impact of an entire production. As early as 1908 the distinguished French composer Camille Saint-Saëns was commissioned to write a special musical score for the first of the Film d'Art productions, *The Assassination of the Duke de Guise.* In the US the great cinema pioneer D. W. Griffith collaborated on scoring his own giant productions *The Birth of a Nation* (1915) and *Intolerance* (1916). Most major silent productions were released with an accompanying score, either an original composition or library selections. In large metropolitan theaters, the scores were played by a full orchestra from a specially constructed orchestra pit. But even the small theaters in the provinces had their own resident pianist with a prepared selection of musical passages to go with every mood.

The arrival of the synchronous sound track imposed new restrictions on the film composer and established a new field of discipline in music art. Stopwatch precision was required of the composer, who now had to subordinate his music not only to the requirements of the plot but also to the complexities of a sound track that included dialogue and sound effects as well as his music. At first, most screen scores were arrangements of existing compositions, but by the mid-30s original music was being composed for the majority of American and European feature productions. Many of the early "original" scores were innocuous pieces of background music designed to interfere as little as possible with the action and the dialogue and to function simply as adhesive material to strengthen the film's continuity. Another popular application, known in the business jargon as "Mickeymousing," was the use of the music score to stimulate the emotions of the audience at every twist in the mood and action of a film.

However, as composers came to terms with the specialized requirements of film music, and filmmakers came to accept the film composer as an essential member of their creative team, the emphasis in film scores shifted from the functions of sketching a background and setting a mood to those of an integrated element in the total effect of a motion picture. Some of the best film scores have resulted from the involvement of the composer in the early phases of production and a close collaboration between composer and director. Advances in recording technology, growing public sophistication, and the evolvement of a professional cadre of screen composers have combined to produce a growing body of film music, adding an important dimension to cinema art.

scoring stage. A sound stage equipped with screening facilities and designed to accommodate a large number of musicians. It is used for scoring a motion picture while it is being screened.

Scorsese, Martin. Director. Born on Nov. 17, 1942, in Flushing, N.Y. The son of a Sicilian immigrant clothes presser, he was raised in a tenement in New York's Little Italy. He was a sickly youth, besieged by asthma, pleurisy, and other physical handicaps, which excluded him from sports, thus depriving him of close associations with other kids in his tough neighborhood. After grade school he entered a seminary, intending to become a priest, but dropped out after one year and then pursued his childhood love, the movies. He enrolled at New York University's Film School, getting a B.S. degree in film communications in 1964 and an M.A. in the same field in 1966 while also serving as an assistant instructor. During this period he made a number of prize-winning student shorts, including *What's a Nice Girl Like You Doing in a Place Like This?* (1963) and *It's Not Just You, Murray* (both 1964), and *The Big Shave* (1967) which won prizes at film festivals. He stayed on at NYU's film department as an instructor through 1970 and during his tenure on the faculty directed his first feature film, *Who's That Knocking at My Door?* (1968), originally titled *I Call First,* a small-scale production about an Italian-American youth which, like several of Scorsese's future films, had autobiographical undertones and an emphasis on character study rather than dramatic plot.

Scorsese was then assigned as co-supervising editor of the documentary *Woodstock* (1970) and was associate producer and post-production supervisor on another documentary, François Reichenbach's *Medicine Ball Caravan* (1971). After working briefly for the CBS-TV election unit covering Hubert Humphrey, Scorsese turned out his second feature film, *Boxcar Bertha* (1972), a blood-and-gore sequel to Roger Corman's *Bloody Mama.* It was a minor exploitation flick, but it gave the young director the opportunity to work within the Hollywood system and paved the way to his phenomenal rise in the coming years.

Mean Streets (1973) was Scorsese's first significant film. Like his first feature, *Who's That Knocking at My Door?,* it was set almost entirely in Little Italy, the scene of the director's own youth, and starred Harvey Keitel as a young Italian-American at odds with his seedy environment. Again the emphasis was on character development rather than conventional plot line, and the visual style characterized by restless, jittery camera movement reflecting the tension of city life, elements that would later find a more elaborate and striking expression in Scorsese's *Taxi Driver* (1976).

Despite ecstatic reviews, *Mean Streets* was a box-office flop, but Scorsese's next film, *Alice Doesn't Live Here Anymore* (1975), a more conventional, commercially inspired Hollywood picture, proved to be the sleeper of the year at the box office, partly because of its feminist women's liberation theme. Then came *Taxi Driver* (1976), a vivid and disturbing summary of Scorsese's impression of the seedy side of city life. The film, which won the International Grand Prize at Cannes, is characterized by the personality and encounters of a psychotic Vietnam-veteran cabbie. Once more, the emphasis is on characterization, this time abetted by a superb performance by Robert DE NIRO, the actor who would loom important in several of Scorsese's future films as an embodiment of the director's vision of urban society's neuroses. Following *New York New York* (1977), an affectionate, nostalgic, glitzy, colorful tribute to the Hollywood musical of the 40s, starring De Niro and Liza MINNELLI, Scorsese chose black-and-white cinematography to render stark realism, brutal vigor, and psychological intensity to the story of former middleweight boxing champion Jake La Motta in *Raging Bull* (1980). The film earned Academy Awards for De Niro in the title role and for editor Thelma Schoonmaker, as well as Oscar nominations for best film and best director.

In a further switch of genres, but in line with his continuing preoccupation with the darker side of urban life, Scorsese next turned out *The King of Comedy* (1983), an incisive black comedy-drama about an obsessively ambitious fan (De Niro) who wreaks freaky havoc while stalking a comic celebrity (Jerry LEWIS) with the help of a zany accomplice (Sandra Bernhard). Other bizarre aspects of city life, during a seemingly endless night, were evoked in *After Hours* (1985), an amusing, stylish, though trivial nightmarish comedy, which earned Scorsese the best director prize at Cannes.

Following *The Color of Money* (1986), a finely crafted but prosaic sequel to Robert Rossen's *The Hustler* (1961), Scorsese finally launched his long-dormant project, *The Last Temptation of Christ* (1988). Faithfully adapted from the novel by Nikos Kazantzakis, the film drew fire from religious groups, which were scandalized by its portrayal of Jesus as a vulnerable, sensual man, tormented by inner conflict, self-doubt, and all-too-human desires. But it went on to win the Film Critics prize at Venice and earned Scorsese another Academy Award nomination. Many critics, though, voiced disappointment in the film's banal dialogue and restrained spiritual fire. Scorsese returned to more familiar grounds with *Goodfellas* (1990), a remarkably vivid portrait of mob life. It earned him another Oscar nomination, the British Academy Awards for best film and best direction, and the Silver Lion as best director at the Venice Festival. He scored another popular success with *Cape Fear* (1991), a graphically violent, blood-chilling reinterpretation of the 1962 screen thriller. He then switched gears with a lush, exquisitely detailed, chilly adaptation of Edith Wharton's *The Age of Innocence* (1993), showcasing subtle performances by Michelle Pfeiffer and Daniel Day-Lewis.

Despite his enormous prestige and frequent commercial success, Scorsese never became part of the Hollywood establishment, which is likely the reason for his never having won the industry's Oscar. Based in New York, he pursues his own path (with Hollywood money), continually turning out films that are utterly personal and often deeply autobiographical. He has interspersed his commercial product with occasional nonfiction films, like *Italianamerican* (1974), a documentary portrait of his parents, or *American Boy* (1978), a portrait of a friend, who was a child of the drug culture of the 60s. In addition, he is active in film preservation, having been involved in the restoration and reissue of *Lawrence of Arabia* and *El Cid*. He has also appeared in several films as an actor, usually in brief cameos. Bold, inventive, versatile, and uncompromising, Scorsese is one of the most intelligent and provocative filmmakers working in cinema today. His second of four marriages was to screenwriter-director Julia Cameron. In 1979 he married actress Isabella ROSSELLINI; they divorced in 1983. In 1985 he married Barbara De Fina, a filmmaker. Autobiography (compiled and edited by David Thompson and Ian Christie): *Scorsese on Scorsese* (1989).

FILMS: *What's a Girl Like You Doing in a Place Like This?* (short; dir., sc.) 1963; *It's Not Just You, Murray* (short; dir., co-sc.) 1964; *The Big Shave* (short; dir., sc.) 1967; *Who's That Knocking at My Door?/J.R./Bring on the Dancing Girls/I Call First* (dir., sc., act.) 1968; *Street Scenes* (doc.; dir.), *Woodstock* (doc.; co-superv. edit., asst. dir.) 1970; *Medicine Ball Caravan* (assoc. prod., superv. edit) 1971; *Boxcar Bertha* (dir., act.), *Elvis on Tour* (doc.; montage superv.) 1972; *Mean Streets* (dir., co-sc., act.) 1973; *Italianamerican* (doc. short; dir., co-sc.) 1974; *Alice Doesn't Live Here Anymore* (dir., act.) 1975; *Taxi Driver* (dir., act.), *Cannonball* (act.) 1976; *New York New York, The Last Waltz* (doc.; dir.), *American Boy: A Profile of Steven Prince* (doc.; dir., personal appearance), *Roger Corman: Hollywood's Wild Angel* (doc.; personal appearance) 1978; *Raging Bull* (dir., act.) 1980; *The King of Comedy* (dir., act.) 1983; *Pavlova* (act.; UK/USSR) 1984; *After Hours* (dir., act.) 1985; *Autour de Minuit/Round Midnight* (act.; US/Fr.), *The Color of Money* (dir.) 1986; *The Last Temptation of Christ* (dir.) 1988; *New York Stories* (dir. "Life Lessons" episode) 1989; *Dreams/Akira Kurosawa's Dreams* (act., as Vincent Van Gogh; Jap.), *Goodfellas* (dir., co-sc.), *The Grifters* (co-prod.) 1990; *Guilty by Suspicion* (act.), *Cape Fear* (dir.) 1991; *The Age of Innocence* (dir., co-sc.), *Mad Dog and Glory* (prod.) 1993; *Naked in New York* (exec. prod. only), *Quiz Show* (act. only), *With Closed Eyes* 1994; *Casino* (also co-sc.), *Clockers* (prod.), *Search and Destroy* (act., ex-prod. only) 1995; *Grace of My Heart* (exec. prod.) 1996; *Rough Magic* (prod. only) 1997.

Scott, Adrian. Producer, screenwriter. *b.* Feb. 6, 1912, Arlington, N.J. *d.* 1973, *ed.* Amherst. A former magazine editor, he entered films in 1940 as screenwriter, becoming an RKO producer three years later. His career ended in 1947, after he refused to testify before the House Un-American Activities Committee on his alleged Communist affiliation. He was sentenced to one year of imprisonment as one of the "Hollywood Ten." According to the official committee report, he was identified in 1951 as a Communist by Edward DMYTRYK, a co-defendant and the director of most of his films. Blacklisted by the industry, he never returned to films.

FILMS: As screenwriter—*Keeping Company* 1940; *The Parson of Panamint, We Go Fast* 1941; *Mr. Lucky* 1943; *My Pal Wolf* 1944; *Miss Susie Slagle's* (adapt.) 1946. As producer—*Murder My Sweet/Farewell My Lovely* 1944; *Cornered, Deadline at Dawn* 1946; *Crossfire, So Well Remembered* 1947.

Scott, Campbell. Actor. Born 1962 in Westchester, N.Y. *ed.* Lawrence University, Appleton, Wis. The son of actors George C. SCOTT and Colleen DEWHURST, this bright, talented leading performer emulated his parents by appearing on and off Broadway and moving on to Hollywood films, primarily in supporting roles to begin with, until a couple of breakthrough performances established him as an intelligent, impressive actor. He expanded his film career to include co-directing the critical favorite *Big Night* (1996) with fellow actor and first-time director Stanley TUCCI.

FILMS: *Five Corners* 1988; *Longtime Companion, The Sheltering Sky* 1990; *Dead Again, Dying Young* 1991; *Singles* 1992; *The Innocent* 1993; *Mrs. Parker and the Vicious Circle* 1994; *Big Night* (co-dir.) 1996; *The Daytrippers* (co-exec. prod.) 1997.

Scott, George C(ampbell). Actor. Born on Oct. 18, 1926, in Wise, Va. *ed.* U. of Missouri. Served four years in the Marines before making the uphill climb from campus productions and summer stock to off Broadway, Broadway, TV ('East Side West Side' series, etc.), and films. A magnetic screen personality, intelligent, instinctive, intense, and vigorous, he has dominated many a scene in both supporting and leading parts. In 1971, after denouncing the Academy Awards as a meaningless, self-serving "meat parade," and announcing that he would refuse to accept an award if he won one, he was declared the winner in the 1970–71 Oscar ceremony for his title role in *Patton,* to the embarrassment of the industry and the delight of the press and the public. Ironically, shortly after this he was also named winner of TV's Emmy Award for his performance in Arthur Miller's 'The Price.' He did not accept either prize. He directed two of his own films in the early 70s. In the 80s, he turned increasingly to television, memorably as Fagin in *Oliver Twist* (1982), as Scrooge in *A Christmas Carol* (1984), and in the title role in the miniseries 'Mussolini—The Untold Story' (1985). But his TV series 'Mr. President' (1987) was not a success. Scott has been married five times, all to actresses: Carolyn Hughes (1951–54), Patricia Reed (1954–60), Colleen DEWHURST (1960–65 and again 1967–72), and Trish VAN DEVERE (from 1972). Of his five children Devon (*b.* 1959) and Campbell SCOTT became actors.

FILMS: *The Hanging Tree, Anatomy of a Murder* 1959; *The Hustler* 1961; *The List of Adrian Messenger* 1963; *Dr. Strangelove* (UK), *The Yellow Rolls-Royce* (UK) 1964; *La Bibbia/The Bible. . . In the Beginning* (as Abraham; It./US), *Not with My Wife You Don't!* 1966; *The Flim-Flam Man* 1967; *Petulia* (UK/US) 1968; *This Savage Land* (feature re-edited from two episodes of the TV series "The Road West," first shown in 1966) 1969; *Patton* (title role) 1970; *Jane Eyre* (as Rochester; UK), *They Might Be Giants, The Last Run, The Hospital* 1971; *The New Centurions, Rage* (also dir.) 1972; *Oklahoma Crude, The Day of the Dolphin* 1973; *Bank Shot, The Savage Is Loose* (also prod., dir.) 1974; *The Hindenburg* 1975; *Islands in the Stream, The Prince and the Pauper/Crossed Swords* (UK) 1977; *Movie* 1978; *Hardcore, Arthur Miller on Home Ground* (doc.) 1979; *The Changeling* (Can.), *The Formula* 1980; *Taps* 1981; *The Indomitable Teddy Roosevelt* (doc., narrator only), *Firestarter* 1984; *The Exorcist III, The Rescuers Down Under* (v/o) 1990; *Malice* 1993; *Angus* 1995.

Scott, Gordon. Actor. Born Gordon M. Werschkul, on Aug. 3, 1927, in Portland, Ore. *ed.* U. of Oregon. A former GI, fireman, cowboy, and lifeguard, he entered films in the mid-50s thanks to his muscular build and starred in a succession of Tarzan movies. In the early 60s he went to Italy, where for several years he appeared in action epics, specializing in Samsonian roles. Formerly (1955–59) married to Vera MILES.

FILMS INCLUDE: In the US—*Tarzan's Hidden Jungle* (title role) 1955; *Tarzan and the Lost Safari* (title role) 1957; *Tarzan's Fight for Life* (title role) 1958; *Tarzan's Greatest Adventure* (title role) 1959; *Tarzan the Magnificent* (title role)1960. In Italy—*Maciste alla Corte del Gran Khan/Samson and the Seven Miracles of the World, Romolo e Remo/Duel of the Titans* (as Remus), *Maciste contro il Vampiro/Goliath and the Vampires* 1961; *Il Gladiatore di Roma/Gladiator of Rome* 1962; *Ercole contro Molock/Conquest of Mycene, Il Leone di San Marco/The Lion of St. Mark* 1964; *Gli Uomini dal Passo Pesante/The Tramplers* 1966.

Scott, Janette. Actress. Born Thora Janette Scott, on Dec. 14, 1938, in Morecambe, England. The daughter of stage and screen actress Thora Hird (*b.* May 28, 1916, Morecambe, England), she began her career in films as a child actress and later played leads in many British and some American screen productions: Her second (1966–77) of three marriages was to singer Mel Torme.

FILMS INCLUDE: *Went the Day Well?/48 Hours* 1942; *2,000 Women* 1944; *No Place for Jennifer* 1949; *The Galloping Major, No Highway/No Highway in the Sky* (UK/US), *The Magic Box* 1951; *Background/Edge of Divorce* 1954; *Now and Forever* 1955; *Helen of Troy* (as Cassandra; US/It.) 1956; *The Good Companions, Happy Is the Bride* 1957; *The Devil's Disciple* (as Judith; UK/US) 1959; *School for Scoundrels* 1960; *Double Bunk* 1961; *Two and Two Make Six* 1962; *The Day of the Triffids, Paranoiac, Siege of the Saxons, The Old Dark House* (US/UK) 1963; *The Beauty Jungle/Contest Girl* 1964; *Crack in the World* (US) 1965; *Bikini Paradise* (US) 1967.

Scott, Lizabeth. Actress. Born Emma Matzo, on Sept. 29, 1922, in Scranton, Pa., of English-Russian parentage. *ed.* Marywood Coll. (Pa.); Alvienne School of Drama, N.Y. Alluring, sexy-voiced star of Hollywood films in the decade following WW II. She began her stage career in stock and got her first break as Tallulah Bankhead's understudy in Broadway's 'The Skin of Our Teeth' (1942). During that period she supplemented her income as a fashion model for *Harper's Bazaar*. She was spotted by Hal Wallis and given a screen test, as a result of which she was given a leading role in her first film *You Came Along* (1945). Her first significant role was in *Dead Reckoning* (1947). During the late 40s and early 50s she was promoted by Paramount as a type similar to Lauren Bacall and Veronica Lake. Her most recent appearance was in the offbeat British film, *Pulp* (1972).

FILMS: *You Came Along* 1945; *The Strange Love of Martha Ivers* 1946; *Variety Girl* (cameo), *Dead Reckoning, Desert Fury* 1947; *I Walk Alone, Pitfall* 1948; *Too Late for Tears, Easy Living* 1949; *Paid in Full, Dark City* 1950; *The Company She Keeps, Two of a Kind, The Racket* 1951; *Red Mountain, Stolen Face* 1952; *Scared Stiff* 1953; *Bad for Each Other, Silver Lode* 1954; *The Weapon* (UK) 1956; *Loving You* 1957; *Pulp* (UK) 1972.

Scott, Martha. Actress. Born on Sept. 22, 1914, in Jamesport, Mo. *ed.* U. of Michigan. After experience in stock, she scored a personal triumph in her very first Broadway play, acting the lead in 'Our Town' (1938). In 1940 she was nominated for an Oscar for repeating the role on the screen. Talented and unglamorous, she alternately starred in films and plays of the 40s, then moved into character parts. She has appeared on numerous TV programs since the early 50s. She also produced a number of plays and was co-producer of the film *First Monday in October.*

FILMS: *Our Town* (as Emily Webb), *The Howards of Virginia* 1940; *Cheers for Miss Bishop, They Dare Not Love, One Foot in Heaven* 1941; *Hi Diddle Diddle, Stage Door Canteen* (cameo), *In Old Oklahoma* 1943; *So Well Remembered* 1947; *Strange Bargain* 1949; *When I Grow Up* 1951; *The Desperate Hours* 1955; *The Ten Commandments* 1956; *Sayonara, 18 and Anxious* 1957; *Ben-Hur* 1959; *Charlotte's Web* (v/o) 1973; *Airport 1975* 1974; *The Turning Point* 1977: *First Monday in October* (co-prod. only) 1981; *Doin' Time on Planet Earth* 1988.

Scott, Randolph. Actor. *b.* George Randolph Crane Scott, Jan. 23, 1898, Orange, Va. *d.* 1987. *ed.* Georgia Tech; U. of North Carolina (engineering). Prototype of the Hollywood cowboy star, tall, rugged, and weathered, he began his adult life at 14, lying about his age and enlisting for WW I combat service. Returning home, he completed his studies, but instead of seeking employment as an engineer, he turned to the stage, joining the Pasadena Community Playhouse. After meeting Howard Hughes on a golf course, he entered films as a bit player late in 1927. He came into his own in the mid-30s, at first with a variety of romantic leads, then as a Western star. For a time, he was a roommate of fellow up-and-coming star Cary GRANT. He made his greatest contribution to the Western genre in the late 50s as the aging cowboy hero of a series of rough B Westerns directed by Budd BOETTICHER for an independent production company, Ranown, headed by Scott and Harry Joe BROWN. A consistent box-office attraction, although his films varied greatly in quality, Scott retired early in the 60s as one of Hollywood's richest men. His personal wealth, in oil wells, real estate, and securities, was estimated at anywhere between 50 and 100 million dollars.

FILMS: *Sharp Shooters* (bit) 1928; *The Far Call, The Black Watch, The Virginian, Dynamite* (all bits) 1929; *Women Men Marry* 1931; *Sky Bride, A Successful Calamity, Hot Saturday, Wild Horse Mesa, Island of Lost Souls* 1932; *Hello Everybody!, Heritage of the Desert, Murders in the Zoo, Supernatural, Sunset Pass, Cocktail Hour, Man of the Forest, To the Last Man, Broken Dreams, The Thundering Herd* 1933; *The Last Round-Up, Wagon Wheels* 1934; *Home on the Range, Roberta, Rocky Mountain Mystery, Village Tale, She* (as Leo Vincey), *So Red the Rose* (as Duncan Bedford) 1935; *Follow the Fleet, And Sudden Death, The Last of the Mohicans* (as Hawkeye), *Go West Young Man* 1936; *High Wide and Handsome* 1937; *Rebecca of Sunnybrook Farm, The Texans, The Road to Reno* 1938; *Jesse James, Susannah of the Mounties, Frontier Marshal* (as Wyatt Earp), *Coast Guard, 20,000 Men a Year* 1939; *Virginia City, My Favorite Wife, When the Daltons Rode* 1940; *Western Union, Belle Starr* (as Sam Starr) 1941; *Paris Calling, To the Shores of Tripoli, The Spoilers, Pittsburgh* 1942; *The Desperadoes, Bombardier, Corvette K-225, Gung Ho!* 1943; *Follow the Boys* (cameo), *Belle of the Yukon* 1944; *China Sky, Captain Kidd* 1945; *Abilene Town, Badman's Territory, Home Sweet Homicide* 1946; *Trail Street, Gunfighters, Christmas Eve* 1947; *Albuquerque, Coroner Creek, Return of the Badmen* 1948; *The Walking Hills, Canadian Pacific, The Doolins of Oklahoma, Fighting Man of the Plains* 1949; *The Nevadan, Colt .45, The Cariboo Trail* 1950; *Sugarfoot/A Swirl of Glory, Santa Fe, Fort Worth, Starlift* (cameo), *Man in the Saddle* 1951; *Carson City, Hangman's Knot* 1952; *Man Behind the Gun, The Stranger Wore a Gun, Thunder Over the Plains* 1953; *Riding Shotgun, The Bounty Hunter*

1954; *Ten Wanted Men, Rage at Dawn, Tall Man Riding, A Lawless Street* 1955; *Seven Men from Now, 7th Cavalry* 1956; *The Tall T, Shoot-Out at Medicine Bend, Decision at Sundown* 1957; *Buchanan Rides Alone* 1958; *Ride Lonesome, Westbound* 1959; *Comanche Station* 1960; *Ride the High Country* 1962.

Scott, Ridley. Director. Born on Nov. 30, 1937, in South Shields, England. *ed.* West Hartlepool Coll. of Art; Royal Coll. of Art, London. He entered BBC-TV in the mid-60s as a set designer and soon moved on to directing, turning out slick episodes for such series as 'Z Cars' and 'The Informer.' He then set up his own production company, Ridley Scott Associates, through which he manufactured TV commercials that became noted for their technical superiority and visual dazzle. Scott brought that flair for sumptuous design to the big screen when he made his debut as a feature director in 1977. His *The Duellists,* winner of the Cannes Festival prize for best first film, was a lavishly mounted if muddled adaptation of a Joseph Conrad story about a feud between two officers during the Napoleonic Wars. Style again won out over substance in Scott's *Alien* (1979), a science-fiction thriller more admired for its technique and startling editing than for originality or profundity. It was a huge box-office hit. *Blade Runner* (1982) was Scott's quintessential film: a boldly designed, visually arresting but structurally somewhat sloppy and narratively fuzzy look at a bleak 21st century L.A. He fused visual flair with dramatic drive in 1991's *Thelma & Louise*, which, with its daring heroines and their determined escape, became a feminist movie standard. He is the brother of director Tony SCOTT.

FILMS: *The Duellists* (UK) 1977; *Alien* (US/UK) 1979; *Blade Runner* 1982; *Legend* (UK) 1985; *Someone to Watch Over Me* (also exec. prod.) 1987; *Black Rain* (US) 1989; *Thelma & Louise* (also co-prod.) 1991; *1492* (also co-prod.) 1992; *The Browning Version* (co-prod. only) 1994; *White Squall* (also ex.-prod.) 1996; *G.I. Jane* (also prod.) 1997.

Scott, Sherman. See NEWFIELD, Sam.

Scott, Tony. Director. Born 1944 in Newcastle, England. *ed.* Leeds Coll. of Art; Royal Coll. of Art, London. Following in the footsteps of his older brother, Ridley SCOTT, he directed numerous commercials before venturing into features in 1983. Like Ridley, Tony is known primarily for his mastery of film technique. After his debut feature, *The Hunger* (1983), a kinky, enigmatic thriller, he went to Hollywood and scored a huge commercial hit with *Top Gun* (1986), a vapid air-action saga about young student pilots. He continued in a commercial, rather than creative vein, until 1993, when *True Romance* gained a young, art-house following.

FILMS: *The Hunger* (UK) 1983; *Top Gun* 1986; *Beverly Hills Cop II* 1987; *Revenge, Days of Thunder* 1990; *The Last Boy Scout* 1991; *True Romance* 1993; *Crimson Tide* 1995; *The Fan* 1996.

Scott, Zachary. Actor. *b.* Zachary Thomson Scott, Jr., Feb. 24, 1914, Austin, Tex. *d.* 1965. The son of a prominent surgeon, he dropped out of the University of Texas after one year and sailed to England, where he began his stage career in the provinces. Returning to the US, he completed his college studies, then resumed acting in stock and later on Broadway. He was signed by Warners and made an auspicious screen debut, playing the ruthless title role in *The Mask of Dimitrios* (1944). On a loan-out to United Artists, he next gave a powerful yet restrained performance in the role of a sharecropper in Jean Renoir's *The Southerner* (1945). He then reverted at Warners to the type of role he played in *Dimitrios,* the sleek, charming heel that audiences love to hate. Scott was effectively typecast as a smooth villain or scoundrel through most of his film career, although he was occasionally seen in sympathetic leads. His film career waned in the 50s, when he freelanced in minor productions, and he devoted more and more of his time to television and the stage. He died of a brain tumor at 51. His widow is stage actress Ruth Ford.

FILMS: *The Mask of Dimitrios, Hollywood Canteen* (cameo) 1944; *The Southerner, Mildred Pierce, Danger Signal* 1945; *Her Kind of Man* 1946; *Stallion Road, The Unfaithful, Cass Timberlane* 1947; *Ruthless, Whiplash* 1948; *Flaxy Martin, South of St. Louis, Flamingo Road, One Last Fling* 1949; *Guilty Bystander, Colt .45, Shadow on the Wall, Born to Be Bad, Pretty Baby* 1950; *Lightning Strikes Twice, The Secret of Convict Lake, Let's Make It Legal* 1951; *Stronghold, Wings of Danger* 1952; *Appointment in Honduras* 1953; *The Treasure of Ruby Hills, Shotgun, Flame of the Islands* 1955; *Bandido* 1956; *The Counterfeit Plan, Man in the Shadow/Violent Stranger, Flight Into Danger, Natchez Trace* 1960; *La Joven/The Young One* (in Mexico, for Buñuel) 1961; *It's Only Money* 1962.

Scott-Thomas, Kristin. Actress. Born in 1961, in England. *ed.* Central School of Speech and Drama, London; Ecole Nationale des Arts et Techniques de Theatre, Paris, France. Dignified, statuesque beauty, of international fame for her convincing, powerful performances on the stage and screen. Her American film career took off in 1996 with the release of director Anthony MINGHELLA's sweeping, epic romance *The English Patient,* earning an Academy Award nomination as best actress.

FILMS: *Under the Cherry Moon* (US) 1985; *A Handful of Dust* (UK), *The Tenth Man* (US) 1988; *Bitter Moon* (Fr./UK) 1992; *Four Weddings and a Funeral* (UK), *An Unforgettable Summer* (Fr./Rom.) 1994; *Angels & Insects* (US), *Richard III* (US/UK) 1995; *Le Confessionale* (Can./Fr./UK), *Mission: Impossible* (US), *The English Patient* (US) 1997.

scraper. A device for removing emulsion from portions of a film so that they can be spliced with cement. The scraper is usually incorporated into a SPLICER but also comes as a separate tool.

scratches. Marks on the surface of film, usually caused by friction with parts of cameras, projectors, viewers, or processing machines, or by careless rewinding and handling. They differ from "abrasions" in that they are deeper and usually penetrate the emulsion surface. Scratches on positive film, which appear in screening as black marks, are common in prints that have been projected many times. Much more serious are negative scratches, which appear in screening as white marks. Since a negative scratch would be duplicated in every print, it is essential that negatives remain scratch-free. To protect the original negative, it is a common practice to make several dupe negatives from which many prints can be made.

scratch print (also **slop print**). 1. A motion picture print duplicated from a completed work print, usually for the purpose of saving time in meeting a deadline. Having two prints of the same film enables an editor to pursue two time-consuming procedures simultaneously. For example, he can send one print to the negative cutter for matching and prepare the other print for a sound mix. Since the scratch print is not intended for subsequent use, little attention is paid to its clarity or overall quality. 2. Library footage used by an editor for inserts in the work print. It often arrives at the cutting room deliberately scratched by the supplier to prevent unauthorized duplication of rare scenes. When the work print is edited to a fine cut, a fresh, usable copy is substituted for the scratched footage from the negative kept by the cautious supplier.

screen. The reflective or translucent material onto whose surface motion pictures are projected. The standard shape of the cinema screen was set in 1906 at an ASPECT RATIO (width in relation to height) of 4:3, or 1.33:1. Over the years, filmmakers have experimented with a variety of screen sizes and shapes, and in the 50s, with the advent of the wide screen, a broad range of shapes was introduced with aspect ratios of up to 2.55:1. It is sometimes necessary to join several sheets of material together to form a large screen. The screens are perforated to allow the transmission into the auditorium of sound from loudspeakers placed behind the screens.

The great majority of cinema screens are opaque rather than translucent. The light rays from the projector fall upon the reflective opaque surface and are reflected and made visible to the spectators. The most common variety of opaque screen is the white matte, which provides uniform brightness from any angle. Other varieties are the aluminum screen, which tends to increase brightness but also contrast and graininess, and the beaded screen, which reflects in narrow angle and is therefore suitable for use only in narrow auditoriums.

Translucent screens are used with BACK PROJECTION systems. They are rarely installed in motion picture theaters and their use is limited mainly to small display and demonstration projection units.

Screen Actors Guild. See SAG.

Screen Extras Guild. See SEG.

screenplay (also called **script** and **scenario**). The written text upon which a film production is based. Unlike a stage play, which is generally produced and performed the way, or close to the way, it was originally written, the screenplay is wide open to interpretation and change and seldom reaches the screen intact. While the playwright communicates with his audience almost as directly as a novelist, the screenwriter communicates through intermediaries. His work is an essential element—but only one element—in a collaborative enterprise that is presided over by the director. Scenes may undergo changes of content, motivation, emphasis, or dialogue at several preproduction stages and even as the filming progresses, at the discretion of the director.

As literature, few screenplays stand on their own, nor are they meant to. A good script is not judged by the way it reads but by its effectiveness as a blueprint for a film. To be successful, it must be conceived in visual terms and should sustain a pace of action and dialogue in keeping with the requirements of a motion picture. Its dialogue must integrate well with other elements of the sound track, such as music and effects.

Screenwriting is a multistage process that begins with an original idea or an acquired published property, such as a novel, short story, or play. Usually, it is first presented to a producer as a brief synopsis that outlines the story, dramatic highlights, and main characters. Variably known as a concept, or an outline, the synopsis usually runs only a few pages in length. The next step is the treatment, an extensive, detailed elaboration of the ideas contained in the synopsis. A good treatment is presented in well-developed narrative form and covers every event and all the major action in the proposed film in proper, though tentative, continuity. The treatment is followed by a first-draft screenplay, written in script form and containing full dialogue. A rewrite or several rewrites may follow before the script is polished into a final screenplay, or shooting script, a fully approved, scene-by-scene document with full dialogue and detailed camera setups.

In the US, screenplays for feature films are usually presented in a format similar to that of a stage play, with dialogue and directions alternating. On the other hand, documentary and industrial films are presented in a two-column format, with the left column containing camera directions and the right column dialogue, narration, music, and sound effects. The latter format is preferred by most European filmmakers for feature films as well as for documentaries.

screen test. A filmed audition to determine a person's ability as an actor or an actor's suitability for a specific part in a motion picture.

screenwriter. A person who writes or participates in the writing of film scripts. Historically, the screenwriter did not come into prominence until the advent of the feature film. Early one-reel and split-reel shorts were usually made extemporaneously with only a vague plot in mind. The responsibility for the story as well as other aspects of production was often that of the cameraman, the formative years' jack-of-all-trades. Gradually, however, as films grew in length and sophistication, the need arose for specialists in every department, including scriptwriting. First came the gag writer, often a vaudeville or music-hall comedian, who supplied ideas for comic situations. As stories became more complicated, writers were hired to develop continuity and to compose title cards.

The arrival of sound eliminated the need for titles but created a demand for experienced dialogue writers, which were initially recruited mainly from the stage. However, it soon became recognized that the art and craft of screenwriting differed in several essential respects from those of playwriting. Before long, special screenwriting techniques had evolved and a corps of professional screenwriters had developed at film studios everywhere. In France, dialogue writing became a specialty all its own. Areas of specialty are less well defined in Hollywood and other film centers, but in these places, too, many writers tend to specialize in particular aspects of screenwriting. Some stand out as idea people, others are known as skilled dramaturgists, while still others are adept at inventing comic situations or excel in writing dialogue or in polishing or "doctoring" other people's scripts. Not all screenwriters possess the visual imagination and technical know-how required for writing final shooting scripts, complete with detailed camera directions. Often this is done by an experienced specialist. Many screenplays are a result of a collaborative effort by two or more writers, with the director or producer frequently participating to one degree or another.

The question of the "authorship" of films has been hotly debated among critics ever since the development in the 50s of the AUTEUR THEORY, which promulgated the notion (some claim myth) that the director is the true author of a work that is essentially visual. While proponents of the *politique des auteurs* claim that the creative director's work is distinguished not only by its visual style but also by a consistency of theme, others point out that theme, as developed through plot, characterization, and dialogue, is primarily the realm of the writer, and unless the director happens to write his own scripts, he interprets rather than creates the theme. Whatever the merits of the debate, there is no questioning the magnitude of the screenwriter's contribution to the essentially collaborative art of film.

Notable Hollywood screenwriters over the years have included George Axelrod, John L. Balderston, Charles Brackett, Leigh Brackett, Richard Brooks, Harry Brown, Sidney Buchman, W. R. Burnett, Niven Busch, Raymond Chandler, Borden Chase, Paddy Chayefsky, Lenore Coffee, Betty Comden and Adolph Green, I. A. L. Diamond, Philip Dunne, Julius Epstein, Joe Eszterhas, Carl Foreman, Jules Furthman, Lowell Ganz and Babaloo Mandel, William Goldman, Frances Goodrich and Albert Hackett, Ben Hecht, Buck Henry, Ruth Prawer Jhabvala, Nunnally Johnson, Garson Kanin, Howard Koch, Norman Krasna, Ring Lardner, Jr., Arthur Laurents, Charles Lederer, Ernest Lehman, Anita Loos, Charles MacArthur, Ben Maddow, John Lee Mahin, Richard Maibaun, Albert Maltz, Herman J. Mankiewicz, Joseph L. Mankiewicz, Frances Marion, Edwin Justus Mayer, Seton I. Miller, Dudley

Nichols, John Paxton, Eleanor Perry, James Poe, Abraham Polonsky, Richard Price, Samson Raphaelson, Robert Riskin, Casey Robinson, Morrie Ryskind, Allan Scott, John Patrick Shanley, Charles Schnee, Robert E. Sherwood, Stirling Silliphant, Donald Ogden Stewart, Jo Swerling, Robert Towne, Dalton Trumbo, Ernest Vajda, Anthony Veiller, Philip Yordan, and Waldemar H. Young. Skilled writers better known as directors include Woody Allen, Delmer Daves, Blake Edwards, John Huston, Neil Jordan, Lawrence Kasdan, Stanley Kubrick, Spike Lee, John Sayles, Ron Shelton, Oliver Stone, Preston Sturges, Frank Tashlin, and Billy Wilder.

In the 90s, a number of stellar young talents have emerged, among them: Ann Biderman, Shane Black, Scott Alexander and Larry Kareszewski, Scott Frank, Jeb Stuart, and Ted Tally.

Screen Writers Guild. See WRITERS GUILD OF AMERICA.

scrim. In films, a translucent screen, usually made of wire gauze, positioned in front of a light source on the set to soften or diffuse emitted light.

script. See SCREENPLAY.

Seagal, Steven. Actor. Born on Apr. 10, 1952, in Detroit. Tall, athletic, hip, bone-crunching hero of action pictures. Fascinated since early childhood by the martial arts, he developed karate skills in Los Angeles, where his family moved when he was nine. At 17 he traveled to Japan, where he studied and later taught aikido. Returning to the US 15 years later, he entered films in the late 80s and promptly emerged as the popular, ponytailed, iron-fisted star of a string of enormously profitable hit-first-ask-later thrillers. His 1990 *Marked for Death* was one of the top grossers of that year. A Sixth-Degree Black Belt, Seagal heads his own company, Streamroller Productions. His second wife is model-actress Kelly LeBrock. He is the father of four.

FILMS: *Above the Law* (also co-prod., co-story, chor.) 1988; *Hard to Kill, Marked For Death* (also co-prod.) 1990; *Out for Justice* (also co-prod.) 1991; *Under Siege* (also co-prod.) 1992; *On Deadly Ground* (also co-prod., dir.) 1994; *Executive Decision, Under Seige 2: Dark Territory* (also co-prod.) 1995; *Glimmer Man* 1996; *Fire Down Below* 1997.

Seagull, Barbara. See HERSHEY, Barbara.

Seale, John. Director of photography, director. Born 1942 in Warwick, Queensland, Australia. Following a start in Australian TV, he freelanced as a camera operator on some notable features—including Peter Weir's *Picnic at Hanging Rock* (1975), *The Last Wave* (1977), and *Gallipoli* (1981)—and as a second-unit cameraman on *The Year of Living Dangerously* (1983). At the same time, he worked on smaller productions as a chief cameraman, gradually establishing a reputation as a highly skilled lighting cinematographer. Working mainly in the US since the mid-80s, he was nominated for Oscars for the brilliant cinematography of *Witness* (1985), *Rain Man* (1988), and *The English Patient* (1996). He turned out his first film as a director in 1991.

FILMS INCLUDE: As director of photography—*Deathcheaters* 1976; *Fatty Finn* 1980; *The Survivor* 1981; *Goodbye, Paradise, Fighting Back* 1982; *Careful, He Might Hear You, BMX Bandits* 1983; *Silver City* 1984; *Witness* (US) 1985; *The Hitcher* (US), *Children of a Lesser God* (US), *The Mosquito Coast* (US) 1986; *Stakeout* (US) 1987; *Gorillas in the Mist* (US), *Rain Man* (US) 1988; *Dead Poets Society* (US) 1989; *The Doctor* (US) 1991; *Ghosts of Mississippi, The English Patient* 1996. As director—*Till There Was You* 1991.

Sears, Fred F. Director. *b.* July 7, 1913, Boston. *d.* 1957. *ed.* Boston Coll. A former stage actor, director, and producer, he entered films as an actor, appearing in such productions as *Down to Earth* (1947) and *The Golden Blade* (1948), then switched to directing in 1949. During the following decade he turned out numerous low-budget Hollywood films, mostly for Columbia Pictures and mainly in the action and fantasy fields, occasionally rising above his unremarkable material. He also directed some live plays for TV and taught drama at Southwestern University.

FILMS: *Desert Vigilante, Horsemen of the Sierra* 1949; *Across the Badlands, Raiders of Tomahawk Creek, Lightning Guns* 1950; *Prairie Roundup, Ridin' the Outlaw Trail, Snake River Desperadoes, Bonanza Town, Pecos River* 1951; *Smoky Canyon, The Hawk of Wild River, The Kid from Broken Gun, Last Train from Bombay* 1952; *Target—Hong Kong, Ambush at Tomahawk Gap, The 49th Man, Mission Over Korea, Sky Commando, The Nebraskan* 1953; *El Alamein, Overland Pacific, The Miami Story, Massacre Canyon, The Outlaw Stallion* 1954; *Wyoming Renegades, Cell 2455—Death Row, Chicago Syndicate, Apache Ambush, Teen-Age Crime Wave* 1955; *Inside Detroit, Fury at Gunsight Pass, Rock Around the Clock, Earth vs. the Flying Saucers, The Werewolf, Miami Exposé, Cha-Cha-Cha Boom!, Rumble on the Docks* 1956; *Don't Knock the Rock, Utah Blaine, Calypso Heat Wave, The Night the World Exploded, The Giant Claw, Escape from San Quentin* 1957; *The World Was His Jury, Going Steady, Crash Landing, Badman's Country, Ghost of the China Seas* 1958.

Seastrom, Victor. See SJÖSTRÖM, Victor.

Seaton, George. Director, producer, screenwriter. *b.* Apr. 17, 1911, South Bend, Ind. *d.* 1979. A former stage actor and producer, he entered films in 1933 as screenwriter. Turning director in the mid-40s, he continued writing his own scripts and won best screenplay Academy Awards for *Miracle on 34th Street* and *The Country Girl.* In 1952 he formed a partnership with William Perlberg, with whom he co-produced many films through the mid-60s. Seaton's films were, on the whole, commercially successful but, with several notable exceptions, predictable and uninspired.

FILMS: *Student Tour* (co-story only) 1934; *The Winning Ticket* (co-story only) 1935; *A Day at the Races* 1937; *The Doctor Takes a Wife* 1940; *This Thing Called Love, Moon Over Miami, Charley's Aunt* 1941; *The Magnificent Dope, Ten Gentlemen from West Point* 1942; *The Meanest Man in the World, Coney Island, The Song of Bernadette* 1943; *The Eve of St. Mark* 1944; *The Cockeyed Miracle* (play basis only) 1946. As director—*Diamond Horseshoe* (also sc.), *Junior Miss* (also sc.) 1945; *The Shocking Miss Pilgrim* (also sc.), *Miracle on 34th Street* (also sc.) 1947; *Apartment for Peggy* (also sc.) 1948; *Chicken Every Sunday* (also co-sc.) 1949; *The Big Lift* (also story, sc.) *For Heaven's Sake* (also sc.) 1950; *Anything Can Happen* (also co-sc.) 1952; *Little Boy Lost* (also sc.) 1953; *The Country Girl* (also co-prod., sc.) 1955; *The Proud and the Profane* (also co-story, sc.) 1956; *Williamsburg: The Story of a Patriot* (doc.) 1957; *Teacher's Pet* 1958; *The Pleasure of His Company* 1961; *The Counterfeit Traitor* (also sc.) 1962; *The Hook* 1963; *36 Hours* (also sc.) 1965; *What's So Bad About Feeling Good?* (also prod., co-story, co-sc.) 1968; *Airport* (also sc.) 1970; *Showdown* (also prod.) 1973. As co-producer with William Perlberg—*Rhubarb* 1951; *Somebody Loves Me* 1952; *The Bridges at Toko-Ri* 1955; *The Tin Star* 1957; *But Not for Me* 1959; *The Rat Race* 1960; *Twilight of Honor* 1963.

Seberg, Jean. Actress. *b.* Nov. 13, 1938, Marshalltown, Iowa. *d.* 1979. A stagestruck small-town Iowa U. freshman, she soared to fame at age 17 when she was selected out of thousands of contenders to play the title role in Otto Preminger's *Saint Joan.* The fanfare of studio publicity made her famous before the shooting even began, but the film turned out be a critical and commercial flop. She fared somewhat better in Preminger's next effort, *Bonjour Tristesse,* but seemed all but washed up in the business when her career took a favorable turn in France. She found new audiences and new respect in the role of an American beatnik in Paris, in Jean-Luc Godard's directorial debut, *Breathless.* Taking a cue from Godard, other directors began tapping Seberg's facility to project an enchanting brand of corruptible innocence. She gave a remarkable performance in Robert Rossen's *Lilith* (1964), as a schizophrenic patient who seduces her novice therapist, and went on to perform in many international productions. Seberg's personal life was marked by tragedy. Politically active in the cause of the Black Panthers, she became the object of real and imagined harassment by the American press and government agencies. With her mental health deteriorating, she suffered a nervous breakdown following a miscarriage. Three of her four husbands directed her in mediocre films: attorney-filmmaker François Moreuil (1958–60) in *La Récreation/Playtime* (1961), novelist Romain Gary (1962–70) in *Kill!* (1971), and director Dennis Berry (1972–78) in *Le Grand Délire* (1975). Although separated but not officially divorced from Berry, Seberg married Algerian-born Ahmed Hasni in May of 1979. Three months and one week later she was found dead of an overdose of barbiturates, a probable suicide.

FILMS INCLUDE: *Saint Joan* (US) 1957; *Bonjour Tristesse* (US) 1958; *The Mouse That Roared* (UK) 1959; *Á Bout de Souffle/Breathless* (Fr.), *Let No Man Write My Epitaph* (US) 1960; *L'Amant de Cinq Jours/The Five Day Lover* (Fr./It.), *Les Grandes Personnes/Time Out for Love* (Fr./It.), *La Récréation/Playtime* (Fr.) 1961; *In the French Style* (US/Fr.) 1963; *Echappement Libre/Backfire* (Fr./It./Sp.), *Lilith* (US) 1964; *Moment to Moment* (US), *A Fine Madness* (US), *La Ligne de Démarcation* (Fr.) 1966; *La Route de Corinthe/Who's Got the Black Box?* (Fr./It./Gr.) 1967; *Les Oiseaux vont mourir au Pérou/Birds in Peru* (Fr.) 1968; *Pendulum* (US), *Paint Your Wagon* (US) 1969; *Airport* (US), *Macho Callahan* (US) 1970; *Kill!/Kill Kill Kill* (Fr./It./Ger./Sp.) 1971; *L'Attentat/The French Conspiracy, La Corruption de Chris Miller/The Corruption of Chris Miller* (Sp.) 1972; *Le Chat et la Souris/Cat and Mouse* (Fr.) 1974; *Le Grand Délire* (Fr.) 1975; *Die Wildente/The Wild Duck* (Ger./Aus.) 1976.

second assistant director. See ASSISTANT DIRECTOR.

second cameraman. See CAMERA OPERATOR.

second feature. The lesser feature in a double bill (double feature).

second unit. A self-contained production unit assigned to film sequences not requiring the presence of the director or the principal players. These may range from routine background shots at remote locations to complex large-scale action sequences requiring the special talents of a SECOND-UNIT DIRECTOR.

second-unit director. An individual especially skilled at the staging of large-scale action sequences that may involve complex special effects and the participation of many extras, horses, etc. The typical second-unit director is not skilled at directing actors or handling intimate dramatic scenes but is superior to most ordinary directors in his ability to organize and handle big action. Some of the most memorable sequences in Hollywood films have been staged by second-unit directors, notably the chariot races in both versions of *Ben-Hur* and the charge in *The Charge of the Light Brigade.* Among the most capable and best-known second-unit directors are B. Reeves Eason, Yakima Canutt, and Andrew Marton.

Sedgwick, Edward. Director. *b.* Nov. 7, 1892, Galveston, Tex. *d.* 1953. Prolific director of silent and sound Hollywood films. He began as a circus and vaudeville performer in a family act, "The Five Sedgwicks," in which he appeared with his parents and twin sisters, Josie and Eileen. He entered films as a comic actor in 1915, making his directorial debut in 1921. At first specializing in Westerns (Tom Mix, Hoot Gibson, etc.), he later turned to comedy. He reached a career peak at MGM in the late 20s and early 30s, notably with a string of Buster KEATON films. But much of his later product was routine. His sister, Eileen Sedgwick (1895–1991), also in films from 1915, became a popular star of silent serials and action pictures. Her twin, Josie (Josephine) Sedgwick (1895–1973), was also a film actress, often in Westerns.

FILMS: *Fantomas* (serial), *Live Wires* (also co-story), *Bar Nothin', The Rough Diamond* (also co-story, sc.) 1921; *The Bearcat, Chasing the Moon* (also co-story), *Boomerang Justice, Do and Dare* (also sc.), *The Flaming Hour* 1922; *The First Degree, Single Handed* (also story), *The Gentleman from America, Romance Land, Dead Game* (also story, sc.), *Blinky* (also sc.), *Out of Luck* (also story), *The Ramblin' Kid, Shootin' for Love, The Thrill Chaser* (also co-story) 1923; *Hook and Ladder* (also co-story), *Broadway or Bust* (also co-story), *Ride for Your Life, 40-Horse Hawkins* (also co-story, co-sc.), *Hit and Run* (also co-story, co-sc.), *The Sawdust Trail, The Ridin' Kid from Powder River* 1924; *The Hurricane Kid, The Saddle Hawk* (also co-story, co-sc.), *Let 'Er Buck* (also co-story, co-sc.), *Spook Ranch* (co-story only), *Lorraine of the Lions, The Phantom of the Opera* (addnl. sequences only), *Two-Fisted Jones* 1925; *Under Western Skies* (also story), *The Flaming Frontier* (also story), *The Runaway Express, Tin Hats* (also story) 1926; *The Bugle Call, Slide Kelly Slide, Spring Fever, West Point* 1927; *Circus Rookies* (also co-story), *The Cameraman* 1928; *Spite Marriage* 1929; *Doughboys, Free and Easy, Remote Control* (addnl. scenes only) 1930; *Parlor Bedroom and Bath, A Dangerous Affair, Maker of Men* (also story) 1931; *The Passionate Plumber, Speak Easily* 1932; *What—No Beer?, Horse Play, Saturday's Millions* 1933; *I'll Tell the World, The Poor Rich, Here Comes the Groom, Death on the Diamond* 1934; *Father Brown—Detective, Murder in the Fleet* (also story), *The Virginia Judge* 1935; *Mister Cinderella* 1936; *Pick a Star, Riding on Air, Fit for a King* 1937; *The Gladiator* 1938; *Burn 'Em Up O'Connor, Beware—Spooks* 1939; *So You Won't Talk* 1940; *Air Raid Wardens* 1943; *A Southern Yankee* 1948; *Ma and Pa Kettle Back on the Farm* 1951.

Sedgwick, Kyra. Actress. Born on Aug. 19, 1965, in New York City. *ed.* USC. Likable, sad-eyed screen lead and character player, in films since the 1980s. Won the Theatre World Award for her performance in 'Ah Wilderness' and received acclaim for the title role in the TV special *Miss Rose White*. She has established herself as a warm, appealing screen actor with impressive performances in *Something to Talk About* (1995) and *Phenomenon* (1996). Married to actor Kevin BACON.

FILMS INCLUDE: *Lemon Sky, Kansas* 1988; *Born on the Fourth of July* 1989; *Mr. & Mrs. Bridge* 1990; *Pirates* 1991; *Singles* 1992; *Heart & Souls* 1993; *Murder in the First, Something to Talk About* 1995; *Losing Chase, The Low Life, Phenomenon* 1996.

Seeber, Guido. Director of photography. *b.* June 22, 1879, Chemnitz, Germany. *d.* 1940. One of the most important lighting cameramen of silent German cinema with hundreds of films to his credit. From 1908 to 1914 he was in charge of all technical operations at the Deutsche Bioscop film company in addition to his duties as a cameraman.

FILMS INCLUDE: *Sumurun* 1908; *Der fremde Vogel, Zigeunerblut* 1911; *Die arme Jenny, Komödianten, Der Totentanz* 1912; *Engelein* (co-phot.), *Die Filmprimadonna* (co-phot.), *Der Streichholzkünstler* (also prod., sc.), *Der Student von Prag* 1913; *Das Feuer, Der Golem, Weisse Rosen* 1914; *Das wandernde Bild* 1920; *Hochstapler* 1921; *Alt-Heidelberg, Fridericus Rex* (co-phot.), *Sylvester/New Year's Eve* (co-phot.), *Wilhelm Tell* (co-phot.) 1923; *Lebende Buddhas* (co-phot.), *Ein Sommernachtstraum/A Midsummer Night's Dream* (co-phot.) 1924; *Die freudlose Gasse/The Street of Sorrow/The Joyless Street* (co-phot.) 1925; *Geheimnisse einer Seele/Secrets of a Soul* (co-phot.) 1926; *Dirnentragödie/Small Town Sinners/Tragedy of the Street* 1927; *Ewiger Wald* (co-phot.) 1936.

Seeley, S. K. See SEKELY, Steve.

SEG. Screen Extras Guild. A union representing the interests of persons regularly employed as extras on the screen. Organized in 1945, it was absorbed by SAG in the mid-90s and is no longer a single organization.

Segal, Alex. Director. *b.* July 1, 1915, Brooklyn, N.Y. *d.* 1977. *ed.* Carnegie Inst. Award-winning stage and TV director, he ventured only occasionally into films, with mixed results. He was chairman of the department of drama at the University of Southern California.

FILMS: *Ransom* 1956; *All the Way Home* 1963; *Joy in the Morning, Harlow* (Carol Lynley version) 1965.

Segal, George. Actor. Born on Feb. 13, 1934, in New York City. *ed.* Columbia. Personable, offbeat leading man of Hollywood films. He staged his own amateur magic act at age eight and while still at school led the "Bruno Lynch and His Imperial Jazz Band" as a conductor-vocalist. After graduating from college, he worked as a janitor, usher, and jazz musician while breaking into show business in New York clubs and on the off-Broadway stage. He has since been seen on Broadway and frequently on TV, in addition to playing a wide range of lead roles, in both dramatic and comic films. He was nominated for an Oscar as best supporting actor for his performance in *Who's Afraid of Virginia Woolf?* (1966). With his moderately successful screen career ebbing in the early 80s, Segal temporarily revived his pursuit of music. In 1981 he performed at Carnegie Hall with his Beverly Hills Unlisted Jazz Band.

FILMS: *The Young Doctors* 1961; *Act One* 1963; *The New Interns, Invitation to a Gunfighter* 1964; *Ship of Fools, King Rat* 1965; *Who's Afraid of Virginia Woolf?, Lost Command, The Quiller Memorandum* (UK/US) 1966; *The St. Valentine's Day Massacre* 1967; *Bye Bye Braverman, No Way to Treat a Lady, Tenderly/The Girl Who Couldn't Say No* (It.) 1968; *L'Etoile du Sud/The Southern Star* (Fr./UK), *The Bridge at Remagen* 1969; *Loving, The Owl and the Pussycat, Where's Poppa?* 1970; *Born to Win* 1971; *The Hot Rock* 1972; *A Touch of Class* (UK), *Blume in Love* 1973; *The Terminal Man, California Split* 1974; *Russian Roulette, The Black Bird* 1975; *The Duchess and the Dirtwater Fox; Midway/The Battle of Midway* 1976; *Fun with Dick and Jane, Rollercoaster* 1977; *Who Is Killing the Great Chefs of Europe?* 1978; *Lost and Found* 1979; *The Last Married Couple in America* 1980; *Carbon Copy* 1981; *Stick, Killing 'Em Softly* (Can.; release delayed from 1982) 1985; *All's Fair, Look Who's Talking* 1989; *The Clearing* (US/USSR), *For the Boys, A Bear Named Arthur, Me Myself and I* 1992; *Army of One* 1994; *The Babysitter, To Die For* (unbilled cameo) 1995; *The Cable Guy, Flirting with Disaster, It's My Party, the Mirror Has Two Faces* 1996.

Segal, Vivienne. Singer, actress. *b.* Apr. 19, 1897, in Philadelphia. *d.* 1992. Star of operetta and Broadway musicals from age 16, she headed the original casts of 'Desert Song' (1926) and 'Pal Joey' (1940), among other memorable shows. She starred briefly in early sound films but was only mildly successful and soon returned to the stage.

FILMS: *Song of the West, Bride of the Regiment, Golden Dawn, Viennese Nights* 1931; *The Cat and the Fiddle* 1934.

Seidelman, Susan. Director. Born on Dec. 11, 1952, Abington, Penn., a suburb of Philadelphia. After studying art and fashion design at Drexel University, she clerked briefly at a Philadelphia UHF TV station, then moved to New York in 1974 for graduate studies at the NYU film school. Her award-winning student films, like *You Act Like One, Too* and *Yours Truly, Andrea G. Stern,* were about women, a favorite subject of this self-declared feminist director, when she turned professional in the early 80s. Seidelman started her first feature, *Smithereens,* in 1980 with $10,000 she had inherited from her grandmother. Completed two years later for a mere $80,000, the film, an astute character study of a punk-rock groupie and her vague ambitious dreams, became the surprise hit of the 1982 Cannes Festival. Seidelman's next film, *Desperately Seeking Susan* (1985), starring Rosanna ARQUETTE as a bored housewife and MADONNA as a kookie rocker in an offbeat parody involving amnesia and mistaken identity, became a huge box-office and critical hit that was later much discussed in college film courses. Seidelman went on to direct several other commercially viable light films focusing mainly on women characters. While affirming a measure of bankability and her directorial skill, none have thus far fulfilled the promise of her first two features.

FEATURE FILMS: *Smithereens* (also prod., co-sc., edit.) 1982; *Desperately Seeking Susan* 1985; *Making Mr. Right* (also co-exec. prod.) 1987; *Cookie* (also co-exec. prod.), *She-Devil* (also co-prod.) 1989; *Erotic Tales* (co-dir.) 1994.

Seigner, Louis. Actor. *b.* June 12, 1903, Saint-Chef, France. *d.* 1991. Dignified character player of the French stage and screen. A veteran member of the Comédie-Française, he played important supporting roles in many films. His daughter, Françoise Seigner, is also an actress.

FILMS INCLUDE: *Chotard & Cie* 1933; *Le Commissaire est Bon Enfant* 1935; *Entente cordiale* 1939; *Nous les Gosses* 1941; *Le Mariage de Chiffon, La Symphonie fantastique* 1942; *Goupi Mains-Rouges, Le Corbeau/The Raven, Les Anges du Péché/Angels of the Street* 1943; *Vautrin/Vautrin the Thief* 1944; *Jéricho, Patrie, Un Revenant/A Lover's Return* 1946; *Les Frères Bouquinquant* 1947; *La Chartreuse de Parme, D'Homme à Hommes* 1948; *Rendez-Vous de Juillet* 1949; *Miquette et sa Mère/Miquette, La Souricière* 1950; *Maître après Dieu, Boîte du Nuit/Hotbed of Sin* 1951; *Le Plaisir/House of Pleasure, Nous sommes tous des Assassins/We Are All Murderers, Adorables Créatures/Adorable Creatures, La Fête à Henriette/Holiday for Henrietta* 1952; *Les Dents longues, Lucrèce Borgia/Sins of the Borgias, L'Esclave* 1953; *Obsession* 1954; *Marguerite de la Nuit* 1956; *Nathalie/The Foxiest Girl in Paris, Les Espions* 1957; *Le Bourgeois Gentilhomme/The Would-Be Gentleman/The Bourgeois Gentleman* (as M. Jourdain), *Les Grandes Familles/The Possessors* 1958; *Le Mariage de Figaro/The Marriage of Figaro* (as Bartholo) 1959; *Le Baron de l'Ecluse, La Vérité/The Truth* 1960; *L'Eclisse/Eclipse* (It./Fr.) 1962; *Les Amitiés particulières/This Special Friendship* 1964; *Soleil noir* 1966; *Section spéciale/Special Section* 1975.

Seiler, Lewis. Director. *b.* 1891, New York City. *d.* 1963. A former assistant director and gagman, he began his career as director in the mid-20s, at first with comedy shorts, then with Tom Mix Westerns. He became established as an action specialist in a variety of genres—Westerns, crime melodramas, and war films—working mostly with low to medium budgets from lowbrow scripts. But he also turned out many comedies and occasional straight dramas.

FEATURE FILMS: *Darwin Was Right* 1924; *No Man's Gold, The Great K & A Train Robbery* 1926; *The Last Trail, Tumbling River, Outlaws of Red River, Wolf Fangs* 1927; *Square Crooks, The Air Circus* (co-dir. with Howard Hawks), 1928; *The*

Ghost Talks, Girls Gone Wild, A Song of Kentucky 1929; *No Greater Love, Deception* 1932; *Frontier Marshal* 1934; *Asegure a su Mujer* (in Spanish), *Charlie Chan in Paris, Ginger, Paddy O'Day* 1935; *Here Comes Trouble, The First Baby, Star for a Night, Career Woman* 1936; *Turn Off the Moon* 1937; *He Couldn't Say No, Crime School, Penrod's Double Trouble, Heart of the North* 1938; *King of the Underworld, You Can't Get Away with Murder, The Kid from Kokomo, Hell's Kitchen* (co-dir. with E. A. Dupont), *Dust Be My Destiny* 1939; *It All Came True, Flight Angels, Murder in the Air, Tugboat Annie Sails Again, South of Suez* 1940; *Kisses for Breakfast, The Smiling Ghost, You're in the Army Now* 1941; *The Big Shot, Pittsburgh* 1942; *Guadalcanal Diary* 1943; *Something for the Boys* 1944; *Doll Face, Molly and Me* 1945; *If I'm Lucky* 1946; *Whiplash* 1948; *Breakthrough* 1950; *The Tanks Are Coming* 1951; *The Winning Team, Operation Secret* 1952; *The System* 1953; *The Bamboo Prison* 1954; *Women's Prison* 1955; *Battle Stations, Over-Exposed* 1956; *The Story of Lynn Stuart* 1958.

Seiter, William A. Director. *b.* June 10, 1892, New York City. *d.* 1964. *ed.* Hudson River Military Acad. A former artist and writer, he broke into films as a Keystone Cop, later becoming assistant director and screenwriter. He became a director in 1918, at first of short subjects and shortly after of feature films. A prolific, sure-handed craftsman, he directed scores of entertaining if insignificant films in a variety of genres through the mid-50s but was most at home with romantic and sentimental light drama. His first wife (1926–32) was actress Laura LA PLANTE; his second (from 1936) Marian NIXON.

FEATURE FILMS: *The Kentucky Colonel* 1920; *Hearts and Masks, Passing Through, The Foolish Age* (also co-sc.), *Eden and Return* 1921; *Boy Crazy, Gay and Devilish, The Understudy, Up and At 'Em* (also co-story), *When Love Comes, The Beautiful and the Damned* 1922; *Bell Boy 13, Little Church Around the Corner* 1923; *Daddies, The White Sin, His Forgotten Wife, Listen Lester* (also co-adapt.), *Helen's Babies, The Family Secret, The Fast Worker* 1924; *The Mad Whirl, Dangerous Innocence, The Teaser, Where Was I?,* 1925; *What Happened to Jones, Skinner's Dress Suit, Rolling Home, Take It from Me* 1926; *The Cheerful Fraud* (also co-sc.), *The Small Bachelor, Out All Night* 1927; *Thanks for the Buggy Ride, Good Morning Judge, Happiness Ahead, Waterfront, Outcast* 1928; *Synthetic Wife, Why Be Good?, Prisoners, Smiling Irish Eyes, Footlights and Fools, The Love Racket* 1929; *Strictly Modern, Back Pay, The Flirting Widow, The Truth About Youth, Going Wild, Sunny* 1930; *Kiss Me Again, Big Business Girl, Too Many Crooks, Full of Notions, Caught Plastered, Peach O'Reno* 1931; *Way Back Home, Girl Crazy, Young Bride/Love Starved, Is My Face Red?, Hot Saturday, If I Had a Million* (co-dir. with several others) 1932; *Hello Everybody!, Diplomaniacs, Professional Sweetheart, Chance at Heaven* 1933; *Sons of the Desert, Rafter Romance, Sing and Like It, Love Birds, We're Rich Again, The Richest Girl in the World* 1934; *Roberta, The Daring Young Man, Orchids to You, In Person, If You Could Only Cook* 1935; *The Moon's Our Home, The Case Against Mrs. Ames, Dimples, Stowaway* 1936; *This Is My Affair, The Life of the Party, Life Begins in College* 1937; *Sally Irene and Mary, Three Blind Mice, Room Service, Thanks for Everything* 1938; *Susannah of the Mounties, Allegheny Uprising* 1939; *It's a Date, Hired Wife* (also prod.) 1940; *Nice Girl?, Appointment for Love* 1941; *Broadway, You Were Never Lovelier* 1942; *Destroyer, A Lady Takes a Chance* 1943; *Four Jills in a Jeep, Belle of the Yukon* (also prod.) 1944; *It's a Pleasure, The Affairs of Susan, That Night with You* 1945; *Little Giant, Lover Come Back* 1946; *I'll Be Yours* 1947; *Up In Central Park, One Touch of Venus* 1948; *Borderline* (also prod.) 1950; *Dear Brat* 1951; *The Lady Wants Mink* (also prod.), *Champ for a Day* (also prod.) 1953; *Make Haste to Live* (also co-prod.) 1954.

Seitz, George B(rackett). Director. *b.* Jan. 3, 1888, Boston. *d.* 1944. An art school graduate, he started as an illustrator but soon turned to the stage as an actor and playwright. He entered films in 1913 as actor and screenwriter for Pathé. His screenplays for features included such major productions as *The Beloved Vagabond, Simon the Jester* (both 1915), *The Light That Failed* (1916), *Blind Man's Luck* (1917), and *The Naulahka* (1918). But his most important early contribution was to the development of the embryonic serial genre, as the screenwriter for Pearl White's groundbreaking *The Perils of Pauline* (1914) and later as the director and producer of numerous other serials. He also appeared in many of these as an actor, sometimes in the starring role. He virtually dominated the serial field until 1925, when he turned exclusively to features. His silent feature output consisted for the most part of action films, often Westerns. His sound films included much of the same but also a great many lighter in theme, including most of the ANDY HARDY series. Seitz had a reputation for uncompromising professionalism in his work, always completing films on or before schedule and well within the limits of his budget. The effectiveness of some of his work in the thriller genre is quite amazing considering the speed at which he turned out his films. He was the brother of John F. SEITZ. His son, George B. Seitz, Jr. (*b.* Sept. 6, 1915, Montclair, N.J.), is a writer-director of documentary and TV films.

FILMS: Serials—*The Exploits of Elaine* (co-dir. with Louis Gasnier), *The New Exploits of Elaine* (also co-sc.), *The Romance of Elaine* (also co-sc.) 1915; *The Iron Claw* (co-dir. with Edward José; also sc., act.) 1916; *Pearl of the Army* (dir. last few episodes only; also sc.) 1916–17; *The Fatal Ring* (also act.) 1917; *The House of Hate* 1918; *The Lightning Raider* (also co-sc., act.), *Bound and Gagged* (also act.) 1919; *The Black Secret* (also act.) 1919–20; *Pirate Gold* 1920; *Velvet Fingers* (also act.) 1920–21; *The Sky Ranger* (also act.), *Hurricane Hutch* 1921; *Go Get 'Em Hutch* (also prod.), *Speed* 1922; *Plunder* (also prod.) 1923; *Way of a Man* (also sc.), *Leatherstocking, The 40th Door, Galloping Hoofs, Into the Net* 1924; *Sunken Silver* (also prod.) 1925. Features—*Rogues and Romance* (also prod., story, sc., act.) 1920; *The 40th Door* (feature version of serial) 1924; *Wild Horse Mesa, The Vanishing American* 1925; *Desert Gold, Pals in Paradise, The Ice Flood* (also co-sc.), *The Last Frontier* 1926; *Jim the Conqueror, The Great Mail Robbery, The Blood Ship, The Tigress, Isle of Forgotten Women, The Warning* (also sc.) 1927; *Ransom* (also story), *Beware of Blondes, Court-Martial, The Circus Kid, Blockade, Hey Rube!* 1928; *Black Magic* 1929; *Murder on the Roof, Guilty?, Midnight Mystery, Danger Lights* 1930; *Drums of Jeopardy, The Lion and the Lamb, Arizona/Men Are Like That, Shanghaied Love, Night Beat* 1931; *Sally of the Subway* (also story, sc.), *Docks of San Francisco, Sin's Pay Day, Passport to Paradise* (also story, sc.), *The Widow in Scarlet* 1932; *Treason, The Thrill Hunter, The Women in His Life* 1933; *Lazy River, The Fighting Rangers* 1934; *Only Eight Hours, Society Doctor, Shadow of Doubt, Times Square Lady, Calm Yourself, Woman Wanted, Kind Lady* 1935; *Exclusive Story, Absolute Quiet, The Three Wise Guys, The Last of the Mohicans, Mad Holiday* 1936; *Under Cover of Night, A Family Affair, The 13th Chair, Mama Steps Out, Between Two Women, My Dear Miss Aldrich* 1937; *You're Only Young Once, Judge Hardy's Children, Yellow Jack, Love Finds Andy Hardy, Out West with the Hardys* 1938; *The Hardys Ride High, Six Thousand Enemies, Thunder Afloat, Judge Hardy and Son* 1939; *Andy Hardy Meets Debutante, Kit Carson, Sky Murder, Gallant Sons* 1940; *Andy*

Hardy's Private Secretary, Life Begins for Andy Hardy 1941; *A Yank on the Burma Road, The Courtship of Andy Hardy, Pierre of the Plains, Andy Hardy's Double Life* 1942; *Andy Hardy's Blonde Trouble* 1944.

Seitz, John F. Director of photography. *b.* June 23, 1893, Chicago. *d.* 1979. A leading Hollywood cameraman in both the silent and sound eras. The younger brother of director George B. SEITZ, he entered films at age 16 as a lab technician, becoming a feature film cameraman in 1916. In the 20s he collaborated with director Rex INGRAM, working on *The Four Horsemen of the Apocalypse* and other major productions. During that period he contributed to the development of MATTE shots and became famous for his characteristic (and at the time innovative) use of intense low-key lighting. In the 40s he was lighting cameraman on many important Hollywood productions, notably those of Preston Sturges and Billy Wilder. He retired in 1960 to pursue independent lab experiments. He held 18 patents on photographic inventions and earned seven Oscar nominations for best cinematography.

FILMS INCLUDE: *Souls in Pawn* 1917; *Beauty and the Rogue* 1918; *The Westerners* 1919; *Hearts Are Trumps, Shore Acres* 1920; *The Conquering Power, The Four Horsemen of the Apocalypse, Uncharted Seas* 1921; *The Prisoner of Zenda, Trifling Women* 1922; *Scaramouche, Where the Pavement Ends* 1923; *The Arab* 1924; *The Magician, Mare Nostrum* 1926; *Adoration, The Patsy* 1928; *The Divine Lady, Saturday's Children* 1929; *Kismet* 1930; *East Lynne, Over the Hill* 1931; *Passport to Hell* 1932; *Adorable* 1933; *Marie Galante* 1934; *Helldorado, Curly Top, The Littlest Rebel* 1935; *The Country Doctor* (co-phot.), *Captain January, Poor Little Rich Girl* 1936; *Madame X, Navy Blue and Gold* 1937; *Lord Jeff, Young Dr. Kildare* 1938; *Huckleberry Finn, Sergeant Madden* 1939; *A Little Bit of Heaven* 1940; *Sullivan's Travels* 1941; *This Gun for Hire, The Moon and Sixpence, Lucky Jordan* 1942; *Five Graves to Cairo* 1943; *The Miracle of Morgan's Creek, Double Indemnity, Hail the Conquering Hero* 1944; *The Unseen, The Lost Weekend* 1945; *Home Sweet Homicide* 1946; *Wild Harvest, Calcutta* 1947; *Saigon, The Big Clock, Night Has a Thousand Eyes* 1948; *The Great Gatsby, Chicago Deadline* 1949; *Sunset Boulevard* 1950; *When Worlds Collide* (co-phot.) 1951; *The Iron Mistress* 1952; *Botany Bay* 1953; *Saskatchewan, Rogue Cop* 1954; *The McConnell Story* 1955; *Santiago* 1956; *The Big Land* 1957; *The Badlanders* 1958; *The Man in the Net* 1959; *Guns of the Timberland* 1960.

Sekely, Steve. Director. *b.* Istvan (Stephan) Szekely, Feb. 25, 1899, Budapest. *d.* 1979. A former journalist and short-story writer, he directed numerous German, Austrian, and Hungarian films before coming to the US in 1938. His American output consisted of routine low-budget films and much TV fare. From the early 50s he worked sporadically in Europe. He was also known as S. K. Seeley.

FILMS INCLUDE: In Europe—*Rhapsodie der Liebe* (Aus.) 1929; *Die grosse Sehnsucht* (Ger.), *Seitensprünge* (Ger.) 1930; *Er und sein Diener* (Ger.) 1931; *Ein steinreicher Mann* (Ger.), *Piri Mindont Tud* (Hung.) 1932; *Skandal in Budapest/Pardon tévedtem/Romance in Budapest* (co-dir. with Geza von Bolvary; German/Hungarian versions), *Rakoczi Marsch/Rakoczi Induló* (German/Hungarian versions) 1933; *Ida Regenye* (Hung.), *Lila Akác* (Hung.), *Ball im Savoy* (Aus./Hung.), *Emmy* (Hung.) 1934; *Café Moszkva* (Hung.), *Szensacio* (co-dir. with Ladislao Vajda; Hung.), *An Affair of Honor* 1936; *Two Prisoners* (Hung.), *Beauty of the Pusta* (Hung.), *I Married for Love* (Hung.) 1937; *Heart to Heart* (Hung.) 1938. In the US (complete)—*A Miracle on Main Street,* 1940; *Behind Prison Walls, Revenge of the Zombies* 1943; *Women in Bondage, Lady in the Death House, Waterfront, My Buddy, Lake Placid Serenade* 1944; *The Fabulous Suzanne* 1946; *Blonde Savage* 1947; *Hollow Triumph/The Scar* 1948; *Amazon Quest* 1949; *Stronghold* (and Spanish version, *Furia Roja*) 1952. In Europe—*Le Avventure di Cartouche* (co-dir. with Gianni Vernuccio; It.) 1954; *The Day of the Triffids* (UK) 1963; *Kenner/Year of the Cricket* (US) 1969; *The Girl Who Liked Purple Flowers* (Hung.) 1973.

Selander, Lesley. Director. *b.* May 26, 1900, Los Angeles. *d.* 1979. He went into films directly out of high school, beginning as a lab technician. He became assistant cameraman in 1920, cameraman in 1922, and assistant director in 1924. He directed some comedy shorts before joining MGM, where he worked as assistant director on such productions as *The Thin Man, A Night at the Opera,* and *Fury.* In 1936 he finally became a feature director, thanks to his friendship with Buck JONES. He piloted many of the cowboy star's later films, as well as those of Tim Holt and a great many Hopalong Cassidy pictures. In all, he directed scores of low-budget action films, mostly Westerns, in addition to hundreds of episodes for TV series.

FILMS INCLUDE: *Ride 'Em Cowboy, Empty Saddles* 1936; *Sandflow, Left-Handed Law, The Barrier, Hopalong Rides Again, Black Aces* 1937; *Heart of Arizona, Pride of the West, The Mysterious Rider, Sunset Trail, The Frontiersmen* 1938; *Heritage of the Desert, Range War* 1939; *Santa Fe Marshal, Hidden Gold, Stagecoach War, The Light of the Western Stars, Cherokee Strip* 1940; *The Roundup, Doomed Caravan, Pirates on Horseback, Thundering Hoofs* 1941; *Undercover Man, Lost Canyon* 1942; *Border Patrol, Colt Comrades* 1943; *Lumberjack, Call of the Rockies, Forty Thieves* 1944; *The Great Stagecoach Robbery, Phantom of the Plains, Jungle Raiders* (serial), *The Trail of Kit Carson, The Vampire's Ghost* 1945; *The Catman of Paris, Passkey to Danger, Traffic in Crime, Night Train to Memphis, Out California Way* 1946; *The Pilgrim Lady, Robin Hood of Texas, Blackmail, The Red Stallion* 1947; *Panhandle, Guns of Hate, Belle Starr's Daughter, Indian Agent* 1948; *Stampede, Sky Dragon, Masked Raiders, The Mysterious Desperado* 1949; *Dakota Lil, Storm Over Wyoming, The Kangaroo Kid, Law of the Badlands* 1950; *Cavalry Scout, I Was an American Spy, The Highwayman, Saddle Legion, Gunplay, Flight to Mars* 1951; *Road Agent, Desert Passage, The Raiders, Battle Zone, Flat Top* 1952; *Fort Vengeance, War Paint, Fort Algiers, Royal African Rifles, Fighter Attack* 1953; *Arrow in the Dust, Return from the Sea, The Yellow Tomahawk, Dragonfly Squadron* 1954; *Shotgun, Tall Man Riding, Desert Sands, Fort Yuma* 1955; *The Broken Star* 1956; *The Wayward Girl, Tomahawk Trail, Revolt at Fort Laramie, Outlaw's Son* 1957; *The Lone Ranger and the Lost City of Gold* 1958; *The Outrage* (2nd-unit dir. only) 1964; *Fort Courageous, Town Tamer* 1965; *Fort Utah* 1967; *Arizona Bushwhackers* 1968.

Selig, William N. Pioneer showman and film producer. *b.* Mar. 14, 1864, Chicago. *d.* 1948. A former magician, he ran a successful minstrel show before entering the fledgling motion picture business in 1896. Impressed by a demonstration of the Edison Kinetoscope in Dallas, in 1895, he had tried to devise an apparatus to project film on a screen. Failing that, he had had the Lumière Cinématographe duplicated in a workshop and with the help of a machinist developed the Selig Standard Camera and the Selig Polyscope, a projector. In 1896 he rented a loft in a midtown Chicago alley and began producing films under the banner of the Selig Polyscope Company. Surviving pressures from the MOTION PICTURE PATENTS COMPANY, he soon prospered in the business.

When Theodore Roosevelt set out on his famous hunt in Africa in 1909, Selig tried unsuccessfully to obtain the former

President's permission to have a motion picture cameraman attached to the expedition. Undaunted, he bought an aging lion at a bargain price and hired an actor to impersonate Roosevelt and a number of Chicago blacks to play African natives. With the help of optical faking and clever cutting, his director created a jungle scene, at the climax of which "Teddy" killed a lion. The film was in the can when the news of Roosevelt's slaying of a lion in Africa hit the headlines. In a matter of days, Selig released his film to motion picture theaters. *Hunting Big Game in Africa* was a smash hit. Encouraged by its success, Selig (who for some reason was addressed as "Colonel" Selig) decided to acquire a whole zoo and began turning out animal and jungle pictures by the dozen. He also financed expeditions to exotic lands to obtain authentic footage for films.

Selig was the first film producer to set up a studio in Hollywood, in 1909, and was among the first to produce films of feature length. His 1914 version of *The Spoilers* was an enormous box-office hit. Earlier in that year he had produced America's first serial, *The Adventures of Kathlyn,* and had begun a series of animated cartoons which he called "Seligettes." He also introduced to the world Tom Mix and his exciting early Westerns. Selig retired from the business in 1922, four years after the Polyscope company folded.

FILMS INCLUDE: *The Tramp and the Dog* 1896; *Trapped by Bloodhounds or Lynching at Cripple Creek* 1905; *The Tramp and the Dog* 1906; *The Count of Monte Cristo, Dr. Jekyll and Mr. Hyde* 1908; *Hunting Big Game in Africa, On the Little Big Horn or Custer's Last Stand, Up San Juan Hill, On the Border* 1909; *The Merry Wives of Windsor, Davy Crockett, Wizard of Oz* 1910; *Zulu-Land, The Two Orphans, Cinderella, Lost in the Jungle* 1911; *The Coming of Columbus, Kings of the Forest* 1912; *The Three Wise Men, Alone in the Jungle* 1913; *The Adventures of Kathlyn* (serial), *The Spoilers, The Fifth Man* 1914; *Pals in Blue, On the Eagle Trail, The House of a Thousand Candles* 1915; *The Ne'er-Do-Well, Sweet Lady Peggy* 1916; *The Garden of Allah* 1917; *A Hoosier Romance* 1918; *The Hunger of the Blood, The Last Chance, Kazan, The Mask* 1921; *The Rosary* (co-prod.) 1922.

Sellars, Elizabeth. Actress. Born on May 6, 1923, in Glasgow, Scotland. On the British stage from age 15, she has also played leads and supporting parts on TV and in films.

FILMS INCLUDE: *Floodtide* 1948; *Madeleine, Guilt Is My Shadow* 1950; *Cloudburst* 1951; *Hunted/The Stranger in Between, The Gentle Gunman* 1952; *The Long Memory* 1953; *The Barefoot Contessa* (US), *Desiree* (US) 1954; *Prince of Players* (US), *Three Cases of Murder* 1955; *Forbidden Cargo, The Last Man to Hang* 1956; *Law and Disorder* 1958; *The Day They Robbed the Bank of England, Never Say Go* 1960; *55 Days at Peking* (US) 1963; *The Chalk Garden* 1964; *The Mummy's Shroud* 1967; *The Hireling* 1973.

Selleck, Tom. Actor. Born on Jan. 29, 1945, in Detroit. Tall (6' 4"), dark, handsome, mustachioed leading man of American TV and films, typically in macho roles. Raised in California, he attended UCLA on a basketball scholarship, also excelling in baseball and football. He then turned to modeling and acting in TV commercials. Guest roles in TV followed, as well as a bit as one of Mae West's studs in *Myra Breckinridge* (1970). After a two-year stint (1974–75) on the daytime soap 'The Young and the Restless' and an assortment of TV and movie roles, he hit the big time as the star of the series 'Magnum P.I.' (1980–88). His big-screen career received a fleeting boost from the box-office success of *Three Men and a Baby* (1987). His second wife (from 1987) is stage actress-dancer Jillie Mack.

FILMS: *Myra Breckinridge* (bit) 1970; *The Seven Minutes* 1971; *Daughters of Satan* 1972; *Terminal Island* 1973; *Midway/The Battle of Midway* (bit) 1976; *Coma* 1978; *High Road to China* 1983; *Lassiter, Runaway* 1984; *Three Men and a Baby* 1987; *Her Alibi, An Innocent Man* 1989; *Quigley Down Under, Three Men and a Little Lady* 1990; *Folks!, Mr. Baseball, Christopher Columbus: The Discovery* 1992; *Open Season* 1996; *In and Out* 1997.

Sellers, Peter. Actor. *b.* Richard Henry Sellers, Sept. 8, 1925, Southsea, England. *d.* 1980. Offbeat character comedian, famous for his diverse personality disguises. On the stage since childhood with his parents' comedy act, he won a talent contest at 13 and joined the RAF at 17, seeing duty as a camp entertainer. Gaining popularity on BBC radio's long-running 'The Goon Show,' he entered British films in the early 50s, appearing in several shorts before making his feature debut. By the end of the decade, his popularity was worldwide and in the 60s he developed into a star of international caliber, working in Hollywood and on the Continent as well as in the London studios. Sellers' career reached its peak in 1964, when he played widely divergent roles in two of his best-remembered films; *Dr. Strangelove,* the brilliant antiwar satire, in which he tripled as the US President, a British officer, and the mad ex-Nazi scientist; and the mystery-comedy *The Pink Panther,* in which he created the character of the inimitable bumbling detective, Inspector Clouseau. The many sequels to the latter role made him rich but hampered his comic invention. With time, his career stagnated into repetition. Of his final films, only *Being There* (1979) was reminiscent of Sellers's best. Deteriorating health presented another late-career problem for Sellers, whose several heart attacks interfered with the schedules of his last few films. The first two and fourth of Sellers's marriage were to actresses: Anne Hayes (1951–63), Britt Ekland (1964–68), and Lynne Frederick, from 1977 till his death of a heart attack at age 54.

FEATURE FILMS: *Penny Points to Paradise* 1951; *Down Among The Z Men* 1952; *Orders Are Orders* 1954; *John and Julie, The Ladykillers* 1955; *The Smallest Show on Earth, The Naked Truth/Your Past Is Showing* 1957; *Up the Creek, Tom Thumb* 1958; *Carlton-Browne of the F.O./Man in a Cocked Hat, The Mouse That Roared, I'm All Right Jack, The Battle of the Sexes* 1959; *Two-Way Stretch, Never Let Go, The Millionairess* 1960; *Mr. Topaze/I Like Money* (also dir.) 1961; *Only Two Can Play, Waltz of the Toreadors, The Dock Brief/Trial and Error, The Road to Hong Kong* (US/UK; cameo), *Lolita* (as Clare Quilty; US/UK) 1962; *The Wrong Arm of the Law, Heavens Above!* 1963; *Dr. Strangelove, The Pink Panther* (US), *The World of Henry Orient* (US), *A Shot in the Dark* (US/UK) 1964; *What's New Pussycat?* (US/Fr.) 1965; *The Wrong Box, Caccia alla Volpe/After the Fox* (It./UK/US) 1966; *Casino Royale, Sept fois Femme/Woman Times Seven* (Fr./It./US), *The Bobo* 1967; *The Party* (US), *I Love You Alice B. Toklas!* (US) 1968; *The Magic Christian* (also co-sc.) 1969; *Hoffman, There's a Girl in My Soup, A Day at the Beach* 1970; *Where Does It Hurt?, Alice's Adventures in Wonderland* (as the March Hare) 1972; *The Optimists of Nine Elms/The Optimists* 1973; *The Blockhouse, Soft Beds Hard Battles/Undercovers Hero* (in six roles, including Hitler), *The Great McGonagall* (as Queen Victoria) 1974; *The Return of the Pink Panther* 1975; *Murder by Death* (US), *The Pink Panther Strikes Again* 1976; *Revenge of the Pink Panther* 1978; *The Prisoner of Zenda, Being There* 1979; *The Fiendish Plot of Dr. Fu Manchu* 1980; *The Trail of the Pink Panther* (a posthumous patchwork of new footage with outtakes from earlier episodes) 1982.

Selsyn motor. Trade name for a self-synchronizing (hence the name) interlocking motor that is used for running two related pieces of motion picture equipment in perfect sync; for example, a camera and a sound recorder during filming, or a camera and a projector during a process shot.

Seltzer, David. Screenwriter, director. Born in 1940, in Highland Park, Ill. A graduate of Northwestern University's School for Film and Television, he started his career in New York on the staff of TV's 'I've Got a Secret.' During that period, he directed a short film, *My Trip to New York.* In 1966 he moved to Los Angeles as a writer, and later also director and producer, of David Wolper documentaries. TV programs which he produced and directed included 'National Geographic Specials' and 'The Underwater World of Jacques Cousteau.' Graduating to feature films as a screenwriter in the early 70s, he enhanced his prestige with the script for the box-office hit *The Omen* (1976). He took a first stab at directing in 1986. He is married to flutist Eugenia Zuckermar.

FEATURE FILMS (as screenwriter): *Willie Wonka and the Chocolate Factory* (co-sc.; uncredited), *The Hellstrom Chronicle* (doc.) 1971; *King Queen Knave* (co-sc.; UK), *One Is a Lonely Number* 1972; *The Other Side of the Mountain* 1975; *The Omen* 1976; *Prophecy* 1979; *Table for Five* 1983; *Six Weeks* 1985; *Lucas* (also dir.) 1986; *Someone to Watch Over Me* (rewrite only; uncredited) 1987; *Punchline* (also dir.) 1988; *Bird on a Wire* (co-sc.) 1990; *Shining Through* (also co-exec. prod., dir.) 1992.

Selwyn, Edgar. Director, producer, screenwriter. *b.* Oct. 12, 1875, Cincinnati. *d.* 1944. A former stage actor and occasional playwright, he founded the All-Star Feature Films Company with his brother in 1912. In 1917 the company merged with that of Samuel Goldfish (later Goldwyn) to form the Goldwyn Pictures Corporation, a forerunner of MGM. Selwyn became independent again in 1920 but in 1929 joined MGM as writer-director. He was a producer of routine films from the mid-30s to the early 40s. His wife, Ruth (Wilcox) Selwyn (1905–54), occasionally appeared in films.

FILMS (as director): *The Girl in the Show* (also sc.) 1929; *War Nurse* 1930; *The Sin of Madelon Claudet, Men Call It Love* 1931; *Skyscraper Souls* 1932; *Men Must Fight, Turn Back the Clock* (also story) 1933; *The Mystery of Mr. X* 1934.

Selznick, David O(liver). Producer. *b.* May 10, 1902, Pittsburgh. *d.* 1965. *ed.* Columbia. Prototype of the creative, independent Hollywood producer whose impact on his films went far beyond the mere financing and administration of production. The son of film magnate Lewis J. SELZNICK and brother of producer and talent agent Myron SELZNICK, he began by assisting his father in film promotion, production, and distribution. In 1923, after his father went bankrupt, David made two short exploitation documentaries, one about boxing, the other showing Rudolph Valentino judging a beauty contest in Madison Square Garden. But he soon lost his profits in publishing and real estate ventures and set out for Hollywood, where he was hired, reluctantly, in 1926, by his father's former partner, Louis B. Mayer, as assistant story editor, then associate producer of MGM's B pictures. A couple of years later he married Mayer's daughter, Irene.

Unsatisfied with his progress at MGM, in 1927 Selznick moved on to Paramount as associate director, and in 1931 he joined the slumping RKO, where he became vice president in charge of production. In 1933, when Irving Thalberg became gravely ill, Mayer brought Selznick back into the MGM fold, this time as vice president and producer. In 1936, after producing a string of highly successful films, David founded his own company, Selznick International. Three years later he produced one of the most profitable films of all time, *Gone With the Wind,* on which he used three main directors and 15 screenwriters, but wrote much of the final script and directed some of the scenes himself.

The following year Selznick brought Alfred Hitchcock from England to direct his first American film, *Rebecca.* In the 40s Selznick launched a number of grand-scale independent productions and in 1949 he married the star of several of these, Jennifer JONES. In the 50s he ventured into European co-productions, then produced his last film, an unsuccessful version of *A Farewell to Arms.* Several subsequent projects remained unrealized, including plans to produce *War and Peace,* on which he was beaten to the punch by the Italian Dino De Laurentiis. A tireless worker, Selznick was famous for his production memos, of which he wrote hundreds during the course of a single filming. The main character in the film *The Bad and the Beautiful,* played by Kirk Douglas, is supposedly patterned after him. Selznick's son, Jeffrey Selznick (*b.* 1932), is a film producer in Europe.

FILMS INCLUDE: *Roulette* 1924; *Spoilers of the West* 1927; *Forgotten Faces* 1928; *The Four Feathers, Chinatown Nights, The Man I Love* 1929; *Street of Chance* 1930; *Bill of Divorcement, What Price Hollywood* 1932; *King Kong, Topaze, Dinner at Eight* 1933; *Viva Villa!, Manhattan Melodrama* 1934; *David Copperfield, Vanessa—Her Life Story, Reckless, Anna Karenina, A Tale of Two Cities* 1935; *Little Lord Fauntleroy, The Garden of Allah* 1936; *A Star Is Born, Nothing Sacred, The Prisoner of Zenda* 1937; *The Adventures of Tom Sawyer, The Young in Heart* 1938; *Made for Each Other, Intermezzo, Gone With the Wind* 1939; *Rebecca* 1940; *Since You Went Away* (also sc.) 1944; *Spellbound* 1945; *Duel in the Sun* (also sc.) 1946; *The Paradine Case* (also sc.), *Portrait of Jennie* 1948; *The Third Man* (co-financed) 1949; *Gone to Earth/The Wild Heart* (co-financed) 1950; *Stazione Termini/Indiscretion of an American Wife* (co-financed) 1953; *A Farewell to Arms* 1957.

Selznick, Lewis J. Executive, film mogul. *b.* Lewis Zeleznik, May 2, 1870, Kiev, Russia. *d.* 1933. One of 18 children of an impoverished Jewish family, he was sent to England at age 12 and worked as a factory hand until he could pay his own passage to America. Settling in Pittsburgh, he started out as a jeweler's apprentice, and by the time he was 24 he owned a chain of jewelry stores. In 1910 he moved to New York and two years later abandoned the safety of the jewelry business for a risky investment in motion pictures. After forcing his way in and out of the Universal hierarchy, he joined the World Film Corporation, which released and distributed films made by independent producers. Before long, however, he walked away with the company's chief asset, the star Clara Kimball Young, and formed the Clara Kimball Young Film Corporation with himself as president and general manager. Within months he had formed the Selznick Company and began releasing prime movies under the slogan "Selznick Pictures Make Happy Hours." His business prospered for a while and he was fast becoming a leading mogul in the industry. But his weakness for gambling and a bitter rivalry with such competitors as Adolph ZUKOR and Louis B. MAYER combined to gradually crumble the Selznick empire. He tried desperately to hang on by forming the Select Pictures Corporation for the release of inexpensive films, in partnership with Zukor, but in 1923 he was forced into bankruptcy and out of the film business. After failing in a Florida land boom venture, he spent the rest of his days in retirement, supported by his sons, David and Myron SELZNICK.

Selznick, Myron. Producer, production executive, talent agent. *b.* Oct. 5, 1898, Pittsburgh. *d.* 1944. The eldest son of Lewis J. SELZNICK, and brother of David O. SELZNICK. He dropped out of Columbia University after only two months and began his career as a scanner of defects in his father's films-examining room. He advanced rapidly through various phases of the business, working as a shipping clerk, purchasing agent, studio manager, and eventually producer. He was the industry's youngest producer and still underage (his mother signed checks for him). At the age of 21 he became chief of production of Selznick Pictures and shortly before the collapse of his father's empire he served as president of Select and Selznick Pictures. Forced out of this lofty position by his father's bankruptcy in 1923, he tried unsuccessfully to survive as an independent producer. In 1928 he became a talent agent and was soon prospering as one of Hollywood's leading agents, exerting great leverage on studio affairs through his control over a roster of top directors, writers, and stars.

FILMS INCLUDE (as producer): *One Week of Love* 1922; *Rupert of Hentzau, The Common Law* 1923; *The Arizona Whirlwind, Topsy and Eva* 1927.

Sembène, Ousmane. Director. Born on Jan. 1, 1923, in Ziguinchor, Senegal. The leading filmmaker of sub-Saharan Africa. The son of a Moslem fisherman, he had little formal education and began his working life as a bricklayer, plumber, and apprentice mechanic. During WW II, he joined the Free French Forces, serving in a unit of African sharpshooters in Africa and Europe. In 1948 he sailed as a stowaway to France, where he briefly held various manual jobs before settling in the Marseilles waterfront as a docker. Before long, he became a union leader and in 1950 joined the French Communist Party. During the 50s he began painting and writing poetry in French. In 1956 he published a first novel, *Le Docker noir,* a semiautobiographical depiction of life among black dockers in France. Following a back injury that forced him out of manual labor, he devoted himself to writing full time, and by the early 60s he had become established as a major novelist and short story writer. He also traveled widely, as far as China and Vietnam. A return trip home convinced him to try film rather than literature as a means of communicating his ideas to his own people. In 1962 he enrolled on a scholarship at the Moscow film school, where he studied under Mark DONSKOY, then worked at Gorki film studios under the tutelage of Sergei GERASIMOV. Returning to Africa, he began directing shorts in 1963, then achieved instant international recognition with his first feature, *La Noire de. . . /Black Girl* (1966). Although technically flawed, this tragic drama about the alienation and eventual suicide of a black servant transplanted to southern France is considered the first major production of the African cinema and won several international awards. But it also upset many in France for its portrayal of European neocolonialism, which included the exploitation of Africans as virtual slaves. Yet Sembène used French subsidies to make his next film, the French-Senegalese co-production *Mandabi/The Money Order* (1968), a comedy of errors spoken in an African dialect. It received a special mention from the jury at the 1968 Venice Festival and was named best film at the 1970 Atlanta Film Festival. Sembène's next film, *Emitai* (1971), a depiction of a confrontation between native Senegalese and French troops over conscription and supplies of rice, won prizes in the Soviet Union but caused resentment in France, where it was deemed politically objectionable. *Xala/Impotence* (1974) was a satire about the Senegalese upper crust and its longstanding imitation of European customs and manners. The East-West clash of cultures also played a significant part in *Ceddo/The People* (1977), which used a Senegalese village as a microcosm of African political and social history. Sembène won the Special Jury Grand Prix at the Venice Film Festival for *Camp de Thiaroye* (1988). He has been married since 1974 to Carrie Moore, an American.

FILMS (as director-screenwriter): Shorts—*Songhays/L'Empire Songhay/The Songhay Empire* (doc.; unreleased), *Borom Sarret* 1963; *Niaye* 1965; *Taun/The Eldest Son* 1970. Features—*La Noire de. . . /Black Girl* 1966; *Mandabi/Le Mandat/The Money Order* 1968; *Emitai* 1971; *Xala/Impotence* 1974; *Ceddo/The People* 1977; *Camp de Thiaroye* (also prod.) 1988.

Semel, Terry. Executive. Born on Feb. 24, 1943 in New York, N.Y. *ed.* Long Island Univ. (accounting). Warner Bros. executive who helped to re-establish the studio in the 1980s and 1990s as a leading American player. Hired as a sales trainee at Warner Bros. in the 1960s, he worked his way up to become branch manager. After a stint at Buena Vista, he returned to Warner Bros., where he was president of domestic sales, and since 1980 president and COO. In 1996 Time-Warner merged with the Ted Turner empire, creating more responsibility for Semel along with fellow executive Robert Daly.

Semler, Dean. Australian director of photography. A former newsreel and documentary cameraman, he moved into features in the mid-70s and first drew international attention with the electrifying cinematography of *Mad Max II/The Road Warrior* (1981). Later in the decade he worked with increasing frequency in Hollywood. He was nominated for an Academy Award for *Dances with Wolves* (1990).

FILMS INCLUDE: *Let the Balloon Go* 1976; *Thirst* 1977; *Hoodwink, Mad Max II/The Road Warrior* 1981; *Kitty and the Bagman* 1982; *Undercover* 1983; *Razorback* 1983; *The Coca Cola Kid, Mad Max—Beyond Thunderdome* 1985; *Bullseye* 1986; *The Lighthorsemen* 1987; *Cocktail* (US), *Young Guns* (US) 1988; *Dead Calm, Farewell to the King* (US), *K-9* (US) 1989; *Impulse* (US), *Young Guns II* (US), *Dances with Wolves* (US) 1990; *City Slickers* 1991; *The Power of One* 1992; *Last Action Hero, Super Mario Bros., The Three Musketeers* 1993; *The Cowboy Way* 1994; *Waterworld* 1995; *Gone Fishing* 1997.

Semon, Larry. Actor, director. *b.* July 6, 1889, West Point, Miss. *d.* 1928. One of the most popular and highest paid Hollywood comedians of the early 20s. The son of a professional magician (Zera the Great), he started out as a cartoonist for the New York *Sun.* In 1916 he was hired by Vitagraph to write and direct comedy shorts. The following year he began starring himself in the company's films, and within a short time his popularity approached that of Chaplin, Keaton, and Lloyd. His films, mostly one- and two-reelers, were loosely structured around inventive sight gags and speedy chase sequences. His screen character was typically that of a white-faced dumbbell with a stupid grin and oversized pants. His popularity extended to Europe, where he was known in France as Zigoto, in Italy as Ridolini, and in Spain as Romasin. He directed most of his own films and was often supported by a villainous Oliver Hardy and by leading ladies Lucille Carlisle and Dorothy Dwan, both of whom he married in succession.

Always an extravagant spender on the set, Semon fell out of favor at Vitagraph in 1922 and took his business elsewhere. He began turning out feature films, which weren't successful enough at the box office to justify their inflated budgets. He tried to resurrect his career with a straight acting role in Von Sternberg's *Underworld* but finally gave up on films, turning briefly to vaudeville. In March 1928 he declared bankruptcy and in October he died of pneumonia after a nervous breakdown.

FILMS INCLUDE (as both director and actor, unless otherwise noted): *The Man from Egypt* (dir. only), *A Villainous Villain* (dir. only), *Love and Loot* (dir. only) 1916; *Footlights and Fakers* (dir. only), *Rough Toughs and Roof Tops* (also sc.), *Boasts and Boldness, Spooks and Spasms* 1917; *Babes and Boobs, Spies and Spills* 1918; *Passing the Buck* (also sc.), *The Simple Life* 1919; *The Stagehand* (co-dir.), *The Suitor* (co-dir.) 1920; *The Sportsman* (co-dir.), *The Fall Guy* (co-dir.) 1921; *The Sawmill* (co-dir.), *The Show* (co-dir.), *The Sleuth* (co-dir.) 1922; *No Wedding Bells, Midnight Cabaret* 1923; *The Girl in the Limousine* 1924; *The Perfect Clown* (act. only), *The Wizard of*

Oz (as the Scarecrow; also co-sc.) 1925; *Stop Look and Listen* (also exec. prod., co-sc.) 1926; *Spuds* (also exec. prod., sc.), *Underworld* (act. only) 1927.

Semple, Lorenzo, Jr. American playwright, screenwriter. His screenplays, ranging from psychological drama to action-packed adventure, have often been laced with humor.

FILMS: *The Honeymoon Machine* (play basis only, 'The Golden Fleecing') 1961; *Batman* 1966; *Pretty Poison* 1968; *Daddy's Gone a-Hunting* (co-sc.) 1969; *The Sporting Club, The Marriage of a Young Stockbroker* 1971; *Papillon* (co-sc.) 1973; *The Supercops, The Parallax View* (co-sc.) 1974; *The Drowning Pool* (co-sc.), *Three Days of the Condor* (co-sc.) 1975; *King Kong* 1976; *Hurricane* 1979; *Flash Gordon* 1980; *Never Say Never Again* 1983; *Sheena* (co-sc.) 1984; *Never Too Young to Die* (co-sc.) 1986.

Semprun, Jorge. Screenwriter, novelist. Born on Dec. 10, 1923, in Madrid. A member of the Spanish Communist Party and combatant against Franco, he was deported in 1942, then fought with the French Resistance and was imprisoned by the Nazis at Buchenwald. After the war he was a journalist for UNESCO and in the 60s began writing novels and screenplays. Disenchanted with the Communist Party, he expressed in his writing loathing of totalitarian regimes of any kind. He won an Oscar nomination for the script of Resnais's *La Guerre est finie* (1966) and later contributed significantly to several political thrillers by COSTA-GAVRAS. He directed one film, *The Two Memories.*

FILMS: *La Guerre est finie/The War Is Over* 1966; *Z* 1969; *L'Aveu/The Confession* 1970; *L'Attentat/The French Conspiracy* 1972; *Les Duex Mémoires/The Two Memories* (also dir.) 1973; *Stavisky* 1974; *Section spéciale/Special Section* 1975; *Une Femme à sa Fenêtre/A Woman at Her Window* 1976; *Les Routes du sud/The Roads to the South* 1978; *Les Trottoirs de Saturne* 1985.

Sen, Marinal. Director. Born on May 4, 1923, in East Bengal (now Bangladesh), into a middle-class Indian family. While studying physics in Calcutta in the early 40s he was influenced by Marxist ideology and at about the same time took an interest in the technical side of cinema and began writing film reviews. In 1943 he joined the Indian People's Theatre Association, a Communist-sponsored group that dispatched stage troupes into the countryside. He earned a meager living as a teacher, journalist, proofreader, and salesman of patent medicines before embarking on his filmmaking career in 1956. Sen's early films, uneven in quality, typically used couples and small family units as microcosms for the ills of Bengali society, particularly the poor and the middle class. He first attracted international attention with *Bhuvan Shome* (1969), a production considered a landmark in Indian cinema's history, signaling the arrival of its "new wave." Made at a modest budget, like all of Sen's films, it was more perceptive and bolder in concept and execution than the director's earlier films. A robust tale about a tradition-rooted bureaucrat whose values are overturned by a simple village girl, it marked Sen as a mature artist who is comfortable with his medium and enjoys experimenting with its tools. Another milestone in Sen's career was *In Search of Famine* (1980), a film within a film in which a camera crew, in the process of making a film on location recalling the Bengal famine of 1943, only manages to upset and deepen the misery of villagers whose plight they purport to expose. The film won the Special Jury Prize (Silver Bear) at the 1981 Berlin Festival. *Kharij/The Case Is Closed* won the Jury Prize at Cannes in 1983.

FILMS: *Raat Bhore/Night's End/The Dawn* 1956; *Neel Akasher Neechey/Under the Blue Sky* 1959; *Baishey Shravana/The Wedding Day* 1960; *Punnascha/Over Again* 1961; *Abasheshey/And a Last* 1962; *Protinidhi/Two Plus One* 1964; *Akash Kusum/Up in the Clouds* 1965; *Matira Manisha/ Two Brothers, Moving Perspectives* (doc.) 1967; *Bhuvan Shome* 1969; *Ichhapuran/Wish Fulfillment* 1970; *Interview, Ek Adhuri Kahani/An Unfinished Story* 1971; *Calcutta '71* 1972; *Patadik/The Guerrilla Fighter* 1973; *Chorus* 1974; *Mrigaya/The Royal Hunt* 1976; *Oka Dorie Katha/The Outsiders* 1977; *Parashuram/The Man with the Axe* 1978; *Ek Din Pratidin/And Quiet Rolls the Dawn/One Day Like Another* 1979; *Aakaler Sandane/In Search of Famine* 1980; *Chaalchitra/The Kaleidoscope* 1981; *Kharij/The Case Is Closed* 1983; *Khandar/The Ruins* 1984; *Tasveer Apni Apni/Their Own Faces/Portrait of a New Man* (orig. for TV) 1985; *Genesis* (Ind./Fr./Belg./Switz.) 1986; *Ek Din Achanak/Suddenly One Day* 1989; *City Life* ("Calcutta, My Eldorado" episode; Hol.) 1990; *Mahaprithivi/World Within World Without* 1992.

senior. A 5,000-watt heavy-duty studio spotlight.

Sennett, Mack. Director, producer, actor. *b.* Michael (Mikall) Sinnott, Jan. 17, 1880, Danville, near Richmond, Quebec, Canada, to working-class Irish immigrants. *d.* 1960. He was blessed with a rich, robust basso voice and had dreams of becoming an opera singer, but when he moved with his parents to East Berlin, Conn., when he was 17, he started his working life as a laborer at the American Iron Works. A chance encounter in 1902 with actress Marie Dressler resulted in a letter of introduction to producer David Belasco and the decision to go to New York to try his luck on the stage. Belasco advised the young aspirant to return home, but Michael stayed in New York to begin what would eventually amount to a minor career as a performer in burlesque and a chorus boy in several Broadway musicals.

Looking to improve his earnings, gain steady employment, and still stay in show business, Mack Sennett (by now his stage name) presented himself at Manhattan's Biograph studios and began acting in films in mid-1908, initially in supporting roles but soon also in leads. Between August of 1908 and July of 1911 he co-starred in many shorts under the direction of D. W. GRIFFITH, opposite such early screen personalities as Florence Lawrence, Linda Arvidsen, Mary Pickford, Blanche Sweet, and Mabel Normand. He also contributed a number of scripts for Griffith films, including *The Lonely Villa* (1909). From the start, he showed great curiosity about filming and editing techniques, grilling Griffith, cameraman Billy BITZER, and anyone else who would answer for clues to the secrets of their art and craft. By late 1910 he was directing Biograph shorts as well as acting in them.

Sennett was an experienced director, specializing in comedy, when he left Biograph in 1912 to enter an association with two former bookies, Charles O. Bauman and Adam Kessel, in a new production company they named Keystone. Under Sennett's direction, Keystone soon became recognized as a leading studio in the slapstick comedy field, a genre that evolved in America to new heights of frenzied madness from its more inhibited beginnings in early French silent comedies. Sennett brought with him from Biograph such leading comic stars as Fred Mace, Ford Sterling, and Mabel Normand. He was particularly fortunate in his association with Miss Normand, who would become not only one of the most gifted comediennes of her day but for several years also Sennett's intimate friend. The rapidly growing roster of regular Keystone performers soon included such comedy stars as Edgar Kennedy, Roscoe "Fatty" Arbuckle, Phyllis Allen, Chester Conklin, Al St. John, Slim Summerville, Alice Davenport, Minta Durfee, Harry McCoy, and Mack Swain. One star who began his film career at

Keystone and went on to much greater heights elsewhere was Charlie CHAPLIN, who starred in 35 comedies at Keystone, all during 1914, some under Sennett's direction, before being lured away by Essanay.

Keystone's growing reputation as the silent screen's foremost comedy mill owed much to Sennett's leadership and gruff but contagiously fun-loving personality. Sennett brought to films an intuitive sense of comic timing, which he had refined through years of experience in burlesque and in the months he had spent in front of the camera under the direction of others. The early Keystones were largely improvisational affairs, made with only the skimpiest of script outlines but timed to perfection by Sennett in the cutting room. The typical Keystone product was a crudely constructed farce that derived its comic force not from the twists of a plot but from a persistent succession of visual gags, a spirited, often vulgar, physical free-for-all that ridiculed anything and everything and merrily thumbed its nose at social conventions and institutions.

Gradually, though, as the Keystone company grew in size and the length of its product steadily increased from split reels to one-reelers and eventually two-reelers, order slowly replaced chaos, planning superseded improvisation, and the wild frenzy that characterized the early Sennett films was considerably tempered. Other directors were brought in to share duties with Sennett on the expanding schedule of production, among them Henry "Pathé" Lehrman, Wilfred Lucas, Dick Jones, Clarence Badger, George Nicholls, and Edward Cline. Production became more diversified. Cheesecake was added in the shapely form of the famed Bathing Beauties, and child appeal with the "Kid Komedies," a kiddie series that preceded Hal Roach's "Our Gang" by almost a decade.

Sennett devoted his energies to supervising the constant flow of production. He spent much of his time in the cutting room, where, with his scissors, he exercised final authority over each and every film. In 1915, Keystone was absorbed into the newly created Triangle Film Corporation, putting under one roof the creative talents of the three biggest names of the American silent screen—D. W. Griffith, Thomas H. INCE, and Mack Sennett. Keystone functioned as an autonomous unit within Triangle. With larger budgets now at his disposal and a less hectic production schedule, Sennett's films became technically more polished. The gradual move away from uninhibited slapstick continued, and his program now included a series of romantic comedies co-starring Gloria Swanson and Bobby Vernon as well as a variety of other comedy material with emphasis on situation humor rather than knockabout physical gags.

In March of 1917, Griffith pulled out of the deal and was soon followed by Ince and Sennett. To gain his freedom, Sennett had to give up the Keystone trademark, but he took along the team that helped make Keystone famous and in June 1917 organized his own company, Mack Sennett Comedies, releasing initially through Paramount, then in the early 20s through Associate Producers and First National. Under the new banner, he continued producing two-reel comedies but from time to time tackled the production of feature-length films, including several that starred Mabel Normand. In 1923, Sennett began a long association with Pathé that lasted through the end of the silent era, in 1928. Here he launched the career of a new comic star, Harry LANGDON, and began three new comedy series, "The Smith Family," "Handy Andy," and "Taxicab."

The advent of sound signified the beginning of the end of the legend of Mack Sennett as the "King of Comedy." In 1929 he associated himself with Educational, a short-subject studio noted for the cheap look of its product, and although he continued producing and directing for several years, his name no longer carried the weight it once did. Although the clumsiness of early sound techniques gravely inhibited his brand of comedy, Sennett quickly adjusted to the requirements of talk and music in films, and when he briefly renewed his association with Paramount in 1932, he produced several comedy shorts that starred W. C. Fields, and a series of musical shorts featuring Bing Crosby. He also experimented with an early color process he called Natural Color and included several color shorts in his repertoire of the late 20s and early 30s, among them *Movie Town,* in which he also appeared as himself. In 1935, Sennett returned to Educational, for whom he directed several shorts, including his only Buster Keaton film, *The Timid Young Man,* before retiring from active filmmaking and returning to Canada, practically broke. He came out of retirement, however, in 1939, for a nominal position as associate producer at 20th Century-Fox. He was technical adviser on *Hollywood Cavalcade* (1939), in which he also appeared as himself. He made another personal appearance in *Down Memory Lane* (1949).

During the Oscar ceremonies for 1937, Sennett was honored with a special Academy Award. Sennett was portrayed by Robert Preston in the 1974 Broadway musical 'Mack and Mabel.'

FILMS INCLUDE (all shorts except as noted): As actor—*Balked at the Altar, The Song of the Shirt, Mr. Jones at the Ball* 1908; *The Curtain Pole, The Politician's Love Story, The Lonely Villa* (also co-sc.), *The Way of a Man, The Slave, Pippa Passes, The Gibson Goddess, Nursing a Viper* 1909; *The Dancing Girl of Butte, In Old California, All on Account of the Milk, The Englishman and the Girl, The Newlyweds, An Affair of Hearts, Never Again, The Call to Arms* 1910; *The Italian Barber, Paradise Lost, The White Rose of the Wilds, The Last Drop of Water* 1911. As director—*The Lucky Toothache* (also sc., act.), *The Masher* (also sc., act.) 1910; *Comrades* (also act.), *Cupid's Joke* (also act.), *The Country Lovers* (also act.), *The Manicure Lady* (also act.), *A Dutch Gold Mine* (also act.), *The Wonderful Eye, The Ghost* (also act.), *The Beautiful Voice* (also act.), *The Village Hero* (also act.), *Too Many Burglars* (also act.), *The Inventor's Secret, Their First Divorce* (also act.), *Resourceful Lovers, Caught with the Goods* (also act.) 1911; *The Joke on the Joker, Brave and Bold, Pants and Pansies, The Fatal Chocolate* (also act.), *A Spanish Dilemma* (also act.), *Hot Stuff* (also act.), *Oh Those Eyes!, Those Hicksville Boys* (also act.), *The Leading Man, When the Fire Bells Rang, Neighbors, The New Baby* (also act.), *One-Round O'Brien, The Speed Demon* (also act.), *Willie Becomes an Artist, The Tourists* (also act.) 1912. As director-producer—*Cohen Collects a Debt, The Water Nymph, The New Neighbor, Pedro's Dilemma* (also act.), *Stolen Glory, The Ambitious Butler* (also act.), *At Coney Island* (also act.), *Mabel's Lovers, The Rivals* (also act.), *Mr. Fixit* (also act.), *Brown's Seance, The Drummer's Vacation, The Duel* (also act.) 1912; *A Double Wedding, The Mistaken Masher* (also act.), *The Elite Ball, The Battle of Who Run* (also act.), *A Red Hot Romance, The Sleuth's Last Stand* (also act.), *A Strong Revenge* (also act.), *At Twelve O'Clock* (also act.), *Her New Beau* (also act.), *Those Good Old Days, A Game of Poker, A Life in the Balance, A Fishy Affair, The Bangville Police, The New Conductor, That Ragtime Band, Algy on the Force, His Ups and Downs, Mabel's Awful Mistake* (also act.), *The Foreman of the Jury, The Gangsters, Barney Oldfield's Race for a Life* (also act.), *The Hansom Driver* (also act.), *The Speed Queen, The Waiters' Picnic, The Tale of a Black Eye, Safe in Jail, The Telltale Light, A Noise from the Deep, Cohen's Outing, The Firebugs, Mabel's New Hero, The Gypsy Queen, The Faithful Taxicab, Schnitz the Tailor, A Healthy Neighborhood, Two Old Tars, A Quiet Little Wedding,*

The Speed Kings, Love Sickness at Sea (also act.), *Cohen Saves the Flag, Zuzu the Band Leader, The Gusher, A Bad Game, Some Nerve* 1913; *Love and Dynamite, In the Clutches of the Gang* (co-dir. with George Nicholls), *Too Many Brides, Mabel's Strange Predicament* (co-dir. with Henry "Pathé" Lehrman), *Tango Tangles, Mack It Again* (also act.), *A Bathing Beauty, Mabel at the Wheel* (co-dir. with Mabel Normand; also act.), *Twenty Minutes of Love, The Fatal Flirtation, The Knockout* (also act.), *Mabel's Latest Prank* (also act.), *He Loved the Ladies, The High Spots on Broadway, Stout Heart but Weak Knees, Tillie's Punctured Romance* (feature), *A Colored Girl's Love* 1914; *Love Speed and Thrills* (prod. only), *Hearts and Planets* (prod. only), *Our Dare Devil Chief* (prod. only), *For Better—But Worse* (also act.), *Those College Girls, The Little Teacher* (also act.), *My Valet* (also sc., act.), *A Favorite Fool* (prod., sc. only), *Stolen Magic* (also sc., act.) 1915; *A Modern Enoch Arden* (prod. only), *A Movie Star* (prod. only), *Bright Lights* (prod. only), *The Moonshiners* (prod. only) 1916; *Teddy at the Throttle* (prod. only), *Cactus Nell* (prod. only), *A Clever Dummy* (prod. only), *The Pullman Bride* (prod. only) 1917; *The Battle Royal* (prod. only), *Mickey* (feature; prod. only), *Sleuths* (prod. only) 1918; *The Foolish Age* (prod. only), *Hearts and Flowers* (prod. only), *A Submarine Pirate* (prod. only), *Yankee Doodle in Berlin* (feature; prod. only), *Uncle Tom Without a Cabin* (prod. only) 1919; *Down on the Farm* (feature; prod. only), *Married Life* (feature; prod. only), *Love Honor and Behave* (feature; prod. only) 1920; *A Small Town Idol* (feature; prod., sc. only), *Home Talent* (feature; co-dir. with James E. Abbe; also sc.), *Molly O'* (feature; prod., story only) 1921; *Oh Mabel Behave* (feature; co-dir. with Ford Sterling; also act.), *The Crossroads of New York* (feature; prod., story, sc. only) 1922; *Suzanna* (feature; prod., sc. only), *The Shriek of Araby* (feature; prod., story, sc. only), *The Extra Girl* (feature; prod., story only) 1923; *Picking Peaches* (prod. only), *The Halfback of Notre Dame* (prod. only), *The Hollywood Kid* (prod., act. only), *The Cat's Meow* (prod. only), *Romeo and Juliet* (prod. only), *The First 100 Years* (prod. only) 1924; *The Wild Goose Chaser* (prod. only), *Boobs in the Woods* (prod. only), *Plain Clothes* (prod. only), *The Marriage Circus* (prod. only), *Lucky Stars* (prod. only) 1925; *Saturday Afternoon* (prod. only), *Gooseland* (prod. only), *The Ghost of Folly* (prod. only), *Hoboken to Hollywood* (prod. only), *The Prodigal Bridegroom* (prod. only) 1926; *Should Sleepwalkers Marry?* (prod. only), *Crazy to Act* (prod. only), *His First Flame* (feature; prod. only), *Fiddlesticks* (prod. only), *Love in a Police Station* (prod. only) 1927; *A Finished Actor, The Beach Club* (prod. only), *The Good-Bye Kiss* (feature; prod. only), *The Campus Carmen* (prod. only), *A Taxi Scandal* (prod. only), *The Lion's Roar* (also story, sc.) 1928; *The Bride's Relations, Whirls and Girls, The Big Palooka, Girl Crazy, Jazz Mamas, The Golfers, A Hollywood Star, Clancy at the Bat* 1929; *Scotch, Sugar Plum Papa, Bulls and Bears, Honeymoon Zeppelin, Radio Kisses* (in color; prod., song only), *Fat Wives for Thin, Campus Crushers, The Chumps, Goodbye Legs, Hello Television* (prod. only), *Midnight Daddies* (feature), *Divorced Sweethearts, Racket Cheers* 1930; *A Poor Fish* (in color), *Dance Hall Marge, Ghost Parade, Monkey Business in Africa, Movie Town* (in color; also act.), *Fainting Lover, I Surrender Dear, Speed, One More Chance* 1931; *Dream House* (prod. only), *The Billboard Girl* (prod. only), *The Candid Camera* (prod. only), *The Giddy Age* (prod. only), *The Dentist* (prod. only), *Hypnotized* (feature; also co-story) 1932; *The Wrestlers* (prod. only), *The Singing Boxer* (prod. only), *The Fatal Glass of Beer* (prod. only), *Sing Bing Sing* (prod. only), *The Pharmacist* (prod. only), *The Barber Shop* (prod. only) 1933; *Ye Old Saw Mill* (also story), *Flicker Fever* (also sc.), *Just Another Murder* (also story), *The Timid Young Man, Way Up Thar* 1935.

sensitometry. The measurement of the light-response characteristics of film emulsions under specified conditions of exposure and development. The testing instrument used in sensitometry is a sensitometer.

Sensurround. Trademark for a special-effects system developed by Universal in 1974 to enhance the impact of tremor scenes in the disaster film *Earthquake.* It is a system that adds air vibrations to the sound track of a film during the dubbing process. A special apparatus installed in theaters decodes control signals on the sound track, triggering a series of audible and subaudible effects. The vibration of air movement against the body and ears of people in the audience creates the illusion of participation in an action-filled event, such as the tremor in *Earthquake* (1974), a battle scene in *Midway* (1976), or a rollercoaster ride in *Rollercoaster* (1977). Only theaters equipped with a decoding unit, a special amplifier, and a series of between 10 and 20 huge speakers can reproduce the effect of Sensurround. The same films are later shown without the effect in smaller, second-run theaters.

sequence. A number of scenes linked together by time, location, or narrative continuity to form a unified episode in a motion picture. It is often likened to a chapter in a book, the scene being the equivalent of a paragraph and the shot the equivalent of a sentence. Traditionally, but not necessarily, a sequence begins with a fade-in and ends with a fade-out or some other optical transitional device. See FADE.

Serandrei, Mario. Film editor. Born on May 23, 1907, in Naples. The most prominent editor of postwar Italian cinema. Serandrei has worked on many of Visconti's films as well as other important Italian productions. He is credited with coining the term "neorealism," which he first used to describe Visconti's emerging new style in *Ossessione* (1942). At times he used pseudonyms, such as Mark Sirandrews or Mark Suran.

FILMS INCLUDE: *Ossessione* 1942; *La Terra Trema* 1947; *Bellissima* 1951; *Senso, Il Bidone* 1955; *Le Notti bianche/White Nights* 1957; *Rocco e i suoi Fratelli/Rocco and His Brothers* 1960; *La Ragazza con la Valigia/Girl with a Suitcase, Salvatore Giuliano* 1961; *Boccaccio '70* 1962; *Il Gattopardo/The Leopard* 1963; *Le Grande Olimpiade/The Grand Olympics* (doc.), *La Donna scimmia/The Ape Woman, Italiano Brava Gente* 1964; *La Battaglia di Algeri/The Battle of Algiers* 1966; *Le Streghe/The Witches* (Visconti episode) 1967.

Serato, Massimo. Actor. *b.* Giuseppe Segato 1917, in Oderzo, Italy. *d.* 1989. Handsome leading man and, later, supporting player of Italian films from the early 40s. He was often seen in costume epics.

FILMS INCLUDE. *L'Ispettore Vargas* 1940; *Piccolo Mondo antico, L'Uomo venuto dal Mare/Man of the Sea* 1941; *Giacomo l'Idealista* 1942; *Il Sole sorge ancora/Outcry* 1946; *La Signora dalle Camelie/La Traviata/The Lost One* (as Alexandre Dumas Fils in prologue) 1947; *La Strada Buia/Fugitive Lady, Domenica d'Agosto, Il Ladro di Venezia/The Thief of Venice* 1949; *Shadow of the Eagle* (UK) 1950; *Il Conte di S. Elmo/The Count of St. Elmo* 1951; *Il Mercante di Venezia/The Merchant of Venice* 1952; *Lucrèce Borgia/Sins of the Borgias* (as the Duke of Aragon; Fr./It.), *Dramma nella Casbah/The Man from Cairo* (It./US) 1953; *Madame Du Barry* (Fr./It.) 1954; *The Silent Enemy* (UK) 1958; *La Maja Desnuda/The Naked Maja* (US/It.) 1959; *David e Golia/David and Goliath* (as Abner), *La Venere dei Pirati/Queen of the Pirates* 1960; *Constantino il Grande/Constantine and the Cross, El Cid* (US/It.) 1961; *Le Secret de D'Artagnan/The Secret Mark of D'Artagnan* (as Cardinal Richelieu; Fr./It.) 1962; *55 Days at Peking* (US) 1963;

Maciste alla Corte delo Zar/Samson vs. the Giant King 1964; *La Decima Vittima/The Tenth Victim* 1965; *I Criminali della Galassia/The Wild Wild Planet* 1966; *Camille 2000* (US) 1969; *The Gamblers* (US) 1970; *Don't Look Now* (UK/Fr./It.) 1973; *Nana* 1982; *Saving Grace* (US) 1986.

serial. A multi-episode film, usually an action-adventure melodrama, presented in theaters one chapter at a time in weekly installments over a period of several months. Each chapter typically ends in a cliff-hanger, a moment of suspense and uncertainty that leaves the audience eager for a resolution that does not come until the next chapter. The serial phenomenon grew out of the tradition of the SERIES, which probably originated in France in 1908 with Victorin JASSET's "Nick Carter" and spread to the US by 1910. The forerunner of the serial genre was the Edison melodrama *What Happened to Mary?* (1912), starring Mary Fuller, which was serialized simultaneously in monthly installments in the magazine *McClure's Ladies World* and on the screen. The first film in the true serial format, each chapter ending with a teasing cliff-hanger, was Selig's *The Adventures of Kathlyn,* starring Kathlyn WILLIAMS and directed by F. J. Grandon, which was completed in 1913 and released in 13 installments from January to May of 1914. The first chapter was three reels long and the following ones two reels long each.

The two-reel chapter remained the standard length of the serial episode in the coming years. The serial that made the genre internationally popular was *The Perils of Pauline* (April–December 1914), a 20-chapter adventure melodrama starring Pearl WHITE, which was directed by Donald Mackenzie under the supervision of Louis GASNIER. The film was produced by the American branch of the Pathé company, which dominated the field for several years. The success of *The Perils of Pauline* prompted the production in the US of many other silent serials featuring female heroines, among them Grace CUNARD, Helen HOLMES, Louise Lorraine, Allene RAY, Ruth ROLAND, and Eileen SEDGWICK. But for several years Miss White remained the most popular of the pack, with such serials as *The Exploits of Elaine* and *The Romance of Elaine* (both 1915), *The Iron Claw* and *Pearl of the Army* (both 1916), *The Fatal Ring* (1917), *The House of Hate* (1918), and *The Black Secret* (1919). The longest-running serial of all time was *The Hazards of Helen.* Its 119 episodes were shown in US theaters from November 1914 through February 1917.

The popularity of the American serial spread quickly to Europe, where France's Louis FEUILLADE, already famous for the series "Fantômas" (1913) and the two-part demiserial *Les Vampires* (1915), ventured into the multiple-episode serial field with such 12-chapter melodramas as *Judex* (completed in 1916 but released early in 1917), *Tih Minh* (1918), and *Barabbas* (1920). In Germany, a six-part serial, *Homunculus,* was directed by Otto Rippert in 1916. In Italy, Emilio GHIONE, the creator of the "Za-la-Mort" series, made the eight-chapter *I Topi Grigi* (1917–18), among other serials. But the serial remained mainly an American phenomenon. By 1920 as many as 20 or 30 serials were being produced annually in the US.

The rate of serial production decreased after the advent of sound, but their popularity was not diminished. The first talkie serial was Universal's *The Ace of Scotland Yard* (1929). Other studios that dominated the field during the sound era were Columbia, Mascot, and Republic. But sound was of little importance in the typical serial of the 30s and 40s, which was short on dialogue and long on action. Appealing mainly to the Saturday matinee kiddie audience, the serial plot was comfortably predictable, despite the many meaningless twists and complications. The speedy chase, the last-minute rescue, the frequent fist- and gunfights, were the main attractions, and it mattered little what the hero and the villain were fighting over—industrial diamonds, secret government formulas, mysterious scientific devices, or a diabolical scheme to dominate the world.

Many of the serial characters and some of the plots were borrowed from popular newspaper comic strips and comic books—*Dick Tracy, Mandrake the Magician, The Green Hornet, Buck Rogers, Red Ryder, The Phantom, Captain Marvel, Terry and the Pirates, Batman, Superman,* etc. The most popular talkie serial, still shown frequently on TV, was the space adventure fantasy *Flash Gordon* (1936), starring Buster CRABBE and Jean ROGERS and featuring Charles MIDDLETON as the archvillain Emperor Ming the Merciless. It was also the most expensive serial ever made, costing about $350,000, three times the budget of the average serial. It was followed by two sequels.

Among the Hollywood players who specialized in the portrayal of serial heroes, the most popular, in addition to Crabbe, were Robert LOWERY, Kane RICHMOND, and Tom TYLER. Among the top villains, in addition to Middleton, were Roy Barcroft, Henry BRANDON, Eduardo CIANNELLI, and Bela LUGOSI. The popularity of the serial gradually diminished after WW II. Columbia's *Blazing the Overland Trail* (1956) was the last serial ever produced.

series. A group of films, each complete on its own but sharing a common cast of main characters with continuing traits and a similar situation format that despite plot variations remains true to a basic premise and develops according to an expected formula. The term is often confused with SERIAL, which actually grew out of the tradition of the screen series. The serial was inspired by the success of the serialized newspaper and magazine story.

The series format seems to have originated concurrently in France and the US. In France it started with Victorin JASSET's "Nick Carter" adventure melodramas. Louis FEUILLADE popularized the format with such series as "Bébé" (1910–13), "Bout-de-Zan" (1912–16), and "Fantômas" (1913–14). Another successful series was Jean DURAND's "Onésime" (1910–14). Other European countries contributed to the format, among them Italy with Emilio GHIONE's "Za la Mort" series (1914).

In the US meanwhile, one of the earliest known attempts at creating a regular series was D. W. GRIFFITH's "Mr. Jones" (1908–9), which starred John Compson, Florence Lawrence, and Mack Sennett. Other early series include G. M. ANDERSON's "Broncho Billy" Westerns (1910–16); "Alkali Ike" (1911–13), starring Augustus Carney; "Bunny" (1912–14), starring John Bunny and Flora Finch; "Billy" (1912–13), starring Billy Quirk; Allan DWAN's "Calamity Anne" (1912–14), starring Louise Lester; "Fatty" (1913–17), starring Roscoe Arbuckle; "Ambrose" (1914–15), starring Mack Swain; and "Sweedie" (1914–15), starring Wallace Beery.

Like the serial, the series format remained more popular in the US than in Europe, although in France Max LINDER continually scored commercially with his "Max" comedy shorts (1910–17). Hollywood produced a number of feature-length series during the silent era, among them "The Cohens and Kellys" comedy series, whose success extended past the advent of sound. But the most productive period of the American feature-length series began in the early 30s in the wake of the Depression and the birth of the B PICTURE. Major as well as minor Hollywood studios started churning out innumerable low-budget quickie formula productions to maintain a constant supply of films for the bottom half of the double-bill presentation. The series films covered a broad range of genres: domestic comedy ("Andy Hardy," "Henry Aldrich," "Blondie," etc.), knockabout farce ("Mexican Spitfire"), lowbrow slapstick ("The Bowery Boys," etc.), cornball comedy ("Ma and Pa Kettle," etc.), romantic situation comedy ("Maisie," etc.), mystery and suspense comedies and dramas ("Boston Blackie," "Charlie Chan," "Crime Doctor," "Ellery Queen," "The Falcon," "Mr. Moto," "The Lone Wolf," "Philo Vance," "The Saint," "Sherlock Holmes," "The Thin Man," etc.), jungle adventures ("Tarzan," "Jungle Jim," "Bomba," etc.), medical dramas ("Dr. Kildare," "Dr. Christian," etc.), Westerns ("Hopalong Cassidy," "The Cisco Kid," "The Three Mesquiteers," etc.), and animal series ("Francis," etc.).

There were also groups of films not planned or released as series but developed as sequels to a successful motion picture, like *Dracula, Frankenstein, The Invisible Man, The Mummy,* and *Lassie.* The series films varied widely in quality from studio to studio. Most were cheaply and speedily made, but the MGM product ("Andy Hardy," "Dr. Kildare," "Maisie," "The Thin Man") stood out for its consistent slickness and polish. Paramount scored a success with the "Road" series, starring Bing Crosby, Bob Hope, and Dorothy Lamour. Several of the studios used the series as a proving ground for untested promising talent, and a good number of future stars began their careers by making appearances in series.

The Hollywood series declined along with the double feature after WW II and all but disappeared by the early 50s, only to reappear as a staple of TV programming. The occasional sequential films produced later, like the Matt Helm espionage adventures and the sequels to *Planet of the Apes,* have mostly been expensive productions individually exploited for top box-office dollar and not truly series in the original sense of the term. The same holds for Britain's James Bond cycle of spy extravaganzas. However, the British successfully carried on the old tradition into the 70s with the low-budget "Carry On . . ." farcical comedy series. The closest representatives of series in the 80s and 90s were the *Superman* and *Rocky* films on the high end, and the *Friday the 13th* and *Police Academy* films on the low end.

Serling, Rod. Screenwriter. *b.* Dec. 25, 1924, Syracuse, N.Y. *d.* 1975. *ed.* Antioch Coll. A paratrooper during WW II, he worked for a Midwest radio station before moving to network TV in the early 50s. He earned high critical praise for his teleplay 'Patterns,' for which he won his first of five Emmy Awards, and which he later adapted for the big screen. Until the mid-60s he remained one of television's most successful writers, reaching a peak of success with his long-running 'Twilight Zone' series, which dealt with science fiction and the supernatural. He created the series, hosted it, and wrote many of its segments. His direct contribution to the cinema was far less abundant and considerably less important. A chain smoker, he died at 50 during open-heart surgery.

FILMS: *The Rack* (teleplay basis only), *Patterns* (from his own teleplay) 1956; *Saddle the Wind* 1958; *Incident in an Alley* (story only), *Requiem for a Heavyweight* (from his own teleplay) 1962; *The Yellow Canary* 1963; *Seven Days in May* 1964; *Assault on a Queen* 1965; *Planet of the Apes* 1968; *The Man* 1972; *Deadly Fathoms* (doc.; commentary only) 1973; *The Outer Space Connection* (doc.; narrator only), *Encounter with the Unknown* (narrator only) 1975.

Sernas, Jacques. Actor. Born on July 30, 1925, in Kaunas, Lithuania. Leading man, then character player, of international films. Educated in Paris, he joined the French Resistance and was caught by the Germans and imprisoned for more than a year in Buchenwald. After the war, he briefly studied medicine but dropped out of school to make his screen debut in 1946. He subsequently appeared in many French and Italian films and received an international buildup when he was chosen among many to portray Paris in the American-Italian production of *Helen of Troy* (1956). An attempt to mold him into a Hollywood star was not successful and he returned to European films, gradually slipping from leading to supporting roles. He was memorable as a fading matinee idol in Fellini's *La Dolce Vita.*

FILMS INCLUDE: *Miroir* (Fr.) 1947; *Gioventù perduta/Lost Youth* (It.) 1948; *La Revoltée* (Fr.), *Il Mulino del Pò/The Mill on the Po* (It.), *Jean de la Lune* (Fr.), *Il Lupo della Sila/Lure of the Sila* (It.) 1949; *Il Cielo è Rosso/The Sky Is Red* (It.), *Golden Salamander* (UK) 1950; *Cuori sul Mare* (It.), *Barbe-Bleu/Bluebeard* (Fr./It.) 1951; *Camicie rosse/Anita Garibaldi* (It.) 1952; *Cento Anni d'Amore* (It.) 1953; *Jump Into Hell* (US) 1955; *Helen of Troy* (as Paris; US/It.) 1956; *Il Segno di Roma/Sign of the Gladiator* (It.), *Vite perdute/Lost Souls* (It.) 1958; *Le Notti di Lucrezia Borgia/The Night of Lucretia Borgia* (It.) 1959; *La Dolce Vita* (It./Fr.), *La Regina dei Tartari/The Huns* (It./Fr.) 1960; *Romolo e Remo/Duel of the Titans* (It.) 1961; *Il Figlio di Spartacus/The Slave* (It.), *Il Conquistatore di Corinto/The Centurion* (It.) 1962; *La Guerre secrète/The Dirty War* (Fr./It./Ger.) 1965; *Midas Run* (US) 1969; *Hornet's Nest* (US) 1970; *Super Fly T.N.T.* (US) 1973; *Children of Rage* 1975; *L'Avaro/The Miser* (It./Fr./Sp.), *L'Africana/The Woman from Africa* (It./Ger./Fr.) 1990.

Sersen, Fred. American special-effects photographer. He set up the trick photography for many 20th Century-Fox films of the late 30s and 40s, winning Academy Awards for *The Rains Came* and *Crash Dive,* and was appointed head of Fox's special-effects department. The giant tank at the Fox studios was named after him because of his expertise at staging exciting ocean scenes on the lot.

FILMS INCLUDE: *In Old Chicago, Suez* 1938; *The Rains Came* 1939; *Brigham Young* 1940; *Crash Dive, Guadalcanal Diary, Lifeboat, The Song of Bernadette, Heaven Can Wait* 1943; *Jane Eyre, Keys of the Kingdom, Laura, The Lodger* 1944; *A Tree Grows in Brooklyn, Hangover Square, Leave Her to Heaven* 1945; *Anna and the King of Siam, My Darling Clementine* 1946; *The Ghost and Mrs. Muir, Forever Amber, Gentleman's Agreement, Nightmare Alley, Boomerang* 1947.

Serrau, Coline. Director. Born in 1947, in France. A former stage and movie actress, she directed a TV short (*Le Rendez-vous*) before venturing into full-length productions in 1977. Although her films usually focused on issues concerning women, she achieved her greatest success with a male-centered motion picture, *Three Men and a Cradle* (1985). Made on a modest budget with little-known players, the brightly entertaining comedy became a huge box-office hit, winning César awards for best film and best screenplay (her own) and prompting a Hollywood remake, *Three Men and a Baby* (1987), on which she served as a technical advisor.

FILMS: As actress—*On s'est trompé d'Histoire d'Amour* (also sc.) 1974; *Sept Morts sur Ordonance* 1976; *Le Fou de Mai* 1977. As director/screenwriter—*Mais qu'est-ce qu'elles veulent?/But What Do These Women Want?* (doc.; also sound) 1977; *Pourquoi pas!/Why Not!* 1978; *Qu'est-ce qu'on attend pour être heureux!* 1982; *Trois Hommes et un Couffin/Three Men and a Cradle* 1985; *Three Men and a Baby* (screenplay basis, tech. advisor only; US) 1977; *Romauld et Juliette/Mama There's a Man in Your Bed* 1989; *Three Men and a Little Lady* (screenplay basis only; US) 1990; *La Crise* 1992; *A Visit to the Green Planet* (also act.) 1996.

Serrault, Michel. Actor. Born in 1928, in Brunoy, France. *ed.* Paris Conservatoire. Superb character star of French films. A former singer and member of Robert Dhéry's theater troupe, he entered films in the mid-50s and often teamed on the stage and screen with Jean Poiret. Best known to American audiences for his poignant portrait of the effeminate Albin in Edouard

Molinaro's *La Cage aux Folles* (1978), the gay farce that outgrossed any other foreign film in the US box office. Exceptionally versatile, he excelled in a wide range of portrayals, dramatic as well as comic. His many awards include a César for *Garde à Vue* (1981).

FILMS INCLUDE: *Les Diaboliques/Diabolique, Cette Sacrée Gamine/Mam'zelle Pigalle* 1955; *Assassins et Voleurs/Lovers and Thieves* 1957; *Candide* 1960; *La Belle Américaine* 1961; *Les Vierqes, Le Repos du Geurrier/Love on a Pillow* 1962; *La Chasse à l'Homme/Male Hunt* 1964; *Le Roi de Coeur/King of Hearts* 1966; *Le Fou de Labo 4* 1967; *A tout casser/Breaking It Up* 1969; *Le Viager, Tous le Monde il est Beau—Tous le Monde il est Gentile, Un Meurtre est un Meurtre/A Murder Is a Murder. . . Is a Murder* 1972; *Les Gapards/The Holes* 1973; *Préparez vos Mouchoirs/Get Out Your Handkerchiefs, La Cage aux Folles* 1978; *L'Associé/The Associate, Buffet froid* 1979; *La Cage aux Folles II, Pile ou Face/Heads or Tails* 1980; *Garde à Vue/Under Suspicion* 1981; *Les Fantomes du Chapelier, Deux Heures moins le quart avant Jésus-Christ* (as Julius Caesar) 1982; *Mortelle randonée* 1983; *Le Bon Plaisir, A Mort l'Arbitre!, Le Bon Roi Daqobert* 1984; *Les Rois du Gaq, Liberté Eqalité Chougroute* (as Louis XVI), *On ne meurt que deux fois/He Died with His Eyes Open, La Cage aux Folles III ("Elles" se marient)/La Cage aux Folles 3: The Wedding* 1985; *Mon Beau-Frère a tué ma Soeur* 1986; *Le Miraculé* 1987 *Ennemis intimes* 1987; *Bonjour, L'Angoisse* 1988; *Comédie d'Amour, Buon Natale buon Anno/Merry Christmas, Happy New Year* (It./Fr.) 1989; *Docteur Petiot* (also co-prod.) 1990; *City for Sale, La Vielle qui marchait dans la Mer/The Old Lady Who Wades in the Sea* 1991; *Haute Époque* 1994.

Servais, Jean. Actor. *b.* Sept. 24, 1910, Angers, Belgium. *d.* 1976. Leading man of the French stage and screen in the 30s who in the 50s developed into a fine character player with an excellent voice and a face that exuded melancholy intelligence. He was at one time married to actress Dominique Blanchar.

FILMS INCLUDE: *Criminel, Mater Dolorosa* 1932; *Les Misérables* (as Marius), *Angèle, Amok* 1934; *Le Dernier Heure* 1935; *Rose* 1936; *Le Schpountz/Heartbeat, La Vie est magnifique* 1938; *Quartier sans Soleil* 1939; *La Danse de Mort* 1946; *Une si Jolie Petite Plage/Riptide* 1949; *Le Château de Verre* 1950; *Le Plaisir/House of Pleasure* 1952; *Rue de l'Estrapade* 1953; *Du Rififi chez les Hommes/Rififi, Les Héros sont fatigués/Heroes and Sinners* 1955; *La Chatelaine du Liban* 1956; *Celui qui doit mourir/He Who Must Die* 1957; *Tamango, Jeux dangereux* 1958; *La Fièvre monte à El Pao/Republic of Sin* (Fr./Mex.) 1960; *Les Menteurs/The Liars* 1961; *Le Crime ne paie pas/Crime Does Not Pay, The Longest Day* (US) 1962; *L'Homme de Rio/That Man from Rio* 1964; *Lost Command* (US) 1966; *Meglio Vedova/Better a Widow* (It.), *Las Vegas—500 Millones/They Came to Rob Las Vegas* (Sp./Fr./It./Ger.), *Seduta alla sua Destra/Black Jesus* (It.) 1968; *Le Seuil du Vide* 1971; *Le Protecteur/The Devil's Nightmare* 1973.

set. A construction representing an interior or exterior locale in which the action of a motion picture takes place. Over the years the task of set design and erection has progressed from the crude painting of backdrops in the tradition of the stage to a complex art requiring the collaboration of many skilled artists and craftsmen. Sets have become not only more lavish but also more realistic and detailed. They may range from a simple interior to an amazingly accurate mock-up of the interior of a jetliner or a ship, and from the standard main street of a Western town to a highly complicated reproduction of a medieval city, complete with castles and authentic props. Many studios have on their grounds permanent built-up areas representing various locales. Although the façade of the buildings is usually a false front with nothing behind it, the illusion of reality may be perfectly achieved through the rudimentary principles of editing.

The person responsible for the overall look of a film, and for each and every set is the ART DIRECTOR. He works in close collaboration with the SET DESIGNER, whose job it is to translate the art director's ideas into actual drawn plans and construction specifications. Other artists and craftsmen involved in the building of sets in the US (they are all members of IATSE, the International Association of Theatrical Stage Employees) are set decorators, mold makers, property craftsmen (prop master, upholsterer, greensman, etc.), set painters, scenic and title artists, ornamental plasterers, and grips.

set decorator. The person responsible for dressing a motion picture set with appropriate decorative furnishings—furniture, rugs, lamps, draperies, wall paintings, books, etc. He is answerable to the set designer and ultimately to the art director.

set designer. The art director's right-hand man. Usually a draftsman with some architectural training, his job is to draw plans and list specifications for the building of sets from the verbal descriptions or rough sketches provided by the art director.

set estimator. An employee of the art department of a motion picture company responsible for preparing cost estimates for the building of sets, the basis being verbal descriptions or drawings of proposed constructions.

setup. In the narrow sense, the positioning of the camera for any particular shot. In a broader sense, the arrangement of camera, lights, sound equipment, and the actors in the correct places in relation to one another and to the area of the scene, before the filming of any shot.

seventh art. The art of motion pictures. The term was coined in 1916 by Italian poet and pioneer film theoretician Ricciotto CANUDO.

Sevilla, Carmen. Actress, dancer, singer. Born Carmen Galisteo, in 1930, in Seville, Spain. A popular stage and nightclub entertainer, she has also starred in many Spanish, Italian, and French films, mostly musicals but sometimes straight dramas.

FILMS INCLUDE: *Jalisco canta en Sevilla* 1948; *La Revoltosa* 1949; *Cuentos de la Alahambra* 1950; *Andalousie* (Fr.), *Le Désir et l'Amour* (Fr.) 1951; *Babes in Bagdad/Muchachas de Bagdad* (US/UK/Sp.), *Violettes impériales* (Fr.) 1952; *Plume au Vent* (Fr.), *La Belle de Cadix* (Fr./Sp.) 1953; *Congreso en Sevilla* 1955; *Don Juan/Pantaloons* (Fr./Sp.) 1956; *Los Amantes del Desierto* (Sp./It.), *La Venganza, Spanish Affair/Flamenco* (US/Sp.), *Pane Amore e Andalusia* (It./Sp.) 1958; *Europa di Notte/European Nights* (entertainment doc.; It./Fr.) 1959; *King of Kings* (as Mary Magdalene; US) 1961; *Camina del Rocio* 1965; *Un Adulterio decente* 1969; *Antony and Cleopatra* (as Octavia; UK/Sp./Switz.) 1972.

Sewell, Vernon. Director. Born in 1903, in London. *ed.* Marlborough Coll. A former assistant cameraman and film editor, he has directed a score of low-budget British thrillers, as well as many TV episodes ('The Avengers,' etc.).

FILMS INCLUDE: *The Medium* 1934; *The Silver Fleet* 1942; *Latin Quarter Frenzy* 1945; *Ghosts of Berkeley Square* 1947; *Jack of Diamonds* 1949; *Black Widow* 1951; *Ghost Ship* 1952; *Counterspy* 1953; *Dangerous Voyage* 1954; *Soho Incident* 1956; *Battle of the V-1* 1958; *Wrong Number* 1959; *Urge to Kill* 1960; *House of Mystery* 1961; *Strongroom* 1962; *A Matter of Choice* 1963; *Some May Live* 1967; *The Blood Beast Terror/The Vampire Beast Craves Blood, Curse of the Crimson Altar/The Crimson Cult* 1968; *Burke and Hare* 1971.

sexploitation films. Motion pictures made to exploit a public taste for erotica. Sex has proven itself a highly exploitable commodity since the earliest days of cinema. "Schlock" producers at the fringe of the industry have been reaping steady profits for years from the making of a wide variety of films whose sole appeal is their depiction of physical intimacy. They have usually been made cheaply and unimaginatively and have been as explicit as the law would allow. Since the late 60s, in the wake of Supreme Court decisions concerning obscenity, sexploitation films shown in theaters of many American cities have been increasingly daring in their explicit depiction of genitalia and sexual activity, a far cry from the innocent striptease and nudie-camp sensations of the previous decades. Popularly known as porno (for pornographic) films, adult films, or skin flicks, sexploitation films fall into two main categories: hard-core porn, those depicting actual intercourse and shown at theaters specializing in this type of fare; and soft-core porn, those faking intercourse but still offering full nudity and much sexual activity and distributed to a tamer general market.

Seyffertitz, Gustav von. Actor. *b.* 1863, Vienna. *d.* 1943. Character actor of numerous Hollywood silent and sound films, after long stage experience in Germany and the US. Archvillain of many a movie, memorably as Moriarty opposite John Barrymore in *Sherlock Holmes* (1922). During WWI he used the screen name G. Butler Clonblough to disguise his Teutonic background. He used that pseudonym as late as 1919, as the director of *The Secret Garden* for Famous Players/Paramount; and the screen credit G. V. Seyffertitz as the director of three films for Vitagraph, all starring Alice Calhoun and all released in 1921: *Princess Jones, Closed Doors,* and *Peggy Puts It Over.*

FILMS INCLUDE: *Down to Earth, The Countess Charming, The Little Princess, The Devil-Stone* 1917; *The Widow's Might, Old Wives for New, Less Than Kin, Till I Come Back to You* 1918; *The Dark Star, The Vengeance of Durand* 1919; *Slaves of Pride, The Sporting Duchess, Madonnas and Men* 1920; *When Knighthood Was in Flower, Sherlock Holmes* (as Moriarty) 1922; *Mark of the Beast* 1923; *The Lone Wolf, Yolanda, The Bandolero* 1924; *The Eagle, The Goose Woman* 1925; *Diplomacy, Sparrows, Don Juan, The Bell* 1926; *The Student Prince, The Gaucho, The Wizard, The Magic Flame* 1927; *The Yellow Lily, Vamping Venus, The Docks of New York, The Mysterious Lady, Me Gangster* 1928; *The Case of Lena Smith, The Canary Murder Case, Chasing Through Europe, His Glorious Night, Seven Faces* 1929; *Dangerous Paradise, The Bat Whispers* 1930; *Dishonored* 1931; *Shanghai Express, Doomed Battalion* 1932; *Queen Christina* 1933; *Mystery Liner* 1934; *She* 1935; *Little Lord Fauntleroy, Mad Holiday* 1936; *In Old Chicago* 1938; *Nurse Edith Cavell* 1939.

Seymour, Jane. Actress. Born Joyce Penelope Wilhelmina Frankenberg, on May 13, 1951, in Wimbledon, England. Lovely, brunette leading lady of the British and American stage and screen. The daughter of a Jewish gynecologist, she trained for the ballet at London's Arts Educational School and at 18 turned to drama. In addition to her film credits, she starred in many TV movies and miniseries ('East of Eden,' 'War and Remembrance,' etc.) and in the Broadway production of 'Amadeus' (1980). She starred in her own dramatic series, 'Dr. Quinn, Medicine Woman' (1993). The first of her three marriages was to Michael Attenborough, the son of Sir Richard. Another Jane Seymour appeared in a few Hollywood films from the late 30s to the early 50s. Author: *Jane Seymour's Guide to Romantic Living* (1986).

FILMS INCLUDE: *Oh! What a Lovely War* 1969; *Young Winston* 1972; *Live and Let Die* 1973; *Sinbad and the Eye of the Tiger* 1974; *Battlestar Galactica* 1979; *Oh Heavenly Dog, Somewhere in Time* 1980; *Lassiter* 1984; *Head Office* 1985; *La Revolution Française/The French Revolution* (as Marie Antoinette; Fr./Ger./It./Can.) 1989; *Keys to Freedom* 1990.

Seyrig, Delphine. Actress. *b.* Apr. 10, 1932, Beirut, Lebanon, to French Alsatian parents. *d.* 1990, of lung disease. Intriguing leading lady of French and international films whose enigmatic screen personality and expressive face enriched several major productions of the 60s and 70s. She won the best actress award at the Venice Festival for her performance in the latter film. An archeologist's daughter, she started her career on the Paris stage in 1952 and in 1956 went to the US, where she studied at the Actors Studio, performed on TV, and made her big-screen debut in a 16 mm underground film, *Pull My Daisy* (1958). Returning to France, she won immediate recognition for her interpretation of a complex Proustian role in Alain Resnais's *Last Year at Marienbad* (1961), her first professional film. She later appeared in many other movies, in roles both large and small and performances always graceful and intriguing. A dedicated feminist, she figured prominently in films by women directors, notably Marguerite Duras's *India Song* and Chantal Akerman's *Jeanne Dielman* (both 1975). In the late 70s she directed a number of experimental videotape shorts and the feature-length film *Soi belle et tais-toi* (1977).

FILMS INCLUDE: *Pull My Daisy* (US) 1958; *L'Année dernière à Marienbad/Last Year at Marienbad* 1961; *Muriel* 1963; *La Musica* 1966; *Accident* (UK) 1967; *Baisers volés/Stolen Kisses* 1968; *Mister Freedom, La Voie Lactée/The Milky Way* 1969; *La Rouge aux Lèvres/Daughters of Darkness* (Fr./US), *Peau d'Ane/Donkey Skin* 1971; *Le Journal d'un Suicide, La Charme discret de la Bourgeoisie/The Discreet Charm of the Bourgeoisie* 1972; *The Day of the Jackal* (UK/Fr.), *A Doll's House* (as Christine Linde; UK) 1973; *The Black Windmill* (UK), *Eulallie quitte les Champs/The Star the Orphan and the Butcher, Aloise* 1974; *India Song, Jeanne Dielman 23 Quai de Commerce 1080 Bruxelles* 1975; *Caro Michele* (It.) 1976; *Der letzte Schrei* (Ger.), *Baxter—Vera Baxter, Repérages/Faces of Love* (Switz./Fr.) 1977: *Le Chemin perdu* (Switz./Fr.) 1979; *Chère Inconnu/I Sent a Letter to My Love* 1980; *Fresh Orlando* (Ger.) 1981; *Le Grain de Sable, Dorian Grey im Spiegel der Boulevardprese/Dorian Grey in the Mirror of the Popular Press* 1983; *Les Années 80/Golden Eighties* 1986; *Seven Women Seven Sins* (Ger./Fr./US/Aus./Belg.) 1987; *Johanna d'Arc of Mongolia/Joan of Arc of Mongolia* (Ger.) 1989; *Window Shopping* (released posthumously) 1994.

SFX. Commonly used abbreviation for SOUND EFFECTS.

Shaffer, Anthony and Peter. Playwrights, screenwriters, novelists. Twin brothers, both born on May 15, 1926, in Liverpool, England, both educated at Cambridge. While pursuing separate early careers, Anthony as a barrister and Peter at the acquisition department of the New York Public Library, they collaborated on several novels in the early 50s, using the pseudonym Peter Anthony. Each later achieved fame separately as a playwright, Anthony with 'Sleuth' (1970) and Peter with 'Five Finger Exercise' (1958), 'The Private Ear and the Public Eye' (1962), 'Equus' (1973), and 'Amadeus' (1980), among other plays. Each also wrote screenplays. Peter was nominated for an Academy Award for his screen adaptation of *Equus* (1979) and won the Oscar for *Amadeus* (1984).

FILMS (as screenwriters): Anthony—*Mr. Forbush and the Penguins* 1971; *Frenzy, Sleuth* (from his own play) 1972; *The Wicker Man* 1973; *Death on the Nile* 1978; *Absolution/Murder by Confession* (release delayed from 1978) 1981; *Evil Under the Sun* 1982; *Appointment with Death* (co-sc.) 1988. Peter—*Equus* (from his own play) 1977; *Amadeus* (from his own play) 1984.

Shaiman, Marc. Composer. Born 1957. He began his career as musical director for a number of Bette MIDLER's stage shows, graduating to music supervisor for many of her films. Twice nominated for an Oscar, for his music in *Sleepless in*

Seattle (1993) and for original music score for *The American President* (1995), he also made his debut as an actor in the James L. Brooks comedy *Broadcast News* (1987).

FILMS: *Divine Madness* (arranger) 1980; *Broadcast News* (act. only) 1987; *Big Business* (mus., mus. superv.) 1988; *When Harry Met Sally. . .* (music arranger) 1989; *Misery* 1990; *The Addams Family, City Slickers, For the Boys* (also act.), *Hot Shots!* (act. only), *Scenes from a Mall* 1991; *A Few Good Men, Mr. Saturday Night, Sister Act* 1992; *Addams Family Values, For Love or Money, Heart and Souls* (also act.), *Hocus Pocus* (act. only), *Sister Act 2: Back in the Habit* (also assoc. prod.), *Sleepless in Seattle* 1993; *City Slickers II: The Legend of Curly's Gold, North, Speechless, That's Entertainment! III* 1994; *The American President, Stuart Saves His Family* 1995; *Bogus, First Wives Club, Ghosts of Mississippi, Mother* 1996.

Shamroy, Leon. Director of photography. *b.* July 16, 1901, New York City. *d.* 1974. *ed.* Cooper Union; CCNY; Columbia. A former mechanical engineer, he entered films as a lab technician, but his off-the-job photography on experimental films soon attracted the attention of producers and he moved behind the camera. A creative, innovative lighting cameraman, he was one of the first to use a zoom lens. He gained an industry-wide reputation for his understated black-and-white photography in the 30s and for his brilliant color work from the 40s. For 30 years his style dominated production quality at Fox. In the 50s he helped many directors at Fox adapt to the requirements of CinemaScope by making sensible use of this and other wide-screen processes. He won Academy Awards for *The Black Swan* (1942), *Wilson* (1944), *Leave Her to Heaven* (1945), and *Cleopatra* (1963). He was married to actress Mary Anderson.

FILMS INCLUDE: *Tongues of Scandal* 1927; *The Last Moment* 1928; *Alma de Gaucho* 1930; *Stowaway* 1932; *Jennie Gerhardt, Three-Cornered Moon* 1933; *Good Dame, Thirty-Day Princess, Kiss and Make Up* 1934; *Private Worlds, She Married Her Boss, Accent On Youth* 1935; *Soak the Rich* 1936; *You Only Live Once* 1937; *Made for Each Other, The Story of Alexander Graham Bell, The Adventures of Sherlock Holmes* 1939; *Little Old New York, Lillian Russell, Four Sons, Down Argentine Way* (co-phot.), *Tin Pan Alley* 1940; *The Great American Broadcast* (co-phot.), *That Night in Rio* (co-phot.), *Moon Over Miami* (co-phot.) 1941; *Roxie Hart, The Black Swan* 1942; *Crash Dive, Stormy Weather, Claudia* 1943; *Buffalo Bill, Wilson* 1944; *A Tree Grows in Brooklyn, State Fair, Leave Her to Heaven* 1945; *Forever Amber, Daisy Kenyon* 1947; *That Lady in Ermine* 1948; *Prince of Foxes, Twelve O' Clock High* 1949; *Cheaper by the Dozen* 1950; *On the Riviera, David and Bathsheba* 1951; *With a Song in My Heart, The Snows of Kilimanjaro* 1952; *Call Me Madam, The Robe* 1953; *The Egyptian* 1954; *Daddy Long Legs, Love Is a Many Splendored Thing* 1955; *The King and I* 1956; *The Desk Set* 1957; *South Pacific, The Bravados* 1958; *Porgy and Bess, The Blue Angel* 1959; *North to Alaska* 1960; *Cleopatra, The Cardinal* 1963; *The Agony and the Ecstasy* 1965; *The Glass Bottom Boat* 1966; *Caprice* 1967; *Planet of the Apes* 1968; *Justine* 1969.

Shane, Maxwell. Director, screenwriter. *b.* Aug. 26, 1905, Paterson, N.J. *d.* 1983. *ed.* UCLA; USC Law School. A former journalist, publicist, and advertising man, he wrote many minor screenplays beginning in 1937. He directed several routine pictures in the late 40s and early 50s, afterward becoming a successful TV producer.

FILMS (as director): *Fear in the Night* (also sc.) 1947; *City Across the River* (also prod., co-sc.) 1949; *The Glass Wall* (also sc.) 1953; *The Naked Street* (also co-sc.) 1955; *Nightmare* (also sc.) 1956.

Shanley, John Patrick. Playwright, screenwriter, director. Born in 1950, in the Bronx, N.Y., the son of a meatpacker and a telephone operator. The author of such esteemed plays as 'Danny and the Deep Blue Sea,' 'Savage in Limbo,' 'A Dreamer Examines His Pillow,' and 'Women of Manhattan,' he branched into screenwriting in the late 80s, winning an Academy Award for his script for *Moonstruck* (1987), a delightful bittersweet romantic comedy. He fared far less successfully with his debut film as a director, *Joe Versus the Volcano* (1990), an overblown shaggy dog comedy. He was seen as an actor in *Crossing Delancey* (1988).

FILMS (as screenwriter): *Moonstruck* 1987; *Five Corners* 1988; *January Man* 1989; *Joe Versus the Volcano* (also dir.) 1990; *Alive* 1992; *Congo* 1995.

Shapiro, Stanley. Screenwriter, producer. *b.* July 16, 1925, New York City. *d.* 1990. A veteran of radio and TV, he scored a succession of hits in the 60s as the writer and later also producer of slick romantic Hollywood comedies. He won an Academy Award for the screenplay of *Pillow Talk* (1959).

FILMS INCLUDE (as screenwriter): *South Sea Woman* 1953; *The Perfect Furlough* 1958; *Pillow Talk, Operation Petticoat* 1959; *Come September* 1961; *That Touch of Mink* 1962; *Bedtime Story* (also prod.) 1964; *A Very Special Favor* (also prod.) 1965; *How to Save a Marriage—and Ruin Your Life* (also prod.) 1968; *Me Natalie* (story basis, prod. only) 1969; *For Pete's Sake* (co-sc., co-prod.) 1974; *Seniors* (co-prod. only) 1978: *Carbon Copy* (also co-prod.) 1981; *Dirty Rotten Scoundrels* (co-sc. from his co-story for *Bedtime Story*) 1988.

Sharaff, Irene. Costume designer. *b.* 1910, in Boston. *d.* 1993. Trained at New York's School of Fine and Applied Arts and the Arts Students League, and at the Grande Chaumière in Paris, she began her career in 1929 with the Civic Repertory Theatre Company. Her stage background proved advantageous in her film work, which included many major Hollywood musicals. She was nominated for 16 Academy Awards, alone or in collaboration, winning five Oscars, for *An American in Paris* (the ballet sequence, 1951), *The King and I* (1956), *West Side Story* (1961), *Cleopatra* (1963), and *Who's Afraid of Virginia Woolf?* (1966).

FILMS INCLUDE: *Girl Crazy* 1943; *Meet Me in St. Louis* 1944; *Yolanda and the Thief* 1945; *The Dark Mirror, The Best Years of Our Lives* 1946; *The Secret Life of Walter Mitty* 1947; *A Song Is Born* 1948; *An American in Paris* 1951; *Call Me Madam* 1953; *A Star Is Born, Brigadoon* 1954; *Guys and Dolls* 1955; *The King and I* 1956; *Les Girls* 1957; *Porgy and Bess* 1959; *Can-Can* 1960; *West Side Story, Flower Drum Song* 1961; *Cleopatra* 1963; *The Sandpiper* 1965; *Who's Afraid of Virginia Woolf?* 1966; *The Taming of the Shrew* 1967; *Funny Girl* 1968; *Hello Dolly!* 1969; *The Great White Hope* 1970; *The Other Side of Midnight* 1977; *Mommie Dearest* 1981.

Sharif, Omar. Actor. Born Michael Shalhoub, on Apr. 10, 1932, in Alexandria, Egypt. *ed.* Victory Coll., Cairo. Romantic star of Egyptian and later international films. The son of a wealthy merchant of Lebanese descent, he converted to Islam and changed his name to Omar El-Sharif shortly after making his Egyptian film debut in 1953. His popularity in the Arab-speaking world increased after he married Faten Hamama (*b.* 1931), then the leading star of Egyptian films, in 1955. Following their 1974 divorce, Sharif married another actress, Sohair Ramzi, in 1977. His casting in David Lean's *Lawrence of Arabia* led to a career in American and international films, notably as the lead in *Doctor Zhivago*. He received an Oscar nomination as best supporting actor for his performance in *Lawrence of Arabia*. Sharif is one of the world's most famous bridge players, the leader of a professional team that has won many international tournaments.

FILMS INCLUDE: In Egypt—*The Struggle in the Valley* 1953; *Devil of the Desert* 1954; *Land of Peace* 1955; *Goha* (Fr.; filmed in Tunis) 1957; *Scandal at Zamalek* 1958; *Struggle on the Nile* 1959; *The Agony of Love* 1960; *The Mameluks* 1963. Abroad—*Lawrence of Arabia* (UK) 1962; *The Fall of the Roman Empire* (US), *Behold a Pale Horse* (US), *The Yellow Rolls-Royce* (UK) 1964; *Genghis Khan* (title role; US/UK/Ger./Yug.), *La Fabuleuse Aventure de Marco Polo/Marco the Magnificent* (Fr./It./Eg./Afghan.), *Doctor Zhivago* (title role; US) 1965; *The Poppy Is Also a Flower* (UN/US) 1966; *La Nuit des Généraux/The Night of the Generals* (Fr./US), *C'era una Volta/More Than a Miracle* (It./Fr.) 1967; *Funny Girl* (as gambler Nick Arnstein; US), *Mayerling* (as Rudolf; UK/Fr.) 1968; *Mackenna's Gold* (US), *Che!* (as Che Guevara; US), *The Appointment* (US) 1969; *The Last Valley* (UK), *The Horsemen* (US), *Le Casse/The Burglars* (Fr.) 1971; *Le Droit d'aimer/The Right to Love* (Fr.) 1972; *L'Ile mystérieuse/The Mysterious Island of Captain Nemo* (as Captain Nemo; Fr./Sp.) 1973; *The Tamarind Seed* (UK), *Juggernaut* (UK) 1974; *Funny Lady* (as Arnstein; US), *An Ace Up My Sleeve* (UK) 1975; *Crime and Passion* (US/Ger.) 1976; *Ashanti* (US), *Bloodline* (US) 1979; *The Baltimore Bullet* (US), *Oh Heavenly Dog!* (US) 1980; *Green Ice* (UK) 1981; *Top Secret!* (US) 1984; *Les Possédés/The Possessed* (Fr.), *Les Pyramides bleues/Paradise Calling* (Fr./Mex.) 1988; *The Rainbow Thief* (UK), *Viaggio D'Amore/Journey of Love* (It./Fr.) 1990; *War in the Land of Egypt* (Egy.), *Mayrig/Mother* (Fr.) 1991; *588 Rue Paradis* (Fr.) 1992.

Sharkey, Ray. Actor. *b.* 1952 in Brooklyn, N.Y. *d.* 1993, of AIDS. Character lead and supporting player of the American screen. Trained at the HB Studio, he began his career in TV and appeared briefly on the stage before breaking into movies in the mid-70s. Memorable on-screen in the title role in *The Idolmaker* and as Phil in *Willie and Phil* (both 1980), and as a supporting player on TV's 'Wiseguy.'

FILMS INCLUDE: *The Lords of Flatbush* 1974; *Trackdown* 1976; *Stunts* 1977; *Hot Tomorrows, Who'll Stop the Rain?, Paradise Alley* 1978; *Heart Beat, Willie and Phil, The Idolmaker* 1980; *Love and Money, Some Kind of Hero* 1982; *Body Rock* 1984; *Hellhole* 1985; *Wise Guys, No Mercy* 1986; *Private Investigations* 1987; *Scenes from the Class Struggle in Beverly Hills, Wired* 1989; *Act of Piracy* (release delayed from 1987), *The Rain Killer* 1990; *Hotel Oklahoma, Relentless 2: Dead On* 1991; *Round Trip to Heaven, Zebrahead* 1992; *Cop-and-a-Half* 1993.

sharp. Describing a motion picture image in accurate focus and rendering a crisp, detailed picture.

Sharp, Don. Director. Born in April, 1922, in Hobart, Tasmania, Australia. An actor on the Australian stage and screen from 1945, he went to London in 1948 and entered British films as a screenwriter the following year. Starting in the mid-50s, he directed many films, at first juvenile fare, then horror pictures. He also directed numerous TV episodes and was second-unit director on such films as *Carve Her Name with Pride* (1958) and *Those Magnificent Men in Their Flying Machines* (1965).

FILMS INCLUDE (as director): *The Stolen Airliner* (also sc.) 1955; *The Professionals* 1960; *It's All Happening/The Dream Maker, The Kiss of the Vampire* 1963; *The Devil-Ship Pirates, Witchcraft* 1964; *The Face of Fu Manchu, Curse of the Fly* 1965; *Rasputin—The Mad Monk, Our Man in Marrakesh/Bang! Bang! You're Dead!, The Brides of Fu Manchu* 1966; *Jules Verne's Rocket to the Moon, Those Fantastic Flying Fools/Blast-Off* 1967; *Taste of Excitement* 1968; *The Violent Enemy* 1969; *Puppet on a Chain* 1971; *Psychomania/The Death Wheelers* 1972; *Dark Places* 1974; *Hennessy* 1975; *The Four Feathers* (TV movie in the US; theatrical in the UK), *The 39 Steps* 1978; *Bear Island* 1980; *What Waits Below* 1984.

Shatner, William. Actor. Born on Mar. 22, 1931, in Montreal. Sturdily built leading man of American TV and films. Resisting his Jewish parents' urgings that he join the family clothing business, he began performing with regional Canadian repertory companies after graduating from McGill. Moving to New York, he performed on Broadway and in early live television plays, then relocated to Los Angeles, where he made a favorable impression in his film debut as Alexei in *The Brothers Karamazov* (1958). But it was on TV that he had his greatest success, as Captain James T. Kirk in the monumental series 'Star Trek' (1966–69). He repeated the role in the series' movie spin-offs, and directed one of them, the disappointing *Star Trek V: The Final Frontier* (1989). Earlier he had directed several episodes of the TV police series 'T. J. Hooker,' in which he also starred in the title role. From 1991 he starred in the series 'Rescue 911.' Shatner parlayed his 'Star Trek' success into a publishing career, authoring several science fiction books, including *Tek War* and *Tek Lords*. His 1993 autobiography is *Star Trek Memories*. Shatner's second wife was actress Marcie Lafferty. His daughter, Melanie, is also a performer.

FILMS: *The Brothers Karamazov* (as Alexei Karamazov) 1958; *Judgment at Nuremberg, The Explosive Generation* 1961; *The Intruder* 1962; *The Outrage* 1964; *Hour of Vengeance* (It.) 1968; *Big Bad Mama, Dead of Night* 1974; *The Devil's Rain, Impulse* 1975; *A Whale of a Tale, Kingdom of the Spiders* 1977; *The Third Walker* (Can.) 1978; *Riel, Star Trek—The Motion Picture* 1979; *The Kidnapping of the President* (Can.) 1980; *The Land of No Return/Snowman/Challenge to Survive* (filmed in 1975; release delayed from 1978) 1981; *Visiting Hours* (Can.), *Star Trek II: The Wrath of Khan, Airplane II: The Sequel* 1982; *Star Trek III: The Search for Spock* 1984; *Star Trek IV: The Voyage Home* 1986; *Star Trek V: The Final Frontier* (also dir., co-story) 1989; *Star Trek VI: The Undiscovered Country* 1991; *National Lampoon's Loaded Weapon I* 1993; *Star Trek: Generations* 1994.

Shavelson, Melville. Screenwriter, director, producer. Born on Apr. 1, 1917, in Brooklyn, N.Y. *ed.* Cornell. A former radio writer, he got into films in the mid-40s through his association with the Bob Hope show. He collaborated on many funny screenplays for Hope, Danny Kaye, and other comedy stars as well as some light musicals. In the mid-50s he also began directing and producing with mixed results. In 1971 he published a book, *How to Make a Jewish Movie,* about his misadventures while filming *Cast a Giant Shadow* in Israel. In 1975 he published *Lualda,* a racy, humorous novel about Hollywood.

FILMS INCLUDE: As screenwriter—*The Princess and the Pirate* 1944; *Wonder Man* 1945; *The Kid from Brooklyn* 1946; *Where There's Life* 1947; *Sorrowful Jones, Always Leave Them Laughing, The Great Lover* 1949; *The Daughter of Rosie O'Grady* 1950; *Double Dynamite, On Moonlight Bay* 1951; *I'll See You in My Dreams, April in Paris* 1952; *Trouble Along the Way* (also prod.) 1953. As director-writer (complete)—*The Seven Little Foys* 1955; *Beau James* 1957; *Houseboat* 1958; *The Five Pennies* 1959; *It Started in Naples* 1960; *On the Double* 1961; *The Pigeon That Took Rome* (also prod.) 1962; *A New Kind of Love* (also prod.) 1963; *Cast a Giant Shadow* (also prod.) 1966; *Yours Mine and Ours* 1968; *The War Between Men and Women* 1972; *Mixed Company* (also prod.) 1974.

Shaver, Helen. Actress. Born on Feb. 24, 1951, in St. Thomas, Ont., Canada. Seductive, husky-voiced, blonde leading lady and supporting player of Canadian and American films and television. The fifth of six girls, she developed a yen for acting during a long convalescence from a childhood heart disease.

After training at the Banff School of Fine Arts in Alberta, she came to Los Angeles but was denied acting jobs for lack of working papers. After five years of stage and screen work back in Canada, she returned to Hollywood in 1978 and has since worked steadily on both sides of the border. In addition to features and TV movies, she starred in the short-lived US TV series 'United States' (1980) and 'Jessica Novak' (1981).

FILMS INCLUDE: *Shoot* 1976; *Outrageous!, Starship Invasions, Who Has Seen the Wind?* 1977; *In Praise of Older Women, High-Ballin'* 1978; *The Amityville Horror* 1979; *Gas* 1981; *Harry Tracy Desperado/Harry Tracy* 1982; *The Osterman Weekend* 1983; *Best Defense* 1984; *Desert Hearts, The Color of Money* 1986; *The Believers* 1987; *The Land Before Time* (v/o) 1988; *Tree of Hands* 1989; *Bethune: The Making of a Hero* 1990; *Zebrahead, One Hot Summer* 1992; *Change of Heart* 1993; *The Craft* 1996.

Shaw, Irwin. Novelist, playwright, screenwriter. *b.* Feb. 27, 1913, Brooklyn, N.Y. to Jewish immigrants from Russia. *d.* 1984. *ed.* Brooklyn Coll. He began as a radio dramatist, adapting episodes for "Dick Tracy" and other popular shows. He saw his first play and screenplay produced in 1936 and his first collection of short stories published in 1940. But it wasn't until the publication of his best-selling WW II novel, *The Young Lions,* in 1948 that he became successful and famous as an author. He continued to write for the screen, and several films were adapted from his fiction.

FILMS: *The Big Game* 1936; *Out of the Fog* (play basis only) 1941; *The Talk of the Town* 1942; *The Commandos Strike at Dawn* 1943; *Easy Living, Take One False Step* (both orig. story only) 1949; *I Want You* 1951; *Act of Love* 1953; *Ulisse/Ulysses* (It.) 1954; *War and Peace* (co-sc., uncredited) 1956; *Tip on a Dead Jockey* (story basis only), *Fire Down Below* 1957; *The Young Lions* (novel basis only), *Desire Under the Elms, Le Diga sol Pacifico/This Angry Age/The Sea Wall* (It.) 1958; *The Big Gamble* 1961; *Two Weeks in Another Town* (novel basis only) 1962; *In the French Style* (also co-prod., from own story US/Fr.) 1963; *Survival* (doc.; also co-prod.; Isr.) 1968; *Three* (story basis only) 1969.

Shaw, Robert. Actor, novelist, playwright. *b.* Aug. 9, 1927, Westhoughton, England. *d.* 1978. The son of a physician whose losing bout with alcoholism led to his suicide when Robert was 12, he was raised in Scotland, then in England's Cornwall, and was drawn to both acting and writing at a young age. After training at the Royal Academy of Dramatic Art, he made his stage debut in 1949 with the Shakespeare Memorial Theatre at Stratford-on-Avon and has subsequently appeared in many plays and films. On the screen from the 50s, he was seen mainly in character roles, often as a nasty villain, in both British and US films, but in the mid-70s, around the age of 50, he suddenly emerged as a highly paid star in such popular films as *The Sting* (1973), *Jaws* (1975), *Swashbuckler* (1976), and *The Deep* (1977). He was nominated for a best supporting actor Oscar for his portrayal of Henry VIII in *A Man for All Seasons* (1966). He wrote a play, 'Off the Mainland,' and several novels, including *The Hiding Place* (1959), *The Sun Doctor* (1961), *The Flag* (1965), and *The Man in the Glass Booth* (1967). He adapted the latter into a play that was presented successfully on the London stage and on Broadway in 1967–68 and was turned into a film in 1975. *The Hiding Place* provided the basis for the screen comedy *Situation Hopeless—But Not Serious* (1965). Shaw, who had made his home on a vast estate in County Mayo, Ireland, with his third wife and ten children, died of a heart attack at 51. His second wife (from 1963 till his death) was actress Mary URE.

FILMS: *The Lavender Hill Mob* (bit) 1951; *The Dam Busters* 1954; *Doublecross, A Hill in Korea/Hell in Korea* 1956; *See Fury* 1958; *Libel* 1959; *The Valiant* 1961; *Tomorrow at Ten* 1962; *From Russia with Love, The Caretaker/The Guest* 1963; *The Luck of Ginger Coffey* (title role; Can./US) 1964; *Battle of the Bulge* (US) 1965; *A Man for All Seasons* (as Henry VIII) 1966; *Custer of the West* (as General Custer; US), *The Birthday Party* 1968; *Battle of Britain, The Royal Hunt of the Sun* (as explorer Francisco Pizarro; US/UK), *Figures in a Landscape* 1970; *A Town Called Hell/A Town Called Bastard* (UK/Sp.) 1971; *Young Winston* (as Lord Randolph Churchill) 1972; *A Reflection of Fear, The Hireling, The Sting* (US) 1973; *The Taking of Pelham 123* (US) 1974; *Jaws* (US), *Diamonds* (Isr./Switz./US), *Das Richter und sein Henker/End of the Game* (Ger./It.) 1975; *Robin and Marian* (as the Sheriff of Nottingham), *Swashbuckler* (title role; US) 1976; *The Deep* (US), *Black Sunday* (US) 1977; *Force 10 from Navarone* 1978; *Avalanche Express* (US) 1979.

Shaw, Run Run. Producer. Born on October 14, 1907, in Shanghai, China. Leading producer of action films for Hong Kong and international markets, including *Five Fingers of Death*. Since 1959 he has been chairman of Shaw Brothers Ltd., which he founded with brother Runme Shaw.

FILMS INCLUDE: *Pai-She Chuan/Madame White Snake* 1963; *Ta Chi/The Last Woman of Shang, Liang Shan-Po Yu Chu Ying-Tai/The Love Eterne* 1964; *Hua Mu-Lan/The Lady General* 1965; *Lovers' Rock* 1966; *Sons of Good Earth* 1967; *Vermillion Door* 1969; *Five Fingers of Death* 1973; *The Sacred Knives of Vengeance/The Killer* 1974; *Cleopatra Jones and the Casino of Gold* 1975; *Big Bad Sis* 1976; *Bruce Lee and I/Bruce and I, The Brotherhood, Shaolin Avenger* 1976; *Innocent Lust, The Mad Monk, The Mad Monk Strikes Again* 1977; *Shaolin Abbot* 1979; *Two Champions of Shaolin* 1980; *Girl with the Diamond Slipper, My Name Ain't Suzie, Carry On Doctors and Nurses* 1985.

Shaw, Susan. Actress. *b.* Patsy Sloots, Aug. 29, 1929, West Norwood, England. *d.* 1978. Leading lady of British films of the late 40s and 50s. A former model, she was groomed as a starlet by the Rank Organisation. Her first of three marriages (1949–53) was to actor Albert LIEVEN and the second (1954–58) to actor Bonar COLLEANO.

FILMS INCLUDE: *London Town/My Heart Goes Crazy* 1946; *The Upturned Glass, Holiday Camp, Jassy, It Always Rains on Sunday* 1947; *My Brother's Keeper, London Belongs to Me/Dulcimer Street, Quartet, Here Come the Huggetts* 1948; *Marry Me, Train of Events* 1949; *The Woman in Question, Pool of London* 1950; *There Is Another Sun/Wall of Death* 1951; *The Killer Walks* 1952; *The Intruder* 1953; *The Good Die Young* 1954; *Fire Maidens from Outer Space* 1956; *The Diplomatic Corpse* 1957; *Chain of Events* 1958; *Carry on Nurse* 1959; *Stranglehold* 1962; *The Switch* 1963.

Shawn, Wallace. Playwright, actor. Born on Nov. 12, 1943, in New York City, the son of William Shawn, former longtime editor of the *New Yorker. ed.* Harvard; Oxford. He taught English in India on a Fulbright scholarship and English, Latin, and drama in New York before embarking on a stage career as a playwright and actor. He won an Obie Award for his first off-Broadway play, 'Our Late Night' (1975). Small-framed, balding, and projecting intellect, he began playing character roles in films in the late 70s. His portrayals ranged from a philosophizing, self-exploring communicator in *My Dinner with Andre* (1981)—for which he also co-wrote the script—to a comically menacing villain in *The Princess Bride* (1987).

FILMS INCLUDE: *Manhattan, Starting Over, All That Jazz* 1979; *Simon, Atlantic City* (Can./Fr.) 1980; *My Dinner with Andre* (also co-sc.) 1981; *A Little Sex* 1982; *Lovesick, The First Time, Strange Invaders, Deal of the Century* 1983; *Crackers,*

The Hotel New Hampshire, The Bostonians, Micki and Maude 1984; *Heaven Help Us* 1985; *Head Office* 1986; *Prick Up Your Ears* (UK), *The Bedroom Window, Radio Days, Nice Girls Don't Explode, The Princess Bride* 1987; *The Moderns* 1988; *She's Out of Control, Scenes from the Class Struggle in Beverly Hills, We're No Angels* 1989; *The Cemetery Club, Shadows and Fog, Mom and Dad Save the World* 1992; *Meteor Man, Nickel and Dime* 1993; *Mrs. Parker and the Vicious Circle, Vanya on 42nd Street* 1994; *Canadian Bacon, Clueless, Toy Story* (v/o) 1995; *All Dogs Go To Heaven 2* (v/o), *The Wife* 1996; *The Designated Mourner* (scr.) 1997.

Shea, John. Actor. Born on Apr. 14, 1949, in North Conway, N.H. *ed.* Bates Coll.; Yale School of Drama (directing). Darkly handsome, curly-haired leading man of the American stage, screen, and television. Memorable as Jack Lemmon's vanished son in Costa-Gavras's *Missing* (1982). On the New York stage, he won a Drama Desk Award for 'American Days' and an Obie for off-Broadway's 'The Ding Room.' He was awarded an Emmy for his performance in the TV movie 'Baby M' (1988) and was a regular on the series 'The Adventures of Lois and Clark.'

FILMS INCLUDE: *Hussy* (UK) 1980; *Missing* 1982; *In Our Hands, Windy City* 1984; *Lune de Miel/Honeymoon* (Fr./Can.) 1985; *Once We Were Dreamers/Unsettled Land* (Isr./US) 1987; *A New Life, Stealing Home* 1988; *Freejack, Honey I Blew Up the Kid* 1992; *Backstreet Justice* 1994.

Shear, Barry. Director. *b.* Mar. 23, 1923, New York City. *d.* 1979. *ed.* U. of Wisconsin. A veteran of American TV from its infancy, he turned to feature directing in the late 60s, gaining some critical attention with several well placed if sensational action dramas with an emphasis on realistic violence.

FILMS: *Wild in the Streets* 1968; *The Todd Killings* (also prod.) 1971; *Across 110th Street* (also co-exec. prod.) 1972; *The Deadly Trackers* (US/Sp.) 1973.

Shearer, Douglas. Sound recording technician. *b.* Nov. 17, 1899, Westmount, Quebec, Canada. *d.* 1971. The brother of Norma SHEARER, he came to Hollywood to visit his sister and was hired by MGM as an assistant in the camera department. During the switch to talkies in the late 20s, he was appointed head of the company's sound department and soon proved himself one of the most inventive technicians in this pioneering field. During his more than 40 years with MGM he contributed more than any other man in Hollywood to the perfection of motion picture sound. He is credited with many technical innovations and with the consistent high quality of sound which distinguished MGM films over the years. He won 12 Academy Awards for "best sound recording" and for such achievements as developing an improved recording system and a method for reducing unwanted noise. In 1959 he received an additional Oscar, in the scientific and technical category, as the co-developer of MGM's Camera 65 wide-screen system. In 1955 he was appointed the company's director of technical research, a position he held until his retirement in 1968. Films for which he won Oscars include: *The Big House* (1930), *Naughty Marietta* (1935), *San Francisco* (1936), *Strike Up the Band* (1940), *30 Seconds Over Tokyo* (1944), *Green Dolphin Street* (1947), and *The Great Caruso* (1951).

Shearer, Moira. Dancer, actress. Born Moira King, on Jan. 26, 1926, in Dunfermline, Scotland. A ballet dancer from age six, she made her professional debut with the International Ballet at 15 and joined the famed Sadler's Wells at 16. She entered films as the ballerina-star of *The Red Shoes* and *Tales of Hoffman,* but her fragile, fairylike beauty later also got her non-dancing roles. She retired early in the 60s, after marrying news analyst and novelist Ludovic Kennedy, but was back on the London stage in 1974, playing a dramatic role in 'Man and Wife.'

FILMS: *The Red Shoes* 1948; *Tales of Hoffman* 1951; *The Story of Three Loves* 1953; *The Man Who Loved Redheads* 1955; *Peeping Tom, Un Deux Trois Quatre!/Les Collants noirs/Black Tights* (Fr.) 1960.

Shearer, Norma. Actress. *b.* Edith Norma Shearer, Aug. 10, 1900, Montreal, Canada. *d.* 1983. The daughter of a wealthy businessman, she was given piano and dance lessons in early childhood, and at 14 she won a beauty contest. When her father's business suddenly failed during WW I, she and her sister were brought to New York by their mother, who was hoping to get them into show business. Failing an audition with Florenz Ziegfeld, Norma modeled and posed for advertising billboards. In 1920 she began appearing in extra and bit parts in films shot in the New York City vicinity. It was in one of these, *The Stealers,* that she was seen by Irving THALBERG, the future "boy wonder" of MGM. While still at Universal, Thalberg tried to track her down but wasn't able to locate her until 1923, when he was looking for star material for the Mayer company. She was signed on a long-term contract and by 1925 was playing leads in major films. However, her rise to top stardom did not start until 1927, the year she married Thalberg. From then on, she had her choice of films and directors and played many of the plum roles in the MGM repertoire.

Norma Shearer was hardly the most beautiful woman on the lot nor the best actress, but she had poise and elegance and, above all, a driving ambition and a thorough understanding of the nature of motion pictures. She wisely refrained from being typecast and with the help of her husband she achieved a varied balance of roles in both comedy and drama. She was nominated for Academy Awards five times (for *Their Own Desire, A Free Soul, The Barretts of Wimpole Street, Romeo and Juliet,* and *Marie Antoinette*) and won the Oscar for her performance in *The Divorcee* (1930). Billed by MGM as "The First Lady of the Screen," Miss Shearer retained her lofty position in the company after Thalberg's death in 1936. But in the absence of her mentor, she made errors of judgment that proved fatal to her career. She turned down the starring roles in *Gone With the Wind* and *Mrs. Miniver* and instead appeared in two successive flops, *We Were Dancing* and *Her Cardboard Lover.* After the release of the latter in 1942, she married a ski instructor 20 years her junior and retired from the screen.

FILMS: *The Flapper, The Restless Sex, Way Down East, The Stealers* 1920; *The Sign on the Door* 1921; *Channing of the Northwest, The Bootleggers, The Man Who Paid* 1922; *The Devil's Partner, A Clouded Name, The Wanters, Pleasure Mad, Lucretia Lombard, Man and Wife* 1923; *Broadway After Dark, Trail of the Law, Blue Waters, The Wolf Man, Empty Hands, Broken Barriers, He Who Gets Slapped, The Snob, Married Flirts* 1924; *Lady of the Night, Waking Up the Town, Pretty Ladies, A Slave of Fashion, Excuse Me, The Tower of Lies, His Secretary* 1925; *The Devil's Circus, The Waning Sex, Upstage* 1926; *The Demi-Bride, After Midnight, The Student Prince* 1927; *The Latest from Paris, The Actress, A Lady of Chance* 1928; *The Trial of Mary Dugan, The Last of Mrs. Cheyney, The Hollywood Revue of 1929, Their Own Desire* 1929; *The Divorcee, Let Us Be Gay* 1930; *The Stolen Jools* (comedy short), *Strangers May Kiss, A Free Soul, Private Lives* (as Amanda Prynne) 1931; *Strange Interlude* (as Nina Leeds), *Smilin' Through* 1932; *Riptide, The Barretts of Wimpole Street* (as Elizabeth Barrett) 1934; *Romeo and Juliet* (as Juliet) 1936; *Marie Antoinette* (title role) 1938; *Idiot's Delight, The Women* 1939; *Escape* 1940; *We Were Dancing, Her Cardboard Lover* 1942.

Sheedy, Ally. Actress. Born Alexandra Sheedy, on June 13,

1962, in New York City. *ed.* USC. Quirky brunette ingenue, then leading lady of the American screen. The daughter of Charlotte Sheedy, a well-known literary agent, she was a precocious child. She danced with the American Ballet Theater at six; published her first book, *She Was Nice to Mice,* at ten; and was writing book and movie reviews for the *New York Times* and *The Village Voice* at 12. Entering films at 20, she was among the brightest of the Hollywood "brat pack" of the mid-80s. Later in the decade, she overcame drug addiction and anorexia before resuming her career as a young adult.

FILMS: *Bad Boys, War Games* 1983, *The Breakfast Club, Oxford Blues* 1984; *St. Elmo's Fire, Twice in a Lifetime* 1985; *Blue City, Short Circuit* 1986; *Maid to Order* 1987; *Heart of Dixie* 1989; *Betsy's Wedding* 1990; *Only the Lonely* 1991; *Home Alone 2: Lost in New York* 1992; *The Pickle, Man's Best Friend, Tattle Tale* 1993; *One Night Stand* 1994.

Sheekman, Arthur. Screenwriter. *b.* Feb. 5, 1901, Chicago. *d.* 1978. *ed.* U. of Minnesota. A former columnist and drama critic, he entered films as screenwriter in the early 30s through his association with Marx Brothers radio broadcasts. He handled some drama but mostly comedy material, often in collaboration. An intimate friend of Groucho Marx, he collaborated on several of the comedian's books. He was married to actress Gloria STUART.

FILMS INCLUDE: *Monkey Business* (addnl. dial.) 1931; *Duck Soup* (addnl. dial.), *Roman Scandals* 1933; *Kid Millions* 1934; *Rose of the Rancho, Dimples, Pigskin Parade, Stowaway* 1936; *The Gladiator* 1938; *Wonder Man* (story only) 1945; *Blue Skies* 1946; *Blaze of Noon, Dear Ruth, Welcome Stranger* 1947; *Hazard, Saigon* 1948; *Dear Wife* 1949; *Mr. Music* 1950; *Young Man with Ideas* 1952; *Call Me Madam* 1953; *Bundle of Joy* 1956; *Some Came Running* 1958; *Ada* 1961.

Sheen, Charlie. Actor. Born Carlos Irwin Estevez, on Sept. 3, 1965, in Los Angeles. Athletic, wholesome leading man of Hollywood films. The son of actor Martin SHEEN, and younger brother of actor Emilio ESTEVEZ, he got his first taste of show business at age nine, as an extra in the TV movie *The Execution of Private Slovik* (1974), starring his father. He also appeared as an extra alongside his father in the feature *Apocalypse Now* (1979) but his true early ambition was to become a professional baseball player. Only after a poor attendance record at high school had prevented him from taking advantage of an athletic scholarship from the University of Kansas did he begin to consider acting seriously. He was among Hollywood's most popular and busiest young stars in the late 80s and early 90s. Sheen writes comically volatile poetry, a proposed book of which made the rounds in bootlegged versions in the early 90s. His work remains unpublished. He wrote, produced, and directed a 35 mm short, *R.P.G. II.*

FILMS: *Red Dawn* 1984; *The Boys Next Door* 1985; *Lucas, Ferris Bueller's Day Off, The Wraith, Platoon, Wisdom* 1986; *Three for the Road, No Man's Land, Wall Street* 1987; *Young Guns, Eight Men Out, Never on Tuesday* (cameo) 1988; *Major League, Courage Mountain, Tale of Two Sisters* (narrator only from own poetry) 1989; *Navy Seals, Men at Work, Cadence, The Rookie, Backtrack* 1990; *Hot Shots!* 1991; *Hot Shots Part: Deux!, The Three Musketeers* 1993; *The Chase, Major League II, Terminal Velocity* 1994; *All Dogs Go To Heaven* (v/o), *The Arrival* 1996; *Money Talks, The Shadow Conspiracy* 1997.

Sheen, Martin. Actor. Born Ramon Estevez, on Aug. 3, 1940, in Dayton, Ohio, to a Spanish immigrant father and Irish mother, the seventh child of a poor family of ten. Charismatic leading man of the American stage, screen, and television. Directly out of high school he went to New York, where he began his acting career at the off-off-Broadway Living Theatre, supplementing his income through such jobs as janitor, car washer, soda jerk, and messenger. His big chance came in 1964, when he played a leading part in the Broadway production of 'The Subject was Roses,' a role he later repeated in the 1968 screen version. He later appeared frequently on TV (the title role in 'The Execution of Private Slovik,' among other lead parts) and made his big screen debut in 1967 as one of two punks terrorizing subway passengers in *The Incident.* He has since played leads in many other films, notably a superlative performance as an alienated youth on a killing spree in Terrence Malick's *Badlands* (1973), a role for which he was named best actor at the San Sebastian (Spain) Film Festival. Surviving a heart attack during the grueling production of *Apocalypse Now* (1979), Sheen performed prolifically on TV as well as in feature films, appearing in numerous productions in leads and character roles. Having impersonated Robert Kennedy in the 1974 teleplay 'The Missiles of October,' he portrayed John F. Kennedy in the miniseries 'Kennedy' (1983). He was seen in numerous TV movies, among them *The Long Road Home* (1981), for which he received an Emmy. Following some experience in TV, Sheen made his debut as a feature director with *Cadence* (1990). An activist for various causes, he was arrested many times for participating in anti-nuke demonstrations. He is the father of screen stars Emilio ESTEVEZ and Charlie SHEEN. His son, Ramon, and daughter, Renée, are also actors, as is his own brother, Joe Phelan.

FILMS: *The Incident* 1967; *The Subject Was Roses* 1968; *Catch-22* 1970; *No Drums No Bugles, When the Line Goes Through* (unreleased) 1971; *The Forests Are Nearly All Gone Now* (unreleased), *Pickup on 101, Rage* 1972; *Badlands* 1973; *The Legend of Earl Durand* 1975; *The Cassandra Crossing, The Little Girl Who Lives Down the Lane* (Can.) 1977; *Eagle's Wing* (UK), *Apocalypse Now* 1979; *The Final Countdown, Loophole* (UK) 1980; *Gandhi* (UK), *That Championship Season, I'm the King of Prussia* 1982; *Enigma* (UK/Fr.), *Man Woman and Child, The Dead Zone* 1983; *Firestarter* 1984; *In the Name of the People* (doc.; narr. only), *Broken Rainbow* (doc.; narr. only) 1985; *A State of Emergency* 1986; *Dear America* (doc.; v/o), *The Believers, Siesta, Wall Street* 1987; *Da* (also co-exec. Prod.), *Judgment in Berlin* (also co-exec. prod.), *Walking After Midnight* (doc.; Can.) 1988; *Personal Choice/Beyond the Stars, Cold Front* (Can.), *Beverly Hills Brats* 1989; *Cadence* (also dir., co-sc.) 1990; *The Maid* (Fr.), *JFK* (narr.) 1991; *Gettysburg* 1993; *The American President, Dead Presidents* 1995; *Entertaining Angels, The War at Home* 1996; *Truth or Consequences, N.M., Spawn* 1997.

Sheffer, Craig. Actor. Born April 23, 1960, in York, Pa. *ed.* East Stroudsburg State College, Pa. Starting out on the stage, this strong, sincere actor got his break on Broadway starring in Harvey FIERSTEIN's 'Torch Song Trilogy.' After doing some television, he landed his first film role, *That Was Then, This Is Now* (1985), and worked steadily without much notice until Robert REDFORD cast him in *A River Runs Through It* (1992).

FILMS: *That Was Then This Is Now* 1985; *Fire with Fire* 1986; *Some Kind of Wonderful* 1987; *Split Decisions* 1988; *Babycakes* 1989; *Nightbreed* 1990; *Eye of the Storm* 1991; *A River Runs Through It* 1992; *Demolition Man* (also ex-prod.), *Fire in the Sky, The Program* 1993; *The Desperate Trail, Sleep with Me* 1994; *In Pursuit of Honor, Wings of Courage* 1995.

Sheffield, Johnny. Actor. Born on Apr. 11, 1931, in Pasadena, Calif. *ed.* UCLA. The son of child-star-turned-character-actor Reginald Sheffield (*b.* Reginald Sheffield Cassan, Feb. 18, 1901, London; *d.* 1957). After appearing at age seven in the original cast of Broadway's 'On Borrowed Time,' he was chosen by MGM to play Tarzan's foundling son, Boy, in the popular jungle films of the 40s. When he grew too old for the role of Johnny Weissmuller's son, he was given his own series, *Bomba the Jungle Boy,* but as he gained in years and size his film career came to an end in the mid-50s. Sheffield played occasional roles fully dressed, but it was in loincloth that he was the envy of every child in the world for more than a decade.

FILMS INCLUDE: *Tarzan Finds a Son, Babes in Arms* 1939; *Little Orvie, Lucky Cisco Kid* 1940; *Tarzan's Secret Treasure, Million Dollar Baby* 1941; *Tarzan's New York Adventure* 1942; *Tarzan Triumphs* 1943; *Tarzan and the Huntress* 1947; *Bomba the Jungle Boy* 1949; *The Lost Volcano* 1950; *The Lion Hunters* 1951; *Bomba and the Jungle Girl* 1952; *Safari Drums* 1953; *The Golden Idol* 1954; *Lord of the Jungle* 1955.

Shelby, Juliet. See MINTER, Mary Miles.

Sheldon, Sidney. Screenwriter, sometime director-producer. Born in 1917, in Chicago. In Hollywood initially as a $24-a-week reader for Universal, he won an Academy Award for the original screenplay of *The Bachelor and the Bobby Soxer* (1947). But most of his scripts were routine and his attempt at direction was unsuccessful. He also shared a Tony Award for the libretto of the Broadway musical 'Redhead' (1959). In the 70s he suddenly emerged as a successful glitz novelist. Three of his several best-sellers, *The Naked Face* (1970), *The Other Side of Midnight* (1974), and *Bloodline* (1977), were adapted to the screen.

FILMS INCLUDE (as screenwriter): *Mr. District Attorney in the Carter Case* 1941; *She's in the Army* 1942; *The Bachelor and the Bobby Soxer* 1947; *Easter Parade* 1948; *Nancy Goes to Rio, Annie Get Your Gun* 1950; *Rich Young and Pretty, Three Guys Named Mike* 1951; *Just This Once* 1952; *Dream Wife* (also dir., prod.), *Remains to Be Seen* 1953; *You're Never Too Young* 1955; *Anything Goes, The Birds and the Bees, Pardners* 1956; *The Buster Keaton Story* (also dir., prod.) 1957; *All in a Night's Work* 1961; *Jumbo* 1962; *The Other Side of Midnight* (novel basis only) 1977; *Sidney Sheldon's Bloodline* (novel basis only) 1979; *The Naked Face* (novel basis only) 1984.

Shelley, Barbara. Actress. Born Barbara Kowin, in 1933, in London. A former model, she began her film career in Italy in 1953. Beginning in the late 50s, she starred in many British films, mostly of the horror genre. She has also done much TV.

FILMS INCLUDE: *Mantrap/Woman in Hiding* 1953; *The Barefoot Contessa* 1954; *Luna nuova* 1955; *Mio Figlio Nerone/Nero's Mistress* 1956; *The Little Hut, Cat Girl* 1957; *The Camp on Blood Island, Blood of the Vampire* 1958; *Bobbykins* 1959; *Village of the Damned* 1960; *The Shadow of the Cat* 1961; *Postman's Knock, Death Trap* 1962; *Blind Corner/Man in the Dark, The Gorgon* 1964; *The Secret of Blood Island* 1965; *Dracula—Prince of Darkness, Rasputin—The Mad Monk* 1966; *Quatermass and the Pit/Five Million Years to Earth* 1967; *Ghost Story/Madhouse Mansion* 1974.

Shelton, Ron. Director, screenwriter. Born on Sept. 15, 1945, in Whittier, Calif. *ed.* Westmont Coll., Santa Barbara (English); U. of Arizona (sculpture). Before entering films in the early 80s he was a college basketball star, then a minor-league second baseman in the Baltimore Orioles' farm system during the late 60s and early 70s. Twenty-five and going nowhere, he gave up on his dream of big-time baseball after five frustrating years and moved back to Los Angeles. He cleaned bars and dressed store-window mannequins, among other odd jobs, while trying to make ends meet as a painter and sculptor. He then turned to screenwriting, eventually attracting the attention of director Roger SPOTTISWOODE. Shelton served as an associate producer on Spottiswoode's *The Pursuit of D. B. Cooper* (1981) and as a second-unit director on two films adapted from his scripts. He made his own auspicious debut as a director-writer with *Bull Durham* (1988), a witty, entertaining behind-the-scenes look at a minor-league baseball team, which earned him an Oscar nomination for best screenplay. He followed this with *Blaze* (1989), a bawdy peek at the love affair between governor of Louisiana Earl Long and Baltimore stripper Blaze Starr. The director then returned to his favorite world of sports with a basketball gem, *White Men Can't Jump* (1992). Shelton's wife, Lois, is a documentary filmmaker.

FILMS: As screenwriter—*Under Fire* (also 2nd-unit dir.) 1983; *The Best of Times* (also 2nd-unit dir.) 1986; *Blue Chips* (co-exec. prod. only) 1994. As director-screenwriter—*Bull Durham* 1988; *Blaze* 1989; *White Men Can't Jump* 1992; *Blue Chips* (also co-exec. prod.), *Cobb* 1994; *Tin Cup* (also co-sc.) 1996.

Shengelaya, Eldar. Director. Born on Jan. 26, 1933, in Tiflis, Georgia, the former USSR. The son of director Nikolai SHENGELAYA, he studied film at Moscow's All-Union State Institute of Cinematography, under Sergei YUTKEVICH. Early in his career, he experimented with co-director Alexei Sakharov on a novel approach to fairy tales, which he later developed on his own into a unique genre of realistic fantasy some Russians called "tragi-farce."

FILMS: *Legend of the Ice Heart* (co-dir.) 1957; *A Snow Fairy Tale* (co-dir.) 1959; *The White Caravan* (co-dir., co-sc.) 1964; *He Did Not Want to Kill/Mikela* 1967; *An Extraordinary Exhibition* 1968; *The Eccentrics, Samanishvili's Grandmother* (also co-sc.) 1974; *The Blue Mountains* (also co-sc.) 1983.

Shengelaya, Nikolai. Director. *b.* 1901, Tiflis, Georgia, USSR. *d.* 1943. A novelist and poet, he turned to films in the late 20s and became a leading force in Georgian production with a number of perceptive, original films. He was the father of Eldar SHENGELAYA.

FILMS: *Giulli* (co-dir.) 1927; *Elliso/Caucasian Love* 1928; *Twenty-Six Commissars* 1933; *Golden Valley* 1937; *Motherland* 1939; *He'll Come Back Again/In the Black Mountains* 1941.

Shepard, Sam. Playwright, actor, screenwriter, director. Born Samuel Shepard Rogers, on Nov. 5, 1943, in Fort Sheridan, Ill. *ed.* Mount St. Antonio Jr. Coll., Walnut, Calif. An "army brat," he was moved around as a child until the family eventually settled in Duarte, California. Showing an early interest in the theater, he joined a local church drama group, and later was appointed playwright-in-residence at the Magic Theatre in San Francisco. He then moved to New York, where he served tables at the Village Gate while starting a career off-off Broadway. He worked at experimental spots like La Mama, Cafe Cino, the Open Theatre, and the American Place Theatre, and in the late 60s began gaining increasing recognition as a playwright. His prolific output included several Obie Award–winning plays and a Pulitzer winner, 'Buried Child' (1979). Shepard has also written and directed for the screen but his main contribution to film was in the acting department. Tall and lanky, with cleft-chinned, blue-eyed, virile good looks, he made occasional screen appearances in the 70s and developed into an appealing leading man in the early 80s, when he appeared in such films as *Frances* (1982) and *The Right Stuff* (1983). He was nominated for an Academy Award for his portrayal of astronaut Chuck Yeager in the latter. He made a less than persuasive debut as a director with *Far North* (1988). Divorced from actress O-Lan Johnson Dark, Shepard shares a home with actress Jessica LANGE, the mother of two of his three children.

FILMS (as actor, unless otherwise noted): *Me and My Brother* (doc. drama; co-sc. only), *Brand X* 1969; *Zabriskie Point* (co-sc. only), *Bronco Bullfrog* (UK) 1970; *Oh Calcutta!*

(co-sc. only) 1972; *Renaldo and Clara, Days of Heaven* 1978; *Resurrection* 1980; *Raggedy Man* 1981; *Frances* 1982; *The Right Stuff* (as Col. Chuck Yeager) 1983; *Paris Texas* (sc. only, from his story 'Motel Chronicles'; Ger./Fr.), *Country* 1984; *Fool for Love* (also sc., from his own play) 1985; *Crimes of the Heart* 1986; *Baby Boom* 1987; *Far North* (dir., sc. only) 1988; *Steel Magnolias* 1989; *Bright Angel, Passagier Faber/Voyager* (Ger./Fr.) 1990; *Defenseless* 1991; *Thunderheart* 1992; *The Pelican Brief* 1993; *Silent Tongue* (dir., sc. only) 1994; *Safe Passage* 1994; *Curse of the Starving Class* 1995.

Shepherd, Cybill. Actress. Born on Feb. 18, 1949, in Memphis, Tenn. *ed.* Hunter Coll.; NYU; USC. Blonde, blue-eyed, seductive leading lady of American films and television. Winner of the Memphis Miss Teenage contest, she failed in her bid for the title of Miss Teenage America but went on to a successful modeling career in New York. She was discovered by Peter BOGDANOVICH, who cast her perfectly as the high school flirt in *The Last Picture Show* (1971). She later starred in several other of the director's films, but his infatuation with his protégée proved disadvantageous to both their careers. An industry outsider, Shepherd enjoyed a comeback on TV in the late 80s as the star of the hit series 'Moonlighting.' She returned to the big screen after a long absence in 1989 and in the following year appeared in *Texasville*, a disappointing sequel to *The Last Picture Show*. She is an outspoken proponent for women's rights, the pro-choice movement, vegetarianism (which got her canned from a commercial promoting beef consumption), and the right to bear arms. She is currently starring in the hit TV series 'Cybill.' Twice divorced, she is the mother of three.

FILMS: *The Last Picture Show* 1971; *The Heartbreak Kid* 1972; *Daisy Miller* 1974; *At Long Last Love* 1975; *Taxi Driver, Special Delivery* 1976; *Silver Bears* 1977; *The Lady Vanishes* (UK) 1979; *The Return/The Alien's Return* 1980; *Chances Are* 1989; *Texasville, Alice* 1990; *Married to It* 1991; *Once Upon A Crime* 1992.

Shepitko, Larissa. Director. *b.* 1939, in Armtervosk, Eastern Ukraine. *d.* 1979. At 16 she went to Moscow, where she enrolled at the VGIK state film school as a pupil of Alexander DOVZHENKO. After the director's death, in 1956, she assisted his widow, Yulia SOLNTSEVA, on the completion of *Poem of the Sea* (1958). In the early 60s Shepitko directed two student shorts and in 1963 turned out a remarkable diploma feature, *Heat* (1963). Critics praised the film's sharp imagery and the director's success in relating the characters to their arid environment. Shepitko was also hailed for her perseverance. The heat during filming at the film's Central Asian location was so intense that at one point the exhausted director had to be carried to the set on a stretcher. A beautiful woman, she was compared in looks and talent to Leni RIEFENSTAHL. Shepitko's reputation was further enhanced by *Wings* (1966) and *You and I* (1971), both noted for their bold treatment of issues concerning modern Soviet society. She reached the peak of her prestige with *The Ascent* (1977), a WW II film dealing with such moral issues as good versus evil and loyalty versus betrayal. The film earned her the Golden Bear at the Berlin Festival and a tentative offer to direct in the US. But in July of 1979, while returning from location scouting for a new film, she and four members of her crew were killed in a car crash near Moscow. The planned film, ironically titled *Farewell,* was completed by Shepitko's husband, director Elem KLIMOV, and released in 1981. The following year Klimov filmed a loving tribute to his departed wife, simply titled *Larissa.*

FILMS (as director-screenwriter): *The Blind Cook* (short) 1961; *Living Water* (short) 1962; *Heat* 1963; *Wings* 1966; *The Homeland of Electricity* (shot in 1967; completed in 1968 and shelved; released in 1987 as part of a two-short feature, *The Beginning of an Unknown Century*) 1968; *The Ascent* 1977; *Farewell* (script concept only; filmed posthumously by Elem Klimov) 1981.

Shepperd, John. See STRUDWICK, Shepperd.

Sher, Jack. Screenwriter, director. *b.* Mar. 16, 1913, Minneapolis. *d.* 1988. *ed.* U. of Minnesota. A former newspaper columnist and the writer of several books and many magazine articles, he began writing for the screen in the early 50s and occasionally also directed later in that decade. After a ten-year absence he returned to films in 1973 as a producer.

FILMS (as screenwriter): *My Favorite Spy* 1951; *Shane* (addnl. dial. only), *Off Limits, The Kid from Left Field* 1953; *World in My Corner, Walk the Proud Land* 1956; *Four Girls in Town* (also dir.), *Joe Butterfly* 1957; *Kathy O'* (also dir.) 1958; *The Wild and the Innocent* (also dir.) 1959; *The 3 Worlds of Gulliver* (also dir.) 1960; *Love in a Goldfish Bowl* (also dir.), *Paris Blues* 1961; *Critic's Choice, Move Over Darling* 1963; *Slither* (prod. only) 1973.

Sheridan, Ann. Actress. *b.* Clara Lou Sheridan, Feb. 21, 1915, Denton, Tex. *d.* 1967. *ed.* North Texas State Teachers Coll. The winner of a "Search for Beauty" contest in 1933, she won as her prize a bit part in a Paramount film by that title. She was then signed to a starlet's contract and given extra and bit roles in a rapid succession of other Paramount films, under her real name. In less than two years she appeared in more than 20 films in roles of little or no consequence. Her career began picking up in 1936 when she switched to Warners. The studio offered her better parts and launched a publicity campaign that billed her as the "Oomph Girl." She was well cast as a wise, down-to-earth gal in several social-crime melodramas of the late 30s, but it wasn't until *Kings Row* (1942) that she was able to prove real ability as an actress. She later had opportunities to exhibit her versatility in comedy and melodrama and to demonstrate a warm contralto in a couple of musicals. She remained a popular star throughout the 40s, but her film career began slipping early in the 50s and was over before the end of the decade. She appeared in some stock and was a regular in the NBC daytime soap opera 'Another World.' She was starring in the nighttime TV series 'Pistols and Petticoats' at the time of her death of cancer. All three of Miss Sheridan's husbands were actors, Edward NORRIS, George BRENT, and Scott McKay.

FILMS: As Clara Lou Sheridan—*Search for Beauty, Bolero, Come On Marines!, Murder at the Vanities, Kiss and Make Up, Shoot the Works, The Notorious Sophie Lang, Ladies Should Listen, Wagon Wheels, Mrs. Wiggs of the Cabbage Patch, College Rhythm, You Belong to Me, Ready for Love, Limehouse Blues, One Hour Late* 1934; *Enter Madame, Home on the Range, Rumba* 1935. As Ann Sheridan—*Behold My Wife, Car 99, Rocky Mountain Mystery, Mississippi, The Glass Key, The Crusades, Red Blood of Courage, Fighting Youth* 1935; *Sing Me a Love Song* 1936; *Black Legion, The Great O'Malley, San Quentin, Wine Women and Horses, The Footloose Heiress, Alcatraz Island* 1937; *She Loved a Fireman, The Patient in Room 18, Mystery House, Cowboy from Brooklyn, Little Miss Thoroughbred, Letter of Introduction, Broadway Musketeers, Angels with Dirty Faces* 1938; *They Made Me a Criminal, Dodge City, Naughty but Nice, Winter Carnival, Indianapolis Speedway, Angels Wash Their Faces* 1939; *Castle on the Hudson, It All Came True, Torrid Zone, They Drive by Night, City for Conquest* 1940; *Honeymoon for Three, Navy Blues* 1941; *The Man Who Came to Dinner, Kings Row* (as Randy Monaghan), *Juke Girl, Wings for the Eagle, George Washington Slept Here* 1942; *Edge of Darkness, Thank Your Lucky Stars* (cameo) 1943; *Shine On Harvest Moon, The Doughgirls* 1944;

One More Tomorrow 1946; *Nora Prentiss, The Unfaithful* 1947; *The Treasure of the Sierra Madre* (unbilled cameo as a streetwalker), *Silver River, Good Sam* 1948; *I Was a Male War Bride* 1949; *Stella, Woman on the Run* 1950; *Steel Town, Just Across the Street* 1952; *Take Me to Town, Appointment in Honduras* 1953; *Come Next Spring, The Opposite Sex* 1956; *Triangle on Safari/Woman and the Hunter* (UK) 1957.

Sheridan, Jim. Director. Born in 1949, in Dublin. Ireland. After graduating from University College, he followed in his father's footsteps and started a small theatrical company called Children's T. and ran the Project Art Centre, Dublin's main alternative theater. Traveling to New York, he served as artistic director of that city's Irish Arts Center and briefly attended the NYU film school. On returning to Ireland, he directed a remarkable first film, *My Left Foot* (1989), a sensitive, often humorous and refreshingly unsentimental adaptation of the autobiography by the late paralyzed writer-painter Christy Brown. Sheridan was nominated for an Academy Award for directing the film.

FILMS: *My Left Foot* (also co-sc.) 1989; *The Field* (also sc.) 1990; *Into the West* (sc. only), *In the Name of the Father* (also prod, co-sc.) 1993; *Some Mother's Son* (co-prod., co-sc.) 1996.

Sheriff, Paul. Art director. *b.* Paul Shouvalov, Nov. 13, 1903, Moscow. *d.* 1965. *ed.* Oxford; Camborne School of Mines. A former architect and mining engineer, he entered British films in the late 30s and under the tutelage of Lazare MEERSON developed into one of England's finest set designers.

FILMS INCLUDE: *Dark Journey* 1937; *French Without Tears* 1939; *Freedom Radio/The Voice in the Night, Quiet Wedding* 1940; *The First of the Few/Spitfire* 1942; *The Gentle Sex* 1943; *Henry V* 1944; *The Way to the Stars/Johnny in the Clouds* 1945; *School for Secrets/Secret Flight* 1946; *Vice Versa* 1947; *Adam and Evelyne/Adam and Evalyn* 1949; *The Black Rose* (UK/US) 1950; *The Crimson Pirate* (UK/US) 1952; *Moulin Rouge* (UK/US) 1953; *Gentlemen Marry Brunettes* (US) 1955; *The Doctor's Dilemma* 1959; *The Millionairess, The Grass Is Greener* 1960.

Sherin, Edwin. Director. Born on Jan. 15, 1930, in Harrisburg, Pa. *ed.* Brown. A noted Broadway director-actor, he turned briefly to films in the early 70s with interesting though unremarkable results.

FILMS: *Valdez Is Coming* 1971; *Glory Boy/My Old Man's Place* 1972.

Sherman, Gary A. American director with a taste for action and an interest in crime and the macabre. He has also directed some made-for-TV films.

FILMS: *Death Line/Raw Meat* 1973; *Phobia* (co-sc. only) 1980; *Dead and Buried* 1981; *Vice Squad* 1982; *Wanted Dead or Alive* (also co-sc.) 1987; *Poltergeist III* (also exec. prod., co-sc., sp. eff. design) 1988; *Lisa* (also co-sc.) 1990.

Sherman, George. Director. *b.* July 14, 1908, New York City. *d.* 1991. Entered films in the early 30s as an assistant director. From 1937 he directed scores of low-budget Westerns for Republic. These included many of "The Three Mesquiteers," starring John Wayne. In the mid-40s he graduated to medium-budget Westerns and other subjects at Columbia and later at Universal and other studios. A competent, prolific craftsman, he directed (and in many cases also produced) more than 100 films as well as some 250 segments of TV series. Sherman's last film, *Big Jake* (1971), provided a nostalgic reunion between the director and his erstwhile star, John Wayne.

FILMS: *Wild Horse Rodeo* 1937; *The Purple Vigilantes, Outlaws of Sonora, Riders of the Black Hills, Heroes of the Hills, Pals of the Saddle, Overland Stage Raiders, Rhythm of the Saddle, Sante Fe Stampede, Red River Range* 1938; *Mexicali Rose, The Night Riders, Three Texas Steers, Wyoming Outlaw, Colorado Sunset, New Frontier/Frontier Uprising, Cowboys from Texas, The Kansas Terrors, Rovin' Tumbleweeds, South of the Border* 1939; *Ghost Valley Raiders, Covered Wagon Days, Rocky Mountain Rangers, One Man's Law, The Tulsa Kid, Under Texas Skies, The Trail Blazers, Texas Terrors, Lone Star Raiders, Frontier Vengeance* (all also assoc. prod.) 1940; *Wyoming Wildcat, The Phantom Cowboy, Two-Gun Sheriff, Desert Bandit, Kansas Cyclone, The Apache Kid, Death Valley Outlaws, A Missouri Outlaw* (all also assoc. prod.), *Citadel of Crime* 1941; *Arizona Terrors, Stagecoach Express, Jesse James Jr., The Cyclone Kid, The Sombrero Kid, X Marks the Spot* (all also assoc. prod.) 1942; *London Blackout Murders, The Purple V* (also assoc. prod.), *The Mantrap* (also assoc. prod.), *The West Side Kid, A Scream in the Dark, Mystery Broadcast* (also assoc. prod.) 1943; *The Lady and the Monster, Storm Over Lisbon* (both also assoc. prod.) 1944; *The Crime Doctor's Courage* 1945; *The Bandit of Sherwood Forest* (co-dir. with Henry Levin), *Talk About a Lady, Renegades, The Gentleman Misbehaves, Personality Kid, Secret of the Whistler* 1946; *Last of the Redmen* 1947; *Relentless, Black Bart, River Lady, Feudin' Fussin' and a-Fightin', Larceny* 1948; *Red Canyon, Calamity Jane and Sam Bass* (also story), *Sword in the Desert, Yes Sir That's My Baby* 1949; *Comanche Territory, Spy Hunt, The Sleeping City* 1950; *Tomahawk, Target Unknown, The Golden Horde, The Raging Tide* 1951; *Steel Town, The Battle at Apache Pass, Back at the Front, Against All Flags* 1952; *Lone Hand, The Veils of Bagdad* 1953; *War Arrow, Border River, Johnny Dark, Dawn at Socorro* 1954; *Chief Crazy Horse, The Treasure of Pancho Villa, Count Three and Pray* 1955; *Comanche, Reprisal!* 1956; *The Hard Man* 1957; *The Last of the Fast Guns, Ten Days to Tulara* (also co-prod.), *Son of Robin Hood* (also prod.; UK) 1958; *The Flying Fontaines* 1959; *Hell Bent for Leather, For the Love of Mike* (also prod.), *The Enemy General, The Wizard of Bagdad* 1960; *The Fiercest Heart* (also prod.), *The Comancheros* (prod. only) 1961; *Panic Button* 1964; *Joaquin Murrieta/Murieta* (Sp.) 1965; *Smoky* 1966; *Hello Down There* (prod. only) 1969; *Big Jake* 1971; *Little Mo* (prod. only; orig. made for TV) 1978.

Sherman, Lowell. Actor, director. *b.* Oct. 11, 1885, San Francisco. *d.* 1934. A descendant of several generations of performers, he was an important Broadway actor before making his screen debut in D. W. Griffith's *Way Down East* (1920). He specialized in the portrayal of smooth lovers and lecherous villains in silent comedies and dramas of the 20s which treated sex rather openly, often via sophisticated double entendres. He was to rely on this mastery of bedroom humor and manners when he turned director as well as actor in talkies of the early 30s. He died during the production of *Becky Sharp* (1935). The film was re-shot from scratch by Rouben MAMOULIAN. Sherman married and divorced actresses Evelyn Booth, Pauline Garon, and Helene COSTELLO.

FILMS INCLUDE: As actor—*Way Down East, Yes or No* 1920; *The Gilded Lily, Molly O', What No Man Knows* 1921; *Grand Larceny, A Face in the Fog* 1922; *Bright Lights of Broadway* 1923; *The Masked Dancer, The Spitfire, The Truth About Women, Monsieur Beaucaire* (as King Louis XV) 1924; *Satan in Sables* 1925; *The Love Toy, The Wilderness Woman, You Never Know Women, Lost at Sea* 1926; *Convoy, The Girl from Gay Paree* 1927; *The Divine Woman, The Whip Woman, The Heart of a Follies Girl, The Garden of Eden, The Mad Hour, The Whip, A Lady of Chance* 1928; *Evidence, General Crack* 1929; *Mammy, He Knew Women, Ladies of Leisure, Midnight Mystery, Oh Sailor Behave!* 1930; *What Price Hollywood* 1932. As director (complete)—*Lawful Larceny* (also act.), *The Pay-*

Off (also act.) 1930; *The Royal Bed* (also act.), *Bachelor Apartment* (also act.), *High Stakes* (also act.) 1931; *The Greeks Had a Word for Them* (also act.), *False Faces* (also act.), *Ladies of the Jury* 1932; *She Done Him Wrong, Morning Glory, Broadway Thru a Keyhole* 1933; *Born to Be Bad* 1934; *Night Life of the Gods* 1935.

Sherman, Richard M. (*b.* June 12, 1928, New York City) and **Robert B.** (*b.* Dec. 19, 1925, New York City). Brother songwriting team. Both were educated at Bard College and after making a name for themselves as a pop composer-lyricist team were hired by Walt Disney studios, for which they wrote many popular songs in the 60s, including the Oscar-winning "Chim Chim Cher-ee" for the film *Mary Poppins.* Freelancing in the early 70s, they began collaborating on screenplays as well as on the music and lyrics of kiddie-market films.

FILMS INCLUDE: *Nightmare* (Richard only) 1956; *The Absent-Minded Professor, The Parent Trap* 1961; *Moon Pilot, Bon Voyage* 1962; *Miracle of the White Stallions, Summer Magic* 1963; *Mary Poppins, Those Calloways* 1964; *That Darn Cat* 1965; *Monkeys Go Home!, The Jungle Book, The Happiest Millionaire* 1967; *The One and Only Genuine Original Family Band, Chitty Chitty Bang Bang* 1968; *The Aristocats, Bedknobs and Broomsticks* 1971; *Snoopy Come Home* 1972; *Charlotte's Web, Tom Sawyer* (also sc.) 1973; *Huckleberry Finn* (also sc.) 1974; *The Slipper and the Rose* (also sc.; UK) 1976.

Sherman, Vincent. Director. Born on July 16, 1906, in Vienna, Ga. *ed.* Oglethorpe U. (Atlanta). Formerly on the stage, he entered films as an actor in 1933, appearing in such productions as 'Counsellor-at-Law' (1933), 'One is Guilty,' and 'Midnight Alibi' (both 1934). Later in the 30s he turned screenwriter, collaborating on such films as *Crime School* (1938) and *King of the Underworld* (1939). A director from 1939, he worked mainly for Warners, establishing a reputation as a highly competent technician with a taste for melodrama. After three decades as a feature director, he turned to TV movies in the 70s.

FILMS: *The Return of Dr. X* 1939; *Saturday's Children, The Man Who Talked Too Much* 1940; *Flight from Destiny, Underground* 1941; *All Through The Night, The Hard Way* 1942; *Old Acquaintance* 1943; *In Our Time, Mr. Skeffington* 1944; *Pillow to Post* 1945; *Janie Gets Married* 1946; *Nora Prentiss, The Unfaithful* 1947; *The Adventures of Don Juan* 1949; *The Hasty Heart* (UK), *The Damned Don't Cry, Harriet Craig, Backfire* 1950; *Goodbye My Fancy* 1951; *Lone Star, Affair in Trinidad* 1952; *Difendo il mio Amore* (It.) 1956; *The Garment Jungle* 1957; *The Naked Earth* 1958; *The Young Philadelphians* 1959; *Ice Palace* 1960; *A Fever in the Blood, The Second Time Around* 1961; *Cervantes/The Young Rebel* (Sp./It./Fr.) 1968.

Sheriff, R(obert) C(edric). Playwright, novelist, screenwriter. *b.* June 6, 1896, Kingston-on-Thames, England. *d.* 1975. *ed.* Oxford. He began as an insurance clerk and turned to writing after returning from WW I service as an infantry captain. He wrote many plays (notably the classic 'Journey's End'), some of which have been adapted to the screen, and a number of novels. From the early 30s he also wrote memorable screenplays, alone and in collaboration. Autobiography: *No Leading Lady* (1968).

FILMS: In the US—*Journey's End* (play basis only) 1930; *The Old Dark House* (addnl. dial. only) 1932; *The Invisible Man* 1933; *One More River* 1934; *The Road Back* 1937; *Four Feathers* (UK), *Goodbye Mr. Chips* (UK/US) 1939; *That Hamilton Woman* 1941; *This Above All, Stand By for Action* (co-story only) 1942; *Forever and a Day* 1943. In the UK—*Odd Man Out* 1947; *Quartet* 1948; *Trio* 1950; *No Highway/No Highway in the Sky, Home at Seven/Murder on Monday* (play basis only) 1951; *The Dam Busters* 1954; *The Night My Number Came Up, Storm Over the Nile* (remake of *Four Feathers*) 1955.

Sherwood, Bill. Director. *b.* 1952, Washington, D.C. *d.* 1990. Raised in Battle Creek, Mich., he studied art in Interlochen, music composition at Juilliard, and film at Hunter College and USC. He made a few shorts and wrote several unproduced scripts before directing an impressive first feature, *Parting Glances* (1986), an incisive drama about gay life in the shadow of AIDS. It was also to be his last film. At age 37 he died of the disease.

Sherwood, Robert E(mmet). Playwright, screenwriter. *b.* Apr. 4, 1896, New Rochelle, N.Y. *d.* 1955. *ed.* Harvard. The noted Pulitzer Prize–winning (several times) dramatist was associated with the cinema in more ways than one. During his early career as editor and journalist, he was motion picture editor and critic for the old *Life* Magazine and the New York *Herald.* Many of his plays were adapted to the screen by others, and he also wrote original stories, adaptations, and screenplays directly for films, alone and in collaboration. He won an Academy Award for the screenplay of *The Best Years of Our Lives.*

FILMS: Based on his plays—*Oh What a Nurse!* 1926; *The Private Life of Helen of Troy* (partly based on his 'Road to Rome') 1927; *The Royal Bed* (from 'The Queen's Husband'), *Le Roi s'ennuie* (French-language version of preceding), *Waterloo Bridge* 1931: *Two Kinds of Women* (from 'This Is New York') 1932; *Reunion in Vienna* 1933; *The Petrified Forest* 1936; *Tovarich* (from his Broadway adaptation) 1937; *Waterloo Bridge* 1940; *Escape in the Desert* (from 'The Petrified Forest') 1945; *Jupiter's Darling* (from 'Road to Rome') 1955; *Gaby* (from 'Waterloo Bridge') 1956. As screenwriter—*The Lucky Lady* (co-sc.) 1926; *Cock of the Air* (co-story, co-sc.) 1932; *Roman Scandals* (co-story) 1933; *The Scarlet Pimpernel* (co-sc.; UK), *The Ghost Goes West* (sc.; UK) 1935; *Thunder in the City* (co-story, co-sc.; UK) 1937; *The Divorce of Lady X* (co-sc.; UK), *The Adventures of Marco Polo* (sc.) 1938; *Idiot's Delight* (sc. from own play), *Over the Moon* (co-story; UK) 1939; *Abe Lincoln in Illinois* (sc. from own play), *Rebecca* (co-sc.) 1940; *The Best Years of Our Lives* (sc.) 1946; *The Bishop's Wife* (co-sc.) 1947; *Man on a Tightrope* (sc.), *Main Street to Broadway* (story) 1953.

Shields, Brooke. Actress. Born on May 1, 1965, in New York City. Exquisitely beautiful young star of Hollywood films. The daughter of a socially prominent cosmetics executive and his ex-model wife (and granddaughter of tennis champion of the 30s, Francis X. Shields, and an Italian princess), she began a modeling career a day short of her second birthday, as an Ivory Soap baby. Driven by her divorced mother, she enjoyed a lucrative career as a child model, decorating advertisements for toothpaste, shampoo, and other products. In 1978 she stunned movie audiences with her seductive performance in the role of a 12-year-old prostitute in Louis Malle's American film *Pretty Baby.* She went on to play a sensual nymphet in several mediocre films, including the box-office hit *The Blue Lagoon* (1980), and in the early 80s earned a fortune appearing in suggestive Calvin Klein jeans commercials ('Nothing comes between me and my Calvins'). She then took a leave of absence from show business to pursue a B.A. degree in French literature at Princeton. Always an advocate of clean living and a vocal believer in the importance of virginity, Shields penned the wholesome *On Your Own* (1985) for kids about to go off to college. After graduating, she returned to the screen in the late 80s in adult roles, and in the mid-90s, made the transition to the small screen, starring in the well-received sitcom 'Suddenly Susan.'

FILMS: *Communion/Alice Sweet Alice/Holy Terror* 1977; *Pretty Baby, King of the Gypsies* 1978; *Tilt, Wanda Nevada, Just You and Me Kid* 1979; *The Blue Lagoon* 1980; *Endless Love* 1981; *Sahara, The Muppets Take Manhattan* (cameo) 1984;

Young Guns (cameo) 1988; *Brenda Starr* (viewing delayed from 1987; US release 1992), *Speed Zone* 1989; *Backstreet Dreams* 1990; *An American Love* (It.) 1992; *Freaked* 1993; *Born Wild, The Seventh Floor* 1994.

Shigeta, James. Actor. Born in 1933, in Hawaii. He played an assortment of Oriental roles in Hollywood films of the 60s, in a leading as well as a supporting capacity.

FILMS INCLUDE: *The Crimson Kimono* 1959; *Walk Like a Dragon* 1960; *Cry for Happy, Bridge to the Sun, Flower Drum Song* 1961; *Paradise Hawaiian Style* 1966; *Nobody's Perfect* 1968; *Lost Horizon* 1973; *The Yakuza* 1975; *Midway* 1976; *Die Hard* 1988; *Cage* 1989; *China Cry* 1990.

Shimkus, Joanna. See POITIER, Sidney.

Shimura, Takashi. Actor. *b.* Mar. 12, 1905, Hyogo, Japan. *d.* 1982. A former stage actor, he was one of the leading character players of the Japanese cinema, appearing frequently in the films of Kurosawa. He is best remembered by Western audiences for his lead role in *Ikiru/Living,* as the woodcutter in *Rashomon,* and as the Samurai leader in *Seven Samurai/The Magnificent Seven,* a rousing epic that was later remade in Hollywood under the title *The Magnificent Seven.*

FILMS INCLUDE: *Chuji Uridasu* 1935; *Osaka Elegy* 1936; *Jigoku no Mushi* 1938; *The Last Days of Edo* 1941; *Judo Saga I* 1943; *The Most Beautiful* 1944; *The Men Who Tread on the Tiger's Tail* 1945; *No Regrets for Our Youth* 1946; *Snow Trail* 1947; *Drunken Angel* 1948; *The Quiet Duel, Stray Dog* 1949; *Scandal, Rashomon* 1950; *The Idiot* (Jap./USSR), *Stolen Love* 1951; *Life of Oharu, Ikiru/Living* 1952; *Eagle of the Pacific* 1953; *Godzilla, Seven Samurai/The Magnificent Seven* 1954; *Last Embrace, No Time for Tears, Record of a Living Being/I Live in Fear* 1955; *I Saw the Killer* 1956; *Throne of Blood, The Mysterians* 1957; *The Hidden Fortress* 1958; *Samurai Saga, Saga of the Vagabonds* 1959; *I Bombed Pearl Harbor, Man Against Man, The Bad Sleep Well* 1960; *Yojimbo* 1961; *Sanjuro, Gorath* 1962; *High and Low* 1963; *Kwaidan, Hoichi the Earless* 1964; *Red Beard* 1965; *Frankenstein Conquers the World* (Jap./US) 1966; *The Emperor and the General* 1967; *The Day the Sun Rose* 1968; *Samurai Banners* 1969; *Zatiochi's Conspiracy* 1973; *Ogin Saga/Love and Faith of Ogin* 1979.

Shindo, Kaneto. Director, screenwriter. Born on Apr. 28, 1912, in Hiroshima, Japan. The son of a farmer, he entered films in 1934 as assistant art director, graduating to art director by the late 30s. In the mid-40s he began the second phase of his career, as a screenwriter, collaborating regularly on the films of Kimibasuro YOSHIMURA but also working for Mizoguchi, Ichikawa, and other leading Japanese directors. In 1950 he established his own company, in partnership with Yoshimura and actress Nobuko Otowa (*b.* Oct. 1, 1924, Osaka), who became Shindo's regular star. The following year he made his debut as director with *The Story of a Beloved Wife,* an autobiographical chronicle of his late spouse, who had died in 1940. He became internationally known in 1952 with *Children of Hiroshima,* an anguished account of the aftermath of the atomic bombardment of his native city. This film has been praised for its idealism and pictorial quality but criticized for its overbearing sentimentality, a critical assessment that has since been shared by several other Shindo films. In 1960, Shindo created a masterpiece, *The Island,* a grim, unadorned account of the barren life of an isolated farmer's family that contained a memorable performance by Otowa. Not a word is spoken throughout the film, as if to suggest that actions and not words best express the existence of man. The film won first prize at the 1960 Moscow Film Festival. Shindo went on to score another international success with *Onibaba/The Demon/The Hole* (1964), a striking period piece about human cruelty and capacity for survival that has been hailed for its great visual beauty and powerful dramatic force. These themes, as well as a growing preoccupation with human sexuality as a life force, characterized several of the director's subsequent films. A prolific screenwriter, Shindo wrote more than 200 scripts for other directors, as well as for his own films.

FILMS (as director-screenwriter): *The Story of a Beloved Wife* 1951; *Avalanche, Children of Hiroshima/Children of the Atom Bomb* 1952; *Epitome, A Woman's Life* 1953; *Gutter* 1954; *Wolves* 1955; *A Geisha's Suicide, The Fishing Boat* 1956; *Harbor Rats* 1957; *Only Women Have Trouble* 1958; *The Lucky Dragon No. 5, The Bride from Japan* 1959; *The Island* 1961; *The Man* 1962; *Mother* 1963; *Onibaba/The Demon/The Hole* 1964; *Conquest* 1965; *Lost Sex* 1966; *Libido/The Origin of Sex* 1967; *Kuroneko/Black Cat* 1967; *Operation Negligee* 1968; *Strange Affinity, Heat Wave Island* 1969; *Live Today—Die Tomorrow* 1971; *The Life of a Film Director* (doc. on Kenji Mizoguchi), *My Way* 1975; *Chikuzan Travels Alone/The Life of Chikuzan* 1977; *Hokusai—Ukiyo-e Master* 1982; *The Horizon* 1984; *Bokudo Kidan/The Strange Story of Oyuki, Tooki Rakujitsu/Faraway Sunset* 1993.

Shinoda, Masahiro. Director. Born on Mar. 9, 1931, in Gifu, Japan. An outstanding representative of the "new wave" of postwar Japanese cinema. An engineer's son, he had planned for a career in science, but instead majored in literature and drama at Tokyo's Waseda University, where he excelled in sports, soon becoming a regional middle-distance running champion. Shortly after graduation he joined the Sochiku-ofuna studios in 1953 as an assistant-director trainee and before long developed a reputation as one of the best in the business. After winning a prize for a screenplay, he was given the chance to direct his first feature, *One-Way Ticket for Love* (1960). Shinoda's early films typically dealt with the world of Japan's youth, often focusing on the cultural generation gap. His first noteworthy production was *Pale Flower* (1964), a psychologically insightful look at Yokohama's crime gangs, which served as a prototype for a wave of *yakura* (gangster) dramas that followed in the 60s. Like many of Shinoda's subsequent films, *Pale Flower* was noted for its striking imagery, sparse dialogue, and pessimistic preoccupation with social pathology. The director's nearly nihilistic view of aspects of Japanese life and custom sharpened after he began producing his films independently for his own company, Hyogensha, in 1967. Sex, violence, and fatalistic despair were typical ingredients in *Clouds at Sunset* (1967), *Double Suicide* (1969), *The Ballad of Orin* (1977), among other of his films. Shinoda married one of his frequent stars, Shima IWASHITA.

FILMS: *One-way Ticket for Love, Dry Lake/Youth in Fury* 1960; *Killers on Parade/My Face Red in the Sunset, Epitaph to My Love, Love Old and New/Shamisen and Motorcycle* 1961; *Our Marriage, Glory on the Summit/Burning Youth, Tears on the Lion's Mane* 1962; *Pale Flower, Assassination/The Assassin* 1964; *With Beauty and Sorrow, Samurai Spy/Sarutobi* 1965; *Punishment Island/Captive's Island* 1966; *Clouds at Sunset* 1967; *Double Suicide* 1969; *Buraikan/The Scandalous Adventures of Buraikan/Outlaws* 1970; *Silence* 1971; *Sapporo Winter Olympics* (doc.) 1972; *The Petrified Forest* 1973; *Himiko* 1974; *Under the Fall of the Cherry Blossoms* 1975; *Nihonmaru Ship* (doc.), *Sado's Ondeko-Za* (doc.) 1976; *The Ballad of Orin/Orin a Blind Woman/Melody in Gray/Banished* 1977; *Demon Pond* 1979; *Devil's Island/Island of Evil Spirits* 1981; *MacArthur's Children* 1984; *Gonza the Spearman* 1986; *Die Tänzerin/The Dancer* (Ger./Jap.), *Takeshi* 1990.

Shire, David. Composer. Born on July 3, 1937, in Buffalo, N.Y. *ed.* Yale. A versatile, prolific musician, he composed scores and songs for the stage and TV as well as for films. He won an Academy Award for the song 'It Goes Like It Goes' from his score for *Norma Rae* (1979). Divorced from Talia SHIRE, he married actress Didi Conn.

FILMS INCLUDE: *One More Train to Rob, Drive He Said, Skin Game* 1971; *To Find a Man* 1972; *Steelyard Blues* (adapt.), *Class of '44* 1973; *The Conversation, The Taking of Pelham 123* 1974; *Farewell My Lovely, The Hindenberg* 1975; *All the President's Men, The Big Bus* 1976; *Saturday Night Fever* 1977; *Straight Time* 1978; *Fast Break, Norma Rae* 1979; *Only When I Laugh* 1981; *The World According to Garp* 1982; *Max Dugan Returns* 1983; *2010* 1984; *Return to Oz* 1985; *Short Circuit, 'Night Mother* 1986; *Backfire* 1987; *Monkey Shines, Vice Versa* 1988; *Bed and Breakfast* 1991; *One Night Stand* 1994.

Shire, Talia. Actress. Born Talia Rose Coppola, on Apr. 25, 1946, in Lake Success, N.Y. The younger sister of director Francis Ford COPPOLA, she attended the Yale School of Drama and appeared in several minor Roger Corman films under her maiden name before getting her first big break in her brother's *The Godfather* (1972). She was nominated for an Academy Award and won the New York Film Critics Award for her performance in that film's sequel, *The Godfather Part II* (1974), in the role of Connie Corleone, Al Pacino's sluttish sister. She gave another memorable performance in *Rocky* (1976), in the role of the film hero's shy, plain girlfriend. Divorced from composer David SHIRE, she married producer Jack Schwartzman, with whom she began producing films under the banner TaliaFilm II.

FILMS: *The Wild Racers* 1968; *The Dunwich Horror, Gas-s-s-s...* 1970; *Un Homme est Mort/The Outside Man* (Fr./It.), *The Godfather* 1972; *The Godfather Part II* 1974; *Rocky* 1976; *Old Boyfriends, Rocky II, Prophecy* 1979; *Windows* 1980; *Rocky III* 1982; *Rocky IV* 1985; *Rad, Hyper Sapien/From Another Star* (also exec. prod.) 1986; *Lionheart* (co-prod. only) 1987; *New York Stories* ("Life Without Zoe" episode) 1989; *Rocky V, The Godfather Part III* 1990; *Bed and Breakfast* 1991; *Cold Heaven* 1992; *Dead Fall* 1993; *One Night Stand* (dir. only) 1994.

Shirley, Anne. Actress. *b.* Dawn Evelyeen Paris, Apr. 17, 1918, New York City. *d.* 1993. In Hollywood films from age five as Dawn O'Day, she changed her name to Anne Shirley in 1934 when she was assigned the title part in *Anne of Green Gables,* and continued her screen career as an ingenue (memorably in *Stella Dallas,* for which she was nominated for an Oscar as best supporting player in 1937) and later as a leading lady. She retired in 1945, after marrying her second husband, producer Adrian SCOTT, one of the HOLLYWOOD TEN. Shortly after their 1948 divorce she married screenwriter Charles LEDERER. Their marriage lasted from 1949 till his death in 1976. Her first husband was actor John PAYNE.

FILMS INCLUDE: As Dawn O'Day—*Moonshine Valley* 1922; *The Spanish Dancer* 1923; *The Fast Set* 1924; *Riders of the Purple Sage* 1925; *The Callahans and the Murphys, Night Life* 1927; *Mother Knows Best, Sins of the Fathers* 1928; *Four Devils* 1929; *City Girl, Liliom* 1930; *Emma, Young America, So Big, Three on a Match, Rasputin and the Empress* (as Anastasia) 1932; *The Life of Jimmy Dolan* 1933. As Anne Shirley—*Anne of Green Gables* (title role) 1934; *Steamboat 'Round the Bend, Chasing Yesterday* 1935; *Chatterbox, M'liss, Make Way for a Lady* 1936; *Too Many Wives, Stella Dallas* 1937; *Law of the Underworld, Mother Carey's Chickens, A Man to Remember, Girls' School* 1938; *Sorority House, Career* 1939; *Vigil in the Night, Saturday's Children, Anne of Windy Poplars* 1940; *West Point Widow, Unexpected Uncle, All That Money Can Buy* 1941; *Mayor of 44th Street, The Powers Girl* 1942; *Lady Bodyguard, Bombardier, Government Girl* 1943; *Man from Frisco, Music in Manhattan, Murder My Sweet/Farewell My Lovely* 1944.

Sholder, Jack. Director. Born on June 8, 1945, in Philadelphia. An electrician's son, he studied chemical engineering at the Drexel Institute of Technology, literature at Antioch College, and English and philosophy at Edinburgh University in Scotland. He began making 16 mm shorts while still at school. After graduation he moved to New York, where he turned out several prize-winning short subjects, notably *The Garden Party* (1973). He also worked as an editor on the documentary feature *King: A Film Record... Montgomery to Memphis* (1970, uncredited) and *The Burning* (1981). A director since the early 80s, he worked mostly with minuscule budgets, yet demonstrated uncommon skill in orchestrating action and sustaining suspense while making his films look more expensive. He won the Grand Prize at the 1988 Avoriaz Festival of Fantasy Films for *The Hidden* (1987).

FEATURE FILMS: *Alone in the Dark* (also sc.) 1982; *A Nightmare on Elm Street Part 2: Freddy's Revenge* 1985; *Where Are the Children?* (sc. only) 1986; *The Hidden* 1987; *Renegades* 1989.

shoot. To photograph a shot, a scene, a sequence, or an entire film with a motion picture camera.

shooting company. The crew working on a particular motion picture.

shooting outline. A sketchily written list of actions and objects to be photographed when a shooting script is not available. Rarely used in the making of feature films, it is quite common with documentaries, when a camera crew may be sent out to cover an event whose outcome cannot be anticipated in detail.

shooting ratio. The ratio of the length of raw film exposed in shooting to the footage actually used in the completed motion picture. A 5:1 ratio is considered economical; a 15:1 ratio outrageously wasteful.

shooting schedule. An advance schedule for work assignments and equipment needed for a filming session. See BREAKDOWN.

shooting script. The approved final screenplay, with full dialogue and detailed camera setups and other instructions, which is used by the director in the production of a film.

Shore, Dinah. Singer, actress. *b.* Frances Rose Shore, Mar. 1, 1917, Winchester, Tenn. *d.* 1994. *ed.* Vanderbilt U. A singing star on radio from the late 30s, she made an unsuccessful bid as a movie star in Hollywood films of the 40s but later enjoyed great popularity on TV. Her first marriage was to actor George MONTGOMERY.

FILMS: *Thank Your Lucky Stars* 1943; *Up in Arms, Follow the Boys, Belle of the Yukon* 1944; *Make Mine Music* (v/o), *Till the Clouds Roll By* 1946; *Fun and Fancy Free* 1947; *Aaron Slick from Punkin Crick* 1952; *Oh God!* (cameo, as herself) 1977; *Health* 1979.

Shore, Howard. Composer. Born in 1947, in Canada. He was the music director of TV's 'Saturday Night Live' before taking on movie scoring full time in 1980. Starting with low-budget films, he gradually advanced to major productions.

FILMS INCLUDE: *I Miss You Hugs and Kisses* 1978; *The Brood* 1979; *Scanners* 1981; *Videodrome* 1983; *Places in the Heart* 1984; *After Hours* 1985; *The Fly* 1986; *Nadine* 1987; *Big, Dead Ringers* 1988; *She-Devil* 1989; *Quick Change* (addnl. music only), *Postcards from the Edge* (superv. mus. numbers only) 1990; *The Silence of the Lambs, A Kiss Before Dying, Naked Lunch* 1991; *Philadelphia* 1993; *Ed Wood* 1994.

Shore, Pauly. Actor, comedian. Born February 1, 1968, in Hollywood. Following in the footsteps of his parents, both comedians who own the famed Comedy Store in Los Angeles, he spent time as a "vj" on MTV, then hosted his own show until his feature film career took off with the comedies *Encino Man*

(1992) and *Jury Duty* (1995). His goofy, popular characterizations have become his trademark.

FILMS: *For Keeps* 1988; *Class Act*, *Encino Man* 1992; *Son in Law* 1993; *In the Army Now* 1994; *Jury Duty* 1995; *Bio-Dome* 1996.

Short, Martin. Actor. Born on Mar. 26, 1950, in Hamilton, Ont., Canada. Diminutive funnyman of American TV and films. The son of an Irish-born steel executive and his concert-violinist wife, he began performing at McMaster University, where he majored in social work. After graduation he moved to Toronto, where he began his professional career in 1972, in a production of 'Godspell.' In 1977 he joined the Second City improvisation troupe and later performed with other members on SCTV. He made his first film appearance in 1979 but he scored his first success on TV as a zany participant in the 1984 season of 'Saturday Night Live.' He returned to the big screen in 1986, by then a popular comedian. His film successes have been modest in recent years. He made his Broadway debut in the musical version of 'The Goodbye Girl' in 1993.

FILMS: *Lost and Found, The Outsider* 1979; *Three Amigos* 1986; *Innerspace, Cross My Heart* 1987; *Three Fugitives, The Big Picture* 1989; *Pure Luck* 1991; *Father of the Bride* 1992; *Captain Ron* 1992; *Clifford* 1994; *Father of the Bride II, The Pebble and the Penguin* (v/o) 1995; *Mars Attacks!* 1996; *A Simple Wish, Jungle 2 Jungle* 1997.

short subject (also **short**). A film whose duration is relatively short. Generally, the term is applied to films of three reels or less and the total running time does not exceed 30 minutes. Early motion pictures were all short subjects, running anywhere from one to several minutes. Sometime during the first decade of this century, the length of the average subject was standardized to one reel, or about ten minutes of running time. Gradually, producers extended the length of their more-important productions to two and even three reels, but the one-reel film remained the standard for quite some time. The international success of such longer European films as *Queen Elizabeth* (1912) and *Cabiria* (1913) prompted a trend toward feature-length films in America. A pacesetter in that trend was D. W. Griffith with *Judith of Bethulia* (1913), *The Birth of a Nation* (1915), and *Intolerance* (1916).

By the end of WW I, the feature film had largely replaced shorts in motion picture theater programs, with the short subject relegated to the status of an added attraction. For a while the great comedians of the American screen continued to work in the short format, but by the mid-20s they too had moved on to features. As an added attraction on the cinema program, shorts of many genres—comedies, dramas, cartoons, newsreels, etc.—continued to be popular until the mid-40s, when they began being gradually phased out in favor of a double-feature program.

The major Hollywood studios used their short-subject departments as training and testing grounds for directors, actors, and other film personnel, as well as for testing such technological advances as color and sound. On the fringes of commercial cinema, amateur and semiprofessional filmmakers used the relatively inexpensive format for experimentation or as a means of breaking through the barriers of the industry. By the early 50s, the short subject had all but disappeared from the program at motion picture theaters. But the short subject has remained the principal tool of the documentarian, the animator, the makers of educational, scientific, and promotional film, and the avant-garde filmmaker experimenting with the medium.

Shostakovich, Dmitri. Composer. *b.* Sept. 25, 1906, St. Petersburg (now Leningrad), Russia. *d.* 1975. The celebrated Soviet composer who created some of the most striking orchestral works in this century despite a cultural straitjacket imposed on him by political commissars, he began his career as a piano accompanist for silent films. In addition to composing symphonies, concertos, chamber music, piano pieces, operas, oratorios, and ballets, he wrote many memorable scores for Soviet films. He saw the role of a film score as ideally being an integral part of the total concept of the film. His music was used in the background of many films posthumously.

FILMS INCLUDE: *The New Babylon* 1929; *Golden Mountains, Alone* 1931; *Counterplan* 1932; *The Youth of Maxim* 1935; *The Return of Maxim* 1937; *The Vyborg Side/New Horizons* 1939; *Zoya* 1944; *The Young Guard* 1947; *Life in Bloom, The Fall of Berlin* 1949; *The First Echelon* 1957; *Khovanschina* 1959; *Song Over Moscow* 1963; *Hamlet* 1964; *Katerina Izmailova* (also sc.) 1967; *King Lear* 1971.

shot. A single continuous TAKE, filmed in a single session from one camera setup. The basic grammatical unit of the language of film, a shot may range from a single frame taken from a fixed position to a setup involving complex camera movement. See also SCENE, SEQUENCE.

Showscan. A high-speed cinematographic process that captures unusually vivid images, creating an illusion of depth without the use of special 3-D glasses by viewing audiences. Invented by Douglas TRUMBULL, the process requires 70 mm film to be shot and projected at 60 frames per second, two and a half times the normal rate of 24 frames per second. A special wall-to-wall, extremely bright curved screen is essential for an effective projection.

shrinkage. The reduction in the dimensions of motion picture film resulting from loss of moisture during drying, processing, or storage. Shrinkage may cause a film print to tear during projection or it may produce poor picture quality on the screen.

Shub, Esther. Film editor, compilation specialist. *b.* Mar. 3, 1894, Chernigovsky District, Ukraine. *d.* 1959. A friend of Mayakovsky and Eisenstein, she was hired by the fledgling Soviet film industry in 1922 to re-cut and re-title foreign films (including American serials) and make them "suitable" for viewing by Soviet audiences. She soon became a very skillful editor. Inspired by Eisenstein's successful employment of montage in *Potemkin,* in 1926 she undertook the editing of old newsreel footage, forming it into a series of compelling compilation films tracing the then-recent history of Russia before, during, and after the Revolution. Her films remain among the finest examples of creative editing in compilation films. Technically, she was considered the director of these films, for most of which she also wrote the narration scripts.

FILMS: *The Fall of the Romanov Dynasty, The Great Road* 1927; *The Russia of Nicholas II and Leo Tolstoy* 1928; *Today/Cannons or Tractors* 1930; *KSE/Komsomol* 1932; *Moscow Builds the Metro* 1934; *Land of the Soviets* 1937; *Spain* 1939; *Twenty Years of Cinema* (co-dir. with Pudovkin) 1940; *Fascism Will Be Destroyed/The Face of the Enemy* 1941; *Native Country* 1942; *Across the Araks* 1947.

Shue, Elizabeth. American actress. Born in 1964. Appealing ingenue of Hollywood films from the late 80s. Always an appealing actress on the fringe, she made her presence known to Hollywood with her stunning performance as a hooker who falls in love a man intent on dying from alcoholism in *Leaving Las Vegas* (1995), receiving an Academy Award nomination as best actress. She also co-starred in the short-lived TV series 'Call for Glory' (1984–85).

FILMS: *The Karate Kid* 1984; *Link* (UK) 1986; *Adventures in Babysitting* 1987; *Cocktail* 1988; *Back to the Future Part II* 1989; *Back to the Future Part III* 1990; *The Marrying Man, Soapdish* 1991; *Twenty Bucks* 1992; *Heart and Souls* 1993;

Leaving Las Vegas, The Underneath 1995; *The Trigger Effect* 1996; *Cousin Bette, The Saint* 1997.

Shuftan, Eugene. See SCHÜFFTAN, Eugen.

Shukshin, Vasily. Director, screenwriter, actor. *b.* July 5, 1929, Strotsky, Siberia. *d.* 1974. Of peasant stock, he closed the gaps in his limited formal education through voracious reading and before long began writing poetry and short stories. Following military service as a sailor with the Black Sea fleet, he briefly held manual jobs in Siberia, then moved to Moscow, where he enrolled in 1954 at the VGIK film school as a directing student of Mikhail ROMM. During that period, he began publishing his stories of Siberian life in major periodicals. He began his film career as an actor in 1958 and had been an established screen performer by the time he made his mark as a director-screenwriter. From the start, he asserted himself as a maverick filmmaker, courageous in his truthful depiction of boorish peasant characters, in their rural home ground or in an alien and corrupting urban environment. He wrote the scripts for all of his own films, sometimes from his own published stories. He won the Golden Lion at the Venice Youth Film Festival for *There Was a Lad* (1964). He achieved his greatest success with *The Red Snowball Tree* (1974), a heavily censored drama about an ex-convict and his underworld milieu, in which he also played the leading role. It was the last film he directed. While performing that same year in Sergei Bondarchuk's *They Fought for Their Country* (released 1975), Shukshin suffered a heart attack and died, at 45, at the peak of his celebrity. He was married to actress Lydia Fedoseyeva.

FILMS: As actor (partial list)—*Two Fyodors* 1958; *The Golden Squadron* 1959; *A Simple Story* 1960; *When the Trees Grew Tall* 1961; *Alenka* 1962; *The Two of Us* 1963; *The Journalist* 1967; *The Three Days of Victor Chernyshev* 1968; *Liberation, By the Lake* 1972; *They Fought for Their Country* 1975. As screenwriter—*A Soldier Came from the Front* 1973; *Fellow Countrymen* 1975. As director-screenwriter (complete)—*Report from Lebiazhe* (also act.) 1960; *There Was a Lad* 1964; *Your Son and Brother* 1966; *Strange People* 1970; *That's the Way It Is/Happy Go Lucky* (also act.; unreleased) 1972; *The Red Snowball Tree/Red Berry* (also act.) 1974.

Shumlin, Herman. Director. *b.* Dec. 6, 1898, Atwood, Colo. *d.* 1979. A former reporter and from 1927 a successful Broadway producer and director, he also directed two films in the 40s.

FILMS: *Watch on the Rhine* 1943; *Confidential Agent* 1945.

shutter. A mechanical device in a camera which is designed to obstruct light from the film while individual frames are moved into position for exposure. Shutters come in various designs, the most common of which are the DIAPHRAGM, the focal plane shutter, and the sector shutter. A variable shutter is one that can be adjusted to admit more or less light.

shuttle. A moving part in a motion picture camera mechanism which carries the film forward and holds each frame in precise registration during exposure.

Shyer, Charles. Director, screenwriter. Born on Oct. 11, 1941, in Los Angeles. Promising filmmaker of light Hollywood fare. The son of Melville Shyer, a founding member of the Directors Guild of America, he began his career as a writer on the 'Combat' TV series and in the late 70s began collaborating on the scripts of comedy features. In 1976 he met Nancy Meyers (*b.* 1949, Philadelphia), an executive story editor for Mowtown Productions, who later became his wife and screenplay collaborator. After sharing an Oscar nomination for the script of *Private Benjamin* (1980), they formed their own production company and turned out several entertaining films that she produced, he directed, and both wrote.

FILMS: As screenwriter—*Smokey and the Bandit* 1977; *Goin' South, House Calls* 1978; *Private Benjamin* 1980; *Once Upon a Crime* 1992. As director-screenwriter (Meyers as producer/co-writer)—*Irreconcilable Differences* 1984; *Baby Boom* 1987; *Father of the Bride* 1991; *I Love Trouble* 1994; *Father of the Bride II* 1995.

Sidney, George. Actor. *b.* Samuel Greenfield, Mar. 18, 1876, New York City. *d.* 1945. Short, stocky comic character star of Hollywood silents and early talkies. A veteran of vaudeville and the legitimate stage, he specialized in ethnic Jewish roles, making his film debut in the role of Abe Potash in *In Hollywood with Potash and Perlmutter* (1924) and gaining popularity as Jacob Cohen in the long-running "The Cohens and Kellys" series of feature comedies.

FILMS INCLUDE: *In Hollywood with Potash and Perlmutter* 1924; *Classified* 1925; *Partners Again, The Cohens and Kellys, Sweet Daddies, The Prince of Pilsen, Millionaires* 1926; *The Auctioneer, Lost at the Front, For the Love of Mike, The Life of Riley, Clancy's Kosher Wedding* 1927; *The Cohens and Kellys in Paris, The Latest from Paris, We Americans, Flying Romeos, Give and Take* 1928; *The Cohens and Kellys in Atlantic City* 1929; *Around the Corner, The Cohens and Kellys in Africa* 1930; *The Heart of New York, The Cohens and Kellys in Hollywood* 1932; *The Cohens and Kellys in Trouble* 1933; *Manhattan Melodrama* 1934; *Diamond Jim* 1935; *Good Old Soak* 1937.

Sidney, George. Director. Born on Oct. 4, 1916, in Long Island City, N.Y. The son of show people, he did some stage acting as a child and appeared in a Tom Mix Western in the early 20s. He joined MGM as a messenger boy in 1933 and moved up to sound technician and film editor the following year. In 1935 he was assistant director and second-unit director and in 1936, when barely 20, he became a director of MGM's screen tests. That same year he submitted a script to Pete Smith of the famed "Pete Smith Specialties" and was assigned to direct it and several other shorts in the series. He subsequently directed numerous shorts for such series as "Crime Does Not Pay" and "Our Gang." After winning two Academy Awards in succession, for the shorts *Quicker 'n a Wink* (in the "Pete Smith Specialties" series, 1940) and *Of Pups and Puzzles* (in the "Passing Parade" series, 1941), he was elevated to feature director.

During his 15-year tenure as a feature director at MGM, Sidney specialized in lavish musicals (*Anchors Aweigh, Annie Get Your Gun, Show Boat,* etc.) and choreographed period adventure films with an accent on parody (*The Three Musketeers, Scaramouche*). He was more heavy-handed in his occasional piloting of straight drama. Beginning in the late 50s, he produced and directed independently for release through Columbia and other companies. He managed to bounce back from such expensive failures as *Pepe* with box-office winners like the musical *Bye Bye Birdie.* For several years, Sidney also acted as president of Hanna-Barbera Productions, animation specialists. In 1978 he married Jane Robinson, the widow of Edward G. Robinson.

FEATURE FILMS: *Free and Easy* 1941; *Pacific Rendezvous* 1942; *Pilot No. 5, Thousands Cheer* 1943; *Bathing Beauty* 1944; *Anchors Aweigh* 1945; *The Harvey Girls, Holiday in Mexico* 1946; *Cass Timberlane* 1947; *The Three Musketeers* 1948; *The Red Danube* 1949; *Key to the City, Annie Get Your Gun* 1950; *Show Boat* 1951; *Scaramouche* 1952; *Young Bess, Kiss Me Kate* 1953; *Jupiter's Darling* 1955; *The Eddy Duchin Story* 1956; *Jeanne Eagels* (also prod.), *Pal Joey* 1957; *Who Was That Lady?, Pepe* (also prod.) 1960; *Bye Bye Birdie, A Ticklish Affair* 1963; *Viva Las Vegas* (also co-prod.) 1964; *The Swinger* (also prod.) 1966; *Half a Sixpence* (also co-prod.) 1968.

Sidney, Sylvia. Actress. Born Sophia Kosow, on Aug. 8, 1910, in the Bronx, N.Y. The daughter of Jewish immigrants from Russia, she trained for the stage at the Theatre Guild School and made her professional debut at 16 in Washington. She made her first New York appearance the following year and almost immediately moved into leading roles on Broadway. She also made a tentative start in films in 1929, playing a screaming witness in a courtroom drama, *Thru Different Eyes.* Two years later she settled in Hollywood as a Paramount star. She soon attained worldwide popularity. Following the release of *Madame Butterfly* (1932) her portrait was used as a trademark for a brand of Japanese condoms that became known as Sylvia Sidneys. Almost invariably she was cast as a downtrodden girl of the working class. There was an intense, vulnerable, waif-like quality about her that made her the perfect screen heroine of the Depression era. Occasionally she would be given an opportunity to demonstrate her versatility as an actress in a different role, even in comedy, but on the whole she was strictly typecast, to her utter discontent. By the early 40s she was devoting more time to the stage than to films, and her screen appearances dwindled down to a trickle. After playing three character parts in films of the 50s, she retired from the screen. She has since been quite busy in the theater, mostly in stock and on the road. She returned to the screen in 1973, in *Summer Wishes, Winter Dreams,* a role for which she was nominated for an Oscar. Her comeback continued on screen in films and on television, and she remained active through the early 90s. Miss Sidney has been married and divorced three times. Her first husband (1935–36) was publisher Bennett A. Cerf; her second (1938–47) was actor Luther ADLER. In 1990 she was honored for life achievement by the Film Society of Lincoln Center.

FILMS: *Broadway Nights* (cameo) 1927; *Thru Different Eyes* 1929; *City Streets, Confessions of a Co-Ed, An American Tragedy* (as Roberta Alden), *Street Scene* (as Rose Maurrant), *Ladies of the Big House* 1931; *The Miracle Man, Merrily We Go to Hell, Make Me a Star* (cameo), *Madame Butterfly* (title role) 1932; *Pick Up, Jennie Gerhardt* (title role) 1933; *Good Dame, Thirty Day Princess* (dual role) 1934; *Behold My Wife, Accent on Youth, Mary Burns—Fugitive* 1935; *The Trail of the Lonesome Pine, Fury, Sabotage/A Woman Alone* (UK) 1936; *You Only Live Once, Dead End* (as Drina) 1937; *You and Me* 1938; *One Third of a Nation* 1939; *The Wagons Roll at Night* 1941; *Blood on the Sun* 1945; *The Searching Wind, Mr. Ace* 1946; *Love from a Stranger* 1947; *Les Misérables* (as Fantine) 1952; *Violent Saturday* 1955; *Behind the High Wall* 1956; *Summer Wishes Winter Dreams* 1973; *God Told Me So* 1976; *I Never Promised You a Rose Garden* 1977; *Damien: Omen II* 1978; *Hammett* 1982; *L'assassino dei poliziotti/Cop Killers/Corrupt* (It.) (1983); *Beetlejuice* 1988; *Used People* 1992; *Mars Attacks!* 1996.

Siegel, Don(ald). Director. *b.* Oct. 26, 1912, Chicago. *d.* 1991. The son of a mandolin virtuoso, he received his education in England, at Cambridge, then trained for the stage at London's Royal Academy of Dramatic Art. After a discouraging start as an actor, he joined Warners in Hollywood in 1933 as an assistant film librarian. He later became an assistant cutter, graduated to head of the insert department, and organized (and headed) the montage department at Warners. In the latter capacity he shot some memorable transition sequences for such films as *City for Conquest, Casablanca,* and *Blues in the Night.* In the early 40s he also directed a number of shorts, two of which won Academy Awards in the same year, 1945, *Star in the Night* and *Hitler Lives?*. The following year he made his debut as a feature director. Siegel specialized in fast-moving crime and action pictures whose protagonists were typically young social outcasts of the loner brand.

Although his output consisted mainly of modestly budgeted B pictures, Siegel periodically transcended the genre. In the powerfully realistic prison drama *Riot in Cell Block 11* (1954), as in several subsequent films, he effectively used non-actors to play themselves in minor roles or in crowd scenes. And he often resorted to on-the-spot improvisation on the set, incurring the wrath of many a screenwriter. His *Invasion of the Body Snatchers* (1956), a harrowing parable of Cold War hysteria, remains one of the screen's most effective science-fiction thrillers. In the late 50s Siegel was discovered by the young critics (and future directors) of the *Cahiers du Cinéma*—among them Godard, Truffaut, and Rohmer—who crowned him a gifted *auteur* with a consistent style and point of view, much to his own surprise. In the late 60s, following a mixed bag of less-than-memorable productions, the director began a fruitful collaboration with actor Clint EASTWOOD that resulted in 1971 in *Dirty Harry,* a riveting action drama that gave the screen one of its toughest, most unscrupulous law-and-order heroes. Some critics labeled that definitive maverick cop saga "fascist," though Siegel insisted he was a liberal. The film's success afforded Siegel access to larger-budget productions, including the critically praised elegiac Western, *The Shootist.* His career ended on a downturn with two successive failures in the early 80s. He played a bartender in Eastwood's *Play Misty for Me* (1971) and made cameo appearances in the remake of *Invasion of the Body Snatchers* (1978) and in *Into the Night* (1985), as well as in several of his own films. Siegel's first marriage (1949–53) to actress Viveca LINDFORS produced actor Kristoffer Tabori (*b.* 1952, Los Angeles). His second (of a total of three) marriages was to actress Doe Avedon.

FEATURE FILMS: *The Verdict* 1946; *Night Unto Night, The Big Steal* 1949; *Duel at Silver Creek* 1952; *No Time for Flowers, Count the Hours, China Venture* 1953; *Riot in Cell Block 11, Private Hell 36* 1954; *An Annapolis Story* 1955; *Invasion of the Body Snatchers, Crime in the Streets* 1956; *Baby Face Nelson* 1957; *Spanish Affair, The Lineup, The Gun Runners* 1958; *Hound Dog Man, Edge of Eternity* (also assoc. prod.) 1959; *Flaming Star* 1960; *Hell Is for Heroes* 1962; *The Killers* (also prod.) 1964; *The Hanged Man* (TV movie) 1965; *Stranger on the Run* (TV movie) 1967; *Madigan, Coogan's Bluff* (also prod.) 1968; *Death of a Gunfighter* (co-dir. with Robert Totten under combined pseudonym of Allen Smithee) 1969; *Two Mules for Sister Sara* 1970; *The Beguiled* (also prod., act.), *Dirty Harry* (also prod.) 1971; *Charley Varrick* (also prod., act.) 1973; *The Black Windmill* (also prod.; UK) 1974; *The Shootist* 1976; *Telefon* 1977; *Escape from Alcatraz* (also prod., act.) 1979; *Rough Cut* 1980; *Jinxed!* 1982.

Siegel, Sol C. Producer. *b.* Mar. 30, 1903, New York City. *d.* 1982. *ed.* Columbia (journalism). A former New York *Herald Tribune* reporter and sales executive for a recording company, in 1934 he went to Hollywood to help organize the corporate merger of four companies into Republic Pictures. He remained with the company as executive producer until 1940 and was responsible for many of Gene Autry's and John Wayne's early Westerns. In 1940 he moved over to Paramount and in 1947 to 20th Century-Fox and soon gained a reputation as a successful producer of entertaining, profitable, and occasionally meritorious films. In 1956 he joined MGM, where he was elevated to vice president in charge of production in 1958, replacing Dore Schary. He became an independent producer in the early 60s.

FILMS INCLUDE: *Army Girl* 1938; *Dark Command* 1940; *World Premier, Buy Me That Town,* 1941; *Sweater Girl* 1942; *Hostages* 1943; *Kiss and Tell* 1945; *Blue Skies* 1946; *The Perils of Pauline, Welcome Stranger* 1947; *The Iron Curtain, Cry of the City* 1948; *A Letter to Three Wives, House of*

Strangers, I Was a Male War Bride, Prince of Foxes 1949; *Panic in the Streets, My Blue Heaven* 1950; *Fourteen Hours, On the Riviera* 1951; *Deadline U.S.A., What Price Glory, Monkey Business* 1952; *Call Me Madam, Gentlemen Prefer Blondes* 1953; *Three Coins in the Fountain, Broken Lance* 1954; *High Society* 1956; *Les Girls* 1957; *Merry Andrew* 1958; *Some Came Running* 1959; *Home from the Hill* 1960; *Walk Don't Run, Alvarez Kelly* 1966; *No Way to Treat a Lady* 1968.

Siemaszko, Casey. Actor. Born on Mar. 17, 1961, in Chicago. Energetic, appealing, slightly built, promising lead and supporting player of American films of the 80s and early 90s. The son of a Polish-born father and an English mother, he performed in many stage productions in Chicago before moving to Hollywood.

FILMS: *Class* 1983; *Back to the Future* 1985; *Stand by Me* 1986; *Gardens of Stone, Three O' Clock High* 1987; *Biloxi Blues, Young Guns* 1988; *Breaking In, Back to the Future Part II* 1989; *The Big Slice, Near Misses* 1991; *Of Mice and Men* 1992; *Milk Money, Theresa's Tattoo* 1994.

Sierck, Detlaf. See SIRK, Douglas.

Sight and Sound. A film quarterly widely acknowledged as the leading cinema publication in the English language. Founded in 1932, it is published in London.

Signoret, Simone. Actress. *b.* Simone Kaminker, Mar. 25, 1921, Wiesbaden, Germany, to French nationals. *d.* 1985. Raised in Paris, she was forced to quit school and help support her mother and two brothers during the Occupation, when her Jewish father, a linguist, fled to London to join De Gaulle's Free French. She worked as a typist, then began appearing as an extra in films. Gaining experience before the camera, she gradually moved into featured parts and, finally, in 1946, into leading roles. She specialized for a while in portraying tarts or lovelorn women—memorably in Jacques Becker's *Casque d'Or* (1952), Marcel Carné's *Thérèse Raquin* (1953), and Henri Clouzot's *Les Diaboliques* (1954)—and eventually matured into matronly roles. An intelligent actress who projected self-awareness, vulnerable strength, and ripe sensuality, she developed into a leading personality of the international screen. She won an Academy Award as best actress for her performance in the British film *Room at the Top* (1958) and was nominated for another for the American *Ship of Fools* (1965). Although overweight and appearing world-weary, Signoret aged gracefully and ended her illustrious career with a string of superb portrayals, notably Moshe Mizrahi's *La Vie devant soi/Madame Rosa* (1977) and *Chère inconnu/I Sent a Letter to My Love* (1980). Briefly (1948–49) married to director Yves ALLÉGRET (their daughter, screen actress Catherine Allégret, was born in 1946), Signoret married actor-singer Yves MONTAND in 1951. They co-starred in several films. She wrote two volumes of memoirs—*La Nostalgie n'est plus ce qu'elle était/Nostalgia Isn't What It Used to Be* (1976) and *Le Lendemain, cela était souriante?* (1979)—and a novel, *Adieu, Volodia* (1985).

FILMS INCLUDE: *Le Prince charmant* (bit), *Les Visiteurs du Soir/The Devil's Envoys* (bit) 1942; *La Bôite aux Rêves* (bit) 1945; *Les Démons de l'Aube, Macadam/Back Streets of Paris* 1946; *Fantômas* 1947; *Against the Wind* (UK), *L'Impasse des Deux Anges, Dedée d'Anvers/Dedee* 1948; *Swiss Tour/Four Days' Leave* (Switz.) 1949; *Manèges/The Cheat, La Ronde* 1950; *Le Traqué/Gunman in the Streets* (Fr./US), *Ombre et Lumière* 1951; *Casque d'Or* 1952; *Thérèse Raquin/The Adulteress* (title role) 1953; *Les Diaboliques/Diabolique* 1955; *La Mort en ce Jardin/Gina/Evil Eden/Death in the Garden* (Fr./Mex.) 1956; *Les Sorcières de Salem/The Witches of Salem/The Crucible* (as Elizabeth Proctor) 1957; *Room at the Top* (UK) 1958; *Adua e le Compagne/Love à la Carte* (It.) 1960; *Le Mauvais Coups/Naked Autumn, Les Amours célèbres* 1961; *Term of Trial* (UK) 1962; *Le Jour et l'Heure/The Day and the Hour* (Fr./It.), *Dragées au Poivre/Sweet and Sour* (Fr./It.) 1963; *Ship of Fools* (US), *Compartiment Tueurs/The Sleeping Car Murder* 1965; *Paris brûle-t-il?/Is Paris Burning?* (US/Fr.) 1966; *The Deadly Affair* (UK), *Games* (US) 1967; *The Sea Gull* (as Irina Arkadina; US/UK) 1968; *L'Armée des Ombres, L'Americain* 1969; *L'Aveu/The Confession* 1970; *Le Chat, La Veuve Couderc/The Widow Couderc* 1971; *Rude Journée pour la Reine* 1973; *Defense de Savoir, La Chair de l'orchidée* 1974; *Police Python 357* 1976; *La Vie devant soi/Madame Rosa* 1977; *Une Femme dangereuse, Judith Therpauve* 1978; *L'Adolescente/ The Adolescent* 1979; *Chère inconnue/I Sent a Letter to My Love* 1980; *L'Etoile du Nord, Guy de Maupassant* 1982; *Des Terroristes à la retraite* (narrator only) 1983.

Silberman, Serge. Producer. Born on May 13, 1917, in Poland. Influential producer of French films and European co-productions. Entering the industry in the mid-50s, he was responsible for many major undertakings, including the later output of Buñuel.

FILMS INCLUDE: *Bob le Flambeur* 1955; *Calle Mayor/Grand'Rue/The Lovemaker* (Sp./Fr.) 1956; *Le Trou* 1959; *Madame Sans-Gêne* 1960; *Le Journal d'une Femme de Chambre/The Diary of a Chambermaid* 1963; *La Voie lactée/ The Milky Way* 1969; *Le Passager de la Pluie/Rider on the Rain* 1970; *Le Charme discret de la Bourgeoisie/The Discreet Charm of the Bourgeoisie* 1972; *Le Fantôme de la Liberté/The Phantom of Liberty* 1974; *Cet Obscur Objet de Désir/That Obscure Object of Desire* 1977; *Exposed* (exec. prod.; US) 1983; *Ran* (Fr./Jap.) 1985; *Max Mon Amour* 1986; *Anna Karamazova* (Fr./USSR) 1991.

silent bit. A bit role in which the player has no lines to deliver.

silent print. See PICTURE PRINT.

silent speed. The rate at which film passes through a motion picture camera when it is not intended to be used with sound accompaniment—usually 16 and sometimes 18 frames per second (f.p.s.), versus 24 frames per second for sound. During the early silent days, when cameras were cranked by hand, the silent speed varied from 12 to 20 f.p.s.

silhouette. The nearly black outline of a subject, appearing on the screen with little or no detail as a result of BACK LIGHTING.

Silliphant, Stirling. Screenwriter, producer. Born on Jan. 16, 1918, in Detroit. *ed.* USC. A former advertising and promotion executive with Disney and Fox, he produced a couple of films early in the 50s, then turned screenwriter, working on both feature films and such successful TV series as 'Naked City' and 'Route 66.' He won an Academy Award for the screenplay of *In the Heat of the Night* (1967).

FILMS INCLUDE (as screenwriter): *The Joe Louis Story* (prod. only) 1953; *Five Against the House* (also co-prod.) 1955; *Nightfall* 1957; *The Lineup* 1958; *Village of the Damned* (UK) 1960; *The Slender Thread* 1965; *In the Heat of the Night* 1967; *Charly* 1968; *Marlowe* 1969; *A Walk in the Spring Rain* (also prod.), *The Liberation of L. B. Jones* 1970; *Murphy's War* (UK) 1971; *Shaft's Big Score* (exec. prod. only), *The New Centurions, The Poseidon Adventure* 1972; *Shaft in Africa* 1973; *The Towering Inferno* 1974; *The Killer Elite* 1975; *The Enforcer* 1976; *Telefon* 1977; *Swarm* 1978; *Circle of Iron/The Silent Flute* 1979; *When Time Ran Out* 1980; *Over the Top, Catch the Heat* (also co-exec. prod.) 1987; *The Grass Harp* (co-sc.) 1996.

Sills, Milton. Actor. *b.* Jan. 12, 1882, Chicago. *d.* 1930. The son of well-to-do parents, he became involved in college dramatics at the University of Chicago. After graduation, he joined his first of several stock companies and made his New York debut in 1908. Entering films in 1914, he soon became a highly popular screen hero. He was tall and rugged and a fine, versatile actor, capable of playing leading roles in a wide range of films—from swashbucklers and Westerns to comedies and melodramas. He remained a popular star through the silent era and was looking forward to continued success in talkies after an impressive performance in the title role of *The Sea Wolf,* when he died at 48 of a heart attack. His widow is actress Doris KENYON, who co-starred in a number of his films.

FILMS INCLUDE: *The Pit* 1914; *The Deep Purple, The Arrival of Perpetua, The Rack* 1915; *Patria* (serial), *The Honor System, Souls Adrift* 1917; *The Yellow Ticket, The Claw, The Hell Cat* 1918; *Shadows, The Stronger Vow, Satan Jr., Eyes of Youth* 1919; *The Weekend, Behold My Wife* 1920; *The Great Moment, The Faith Healer, At the End of the World, Salvage* 1921; *One Clear Call, Skin Deep, Borderland, Environment, The Forgotten Law, Burning Sands* 1922; *Adam's Rib, The Last Hour, Souls for Sale, Legally Dead, The Isle of Lost Ships, The Spoilers, Flaming Youth* 1923; *The Heart Bandit, Flowing Gold, Single Wives, Madonna of the Streets, The Sea Hawk* 1924; *As Man Desires, I Want My Man, The Knockout, The Unguarded Hour* 1925; *Puppets, Men of Steel, Paradise, The Silent Lover* 1926; *The Sea Tiger, Framed, The Valley of the Giants* 1927; *Burning Daylight, The Hawk's Nest, The Crash, The Barker* 1928; *Love and the Devil, His Captive Woman* 1929; *Man Trouble, The Sea Wolf* 1930.

Silva, Henry. Actor. Born in 1928, in Brooklyn, N.Y., of Puerto Rican parentage. He worked as a delivery boy and longshoreman before training for the stage with Group Theatre and at the Actors Studio. Beady-eyed and high-cheekboned, he often played Indians, Mexicans, or Orientals in films but has been mostly typecast as a sadistic villain. He played the lead, a gangster, in *Johnny Cool* (1963) and starred in a number of Italian films.

FILMS INCLUDE: *Viva Zapata!* 1952; *Crowded Paradise* 1956; *A Hatful of Rain* 1957; *The Law and Jake Wade, The Bravados* 1958; *Green Mansions* 1959; *Cinderfella* 1960; *Sergeants 3, The Manchurian Candidate* 1962; *A Gathering of Eagles, Johnny Cool* 1963; *The Secret Invasion* 1964; *Je vous salve Mafia/Hail! Mafia* (Fr./It.), *The Return of Mr. Moto* (title role), *Un Fiume di Dollari/The Hills Run Red* (It.), *The Reward* 1965; *The Plainsman* 1966; *Matchless* (It.), *Assassination* (It.), 1967; *Never a Dull Moment* 1968; *The Animals* 1971; *Man and Boy, La Mala Ordina/The Italian Connection* 1972; *Les Hommes* (Fr.) 1973; *The Kidnap of Mary Lou* (It.) 1974; *L'Uomo della Strada Fa Giustizia* (It.), *Shoot* (Can.), *Eviolenti* (It.) 1976; *Love and Bullets* (UK), *Buck Rogers in the 25th Century, Thirst* (Austral.) 1979; *Alligator* 1980; *Sharky's Machine* 1981; *Wrong is Right* 1982; *Bronx Warriors 2* (It./US) 1984; *Allan Quatermain and the Lost City of Gold, Amazon Women on the Moon* 1987; *Bulletproof, Above the Law* 1988; *Dick Tracy* 1990; *Fists of Steel* 1991; *Trained to Kill* 1992; *The End of Violence* 1997.

Silver, Joan Micklin. Director, screenwriter. Born Joan Micklin on May 24, 1935, in Omaha, Neb. The daughter of Russian Jewish immigrants, she studied music and literature at Sarah Lawrence, then married and moved to Cleveland, where she taught music to disturbed children and wrote and directed for community theaters. In 1967 she moved with her husband and three daughters to New York, where she contributed to the *Village Voice* and later began writing scripts for educational films produced by the *Encyclopedia Britannica.* In 1972, she collaborated with James Bridges on the screenplay for the feature *Limbo,* a drama about women whose husbands were captured or missing in Vietnam, which was directed indifferently by Mark Robson. Determined to take full charge of her subsequent film work, she began directing shorts, in preparation for her first feature as a director. *Hester Street* (1985) proved to be an enchanting debut film, a delicately observed period piece about a Jewish immigrant couple's pains of adjusting to the ways of the New World in Manhattan's Lower East Side during the 20s. She returned wistfully, and again successfully, to that scene, this time in a modern setting, in the charming *Crossing Delancey* (1988). Her husband, real-estate businessman Raphael D. Silver (*b.* 1930, Cleveland), produced several of her films and directed two of his own. Their daughter, Marisa SILVER, is a budding film director. Another daughter, Dina Silver, is a producer.

FEATURE FILMS (as director): *Limbo/Women in Limbo* (co-sc. only) 1972; *Hester Street* (also sc.) 1975; *Between the Lines* 1977; *On the Yard* (prod. only), *Head Over Heels/Chilly Scenes of Winter* (also sc.) 1979; *Crossing Delancy* 1988; *Loverboy* 1989; *Big Girls Don't Cry. . . They Get Even* 1992.

Silver, Joel. Producer. Born on July 14, 1952, in South Orange, N.J. The son of a public-relations executive and a former reporter, he became addicted to movies in childhood and helped organize a film festival at his high school, where he also directed stage plays. After attending the NYU film school, he moved to Los Angeles, where, following an assortment of entry-level jobs, he began his career as an assistant to producer Lawrence Gordon, and worked in that capacity on the Burt Reynolds box-office hits *The End* and *Hooper* (both 1978). An ebullient, dynamic, combative workaholic, he eventually (after briefly working at Universal and Polygram) assumed the presidency of Lawrence Gordon Productions, then attained total independence as head of his own company, Silver Pictures. He achieved a position of power in the industry as the producer of highly profitable, mostly action-based movies. A throwback to the studio moguls of old Hollywood, he was described by a magazine writer as "the Selznick of Shlock." He is credited with being instrumental in motivating the trend for glitzy, cartoon-like violence in the Hollywood action movies of the 80s. Several became megahits, helping the cumulative earnings of his films of that decade to exceed a billion dollars. He played the role of a director in *Who Framed Roger Rabbit?* (1988).

FILMS INCLUDE (as producer, alone or in collaboration): *The Warriors* (assoc. prod.) 1979; *Xanadu* 1980; *48 Hours, Jekyll & Hyde. . . Together Again* (exec. prod.) 1982; *Streets of Fire* 1984; *Brewster's Millions, Weird Science, Commando* 1985; *Jumpin' Jack Flash* 1986; *Lethal Weapon, Predator* 1987; *Action Jackson, Die Hard* 1988; *Lethal Weapon 2, Road House* 1989; *Ford Fairlane, Die Hard 2* 1990; *Hudson Hawk, Ricochet, The Last Boy Scout* 1991; *Lethal Weapon 3* 1992; *Demolition Man* (co-pr.) 1993; *Richie Rich* 1994; *Assassins* 1995; *Executive Decision* 1996; *Father's Day* 1997.

Silver, Marisa. Director. Born on April 23, 1960, in Cleveland. *ed.* Harvard. Up-and-coming filmmaker, the daughter of director Joan Micklin SILVER and producer Raphael D. Silver.

FILMS: *Old Enough* 1984; *Permanent Record* 1988; *Vital Signs* 1990; *He Said She Said* (co-dir. with Ken Kwapis) 1991.

Silver, Ron. Actor. Born July 1946, in New York City, he grew up on the Lower East Side. Expressive, intense leading man of the American stage and screen. After graduating from the University of Buffalo, he received his master's degree in Chinese from St. John's University and the College of Chinese Culture in Taiwan. Returning to New York, he trained at the Herbert Berghof Studio and the Actors Studio, making his theatrical debut in 1972 and his first cinematic appearance in 1976. He won a Tony Award for his performance on Broadway in

David Mamet's 'Speed-the-Plow' (1988) and received accolades for his portrayal of defense attorney Alan Dershowitz in the film *Reversal of Fortune* (1990). A dedicated political activist, in 1989 he became founding president of the Creative Coalition, a group calling for the involvement of artists in pressing social issues. In 1991 he succeeded the late Colleen Dewhurst as president of the Actors' Equity Association, the stage performers' union.

FILMS: *Tunnelvision* 1976; *Semi-Tough* 1977; *Silent Rage, Best Friends* 1982; *The Entity, Lovesick, Silkwood* 1983; *Garbo Talks, Oh God! You Devil, The Goodbye People* 1984; *Eat and Run* 1986; *Enemies A Love Story* 1989; *Fellow Traveller,* (UK/US), *Blue Steel, Reversal of Fortune* (as Alan Dershowitz) 1990; *Married to It* 1991; *Mr. Saturday Night* 1992; *Timecop* 1994; *The Arrival, Girl 6* 1996.

Silvera, Frank. Actor. *b.* July 24, 1914, Kingston, Jamaica. *d.* 1970. *ed.* Northeastern Law School. A veteran of the stage, he played character parts in Hollywood films of the 50s and 60s, often as a Mexican, Indian, or Oriental heavy. He played the lead in two early Stanley Kubrick productions, *Fear and Desire* (1953) and *Killer's Kiss* (1955), and co-starred in the TV series 'The High Chaparral' (1967–70). He died at 56, in an accident in which he was electrocuted by a home appliance.

FILMS INCLUDE: *The Cimarron Kid* 1951; *Viva Zapata!, The Fighter, The Miracle of Our Lady of Fatima* 1952; *Fear and Desire* 1953; *Killer's Kiss* 1955; *Crowded Paradise* 1956; *Crime and Punishment USA* 1959; *The Mountain Road, Key Witness* 1960; *Mutiny on the Bounty* 1962; *Toys in the Attic, Lonnie* 1963; *The Greatest Story Ever Told* 1965; *The Appaloosa* 1966; *Hombre, The St. Valentine's Day Massacre* 1967; *Uptight* 1968; *The Stalking Moon, Che!, Guns of the Magnificent Seven* 1969; *Valdez Is Coming!* 1971.

Silverheels, Jay. Actor. *b.* Harold J. Smith, May 26, 1919, Six Nations Indian Reservation, Ontario, Canada. *d.* 1980. The son of a Mohawk chief, he made a name for himself as a lacrosse player and amateur boxer before entering films in the 40s. He went on to play supporting parts in numerous pictures and gained popularity on TV in the role of Tonto, John Hart's, and then Clayton MOORE's, loyal sidekick in the long-running (1949–57) series 'The Lone Ranger,' and two spin-off feature films. In 1974 he started a new career as a harness racing driver. He was credited as Silverheels Smith on some of his early films.

FILMS INCLUDE: *Too Many Girls* 1940; *Valley of the Sun* 1942; *Captain from Castille* 1947; *Key Largo, Yellow Sky* 1948; *Lust for Gold, Sand* 1949; *Broken Arrow* (as Geronimo) 1950; *The Battle at Apache Pass, The Pathfinder* 1952; *Saskatchewan* 1954; *Walk the Proud Land* (again as Geronimo), *The Lone Ranger* (as Tonto) 1956; *The Lone Ranger and the Lost City of Gold* (again as Tonto) 1958; *Alias Jesse James* 1959; *Indian Paint* 1965; *Smith!* 1969; *The Phynx* (cameo) 1970; *The Man Who Loved Cat Dancing, One Little Indian, Santee* 1973.

Silvers, Phil. Actor. *b.* May 11, 1912, Brooklyn, N.Y. *d.* 1985. A boy singer in vaudeville from age 13, he appeared in some early Warners musical two-reelers before joining Minsky's burlesque troupe in 1934 as third-banana comedian. He made his feature film debut in 1940 and for a decade enlivened many a Hollywood musical and light film with pleasant comic relief, usually playing the part of the hero's friend. He achieved stardom on Broadway in 1951 with the musical comedy 'Top Banana' and repeated the role in the subsequent screen version. He enjoyed enormous popularity on TV in the late 50s as the rascally Sergeant Bilko in TV's hit series 'The Phil Silvers Show' (initially called 'You'll Never Get Rich'), for which he won an Emmy Award. Autobiography: *The Laugh Is on Me* (1973).

FILMS INCLUDE: *Hit Parade of 1941* 1940; *The Penalty, Tom Dick and Harry, Lady Be Good, Ice-Capades, You're in the Army Now* 1941; *All Through the Night, Roxie Hart, My Gal Sal, Just Off Broadway, Footlight Serenade* 1942; *Coney Island, A Lady Takes a Chance* 1943; *Cover Girl, Four Jills in a Jeep, Something for the Boys* 1944; *Diamond Horseshoe, A Thousand and One Nights, Don Juan Quilligan* 1945; *If I'm Lucky, Summer Stock* 1950; *Top Banana, Lucky Me* 1954; *40 Pounds of Trouble, It's a Mad Mad Mad Mad World* 1963; *A Funny Thing Happened on the Way to the Forum* 1966; *A Guide for the Married Man, Follow that Camel* (UK) 1967; *Buona Sera Mrs. Campbell* 1968; *The Boatniks* 1970; *The Strongest Man in the World* 1975; *Won Ton Ton—The Dog Who Saved Hollywood* 1976; *The Chicken Chronicles* 1977; *The Cheap Detective* 1978; *Racquet* 1979; *The Happy Hooker, There Goes the Bride* (UK) 1980.

Silverstein, Elliot. Director. Born on Aug. 3, 1927, in Boston. A product of the Yale Drama School, he taught at the Theater Arts Department of Brandeis University, then directed plays for TV. After making his feature film debut in the early 60s, he scored a hit in 1965 with *Cat Ballou,* an entertaining spoof of the Hollywood Western that boasted an Oscar-winning performance by Lee Marvin. But Silverstein was far less successful with his subsequent films.

FILMS: *Belle Sommers* 1962; *Cat Ballou* 1965; *The Happening* 1967; *A Man Called Horse* 1970; *Deadly Honeymoon* 1974; *The Car* (also co-prod.) 1977.

Silverstone, Alicia. Actress. Born 1977 in San Francisco. Although labeled an overnight star for her runaway performance in *Clueless* (1995), this precocious young leading lady was already a well-known presence, primarily for her appearances in popular music videos on MTV. Today she commands a major salary and has been given a film production deal at Columbia Pictures.

FILMS: *The Crush* 1993; *The Babysitter, Clueless, Hideaway* 1995; *Excess Baggage* 1997.

Silvestri, Alan. Composer. Born on Mar. 26, 1950, in New York City. *ed.* Berklee Coll. of Music, Boston. Prolific, dynamic scorer of American films of the 80s and early 90s, with penchant for breezy music.

FILMS INCLUDE: *Las Vegas Lady, The Amazing Dobermans* 1976; *Romancing the Stone* 1984; *Fandango, Cat's Eye, Back to the Future, Summer Rental* 1985; *The Clan of the Cave Bear, The Delta Force, American Anthem, Flight of the Navigator/Take It Easy, No Mercy* 1986; *Critical Condition, Outrageous Fortune, Predator, Overboard* 1987; *Who Framed Roger Rabbit?, My Stepmother Is an Alien* 1988; *She's Out of Control, The Abyss, Back to the Future Part II* 1989; *Back to the Future Part III, Young Guns II* 1990; *Soapdish, Dutch, Ricochet, Shattered, Father of the Bride* 1991; *Stop! Or My Mom Will Shoot, Ferngully: The Last Rainforest, Death Becomes Her* 1992; *Grumpy Old Men, Judgment Night* 1993; *Blown Away, Forrest Gump* 1994; *Father of the Bride II, Judge Dredd, The Quick and the Dead* 1995; *The Long Kiss Goodnight* 1996; *Contact, Volcano* 1997.

Sim, Alastair. Actor. *b.* Oct. 9, 1900, Edinburgh, Scotland. *d.* 1976. *ed.* Edinburgh U. A former professor of elocution, he was 30 when he made his stage debut in London and 35 when he entered British films. A highly gifted character actor with wonderfully expressive doleful eyes and a penchant for portraying eccentric types, he delighted film audiences for years with his droll wit and sly comic characterizations, memorably in *Laughter in Paradise, The Belles of St. Trinian's,* and *The Green Man.* He was equally adept at expressing irony in dramatic roles (in *Scrooge, An Inspector Calls,* etc.). He also appeared in numerous plays, many of which he produced or directed.

FILMS: *Riverside Murder, The Case of Gabriel Perry, A Fire Has Been Arranged, The Private Secretary, Late Extra* 1935; *Troubled Waters, Wedding Group/Wrath of Jealousy, The Big Noise, The Man in the Mirror, Keep Your Seats Please, The Mysterious Mr. Davis/My Partner Mr. Davis, She Knew What She Wanted* 1936; *Strange Experiment, Clothes and the Woman, Gangway, The Squeaker/Murder on Diamond Row, Romance in Flanders/Lost on the Western Front, Melody and Romance* 1937; *Sailing Along, The Terror, Alf's Button Afloat, This Man Is News* 1938; *Climbing High, Inspector Hornleigh, This Man in Paris, Inspector Hornleigh on Holiday* 1939; *Law and Disorder* 1940; *Inspector Hornleigh Goes to It/Mail Train, Cottage to Let/Bombsight Stolen* 1941; *Let the People Sing* 1942; *Waterloo Road* 1944; *Journey Together* 1945; *Green for Danger* 1946; *Hue and Cry, Captain Boycott* 1947; *London Belongs to Me/Dulcimer Street* 1948; *The Happiest Days of Your Life, Stage Fright* 1950; *Laughter in Paradise, Lady Godiva Rides Again* (cameo), *Scrooge/A Christmas Carol* (as Scrooge) 1951; *Folly to Be Wise* 1952; *Innocents in Paris* 1953; *An Inspector Calls, The Belles of St. Trinian's* (dual role as headmistress [!] and her brother) 1954; *Escapade, Geordie/Wee Geordie* 1955; *The Green Man* 1956; *Blue Murder at St. Trinian's* 1957; *The Doctor's Dilemma, Left Right and Centre* 1959; *School for Scoundrels, The Millionairess* 1960; *The Anatomist* 1961; *The Ruling Class* 1972; *Royal Flash* 1975; *Escape from the Dark/The Littlest Horse Thieves* 1976.

Simmons, Jean. Actress. Born on Jan. 31, 1929, in London. Beautiful and talented star of British and American films. She was only 14 when she was chosen from among a group of dance students to play Margaret Lockwood's sister in the British film *Give Us the Moon* (1944). A graceful and delicate beauty, she gained popularity as the spoiled young Estella in Lean's *Great Expectations* (1946) and became an established star after she was selected by Laurence Olivier to play Ophelia in his screen production of *Hamlet* (1948). She was awarded the best actress prize at the Venice Festival and was nominated for an Oscar for her performance in that role. In 1950 she married actor Stewart GRANGER and accompanied him to Hollywood, where she became a successful star at Fox after freeing herself in the courts from the legal binds of a Howard Hughes contract. She divorced Granger in 1960 and that same year married Richard BROOKS, who directed her in *Elmer Gantry,* a film memorable for, among other things, her excellent performance. She continued her career in the 60s, giving many splendid performances in roles that often wasted her talent, and was nominated again for an Oscar for *The Happy Ending* (1969). She semiretired from films in the early 70s but after touring for two years with the play 'A Little Night Music,' she returned to regular work in front of the cameras, mostly in TV movies. She divorced Brooks in 1977.

FILMS: In the UK—*Give Us the Moon, Mr. Emmanuel, Kiss the Bride Goodbye, Meet Sexton Blake* 1944; *The Way to the Stars/Johnny in the Clouds, Caesar and Cleopatra,* 1945; *Great Expectations* (as Estella), *Hungry Hill* 1946; *Black Narcissus, Uncle Silas/The Inheritance* (as Miss Ruthyn), *The Woman in the Hall* 1947; *Hamlet* (as Ophelia) 1948; *The Blue Lagoon, Adam and Evelyne/Adam and Evelyn* 1949; *So Long at the Fair, Cage of Gold, Trio, The Clouded Yellow* 1950. In the US—*Androcles and the Lion* (as Lavinia), *Angel Face, Young Bess* (as Queen Elizabeth I), *Affair with a Stranger, The Robe, The Actress* (as actress Ruth Gordon) 1953; *She Couldn't Say No, The Egyptian, A Bullet Is Waiting, Desiree* (title role, to Brando's Napoleon) 1954; *Footsteps in the Fog* (UK), *Guys and Dolls* (as Sarah Brown) 1955; *Hilda Crane* 1956; *This Could Be the Night, Until They Sail* 1957; *The Big Country, Home Before Dark* 1958; *This Earth Is Mine* 1959; *Elmer Gantry, Spartacus, The Grass Is Greener* (UK) 1960; *All the Way Home* 1963; *Life at the Top* (UK) 1965; *Mister Buddwing* 1966; *Divorce American Style, Rough Night in Jericho* 1967; *The Happy Ending* 1969; *Say Hello to Yesterday* (UK) 1971; *Mr. Sycamore* 1975; *Dominique* (UK) 1978; *Yellow Pages/Going Undercover* (UK) 1985; *The Dawning* 1988; *How To Make an American Quilt* 1995.

Simon, Michel. Actor. *b.* François Simon, Apr. 9, 1895, Geneva, Switzerland. *d.* 1975. Large, homely, crude-looking character star of the French stage and films. The son of a sausage maker, he went to Paris at 16 and earned his living as a boxer, photographer, and music hall clown-acrobat-dancer before making his legitimate stage debut in 1918. He began appearing in films in 1925, but it wasn't until the advent of sound that he established himself as an outstanding actor. He achieved his first big success with Marcel Achard's *Jean de la Lune,* which he played on the Paris stage in 1929 and in Jean Choux's subsequent film version in 1931. Among the many other important French films that benefited from his powerful performances were Jean Renoir's *La Chienne* (1931) and *Boudu sauvé des Eaux/Boudu Saved from Drowning* (1932), Jean Vigo's *L'Atalante* (1934), Marcel Carné's *Drôle de Drame/Bizarre Bizarre* (1937) and *Quai des Brumes/Port of Shadows* (1938), Julien Duvivier's *La Fin du Jour/The End of a Day* (1939) and *Panique/Panic* (1946), and René Clair's *La Beauté du Diable/Beauty and the Devil* (1950).

Simon's gross physique and matching deep gravel voice were perfectly suited for his earthy characterizations of common people. He often played those with a natural pathos that exposed bare the depths of a character's tormented soul. He demonstrated virtuosic versatility by often portraying droll or grotesque figures, in addition to his many tragic roles.

Simon's prominence in French films declined in the 50s. His career was threatened by the effects of a makeup dye he used for a role in 1957 which disabled his central nervous system, paralyzing part of his body and face. He recuperated, however, and after several secondary roles made a triumphant comeback as an important star with a magnificent performance in *Le Vieil Homme et l'Enfant/The Two of Us* (1967), as an anti-Semitic peasant whose true humanistic nature is revealed through a wartime relationship with a Jewish boy. Except for a brief marriage, Simon lived alone in a country home with four apes and a parrot as his only companions. His son, François, is also an actor.

FILMS INCLUDE: *Feux Mathias Pascal/The Late Matthew Pascal* 1925; *La Passion de Jeanne d'Arc/The Passion of Joan of Arc, Tire-au-Flanc* 1928; *L'Enfant de l'Amour* 1930; *Jean de la Lune, On purge Bébé, La Chienne* 1931; *Boudu sauvé des Eaux/Boudu Saved from Drowning* 1932; *Du Haut en Bas* 1933; *L'Atalante, Le Lac aux Dames, Le Bonheur* 1934; *Sous les Yeux d'Occident/Razumov* 1936; *Dréole de Drame/Bizarre Bizarre, Naples au baiser de Feu/The Kiss of Fire* 1937; *Les Disparus de Saint-Agil/Boys' School, Quai des Brumes/Port of Shadows, La Belle Etoile* 1938; *Derrière la Façade/32 Rue Montmartre, La Fin du Jour/The End of a Day, Fric-Frac, Circonstances atténuantes/Extenuating Circumstances* 1939; *Les Musiciens du Ciel, La Comédie du Bonheur, La Tosca/The Story of Tosca* (as Scarpia; It.) 1940; *Il Re si Diverte/The King's Jester* (as Rigoletto; It.) 1941; *Au Bonheur des Dames/Shop-Girls of Paris* 1943; *Vautrin/Vautrin the Thief* (title role) 1944; *Un Ami viendra ce Soir/A Friend Will Come Tonight, Panique/Panic* 1946; *Non Coupable/Not Guilty* 1947; *Fabiola* (It.) 1948; *La Beauté du Diable/Beauty and the Devil* (as Prof. Faust/Mephistopheles) 1950; *Le Poison* 1951; *Il Mercante di*

Venezia/The Merchant of Venice (as Shylock; It.) 1952; *La Vie d'un Honnête Homme/The Virtuous Scoundrel* (dual role) 1953; *Saadia* (US, filmed in Morocco) 1954; *Un Certain M. Jo, Es geschah am hellichten Tag/It Happened in Broad Daylight* (Ger./Switz.) 1958; *Austerlitz, Candide* 1960; *Cyrano et d'Artagnan* 1963; *Le Train/The Train* (Fr./It./US) 1964; *Le Vieil Homme et l'Enfant/The Two of Us* 1967; *La Maison* 1970; *Blanche* 1971; *La piú Bella Serata della mia Vita* (It.) 1972; *Eulallie quitte les Champs* 1974; *L'Ibis Rouge* 1975.

Simon, Neil. Playwright, screenwriter. Born Marvin Neil Simon, on July 4, 1927, in the Bronx, N.Y. *ed.* NYU. He wrote material for TV and stage comedians before scoring his first success as a playwright with 'Come Blow Your Horn' in 1961. He has since written a succession of other hit Broadway plays, mostly comedies, becoming the financially most successful playwright in the history of the American theater. Several of his plays were adapted to the screen by himself or by others. He has also written a number of original screenplays. He was nominated for Academy Awards for the scripts of *The Odd Couple* (1968), *The Sunshine Boys* (1975), *The Goodbye Girl* (1977), and *California Suite* (1978). In 1991 he was awarded the Pulitzer Prize for the play 'Lost in Yonkers.' His second wife (1973–83) was actress Marsha MASON.

FILMS (as screenwriter): *Come Blow Your Horn* (play basis only) 1963; *Caccia alla Volpe/After the Fox* (co-sc.; It./US/UK) 1966; *Barefoot in the Park* (from own play) 1967; *The Odd Couple* (from own play) 1968; *Sweet Charity* (co-musical-play basis only) 1969; *The Out-of-Towners* 1970; *Plaza Suite* (from own play), *Star Spangled Girl* (play basis only) 1971; *Last of the Red Hot Lovers* (from own play), *The Heartbreak Kid* 1972; *The Prisoner of Second Avenue* (from own play), *The Sunshine Boys* (from own play) 1975; *Murder by Death* 1976; *The Goodbye Girl* 1977; *The Cheap Detective, California Suite* (from own play) 1978; *Chapter Two* (from own play) 1979; *Seems Like Old Times* 1980; *Only When I Laugh* (from own play, 'The Gingerbread Lady'; also co-prod.) 1981; *I Ought to Be in Pictures* (from own play; also co-prod.) 1982; *Max Dugan Returns* (also co-prod.) 1983; *The Lonely Guy* (adapt. only) 1984; *The Slugger's Wife* 1985; *Brighton Beach Memoirs* (from own play) 1986; *Biloxi Blues* (from own play) 1988; *The Marrying Man* (also co-exec. prod.) 1991.

Simon, Simone. Actress. Born on Apr. 23, 1911, in Béthune, France. The daughter of a French engineer and an Italian housewife, she grew up in Marseilles. In 1930 she went to Paris, where she worked briefly as a fashion designer and a model before making her film debut in 1931. Petite and kittenish, with a child-woman sensuality á la Bardot, she was summoned to Hollywood in 1936. But she didn't get along with her employers at Fox, and despite growing popularity she returned to France within two years. However, a glowing performance opposite Jean Gabin in Renoir's *La Bête humaine/The Human Beast* (1938) resulted in another Hollywood invitation, and in her most memorable role in American films, the mysterious lead in the horror classic *Cat People* and later in *The Curse of the Cat People.* She returned to France at the end of WW II.

FILMS INCLUDE: In France—*Le Chanteur inconnu, Mam'zelle Nitouche* 1931; *Tire-au-Flanc* 1933; *Le Lac aux Dames* 1934; *Les Yeux noirs/Dark Eyes, Les Beaux Jours* 1935. In the US—*Girls' Dormitory, Ladies in Love* 1936; *Seventh Heaven, Love and Hisses* 1937; *Josette, La Bête humaine/The Human Beast* (Fr.) 1938; *All That Money Can Buy* 1941; *Cat People* 1942; *Tahiti Honey* 1943; *The Curse of the Cat People, Mademoiselle Fifi* 1944. In Europe—*Pétrus* (Fr.) 1946; *Temptation Harbor* (UK) 1947; *Donne senza Nome/Women Without Names* (It.), *La Ronde* (Fr.), 1950; *Olivia/Pit of Loneliness* (Fr.) 1951; *Le Plaisir/House of Pleasure* (Fr.) 1952; *Double Destin* (Fr.) 1955; *The Extra Day* (UK) 1956; *La Femme en Bleu* 1973.

Simon, S. Sylvan. Director. *b.* Mar. 9, 1910, Chicago. *d.* 1951. *ed.* U. of Michigan; Columbia. A former drama instructor and radio executive, he began directing for the stage in 1933, and in 1935 he joined Warners as director of screen tests. From 1937 he directed numerous routine thrillers and light romances and comedies for Universal, then MGM. He ended his directing career with a strong melodrama, *Lust for Gold* (1949), and began producing not long before his sudden death at 41.

FILMS: As director—*A Girl with Ideas, Prescription for Romance* 1937; *The Crime of Dr. Hallet, Nurse from Brooklyn, The Road to Reno, Spring Madness* 1938; *Four Girls in White, The Kid from Texas, These Glamour Girls, Dancing Co-Ed* 1939; *Two Girls on Broadway, Sporting Blood, Dulcy* 1940; *Keeping Company, Washington Melodrama, Whistling in the Dark* 1941; *The Bugle Sounds, Rio Rita, Grand Central Murder, Tish, Whistling in Dixie* 1942; *Salute to the Marines, Whistling in Brooklyn* 1943; *Song of the Open Road* 1944; *Son of Lassie, Abbott and Costello in Hollywood* 1945; *Bad Bascomb, The Thrill of Brazil, The Cockeyed Miracle* 1946; *Her Husband's Affairs* 1947; *I Love Trouble* (also prod.), *The Fuller Brush Man* (also prod.) 1948; *Lust for Gold* (also prod.) 1949. As producer—*Shock-proof, Miss Grant Takes Richmond* 1949; *The Good Humor Man, Born Yesterday* 1950.

Simpson, Claire. American film editor. She won an Academy Award for *Platoon* (1986). Also billed as Claire Simpson-Crozier.

FILMS INCLUDE: *C.H.U.D.* 1984; *Salvador, Platoon* 1986; *Someone to Watch Over Me, Wall Street* 1987; *Tequila Sunrise* 1988; *Hell High* 1989; *State of Grace* 1990; *The Mambo Kings* 1992.

Simpson, Don. Producer. *b.* Donald C. Simpson, on Oct. 25, 1945, in Anchorage, Alaska. *d.* 1996. A Phi Beta Kappa graduate of the University of Oregon, he began his working career as an account executive in advertising, and later joined Warner Bros. as a marketing executive, specializing in youth-oriented films. In 1975 he moved to Paramount, where he rapidly rose through the ranks to become president of worldwide production in 1981. Two years later he formed Simpson-Bruckheimer Productions with Detroit-born Jerry BRUCKHEIMER. Operating under a special deal with Paramount, the partners went on to produce a string of box-office hits. Early in the 90s they shifted their allegiance to Disney. Simpson appeared as an actor in several films.

FILMS INCLUDE: *Cannonball* (co-sc., act. only) 1976; *Flashdance* 1983; *Beverly Hills Cop, Thief of Hearts* 1984; *Top Gun* 1986; *Beverly Hills Cop II* 1987; *The Big Bang* (act. only), *Days of Thunder* (also act.), *Young Guns II* (act. only) 1990; *Bad Boys, Crimson Tide, Dangerous Minds* 1995.

Sinatra, Frank. Actor, singer. Born Francis Albert Sinatra, on Dec. 12, 1915, in Hoboken, N.J. The son of an Italian immigrant fireman, he started out as a copyboy at a local newspaper, then organized a singing group, "The Hoboken Four." His first break came when he won first prize on radio's 'Major Bowes Amateur Hour.' This led to appearances on radio, engagements in small nightclubs, and eventually the position of a vocalist with the Harry James and the Tommy Dorsey bands. He struck out on his own in the early 40s and soon emerged as the idol of swooning, screaming bobby-soxers across America. A scrawny little baritone with hollow cheeks, a hungry look, and a casual singing style marked by a careful phrasing of lyrics, he was dubbed "The Voice" by his admirers and for several years enjoyed enormous popularity on the stage, on radio, in nightclubs, and in light musical films.

But when his vocal cords abruptly hemorrhaged in 1952, Sinatra was dropped by MCA, the giant talent agency, and his career seemed finished. He fought back courageously, however. He begged Columbia to cast him in the role of Maggio in *From Here to Eternity* and agreed to play the part for an insulting fee of $8,000. He won the best supporting actor Academy Award for his sensitive portrayal in the dramatic role. In 1955 he was nominated for an Oscar as best actor for his dramatic performance as a drug addict in *The Man with the Golden Arm* and in next to no time he was on his way not only to a complete recovery of his former success but also to new heights of status as the "Chairman of the Board of Show Business."

Besides his having gained respect as an actor, Sinatra's voice returned to top form and his singing style became more mature and more sophisticated than ever. Within a few years he was a superstar of films, TV, recordings, and nightclubs, and he had accumulated a fortune that he invested in a diversity of business ventures, from industry and real estate to gambling casinos and racetracks.

Sinatra has been often criticized for association with underworld figures in connection with some of his business affairs. He is one of the wealthiest men in show business; he is also among the most volatile. On the one hand, he has been known as an arrogant and quick-tempered man who gets into frequent fistfights and who on several occasions has physically attacked news photographers prying into his amorous escapades; on the other, he has a reputation for kindness and generosity which has expressed itself in magnanimous acts of philanthropy for individuals and organizations. At the 1971 Oscar ceremony he was honored with the Jean Hersholt Humanitarian Award. Shortly after, he announced his retirement "from the entertainment world and public life," but soon resumed his hectic activities as entertainer and man in the news. In 1983 he was the recipient of Kennedy Center honors for life achievement and in 1985 he was awarded the Medal of Freedom, America's highest civilian honor, from President Ronald Reagan at the White House. Later in the decade he launched an enormously successful concert tour with Sammy DAVIS, JR., and Liza MINNELLI, and in 1993 released an album of duets with an array of younger recording stars. His stormy life was the subject of an unauthorized biography by Kitty Kelley, *Sinatra*, and was depicted in the TV miniseries 'Sinatra' (1992). One of the entertainment world's most enduring artists and most visible celebrities, Sinatra has been linked romantically with many glamorous women. He has been married four times. Two of his three children from his first marriage (1939–1951), to Nancy Barbato, singer Nancy Sinatra (*b.* 1940) and singer Frank Sinatra, Jr. (*b.* 1944), have appeared in films. His second wife (1951–57) was actress Ava GARDNER and his third (1966–68) actress Mia FARROW. In 1976 he married Barbara Marx (née Blakely), the widow of Zeppo Marx.

FILMS: *Las Vegas Nights* (as vocalist with Tommy Dorsey's band) 1941; *Ship Ahoy* (as Dorsey vocalist) 1942; *Reveille with Beverly* (as vocal soloist), *Higher and Higher* (first acting role) 1943; *Step Lively* 1944; *The House I Live in* (Oscar-winning short), *Anchors Aweigh* 1945; *Till the Clouds Roll By* (cameo) 1946; *It Happened in Brooklyn* 1947; *The Miracle of the Bells, The Kissing Bandit* 1948; *Take Me Out to the Ball Game, On the Town* 1949; *Double Dynamite* 1951; *Meet Danny Wilson* 1952; *From Here to Eternity* (as Angelo Maggio) 1953; *Suddenly* 1954; *Young at Heart, Not as a Stranger, Guys and Dolls* (as Nathan Detroit), *The Tender Trap, The Man with the Golden Arm* 1955; *Meet Me in Las Vegas* (cameo), *High Society, Johnny Concho, Around the World in 80 Days* (cameo) 1956; *The Pride and the Passion, The Joker Is Wild* (as entertainer Joe E. Lewis), *Pal Joey* 1957; *Kings Go Forth* 1958; *Invitation to Monte Carlo* (travelogue; UK), *Some Came Running, A Hole in the Head, Never So Few* 1959; *Can-Can, Ocean's Eleven, Pepe* (cameo) 1960; *The Devil at 4 O'Clock* 1961; *Sergeants 3* (also prod.), *The Road to Hong Kong* (cameo; UK/US), *The Manchurian Candidate* 1962; *The List of Adrian Messenger* (cameo), *Come Blow Your Horn, 4 for Texas* 1963; *Robin and the 7 Hoods* (also prod.) 1964; *None but the Brave* (also dir., prod.), *Von Ryan's Express, Marriage on the Rocks* 1965; *The Oscar* (cameo), *Cast a Giant Shadow* (cameo), *Assault on a Queen* 1966; *The Naked Runner, Tony Rome* 1967; *The Detective, Lady in Cement* 1968; *Dirty Dingus Magee* 1970; *That's Entertainment* (on-screen narr.) 1974; *The First Deadly Sin* (also co-prod.) 1980; *Cannonball Run II* 1984; *Who Framed Roger Rabbit?* (v/o) 1988; *Entertaining the Troops* (doc.) 1989; *Listen Up* (doc.) 1990.

Sinclair, Robert B. Director. *b.* May 24, 1905, Toledo, Ohio. *d.* 1970. *ed.* U. of Pennsylvania. A former stage actor, he directed many successful Broadway productions of the 30s, including 'Life Begins,' 'Dodsworth,' 'Pride and Prejudice,' 'The Postman Always Rings Twice,' 'The Women,' 'Babes in Arms,' and 'The Philadelphia Story.' He then joined MGM as a director of B pictures, and his achievements as a film director were modest. He was at one time married to Heather ANGEL.

FILMS: *Woman Against Woman, Dramatic School* 1938; *Joe and Ethel Turp Call on the President* 1939; *And One Was Beautiful, The Captain Is a Lady* 1940; *Wild Man of Borneo, I'll Wait for You, Down in San Diego* 1941; *Mr. and Mrs. North* 1942; *Mr. District Attorney* 1947; *That Wonderful Urge* 1948.

Sinden, Donald. Actor. Born Oct. 9, 1923, in Plymouth, England. Colorless leading man of the British stage (from early 40s) and screen (from early 50s), he has appeared in character roles since the late 60s.

FILMS INCLUDE: *Portrait from Life/The Girl in the Painting* (bit) 1948; *The Cruel Sea, Mogambo* (US) 1953; *Doctor in the House, The Beachcomber* 1954; *Simba, Above Us the Waves, An Alligator Named Daisy* 1955; *Rockets Galore/Mad Little Island, The Captain's Table* 1958; *Operation Bullshine* 1959; *Your Money or Your Wife, The Siege of Sidney Street* 1960; *Decline and Fall. . . of a Bird Watcher* 1968; *Villain* 1971; *The Day of the Jackal* 1973; *The Island at the Top of the World* 1974; *The Lucky Touch* 1975; *Helicopter* 1981; *The Children* 1990.

Singer, Alexander. Director. Born in 1932, in New York City. A former magazine photographer, he gained filmmaking experience during his military service. Returning to civilian life, he broke into films as assistant director to schoolmate Stanley Kubrick on *The Killing* (1956). After some TV work, he made a promising debut as feature film director with the breezy, offbeat *A Cold Wind in August,* but his handful of subsequent films were routine, murky melodramas.

FILMS: *A Cold Wind in August* 1961; *Psyche 59* (UK) 1964; *Love Has Many Faces* 1965; *Captain Apache* 1971; *Glass Houses* (also co-sc.) 1972.

Singer, Lori. Actress. Born on Nov. 6, 1962, in Corpus Christi, Tex. *ed.* Juilliard. Attractive, blue-eyed leading lady of Hollywood films. The daughter of symphony conductor Jacques Singer, she was a concert cellist before landing a co-starring role in the TV series 'Fame' (1982–83) which, in turn, led to a promising film career. Her older brother, Vancouver-born Marc Singer, is an athletically built leading man who made his debut in *Go Tell It to the Spartans* (1978), but is most closely identified with his title role in *The Beastmaster* (1982).

FILMS: *Footloose* 1984; *The Falcon and the Snowman, The Man with One Red Shoe, Trouble in Mind* 1985; *Summer*

Heat 1987; *Made in USA* 1988; *Warlock* 1991; *Equinox, Short Cuts* 1993; *F.T.W.* 1994.

single broad. See BROAD.

single-frame exposure. The method of exposing motion picture film frame by frame rather than at a continuous rate of speed. The method is applied in STOP MOTION and TIME LAPSE cinematography.

single-system recording. The process of recording picture and sound simultaneously on the same film. The system is used mostly for newsreels and inexpensive documentaries, where the quality of sound is secondary to considerations of mobility and speed. The picture and the sound are both recorded by the camera, providing automatic synchronization and eliminating the need for a separate recording unit. The disadvantage, in addition to the poorer sound quality, is that the preset synchronization allows the editor little freedom in manipulating the picture and the sound in relation to each other. See also DOUBLE SYSTEM.

Singleton, John. Director. Born in 1967, in Los Angeles, the son of a real-estate agent. As a film student at USC, he wrote a semi-autobiographical script, which earned him the school's prestigious Jack Nicholson Award. Shortly after, he exploded on the Hollywood scene with a powerful film based on that screenplay, *Boyz N the Hood,* a gritty, behind-the-scenes look at the street life in the gang-infested black ghetto of south-central Los Angeles. At age 24 he became the youngest person ever nominated for an Academy Award for best director. He received another Oscar nomination for the screenplay and the New York Film Critics voted him best new director. His next effort, *Poetic Justice* (1993), was, despite the presence of singer Janet Jackson and the poetry of Maya Angelou, a critical and box-office disappointment.

FILMS: *Boyz N the Hood* (also sc.) 1991; *Poetic Justice* (also sc.) 1993; *Higher Learning* 1995; *Rosewood* 1997.

Singleton, Penny. Actress. Born Mariana Dorothy McNulty, on Sept. 15, 1908, in Philadelphia. *ed.* Columbia. A niece of former Postmaster General James Farley. She made her professional debut as a singer-acrobat in the Broadway musical 'Good News' (1927) and appeared also in the screen version in 1930. A contract player in Hollywood from 1936, she played comic supporting parts in a number of films, at first under her maiden name, then under her married name, Singleton, before soaring to popularity in the title role of the long-running (1938–50) "Blondie" feature series, opposite Arthur LAKE. She also played the part on radio for many years. After the series came to an end, she appeared briefly in nightclubs, then became active in union affairs. As vice president and executive secretary of AGVA, she organized the Rockettes' strike against Radio City Music Hall in 1966. She returned to Broadway briefly in 1971, replacing Ruby Keeler in 'No No Nanette.' Her second husband is B-film producer Robert Sparks.

FILMS INCLUDE: As Dorothy McNulty—*Good News, Love in the Rough* 1930; *After the Thin Man* 1936; *Vogues of 1938, Sea Racketeers* 1937. As Penny Singleton—*Swing Your Lady, Racket Busters, Boy Meets Girl, Secrets of an Actress, The Mad Miss Manton, Hard to Get, Blondie* 1938; Numerous "Blondie" episodes 1938–50; *Go West Young Lady* 1941; *Footlight Glamour* 1943; *Young Widow* 1946; *The Best Man* 1964; *Jetsons: The Movie* (v/o) 1990.

Sinise, Gary. Director, actor. Born in 1955, near Chicago. The co-founder and former artistic director of Chicago's highly regarded Steppenwolf Theatre Company, he made a tentative start as a film director in 1988 with *Miles from Home,* about the rise and fall of a family of Iowa farmers. He followed it with a remake of John Steinbeck's *Of Mice and Men* (1992), in which he also co-starred in the role of George. His career took a huge leap forward with his role as Lt. Dan in *Forrest Gump* (1994), receiving a supporting actor Academy Award nomination. He was praised for his work on Broadway in 'The Grapes of Wrath.'

FILMS: *Miles from Home* (dir.) 1988; *Jack the Bear* (act.) 1991; *Of Mice and Men* (dir., act.), *A Midnight Clear* (act.) 1992; *Jack the Bear* (act.) 1993; *Forrest Gump* 1994; *Apollo 13, The Quick and the Dead* 1995; *Ransom* 1996; *Albino Alligator* 1997.

Siodmak, Curt. Screenwriter, sometime director. Born on Aug. 10, 1902, in Dresden, Germany. *ed.* U. of Zurich. The younger brother of Robert SIODMAK, he started out as a reporter and began his association with the cinema as co-scripter (with Billy Wilder) of his brother's *Menschem am Sonntag/People on Sunday.* He also wrote scripts for several of Robert's subsequent films but worked mostly on his own after arriving in Hollywood in 1938. In addition to turning out many scripts, often dealing with the fantastic, he also wrote several horror novels, including *Donovan's Brain,* and short stories that have been adapted to the screen. He also tried his hand at directing, with humdrum results.

FILMS INCLUDE: As screenwriter (alone or in collaboration)—*Menschen am Sonntag/People on Sunday* (doc.; Ger.) 1929; *Der Mann der seinen Mörder sucht/Looking for His Murderer* (Ger.) 1931; *F.P.1 antwortet nicht/F.P.1* (Ger.) 1932; *La Crise est finie* (Fr.) 1934; *The Tunnel/Transatlantic Tunnel* (UK) 1935; *Her Jungle Love* (co-story only) 1938; *The Invisible Man Returns, Black Friday, The Ape* 1940; *Aloma of the South Seas* (co-story only), *The Wolf Man* 1941; *Pacific Blackout* (co-story only), *Invisible Agent* 1942; *Frankenstein Meets the Wolf Man, I Walked with a Zombie, Son of Dracula* (co-story only) 1943; *The Lady and the Monster* (novel basis, *Donovan's Brain*), *House of Frankenstein* (story only), *The Climax* 1944; *Frisco Sal, Shady Lady* 1945; *The Return of Monte Cristo* (co-story only) 1946; *The Beast with Five Fingers* 1947; *Berlin Express* (story only) 1948; *Tarzan's Magic Fountain, Swiss Tour/Four Days' Leave* (Switz./US) 1949; *Donovan's Brain* (novel basis only) 1953; *Riders to the Stars* 1954; *Earth vs. the Flying Saucers* 1956. As director—*Bride of the Gorilla* (also sc.) 1951; *The Magnetic Monster* (also co-sc.) 1953; *Curucu—Beast of the Amazon* (also sc.) 1956; *Love Slaves of the Amazon* (also prod., sc.) 1957; *Liebesspiele im Schnee/Ski Fever* (Aus./Czech./US) 1967.

Siodmak, Robert. Director. *b.* Aug. 8, 1900, Memphis, Tenn. *d.* 1973. The son of a Leipzig banker in the US on a business trip, he was brought to Germany while still an infant. After graduating from the University of Marburg, he began acting in German repertory, but financial pressures forced him into a job as a bank clerk and several unsuccessful business ventures. In 1925 he entered the German film industry as a title writer for imported US films. The following year he became a film editor and in 1929 he made his directorial debut, co-directing with Edgar G. Ulmer the noted feature documentary *Menschen am Sonntag/People on Sunday.* The film also marked the starting point of the careers of Curt SIODMAK, Robert's brother, of Billy Wilder, who collaborated on the script, and of Eugen Schüfftan and Fred Zinnemann, who collaborated on the photography. Siodmak went on to direct several German films, mostly suspense thrillers, but being Jewish, he was forced into exile in Paris after the Nazi takeover in 1933. He managed to leave Paris just before its occupation and in 1940 he headed for Hollywood.

After directing a string of B pictures for various studios, Siodmak attracted attention beginning in 1944 with a succession of atmospheric psychological thrillers for Universal, which were aptly described by critic Andrew Sarris as "more Germanic than his German [films]." He put the mysterious features of Ella Raines to excellent advantage in *Phantom Lady, The Suspect,* and *Uncle Harry,* successfully cast Deanna Durbin and Gene Kelly out of character in *Christmas Holiday,* and drew out the most interesting performance of Burt Lancaster's career in the actor's screen debut, *The Killers,* a taut adaptation of the Hemingway short story. Siodmak's Hollywood films of the early 50s were far less interesting, except for the lively costume adventure comedy *The Crimson Pirate.* He then reversed his exile route by returning to France in 1953 and to Germany the following year.

FILMS: In Germany—*Menschen am Sonntag/People on Sunday* (doc.; co-dir. with Edgar G. Ulmer) 1929; *Abschied* 1930; *Der Mann der seinen Mörder sucht/Looking for His Murderer, Voruntersuchung/Inquest* 1931; *Stürme der Leidenschaft/Tempest, Quick/Quick—König der Clowns* 1932; *Brennendes Geheimnis/The Burning Secret* 1933. In France—*Le Sexe faible* 1933; *La Crise est finie* 1934; *La Vie parisienne, Le Grand Refrain/Symphonie d'Amour* (superv. only), *Mister Flow/Compliments of Mr. Flow* 1936; *Cargaison blanche/Traffic in Souls/Woman Racket* 1937; *Mollenard/Hatred, Ultimatum* (completed for Robert Wiene) 1938; *Pièges/Personal Column* 1939. In the US—*West Point Widow* 1941; *Fly by Night, The Night Before the Divorce, My Heart Belongs to Daddy* 1942; *Someone to Remember, Son of Dracula* 1943; *Phantom Lady, Cobra Woman, Christmas Holiday* 1944; *The Suspect, Conflict* (co-story only), *Uncle Harry/The Strange Affair of Uncle Harry, The Spiral Staircase* 1945; *The Killers, The Dark Mirror* 1946; *Time Out of Mind* (also prod.) 1947; *Cry of the City* 1948; *Criss Cross, The Great Sinner* 1949; *Thelma Jordan, Deported* 1950; *The Whistle at Eaton Falls* 1951; *The Crimson Pirate* (UK/US) 1952; *Le Grand Jeu/Flesh and Woman* (Fr.) 1954. In Germany—*Die Ratten* 1955; *Mein Vater der Schauspieler* 1956; *Nachts wenn der Teufel Kam/The Devil Strikes at Night* 1957; *Dorothea Angermann, The Rough and the Smooth/Portrait of a Sinner* (UK) 1959; *Katia/Une Jeune Fille un Seul Amour/Magnificent Sinner* (Fr.), *Mein Schulfreund* 1960; *L'Affaire Nina B* (Fr./Ger.), *Tunnel 28/Escape from East Berlin* (Ger./US) 1962; *Der Schut* 1964; *Der Schatz der Azteken* (Ger./It./Sp.), *Die Pyramide des Sonnengottes* (Ger./It./Sp.) 1965; *Custer of the West/A Good Day for Fighting* (US) 1968; *Der Kampf um Rom* (in two parts; Ger./It.) 1968–69.

Sirk, Douglas (Sierck, Detlef). Director. *b.* Claus Detlev Sirk, Apr. 26, 1900, Skagen, Denmark (possibly in Hamburg to Danish parents). *d.* 1987. He went to Germany in his teens to study art and drama and stayed to become a successful stage producer and director, germanizing his name to Detlef Hans Sierck. A leftist in political orientation, he came under increasing pressure from the authorities after the Nazi rise to power and as a result decided in 1934 to switch to films, an industry that because of its international market was less subjected to rigorous control by the Nazi regime than was the theater. After directing several shorts, he turned to features in 1935 and soon acquired a reputation for the visual excellence of his films. In 1937 he left Germany with his Jewish wife and emigrated to the US via Spain, South Africa, and Australia. He was virtually unknown in Hollywood and despite his notable achievements in Europe he had to begin building his reputation from scratch. Since German-sounding names were anathema during WW II, he changed his to Douglas Sirk.

Most of the projects assigned to him were unpromising in content and minuscule in budget. He was often forced to contend with ridiculous scripts, ranging in genre from thrillers to maudlin soap operas. That he managed to overcome the handicap and end up with a good number of thoroughly enjoyable films is a tribute to his personal taste and the formal excellence of his visual style. Although based on a painfully foolish plot, *Magnificent Obsession* (1954) was the first of a string of Sirk melodramas that became box-office hits. Among these, *All That Heaven Allows* (1955) and *Written on the Wind* (1956), were also critically well received. *Imitation of Life* (1959) enjoyed the greatest commercial success. For reasons of health, he was forced to retire from activity in the cinema in 1959. He returned to Germany and settled in Munich.

FILMS: In Germany—*April April, Stützen der Gesellschaft, Das Mädchen von Moorhof* 1935; *Das Hofkonzert/La Chanson du Souvenir* (also co-sc.; German- and French-language versions), *Schlussakkord/Final Accord/Ninth Symphony* (also co-sc.) 1936; *La Habañera, Liebling der Matrosen* (also co-sc.), *Zu neuen Ufern/To New Shores, Die Heimat ruft/Home Is Calling* 1937. In South Africa—*Wilton's Zoo* 1938. In the US—*Hitler's Madman* 1943; *Summer Storm* (also co-sc.) 1944; *A Scandal in Paris* 1946; *Lured* 1947; *Sleep My Love* 1948; *Slightly French, Shockproof* 1949; *Mystery Submarine* 1950; *The First Legion* (also co-prod.), *Thunder on the Hill, The Lady Pays Off, Weekend with Father* 1951; *No Room for the Groom, Has Anybody Seen My Gal? Meet Me at the Fair* 1952; *Take Me to Town, All I Desire* 1953; *Taza Son of Cochise, Magnificent Obsession, Sign of the Pagan* 1954; *Captain Lightfoot* 1955; *There's Always Tomorrow, All That Heaven Allows* 1956; *Written on the Wind, Battle Hymn, Interlude* 1957; *The Tarnished Angels, A Time to Love and a Time to Die* 1958; *Imitation of Life* 1959.

16 mm. A film gauge widely in use by paraprofessional filmmakers. Introduced in 1923 for the amateur market, 16 mm film and equipment have gradually evolved as the tools of filmmakers whose work is not intended for theatrical release. The greater mobility of the equipment and the less-expensive cost of raw stock and processing have made 16 mm ideal for use in the production of documentaries and scientific, educational, industrial, and promotional films, as well as by avant-garde filmmakers and serious amateurs. It has also been widely in use in TV production.

Sixteen mm film contains 40 frames per foot. The film is perforated along both edges for silent use, but along only one for sound, the other edge being reserved for the sound track. A wide variety of cameras, projectors, and printing and editing equipment is available, some of it every bit as sophisticated as the equipment for the professional 35 mm gauge.

Sizemore, Tom. Actor. Born in 1964 in Detroit, Mich. *ed.* Wayne State University, Detroit; Temple University, Philadelphia, Pa. With a film career on the fast track due to his quick-witted, engaging persona, Sizemore started out on the stage in New York and in regional theater before being discovered by Hollywood. He steadily turns in gutsy, powerful performances.

FILMS: *Born On the Fourth of July, Lock Up, Rude Awakenings* 1989; *Blue Steel, Flight of the Intruder, Guilty By Suspicion, Harley Davidson and the Marlboro Man* 1991; *Passenger 57* 1992; *Heart and Souls, Striking Distance, True Romance, Watch It* 1993; *Natural Born Killers, Wyatt Earp* 1994; *Devil in a Blue Dress, Heat, Strange Days* 1995; *The Relic* 1997.

Sjöberg, Alf. Director. *b.* June 21, 1903, Stockholm. *d.* 1980. He began staging class plays while still a high school student. After training at the Royal Dramatic Theater, he began acting professionally in 1925 and directing for the stage in 1927. Stimulated by the expressive visual power of the cinema after viewing an Eisenstein film, he ventured successfully into film directing in 1929 with the silent *The Strongest.* But with the advent of sound and the abundance of stagy films on the

Swedish screen, he became disillusioned with cinema and returned to stage directing. In 1930 he was appointed head director of the Royal Dramatic Theater. During the next decade he gained a reputation as one of Sweden's most accomplished stage directors. In the 40s he returned to filmmaking and was instrumental in the renaissance of Swedish cinema, dormant since the silent era.

Sjöberg was Sweden's most important director before the advent of Ingmar Bergman, who began his film career as screenwriter for Sjöberg's internationally successful drama *Hets* (known as *Torment* in the US and as *Frenzy* in England). Sjöberg's remarkable screen adaptation of Strindberg's 'Miss Julie' won the grand prize (in a tie with De Sica's *Miracle in Milan*) at the 1951 Cannes Film Festival. His other important films were *Himlaspelet/The Road to Heaven* (1942) and *Bare en Mor/Only a Mother* (1949), but generally after *Miss Julie,* his screen work was uneven. Famous for his elegant adaptations from the stage and literature, he collaborated on most of his own scripts.

FILMS: *The Strongest* (also story) 1929; *They Staked Their Lives* (also co-sc.), *Blossom Time* (also sc.) 1940; *Home from Babylon* (also co-sc.) 1941; *Himlaspelet/The Road to Heaven* (also co-sc.) 1942; *Hets/Torment/Frenzy, The Royal Hunt* 1944; *Journey Out* (also sc.) 1945; *Iris and the Lieutenant* (also sc.) 1946; *Bare en Mor/Only A Mother* (also co-sc.) 1949; *Miss Julie* (also sc.) 1951; *Barabbas* (also co-sc.) 1953; *Karin Daughter of Man* (also sc.) 1954; *Wild Birds* (also co-sc.) 1955; *Last Pair Out* 1956; *The Judge* (also co-sc.) 1960; *The Island* (also co-sc.) 1966; *The Father* (also sc.) 1969.

Sjöman, Vilgot. Director. Born David Harald Vilgot Sjöman, on Dec. 2, 1924, in Stockholm. The son of a construction worker, he began working at 15, at first as a clerk with a cereal company, then as an orderly in a local prison. In his spare time he wrote several plays, which he was unable to have produced on the stage. He then adapted one of these into a novel and eventually a screenplay for Gustaf Molander's *Trots/Defiance* (1952). In 1956, Sjöman came to the US, on a scholarship to UCLA, where he attended a six-month film course, at the end of which he worked as an apprentice on *The Proud and the Profane.* After returning to Sweden, he wrote an incisive sociological study of the American film colony which was published in 1961 under the title *In Hollywood.* The following year he worked as Ingmar Bergman's assistant on *Winter Light* (1963) and later published a report on the making of the film, *Diary with Ingmar Bergman.* His professional association with Bergman dated back to the late 40s. In 1968 he appeared in the director's *Shame,* in the role of a TV interviewer.

Despite Sjöman's long association with the industry, his career as director did not begin until 1962, when he was 38. His films have typically dealt with Swedish society's morals and mores, revealing primarily a concern with sexual taboos and a fascination with violent and perverse aspects of sexuality. Both his *491* (1964) and *I Am Curious—Yellow* (1967) ran into censorship trouble in Sweden and abroad. The latter film was seized by US customs and released after a stormy legal battle. The publicity about its sensational aspects made the film a huge moneymaker when it was finally released in New York in 1969. The film's clearance by the court and its success at the box office helped open the way for explicit sex on the American screen in the 70s. Sjöman is a director in constant search of new styles and new things to say. Unfortunately, his reputation among filmgoers derives mainly from the sordid aspects of his films.

FILMS: *The Swedish Mistress* (also sc.) 1962; *491, The Dress* 1964; *Sysskonbädd/My Sister My Love* (also sc.) 1966; *Stimulantia* ("The Negress in the Wardrobe" episode; also sc.), *I Am Curious—Yellow* (also sc.) 1967; *I Am Curious—Blue* (also sc.), *Journey with Father* (short; also sc.) 1968; *You're Lying* (also sc.) 1969; *Lyckliga Skitar/Blushing Charlie* (also co-sc.) 1970; *The Karlsson Brothers* (also sc.) 1972; *Troll/Till Sex Do Us Part* (also co-sc.) 1973; *A Handful of Love* (also sc.) 1974; *The Garage* (also sc.) 1975; *Tabu/Taboo* (also sc.) 1977; *Linus and the Mysterious Red Brick House/Linus* (also sc. from own book) 1979; *I Am Blushing* (also sc.) 1981; *Malacca* (also prod., sc.) 1986; *The Pitfall* (also sc.) 1989.

Sjöström, Victor (known in the US as **Seastrom).** Director, actor. *b.* Sept. 20, 1879, Silbodal, Sweden. *d.* 1960. His father, once a prosperous lumber manufacturer, lost his entire fortune during a crisis in the industry. He worked for a while as a simple laborer, then brought his family to the US in the hope of starting a new life. Business in America was good and the father was soon able to regain his fortune. But little Victor, who received his education at various public schools, was unhappy, for his father's character had undergone a strange transformation. He had become a religious fanatic and ruled the household with puritan tyranny. Victor began detesting him, and when his mother, a former minor actress, died, he returned alone to Sweden. He attended high school at Uppsala and began participating in amateur dramatics. When his father died, Victor decided to become a professional actor. He was 16 at the time. He found employment in Finland and in four years had gained enough experience to return to Sweden as an established actor and director of small theaters. He appeared and directed in the provinces and the cities with varying success.

In 1911, Sjöström attempted a novel idea: presenting motion pictures in a theater in conjunction with live shows. But the experiment wasn't commercially successful. In the hope of making enough money to revive his project, he accepted an offer to join Svenska Bio, the film company, at a substantial salary. Another new employee at the studio, hired several months earlier, was Mauritz STILLER. Together, the two young men were destined to lead the fledging Swedish film industry to a preeminent position in world cinema. Sjöström made his debut as an actor in Stiller's *The Black Masks* (1912) but soon made his own mark as a director. In 1913 he directed his first major film, *Ingeborg Holm,* which drew raves from the European intellectual community. His reputation was further established with such films as *Terje Vigen/A Man There Was* (1917), *The Outlaw and His Wife* (1918), *A Girl from the Marsh Croft* (1919), *The Sons of Ingmar* (1919), and *The Phantom Carriage* (1921; also known as *The Stroke of Midnight* or *Thy Soul Shall Bear Witness*).

In contrast to Stiller's vivid, technically virtuosic style, Sjöström's work was characteristically more restrained, solemn, and ponderous. Sjöström shot many of his films on location, as did Stiller, and enhanced the dramatic effect of his films by integrating characters and landscapes. Of the two directors, Sjöström was the first to go Hollywood, partly because the Swedish film industry underwent a long period of decline in the early 20s, the result of growing competition from foreign films, especially American. In 1923, following a number of commercial failures, Sjöström arrived in Hollywood to study American methods of production. He was signed by the Goldwyn company as a director and remained on the payroll when the film merged into MGM the following year. His surname was changed to Seastrom.

The masterpiece of Sjöström's American period was *The Wind* (1928), starring Lillian Gish, a powerful drama of mental disintegration in an alien environment which derived much of its force from the interplay between the characters and the elements of nature. Other notable Sjöström achievements in Hollywood were *He Who Gets Slapped* and *The Tower of Lies,* both starring Lon Chaney; *The Scarlet Letter,* starring Lillian Gish; and *The Divine Woman,* with Greta Garbo in the title role. Sjöström returned to Sweden late in 1928, in time to attend the deathbed of his longtime friend Mauritz Stiller.

Thanks to his brief Hollywood experience with talkies, Sjöström was able to assist Swedish studios with technical advice during the transition to sound, but he himself directed only one film, in Swedish and German versions. After a long period of semiretirement he directed his last film, *Under the Red Robe* (1937), in England. During WW II he was appointed director of production for Svensk Film Industri. Sjöström, who had collaborated on the scripts and acted in many of his own films as well as in those of other directors, now also made occasional appearances in major films and closed his screen career in 1957 with a striking performance as the old scholar in Ingmar Bergman's *Wild Strawberries* (1957). Sjöström's second (1911–16) of three marriages was to actress Lily Bech (*b.* Lili Beck Magnussen, Dec. 25, 1885, Denmark; deceased). The third (1922–45) was to actress Edith Erastoff (*b.* 1887, Helsinki; *d.* 1945). Each starred in several of his films.

FILMS: In Sweden—*The Gardener* (also act.), *A Secret Marriage, A Summer Tale* (never released) 1912; *The Marriage Bureau* (also sc.), *Smiles and Tears, Lady Marion's Summer Flirtation, The Voice of Blood* (also act.), *Ingeborg Holm* (also sc.), *Life's Conflicts* (also act.) 1913; *The Clergyman, Love Stronger Than Hate, Half-Breed, The Miracle, Do Not Judge, A Good Girl Should Solve Her Own Problems* (also sc.), *Children of the Street, Daughter of the High Mountain* (also sc., act.), *Hearts That Meet* 1914; *The Strike* (also co-sc., act.), *One Out of Many* (also sc.), *Expiated Guilt* (also co-sc.), *It Was in May* (also sc.), *Keep to Your Trade* (also sc.), *Judas Money* 1915; *The Governor's Daughters* (also sc.), *Sea Vultures, At the Moment of Trial* (also sc., act.), *Ships That Meet, She Was Victorious* (also sc., act.), *Therese* (also co-sc.) 1916; *The Kiss of Death* (also co-sc., act.), *Terje Vigen/A Man There Was* (also act.) 1917; *The Outlaw and His Wife* (also sc., act.) 1918; *The Sons of Ingmar* (in two parts; also sc., act.), *A Girl from the Marsh Croft* (also co-sc.), *His Grace's Will* (also co-sc.) 1919; *The Monastery of Sendomir* (also sc.), *Karin Daughter of Ingmar* (also co-sc., act.), *The Executioner* (also act.) 1920; *The Phantom Carriage/The Stroke of Midnight/Thy Soul Shall Bear Witness* (also sc., act.) 1921; *Vem Dômer?/Love's Crucible* (also co-sc.), *The Surrounded House* (also co-sc., act.) 1922; *Fire on Board/The Hell Ship* (also act.). In the US—*Name the Man, He Who Gets Slapped* (also co-sc.) 1924; *Confessions of a Queen, The Tower of Lies* 1925; *The Scarlet Letter* 1926; *The Divine Woman, The Wind, The Masks of the Devil* 1928; *A Lady to Love* (and German-language version, *Die Sehnsucht jeder Frau*) 1930. In Sweden—*Markurells i Wadkôping* (and German-language version, *Väter und Söhne/Father and Son;* also act. in Swedish version only) 1930–31. In the UK—*Under the Red Robe* 1937.

Skelton, Red. Actor. *b.* Richard Bernard Skelton, on July 18, 1910, in Vincennes, Ind. *d.* 1997. Orphaned from his circus-clown father before he was born and raised in dire poverty by his overworked charwoman-mother, he was singing for pennies on the streets of his home town at the age of seven. At ten he quit school to join a medicine show and spent the rest of his childhood and early youth entertaining on show boats, in circuses, burlesque, and vaudeville. He was a small-time comic, appearing mostly in one night stands until the early 30s, when he developed a doughnut-dunking routine that eventually got him a booking at New York's Paramount Theater. Success on radio followed and in 1938 he made his debut in films. In the 40s and early 50s, Skelton developed into a popular comedy star of many MGM productions. He later capped his screen success with TV superstardom, showcasing his pantomime routines and such famous characterizations as Freddie the Freeloader and Clem Kadiddlehopper. He also wrote music, including the theme song 'My True Love' for the film *Made in Paris* (1966). Although he disappeared from the screen in the late 60s, Skelton continued performing in clubs and comedy concerts, and in 1990, at 80, he brought his nostalgic act to Carnegie Hall. His third wife (since 1973) was Lothian Toland, 25 years his junior, the daughter of cinematographer Gregg Toland of *Citizen Kane* fame.

FILMS: *Having Wonderful Time* 1938; *Flight Command, The People vs. Dr. Kildare, Whistling in the Dark, Dr. Kildare's Wedding Day, Lady Be Good* 1941; *Ship Ahoy, Maisie Gets Her Man, Panama Hattie, Whistling in Dixie* 1942; *Du Barry Was a Lady, Thousands Cheer, I Dood It, Whistling in Brooklyn* 1943; *Bathing Beauty* 1944; *Ziegfeld Follies, The Show-Off* 1946; *Merton of the Movies* 1947; *The Fuller Brush Man, A Southern Yankee* 1948; *Neptune's Daughter* 1949; *The Yellow Cab Man, Duchess of Idaho* (cameo), *Three Little Words* (as songwriter Harry Ruby), *The Fuller Brush Girl* (cameo), *Watch the Birdie* 1950; *Excuse My Dust, Texas Carnival* 1951; *Lovely to Look At* 1952; *The Clown, Half a Hero* 1953; *The Great Diamond Robbery, Susan Slept Here* (cameo) 1954; *Around the World in 80 Days* (cameo) 1956; *Public Pigeon No. 1* 1957; *Ocean's Eleven* (cameo) 1960; *Those Magnificent Men in Their Flying Machines* (UK) 1965.

Skerritt, Tom. Actor. Born on Aug. 5, 1933, in Detroit. *ed.* Wayne State U.; UCLA. Robust leading man and supporting player of American films and television, typically in cool, macho roles. His long-lingering film career picked up momentum after *Alien* (1979). He won acclaim, newfound popularity, and a best actor Emmy in 1993 for his performance on the television series 'Picket Fences.'

FILMS INCLUDE: *War Hunt* 1962; *One Man's Way* 1964; *Those Calloways* 1965; *M*A*S*H* 1970; *Wild Rovers* 1971; *Fuzz* 1972; *Thieves Like Us, Big Bad Mama* 1974; *The Devil's Rain* 1975; *The Turning Point* 1977; *Up in Smoke* 1978; *Alien, Ice Castles* 1979; *Savage Harvest, The Burning Man/A Dangerous Summer* (Austral.), *Silence of the North* (Can.) 1981; *Fighting Back* 1982; *The Dead Zone* (Can.) 1983; *Top Gun, Hell Camp/Opposing Force, Spacecamp, Wisdom* 1986; *Maid to Order, The Big Town* 1987; *Poltergeist III* 1988; *Big Man on Campus, Steel Magnolias* 1989; *Honor Bound, The Rookie* 1990; *Poison Ivy, Wild Orchid II: Two Shades of Blue, A River Runs Through It, Singles* 1992; *Knight Moves* 1993; *Contact* 1997.

skin flicks. Slang for pornographic motion pictures.

skip framing. A method of optical printing in which only every other or every third frame on the negative is printed, to give the effect of speeded-up action. When alternate frames are printed the action is accelerated to twice the normal speed; when every third frame is printed, to three times the normal speed, etc. The opposite of skip framing is "double framing," which slows down the action by repeating a frame two or more times.

Skipworth, Alison. Actress. *b.* Alison Groom, July 25, 1863, London. *d.* 1952. A regal beauty in her youth, she went on the London stage at the age of 31 to help supplement the meager income of her artist husband. She made her Broadway debut the following year, 1895, and later appeared in numerous American stage productions in leads, then in supporting roles. Excluding an isolated film appearance in 1921, she began her film career in 1930 and for nearly a decade played character roles in numerous Hollywood productions, specializing in the portrayal of lofty matrons and grand dames. She is best remembered as the hefty, indomitable foil to W. C. Fields's antics in *If I Had a Million* (1932), *Tillie and Gus* (1933), and *Six of a Kind* (1934).

FILMS INCLUDE: *Handcuffs or Kisses* 1921; *Raffles, Outward Bound, Du Barry—Woman of Passion* 1930; *Virtuous Husband, The Night Angel, Devotion* 1931; *Madame Racketeer, Night After Night, If I Had a Million* 1932; *Tonight Is Ours, A Lady's Profession, Song of Songs, Midnight Club, Tillie and Gus, Alice in Wonderland* 1933; *Six of a Kind, Wharf Angel, The Notorious Sophie Lang, The Captain Hates the Sea, Here Is My Heart* 1934; *The Casino Murder Case, The Devil Is a Woman, Becky Sharp* (as *Vanity Fair's* Miss Crawley), *Doubting Thomas, Shanghai* 1935; *The Princess Comes Across, Satan Met a Lady, The Gorgeous Hussy* 1936; *Stolen Holiday, Two Wise Maids* 1937; *King of the Newsboys, Ladies in Distress, Wide Open Faces* 1938.

Skirball, Jack H. Producer. *b.* June 23, 1896, in Homestead, Pa. *d.* 1985. Formerly a motion picture business executive, he was put in charge of production and distribution at Educational Pictures in 1932. He resigned the post in 1939 to become an independent producer, notably of two Hitchcock films, *Saboteur* (co-prod., 1942) and *Shadow of a Doubt* (1943).

FILMS INCLUDE: *Miracle on Main Street* 1939; *The Howards of Virginia* (assoc. prod.) 1940; *Saboteur* (co-prod.) 1942; *Shadow of a Doubt* 1943; *It's in the Bag, Guest Wife* 1945; *So Goes My Love, Magnificent Doll* 1946; *Bride for Sale* 1949; *The Secret Fury* 1950; *Payment on Demand* 1951; *A Matter of Time* (co-prod.; US/It.) 1976.

Skladanowsky, Max. Inventor, pioneer of German cinema. *b.* Apr. 30, 1863, Berlin. *d.* 1939. The son of a magic lantern showman, he became involved with the presentation of optical shows in his early youth. Between 1892 and 1895, with the aid of his brother Emil (1859–1945), he designed a projection apparatus they called the Bioskop (or Bioscope). He patented the invention in 1895 and on November 1 of that year gave the first public presentation of projected motion pictures in Germany. Since the brothers Skladanowsky's public presentation preceded that of the brothers Lumière in Paris by a few weeks, the Germans have claimed for Max the title of the true inventor of cinema, conveniently disregarding the fact that the Lumières had been showing their films for months before that date in private presentations to a nonpaying public. In any case, the Skladanowsky apparatus was a crude machine, employing a dual lens system to project two sets of film strips alternately, each running at the speed of eight frames per second. It projected series of pictures and not continuous motion pictures in the true sense. It was soon abandoned.

Skolimowski, Jerzy (Yurek). Director. Born on May 5, 1938, in Warsaw. Even before graduating from Warsaw University in 1959, he had published a collection of short stories and two volumes of poetry. He also played jazz drums and dabbled in amateur boxing. A chance encounter with the director led the young writer to a collaboration on the screenplay of Andrzej WAJDA's *Innocent Sorcerers* (1960). On the recommendation of Wajda, he was accepted the following year as a student at the famous state film school in Lodz. During his four-year term of studies he collaborated on the script of Polanski's *Knife in the Water* and directed a medium-length film, *Boxer,* featuring himself in the title role. Since his graduation in 1964, he has emerged as one of the brightest and most inventive talents of the East European cinema.

The protagonist of Skolimowski's first feature film, *Rysopis/Identification Marks: None* (1964), like the typical nonhero of his subsequent early films, is an outsider, again played by Skolimowski himself, who seems to drift as aimlessly as the haphazard structure of the film. But Skolimowski's style matured rapidly, reaching an assertive peak with *Deep End* (US/Ger.; 1970), one of several productions he has filmed in the West since Polish authorities banned his anti-Stalinist film *Hands Up!* (1967). He scored international successes with the British-made *The Shout* (1978), sharing the Special Jury Prize at Cannes, and *Moonlighting* (1982), which earned him the best screenplay award at the same festival. Known by film crews as a swift-paced, decisive director, Skolimowski is endowed with visual imagination, genuine compassion for characters, and a near surrealistic sense of humor. He is one of only a few directors who have managed to pursue concurrently successful careers on both sides of the erstwhile Iron Curtain. He has written or collaborated on all his scripts and has appeared as an actor in several of his own films.

FEATURE FILMS: *Innocent Sorcerers* (co-sc. only) 1959; *Knife in the Water* (co-sc. only), *A Friend* (co-sc. only) 1960; *Rysopis/Identification Marks: None* (also prod., sc., art dir., edit., act.) 1964; *Walkover* (also sc., act.) 1965; *Barrier* (also sc.) 1966; *Le Départ* (also co-sc., Belg.), *Hands Up!* (also sc., art dir., act.) 1967; *Dialogue* (one episode; also sc.; Czech.) 1968; *The Adventures of Gerard* (also co-sc.; UK/Switz.), *Deep End* (also co-sc.; US/Ger.) 1970; *Herzbube/King Queen Knave* (also co-sc.; Ger./US) 1972; *The Shout* (also co-sc.; UK) 1978; *Die Falschung/Circle of Deceit* (act. only; Ger./Fr.) 1981; *Moonlighting* (also co-prod., UK) 1982; *Success Is the Best Revenge* (also co-sc.; UK) 1984; *White Nights* (act. only; US), *The Lightship* (US/Ger.) 1985; *Mesmerized* (orig. treatment only; UK/Austral./NZ) 1986; *Big Shots* (act. only; US) 1987; *Les Eaux printaniers/Torrents of Spring* (also co-sc., act.; It./Fr.) 1989; *Before and After Death* (also sc.) 1992; *The Hollow Men* (prod.) 1993; *Mars Attacks!* (act. only) 1996.

Skouras, Spyros P. Movie mogul. *b.* Mar. 28, 1893, Skourohorion, Greece. *d.* 1971. One of ten children of a poor Greek shepherd, he made his way to the US in 1910 with two of his brothers, Charles and George. The three worked as busboys in a St. Louis hotel and moonlighted as newsboys. Working diligently and living frugally, they were able to save $4,000, which they invested in a share of a St. Louis motion picture theater. Eventually they bought out their partners and gradually took over control of all St. Louis cinemas. In the late 20s the brothers sold their growing chain of theaters to Warners, and Spyros took over the management of the entire Warners circuit. In 1930 he left Warners to join Paramount. In 1932 he took over the Fox Metropolitan chain, rescued it from bankruptcy, and in 1935 helped engineer Fox's merger with 20th Century.

In 1942, Skouras became president of 20th Century-Fox, and with the help of production chief Darryl Zanuck, he moved the studio into a dominant position in the industry, despite his notoriously limited knowledge of the English language. During the postwar years, when Hollywood was facing the crisis of television, he was the driving force behind the publicity campaign "Movies Are Better Than Ever." Refusing to concede to the competition from the small tube, he launched the wide-screen era in 1953 with the acquisition of CinemaScope. But when Fox faltered financially in the early 60s, he was made the scapegoat for the $30-million *Cleopatra* fiasco and in 1962 he was kicked upstairs to the position of board chairman. He resigned the post in 1969 to look after his own diversified investments, including a shipping line.

sky filter. A graduated light filter used to darken the sky area of a picture without affecting the rest of the scene. It is used mostly in black-and-white cinematography.

Skye, Ione. Actress. Born Ione Skye Leitch, in 1971, in

London. Bright, fresh-faced young lead of Hollywood films. The out-of-wedlock daughter of 60s folk-rock singer Donovan (Leitch), whom she never met, she was raised by her mother in Los Angeles. She got into films by chance, when director Tim Hunter spotted her picture in a fashion article in *L.A. Weekly* and cast her in *River's Edge* (1987) in the role of a confused high-school kid. Her older brother, Donovan Leitch (*b.* 1967), is also a movie actor.

FILMS: *River's Edge, Stranded* 1987; *A Night in the Life of Jimmy Reardon* 1988; *The Rachel Papers* (UK), *Say Anything. . .* 1989; *Mindwalk* 1990; *Samantha* 1991; *Gas Food and Lodging, Wayne's World* (bit) 1992; *Four Rooms* 1995.

slate. A small board marked with information pertinent to the identification of film in the cutting room, such as the title of the film, the names of the director and director of photography, the number of the scene and the take, and the date. At the beginning or the end of each take, the slate is held in front of the camera and exposed for several frames. When shooting sound, the slate used has a hinged section attached which can be snapped quickly to produce a loud crack, providing an aural-visual cue for the purpose of synchronization. When used in this fashion the slate is called "clapper boards," or CLAPSTICKS.

Slater, Christian. Actor. Born on Aug. 18, 1969, in New York City. Sly, confident young lead of Hollywood films. The son of stage actor Michael Hawkins and movie casting director Mary Jo Slater (now v.p. of talent at MGM), he began his career at age seven in the TV soap opera 'One Life to Live' and later performed with a touring company of 'The Music Man.' He entered films in the mid-80s, establishing a presence as the crazed teen obsessed with Winona Ryder in the pitch-black comedy *Heathers* (1989). Slater's offbeat, shady delivery reminded many of a young Jack Nicholson, and his sex appeal made him a popular—if not always bankable—leading man.

FILMS: *The Legend of Billie Jean* 1985; *The Name of the Rose* (Ger./It./Fr.) 1986; *Personal Choice, Tucker: The Man and His Dream* 1988; *Gleaming the Cube, Heathers, The Wizard* 1989; *Tales from the Darkside: The Movie, Young Guns II, Pump Up the Volume* 1990; *Robin Hood: Prince of Thieves, Mobsters, Star Trek VI: The Undiscovered Country* (cameo) 1991; *Kuffs, Ferngully. . . The Last Rainforest* (v/o), *Where the Day Takes You, Untamed Heart* (v/o) 1992; *True Romance* 1993; *Interview with the Vampire, Jimmy Hollywood* 1994; *Murder in the First* 1995; *Bed of Roses, Broken Arrow* 1996; *The Flood* 1997.

Slater, Helen. Actress. Born on Dec. 15, 1963, in New York City. Strapping, blonde leading lady of the American stage and screen. A graduate of Manhattan's High School for the Performing Arts, she got her big break in the lead role of *Supergirl* (1984), but has yet to achieve major stardom.

FILMS: *Supergirl* 1984; *The Legend of Billie Jean* 1985; *Ruthless People* 1986; *The Secret of My Success* 1987; *Sticky Fingers* 1988; *Happy Together* 1990; *City Slickers* 1991; *Chantilly Lace* 1993; *Lassie* 1994.

Slezak, Walter. Actor. *b.* May 3, 1902, Vienna. *d.* 1983. The son of noted operatic tenor and later film character comedian Leo Slezak (1873–1946), he was studying medicine and working as a bank clerk when he was discovered by film director Michael Kertesz (Curtiz) in 1922. He played romantic leads on the stage and in German films, but his tendency to gain weight soon forced him into character parts. In the US since 1930, he made his Broadway debut the following year but did not start in films until 1942. Hollywood typecast him either as a menacing heavy or a bumbling idiot, often as both in the same film. While pursuing a successful screen career, he continued appearing on the stage. In 1955 he won both the Tony and the New York Critics awards for his role in the Broadway musical "Fanny." In 1957 he sang in the operetta "The Gypsy Baron" at the Metropolitan Opera, the first of several operatic engagements. Long a resident of Switzerland, he appeared mainly in European-based productions in the late phases of his film career. His daughter Erika Slezak has starred in TV soap operas.

FILMS INCLUDE: In Germany—*Sodom und Gomorra/Queen of Sin and the Spectacle of Sodom and Gomorrah* 1922; *Mikaël/Michael/Chained* 1924; *Junges Blut* 1926; *Die grosse Pause, Die Lorelei* 1927; *Eros in Ketten* 1930. In the US—*Once Upon a Honeymoon* 1942; *This Land is Mine, The Fallen Sparrow* 1943; *Lifeboat, Step Lively, Till We Meet Again* 1944; *The Princess and the Pirate, Salome—Where She Danced, The Spanish Main, Cornered* 1945; *Sinbad the Sailor, Riff-Raff* 1947; *The Pirate* 1948; *The Inspector General* 1949; *The Yellow Cab Man, Spy Hunt* 1950; *Bedtime for Bonzo, People Will Talk* 1951; *Call Me Madam, White Witch Doctor* 1953; *Ten Thousand Bedrooms* 1957; *The Miracle* 1959; *Come September* 1961; *The Wonderful World of the Brothers Grimm* 1962; *Emil and the Detectives* 1964; *A Very Special Favor* 1965; *El Fantastico Mundo del Dr. Coppelius/Dr. Coppelius* (title role; Sp./US) 1966; *The Caper of the Golden Bulls* 1967; *Black Beauty* (UK/Ger.) 1971; *Treasure Island* (as Squire Trelawney, UK/Fr./Ger./Sp.) 1972; *The Mysterious House of Dr. C.* (again as Dr. Coppelius) 1976.

Sloane, Everett. Actor. *b.* Oct. 1, 1909, New York City. *d.* 1965. *ed.* U. of Pennsylvania. Having lost his job as Wall Street runner in the 1929 crash, he turned to acting on the stage as well as in thousands of radio dramas. He made his Broadway debut in 1935, then joined Orson Welles's Mercury Theatre. He followed Welles to Hollywood and made an impressive film debut as Bernstein in *Citizen Kane* (1941). A formidable character actor despite his diminutive size, he played powerful key parts in many films, memorably in Welles's *The Lady from Shanghai* (1948) and in Fielder Cook's *Patterns* (1956). He took his own life by an overdose of sleeping pills.

FILMS INCLUDE: *Citizen Kane* 1941; *Journey Into Fear* 1943; *The Lady from Shanghai* 1948; *Prince of Foxes* 1949; *The Men* 1950; *The Enforcer, Sirocco, The Desert Fox, The Blue Veil* 1951; *The Big Knife* 1955; *Patterns, Somebody Up There Likes Me, Lust for Life* 1956; *Marjorie Morningstar* 1958; *Home from the Hill* 1960; *By Love Possessed* 1961; *The Patsy, The Disorderly Orderly* 1964.

Sloane, Paul. Director. Born on Apr. 16, 1893, in New York City. *ed.* NYU. In films from 1914 as screenwriter for Edison, then Fox and Paramount, he turned director in 1925. Following a seesaw Hollywood career, he settled in Japan in the early 50s as an independent producer.

FILMS INCLUDE: *A Man Must Live, Too Many Kisses, The Shock Punch, The Coming of Amos* 1925; *Made for Love, Eve's Leaves, The Cling Vine, Corporal Kate* 1926; *Turkish Delight* 1927; *The Blue Danube* (also co-sc.) 1928; *Hearts in Dixie* 1929; *The 3 Sisters, The Cuckoos, Half Shot at Sunrise* 1930; *Traveling Husbands, Consolation Marriage* 1931; *War Correspondent* 1932; *The Woman Accused* 1933; *Straight Is the Way, Down to Their Last Yacht* 1934; *Here Comes the Band* 1935; *Geronimo* (also sc.) 1940; *The Sun Sets at Dawn* (also sc.) 1951.

Slocombe, Douglas. Director of photography. Born on Feb. 10, 1913, in London. A former journalist and still photographer, he began his association with films as a WW II newsreel cameraman. After the war, he joined the Ealing studios as director of photography. Remaining with the company for 17 years, he was behind the camera on some of the studio's most important productions. He has been freelancing since the early 60s, and from the early 70s has also worked on high-budget

Hollywood films. He was nominated for Academy Awards for the cinematography of *Travels with My Aunt* (1972), *Julia* (1977), and *Raiders of the Lost Ark* (1981).

FILMS INCLUDE: *Lights Out in Europe* (doc. on invasion of Poland) 1940; *The Big Blockade* 1941; *For Those in Peril* 1943; *Dead of Night* 1945; *The Captive Heart* 1946; *Hue and Cry, It Always Rains on Sunday* 1947; *Saraband for Dead Lovers/Saraband* 1948; *Kind Hearts and Coronets* 1949; *Cage of Gold* 1950; *The Lavender Hill Mob, The Man in the White Suit* 1951; *Mandy/The Story of Mandy/Crash of Silence, The Titfield Thunderbolt* 1952; *Ludwig II* (Ger.), *Lease on Life* 1954; *The Smallest Show on Earth* 1958; *The Mark* 1961; *The L-Shaped Room, Freud* (US) 1962; *The Servant* 1963; *A High Wind in Jamaica* 1965; *The Blue Max* 1966; *Dance of the Vampires/The Fearless Vampire Killers* 1967; *Boom, The Lion in Winter* 1968; *The Italian Job* 1969; *The Buttercup Chain* 1970; *The Music Lovers, Murphy's War* 1971; *Travels with My Aunt* 1972; *Jesus Christ Superstar* (US) 1973; *The Great Gatsby* (US), *The Marseille Contract/The Destructors* 1974; *Rollerball* (US), *The Maids, Hedda* 1975; *The Sailor Who Fell from Grace with the Sea, Nasty Habits* 1976; *Julia* (US), *Close Encounters of the Third Kind* (co-phot.; US) 1977; *Caravans* (US/Iran) 1978; *The Lady Vanishes, Lost and Found* (US) 1979; *Nijinsky* 1980; *Raiders of the Lost Ark* (US) 1981; *The Pirates of Penzance* (US), *Never Say Never Again* 1983; *Indiana Jones and the Temple of Doom* (US), *Water* 1984; *Lady Jane* 1986; *Indiana Jones and the Last Crusade* (US) 1989.

Sloman, Edward. Director. *b.* July 19, 1887, London. Deceased. A former stage and screen actor, he directed numerous Hollywood silents and early talkies, mainly routine, in a variety of genres.

FILMS INCLUDE: *A Woman's Daring, The Twinkler, Lying Lips* 1916; *Pride and the Man, The Fighting Gentleman, The Sea Master, Snap Judgment, Frame-Up, New York Luck* 1917; *The Midnight Trail, Mantle of Charity, Social Briars, Money Isn't Everything* 1918; *Molly of the Follies, The Westerners* 1919; *Slam Bang Jim, Burning Daylight, Blind Youth, The Mutiny of the Elsinore* 1920; *The Marriage of William Ashe, Quick Action, The Other Woman, Pilgrims of the Night* (also sc.), *The Ten Dollar Raise* 1921; *Shattered Idols, The Woman He Loved* 1922; *The Last Hour* (also prod.), *Backbone, The Eagle's Feather* 1923; *Up the Ladder, The Price of Pleasure, The Storm Breaker, His People/Proud Heart* 1925; *The Beautiful Cheat, Old Soak, Butterflies in the Rain* 1926; *Alias the Deacon, Surrender* 1927; *We Americans* (also co-sc.), *The Foreign Legion* 1928; *The Girl on the Barge, The Lost Zeppelin* 1929; *The Kibitzer, Hell's Island, Puttin' on the Ritz, Soldiers and Women* 1930; *Gun Smoke, The Conquering Horde, Murder by the Clock, Caught, His Woman* 1931; *Wayward* 1932; *There's Always Tomorrow* 1934; *A Dog of Flanders* 1935; *The Jury's Secret* 1938.

slop print. See SCRATCH PRINT.

slow motion. An effect resulting from running film through a camera at faster-than-normal speed. When the film is projected at the standard rate of speed, action on the screen seems slowed down. The effect is often used in coverage of sports events, such as diving, to demonstrate skill and style, or to recapture a key moment in a ball game. It has also been widely used for artistic effect, to create a romantic aura or stress a moment in time. Pudovkin, for instance, used slow motion in a suicide scene in *The Deserter,* in which a man jumping into a river seems sucked down by the slowly splashing waves. The opposite of slow motion is fast motion, or ACCELERATED MOTION.

slug. A piece of blank LEADER inserted in a work print to replace damaged or missing footage temporarily.

Small, Edward. Producer. *b.* Feb. 1, 1891, Brooklyn, N.Y. *d.* 1977. A former actor and impresario, he set up a talent agency in Hollywood in the early 20s. At the same time, he began producing films. In 1932 he co-founded Reliance Pictures, distributing through United Artists. In 1938 he organized Edward Small Productions. He produced many commercially successful films as well as numerous TV programs.

FILMS INCLUDE: *Passion's Pathway* (co-prod.) 1924; *The Sporting Lover* (co-prod.) 1926; *McFadden's Flats, The Gorilla* (co-prod.) 1927; *The Song of Love* (exec. prod.) 1929; *Clancy in Wall Street* 1930; *I Cover the Waterfront* 1933; *The Count of Monte Cristo, Transatlantic Merry-Go-Round* 1934; *Let 'Em Have It* 1935; *The Last of the Mohicans* 1936; *Sea Devils, Super-Sleuth, The Toast of New York* 1937; *The Duke of West Point* 1938; *The Man in the Iron Mask* 1939; *My Son My Son!, South of Pago-Pago, Kit Carson, The Son of Monte Cristo* 1940; *The Corsican Brothers* 1941; *Miss Annie Rooney, Friendly Enemies* 1942; *Up in Mabel's Room, Abroad with Two Yanks* 1944; *Brewster's Millions, Getting Gertie's Garter* 1945; *Temptation* 1946; *The Fuller Brush Man* (exec. prod.), *Raw Deal, The Black Arrow* (exec. prod.) 1948; *Black Magic* (exec. prod.) 1949; *Davy Crockett—Indian Scout* 1950; *Valentino, Lorna Doone* 1951; *Scandal Sheet, Kansas City Confidential* 1952; *Southwest Passage* 1954; *The Naked Street* 1955; *Monkey on My Back* 1957; *Witness for the Prosecution* (exec. prod.) 1958; *Solomon and Sheba* (exec. prod.) 1959; *Jack the Giant Killer* 1962; *I'll Take Sweden* 1965; *Boy! Did I Get a Wrong Number!* 1966; *The Wicked Dreams of Paula Schultz* 1968; *The Christine Jorgensen Story* 1970.

Small, Michael. American composer. Born in 1939. In films since the late 60s.

FILMS INCLUDE: *Out of It* 1969; *Puzzle of a Downfall Child, The Revolutionary* 1970; *Klute* 1971; *Child's Play, Dealing* 1972; *Love and Pain and the Whole Damned Thing* 1973; *The Parallax View* 1974; *The Stepford Wives, Night Moves* 1975; *Marathon Man* 1976; *Pumping Iron* (doc.), *Audrey Rose* 1977; *Girlfriends, The Driver, Comes a Horseman* 1978; *Going in Style* 1979; *Those Lips Those Eyes* 1980; *The Postman Always Rings Twice, Continental Divide, Rollover* 1981; *The Star Chamber* 1983; *Firstborn* 1984; *Target* 1985; *Brighton Beach Memoirs* 1986; *Black Widow, Orphans, Jaws the Revenge* 1987; *1969* 1988; *See You in the Morning* 1989; *Mountains of the Moon* 1990.

Smalley, Phillips. Actor, director. *b.* Wendell Phillips Smalley, Aug. 7, 1875, Brooklyn, N.Y. *d.* 1939. *ed.* Oxford; Harvard Law School. A veteran of the stage, he entered films in 1909 and co-starred with his first wife, Lois WEBER, in many early Rex productions. Between 1912 and 1916 he directed many shorts starring Pearl White and co-directed with Weber several more ambitious productions, sometimes starring himself. By the early 20s he had been relegated to character roles.

FILMS INCLUDE: As director—*Bella's Beau, The Chorus Girl, The Mind Cure* 1912; *Heroic Harold, That Other Girl, Accident Insurance, Pearl's Admirers, Where Charity Begins, The Girl Reporter, The Broken Spell, Willie's Great Scheme, The Jew's Christmas* (co-dir. with Lois Weber; also act.) 1913; *The Ring, Lizzie and the Iceman, The Spider and Her Web* (also act.), *Behind the Veil* (co-dir. with Weber; also act.), *The Merchant of Venice* (co-dir. with Weber; also act. as Shylock), *Shadowed, Willie's Disguise, False Colors* (co-dir., co-sc. with Weber; also act.) 1914; *Sunshine Molly* (co-dir. with Weber; also act.), *Scandal* (co-dir. with Weber; also act.), *The Yankee Girl, A Cigarette—That's All* (also act.) 1915; *Hop the Devil's Brew* (co-dir. with Weber; also act.), *The Dumb Girl of Portici* (co-dir. with Weber), *Where Are My Children?* (co-dir. with Weber), *The Flirt* (co-dir. with Weber) 1916. As actor—*The Armorer's Daughter* 1910; *Fate, On the Brink* 1911; *Angels Unaware* 1912; *A Fool and His Money* 1914; *Too Wise Wives* 1921; *The Power of a Lie* 1922; *Cameo Kirby, Temptation, Flaming Youth* 1923; *Daughters of Today, For Sale, Single Wives, Cheap Kisses* 1924; *Charley's Aunt, The Awful Truth, The Fate of a Flirt, Soul Mates, Stella Maris* 1925; *Money Talks, The Taxi Mystery* 1926; *The Broken Gate, Sensation Seekers, Stage Kisses, Man Crazy, Tea for Three* 1927; *Broadway Daddies, Sinners in Love, The Border Patrol* 1928; *High Voltage, True Heaven* 1929; *Peacock Alley, Charley's Aunt* (remake) 1930; *A Free Soul* 1931; *The Greeks Had a Word for Them, Escapade* 1932; *Cocktail Hour* 1933; *Madame Du Barry, Bolero* 1934; *Night Life of the Gods, All the King's Horses, A Night at the Opera* (bit) 1935.

Smell-O-Vision. A process of aromatic cinema which Mike Todd, Jr., tried unsuccessfully to exploit in 1960. Unlike the competing system, Aroma-Rama, in which the odors were circulated through the theater's regular ventilating system, Smell-O-Vision directed its scents directly to each individual seat in the house through a tubing system. Each scent was contained in a vial on a rotating drum and was triggered by a signal from a "smell track" on the film. Only one film was made in Smell-O-Vision, *Scent of Mystery.* It was only mildly successful and, as *Variety* had predicted, the aroma gimmick was nothing more than a passing whiff. A new system of film aromatics, Odorama, was developed for use in offbeat filmmaker John Waters's suburban satire *Polyester*.

Smight, Jack. Director. Born on Mar. 9, 1926, in Minneapolis. Technically efficient director of slick Hollywood entertainment with no evident personal style or point of view. A veteran of television, he turned to feature films in 1964 but has since returned periodically to the small screen as director of TV movies or episodes of such TV series as 'Banacek' and 'Columbo.'

FILMS: *I'd Rather Be Rich* 1964; *The Third Day* (also prod.) 1965; *Harper, Kaleidoscope* (UK) 1966; *The Secret War of Harry Frigg, No Way to Treat a Lady* 1968; *Strategy of Terror* (orig. made for TV), *The Illustrated Man* 1969; *The Traveling Executioner* (also prod.), *Rabbit Run* 1970; *Airport 1975* 1974; *Midway* 1976; *Damnation Alley/Survival Run* 1977; *Fast Break* 1979; *Loving Couples* 1980; *Number One with a Bullet* 1987; *The Favorite* (Switz.) 1989.

Smith, Alexis. Actress. *b.* Gladys Smith, June 8, 1921, in Penticton, British Columbia, Canada. *d.* 1993. Leading lady and second lead of Hollywood films of the 40s and 50s. Having gained some acting experience in Canadian summer stock during her teens, she was given the lead in a production of Los Angeles City College, which she was attending. She was seen by a Warner Bros. talent agent and signed on a long-term contract following a screen test. She remained with the studio for ten years, playing charming, resourceful, often cool and calculating leading ladies with aloof magnetism. At her best as "the other woman." In the 50s she freelanced for various studios, then retired from the screen at the end of the decade. She looked as youthful and alluring as ever in the early 70s when she made a Broadway comeback as the star of the musical 'Follies.' On the strength of her new popularity, she returned to the screen in 1975 after an absence of 16 years. She was married from 1944 until her death to actor Craig Stevens.

FILMS INCLUDE: *The Lady with Red Hair* 1940; *Steel Against the Sky, Dive Bomber* 1941; *Gentleman Jim* 1942; *The Constant Nymph* 1943; *The Adventures of Mark Twain* (as Mrs. Samuel Clemens), *The Doughgirls* 1944; *The Horn Blows at Midnight, Conflict, Rhapsody in Blue, San Antonio* 1945; *Of Human Bondage* (as Nora Nesbitt), *Night and Day* (as Mrs. Cole Porter) 1946; *Stallion Road, The Two Mrs. Carrolls* 1947; *The Woman in White, The Decision of Christopher Blake, Whiplash* 1948; *South of St. Louis, Any Number Can Play, One Last Fling* 1949; *Montana, Undercover Girl* 1950; *Here Comes the Groom* 1951; *The Turning Point* 1952; *Split Second* 1953; *The Sleeping Tiger* (UK) 1954; *The Eternal Sea* 1955; *Beau James* 1957; *This Happy Feeling* 1958; *The Young Philadelphians* 1959; *Jacqueline Susann's Once Is Not Enough* 1975; *The Little Girl Who Lives Down the Lane* (Can.) 1977; *Casey's Shadow* 1978; *La Truite/The Trout* (Fr.) 1982; *Tough Guys* 1986.

Smith, Sir C. Aubrey. Actor. *b.* Charles Aubrey Smith, July 21, 1863, London. *d.* 1948. *ed.* Cambridge. A member of England's national cricket team, he made his stage debut at the age of 30. From 1896 he also frequently appeared on the American stage and in 1915 he made his film debut in the US. Tall and imposing, he played leads in several American and British silents but is best known for his work as a jutty-eye-browed character actor in numerous Hollywood talkies of the 30s and 40s, in which he typically represented a benevolent British gentleman of prominence. He was knighted in 1944.

FILMS INCLUDE: *Builder of Bridges* 1915; *The Witching Hour* 1916; *Castles in Spain* (UK) 1920; *The Bohemian Girl* (UK) 1922; *The Rejected Woman* 1924; *Birds of Prey/The Perfect Alibi* (UK) 1930; *Trader Horn, The Bachelor Father* (title role), *Daybreak, Never the Twain Shall Meet, Just a Gigolo, Son of India, Surrender* 1931; *Polly of the Circus, Tarzan the Ape Man, Love Me Tonight, Trouble in Paradise* 1932; *Secrets, The Barbarian, Adorable, Morning Glory, Bombshell* 1933; *Queen Christina, The House of Rothschild* (as the Duke of Wellington), *One More River, Bulldog Drummond Strikes Back, Cleopatra* (as Enobarbus), *The Scarlet Empress, Caravan, We Live Again* (as Prince Korchagin of Tolstoy's *Resurrection*) 1934; *The Lives of a Bengal Lancer, Clive of India, The Gilded Lily, China Seas, The Crusades, Jalna, The Tunnel/Transatlantic Tunnel* (UK) 1935; *Little Lord Fauntleroy, Romeo and Juliet* (as Lord Capulet), *The Garden of Allah, Lloyds of London* (as Queensberry) 1936; *Wee Willie Winkie, The Prisoner of Zenda* (as Colonel Zapt), *The Hurricane* 1937; *Sixty Glorious Years* (again as the Duke of Wellington; UK), *Four Men and a Prayer, Kidnapped* (as the Duke of Argyle) 1938; *The Four Feathers* (UK), *The Sun Never Sets, The Under-Pup, Another Thin Man, Balalaika* 1939; *Rebecca* (as Colonel Julyan), *Waterloo Bridge* 1940; *Dr. Jekyll and Mr. Hyde* 1941; *Forever and a Day, Flesh and Fantasy, Madame Curie* (as Lord Kelvin) 1943; *The Adventures of Mark Twain, The White Cliffs of Dover* 1944; *And Then There Were None* 1945; *Cluny Brown* 1946; *Unconquered, An Ideal Husband* (as Lord Caversham; UK) 1947; *Little Women* (as Mr. Lawrence) 1949.

Smith, Bud. Film editor. Born in Tulsa, Okla. A former champion race-car driver, he turned to film editing in the late 60s and subsequently earned Oscar nominations for *The Exorcist* (1973) and *Flashdance* (1983), both in collaboration. He shared the British Academy Award for the latter. He occasionally ventured into producing and in 1988 took a first, not-too-promising stab at directing with the teen comedy *Johnny Be Good.*

FILMS INCLUDE: *Putney Swope* 1969; *Pound* 1970; *The Exorcist* (co-edit.) 1973; *Rhinoceros* 1974; *Sorcerer* 1977; *The Brink's Job* (co-edit.) 1978; *Cruising* 1980; *Personal Best, Cat People* (co-edit.; also 2nd-unit dir.) 1982; *Flashdance* (co-edit.), *Deal of the Century* (co-edit.) 1983; *The Karate Kid* (co-edit.; also assoc. prod.) 1984; *To Live and Die in L.A.* (also co-prod.) 1985; *Some Kind of Wonderful* (co-edit.) 1987; *Johnny Be Good* (dir. only) 1988; *Sing* (co-edit.), *Gross Anatomy* (co-edit.) 1989; *Darkman* (co-edit.) 1990.

Smith, Charles Martin. Actor. Born on Oct. 30, 1953, in Van Nuys, Calif. *ed.* California State U. Small-framed, earnest-looking character lead and supporting player of American films. He made a vivid impression as a baby-faced intense youngster in *American Graffiti* (1973), then re-emerged from a decade of relative obscurity (changing his billing from Charlie to Charles in the process) with a memorable, near-solo performance in the man-in-the-wilderness saga *Never Cry Wolf* (1983). In 1986 he made an adequate debut as a director with the rock-theme movie *Trick or Treat.* His son, Frank Smith, is an animation artist.

FILMS: *The Culpepper Cattle Company, Fuzz* 1972; *Pat Garrett and Billy the Kid, American Graffiti* 1973; *The Spikes Gang* 1974; *Rafferty and the Gold Dust Twins* 1975; *No Deposit No Return* 1976; *The Hazing, The Buddy Holly Story* 1978; *Herbie Goes Bananas* 1980; *Never Cry Wolf* 1983; *Starman* 1984; *Trick or Treat* (cameo; also dir.) 1986; *The Untouchables* 1987; *The Experts* 1989; *The Hot Spot* 1990; *Deep Cover* 1992; *Fifty-Fifty* 1993; *Speechless* 1994; *Wedding Bell Blues* 1996; *Air Bud* (dir. only) 1997.

Smith, Cliff(ord). Director. *b.* Aug. 22, 1894, Richmond, Ind. *d.* 1937. A leading director of Westerns during the Hollywood silent era, he handled many of the early films of William S. HART and later directed other cowboy stars, including Tom Mix. In the early 20s he had his own production company, but later worked for other producers and became unemployed at the advent of sound. He returned to work briefly as a serial director at Universal during the last two years of his life.

FILMS INCLUDE: *The Scourge of the Desert* (co-dir. with William S. Hart), *Mr. Silent Haskins* (co-dir. with Hart), *The Darkening Trail* (co-dir. with Hart), *The Taking of Luke McVane* (co-dir. with Hart), *The Ruse, The Conversion of Frosty Blake, The Roughneck, Keno Bates—Liar, The Disciple* 1915; *The Aryan* (co-dir. with Hart; also act.), *Hell's Hinges* (co-dir. with Hart; also act.) 1916; *The Devil Dodger, The Medicine Man* 1917; *Paying His Debt, Wolves of the Border, A Red-Haired Cupid, The Fly God, By Proxy, The Pretender, Silent Rider, Untamed* 1918; *The She-Wolf* 1919; *The Cyclone, Three Gold Coins, The Girl Who Dared* 1920; *Western Hearts* (also prod., co-story, co-sc.), *Crossing Trails* (also prod.) 1921; *Daring Danger* (also prod.), *My Dad* (also prod.) 1922; *Scarred Hands* (also act.), *Wild Bill Hickok* 1923; *The Western Wallop, The Back Trail, Daring Chances* (also prod.), *Fighting Fury* 1924; *The Call of Courage, The Red Rider, A Roaring Adventure* 1925; *The Demon, The Desert's Toll/The Devil's Toll, The Fighting Peacemaker, The Phantom Bullet, The Set-Up, The Terror* 1926; *The Valley of Hell, Spurs and Saddles, Open Range* 1927; *The Three Outcasts* 1929; *Ace Drummond* (serial; co-dir. with Ford Beebe), *The Adventures of Frank Merriwell* (serial) 1936; *Jungle Jim* (serial; co-dir. with Beebe), *Wild West Days* (serial; co-dir. with Beebe) 1937.

Smith, George Albert. Inventor, pioneer film director. *b.* 1864, Brighton, England. *d.* 1959. An established portrait photographer, he built his own movie camera in 1896 and began making films the following year. A prodigious innovator, he rivaled France's Méliès in devising special effects for his trick films. As early as 1897 he patented double exposure as a filmic device and in 1900 pioneered in the use of the close-up as an intercut. In 1900, forming a partnership with Charles URBAN, he built one of the world's first motion picture studios, in Brighton. Almost from the beginning of his involvement with film, he sought to develop a satisfactory color technique. In 1906 he patented KINEMACOLOR and in 1908 he formed with Urban the Natural Color Kinematograph Company for the commercial exploitation of the two-color process.

FILMS INCLUDE: *The Haunted Castle, The Corsican Brothers* 1897; *Waves and Spray, The Miller and the Sweep, Cinderella, Faust and Mephistopheles* 1898; *The Legacy, Aladdin and the Wonderful Lamp* 1899; *The House That Jack Built, Grandma's Reading Glass* 1900; *Mother Goose Nursery Rhymes* 1902; *Dorothy's Dream* 1903; *Kinemacolor Puzzle* 1909.

Smith, Harry. Avant-garde animator. Born in 1923, in Portland, Ore. Eccentric, enigmatic filmmaker who began experimenting with unorthodox forms of film animation in the early 40s. His output includes batiked abstractions, hand-painted directly on film; optically printed imagery; and cut-and-paste collages. He spent years working on his best-known piece, *Heaven and Earth Magic,* a hallucinatory animated film originally running three hours and later cut down to 66 minutes. A devout occultist and expert on Kiowa peyote rituals, Smith is a respected ethnomusicologist and an authority on Ukrainian painted Easter eggs.

Smith, Kent. Actor. *b.* Frank Kent Smith, Mar. 19, 1907, New York City. *d.* 1985. *ed.* Harvard. A serious, intelligent actor with much Broadway experience, he was an atypical Hollywood leading man, making up in sincerity for a complete lack of sex appeal. In the late 50s he switched to character roles. He co-starred in the TV series 'Peyton Place' (1964–65) and 'The Invaders' (1967–68). His second wife (from 1962) was Broadway star and movie actress Edith Atwater (*b.* Apr. 22, 1911, Chicago; *d.* 1986), who had been previously married to actor Hugh Marlowe.

FILMS INCLUDE: *The Garden Murder Case* 1936; *Back Door to Heaven* 1939; *Cat People* 1942; *Hitler's Children, Forever and a Day, This Land Is Mine* 1943; *Three Russian Girls, The Curse of the Cat People, Youth Runs Wild* 1944; *The Spiral Staircase* 1946; *Nora Prentiss, Magic Town, The Voice of the Turtle* 1947; *The Fountainhead* 1949; *My Foolish Heart, The Damned Don't Cry, This Side of the Law* 1950; *Paula* 1952; *Comanche* 1956; *Sayonara* 1957; *Imitation General, The Badlanders, Party Girl, The Mugger* 1958; *This Earth Is Mine* 1959; *Strangers When We Meet* 1960; *Susan Slade* 1961; *Moon Pilot* 1962; *The Balcony* 1963; *A Distant Trumpet, Youngblood Hawke* 1964; *The Trouble with Angels* 1966; *Games* 1967; *Kona Coast* 1968; *Death of a Gunfighter* 1969; *The Games* 1970; *Pete 'n' Tillie* 1972; *Lost Horizon* 1973.

Smith, Kurtwood. Actor. Born on July 3, 1942, in New Lisbon, Wis. Versatile, mild-mannered, balding character player of the American stage, screen, and television. The holder of a master's degree in drama from Stanford, he taught in colleges and performed on the San Francisco stage before moving to Hollywood in the early 80s. Memorable for his against-type role as a menacing drug overlord in *Robocop* (1987). He co-starred in the TV police series 'The Renegades' (1983).

FILMS INCLUDE: *Roadie* (bit) 1980; *Zoot Suit* 1981; *Going Berserk* 1983; *Flashpoint* 1984; *Robocop* 1987; *Rambo III* 1988; *True Believer, Dead Poets Society, Heart of Dixie* 1989; *Quick Change* 1990; *Oscar, Star Trek VI: The Undiscovered Country, Company Business* 1991; *Shadows and Fog* 1992; *Fortress* 1993; *Last of the Dogmen, To Die For* 1995; *Broken Arrow* 1996.

Smith, Dame Maggie. Actress. Born on Dec. 28, 1934, in Ilford, England. Supremely gifted comedienne and dramatic player of the British stage and films. The daughter of a pathologist for Oxford University, she trained for the stage at the Oxford Playhouse School. She made her London debut in a revue in 1952 and her first Broadway appearance in 'New Faces' in 1956. She has since appeared in numerous plays on both sides of the Atlantic, generally reaping rave reviews from critics. She has made relatively few film appearances but has enjoyed a high "batting average" as a screen actress in public and critical esteem. She won Academy Awards for her performances in *The Prime of Miss Jean Brodie* (best actress, 1969) and *California Suite* (best supporting actress, 1978) and was nominated for Oscars for *Othello* (best supporting actress, 1965), *Travels with My Aunt* (best actress, 1972), and *A Room with a View* (best supporting actress, 1986). She won the British Film Academy Award as best actress for *A Private Function* (1984) and *The Lonely Passion of Judith Hearne* (1987). She was awarded a Tony in 1990 for her Broadway performance in 'Lettice and Lovage,' and in 1993 was nominated for an Emmy for best actress for her role in the PBS version of 'Suddenly, Last Summer.' Her first husband (1967–75) was actor Robert STEPHENS; her second (from 1975) screenwriter Beverley Cross.

FILMS: *Child in the House* (bit) 1956; *Nowhere to Go* 1958; *Go to Blazes* 1962; *The V.I.P.s* 1963; *The Pumpkin Eater* 1964; *Young Cassidy* (UK/US), *Othello* (as Desdemona) 1965; *The Honey Pot* (US/UK) 1967; *Hot Millions* 1968; *The Prime of Miss Jean Brodie, Oh! What a Lovely War* 1969; *Travels with My Aunt* 1972; *Love and Pain and the Whole Damn Thing* 1973; *Murder by Death* (US) 1976; *Death on the Nile, California Suite* (US) 1978; *Clash of the Titans, Quartet* 1981; *Evil Under the Sun, Ménage à Trois/Better Late than Never, The Missionary* 1982; *Lily in Love/Fitz and Lily* 1983; *A Private Function* 1984; *A Room with a View* 1986; *The Lonely Passion of Judith Hearne* 1987; *Romeo-Juliet* (v/o; Belg.) 1990; *Hook* 1991; *Sister Act* 1992; *The Secret Garden, Sister Act 2: Back in the Habit* 1993; *Richard III* 1995; *First Wives Club* 1996; *Washington Square* 1997.

Smith, Pete, Producer of shorts. *b.* Peter Schmidt, Sept. 4, 1892, New York City. *d.* 1979. The son of a brewery cooper, he dropped out of school at 13 to begin a low-paying career as a stenographer-typist. He made his first contact with show business in 1912 as a secretary of a vaudeville players' union and later as a reviewer for *Billboard* magazine. He then began a successful stint as a press agent and eventually wound up with MGM as publicity director and head of the advertising department. In 1931 he began producing and narrating shorts for the studio, which soon became popular with audiences for their folksy and inventive style. They comprised a wide variety of subjects, from sports wrap-ups to entertaining educational shorts. Some were in color and others, presented as Audioscopics, utilized a 3-D technique.

In 1936, Smith began producing his most celebrated series of shorts, the "Pete Smith Specialties," which enjoyed a great popular success. "A Smith named Pete," as he introduced himself, produced and narrated some 300 shorts in all. Two of these, *Penny Wisdom* (about cooking, 1937) and *Quicker'n a Wink* (in ultra-slow motion, 1940) won Academy Awards. More than 20 others were nominated for Oscars. In 1955, the year of his retirement, Smith was presented with a special Academy Award "for his witty and pungent observations of the American scene."

At age 86, despondent over his deteriorating health, Smith jumped to his death from the roof of a Los Angeles convalescent hospital.

Smith, Will. Actor, comedian, musician. Born 1970. This winning, versatile actor-singer is at his best typically in comedies. He made a name for himself as an actor with his hit television sitcom 'The Fresh Prince of Bel-Air.' Willing to take on a variety of roles, he signed on to co-star in *Six Degrees of Separation* (1993) as a young, gay con man posing as the son of Sidney POITIER. He has since gone on to become a major box office star with the films *Bad Boys* (1995) and the blockbuster *Independence Day* (1996).

FILMS: *Where the Day Takes You* 1992; *Made in America, Six Degrees of Separation* 1993; *Bad Boys* 1995; *Independence Day* 1996; *Men in Black* 1997.

Smithee, Allen (also **Alan**). Pseudonym designated by the Directors Guild of America as the only name permitted as a screen credit by a director who wishes to remove his name from a film, often in reaction to interference by producers with the film's final cut. The designation originated in 1967, after Don Siegel replaced Robert Totten as the director of *Death of a Gunfighter* 25 days into the shooting. Both were dissatisfied with the way the movie turned out and neither wanted his name associated with it. Ironically, when the film was released in 1969 a New York Times critic singled out for praise the fictitious director: ". . . the film has been sharply directed by Allen Smithee . . ." Screenwriter Joe Eszterhas used it as the subject of his screenplay *An Allen Smithee Film* (1997).

FILMS INCLUDE (real director/s in parentheses): *Death of a Gunfighter* (Don Siegel/Robert Totten; released in 1969) 1967; *Fade In* (Jud Taylor) 1968; *Stitches* (Rod Holcomb) 1985; *Let's Get Harry* (Stuart Rosenberg) 1986; *Morgan Stewart's Coming Home* (Terry Winsor/Paul Aaron), *Ghost Fever* (Lee Madden) 1987; *I Love N.Y.* (Gianni Bozzacchi) 1988; *The Shrimp on the Barbie* (Michael Gottlieb) 1990.

smoke and fog effects. In the past, such effects were usually produced by crude but rather effective methods, such as pouring water over dry ice or burning kerosene. Today the effects are achieved with remarkable ease and efficiency by a variety of portable devices that produce realistic smoke, fog, mist, and haze effects with the flick of a finger. The various fog makers and smoke pots available in the market produce safe, odorless, and long-lasting vapors.

Smoktunovsky, Innokenti. Actor. Born on Mar. 28, 1925, in Tomski Oblast, Siberia. Leading star of the Soviet stage and screen. A WW II veteran, he trained at the Pushkin Theater Studio in Karsonyarsk and in the 50s developed into a major artist, gaining fame after a superb portrayal of Prince Myshkin in a 1958 production of Dostoyevsky's 'The Idiot' at the Bolshoi Theater in Leningrad. He virtually dominated the Soviet screen with his powerful portraits in the 60s and 70s. He won the Lenin Prize in 1964 and was named People's Artist of the USSR in 1974.

FILMS INCLUDE: *Murder on Dante Street* 1956; *Soldiers, The Storm* 1957; *The First Day* 1958; *The Letter That Was Never Sent* 1960; *Next Spring* 1961; *Nine Days of One Year, Mozart and Salieri/Requiem for Mozart* (as Mozart) 1962; *Hamlet* (title role) 1964; *The First Visitor* (as Lenin), *One Planet* (as Lenin) 1966; *The Living Corpse* 1969; *Tchaikovsky* (title role), *Crime and Punishment* (as Porfiry Petrovich) 1970; *Uncle Vanya* (as Voinitsky) 1971; *Taming of the Fire* 1972; *Mothers and Daughters* 1974; *A Lover's Romance, They Fought for Their Country, Choosing Your Aim* (as Franklin D. Roosevelt) 1975; *The Legend of Till* (as Karl I) 1976; *The Steppe* 1977; *Barrier* 1978; *Moscow Doesn't Believe in Tears* (as himself) 1980; *Krazha* 1982; *Oci Ciornie/Dark Eyes* (It./USSR) 1986.

SMPTE (Society of Motion Picture and Television Engineers). Organized in 1916 as the Society of Motion Picture Engineers, this authoritative professional association sets and defines technical standards in the motion picture and TV industries. The word Television was added to the organization's name in 1950. Publishes *SMPTE Journal.* In England, the British Kinematograph Society was originally created as a branch of the SMPTE but is now independent, fulfilling similar functions in England to those of SMPTE in the US.

sneak preview. A screening of a motion picture in advance of its general release to test audience reaction. It is usually unannounced but is sometimes advertised without mention of the film's title. Unfavorable audience reaction may lead to re-editing of the film and in extreme cases to its being shelved. Irving Thalberg, the "boy wonder" of MGM, habitually attended the sneak previews of his productions and on several occasions ordered a picture to be rewritten and re-shot from scratch, at great expense to the company.

Snipes, Wesley. Actor. Born in 1963, in the Bronx, N.Y. Tall, imposing, black leading man of the American screen. He dropped out of Manhattan's High School for the Performing Arts when his family moved to Florida, but he resumed the study of acting at the State University of New York at Purchase. He earned his living as a telephone installer before breaking into films in 1986. An impressive moment in the 1987 Michael Jackson video 'Bad' led to groundbreaking exposure in *New Jack City* (1991) and caught the eye of director Spike LEE, who catapulted Snipes to stardom in *Jungle Fever* (1991).

FILMS: *Wildcats, Streets of Gold* 1986; *Critical Condition* 1987; *Major League* 1989; *King of New York* (It./US), *Mo' Better Blues* 1990; *New Jack City, Jungle Fever* 1991; *The Waterdance, White Men Can't Jump, Passenger 57* 1992; *Boiling Point, Rising Sun, Demolition Man* 1993; *Drop Zone, Sugar Hill* 1994; *Money Train, To Wong Foo Thanks for Everything Julie Newmar, Waiting to Exhale* 1995; *The Fan* 1996; *Murder at 1600, One Night Stand* 1997.

Snodgress, Carrie. Actress. Born on Oct. 27, 1946, in Chicago. *ed.* Northern Illinois U.; Goodman Theatre School, Chicago (M.A.). Talented leading lady of the American stage, TV, and films. After gaining a nomination for an Oscar as best actress for her screen-debut performance in Frank Perry's *Diary of a Mad Housewife* (1970), she disappeared from the screen for several years, during which she set up house with rock star Neil Young and gave birth to their son, Zeke.

FILMS: *Diary of a Mad Housewife, Rabbit Run* 1970; *The Fury* 1978; *The Attic* 1979; *Homework, Trick or Treats* 1982; *A Night In Heaven* 1983; *Pale Rider* 1985; *Murphy's Law, Rainy Day Friends* 1986; *Blueberry Hill* 1988; *The Chill Factor* 1989; *Across the Tracks* 1990; *The Ballad of Little Jo* 1993; *8 Seconds, Blue Sky* (release delayed from 1992) 1994; *White Man's Burden* 1995.

snoot. A conelike attachment for a studio lamp, designed to direct its light to a specific area of a set.

Snow, Marguerite. American actress. *b.* 1889. *d.* 1958. Beautiful brunette leading lady of Hollywood silents. She entered films in 1911 and played an assortment of leads in a variety of productions, often opposite James CRUZE, who became her husband (they later divorced) and Francis X. BUSHMAN. She sometimes portrayed "vampy" parts, like the title role in *Carmen* (1913) and the villainess Princess Olga in the serial *The Million Dollar Mystery* (1914). She retired from the screen in 1925.

FILMS INCLUDE: *The Pied Piper of Hamelin, She, The Tomboy, The Honeymooners* 1911; *Lucile, And the Greatest of These Is Charity, Undine, Forest Rose, A Militant Suffragette* 1912; *Carmen* (title role), *The Caged Bird* 1913; *Joseph in the Land of Egypt, The Million Dollar Mystery* (serial) 1914; *Zudora/20 Million Dollar Mystery* (serial) 1914–15; *The Angel in the Mask, The Patriot and the Spy, The Second in Command, The Silent Voice, Rosemary, Daughter of Kings* 1915; *Marble Heart, The Half-Million Bride* 1916; *Broadway Jones, Hunting of the Hawk* 1917; *The Eagle's Eye* (serial), *The First Law* 1918; *In His Brother's Place* 1919; *Felix O'Day, The Woman in Room 13* 1920; *Lavender and Old Lace* 1921; *The Veiled Woman* 1922; *Chalk Marks* 1924; *Savages of the Sea, Kit Carson Over the Great Divide* 1925.

Snow, Michael. Experimental artist and filmmaker. Born on Dec. 10, 1929, in Toronto. The son of an English-speaking civil engineer and a pianist of French-Canadian origin, he demonstrated early talent as both a jazz musician and an artist. After his 1953 graduation from the Ontario College of Art with a degree in design, he worked briefly in advertising, traveled extensively in Europe, married filmmaker Joyce Wieland, and began exploring varied novel means of artistic endeavor. Although he had made an isolated animated short in 1956, it was only after he moved to New York in the early 60s that he began gravitating to film as a medium of personal expression. He made *New York Eye and Ear Control* (1964)—now famous for its Walking Woman framing silhouette—as an extension of his complex graphic concepts and exercises with real and imagined space. He is best known for his next film, *Wavelength* (1967), a 45-minute zoom lens–aided exploration of pure time and space that strongly influenced the structural movement of the avant-garde and became a standard item in film school screenings. Pans, tilts, zooms, and camera movement remained basic tools in Snow's unrelenting pursuit of the essence of cinematic space. The complexities of his films' soundtracks bear evidence of his musical background. He was seen in the documentaries *Fire: The Work of Joyce Wieland* (1987) and *I Will Not Make Any More Boring Art* (1988).

FILMS: *A to Z* (animated short) 1956; *New York Eye and Ear Control/A Walking Woman Work* 1964; *Short Shave* 1965; *Wavelength, Standard Time* 1967; *Back and Forth, One Second in Montreal, Dripping Water* (co-dir. with Joyce Wieland) 1969; *Side Seat Paintings Slides Sound Film* 1970; *La Région centrale/The Central Region* 1971; *Rameau's Nephew by Diderot (Thanks to Dennis Young) by Wilma Schoen, Two Sides to Every Story* 1974; *Breakfast/Table Top Dolly* (begun in 1972) 1976; *Presents, This Is It* 1982; *So Is This* 1983; *Sealed Figures* 1989.

snow effects. Shredded feathers or plastic flakes used in the making of motion pictures to produce the effect of light falling snow. For heavy snow effects, gypsum and asbestos are commonly used. The "snow" is dispensed by mechanical hoppers and distributed over a set by giant fans.

Sobocinski, Witold. Director of cinematography. Born on Oct. 15, 1929, in Ozorkow, Poland. Leading Polish cinematographer. Trained at the Lodz Film School, he contributed memorable images to films of Skolimowski, Wajda, Zanussi, and Polanski, among other directors.

FILMS INCLUDE: *Hands Up!* 1967; *Everything for Sale* 1968; *The Adventures of Gerard* (UK/Switz.) 1970; *Family Life* 1971; *The Wedding* 1972; *The Hourglass Sanatorium* 1973; *The Catamount Killing* (Ger.) 1974; *Land of Promise/Promised Land* (co-phot.) 1975; *Death of a President* 1978; *Wege in der Nacht/Ways in the Night/Night Paths* (Ger.) 1979; *Pirates* (Fr./Tunis) 1986; *Frantic* (US) 1988; *Torrents of Spring* (co-phot.; It./Fr./UK) 1989; *Bronsteins Kinder* (Ger.) 1991; *Red* 1994; *Marvin's Room, Ransom* 1996.

Soderbergh, Steven. Director. Born on January 14, 1963, in Atlanta. Raised in Louisiana, he was attending a Baton Rouge high school when he enrolled in a film animation class at Louisiana State University, where his father was dean of the College of Education. Soon he began making film shorts with equipment he had borrowed from students at the university. After completing high school at 17, he decided to skip college and headed for Hollywood in a frustrated pursuit of a movie career. Back in Baton Rouge, he worked as a coin-changer at an arcade and in his spare time made a humorous short called *Rapid Eye Movement* about his Hollywood non-experience. Eventually he landed a job with a video production house and enjoyed some success as the director of a music video for the rock group Yes, which was nominated for a Grammy Award. He began writing screenplays speculatively and at one point of frustration retreated into a prolonged, self-destructive drinking binge. On recovering, he directed *Winston*, a short about sexual deception, a theme that he would later develop as the core of his first feature, *sex, lies and videotape* (1989), based on a script he had written in one eight-day burst. Directed with a modest budget of only $1.2 million, *sex, lies, and videotape*, an intriguing modern-day morality tale, proved the hit of the 1989 Cannes Film Festival, winning the Palme d'Or as best film, as well as the International Critics Prize and the best actor prize for James Spader. It was later nominated for an Oscar for best screenplay. Soderbergh followed this triumph with *Kafka* (1991), a well directed but conventional screen biography of the Czech author, and *King of the Hill*, a Depression-era coming-of-age tale.

FILMS: *sex lies and videotape* (also sc., edit.) 1989; *Kafka* 1991; *King of the Hill* 1993; *The Underneath* (also sc.) 1994; *Gray's Anatomy*, *Nightwatch* (sc. only), *Schizopolis* (sc., dir., act.) 1996.

soft focus. An effect obtained by shooting slightly out of focus, by using a special filter, or by placing gauze or other diffusing material in front of the lens. The technique causes an image to appear diffused and lacking in sharp definition. It has been frequently employed to create a romantic aura or to obliterate harsh lines from the faces of aging actresses.

soft light. A light source producing a diffused illumination on a set, minimizing shadows.

Sokoloff, Vladimir. Actor. *b.* Dec. 26, 1889, Moscow. *d.* 1962. *ed.* U. of Moscow. A veteran of the Moscow Art Theatre, he left Russia in 1923 and continued his acting career in Berlin and Paris, on the stage and in films. In 1937 he left Europe for Hollywood, where he played numerous character parts, typically portraying a Slav or a member of some other foreign nationality, as a sort of male counterpart of Maria OUSPENSKAYA.

FILMS INCLUDE: In Europe—*Die Abenteuer eines Zehnmarkscheines/Uneasy Money* (Ger.) 1926; *Napoléon* (Fr.), *Die Liebe der Jeanne Ney/The Love of Jeanne Ney* (Ger.) 1927; *Liebling der Götter/Der grosse Tenor/Darling of the Gods* (Ger.) 1930; *Die Dreigroschenoper/The Threepenny Opera* (Ger./US), *Niemandsland/Hell on Earth* (lead; Ger.) 1931; *Die Herrin von Atlantis* (and in French-language version, *L'Atlantide;* Ger.), *Gehetzte Menschen* (Ger.) 1932; *Dans les Rues/Song of the Street* (lead; Fr.) 1933; *Le Lac aux Dames* (Fr.) 1934; *Mayerling* (Fr.), *Mister Flow/Compliments of Mr. Flow* (Fr.), *Les Bas-Fonds/The Lower Depths* (Fr.) 1936. In the US—*The Life of Emile Zola* (as Paul Cézanne), *West of Shanghai, Conquest* 1937; *Blockade, The Amazing Dr. Clitterhouse, Spawn of the North* 1938; *Juarez, The Real Glory* 1939; *Comrade X* 1940; *Love Crazy* 1941; *Crossroads, Road to Morocco* 1942, *Mission to Moscow* (as Kalinin), *For Whom the Bell Tolls* (as Anselmo), *Mr. Lucky* 1943; *Song of Russia, Passage to Marseille, Till We Meet Again, The Conspirators* 1944; *A Royal Scandal, Paris Underground* 1945; *Scarlet Street, Cloak and Dagger* 1946; *To the Ends of the Earth* 1948; *The Baron of Arizona* 1950; *Macao* 1952; *While the City Sleeps* 1956; *Twilight for the Gods* 1958; *Man on a String, The Magnificent Seven* 1960; *Mr. Sardonicus* 1961; *Taras Bulba* 1962.

Solanas, Fernando E. Director. Born on Feb. 16, 1936, in Olivos, Argentina. Following studies of law, drama, and music in Buenos Aires, he worked in advertising. In 1966 he joined the Ciné Liberación collective, a group of leftist-leaning, pro-Peronist filmmakers dedicated to fighting Argentina's military regime with cameras. There he joined with Spanish-born Octavia Getino to make *The Hour of the Furnaces* (1968), a remarkable, militantly polemic, four-hour-plus documentary that prompted spectators to rise against their oppressors. Made clandestinely, the film presented a dazzlingly vivid collage of newly shot material—action, graphics, interviews, and poems, mixed with newsreel footage and excerpts from old fact and fiction films, and still photographs—in a searing indictment of the effects of neocolonialism on Argentina. Solanas continued his propagandistic collaboration with Getino on behalf of the Peronist movement until the dictator's return to power in 1973, then turned with equal vigor and imagination to fiction films. In the wake of the military coup against Peron in 1976, the director went into exile in Paris, where he remained until 1983. The experience inspired *Tangos—The Exile of Gardel* (1985), a delightful film about cultural nostalgia among Argentine expatriates in France that won the Special Jury Prize at the Venice Film Festival. Solanas was then named best director at Cannes for *South* (1988), another memoir of the past which, like its predecessor, used tango music at its evocative core.

FILMS: *La Hora del los Hornos/The Hour of the Furnaces* (also co-sc., co-phot., edit., co-songs) 1968; *Peron: Actualización politica y doctrinaria para la Toma del Poder, La Revolución justicialista* 1971; *Los Hijos de Fierro* 1976; *La Mirada de los Otros/Régard des Autres* (doc.) 1979; *Tangos—el Exilio de Gardel/Tangos—The Exile of Gardel* (also sc., co-prod., co-songs, act.; Arg./Fr.) 1985; *Sur/South* (also sc., des., song; Arg./Fr.) 1988; *El Viaje/The Journey* (also sc., des., co-edit.; Arg./Fr.) 1992.

Solas, Humberto. Director. Born in December, 1942, in Havana. A leading figure in contemporary Cuban revolutionary cinema. He dropped out of school at 14 to join the struggle against the dictatorship of Batista. In 1959 he joined the Cuban Film Institute, where he made a number of documentary and fiction shorts. He is best known for *Lucia* (1968), a film that traces phases of Cuban history through the lives of female characters.

FILMS INCLUDE: *Casablanca* 1961; *Variaciones* 1963; *El Acoso* 1964; *Manuela* 1966; *Lucia* 1968; *Una Dia de Noviembre* 1972; *Simparele* 1974; *Cantata de Chile* 1976; *Wilfredo Lam* 1978; *Cecilia Valdés* 1982; *Amada* 1983; *Un Hombre de Exito* 1986.

Soldati, Mario. Director, screenwriter, novelist. Born on Nov. 17, 1906, in Turin, Italy. A graduate of the University of Turin, he came to the US in the late 20s to study, and later teach, at Columbia University, while doubling as a correspondent for a Genoa newspaper. Returning to Italy, he began a literary career that has consisted of short stories, novels, and nonfiction, including *America—Primo Amore/America—First Love.* At the same time, he pursued a parallel career in films, at first (from 1931) as screenwriter, then (from 1938) also as director. He made an important contribution to Italian cinema in the early 40s with several intelligent films, notably *Piccolo Mondo Antico* (1941) and *Malombra* (1942), but most of his subsequent ones were commercially inspired and routine. He was second-unit director on the American-Italian co-productions of *War and Peace* (1956) and *Ben-Hur* (1959). Since the late 50s he has been devoting most of his time to writing. He collaborated on the scripts of most of his own films, as well as on some films of other directors.

FILMS (as director and co-screenwriter): *La Principessa Tarakanova* (co-dir. with Fedor Ozep); *La Signora di Montecarlo* (co-dir. with André Berthomieu) 1938; *Due Milioni per un Sorriso* (co-dir. with Carlo Borghesio), *Dora Nelson* 1939; *Tutto per la Donna* 1940; *Piccolo Mondo Antico/Old-Fashioned World, Tragica Notte* 1941; *Malombra* 1942; *Quartieri Alti* 1943; *Le Miserie del Signor Travet/His Young Wife* 1945; *Eugenia Grandet* 1946; *Daniele Cortis* 1947; *Fuga in Francia/Flight Into France* 1948; *Quel Bandito sono io!* 1949; *Botta e Risposta, Donne e Briganti/Of Love and Bandits*

1950; *Il Sogno di Zorro, E l'Amor che mi rovina, O.K. Nerone/OK Nero* 1951; *Le Avventure di Mandrin, I Tre Corsari, Jolanda—La Figlia del Corsaro nero* 1952; *La Provinciale/The Wayward Wife, La Mano dello Straniero/The Stranger's Hand* 1953; *Questa è la Vita/Of Life and Love* ("Il Ventaglino" episode) 1954; *La Donna del Fiume/Woman of the River* 1955; *Era di Venerdi 17/The Virtuous Bigamist, Italia Piccola* 1957; *Policarpo—Ufficiale di Scrittura* 1959; *Il Maestro* (novella basis only; Fr./Bel.) 1989.

Solntseva, Yulia. Director. Born in 1901, in Russia. A former actress, she made her screen debut in 1924, in Protazanov's *Aelita.* In 1930 she met director Alexander DOVZHENKO and became his assistant and later his wife. She co-directed several of Dovzhenko's films and after his death directed a number of films from his unfinished scripts.

FILMS: *Schors* (assoc. dir. to Alexander Dovzhenko) 1939; *Liberation* (assoc. dir. to Dovzhenko) 1940; *The Fight for Our Soviet Ukraine/Ukraine in Flames* (compilation film; co-dir. with Y. Avdeyenko under Dovzhenko's supervision) 1943; *Victory in the Ukraine and the Expulsion of the Germans from the Boundaries of the Ukrainian Soviet Earth* (compilation film; co-dir. with Dovzhenko) 1945; *Michurin/Life in Bloom* (assoc. dir. to Dovzhenko) 1948; *Igor Bulichov* (in two parts) 1952–53; *The Reluctant Inspectors* (medium length) 1955; *Poem of the Sea* 1958; *The Flaming Years* 1961; *The Enchanted Desna* 1965; *Unforgettable* 1969.

Sologne, Madeleine. Actress. Born Madeleine Vouillon, on Oct. 27, 1912, in La Ferté-Imbault, France. A popular leading lady of French films of the 40s, when she represented the contemporary ideal of feminine beauty.

FILMS INCLUDE: *Adrienne Lecouvreur, Les Gens du Voyage* 1938; *Raphaël le Tatoué* 1939; *Le Danube bleu* 1940; *Fièvres* 1941; *L'Eternel Retour/The Eternal Return* 1943; *Vautrin/Vautrin the Thief* 1944; *Mademoiselle X* 1944; *Un Ami viendra ce Soir/A Friend Will Come Tonight, La Foire aux Chimères/The Devil and the Angel* 1946; *Une Grande Fille toute simple/Just a Big Simple Girl* 1948; *Les Naufrageurs* 1959; *Il suffit d'aimer/Bernadette of Lourdes* 1961; *Le Temps des Loups* 1969.

Sommer, Elke. Actress. Born Elke Schletz, on Nov. 5, 1940, in Berlin. Sexy blonde leading lady of American and international films. The daughter of a Lutheran minister who died when she was 14, she attended a German university, planning to become a linguist and a diplomatic interpreter, but got sidetracked by modeling and eventually by a thriving international screen career, mainly in minor films. A bright and frequent guest on TV talk shows, she speaks seven languages fluently. She has been married since 1964 to writer Joe Hyams and is a resident of southern California.

FILMS INCLUDE: *Das Totenschiff* (Ger.), *I Ragazzi del Juke Box* (It.) 1959; *Femmine di Lusso/Love the Italian Way/Love Italian Style* (It.) 1960; *De quoi tu mêles Daniela?/Daniella by Night* (Fr./Ger.), *Geliebte Hochstaplerin* (Ger.), *Don't Bother to Knock/Why Bother to Knock* (UK) 1961; *Douce Violence/Sweet Ecstasy* (Fr.), *Auf Wiedersehn* (Ger.), *Bahia de Palma* (Sp.) 1962; *The Victors* (UK/US), *The Prize* (US) 1963; *A Shot in the Dark* (US/UK) 1964; *Le Bambole/The Dolls* (It./Fr.), *The Art of Love* (US) 1965; *The Money Trap* (US), *The Oscar* (US), *Boy Did I Get a Wrong Number!* (US), *Deadlier Than the Male* (UK) 1966; *The Venetian Affair* (US) 1967; *The Wicked Dreams of Paula Schultz* (US) 1968; *The Wrecking Crew* (US) 1969; *The Invincible Sex* (US) 1970; *Percy* (UK), *Zeppelin* (UK/Fr.) 1971; *Gli Orrori del Castello di Norimberga/Baron Blood* (It./Fr.) 1972; *Percy's Progress/It's Not the Size That Counts* (UK) 1974; *Ten Little Indians* (UK/Fr./It./Ger./Sp.), *House of Exorcism* (It.) 1975; *Das Netz* (Ger.) 1976; *The Swiss Conspiracy* 1977; *I Miss You—Hugs and Kisses* (Can.) 1978; *The Prisoner of Zenda* (US), *The Double McGuffin* (US) 1979; *Der Mann in Pyjama* (Ger.) 1981; *Invisible Strangler* (US) 1984; *Lily in Love* (Hung./US) 1985; *Adventures Beyond Belief/Neat and Tidy* 1988; *Himmelsheim* (Ger.) 1989; *Severed Ties* (US) 1992.

Sommer, Josef. Actor. Born Maximilian Josef Sommer, on June 26, 1934, Greifswald, Germany. *ed.* Carnegie-Mellon U. In the US from youth, he served in the Army, then trained for the stage at the American Shakespeare Festival in Stratford, Connecticut, where he made his professional debut in 1970. The following year he entered films and has since played key character roles in many major productions.

FILMS INCLUDE: *Dirty Harry* 1971; *Man on a Swing* 1974; *The Front* 1976; *Close Encounters of the Third Kind* 1977; *Hide in Plain Sight* 1980; *Absence of Malice, Rollover, Reds* 1981; *Hanky Panky, Still of the Night, Sophie's Choice* (narr.) 1982; *Silkwood* 1983; *Iceman* 1984; *Witness, Target* 1985; *The Rosary Murders* 1987; *Dracula's Widow* 1987; *Chances Are, Bloodhounds of Broadway* 1989; *Shadows and Fog, The Mighty Ducks* 1992; *Nobody's Fool* 1994; *Moonlight and Valentino, Strange Days* 1995; *The Chamber* 1996.

Sondergaard, Gale. Actress *b.* Edith Holm Sondergaard, Feb. 15, 1899. *d.* 1985. *ed.* U. of Minnesota. A professor's daughter, she turned to the stage after graduating from college. After several years in stock, she made it to Broadway in the late 20s. In the mid-30s she followed her second husband (from 1930), director Herbert BIBERMAN, to Hollywood and reluctantly accepted her first film role, in *Anthony Adverse* (1936). She won the best supporting actress Academy Award, the first ever given in this category, for her performance in the film. She subsequently played character parts in many films, typically cast as a catty, cunning, or vicious woman. By the late 40s she was well established as Hollywood's number one female villain, but her career was cut short by blacklisting, following the House Un-American Activities Committee hearings. Neither she nor her husband, who was one of the HOLLYWOOD TEN, could obtain work in films. After a long layoff period, she emerged from retirement in 1965 with a one-woman off-Broadway show entitled 'Woman'. She returned to the screen in 1969, and after another long absence made another comeback in 1976.

FILMS: *Anthony Adverse* (as Faith Paleologus) 1936; *Maid of Salem, Seventh Heaven, The Life of Emile Zola* (as Mrs. Alfred Dreyfus) 1937; *Lord Jeff, Dramatic School* 1938; *Never Say Die, Juarez* (as Empress Eugenie), *The Cat and the Canary* 1939; *The Llano Kid, The Blue Bird* (as Tylette/The Cat), *The Mark of Zorro, The Letter* 1940; *The Black Cat* 1941; *Paris Calling, My Favorite Blonde, Enemy Agents Meet Ellery Queen* 1942; *A Night to Remember, Appointment in Berlin, The Strange Death of Adolf Hitler, Isle of Forgotten Sins* 1943; *Spider Woman* (title role), *Follow the Boys, The Invisible Man's Revenge, Christmas Holiday, Gypsy Wildcat, Enter Arsene Lupin, The Climax* 1944; *The Spider Woman Strikes Back* (title role), *Night in Paradise, Anna and the King of Siam, The Time of Their Lives* 1946; *Pirates of Monterey, Road to Rio* 1947; *East Side West Side* 1949; *Slaves* 1969; *Pleasantville, The Return of a Man Called Horse* 1976; *Echoes* 1983.

Sondheim, Stephen. Composer, lyricist. Born on Mar. 22, 1930, in New York City. *ed.* Williams Coll. (magna cum laude). Several of the works of this brilliantly inventive, boldly experimental, Oscar-, Tony-, Grammy-, and Pulitzer Prize–winning author-composer of Broadway musicals have been adapted by others for the screen. In addition, he occasionally contributed material directly to films.

FILMS: *West Side Story* (lyr.) 1961; *Gypsy* (co-lyr.) 1962; *A Funny Thing Happened on the Way to the Forum* (mus., lyr.) 1966; *The Last of Sheila* (co-sc.) 1973; *Stavisky* (mus.; Fr.) 1974; *The Seven-Percent Solution* (song) 1976; *A Little Night Music* (mus., lyr.) 1977; *Airplane!* (song) 1980; *Reds* (theme mus.) 1981; *Terms of Endearment* (song) 1983; *Dick Tracy* (songs), *Postcards from the Edge* (song) 1990; *The Birdcage* 1996.

Sonnenfeld, Barry. Director of photography, director. Born in 1953, in New York City. Having graduated from NYU with a degree in political science, he worked as a photo technician, mixing chemicals in a lab, then returned to the university as a student in the film department. After demonstrating his skills as a cameraman on the Oscar-nominated documentary *In Our Water* (1982), he joined classmates Joel and Ethan COEN in their venture into features. He made his debut as a director in 1991 with *The Addams Family,* a huge box-office hit.

FILMS INCLUDE: As director of photography—*In Our Water* (doc.) 1982; *Blood Simple* 1984; *Compromising Positions* 1985; *Raising Arizona, Three O' Clock High, Throw Momma from the Train* 1987; *Big* 1988; *When Harry Met Sally. . .* 1989; *Miller's Crossing, Misery* (also 2nd-unit dir.) 1990. As director—*The Addams Family* 1991; *For Love or Money, Addams Family Values* (also cameo) 1993; *Get Shorty* (also ex-prod.) 1995; *Men in Black* 1997.

Sony Pictures Entertainment. See COLUMBIA PICTURES, TRISTAR PICTURES.

Sordi, Alberto. Actor, sometime director. Born on June 15, 1919, in Rome. At 13 he won an MGM contest for imitating Oliver Hardy and subsequently he became a comedian on the Italian music-hall and legitimate stage. In films since 1938, he developed in the 50s into one of the Italian screen's most beloved personalities, a comedian capable of a broad emotional range. He was named best actor at the 1972 Berlin Festival for *Why*. Since the early 60s he has been directing and co-scripting his own films with increasing frequency.

FILMS INCLUDE (as actor): *La Principessa Tarakanova* 1938; *La Notte delle Beffe* 1940; *La Signorina* 1942; *Le Miserie del Signor Travet/His Young Wife* 1946; *Il Delitto de Giovanni Episcopo* 1947; *Lo Sceicco bianco/The White Sheik, Toto e i Re di Roma* 1952; *I Vitelloni* 1953; *Un Giorno in Pretura/A Day in Court* (also co-sc.), *Due Notti con Cleopatra/Two Nights with Cleopatra, Tempi Nostri, Le Rouge et le Noir* (Fr.), *Un Americano a Roma, Il Seduttore, Gran Varietà, Il Matrimonio* 1954; *Il Segno di Venere, Un Eroe di Nostri Tempi, La Bella di Roma* 1955; *Mio Figlio Nerone/Nero's Mistress/Nero's Weekend, Era di Venerdi 17/The Virtuous Bigamist, Lo Scapolo* 1956; *A Farewell to Arms* (US) 1957; *Fortunella, Ladro lui Ladra lei, Racconti d'Estate/Love on the Riviera, Il Marito, Domenica è sempre Domenica* (also co-sc.), *Nella Città l'Inferno/. . . And the Wild Wild Women/Hell in the City* 1958; *I Magliari, Il Moralista/The Moralist, Il Vedovo, La Grande Guerra/The Great War* 1959; *Tutti a Casa/Everybody Go Home!, Il Vigile, Crimen/. . . And Suddenly It's Murder* 1960; *Il Giudizio Universale, I Due Nemici/The Best of Enemies* (It./UK) 1961; *Il Mafioso/Mafioso* 1962; *Il Boom, Il Maestro di Vigevano, Il Diavolo/To Bed or Not to Bed* 1963; *I Tre Volti, Those Magnificent Men in Their Flying Machines* (UK), *Made in Italy* 1965; *Fumo di Londra* (also dir., co-story, co-sc.), *Scusi—Lei è Favorevole o Contrario?* (also dir., co-story, co-sc.) 1966; *Un Italiano in America* (also dir., co-story, co-sc.), *Le Streghe/The Witches, Le Fate/The Queens* 1967; *Amore Mio Aiutami* (also dir.) 1969; *Le Coppie* ("La Camera" episode; also dir., sc.), *Contestazione Generale* 1970; *Detenuto in Attesa di Giudizio/Why* 1971; *La più Bella Serata de Mia Vita* 1972; *Polvere di Stelle* (also dir., co-sc.) 1973; *Finchè c'è Guerra c'è Speranza* (also dir.), *To Love Perhaps to Die* (Sp.) 1975; *Il Commune Senso del Pudore* (also dir.) 1976; *Quelle Strane Occasioni, Un Borghese Piccolo Piccolo, I Nuovi Mostri/Viva Italia!, Tra Moglie e marito* 1977; *Le Temoin* (Fr./It.), *Dove vai in Vacanza?* (also dir. "Le Vacanze intelligenti" episode) 1978; *L'Ingorgo—una Storia impossibile/Traffic Jam/Bottleneck* 1979; *Il Malato immaginario/The Hypochondriac* (also co-sc.) 1980; *Io e Caterina* (also dir., co-sc.) 1981; *Il Marchese del Grillo* (also co-sc.), *Io so che tu sai che Io so* (also dir., co-sc.) 1982; *In Viaggio con Papá* (also dir., co-sc.), *Il Tassinaro* (also dir., co-sc.) 1983; *Bertoldo Bertolino e Cacasenno, Tutti Dentro* (also dir., co-sc.) 1984; *Sono un Fenomeno paranormale* (also co-sc.) 1985; *Troppo Forte* (also co-sc.) 1986; *Un Tassinaro a New York* (also dir., co-sc.) 1987; *Una Botta di Vita/A Taste of Life* 1989; *L'Avaro/The Miser* (also co-sc.) 1990; *Vacanze Di Natale '91* (also co-sc.), *Assolto per aver commesso il Fatto* (also dir., co-sc.) 1992.

Sorvino, Mira. Actress. Born 1969. *ed.* Harvard. A striking beauty, she is the daughter of actor Paul SORVINO. She quickly showed her talents as an actress in her early films, from portraying a Spanish translator and a Jewish intellectual to being a 19th century Brazilian beauty in England. Her chameleon-like approach to developing unique, individual characters earned her the supporting actress Academy Award for her comedic turn in Woody ALLEN's *Mighty Aphrodite* (1995).

FILMS: *Amongst Friends* (also assoc. prod.) 1993; *Barcelona, Parallel Lives, Quiz Show* 1994; *Blue in the Face, Mighty Aphrodite* 1995; *Beautiful Girls* 1996; *Romy and Michele's High School Reunion, Mimic* 1997.

Sorvino, Paul. Actor. Born in 1939, in Brooklyn, N.Y. Tall, heavyset, versatile character lead and supporting player of the American stage and screen. A frustrated opera singer, he took vocal lessons for 18 years before conceding to a career on the dramatic stage. Trained at the AADA, he appeared in a couple of Broadway plays of the 60s before entering films. Also seen frequently on TV. His daughter is actress Mira SORVINO.

FILMS: *Where's Poppa?* 1970; *The Panic in Needle Park, Cry Uncle, Made for Each Other* 1971; *A Touch of Class* (UK), *The Day of the Dolphin* 1973; *The Gambler, Shoot It Black Shoot It Blue* 1974; *I Will I Will. . . for Now* 1976; *Oh God!* 1977; *Bloodbrothers, Slow Dancing in the Big City* 1978; *Lost and Found* 1979; *Cruising* 1980; *Reds* 1981; *Melanie* (Can.), *I the Jury, That Championship Season* 1982; *Off the Wall* 1983; *The Stuff, Turk 182* 1985; *Very Close Quarters* (filmed in 1983), *A Fine Mess, Vasectomy, A Delicate Matter* 1986; *Dick Tracy, Goodfellas* 1990; *The Rocketeer, Age Isn't Everything* 1991; *Life in the Food Chain* 1992; *Nixon* 1995; *Love Is All There Is, Romeo and Juliet* 1996; *Money Talks* 1997.

Sothern, Ann. Actress. Born Harriette Lake, on Jan. 22, 1909, in Valley City, N. Dak. *ed.* U. of Washington. Trained as a vocalist by her concert-soprano mother, she made her film debut under her real name, playing a bit in the early Warners sound musical *The Show of Shows* (1929). She played another bit in the MGM Buster Keaton vehicle *Doughboys* (1930), and two other films, then headed for Broadway, where she quickly rose from small parts to leads. She returned to Hollywood in 1933 and was signed to a Columbia contract, this time as Ann Sothern, and soon found her niche as a lighthearted heroine of B pictures of Columbia and RKO. Moving to MGM in 1939, she rapidly gained popularity as the bouncy, scatterbrained blonde heroine of the comedy-adventure series "Maisie," in which she starred ten times in a span of eight years.

Miss Sothern was also given the opportunity to showcase her pleasant voice and comic energy as the star of such lively musical comedies as *Lady Be Good* and *Panama Hattie.* And she demonstrated undeniable dramatic talent in such films as *Cry Havoc* and *A Letter to Three Wives.* Her warmth and vitality kept her a popular minor star until the early 50s, when she quit films to pursue a successful career on TV as the star of her own shows, 'Private Secretary' (1953–57) and, later, 'The Ann Sothern Show' (1958–61). She also toured with stage plays. She returned to the screen in the mid-60s in occasional character roles. She was nominated for an Academy Award as best supporting actress for *The Whales of August* (1987). She was formerly married to actors Roger PRYOR (1936–42) and Robert STERLING (1943–49). Her daughter by the latter, Tisha Sterling (*b.* Patricia Ann Sterling, Dec. 10, 1944), is an actress.

FILMS INCLUDE: *The Show of Shows* 1929; *Doughboys* 1930; *Broadway Through a Keyhole, Let's Fall in Love* 1933; *The Hell Cat, Blind Date, Kid Millions* 1934; *Folies Bergère, Hooray for Love, The Girl Friend, Grand Exit* 1935; *You May Be Next, Don't Gamble with Love, My American Wife, Walking on Air, The Smartest Girl in Town* 1936; *Dangerous Number, Fifty Roads to Town, There Goes My Girl, Super-Sleuth, Danger—Love at Work, There Goes the Groom, She's Got Everything* 1937; *Trade Winds, Maisie* (first in series), *Hotel for Women, Fast and Furious, Joe and Ethel Turp Call on the President* 1939; *Congo Maisie, Brother Orchid, Dulcy* 1940; *Maisie Was a Lady, Lady Be Good* 1941; *Maisie Gets Her Man, Panama Hattie* 1942; *Three Hearts for Julia, Thousands Cheer, Cry Havoc* 1943; *Maisie Goes to Reno* 1944; *Up Goes Maisie* 1946; *Undercover Maisie* (last in series) 1947; *April Showers, Lords and Music* 1948; *A Letter to Three Wives, The Judge Steps Out* 1949; *Nancy Goes to Rio, Shadow on the Wall* 1950; *The Blue Gardenia* 1953; *The Best Man, Lady in a Cage* 1964; *Sylvia* 1965; *Chubasco* 1968; *The Killing Mind* 1973; *Golden Needles* 1974; *Crazy Mama* 1975; *The Manitou* 1978; *The Little Dragons* 1980; *The Whales of August* 1987.

Southern, Terry. Novelist, screenwriter. Born on May 1, 1926, in Alvarado, Tex. *ed.* SMU; U. of Chicago; Northwestern; Sorbonne. A no-holds-barred satirist who thrives on outrageous humor, he gained notoriety in the late 50s as the co-author (under the pseudonym Maxwell Kenton, with Mason Hoffenberg) of the first-published-in-Paris erotic novel *Candy,* a modern-day parody of Voltaire's *Candide.* He collaborated on a number of screenplays, sharing Academy Award nominations for *Dr. Strangelove* (1964) and *Easy Rider* (1969).

FILMS: *Dr. Strangelove or How I Learned to Stop Worrying and Love the Bomb* 1964; *The Cincinnati Kid, The Loved One* 1965; *Barbarella* (Fr./It.), *Candy* (co-novel basis only) 1968; *Easy Rider, The Magic Christian* (from own novel; UK) 1969; *End of the Road* 1970; *The Telephone* 1988.

sound. The sound era in the history of motion pictures traditionally begins in 1927, the year of *The Jazz Singer* and the talkie revolution. But attempts to give film a voice date back to the earliest days of cinema.

The most primitive of the early sound methods consisted of simply placing actors, singers, and noisemakers behind the screens of motion picture theaters and having them simulate dialogue, music, and sound effects more or less in synchronization with the film being shown. Imperfect as it was, this sound "system" was utilized as late as 1915 in special presentations of D. W. Griffith's *The Birth of a Nation.* More complex and more dependable were the early sound systems that used phonograph records in synchronization with lip movement on the screen. Even before he patented his motion picture machine, the KINETOSCOPE, Thomas EDISON had directed his assistant, W. K. Laurie DICKSON, to develop an apparatus that would combine the new invention with an earlier one, the Edison phonograph. As early as 1889, Dickson was able to demonstrate to Edison the result of his effort, which they christened the Kinetophonograph (also known as the Kinetophone). It was basically a regular Kinetoscope linked with a gramophone, which piped in sounds for personal listening through a stethoscope-like device. It was introduced into a number of peep-show parlors, but the novelty enjoyed only limited success. A more advanced and complicated version of the Kinetophone was later tried out at several American and British motion picture theaters, but a fire at the Edison labs in 1914 ended for all time that company's experiments with sound films. Experiments with various sound systems coupled with phonographs were continued, however, by others in Europe as well as in the US. Among the more successful systems were the French Chronophone and the American Cinephone.

Concurrent with the experiments in sound systems linked to phonographs, inventors here and abroad developed sound reproduction processes in which sound was registered directly on film. The first patent for a sound system using a photoelectric cell as a means of recording was issued as early as 1900. In 1904, Eugene LAUSTE, a former Edison employee, built a rather advanced sound-on-film recording device, but like other inventors of the time he was unable to develop a reliable amplifying system, and he abandoned his experiments at the outbreak of WW I. More persistent was Lee DE FOREST, an American scientist and wireless pioneer, who after many setbacks perfected his Phonofilm system in 1923. The system was demonstrated in various motion picture theaters throughout the US. Despite initial public apathy, the system was acquired by Fox and was eventually integrated into that studio's own MOVIETONE process in 1927.

In 1926, Warner Brothers, one of Hollywood's smallest and financially least stable studios, had formed the Vitaphone Company, in partnership with Western Electric, to develop a sound system for motion pictures. In August of 1926, Vitaphone premiered in New York a series of demonstration shorts along with a feature film, *Don Juan,* starring John Barrymore. The score for the feature, played by the New York Philharmonic, was recorded on discs. The playing time for each record equaled the projection time of one reel. Four projectors were used to provide immediate substitution in case one machine got out of sync with the recording apparatus. Despite the precaution, presentations of the new system were frequently disrupted by breakdowns in synchronization. Yet the Warner brothers, on the verge of bankruptcy, decided to gamble everything they had on their conviction that sound was going to revolutionize the industry and salvage their company. They acquired full interest in Vitaphone and launched an all-out publicity and sales campaign for their sound system. Their gamble paid off in October of 1927, when they made motion picture history by releasing *The Jazz Singer,* the film that set the industry on an irreversible new course.

The Jazz Singer was basically a silent picture with occasional awkwardly synchronized musical passages and several sentences of spoken words, but when Al Jolson spoke the now-historic phrase "Wait a minute; wait a minute. You ain't heard nothing yet," audiences stood up and cheered. The film became a tremendous box-office hit. Encouraged by their success, the Warners released their first all-talking film, *Lights of New York,* in 1928. Reluctantly, other studios began switching to sound and within months silent cinema was a thing of the past. But the Vitaphone system that started it all was heading for rapid oblivion. The imperfections inherent in the disc-synchronization process rendered this and similar systems unreliable and to many studios unacceptable. Within a couple of years disc synchronization had been completely replaced by sound-on-film systems.

The first system to employ successfully the direct recording of sound on film, utilizing a photoelectric cell, was Fox's Movietone. Other systems quickly followed. Before long there were not one but two separate systems for recording sound on film optically—the VARIABLE-AREA SOUND TRACK and the VARIABLE-DENSITY SOUND TRACK. In both systems, sound patterns recorded along the edge of film (see SOUND TRACK) are scanned during projection by a light-sensitive photoelectric cell and converted into electric impulses. These are "decoded," amplified, and transmitted into loudspeakers to reach the spectators as sound waves through perforations in the screen.

The initial effect of the sound revolution on the development of cinema art was regressive. The camera, which had achieved a high degree of freedom of mobility toward the end of the silent era, was suddenly enchained again. Much as in the early days of cinema, it functioned passively and statically as actors moved mechanically from one strategically placed microphone to another. The vacuum-tube microphones were sensitive in only one direction and actors were required to speak into vases and umbrella stands to register their voices clearly. But the quality of sound recording improved rapidly and by the early 30s directors in both the US and Europe were using the sound track creatively to give their films an added dimension.

There were other side effects to the advent of sound. For one thing, the spoken dialogue effectively ended the era of truly international films. To gain entry into the international market, films had to be produced in several foreign-language versions, a costly and time-consuming practice. Later on, subtitles and dubbing solved the problem more practically. Other victims of "the talkies" were numerous actors and actresses whose voices proved inadequate to the requirements of the microphone. The careers of many established stars whose faces were their fortune ended suddenly. Conversely, the advent of sound heralded a mass importation to Hollywood and other film capitals of stage actors with trained voices. Theater directors were also recruited, mainly as dialogue directors to assist action-oriented film directors with no experience at coaching speaking actors.

A true revolution in quality came immediately after the war with the commercial introduction of recording tape. By 1950 the process of recording sound optically directly on film was virtually abandoned in favor of a magnetic tape sound track, which could be reproduced without loss of quality and transferred to film to create a high-fidelity composite print. Several separate sound tracks—for dialogue, music, sound effects, narration, etc.—can be recorded and later mixed at a console to create a combined balanced sound track, providing filmmakers with great flexibility and creative control.

A source of further improvement in sound quality is the Dolby noise-reduction system, originally developed by DOLBY LABORATORIES for tape-recording equipment. It reduced hisses and other unwanted noise electronically, making motion picture sound tracks clearer and smoother than ever before. STEREOPHONIC SOUND became a by-product of the wide-screen vogue of the 50s and has remained an ear-filling staple at specially equipped theaters whenever large-scale film spectacles are shown. The Dolby stereo system, popular since the late 70s, made stereophonic sound cheaper and more widely available. DIGITAL SOUND TRACKS, introduced for some films in the 90s, yield greater range and crispness than optical sound tracks.

sound camera. A camera designed and equipped for shooting sound pictures. It is usually blimped to prevent the noise of its mechanism from being picked up by the microphone during sound recording. See BARNEY; BLIMP; CAMERA, MOTION PICTURE; SOUND.

sound crew. Personnel in a film production unit responsible for the recording of sound during shooting. In documentary or industrial film production this task is often carried out by a single person, simply known as the "sound man," but in feature film production several people are involved. The ultimate responsibility for the quality of the sound lies with the "sound mixer" or "floor mixer," not to be confused with the specialist who synthesizes the sound tracks during the mix. The sound mixer is to the sound crew what the director of photography is to the camera crew, a highly qualified and experienced sound technician or engineer who has the final say on the set on matters concerning sound. In the actual operation of the sound recording equipment, he is usually assisted by a "sound recorder." Another important member of the crew is the BOOM MAN, or boom operator, who manipulates the MICROPHONE BOOM to achieve optimum sound while keeping his equipment out of the camera's field of view. The CABLEMAN (sometimes there is more than one) is another member of the sound crew; it is his duty to run and maintain cables among the separate pieces of sound equipment on the set. The sound crew may also include one or more "operators" who perform a variety of duties, from monitoring playback machines to maintaining the p.a. (public address) system and loading and unloading tape spools.

sound editor. Also known as the "sound effects editor," this person prepares the DIALOGUE TRACK (or production track) for DUBBING and adds SOUND EFFECTS to the film. The sound editor must solve such problems on the dialogue track as unwanted background noise, clipped words of dialogue, and differences in recorded level of dialogue. He or she coordinates the creation of sound effects or their retrieval from a library. The sound editor typically has an assistant sound editor; on large films, several sound editors may work under a supervising sound editor.

sound effects. Natural or artificially created sounds, other than speech or music, that become part of a motion picture's sound track. Such sounds (a gun popping, a door slamming, a glass breaking, thunder rolling, etc.) are recorded during filming or separately (sound not recorded synchronously with film is known as "wild sound") or borrowed from a library of stock sound effects. Certain large film and TV studios are equipped with a sophisticated sound-effects console that stores hundreds of prerecorded sounds and enables the operator to scan, locate, and introduce directly into the sound track any desired effect within seconds. The person in charge of obtaining and adding sound effects to a film is called the SOUND EDITOR or sound effects editor. See also EFFECTS TRACK; WILD TRACK.

sound speed. The rate at which film passes through a motion picture camera when it is intended to be accompanied by sound. It has been standardized since the advent of sound at 24 frames per second. See also SILENT SPEED.

sound stage. A soundproof studio equipped for the production of sound films.

sound track. A narrow band on the left side of sound film (when the emulsion faces the viewer) which carries recorded patterns of dialogue, narration, music, and sound effects. It is activated during projection to provide "talkies" with their voice (see SOUND). The sound track on a strip of film is printed a number of frames ahead of the corresponding picture so that the sound and picture can be synchronized during projection, compensating for the physical distance on a projector between the picture gate and the sound head. See ADVANCE, OPTICAL SOUND TRACK, DIGITAL SOUND TRACK.

soup. A slang term for the developing solution used in processing film.

Sovcolor. A color film process adapted by the Soviets from the German AGFACOLOR after their troops occupied the Agfa plant at Wolfen toward the end of WW II. It is still widely used in the production of Russian films.

Soviet Union (USSR). For most of the twentieth century, Russia and the 14 republics it dominated were part of a single political entity, the Soviet Union, encompassing 14 percent of the earth's land area and comprising over 100 ethnic groups. Soviet cinema was so closely associated in the eyes of Westerners with Marxist themes of political, social, and economic struggle that many forgot that a thriving "capitalist" film industry existed in czarist Russia for a full decade before the October 1917 Revolution. Since the collapse of the Soviet Union in 1991, a non-Soviet Russian cinema has been restored and a number of autonomous film industries have been created in the newly independent republics.

The Russians claim that two of their nationals, Alexei Sanarski and Ivan Akimov, invented a film apparatus, independently of other pioneers, as early as 1896. But film production of any consequence did not begin in Russia until 1907. Meanwhile, foreign entrepreneurs had dominated the scene. The Lumière brothers were the first to show films to Russians in St. Petersburg in May of 1896. They were followed by England's Robert W. Paul and American representatives of the Edison company. Later France's Gaumont and Pathé opened permanent branches in Russia. Local amateur cameramen occasionally submitted newsreel footage for inclusion in the film programs of the foreign companies, but no organized filmmaking by Russians took place until 1907.

It was during that year that Alexander Drankov, the official photographer of the Duma, the Czar's legislature, announced the opening of Russia's first film studio and embarked on his first production, a screen adaptation of Pushkin's *Boris Godunov.* But the project was scrapped in mid-production when the leading actor changed his mind about appearing in the lowly regarded medium of film. In the meantime, Pathé rushed into production *Cossacks of the Don,* a nonfiction film about Cossack life, which was directed by a Frenchman, Maurice Maître. Released in February of 1908, it is considered by some to be Russia's first film, although others reserve that distinction for Drankov's *Stenka Razin,* which was released ten months later but was truly a story film, adapted from a popular novel, and was directed by a Russian, Vladimir Romashkov.

By 1910 there were 15 large and small film companies operating in Russia, mainly in Moscow. Their catalogs covered a variety of genres, but most prevalent were adaptations of literature and drama, both classical and modern, and elaborate but stagy costume spectacles. The scarcity of films dealing with contemporary issues was partly the result of strict czarist censorship.

Representative examples of the pre-Revolutionary output included Vasili Goncharov's *The Death of Ivan the Terrible* (1909), *Peter the Great* (1910), *The Life and Death of Pushkin* (1910), *Yevgeni Onegin* (1911), the highly successful *The Defense of Sebastopol* (1911), *1812* (1912), *The Accession of the Romanov Dynasty* (1913), and *Volga and Siberia* (1914); Pyotr Chardynin's *Queen of Spades* (1911), *The Kreutzer Sonata* (1911), *Woman of Tomorrow* (1914), *Chrysanthemums* (1914), *Natasha Rostova* (1915), and *Flood* (1915); Yakov PROTAZANOV's *The Prisoner's Song* (1911), *Departure of a Grand Old Man* (1912), *The Shattered Vase* (1913), *War and Peace* (in collaboration with Vladimir GARDIN, 1915), *Nikolai Stavrogin* (1915), *Sin* (1916), and *The Queen of Spades* (1916); Wladyslaw STAREWICZ's *The Beautiful Leukanida* (animated puppet film, 1912), *Christmas Eve* (1913), *A Terrible Revenge* (1913), and *Ruslan and Ludmila* (1915); Gardin's *Keys to Happiness* (1913), *Anna Karenina* (1914), *Days of Our Life* (1914), *Ghosts* (1915), and *Petersburg Slums* (in collaboration with Protazanov, 1915); and Yevgeni BAUER's *Freed Bird* (1914), *Tears* (1914), *Life in Death* (1914), *Song of Triumphant Love* (1915), *Singed Wings* (1915), *Queen of the Screen* (1916), and *A Life for a Life* (1916). There were also many lowbrow comedies made in imitation of popular imports, as well as occasional outstanding dramatic productions like Vsevolod Meyerhold's *The Picture of Dorian Gray* (1915).

Although foreign films dominated the market, domestic products were increasingly popular, especially those featuring Russia's own stars, like Ivan MOZHUKHIN, Natalia Lisenko, Olga BACLANOVA, and Vera Kholodnaya, and the Polish-born Pola NEGRI. The last and most important pre-Revolutionary production—according to historian Jay Leyda—was Protazanov's *Father Sergius,* an adaptation of a Tolstoy story starring Mozhukhin and Lissenko. This compelling anticlerical drama, set against an authentic background of events at the court of Czar Nikolai II, was completed before October 1917 but for some reason not released until May of the following year. Its production had been made possible by a considerable relaxation in censorship that followed the temporary assumption of power by the Kerenski government.

The October Revolution brought in its wake significant changes in the Russian cinema. Many of its veteran directors, actors, and technicians emigrated to France, Germany, and the US, among other countries. Only a few of the old-timers became integrated into the newly emerging Soviet cinema. The chaotic conditions that disrupted all areas of life during the period of violent transition made normal film production virtually impossible. Yet, despite civil war and famine, the foundations of a new industry were laid. True to Lenin's credo that the cinema was a significant tool of the Revolution, the Bolsheviks set up a film subsection on November 9, 1917, as part of the newly formed State Department of Education. The subsection was headed by Lenin's wife, Nadezhda Krupskaya. Its main purpose was to reconstruct the film industry and transform it into a potent weapon for the enlightenment of the working masses. The foreign blockade effectively cut off all importation of films, new film stock, and equipment. But before supplies had completely dried up, production was continuing, with the cooperation of the less defiant commercial producers and under the guidance of state cinema committees that were set up in Moscow and Petrograd. There was a gradual transformation of film content from vaguely defined ideology to full-fledged Socialist propaganda. In the summer of 1918 the first agit-train left for the Eastern front. The agit-trains (or agitprop trains, as they were also known) were self-contained mobile propaganda centers, especially equipped to disseminate agitational "message" entertainment and information to faraway posts. Their crews presented movies, plays, and other forms of culture with political commentary and often included filming units that recorded events during the trip for use in *agitki,* films expressly made for propaganda. Edward TISSÉ, who would later become famous as Eisenstein's cameraman, was aboard the first agit-train. The footage he shot was sent back to Moscow, where it was edited by another future great of the Soviet cinema, Dziga VERTOV.

The change in the content of films during 1918 is easily discernible through their titles. Releases of the first six months included *Creation Can't Be Bought* (an adaptation of Jack London's *Martin Eden*), *The Young Lady and the Hooligan, Shackled by Film, The Woman Who Invented Love,* and *Maids of the Mountain.* Films released later in the year included *Bread, Signal, Underground,* and *Uprising.*

An important step in the process of rebuilding was the establishment of the VGIK, the State Institute of Cinematography, in Moscow, and another school, for training film technicians and actors, in Petrograd. But in the immediate range, a practical training ground was provided by the civil war itself, offering to dozens of inexperienced cameramen an opportunity to develop as technicians and artists on the battlefields and to numerous editors back home a constant flow of filmed material with which to sharpen their skills. Much of the scarce raw stock was used for the production of *agitki.* Typical of these were *Daredevil* and *For the Red Banner,* both released early in 1919. But a number of nonpolitical feature films were also made during that year, including Yuri Zheliabuzhsky's screen version of Andersen's *The Emperor's New Clothes,* Protazanov's *The Queen's Secret,* which was adapted from Elinor Glyn's *Three Weeks,* and Alexander Sanin's *Polikushka,* an impressive adaptation of a Tolstoy story which was withheld from release until 1922.

Conditions for filming having deteriorated rapidly (equipment and raw stock were mysteriously scarce), in August of 1919 the government decreed the nationalization of the film industry, effective in January of the following year. By 1920–21 production had dwindled to a trickle and only half the country's movie theaters remained open. Of the original 143 cinemas in Moscow, only ten were functioning regularly. There were weeks when not a single theater was operating, because of malfunctioning equipment, electricity blackouts, or the unavailability of films. The few films released during this period dealt mostly with revolutionary themes. Typical titles included *Domestic Agitator, Village in Crisis, On the Red Front,* and *In the Days of Struggle* (all 1920), *Sickle and Hammer* and *Hunger—Hunger—Hunger* (both 1921), and *Infinite Sorrow* and *Whirlwind of Revolution* (1922). More ambitious in scope were Alexander Rasumny's adaptation of Gorky's *Mother* (1920) and Dziga Vertov's 13-reel compilation film *History of the Civil War* (1922).

Conditions began improving late in 1921 as a result of Lenin's New Economic Plan, which allowed a partial return to private enterprise. Film equipment and raw stock resurfaced suddenly and as mysteriously as they had earlier disappeared, but not in quantities large enough to make resumption of normal production possible. It was only in 1922, with the Soviet-German trade agreement that followed the Rapallo Treaty, that fresh film stock was imported and once again widely available. Production jumped from 11 features in 1921 to 157 in 1924. The importation of foreign films was also resumed, and profits from their exhibition were diverted to domestic production. In December of 1922 the government reorganized the scattered cinema committees into a centralized body, Goskino (the State Cinema Enterprise). Goskino became the Sovkino Trust in 1925, with a monopoly over film production, distribution, and rental in Russia proper and over film imports and exports in both Russia and the autonomous republics. However, the "ideological direction" of production remained the responsibility of the Commissariat of Education. Certain companies, like Mezharbpom and Leningradkino, were allowed a degree of autonomy within the new setup. A special unit, Proletkino, was put together in 1923 to undertake the production of political films, in line with party ideology.

Curiously, the spirit of wild experimentation that permeated Russian literature and drama in the early post-Revolutionary years. Few if any departed from the conventional norms in style. Within the party, opinion was sharply divided on whether to permit and support nonnaturalistic, avant-gardist expression in film and other arts. A decision was formalized as policy by a Politburo resolution in July of 1925, paving the way for a burst of creative freedom and heralding the most exciting period in the history of Soviet cinema. But even before the official sanction, some experimentation went on, especially in the work of Dziga Vertov, who began making his unorthodox Kino-Pravda newsreels in mid-1922, and in the workshop experiments in montage by Lev KULESHOV early in 1923. April of 1924 saw the release of the Kuleshov collective's *The Extraordinary Adventures of Mr. West in the Land of the Bolsheviks,* a satirical comedy about the bewildered impressions of an American in Russia. A young filmmaker, Vsevolod PUDOVKIN, who assisted on Kuleshov's direction, collaborated on the script and played one of the leading roles. Other notable films during this time included Gardin's *Locksmith and Chancellor* (1923), Rasumny's *Kombrig Ivanov/Beauty and the Bolshevik* (1923), Ivan Perestiani's *Red Imps* (1923), Alexander Ivanovsky's *Palace and Fortress* (1924), Protazanov's futurist fantasy *Aelita* (1924), and Grigori KOZINTSEV and Leonid TRAUBERG's *The Adventures of Oktyabrina* (1924).

The mid-20s was also a period of enthusiastic theoretical thinking and writing, which found its expression in lectures, debates, and magazine articles. Two theatrical figures who had considerable influence on the young filmmakers emerging at this time were Vladimir Mayakovsky and Vsevolod Meyerhold. Both were instrumental in the artistic development of Sergei EISENSTEIN, who in 1925 made a momentous transition from the stage to films with *Strike* and *The Battleship Potemkin/Potemkin.* Eisenstein and two other young directors, Pudovkin and Alexander DOVZHENKO, formed a formidable triumvirate of talent and originality that helped place Soviet film in the forefront of the international cinema during the final years of the silent era.

Creative versatility and adventurous exuberance characterized the Soviet cinema of the late 20s, with avant-garde and traditional forms of filmmaking co-existing and thriving. Among the many notable films of the period were Eisenstein's *October/Ten Days That Shook the World* (1928) and *The General Line/Old and New* (1929); Pudovkin's *Mother/Mother 1905* (1926), *The End of St. Petersburg* (1927), and *Storm Over Asia/The Heir to Genghis Khan* (1929); Dovzhenko's *Zvenigora* (1928), *Arsenal* (1929), and *Earth/Soil* (1930); Vertov's *Stride Soviet!* (1926), *A Sixth of the World* (1926), and *The Man with a Movie Camera* (1929); Esther SHUB's compilation films *The Fall of the Romanov Dynasty* (1927) and *The Russia of Nikolai II and Lev Tolstoy* (1928); Kuleshov's *Dura Lex/By the Law* (1926); Grigori Kozintsev and Leonid Trauberg's *The Cloak/The Overcoat* (1926), *S.V.D./The Club of the Big Deed* (1927), and *The New Babylon* (1929); Abram ROOM's *Bed and Sofa* (1926); Boris BARNET's *Girl with a Hat Box/When Moscow Laughs* (1927) and *The House on Trubyana Square* (1928); Protazanov's *The Forty-First* (1927); Friedrich ERMLER's *Katka's Reinette Apples* (in collaboration with Eduard Johanson, 1926) and *Fragment of an Empire* (1929); Nikolai OKHLOPKOV's *The Sold Appetite* (1928); Yakov Bliokh's *The Shanghai Document* (documentary, 1928); Sergei YUTKEVICH's *Lace* (1928); Nikolai SHENGELAYA's *Elliso/Caucasian Love* (1928); Fedor OZEP's *Earth in Chains/The Yellow Pass/The Yellow Ticket* (1928); Mikhail CHIAURELI's *Saba* (1929); Victor Turin's *Turksib* (documentary, 1929); Ilya TRAUBERG's *Blue Express/The China Express* (1929); and Mikhail KALATOZOV's *Salt for Svanetia* (documentary, 1930).

Regrettably, the spirit of creative liberty and experimentation in the Soviet cinema was stifled before it could extend into the sound era. Eisenstein was among the first to feel the effects of the change that was taking place in the Bolshevik hierarchy early in 1928, when the release of his *October* was received with hostile suspicion by the party leadership, who adopted the term "formalism" as a derogatory description of the director's use of symbolism and exercises in rhythm and visual style. Stalin's increasing stranglehold on the Party soon embraced the cinema, as it did all other areas of Soviet life. The All-Union Party Conference on the cinema which assembled on March 15, 1928, under the sponsorship of the Department of Propaganda and Agitation, sprinkled its resolutions with references to "remnants of bourgeois influence" and warnings against "formalistic" tendencies by directors. The conference resolved that "the basic criterion for evaluating the art qualities of a film is the requirement that it be presented in a form which can be understood by the millions," thus setting the tone for the doctrine of socialist realism that would dominate the Soviet cinema, as well as the other arts, until Stalin's death and beyond.

Further effects of Stalin's ascendancy were a decree of December 7, 1929, that all filmmaking units allocate 30 percent of their budgets to the production of documentaries to augment the industrial objectives of the dictator's first Five Year Plan. The Soviet cinema was entering a protracted period of creative drought.

Although the Russians claim to have developed sound-on-film recording systems as early as 1926, it wasn't until late in 1930 that the Soviet's first true talkie was made, Yuli RAIZMAN's *The Earth Thirsts.* Of two competing sound systems, Tager's variable density and Shorin's variable area, the former was the only one adopted by the industry. The conversion to sound was not total and some silent films continued to be made through the mid-30s for distribution in remote areas lacking sound projectors. Generally, the early talkies were timid and conventional in their use of sound, although there were instances of imaginative integration of music with film, notably in Vertov's *Enthusiasm/Symphony of the Donbas* (1931) and *Three Songs About Lenin* (1934). Other notable early talkies included Nikolai Ekk's *Road to Life* (1931), Olga Preobrazhenskaya's *The Quiet Don/Cossacks of the Don* (1931), Kozintsev and Trauberg's *Alone* (1931), Yutkevich's *Golden Mountains* (1931), Chiaureli's *Out of the Way!* (1931), Dovzhenko's *Ivan* (1932), Ermler and Yutkevich's *Counterplan/Pozor/Shame* (1932), Pudovkin's *A Simple Case/Life Is Beautiful* (1932) and *Deserter* (1933), Barnet's *Outskirts/Patriots* (1933), and Kuleshov's *The Great Console*r (1933).

By the mid-30s the Soviet cinema had settled into comfortable mediocrity, with few if any traces of the social concern and artistic vitality that had characterized it in the past. Output became compartmentalized into standard genres. Musical films enjoyed a vogue, led by such escapist productions as Igor Savchenko's *Accordion* (1934); Grigori ALEXANDROV's *Jazz Comedy/Jolly Fellows/Moscow Laughs* (1934), *Circus* (1936), and *Volga-Volga* (1938); and Ivan PYRIEV's *The Rich Bride/Country Bride* (1938) and *Tractor Drivers* (1939).

There was also a revival of literary adaptations, exemplified by such films as Grigori ROSHAL and Vera STROYEVA's *Petersburg Nights* (1934), Roshal's *The Oppenheim Family* (1939), Vladimir PETROV's *Thunderstorm* (1934), ROMM's *Pushka/Boule de Suif* (1934), Protazanov's *Without Dowry* (1937), and Mark DONSKOY's "Gorky Trilogy" (1938–40), which was based on the author's memoirs. A genre that vividly reflected the political conformity of the Soviet filmmakers was the hero-worship film that paid overblown tribute to the amplified deeds of revolutionary figures and events. The film that set the pattern for the genre was Sergei and Georgy VASILIEV's *Chapayev* (1934). Among the films that followed were Kozintsev and Trauberg's "Maxim Trilogy" (1935–39), Yefim DZIGAN's *We Are from Kronstadt* (1936), Alexander ZARKHI and Josef HEIFITZ's *Baltic Deputy* (1937), Dovzhenko's *Shchors/Schors* (1939), and Ermler's *The Great Citizen* (in two parts, 1938–39).

Stalin's espousal of the "personality cult" resulted in a wave of films lauding the achievements of Lenin and Stalin himself. The growing menace from Germany in the late 30s gave rise to a number of films extolling heroic figures from Russia's past, among them Petrov's two-part *Peter the First* (1937–39) and Eisenstein's *Alexander Nevsky* (1938). *Nevsky* was Eisenstein's first sound film, noted for the contrapuntal effect of the director's visual rhythms and the music of Sergei Prokofiev. It was also Eisenstein's first finished film since his return from his unhappy sojourn in the US and Mexico.

The abuse Eisenstein suffered at the hands of Shumyatsky, who had consistently foiled the director's film projects and aborted the promising *Bezhin Meadow* in midproduction, was a sad illustration of the sorry state of the Soviet cinema during Stalin's dictatorship. It wasn't until Eisenstein had been tamed into submission, confessing in print his artistic "errors," that he was trusted with the direction of *Nevsky,* and even then only under the watchful supervision of government-appointed associates. Political and artistic compliance became the key to employment, in a system that rewarded mediocrity and discouraged creative originality.

After the signing of the Soviet-German non-aggression pact, on August 23, 1939, anti-Nazi films like Adolf Minkin and Herbert Rappaport's *Professor Mamlock* (1938) and Grigori Roshal's *The Oppenheim Family*, and even Eisenstein's historic but politically sensitive *Alexander Nevsky,* were discreetly withdrawn from circulation. Instead, there was a brief flirtation with pro-German films, an example of which was Dovzhenko's *Liberation* (1940).

The German invasion of Russia, on June 22, 1941, brought about a revival of the documentary, a field that had been relatively dormant for a number of years. Cameramen were dispatched to the fronts and the material they sent back was edited into morale-boosting COMPILATION FILMS. Among the most ambitious of these were Leonid Varlamov and Ilya Kopalin's *The Defeat of the German Armies Near Moscow* (1942), Roman KARMEN's *Leningrad in Combat* (1942), Mikhail Slutsky's *Day of War* (1942), Varlamov's *Stalingrad* (1943), Vasili Belayev's *The People's Avengers* (1943), Dovzhenko and Yulia SOLNTSEVA's *The Fight for Our Soviet Ukraine* (1943) and *Victory in the Ukraine. . .* (1945), and Raizman's *Berlin/The Fall of Berlin* (1945). A novel format during the war was the "Fighting Film Album," an anthology of propaganda and morale shorts issued at periodic intervals in 1941 and 1942 (see DOCUMENTARY).

Feature film production was affected by the evacuation of personnel from the film centers in Moscow and other big cities to remote facilities in the Asian republics of the USSR. The curtailed wartime feature catalog comprised themes that related to the conflict as well as general themes and even light entertainment productions. Notable titles of the period included Pyriev's *Swineherd and Shepherd/They Met in Moscow* (1941) and *At 6 P.M. After the War/Six P.M.* (1944); Donskoy's *How the Steel Was Tempered/Heroes Are Made* (1942), *The Rainbow* (1944), and *Unconquered/The Taras Family* (1945); Ermler's *She Defends Her Country/No Greater Love* (1943); Yutkevich's *The New Adventures of Schweik* (1943) and *Hello Moscow!* (1946); Petrov's *Kutuzov/1812* and *Jubilee* (both 1944); Raizman's *Mashenka* (1942) and *Moscow Sky* (1944); Lev ARNSHTAM's *Zoya* (1944); Gerasimov's *The Great Earth* (1944); Romm's *Girl No. 217* (1944); Abram Room's *Invasion* (1945); Barnet's *One Night/Dark Is the Night* (1945); and Alexander Stolper's *Days and Nights* (1945). The outstanding production of the war period was Eisenstein's *Ivan the Terrible, Part I,* which was released early in 1945.

The postwar years represented the low point in the history of the Soviet cinema, in both quality and quantity. Fanned by the hysteria of the Cold War, the Stalinist repression reached a peak level. Charges of formalism abounded, and several of the leading directors were reprimanded for deviations from socialist realism and compelled to revise their films drastically. Some films were totally banned and withheld from release for a number of years, among them Kozintsev and Trauberg's *Plain People* (1945/release delayed to 1956), Eisenstein's *Ivan the Terrible Part II/The Boyars' Plot* (1946/1958), and Leonid Lukov's *A Great Life, Part II* (1946/1958). Yutkevich's *Light Over Russia* (1947) was banned altogether, and Pudovkin's *Admiral Nakhimov* (1946), Gerasimov's *Young Guard* (1947–48), and Dovzhenko's *Michurin/Life in Bloom* (1947) won a seal of approval only after considerable "cleansing."

Several films of the late 40s and early 50s were blatant anti-Western propaganda pieces, among them Romm's *The Russian Question* (1948), Alexandrov's *Meeting on the Elbe* (1949), and Kalatozov's *Conspiracy of the Doomed* (1950). Other films of the period included Ermler's *The Turning Point* (1946); Chiaureli's *The Vow* (1946), *The Fall of Berlin* (1949–50), and *The Unforgettable Year 1919* (1952); Alexander PTUSHKO's enchanting legends *The Stone Flower* (1946), Russia's first color feature, and *Sadko* (1953); Alexander Andryevsky's version of *Robinson Crusoe* (1946), the first of several productions in an experimental stereoscopic system not requiring special glasses; Zarkhi and Heifitz's *In the Name of Life* (1947); Arnshtam's *Glinka/The Great Glinka* (1947); Pyriev's *Tales of the Siberian Land/Song of Siberia/Symphony of Life* (1947); Donskoy's *Village Teacher* (1947); Barnet's *The Scout's Exploit/Secret Agent* (1947) and *Bountiful Summer* (1951); Stolper's *The Story of a Real Man* (1948); Raizman's *The Train Goes East* (1948) and *Dream of a Cossack/Cavalier of the Golden Star* (1951); Petrov's two-part *Battle of Stalingrad/The First Front/The Victors and the Vanquished* (1949–50) and *Revizor/The Inspector General* (1952); Roshal's *Academician Ivan Pavlov* (1949) and *Mussorgsky* (1950); Savchenko's *Taras Schevchenko* (1951); Alexandrov's *Glinka/Man of Music* (1952); Gerasimov's *The Country Doctor* (1952); Pudovkin's *Vasili's Return/The Return of Vasili Bortnikov* (1953); and Romm's *Admiral Ushakov* (1953).

Subtle but perceptible changes began showing in the Soviet cinema within a year of Stalin's death in 1953. Heifitz's *A Big Family* (1954) examined the gray shades of the personalities of its characters with an honesty and humanistic sincerity that had been absent from the Soviet screen for many years. But it wasn't until after Khrushchev's famous speech at the 20th Party Congress in 1956, in which he denounced the personality cult and other aspects of Stalinism, that the liberalizing impact of the political transformation could fully reach the screen.

The effects of the change were first clearly noticed in Grigori CHUKHRAI's *The Forty-First* (1956) and found their fuller expression in Kalatozov's *The Cranes Are Flying* (1957) and Chukhrai's *Ballad of a Soldier* (1959), films that broke away from the patterns of conventional propaganda and stereotypical heroics and reintroduced lyricism and emotional truth to the Soviet screen. *Cranes* was a big international success and won the Grand Prize at the Cannes Festival. Other notable films of the post-Stalin 50s included Yutkevich's *Skanderbeg* (1954), *Othello* (1956), and *Stories About Lenin* (1958); Konstantin Yudin's *The Safety Match* (1954); Kalatozov's *True Friends* (1954) and *The First Echelon* (1956); Alexander ALOV and Vladimir NAUMOV's *Restless Youth* (1955), *Pavel Korchagin* (1957), and *The Wind* (1959); Arnshtam's *Romeo and Juliet/The Ballet of Romeo and Juliet* (1955); Samson Samsonov's *The Grasshopper* (1955); Raizman's *Conflict/Lesson of Life* (1955) and *The Communist* (1958); Ermler's *An Unfinished Story* (1955); Donskoy's *Mother/1905* (1956), *At Great Cost/The Horse That Cried* (1957), and *The Gordeyev Family* (1959); Heifitz's *The Rumiantsev Affair* (1956) and *My Beloved* (1958); Eldar Ryazanov's *Carnival Night/Carnival in Moscow* (1957); Kozintsev's *Don Quixote* (1957); Gerasimov's *And Quiet Flows the Don* (1957); Zarkhi's *The Heights* (1957); and Lev KULIJANOV's *The House I Live In* (co-dir. with Yakov Segel, 1957) and *Our Father's House/A Home for Tanya* (1959). Eisenstein's *Ivan the Terrible Part II* and Dovzhenko's *Poem of the Sea* were released posthumously in 1958. Unfortunately neither was around to enjoy to the full the rebirth of the Soviet cinema the two had worked so vigorously to bring about.

The liberalized spirit continued into the early 60s, with both veteran and young directors participating in a revitalized program of production. Notable contributions by the "old guard" included Heifitz's *The Lady with the Dog* (1960); Kalatozov's *The Letter That Was Never Sent* (1960); Pyriev's *White Nights* (1960); Romm's *Nine Days of One Year* (1962) and *Ordinary Fascism/Triumph Over Violence* (1964); Gerasimov's *Men and Beasts* (1962); Yutkevich's *The Bath House* (co-dir. with Anatoly Karanovich, 1962); and Kozintsev's *Hamlet* (1964). The middle-generation directors were best represented by Chukhrai's anti-Stalinist *Clear Skies* (1961). New talent emerged in the persons of Sergei BONDARCHUK (*Fate of a Man/Destiny of a Man,* 1959), Mikhail (Moisei) Kalik (*Lullaby,* 1961), Gregory Danelia and Igor Talankin (*Seryozha/A Summer to Remember,* 1960), Vladimir Fetin (*The Colt,* 1960), Andrei TARKOVSKY (*Ivan's Childhood/My Name is Ivan,* 1962), Mikhail Schweitzer (*Resurrection,* 1962–63), Gennadi Gabai (*Forty-Nine Days,* 1962), Larissa Shepitko (*Heat,* 1963), Marlen Khutziev (*I Am 20,* 1963), Ilya Klimov (*Welcome Kostya!,* 1964), and Sergei Paradzhanov (*Shadows of Our Forgotten Ancestors,* 1965).

Just when it seemed that the Soviet cinema was again on the path of creative health, political events undermined its recovery once more. Khrushchev's forced retirement in 1964 was followed by a gradual regression and by the re-tightening of state control over films. Official intervention in production and distribution did not reassume the ugly proportions of the Stalinist era, but it once again became a major stumbling block to individual expression. But even such caution failed to guarantee freedom from scrutiny. Tarkovsky's *Andrei Rublev,* a biography of a 14th-century icon painter, was completed in 1966 but withheld from release in the Soviet Union until 1971. Many other films were drastically revised or altogether shelved.

Soviet films approved and released in the late 60s and the 70s included Alov and Naumov's *The Flight* (1971) and *The Legend of Til Eulenspiegel* (1975); Tengiz Abuladze's *The Wishing Tree* (1977); Alexei Batalov's *The Gambler* (1973); Ilya Averbakh's *Monologue* (1972) and *Confession of Love* (1978); Bondarchuk's four-part *War and Peace* (1966–67), *They Fought for Their Country* (1975), and *The Steppe* (1977); Mikhail Bogin's *Sozya* (1967); Alexander Chakovsky's *Blockade* (1975); Vitali Chetrika's *Flames* (1975); Chukhrai's *Stalingrad/Battle of Stalingrad/Memory* (documentary, 1970) and *Untypical Story* (1977); Vadim Derbenyov and Yuri Grigorovich's ballet films *Spartacus* (1976) and *Ivan the Terrible* (1978); Danelia's *Afonya* (1975); Donskoy's *A Mother's Heart/Sons and Mothers* (1966) and *Chaliapin* (1970); Leonid Gaidai's *The 12 Chairs* (1971), *Ivan Vasilievich* (1973), and *Impossible!* (1976); Gerasimov's *The Journalist* (1967), *By the Lake* (1970), *Mothers and Daughters* (1974), and *The Red and The Black* (1976); Boris Grigoryev's *Beginning of a Legend*

(1975); Heifitz's *The Only One* (1976) and *Asya* (1978); Elyar Ishmukhmedon's *Meeting and Partings* (1974); Kalik's *Goodbye Boys* (1965); Yuli Karasik's *The Sixth of July* (1968), *The Seagull* (1971), and *Personal Opinion* (1977); Karmen's *Death of a Commissar* (1966–68); Danil Khrabovitsky's *Taming of the Fire* (1972); Khutziev's *Rain in July* (1967); Elim Klimov's *Agony* (1974); Kozintsev's *King Lear* (1972); Kulijanov's *Crime and Punishment* (1969); Yevgeny Matevyev's *Earthly Love* (1975); Vladimir Menshov's *Moscow Does Not Believe in Tears* (1979; Oscar for best foreign language film, 1980); Nikita MIKHALKOV's *A Slave of Love* (1976) and *Oblomov* (1979); Andrei KONCHALOVSKY's *The First Teacher* (1965), *Asya's Happiness* (release delayed from 1966 to 1969), *Uncle Vanya* (1971), *Lovers' Romance* (1974), *Land of the Giants* (1975), and four-part *Siberiade* (1979); Tolomush Okeyev's *The Skies of Our Childhood* (1967), *Worship the Fire* (1972), and *The Red Apple* (1975); Vasili Ordynsky's *Red Square* (1971); Yuri Ozerov's *Communists* (1975); Gleb PANFILOV's *The Beginning* (1971) and *Peace—Bread—Freedom* (1977); Sergei PARADJANOV's *Sayat Nova* (1978); Margarita Pilkhina's *Anna Karenina* (1974); Pyriev's *Light of a Distant Star* (1965) and *The Brothers Karamazov* (1968); Raizman's *Your Contemporary* (1967); Room's *The Untimely Man* (1973); Stanislav Rostotsky's *And the Dawns Are Quiet Here* (1972); Alexei Saltikov's *The Chairman* (1968), *The Director* (1969), and *Breakup* (1971); Schweitzer's *Carousel* (1971); Eldar SHENGELAYA's *An Unusual Exhibition* (1968); Gregory Shengelaya's *Melodies of the Verisky Neighborhood* (1975); SHEPITKO's *Wings* (1966), *You and I* (1973), and *Sotnikov* (1977); Vasili SHUSHKIN's *There Was a Lad* (1964) and *The Red Snowball Tree* (1974); Talankin's *Choice of Goal* (1974); Tarkovsky's *Solaris* (1972) and *The Mirror* (1975–78); Yutkevich's *Lenin in Poland/Portrait of Lenin* (1966), *Theme for a Short Story* (1969), and *Mayakovsky Laughs* (co-dir. with Anatoly Karanovich, 1976); and Zarkhi's *Anna Karenina* (1967) and *Towns and Years* (1973).

In the late 60s the Soviet Union embarked on a program of ambitious co-production that resulted in such films as Bondarchuk's *Waterloo* (with Italy, 1970); Kalatozov's *I Am Cuba!* (with Cuba, 1963–66) and *The Red Tent* (with Italy, 1971), Alexander Zguridi's *Black Mountain* (with India, 1971), Alexander Mita's *Moscow My Love* (with Japan, 1974), Akira Kurosawa's *Dersu Uzala* (with Japan, 1975), and George Cukor's *The Blue Bird* (with the US, 1976).

By the late 70s, there were 43 film studios scattered around Russia and the other constituent republics, 19 for feature production and 24 for documentaries. The decade saw a trend toward decentralization of production; by the late 70s about 50 percent of all films made in the Soviet Union originated in the republics. Relatively few foreign films were imported, mostly from the Eastern Bloc. Films from the West were relatively scarce in general distribution but were shown regularly to small, privileged audiences. Both foreign and domestic films were carefully censored and classified on a scale of 1 to 4 as to their suitability for general release. Grade 3 films were shown to closed audiences and grade 4 films were not shown at all.

In the early 80s, a number of internationally known Soviet directors, many of them long-time veterans, were creating films of high artistic merit: Ilya Averbach (*Declaration of Love*, 1981); Gregori Chukrai (*Life Is Wonderful*, 1980); Georgi Danelia (*Autumn Marathon*, 1981); Anatoli Efros (*Thursdays Never Again*, 1983); Ali Khamrayev from Uzbekistan (*Bodyguard*, 1980); Elem Klimov (*Come and See*, 1985); Nikita Mikalkov (*A Private Conversation*, 1983); Gleb Panfilov (*Vassa*, 1983); and Andrei Tarkovsky (*Nostalgia*, 1983). However, by the middle of the decade, Soviet cinema had mostly stagnated, with a resurgence of ponderous epics in the socialist realist style (such as Sergei Gerasimov's *Leo Tolstoy*, 1984) and continuing censorship of politically objectionable, long-completed films, such as Elem Klimov's *Agonia* and Otar Yoseliani's *Pastorale*. In 1984, the great master Tarkovsky officially defected to the West, where he had been working for some time. His defection marked the end of an era in Soviet film. The following year, Mikhail Gorbachev's accession as Soviet leader marked the beginning of a new one.

Gorbachev began to institute policies of liberalization and democratic reform. His policies of *perestroika* ("restructuring") and *glasnost* ("openness") were a boon to filmmakers who had yearned for decades to practice their art freely, without fear of censorship. In 1986, the Fifth Congress of Soviet Filmmakers laid the groundwork for a revitalized and open cinema, one that could honestly explore contemporary social problems and the "blank spaces" that Soviet censorship had long enforced in people's knowledge of their own history. The Soviet Filmmakers Union was transformed from a monolithic organization to an association of independent guilds. In the years that followed, Soviet studios gained virtual independence to finance and distribute their product and arrange co-productions with the West; film units within studios were free to make what they wanted, as long as they could turn a profit.

Films that had been banned for as long as 20 years were finally released, including Andrei Konchalovsky's *Assya's Happiness* and Vladimir Naumov's *A Bad Anecdote*. Alexander Askoldov's debut film *The Commissar*, made in 1967, went unreleased until 1988, when it won several prizes at the Berlin Film Festival. A new generation of Soviet filmmakers treated subjects that were previously taboo, such as sex and drugs among alienated young people in Vasily Pichul's popular debut film *Little Vera* (1988). Critically acclaimed films released in 1986–88 included Vadim Abdrashitov's *Plumbum/Dangerous Game*, Nanni Dzhordzhadze's *My English Granddad*, Irakly Kvirikadze's *The Swimmer*, Panfilov's *The Theme*, Sergei Paradjanov and Dodo Abashidze's *Ashik Kerib*, Karen Shakhnazarov's *Courier*, and Tarkovsky's last film, *The Sacrifice* (released abroad in 1986).

A recurring theme in the "cinema of *glasnost*" was the moral tragedy of those who had conformed politically to escape repercussions. Films on this subject included Eldar Ryazanov's satirical *A Forgotten Melody for the Flute*, V. Bortko's *Having Lied Only Once*, and R. Odzhagov's *The Other Life*. Other motion pictures of the late 80s addressed the problems and motivations of young people, including Sergei Soloviev's *Assa!*, an evocative melodrama with rock music; Valery Orodnikov's rock-inspired *Challenge to the Logic of Things* and *Burglar*; and the documentary *Is It Easy To Be Young?* by Latvian filmmakers Herz Frank and Juris Podnieks.

In 1989, the Soviet Filmmakers Union celebrated the new Soviet cinema by establishing the Nikes, or "Soviet Oscars," awards honoring individual achievements as determined by the votes of peers in the industry. In the first awards ceremony, honoring films of 1987, the prize for best film went to Georgian director Tengiz Abuladze's *Repentance*, a darkly comic, avant-garde condemnation of Stalinism that had been kept on the shelf from 1984 to 1987, when *glasnost* made its release possible.

After the demise of the Soviet Union in 1991, Soviet cinema officially ceased to exist. Replacing it were the cinemas of numerous former constituent republics, of which Russia was the most productive. Throughout the former empire, film industries struggled to survive economic chaos and the woes of rapid privatization and decentralization. No longer could studios and filmmakers depend on vertical state control of financing, production, distribution, and exhibition. In 1991, private financing led to the production of over 400 films, a new record. But the following year, fewer than 70 films were begun, and most faced poor prospects for completion. Adding to its difficulties, the film industry in the former Soviet Union began to suffer, as the European cinema had for years, from the stiff competition of American productions and the continuing popularity of television.

Major studios, most notably Mosfilm, Lenfilm, and Gorky Studio, responded by restructuring as quickly as possible, stepping up the number of co-productions, and seeking to attract location filming of foreign productions. The Soviet Filmmakers Union re-titled itself the Federation of Independent Filmmakers Union. Many filmmakers tried to do as the capitalists do, producing slick, commercial films laden with sex and violence, in sharp contrast to the art-house cinema dominating the recent past.

Despite the turmoil, films of artistic merit continued to be made in the 90s. Russian films of the 90s include Nijole Adomenaite's *The House Built on Sand* (1991); Igor and Gleb Aleinikov's *Tractor Drivers* (1992); Victor Aristov's *Satan* (1991); Lidia Bobrova's *Hey, You, Geese!* (1992); Nikolai Dostal's *Cloud Paradise* (1992); Karen Gevorkain's *Spotted Dog Running Along the Seashore* (1991); Oleg Kovalov's *The Scorpion's Gardens* (1992); Viacheslav Krishtofovich's *Adam's Rib* (1991); Pavel Lounguine's *Taxi Blues* (1990); Alexander Mitta's *Lost in Siberia* (1991); Kira Muratova's *Asthenic Syndrome* (1990); Alexander Rogozhikin's *The Guard* (1990); Eldar Ryazanov's *The Promised Heavens* (1991); Karen Shakhnazarov's *The Tsar's Assassin* (1991); Sergei Soloviev's *The House Under the Starry Sky* (1991); Yevgeny Tsymbal's *The Tale of the Unextinguished Moon* (1991); Yevgeny Yevtushenko's *Stalin's Funeral* (1991); Nikita Mikhalkov's Oscar-winning film *Burnt By the Sun* (1994), and young director Sergei Bobrov's *Prisoner of the Mountains* (1996).

Filmmaking has continued on a smaller scale in the other former Soviet republics. The number of features released per year in each new nation—typically fewer than five or ten—reflects their smaller population base; government financing is often essential for domestic film industries to survive. The Baltic nations have been among the most committed to production of artistic films. In Estonia, directors of the 90s include Roman Baskin (*Peace Street*), Arvo Iho (*The Observer*), Jaan Kolberg (*This Lost Way*), Jüri Sillart (*The Sunny Kids*), and Tõnu Virve (*Dance Macabre*); in Latvia, Vasilyy Mass (*The Spider*) and Janis Streics (*The Child of Man*); in Lithuania, Sarunas Bartas (*To the Memory of the Day Passed*), Algimantas Puipa (*The Ticket to Taj Mahal*), and Jonas Vaitkus (*A Thrush, A Green Bird*).

The film industries in some former Soviet republics have been plagued and in some cases halted by political turmoil and civil war. This has been true in Georgia, home of veteran directors like Tengiz Abuladze, Lana Gogoberidze, Sergei Paradzhanov, Eldar Shenghelaya, and Rezo Tchkeidze. Other film industries have been enriched as filmmakers become more free to explore what is distinctive in their nations' identities. This has been the case in Central Asia, particularly in Tadzhikistan, where notable directors of the 90s include Tolib Khamidov (*Identification of Wishes*), Bakhtia Khudonazarov (*Brothers*), and Bako Sadykov (*Blessed Bukhara*). Prominent directors in Kazakhstan include Ardak Amirkulov, Amir Karakulov, and Yermek Shinarbaev; in Uzbekistan, Samir Abbasov, Shukhara Abbasov, Dzhakangir Faiziyev, Yuri Sabitov, and Mairam Yusupova.

Spaak, Charles. Screenwriter. *b.* May 25, 1903, Brussels, to a prominent Belgian family. *d.* 1975. His father was a noted playwright and poet; his mother a member of the Belgian Senate; his brother, Paul-Henri Spaak, the world-famous statesman. Charles arrived in Paris in 1928 as director Jacques FEYDER's secretary and soon began writing scripts for his employer's films, as well as those of other directors. Next to Jacques Prévert, he contributed more than any other screenwriter to the resurgence of French cinema in the 30s and had much to do with the success of some of the most notable "poetic realism" films of Feyder, RENOIR, and DUVIVIER. In the early 50s he was instrumental in the screen work of director André CAYATTE. Spaak directed one film, *Le Mystère Barton* (1949). His daughters, Agnès Spaak (*b.* 1944) and Catherine Spaak (*b.* 1945, Paris), are both well-known screen actresses.

FILMS INCLUDE: *Les Nouveaux Messieurs* 1929; *Le Grand Jeu* 1934; *Pension Mimosa, La Kermesse héroïque/Carnival in Flanders, Les Beaux Jours, La Bandera/Escape from Yesterday* 1935; *La Belle Equipe/They Were Five, La Porte du Large/The Great Temptation, Les Bas-Fonds/The Lower Depths* 1936; *L'Homme du Jour/The Man of the Hour, La Grande Illusion/Grand Illusion* 1937; *L'Etrange M. Victor, Mollenard/Hatred* 1938; *La Fin du Jour/The End of a Day* 1939; *L'Assassinat du Père Noël/Who Killed Santa Claus? Premier Bal* 1941; *Untel Père et Fils/The Heart of a Nation, Le Ciel est à vous/The Woman Who Dared* 1943; *La Part de l'Ombre/Blind Desire* 1945; *Panique/Panic, L'Idiot/The Idiot, Jéricho, L'Homme au Châpeau rond/The Eternal Husband, L'Affaire du Colier de la Reine/The Queen's Necklace* 1946; *D'Homme à Hommes/Man to Men* 1948; *Le Mystère Barton* (also dir.), *Retour à la Vie* 1949; *Justice est faite/Justice Is Done* 1950; *Adorables Créatures/Adorable Creatures, Nous sommes tous des Assassins/We Are All Murderers* 1952; *Le Grand Jeu, Thérèse Raquin/The Adulteress* 1953; *Avant le Déluge* 1954; *Le Dossier noir* 1955; *Paris Palace Hôtel/Paris Hotel, Crime et Châtiment/Crime and Punishment* 1956; *Charmants Garçons* 1957; *Les Tricheurs/The Cheaters* 1958; *La Française et l'Amour/Love and the Frenchwoman, Katia/Magnificent Sinner* 1960; *La Chambre ardente/The Burning Court, Cartouche, Germinal* 1962; *Le Glaire et la Balance/Two Are Guilty* 1973; *La Main à couper* 1974.

Spacek, Sissy. Actress. Born Mary Elizabeth Spacek, on Dec. 25, 1949, in Quitman, Tex. Fair-haired, blue-eyed, slim leading lady of Hollywood films. A cousin of actor Rip TORN, she came to films via the Actors Studio, where she studied for eight months under Lee STRASBERG. Early in her career she specialized in impersonating weird teenagers. She made a strong impression in *Badlands* (1973), in which at the age of 24 she gave a convincing portrayal of a 15-year-old on an intense crime spree with a psychotic boyfriend. She was 27 when she gave an equally believable performance in the role of a tormented high-school senior who gets even with her taunters through telekinetic powers in *Carrie* (1976). And she was 31 when she portrayed country singer Loretta Lynn from age 13 to maturity in *Coal Miner's Daughter* (1980), then proved herself equally superior in adult roles. She won an Academy Award as best actress for the latter film and earned Oscar nominations for *Carrie, Missing* (1982), *The River* (1984), and *Crimes of the Heart* (1986). Married to art director Jack Fisk since 1974, Spacek worked as a set decorator on such films as *Phantom of the Paradise* (1974) and *Death Game/The Seducers* (1977).

FILMS: *Prime Cuts* 1972; *Ginger in the Morning, Badlands* 1973; *Carrie, Welcome to L.A., Three Women* 1976; *Heartbeat, Coal Miner's Daughter* (as country singer Loretta Lynn) 1980; *Raggedy Man* 1981; *Missing* 1982; *The River* 1984;

Marie 1985; *Violets Are Blue, 'Night Mother, Crimes of the Heart* 1986; *The Long Walk Home* 1990; *Hard Promises, JFK* 1991; *Trading Mom* 1994; *The Grass Harp* 1996; *L.A. Confidential* 1997.

Spacey, Kevin. Actor. Born on July 26, 1959, in South Orange, N.J. *ed.* L.A. Valley Coll., Juilliard. Appealing character player of stage and screen. A veteran of comedy clubs, he has appeared widely at leading repertory theaters and on Broadway, where he won a Tony for his performance in 'Lost in Yonkers.' Active in film since 1986, he was awarded the Oscar as best supporting actor for his performance in *The Usual Suspects* (1995).

FILMS INCLUDE: *Heartburn* 1986; *Rocket Gibraltar, Working Girl* 1988; *Dad, See No Evil Hear No Evil* 1989; *Henry & June, A Show of Force* 1990; *Glengarry Glen Ross, Consenting Adults* 1992; *Iron Will, The Ref* 1994; *Outbreak, Seven, Swimming with Sharks* (also co-prod.), *The Usual Suspects* 1995; *A Time to Kill* 1996; *Albino Alligator* (dir.), *L.A. Confidential* 1997.

Spade, David. Actor, comedian. Born July 22, 1965, in Birmingham, Mich. This youthful, dry-witted stand-up comedian toured the club circuit before landing guest shots on television, eventually leading to his memorable stint on NBC's 'Saturday Night Live.' He developed a friendship with fellow SNL'er Chris Farley, with whom he's often teamed on the big screen.

FILMS: *Police Academy 4: Citizens on Patrol* 1987; *Light Sleeper* 1992; *Coneheads* 1993; *PCU* 1994; *Tommy Boy* 1995; *Black Sheep* 1996.

Spader, James. Actor. Born on February 7, 1960, in Boston, into a family of educators. Clean-cut leading man and supporting player of the American stage, screen, and TV. He dropped out of Phillips Academy prep school to train for the theater at New York's Michael Chekhov Studio. Between occasional acting jobs on the stage and TV he supported himself as a railroad car loader, truck driver, soda jerk, and stable boy. Entering films in the early 80s, he was often cast as a spoiled or villainous yuppie. But eventually he landed more versatile roles, culminating in the complex part of the video snooper in *sex, lies, and videotape* (1989), for which he won the best actor prize at the Cannes Festival.

FILMS: *Endless Love* 1981; *The New Kids, Tuff Turf* 1985; *Pretty in Pink* 1986; *Mannequin, Baby Boom, Less Than Zero, Wall Street* 1987; *Jack's Back* 1988; *sex lies and videotape, The Rachel Papers* (US/UK) 1989; *Bad Influence, White Palace* 1990; *True Colors* 1991; *Storyville, Bob Roberts* 1992; *The Music of Chance* 1993; *Dream Lover, Stargate, Wolf* 1994; *2 Days in the Valley* 1996; *Crash, Keys to Tulsa* 1997.

Spain. Spanish film has only recently been accorded the international recognition of its Eastern neighbors, France and Italy. For many outside of Spain, the study of that nation's cinema began and ended with Luis BUÑUEL, a Spanish native; but he made only a few films in his native land (opting for more welcoming locations in France, Mexico, and the US) and thus cannot serve as the sole exemplar of the national cinema. Spain's cinematic history from 1939 to 1975 was also decisively influenced by the dictatorship of Generalissimo Francisco Franco and the regime's oppressive control of the film industry. This circumstance led to long periods of outright exclusion of Spain from the world film market; it also casts a pall today over any attempt to re-evaluate the film output of this period, long stereotyped as bleak and uninspired. But through the efforts of critics and scholars a new history of Spanish cinema is emerging, revealing the formerly unheralded successes of the Franco period. The years since Franco's death have witnessed the development of an artistic and commercially successful film community in Spain.

Film was introduced to the Spanish public in 1896 through screenings in Madrid. Among the founding figures of the national cinema were Fructuoso Gelabert, who filmed *Riña en un café* (*Quarrel in a Café*, 1897), a pioneering film with a story line, and later an important series of documentaries; Segundo de Chomón, a prolific "trick" cinematographer in the mold of MÉLIÈS; and Eduard Jimeno, Jr. and Sr., who followed the Lumière fashion of filming "realities."

A maturation came in the late teens and 20s with the local development of feature films. By 1932, a production company was organized—Compañia Industrial del Film Español, S.A. (CIFESA)—that dominated the Spanish industry for decades to come. Among the creative personnel of the era was performer and director Floriàn Rey. Important films in Rey's early career (which continued into the 40s) include two versions of *La verbena de la Paloma* (*The Feast of the Dove*, 1919 and 1935), *La hermana San Sulpicio* (*Sister St. Sulpice*, 1934), *Morena Clara* (*Fair Brunette*, 1936), and the famed *La aldea maldita* (*The Accursed Village*, 1929), a drama of rural farmers migrating to the city. Other notable films of the 20s and early 30s include *La casa de La Troya* (*The House of La Troya*, d. Manuel Noriega and Alejandro Pérez Lugín, 1924); *Zalacaín el aventuerero* (*Zalacaín, the Adventurer*, d. Francisco Camacho, 1930); *La malcasada* (d. Gómez Hidalgo, 1926); *Bolche* (d. Francisco Elías, 1933); and Alejandro Pérez Lugín's *Nobleza baturra* (*Rustic Nobility*, 1926).

Censorship long preceded the Franco regime in Spain; it was in place in Barcelona by 1913. One victim of this institution was Buñuel, whose maiden project in Spain (after an absence of many years in Paris) was a documentary on the extreme poverty of Las Hurdes mountain region on the border of Portugal (*Las Hurdes*, 1932). The film was banned by the Spanish government for decades for its grim portrait of suffering within this remote community.

The Spanish Civil War (1936–39) ended in the elevation of the Francoist regime. The regime succeeded early at bringing film production entirely under its control. Even by 1937, Spanish films had to be licensed through the nationalist forces and were subjected to rigorous censorship before distribution. By 1941, filmmakers were ordered to submit their screenplays to censors before production started. Censorship concerns included not only political matters (loyalty to the regime), but treatment of domestic life (for instance, women were expected to be docile servants and housewives), the church (anti-clericalism was not permitted), and miscellaneous moral issues. Also by 1941, foreign films, which were highly popular with Spanish audiences, were not permitted to be screened commercially in Spain unless dubbed locally into Spanish and heavily censored. The regime financed film production as part of its propaganda efforts, paying up to half the production costs outright for projects determined to be in the "national interest." In 1942, the government monopolized newsreel and documentary production under the No-Do (Noticiario Cinematografico Español). From 1944 until 1973, film production in Spain became the individual province of the Minister of Culture, Admiral Luis Carrero Blanco.

Above all, Franco's regime demanded self-celebration in film. Franco (according to legend) himself authored the screenplay of the fantastically popular *Raza* (*Race*, d. Jose Saenz de Heredia, 1941), a tale of bravery set in the recently concluded Civil War. Other pictures of this period with Civil War themes include *Sín novedad en el alcazar* (*Siege of the Alcazar*, d. Augusto Genina, 1940), *Escuadrilla* (*Squadron*, 1941), and *Servicio al mar* (*The Naval Service*, 1950). Still other films glorified Spain's history, notably *Los ultimos de Filipinas* (*The Last*

Stand in the Philippines, d. Antonio Roman, 1945), honoring the armed resistance of the last stand of Spanish troops against the American occupation of the Philippines after the Spanish-American War; *Locura de amor* (*Love Madness*, d. Juan de Orduña, 1948), a tale of imperial-era royalty; and *Agustina de Aragón* (1950), about Spain's war with Napoleonic France.

Despite the coercion of the Franco regime, Spanish filmmakers were able to make some artful and even enduring commercial films. As with US cinema, some of the finest films were simple genre works. Playwright Enrique Jardiel Poncela contributed the dark, absurdist 1943 comedy *Eloisa esta debajo de un almendra* (*Eloisa is Underneath an Almond Tree*), directed by Rafael Gil, which is plotted as a murder mystery set in a Moorish castle. A popular ghost story, *La torre de los siete jorobados* (*The Tower of the Seven Hunchbacks*, d. Edgar Neville, 1944), was also a beautiful, highly stylized gothic work. Among the many religious films, one of the most memorable was *Marcelino, pan y vino* (*Marcelino, Bread and Wine*, d. Ladislav Vajda, 1954), a tale of an orphan's visits to a long-forgotten image of Jesus Christ. This film featured the performance of six-year-old Pablito Calvo; it was the first of many child-star films that filled Spanish screens for the next decade. Musicals were perennially popular; among the most famous were *La Dolores* (d. Florian Rey, 1940) and *El ultimo cuple* (*The Last Song*, d. Juan de Orduna, 1957).

Spanish cinema under Franco was also not without its subversive elements. A movement of Barcelona-based film artists called the "telurico" (essentialists) produced a series of formally intriguing, noncommercial features in the late 40s and 50s. Among the greatest of these was *Vida en Sombras* (*Life in Shadows*, d. Lorenzo Llobet Gracia, 1948), which centered on the obsessions and hallucinations of a cinematographer who believes he his responsible for a woman's death. A Spanish realist cinema also emerged during the 50s. The key work of this cycle was *Surcos* (*Furrows*, d. Jose Antonio Nieves Conde, 1951), a portrait of hardscrabble rural life and the corruption of the cities.

By general acclaim, the 50s marked the beginning of Spain's contemporary cinema, with the first films of three of Spain's brightest talents: Juan Antonio BARDEM, Luis BERLANGA, and Carlos SAURA. A defining moment of the decade came in 1951, when the Institute of Italian cultures held an Italian film festival, featuring the neorealist titles long unavailable even to Spaniards in the film industry. In the same year, Bardem and Berlanga collaborated on their first feature, the neorealist drama *Esa Pareja feliz* (*The Happy Family*, 1951). After this auspicious debut, the two filmmakers pursued distinct careers. Berlanga continued to mine the neorealist vein, salted with irony and wry social commentary. His solo debut was *Bienvenido, Mr. Marshall* (*Welcome, Mr. Marshall*, 1952), a pointed critique of US foreign policy in Europe (the title refers to the Marshall Plan). Other films directed by Berlanga included *Calabuch* (1956) and *Los jueves, milagro* (*A Miracle Every Thursday*, 1957). Bardem debuted with *Cómicos* (*Comics*, 1953), a fictionalized memoir of his childhood spent among show people. His later pictures tended toward the political (particularly opposition to Francoism), but included a good many genre and other commercial pieces. His other pictures from this period include *Calle mayor* (*Main Street*, 1956) and *Muerte de un ciclista* (*Death of a Cyclist*, 1955).

At the end of the decade, Carlos Saura shot the NOUVELLE VAGUE-influenced *Los Golfos* (1960), a modern drama about adolescent gangsters. Through the government's efforts, the film failed commercially (its domestic release was delayed two years), although it was screened successfully at the 1960 Cannes Film Festival. Saura achieved stature abroad and at home as a personal filmmaker, whose films are marked by their introspection, a discomfit with the past and elliptical "art film" narratives. His career has continued successfully, with at least one picture a year since the mid-60s. Some of his features include *La caza* (*The Hunt*, 1966), *El jardin de las delicias* (*The Garden of Delights*, 1970), *Ana y los lobos* (*Ana and the Wolves*, 1972), *La prima Angélica* (*Cousin Angelica*, 1973), and *Cría cuervos* (*Raise Ravens*, 1975).

The 60s cinema of Spain was bracketed by appearances of the famous expatriate Buñuel. In 1960, he returned to direct *Viridiana* (1961). Though the Spanish government entered the completed film at Cannes, where it became the first Spanish production to win the Palme d'Or, it was immediately suppressed domestically by the regime for perceived anti-clericalism and blasphemy. This caused much rancor among Spanish film critics and in the film industry. The ban on the film remained until after Franco's death.

The 60s introduced a younger generation of Spanish film directors, situated to challenge the dulling effect of the regime's mandates. This decade saw the advent of the "New Spanish Cinema" (said to fall between 1962 and 1966), a metaphoric style of filmmaking that engaged in oblique social criticism of the Franco era. This wave included such films as Francisco Regueiro's *El buen amor* (*The Good Love*, 1963), Basilo M. Patino's *Nueve cartas a Berta* (*Nine Letters to Berta*, 1965), Mario Camus's *Con el vento solano* (*With the East Wind*, 1965), Miguel Picazo's *La tia Tula* (*Aunt Tula*, 1964), and Angelino Fons's *La busca* (*The Search*, 1966). Such films reached a very limited audience in Spain, due to government control of theater booking. Another group of directors known as the "Barcelona School," which included Jamie Camino, Vicente Aranda, and Gonzalo Suarez, emphasized fantasy over social realism. Finally, there were many Westerns, spy thrillers, farces, and other genre works, produced primarily to fill domestic theaters, that could occasionally convey a wry disapproval of Spanish social conservatism (particularly the comedies of Manuel Summers).

These efforts brought a high level of production during the 60s, along with a gradual lifting of the taboos of the previous decades. The cultural climate warmed to the point that, by the end of the decade, even Buñuel could return with the regime's blessing to direct *Tristana* (released in 1970). Additional notable films of the 60s include Vincente Aranda's *Fata Morgana*, 1966; Bardem's *A las Cinco de la Tarde* (*At Five O' Clock in the Morning*, 1960); Berlanga's *El Verdugo* (*The Executioner*, 1963); Mario Camus's *Con el* in 1973 and the death of Franco himself in 1975. This period ushered in the greatest period of "apertura" (liberalization) in the nation's recent cultural history. José Luis BORAU, who had been a critic, producer, and director since the 60s, emerged as a central figure during this transition. The films released by his production company El Iman often had a political bent, but were narrated with the efficiency and verve of classical Hollywood. During the 70s, Borau wrote screenplays for and produced *Mi querida senorita* (*My Dearest Lady*, d. Jamie De Armiñan, 1971), which was nominated for an Academy Award, and *Camada Negra* (*Black Brood*, d. Mañuel Gutiérrez ARAGÓN, 1977). He directed and served as co-writer on *Hay que Matar a B.* (*B. Must Die*, 1974), *Furtivos* (*Poachers*, 1975), and *La Sabina* (*The She Dragon*, 1979). Borau often collaborated with Mañuel Gutiérrez Aragón, former student and first-rate filmmaker in his own right. The 70s saw a new wave of nationalist cinema, with Catalonian directors Antoni Ribas and Jamie Camino making their first feature films, and some furtive avant-garde experiments that included Alvaro Del Amo's notorious 1979 comedy *Dos* (*Two*). Other notable figures from this period include directors Jamie Chavarri, Victor ERICE, Ricardo Franco, and José Luis Carol.

Films from the 70s include Aranda's *Cambio de sexo* (*Change of Sex*, 1977); Armiñan's *El amor del Capitan Brando* (*The Love of Captain Brando*, 1974), and *Al servicio del la mujer española* (*At the Service of the Spanish Woman*, 1978); Bardem's *El puente* (*The Long Weekend*, 1976); Berlanga's *La Escopeta Nacional* (*National Shotgun*, 1978), Bellment's *L'orgía* (*The Orgy*, 1978); Antonio Betancor's *Sentados al borde de la mañana* (*Sitting at the Edge of Dawn*, 1978); Jose Juan Bigas Luna's *Tatuaje* (*Tattoo*, 1976), *Caniche* (1979), and *Bilbao, una historia del amor* (*Bilbao, A Love Story*, 1978); Roberto Bodegas's *Los nuevos españoles* (*The New Spaniards*, 1974), Camino's *La largas vaciones del 36* (*The Long Vacations of '36*, 1975); Camus's *Los pajaros de Baden-Baden* (*The Birds of Baden-Baden*, 1974); Jamie Chavarri's *El desencanto* (*The Disenchantment*, 1976), and *A un Dios desconocido* (*To an Unknown God*, 1977); Antonio Drove's *La verdad sobre el caso Salvota* (*The True Story of the Savolta Case*, 1978); Erice's *El espíritu de la colmena* (*The Spirit of the Beehive*, 1973; Ricardo Franco's *Pascual Duarte* (1975); Antonio Giménez-Rico's *Retrato de familia* (*Family Portrait*, 1976); Emilio Martinez Lazaro's *Las palabras de Max* (*Max's Speech*, 1977); Josefina Molina's *Vera, un cuentro cruel* (*Vera, Her Cruel Story*, 1973); Ribas's *La ciutat cremada* (*Burnt City*, 1976); Gonzalo Suarez's *La regenta* (*The Director*, 1975), *Beatriz* (1976), and *Parranda* (*Binge*, 1977); Immanol Uribe's *Elproceso de Burgos* (*The Burgos Trial*, 1979).

In the 80s and 90s, filmmakers continued to expand on the liberty afforded them by the change in government, including the election of a socialist government. The popularity of comic director Pedro ALMODÓVAR, confirmed with his 1984 release *Qué he hecho yo para merecer esto?* (*What Have I Done To Deserve This?*), gave Spanish cinema renewed exposure in non-Spanish-speaking markets. Notable films of the 80s and 90s include Luis ALCORIZA's *Tac-tac* (1981); Almodóvar's *Matador* (1985), *Tie Me Up, Tie Me Down* (1989), and *High Heels* (1991); Aranda's *La muchacha de las bragas de loro* (*The Girl with the Golden Panties*, 1980), *Asesinato en el comité central* (*Murder in the Central Committee*, 1983), and *Si te dicen que caí* (1990); Armiñan's *El nido* (*The Nest*, 1980); Jose and Cecilia Bartolome's *Después de...* (*After...*, 1981); Berlanga's *Patrimmonio nacional* (*National Patrimony*, 1981), *Nacional III* (1982), and *La Vaguilla* (*The Young Bull*, 1985); Francesc Betriu's *Los fieles sirvientes* (*The Faithful Servants*, 1980) and *Placa del Diamante* (*Diamond Square*, 1982); Alberto Bermejo's *Vencinos* (*Neighbors*, 1981); Betancor's *1919: Crónica del alba* (*1919: Days of Dawn*, 1982); Borau's *Río Abajo* (*On the Line*, 1984) and *Tata Mia* (*Dearest Nanny*, 1986); Camino's *El largo inverno* (*The Long Winter*, 1992); Camus's *La Colema* (*The Beehive*, 1982), *Guerrilla—los desastres del a guerra* (*Guerrilla—The Disaster of War*, 1983), and *El sol del membrillo* (*The Sun of the Quince Tree*, 1992); Aragon's *Demonios en el jardín* (*Demons in the Garden*, 1982), and *La noche mas hermosa* (*The Most Beautiful Night*, 1984); Oscar Ladoire's *Opera prima* (1980) and *A contratiempo* (*Syncopated Time*, 1981); Lazaro's *Sus años doradas* (*Her Golden Years*, 1980); Pilar Miró's *Cuenca's Crime* (1980) and *Gary Cooper que estas en los cielos* (*Gary Cooper Who Art in Heaven*, 1981); Molina's *Función de noche* (*Evening Performance*, 1981) and *Esquilache*, (1989); Basilio Martín Patino's *Caudillo* (*Leader*, 1976); Jose A. Salgot's *Mater Amatisima* (*Beloved Mother*, 1982); Saura's *Dulces horas* (*Sweet Hours*, 1981); Suarez's *Epiligo* (*Epilogue*, 1984); Summers's *Angeles gordos* (*Fat Angels*, 1980); Uribe's *La fuga de Segovia* (*Escape from Segovia*, 1981), *La muerte de Mikel* (*The Death of Mikel*, 1983), and *El rey pasmado*, 1992; and Ivan Zulueta's *Arrebato* (*Rapture*, 1980).

Spano, Vincent. Actor. Born on Oct. 18, 1962, in Brooklyn, N.Y. Swarthy leading man of American and international films. On the stage from early youth, he left his first mark on Broadway at age 14, in 'Shadow Box'. In films from the late 70s, memorably as 'Sheik' in John Sayles's *Baby, It's You* (1983).

FILMS: *Over the Edge, The Double McGuffin* 1979; *The Black Stallion Returns, Baby It's You, Rumble Fish* 1983; *Alphabet City* 1984; *Maria's Lovers, Creator* 1985; *Good Morning Babilonia/Good Morning Babylon* (It./Fr./US) 1987; *Aquarium/High Frequency* (It.), *And God Created Woman* 1988; *Venezia Rosso Sangue/Venice Blood Red/Venetian Red* (as playwright Carlo Goldoni; It./Fr.) 1989; *City of Hope, Oscar* 1991; *Alive* 1992; *The Tie That Binds* 1995.

sparks. A slang term for a studio electrician.

Sparks, Ned. Actor. *b.* Edward A. Sparkman, 1883, Ontario. *d.* 1957. Dour-faced, rasping-voiced, much-mimicked character comedian of numerous Hollywood silents and talkies, following a long career on the stage.

FILMS INCLUDE: *A Wide-Open Town* 1922; *The Boomerang, Seven Keys to Baldpate, Bright Lights, Soul Mates* 1925; *Mike, The Auction Block* 1926; *The Secret Studio, Alias the Lone Wolf, Alias the Deacon* 1927; *The Big Noise, The Magnificent Flirt* 1928; *The Canary Murder Case, Nothing but the Truth, Street Girl* 1929; *Love Comes Along, The Devil's Holiday, The Fall Guy, Leathernecking, Conspiracy* (lead role) 1930; *Iron Man* 1931; *The Miracle Man, Big City Blues* 1932; *42nd Street, Secrets, Gold Diggers of 1933, Lady for a Day, Too Much Harmony, Going Hollywood, Alice in Wonderland* (as the Caterpillar) 1933; *Hi Nellie!, Sing and Like It, Private Scandal, Down to Their Last Yacht, Servants' Entrance, Marie Galante, Imitation of Life* 1934; *Sweet Adeline, Sweet Music* 1935; *Collegiate* 1936; *One in a Million, Wake Up and Live* 1937; *Hawaii Calls* 1938; *The Star Maker* 1939; *For Beauty's Sake* 1941; *Stage Door Canteen* 1943; *Magic Town* 1947.

Sparkuhl, Theodor. Director of photography. *b.* Oct. 7, 1894, Hannover, Germany. *d.* 1945. *ed.* U. of Goettingen; U. of Bonn. He entered films in 1911 as projectionist, became a newsreel cameraman for Gaumont the following year, and in that capacity covered WW I in Russia and the Middle East. A director of photography since 1918, he worked almost exclusively for Ernst Lubitsch until the director's departure for the US in 1921. In 1930, Sparkuhl left for England and France, en route to Hollywood, where he signed up with Paramount in 1933.

FILMS INCLUDE: In Germany—*Die Augen der Mumie Ma/The Eyes of the Mummy, Carmen/Gypsy Blood* 1918; *Die Austernprinzessin/The Osyter Princess, Rausch/Intoxication, Madame Dubarry/Passion, Die Puppe/The Doll* 1919; *Sumurun, Anna Boleyn/Deception* 1920; *Die Bergkatze* 1921; *Das Weib des Pharao/The Loves of Pharaoh, Die Flamme/Montmartre* 1922; *Dekameron Nächte* 1924; *Manon Lescaut* 1926; *Abwege* 1928. In France—*La Chienne* 1933. In the US—*Midnight Club* 1933; *Caravan* 1934; *The Last Outpost* 1935; *The Big Broadcast of 1937* 1936; *High Wide and Handsome* 1937; *Beau Geste* 1939; *Wake Island, The Glass Key* 1942; *Star Spangled Rhythm* 1943; *Till We Meet Again* 1944; *Blood on the Sun* 1945; *The Bachelor's Daughters* 1946.

special effects (SP-EFX, FX, SFX). Artificially devised effects used to create illusory impressions in a motion picture. The term encompasses both photographic or VISUAL EFFECTS, which are achieved through manipulation of the film image, and physical or MECHANICAL EFFECTS, which are staged through physical means on a set during filming. Visual effects include such basic techniques as the DISSOLVE, the FADE, and the WIPE, as well as more glamorous processes used to simulate bizarre, spectacular, or dangerous phenomena. The earliest visual effects were done "in-camera," before developing the film. For example, in a GLASS SHOT, the camera filmed a partially clear glass sheet; actors were visible through the clear part, while the rest was obscured by background scenery painted on the glass. Rudimentary MATTE SHOTS were done by masking part of the camera lens, filming the actors, rewinding the film, masking the part that had previously been exposed, and filling the unexposed part with MATTE PAINTINGS or STOP MOTION puppets. Another in-camera technique, BACK PROJECTION or process photography, was done by projecting moving scenery through a translucent screen behind the actors on the set. An analogous process, FRONT PROJECTION, became possible with the invention of highly reflective materials for background screens.

The development of the OPTICAL PRINTER, a machine that employs a camera and projector to re-photograph and combine separate pieces of film, gave special effects artists more flexibility. No longer did visual effects need to be done in-camera; they could be created by compositing elements photographed at different times on separate rolls of film. Various TRAVELING MATTE techniques have been developed so that numerous components can be joined in a single image: actors filmed on a sound stage, backgrounds filmed on location, miniature buildings filmed on a back lot, and puppet monsters filmed in an animator's studio. The most commonly used traveling matte technique since the 1950s has been the BLUE SCREEN PROCESS.

Effects produced through the use of optical printers are known as "opticals," a term sometimes used loosely to refer to all visual effects. A film's visual effects may also include ANIMATION techniques, such as ROTOSCOPE, in which elements of live action footage are transformed into hand-painted animated elements.

Viewers are often unaware of mechanical effects in action, such as the wires that help an actor carry his leading lady or the cigarette ash dropping at just the right comic moment from the prop cigarette. More noticeable are the weather conditions produced by wind fans, snow and rain machines, and fog makers. Mechanical effects include explosions set off by remote detonation, gunshot holes simulated through explosive SQUIBS on actors' clothing, functioning weapons, fires, cave-ins, car crashes, train derailments, shipwrecks, and earthquakes. Epic disasters and battles are often staged through the use of MINIATURES, typically filmed in slow motion to compensate for their smaller scale. Full-scale mechanical effects filmed on the set are known as "floor effects."

Mechanical effects also include dummies and PUPPETS of every variety. Some puppets are miniature, some full scale. Some are animated by old-fashioned hand, rod, and marionette techniques; some are sophisticated costumes manipulated from inside by actors; some are animated by stop motion (filmed one frame at a time) or GO-MOTION (stop motion enhanced by computer control). Some are small animatronic creatures activated by electronic mechanisms; others are large monsters moved by hydraulic pulleys. Makeup effects such as latex monster masks and facial appliances, fake wounds, body suits, or makeup to simulate aging, may also contribute to the creating of illusions.

A given special effects sequence may include a number of mechanical and optical effects. A miniature of a spaceship is matted against the backdrop of space through the use of an optical printer. A flying actor is suspended by wires on a soundstage, matted against a sky through the blue screen process, and simulated in long shot by a miniature puppet. An earthquake sequence may include falling rocks suspended on wires, fake floors caving in, smoke and fire effects, falling people simulated by stunt players and puppets, miniatures of collapsing buildings, and matte paintings of background devastation.

Computer technology has revolutionized the special effects industry. Computerized MOTION CONTROL systems allow for precise repetition of motion, important for the multiple camera passes used to create traveling matte effects. Puppets are often remotely controlled by computerized "waldos," replicas manipulated offstage by puppeteers. Most significant has been the development of COMPUTER-GENERATED IMAGERY, COMPUTER ANIMATION, and DIGITAL EFFECTS. Elements created or manipulated on a computer—monsters, spaceships, scenery, shadows, snow and rain effects—can now be seamlessly integrated with photographed images. Filmed images themselves, once converted to digital form, can be manipulated on computers. Unwanted elements such as wires or rods can be erased; other elements can be transformed through techniques such as MORPHING.

In the days of the STUDIO SYSTEM, from the 20s to the early 50s, each major studio had its own special effects department to create the magic for its films. With the collapse of the studio system, these departments were disbanded, and special effects artists became freelancers. The age of the modern special effects company began with George Lucas's founding of INDUSTRIAL LIGHT & MAGIC (ILM) to create the effects for his film *Star Wars* (1977). The phenomenal success of *Star Wars*, with its abundance of eye-filling special effects, led to a wave of science fiction/fantasy blockbusters in which the special effects were the true star. An increasing number of special effects were employed even in other genres—comedies, action films, horror films. Producing these effects were independent special effects artists and a number of independent companies, of which ILM was the most prestigious. Other special effects companies include Apogee, Boss Film Studios, Dreamquest, Pacific Data Images, Stan Winston Studios, and Visual Concept Engineering.

speed. 1. The rate at which film travels through a camera, a projector, or a printer. It may be expressed in frames per second (normally 24) or in feet per minute (90 for 35 mm film; 36 for 16 mm film). See SILENT SPEED; SOUND SPEED. 2. The relative sensitivity of raw film stock to exposure, expressed in ASA numbers in the US and in DIN numbers in part of Europe. 3. The relative optical sensitivity of a lens to light, expressed in f-numbers or T-numbers and calibrated by F-STOP or T-STOP settings.

"Speed!" The cue that lets the director know that the camera and sound recorder are running at the proper operational speed and in sync and that the shooting of action can begin.

SP-EFX. Commonly used abbreviation for SPECIAL EFFECTS.

Spencer, Bud. Actor. Born Carlo Pedersoli, in 1929, in Italy. Hulking strongman of spaghetti Westerns and cheap action pictures. A former national swimming champion, he teamed with Terence HILL (Mario Girotti) in the late 60s to form a formidable fighting duo, both actors assuming Anglo-Saxon names to appeal to Hollywood-crazed Italian audiences. The stars later pursued separate careers.

FILMS INCLUDE: *Dio perdona Io no/God Forgives, I Don't/Blood River* 1967; *I Quattro dell'Ave Maria/Ace High/ Revenge in El Paso* 1968; *Un Esercito di 5 Uomini/The Five Man Army, La Colina degli Stivali/Boot Hill* 1969; *Lo chiamavano Trinità/They Call Me Trinity, Si puo fare. . . Amigo/The Big and the Bad, Quattro Mosche di Veluto grigio/Four Flies on Grey Velvet* 1971; *Una Ragione per vivere una Ragione per morire/A Reason to Live A Reason to Die, E poi lo chiamrono il Magnifico/A Man from the East* 1972; *Più forte Ragazzi! All the*

Way Boys 1973; *Piedone lo Sbiro* 1974; *Il Soldato di Ventura* 1975; *Charleston* 1976; *I Due Superpiedi quasi Piatti/Two Super Cops* 1977; *Piedone l'Africano, Lo chiamavano/ Bulldozer* 1978; *Occhio alla Penna* 1980; *Bomber, Banana Joe* 1982; *Go for It* 1983; *Miami Super Cops* 1985; *Aladdin* 1986.

Spencer, Dorothy. Film editor. Born on Feb. 2, 1909, in Covington, Ky. A highly skilled cutter whose illustrious Hollywood career spanned five decades, mainly at 20th Century-Fox. Associated with numerous major productions, she collaborated with Ford, Hitchcock, Lubitsch, and Kazan, among other directors. She was nominated for Oscars for *Stagecoach* (1939), *Decision Before Dawn* (1951), *Cleopatra* (1963), and *Earthquake* (1974).

FILMS INCLUDE: *Married in Hollywood* 1929; *The Case Against Mrs. Ames* 1936; *Blockade* 1938; *Trade Winds, Stagecoach* 1939; *Foreign Correspondent* 1940; *Sundown* 1941; *To Be or Not to Be* 1942; *Heaven Can Wait* 1943; *Lifeboat* 1944; *A Tree Grows in Brooklyn, A Royal Scandal* 1945; *Dragonwyck, Cluny Brown, My Darling Clementine* 1946; *The Ghost and Mrs. Muir* 1947; *That Lady in Ermine, The Snake Pit* 1948; *Down to the Sea in Ships* 1949; *Three Came Home, Under My Skin* 1950; *Fourteen Hours, Decision Before Dawn* 1951; *Lydia Bailey* 1952; *Man on a Tightrope* 1953; *Night People, Demetrius and the Gladiators, Broken Lance* 1954; *Prince of Players, Soldier of Fortune, The Left Hand of God, The Rains of Ranchipur* 1955; *The Man in the Gray Flannel Suit* 1956; *A Hatful of Rain* 1957; *The Young Lions* 1958; *The Journey* 1959; *From the Terrace, North to Alaska* 1960; *Wild in the Country* 1961; *Cleopatra* 1963; *Circus World* 1964; *Von Ryan's Express* 1965; *The Lost Command* 1966; *A Guide for the Married Man, Valley of the Dolls* 1967; *Daddy's Gone a-Hunting* 1969; *Happy Birthday, Wanda June* 1971; *Earthquake* 1974; *The Concorde—Airport '79* 1979.

Sperling, Milton. Producer, screenwriter. Born on July 6, 1912, in New York City. *ed.* CCNY. He entered films as a messenger boy and shipping clerk at Paramount's Astoria studios in Long Island City. In Hollywood since the early 30s, he was secretary to Darryl F. Zanuck and Hal B. Wallis and associate producer for Edward Small before becoming a screenwriter at Fox in 1936 and a producer in 1941. After WW II service as a Marine captain, he formed an independent production company, US Films.

FILMS INCLUDE: As screenwriter—*Sing Baby Sing* 1936; *Thin Ice* 1937; *The Great Profile* 1940. As producer—*Sun Valley Serenade* 1941; *I Wake Up Screaming* 1942; *Crash Dive* 1943; *Cloak and Dagger* 1946; *Pursued* 1947; *My Girl Tisa* 1948; *South of St. Louis* 1949; *Three Secrets* 1950; *The Enforcer, Distant Drums* 1951; *Retreat Hell!* (also story, sc.), *Blowing Wild* 1953; *The Court-Martial of Billy Mitchell* (also co-story, co-sc.) 1955; *Marjorie Morningstar* 1958; *The Bramble Bush* (also co-sc.), *The Rise and Fall of Legs Diamond* 1960; *Merrill's Marauders* (also co-sc.) 1962; *Battle of the Bulge* (co-prod., co-sc.) 1965; *Captain Apache* (co-prod., co-sc.) 1971.

Spewack, Samuel. Playwright, screenwriter, novelist. *b.* Sept. 16, 1899, Ukraine, Russia. *d.* 1971. *ed.* Columbia. In the US from childhood, he began his career as a reporter for the New York *World.* In 1922 he married Bella Cohen (*b.* 1899, Bucharest; *d.* 1990), also a reporter. As Samuel and Bella Spewack, they collaborated from the late 20s on many slam-bang comedies, some of which enjoyed great success on the Broadway stage and in films. In 1942 Spewack wrote and produced a grim compilation documentary, *The World at War,* for the US Office of War Information. Later in the war he served as information officer of the US Embassy in Moscow. The Spewacks won both a Tony Award and a Page One Award for their book for Cole Porter's musical 'Kiss Me, Kate' (1948–49). They shared an Oscar nomination for the screenplay of *My Favorite Wife* (1940).

FILMS INCLUDE: *The Secret Witness* (play basis only) 1931; *Clear All Wires* (play basis only), *The Nuisance* 1933; *The Gay Bride* (play basis only), *The Cat and the Fiddle* 1934; *Rendezvous* 1935; *Vogues of1938* 1937; *Boy Meets Girl* 1938; *My Favorite Wife* 1940; *The World at War* (doc.; also prod.) 1942; *Week-End at the Waldorf* 1945; *Kiss Me Kate* (play basis only) 1953; *Move Over Darling* 1963.

Spheeris, Penelope. Director. Born in 1945, in New Orleans. The eldest child of the owners of a traveling carnival, she endured a difficult youth. When she was seven, her father, a onetime Olympic wrestler and the troupe's strongman, was killed in a knife fight. Her alcoholic mother, nicknamed Gypsy for her penchant for frequent marriages (nine), moved with her four children to California. Tragedy followed Spheeris into adulthood, when she lost the father of her own daughter, Anna, to a drug overdose. Bulldozing through these and other obstacles, Spheeris toiled for years as a waitress, till she graduated from UCLA with a master's degree in film. She then began producing short films for satirist Albert Brooks on TV's 'Saturday Night Live.' After producing Brooks's first feature, *Real Life* (1978), she made her own debut as a director with *The Decline of Western Civilization* (1981), an eye-popping documentary on the punk rock scene. A 1988 follow-up on the heavy metal counterculture was equally illuminating. The low-budget dramatic features she directed in between, typically depressing affairs, dealing with troubled youths, were, however, far less inspired. In 1992 she enjoyed sudden success with her first comedy, *Wayne's World,* a feature-length expansion of a 'Saturday Night Live' skit, which became a huge sleeper hit at the box office. It led to a more high-budget mainstream entry, *The Beverly Hillbillies.*

FILMS: *Real Life* (prod. only) 1978; *The Decline of Western Civilization* (doc.; also prod., sc.) 1981; *Suburbia/The Wild Side* (also sc.) 1984; *The Boys Next Door* 1985; *Hollywood Vice Squad* 1986; *Summer Camp Nightmare/The Butterfly Revolution* (co-sc. only), *Dudes* 1987; *The Decline of Western Civilization II: The Metal Years* (doc.; also sc.) 1988; *Wedding Band* (act.) 1990; *Wayne's World* 1992; *The Beverly Hillbillies* 1993; *The Little Rascals* 1994; *Black Sheep* 1996.

spider. A three-armed metal device that opens to form a horizontal Y shape to support the legs of a camera tripod on a slippery or delicate surface. See also TRIANGLE.

spider box. Film studio term for what is known in the electrical industry as a junction box, a multi-outlet receptacle into which a number of lighting units can be plugged.

Spiegel, Sam. Producer. *b.* Nov. 11, 1903, Jaroslau, Austria (now Jaroslaw, Poland). *d.* 1985. *ed.* U. of Vienna. After a period of service with a youth group in Palestine, he entered films as a story translator during a 1927 visit to Hollywood, then returned to Europe as a producer of German and French versions of Universal Films in Berlin. A fugitive from Hitler's Germany in 1933, he produced a number of films independently elsewhere in Europe before migrating to the US in 1935. As a Hollywood producer from the early 40s, he used the pseudonym S. P. Eagle until 1954, intending to give his name a more distinguished ring, but after a string of successes as an independent producer, both here and in England, he reverted to his real name. In his heyday, Spiegel was one of the world's few truly independent producers and one of the few consistently successful ones. Working closely with his directors and screenwriters, he produced many films of both artistic quality and box-office appeal. Three of his productions, *On the Waterfront* (1954), *The Bridge on the River Kwai* (1957), and *Lawrence of Arabia* (1962), won "best picture" Academy Awards. In addition, he received the Irving Thalberg Memorial Award at the 1963 Oscar ceremonies.

FILMS INCLUDE: *Unsichtbare Gengner/Invisible Opponent* (Aus.) 1933; *The Invader/An Old Spanish Custom* (co-prod.; UK) 1936; *Tales of Manhattan* (co-prod.) 1942; *The Stranger* 1946; *We Were Strangers* 1949; *The Prowler* 1951; *The African Queen* (UK/US) 1952; *On the Waterfront* 1954; *The Strange One, The Bridge on the River Kwai* (UK) 1957; *Suddenly Last Summer* 1959; *Lawrence of Arabia* (UK) 1962; *The Chase* 1966; *La Nuit des Généaux/The Night of the Generals* (Fr./UK) 1967; *Nicholas and Alexandra* (UK) 1971; *The Last Tycoon* 1976.

Spielberg, Steven. Director, producer. Born on Dec. 18, 1947, in Cincinnati, of Jewish descent. The introverted son of an emotionally distant electric engineer father, specializing in computers, and a doting concert-pianist mother, he moved with his family to New Jersey, then on to Phoenix, Arizona, while still a tot. A film enthusiast since early childhood, he gained production experience with home movies and by the age of 12 had turned out his first scripted amateur film with actors. At 13 he won a contest with a 40-minute war film, *Escape to Nowhere,* and three years later completed *Firelight,* an ambitious 140-minute-long amateur production. He turned out five films during his studies in the film department of California State College and made his professional debut with a 24-minute short, *Amblin',* which was shown at the 1969 Atlanta Film Festival. Its success led to a contract with Universal and to much television work, including the TV movies *Duel* and *Something Evil.* He made his debut as a feature film director with *The Sugarland Express* in 1974 and was then assigned to direct a film that would become not only a milestone in the young director's own career but a launching pad for a significant new trend in the American movie industry. Brilliantly adapted from a Peter Benchley bestseller, *Jaws* (1975), a nail-biting thriller about a shark terrorizing a New England beach community, cost only \$8.5 million to make. It eventually reaped \$130 million in North American rentals, changing the way Hollywood viewed its business. The era of the megabuck movie dawned, and a new math evolved in which costs would be measured against potential returns.

Now buttressed by phenomenally generous budgets, Spielberg went on to write page after glorious page in Hollywood's spreadsheet logs. He scored another critical and commercial triumph with *Close Encounters of the Third Kind* (1977), an arresting science-fiction drama that earned him his first Academy Award nomination as best director. Surviving the grand folly of *1941* (1979), a grossly inflated gag- and trick-filled farce about WW II panic in L.A., he soon solidified his formidable position in the industry. Spielberg and his friend George LUCAS redefined the demographics of the movie audience and for a good number of years virtually dominated the commercial side of the Hollywood scene.

Spielberg reached a dizzying apex of success at the start of the 80s. His hit parade began with *Raiders of the Lost Ark* (1981), an exhilaratingly paced adventure thriller inspired by old matinee cliff-hanger serials that had excited the director and producer (Lucas) in childhood. A masterpiece of technical craftsmanship and a fine example of storytelling at a rudimentary, diverting level, the film, budgeted at \$20 million, went on to earn \$116 million in North American rentals. It earned Spielberg a second Oscar nomination as best director and universal accolades and went on to spawn two successful "Indiana Jones" sequels, both directed by Spielberg. But the success of *Raiders* was dwarfed in 1982 by *E.T. The Extra-Terrestrial,* a film that for many years remained the box-office champion of all times—\$228 million in North American rentals—and earned Spielberg a third Oscar nomination. Perhaps more than any other of his films, this imaginative, heartfelt, enchanting, science-fiction tale of a little boy's love of an alien creature, echoes the inner mind of the director's personality.

Spielberg entertains others the way *he* would like to be entertained, and uses the medium of film as an ultimate toy through which he can communicate with other kids of all ages while keeping himself shyly remote.

Increasingly expanding his activity as a producer, while continuing to direct, he rapidly amassed a huge fortune, becoming one of filmdom's wealthiest men. For a couple of weeks in 1982 he collected a cool \$1 million each day in personal profits from *E.T.* and *Poltergeist.* In 1984 he formed Amblin Entertainment, one of Hollywood's largest independent companies. Located in a luxurious compound on the lot of Universal Studios, the highly productive, hugely profitable company wields enormous power in the industry. Among his successes as co-executive producer were *Gremlins* (1984), *Back to the Future* (1985), and the animated feature *An American Tail* (1986), all of which led to sequels. Spielberg collaborated with Disney in producing *Who Framed Roger Rabbit?* (1988), a visually innovative blend of animation and live action that helped revive the animation genre. As an executive producer, Spielberg shepherded the careers of such directors as Robert ZEMECKIS, Joe DANTE, and animator Don BLUTH.

As a director, Spielberg continued to impress. In a distinct departure from his typical work, he turned out *The Color Purple* (1985), an emotionally charged, sensitively told adaptation of Alice Walker's Pulitzer Prize–winning novel about the tribulations of a black girl in the traditional South. It was Spielberg's first adult film and in many ways a superior production. Although some critics faulted the director for sweetening the harshness of the original book and replacing its earthy passion with superficial sentimentality, most found the film touching and exhilarating, magnificently shot, and beautifully played. It was nominated for an Oscar as best picture, but in what seemed like intentional snubbing, members of the Academy refrained from nominating Spielberg for best director. Possibly by way of an apology, the Academy bestowed on Spielberg the honorary Irving G. Thalberg Award, for the body of his work, during the 1987 Oscar ceremony.

Spielberg was less successful with his next "adult" film, *Empire of the Sun* (1987), which was a splendid recreation of colonial life in China at the outset of WW II, but marred by lack of emotional fire. He used plenty of physical fire but barely any true passion in attempting to recapture the magic of Victor Fleming's *A Guy Named Joe* (1943) with his technically spectacular but unconvincing remake *Always* (1989). The director confronted his own duality in *Hook* (1991), a spectacular updating of *Peter Pan* in which the protagonist, a hard-driving takeover lawyer who was once Peter Pan, struggles to balance inner conflicts between creativity and ambition. Though the film was among the top-grossers of its year, it received mixed reviews and was considered a box-office disappointment, given Spielberg's earlier track record.

Just when it seemed that Spielberg's directorial career was in decline, he reached a new height of commercial success with *Jurassic Park* (1993), a visually astonishing science fiction thriller about a theme park where genetically engineered dinosaurs run amok. The film restored Spielberg's reputation for roller-coaster terror and the blending of special effects wizardry with spellbinding, if two-dimensional, storytelling. It set new speed records for grossing $100 million at the box office (in 9 days) and $200 million (in 23 days), and surpassed Spielberg's own *E.T.* as the all-time rental champion.

Having reaffirmed his position as the premier director of summer blockbusters, he turned again to serious films with *Schindler's List*. Set, like many of his films, during World War II, it was his most ambitious effort yet in subject and treatment: a story of the Holocaust photographed in documentary-style black and white. In recognition of this achievement, he received his first Academy Award as best director.

In the late 80s, Spielberg branched into TV production with a less than successful anthology series, 'Amazing Stories,' for which he directed two episodes. He returned to TV production in the 90s with the futuristic underwater adventure 'SeaQuest DSV.' In 1994, joining fellow Hollywood moguls David Geffen and Disney alum Jeffrey Katzenberg in partnership, Spielberg created a new motion picture studio eventually named DREAMWORKS SKG (*S*pielberg *K*atzenberg *G*effen). The first of its kind in decades, the studio was developed to produce not only feature films but television, music, and interactive computer entertainment.

Spielberg's 1985 marriage to actress Amy IRVING ended in divorce in 1989. He later married actress Kate CAPSHAW. His sister, Anne Spielberg, is a screenwriter who shared an Oscar nomination for *Big*.

FILMS: *Duel* (TV movie, released theatrically in 1983; dir.) 1971; *Ace Eli and Rodger of the Skies* (story) 1973; *The Sugarland Express* (dir., co-story) 1974; *Jaws* (dir.) 1975; *Close Encounters of the Third Kind* (dir., story, sc.) 1977; *I Wanna Hold Your Hand* (exec. prod.) 1978; *1941* (dir.) 1979; *The Blues Brothers* (act.), *Used Cars* (co-exec. prod.) 1980; *Raiders of the Lost Ark* (dir.), *Continental Divide* (co-exec. prod.) 1981; *E.T. The Extra-Terrestrial* (dir., co-prod.), *Poltergeist* (co-prod., co-story, co-sc.) 1982; *Twilight Zone—The Movie* (dir. one segment, co-prod.) 1983; *Indiana Jones and the Temple of Doom* (dir.), *Gremlins* (co-exec. prod.) 1984; *The Goonies* (co-exec. prod., story), *Back to the Future* (co-exec. prod.), *Young Sherlock Holmes* (co-exec. prod.), *The Color Purple* (dir., co-prod.) 1985; *The Money Pit* (co-exec. prod.), *An American Tail* (co-exec. prod.) 1986; *Innerspace* (co-exec. prod.), *Batteries Not Included* (co-exec. prod.), *Empire of the Sun* (dir., co-prod.) 1987; *Who Framed Roger Rabbit?* (co-exec. prod.), *The Land Before Time* (co-exec. prod.) 1988; *Indiana Jones and the Last Crusade* (dir.), *Dad* (co-exec. prod.), *Back to the Future Part II* (co-exec. prod.), *Always* (dir., co-prod.) 1989; *Arachnophobia* (co-exec. prod.), *Joe Versus the Volcano* (co-exec. prod.), *Back to the Future Part III* (co-exec. prod.), *Gremlins 2: The New Batch* (co-exec prod.), *Listen Up* (doc.; personal appearance) 1990; *Cape Fear* (co-exec. prod.), *An American Tail: Fievel Goes West* (co-prod.), *Hook* (dir.) 1991; *Jurassic Park* (dir., co-exec. prod.), *Schindler's List* (dir., co-exec. prod.), *We're Back: A Dinosaur's Tale* (co-exec. prod.) 1993; *Casper* (exec. prod.), *Balto* (exec. prod.) 1995; *Twister* (exec. prod.) 1996; *Amistad* (also prod.), *The Lost World* 1997.

Spigelgass, Leonard. Screenwriter, playwright. *b.* Nov. 26, 1908, Brooklyn, N.Y. *d.* 1985. After graduating from NYU, he started his film career as a reader and story editor. From 1933, he wrote many screenplays, alone and in collaboration, specializing in comedy and light fare, like Howard Hawks's *I Was a Male War Bride* (1949). But he also wrote a number of incisive dramas, one of which—*Mystery Street* (1950)—earned him an Academy Award nomination. Several of his plays reached Broadway, notably 'A Majority of One' (1959).

FILMS INCLUDE: *Hello Sister* 1933; *Princess O'Hara* (assoc. prod. only) 1935; *A Letter of Introduction* 1938; *Unexpected Father* 1939; *Boys from Syracuse, One Night in the Tropics* 1940; *Million Dollar Baby* 1941; *All Through the Night, The Big Street* 1942; *They Got Me Covered* 1943; *The Perfect Marriage* 1946; *So Evil My Love* 1948; *I Was a Male War Bride* 1949; *Mystery Street* 1950; *Night Into Morning* 1951; *Because You're Mine* 1952; *Scandal at Scourie* 1953; *Deep in My Heart* 1954; *Silk Stockings* 1957; *Pepe* 1960; *A Majority of One* (from his own play) 1961; *Gypsy* 1962.

Spinotti, Dante. Director of photography. Born in 1943, in Tolmezzo, Italy. A superior craftsman with a bold vision and his own distinctive style, he was behind the camera on many Italian films and international co-productions of the 80s and early 90s, and, with increasing frequency, also Hollywood movies.

FILMS INCLUDE: In Italy—*Il Minestrone* 1980; *La Disubbidienza* 1981; *I Paladini, Sogno di una Notte d'Estate/ Summer Night's Dream* 1983; *Quartetto Basileus/Basileus Quartet, Sotto. . . Sotto* 1984; *Interno Berlinese/The Berlin Affair* 1985. In the US—*Choke Canyon/On Dangerous Ground, Manhunter, Crimes of the Heart* 1986; *From the Hip* 1987; *Illegally Yours, La Leggenda Del Santo Bevitore* (It./Fr.), *Mamba/ Fair Game/Fair Game* (It.), *Beaches* 1988; *Torrents of Spring* (co-phot.; It./Fr.) 1989; *True Colors, Hudson Hawk, Frankie and Johnny* 1991; *Blink, Nell* 1994; *Heat, The Quick and the Dead* 1995; *The Mirror Has Two Faces* 1996; *L.A. Confidential* 1997.

spill light. Undesirable or excessive illumination falling on a subject or on a set.

splice. To join two lengths of film, welding or butting them. In the most common method of splicing, the emulsion is removed from the surface of one end of film by scraping; cement (acetic acid) is then applied to the scraped surface, and the two ends are overlapped and welded together. Less common, but rapidly growing in acceptance, is the dry splice method, by which the two film ends are cut to form a butt joint without overlapping. The splice is made with transparent adhesive tape.

splicer. A mechanical device for splicing film. The three basic types are the hand splicer, operated entirely by hand; the machine splicer, operated by both hands and feet; and the hot splicer, a heavy-duty device utilizing heat for rapid drying of the adhesive cement.

split focus. The focusing of a lens on a point between two widely separated objects, one in the foreground and the other in the background, so that both are within the acceptable depth of field for sharp definition.

split reel. 1. A film spool with a removable side, widely in use in cutting rooms. It allows an editor to mount or remove film without winding or rewinding. 2. In early silent films a single reel containing two short subjects, each running less than five minutes.

split screen. An effect shot in which two or more different images appear on the same frame. The effect is achieved by a matte process and multiple exposures. An image is exposed on a preselected portion of the frame while the rest of the frame is masked. The exposed portion of the frame is then masked and another image is printed on the remainder of the frame. When more than two images are desired, the process is repeated as many times as necessary. Each image is exposed in its proper position in the frame while the rest of the frame is masked.

spotlight. Or "spot." A focused light that projects an intense and narrow beam that can be directed to a specific part of a set. Most studio lights are spotlights.

Spottiswoode, Raymond. Film theoretician and technical expert. *b.* 1913, London. *d.* 1970. After an apprenticeship with John GRIERSON's documentary unit in England, he worked for

MGM in Hollywood in the late 30s. During WW II he produced Canadian war-effort documentaries and was appointed technical supervisor on the National Film Board of Canada. His books on the theory and practice of cinema, *A Grammar of Film* (1935) and *Film and Its Techniques* (1951), are required reading in cinema courses throughout the English-speaking world. He has lectured on film at several American and British universities. In the 50s he was engaged in a thorough research into the potential development of 3-D systems of cinematography and co-authored the book *Theory of Stereoscopic Transmission* (1953).

Spottiswoode, Roger. Director. Born in 1943, in England. He was cutting British documentaries and TV commercials before starting his feature career in the early 70s in Hollywood as a film editor for Sam Peckinpah. A decade later he turned to directing with workmanlike but unspectacular consequences.

FILMS: As editor—*Straw Dogs* (co-edit.) 1971; *The Getaway* (co-edit.) 1972; *Pat Garrett and Billy the Kid* (co-edit.) 1973; *The Gambler* 1974; *Hard Times* 1975. As associate producer—*Who'll Stop the Rain?* 1978. As director—*Terror Train* (Can.) 1980; *The Pursuit of D. B. Cooper* 1981; *48 Hrs.* (co-sc. only) 1982; *Under Fire* 1983; *Baby. . . Secret of the Lost Legend* (exec. prod. only) 1985; *The Best of Times* 1986; *Shoot to Kill* 1988; *Turner & Hooch* 1989; *Air America* 1990; *Stop! Or My Mom Will Shoot* 1992; *Mesmer* 1994.

Springsteen, R. G. (Bud). Director. Born on Sept. 8, 1904, in Tacoma, Wash. *ed.* U. of Washington. In films as assistant director since 1930, he began directing Wild Bill Elliott and Allan Lane Westerns for Republic in 1945. He later branched out into films of other genres, mostly unambitious low-budget productions with the notable exception of *Come Next Spring* (1956), a fine rural drama.

FILMS INCLUDE: *Marshal of Laredo, Wagon Wheels Westward* 1945; *California Gold Rush, Home on the Range, Conquest of Cheyenne, Santa Fe Uprising, Stagecoach to Denver* 1946; *Marshal of Cripple Creek, Along the Oregon Trail, Under Colorado Skies* 1947; *The Main Street Kid, Heart of Virginia, Secret Service Investigator, Out of the Storm* 1948; *Death Valley Gunfighters, Hellfire, The Red Menace, Flame of Youth* 1949; *Singing Guns, Harbor of Missing Men, The Arizona Cowboy, Hills of Oklahoma* 1950; *Million Dollar Pursuit, Honeychile, Street Bandits* 1951; *The Fabulous Señorita, Oklahoma Annie, Gobs and Gals, Tropical Heat Wave* 1952; *A Perilous Journey* 1953; *Geraldine* 1954; *I Cover the Underworld, Double Jeopardy, Track That Man Down* (UK) 1955; *Come Next Spring, When Gangland Strikes* 1956; *Affair in Reno* 1957; *Cole Younger—Gunfighter, Revolt in the Big House* 1958; *Battle Flame, King of the Wild Stallions* 1959; *Operation Eichmann* 1961; *Showdown* 1963; *He Rides Tall, Bullet for a Badman, Taggart* 1964; *Black Spurs* 1965; *Apache Uprising, Johnny Reno, Waco* 1966; *Red Tomahawk, Hostile Guns* 1967; *Tiger by the Tail* 1970.

sprocket holes. Perforations along either or both edges of a film which are spaced so that they can be accurately engaged and held in precise alignment by the SPROCKETS of the transport mechanisms of cameras, projectors, and other motion picture equipment.

sprockets. Toothed wheels inside a camera, projector, or other mechanisms which drive the film by engaging its perforations, or SPROCKET HOLES.

squeeze lens. See ANAMORPHIC LENS.

squib. In films, an electrical firing device used for the simulation of bullet hits. When it is activated, preselected targets appear to have been hit by a bullet although no gun has really been fired.

Stack, Robert. Actor. Born on Jan. 13, 1919, in Los Angeles. *ed.* USC. Tall, ruggedly handsome leading man of Hollywood films. His film career was launched when he was 20 with a splash of publicity as "the first boy to kiss Deanna Durbin" in *First Love* (1939). He subsequently played routine youthful romantic leads and resumed his career in similar roles after returning from WW II service with the Navy. His first challenging part was the lead in Budd Boetticher's *The Bullfighter and the Lady* (1951). In 1954 he gave a solid performance in *The High and the Mighty* and in 1957 he was nominated for an Oscar as best supporting player for *Written on the Wind.* But it was his role as Eliot Ness in the long-running TV series 'The Untouchables' (1959–63; Emmy Award in 1960) with which he became most closely identified by American audiences. He later starred in the series 'The Name of the Game' (1968–71), 'Most Wanted' (1976–77), 'Strike Force' (1981–82), and 'Unsolved Mysteries' (ongoing, since 1991). Autobiography: *Straight Shooting* (1980).

FILMS INCLUDE: *First Love* 1939; *The Mortal Storm, A Little Bit of Heaven* 1940; *Nice Girl?, Badlands of Dakota* 1941; *To Be or Not to Be, Men of Texas, Eagle Squadron* 1942; *A Date with Judy, Fighter Squadron, Miss Tatlock's Millions* 1948; *Mr. Music* 1950; *The Bullfighter and the Lady* 1951; *Bwana Devil, War Paint, Sabre Jet* 1953; *The High and the Mighty, The Iron Glove* 1954; *House of Bamboo, Good Morning Miss Dove* 1955; *Great Day in the Morning* 1956; *Written on the Wind* 1957; *The Tarnished Angels, The Gift of Love* 1958; *John Paul Jones* (title role) 1959; *The Last Voyage* 1960; *The Scarface Mob* (re-edited feature version of TV episodes) 1962; *The Caretakers* 1963; *Paris brûle-t-il?/Is Paris Burning?, Il Sigillo de Pechino/Die Holle von Macao/Les Corrumpus/The Corrupt Ones* (It./Ger./Fr.) 1966; *Le Soleil des Voyous/Il più grande Colpo del Secolo/Action Man* (Fr./It.) 1967; *Storia di una Donna/Story of a Woman* (It./US) 1969; *Un Second Souffle/A Second Wind* (Fr.) 1978; *1941* 1979; *Airplane!* 1980; *Uncommon Valour* 1983; *Big Trouble, The Transformers* (v/o) 1986; *Plain Clothes, Caddyshack II* 1988; *Joe Versus the Volcano* 1990.

stage. The area of a studio in which sets are constructed and filming takes place. A stage equipped for sound recording (as most are today) is called a SOUND STAGE. A large studio contains a number of stages.

stagehand. A general term for a studio employee who helps prepare a set for filming by moving scenery and props and performing other manual tasks.

Stahl, John M. Director, producer. *b.* Jan. 21, 1886, New York City. *d.* 1950. A former stage actor, he entered films in 1913 as a bit player and turned director the following year. There is no reliable record of his early work (1914–17), and many of his silent films are not available for evaluation. But his list of sound films shows a remarkable consistency of style, marked by a vivid visual sense and a capacity for treating mundane melodramatic material with intelligence and sensitivity. Between 1927 and 1929, Stahl produced numerous films in partnership with the Tiffany company, a studio specializing in low-budget fare. Joining Universal in 1930, Stahl soon emerged as the highly skilled director of a popular string of stylish, tearful "women's pictures": *Back Street* (1932), *Only Yesterday* (1933), *Imitation of Life* (1934), and *Magnificent Obsession* (1935). Moving over to Fox in 1943, he was responsible for such lavish productions as *The Keys of the Kingdom* (1944), *Leave Her to Heaven* (1945), and *The Foxes of Harrow* (1947).

FEATURE FILMS: *The Lincoln Cycle* (series of seven two-reelers distributed sequentially) 1917; *Wives of Men* (also story, sc.), *Suspicion* 1918; *Her Code of Honor, The Woman Under Oath* 1919; *Greater Than Love, Women Men Forget, The Woman in His House* 1920; *The Child Thou Gavest Me* (also prod.), *Sowing the Wind, Suspicious Wives* 1921; *The Song of Life, One Clear Call* 1922; *The Dangerous Age, The Wanters* 1923; *Why Men Leave Home, Husbands and Lovers* (also co-story) 1924; *Fine Clothes* 1925; *Memory Lane* (also prod., co-story, co-sc.), *The Gay Deceiver* 1926; *Lovers?* (also prod.), *In Old Kentucky* (also prod.) 1927; *A Lady Surrenders* 1930; *Seed, Strictly Dishonorable* 1931; *Back Street* 1932; *Only Yesterday* 1933; *Imitation of Life* 1934; *Magnificent Obsession* 1935; *Parnell* (also prod.) 1937; *Letter of Introduction* (also prod.) 1938; *When Tomorrow Comes* (also prod.) 1939; *Our Wife* 1941; *Immortal Sergeant, Holy Matrimony* 1943; *The Eve of St. Mark, The Keys of the Kingdom* 1944; *Leave Her to Heaven* 1945; *The Foxes of Harrow* 1947; *The Walls of Jericho* 1948; *Father Was a Fullback, Oh You Beautiful Doll* 1949.

Stallings, Laurence. Playwright, screenwriter, novelist. *b.* 1894, Macon, Ga. *d.* 1968. *ed.* Wake Forest (B.A.), Georgetown (M.S.). A former reporter and literary editor for the New York *World,* he lost a leg during his WW I service as a captain in the Marines. His war experience provided the background for his most famous play, 'What Price Glory' which he co-authored with Maxwell Anderson, and for some of his other plays, novels, and screenplays. He also wrote scripts for several quality Westerns.

FILMS INCLUDE: *The Big Parade* (story only) 1925; *What Price Glory* (play basis only), *Old Ironsides* (story only) 1926; *Show People* (co-treatment) 1928; *The Cock-Eyed World* (play basis only) 1929; *Billy the Kid* (dial.), *Way for a Sailor* 1930; *So Red the Rose* 1935; *Too Hot to Handle* 1938; *Northwest Passage* 1940; *Jungle Book* 1942; *Salome—Where She Danced* 1945; *Christmas Eve* 1947; *A Miracle Can Happen* 1948; *Three Godfathers, She Wore a Yellow Ribbon* 1949; *What Price Glory* (remake; play basis only) 1952; *The Sun Shines Bright* 1954.

Stallone, Sylvester. Actor, director, screenwriter. Born Michael Sylvester Stallone, on July 6, 1946, in New York City. A product of a poor, broken home, he grew up in New York's rough Hell's Kitchen section, then in Silver Spring, Maryland, and a sleazy section of Philadelphia, spending several years at the homes of foster parents. He was booted out of 14 schools in 11 years but thanks to his muscular physique was able to attend the American College in Switzerland on an athletic scholarship. He also briefly attended the drama department at the University of Miami, where instructors discouraged him from entertaining any ideas of a future acting career. He tried his hand at a variety of jobs, including zoo attendant and pizza chef, and in 1970 worked as an usher at New York's Baronet movie theater. Still determined to become an actor, he appeared in the nude off-Broadway drama 'Score' and the porno movie *Party at Kitty and Studs/The Italian Stallion* (both 1970), and was able to land small parts in occasional films. In 1974 he played one of the leads in the low-budget New York–made film *The Lords of Flatbush* and in the following year played supporting roles in such Hollywood films as *Farewell My Lovely, Capone,* and *Death Race 2000.* Still, he considered his career at a dead end. Nearly broke and his wife pregnant, he determined to create his own opportunity to become a star by writing his own screenplay. In three days he completed the first draft for *Rocky,* a story of a down-and-out boxer who triumphs against heavy odds. He sold the script to producers Irwin Winkler and Robert Chartoff for a relatively small sum of money but for a large share of the profits on the condition that he be assigned the starring role in the film. The film turned out to be the "sleeper" of 1976, winning the best picture Academy Award as well as the best director (John Avildsen) and best editing Oscars. Stallone, who was nominated for both best actor and best screenplay awards, won neither, but he became established overnight as a leading screen personality and stood to gain a great deal of money as his share of the profits of *Rocky,* which quickly became a solid box-office hit. Sly, as Stallone is known to his friends, went on to become one of Hollywood's most successful star-entrepreneurs, taking personal control of his movie vehicles, frequently writing or collaborating on their scripts, and occasionally directing them. He scored powerfully at the box office with four sequels to *Rocky* and with a reactionary three-movie saga depicting the incredible physical feats of a Vietnam vet named John Rambo, starting with *First Blood* (1982). Although many critics say he still can't act, and stand-up comics keep imitating his macho bluster and slurred speech, Stallone has persevered as a popular superstar. Other than the Rocky and Rambo series, however, his films sometimes fared only modestly at the box office. In the early 90s he attempted comedy films, with little success. His 1993 return (with *Cliffhanger* and *Demolition Man*) to the action genre he helped define put him back on a winning streak. Offscreen, he has displayed a gentle side, collecting art, painting in a surrealist style and giving freely of his time to charitable causes. He divorced his first wife, a fellow usher at the Baronet, in 1985, after an 11-year union and two sons. That same year he married Danish-born actress-model Brigitte Nielsen. That marriage ended in 1988. He has since married again.

FILMS (as actor): *Party at Kitty and Studs/The Italian Stallion* (porno movie) 1970; *Bananas* (unbilled bit) 1971; *Klute* (unbilled bit) 1972; *The Lords of Flatbush* 1974; *No Place to Hide, The Prisoner of Second Avenue* (bit), *Capone* (as Frank Nitti), *Death Race 2000, Farewell My Lovely* 1975; *Cannonball* (cameo), *Rocky* (also sc.) 1976; *F.I.S.T.* (also co-sc.), *Paradise Alley* (also dir., sc., lyr.) 1978; *Rocky II* (also dir., sc.) 1979; *Nighthawks, Victory/Escape to Victory* 1981; *Rocky III* (also dir., sc.), *First Blood* (Can.) 1982; *Staying Alive* (dir., co-prod., co-sc. only) 1983; *Rhinestone* (also co-sc., lyr.) 1984; *Rambo: First Blood Part II* (also co-sc.), *Rocky IV* (also dir., sc.) 1985; *Cobra* (also sc.) 1986; *Over the Top* (also co-sc.) 1987; *Rambo III* (also co-sc.) 1988; *Lock Up, Tango & Cash* 1989; *Rocky V* (also sc.) 1990; *Oscar* 1991; *Stop! or My Mom Will Shoot* 1992; *Cliffhanger, Demolition Man* 1993; *The Specialist* 1994; *Assassins, Judge Dredd* 1995; *Daylight* 1996; *Cop Land* 1997.

Stamp, Terence. Actor. Born on July 22, 1939, in London. Brooding, handsome leading man, and later supporting player, of British and international films. A cockney tug-master's son, he performed briefly on the stage before making an auspicious, Oscar-nominated screen debut playing the title role in *Billy Budd* (1962). Three years later he was named best actor at Cannes for his chilling portrayal of a psychotic in *The Collector.* But at the height of his success, bored by fame and broken-hearted over an aborted love affair with model Jean Shrimpton, he went in 1969 into a five-year exile in India, in quest of peace and happiness, occasionally commuting to continental Europe for appearances in films. In the late 70s he resumed a fuller screen career in character roles, at times menacing, memorably as the gaunt, evil General Zod in *Superman II* (1981). He made his debut as a director with *Stranger in the House* (1991). Autobiography: *Coming Attractions* (1988).

FILMS: *Billy Budd* (title role), *Term of Trial* 1962; *The Collector* (US/UK) 1965; *Modesty Blaise* 1966; *Far from the Madding Crowd, Poor Cow* 1967; *Blue* (US), *Histoires extraordinaires/Spirits of the Dead* (Fellini episode; Fr./It.), *Teorema* (It.) 1968; *The Mind of Mr. Soames* 1970; *Una Stagione all' Inferno* (It.) 1971; *Hu-Man* (Fr.) 1975; *Strip-Tease* (It.), *La Divina Creatura/The Divine Nymph* (It.) 1976; *The Thief of Bagdad* (TV movie; theatrical in Europe), *Superman* 1978; *Meetings with Remarkable Men, Amo non amo/I Love You I*

Love You Not (It.) 1979; *Mistero en la Isla de los Monstruos/Monster Island* (Sp./US), *Superman II* (US/UK) 1980; *Morte in Váticano/Death in the Vatican* (It.) 1981; *The Hit, The Company of Wolves* 1984; *Link, Legal Eagles* (US), *Directed by William Wyler* (doc.; US), *Hud/Skin* 1986; *The Sicilian* (US), *Wall Street* (US) 1987; *Young Guns* (US), *Alien Nation* (US) 1988; *Genuine Risk* 1990; *Stranger in the House* (also dir.) 1991; *Beltenebros* (Sp.) 1992; *The Real McCoy* 1993; *The Adventures of Priscilla, Queen of the Desert* 1994; *Limited Edition* 1996; *Bliss, Dream with Fishes, Wings of a Dove* 1997.

standard leader. See ACADEMY LEADER.

standard stock. Thirty-five millimeter motion picture film. Films of narrower gauge (16 mm, 8 mm, etc.) are known as "substandard."

Stander, Lionel. Actor. *b.* Jan. 11, 1908, in New York City. *d.* 1994. *ed.* U. of North Carolina. On the stage from age 19, he began appearing in film shorts in 1932 and in features in 1935. A gravel-voiced comedian, he specialized in eccentric, semi-heavy character roles and was an established Hollywood supporting player when his career was suddenly interrupted by blacklisting in the early 50s, as a result of his uncooperative testimony before the House Un-American Activities Committee. He worked for a while in summer stock, then as a Wall Street broker, and did not return to the screen until the late 60s. He lived for a long period in Rome, where he enjoyed great popularity as a co-star of several spaghetti Westerns and a variety of Continental co-productions. In 1979–84 he appeared as an eccentric chauffeur in the TV adventure series 'Hart to Hart.'

FILMS INCLUDE: *The Scoundrel, Page Miss Glory* 1935; *Soak the Rich, The Milky Way, Mr. Deeds Goes to Town, Meet Nero Wolfe* 1936; *A Star is Born, The League of Frightened Men, The Last Gangster* 1937; *Professor Beware, The Crowd Roars* 1938; *What a Life* 1939; *The Bride Wore Crutches* 1941; *Hangmen Also Die, Guadalcanal Diary* 1943; *The Kid from Brooklyn, Specter of the Rose* 1946; *Mad Wednesday* 1947; *Call Northside* 777, *Unfaithfully Yours* 1948; *St. Benny the Dip* 1951; *The Loved One* 1965; *Cul-de-Sac* (UK), *Promise Her Anything* 1966; *A Dandy in Aspic* (UK), *C'era Ona Volta il West/Once Upon a Time in the West* (It.) 1968; *Per Grazia Ricevuta/The Cross-Eyed Saint* (It.), *The Gang That Couldn't Shoot Straight* 1971; *Treasure Island* (UK/Ger.), *Pulp* (UK), *Don Camillo e i Giovanni d'Oggi* (It./Fr.), *Tedeum* (It./Sp.) 1972; *Mordi e Fuggi* (It.), *Paolo el Caldo/The Sensuous Sicilian/The Sensual Man* (It.) 1973; *The Black Bird, Ah si?. . . e io lo dico a Zorro* (It.) 1975; *The Cassandra Crossing, New York New York* 1977; *Matilda* 1978; *1941* 1979; *The Rip-Off/The Squeeze* (It.) 1980; *The Transformers* (v/o) 1986; *Wicked Stepmother, Cookie* (bit) 1989; *Joey Takes a Cab* 1990.

stand-in. A substitute for a motion picture star during the tedious process of preparing scenes, setting up the camera, taking light-meter readings, adjusting lights, etc. The men or women in question are chosen for their physical resemblance to a particular star, in size, coloring, and facial features. The stand-in may occasionally be used to substitute for the star in long shots or crowd scenes that require no acting. When a stand-in is used as a substitute for the star in potentially hazardous situations or in stunts requiring specialized physical agility, he or she is better known as a DOUBLE. See also STUNTMAN.

Standing, Sir Guy. Actor. *b.* Sept. 1, 1873, London. *d.* 1937. A prominent performer of the British and American stage, he played some key character parts in Hollywood films of the 30s. He was the father of actress Kay HAMMOND. His brother, Herbert Standing (1884–1955), appeared in many Hollywood silents.

FILMS INCLUDE: *The Story of Temple Drake, The Eagle and the Hawk, Cradle Song* 1933; *Death Takes a Holiday, The Witching Hour, Now and Forever* 1934; *The Lives of a Bengal Lancer* 1935; *I'd Give My Life, Lloyds of London* 1936; *Bulldog Drummond Escapes* 1937.

Stang, Arnold. Actor. Born on Sept. 28, 1925, in Chelsea, Mass. Bespectacled, impish comedian on radio from age ten. Later also on the stage, on TV, and in films. Memorable as the pathetic derelict Sparrow in *The Man with the Golden Arm* (1955). His extensive TV credits include regular appearances as a stagehand on 'The Milton Berle Show' (1953–55).

FILMS INCLUDE: *Seven Days' Leave* 1942; *So This Is New York* 1948; *The Man with the Golden Arm* 1955; *Dondi* 1961; *The Wonderful World of the Brothers Grimm* 1962; *It's a Mad Mad Mad Mad World* 1963; *Second Fiddle to a Steel Guitar* 1965; *Skidoo* 1968; *Hello Down There!* 1969; *Raggedy Ann and Andy* (v/o) 1977.

Stanley, Kim. Actress. Born Patricia Kimberly Reid, Feb. 11, 1925, Tularosa, N.M. *ed.* U. of New Mexico; Texas State. She began acting in college and in stock. Arriving in New York, she worked as a model while training at the Actors Studio under Kazan and Strasberg. An intense Method actress, she won praise and awards for her performances on Broadway and the London stage. She has appeared in only three films, but her screen performances were remarkable and memorable. She was nominated for an Oscar as best actress for *Seance on a Wet Afternoon* (1964) but shortly after suffered a breakdown and temporarily retired from the screen. She later taught drama at the College of Santa Fe, N.M. She made a memorable movie comeback in *Frances* (1982), gaining her second Oscar nomination for the supporting role of the heroine's crazed mother.

FILMS: *The Goddess* 1958; *Seance on a Wet Afternoon* 1964; *The Three Sisters* 1977; *Frances* 1982; *The Right Stuff* 1983.

Stanley, Richard. See MORGAN, Dennis.

Stanton, Harry Dean. Actor. Born on July 14, 1926, in West Irvine. Ky. *ed.* U. of Kentucky. Lean, gaunt, dour-faced character player of the American screen. Following WW II service with the Navy, he trained at the Pasadena Playhouse and for many years performed modestly on the stage before entering films in the late 50s. Before long he emerged as one of Hollywood's most convincing character players, a versatile performer with a broad repertoire of roles, from psychos and villains to sympathetic, even good-humored leading men. During much of the 60s he was billed Dean Stanton.

FILMS INCLUDE: *The Wrong Man, Tomahawk Trail* 1957; *The Proud Rebel* 1958; *Pork Chop Hill* 1959; *The Adventures of Huckleberry Finn* 1960; *How the West was Won* 1962; *The Man from the Diner's Club* 1963; *The Hostage* 1966; *Cool Hand Luke* 1967; *Kelly's Heroes* 1970; *Cisco Pike* 1971; *Pat Garrett and Billy the Kid, Dillinger* 1973; *Born to Kill/Wild Drifter/Gamblin Man/Cockfighter, Zandy's Bride/For Better for Worse, The Godfather Part II* 1974; *Rancho Deluxe, 92 in the Shade, Farewell My Lovely* 1975; *The Missouri Breaks* 1976; *Straight Time* 1978; *Wise Blood, Alien, The Rose* 1979; *La Mort en Direct/Death Watch* (Fr./Ger.), *The Black Marble, Private Benjamin* 1980; *Escape from New York* 1981; *One from the Heart, Young Doctors in Love* 1982; *Christine* 1983; *Repo Man, Red Dawn, The Bear, Paris Texas* (Ger./Fr.) 1984; *Uforia, One Magic Christmas, Fool for Love* 1985; *Pretty in Pink* 1986; *Slamdance* 1987; *Stars and Bars, Mr. North, The Last Temptation of Christ* 1988; *Dream a Little Dream, Twister* 1989; *The Fourth War, Wild at Heart* 1990; *Payoff* 1991; *Man Trouble, Twin Peaks: Fire Walk with Me* 1992; *Never Talk to Strangers* 1995; *Down Periscope* 1996; *Fire Down Below, She's So Lovely* 1997.

Stanwyck, Barbara. Actress. *b.* Ruby Stevens, July 16, 1907, Brooklyn, N.Y., of Irish-Scottish ancestry. *d.* 1990, of congestive heart failure. Orphaned at age four, she was raised by an older sister and boarded with various friends of the family. She quit school at 13 to work as a parcel wrapper in a Brooklyn department store and at other unskilled, low-paying jobs. All the while, she trained herself as a dancer and at 15 began her show business career as a chorus girl, appearing with the Ziegfeld Follies and other stage revues. She gradually worked her way up to the lead part in a straight play, 'The Noose,' which ran for nine months on Broadway in 1926. The following year she made her screen debut, playing a minor role in a silent film shot in New York. She then returned to Broadway and in 1928 married vaudeville headliner Frank Fay. She followed Fay to Hollywood when he was signed to a Warners contract and was herself signed to nonexclusive contracts by both Columbia and Warners.

From the start, Stanwyck impressed her employers and the public with her thorough professionalism. She was neither a great actress nor did she ever give a bad performance. She was simply a disciplined, hard-working actress who responded to every challenge with total commitment. Barbara's early career was guided for the most part by Frank CAPRA and William WELLMAN. By the late 30s she was firmly entrenched as a dependable leading lady and in the early 40s she reached a career peak with winning performances in such films as *The Lady Eve, Meet John Doe, Ball of Fire,* and *Double Indemnity.* In 1944 she was announced by the Internal Revenue Service to be the highest paid woman in the United States, slightly ahead of Bette Davis.

Barbara Stanwyck proved herself equally at ease with comedy and drama, in a broad range of roles, but became most closely identified with her characterizations as an aggressive, take-charge, hard-as-nails dame. Her film career faltered in the 50s, when she was cast in many second-rate vehicles and ended by the mid-60s. But she did well on TV as the star of 'The Barbara Stanwyck Show' (1960–61; Emmy Award 1961), 'The Big Valley' (1965–69; Emmy 1966), the miniseries 'The Thorn Birds' (Emmy Award 1983), and 'The Colbys,' as well as in many guest appearances. Divorced from Frank Fay in 1935, she married Robert TAYLOR in 1939. They divorced in 1951. She was nominated for an Oscar four times (for *Stella Dallas, Ball of Fire, Double Indemnity,* and *Sorry, Wrong Number)* but never won; however, she was awarded an honorary Academy Award for lifetime achievement in 1981.

FILMS: *Broadway Nights* 1927; *The Locked Door, Mexicali Rose* 1929; *Ladies of Leisure* 1930; *Illicit, Ten Cents a Dance, Night Nurse, The Miracle Woman* 1931; *Forbidden, Shopworn, So Big, The Purchase Price* 1932; *The Bitter Tea of General Yen, Ladies They Talk About, Baby Face, Ever in My Heart* 1933; *Gambling Lady, A Lost Lady* 1934; *The Secret Bride, The Woman in Red, Red Salute, Annie Oakley* (title role) 1935; *A Message to Garcia, The Bride Walks Out, His Brother's Wife, Banjo on My Knee* 1936; *The Plough and the Stars* (as Nora), *Interns Can't Take Money, This Is My Affair, Stella Dallas* (title role), *Breakfast for Two* 1937; *Always Goodbye, The Mad Miss Manton* 1938: *Union Pacific, Golden Boy* (as Lorna Moon) 1939; *Remember the Night* 1940; *The Lady Eve, Meet John Doe, You Belong to Me* 1941; *Ball of Fire, The Great Man's Lady, The Gay Sisters* 1942; *Lady of Burlesque, Flesh and Fantasy* 1943; *Double Indemnity, Hollywood Canteen* 1944; *Christmas in Connecticut* 1945; *My Reputation, The Bride Wore Boots, The Strange Love of Martha Ivers* 1946; *California, The Two Mrs. Carrolls, The Other Love, Cry Wolf* 1947; *B.F.'s Daughter, Sorry Wrong Number* 1948; *The Lady Gambles, East Side West Side* 1949; *Thelma Jordan, No Man of Her Own, The Furies, To Please a Lady* 1950; *The Man with a Cloak* 1951; *Clash by Night* 1952; *Jeopardy, Titanic, All I Desire, The Moonlighter, Blowing Wild* 1953; *Witness to Murder, Executive Suite, Cattle Queen of Montana* 1954; *The Violent Men, Escape to Burma* 1955; *There's Always Tomorrow, The Maverick Queen, These Wilder Years* 1956; *Crime of Passion, Trooper Hook, Forty Guns* 1957; *Walk on the Wild Side* 1962; *Roustabout* 1964; *The Night Walker* 1965.

Stapleton, Maureen. Actress. Born on June 21, 1925, in Troy, N.Y. She arrived in Manhattan directly out of high school in 1943 and worked in a variety of odd jobs (waitress, model for Raphael Sawyer and Reginald Marsh) while training for the stage evenings at the Herbert Berghof Acting School. She made her Broadway debut in 1946 and scored a personal triumph in 1951 in 'The Rose Tattoo.' She then starred in several other Tennessee Williams plays as well as in many other Broadway productions. An excellent performer, capable of projecting vitality and fatigue, vulnerability and strength at the same time, she was nominated for a supporting Oscar for her very first film performance, in *Lonelyhearts,* and again for *Interiors* (1978). She won an Academy Award for her portrayal of Emma Goldman in *Reds* (1981). Her numerous TV appearances included an Emmy-winning performance in the drama 'Among the Paths to Eden' (1968). But she remained primarily a stage actress. Because of her earthiness, and the frowzy, disheveled characters she often played at the height of her career, she has been called "the American Anna Magnani." Her second husband was playwright David Rayfiel.

FILMS: *Lonelyhearts* 1959; *The Fugitive Kind* 1960; *Vu du Pont/A View from the Bridge* (Fr./It.) 1962; *Bye Bye Birdie* 1963; *Trilogy* 1969; *Airport* 1970; *Plaza Suite* 1971; *Interiors* 1978; *The Runner Stumbles, Lost and Found* 1979; *The Fan, On the Right Track, Reds* (as Emma Goldman) 1981; *Johnny Dangerously* 1984; *Cocoon, The Cosmic Eye* (v/o) 1985; *The Money Pit, Heartburn* 1986; *Hello Actors Studio* (doc.), *Sweet Lorraine, Made in Heaven, Nuts* 1987; *Doin' Time on Planet Earth, Cocoon: The Return* 1988; *Passed Away* 1992; *Trading Mom* 1994.

star. 1. An actor or actress who has wide recognition and appeal and is cast regularly in lead roles in major productions. See also STAR SYSTEM. 2. The lead actor or actress in a film.

Starewicz, Wladyslaw. Director, animator. *b.* Aug. 6, 1892, Vilna, Poland (later, Russia). *d.* 1965. A former bookkeeper and art student, he entered films in Moscow in 1912, and with no previous experience soon distinguished himself as a brilliant film technician and an inventive animator. He directed live-action films as well as animated cartoons but did his most original work in stop-motion puppet animation. Shortly after the Revolution, he emigrated to France, where he continued his work, winning several international awards for his animated films (in France, the spelling of his name was simplified to Ladislas Starevitch). He usually wrote his own scripts and was his own cameraman and art director. His most ambitious and best-known work was *Le Roman de Renard/The Tale of the Fox,* a feature-length puppet-animation film that he made over a period of years, starting in 1928. A German-language version was released in 1937. A full-blown version with a music score and the dubbed voices of famous French stars opened in Paris in the spring of 1941.

FILMS INCLUDE: In Russia—*The Beautiful Leukanida, Happy Scenes from Animal Life, The Cameraman's Revenge, The Grasshopper and the Ant* 1912; *The Four Devils, Christmas Eve, A Terrible Revenge* 1913; *Ruslan and Ludmila* 1915; *On the Warsaw Highway* 1916. In France—*L'Epouvantail* 1921; *La*

Voix du Rossignol 1923; *Le Rat de Ville et le Rat des Champs* 1927; *Amour noir et Amour blanc* 1928; *Le Roman de Renard/The Tale of the Fox* (feature) 1928–41; *Zanzabelle à Paris* 1949; *Fleur de Fougère* 1950.

Stark, Ray. American producer. Born ca. 1910. *ed.* Rutgers. A former newsman and publicity writer, he started his business career after WW II as a representative of radio writers, then flourished as a literary agent, representing such authors as Hecht, Costain, and Marquand. He later joined Famous Artists as a talent agent and represented such stars as Marilyn Monroe, Richard Burton, and Kirk Douglas. In 1957 he formed with production executive Eliot Hyman (*b.* Aug. 28, 1904, New York) the Seven Arts Productions company, which became a major factor in films-for-TV production, packaging, and sales. He resigned his post as executive vice president in charge of production in 1966 to pursue independent projects. As a longtime son-in-law of the legendary Fanny Brice (his wife, Frances, died in 1992), he struck it big as the producer of her screen biography, *Funny Girl* (1968), starring Barbra Streisand, and went to score several other box-office bonanzas. He was honored with the Irving Thalberg Award during the 1980 Academy Award ceremony. As head of Rastar Productions and Ray Stark Productions, he remained a powerful presence in Hollywood through the late 80s.

FILMS INCLUDE: *The World of Suzie Wong* 1960; *The Night of the Iguana* 1964; *Oh Dad Poor Dad. . .* (co-prod.), *Reflections in a Golden Eye* 1967; *Funny Girl* 1968; *The Owl and the Pussycat* 1970; *Fat City* 1972; *The Way We Were* 1973; *Funny Lady, The Sunshine Boys* 1975; *Murder by Death* 1976; *The Goodbye Girl* 1977; *Casey's Shadow, The Cheap Detective, California Suite* 1978; *Chapter Two, The Electric Horseman* 1979; *Seems Like Old Times* 1980; *Annie* 1982; *The Slugger's Wife* 1985; *Brighton Beach Memoirs, Nothing in Common, Peggy Sue Got Married* 1986; *Biloxi Blues* 1988; *Steel Magnolias* 1989; *Lost in Yonkers* 1993.

Starke, Pauline. Actress. *b.* Jan. 10, 1900, Joplin, Mo. *d.* 1977. She entered films with no previous acting experience in 1916, making her debut as a dancing extra in D. W. Griffith's *Intolerance.* Late in 1917, after a period as a bit and supporting player, she began playing leads in films of Frank Borzage, then of Maurice Tourneur. In the 20s she starred in several major silent productions, as well as in many routine pictures. She retired from the screen shortly after the advent of sound.

FILMS INCLUDE: *Intolerance, The Rummy* 1916; *Until They Get Me* 1917; *The Shoes That Danced, Innocents Progress, Alias Mary Brown, Daughter Angele, The Atom* 1918; *Whom the Gods Would Destroy, The Life Line, The Broken Butterfly, Eyes of Youth, Soldiers of Fortune* 1919; *A Connecticut Yankee at King Arthur's Court, The Little Shepherd of Kingdom Come, Dangerous Days, The Untamed* 1920; *Salvation Nell, Wife Against Wife, Flower of the North* 1921; *My Wild Irish Rose, The Kingdom Within* 1922; *Lost and Found/Lost and Found on a South Sea Island, The Little Girl Next Door, His Last Race, In the Palace of the King, Eyes of the Forest* 1923; *Dante's Inferno, Hearts of Oak, Forbidden Paradise* 1924; *The Man Without a Country/As No Man Has Loved, The Devil's Cargo, Adventure* 1925; *War Paint, Love's Blindness* 1926; *Women Love Diamonds, Captain Salvation, Dance Magic* 1927; *Streets of Shanghai, Man Woman and Wife, The Viking* 1928; *A Royal Romance, What Men Want* 1930; *$20 a Week* 1935; *She Knew All the Answers* 1941.

starlet. A young actress promoted and publicized as a future star. Starlets abounded in Hollywood in the heyday of the studio system. Pretty girls by the hundreds were signed on low-paying, long-term contracts and given training, publicity, and minor roles in major films, in the hope that they would develop into bona fide stars. Only a few ever made it.

Starr, Ringo. See BEATLES, The.

Starrett, Charles. Actor. *b.* Mar. 28, 1903, Athol, Mass. *d.* 1986. A football star at Dartmouth, he was bitten by the acting bug when, along with fellow athletes at the college, he was selected to appear as an extra in a 1926 Richard Dix film, *The Quarterback,* part of the action of which was shot on campus. After graduation, he gained acting experience in stock and in a couple of supporting parts on Broadway before beginning his film career in 1930 with Paramount. He played youthful romantic leads until 1936, when he became a cowboy star at Columbia. Handsome and athletic, he appeared in numerous low-budget Westerns through the early 50s with undiminishing popularity, often as a character known as the Durango Kid. His frequent sidekick was Smiley BURNETTE.

FILMS INCLUDE: *Fast and Loose* 1930; *The Royal Family of Broadway, Damaged Love, The Viking, Silence, The Age for Love, Touchdown* 1931; *Sky Bride, Lady and Gent, The Mask of Fu Manchu* 1932; *Our Betters, Jungle Bride, The Sweetheart of Sigma Chi, Mr. Skitch* 1933; *This Man Is Mine, Call It Luck, Desirable, Gentlemen Are Born, The Silver Streak* 1934; *Sons of Steel, A Shot in the Dark, Make a Million, So Red the Rose* 1935; *Mysterious Avenger, Secret Patrol, Stampede, Along Came Love* 1936; *Two Gun Law* 1937; *Outlaws of the Prairie, Start Cheering, Law of the Plains, South of Arizona, The Colorado Trail* 1938; *Spoilers of the Range, Western Caravans, The Man from Sundown, The Stranger from Texas* 1939; *Blazing Six Shooters, The Durango Kid* 1940; *The Pinto Kid, Thunder Over the Prairie* 1941; *West of Tombstone, Pardon My Gun* 1942; *Fighting Buckaroo, Robin Hood of the Range, Cowboy in the Clouds* 1943; *Sundown Valley* 1944; *Sagebrush Heroes, Return of the Durango Kid, Lawless Empire* 1945; *Gunning for Vengeance, Desert Horsemen, Terror Trail* 1946; *Riders of the Lone Star* 1947; *Phantom Valley, Last Days of Boot Hill* 1948; *The Blazing Trail* 1949; *Texas Dynamo* 1950; *The Kid from Amarillo* 1951; *Rough Tough West* 1952.

Starrett, Jack. Director. *b.* Nov. 2, 1936, Refugio, Tex. *d.* 1989. He entered films in the mid-60s as an actor and jack-of-all-trades in low-budget motorcycle sagas and began directing films in that same genre in 1969. He broadened his range in the 70s, but the main ingredients of his films remained rough action and violence. He appeared as an actor in several of his own productions. His acting credits in films of other directors included *Like Father Like Son* (1961), *The Young Sinner* (1965), *Hell's Angels on Wheels* (1967), *The Gay Deceivers* (1969), *The Rose* (1979), *First Blood* (1982), and *The River* (1984). He died at 52 of kidney failure.

FILMS (as director): *Run Angel Run!* 1969; *The Losers* (also act.), *Cry Blood Apache* (also act.) 1970; *The Strange Vengeance of Rosalie, Slaughter* 1972; *Cleopatra Jones* 1973; *Gravy Train/The Dion Brothers* (also act.) 1974; *Race with the Devil* (also act.) 1975; *A Small Town in Texas* 1976; *Final Chapter—Walking Tall* 1977; *Kiss My Grits/A Texas Legend/Summer Heat* 1982.

star system. The set of practices by which a few actors and actresses are cast regularly in lead roles, developing mass followings that help ensure the success of their films. The system first came into being in the silent era when movie audiences clamored to know the names of their favorite performers. At first movie studios refused to reveal the names, fearing correctly that the performers would ask for more money. The first movie star to be known by her real name appeared not in America but in Germany: Henny Porten, star of *The Love of the Blind Girl* (1909). The first American movie star was Florence Lawrence in

1910, previously known as the "Biograph Girl" for the studio that had produced her films before Carl Laemmle of IMP (Independent Motion Picture Company of America) lured her away. Despite having to pay more for stars with names, studios soon realized the commercial value of stars: people would see a film if it featured performers they knew and liked. By 1919, the popularity and high salaries of performers such as Mary Pickford, Charles Chaplin, and Douglas Fairbanks had permanently established the Hollywood star system.

From the 20s to the early 50s, the major studios exerted tight control over the star system, each carefully grooming a stable of stars, strategically placing them in film roles, monitoring their offscreen lives, and generating publicity to keep them in the popular eye. Though stars were given large salaries, the studios limited their ability to seek raises and greater power by signing them to long contracts and sticking together against actors' demands.

When studio power declined in the mid-50s (see STUDIO SYSTEM), movie stars, through their talent agents, were able to demand and get more money and more control over their careers. No longer bound by multi-year contracts, stars in the decades since have been free to move from studio to studio. One result is that there are many fewer stars, as studios have made fewer films and increasingly relied on other means to get the public into the theaters, such as dazzling special effects and "high concept" story ideas. However, a handful of stars continue to exert enormous power in Hollywood, measured in their hefty incomes (often including a share of a film's gross receipts) and their ability to get studios to "green-light" projects on the basis of their participation. See also ACTING, IN CINEMA.

START. Polish acronym for Society of the Devotees of the Artistic Film. An avant-garde film society established in Poland in 1929–30 by a group of students including future film directors Wanda Jakubowska and Alexander Ford. Its members pressed for the development of a "socially relevant" cinema in Poland. Their immediate impact was negligible, but their doctrine helped lay the theoretical foundations of Polish cinema after WW II.

start mark. A mark, usually in the form of an X, on a film's leader and on the leaders of its corresponding sound tracks to indicate a common synchronization point. Start marks also appear on composite release prints at a certain distance from the first frame as an aid to a projectionist in threading a film for projection.

static marks. Dark streaks on film resulting from a discharge of static electricity through friction in the camera or careless handling, especially in cold weather.

Staudte, Wolfgang. Director. Born on Oct. 9, 1906, in Saarbrucken, Germany. The son of a stage and screen director, he was trained for the stage by REINHARDT and Piscator. He began appearing on the German stage in the late 20s and in films in 1933. Among the many films in which he appeared was the infamous anti-Semitic propaganda piece *Jud Süss/Jew Suess* (1940). He made his debut as director in 1943. Upon Germany's surrender, he found himself in the Eastern sector, where he contributed importantly to the reconstruction of German cinema with a number of films, notably the anti-Nazi *Die Mörder sind unter uns/Murderers Among Us* (1946). He has been working in West Germany since 1953. He often writes his own scripts.

FILMS (as director): *Akrobat schö-ö-ön* (also sc.) 1943; *Ich hab' von Dir geträumt* 1944; *Frau über Bord* 1945; *Die Mörder sind unter uns/Murderers Among Us* (also sc.) 1946; *Die seltsamen Abenteuer des Herrn Fridolin B* (also sc.) 1948; *Rotation* (also co-sc.), *Schicksal aus zweiter Hand* (also sc.) 1949; *Der Untertan/The Underdog* (also co-sc.) 1951; *A Tale of Five Cities/A Tale of Five Women* ("Wird Europa wieder lachen?" episode; European co-production) 1952; *Die Geschichte des kleinen Muck/Little Mook* (also co-sc.) 1953; *Leuchtfeur* 1954; *Mutter Courage und ihre Kinder* (also co-sc. with Berthold Brecht; unfinished), *Ciske—Ein Kind braucht Liebe/Ciske* (also sc.) 1955; *Rose Bernd/The Sins of Rose Bernd* 1957; *Kanonen-Serenade/Always Victorious* (also co-sc.), *Madeleine und der Legionär, Der Maulkorb* 1958; *Rosen für den Staatsanwalt/Roses for the Prosecutor* (also story) 1959; *Kirmes* (also sc.), *Der letzte Zeuge/The Last Witness* 1960; *Die glücklichen Jahre der Thorwalds* (co-dir. with John Olden), *Die Rebellion* (also co-sc.) 1962; *Die Dreigroschenoper/Three Penny Opera* (also co-sc.) 1963; *Herrenpartie* (also co-sc.), *Das Lamm* 1964; *Ganovenehre* 1966; *Heimlichkeiten/Secrets* (also co-sc.) 1968; *Die Herren mit der weissen Weste* 1970; *Heisse Spur St. Pauli/Fluchtweg St. Pauli* 1971; *The Sea Wolf* 1973; *Zwischengleis* (orig. made for TV) 1978.

Steadicam. Trade name for a device that helps stabilize handheld cameras. Its developers were awarded a special Oscar for 1977, for achievement in the scientific and technical field.

Steadman, Alison. Actress. Born on Aug. 26, 1946, in Liverpool, England. Talented character player of stage and screen. After studying acting at the East 15 Acting School in England, she debuted on the stage in 1969 and has since appeared in various classic and modern plays. Active in film since the 1980s, she distinguished herself in *The Singing Detective* (a TV miniseries in Britain, theatrical release in the US) and *Life is Sweet*, among other works. Married director Mike LEIGH.

FILMS INCLUDE: *Kipperbang* 1982; *Champions* 1983; *A Private Function* 1984; *Clockwise* 1986; *The Singing Detective, Stormy Monday* 1988; *The Adventures of Baron Munchausen* 1989; *Blame It On the Bellboy* 1992.

Steel, Anthony. Actor. Born on May 21, 1920, in London. *ed.* Cambridge. Tall, robust leading man of British films. He made his screen debut in 1948, following three years of stage experience and in the early 50s enjoyed considerable popularity in England and abroad. After marrying movie sex goddess Anita EKBERG in 1956 (they divorced in 1962) he began appearing indiscriminately in run-of-the-mill Italian films and Continental co-productions, gradually fading from prominence, disappearing altogether from the screen by the end of the 70s.

FILMS INCLUDE: *Saraband for Dead Lovers/Saraband* 1948; *The Blue Lamp, The Wooden Horse, The Mudlark* 1950; *Laughter in Paradise, Where No Vultures Fly/Ivory Hunter* 1951; *Another Man's Poison, The Planter's Wife/Outpost in Malaya, Emergency Call/Hundred Hour Hunt* 1952; *The Master of Ballantrae, Something Money Can't Buy, The Malta Story, Albert R.N./Break to Freedom* 1953; *West of Zanzibar, The Sea Shall Not Have Them* 1954; *Storm Over the Nile, Out of the Clouds* 1955; *The Black Tent, Checkpoint* 1956; *Harry Black/Harry Black and the Tiger, A Question of Adultery* 1958; *Honeymoon* (Sp.) 1959; *La Tigre dei Sette Mari/Tiger of the Seven Seas* (It./Fr.), *A Matter of Choice* 1963; *Le Fate/The Queens* (It./Fr.) 1966; *Lo Sbarco di Anzio/Anzio* (It.) 1968; *Run Rabbit Run, The Story of O* 1975; *The Night of the High Tide* 1976; *The World Is Full of Married Men* 1979; *The Mirror Crack'd, The Monster Club* 1980.

Steel, Dawn. Executive. Born on Aug. 19, 1946, in New York City. The first woman ever appointed president of a major Hollywood studio. The granddaughter of Russian Jewish immigrants named Spielberg (her father, an unsuccessful businessman, changed the name to Steel), she was raised in Little Neck, Long Island. At 14, while attending the local high school, she began working at a shoe store to earn spending money. Shortage of funds later forced her to drop out of Boston University, where she studied marketing for one year. She spent another year at NYU, supporting herself as a bookkeeper, then plunged into the job market as a receptionist, then as a statistician for a sports publisher. She then moved on to *Penthouse*, where she spent four years as a writer, editorial assistant, and eventually merchandising director. On her own, she started a novelty mail-order operation, specializing in "designer" toilet paper. Moving to Los Angeles in 1978, she landed a job in Paramount's merchandising department and soon dazzled her employers with her inventive campaign for *Star Trek—The Motion Picture* (1979). Within a year she was promoted to vice president of production. As senior vice president from 1983 and president of production from 1985, she was responsible for many of the studio's box-office hits, including *Flashdance, Top Gun, Beverly Hills Cop II, The Untouchables, Fatal Attraction,* and *The Accused.* She left Paramount in 1987 to become president of Columbia Pictures, the first woman to reach such rank in the Hollywood hierarchy. Vacating the post in the wake of Sony's takeover of Columbia, Steel ventured in the early 90s into independent production in association with the Disney company. In 1993, she published an eye-opening account of her career, *They Can Kill You, But They Can't Eat You.* Her second husband is producer Charles Roven.

Steele, Barbara. Actress. Born on Dec. 29, 1937, in Trenton Wirrall, England. Photogenic, raven-haired heroine of numerous horror thrillers. Although trained as a painter, she began acting in repertory in 1957 and in British films the following year. During the 60s she appeared mainly in cheap Italian scare quickies. She was seen in several American productions of the late 70s, before retiring from the screen after the death of her husband, screenwriter James POE.

FILMS INCLUDE: *Bachelor of Hearts* (UK) 1958; *Sapphire* (UK) 1959; *La Maschera del Demonio/Black Sunday* (It.) 1960; *The Pit and the Pendulum* (US) 1961; *L'Orribile Segreto del Dr. Hitchcock/The Horrible Dr. Hitchcock* (It.) 1962; *Otto e Mezzo/8½* (It.), *Lo Spetro/The Ghost, Le Ore dell'Amore/The Hours of Love* (It.) 1963; *Danse Macabre/ Danza Macabra/Castle of Blood* (Fr./It.), *Le Voci bianche/White Voices* (It./Fr.) 1964; *Amanti d'Oltretomba/Nightmare Castle* (It.) 1965; *Revenge of the Blood Beast/The She Beast* (UK/It.), *Terror-Creatures from the Grave* (US/It.), *Der junge Törless/ Young Torless* (Ger./Fr.) 1966; *Curse of the Crimson Altar/The Crimson Cult* (UK) 1968; *Caged Heat* (US) 1974; *They Came from Within* (Can.) 1976; *I Never Promised You a Rose Garden* (US) 1977; *Pretty Baby* (US), *Piranha, La Clé sur la Porte* (Fr.) 1978; *The Silent Scream* (US) 1980.

Steele, Bob. Actor. *b.* Robert North Bradbury, Jr., Jan. 23, 1906, Pendleton, Ore. *d.* 1988. The son of Robert North BRADBURY, a prolific director of silent action films, he began his screen career at 14, appearing with his twin brother Bill in *The Adventures of Bob and Bill,* a series of semidocumentary nature shorts directed by their father. The experience Bob gained in the series, as well as in juvenile parts in a number of his father's feature Westerns as Bob Bradbury, Jr., proved helpful when he began his career as a cowboy star in 1927. A dynamic two-fisted man of action, he projected strength and virility despite his small size. He starred in numerous Westerns for various studios through the mid-40s and was popular as one of the "Three Mesquiteers." Occasionally he appeared in films of other genres, memorably as Curly in *Of Mice and Men.* From the mid-40s he played character parts. In the 60s he was a regular in the cast of the TV series 'F Troop' (1965–67).

FILMS INCLUDE: *Davy Crockett at the Fall of the Alamo* 1926; *Sitting Bull at the Spirit Lake Massacre, The Mojave Kid* 1927; *Captain Careless, Man in the Rough, The Ridin' Renegade, Driftin' Sands* 1928; *The Amazing Vagabond, Come and Get It!, The Invaders, Laughing at Death, The Cowboy and the Outlaw* 1929; *The Land of Missing Men, Breezy Bill, Hunted Men, The Oklahoma Sheriff, The Man from Nowhere* 1930; *Sunrise Trail* 1931; *Riders of the Desert, Law of the West, Hidden Valley* 1932; *Mystery Squadron* (serial), *Young Blood, Galloping Romeo* 1933; *Powdersmoke Range* 1935; *The Kid Ranger, Cavalry* 1936; *Border Phantom, Doomed at Sundown* 1937; *Desert Patrol* 1938; *Of Mice and Men* (as Curly) 1940; *The Great Train Robbery* 1941; *Westward Ho!* 1942; *Revenge of the Zombies* 1943; *The Big Sleep* 1946; *Killer McCoy* 1947; *South of St. Louis* 1949; *The Enforcer* 1951; *The Lion and the Horse* 1952; *The Steel Jungle* 1956; *Rio Bravo* 1959; *The Comancheros* 1961; *Taggart* 1964; *Requiem for a Gunfighter* 1965; *Hang 'Em High* 1968; *The Great Bank Robbery* 1969; *Rio Lobo* 1970; *Something Big* 1971.

Steele, Tommy. Actor, singer. Born Thomas Hicks, on Dec. 17, 1936, in London. A former merchant seaman, he became popular in 1956 as a pop singer. He later developed into an all-around entertainer, noted for his cockney zest. He starred in the musical 'Half a Sixpence' in London and on Broadway and in British as well as American films.

FILMS: *Kill Me Tomorrow, The Tommy Steele Story/Rock Around the World* 1957; *The Duke Wore Jeans* 1958; *Tommy the Toreador* 1959; *Light Up the Sky* 1960; *It's All Happening/The Dream Maker* 1963; *The Happiest Millionaire* (US), *Half a Sixpence* (UK/US) 1967; *Finian's Rainbow* (US) 1968; *Where's Jack?* 1969.

Steenburgen, Mary. Actress. Born in 1953, in Newport, Ark. Charming, vivacious, offbeat leading lady of American films. Raised in North Little Rock, Ark., where her father was a lifelong employee of the Missouri Pacific Railroad, she discovered drama at Hendrix College. On the recommendation of a teacher, she headed at 19 to New York, enrolling at the Neighborhood Playhouse, where she studied under Sanford Meisner, supporting herself as a waitress. She was performing with a comedy improvisational group when she was discovered by Jack Nicholson, who chose her as his leading lady in *Goin' South* (1978). Two years later she won the Academy Award as best supporting actress for *Melvin and Howard.* She is active in political causes and in 1992 campaigned for President Bill Clinton. From 1980 to 1990 she was married to Malcolm McDOWELL, her co-star in *Time After Time* (1979). She is now married to actor Ted DANSON.

FILM: *Goin' South* 1978; *Time After Time* 1979; *Melvin and Howard* 1980; *Ragtime* 1981; *A Midsummer Night's Sex Comedy* 1982; *Cross Creek, Romantic Comedy* 1983; *One Magic Christmas* 1985; *Dead of Winter, End of the Line* (also exec. prod.), *The Whales of August* 1987; *Miss Firecracker, Parenthood* 1989; *Back to the Future Part III, The Long Walk Home* (v/o) 1990; *The Butcher's Wife* 1991; *Philadelphia, What's Eating Gilbert Grape* 1993; *Clifford, Pontiac Moon* 1994; *Mi Familia/My Family, Powder* 1995; *The Grass Harp* 1996.

Steiger, Rod. Actor. Born Rodney Stephen Steiger, on Apr. 14, 1925, in Westhampton, N.Y. Character star of the American screen. He quit high school at 16 to join the Navy and served for the duration of WW II on a destroyer in the Pacific. After his discharge he stayed on with the Navy as a civilian clerk with the Department of Dependents and Beneficiaries. While there, he began acting with an amateur group and soon decided to apply his GI Bill scholarship toward an education in drama. He enrolled at the Dramatic Workshop of the New School for Social Research and after two years went on to the New York Theatre

Wing and from there to the Actors Studio. He emerged at the end of his studies as one of the most imposing exponents of "the Method," a highly gifted actor with an enormous stage and screen presence.

He gained most of his early professional experience on the stage and in TV drama, winning plaudits for his portrayal of the title role in the original television production of 'Marty' that preceded the film version. Apart from an isolated screen role in *Teresa* (1951), he started his film career in 1954 with an immensely impressive characterization as Marlon Brando's older brother in *On the Waterfront,* a performance that won him a nomination for an Oscar. He won another Oscar nomination for *The Pawnbroker* (1965) and received the Academy Award for his portrayal of a police officer in *In the Heat of the Night* (1967). Despite a sometime tendency to overact, Steiger remains one of the most effective of American and international screen actors, both as a character heavy and a powerful proponent. Formerly married to Claire BLOOM (second of three, 1959–69), Steiger is a self-confessed "bum" and "wino," with a gargantuan appetite and a preference for solitude.

FILMS: *Teresa* 1951; *On the Waterfront* 1954; *Oklahoma!* (as Jud), *The Big Knife, The Court-Martial of Billy Mitchell* 1955; *Jubal, The Harder They Fall, Back from Eternity* 1956; *Run of the Arrow, Across the Bridge* (UK), *The Unholy Wife* 1957; *Cry Terror* 1958; *Al Capone* (title role) 1959; *Seven Thieves* 1960; *The Mark* (UK) 1961; *The World in My Pocket, 13 West Street, Convicts 4, The Longest Day* 1962; *Le Mani sulla Città/Hands Over the City* (It.) 1963; *Gli Indifferenti/Time of Indifference* (It.) 1964; *E venne un Uomo/And There Came a Man* (It./Fr.), *The Pawnbroker, The Loved One, Doctor Zhivago* 1965; *La Ragazza e il Generale/The Girl and the General* (It./Fr.), *In the Heat of the Night* 1967; *No Way to Treat a Lady, The Sergeant* 1968; *Three Into Two Won't Go* (UK), *The Illustrated Man* 1969; *Waterloo* (as Napoleon; USSR/It.) 1970; *Happy Birthday Wanda June* 1971; *Giu la Testa/Duck You Sucker!* (It.) 1972; *A Proposito Luciano/Re: Lucky Luciano* (It.), *Lolly-Madonna XXX, Gli Eroi/The Heroes* (It.) 1973; *Mussolini: Ultimo Atto/Last Days of Mussolini/The Last Four Days* (title role; It.) 1974; *Les Innocents aux Mains sales/Dirty Hands* (Fr.), *Hennessy* (UK) 1975; *W. C. Fields and Me* (as W. C. Fields) 1976; *Jim Buck/Portrait of a Hitman, F.I.S.T.* 1978; *Love and Bullets* (UK), *Steiner-das eiserne Kreuz II/Sergeant Steiner/ Breakthrough* (Ger.), *The Amityville Horror, Wolf Lake/The Honor Guard* (release delayed to 1981; Can.) 1979; *The Lucky Star* (Can.), *Klondyke Fever/Jack London's Klondyke Fever* 1980; *Lion of the Desert* (as Benito Mussolini; Libya/UK), *Cattle Annie and Little Britches, The Chosen* 1981; *Der Zauberberg/The Magic Mountain* (Ger.) 1982; *The Naked Face* (UK) 1984; *The Kindred, Feel the Heat/Catch the Heat, Hello Actors Studio* (doc.), *American Gothic* (UK) 1987; *The January Man, The Summer of White Roses* (UK/Yug.), *Tennessee Nights* 1989; *Men of Respect* 1990; *The Ballad of the Sad Cafe, Guilty as Charged* 1991; *The Player* (cameo) 1992; *The Specialist* 1994; *Carpool, Mars Attacks!,* 1996; *Shiloh, Truth or Consequences, N.M.,* 1997.

Stein, Paul L(udwig). Director. *b.* Feb. 4, 1892, Vienna. *d.* 1951. Educated in Vienna and Berlin, he first arrived in the US at the age of 18 and started his film career as a screenwriter for various East Coast studios while being employed as a Broadway stage manager. He then returned to Europe and for two years appeared as an actor on the Vienna stage and in Austrian and German films. After directing two films for his own production company, he joined UFA as a director in 1920 and turned out a dozen or so German films before going to Hollywood in 1926. His American films, like his German ones, were for the most part romantic or domestic dramas and comedies, often from the woman's viewpoint. In the early 30s he moved on to England, where he continued directing romantic films and occasionally musicals and mysteries.

FILMS INCLUDE: In Germany—*Der Teufel der Liebe* (also prod.) 1919; *Das Martyrium, Die geschlossene Kette, Arme Violetta/The Red Peacock* 1920; *Das Opfer der Helen, Der ewige Kampf* 1921; *Ein Traum vom Glück* 1924; *Ich liebe Dich, Liebesfeuer, Die Insel der Träume* 1925. In the US (complete)—*My Official Wife* 1926; *Don't Tell the Wife, The Climbers, The Forbidden Woman* 1927; *Man-Made Woman, Show Folks* 1928; *Her Private Affair, The Office Scandal, This Thing Called Love* 1929; *One Romantic Night, Sin Takes a Holiday, The Lottery Bride* 1930; *Born to Love, The Common Law* 1931; *A Woman Commands* 1932. In the UK (complete)—*Lily Christine* 1932; *The Song You Gave Me* 1933; *Red Wagon, Blossom Time/April Romance* 1934; *Mimi, Heart's Desire* 1935; *Faithful* 1936; *Cafe Colette* 1937; *Just Like a Woman, Jane Steps Out, Black Limelight* 1938; *Poison Pen, The Outsider* 1939; *Gentleman of Venture/It Happened to One Man* 1940; *The Saint Meets the Tiger* 1941; *Talk About Jacqueline* 1942; *Kiss the Bride Goodbye, Twilight Hour* 1944; *Waltz Time* 1945; *The Laughing Lady, The Lisbon Story* 1946; *Counterblast/Devil's Plot* 1948; *The Twenty Questions Murder Mystery* 1950.

Steinbeck, John. Novelist, screenwriter. *b.* Feb. 27, 1902, Salinas, Calif. *d.* 1968. The Nobel Prize–winning author of *The Grapes of Wrath* and several other novels that have been successfully adapted into films, also contributed a number of stories and screenplays directly for the screen.

FILMS: Adapted from his novels or stories by others—*Of Mice and Men, The Grapes of Wrath* 1940; *Tortilla Flat* 1942; *The Moon Is Down* 1943; *Lifeboat* (story) 1944; *A Medal for Benny* (co-story) 1945; *East of Eden* 1955; *The Wayward Bus* 1967; *Cannery Row* 1982; *Of Mice and Men* 1992. Screenplays by Steinbeck—*The Forgotten Village* (doc.; also story) 1941; *La Perla/The Pearl* (co-sc. from own novelette; Mex.) 1946; *The Red Pony* (from own novel) 1949; *Viva Zapata!* 1952.

Steiner, Max. Composer. *b.* Maximilian Raoul Steiner, May 10, 1888, Vienna. *d.* 1971. A musical prodigy, he graduated from Vienna's Imperial Academy of Music at 13, after completing the eight-year course in one year. The following year he wrote the book and lyrics and composed the score for a musical that played Vienna for two years. Studying under Mahler, he was a professional conductor at 16. In 1914 he emigrated to the US, where he became conductor and orchestrator of Broadway musicals for George White, Florenz Ziegfeld, and Victor Herbert. With the advent of sound, he went to Hollywood in 1929 and exerted an enormous influence on the development of the musical score as a functional element in films. His scores were typically melodious and full-bodied and closely linked with the visual images. He won Academy Awards for the scores of *The Informer* (1935), *Now, Voyager* (1942), and *Since You Went Away* (1944) and was nominated for 15 other Oscars. His score for *The Treasure of the Sierra Madre* (1948) won the top prize at Venice. His best-known music is probably the score of *Gone With the Wind* (1939), one of the richest and longest in screen history. In all, he scored more than 200 films, mostly for RKO and Warners. Excerpts from his music have been used in many films since his death.

FILMS INCLUDE: *Rio Rita* 1929; *Dixiana* 1930; *Cimarron* 1931; *Symphony of Six Million, A Bill of Divorcement* 1932; *King Kong, Morning Glory, Little Women* 1933; *The Lost Patrol, Of Human Bondage* 1934; *Roberta, The Informer, She, Top Hat, Alice Adams* 1935; *Follow the Fleet, The Garden of Allah, The Charge of the Light Brigade, Winterset* 1936; *A Star*

Is Born, The Life of Emile Zola 1937; *Jezebel, The Dawn Patrol, Four Daughters, The Sisters* 1938; *Dodge City, Dark Victory, Gone With the Wind* 1939; *The Letter* 1940; *The Great Lie, Sergeant York, They Died with Their Boots On* 1941; *Now Voyager* 1942; *Casablanca* 1943; *Since You Went Away* 1944; *Mildred Pierce, Rhapsody in Blue* 1945; *The Big Sleep, Cloak and Dagger* 1946; *The Treasure of the Sierra Madre, Key Largo, Johnny Belinda* 1948; *The Fountainhead, White Heat* 1949; *The Flame and the Arrow, The Glass Menagerie* 1950; *So Big* 1953; *The Caine Mutiny* 1954; *Battle Cry* 1955; *The Searchers* 1956; *A Summer Place* 1959; *The Dark at the Top of the Stairs* 1960; *Parrish, Susan Slade* 1961; *A Majority of One, Rome Adventure* 1962; *Spencer's Mountain* 1963; *A Distant Trumpet, Youngblood Hawke* 1964; *Two on a Guillotine* 1965.

Steinhoff, Hans. Director. *b.* Mar. 10, 1882, Pfaffenhofen, Germany. *d.* 1945, in a plane crash. He quit medical studies to become a stage actor and director. Helming German films from the early 20s he rose to importance after the advent of the Nazis, when he was entrusted by Goebbels with the direction of some key propaganda films. The films he made during WW II, most notoriously *Ohm Krüger* (1941), were ruthlessly inflammatory and virulently anti-Semitic.

FILMS INCLUDE: *Bräutigam auf Kredit* 1921; *Der Bettelstudent, Birbi* (also sc.), *Der falsche Dimitri* (also co-sc.), *Kleider machen Leute* (also co-sc.) 1922; *Inge Larsen* 1923; *Mensch gegen Mensch* 1924; *Gräfin Mariza* 1925; *Der Herr des Todes, Die Tragödie eines Verlorenen, Wien-Berlin* 1926; *Das Frauenhaus von Rio* 1927; *Nachtgestalten* 1929; *Rosenmontag* 1930; *Die Pranke, Mein Leopold, Der wahre Jakob* 1931; *Scampolo—Ein Kind der Strasse* 1932; *Mutter und Kind, Madame wünscht keine Kinder, Hitlerjunge Quex* 1933; *Freut Euch des Lebens, Die Insel, Lockvogel* 1934; *Der alte und der junge König* 1935; *Eine Frau ohne Bedeutung* 1936; *Ein Volksfeind* (also co-sc.) 1937; *Tanz auf dem Vulkan* (also co-sc.) 1938; *Robert Koch* 1939; *Die Geierwally* 1940; *Ohm Krüger* 1941; *Rembrandt* (also co-sc.) 1942; *Gabriele Dambrone* 1943; *Shiva und die Galgenblume* (also co-sc.) 1945.

Steinkamp, Fredric. Film editor. Born on Aug. 22, 1928, in Los Angeles. *ed.* UCLA (marketing). The son of William Steinkamp, a veteran Fox employee (from 1919), who ran the studios camera and sound departments and would later dub musicals at MGM, he began performing odd jobs in the movie industry during high school vacations. He joined MGM as an apprentice cutter in 1952, becoming a full editor in 1960. He shared an Academy Award for *Grand Prix* (1966) and was nominated for Oscars four more times, twice sharing the honor with his son and frequent collaborator, William Steinkamp (*b.* June 9, 1953). Two other sons, Karl and Robert, are budding editors.

FILMS INCLUDE (alone or in collaboration): *The Adventures of Huckleberry Finn* 1960; *All Fall Down, Period of Adjustment* 1962; *Sunday in New York* 1963; *The Unsinkable Molly Brown,* 1964; *Grand Prix* 1966; *Charly* 1968; *They Shoot Horses Don't They?* 1969; *A New Leaf* 1971; *Freebie and The Bean* 1974; *The Yakuza, Three Days of the Condor* 1975; *Bobby Deerfield* 1977; *Fedora* 1979; *Hide in Plain Sight* 1980; *Tootsie* 1982; *Against All Odds* 1984; *White Nights, Out of Africa* 1985; *Burglar, Adventures in Babysitting* 1987; *Scrooged* 1988; *Havana* 1990; *Blood in Blood Out* 1992; *The Firm* 1993.

Sten, Anna. Actress. *b.* Annel (Anjuschka) Stenskaja Sudakevich, on Dec. 3, 1908, in Kiev, Russia. *d.* 1993. The daughter of a Russian ballet master and a Swedish mother, she worked briefly as a waitress before beginning her acting career with Stanislavsky's Moscow Art Theatre. She appeared in a number of Soviet films (1927–28) before departing for Germany. Her performance in the German film *The Murderer Dmitri Karamazov* brought her to the attention of American producer Sam Goldwyn, who brought her to Hollywood in the early 30s amid an intensive publicity campaign, hoping to create another Garbo or Dietrich. But she somehow failed to appeal to American audiences and soon became known in the industry as "Goldwyn's Folly." After poor box-office response to several of her films, Goldwyn conceded he had made an expensive error, a rare one in his career, and terminated her contract. She continued appearing in occasional films but devoted most of her time to a semiprofessional career as a painter. In 1960 she appeared briefly as Jenny in the long-running New York production of 'The Threepenny Opera' and later toured with that play. Her first husband was director Fedor OZEP; her second, director-producer Dr. Eugene Frenke.

FILMS INCLUDE: In the USSR—*The Girl with the Hat Box/When Moscow Laughs* 1927; *Earth in Chains/The Yellow Ticket/The Yellow Pass, The House on Trubnaya Square, The White Eagle/The Lash of the Czar, The Heir to Genghis Khan/Tempest Over Asia/Storm Over Asia* 1928. In Germany—*Der Mörder Dimitri Karamasoff/Karamazov/The Murderer Dmitri Karamazov/The Brothers Karamazov* (as Grushenka), *Bomben auf Monte Carlo/Monte Carlo Madness, Salto Mortale/Trapeze* 1931; *Stürme der Leidenschaft/Tempest* 1932. In the US—*Nana* (title role), *We Live Again/Resurrection* (as Katusha) 1934; *The Wedding Night* 1935; *A Woman Alone/Two Who Dared* (UK) 1936; *Exile Express* 1939; *The Man I Married* 1940; *So Ends Our Night* 1941; *Chetniks, They Came to Blow Up America* 1943; *Three Russian Girls* 1944; *Let's Live a Little* 1948; *Soldier of Fortune* 1955; *Runaway Daughters* 1956; *The Nun and the Sergeant* 1962.

Steno. Director, screenwriter. *b.* Stefano Vanzina, Jan. 19, 1915, Rome. *d.* 1988. He attended the Centro Sperimentale di Cinematografia while completing his law studies at the University of Rome. After working briefly as a writer and cartoonist for a humor magazine, he entered films in 1939 as an assistant director and script collaborator. After WW II he began directing as well as writing for films, initially in collaboration with Mario MONICELLI, then, from 1953, on his own. Although he worked in a number of genres, his most successful films were comedies, at times excessively vulgar. Sometimes billed as Stefano Vanzina, his real name.

FILMS (as director and co-screenwriter): In collaboration with Mario Monicelli—*Al Diavolo la Celebrità* 1949; *Totò cerca Casa, Vita da Cani, E arrivato il Cavaliere* 1950; *Guardie e Ladri/Cops and Robbers* 1951; *Totò e i Re di Roma* 1952; *Le Infedeli, Totò e le Donne* 1953. Directing alone—*Totò a Colori, L'Uomo la Bestia e la Virtù* 1953; *Cinema d'Altri Tempi, Un Giorno in Pretura/A Day in Court, Un Americano a Roma, Le Avventure di Giacomo Casanova/Sins of Casanova* 1954; *Piccola Posta, Mio Figlio Nerone/Nero's Mistress* 1956; *Femmine Tre Volte, Susanna tutta Panna* 1957; *Mia Nonna Polizziota, Guardia Ladro e Cameriera* 1958; *Totò nella Luna, I Tartassati, Totò Eva e il Pennello Proibito, Tempi Duri per i Vampiri* 1959; *A noi piace Freddo!, Un Militare e Mezzo, Letto a Tre Piazze* 1960; *Psycosissimo* 1961; *I Moschettieri del Mare, La Ragazza di Mille Mesi, Totò Diabolicus, Copacabana Palace/Girl Game* 1962; *I Due Colonnelli/Two Colonels, Totò Contro I Quattro* 1963; *Gli Eroi del West, I Gemelli del Texas* 1964; *Letti Sbagliati* 1965; *Rose rosse per Angelica, Amore all'Italiana/I Superdiabolici* 1966; *Arriva Dorellik* 1967; *La Feldmarescialla, Capriccio all'Italiana* ("Il Mostro della Domenica" episode) 1968; *Il Trapianto* 1969; *Cose di Cosa Nostra, Il Vichingo venuto dal Sud* 1971; *La Polizia Ringrazia/Execution Squad, Il Terrore con gli Occhi Storti, L'Uccello Migratore* 1972; *Piedone lo sbirro/Flatfoot, Anastaia mio Fratello* 1973; *La Polizlotta* 1974; *Piedone a Hong Kong, Il Padrone e l'Operaio* 1975; *L'Italia s'è rotta, Febbre de Cavallo* 1976; *Tre Tigri contro Tre Tigri* (co-dir.) 1977; *Doppio Delitto, Piedone l'Africano, Piedone d'Egitto/Flatfoot on the Nile, Amori miei* 1978; *Dottor Jekyll e Gentile Signora/Il Dottor Jekyll Jr., Amici diversi* 1979; *Banana Joe* 1982.

Stephens, Sir Robert. Actor. *b.* July 14, 1931, in Bristol, England. *d.* 1994. Leading man and supporting player of the British (and occasionally American) stage, TV, and films. He has also directed a number of plays. His second wife was actress Maggie SMITH. Their son is actor Toby Stephens.

FILMS INCLUDE: *Circle of Deception, Pirates of Tortuga* (as Pirate Henry Morgan; US), *A Taste of Honey* 1961; *The Inspector/Lisa* (UK/US) 1962; *The Small World of Sammy Lee, Cleopatra* (as Germanicus; US/UK) 1963; *Morgan—A Suitable Case for Treatment/Morgan!* 1966; *Romeo and Juliet* (as the Prince of Verona; UK/It.) 1968; *The Prime of Miss Jean Brodie* 1969; *The Private Life of Sherlock Holmes* (title role; UK/US) 1970; *Travels with My Aunt* (UK/US) 1972; *Luther* (UK/US) 1973; *The Shout* 1978; *High Season, Testimony* 1987; *Henry V* 1989; *Wings of Fame* 1990; *The Pope Must Die/The Pope Must Diet* 1991; *Chaplin* 1992; *Searching for Bobby Fischer, The Secret Rapture* 1993; *Century* (UK) 1994.

Stephenson, Henry. Actor. *b.* Henry S. Garroway, Apr. 16, 1871, Granada, British West Indies. *d.* 1956. *ed.* Rugby. A veteran of the London and New York stage, he played character parts in occasional silent and numerous sound Hollywood productions, typically portraying genial gentlemen of good breeding and lending distinction to many historical dramas and literary adaptations.

FILMS INCLUDE: *The Spreading Dawn* 1917; *The Black Panther's Cub* 1921; *Men and Women, Wild Wild Susan* 1925; *Red Headed Woman, A Bill of Divorcement, Cynara, The Animal Kingdom* 1932; *Double Harness, Little Women* (as Mr. Laurence) 1933; *Man of Two Worlds, Thirty Day Princess, Stingaree, One More River, What Every Woman Knows* 1934; *Vanessa: Her Love Story, Reckless, Mutiny on the Bounty* (as Sir Joseph Banks), *Captain Blood* (as Lord Willoughby) 1935; *Little Lord Fauntleroy, The Charge of the Light Brigade, Beloved Enemy* 1936; *The Prince and the Pauper* (as the Duke of Norfolk), *The Emperor's Candlesticks, Conquest* (as Count Walewski) 1937; *Marie Antoinette, Suez* (as Count Mathieu de Lesseps) 1938; *Tarzan Finds a Son, The Adventures of Sherlock Holmes, The Private Lives of Elizabeth and Essex* (as Lord Burghley) 1939; *Little Old New York* (as New York State's first chancellor, Robert R. Livingston), *Spring Parade, Down Argentine Way* 1940; *This Above All* (as General Cathaway) 1942; *Mr. Lucky* 1943; *The Hour Before Dawn* 1944; *The Green Years, Of Human Bondage, Night and Day* 1946; *The Locket, Song of Love* (as King Albert) 1947; *Oliver Twist* (as Mr. Brownlow; UK), *Enchantment* 1948; *Challenge to Lassie* 1949.

step outline. A synopsis; a brief step-by-step outline of the narrative progression and dramatic structure of a proposed film story, submitted for approval before the writing of a screenplay.

step printing. A method of printing in which the film is advanced intermittently, each frame being exposed in a stationary state. This method is often preferred to the more common continuous-motion printing when optical effects are desired.

stereophonic sound. A system of sound reproduction designed to add depth to sound and increase its realism. Sounds are picked up by several microphones and recorded on separate tracks. They are then played back on separate channels through speakers placed in positions corresponding to those of the microphones. Stereophonic sound has played an important part in the presentation of wide-screen productions in motion picture theaters since the early 50s. The system developed by DOLBY LABORATORIES in the 1970s made stereophonic sound more widely available. The Dolby stereo system, which requires theaters to be equipped with a decoding box, produces realistic four-channel sound using an optical sound track on standard 35 mm prints.

stereoscopic cinema. A method of producing and projecting films in such a way that an illusion of three-dimensional vision is achieved. The process is known popularly as "3-D." Experimentation with various still-photography stereoscopic devices began in the latter part of the 19th century. By the advent of the cinema at the turn of the century, projectors for stereoscopic still pictures were in wide use throughout the world. Around 1900, three-dimensional motion picture processes were patented in Great Britain, France, and the US, but they never went beyond the experimental stage. A resurgence of interest in the process in the 20s brought in its wake some technological advances and a number of successful theatrical presentations of 3-D motion pictures. But as soon as public curiosity waned, the various systems were abandoned. By the end of the silent era, no fewer than 200 different stereoscopic movie systems had been patented and tried, but none proved technically and commercially viable beyond its initial impact.

Experiments with various stereoscopic systems continued after the advent of sound in Europe as well as in the US. Every now and then a "wholly revolutionary" three-dimensional motion picture process was announced. However, most presentations were only variations of several basic methods that changed little over the years. In some, the images were shown on the screen side by side and converged into one when viewed through a special device; in others, two images appeared on the same frame separated by a distance identical to that separating the human eyes; in still others, two images were alternately projected on the screen with a shutter device. Then there was the anaglyph color process in which red and green images fused into a single image in depth when viewed through red and green glasses. During New York's World's Fair in 1939, a color stereoscopic process was introduced that utilized a polarized filter on the projector and polaroid glasses for the audience. Two years later the Soviets premiered a "parallax stereogram" system that required no glasses but was far from perfect in reproduction respects.

Interest in the various 3-D processes was awakened in the US in the early 50s when Hollywood found itself faced with a king-size crisis as a result of competition from TV. Along with CinemaScope, Cinerama, and other wide-screen processes, films in depth re-emerged as a possible attraction to dwindling cinema audiences. First came *Bwana Devil,* premiered late in 1952, then a virtual avalanche of 3-D films from every major studio and many small ones. Among the more successful were Warners' *House of Wax* and MGM's *Kiss Me Kate,* but most films of the 3-D crop were low-quality quickies whose sole attraction was technical gimmickry. Within a year or two the 3-D frenzy had subsided in the face of growing public apathy.

But inventors and entrepreneurs still haven't given up. Despite a 70-year-old failure to produce a wholly satisfactory 3-D process, research continues. One system that holds great promise is the yet unexplored process of holography, which would employ a laser beam to produce three-dimensional images. It is hoped that holography will make possible stereoscopic films of good technical quality and considerable depth. When perfected, the process should do away with the necessity to equip audiences with special glasses.

Sterling, Ford. Actor. *b.* George Ford Stitch, Nov. 3, 1883, LaCrosse, Wis. *d.* 1939. In his teens he ran away from home to join a circus, which featured him as "Keno, the Boy Clown." He later performed in vaudeville and on the legitimate stage and in 1911 he joined Mack SENNETT's unit at Biograph. In 1912 he followed Sennett to Keystone, where with Mabel Normand and Fred Mace he provided the nucleus of the early Keystone comedies. He appeared in innumerable shorts, typically as a comic villain, most memorably as Chief Teheezal of the Keystone Cops. Sterling wandered in and out of Sennett's films for several years and for a while starred in his own series, the Sterling Comedies. He finally broke with Sennett in 1921. He then played character parts and occasional leads in feature films, but his knockabout slapstick was often out of keeping with the more disciplined comedy style of features. His activity was curtailed in the 30s following the loss of a leg in an accident.

FILMS INCLUDE: *Abe Gets Even with Father* 1911; *Cohen Collects a Debt, The Flirting Husband, The Ambitious Butler, The Beating He Needed, A Bear Escape, The Deacon's Troubles* 1912; *On His Wedding Day, Hide and Seek, The New Conductor, That Rag Time Band, Safe in Jail, The Firebugs, Zuzu the Band Leader, The Gusher* 1913; *Love and Dynamite, In the Clutches of the Gang, Raffles Gentleman Burglar, Between Showers, Tango Tangles* 1914; *Our Dare Devil Chief, Court House Crooks, Only a Messenger Boy, His Father's Footsteps* (also co-dir. with Charles Parrott), *The Hunt* (also co-dir. with Parrott) 1915; *His Pride and Shame* (also co-dir. with Parrott), *His Wild Oats* (also co-dir. with Clarence Badger), *His Lying Heart* (also dir.), *The Manicurist* (also dir.) 1916; *Stars and Bars* (also dir.), *Pinched in the Finish, Her Torpedoed Love* 1917; *Her Screen Idol, Beware of Boarders* 1918; *Hearts and Flowers, Yankee Doodle in Berlin, His Last False Step* 1919; *Married Life, Don't Weaken, Love Honor and Behave* 1920; *An Unhappy Finish* 1921; *Oh Mabel Behave* (also co-dir. with Mack Sennett), *The Stranger's Banquet* 1922; *The Brass Bottle, The Day of Faith, The Spoilers* 1923; *Wild Oranges, Love and Glory, Galloping Fish, He Who Gets Slapped, So Big* 1924; *Daddy's Gone a-Hunting, The Trouble with Wives, Stage Struck, Steppin' Out* 1925; *The American Venus, The Road to Glory, Miss Brewster's Millions, Good and Naughty, The Show-Off, Everybody's Acting, Stranded in Paris* 1926; *Casey at the Bat, For the Love of Mike* 1927; *Gentlemen Prefer Blondes, Wife Savers, Sporting Goods, Oh Kay!* 1928; *The Fall of Eve, Sally* 1929; *Showgirl in Hollywood, Bride of the Regiment, Kismet* 1930; *Her Majesty Love* 1931; *Alice in Wonderland* (as the White King) 1933; *Black Sheep* 1935.

Sterling, Jan. Actress. Born Jane Sterling Adriance, on Apr. 3, 1923, in New York City, into a socially prominent family. She trained for the stage at Fay Compton's school in England and made her Broadway debut in 1938 (at 15) and her first motion picture appearance a decade later. A cool blonde, she often played high-class floozies in films. She was nominated for an Oscar for her work in that vein in *The High and the Mighty.* The widow of actor Paul DOUGLAS, she now lives in London with actor Sam WANAMAKER. After a long absence, she returned to the screen in 1976.

FILMS INCLUDE: *Johnny Belinda* 1948; *Caged, Mystery Street, Union Station* 1950; *Appointment with Danger, Ace in the Hole/The Big Carnival, Rhubarb* 1951; *Flesh and Fury* 1952; *Split Second, The Vanquished, Pony Express* 1953; *Alaska Seas, The High and the Mighty, The Human Jungle* 1954; *Women's Prison, Female on the Beach, Man with the Gun* 1955; *The Harder They Fall, 1984* 1956; *Slaughter on Tenth Avenue* 1957; *Kathy O'* 1958; *Love in a Goldfish Bowl* 1961; *The Incident* 1967; *The Angry Breed* 1968; *The Minx* 1969; *Sammy Somebody* 1976; *First Monday in October* 1981.

Sterling, Robert. Actor. Born William Hart, on Nov. 13, 1917, in New Castle, Pa. *ed.* U. of Pittsburgh. Second-string leading man of Hollywood films of the 40s. The son of a Chicago Cubs catcher, Walter S. Hart, he worked as a clothes salesman before breaking into films in the late 30s. Tall, handsome, boyish, and bland, he usually played leads in B pictures and second leads in A's. He retired from acting in the mid-60s and later entered the computer business. His marriage (1943–49) to actress Ann SOTHERN produced actress Tisha (Patricia) Sterling. In 1951 he married Anne JEFFREYS, his co-star in the TV series 'Topper' (1953–55).

FILMS INCLUDE: *Only Angels Have Wings* 1939; *Manhattan Heartbeat, Yesterday's Heroes, The Gay Caballero* 1940; *The Penalty, I'll Wait for You, The Get-Away, Ringside Maisie, Two-Faced Woman* 1941; *Johnny Eager, This Time for Keeps, Somewhere I'll Find You* 1942; *The Secret Heart* 1946; *Roughshod* 1949; *The Sundowners* 1950; *Show Boat* 1951; *Column South* 1953; *Return to Peyton Place, Voyage to the Bottom of the Sea* 1961; *A Global Affair* 1964.

Stern, Daniel. Actor. Born on Aug. 28, 1957, in Bethesda, Md. Likeable leading man, second lead, and supporting player of the American screen. Trained at the H. B. Studios, he also performed on the stage and in such TV series as 'Hometown' (1985) and 'The Wonder Years' (1991–92). He directed some episodes of the latter.

FILMS INCLUDE: *Breaking Away, Starting Over* 1979; *It's My Turn, Stardust Memories* 1980; *I'm Dancing as Fast as I Can, Diner* 1982; *Blue Thunder, Get Crazy* 1983; *C.H.U.D.* 1984; *Key Exchange* 1985; *Hannah and Her Sisters, The Boss' Wife* 1986; *Born in East L.A.* 1987; *The Milagro Beanfield War, D.O.A.* 1988; *Leviathan, Little Monsters* 1989; *Coupe De Ville, My Blue Heaven, Home Alone* 1990; *City Slickers* 1991; *Home Alone 2* 1992; *Rookie of the Year* (also dir.) 1993; *City Slickers 2: The Legend of Curly's Gold* 1994; *Bushwacked* 1995; *Celtic Pride* 1996.

Stern, Steven Hilliard. Director. Born on Nov. 1, 1937, in Timmins, Ontario, Canada. *ed.* Ryerson Institute of Technology. Competent helmer of numerous TV movies and a handful of pedestrian American and Canadian features.

FEATURE FILMS: *P.S. I Love You* 1971; *Neither by Day Nor by Night* (US/Isr.) 1972; *The Harrad Summer* 1974; *Running* 1979; *The Devil and Max Devlin* 1982; *Rolling Vengeance* 1987; *Love & Murder* 1990; *Money* (Fr./It./Can.) 1991.

Stern, Stewart. Screenwriter. Born on Mar. 22, 1922, in New York City. *ed.* U. of Iowa. A former stage actor, he began writing for films and TV after his WW II service in the infantry. He has collaborated on a number of notable Hollywood films.

FILMS INCLUDE: *Teresa* 1951; *Rebel Without a Cause* 1955; *The Rack* 1956; *The Outsider* 1962; *The Ugly American* 1963; *Rachel Rachel* 1968; *The Last Movie* 1971; *Summer Wishes Winter Dreams* 1973.

Sternberg, Josef von. Director. *b.* Josef Sternberg, May 29, 1894, Vienna. *d.* 1969. Born into a poor, Orthodox Jewish family—the aristocratic "von" was added to his name by a Hollywood producer who thought it would look better on a cinema marquee—he was brought to the US at the age of seven, where he received part of his early education in Jamaica, Queens, New York. He subsequently returned to Vienna to complete his schooling but was back in New York at the age of 17, when he found a job as a film patcher for the World Film Company in Fort Lee, New Jersey. He gradually advanced to film cutter, writer, assistant director, and advisor to the company's boss, William S. Brady. In 1917 he joined the Army Signal Corps and made a number of training films. After the Armistice, he traveled about the US and Europe, working as an assistant to various directors. He finally settled in Hollywood in 1924.

After gaining some experience directing scenes unfinished by other directors, von Sternberg got together with a young British stage actor, George K. Arthur, who wanted to invest $5,000 to subsidize his own screen debut. Von Sternberg had a screenplay ready for just such an occasion. He shot *The Salvation Hunters* on location, at the docks of San Pedro Bay, on a shoestring budget and with no name stars. His naturalistic depiction of the world of the waterfront derelicts was a novelty in American cinema and the film had Hollywood buzzing with interest in the new director, who in his very first production was able to demonstrate a completely original visual style, noted for its interplay of light and shade.

Mary Pickford wanted him to direct her next picture, but they couldn't agree on a subject and on an approach and the project was abandoned. Von Sternberg signed up with MGM, but the studio didn't like the way he directed his first film there, *The Exquisite Sinner,* and had it remade by another director. The same happened to his second assignment, *The Masked Bride,* and his contract was discontinued by mutual consent. Next, Charlie Chaplin asked him to direct a vehicle for his protégée, Edna Purviance, alternately titled *The Sea Gull* and *A Woman of the Sea.* Von Sternberg completed the production to his own satisfaction, but Chaplin found the film too sophisticated for general audiences and it was never released. According to persons who saw the unreleased print, this was one of the most exquisitely beautiful pictures ever filmed in Hollywood.

Von Sternberg's cycle of misfortune was finally broken late in 1926, when he joined Paramount as assistant director. Impressing producers with a clever salvage job on another director's film, he was assigned to direct *Underworld,* from a story by Ben Hecht. It was Hollywood's first serious look at the world of the gangster and it was executed in the inimitable von Sternberg style, characterized by bold pictorialism and a rather flimsy plot structure. In this and subsequent von Sternberg films the visual form itself rather than a conventional plot express the content. Pictorial compositions and light and shadow effects are used to illuminate the characters and to express their motivations; von Sternberg used the camera as a painter's brush or a poet's pen.

Von Sternberg has been criticized as a mannered, self-indulgent stylist with a trivial, detached vision of the world. But not even his detractors have denied the dramatic power of his plastic vision and the validity of his experimentation in the juxtaposition of shadow and light to express shifts of mood and inner action. During his peak years (1927–35) he was the undisputed great master of the American screen, an inspired artist and a superb technician.

In 1930, von Sternberg went to Germany to direct Emil Jannings in UFA's first talkie, *The Blue Angel.* Searching for an actress who could exude the raw sexuality of the film's seductive vamp, Lola Lola, he discovered Marlene DIETRICH on the Berlin stage. It was the beginning of a five-year Pygmalion-Galatea (some say Svengali-Trilby) association during which von Sternberg molded Marlene's on- and offscreen personality to conform to an image of his conception, thus transforming her from a plump *fräulein* into a glamorous, sensuous star. *The Blue Angel,* a classic of screen erotica, was a tremendous international success. Dietrich followed von Sternberg to Hollywood, leaving behind her husband and child. The six Dietrich films von Sternberg directed there—*Morocco, Dishonored, Shanghai Express, Blonde Venus, The Scarlet Empress,* and *The Devil Is a Woman*—constituted cumulatively the peak achievement of his career. They all bore his unmistakable personal signature, all characterized by his visual bravura and the ever present scrims, veils, nets, fog, or smoke between subject and camera.

Von Sternberg was among the most enigmatic of Hollywood's directors, a volatile man of mystery and contradiction, proud and arrogant, stubborn and secretive. He was the last of the Hollywood directors who dressed the part, complete with boots and sometimes even a turban. His films rarely had wide commercial appeal and after his working relationship with Dietrich and Paramount ended in 1935 he found the major studios unresponsive to his ideas. After making two films for Columbia—an interesting version of *Crime and Punishment* and an adaptation of an operetta, *The King Steps Out*—he went to England in 1937. There he began his most ambitious production, an adaptation of Robert Graves's historical novel *I Claudius,* starring Charles Laughton in the title role. The production, under the aegis of Alexander Korda, was ill fated from the start. After several weeks of filming, the production was halted as a direct result of an injury suffered by its feminine lead, Merle Oberon, in an automobile accident. For reasons that remain clouded in mystery to this day, the production was never resumed and the film remained unfinished. In the late 60s, BBC-TV in England produced a feature-length documentary about the *I Claudius* mystery, entitled 'The Epic That Never Was.' It was shown in the US on educational television. The many excerpts from the unfinished film which were shown in the documentary suggest that this might have been not only von Sternberg's greatest work but one of the finest pictorial symphonies in the history of the cinema.

Returning to the US in 1938, von Sternberg agreed to make two films for MGM. On the first, he was replaced by another director after several days of shooting. He completed the second with mediocre results. Von Sternberg re-attained his form with *The Shanghai Gesture* (1941), but his subsequent Hollywood films, made unhappily and halfheartedly for Howard Hughes, were infrequent and rather routine. The most important achievement in the latter phase of his career was a film he made in 1953 in Japan. *Ana-Ta-Han* (or *The Saga of Anatahan*) was a remarkable dramatized re-creation of a true WW II incident about a group of Japanese marines who continued to man their positions on an island for seven years after the conclusion of WW II, because they refused to believe that the war had ended in Japan's defeat.

In the mid-50s, von Sternberg went into semiretirement in his modern Los Angeles mansion and spent much of his last years traveling to international film festivals and lecturing in universities in the US and abroad. In 1965 he published a bitter autobiography, *Fun in a Chinese Laundry.* He died of a heart ailment at the age of 75.

FILMS (as director): *The Salvation Hunters* (also prod., sc.), *The Masked Bride* (completed by Christy Cabanne) 1925; *The Exquisite Sinner* (also co-sc.; completed by Phil Rosen), *A Woman of the Sea/The Sea Gull* (also sc.; shown only once but never released) 1926; *Children of Divorce* (several sequences only for Frank Lloyd; uncredited), *It* (several sequences only for Clarence Badger; uncredited), *Underworld* 1927; *The Last Command* (also sc.?), *The Dragnet, The Docks of New York* 1928; *The Case of Lena Smith, Thunderbolt* 1929; *Der blaue Engel/The Blue Angel* (also sc.; Ger.), *Morocco* 1930; *Dishonored* (also story), *An American Tragedy* (also co-adapt., sc.) 1931; *Shanghai Express, Blonde Venus* (also story) 1932; *The Scarlet Empress* 1934; *The Devil Is a Woman* (also phot.), *Crime and Punishment* 1935; *The King Steps Out* 1936; *I Claudius* (also sc.; unfinished) 1937; *Sergeant Madden* 1939; *The Shanghai Gesture* (also sc.) 1941; *The Town* (doc. short) 1944; *Duel in the Sun* (directed some scenes during brief illness of King Vidor while on the set as a color consultant; uncredited) 1946; *Macao* 1952; *The Saga of Anatahan/Ana-Ta-Han* (also prod., sc., phot., narr. of English version; Jap.) 1953; *Jet Pilot* (made in 1950; release delayed by Howard Hughes) 1957.

Sternhagen, Frances. Actress. Born on Jan. 13, 1930, Washington, D.C. Capable character player of the American stage and screen. Trained at the drama department of Vassar College, at the Perry-Mansfield School of the Theatre, and with Stanford Meisner at New York's Neighborhood Playhouse, she began her professional career in 1953 with the Arena Stage in her hometown and made her New York debut off Broadway in 1955. She later performed in many Broadway productions, winning a Tony Award for 'The Good Doctor' (1973), and accolades in such plays as 'Equus' (1974) and 'On Golden Pond' (1979). She played a broad range of roles in films from the late 60s.

FILMS: *Up the Down Staircase, The Tiger Makes Out* 1967; *The Hospital* 1971; *Two People* 1973; *Fedora* 1978; *Starting Over* 1979; *Outland* 1981; *Independence Day, Romantic Comedy* 1983; *Bright Lights Big City* 1988; *Communion, See You in the Morning* 1989; *Sibling Rivalry, Misery* 1990; *Doc Hollywood* 1991; *Raising Cain* 1992; *The Grass Harp* 1996.

Stevenin, Jean-Francois. Director, actor. Born in 1943 in France. An actor in films of Francois TRUFFAUT and others, he turned to directing in the 1980s.

FILMS INCLUDE (as actor): *The Wild Child* 1970; *Day for Night* 1973; *Small Change* 1976; *Mais Ou Et Donc Ornicar* 1979; *The Dogs of War* (UK) 1980; *Like a Turtle on Its Back* 1981; *Passion* (Fr./Switz.) 1983; *Parole de Flic* 1985; *Je Hais Les Acteurs, Menage, Salome* 1986; *Sale Destin!* 1987; *36 Fillette, Y'a Bon Les Blancs, Les Maris, Les Femmes, Les Amants* 1988. As director: *Passe Montagne* 1979; *Double Messieurs* (also prod., sc.) 1986.

Stevens, Andrew. See STEVENS, Stella.

Stevens, Connie. Actress, singer. Born Concetta Rosalie Ann Ingolia, on Aug. 8, 1938, in Brooklyn, N.Y. Perky, blonde leading lady of Hollywood films. She made her debut as ingenue in teen-oriented films after winning several talent contests. She also made a number of popular recordings and starred on TV ('Hawaiian Eye,' etc.) and on Broadway ('Star Spangled Girl'). Formerly married to actor James Stacy and to Eddie FISHER.

FILMS INCLUDE: *Young and Dangerous* 1957; *Rock-a-Bye Baby, The Party Crashers* 1958; *Parrish, Susan Slade* 1961; *Palm Springs Weekend* 1963; *Two on a Guillotine, Never Too Late* 1965; *Way... Way Out* 1966; *The Grissom Gang* 1971; *Scorchy* 1976; *Sgt. Pepper's Lonely Hearts Club Band* 1978; *Grease 2* 1982; *Back to the Beach* 1987; *Tapeheads* 1988.

Stevens, Craig. Actor. Born Gail Shikles, Jr., on July 8, 1918, in Liberty, Mo. A schoolteacher's son, he was headed for a career in dentistry when he got the acting bug in dramatic classes at the University of Kansas. After some training at Paramount's acting school and the Pasadena Playhouse and brief experience in stock, he was signed by Warners in 1941 and for the next two decades played routine leads in second features and supporting roles in major productions of that and other studios. But it was on TV that he gained stardom in the late 50s, playing the title role in the popular series 'Peter Gunn' (1959–63). He later appeared in many other TV productions as well as in occasional stage plays, sometimes opposite his wife (from 1944 until her death in 1993), Alexis SMITH.

FILMS INCLUDE: *Affectionately Yours, Dive Bomber, Steel Against the Sky* 1941; *Spy Ship, Secret Enemies, The Hidden Hand* 1942; *The Doughgirls, Since You Went Away* 1944; *Roughly Speaking* 1945; *Humoresque* 1946; *The Man I Love* 1947; *Night Unto Night* 1949; *Where the Sidewalk Ends* 1950; *Drums in the Deep South* 1951; *Phone Call from a Stranger* 1952; *Murder Without Tears, Abbott and Costello Meet Dr. Jekyll and Mr. Hyde* 1953; *The French Line* 1954; *The Deadly Mantis* 1957; *Buchanan Rides Alone* 1958; *Gunn* 1967; *S.O.B.* 1981; *La Truite/The Trout* (Fr.) 1982.

Stevens, George. Director. *b.* Dec. 18, 1904, Oakland, Calif. *d.* 1975. Both his parents were actors and he made his debut on the stage at the age of five, performing in his father's traveling company. He entered films in 1921 as an assistant cameraman. In 1927 he joined Hal Roach as a cameraman and worked on many of the Laurel and Hardy comedy shorts. Late in 1930 he was assigned by Roach to direct the two-reel comedy series "The Boy Friends." In 1932 he moved on to Universal and from there to RKO, still as a director of shorts. The following year he graduated to feature films. After several routine comedies, he scored his first big success with *Alice Adams,* a fine piece of small-town Americana noted for an inspired performance by Katharine Hepburn. His reputation was further enhanced in 1936 with *Swing Time,* one of the best of the Fred Astaire-Ginger Rogers cycle of screen musicals.

Stevens then demonstrated his versatility with *Gunga Din,* one of the most exciting of Hollywood's British Empire–theme adventure pictures.

During WW II, Stevens served as a major at the head of an Army Signal Corps film unit and was responsible for the coverage of such events as the liberation of Denmark, the freeing of the inmates of the Dachau concentration camp, and the capture of Hitler's Berchtesgaden hideaway. Stevens was released from the service in 1945 as a lieutenant colonel.

Stevens's reputation reached its apex in the early 50s with *A Place in the Sun* (1951), an excellently played screen adaptation of Dreiser's *An American Tragedy,* which won Stevens his first best director Oscar. He won an Irving Thalberg Memorial Academy Award "for high quality of production" in 1953, the year he directed his famous idyllic Western, *Shane.* He received his second best director Academy Award for *Giant* (1956), an adaptation of the sprawling Ferber novel.

Stevens was one of Hollywood's least productive directors in the quantitative sense. Intent on perfection and visual authenticity, he would spend many months, sometimes years, on pre- and postproduction. He reportedly covered every scene from any possible angle, shooting at a ratio much greater than deemed necessary by most Hollywood directors. But the results, more often than not, justified the extra investment in time and money and Stevens scored a remarkably high average both with critics and with ticket buyers. For most of his career his work was held in continuous high esteem by the American critical establishment, although his reputation suffered a decline in the 60s, following his uninspired handling of the superspectacle *The Greatest Story Ever Told* (1965), which he took five years to complete. His son is George STEVENS, JR.

FEATURE FILMS: *The Cohens and Kellys in Trouble* 1933; *Bachelor Bait, Kentucky Kernels* 1934; *Laddie, The Nitwits, Alice Adams, Annie Oakley* 1935; *Swing Time* 1936; *Quality Street, A Damsel in Distress* 1937; *Vivacious Lady* (also prod.) 1938; *Gunga Din* (also prod.) 1939; *Vigil in the Night* (also prod.) 1940; *Penny Serenade* (also prod.) 1941; *Woman of the Year, The Talk of the Town* (also prod.) 1942; *The More the Merrier* (also prod.) 1943; *I Remember Mama* (also exec. prod.) 1948; *A Place in the Sun* (also prod.) 1951; *Something to Live For* (also prod.) 1952; *Shane* (also prod.) 1953; *Giant* (also co-prod.) 1956; *The Diary of Anne Frank* (also prod.) 1959; *The Greatest Story Ever Told* (also prod.) 1965; *The Only Game in Town* 1970.

Stevens, George, Jr. Executive. Born on Apr. 3, 1932, in Los Angeles. *ed.* Occidental Coll. A former TV producer-director, he assisted his father, director George STEVENS, on several productions of the late 50s and early 60s. From 1962 to 1967 he served as chief of the Motion Picture Service of the USIA and in that capacity produced the celebrated documentary *John F. Kennedy: Years of Lightning—Day of Drums.* From 1967 through 1979 he was the director of the AMERICAN FILM INSTITUTE. In 1976 he produced the institute's compilation film *America at the Movies.* He wrote, produced, and directed a loving tribute to his father, *George Stevens: A Filmmaker's Journey* (1984) and in 1991 won an Emmy as co-executive producer of the TV miniseries 'Separate But Equal.'

Stevens, Inger. Actress. *b.* Inger Stensland, Oct. 18, 1934, Stockholm. *d.* 1970. The product of a broken home, she arrived in the US at age 13 with her father, who was attending Harvard on a Fulbright scholarship. When her father remarried and moved to Manhattan, Kans., she ran away from home and at 16 made her show business debut in Kansas city burlesque. At 18 she arrived in New York, where she worked in the garment center and as a chorus girl in the Latin Quarter while studying at the Actors Studio and making the rounds of Broadway agents. Several TV commercials led to assignments in TV plays and in 1956 she finally made her Broadway debut in a short-lived play called 'Debut.' The following year she broke into films and gradually gained popularity as a star, especially after her success in the TV series 'The Farmer's Daughter' (1963–66). Her professional success was constantly overshadowed by personal unhappiness, however. In 1955 she married her agent, but they separated after four months. Her fractured romances with Bing Crosby (just before his last marriage) and a famous married star contributed to the depression that led her to attempt suicide in 1959, after which she remained blind for two weeks. After her death of an overdose of barbiturates at the age of 36 it was revealed that she had been secretly married (from 1961) to black musician Isaac (Ike) Jones.

FILMS: *Man on Fire* 1957; *Cry Terror, The Buccaneer* 1958; *The World The Flesh and the Devil* 1959; *The New Interns* 1964; *A Guide for the Married Man, A Time for Killing* 1967; *Firecreek, Madigan, 5 Card Stud, Hang 'Em High* 1968; *House of Cards, A Dream of Kings* 1969.

Stevens, Leith. Composer-arranger-conductor. *b.* 1909, Mount Moriah, Mo. *d.* 1970. A child prodigy, he started his professional career at the age of 11 as an accompanist to vocalists in Kansas City and made his debut as a conductor there at 16. In 1927 he was awarded a Juilliard Foundation Fellowship and three years later joined CBS radio as an arranger and later conductor and composer. His first film score, for RKO's *Syncopation* (1942), included his 'American Rhapsody,' which was later performed in concert halls. After returning from WW II service as radio director for the Southwest Pacific Area with the Office of War Information, he composed scores for many other films and numerous TV shows. He died at 60 of a heart attack just minutes after having learned that his wife had been killed in a traffic accident.

FILMS INCLUDE: *Syncopation* 1942; *Night Song* 1947; *All My Sons* 1948; *Destination Moon* 1950; *When Worlds Collide* 1951; *Beware My Lovely, Eight Iron Men* 1952; *The Hitch-Hiker* 1953; *The Wild One* 1954; *The Scarlet Hour, Julie* 1956; *The Garment Jungle, The James Dean Story* 1957; *Bullwhip* 1958; *The Five Pennies, The Gene Krupa Story* 1959; *Hell to Eternity* 1960; *Man-Trap, On the Double* 1961; *The Interns* 1962; *A New Kind of Love* 1963; *The Night of the Grizzly* 1966; *Chuka* 1967.

Stevens, Leslie. Director, producer, screenwriter, playwright. Born Feb. 3, 1924, Washington, D.C. *ed.* Yale Drama School. At the age of 15 he sold his first play, 'The Mechanical Rat,' to Orson Welles's Mercury Theater. He then wrote a number of other plays, and after returning from WW II service as a captain in the Air Force, he began producing and directing plays as well. He began his association with cinema in the late 50s, at first as a screenwriter, then director-producer-writer of two offbeat films that starred his former wife (she later committed suicide) Kate Manx. One of his features, the occult-theme *Incubus* (1966), had the distinction of possibly being the only film whose entire dialogue was spoken in Esperanto! He has written prolifically for TV and created, produced, and directed such series as 'Stoney Burke,' 'Outer Limits,' 'It Takes a Thief,' 'McCloud,' and 'The Name of the Game.' He has also directed a number of TV movies.

FILMS: *The Left-Handed Gun* (sc.) 1958; *Private Property* (dir., sc., co-prod.) 1960; *Marriage-Go-Round* (sc., from own play) 1961; *Hero's Island* (dir., sc., prod.) 1962; *The War Lord* (play basis, 'The Lovers') 1965; *Incubus* (dir., sc.) 1966; *Buck Rogers in the 25th Century* (superv. prod., co-sc.), *Battlestar Galactica* (superv. prod.) 1979; *Three Kinds of Heat* (dir., sc.) 1987; *Return to the Blue Lagoon* (sc.) 1991.

Stevens, Mark. Actor. Born Richard Stevens, on Dec. 13, 1915, in Cleveland. Trained as a painter but began an acting career in Canada, on the stage and on radio. After a stint as an announcer and production manager in an Akron, Ohio, radio station, he entered films in the early 40s, briefly using the pseudonym Stephen Richards. He was making headway as a leading man in several better-than-average productions of the late 40s but was later victimized by poor vehicles. He also directed and produced several mediocre films. Not to be confused with a porno film star who spells his name both Marc and Mark Stevens.

FILMS INCLUDE: *Passage to Marseille* 1944; *Objective Burma, Within These Walls, Pride of the Marines* 1945; *From This Day Forward, The Dark Corner* 1946; *I Wonder Who's Kissing Her Now* 1947; *The Street with No Name, The Snake Pit* 1948; *Sand, Oh You Beautiful Doll, Dancing in the Dark* 1949; *Please Believe Me, Between Midnight and Dawn* 1950; *Target Unknown, Reunion in Reno, Little Egypt* 1951; *Mutiny, Torpedo Alley* 1952; *Jack Slade* 1953; *Cry Vengeance* (also dir., prod.) 1954; *Timetable* (also dir., prod.) 1956; *Gunsmoke in Tucson* 1958; *September Storm* 1960; *Fate Is the Hunter* 1964; *Tierra del Fuego/Sunscorched* (also dir., co-sc.; Sp./Ger.) 1965; *Frozen Alive* (UK/Ger.) 1966.

Stevens, Onslow. Actor. *b.* Onslow Ford Stevenson, Mar. 29, 1902, Los Angeles. *d.* 1977. A second-generation actor (his father was character player Houseley Stevenson), he made his debut in 1926 at the Pasadena Community Playhouse, where he later directed and appeared in numerous plays in the intervals between his occasional leads and many character parts on Broadway and in numerous films. Often played heavies.

FILMS INCLUDE: *Heroes of the West* (serial), *Once in a Lifetime* 1932; *Peg o' My Heart* (lead opposite Marion Davies), *The Secret of the Blue Room, Only Yesterday, Counsellor-at-Law* 1933; *Bombay Mail, The Vanishing Shadow* (serial; lead), *In Love with Life* (lead) 1934; *The Three Musketeers* (as Aramis), *Grand Exit* 1935; *Under Two Flags, Three on the Trail, Murder with Pictures* 1936; *You Can't Buy Luck* (lead), *Flight from Glory* 1937; *When Tomorrow Comes, Those High Grey Walls* 1939; *The Man Who Wouldn't Talk, Mystery Sea Raider* 1940; *The Monster and the Girl* 1941; *Appointment in Berlin* 1943; *House of Dracula* 1945; *O.S.S., Angel on My Shoulder* 1946; *Night Has a Thousand Eyes, Walk a Crooked Mile* 1948; *Red Hot and Blue* 1949; *Mark of the Gorilla* 1950; *Sealed Cargo, Sirocco* 1951; *A Lion Is in the Streets* 1953; *Them* 1954; *New York Confidential* 1955; *Tribute to a Bad Man* 1956; *The Buccaneer* 1958; *Lonelyhearts* 1959; *All the Fine Young Cannibals* 1960; *The Couch* 1962.

Stevens, Stella. Actress. Born Estelle Egglestone, on Oct. 1, 1936, in Hot Coffee, Miss. *ed.* Memphis State. A delectable blonde projecting a mixture of sensuality and innocence as a *Playboy* centerfold, she first gained motion picture attention in the role of Appassionata von Climax in the film version of *Li'l Abner.* For a decade or so she remained a popular star. In 1979 she produced and directed a 90-minute documentary, *The American Heroine,* and in 1989 directed a Canadian feature, *The Ranch.* Her son, Andrew Stevens (*b.* June 10, 1955, Memphis, Tenn.), is also a film actor.

FILMS INCLUDE: *Say One for Me, Li'l Abner* 1959; *Man-Trap* 1961; *Too Late Blues* 1962; *The Courtship of Eddie's Father, The Nutty Professor* 1963; *Advance to the Rear* 1964; *Synanon* 1965; *The Silencers* 1966; *How to Save a Marriage—And Ruin Your Life, Sol Madrid* 1968; *The Mad Room* 1969; *The Ballad of Cable Hogue* 1970; *A Town Called Hell* (Sp.) 1971; *Slaughter, The Poseidon Adventure* 1972; *Arnold* 1973; *Cleopatra Jones and the Casino of Gold* 1975; *Las Vegas Lady, Nickelodeon* 1976; *The Manitou* 1978; *The American Heroine* (doc.; prod., dir. only) *Wacko, Chained Heat* 1983; *The Longshot, Monster in the Closet* 1986; *Adventures Beyond Belief/Neat and Tidy* 1988; *The Ranch* (dir. only; Can.) 1989; *The Terror Within II* 1991; *Molly and Gina* 1994.

Stevenson, Juliet. Actress. Born Juliet Stevens on October 30, 1956, in Essex, England. *ed.* Royal Academy of Dramatic Arts, London. Classically trained, charming British actress, a favorite on the stages of London's West End. Her performance in 'Death and the Maiden' (1991) won praise from critics. Her film career took flight with her role as a woman unwilling to accept the death of her lover in *Truly, Madly, Deeply* (1991).

FILMS: *Drowning by the Numbers* 1987; *Truly Madly Deeply* 1991; *The Secret Rapture, The Trial* 1993; *Emma* 1996.

Stevenson, Robert. Director. *b.* 1905, London. *d.* 1986. The son of a successful businessman, he studied science at Cambridge, excelling in aerodynamics. Graduate studies in psychology at that university led to his interest in film. He entered the industry as a screenwriter in 1930 and began directing two years later. Proving himself a skillful craftsman with sumptuous productions like *Tudor Rose* (1936, seen in the US as *Nine Days a Queen*) and *King Solomon's Mines* (1937), he soon moved into the forefront of British cinema. In 1939 he was brought to Hollywood by David O. Selznick, who kept him under contract until 1949 but never used him to direct any of his productions and instead loaned him out to various studios. In 1949 he joined RKO and from 1956 he worked at the Walt Disney studios. An elegant stylist and a proficient technician, he directed such diverse films as the period romance *Jane Eyre,* the documentary-style crime drama *To the Ends of the Earth,* and the commercially successful fairy tale *Mary Poppins.* Married and divorced actress Anna LEE.

FILMS: In the UK—*Happy Ever After* (co-dir. with Paul Martin; UK/Ger.) 1932; *Falling for You* (co-dir. with Jack Hulbert) 1933; *Jack of All Trades/The Two of Us* (co-dir. with Hulbert) 1934; *Tudor Rose/Nine Days a Queen* (also sc.), *The Man Who Changed His Mind/The Man Who Lived Again* (also sc.) 1936; *King Solomon's Mines, Non-Stop New York* 1937; *Owd Bob/To the Victor* 1938; *The Ware Case* (also prod.), *A Young Man's Fancy* (also story), *Return to Yesterday* 1939. In the US—*Tom Brown's Schooldays* 1940; *Back Street* 1941; *Joan of Paris* 1942; *Forever and a Day* (co-dir., co-prod.) 1943; *Jane Eyre* (also co-sc.) 1944; *Dishonored Lady* 1947; *To the Ends of the Earth* 1948; *The Woman on Pier 13/I Married a Communist* 1949; *Walk Softly Stranger* 1950; *My Forbidden Past* 1951; *The Las Vegas Story* 1952; *Johnny Tremain, Old Yeller* 1957; *Darby O'Gill and the Little People* 1959; *Kidnapped* (UK) 1960; *The Absent-Minded Professor* 1961; *In Search of the Castaways* (US/UK) 1962; *Son of Flubber* 1963; *The Misadventures of Merlin Jones, Mary Poppins* 1964; *The Monkey's Uncle, That Darn Cat* 1965; *The Gnome-Mobile* 1967; *Blackbeard's Ghost* 1968; *The Love Bug* 1969; *Bedknobs and Broomsticks* 1971; *Herbie Rides Again, The Island at the Top of the World* 1974; *One of Our Dinosaurs Is Missing* (US/UK) 1975; *The Shaggy D.A.* 1976.

Stewart, Alexandra. Actress. Born on June 10, 1939, in Montreal. Intriguing leading lady and second lead of French and international films since the late 50s, following studies in Paris.

FILMS INCLUDE: *Les Motards* 1958; *Les Liaisons dangereuses* (bit) 1959; *L'Eau à la Bouche/A Game for Six Lovers, Tarzan the Magnificent* (UK), *Exodus* (US) 1960; *La Mort de Belle/The Passion of Slow Fire, Les Mauvais Coups/Naked Autumn, La Morte-Saison des Amours/The Season for Love* 1961; *Dragées au Poivre/Sweet and Sour* (Fr./It.), *Le Feu Follet/The Fire Within* (Fr./It.), *Das grosse Liebesspiel/And So to Bed* (Aus./Ger.) 1963; *Mickey One* (US), *Marcia Nuziale* (It.) 1965; *Maroc 7* (UK) 1966; *Waiting for Caroline* (originally made for Canadian TV) 1967; *La Mariée était en Noir/The Bride Wore Black* (Fr./It.), *Only When I Larf* (UK) 1968; *The Man Who Had Power Over Women* (UK) 1970; *Zeppelin* (Fr./UK) 1971; *Les Soleils de l'Ile de Pâques* 1972; *La Nuit américaine/Day for Night* 1973; *The Marseilles Contract/The Destructors* (UK/Fr.) 1974; *Black Moon* 1975; *Julie Pot de Colle* 1977; *Goodbye Emmanuelle, La Petite Fille en Velours bleu, In Praise of Older Women* (Can.) 1978; *Phobia* (Can.) 1980; *Agency* (Can.), *The Last Chase* (Can.), *Chanel Solitaire* (US/Fr.), *Madame Claude 2/Intimate Moments, Aiutami a sognare/Help Me Dream* (It.) 1981; *Au-delà de cette Limite votre Ticket n'est plus valable/Your Ticket Is No Longer Valid* (Can./Fr.), *Cercasi Gesù* (It.), *La Guerillera* (Fr./It./Sp./Port.) 1982; *Femmes* (Fr./Sp.) 1983; *Le Bon Plaisir, Le Sang des autres/The Blood of Others* 1984; *Peau d'Ange/Angel Skin, Under the Cherry Moon* (US) 1986; *Der Passagier/Welcome to Germany* 1988.

Stewart, Anita. Actress. *b.* Anna M. Stewart, Feb. 7, 1895, Brooklyn, N.Y. *d.* 1961. The sister-in-law of director-actor Ralph INCE, she entered films with Vitagraph in 1911 and then starred in many of the company's productions. She was sometimes billed as Anna Stewart early in her career. When she signed with Louis B. Mayer in 1917 before the expiration of her Vitagraph contract, the latter company sued and won a landmark case in studio-actor labor relations. She remained an important star until the advent of the talkies, when she retired. For a while she headed her own production company with L. B. Mayer as her production executive. Her brother, George Stewart, was also an actor in silent films. She authored a novel, *The Devil's Toy.*

FILMS INCLUDE: *Her Choice, The Godmother, The Wood Violet, The Song of the Shell* 1912; *The Moulding, Two's Company Three's a Crowd, The Song Bird of the North, Sweet Deception, The Swan Girl, The Wreck* 1913; *A Million Bid, Shadows of the Past, Wife Wanted, The Painted World, Lincoln the Lover* 1914; *The Sins of the Mothers, The Juggernaut, The Goddess* (serial) 1915; *My Lady's Slipper, The Suspect, The Daring of Diana, The Combat* 1916; *The Girl Philippa, The Glory of Yolanda, The Message of the Mouse* 1917; *Virtuous Wives* 1918; *A Midnight Romance, Mary Regan, Her Kingdom of Dreams, The Mind-the-Paint Girl, In Old Kentucky* 1919; *The Fighting Shepherdess, The Yellow Typhoon* 1920; *Playthings of Destiny, The Invisible Fear, Sowing the Wind, Her Mad Bargain* 1921; *A Question of Honor, Rose o' the Sea, The Woman He Married* 1922; *The Love Piker* 1923; *The Great White Way* 1924; *The Boomerang, Never the Twain Shall Meet* 1925;

Rustling for Cupid, The Prince of Pilsen 1926; *Wild Geese* 1927; *Romance of a Rogue, Name the Woman, Sisters of Eve* 1928.

Stewart, Donald Ogden. Screenwriter, playwright, novelist. *b.* Nov. 30, 1894, Columbus, Ohio. *d.* 1980. *ed.* Yale. After WW I service in the Navy and travels in Europe, he settled in New York and began writing satirical novels, which were quite popular in the 20s. In 1928 he was introduced to the theater by a college chum, Philip Barry, who wrote the part of socialite Nick Potter in his play 'Holiday' with Stewart in mind. Stewart played the part on Broadway. Fascinated with stage life, he wrote his first play, 'Rebound' (1930), in which he also played one of the leading parts, and followed this with a musical 'Fine and Dandy' (1930). As early as 1925, Stewart had been assigned to adapt one of his own novels for the screen, but the project was shelved and instead he wrote an adaptation of the play 'Brown of Harvard,' which was released in 1926. In 1930, Stewart settled in Hollywood as a screenwriter, following an appearance in a supporting part in the film *Not So Dumb.* He soon gained a reputation for his sophisticated screenplays and sparkling dialogue. He won an Academy Award for the script of *The Philadelphia Story,* which he adapted from the Philip Barry play. After Hitler's rise to power he became involved in the political activities of the Hollywood Anti-Nazi League. This association came back to haunt him during the McCarthy era, when it was claimed the organization had been a cover-up for a Communist cell. Blacklisted, he left Hollywood for good in 1951 and settled in London, where he wrote his autobiography in 1970.

FILMS: *Brown of Harvard* (adapt.) 1926; *Laughter* (dial.) 1930; *Finn and Hattie* (novel basis, *Mr. and Mrs. Haddock Abroad*), *Rebound* (dial.; from own play), *Tarnished Lady* (sc., from own story) 1931; *Smilin' Through* (dial.) 1932; *The White Sister* (sc.), *Another Language* (addnl. dial.), *Going Hollywood* (sc.) 1933; *Dinner at Eight* (addnl. dial.), *The Barretts of Wimpole Street* (co-sc.) 1934; *No More Ladies* (co-sc.) 1935; *The Prisoner of Zenda* (co-sc., addnl. dial.) 1937; *Holiday* (co-sc.), *Marie Antoinette* (co-sc.) 1938; *Love Affair* (co-sc.), *The Night of Nights* (story, sc.) 1939; *Kitty Foyle* (co-sc.), *The Philadelphia Story* (sc.) 1940; *That Uncertain Feeling* (sc.), *A Woman's Face* (co-sc.), *Smilin' Through* (co-sc.) 1941; *Tales of Manhattan* (co-sc.), *Keeper of the Flame* (sc.) 1942; *Without Love* (sc.) 1945; *Life with Father* (sc.), *Cass Timberlane* (sc.) 1947; *Edward My Son* (sc.) 1949; *Escapade* (sc., under pseudonym Gilbert Holland; UK) 1955; *Moment of Danger/Malaga* (co-sc.; UK) 1960.

Stewart, Elaine. Actress. Born Elsa Steinberg, on May 31, 1929, in Montclair, N.J. Striking leading lady of Hollywood films of the 50s. She worked as usherette-cashier in her hometown movie house and modeled before breaking into films. In the 70s she was seen as a blackjack dealer in a TV game show, which her husband produced.

FILMS INCLUDE: *Sailor Beware* 1951; *Everything I Have Is Yours, The Bad and the Beautiful* 1952; *Young Bess* (as Anne Boleyn), *Take the High Ground* 1953; *Brigadoon, The Adventures of Haji Baba* 1954; *The Tattered Dress, Night Passage* 1957; *High Hell* 1958; *Escort West* 1959; *The Rise and Fall of Legs Diamond* 1960; *Le Sette Sfide/The Seven Revenges* (It.), *Most Dangerous Man Alive* 1961.

Stewart, James. Actor. *b.* May 20, 1908, in Indiana, Pa. *d.* 1997. An amateur magician and accordionist from boyhood, he made his acting debut in a Boy Scout play and later appeared in shows of the Princeton Triangle Club. After graduating from Princeton in 1932 with a degree in architecture, he was persuaded by classmate Joshua Logan to join the University Players at Falmouth, Mass., whose members included such future stars as Henry FONDA and Margaret SULLAVAN. Stewart and Fonda were roommates when they both took their first steps on Broadway later that year and also when they first arrived in Hollywood in 1935. They remained good friends, although in the ensuing years they drifted apart in their political and social views as Stewart became a spokesman for the conservative cause. Miss Sullavan, Fonda's ex-wife, was instrumental in Stewart's early screen career by insisting time and again that he be given parts in her films.

A gawky, gangling young man with a slow, hesitant drawl and a shy country-boy manner, Stewart was an oddity among Hollywood's leading men and a challenge to casting directors. But the oddity was soon revealed as a unique asset, when Stewart's clod-kicking embarrassment and pleasantly nasal delivery were put to work in W. S. Van Dyke's *It's a Wonderful World* (1939) and in Frank Capra's sentimental social comedies *You Can't Take It with You* (1938) and *Mr. Smith Goes to Washington* (1939). He won the New York Film Critics best actor award for the last of these three films. The following year, 1940, he won an Academy Award for *The Philadelphia Story* and took his place among Hollywood's leading stars.

During WW II, Stewart flew 20 missions over Germany as a bomber pilot, rising from a private to a full colonel. Until his retirement from the service in 1968, he was a brigadier general in the Air Force Reserve, the highest ranking entertainer in the US military. After the war, Stewart's screen personality matured and his roles became more diversified. He played detectives, Western heroes, and other masculine types and only occasionally returned to the shy, absentminded characters he had played in the past. In the early 50s he became one of the first Hollywood stars to elect to work for a percentage of the profits, a decision that proved fortuitous when he appeared in several box-office hits by Hitchcock and other leading directors.

Stewart was cited again by the New York Film Critics in 1959 for his performance in Preminger's *Anatomy of a Murder.* He was nominated for an Oscar for that film as well as for *Mr. Smith Goes to Washington, It's a Wonderful Life* (his favorite film), and *Harvey.* Stewart's career as a leading star extended into the early 70s, when he also made a Broadway comeback, in 'Harvey,' and headed the cast in two TV shows, the comedy series 'The James Stewart Show' (1971–72) and the drama series 'Hawkins' (1973–74). But he sustained the adulation of the public for many years after, his fans increasing in number with the proliferation of videotape releases and TV screenings of his old films. He was honored for life achievement by the American Film Institute in 1980, by the Kennedy Center in 1983, and by the Film Society of Lincoln Center in 1990. During the 1985 Oscar Ceremony he was honored with a special Academy Award "for 50 years of meaningful performances, for his high ideals, both on and off the screen, with the respect and affection of his colleagues." That same year he received the Medal of Freedom, America's highest civilian honor. A superpatriot, he was a hawk on Vietnam and has allied himself with various conservative groups on political and economic issues as well. His personal life has been well shielded from adverse publicity. After many years as Hollywood's most eligible bachelor, he married at the age of 41, and remained an exemplary husband through 45 years of marriage, which ended with his wife Gloria's death in 1994. Together they had four children. Author: *Jimmy Stewart and His Poems* (1989).

FILMS: *The Murder Man* 1935; *Next Time We Love, Rose Marie, Wife vs. Secretary, Small Town Girl, Speed, The Gorgeous Hussy, Born to Dance, After the Thin Man* 1936; *Seventh Heaven, The Last Gangster, Navy Blue and Gold* 1937; *Of Human Hearts, Vivacious Lady, The Shopworn Angel, You*

Can't Take It with You 1938; *Made for Each Other, Ice Follies of 1939, It's a Wonderful World, Mr. Smith Goes to Washington, Destry Rides Again* 1939; *The Shop Around the Corner, The Mortal Storm, No Time for Comedy, The Philadelphia Story* 1940; *Come Live with Me, Pot o' Gold, Ziegfeld Girl* 1941; *It's a Wonderful Life, Magic Town* 1947; *On Our Merry Way/A Miracle Can Happen, Call Northside 777, Rope* 1948; *You Gotta Stay Happy, The Stratton Story* (as baseball player Monty Stratton) 1949; *Malaya, Winchester 73, Broken Arrow, The Jackpot, Harvey* 1950; *No Highway/No Highway in the Sky* (UK) 1951; *The Greatest Show on Earth, Bend of the River, Carbine Williams* 1952; *The Naked Spur, Thunder Bay* 1953; *The Glenn Miller Story* (title role), *Rear Window* 1954; *The Far Country, Strategic Air Command, The Man from Laramie* 1955; *The Man Who Knew Too Much* 1956; *The Spirit of St. Louis* (as aviator Charles A. Lindbergh), *Night Passage* 1957; *Vertigo, Bell Book and Candle* 1958; *Anatomy of a Murder, The FBI Story* 1959; *The Mountain Road* 1960; *X-15* (narrator only), *Two Rode Together* 1961; *The Man Who Shot Liberty Valance, Mr. Hobbs Takes a Vacation, How the West Was Won* 1962; *Take Her She's Mine* 1963; *Cheyenne Autumn* (as Wyatt Earp) 1964; *Dear Brigitte, Shenandoah* 1965; *The Flight of the Phoenix, The Rare Breed* 1966; *Firecreek, Bandolero!* 1968; *The Cheyenne Social Club* 1970; *Fools' Parade* 1971; *That's Entertainment* (on-screen co-narr.) 1974; *The Shootist* 1976; *Airport 77* 1977; *The Big Sleep* (UK), *The Magic of Lassie* 1978; *Afurika Monogatari/A Tale of Africa/The Green Horizon* (Jap.) 1981; *An American Tail 2: Fievel Goes West* (v/o) 1991.

Stewart, Paul. Actor, TV director. *b.* Mar. 13, 1908, New York City. *d.* 1986. *ed.* Columbia. On the stage since his early teens, he joined Orson Welles's Mercury Theater in 1938 and appeared in several of its stage and radio productions, including the famous 'War of the Worlds' broadcast. He made his screen debut in Welles's *Citizen Kane* (1941), in the role of Kane's oily valet. He subsequently played many character parts in films, typically as a cold-blooded, skeptical type, often a gangster. From the mid-50s he directed for TV but also continued working as an actor both on TV and in films. Another Paul Stewart is a special effects artist associated with the disaster that occurred during filming of John LANDIS's segment of *Twilight Zone—The Movie* (1983).

FILMS INCLUDE: *Citizen Kane* 1941; *Johnny Eager* 1942; *Mr. Lucky* 1943; *Champion, The Window* 1949; *Twelve O' Clock High, Edge of Doom, Walk Softly Stranger* 1950; *Appointment with Danger* 1951; *Deadline U.S.A., Carbine Williams, The Bad and the Beautiful* 1952; *The Juggler* 1953; *Chicago Syndicate, The Cobweb* 1955; *Hell on Frisco Bay* 1956; *Top Secret Affair* 1957; *A Child Is Waiting* 1963; *The Greatest Story Ever Told* 1965; *In Cold Blood* 1967; *Jigsaw* 1968; *How to Commit Marriage* 1969; *The Day of the Locust, Bite the Bullet* 1975; *W. C. Fields and Me* (as Florenz Ziegfeld) 1976; *Opening Night, Revenge of the Pink Panther* 1978; *S.O.B., Nobody's Perfekt* 1981; *Tempest* 1982.

Stewart, Peter. See NEWFIELD, Sam.

still. A single photograph taken with an ordinary camera, as opposed to a succession of pictures taken with a motion picture camera. More specifically, a still is a glossy photograph blown up from a frame of a motion picture (action still) or taken by a still photographer on the motion picture set for the purpose of promotion and publicity.

Stiller, Ben. Actor, writer, director. Born 1966 in New York City. *ed.* UCLA Film School, Los Angeles. Creative and gifted comedic actor of television and film. Equally talented as a director-writer, he made a name for himself with the Gen-X comedy *Reality Bites* (1994) and garnered critical kudos for his performance as a young man searching for his biological parents in *Flirting with Disaster* (1996). He is the son of comedy team Stiller and Meara.

FILMS: *Empire of the Sun* 1987; *Fresh Horses* 1988; *Next of Kin* 1989; *Stella* 1990; *Highway to Hell* 1992; *CB4* 1993; *Heavyweights, Reality Bites* (also dir.) 1994; *Flirting with Disaster, If Lucy Fell* 1996.

Stiller, Mauritz. Director. *b.* Moshe Stiller, July 17, 1883, Helsinki, to Russian-Polish parents of the Jewish faith. *d.* 1928. Orphaned at age four, he was raised by a Katzman family, whose name he used until coming of age. He attended Hebrew school, took violin lessons, and was trained to enter his adopters' haberdashery business. Finland was under Russian domination during that period, and, when Stiller was conscripted into the Czar's army, he fled to Sweden with a false passport. Having gained a modest reputation as an actor and director of the avant-garde, he entered Swedish cinema in 1912 on the recommendation of a famous stage star of the period. Within several years he had established himself alongside Victor SJÖSTRÖM (Seastrom) as the greatest director of the "golden age" of the silent Swedish cinema. He and Sjöström brought to their films a sophistication and a sense of visual lyricism that catapulted Swedish cinema into a leading position in Europe during a period that extended into the early 20s.

During his early career, Stiller specialized in elegant, well-paced, satirical social comedies marked by bright visual gags and the spontaneous acting of their players. After WW I he became identified more closely with epic films, notably his free adaptations of several Selma Lagerlöf novels. He wrote the scripts, alone or in collaboration, for many of his films and appeared in several as an actor. Among his more successful comedies were *Love and Journalism* and *Thomas Graal's First Child.* In 1920, Stiller scored an international hit with *Erotikon,* a sumptuous sex epic. His international reputation was further enhanced by the Lagerlöf-based epics *Sir Arne's Treasure/The Three Who Were Doomed, Gunnar Hede's Saga,* and *The Story of Gösta Berling* (also known as *The Atonement of Gösta Berling, The Legend of Gösta Berling,* or *The Gösta Berling Saga*).

The latter film introduced to the world one of its great future superstars, Greta GARBO. Stiller, who had discovered Garbo at the training school of Stockholm's Royal Dramatic Theater, became her mentor, teacher, and inseparable companion. Friends called them Pygmalion and Galatea, Beauty and the Beast, or Svengali and Trilby. In 1924, Stiller was approached by Louis B. Mayer, who offered him work in Hollywood. Stiller insisted that Garbo be part of the deal, and the following year they both arrived in the US. However, once in Hollywood, their positions became reversed. Garbo was immediately groomed and launched into stardom, while Stiller couldn't get started. He and Mayer were both outspoken and quick-tempered men and detested each other. On Garbo's first film Stiller functioned only as assistant director and interpreter for the star. She insisted he be assigned as director of her second MGM picture, *The Temptress,* but after a series of clashes with company personnel he was replaced by Fred Niblo.

Stiller next moved over to Paramount, where he directed *Hotel Imperial* (1927), an impressive film, strong on atmosphere and camera manipulation. He subsequently directed *The Woman on Trial* for Paramount. Like *Hotel Imperial,* the film starred Pola Negri. Then Stiller began *The Street of Sin,* starring Emil Jannings, from a script by Josef von Sternberg. But a quarrel with studio brass forced Stiller to quit the project in midproduction. The film was completed by von Sternberg. Stiller, who by this time was showing the symptoms of a respiratory illness, left

Hollywood for Europe, a broken man. Doctors recommended that he go to Switzerland for mountain air, but he returned to Sweden instead, where he directed a successful stage musical, 'Broadway.' A few months after the opening, in November of 1928, he died, at the age of 45.

FILMS: In Sweden—*Mother and Daughter* (also sc., act.), *The Black Masks* (also co-sc.), *The Tyrannical Fiancée* (also sc., act.) 1912; *The Vampire* (also sc.), *When Love Kills* (also story, co-sc.), *When the Alarm Bell Rings, The Child, The Unknown Woman* (also sc.), *On the Fateful Roads of Life* (also sc.), *The Modern Suffragette* (also sc.), *The Model* (also sc.; never released) 1913; *When the Mother-in-Law Reigns* (also sc., act.), *Brothers* (also story, co-sc.), *People of the Border, Because of Her Love* (also sc.), *The Chamberlain* (also sc.), *Stormy Petrel, The Shot, The Red Tower* (also co-sc.) 1914; *When Artists Love, Playmates* (also sc.), *His Wife's Past, Ace of Thieves, The Dagger* (banned by Swedish censors but shown successfully abroad), *Madame de Thebes* 1915; *The Avenger, The Mine Pilot, His Wedding Night, The Lucky Brooch, Love and Journalism, The Wings* (also sc.), *The Fight for His Heart* (also sc.), *The Ballet Primadonna* 1916; *Thomas Graal's Best Film, Alexander the Great* (also sc.) 1917; *Thomas Graal's First Child* (also co-sc.) 1918; *Song of the Scarlet Flower* (also co-sc.), *Sir Arne's Treasure/The Three Who Were Doomed* (also co-sc.) 1919; *The Fishing Village, Erotikon* (also co-sc.) 1920; *Johan* (co-dir., co-sc. with Arthur Nordeen), *The Exiles* (also co-sc.) 1921; *Gunnar Hede's Saga* (also sc.) 1923; *The Story of Gösta Berling/The Atonement of Gösta Berling/The Legend of Gösta Berling/The Gösta Berling Saga* (also co-sc.) 1924. In the US—*The Temptress* (completed by and credited to Fred Niblo) 1926; *Hotel Imperial, The Woman on Trial* 1927; *The Street of Sin* (completed by Josef von Sternberg but credited solely to Stiller) 1928.

stock. Unexposed negative film. Also called "raw stock."

stock footage. Existing film footage, previously shot, that is taken from the company's archives or a newsreel library and incorporated into a new production. Also called "library footage." A single unit of stock footage is known as a "stock shot" or a LIBRARY SHOT. Stock footage often consists of coverage of important historic events or of shots that are difficult or too expensive to duplicate, such as planes crashing, boats sinking, cities being bombed, or a variety of other man-made or natural disasters. COMPILATION FILMS are made entirely of stock footage.

Stockwell, Dean. Actor. Born on Mar. 5, 1936, in North Hollywood, Calif. Curly-haired, twinkly-eyed child star of the 40s, he grew up into a sensitive, intense leading man. The son of Broadway performers, he made his stage debut at age seven, appearing in the Theatre Guild production of 'The Innocent Voyage,' alongside his brother, Guy Stockwell (*b.* 1938). Two years later he charmed movie audiences in the screen musical *Anchors Aweigh* and for several years remained a popular child performer in other MGM films. He successfully survived the awkward adolescent years but was at first given better acting opportunities as an adult on TV than in films. After sporadic film appearances, his career received a boost with a deranged role in David Lynch's *Blue Velvet* (1986). He was nominated for a best supporting actor Oscar for his role as a Mafia Don in *Married to the Mob* (1988). Later, he co-starred on TV in 'Quantum Leap' (1991–93). He was formerly married to actress Millie PERKINS.

FILMS INCLUDE: *Valley of Decision, Anchors Aweigh* 1945; *The Green Years, Home Sweet Homicide* 1946; *The Mighty McGurk, Song of the Thin Man, The Romance of Rosy Ridge, Gentleman's Agreement* 1947; *Deep Waters, The Boy with Green Hair* 1948; *Down to the Sea in Ships, The Secret Garden* 1949; *The Happy Years, Kim* (title role), *Stars in My Crown* 1950; *Cattle Drive* 1951; *The Careless Years* 1957; *Compulsion* 1959; *Sons and Lovers* (as Paul Morel; UK) 1960; *Long Day's Journey Into Night* (as Edmund Tyrone) 1962; *Rapture* (US/Fr.) 1965; *Psych-Out* 1968; *The Dunwich Horror* 1970; *The Last Movie* (bit) 1971; *The Loners* 1972; *Werewolf of Washington* 1973; *Win Place or Steal* 1975; *Tracks* 1977; *She Came to the Valley* 1979; *One Away* 1980; *Wrong is Right* 1982; *Paris Texas, Alsino and the Condor* (Nic.) 1983; *Dune* 1984; *The Legend of Billie Jean, To Live and Die in L.A.* 1985; *Blue Velvet* 1986; *Beverly Hills Cop 2, Gardens of Stone, The Time Guardian* 1987; *Tucker: The Man and His Dream, The Blue Iguana, Married to the Mob* 1988; *Limit Up, Stickfighter, Buying Time* 1989; *Smokescreen* 1990; *Back Track* 1991; *Chasers* 1994; *Mr. Wrong* 1996; *McHale's Navy* 1997.

Stokowski, Leopold. Conductor. *b.* Leopold Boleslawawicz Antoni Stanislaw Stokowski, Apr. 18, 1882, in London. *d.* 1977. The son of a Polish cabinetmaker and his Irish-born wife, he made his professional musical debut at 18 as an organist of London's St. James's Church and later developed into one of the world's foremost symphony orchestra conductors. An American citizen since 1915, he is credited with molding the Philadelphia Orchestra into one of the world's finest. A tireless innovator who introduced many controversial compositions, he was also dedicated to bringing classical music to the masses and for that purpose agreed to appear as himself in several films. A handsome man of aristocratic features and a photogenic white mane, he co-starred with Deanna Durbin in one of her most successful films, *100 Men and a Girl* (1937), and later persuaded Walt Disney to create the musical animation film *Fantasia* (1940), with Stokowski as music advisor and on- and off-camera conductor. At the age of 80, Stokowski launched the American Symphony Orchestra, with which he toured successfully throughout the US and abroad. He received a special Oscar in 1941 "for unique achievement in creating a new form of visualized music in Walt Disney's production *Fantasia*." At his death at 95 in England, he was still making recordings.

FILMS: *The Big Broadcast of 1937* 1936; *100 Men and a Girl* 1937; *Fantasia* 1940; *Carnegie Hall* 1947.

Stoll, George. Music director, conductor. *b.* May 7, 1905, in Minneapolis. *d.* 1985. After radio experience, he orchestrated numerous MGM musicals from the late 30s, winning an Academy Award for the score of *Anchors Aweigh* (1945).

FILMS INCLUDE: *Broadway Melody of 1938* 1937; *Babes in Arms* 1939; *Strike Up the Band* 1940; *Ziegfeld Girl* 1941; *For Me and My Gal* 1942; *Cabin in the Sky* 1943; *Meet Me in St. Louis, Music for Millions, Anchors Aweigh* 1945; *The Kissing Bandit* 1949; *The Toast of New Orleans* 1950; *The Student Prince* 1954; *Meet Me in Las Vegas* 1956; *Jumbo* 1962; *The Courtship of Eddie's Father* 1963; *Viva Las Vegas* 1964; *Girl Happy* 1965; *Made in Paris* 1966.

Stoll, John. Art director. Born on Dec. 12, 1913, in London. In British films from the mid-40s, he became established in the 60s as one of England's leading motion picture designers, particularly after his work on *Lawrence of Arabia* (1962), for which he shared an Academy Award with John Box.

FILMS INCLUDE: *The Snorkel* 1958; *Ferry to Hong Kong* 1959; *The Greengage Summer/Loss of Innocence* 1961; *Lawrence of Arabia* (co-art dir.) 1962; *The Running Man* 1963; *The Seventh Dawn* (UK/US) 1964; *The Collector* (US/UK) 1965; *Lost Command* (US) 1966; *How I Won the War* 1967; *A Twist of Sand* 1968; *Hannibal Brooks* 1969; *Cromwell* 1970; *Living Free* 1971; *Shaft in Africa* (US), *The Golden Voyage of Sinbad* 1973; *The Beat Must Die* 1974; *Seven Nights in Japan* (UK/Fr.) 1976; *Firepower* (co-art dir.) 1979.

Stoloff, Ben(jamin). Director. *b.* 1895, Philadelphia. *d.* 1960. *ed.* USC. A feature film director from the late 20s, following long experience with short subjects. He specialized in light musicals and B mysteries and action pictures. He also produced a number of low-budget films in the late 40s.

FILMS INCLUDE: *The Canyon of Light* 1926; *The Circus Ace, Silver Valley, The Gay Retreat* 1927; *A Horseman of the Plains, Plastered in Paris* 1928; *Protection, The Girl from Havana, Speakeasy* 1929; *Happy Days, Fox Movietone Follies of 1930, Soup to Nuts* 1930; *Three Rogues, Goldie* 1931; *The Night Mayor, The Devil Is Driving, Destry Rides Again* (Tom Mix version) 1932; *Obey the Law, Night of Terror* 1933; *Palooka, Transatlantic Merry-Go-Round* 1934; *To Beat the Band* 1935; *Two in the Dark* 1936; *Sea Devils, Super Sleuth, Fight for Your Lady* 1937; *Radio City Revels, The Affairs of Annabel* 1938; *The Marines Fly High* 1940; *The Hidden Hand* 1942; *Secret Enemies, The Mysterious Doctor* 1943; *Bermuda Mystery, Take It or Leave It* 1944; *Johnny Comes Flying Home* 1946; *It's a Joke Son* 1947.

Stoloff, Morris. Music director, conductor. *b.* 1893, Philadelphia. *d.* 1980. A child-prodigy violinist, he played with the Los Angeles Philharmonic before joining Paramount in 1928 as a concert master. With Columbia as music director from 1936, he became head of the studio's music department in the 40s. He won Academy Awards for orchestrating *Cover Girl* (1944), *The Jolson Story* (1946), and *Song Without End* (1960).

FILMS INCLUDE: *Craig's Wife* 1936; *The Awful Truth* 1937; *Cover Girl* 1944; *A Song to Remember* 1945; *The Jolson Story, Gilda* 1946; *Born Yesterday* 1950; *From Here to Eternity, The 5000 Fingers of Dr. T* 1953; *The Long Gray Line, My Sister Eileen* 1955; *Picnic, The Eddy Duchin Story* 1956; *Pal Joey* 1957; *Song Without End* 1960; *Fanny* 1961; *Lawrence of Arabia* (UK) 1962; *None but the Brave* (US/Jap.) 1965; *The Naked Runner* (UK) 1967.

Stolper, Alexander. Director. Born in 1907, in Russia. A former journalist and stage director, he began directing Soviet films in the early 30s. Many of his films have dealt with themes related to WW II.

FILMS INCLUDE: *A Simple Story* 1930; *The Law of Life* 1940; *A Lad from Our Town, Wait for Me!* 1943; *Days and Nights* 1945; *Our Heart* 1946; *The Story of a Real Man* 1948; *Far from Moscow* 1950; *The Road* 1955; *The Living and the Dead* 1964; *Soldiers Aren't Born* 1968.

Stoltz, Eric. Actor. Born in 1961, in American Samoa. *ed.* USC. Deceptively easygoing film lead of the 1980s and 1990s. Leaving college after two years, he studied with Stella Adler and others, and began appearing widely on the stage. He was nominated for a Tony in his Broadway debut in 'Our Town.' Debuted in films in 1982, with several praised performances mainly in independent films.

FILMS INCLUDE: *Fast Times at Ridgemont High* 1982; *Running Hot, Surf II, The Wild Life* 1984; *Code Name: Emerald, The New Kids, Mask* 1985; *Sister Sister, Lionheart, Some Kind of Wonderful* 1987; *Haunted Summer, Manifesto* (US/Yug.) 1988; *Say Anything* (also prod. asst.), *The Fly II* 1990; *Memphis Belle* 1990; *Singles* (cameo), *The Waterdance* 1992; *Bodies Rest and Motion* 1993; *Killing Time, Naked in New York, Pulp Fiction, Sleep with Me* 1994; *Fluke, The Prophecy, Rob Roy, Screaming* 1995; *2 Days in the Valley, Grace of My Heart, Jerry Maguire* 1996; *Anaconda, Inside, Keys to Tulsa* 1997.

Stone, Andrew L. Director-producer-screenwriter. Born on July 16, 1902, in Oakland, Calif. *ed.* U. of California. He entered the film industry while still a student, working for a San Francisco film exchange for four years. Moving to Hollywood in the mid-20s, he worked in a film laboratory, then in Universal's prop department, before becoming a director of two-reel dramas at Paramount in 1927. He directed his first feature the following year. During the first phase of his career as a director (through the 40s) his films were for the most part pleasant but routine comedies and light musicals. In the 50s and 60s he made neat little thrillers and mostly melodramas, characteristically emphasizing authenticity of location and action. But his reputation suffered in the early 70s as a result of two poor screen biographies of Grieg and Johann Strauss. He has produced and scripted most of his own films. His wife, Virginia, has been his co-producer and editor since the late 50s.

FEATURE FILMS: *Dreary House* (also prod.) 1928; *Sombras de Gloria* (Spanish version of *Blaze o' Glory*) 1930; *Hell's Headquarters* 1932; *The Girl Said No* (also prod., story) 1937; *Stolen Heaven* (also prod., story), *Say It in French* (also prod.) 1938; *The Great Victor Herbert* (also prod., co-story) 1939; *The Hard-Boiled Canary/There's Magic in Music* (also prod., co-story) 1941; *Stormy Weather, Hi Diddle Diddle* (also prod.) 1943; *Sensations of 1945* (also prod., co-sc.) 1944; *Bedside Manner* (also prod.) 1945; *The Bachelor's Daughters* (also prod., sc.) 1946; *Fun on a Weekend* (also prod., sc.) 1947; *Highway 301* (also story, sc.) 1950; *Confidence Girl* (also prod., story, sc.), *The Steel Trap* (also story, sc.) 1952; *A Blueprint for Murder* (also story, sc.) 1953; *The Night Holds Terror* (also prod., story) 1955; *Julie* (also sc.) 1956; *Cry Terror* (also co-prod., sc.), *The Decks Ran Red* (also co-prod., sc.) 1958; *The Last Voyage* (also co-prod., sc.) 1960; *Ring of Fire* (also co-prod., sc.) 1961; *The Password Is Courage* (also co-prod., sc.; UK) 1962; *Never Put It in Writing* (also co-prod., sc.; UK) 1964; *The Secret of My Success* (also co-prod., sc.; UK) 1965; *Song of Norway* (also co-prod., story, sc.) 1970; *The Great Waltz* (also prod., sc.) 1972; *Rollercoaster* (asst. dir. only) 1977.

Stone, Fred. Actor. *b.* Aug. 19, 1873, Denver. *d.* 1959. Entered show business at nine as a circus tightrope walker. Teaming with David Montgomery in 1894, he became a very popular entertainer in vaudeville and in stage musicals. He played the Scarecrow in the original Broadway presentation of 'The Wizard of Oz' in 1903. Appearing only occasionally in films, he starred in a number of silents and played key character parts in several talkies, memorably as Katharine Hepburn's father in *Alice Adams* (1935). His daughters, Dorothy (1905–74), Carol (*b.* 1915), and Pamela (*b.* 1916), appeared in a few films.

FILMS INCLUDE: *The Goat* 1918; *Under the Top, Johnny Get Your Gun* 1919; *The Duke of Chimney Butte* 1921; *Billy Jim* 1922; *Broadway After Dark* 1924; *Smiling Faces* 1932; *Alice Adams* 1935; *The Trail of the Lonesome Pine, My American Wife* 1936; *Life Begins in College* 1937; *The Westerner* 1940.

Stone, George E. ("Georgie"). Actor. *b.* George Stein, May 23, 1903, Lodz, Poland. *d.* 1967. In the US from childhood, he began his show business career as a song-and-dance kid in vaudeville and on the legitimate stage and made many screen appearances since his teens. He gave a memorable adult performance as the Sewer Rat in *Seventh Heaven* (1927). He then played character roles in nearly 200 films, typically as a Runyonesque gangster (he was a close friend of Runyon). He played The Runt, Chester Morris's dumb but amiable pal, in a dozen "Boston Blackie" movies. He also was a regular on the long-running TV series 'Perry Mason.'

FILMS INCLUDE: *Children of the Feud* 1916; *Till I Come Back to You* 1918; *Just Pals* 1920; *Jackie, Desperate Trails, The Whistle* 1921; *The Fourth Musketeer* 1923; *Seventh Heaven, Brass Knuckles* 1927; *San Francisco Nights, Tenderloin, The Racket, State Street Sadie* 1928; *The Redeeming Sin, Melody Lane, Skin Deep* 1929; *Under a Texas Moon* 1930; *Little Caesar,*

Cimarron, The Front Page, The Spider, Five Star Final 1931; *Taxi!, The Last Mile* 1932; *The Vampire Bat, 42nd Street, The Big Brain* (lead), *Penthouse* 1933; *Viva Villa!, The Dragon Murder Case* 1934; *Hold 'Em Yale, Frisco Kid* 1935; *Bullets or Ballots, Rhythm on the Range, Anthony Adverse* 1936; *Alcatraz Island* 1937; *Mr. Moto's Gamble, You and Me, Submarine Patrol* 1938; *The Night of Nights* 1939; *I Take This Woman, Island of Doomed Men, North West Mounted Police* 1940; *Confessions of Boston Blackie* 1941; *The Devil with Hitler* 1942; *Roger Touhy—Gangster* 1944; *Suspense, Abie's Irish Rose* 1946; *Bloodhounds on Broadway* 1952; *Pickup on South Street* 1953; *Guys and Dolls, The Man with the Golden Arm* 1955; *Some Like It Hot* 1959; *Pocketful of Miracles* 1961.

Stone, Lewis. Actor. *b.* Nov. 15, 1879, Worcester, Mass. *d.* 1953. A matinee idol on Broadway, he made his film debut in 1915, but his career was soon interrupted by WW I service as a major in the cavalry. Returning to films after the Armistice, he soon developed into a popular leading man. During the silent era he played dignified, gentlemanly romantic heroes. Among his more notable screen parts in the 20s were the dual lead role of Rudolf Rassendyll and King Rudolf in Rex Ingram's *The Prisoner of Zenda* (1922), the adversary role to Ramon Novarro in Ingram's *Scaramouche* (1923), and one of the leads in the successful screen adaptation of Conan Doyle's *The Lost World* (1925). He was nominated for an Oscar as best actor for *The Patriot* (1928). Although he was fifty at the advent of sound, he continued playing mature leads, notably in several films opposite Greta Garbo, but gradually and gracefully eased into solid character parts. Later in his career he typically played genial senior citizens, memorably as Judge Hardy in the ANDY HARDY film series. He spent his entire sound-film career with MGM. In all he appeared in nearly 200 films. He died of a heart attack at 73 while chasing vandals from his property.

FILMS INCLUDE: *The Man Who Found Out* 1915; *The Havoc, Honor's Altar* 1916; *Man of Bronze* 1918; *Man's Desire* 1919; *Milestones, Nomads of the North, Held by the Enemy, The River's End* 1920; *The Concert, The Golden Snare, Beau Revel, Pilgrims of the Night* 1921; *The Dangerous Age, The Rosary, A Fool There Was, The Prisoner of Zenda* (dual role, as Rudolf Rassendyll/King Rudolf), *Trifling Women* 1922; *The World's Applause, You Can't Fool Your Wife, Scaramouche* (as the Marquis de la Tour d'Azyr) 1923; *The Stranger, Cytherea, Why Men Leave Home, Husbands and Lovers, Inez from Hollywood* 1924; *The Talker, Confessions of a Queen, Fine Clothes, The Lady Who Lied, The Lost World, What Fools Men* 1925; *The Girl from Montmartre, Midnight Lovers, Old Loves and New, Don Juan's Three Nights* 1926; *An Affair of the Follies, Lonesome Ladies, The Private Life of Helen of Troy* (as Menelaus) 1927; *The Foreign Legion, The Patriot, Freedom of the Press, A Woman of Affairs* 1928; *The Trial of Mary Dugan, Wild Orchids, Madame X, The Wonder of Women, Their Own Desire* 1929; *The Big House, Romance, The Office Wife, Passion Flower* 1930; *Inspiration, Father's Son, My Past/Ex-Mistress, The Secret Six, Always Goodbye, The Bargain/You and I, The Sin of Madelon Claudet, The Phantom of Paris, Mata Hari* 1931; *Grand Hotel* (as Dr. Otternschlag), *The Wet Parade, Letty Lynton, Red Headed Woman, The Mask of Fu Manchu* 1932; *Men Must Fight, The White Sister, Looking Forward/The New Deal, Bureau of Missing Persons, Queen Christina* (as Chancellor Oxenstierna) 1933; *Treasure Island* (as Captain Smollett) 1934; *David Copperfield* (as Mr. Wickfield), *Vanessa: Her Love Story* (as Adam), *China Seas, Shipmates Forever* 1935; *Small Town Girl, Suzy* 1936; *The Thirteenth Chart, You're Only Young Once* (and numerous subsequent "Andy Hardy" films through 1946) 1937; *Yellow Jack* 1938; *Sporting Blood* 1940; *The Bugle Sounds* 1942; *The Hoodlum Saint, Three Wise Fools* 1946; *State of the Union* 1948; *Any Number Can Play* 1949; *Key to the City, Stars in My Crown* 1950; *Night Into Morning* 1951; *It's a Big Country, Scaramouche* (remake; as George de Valmorin), *The Prisoner of Zenda* (remake; as the Cardinal) 1952; *All the Brothers Were Valiant* 1953.

Stone, Milburn. Actor. *b.* July 5, 1904, Burton, Kans. *d.* 1980. Leading man and supporting player of mainly minor Hollywood films. He toured with various rep companies for ten years before making his screen debut in 1936. For several years he played leads in low-budget action films and serials as well as featured roles in more expensive productions, but eventually he settled on a career as a character player, typically in villainous roles. Familiar as the gruff Doc Adams in the long-running TV series 'Gunsmoke,' for which he won an Emmy in 1968.

FILMS INCLUDE: *The Milky Way, China Clipper* 1936; *Atlantic Flight, Federal Bullets* 1937; *The Port of Missing Girls, Crime School, Sinners in Paradise* 1938; *Tail Spin, Mystery Plane/Sky Pilot, Young Mr. Lincoln* (as Stephen A. Douglas), *Tropic Fury, Nick Carter—Master Detective* 1939; *Enemy Agent, Give Us Wings* 1940; *The Great Train Robbery* 1941; *Frisco Lil, Reap the Wild Wind* 1942; *Captive Wild Woman, Sherlock Holmes Faces Death, The Mad Ghoul, Gung Ho!* 1943; *The Imposter, Jungle Woman, The Great Alaskan Mystery* (serial), *Phantom Lady* 1944; *The Master Key* (serial), *She Gets Her Man, The Frozen Ghost, Strange Confession* 1945; *The Spider Woman Strikes Back, Inside Job* 1946; *Calamity Jane and Sam Bass* 1949; *Branded* 1951; *The Atomic City* 1952; *Pickup on South Street, Arrowhead, The Sun Shines Bright* 1953; *The Siege at Red River* 1954; *Black Tuesday, The Long Gray Line* 1955; *Drango* 1957.

Stone, Oliver. Director, writer, producer. Born on Sept. 15, 1946, in New York, N.Y. *ed.* Yale; NYU (B.F.A.). A foremost director since the 1980s, known for his consistently controversial films. Enlisting in the Army, he spent a formative young adulthood in Vietnam, working as a teacher in Cholon and becoming a highly decorated US infantry specialist fourth class. Following his years in Vietnam, he studied film at New York University and began writing and directing his first commercial feature, the shocker *Seizure*. His screenplays for the charged, violent films that followed (*Midnight Express*, *Scarface*, *Year of the Dragon*), established an important commercial presence and pointed to his penchant for creating male personal dramas built upon explorations of violence and self-betrayal, themes that would come to drive his future films. These explorations would also come to center on unresolved contemporary national experiences, beginning with the conflict in El Salvador in *Salvador*. Praised both for its performances and its early focus on the varieties of corruption in that country, the film was followed in the same year by his first major commercial success, *Platoon*. Winning for Stone the Academy Award for best director and the Directors Guild Award, the disturbing first-person chronicle of life on the front line in Vietnam rekindled national interest in a war that ended a decade earlier. *Wall Street* focused on a perhaps even more timely topic, as it both lionized and condemned the stereotypic 1980s passion for greed; *Born on the Fourth of July* returned to the Vietnam War, this time viewing the experience through the eyes of a vet who has been paralyzed and must readjust to civilian life. Based on the autobiography of the same name by Ron Kovic, it gave actor Tom Cruise his first major serious dramatic role and won for Stone his second Academy Award for best director. Stone's next film, *The Doors*, a direct but not compelling view of the rock and drug culture of the 1960s and 1970s, generated new interest in the already media-sapped period, as did *JFK*, his driving documentary-saga of the investigation of the Kennedy assassination. The film, which recreated (and sometimes reformulated) history through the inquiry of New Orleans D.A. Jim Garrison, fed another half-decade of speculations about the reasons and people behind the assassination. His *Heaven and Earth*, based on the memoirs of Vietnamese woman Le Ly Hayslip, completed a trilogy of Vietnam films. Since the 1980s, he has also produced several Hollywood dramas.

FILMS INCLUDE: As director—*Seizure* (also sc., ed.) 1974; *Midnight Express* (sc. only) 1978; *The Hand* (also act., sc.) 1981; *Conan the Barbarian* (sc. only) 1982; *Scarface* (sc. only) 1983; *Year of the Dragon* (sc. only) 1985; *8 Million Ways to Die* (sc. only) 1985; *Platoon* (also sc., act.), *Salvador* (also sc., prod.) 1986; *Wall Street* (also sc., act.) 1987; *Talk Radio* (also sc.) 1988; *Born on the Fourth of July* (also sc., prod., act.) 1989; *The Doors* (also sc.) 1991; *JFK* (also sc.) 1991; *Heaven and Earth* (also sc., prod.) 1993; *Natural Born Killers* (also co-sc., co-prod.) 1994; *Nixon* (also co-sc., co-prod.) 1995. As producer—*Blue Steel* 1989; *Reversal of Fortune* 1990; *Iron Maze* (US/Jap., co-exec. prod.) 1991; *Zebrahead* (co-exec. prod.) 1992; *The New Age* (exec. prod. only) 1994; *Evita* (co-sc. only), *Killer* (co-exec. prod.), *The People vs. Larry Flynt* (co-prod. only) 1996; *U-Turn* 1997.

Stone, Peter. Playwright, screenwriter. Born on Feb. 27, 1930, in Los Angeles. *ed.* Bard Coll.; Yale. The holder of a doctorate in literature, he became established in the 60s as a successful writer for both the stage and screen. For Broadway he authored such musicals as 'Kean' (1961), 'Skyscraper' (1965), '1776' (1969), and 'Two by Two' (1970). In Hollywood, he made an impressive start with the script of *Charade* (1963), which he based on a novel he had co-authored, and in 1964 he shared an Academy Award for the screenplay of *Father Goose*. He has also written for TV, winning an Emmy Award in 1963. He sometimes uses the pseudonym Pierre Marton.

FILMS: *Charade* (from own co-novel, *The Unsuspecting Wife*) 1963; *Father Goose* (co-sc.) 1964; *Mirage* 1965; *Arabesque* (co-sc.) 1966; *The Secret War of Harry Frigg* (co-sc.), *Jigsaw* (based on his screenplay for *Mirage*) 1968; *Sweet Charity* 1969; *Skin Game* 1971; *1776* (from his own Broadway musical) 1972; *The Taking of Pelham 123* 1974; *Silver Bears* 1977; *Someone Is Killing the Great Chefs of Europe* 1978.

Stone, Sharon. Actress. Born on Mar. 10, 1958, in Meadville, Pa. *ed.* Edinboro Univ. Dangerously sultry screen lead. After competing in a local beauty contest, she moved to New York, where her well-scrubbed beauty brought her work in commercials. Shortly after settling in Hollywood, she debuted in her first film, *Stardust Memories*, but it was not until ten years and several varying performances later that she established herself as a screen presence in her role as an overaggressive wife in *Total Recall*. Notorious for the way she uncrossed her legs in the interrogation scene in *Basic Instinct*, her performance as the icy femme fatale in that movie made her one of Hollywood's leading female box-office attractions. Her career took a turn when Martin SCORSESE cast her as the doped-up mob wife in *Casino* (1995), a role many felt confirmed her as a serious actress, earning an Academy Award nomination as best actress.

FILMS INCLUDE: *Stardust Memories* 1980; *Deadly Blessing* 1981; *Bolero* 1982; *Irreconcilable Differences* 1984; *King Solomon's Mines* 1985; *Allan Quatermain and the Lost City of Gold, Police Academy 4: Citizens on Patrol* 1987; *Cold Steel, Above the Law, Action Jackson* 1988; *Personal Choice, Blood and Sand* 1989; *Total Recall* 1990; *He Said She Said, Scissors, Year of the Gun* 1991; *Basic Instinct, Diary of a Hitman* 1992; *Sliver* 1993; *Intersection, The Specialist* 1994; *Casino, The Quick and the Dead* 1995; *Diabolique, Last Dance* 1996.

Stonehouse, Ruth. American actress. *b.* 1893. *d.* 1941. She entered films with Essanay in 1911 and before long became one of the studio's leading stars (often opposite Francis X. BUSHMAN) as well as a part share owner. She later played leads for Universal and other studios but ended her career in 1928 as a supporting player.

FILMS INCLUDE: *The Papered Door* 1911; *Sunshine, Billy McGrath's Love Letters, From the Submerged, Twilight, Neptune's Daughter, Chains* 1912; *The Spy's Defeat, The Pathway of Years, Broken Threads United, Home Spun, Thy Will Be Done, A Woman's Way, In Convict's Garb* 1913; *The Hand That Rocks the Cradle, The Other Girl, Ashes of Hope, Trinkets of Tragedy, Night Hawks, Blood Will Tell, An Angel Unaware, Sparks of Fate, Splendid Dishonor, The Battle of Love* 1914; *An Amateur Prodigal, The Slim Princess, The Fable of the Galumptious Girl, A Night in Kentucky, Above the Abyss, The Romance of an American Duchess, When My Lady Smiles* 1915; *The Adventures of Peg o' the Ring* (serial) 1916; *Follow the Girl, The Phantom Husband* 1917; *The Master Mystery* (serial), *The Masked Rider* (serial), *Puppy Love* 1919; *Hope, Are All Men Alike?, Parlor Bedroom and Bath* 1920; *I Am Guilty, Don't Call Me Little Girl* 1921; *The Flash, Flames of Passion, Lights Out, The Way of the Transgressor* 1923; *A Girl of the Limberlost, Broken Barriers* 1924; *A Two-Fisted Sheriff, Fifth Avenue Models, The Fugitive* 1925; *The Wives of the Prophet, Broken Homes* 1926; *Poor Girls, The Satin Woman* 1927; *The Ape, The Devil's Cage* 1928.

Stooges, The Three. Comedy team specializing in violent, vulgar slapstick. Formed in vaudeville in 1923, its original members were Moe Howard (*b.* 1897, Brooklyn, N.Y.; *d.* 1975) and his brother Shemp Howard (*b.* Samuel Howard, Mar. 17, 1900, Brooklyn, N.Y.; *d.* 1955), who played second bananas to vaudevillian Ted Healy in an act billed as "Ted Healy and His Stooges." In 1928 the brothers were joined by Larry Fine (*b.* 1911, Philadelphia; *d.* 1974). Following their success in vaudeville, the three appeared in several Broadway revues and in 1930 supported Healy in the feature film *Soup to Nuts*, in which they were billed as "The Racketeers." Shortly after, Shemp left the act and was replaced by his brother Curly (*b.* Jerome Howard, 1906, Brooklyn, N.Y.; *d.* 1952). The Three Stooges continued appearing in occasional feature films and in 1934 began the longest-running series of two-reel comedies in the history of sound films.

Some 200 Three Stooges shorts were produced by Columbia between 1934 and 1958, under such directors as Del Lord, Charlie (Charley) Chase, Jules White, and Edward Bernds. The "comic" action of these films consisted mainly in depicting members of the team brutally bopping each other on the head with mallets, tweaking one another's noses, gouging eyes, and kicking shins. In 1946 Curly left the team after suffering a stroke, and brother Shemp was recalled to take his place. After Shemp's death in 1955, he was replaced by Joe Besser, who in turn was replaced by Joe De Rita ("Curly Joe") in 1959, when the team ventured into feature films, capitalizing on a renewed popularity that resulted from the release on TV of their old shorts.

FEATURE FILMS INCLUDE: *Soup to Nuts* 1930; *Dancing Lady* 1933; *Gift of Gab, The Captain Hates the Sea* 1934; *Start Cheering* 1938; *My Sister Eileen* 1942; *Swing Parade of 1946* 1946; *Have Rocket Will Travel* 1959; *Stop Look and Laugh* (compilation of their shorts) 1960; *Snow White and the Three Stooges* 1961; *The Three Stooges in Orbit* 1962; *It's a Mad Mad Mad Mad World, Four for Texas* 1963; *The Outlaws Is Coming!* 1965.

stop. See APERTURE; F-STOP; T-STOP.

stop frame. See FREEZE FRAME.

stop motion. A cinematographic technique by which inanimate objects may appear to be moving on the screen. It is achieved by the manipulation of the objects between successive takes of individual frames. A scene is photographed frame by frame. Objects are moved slightly between exposures but remain stationary during exposure. When the film is projected an illusion of motion is created. The technique may be easily accomplished by any amateur with a camera capable of taking single frames. Special devices have been developed over the years to assure precision and accuracy in professional stop-motion cinematography. Stop motion is an essential technique in PUPPET animation and SPECIAL EFFECTS. It is also widely used in the production of television commercials. See also GO-MOTION.

Stoppa, Paolo. Actor. Born on June 16, 1906, in Rome. For many years, one of Italy's foremost stage and screen character actors, since 1935 he has appeared in scores of Italian and many international films. He founded and managed a theater that frequently employed Visconti as a director in the early stage of his career.

FILMS INCLUDE: *Re Burlone* 1935; *Marcella* 1937; *Frenesia* 1939; *Mélodie eterne/Eternal Melodies, La Corona di Ferro/Iron Crown* 1940; *Rossini* 1941; *Don Giovanni/The Loves of Don Juan* 1942; *Aquila nera* 1946; *Fabiola* 1949; *La Beauté du Diable/Beauty and the Devil* (Fr.) 1950; *Donne e Briganti/Of Love and Bandits, Miracolo a Milano/Miracle in Milan* 1951; *Altri Tempi/Times Gone By, Les Sept Péchés capitaux/Seven Capital Sins* (Fr.), *Les Belles de Nuit/Beauties of the Night* (Fr.), *Roma Ore 11/Rome 11 O' Clock* 1952; *Destinées/Daughters of Destiny* (Fr./It.), *Puccini, Le Retour de Don Camillo/The Return of Don Camillo* (Fr./It.), *Statzione Termini/Indiscretion of an American Wife* 1953; *Carosello Napoletano/Neapolitan Carousel, Casa Ricordi/House of Ricordi* (lead, as Giovanni Ricordi), *Pane Amore e Gelosia/Frisky, L'Oro di Napoli/Gold of Naples* 1954; *La Bella Mugnaia/The Miller's Beautiful Wife* 1955; *Pepote* (Sp./It.) 1956; *Vacanze a Ischia/Holiday Island* 1958; *La Loi/Where the Hot Wind Blows* (Fr./It.) 1959; *Cartagine in Fiamme/Carthage in Flames, Rocco e i suoi Fratelli/Rocco and His Brothers, La Giornata Balorda/From a Roman Balcony* 1960; *Boccaccio '70* 1962; *Il Gattopardo/The Leopard* 1963; *Becket* (as Pope Alexander III; UK/US), *Behold a Pale Horse* (US), *Der Besuch/The Visit* (Ger./Fr./It./US) 1964; *Caccia alla Volpe/After the Fox* (It./US/UK) 1966; *C'era una Volta il West/Once Upon a Time in the West* (It./US) 1968; *La Matriarca/The Libertine* 1969; *Jus Primae Noctis* 1972; *Il Casotto* 1977; *La Mazetta* 1978; *Suor Omicidi* 1979.

Stoppard, Tom. Playwright, screenwriter. Born Tomas Straussler on July 3, 1937, in Zlin, Czechoslovakia. Inventive English-language playwright praised for his experimentation with language, the dramatic form, and philosophy. Much of his film work has involved the adaptation of leading novelists to the screen, including Nabokov (*Despair*) and Graham Greene (*The Human Factor*). He adapted and directed the screen version of his own play, the *Hamlet*-inspired 'Rosencrantz and Gildenstern Are Dead,' in 1990.

FILMS INCLUDE: *The Engagement* 1970; *The Romantic Englishwoman* 1975; *Despair* 1978; *The Human Factor* 1979; *Squaring the Circle* 1983; *Brazil* 1985; *Empire of the Sun* 1987; *Rosencrantz and Guildenstern Are Dead* (also dir.), *The Russia House* 1990; *Billy Bathgate* 1991.

stopping down. Reducing the aperture of a lens.

Storaro, Vittorio. Director of cinematography. Born in 1940 in Rome. *ed.* Duca D'Aosta Technical Photographic Institute; Italian Cinemagraphic Training Center; Centro Sperimental di Cinematografia. Leading cinematographer since the 1970s. His sweep and ability to convey the sensuousness of surroundings has been highlighted well in the works of modern saga makers COPPOLA, BEATTY, and particularly BERTOLUCCI, the look of whose films he has helped to define. He won Academy Awards in photography for *Apocalypse Now, Reds*, and *The Last Emperor*. He was the photographic consultant on the Disney short *Captain EO*.

FILMS INCLUDE: *Delitto al Circolo del Tennis, L'Uccello dalle Piume di Cristallo* 1969; *Il Conformista/The Conformist, Giovinezza Giovinezzza, La Strategia del Ragno/The Spider's Strategem* 1970; *Addio, Fratello Crudele, Orlando Furioso* 1971; *Corpo d'Amore, Last Tango in Paris* 1972; *'Tis a Pity She's a Whore, Giordano Bruno, Malizia* 1973; *Novecento/1900* 1976; *Submission* 1977; *Agatha, Apocalypse Now, La Luna* 1979; *Reds* 1981; *One from the Heart* 1982; *Wagner* 1983; *Ladyhawke* 1985; *Ishtar, The Last Emperor* 1987; *Tucker: The Man and His Dream* 1988; *New York Stories* ("Life Without Zoe") 1989; *Dick Tracy, The Sheltering Sky* 1990; *Little Buddha* 1993; *Flamenco* 1997.

Storck, Henri. Documentary director. Born on Sept. 5, 1907, in Ostende, Belgium. A film enthusiast from adolescence, he founded a film club in his hometown in 1928 and the following year began making amateur films. After a period of apprenticeship in Paris, which culminated with work as an assistant to Jean Vigo on *Zéro de Conduite/Zero for Conduct* (1933), he returned to Belgium and soon established himself as his country's foremost documentary filmmaker and one of the leading nonfiction directors in Europe. His output has been prolific and diversified in theme and style, ranging through the entire gamut of the documentary genre, from the experimental and the avant-garde to the poetic view of life, the aesthetic exploration of art, and the grim exposition of social conditions. In addition, he has made many industrial and publicity shorts on assignment. Several of his shorts and feature-length films won international awards and his work has influenced documentary filmmakers everywhere. Storck, who was among the founders of Belgium's Royal Film Archive in 1938 and the International Association of Documentary Filmmakers in 1964, is teaching film production at the Institut des Arts de Diffusion in Brussels. He authored *Le Film récréatif pour Spectateurs Juveniles (The Entertainment Film for Juvenile Audiences),* which was published by UNESCO in 1950.

FILMS INCLUDE: *Pour vos Beaux Yeux, Images d'Ostende, La Mort de Vénus* 1930; *Une Idylle à la Plage* 1931; *Histoire du Soldat inconnu* 1932; *Borinage* (co-dir., co-sc., co-phot., co-edit. with Joris Ivens) 1933; *L'Ile de Pâques* (prod., edit. only) 1935; *Regards sur la Belgique ancienne* 1936; *Les Maisons de la Misère* 1937; *Symphonie Paysanne* (in five parts) 1944; *Le Monde de Paul Delvaux* 1946; *Rubens* 1948; *Au Carrefour de la Vie* 1949; *Le Banquet des Fraudeurs* 1951; *La Fenêtre ouverte* 1952; *Le Trésor d'Ostende* 1955; *Décembre—Mois des Enfants* 1956; *Couleur de Feu* 1957; *Les Seigneurs de la Forêt/Masters of the Congo Jungle* 1958; *Les Gestes du Silence* 1960; *Les Dieux du Feu* 1961; *Le Bonheur d'être aimee* 1962; *Matières nouvelles* 1964; *Jeudi on chantera comme Dimanche* 1966; *Paul Delvaux ou les Femmes défendues* 1971; *Fêtes de Belgique* (co-dir., co-sc.) 1973.

Storey, Edith. American actress. Born in 1892. Popular star of early silent films, noted for her beauty and athletic prowess. She began her career with Vitagraph, then played leads for Metro and other studios. She retired from the screen in 1921.

FILMS INCLUDE: *Barbara Frietchie* 1908; *Mogg Megone, Les Miserables* (in four parts), *Onawanda* 1909; *The Life of Moses* (in five parts) 1919–10; *Saved by the Flag* 1910; *A Tale of Two Cities, Billy the Kid* 1911; *The Telephone Girl,*

The Victoria Cross, The Serpents, The Lady of the Lake, Lincoln's Gettysburg Address, The Troublesome Step-Daughters, Two Women and Two Men 1912; *The Vengeance of Durand, A Regiment of Two, The Next Generation, The Cure* 1913; *Children of the Feud, The Christian, Captain Alvarez, Hearts of the First Empire, Hope's Foster Mother, The Old Flute Player, In the Latin Quarter* 1914; *The Quality of Mercy, The Island of Regeneration, Love's Way, The Ruling Power, The Dust of Egypt, On Her Wedding Night* 1915; *The Tarantula, An Enemy to the King* 1916; *Money Magic, Captain of the Grey Horse Troop* 1917; *Eyes of Mystery, Revenge, The Claim, Treasure of the Sea, The Demon, Legion of Death* 1918; *As the Sun Went Down, The Silent Woman* 1919; *Moon Madness* 1920; *Beach of Dreams, The Greater Profit* 1921.

Storm, Gale. Actress, singer. Born Josephine Owaissa Cottle, on Apr. 5, 1922, in Bloomington, Tex. Wholesome leading lady of minor Hollywood films of the 40s, after winning a "Gateway to Hollywood" contest while still at high school. She soared into big-time stardom on TV in the 50s in the series 'My Little Margie' and 'The Gale Storm Show' (originally 'Oh Susanna!'). She retired from performing in the 60s amid personal problems, recounted in her 1981 memoir *I Ain't Down Yet*. She is married to former screen actor Lee Bonnel, who appeared in a few minor films, sometimes billed as Terry Belmont, and is now an insurance executive.

FILMS INCLUDE: *Tom Brown's School Days* 1940; *Jesse James at Bay* 1941; *Foreign Agent, Rhythm Parade* 1942; *Revenge of the Zombies, Nearly 18, Campus Rhythm* 1943; *Where Are Your Children?* 1944; *Forever Yours, Sunbonnet Sue* 1945; *Swing Parade of 1946* 1946; *It Happened on Fifth Avenue* 1947; *The Dude Goes West* 1948; *Stampede, Abandoned* 1949; *The Underworld Story, Curtain Call at Cactus Creek, Between Midnight and Dawn* 1950; *Al Jennings of Oklahoma, The Texas Rangers* 1951; *Woman of the North Country* 1952.

story analyst. A studio employee whose job it is to read, evaluate, and synopsize dramatic and other literary properties that might be considered for screen adaptation. Also known as a READER.

storyboard. A layout of sketches, drawings, or still photographs in continuity which outlines the main action and the narrative progression of a sequence or an entire film. Storyboards are widely used in planning animation films and in the presentation of proposed TV commercials to prospective clients. Some feature film directors who like to prepare their scenes carefully in advance of production also use this technique.

story editor. An employee of a studio's scenario department who reviews synopses and evaluations of dramatic and other literary properties made by his staff of readers (or story analysts). He or she recommends to a producer that a certain property should or should not be made into a motion picture.

Stossel, Ludwig. Actor. *b.* Feb. 12, 1883, Lockenhaus, Austria. *d.* 1973. On the Austrian and German stage from age 17, he acted for Reinhardt and Preminger, among other directors. In Hollywood from 1940, after a stopover in London, he played character parts in numerous films, generally portraying amiable Germanic types, memorably as Lou Gehrig's father in *The Pride of the Yankees* (1942) and as Albert Einstein in *The Beginning or the End* (1947). He was popular in the 60s as "the little old winemaker" in a long series of TV commercials.

FILMS INCLUDE: In Germany—*Bockbierfest, Skandal um Eva* 1930; *Elisabeth von Oesterreich* 1931; *Strich durch die Rechnung* 1932. In Austria—*O Schwarzwald! O Heimat!* 1936. In the US—*Four Sons, The Man I Married* 1940; *Man Hunt, Underground, Great Guns* 1941; *All Through the Night, Woman of the Year, The Pride of the Yankees* (as Lou Gehrig's father), *Iceland, Pittsburgh* 1942; *Casablanca, They Came to Blow Up America, Action in the North Atlantic, Hers to Hold, Hitler's Madman, The Strange Case of Adolf Hitler* 1943; *The Climax* 1944; *Dillinger* 1945; *Cloak and Dagger* 1946; *The Beginning or the End* (as Dr. Albert Einstein), *Song of Love, This Time for Keeps* 1947; *A Song Is Born* 1948; *The Merry Widow* 1952; *Call Me Madam* 1953; *The Sun Shines Bright* 1954; *Me and the Colonel* 1958; *The Blue Angel* 1959.

Stothart, Herbert. Composer, arranger, music director. *b.* Sept. 11, 1885, Milwaukee. *d.* 1949. He began composing for varsity shows while a student at the University of Wisconsin. He composed for Broadway from the early 20s and scored a huge success with the operetta 'Rose Marie,' which he co-wrote with Rudolf Friml. He composed his first film score in 1928, providing the music for the US presentation of the Soviet silent film *The End of St. Petersburg.* He subsequently scored or orchestrated numerous films for MGM, winning an Academy Award for the original score of *The Wizard of Oz.* Recovering from a severe heart attack in 1947, he composed 'Heart Attack: A Symphonic Poem.' Two years later he died of cancer.

FILMS INCLUDE: *Rose Marie* 1928; *Dynamite* 1929; *In Gay Madrid, Madame Satan, The Rogue Song* 1930; *New Moon* 1931; *Rasputin and the Empress* 1933; *Queen Christina, Viva Villa!, The Barretts of Wimpole Street, The Merry Widow* 1934; *David Copperfield, Naughty Marietta, Anna Karenina, Mutiny on the Bounty, A Night at the Opera, Ah Wilderness!, A Tale of Two Cities* 1935; *Rose Marie, San Francisco* 1936; *Camille, The Good Earth, Maytime, Romeo and Juliet, Conquest, The Firefly* 1937; *The Girl of the Golden West, Marie Antoinette, Sweethearts* 1938; *Idiot's Delight, The Wizard of Oz* 1939; *Waterloo Bridge, New Moon, Bitter Sweet* 1940; *Ziegfeld Girl* 1941; *Rio Rita, Mrs. Miniver* 1942; *Random Harvest, Thousands Cheer* 1943; *Madame Curie* 1944; *National Velvet, They Were Expendable* 1945; *The Green Years* 1946; *The Yearling* 1947; *The Three Musketeers* 1948; *Big Jack* 1949.

Stout, Archie (Archibald). Director of photography. *b.* Mar. 30, 1886, in Renwick, Iowa. *d.* 1965. A former hotel manager and forest ranger, he entered films in 1914 as assistant cameraman at Sennett's Keystone. He subsequently worked on numerous films, specializing in outdoor cinematography. In 1952 he won an Academy Award (in collaboration) for Ford's *The Quiet Man* but retired two years later after a heart attack.

FILMS INCLUDE: *His Nibs* (co-phot.) 1921; *The Ten Commandments* (co-phot.) 1923; *Feet of Clay* (co-phot.) 1924; *Varsity* 1928; *Darkened Rooms* 1929; *Dangerous Paradise, Young Eagles, The Benson Murder Case, The Return of Dr. Fu Manchu, Derelict, Manslaughter, The Sea God* 1930; *It Pays to Advertise* 1931; *Sunset Pass* 1933; *Borderland* 1937; *Professor Beware* 1938; *Rulers of the Sea* (co-phot.) 1939; *It Happened Tomorrow, Summer Storm* 1944; *Captain Kidd* 1945; *Angel and the Badman* 1947; *Fort Apache* 1948; *Outrage* 1950; *Hard Fast and Beautiful* 1951; *The Quiet Man* (co-phot.), *Big Jim McLain* 1952; *The Sun Shines Bright, Island in the Sky* 1953; *Hondo* (co-phot.), *The High and the Mighty* 1954.

Stowe, Madeleine. Actress. Born on Aug. 18, 1958, in Los Angeles, Calif. *ed.* USC. Attractive, dark-haired screen lead, in films since the 1980s. Began career in the theater in California.

FILMS INCLUDE: *Stakeout* 1987; *Worth Winning* 1989; *Revenge, The Two Jakes* 1990; *Closet Land* 1991; *The Last of the Mohicans, Unlawful Entry* 1992; *Another Stakeout, Short Cuts* 1993; *Bad Girls, Blink, China Moon* 1994; *12 Monkeys* 1995.

Stradling, Harry. Director of photography. *b.* 1902, England. *d.* 1970. In the US from his teens, he began his film career in the early 20s as cameraman of shorts and of routine Hollywood features. However, it was in France in 1934–35 that he first gained prominence as a gifted lighting cameraman, especially after working on Jacques Feyder's *La Kermesse héroïque/Carnival in Flanders.* He later worked on several distinguished British films before returning to Hollywood in 1940. For the following 30 years he was responsible for the cinematography of many important American productions, winning Academy Awards for *The Picture of Dorian Gray* (1945) and *My Fair Lady* (1964). He was particularly noted for his lavish color photography. He died while shooting *The Owl and the Pussycat.* He was the father of Harry STRADLING, JR.

FILMS INCLUDE: In the US—*The Devil's Garden* 1920; *The Great Adventure* (co-phot.) 1921; *The Secrets of Paris* (co-phot.) 1922; *The Substitute Wife* 1925; *Burnt Fingers* 1927; *Mother's Boy* (co-phot.) 1929. In France—*Le Grand Jeu* 1934; *Quelle Drôle de Gosse, La Kermesse heroïque/Carnival in Flanders* 1935. In the UK—*Knight Without Armor* 1937; *The Divorce of Lady X, South Riding, Pygmalion, The Citadel* 1938; *Jamaica Inn* (co-phot.), *Q Planes, Over the Moon, The Lion Has Wings* (co-phot.) 1939. In the US—*My Son My Son, They Knew What They Wanted* 1940; *Suspicion, The Devil and Miss Jones, Mr. and Mrs. North, The Corsican Brothers* 1941; *Nazi Agent* 1942; *The Human Comedy* 1943; *Song of Russia, Bathing Beauty* 1944; *The Picture of Dorian Gray* 1945; *Easy to Wed, Holiday in Mexico* 1946; *Till the Clouds Roll By, Sea of Grass, Song of Love* 1947; *The Pirate, Easter Parade, Words and Music* 1948; *The Barkleys of Broadway, In the Good Old Summertime* 1949; *Valentino, A Streetcar Named Desire* 1951; *Androcles and the Lion* 1953; *Johnny Guitar* 1954; *Guys and Dolls* 1955; *Helen of Troy, The Eddy Duchin Story* 1956; *A Face in the Crowd* (co-phot.), *The Pajama Game* 1957; *Marjorie Morningstar, Auntie Mame* 1958; *The Young Philadelphians, A Summer Place* 1959; *Who Was That Lady?, The Dark at the Top of the Stairs* 1960; *Parrish, On the Double* 1961; *A Majority of One, Gypsy* 1962; *Mary Mary* 1963; *My Fair Lady* 1964; *How to Murder Your Wife* 1965; *Who's Afraid of Virginia Woolf?* 1966; *Funny Girl* 1968; *Hello Dolly!* 1960; *On a Clear Day You Can See Forever, The Owl and the Pussycat* (completed by Andrew Laszlo) 1970.

Stradling, Harry, Jr. American director of photography. The son of Harry STRADLING, he entered the film industry as camera assistant and, after a period as camera operator, developed in the late 60s and early 70s into a leading Hollywood cinematographer. At his best with outdoor color photography.

FILMS INCLUDE: *Welcome to Hard Times* 1967; *With Six You Get Eggroll* 1968; *Support Your Local Sheriff, Young Billy Young, The Good Guys and the Bad Guys* 1969; *There Was A Crooked Man, Dirty Dingus Magee, Little Big Man* 1970; *Fools' Parade, Something Big* 1971; *Skyjacked, 1776* 1972; *The Man Who Loved Cat Dancing, The Way We Were* 1973; *McQ, Bank Shot* 1974; *Bite the Bullet, Rooster Cogburn* 1975; *Midway, The Big Bus, Special Delivery* 1976; *The Greatest, Damnation Alley* 1977; *Convoy, Go Tell the Spartans, Born Again* 1978; *Prophecy* 1979; *Up the Academy, Carny* 1980; *S.O.B., The Pursuit of D. B. Cooper, Buddy Buddy* 1981; *Micki and Maude* 1984; *A Fine Mess* 1986; *Blind Date* 1987; *Caddyshack II* 1988.

Straight, Beatrice. Actress. Born on August 2, 1918, in Old Westbury, N.Y. Classically stage-trained character player, best known in film for her Academy Award–winning performance as the spurned spouse in *Network.* Won a Tony for her performance in 'The Crucible.'

FILMS INCLUDE: *Phone Call from a Stranger* 1952; *Patterns* 1956; *The Nun's Story* 1959; *Network* 1976; *Bloodline, The Promise* 1979; *The Formula* 1980; *Endless Love* 1981; *Poltergeist* 1982; *Two of a Kind* 1983; *Power, Under Seige* 1986; *Deceived* 1991.

straight cut. A direct transition from one shot to another without resorting to any optical effects. The meaning of the term is the same as CUT, but the indication is more emphatic.

straight man. An entertainer who plays a foil for a comedian, as Bud Abbott for Lou Costello or Dean Martin for Jerry Lewis.

straight part. An ordinary, straightforward dramatic part, not played for comedy, villainy, or any other specific effect.

Strand, Paul. Documentary filmmaker. *b.* Oct. 16, 1890, New York City. *d.* 1976. A noted still photographer who exerted great influence on the contemporary art of photography. He stunned film audiences in the mid-30s with a beautifully photographed and deeply moving documentary about fishermen, *Redes/The Wave,* which he had written, produced, and photographed (Fred Zinnemann had directed) in Mexico. Returning to the US, he became the leader of a group of enthusiastic, socially conscious New York–based writers, artists, and filmmakers, a group that included such personalities as Zinnemann, Elia Kazan, Ralph Steiner, Willard Van Dyke, Pare Lorentz, Sydney Myers, Leo Hurwitz, and John Howard Lawson. In 1937 he founded Frontier Films with the help of John Dos Passos, Lillian Hellman, Archibald MacLeish, Clifford Odets, and Lewis Milestone, among others, for the purpose of producing "meaningful and progressive" documentary films. The group's activity was cut short by WW II. Later, several of its members became victims of the McCarthy era. In 1948, Strand retired from his cinematic activities and returned to still photography. However, by this time he had made an enormous contribution to the development of the American documentary.

FILMS INCLUDE: *Manhattan* (co-dir., phot.) 1921; *The Live Wire* (co-phot.) 1925; *Redes/The Wave* (prod., co-sc., phot.), *The Plow That Broke the Plains* (co-phot.) 1936; *The Heart of Spain* (co-prod., co-edit.) 1937; *Return to Life* (co-prod.) 1938; *China Strikes Back* (co-prod.) 1939; *Native Land* (co-dir., so-sc., phot.) 1942.

Strange, Glenn. Actor. *b.* Aug. 16, 1899, Weed, N.M., of Irish-Cherokee Indian parentage. *d.* 1973. A former rancher, deputy sheriff, and rodeo performer, he entered show business as a member of the Arizona Wranglers radio group. He entered films in the mid-30s and played supporting roles in many low-budget productions, mostly Westerns, often as the bad guy. He won a measure of fame among horror film devotees after portraying Frankenstein's monster in several films. Late in his career he became familiar to TV viewers as the bartender, Sam, in the long-running 'Gunsmoke' series.

FILMS INCLUDE: *New Frontier* 1935; *Arizona Days* 1937; *Mysterious Rider* 1938; *Range War* 1939; *Wagon Train* 1940; *The Mad Monster* 1942; *Action in the North Atlantic, Mission to Moscow* 1943; *The Monster Maker* 1944; *House of Frankenstein, House of Dracula* 1945; *Abbott and Costello Meet Frankenstein, Red River* 1948; *Double Crossbones, Texas Carnival, The Red Badge of Courage* 1951; *The Lawless Breed* 1952; *The Vanishing American* 1955; *Quantrill's Raiders* 1958.

Strasberg, Lee. Actor, stage director. *b.* Nov. 17, 1901, Budzanow, Austria. *d.* 1982. In the US from age nine, he trained under Boleslavsky and Ouspenskaya at the American Laboratory Theatre, making his acting debut in 1925. He was among the founders in 1930 of the Group Theatre in New York, for which he directed many plays through 1937. In 1949 he became the artistic director of the ACTORS STUDIO and in that capacity exerted great influence on the contemporary American theater and cinema. In 1969 he established the Lee Strasberg Institute of the Theatre in New York and Los Angeles. He made an auspicious debut as a screen actor in *The Godfather Part II* (1974), playing the role of mobster Hyman Roth, for which he was nominated for an Oscar as best supporting player. He was the father of Susan STRASBERG.

FILMS: *The Godfather Part II* 1974; *The Cassandra Crossing* 1977; *Boardwalk, And Justice for All, Going in Style* 1979.

Strasberg, Susan. Actress. Born on May 22, 1938, in New York City. The daughter of Lee and Paula STRASBERG, founders and directors of the Actors Studio, she was raised in the limelight of the stage but never attended her parents' famous school. She made her stage debut at 14 off Broadway. In 1955 she won laurels for her performance in the title role in the Broadway production of 'The Diary of Anne Frank.' She made her screen debut the same year and has since played gentle leads in a number of films. Formerly married to actor Christopher Jones. Author: *Marilyn and Me* (1992) about her friendship with Marilyn Monroe.

FILMS: *The Cobweb* 1955; *Picnic* 1956; *Stage Struck* 1958; *Kapo* (It./Fr./Yug.) 1960; *Taste of Fear/Scream of Fear* (UK) 1961; *Il Disordine/Disorder* (It./Fr.), *Hemingway's Adventures of a Young Man* 1962; *The High Bright Sun/McGuire Go Home!* (UK) 1965; *The Trip* 1967; *Psych-Out, Chubasco, The Name of the Game Is Kill!, The Brotherhood* 1968; *Sweet Hunters* 1969; *Who Fears the Devil/Legend of Hillbilly John* 1973; *Sammy Somebody* 1976; *Rollercoaster* 1977; *The Manitou, In Praise of Older Women* (Can.) 1978; *Bloody Birthday* 1980; *Sweet 16* 1981; *Delta Force* 1986; *Prime Suspect* 1988; *The Runnin' Kind* 1989; *The Light in the Jungle* 1991.

Strathairn, David. Actor. Born in 1949 in San Francisco, Calif. *ed.* Williams Coll., Ringling Bros. Clown Coll. A featured player on and off Broadway, he has appeared in several films of his Williams classmate John SAYLES, including his own and Sayles's directorial debut, *The Return of the Secaucus Seven*. Regular on the TV series 'The Days and Nights of Molly Dodd.'

FILMS INCLUDE: *The Return of the Secaucus Seven* 1979; *When Nature Calls* 1982; *Enormous Changes at the Last Minute, Lovesick, Silkwood* 1983; *The Brother from Another Planet, Iceman* 1984; *At Close Range* 1986; *Matewan* 1986; *Call Me, Dominick and Eugene, Eight Men Out, Stars and Bars* 1988; *The Feud* 1989; *Memphis Belle* 1990; *City of Hope* 1991; *Big Girls Don't Cry... They Get Even, Bob Roberts, Sneakers, Shadows and Fog, A League of Their Own* 1992; *Lost in Yonkers, The Firm, A Dangerous Woman* 1993; *The River Wild* 1994; *Dolores Claiborne, Losing Isaiah* 1995; *Mother Night* 1996; *L.A. Confidential* 1997.

Straub, Jean-Marie. Director. Born in 1933, in Metz, France. As a teenager he organized a film society in Metz. After literature studies in Strasbourg and Nancy, he went to Paris, where he worked as an assistant to Abel Gance, Jean Renoir, and Robert Bresson, among other directors. In 1958 he left France to avoid the draft, settling in Munich, Germany. He began directing in the early 60s and soon became recognized as a leading voice in the New German Cinema. His style is typically sparse, minimal, elliptical, and austere. His wife, Danièle Huillet, collaborates on his films as producer and writer.

FILMS INCLUDE: *Machorka-Muff* (short) 1963; *Nicht versohnt oder Es hilft nur Gewalt wo Gewalt herrscht/Not Reconciled or Only Violence Helps Where It Rules/Unreconciled* (also co-prod., co-sc.) 1965; *Chronik der Anna Magdalena Bach/Chronicle of Anna Magdalena Bach* (also co-sc., co-edit.) 1967; *Der Brautigam die Komödiantin und der Zuhalter/The Bridegroom the Comedienne and the Pimp* (short) 1968; *Othon* (co-dir., co-sc., co-edit. with Danièle Huillet; also act. under pseudonym Jubarithe Semaran) 1971; *Geschichtsunterricht/History Lessons* (also co-prod., co-sc., co-edit.) 1973; *Moses and Aaron* (co-dir., co-sc., co-edit. with Huillet) 1975; *Della Nube alla Resistenza* (co-dir. with Huillet) 1979.

Strauss, Robert. Actor. *b.* Nov. 8, 1913, New York City. *d.* 1975. Burly character actor and comedian of the American stage and screen, he was outstanding as "Animal" in both the Broadway and Hollywood versions of *Stalag 17*, a role for which he was nominated for an Oscar. The son of a theater costume designer, he had worked as a busboy, a salesman, and a singing waiter, among other occupations, before starting his acting career. In addition to acting in many plays and films, he also appeared in numerous TV shows.

FILMS INCLUDE: *Native Land* (doc.) 1942; *Sailor Beware, Jumping Jacks* 1952; *Stalag 17* 1953; *Act of Love, Money from Home* 1954; *The Bridges of Toko-Ri, The Seven Year Itch, The Man with the Golden Arm* 1955; *Attack!* 1956; *Li'l Abner* 1959; *Wake Me When It's Over* 1960; *The George Raft Story* 1961; *The Wheeler Dealers, The Thrill of It All* 1963; *Harlow* 1965; *Frankie and Johnny* 1966; *Fort Utah* 1967; *Dagmar's Hot Pants* (Den.) 1971.

Strayer, Frank. Director. *b.* Sept. 21, 1891, Altoona, Pa. *d.* 1964. *ed.* Penn. Military Acad.; Carnegie Tech. After WW I service as an ensign with the Navy, he joined Metro as assistant director and occasionally actor. From the mid-20s he directed for Columbia and other studios, mostly routine second features. He was responsible for many of the early episodes of the popular comedy series "Blondie."

FILMS INCLUDE: *An Enemy of Men, The Fate of a Flirt, The Lure of the Wild* 1925; *When the Wife's Away, Sweet Rosie O'Grady* 1926; *The Bachelor's Baby, Pleasure Before Business, Rough House Rosie, Now We're in the Air* 1927; *Partners in Crime, Just Married, Moran of the Marines* 1928; *The Fall of Eve, Acquitted* 1929; *Let's Go Places, Borrowed Wives* 1930; *Caught Cheating, Murder at Midnight, Anybody's Blonde, Soul of the Slums* 1931; *The Monster Walks, Gorilla Ship, Manhattan Tower, The Crusader* 1932; *The Vampire Bat, By Appointment Only, Dance Girl Dance* 1933; *In Love with Life, Cross Streets, Fugitive Road, Once in a Million, In the Money* 1934; *Port of Lost Dreams, The Ghost Walks, Public Opinion, Symphony of Living, Society Fever* 1935; *Hitchhike to Heaven, Sea Spoilers* 1936; *Off to the Races, Big Business, Hot Water* 1937; *Blondie* (and a dozen subsequent episodes in the series through 1943) 1938; *Go West Young Lady* 1941; *The Daring Young Man* 1943; *Mama Loves Papa, Senorita of the West* 1945; *The Sickle or the Cross* 1951.

Streep, Meryl. Born in 1951, in Basking Ridge, N.J. Radiant, expressive, talented leading lady of the American stage and screen. At 12 she took voice lessons for opera but developed an interest in acting while attending high school and began playing leads in school productions. She later majored in drama at Vassar, spent a term at Dartmouth studying costume design and playwriting, and went on to graduate work at the Yale School of Drama. After playing leads in several productions of the Yale Repertory Theater, she came to New York and appeared successfully in a number of Broadway plays, including Tennessee Williams's '27 Wagons Full of Cotton,' for which she was nominated for a Tony Award. In 1976 she joined the New York Shakespeare Festival, and in the following year made her screen debut in *Julia*. She was nominated for an Oscar as best supporting actress for *The Deer Hunter* (1978) and won the National Society of Film Critics Award for that role. It was her first of many Oscar nominations. She first won for best supporting actress for her work in the divorce drama *Kramer vs. Kramer*

(1979). She then won for best actress for her role as a Polish woman who must choose which of her children lives in *Sophie's Choice* (1982). Throughout the 80s, Streep tackled a wide variety of dramatic roles, becoming well known for her uncanny ability to mimic accents. She turned to comedic roles in the late 80s and early 90s. She excelled as a comedienne, from her first, semisuccessful effort *She-Devil* (1989) to the special effects-laden blockbuster *Death Becomes Her* (1992). Nominated for ten Academy Awards throughout her career so far, she is one of Hollywood's most esteemed actresses, also winning the Emmy Award for her performance in the 1978 TV drama 'Holocaust.'

FILMS: *Julia* 1977; *The Deer Hunter* 1978; *Manhattan, The Seduction of Joe Tynan, Kramer vs. Kramer* 1979; *The French Lieutenant's Woman* 1981; *Still of the Night, Sophie's Choice* 1982; *Silkwood* 1983; *Falling in Love* 1984; *Plenty, Out of Africa* 1985; *Heartburn* 1986; *Ironweed* 1987; *A Cry in the Dark* 1988; *She-Devil* 1989; *Postcards from the Edge* 1990; *Defending Your Life* 1991; *Death Becomes Her* 1992; *The House of the Spirits* 1993; *The River Wild* 1994; *Before and After, The Bridges of Madison County* 1995; *Marvin's Room* 1996.

street films. See GERMANY.

Streisand, Barbra. Actress, singer, director. Born Barbara Joan Streisand, on Apr. 24, 1942, in Brooklyn, N.Y. Superstar entertainer of the American stage, TV, recordings, and films. Harboring show-business ambitions since early childhood, she worked as a switchboard operator and theater usherette while struggling to make headway in the world of entertainment. She finally made a modest breakthrough by winning a Greenwich Village nightclub contest and after gaining some recognition on the nightclub circuit and appearing in an off-Broadway revue, she made her Broadway debut in 'I Can Get It for You Wholesale' in 1962. The musical wasn't very successful and her role in it, as Yetta Tessye Marmelstein, not too big. But she stole the show with her clowning and singing, won the New York Critics Award, and almost overnight was catapulted to superstardom. Compensating for an imperfect face and a kookie Brooklynese personality with a throbbing, ranging voice and glowing magnetism, she became enormously popular in supper clubs and in TV guest appearances, capping her success in 1964 with a glittering performance in the role of Fanny Brice in the Broadway musical 'Funny Girl.' She was signed by CBS on a multi-year, multimillion-dollar contract and enjoyed tremendous success with a string of recordings and elaborate TV specials.

Streisand was firmly entrenched at the apex of the American entertainment industry by the time she made her film debut in 1968, repeating her stage role in *Funny Girl.* She proved herself equally in command of the film medium as she had been as a stage and recording star and won an Academy Award for her performance, in a tie with Katharine Hepburn. In 1970 she was presented with a special Broadway Tony Award as "Actress of the Decade." Other films followed, all dominated by her vibrant personality and enormous talent. Despite the mediocrity of most of her vehicles of the 70s, and the growing criticism of her as a megalomaniac and a tyrant on the set who interferes with every detail of production, she remained a top box-office attraction and the leading female screen personality. She won an Oscar in 1977 for composing the music for the song "Evergreen" for the film *A Star Is Born.*

In the 80s, Streisand turned her hand to directing. Directing herself in an adaptation of Isaac Bashevis Singer's *Yentl* (1983), she played a young Jewish woman who longs to study the Talmud and so disguises herself as a man. Her appearance is so convincing she attracts romantic interest from Amy Irving, and goes through with a comic marriage. After *Yentl*, Streisand concentrated on projects with her production company, Barwood Films. She starred in *Nuts* (1987), playing a high-class prostitute whose sanity is in question, then again directed herself in 1991's *The Prince of Tides*. The latter was widely praised and received several Oscar nominations including one for best film. The best director nomination, however, has proven elusive; she, along with her supporters, has accused the academy of overlooking her for her sex and her maverick sensibilities. She is active in liberal political causes. Despite a well-known problem with stage fright, she has begun to make more concert appearances in the 90s, including an appearance at the inaugural concert for President Bill Clinton. She is divorced from Elliott GOULD, who was her co-star in 'I Can Get It for You Wholesale,' the musical that started it all. Her son, actor Jason Gould, appeared with his mother in *The Prince of Tides*.

FILMS: *Funny Girl* (as Fanny Brice) 1968; *Hello Dolly!* 1969; *On a Clear Day You Can See Forever, The Owl and the Pussycat* 1970; *What's Up Doc?, Up the Sandbox* 1972; *The Way We Were* 1973; *For Pete's Sake* 1974; *Funny Lady* (again as Fanny Brice) 1975; *A Star Is Born* (also song composer) 1976; *The Main Event* (also co-exec. prod.) 1979; *All Night Long* 1981; *Yentl* (also dir., prod., co-sc., songs) 1983; *Nuts* (also prod., songs) 1987; *The Prince of Tides* (also dir., co-prod.) 1991; *The Mirror Has Two Faces* (also dir.) 1996.

stress marks. Streaks on a film print which usually are caused by undue mechanical friction or pressure in the negative stage.

Strick, Joseph. Director, producer, screenwriter. Born in 1923, in Pittsburgh. His studies at UCLA were interrupted by WW II, which he spent as a cameraman with the USAAF. Returning to civilian life, he made his first film, the documentary *Muscle Beach* (co-directed with Irving Lerner, 1948), on weekends while working as a copyboy at the Los Angeles *Times.* Later, while working for TV, he took five years to complete in his spare time *The Savage Eye* (1959), an innovative semidocumentary feature about urban life, which he co-directed with Ben Maddow and Sidney Meyers. The film won several international awards. Venturing into literary adaptations in the 60s, he drew much praise but also some criticism for his courageous undertaking of converting to the screen James Joyce's complex stream-of-consciousness novel *Ulysses* (1967). In 1970 he won an Oscar for his documentary short *Interviews with My Lai Veterans.*

FILMS: *Muscle Beach* (doc.; co-dir. with Irving Lerner) 1948; *Jour de Fête* (doc. short; Fr.) 1949; *The Big Break* (doc.; dir., prod.) 1953; *The Savage Eye* (co-dir., co-prod., co-sc., co-edit. with Ben Maddow and Sidney Meyers) 1959; *An Affair of the Skin* (assoc. prod.), *The Balcony* (dir., co-prod.) 1963; *The Hecklers* (dir. for British TV) 1966; *Ulysses* (dir., prod., co-sc.), *The Legend of the Boy and the Eagle* (co-assoc. prod.) 1967; *Justine* (replaced by George Cukor as director early in the filming), *Ring of Bright Water* (prod.) 1969; *Tropic of Cancer* (dir., prod., co-sc.), *Interviews with My Lai Veterans* (doc. short; dir., prod., sc.) 1970; *Road Movie* (dir., prod.) 1974; *A Portrait of the Artist as a Young Man* (dir.) 1979; *Criminals* 1996.

strike. To dismantle a set after filming has been completed.

striping. The process of applying a band of magnetic coating, or a stripe, to motion picture film for the purpose of sound recording.

Stritch, Elaine. Actress. Born on Feb. 2, 1926, in Detroit. Character comedienne of the American stage, screen, and TV. Educated at a finishing school, she prepared for the stage with Erwin Piscator at the Dramatic Workshop of the New School, making her debut in a school production in 1944. She made her first Broadway appearance two years later and subsequently appeared in numerous stage productions in New York and on tour. She also appeared frequently on TV and co-starred as Ruth in the 1960–61 series 'My Sister Eileen.' Her film roles have been sporadic. In 1973 she married an English actor, John Bay, and moved to London.

FILMS: *The Scarlet Hour* 1956; *Three Violent People, Farewell to Arms* (as Helen Ferguson) 1957; *The Perfect Furlough* 1959; *Who Killed Teddy Bear?* 1965; *The Sidelong Glances of a Pigeon Kicker/Pigeons* 1970; *Providence* (Fr.) 1977; *September, Cocoon: The Return* 1988; *Cadillac Man* 1990; *Out to Sea* 1997.

stroboscopic effects. Undesirable optical effects resulting from the relationship between the speed of the subject being filmed and the interval between camera exposures. The most common example of the stroboscopic effect, or strobing, is the illusion of spoked wheels revolving backward while in reality they are rolling forward. The effect can be minimized by reducing the number of spokes on the wheel, increasing the shooting speed, slowing camera movement, changing the camera angle, etc.

Strock, Herbert L. Director. Born on Jan. 13, 1918, in Boston. A former publicist and film editor, he turned out a number of inexpensive, rather shrill Hollywood horror and action melodramas in the 50s and 60s.

FILMS: *Storm Over Tibet* 1952; *Gog* 1954; *Battle Taxi* 1955; *I Was a Teenage Frankenstein, Blood of Dracula* 1957; *Rider on a Dead Horse, The Devil's Messenger* (partly re-edited from 1959 Swedish TV series, 'No. 13 Demon Street,' which Strock directed from a script by Curt Siodmak) 1962; *The Crawling Hand* 1963.

Strode, Woody (Woodrow). Actor. *b.* 1914, in Los Angeles. *d.* 1995. *ed.* UCLA. A former star end in the Canadian Football League, and later a professional wrestler, he made his first film appearance in 1941 and in the 50s was seen regularly on the screen as Hollywood's perennial black muscleman. A rangy athlete with a powerful physique, he was used mostly in decorative supporting roles, which required little more of him than baring his chest, flashing his teeth, and flexing his muscles. But in 1960 he was finally given a real opportunity to act in the role of a black soldier on trial for murder and rape in John Ford's *Sergeant Rutledge.* He subsequently played meatier roles in other films, both in Hollywood and in Europe, and scored a personal triumph as the star of the Italian production *Seduta alla sua Destra/Black Jesus* (1968), in which he portrayed a hero patterned after the African leader Patrice Lumumba.

FILMS INCLUDE: *Sundown* 1941; *The Lion Hunters* 1951; *The City Beneath the Sea* 1953; *The Gambler from Natchez* 1954; *The Ten Commandments* 1956; *Tarzan's Fight for Life* 1958; *Pork Chop Hill* 1959; *The Last Voyage, Sergeant Rutledge, Spartacus* 1960; *The Sins of Rachel Cade, Two Rode Together* 1961; *The Man Who Shot Liberty Valance* 1962; *Tarzan's Three Challenges* 1963; *Genghis Khan* (US/UK/Ger./Yug.) 1965; *Seven Women, The Professionals* 1966; *Seduto alla sua Destra/Black Jesus* (It.), *C'era una volta il West/Once Upon a Time in the West* (It./US), *Shalako* (UK) 1968; *Che!* 1969; *La Spina dorsale del Diavolo/The Deserter* (It./Yug.), *The Last Rebel* 1971; *Black Rodeo* (guest star-narrator), *The Revengers, La Mala Ordina/The Italian Connection* (It.) 1972; *The Gatling Gun* 1973; *Winter Hawk* 1975; *Oil* (It.), *Kingdom of the Spiders* 1977; *Ravagers, Jaguar Lives, Kill Castro/Assignment: Kill Castro/Key West Crossing/Cuba Crossing/Sweet, Dirty Tony/The Mercenaries* 1979; *The Final Executioner, Vigilante, The Black Stallion Returns, Scream, Violent Breed* 1983; *Jungle Warriors, The Cotton Club* 1984; *Lust in the Dust* 1985; *Super Brother* 1990; *Storyville* 1992; *Posse* 1993; *The Quick and the Dead* 1995.

Stroheim, Erich Von. Director, actor. *b.* Sept. 22, 1885, Vienna. *d.* 1957. Contrary to a widely accepted myth, he was not born Erich Hans Carl Maria Stroheim von Nordenwall, a descendant of a noble Prussian military family, but Erich Oswald Stroheim, the son of a Jewish hatter from Gleiwitz in Prussian Silesia who had settled in Vienna. Contrary to another myth, which he himself initiated, Stroheim was not a career officer in the cavalry, although he did serve briefly in the Austro-Hungarian army, where he acquired a skill at fencing. His true early career was that of a supervisor in his father's small straw hat manufacturing plant.

Von Stroheim emigrated to the US sometime between 1906 and 1909. He worked at a variety of odd jobs before arriving in Hollywood in 1914. After playing bit roles in a number of films, he established himself as a regular member of D. W. Griffith's company as a bit player, assistant director, and military advisor. In 1917, the year in which America entered WW I, he played for the first time the role with which he was to become identified in years to come, that of the Prussian officer, a rigid and autocratic Hun with cruel thin lips and a sarcastic, monocled gaze.

After the Armistice, there was little demand for Von Stroheim's services as an actor and he began actively seeking an opportunity to direct. He finally succeeded in convincing Carl Laemmle of Universal to let him direct *Blind Husbands,* an adaptation of Von Stroheim's own short story "The Pinnacle." Von Stroheim wrote the script, designed the sets, directed, and played the lead role of Lieutenant von Steuben in *Blind Husbands.* The film's plot, a sex triangle melodrama, was rather trite and insignificant. But critics noticed the careful attention to detail in the décor, the costumes, the gestures of the actors, and the keen psychological observation of the characters and their motivations. *Blind Husbands* was acknowledged as the subtlest, wittiest, and most sophisticated sex drama presented on the American screen to that date. The film was a commercial as well as a critical success.

The sex triangle also provided the central motif for Von Stroheim's next two films, *The Devil's Pass Key* and *Foolish Wives,* which, together with *Blind Husbands,* formed an urbane and mature trilogy of adultery rich in realistic detail. The plots of all three films concerned the sexual awakening of a neglected American wife in Europe who responds to the attention of a courtly Continental, twice played by Von Stroheim himself. *Foolish Wives* was Von Stroheim's first important film and the first to establish his reputation as both a creative genius and a profligate spendthrift. He spent close to a million dollars of Universal's money on *Foolish Wives,* an extravagant sum in the early 20s.

Von Stroheim's insistence on authentic detail caused production to take nearly a year. He demanded the studio build for him a life-size replica of Monte Carlo and insisted on shooting the exteriors on remote locations. This extravagance became a source of annoyance to the studio's young production head, Irving Thalberg. Although *Foolish Wives* turned out to be Universal's biggest box-office hit to date, it was also the most expensive and the margin of profit was slight. In addition, Von Stroheim developed a tendency to make his films very long, so that he could explore the psychology of the characters at a leisurely pace.

As a result of this last extravagance, the studio handed the final cutting of his films to others. *Foolish Wives* was released in a mutilated version, about a third shorter than Von Stroheim had intended, much to his chagrin. From that point on, none of his films appeared on the screen as he had made them. He was fired by Thalberg midway through the production of his next film, *Merry-Go-Round,* which was eventually finished by Rupert Julian. Ironically, Von Stroheim was working for Thalberg again on his very next assignment, *Greed.* He had started the film under the Goldwyn banner and found himself working for Thalberg when the Goldwyn and Metro companies merged to form MGM. *Greed* was Von Stroheim's great masterpiece and his greatest folly. He adapted it from Frank Norris's naturalist novel *McTeague* with an obsessive commitment to a literal transcription of every detail in the author's book. The result was a monumental production of staggering proportions.

An intensely realistic drama of avarice and human degradation, *Greed* was completed by Von Stroheim as a 42-reel film, which would have required seven hours of continuous showing. Reluctantly, he cut the film down to 24 reels. It was still much too long for commercial release, but he refused to cut any more. The cutting was then turned over to director Rex Ingram, who brought it down to 18 reels. *Greed* was finally released in ten reels to extremely mixed notices. The few who had seen Von Stroheim's 42-reel original version acclaimed it as one of the great masterpieces of cinema art. The complete version is said to be preserved in the MGM vaults, but it hasn't been seen by anyone in several decades.

The *Greed* affair irreparably damaged Von Stroheim's reputation among budget-conscious Hollywood producers, but MGM recognized his talent and assigned him to direct one more film, *The Merry Widow,* from the operetta by Franz Lehár. Von Stroheim used the operetta libretto only as an outline and turned the film into an orgiastic black comedy replete with descriptions of sadism, perversion, and debauchery behind the bittersweet façade of Hapsburg society. Decadent life in Imperial Vienna was also the theme of *The Wedding March,* which Von Stroheim directed for Paramount. He conceived it as part of a trilogy that had begun with his *Merry-Go-Round.* Again the completed film was so long that, even after severe cutting, it had to be released in Europe in two parts, the second exhibited as a separate film entitled *The Honeymoon.*

Von Stroheim's history of extravagances and martyrdom repeated itself with *Queen Kelly* (1928). The film starred Gloria Swanson, who also produced, with the financial backing of Joseph P. Kennedy. Miss Swanson didn't care much for Von Stroheim's flamboyance and she fired him midway through production, with $600,000 gone down the drain. Eventually, she salvaged the filmed footage by having it re-cut at an additional cost of $200,000. The released version, repudiated by Von Stroheim, was shown in Europe but never exhibited in the US.

Von Stroheim's silent films anticipated the sound era in their meticulous realism. But the director was destined never to make a sound film. He did begin the talkie *Walking Down Broadway* in 1932, but the film was shelved by the studio and later completely re-shot by Alfred Werker as *Hello Sister.* Hollywood's *homme terrible* was forced to abandon directing and reluctantly return to his former specialty as an actor, playing ramrod-spined Prussians in both American and European productions, most memorably perhaps as the commandant of the German prisoner-of-war camp in Jean Renoir's *La Grande Illusion/Grand Illusion* (1937). He also collaborated on a number of scripts and wrote three novels. Until his death in Paris, in 1957, Von Stroheim remained one of cinema's tragic figures, a man in constant quest of directing projects that no longer materialized.

FILMS: As director—*Blind Husbands* (also story, sc., art dir., act.) 1919; *The Devil's Pass Key* (also co-story, sc., art dir.) 1920; *Foolish Wives* (also story, sc., co-art dir., co-costumes, act.) 1922; *Merry-Go-Round* (also story, sc., co-art dir., co-costumes completed by Rupert Julian) 1923; *Greed* (also sc., co-art dir.) 1923–25; *The Merry Widow* (also co-sc., co-art dir., co-costumes) 1925; *The Wedding March* (also co-sc., co-art dir., co-costumes, act.), *Queen Kelly* (also story, sc., co-art dir.; unfinished) 1928; *Walking Down Broadway* (also co-sc.; never released, 1932–33). As actor—In the US: *Captain McLean* 1914; *The Birth of a Nation* (bit), *The Failure* (participation unconfirmed), *Ghosts, A Bold Impersonation* (participation unconfirmed), *Old Heidelberg* (also asst. dir.) 1915; *His Picture in the Papers* (also asst. dir.), *Macbeth* (also art. dir., asst. dir.), *Intolerance* (bit; also asst. dir.), *The Social Secretary* (also asst. dir.), *Less Than Dust* (also asst. dir.) 1916; *Panthea* (also asst. dir.), *In Again—Out Again* (also art dir., asst. dir.), *For France, Reaching for the Moon, Sylvia of the Secret Service* 1917; *The Unbeliever, Hearts of the World* (also tech. advisor, asst. dir.), *The Hun Within, The Heart of Humanity* (also tech. advisor) 1918; *Souls for Sale* (cameo) 1923; *The Great Gabbo* 1929; *Three Faces East* 1930; *Friends and Lovers* 1931; *The Lost Squadron, As You Desire Me* 1932; *Crimson Romance* (also tech. advisor), *Fugitive Road* (also co-sc., tech. advisor) 1934; *The Crime of Dr. Crespi* 1935. In France: *Marthe Richard, La Grande Illusion/Grand Illusion, Mademoiselle Docteur* (UK version), *L'Alibi* 1937; *Les Pirates du Rail, L'Affaire Lafarge, Les Disparus de Saint-Agil/Boys' School, Ultimatum, Gibraltar/It Happened in Gibraltar* 1938; *Derrière la Façade/32 Rue de Montmartre, Rappel Immédiat/Thunder Over Paris, Pièges/Personal Column, Le Monde tremblera ou La Révolte des Vivants, Tempête sur Paris* 1939; *Menaces, Paris—New York* 1940. In the US: *I Was an Adventuress* 1940; *So Ends Our Night* 1941; *Five Graves to Cairo, The North Star/Armored Attack* 1943; *The Lady and the Monster, Storm Over Lisbon* 1944; *The Great Flammarion, Scotland Yard Investigator* 1945; *The Mask of Dijon* 1946; *Sunset Boulevard* (US) 1950. In France: *La Foire aux Chimères/The Devil and the Angel, On ne meurt pas comme ça* 1946; *La Danse de Mort* (also co-adapt., co-dial.) 1947; *Le Signal rouge* (Fr./Aus.), *Portrait d'un Assassin* 1949; *Alraune/Mandrake* (Ger.) 1952; *Minuit—Quai de Bercy, L'Envers du Paradis, Alerte au Sud* 1953; *Napoléon* (as Beethoven), *Série noire, La Madonne des Sleepings* 1955.

Stromberg, Hunt. Producer. *b.* 1894, Louisville, Ky. *d.* 1968. A former sports reporter for the St. Louis *Times,* he entered films in his early 20s as publicity director for the Goldwyn company in New York. In 1919 he went to Hollywood as personal representative of Thomas Ince and in 1921 began producing independently and occasionally directing his own product. In 1925 he joined the staff of MGM, where he became one of the several talented producers working as "supervisors" under the leadership of Irving Thalberg. He remained with the studio for 17 years, producing many of the company's profitable properties, including Joan Crawford's and Jean Harlow's pictures. The Nelson Eddy-Jeanette MacDonald cycle, and "The Thin Man" series. His *The Great Ziegfeld* won the best picture Oscar in 1936. From the early 40s he produced independently, releasing through United Artists. He retired in 1951.

FILMS INCLUDE: *The Foolish Age* (also sc.) 1921; *Boy Crazy* 1922; *Breaking Into Society* (also dir., sc.) 1923; *The Night Hawk, The Fire Patrol* (also dir.), *The Siren of Seville* (also co-dir.), *A Cafe in Cairo* 1924; *Soft Shoes* (also co-sc.), *The Bad Lands, Paint and Powder* (also dir.) 1925; *Our Dancing Daughters, The Torrent, White Shadows of the South Seas* 1928; *Thunder, The Bridge of San Luis Rey* 1929; *Our Blushing Brides* 1930; *Letty Lynton, Red Dust* 1932; *The White Sister, Bombshell* 1933; *The Thin Man, Treasure Island, The Painted Veil* 1934; *Naughty Marietta, Ah Wilderness!* 1935; *Rose Marie, Wife vs.*

Secretary, The Great Ziegfeld 1936; *Maytime, Night Must Fall, The Firefly* 1937; *Marie Antoinette, Sweethearts* 1938; *Idiot's Delight, The Women* 1939; *Northwest Passage, Susan and God, Pride and Prejudice* 1940; *They Met in Bombay* 1941; *I Married an Angel* 1942; *Lady of Burlesque* 1943; *Guest in the House* 1944; *Lured* (exec. prod.) 1947; *Too Late for Tears* 1949; *Between Midnight and Dawn* 1950; *Mask of the Avenger* 1951.

Strong, Arnold. See SCHWARZENEGGER, Arnold.

Stroud, Don. Actor. Born in 1937, in Hawaii. Sturdy leading man and supporting player of Hollywood films from the late 60s. Typically in tough, gutsy roles.

FILMS INCLUDE: *Games* 1967; *Madigan, Journey to Shiloh, Coogan's Bluff* 1968; *Explosion* (Can.), *Bloody Mama, Angel Unchained* 1970; *Von Richthofen and Brown* 1971; *Joe Kidd* 1972; *Slaughter's Big Ripoff, Scalawag* (Yug./It./US) 1973; *Live a Little—Steal a Lot* 1975; *The Killer Inside Me, Death Weekend/The House by the Lake* (Can.) 1976; *Sudden Death, The Choirboys* 1977; *Search and Destroy/Striking Back* 1978; *The Amityville Horror* 1979; *The Night the Lights Went Out in Georgia, Sweet 16* 1981; *Armed and Dangerous* 1986; *Two to Tango* 1988; *Down the Drain, Twisted Justice* 1989; *The Divine Enforcer, Prime Target, The King of the Kickboxers* 1991; *Wild America* 1997.

Stroyeva, Vera. Director. Born in 1903, in Kiev, Russia. The wife of director Grigori ROSHAL, she entered Soviet films in 1926 as screenwriter. After collaborating with her husband on a number of films, she became a director in her own right, specializing in lavish musicals and screen adaptations of operas.

FILMS: *The Right of Fathers* 1931; *The Man Without a Case* (also co-sc.) 1932; *Petersburg Nights* (co-dir. with Grigori Roshal; also co-sc.) 1934; *A Generation of Conquerors/ Revolutionists* (also co-sc.) 1936; *In Search of Happiness* (co-dir., co-sc. with Roshal) 1940; *Marite* 1947; *The Grand Concert* 1951; *Variety Stars* 1954; *Boris Godunov* (also co-sc.) 1955; *Plains—My Plains* 1957; *Khovanschina* (also co-sc.) 1959.

Strudwick, Shepperd. Actor. *b.* Sept. 22, 1907, Hillsboro, N.C. *d.* 1983. *ed.* U. of North Carolina. Cultivated, gentlemanly leading man and character player of the American stage (from 1928) and screen; a member of the Actors Studio. In the early 40s used the pseudonym John Shepperd.

FILMS INCLUDE: As Shepperd Strudwick—*Fast Company* 1938; *Congo Maisie* 1940. As John Shepperd—*Belle Starr, The Men in Her Life, Remember the Day* 1941; *Rings on Her Fingers, Ten Gentlemen from West Point, The Loves of Edgar Allan Poe* (title role), *Dr. Renault's Secret* 1942; *Chetniks* 1943; *Home Sweet Homicide* 1946. As Shepperd Strudwick—*Joan of Arc, Enchantment* 1948; *The Red Pony, Chicago Deadline, All the King's Men, The Reckless Moment* 1949; *Let's Dance, Three Husbands* 1950; *A Place in the Sun* 1951; *The Eddy Duchin Story, Autumn Leaves, Beyond a Reasonable Doubt* 1956; *The Sad Sack* 1957; *Violent Midnight/Psychomania* 1963; *Daring Game* 1968; *Slaves* 1969; *Cops and Robbers* 1973.

Struss, Karl. Director of photography. *b.* 1891, New York City. *d.* 1981. The son of a bonnet-wire manufacturer, he worked in his father's plant while taking photography courses at Columbia University in the evenings. In 1914 he set up his own photographic studio in Manhattan, where he did portraits and magazine and advertising work. In 1919 he went to Hollywood, where he was hired as a cameraman by Cecil B. DE MILLE. He freelanced after his three-year contract expired and was one of the leading cameramen among the 13 employed on the set of *Ben-Hur* (1926). By devising a special filter technique, he was able to achieve a visual transformation of lepers into people with healthy skins without resorting to optical transitions. (Five years later he employed the same technique to transform Fredric March from Dr. Jekyll to Mr. Hyde.) In 1927, after sharing the very first Academy Award with Charles Rosher for *Sunrise*, Struss went to work for D. W. GRIFFITH and in 1931 he joined Paramount, where he remained for 18 years. An innovative technician and an inspired craftsman, Struss was among Hollywood's foremost creative cameramen until his retirement in the late 50s.

FILMS INCLUDE: *Something to Think About* (co-phot.) 1920; *The Affairs of Anatol* (co-phot.), *Fool's Paradise* (co-phot.) 1921; *Saturday Night* (co-phot.), *Rich Men's Wives* (co-phot.) 1922; *The Hero, Maytime* 1923; *Poisoned Paradise, The Legend of Hollywood, Idle Tongues* 1924; *The Winding Stair* 1925; *Meet the Prince, Sparrows* (co-phot.), *Ben-Hur* 1926; (co-phot.), *Sunrise* (co-phot.) 1927; *Drums of Love, The Night Watch, The Battle of the Sexes* (co-phot.) 1928; *Lady of the Pavements, Coquette, Taming of the Shrew* 1929; *One Romantic Night, The Bad One, Abraham Lincoln* 1930; *Kiki, Skippy* 1931; *Dr. Jekyll and Mr. Hyde, The Sign of the Cross, Island of Lost Souls* 1932; *Tonight Is Ours* 1933; *Four Frightened People, Belle of the Nineties* 1934; *Two for Tonight, Goin' to Town* 1935; *Anything Goes, Go West Young Man, Hollywood Boulevard* 1936; *Waikiki Wedding* 1937; *Sing You Sinners* 1938; *The Great Dictator* (co-phot.) 1940; *Aloma of the South Seas* (co-phot.) 1941; *Journey Into Fear* 1942; *Rainbow Island* 1944; *The Macomber Affair* (co-phot.) 1947; *Rocketship XM* 1950; *Limelight* 1952; *Cavalleria Rusticana* (co-phot.; It.), *Attila* (co-phot.; It.) 1954; *Mohawk* 1955; *The Fly* 1958; *The Rebel Set* 1959.

Stuart, Gloria. Actress. Born on July 14, 1910, in Santa Monica, Calif. *ed.* U. of California. Glamorous blonde leading lady of Hollywood films of the 30s, following some stage experience. Even before she made her first film, her contract was a cause of a dispute between Paramount and Universal. After arbitration by the Motion Picture Association, she was awarded to the latter but later worked for Fox and other studios. In 1934 she married screenwriter Arthur SHEEKMAN, her second husband. After retiring from the screen in the mid-40s, she took up painting. She had a one-woman show in New York in 1961.

FILMS INCLUDE: *Street of Women, The All American, The Old Dark House, Air Mail, Back Street* 1932; *Laughter in Hell, Sweepings, Private Jones, The Kiss Before the Mirror, Girl in 419, The Secret of the Blue Room, The Invisible Man, Roman Scandals* 1933; *Beloved, I'll Tell the World, The Love Captive, Here Comes the Navy, Gift of Gab* 1934; *Maybe It's Love, Gold Diggers of 1935, Laddie* 1935; *Professional Soldier, The Prisoner of Shark Island, The Poor Little Rich Girl, The Crime of Dr. Forbes, 36 Hours to Live, The Girl on the Front Page* 1936; *Girl Overboard, Life Begins in College* 1937; *Rebecca of Sunnybrook Farm, Keep Smiling, Time Out for Murder* 1938; *The Three Musketeers* (as the Queen) 1939; *The Whistler* 1944; *She Wrote the Book* 1946.

Stuart, John. Actor. *b.* John Croall, July 18, 1898, Edinburgh, Scotland. *d.* 1979. After WW I service as an officer in the Black Watch, he made his stage debut in 1919 and his first film the following year. During the 20s and 30s, he was among England's most popular stars. He was later seen in character parts or cameos and in all appeared in hundreds of films. His first wife was actress Muriel Angelus.

FILMS INCLUDE: *Her Son* 1920; *Sinister Street* 1922; *This Freedom, School for Scandal* 1923; *The Pleasure Garden, Mademoiselle from Armentieres* 1926; *Hindle Wakes/Fanny Hawthorn, The Flight Commander* 1927; *Kitty, Atlantic* 1929; *Children of Chance* 1930; *Midnight, The Hound of the*

Baskervilles 1931; *In a Monastery Garden, Number 17, Men of Steel* 1932; *The Wandering Jew, The Pointing Finger* 1933; *Bella Donna* 1934; *Abdul the Damned* 1935; *The Secret Voice* 1936; *Ships with Wings, Penn of Pennsylvania/The Courageous Mr. Penn* 1941; *Madonna of the Seven Moons* 1944; *Mrs. Fitzherbert, Mine Own Executioner* 1947; *The Magic Box* 1951; *The Naked Truth/Your Past Is Showing* 1957; *Blood of the Vampire* 1958; *Too Many Crooks* 1959; *Sink the Bismarck, Village of the Damned* 1960; *Paranoiac* 1963; *Son of the Sahara* 1966.

Stuart, Nick. Actor. *b.* Nicholas Pratza, 1904, Abrud, Rumania. *d.* 1973. Boyish athletic leading man of late silent and early sound Hollywood B films. Raised and educated in Dayton, Ohio, he worked as a shipping clerk before entering films as a prop boy in the mid-20s. He later held jobs as a script clerk and assistant cameraman, then turned to acting in 1927. After retiring from the screen in the mid-30s, he became a bandleader but broke up his orchestra in the early 60s and opened a men's store in Biloxi, Miss. He made brief cameo appearances in two films of the mid-60s. He was at one time married to Sue CAROL.

FILMS INCLUDE: *The Cradle Snatchers, High School Hero* 1927; *The News Parade, The River Pirate* 1928; *Girls Gone Wild, Joy Street, Chasing Through Europe, Why Leave Home?* 1929; *Swing High, The Fourth Alarm* 1930; *The Mystery Train* 1931; *Police Call, Secret Sinners* 1933; *Secrets of Chinatown* 1935; *Underworld Terror* 1936; *It's a Mad Mad Mad Mad World* (cameo) 1963; *This Property Is Condemned* (cameo) 1966.

Studi, Wes. Actor. Born December 17, 1947, in Nofire Hollow, Okla. *ed.* Tulsa Junior College (Okla.). A full-blooded Cherokee Indian, Studi served in the Vietnam War. Upon his return, he became involved with Native American politics, started a newspaper, and began teaching as well as ranching. After touring a one-man show, he was brought to Hollywood where he has performed in a wide range of character roles in many major films.

FILMS: *Powwow Highway* 1989; *Dances with Wolves* 1990; *The Doors* 1991; *The Last of the Mohicans* 1992; *The Broken Chain, Geronimo: An American Legend* 1993; *Street Fighter* 1994; *Heat* 1995.

studio. 1. A company that finances, produces, and distributes movies. See also STUDIO SYSTEM. 2. A stage, building, or complex of buildings where movies are produced.

studio manager. An administrative executive responsible for supervising personnel and co-ordinating the business activities of a studio but not directly involved in film production.

studio system. The set of practices by which a few companies controlled most aspects of the American movie industry from the 1920s to the early 1950s. The major studios of the era were COLUMBIA, METRO-GOLDWYN-MAYER, PARAMOUNT, RKO, 20TH CENTURY-FOX, WARNER BROS., and UNIVERSAL. Each company maintained vertical control over production, distribution, and exhibition by owning both the studio complexes in Hollywood where movies were made and the national chains of theaters in which they were exhibited. Financed by bankers in New York, movies were conceived, scripted, and produced with factory-like efficiency. Studio heads governed all aspects of production through their production managers and the producers under them; labor was divided into separate departments such as costumes, art direction, special effects, and editing; directors, screenwriters, and actors worked under contract as employees with severely limited creative power (see STAR SYSTEM). Popular genres such as Westerns, melodramas, and mysteries were developed to keep production costs down and build presold audiences for new films. Though a few popular directors, such as John Ford, Howard Hawks, Frank Capra, Billy Wilder, and Alfred Hitchcock, were able to retain a considerable degree of independence, the greater number subsumed their individual identities to the demands of the studio, each of which came to exhibit a characteristic "house style."

The major studios had some competitors, chiefly low-budget companies like REPUBLIC and MONOGRAM and independent producers like David O. SELZNICK and Samuel GOLDWYN. But by the end of the 1930s, the majors produced and released more than 75 percent of each year's films; each released over 50 films annually. Each studio's output included high-budget 'A' pictures with top stars and low-budget, second-feature 'B' pictures with lesser stars.

The beginning of the end of the studio system came in 1948, when the Supreme Court ordered the companies to divest themselves of their theater chains, thus ending their vertical monopoly over exhibition. The decline was hastened by the rise of television in the years that followed. The studios scrambled to meet the competition from the small screen with fewer and more expensive wide-screen productions, but found it economically unfeasible to maintain the studio complexes with their large payrolls of permanent staff. Departments were dismantled, contracts lapsed, and, by the end of the 50s, the studio system had come to an end. The major studios themselves survived (except for RKO), but changed hands frequently, bought by a succession of business conglomerates. They now function chiefly as financing and distribution entities that approve and release projects executed by independent production companies. See also INDEPENDENT.

stunt player. A person hired to double for a motion picture actor in action scenes requiring special physical skills or involving risk to body and limb. Stuntmen and stuntwomen are usually selected for a particular shot because of their ability to perform specialized stunts (jumping off a train, falling off a galloping horse, crashing in a car, etc.) and their superficial resemblance to the actor or actress for whom they substitute. They must be of similar height, body build, and coloring and of course must be outfitted in exactly the same costume as that worn by the star. Hollywood's regular core of stuntmen, numbering fewer than 100, is organized in the Hollywood Stuntsmen Association. They are also members of the Screen Actors Guild. They are usually paid by the stunt, the fee depending on the difficulty and risk involved. For large-budget productions requiring a great number of stunts, a stunt co-ordinator is hired to organize and supervise the work of several stuntmen. Considering the nature of their work, stuntmen seem to have been relatively immune to severe injury. Still, the hazards are great. Four stuntmen were killed in the decade between 1955 and 1965 and many others were injured, but only a few seriously.

Sturges, John. Director. *b.* Jan. 3, 1911, Oak Park, Ill. *d.* 1992. He entered films in 1932 as an assistant in the blueprint department of RKO. He continued his apprenticeship in the art department and in the cutting room and later worked as a production assistant for Selznick. He had worked his way up to film editor by the time the US entered WW II. Serving as a captain with the Air Corps, he directed and edited some 45 documentaries and training films, including the feature-length documentary *Thunderbolt* (1945), which he co-directed with Lt. Col. William WYLER. Returning to Hollywood, he made his debut as a feature film director in 1946. In the 50s, Sturges acquired a reputation as a solid director of Western action on the basis of several taut productions such as *Escape from Fort Bravo, Bad Day at Black Rock, Gunfight at the O.K. Corral,* and *Last Train from Gun Hill.* In the early 60s he had solid hits with *The Magnificent Seven* and *The Great Escape.* But it was form rather than substance that characterized his work. Overall, his misses outnumbered his hits, and his successes or failures were often correlated to the quality of the scripts given him.

FILMS: *Thunderbolt* (doc.; co-dir. with William Wyler) 1945; *The Man Who Dared, Shadowed, Alias Mr. Twilight* 1946; *For the Love of Rusty, Keeper of the Bees* 1947; *Best Man Wins, The Sign of the Ram* 1948; *The Walking Hills* 1949; *The Capture, Mystery Street, Right Cross* 1950; *The Magnificent Yankee, Kind Lady, The People Against O'Hara* 1951; *It's a Big Country* (co-dir.), *The Girl in White* 1952; *Jeopardy, Fast Company, Escape from Fort Bravo* 1953; *Bad Day at Black Rock, Underwater, The Scarlet Coat* 1955; *Backlash* 1956; *Gunfight at the O.K. Corral* 1957; *The Law and Jake Wade, The Old Man and the Sea* 1958; *Last Train from Gun Hill, Never So Few* 1959; *The Magnificent Seven* (also prod.) 1960; *By Love Possessed* 1961; *Sergeants 3* 1962; *A Girl Named Tamiko, The Great Escape* (also prod.) 1963; *The Satan Bug* (also prod.), *The Hallelujah Trail* (also prod.) 1965; *Hour of the Gun* (also prod.) 1967; *Ice Station Zebra* 1968; *Marooned* 1969; *Joe Kidd* 1972; *Valdez il Mezzosangue/Chino/The Valdez Horses* (It./Sp./Fr.) 1973; *McQ* 1974; *The Eagle Has Landed* (UK) 1976.

Sturges, Preston. Director, screenwriter, playwright. *b.* Edmond P. Biden, Aug. 29, 1898, Chicago. *d.* 1959. The son of wealthy socialites, he received his education in France, Germany, and Switzerland, as well as in American private schools. At 16 he became the manager of the Deauville branch of his mother's cosmetics firm. He returned home after the outbreak of WW I and when the US entered the war he joined the Air Corps. After the Armistice he returned to the cosmetics business and invented a kissproof lipstick. He later tried a career as an inventor in other fields with modest success. He turned a new leaf in the late 20s when he wrote his first of several plays during a prolonged stay in hospital following the removal of his appendix. His second play, 'Strictly Dishonorable,' was a Broadway hit, the most popular comedy of the 1929–30 season. It was adapted to the screen in 1931 and again in 1951.

Sturges, who had written dialogue for two 1930 Paramount films, settled in Hollywood as a screenwriter in 1933 following a couple of Broadway flops. He soon acquired a reputation as an urbane, cultured writer of polished, sophisticated scripts. Not content with having his material directed by others, he pressed Paramount in 1940 into letting him direct his own screenplay, *The Great McGinty.* The film turned out to be an unexpected critical and commercial success and propelled Sturges into one of the most meteoric directorial careers in the history of Hollywood. During a brief span (1940–44) he was widely acknowledged as Hollywood's most brilliant satirist, a worthy successor to Lubitsch and Capra in social comedy.

Sturges's films of that period parodied with pungent wit various aspects of American life, from politics and advertising to sex and hero worship. They were marked by their verbal wit, opportune comic timing, and eccentric, outrageously funny cameo characterizations. His success led to a whole movement of Hollywood screenwriters toward careers as directors. But it was short-lived. Sturges's decline was as meteoric as his rise. In 1944 he left Paramount to go into a disastrous association with Howard Hughes from which Sturges never fully recovered. His films of the late 40s lacked the timing and satiric bite that had characterized his earlier productions.

After being removed by Hughes from the helm of the ill-fated film *Vendetta,* Sturges went into a long self-exile in Europe. Several years passed before he got a chance to direct his next and last film in France, *Les Carnets du Major Thompson/The French They Are a Funny Race,* a sad epilogue to a career that had begun so brilliantly 15 years earlier. In addition to the films he wrote and directed, Sturges's screen credits also include song lyrics for the film *One Rainy Afternoon* (1936) and personal appearances in the pictures *Star Spangled Rhythm* (1942) and *Paris Holiday* (1958). He won an Oscar for the script of *The Great McGinty.*

FILMS: As screenwriter—*The Big Pond* (dial. only), *Fast and Loose* (addnl. dial. only) 1930; *Strictly Dishonorable* (play basis only) 1931; *Child of Manhattan* (play basis only), *The Power and the Glory* 1933; *Thirty-Day Princess, Imitation of Life* (uncredited), *We Live Again* 1934; *The Good Fairy, Diamond Jim* 1935; *Next Time We Love* (uncredited) 1936; *Hotel Haywire, Easy Living* 1937; *Port of Seven Seas, If I Were King* 1938; *Never Say Die* 1939; *Remember the Night* 1940; *The Birds and the Bees* 1956; *Rock-a-Bye Baby* (story only) 1958. As director-screenwriter—*The Great McGinty, Christmas in July* (also prod.) 1940; *The Lady Eve, Sullivan's Travels* 1941; *The Palm Beach Story* 1942; *The Miracle of Morgan's Creek, Hail the Conquering Hero, The Great Moment* 1944; *Mad Wednesday* (also prod.) 1947; *Unfaithfully Yours* (also prod.) 1948; *The Beautiful Blonde from Bashful Bend* (also prod.) 1949; *Les Carnets du Major Thompson/The French They Are a Funny Race* (Fr.) 1955.

Styne, Jule. Composer, songwriter. *b.* Jules Stein, on Dec. 31, 1905, in London. *d.* 1994. In the US from early childhood, he was a concert pianist at age eight and a piano soloist with the Chicago Symphony before he reached nine. In 1931 he organized and led his own band. Gaining a reputation as a vocal arranger, he went to Hollywood in the mid-30s as a voice coach to Alice Faye and Shirley Temple, among others. He began composing for films in 1938 and has since written numerous popular songs and scores for Tin Pan Alley, Hollywood, TV, Broadway, and ballet, in collaboration with Frank LOESSER and Sammy CAHN, among others. He won an Academy Award for the title song of *Three Coins in the Fountain* (1954).

FILMS INCLUDE: *Hold That Co-Ed* 1938; *Sweater Girl* ('I Don't Want to Walk Without You,' etc.), *Youth on Parade* ('I've Heard That Song Before,' etc.) 1942; *Step Lively* ('Come Out Come Out Wherever You Are,' etc.), *Follow the Boys* ('I Walk Alone,' etc.) 1944; *Anchors Aweigh, The Stork Club* ('Love Me') 1945; *The Sweetheart of Sigma Chi* ('Five Minutes More') 1946; *It Happened in Brooklyn* 1947; *Romance on the High Seas* ('It's Magic,' etc.) 1948; *Gentlemen Prefer Blondes* 1953; *Three Coins in the Fountain* 1954; *My Sister Eileen* 1955; *Bells Are Ringing* 1960; *Gypsy* 1963; *Funny Girl* 1968; *Thieves* (co-composer) 1977.

subjective camera. Camera angle that views action through the eyes of a particular observer, rather than through the usual objective, impersonal point of view. Subjective camera angles are common in films. Whenever a close-up of a particular player is followed by a bit of action, we assume we are seeing the action through that person's eyes. But rarely is an entire sequence, let alone en entire film, shot this way, An extreme and outstanding example of a film shot totally on the subjective camera premise is Robert Montgomery's suspense drama *Lady in the Lake* (1947). Montgomery directed and starred in this offbeat film, playing the role of Raymond Chandler's private eye Philip Marlowe. The film is told in the first person with nearly all the action seen through the hero's eyes. The audience sees Montgomery only when he is first introduced and whenever his image is reflected in a mirror. When the other actors in the film address Montgomery they look directly into the camera as if looking into his eyes. His reactions are never seen, only heard.

substandard film. Film of narrower gauge than the standard 35 mm, such as 16 mm or 8 mm. The term does *not* refer to the quality of the film, just its width.

subtitles. Lines superimposed on the lower part of a print of a foreign-language motion picture for the purpose of translating dialogue.

subtractive process. A method of reproducing color on film by filtering out certain tints from any of the three primary colors. The negative film is coated with three layers of emulsion, each sensitive to one particular primary color. Thus any of the colors can be removed or subtracted to achieve the desired color balance in the final print. See also COLOR CINEMATOGRAPHY.

Sucksdorff, Arne. Documentary director. Born on Feb. 3, 1917, in Stockholm. After studies of natural history and art in Stockholm and Berlin, he went on a tour of Italy. His still photographs of the trip won first prize in a contest by a Swedish film magazine. He then bought himself a motion picture camera, with which he toured Sweden, exalting the beauties of its natural life in a series of lyrical short films. Since the early 50s he has ventured into feature length films and extended his vision into foreign lands. He won awards at the Cannes Film Festival for his short *Indian Village* and feature *The Flute and the Arrow.* Sucksdorff, who writes all his own scripts and executes his own cinematography, is among the world's leading documentarians.

FILMS: Shorts—*An August Rhapsody* 1939; *Your Own Land* 1940; *A Summer Tale* 1941; *West Wind, Reindeer Time* 1943; *The Gull* 1944; *Dawn, Shadows on the Snow* 1945; *Rhythm of a City, Dream Valley* 1947; *The Open Road, A Divided World* 1948; *Going Ashore, The Living Stream* 1950; *Indian Village, The Wind and the River* (both in India) 1951. Features—*The Great Adventure* 1953; *The Flute and the Arrow* 1957; *The Boy in the Tree* 1961; *My Home Is Copacabana* (in Brazil) 1966.

Sullavan, Margaret. Actress. *b.* Margaret Brooke, May 16, 1911, Norfolk, Va. *d.* 1960. The daughter of a well-to-do family, she studied dance and drama from childhood and at 17 made her professional stage debut with the famed University Players along with other young aspirants, including Henry Fonda and James Stewart. In 1931 she made it to Broadway and in 1933 she signed a lucrative film contract with Universal. Her magnetic, winning personality made her a successful movie star right from the start, but her quick temper and disdainful attitude toward Hollywood soon led to frequent clashes with the studio and occasional flights back to Broadway. A versatile and subtle actress, she excelled at both drama and sophisticated comedy but was most typically used by Hollywood in tearful melodramas. She won the New York film critics best actress award for her role as Robert Taylor's tubercular wife in *Three Comrades* (1938) and the Drama Critics Award for her performance on Broadway in 'The Voice of the Turtle' in 1943. She retired from the screen that same year and returned only once, in 1950. From the late 40s she suffered from increasing deafness but continued her stage work with great success until her death. The first three of her four husbands were actor Henry FONDA, director William WYLER, and producer-agent Leland HAYWARD. She died tragically at the age of 49 of an accidentally administered medication. Her daughter by Hayward is Brooke Hayward, author of *Haywire,* a tragic memoir of the family and the events that led to Sullavan's death.

FILMS: *Only Yesterday* 1933; *Little Man What Now?* 1934; *The Good Fairy, So Red the Rose* (as Valette Bedford) 1935; *Next Time We Love, The Moon's Our Home* 1936; *Three Comrades, The Shopworn Angel, The Shining Hour* 1938; *The Shop Around the Corner, The Mortal Storm* 1940; *Back Street* (as Ray Smith), *So Ends Our Night, Appointment for Love* 1941; *Cry Havoc* 1943; *No Sad Songs for Me* 1950.

Sullivan, Barry. Actor. Born Patrick Barry, on Aug. 29, 1912, in New York City. *ed.* NYU; Temple U. Worked as a theater usher and department store buyer before making his Broadway debut in 1936. In Hollywood since the early 40s, he has been a solid leading man in numerous films of all genres, often thrillers and gangster pictures. He has also played much TV.

FILMS INCLUDE: *The Woman of the Town* 1943; *Lady in the Dark, And Now Tomorrow* 1944; *Getting Gertie's Garter* 1945; *Suspense* 1946; *Framed, The Gangster* 1947; *Smart Woman* 1948; *Bad Men of Tombstone, Any Number Can Play, The Great Gatsby* (as Tom Buchanan), *Tension* 1949; *The Outriders, Nancy Goes to Rio* 1950; *Payment on Demand, Three Guys Named Mike, Cause for Alarm, No Questions Asked* 1951; *Skirts Ahoy!, The Bad and the Beautiful* 1952; *Jeopardy* 1953; *Loophole, Playgirl, The Miami Story* 1954; *Queen Bee* 1955; *The Maverick Queen* 1956; *Forty Guns* 1957; *Wolf Larsen, Another Time Another Place* 1958; *The Purple Gang* 1960; *The Light in the Piazza* 1962; *A Gathering of Eagles* 1963; *Man in The Middle, Stage to Thunder Rock* 1964; *My Blood Runs Cold, Harlow* (Carol Lynley version) 1965; *An American Dream* 1966; *Buckskin* 1968; *This Savage Land* 1969; *Tell Them Willie Boy Is Here* 1970; *Earthquake* 1974; *The Human Factor* 1975; *Oh God!* 1977; *Caravans* 1978.

Sullivan, C. Gardner. Screenwriter. *b.* Sept. 18, 1879, Stillwater, Minn. *d.* 1965. *ed.* U. of Minnesota. A former newspaper reporter and feature writer, he began writing occasional scripts in 1911 and in the following year he began to work for Thomas H. Ince's organization, where he rapidly established himself as head of the scenario department. He wrote numerous screenplays based on incidents from US history and more than any writer contributed to the development of the Western genre in American films with his authentic scripts for William S. Hart's pictures. In the mid-20s Sullivan also produced a number of films for Cecil B. De Mille and for his own company. He remained an important screenwriter well into the sound era, when he worked on several De Mille spectaculars, among other films.

FILMS INCLUDE: *Her Polished Family, The Altar of Death, The Army Surgeon, The Invaders* 1912; *A Shadow of the Past, The Boomerang, The Sea of Silence, Days of '49, The Witch of Salem* 1913; *The Battle of Gettysburg, One of the Discard* (also co-dir. with Thomas H. Ince), *The Bargain, The Passing of Two-Gun Hicks* 1914; *The Italian, Satan McAllister's Heir, The Last of the Line, On the Night Stage, The Roughneck, The Ruse, Pinto Ben* 1915; *Hell's Hinges, The Aryan, The Iron Strain, Peggy, Civilization* 1916; *Gates of Doom* 1917; *Carmen of the Klondyke, Branding Broadway, Midnight Patrol, Shark Monroe* 1918; *Wagon Track, Sahara, Happy Though Married* 1919; *Hairpins, Behind the Door* 1920; *Greater Than Love, Hail the Woman* 1921; *Soul of the Beast, Human Wreckage, Dulcy, Strangers in the Night* 1923; *The Goldfish, The Marriage Cheat, Wandering Husbands, The Only Woman, Dynamite Smith, The Mirage, Cheap Kisses* 1924; *The Monster* (titles only), *Playing with Souls, Tumbleweeds* 1925; *Gigolo* (prod. only), *The Clinging Vine* (prod. only), *Sparrows* 1926; *White Gold* (prod. only), *Vanity* (prod. only) 1927; *Sadie Thompson* (prod. only), *Tempest, The Woman Disputed* 1928; *Alibi, The Locked Door* 1929; *The Cuban Love Song* (story only) 1931; *Strange Interlude* 1932; *Men Must Fight* 1933; *Father Brown—Detective* 1934; *Car 99* 1935; *Three Live Ghosts* 1936; *The Buccaneer* 1938; *Union Pacific* 1939; *North West Mounted Police* 1940; *The Buccaneer* (remake) 1958.

Sullivan, Francis L. Actor. *b.* Jan. 6, 1903, London. *d.* 1956. Rotund character actor of the stage and British and American films, often in villainous roles.

FILMS INCLUDE: *The Missing Rembrandt* 1932; *The Wandering Jew* 1933; *Great Expectations* (US), *Cheating*

Cheaters (US) 1934; *The Mystery of Edwin Drood* (as Mr. Crisparkle; US) 1935; *Spy of Napoleon, A Woman Alone/Two Who Dared* 1936; *Non-Stop New York, Dinner at the Ritz* 1937; *The Drums/Drums, The Citadel* 1938; *Climbing High, Four Just Men/The Secret Four* 1939; *21 Days/21 Days Together* 1940; *Pimpernel Smith/Mister V* 1941; *The Day Will Dawn/The Avengers* 1942; *Caesar and Cleopatra* (as Pothinus) 1945; *Great Expectations* (as Mr. Jaggers) 1946; *The Man Within/The Smugglers* 1947; *Oliver Twist* (as Mr. Bumble), *Joan of Arc* (as Pierre Cauchon; US), *The Winslow Boy, Broken Journey* 1948; *Christopher Columbus* (as Francisco de Bobadilla), *The Red Danube* (US) 1949; *Night and the City* (US/UK) 1950; *Behave Yourself* (US), *My Favorite Spy* (US) 1951; *Caribbean* (US) 1952; *Sangaree* (US), *Plunder of the Sun* (US) 1953; *Drums of Tahiti* (US) 1954; *The Prodigal* (US) 1955.

Sullivan, Pat. Animator. *b.* 1887, Sydney, Australia. *d.* 1933. Emigrating to the US, he began drawing comic strips for newspapers in 1914. Soon after, he transferred his most popular cartoon character, Felix the Cat, to the screen. The cartoon series enjoyed universal popularity long before the advent of Disney's Mickey Mouse. Sullivan's son, Pat, Jr. (*b.* Mar. 7, 1915, Sydney), heads Felix the Cat Creations, Inc., a company set up to produce cartoons for TV and various products carrying the famous cat's name.

Summers, Walter. Director. *b.* 1896, in Barnstaple, England. *d.* 1973. The son of show people, he went on the stage as a boy. At the age of 17 he became an assistant director and in 1918 began writing screenplays for director Cecil HEPWORTH. A director from 1923, he wrote most of his own scripts. His films are noted for their realism. His son, Jeremy Summers (*b.* 1931, St. Albans, England), has been a director of British films since the early 60s, specializing in low-budget thrillers.

FILMS INCLUDE: *I Pagliacci* (co-dir.) 1923; *The Unwanted* 1924; *Ypres* (doc.) 1925; *Mons/The Battle of Mons* (doc.), *Nelson* 1926; *The Battles of Coronel and Falkland Islands* (doc.) 1927; *Bolibar/The Betrayal* 1928; *The Lost Patrol, Chamber of Horrors* 1929; *Suspense, The Man from Chicago* 1930; *The Flying Fool* 1931; *The Return of Bulldog Drummond* 1934; *Ourselves Alone/River of Unrest* (co-dir. with Brian Desmond Hurst), *The Limping Man* 1936; *The Price of Folly* 1937; *Premiere* 1938; *At the Villa Rose, Dark Eyes of London* 1939; *Traitor Spy* 1940.

Summerville, Slim (George). Actor. *b.* George J. Sommerville, July 10, 1892, Albuquerque, N.M. *d.* 1946. Raised in Canada and Oklahoma, he ran away from home in his early teens and for several years tramped about the country, making a living at a variety of odd jobs. In 1913 he joined Mack Sennett's Keystone comedies, thanks to an introduction by Edgar Kennedy. He became one of the celebrated Keystone Cops and soon gained popularity as a character comedian in numerous Sennett shorts. Lanky and naïve-looking, he typically personified rural characters. In 1918 he moved to the Sunshine Comedies at Fox, where he switched from comedian to director of comedy shorts in the early 20s. He continued in the same capacity at FBO and Universal until the late 20s, when he returned to acting in feature films, memorably as Tjaden in *All Quiet on the Western Front* (1930) and in a series of feature comedies co-starring ZaSu PITTS.

FILMS INCLUDE: *The Knockout, Mabel's Busy Day, Laughing Gas, Gentlemen of Nerve, Cursed by His Beauty, Dough and Dynamite, Tillie's Punctured Romance, Ambrose's First Falsehood* 1914; *Her Winning Punch, The Home Breakers, Their Social Splash, Beating Hearts and Carpets, Those Bitter Sweets, Her Painted Hero, Those College Girls, A Game Old Knight, The Great Vacuum Robbery* 1915; *His Bread and Butter, His Busted Trust, The Three Slims* 1916; *Villa of the Movies, Her Fame and Shame, The Dog Catcher's Love, Roping Her Romeo* 1917; *The Kitchen Lady* 1918; *Skirts* 1921; *The Texas Streaks* 1926; *The Beloved Rogue, The Chinese Parrot* 1927; *Riding for Fame* (also co-sc.) 1928; *King of the Rodeo, One Hysterical Night, Strong Boy, Tiger Rose, The Last Warning* 1929; *Troopers Three, All Quiet on the Western Front, The King of Jazz, Under Montana Skies, The Spoilers, See America Thirst* 1930; *The Front Page, Bad Sister* 1931; *Tom Brown of Culver, Air Mail, The Unexpected Father* 1932; *They Just Had to Get Married, Out All Night, Her First Mate, Love Honor and Oh Baby!* 1933; *Love Birds, Their Big Moment* 1934; *Love Begins at 40, The Farmer Takes a Wife, Way Down East* 1935; *The Country Doctor, Captain January, White Fang, Pepper, Reunion* 1936; *Off to the Races, Love Is News, The Road Back* 1937; *Rebecca of Sunnybrook Farm, Kentucky Moonshine, Submarine Patrol* 1938; *Jesse James* 1939; *Gold Rush Maisie* 1940; *Western Union, Tobacco Road* 1941; *I'm from Arkansas* 1944; *The Hoodlum Saint* 1946.

Sundance Institute. Organization founded by Robert REDFORD in 1980 to discover, develop, and train young film-makers and support the artistic vitality of American cinema. Each year, the Institute offers financial support and laboratory training for directors and screenwriters who apply and are chosen. The Institute also pursues international cultural exchanges and sponsors the annual Sundance Film Festival, which focuses on new American independent films.

Sundberg, Clinton. Actor. *b.* Dec. 7, 1906, in Appleton, Minn. *d.* 1987. *ed.* Hamline U. (St. Paul). A former teacher, he made his debut in stock and later appeared in London and on Broadway. From the late 40s, he played light character parts in Hollywood films, typically as a sympathetic butler, memorably in a number of popular MGM musicals.

FILMS INCLUDE: *Undercurrent* 1946; *The Hucksters, Good News* 1947; *Easter Parade, A Date with Judy, The Kissing Bandit, Words and Music* 1948; *Command Decision, The Barkleys of Broadway, In the Good Old Summertime* 1949; *Annie Get Your Gun, The Toast of New Orleans* 1950; *On the Riviera, As Young As You Feel* 1951; *The Belle of New York* 1952; *Main Street to Broadway, The Caddy* 1953; *The Birds and the Bees* 1956; *The Wonderful World of the Brothers Grimm* 1962; *Hotel* 1967.

sun gun. A portable, handheld, battery-powered lighting unit. It is used mostly for documentary and news work, where mobility is of the essence and time does not allow the setting up of standard lighting equipment.

sunlight. In film terminology, light reaching a photographed object directly from the sun, as compared with the more inclusive DAYLIGHT, which encompasses a variety of natural light sources available for filming during the day, including light emanating from the sky as well as light attained through reflection.

sunshade. See MATTE BOX.

Sunshine, Marion. Actress, singer, songwriter. *b.* Mary Tunstall Ijames, May 15, 1894, Louisville, Ky. *d.* 1963. On the stage from age five, she appeared in several dramas, toured in vaudeville in a sister act, Tempest & Sunshine, and at 13 performed in the very first presentation of 'The Ziegfeld Follies' (1907). She entered films in 1908 and for several years played child and ingenue roles in many early silents, sometimes in support of Mary Pickford. Retiring from the screen around 1915, she returned to the stage and became a vaudeville headliner, often writing her own material. She helped popularize Latin American music in the US and herself wrote music and lyrics to a number of songs, among them the famous 'The Peanut

Vendor,' for which she co-wrote the English lyrics. She returned to films only once, playing a supporting role in *I'm from Arkansas* (1944).

FILMS INCLUDE: *The Tavern-Keeper's Daughter* 1908; *In the Season of Buds* 1910; *The Italian Barber, Three Sisters, A Decree of Destiny, The Rose of Kentucky, The Stuff Heroes Are Made Of, Dan the Dandy, Her Awakening* 1911; *Heredity* 1912; *Sunshine and Tempest* 1915; *I'm from Arkansas* 1944.

superimposition. The technique of photographing or printing one (or more) image(s) on top of another so that both (all) may be seen simultaneously in screening. The effect may be achieved in any of several ways, including by the exposure of the same piece of film more than once in the camera, by a glass shot, or by double or multiple printing. Sequences composed of a succession of superimpositions are known in Hollywood as MONTAGE sequences, but the meaning of the term "montage" is quite different in the theories and films of Eisenstein and other Soviet directors, in which it is used to describe a dynamic style of editing. Superimposition has been used frequently for dream sequences or for transitional scenes emphasizing the passage of time. But the technique is most commonly employed in the printing of subtitles over foreign-language films.

Surtees, Bruce. American director of photography. The son of Robert L. SURTEES, he asserted himself in the early 70s as a highly skilled cinematographer. He has been busy ever since. Nominated for an Oscar for the black-and-white photography of *Lenny* (1974).

FILMS INCLUDE: *The Beguiled, Play Misty for Me, Dirty Harry* 1971; *The Great Northfield Minnesota Raid, Conquest of the Planet of the Apes, Joe Kidd* 1972; *Blume in Love, The Outfit* 1973; *Lenny* 1974; *Night Moves* 1975; *Leadbelly, The Outlaw Josey Wales, The Shootist* 1976; *The Turning Point* 1977; *Escape from Alcatraz* 1979; *Ladies and Gentleman the Fabulous Stains* 1980; *White Dog, Firefox, Inchon, Honkytonk Man, Risky Business* 1982; *Bad Boys, Sudden Impact* 1983; *Tightrope, Beverly Hills Cop* 1984; *Pale Rider* 1985; *Psycho 3, Out of Bounds, Ratboy* 1986; *Back to the Beach* 1987; *License to Drive* 1988; *Men Don't Leave* 1989; *Run* 1990; *The Super* 1991; *One Hot Summer* 1992; *Stars Fell on Henrietta* 1995.

Surtees, Robert L. Director of photography. *b.* on Aug. 9, 1906, in Covington, Ky. *d.* 1985. In Hollywood since 1927, he began as assistant cameraman to Gregg Toland, Joseph Ruttenberg, and others. Since the 40s he has distinguished himself as one of the most reliable of Hollywood cameramen, a specialist in lush color cinematography. He won Academy Awards for *King Solomon's Mines* (1950), *The Bad and the Beautiful* (1952), and *Ben-Hur* (1959). He is the father of Bruce SURTEES.

FILMS INCLUDE: *Lost Angel, Two Girls and a Sailor, Music for Millions, Thirty Seconds Over Tokyo* 1944; *Our Vines Have Tender Grapes* 1945; *Two Sisters from Boston* 1946; *Unfinished Dance* 1947; *The Kissing Bandit, A Date with Judy, Act of Violence* 1948; *That Midnight Kiss* 1949; *Intruder in the Dust, King Solomon's Mines* 1950; *Quo Vadis* (co-phot.) 1951; *The Merry Widow, The Bad and the Beautiful* 1952; *Mogambo* (co-phot.), *Escape from Fort Bravo* 1953; *Trial, Oklahoma!* 1955; *The Swan* 1956; *Les Girls, Raintree County* 1957; *Ben-Hur* 1959; *Mutiny on the Bounty* 1962; *The Collector* (co-phot.), *The Hallelujah Trail* 1965; *Lost Command* 1966; *Doctor Dolittle, The Graduate* 1967; *Sweet Charity, The Arrangement* 1969; *Summer of '42, The Last Picture Show* 1971; *The Cowboys, The Other* 1972; *Lost Horizon, Oklahoma Crude, The Sting* 1973; *The Great Waldo Pepper, The Hindenburg* 1975; *A Star Is Born* 1976; *The Turning Point* 1977; *Bloodbrothers, Same Time Next Year* 1978.

Suschitzky, Peter. British director of photography. Son of Wolfgang SUSCHITZKY.

FILMS INCLUDE: *It Happened Here* 1966; *Privilege* 1967; *The Charge of the Light Brigade* (2nd-unit phot. only), *Charlie Bubbles* 1968; *The Gladiators* (Sw.), *Lock Up Your Daughters* 1969; *Leo the Last* 1970; *The Pied Piper* (UK/Ger.) 1972; *Henry VIII and His Six Wives* 1973; *All Creatures Great and Small* 1974; *Lisztomania* 1975; *Valentino* 1977; *The Empire Strikes Back* 1980; *Krull* 1983; *Falling in Love* 1984; *In Extremis* 1985; *Dead Ringers* 1988; *Where the Heart Is* 1990; *Naked Lunch* 1991; *M. Butterfly* 1993; *The Vanishing* 1994.

Suschitzky, Wolfgang. Director of photography. Born in 1912, in Vienna. A longtime resident in Britain, he has worked on documentaries and TV films as well as on features. He is the father of Peter SUSCHITZKY.

FILMS INCLUDE: *No Resting Place* 1951; *Cat and Mouse* 1957; *The Small World of Sammy Lee* 1963; *Ulysses* 1967; *The Vengeance of She* 1968; *Ring of Bright Water* 1969; *Entertaining Mr. Sloane* 1970; *Get Carter, Living Free* 1971; *Theatre of Blood* 1973; *Something to Hide* 1976.

Susskind, David. *b.* Dec. 19, 1920, in New York City. *d.* 1987. *ed.* U. of Wisconsin; Harvard. A former press agent for Warners and a talent agent for MCA, he formed his own agency, Talent Associates, in 1948, and soon after began producing for TV and, from the mid-50s, for Broadway and Hollywood. In addition, he was the moderator of a long-running talk show on syndicated TV.

FILMS INCLUDE: *Edge of the City* 1957; *A Raisin in the Sun* 1961; *Requiem for a Heavyweight* 1962; *All the Way Home* 1963; *Lovers and Other Strangers* 1970; *The Pursuit of Happiness* 1971; *All Creatures Great and Small* (co-prod.; UK) 1974; *Alice Doesn't Live Here Anymore* (co-prod.) 1975; *It Shouldn't Happen to a Vet* (exec. prod.; UK), *Buffalo Bill and the Indians* 1976.

Sutherland, Donald. Actor. Born on July 17, 1934, in Saint John, N.B., Canada. *ed.* U. of Toronto. A disc jockey at a Nova Scotia radio station at age 14, he began acting with local groups during his college days. After graduating, in 1956, he went to England to study at the London Academy of Music and Dramatic Art. He made several appearances on the London stage before making his screen debut in 1964, playing a dual role in an Italian horror picture. Tall (6' 4") and imposing, he played low-keyed supporting parts of amazing versatility in a succession of British and American films, then soared to stardom on the strength of his characterization of the irreverent Army surgeon Hawkeye Pierce in *M*A*S*H*. He for many years remained one of the screen's most popular personalities. A political activist, he was once a close associate of Jane Fonda and was a star member of her antiwar troupe. His son is actor Kiefer SUTHERLAND.

FILMS INCLUDE: *Il Castello dei Morti Vivi/Castle of the Living Dead* (It.) 1964; *The Bedford Incident* (UK/US), *Dr. Terror's House of Horrors* (UK/US), *Fanatic/Die! Die! My Darling!* (UK) 1965; *Promise Her Anything* (bit; UK) 1966; *The Dirty Dozen* (US/UK) 1967; *Sebastian* (UK), *Interlude* (UK), *Oedipus the King* (UK), *The Split, Joanna* (UK) 1968; *M*A*S*H, Start the Revolution Without Me, Kelly's Heroes* (US/Yug.), *Alex in Wonderland, Act of the Heart* (Can.) 1970; *Little Murders, Klute, Johnny Got His Gun* (as Christ) 1971; *F.T.A.* (filmic record of anti-Vietnam War show; also co-prod., co-dir., co-sc.) 1972; *Steelyard Blues, Lady Ice, Don't Look Now* (UK/Fr./It.) 1973; *S*P*Y*S* (UK/US) 1974; *Alien Thunder/Dan Candy's Law* (Can.), *Der Richter und sein Henker/End of the Game* (cameo, as a corpse; Ger./It.), *The Day of the Locust* 1975; *1900* (It.), *Fellini's Casanova* (lead; It.), *The Eagle Has*

Landed (UK) 1976; *The Kentucky Fried Movie* (cameo), *Disappearance* (Can.) 1977; *Les Liens de Sang* (Fr./Can.), *National Lampoon's Animal House* (cameo), *Invasion of the Body Snatchers, The Great Train Robbery* (UK) 1978; *Murder by Decree* (UK/Can.), *Very Big Withdrawal* (Can.), *Bear Island* (UK/Can.), *Nothing Personal* 1979; *Ordinary People* 1980; *Gas, Disappearance, Eye of the Needle* 1981; *Max Dugan Returns, Threshold* 1983; *Crackers, Ordeal by Innocence* 1984; *Heaven Help Us, Revolution* 1985; *The Wolf at the Door* (Den./Fr.), *The Rosary Murders, Bethune: The Making of a Hero, The Trouble with Spies* 1987; *Apprentice to Murder* 1988; *Lost Angels, Lock Up, A Dry White Season* 1989; *Eminent Domain, Backdraft, JFK* 1991; *Buffy the Vampire Slayer* 1992; *Six Degrees of Separation, Benefit of the Doubt, Younger and Younger* 1993; *Disclosure, The Puppet Masters* 1994; *Outbreak* 1995; *A Time to Kill* 1996; *The Shadow Conspiracy* 1997.

Sutherland, Edward. Director. *b.* Jan. 5, 1895, London, to American parents. *d.* 1974. Also known as A. Edward Sutherland or Eddie Sutherland. A vaudeville and stage player from childhood, he entered films in 1914 as a stuntman and actor, making his debut in a serial starring Helen Holmes. He later appeared in Keystone comedies and played juvenile leads and supporting roles in feature films. In 1923 he was Chaplin's assistant director on *A Woman of Paris.* Turning director late in the following year, he has specialized in above-par comedy and light, entertaining films, notably several W. C. Fields vehicles. Began directing and producing for TV in the late 40s. At one time he was married to Louise BROOKS.

FILMS: *Coming Through, Wild Wild Susan, A Regular Fellow* 1925; *Behind the Front, It's the Old Army Game, We're in the Navy Now* 1926; *Love's Greatest Mistake, Fireman Save My Child, Figures Don't Lie* 1927; *Tillie's Punctured Romance, The Baby Cyclone, What a Night!* 1928; *Close Harmony* (co-dir. with John Cromwell), *The Dance of Life* (co-dir. with Cromwell), *Fast Company, The Saturday Night Kid, Pointed Heels* 1929; *Paramount on Parade* (co-dir. with ten others), *Burning Up, The Social Lion, The Sap from Syracuse* 1930; *The Gang Buster, June Moon, Up Pops the Devil, Palmy Days* 1931; *Sky Devils, Mr. Robinson Crusoe, Secrets of the French Police* 1932; *Murders in the Zoo, International House, Too Much Harmony* 1933; *Mississippi, Diamond Jim* 1935; *Poppy* 1936; *Champagne Waltz* 1937; *Every Day's a Holiday* 1938; *The Flying Deuces* 1939; *The Boys from Syracuse, Beyond Tomorrow, One Night in the Tropics* 1940; *The Invisible Woman, Nine Lives Are Not Enough, Steel Against the Sky* 1941; *Sing Your Worries Away, Army Surgeon, The Navy Comes Through* 1942; *Dixie* 1943; *Follow the Boys, Secret Command* 1944; *Having Wonderful Crime* 1945; *Abie's Irish Rose* (also prod.) 1946; *Bermuda Affair* 1957.

Sutherland, Kiefer. Actor. Born on Dec. 18, 1966, in London. Puckish screen lead, often in off-kilter roles. Son of actor Donald SUTHERLAND and actress Shirley Douglas, he studied theater in Toronto, where he spent part of his youth, and played his first starring role in 1984 with *The Bay Boy*, for which he gained the Canadian version of an Academy Award.

FILMS INCLUDE: *Max Dugan Returns* 1983; *The Bay Boy* 1984; *At Close Range, Crazy Moon, Stand By Me* 1986; *The Killing Time, The Lost Boys, Promised Land* 1987; *1969, Bright Lights Big City, Young Guns* 1988; *Renegades* 1989; *Chicago Joe and the Showgirl, Flashback, Flatliners, The Nutcracker Prince* (v/o), *Young Guns II* 1990; *Article 99, A Few Good Men, Twin Peaks: Fire Walk with Me, The Vanishing* 1992; *The Three Musketeers* 1993; *The Cowboy Way* 1994; *Eye for an Eye, Freeway, A Time to Kill* 1996; *Truth or Consequences, N.M.* (also dir.) 1997.

Sutton, Grady. Actor. Born on Apr. 5, 1908, in Chattanooga, Tenn. Flabby character comedian, typically playing slow-witted rural yokels. In Hollywood from age 16, he became popular in the early 30s in a series of comedy shorts, "The Boy Friends," which were directed by George Stevens early in his career. He later appeared in numerous features, memorably in several W. C. Fields films, and in countless TV episodes.

FILMS INCLUDE: *The Mad Whirl* (bit), *The Freshman* (bit) 1925; *Skinner's Dress Suit* (bit) 1926; *The Sophomore* (bit) 1929; *This Reckless Age, Pack Up Your Troubles, Hot Saturday* 1932; *The Pharmacist* (short), *Only Yesterday, College Humor* 1933; *Laddie, The Man on the Flying Trapeze, Alice Adams* 1935; *My Man Godfrey, Pigskin Parade* 1936; *Waikiki Wedding, Stage Door* 1937; *Vivacious Lady, Having Wonderful Time, Alexander's Ragtime Band* 1938; *You Can't Cheat an Honest Man, It's a Wonderful World* 1939; *Torrid Zone, The Bank Dick* 1940; *Bedtime Story* 1941; *A Lady Takes a Chance* 1943; *The Great Moment, Since You Went Away* 1944; *A Royal Scandal, A Bell for Adano, Anchors Aweigh* 1945; *Nobody Lives Forever* 1946; *My Wild Irish Rose* 1947; *A Star Is Born, White Christmas* 1954; *Jumbo* 1962; *My Fair Lady* 1964; *Paradise Hawaiian Style* 1966; *I Love You Alice B. Toklas!* 1968; *Myra Breckinridge* 1970; *Support Your Local Gunfighter* 1971.

Sutton, John. Actor. *b.* Oct. 22, 1908, Rawalpindi, India, of British parents. *d.* 1963. After spending a decade in various British colonies as hunter, rancher, and plantation manager, he arrived in Hollywood in the mid-30s as a technical consultant on films with a British Empire background. Darkly handsome, he began appearing in films in 1937, typically playing the hero's romantic rival or dashing, dangerous, often cruel, swashbuckling adversary.

FILMS INCLUDE: *Bulldog Drummond Comes Back* 1937; *Four Men and a Prayer* 1938; *Tower of London* 1939; *The Invisible Man Returns* 1940; *Hudson's Bay* (as Lord Crewe), *A Yank in the R.A.F., Moon Over Her Shoulder* (lead) 1941; *My Gal Sal, Ten Gentlemen from West Point, Thunder Birds* 1942; *Tonight We Raid Calais* (lead) 1943; *Jane Eyre* (as Dr. Rivers), *The Hour Before Dawn* 1944; *Claudia and David* 1946; *Captain from Castile, Adventures of Casanova, The Three Musketeers* (as the Duke of Buckingham) 1948; *The Fan, Bride of Vengeance, Bagdad* 1949; *The Second Woman, Payment on Demand, David and Bathsheba* 1951; *My Cousin Rachel* 1952; *Sangaree* 1953; *Death of a Scoundrel* 1956; *The Bat, The Return of the Fly, Beloved Infidel* 1959; *The Canadians* (Can./US/UK) 1961; *Of Human Bondage* 1964.

Suzuki, Seijun. Director. Born in 1923 in Japan. Stylish director who broke boundaries in Japanese genre films. In the 1950s, he became a contract director for the then-downtrodden genre-driven Nikkatsu Studios. There, he defined each of his assignments, be they *yakuza* (gangster), soft-core porno, or other genre type, with strong visuals and outlandish narratives that reflected his perceived tension betwen *mu* (nothingness) and *keren* (artiface). Although by the 1960s he had developed a following, he was let go from the studio in 1967, on the grounds of making "incomprehensible and unprofitable films." Supported by critics and filmmakers, he eventually won a settlement. However, his career did not rebound for over a decade.

FILMS INCLUDE: *Rabu retaa/Love Letter* 1959; *Akutaro/The Bastard, Kanto mushuku/Kanto Wanderer, Tantei Jimosho 23—kutabare akutödomo/Detective Bureau 23: Down with the Wicked* 1963; *Nikudai no mon/Gate of Flesh* 1964; *Irezumi Ichidai/One Generation of Tattoos, Shunpuden/Story of a Prostitute* 1965; *Tokyo nagaremono/Tokyo Drifter, Kenka Erejii/Elegy to Violence* 1966; *Koroshi no rakuin/Branded to*

Kill, Kawachi Karumen/Carmen from Kawachi 1967; *Zigeunerweisen* 1980; *Kageroza/Heat Shimmer Theater* 1981; *Yumeji* 1991.

Swain, Mack. Actor. *b.* Feb. 16, 1876, Salt Lake City. *d.* 1935. A 22-year veteran of minstrel shows, vaudeville, and the legitimate stage, he joined Mack Sennett's Keystone comedies late in 1913. A robust, massive (6' 2", 280 lbs.) knockabout comedian, he was a welcome addition to the roster of the Keystone slapstick talent. During 1914 he supported Charlie Chaplin in many of his early shorts. Late that year Swain began starring in his own comedy series, portraying a boisterous, lecherous character called Ambrose, with a huge mustache and heavy makeup. Swain remained with Keystone for four years, appearing in innumerable comedy shorts. In 1917 he moved on to L-KO and later to other comedy-producing studios. When his fortunes declined in the early 20s, he was rescued from oblivion by Chaplin and returned the favor with marvelous characterizations in such feature films as *The Pilgrim* and especially *The Gold Rush.* He played his most memorable role in the latter as Big Jim McKay, the giant prospector who fancies Chaplin a chicken in a delirium of starvation and then shares his shoe dinner. He later played character parts and occasional leads in many feature films until shortly before his death of an internal hemorrhage.

FILMS INCLUDE: *Caught in a Cabaret, A Busy Day, Caught in the Rain, The Knockout, Mabel's Married Life, Laughing Gas, Tillie's Punctured Romance, Getting Acquainted, His Prehistoric Past, Ambrose's First Falsehood* 1914; *Love Speed and Thrills, The Home Breakers, Ambrose's Sour Grapes, Ambrose's Fury, Our Dare Devil Chief, The Battle of Ambrose and Walrus* 1915; *A Modern Enoch Arden, A Movie Star, By Stork Delivery, His Bitter Pill, Vampire Ambrose, The Danger Girl* 1916; *His Naughty Thought, Thirst, The Pullman Bride* 1917; *The Idle Class* 1921; *Pay Day* 1922; *The Pilgrim* 1923; *The Gold Rush* 1925; *Hands UP!, Sea Horses, Footloose Widows, The Torrent, Kiki* 1926; *The Shamrock and the Rose* (lead), *Finnegan's Ball* (lead), *Mockery, The Beloved Rogue* 1927; *Tillie's Punctured Romance, Gentlemen Prefer Blondes, Caught in the Fog* 1928; *The Last Warning, The Cohens and Kellys in Atlantic City* (lead) 1929; *Redemption, The Sea Bat* 1930; *Finn and Hattie* 1931; *Midnight Patrol* 1932.

Swanson, Gloria. Actress. *b.* Gloria Josephine Mae Swenson, Mar. 27, 1897, Chicago, of Swedish-Italian descent. *d.* 1983. The daughter of an Army officer, she attended more than a dozen schools in various locations before resettling in her native city in her early teens. A chance visit to Chicago's Essanay studios in 1913 resulted in her employment as an extra player and in her acquaintance with actor Wallace BEERY, whom she married in 1916. That same year they both went to Hollywood, where Beery accepted an offer from Mack Sennett's Keystone company on the condition that his wife also be hired. Contrary to persistent references in various sources, Miss Swanson was never a Sennett "Bathing Beauty" (she said she never could swim). Neither was she part of the wild slapstick of the Keystone Kops. Rather, she was teamed with Bobby Vernon in a series of romantic comedies. Early in her career she was occasionally billed as Gloria Mae.

When Sennett pulled out of the Triangle organization in 1917 to join Paramount, Miss Swanson followed him, but she soon tired of comedy and returned to Triangle, where she starred in a succession of tearful dramas. In 1919, following Triangle's debacle, she moved over to Cecil B. De Mille's unit at Paramount and rapidly rose to top stardom in a group of slick, suggestive bedroom farces. By the mid-20s she ranked among Hollywood's reigning queens of the silent screen. A born showwoman, she knew full well the value of publicity. Every dress she wore on- or offscreen was carefully depicted in fashion magazines and every move she made received wide press coverage. Never more so perhaps than in 1925 when, after filming *Madame Sans-Gêne* in France, she returned to Hollywood with a genuine marquis as her third husband and was welcomed by a brass band and, like royalty, driven home in a motorcade. (She had divorced Beery in 1916, then married and divorced and married again.) For many American women she was glamour personified.

Swanson remained with Paramount until 1926, now specializing mostly in drama. The following year, bankrolled by Joseph P. KENNEDY, father of the late President, she struck out on her own, producing her own films for release through United Artists. She lost much of her own money as a result of director Erich Von STROHEIM's extravagance in the production of *Queen Kelly* (1928). She fired Stroheim in midproduction, then tried to salvage the film by sinking even more of her own money into reediting the footage and tacking on a forced ending. The final product was shown in Europe and South America but was not released in the US, where it ran into censorship trouble. During the transition period to sound, Miss Swanson proved she could not only talk effectively but even sing. However, her early talkies were mostly unsuccessful and in 1934 she retired from the screen.

She came back for one comedy opposite Adolphe Menjou in 1941, then made a memorable second comeback in 1950, giving an outstanding performance in *Sunset Boulevard,* in the role of a neurotic, faded silent screen star. Ironically, Von Stroheim played her former director. She was nominated for an Oscar as best actress for her role in that film (she had two earlier nominations, for *The Trespasser* and *Sadie Thompson*). She subsequently appeared in two poor films, one in Italy, then slipped back into semiretirement. She lent her name to a now-defunct cosmetics line and served as an advisor to a dress company, but her public appearances were restricted mostly to occasional guest spots on TV talk shows, in which she promoted the consumption of health foods. In 1971 she made a third comeback, this time on Broadway, as the star of the play 'Butterflies Are Free.' She returned to the screen once more in 1974, playing a key character role in *Airport 1975.* She married for the sixth time in 1976.

FILMS: Shorts—*At the End of a Perfect Day, The Ambition of the Baron, The Fable of Elvira and Farina and the Meal Ticket, His New Job* (bit), *Sweedie Goes to College, The Romance of an American Duchess, The Broken Pledge* 1915; *A Dash of Courage, Hearts and Sparks, A Social Cub, The Danger Girl, Love on Skates, Haystacks and Steeples* 1916; *The Nick-of-Time Baby, Teddy at the Throttle, Baseball Madness, Dangers of a Bride, The Sultan's Wife, The Pullman Bride* 1917. Features—*Society for Sale, Her Decision, You Can't Believe Everything, Everywoman's Husband, Shifting Sands, Station Content, Secret Code, Wife or Country* 1918; *Don't Change Your Husband, For Better for Worse, Male and Female* 1919; *Why Change Your Wife?, Something to Think About* 1920; *The Great Moment, The Affairs of Anatol, Under the Lash, Don't Tell Everything* 1921; *Her Husband's Trademark, Beyond the Rocks, Her Gilded Cage, The Impossible Mrs. Bellew* 1922; *My American Wife, Hollywood* (cameo), *Prodigal Daughters, Bluebeard's 8th Wife, Zaza* 1923; *The Humming Bird, A Society Scandal, Manhandled, Her Love Story, Wages of Virtue* 1924; *Madame Sans-Gêne, The Coast of Folly, Stage Struck* 1925; *The Untamed Lady, Fine Manners* 1926; *The Love of Sunya* 1927; *Sadie Thompson, Queen Kelly* 1928; *The Trespasser* 1929; *What a Widow!* 1930; *Indiscreet, Tonight or Never* 1931; *Perfect Understanding* (UK)

1933; *Music in the Air* 1934; *Father Takes a Wife* 1941; *Sunset Boulevard* 1950; *Three for Bedroom C* 1952; *Mio Figlio Nerone/Nero's Mistress* (It./Fr.) 1956; *Airport 1975* 1974.

Swarthout, Gladys. Singer, actress. *b.* Dec. 25, 1904, Deepwater, Mo. *d.* 1969. Singing in a church choir from the age of 12, she studied at Chicago's Bush Conservatory and made her professional debut with the Chicago Civic Opera Company in 1924. She appeared with other companies and toured in concert before joining New York's Metropolitan Opera in 1929. She sang with the Met for five seasons, lending her lustrous mezzo-soprano to *Norma, Carmen,* and *Lakme,* among many other notable operatic staples. Beautiful as she was talented, she was brought to Hollywood by Paramount in the mid-30s as competition to Columbia's Grace MOORE and MGM's Jeanette MACDONALD. However, her box-office appeal was limited, and she retired from the screen after only five starring roles. She fared much better later on, on radio and some TV. Her career was hampered by a heart condition caused by rheumatic fever, which she had suffered in her childhood. She was felled by the illness in July of 1969, at her villa, near Florence, Italy.

FILMS: *Rose of the Rancho, Give Us This Night* 1936; *Champagne Waltz* 1937; *Romance in the Dark* 1938; *Ambush* 1939.

Swayze, Patrick. Actor, dancer. Born on Aug. 18, 1954, in Houston, Tex. *ed.* Harkness Ballet School, Joffrey Ballet School, San Jacinto Coll. Affable, graceful romantic lead of 1980s and 1990s. Son of choreographer Patsy Swayze, he began performing as a dancer in Disney on Parade. After appearing in the Broadway production of 'Grease,' he made his film debut in 1979 and established himself as a lead in the steamy musical-drama *Dirty Dancing.* As the sincere ghost lover in the hugely successful *Ghost,* he became a box-office draw.

FILMS INCLUDE: *Skatetown, U.S.A.* 1979; *The Outsiders, Uncommon Valor* 1983; *Grandview U.S.A.* (also chor.), *Red Dawn* 1984; *Youngblood* 1986; *Dirty Dancing* (also songs), *Steel Dawn* 1987; *Tiger Warsaw* 1988; *Next of Kin, Road House* (also songs) 1989; *Ghost* 1990; *Point Break* 1991; *City of Joy* (UK./Fr.) 1992; *Father Hood* 1993; *To Wong Foo Thanks for Everything Julie Newmar, Three Wishes* 1995.

Sweden. Considering the small size of its population (about 8.5 million), this Scandinavian kingdom's contribution to the art of cinema has been astounding. As elsewhere in Europe, domestic production was preceded by early exhibitions of Lumière and Edison shorts. The first known local film entrepreneur was Numa Peterson, a still photographer who began exhibiting and manufacturing films under exclusive license from Lumière. A Lumière agent, Georges Promio, trained a Peterson employee, Ernest Florman, who in 1898 began filming local news events as well as brief comedies and scenes from dramatic stage productions, including Ibsen plays. But the domination of the Swedish market by foreign production companies continued for several years.

In 1905 a young man by the name of Charles Magnusson, who was to have a profound influence on the Swedish silent cinema, entered the industry as a newsreel cameraman. In 1909 he joined Svenska Bio (Ab Svenska Biografteatern), a two-year-old company, as production manager and director. Under his guidance, the company, which was incorporated in 1919 into Svensk Filmindustri, became a leading force in national production. It has remained an industry leader to this day. Magnusson himself also directed a number of films between 1909 and 1912, but his main importance was as a discoverer and inspirer of talent. Another former newsreel cameraman who joined Svenska Bio in 1911 was Julius Jaenzon, whose brilliant cinematography would become a significant factor in the success of many films during the "golden age" of the Swedish cinema (1914–21). Jaenzon also directed a number of films, including a notable collaborative effort with Magnusson, *The Vagabond's Galoshes* (1912), an ambitious adaptation of a Hans Christian Andersen tale that was partly shot in France and the United States and included impressive tracking shots taken from a New York City trolley. Svenska Bio's main competition in the early years came from producer Erik Dahlberg, who specialized in historical films, and from the Svea company, which concentrated on adaptations of stage plays, notably Strindberg's *Miss Julie* and *The Father* (both 1912).

The year 1912 was a pivotal one in the history of the Swedish cinema. In that year Magnusson signed as directors two men whose talents would carry the young industry into a glorious creative period at the outset of WW I. They were former stage actors Victor SJÖSTRÖM and the Finnish-born Russian-Jewish émigré Mauritz STILLER. Stiller was noted for his style of ironic comedy, but he was equally at home with comedy and drama. Sjöström (known in the US as Seastrom) was famous for social comment. Both men achieved some of their most impressive work with literary adaptations, especially from the works of Selma Lagerlöf and Ibsen.

Sweden's neutrality in WW I provided the country's film industry with a distinct advantage during the conflict. While other European film industries were hampered by international blockades and disruption of production, the Swedish cinema continued to thrive. Not only could it export its films to program-starved countries, but the industry's position solidified at home as a result of curbed competition from abroad. These privileged conditions helped draw worldwide attention to the high quality of the films of Sjöström, Stiller, and other directors of the period.

Outstanding films of the war period included Sjöström's *Terje Vigen, The Girl of the Marsh Croft/The Girl from Stormy Croft* (both 1919), and *The Sons of Ingmar* (1919) and Stiller's *Love and Journalism* (1916), *Thomas Graal's Best Film* (1917), and *Thomas Graal's First Child* (1918). Sjöström's films in particular were notable for their penetrating examination of psychological conflicts within characters and between characters and their physical environment, elements prevalent in Swedish literature and drama that would later find their supreme expression in the films of Ingmar BERGMAN.

The prosperity of the Swedish cinema continued briefly after the war ended, as the "golden age" reached its peak with such productions as Stiller's *Sir Arne's Treasure* (1919) and *Johan* (1921) and Sjöström's *The Phantom Carriage/Thy Soul Shall Bear Witness* (1921). But as conditions in Europe returned to normalcy, there was a rapid escalation of competition from abroad, especially from the United States, whose films increasingly gained a dominant position on European screens. Forced into a defensive position, the Swedish film industry began compromising the distinctive qualities that had made it successful for the sake of a share of the box office, abandoning the themes that gave the national industry its special flavor for standard entertainment aimed to please popular taste. To increase its competitive edge, Svenska Bio merged with Skandinaviska Filmcentralen in 1919 to form the Svensk Filmindustri. Under Magnusson's direction, the company began a policy of ambitious commercial productions, but the box-office performance of many of these did not justify their high cost.

The sacrifice of identity failed to save the Swedish film industry from the throes of a full-fledged crisis that would last through the 20s and 30s. Some of the blame was placed at Hollywood's doorstep. The American movie capital was seen not only as the main nemesis at the box office but also as the magnet that drained Sweden's top film talent. Sjöström migrated to America in 1923, followed in 1925 by Stiller and the stars of his *The Legend of Gösta Berling/The Story of Gösta Berling/The Gosta Berling Saga* (1924), Lars HANSON and Greta GARBO. With the exception of some valiant tries by such new directors as Per Lindberg and the brothers Olof and Gustaf MOLANDER, the Swedish cinema of the 20s was chronically ailing. The situation worsened in the 30s after the advent of sound, when language barriers added yet another obstacle to the exportation of Swedish films. Co-production with Germany and other countries was attempted to no avail. The only Swedish film of the 30s that enjoyed international success was Gustaf Molander's *Intermezzo* (1936), which led to the Hollywood career of its female star, Ingrid BERGMAN. That film was remade in Hollywood by Gregory Ratoff in 1939 as Bergman's first vehicle there.

Sweden's traditional neutrality once again proved beneficial to the country's film industry when WW II broke out. The gradual revival began in the early 40s, partly stimulated by the return to Sweden of Sjöström, who was appointed "artistic consultant" to Svensk Filmindustri and the resumption of the interrupted film career of another gifted director, Alf SJÖBERG, who had returned to the theater for a full decade after having made only one film, the impressive *The Strongest* (1929). Sjöberg's *Hets/Torment/Frenzy* (1944), from a script by young Ingmar Bergman, was a key production in the revival of the Swedish cinema, an effective study of the psychology of sexuality and cruelty. Bergman turned to directing with *Crisis* in 1945 and in the 50s became increasingly recognized as one of world cinema's leading filmmakers.

Other Swedish directors who established their reputations during the 40s included Hasse Ekman (*Changing Trains/Unexpected Meeting,* 1943; *In the Waiting Room of Death/Interlude,* 1946); Erik "Hampe" Faustman (*Night in the Harbor,* 1943; *When Meadows Bloom,* 1946; *Lars Hard,* 1948); Anders HENRIKSON (*A Crime,* 1940; *Blood and Fire,* 1945); Lars-Eric Kjellgren (*Private Bom,* 1948); Arne MATTSON (*Bad Eggs/Incorrigible,* 1946); Ake Ohberg (*People of Simlangen Valley,* 1948); and comedian-director Nils Poppe (*Money,* 1946; *The Balloon,* 1948). Notable films of the 40s made by veteran directors included Gustaf Edgren's *Katrina* (1943) and *Sunshine Follows Rain* (1946); Gustaf Molander's *Ride Tonight!* (1942) and *Ordet/The Word* (1943); Olof Molander's *Appassionata* (1944); and Alf Sjöberg's *Himlaspelet/The Road to Heaven* (1942) and *Only a Mother* (1949).

The periodic international successes of Swedish films of the 40s and 50s masked the essentially isolationist character of the domestic film industry. Because of the relatively small potential audience size, foreign-language films in Sweden are frugally subtitled rather than dubbed. This apparent self-sufficiency helped the Swedish cinema retain its distinctive national flavor, but in financial terms it placed the industry in a constantly precarious position, putting producers at the mercy of a potential audience of limited size. The Swedish cinema entered one of its periodical crises in the early 50s when the imposition of a very high entertainment tax considerably increased the hazard of production, and the competition from television further reduced attendance at the movies.

Despite the financial difficulties a number of excellent films were turned out during the 50s. Ingmar Bergman emerged as the dominant figure among the directors, with such films as *Illicit Interlude/Summer Interlude* (1950), *Monika/Summer with Monika* (1953), *The Naked Night/Sawdust and Tinsel* (1953), *Dreams/Journey Into Autumn* (1954), *Smiles of a Summer Night* (1955), *The Seventh Seal* (1957), and *Wild Strawberries* (1957). Other notable productions included Arne Mattson's *One Summer of Happiness* (1951), *Salka Valka* (1954), and *The Phantom Carriage* (1958); Sjöberg's *Miss Julie* (1951) and *Karin Mansdotter/Karin Daughter of Man* (1954); and Arne SUCKSDORFF's fictionalized documentary *The Great Adventure* (1953).

By the early 60s feature production had dropped from an annual average of 40 during the peak WW II years to only 15. There was clearly a need for measures to reinvigorate the film industry. One significant step forward was the establishment in 1963 of the Swedish Film Institute with the aim of encouraging quality film through a system of monetary awards for worthy projects. A name closely associated with the Institute is Harry Schein, the organization's first president, whose personality figured prominently in the direction of the Swedish cinema in the 60s and 70s. He was replaced in 1978 by Finnish-born producer-director Jörn DONNER.

The 60s also saw a growing trend among young Swedish filmmakers away from the soul-searching themes focusing on the individual and toward social and political concerns that affect society as a whole. Among the directors who represented these preoccupations are Bo Widerberg (*Raven's End,* 1963; *Elvira Madigan,* 1967; *Adalen 31,* 1969); Vilgot SJÖMAN (*491,* 1964; *I Am Curious—Yellow,* 1967); Jörn Donner (*A Sunday in September,* 1963; *Adventure Starts Here,* 1965); and former actress Mai ZETTERLING (*Loving Couples,* 1964; *Night Games,* 1966; *The Girls,* 1968). Other notable films of the 60s included Hans Abramson's *The Serpent* (1966); Bergman's *The Virgin Spring* (1960), *Through a Glass Darkly* (1961), *Winter Light* (1963), *The Silence* (1963), *Hour of the Wolf* (1968), and *Shame* (1968); Bjorkman's *I Love You Love* (1968); Jonas Cronell's *Hugs and Kisses* (1967); Ake Falck's *Swedish Wedding Night* (1964); Kjell GREDE's *Hugo and Josefin* (1967); Jan Halldoff's *A Dream of Freedom* (1969); Alf Kjellin's *Pleasure Garden* (1961); Jarl Kulle's *The Bookseller Who Gave Up Bathing* (1969); Peter Kylberg's *I* (1966); Lars Magnus Lindgren's *Dear John* (1964); Mattson's *Bamse/The Teddy Bear* (1969); Stellan Olsson's *It's Up to You* (1969); Sjöberg's *The Island* (1966) and *The Father* (1969); and Jan Troell's *Here's Your Life* (1966).

The upsurge in quality production in the wake of the founding of the Swedish Film Institute was not accompanied, however, by a similar improvement in the industry's financial base. Problems of financing and distribution carried on into the 70s, when feature production stabilized at 20 to 25 annually. With the exception of occasional ambitious projects like Jan Troell's *The Emigrants* (1971) and *The New Land* (1973), the typical Swedish product was hampered by minimal budgets. An unusually high percentage of the films was of a quality that assured attention at international film festivals, but most performed poorly at the box office and relatively few enjoyed wide distribution abroad. One major obstacle to growth was removed in the mid-70s, when the traditional feud between the Swedish film and TV industries was finally patched up and an era of cooperation between the two media began, to the benefit of both.

Notable films of the 70s included Roy Andersson's *Giliap* (1976); Mats Arehn's *Maria* (1975) and *The Assignment* (1976); Johan Bergenstahle's *A Baltic Tragedy* (1971) and *Hello Baby!* (1975); Per Berglund's *Beyond the Line of Duty* (1971); Bergman's *Cries and Whispers* (1972), *Scenes from a Marriage* (1973), *The Magic Flute* (1975), and *Face to Face* (1976); Ivo Dvorak's *Metamorphosis* (1975); Bengt Forslund's *The Air Cage* (1972); Kjell Grede's *A Simple Melody* (1974) and *A Madman's Defense* (1976); Jan Halldoff's *Dog Days* (1971), *The Office Party* (1972), *The Last Adventure* (1975), and *Buddies* (1976); Michael Meschke's *Purgatory* (1975); Vilgot

Sjöman's *Troll* (1973), *A Handful of Love* (1974), and *Siesta Samba* (1976); Ingvar Skogsberg's *The City of My Dreams* (1977); Jiri Tirl's *Pistols* (1974); Troell's *Bang!* (1977); and Widerberg's *Joe Hill* (in the US, 1971), *Stubby* (1974), *Man on the Roof* (1977), and *Victoria* 1979.

A technician's strike in 1975 and Ingmar Bergman's self-exile in 1976, following a confrontation with internal revenue authorities, were among the events that affected the Swedish cinema in the 70s. During the decade, the Swedish Film Institute became increasingly involved in film production, in addition to fulfilling its traditional functions. The appointment of Jörn Donner, an experienced director and producer, as president of the Institute in 1978 was seen as a constructive step toward fortifying the film industry for the challenges of the future.

Regrettably, the 80s proved a thin period for the release of notable films and the emergence of new creative personalities. Production plateaued at 15 to 20 features per year. Although Swedish studios continued to turn out comedies and dramas for domestic consumption (Swedish films regularly appear in that nation's annual top box-office lists), few of these films successfully entered the commercial export market. Notable international successes from this period include Lasse Hallström's childhood comedy *My Life as a Dog* (1985), which was followed by his move to Hollywood and the romantic comedy *Once Around* (1991); Bille August's Danish-Swedish co-production *Pelle the Conqueror* (1988), which garnered a foreign film Oscar; and Bergman's *Fanny and Alexander* (1983), a multiple Oscar winner. Young talent who enjoyed film festival exposure during this period included Agenta Elers-Jarleman (*Beyond Sorry, Beyond Pain*, 1983); Carl Gustaf Kykvist (*The Woman on the Roof*, 1989; *Shining Weapon*, 1991); Stig Larsson (*Angel*, 1990; *The Rabbit Man*, 1991) and Lars Von Trier (*Nocturne*, 1981; *Epidemic*, 1987; *Europa*, 1991; *Breaking the Waves*, 1996).

Sweeney, D. B. Actor. Born Daniel Bernard Sweeney on November 14, 1961, in Shoreham, Long Island, N.Y. This energetic, agile actor had designs on a career in pro baseball but an injury cut his dreams short. Turning to acting, his strong but sensitive television performances led to a feature film career instead. Ironically, he is perhaps best known for his role as the former pro hockey hopeful who turns to figure skating after an injury in *The Cutting Edge* (1992).

FILMS: *Fire with Fire, Power* 1986; *Gardens of Stone, No Man's Land* 1987; *Eight Men Out* 1988; *A Day in October, Memphis Belle* 1990; *Leather Jackets* 1991; *The Cutting Edge* 1992; *Fire in the Sky, Hear No Evil* 1993; *Roommates, Three Wishes* 1995.

Sweet, Blanche. Actress. *b.* June 18, 1895, in Chicago. *d.* 1986. The daughter of show people, she went on the stage before reaching the age of four and was a seasoned veteran by the time she entered films in 1909, at the age of 14. Working for Biograph, she soon became a favorite Griffith heroine. Unlike his other top leading ladies (Lillian GISH, Mae MARSH, etc.), she wasn't the fragile, helpless type but a strong and determined heroine, confident and resourceful in the clutch. Her most memorable roles for Griffith were in the title roles of *The Lonedale Operator* (a landmark Griffith film, noted for its advanced cutting techniques) and *Judith of Bethulia,* Griffith's most ambitious production before *The Birth of a Nation.* In 1915 she left Griffith for the Lasky company, where she starred in the films of De Mille and other directors. In 1922 she married one of her frequent directors at Famous Players-Lasky, Marshall NEILAN. They were divorced in 1929. Among her best performances in the post-Griffith period were her roles in *Anna Christie* (1923), the first screen adaptation of an O'Neill play, directed by John Griffith Ray, and *Tess of the D'Urbervilles* (1924), directed by Neilan. Her career declined towards the end of the silent period. She appeared in three early talkies but soon retired to a modest career in vaudeville and stock. In 1936 she married her stage co-star, screen veteran Raymond HACKETT. She was widowed in 1958 and in the following year she returned fleetingly to the screen, playing a bit in a Danny Kaye vehicle, *The Five Pennies.*

FILMS INCLUDE: *A Man with Three Wives, A Corner in Wheat, Choosing a Husband, The Day After* 1909; *The Rocky Road, All on Account of the Milk, A Romance of the Western Hills* 1910; *Was He a Coward?, The Lonedale Operator, How She Triumphed, The White Rose of the Wilds, The Country Lovers, The Primal Call, The Last Drop of Water, Fighting Blood, A Country Cupid, Out of the Shadow, The Blind Princess and the Poet, The Stuff Heroes Are Made Of, The Long Road, Love in the Hills, The Battle, A Woman Scorned* 1911; *The Eternal Mother, A Sister's Love, Under Burning Skies, The Goddess of Sagebrush Gulch, The Punishment, The Lesser Evil, The Spirit Awakened, Man's Lust for Gold, The Painted Lady, Blind Love, The God Within* 1912; *Pirate Gold, Oil and Water, A Chance Deception, Love in an Apartment Hotel, Near to Earth, The Hero of Little Italy, The Stolen Bride, Death's Marathon, The Mistake, The Coming of Angelo, The Vengeance of Galora, The House of Discord, Three Friends* 1913; *The Massacre, Classmates, The Soul of Honor, Ashes of the Past, Home Sweet Home, Judith of Bethulia, The Escape, The Tear That Burned, Strongheart, For Those Unborn, Men and Women, The Avenging Conscience/Thou Shalt Not Kill, Her Awakening, For Her Father's Sins, The Little Country Mouse, The Old Maid/Dorothy in the Garret* 1914; *The Warrens of Virginia, The Captive, Stolen Goods, The Clue, The Secret Orchard, The Case of Becky, The Secret Sin* 1915; *The Ragamuffin, The Black List, The Sowers, The Thousand-Dollar Husband, The Dupe, Public Opinion, The Storm* 1916; *The Evil Eye, Those Without Sin, The Silent Partner* 1917; *The Unpardonable Sin, The Hushed Hour, A Woman of Pleasure* 1919; *The Deadlier Sex, Simple Souls, A Girl in the Web, Her Unwilling Husband* 1920; *That Girl Montana* 1921; *Quincy Adams Sawyer* 1922; *The Meanest Man in the World, In the Palace of the King, Anna Christie* (title role) 1923; *Those Who Dance, Tess of the D'Urbervilles* (title role) 1924; *His Supreme Moment, The Sporting Venus, Why Women Love, The New Commandment* 1925; *Bluebeard's Seven Wives, The Lady from Hell, The Far Cry, Diplomacy* 1926; *Singed* 1927; *The Woman in White* (UK) 1929; *The Woman Racket, Show Girl in Hollywood, The Silver Horde* 1930; *The Five Pennies* (bit) 1959.

Swerling, Jo (Joseph). Screenwriter, playwright. Born on April 8, 1897, in Russia. In the US from childhood, he was a newspaper and magazine writer before turning to the stage and films. Among his plays are 'The Kibitzer' and 'Guys and Dolls,' both in collaboration. He has written numerous quality screenplays for Capra, Borzage, Ford, Mamoulian, Hitchcock, Wyler, and other distinguished Hollywood directors.

FILMS INCLUDE (as screenwriter, alone or in collaboration): *Melody Lane* (play basis only, 'The Understander') 1929; *Ladies of Leisure, The Kibitzer* (play basis only, in collaboration with Edward G. Robinson), *Sisters, Rain or Shine, Hell's Island* 1930; *The Last Parade, Dirigible, Ten Cents a Dance, Platinum Blonde, Miracle Woman* 1931; *Forbidden, Behind the Mask, War Correspondent, Washington Merry-Go-Round* 1932; *Man's Castle* 1933; *No Greater Glory, Lady by Choice* 1934; *Love Me Forever, The Whole Town's Talking* 1935; *Pennies from Heaven* 1936; *Double Wedding* 1937; *Doctor Rhythm, I Am the Law* 1938; *Made for Each Other, The Real Glory* 1939; *The Westerner* 1940; *Blood and Sand, Confirm or Deny* 1941; *The*

Pride of the Yankees 1942; *Crash Dive* 1943; *Lifeboat* 1944; *Leave Her to Heaven* 1945; *It's a Wonderful Life* 1946; *Thunder in the East* 1953; *Guys and Dolls* (play basis only) 1955; *King of the Roaring Twenties* 1961.

Swift, David. Director, screenwriter, producer. Born in 1919, in Minneapolis. He entered films as an animator at the Walt Disney studios. Following WW II service with the Air Force, he began writing comedy for radio and, later, drama for TV. Having gained directing experience on TV during the 50s, he ventured into feature films in the 60s.

FILMS (as director-screenwriter): *Pollyanna* 1960; *The Parent Trap* 1961; *The Interns* 1962; *Love Is a Ball, Under the Yum Yum Tree* 1963; *Good Neighbor Sam* (also prod.) 1964; *How to Succeed in Business Without Really Trying* (also prod.) 1967; *The Black Panther* (act. only; UK) 1977; *Candleshoe* (sc. only) 1978; *Foolin' Around* (co-sc. only) 1979.

Swinburne, Nora. Actress. Born Elinore Johnson, on July 24, 1902, in Bath, England. *ed.* Rosholme Coll; RADA. The daughter of a toy manufacturer, she began her stage career as an actress and a dancer at the age of ten. Developing into an attractive leading lady, she starred in British silent films of the 20s and has since been seen in many supporting parts, on the stage as well as in sound films.

FILMS INCLUDE: *Branded* 1920; *The Fortune of Christina McNab* 1921; *Red Trail* (US), *Hornet's Nest* 1923; *A Girl of London* 1925; *Alf's Button* 1930; *Potiphar's Wife* 1931; *White Face, Mr. Bill the Conqueror/The Man Who Won* 1932; *Perfect Understanding* 1933; *Dinner at the Ritz* 1937; *The Citadel* 1938; *A Gentleman of Venture/It Happened to One Man* 1940; *They Flew Alone/Wings and the Woman* 1942; *The Man in Grey* 1943; *Fanny by Gaslight/Man of Evil* 1944; *Jassy* 1947; *Quartet, The Blind Goddess* 1948; *Christopher Columbus* 1949; *My Daughter Joy/Operation X* 1950; *The River* (for Jean Renoir, in India), *Quo Vadis* (as Pomponia; US) 1951; *Betrayed* (US) 1954; *The End of the Affair* 1955; *Helen of Troy* (as Hecuba; US/It.) 1956; *Conspiracy of Hearts* 1960; *Interlude* 1968; *Anne of the Thousand Days* 1969.

swish pan. Also known as "zip pan" or "whip shot." A rapid panning of a camera on its vertical axis from one point to another, causing a blurred sensation when the image is viewed on the screen. The swish pan is sometimes used for a dramatic transition from one scene to another.

Switzer, Carl ("Alfalfa"). Actor. *b.* Aug. 8, 1926, Paris, Ill. *d.* 1959. Freckled, squeaky-voiced, lovable member of "Our Gang" comedy series. A performer from early childhood, he joined the series in 1935 and stayed with it until 1942. He made an art of atrocious off-key singing, although he actually had a trained voice and started out in show business as a singer. He also appeared in many feature films. As he advanced in age, his film roles declined and he was relegated mostly to bits. To supplement his income, he became a hunting and fishing guide in northern California and eventually a bartender. He was shot in January of 1959 in a drinking brawl with a former hunting-venture partner over a $50 debt. The slaying was ruled "justifiable homicide."

FILMS INCLUDE: *Too Many Parents, Easy to Take, General Spanky* 1936; *Wild and Woolly* 1937; *I Love You Again* 1940; *The Human Comedy* 1943; *Going My Way* 1944; *The Gas House Kids, Courage of Lassie* 1946; *State of the Union* 1948; *A Letter to Three Wives* 1949; *Pat and Mike* 1952; *Island in the Sky* 1953; *The High and the Mighty, Track of the Cat* 1954; *Motorcycle Gang* 1957; *The Defiant Ones* 1958.

Sydney, Basil. Actor. *b.* Apr. 23, 1894, St. Osyth, England. *d.* 1968. On the stage from age 15, he first came to the US in 1920 and in that year made his screen debut in the Hollywood version of his London stage success *Romance.* He starred in another Hollywood silent and spent an entire decade in America, appearing in numerous plays on Broadway and on tour. In the early 30s he commuted between London and New York but thereafter settled permanently back in England where he appeared in many plays and played strong character roles in films, returning to Hollywood only on sporadic occasions. All three of his wives were actresses, Doris Keane, Mary Ellis, and Joyce Howard.

FILMS INCLUDE: *Romance* (US) 1920; *Red Hot Romance* (US) 1922; *The Tunnel/Transatlantic Tunnel* 1935; *Rhodes of Africa/Rhodes, The Amateur Gentleman, Accused, Talk of the Devil, Crime Over London* 1936; *Four Just Men/The Secret Four* 1939; *Ships with Wings* 1941; *Went the Day Well?/48 Hours* 1942; *Caesar and Cleopatra* (as Rufio) 1945; *Meet Me at Dawn* 1946; *Jassy, The Man Within/The Smugglers* 1947; *Hamlet* (as Claudius) 1948; *Angel with the Trumpet* 1949; *Treasure Island* (as Captain Smollett; UK/US) 1950; *The Magic Box* 1951; *Ivanhoe* (as Waldemar Fitzurse; UK/US) 1952; *Salome* (as Pontius Pilate; US) 1953; *Hell Below Zero, The Dam Busters* 1954; *Simba* 1955; *Star of India* (as Louis XIV; US), *Around the World in 80 Days* (cameo; US) 1956; *Island in the Sun, Sea Wife* 1957; *A Question of Adultery* 1958; *John Paul Jones* (US), *The Devil's Disciple* (UK/US) 1959; *The Three Worlds of Gulliver* (as the Emperor of Lilliput; US/UK/Sp.) 1960; *Les Mains d'Orlac/The Hands of Orlac* (Fr./UK) 1961.

Sydow, Max von. Actor. Born Carl Adolf von Sydow, on Apr. 10, 1929, Lund, Sweden. The son of a university professor, he was trained for the stage at Stockholm's Royal Dramatic Theater School. After making his screen debut in 1949, he acquired a reputation for excellence on the Swedish stage which he has extended into films since the late 50s under the guidance of Ingmar BERGMAN. Tall gaunt, blond, and imposing, with an authoritative voice, he made his strong screen presence felt in many of Bergman's films, in which he typified the struggling modern man, as well as in several Hollywood and international productions. He portrayed Christ in George STEVENS's *The Greatest Story Ever Told* and received an Academy Award nomination for Best Actor in *Pelle the Conqueror* (1988).

FILMS INCLUDE: *Only a Mother* 1949; *Miss Julie* 1951; *No Man's Woman* 1953; *The Seventh Seal, Wild Strawberries* 1957; *Brink of Life, The Magician* 1958; *The Virgin Spring* 1960; *Through a Glass Darkly* 1961; *The Swedish Mistress* 1962; *Winter Light* 1963; *The Greatest Story Ever Told* (as Jesus Christ; US), *The Reward* (US) 1965; *Hawaii* (US), *The Quiller Memorandum* (UK/US), *Here Is Your Life* 1966; *Hour of the Wolf, Shame* 1968; *Made in Sweden* 1969; *The Kremlin Letter* (US), *The Passion of Anna* 1970; *The Emigrants, The Touch* (Sw./US), *The Night Visitor* (UK/Sw.) 1971; *Embassy* (UK/US) 1972; *The New Land, The Exorcist* (US) 1973; *Steppenwolf* (UK/Fr./It./Ger.) 1974; *Three Days of the Condor* (US), *Il Contesto* (It.) 1975; *Cadaveri Eccelenti/Illustrious Corpses* (It.), *Cuore di Cane* (It.), *Foxtrot/The Other Side of Paradise* (Mex./Switz.), *Voyage of the Damned* (UK), *Il Deserto dei Tartari/Le Désert des Tartares* (It./Fr./Iran) 1976; *Exorcist II: The Heretic* (US), *March or Die* (UK), *Gran Bollito* (It.) 1977; *Brass Target* (US) 1978; *The Hurricane* (US) 1979; *Flash Gordon* (US; as Ming the Merciless), *Death Watch* (Fr./Ger.) 1980; *Victory* (US) 1981; *Conan the Barbarian* (US) 1982; *Strange Brew* (Can.), *Never Say Never Again* (US) 1983; *Dune* (US), *Dreamscape* (US), *Target Eagle* (Sp./Mex.), *Soldier's Tale* (v/o; US) 1984; *Quo Vadis* (It.) 1985; *Hannah and Her Sisters* (US), *Duet for One* (US) 1986; *The Wolf at the Door* (Den./Fr.) 1987; *Pelle the Conqueror* (Sw.) 1988; *Hiroshima: Out of the Ashes* (US), *Awakenings* (US) 1990; *A Kiss Before Dying* (US)

1991; *Needful Things* 1993; *Judge Dredd,* 1995; *Hansum, Jerusalem* 1996.

Sylvie. Actress. *b.* Louise Sylvain, Jan. 3, 1883, Paris. *d.* 1970. A veteran character player of the French stage and screen, she gained sudden "stardom" at the age of 81, playing the title role in *The Shameless Old Lady* to rave reviews.

FILMS INCLUDE: *Britannicus* 1912; *Germinal* 1918; *Crime et Châtiment/Crime and Punishment* 1935; *Un Carnet de Bal* 1937; *L'Esclave blanche/The Pasha's Wives, La Fin du Jour/The End of a Day* 1939; *Le Corbeau/The Raven, Les Anges du Péché/Angels of the Streets* 1943; *Le Père Goriot* 1944; *L'Idiot/The Idiot* 1946; *Le Diable au Corps/Devil in the Flesh* 1947; *Dieu a besoin des Hommes/God Needs Men* 1950; *Sous le Ciel de Paris/Under the Paris Sky, Le Fruit défendu/Forbidden Fruit* 1951; *Le Petit Monde du Don Camillo/The Little World of Don Camillo, Nous sommes tous des Assassins/We Are All Murderers* 1952; *Tempi Nostri/Anatomy of Love* (It.), *Thérèse Raquin/The Adulteress* (as Mme. Raquin) 1953; *Ulisse/Ulysses* (as Eurycleia; It.) 1954; *Le Miroir a Deux Faces/The Mirror Has Two Faces* 1958; *Cronaca familiare/Family Diary* (It.) 1962; *La Vieille Dame indigne/The Shameless Old Lady* 1965; *J'ai tué Raspoutine* 1967.

Syms, Sylvia. Actress. *b.* Jan. 6, 1934, in London. *d.* 1992. *ed.* RADA. Blonde leading lady of British films and TV, following some stage experience.

FILMS INCLUDE: *My Teenage Daughter* 1956; *No Time for Tears, Woman in a Dressing Gown* 1957; *Ice Cold in Alex/Desert Attack, The Moonraker, Bachelor of Hearts* 1958; *Ferry to Hong Kong, Expresso Bongo* 1959; *Conspiracy of Hearts, The World of Suzie Wong* 1960; *Le Vergini di Roma* (It./Fr.), *Flame in the Streets, Victim* 1961; *The Quare Fellow* 1962; *The World Ten Times Over/Pussycat Alley* 1963; *East of Sudan* 1964; *Operation Crossbow* (UK/It.) 1965; *Danger Route* 1967; *Hostile Witness* 1968; *The Desperados* (US), *Run Wild Run Free* 1969; *Born to Win* (US) 1971; *Asylum* 1972; *There Goes the Bride* 1979; *Nancy Astor* 1982; *Absolute Beginners* 1986; *A Chorus of Disapproval, Shirley Valentine* 1989; *Shining Through* (US), *Dirty Weekend* 1991.

sync. Abbreviation for "synchronization," "synchronism," etc. When a motion picture and its accompanying sound track are aligned in proper SYNCHRONIZATION, the film is said to be "in sync." When they are out of alignment the film is said to be "out of sync."

synchronization. In motion pictures the process of aligning a picture and sound track in correct relationship so that an action and its corresponding sound coincide.

synchronizer. A cutting-room device with linked sprocket wheels by means of which an editor can keep a film and several sound tracks in synchronization. The sprocket wheels are attached to a revolving shaft. Once the perforations of the film and sound tracks are engaged in their proper positions, their proper relationship is maintained while the film is moved along by REWINDS.

synchronous sound. Motion picture sound timed to coincide with a correspondent image. The opposite is asynchronous sound, which is used as a counterpoint to the image. See also ASYNCHRONISM.

synchronous speed. The identical speed at which cameras, sound recorders, and projectors should run in order to ensure a faithful reproduction of a sound scene being filmed. This speed is standardized at 24 frames per second, or 90 feet per minute for 35 mm film, and 36 feet per minute for 16 mm film.

sync mark. Same as START MARK.

synopsis. A brief written outline of the plot and main action of a proposed motion picture. It usually precedes the writing of a TREATMENT, which in turn precedes the writing of the SCREENPLAY, or shooting script.

Szabó, István. Director. Born in 1938, in Budapest. A leading director of the Hungarian new cinema. A graduate of Budapest's Academy of Film Art, he drew attention at various international festivals in the early 60s with three attractive shorts, then turned to feature films with equal success. His *Confidence* (1979) won the Berlin Film Festival Silver Bear, and for *Mephisto* (1981) he received the Hungarian Film Critics Award, an award for best screenplay at Cannes, and the Oscar for best foreign film. His work is characterized by both technical proficiency and innocent charm.

FILMS: Shorts—*Concert, Variations on a Theme* 1961; *You* 1963; *Piety* 1968; *Why I Love It* (collection of shorts) 1970; *City Map* 1978. Features—*Age of Illusions* 1964; *Father* 1966; *A Film About Love* 1970; *25 Firemen's Street* 1974; *Premiere* 1976; *Tales of Budapest* 1977; *The Hungarians* 1978; *Confidence* 1979; *The Green Bird* 1980; *Mephisto* 1981; *Colonel Redl* 1984; *Hanussen* (also co-sc.) 1989; *Opera Europa, Tusztortenet/Stand Off* (act only) 1990; *Meeting Venus* 1991; *Sweet Emma, Dear Bob* 1992.

Szakall, Szöke. See SAKALL, S. Z.

Szekely, Istvan. See SEKELY, Steve.

Szwarc, Jeannot. Director. Born on Nov. 21, 1939, in Paris. Director of commercial, often fantasy-oriented, Hollywood fare. Active since the 1970s. Has also directed several TV movies and episodes of action shows.

FILMS INCLUDE: *Extreme Close-Up* 1973; *Bug* 1975; *Jaws 2* 1978; *Somewhere in Time* 1980; *Enigma* 1982; *Supergirl* 1984; *Santa Claus: The Movie 1985.*

T

Tacchella, Jean-Charles. Director. Born in 1925, in France. A former journalist and film critic, he began writing scripts for movies and TV in the early 60s and in the early 70s turned to directing with two prize-winning shorts. He piloted his first feature in 1973 and in 1976 enjoyed unexpected success in the American market with *Cousin Cousine,* a story of adultery among married couples which was nominated for an Oscar as best foreign picture and won the Louis Delluc Prize in France in 1975. Although he is regarded at home as a capable filmmaker, skilled at blending tenderness and humor in the facile texture of his films, he has never matched the international success he had achieved with that film. He writes his own scripts. His *Travelling-avant* ("Tracking shot" or "Do In") was largely autobiographical.

FILMS (as director-screenwriter): Shorts—*Les Derniers Hiver* 1971; *Une Belle Journée* 1972. Features—*Voyage en Grande Tartarie/Voyage to Grand Tartarie* 1974; *Cousin Cousine* 1975; *Pays bleu/Blue Country* 1977; *Il y a longtemps que je t'aime/It's a Long Time That I've Loved You/Soupçon* 1979; *Croque la Vie* 1981; *Escalier C* 1985; *Travelling-avant* 1987; *Cousins* (screenplay basis only, *Cousin, Cousine;* US) 1989; *Dames galantes/Gallant Ladies* 1990; *The Man of My Life* 1993; *Tous les Jour Dimanche* 1994.

tachometer. A speed-measuring device, often used in conjunction with a motion picture camera to indicate the actual operating speed of its motor. The speed is indicated in terms of frames per second.

tail. A length of blank leader attached to the end of a roll of film to facilitate the projection of the last frames and to protect them from damage.

tails up (or **tails out).** Describing film so wound that its first frame is nearest to the inner core. It must be rewound before projection. The opposite of HEAD UP.

Taiwan. The film industry of Taiwan arose, curiously enough, largely through the efforts of foreign nationals. During WW II, the Japanese occupation government founded the Taiwan Motion Picture Association (which in 1945 became the Taiwan Film Studio), placed under the authority of the Taiwan Provincial Department of Information. As might be imagined, its output was largely war-related propaganda. With the advent of the Chinese Revolution in 1949, a new cultural force, the mainland Chinese, introduced commercial filmmaking to the island. China Movie Studio relocated in Taiwan by 1949, and China Educational Film Studio followed in 1956. The national studio, Central Motion Picture Corporation (CMPC), emerged from a consolidation of the Agricultural Film Corporation and Taiwan Motion Picture in 1954. By the latter half of the 50s, production of Taiwanese features exploded: 21 films in 1956, 110 in 1957. Most of the new productions were Taiwanese dialect films that dealt with local issues, personalities, and folklore.

The industry slumped during the early 60s. The Republic of China tried, largely unsuccessfully, to boost production through the CMPC by directly financing some features for export and loaning money to local companies to encourage production of high quality films. It also founded the annual Golden Horse Awards to honor Taiwanese productions.

But it was the intervention of Hong Kong producers that revived the domestic box office. Lee Han-Hsiang of Shaw Brothers studio established the Grand Movie Company, famous for popular costume dramas during the 60s. Hu Chin-Chuan, who introduced the "swordsman" genre to Taiwan, founded International Motion Picture Studio. By the end of the 60s, Taiwanese studios released some 200 features per year, although by the mid-70s that number had declined by half.

Taiwan enjoyed international critical renown in the 80s and 90s for the works of its *hsin-jui* (new wave). The government initially boosted the careers of Taiwan's new generation of directors through CMPC financing. The 1982 CMPC production *In Our Time* introduced first works by four directors: Jim T'ao, Edward Yang, K'o Yi-cheng, and Chang Yi. A succeeding CMPC feature, *The Sandwich Man* (1983), presented new works by HOU HSIAO-HSIEN, Tseng Chuang-hsiang, and Wan Jen. Dozens of successful feature films followed in the wake of these two films. The recurring themes of new wave films were socially conscious, verging on social criticism (particularly in the films of Hou Hsiao-Hsien and Edward Yang), and elegiac, often expressing nostalgia for the nation's recent agrarian past. Their films also differed in style from their antecedents because they used less well known and nonprofessional actors, elliptical narratives, and generally higher production values.

Notable among the new wave personalities and their films are writer-director Chang Yi (*Jade Love*, 1984; *Kuei-Mei, A Woman*, 1985); director-cinematographer Ch'en K'un-Hou (*Growing Up*, 1983; *The Matrimony*, 1985); writer-director-producer Hou Hsiao-Hsien (*A Time to Love and a Time to Die*, 1985; *Dust in the Wind*, 1987; *City of Sadness*, 1989); and writer-director Edward Yang (*That Day, On the Beach*, 1983; *Taipei Story*, 1984; *Brighter Summer Day*, 1991). Of these directors, Hou has achieved the greatest success outside of his native country, garnering awards at the Venice and Cannes festivals and serving as executive producer for Zhang Yimou of the People's Republic of China (*Raise the Red Lantern*, 1991).

A constant of the Taiwanese film industry has been strict government regulation through the Motion Picture Department of the Government Information Office. Its jurisdiction extends not only to censorship laws, which require all films to be screened and licensed by the government before release, but to all aspects of the business as well. Producers, distributors, and exhibitors must all be licensed and meet demanding conditions to operate. In support of its local industry, the government also enforces import quotas of foreign productions and finances the nation's export business.

take. A single continuous shot taken by a motion picture camera without any interruption or break. A film director may order any number of successive takes of the same action until he is satisfied he has got a perfect shot. Each take of a scene is numbered sequentially on a SLATE which is held in front of the camera and photographed for the purpose of identification in the cutting room. The selected take is printed and incorporated into the work print.

take-up reel. The reel onto which film is wound after exposure in the camera or after passing through the picture gate in a projector.

Talankin, Igor. Director. Born in 1927, in Russia. He entered Soviet films in 1960 after stage experience and training at Mosfilm. Noted for his lyrical style.

FILMS INCLUDE: *Seryozha/A Summer to Remember* (co-dir. with Georgi Daneliya) 1960; *The Entry* 1962; *Day Stars* 1969; *Tchaikovsky* (USSR/US) 1970; *Choice of Goal* 1974; *Father Serge* (also sc.) 1978.

Talbot, Lyle. Actor. Born Lysle Hollywood Henderson, on Feb. 8, 1902, in Pittsburgh. He started his show business career directly out of high school, touring with his parents in tent shows as a magician. Broadening his scope to include acting, he traveled extensively with various stock and rep companies, then founded his own company, The Talbot Players, in Memphis. He entered films in the early 30s, with Warner Bros., and for many years pursued a dual career, as a leading man in B pictures and a heavy in both B's and A's, often portraying underworld characters. He also performed on Broadway and in many TV shows, including 'Ozzie and Harriet' and the 'Burns and Allen Show.'

FILMS INCLUDE: *Love Is a Racket, The Purchase Price, Three on a Match, The 13th Guest, No More Orchids* 1932; *20,000 Years in Sing Sing, Ladies They Talk About, The Life of Jimmy Dolan, A Shriek in the Night, She Had to Say Yes, Mary Stevens M.D., Havana Widows* 1933; *Heat Lightning, Fog Over Frisco, Return of the Terror, The Dragon Murder Case, One Night of Love, Murder in the Clouds* 1934; *It Happened in New York, Chinatown Squad, Oil for the Lamps of China, Page Miss Glory, The Case of the Lucky Legs* 1935; *The Singing Kid, Murder by an Aristocrat, Trapped by Television, Go West Young Man* 1936; *Second Honeymoon* 1937; *Gateway* 1938; *Second Fiddle, Torture Ship* 1939; *Parole Fixer* 1940; *They Raid by Night* 1942; *A Night for Crime* 1943; *Up in Arms, Mystery of the River Boat* (serial), *Are These Our Parents?* 1944; *Chick Carter Detective* (serial) 1946; *The Vigilante* (serial) 1947; *The Vicious Circle* 1948; *Batman and Robin* (serial) 1949; *Champagne for*

Caesar, Atom Man vs. Superman (serial; as Atom Man), *The Jackpot* 1950; *Purple Heart Diary* 1951; *With a Song in My Heart, Untamed Women* 1952; *Trader Tom of the China Seas* (serial), *There's No Business Like Show Business* 1954; *The Great Man* 1957; *City of Fear* 1959; *Sunrise at Campobello* 1960.

talent scout. An elusive connoisseur of talent by whom aspiring actors and actresses hope one day to be discovered for a career in films.

Taliaferro, Mabel. Actress. *b.* 1887, New York City. *d.* 1979. On the stage from early childhood, she played juvenile leads in a number of Broadway productions before making her film debut in the title role of the 1911 Selig production of *Cinderella.* She later played youthful, innocent roles in other films and was known as "The Sweetheart of American Movies" before Mary PICKFORD laid claim to the title "America's Sweetheart." Mabel retired from the screen in 1921, returning only once, in 1940. Her sister, Edith Taliaferro (1894–1958), was also a stage and screen actress. Both were cousins of actress Bessie BARRISCALE.

FILMS INCLUDE: *Cinderella* (title role) 1911; *When Rome Ruled The Three of Us* 1914; *Her Great Price, The Snowbird, God's Half Acre, The Dawn of Love, The Sunbeam* 1916; *A Wife by Proxy, The Barricade, A Magdalene of the Hills, Peggy Leads the Way, Peggy, the Will o' the Wisp, Draft 258* 1917; *The Rich Slave* 1920; *Sentimental Tommy* 1921; *My Love Came Back* 1940.

talkies. Popular term for sound motion pictures, widely used during and shortly after the introduction of sound. Now nearly obsolete, the term is still useful in distinguishing between silent and sound films. See SOUND.

Talmadge, Constance. Actress. *b.* Apr. 19, 1898, Brooklyn, N.Y. *d.* 1973. The younger sister of Natalie and Norma TALMADGE, she entered films in 1914 and for two years appeared in many comedy shorts opposite Billy QUIRK. She got her big break in D. W. Griffith's *Intolerance* (1916), in which she was aptly cast as the spirited, tomboyish Mountain Girl in the Babylonian episode. The role revealed her natural talent for comedy which was to establish her as a leading star, a position she held throughout the silent era. Abetted by the guidance and the influence of her brother-in-law Joseph Schenck, she was nearly as successful as her more famous sister Norma. The two were never in competition. While Norma cornered the market on tear-jerking melodramas, Constance's forte was the sophisticated comedy, a field in which she had few rivals in the 20s. At the height of her success she had her own production company. The four-times-married Constance retired from the screen during the transition to sound without making a single talkie. She and her sisters are the subjects of an Anita Loos biography, *The Talmadge Girls* (1978).

FILMS INCLUDE: *Buddy's First Call, The Mysterious Lodger, The Peacemaker, In Bridal Attire, In the Latin Quarter, The Egyptian Mummy* 1914; *Billy's Wager, The Green Cat, The Master of His House, The Lady of Shalott, The Vanishing Vault, Spades Are Trump, Captivating Mary Carstairs* 1915; *The Missing Links, The Matrimaniac, Intolerance* 1916; *Betsy's Burglar, Scandal, The Honeymoon* 1917; *The Studio Girl, A Pair of Silk Stockings, A Lady's Name* 1918; *The Veiled Adventure, The Fall of Babylon* (expanded version of Babylonian scene from *Intolerance*), *A Temperamental Wife, A Virtuous Vamp, Happiness a la Mode* 1919; *Two Weeks, In Search of a Sinner, The Love Expert, The Perfect Woman, Dangerous Business* 1920; *Mama's Affair, Wedding Bells, Lessons in Love, Woman's Place* 1921; *The Primitive Lover, Polly of the Follies, East Is West* 1922; *Dulcy, The Dangerous Maid* 1923; *The Goldfish, Her Night of Romance* 1924; *Learning to Love, Her Sister from Paris* 1925; *The Duchess of Buffalo* 1926; *Venus of Venice, Breakfast at Sunrise* 1927; *Venus* (in France) 1929.

Talmadge, Natalie. See KEATON, Buster; TALMADGE, Norma.

Talmadge, Norma. Actress. *b.* May 26, 1893 *d.* 1957. The eldest of three Brooklyn sisters driven to screen stardom by a determined stage mother, she was also the first to break into movies, making her debut with Vitagraph in 1910. Both she and Constance TALMADGE rose to superstardom in silent films. The third sister, Natalie Talmadge (1897–1969), was more famous as the wife of Buster KEATON, although she appeared successfully in a number of silent comedies, including Keaton's *Our Hospitality* (1923). Norma was barely 18 when she played the leading lady in her first important film, the original screen version of *A Tale of Two Cities* (1911). She later starred in innumerable films for Vitagraph and Triangle, among other companies. But her future as a star really began shaping up after she married the influential producer Joseph SCHENCK, who took charge of her career in 1916. He set up the Norma Talmadge Film Corporation, releasing through First National and later through United Artists.

Norma's career reached a peak in the early 20s, when she ranked among the most popular idols of the American screen. Her specialty was the suffering heroine of tearful melodramas, and as long as these kept drawing audiences to the box office she remained at the top. She separated from Schenck in 1928 (they would divorce six years later), but he briefly continued to manage her career as well as that of her sister Constance. Norma, who wasn't a particularly good actress, tried bravely to make a transition to sound films, but after two disheartening attempts she retired from the screen to live off her considerable fortune. She returned to the headlines twice in the 30s: in 1934, when she divorced Schenck and married George JESSEL; and in 1939, when she divorced Jessel. Her third marriage, to a Beverly Hills physician, lasted until her premature death of complications from a long bout with arthritis aggravated by drug abuse.

FILMS INCLUDE: *Love of Chrysanthemum, In Neighboring Kingdoms, A Broken Spell, Uncle Tom's Cabin, A Dixie Mother* 1910; *A Tale of Two Cities, The Sky Pilot, The General's Daughter, The Thumb Print, Her Hero, The Child Crusoes* 1911; *The First Violin, Captain Barnacle's Messmate, Mrs. 'Enry 'Awkins, Fortunes of a Composer, The Troublesome Stepdaughters, O'Hara—Squatter and Philosopher, Casey at the Bat* 1912; *Omens and Oracles, The Midget's Revenge, 'Arriet's Baby, An Old Man's Love Story, Solitaires, Under the Daisies, The Other Woman, Extremities, The Doctor's Secret, The Blue Rose, His Silver Bachelorhood, Fanny's Conspiracy* 1913; *Sawdust and Salome, Cupid Versus Money, The Sacrifice of Kathleen, A Helpful Sisterhood, John Rance—Gentleman, Goodbye Summer, The Peacemaker, The Mill of Life, Sunshine and Shadows, A Daughter of Israel* 1914; *The Barrier of Faith, A Daughter's Strange Inheritance, A Pillar of Flame, Captivating Mary Carstairs, The Battle Cry of Peace* 1915; *The Missing Links, The Crown Prince's Double, The Children in the House, Going Straight/Corruption, The Devil's Needle, The Social Secretary, Fifty-Fifty* 1916; *Panthea, Poppy, The Moth, The Secret of the Storm Country* 1917; *The Ghosts of Yesterday, De Luxe Annie, Her Only Way, The Forbidden City* 1918; *The New Moon, The Way of a Woman, Probation Wife, The Isle of Conquest* 1919; *She Loves and Lies, The Woman Gives, The Branded Woman, A Daughter of Two Worlds* 1920; *The Passion Flower, The Sign on the Door, The Wonderful Thing, Love's Redemption* 1921; *Smilin' Through, The Eternal Flame* 1922; *The Voice from the Minaret, Within the Law, Ashes of Vengeance*

1923; *The Song of Love, Secrets, The Only Woman* 1924; *The Lady, Graustark* 1925; *Kiki* 1926; *Camille* (title role) 1927; *The Dove, The Woman Disputed* 1928; *New York Nights* 1929; *Du Barry—Woman of Passion* (title role) 1930.

Tamblyn, Russ. Actor, dancer. Born Russell Tamblyn, on Dec. 30, 1934, in Los Angeles. A radio, stage, and screen performer since early childhood (as Rusty Tamblyn), he demonstrated dazzling acrobatic dancing ability in such Hollywood musicals as *Seven Brides for Seven Brothers* (1954) and *West Side Story* (1961) and played juvenile leads in nonmusical films. He was nominated for an Academy Award as best supporting player for his performance in *Peyton Place* (1957). Recently seen mostly in low-budget productions. Was a regular on the TV drama series 'Twin Peaks.'

FILMS INCLUDE: *The Boy with Green Hair* 1948; *The Kid from Cleveland, Samson and Delilah* 1949; *Captain Carey USA, Father of the Bride* 1950; *As Young As You Feel* 1951; *Retreat Hell!* 1952; *Take the High Ground* 1953; *Seven Brides for Seven Brothers* 1954; *Hit the Deck* 1955; *The Fastest Gun Alive, Young Guns* 1956; *Peyton Place* 1957; *High School Confidential, Tom Thumb* 1958; *West Side Story* 1961; *The Wonderful World of the Brothers Grimm, How the West Was Won* 1962; *Follow the Boys, The Haunting* 1963; *The Long Ships* 1964; *War of the Gargantuans* (Jap./US), *Son of a Gunfighter* 1966; *Satan's Sadists* 1970; *The Last Movie* (cameo) 1971; *Dracula vs. Frankenstein* 1973; *Win Place or Steal* 1975; *Black Heat* 1976; *Human Highway* (also co-sc.) 1982; *Los Monjes sangrientos/Blood Screams* (Mex.) 1986; *Cyclone, Commando Squad* 1987; *Wizards of the Demon Sword* 1991; *Cabin Boy* 1994.

Tamiroff, Akim. Actor. *b.* Oct. 29, 1899, Baku, Russia. *d.* 1972. Trained for the stage at the Moscow Art Theater drama school, he arrived in the US in 1923 on a tour with a troupe of actors and decided to stay. He appeared on the stage in several New York Theatre Guild productions and from the early 30s played character parts in numerous Hollywood productions. A flamboyant actor with a strong screen presence, he played some character leads, as in *The Way of All Flesh,* in which he portrayed an Emil Jannings type of tragic role, but for the most part he was cast in villainous or eccentric supporting parts, often as an unsavory, mysterious foreigner with a heavy Slavic accent. He was equally effective in broad comedy roles and in the late 50s he appeared mostly in European films. He played Sancho Panza in Orson Welles's unfinished *Don Quixote* and played the lead in the 1959 Broadway adaptation of 'Rashomon.' He was nominated for Oscars for his performances in *The General Died at Dawn* (1936) and *For Whom the Bell Tolls* (1943).

FILMS INCLUDE: *Okay America* 1932; *Queen Christina* 1933; *Sadie McKee, The Great Flirtation, Whom the Gods Destroy, Chained* 1934; *The Lives of a Bengal Lancer, Naughty Marietta, Black Fury, Go Into Your Dance, China Seas, The Last Outpost, The Gay Deception* 1935; *The Story of Louis Pasteur, Woman Trap, Desire, Anthony Adverse, The General Died at Dawn* (title role), *The Jungle Princess* 1936; *The Soldier and the Lady/Michael Strogoff, King of Gamblers, The Great Gambini* (title role), *High Wide and Handsome* 1937; *The Buccaneer, Dangerous to Know* (lead), *Spawn of the North, Ride a Crooked Mile* (lead) 1938; *Paris Honeymoon, King of Chinatown* (title role), *Union Pacific, The Magnificent Fraud* (lead, in multiple roles), *Disputed Passage* (lead) 1939; *The Way of All Flesh* (lead), *Untamed, The Great McGinty, North West Mounted Police* 1940; *New York Town, The Corsican Brothers* (as Colonna) 1941; *Tortilla Flat* (as Pablo) 1942; *Five Graves to Cairo, For Whom the Bell Tolls* (as Pablo), *His Butler's Sister* 1943; *The Miracle of Morgan's Creek, The Bridge of San Luis Rey* (as Uncle Pio), *Dragon Seed* (as Wu Lien), *Can't Help Singing* 1944; *A Scandal in Paris* 1946; *Fiesta, The Gangster* 1947; *My Girl Tisa, Relentless* 1948; *Outpost in Morocco, Black Magic/Cagliostro* 1949; *You Know What Sailors Are* (UK), *Desert Legion* 1953; *Don Quixote* (as Sancho Panza; unfinished), *Mr. Arkadin/Confidential Report* (Switz./Sp.) 1955; *Anastasia* (UK) 1956; *Yangtse Incident/Battle Hell* (UK) 1957; *Touch of Evil, Me and the Colonel* 1958; *Ocean's Eleven* 1960; *Romanoff and Juliet* 1961; *Le Procès/The Trial* (as Block; Fr./It./Ger.), *The Reluctant Saint* 1962; *Panic Button, Topkapi* 1964; *Le Bambole* (Bolognini episode; It./Fr.), *Lord Jim* (UK/US), *Alphaville* (Fr./It.), *La Fabuleuse Aventure de Marco Polo/Marco the Magnificent* (Fr./It./Yug./Eg./Afghan.) 1965; *Lt. Robinson Crusoe U.S.N., The Liquidator* (UK), *Hotel Paradiso* (UK/US), *Caccia alla Volpe/After the Fox* (It./US/UK) 1966; *Una Rosa per tutti/A Rose for Everyone* (It.), *The Vulture* (US/UK/Can.) 1967; *Great Catherine* (UK) 1968; *The Great Bank Robbery* 1969; *Sabra/Death of a Jew* (Fr./It.) 1970.

Tanaka, Kinuyo. Actress, director. *b.* Nov. 29, 1909, Shinomoseki, Japan. *d.* 1977. In Japanese films from the age of 14, after brief experience in light opera, she starred in numerous productions, notably Mizoguchi's *Life of Oharu* and *Ugetsu,* Ozu's *Equinox Flower,* and Kinoshita's *Ballad of Narayama.* She won the best actress prize at the 1975 Berlin Festival for *Sandakan 8.* In 1953 she became the first woman to direct a Japanese film, the lyrical *Love Letter.* She married director Hiroshi Shimizu in 1929. They later divorced.

FILMS INCLUDE: As actress—*A Woman from the Genroku Era* 1924; *Ochimusha* 1925; *Torrent* 1926; *Intimate Dream* 1927; *Tales from a Land by the Sea, The Village Bride* 1928; *I Graduated But. . .* 1929; *Oyosan* 1930; *I Flunked But. . .* 1931; *The Loyal 47 Ronin* 1932; *A Woman of Tokyo* 1933; *An Innocent Maid* 1935; *New Way* 1936; *The Tree of Love* 1937; *Woman of Osaka* 1940; *Musashi Miyamoto* 1944; *The Victory of Women* 1946; *The Love of the Actress Sumako* 1947; *Women of the Night* 1948; *My Love Has Been Burning* 1951; *Miss Oyu* 1951; *Mother, Life of Oharu* 1952; *Four Chimneys, Ugetsu* 1953; *Sansho the Bailiff/The Bailiff* 1954; *Flowing* 1956; *Ballad of Narayama, Equinox Flower* 1958; *Eternity of Love* 1961; *Lonely Lane* 1962; *Alone on the Pacific/My Enemy the Sea* 1963; *Red Beard* 1965; *Judo Champion* 1967; *Sandakan 8* 1975; *Daichi no Komori-uta* 1976. As director—*Love Letter* (also act.) 1953; *The Moon Rises* (also act.) 1955; *A Wandering Princess* (also act.), *Love Under the Crucifix* 1960.

Tandy, Jessica. Actress. *b.* June 7, 1907, in London. *d.* 1994. *ed.* U. of Western Ontario (law). Superb, versatile dramatic performer of the British and American stage and screen. Raised from age 12 by her widowed mother, a headmistress at a school for retarded children, she trained at the Ben Greet Academy of Acting, making her professional debut at 16, and her first New York performance at 21. She rapidly gained prominence on both sides of the Atlantic, eventually inheriting from Helen Hayes the unofficial title "The First Lady of Broadway." She won her first Tony Award as the original Blanche du Bois, opposite Marlon Brando, in Tennessee Williams's 'A Streetcar Named Desire' (1948). It was followed by Tonys for 'The Gin Game' (1978) and 'Foxfire' (1982). Tandy's screen appearances, spanning five decades, were more sporadic but no less memorable. Heavily in demand by Hollywood in the 80s and early 90s, she won the Academy Award as best actress for *Driving Miss Daisy* (1989) and gained an Oscar nomination as best supporting actress for *Fried Green Tomatoes* (1991). Her busy acting schedule still permitted her to earn a law degree from the University of Western Ontario in 1974. Formerly (1932–40) the wife of actor Jack HAWKINS, she was married to Hume CRONYN, with whom she frequently teamed on the stage, from 1942 until her death in 1994.

FILMS: *The Indiscretions of Eve* (UK) 1932; *Murder in the Family* (UK) 1938; *The Seventh Cross* 1944; *The Valley of Decision* 1945; *The Green Years, Dragonwyck* 1946; *Forever Amber* 1947; *A Woman's Vengeance* 1948; *September Affair, The Desert Fox* 1951; *The Light in the Forest* 1958; *Hemingway's Adventures of a Young Man* 1962; *The Birds* 1963; *Butley* (UK/US) 1974; *Honky Tonk Freeway* 1981; *The World According to Garp, Still of the Night, Best Friends* 1982; *The Bostonians* 1984; *Cocoon* 1985; *Batteries Not Included* 1986; *The House on Carroll Street, Cocoon: The Return* 1988; *Driving Miss Daisy* 1989; *Fried Green Tomatoes* 1991; *Used People* 1992; *Camilla, Nobody's Fool* 1994.

Tanner, Alain. Director. Born on Dec. 6, 1929, in Geneva, to a writer-painter father and an actress mother. He studied economics at Geneva's Calvin College but took an early interest in films and, after graduating, went to London, where he worked as an apprentice at the British Film Institute. While there he co-directed with fellow countryman Claude GORETTA the hidden camera documentary short *Nice Time,* about night life in Piccadilly Circus, which won the experimental film prize at the 1957 Venice Festival. The following year he joined the BBC briefly as an assistant producer of TV documentaries. After a disappointing stopover in Paris, he returned home, where he began directing for the French-language network of Swiss TV. With four other young filmmakers, Tanner co-founded in 1966 Groupe Cinq, and two years later proceeded to direct the co-operative's, and his own, first feature, *Charles—Dead or Alive.* Considered a pivotal production in the rebirth of Swiss cinema, the film, a probing look at a critical moment in the life a wealthy industrialist, won the first prize at the 1969 Loc Festival. Tanner has since asserted himself as Switzerland's best-known and most-talented director, a politically oriented leftist filmmaker who in just a few years has become a most familiar name on the international festival circuit. He advocates a distanced Brechtian cinema that calls attention to its artificiality and attempts to engage the audience in a kind of dialogue. He writes his own scripts, alone or in collaboration, mainly with John Berger. The two shared the best screenplay award from the US National Society of Film Critics for *Jonah Who Will Be 25 in the Year 2,000* (1976), a humorous account on the effect of the '68 Paris unrest on the lives of eight characters. Tanner won the Special Jury Prize at Cannes for a follow-up film, *Light Years Away* (1981). Most of his films are French-Swiss co-productions. His work is the subject of the documentary *Cinema—Dead or Alive,* made by the Zurich Film-collective in the late 70s. His wife, Jeannine, is a former actress.

FEATURE FILMS (as director-screenwriter): *Charles—Mort ou vif/Charles—Dead or Alive* 1969; *La Salamandre/The Salamander* 1971; *La Rétour d'Afrique/Return from Africa* 1972; *Le Milieu du Monde/The Middle of the World* 1974; *Jonas qui aura 25 Ans en l'An 2000/Jonah Who Will Be 25 in the Year 2000* 1976; *Messidor* 1979; *Les Années lumière/Light Years Away* 1981; *Dans la Ville blanche/In The White City* (also co-prod.; Switz./Port.) 1983; *No Man's Land* (also prod.) 1985; *Flamme dans mon Coeur/A Flame in My Heart, La Vallée fantôme* 1987; *La Femme de Rose Hill* (also co-prod.; Switz./Fr./Ger.) 1989; *The Man Who Lost His Shadow* 1991; *The Diary of Lady M.* 1994.

tape. See MAGNETIC TAPE.

tape splice. See HOT SPLICE.

Taradash, Daniel. Screenwriter. Born on Jan. 29, 1913, in Louisville, Ky. *ed.* Harvard; Harvard Law School. He passed his New York Bar examinations in 1937 but gave up his law practice after winning a nationwide playwriting contest the following year. In Hollywood since 1939, he has written infrequent but usually intelligent screenplays, winning an Academy Award for *From Here to Eternity* (1953). In 1956 he made an unsuccessful stab at directing with *Storm Center.*

FILMS INCLUDE: *Golden Boy* (co-sc.) 1939; *A Little Bit of Heaven* 1940; *Knock on Any Door* (co-sc.) 1949; *Rancho Notorious, Don't Bother to Knock* 1952; *From Here to Eternity* 1953; *Desiree* 1954; *Storm Center* (also dir.), *Picnic* 1956; *Bell Book and Candle* 1958; *Morituri/Saboteur: Code Name Morituri* 1965; *Hawaii* (co-sc.) 1966; *Castle Keep* (co-sc.) 1969; *Doctors' Wives* 1971; *The Other Side of Midnight* 1977.

Tarantino, Quentin. Screenwriter, director, producer, actor. Born March 27, 1963, in Knoxville, Tenn. He moved to Los Angeles with his mother at an early age. Having never finished high school, he found himself working as a clerk at a video store where his knowledge of obscure and well-known movies enabled him to cultivate relationships with customers who happened to be in the film industry. After making his debut as a director-screenwriter-actor with *Reservoir Dogs* (1992), he quickly established himself as a filmmaker of blistering wit, memorable characters, and a penchant for violence. He received numerous awards for *Pulp Fiction* (1994), including an Oscar for his screenplay, and a nomination as best director, proving that dreams do come true in Hollywood.

Through his relationship with Miramax Films, Tarantino and his distribution company Rolling Thunder, bring to the American screen little-known genre films, the first of which was the slick, made-in-Hong Kong crime comedy *Chungking Express* (1994; US release in 1996). He is romantically linked to actress Mira SORVINO.

FILMS: *Reservoir Dogs* (sc., dir., act.) 1992; *The Coriolis Effect* (act. only), *True Romance* (sc. only) 1993; *Killing Zoe* (exec. prod. only), *Natural Born Killers* (story only), *Pulp Fiction* (dir., sc.) *Sleep with Me* (act. only), *Somebody to Love* (act. only) 1994; *Crimson Tide* (uncredited sc.), *Desperado* (act. only), *Destiny Turns on the Radio* (act. only), *Four Rooms* (dir., sc., act.) 1995; *From Dusk Till Dawn* (exec. prod., sc., act.), *Girl 6* (act. only) 1996.

target. A small circular FLAG used in shading a camera lens from direct light.

Tarkovsky, Andrei. Director. *b.* Apr. 4, 1932, Lavorazhe, Russia. *d.* 1986. The son of Arseny Tarkovsky, a well-known poet, he studied at Moscow's Institute of Oriental Languages, majoring in Arabic. He then enrolled at the Soviet State Film School (VGIK), where he was tutored by Mikhail ROMM. He showed much promise with his prize-winning diploma film, *Steamroller and the Violin* (1960). He won international acclaim and the Golden Lion at the Venice Festival for his first feature film, *Ivan's Childhood/My Name Is Ivan* (1962), a tribute to the heroism of an orphan boy in WW II action behind enemy lines. The film was uncommonly lyrical in its sincere sentiment and visual beauty, though it conformed in story and outlook with the official Soviet cultural line. This was not the case with Tarkovsky's next film, *Andrei Rublev,* a grimly realistic portrayal of a 15th-century Russian monk which was made in 1966 but was banned in Russia until 1971, a year after it won a prize at the Cannes Film Festival. Tarkovsky's third feature, *Solaris* (1972), a parable of love and life masquerading in the guise of a science fiction film, was less controversial but still drew official criticism as being too arcane and whimsical for average audiences to understand. It won the Jury Prize at Cannes. Tarkovsky became widely known abroad as the Soviet Union's most unorthodox filmmaker, but his films enjoyed only limited distribution at home. In 1975 he shocked Muscovites with his most controversial film yet, the autobiographical *The Mirror,* in which he employed an open-ended plot structure and unorthodox cinematic techniques familiar to Western audiences but radically revolutionary as far as Soviet filmgoers were concerned. Venturing abroad, Tarkovsky shared the Grand Prix de Création and the International Critics Prize at the Cannes Festival for *Nostalgia* (1983), a pictorially haunting if curiously enigmatic film about a Russian in search of his cultural past in Italy. He then proceeded to London, where he directed a stage production of 'Boris Gudonov' at Covent Garden. Having officially defected to the West in 1984, Tarkovsky made his last film under Swedish-French auspices. Beautifully shot by Sven Nykvist on the Baltic Sea island of Gotland, off the coast of Sweden, *The Sacrifice* (1986) offered an intimately personal statement by the director about the value to humanity of selfless spiritual commitment. The film was well received at Cannes, gaining the Grand Special Jury Prize, the International Critics Prize, and the Ecumenical Prize. Shortly after the triple win, Tarkovsky died of lung cancer at age 54. His career was the subject of the documentary *Directed by Andrei Tarkovsky* (1988).

FILMS: *There Will Be No Leave Today* (short) 1959; *The Steamroller and the Violin* (also co-sc.; medium-length) 1960; *Ivan's Childhood/My Name Is Ivan* 1962; *Andrei Rublev* (also co-sc.; release delayed to 1971) 1966; *Solaris* (also co-sc.) 1972; *The Mirror* (also co-sc.) 1975; *Stalker* 1979; *Nostalghia/Nostalgia* (also co-sc.; It.) 1983; *Offret/Sacrificatio/Le Sacrifice/The Sacrifice* (also sc., co-edit.; Sw./Fr.) 1986.

Tashlin, Frank. Director, screenwriter. *b.* Feb. 19, 1913, Weehawken, N.J. *d.* 1972. A school dropout at 13, he worked at a variety of jobs before entering films in 1930 as a cartoonist on Paul TERRY's "Aesop's Film Fables" series. In 1933 he worked briefly as a gagman for Hal ROACH and in the following year he began a syndicated comic strip, "Van Boring," which ran in a string of newspapers for four years. In 1939 he became a story editor at the Walt Disney studios; in the mid-40s he abandoned animation completely for a career as a screenwriter for films starring Bob Hope, Red Skelton, and other comedians. Turning director in the early 50s, he naturally veered toward comedy. His background as a cartoonist became evident in the inventiveness and the frenzy of his farces, and the exaggerated, sometimes vulgar tone of his social parodies. Tashlin was greatly admired for awhile by some French critics for directing several of the more successful comedies of Jerry LEWIS as well as a couple of risqué romps featuring the ample loveliness of Jayne MANSFIELD. Jean-Luc GODARD saw in Tashlin's work the vanguard of a truly modern style in film comedy.

FILMS: As screenwriter (alone or in collaboration)—*Delightfully Dangerous* (co-story only) 1945; *Variety Girl* 1947; *One Touch of Venus, The Paleface, The Fuller Brush Man* 1948; *Miss Grant Takes Richmond* 1949; *Love Happy, A Woman of Distinction, Kill the Umpire, The Good Humor Man, The Fuller Brush Girl* 1950; *The Scarlet Hour* 1956; *The Shakiest Gun in the West* (co-screenplay basis only, *The Paleface*) 1972. As director-screenwriter—*The Lemon Drop Kid* (co-dir. with Sidney Lanfield; uncredited) 1951; *The First Time, Son of Paleface* 1952; *Marry Me Again* 1953; *Susan Slept Here* (dir. only) 1954; *Artists and Models* 1955; *The Lieutenant Wore Skirts, Hollywood or Bust* (dir. only), *The Girl Can't Help It* (also prod.) 1956; *Will Success Spoil Rock Hunter?* (also prod.) 1957; *Rock-a-Bye Baby, The Geisha Boy* 1958; *Say One for Me* (dir., prod. only) 1959; *Cinderfella* 1960; *Bachelor Flat, It's Only Money* (dir. only) 1962; *The Man from the Diners' Club* (dir. only), *Who's Minding the Store?* 1963; *The Disorderly Orderly* 1964; *The Alphabet Murders* (dir. only; UK), *The Glass Bottom Boat* (dir. only) 1966; *Caprice* 1967; *The Private Navy of Sgt. O'Farrell* 1968.

Tashman, Lilyan. Actress. *b.* Lillian Tashman, Oct. 23, 1899, Brooklyn, N.Y. *d.* 1934. Elegant leading lady and second lead of Hollywood silents and early talkies. The daughter of a children's clothing manufacturer, she was a model and a Ziegfeld Girl before her film debut in 1921. In films she was usually cast as a sophisticated, sarcastic blonde. She was considered one of Hollywood's best-dressed women and was one of the film colony's social leaders. Her second husband was actor Edmund LOWE. She died at 35 following an emergency operation for a tumorous condition.

FILMS INCLUDE: *Experience* 1921; *Manhandled, The Garden of Weeds, The Dark Swan* 1924; *A Broadway Butterfly, The Parasite, Déclassée, Pretty Ladies, Bright Lights* 1925; *Rocking Moon, Siberia, For Alimony Only, Love's Blindness, So This Is Paris* 1926; *Camille, The Stolen Bride, French Dressing* 1927; *Happiness Ahead, Manhattan Cocktail, Craig's Wife* 1928; *The Trial of Mary Dugan, Bulldog Drummond, New York Nights, The Marriage Playground* 1929; *No No Nanette, Puttin' on the Ritz, On the Level, The Matrimonial Bed, The Cat Creeps* 1930; *One Heavenly Night, Millie, Murder by the Clock, The Mad Parade, Girls About Town* 1931; *The Wiser Sex, Scarlet Dawn, Those We Love* 1932; *Too Much Harmony* 1933; *Wine Women and Song, Riptide* 1934; *Frankie and Johnny* 1936.

Tati, Jacques. Director, actor. *b.* Jacques Tatischeff, Oct. 9, 1908, Le Pecq, France, of Russian-Dutch-Italian-French descent. *d.* 1982. The grandson of the Russian Czar's former ambassador to Paris, he received art training so that he could enter his father's art restoration and picture-framing business. But he was drawn by sports, especially rugby, which he played professionally for a brief spell with the famous Racing Club team. He utilized this interest and experience in the early 30s when he turned cabaret and music hall entertainer with an act in which he pantomimed the top sports figures of the time. His success was immediate, and several of his routines were made into short films, which he wrote and in which he starred. But his film career did not begin in earnest until after WW II.

After playing small parts in two feature films of Claude Autant-Lara, Tati directed a short film featuring himself, *L'Ecole des Facteurs,* in 1947. The result was so successful that his producer decided to expand it into a feature film. The outcome was *Jour de Fête* (1949), a milestone in French screen comedy. Tati emphasized visual humor and employed an entertaining mélange of comic styles in satirizing the modern obsession with speed through the tribulations of a village postman (played by Tati) who is inspired by a film dealing with speedy American postal techniques into virtuosic time-saving feats. The film won the best script award at the Venice Festival and was a critical and commercial success. But Tati admirers had to wait four years before the release of his next comic masterpiece, *Mr. Hulot's Holiday.* The delay was the combined result of Tati's difficulties in raising money for the project and the kind of painstaking, time-consuming preproduction preparations that have characterized all his work.

In Mr. Hulot, Tati created a gangling, awkward character whose peculiar gait and odd misadventures set him apart from the gadget-obsessed world around him. Mr. Hulot remained Tati's alter ego in his three subsequent productions, an island of sanity and warm humanity surrounded by a sea of antiseptic modernity. Tati was a meticulous director who devoted exorbitant stretches of time to the painstaking preparation for each film. With revenues and funding in short supply, he was unable to turn out films with any regularity. Despite the success of such comedies as *Mon Oncle* (1958) and *Playtime* (1968), he found himself constantly beset by financial problems. His old films were frequently impounded by banks as collateral against his large debts, thus restricting the cash flow that he so desperately needed to produce more films. Following the release of his last film, *Parade* (1974), he announced plans in 1977 to start a new production, *Confusion.* But it never materialized. In a career spanning three decades, Tati made only six feature films, but the originality and the unique quality of his work assured him of a leading position in the pantheon of movie comedy.

FILMS: Shorts—*Oscar Champion de Tennis* (sc., act.) 1932; *On demande une Brute* (co-sc., act.) 1934; *Gai Dimanche* (co-sc., act.) 1935; *Soigné ton Gauche* (sc., act.) 1936; *Retour à la Terre* (sc., act.) 1938; *L'Ecole des Facteurs* (dir., sc., act.) 1947. Features—*Sylvie et le Fantôme/Sylvie and the Phantom* (act. only) 1946; *Le Diable du Corps* (act. only) 1947; *Jour de Fête* (dir., co-sc., act.) 1949; *Les Vacances de Monsieur Hulot/Mr. Hulot's Holiday* (dir., co-sc., act.) 1953; *Mon Oncle/My Uncle* (dir., co-sc., act.) 1958; *Play-Time/Playtime* (dir., sc., act.) 1968; *Trafic/Traffic* (dir., sc., act.) 1971; *Parade* (dir., sc., act.; for TV) 1974.

Tauber, Richard. Singer, actor. *b.* May 16, 1893, Linz, Austria. *d.* 1948. The internationally famous operatic tenor starred in a number of German films of the early 30s. After the Nazi takeover in 1933, he emigrated to Great Britain, where he enjoyed great success as a singing screen personality.

FILMS INCLUDE: In Germany—*Das lockende Ziel* (also prod.), *Das Land des Lächelns* (also prod.) 1930; *Die grosse Attraktion* 1931; *Melodie der Liebe* 1932. In the UK—*Blossom Time, April Romance* 1934; *Heart's Desire* (also song-writer) 1935; *Land Without Music/Forbidden Music* 1936; *Pagliacci/A Clown Must Laugh* 1937; *Waltz Time* 1945; *The Lisbon Story* 1946.

Taurog, Norman. Director, actor. *b.* Feb. 23, 1899, Chicago. *d.* 1981. On the stage from childhood, he entered films in 1913 as a boy actor at the Ince studios. In 1919 he began directing Larry Semon comedy shorts at Vitagraph. He later directed Lloyd Hamilton shorts for Educational, among other comedy series. A prolific feature director since 1928, he specialized in comedy and light fare but also turned out a number of films in a more serious vein. In four decades of entertaining feature work, mainly for MGM and Paramount, Taurog proved himself the ideal studio director, an excellent craftsman with no particular style or theme who was capable of turning almost any assignment into an attractive box-office package. He won the best director Academy Award for *Skippy* (1931), a Jackie Cooper vehicle, and was nominated for another Oscar for *Boys Town* (1938), starring Spencer Tracy and Mickey Rooney.

FEATURE FILMS: *The Farmer's Daughter* (co-dir. with Arthur Rosson) 1928; *Lucky Boy* (co-dir. with Charles C. Wilson) 1929; *Troopers Three* (co-dir. with Reeves Eason), *Sunny Skies, Hot Curves, Follow the Leader* 1930; *Finn and Hattie* (co-dir. with Norman Z. McLeod), *Skippy, Newly Rich, Huckleberry Finn, Sooky* 1931; *Hold 'Em Jail!, The Phantom President, If I Had a Million* (W. C. Fields episode) 1932; *A Bedtime Story, The Way to Love* 1933; *We're Not Dressing, Mrs. Wiggs of the Cabbage Patch, College Rhythm* 1934; *The Big Broadcast of 1936, Strike Me Pink, Rhythm on the Range, Reunion* 1936; *Fifty Roads to Town, You Can't Have Everything* 1937; *The Adventures of Tom Sawyer, Mad About Music, Boys Town, The Girl Downstairs* 1938; *Lucky Night* 1939; *Young Tom Edison, Broadway Melody of 1940, Little Nellie Kelly* 1940; *Men of Boys Town, Design for Scandal* 1941; *Are Husbands Necessary?, A Yank at Eton* 1942; *Presenting Lily Mars, Girl Crazy* 1943; *The Hoodlum Saint* 1946; *The Beginning or the End* 1947; *Big City, The Bride Goes Wild, Words and Music* 1948; *That Midnight Kiss* 1949; *Please Believe Me, The Toast of New Orleans, Mrs. O'Malley and Mr. Malone* 1950; *Rich Young and Pretty* 1951; *Room for One More, Jumping Jacks* 1952; *The Stooge, The Stars Are Singing, The Caddy* 1953; *Living It Up* 1954; *You're Never Too Young* 1955; *The Birds and the Bees, Pardners, Bundle of Joy* 1956; *The Fuzzy Pink Nightgown* 1957; *Onionhead* 1958; *Don't Give Up the Ship* 1959; *Visit to a Small Planet, G.I. Blues* 1960; *All Hands on Deck, Blue Hawaii* 1961; *Girls! Girls! Girls!* 1962; *It Happened at the World's Fair, Palm Springs Weekend* 1963; *Tickle Me, Sergeant Deadhead, Dr. Goldfoot and the Bikini Machine* 1965; *Spinout* 1966; *Double Trouble* 1967; *Speedway, Live a Little Love a Little* 1968.

Tavernier, Bertrand. Director. Born on Apr. 25, 1941, in Lyons, France. The son of noted poet-journalist René Tavernier (1915–89), he studied law for a year or two but gave in to his passion for cinema and began writing interviews with directors and film reviews for various French publications, including *Cahiers du Cinéma.* An unabashed film buff, he co-founded a cine club, the Nickel-Odéon, collaborated on a number of books, including *Trente Ans de Cinéma américain (Thirty Years of American Cinema),* and entered the film industry proper as a publicist. He also collaborated on a number of scripts and in 1963 directed the first of several shorts. It wasn't until 1974 that he turned out his first feature, *L'Horloger de Saint-Paul,* a taut, atmospheric character study based on a novel by Simenon, for which he won the French cinema's most coveted award, the Prix Louis Delluc. The film featured veteran actor Philippe Noiret, who would play the protagonist in nearly all of Tavernier's subsequent productions. "He is my autobiographical actor," the director has often said. On the whole, Tavernier developed closer relationships with actors than his contemporaries of the French New Wave. "Actors like to work with me because I'm a good public—I like to be astonished," he said. He also sees his films as being more deeply rooted in political and social themes. Although he sees himself as a thoroughly French director, providing in his films a narrative and stylistic link between the traditional national cinema of the 30s and 40s and the New Wave, Tavernier acknowledges a debt to American movies, the dynamic visual style of which he tries to emulate in his own productions. He is a proven master of balancing grand-scale action and intimacy. Thematically the director is frequently preoccupied with the struggle between good and evil. His films, while not truly autobiographical, are intimately personal. "My childhood was marked by loneliness because my parents didn't get along," he once confessed. "And it's coming out in every movie. I've practically never had a couple in my films." Tavernier experienced the agony of the breakup of his own marriage (from 1965) to English-born Colo O'Hagan Tavernier, who became his script collaborator only after their 1980 separation, retaining his name. Their son, Nils Tavernier, is an actor.

FILMS (as director): *La Chance et l'Amour* ("Une Chance explosive" episode) 1964; *Les Baisers* ("Le Baiser de Judas" episode) 1965; *L'Horloger de Saint-Paul/The Clockmaker* (also sc.) 1974; *Que la Fête commence/Let Joy Reign Supreme* (also sc.) 1975; *Le Juge et l'Assassin/The Judge and the Assassin* (also co-sc.) 1976; *Des Enfants gâtés/Spoiled Children* (also sc.) 1977; *La Mort en direct/Death Watch* (in English; also co-prod., co-sc.), *Une Semaine de Vacances/A Week's Vacation* (a co-prod., co-sc.) 1980; *Coup de Torchon/Clean Slate* (also co-sc.) 1981; *La Trace* (co-prod, co-sc. only) 1983; *Mississippi Blues* (doc.; co-dir. with Robert Parrish, co-prod.), *Un Dimanche â la Campagne/A Sunday in the Country* (also co-sc.) 1984; *Au de Minuit/Round Midnight* (also co-sc.; US/Fr.) 1986; *Les Moi d'Avril sont meurtriers* (co-sc. only) 1987; *La Passion Béatrice/Beatrice* 1988; *La Vie est rien d'autre/Life and Nothing*

But (also co-sc.) 1990; *Daddy Nostalgie* 1991; *La Guerre sans Nom/The Undeclared War* (doc.; also co-sc.) 1992; *D'Artganon's Daughter* 1994; *L'Appat* 1995; *Captain Conan* 1996.

Taviani, Paolo and **Vittorio.** Brother team of directors, both born in San Miniato, Italy, Paolo on Nov. 8, 1931, and Vittorio on Sept. 20, 1929, the sons of a lawyer persecuted by the authorities as an anti-Fascist. They both studied at the University of Pisa, Paolo liberal arts and Vittorio law. During their student days they took an interest in the cinema, initially as club organizers and film critics. They wrote and produced several experimental plays and directed a number of film shorts before turning out their first feature in 1962. Their first two features were made in collaboration with Valentino Orsini (*b.* 1926, Pisa). The brothers work in perfect harmony as a synchronized unit, planning and writing their films together and taking turns at directing scenes. Their films have typically dealt with social problems in southern Italy. Their *Padre Padrone* (1977), an austere yet intense true drama about a child who overcomes brutalization by his peasant father to emerge as a gifted scholar, was the first film ever to win both the Palme d'Or (first prize) and the International Critics Prize at the Cannes Film Festival. Following the prettily photographed but heavy-handed *The Meadow* (1979), the Tavianis triumphed again with *Night of the Shooting Stars* (1982), a richly textured, ballad-like film about the predicament of Tuscan peasants awaiting liberation by advancing US forces. Their international reputation steadily growing, the brothers won the Special Jury Prize at Cannes (Silver Palm) for that film, which also earned them the American National Society of Film Critics Award for best directing. The Tavianis traveled to the US in 1987 to film *Good Morning, Babylon,* an enchanting valentine to Hollywood's nascent years, about two Italian brothers who help build the massive sets for D. W. Griffith's *Intolerance.*

FEATURE FILMS (as directors-writers): *Un Uomo da bruciare/A Man for Burning* (co-dir. with Valentino Orsini) 1962; *I Fuorilegge del Matrimonio* (co-dir. with Orsini) 1963; *Sovversivi* 1968; *Sotto il Segno dello Scorpione/Under the Sign of Scorpio* 1969; *San Michele aveva un Gallo* 1972; *Allonsanfan* 1974; *Padre Padrone/Father Master* 1977; *Il Prato/The Meadow* 1979; *La Notte di San Lorenzo/The Night of the Shooting Stars* 1982; *Kaos* 1984; *Good Morning, Babilonia/ Good Morning, Babylon* (It./Fr./US) 1987; *Il Sole a di Notte/The Sun Also Shines at Night* 1990; *Wild Flower* 1994.

Tavoularis, Dean. Production designer. Born in 1932, in Lowell, Mass. Trained in architecture at the Otis Art Institute, he began his film career with Disney's animation department, later switching to live-action productions. After a stopover at Columbia, he joined Warner Bros. as an assistant art director and worked in that capacity on *Ship of Fools* (1965) and other films. Following an impressive debut as a designer with Arthur Penn's *Bonnie and Clyde* (1967) and a collaboration with Antonioni on *Zabriskie Point,* he became associated mainly with Francis Ford Coppola, for whom he designed many striking sets. He won an Academy Award for *The Godfather, Part II* (1974) and Oscar nominations for *The Brink's Job* (1978), *Apocalypse Now* (1979), *Tucker: The Man and His Dream* (1988), and *The Godfather, Part III* (1990). He is married to French actress Aurore CLÉMENT. His brother, Alex Tavoularis, is also an art director/production designer.

FILMS INCLUDE: *Bonnie and Clyde* 1967; *Candy* 1968; *Zabriskie Point, Little Big Man* 1970; *The Godfather* 1972; *The Godfather, Part II, The Conversation* 1974; *Farewell My Lovely* 1975; *The Brink's Job* 1978; *Apocalypse Now* 1979; *Hammett, One from the Heart, The Escape Artist* 1982; *The Outsiders, Rumble Fish* 1983; *Peggy Sue Got Married* 1986; *Un Homme amoureux/A Man in Love* (Fr./It.), *Gardens of Stone* 1987; *Tucker: The Man and His Dream* 1988; *New York Stories* ("Life Without Zoe" episode) 1989; *The Godfather Part III* 1990; *Final Analysis* 1992; *Rising Sun* 1993; *I Love Trouble* 1994; *Jack* 1996.

Taylor, Alma. Actress. *b.* Jan. 3, 1895, London. *d.* 1974. Child star, then popular leading lady of British silent films. Later in occasional character parts.

FILMS INCLUDE: *His Daughter's Voice* 1906; *The Little Flower Girl* 1908; *Tilly the Tomboy Goes Boating* 1910; *The Smuggler's Stepdaughter* 1911; *Oliver Twist* 1912; *David Copperfield, The Old Curiosity Shop* 1913; *The Girl Who Lived in Straight Street* 1914; *Sweet Lavender, Iris* 1915; *Annie Laurie* 1916; *The Cobweb, The American Heiress* 1917; *Sheba* 1919; *Alf's Button, Anna the Adventuress* 1920; *The Tinted Venus* 1921; *The Shadow of Egypt* 1924; *A South Sea Bubble* 1928; *Deadlock* 1931; *Everybody Dance* 1936; *Lilacs in the Spring/ Let's Make Up* 1954; *Lost/Tears for Simo* 1956; *Blue Murder at St. Trinian's* 1957.

Taylor, Don. Actor, director. Born on Dec. 13, 1920, in Freeport, Pa. *ed.* Pennsylvania State U. Amiable leading man and second lead of Hollywood films. After playing bits in a couple of movies, he got his break in the Army Air Force stage production of 'Winged Victory,' in a role he later repeated on the screen. He has written a number of one-act plays, radio dramas, and short stories and in the 60s turned to directing TV programs and feature films. Divorced from actress Phyllis Avery, he is married to actress Hazel COURT. His credits are sometimes confused with those of British producer-screenwriter Donald Taylor, who has also directed several films.

FILMS INCLUDE: As actor—*Girl Crazy* (bit) 1943; *Winged Victory* 1944; *Song of the Thin Man* 1947; *The Naked City, For the Love of Mary* 1948; *Battleground* 1949; *Father of the Bride* 1950; *Father's Little Dividend, Flying Leathernecks, The Blue Veil* 1951; *Japanese War Bride* 1952; *Destination Gobi, Stalag 17* 1953; *I'll Cry Tomorrow* 1955; *The Bold and the Brave, Ride the High Iron* 1956; *The Savage Guns* 1962. As director—(complete) *Everything's Ducky* 1961; *Ride the Wild Surf* 1964; *Jack of Diamonds* 1967; *The Five Man Army* 1970; *Escape from the Planet of the Apes* 1971; *Tom Sawyer* (also act.) 1973; *Echoes of a Summer/The Last Castle* (US/Can.) 1975; *The Great Scout and Cathouse Thursday* 1976; *The Island of Dr. Moreau* 1977; *Damien: Omen II* 1978; *The Final Countdown* 1979.

Taylor, Elizabeth. Actress. Born on Feb. 27, 1932, in London, to American parents long in residence in Britain. As soon as she could walk she was given ballet lessons, and at the age of three she danced with her class before the Royal Family. In 1939, just before the outbreak of WW II, the Taylors returned to the US and settled in Los Angeles, where Mr. Taylor opened an art gallery at the Beverly Hills Hotel. Little Elizabeth, a striking beauty at the age of ten, soon attracted the attention of movie scouts and in 1942 she made her screen debut at Universal in *There's One Born Every Minute,* a lowbrow comedy in which she was teamed with Carl ("Alfalfa") Switzer. The following year she was signed by MGM on a long-term contract that tied her to the studio until the early 60s. In the decade that followed she blossomed from a pretty little child star into, in the opinion of many, the world's most beautiful woman, and one of the most popular screen personalities of all time. A perfect beauty with unique violet eyes, she skipped by the awkward adolescent stage, maturing almost directly from child roles to romantic leads.

In her personal life, too, she ripened early, dating Howard Hughes at 17 and taking her first marriage vows, to hotelier Nick Hilton, before she reached 18. The marriage lasted but a few months, long enough to be exploited by MGM for publicity of her then-current Taylor-made picture *Father of the Bride.* In 1952 she married actor Michael WILDING. After their 1957 divorce, she converted to Judaism to marry flamboyant showman Mike TODD. This marriage is said to have had a profound influence on her maturation both as a woman and an actress, but it came to a tragic end the following year when Todd was killed in the crash of his private airplane, which he had named "The Lucky Liz" after her. The best man at their wedding, singer Eddie FISHER, was the first to rush to her side to comfort her in her grief. When they were married in 1959, she was ostracized by outraged fans for breaking up Fisher's marriage to another favorite, Debbie REYNOLDS. She won back the public's affection in the early 60s when she almost died of pneumonia while filming in London. The wave of sympathy helped her win her first Academy Award, for *Butterfield 8,* in which she did not give one of her best performances. She had been nominated for an Oscar for *Raintree County* (1957), *Cat on a Hot Tin Roof* (1958), and *Suddenly Last Summer* (1959). She was again in the headlines when her on-screen romance with Richard BURTON on the set of *Cleopatra,* one of Hollywood's most extravagant flops, developed into a sizzling offscreen affair. They married in 1964, shortly after her divorce from Fisher, and later appeared together in several productions.

Miss Taylor, one of the world's highest-paid performers, won a second Academy Award, for her performance in *Who's Afraid of Virginia Woolf?* (1966). In 1972, as beautiful as ever, if somewhat plumper, she celebrated her fortieth birthday and the birth of her first grandchild. Her marriage to Burton faltered in the early 70s. After several well-publicized separations and reconciliations, a divorce, and a remarriage, they finally redivorced in 1976. Miss Taylor then went through a seventh marriage ceremony, to John Warner, a former Secretary of the Navy who was elected a US senator (from Virginia) in 1978. That marriage ended in 1982. Glamorous and popular as ever despite her bouts with liquor, food, and weight gain, Taylor remained one of the world's most photographed and most publicized celebrities in the 80s and 90s. As her film roles dwindled, she used her celebrity to launch a successful line of perfumes and to raise millions of dollars for AIDS research. She became active in television, starring in several telefilms and in the miniseries 'North and South,' during which she aggravated a lifelong back injury. She lent her voice to the animated 'The Simpsons' television show as Baby Maggie. In October of 1991, just four months short of her 60th birthday, she married for the eighth time in an opulent ceremony on the grounds of a ranch owned by entertainer Michael Jackson, a close confidante. She had met the groom, construction worker Larry Fortensky, 20 years her junior, at a treatment center for drug and alcohol abuse. That marriage ended in a difficult, very public divorce in 1995. She now focuses all of her attention on fighting the battle against AIDS, traveling the country and the world, vowing to do so until a cure is discovered.

FILMS: *There's One Born Every Minute* 1942; *Lassie Come Home* 1943; *Jane Eyre* (as Helen), *The White Cliffs of Dover, National Velvet* (as Velvet Brown) 1944; *Courage of Lassie* 1946; *Cynthia, Life with Father* 1947; *A Date with Judy, Julia Misbehaves* 1948; *Little Women* (as Meg) 1949; *Conspirator* (UK/US), *The Big Hangover, Father of the Bride* 1950; *Quo Vadis* (unbilled cameo), *Father's Little Dividend, A Place in the Sun, Callaway Went Thataway* (cameo) 1951; *Love Is Better Than Ever, Ivanhoe* (as Rebecca, UK/US) 1952; *The Girl Who Had Everything* 1953; *Rhapsody, Elephant Walk, Beau Brummel, The Last Time I Saw Paris* 1954; *Giant* 1956; *Raintree County* 1957; *Cat on a Hot Tin Roof* (as Maggie) 1958; *Suddenly Last Summer* 1959; *Scent of Mystery* (unbilled cameo), *Butterfield 8* 1960; *Cleopatra* (title role, US/UK), *The V.I.P.s* (UK) 1963; *The Sandpiper* 1965; *Who's Afraid of Virginia Woolf?* 1966; *The Taming of the Shrew* (as Katharina; also co-prod.; US/It.), *Doctor Faustus* (as Helen of Troy; UK/It.), *Reflections in a Golden Eye, The Comedians* (US/Fr.) 1967; *Boom!* (US/UK), *Secret Ceremony* (UK) 1968; *The Only Game in Town* 1970; *Under Milk Wood* (UK) 1971; *Zee & Co./X Y & Zee* (UK), *Hammersmith Is Out* 1972; *Divorce His Divorce Hers* (three-hour, two-part TV drama), *Night Watch* (UK), *Ash Wednesday* (Fr./It./UK/US); *That's Entertainment* (on-screen co-narrator), *Identikit/The Driver's Seat* (It.) 1974; *The Blue Bird* (US/USSR) 1976; *A Little Night Music* (Aus./Ger./US) 1977; *Winter Kills* 1979; *The Mirror Crack'd* (UK) 1980; *Genocide* (doc.; narr. only) 1981; *Il Giova Toscanini/Young Toscanini/Toscanini* (It./Fr.) 1988; *The Flintstones* 1994.

Taylor, Estelle. Actress. *b.* Estelle Boylan, May 20, 1899, Wilmington, Del. *d.* 1958. Beautiful brunette star of silent and early sound Hollywood films. A former typist, she married a local banker at 14 and separated from him four years later when she went to New York to study acting at Sargent's Dramatic School. She modeled for artists and appeared in the chorus of a couple of Broadway musicals before making her screen debut in 1920. She starred in many silent films, including several prestigious productions, such as C. B. De Mille's *The Ten Commandments* (1923), in which she played Miriam, sister of Moses, and Alan Crosland's *Don Juan* (1926), in which she portrayed Lucretia Borgia opposite John Barrymore. In 1925 she co-starred with world champion heavyweight boxer Jack Dempsey in *Manhattan Madness* and married him that same year, and in 1928 they appeared together on Broadway in 'The Big Fight.' But they divorced in 1931. Miss Taylor, who was often seen in vampy or exotic roles, survived the transition to sound and played leads and character roles in a number of talkies, memorably as Sylvia Sidney's tenement mother in King Vidor's *Street Scene* (1931). She made her last screen appearance in 1945.

FILMS INCLUDE: *The Golden Shower* 1919; *The Adventurer, The Return of Tarzan, While New York Sleeps, Blind Wives* 1920; *Foot-falls* 1921; *A Fool There Was, Monte Cristo, The Lights of New York, Thorns and Orange Blossoms, Only a Shop Girl, A California Romance* 1922; *Desire, Forgive and Forget, Bavu, The Ten Commandments* (as Miriam, sister of Moses) 1923; *Tiger Love, Passion's Pathway, Dorothy Vernon of Haddon Hall* (as Mary, Queen of Scots), *The Alaskan, Playthings of Desire* 1924; *Manhattan Madness, Wandering Footsteps* 1925; *Don Juan* (as Lucretia Borgia) 1926; *New York* 1927; *The Whip Woman, Honor Bound, Lady Raffles* 1928; *Where East Is East* 1929; *Liliom* 1930; *Cimarron, Street Scene, The Unholy Garden* 1931; *Call Her Savage, Western Limited* 1932; *The Southerner* 1945.

Taylor, Gil(bert). Director of photography. Born on Apr. 12, 1914, in Bushey Heath, England. In British films as camera assistant from age 15, he became a highly competent lighting cameraman in the late 40s, in both black and white and color. During the 60s he was responsible for the superior cinematography of such films as *Dr. Strangelove* and *A Hard Day's Night* and in the late 70s he was entrusted with several top-budget Hollywood productions.

FILMS INCLUDE: *Brighton Rock/Young Scarface* 1947; *The Guinea Pig/The Outsider* 1948; *Seven Days to Noon* 1950; *The Yellow Balloon* 1952; *The Weak and the Wicked* 1953; *Front Page Story* 1954; *The Dam Busters* 1955; *The Good Companions* 1957; *Ice Cold in Alex/Desert Attack* 1958; *The Rebel/Call Me Genius* 1961; *Dr. Strangelove, A Hard Day's*

Night 1964; *Repulsion, The Bedford Incident* 1965; *Cul-de-Sac* 1966; *Before Winter Comes* 1969; *Macbeth* 1971; *Frenzy* 1972; *Soft Bed Hard Battles/Undercover Hero* 1974; *The Omen* (US) 1976; *Star Wars* (US) 1977; *Dracula* (US) 1979; *Flash Gordon* (US) 1980; *Green Ice* 1981; *Venom* 1982; *Losin' It* (US) 1983; *Lassiter* (US) 1984; *The Bedroom Window* (US) 1987.

Taylor, Kent. Actor. *b.* Louis Weiss, May 11, 1906, on a ranch near Nashua, Iowa. *d.* 1987. Dandy leading man of numerous Hollywood B pictures of the 30s and 40s. Sporting a pencil-thin mustache, he also played second leads in many A productions. On TV, he played the title role in the 'Boston Blackie' series (1951–53) and co-starred in 'The Rough Riders' (1958–59). His movie career extended into the early 70s.

FILMS INCLUDE: *Road to Reno* 1931; *Devil and the Deep, Merrily We Go to Hell, Blonde Venus, The Sign of the Cross* 1932; *A Lady's Profession, The Mysterious Rider, I'm No Angel, White Woman, Cradle Song* 1933; *Death Takes a Holiday, David Harum* (as John Lenox), *Double Door, Mrs. Wiggs of the Cabbage Patch* 1934; *The County Chairman, Two Fisted* 1935; *My Marriage, Florida Special, Ramona* 1936; *When Love Is Young* 1937; *The Jury's Secret, The Last Express* 1938; *The Gracie Allen Murder Case, Five Came Back, Sued for Libel* 1939; *I Take This Woman, I'm Still Alive* 1940; *Washington Melodrama* 1941; *Frisco Lil, Tombstone* (as Doc Halliday), *Gang Busters* (serial) 1942; *Halfway to Shanghai* 1943; *Alaska* 1944; *The Daltons Ride Again* (as Bob Dalton) 1945; *Tangier, Deadline for Murder, Smooth as Silk, Young Widow, Dangerous Millions* 1946; *Second Chance, The Crimson Key* 1947; *Half Past Midnight* 1948; *Western Pacific Agent* 1950; *Payment on Demand* 1951; *Playgirl* 1954; *Secret Venture* (UK) 1955; *Ghost Town, Slightly Scarlet* 1956; *Gang War* 1958; *The Purple Hills* 1961; *The Day Mars Invaded Earth, Harbor Lights* 1963; *Brides of Blood* 1968; *Satan's Sadists* 1969; *Hell's Bloody Devils* 1970.

Taylor, Laurette. Actress. *b.* Helen Laurette Magdalene Cooney, Apr. 1, 1884, New York City. *d.* 1946. The famous Broadway star who was the toast of New York in the 1910s and 1920s, appeared in only three films, notably *Peg o' My Heart* (1922), in which she repeated one of her greatest stage successes.

FILMS: *Peg o' My Heart* 1922; *Happiness, One Night in Rome* 1924.

Taylor, Lili. Actress. Born in 1967, in Glencoe, Ill. Appealing, promising young lead of American films from the late 80s. The second youngest of six children, she grew up in a North Shore Chicago suburb. She dropped out of DePaul University after less than a year of theater studies and after performing briefly on the stage in Chicago and Louisville, Kentucky, moved to New York, where she appeared in a play and made her screen debut in 1988. Since, she has continued to work, primarily in independent, art-house films, establishing a strong reputation as a quirky, loveable, capable screen actor.

FILMS: *She's Having a Baby* (bit), *Mystic Pizza* 1988; *Say Anything. . . , Born on the Fourth of July* 1989; *Bright Angel* 1990; *Dogfight* 1991; *Household Saints, Short Cuts* 1993; *Mrs. Parker and the Vicious Circle, Ready to Wear* 1994; *The Addiction, Four Rooms* 1995; *Girls Town, Illtown, I Shot Andy Warhol, Killer* (unbilled cameo) 1996; *Kicked in the Head* 1997.

Taylor, Ray. Director. *b.* Dec. 1, 1888, Perham, Minn. *d.* 1952. A former actor and stage manager, he entered films after WW I service as assistant director to John FORD at Fox. He then moved to Universal, where he became director of shorts, serials, and eventually also low-budget action features. A prolific director, he turned out scores of silent and sound serials and features. Serials are designated "S" in the credits below.

FILMS INCLUDE: *Fighting with Buffalo Bill* (S) 1926; *Whispering Smith Rides* (S) 1927; *The Vanishing Rider* (S), *The Avenging Shadow, Beauty and Bullets, Quick Triggers* 1928; *The Ace of Scotland Yard* (S), *Eyes of the Underworld* (co-dir. with Leigh Jason), *Come Across* 1929; *The Jade Box* (S) 1930; *Danger Island* (S) 1931; *The Airmail Mystery* (S) 1932; *Clancy of the Mounted* (S), *Gordon of Ghost City* (S) 1933; *The Return of Chandu* (S) 1934 (also made as a feature in 1935); *The Roaring West* (S), *Outlawed Guns, Call of the Savage* 1935; *The Phantom Rider* (S), *The Three Mesquiteers* 1936; *Dick Tracy* (S; co-dir. with Alan James), *Drums of Destiny* 1937; *The Spider's Web* (S; co-dir. with James W. Horne), *Rawhide* 1938; *Flash Gordon Conquers the Universe,* (S; co-dir. with Ford Beebe), *The Green Hornet* (S; co-dir. with Beebe), *West of Carson City* 1940; *Riders of Death Valley* (S; co-dir. with Beebe) 1941; *Gang Busters* (S; co-dir. with Beebe), *Destination Unknown* 1942; *Mystery of the River Boat* (S; co-dir. with Lewis D. Collins) 1944; *Jungle Queen* (S; co-dir. with Collins), *The Daltons Ride Again* 1945; *Lost City of the Jungle* (S; co-dir. with Collins) 1946; *The Vigilantes Return* 1947; *Mark of the Lash* 1948; *Son of Billy the Kid* 1949.

Taylor, Renee. See BOLOGNA, Joseph.

Taylor, Robert. Actor. *b.* Spangler Arlington Brugh, Aug. 5, 1911, Filley, Nebr. *d.* 1969. The son of a country doctor, he attended Doane College in Nebraska, where he majored in music, then followed his cello teacher to Pomona College in California. His performance in a college production led to a screen test and a long-term contract with MGM. Handsome to the point of prettiness, and billed as "The Man with the Perfect Profile," he vied with Clark Gable for popularity as the screen's top romantic star. He made his first real impact on a loan-out to Universal in *Magnificent Obsession* in 1935, and for the next 30 years he remained one of MGM's principal players, starring opposite some of the screen's most glamorous leading ladies, from Garbo and Harlow to Ava Gardner and Elizabeth Taylor.

Taylor gradually got rid of the glamour-boy image and developed into a mature actor of solid character. He also acquired a reputation among directors as a no-nonsense professional who made up for any lack of depth in his acting with his serious attitude and hard work. During WW II he served as a flight instructor with the Navy's Air Transport. He also directed 17 Navy training films and narrated the feature-length documentary *The Fighting Lady.* His personal life was as earnest and scandal-free as his professional career. He was married twice, to Barbara STANWYCK from 1939 till 1952, and to Ursula Thiess from 1954 until his death of lung cancer at the age of 57.

FILMS: *Handy Andy, There's Always Tomorrow, A Wicked Woman* 1934; *Buried Loot* (short in "Crime Does Not Pay" series), *Society Doctor, Times Square Lady, West Point of the Air, Murder in the Fleet, Broadway Melody of 1936, Magnificent Obsession* (as Robert Merrick) 1935; *Small Town Girl, Private Number, His Brother's Wife, The Gorgeous Hussy* 1936; *Camille* (as Armand), *Personal Property, This Is My Affair, Broadway Melody of 1938, Lest We Forget* (short in memory of Will Rogers) 1937; *A Yank at Oxford, Three Comrades* (as Erich), *The Crowd Roars* 1938; *Stand Up and Fight, Lucky Night, Lady of the Tropics, Remember?* 1939; *Waterloo Bridge, Escape* 1940; *Flight Command, Billy the Kid* (title role), *When Ladies Meet* 1941; *Johnny Eager, Her Cardboard Lover* 1942; *Stand By for Action, Bataan, The Youngest Profession* (cameo) 1943; *Song of Russia, The Fighting Lady* (doc.; narrator) 1944; *Undercurrent* 1946; *High Wall* 1947; *The Bribe* 1949; *Ambush, Conspirator* (UK/US), *Devil's Doorway* 1950; *Quo Vadis* (as Marcus Vinitius) 1951; *Westward the Women, Ivanhoe* (title role; UK/US) 1952; *Above and Beyond, I Love Melvin* (cameo), *Ride Vaquero, All the Brothers Were Valiant* 1953; *Knights of the*

Round Table (as Lancelot; UK/US), *Valley of the Kings, Rogue Cop* 1954; *Many Rivers to Cross, The Adventures of Quentin Durward/Quentin Durward* (title role; UK) 1955; *The Last Hunt, D-Day the Sixth of June, The Power and the Prize* 1956; *Tip on a Dead Jockey* 1957; *Saddle the Wind, The Law and Jake Wade, Party Girl* 1958; *The Hangman, The House of the Seven Hawks* 1959; *Killers of Kilimanjaro* 1960; *Miracle of the White Stallions, Cattle King* 1963; *A House Is Not a Home* 1964; *The Night Walker* 1965; *Pampa Salvaje/Savage Pampas* (Sp./Arg./US), *Johnny Tiger* 1966; *Return of the Gunfighter* (TV movie), *Hondo* (cameo), *La Sfinge d'Oro/The Glass Sphinx* (It./Eg./US) 1967; *Where Angels Go Trouble Follows, Le Rouble à Deux Faces/The Day the Hot Line Got Hot* (Fr./Sp.) 1968.

Taylor, Rod. Actor. Born Robert Taylor, on Jan. 11, 1929, in Sydney, Australia. Husky, square-jawed leading man of American and international films. Trained as a painter, he turned to acting instead. He appeared in several Australian stage productions and two films before making it to Hollywood in 1955. He progressively rose from supporting parts to rugged-hero roles. Early in his career he was billed Rodney Taylor.

FILMS INCLUDE: *The Stuart Expedition* (Austral.) 1951; *Long John Silver* (as Israel Hands; Austral./US) 1954; *The Virgin Queen* 1955; *The Catered Affair, Giant* 1956; *Raintree County* 1957; *Separate Tables* 1958; *Ask Any Girl* 1959; *The Time Machine* (as the Time Traveler) 1960; *The Birds, A Gathering of Eagles, The V.I.P.s* (UK) 1963; *Sunday in New York, Fate Is the Hunter* 1964; *36 Hours, Young Cassidy* (US/UK in Ireland), *Do Not Disturb* 1965; *The Glass Bottom Boat, The Liquidator* (UK) 1966; *Hotel, Chuka* (also co-prod.) 1967; *Dark of the Sun* (UK), *The Hell with Heroes, Nobody Runs Forever/The High Commissioner* (UK/US) 1968; *Zabriskie Point, The Man Who Had Power Over Women* (UK), *Darker Than Amber* 1970; *The Train Robbers, Trader Horn, The Deadly Trackers* 1973; *Gli Eroi/The Heroes* (It.), *Partisani/Hell River* (Yug./US) 1974; *The Picture Show Man* (Austral.) 1977; *An Eye for an Eye* (Ire.) 1978; *On the Run* (Austral.) 1982; *Time to Die/Seven Graves for Rogan* (filmed in 1979) 1983; *A Rage in Harlem* (UK/US) 1991.

Taylor, Sam. Director, screenwriter. *b.* Aug. 13, 1895, New York City. *d.* 1958. He entered films in 1916, straight out of Fordham University, as a gagman and screenwriter of Kalem comedies. He rose to prominence in the early 20s as the director (mostly in collaboration with Fred NEWMEYER) and co-scripter of some of Harold Lloyd's most successful shorts and feature length comedies. In the late 20s and early 30s he widened his scope with dramas and sophisticated comedies that starred such personalities as John BARRYMORE, Norma TALMADGE, Douglas FAIRBANKS, and Mary PICKFORD. For the last two he directed an adaptation of *The Taming of the Shrew* (1929) that became famous for the credit line: "By William Shakespeare, with additional dialogue by Sam Taylor." He retired from films in 1935 to enter the publicity business but returned in the mid-40s to direct a rather weak Laurel and Hardy feature comedy, *Nothing but Trouble.*

FILMS (as director): *Now or Never, I Do, Among Those Present, Never Weaken* (all shorts; all co-dir. with Fred Newmeyer, co-sc.) 1921; *Safety Last* (co-dir. with Newmeyer, co-sc.), *Why Worry?* (co-dir. with Newmeyer, sc.) 1923; *Girl Shy, Hot Water* (both co-dir. with Newmeyer, co-sc.) 1924; *The Freshman* (co-dir. with Newmeyer, co-sc.) 1925; *For Heaven's Sake, Exit Smiling* (also co-sc.) 1926; *My Best Girl* 1927; *Tempest, The Woman Disputed* (co-dir. with Henry King) 1928; *Coquette* (also dial.), *The Taming of the Shrew* (also adapt., addnl. dial.) 1929; *Du Barry Woman of Passion* (also adapt.) 1930; *Kiki* (also sc.), *Skyline, Ambassador Bill* 1931; *Devil's Lottery* 1932; *Out All Night* 1933; *The Cat's Paw* 1934; *The Vagabond Lady* (also prod.) 1935; *Nothing but Trouble* 1945.

Taylor, William Desmond. Director. *b.* William Cunningham Dean Tanner, Apr. 26, 1877, Ireland. *d.* 1922, in Hollywood, a victim of homicide. A former stage and screen actor, and one of Hollywood's most colorful personalities during its "age of innocence," he made his directorial debut late in 1914 and before long rose to prominence as the director of several Mary Pickford vehicles and films of other noted stars on the Famous Players-Lasky lot. A suave, handsome man-about-town, he gained wide social acceptance, especially among lady stars, and was elected president of the Screen Directors Guild. On the night of February 2, 1922, he was shot to death in his Hollywood mansion in circumstances that remain mysterious to this day. The inquest that followed his murder revealed his intimate involvement with several popular stars, among them Mabel NORMAND and Mary Miles MINTER, both of whom had visited him on the tragic night. Although neither star was suspected of the killing, the scandal promptly ended their screen careers. The use of narcotics was also mentioned in the case. Coming as it did just several months after the "Fatty" Arbuckle scandal, the Taylor murder resulted in increased pressure on the Hollywood community by various citizens' groups. It was pressure of this kind that eventually led the studios to initiate the self-regulatory Hays Office to improve its image both on and off the screen. The Taylor mystery always intrigued director King VIDOR, who 45 years after the event, in 1967, began a thorough investigation of the murder. After Vidor's death in 1982, his authorized biographer, Sidney Kirkpatrick, gained access to the evidence and published the director's sleuthing conclusions in the book *A Cast of Killers* (1986).

FILMS INCLUDE: *The Criminal Code* (also act.), *The Beggar Child* 1914; *An Eye for an Eye* (also act.), *The Last Chapter, The Diamond from the Sky* (serial; co-dir. with Jacques Jaccard), *The Last Chapter, The High Hand* 1915; *The American Beauty, Davy Crockett, He Fell in Love with His Wife, Ben Blair, Her Father's Son, The House of Lies, Pasquale, The Parson of Panamint* 1916; *Redeeming Love, The Happiness of Three Women, The Varmint, World Apart, Tom Sawyer, Jack and Jill* 1917; *The Spirit of '17, Huck and Tom, Up the Road with Sally, His Majesty Bunker Bean, Mile-a-Minute Kendall, How Could You Jean?, Johanna Enlists* 1918; *Captain Kidd Jr., Anne of Green Gables* 1919; *Judy of Rogue's Harbor, Nurse Marjorie, Jenny Be Good, The Furnace, Huckleberry Finn, The Soul of Youth* 1920; *The Witching Hour, Sacred and Profane Love, Beyond, Wealth, Morals* 1921; *The Green Temptation, The Top of New York* 1922.

Taylor-Young, Leigh. Actress. Born on Jan. 25, 1944, in Washington, D.C. *ed.* Northwestern. Well-built, fresh-faced leading lady of American films of the late 60s and early 70s. On the screen from the late 60s following popularity in the TV series 'Peyton Place' (1966–67) in which she co-starred with her first husband (1967–73), Ryan O'NEAL. In 1978 she married Columbia Pictures executive Guy McElwaine. After a long absence to raise a family, she returned to acting in the early 80s.

FILMS: *I Love You Alice B. Toklas* 1968; *The Big Bounce* 1969; *The Games* (cameo; UK), *The Buttercup Chain* (UK), *The Adventurers* 1970; *The Horsemen, The Gang That Couldn't Shoot Straight* 1971; *Soylent Green* 1973; *Can't Stop the Music, Looker* 1981; *Secret Admirer, Jagged Edge* 1985; *Accidents* (Austral.) 1988; *Honeymoon Academy* 1990.

Tcherina, Ludmilla. Dancer, actress. Born Monique Tchemerzine, on Oct. 10, 1925, in Paris. A former prima ballerina of the Monte Carlo Ballet, she played feminine leads in French and foreign films from the mid-40s.

FILMS INCLUDE: *Un Revenant/A Lover's Return* 1946; *The Red Shoes* (UK) 1948; *La Belle que voilà* 1949; *The Tales of Hoffman* (UK), *The Legend of Parsifal* (Sp.) 1951; *Spartaco/Spartacus* (It.) 1952; *La Figlia di Mata Hari/The Daughter of Mata Hari* (It./Fr.), *Sign of the Pagan* (US/It.) 1954; *Oh Rosalinda!* (UK) 1955; *Lune de Miel* (Sp.) 1959; *Les Amants de Teruel/The Lovers of Teruel* (also prod.) 1962; *Une Ravissante Idiote/A Ravishing Idiot* 1963.

Teague, Lewis. Director. Born on Mar. 8, 1938, in Brooklyn, N.Y. A former editor of low-budget Roger Corman thrillers, he gradually moved into directing in the 70s and scored a comedy hit with *The Jewel of the Nile* in 1985. He is skilled at film action.

FILMS (as director): *Dirty O'Neil* (co-dir.) 1974; *Death Race 2,000* (2nd-unit dir.) 1975; *Thunder and Lightning* (2nd-unit dir.) 1977; *Avalanche* (2nd-unit dir.) 1978; *Fast Charlie... the Moonbeam Rider* (2nd-unit dir.), *The Lady in Red/Guns Sin and Bathtub Gin* (also edit.) 1979; *The Big Red One* (2nd-unit dir.), *Alligator* 1980; *Fighting Back/Death Vengeance* 1982; *Cujo* 1983; *Cat's Eye/Stephen King's Cat's Eye, The Jewel of the Nile* 1985, *Collision Course* (filmed in 1988), *Navy Seals* 1990.

Teal, Ray. Actor. *b.* Jan. 12, 1902, Grand Rapids, Mich. *d.* 1976. *ed.* U. of Texas; U. of California. He worked his way through college playing a saxophone and after graduation led his own small band. Switching to acting, he appeared in stock before his Hollywood debut in 1938. He played character parts in numerous films, mostly Westerns, both as a mean heavy and a good guy, often as a sheriff. He was seen regularly as Sheriff Coffee in the TV series 'Bonanza.'

FILMS INCLUDE: *Western Jamboree* 1938; *Northwest Passage, Cherokee Strip* 1940; *Wild Bill Hickok Rides* 1942; *None Shall Escape* 1944; *Along Came Jones* 1945; *The Best Years of Our Lives, Canyon Passage* 1946; *Brute Force* 1947; *Whispering Smith, Joan of Arc* 1948; *The Men* 1950; *Along the Great Divide, Ace in the Hole/The Big Carnival* 1951; *The Captive City, Carrie, Hangman's Knot, The Wild North* 1952; *The Wild One* 1954; *Run for Cover, The Desperate Hours* 1955; *Band of Angels* 1957; *Saddle the Wind* 1958; *Home from the Hill, Inherit the Wind* 1960; *One-Eyed Jacks, Judgment at Nuremberg* 1961; *Cattle King* 1963; *Taggart* 1964; *Chisum* 1970.

Tearle, Conway. Actor. *b.* Frederick Levy, May 17, 1878, New York City. *d.* 1938. *ed.* West Point. The half brother of Sir Godfrey TEARLE. He received his early education in England, where he gained some experience on the stage from 1892. Returning to the US in 1905, he pursued a successful career on Broadway before entering films in 1914. He starred in numerous silent and early sound pictures, usually playing dependable, worldly heroes.

FILMS INCLUDE: *The Nightingale, Shore Acres* 1914; *Seven Sisters, Helene of the North* 1915; *The Common Law, The Heart of the Hills* 1916; *The Foolish Virgin, The Fall of the Romanoffs* 1917; *Stella Maris, Virtuous Wives* 1918; *The Way of a Woman, Atonement, A Virtuous Vamp* 1919; *Two Weeks, The Forbidden Woman* 1920; *The Oath, Society Snobs, The Man of Stone, After Midnight, The Fighter* 1921; *The Eternal Flame, Love's Masquerade, Shadows of the Sea, One Week of Love* 1922; *Bella Donna, Ashes of Vengeance, The Rustle of Silk, The Common Law* 1923; *Black Oxen, Lilies of the Field, The White Moth, Flirting with Love* 1924; *The Great Divide, Bad Company, School for Wives, The Heart of a Siren, The Mystic, Morals for Men* 1925; *Dancing Mothers, The Dancer of Paris, My Official Wife, The Sporting Lover, The Greater Glory* 1926; *Moulders of Men, Altars of Desire* 1927; *The Gold Diggers of Broadway, Evidence, The Lost Zeppelin* 1929; *The Truth About Youth* 1930; *Captivation, Pleasure, Morals for Women* 1931; *Her Mad Night, Vanity Fair* 1932; *Should Ladies Behave?* 1933; *Stingaree* 1934; *Sing Sing Nights* 1935; *Klondike Annie, Romeo and Juliet* (as the Prince of Verona) 1936.

Tearle, Sir Godfrey. Actor. *b.* Oct. 12, 1884, New York City. *d.* 1953. The half brother of Conway TEARLE. He was brought up in England by his actor parents and made his stage debut at nine. He later rose to distinction in numerous London plays. He starred in occasional British silents and played character parts in talkies. Memorable as the enemy master spy with the missing finger in Hitchcock's *The 39 Steps* (1935) and as a gallant R.A.F. aviator, the lead, in *One of Our Aircraft Is Missing* (1942).

FILMS INCLUDE: *Romeo and Juliet* 1908; *The Fool* 1913; *A Sinless Sinner, Queen's Evidence* 1919; *Salome of the Tenements* (US) 1925; *Infatuation* 1930; *The 39 Steps, The Last Journey* 1935; *East Meets West* 1936; *One of Our Aircraft Is Missing, Tomorrow We Live/At Dawn We Die* 1942; *The Rake's Progress/Medal for the General/The Gay Intruders* 1944; *Notorious Gentleman* 1945; *The Beginning or the End* (as President Franklin D. Roosevelt; US) 1947; *White Corridors* 1951; *Mandy/The Story of Mandy/Crash of Silence* 1952; *Decameron Nights* (in two roles; US/UK), *The Titfield Thunderbolt* 1953.

Teasdale, Verree. Actress. *b.* Mar. 15, 1904, Spokane, Wash. *d.* 1987. Trained for the stage at the New York School of Expression, she appeared in many Broadway productions from 1924 and made her screen debut in 1929. She played leads and supporting roles in many Hollywood films through the early 40s, typically portraying glamorous, and sometimes bitchy, blondes. She was married to Adolphe MENJOU from 1934 till his death in 1963.

FILMS INCLUDE: *Syncopation* 1929; *The Sap from Syracuse* 1930; *Skyscraper Souls, Payment Deferred* 1932; *Luxury Liner, Roman Scandals* 1933; *Fashions of 1934, A Modern Hero, Dr. Monica, Desirable, Madame Du Barry* 1934; *A Midsummer Night's Dream* (as Hippolyta, Queen of the Amazons) 1935; *The Milky Way* 1936; *First Lady* 1937; *Topper Takes a Trip, Fifth Avenue Girl* 1939; *I Take This Woman, Love Thy Neighbor* 1940; *Come Live with Me* 1941.

Téchiné, André. Director. Born in 1943, in France. A former film critic and professor at IDHEC, he turned out his first feature film in 1969. After directing a TV series, several plays, and a short, he returned to features with *Souvenirs d'en France,* a Jeanne Moreau vehicle, in 1975. He drew critical praise with *Barocco* (1977), an elegant stylistic exercise notable for its imaginative use of color. He elicited marvelous performances from Isabelle Adjani, Marie-France Pisier, and Isabelle Huppert in the literary biography *The Brontë Sisters* (1979) and won the best director prize at Cannes for his deft handling of *Rendez-vous* (1985), a stylish, atmospheric, sensual backstage melodrama.

FEATURE FILMS: *Paulina s'en va* (also sc.) 1969; *Souvenirs d'en France/French Provincial* (also co-sc.) 1975; *Barocco* (also co-story) 1977; *Les Soeurs Brontë/The Brontë Sisters* (also co-sc.) 1979; *Hôtel des Amériques* (also co-sc.) 1981; *La Matiouette ou L'Arrière-Pays* (medium-length; also co-sc.) 1983; *Rendez-vous* (also co-sc.) 1985; *Le Lieu du Crime/Scene of the Crime* (also co-sc.) 1986; *Les Innocents* (also co-sc.) 1987; *J'embrasse Pas* (also co-sc.) 1991; *Wild Reeds* 1994; *My Favorite Season* 1995; *Les Voleurs* 1996.

technical advisor. An expert in any particular field who is hired as a consultant on a motion picture set to ensure the authenticity of details in his specialized area. A retired naval officer may be asked to offer advice on the workings of a submarine, or a native of Nepal to authenticate background details concerning his country from customs to costumes.

Technicolor. Trademark for a color process invented by Herbert T. Kalmus and Daniel F. Comstock during WW I. The first film in the process, *The Gulf Between,* was produced by the inventors in 1917. Technicolor was incorporated in 1922 with Kalmus as president.

Originally, Technicolor was a two-color system in which superimposed red and green images were thrown on the screen at the same time by a special projector. The process was continually improved and was used successfully in *The Black Pirate* (1926) starring Douglas Fairbanks. Several other Technicolor features were released in the late 20s, but since the process was highly expensive and far from perfect, most studios preferred to limit the use of color to selected sequences rather than produce entire features in color. As public interest in the novelty waned, the number of color films produced in the early 30s dwindled to nearly zero.

Then, in 1932, Technicolor introduced its three-color process, a markedly improved system that produced accurate and eye-pleasing images by way of marrying negatives individually sensitive to red, green, and blue. After the system was tried out on a number of shorts, it was used successfully in 1935 on Rouben Mamoulian's feature *Becky Sharp.* Other features in Technicolor followed in the late 30s, culminating in the sumptuous color production of *Gone With the Wind* (1939). Technicolor continued to improve and despite increasing competition has remained an important factor in present day color cinematography. See also COLOR CINEMATOGRAPHY; KALMUS, Herbert T.

telecine. Apparatus used for projecting film on a television screen.

telefoni bianchi. See ITALY.

telephoto lens. A long-focus lens that magnifies like a telescope, making it possible to take close shots of distant objects. The lens tends to reduce perspective and flatten images.

Tellegen, Lou. Actor. *b.* Isidor Van Dameler, 1881, Holland. *d.* 1934, a suicide. He made his stage debut in Amsterdam in 1903 and gained prominence on the Paris stage from 1909 as Sarah BERNHARDT's leading man. He accompanied "the Divine Sarah" on her American tour in 1910 and later co-starred in her three highly successful productions for the Film d'Art company, *La Dame aux Camélias, Adrienne Lecouvreur,* and *Queen Elizabeth.* The latter was a huge hit in the American market and the profits from its importation helped start Adolph ZUKOR in the film business. Tellegen, who was considered one of the most handsome stage and screen lovers of his day, then made a second trip to the US, in 1913, and after starring in a couple of Broadway productions, he settled in Hollywood, where he played ultra-sophisticated leading men in many silent films. In 1916 he married opera and screen star Geraldine FARRAR. They divorced in 1923. His other three marriages also ended in divorce. In 1931 he published a volume of memoirs, *Women Have Been Kind.* He also directed a number of films.

FILMS INCLUDE: In France—*La Dame aux Camélias* 1911; *Queen Elizabeth, Adrienne Lecouvreur* 1912. In the US—*The Explorer, The Unknown* 1915; *The Victoria Cross, The Victory of Conscience* 1916; *What Money Can't Buy* (dir. only), *The Black Wolf, The Long Trail* 1917; *The Things We Love* (dir. only) 1918; *The World and Its Woman, Flame of the Desert* 1919; *The Woman and the Puppet* 1920; *Let Not Man Put Asunder, Between Friends, Greater Than Marriage, Those Who Judge, Single Wives, The Breath of Scandal* 1924; *The Redeeming Sin, The Verdict, Parisian Nights, After Business Hours, The Sporting Chance, Parisian Love, East Lynne* 1925; *The Outsider, Siberia, Three Bad Men, Womanpower* 1926; *Stage Madness, The Prince from Hoboken, Married Alive* 1927; *No Other Woman* (dir. only) 1928; *Enemies of the Law* 1931.

Temple, Julien. Director. Born on Nov. 26, 1953, in London. He majored in architecture and history at Cambridge but, following training at London's National Film School, he focused his professional work on camp, pop culture, and loud music. A specialist in music videos and rock-concert fare, he turned in a number of dynamic, wildly rambling, choppily edited performance and music-related films.

FEATURE FILMS: *The Great Rock 'n' Roll Swindle* 1979; *The Secret Policeman's Other Ball* 1982; *Undercover* (also sc.) 1983; *Man* (also sc.) 1984; *Running Out of Luck* (also sc.) 1985; *Absolute Beginners* 1986; *Aria* ("Rigoletto" segment; also sc.) 1987; *Earth Girls Are Easy* 1989; *At the Max* (creative consultant/location dir. only) 1991.

Temple, Shirley. Actress. Born on Apr. 23, 1928, in Santa Monica, Calif., the daughter of a bank teller. She began taking dancing classes at the age of three and was chosen from among her classmates to appear in a series of one-reel films before she reached four. The series, called "Baby Burlesks," consisted of takeoffs on popular movies of the time, with Shirley playing the leading lady roles, imitating Marlene Dietrich and other famous stars. At the same time, she began playing bit parts in feature films. She first attracted attention in 1934 in a song-and-dance number, 'Baby Take a Bow,' which she performed admirably in the film *Stand Up and Cheer.* She was consequently signed by Fox and within months reached unprecedented heights of popularity. At the end of her first year as a child star, she received a special Academy Award "in grateful recognition of her outstanding contribution to screen entertainment during the year 1934."

By 1938 she had topped all other Hollywood stars as the number one box-office attraction. A cute, doll-like, precocious child, complete with dimples and curls, she provided a bright little spot in the Depression years of the 30s. At the height of her success she was virtually a national institution, a model for the child every mother wanted and every little girl tried to imitate. A whole industry developed around the Shirley Temple phenomenon: dolls, coloring books, dresses, etc. No child star before or after her enjoyed so great a popularity or was able to display a wider range of natural talents, as an actress, a dancer, and a singer. But by 1940 she was quickly approaching the status of a has-been. She terminated her Fox contract, following two flops, but fared no better at MGM, which let her go after only one production. She continued appearing in films of various studios through the late 40s, but she simply did not hold the same appeal as an adolescent and an ingenue that she had held as a child.

She attempted a comeback on TV in 1958 as the hostess of 'The Shirley Temple Storybook,' but the show was not renewed after its initial year. She tried again with 'The Shirley Temple Show' in 1960, but the results were similarly discouraging. In the late 60s she entered politics and ran unsuccessfully for the vacant Republican congressional seat of her home district of San Mateo, California. In 1968 she was appointed by President Nixon as a US representative at the United Nations. She served as US ambassador to Ghana from 1974 till 1976, when she became US chief of protocol. In 1989 President George Bush appointed her ambassador to Czechoslovakia. Divorced in 1949 from actor John AGAR, whom she had married at 17 in 1946, Miss Temple married TV executive Charles Black in 1950 and is officially known as Shirley Temple Black. Autobiography: *Child Star* (1988).

FEATURE FILMS: *The Red-Haired Alibi* 1932; *To the*

Last Man, Out All Night 1933; *Carolina, Mandalay, Stand Up and Cheer, Now I'll Tell, Change of Heart, Little Miss Marker, Baby Take a Bow, Now and Forever, Bright Eyes* 1934; *The Little Colonel, Our Little Girl, Curly Top, The Littlest Rebel* 1935; *Captain January, Poor Little Rich Girl, Dimples, Stowaway* 1936; *Wee Willie Winkie, Heidi* 1937; *Rebecca of Sunnybrook Farm, Little Miss Broadway, Just Around the Corner* 1938; *The Little Princess, Susannah of the Mounties* 1939; *The Blue Bird, Young People* 1940; *Kathleen* 1941; *Miss Annie Rooney* 1942; *Since You Went Away* 1944; *I'll Be Seeing You, Kiss and Tell* 1945; *Honeymoon, The Bachelor and the Bobby-Soxer, That Hagen Girl* 1947; *Fort Apache* 1948; *Mr. Belvedere Goes to College, Adventure in Baltimore, The Story of Seabiscuit, A Kiss for Corliss* 1949.

tempo. The pace and timing of a motion picture resulting from movement in front of the camera, movement of the camera, and the rhythm of the cutting.

tener. A heavy-duty spotlight that utilizes a 10,000-watt lamp.

Tennant, Victoria. Actress. Born on September 30, 1950, in London. Sophisticated leading lady of the British and American screen. The daughter of talent agent Cecil Tennant and ballerina Irene Baranova, she trained at London Central School of Speech and Drama and performed in British plays and films before moving to Hollywood in 1983 in the wake of her success in the TV miniseries 'Winds of War.' She was married to actor Steve MARTIN (1986–1994).

FILMS INCLUDE: *The Ragman's Daughter* (UK) 1972; *Sphinx, The Winds of War* (US/UK) 1981; *Horror Planet/ Inseminoid* (UK) 1982; *Stranger's Kiss, All of Me* 1984; *The Holcroft Covenant* (UK) 1985; *Best Seller, Flowers in the Attic* 1987; *The Handmaid's Tale, Whispers* (Can.) 1990; *L.A. Story* 1991; *The Plague* 1992.

Terry, Alice. *b.* Alice Frances Taafe, July 24, 1899, Vincennes, Ind. *d.* 1987. Actress. She entered films in 1916 with Triangle, at first using her real name professionally, but it wasn't until the early 20s that she became an important star in the films of her husband, director Rex INGRAM. Her cool beauty and poised elegance served to counterbalance the flamboyance of such Latin-lover leading men as Rudolph Valentino, in *The Four Horsemen of the Apocalypse,* and Ramon Novarro, in *The Arab.* Since she appeared mostly in her husband's films, Miss Terry's screen career was somewhat irregular and she did not enjoy the kind of frequent exposure that made lesser actresses and movie stars much more popular. In the mid-20s, Ingram and Terry settled in Nice, on the French Riviera, where the director set up his own studio, releasing through MGM. Sound ended the career of both. After Ingram's death in 1950, Miss Terry lived in retirement in Hollywood, where she died of pneumonia at 87.

FILMS INCLUDE: *The Bugle Call, Not My Sister* 1916; *Strictly Business, The Bottom of the Well* 1917; *Old Wives for New* 1918; *Thin Ice, The Love Burglar, The Valley of the Giants* 1919; *Hearts are Trumps* 1920; *The Four Horsemen of the Apocalypse, The Conquering Power* 1921; *Turn to the Right, The Prisoner of Zenda* 1922; *Where the Pavement Ends, Scaramouche* 1923; *The Arab* 1924; *Sackcloth and Scarlet, The Great Divide, Confessions of a Queen, Any Woman* 1925; *Mare Nostrum, The Magician* 1926; *Lovers?, The Garden of Allah* 1927; *The Three Passions* 1929; *Baroud/Love in Morocco* 1930; *Asilo Naval* (Sp.) 1935.

Terry, Paul. Animator. *b.* Feb. 19, 1887, San Mateo, Calif. *d.* 1971. A former news photographer and syndicated cartoonist for the Hearst chain, he began producing animated cartoons in 1915 and pioneered in many animation techniques. In the 20s he produced the famous cartoon series "Aesop's Film Fables." In the 30s he created his long-running Terrytoon series, featuring such animated cartoon characters as Mighty Mouse and Heckle and Jeckle. In 1955, Terry sold his New Rochelle, N.Y., studio, and his stock of more than 1,100 animated shorts, to CBS and retired from the business.

Terry, Phillip (or **Phil**). American actor. Born in 1909. Leading man and second lead of Hollywood films from the late 30s; mostly seen in B pictures. He was the third (1942–46) husband of Joan CRAWFORD.

FILMS INCLUDE: *Navy Blue and Gold* 1937; *Yellow Jack* 1938; *Calling Dr. Kildare, On Borrowed Time, Balalaika* 1939; *Those Were the Days* 1940; *The Monster and the Girl, The Parson of Panamint, Public Enemies* 1941; *Are Husbands Necessary?, Sweater Girl, Wake Island* 1942; *Bataan* 1943; *Ladies Courageous, Music in Manhattan* 1944; *Pan-Americana, The Lost Weekend* 1945; *The Dark Horse, To Each His Own* 1946; *Born to Kill, Seven Keys to Baldpate* 1947; *Deadline U.S.A.* 1952; *The Leech Woman* 1960; *The Explosive Generation* 1961; *The Navy vs. the Night Monsters* 1966.

Terry-Thomas. Actor. *b.* Thomas Terry Hoar-Stevens, July 14, 1911, London, to an upper-crust family. *d.* 1990. *ed.* Ardingly Coll. Mustached, gap-toothed comedian of British and American films. He worked as a clerk, then a meat salesman for a cold storage company, with whose amateur dramatic society he began performing in the early 30s. Turning professional, he became a bandleader, then dancer and vaudeville impersonator, gradually gaining popularity in cabaret, music halls, radio, and movies. It wasn't until the mid-50s, however, that his film career took off. His exuberant, frenzied style of comedy, in roles ranging from the silly to malevolent, enlivened numerous international productions through the late 60s. In 1971 he was diagnosed with Parkinson's disease. For several years he continued performing in films in a curtailed schedule but in 1977 was forced into retirement. He lived with his second wife on the Balearic Island of Ibiza but returned to London in 1984.

FILMS INCLUDE: *It's Love Again* 1936; *Racketeer* 1937; *For Freedom* 1940; *The Brass Monkey* 1947; *Helter Skelter* 1949; *Private's Progress, The Green Man* 1956; *Brothers in Law, Blue Murder at St. Trinian's, The Naked Truth, Your Past Is Showing* 1957; *Tom Thumb, Too Many Crooks* 1958; *Carlton-Browne of the F.O./Man in a Cocked Hat, I'm All Right Jack* 1959; *School for Scoundrels, Make Mine Mink* 1960; *A Matter of Who* 1961; *Kill or Cure* (US), *Bachelor Flat* (US), *Operation Snatch, The Wonderful World of the Brothers Grimm* (US) 1962; *The Mouse on the Moon, It's a Mad Mad Mad Mad World* (US) 1963; *How to Murder Your Wife* (US), *Strange Bedfellows* (US), *Those Magnificent Men in Their Flying Machines* 1965; *La Grande Vadrouille/Don't Look Now* (Fr./UK), *Our Man in Marrakesh/Bang! Bang! You're Dead!* 1966; *A Guide for the Married Man* (US), *The Perils of Pauline* (US) 1967; *Danger: Diabolik* (Fr./It.), *Where Were You When the Lights Went Out?* (US), *Arabella* (It.) 1968; *2000 Years Later, Monte Carlo or Bust/Those Daring Young Men in Their Jaunty Jalopies* (UK/Fr./It.) 1969; *The Abominable Dr. Phibes* 1971; *Dr. Phibes Rises Again* 1972; *Gli Eroi/The Heroes* (It.) 1974; *The Adventures of Tom Jones/The Bawdy Adventures of Tom Jones, Spanish Fly* 1976; *The Last Remake of Beau Geste* (US) 1977; *The Hound of the Baskervilles* 1978.

Teshigahara, Hiroshi. Director. Born on Jan. 28, 1927, in Tokyo. The son of a painter who specialized in floral designs, he studied painting at the Tokyo Art Institute and made his first contact with film as a critic. He began directing documentary shorts in the early 50s and moved on to features in the 60s. His first feature-length film, *The Pitfall* (1961), was by his own definition a "documentary fantasy." It revealed a preoccupation with the bizarre which blossomed into a compelling abstract experience in *Woman in the Dunes* (1964). The latter film, made independently for a mere $100,000, made a strong impression on Western audiences with its bold imagery and enormous close-ups and won the Jury Prize at Cannes. Teshigahara's subsequent films, mainly psychological thrillers, have been less daring or innovative. After recovering from injuries in a 1970 car crash, Teshigahara turned out one of his most controversial films, *Summer Soldiers* (1972), the story of GI deserters fleeing the war in Vietnam into a life of depravity in Japan. The director then withdrew from filmmaking for 17 years, during which he turned his attention to the art of flower arranging and the study of ceramics. He became a driving force in the activities of Sogetsu, the flower-arranging school his father had established in the 20s, and in Japan's arts avant-garde. During that period he also made several TV documentaries. Teshigahara returned to features in 1989 with *Rikyu,* a sumptuous 16th-century costume drama.

FEATURE FILMS: *The Pitfall* 1961; *Woman in the Dunes, La Fleur de l'Age ou les Adolescentes/The Adolescents/That Tender Age* ("Ako" episode, deleted from American release print; Can./Fr./It./Jap.) 1964; *The Face of Another* 1966; *The Man Without a Map* 1968; *Summer Soldiers* (also phot.) 1972; *Rikyu* 1989.

Tesich, Steve. Screenwriter, playwright. *b.* Stoyan Tesich, Sept. 29, 1942, in Titovo Utice, Yugoslavia. *d.* 1996. *ed.* Indiana U. (B.A., Phi Beta Kappa); Columbia (M.A.). It wasn't until 1959, when he arrived with his mother in the US, that he first met his father, who had emigrated to America many years ahead of the rest of the family. He became a naturalized citizen in 1961. After receiving his master's degree in Russian literature from Columbia in 1967, he turned to playwriting, with increasing success. He won an Academy Award for his first screenplay, *Breaking Away* (1979). His script for *Four Friends* (1981) was largely autobiographical.

FILMS: *Breaking Away* 1979; *Eyewitness, Four Friends* 1981; *The World According to Garp* 1982; *American Flyers, Eleni* 1985.

Tetzlaff, Ted (Theodore). Director, director of photography. Born on June 3, 1903, in Los Angeles. He entered films in the early 20s as a lab, then camera, assistant, graduating to director of photography in 1926. He was behind the camera on several of Frank Capra's early films at Columbia and was responsible for the cinematography of several prestigious Paramount productions of the 30s. He made his debut as director in 1941 with *World Premiere,* a comedy starring John BARRYMORE, but his new career was interrupted by WW II, in which he served with the rank of major. Returning to Hollywood, he resumed working, briefly as lighting cameraman on such films as *The Enchanted Cottage* and *Notorious,* then directing a number of well-made suspense thrillers, of which *The Window* was by far the best. But after turning out a couple of mediocre adventure yarns, he retired from films in the late 50s.

FILMS INCLUDE: As director of photography—*Atta Boy* (co-phot.) 1926; *Eager Lips, Ragtime, Polly of the Movies* 1927; *The Apache, Comrades, The Power of the Press* (co-phot.) 1928; *The Younger Generation, The Donovan Affair, Father and Son, Wall Street, Mexicali Rose* 1929; *Sisters, The Squealer, Tol'able David, Hurricane* 1930; *Brief Moment* 1933; *Fugitive Lovers* 1934; *Paris in Spring* 1935; *My Man Godfrey, The Princess Comes Across* 1936; *Easy Living* 1937; *Fools for Scandal* 1938; *Remember the Night* 1940; *Road to Zanzibar* 1941; *I Married a Witch* 1942; *The Enchanted Cottage* 1945; *Notorious* 1946. As director (complete)—*World Premiere* 1941; *Riff-Raff* 1947; *Fighting Father Dunne* 1948; *Johnny Allegro, The Window, Dangerous Profession* 1949; *The White Tower* 1950; *Under the Gun, Gambling House* 1951; *The Treasure of Lost Canyon* 1952; *Terror on a Train/Time Bomb* (UK) 1953; *Son of Sinbad* 1955; *Seven Wonders of the World* (co-dir.) 1956; *The Young Land* 1959.

Tewkesbury, Joan. Screenwriter, director. Born on Apr. 8, 1936 in Redlands, Calif. *ed.* USC. Trained as a dancer from early childhood, she appeared at age 11 as one of the ballet rats in *The Unfinished Dance* (1947), a backstage movie starring Margaret O'Brien. She also performed on the stage and understudied for Mary Martin in 'Peter Pan' in 1954–55. She later directed and choreographed Little Theatre productions in the Los Angeles area and taught dance at the American School of Dance, drama at USC, and film at UCLA. She entered films as a protégée of Robert Altman, at first as script supervisor on *McCabe and Mrs. Miller* (1971), then as screenwriter, notably of *Nashville* (1976). Her first attempt at directing, *Old Boyfriends* (1979), met with critical disapproval. She also directed a number of TV dramas and wrote and directed the off-Broadway play 'Cowboy Jack' (1978).

FILMS: *The Unfinished Dance* (act.) 1947; *Man's Favorite Sport* (bit) 1964; *Thieves Like Us* (co-sc.) 1974; *Hempstead Center* (on Anna Freud; dir., sc.), *Nashville* (sc.) 1976; *Old Boyfriends* (dir.) 1979; *A Night in Heaven* (sc.) 1986; *The Player* (cameo; act. only) 1992.

Tewksbury, Peter. American director. Born in 1924. He brought to films an elegant, sure touch, the result of several years of experience in TV on such series as 'Father Knows Best' and 'My Three Sons.' But he was hampered for the most part by poor material, and in the late 60s returned to TV.

FILMS: *Sunday in New York, Emil and the Detectives* 1964; *Doctor You've Got to Be Kidding* 1967; *Stay Away Joe* 1968; *The Trouble with Girls* 1969.

Thalberg, Irving G. Production executive. *b.* May 30, 1899, Brooklyn, N.Y., of Jewish-German parentage. *d.* 1936. Frail and sickly as a child, he spent many months away from school, bedridden with a succession of ailments that threatened to aggravate his rheumatic heart condition. Since he had been told by doctors he might not live to be 30, he did not bother with college after graduating from high school but instead applied himself to shorthand and speed typing and took a job with a small trading company. In 1918 he began to work for a friend of the family, Carl LAEMMLE, head of the Universal Film Manufacturing company, initially as secretary to Laemmle's assistant, then as private secretary to Laemmle himself. Thalberg's secretarial skills and his rapid grasp of the film business soon made him an indispensable confidant of Laemmle at the company's Broadway headquarters. When the management of the company's production center, Hollywood's Universal City, fell into disarray, Laemmle appointed his trusted secretary as head of production.

Although barely 20, with a slight build and an innocent face that made him look even younger, Thalberg soon took firm hold of Universal City, establishing a reputation as a capable administrator, a tough taskmaster, and an intuitive judge of story material that would please the public. Around Hollywood they began calling him "The Boy Wonder," after the title of a short story in *The Saturday Evening Post,* by a former Universal writer, whose producer hero seemed patterned after Thalberg. Years later Thalberg would become the model for the hero of F. Scott Fitzgerald's unfinished novel, *The Last Tycoon.*

Thalberg's reputation was enhanced by the way he handled Erich von STROHEIM, Hollywood's *enfant terrible,* in stormy confrontations over the production of *Foolish Wives* (1922) and *Merry-Go-Round* (1923). In February of 1923, Thalberg severed his association with Laemmle on personal grounds (their relationship became untenable when Thalberg turned down a proposition that he marry the boss's daughter Rosabelle) and joined the small company of Louis B. MAYER as vice president and head of production. In April of 1924, Mayer's studio was absorbed into a mammoth new production company, METRO-GOLDWYN-MAYER (MGM), with Mayer assuming the position of first vice president and general manager and Thalberg that of vice president and supervisor of production. Ironically, one of the first projects Thalberg inherited with his new job was yet another von Stroheim production, *Greed,* which mushroomed through the director's extravagance and excessive attention to detail into a 42-reel epic requiring seven hours of viewing. Once again the two men locked horns. When von Stroheim refused to cut the film to manageable size, Thalberg removed him from the helm and had the film pared by others under his own supervision.

Under Mayer's management and Thalberg's artistic direction, MGM grew and prospered rapidly, becoming by the early 30s Hollywood's most prestigious and most glamorous film factory, with "more stars than there are in the heavens." One of the company's leading stars was Norma SHEARER, whom Thalberg had married in 1927. Despite his failing health, Thalberg personally supervised many of the studio's top productions from inception through completion. He spared no money or effort in his quest of the polished craftsmanship for which MGM's films became famous, often re-shooting scenes and re-editing whole sections before approving a production for release. He instituted the SNEAK PREVIEW, requiring that each one of his major films be first shown to an unsophisticated audience in a small community to determine public reaction before the general release. An unfavorable reaction usually meant a major overhaul.

During his 12-year tenure at MGM, Thalberg personally supervised the production of such films as *He Who Gets Slapped* (1924), *The Merry Widow, The Big Parade* (both 1925), *Ben-Hur* (1926), *Flesh and the Devil* (1927), *The Crowd* (1928), *Hallelujah* (1929), *Anna Christie, The Big House* (both 1930), *Private Lives* (1931), *Freaks, Strange Interlude* (both 1932), *The Merry Widow, The Barretts of Wimpole Street* (both 1934), *Mutiny on the Bounty, China Seas, A Night at the Opera* (all 1935), *Romeo and Juliet* (1936), and *The Good Earth* (released posthumously in 1937). But Thalberg's name rarely appeared on the screen. "Credit you give yourself isn't worth having," he said.

During a Christmas party in 1932, Thalberg was stricken with a severe heart attack. After recovering, he took leave of his duties for further recuperation in Europe. When he returned, he found that much of his power had been taken away, and although he was allowed to keep his position near the top of the MGM pyramid, his authority and influence were considerably reduced. He died of pneumonia at 37. In 1937 the Academy of Motion Picture Arts and Sciences instituted the Irving G. Thalberg Memorial Award, which has since been given each year during the Oscar presentations "for the most consistent high level of production achievement by an individual producer."

Thatcher, Torin. Actor. *b.* Jan. 15, 1905, Bombay, India, to British parents. *d.* 1981. A former teacher, he trained for the stage at the Royal Academy of Dramatic Art and made his London debut in 1927 and his British film debut in 1934. A powerfully built man, he played tough, commanding character parts in many films, at first in England and from the early 50s in Hollywood.

FILMS INCLUDE: In the UK—*General John Regan* 1934; *Sabotage* 1936; *Knight Without Armor* 1937; *Climbing High, The Spy in Black/U-Boat 29* 1939; *Let George Do It* 1940; *Major Barbara* 1941; *Next of Kin* 1942; *The Captive Heart, Great Expectations* (as Bentley Drummle "The Spider") 1946; *The Fallen Idol* 1948. In the US—*Affair in Trinidad, The Crimson Pirate* (US/UK), *The Snows of Kilimanjaro, Blackbeard the Pirate* (as Sir Henry Morgan) 1952; *The Desert Rats, Houdini, The Robe* 1953; *Knock on Wood, The Black Shield of Falworth* 1954; *Love Is a Many Splendored Thing, Lady Godiva* 1955; *Helen of Troy* (as Ulysses; US/It.) 1956; *Band of Angels* 1957; *The 7th Voyage of Sinbad, Witness for the Prosecution* 1958; *The Miracle* (as the Duke of Wellington) 1959; *Mutiny on the Bounty* 1962; *The Sandpiper* 1965; *Hawaii* 1966; *The King's Pirate* 1967.

Thaxter, Phyllis. Actress. Born Phyllis St. Felix Thaxter, on Nov. 20, 1921, in Portland, Me. Leading lady of the American stage and films. The daughter of a Maine Supreme Court justice and a former Shakespearean actress, she trained for the stage at the Montreal Repertory Theatre and made her Broadway debut in 1938. In Hollywood from the mid-40s, she usually played sincere, unglamorized types, often faithful wives. Her career was set back by an attack of infantile paralysis in 1952. Her first husband (1944–62) was James Aubrey, who later became president of CBS-TV, then MGM. Their daughter, Skye Aubrey (*b.* Schuyler Aubrey, 1945) is an actress.

FILMS INCLUDE: *Thirty Seconds Over Tokyo* 1944; *Bewitched, Week-End at the Waldorf* 1945; *The Sea of Grass* 1947; *The Sign of the Ram, Blood on the Moon* 1948; *Act of Violence* 1949; *The Breaking Point* 1950; *Jim Thorpe—All American, Come Fill the Cup* 1951; *Springfield Rifle, Operation Secret* 1952; *Women's Prison* 1955; *Man Afraid* 1957; *The World of Henry Orient* 1964; *Superman* 1978.

theme. 1. The subject of a film or its basic idea. 2. A musical passage associated with a character or a place in a film, such as "Tara's Theme" in *Gone With the Wind.*

Theodorakis, Mikis. Composer. Born in 1925, in Khios (island), Greece. The son of a minor civil servant, he began his musical education as a small boy, at the Conservatory of Patras. When he was 14 the family moved to the city of Tripolis, where he organized musical groups and gave his first public concert. In 1943 he enrolled at the Athens Conservatory and that same year was arrested for membership in the resistance against the German-Italian occupation. It was the beginning of a stormy political life as a nationalist and leftist, which was to interfere with his musical career for many years. He was imprisoned, tortured, and finally deported in the civil war of 1947–52. In 1953 he moved to Paris, where he enrolled at the Conservatoire and before long gained recognition as a composer of orchestral music, oratorios, ballets, and theater and film scores. He returned to Greece in 1961 and as leader of the Lambrakis youth movement was elected to parliament two years later. He continued composing for films and in 1964 gained international fame for his memorable score for *Zorba the Greek.* In 1967 he was arrested for political activity by the military junta that took over the Greek government and was not released until 1970, when he went into exile to France. In 1972 he resigned from the Communist Party and in 1974, with the restoration of democratic rule, returned to Greece.

FILMS INCLUDE: *Eva* (Gr.) 1953; *Ill Met by Moonlight/Night Ambush* (UK) 1956; *Luna de Miel/Honeymoon* (Sp.) 1959; *The Shadow of the Cat* (UK) 1961; *Les Amants de Teruel/The Lovers of Teruel* (co-composer; Fr.), *Electra* (Gr.), *Phaedra* (Gr./US/Fr.), *Five Miles to Midnight* (US/Fr./It.) 1962; *Zorba the Greek* (US/Gr.) 1964; *The Day the Fish Came Out* (UK/Gr.) 1967; *Z* (Fr./Alg.) 1969; *The Trojan Women* (Gr./UK /US) 1971; *Etat de Siège/State of Siege* (Fr.), *Serpico* (US) 1973; *Partisani/Hell River* (Yug./US) 1974; *Actas de Marusia* (Mex.) 1976; *Iphigenia* 1977; *Easy Road* (Gr.) 1979; *The Man with the Red*

Carnation (Gr.) 1980; *Les Clowns de Dieu* (Fr.) 1987; *Sis* (Gr.) 1989.

theory, film. A theory of film attempts to explain the nature of cinema and analyze how films produce emotional and cognitive effects. Often, film theories place cinema in a broader context (social, political, philosophical) and provide a framework for evaluating artistic merit. Unlike practical criticism, which is concerned with interpretation and judgment of specific films, film theory seeks to establish principles applicable to all films.

As a distinct field of inquiry, film theory had its origins within the first two decades after the invention of motion pictures. At a time when many people assumed that film was a mere record of real or theatrical events, the first film theorists were concerned with showing that film was a new, distinct, and valid art form, though one that shared the properties of many other arts (theater, music, painting). German-born American philosopher Hugo Münsterburg, a close predecessor of the Gestalt school of psychology, was among those who argued that cinema was a new artistic medium. In the first major text in film theory, *The Photoplay: A Psychological Study* (1916), he maintained that films do not reproduce objective reality but mental experience. The cinema is mental in its very essence, because the activity of the spectator's mind is required to construct the illusion of motion from a succession of static film frames. Camera angles and frame compositions are organized by the same principle of "attention" that is at work when a perceiver's eye focuses on particular details of sensory experience.

Rudolf ARNHEIM, a German Gestalt psychologist who, like Münsterburg, emigrated to the US, developed a theory of film that shared much in common with Münsterburg's but proved much more influential. In *Film as Art* (1932), Arnheim emphasized the differences between the perception of experience in film and in life, arguing that the strength of film lay in its deviations from reality, including the two-dimensionality of the screen, the limitations of the frame, and the fragmentation and rearranging of space and time. Many theorists came to share his view that cinema achieves its effects by using its unique tools to transform ordinary reality into something more meaningful and expressive. This school of thought is broadly known as formalist or formative film theory.

Formalism was the position of two Russian theorists and directors of the 1920s, V.I. PUDOVKIN and Sergei EISENSTEIN, who established a theoretical basis for the techniques of thematic editing, or MONTAGE, that they employed in their films. Author of *Film Technique* (1929), Pudovkin argued that the "foundation of film art is editing" because meaning in cinema is constructed from the juxtaposition of shots. He argued for a style of editing in which each shot makes a new point through its relation to other shots. Eisenstein, author of *Film Sense* (1942) and *Film Form* (1947), went further, arguing that meaning emerges from the dialectical conflict between shots with opposing tendencies. While Pudovkin focused on how editing could heighten drama and communicate narrative, Eisenstein argued that montage could express abstract intellectual ideas as well.

Broadly opposed to formalist theories are realist ones. Realist theories locate the power of film in its ability to capture objective material reality. These theories bear a close connection to cinematic styles such as socialist realism (the official style of Soviet-bloc countries beginning in the 1930s) and Italian NEOREALISM (employed in the 1940s by directors such as Roberto ROSSELINI and Vittorio DE SICA). Hungarian aesthetician George Lukács developed the theoretical foundation of socialist realism; fellow Hungarian Béla BALÁZS, in *The Theory of Film* (1945), took a middle position between formalism and realism, arguing that artistic manipulation must be balanced with the presentation of concrete reality. Cesare ZAVATTINI, who wrote the screenplay for De Sica's neorealist film *The Bicycle Thief* (1948), theorized that the purpose of cinema is to explore the "dailiness" of events, and thereby build compassion and understanding for ordinary human beings.

German-born American Siegfried KRACAUER made a strong case for realism in his *Theory of Film: The Redemption of Physical Reality* (1960). He argued that cinema favors the appearance of unstaged reality, "found" moments, nature caught in the act, with loose, open narratives suggesting the indeterminacy of life. In turn, he opposed the formative or expressionistic tendency of films that emphasized plotting, patterning, and stylized sets.

Kracauer's ideas bear affinities to those of French critic André BAZIN, who became one of the most influential film theorists through his editorship of CAHIERS DU CINÉMA, the film journal he co-founded in 1951. In numerous essays, collected posthumously in *What Is Cinema*? (1967), he argued that the artist's vision should be in balance with the objective materials presented on the screen. He was suspicious of the editing techniques of Pudovkin and Eisenstein, which depended heavily on close-ups that allowed the filmmaker tight control over the spectator's experience. Bazin preferred the use of long takes and camera pans to preserve the continuity of real time and space; he celebrated DEEP FOCUS photography, which freed spectators to make choices as they observed simultaneous planes of action. He praised the deep-focus work of directors such as Jean RENOIR, Orson WELLES and William WYLER and the neorealism of De Sica and Rossellini.

Beginning in the mid-50s, a number of Bazin's disciples, contributors to *Cahiers du Cinéma*, took the study of film in a new direction known as AUTEUR THEORY. Less a theory of the nature of film than a method of criticism, it held that the best movies are dominated by the personal vision and style of the director. The auteurists were eclectic in that they evaluated films not by universal criteria but by the strength and originality of individual directors. Auteurism was advanced by such French critics as François TRUFFAUT, Jean-Luc GODARD, Claude CHABROL, Eric ROHMER, and Jacques RIVETTE, who went on to become auteurist directors in their own right in the cinematic movement known as the NOUVELLE VAGUE, or New Wave. American critic Andrew SARRIS, who coined the term "auteur theory" in the early 60s, helped to spread auteurism in the US.

In Europe and the US, Bazinian realism and auteurism were significant in fostering the rapid expansion of film studies as a university discipline. Bazin contributed a persuasive view of the nature and history of film and the idea of a classical style of filmmaking that balances realistic and expressionistic elements. By centering on great directors, auteurism contributed a principle for organizing film history and selecting films to research. However, Bazin's work was criticized for its weakness in explaining the power of expressionistic films and for its focus on aesthetic effects to the exclusion of political concerns. Auteurism, too, had weaknesses, not least its tendency to condemn worthwhile films and glorify bad ones solely on the basis of the director's reputation. The heyday of auteurism was brief, ending in the early 70s, though it left a lasting legacy in the tendency to consider the director the principal author of a film.

French theorist Jean MITRY, the first recognized film professor at the University of Paris, attempted to synthesize Bazin's ideas with those of the formalists, in *Esthétique et psychologie du cinéma* (1963), a scholarly, comprehensive work that organized all the theoretical problems of the first 50 years of film theory. Mitry advanced an eclectic range of new insights from the disparate fields of philosophy, linguistics, and psychology. Mitry's work marked the end of an era, for afterwards, film theory took a new turn, one based on semiology or semiotics, the study of signs.

Cinema semiology was inaugurated by French theorist Christian METZ, author of *Film Language: A Semiotics of the Cinema* (France, 1968; English trans., 1974). Drawing on the linguistics of early 20th-century Swiss scholar Ferdinand de Saussure, Metz developed the proposition that cinema communicates through a network of signs interpreted through overlapping systems of codes. Whereas earlier theorists had posited the shot as the basic unit of film meaning, Metz argued that the shot was much too large to be basic. He considered the sign the minimal unit of meaning, with each shot containing dozens, even hundreds of signs. These, he argued, could be analyzed by identifying a set of master codes (photography, language, spatial composition) and dividing them into more specific subcodes (photography into shots, angles, colors, etc.) and subdivisions of subcodes (shots into long shots, medium shots, close-ups). From these theoretical foundations, Metz developed a systematic, rigorous methodology for analyzing film meaning.

In the 70s and 80s, semiology became the most prominent school of film theory, elaborated by ideas from diverse sources. Drawing on the structural anthropology of Claude Lévi-Strauss, cinema structuralists argued that films, like myths and folk tales, contain deep structures of symbolic meaning that can be analyzed in terms of antinomies or opposites in dialectical conflict. Structuralism, in turn, intersects with genre studies, which focuses on the characteristic narratives of commercial cinema (Westerns, thrillers, musicals, comedies, etc.). Peter WOLLEN, who contributed to the development of semiology with *Signs and Meaning in the Cinema* (1969), took a structuralist approach to the study of Westerns; Conin MacArthur applied structuralism to the FILM NOIR style in *Underworld USA*.

Beginning in the mid-70s, cinema semiology was amplified by ideas from Marxism and psychoanalysis, first in the works of Metz and Jean-Louis Baudry, and later in those of such critics as Jean-Pierre Oudart, Stephen Heath, and Philip Rosen. While Marxism has influenced film theory since the days of Pudovkin and Eisenstein, the particular approach of these theorists draws on the work of Louis Althusser, who believed that artistic media reinforce a society's ideology by "subject positioning"—using emotional effects to guide the spectator (or subject) into the ideological position required by the social order. The techniques of psychoanalysis devised by Jacques Lacan are used to analyze how films accomplish these effects.

Despite its widespread influence, semiology has shortcomings, particularly its dependence on jargon, its totalizing tendencies, and its remoteness from the actual experience of viewing a film. Some critics have investigated the organic experience of watching films by introducing concepts from the philosophical field of phenomenology. These have included French critics Amédée Ayfre, Henri Agel, and Roger Munier. American Stanley Cavell drew on phenomenology in *The World Viewed: Reflections on the Ontology of Film* (1971).

Many critics favor an eclectic approach to the study of cinema, drawing not on one theory but many in order to address different issues and illuminate different types of films. Leo Braudy's *The World in a Frame: What We See in Films* (1976) analyzes the significance of genre while also attending to such matters as visual style (in terms of "open" worlds, associated with realistic cinema, and "closed" worlds, associated with expressionistic cinema). David BORDWELL, in works like *Film Art: An Introduction* (1985), applies cognitive psychology to examine how meaning is constructed from films.

Feminist critics such as Molly Haskell, Julia Lesage, and Laura MULVEY have applied diverse theoretical tools to study the image of women in films and the ways in which cinema reinforces the position of women in society. Haskell's seminal work in this field is *From Reverence to Rape* (1974). Laura Mulvey, who has frequently collaborated with Peter Wollen, wrote the influential essay "Visual Pleasure and Narrative Cinema" (1975).

Film historians and historically oriented critics develop theories of film in the context of technological, economic, or social history. Significant film histories include Gerald Mast's *A Short History of the Movies* (1976) and Robert Sklar's *Movie-Made America: A Cultural History of American Movies* (1975). Social history and genre studies are combined in such works as Robert Warshow's *The Immediate Experience* (1962) and Andrew Bergman's *We're in the Money: Depression America and Its Films* (1971).

Thesiger, Ernest. Actor. *b.* Jan. 15, 1879, London. *d.* 1961. Character player of British and occasional American films, often in eccentric roles. Memorable as the effeminate mad scientist Dr. Praetorius in *The Bride of Frankenstein* (1935).

FILMS INCLUDE: *Nelson* 1918; *The Pickwick Papers* 1921; *The Old Dark House* (US) 1932; *The Ghoul* 1933; *My Heart Is Calling* 1934; *The Bride of Frankenstein* (US) 1935; *The Man Who Could Work Miracles* 1936; *Henry V* (as the Duke of Beri) 1944; *Caesar and Cleopatra* (as Theodotus) 1945; *Beware of Pity* 1946; *The Man Within/The Smugglers* 1947; *Quartet, The Winslow Boy* 1948; *Last Holiday* 1950; *The Man in the White Suit, Scrooge/A Christmas Carol, Laughter in Paradise* 1951; *The Robe* (as Emperor Tiberius; US) 1953; *Father Brown/The Detective* 1954; *The Adventures of Quentin Durward/Quentin Durward* (as Lord Crawford) 1955; *The Horse's Mouth* 1958; *The Battle of the Sexes* 1959; *Sons and Lovers* 1960; *The Roman Spring of Mrs. Stone* 1961.

Thewlis, David. Actor. Born 1963 in Blackpool, England. *ed.* Guildhall School of Music and Drama, London. A tall, slim, and striking actor who began his career as a punk guitarist while gaining experience on the London stage and several regional theaters. He eventually appeared on British television, notably on the series 'Prime Suspect.' His major successes came with his roles in the Mike Leigh films *Life Is Sweet* (1991) and *Naked* (1993).

FILMS: *Little Dorrit* 1988; *Life Is Sweet* 1991; *Afraid of the Dark, Damage* 1992; *Naked, The Trial* 1993; *Black Beauty* 1994; *Restoration, Total Eclipse* 1995; *Dragonheart, James and the Giant Peach* (v/o), *The Island of Dr. Moreau* 1996; *Seven Years in Tibet* 1997.

Thiele, Rolf. Director, producer, screenwriter. *b.* Mar. 7, 1918, Redlice, Czechoslovakia, to German parents. *d.* 1982. *ed.* U. of Göttingen. Immediately after WW II he co-founded a production company in Berlin through which he produced many successful films. Directing since the early 50s, he made a name for himself abroad with *Das Mädchen Rosemarie/Rosemary* (1958) and *Tonio Kröger* (1964), both featuring his favorite actress, Nadja TILLER. His films often dealt with mildly erotic themes.

FILMS INCLUDE (as director): *Primanerinnen* (also prod., sc.) 1951; *Der Tag vor der Hochzeit* (also prod., sc.) 1952; *Geliebtes Leben* (also prod., sc.) 1963; *Sie* (also prod., sc.) 1954; *Die Barrings* (also co-sc.) 1955; *Friedrike von Barring* (also sc.) 1956; *Skandal in Ischl* 1957; *Das Mädchen Rosemarie/Rosemary* (also co-sc.) 1958; *Labyrinth* (also co-sc.) 1959; *Der liebe Augustin* 1960; *Lulu* (also sc.) 1962; *Moral 63* (also sc.) 1963; *Tonio Kröger* 1964; *Das Liebeskarussell* (in two parts) 1965; *Ohrfeigen* (also sc.) 1969; *Gelöbt sei was hart macht* (also prod.) 1972; *Slap in the Face* 1975; *Ondine* 1976; *Schöner Gigolo—armer Gigolo/Just a Gigolo* (prod. only) 1978.

Thiele, Wilhelm (also known as **William** in the US). Director. *b.* May 10, 1890, Vienna. *d.* 1975. A graduate of the Vienna Conservatory, he went on the stage at 19 and began directing plays shortly after. He made his debut as a film director in 1923 in Austria, and in 1926 joined UFA in Berlin. Most of his films were light, entertaining, and unpretentious. The best known of these, *Die Drei von der Tankstelle/The Three from the Gas Station* (1930), enjoyed an international commercial success. In the early 30s he also worked in France and after the Nazi rise to power, he left for England, en route to the US. His Hollywood output (1935–46) was mostly routine and included a couple of Tarzan pictures. He was Josef von Sternberg's assistant on *The King Steps Out* (1936). He eventually returned to Germany.

FILMS INCLUDE: In Austria and Germany—*Märchen aus Alt-Wien* (also co-sc.), *Franz Léhar* (co-dir. with Hans Torre) 1923; *Orientexpress* (also sc.), *Die selige Exzellenz/His Late Excellency* (also co-sc.) 1927; *Die Dame mit der Maske, Hurra! ich lebe!/Hurrah! I'm Alive!* 1928; *Adieu Mascotte* 1929; *Die Drei von der Tankstelle/The Three from the Gas Station* (and French version, *Le Chemin du Paradis*), *Liebeswalzer* 1930. In France—*L'Amoureuse Aventure* (and German version, *Madame hat Ausgang), Le Bal* (and German version, *Der Ball*) 1931; *La Fille et le Garçon/The Girl and the Boy* (and German version, *Zwei Herzen und ein Schlag*) 1932. In Germany—*Grossfürstin Alexandra* 1933. In the UK—*Waltz Time* 1933. In the US (complete)—*Lottery Lover* 1935; *Don't Get Personal* (also story), *Jungle Princess* 1936; *London by Night, Beg Borrow or Steal* 1937; *Bad Little Angel, Bridal Suite* 1939; *The Ghost Comes Home* 1940; *Tarzan Triumphs, Tarzan's Desert Mystery* 1943; *The Madonna's Secret* (also co-story, co-sc.) 1946. In Germany—*Der letzte Füssganger* (also co-sc.), *Sabine und die 100 Männer* 1960.

Thiess, Ursula. See TAYLOR, Robert.

thin print. A film print lacking in density.

Thirard, Armand. Director of photography. *b.* Oct. 25, 1899, Mantes, France. A sometime actor during the silent era, he became a lighting cameraman in the late 20s. Working through four decades with such leading French directors as DUVIVIER, CHRISTIAN-JAQUE, CLOUZOT, and VADIM, he achieved some notable cinematography in both black and white and color. He retired late in the 60s.

FILMS INCLUDE: *Maman Colibri* 1929; *David Golder, Le Bal* 1931; *Poil de Carotte* 1932; *L'Equipage/Flight Into Darkness* 1935; *Mayerling* 1936; *Gribouille/Heart of Paris* 1937; *Hôtel du Nord* (co-phot.) 1938; *Remorques/Stormy Waters, L'Assassinat du Père Noël/Who Killed Santa Claus?* 1941; *La Symphonie fantastique* 1942; *La Symphonie pastorale* 1946; *Le Silence est d'Or/Man About Town, Quai des Orfèvres/Jenny Lamour* 1947; *Manon* 1949; *Les Belles de Nuit/Beauties of the Night* 1952; *Le Salaire de la Peur/The Wages of Fear* 1953; *Les Diaboliques* 1955; *Et Dieu créa la Femme/And God Created Woman* 1956; *Sait-on jamais?/No Sun in Venice* 1957; *Babette s'en va-t-en Guerre/Babette Goes to War* 1959; *La Vérité/The Truth* 1960; *Aimez-vous Brahms?/Goodbye Again* (Fr./US) 1961; *Le Repos du Guerrier/Love on a Pillow* 1962; *Les Bonnes Causes/Don't Tempt the Devil, Château en Suede/Nutty Naughty Chateau* 1963; *La Fabuleuse Aventure de Marco Polo/Marco the Magnificent* 1965; *Guns for San Sebastian* (US/Fr./It./Mex.) 1967; *Le Cerveau/The Brain* (tech. advisor only) 1969.

Thiriet, Maurice. Composer. Born on May 2, 1906, in Meulan, France. A graduate of the Paris Conservatory, he composed a variety of musical works, including scores for many French films since the early 30s. Many of his scores are noted for their light, catchy tunes with a melancholy edge.

FILMS INCLUDE: *Il était une Fois* 1933; *Adrienne Lecouvreur* 1938; *Les Visiteurs du Soir/The Devil's Envoys, La Nuit fantastique* 1942; *Les Enfants du Paradis/Children of Paradise* 1945; *L'Idiot/The Idiot* 1946; *Une si Jolie Petite Plage/Riptide* 1949; *Fanfan la Tulipe/Fanfan the Tulip* 1952; *Thérèse Raquin/The Adulteress* 1953; *L'Air de Paris* 1954; *Crime et Châtiment/Crime and Punishment* 1956; *Il suffit d'aimer/Bernadette of Lourdes* 1961.

35 mm. The standard gauge of film and equipment used in professional cinematography since the earliest days of cinema.

Thomas, Anna. See NAVA, Gregory.

Thomas, Betty. Actress, director. Born Betty Thomas Neinhauser on July 27, 1948, in St. Louis, Mo. *ed.* University of Ohio. Tall and slim, she started as a high school teacher but a waitressing job at Chicago's Second City improv club turned her on to acting. Eventually finding her way to television and into a long-running, Emmy Award–winning role on 'Hill Street Blues,' the show's producer Steven Bochco offered her the chance to direct a sitcom. She has since become a successful feature film director of mainly comedies.

FILMS: *Chesty Anderson, USN, Jackson County Jail, Tunnelvision* 1976; *Outside Chance* 1978; *Used Cars* 1980; *Homework* 1982; *Troop Beverly Hills* 1989; *Only You* (dir. only) 1992; *The Brady Bunch Movie* (dir.) 1995; *Private Parts* 1997.

Thomas, Danny. Actor, singer. *b.* Muzyad Yakhoob (later changed to Amos Jacobs), Jan. 6, 1912, Deerfield, Mich., the fifth of nine children of Catholic immigrants from Lebanon. *d.* 1991, of a heart attack. After getting a taste of show business as a candy butcher at a burlesque theater, he began his professional career in 1932 as a singer at a Detroit radio station. In 1938 he began appearing in nightclubs as an MC-comedian. Steadily gaining popularity during WW II, he began a brief film career in the late 40s in rather schmaltzy leads or comic supporting roles. He later had great success on TV as the star of the long-running (1953–64) 'Make Room for Daddy' (later renamed 'The Danny Thomas Show'), for which he won an Emmy in 1954. He also starred in many specials and made numerous guest appearances in variety shows. In the late 50s he branched into production, forming a partnership with Sheldon Leonard and later with Aaron Spelling, and reaping huge profits from such hit series as 'The Andy Griffith Show,' 'The Dick Van Dyke Show,' 'Gomer Pyle,' and 'The Mod Squad.' He was less successful in attempting to revive his career as a performer with 'The Danny Thomas Hour' (1967–68) and 'Make Room for Granddaddy' (1970–71). He was the father of actress Marlo Thomas (*b.* Margaret Julia Thomas, Nov. 21, 1938, in Detroit), who starred in the TV series 'That Girl' (1966–71) and several films and married TV talk show host Phil Donahue. Autobiography: *Make Room for Danny* (1990).

FILMS: *The Unfinished Dance* 1947; *Big City* 1948; *Call Me Mister, I'll See You in My Dreams* (as Gus Kahn) 1951; *The Jazz Singer* 1953; *Looking for Love* (cameo) 1964; *Don't Worry We'll Think of a Title* (cameo) 1966; *Journey Back to Oz* (v/o) 1974.

Thomas, Gerald. Director. Born on Dec. 10, 1920, in Hull, England. The younger brother of Ralph THOMAS, he entered British films in 1946 as assistant editor, graduating to editor in 1950. A director since the mid-50s, he began with a string of suspense films, then found his niche in lowbrow comedy, especially with the commercially successful low-budget "Carry On" series.

FILMS INCLUDE: *Circus Friends* 1956; *Time Lock, The*

Vicious Circle/The Circle 1957; *Chain of Events, Carry On Sergeant* 1958; *Carry On Nurse, Please Turn Over* 1959; *Watch Your Stern, No Kidding/Beware of Children, Carry On Constable* 1960; *Raising the Wind/Roommates* 1961; *Carry On Cruising, The Iron Maiden* 1962; *Nurse on Wheels* 1963; *Carry On Spying, Carry On Cleo* 1964; *The Big Job* 1966; *Follow That Camel* 1967; *Carry On at Your Convenience* 1971; *Carry On England* 1976; *Carry On Emmanuelle* 1978; *The Second Victory* (Austral.) 1986.

Thomas, Henry. Actor. Born on Sept. 8, 1971, in San Antonio, Tex. He earned his place in film history as Steven Spielberg's choice for the pivotal role of the ten-year-old boy who befriends a creature from another planet in *E.T., The Extra-Terrestrial* (1982). Within seven years he matured on the screen, assuming the role of a young paramour in Milos Forman's *Valmont* (1989).

FILMS: *Raggedy Man* 1981; *E.T., The Extra-Terrestrial* 1982; *Misunderstood, Cloak and Dagger* 1984; *The Quest* (Austral.), *Murder One* (Can.) 1988; *Valmont* (Fr./UK) 1989; *Psycho IV: The Beginning* 1990; *Get Back* (prod.) 1991; *Fire in the Sky* 1993; *Curse of the Starving Class, Legends of the Fall* 1995.

Thomas, Jameson. Actor. *b.* Mar. 24, 1889, London. *d.* 1939. On the British stage from his teens, he starred in silent British films. He came to Hollywood in 1930, played a number of dashing leads, then mostly supporting parts, among them the man Claudette Colbert almost married in *It Happened One Night* (1934). He died at 49 of tuberculosis.

FILMS INCLUDE: In the UK—*Chu Chin Chow* 1923; *Decameron Nights* 1924; *The Apache, The Gold Cure* 1925; *Pearl of the South Seas* 1926; *Blighty* 1927; *The White Sheik/Kings Mate, The Farmer's Wife, Tesha/A Woman in the Night* 1928; *Piccadilly, Power Over Men, The Feather, High Treason* 1929; *The Hate Ship, Night Birds, Elstree Calling* 1930. In the US—*Extravagance* 1930; *Convicted, Night Life in Reno* 1931; *Three Wise Girls, The Phantom President, No More Orchids* 1932; *Brief Moment* 1933; *It Happened One Night, The Scarlet Empress, Now and Forever* 1934; *The Lives of a Bengal Lancer, The World Accuses, Charlie Chan in Egypt, The Last Outpost* 1935; *Mr. Deeds Goes to Town* 1936; *The League of Frightened Men, 100 Men and a Girl* 1937; *Death Goes North* 1939.

Thomas, Jeremy. See THOMAS, Ralph.

Thomas, Olive. Actress. *b.* Oliveretta Elaine Duffy, Oct. 29, 1884, Charleroi, Pa. *d.* 1920, a suicide. She ran away from poverty and a teenage marriage to live with a cousin in New York and wound up as a sales clerk in a Harlem department store. After entering and winning a newspaper beauty contest for "The Perfect Model," she gained sudden fame and found herself modeling for *Vogue* and *Vanity Fair* and starring in the 'Ziegfeld Follies' of 1915. In next to no time she was the toast of Broadway, widely admired as "the world's most beautiful girl." She was signed to a film contract by Triangle and later became the star attraction of Myron Selznick's newly formed production company. She married film actor Jack PICKFORD, Mary Pickford's brother, in 1917, and was at the height of her fame and success when she was found dead in a Paris hotel of an overdose of barbiturates.

FILMS INCLUDE: *Beatrice Fairfax* 1916; *Indiscreet Corinne, A Girl Like That, Madcap Madge, Broadway Arizona, Betty Takes a Hand* 1917; *An Heiress for a Day, Limousine Life, The Follies Girl* 1918; *The Glorious Lady, Love's Prisoner, Prudence on Broadway, Out Yonder, Toton, The Spiteful Bride, Upstairs and Down* 1919; *Footlights and Shadows, Youthful Folly, The Flapper, Darling Mine, Everybody's Sweetheart* 1920.

Thomas, Pascal. Director. Born on Apr. 2, 1945, in Montargis, France. A former journalist and film critic for some of France's leading mass-circulation magazines, he directed his first feature film in 1972 and has since scored several commercial and critical successes. His films, usually unassuming, simple stories set against a provincial background, signify a return to the poetic naturalism that dominated the best of the French cinema in the 30s. Some see him as a successor to Jean RENOIR. Inactive through much of the 80s, he resumed his film career with a gentle sex comedy, *Les Maris, les femmes, les Amants* (trade shown 1988, released 1989).

FEATURE FILMS: (as director/co-screenwriter) *Les Zozos* 1972; *Pleure pas la Bouche pleine/Don't Cry with Your Mouth Full* 1973; *Le Chaud Lapin* 1974; *Nono Nenesse* (co-dir. with Jacques Rozier; unreleased) 1975; *La Surprise du Chef* 1976; *Un Oursin dans la Poche* 1977; *Confidences pour Confidences* 1979; *Celles qu'on n'a pas eues* 1981; *Les Maris, les Femmes, les Amants* (also act.) 1989; *Pagaille* 1991.

Thomas, Ralph. Director. Born on Aug. 10, 1915, in Hull, England. *ed.* Middlesex University Coll. Older brother of Gerald THOMAS. He made his start in British films as a clapper boy while still a student in 1932. In 1934 he rose to assistant editor, then left the industry to begin a career in journalism. After WW II service with the 9th Lancers, he returned to films as supervisor of the trailer department at Rank. A director since the late 40s, he has demonstrated proficiency in a variety of genres, from comedy and adventure to drama and suspense. He wound up his career in the late 70s on a low note with a string of trashy sex comedies. He shouldn't be confused with Ralph L. Thomas, a Brazilian-born director of Canadian movies. The British Thomas's son, Jeremy Thomas (*b.* 1949, London) is a former film editor who turned producer in the late 70s and lists among his credits Bernardo Bertolucci's Oscar-winning epic *The Last Emperor* (1987).

FILMS: *Helter Skelter, Once Upon a Dream, Traveller's Joy* 1949; *The Clouded Yellow* 1950; *Appointment with Venus/Island Rescue* 1951; *The Venetian Bird/The Assassin* 1952; *The Dog and the Diamonds, A Day to Remember* 1953; *Doctor in the House, Mad About Men* 1954; *Doctor at Sea, Above Us the Waves* 1955; *The Iron Petticoat, Checkpoint* 1956; *Doctor at Large, Campbell's Kingdom* 1957; *A Tale of Two Cities, The Wind Cannot Read* 1958; *The 39 Steps, Upstairs and Downstairs* 1959; *Conspiracy of Hearts, Doctor in Love* 1960; *No Love for Johnnie, No My Darling Daughter* 1961; *A Pair of Briefs, The Wild and the Willing/Young and Willing* 1962; *Doctor in Distress* 1963; *Hot Enough for June/Agent 8¾* 1964; *The High Bright Sun/McGuire Go Home!* 1965; *Doctor in Clover/Carnaby M.D., Deadlier Than the Male* 1966; *Some Girls Do, Nobody Runs Forever/The High Commissioner* (UK/US) 1968; *Doctor in Trouble* 1970; *Percy, Quest for Love* 1971; *It's a 2'6" Above the Ground World/The Love Ban* 1973; *Percy's Progress/It's Not the Size That Counts* 1974; *A Nightingale Sang in Berkeley Square* 1979 Other films produced by Jeremy include: *The Sheltering Sky* 1990; *Naked Lunch* 1991; *Little Buddha* 1994.

Thomas, William C. Producer, director. *b.* Aug. 11, 1903, Los Angeles. *d.* 1984. *ed.* USC. A former publicity writer, he contributed occasional screen stories in the 30s. He began producing in 1938. From the early 40s to the late 50s he co-produced with William H. Pine (*b.* Feb. 15, 1896, Los Angeles; Deceased), and occasionally also directed, numerous low-budget action and suspense films, releasing through Paramount. Because of the bargain-basement budget of many of their early productions they were nicknamed "Dollar Bills."

FILMS INCLUDE (as producer, mostly in collaboration):

King of Alcatraz 1938; *Some Like It Hot* 1939; *The Farmer's Daughter* 1940; *No Hands on the Clock, Power Dive* 1941; *Wildcat* 1942; *Tornado, Gunner* (dir. by Pine) 1943; *Double Exposure* 1944; *Tokyo Rose, One Exciting Night/Midnight Manhunt* (also dir.) 1945; *Swamp Fire* (dir. by Pine), *They Made Me a Killer* (also dir.) 1946; *Big Town* (also dir.), *Big Town Scandal* (also dir.), *I Cover Big Town* (also dir.), *Big Town After Dark/Underworld After Dark* (also dir.) 1947; *Albuquerque* 1948; *Special Agent* (also dir.), *El Paso* 1949; *The Lawless, The Eagle and the Hawk* 1950; *The Last Outpost* 1951; *Hong Kong, Caribbean* 1952; *The Vanquished, Sangaree* 1953; *Jivaro* 1954; *Run for Cover, The Far Horizons, Lucy Gallant* 1955; *Nightmare* 1956; *The Big Caper* 1957.

Thompson, Carlos. Actor. *b.* Juan Carlos Mundin Schafter (or Mundanschaffter), June 7, 1916, Buenos Aires, of German descent *d.* 1990. *ed.* U. of Buenos Aires. A leading man of the Argentinian stage and screen, he played Continental-lover leads in a number of Hollywood films of the 50s, then continued his career in Europe, mostly in German films. In 1957 he married actress Lilli PALMER and settled with her in Switzerland. Several years later he quit acting and turned to writing and TV production. After Palmer's death of a heart attack in 1986, he became increasingly depressed. In September of 1990 he returned to Argentina, ending 37 years of self-exile. A month later he shot himself to death.

FILMS INCLUDE: In Argentina—*Y Magnana seran Hombres* 1939; *Los Verdes Paradisos* 1947; *Abuzo de Confianza* 1949; *El Crimen de Orib* 1950; *La Indesable* 1951; *El Tunnel* 1952. In the US—*Fort Algiers* 1953; *The Flame and the Flesh, Valley of the Kings* 1954; *El Ultimo Rebelde/The Last Rebel* (Mex.), *Magic Fire* (as Franz Liszt) 1956; *Raw Wind in Eden* 1958. In Europe—*Das Wirtshaus im Spessart/The Spessart Inn* (Ger.), *Stephanie* (Ger.) 1958; *Eva* (Aus.) 1959; *Frau Cheneys Ende/The Last of Mrs. Cheyney* (Ger.) 1961; *La Vie de Château* (Fr.) 1966.

Thompson, Emma. Actress. Born in 1959, in London, into a long line of theater folk. Gently radiant leading lady of the British stage and screen. The daughter of stage and TV director Eric Thompson and actress Phyllida Law, she began her acting life when a child. While studying English literature at Cambridge, she joined the Footlights, the school's variety group, and began writing for and performing in an all-woman program of comedy sketches. After graduating, she briefly performed as a bawdy stand-up comic, then began attracting widening attention through appearances on TV and West End stage productions. During that formative stage of her career she met actor-director Kenneth BRANAGH, who became her husband until their divorce in 1994. On the screen since the late 80s, she wowed critics with her intelligent performances, especially in James Ivory's *Howards End* (1992), for which she won the Academy Award as best actress. She was again in the Oscar spotlight, this time with dual nominations for *In the Name of the Father* (best supporting actress) and *The Remains of the Day* (best actress), both in 1993. Turning her attentions to screenwriting, she undertook the task of adapting Jane Austen's classic novel *Sense and Sensibility* (1995), taking the screenplay Oscar and yet another nomination as best actress for the same film.

FILMS: *The Tall Guy, Henry V* (as Katherine) 1989; *Impromptu* (US/Fr.) 1990; *Dead Again* (US) 1991; *Howards End, Peter's Friends* 1992; *Much Ado About Nothing* (UK), *The Remains of the Day* (UK), *In the Name of the Father* 1993; *Junior, My Father the Hero* (unbilled cameo) 1994; *Carrington, Sense and Sensibility* (also sc.) 1995; *The Winter Guest* 1997.

Thompson, J. Lee. See LEE THOMPSON, J.

Thompson, Jack. Actor. Born John Payne, on Aug. 31, 1940, in Sydney, Australia. Stalwart leading man and supporting player of Australian and international films. He turned to acting at the drama workshop of his alma mater, Queensland University. Memorable as the defending military attorney in *Breaker Morant* (1980). He formed his own production company, Pan Film Enterprises, and in 1988 was appointed to the board of the Australian Film Finance Corporation.

FILMS INCLUDE: *The Savage Wild* 1970; *Wake in Fright/Outback* 1971; *Libido* 1973; *Petersen* 1974; *Sunday Too Far Away* 1975; *Scobie Malone, Caddie, Mad Dog Morgan/Mad Dog* 1976; *The Chant of Jimmie Blacksmith* 1978; *The Journalist* 1979; *Breaker Morant, Earthling* 1980; *Bad Blood* (NZ/UK) 1981; *The Man from Snowy River* 1982; *Merry Christmas Mr. Lawrence* (UK/Jap.) 1983; *Burke and Wills* (as Burke), *Flesh and Blood* (US/Hol.) 1985; *Ground Zero* 1987; *Waterfront* 1988; *Turtle Beach, Wind* 1992; *The Sum of Us* 1994; *Last Dance* 1996.

Thompson, Lea. Actress. Born on May 31, 1961, in Rochester, Minn. Versatile young lead of the American screen. A professional dancer from age 14, she trained on scholarships to the Pennsylvania Ballet Company, the American Ballet Theatre, and the San Francisco Ballet before converting to acting in Burger King commercials of the early 80s. In films from 1983, she portrayed a wide range of characterizations, memorably as Lorraine Bates/McFly in *Back to the Future* (1985) and its sequels.

FILMS: *Jaws 3-D, All The Right Moves* 1983; *Red Dawn, The Wild Life* 1984; *Back to the Future, Yellow Pages/Going Undercover* (UK) 1985; *Spacecamp, Howard the Duck* 1986; *Some Kind of Wonderful* 1987; *The Wizard of Loneliness, Casual Sex?* 1988; *Back to the Future Part II* 1989; *Back to the Future Part III* 1990; *Article 99* 1992; *Dennis the Menace* 1993; *Little Rascals* 1994.

Thompson, Marshall. Actor. *b.* James Marshall Thompson, Nov. 27, 1925, Peoria, Ill. *d.* 1992. A descendant of Supreme Court Chief Justice John Marshall, he trained briefly for the clergy at Occidental College before opting for an acting career. Because of his lanky body and boyish face he was cast primarily in naïve juvenile roles in MGM films of the 40s and it wasn't until the 50s that he began tackling mature leads and second leads, as a freelance actor, at times even portraying psychopaths. More often, however, he was seen in a GI uniform or a space suit. In 1964 he directed himself in a mediocre war film, *A Yank in Vietnam,* a film also known as *Year of the Tiger.* He also appeared frequently on TV. In the early 60s he starred in the short-lived series 'The World of Giants' and 'Angel' and joined the staff of Ivan Tors productions as an actor and occasionally director of animal shorts. He starred in Tors's popular feature *Clarence the Cross-Eyed Lion* (1964) and subsequently (1966–69) in the derivative 'Daktari' TV series. He also directed several of the series' episodes. Thompson spent much of the 80s in Africa, where he produced, directed, and acted in the documentary series 'Orphans of the Wild.'

FILMS INCLUDE: *Reckless Age, The Purple Heart* 1944; *The Clock, The Valley of Decision, They Were Expendable* 1945; *Gallant Bess, The Secret Heart* 1946; *The Romance of Rosy Ridge* 1947; *Homecoming, Words and Music* 1948; *Command Decision, Roseanna McCoy, Battleground* 1949; *Mystery Street, Devil's Doorway, Dial 1119* 1950; *The Tall Target* 1951; *My Six Convicts, The Rose Bowl Story* 1952; *The Caddy* 1953; *To Hell and Back, Good Morning Miss Dove, Cult of the Cobra* 1955; *La Grande Caccia/East of Kilimanjaro* (It./US/UK) 1957; *The Fiend Without a Face, It! The Terror from Beyond Space* 1958; *The First Man Into Space* (UK) 1959; *Flight of the Lost Balloon* 1961; *No Man Is an Island* 1962; *A Yank in Vietnam* (also dir.)

1964; *Clarence the Cross-Eyed Lion* 1965; *To the Shores of Hell, Around the World Under the Sea* 1966; *George* (also prod.; Ger./Switz.) 1973; *The Turning Point* 1977; *Bog* 1978; *The Formula* 1980; *White Dog* 1982.

Thomson, Alex. Director of photography. Born on Jan. 12, 1923 in London. He entered British films in 1946. After a long period of apprenticeship, he became Nicolas ROEG's camera operator in the early 60s, working in that capacity on such films as *The Masque of the Red Death* (1964), *Fahrenheit 451* (1966), and *A Funny Thing Happened on the Way to the Forum* (also 1966). Elevated to a lighting cameraman in 1968, he went on to establish his own reputation as a cinematographer with a bold visual eye. He was nominated for an Oscar for *Excalibur* (1981).

FILMS INCLUDE: *Here We Go 'Round the Mulberry Bush* 1968; *Alf the Great* 1969; *The Night Digger* 1971; *Dr. Phibes Rises Again, Fear Is the Key* 1972; *The Man Who Would Be King* (2nd-unit phot.) 1975; *The Class of Miss MacMichael, The Cat and the Canary, Superman* (addnl. phot.) 1978; *Excalibur* 1981; *Eureka, The Keep* 1983; *Electric Dreams* (US) 1984; *Year of the Dragon* (US), *Legend* 1985; *Labyrinth, Raw Deal* (US), *Duet For One* (US/UK) 1986; *The Sicilian* (US), *Date with an Angel* (US) 1987; *Track 29, High Spirits* 1988; *Leviathan* (US/It.), *The Rachel Papers* 1989; *The Krays, Mr. Destiny* (US) 1990; *Alien 3* 1992; *Cliffhanger, Demolition Man* 1993; *Black Beauty* 1994; *Executive Decision* 1995; *Hamlet* 1996.

Thomson, Fred. Actor. *b.* Frederick Clifton Thomson, Feb. 26, 1890, Pasadena, Calif. *d.* 1928. The son of a Presbyterian minister, he was trained for the clergy at Occidental College in Los Angeles and at the Princeton Theological Seminary, where he excelled in various sports. He was ordained a minister in 1913 and appointed a pastor in Los Angeles and later in Nevada. Enlisted as a chaplain in WW I, he was recuperating from a broken leg at an Army hospital that was visited by film star Mary Pickford and famous screenwriter Frances MARION. After the war he saw much of Miss Marion and married her in 1919. Becoming a Hollywood resident, he left the ministry to enter films in a Mary Pickford vehicle, *The Love Light* (1921). Handsome, rugged, and athletic, he was soon signed by FBO as a cowboy star. His Westerns were slickly made and boasted excellent photography and good production values. They emphasized rapid action and dazzling stunts, with Thomson riding his famous horse, Silver King, and performing most of the acrobatics himself, rarely resorting to doubles. He quickly became one of the top cowboy stars of the 20s, rivaling Tom Mix in popularity. His career at FBO and later at Paramount lasted only seven years. He died of pneumonia at the height of his success on Christmas night 1928. He was only 38. Not to be confused with Fred or Frederick A. Thomson, a director of American silent films.

FILMS INCLUDE: *The Love Light, Just Around the Corner* 1921; *Penrod, Oath-Bound* 1922; *The Eagle's Talons* (serial) 1923; *The Mask of Lopez, Galloping Gallagher, The Silent Stranger, The Dangerous Coward, The Fighting Sap* 1924; *That Devil Quemado, The Wild Bull's Lair, Ridin' the Wind* 1925; *The Tough Guy, Hands Across the Border, The Two-Gun Man, Lone Hand Saunders* 1926; *Don Mike, Arizona Nights, Jesse James* 1927; *The Pioneer Scout, The Sunset Legion, Kit Carson* 1928.

Thorndike, Dame Sybil. Actress. *b.* Oct. 24, 1882, Gainsborough, England. *d.* 1976. Preeminent actress of the British stage and occasional films. She began her performing career as a concert pianist, but, after breaking a wrist, turned to acting, making her stage debut in 1904. She gained prominence in the 20s in the title role of 'Saint Joan,' a role said to have been tailored especially for her by G. B. Shaw, and for her portrayals of Greek tragedy heroines. In recognition of her achievements she was created Dame Commander of the British Empire in 1931. She often appeared with her husband, Lewis Casson, whom she married in 1908. He died in 1969. Her screen career was sporadic but replete with memorable performances.

FILMS INCLUDE: *Moth and Rust* 1921; *Dawn* (as Nurse Edith Cavell) 1928; *To What Red Hell* 1929; *Hindle Wakes* 1931; *Tudor Rose/Nine Days a Queen* 1936; *Major Barbara* (as Gen. Baines) 1941; *Nicholas Nickleby* (as Mrs. Squeers) 1947; *Britannia Mews/The Forbidden Street* (UK/US) 1949; *Stage Fright, Gone to Earth/The Wild Heart* 1950; *The Magic Box* 1951; *Melba* (as Queen Victoria; US) 1953; *The Prince and the Showgirl* 1957; *Alive and Kicking* 1958; *Shake Hands with the Devil* (Ire./US), *Jet Storm* 1959; *Hand in Hand, The Big Gamble* (US) 1961; *Uncle Vanya* (filmed theater) 1963.

Thornton, Billy Bob. Actor, director, writer. Multitalented character actor whose intelligent, heart-wrenching performance as a mentally retarded man in *Sling Blade* (1996) earned an Academy Award nomination in the best actor category as well as best adapted screenplay (from his story). Until that time, Thornton had worked mostly on the periphery of mainstream Hollywood, appearing in bit and supporting roles.

FILMS INCLUDE: *South of Reno* (bit) 1988; *For the Boys, One False Move* 1991; *Bound By Honor, Indecent Proposal, Tombstone* 1993; *Floundering, On Deadly Ground, The Stars Fell on Henrietta* 1994; *Dead Man* 1995; *Sling Blade* 1996; *Boogie Nights, U-Turn* 1997.

Thornton, Sigrid. Actress. Born in 1959, in Canberra, Australia. Personable, brunette leading lady of Australian films. On the stage from age nine and television from 13, she began appearing in feature films in 1977 and quickly became established as one of her country's premier screen heroines.

FILMS INCLUDE: *The Getting of Wisdom* 1977; *Snapshot* 1979; *Partners* 1981; *Duet for Four, The Man from Snowy River* 1982; *Street Hero* 1984; *Niel Lynne* 1985; *The Lighthorsemen, Slate & Me* 1987; *Return to Snowy River* 1988; *Great Expectations* (also assoc. prod.) 1990; *Over the Hill* 1992; *Trapped in Space* 1994.

Thorpe, Richard. Director. *b.* Rollo Smolt Thorpe, Feb. 24, 1896, Hutchinson, Kans. *d.* 1991. A former actor in vaudeville, stock, and musical comedy, he entered films in 1921 and appeared in various short and feature productions. He turned to directing in 1923 with a string of Charlie MURRAY comedy shorts, then turned out scores of low-budget Westerns, dramas, and comedies for various studios in the late silent and early sound era. His career began to pick up in the mid-30s, after he joined MGM. A prolific, technically proficient filmmaker, he rapidly advanced from second features to prestige productions. Over the next 30 years he proved himself to be a reliable director of all genres, ideally suited in his ability and temperament for working within the Hollywood studio system. Although he lacked a particular personal style and never directed a "great" picture, he had a consistently acceptable batting average as a director of fine, unpretentious entertainment, ranging from drama and polished adventure to comedy and musicals. In all he directed hundreds of films in some 45 years, retiring in 1967. His son, Jerry Thorpe (*b.* 1930), is a director and producer of features and TV movies.

FILMS INCLUDE (sound films complete): *Rough Ridin'* (also act.), *Battling Buddy, Fast and Fearless* 1924; *The Desert Demon, Saddle Cyclone, Full Speed* 1925; *The Bandit Buster* (also sc.), *College Days, Double Daring, The Fighting Cheat, Rawhide, Josselyn's Wife* 1926; *Between Dangers* (also sc.), *The Cyclone Cowboy, The Desert of the Lost, The First Night, Soda*

Water Cowboy, White Pebbles 1927; *The Vanishing West* (serial), *Vultures of the Sea* (serial), *The Cowboy Cavalier, Desperate Courage, The Valley of Hunted Men* 1928; *The Fatal Warning* (serial), *King of the Kongo* (serial), *The Bachelor Girl* 1929; *The Lone Defender* (serial), *Border Romance, The Dude Wrangler, Wings of Adventure, Under Montana Skies, The Utah Kid* 1930; *King of the Wild* (serial), *The Lawless Woman* (also co-sc.), *The Lady from Nowhere, Wild Horse* (co-dir. with Sidney Algier), *The Sky Spider, Grief Street, Neck and Neck, The Devil Plays* 1931; *Cross Examination, Murder at Dawn, Forgotten Women, Probation, The Midnight Lady, Escapade, Forbidden Company, Beauty Parlor, The King Murder, The Thrill of Youth, Slightly Married* 1932; *Women Won't Tell, The Secrets of Wu Sin, Love Is Dangerous, Forgotten, Strange People, I Have Lived, Notorious but Nice, Man of Sentiment, Rainbow Over Broadway* 1933; *Murder on the Campus, The Quitter, City Park, Stolen Sweets, Green Eyes, Cheating Cheaters* 1934; *Secret of the Chateau, Strange Wives, Last of the Pagans* 1935; *The Voice of Bugle Ann, Tarzan Escapes* 1936; *Dangerous Number, Night Must Fall, Double Wedding* 1937; *Man-Proof, Love Is a Headache, The First 100 Years, The Toy Wife, The Crowd Roars, Three Loves Has Nancy* 1938; *The Adventures of Huckleberry Finn, Tarzan Finds a Son* 1939; *The Earl of Chicago, Twenty-Mule Team, Wyoming* 1940; *The Bad Man, Barnacle Bill, Tarzan's Secret Treasure* 1941; *Joe Smith American, Tarzan's New York Adventure, Apache Trail, White Cargo* 1942; *Three Hearts for Julia, Above Suspicion, Cry Havoc* 1943; *Two Girls and a Sailor* 1944; *The Thin Man Goes Home, Thrill of a Romance, Her Highness and the Bellboy, What Next Corporal Hargrove?* 1945; *Fiesta, This Time for Keeps* 1947; *On an Island with You, A Date with Judy* 1948; *The Sun Comes Up, Big Jack, Challenge to Lassie* 1949; *Malaya, Black Hand, Three Little Words* 1950; *Vengeance Valley, The Great Caruso, The Unknown Man* 1951; *It's a Big Country* (co-dir.), *Carbine Williams, Ivanhoe, The Prisoner of Zenda* 1952; *The Girl Who Had Everything, All the Brothers Were Valiant* 1953; *Knights of the Round Table, The Flame and the Flesh, The Student Prince, Athena* 1954; *The Prodigal, Quentin Durward* 1955; *Ten Thousand Bedrooms, Tip on a Dead Jockey, Jailhouse Rock* 1957; *The House of the Seven Hawks* 1959; *Killers of Kilimanjaro* 1960; *I Tartari/The Tartars* (It./Yug.), *The Honeymoon Machine* 1961; *The Horizontal Lieutenant* 1962; *Follow the Boys, Fun in Acapulco* 1963; *The Golden Head* (Hung./US), *The Truth About Spring, That Funny Feeling* 1965; *The Scorpio Letters* (made for TV), *The Last Challenge* (also prod.) 1967.

threading. The proper placing of film over the sprockets and through the guides and paths of a camera, projector, or other motion picture apparatus before it is put into operation.

3-D. Three-dimensional films. See STEREOSCOPIC CINEMA.

Three Stooges, The. See STOOGES, THE THREE.

throw. The distance between a projector lens and the screen on which a film is shown.

Thulin, Ingrid. Actress. Born on Jan. 27, 1929, in Solleftea, Sweden. After ballet studies, she trained for the stage at Stockholm's Royal Dramatic Theater and took up pantomime with Etienne Decroux in Paris. She began her film career while still a student, in 1948, but it wasn't until she began working for director Ingmar BERGMAN, at the Malmö Municipal Theater and in films from the mid-50s, that she emerged as one of the finest dramatic stage and screen actresses of her country. A cool, aloof blonde beauty with both an intellectual and intuitive grasp of her roles, she ventured into international films in the early 60s, appearing notably in Alain Resnais's *La Guerre est finie* (France) and Luchino Visconti's *The Damned* (Italy). She shared the best actress award at Cannes in 1958 for her role in Bergman's *Brink of Life.* She is married to Harry Schein, the founder of the Swedish Film Institute. She directed a short and two features.

FILMS INCLUDE: *Where the Winds Blow* 1948; *Love Will Conquer* 1949; *Jack of Hearts* 1950; *Foreign Intrigue* (US) 1956; *Wild Strawberries* 1957; *Brink of Life, The Magician* 1958; *The Judge* 1960; *The Four Horsemen of the Apocalypse* (US) 1962; *Winter Light, The Silence* 1963; *Die Lady/Games of Desire* (Ger./Fr.), *Sextet* (Den.) 1964; *Return from the Ashes* (US/UK) 1965; *La Guerre est finie* (Fr./Sw.), *Night Games* 1966; *Adélaide* (Fr./It.), *Hour of the Wolf* 1968; *The Ritual, La Caduta degli Dei/Götterdämmerung/The Damned* (It./Ger.) 1969; *Cries and Whispers* 1972; *A Handful of Love* 1974; *Devotion* (short; also dir.), *Catalepsis* (It.), *La Cage* (Fr.) 1975; *Moses* (as Miriam; UK/It.), *Salon Kitty/Madam Kitty* (It./Ger./Fr.) 1976; *The Cassandra Crossing* (US), *E Comincio il Viaggio nella Vertigini* (It.) 1977; *One and One* (also co-dir.) 1978; *Brusten Himmel/Broken Sky* (dir. only) 1982; *At the Rehearsal* 1984; *Il Giorno Prima/Control* (It./Fr./Can.) 1987; *La Casa Del Sorriso/House of Smiles* (It.) 1991.

Thundercloud, Chief. Actor. *b.* Victor Daniels, Apr. 12, 1899, Muskogee, Okla. *d.* 1955. *ed.* U. of Arizona. A full-blooded Indian but not really a chief, he worked as a cowpuncher, miner, and rodeo performer, among other occupations, before entering films in the late 20s. For several years he performed stunts and played extra and bit parts. He gained some popularity among young crowds in the late 30s when he played Tonto in a couple of "Lone Ranger" serials and a feature film. He later played Indian chiefs and exotic natives in many films, including the title role in *Geronimo* (1950). Another Chief Thundercloud (1901–67) appeared in some B Westerns of the 30s.

FILMS INCLUDE: *The Big Trail* 1930; *Ramona* 1936; *The Lone Ranger* (serial) 1938; *Geronimo, Typhoon, Hi-Yo Silver, North West Mounted Police* 1940; *Hudson's Bay, Western Union* 1941; *Buffalo Bill* 1944; *The Senator Was Indiscreet* 1947; *Ambush, Davy Crockett Indian Scout, Colt .45, I Killed Geronimo* 1950; *Buffalo Bill in Tomahawk Territory* 1952.

Thurman, Uma. Actress. Born on Apr. 29, 1970, in Boston. Tall, willowy, enticing young lead of the late 80s and early 90s. She grew up on the campus of Amherst College, where her father is professor of Buddhism and comparative literature and her Swedish-born mother practices psychotherapy. She began modeling while still in high school and deferred college to launch her screen career at 17. She impressed the following year in the role of the seduced virgin in Stephen Frears's *Dangerous Liaisons* (1988). In *Pulp Fiction* (1994), she played a mobster's girlfriend who mistakes heroin for cocaine and suffers a seriously horrifying rescue from her overdose abyss. Her performance earned a supporting actress Academy Award nomination. She is divorced from actor Gary OLDMAN.

FILMS: *Kiss Daddy Goodnight* 1987; *Johnny Be Good, Dangerous Liaisons* 1988; *Adventures of Baron Munchausen* 1989; *Where the Heart Is, Henry & June* (as June Miller) 1990; *Final Analysis, Jennifer Eight, Mad Dog and Glory* 1992; *Even Cowgirls Get the Blues, A Month By the Lake, Pulp Fiction* 1994; *The 8th Day, Beautiful Girls, The Truth About Cats and Dogs* 1996; *Batman and Robin* 1997.

Tibbett, Lawrence. Singer, actor. *b.* Nov. 16, 1896, Bakersfield, Calif. *d.* 1960. The son of a sheriff who was killed in a battle with cattle rustlers, he helped support the family while attending high school in Los Angeles. He also took voice lessons and began a professional singing career that led to a contract with the Metropolitan Opera in New York in 1923. He soon gained a reputation as one of the world's finest baritones. He remained with the Met for 28 years. In the early 30s he starred in a number of early sound musical films. He was nominated for an Academy Award as best actor for his performance in his film debut, *The Rogue Song* (1930).

FILMS: *The Rogue Song, New Moon* 1930; *The Prodigal, The Cuban Love Song* 1931; *Metropolitan* 1935; *Under Your Spell* 1936.

Ticotin, Rachel. Actress. Born on Nov. 1, 1958, in the Bronx, N.Y., of Hispanic descent. Brunette leading lady of American films and television. She is married to actor David CARUSO.

FILMS INCLUDE: *King of the Gypsies* (bit) 1978; *Fort Apache the Bronx, Four Friends* 1981; *Critical Condition* 1987; *Total Recall* 1990; *F/X2, One Good Cop* 1991; *Where the Day Takes You* 1992; *Falling Down* 1993; *Don Juan DeMarco, Steal Big Steal Little* 1995; *ConAir* 1997.

Tierney, Gene. Actress. *b.* Nov. 20, 1920, Brooklyn, N.Y. *d.* 1991, of emphysema. The daughter of a prosperous broker, she was educated in private schools in Connecticut and Switzerland. When she expressed an interest in an acting career after her society debut, her father formed a family owned corporation, Belle-Tier, to develop, promote, and exploit her untried talent. Exquisitely etched cheekbones, slanted blue-green eyes, and an exotic feline beauty helped her break into Broadway in 1939. She played supporting parts in several plays, including 'The Male Animal' (1940). The latter play was seen by Darryl F. Zanuck, who signed her to a 20th Century-Fox contract. The agreement guaranteed her the right to return to Broadway once a year, an option she never did or never was able to exercise. Instead, she settled on a film career that consisted for the most part of routine feminine leads but included a number of high points that made her an important Hollywood star. Among these were the mysterious title role in *Laura* and her portrayal of a murderous vixen in *Leave Her to Heaven,* for which she received her only Oscar nomination.

In 1941, Miss Tierney married designer Oleg Cassini. Two years later they suffered a personal tragedy when their first daughter was born mentally retarded as a result of the German measles Gene had contracted during her pregnancy. After her divorce from Cassini in 1952, Miss Tierney was seeing a lot of Aly Khan, Rita Hayworth's former husband. But their marriage plans were strongly opposed by the Aga Khan. When Aly left her, Gene suffered a nervous breakdown and was admitted to a Hartford, Conn., sanitarium. She was discharged after a year and a half but was later committed to another institution for a period of eight months. After her marriage to a Houston oilman (an ex of Hedy Lamarr) in 1960, she returned to acting on a part-time basis and subsequently played character parts in occasional films and made several appearances on TV. Her autobiography, *Self Portrait* (1979), reveals that she regularly dated John F. Kennedy during his Navy days and frankly discusses her past misfortunes.

FILMS: *The Return of Jesse James* 1940; *Hudson's Bay, Tobacco Road* (as Ellie May), *Belle Starr* (title role), *Sundown* 1941; *The Shanghai Gesture, Son of Fury, Rings on Her Fingers, Thunder Birds* 1942; *China Girl, Heaven Can Wait* 1943; *Laura* 1944; *A Bell for Adano, Leave Her to Heaven* 1945; *Dragonwyck, The Razor's Edge* 1946; *The Ghost and Mrs. Muir* 1947; *The Iron Curtain, That Wonderful Urge* 1948; *Whirlpool, Night and the City, Where the Sidewalk Ends* 1950; *The Mating Season, On the Riviera, The Secret of Convict Lake, Close to My Heart* 1951; *Way of a Gaucho, Plymouth Adventure* 1952; *Never Let Me Go* 1953; *Personal Affair* (UK), *Black Widow, The Egyptian* 1954; *The Left Hand of God* 1955; *Advise and Consent* 1962; *Toys in the Attic* 1963; *The Pleasure Seekers* 1964.

Tierney, Lawrence. Actor. Born on Mar. 15, 1919, in Brooklyn, N.Y. *ed.* Manhattan Coll., where he excelled in track athletics. The older brother of Scott BRADY, he had a brief stage career before entering films in 1943. He has played both leads and supporting parts, typically as a tough, ruthless character. He is best remembered for the title role in *Dillinger* (1945). Tough ruthlessness has characterized his private life as well. His frequent brushes with the law on charges of drunken driving and disorderly conduct have been widely publicized. In 1973 he was stabbed in a barroom brawl in Manhattan.

FILMS INCLUDE: *The Ghost Ship* 1943; *Youth Runs Wild* 1944; *Dillinger* (title role), *Back to Bataan* 1945; *Badman's Territory, Step by Step, San Quentin* 1946; *Born to Kill* 1947; *Bodyguard* 1948; *Shakedown, Kill or Be Killed* 1950; *The Hoodlum* 1951; *The Greatest Show on Earth* 1952; *The Steel Cage* 1954; *Female Jungle* 1956; *A Child Is Waiting* 1963; *Custer of the West* 1968; *Abduction* 1975; *Andy Warhol's Bad* 1977; *Arthur, Midnight/Backwoods Massacre* 1981; *Prizzi's Honor, Silver Bullet* 1985; *Murphy's Romance* 1986; *Tough Guys Don't Dance* 1987; *Wizards of the Demon Sword* 1991; *Reservoir Dogs, The Runestone* 1992.

Tiffin, Pamela. Actress. Born Pamela Wonso, on Oct. 13, 1942, in Oklahoma City, Okla. *ed.* Hunter Coll. (NYC). A model in her teens, she trained for the stage with Stella Adler, entered films in the early 60s, and for a decade played cute ingenues and feminine leads in Hollywood productions. She then settled in Rome, where for several years she starred in routine Italian films. At one time she was married to magazine publisher Clay Felker.

FILMS INCLUDE: *Summer and Smoke, One Two Three* 1961; *State Fair* 1962; *Come Fly with Me* 1963; *For Those Who Think Young, The Lively Set, The Pleasure Seekers* 1964; *Oggi Domani e Dopodomani/Kiss the Other Sheik* (It./Fr.), *The Hallelujah Trail* 1965; *Harper* 1966; *Viva Max!* 1969; *Cose di Cosa Nostra/The Godson* (It./Fr.), *Giornata Nera per l'Ariete* (It.) 1971; *Los Amigos/Deaf Smith and Johnny Ears* (Sp./It.), *Punto e a Capo* (It.) 1973; *Evil Fingers* (It.) 1974.

tight shot. A shot in which the subject matter fills almost the entire frame.

Tiller, Nadja. Actress. Born on Mar. 16, 1929, in Vienna, the daughter of an actor and an opera-singer mother. A former model and bit player on the stage, she entered films in 1949 after winning the Miss Austria beauty crown. She exuded raw sexuality in many German and international films, often in productions directed by Rolf THIELE. She is married to German screen actor Walter Giller.

FILMS INCLUDE: *Eroica* 1949; *Illusion in Moll* 1952; *Sie, Der letzte Sommer* 1954; *Die Barrings, Ball im Savoy* 1955; *Mozart/The Life and Loves of Mozart* (Aus.), *Friedrike von Barring, Ich suche Dich* 1956; *Le Désordre et la Nuit/Night Affair* (Fr.), *Das Mädchen Rosemarie/Rosemary* 1958; *Du Rififi chez les Femmes/Riff Raff Girls* (Fr./It.), *The Rough and the Smooth/Portrait of a Sinner* (UK), *Labyrinth, Die Buddenbrooks* 1959; *La Chambre ardente/The Burning Court* (Fr./Ger./It.), *Lulu* (Aus.), *Anima nera* (It.) 1962; *Das grosse Libesspiel/And So to Bed* 1963; *Tonio Kröger* (Ger./Fr.) 1964; *Du Rififi à Paname/The Upper Hand* (Fr./It./Ger.), *The Poppy Is Also a Flower* (originally made for TV; US), *Tendre Voyou/Tender Scoundrel* (Fr./It.) 1966; *Lady Hamilton* (Fr./It./Ger.) 1968; *Ohrfeigen* 1969; *L'Etrusco uccide ancora/The Dead Are Alive* (It./Yug./Ger.) 1972; *Slap in the Face, The Silkworm, Babysitter* (It./Fr./Ger.) 1975.

Tilly, Jennifer. Actress. Born September 10, 1958, in British Columbia, Canada. *ed.* Stephens College. Appealing, offbeat, comedically gifted actress of stage, television, and films. Starting out on the stage then on to episodic television, she has worked consistently in films since her debut in *No Small Affair* (1984). She earned a supporting actress Academy Award nomination for her star turn in Woody Allen's *Bullets Over Broadway* (1994). Her sister is actress Meg TILLY.

FILMS: *No Small Affair* 1984; *Moving Violations* 1985; *Inside Out* 1986; *He's My Girl, Rented Lips* 1987; *High Spirits, Johnny Be Good, Remote Control* 1988; *The Fabulous Baker Boys, Far from Home, Let It Ride* 1989; *Scorchers* 1991; *Made in America, Shadow of the Wolf* 1993; *Bullets Over Broadway, The Getaway* 1994; *Bound* 1996.

Tilly, Meg. Actress. Born in 1960, in California. Delicate, quietly elegant, brunette leading lady of the American screen. Publicity shy, she released no information concerning her background. Apparently raised in Texada, Canada, she began her career in her teens as a dancer with a local community troupe but switched to acting after a back injury. She arrived in New York at age 16 and following some TV work made an unassuming film debut with a fleeting appearance in *Fame* (1980). Becoming rapidly established as a fine young actress, she won an Oscar nomination for best supporting actress for her portrait of a possessed nun in *Agnes of God* (1985). She is married to studio executive John Calley. Her sister, Jennifer TILLY is also a screen actress.

FILMS: *Fame* (bit) 1980; *Tex* 1982; *One Dark Night, The Big Chill, Psycho* II 1983; *Impulse* 1984; *Agnes of God* 1985; *Beat* 1986; *Masquerade, The Girl in a Swing* (UK/US) 1988; *Valmont* (Fr./UK) 1989; *The Two Jakes* 1990; *Leaving Normal* 1992; *Body Snatchers*, *Sleep with Me* 1994.

tilt. The pivotal movement of a camera in a vertical plane. In a tilt shot, the camera is moved up (tilt up) or down (tilt down), in contrast with a PAN shot, in which the camera is moved horizontally.

time lapse. A cinematographic technique in which individual frames of film are exposed at predetermined intervals. When the film is projected at normal speed it produces a compressed visual record of events occurring over long periods of time, such as flowers blooming or a chick emerging from its egg. When used in conjunction with a microscope, the technique can aid in the analysis of chemical processes and other scientific phenomena. Time lapse, which was used to great effect in the French film *Farrebique,* can be accomplished with any motion picture camera designed to take single frames. To ensure accuracy, cameras are linked to timing devices that turn them on and off at regular intervals.

timing. 1. The manipulation of action by a director or an actor to achieve a desired tempo or a certain effect in a scene. 2. In laboratory procedures, the evaluation by technicians of the density and tonal value of each frame of film, against a predetermined standard, before the actual printing. Experienced timers use a subjective visual approach in evaluating tonal value. Their objective is to achieve a consistent tonal balance throughout an entire film. Recommendations for corrections are listed in detail on *timing cards.*

Tinling, James. Director. *b.* May 8, 1889, Seattle. *d.* 1967. *ed.* U. of Washington. He entered films in the early 20s as a prop boy and occasional stuntman. He later worked in the script department at Fox and served his apprenticeship as assistant director under Howard HAWKS. From the late 20s to the late 40s he directed many films, mostly routine B pictures, typically minor thrillers and light fare. In the early 50s he quit films for TV.

FILMS: *Very Confidential* 1927; *Soft Living, Don't Marry* 1928; *True Heaven, The Exalted Flapper, Words and Music* 1929; *One Mad Kiss* (co-dir. with Marcel Silver), *For the Love of L'il* 1930; *The Flood* 1931; *El Ultime Varon sobre la Tierra* (in Spanish), *Arizona to Broadway, The Last Trail, Jimmy and Sally* 1933; *Three on a Honeymoon, Call It Luck, Love Time* 1934; *Señor Casada necesita marido* (in Spanish), *Under the Pampas Moon, Welcome Home, Charlie Chan in Shanghai* 1935; *Every Saturday Night, Champagne Charlie, Educating Father, Pepper, Back to Nature* 1936; *The Holy Terror, Angel's Holiday, Sing and Be Happy, The Great Hospital Mystery, 45 Fathers* 1937; *Change of Heart, Mr. Moto's Gamble, Passport Husband, Sharpshooters* 1938; *Boy Friend* 1939; *Last of the Duanes, Riders of the Purple Sage* 1941; *Sundown Jim, The Lone Star Ranger* 1942; *Cosmo Jones—Crime Smasher* 1943; *Rendezvous 24, Deadline for Murder, Dangerous Millions* 1946; *Strange Journey, Second Chance, Roses Are Red* 1947; *Night Wind, Trouble Preferred* 1948; *Tales of Robin Hood* 1951.

Tiomkin, Dimitri. Composer, music director. *b.* May 10, 1899, near St. Petersburg, Russia. *d.* 1979. A graduate of the St. Petersburg Conservatory of Music and St. Petersburg University, and the holder of a doctor of law degree from the University of St. Mary's, he began his musical career in 1919 as a concert pianist and conductor. In the 20s he introduced George Gershwin's music to Europe in a successful concert tour. He emigrated to the US in 1925 and was naturalized in 1937. In Hollywood since the early 30s, he scored numerous films in a wide range of genres and styles. He was perhaps the most versatile and certainly the best known of the American screen's composers. His melodious scores combined elements from both the European and American cultures, and he admitted to generous borrowing from the classical and folk repertoire of both continents. In 40 years as a screen composer, he contributed memorable scores and theme songs for many important films, ranging from a lone harmonica sound in *High Noon* (1952) to a 100-piece orchestra in *Giant* (1956). He won Academy Awards for the scores of *High Noon* (two Oscars: for best score and best theme song), *The High and the Mighty* (1954), and *The Old Man and the Sea* (1958), and was nominated for several other Oscars. He also won many other international awards and citations. He authored an autobiography, *Please Don't Hate Me* (1960), and produced and directed the Soviet-American co-production *Tschaikovsky* (1970).

FILMS INCLUDE: *Devil-May-Care* (ballet music) 1929; *Lord Byron of Broadway* (ballet music), *The Rogue Song* (ballet music) 1930; *Resurrection* 1931; *Alice in Wonderland* 1933; *Mad Love* 1935; *Lost Horizon* 1937; *Spawn of the North, The Great Waltz, You Can't Take it with You* 1938; *Mr. Smith Goes to Washington, Only Angels Have Wings* 1939; *The Westerner* 1940; *The Corsican Brothers, Meet John Doe* 1941; *The Moon and Sixpence* 1942; *Shadow of a Doubt* 1943; *Why We Fight* (WW II doc. series) 1943–44; *The Battle of St. Pietro* (doc.), *The Bridge of San Luis Rey* 1944; *Dillinger* 1945; *It's a Wonderful Life, The Dark Mirror* 1946; *Duel in the Sun, The Long Night* 1947; *Red River, Portrait of Jennie* 1948; *Champion, Home of the Brave* 1949; *The Men* 1950; *Cyrano de Bergerac, Strangers on a Train, The Thing* 1951; *The Big Sky, High Noon* 1952; *Blowing Wild, I Confess* 1953; *Dial M for Murder, The High and the Mighty* 1954; *Giant, Friendly Persuasion* 1956; *Wild Is the Wind, Gunfight at the O.K. Corral* 1957; *The Old Man and the Sea* 1958; *Rio Bravo* 1959; *The Alamo, The Sundowners, The Unforgiven* 1960; *Town Without Pity, The Guns of Navarone* 1961; *55 Days at Peking* 1963; *The Fall of the Roman Empire* 1964; *The War Wagon* 1967; *Mackenna's Gold* (co-prod. only) 1969; *Tschaikovsky* (prod., dir., orchestrated; US/USSR) 1970.

Tippett, Phil. Special effects artist. Born in 1951 in Berkeley, Calif. As a child he was mesmerized by Ray Harryhausen's STOP MOTION animation in *The Seventh Voyage of*

Sinbad (1958). At age 13, he bought an 8 mm camera and taught himself the technique. After a stint in art school, he animated puppets for low-budget films and TV commercials, including the Pillsbury Doughboy. His big break in feature films came when he joined INDUSTRIAL LIGHT & MAGIC (ILM) to animate the miniature chess game in *Star Wars* (1977). He has stayed almost continuously with ILM since then, designing and animating creatures for numerous projects and sharing an Oscar for *Return of the Jedi* (1983). He helped develop the technique of GO-MOTION to bring to life the dragon in *Dragonslayer* (1981).

FILMS INCLUDE: *Star Wars* 1977; *The Empire Strikes Back* 1980; *Dragonslayer* 1981; *Return of the Jedi* 1983; *Indiana Jones and the Temple of Doom* 1984; *Willow* 1988; *Robocop 2* 1990; *Jurassic Park, Robocop 3* 1993.

Tissé, Edward. Director of photography. *b.* Apr. 1, 1897, Lithuania, to a Swedish father and a Russian mother. *d.* 1961. A newsreel cameraman during the Russian Revolution, he rose to international prominence in the 20s as Sergei EISENSTEIN's regular cameraman. He was the director of photography on all Eisenstein's films and contributed much to the visual quality of the Soviet master's work. He accompanied Eisenstein on his American trip in the late 20s and shot the exquisite footage for the unfinished *Que Viva Mexico!* He also collaborated with other Soviet directors, with less remarkable results.

FILMS INCLUDE: *Signal* (co-phot.) 1918; *Sickle and Hammer, Hunger Hunger Hunger* 1921; *Elder Vasili Gryaznov* 1924; *Jewish Luck* (co-phot.), *Strike* (co-phot.), *Potemkin* 1925; *Ten Days That Shook the World/October* 1927; *Old and New/The General Line* 1929; *Romance sentimentale* (Fr.), *Frauennot-Frauengluck* (doc.; also dir.; Switz.) 1930; *Que Viva Mexico!* (unfinished, 1931; footage used in Sol Lesser's *Thunder Over Mexico,* 1934, and in two other films), *Aerogard* 1935; *Alexander Nevsky* 1938; *Ivan the Terrible* (Pt. I, II; co-phot., 1944–46; Pt. II not released until 1958); *Meeting on the Elbe* 1949; *Glinka* 1952; *The Immortal Garrison* (co-dir. with Z. Agranenko) 1956.

Tissier, Jean. Actor. *b.* Apr. 1, 1896, Paris. *d.* 1973. Character player of hundreds of French films, mostly routine, since 1934, following stage experience from the early 20s; often in comic roles. A former journalist, he wrote an autobiography, *Sans Maquillage* (1945).

FILMS INCLUDE: *Voyage imprévu/The Slipper Episode* 1934; *La Garçonne* 1936; *L'Affaire du Courrier de Lyon/The Courier of Lyons* 1937; *Carrefour/Crossroads* 1938; *Battement de Coeur* 1939; *Fausse Alerte/The French Way* 1940; *Nous les Gosses, Premier Rendez-Vous/Her First Affair* 1941; *Les Inconnus dans la Maison/Strangers in the House, L'Assassin habite au 21/The Murderer Lives at Number 21* 1942; *Au Bonheur des Dames/Shop-Girls of Paris* 1943; *Les Aventures de Casanova/Loves of Casanova* 1947; *Les Casse-Pieds/The Spice of Life, Gigi* 1949; *Prima Communione/Father's Dilemma* (It.), *Quai de Grenelle/The Strollers* 1950; *Papa Maman la Bonne et moi/Mama Papa the Maid and I* 1954; *Boulevard du Crime* 1955; *Et Dieu créa la Femme/And God Created Woman, Notre Dame de Paris/The Hunchback of Notre Dame* (as Louis XI) 1956; *Candide* (as Dr. Jacques) 1960; *Strip-Tease/Sweet Skin* 1963; *Le Voci bianche/White Voices* (It./Fr.) 1964; *Deux Billets pour Mexico/Dead Run* 1967; *La Veuve Couderc* 1971.

titles. Written matter inserted into a film for introductory or explanatory purpose. In modern films, titles appear most often in the form of the opening and closing credits. The title spelling out the name of the picture is known as the "main title." The others are simply known as "credit titles" or "secondary credit titles." The title announcing the end of a film is naturally called the "end title." Titles superimposed on the bottom of the frame as translation of foreign dialogue are known as SUBTITLES.

In the early Nickelodeon days, beautifully lettered titles were used not only to explain the action but also as a substitute for spoken dialogue and as a means of communication with an uninitiated audience ("Would the ladies please remove their hats," etc.). As the star system began to emerge, credit titles assumed major importance. The order of billing and the size of lettering were regulated by a complicated set of rules. The actor or actress whose name appeared before or above the main title had formal proof of his or her status as a big star. After the transition to sound, when explanatory and dialogue titles were largely disposed of, the attention of title artists focused on variations in the design of the credit titles. Not only did the lettering become more ornate, but an effort was often made to decorate titles in accordance with the particular theme of the film—scrolls for Biblical epics, cartoon characters for comedies, etc. In the 50s graphics designer Saul Bass introduced an exciting new style of credit titles, combining live action with imaginative graphic designs in such films as *Carmen Jones, The Man with the Golden Arm,* and *Anatomy of a Murder.* His title sequence for *Around the World in 80 Days* was a colossal production in its own right.

In the 60s split screens and other complex optical effects were introduced into titles. By the 70s the trend was away from the ornate and toward simple block lettering superimposed during the opening scene of a film. Credit titles were often introduced well after the beginning of the film to allow the plot and the action to seize the attention of the viewer in a segment known as a teaser. In the late 70s and 80s, films like *Star Wars*, with its serial-like "title crawl" stating the action so far, and *Indiana Jones and the Temple of Doom*, with opening titles integrated into a dance number, marked a renewed interest in title design as a way of establishing a film's individual style. The comedy *Soapdish* featured Bass-inspired graphic design in its opening credits, while the kinetic title sequences in Spike Lee's *Do the Right Thing* and *Jungle Fever* helped set a tone of urban excitement and tension.

T-numbers. See T-STOP.

Toback, James. Screenwriter, director, producer. Born on Nov. 23, 1944, in New York, N.Y. *ed.* Harvard, Columbia. Former teacher of literature at the City College of New York and widely published journalist who became a screenwriter in the 70s and later a director. He was nominated for an Academy Award for his screenplay for *Bugsy*. Author: *Jim*, on former football player Jim Brown.

FILMS INCLUDE (as screenwriter): *The Gambler* 1974; *Fingers* (also dir.) 1977; *Love & Money* (also dir., prod.) 1980; *Exposed* (also dir., prod., act.) 1983; *The Pick-Up Artist* (also dir.) 1987; *The Big Bang* (doc., also dir., act.) 1989; *Alice* (act. only) 1990; *Bugsy* (also act.) 1991.

Tobias, George. Actor. *b.* 1901, New York City. *d.* 1980. A veteran of the stage (Provincetown Players, Theatre Guild, etc.), he entered films in the late 30s and went on to play character parts, both nice guys and heels, both comic and dramatic, in many film and television productions. He had his best film roles at Warners in the 40s, but gained still greater recognition as neighbor Abner Kravitz on the TV sitcom 'Bewitched' (1964–72).

FILMS INCLUDE: *Maisie, Ninotchka, The Hunchback of Notre Dame, Balalaika* 1939; *Saturday's Children, Torrid Zone, They Drive by Night, City for Conquest, South of Suez* 1940; *Strawberry Blonde, Out of the Fog, Sergeant York* 1941; *Captains of the Clouds, Yankee Doodle Dandy, Wings for the Eagle, My Sister Eileen* 1942; *Air Force, Mission to Moscow, This Is the Army* 1943; *Passage to Marseille, Between Two*

Worlds 1944; *Objective Burma, Mildred Pierce* 1945; *Nobody Lives Forever* 1946; *Sinbad the Sailor, My Wild Irish Rose* 1947; *The Set-Up* 1949; *Southside 1-1000* 1950; *Rawhide, Ten Tall Men* 1951; *The Glenn Miller Story* 1954; *The Seven Little Foys* 1955; *Silk Stockings* 1957; *Marjorie Morningstar* 1958; *A New Kind of Love* 1963; *The Glass Bottom Boat* 1966; *The Phynx* (cameo) 1970.

Tobin, Genevieve. Actress. Born on Nov. 29, 1901, in New York City. Lively blonde, green-eyed leading lady of the American stage and screen. On the stage as a child, she interrupted her career to complete her schooling in New York and Paris, then returned to Broadway as a young adult in 1928. She appeared in a single silent film but remained primarily a stage actress until the early 30s, when she settled in Hollywood. She spent most of her screen career at Warner Bros., where she played leads and second leads in many films, often in roguish or flirtatious roles. She married director William KEIGHLEY in 1938 and a couple of years later retired from the screen. Widowed in 1972, she has residences in New York and Paris.

FILMS INCLUDE: *No Mother to Guide Her* 1923; *A Lady Surrenders, Free Love* 1930; *Seed, Up for Murder, The Gay Diplomat* 1931; *One Hour with You, Hollywood Speaks* 1932; *Perfect Understanding, Pleasure Cruise, Infernal Machine, The Wrecker, Goodbye Again, I Loved a Woman* 1933; *Easy to Love, Dark Hazard, The Ninth Guest, Success at Any Price, Kiss and Make-Up, Uncertain Lady* 1934; *The Woman in Red, The Goose and the Gander, Here's to Romance, The Case of the Lucky Legs, Broadway Hostess* 1935; *The Petrified Forest, Snowed Under* 1936; *The Great Gambini* 1937; *Dramatic School* 1938; *Zaza* 1939; *No Time for Comedy* 1940; *Queen of Crime* 1941.

Tobolowsky, Stephen. Actor. Born on May 30, 1951, in Dallas, Tex. *ed.* Southern Methodist U. Portly, balding character player adept at villainous or comedic everyman roles. Active in films since 1984. Has appeared widely on TV.

FILMS INCLUDE: *Swing Shift* 1984; *True Stories* (also co-sc.), *Nobody's Fool* 1986; *Spaceballs* 1987; *Mississippi Burning* 1988; *Checking Out, Two Idiots in Hollywood* (also dir., sc.), *Great Balls of Fire, In Country, Breaking In* 1989; *Bird on a Wire, Funny About Love, Welcome Home, Roxy Carmichael, The Grifters* 1990; *Thelma & Louise, Memoirs of an Invisible Man* 1991; *Basic Instinct, Roadside Prophets, Single White Female, Where the Day Takes You, Sneakers, Hero* 1992; *The Pickle, Groundhog Day, Josh and S.A.M.* 1993; *My Father the Hero, Radioland Murders* 1994; *Dr. Jekyll and Ms. Hyde, Murder in the First* 1995.

Todd, Ann. Actress. *b.* Jan. 24, 1909, in Hartford, England. *d.* 1993. On the British stage from 1928, she entered films in the early 30s and became an internationally popular star in the mid-40s as a result of her role as a vulnerable pianist in the highly romantic drama *The Seventh Veil.* Her third husband (1949–57) was David LEAN, who directed several of her pictures. In the 60s she produced, wrote, and directed several travel documentaries.

FILMS: *Keepers of Youth, These Charming People, The Ghost Train* 1931; *The Water Gypsies* 1932; *The Return of Bulldog Drummond* 1934; *Things to Come* 1936; *Action for Slander, The Squeaker/Murder on Diamond Row* 1937; *South Riding* 1938; *Poison Pen* 1939; *Danny Boy, Ships with Wings* 1941; *The Seventh Veil* 1945; *Gaiety George/Showtime* 1946; *Daybreak* 1947; *The Paradine Case* (US), *So Evil My Love* (US/UK) 1948; *The Passionate Friends/One Woman's Story* 1949; *Madeleine* 1950; *The Sound Barrier/Breaking Through the Sound Barrier* 1952; *The Green Scarf* 1954; *Time Without Pity* 1957; *Taste of Fear/Scream of Fear* 1961; *The Son of Captain Blood* (It./Sp./US) 1962; *90 Degrees in the Shade* (Czech./UK) 1965; *The Fiend/Beware of the Brethren* 1971; *The Human Factor* (UK) 1979; *Ingrid* (UK), *Hitchcock Il Brivido del Genio* (It.), *The McGuffin* (UK) 1985.

Todd, Ann (E.). American actress. Born Anne Todd Mayfield in 1932. Moderately popular child star of Hollywood films of the 30s and 40s. She added the middle initial "E" to her screen name in the mid-40s to avoid confusion with the British actress Ann Todd.

FILMS INCLUDE: *Stronger Than Desire, Intermezzo, Destry Rides Again* 1939; *The Blue Bird, All This and Heaven Too, Brigham Young* 1940; *Blood and Sand, How Green Was My Valley, Remember the Day* 1941; *Kings Row* 1942; *Roughly Speaking, Pride of the Marines* 1945; *My Reputation, The Jolson Story, Margie* 1946; *Three Daring Daughters* 1948; *Cover-Up* 1949; *The Lion Hunters* 1951.

Todd-AO. See TODD, Michael; WIDE-SCREEN PROCESSES.

Todd, Michael ("Mike"). Producer, promoter, showman. *b.* Avram Goldenbogen, June 22, 1907, Minneapolis. *d.* 1958, in a plane crash. After trying his hand at a variety of business ventures, he began producing Broadway plays in 1936. He entered the film business in 1945, forming Michael Todd Productions. In 1951 he organized Thomas-Todd Productions with Lowell Thomas. In the early 50s he played an important role in Hollywood's wide-screen rush in the wake of TV competition. One of the original partners of the Cinerama corporation, he sold his shares in the company in 1953 and announced the formation of the Magna Corporation, in partnership with movie mogul Joseph M. SCHENCK, to exploit a 65 mm wide-screen process he had named Todd-AO. Their first production, *Oklahoma!* (1955), was a smash hit, but its success was overshadowed by the spectacular box-office returns of Todd's next project, the star-studded multimillion-dollar spectacle *Around the World in 80 Days* (1956). In March of 1958, while he was en route to New York for a dinner of the National Association of Theater Owners, at which he was to be named "Showman of the Year," his private plane crashed, killing all aboard. The plane was named "The Lucky Liz" after his wife, film star Elizabeth TAYLOR. They had been married the previous year after she had converted to Judaism.

Todd, Richard. Actor. Born Richard Andrew Palethorpe-Todd, on June 11, 1919, in Dublin. Dynamic yet somewhat stiff leading man of British and some American films. On the stage from 1937, he was a founder-member of the Dundee Repertory Theatre in 1939. After distinguished WW II service with the King's Own Light Infantry and the Parachute Regiment, he returned briefly to the stage before launching a modestly successful film career in the late 40s, highlighted by a memorable performance in *The Hasty Heart* (1949), for which he was nominated for an Academy Award as best actor.

FILMS INCLUDE: *For Them That Trespass, Interrupted Journey, The Hasty Heart* 1949; *Stage Fright, Portrait of Clare* 1950; *Lightning Strikes Twice* (US), *Flesh and Blood* 1951; *The Story of Robin Hood* (title role; UK/US), *24 Hours of a Woman's Life, The Venetian Bird/The Assassin* 1952; *The Sword and the Rose* (UK/US), *Rob Roy—The Highland Rogue* (title role; UK/US) 1953; *Secrets d'Alcove/Il Letto/The Bed* (Fr./It.) 1954; *A Man Called Peter* (as US Senate Chaplain Peter Marshall; US), *The Virgin Queen* (as Sir Walter Raleigh; US), *The Dam Busters* 1955; *D-Day the Sixth of June* (US) 1956; *Saint Joan* (as Dunois, Bastard of Orleans), *Yangtse Incident/Battle Hell* 1957; *Chase a Crooked Shadow, Naked Earth, Intent to Kill* 1958; *Danger Within/Breakout* 1959; *Never Let Go* 1960; *Don't Bother to Knock/Why Bother to Knock* (also exec. prod.), *The Long and the Short and the Tall/Jungle Fighters, The Hellions* 1961; *The Boys, The Longest Day* (US) 1962; *Operation Crossbow* (UK/It.), *The Battle of the Villa Fiorita* (US/UK)

1965; *The Love-Ins* (US) 1967; *Subterfuge* (US/UK) 1969; *Il Dio Chiamato Dorian/Dorian Gray* (It./Ger.) 1970; *Asylum* 1972; *The Big Sleep* 1978; *Home Before Midnight* 1979; *House of the Long Shadows* (US) 1983.

Todd, Thelma. Actress. *b.* July 29, 1905, Lawrence, Mass. *d.* 1935. Vivacious blonde comedienne of numerous Hollywood shorts and feature films. A former schoolteacher and part-time model, she entered films in the mid-20s after winning a beauty contest. Her popularity reached a peak in the early 30s, when she starred in comedy shorts opposite Charlie CHASE and later in her own comedy series, with ZaSu PITTS and Patsy KELLY successively. As beautiful as she was talented, she also did well in both comic and dramatic feature films, in which she usually played wisecracking types. Memorable in two Marx Brothers comedies and two Laurel and Hardy vehicles. She died in her parked car of carbon monoxide poisoning, in circumstances that remain mysterious to this day.

FILMS INCLUDE: *Fascinating Youth* 1926; *Rubber Heels, Nevada, The Gay Defender* 1927; *The Noose, Heart to Heart, Vamping Venus, The Crash, The Haunted House* 1928; *Naughty Baby, Seven Footprints to Satan, Careers, The House of Horror* 1929; *Command Performance, Follow Thru* 1930; *The Hot Heiress, Swanee River, Aloha, The Maltese Falcon, Monkey Business, Corsair* 1931; *This is the Night, Horse Feathers, Speak Easily, Call Her Savage, Klondike* 1932; *Cheating Blondes, Fra Diavolo/The Devil's Brother, Son of a Sailor, Sitting Pretty, Counsellor-at-Law, You Made Me Love You* 1933; *Hips Hips Hooray, Palooka, Bottoms Up, Cockeyed Cavaliers, Take the Stand* 1934; *Lightning Strikes Twice, Two for Tonight* 1935; *The Bohemian Girl* 1936.

Tognazzi, Ugo. Actor. *b.* Mar. 23, 1922, in Cremona, Italy. *d.* 1990. A former accountant, he entered Italian films in 1950 following amateur stage experience. But it was not until the 60s that he emerged as a leading screen personality, capable of playing both comic and dramatic leads and supporting parts with equal facility. He was especially effective, however, with comedy roles of the black-humor variety. He occasionally directed.

FILMS INCLUDE: *I Cadetti di Guascogna* 1950; *Milanesi a Napoli* 1954; *Quelle Joie de Vivre* 1960; *Il Mantenuto* (also dir.), *Psycosissimo, Il Federale/The Fascist* 1961; *La Voglia Matta/Crazy Desire* 1962; *I Mostri/Opiate '67, Le Ore dell' Amore/The Hours of Love, Una Storia moderna: L'Ape Regina/ The Conjugal Bed* 1963; *Alta Infedeltà/High Infidelity, La Donna Scimmia/The Ape Woman, Il Magnifico Cornuto/The Magnificent Cuckold, Liola/A Very Handy Man* 1964; *Una Moglie Americana/Run for Your Wife* 1965; *Il Fischio al Naso* (also dir., co-sc.), *L'Immorale/The Climax* 1967; *Il Padre di Famiglia/The Head of the Family, Sissignore* (also dir., co-sc.), *Barbarella* 1968; *Porcile/Pigsty* 1969; *La Califfa* 1970; *L'Udienza* 1971; *In Nome del Popolo Italiano, Il Maestro e Margherita* 1972; *La Grande Bouffe* (Fr./It.), *Vogliamo i Colonnelli* 1973; *Amici Miei/My Friends, Romanzo Popolare* 1975; *L'Anatra all'Arancia, Signore e Signori Buonanotte* 1976; *La Stanza del Vescovo, Il Casotto, I Nuovi Mostri/Viva Italia!* 1977; *Il Gatto, La Mazzetta, Primo Amore/First Love, La Cage aux Folles* (Fr./It.) 1978; *Due Pezzi di Pane, L'Ingorgo/ Bottleneck/Traffic Jam, Dove vai in Vacanza?, I Viaggiatori della Sera* (also dir.) 1979; *La Cage aux Folles II* (Fr./It.), *Sono Fotogenico, Sunday Lovers* 1980; *La Tragedia di un Uomo Ridicolo/Tragedy of a Ridiculous Man* 1981; *Amici miei atto II, Il Petomane, Scherzo del Destino in Agguato Dietro L'Angolo Come un Brigante di Strada, Scusa se e poco, Trenta Minuti D'Amore* 1983; *Bertoldo, Bertoldino e Cacasenno, Le Bon Roi Dagobert* (Fr.) 1984; *La Cage aux Folles III: "Elles" se marient* (Fr./It.) 1985; *Amici Miei Atto III, Yiddish Connection* 1986; *Ultimo Momento* 1987; *Arrivederci e Grazie, I Giorni del commissario Ambrosio* 1988; *Tolerance* 1989; *La Batalla de los Tres Reyes* 1990.

Tokar, Norman. Director. *b.* 1920, Newark, N.J. *d.* 1979. A former actor, he played juveniles on Broadway and was the voice of Henry Aldrich in the radio series. After WW II service, he began writing, then also directing for radio and TV. From the early 60s, he directed feature films for the Walt Disney studios.

FILMS: *Big Red* 1962; *Savage Sam* 1963; *A Tiger Walks* 1964; *Those Calloways* 1965; *The Ugly Dachshund, Follow Me Boys!* 1966; *The Happiest Millionaire* 1967; *The Horse in the Gray Flannel Suit* 1968; *Rascal* 1969; *The Boatniks* 1970; *Snowball Express* 1972; *Where the Red Fern Grows* 1974; *The Apple Dumpling Gang* 1975; *No Deposit No Return* 1975; *The Cat from Outer Space* (also co-prod.), *Candleshoe* 1978.

Toland, Gregg. Director of photography. *b.* May 29, 1904, Charleston, Ill. *d.* 1948. He entered films at 15 as an office boy and became an assistant cameraman the following year. Graduating to lighting cameraman in 1929, he soon distinguished himself as one of the most inventive and creative artists in his field. He worked for various studios, but mainly for independent producer Sam GOLDWYN, who allowed him a great deal of creative freedom. Toland's experiments with lighting and optics did much to advance the state of the art of cinematography in Hollywood. His beautifully balanced high-key photography set the technical standard for the industry for years to come. Perhaps his most famous achievement was the deep-focus technique, involving complex compositions, which he developed to perfection in the 40s for Orson Welles's *Citizen Kane* (1941), and for William Wyler's *The Best Years of Our Lives* (1946). More than any other cameraman, Toland left his unmistakable signature on the films he photographed. He won an Academy Award for the cinematography of Wyler's *Wuthering Heights* (1939). During WW II, as a lieutenant in the Navy's camera department, he co-directed a war documentary, *December 7th* (1943), with Lt. John Ford. He died of a heart attack at the age of 44.

FILMS INCLUDE: *Bulldog Drummond* (co-phot.), *The Trespasser* (co-phot.), *Condemned* (co-phot.) 1929; *Raffles* (co-phot.), *Whoopee!* (co-phot.) 1930; *The Devil to Pay* (co-phot.), *Tonight or Never* (co-phot.), *Palmy Days* 1931; *Play Girl, Man Wanted, The Kid from Spain* 1932; *Tugboat Annie, The Masquerader, Roman Scandals* 1933; *Nana, We Live Again* 1934; *Mad Love* (co-phot.), *The Dark Angel, Les Miserables* 1935; *Come and Get It* (co-phot.), *Strike Me Pink* (co-phot.), *These Three, The Road to Glory, Beloved Enemy* 1936; *History is Made at Night, Dead End* 1937; *The Cowboy and the Lady, Kidnapped, The Goldwyn Follies, Wuthering Heights, Intermezzo* 1939; *The Westerner, The Grapes of Wrath, The Long Voyage Home* 1940; *Citizen Kane, Ball of Fire, The Little Foxes* 1941; *December 7th* (doc.; also co-dir. with John Ford) 1943; *The Outlaw* (co-phot.) 1943; *Song of the South* (live-action sequences only), *The Kid from Brooklyn, The Best Years of Our Lives* 1946; *The Bishop's Wife, A Song Is Born* 1948; *Enchantment* 1949.

Toler, Sidney. Actor. *b.* Apr. 28, 1874, Warrensburg, Mo. *d.* 1947. *ed.* U. of Kansas. Formerly on the stage, he entered films early in the sound era and played character parts in numerous Hollywood productions. In 1938, after the death of Warner OLAND, he took over the title role of the "Charlie Chan" series. He played the clever Oriental detective in many films until his own death, when he was replaced by Roland WINTERS.

FILMS INCLUDE: *Madame X* 1929; *Strictly Dishonorable* 1931; *Strangers in Love, Speak Easily, Blonde Venus, The Phantom President* 1932; *The King of the Jungle, The World*

Changes 1933; *Spitfire, The Trumpet Blows* 1934; *The Daring Young Man, Call of the Wild* 1935; *Give Us This Night, The Gorgeous Hussy* (as Daniel Webster), *Our Relations* 1936; *That Certain Woman, Double Wedding* 1937; *If I Were King, Charlie Chan in Honolulu* 1938; *King of Chinatown* 1939; *Murder Over New York* 1940; *Dead Men Tell* 1941; *Castle in the Desert* 1942; *A Night to Remember, White Savage* 1943; *Charlie Chan in the Secret Service, The Chinese Cat* 1944; *The Scarlet Clue, The Red Dragon* 1945; *Dark Alibi* 1946; *The Trap* 1947.

Tolkan, James. Actor. Born on June 20, 1931, in Calumet, Mich. *ed.* Univ. of Iowa. Versatile character actor, active since the 60s. Trained with Stella Adler and appeared widely in theater.

FILMS INCLUDE: *Stiletto* 1969; *They Might Be Giants* 1971; *The Friends of Eddie Coyle* 1973; *Love and Death* 1975; *The Amityville Horror* 1979; *Wolfen, Prince of the City* 1981; *Author! Author!, Hanky Panky* 1982; *Nightmares* (v/o), *WarGames* 1983; *Iceman, The River* 1984; *Turk 182!, Back to the Future* 1985; *Off Beat, Top Gun, Armed and Dangerous* 1986; *Masters of the Universe, Made in Heaven* 1987; *Split Decisions* 1988; *Second Sight, Back to the Future Part II, Family Business* 1989; *Opportunity Knocks, Back to the Future III, Dick Tracy* 1990; *Problem Child 2* 1991; *Sketch Artist* 1992; *Boiling Point* 1993.

Tolkin, Michael. Screenwriter, director, novelist. Born in 1950 in New York, N.Y. *ed.* Middlebury Coll. The son of TV writer Mel Tolkin, he was a widely published journalist (*Village Voice, L.A. Times*) before becoming a TV story editor and then a screenwriter. Author of *Among the Dead,* a novel, and *The Player*, the inventive screenplay that gained him notice in the film world.

FILMS INCLUDE: *Gleaming the Cube* 1989; *The Rapture* (also dir.); *The Player* (also act., co-prod.); *Deep Cover* (co-sc., also story) 1992; *The New Age* 1994.

Tomei, Marisa. Actress. Born on Dec. 4, 1964, in Brooklyn, N.Y. *ed.* Boston U. Spirited comedic and dramatic film lead. After training in daytime serials, she debuted in film in 1984 and came to prominence with her Academy Award—winning performance as the smart, wisecracking girlfriend in *My Cousin Vinny*.

FILMS: *The Flamingo Kid* 1984; *Oscar* 1991; *My Cousin Vinny, Chaplin* (US/UK) 1992; *Equinox* 1993; *Only You, The Paper* 1994; *Four Rooms, The Perez Family* 1995; *Unhook the Stars* 1996; *A Brother's Kiss, Welcome to Sarajevo* 1997.

Tomlin, Lily. Actress. Born Mary Jean Tomlin, in September, 1939, in Detroit, where her parents had migrated from the Kentucky Hill country during the height of the Depression. She began working as a dime store clerk at 14, while attending high school, to supplement the income of her father, a toolmaker in a brass factory. She later attended Detroit's Wayne State University as a premed student but soon dropped out to become a performer in a local cabaret. In 1966 she went to New York, where she performed comedy routines on the coffee-house circuit, did commercials, and appeared regularly on the last and least successful version of TV's 'The Garry Moore Show.' After the show folded early in 1967 she returned to the cabaret circuit for nearly three years, but in December of 1969 she joined the cast of TV's 'Laugh-In' and soon rose to popularity with her series of clever impersonations, most notably those of the telephone operator Ernestine and the devilish little five-year-old Edith Ann. By the time she left the show in 1972, Miss Tomlin had established herself as a masterful entertainer with an uncanny ability to capture detailed characterizations. She has since starred in her own Emmy Award—winning TV specials, released several hit records, triumphed with two one-woman stage shows done in collaboration with writer Jane Wagner, and proved herself an actress of tremendous range in such disparately styled films as *Nashville* and *The Late Show.* She was voted best supporting actress by the New York Film Critics for her sympathetic portrayal of a distressed gospel singer in the *Nashville* and won kudos for her unrestrained comic portrait of Margo, a zany, unpredictable whacko, in *The Late Show*. Her career remains active in the 90s, with regular film roles that include a spirited Miss Hathaway in *The Beverly Hillbillies*, as well as an appearance in HBO's *And the Band Played On* (1993) and is a regular on the 'Murphy Brown' TV series.

FILMS: *Nashville* 1975; *The Late Show* 1977; *Moment by Moment* 1978; *Nine to Five* 1980; *The Incredible Shrinking Woman* 1981; *All of Me* 1984; *Big Business* 1988; *The Search for Signs of Intelligent Life in the Universe, The Player* (cameo), *Shadows and Fog* 1992; *The Beverly Hillbillies, Short Cuts* 1993; *Blue in the Face* 1995; *Flirting with Disaster, Getting Away with Murder* 1996.

Tomlinson, David. Actor. Born on May 7, 1917, in Henley-on-Thames, England. Light leading man and character comedian of British films, following stage experience from 1935. Usually seen in amiable roles. His career was interrupted at an early stage by his WW II service as an RAF pilot.

FILMS INCLUDE: *Quiet Wedding* 1940; *Pimpernel Smith/Mister V* 1941; *The Way to the Stars/Johnny in the Clouds, Journey Together* 1945; *School for Secrets/Secret Flight* 1946; *Master of Bankdam, Fame is the Spur* 1947; *My Brother's Keeper, Easy Money, Sleeping Car to Trieste, Miranda, Broken Journey* 1948; *The Children Hundreds/The Amazing Mr. Beecham, Marry Me, Landfall* 1949; *So Long at the Fair, The Wooden Horse* 1950; *Hotel Sahara, The Magic Box* 1951; *Castle in the Air* 1952; *Three Men in a Boat* 1956; *Carry On Admiral/The Ship Was Loaded* 1957; *Up the Creek* 1958; *Follow That Horse!* 1960; *Tom Jones* (as Lord Fellamar) 1963; *Mary Poppins* (as Mr. Banks; US) 1964; *The Truth About Spring, War-Gods of the Deep/City Under the Sea* (US/UK) 1965; *The Liquidator* 1966; *The Love Bug* (US) 1969; *Bedknobs and Broomsticks* (US) 1971; *Bon Baisers de Hong Kong* (Fr.) 1975; *The Water Babies* 1979; *The Fiendish Plot of Dr. Fu Manchu* 1980.

tonal key. The balance of light or dark tones in a photographed image. When the tones are on the light side, the image is said to be in "high key." Conversely, when the tones are relatively dark, the picture is termed "low key."

Tone, Franchot. Actor. *b.* Stanislas Pascal Franchot Tone, Feb. 27, 1905, Niagara Falls, N.Y. *d.* 1968. The son of a socially prominent industrialist, he was drawn to acting while studying at Cornell, where he became president of the Dramatic Club. He made his professional stage debut in 1927, in stock, and before long reached Broadway. In films from the early 30s, he was generally typecast in playboy or successful man-about-town roles that agreed with his well-bred looks and manners. He spent most of the 30s with MGM, in films that ranged from good to routine, playing both comedy and drama with ease and mild conviction. By 1937 he had climbed to seventh place in the list of Hollywood's top box-office stars. He played second leads in three of his best films of this period: *Mutiny on the Bounty* (Oscar-nominated as best actor), *The Lives of a Bengal Lancer,* and *Three Comrades.* In the 40s, Tone freelanced among several studios and returned periodically to the stage. Apart from *Five Graves to Cairo* and *Phantom Lady,* his films of the decade ranged from mediocre to poor.

His screen career petered out in the early 50s and he returned to the stage. In 1958 he co-produced, co-directed, and starred in *Uncle Vanya,* an uninspired screen adaptation of his off-Broadway production. He played occasional character parts in films of the 60s and received good notices for his role in the 1963 New York revival of 'Strange Interlude.' He co-starred in the 'Ben Casey' TV series in 1965–66. At the time of his death, of lung cancer, he was negotiating for the rights to film Jean Renoir's biography *Renoir My Father.* Tone was married and divorced four times. His wives were all actresses: Joan CRAWFORD (1935–39), Jean WALLACE (1941–48), Barbara PAYTON (1951–52), and Dolores Dorn-Heft (1956–59). He made headlines when he was roughed up by actor Tom NEAL in a barroom brawl over Miss Payton.

FILMS: *The Wiser Sex* 1932; *Gabriel Over the White House, Today We Live, Midnight Mary, The Stranger's Return, Stage Mother, Bombshell, Dancing Lady* 1933; *Moulin Rouge, Sadie McKee, The World Moves On, The Girl from Missouri, Straight Is the Way, Gentlemen Are Born* 1934; *The Lives of a Bengal Lancer, Reckless, One New York Night, No More Ladies, Mutiny on the Bounty* (as Roger Byam), *Dangerous* 1935; *Exclusive Story, The Unguarded Hour, The King Steps Out* (as Emperor Franz Josef of Austria), *Suzy, The Gorgeous Hussy, Love on the Run* 1936; *Quality Street, They Gave Him a Gun, Between Two Women, The Bride Wore Red* 1937; *Man-Proof, Love Is a Headache, Three Comrades, Three Loves Has Nancy* 1938; *The Girl Downstairs, Thunder Afloat, Fast and Furious* 1939; *Trail of the Vigilantes* 1940; *Nice Girl?, She Knew All the Answers, This Woman Is Mine* 1941; *The Wife Takes a Flyer, Star Spangled Rhythm* 1942; *Five Graves to Cairo, Pilot No. 5, True to Life, His Butler's Sister* 1943; *Phantom Lady, The Hour Before Dawn, Dark Waters* 1944; *That Night with You* 1945; *Because of Him* 1946; *Honeymoon, Lost Honeymoon, Her Husband's Affairs* 1947; *I Love Trouble, Every Girl Should Be Married* 1948; *Jigsaw* 1949; *The Man on the Eiffel Tower, Without Honor* 1950; *Here Comes the Groom* 1951; *Uncle Vanya* (as Dr. Mikhail Astroff; also co-dir. with John Goetz, co-prod.) 1958; *Advise and Consent* (as "The President") 1962; *La Bonne Soupe* (Fr./It.) 1964; *In Harm's Way, Mickey One* 1956; *Nobody Runs Forever/The High Commissioner* (UK/US) 1968.

toning. The chemical process by which the brightness of a print is increased or its colors corrected.

Tonti, Aldo. Director of photography. *b.* Mar. 2, 1910, Rome. *d.* 1988. In Italian films as camera assistant from 1934, he graduated to lighting cameraman in 1939. In the early 40s he contributed to the emergence of neorealism in Italian cinema as Luchino Visconti's cameraman on *Ossessione* (*Obsession*). Most of his subsequent films were routine, but his list of credits includes some important films of ROSSELLINI, LATTUADA, and FELLINI. He also played comic roles in occasional films.

FILMS INCLUDE: *Sei Bambine e il Perseo* 1939; *Caravaggio* 1940; *Nozze di Sangue* 1941; *Bengasi, Ossessione* (co-phot.) 1942; *La Porta del Cielo, Roma Città Libera, Il Bandito* 1946; *Il Delitto di Giovanni Episcopo, La Figlia del Capitano* 1947; *Proibito Rubare, Senza Pietà/Without Pity, Amore* ("Il Miracolo" episode), *Molti Sogni per le Strade* 1948; *Il Mulino del Po/The Mill on the Po, Il Lupo della Sila/Lure of the Sila* 1949; *Signorinella, Napoli Milionaria, Side Street Story, Il Brigante Musolino* 1950; *Romanticismo* 1951; *Sensualità, Europa '51* 1952; *Le Infedeli, Dov'è la Libertà?, La Lupa* 1953; *Attila* (co-phot.), *Proibito, Ulisse/Ulysses* (co-phot.) 1954; *War and Peace* (2nd-unit phot.; US/It.), *Le Notti di Cabiria/Nights of Cabiria/Cabiria* (co-phot.) 1956; *Fortunella, India* (doc.), *La Tempesta/Tempest* 1958; *Serenade einer grossen Liebe/For the First Time* (Ger./US) 1959; *Ombre bianche/The Savage Innocents, Il Gobbo/The Hunchback of Rome* (co-phot.) 1960; *Barabba/Barabbas* 1961; *Il Diavolo/To Bed or Not to Bed* 1963; *La Donna Scimmia/The Ape Woman* 1964; *Casanova '70* 1965; *Cast a Giant Shadow* (US), *L'Arcidiavolo/The Devil in Love* 1966; *Reflections in a Golden Eye* (US) 1967; *Città Violenta* 1970; *La Spina Dorsa del Diavolo/The Deserter* (It./Sp./US) 1971; *Joe Valachi: I Segreti di Cosa Nostra/The Valachi Papers* 1972; *Crazy Joe* 1973; *The Count of Monte Cristo* (UK), *Une Femme à sa Fenêtre/A Woman at Her Window* (Fr.) 1976; *René la Canne* (Fr./It.), *Quelle Strane Occasioni* (co-phot.) 1977; *Ashanti* 1979.

Toomey, Regis. Actor. *b.* Aug. 13, 1902, in Pittsburgh. *d.* 1991. *ed.* U. of Pittsburgh. After five years of stage work he switched to films. In a career that spanned four decades, he appeared in more than 150 films, playing occasional leads and numerous character roles, typically as a man of action on either side of the law. He also appeared on innumerable TV programs including regular stints in the series 'Dante's Inferno,' 'Hey, Mulligan,' 'Richard Diamond,' and 'Burke's Law.'

FILMS INCLUDE: *Alibi, Illusion* 1929; *Rich People, Street of Chance, Framed, The Light of Western Stars, A Man from Wyoming* 1930; *Finn and Hattie, The Finger Points, Kick In, Touchdown!, Under Eighteen* 1931; *Shopworn, The Midnight Patrol, They Never Come Back* 1932; *State Trooper, Soldiers of the Storm* 1933; *Murder on the Blackboard* 1934; *G-Men* 1935; *Big City, Shadows of the Orient* 1937; *The Invisible Menace* 1938; *The Phantom Creeps* (serial), *Union Pacific, Thunder Afloat* 1939; *His Girl Friday, Northwest Passage, North West Mounted Police, Arizona* 1940; *Meet John Doe, The Nurse's Secret, Dive Bomber, They Died with Their Boots On* 1941; *Bullet Scars, The Forest Rangers, Tennessee Johnson* 1942; *Destroyer, Jack London* 1943; *Phantom Lady, Follow the Boys, The Doughgirls* 1944; *Spellbound* 1945; *The Big Sleep, Magic Town, The Bishop's Wife* 1947; *The Boy with Green Hair* 1948; *Mighty Joe Young, Come to the Stable* 1949; *Cry Danger, Show Boat* 1951; *My Six Convicts, Just for You* 1952; *The High and the Mighty, The Human Jungle* 1954; *Guys and Dolls* 1955; *Dakota Incident* 1956; *Warlock* 1959; *The Last Sunset, Voyage to the Bottom of the Sea, King of the Roaring Twenties* 1961; *Man's Favorite Sport?* 1964; *Gunn* 1967; *Change of Habit* 1969; *Cover Me Babe* 1970; *The Carey Treatment* 1972; *God Bless Dr. Shagetz* 1977.

top hat. A squat camera mount used in filming low-angle shots.

Topol. Actor. Born Haym Topol, on Sept. 9, 1935, in Tel Aviv. After gaining acting experience during his military service with an Israeli army entertainment unit, he began performing professionally on the stage and in films. He made his name on the London stage playing Tevye in 'Fiddler on the Roof,' a role he later repeated in the screen production and for which he was nominated for an Oscar. Later seen in such TV miniseries as' The Winds of War' (1983) and 'Queenie' (1987).

FILMS INCLUDE: *Sallah* (Isr.) 1964; *Cast a Giant Shadow* (US) 1966; *Every Bastard a King* (Isr.) 1968; *Before Winter Comes* (UK) 1969; *A Talent for Loving* (UK) 1970; *The Rooster* (Isr.), *Fiddler on the Roof* (US) 1971; *Follow Me/The Public Eye* (UK) 1972; *Galileo* (title role; UK/US) 1975; *The House on Garibaldi Street* (TV) 1979; *Flash Gordon* 1980; *For Your Eyes Only* 1981; *Roman Behemshechim* (Isr.) 1985.

Topper, Burt. Producer. Born in 1928. American producer-director-screenwriter of mostly shrill low-budget action pictures. For some reason, his films have been discussed in some depth by critics of the leading French film magazine *Cahiers du Cinéma.* He has also produced a number of films directed by others. He was executive producer on *Wild in the Streets* (1968).

FILMS (as director): *Hell Squad* (also prod., sc.) 1958; *Tank Commandos* (also prod., sc.), *The Diary of a High School*

Bride (also prod., co-sc.) 1959; *War Is Hell* (also prod., sc., act.), *The Strangler* 1964; *The Devil's 8* (also prod.) 1969; *The Hard Ride* (also exec. prod., sc.) 1971; *The Day the Lord Got Busted* (also prod., sc.) 1976.

Torn, Rip. Actor. Born Elmore Rual Torn, on Feb. 6, 1931, in Temple, Tex. *ed.* Texas A & M; U. of Texas. Explosive, unpredictable leading man and character player of the stage, TV, and films. He studied animal husbandry, intending to become a rancher, then decided to become an actor so that he could buy a ranch. He hitchhiked to Hollywood, hoping for immediate stardom, but instead found himself a dishwasher and a short-order cook. He eventually began getting roles on TV and in occasional films, then set out for New York, where he studied under Lee Strasberg at the Actors Studio and took up dancing under Martha Graham. In 1963 he married actress Geraldine PAGE, from whom he was later divorced. In films he has often been cast as a surly, violent, unbalanced, and deceptively sensitive character, memorably as Finley Jr. in *Sweet Bird of Youth.* But he has also played some comic roles and in 1970 he portrayed Henry Miller in *Tropic of Cancer.* He made a stab at directing with *The Telephone* (1988) and currently stars on 'The Larry Sanders Show' TV series.

FILMS INCLUDE: *Baby Doll* 1956; *A Face in the Crowd, Time Limit* 1957; *Pork Chop Hill* 1959; *King of Kings* (as Judas) 1961; *Sweet Bird of Youth* 1962; *Critic's Choice* 1963; *The Cincinnati Kid* 1965; *One Spy Too Many* 1966; *You're a Big Boy Now, Beach Red* 1967; *Sol Madrid, Beyond the Law* 1968; *Coming Apart* 1969; *Tropic of Cancer* 1970; *Maidstone* 1971; *Slaughter* 1972; *Payday, Crazy Joe* (It./US) 1973; *The Man Who Fell to Earth* (UK), *Birch Interval, Nasty Habits* (UK) 1976; *The Private Files of J. Edgar Hoover* 1977; *Coma* 1978; *The Seduction of Joe Tynan* 1979; *One-Trick Pony, The First Family* 1980; *Heartland* 1981; *Jinxed, Airplane 2: The Sequel, The Beastmaster, A Stranger is Watching* 1982; *Cross Creek* 1983; *City Heat, Songwriter, Flashpoint, Misunderstood* 1984; *Beer, Summer Rental* 1985; *Nadine, Extreme Prejudice* 1987; *The Hit List, Blind Curve* (short), *The Telephone* (dir. only) 1988; *Cold Feet, Hit List, Zwei Frauen* (Ger.) 1989; *Silence Like Glass, Beautiful Dreamers, The Hunt for Red October* 1990; *Defending Your Life, Another Pair of Aces: Three of a Kind* (TV, released theatrically with added footage), *My Son Johnny* 1991; *Finnegan's Wake, Dolly Dearest, Hard Promises* 1992; *Robocop 3* 1993; *North* 1994; *Canadian Bacon, How To Make an American Quilt* 1995; *Down Periscope* 1996; *Hercules* (v/o), *Trial and Error* 1997.

Tornatore, Giuseppe. Director, screenwriter. Born in 1956 in Bagheria, Italy. Former photographer and documentary director who began directing feature films in the mid-80s. His evocative view of postwar childhood and movie enthrallment, *Cinema Paradiso*, won an Academy Award for best foreign film.

FILMS INCLUDE (as dir.): *Il Camorrista/The Professor* (also sc.) 1986; *Nuova Cinema Paradiso/Cinema Paradiso* (also sc., story; It./Fr.) 1988; *Stanno Tutti Bene/Everybody's Fine* (also sc.) 1990; *La Domenica Specialmente/Especially on Sundays* (co-dir.) 1991; *A Pure Formality* 1994.

Torrence, David. Actor *b.* David Torrence Tayson, 1880, Edinburgh, Scotland. *d.* 1942. The younger brother of Ernest TORRENCE, he performed on Broadway early in the century and appeared in several films shortly before the outbreak of WW I. However, his main screen career did not start until the early 20s, after he had experienced unfortunate misadventures as a cattle rancher in Mexico. Tall and distinguished, he played severe, often domineering, sometimes menacing, character parts in numerous silent and sound films.

FILMS INCLUDE: *The Prisoner of Zenda, Tess of the D'Urbervilles* 1913; *The Inside of the Cup* 1921; *Sherlock Holmes, Tess of the Storm Country, Forsaking All Others* 1922; *The Power of a Lie, The Man Next Door, The Light That Failed, The Drums of Jeopardy* 1923; *The Dawn of a Tomorrow, Tiger Love, Idle Tongues* 1924; *Her Husband's Secret, The Mystic, The Wheel, The Tower of Lies* 1925; *Brown of Harvard, The Man in the Shadow, Forever After, The Unknown Cavalier* 1926; *The Third Degree, The Mysterious Rider, Annie Laurie, Rolled Stockings, On the Stroke of Twelve* 1927; *The Little Shepherd of Kingdom Come, Undressed, City of Purple Dreams* 1928; *Strong Boy, The Black Watch, Disraeli* 1929; *City Girl, Raffles, Scotland Yard, River's End* 1930; *The Bachelor Father, East Lynne, Five Star Final* 1931; *A Successful Calamity, Smilin' Through, The Mask of Fu Manchu* 1932; *Voltaire, The Masquerader, Berkeley Square* 1933; *Queen Christina, Madame Spy, What Every Woman Knows* 1934; *Black Sheep, The Dark Angel, Captain Blood* 1935; *The Country Doctor, Mary of Scotland* 1936; *Lost Horizon, Ebb Tide* 1937; *Stanley and Livingstone, Rulers of the Sea* 1939.

Torrence, Ernest. Actor. *b.* June 26, 1878, Edinburgh, Scotland. *d.* 1933. A graduate of the Edinburgh Academy of Music, the Stuttgart (Germany) Conservatory, and London's Royal Academy of Music, he was a noted operatic baritone before entering Hollywood films in the early 20s. He played occasional leads and numerous character parts of importance in silents and early talkies, often villainous, sometimes demented. He was the older brother of David TORRENCE.

FILMS INCLUDE: *Tol'able David* 1921; *The Prodigal Judge, Singed Wings, Broken Chains* 1922; *The Brass Bottle, The Covered Wagon, The Trail of the Lonesome Pine, The Hunchback of Notre Dame, Ruggles of Red Gap* 1923; *The Heritage of the Desert, The Fighting Coward, The Side Show of Life, Peter Pan* (as Captain Hook) 1924; *The Dressmaker from Paris, Night Life of New York, The Wanderer, The Pony Express* 1925; *The American Venus, The Blind Goddess, The Rainmaker, Mantrap, The Lady of the Harem* 1926; *The King of Kings* (as Peter), *Captain Salvation, Twelve Miles Out* 1927; *Across to Singapore, Steamboat Bill Jr., The Cossacks* 1928; *The Bridge of San Luis Rey* (as Uncle Pio), *Desert Nights/Thirst, The Unholy Night, Untamed* 1929; *Officer O'Brien, Sweet Kitty Bellairs, Call of the Flesh* 1930; *Fighting Caravans, Shipmates, Sporting Blood, The Great Lover, The Cuban Love Song* 1931; *Sherlock Holmes* (as Moriarty) 1932; *Hypnotized, I Cover the Waterfront* 1933.

Torre Nilsson, Leopoldo. Director, screenwriter. *b.* May 5, 1924, Buenos Aires. *d.* 1978. The son of veteran Argentinian film director Leopoldo Torres-Rios (1899–1960) and a Swedish mother, he began his film career at the age of 15 as an assistant to his father and other directors. In his early 20s he was drawn away from cinema by literature and wrote a play, a collection of poems, and a novel. In 1947 he directed a short, *La Mura,* but it wasn't until 1950 that he re-oriented himself completely toward the cinema. His first two films as director were made in collaboration with his father. On his own from 1954, he rapidly established himself as one of his country's leading directors and in 1957 he burst upon the international scene with *La Casa del Angel/The House of the Angel/End of Innocence,* which was received enthusiastically at the Cannes Film Festival. Torre Nilsson's subsequent films confirmed his reputation as a brilliant stylist. His work benefited much from the collaboration of his wife, novelist-playwright Beatriz Guido, on many of his scripts. A recurrent theme in their films was the corruption of innocence and the hypocrisy of the institutions of the Establishment.

FEATURE FILMS (as director-writer): *El Crimen de*

Oribe (co-dir., with Leopoldo Torres-Rios) 1950; *El Hijo del Crack* (co-dir. with Torres-Rios) 1953; *Días de Odio/Days of Hatred, La Tigra* 1954; *Para vestir Santos* 1955; *Graciela, El Protegido* 1956; *La Casa del Angel/The House of the Angel/End of Innocence* 1957; *El Secuestrador/The Kidnapper* 1958; *La Caida/The Fall* 1959; *Fin de Fiesta/The Blood Feast/The Party Is Over, Un Guapo del 900* (also co-prod.) 1960; *La Mano en la Trampa/The Hand in the Trap, Piel de Verano/Summerskin* (also prod.) 1961; *Setenta Veces Siete/The Female: Seventy Times Seven, Homenaje a la Hora de la Siesta/Homage at Siesta Time* 1962; *La Terraza/The Terrace* 1963; *El Ojo de la Cerradura/The Eavesdropper* (Arg./US) 1964; *Cavar un Foso/To Dig a Pit, La Chica del Lunes/Monday's Child* (Puerto Rico) 1966; *Los Traidores de San Angel/Traitors of San Angel* (Puerto Rico) 1967; *Martin Fierro* 1968; *El Santo de la Espada/The Knight of the Sword* 1970; *La Maffia/The Mafia, Guemes—La Tierra en Armas* 1972; *Los Siete Locos/The Seven Madmen* 1973; *Boquitas Pintadas/Painted Lips* 1974; *Los Gauchos Judíos/Jewish Gauchos* (co-prod. only), *Diario de la Guerra del Cerdo/Diary of the Pig War* 1975; *El Pibe Cabeza, Piedra Libre* 1976.

Torres, Raquel. Actress. *b.* Nov. 11, 1908, in Hermosillo, Mexico. *d.* 1987. Educated in a Los Angeles convent, she made a vivid impression in W. S. Van Dyke's *White Shadows of the South Seas,* a film effectively combining elements of fiction and documentary styles. Her exotic beauty was her main asset in several subsequent early sound films. She retired from the screen to marry a wealthy businessman. Widowed, she married actor Jon HALL in 1959.

FILMS INCLUDE: *White Shadows of the South Seas* 1928; *The Bridge of San Luis Rey* (as Pepita), *The Desert Rider* 1929; *Under a Texas Moon, The Sea Bat* 1930; *Aloha* 1931; *So This Is Africa!, The Woman I Stole, Duck Soup* 1933; *Red Wagon* (UK) 1934.

Torres Contreras, Miguel. Mexican director, producer, screenwriter, actor. A leading figure in the Mexican film industry since the early 20s, he independently produced and directed many films of quality through the late 50s and appeared in several as an actor. In the late 20s he spent some time in Hollywood, learning the new sound techniques and producing some film for the Spanish-speaking market. In 1960 he published *The Black Book of Mexican Cinema,* an indictment of the control by Americans of his country's means of film distribution and exhibition.

FILMS INCLUDE: *El Caporal* (co-dir.) 1921; *El Hombre sin Patria* 1922; *Almas Tropicales* 1923; *Oro Sangre y Sol* 1925; *El Relicario* 1926; *La Sombra de Pancho Villa* 1932; *Juarez y Maximiliano, La Noche del Pecado* 1933; *Tribu* 1934; *No te Enganes Corazon/Don't Fool Thyself—Heart* 1936; *La Paloma* 1937; *La Golondrina/The Swallow* 1938; *Hombre o Demonio/The Mad Empress* 1940; *Simón Bolívar/The Life of Simon Bolivar* 1941; *El Padro Morelos, Carabelleria del Imperio* 1942; *La Vida inutil de Tito Perez* 1943; *Bamba* 1948; *Vuelva Pancho Villa/Pancho Villa Returns* 1949; *Amor a la Vida* 1950; *Viva la Soldera!* 1958.

Tors, Ivan. Producer, screenwriter, sometimes director. *b.* June 12, 1916, Budapest. *d.* 1983. *ed.* U. of Budapest; Fordham. He was a playwright in Europe before emigrating to the US in the late 30s. After WW II service with the US Army Air Force and the OSS, he entered films as a screenwriter. In the 50s he produced and wrote a number of science fiction films. From the early 60s he specialized in films featuring animals, mostly spin-offs of his popular kiddie TV series ('Flipper,' 'Gentle Ben,' etc.). His company operated from Miami, Fla., where he set up an extensive menagerie of animal "stars," and Los Angeles, near which he created a 260-acre wildlife preserve known as "Africa, U.S.A."

FILMS INCLUDE: As screenwriter—*Song of Love* 1947; *In the Good Old Summertime, That Forsyte Woman* 1949; *Watch the Birdie* 1950. As producer-writer—*The Magnetic Monster, The Mask of the Himalayas* 1953. As producer—*Riders to the Stars, Gog* 1954; *Underwater Warrior* 1958; *Flipper* 1963; *Rhino!* (dir. only) 1964; *Clarence the Cross-eyed Lion* (exec. prod.), *Zebra in the Kitchen* (also dir.) 1965; *Namu the Killer Whale* (exec. prod.) 1966; *Africa—Texas Style* (exec. prod.), *Gentle Giant* 1967; *Daring Game* (exec. prod.) 1968; *Hello Down There* (exec. prod.) 1969; *Escape from Angola* (co-exec. prod.) 1976.

Totheroh, Rolland H. ("Rollie"). Director of photography. *b.* 1890, San Francisco. *d.* 1967. He worked briefly as a newspaper illustrator before joining the Essanay studios in Chicago as cameraman in 1910. When Charlie CHAPLIN moved to Essanay from Keystone in 1915, Totheroh was assigned to photograph his films. They got along well and when Chaplin left Essanay he took Totheroh along. Their collaboration continued through the 40s.

FILMS INCLUDE: *His New Job, The Champion, The Tramp, The Bank, A Night in the Show* 1915; *Carmen, The Vagabond, The Pawnshop, The Rink* (last two co-phot.) 1916; *Easy Street, The Cure, The Immigrant, The Adventurer* (all co-phot.) 1917; *Shoulder Arms* 1918; *The Kid* 1921; *The Pilgrim, A Woman of Paris* (co-phot.) 1923; *The Gold Rush* 1925; *The Circus* 1928; *City Lights* (co-phot.) 1931; *Modern Times* (co-phot.) 1936; *The Great Dictator* (co-phot.) *Monsieur Verdoux* (co-phot.) 1947; *Song of My Heart* 1948.

Totò. Actor. *b.* Antonio de Curtis Gagliardi Ducas Comneno di Bisanzio, Feb. 15, 1898, Naples. *d.* 1967. Born into a distinguished but impoverished family. After completing his military service in WW I, he began playing comic roles in music hall revues and on the legitimate stage. He gradually gained popularity and was an accomplished comedy star by the time he made his screen debut in 1936. The broad exposure he obtained through films rapidly made him one of the most beloved comic personalities in Italy, where his status was similar to that of FERNANDEL in France. Totò appeared in scores of Italian films with undiminishing success until his death of a heart attack.

FILMS INCLUDE: *Fermo con le Mani* 1937; *Animali Pazzi* 1939; *L'Allegro Fantasma* 1941; *Il Ratto delle Sabine* 1945; *I Due Orfanelli* 1947; *Totò al Giro d'Italia* 1949; *Totò le Moko, Napoli Milionaria/Side Street Story, Figaro qua Figaro là* 1950; *Totò Tarzan, Guardie e Ladri/Cops and Robbers* 1951; *Totò e i Re di Roma* 1952; *Tempi Nostri/The Anatomy of Love* 1953; *Questa è la Vita/Of Life and Love, L'Oro di Napoli/Gold of Naples* 1954; *Totò all'Inferno, Racconti Romani* 1955; *La Loi c'est la Loi/The Law Is the Law* (Fr./It.), *I Soliti Ignoti/Big Deal on Madonna Street* 1958; *Totò nella Luna, I Tartassati* 1959; *Risota di Gioia/The Passionate Thief* 1960; *Totò Diabolicus* 1962; *I Due Colonnelli/Two Colonels* 1963; *Le Belle Famiglie* 1964; *La Mandragola* 1965; *Operazione San Gennaro/Treasure of San Gennaro, Uccellacci e Uccellini/The Hawks and the Sparrows* 1966; *Le Streghe/The Witches* 1967; *Capriccio all'Italiana* 1968.

Totter, Audrey. Actress. Born on Dec. 20, 1918, in Joliet, Ill. She joined a theater group directly out of high school and from 1939 played in many radio dramas and soap operas. In Hollywood since the mid-40s, she has played leads and second leads in numerous films, often on the action and suspense side. She typically portrayed detached, hardened, humorless, and somewhat mysterious blondes. Her career declined after she left MGM in the late 40s. She came out of retirement in 1972 to appear regularly in the role of a nurse in the TV series 'Medical Center.'

FILMS INCLUDE: *Main Street After Dark, Dangerous Partners* 1945; *The Sailor Takes a Wife, The Postman Always Rings Twice, The Cockeyed Miracle* 1946; *Lady in the Lake, The Beginning or the End, The Unsuspected, High Wall* 1947; *The Saxon Charm* 1948; *Alias Nick Beal, The Set-Up, Any Number Can Play, Tension* 1949; *Under the Gun, FBI Girl, The Blue Veil* 1951; *The Sellout, My Pal Gus, Assignment—Paris* 1952; *Man in the Dark* 1953; *Women's Prison, A Bullet for Joey* 1955; *Man or Gun* 1958; *The Carpetbaggers* 1964; *Harlow* (Carol Lynley version) 1965; *Chubasco* 1968; *The Apple Dumpling Gang Rides Again* 1979.

Touchstone Films. See DISNEY CO., The Walt.

Tourjansky, Victor. Director. *b.* Vyacheslav Turzhansky, in 1891, in Kiev, Russia. A pupil of Stanislavsky at Moscow's Academy of Dramatic Art, he entered films as an actor in 1912 and switched to directing in 1914. In 1919, after the Bolshevik Revolution, he emigrated to France with his wife, actress Nathalie Kovanko. He subsequently directed numerous films, mostly routine, in France, Germany, and Italy, and worked in Hollywood in the late 20s. He was Abel GANCE's assistant on *Napoléon* (1927) and Michael Anderson's on *The Shoes of the Fisherman* (1968).

FILMS INCLUDE: In Russia—*Symphony of Love and Death* 1914; *The Brothers Karamazov, Wanderer Beyond the Grave* 1915; *Isle of Oblivion* (also act.) 1917; *Paradise Without Adam* 1918. In France—*L'Ordonnance, Les Contes des Mille et Une Nuits/Tales of 1001 Nights* 1921; *Le 15e Prélude de Chopin, La Nuit du Carnaval* 1922; *Le Chant de l'Amour triomphant* 1923; *Ce Cochon de Morin, La Dame masquée* 1924; *Le Prince charmant* 1925; *Michel Strogoff/Michael Strogoff* 1926. In the US—*The Adventurer* 1928. In Germany—*Wolga-Wolga* 1928; *Manolescu* 1929; *Der Herzog von Reichstadt* (and French-language version, *L'Aiglon;* Ger./Fr.) 1931. In France—*Le Chanteur inconnu* 1931; *Hôtel des Etudiants* 1932; *L'Ordonnance* (remake) 1933; *Volga en Flammes* 1934; *Les Yeux noirs/Dark Eyes* 1935. In Germany—*Die ganze Welt dreht sich um Liebe/The World's in Love* 1935; *Stadt Anatol* 1936. In France—*Vertige d'un Soir* 1936; *Le Mensonge de Nina Petrovna/The Lie of Nina Petrovna, Nostalgie/The Postmaster's Daughter* 1937. In Germany—*Der Blaufuchs, Verklungene Melodie* 1938; *Eine Frau wie Du, Der Gouverneur* 1939; *Feinde* (also co-sc.) 1940; *Illusion* (also co-sc.) 1941; *Liebesgeschichten, Tonelli* (also co-sc.) 1943; *Orient-Express* (also co-sc.) 1944; *Dreimal Komödie* (also co-sc.) 1945; *Der blaue Strohut* (also co-sc.) 1949; *Vom Teufel gejagt* (also co-sc.) 1950; *Ehe für eine Nacht* 1952; *Salto Mortale* 1953; *Morgengrauen* 1954; *Die Toteninsel* (also co-sc.), *Königswalzer* 1955; *Herz ohne Gnade* 1958. In Italy—*La Venere di Cheronea* (co-dir. with Fernando Cerchio; It./Fr.) 1958; *I Battellieri del Volga/Prisoner of the Volga* (also co-sc.; It./Fr.), *Erode il Grande/Herod the Great* (It./Fr.) 1959; *I Cosacchi/The Cossacks* (co-dir. with Giorgio Rivalta; also co-sc.; It./Fr.) 1960; *Le Triomphe de Michel Strogoff* (Fr./Ger.) 1961; *Una Regina per Cesare* (co-dir. with Piero Pierotti; It./Fr.) 1962.

Tourneur, Jacques. Director. *b.* Nov. 12, 1904, Paris. *d.* 1977. The son of director Maurice TOURNEUR, he accompanied his celebrated father to the US in 1914 and became an American citizen in 1919. He grew up in the Hollywood milieu and in 1924 joined MGM as an office boy. He later acted in a number of films and worked as a script clerk on his father's productions. In 1928 he returned to Paris as his father's film editor and in 1931 he made his debut there as director. Back in Hollywood in 1935, he rejoined MGM, as a second-unit director on *A Tale of Two Cities.* The following year he was made a short-subject director and in 1939 he began directing B features. It was at RKO in the early 40s, under the guidance of producer Val LEWTON, that Tourneur emerged as a worthy successor to his famous father as a master of the horror and fantasy genre.

Cat People and *I Walked with a Zombie* are two fine examples of literate, low-keyed suspense films in which the horror is implicit, looming ominously in the background but rarely seen. Shock comes in small and effective doses and is enhanced by a sustained ominous mood. The same restraint and cultured taste have been characteristic of Tourneur's subsequent films in other genres, but with the passage of time his misses outnumbered his hits and he turned to television for many of his assignments.

FEATURE FILMS: In France—*Un Vieux Garçon, Tout ça ne vaut pas l'Amour* 1931; *La Fusée, Toto, Pour être aimée* 1933; *Les Filles de la Concierge* 1934. In the US—*They All Came Out, Nick Carter—Master Detective* 1939; *Phantom Raiders* 1940; *Doctors Don't Tell* 1941; *Cat People* 1942; *I Walked with a Zombie, The Leopard Man* 1943; *Days of Glory, Experiment Perilous* 1944; *Canyon Passage* 1946; *Out of the Past* 1947; *Berlin Express* 1948; *Easy Living* 1949; *The Flame and the Arrow, Stars in My Crown* 1950; *Circle of Danger* (UK), *Anne of the Indies* 1951; *Way of a Gaucho* 1952; *Appointment in Honduras* 1953; *Stranger on Horseback, Wichita* 1955; *Great Day in the Morning* 1956; *Nightfall, Night of the Demon/Curse of the Demon* (UK) 1957; *The Fearmakers* 1958; *Timbuktu, La Battaglia di Maratona/The Giant of Marathon* (It.), *Frontier Rangers* (originally made for TV) 1959; *The Comedy of Terrors* 1963; *War Gods of the Deep/City Under the Sea* (US/UK) 1965.

Tourneur, Maurice. Director. *b.* Maurice Thomas, Feb. 2, 1876, Paris. *d.* 1961. The son of a jewel merchant, he began his career as a decorator and a book illustrator. After returning from military service with the French artillery in North Africa, he went to work as an assistant at the atelier of the sculptor Auguste Rodin. In 1900 he was introduced into theatrical circles by his artist friends and became an actor with the Réjane and André Antoine companies, among others. He quit the stage after a quarrel with Antoine and became an assistant director at the Eclair film company in 1911. The following year he graduated to director and soon gained a reputation for the pictorial quality of his work. In 1914 he was sent to the US to direct the American productions of Eclair at its Fort Lee, N.J., studios. Tourneur, who spoke English quite well, soon emerged as one of the great stylists of the early American cinema. He directed numerous productions of exquisite visual beauty for Eclair, then World, Paragon, Equitable, Paramount, and other studios.

Tourneur's films are noted for their subtlety, restraint, and sustained mood. He did particularly well with themes of mystery and fantasy. In 1926, after a dispute with MGM over the production of Verne's *The Mysterious Island,* he returned to France, where he met with some resentment for having dodged the draft during WW I. He continued making films until 1949, when he lost a leg in a car accident. He spent the rest of his years as a translator of American mystery novels into French. He died at the age of 83. Father of director Jacques TOURNEUR.

FILMS: In France—*Le Friquet* (also sc.), *Jean la Poudre* (also sc.), *Le Système du Docteur Goudron et du Professeur Plume/The Lunatics, Figures de Cire* 1912; *Le Dernier Pardon, Le Puits mitoyen, Le Camée, Soeurette* (also sc.), *Le Corso rouge, Mademoiselle 100 Millions, Les Gaîtés de l'Escadron* (also sc.), *La Dame de Montsoreau* (also sc.) 1913; *Monsieur Lecocq* (also sc.), *Rouletabille* (in two parts: 1. *Le Mystère de la Chambre jaune;* 2. *La Dernière Incarnation de Larsan*) 1914. In the US—*The Man of the Hour* (also sc.), *Mother* (also sc.), *The Wishing Ring* (also sc.), *The Pit* (also sc.) 1914; *Alias Jimmy*

Valentine (also sc.), *The Cub* (also sc.), *The Ivory Snuff Box, Trilby, The Butterfly on the Wheel* 1915; *Human Driftwood* (co-dir. with Emile Chautard), *The Pawn of Fate, The Hand of Peril* (also prod., sc.), *The Closed Road* (also prod., sc.), *The Rail Rider, The Velvet Paw* 1916; *A Girl's Folly, The Whip, The Undying Flame, Exile, The Law of the Land* (also sc.), *The Pride of the Clan, The Poor Little Rich Girl, Barbary Sheep, The Rise of Jenny Cushing* 1917; *Rose of the World, A Doll's House, The Blue Bird, Prunella, Woman* (also prod.), *Sporting Life* (also prod.) 1918; *The White Heather* (also prod.), *The Life Line* (also prod.), *The Broken Butterfly* (also co-sc.), *Victory* (also prod.) 1919; *The County Fair* (co-dir. with Edward J. Mortimer), *My Lady's Garter* (also prod.), *Treasure Island* (also prod.), *The Great Redeemer* (also prod.), *The White Circle* (also prod.), *Deep Waters* (also prod., sc.), *The Last of the Mohicans* (co-dir. with Clarence Brown; also prod.) 1920; *The Bait, The Foolish Matrons* (co-dir. with Brown; also prod.) 1921; *Lorna Doone* (also prod., co-sc.) 1922; *While Paris Sleeps/The Glory of Love* (also prod.; release delayed from 1920), *The Christian, The Isle of Lost Ships* (also exec. prod.), *The Brass Bottle* (also prod.), *Jealous Husbands* (also exec. prod.) 1923; *Torment* (also exec. prod.), *The White Moth* (also exec. prod.) 1924; *Sporting Life, Never the Twain Shall Meet, Clothes Make the Pirate* 1925; *Old Loves and New, Aloma of the South Seas, The Mysterious Island* (replaced on set after shooting only a number of scenes; film completed and credited to Lucien Hubbard and released in 1929) 1926. In France—*L'Equipage/The Last Flight* 1928. In Germany—*Das Schiff der verlorene Menschen* 1929. In France—*Accusee—Levez-vouz!* 1930; *Maison de Danses, Partir* 1931; *Au Nom de la Loi, Les Gaîtés de l'Escadron* (also co-sc.), *Lidoire* (also co-sc.) 1932; *Les Deux Orphelines* (also co-sc.), *L'Homme Mysterieux/ Obsession* 1933; *Le Voleur* 1934; *Justin de Marseilles* 1935; *Koenigsmark* (and English version, *Crimson Dynasty*), *Samson, Avec le Sourire/With a Smile* 1936; *Le Patriote/The Mad Emperor, Katia* 1938; *Volpone, Péchés de Jeunesse* 1941; *Mam'zelle Bonaparte* 1941; *La Main du Diable/Carnival of Sinners, Le Val d'Enfer* 1943; *Cécile est Morte* 1944; *Après l'Amour, L'Impasse des Deux Anges* 1948.

Tover, Leo. Director of photography. *b.* Dec. 6, 1902, New Haven, Conn. *d.* 1964. He entered films at age 16 and worked his way up from clapper boy and camera assistant to a highly respected lighting cameraman of both silent and sound Hollywood films, mainly for Paramount and Fox.

FILMS INCLUDE: *Fascinating Youth, The Great Gatsby* 1926; *Love's Greatest Mistake* 1927; *Street Girl, The Vagabond Lover* 1929; *The Silver Horde* 1930; *The Royal Bed, The Gay Diplomat* 1931; *Lost Squadron* (co-phot.), *Symphony of Six Million* 1932; *College Humor, I'm No Angel* 1933; *Bolero* 1934; *The Big Broadcast of 1936* 1935; *Rose of the Rancho, Valiant Is the Word for Carrie* 1936; *Maid of Salem, I Met Him in Paris* 1937; *Bluebeard's Eighth Wife* 1938; *Never Say Die, Invitation to Happiness* 1939; *Untamed* 1940; *I Wanted Wings, Hold Back the Dawn, Bahama Passage, The Major and the Minor* 1941; *Star Spangled Rhythm* (co-phot.) 1942; *The Crystal Ball, China* 1943; *Dead Reckoning, Woman on the Beach* 1947; *I Walk Alone, Sealed Verdict, The Snake Pit* 1948; *The Heiress* 1949; *When Willie Comes Marching Home, Secret Fury* 1950; *The Secret of Convict Lake, The Day the Earth Stood Still* 1951; *The Pride of St. Louis* 1952; *The President's Lady, A Blueprint for Murder* 1953; *Untamed, Soldier of Fortune, The Tall Men* 1955; *The Conqueror, The Revolt of Mamie Stover, Love Me Tender* 1956; *The Sun Also Rises* 1957; *In Love and War* 1958; *Blue Denim, Journey to the Center of the Earth* 1959; *From the Terrace* 1960; *Sunday in New York* 1963; *Strange Bedfellows, A Very Special Favor* 1965.

Towne, Robert. Screenwriter, director, producer, actor. Born in 1936. *ed.* Pomona College. Leading screenwriter and script doctor since the 1970s. After training as a writer with Roger CORMAN, he wrote several trenchant screenplays that defined the moral ambiguities of modern society, including *The Last Detail, Shampoo*, and *Chinatown*, for which he won an Academy Award. Beginning in the 80s, his directorial efforts have been claimed interesting but have largely failed to generate great box-office success. Well known for his strengths in developing urban characters and maintaining suspense, he has worked often as a script doctor, contributing without credit to several mainstream successes, such as *Marathon Man* and *The Godfather*, for which he wrote the scene in the garden between Al Pacino and Marlon Brando. Also nominated for Academy Awards for *The Last Detail* and *Shampoo*.

FILMS INCLUDE (as screenwriter): *The Last Woman on Earth* (also act. under pseudonym Edward Wain) 1960; *Creature from the Haunted Sea* (act. only under pseudonym Edward Wain) 1961; *The Tomb of Ligeia* 1964; *Bonnie and Clyde* (consultant), *Villa Rides* 1967; *Drive, He Said* (act. only) 1971; *The Last Detail* 1973; *Chinatown* 1974; *Shampoo, The Yakuza* 1975; *Personal Best* (also dir.) 1981; *Greystoke: The Legend of Tarzan of the Apes* (under pseudonym P. H. Vazak) 1984; *The Bedroom Window* (also exec. prod.), *The Pick-Up Artist* (act. only), *Tough Guys Don't Dance* (consultant) 1987; *Tequila Sunrise* (also dir.) 1988; *Days of Thunder* (also story), *The Two Jakes* 1990; *The Firm* (co-sc.) 1993; *Love Affair* 1994; *Mission: Impossible* 1996.

Townsend, Robert. Director, actor, writer, producer. Born on Feb. 6, 1957, in Chicago, Ill. *ed.* Illinois State U., Hunter Coll. Craftily inventive comedic filmmaker and player. After abandoning a career in baseball, he performed on the stage with Second City and the Experimental Black Actors Guild. After several strong performances as an actor, he debuted as a director in 1987. His first feature, *Hollywood Shuffle*, based on his encounters on the job hunt, was praised for its funny but pungent barbs at black stereotyping. Subsequent efforts have been uneven but imaginative.

FILMS INCLUDE: As director—*Hollywood Shuffle* (also act., sc., prod.) *Eddie Murphy Raw* 1987; *The Five Heartbeats* (also act., sc., prod.) 1991; *Meteor Man* (also act., sc.) 1993. As actor—*Willie & Phil* 1980; *A Soldier's Story, Streets of Fire* 1984; *American Flyers* 1985; *Odd Jobs, Ratboy* 1986; *The Mighty Quinn, I'm Gonna Git You Sucka* (uncredited) 1989; *Meteor Man* (also sc., co-prod.)1993; *B.A.P.S.* (dir.) 1997.

Toye, Wendy. Director. Born on May 1, 1917, in London. A professional dancer from age four, she staged a ballet at the London Palladium when she was only ten. She subsequently choreographed, danced, and acted in numerous stage productions. Since 1946 she has produced and directed many highly successful plays, musicals, and ballets for the Old Vic, Sadler's Wells, and other companies. During the 50s and early 60s she also directed films, with somewhat lesser success. She has also done much directing for British TV.

FILMS: *The Stranger Left No Card* (short) 1953; *The Teckman Mystery* 1954; *Three Cases of Murder* (one episode), *Raising a Riot, All for Mary* 1955; *On the Twelfth Day* (short) 1956; *True as a Turtle* 1957; *We Joined the Navy* 1962; *The King's Breakfast* (short) 1963.

Toyoda, Shiro. Director. Born on Jan. 3, 1906, in Kyoto, Japan. In films from the age of 19, as screenwriter and assistant to director Yasujiro SHIMAZU, he began directing in the late 20s. He has acquired a reputation as a good actors' director. His films have often dealt, sometimes humorously, with the question of individual freedom versus social conformity.

FILMS INCLUDE: *Painted Lips* 1929; *Three Women* 1935; *Young People* 1937; *Nightingale* 1938; *Spring on Lepers' Island* 1940; *Young Figure* 1943; *The Four Seasons of Woman* 1950; *Whisper of Spring* 1952; *The Mistress/Wild Geese* 1953; *Grass Whistle, Marital Relations* 1955; *Madame White Snake* 1956; *Snow Country, Evening Calm* 1957; *Pilgrimage at Night* 1959; *The Twilight Story* 1960; *The Diplomat's Mansion* 1961; *Till Tomorrow Comes* 1962; *Madame Aki* 1963; *Sweet Sweat* 1964; *Illusion of Blood, Tale of a Carpenter* 1965; *River of Forever* 1967; *Portrait of Hell* 1969.

track. See SOUND TRACK.

tracking shot (also **trucking shot, traveling shot, dolly shot**). A shot in which a camera—mounted on tracks, on a vehicle, or on a dolly—moves forward, backward, or sideways, to follow the action and the movements of performers. The camera is said to "track in" when moving closer to the subject and to "track out" when moving away from the subject.

track laying. The process of fitting sound tracks to a motion picture. The job is usually done by a sound cutter.

tracks. Rails attached to the floor of a studio set or to the ground on an exterior location to facilitate the moving of a camera from one position to another during the filming of a shot.

Tracy, Lee. Actor. *b.* William Lee Tracy, Apr. 14, 1898, Atlanta. *d.* 1968. *ed.* Union Coll. (Schenectady, N.Y.). He worked briefly on the railroad before making his stage debut in stock in 1921. He moved up to Broadway in 1924 and made his screen debut in 1929. Following his success as Hildy Johnson on Broadway in 'The Front Page' (1930), he was frequently cast in films as a fast-talking crack reporter. He also played a variety of other dynamic types, in both lead and supporting roles, in films of the 30s and early 40s. He was nominated for an Oscar for his last film role, in *The Best Man* (1964). He starred in the TV series 'Martin Kane—Private Eye' and appeared in many other television programs.

FILMS INCLUDE: *Big Time* 1929; *Born Reckless, Liliom, She Got What She Wanted* 1930; *The Strange Love of Molly Louvain, Love Is a Racket, Doctor X, Blessed Event, Washington Merry-Go-Round, The Night Mayor, The Half-Naked Truth* 1932; *Clear All Wires, Private Jones, The Nuisance, Dinner at Eight, Turn Back the Clock, Bombshell, Advice to the Lovelorn* 1933; *I'll Tell the World, You Belong to Me, The Lemon Drop Kid* 1934; *Carnival, Two Fisted* 1935; *Sutter's Gold, Wanted: Jane Turner* 1936; *Criminal Lawyer, Behind the Headlines* 1937; *Crashing Hollywood* 1938; *Fixer Dugan, The Spellbinder* 1939; *Millionaires in Prison* 1940; *The Payoff, Power of the Press* 1943; *Betrayal from the East* 1945; *High Tide* 1947; *The Best Man* 1964.

Tracy, Spencer. Actor. *b.* Apr. 5, 1900, Milwaukee. *d.* 1967. The son of a truck salesman, he was educated at a Jesuit prep school and intended to study for the priesthood, but he quit school in 1917 to join the Navy. After WW I ended, he resumed his studies at Northwestern Military Academy and in 1921 enrolled at Ripon College (Wis.). At Ripon he scored an unexpected triumph playing the lead in a college play and made up his mind to become an actor. In 1922 he enrolled at the American Academy of Dramatic Arts in New York and that same year landed his first bit role on Broadway as one of the robots in Karel Capek's 'R.U.R.' But after graduating the following year he found the going rough and was forced into a series of odd jobs to survive—as bellhop, janitor, door-to-door salesman, etc. He finally found employment in stock and gradually built himself a reputation as a solid, dependable leading man whose acting ability overshadowed his moodiness, rudeness, and short temper.

He began appearing on Broadway with increasing frequency and, finally, in 1930 landed the lead role in 'The Last Mile,' a successful prison drama that led to his career in films. Impressed with Tracy's performance in the play, director John Ford chose him for the lead in the Hollywood gangster drama *Up the River.* Tracy was signed by Fox and for several years he was typecast in "tough guy" roles. Stocky and craggy-faced, he wasn't handsome in the conventional Hollywood way and was rarely cast as a typical leading man. Yet in just a few years he was to become one of the top stars in the business, admired by the public for his unpretentious humor and his ability to project sincerity and straightforward manliness, and by the critics for his seemingly effortless, completely natural, and restrained performances. Some wags called him "The Prince of Underplayers."

Through much of his career, Tracy was widely acknowledged as one of Hollywood's greatest screen actors. Laurence Olivier once commented: "I've learned more about acting from watching Tracy than in any other way. He has great truth in everything he does." Tracy's big break came in 1935, when he switched to MGM and was assigned roles that allowed him to demonstrate his versatility. He won Academy Awards for *Captains Courageous* (1937) and *Boys Town* (1938), the first actor to win two Oscars in succession. In addition he received Oscar nominations for *San Francisco* (1936), *Father of the Bride* (1950), *Bad Day at Black Rock* (1955), *The Old Man and the Sea* (1958), *Inherit the Wind* (1960), *Judgment at Nuremberg* (1961), and *Guess Who's Coming to Dinner* (1967). With the passage of years he gradually moved into warm and dignified but irascible fatherly roles. Tracy, who had been married since 1923 to former stage actress Louise Treadwell, received much unwanted publicity in the early 30s as a result of a romantic interlude with Loretta Young. In 1942 he began a lifelong close relationship with actress Katharine HEPBURN, his co-star in nine films. Their intimate friendship became a Hollywood legend and by silent consent was never exploited by the scandalmongers of the gossip columns. A devout Catholic, Tracy never divorced his wife, although they lived separately for years. In the early 60s, when Tracy was felled by lung congestion, Miss Hepburn interrupted her own career to be at his bedside. They returned to the screen together, after several years of absence, as co-stars of *Guess Who's Coming to Dinner* (1967). Tracy appeared very ill throughout the production but carried on with his role with admirable courage. Several weeks after the completion of shooting, he died. The Tracy-Hepburn affair was the subject of a 1971 best-seller by Garson Kanin, *Tracy and Hepburn.*

FILMS: Shorts—*Taxi Talks, The Strong Arm, The Hard Guy* 1930. Features—*Up the River* 1930; *Quick Millions, Six Cylinder Love, Goldie* 1931; *She Wanted a Millionaire, Sky Devils, Disorderly Conduct, Young America, Society Girl, The Painted Woman, Me and My Gal* 1932; *20,000 Years in Sing Sing, Face in the Sky, Shanghai Madness, The Power and the Glory, The Mad Game, A Man's Castle* 1933; *The Show-Off, Looking for Trouble, Bottoms Up, Now I'll Tell, Marie Galante* 1934; *It's a Small World, The Murder Man, Dante's Inferno, Whipsaw* 1935; *Riffraff, Fury, San Francisco, Libeled Lady* 1936; *They Gave Him a Gun, Captains Courageous* (as Manuel), *Big City* 1937; *Mannequin, Test Pilot, Boys Town* (as Father Flanagan) 1938; *Stanley and Livingstone* (as Stanley) 1939; *I Take This Woman, Northwest Passage, Edison the Man* (as Thomas A. Edison), *Boom Town* 1940; *Men of Boys Town* (again as Father Flanagan), *Dr. Jekyll and Mr. Hyde* (title role) 1941; *Woman of the Year, Tortilla Flat* (as Pilon), *Keeper of the Flame* 1942; *A Guy Named Joe* 1943; *The Seventh Cross, Thirty Seconds Over Tokyo* 1944; *Without Love* 1945; *The Sea of Grass, Cass Timberlane* (title role) 1947; *State of the Union*

1948; *Edward My Son* (as Arnold Boult), *Adam's Rib* 1949; *Malaya, Father of the Bride* 1950; *Father's Little Dividend, The People Against O'Hara* 1951; *Pat and Mike, Plymouth Adventure* 1952; *The Actress* 1953; *Broken Lance* 1954; *Bad Day at Black Rock* 1955; *The Mountain* 1956; *Desk Set* 1957; *The Old Man and the Sea* (title role), *The Last Hurrah* 1958; *Inherit the Wind* (as a renamed Clarence Darrow) 1960; *The Devil at 4 O' Clock, Judgment at Nuremberg* 1961; *It's a Mad Mad Mad Mad World* 1963; *Guess Who's Coming to Dinner* 1967.

Tracy, William. Actor. *b.* Dec. 1, 1917, Pittsburgh. *d.* 1967. Trained for the stage at the American Academy of Dramatic Arts, he appeared in a number of Broadway plays and musicals. He went to Hollywood in 1938 to repeat his stage role in *Brother Rat* and stayed to play in many films of the late 30s and 40s, often as a dull-witted juvenile or immature adult.

FILMS INCLUDE: *Brother Rat, Angels with Dirty Faces* 1938; *Million Dollar Legs* 1939; *The Shop Around the Corner, Strike Up the Band, Terry and the Pirates* (serial; title role), *Gallant Sons* 1940; *Tobacco Road* (as Dude Lester), *Mr. and Mrs. Smith, Tanks a Million, Tillie the Toiler* 1941; *Hayfoot, Young America, To the Shores of Tripoli, About Face* 1942; *Fall In, Yanks Ahoy* 1943; *Here Comes Trouble* 1948; *As You Were* 1951; *Mr. Walkie Talkie* 1952; *The Wings of Eagles* 1957.

trailer. 1. A short publicity film, shown as part of a regular program at a theater, advertising the merits of a forthcoming motion picture. Often preceded by the title "Coming Attractions," the trailer consists of highlight scenes from the forthcoming attraction, appropriately cut to create an impression of excitement and accompanied by superimposed titles or narration worded in superlatives. 2. Another name for TAIL, a length of blank leader at the end of a reel.

training films. Motion pictures produced for the purpose of instructing personnel in the military, industry, etc., on methods, procedures, and techniques concerning specific tasks.

transfer. The process of re-recording a sound track from the original tape to magnetic film.

transitional effects. Effects produced by a motion picture camera or added optically in the lab which allow a smooth flow of film narrative by providing a link between separate scenes. The most common transitional effects are the FADE, the DISSOLVE, and the WIPE. Other variations include the SWISH PAN, out-of-focus effects, and the moving of a body or an object toward or away from the camera lens.

translucent screen. A semitransparent screen often used in BACK PROJECTION.

transparency. A picture printed on glass, celluloid, or other transparent material which is made visible by transmitted light. Still transparencies are often used in process shots, to project a background for a scene.

Trauberg, Ilya. Director. *b.* Nov. 20, 1905, Odessa, Russia. *d.* 1948. The younger brother of Leonid TRAUBERG, he made his directorial debut in 1927 with a documentary, *Leningrad Today.* After being engaged as one of the three assistants on Sergei Eisenstein's *October/Ten Days That Shook The World,* he was assigned his first feature film, *Blue Express/The China Express,* which he turned into a masterpiece of montage. Using a trans-Asiatic train and its passengers as a microcosm of Chinese social and political life, he brilliantly employed rhythmic cutting in presenting his revolutionary theme. He later made only a handful of films, but the influence of his *China Express* on contemporary Soviet filmmakers was considerable.

FILMS: *Leningrad Today* (doc.) 1927; *Blue Express/The China Express* (also co-sc.) 1929; *Kites* (short) 1931; *We Work for You* 1932; *An Unusual Case* (also co-sc.) 1934; *Son of Mongolia* 1936; *The Year 1919* (compilation film; also co-sc.) 1938; *Concert Waltz* (co-dir. with M. Dubson, co-sc.) 1940; *We Expect Victory There* (war propaganda film) 1941; *The Spider* (co-dir. with I. Zemgano) 1942.

Trauberg, Leonid. Director. Born in 1902, in Odessa, Russia. A co-founder of FEX (Factory of the Eccentric Actor) in 1922, he collaborated from 1924 with Grigori KOZINTSEV on the direction of a number of important Soviet films, notably "The Maxim Trilogy." Their collaboration lasted through the mid-40s, when each began directing films on his own. Older brother of Ilya TRAUBERG.

FILMS: For full credit list of films made in collaboration with Grigori Kozintsev, see KOZINTSEV, Grigori. Alone—*The Actress* 1943; *Plain People* 1945 (release delayed until 1956); *Soldiers Were Marching* (also sc.) 1958; *Dead Souls* (also sc.) 1960. In collaboration with A. Tontichkin—*Free Wind* 1961.

Trauner, Alexander (Alexandre). Art director. Born on Aug. 3, 1906, in Budapest. A promising young painter, he arrived in Paris to exhibit his works and stayed to become an assistant of the famed French art director Lazare MEERSON. He followed the Meerson tradition of studio-controlled realism when he became an art director in his own right, most notably in the films of Marcel CARNÉ. During the Nazi Occupation, the Jewish Trauner continued his film work from various hiding places, yet during this period he was able to produce some of his most memorable sets, anonymously for such films as *Les Visiteurs du Soir/The Devil's Envoys* and *Les Enfants du Paradis/Children of Paradise.* Since the late 50s he has worked frequently on American films, especially those requiring European backgrounds.

FILMS INCLUDE: *L'Affaire est dans le Sac* (asst. art dir.) 1932; *Ciboulette* (asst. art dir.) 1933; *L'Hôtel du Libre Echange* (asst. art dir.) 1934; *Drôle de Drame/Bizarre Bizarre* 1937; *Quai des Brumes/Port of Shadows, Entrée des Artistes/The Curtain Rises, Hôtel du Nord* 1938; *Le Jour se lève/Daybreak* 1939; *Remorques/Stormy Waters* 1941; *Les Visiteurs du Soir/The Devil's Envoys* (co-art dir.; uncredited) 1942; *Lumière d'Eté* (co-art dir.; uncredited) 1943; *Les Enfants du Paradis/Children of Paradise* (co-art dir.; uncredited) 1945; *Les Portes de la Nuit/Gates of the Night* 1946; *Voyage-Surprise* (co-art dir.) 1947; *Manèges/The Cheat, La Marie du Port* (co-art dir.) 1950; *Juliette ou la Clé des Songes/Juliette* 1951; *Othello* (for Orson Welles), *La Jeune Folle/Desperate Decision* 1952; *L'Amant de Lady Chatterley/Lady Chatterley's Lover, Land of the Pharaohs* (US) 1955; *Love in the Afternoon* (US) 1957; *Witness for the Prosecution* (US) 1958; *The Nun's Story* (US) 1959; *Once More with Feeling* (US), *The Apartment* (US) 1960; *Aimez-vous Brahms?/Goodbye Again* (Fr./US), *Paris Blues* (US), *One Two Three* (US) 1961; *Gigot* (US) 1962; *Irma La Douce* (US) 1963; *Behold a Pale Horse* (US), *Kiss Me Stupid* (US) 1964; *How to Steal a Million* (US) 1966; *La Nuit des Généraux/The Night of the Generals* (Fr./UK) 1967; *A Flea in Her Ear* (US/Fr.), *Uptight* (US) 1968; *La Promèsse de l'Aube/Promise at Dawn* (Fr./US), *The Private Life of Sherlock Holmes* (US/UK) 1970; *L'Impossible Objet/Impossible Object* 1973; *The Man Who Would Be King* (UK) 1975; *Mr. Klein* 1976; *Les Routes du Sud* 1978; *The Fiendish Plot of Dr. Fu Manchu* (UK), *Don Giovanni* (It.) 1980; *Coup de Torchon* 1981; *La Truite* 1982; *Tchao Pantin* 1983; *Vive les Femmes!* 1984; *Harem, Subway* 1985; *Round Midnight* (US) 1986; *Le Moustachu* 1987; *La Nuit Bengali* 1988; *Comedie d'amour, Reunion* (US) 1989.

traveling matte. An elaborate MATTE or masking technique that makes it possible to combine elements photographed under different circumstances, such as actors on a soundstage, background scenes on location, and MINIATURES and MATTE PAINTINGS in a SPECIAL EFFECTS workshop. The procedure most often employed is the BLUE SCREEN PROCESS, which involves the use of colored screens and colored filters, multiple maskings with moving silhouettes, and an OPTICAL PRINTER. Computer compositing (see DIGITAL EFFECTS) can yield more seamless results and has begun to gain favor as an alternative.

traveling shot. A shot requiring camera movement. See DOLLY SHOT; TRACKING SHOT.

travelogue. A short film describing a people or a place, often superficially. Hundreds of travelogues were produced by Hollywood in its heyday as fillers in motion picture theater programs. They typically emphasized the glamorous aspects of life in faraway places, completely avoiding any visual or verbal reference to such realities as slums and poverty. Many ended with stock lines: "As the sun sinks slowly in the west, we bid farewell. . . ."

Travers, Bill. Actor. *b.* Jan. 3, 1922, in Newcastle-upon-Tyne, England. *d.* 1994. Tall, brawny leading man of British stage, screen, and TV. At his most comfortable in outdoor settings. He married Virginia MCKENNA, with whom he co-starred in *Born Free* and a number of other films.

FILMS INCLUDE: *The Wooden Horse* 1950; *The Browning Version* 1951; *Romeo and Juliet* (as Benvolio) 1954; *Geordie/Wee Geordie, Footsteps in the Fog* 1955; *Bhowani Junction* (US/UK) 1956; *The Barretts of Wimpole Street* (as Robert Browning), *The Seventh Sin* (US), *The Smallest Show on Earth* 1957; *The Bridal Path* 1959; *Gorgo* 1960; *The Green Helmet, Invasion Quartet* 1961; *Duel at Diablo* (US), *Born Free* 1966; *A Midsummer Night's Dream* 1968; *Ring of Bright Water* 1969; *An Elephant Called Slowly* (also co-prod., co-sc.) 1970; *Boulevard du Rhum* (Fr.) 1971; *The Belstone Fox* 1973; *Christian the Lion* (also co-prod., co-dir., co-sc.) 1976.

Travers, Henry. Actor. *b.* Travers Heagerty, 1874, Ireland. *d.* 1965. A veteran of the British stage, he played character parts in Broadway plays from the early 20s and in Hollywood films from the early 30s. Typically cast as a dignified and amiable senior citizen, he appeared in an unusually high number of top-quality productions; his best-known role may be that of Clarence Odbody, the Angel Second Class, in *It's a Wonderful Life*. He was nominated for an Oscar as best supporting actor for his performance in *Mrs. Miniver* (1942).

FILMS INCLUDE: *Reunion in Vienna, Another Language, The Invisible Man* 1933; *Death Takes a Holiday* 1934; *After Office Hours, Escapade, Seven Keys to Baldpate* 1935; *The Sisters* 1938; *Dodge City, Dark Victory, On Borrowed Time, Stanley and Livingstone, The Rains Came* 1939; *Primrose Path, Edison the Man* 1940; *High Sierra, The Bad Man* 1941; *Ball of Fire, Mrs. Miniver, Random Harvest* 1942; *Shadow of a Doubt, The Moon Is Down, Madame Curie* 1943; *None Shall Escape, Dragon Seed* 1944; *Thrill of a Romance, The Bells of St. Mary's* 1945; *It's a Wonderful Life, The Yearling* 1946; *Beyond Glory* 1948; *The Girl from Jones Beach* 1949.

Travolta, John. Actor. Born on Feb. 18, 1954, in Englewood, N.J., of Italian-Irish descent. Highly popular young star of American TV and movies of the late 70s, and later a likeable lead of the 90s. A high school dropout at 16, he began his acting career in summer stock in New Jersey. After a period of training in acting and dancing he began doing commercials and off Broadway. He moved to Hollywood, where he got occasional small roles on TV, then joined the national touring company of 'Grease,' eventually making the Broadway casts of 'Grease' and the Andrews Sisters' musical 'Over Here!' He got his big break in 1975 when he joined the cast of the TV series 'Welcome Back, Kotter,' in the role of the dimwitted but lovable Vinnie Barbarino. Although his role in the series was secondary, he immediately attracted an enthusiastic following and soon became one of television's top stars. Film assignments quickly followed. An appealing young man with a dazzling grin, luminous blue eyes, and a characteristic cleft chin, he extended his popularity to the big screen with a convincing performance in the role of Tony Manero, king of the Brooklyn disco scene, in the film *Saturday Night Fever* (1977) and enjoyed another success with the screen version of *Grease* (1978), and with *Urban Cowboy* (1980), which helped popularize Western wear in the early 80s. During this period, he also released a few hit records, having done all his own singing in *Grease*.

Travolta's film career sagged in the 80s and he never regained the critical buzz from his first few films, but by the early 90s his popularity was rebounding thanks to the successful *Look Who's Talking* series (from 1989) and the critical and box-office success of his turn in *Pulp Fiction* (1994). He is again one of the highest paid and most popular actors working today. He credits Scientology with his comeback and his self-actualization. Sister Ellen and brother Joey are also actors. He is married to actress Kelly Preston.

FILMS: *The Devil's Rain* 1975; *The Boy in the Plastic Bubble* (TV movie), *Carrie* 1976; *Saturday Night Fever* 1977; *Grease, Moment by Moment* 1978; *Urban Cowboy* 1980; *Blow Out* 1981; *Staying Alive* 1983; *Two of a Kind* 1984; *Perfect* 1985; *The Experts* 1989; *Look Who's Talking* 1989; *Look Who's Talking, Too* 1990; *Shout* 1991; *Look Who's Talking Now* 1993; *Eyes of an Angel* (filmed in 1990), *Pulp Fiction* 1994; *Broken Arrow, White Man's Burden* 1995; *Phenomenon, Michael* 1996; *Face/Off, Mad City, She's So Lovely* 1997.

Treacher, Arthur. Actor. *b.* Arthur Veary, July 23, 1894, Brighton, England. *d.* 1975. Trained for a career in law, in the footsteps of his father, he turned to acting on the London stage after completing his WW I military service. Arriving in the US in 1926, he appeared in a number of revues and Broadway plays before switching to films. Tall and well mannered, he was soon typecast by Hollywood as the perfect butler—meticulous, impeccably dressed, and often haughty, dour-faced, and disdainful. He played the role numerous times in the 30s and 40s and only rarely was given a chance to step out of character. In the early 60s he acted as Merv Griffin's sidekick in a nightly TV talk show. Later, he lent his name to a nationwide household help agency and in the early 70s he was associated with the Arthur Treacher's Fish and Chips fast-food chain.

FILMS INCLUDE: *Battle of Paris* 1929; *Gambling Lady, The Key, Viva Villa!, Madame Du Barry* 1934; *Bordertown, David Copperfield, No More Ladies, Curly Top, A Midsummer Night's Dream, Splendor* 1935; *Magnificent Obsession, Anything Goes, Satan Met a Lady, Thank You Jeeves, Under Your Spell, Stowaway* 1936; *Step Lively Jeeves, Thin Ice, Heidi* 1937; *Mad About Music, My Lucky Star, Always in Trouble* 1938; *The Little Princess, Barricade* 1939; *Irene* 1940; *Forever and a Day* 1943; *National Velvet* 1944; *Delightfully Dangerous* 1945; *That Midnight Kiss* 1949; *Love That Brute* 1950; *Mary Poppins* 1964.

treatment. The intermediate stage in the development of a script; it occurs between the SYNOPSIS (or step outline) and the SCREENPLAY, or shooting script. It consists of a fully developed narrative covering all the principal situations and may include certain key passages of dialogue.

Tree, Dorothy. Actress. *b.* May 21, 1909, in Brooklyn, N.Y. *d.* 1992. *ed.* Cornell. Leading lady, second lead, and supporting player of Hollywood films, following stage experience, including much Broadway. Later a voice teacher, she authored *A Woman's Voice,* a guide for public speaking.

FILMS INCLUDE: *Just Imagine* 1930; *Husband's Holiday*

1931; *Life Begins* 1932; *East of Fifth Avenue* 1933; *Here Comes the Navy, The Dragon Murder Case, Madame Du Barry, The Firebird* 1934; *The Woman in Red, Four Hours to Kill, A Night at the Ritz* 1935; *Three Godfathers* 1936; *The Great Garrick* 1937; *Trade Winds, Confessions of a Nazi Spy* 1939; *Abe Lincoln in Illinois, Knute Rockne—All American* 1940; *Nazi Agent* 1942; *Hitler—Dead or Alive, Crime Doctor* 1943; *No Sad Songs for Me, The Asphalt Jungle, The Men* 1950.

Treen, Mary. Actress. *b.* 1907, in St. Louis, Mo. *d.* 1989. Trained as a dancer, she appeared in many revues and stage musicals. Beginning in 1934 she provided comedy relief in numerous Hollywood films, often in the role of a plain-looking working girl.

FILMS INCLUDE: *Happiness Ahead, Babbitt* 1934; *Traveling Saleslady, G-Men, A Night at the Ritz, Don't Bet on Blondes, Page Miss Glory, Shipmates Forever, The Case of the Lucky Legs* 1935; *Colleen, Life Begins at 20* 1936; *God's Country and the Woman, They Gave Him a Gun, Ever Since Eve, Second Honeymoon* 1937; *Sally Irene and Mary, Kentucky Moonshine* 1938; *First Love* 1939; *Kitty Foyle* 1940; *You Belong to Me* 1941; *The Great Man's Lady, They All Kissed the Bride* 1942; *They Got Me Covered, The Powers Girl, Hit Parade of 1943* 1943; *Casanova Brown, I Love a Soldier* 1944; *Don Juan Quilligan* 1945; *From This Day Forward* 1946; *It's a Wonderful Life* 1947; *Let's Live a Little* 1948; *Sailor Beware* 1952; *The Caddy, Let's Do It Again* 1953; *The Birds and the Bees* 1956; *The Sad Sack* 1957; *All in a Night's Work* 1961; *Who's Minding the Store?* 1963; *Paradise Hawaiian Style* 1966; *The Strongest Man in the World* (bit) 1975.

Trenker, Luis. Actor, director, screenwriter. *b.* Oct. 4, 1893, in Ortisei, Italy, of German parents. *d.* 1990. After WW I service as a pilot, he worked as a mountain guide and was hired in 1921 to guide Arnold FANCK's production unit, shooting *Marvels of Ski,* in the Alps. A robust, handsome athlete, he found himself playing the lead part in the film and further Fanck MOUNTAIN FILMS, often opposite Leni RIEFENSTAHL. From the early 30s he also directed and wrote films in that and other genres.

FILMS INCLUDE: As actor—*Das Wunder des Schneeschuhs/Marvels of Ski* (doc.) 1921; *Der Berg des Schicksals/Peak of Fate* 1924; *Der heilige Berg/Peaks of Destiny* 1926; *Der grosse Sprung/The Big Jump* 1927; *Der Kampf ums Matterhorn/The Fight for the Matterhorn* 1928; *Der Ruf des Nordens/Call of the North* (also prod.) 1929; *Der Sohn der Weissen Berge* 1930; As director-actor-writer—*Berge in Flammen/The Doomed Battalion* (co-dir. with Karl Hartl; English-language version dir. by Cyril Gardner) 1931; *Der Rebell/The Rebel* (co-dir. with Curtis Bernhardt; English-language version co-dir. with Edwin H. Knopf) 1932; *Der verlorene Sohn* 1934; *Der Kaiser von Kalifornien* 1936; *Condottieri/ Giovanni de Medici—The Leader* (It./Ger.), *Der Berg ruft/The Challenge* (English-language version co-dir. with Vincent Korda) 1937; *Liebesbriefe aus dem Engadin* 1938; *Der Feuerteufel* 1940; *Monte Miracolo* (It.) 1943; *Im Banne des Monte Miracolo* 1945; *Duell in den Bergen* 1949; *Flucht in die Dolomiten* 1955; *Wetterleuchten und Maria* 1957; *Sein bester Freund* 1962.

Trevor, Claire. Actress. Born Claire Wemlinger, on Mar. 8, 1909, in New York City. She began her acting career in stock in the late 20s after attending Columbia and the American Academy of Dramatic Arts. By 1932 she was starring on Broadway opposite Edward Arnold and appearing in Vitaphone shorts, which were filmed in the Flatbush section of Brooklyn. Making her feature film debut the following year, she soon found herself typecast as a gang moll, a saloon girl, or an assortment of other cynical but golden-hearted floozies. She was put mainly in B pictures but proved herself a highly gifted actress in her occasional A's, notably in *Dead End, Stagecoach, Key Largo,* and *The High and the Mighty.* She was nominated for Oscars for her roles in the first and the fourth and won the best supporting actress Academy Award for the third. Since the 50s she has also appeared much on TV, and won an Emmy in 1956 for her performance in 'Dodsworth,' opposite Fredric March.

FILMS INCLUDE: *Life in the Raw, The Last Trial, The Mad Game, Jimmy and Sally* 1933; *Hold That Girl, Baby Take a Bow, Wild Gold* 1934; *Black Sheep, Dante's Inferno, Navy Wife* 1935; *My Marriage, Song and Dance Man, Human Cargo, To Mary—With Love, Star for a Night, 15 Maiden Lane, Career Woman* 1936; *Time Out for Romance, King of Gamblers, One Mile from Heaven, Dead End, Second Honeymoon, Big Town Girl* 1937; *Walking Down Broadway, The Amazing Dr. Clitterhouse, Valley of the Giants, Five of a Kind* 1938; *Stagecoach, I Stole a Million, Allegheny Uprising* 1939; *Dark Command* 1940; *Honky Tonk, Texas* 1941; *The Adventures of Martin Eden, Crossroads, Street of Chance* 1942; *The Desperadoes, The Woman of the Town* 1943; *Murder My Sweet* 1944; *Johnny Angel* 1945; *Crack-Up, The Bachelor's Daughters* 1946; *Born to Kill* 1947; *Raw Deal, Key Largo, The Babe Ruth Story, The Velvet Touch* 1948; *The Lucky Stiff* 1949; *Borderline* 1950; *Hard Fast and Beautiful, Best of the Badmen* 1951; *Hoodlum Empire, My Man and I* 1952; *Stop—You're Killing Me, The Stranger Wore a Gun* 1953; *The High and the Mighty* 1954; *Man Without a Star, Lucy Gallant* 1955; *The Mountain* 1956; *Marjorie Morningstar* 1958; *Two Weeks in Another Town* 1962; *The Stripper* 1963; *How to Murder Your Wife* 1965; *The Cape Town Affair* (South Africa) 1967; *Kiss Me Goodbye* 1982.

Triangle. A film corporation formed in 1915 by Harry Aitken, formerly of Mutual, in association with Adam Kessel and Charles Bauman. It combined under one roof the talents of three formidable filmmakers, after which the company was named: D. W. GRIFFITH, Thomas INCE, and Mack SENNETT. For three years Triangle was a dominant factor in American cinema, producing prestige pictures and gaining exclusive bookings to thousands of motion picture theaters at higher than usual ticket prices. But the company, suffering from the financial losses of Griffith's *Intolerance* and the departure in 1917 of both Griffith and Sennett, was dissolved in 1918.

triangle. A foldable three-pointed device designed to hold the legs of a tripod and prevent them from slipping apart. Its function is similar to that of a SPIDER.

trick photography. See SPECIAL EFFECTS.

Triesault, Ivan. Actor. *b.* 1902, Talinn, Estonia. *d.* 1980. On his hometown stage from the age of 14, he emigrated to the US at 18 and after a period of acting and dance training in New York and London, he appeared as a pantomimist and dancer on the stage of the Radio City Music Hall and other auditoriums. After acting in stock and briefly on Broadway, he went to Hollywood, where he played character parts in many films, typically as a Nazi, a Communist agent, or some other undesirable foreigner.

FILMS INCLUDE: *Mission to Moscow* 1943; *In Our Time, Uncertain Glory, The Hitler Gang* (as Pastor Niemöller), *Days of Glory* 1944; *Counter-Attack* 1945; *Notorious* 1946; *Golden Earrings* 1947; *To the Ends of the Earth* 1948; *Johnny Allegro* 1949; *Kim* 1950; *Five Fingers, The Bad and the Beautiful* 1952; *Young Bess* 1953; *Her Twelve Men* 1954; *Jet Pilot* 1957; *Fraulein, The Amazing Transparent Man* 1960; *Barabba/Barabbas* (It.) 1961; *The 300 Spartans* 1962; *Von Ryan's Express* 1965; *Batman* (bit) 1966.

trim. To cut or shorten in editing.

trim bin. See BIN.

Trimble, Laurence ("Larry"). Also billed as Lawrence Trimble. Director. *b.* 1885, Robbinston, Me. *d.* 1954. A short-story writer of adventure tales, he came to New York in quest of material in 1910 and found himself working as actor-screenwriter at the Vitagraph studios. His big chance came when Vitagraph hired his dog, Jean, and turned her into a popular animal star, "Jean the Vitagraph Dog." Trimble was asked to guide the dog during the shooting and he soon took over as the director of a whole series of films co-starring Jean with "The Vitagraph Girl," Florence TURNER. He rapidly gained recognition as one of the most capable directors on the lot and was also assigned to direct the films starring John BUNNY and Flora FINCH. In 1913 he and Miss Turner went to England, where they appeared together in London music halls and ventured into independent production of films for release through Cecil Hepworth. Trimble directed some of Britain's best features of the WW I period. He returned to American films in the early 20s with a series of successful films starring his newest discovery, the dog Strongheart, a popular animal in the silent screen era.

FILMS INCLUDE: In the US—*Saved by the Flag* 1910; *The Battle Hymn of the Republic* 1911; *The French Spy, Cardinal Wolsey* (co-dir. with J. Stuart Blackton) 1912; *The Pickwick Papers, Sisters All, Checkmated, The Deerslayer* (co-dir. with Hal Reid), *There's Music in the Hair, Under the Make-Up* (also sc.) 1913. In the UK—*The Harper Mystery* 1913; *Through the Valley of Shadows, The Murdock Trial, For Her People* 1914; *My Old Dutch, Caste, Far from the Madding Crowd, The Great Adventure* 1915; *Sally in Our Alley, A Place in the Sun* 1916. In the US—*The Silent Call* 1921; *Brawn of the North* (also co-prod., co-sc.) 1922; *The Love Master* (also co-prod., sc.), *Sundown* (co-dir. with Harry O. Hoyt) 1924; *White Fang* 1925; *My Old Dutch* (also sc.) 1926.

trims. Sections of film cut from a scene by the editor and left over after he has made his selection of the footage he wants used in the work print. Trims, also called OUT-TAKES or "outs," must be carefully classified and preserved in the event that they will be needed for incorporation into the final film. Contrary to the famous phrase, trims are not left "on the cutting-room floor" but placed in a BIN after being marked and numbered.

Trintignant, Jean-Louis. Actor. Born on Dec. 11, 1930, in Fiolenc, France. The son of a manufacturer, he left law school at age 20 and went to Paris to study acting. Overcoming personal shyness and a thick provincial accent, he made his stage debut in 1951 and has since appeared in many plays. He made his first screen appearance in 1956 in a supporting part, and became known to international film audiences later that year for his role as Brigitte Bardot's timid husband in Vadim's *Et Dieu créa la Femme/And God Created Woman.* His rise to fame seemed to accelerate as the result of his well-publicized offscreen romance with the sex kitten. But just when he seemed on the threshold of success, he was recruited into military service in Algeria. Returning to the screen after a three-year absence, he re-plodded his way up to the top through a succession of mostly routine films interspersed with occasional good roles in both French and Italian productions.

In 1966, Trintignant was "rediscovered" by international cinema audiences as Anouk Aimée's love interest in the highly successful box-office production of Claude Lelouche's *Un Homme et une Femme/A Man and a Woman.* A car-racing enthusiast, it was he who suggested that Lelouche make the protagonist a racer, rather than a doctor as originally planned. He has since remained one of the leading personalities of the European cinema, a star whose appeal seems to stem largely from his economy of expression and the sense of ambiguity and mystery he projects on the screen. He garnered wide praise for his performance in such films as *Ma Nuit chez Maud/My Night at Maud's, Z,* and *Il Conformista/The Conformist.* In 1969 he won the best actor award at Cannes for *Z.* Divorced from actress Stephane AUDRAN (now the wife of Claude Chabrol), Trintignant is married to director Nadine TRINTIGNANT, who directed several of his films. He directed his own first film in 1973.

FILMS INCLUDE: *Si tous les Gars du Monde/If All the Guys in the World* 1956; *Et Dieu créa la Femme/And God Created Woman* 1956; *Les Liaisons dangereuses, Estate Violenta/Violent Summer* (It./Fr.) 1959; *Austerlitz, Le Coeur battant/The French Game* 1960; *L'Atlantide/Journey Beneath the Desert* (It./Fr.) 1961; *Les Sept Péchés capitaux/Seven Capital Sins, Il Sorpasso/The Easy Life* (It.) 1962; *Château en Suède/Nutty Naughty Chateau, Il Successo* (It.) 1963; *Mata Hari—Agent H-21, Compartiment tueurs/The Sleeping Car Murder* 1965; *Paris brûle-t-il?/Is Paris Burning?* (Fr./US), *La Longue Marche, Un Homme et une Femme/A Man and a Woman* 1966; *Trans-Europ Express, Col Cuore in Gola/Deadly Sweet* (It./Fr.), *L'Homme qui ment/The Man Who Lies* (Czech./Fr.) 1967; *Les Biches,* 1968; *Z, Ma Nuit chez Maud/My Night at Maud's, La Matriarca/The Libertine* (It.) 1969; *Il Conformista/The Conformist, Le Voyou/The Crook, L'Américain* 1970; *Sans mobile apparent/Without Apparent Motive* 1971; *La Course du Lièvre à travers les Champs/And Hope to Die, L'Attentat/The French Conspiracy, Un Homme est Mort/The Outside Man* (Fr./US) 1972, *Une Journée bien remplie* (also dir.), *Défense de Savoir, Le Train* 1973; *Les Violons du Bal, Le Mouton enragé/The French Way/Love at the Top, Le Secret, Le Jeu avec le Feu* 1974; *L'Aggression/Act of Aggression, Flic Story, Il Pleut sur Santiago/It Is Raining on Santiago* 1975; *La Donna della Domenica* (It./Fr.), *Le Voyage de Noces, L'Ordinateur des Pompes Funebres, Le Désert des Tartares* 1976; *Les Passagers, Repérages/Faces of Love* (Switz./Fr.) 1977; *L'Argent des autres* 1978; *Le Maitre-Nageur/The Lifeguard* (also dir., sc.), *Melancolie Baby, La Terrazza* 1979; *La Banquiere, Je vous aime* 1980; *Une Affaire d'Hommes, Eaux Profondes, Passione d'amore* 1981; *Colpire Al Cuore, La Nuit de Varennes, Vivement Dimanche/Confidentially Yours* 1982; *Le Bon Plaisir, La Crime, Femmes de personne, Under Fire* (US) 1983; *L'Ete Prochain/Next Summer, Partir Revenir, Surtuz Egy Fekete Bivalyert, Viva la Vie!* 1984; *L'Homme aux yeux d'argent, Rendezvous* 1985; *La Femme de ma vie, Un Homme et une femme: Vingt ans deja/A Man and a Woman: 20 Years Later, Quinze Aout* (short) 1986; *Le Moustachu, La Vallee fantome* 1987; *Bunker Palace Hotel* (UK), *Club Extinction/Dr. M* (Ger.) 1989; *Merci, la vie* 1991; *L'Oeil Ecarlate* 1992; *Red* 1994; *City of Lost Children* 1995; *Self Made Hero, Tykho Moon* 1997.

Trintignant, Nadine. Director. Born Nadine Marquand, on Nov. 11, 1934, in Nice, France. The sister of actors Serge and Christian Marquand, she dropped out of high school at 15 to enter the film industry as a lab assistant. After gaining experience as an assistant editor and script clerk she became a highly regarded film editor for such directors as Jacques Doniol-Valcroze, Serge Bourguignon, and Jean-Luc Godard. She directed a short and a number of TV programs before turning feature director in the late 60s. Most of her films have starred Jean-Louis TRINTIGNANT, whom she married in 1960. She writes her own scripts.

FILMS: *Fragilité—ton Nom est Femme* (short; also sc.) 1965; *Mon Amour mon Amour* (also sc.) 1967; *Le Voleur de Crimes* (also sc.) 1969; *Ça n'arrive qu'aux autres/It Only Happens to Others* (also sc.) 1971; *Defense de savoir* (also co-sc.) 1973; *Le Voyage de Noces/Jalousie 1976* (also sc.) 1976; *Premier Voyage* (also sc.) 1979; *L'Ete Prochain/Next Summer* (also sc.) 1984; *La Maison de Jade* (also sc.) 1988.

tripack. Film coated with three layers of emulsion for use in color photography.

trip gear. An automatic apparatus that, by means of a clutch and an electric motor, enables an unmanned camera to expose single frames of film, or a succession of single frames, at a constant speed. It is used in animation and time-lapse cinematography.

tripod. A three-legged camera support, adjustable for height. Tripods come in a variety of sizes. Their legs are usually made of wood, but sometimes of metal. The wood tripod is tipped with an aluminum shoe to prevent it from sliding. An important part of the tripod is the "head," or "tripod head," on which the camera is mounted. There are several types of heads, the most common of which is the friction head. Other types include the gear head, the fluid head, and the gyroscopic head. The function of the head is to permit the camera to swivel in all planes, for panning, tilting, etc., in the smoothest possible manner. There are a number of special-purpose tripods, including the BABY TRIPOD, which is used for low-angle shooting.

tripod head. See TRIPOD.

Tripplehorn, Jeanne. Actress. Born 1963 in Tulsa, Okla. *ed.* Juilliard School of Drama, New York City. She began her career on the stage, appearing in a number of New York productions including ''Tis Pity She's A Whore' for the Public Theatre in 1992. She delved into television briefly but it was her performances on the silver screen that gained critical attention, beginning with *The Firm* (1993).

FILMS: *The Perfect Tribute* 1991; *Basic Instinct* 1992; *The Firm, The Night We Never Met* 1993; *Reality Bites* 1994; *Waterworld* 1995; *Till There Was You* 1997.

TriStar Pictures. Motion picture production and distribution company. Its logo a white-winged horse, the company was founded in 1982 by CBS, Home Box Office (HBO), and COLUMBIA PICTURES, each representing a different venue (broadcast TV, cable TV, and theatrical release). However, over the years, Columbia became the dominant owner, as CBS left the partnership and HBO reduced its share. Under its first president, Gary Hendler (1982–84), TriStar released its first productions, *The Natural* and *Places in the Heart*, in 1984. That same year, it began a practice of distributing independent features as well, including *Supergirl* and *Silent Night, Deadly Night*. Since then, TriStar has released a diverse group of films, including action blockbusters such as *Rambo* (1985), *Total Recall* (1990), *Terminator 2* (1991), and *Cliffhanger* (1993), comedies such as *Look Who's Talking* (1989), *Sleepless in Seattle* (1993), and *Jerry Maguire* (1996), and art films such as Francis Ford Coppola's *Peggy Sue Got Married* (1986) and Woody Allen's *Husbands and Wives* (1992).

In 1987, TriStar merged with Columbia to form Columbia Pictures Entertainment, then controlled by the Coca-Cola Company. In 1989, Japan's Sony Corporation purchased both TriStar and Columbia, which became self-contained financier-distributors under the umbrella of Sony Pictures Entertainment, as the parent company was renamed in 1991. Loews Theaters, acquired by TriStar in 1986, also passed into Sony's hands. From 1990 through 1993, TriStar was chaired by Mike Medavoy. In January 1994, Medavoy resigned and Columbia chairman Mark Canton was named chairman of the Columbia TriStar Motion Picture Companies.

Big changes were again in order for TriStar in 1996 when heavy losses forced a sweeping expulsion of executives, including Canton. Operation of the studio is now headed by Sony topper John Calley.

Trivas, Victor. Screenwriter, director, art director, *b.* 1896, Russia. *d.* 1970. He entered German cinema in the late 20s as an art director for PABST and worked in this capacity on several films, notably *The Loves of Jeanne Ney.* In 1931 he wrote and directed *Niemandsland* (*No Man's Land,* shown in the US as *Hell on Earth*), a strong plea for pacifism, all copies of which were destroyed when the Nazis came to power. In 1933 he found refuge in France, then continued to the US, where he wrote a number of scripts, and the original story for Orson Welles's *The Stranger,* for which he was nominated for an Academy Award. He was the author of a novel, *The 32nd Day.*

FILMS INCLUDE (as screenwriter, alone or in collaboration): In Germany—*Aufruhr des Blutes* (also art dir.) 1929; *Niemandsland/Hell on Earth* (also dir.), *Der Mörder Dimitri Karamasoff, Das Lied vom Leben/The Song of Life* 1931; *Grosstadtnacht* 1933. In France—*Dans les Rues/Song of the Street* (also dir.) 1933; *Les Otages/The Mayor's Dilemma* 1939. In the US—*Song of Russia* (co-story only) 1942; *The Stranger* (co-story only) 1946; *Where the Sidewalk Ends* 1950; *The Secret of Convict Lake* 1951. In Germany—*Die Nackte und der Satan/The Head* (also dir.) 1959.

Trnka, Jiří. Animator. *b.* Feb. 24, 1912, Pl'zen (Pilsen), Czechoslovakia. *d.* 1969. A graduate of Prague's School of Arts and Crafts, in 1936 he created a puppet theater, which was disbanded after the outbreak of WW II. During the war he designed stage sets and illustrated children's books. In 1945 he set up an animation unit with several collaborators at the Prague film studio; they called the unit "Trick Brothers." Trnka specialized in puppet animation, a traditional Czech art form, of which he became the undisputed master. He also created animated cartoons, but it was his puppet animation that made him an internationally recognized artist and the winner of film festival awards at Venice and elsewhere. He wrote the scripts for most of his own films.

FILMS INCLUDE: *Grandpa Planted a Beet* 1945; *The Gift, The Animals and the Brigands* 1946; *The Czech Year* 1947; *The Emperor's Nightingale* 1948; *Song of the Prairie* 1949; *Prince Bayaya* 1950; *The Golden Fish* 1951; *Old Czech Legends* 1953; *The Good Soldier Schweik* 1954; *A Midsummer Night's Dream* 1959; *Obsession* 1961; *Cybernetic Grandma* 1962; *The Archangel Gabriel and Mrs. Goose, The Hand* 1965.

Troell, Jan. Director. Born on July 23, 1931, in Limhamm, Skåne, Sweden. A dentist's son, he worked as a schoolteacher for nine years before embarking on a film career in the early 60s. He turned out a number of shorts and assisted Bo Widerberg as a cameraman and co-editor on several projects before directing his first feature in 1966. He has since established himself as one of Sweden's leading directors, a sensitive, keen-eyed interpreter for the screen of his country's literature and lore. In 1974 he directed *Zandy's Bride* in the US. He has photographed, edited, and co-scripted all but that one of his own films.

FEATURE FILMS (as director): *4 X 4* ("Stopover in the Marshland" episode; also co-sc., phot., edit.; Sw./Fin./Nor./Den.) 1965; *Here's Your Life* (also co-sc., phot., edit.) 1966; *Who Saw Him Die?/Eeny Meeny Miny Moe* (also co-sc., phot., edit.) 1968; *The Emigrants* (also co-sc., phot., edit.) 1971; *The New Land* (also co-sc., phot., edit.) 1973; *Zandy's Bride* (US) 1974; *Bang!* (also co-sc., phot., edit.) 1977; *The Flight of the Eagle* 1978; *Hurricane* (US) 1979; *Ingenjor Andrees Luftfard* (also sc., phot., ed.) 1982; *Sagolandet* (also act., sc., phot., ed.) 1986; *Il Capitano/A Swedish Requiem* (also sc., phot., ed.) 1991; *Dancing* 1994; *Hamsun* 1997.

trombone. On a motion picture set, a bracket to which lights may be attached.

Trotta, Margarethe von. Director, screenwriter, actress. Born on Feb. 21, 1942, in Berlin. After studying German and Latin literature in Paris and Munich, she embarked on an acting career, appearing on the stage and in films by leading European directors, including her future husband, Volker SCHLÖNDORFF. Through him she came to direct; her first effort, *The Lost Honor of Katerina Blum*, was a directorial collaboration with him. On the whole, her works, such as *Sisters, or the Balance of Happiness* and *The German Sisters*, have been praised for their subtle yet straightforward examinations of psychological and political complexities.

FILMS INCLUDE: As director—*Die Verlorene Ehre der Katharina Blum/The Lost Honor of Katerina Blum* (co-dir., co-sc.) 1975; *Das Zweite Erwachen der Christa Klages/The Second Awakening of Krista Clarges* 1977; *Schwestern, Oder Die Balance Des Gluecks/Sisters, or the Balance of Happiness* (also sc.) 1979; *Die Bleierne Zeit/The German Sisters* (also sc.) 1981; *Friends and Husbands* (also sc.) 1983; *Rosa Luxemburg* (also sc.) 1985; *Paura e Amore/The Three Sisters* (also sc.) 1990; *L'Africana/The African Woman* 1990; *Anni del Muro* 1992. As actress—*Der amerikanische Soldat/The American Soldier* 1970; *Dër Plözliche Reichtum der Armen Leute Von Kombach/The Sudden Wealth of the Poor People of Kombach* (also sc.) 1971; *Coup de Grace* (Fr./Ger., also sc.) 1976; *The Promise, Zeit des Zorns* 1994.

Trotti, Lamar. Screenwriter, producer. *b.* Oct. 18, 1900, Atlanta. *d.* 1952. *ed.* U. of Georgia. A former newspaper reporter, he published and edited a motion picture trade magazine before entering films as an assistant to a Fox executive. He began writing screenplays in the early 30s (initially in collaboration with Dudley NICHOLS) and producing in the early 40s. His credits, alone or in collaboration, include many important 20th Century-Fox productions, notably John Ford's *Young Mr. Lincoln* (1939) and William Wellman's *The Ox-Bow Incident* (1943).

FILMS INCLUDE: As screenwriter alone or in collaboration—*The Man Who Dared* 1933; *You Can't Buy Everything* (co-story only), *Hold That Girl* 1934; *Life Begins at 40, Steamboat 'Round the Bend* 1935; *The Country Beyond, Pepper, Romana* 1936; *This Is My Affair, Slave Ship, Wife Doctor and Nurse* 1937; *In Old Chicago, The Baroness and the Butler, Alexander's Ragtime Band, Gateway, Kentucky* 1938; *The Story of Alexander Graham Bell, Young Mr. Lincoln, Drums Along the Mohawk* 1939; *Brigham Young—Frontiersman* 1940; *Hudson's Bay, Belle Starr* 1941; *To the Shores of Tripoli, Tales of Manhattan, Thunder Birds* (also prod.) 1942; *The Immortal Sergeant* (also prod.), *The Ox-Bow Incident* (also prod.), *Guadalcanal Diary* 1943; *Wilson* 1944; *A Bell for Adano* 1945; *The Razor's Edge* 1946. As producer-screenwriter—*Mother Wore Tights* 1947; *Captain from Castile, The Walls of Jericho* 1948; *Yellow Sky, You're My Everything* 1949; *Cheaper by the Dozen, An American Guerrilla in the Philippines* 1950; *I'd Climb the Highest Mountain, As Young as You Feel* 1951; *With a Song in My Heart, O. Henry's Full House, Stars and Stripes Forever* 1952; *There's No Business Like Show Business* (story basis only) 1954.

trucking shot. Essentially the same as TRACKING SHOT, but more specifically used to describe a shot taken from a moving truck, van, or some other motorized vehicle rather than a dolly.

Truex, Ernest. Actor. *b.* Sept. 19, 1890, Kansas City, Mo. *d.* 1973. On the stage from early childhood, he played impish little heroes in some silent films, initially co-starring with Mary Pickford, and meek, little middle-aged men, often henpecked husbands, in many talkies. Also much on TV, including a regular role in the series 'Mr. Peepers.'

FILMS INCLUDE: *Caprice* 1913; *An American Citizen, A Good Little Devil* 1914; *Come On In* 1918; *Oh You Women!* 1919; *The Night of the Pub* (short) 1920; *Six Cylinder Love* 1923; *Whistling in the Dark, The Warrior's Husband* 1933; *Everybody Dance* (UK) 1936; *Start Cheering, Mama Runs Wild, The Adventures of Marco Polo* 1938; *It's a Wonderful World, Bachelor Mother, Island of Lost Men* 1939; *His Girl Friday, Slightly Honorable, Lillian Russell, Christmas in July, Little Orvie, Calling All Husbands* 1940; *Private Buckaroo* 1942; *The Crystal Ball, True to Life* 1943; *Her Primitive Man* 1944; *A Night in Paradise* 1946; *The Leather Saint* 1956; *Twilight for the Gods* 1958; *Fluffy* 1965.

Truffaut, François. Director. *b.* Feb. 6, 1932, in Paris. *d.* 1984. He had a childhood as lonely and unhappy as that of the little hero of his first feature film, *The 400 Blows.* Neglected at home and misunderstood at school, he spent a spell in a reformatory and was working in a factory at the age of 15. He found his main solace in the darkness of movie theaters and while still in his teens became active in the organization of ciné clubs. His enthusiasm for the cinema brought him to the attention of critic André BAZIN, who invited him to join the staff of his film magazine, *Cahiers du Cinéma.* His career as a young film critic was interrupted by military service, which ended in desertion, a prison sentence, and a dishonorable discharge. Back at *Cahiers,* Truffaut quickly gained a reputation as the most ferocious and caustic among the young film critics who were eventually to become the core of the French New Wave. He led the attack on conventional French cinema as pretentious and artificial and was influential in the development of the AUTEUR THEORY, which exalted the works of commercial American directors and made celebrities of obscure directors of action B pictures.

Truffaut made his first film, a 16 mm amateur short, in 1954, but it was with his second short, *Les Mistons* (1957), that he made his mark as a filmmaker. Oddly, this charming, evocative little film about the arousal of sexual feelings in a group of boys during a summer holiday was quite conservative in style, much in the tradition of the romantic realism in French cinema which Truffaut had criticized so vehemently. The same is true of Truffaut's first feature film, *The 400 Blows,* which owed more to Vigo and Renoir than to the technical stylists he had admired in his critical writings.

Like many an author's novel, *The 400 Blows* was largely autobiographical. Its hero, the 12-year-old Antoine Doinel (Jean-Pierre LÉAUD), is the same misunderstood and troubled child Truffaut was. He too is arrested for truancy and confined to a juvenile prison and he too ends that difficult period of his life on a troubled, hopeful note, in a memorable final freeze-frame shot at the ocean. One of cinema's most sincere and sensitive evocations of childhood, *The 400 Blows* was received enthusiastically by international audiences and did much to advance Truffaut's personal career as well as the prestige of the Nouvelle Vague.

Intermittently throughout his later career, Truffaut returned to his mirror-image hero, continuing the adventures of Antoine Doinel into adolescence and adult life in an episode in *Love at Twenty* and in the films *Stolen Kisses, Bed and Board,* and *Love on the Run.* The role continued to be played by a maturing Léaud, who developed into an important actor of the new French cinema. With his second feature, *Shoot the Piano Player,* Truffaut revealed the other side of his artistic personality, the one awed by the stylistics of his favored American directors. He blended suspense and humor and a variety of technical styles into his oddly jointed *série noire* thriller. He changed pace again with *Jules and Jim,* an evocative romantic triangle in which he sacrificed camera dynamics for character study and period atmosphere.

Truffaut's artistic "schizophrenia" remained evident in all his subsequent films. Throughout the rest of his career, he continued to waver between the influences of two great masters, RENOIR and HITCHCOCK. A passionately romantic humanist like Renoir, Truffaut was also a devout admirer of the skills of Hitchcock, which he attempted to emulate in several of his own thrillers.

Truffaut nearly allowed his professional dichotomy to enter his personal life when he hesitated for a while between marrying Hitchcock's daughter Patricia and one of Renoir's nieces. He finally married the daughter of a French producer named Morgenstern. It was with her dowry that he was able to produce most of his films under his own banner. As an homage to Renoir, he called his production company Les Films du Carrosse, after the French director's famous film *La Carrosse d'Or/The Golden Coach.* Truffaut is acknowledged as having been among the most gifted and sincere representatives of the new French cinema, an apolitical director whose love affair with cinema was contagious. He tried to share this love of film with his audience in his behind-the-scenes film about film, *Day for Night* (1973), in which he also appeared in the role of the director. It won an Oscar as best foreign film for 1973.

In addition to scripting or co-scripting all his films as director, Truffaut collaborated on the scripts or produced through his company a number of films of other directors. Among his collaborations as a writer was the story framework for GODARD's *Á Bout de Souffle/Breathless* (1960) and the scripts of such films as Claude de Givray's *Tire au Flanc/The Army Game* (also exec. prod.; 1961) and Jean-Louis Richard's *Mata Hari—Agent H-21* (also co-exec. prod.; 1965). His films as a producer, co-producer, or executive producer include Jacques Rivette's *Paris nous appartient* and Jean Cocteau's *Le Testament d'Orphée/The Testament of Orpheus* (both 1960), Jean-Luc Godard's *Deux ou Trois Choses que Je Sais d'Elle* (1967), Maurice Pialat's *L'Enfance nue/Naked Childhood/Me* (1968), Eric Rohmer's *Ma Nuit chez Maud/My Night at Maud's* (1969), and Bernard Dubois's *Les Lolos de Lola* (1976). He played one of the leading roles, that of a French scientist, in Steven Spielberg's American production *Close Encounters of the Third Kind* (1977). With Claude de Givray, he co-wrote the story for *La Petite voleuse/The Little Thief* (1988), which was filmed posthumously by Truffaut's longtime assistant, Claude Miller. His daughters with ex-wife Madeleine Morgenstern, Laura and Eva Truffaut, appeared in *L'Argent de Poche/Small Change* (1976). He was also the father of another daughter, Joséphine, with French actress Fanny Ardant. He died in Neuilly, France, of a brain tumor. Author: *Les Films de ma Vie* (1975); *Hitchcock/Truffaut* (1983); *Francois Truffaut Correspondence* (posthumous collection of letters, 1990).

FILMS: Shorts—*Une Visite* 1954; *Les Mistons/The Mischief Makers* (also sc., dial.) 1958; *Histoire d'Eau* (co-dir. with Jean-Luc Godard; also sc.) 1959. Features—*Les Quatre Cents Coups/The 400 Blows* (also sc.) 1959; *Tirez sur le Pianiste/Shoot the Piano Player* (also co-sc., dial.) 1960; *Jules et Jim/Jules and Jim* (also co-sc., co-dial.) 1961; *L'Amour à Vingt Ans/Love at Twenty* ("France" episode; also sc., act.) 1962; *La Peau douce/The Soft Skin* (also co-sc., dial.) 1964; *Fahrenheit 451* (also co-sc., co-dial.; UK) 1966; *La Mariée était en Noir/The Bride Wore Black* (also co-sc., co-dial.), *Baisers volés/Stolen Kisses* (also co-sc., co-dial.) 1968; *La Sirène du Mississippi/Mississippi Mermaid* (also sc., dial.) 1969; *L'Enfant sauvage/The Wild Child* (also co-sc., co-dial., act.), *Domicile conjugal/Bed and Board* (also co-sc.) 1970; *Les Deux Anglaises et le Continent/Two English Girls* (also co-sc., co-dial.) 1971; *Une Belle Fille comme moi/Such a Gorgeous Kid Like Me* (also co-sc., co-dial.) 1972; *La Nuit américaine/Day for Night* (also co-sc., dial., act.) 1973; *L'Histoire d'Adèle H./The Story of Adele H.* (also co-sc., co-dial.) 1975; *L'Argent de Poche/Small Change* (also co-sc.) 1976; *Close Encounters of the Third Kind* (act. only; US), *L'Homme qui aimait les Femmes/The Man Who Loved Women* (also co-sc.) 1977; *La Chambre verte/The Green Room* (also co-sc., act.) 1978; *L'Amour en fuite/Love on the Run* (also co-sc.) 1979; *Close Encounters of the Third Kind: Special Edition* (act. only; US), *Le Dernier Metro/The Last Metro* (also sc.) 1980; *La Femme d'a cote/The Woman Next Door* (also sc.) 1981; *Vivement Dimanche/Confidentially Yours* (also prod., sc.) 1982; *Breathless* (from film; US), *The Man Who Loved Women* (from film; US) 1983; *Vivement Truffaut* (doc.; act.) 1985; *La Petite voleuse/The Little Thief* (co-story) 1988.

Trumbo, Dalton. Screenwriter, novelist. *b.* James Dalton Trumbo, Dec. 9, 1905, Montrose, Colo. *d.* 1976. *ed.* U. of Colorado; UCLA; USC. A former newspaper reporter and editor, he entered films as a screenwriter in 1935. In 1947 he became one of the HOLLYWOOD TEN, who were sentenced to a jail term by a grand jury for contempt of Congress for refusing to testify before the House Un-American Activities Committee about their alleged membership in the Communist Party. After he was blacklisted by the industry, his income was reduced from $3,000 weekly (or $75,000 a script, as his MGM contract stipulated) to zero. But he began an arduous climb back even while serving his ten-month jail sentence at the Federal penitentiary in Ashland, Ky., smuggling out a script for sale "underground," using a pseudonym. After his release, he sold his California ranch and moved to Mexico, where he continued writing scripts at cut-rate fees for the thriving "black market" that opened up for blacklisted writers. He wrote 18 screenplays under various pseudonyms. His story for *The Brave One* (1956) won an Academy Award for an elusive Robert Rich, who turned out to be none other than Trumbo, to the utter embarrassment of the industry.

Trumbo was the first of the blacklisted writers to emerge from the underground, thanks to the insistence of Kirk Douglas and Otto Preminger that his name appear in the screen credits of their respective 1960 productions *Spartacus* and *Exodus.* The American Legion picketed the showings of both films to no avail. In the early 70s, Trumbo realized an old dream in bringing to the screen his grim 1939 antiwar novel *Johnny Got His Gun.* He directed the production himself, making his debut in what might have become a new phase in his career. The film won a prize at the Cannes Festival. But Trumbo's comeback was hampered by illness. He underwent surgery for lung cancer and died three years later of a heart attack, at 70. In 1970 a collection of his letters in the years 1942–62 was published under the title *Additional Dialogue.* The letters were compared by one critic to Thoreau's *Journals.*

FILMS INCLUDE: *Road Gang, Love Begins at 20* 1936; *Devil's Playground* 1937; *Fugitives for a Night, A Man to Remember* 1938; *The Flying Irishman, Five Came Back, Career* 1939; *The Lone Wolf Strikes* (story only), *Curtain Call, A Bill of Divorcement, We Who Are Young, Kitty Foyle* 1940; *You Belong to Me* (story only) 1941; *The Remarkable Andrew* 1942; *A Guy Named Joe* 1943; *Tender Comrade, Thirty Seconds Over Tokyo* 1944; *Our Vines Have Tender Grapes* 1945; *Emergency Wedding* (story only) 1950; *The Brave One* (under pseudonym Robert Rich) 1956; *Spartacus, Exodus* 1960; *The Last Sunset* 1961; *Lonely Are the Brave* 1962; *The Sandpiper* 1965; *Hawaii* 1966; *The Fixer* 1968; *Johnny Got His Gun* (also dir.), *The Horsemen* 1971; *F.T.A.* 1972; *Executive Action, Papillon* 1973.

Trumbull, Douglas. Special effects artist, director of photography, director. Born on April 8, 1942, in Los Angeles. *ed.* El Camino Coll., Torrence, Calif. He did technical illustrations for advertising firms before joining Graphic Films to work on animated promotional films about space for NASA and the Air Force. Director Stanley Kubrick saw one of these films, *To the Moon and Beyond* (1964), and hired Trumbull as one of the special effects supervisors on *2001: A Space Odyssey* (1968). The visual wonders in that film established Trumbull's reputation as a special effects wizard, leading to his directorial debut three years later with another space film, *Silent Running* (1971). He won Academy Award nominations for his special effects in *Close Encounters of the Third Kind* (1977), *Star Trek: The Motion Picture* (1979), and *Blade Runner* (1982). The second feature he directed, *Brainstorm*, featured Natalie Wood's last performance. Later Trumbull turned to designing interactive entertainments and theme park attractions, including the effects for Universal Studios' "Back to the Future: The Ride". He also invented the slit-scan photography process, used to create the impression of headlong motion, and the SHOWSCAN film process.

FILMS INCLUDE (as special effects artist or supervisor): *Candy* (It./Fr.), *2001: A Space Odyssey* (US/UK) 1968; *The Andromeda Strain, Silent Running* (also dir.) 1971; *Close Encounters of the Third Kind* 1977; *Star Trek: The Motion Picture* 1979; *Blade Runner* 1982; *Brainstorm* (also dir., prod.) 1983.

Tryon, Glenn. Actor, director, producer, screenwriter. *b.* Sept. 14, 1894, Julietta, Idaho. *d.* 1970. On the stage from boyhood, he appeared in tent and medicine shows and in scores of plays in stock before breaking into films in 1924. A handsome "all-American" young man, he played light leads in many silents and early talkies. In the mid-30s he turned to writing, producing, and directing routine B films.

FILMS INCLUDE: As actor—*The White Sheep, The Battling Orioles* 1924; *The Denver Dude, The Poor Nut, Painting the Town, A Hero for a Night* 1927; *Thanks for the Buggy Ride, Hot Heels, Lonesome, The Gate Crasher, How to Handle Women* 1928; *Broadway, It Can Be Done, Skinner Steps Out, Barnum Was Right* 1929; *Dames Ahoy!, The King of Jazz, The Midnight Special* 1930; *Daybreak, The Sky Spider, Dragnet Patrol* 1931; *The Big Payoff* 1933; *George White's Scandals* 1945; *Variety Girl* 1947; *The Hometown Story* 1951. As screenwriter—*Bachelor Bait* 1934; *Roberta, The Daring Young Man, Orchids to You, Seven Keys to Baldpate* (all addnl. dial. only) 1935. As director—*Gridiron Flash* (also sc.), *The Richest Girl in the World* (also sc.) 1934; *Two in Revolt* 1936; *The Law West of Tombstone* 1938; *Beauty for the Asking* 1939; *That Nazty Nuisance* (also prod.), *Calaboose* 1943. As associate producer—*Hold That Ghost, Hellzapoppin* 1941. As producer—*The Devil with Hitler* 1942.

Tryon, Tom. Actor. *b.* Jan. 14, 1926, Hartford, Conn. *d.* 1991. *ed.* Yale. After WW II service with the Navy he studied painting at Yale and attended New York's Art Students League, then joined a stock company as a set designer and actor. Early in the 50s he broke into TV as production assistant and soon switched to acting. He moved on from there to leads in films, reaching his peak in the title role in Preminger's *The Cardinal* (1963). He gave up acting in the late 60s for a writing career and wrote several best-selling novels. One of these, *The Other,* was made into a film in 1972 with Tryon as screenwriter and executive producer. Another of his books, *Crowned Heads,* was adapted in part to the screen in 1978 as *Fedora.*

FILMS INCLUDE: *The Scarlet Hour, Screaming Eagles* 1956; *Three Violent People* 1957; *The Story of Ruth* 1960; *Marines Let's Go!* 1961; *Moon Pilot, The Longest Day* 1962; *The Cardinal* 1963; *In Harm's Way, The Glory Guys* 1965; *Color Me Dead* 1969.

T-stop. A setting on a camera lens calibrating the true amount of light *transmitted through* the lens (the "T" stands for "transmission"), unlike the *f*-stop numbering system, which indicates only the amount of light *entering* a lens and does not take into account the loss of light through absorption or reflection.

Tsuburaya, Eiji. Special-effects director. *b.* July 7, 1901, Fukushuna, Japan. *d.* 1970. In Japanese films as cameraman from 1922, he gained a reputation in the West in the 50s and 60s for his remarkable trick effects in many Japanese science fiction films.

FILMS INCLUDE: *The Invisible Man, Godzilla* 1954; *Radon* 1956; *The Mysterians* 1957; *Battle in Outer Space* 1959; *The Human Vapor, I Bombed Pearl Harbor* 1960; *Mothra, The Last War* 1961; *Gorath, King Kong vs. Godzilla* 1962; *Dogora the Space Monster* 1964; *Ghidra—The Three-Headed Monster* 1968; *The War of the Gargantuas, Frankenstein Conquers the World* 1966; *Ultraman, King Kong Escapes* 1967; *Admiral Yamamoto, Destroy All Monsters* 1968; *Battle of the Japan Sea, Latitude Zero* 1969.

Tsui Hark. Director, producer, screenwriter. Born in 1951 in Vietnam. *ed.* Southern Methodist Univ., Univ. of Texas. Creator of popular Hong Kong action and fantasy films. Like many Asian directors, he began his career in the US, first attending American colleges, then moving to New York City to work in Chinese-language arts and media—a newspaper, community theater, and cable television production. Relocating to Hong Kong in 1977, he directed television dramas and in 1979, his first feature, *Butterfly Murders*.

Within the Asian cinema, he has achieved a fame comparable to American producer and director Steven Spielberg. His directorial signature is an antirealist visual style, bordering on the hallucinatory, with rapid action. While most of his films have been energetic genre works—war and espionage, gangster films and ghost stories (wildly popular in Asia)—he also produced and co-directed (with Yim Ho) a notable drama, *The King of Chess*. As producer his credits include a trio of films directed by John Woo and starring Chow Yun-Fat (*A Better Tomorrow, A Better Tomorrow II*, and *The Killer*) and the *Chinese Ghost Story* series.

FILMS INCLUDE (as director/co-director): *Butterfly Murders* 1979; *Dangerous Encounters of the First Kind, Don't Play With Fire, We're Going to Eat You* 1980; *All the Wrong Clues (for the Right Solution)* 1981; *Zu: Warriors from the Magic Mountain* 1983; *Aces Go Places III: Our Man from Bond Street, Shanghai Blues* 1984; *Working Class* 1985; *Peking Opera Blues* 1986; *A Better Tomorrow III: Love and Death in Saigon* 1989; *Swordsman* (co-dir.); *The Master, King of Chess* (co-dir.) 1990; *Once Upon A Time In China, The Raid, A Chinese Ghost Story III* 1991; *Once Upon A Time In China II* 1992.

Tsukasa, Yoko. Actress. Born on Aug. 20, 1934, in Tottori, Japan. Delicate leading lady of Japanese films; formerly a cover girl.

FILMS INCLUDE: *Forever Be Mine* 1954; *Marital Relations* 1955; *Brother and Sister* 1956; *The Blue Mountains* 1957; *The Flower, Summer Clouds* 1958; *Samurai Saga, The Young Lovers* 1959; *Late Autumn, The Angry Sea* 1960; *Yojimbo, Eternity of Love, Challenge to Live, Early Autumn* 1961; *The Wiser Age, Chushingura, The Loyal 47 Ronin* 1962; *Twilight Path* 1964; *Moment of Terror* 1966; *Kojiro, Two in the Shadow, Rebellion* 1967; *Battle of the Japan Sea* 1969; *Band of Assassins* 1970; *The Steel Edge of Revenge* 1974.

Tucci, Stanley. Actor, director. *b.* January 11, 1960, in Katonah, N.Y. *ed.* SUNY (Purchase, N.Y.). Dependable, versatile actor with an often imposing screen presence. For years he has had an active television and film career without much notoriety until the 90s when more substantial, challenging roles came his way. He astounded critics with his writing and directing debut *Big Night* (1996).

FILMS: *Prizzi's Honor* 1985; *Who's That Girl?* 1987; *Monkey Shines* 1988; *The Feud, Slaves of New York* 1989; *Quick Change* 1990; *Billy Bathgate, Men of Respect* 1991; *Beethoven, In the Soup, Prelude To a Kiss, The Public Eye* 1992; *The Pelican Brief, Undercover Blues* 1993; *It Could Happen To You, Mrs. Parker and the Vicious Circle* 1994; *Jury Duty, Kiss of Death* 1995; *Big Night* (also co-sc., co-dir.), *A Modern Affair* 1996; *A Life Less Ordinary* 1997.

Tucker, Forrest. Actor. *b.* Feb. 12, 1919, in Plainfield, Ind. *d.* 1986. *ed.* George Washington U. Husky blond leading man of numerous Hollywood films, often Westerns and action pictures. He started out in the early 40s, playing mostly bullies and villains, but in the 50s he typically played the hero. Character roles followed until his death. Regular on television sitcom 'F Troop.'

FILMS INCLUDE: *The Westerner* 1940; *Emergency Landing, New Wine* 1941; *Counter-Espionage, Keeper of the Flame* 1942; *Renegades, Dangerous Business, Never Say Goodbye, The Yearling* 1946; *Gunfighters* 1947; *The Plunderers, Coroner Creek* 1948; *Hellfire, Brimstone, Sands of Iwo Jima* 1949; *The Nevadan, Rock Island Trail, California Passage* 1950; *Oh Susanna!, Fighting Coast Guard, Warpath, The Wild Blue Yonder* 1951; *Bugles in the Afternoon, Hoodlum Empire, Montana Belle* 1952; *Pony Express, Laughing Anne* (UK) 1953; *Trouble in the Glen* (UK), *Flight Nurse, Jubilee Trail* 1954; *Finger Man, Night Freight* 1955; *Break in the Circle* (UK), *Stagecoach to Fury* 1956; *The Abominable Snowman* (UK), *The Quiet Gun, Three Violent People* 1957; *Auntie Mame, Fort Massacre, The Strange World of Planet X/The Cosmic Monster* (UK), *The Trollenberg Terror/The Crawling Eye* (UK) 1958; *Counterplot* 1959; *The Night They Raided Minsky's* 1968; *Barquero, Chisum* 1970; *Cancel My Reservation* 1972; *The Wild McCullochs* 1975; *The Wackiest Wagon Train in the West* 1976; *Final Chapter—Walking Tall* 1977; *A Rare Breed* 1981; *Outtakes* (compilation of genre scenes), *Thunder Run* 1985; *Timestalkers* (TV) 1987.

Tucker, George Loane. Director. *b.* 1881, Chicago. *d.* 1921. A former railroad clerk, he entered films in 1908 as an actor. A director from 1910, he turned out numerous one-reelers at IMP and Reliance-Majestic before making a name for himself in 1913 with *Traffic in Souls,* a sensational six-reel exposé of white slavery. Tucker and several other directors at IMP, including Herbert BRENON and King BAGGOT, financed the film out of their own pockets since it had not been authorized by studio boss Carl LAEMMLE. It cost $7,500 to make and reaped half a million dollars at the box office within days, a fact that started a Hollywood vogue of sex films. Before the film's release, Tucker was on his way to England, where he was to enjoy considerable success as a director of quality films and marry one of his stars, Elizabeth Risdon. He returned to the US in 1917. Before his untimely death, he directed several films in Hollywood, including *The Miracle Man* (1919), the film that launched the starring career of Lon CHANEY after years in secondary roles. *Photoplay* headlined its tribute to Tucker after his death: "First of the Immortals."

FILMS INCLUDE: In the US—*Their First Misunderstanding* (co-dir. with Thomas H. Ince), *The Dream* (co-dir. with Ince), *Behind the Stockade* (co-dir. with Ince; also sc.), *The Aggressor* (co-dir. with Ince), *Over the Hills* (co-dir. with Joseph Smiley), *The Rose's Story* (co-dir. with Smiley) 1911; *Traffic in Souls* (also co-sc.) 1913. In the UK—*She Stoops to Conquer, England Expects, On His Majesty's Service, The Fringe of War, The Revenge of Mr. Thomas Atkins* 1914; *The Middleman, The Prisoner of Zenda, Rupert of Hentzau, Sons of Satan, The Shulamite, The Christian* 1915; *The Morals of Weybury/The Hypocrites, The Game of Liberty, Arsene Lupin, The Man Without a Soul, The Manxman* 1916; *A Mother of Dartmoor, A Mother's Influence* 1917. In the US—*A Man of His Word, The Cinderella Man* 1917; *Dodging a Million, Joan of Plattsburg* (co-dir. with William Humphreys), *Virtuous Wives* 1918; *The Miracle Man* 1919; *Ladies Must Live* (also sc.) 1921.

Tucker, Richard. Actor. *b.* 1869, Brooklyn, N.Y. *d.* 1942. A seasoned stage actor, he joined the Edison company in 1913 and played leads in numerous silent films before easing into dominating character roles. Except for a stint in WW I military service, he remained active through the late 30s, appearing in hundreds of films in all.

FILMS INCLUDE: *An Almond-Eyed Maiden, Mercy Merrick, The Pied Piper of Hamelin* 1913; *The Midnight Ride of Paul Revere, The Stuff That Dreams Are Made Of* 1914; *Vanity Fair* 1915; *The Woman in Room 13, Dollars and Sense, The Branding Iron, The Great Lover* 1920; *A Voice in the Dark, Roads of Destiny, The Old Nest, The Night Rose* 1921; *Grand Larceny, When the Devil Drives, Remembrance* 1922; *Is Divorce a Failure?, The Broken Wing, Cameo Kirby* 1923; *Beau Brummel, The Tornado* 1924; *The Man Without a Country, The Air Mail, The Bridge of Sighs* 1925; *The Blind Goddess, The Lily, Shameful Behavior?, Devil's Island* 1926; *Matinee Ladies, Dearie, Wings, The Desired Woman, The Jazz Singer* 1927; *Thanks for the Buggy Ride, Beware of Married Men, Loves of an Actress, Show Girl, On Trial, Love Over Night, My Man* 1928; *Daughters of Desire, Lucky Boy, The Dummy, The Squall, This Is Heaven, The Unholy Night, Painted Faces* 1929; *Puttin' on the Ritz, The Benson Murder Case, Courage, Shadow of the Law, Manslaughter, The Bat Whispers* 1930; *Inspiration, Seed, The Black Camel, The Deceiver, X Marks the Spot* 1931; *Careless Lady, A Successful Calamity, Pack Up Your Troubles* 1932; *The World Gone Mad, Saturday's Millions* 1933; *The Countess of Monte Cristo, A Modern Hero, Baby Take a Bow* 1934; *Sing Sing Nights, Shadow of Doubt* 1935; *The Plot Thickens* 1936; *Something to Sing About* 1937; *The Texans* 1938; *The Great Victor Herbert* 1939.

Tufts, Sonny. Actor. *b.* Bowen Charlton Tufts III, July 16, 1911, Boston, to prominent banking family. *d.* 1970. *ed.* Yale. Determined as a child to become a singer, he joined a church choir and while at Yale formed a band, appointing himself the vocalist. After operatic training in New York and Paris, he was auditioned at New York's Metropolitan Opera and won a year's tuition for further voice training. Meanwhile, he supported himself as a clerk and later an icebox salesman. In 1938–39 he landed parts in two Broadway musicals and in 1939 he played a small supporting part in a low-budget film, *Ambush.* After several years of singing in night spots, he returned to the screen as a leading man. The year was 1943 and most male stars were away on military service. A college football injury kept Tufts out of uniform and for a brief spell he became a star. Tall (6' 4"), blond, and blue-eyed, he typically played amiable, easygoing, innocuous leading men. But by the end of the 40s his screen career began to sag and he was soon reduced to secondary roles or to leads in bottom-budget pictures.

In the 50s, Tufts was sued by several showgirls for allegedly biting them in the thigh and unsuccessfully fought a drinking problem. He became a camp figure. His very name became a joke and the mere mention of it in a nightclub or on a TV talk show brought down the house in gales of laughter. He made several unsuccessful bids at comebacks in the 60s before his death of pneumonia.

FILMS: *Ambush* 1939; *So Proudly We Hail, Government Girl* 1943; *I Love a Soldier, Here Come the Waves, In the Meantime Darling* 1944; *Duffy's Tavern, Bring on the Girls* 1945; *Miss Susie Slagle's, The Well-Groomed Bride, The Virginian, Cross My Heart* 1946; *Swell Guy, Variety Girl, Easy Come Easy Go, Blaze of Noon* 1947; *The Untamed Breed* 1948; *The Crooked Way, Easy Living* 1949; *The Gift Horse/Glory at Sea* (UK) 1952; *No Escape, Run for the Hills, Cat Women of the Moon* 1953; *Serpent Island* 1954; *The Seven Year Itch* 1955; *Come Next Spring* 1956; *The Parson and the Outlaw* 1957; *Town Tamer* 1965; *Cotton-pickin' Chickenpickers* 1967.

Tugend, Harry. Screenwriter, producer. Born on Feb. 17, 1898, in Brooklyn, N.Y. Formerly a radio and vaudeville singer-actor, he began his writing career with sketches for the Ziegfeld Follies, then wrote and directed many of Fred ALLEN's radio shows. In Hollywood since the mid-30s, he wrote many light screenplays, alone or in collaboration. He also produced a number of films from the mid-40s and is the author of a Broadway-produced play, 'The Wayward Stork' and of much TV material.

FILMS INCLUDE (as screenwriter): *The Littlest Rebel, Thanks a Million* 1935; *King of Burlesque, Captain January, The Poor Little Rich Girl* 1936; *Wake Up and Live, You Can't Have Everything, Ali Baba Goes to Town* 1937; *Sally Irene and Mary, Little Miss Broadway* 1938; *Second Fiddle, Little Old New York* 1939; *Seven Sinners* (co-story only) 1940; *Caught in the Draft, Birth of the Blues* 1941; *Star Spangled Rhythm* 1942; *True to Life* 1943; *Cross My Heart* (also prod.), *Golden Earrings* (prod. only) 1947; *A Song Is Born. A Southern Yankee* 1948; *Take Me Out to the Ball Game* 1949; *Wabash Avenue* 1950; *Road to Bali* (prod., co-story only) 1953; *Public Pigeon No. 1* (also prod.) 1957; *Pocketful of Miracles* 1961; *Who's Minding the Store?* 1963.

Tully, Montgomery. Director. Born on May 6, 1904, in Dublin. *ed.* U. of London. A director of documentaries from 1929, he turned to feature films in the mid-40s and has specialized in crime and suspense subjects. He often writes his own scripts and sometimes contributes screenplays to films of other directors. He has also written novels and plays and directed for British TV.

FILMS INCLUDE: *Murder in Reverse* 1945; *Spring Song* 1946; *Mrs. Fitzherbert* 1947; *Boys in Brown* 1950; *A Tale of Five Cities* (co-dir. with four others; UK/Fr./It./Ger.) 1951; *Small Town Story* 1953; *The Diamond, 36 Hours* 1954; *Dial 999, The Glass Cage* 1955; *The Counterfeit Plan, The Hypnotist, Man in the Shadow* 1957; *Escapement, The Strange Awakening, The Long Knife, Man With a Gun, The Diplomatic Corpse* 1958; *Man Accused* 1959; *Jackpot, The Price of Silence, Dead Lucky* 1960; *The Third Alibi* 1961; *Out of the Fog* 1962; *Master Spy* 1963; *Clash by Night/Escape by Night* 1964; *The Terrornauts* 1967; *Battle Beneath the Earth* 1968; *The Hawks* 1969.

Tully, Tom. Actor. *b.* 1908, Durango, Colo. *d.* 1982. A veteran of the US Navy, and of radio and the legitimate stage, he played character parts in many Hollywood films, typically on the tough-but-nice side. He was nominated for an Oscar as best supporting actor for his performance in *The Caine Mutiny* (1954).

FILMS INCLUDE: *Northern Pursuit* 1943; *Destination Tokyo, Secret Command* 1944; *The Unseen* 1945; *Adventure, The Virginian, Till the End of Time* 1946; *Lady in the Lake* 1947; *Killer McCoy, Rachel and the Stranger, June Bride, Blood on the Moon* 1948; *Where the Sidewalk Ends* 1950; *Love Is Better Than Ever, Ruby Gentry* 1952; *The Jazz Singer, The Moon Is Blue* 1953; *The Caine Mutiny* 1954; *Love Me or Leave Me, Soldier of Fortune* 1955; *Ten North Frederick* 1958; *The Wackiest Ship in the Army* 1960; *The Carpetbaggers* 1964; *Coogan's Bluff* 1968; *Charley Varrick* 1973.

Tunberg, Karl. Screenwriter, sometimes producer. *b.* Mar. 11, 1907, in Spokane, Wash. *d.* 1992. In Hollywood from 1937, he wrote numerous screenplays, alone or in collaboration, mostly on the light side. Occasionally ventured into producing.

FILMS INCLUDE (as screenwriter): *You Can't Have Everything, Life Begins in College* 1937; *Rebecca of Sunnybrook Farm* 1938; *Down Argentine Way* 1940; *A Yank in the R.A.F., Weekend in Havana* 1941; *My Gal Sal* 1942; *Dixie* 1943; *Masquerade in Mexico* (also prod.) 1945; *Kitty* (also prod.) 1946; *Up in Central Park, You Gotta Stay Happy* (both also prod.) 1948; *Night Into Morning* 1951; *Because You're Mine* 1952; *Beau Brummel* 1954; *Count Your Blessings* (also prod.), *Libel* (UK), *Ben-Hur* 1959; *Taras Bulba* 1962; *The Seventh Dawn* (also prod.) 1964; *Harlow* (Carol Lynley version) 1965; *Where Were You When the Lights Went Out?* 1968; *How Do I Love Thee?* 1970.

Turman, Lawrence. Producer. Born in 1926, in Los Angeles. *ed.* UCLA. He was in the textile business and with a talent agency before becoming an independent producer. Several of his films enjoyed critical and commercial success.

FILMS INCLUDE: *The Young Doctors* 1961; *I Could Go on Singing* 1963; *The Best Man* 1964; *The Flim-Flam Man, The Graduate* 1967; *Pretty Poison* 1968; *The Great White Hope* 1970; *The Marriage of a Young Stockbroker* (also dir.) 1971; *The Nickel Ride* (co-exec. prod.) 1974; *The Drowning Pool* (co-prod.) 1975; *Heroes* (co-prod.), *First Love* (co-prod.) 1977; *Walk Proud* 1979; *Tribute* 1980; *Caveman* 1981; *The Thing* 1982; *Second Thoughts* (also dir.) 1983; *Mass Appeal* 1984; *The Mean Season* 1985; *Short Circuit, Running Scared* 1986; *Short Circuit 2, Full Moon in Blue Water* 1988; *Gleaming the Cube* 1989; *The Getaway, The River Wild* 1994.

Turner, Florence. Actress. *b.* 1885, New York City. *d.* 1946. On the stage from the age of three, she joined Vitagraph in 1906 as actress–wardrobe mistress and became the studio's leading star, known to millions as the "Vitagraph Girl." She appeared in the company's most prestigious early silents, co-starring with Maurice COSTELLO and other matinee idols. In 1913 she went to England with her frequent director and lifelong friend Laurence ("Larry") TRIMBLE. They appeared together in London music halls and formed their own production company, Turner Films, Ltd., releasing, through Cecil Hepworth, some of the best films made in Britain during the period. She occasionally collaborated on the screenplays and sometimes directed her own films. In 1916 she returned to the US, but by 1920 she was again starring in British pictures. She finally settled in Hollywood in 1924, but her career quickly faltered and she found herself relegated to secondary roles and eventually begging for work. In the 30s she was among the silent stars who were put on the MGM payroll as a gesture of charity and used from time to time in extra and bit parts.

FILMS INCLUDE: In the US—*How to Cure a Cold* 1907; *The New Stenographer* (Edison version), *Richard III, The Merchant of Venice* 1908; *His Masterpiece* 1909; *A Dixie Mother, St. Elmo, How Championships Are Won—And Lost, Twelfth Night, Francesca da Rimini* 1910; *A Tale of Two Cities* (as Lucie Manette), *The New Stenographer* (Vitagraph version), *The Show Girl, Jean Rescues, The Prejudice of Pierre Marie, Cherry Blossoms, Answer of the Roses, Jealousy, Auld Lang Syne, The Path of True Love* 1911; *Jean Intervenes, An Indian Romeo and Juliet, She Cried, Aunty's Romance* 1912; *The Deerslayer, Under The Make-Up, The House in Suburbia, Checkmated* 1913. In the UK—*The Rose of Surrey, The Harper Mystery* 1913; *Flotilla the Flirt, Polly's Progress, Snobs, The*

Murdock Trial, For Her People, Through the Valley of Shadows (also co-sc.) 1914; *My Old Dutch, Far from the Madding Crowd, East Is East, Grim Justice, Alone in London* 1915. In the US—*Fool's Gold* 1919; *The Brand of Lopez* 1920; *All Dolled Up, Passion Fruit* 1921. In the UK—*The Ugly Duckling, The Old Wives' Tale* 1921; *The Little Mother* 1922; *Sally Bishop* 1923; *Women and Diamonds* 1924. In the US—*The Mad Marriage, Never the Twain Shall Meet, The Dark Angel* 1925; *The Gilded Highway, The Last Alarm, Padlocked* 1926; *College, The Chinese Parrot, Stranded* 1927; *Jazzland, The Road to Ruin* 1928; *The Kid's Clever* 1929; *The Rampant Age* 1930; *Ridin' Fool* 1931.

Turner, Kathleen. Actor. Born on June 19, 1954, in Springfield, Mo. *ed.* Missouri State U.; Univ. of Md.; Central School of Speech and Drama, London. Sensual, husky-voiced, authoritative screen lead. After training in the daytime soap opera 'The Doctors,' she established herself as a screen *femme fatale* in the *noir*-influenced thriller *Body Heat* and displayed an able flair for light comedy (*Romancing the Stone, The Jewel of the Nile*) and dark (*Prizzi's Honor, The War of the Roses*). Her roles in the 90s have largely lacked the easy depth and spark of her previous major performances. Nominated for an Academy Award for her subtle performance as a settled woman who re-experiences her teenage life in *Peggy Sue Got Married*. She made an acclaimed Broadway debut as Maggie in a revival of 'Cat on a Hot Tin Roof.'

FILMS INCLUDE: *Body Heat* 1981; *The Man With Two Brains* 1983; *A Breed Apart, Crimes of Passion, Romancing the Stone* 1984; *The Jewel of the Nile, Prizzi's Honor* 1985; *Peggy Sue Got Married* 1986; *Dear America* (narration), *Julia and Julia* 1987; *The Accidental Tourist, Switching Channels, Who Framed Roger Rabbit* (v/o) 1988; *The War of the Roses* 1989; *V.I. Warshawski* 1991; *House of Cards, Undercover Blues* 1993; *Naked in New York, Serial Mom* 1994; *Moonlight and Valentino* 1995; *A Simple Wish* 1997.

Turner, Lana. Actress. Born Julia Jean Mildred Frances Turner, on Feb. 8, 1920, in Wallace, Idaho. When she was nine her father, a mine foreman, was the victim of a robbery murder, whereupon her mother, a beautician, moved to California in search of employment. Julia Jean attended a convent in San Francisco and Hollywood High School in Los Angeles. According to Hollywood legend, she was playing hooky from school and sipping soda at Schwab's Drugstore on Sunset Boulevard when she was discovered by an editor of *The Hollywood Reporter,* who recommended her to director Mervyn LeRoy. The place has since been a favorite hangout for Hollywood's hopefuls. As the legend continues, she was wearing at the time of her discovery a tight sweater that emphasized her main qualifications. Accordingly, she was publicized early in her career as "The Sweater Girl." During WW II she ranked among the nation's top pinup girls. After several years as just another stacked starlet, she was manufactured by the MGM glamour machine in the 40s into a glittering star.

After assaying a variety of roles, she found her niche in melodrama. Occasionally, she turned in a creditable performance, as in *The Postman Always Rings Twice* (1946) and *Peyton Place* (Oscar-nominated as best actress, 1957), but it was mainly her elegance and poise and her ability to project a promise of promiscuity that made her one of Hollywood's most durable stars. Her personal life has often been as stormy as the most melodramatic of her films. By 1972 she had been married and divorced seven times, eight if one would count her remarriage to former actor (turned restaurateur) Stephen Crane, her second husband, only weeks after obtaining an annulment. The first of the seven (1940–41) was bandleader Artie Shaw; the third (1948–52) was playboy millionaire Bob Topping; the fourth (1953–57) movie Tarzan Lex BARKER. The other three were less famous. In addition, her name was romantically linked with many Hollywood personalities, including mystery millionaire Howard Hughes.

In 1958, Miss Turner's name exploded into the headlines when her teenage daughter, Cheryl Crane (*b.* 1943), stabbed to death underworld hoodlum Johnny Stompanato, her mother's longtime boyfriend. In the ensuing inquest, the killing was pronounced a justifiable homicide on the ground that the girl was trying to protect her mother from what she believed had been an actual threat to her life. Oddly, the adverse publicity, which included public readings from her torrid love letters to Stompanato, hardly affected Miss Turner's career. She continued starring in films until the early 70s. In 1970 she starred in the short-lived TV series 'The Survivors' and was later a semi-regular on 'Falcon Crest.' In 1971 she made her stage debut in an out-of-town production of 'Forty Carats.'

FILMS: *A Star Is Born* (bit), *They Won't Forget, The Great Garrick* 1937; *The Adventures of Marco Polo, Four's a Crowd, Love Finds Andy Hardy, The Chaser* (bit), *Rich Man Poor Girl, Dramatic School* 1938; *Calling Dr. Kildare, These Glamour Girls, Dancing Co-Ed* 1939; *Two Girls on Broadway, We Who Are Young* 1940; *Ziegfeld Girl, Dr. Jekyll and Mr. Hyde, Honky Tonk* 1941; *Johnny Eager, Somewhere I'll Find You* 1942; *Slightly Dangerous, The Youngest Profession, Du Barry Was a Lady* (cameo) 1943; *Marriage Is a Private Affair* 1944; *Keep Your Powder Dry, Week-End at the Waldorf* 1945; *The Postman Always Rings Twice* 1946; *Green Dolphin Street, Cass Timberlane* 1947; *Homecoming, The Three Musketeers* (as Lady de Winter) 1948; *A Life of Her Own* 1950; *Mr. Imperium* 1951; *The Merry Widow, The Bad and the Beautiful* 1952; *Latin Lovers* 1953; *Flame and the Flesh, Betrayed* 1954; *The Prodigal, The Sea Chase, The Rains of Ranchipur* 1955; *Diane* 1956; *Peyton Place* 1957; *The Lady Takes a Flyer, Another Time Another Place* 1958; *Imitation of Life* 1959; *Portrait in Black* 1960; *By Love Possessed, Bachelor in Paradise* 1961; *Who's Got the Action?* 1962; *Love Has Many Faces* 1965; *Madame X* 1966; *The Big Cube* (US/Mex.) 1969; *Persecution/The Terror of Sheba/The Graveyard* (UK) 1974; *Bittersweet Love* 1976; *Witches' Brew* 1979.

Turner, Robert Edward (Ted). Executive. Born on November 19, 1938, in Cincinnati, Ohio. *ed.* Brown U. Flamboyant, outspoken communications magnate. His father ran an outdoor advertising business in Savannah, Georgia, which Ted Turner inherited in 1963 when his father committed suicide. In 1970 he went into broadcasting by buying an Atlanta UHF-TV station, which he called WTBS for Turner Broadcasting System, Inc., the company of which he is president and chairman. Building on the growing cable market, he turned WTBS into a "superstation," the first station distributed nationally to cable systems via satellite. By the mid-80s it reached more than half of all viewers nationwide. In 1980 he founded CNN, the Cable News Network, the model for all subsequent 24-hour news stations. In 1986, his Turner Broadcasting System purchased MGM/UA (see METRO-GOLDWYN-MAYER) for about \$1.5 billion in cash and stock. Turner sold MGM's production, processing, and distribution facilities but kept the historically invaluable library of more than 3,300 films made not only by MGM but by Warner Bros. and RKO. These became programming for his cable stations, which expanded to include TNT (Turner Network Television) in 1988. The frequent airing of vintage movies on Turner's stations endeared him to film fans nearly as much as his computer colorization of black-and-white movies alienated them. Turner's personal devotion to movies is clear from the white-pillared mansion on his South Carolina plantation that is reminiscent of Tara in *Gone With the Wind*. Turner became a theatrical motion picture executive when he purchased New Line Cinema and Castle Rock Entertainment in 1993. His own production company, Turner Pictures, released its first feature, *Gettysburg*, the same year.

A spokesperson for environmentalism and global interdependence, Turner founded the Better World Society and the Goodwill Games. He is also a championship yachtsman who won the America's Cup in 1977 and co-owns two Atlanta pro sports teams, the Braves (baseball) and the Hawks (basketball). After two previous marriages ended in divorce, he married actress Jane FONDA in 1991. In 1996 he sold his companies to Time-Warner, where he now occupies a major position.

Turpin, Ben. Actor. *b.* Sept. 17, 1874, New Orleans. *d.* 1940. Cross-eyed slapstick comedian of the silent screen. Raised in New York, he began his career as a burlesque comedian. He entered films in 1907, joining Essanay shortly after the company began operating in Chicago. For two years he appeared in many Essanay shorts, but he failed to attract much attention and returned to burlesque, in which he enjoyed some success as a character named Happy Hooligan. Turpin returned to Essanay in 1914, but again he remained an obscure comedian until he was cast as a foil to Charlie CHAPLIN the following year. The two comedians did not get along, and in 1916, Turpin joined the newly formed Vogue company. He was now top banana but still a small-time comic.

It wasn't until the latter part of 1917, when he joined Mack SENNETT, that Turpin became a leading comedy star. He enjoyed his greatest success in a series of parodies of hit movies of the period, lampooning such screen personalities as VALENTINO and Erich von STROHEIM. He derived much laughter from the contrast between his small size and ludicrous face and the dashing, sophisticated characters he purported to portray (he had insured his eyes with Lloyds of London against uncrossing). During the sound era, Turpin played cameo roles in occasional films.

FILMS INCLUDE: *Midnight Disturbance, Mr. Flip* 1909; *Golf Champion Chick, Evans Links with Sweedie* 1914; *Snakeville's Hen Medic, His New Job, A Night Out* 1915; *Carmen, Hired and Fired, Lost and Found, The Wicked City* 1916; *The Butcher's Nightmare, A Studio Stampede, Caught in the End, A Clever Dummy, A Pawnbroker's Heart, Roping Her Romeo* 1917; *The Battle Royal, She Loved Him Plenty, Hide and Seek Detectives* 1918; *Cupid's Day Off, When Love Is Blind, Yankee Doodle in Berlin, Uncle Tom Without the Cabin, Sleuths* 1919; *The Star Boarder, Down on the Farm, Married Life* 1920; *A Small Town Idol, Home Talent, Love and Doughnuts* 1921; *Bright Eyes, Home Made Movies* 1922; *The Shriek of Araby, Hollywood, The Daredevil* 1923; *Yukon Jake, Romeo and Juliet, The Reel Virginian* 1924; *Wild Goose Chaser, The Marriage Circus, Hogan's Alley* 1925; *When a Man's a Prince, A Prodigal Bridegroom, Steel Preferred, A Harem Knight* 1926; *A Hollywood Hero, Broke in China, Pride of Pikeville, Love's Languid Lure, The College Hero* 1927; *The Wife's Relations* 1928; *The Show of Shows* 1929; *The Love Parade, Swing High* 1930; *Cracked Nuts* 1931; *Make Me a Star, Million Dollar Legs* 1932; *Hollywood Cavalcade* 1939; *Saps at Sea* 1940.

turret. A revolving lens mount attached to the front of a camera. Lenses mounted on a turret can be swung rapidly into position for filming by rotating the mount.

Turturro, John. Actor, director. Born on Feb. 28, 1957, in Brooklyn, N.Y. *ed.* SUNY (New Paltz, N.Y.); Yale (M.F.A., Drama). Edgy, brooding supporting player of screen and stage. Son of a carpenter, he established himself in a variety of regional and off-Broadway performances, including 'Danny and the Deep Blue Sea,' for which he won an Obie. Since his film debut in 1980, he has specialized in simmering urban types, notably the bigoted Brooklyn pizza man in *Do the Right Thing* and the haunted New York playwright in *Barton Fink*. His directorial debut *Mac*, based on his father's experiences as a Queens home builder in the 1950s, was widely praised. He is married to actress Katherine Borowitz. His brother, Nicholas, is also an actor.

FILMS INCLUDE: *Raging Bull* 1980; *Exterminator 2, The Flamingo Kid* 1984; *Desperately Seeking Susan, To Live and Die in L.A.* 1985; *Gung Ho, The Color of Money, Off Beat, Hannah and Her Sisters* 1986; *The Sicilian* 1987; *Five Corners* 1988; *Do the Right Thing* 1989; *Mo' Better Blues, State of Grace, Miller's Crossing* 1990; *Men of Respect, Jungle Fever, Barton Fink* 1991; *Brain Donors, Mac* (also dir.) 1992; *Fearless* 1993; *Being Human, Quiz Show* 1994; *Clockers, Search and Destroy, Unstrung Heroes* 1995; *Girl 6, Grace of My Heart* 1996; *Box of Moonlight* 1997.

Tushingham, Rita. Actress. Born on Mar. 14, 1942, in Liverpool, England, a pharmacist's daughter. She began acting in plays staged at the convent she was attending in her hometown. After training at the Liverpool Playhouse, she made her professional stage debut in 1960. The following year she made a splendid screen debut in *A Taste of Honey,* for which she won the British Academy Award, the New York Film Critics Award, and the Cannes Festival Award, among other citations. Plain, wide-eyed, and sincere, she has since played modern-day nonheroines, often offbeat, in films of the British realist school. In 1970 she formed her own production company with director Desmond DAVIS, but her career has subsequently suffered from the scarcity of suitable roles and since the 70s she has appeared mainly in routine Italian productions.

FILMS INCLUDE: *A Taste of Honey* 1961; *The Leather Boys, A Place to Go* 1963; *Girl with Green Eyes* 1964; *The Knack, Doctor Zhivago* (US) 1965; *The Trap* 1966; *Smashing Time* 1967; *Diamonds for Breakfast* 1968; *The Guru* (US/Ind.), *The Bed Sitting Room* 1969; *The Case of Laura C.* (It.) 1971; *Where Do You Go from Here?* (Norw.), *Straight On Till Morning* 1972; *The Human Factor, Rachel's Man* (UK/Isr.) 1975; *Ragazzo di Borgata* (It.) 1976; *Gran Bollito* (It.) 1977; *Sotto Choc* (It.) 1978; *Mysteries* (Holl.) 1979; *Judgment in Stone, The Housekeeper, Flying* (Can.) 1986; *Hard Days and Hard Nights, Resurrected* 1988; *Paper Marriage* 1993; *An Awfully Big Adventure* 1995.

Tuttle, Frank. Director. *b.* Aug. 6, 1892, New York City. *d.* 1963. *ed.* Yale. He gained acting and directing experience at college, where he served as president of the Yale Dramatic Association. After graduation, he was assistant editor on *Vanity Fair* and later a publicity writer. He entered films in the early 20s as a screenwriter for Paramount and soon turned to directing. A prolific, dependable filmmaker, he directed many silent and sound entertainment films of better than average quality in a variety of genres. During the McCarthy era he was a star witness at the hearings of the House Un-American Activities Committee. Admitting past membership in the Communist Party, he named many of his Hollywood colleagues as fellow travelers. Although he was not blacklisted, his career went into a sharp decline after his testimony.

FILMS: *The Cradle Buster* (also sc.) 1922; *Second Fiddle* (also co-sc.), *Youthful Cheaters, Puritan Passions* (also co-sc.) 1923; *Grit, Dangerous Money* 1924; *Miss Bluebeard, A Kiss in the Dark, The Manicure Girl, Lucky Devil, Lovers in Quarantine* 1925; *The American Venus, The Untamed Lady, Kid Boots, Love 'Em and Leave 'Em* 1926; *Blind Alleys, Time to Love, The Spotlight, One Woman to Another* 1927; *Easy Come*

Easy Go, His Private Life, Varsity, Something Always Happens (also story), *Love and Learn* 1928; *Marquis Preferred, The Studio Murder Mystery, The Green Murder Case, Sweetie, Men Are Like That* 1929; *Only the Brave, The Benson Murder Case, True to the Navy, Love Among the Millionaires, Paramount on Parade* (co-dir. with ten others), *Her Wedding Night* 1930; *No Limit, It Pays to Advertise, Dude Ranch* 1931; *This Reckless Age, This Is the Night, The Big Broadcast* 1932; *Dangerously Yours, Pleasure Cruise, Roman Scandals* 1933; *Ladies Should Listen, Springtime for Henry, Here Is My Heart* 1934; *All the King's Horses* (also co-sc.), *The Glass Key, Two for Tonight* 1935; *College Holiday* 1936; *Waikiki Wedding* 1937; *Doctor Rhythm* 1938; *Paris Honeymoon, Charlie McCarthy—Detective* (also prod.), *I Stole a Million* 1939; *This Gun for Hire, Lucky Jordan* 1942; *Hostages* 1943; *The Hour Before Dawn* 1944; *The Great John L., Don Juan Quilligan* 1945; *Suspense, Swell Guy* 1946; *Le Traqué/Gunman in the Streets* (Fr.) 1950; *The Magic Face* 1951; *Hell on Frisco Bay, A Cry in the Night* 1956; *Island of Lost Women* 1959.

Tuttle, William J. American makeup artist. MGM's makeup director in the 50s and 60s, he designed the horrific Morlock makeup for *The Time Machine* and the diverse guises of Tony Randall in *Seven Faces of Dr. Lao*.

FILMS INCLUDE: *To Please a Lady, Pagan Love Song, Kim, A Life of Her Own* 1950; *Royal Wedding, Show Boat, The People Against O'Hara, The Strip* 1951; *The Bad and the Beautiful, Pat and Mike, Scaramouche* 1952; *Julius Caesar, Lili* 1953; *Executive Suite* 1954; *It's Always Fair Weather, The Tender Trap* 1955; *Forbidden Planet, High Society, The Opposite Sex* 1956; *Jailhouse Rock, Raintree County, Silk Stockings* 1957; *Cat on a Hot Tin Roof, Gigi, High School Confidential* 1958; *North by Northwest, Some Came Running* 1959; *Please Don't Eat the Daisies, The Time Machine* (US/UK) 1960; *Two Loves* 1961; *How the West Was Won, Jumbo, Mutiny on the Bounty, Ride the High Country, Sweet Bird of Youth, The Wonderful World of the Brothers Grimm* 1962; *Honeymoon Hotel, Kissin' Cousins, The Unsinkable Molly Brown, Viva Las Vegas, Seven Faces of Dr. Lao* 1964; *Harum Scarum, A Patch of Blue* 1965; *The Glass Bottom Boat, The Singing Nun* 1966; *Hot Rods to Hell, The Last Challenge, Welcome to Hard Times* 1967; *The Power, The Split, Where Were You When the Lights Went Out?* 1968; *The Gypsy Moths, The Maltese Bippy* 1969; *The Life and Times of Judge Roy Bean, Necromancy, What's Up Doc?* 1972; *Young Frankenstein* 1974; *Silent Movie, Silver Streak* 1976; *The Greatest* (US/UK) 1977; *The Fury, Same Time Next Year* 1978.

Twelvetrees, Helen. Actress. *b.* Helen Marie Jurgens, Dec. 25, 1907, Brooklyn, N.Y. *d.* 1958, a suicide. Trained for the stage at the American Academy of Dramatic Arts, she arrived in Hollywood in the late 20s following some stage experience and was immediately put into leads, mainly in melodramas. Specializing in tearful roles, she was moderately popular among soap-opera lovers through the mid-30s, when her career suddenly collapsed.

FILMS INCLUDE: *The Ghost Talks, Blue Skies, Words and Music* 1929; *The Grand Parade, Swing High, Her Man, The Cat Creeps* 1930; *Millie, The Painted Desert, A Woman of Experience, Bad Company* 1931; *Panama Flo, Love Starved, State's Attorney, Is My Face Red, Unashamed* 1932; *A Bedtime Story, Disgraced, My Woman, King for a Night* 1933; *Now I'll Tell, She Was a Lady* 1934; *Times Square Lady, She Gets Her Man* 1935; *Hollywood Round-Up* 1937; *Unmarried* 1939.

20th Century-Fox. An American film production and distribution company formed in 1935 as a result of a merger between the veteran Fox company and a new corporation, Twentieth Century. The company's history can be traced back to nickelodeon days, when William Fox, an immigrant from Hungary, opened a penny arcade in Brooklyn, N.Y. He had soon so developed his business that it encompassed a chain of theaters and a film exchange, the Greater New York Film Rental Company. In 1912 he moved into production and in 1915 founded the Fox Film Corporation, a production, distribution, and exhibition firm. The Fox studio's first superstar was the celebrated screen vamp Theda Bara. Other early stars included William Farnum, Betty Blythe, Annette Kellerman, and cowboy favorite Tom Mix. Fox's chief of production was Winfield Sheehan.

In 1921 the studio acquired the services of director John Ford, who worked exclusively for Fox in the next decade. Other Fox directors of the 20s included Herbert Brenon, J. Gordon Edwards, Raoul Walsh, and Frank Borzage. Occasionally the studio invested some of its profits from box-office hits like the Janet Gaynor-Charles Farrell romantic dramas in top-quality productions. Thus, F. W. Murnau was imported from Germany to direct his masterpiece *Sunrise* (1927) and several other films at Fox. By the end of the silent era, Fox was a highly profitable corporation and a major Hollywood studio. When Warner Bros. launched the sound era with its Vitaphone sound-on-disc system in 1926–27, Fox immediately responded with its own system, Movietone, a sound-on-film process it had developed in association with General Electric.

Movietone was the first popular system to employ a sound track directly on film and it set the standard for sound films to this day. At the same time, Fox began a systematic acquisition of motion picture theaters and entered negotiations to take over the assets of Loew's, Inc., a giant organization that owned hundreds of cinemas and was the parent company of MGM. But the deal was nullified as a result of the stock market crash. In addition, the Wall Street disaster, combined with the pressure of government antitrust action, caused Fox stock to drop from $119 to $1 a share in only two days. The company was taken over by a group of bankers but fell on hard times and was saved from bankruptcy thanks only to the high profits reaped from the films of Fox's new child star, Shirley Temple.

In 1935, Fox merged with Twentieth Century, a production firm established two years earlier by Joseph M. Schenck and Darryl F. Zanuck, the former chief of production at Warners. The new corporation was named 20th Century-Fox. Schenck became its president and Zanuck vice president in charge of production. The new company embarked on an ambitious program of production that emphasized technical polish and visual gloss. The photography in 20th Century-Fox films was typically brassy and in sharp focus; the color of its Faye-Grable-Miranda cycle of musicals was gorgeously brilliant. The company's productions varied widely in genre and in artistic level but never in technical quality. Among its contract directors in the 30s, 40s, and 50s were Ernst Lubitsch, Joseph Mankiewicz, Otto Preminger, Henry King, Henry Hathaway, Walter Lang, Anatole Litvak, George Seaton, and Elia Kazan. Its roster of stars included such actresses as Shirley Temple, Alice Faye, Loretta Young, Sonja Henie, Linda Darnell, Betty Grable, Gene Tierney, and Marilyn Monroe, and such actors as Tyrone Power, Don Ameche, Warner Baxter, Henry Fonda, Gregory Peck, and Richard Widmark.

In the 50s the company led the industry in countering the TV threat with the CinemaScope wide-screen system. In the middle of the decade, Zanuck resigned his position to become an independent producer and Spyros Skouras took charge of 20th Century-Fox. But a succession of commercial failures, culminating in the famous *Cleopatra* disaster, led to the ouster of

Skouras in 1962 and to the return to power of Zanuck as president. He brought in his son Richard as production chief, and together they oversaw the phenomenal success of *The Sound of Music* (1965). In 1969, Darryl Zanuck became chairman of the board and Richard succeeded him as president. But in December of 1970, at the end of a stormy stockholders' campaign, Richard was forced out of the company by his own father, who retained his own position at the helm. His victory was short-lived, since he resigned as chief executive in May of 1971, becoming chairman emeritus. Dennis C. Stanfill became chairman and CEO.

In the 70s, 20th Century-Fox enjoyed several major successes, including *The French Connection* (1971) and *The Poseidon Adventure* (1972), but its greatest coup of the decade was *Star Wars* (1977), which generated two sequels and remained one of the top two all-time box-office champions for many years. In 1981, the studio's independent status ended when oil billionaire Marvin Davis bought the company, with Alan J. Hirschfield replacing Stanfill as chairman and CEO. Davis resold it in 1985 to Australian publishing magnate Rupert Murdoch. Murdoch formed Fox Inc., which comprised 20th Century-Fox Film Corporation, Fox Television Stations Inc., and Fox Broadcasting Company. In 1989, the company announced plans to increase movie production with the appointment of independent producer and director Joe ROTH as chairman of Fox Film Corporation. Roth oversaw the enormous success of *Home Alone* (1990) before departing in 1993 to head a production unit at the Walt DISNEY CO.

Barry DILLER, who was named chairman and CEO of Fox, Inc. in 1985, resigned in 1992, at which point Murdoch himself took over those positions. As a result of executive changes, the studio is now headed by Peter Chernin. With tremendous success at the box office from films like *Independence Day* as well as the unexpected smash of the *Stars Wars* trilogy reissue in, optimism and a prosperous outlook have eased tensions in the now revived studio.

Twist, John (or **John Stuart Twist).** Screenwriter. *b.* July 14, 1898, Albany, Mo. *d.* 1976. *ed.* U. of Chicago. He entered films in 1926 as a reader and began writing stories and screenplays in 1927. He often worked on Westerns and action pictures.

FILMS INCLUDE: *Breed of Courage* (story only) 1927; *Blockade* (adapt.) 1928; *The Big Diamond Robbery* 1929; *La Cucaracha* (Oscar-winning short), *West of the Pecos* 1934; *Annie Oakley* 1935; *Yellow Dust, The Last Outlaw* 1936; *We Who Are About to Die, Sea Devils, The Outcasts of Poker Flat, The Toast of New York, Flight from Glory* 1937; *Next Time I Marry* 1938; *The Great Man Votes, The Saint Strikes Back, Three Sons, Reno* 1939; *Too Many Girls* 1940; *Parachute Battalion* 1941; *The Navy Comes Through* 1942; *Bombardier* 1943; *Sinbad the Sailor, Tycoon* 1947; *Colorado Territory* 1949; *Dallas* 1951; *The Big Trees* 1952; *So Big* 1953; *King Richard and the Crusaders* 1954; *The Sea Chase* 1955; *Helen of Troy, Serenade* 1956; *Band of Angels* 1957; *The Deep Six* 1958; *The FBI Story* 1959; *A Distant Trumpet* 1964; *None but the Brave* 1965.

two-shot. A close camera shot just wide enough to keep two persons within the limits of the frame.

Tyler, Tom. Actor. *b.* Vincent Markowski, Aug. 9, 1903, Port Henry, N.Y. *d.* 1954. A former coal miner, seaman, lumberjack, prizefighter, and champion weight lifter, he entered films in 1924 as a stuntman and extra. After playing supporting parts in several films, he was signed up by FBO as a star of Westerns. Handsome and athletic, he rapidly gained popularity as a screen cowboy. He benefited from good production values, frequent action scenes, and the presence of a fetching sidekick, little Frankie DARRO. Tyler made a smooth transition to sound, and although his films declined in quality, he remained popular through the early 40s, thanks mainly to starring roles in a number of highly successful serials. Occasionally, he played supporting parts in major films, sometimes as a villain. In 1943, after completing the serial *The Phantom* and a succession of "Three Mesquiteers" Westerns, Tyler was felled by a crippling rheumatic condition that was to have a devastating effect on his career. He was soon reduced to minor roles and by the early 50s he was broke and hardly working at all. He died of a heart attack at the age of 50.

FILMS INCLUDE: *Galloping Gallagher* (bit) 1924; *Let's Go Gallagher, The Cowboy Musketeer* 1925; *Born to Battle, Masquerade Bandit, The Arizona Streak* 1926; *Cyclone of the Range, The Cowboy Cop, The Cherokee Kid, The Desert Pirate, The Sonora Kid* 1927; *The Avenging Rider, Terror, The Texas Tornado* 1928; *Lone Horseman, The Phantom Rider, The Man from Nevada, Pioneers of the West* 1929; *The Canyon of Missing Men* 1930; *Battling with Buffalo Bill* (serial) 1931; *The Jungle Mystery* (serial), *Two-Fisted Justice* 1932; *Clancy of the Mounted* (serial) 1933; *The Last Outlaw* 1936; *Frontier Marshal, Stagecoach, Gone With the Wind* 1939; *Brother Orchid, The Mummy's Hand, The Westerner* 1940; *Adventures of Captain Marvel* (serial), *West of Cimarron* 1941; *Valley of the Sun, The Talk of the Town* 1942; *The Phantom* (serial), *Riders of the Rio Grande* 1943; *Sing Me a Song of Texas, San Antonio* 1945; *Badman's Territory* 1946; *Blood on the Moon* 1948; *I Shot Jesse James, Lust for Gold, She Wore a Yellow Ribbon* 1949; *Cow Country* 1953.

typecasting. The casting of an actor in roles that conform to the image he has created in previous performances. A classic example is actor Jack NORTON, who played drunks in numerous films and was rarely seen in any other role.

Tyrrell, Susan. Actress. Born in 1946, in San Francisco. Raised in New Canaan, Conn., she began her professional career as a teenager, playing ingenues in summer stock, but later specialized in portraying lushes and whores in off-Broadway and Lincoln Center Repertory productions. She made her screen debut in 1971 and shortly after was nominated for an Oscar as best supporting actress for her performance as a drunken floozy in John Huston's *Fat City* (1972). She has since played character leads and supporting roles in several other films.

FILMS INCLUDE: *The Steagle, Been Down So Long It Looks Like Up to Me, Shoot Out* 1971; *Fat City* 1972; *Catch My Soul, Zandy's Bride* 1974; *The Killer Inside Me* 1976; *Un Autre Homme une Autre Chance/Another Man Another Chance* (Fr.), *Islands in the Stream, Andy Warhol's Bad, I Never Promised You a Rose Garden* 1977; *Racquet, The Forbidden Zone* 1979; *Loose Shoes* 1980; *Night Warning* 1981; *Fast-Walking, Liar's Moon* 1982; *Fire and Ice* (voice) 1983; *Tales of Ordinary Madness* 1983; *Angel* 1984; *Flesh and Blood, Avenging Angel* 1985; *The Offspring/From a Whisper to a Scream* 1987; *The Underachievers, Big Top Pee-Wee* 1988; *Far from Home, Tapeheads* 1989; *Cry-Baby, Rockula* 1990; *Motorama* 1992; *Powder* 1995.

Tyson, Cicely. Actress. Born Dec. 19, 1933, in New York City. She grew up in Harlem, where her parents had moved from the island of Nevis in the Caribbean. Her father operated a pushcart and her mother was a domestic. When they separated, mother and daughter went on welfare and Cicely earned some extra money by selling shopping bags on the street. After she graduated from high school she became a typist at the American Red Cross, then took up modeling, with considerable success. She made her acting debut in a Harlem YMCA production of 'Dark of the Moon' and went from there to the 1971 off-Broadway staging of 'The Blacks.' In 1963–64 she was featured regularly in the role of a secretary in the TV series 'East Side West Side.'

She then began appearing in films, reaching stardom with *Sounder* (1972), for which she was nominated for an Academy Award as best actress. Largely seen on TV from the 70s, she won acclaim for her performances in such TV dramas as 'The Autobiography of Miss Jane Pittman' and 'Roots.'

FILMS: *A Man Called Adam* 1966; *The Comedians* 1967; *The Heart Is a Lonely Hunter* 1968; *Sounder* 1972; *The River Niger, The Blue Bird* (as Cat; US/USSR) 1976; *A Hero Ain't Nothin' but a Sandwich* 1977; *The Concorde—Airport '79* 1979; *Bustin' Loose* 1981; *Fried Green Tomatoes* 1991; *The Grass Harp* 1996; *Hoodlum* 1997.

Tzavellas, George. Director. *b.* 1916, Athens. *d.* 1976. Next to Michael CACOYANNIS and Nikos Kounduros, the most important director of postwar Greek cinema. He studied law but turned to the theater with considerable success before switching to films after WW II. With the notable exception of *Antigone,* he has dealt mostly in popular comedy and melodrama.

FILMS INCLUDE: *Marinos Kontaras* 1947; *The Drunkard* 1949; *Lily of the Harbor* 1952; *The Taxi Driver* 1953; *The Counterfeit Coin/The False Pound Sterling* 1954; *The Grouch* 1956; *We Have Only One Life* 1958; *Antigone* 1961; *A Woman Must Be Afraid of Man* 1965.

U

Uchida, Tomu. Director *b.* Apr. 26, 1898, Okayama, Japan. *d.* 1970. He entered Japanese silent films in 1920 as an actor. From 1923 he apprenticed as an assistant to MIZOGUCHI and other directors and in 1927 he made his directorial debut. His early films were often light parodies and farces, but gradually he moved toward a painstaking realistic style that found its ultimate expression in his best-known film, the semidocumentary *The Earth* (1939). During WW II he fell into disfavor with the militaristic regime and went into self-exile in Manchuria. He crossed over to the Chinese side and became a member of the Communist Party. He did not return to Japan until the mid-50s, when he resumed his work in films, specializing in period drama.

FILMS INCLUDE: *Pain* 1927; *Spinning Earth, Wind of This World* 1928; *A Living Doll, Sweat* 1929; *Return to Heaven* 1930; *Jean Valjean, Miss Nippon* 1931; *Mother Earth Rises* 1932; *Asia Calling* 1933; *Hot Wind* 1934; *Theater of Life* 1936; *Unending Advance* 1937; *The Earth* 1939; *History* 1940; *A Bloody Spear on Mount Fuji* 1955; *The Eleventh Hour* 1957; *Outsiders* 1958; *Murder in Yoshiwara* 1960; *Untamed Fury* 1961; *Duel Without End* 1962; *The Last Duel* 1965; *Kaku and Tsune* 1968; *Swords of Death* (released posthumously) 1972.

UFA (Universum Film Aktien Gesellschaft). Giant film production combine created in GERMANY in 1917 with the help of government funds, initially for the purpose of presenting a positive image of Germany and its political viewpoint and counteracting the wartime impact of the American film on European minds. Several major studios were merged to form UFA, in an effort to elevate the production standards of the German cinema, among them Nordisk-Film, Messter-Film, Union, and the Viennese Sascha-Film. Other film companies were absorbed into UFA in the years following, including Terra and Decla-Bioscop. The company continued to expand for several years, gradually branching into distribution and exhibition as well as production.

After the Armistice, the government's shares of UFA were acquired by the Deutsche Bank, but the company continued enjoying a semi-official status and prestige and, under the leadership of Erich POMMER, played a central role in the postwar "golden age" of the German cinema. However, financial difficulties accentuated by competition from Hollywood in the mid-20s forced UFA into a diminished role and into contracts with Famous Players-Lasky and MGM, which eventually resulted in a further attrition of the German company's former position. UFA sank more deeply into debt and in 1927 was saved from bankruptcy by a trust headed by Dr. Alfred Hugenberg, a Nazi sympathizer, who became chairman of the film company's board of directors. Under Hugenberg's influence, UFA increasingly became an outlet for nationalist propaganda, although the company continued producing prestigious nonpolitical features, including Von Sternberg's *The Blue Angel* (1930).

In 1937, UFA became state-owned. To mark the company's 25th anniversary in 1943, the most spectacular film of the Nazi era, *Münchhausen,* was produced. UFA ceased to exist in 1945, and its large Neubabelsberg studios were taken over by DEFA, the East German production company. An attempt to resurrect the venerated name came in 1956, when a new UFA was refounded in West Germany, but the company later failed.

Uhry, Alfred H. Playwright and screenwriter. Born in 1937. Accomplished American dramatist who became a screenwriter in the 1980s and won an Academy Award for his screenplay of *Driving Miss Daisy*.

FILMS INCLUDE: *Mystic Pizza* 1988; *Driving Miss Daisy* 1989; *Rich in Love* 1992.

Ullman, Tracey. Comedienne, actress. Born on Dec. 29, 1959, in Hackbridge, England. Boisterous, original player of screen, stage, and TV. *ed.* Italia Conti School. She began training as a performer after winning a scholarship to an arts school when she was 12 and later appeared widely on British TV and at London's Royal Court Theatre. Debuted in film in 80s, moving quickly from comedic support to lead. Awarded an Emmy for the TV comedy series, 'The Tracey Ullman Show'; earned gold record for album 'You Broke My Heart in Seventeen Places.' Married to British TV producer Allan McKeown; they have a daughter.

FILMS INCLUDE: *Give My Regards to Broad Street* 1983; *Plenty* 1985; *Jumpin' Jack Flash* 1986; *I Love You to Death* 1990; *Death Becomes Her* 1992; *Robin Hood: Men in Tights, Household Saints* 1993; *Bullets Over Broadway, I'll Do Anything, Ready to Wear* 1994.

Ullmann, Liv. Actress. Born on Dec. 16, 1939, in Tokyo, to Norwegian parents. Outstanding dramatic actress of Swedish and international films whose splendidly expressive face and subtle acting have figured prominently in several Ingmar BERGMAN productions. The daughter of a Norwegian engineer stationed in Japan, she moved with her family to Canada at the outbreak of the Pacific hostilities of WW II. They later lived briefly in New York, where her father died. Returning to Norway with her mother, Liv completed her high school education, then joined a provincial theatrical group and several years later gained prominence on the Oslo stage and in Norwegian films. She achieved international fame in the late 60s and in the 70s as the emotionally strained protagonist of such Bergman films as *Persona* (1966), *Hour of the Wolf* (1968), *Shame* (1968), *The Passion of Anna/Passion* (1969), *Cries and Whispers* (1972), *Scenes from a Marriage* (1973), *Face to Face* (1976), and *Autumn Sonata* (1978). The intimate professional relationship between the director and the actress extended into their private lives. Divorcing their respective mates, they lived together for five years, a union that produced a daughter. Miss Ullmann's radiant beauty and her reputation as an actress of extraordinary emotional range brought her offers of starring roles in international productions, including Hollywood's musical *Lost Horizon* and comedy *40 Carats* (both 1973), in both of which she was woefully miscast. She has also starred on Broadway and the European stage. In the 90s, she co-wrote and directed a film, *Sofie* (1993). Her autobiography, *Changing,* was published in 1977. That same year she was the subject of a feature-length documentary film, *A Look at Liv.*

FILMS: *Fjols til Fjells* (Nor.) 1957; *Tonny* (Nor.), *Kort ar Sommaren/Pan/Short Is the Summer* (Nor./Sw.) 1962; *De kalte ham skarven* (Nor.) 1964; *Ung Flukt* (Nor.), *Persona* (Sw.) 1966; *Hour of the Wolf* (Sw.), *Shame* (Sw.) 1968; *Ann-Magritt* (Nor./Sw.), *The Passion of Anna/Passion* (Sw.) 1969; *De la Part des Copains/Cold Sweat* (Fr./It.) 1970; *The Night Visitor* (Sw./Den./US), *The Emigrants* (Sw.) 1971; *Pope Joan* (UK), *Cries and Whispers* (Sw.) 1972; *Scenes from a Marriage* (orig. on Swedish TV), *Lost Horizon* (US), *40 Carats* (US), *The New Land* (Sw.) 1973; *Zandy's Bridge* (US), *The Abdication* (UK) 1974; *Léonor* (Fr.) 1975; *Face to Face* (Sw.) 1976; *Couleur Chair* (Belg./Fr.), *A Bridge Too Far* (UK), *The Serpent's Egg* (US/Ger.) 1977; *Autumn Sonata* (Sw.) 1978; *Players* 1979; *Richard's Things* (TV; UK) 1980; *The Wild Duck* (Austral.) 1982; *Bay Boy* (Can.), *Dangerous Moves* (Switz.); *Ingrid* (UK), *Let's Hope It's a Girl* 1985; *Gaby—A True Story* (US), *Moscow Adieu, A Time of Indifference, La Amiga* 1988; *The Rose Garden* (US) 1989; *Mindwalk* (US) 1990; *The Ox/Oxen* 1991; *The Long Shadow* 1992; *Sofie* (co-sc., dir. only) 1993; *Dream Play* 1994.

Ulmer, Edgar G. Director. *b.* Sept. 17, 1904, Vienna. *d.* 1972. While studying architecture at Vienna's Academy of Arts and Sciences and philosophy at the University of Vienna, he was employed as actor and assistant set designer at the famous Burg Theater. He later worked as set designer and assistant director on stage productions of Max REINHARDT and on films of the Decla company in Berlin. In 1923 he came to the US with Reinhardt's 'The Miracle' and stayed to design sets for Martin Beck on Broadway and for Universal in Hollywood. Returning to Germany in 1925, he became the assistant of F. W. MURNAU, working on *The Last Laugh, Faust,* and others of the director's notable productions. He accompanied Murnau on his Hollywood venture and assisted on the director's American films, including *Sunrise* and *Tabu.* He returned to Berlin in 1929, just long enough to collaborate with Robert Siodmak on the direction of the documentary *Menschen am Sonntag/People on Sunday,* then settled in Hollywood the following year as an art director. Began as a director in 1933.

Throughout his career, Ulmer worked with minuscule budgets and often with impossible scripts, mostly at the service of Poverty Row studios in the US as well as in Mexico, Italy, and Spain. Some of his films were made for such obscure producers (including several Yiddish and Ukrainian productions) that an accurate and full chronology of his work is almost impossible to compile. Amazingly, an unmistakable mark of a personal style can be discerned throughout much of his grade-Z body of work. One of his first films, *The Black Cat,* has been long recognized as a masterpiece of the horror genre. But most of his subsequent films were largely ignored by American critics until their French colleagues declared him a minor *auteur* and started an Edgar G. Ulmer mystique that crossed the Atlantic. In the 60s, Ulmer served as chief of European operations for Martin Melcher Productions.

FILMS INCLUDE: *Menschen am Sonntag/People on Sunday* (doc.; co-dir. with Robert Siodmak, co-sc.; Ger.) 1929; *Damaged Lives* (also co-sc.), *Mr. Broadway* 1933; *The Black Cat* (also co-sc.), *Thunder Over Texas* (under pseudonym of John Warner) 1934; *From Nine to Nine* (under pseudonym of John Warner) 1935; *Natalka Poltavka* (in Ukrainian), *Greene Felde/Green Fields* (co-dir. with Jacob Ben-Ami; in Yiddish) 1937; *Yankel dem Schmidt/The Singing Blacksmith* (in Yiddish) 1938; *Zaprosh za Dunayem/Cossacks in Exile* (in Ukrainian), *Die Klatsche/The Light Ahead* (in Yiddish), *Fishke der Drume/Fishke the Lame One* (in Yiddish), *Moon Over Harlem* 1939; *Americaner Schadchen/American Matchmaker* (in Yiddish), *Cloud in the Sky* (doc. short about hazards of tuberculosis) 1940; *Another to Conquer* (doc. short, as above) 1941; *Let My People Live* (doc. short about tuberculosis among blacks), *Tomorrow We Live* 1942; *My Son the Hero* (also co-sc.), *Girls in Chains* (also story), *Isle of Forgotten Sins/Monsoon* (also story), *Jive Junction* 1943; *Bluebeard* 1944; *Strange Illusion/Out of the Night, Club Havana* 1945; *Detour, The Wife of Monte Cristo* (also co-story), *Her Sister's Secret, The Strange Woman* 1946; *Carnegie Hall* 1947; *Ruthless* 1948; *I Pirati di Capri/The Pirates of Capri/Captain Sirocco* (It.) 1949; *St. Benny the Dip, The Man from Planet X* 1951; *Babes in Bagdad* 1952; *Murder Is My Beat/Dynamite Anchorage, The Naked Dawn* 1955; *The Daughter of Dr. Jekyll* 1957; *Hannibal* (English-language version of *Annibale;* It.), *The Amazing Transparent Man, Beyond the Time Barrier* 1960; *L'Atlantide/Antinea L'Amante della Città Sepolta/Journey Beneath the Desert* (co-dir. with Giuseppe Masini, both replacing Frank Borzage; Fr./It.) 1961; *Sette contro la Morte/The Cavern* (also prod.; It./Ger.) 1965.

Ulric, Lenore. Actress. *b.* Lenore Ulrich, July 21, 1892, New Ulm, Minn. *d.* 1970. She made her stage debut in stock while still attending high school. In 1911 she joined Essanay in Chicago and starred (initially under her real name, Lenore Ulrich) in many of the company's films, typically as a fiery femme fatale, and was billed as "the magic mistress of a thousand emotions." In 1915 she became a protégée of stage producer David Belasco, who made her into an important Broadway star in the same type of tempestuous roles that had made her popular in her early films. While appearing on the stage, she continued starring in occasional silent and early sound films. In the 30s and 40s she played supporting parts—often as "the other woman"—in Garbo's *Camille* and several other films. Her marriage to actor Sidney BLACKMER lasted four years.

FILMS INCLUDE: *Kilmeny, Capital Punishment, The Better Woman* 1915; *The Heart of Paula, Intrigue, The Road to Love* 1916; *Her Own People* 1917; *Tiger Rose* 1923; *Frozen Justice, South Sea Rose* 1929; *Camille* 1937; *Temptation, Notorious* 1946; *Two Smart People, Northwest Outpost* 1947.

umbrella. An umbrella-shaped reflector used in filming to obtain bounced illumination.

Umeki, Miyoshi. Actress. Born in 1929, in Otaru, Hokkaido, Japan. A radio and nightclub vocalist since her teens, she came to the US in the 50s and through TV exposure landed an Oscar-winning part in the film *Sayonara.* She has since been seen on Broadway ('Flower Drum Song') and on TV ('The Courtship of Eddie's Father' series) but in only a handful of films.

FILMS: *Sayonara* 1957; *Cry for Happy, Flower Drum Song* 1961; *The Horizontal Lieutenant* 1962; *A Girl Named Tamiko* 1963.

undercrank. To operate a camera at a slower than normal speed so that the action appears accelerated on the screen. The term has remained in use since the early silent days, when cameras were cranked by hand.

underdeveloped. An adjective describing negative film that has not been allowed enough time in the developing bath or has been developed with solutions of improper temperature. The resultant print will have a washed-out appearance, lacking in contrast and detail.

underexposed. An adjective describing film exposed either to insufficient light or for too short a duration. Underexposure, usually caused by human error—the setting of a lens incorrectly or filming at excessive speed, for example—results in unusually light prints, lacking distinct tonal gradation.

undershoot. To shoot too little footage for satisfactory coverage of a particular scene. The problem usually becomes evident in the cutting room, when it may be too late or too expensive to go back to the scene for additional footage. Less severe but quite expensive is the tendency by some inexperienced directors to "overshoot," or to take too much footage lest they miss something.

underwater cinematography. The filming of underwater action has always presented special problems for the cinematographer. Beyond the obvious need to protect cameras and other equipment from water seepage, he has to cope with distortion of distance, size, and shape and the limitation of visibility under water. In addition, in the past, camera housings, while they protected an apparatus from damage, actually complicated the work of the cinematographer, who had to compensate for the distance between the camera lens and the housing window in his focusing calculations. This problem has been largely solved by modern underwater cameras that are equipped with special lenses and do not require waterproof and pressureproof housing. But distortion is still unavoidable, especially when filming in great depths. To minimize distortion, wide-angle lenses are usually used in underwater cinematography, whether the action actually takes place in the ocean or, as is often the case, in a studio tank. Many advances in underwater cinematography can be credited to research by the US Navy and to French oceanographer Commander Jacques-Yves COUSTEAU.

Underwood, Ron. Director. Born on Nov. 6, 1953, in Glendale, Calif. *ed.* USC. Peabody Award–winning TV director ('The Mouse and the Motorcycle') who turned to films in the 1980s. Known for offering light twists on familiar themes.

FILMS: *Tremors* (also co-story) 1990; *City Slickers* 1991; *Heart and Souls* 1993; *Speechless* 1994.

Unipod. Trade name for a camera support, used mostly for a newsreel work, where quick setups are desired.

unit. The technical crew assigned to the production of a particular motion picture or a distinct portion thereof.

United Artists. A production, releasing, and distribution company founded in 1919 by Charlie Chaplin, D. W. Griffith, Mary Pickford, and Douglas Fairbanks at the urging of William McAdoo, a former Secretary of the Treasury in the Wilson cabinet, and his publicity assistant, Oscar Price. Price became the company's first president, but he and McAdoo soon left the company, and management passed into the hands of a succession of executives, including Joseph M. SCHENCK at one period. During the silent era, United Artists gained much prestige and earned sizable profits from the release of the films of its founders and other famous directors and stars, including Keaton, Valentino, and Swanson. In the 30s, it released the productions of Sam Goldwyn and British imports produced by Alexander Korda, and packaged many other major films.

Both Goldwyn and Korda, who were important stockholders, pulled out of United Artists in the early 40s. Late in that decade the company fell on bad times, but it returned to the black early in the 50s after it was taken over in 1950 by a syndicate headed by Arthur Krim and Robert Benjamin. Formerly handicapped because it never had its own studio, United Artists in the 50s and 60s was spared the overhead that burdened other Hollywood companies with studios in that period, when location shooting and independent production became trends. United Artists also reaped the benefits of the government-decreed separation of distribution from exhibition (see STUDIO SYSTEM). Theater managers who had formerly been constrained by studio ownership were now free to bid for any features they chose, including those of United Artists. Successful releases by United Artists during this period included *The African Queen* (1951), *High Noon* (1952), *The Night of the Hunter* and *Marty* (both 1955), *Witness for the Prosecution* (1957), *Some Like It Hot* (1959), *The Apartment* and *The Magnificent Seven* (both 1960), *Tom Jones* (1963), and the James Bond films.

In 1957 United Artists became a public company, which in 1967 became a subsidiary of TransAmerica Corporation. The company continued to do well in the 70s, with three best picture Academy Awards in a row for *One Flew Over the Cuckoo's Nest* (1975), *Rocky* (1976), and *Annie Hall* (1977). The beginning of the end for United Artists came when five of its top executives—Krim, Benjamin, William Bernstein, Mike Medavoy, and Eric Pleskow—left in a disagreement over policy to found ORION PICTURES. The company was further crippled by the expensive box-office debacle *Heaven's Gate* (1980).

In 1981 Transamerica sold the ailing company to METRO-GOLDWYN-MAYER (MGM), whose films United Artists had been distributing since 1973. In 1983, MGM and United Artists merged as MGM/UA Entertainment. After several changes of ownership, MGM/UA was acquired in 1992 by the French bank Credit Lyonnais, which restored the name Metro-Goldwyn-Mayer Inc., removing the last vestige of what was once United Artists.

United Kingdom. Britain's contribution to the early development of the cinema was considerable. An important figure in the prehistory of the movies was William G. HORNER, the inventor of the Zoetrope, an apparatus that simulated motion by mounting a series of still pictures inside a drum. Other pioneers included Louis Le Prince, a Leeds resident of French descent who invented a workable motion picture camera before mysteriously disappearing from a train in 1890; Wordsworth Donisthorpe, who filmed a view of Trafalgar Square on a circular frame with a camera he had constructed in 1889; and William FRIESE-GREENE, a persistent dreamer, several of whose many inventions came close to actual cinematography in the late 1880s.

Birt ACRES, an American-born Englishman, launched cinema proper in Britain in 1895 when he filmed with his "Kinetic Lantern" such actuality items as the Derby at Epsom, the Oxford-Cambridge boat race, and the opening of Germany's Kiel Canal, giving the world its first newsreels. But Acres could not show his films for lack of means of projection until January of 1896, when he demonstrated his camera and projector to the Royal Photographic Society. In the interim, the LUMIÈRE brothers had made their historic first showing of films to a paying audience in Paris, on December 28, 1895. In February of 1896 they demonstrated their work to paying customers at London's Polytechnic Hall on Regent Street. Acres gave the first Royal Command Performance of film in July of 1896, but it was another pioneer, Robert W. PAUL, who was the first to exhibit British-made films to a paying audience at the Olympia in March of that year. The title of his first film was *Rough Sea at Dover.* A former optical-instrument maker, Paul was more a technician than an artist. He delighted his audiences with such feats of showmanship as showing a film record of the 1895 Derby on the very night of the event. Also during that year he produced Britain's first story film, the minute-long *The Soldier's Courtship.* Paul made many other short films, mainly comedies, at his rooftop studio above the Alhambra Theatre before moving in 1899 to a studio at Southgate which he specially equipped for trick effects, including a trolley-mounted camera for tracking shots.

The most creative of the early British pioneer filmmakers was Cecil HEPWORTH, who entered the business in 1896, at the age of 21, as a supplier of arc lamps and other motion picture equipment of his own design and a traveling exhibitor of a mixed-media program of films and Magic Lantern slides. In 1898 he published *Animated Photography or The ABC of the Cinematography,* the world's first known film textbook. He went into production in 1899, starting with the short *Express Trains in a Railway Cutting.* Another pioneer was Charles Urban, an American who settled in Britain and began production in 1898. At about the same time, filming activity was begun in Brighton by several filmmakers, including Esme Collings, A. G. SMITH, and James WILLIAMSON. The French Gaumont company opened a London branch in 1898 and was later followed by its chief rival, Pathé. Before long, a rudimentary organization of rental, exhibition, and distribution began to develop, and by the turn of the century the foundations of a thriving film industry had been laid. The artistic level of the early productions was generally rather poor, but technical innovations abounded, especially in the work of Paul, Smith, and Williamson. An early example of the use of the close-up appears in Paul's *The Twins' Tea Party* (1897) and of the extreme close-up in Smith's *Grandma's Reading Glass* (1900). Williamson demonstrated tracking shots in *The Big Swallow* (1901) and rudimentary editing in *Fire!* (1901), in which he intercut exterior and interior shots to advance the story. Some of the scenes were tinted red to heighten realism.

Hepworth emerged as both a technical innovator and a true cinema artist, his films dealing with a variety of themes in a manner far more sophisticated than that of his rivals. The growing scale and ambition of his work set the pace for the others. His *Alice in Wonderland* (1903) was 800 feet long with 16 scenes dissolving into one another. *Rescued by Rover* (1905) surpassed all other British films of the period in its imaginative use of the narrative tools of the cinema. It was complex in structure, utilizing advanced continuity and editing techniques, and included a number of pans and low-angle shots. Hepworth developed a crude sound recording system, the Vivaphone, in 1907. Also in that year, Charles Urban began exploiting KINEMACOLOR, the world's first successful color process, which had been patented by G. A. Smith in 1906.

By 1908 the Bijou type of movie theater had begun to operate, accommodating up to 300 spectators and offering musical accompaniment by a pianist or a small band. Soon theater circuits were formed, and film exchanges replaced the open-market methods of outright film sales. In 1909, Parliament passed the first Cinematograph Films Act, which became law in January of 1910. It marked the beginning of a long history of government meddling in film industry affairs.

By 1910 it was becoming increasingly evident that the British cinema, despite the promising start, had not been keeping pace with the rapid development of motion pictures elsewhere. American and French films were dominating the British screens, with the British product shrinking to just 15 percent of theater programming. On the other hand, British producers repeatedly failed in their attempts to penetrate foreign markets.

To be sure, occasional worthy productions continued to be made, among them W. G. BARKER's ambitious screen adaptation of *Henry VIII* (1911), for which Sir Herbert Tree received a record fee of £1,000 to play the lead role; and Hepworth's *Rachel's Sin* (1911), a domestic drama featuring Britain's first movie star, Gladys Sylvani. But even the most ambitious productions of the time tended to be cautious, unadventurous adaptations from the stage or literary classics, typified by two Hepworth releases of 1913, *Hamlet* and *David Copperfield,* which respectively were directed by Hay Plumb and Thomas Bentley. Both films employed stage actors and many of the conventions of the theater.

The outbreak of WW I further undermined Britain's ability to deal with competition from abroad, especially from the increasingly popular American film, which was now dominating European screens. As part of the war effort, the government imposed an import tax on all goods, including films, which eventually resulted in restrictions on film exports as well. In 1916 an entertainments tax was levied, adversely affecting business at movie theaters, especially in the poorer districts, where many theaters were forced to close down. On the positive side, the war provided the impetus for exciting innovation in the production of newsreels and documentaries, an area in which the British film was to excel throughout its history. In 1914, Britain's first animated cartoons were made. In the feature film field, George PEARSON emerged as a talented director with such films as *A Study in Scarlet* (1914), the cinema's first Sherlock Holmes mystery; and *Ultus—The Man from the Dead* (1915), the first in a series of action adventures in the style of the French *Fantômas.* Other interesting features of the war period included Bert Haldane and F. Martin Thornton's *Jane Shore* (1915), Larry TRIMBLE's *My Old Dutch* (1915), Hepworth's *Sweet Lavender* (1915) and *Comin' Thro' the Rye* (1916), George Loane TUCKER's *Arsene Lupin* (1916), Will Barker's *She* (1916), Fred Paul's *Masks and Faces* (1917), and Maurice ELVEY's *Hindle Wakes* (1918).

The problems that beset the British film industry before and during WW I intensified into a veritable crisis after the war. American films continued to dominate the British screens, while only a few British productions ever reached the American market. By 1926 only 5 percent of the films shown in the United Kingdom were British made. Typical of the industry's distress was the fate of Cecil Hepworth, who in the early 20s continued as a leading figure in the business with *Alf's Button* (1920) and several other successes. Attempting to expand his small studio, Hepworth offered shares in his company to the public. But he could not raise enough cash to meet his obligations and was forced into bankruptcy in 1924. Sadly, the negatives of his films were sold along with other assets and were melted down for their chemical content.

Hepworth's main rival in the early 20s continued to be George Pearson, who scored big commercial hits with *Nothing Else Matters* (1920) and *Squibs* (1921), *Love Life and Laughter* (1923), and *Reveille* (1924), launching the career of Betty BALFOUR as the most popular British star of the silent era. The success of *Squibs* led to several sequels. Another popular film was Harold Shaw's *Kipps* (1921). But the most outstanding commercial success of the decade was Graham CUTTS's *Woman to Woman* (1923), one of the few silent British films to score well at the American box office, partly because it featured a popular Hollywood star, Betty COMPSON. The film launched several important careers. It was the first venture by producer Michael BALCON, who would become a moving force in the British cinema for many years, in association with Victor SAVILLE, who went on to become a leading director and producer in England and later in Hollywood. The script was written by Cutts in collaboration with his young assistant director, Alfred HITCHCOCK. The film was edited by Alma REVILLE, Hitchcock's future wife and script collaborator. It also led to the Hollywood career of its male star, Clive BROOK.

In 1924, Balcon formed Gainsborough Pictures, under which banner Hitchcock began his directing career with *The Pleasure Garden* (1925) and *The Lodger* (1926). Notable silent productions from Gainsborough also included Graham Cutts's *The Rat* (1925) and Adrian BRUNEL's *Blighty* (1927) and *The Constant Nymph* (1928). Another important new figure during this period was director-producer Herbert WILCOX, who made his debut with *Chu Chin Chow* (1923) and enjoyed commercial successes with *Decameron Nights* (1924), *The Only Way* (1925), *Nell Gwynn* (1926), and *Dawn* (1928).

After much debate, the Cinematograph Films Act of 1927 was legislated. It set a quota system that required a gradual increase in the share of domestic products on British screens to a ceiling of 20 percent by 1935. It also made illegal the practice of BLOCK BOOKING, which enabled Hollywood companies to force on British exhibitors a package of films, containing poor films along with good ones, and the even more preposterous practice of "blind booking," which required the buyer to purchase unfinished films as part of the package without the opportunity to see them before the purchase.

The initial impact of the act was dramatically invigorating. In one year the production of British films jumped from 26 to 128. New companies entered the field, and a trend began toward vertical integration, concentrating control of production, distribution, and exhibition in the hands of large corporations, among them Associated British, Gaumont British, British International Pictures, and British Lion. Major theater circuits began a spectacular growth in size and influence. More money was now being spent on prestige productions, resulting in such technically polished silent films as Hitchcock's *The Ring* (1927), Anthony ASQUITH's *Shooting Stars* and *Underground* (both 1928), and E. A. Dupont's *Piccadilly* (1929). But the long-range effect of the quota, which was to become increasingly evident in the 30s, was the inundation of the British cinema by a flood of cheaply made, inferior films.

The coming of sound presented problems in Britain similar to those experienced in other countries. The crude recording methods and the cumbersome equipment caused most films to be static and stagy, and the novelty of the talkies induced filmmakers to crowd their films with wall-to-wall dialogue or endless songs. Significantly, Britain's first talkie, Hitchcock's *Blackmail* (1929), which was converted to sound after starting out as a silent, was more inventive in its use of sound than most films that immediately followed it. Other quality early talkies included Hitchcock's *Murder* (1930); Asquith's *A Cottage on Dartmoor/Escape from Dartmoor* (1930), *Tell England/The Battle of Gallipoli* (1931), and *Dance Pretty Lady* (1931); Saville's *The W Plan* (1931) and *Sunshine Susie/Office Girl* (1932); Walter FORDE's *Rome Express* (1932); and Wilcox's *Goodnight Vienna/Magic Night* (1932). The Entertainments Act of 1932, which permitted Sunday exhibition at the discretion of local authorities, provided that part of the proceeds be given to charity. As a result, exhibitors for many years tended to show their cheapest and worst films on Sundays.

The early 30s saw the birth and growth of the British DOCUMENTARY movement, which, under the leadership and guidance of John GRIERSON, was to exert an enormous influence on the development of the nonfiction film everywhere. In the feature film field, an auspicious event was the entry into the British film business of Alexander KORDA, a Hungarian immigrant who early in 1932, just months after his arrival in the country, had founded London Films. After releasing a number of QUOTA QUICKIES, he produced and directed *The Private Life of Henry VIII* (1933), a film that gained the British cinema international prestige on a scale it had never known before. Korda's exuberance and flamboyance infused the industry with a new spirit of energy and optimism. Korda produced such later successes as Paul CZINNER's *Catherine the Great* (1934), Harold YOUNG's *The Scarlet Pimpernel* (1934), Zoltán KORDA's *Sanders of the River* (1935), René CLAIR's *The Ghost Goes West* (1935), and William Cameron MENZIES' *Things to Come* (1936), and he himself directed the impressive *Rembrandt* (1936).

Encouraged by Korda's success, other British producers, most notably Michael Balcon, undertook more ambitious and expensive ventures, leading the industry into a brief period of unprecedented boom. Among the successful productions of this period of the mid-30s were Saville's *The Good Companions* (1933), *Evergreen* (1934), and *The Iron Duke* (1934); Hitchcock's *The Man Who Knew Too Much* (1934), *The 39 Steps* (1935), and *Sabotage/The Woman Alone* (1937); Wilcox's *Nell Gwyn* (1934), *Peg of Old Drury* (1935), and *Victoria the Great* (1937); Lothar MENDES' *Jew Suss* (1934); Thomas Bentley's *The Old Curiosity Shop* (1935); Robert STEVENSON's *Tudor Rose/Nine Days a Queen* (1936); and Berthold VIERTEL's *Rhodes of Africa/Rhodes* (1936). But with the exception of these and a few other productions, the British film output continued to be depressingly mediocre.

The only action taken to halt the slump was the legislation of a new Cinematograph Films Act (1938), which increased the quota ceiling of the 1927 act and contained enough incentives for domestic production to attract large Hollywood companies like MGM and 20th Century-Fox into several expensive Anglo-American ventures. Fox's *Wings of the Morning* (1937), Britain's first three-color Technicolor production, and MGM's *A Yank at Oxford* (1938), *The Citadel* (1938), and *Goodbye Mr. Chips* (1939) were all directed by Americans with mostly Hollywood stars, but they utilized British studios and employed British technical crews, who gained experience and confidence from their involvement in these highly polished Hollywood-style productions.

Several superior British productions saw the light of day as the decade drew to a close and the clouds of war began to gather, among them Asquith's *Pygmalion* (1938), Hitchcock's *The Lady Vanishes* (1938), Carol REED's *Bank Holiday/Three on a Weekend* (1938) and *The Stars Look Down* (1939), and Zoltán Korda's *The Four Feathers* (1939).

The outbreak of WW II disrupted normal production and diverted much of the film industry's resources to the war effort. Briefly, all movie theaters were closed for fear of an enemy bombing, but they soon reopened and attracted increasingly larger audiences.

The experience gained in peacetime by Britain's documentarians was now put to advantage in the production of propaganda films. The GPO Film Unit was absorbed by the Ministry of Information and became the Crown Film Unit. Notable wartime documentaries included Alberto CAVALCANTI's *The First Days* (1939), Humphrey JENNINGS and Harry WATT's *London Can Take It* (1940), Watt's *Target for Tonight* (1941), Jack Holmes's *Coastal Command* (1942), Jennings's *Fires Were*

Started (1943), Roy BOULTING's *Desert Victory* (1942), Paul ROTHA's *World of Plenty* (1942), Pat JACKSON's *Western Approaches* (1944), and the Anglo-American *The True Glory* (1945), directed jointly by Carol Reed and Garson Kanin. The documentary influence was also strong in several of the wartime fiction feature films, many of which were overtly propagandistic, notably Michael POWELL, Brian Desmond HURST, and Brunel's *The Lion Has Wings* (1939), Powell's *49th Parallel/The Invaders* (1941), Noel COWARD and David LEAN's *In Which We Serve* (1942), Thorold DICKINSON's *Next of Kin* (1942), Powell's *One of Our Aircraft Is Missing* (1942), Charles FREND's *The Foreman Went to France* (1942), Cavalcanti's *Went the Day Well?/48 Hours* (1942), Leslie HOWARD's *The First of the Few/Spitfire* (1942), Watt's *Nine Men* (1943), Frank LAUNDER and Sidney GILLIAT's *Millions Like Us* (1943), Reed's *The Way Ahead* (1944), and Asquith's *The Way to the Stars/Johnny in the Clouds* (1945). More marginally connected to the war were such films as Asquith's *The Demi-Paradise/Adventure for Two* (1943) and Powell and Pressburger's *The Life and Death of Colonel Blimp* (1943).

There were also some excellent films produced in wartime Britain on themes other than the conflict. Producer Alexander Korda completed in Hollywood the lavish *The Thief of Bagdad* (1940). Other prestige films included Dickinson's *Gaslight* (1940) and *The Prime Minister* (1941), Basil DEAN's *Twenty-One Days/21 Days Together* (1940), Gabriel PASCAL's *Major Barbara* (1941), Reed's *Kipps* (1941), Leslie ARLISS's *The Man in Grey* (1943), Laurence OLIVIER's *Henry V* (1944), Coward's *Brief Encounter* (1945), Gilliat's *The Rake's Progress/Notorious Gentleman* (1945), the multi-episode *Dead of Night* (1945), and Pascal's extravagant folly *Caesar and Cleopatra* (1945).

A man who emerged as a leading figure in the British cinema during the war was J. Arthur RANK, who had entered the business in the early 30s as a producer of religious shorts. By the end of the war the Rank Organisation had developed into a powerful combine with control over large chunks of Britain's production, distribution, and exhibition. He was in the US negotiating the sale of his films in 1947 when the British government unexpectedly imposed a 75 percent tax on foreign film imports. In retaliation, American producers embargoed the exportation of Hollywood productions to Britain. Not only did the rift shatter Rank's big sales hopes, but he now found his huge circuit of theaters cut off from a supply of fresh American product.

The British government tried to amend its error by urging Rank and other producers to increase domestic production to fill the void created in theater programming by the American embargo. While theaters were showing reissues of old Hollywood movies, British producers were bravely trying to raise money for a crash program of quality productions. But financing proved difficult, and few of the expensive films made under the plan recouped their costs. When the tax on imported films was repealed in May of 1948, American productions suddenly flooded the screens, knocking British films out of competition. To make things worse, the law required that a high percentage of American profits in Britain be reinvested in domestic film activity. Little wonder that the British cinema was soon once again in the throes of one of its perennial deep crises.

Rising above the economic difficulties and the general mediocrity of production, a number of outstanding films were made during the late 40s which greatly enhanced the reputation of the British cinema overseas. Among these were Lean's *Great Expectations* (1946) and *Oliver Twist* (1948); Powell and Pressburger's *A Matter of Life and Death/Stairway to Heaven* (1946), *Black Narcissus* (1947), and *The Red Shoes* (1948); Reed's *Odd Man Out* (1947), *The Fallen Idol* (1948), and *The Third Man* (1949); Robert HAMER's *It Always Rains on Sunday* (1947); Olivier's *Hamlet* (1948); and Dickinson's *The Queen of Spades* (1949). The late 40s also witnessed the emergence of the EALING COMEDIES—famous for poking fun at authority, the established order, and English manners in an understated satirical style that was unmistakably British. Among the best of these were Charles CRICHTON's *Hue and Cry* (1947), *The Lavender Hill Mob* (1951), and *The Titfield Thunderbolt* (1953); Henry CORNELIUS's *Passport to Pimlico* (1949); Hamer's *Kind Hearts and Coronets* (1949); and Alexander MACKENDRICK's *Whisky Galore/Tight Little Island* (1949), *The Man in The White Suit* (1951), and *The Ladykillers* (1955).

The occasional successes only served to call greater attention to the generally depressed state of the British cinema in the postwar years. The major stumbling block continued to be the elusiveness of foreign markets, particularly the United States. In 1949 the government tried to encourage production by establishing the National Film Finance Corporation to channel loans to the industry, and in 1950 the government set up the British Film Production Fund to administer a pool of money derived from a portion of taxation on tickets for the purpose of subsidizing production. But the decline continued as, along with the rising popularity of television, attendance at movie theaters began dwindling down at an alarming rate.

Some penetration of the US market was accomplished from the late 40s through Anglo-American co-productions and resumption of activity by American companies at Britain's studios because of a favorable tax situation and the need to reinvest "frozen" dollars domestically. Among the more successful Anglo-American productions of the 50s were Jean Negulesco's *The Mudlark* (1950); Raoul Walsh's *Captain Horatio Hornblower* (1951); John Huston's *The African Queen* (1951), *Moulin Rouge* (1953), and *Moby Dick* (1956); Lean's *Summer Madness/Summertime* (1955); and several Disney productions. American money was also involved in Lean's *The Bridge on the River Kwai* (1957), Britain's most spectacular box-office hit of the 50s. An unintended Hollywood investment in England was the talent of director Joseph LOSEY, who settled in London after being blacklisted in America in the wake of the hearings of the House Un-American Activities Committee. On his way to self-exile, Chaplin directed in England the disappointing *A King in New York* (1957).

Other notable British productions of the 50s included John BOULTING's *Seven Days to Noon* (1950) and *I'm All Right, Jack* (1959), Basil DEARDEN's *The Blue Lamp* (1950) and *Sapphire* (1959), Asquith's *The Browning Version* (1951) and *Orders to Kill* (1958), Powell and Pressburger's *Tales of Hoffmann* (1951), Reed's *Outcast of the Islands* (1951), Lean's *The Sound Barrier/Breaking Through the Sound Barrier* (1952), Mackendrick's *Mandy/The Story of Mandy/A Crash of Silence* (1952), Ronald NEAME's *The Card/The Promoter* (1952), Cornelius's *Genevieve* (1953), Frend's *The Cruel Sea* (1953) and *The Long Arm/The Third Key* (1956), Peter BROOK's *The Beggar's Opera* (1953), John HALAS and Joy BATCHELOR's animated *Animal Farm* (1954), Guy HAMILTON's *The Colditz Story* (1954), Hamer's *Father Brown/The Detective* (1954), Olivier's *Richard III* (1955), Michael ANDERSON's *The Dam Busters* (1955), Roy Ward BAKER's *A Night to Remember* (1958), and J. LEE THOMPSON's *Tiger Bay* (1959). Two successful comedy series were launched in the 50s with Ralph THOMAS's *Doctor in the House* (1954) and Gerald THOMAS's *Carry On, Sergeant* (1958). The late 50s also saw a spate of rock 'n' roll movies and the beginning of a trend toward horror films, a genre that became the specialty of the HAMMER FILMS company.

The continuing lethargy of the British film industry

aroused a movement of young filmmakers who in the late 50s challenged the mainstream of the movie establishment with printed manifestos and a series of films, partly sponsored by the BRITISH FILM INSTITUTE, which were shown at London's National Film Theatre between 1956 and 1959. The leaders of the movement, which came to be known as FREE CINEMA, were Lindsay ANDERSON, Tony RICHARDSON, and Karel REISZ. The movement was loosely associated with a broader revolt against traditional values in literature and the theater which first found its expression in the 1956 West End stage production of John Osborne's 'Look Back in Anger.' The combined impact of the Free Cinema and the "angry young men" movements infused the British cinema of the late 50s with a refreshing sense of purpose and social responsibility. The first film to reflect the new, honest approach in the British cinema was Jack CLAYTON's *Room at the Top* (1958), which represented a breakthrough in its frank treatment of sex and its honest depiction of British attitudes toward class, money, and position. The trend toward a realistic treatment of themes hitherto shunned in British films, particularly the life of the working classes, continued in such films as Tony Richardson's screen version of *Look Back in Anger* (1959), *A Taste of Honey* (1961), and *The Loneliness of the Long Distance Runner* (1962); Reisz's *Saturday Night and Sunday Morning* (1960); John SCHLESINGER's *A Kind of Loving* (1962) and *Billy Liar* (1963); and Lindsay Anderson's *This Sporting Life* (1963).

The 60s were marked by the infusion of American money and talent into British film production on an unprecedented scale. Veteran expatriate Joseph Losey, by now established as a leading British director, contributed such fine films as *The Damned* (1961), *The Servant* (1963), *King and Country* (1964), and *Accident* (1967). Another American who made London his regular home was Richard LESTER, who flaunted his dazzling visual style in the BEATLES' films *A Hard Day's Night* (1964) and *Help!* (1965) and in *The Knack* (1965). Stanley KUBRICK went to England to make *Lolita* (1962), *Dr. Strangelove* (1964), and *2001: A Space Odyssey* (1968). Sidney LUMET made *The Hill* (1965) and *The Deadly Affair* (1967). Roger Corman directed *The Masque of the Red Death* and *The Tomb of Ligeia* (both 1964). John Huston was on hand for *The List of Adrian Messenger* (1963) and *Sinful Davey* (1969). Robert Wise made *The Haunting* (1963), and Carl Foreman *The Victors* (1963). Martin Ritt directed *The Spy Who Came in from the Cold* (1965), and Fred Zinnemann *A Man for All Seasons* (1966). Otto Preminger turned out *Bunny Lake Is Missing* (1965). Stanley Donen, the veteran of MGM musicals, helmed in England *The Grass Is Greener* (1960), *Arabesque* (1966), *Two for the Road* (1967), and *Bedazzled* (1967). George Sidney was responsible for *Half a Sixpence* (1967). Among foreign directors from other countries working in England were Italy's Michelangelo Antonioni (*Blow-Up,* 1966), France's François Truffaut (*Fahrenheit 451,* 1966), and Poland's Roman Polanski (*Repulsion,* 1965; *Cul-de-Sac,* 1966; *Dance of the Vampires/The Fearless Vampire Killers,* 1967).

American money was behind most of the high-budget British productions of the 60s, including such international box-office hits as J. Lee Thompson's *The Guns of Navarone* (1961), Lean's *Lawrence of Arabia* (1962), Terence YOUNG's *Dr. No* (1962) and subsequent films in the James Bond series, Don CHAFFEY's *Jason and the Argonauts* (1963), Peter GLENVILLE's *Becket* (1964), John GUILLERMIN's *Guns at Batasi* (1964), Reed's *Oliver!* (1968), and Anthony HARVEY's *The Lion in Winter* (1968). A notable domestically financed hit was Tony Richardson's *Tom Jones* (1963). Other fine British films of the 60s included Guy GREEN's *The Angry Silence* (1960); Jack CARDIFF's *Sons and Lovers* (1960); Ken HUGHES's *The Trials of Oscar Wilde* (1960); Dearden's *The League of Gentlemen* (1960) and *Victim* (1961); Wolf RILLA's *Village of the Damned* (1960); Clayton's *The Innocents* (1961) and *The Pumpkin Eater* (1964); Bryan FORBES's *Whistle Down the Wind* (1961), *The L-Shaped Room* (1962), *Seance on a Wet Afternoon* (1964), and *The Wrong Box* (1966); Gilliat's *Only Two Can Play* (1962); Glenville's *Term of Trial* (1962); Clive DONNER's *The Caretaker/The Guest* (1963) and *Nothing but the Best* (1964); Schlesinger's *Darling* (1965) and *Far from the Madding Crowd* (1967); Lewis GILBERT's *Alfie* (1966); Ken Loach's *Poor Cow* (1967); Kevin Brownlow and Andrew Mollo's *It Happened Here* (1966); Michael WINNER's *The Jokers* (1966); Silvio NARRIZANO's *Georgy Girl* (1966); Lindsay Anderson's *If. . .* (1968); Jack GOLD's *The Bofors Guns* (1968); Albert FINNEY's *Charlie Bubbles* (1968); Richard ATTENBOROUGH's *Oh! What a Lovely War* (1969); Ken RUSSELL's *Women in Love* (1969); and Neame's *The Prime of Miss Jean Brodie* (1969).

In 1970 a new films act was passed in Parliament; it maintained the quota at 30 percent and increased the budget of the Film Finance Corporation. Meanwhile, the infusion of American money into British films had gradually come to a halt and various steps were taken by British studios to pick up the production slack, among them the appointment of a respected filmmaker, Bryan Forbes, as head of production at Elstree. As usual, a handful of noteworthy productions were issued by the studios each year, but the perennial saga of crisis and struggle for survival continued in the 70s. The British government set up sundry commissions to investigate ways of resuscitating the industry but in 1976 seemed to be defeating its own noble purpose by legislating a tax law that required foreign producers resident in Britain to pay a levy of 75 percent on their worldwide earnings, in effect discouraging foreign investment. Britain's film output declined considerably in the late 70s, but the country's excellent studio facilities and reliable technical crews kept active by attracting outsiders, including American TV producers and the makers of such Hollywood spectacles as *Star Wars* (1977) and *Superman* (1978).

Notable British films of the 70s (many of which were produced or directed by Americans) included Lean's *Ryan's Daughter* (1970), Christopher Miles's *The Virgin and the Gypsy* (1970), Jerome Epstein's *The Adding Machine* (1970), Losey's *The Go-Between* (1971), Reginald Mills's *Tales of Beatrix Potter/Peter Rabbit and Tales of Beatrix Potter* (1971), Schlesinger's *Sunday Bloody Sunday* (1971) and *Yanks* (1979), Lionel JEFFRIES's *The Railway Children* (1971), Kubrick's *A Clockwork Orange* (1971) and *Barry Lyndon* (1975), Roman Polanski's *Macbeth* (1971), Peter MEDAK's *A Day in the Death of Joe Egg* and *The Ruling Class* (both 1972), Hitchcock's *Frenzy* (1972), Attenborough's *Young Winston* (1972), Joseph L. Mankiewicz's *Sleuth* (1972), Fred Zinnemann's Anglo-French *The Day of the Jackal* (1973), Lindsay Anderson's *O Lucky Man!* (1973), Melvin Frank's *A Touch of Class* (1973), Peter Duffell's *England Made Me* (1973), Nicolas Roeg's *Don't Look Now* (1973) and *The Man Who Fell to Earth* (1976), Sidney Lumet's *Murder on the Orient Express* (1974), Michael Anderson's *Conduct Unbecoming* (1975) and *Dominique* (1979), John Huston's *The Man Who Would Be King* (1975), Terry GILLIAM's *Monty Python and the Holy Grail* (1975) and Terry Jones's *Monty Python's Life of Brian* (1979), Richard Lester's *Robin and Marian* (1976), Blake Edwards's *The Pink Panther Strikes Again* (1976), Forbes's *The Slipper and the Rose* (1976), Richardson's *Joseph Andrews* (1977), Stuart ROSENBERG's *Voyage of the Damned* (1976), Ridley SCOTT's *The Duellists* (1977) and *Alien* (1979), John STURGES's *The Eagle Has Landed* (1977), Andrew V. McLaglen's *The Wild Geese*

(1978), Alan PARKER's *Midnight Express* (1978), Jerzy SKOLIMOWSKI's *The Shout* (1978), Peter Brook's *Meetings with Remarkable Men* (1979), and American-born James IVORY's *The Europeans* (1979).

British film production revived in the early 80s, with best picture Oscars and worldwide critical and commercial success for Hugh HUDSON's *Chariots of Fire* (1981) and Attenborough's *Gandhi* (1982). Behind these hits was executive David PUTTNAM, who produced the former and helped to found Goldcrest Films, which co-produced the latter. British television's Channel Four also stoked the industry's fires by financing low-budget, independently produced dramatic films for theatrical release followed by TV exhibition, including Skolimowski's *Moonlighting* (1982), Peter GREENAWAY's *The Draughtsman's Contract* (1982), and Richard Eyre's *The Ploughman's Lunch* (1983). The independent company Handmade Films, founded by former Beatle George Harrison in 1978, found success with modestly budgeted comedies, including Gilliam's *Time Bandits* (1981) and Malcolm Mowbray's *A Private Function* (1984). The 80s also brought international recognition for the lavish literary adaptations of producer Ismail MERCHANT, director Ivory, and screenwriter Ruth Prawer Jhabvala, including *Heat and Dust* (1983), *The Bostonians* (1984), and *A Room with a View* (1985).

Despite these success stories, the decade was also a time of turmoil for many in the British film industry. State subsidies virtually came to an end, old established companies also faced hard times. Thorn-EMI, which had inherited the assets of the once mighty ASSOCIATED BRITISH, was forced to sell its film and television interests, including the historic Elstree Studios, to the CANNON GROUP in 1986. Cannon, suffering its own financial problems, was forced to resell the studios the following year. In 1987, the Pinewood Studios, which had been operating as a full-service operation within the Rank Organisation, became a less ambitious rental facility.

American expatriate producer Sam SPIEGEL made his last feature in the 80s (*Betrayal*, directed by David Jones, 1982) as did director David Lean (*A Passage to India*, 1984). Other notable films of the decade were Kubrick's *The Shining* (1980) and *Full Metal Jacket* (1987); Desmond Davis's *Clash of the Titans* (1981); Reisz's *The French Lieutenant's Woman* (1981); Bill FORSYTH's *Gregory's Girl* (1981), *Local Hero* (1983), and *Comfort and Joy* (1984); Anderson's *Britannia Hospital* (1982); Blake Edwards's *Victor/Victoria* (1982); Neil JORDAN's *Angel* (1982), *The Company of Wolves* (1984), and *Mona Lisa* (1986); Peter Duffell's *Experience Preferred... But Not Essential* (1983); Lewis Gilbert's *Educating Rita* (1983); Nagisa Oshima's *Merry Christmas Mr. Lawrence* (1983); Peter YATES's *The Dresser* (1983); Stephen FREARS's *The Hit* (1984), *My Beautiful Laundrette* (1985), and *Sammy and Rosie Get Laid* (1987); Mike NEWELL's *Dance with a Stranger* (1985) and *The Good Father* (1986); Chris Bernard's *Letter to Brezhnev* (1985); Roeg's *Insignificance* (1985); David Drury's *Defence of the Realm* (1985); John IRVIN's *Turtle Diary* (1985); Losey's *Steaming* (1985); Alex Cox's *Sid and Nancy* (1986); Julien Temple's *Absolute Beginners* (1986); Derek JARMAN's *Caravaggio* (1986); Attenborough's *Cry Freedom* (1987); Russell's *Gothic* (1987); David Leland's *Wish You Were Here* (1987); Jack Clayton's *The Lonely Passion of Judith Hearne* (1987); Terence DAVIES's *Distant Voices, Still Lives* (1988); Christine EDZARD's *Little Dorrit* (1988); Mike FIGGIS's *Stormy Monday* (1988); Greenaway's *Drowning by Numbers* (1988) and *The Cook, The Thief, His Wife & Her Lover* (1989); Schlesinger's *Madame Sousatzka* (1988); Michael Radford's *White Mischief* (1988); Gilliam's *The Adventures of Baron Munchausen* (1989); Michael CATON-JONES's *Scandal* (1989); Mike LEIGH's *High Hopes* (1988); Jim SHERIDAN's *My Left Foot* (1989); and Kenneth BRANAGH's *Henry V* (1989).

In the 90s, television companies such as Channel Four and the BBC have expanded their film-financing ventures, while direct government support of the British movie industry has remained minimal. Though cinema admissions passed the 100 million mark in 1991 for the first time since 1980, film production in Britain remains an exceedingly risky venture, as was made clear by the collapse of Palace Films, a major production company that had enjoyed great success in the 80s.

Notable British films of the early 90s include Medak's *The Krays* (1990) and *Let Him Have It* (1991); Parker's *The Commitments* (1991) and *Evita* (1996); Figgis's *Liebestraum* (1991); Anthony Minghella's *Truly Madly Deeply* (1991) and *The English Patient* (1996); Jarman's *Edward II* (1991); Stephen Poliakoff's *Close My Eyes* (1992); Newell's *Enchanted April* (1992); Jordan's *The Crying Game* (1992); Ivory's *Howards End* (1992) and *The Remains of the Day* (1993); Branagh's *Peter's Friends* (1992), *Much Ado About Nothing* (1993), and *Hamlet* (1996); Davies's *The Long Day Closes* (1993); and Sally Potter's *Orlando* (1993). Among the rising new directors in the late 90s are: Pen Densham, Philip Haas, Nicholas Hytner, Beeban Kidron, Charles Sturridge and Trevor Nunn.

United States. Although the birth of cinema and the development of the technical, aesthetic, and commercial aspects of motion pictures came about as a result of parallel advances in several countries, no one nation has contributed more than America to the growth of the SEVENTH ART. The contribution began in the "prehistoric" era of film, when in 1861 Coleman Sellers, a Philadelphia machinist, patented a device for showing serial photographs mounted on a paddle-wheel machine. He called his invention the Kinematoscope. Next a photographer, Henry Heyl, on February 5, 1870, at the Young Men's Society of Saint Mark's Evangelical Church in Philadelphia, demonstrated his Phasmotrope, with which he projected a rapid series of still photographs of dance scenes, creating an impression of motion. But these photographs had been taken individually, not serially, by an ordinary still camera. Another American, Jean-Aimé LE ROY, improved on Heyl's device in 1876.

But it remained for Eadweard MUYBRIDGE, an English-born American photographer, to take the first truly significant step toward the goal of real moving pictures. In 1872, Muybridge began a series of photographic studies of animal locomotion for Governor Leland Stanford of California. In the course of his studies he developed various methods of shooting serial photographs. In 1877 he was able to demonstrate—as a way of settling a $25,000 wager for Stanford, legend says—that a galloping horse indeed had all four legs momentarily off the ground at the same time. Muybridge did this by arranging a battery of 24 still cameras in a row along a track and attaching the shutter mechanism of each camera to wires that were stretched across the tracks and tripped by a galloping horse as it went past the cameras. Muybridge's serial photographs were not motion pictures in the strict sense of the term, but his experiments provided the essential link between still photography and the movies and brought the invention of the cinema an important step closer.

Another essential link in the realization of motion pictures was provided in the mid-1880s through the adaptation of celluloid as a base for a film strip's light-sensitive emulsion by Hannibal Goodwin, an American clergyman, and the exploitation of the same idea by another American, industrialist George EASTMAN. Neither man, however, had intended the invention for motion pictures, envisioning only still-photography use.

A crucial phase in the development of the cinema began in 1887, when inventor Thomas Alva EDISON, "The Wizard of Menlo Park," assigned one of his assistants, William Kennedy Laurie DICKSON, to devise an instrument that would record and reproduce motion in conjunction with the Edison phonograph. In 1889, Dickson demonstrated before Edison the Kinetophonograph, a voice-picture apparatus that produced an inferior visual image on sheets of sensitized celluloid. But in 1891, utilizing perforated strips of film, Dickson perfected for Edison a motion picture camera, the KINETOGRAPH, and a motion picture viewer, the KINETOSCOPE. Patents for both machines were granted Edison in 1893. During the same year, Dickson designed for Edison the world's first film studio (some production had earlier taken place in a converted section of Edison's plant), popularly known as BLACK MARIA, on the grounds of the Edison plant in West Orange, N.J. Although Edison's Kinetoscope was a peep-show device for individual viewing, and could not project films for an audience, it reproduced the world's first true moving pictures and its birth marked the beginning of the history of the cinema.

The commercial exploitation of Edison's "new toy" began on April 14, 1894, when Andrew M. Holland, a Canadian, opened a Kinetoscope parlor in a converted shoe store at 1155 Broadway in New York City. Ten machines were set up in two rows, each machine loaded with a 55-foot film made outdoors or at the Black Maria studio with the Kinetograph apparatus. For 25 cents a customer was entitled to view one row of five machines. The original program comprised the titles *Sandow, Horse Shoeing, Barber Shop, Mouth Support, Wrestling, Table Contortion, Blacksmiths, Highland Dance, Trapeze,* and *Roosters*. The novelty proved an immediate success, and similar Kinetoscope parlors soon opened in Chicago, San Francisco, and Atlantic City.

Business was expanding so rapidly that in August of 1894 the Kinetoscope Company was set up by Messrs. Norman C. Raff and Frank G. Gammon specifically for the purpose of marketing Edison's peep machine under exclusive license throughout the United States. The following month, a similar marketing agreement was reached with a firm headed by Frank Z. Maguire and Joseph D. Baucus for distribution in Europe. The first parlors were established in London and Paris. The early Raff and Gammon catalog included a film clip demonstrating the sharpshooting of Annie Oakley and an excerpt from the finale of the stage play 'Milk White Flag' boasting a cast of 34.

Raff and Gammon's main competition came from the brothers Otway and Gray Latham, who in August of 1894 opened a Kinetoscope parlor at 83 Nassau Street in Lower Manhattan which specialized in the exhibition of filmed prizefights, an abbreviated round per machine. To accommodate the extra length of film required for such an exhibition, Otway and Gray enlisted the help of their father, Major Woodville LATHAM, who devised means for expanding the loading capacity of Edison's machine and later invented the Latham Loop to slacken the tension of wound film and thus lessen its wear and tear.

The Kinetoscope presentations enjoyed an enormous popularity for several months, but the public's initial curiosity and enthusiasm soon began to wane and business at the parlors diminished at a discouraging rate for the many investors who had entered the business with high hopes. It became increasingly evident that the future of motion pictures hinged on the successful development of a projection device.

Many inventors, entrepreneurs, and dreamers participated in the ensuing race to develop a satisfactory projection system. The race went on simultaneously in several countries, with France, England, Germany, and the United States leading the way. In the US one of the early frontrunners was Jean-Aimé Le Roy, who after 20 years of experimentations with various devices founded the Cinematograph Novelty Company in February of 1894 in partnership with Eugene LAUSTE and during the same month began demonstrating a projecting device to prospective investors. In December of the same year, the Latham family founded the Lambda Company. The Lathams gave a public demonstration of their Panopticon projector at a Broadway theater on May 20, 1895, and demonstrated a similar apparatus, the Eidoloscope, for a week's run beginning in August 1895 at Chicago's Olympic Theater. But public and critical reception of both presentations was poor, and the machines were never heard of again.

Other projection devices proliferated, making the rounds under such colorful names as Phantasmagoria or Get-the-moneygraph. None produced acceptable results. The first breakthrough came in September of 1895, when Thomas ARMAT unveiled his Phantoscope at Atlanta's Cotton States Exposition. But several months were to go by before Armat's machine went into commercial exploitation. In the meantime, the brothers Max and Emil SKLADANOWSKY successfully projected intermittent photographs with their Bioscope at Berlin's Wintergarten on November 1, 1895, and the brothers Louis and Auguste LUMIÈRE showed a program of films at the Grand Café in Paris, on December 28, 1895, claiming for themselves the world's first regular exhibition of projected motion pictures to a paying public.

Early in 1896, Thomas Edison acquired the manufacturing and distribution rights to Armat's Phantoscope and, presenting it as his own invention, re-christened the device the Vitascope. A gala premiere of the Vitascope projection system was held at New York's Koster and Bial's Music Hall on April 23. The program consisted of a group of hand-tinted color shorts, including a variety show umbrella dance, a burlesque boxing match, a comic allegory on the Monroe Doctrine, and a scene of waves breaking against a pier which, according to *The New York Times,* "caused the spectators to cheer and marvel most of all." The New York *Dramatic Mirror* reported that some of the spectators in the front rows "seemed to be afraid they were going to get wet. . . ." On June 29, 1896, just two months after the public introduction of the Vitascope, the Lumière Cinematographe made its New York bow at Keith's Union Square Theatre. On October 12 of the same year another projector, the American BIOGRAPH, was introduced, its promoters boasting pictures "larger, brighter, steadier, and more interesting" than their competitors'. Early programs included scenes from the play 'Rip Van Winkle' with Joseph Jefferson in the title role and what was probably the first example of a TRACKING SHOT, taken in North Wales from a moving train. The presentation was an instant success. For several years the Kinetoscope parlors continued to coexist with the new projection auditoriums. But by the beginning of the 20th century they had all but passed from the American scene.

Initially, films in American cities were shown at established music halls, as part of a vaudeville program. But before long, enterprising exhibitors, spurred in part by a vaudeville strike in 1900, began showing film programs in specialized structures, typically converted small stores or enclosed sections of amusement arcades. Small towns were serviced by traveling showmen who exhibited their wares anywhere they could find a vacant hall and a power supply. Audiences were easy to please and nearly anything that moved on the screen brought cheers of enthusiasm. Early films ran an average of 50 feet, allowing no time for story development. Typically they each consisted of a single scene, shot from one fixed camera setup. Plots were elementary—little dramatic incidents or one-gag comic situations. Most of the early crop of films was supplied by one of the three companies that dominated the field—Edison, BIOGRAPH, and VITAGRAPH—which sold the product to exhibitors outright at a dime or so per foot. The margin of profit from film sales was low, but the producers realized high gains from the sale of projection equipment to exhibitors.

The early growth of the American movie business was rapid and would have been even more spectacular were it not for the "patent war," an incessant court battle that had been started by Edison in 1897 and involved hundreds of law suits over patent infringements before it ended in 1908 with the establishment of the MOTION PICTURE PATENTS COMPANY.

As an art, however, the cinema in America, as elsewhere, developed tentatively and gradually. The first important milestone came in January of 1903 with the release of Edwin S. PORTER's *The Life of an American Fireman.* While still a crude production, it represented a first conscious attempt by an American director to create a film in the cutting room. Not only did Porter assemble individual shots into a cohesive narrative, but by intercutting the footage he was able to achieve dramatic sequences of an intensity never before experienced on the screen.

Even more revolutionary in its storytelling techniques was Porter's *The Great Train Robbery,* which was made later in the same year. Although some of the many firsts attributed by film historians to this production have since proved erroneous, it remains a monumental achievement for its time. It was nearly 12 minutes long, an "epic" by the standards of the day, and through the sophisticated use of parallel and overlapping action briskly advanced a logical, semiscripted narrative toward a suspenseful climax. Since most production in those early days took place in and around New York City, few noticed or cared that this first grand Western was entirely shot in the "wilds" of New Jersey.

The phenomenal box-office success of *The Great Train Robbery* gave further impetus to the ongoing expansion of the American film industry. One of the organizational by-products of this growth was the establishment of the EXCHANGE, a regional bureau for the distribution of films to motion picture theaters. As films grew in number and length, exhibitors found the practice of purchasing prints outright inconvenient and uneconomical. The exchange, functioning as a middleman, offered the same films to exhibitors for rental, at a fraction of the purchase price. The first exchange was formed in San Francisco in 1902. By 1907 nearly 150 exchanges were operating from coast to coast.

Another phenomenon that reflected the rapid growth of the film business in the first decade of the 20th century was the flourishing of the NICKELODEON, the makeshift motion picture theater that popularized movies among America's masses from 1905 to 1908, catapulting film into a thriving major industry. The pacesetters in this success story were two Pittsburgh real estate operators, Harry Davis and John P. Harris, who converted a vacant storeroom into a motion picture theater by decorating it pretentiously with discards from the local opera house and installing some 100 seats and a piano. Since they planned to charge five cents for admission, they called their theater the Nickelodeon. So spectacular was the financial success of their venture that within a year imitators operated more than a thousand similar establishments across the country. By 1908 the number of nickelodeons neared 10,000. By this time most establishments were charging their customers a dime. Estimated attendance in 1910, the year in which the nickelodeon craze had reached its peak, was 26 million weekly, just about 20 percent of the total national population.

Most of the nickelodeons were situated in or around the blue-collar districts of the big cities, and the great majority of their audiences came from the working class and the immigrant population. Immigrants in particular were drawn by the lure of film, which during the silent days presented for them no language barrier. Film plots were kept deliberately simple and the action swift to satisfy a public taste that ran the gamut from chase melodrama to chase comedy. Live vaudeville acts were added to the programs, sing-alongs were instituted, films were kept clean and "respectable," and at many establishments women and children were admitted free or at half price. The content of films, too, underwent a gradual change, with growing emphasis on women's stories and adaptations from the classics. By the time the US entered WW I the sleazy nickelodeon had become a thing of the past.

The demise of the nickelodeon coincided with the collapse of the Motion Picture Patents Company. The MPPC constituted a pool of 16 patents for which rights were held by four companies—Edison, Biograph, Vitagraph, and the Armat Moving Picture Company. Six other companies joined the group as licensees, but only Edison and Biograph held stock voting rights. In control of virtually every important patent on cameras, projectors, and film, the Trust, as the organization came to be called, secured and maintained for several years a stranglehold on every aspect of film production, distribution, and exhibition. Through a complex set of interlocking agreements, the Trust protected its interests from outside interlopers, the so-called independents. Only members were permitted to purchase raw film stock from Eastman Kodak. Only licensed exchanges that dealt exclusively with the Trust and agreed to its arbitrary scale of fixed prices were leased films by the major producers, and they could rent pictures only to exhibitors using licensed projectors. An elaborate royalty scheme was devised to assure a constant flow of cash from licensees to the Trust's coffers, with Edison and Biograph enjoying the lion's share.

Despite constant harassment by the Trust, which employed a network of detectives to spy on patent violators and called on federal marshals to arrest violators and confiscate their wares, independent film producers somehow continued to operate and thrive. Motivated by high potential profits, outlaw filmmakers evaded the grip of the Trust by ingenious clandestine tactics. Much of the filming took place away from established production centers like New York and Chicago. Independent producers are partly credited with the discovery of Southern California as a filming locale, conveniently far from the spying eye of the trust and ideally near the Mexican border for quick escape from pursuing lawmen.

The independents are also credited with the initiation of the STAR SYSTEM in movies. In the early days, performers in films were not publicized by name, presumably because the established Patents Company producers feared that the personal popularity of players would lead to high salary demands. In 1910 one of the more defiant of the rebel producers, Carl LAEMMLE, head of the Independent Motion Picture Company of America (IMP), lured away from Biograph its most popular player, Florence LAWRENCE, then known simply as "The Biograph Girl." Laemmle enhanced the impact of the acquisition through a clever publicity stunt that resulted in much personal press coverage for his new star. He similarly conducted a personal publicity campaign for another acquisition, Mary PICKFORD, who would become the most popular player of the American silent screen.

On the whole, the Trust's attempted stranglehold on the industry proved ineffective, and within a few years of its formation there were clear signs that the elaborate structure of the

MPPC was gradually crumbling. The Trust's demise was hastened by its creation of a distribution arm, the General Film Company, in 1910. Through a series of acquisitions and legally questionable practices that drove competitors out of business, General Film within a year controlled all but one of the nation's exchanges. The sole exception was William Fox's Greater New York Film Rental Company. Fox not only refused to sell out but, finding himself cut off from program supply, began producing his own films and in 1912 instituted a suit against the MPPC under the provisions of the Sherman Antitrust Act. The case dragged on from January of 1913 through October of 1915, when a federal district court in Pennsylvania declared the MPPC guilty of illegal practices in restraint of trade. A subsequent appeal was dismissed in 1918, and the MPPC was deemed legally dead.

As the fortunes of the Trust declined, the independents grew in prominence and influence. With a lesser stake in stability and standardized practices, the independents tended to be more adventurous and innovative in their approach to filmmaking and often set production precedents that members of the Trust were forced to follow in order to maintain their competitive edge. In addition to initiating the star system, independent producers were also instrumental in the move toward longer and more ambitious films. The conservative Trust members were reluctant to tamper with the established program composed of several one-reelers, but opportunistic independents, taking note of the box-office success of European films of greater length, were more responsive to the growing demand by exhibitors for feature productions. After scoring a big commercial hit in 1912 with *Queen Elizabeth,* a French import starring Sarah BERNHARDT, Adolph ZUKOR, a nickelodeon owner who had been turned down by the Trust, formed his own production company, FAMOUS PLAYERS, and began producing ambitious literary adaptations starring top Broadway personalities. Other producers soon followed with features of their own.

By 1915 the corporate face of the American movie industry had undergone a complete change. Dozens of new companies had entered the business, and powerful new organizations were being formed. Zukor joined forces with Jesse L. LASKY, distributing through PARAMOUNT. Carl Laemmle had built Universal City to accommodate his vastly expanding program of production. The Fox Film Corporation was developing into a major producer, and the Metro Picture Corporation and the Goldwyn Pictures Corporation were only a year away from launching their own success story. One- and two-reel films were quickly becoming obsolete, except as program fillers, at the same time dooming to oblivion the small, uncomfortable nickelodeon. Elaborate movie palaces were springing up everywhere to provide a fitting surrounding for prestigious feature presentations. By the outbreak of WW I the motion picture business was rapidly heading toward the status of a major growth industry.

On the creative level, too, significant strides forward were made in the early 1910s. Several important film artists emerged who were to leave their mark on the American cinema for many years. At Biograph, David Wark GRIFFITH directed his first film, *The Adventures of Dollie,* in 1908 and within a few years revolutionized filmmaking through his innovative use of the cinema's narrative techniques, his intelligent and versatile selection of themes, and his instinctive grasp of the specific requirements of screen acting in which he coached a whole stable of talented players. Highly prolific as well as creative, Griffith had turned out hundreds of shorts in a wide range of genres before releasing the ambitious four-reel historic spectacle *Judith of Bethulia* in 1914.

Another prominent figure of the period was Mack SENNETT, who started his career in 1908 at Biograph as an actor for Griffith. He turned to directing late in 1910 and soon established his mastery of slapstick comedy. As director and head of production at KEYSTONE from 1912, he created a spontaneous and highly successful factory of zany humor which had a lasting influence on screen comedy. It was at Keystone that the screen's most famous comic personality, Charlie CHAPLIN, started his career in 1914. Also influential during those formative days of the American cinema was Thomas H. INCE, who as a director and later producer was instrumental in streamlining methods of production and developing the discipline of detailed shooting scripts. Ince was particularly adept at creating sprawling Westerns, and it was under his supervision that William S. HART thrived as a director and one of the silent screen's great cowboy stars. Hart, who entered films in 1914, added authenticity and mature themes to a successful formula that had been pioneered by an earlier producer-director-star of the Western genre, G. M. ("Broncho Billy") ANDERSON.

The release in 1915 of Griffith's masterpiece *The Birth of a Nation* was a momentous event for the American cinema. It signified the maturation of film as an art and signaled the advent of the big prestige picture of mass appeal which brought the cinema respect and would soon help American producers dominate markets overseas. The following year saw the release of another towering Griffith masterpiece, *Intolerance,* and a similarly ambitious Ince production, *Civilization.* Griffith, Ince, and Mack Sennett were temporarily grouped together during this period, forming a formidable triumvirate of producers in the services of the short-lived TRIANGLE Film Corporation. Other notable directors of the era included John ADOLFI, Oscar C. APFEL, George D. BAKER, Reginald BARKER, J. Stuart BLACKTON, Herbert BRENON, Van Dyke BROOKE, Christy CABANNE, J. Searle DAWLEY, Cecil B. DE MILLE, Allan DWAN, John EMERSON, Lloyd INGRAHAM, Frank LLOYD, Sidney OLCOTT, Maurice TOURNEUR, Otis Turner, Raoul WALSH, and Lois WEBER.

Actors and actresses became increasingly important in the fortunes of the industry as the star system flourished. Among the popular stars of the early American screen not mentioned previously were Roscoe "Fatty" ARBUCKLE, Theda BARA, John and Lionel BARRYMORE, Beverly BAYNE, Hobart BOSWORTH, John BUNNY, Mae BUSCH, Francis X. BUSHMAN, Lon CHANEY, Maurice COSTELLO, Donald CRISP, Douglas FAIRBANKS, Dustin and William FARNUM, Dorothy and Lillian GISH, Robert (Bobby) HARRON, Bessie LOVE, Mae MARSH, Mary Miles MINTER, Tom MIX, Owen and Tom MOORE, Anna Q. NILSSON, Mabel NORMAND, Charles RAY, Wallace REID, Marguerite SNOW, Gloria SWANSON, Blanche SWEET, Constance and Norma TALMADGE, Florence TURNER, Bobby VERNON, Henry B. WALTHALL, Pearl WHITE, and Clara Kimball YOUNG.

The expansion and consolidation of the film business in the late 1910s was exemplified by the merger of the Famous Players–Lasky Corporation with its distributor, Paramount. Under the aggressive leadership of Adolph Zukor the organization became a formidable force in all three branches of the motion picture business—production, distribution, and exhibition—leading the industry in a rapidly developing trend toward vertical integration and eventually to a new phase of monopolistic control. Zukor perfected the infamous practice of BLOCK-BOOKING, which coerced exhibitors to accept inferior pictures along with desirable ones. Exhibitor resentment resulted in the formation of the FIRST NATIONAL Exhibitors Circuit in 1917 as a purchasing agent for some of America's leading theater owners. First National promptly set up its own production facilities and in 1918 lured Charlie Chaplin from Mutual and Mary Pickford from Paramount. Paramount counteracted by a sweeping investment in the purchase and control of hundreds of theaters.

Reacting against the growing corporate control of the film industry, five of the top names in the business—D. W. Griffith, Charles Chaplin, Mary Pickford, Douglas Fairbanks, and William S. Hart—issued a "declaration of independence" against the movie establishment in January of 1919 and announced the formation of their own distribution organization, UNITED ARTISTS. Hart later withdrew, but the others persevered and despite wide skepticism in the industry went on to make United Artists a highly successful venture.

Overcoming a sharp but brief economic crisis as an aftermath of WW I, the American film industry continued to grow, consolidate, and solidify. Despite the proliferation of companies in all areas of the business, more and more power came to be concentrated in the hands of fewer and fewer giants. By the mid-20s four organizations had emerged supreme—Paramount, First National, Fox, and Loew's—the latter soon emerging as a formidable power through its newly formed production subsidiary, METRO-GOLDWYN-MAYER (MGM). Within several years these big four would be joined by two more—WARNER BROS. and RKO—to form the nucleus of the industry for the next two decades. The corporate headquarters of all these organizations were situated in New York City while production took place mostly in Hollywood, which by this time had become the undisputed capital of the American movie.

Movie producers responded to the "New Morality" that was sweeping the nation with films that echoed the prevailing cynicism, relaxed sexual codes, and ostensible sophistication and introduced to the screen a new breed of hero and heroine, more liberated, daring, and carefree than their morality-bound counterparts in the bygone Victorian-flavored movie years. Cecil B. De Mille was among the pacesetters in this trend, with a cycle of titillating melodramas of passion and infidelity that included *Old Wives for New* (1918), *You Can't Have Everything* (1918), *Don't Change Your Husband* (1919), *For Better for Worse* (1919), *Why Change Your Wife?* (1920), and *The Affairs of Anatol* (1921). Although the imposition of industry self-censorship in 1922, in the wake of the Roscoe "Fatty" Arbuckle affair and other scandals, restrained further incursions into the "new sexuality," the frank exploration of illicit male-female relations continued for some years. Two immigrant directors from Europe, Erich von STROHEIM and Ernst LUBITSCH, excelled in their sophisticated handling of screen eroticism, the former through psychological probing and bold dramatic means (*Blind Husbands,* 1919; *Foolish Wives,* 1922; *Greed,* 1923–25; etc.) and the latter through a satirical, light, and polished touch (*The Marriage Circle,* 1924; *Lady Windermere's Fan,* 1925; *So This Is Paris,* 1926). The American female's quest for sexual liberation and personal fulfillment found its expression toward the late 20s in a virtual flood of films celebrating the flapper and the "It" girl of the spirited Jazz Age. Clara BOW, Colleen MOORE, and Joan CRAWFORD gained enormous popularity by typifying this role on the screen.

The Western, an original American creation, continued to dominate much of the screen repertoire in the 20s, with William S. Hart, Tom Mix, Ken MAYNARD, Harry CAREY, Buck JONES, and Hoot GIBSON emerging as the most popular cowboy stars. Most Westerns were quickly and cheaply made, following a predictable formula, but there were many interesting exceptions and several high-budgeted spectacular epics, notably De Mille's two versions of *The Squaw Man* (1914 and 1918), the two silent versions of *The Spoilers* (Colin CAMPBELL's in 1914 and Lambert HILLYER's in 1923), James CRUZE's *The Covered Wagon* (1923) and *The Pony Express* (1925), John FORD's *The Iron Horse* (1924), King BAGGOT's *Tumbleweeds* (1925), and Irvin WILLAT's *North of 36* (1924).

The costume epic spectacular required a large investment but paid handsome dividends at the box office. Among the most successful in that genre were J. Gordon EDWARD's *Cleopatra* (starring Theda Bara, 1917) and *The Queen of Sheba* (1921); C. B. De Mille's *Joan the Woman* (1917), *The Ten Commandments* (1923), and *The King of Kings* (1927); D. W. Griffith's *Orphans of the Storm* (1922) and *America* (1924); Rex INGRAM's *The Four Horsemen of the Apocalypse* (1921), *The Prisoner of Zenda* (1922), and *Scaramouche* (1923); Allan DWAN's *Robin Hood* (1922); Raoul Walsh's *The Thief of Bagdad* (1924), *The Wanderer* (1925), and *Loves of Carmen* (1927); Fred NIBLO's *The Three Musketeers* (1921), *Blood and Sand* (1922), and *Ben-Hur* (1926); Henry KING's *Romola* (1924); James Cruze's *Old Ironsides* (1926); Wallace Worsley's *The Hunchback of Notre Dame* (1923); Harry BEAUMONT's *Beau Brummel* (1924); and Herbert Brenon's *Beau Geste* (1926). There was a briefly fervent vogue, especially among female audiences, for costume adventures set against Arabian desert backgrounds which was augmented by the wide adulation of Rudolph VALENTINO (*The Sheik,* 1921; *The Son of the Sheik,* 1926). Valentino's success spawned several imitators, among them John GILBERT (*Arabian Love,* 1922) and Ramon NOVARRO (*The Arab,* 1924).

Comedy was a genre in which the American screen achieved some of its greatest moments during the 20s. Chaplin ventured successfully into features with *The Kid* (1921), *The Gold Rush* (1925), and *The Circus* (1928). Buster KEATON came into his own, creating such masterpieces as *Our Hospitality* (1923), *Sherlock Jr.* and *The Navigator* (both 1924), *The General* (1927), and *The Cameraman* (1928). Harold LLOYD flaunted his talent in *A Sailor-Made Man* (1921), *Grandma's Boy* (1922), *Safety Last* and *Why Worry?* (both 1923), *Girl Shy* (1924), and *The Freshman* (1925). And Harry LANGDON joined the ranks of the top screen clowns with *Tramp Tramp Tramp* and *The Strong Man* (both 1926), and *Long Pants* (1927). A genre that began gaining popularity in the late 20s was the gangster film. Underworld themes had been common earlier in the decade, but it wasn't until Josef Von STERNBERG's *Underworld* (1927) and *The Dragnet* (1928) that the genre found its definitive atmosphere and style, setting the stage for the successful Warner Bros. gangster cycle of films of the 30s. Important milestones in the development of the American DOCUMENTARY were two remarkable fact films by Robert FLAHERTY, *Nanook of the North* (1922) and *Moana* (1926).

Other notable films of the postwar silent years included Frank BORZAGE's *Seventh Heaven* (1927); Herbert Brenon's *Peter Pan* (1924); Clarence BROWN's *Flesh and the Devil* (1927); Tod BROWNING's *The Unholy Three* (1925); Chaplin's *A Woman of Paris* (1923); James Cruze's *Ruggles of Red Gap* (1923); Harry d'Abbadie D'ARRAST's *A Gentleman of Paris* (1927); Victor FLEMING's *The Way of All Flesh* (1927); John Ford's *Lightnin'* (1925) and *Mother Machree* (1928); D. W. Griffith's *Broken Blossoms* (1919) and *Way Down East* (1920); Rupert JULIAN's *Merry-Go-Round* (begun by Erich von Stroheim, 1923) and *The Phantom of the Opera* (1925); Henry King's *Tol'able David* (1921) and *Stella Dallas* (1925); Frank Lloyd's *The Sea Hawk* (1924); F. W. MURNAU's *Sunrise* (1927); Fred Niblo's *The Mark of Zorro* (1920) and *Camille* (1927); John S. ROBERTSON's *Dr. Jekyll and Mr. Hyde* (John Barrymore version, 1920); Malcolm ST. CLAIR's *Gentlemen Prefer Blondes* (1928); Josef von Sternberg's *The Salvation Hunters* (1925), *The Last Command,* and *The Docks of New York* (both 1928); King VIDOR's *The Big Parade* (1925) and *The Crowd* (1928); Raoul Walsh's *What Price Glory* (1926); and William WELLMAN's *Wings* (1927).

Great strides forward were made by Hollywood in the 20s

in streamlining production and refining film techniques. And there was a continuing search for innovations that would further expand the immense popularity of the cinema. Experimentation with COLOR CINEMATOGRAPHY processes which had dated back to the earliest days of motion pictures culminated in November of 1922 with the successful New York premiere of Chester M. Franklin's *The Toll of the Sea,* the first feature in the subtractive two-color TECHNICOLOR process. Even more striking and technically improved Technicolor productions were Irvin Willat's *Wanderer of the Wasteland* (1924) and Albert PARKER's *The Black Pirate* (1926). Color sequences were used in several large-scale productions of the period, including *The Phantom of the Opera, Ben-Hur,* and *The King of Kings.*

A far more significant development than the arrival of quality color was the advent of SOUND in the late 20s. Considering that Edison's Kinetophone (Kinetophonograph) was designed with sound in mind as early as 1889, it is surprising that talkies did not reach the screen sooner. There were many attempts to marry sight and sound in the intervening years, including Edison's own nearly successful entry in 1913 and Lee DE FOREST's promising Phonofilm system in 1923. But for various reasons, not the least of which were industry skepticism, resistance, and apathy, none of the experimental systems was adopted. It took an alliance between the engineering capacity of the Western Electric company and the adventurous business acumen of the Warner Bros. company—a smaller Hollywood studio with little to lose and everything to gain by a risky adventure—to bring about the sound revolution. The two corporations formed the Vitaphone Company on April 20, 1926, and on August 6 of that year presented at the Warners' Theater in New York a program of several shorts with synchronized sound and the feature *Don Juan,* directed by Alan CROSLAND and starring John Barrymore, with sound effects and a musical score played on discs by the New York Philharmonic.

The critics and the public reacted enthusiastically to the first demonstration of sound on the screen, but Warners' competitors took a cautious wait-and-see attitude. The only exception was the Fox Film Corporation, which, shortly after, began developing its own MOVIETONE sound system for use in its newsreels. On Christmas Day of 1926, Warner Bros. presented a program of all-talking short subjects, and on October 6, 1927, film history was made with the world premiere of Crosland's *The Jazz Singer,* starring Al JOLSON, the first full-length feature with passages of dialogue. This was followed on July 6, 1928, by Warners' first all-talking feature, Bryan FOY's *Lights of New York.*

The public's response to the new invention was so intense that exhibitors began clamoring for talkies, inducing a frantic race among Warners' competitors to convert to sound. Enjoying a head start thanks to its development of the Movietone talking newsreel, Fox led the pack. In January of 1929 that studio released *In Old Arizona,* directed jointly by Raoul Walsh and Irving CUMMINGS, which was not only the first talkie partly shot outdoors but also the first to utilize the sound-on-film system, which proved quite superior to Warners' not-too-reliable sound-on-disc system. Warners countered on May 28, 1929, with Crosland's *On with the Show,* the first talkie in Technicolor. By the end of 1929 nearly half of all movie theaters in America, and nearly all in the big cities, had been wired for sound. By 1930 the transformation had been complete. Among American filmmakers only Charlie Chaplin continued producing silent films for several years.

The hasty conversion to sound affected the American film industry in several ways. It immediately drove up the cost of production by a considerable margin, forcing some of the smaller companies out of the business. It also undermined the lucrative foreign market sales, ending once and for all the special status of an "international art" the cinema had enjoyed all through its silent days. Initially, the major studios resorted to making several foreign-language versions of every important film they produced, but the practice proved too costly and time-consuming and before long was dropped in favor of DUBBING. SUBTITLES became a later alternative (see FOREIGN VERSION).

On the positive side, the novelty of sound helped the major studios weather the aftermath of the 1929 Wall Street crash by keeping audience interest alive during the difficult Depression years. On the personal level, sound effectively ended many Hollywood careers and helped launch many new ones. Actors and actresses with heavy accents or speech impediments found themselves suddenly without jobs, while a huge demand for stage performers with trained voices brought about a mass hegira from Broadway to Hollywood. Many early talkies were made in New York; Paramount maintained a busy East Coast studio in Astoria, Queens, to permit stage players to work in films while carrying out Broadway engagements. Old time scriptwriters, too, whose main talent was depicting action or writing titles, were being replaced or supplemented by writers with experience in dramatic construction and dialogue. Stage directors were recruited as dialogue directors to assist or replace veteran filmmakers with an eye for composition and action but no experience with guiding vocal performances.

Technically as well as artistically, the conversion to sound initially presented obstacles to filmmakers. Gradually, however, sound techniques improved, and the invention of the BLIMP and the sophisticated microphone once again brought freedom to camera and players alike. Even during the technically awkward early stages, some directors showed a remarkable capacity to utilize sound as well as sight creatively. Among the most inventive of these was Rouben MAMOULIAN, who put the camera booth on wheels to achieve mobility in *Applause* (1929). He also introduced superimposed sound tracks in that film and used ASYNCHRONISM effectively in *City Streets* (1931). Mamoulian later experimented with the SUBJECTIVE CAMERA in *Dr. Jekyll and Mr. Hyde* (1932), used nonrealistic sound in *Love Me Tonight* (also 1932), and in 1935 directed Hollywood's first three-color Technicolor feature, *Becky Sharp.*

Another director who adapted well to sound was Lewis MILESTONE, who achieved his best screen work during the early talkie era with *All Quiet on the Western Front* (1930), *The Front Page* (1931), *Rain* (1932), and *Hallelujah I'm a Bum* (1933). The creative use of sound was also brilliantly evident in King Vidor's *Hallelujah!* (1929) and Ernst Lubitsch's sophisticated light musical romances *The Love Parade* (1929), *Monte Carlo* (1930), and *The Smiling Lieutenant* (1931).

The musical film was a natural consequence of the advent of sound, and like those of the Western the format and style of this new genre were wholly American in origin. The prototype of the early musicals was MGM's *The Broadway Melody* (1929), directed by Harry BEAUMONT, which was promoted as America's first "100% All-Talking, 100% All-Singing, 100% All-Dancing" motion picture. The other major studios responded with their own musical extravaganzas, Warner Bros. with Roy DEL RUTH's *Gold Diggers of Broadway* (1929) and John G. ADOLFI's *The Show of Shows* (1929); Fox with David BUTLER's *Fox Movietone Follies of 1929* (1929); Paramount with *Paramount on Parade* (1930), on which 11 directors collaborated; and Universal with John Murray Anderson's *The King of Jazz* (1930).

The musical boom of the 30s continued with a string of light romances and adapted operettas and reached a lively peak with the Warner Bros. cycle of backstage song-and-dance entertainments, all highlighted by the boldly imaginative choreography of Busby BERKELEY. Among the most memorable of these were Lloyd BACON's *42nd Street* and *Footlight Parade* (both 1933) and *Wonder Bar* (1934); Mervyn LEROY's *Gold Diggers of 1933* (1933); William DIETERLE's *Fashions of 1934* (1934); and Delmer DAVES's *Dames* (1934). Dick POWELL, Ruby KEELER, and Joan BLONDELL starred in several of these. Equally delightful were the Fred ASTAIRE-Ginger ROGERS musicals of the period for RKO, among them Thornton FREELAND's *Flying Down to Rio* (1933), Mark SANDRICH's *The Gay Divorcee* (1934), *Top Hat* (1935), *Follow the Fleet* (1936), and *Shall We Dance?* (1937), and George STEVENS's *Swing Time* (1936). An even more brilliant chapter in the history of screen musicals would be written at MGM in the 40s and early 50s.

The switch to sound was initially accompanied by a boom in cinema attendance, which jumped from 57 million weekly admissions in 1927 to almost double that figure in 1930. The sudden prosperity attracted heavy investments from Wall Street and the banking industry, which resulted not only in further expansion and consolidation of the industry but also in an increasingly tight domination of film production by financiers. Five major studios became established atop the Hollywood corporate hierarchy: Paramount, Fox (later 20TH CENTURY-FOX), MGM, Warner Bros., and RKO. With the exception of MGM, itself a subsidiary of the wealthiest film-industry giant, Loew's, each of these was a fully integrated company with many subsidiaries controlling production, distribution, and exhibition in the US and abroad. In addition to the "Big Five," there were the "Little Three": UNIVERSAL, COLUMBIA, and UNITED ARTISTS. The first two specialized in low-budget production, while the last had no studio of its own, operating instead as a distribution outlet for independent producers.

The euphoria that followed the prosperity of the early talkie days was short-lived as the persistent effects of the Depression eroded the initial enthusiasm of audiences for sound. Attendance at the nation's cinemas plummeted sharply in 1931 and reached a weekly low of 80 million in 1932 and 1933. Many theaters went dark, and many others slashed admission prices and began showing double bills to attract patrons, introducing the B PICTURE to the screen as a regular part of the program. Promotion come-ons included such giveaway gimmicks as "dish nights" and "bank nights." Most of the major studios saw their earnings drop sharply and soon turn into deficits. Paramount filed for bankruptcy, Fox fell to the brink of financial disaster, and RKO and Universal went into receivership. But the industry prevailed, and through corporate re-organizations and further infusion of investment funds emerged from the crisis virtually intact. By 1935, Hollywood was back on its feet, again prosperous, and on the threshold of a glorious period many have dubbed its "golden age."

Each of the major studios developed its own characteristic style of film and its own roster of directors and stars. MGM, with its immense financial resources, was the most glamorous of all, boasting luxuriously polished production values and "More Stars Than There Are in Heaven." Under the combined leadership of Louis B. MAYER and Irving THALBERG, the studio specialized in quality escapist entertainment with only rare excursions into controversial themes. Among its most successful productions of the 30s were Clarence Brown's *Anna Christie* (Greta GARBO's first talkie, 1930); Jack CONWAY's *Red Headed Woman* (1932) and *Viva Villa!* (1934); George CUKOR's *Dinner at Eight* (1933) and *Camille* (1937); Victor Fleming's *Treasure Island* (1934), *Captains Courageous* (1937), *The Wizard of Oz* and *Gone With the Wind* (both 1939); Sidney FRANKLIN's *The Good Earth* (1937); Edmund GOULDING's *Grand Hotel* (1932); Fritz LANG's *Fury* (1936); Robert Z. LEONARD's *The Great Ziegfeld* (1936); Ernst Lubitsch's *The Merry Widow* (1934) and *Ninotchka* (1939); W. S. VAN DYKE's *Trader Horn* (1931) and *The Thin Man* (1934); King Vidor's *The Champ* (1931) and *Northwest Passage* (1940); and Sam WOOD's two Marx Brothers vehicles, *A Night at the Opera* (1935) and *A Day at the Races* (1937), and his *Goodbye Mr. Chips* (1939).

Decorative opulence more artistic in bent was the mark of MGM's nearest rival in the 30s, Paramount. That studio's output was variable, ranging from high-quality prestige productions, to standard light entertainment fare. Paramount's top directors seemed to enjoy greater freedom than their colleagues at other studios, and their films often carried their unmistakable personal signature. De Mille continued in the 30s with his staples of the silent days: Western epics (the third version of *The Squaw Man,* 1931; *The Plainsman,* 1937; and *Union Pacific,* 1939), and gaudy but eye-filling and often erotic costume extravaganzas masquerading as history (*The Sign of the Cross,* 1932; *Cleopatra,* 1934; *The Crusades,* 1935; *The Buccaneer,* 1938). Lubitsch sustained his famous "touch" for sophisticated comedy with *Monte Carlo* (1930), *The Smiling Lieutenant* (1931), *Trouble in Paradise* (1932), *Design for Living* (1933), and *Angel* (1937). He atypically also directed a deeply felt drama, *The Man I Killed/Broken Lullaby* (1932).

Von Sternberg displayed his superb artistry with *Morocco* (1930), *Dishonored* (1931), *Shanghai Express* (1932), *The Scarlet Empress* (1934), and *The Devil Is a Woman* (1935)—all starring Marlene DIETRICH—and with *An American Tragedy* (1931) with Sylvia SIDNEY. Mamoulian's contribution has already been described earlier in this entry. Leisen's decorative touch was evident in such films as *Death Takes a Holiday* (1934), *Hands Across the Table* (1935), *Easy Living* (1937), and *Midnight* (1939). Among the lesser luminaries at Paramount were Henry HATHAWAY, Leo MCCAREY, Ben HECHT and Charles MACARTHUR, Frank LLOYD, Norman Z. MCLEOD, Elliott NUGENT, Wesley RUGGLES, Norman TAUROG, and Frank TUTTLE.

In sharp contrast to the glitter and opulence of MGM and Paramount stood the operations of Warner Bros., a studio notorious for its parsimony and tight discipline. Constantly struggling to stay financially solvent, the brothers instituted frugal hiring methods that brought them into frequent legal clashes with their underpaid and overworked talent, most famously with the headstrong Bette DAVIS. Production, under the iron-fisted supervision of Hal WALLIS and Henry BLANKE, was equally penurious. Cutting corners became an art and limitations an advantage.

The typical Warner Bros. film of the 30s was a lowlife melodrama with protagonists that more often than not were losers and social outcasts. Even the Warner Bros. musicals had a distinct Depression flavor, their heroes and heroines struggling to survive and succeed. But the genres that best characterized the Warner Bros. product of the period were the gangster film and the social-concern drama.

The first of the Warner Bros. sound gangster films was Bryan FOY's *Lights of New York* (1928), but the vogue really started in January of 1931 with the release of Mervyn LeRoy's *Little Caesar,* starring Edward G. ROBINSON. This was followed three months later by William Wellman's *The Public Enemy,* which launched the starring career of another tough screen gangster, James CAGNEY.

Another Warner Bros. personality, Paul MUNI, made his mark away from the studio, for producer Howard HUGHES, in Howard HAWKS's *Scarface* (1932); and a fourth top screen gangster, Humphrey BOGART, became established in 1936 through a memorable performance in Archie MAYO's *The Petrified Forest.*

The gangster cycle continued, with a change of emphasis, into the early 40s. Notable films in the cycle included William KEIGHLEY's *G-Men* (1935) and *Bullets or Ballots* (1936); William WYLER's *Dead End* (1937); Michael CURTIZ's *Angels with Dirty Faces* (1938); and Raoul Walsh's *The Roaring Twenties* (1939) and *High Sierra* (1941).

Closely related to the gangster films were Warner Bros.'s prison melodramas, which took their cue from a 1930 MGM production, George HILL's *The Big House.* Both of these genres were also interrelated with another Warner Bros. staple, the social injustice film. The film that best expressed the combined outcry against prison conditions and society's role in the breeding of crime was LeRoy's *I Am a Fugitive from a Chain Gang* (1932). Other prison melodramas included Curtiz's *20,000 Years in Sing Sing* (1933), Lloyd BACON's *San Quentin* (1937) and *Invisible Stripes* (1940), Anatole LITVAK's *Castle on the Hudson* (1939), and Keighley's *Each Dawn I Die* (1939). John GARFIELD specialized in the portrayal of tough but vulnerable and appealing social victims in Busby Berkeley's *They Made Me a Criminal* (1939) and other films. William Wellman lamented the neglect of youth in *Wild Boys of the Road* (1933). The plight of coal miners was powerfully exposed in Curtiz's *Black Fury* (1935) and mob lynching was condemned in LeRoy's *They Won't Forget* (1937).

Curtiz, LeRoy, and their colleagues were equally proficient in handling the lighter fare of the studio's immense output as they were with the social-theme dramas. One popular Warner Bros. genre was the swashbuckling romantic adventure. Errol FLYNN was the dashing hero and Olivia DE HAVILLAND the demure heroine in such popular period sagas as Curtiz's *Captain Blood* (1935), *The Charge of the Light Brigade* (1936), and *The Adventures of Robin Hood* (co-directed with Keighley, 1938). Also popular were the romanticized screen biographies that at first starred George ARLISS (*Disraeli,* 1929; *Alexander Hamilton,* 1931; *Voltaire,* 1933), then Paul Muni (*The Story of Louis Pasteur,* 1936; *The Life of Emile Zola,* 1937; *Juarez,* 1939) and Edward G. Robinson (*Dr. Ehrlich's Magic Bullet, Dispatch from Reuters,* both 1940). Women's pictures also enjoyed a following, with Bette Davis often representing the emancipated breed and Kay FRANCIS the traditional suffering kind.

Another influential genre of the 30s, the horror and fantasy film, meanwhile thrived at Universal, one of the oldest and in the early 30s one of the poorest of Hollywood's studios. The horror and fantasy genre had its roots in the German cinema of the 1910s and 20s, but it was at Universal that it developed into a Hollywood staple. The studio's top two horror specialists were directors Tod BROWNING and James WHALE. Browning had established his reputation during the 20s with several suspense thrillers starring Lon CHANEY. Universal then imported Paul LENI from Germany to direct the silent *The Cat and the Canary* (1927) and followed this with a sound version, *The Cat Creeps* (1930), which was entrusted to director Rupert Julian of *The Phantom of the Opera* (1925) fame. The formula horror cycle of the 30s began with Browning's *Dracula* (1931), starring Bela LUGOSI, and was followed several months later by Whale's superior *Frankenstein,* which starred Boris KARLOFF. Karloff and Lugosi, and to a lesser extent Lon CHANEY, JR., became the dominant personalities in the demented gallery of Universal's horror creatures. Key films in the cycle included Karl FREUND's *The Mummy* (1932); Whale's *The Old Dark House* (1932), *The Invisible Man* (1933), and *The Bride of Frankenstein* (1935); Stuart WALKER's *The Werewolf of London* (1935); and George WAGGNER's *The Wolf Man* (1941).

Most of the product at Universal was of the B-picture variety; only occasionally did the studio turn out ambitious, high-budget productions. Notable among these were Lewis Milestone's adaptation of Erich Maria Remarque's pacifist novel *All Quiet on the Western Front* (1930) and two versions of Edna Ferber's *Show Boat,* one directed by Harry POLLARD in 1929 and the other by James Whale in 1936. Some commercial success was achieved by such popular tearjerkers as John M. STAHL's *Back Street* (1932), *Imitation of Life* (1934), and *Magnificent Obsession* (1935). But on the whole, the studio's financial foundation was shaky, and only the emergence of Deanna DURBIN as a singing star in 1936 saved the company from bankruptcy. Durbin's films were made by the successful team of producer Joe PASTERNAK and director Henry KOSTER.

A child star also changed around the profit-and-loss picture at Fox (20th Century-Fox from 1935). Shirley TEMPLE was the studio's most treasured revenue source in the mid- to late-30s period, when she reigned as the nation's top box-office attraction. The emphasis at Fox was on slick entertainment, and the majority of the studio's product was light escapist fare. But there were many outstanding exceptions, notably the work of John Ford, who released most of his pre–WW II films through Fox. Among these were *Men Without Women* and *Up the River* (both 1930), *Doctor Bull* (1933), *Steamboat 'Round the Bend* (1935), *The Prisoner of Shark Island* (1936), *Young Mr. Lincoln* (1939), *The Grapes of Wrath* (1940), and *Tobacco Road* and *How Green Was My Valley* (both 1941).

Other quality Fox films in the first decade of sound included Frank Borzage's *The River* (1929) and *Bad Girl* (1931); David Butler's *Sunny Side Up* (1929), *A Connecticut Yankee* (1931), *Handy Andy* (1934), and *Kentucky* (1938); Irving CUMMINGS's *In Old Arizona* (co-directed with Raoul Walsh, 1929) and *The Story of Alexander Graham Bell* and *Hollywood Cavalcade* (both 1939); Allan Dwan's *Suez* (1938) and *Frontier Marshal* (1939); Tay GARNETT's *Slave Ship* (1937); William K. Howard's *The Power and the Glory* (1933); Henry King's *State Fair* (1933), *One More Spring* (1935), *Lloyds of London* (1936), *Alexander's Ragtime Band* (1938), and *Jesse James* (1939); Sidney LANFIELD's *The Hound of the Baskervilles* (1939); and Frank Lloyd's *Cavalcade* and *Berkeley Square* (both 1933).

RKO's repertoire was erratic, ranging from superior culturally ambitious films to run-of-the-mill PROGRAMMERS. Among the highlights of the studio's production in the 30s were Merian C. COOPER and Ernest B. SCHOEDSACK's *King Kong* (1933); John CROMWELL's *Of Human Bondage* (1934); George Cukor's *What Price Hollywood* and *A Bill of Divorcement* (both 1932), *Dinner at Eight* and *Little Women* (both 1933), and *Sylvia Scarlett* (1936); Harry D'Abbadie D'Arrast's *Topaze* (1933); John Ford's *The Lost Patrol* (1934), *The Informer* (1935), *Mary of Scotland* (1936), and *The Plough and the Stars* (1937); Garson KANIN's *A Man to Remember* (1938), *The Great Man Votes* and *Bachelor Mother* (both 1939), *My Favorite Wife* (1940), and *Tom Dick and Harry* (1941); Gregory LA CAVA's *The Half-Naked Truth* (1932), *She Married Her Boss* (1935), and *Stage Door* (1937); Wesley Ruggles's *Cimarron* (1931); and George Stevens's *Alice Adams* (1935) and *Gunga Din* (1939). RKO also released the films of Walt DISNEY from 1937, beginning with the feature *Snow White and the Seven Dwarfs.*

Harry COHN's Columbia relied on the considerable talent of director Frank CAPRA, the master of Hollywood's sentimental comedy, for much of its reputation and financial survival. Among Capra's contributions were *Platinum Blonde* (1931), *American Madness* (1932), *The Bitter Tea of General Yen* and *Lady for a Day* (both 1933), *It Happened One Night* (1934), *Mr. Deeds Goes to Town* (1936), *Lost Horizon* (1937), *You Can't*

Take It with You (1938), *Mr. Smith Goes to Washington* (1939), and *Meet John Doe* (1941). Columbia seldom put directors or actors under contract and more often than not borrowed talent from other studios for particular projects. This policy paid dividends in such films as John G. BLYSTONE's *Tol'able David* (1930); Richard BOLESLAWSKI's *Theodora Goes Wild* (1936); Frank Borzage's *No Greater Glory* (1934); George Cukor's *Holiday* (1938); John Ford's *The Whole Town's Talking* (1935); Howard Hawks's *Twentieth Century* (1934), *Only Angels Have Wings* (1939), and *His Girl Friday* (1940); Ben Hecht and Lee GARMES's *Angels Over Broadway* (1940), Gregory La Cava's *She Married Her Boss* (1935); Leo McCarey's *The Awful Truth* (1937); Rouben Mamoulian's *Golden Boy* (1939); Victor SCHERTZINGER's *One Night of Love* (1934); and William Wyler's *The Gay Deception* (1935). Columbia's own directors were busy turning out the studio's prodigious output of cheap B pictures and serials. Studios that produced B pictures almost exclusively included Monogram and Republic, which boasted such action stars as Gene AUTRY, Roy ROGERS, and John WAYNE. Wayne broke out of B pictures in 1939 with John Ford's independent release *Stagecoach*, becoming one of the most popular movie stars of all time.

Among other Hollywood stars of the 30s and early 40s not previously mentioned were Freddie BARTHOLOMEW, Wallace BEERY, Claudette COLBERT, Ronald COLMAN, Gary COOPER, Bing CROSBY, Joan CRAWFORD, Marie DRESSLER, Alice FAYE, W. C. FIELDS, Henry FONDA, Clark GABLE, Cary GRANT, Jean HARLOW, Walter HUSTON, Katharine HEPBURN, Carole LOMBARD, Myrna LOY, Fredric MARCH, Joel McCREA, William POWELL, Tyrone POWER, George RAFT, Luise RAINER, Mickey ROONEY, Rosalind RUSSELL, Norma SHEARER, Barbara STANWYCK, James STEWART, Robert TAYLOR, Spencer TRACY, Mae WEST, and Jane WITHERS.

By the late 30s Hollywood's major studios not only had fully recovered from the jitters of the Depression days but were solidly entrenched as vertically integrated monopolies under the protection of the US Government's Code of Fair Competition for the Motion Picture Industry, which had been signed into law in 1933. Representing a united front through their powerful trade association, the MPPDA (later renamed the MPAA), they controlled every aspect of the business, assuring themselves secure profit levels, discouraging independent production, and attempting in vain to stem the tide of unionization among motion picture actors, technicians, and creative personnel. Charges of monopolistic practices in restraint of trade in the film industry were increasingly heard, and in 1938 the Justice Department filed an antitrust court case, *The United States vs. Paramount Pictures, Inc., et al.,* which was to have far-reaching effects on the industry ten years later.

Meanwhile, however, the film business in America continued to thrive. Not even the outbreak of WW II could dampen the prosperity. Although foreign markets shrank drastically with the spread of hostilities in Europe and the Far East, the growing strength of the domestic market for films more than compensated for the loss. Attendance increased sharply after America entered the war, when cash became plentiful but commodities scarce.

Hollywood's interest in the growing turmoil in Europe was initially mild. The Spanish Civil War was depicted in a detached, noncontroversial manner in James HOGAN's *The Last Train from Madrid* (1937) and as a bland statement against all forms of war in William DIETERLE's equally neutral *Blockade* (1938). The first clear anti-Fascist stand in a film of a major studio was made in Anatole LITVAK's *Confessions of a Nazi Spy* (1939), for Warners, which warned Americans of the Nazi menace. War-related themes increased and intensified after the actual outbreak of hostilities in Europe. Among the anti-Nazi films made in America between the outbreak of WW II and Pearl Harbor were Charlie Chaplin's satire *The Great Dictator* (1940), Archie MAYO's *Four Sons* (1940), Frank Borzage's *The Mortal Storm* (1940), Alfred HITCHCOCK's *Foreign Correspondent* (1940), Mervyn LeRoy's *Escape* (1940), and Fritz Lang's *Man Hunt* (1941). An appeal to American patriotism was made in such films of WW I heroics as William Keighley's *The Fighting 69th* (1940) and Howard Hawks's *Sergeant York* (1941). Enlistment was encouraged through such productions as Mitchell Leisen's *I Wanted Wings* (1941), made in cooperation with the Army Air Corps, and Michael Curtiz's *Dive Bomber* (1941), produced with the assistance of the Navy. The comic side of barracks life was shown by ABBOTT AND COSTELLO in Arthur LUBIN's *Buck Privates* (1941) and by Bob HOPE in David BUTLER's *Caught in the Draft* (1941). Solidarity with the British cause was expressed in LeRoy's *Waterloo Bridge* (1940) and Henry King's *A Yank in the RAF* (1941), among other films.

Soon after America entered the war, some 40,000 of the industry's 240,000 employees and executives (among them 132 directors) donned the uniforms of the various branches of the Armed Forces. Several hundred were recruited by the Signal Corps, among them Colonel Frank Capra, who as head of the film unit was assigned to produce the famous "Why We Fight" series (see DOCUMENTARY), Major John HUSTON, Lieutenant Colonel Anatole Litvak, and Lieutenant Colonel Darryl F. ZANUCK. The highest ranked Hollywood personality in combat duty was James Stewart, who flew 20 missions over Germany as a bomber pilot. He was demobilized a full colonel, then reactivated in the Air Force Reserve as a brigadier general. In addition, thousands of performers participated in morale-boosting camp shows and USO diversions. Among the most active of these were Joe E. BROWN, Paulette GODDARD, Bob HOPE, Frances LANGFORD, Martha RAYE, and Dinah SHORE. Bette Davis became the president of the famed HOLLYWOOD CANTEEN, which opened in October of 1942.

In June of 1942, the government established the Office of War Information to coordinate wartime propaganda and training production and maintain a link with the commercial film industry. By a special arrangement, copies of all feature films were made available to the Armed Forces overseas free of charge. In addition to direct propaganda and inspirational films, there were many routine escapist productions onto which a war angle was arbitrarily tacked.

The typical wartime film, especially in the early years, tended to be simple-minded, cliché-ridden, and sentimental and has not happily survived the test of time. Seen today, even the grandest success of the period, William Wyler's *Mrs. Miniver* (1942), seems little more than well-made mawkish claptrap. But at the time this tribute to the courage of Britain under the Blitz performed a tremendous service for the national morale and to America's commitment to its closest ally. Screen tributes to another ally, the Soviet Union—among them Michael Curtiz's *Mission to Moscow* (1943), Lewis Milestone's *The North Star* (1943), and Gregory RATOFF's *Song of Russia* (1944)—seemed natural enough at the time, but were to cause a great deal of embarrassment to their makers several years later, during the hearings of the House Un-American Activities Committee.

Relatively few of the hundreds of films produced by Hollywood about the war have had enduring qualities beyond their contemporary propaganda value. Among the best of these were Ernst Lubitsch's satirical *To Be or Not to Be,* Alfred Hitchcock's *Saboteur,* John Huston's *Across the Pacific,* Michael Curtiz's *Casablanca* (all 1942, although the last was not released until the following year); Irving PICHEL's *The Moon Is Down,* Fritz Lang's *Hangmen Also Die,* Billy WILDER's *Five Graves to Cairo,* Herman SHUMLIN's *Watch on the Rhine,* Zoltan KORDA's *Sahara* (all 1943); Hitchcock's *Lifeboat,* Mervyn LeRoy's *Thirty Seconds Over Tokyo* (both 1944); and Raoul Walsh's *Objective Burma!* (1945). Two sober, realistic combat dramas were released just after the cessation of hostilities: William Wellman's *The Story of G.I. Joe* (1945) and Lewis Milestone's *A Walk in the Sun* (1946).

Among the many home-front films of the period, three were particularly fetching: George Stevens's hilarious comedy about the apartment shortage, *The More the Merrier* (1943); Preston STURGES's satire on hero worship, *Hail the Conquering Hero* (1944); and John Cromwell's sentimental but superbly crafted *Since You Went Away* (1944). Patriotism of the WW I variety was brought to bear in such diverting musicals as Michael Curtiz's *Yankee Doodle Dandy* and Busby Berkeley's *For Me and My Gal* (both 1942).

During the war years, the Hollywood studios turned out hundreds of assembly-line escapist films—melodramas, comedies, Westerns, and musicals. Particularly popular were the films starring the GIs' favorite pinup girls, among them Betty Grable, Rita Hayworth, Veronica Lake, Hedy Lamarr, Dorothy Lamour, Ann Sheridan, and Lana Turner.

An astonishing number of superior films were made during the early 40s. Among the best achievements were John Ford's *The Grapes of Wrath,* Lewis Milestone's *Of Mice and Men,* Alfred Hitchcock's *Rebecca,* George Cukor's *The Philadelphia Story,* Walt Disney's *Fantasia,* Rouben Mamoulian's *The Mark of Zorro,* King Vidor's *Northwest Passage,* and Michael Curtiz's *The Sea Hawk* (all 1940); Orson WELLES's *Citizen Kane,* John Huston's *The Maltese Falcon,* Ford's *How Green Was My Valley,* William Wyler's *The Little Foxes,* Preston Sturges's *Sullivan's Travels,* and Alexander HALL's *Here Comes Mr. Jordan* (all 1941); Welles's *The Magnificent Ambersons,* Sturges's *The Palm Beach Story,* Sam Wood's *Kings Row* and *The Pride of the Yankees,* and George Stevens's *The Talk of the Town* (all 1942); William Wellman's *The Ox-Bow Incident,* Hitchcock's *Shadow of a Doubt,* and Ernst Lubitsch's *Heaven Can Wait* (all 1943); Leo McCarey's *Going My Way* and Otto Preminger's *Laura* (both 1944); and Billy Wilder's *The Lost Weekend* (1945).

The wartime boom continued, and 1946 proved the most profitable year in the industry's history. Attendance at cinemas reached an all-time high, and few foresaw or suspected the trouble and decline ahead. The sudden new rise in production costs, caused by inflation, and a labor dispute in 1946 which resulted in a 25 percent raise for studio employees were seen as a minor nuisance. But a succession of graver problems could not be so easily dismissed, and by the time they were all sorted out the face of Hollywood had been forever changed.

The floodgates of disaster opened from several directions at about the same time, making an orderly chronology of the events an all but impossible task. As good a starting point as any are the general economic conditions that prevailed in the nation in the immediate postwar years. With goods and services again available and plentiful, the disposable income of Americans was diverted to the purchase of homes, automobiles, and appliances, cutting deeply into cash available for movie-going. The wider choice of leisure activities was reflected in the gradually declining box-office receipts. The preoccupation of returning servicemen with education and career building cut into the leisure activity of that segment of the population, and the postwar baby boom kept many young families homebound. And then came television—and for the movies, business was never the same again.

Facing a dwindling home market that saw attendance and revenues drop in direct proportion to the spread of commercial TV, the film companies looked abroad, hoping to recapture the overseas markets that had been lost during the war. Struggling to reconstruct their postwar economies, the European governments began instituting protective measures to stem the outflow of the dollar, at that time the world's most stable hard currency.

Great Britain, Hollywood's biggest overseas client, was first to act when, on August 8, 1947, its Labour government levied a massive 75 percent import duty on all films from the dollar area. Stunned and angered, American producers reacted by setting an embargo on all new film exportation to Britain. In May of 1948, the British government repealed the tax and instead set a limit of $17 million that American companies could take out of the country annually. Other European countries legislated similar measures, in effect freezing most of the funds earned abroad by the Hollywood firms. After the initial shock, American producers adjusted to the new reality and began using the frozen funds to manufacture films abroad. By the early 70s nearly half of all American films were being made abroad. By this time, too, foreign markets accounted for more than half the revenues generated by American films.

The Hollywood horror show of the late 40s and early 50s was provided by the House Un-American Activities Committee and its hearings into alleged infiltration of the movie industry by Communists. The hearings, which began in 1947, resulted in the jailing of the HOLLYWOOD TEN and the ruination of many other careers through an unofficial but monstrously effective blacklist. The psychological effects of this dark chapter in the Hollywood story were to last long after the hysteria and the blacklisting had ceased.

A more pressing concern for the industry at the time was the government's ongoing antitrust case against Paramount and the other major studios. After a long series of hearings, appeals, and cross-appeals on several judicial levels, the Supreme Court, in May of 1948, handed down a landmark decision declaring the majors guilty of monopolistic practices in restraint of trade. Block booking, discriminatory pricing and exhibition arrangements, and the fixing of admission prices were found illegal and their future use by film companies was prohibited. In addition, the Big Five were ordered to divest themselves of their theater holdings, the main source of their power and income. The process of divestiture was gradual and slow, but even before the divorcements were completed in the 50s, the structure of the industry and its distribution and exhibition systems had been drastically overhauled. Newly formed organizations took over the theatrical chains and, amid declining attendance, began selling many of their houses. The trimmed-down production companies, no longer obligated to produce enough films to meet the needs of their own theaters, began cutting down on output and personnel.

The films produced by Hollywood in the late 40s and early 50s reflected both the great upheavals in the industry and the general social conditions of the postwar years. The painful readjustment of returning GIs to civilian life was strongly depicted in such films as William Wyler's *The Best Years of Our Lives* (1946) and Fred ZINNEMANN's *The Men* (1950). Racial issues were touched upon in Edward DMYTRYK's *Crossfire* (1947), Elia KAZAN's *Gentleman's Agreement* (1947) and *Pinky* (1949), Clarence Brown's *Intruder in the Dust* (1950), and Joseph LOSEY's *The Lawless* (1950).

The 40s and early 50s also saw the flowering of the FILM NOIR and the proliferation of psychological melodramas reflecting the breakdown of the traditional social fiber and the alienation of the individual in a hostile, or at best indifferent, environment. The milieu was tawdry and the atmosphere dark in such relatively inexpensive black-and-white melodramas as Billy Wilder's *Double Indemnity* (1944); Robert SIODMAK's *Phantom Lady* (1944); *The Spiral Staircase* (1946), and *The Killers* (1946); Fritz Lang's *The Woman in the Window* (1944) and *The Big Heat* (1953); Edward Dmytryk's *Murder My Sweet/Farewell My Lovely* (1944); Michael Curtiz's *Mildred Pierce* (1945); Tay Garnett's *The Postman Always Rings Twice* (1946); Howard Hawks's *The Big Sleep* (1946); Orson Welles's *The Lady from Shanghai* (1948); Nicholas RAY's *In a Lonely Place* (1950); and Robert ALDRICH's *Kiss Me Deadly* (1955).

During the very years of the great Hollywood decline, MGM was writing one of the most glorious chapters in its history with a memorable cycle of lavish screen musicals that elevated the genre to an art. The visual-aural feast was guided by producer Arthur FREED and directors Vincente MINNELLI, Stanley DONEN, and Gene KELLY, the last of whom doubled as the dominant star. Other faces, voices, and legs in the galaxy included Fred Astaire, Judy GARLAND, Cyd CHARISSE, Leslie CARON, Ann MILLER, and Esther WILLIAMS. Among the best of these best of musicals were *Meet Me In St. Louis* (Minnelli, 1944), *On the Town* (Donen-Kelly, 1949), *An American in Paris* (Minnelli, 1951), *Singin' in the Rain* (Donen-Kelly, 1952), and *The Band Wagon* (Minnelli, 1953).

Several superior Westerns were also produced during this period at other studios, among them John Ford's *My Darling Clementine* (1946) and *She Wore a Yellow Ribbon* (1949); King Vidor's *Duel in the Sun* (1947); Howard Hawks's *Red River* (1948); Henry King's *The Gunfighter* (1950); Fred Zinnemann's *High Noon* (1952); Anthony Mann's *The Naked Spur* (1953); and George Stevens's *Shane* (1953). The early 50s also saw the beginning of a vogue for science-fiction films, including George PAL's *Destination Moon* (1950), Robert WISE's *The Day the Earth Stood Still* (1951), Christian NYBY's *The Thing* (1951), Byron HASKIN's *The War of the Worlds* (1953), Joseph NEWMAN's *This Island Earth* (1955), and, slightly later, Fred M. WILCOX's *Forbidden Planet* (1956). Universal's classic horror cycle petered out in self-parody in a series of comedies where Abbott and Costello met the monsters, but new monsters began to emerge in films such as Jack ARNOLD's *Creature from the Black Lagoon* (1954) and Gordon DOUGLAS's *Them!* (1954). In the comedy field, the most exceptional production of the immediate postwar era was significantly a cynical satire, Charlie Chaplin's *Monsieur Verdoux* (1947). Enjoyable comedies on the lighter side included Walter LANG's *Sitting Pretty* (1948), starring Clifton WEBB; two Danny KAYE vehicles, Bruce HUMBERSTONE's *Wonder Man* (1945) and Norman Z. McLeod's *The Secret Life of Walter Mitty* (1947); and two Western spoofs starring Bob Hope and Jane RUSSELL, McLeod's *The Paleface* (1948) and Frank TASHLIN's *Son of Paleface* (1952). Hope also continued his successful teaming with Bing Crosby and Dorothy LAMOUR in Paramount's popular "Road" series, which had started early in the 40s. The immensely popular comedy team of Dean MARTIN and Jerry LEWIS made their film debut in George MARSHALL's *My Friend Irma* (1949).

Besides those previously mentioned, movie stars of the late 40s and 50s included June ALLYSON, Ingrid BERGMAN, Marlon BRANDO, Yul BRYNNER, Montgomery CLIFT, Tony CURTIS, Doris DAY, James DEAN, Kirk DOUGLAS, Glenn FORD, Ava GARDNER, Greer GARSON, Susan HAYWARD, Audrey HEPBURN, Charlton HESTON, William HOLDEN, Judy HOLLIDAY, Rock HUDSON, Van JOHNSON, Grace KELLY, Alan LADD, Burt LANCASTER, Victor MATURE, Kim NOVAK, Maureen O'HARA, Gregory PECK, Elvis PRESLEY, Debbie REYNOLDS, Jane RUSSELL, Eva Marie SAINT, Randolph SCOTT, Frank SINATRA, Elizabeth TAYLOR, Richard WIDMARK, Cornel WILDE, Joanne WOODWARD, and Jane WYMAN.

Notable films of the immediate postwar years, in addition to those previously mentioned, included Alfred E. GREEN's *The Jolson Story* (1946); Charles VIDOR's *Gilda* (1946); Clarence BROWN's *The Yearling* (1946); Jules Dassin's *Brute Force* (1947); H. C. POTTER's *The Farmer's Daughter* (1947); George SEATON's *Miracle on 34th Street* (1947); Jean NEGULESCO's *Johnny Belinda* (1948); John Huston's *The Treasure of the Sierra Madre* (1948), *The Asphalt Jungle* (1950), and *The African Queen* (US/UK; 1951); Anatole Litvak's *Sorry Wrong Number* and *The Snake Pit* (both 1948); William Dieterle's *Portrait of Jennie* (1949); Robert ROSSEN's *All the King's Men* (1949); Raoul Walsh's *White Heat* (1949); William Wyler's *The Heiress* (1949) and *Detective Story* (1951); Mark ROBSON's *Champion* (1949); Henry KING's *Twelve O' Clock High* (1949); Joseph L. MANKIEWICZ's *All About Eve* (1950) and *Julius Caesar* (1953); Billy Wilder's *Sunset Boulevard* (1950), *Ace in the Hole/The Big Carnival* (1951), and *Stalag 17* (1953); George Cukor's *Born Yesterday* (1950); George Stevens's *A Place in the Sun* (1951); Elia Kazan's *A Streetcar Named Desire* (1951), *Viva Zapata!* (1952), and *On the Waterfront* (1954); John Ford's *The Quiet Man* (1952); Vincente Minnelli's *The Bad and the Beautiful* (1952); and Fred Zinnemann's *From Here to Eternity* (1953).

An important contribution was made during this difficult period by the ever-growing number of independent producers—men like Stanley KRAMER and Otto Preminger—who introduced to the screen novel, and sometimes controversial, themes that defied the industry's traditional tameness. Preminger set an important precedent by releasing *The Moon Is Blue* (1953) without the seal of approval of the MPAA Production Code. The film, which shocked some Americans by the utterance of the word "virgin" on the screen, proved popular with many others and set the stage for a revision of the code in 1956.

Looking for ways to beat the competition from television, the majors in the early 50s came up with a battery of projection systems that could not be matched by the small home TV screen. Wide screens and three-dimensional systems had been experimented with on and off since the earliest days of cinema. Now a concerted effort was made to convert these systems from the "nice toy" category to commercial use. The least successful of the novelties proved to be the 3-D system, which ran out of steam a short time after its resurrection in 1952. The three-screen CINERAMA enjoyed a successful run in big cities, but the expense of converting theaters to its use limited its expansion, and it, too, disappeared after a while. Much more durable have been wide-screen systems like 20TH CENTURY-FOX's CINEMASCOPE and Paramount's Vista Vision, which paved the way for MGM's PANAVISION, still in extensive use today. The public thumbed their noses, however, at two systems designed to appeal to their sense of smell, AROMA-RAMA and SMELL-O-VISION. Universal met some success with SENSURROUND, which created vibrations in the air that drew audiences into the on-screen terrors of *Earthquake* (1974). In the late 70s, DOLBY stereophonic sound became standard for big-budget spectacles, while the DIGITAL SOUND TRACK became increasingly common in the 90s.

The collapse of the Hollywood studio system, the rise of the independent producer, and the coincidental infiltration of the American screen by imported European films were some of the factors that combined to bring about a gradual maturation of public taste and a growing acceptance of adult themes in films. The lifting of censorship restrictions was another vital factor. In a landmark decision involving alleged blasphemy in Roberto

ROSSELLINI's *The Miracle,* the US Supreme Court, on May 26, 1952, ruled that motion pictures were "a significant medium for the communication of ideas" and a means of information as well as entertainment, thereby reversing a 1915 Supreme Court ruling that movies were "business, pure and simple," and extending to film the protection of the First Amendment. The effect of this and subsequent court decisions on obscenity which contained such key phrases as "redeeming social value" and "community standards" was to free the movies by and large from the authority of state and local boards of censors and pressure from self-appointed cultural vigilante groups like the Legion of Decency. The MPAA's Production Code has also, meanwhile, undergone considerable revisions, eventually replacing its complex rules of do's and don't's with a RATING system that protects the young while setting virtually no standards on what adult audiences are permitted to see. All this resulted in far-reaching gains of freedom of expression for film producers, which in the permissive social climate of the 70s, reached its extreme manifestation in a flood of hard-core pornographic movies on America's screens.

Many of Hollywood's old-time directors remained active behind the camera alongside a new generation of filmmakers who gradually emerged to prominence, mainly via TV, the stage, and the proliferating film schools. Much of the new talent was absorbed into the Hollywood mainstream, creating technically polished escapist films in proven formulas. But a good number of the younger directors brought to the screen not only an infusion of new vitality but often also new ideas and intriguing personal styles. Their films appealed especially to the younger and more knowledgeable audiences who now comprised the majority of regular filmgoers. During the 60s there was a discernible shift of focus among American audiences away from the adulation of stars and toward a greater appreciation of the director's contribution to film, a trend that was influenced by the French AUTEUR THEORY.

Among the American directors of the 60s and 70s who enjoyed this newly found status, including some foreign-born directors working in the US, were Robert Aldrich, Woody ALLEN, Robert ALTMAN, Hal ASHBY, John AVILDSEN, John BADHAM, Warren BEATTY, Peter BOGDANOVICH, Mel BROOKS, John CASSAVETES, Francis Ford COPPOLA, Roger CORMAN, Brian DE PALMA, Richard DONNER, Clint EASTWOOD, Milos FORMAN, John FRANKENHEIMER, William FRIEDKIN, George Roy HILL, Walter HILL, John HUSTON, Norman JEWISON, Stanley KUBRICK, George LUCAS, Sidney LUMET, David LYNCH, Terrence MALICK, Mike NICHOLS, Alan J. PAKULA, Sam PECKINPAH, Arthur PENN, Roman POLANSKI, Sidney POLLACK, Nicholas Ray, Michael RITCHIE, Martin RITT, George A. ROMERO, Franklin SCHAFFNER, John SCHLESINGER, Martin SCORSESE, Steven SPIELBERG, John STURGES, and John WATERS.

American movie stars of the 60s and 70s included ANN-MARGRET, Anne BANCROFT, Warren Beatty, Charles BRONSON, Ellen BURSTYN, James CAAN, Jill CLAYBURGH, Sandra DEE, Robert DE NIRO, Richard DREYFUSS, Faye DUNAWAY, Robert DUVALL, Clint Eastwood, Jane FONDA, Gene HACKMAN, Goldie HAWN, Dustin HOFFMAN, Elliott GOULD, Diane KEATON, Jack LEMMON, Sophia LOREN, Shirley MACLAINE, Lee MARVIN, Walter MATTHAU, Steve MCQUEEN, Paul NEWMAN, Jack NICHOLSON, Ryan O'NEAL, Al PACINO, Sidney POITIER, Robert REDFORD, Roy SCHEIDER, George C. SCOTT, Cybill SHEPHERD, Sylvester STALLONE, Barbra STREISAND, Donald SUTHERLAND, John TRAVOLTA, Jon VOIGHT, Raquel WELCH, and Natalie WOOD.

As the era of the MULTIPLEX dawned, many big movie houses were converted into two or more little theaters while new theaters were constructed with multiple screens. The art house began attracting specialized audiences in metropolitan areas. For suburbanites, the drive-in proved an accessible and convenient showcase for young couples and entire families. Serious films as well as escapist ones were attracting sizeable crowds. And although attendance never regained its former heights, the profit outlook for film producers steadily improved.

Although most films continued to fall neatly into the traditionally popular genres, audiences were being offered a wider choice of topics and styles. A CINÉMA VÉRITÉ movement developed as an important branch of the American documentary. An avant-garde movement emerged from the underground in the early 60s, when experimental, offbeat productions began reaching the big screens, films like John Cassavetes' improvisational *Shadows* (1961) and Shirley CLARKE's *The Connection* (1962). Later in the period, Jed Johnson's *Andy Warhol's Bad* (1971), John Waters's *Pink Flamingos* (1972), and David Lynch's *Eraserhead* (1978) became cult favorites.

Original musicals of high artistic quality were occasionally made, such as Stanley Donen's *Funny Face* (1957) and Martin Scorsese's *New York, New York* (1977). But most musicals were lifted from the Broadway stage with little change of pace or spirit. Among the most successful adaptations were Robert WISE and Jerome ROBBINS's *West Side Story* (1961), George Cukor's *My Fair Lady* (1964), Wise's *The Sound of Music* (1965), William Wyler's *Funny Girl* (1968), Bob FOSSE's *Cabaret* (1972), Randal KLEISER's *Grease* (1978), and Milos FORMAN's *Hair* (1979).

By the early 60s the gangster film had become an anachronism, with occasional exceptions such as Budd Boetticher's inexpensive *The Rise and Fall of Legs Diamond* (1960). In the late 60s, the genre began to revive with Arthur Penn's *Bonnie and Clyde* (1967), one of the most influential films of the decade. Francis Ford Coppola infused the gangster film with new life and mythic stature in his high-budget *The Godfather* (1972) and *The Godfather Part II* (1974), widely considered among the best films of all time.

Another influential film of the late 60s was Dennis HOPPER's *Easy Rider* (1969). The inexpensive production, which echoed the "hippie" culture, proved a stunning box-office sleeper and affirmed for the major studios the existence of a potent youth market responsive to themes associated with the frustrations of the Vietnam War generation. Curiously, the conflict itself was not the subject of any major film during its duration, if one discounts John Wayne's vapid tribute to the valor of the American Special Forces in Southeast Asia in *The Green Berets* (1968). Evidently, a more distant perspective on the complex social, personal, and moral issues of the war was needed. It wasn't until the late 70s that these painful issues reached the screen with the release of Hal Ashby's *Coming Home* (1978), Michael CIMINO's *The Deer Hunter* (1978), and Francis Ford Coppola's *Apocalypse Now* (1979). The perspective was readily there for a number of interesting Hollywood films about earlier wars, notably Stanley Kubrick's critical look at WW I, *Paths of Glory* (1957); Franklin SCHAFFNER's study of a WW II hero, *Patton* (1970); and Robert Altman's black-humor treatise on the Korean War, *M*A*S*H* (1970). Cold War tensions and distrust of America's politicians were reflected in political thrillers, including John Frankenheimer's *The Manchurian Candidate* (1962) and Alan J. Pakula's *All the President's Men* (1976).

Billy Wilder was among the pathfinders in the satirical trend with *Some Like It Hot* (1959) and *One Two Three* (1961). Kubrick's nightmarish political black comedy, the British-made *Dr. Strangelove* (1964), exerted enormous influence on the genre. Later came such films as Tony RICHARDSON's *The Loved*

One (1965), Mike Nichols's *The Graduate* (1967) and *Catch-22* (1970), Arthur HILLER's *The Tiger Makes Out* (1967), Robert DOWNEY's *Putney Swope* (1969), and Alan ARKIN's *Little Murders* (1971). The American screen comedy of the 70s was dominated by the brilliant philosophic humor of Woody Allen (*Sleeper,* 1973; *Annie Hall,* 1977, etc.) and the lunatic inventiveness of the comic mind of Mel BROOKS (*Blazing Saddles,* 1974; *Silent Movie,* 1976, etc.). There was also a vogue for films scripted by or adapted from the plays of Neil SIMON.

The 70s also saw a mild revival of romantic drama in the wake of the unexpected commercial success of Arthur Hiller's *Love Story* (1970), a trend that also resulted in Sydney Pollack's *The Way We Were* (1973). A wave of nostalgia, sometimes enhanced by a rekindled interest in personal relationships of the young, was responsible for the success of such films as Peter Bogdanovich's *The Last Picture Show* (1971) and *Paper Moon* (1973), Robert MULLIGAN's *Summer of '42* (1971), George Lucas's *American Graffiti* (1973), George Roy Hill's *The Sting* (1973), and Terrence Malick's *Badlands* (1973) and *Days of Heaven* (1978).

The seamier side of life was graphically and powerfully depicted in such dramas as John Schlesinger's *Midnight Cowboy* (1969) and Martin Scorsese's *Mean Streets* (1973) and *Taxi Driver* (1976). The big-city skyline also provided the background for police thrillers such as William Friedkin's *The French Connection* (1971) and for a new hybrid genre of the 70s: films about black heroes, made and played by blacks for a primarily black audience. The trend was set by Gordon PARKS's *Shaft* (1971) and Gordon Parks, Jr.'s *Superfly* (1972), the success of which led to a string of shoddy imitations that have been tagged "blaxploitation" pictures. The cause of women's liberation was echoed more faintly in such films as Robert Altman's *Three Women* (1977), Fred Zinnemann's *Julia* (1977), Claudia WEILL's *Girlfriends* (1978), and Paul MAZURSKY's *An Unmarried Woman* (1978).

The horror film tradition was maintained in the early 60s by Roger Corman through a series of visually striking if dramatically less than perfect adaptations from Edgar Allan Poe, a cycle that began with *The House of Usher* (1960) and ended with *The Masque of the Red Death* (1964). The genre was elevated to cinematic art in Alfred Hitchcock's brilliant exercise in horrific suspense, *Psycho* (1960). Other significant contributions included Robert Wise's *The Haunting* (1963) and Roman Polanski's *Rosemary's Baby* (1968). Graphic violence and gore entered the genre with George A. Romero's *Night of the Living Dead* (1968), predecessor of such slasher films as Tobe Hooper's *The Texas Chainsaw Massacre* (1974) and John Carpenter's *Halloween* (1978). A return to surface style characterized such tales of the supernatural in the 70s as Friedkin's *The Exorcist* (1973), Richard Donner's *The Omen* (1976), and Brian De Palma's *Carrie* (1976). The genre was satirized in the cult musical adaptation *The Rocky Horror Picture Show* (1975).

The big Hollywood spectacle also continued to thrive, making fortunes for some (Michael ANDERSON's *Around the World in 80 Days* for Mike TODD, 1956) and losing fortunes for others (Joseph L. Mankiewicz's *Cleopatra* for Fox, 1963). Among the commercially most successful of mammoth new ventures were remakes of proven box-office attractions: Cecil B. De Mille's *The Ten Commandments* (1956), William Wyler's *Ben-Hur* (1959), and John GUILLERMIN's *King Kong* (1976). Science fiction epics included Kubrick's British-made *2001: A Space Odyssey* (1968), Schaffner's *Planet of the Apes* (1968), Wise's *The Andromeda Strain* (1971), and Douglas Trumbull's *Silent Running* (1971). A popular subgenre of the Hollywood epic in the 70s was the disaster film with spectacular special effects of "natural" or man-made catastrophes. Among the most profitable of these were George SEATON's *Airport* (1970) and its sequels, Ronald NEAME's *The Poseidon Adventure* (1972), Mark ROBSON's *Earthquake* (1974), and Guillermin's *The Towering Inferno* (1974).

The unprecedented box-office success of Steven Spielberg's shark thriller *Jaws* (1975) and George Lucas's science fiction adventure *Star Wars* (1977) signaled the beginning of a new class of Hollywood films: the youth-oriented blockbuster laden with action and special effects. Made on relatively modest budgets, *Star Wars* and *Jaws* were the first films to break the $100 million rental mark and soon climbed respectively to the number one and two spots on the list of all-time top moneymakers. They also generated rich additional revenues from merchandising of associated toys, books, posters, T-shirts, and so on. The result was that studios in the 80s and 90s produced spectacles that were ever more action-packed, eye-filling, and expensive, each costing tens of millions of dollars but promising still greater financial bonanzas. Usually released in the summer or at Christmas time, these films, aimed especially at teenage males, typically fell into the science fiction, fantasy, horror, thriller, or adventure genres. If successful, they usually generated sequels, each more baroque than the one before. They were often criticized for their two-dimensional characters and simplistic narratives but praised for their amazing stunts and SPECIAL EFFECTS. These special effects, increasingly enhanced by COMPUTER-GENERATED IMAGERY, were supplied by a burgeoning, high-tech industry of independent companies such as Lucas's INDUSTRIAL LIGHT & MAGIC, the Stan WINSTON Studio, and Richard EDLUND's Boss Film Studios.

Spielberg and Lucas, the inventors of the modern fantasy blockbuster, remained its undisputed champions into the 90s. Their hits included Spielberg's *E.T.* (1982) and *Jurassic Park* (1993), the top two moneymakers of all time; Spielberg's *Close Encounters of the Third Kind* (1977); the Indiana Jones series masterminded by Lucas and directed by Spielberg, beginning with *Raiders of the Lost Ark* (1981); Irvin KERSHNER's *The Empire Strikes Back* (1980) and Richard Marquand's *Return of the Jedi* (1983), sequels to *Star Wars* that were produced by Lucas's company, Lucasfilm; and a number of films produced by Spielberg's Amblin Entertainment, including Tobe Hooper's *Poltergeist* (1982), Joe DANTE's *Gremlins* (1984), and Robert ZEMECKIS's *Back to the Future* (1985) and *Who Framed Roger Rabbit* (1988).

Other fantasy/science fiction blockbusters of the period included Richard Donner's *Superman* (1978) and sequels, Robert Wise's *Star Trek: The Motion Picture* (1979) and sequels, Ridley SCOTT's *Alien* (1979) and sequels, James Cameron's *The Terminator* (1984) and *Terminator 2: Judgment Day* (1991), Paul VERHOEVEN's *Robocop* (1987) and *Total Recall* (1990), and Tim BURTON's *Batman* (1989) and *Batman Returns* (1992). Action-adventure blockbusters included Martin BREST's *Beverly Hills Cop* (1984) and its sequel, George P. COSMATOS's *Rambo: First Blood Part II* (1985), Tony Scott's *Top Gun* (1986), Donner's *Lethal Weapon* (1987) and sequels, Ron HOWARD's *Backdraft* (1991), John MCTIERNAN's *Die Hard* (1988), and Renny HARLIN's *Die Hard 2* (1990) and *Cliffhanger* (1993).

Blockbusters were no guarantee of box-office success, as witnessed by such expensive flops as Willard Huyck's *Howard the Duck* (1986) and Michael Lehmann's *Hudson Hawk* (1991). But the potential payoff was so great that studios risked ever mightier sums in search of it. To hedge their bets, they sought to hire the stars, directors, screenwriters, and producers who had been most successful on their last outing. The power of the top rank of talent, and of their agents at companies like CREATIVE ARTISTS AGENCY (CAA) and INTERNATIONAL CREATIVE MANAGEMENT (ICM), increased accordingly. In an escalating spiral, the rising costs of talent drove movie budgets even higher, thus ensuring that studios would be even hungrier for big payoffs and more skittish about trying anything very different.

The opportunity for profits increased with the introduction of the home videocassette recorder (VCR) in the mid-1970s (see VIDEO). At first, many in the movie industry feared the new technology as a potentially dangerous competitor analogous to television. In 1984, the Supreme Court ruled in favor of Sony, establishing the principle that home videotaping of copyrighted programs without royalty payments was permissible. In fact, the studios' fear of competition was baseless, since home video actually opened up a profitable new market for studio releases, as did the spread of premium cable channels and pay-per-view systems. All of these exhibition outlets increased the chances that a studio release would recoup its costs and turn a profit. Some films that did poorly at the box office did well enough in home video to justify a sequel. Foreign sales also helped extend a film's potential to turn a profit. In an age of reduced state subsidies for national cinemas, American films increasingly dominated the box office in Europe and other countries, despite protests from foreign filmmakers and critics.

The big potential profits to be made from the movie industry enticed corporate conglomerates to shop for studios, resulting in the Japanese takeovers of Columbia and Universal, the merger of Time Inc. with Warner Communications, and the bidding war in the 1990s over Paramount. However, the potential risks were nearly as great as the rewards. This was made clear from such high-profile failures as the destruction of United Artists (partly due to the expensive failure of Michael Cimino's *Heaven's Gate* in 1980), the continuing debility of MGM, and the bankruptcy of ORION PICTURES, a once-successful company that had been founded in 1978 with hopes of becoming a new major studio. Troubled independents included Atlantic, Cannon, Cinecom, Island Alive, Skouras, and Vestron. Other "indies" succeeded so impressively that they were purchased by larger companies; this was the case with New Line Cinema and Miramax, acquired, respectively, by Turner Entertainment and the Walt Disney Company.

One of the ironies of the period was that the movie industry turned to its old nemesis, television, for products that could be considered presold—vintage TV series turned into big-budget blockbusters. Varying in quality, this class of films included Brian De Palma's *The Untouchables* (1987), Barry Sonnenfeld's *The Addams Family* (1991), Andrew DAVIS's *The Fugitive* (1993), Penelope SPHEERIS's *The Beverly Hillbillies* (1993), and De Palma's *Mission: Impossible* (1996).

Since the studios saw children and young adults as their principal target, movies of all genres were increasingly tailored to this age group. Movie genres that had been mostly dormant were revived with charismatic young casts, including Westerns. The Walt Disney Studios, rejuvenated after a period of decline and now one of Hollywood's most powerful production houses, released a popular new series of musical animated features, including *Beauty and the Beast* (1991) and *Aladdin* (1992), in addition to providing live-action children's fare with such films as Joe Johnston's *Honey, I Shrunk the Kids* (1989).

Disney's adult-oriented subsidiary, Touchstone Films, founded in 1984, was one of the success stories of the period. Turning away for the first time in Disney's history from the family market to an older, more sophisticated audience, Touchstone did well with comedies such as Ron HOWARD's *Splash* (1984) and Emile ARDOLINO's *Sister Act* (1992) and comedy-dramas such as Barry LEVINSON's *Good Morning, Vietnam* (1987) and Peter WEIR's *Dead Poets Society* (1989), both of which starred stand-up comedian turned leading man Robin WILLIAMS.

Comedies generally were a strong genre from the late 70s to the 90s, dominated by graduates of the 'Saturday Night Live' TV series, including Bill MURRAY, Chevy CHASE, Dan AYKROYD, John BELUSHI, Eddie MURPHY, Dana CARVEY, Mike Myers, David SPADE and Chris FARLEY. Successful films in which they appeared included John LANDIS's *National Lampoon's Animal House* (1978) and *Trading Places* (1983), Ivan REITMAN's *Ghostbusters* (1984), and Penelope SPHEERIS's *Wayne's World* (1992), itself based on a 'Saturday Night Live' skit. In a separate development, the directing-producing-writing team of Jerry and David ZUCKER and Jim ABRAHAMS proved themselves heirs to the zany humor of Mel Brooks with joke-filled parodies such as *Airplane!* (1980) and *The Naked Gun* (1988). Other successful comedies of the period included Sydney Pollack's *Tootsie* (1982), Lawrence KASDAN's *The Big Chill* (1983), James L. BROOKS's *Broadcast News* (1987), Norman Jewison's *Moonstruck* (1987), Mike Nichols's *Working Girl* (1988), Ron Shelton's *Bull Durham* (1988), Andrew BERGMAN's *The Freshman* (1990), Penny MARSHALL's *A League of Their Own* (1992), and several films scripted by Lowell Ganz and Babaloo Mandel, including Ron Howard's *Parenthood* (1989) and Ron Underwood's *City Slickers* (1991).

A popular genre of the period was the suspense thriller, often laced with sex and feeding off contemporary urban fears. Examples included Adrian LYNE's *Fatal Attraction* (1987), Joseph Ruben's *Sleeping with the Enemy* (1991), Curtis Hanson's *The Hand That Rocks the Cradle* (1992), and Paul Verhoeven's *Basic Instinct* (1992). The film noir tradition was kept alive by films like Lawrence Kasdan's *Body Heat* (1981), Stephen FREARS's *The Grifters* (1990), John DAHL's *The Last Seduction* (1994) and Bryan Singer's *The Usual Suspects* (1995).

Musicals in which popular songs provide the backdrop for the action, such as John BADHAM's *Saturday Night Fever* (1977), Lyne's *Flashdance* (1983), and Alan Parker's *Evita* (1996), were popular though the influence of music videos in motion picture pacing and rhythm was more widely pervasive. Another popular subgenre was created by John Avildsen's boxing drama *Rocky* (1976), which spawned many sequels and made a star of its leading man and screenwriter Sylvester STALLONE. This category of film, in which underdog athletes triumphed over more polished opponents, also included Avildsen's *The Karate Kid* (1984) and its sequels.

The horror film was increasingly a genre of gore and gross-out makeup effects, seen at their crudest in Sean S. CUNNINGHAM's *Friday the Thirteenth* (1980) and its numerous sequels. Wes CRAVEN's *A Nightmare on Elm Street* (1984) was more imaginative, as was the work of Sam RAIMI (*The Evil Dead*, 1983), Stuart GORDON (*Re-Animator*, 1985), and Canadian-born David CRONENBERG (*The Fly*, 1986). Jonathan DEMME ventured into the genre with the horror-suspense thriller *The Silence of the Lambs* (1991), a critical and commercial success that won a best picture Oscar.

Despite the continuing domination of the industry by men, the period saw the launching of the careers of several major female directors, including Nora EPHRON, Penny Marshall, Susan SEIDELMAN, Joan Micklin SILVER, Penelope Spheeris, and Barbra STREISAND. However, most films aimed primarily at female audiences continued to be directed by men, as they had in the past. These included such lavish dramas as James L. Brooks's *Terms of Endearment* (1983), Sydney Pollack's *Out of Africa* (1985), Streisand's *The Prince of Tides* (1991), and

Wayne WANG's *The Joy Luck Club* (1993). Romantic comedies included Silver's *Crossing Delancey* (1988), Rob REINER's *When Harry Met Sally...* (1989), Garry Marshall's *Pretty Woman* (1990), and Ephron's *Sleepless in Seattle* (1993). Other films that appealed to female audiences included Silver's *Head Over Heels/Chilly Scenes of Winter* (1979), Taylor Hackford's *An Officer and a Gentleman* (1982), Peter Weir's *Witness* (1985), Jerry Zucker's *Ghost* (1990), and Jon Avnet's *Fried Green Tomatoes* (1991). A new spin on the women's picture came with Ridley Scott's *Thelma & Louise* (1991), a feminist buddy movie about two outlaw women on the run.

The Western genre received original and serious treatment in Kevin COSTNER's *Dances with Wolves* (1990) and Clint Eastwood's *Unforgiven* (1992), both of which won best picture Oscars. Also winning best picture awards were stage adaptations such as Milos Forman's *Amadeus* (1984) and Bruce Beresford's *Driving Miss Daisy* (1989).

A new generation of African-American directors created films in many genres that dealt thoughtfully with racism and African-American culture. The most influential of these was Spike LEE, whose films included *She's Gotta Have It* (1986), *Do the Right Thing* (1989), *Jungle Fever* (1991), and *Malcolm X* (1992). Others included Robert Townsend (*Hollywood Shuffle*, 1987); Mario VAN PEEBLES (*New Jack City*, 1991); John SINGLETON (*Boyz N the Hood*, 1991); and the HUGHES BROTHERS (*Menace II Society*, 1993).

Many avant-garde directors continued to do interesting work outside the mainstream, including Todd HAYNES (*Poison*, 1991) and Lizzie BORDEN (*Working Girls*, 1986). Other avant-garde filmmakers joined the mainstream while retaining elements of their peculiar vision, including David Lynch (*Blue Velvet*, 1986) and John Waters (*Hairspray*, 1988). A few directors managed to gain wide recognition while creating and distributing most of their work independently of the major studios, including Henry JAGLOM (*Eating*, 1990), Jim JARMUSCH (*Stranger Than Paradise*, 1984; *Down by Law*, 1986), John SAYLES (*Return of the Secaucus Seven*, 1980; *Matewan*, 1987; *Eight Men Out*, 1988), Gus VAN SANT, JR. (*Drugstore Cowboy*, 1989; *My Own Private Idaho*, 1991), and Wayne WANG (*Chan Is Missing*, 1982; *Dim Sum*, 1985).

Despite Hollywood's fear of originality and taste for glossy escapism, a number of directors continued to do serious films while working with the major studios. These included Woody Allen (*Broadway Danny Rose*, 1984; *Hannah and Her Sisters*, 1986; *Crimes and Misdemeanors*, 1989), Robert Altman (*The Player*, 1992; *Short Cuts*, 1993), Robert BENTON (*Kramer vs. Kramer*, 1979; *Places in the Heart*, 1984), Francis Ford Coppola (*Peggy Sue Got Married*, 1986; *The Godfather Part III*, 1990; *Bram Stoker's Dracula*, 1992), Jonathan Demme (*Something Wild*, 1986; *Married to the Mob*, 1988), Clint Eastwood (*Bird*, 1988; *White Hunter, Black Heart*, 1990; *A Perfect World*, 1993), Philip Kaufman (*The Unbearable Lightness of Being*, 1988; *Henry and June*, 1990), Barry Levinson (*Diner*, 1982; *Tin Men*, 1987; *Rain Man*, 1988), Sidney Lumet (*The Verdict*, 1982; *Running on Empty*, 1988; *Q and A*, 1990), Martin Scorsese (*Raging Bull*, 1980; *The King of Comedy*, 1983; *The Last Temptation of Christ*, 1988; *GoodFellas*, 1990; *The Age of Innocence*, 1993), and Oliver STONE (*Platoon*, 1986; *Born on the Fourth of July*, 1989; *JFK*, 1991).

Among the rising new directors of the 90s are: Allison Anders, Michael Bay, Antonia Bird, Edward Burns, Glenn Gordon Caron, Ted Demme, Uli Edell, Gregory Hoblit, Michael Hoffman, Luis Mandoki, John Mangold, Douglas McGrath, Charles Russell, David O. Russell, Tom Shadyac, Todd Solondz, Whit Stillman, Lee Tamahori, John Turtletaub, and Robert M. Young, among others.

Hollywood stars of the 80s and 90s include Ellen BARKIN, Annette BENING, Jeff BRIDGES, Nicolas CAGE, Jim CARREY, Chevy CHASE, CHER, Glenn CLOSE, Kevin COSTNER, Tom CRUISE, Geena DAVIS, Laura DERN, Michael DOUGLAS, Sally FIELD, Bridget FONDA, Harrison FORD, Jodie FOSTER, Michael J. FOX, Richard GERE, Mel GIBSON, Whoopi GOLDBERG, Melanie GRIFFITH, Tom HANKS, Daryl HANNAH, William HURT, Anjelica HUSTON, Michael KEATON, Kevin KLINE, Jessica LANGE, Steve MARTIN, Bette MIDLER, Demi MOORE, Eddie MURPHY, Bill MURRAY, Chuck NORRIS, Michelle PFEIFFER, Dennis QUAID, Keanu REEVES, Julia ROBERTS, Meg RYAN, Susan SARANDON, Arnold SCHWARZENEGGER, Wesley SNIPES, Sissy SPACEK, Sharon STONE, Meryl STREEP, Kiefer SUTHERLAND, Patrick SWAYZE, Kathleen TURNER, Denzel WASHINGTON, Sigourney WEAVER, Robin WILLIAMS, Bruce WILLIS, and Debra WINGER.

unit production manager. A producer's executive officer, assigned to the production of a particular motion picture. He is responsible for co-ordinating and supervising all the administrative and technical details of the production, from budgeting and scheduling to picking locations and overseeing the activities of the entire crew.

Universal. A motion picture production company founded in 1912 by film pioneer Carl LAEMMLE, following the amalgamation of his IMP company with Bison 101, Nestor, Powers, and several other corporations. In 1915, the company launched Universal City, a 230-acre municipality in the San Fernando Valley equipped to meet the requirements of both studio and exterior shooting. Among the many stars who made Universal City their home in the silent era were Rudolph Valentino, Wallace Reid, and Lon Chaney. It was at Universal that MGM's boy wonder, Irving Thalberg, and Columbia's boss Harry Cohn started out as secretaries to Laemmle and that Erich von Stroheim directed his most successful productions.

In the early 30s Universal gained much prestige from the production of *All Quiet on the Western Front* and box-office success with a superb cycle of horror films (*Frankenstein, Dracula, The Invisible Man,* etc.) featuring Boris KARLOFF and Bela LUGOSI, among others. But by the middle of the decade the company had dipped into financial difficulties and was saved from bankruptcy only in the nick of time, thanks to the enormous success of a series of musicals starring Deanna Durbin. In the 40s, Universal's fortunes hinged on the success of a series of Arabian Nights adventure pictures starring such exotics as Maria Montez, Jon Hall, Turhan Bey, and Sabu. In the early 50s the company remained in the black, thanks mainly to the comedies of Abbott and Costello and the marginal appeal of Donald O'Connor, Jeff Chandler, and a novice, Tony Curtis.

In 1946, Universal merged with International Films and for the next six years was known as Universal International. After the acquisition of controlling interest in Universal by Decca Records and the ascension of Decca's head, Milton Rackmil, to the presidency, the company gradually dropped its B picture line and shifted the emphasis to fewer productions of greater technical polish. The new policy manifested itself in a succession of glossy soap operas produced by Ross Hunter and directed by Douglas Sirk, followed by a series of slick bedroom farces starring Doris Day and Rock Hudson.

In 1962, Decca Records and Universal became subsidiaries of MCA Inc., an entertainment conglomerate that had been founded as the talent agency Music Corporation of America by Jules Stein in Chicago in 1924. Following an antitrust investigation, a 1962 consent decree forced MCA, then headed by Stein and Lew Wasserman, to divest itself of its talent agency interests, but it retained Universal, Decca Records, and the television production company Revue.

In 1966, Universal became the feature film production division of Universal City Studios, Inc., Hollywood's busiest TV series factory. In the 70s, Universal scored several huge box-office triumphs with such films as *Airport* (1970), *The Sting* and *American Graffiti* (both 1973), *The Deer Hunter* and *National Lampoon's Animal House* (both 1978), and above all *Jaws* (1975), which long remained one of the top ten all-time moneymakers. The latter film marked a turning point in Universal's long association with director-producer Steven SPIELBERG, dating back to his debut theatrical release, *The Sugarland Express* (1974). With his Amblin Entertainment production company headquartered on the Universal lot, Spielberg has brought Universal numerous successes, including *Back to the Future* (1985) and the number one and two all-time moneymakers, *Jurassic Park* (1993) and *E.T.: The Extra-Terrestrial* (1982). Other Universal hits of the 80s and 90s have included *Twins* (1988), *Field of Dreams* and *Parenthood* (both 1989), and *Fried Green Tomatoes* (1991).

By the 70s, Universal City had become a popular tourist attraction where visitors peeked behind the scenes of motion picture and video production, shrieked at animatronic monsters, and witnessed stunts and gun duels by a team of well-rehearsed performers. In 1990, the company opened the even more elaborate Universal Studios Florida theme park in Orlando.

Japan's Matsushita Electrical Industrial Company purchased MCA Inc. in 1990, and with it Universal, for an estimated $6.6 billion, the most expensive sale yet of an American company to the Japanese. Wasserman was the chairman and CEO of MCA Inc., while the MCA motion picture group was headed by Thomas Pollock. However, changes were still on the horizon. Unable to get support from its Matsushita owners, the studio was sold to Seagrams Co. head Edgar Bronfman, Jr. As a result, Lew Wasserman, Sid Sheinberg, and Tom Pollock were compensated for their contributions to the studio, but the day-to-day reins were given to former CAA topper Ron Meyer in 1996.

universal leader. A standardized length of film at the beginning and end of release prints. It is marked with identification words, numbers, and symbols as a guide to the projectionist in changing over from one reel to another. Devised by the SMPTE, the universal leader has become the industry standard, replacing the ACADEMY LEADER.

Unsworth, Geoffrey. Director of photography. *b.* 1914, London. *d.* 1978. He entered British films in 1932 as camera assistant and worked his way up to camera operator in 1937. He operated the camera on such noted films as *The Drum/Drums* (1938), *The Four Feathers* (1939), *The Thief of Bagdad* (1940), *The Life and Death of Colonel Blimp* (1943), and *A Matter of Life and Death/Stairway to Heaven* (1946). Graduating to director of photography in 1946, he rapidly developed into one of Britain's best, especially in color cinematography. From the early 60s he also worked on US and international productions. He is credited with collaboration on several technical innovations, including a special front-projection technique devised for effects in *2001: A Space Odyssey* (1968). He won an Oscar for the cinematography of *Cabaret* (1972). The film *Superman* (1978), one of his last credits, is dedicated to his memory.

FILMS INCLUDE: *The Laughing Lady* 1946; *Jassy* 1947; *Blanche Fury* (co-phot.) 1948; *The Blue Lagoon, Scott of the Antarctic* 1949; *Trio* (co-phot.), *The Clouded Yellow* 1950; *The Planter's Wife/Outpost in Malaya* 1952; *The Sword and the Rose, The Million Pound Note/Man with a Million* 1953; *The Purple Plain* 1954; *Simba* 1955; *A Town Like Alice/Rape of Malaya* 1956; *A Night to Remember* 1958; *North West Frontier/Flame Over India* 1959; *The World of Suzie Wong* (US) 1960; *On the Double* (US) 1961; *The 300 Spartans* (US) 1962; *An Evening with the Royal Ballet* 1963; *Becket* 1964; *Genghis Khan* (US/UK/Ger./Yug.) 1965; *Othello* 1966; *Half a Sixpence* (US/UK), *2001: A Space Odyssey* 1968; *The Assassination Bureau* 1969; *Cromwell, The Magic Christian, Three Sisters* 1970; *Unman Wittering and Zigo* 1971; *Cabaret* (US), *Alice's Adventures in Wonderland* 1972; *Baxter, Love and Pain, Don Quixote* 1973; *The Internecine Project, The Abdication, Murder on the Orient Express* 1974; *The Return of the Pink Panther, Royal Flash, Lucky Lady* (US) 1975; *A Matter of Time* (US/It.) 1976; *A Bridge Too Far* 1977; *Superman* (US) 1978; *Tess* (Fr./UK), *The Great Train Robbery* 1979.

UPA (United Productions of America). A film production company formed in 1943 by a group of young animators who broke away from the Disney fold following an artists' strike in 1941. The group, headed by Stephen BOSUSTOW, sought freer modes of expression in the field of animated film. Breaking away from the traditional Disney style that dominated the industry for many years, UPA delighted sophisticated audiences with cartoon series that were simpler in drawing techniques, but more inventive and creative than the standard cartoon fare in motion picture theaters. Among the most famous animators in the group were Pete Burns (*Mr. Magoo*), Bob Cannon (*Gerald McBoing Boing*), John Hubley, Gene Daitch, and Ernest Pintoff.

upstage. The background portion of a set; the part of a set farthest from the camera.

Urban, Charles. American-born pioneer of British cinema. *b.* 1871. *d.* 1942. In 1897 he developed a projector he called the Bioscope, and after running into patent difficulties with Edison, he carried his business to England. In London, he took over the Warwick company, through which he produced newsreels, documentaries, and scientific films from 1902. The following year he formed his own firm, the Charles Urban Trading Company, and began exploring the potential of color cinematography, at first with a chemist, Edward R. Turner, then with a photographer, George Albert SMITH. In 1908 he formed with the latter the Natural Colour Kinematograph Company to exploit their invention, Kinemacolor, a three-color additive process. He produced a number of color shorts and feature films, notably *The Durbar at Delhi* (1911). In 1912 he came to the US to exploit the invention. He set up color studios on Long Island, N.Y., and in Los Angeles, and produced a number of color films, including *The Scarlet Letter* (1913). But his success was limited and his color system was soon abandoned. In the early 20s he directed a series of entertaining science features with such titles as *Science of the Soap Bubbles, From Egg to Chick,* and *Ancient Customs of Egypt* (all 1921).

Ure, Mary. Actress. *b.* Feb. 18, 1933, Glasgow. *d.* 1975. Leading lady of the British stage and infrequent films. She was nominated for an Oscar for her role in *Sons and Lovers.* Divorced from John OSBORNE, she married Robert SHAW. She died at 42, hours after opening a new London play, of an accidental mixture of alcohol and barbiturates.

FILMS: *Storm Over the Nile* 1955; *Windom's Way* 1958; *Look Back in Anger* 1959; *Sons and Lovers* (as Clara Dawes) 1960; *The Mind Benders* 1963; *The Luck of Ginger Coffey* (US/Can.) 1964; *Custer of the West* (as Mrs. Custer; US) 1968; *Where Eagles Dare* 1969; *A Reflection of Fear* 1973.

Urioste, Frank J. Editor specializing in action/adventure films, many of them visually arresting blockbusters of the 80s and 90s. Won Academy Award for work in *Die Hard*.

FILMS INCLUDE: *Whatever Happened to Aunt Alice* 1969; *The Grissom Gang* 1971; *Midway* 1976; *Damnation Alley* 1977; *The Boys in Company C* 1978; *Fast Break* 1979; *Loving*

Couples, The Jazz Singer 1980; *The Entity, Trenchcoat, Amityville 3-D* 1983; *Conan the Destroyer* 1984; *Red Sonja* 1985; *The Hitcher* 1986; *Robocop* 1987; *Die Hard, Road House* 1989; *Total Recall* 1990; *Basic Instinct* 1992; *Cliffhanger* 1993; *Tombstone* 1994.

US Film Service. See DOCUMENTARY.

USSR. See SOVIET UNION.

Ustinov, Peter. Actor, director, playwright, screenwriter, novelist. Born on Apr. 16, 1921, in London, to a journalist-father of Russian descent and an artist-mother of French descent. Trained for the stage at the London Theatre Studio, he made his acting debut at 17. He soon emerged as one of the most versatile talents of the British and American stage and screen: an accomplished actor, a literate author, a cultivated wit, and a delightful conversationalist and raconteur of TV talk shows. He won Academy Awards for his memorable characterizations in *Spartacus* (1960) and *Topkapi* (1964). He also won a TV Emmy for his portrayal of Dr. Johnson in 'The Life of Samuel Johnson.' Seen in several TV productions in the 80s. He portrayed Agatha Christie sleuth Hercule Poirot in three films. In 1971 he divorced actress Suzanne CLOUTIER after 17 years of marriage. Memoirs: *Dear Me* (1977).

FILMS (as actor): *Hullo Fame, Mein Kampf My Crimes* 1940; *One of Our Aircraft Is Missing, The Goose Steps Out* 1942; *The Way Ahead* (also co-sc.), *Carnival* (sc. only) 1944; *School for Secrets/Secret Flight* (dir., sc., co-prod. only) 1946; *Vice Versa* (dir., story, sc., co-prod. only) 1947; *Private Angelo* (also co-dir. with Michael Anderson, sc., co-prod.) 1949; *Odette* 1950; *Hotel Sahara, The Magic Box, Quo Vadis* (as Nero; US) 1951; *Le Plaisir/House of Pleasure* (narrator of English-language version only; Fr.) 1952; *The Egyptian* (US), *Beau Brummel* (as the Prince of Wales; US/UK) 1954; *We're No Angels* (US), *Lola Montès/The Sins of Lola Montes* (Fr./Ger.) 1955; *I Girovaghi* (It.) 1956; *Un Angel pasò por Brooklyn/The Man Who Wagged His Tail* (Sp./It.), *Les Espions* (Fr.) 1957; *School for Scoundrels* (adapt. only), *Spartacus* (US), *The Sundowners* (US/UK/Austral.) 1960; *Romanoff and Juliet/Dig That Juliet* (also prod., dir., sc., from own play; US) 1961; *Billy Budd* (as Captain Edward Fairfax Vere; also prod., dir., co-sc.) 1962; *La Donna nel Mondo/Women of the World* (doc.; narr. only; It.) 1963; *Peaches* (short; narr. only), *Topkapi* (US) 1964; *John Goldfarb Please Come Home* (US), *Lady L* (also dir., sc.; It./Fr./US) 1965; *The Comedians* (US/Fr.), *Blackbeard's Ghost* (as Captain Blackbeard; US), *Hot Millions* (also co-sc.) 1968; *Viva Max!* (US) 1969; *Hammersmith Is Out* (also dir.; US) 1972; *Robin Hood* (v/o, as Prince John; US) 1973; *One of Our Dinosaurs Is Missing* (US/UK) 1975; *Logan's Run* (US), *Treasure of Matecumbe* (US) 1976; *Un Taxi mauve/The Purple Taxi* (Fr./It./Ire.), *The Mouse and His Child* (v/o; US), *The Last Remake of Beau Geste* (US) 1977; *Doppio Delitto* (It./Fr.), *Death on the Nile* 1978; *Ashanti—Land of No Mercy* (US), *Players* (US), *Tarka the Otter* (narr.; US), *Nous maigrirons ensemble* (Fr.) 1979; *Grendel, Grendel, Grendel* (Austral.), *Charlie Chan and the Curse of the Dragon Queen* (US), *The Great Muppet Caper* (cameo; US) 1981; *Evil Under the Sun* (UK) 1982; *Memed My Hawk* (also dir., sc.; UK) 1983; *Peep and the Big Wide World* (short; UK), *Appointment with Death* (US) 1988; *La Revolution Francaise* (Fr.) 1989; *C'era un Castello con 40 Cani* (Fr.) 1990; *Lorenzo's Oil* (US) 1992.

utility man. The lowest-ranking member of a film production crew. He runs errands and carries out a variety of manual duties.

Uys, Jamie. Director, producer, screenwriter. Born Jacobus Johannes Uys in 1921 in Boksburg, South Africa. *ed.* Pretoria Univ. Leading South African filmmaker best known to Western audiences for the broad cultural comedy *The Gods Must Be Crazy*, which became the top foreign box-office success in US history. Sequel: *The Gods Must Be Crazy II*.

FILMS INCLUDE (as director, producer, screenwriter): *The Hellions* (act. only; UK) 1962; *Dingaka* 1965; *After You, Comrade* (also act.; S. Afr.) 1967; *Animals Are Beautiful People* (also phot., ed.) 1974; *The Gods Must Be Crazy* (also act., phot., ed.; Botsw.) 1981; *The Gods Must Be Crazy II* (dir., sc., exec. prod. only; US/Botsw.) 1989.

Vacano, Jost. Director of photography. Born on March 15, 1934, in Germany. Stylized, versatile cinematographer, strong on color and movement. Known for creating harsh, ingenious, futuristic worlds for Paul VERHOEVEN films *Robocop* and *Total Recall*. Working on US films since the mid-80s. Nominated for Academy Award for *Das Boot*.

FILMS INCLUDE: *Die Verlorene Ehre der Katharina Blum/The Lost Honor of Katherina Blum* (Ger.) 1975; *Soldaat van Oranje/Soldier of Orange* (Dutch) 1979; *Das Boot/The Boat* 1981; *Spetters* (Holl.) 1983; *The Neverending Story* 1984; *52 Pick-Up* 1986; *Robocop* 1987; *Rocket Gibraltar* 1988; *Total Recall* 1990.

Vaccaro, Brenda. Actress. Born on Nov. 18, 1939, in Brooklyn, N.Y. Leading lady of the American stage, screen, and television. Raised in Dallas, Tex., she began performing there in high school productions. After training at New York's Neighborhood Playhouse, she started her professional career in the early 60s and has since appeared in many stage productions, on Broadway, and on the road. She has also appeared on TV in numerous programs and commercials and in a number of telefilms. She was nominated for an Oscar as best supporting actress for her performance in *Jacqueline Susann's Once Is Not Enough* (1975). Since the 80s her screen appearances have been limited and of mixed quality.

FILMS: *Where It's At, Midnight Cowboy* 1969; *I Love My Wife* 1970; *Summertree, Going Home* 1971; *Jacqueline Susann's Once Is Not Enough* 1975; *Death Weekend/The House by the Lake* (Can.) 1976; *Airport '77* 1977; *Capricorn One* 1978; *Fast Charlie, The Moonbeam Rider* 1979; *The First Deadly Sin* 1980; *Zorro the Gay Blade* 1981; *Supergirl* 1984; *Water* (UK) 1985; *Heart of Midnight* 1988; *Cookie* 1989; *Ten Little Indians* 1990; *The Masque of the Red Death* 1991; *Love Affair* 1994; *The Mirror Has Two Faces* 1996.

Vadim, Roger. Director. Born Roger Vadim Plemiannikov, on Jan. 26, 1928, in Paris, of Ukrainian-French descent. A stage actor from the age of 16, he served his apprenticeship in films (1947–55) as assistant to director Marc ALLÉGRET and occasional screenwriter. Between 1953 and 1955 he also worked as a journalist for *Paris Match* and directed a number of TV programs. In 1956 he made a sensational debut as a motion picture director with *Et Dieu créa la Femme/And God Created Woman,* a daringly erotic film that challenged conventional views of romanticism. The film, in which Vadim presented the nude body of his young wife, Brigitte BARDOT, in unabashed CinemaScope and blushless Eastman Color, enjoyed a spectacular commercial success, particularly in America. Its prosperity at the box office helped pave the way for other young filmmakers into the mainstream of French cinema and thus made possible the emergence of the New Wave.

Vadim's subsequent films revealed him to be an accomplished technical craftsman with an eye for visual plushness and decorative elegance, but in content, his films have often been superficial and lacking in narrative strength. Sexual relations have been a recurrent theme in his films, the plots of which have often revolved around the unclad beauty of his succession of wives—Bardot, Annette Stroyberg, Jane FONDA—and mistresses. He has collaborated on most of his own scripts and occasionally on scripts of other directors and has appeared as an actor in such films as *The Testament of Orpheus* (1959), *Sweet and Sour* (1963), *Ciao Manhattan* (1973), and *Into the Night* (1985). Author: *Bardot, Deneuve and Fonda: My Life with the Three Most Beautiful Women in the World* (1986).

FILMS: *Et Dieu créa la Femme/And God Created Woman* (also co-sc.) 1956; *Sait-on jamais?/No Sun in Venice* (also sc.) 1957; *Les Bijoutiers du Clair de Lune/The Night Heaven Fell* (also co-sc.) 1958; *Les Liaisons dangereuses* (also co-sc.) 1959; *Et mourir de Plaisir/Blood and Roses* (also co-sc.) 1960; *La Bride sur le Cou/Please Not Now!* (also co-sc.) 1961; *Les Sept Péchés capitaux/Seven Capital Sins* ("Pride" episode; also co-sc.), *Le Repos du Guerrier/Love on a Pillow* (also co-sc.) 1962; *Le Vice et la Vertu/Vice and Virtue* (also prod., co-sc.), *Château en Suede/Nutty Naughty Chateau* (also co-sc.) 1963; *La Ronde/Circle of Love* (also co-adapt.) 1964; *La Curée/The Game Is Over* (also prod., co-sc.) 1966; *Histoires extraordinaires/Spirits of the Dead* ("Metzengerstein" episode; also co-sc.), *Barbarella* (also co-sc.) 1968; *Pretty Maids All in a Row* (US) 1971; *Hellé* (also story) 1972; *Don Juan 1973 ou si Don Juan était une Femme/Ms. Don Juan* (also story, co-sc.) 1973; *La Jeune Fille Assassinée/Charlotte* (also prod., sc., act.) 1974; *Une Femme fidèle* (also co-sc.) 1976; *Night Games* (US) 1980; *Rich and Famous* (act. only; US), *Hot Touch* (US) 1981; *Surprise Party* (US) 1982; *Come Back* (US) 1983; *Into the Night* (act. only; US) 1985; *And God Created Woman* (US) 1988; *The Mad Lover* (US) 1991.

Vajda, Ernest (Ernö). Screenwriter, playwright, novelist. *b.* 1887, Komarom, Hungary. *d.* 1954. The author of successful Broadway plays, a number of novels (which he sometimes signed Sidney Garrick), and an opera libretto, he also wrote, alone or in collaboration, stories and screenplays for numerous Hollywood films. His contribution was greatest in the late 20s and early 30s, when he collaborated on some of Hollywood's most sophisticated romantic comedies (and less frequently on dramas) with such directors as Harry D'ARRAST and Ernst LUBITSCH.

FILMS INCLUDE: *Grounds for Divorce* (play basis only) 1925; *The Crown of Lies* (story), *The Cat's Pajamas* (story), *You Never Know Women* (story) 1926; *Service for Ladies* (story), *The Woman on Trial* (play basis only, 'Confession'), *Serenade* (story, sc.) 1927; *A Night of Mystery* (sc.), *His Tiger Lady* (sc.), *Loves of an Actress* (story), *Manhattan Cocktail* (story) 1928; *Innocents of Paris* (adapt., dial.), *Marquis Preferred* (co-sc.), *The Love Parade* (adapt.) 1929; *Such Men Are Dangerous* (adapt., dial.), *Monte Carlo* (sc.) 1930; *Son of India* (sc., co-dial.), *The Guardsman* (co-sc., co-dial.), *Tonight or Never* (sc.), *The Smiling Lieutenant* (co-sc., co-dial.) 1931; *Smilin' Through* (co-sc.), *Broken Lullaby/The Man I Killed* (co-sc., co-dial.), *Payment Deferred* (co-sc.) 1932; *Reunion in Vienna* (co-sc.) 1933; *The Merry Widow* (co-sc.), *The Barretts of Wimpole Street* (co-sc.) 1934; *A Woman Rebels* (co-sc.), 1936; *Personal Property* (co-sc.), *The Great Garrick* (story, sc.) 1937; *Marie Antoinette* (co-sc.), *Dramatic School* (co-sc.) 1938; *He Stayed for Breakfast* (co-sc.) 1940; *They Dare Not Love* (co-sc.) 1941; *Stars and Stripes Forever* (story) 1952.

Vajda, Ladislao. Director. *b.* Lászlo Vajda, Aug. 18, 1906, Budapest. *d.* 1965. The son of screenwriter Ladislaus VAJDA, he entered Hungarian films in his teens and worked his way up from cutter and cameraman to director in the mid-30s. After directing two Italian films in 1941, he settled in Spain, where he directed many mediocre but commercially successful films. He occasionally also worked in England and Germany, gaining increasing recognition from the early 50s. He died of a heart attack while shooting *La Signora di Beirut,* starring Sarita Montiel.

FILMS INCLUDE: In the UK—*Where Is This Lady?* (co-dir. with Victor Hanbury) 1933. In Hungary—*Hello Budapest!* 1935; *Szensacio* (co-dir. with Steve Sekely), *The Three Spinsters, The Man Under the Bridge* 1936; *My Daughter Is Different, The Wife of General Ling* (UK), *The Borrowed Castle* 1937; *The Crucial Moment, Magda Is Expelled, Friday Rose* 1938. In Italy—*Giuliano de' Medici* 1940; *La Zia Smemorata* (also co-sc.) 1941. In Spain—*Se Vende un Palacio* 1943; *Dolce Lunas de Miel, Testament del Virrey* 1944; *Cinquo Lobitos* 1945; *Barrio* 1947; *Sin Uniforme* 1948. In the UK—*The Golden Madonna* 1949; *The Woman with No Name/Her Panelled Door* (also co-sc.) 1950. In Spain—*Ronda Española* 1951; *Doña Francisquitta* (also co-sc.) 1952; *Carne de Horca* 1953; *Aventuras del Barbero de Sevilla* 1954; *Marcelino Pan y Vino/Marcelino* (also co-sc.), *Tarde de Toros* 1955; *Mio Tio Jacinto* (also co-sc.) 1956; *Un Angel pasó por Brooklyn/Un Angelo è sceso a Brooklyn/The Man Who Wagged His Tail* (also co-adapt.; Sp./It.) 1957. In Germany—*Es geschah am hellichten Tag/It Happened in Broad Daylight* (also co-sc.; Ger./Switz.) 1958; *Ein Mann geht durch die Wand/The Man Who Walked Through the Wall* 1959; *Der Lügner, Die Schatten werden länger/The Shadows Grow Longer* (Ger./Switz.) 1961; *Das Feuerschiff* 1963.

Vajda, Ladislaus. Screenwriter. b. László Vajda, 1880(?), Budapest. *d.* 1933. Father of Ladislao VAJDA. The director of the Hungarian National Theater in Budapest, he also wrote occasional scripts for Michael Kertesz (later CURTIZ) and other Hungarian directors. In Germany from the mid-20s, he wrote screenplays, alone or in collaboration, for a number of important productions, for PABST and others.

FILMS INCLUDE: *Sodom und Gomorra* 1922; *Die Czardasfürstin, Die Liebe der Jeanne Ney/The Loves of Jeanne Ney* 1927; *Abwege* 1928; *Die Büchse der Pandora/Pandora's Box, Die weisse Hölle vom Piz Palü/The White Hell of Pitz Palu, Das Land ohne Frauen/Land Without Laughter* 1929; *Westfront 1918* 1930; *Die Dreigroschenoper/The Threepenny Opera, Kameradschaft, Die Liebesexpress* 1931; *Die Herrin von Atlantis* 1932.

Valdez, Luis. Director, playwright, screenwriter, actor. Born on July 26, 1940, in Delano, Calif. *ed.* San Jose State University (theater). Born to parents of Mexican descent, he spent his childhood as a migrant farm worker. After graduating from college, he worked with the San Francisco Mime Troupe, culminating in a cultural exchange trip to Cuba. Valdez returned to his hometown in 1965, where he joined Cesar Chavez's United Farmworkers and founded a Farmworker's Theater

Company, "El Teatro Campesino," in support of Delano's grape strike and boycott. He created short "actos" or scenarios that dramatized the plight of the farm laborers and short films of their plays. After several years with the company, he wrote and directed the musical drama *Zoot Suit* (1978), which he later filmed and released in 1981. The film garnered critical attention not only as a stylized musical but as a comment on the racist implications of the infamous Sleepy Lagoon case in 1942 Los Angeles. Valdez's second feature, *La Bamba*, a biography of Mexican-American rock star Richie Valens that depicted Hispanic culture in an American context, was successful in both mainstream and Hispanic markets.

FILMS INCLUDE (as director): *Which Way Is Up?* (act. only) 1977; *Zoot Suit* (also sc.) 1981; *La Bamba* (also sc.) 1987.

Valenti, Jack. Executive. Born on Sept. 5, 1921, in Houston, Tex. *ed.* U. of Houston; Harvard (M.B.A.). A combat pilot during WW II. He was heading an advertising and public relations business in Houston when he was appointed special advisor to President Johnson in 1963. In 1966 he was elected president of the Motion Picture Association of America. During his long-term office, which has extended into the 90s, the industry adopted the rating system and a more tolerant attitude in matters of self-censorship. In 1988, he was named the Motion Picture Pioneer of the Year.

Valentine, Joseph A. Director of photography. *b.* Giuseppe Valentino, July 24, 1900, New York City. *d.* 1949. In films from 1920, he was elevated to lighting cameraman in 1924. After years behind the camera on routine productions at Fox, he established a reputation in the 30s for high-quality "glamour" cinematography at Universal and was assigned to photograph many of the studio's expensive Deanna DURBIN vehicles. He later worked on three HITCHCOCK films and shared an Academy Award for the cinematography of Victor Fleming's *Joan of Arc* (1948).

FILMS INCLUDE: *My Husband's Wives, Curlytop* 1924; *The Scarlet Honeymoon* 1925; *The News Parade* (co-phot.) 1928; *Speakeasy* 1929; *Cheer Up and Smile, Soup to Nuts* 1930; *Night of Terror* 1933; *The Gay Deception, Remember Last Night* 1935; *The Unguarded Hour, The Moon's Our Home, Two in a Crowd, Three Smart Girls* 1936; *100 Men and a Girl* 1937; *Mad About Music, The Rage of Paris, That Certain Age* 1938; *First Love* 1939; *My Little Chickadee, It's a Date, The Boys from Syracuse, Spring Parade* 1940; *Nice Girl?, In the Navy, Hold That Ghost* (co-phot.), *Unfinished Business, Appointment for Love, The Wolf Man* 1941; *Saboteur, Eyes of the Underworld* 1942; *Shadow of a Doubt* 1943; *Guest Wife* 1945; *Tomorrow Is Forever, So Goes My Love, Heartbeat, Magnificent Doll* 1946; *Possessed* 1947; *Sleep My Love, Rope* (co-phot.), *Joan of Arc* (co-phot.) 1948; *Bride for Sale* 1949.

Valentino, Rudolph (also **Rodolph**). Actor. *b.* Rodolfo Alfonzo Raffaele Pierre Philibert Guglielmi, May 6, 1895, Castellaneta, Italy. *d.* 1926. The son of an army veterinarian, he was sent to a military academy at 13 but failed to qualify as officer material. When his application to enter a naval academy was turned down, he settled for agricultural studies. In 1912 he traveled to Paris in search of another vocation but instead found himself begging for coins on street corners. Late in 1913 he arrived in New York, certain of a bright future in the land of opportunity. He found room and board among Italian immigrants in Brooklyn and began the American phase of his life as a landscape gardener. He promptly lost his job and resorted to a succession of odd jobs, including dishwashing and table waiting. He got into trouble with the law and was booked by the New York police on a number of occasions on suspicions of petty theft and blackmail.

Drawn by the glitter of the Broadway district, Valentino became a taxi dancer and eventually began exhibiting his skills with various partners in dance halls and nightclubs. He broke into the big time when he replaced Clifton WEBB as the partner of Bonnie Glass, a popular dancer of the period. He later changed partners but not his bad luck. He was again arrested and spent several days in the Tombs, a notorious detention center. After being released, thanks to the intervention of NAZIMOVA, he left New York in the cast of a musical that folded in Ogden, Utah. He continued on his own to San Francisco, where he resumed his career as a dancer. Finally, in 1917, he arrived in Hollywood.

Valentino made the rounds of the casting offices and was soon landing extra and bit parts in films, mostly in the roles of an exotic dancer or a greasy villain. Gradually, his roles improved, but he was still a minor player by 1920. Around this time he married an actress named Jean Acker, but she locked him out of a hotel bridal suite on their wedding night and the marriage was never consummated. Valentino's big break came in 1921 when screenwriter June MATHIS, an influential figure at Metro, insisted that he be given the lead in *The Four Horsemen of the Apocalypse*. The film was a tremendous box-office hit and Valentino was catapulted into instant stardom. Within a couple of years he was a national phenomenon, a male star of unprecedented sensual appeal to women.

Darkly handsome and solidly built yet lithe, Valentino moved gracefully and gazed at his heroines with a mixture of passion and melancholy that sent chills down female spines. To the American woman he represented a symbol of mysterious, forbidden eroticism, a vicarious fulfillment of dreams of illicit love and inhibited passions. But male audiences found his acting ludicrous, his manner foppish, and his screen character effeminate. Nevertheless, the Valentino craze reached new heights with *The Sheik* (1921), at Paramount. During the film's exhibition women fainted in the aisles and Arab motifs began to infiltrate fashions and interior design.

Valentino scored sensationally at the box office with *Blood and Sand* (1922) and *Monsieur Beaucaire* (1924), and in 1923 his small volume of mushy poetry, *Day Dreams*, sold hundreds of thousands of copies, but his career was beginning to take a downturn. In contrast to his strong male image on the screen, Valentino played the weaker-sex role in relation to the women in his life. His ambitious second wife, actress (one film, *When Love Grows Cold*, in 1925) and set designer Natasha Rambova (*b.* Winifred Shaunessy, Jan. 19, 1897; *d.* 1969), took charge of his career and misguided it pitiably. Under her guidance, the Valentino screen image became more and more effeminate. Her constant interference strained his relationship with studio executives to the point that her absence from the set became a condition to his further employment. To add to his troubles, he was arrested on a charge of bigamy for having married Rambova before the dissolution of his first marriage became final. Just when he seemed to be recovering his popularity with two successful United Artists productions, *The Eagle* (1925) and *The Son of the Sheik* (1926), Valentino was blasted in a strongly worded editorial in the Chicago *Tribune*, headlined "Pink Powder Puff." Lamented the writer: "When will we be rid of all these effeminate youths, pomaded, powdered, bejeweled and bedizened, in the image of Rudy—that painted pansy?"

A few months later he was taken to a New York hospital with a perforated ulcer. His sudden death, on August 23, 1926, at the age of 31, brought on a wave of mass hysteria among female fans. Thousands of women lined the streets during his funeral, causing a near riot. Rumors began spreading that he had been poisoned by a discarded mistress, and a Valentino cult sprang up that had sinister necrophilic overtones. Years after his death, Valentino fan clubs around the country were as active in glorifying their hero as they has been during the peak of his career. Every year on the anniversary of his death, a mysterious woman in black has been seen laying a wreath of flowers on his grave, adding a sense of drama to the life and death of a screen legend. Several Valentino biographies have since been published, including one by Rambova. A brief biography of Valentino, "Adagio Dancer," was included in John Dos Passos's famous trilogy *U.S.A.* (1936). The star was portrayed by Anthony Dexter in a film biography in 1951 and by Rudolf Nureyev in another in 1977. In 1978 a section of Irving Boulevard in Hollywood was renamed Rudolph Valentino Street.

FILMS: *Alimony, A Society Sensation, All Night* 1918; *The Delicious Little Devil, A Rogue's Romance, The Home Breaker, Virtuous Sinners, The Big Little Person, Out of Luck, Eyes of Youth* 1919; *The Married Virgin/Frivolous Wives, An Adventuress, The Cheater, Passion's Playground, Once to Every Woman, Stolen Moments, The Wonderful Chance* 1920; *The Four Horsemen of the Apocalypse, Uncharted Seas, The Conquering Power, Camille* (as Armand Duval), *The Sheik* 1921; *Moran of the Lady Letty, Beyond the Rocks, The Isle of Love* (revised version of *An Adventuress,* padding Valentino's small 1920 role with out-takes), *Blood and Sand, The Young Rajah* 1922; *Monsieur Beaucaire* (title role), *A Sainted Devil* 1924; *Cobra, The Eagle* 1925; *The Son of the Sheik* 1926.

Vallee, Rudy. Singer, actor. *b.* Hubert Prior Vallee, July 28, 1901, at Island Point, Vt. *d.* 1986. He intended to become a pharmacist, like his father, but changed his mind when he discovered the saxophone. While attending the University of Maine, he organized his own band. He continued playing the saxophone in local night spots when he transferred to Yale, and after graduation he formed his own band, The Connecticut Yankees. He soon gained popularity as a vocalist on radio, in nightclubs, and on the stage. He was the first pop singer to be termed a "crooner," the first to induce mass swooning in audiences, young and old. One of his most successful songs was "The Vagabond Lover," the title of which stuck for a while as his nickname and was chosen for the title of his first feature film in 1929. He starred in many light romantic films of the 30s, as well as in a number of shorts, often seen clutching his trademark, a megaphone. Later as a character actor he specialized in caricaturing stuffy, eccentric millionaires, notably in *The Palm Beach Story*. In the early 70s he failed in his bid to have the Los Angeles street on which he lived renamed Rue de Vallee. His third wife (1943–44) was actress Jane GREER. Author: *Let the Chips Fall* (1975).

FEATURE FILMS: *The Vagabond Lover, Glorifying the American Girl* (cameo as himself) 1929; *International House* 1933; *George White's Scandals* 1934; *Sweet Music* 1935; *Gold Diggers in Paris* 1938; *Second Fiddle* 1939; *Time Out for Rhythm, Too Many Blondes* 1941; *The Palm Beach Story* 1942; *Happy Go Lucky* 1943; *It's in the Bag, Man Alive* 1945; *People Are Funny, The Fabulous Suzanne* 1946; *The Bachelor and the Bobby-Soxer, Mad Wednesday* 1947; *I Remember Mama, So This Is New York, My Dear Secretary, Unfaithfully Yours* 1948; *Mother Is a Freshman, The Beautiful Blonde from Bashful Bend, Father Was a Fullback* 1949; *The Admiral Was a Lady* 1950; *Ricochet Romance* 1954; *Gentlemen Marry Brunettes* 1955; *The Helen Morgan Story* 1957; *How to Succeed in Business Without Really Trying* 1967; *Live a Little Love a Little, The Night They Raided Minsky's* (narrator only) 1968; *The Phynx* (cameo) 1970; *Sunburst* 1975; *Won Ton Ton—The Dog Who Saved Hollywood* 1976.

Valli, Alida. Actress. Born Alida Maria Altenburger, on May 3, 1921, in Pola, Italy, the daughter of a journalist of Austrian descent and an Italian mother. After some training at Rome's Centro Sperimentale di Cinematografia, she entered films at 15. Although she appeared mainly in routine productions, she soon became one of the Italian screen's leading young stars, thanks to her unusual beauty and natural charm. In 1944 she married pianist-composer Oscar de Mejo (they have since separated) and temporarily retired from the screen rather than appear in Fascist propaganda films. Resuming her work after the war, she came to Hollywood on a contract with David O. Selznick but failed to impress in her few American films. With England's *The Third Man* (1949) she began an international career that saw her gradually mature from romantic roles to strongly etched character parts. Her career suffered a temporary setback as a result of her involvement in 1954 in a drug, sex, and murder scandal of the "dolce vita" variety that rocked Italy for a couple of years. She was sometimes billed simply as Valli.

FILMS INCLUDE: *I Due Sergenti* 1936; *L'Ultima Nemica, Sono stato io* 1937; *Ma l'Amor mio non muore, La Casa del Peccato* 1938; *Assenza ingiustificata, Manon Lescaut* (title role) 1939; *Oltre l'Amore* 1940; *Piccolo Mondo antico, L'Amante segreta, Ore 9—Lezione di Chimica/Schoolgirl Diary* 1941; *Le Due Orfanelle/The Two Orphans, Noi Vivi/Addio Kira, I Pagliacci/ Laugh Pagliacci* 1942; *T'amerò sempre, Apparizione* 1943; *La Vita ricomincia/Life Begins Anew, Il Canto della Vita* 1945; *Eugenia Grandet* (title role) 1946; *The Paradine Case* (US), *The Miracle of the Bells* (US) 1948; *The Third Man* (UK) 1949; *The White Tower* (US), *Walk Softly Stranger* (US) 1950; *Les Miracles n'ont lieu qu'une fois* (Fr./It.), *Ultimo Incontro* 1951; *Les Amants de Tolède/The Lovers of Toledo* (Fr./It./Sp.), *Siamo Donne, La Mano dello Straniero/The Stranger's Hand* (It./UK) 1953; *Senso/The Wanton Contessa* 1954; *Il Grido/The Outcry* 1957; *La Diga sul Pacifico/This Angry Age/The Sea Wall, Les Bijoutiers du Clair de Lune/The Night Heaven Fell* (Fr./It.) 1958; *Les Yeux sans Visage/The Horror Chamber of Dr. Faustus* (Fr.), *Le Dialogue des Carmélites* (Fr.) 1960; *Une aussi Longue Absence/The Long Absence* (Fr./It.) 1961; *Il Disordine/Disorder, The Happy Thieves* (US), *Ophélia* (Fr.) 1962; *El Valle de las Espadas/The Castilian* (Sp./US) 1963; *Edipo Re/Oedipus Rex* 1967; *Le Champignon* (Fr.), *La Strategia del Ragno/The Spider's Stratagem* 1970; *La Prima Notte di Quiete* 1972; *Tendre Dracula/Tender Dracula* (Fr.) 1974; *Ce Cher Victor* (Fr.) 1975; *1900, Le Jeu de Solitaire* (Fr.) 1976; *The Cassandra Crossing* (US), *Berlinguer ti voglio bene, Suspiria* 1977; *Un Cuore semplice, L'Anti Cristo/The Tempter* 1978; *La Luna/Luna* (Fr.), *Inferno* 1979; *Aquella Casa En Las Afueras* (Sp.), *Puppenspiel mit toten Augen* (Ger./It./Sp.) 1980; *Aspern* 1982; *Sogni Mostruosamente Proibiti* (It.) 1983; *Segreti Segreti* (It.) 1984; *Hitchcock, Il Brivido del Genio* (It.) 1985; *Le Jupon rouge* (Fr.) 1987; *A notre regrettable epoux* (Fr.) 1988.

Vallone, Raf. Actor. Born Raffaele Vallone, on Feb. 17, 1917, in Tropea, Italy. *ed.* U. of Turin. A former soccer player, sports reporter, and music and film critic, he entered Italian films in the late 40s and immediately established himself as one of the country's top leading men. His sturdy physique and virile good looks soon led to an international starring career that has included some Hollywood films. In later years, his character roles included the sympathetic pope in *The Godfather Part III* (1990). He is married to a former co-star, Elena Varzi (*b.* 1920, Rome).

FILMS INCLUDE: *Riso Amaro/Bitter Rice* 1948; *Non ç'è Pace tra gli Ulivi/No Peace Under the Olive Tree, Cuori senza Frontiere/The White Line, Il Camino della Speranza/The Path of*

Hope 1950; *Il Cristo Proibito/Strange Deception, Anna* 1951; *Roma Ore 11/Rome 11 O'Clock, Camicie Rosse/Anita Garibaldi* (as Giuseppe Garibaldi) 1952; *Destinées/Daughters of Destiny* ("Lysistrata" episode; Fr./It.), *Gli Eroi della Domenica, Thérèse Raquin/The Adulteress* (Fr.) 1953; *Obsession* (Fr.) 1954; *Il Segno di Venere/The Sign of Venus, Andrea Chenier* (title role) 1955; *Les Possédées/Passionate Summer* 1956; *Rose Bernd/The Sins of Rose Bernd* (Ger.), *Guendalina* 1957; *La Venganza/Vengeance* (Sp.), *La Violetera* (Sp.), *Le Piège/No Escape* (Fr.) 1958; *La Ciociara/Two Women* 1960; *El Cid* (US/It.) 1961; *Vu du Pont/A View from the Bridge* (Fr./It.), *Phaedra* (Gr./US) 1962; *The Cardinal* (US) 1963; *The Secret Invasion* (US) 1964; *Harlow* (Carroll Baker version; US) 1965; *Nevada Smith* (US) 1966; *The Italian Job* (UK) 1969; *The Kremlin Letter* (US), *Cannon for Cordoba* (US) 1970; *A Gunfight* (US) 1971; *Histoire de l'Oeil* (Belg./It.) 1974; *Rosebud* (US), *The Human Factor* (US) 1975; *L'Avvocato del Diavolo/The Devil's Advocate, The Other Side of Midnight* (US) 1977; *The Greek Tycoon* (US) 1978; *An Almost Perfect Affair, Retour à Marseilles* (Fr.), *Omar Mukhtar—Lion of the Desert* (UK), *A Time to Die* (US) 1979; *Le Pouvoir du Mal/Power of Evil* (Fr.) 1985; *The Godfather Part III* (US), *La Leyenda del Cura Bargota* (It.) 1990.

vamp. A seductive, often unscrupulous woman; a femme fatale. The term came into wide use in the US and abroad after Theda BARA played such a character in the film *A Fool There Was* (1914), which was based on Rudyard Kipling's *The Vampire.* But the type had been introduced to the screen several years earlier in the Danish film *Vampirish Dance* (1911). As a screen character, the vamp remained popular through the mid-20s.

Van Cleef, Lee. Actor. *b.* Jan. 9, 1925, in Somerville, N.J. *d.* 1989. After WW II service in the Navy and a brief stint as an accountant, he joined a little theater group and went on from there into films. His sharp features and narrow steely eyes made him an ideal villain and he was typecast as a mean evildoer in numerous Hollywood Westerns and action pictures. In the mid-60s he suddenly soared to stardom as the cruel hero of some top-box-office spaghetti Westerns. He starred as a Ninja martial-arts master in the TV series 'The Master' in 1984.

FILMS INCLUDE: *High Noon, Untamed Frontier* 1952; *Kansas City Confidential, Arena, Vice Squad* 1953; *Rails Into Laramie* 1954, *The Big Combo, A Man Alone* 1955; *The Conqueror, Tribute to a Bad Man, Pardners* 1956; *China Gate, Gunfight at the O.K. Corral, The Tin Star* 1957; *The Young Lions, The Bravados* 1958; *Ride Lonesome* 1959; *Posse from Hell* 1961; *How the West Was Won, The Man Who Shot Liberty Valance* 1962; *Per qualche Dollaro in Più/For a Few Dollars More* (It./Sp./Ger.), *Il Buono il Brutto il Cattivo/The Good the Bad and the Ugly* (It.) 1966; *Da Uomo a Uomo/Death Rides a Horse* (It.), *I Giorni dell'Ira/Day of Anger* (It./Ger.) 1967; *La Resa dei Conti/The Big Gundown* (It.) 1968; *Ehi Amico... C'é Sabata hai chiuso/Sabata* (It.) 1969; *Barquero, El Condor* 1970; *Captain Apache* (US/Sp.), *E Tornato Sabata/Return of Sabata* (It.) 1971; *The Magnificent Seven Ride* 1972; *Johnny le Fligueur/Mean Frank and Crazy Tony* (Fr./It.) 1973; *Take a Hard Ride* 1975; *The Stranger and the Gunfighter, Crime Boss* 1976; *Killers* 1977; *The Rip-Off* 1978; *The Hard Way* (Ire.) 1979; *The Octagon* 1980; *Escape from New York* 1981; *The Squeeze* 1982; *Geheimcode Wildganse/Codename: Wildgeese* (Ger.), *Jungle Raiders* 1984; *Killing Machine* 1985; *Armed Response* 1986; *The Heist, Speed Zone* 1988; *Thieves of Fortune* 1989.

Van Damme, Jean-Claude. Actor. Born Jean-Claude Van Varenbeerg in 1961, in Brussels, Belgium. Powerfully built star of popular Hollywood action films. A former European karate champion, he began studying martial arts at 11 and soon won the European Professional Karate Association's middleweight championship. Profiting from his black belt title, he ran the California Gym in Brussels before coming to the US in 1981. After a series of odd jobs as a limo driver, carpet layer, bouncer, and trainer, he got his first break in a bit part opposite fellow action star Chuck Norris in *Missing in Action* (1984). His well-muscled physique and martial arts skills led to a contract with Cannon Films. Under the guidance of Menahem Golan, he starred in a string of low budget action-adventure films, notably *Bloodsport* (1988), where he played American Ninja Frank Dux. These movies proved his marketability as a leading movie hero and led to his nickname, "Muscles from Brussels."

FILMS INCLUDE: *Missing in Action* 1984; *Rue Barbar, No Retreat, No Surrender* 1986; *Bloodsport, Black Eagle* 1988; *Cyborg, Kickboxer* (also co-story), *Marquis* 1989; *Death Warrant, Lionheart* (also co-story) 1990; *Double Impact* (also co-prod., co-story) 1991; *Universal Soldier, Crossing the Line, Kidd Kickboxer* 1992; *Hard Target* 1993; *Timecop* 1994; *Sudden Death* 1995; *The Quest* (also dir.), *Maximum Risk* 1996; *Double Team* 1997.

Van Devere, Trish. Actress. Born Patricia Dressel, on Mar. 9, 1945, in Englewood Cliffs, N.J. *ed.* Ohio Wesleyan. Leading lady of the American stage, TV, and screen. Married to George C. SCOTT, with whom she co-starred in several productions of the 70s.

FILMS: *The Landlord, Where's Poppa?* 1970; *The Last Run* 1971; *One Is a Lonely Number* 1972; *Harry in Your Pocket, The Day of the Dolphin* 1973; *The Savage Is Loose* 1974; *Movie Movie* 1978; *The Changeling* 1979; *The Hearse* 1980; *Hollywood Vice Squad* 1986; *Messenger of Death* 1988.

Van Doren, Mamie. Actress. Born Joan Lucille Olander, on Feb. 6, 1931, in Rowena, S.D. Platinum blonde sexpot of Hollywood B features; a poor man's Marilyn Monroe. A former secretary, she began her career as a band singer and entered films after a warm-up period in stock. Ever glamorous, she still attends public functions in various states of undress. Author: *Playing the Field* (1987).

FILMS INCLUDE: *The All American* 1953; *Forbidden, Yankee Pasha* 1954; *Ain't Misbehavin', Running Wild* 1955; *The Second Greatest Sex* 1956; *Untamed Youth* 1957; *Teacher's Pet, High School Confidential* 1958; *Guns Girls and Gangsters, The Beat Generation, Girls Town, Born Reckless, The Big Operator* 1959; *Sex Kittens Go to College, The Private Lives of Adam and Eve, College Confidential* 1960; *The Candidate, Three Nuts in Search of a Bolt* 1964; *The Navy vs. the Night Monsters, Las Vegas Hillbillies* 1966; *You've Got to Be Smart* 1967; *Voyage to the Planet of the Prehistoric Women* 1968; *Free Ride* 1985.

Van Dyke, Dick. Actor. Born on Dec. 13, 1925, in West Plains, Mo. After WW II service with the Air Force, during which he did some radio announcing, he ran a small advertising agency that soon folded. He then joined with one Phil Erickson in a nightclub pantomime act billed as "The Merry Mutes." Work on local TV stations eventually led to network programs and to stardom in both the Broadway and Hollywood versions of the musical 'Bye Bye Birdie.' A lithe, likable, multitalented entertainer, he gained popularity as the light leading man of subsequent films and the highly successful 'Dick Van Dyke Show,' for which he won TV's Emmy Award three successive years (1964–66). Since then, he has appeared in numerous TV programs and series. His brother Jerry Van Dyke (*b.* 1931) is also in films and on TV.

FILMS: *Bye Bye Birdie* 1963; *What a Way to Go!, Mary Poppins* 1964; *The Art of Love* 1965; *Lt. Robinson Crusoe USN* 1966; *Divorce American Style, Fitzwilly* 1967; *Never a Dull*

Moment, Chitty Chitty Bang Bang (UK) 1968; *Some Kind of a Nut, The Comic* 1969; *Cold Turkey* 1971; *The Runner Stumbles* 1979; *Dick Tracy* 1990.

Van Dyke, Willard. Documentary director. *b.* Dec. 5, 1906, Denver, Colo. *d.* 1986. *ed.* U. of California. A former bank clerk, insurance salesman, X-ray technician, and still photographer, he began his film career as one of the three cameramen on Pare Lorentz's famous documentary *The River* (1937). Two years later he made his debut as director, collaborating with Ralph Steiner on *The City,* a documentary on urban planning. During WW II he was a producer with the Office of War Information's Overseas Motion Picture Bureau. His *San Francisco* (1945) was the official film on the foundation of the United Nations. After the war he made many documentaries for TV, the USIA, industry, and various foundations. From 1965 to 1973 he was the director of the film department of the Museum of Modern Art. He also served as the vice president of the International Federation of Film Archives.

FILMS (as director): *The City* (co-dir., co-prod., co-phot. with Ralph Steiner) 1939; *Valley Town* (also co-sc.), *The Children Must Learn* (also sc.), *Sarah Lawrence* 1940; *To Hear Your Banjo Play, Tall Tales* 1941; *The Bridge* 1942; *Oswego, Steeltown* 1943; *Pacific Northwest* (also co-phot.) 1944; *San Francisco* (official film on the establishment of the UN) 1945; *Journey Into Medicine* 1946; *The Photographer* 1947; *This Charming Couple, Mount Vernon* 1949; *Years of Change* 1950; *New York University* 1952; *Working and Playing to Health, There Is a Season, Recollections of Boyhood, Cabos Blancos* (co-dir. with Angel Rivera), *Excursion House* 1954; *Life of the Molds* 1957; *Skyscraper* (co-dir. with Shirley Clarke), *Tiger Hunt in Assam, Mountains of the Moon* 1958; *Land of White Alice, The Procession* 1959; *Ireland—the Tear and the Smile, Sweden* 1960; *So That Men Are Free, Harvest* 1962; *Depressed Area* 1963; *Rice* (co-dir. with Wheaton Galentine), *Frontiers of News* (also phot.) 1964; *Pop Buell—Hoosier Farmer in Laos, Taming the Mekong, The Farmer—Feast or Famine* (co-dir. with Roger Barlow), *Frontline Cameras 1935–1965* (also prod.) 1965; *Shape of Films to Come* 1968; *Conversations with Willard Van Dyke* (doc.; act. only) 1981; *He Stands in the Desert Counting the Seconds of His Life* (act. only) 1985.

Van Dyke, W. S. ("Woody"). Director. *b.* William S. Van Dyke II, 1889, Seattle. *d.* 1943. Orphaned from his father before birth, he accompanied his actress mother on her travels and began acting in vaudeville and stock while still a child. He entered films as one of D. W. GRIFFITH's six assistants on *Intolerance* (1916) and the following year began a long and prolific career as a screen director. During the 20s he directed many Westerns and later in his career he returned often to the outdoors. He gained prominence in the late 20s when he successfully took over the direction of *White Shadows of the South Seas* from Robert FLAHERTY. In the 30s he developed into one of MGM's most reliable and versatile directors. His facility and reputation for casual, sometimes sloppy handling of his films earned him the nickname "One Shot Woody" but also resulted in spontaneous performances from his actors. A sure-handed director and skillful technician, he rarely overshot material and often completed his films ahead of schedule. His films were rarely important but frequently entertaining and commercially successful.

FILMS: *The Land of Long Shadows, The Range Boss, Open Places, Men of the Desert, Gift o' Gab* 1917; *The Lady of the Dugout* 1918; *The Hawk's Trail* (serial), *Daredevil Jack* (serial) 1920; *Double Adventure* (serial), *The Avenging Arrow* (serial; co-dir. with William J. Bowman) 1921; *White Eagle* (serial), *According to Hoyle, The Boss of Camp 4, Forget-Me-Not* 1922; *The Little Girl Next Door, You Are in Danger, The Destroying Angel, The Miracle Makers* 1923; *Loving Lies, The Beautiful Sinner, Half-a-Dollar Bill, Winner Take All, The Battling Fool, Gold Heels* 1924; *Barriers Burned Away, Hearts and Spurs, The Trail Rider, Ranger of the Big Pines, Timber Wolf, The Desert's Price* 1925; *The Gentle Cyclone, War Paint* 1926; *Winners of the Wilderness, California, The Heart of the Yukon, Eyes of the Totem, Spoilers of the West, Foreign Devils* 1927; *Wyoming* (also story), *Under the Black Eagle, White Shadows of the South Seas* 1928; *The Pagan* 1929; *Trader Horn, Never the Twain Shall Meet, Guilty Hands, The Cuban Love Song* 1931; *Tarzan the Ape Man, Night Court* 1932; *Penthouse, The Prizefighter and the Lady* (also prod.), *Eskimo* 1933; *Laughing Boy, Manhattan Melodrama, The Thin Man, Hide-Out, Forsaking All Others* 1934; *Naughty Marietta, I Live My Life* 1935; *Rose Marie, San Francisco* (also co-prod.), *His Brother's Wife* (also co-prod.), *The Devil Is a Sissy, Love on the Run, After the Thin Man* 1936; *Personal Property, They Gave Him a Gun, Rosalie* 1937; *Marie Antoinette, Sweethearts* 1938; *Stand Up and Fight, It's a Wonderful World, Andy Hardy Gets Spring Fever, Another Thin Man* 1939; *I Take This Woman, I Love You Again, Bitter Sweet* 1940; *Rage in Heaven, Shadow of the Thin Man, The Feminine Touch* 1941; *Dr. Kildare's Victory, I Married an Angel, Cairo, Journey for Margaret* 1942.

Vanel, Charles. Actor. *b.* Aug. 21, 1892, in Rennes, France. *d.* 1989. On the Paris stage from age 16, he entered films in 1912 and went on to play key character roles in nearly 200 productions in France and elsewhere. A disciplined actor with a powerful screen presence, he often portrayed tragic roles. Memorable in such films as *The Wages of Fear* and *Les Diaboliques.* He also directed two films, *Dans la Nuit* (1929) and *Le Coup de Minuit* (1935). A special tribute was paid him at the Cannes Festival of 1970.

FILMS INCLUDE: *Jim Crow* 1912; *Miarka la Fille à l'Ourse/Miarka the Daughter of the Bear* 1920; *La Maison du Mystère* 1922; *Tempêtes* 1923; *Pêcheur d'Islande* 1924; *Le Réveil, Ame d'Artiste* 1925; *Nitchevo* 1926; *La Proie du Vent, Die weisse Sklavin* (Ger.; and French-language version, *L'Esclave blanche*) 1927; *Feu!, Waterloo* (as Napoleon; Ger.) 1928; *Dans la Nuit* (also dir.) 1929; *Accusée levez-vous* 1930; *Maison de Danses, L'Arlésienne* 1931; *Faubourg Montmartre, Le Croix de Bois* 1932; *Les Misérables* (as Javert), *Le Grand Jeu* 1934; *L'Equipage/Flight Into Darkness, Le Coup de Minuit* (also dir.) 1935; *Port-Arthur/I Give My Life, Jenny, La Belle Equipe/They Were Five, Michel Strogoff* 1936; *Abus de Confiance/Abused Confidence, L'Occident* 1937; *Les Pirates du Rail, La Femme du Bout du Monde* 1938; *Carrefour/ Crossroads, La Brigade sauvage/Savage Brigade* 1939; *L'Or de Cristobal, Le Diamant noir* 1940; *La Loi du Nord* (release delayed) 1942; *Le Ciel est à vous/The Woman Who Dared* 1944; *Le Diable souffle* 1947; *In Nome della Legge/Mafia* (It.) 1949; *Le Salaire de la Peur/The Wages of Fear* 1953; *Si Versailles m'était conté/Royal Affairs in Versailles* (as Comte de Vergennes), *L'Affaire Maurizius/On Trial* 1954; *Les Diaboliques/Diabolique, To Catch a Thief* (US) 1955; *La Mort en ce Jardin/Gina* (Fr./Mex.) 1956; *Le Feu aux Poudres* 1957; *Rafles sur la Ville/Sinners of Paris, Le Piège/No Escape* 1958; *Pêcheur d'Islande* (remake) 1959; *La Vérité/The Truth* 1960; *L'Aîné des Ferchaux* 1962; *La Steppa/The Steppe* (It./Fr.), *Rififi à Tokyo/Rififi in Tokyo, Symphonie pour un Massacre/Symphony for a Massacre* 1963; *Le Chant du Monde* 1965; *Un Homme de trop/Shock Troops* 1967; *Ballade pour un Chien* 1969; *Ils* 1970; *La più Bella Serata della mia Vita* (It.) 1972; *Sept morts sur Ordonnance, Il Contesto* (It.) 1975; *Cadaveri eccelenti/Illustrious Corpses/The Context* (It.), *Es herrscht Ruhe im Land/Calm Prevails Over the*

Country (Ger.), *Nuit d'Or* 1976; *Alice ou la Dernière Fugue* 1977; *Ne pleure pas* 1978; *La Puce et le Prive* (Fr.) 1979; *Three Brothers* (It.) 1980.

Van Eyck, Peter. Actor. *b.* Götz von Eick, July 16, 1913, Steinwehr, Germany. *d.* 1969. A musician, he came to the US in 1932 and worked as an arranger for Irving Berlin and others. A tall, handsome actor, he made his screen acting debut in 1943, the year he became an American citizen. He played Nazis, in and out of uniform, in several wartime Hollywood productions, then continued his career in Europe, where he became a busy leading man in French and German films.

FILMS INCLUDE: *The Moon Is Down, Five Graves to Cairo* 1943; *The Impostor, Address Unknown* 1944; *The Desert Fox* 1951; *Le Salaire de la Peur/The Wages of Fear* (Fr./It.), *Alerte au Sud* (Fr.), *La Chair et le Diable/Flesh and Desire* (Fr./It.), *Singlehanded/Sailor of the King* (UK) 1953; *Le Grand Jeu* (Fr.), *Night People* 1954; *Mr. Arkadin/Confidential Report* (Sp./Switz.), *A Bullet for Joey, Jump Into Hell, Sophie et le Crime/The Girl on the Third Floor* (Fr.) 1955; *The Rawhide Years, Run for the Sun, Attack!* 1956; *Le Feu aux Poudres* (Fr.), *Retour de Manivelle/There's Always a Price Tag* (Fr.), *Der gläserne Turm/The Glass Tower* (Ger.) 1957; *Das Mädchen Rosemarie/Rosemary* (Ger.), *The Snorkel* (UK) 1958; *Labyrinth* (Ger.), *Der Rest ist Schweigen/The Rest Is Silence* (Ger.) 1959; *Die tausend Augen des Dr. Mabuse/The 1000 Eyes of Dr. Mabuse* (Ger./Fr./It.), *Foxhole in Cairo* (UK) 1960; *La Fête espagnole/No Time for Ecstasy* (Fr.) 1961; *Ein Toter sucht seinen Mörder/Vengeance/The Brain* (Ger./UK), *The Longest Day* 1962; *Das grosse Liebesspiel/And So to Bed* (Ger./Aus.), *Station Six—Sahara* (UK/Ger.) 1963; *The Spy Who Came in from the Cold* (UK), *Guerre secrète/The Dirty Game* (Fr./It./Ger.) 1965; *Shalako* (UK) 1968; *The Bridge at Remagen* 1969.

Van Fleet, Jo. Actress. Born on Dec. 30, 1919, in Oakland, Calif. *ed.* U. of the Pacific. Trained for the stage at New York City's Neighborhood Playhouse, she made her professional debut in 1944 and her first New York appearance in 1946. She rose to prominence on Broadway, winning a number of awards for her strong character portrayals. She won the best supporting actress Academy Award for her very first screen role, as James Dean's brothel-madam mother in *East of Eden* (1955). She appeared sporadically but prominently in other films, achieving her best performances in portraying women much older than herself. She is a member of the Actors Studio.

FILMS: *East of Eden* (as Kate), *The Rose Tattoo, I'll Cry Tomorrow* 1955; *The King and Four Queens* 1956; *Gunfight at the O.K. Corral* 1957; *La Diga sul Pacifico/This Angry Age/The Sea Wall* (It./Fr.) 1958; *Wild River* 1960; *Cool Hand Luke* 1967; *I Love You Alice B. Toklas!* 1968; *80 Steps to Jonah* 1969; *The Gang That Couldn't Shoot Straight* 1971; *Le Locataire/The Tenant* (Fr.) 1976.

Vangelis. Composer, conductor. Born Vangelis Papathanassiou on March 23, 1943 in Athens, Greece. Specialist in synthesizer-driven music scores. He began playing the piano at 4 and performed his own compositions at 6. He received his first electronic instrument, an organ, at 14 and by the late 1960s moved to Paris, where he recorded an album *Terra* and wrote music scores for French television documentaries. In 1974 he moved to London and developed his art as an electronic musician, eschewing self-consciously futuristic computer music for atmospheric melodies on the keyboards. He enjoyed his greatest popular success to date with *Chariots of Fire* (1981), for which he won an Academy Award.

FILMS INCLUDE: *Salut, Jerusalem* (Fr.) 1972; *Amore* (Fr.) 1973; *No Oyes Ladrar los Perros?* 1975; *Chariots of Fire, Antarctica* 1981; *Blade Runner, Missing, Pablo Picasso, The Year of Living Dangerously* 1982; *Wonders of Life* 1983; *The Bounty, Sauvage et Beau* 1984; *Nosferatu a Venezia* (Fr.), *Someone to Watch Over Me* (song composer only) 1987; *Le Diner des Bustes* (short; Fr.) 1988; *Francesco, Russicum* 1989; *Bitter Moon, Starwatcher, 1492: The Conquest of Paradise* 1992; *Bitter Moon* 1994.

Van Heusen, James ("Jimmy"). Composer, songwriter. *b.* Edward Chester Babcock, Jan. 26, 1913, Syracuse, N.Y. *d.* 1990. He began his working career at 15, playing the piano for a music publishing house. Later, while attending Syracuse University, where he studied piano and voice, he worked as an announcer on a local radio station. In 1940 he was signed to a Paramount contract, and he went on to compose some scores and many songs, mostly in collaboration with lyricist Johnny BURKE and later Sammy CAHN. Some of his best songs were written for Bing Crosby and Frank Sinatra. He won Academy Awards for the songs 'Swinging on a Star' in *Going My Way* (1944), 'All the Way' in *The Joker Is Wild* (1957), 'High Hopes' in *A Hole in the Head* (1959), and 'Call Me Irresponsible' in *Papa's Delicate Condition* (1963). He headed his own music-publishing company. During WW II, while composing for films, he doubled as a test pilot for Lockheed Aircraft.

FILMS INCLUDE: *Love Thy Neighbor* 1940; *Road to Zanzibar* 1941; *My Favorite Spy, Road to Morocco* ('Moonlight Becomes You,' etc.) 1942; *Dixie* ('Sunday, Monday and Always,' etc.) 1943; *Lady in the Dark* ('Suddenly It's Spring'), *Going My Way, And the Angels Sing* 1944; *Duffy's Tavern* 1945; *Welcome Stranger* 1947; *The Emperor Waltz* 1948; *Riding High* ('Sunshine Cake,' etc.) 1950; *Young at Heart* 1954; *The Tender Trap* 1955; *Anything Goes* 1956; *The Joker Is Wild* 1957; *A Hole in the Head* 1959; *High Time* ('The Second Time Around,' etc.) 1960; *Pocketful of Miracles* 1961; *Papa's Delicate Condition* 1963; *Robin and the 7 Hoods* ('My Kind of Town,' etc.) 1964; *Thoroughly Modern Millie* 1967; *Star* 1968; *The Great Bank Robbery* 1969; *Journey Back to Oz* 1974.

Van Horn, Buddy. Director, stuntman. Came to direct a number of Clint Eastwood vehicles after working on his films for years as a stuntman.

FILMS INCLUDE: As director—*Any Which Way You Can* 1980; *Date with an Angel* 1987; *The Dead Pool* 1988; *Pink Cadillac* 1991. As stuntman—*Two Mules for Sister Sara* 1970; *Joe Kidd* 1972; *High Plains Drifter* (also act.) 1973; *Thunderbolt and Lightfoot* 1974; *Swashbuckler* 1976; *The Last Remake of Beau Geste* 1977; *Yellowbeard* 1983.

Van Parys, Georges. Composer. *b.* June 7, 1902, Paris. *d.* 1971. Immensely prolific, he wrote more than 200 film scores, as well as many chansons, several operettas, and music for the theater. He did his best work for films of René Clair.

FILMS INCLUDE: *Le Million, Un Soir de Raffle* 1931; *Cette Vieille Canaille* 1933; *L'Or dans la Rue* 1934; *Quelle drôle de Gosse* 1935; *Abus de Confiance/Abused Confidence* 1937; *Café de Paris* 1938; *Premier Bal* 1941; *Le Silence est d'Or/Man About Town, La Vie en Rose* 1947; *Jean de la Lune* 1949; *Fanfan la Tulipe/Fanfan the Tulip, Casque d'Or, Les Belles de Nuit/Beauties of the Night, Adorables Créatures/Adorable Creatures* 1952; *Madame de. . ./The Earrings of Madame De* 1953; *Avant le Deluge, Le Grand Jeu, Mam'zelle Nitouche, L'Affaire Maurizius/On Trial, Madame du Barry* 1954; *Les Diaboliques/Diabolique, Nana, French Cancan/Only the French Can, Les Grandes Manoeuvres/The Grand Maneuver* 1955; *The Happy Road* (US/Fr.) 1957; *Les Misérables, Maxime* 1958; *Nathalie Agent secret* 1959; *The Millionairess* (UK) 1960; *Mr. Topaze* 1961; *Les Fêtes galantes* 1965; *Elle bois pas. . . Elle drague pas. . . mais Elle cause* 1970.

Van Peebles, Mario. Actor, director, screenwriter. Born on Jan. 15, 1957, in Mexico. *ed.* Columbia U. (economics). Son of director Melvin VAN PEEBLES, he debuted in film as a teen in his father's *Sweet Sweetback's Baadasssss Song*. In his peripatetic early adulthood, he studied acting with Stella Adler, worked as a budget analyst for New York Mayor Edward I. Koch, and was a Ford model. His film acting career began in earnest in the mid-80s; his first directorial effort, *New Jack City*, was praised for its unflinching view of simmering urban youth. Has also appeared widely on TV and on stage.

FILMS INCLUDE: *The Cotton Club, Exterminator II* 1984; *Rappin'* (also songs) 1985; *Heartbreak Ridge* (also songs), *3:15, Delivery Boys, Last Resort* 1986; *Jaws the Revenge* 1987; *Identity Crisis* (also sc.) 1990; *New Jack City* (also dir.) 1991; *Posse* 1993; *Gunmen, Highlander: The Final Dimension* 1994; *Panther* (also prod., dir.) 1995.

Van Peebles, Melvin. Director, producer, writer, composer. Born Melvin Peebles, in 1932, in Chicago, a tailor's son. He joined the Air Force after graduating from Ohio Wesleyan and for three years served as a navigator on a B-47. Returning to civilian life, he painted and made several film shorts but earned his living as a grip on a San Francisco cable car and later as a post office employee. He then attended graduate school in Holland and went to Paris, where he was arrested several times for dancing and singing on the streets for pennies. But following a period of adjustment, he began writing, at first in English, then in French. He had five novels published, one of which, *La Permission,* became the basis of his first feature film, *The Story of a Three-Day Pass* (1968), about a black soldier's weekend with a white French girl. The film was selected as the French entry in the San Francisco Film Festival. Back in the US, he was assigned by Columbia to direct *Watermelon Man* (1970) and invested his salary from that film into a privately financed production, the X-rated *Sweet Sweetback's Baadasssss Song* (1971), which he produced, directed, scored, edited, and starred in. The film was panned by most critics but went on to become a big moneymaker among black audiences, whose culture it reflected. Van Peebles also made several successful recordings and used some of the musical material for a Broadway show, 'Ain't Supposed to Die a Natural Death,' which again was more appreciated by black audiences than by the critical establishment—the result, Van Peebles claims, of a cultural gap. He says he would like white audiences to view his films as they do films of other cultures, such as Italian or Japanese. His son Mario VAN PEEBLES is an actor and director.

FILMS: *La Permission/The Story of a Three-Day Pass* (dir., sc., co-composer; Fr.) 1968; *Watermelon Man* (dir., co-composer) 1970; *Sweet Sweetback's Baadasssss Song* (dir., prod., sc., edit., composer, act.) 1971; *Greased Lightning* (co-sc. only) 1977; *Identity Crisis* (dir., prod., act.) 1989; *True Identity* (act.) 1991; *Boomerang* (act.) 1992; *Posse* (act. only) 1993; *Terminal Velocity* 1994; *Panther* 1995.

Van Rooten, Luis. Actor. *b.* Nov. 29, 1906, Mexico City. *d.* 1973. *ed.* U. of Pennsylvania. A former architect, he turned to acting on stage and in radio serials. From 1944 he played character parts in many Hollywood films, often as a tough-luck badman. He portrayed Nazi Heinrich Himmler in his first (1944) and last (1961) film roles. Later on TV. He was an authority on horticulture.

FILMS INCLUDE: *The Hitler Gang* (as Himmler) 1944; *Two Years Before the Mast* 1946; *To the Ends of the Earth, Saigon, The Big Clock, Beyond Glory, Night Has a Thousand Eyes* 1948; *City Across the River, Champion* 1949; *Detective Story, My Favorite Spy* 1951; *Lydia Bailey* 1952; *Fraulein* 1958; *Operation Eichmann* (again as Himmler) 1961.

Van Runkle, Theadora. Costume designer. Born ca. 1940. *ed.* Chouinard Art Inst., L.A. Prolific designer who came to prominence designing the trend-setting wardrobe for *Bonnie and Clyde*. Although accomplished as a designer for contemporary films, her strongest contributions are in period works (*The Godfather Part II, New York New York*) in which both the feel for the fashion and filmmaking of the era are evoked. Nominated three times for an Academy Award.

FILMS INCLUDE: *Bonnie and Clyde* 1967; *I Love You Alice B. Toklas!, The Thomas Crown Affair, Bullitt* 1968; *The Reivers* 1969; *Ace Eli and Rodger of the Skies* 1973; *The Godfather Part II, Mame* 1974; *Nickelodeon* 1976; *New York New York* 1977; *Heaven Can Wait, Same Time Next Year* 1978; *The Jerk* 1979; *Heartbeeps, S.O.B.* 1981; *The Best Little Whorehouse in Texas* 1982; *Rhinestone* 1984; *Native Son, Peggy Sue Got Married* 1986; *Everybody's All-American* 1988; *Troop Beverly Hills* 1989; *Stella* 1990; *The Butcher's Wife* 1991; *Leap of Faith* 1992; *Kiss of Death* 1995.

Van Sant, Gus. Director, screenwriter. Born Gus Van Sant, Jr., in 1953 in Louisville, Ky. *ed.* Rhode Island School of Design. Directorial avatar of the post-postwar generation. After producing commercials and working as an assistant to Roger Corman, he debuted as a director in the mid-80s with *Mala Noche*, the story of an ill-fated love affair between a homosexual clerk and a migrant worker. The work established him as an original voice and won the Los Angeles Film Critics Award for best independent film. *Drugstore Cowboy*, his following film, an unapologetic look at a drug-addicted group that supports itself by robbing pharmacies, was a critical and art-house hit and set him as a voice for the young. His study of a gay hustler, *My Own Private Idaho*, like his previous features, was praised for its lyricism, fine performances, and contribution to the canon of GAY AND LESBIAN CINEMA. He has compiled a collection of annual autobiographical shorts (*Five Ways to Kill Yourself, My New Friends*, and others) that is to be made into a larger, chronicle-like work.

FILMS INCLUDE: *Property* (sound only) 1979; *Mala Noche* (also ed., prod., sc.) 1985; *Drugstore Cowboy* (co-sc.) 1989; *My Own Private Idaho* 1991; *Even Cowgirls Get the Blues* 1994; *To Die For* 1995.

Van Sloan, Edward. Actor. *b.* 1882, San Francisco. *d.* 1964. A former commercial artist and a veteran of the stage, he played character parts in numerous Hollywood films of the 30s and early 40s, usually portraying doctors, professors, or other intellectuals. Memorable as the fearless vampire killer in *Dracula* and *Dracula's Daughter* and in several other horror pictures.

FILMS INCLUDE: *Dracula, Frankenstein* 1931; *Behind the Mask, Forgotten Commandments, The Last Mile, The Mummy, The Death Kiss* 1932; *Infernal Machine, The Working Man, Deluge* 1933; *Death Takes a Holiday, The Scarlet Empress* 1934; *A Shot in the Dark, The Last Days of Pompeii* 1935; *The Story of Louis Pasteur, Sins of Man, Dracula's Daughter* 1936; *Penitentiary* 1938; *The Phantom Creeps* (serial) 1939; *The Secret Seven, Before I Hang* 1940; *The Mask of Dijon* 1946; *Betty Co-Ed* 1947.

Van Upp, Virginia. Screenwriter, producer. *b.* 1902, Chicago. *d.* 1970. A child actress in early silent films, she later worked her way up from script girl, cutter, reader, and casting director to screenwriter at Paramount in the mid-30s and to executive producer at Columbia in 1945. A close confidante of Columbia boss Harry COHN, she was entrusted with the shaping of Rita HAYWORTH's career, as writer, producer, and advisor on affairs of the heart.

FILMS INCLUDE (as screenwriter): *The Pursuit of Happiness* 1934; *So Red the Rose* 1935; *Poppy* 1936; *Swing High*

Swing Low 1937; *You and Me* 1938; *Cafe Society, Honeymoon in Bali* 1939; *Virginia, One Night in Lisbon* 1941; *Bahama Passage* 1942; *The Crystal Ball* 1943; *Cover Girl, The Impatient Years, Together Again* (also prod.) 1944; *She Wouldn't Say Yes* (also prod.) 1945; *Gilda* (prod. only) 1946; *Here Comes the Groom* 1951; *Affair in Trinidad* (co-story, assoc. prod. only) 1952.

Van Zandt, Philip. Actor. *b.* Oct. 3, 1904, Amsterdam. *d.* 1958. From 1927 he appeared in many American plays, in stock, on the road, and on Broadway. He played many character parts, often shifty or villainous, in Hollywood films of the 40s and 50s. He died at 53 of an overdose of sleeping pills.

FILMS INCLUDE: *Those High Grey Walls* 1939; *Citizen Kane* 1941; *Wake Island, The Hard Way* 1942; *Hostages, Sherlock Holmes and the Secret Weapon, Air Raid Wardens* 1943; *House of Frankenstein, Sudan, A Thousand and One Nights* 1945; *Somewhere in the Night* 1946; *Slave Girl* 1947; *The Loves of Carmen, The Big Clock, Street with No Name* 1948; *The Lady Gambles* 1949; *Cyrano de Bergerac* 1950; *His Kind of Woman* 1951; *Viva Zapata!* 1952; *Yankee Pasha, Knock on Wood* 1954; *Man of a Thousand Faces* 1957.

Vanzina, Stefano. See STENO.

Varconi, Victor. Actor. *b.* Mihaly Varkonyi, Mar. 31, 1896, Kisvarda, Hungary, on the Rumanian border, to a family of farmers. *d.* 1976. He began his career on the Transylvanian stage and before long he was a matinee idol with the Hungarian National Theater in Budapest. He appeared in several Hungarian and German films before arriving in Hollywood in 1923 on a De Mille contract. He played leads and second leads in many silents and early talkies, typically as a smooth Continental, then eased into character parts, often villainous.

FILMS INCLUDE: *Sodom und Gomorra* (Ger.) 1922; *Triumph, Changing Husbands, Poisoned Paradise, Feet of Clay* 1924; *The Volga Boatman, For Wives Only* 1926; *The King of Kings* (as Pontius Pilate), *Fighting Love, The Angel of Broadway, The Forbidden Woman* 1927; *Chicago, Tenth Avenue, Sinners' Parade* 1928; *The Divine Lady* (as Lord Nelson), *Eternal Love* 1929; *Captain Thunder* 1930; *Doctors' Wives, The Black Camel, Men in Her Life* 1931; *The Doomed Battalion* (English-language version of 1931's *Berge in Flammen;* Ger.), *The Rebel* (English-language version of *Der Rebell;* Ger.) 1932; *The Song You Gave Me* (UK) 1933; *Roberta, Mr. Dynamite, A Feather in Her Hat* 1935; *Dancing Pirate* 1936; *The Plainsman, Big City* 1937; *Suez* (as Victor Hugo), *Submarine Patrol* 1938; *The Story of Vernon and Irene Castle, Mr. Moto Takes a Vacation, Everything Happens at Night* 1939; *Strange Cargo, The Sea Hawk* 1940; *My Favorite Blonde* 1942; *For Whom the Bell Tolls* (as Primitivo) 1943; *The Hitler Gang* (as Rudolph Hess) 1944; *Unconquered* 1947; *Samson and Delilah* 1949; *The Atomic Submarine* 1959.

Varda, Agnès. Director. Born on May 30, 1928, in Brussels, to Greek-French parents. Raised in France, she studied at the Sorbonne and the Ecôle du Louvre, intending to become a museum curator. Instead she became a still photographer. It was her work as the official photographer of the Théâtre National Populaire that awakened her interest in the theater and eventually in films. She knew next to nothing about cinema and had seen only a handful of films before she made her first picture, *La Pointe courte,* in 1954. In many ways it was a precursor of the NOUVELLE VAGUE and particularly of the films of Alain RESNAIS, who edited the film. *La Pointe courte* and Varda's subsequent features and shorts have revealed her as an original artist with an instinctive awareness of and a photographer's eye for visual detail. She established her reputation with *Cléo de 5 à 7/Cleo from 5 to 7* (1962), an intimate account of a pop singer who views the world around her with heightened perception during the two hours she spends in suspense, awaiting the results of a medical examination which will determine whether or not she is suffering from a terminal illness.

Varda's next feature, *Le Bonheur* (1965), an ironic study of happiness, was more decorative than the rest of her films, perhaps because of the stylistic influence of her husband, director Jacques DEMY. In 1968 she came to the US, where she directed two shorts and a feature consistent with her leftist orientation and revealing her ambivalent critical-affectionate view of America. She achieved international acclaim for *Vagabond* (1985), a hugely successful pseudo-documentary about a homeless young wanderer. She has written the screenplays for all her own films.

FILMS (as director-screenwriter): *La Pointe courte* 1954; *O Saisons ô Châteaux* (short) 1957; *L'Opéra Mouffe* (short), *Du Côté de la Côte* (short) 1958; *Cléo de 5 à 7/Cleo from 5 to 7* 1962; *Salut les Cubains* (short) 1963; *Le Bonheur/Happiness* 1965; *Les Créatures* 1966; *Elsa* (short), *Loin du Vietnam/Far from Vietnam* (film essay; co-dir. with several others) 1967; *Uncle Yanko/Uncle Janco* (short; US), *Black Panthers* (short; US) 1968; *Lions Love* (also prod.; US) 1969; *Nausicaa* (semi-doc. about Greeks in France; orig. made for TV) 1970; *Daguerréotypes, Réponses de Femmes* (8 mm film essay) 1975; *L'Une chante l'autre pas/One Sings the Other Does Not* 1977; *Sans Toit ni Loi/Vagabond* (also ed.) 1985; *Le Petit Amour/Kung Fu Master!* (also prod.) 1987; *Jane B. par Agnes V.* (also act., prod., ed.) 1988; *Jacquot de Nantes* 1991; *101 Nights* 1995.

variable-area sound track. A type of optical sound track in which the modulations appear on the film in the form of dark oscillating ridges.

variable-density sound track. A type of sound track in which the modulations appear on the film as horizontal bars, graduating in density from black to the lightest of grays.

variable-focus lens. See ZOOM LENS.

variable shutter. A camera shutter having two metal plates, one fixed and the other adjustable. The plates rotate simultaneously during exposure to allow light to reach the film. This type of shutter is useful in making fades and cross-dissolves in the camera. It also allows the cameraman to control exposure and vary the depth of field without changing the lens settings.

variable-speed motor. Also called a "wild motor." A camera motor that allows the operator to select any one of a range of speeds by turning a selector dial. It is used only in shooting silent sequences, since sound recording requires a constant speed rate.

Variety. The entertainment industry's most important trade journal, published weekly in New York City. In addition to covering stage, television, and recordings, it reports on all aspects of the motion picture industry, including deals, films in production, and box-office results, and publishes reviews and obituaries. A separate publication, *Daily Variety*, is published in Hollywood and offers daily news and commentary on the entertainment industry.

Varnel, Marcel. Director. *b.* Oct. 16, 1894, Paris. *d.* 1947. A pint-sized actor on the Paris stage, he turned director early in the 20s. In 1925 he came to the US, where he directed operettas, musicals, and dramatic plays for the Schuberts on Broadway. He went to Hollywood in the early 30s and directed a number of low-budget thrillers for Fox. In 1933 he moved to London and later directed some of the funniest British comedies of the 30s and early 40s. His son, Max Varnel (*b.* Mar. 21, 1925, Paris), is a director of routine British crime and action pictures and TV films.

FILMS INCLUDE: In the US—*The Silent Witness,*

Chandu the Magician 1932; *Infernal Machine* 1933. In the UK—*Freedom of the Seas* 1934; *Dance Band* 1935; *All In* 1936; *Oh Mr. Porter* 1937; *Alf's Button Afloat, Hey Hey USA* 1938; *Let George Do It* 1940; *Hi Gang* 1941; *Get Cracking* 1943; *He Snoops to Conquer* 1944; *This Man Is Mine* 1946.

Varsi, Diane. Actress. *b.* 1937, in San Mateo, Calif. *d.* 1992. The product of a broken home, she was brought up by strangers and educated in various West Coast convents. She married briefly at 15 and again at 17. By the time she was 21, she had two divorces behind her. Before coming to Hollywood she was variously employed as an apple picker, a waitress, and a factory worker. Determined on a career in show business, she tried folksinging and was a drummer with a band. She enrolled in Jeff COREY's acting classes and had barely begun her studies when she was tested and selected to play Lana Turner's mixed-up daughter in *Peyton Place,* a role for which she was nominated for an Oscar. She subsequently starred in a number of films and seemed ensured of a bright future, when, in 1959, she left Hollywood abruptly, for peaceful retirement in Vermont, stating that she was "running away from destruction." When she ran short on funds she tried to get back into films but was barred from work because she had walked out on her contract with Fox. She finally returned briefly to the screen in the late 60s, and after another long absence reappeared in films once more in the late 70s.

FILMS: *Peyton Place* 1957; *Ten North Frederick, From Hell to Texas* 1958; *Compulsion* 1959; *Sweet Love Bitter* 1967; *Wild in the Streets, Killers Three* 1968; *Bloody Mama* 1970; *Johnny Got His Gun* 1971; *I Never Promised You a Rose Garden* 1977.

Vasiliev, Sergei and **Georgy.** Soviet directors. Sergei (*b.* Nov. 4, 1900, Moscow; *d.* 1959) served in the Red Army during the revolutionary war and remained in uniform until 1924, when he entered films as an editor. In 1928 he met Georgy (*b.* 1899; *d.* 1945), who became his collaborator in editing and from 1930 in directing. They were not related, but because they shared the same surname and worked closely together they came to be known as the Brothers Vasiliev. Their most celebrated film was *Chapayev,* the story of a revolutionary hero, remarkable at its time for presenting the protagonist as a less-than-perfect character. After Georgy's death in 1945, Sergei was appointed head of the Leningrad film studios. He directed two solo films before he died.

FILMS: Sergei and Georgy—*Sleeping Beauty* 1930; *A Personal Affair* 1932; *Chapayev* 1934; *Volotchayevsk Days/The Defense of Volotchayevsk* 1938; *The Defense of Tsaritsin* 1942; *The Front* 1943. Sergei alone—*Heroes of Shipka* 1955; *October Days* 1958.

Vaughn, Robert. Actor. Born on Nov. 30, 1932, in New York City; raised in Minneapolis. A serious-minded leading man, he entered films in 1957 with a B.A. in drama, then worked at L.A. City College on master's and Ph.D. degrees in political science while pursuing an increasingly successful screen career. He was nominated for an Oscar in the supporting category for his role in *The Young Philadelphians* (1959), but the swiftest boost to his career came from his portrayal of Napoleon Solo in the highly successful TV series 'The Man from U.N.C.L.E.' Actively engaged in politics, on the liberal side, in 1972 he wrote *Only Victims,* a detailed record of the Hollywood purge resulting from the investigations of the House Un-American Activities Committee.

FILMS INCLUDE: *No Time to Be Young* 1957; *Teenage Cave Man* 1958; *The Young Philadelphians* 1959; *The Magnificent Seven* 1960; *The Big Show* 1961; *The Caretakers* 1963; *To Trap a Spy, One Spy Too Many* 1966; *The Venetian Affair* 1967; *Bullitt* 1968; *The Bridge at Remagen* 1969; *The Mind of Mr. Soames* (UK), *Julius Caesar* (as Casca; UK) 1970; *La Statua/The Statue* (It./UK), *Clay Pigeon* 1971; *The Towering Inferno* 1974; *Babysitter* (It./Fr./Ger.) 1975; *Demon Seed, Starship Invasion* (Can.) 1977; *Atraco en la Jungla* (release delayed; Sp./Ven.), *Brass Target* 1978; *Good Luck Miss Wyckoff, Key West Crossing/Cuba Crossing/Kill Castro/Assignment: Kill Castro/The Mercenaries/Sweet Dirty Tony* 1979; *Hangar 18/Invasion Force, City in Fear, Battle Beyond the Stars* 1980; *S.O.B.* 1981; *Fukkatsu no Hi/Virus* (Jap.) 1982; *Superman III* 1983; *The Last Bastion* (Austral.) 1984; *Delta Force* 1985; *Black Moon Rising* 1986; *Nightstick, Hour of the Assassin* (US/Peru) 1987; *Captive Rage* 1988; *Emissary, C.H.U.D. II: Bud the Chud, River of Death, Brutal Glory, Skeleton Coast/Fair Trade, Buried Alive, Transylvania Twist* 1989; *Nobody's Perfect, That's Adequate* 1990; *Blind Vision* 1991; *Little Devils* 1992; *Joe's Apartment* 1996.

vault. A fireproof chamber for the long-term storage of film. Vaults should be equipped with provisions for temperature and humidity control to protect the film from deterioration. Extra fire-protection precautions are taken when the stored film has a cellulose nitrate base.

Vávra, Otakar. Director. Born in 1911, in Hradec Králové, Czechoslovakia. He studied architecture at Brno and Prague universities but turned instead to writing as a publicist and later film critic. He made several experimental shorts in the early 30s, before entering Czech films as screenwriter and assistant director in 1933, and turned out his first feature as director in 1937. His third feature, *Guild of the Kutna Hora Virgins/The Merry Wives* (1938), won a prize at the Venice Film Festival but was banned by the Nazis when they entered Czechoslovakia that same year. Vávra, whose films have typically been adaptations from Czech and foreign literature, was able to continue his work during the Occupation and to survive cultural purges of the subsequent Communist regime by drawing his plots from past history and for the most part avoiding contemporary themes. He has written most of his own scripts, alone or in collaboration. He was among the founders of the FAMU film school in Prague and as a professor there exerted considerable influence on the postwar generation of Czech filmmakers for many years. He was fired from his teaching post at FAMU in 1970 after one of his students turned out a film that displeased the authorities but has since resumed his work as a film director.

FEATURE FILMS: *A Philosophical Story, Virginity* 1937; *Guild of the Kutna Hora Virgins/The Merry Wives* 1938; *Humoresque* 1939; *Romance/A Fable of May, The Masked Lover* 1940; *The Turbine* 1941; *I Shan't Be Long* 1942; *Happy Journey* 1943; *Rosina the Foundling* 1945; *The Mischievous Tutor* 1946; *Presentiment* 1947; *Krakatit* 1948; *The Silent Barricade* 1949; *Fall-In* 1952; *Jan Hus* 1955; *Jan Zizka* 1956; *Against All/All Our Enemies* (last three films comprise the *Hussite Trilogy*) 1957; *Citizen Brych* 1958; *The First Rescue Party* 1959; *The Closing Hour, A Sunday in August* 1960; *A Night Guest* 1961; *The Burning Heart/The Ardent Heart* 1962; *The Golden Rennet* 1965; *Romance for Trumpet* 1966; *Witchhammer, The 13th Room* 1969; *Days of Treason* 1973; *Liberation of Prague* 1977.

Védrès, Nicole. Director, novelist, essayist. *b.* Sept. 4, 1911, Paris. *d.* 1965. A distinguished member of the Paris intelligentsia, she made a fine contribution to the art of the compilation film with a nostalgic, humorous, literate feature-length documentary, *Paris 1900.* She then made another impressive feature documentary and two shorts.

FILMS: *Paris 1900* 1947; *La Vie commence Demain/Life Begins Tomorrow* 1949; *Amazone* (short) 1951; *Aux Frontières de l'Homme* (short; co-dir. with Jean Rostand) 1953.

Veidt, Conrad. Actor. *b.* Jan. 22, 1893, Potsdam, near Berlin, Germany. *d.* 1943, in Hollywood. A student of Max REINHARDT, he made his stage debut in 1913 at the latter's Deutsches Theater in Berlin. He entered German cinema in 1917 and soon rose to prominence in films of the expressionist movement. Specializing in demoniacal roles, he often portrayed demented or tormented characters (notably Cesare, the somnambulist, in *The Cabinet of Dr. Caligari*), in keeping with the morbid, perverse world that characterized German films of the period. By the mid-20s, after portraying a succession of historical and literary personalities, and especially after his performance in the title role of *The Student of Prague,* he was world famous and was brought to Hollywood for a series of films. He returned to Germany with the switch to sound, in 1929, but with the advent of the Nazis, he went into exile in England with his Jewish wife. He went back to Germany on a visit the following year and an international incident nearly ensued when he was held by the Nazis on the pretext that he was too ill to travel. His employers, Gaumont British, sent over their own doctors to rescue him. He became a British citizen in 1939. The following year he went to Hollywood to complete *The Thief of Bagdad* and remained to play a succession of commanding Nazis, memorably in *Casablanca* (1943). He died of a heart attack.

FILMS INCLUDE: In Germany—*Der Spion, Furcht, Das Rätsel von Bangalore* 1917; *Es werde Licht, Das Tagebuch einer Verlorenen/Diary of a Lost Girl, Das Dreimäderlhaus, Nocturno der Liebe* (as Frederic Chopin), *Opium* 1918; *Die Reise um die Erde in 80 Tagen/Around the World in 80 Days* (as Phileas Fogg), *Peer Gynt* (as the Button Moulder), *Die Prostitution, Prinz Kuckuck/Prince Cuckoo, Unheimliche Geschichten* (as Death), *Wahnsinn* (also dir.), *Die Nacht auf Goldenhall* (also dir.), *Das Kabinett des Dr. Caligari/The Cabinet of Dr. Caligari* (as Cesare) 1919; *Satanas* (as Lucifer, among other roles), *Der Reigen, Patience, Der Januskopf* (in the dual role of Dr. Jekyll and Mr. Hyde here named Dr. Warren and Mr. O'Connor), *Kurfürstendamm* (as the Devil), *Muriturus, Abend—Nacht—Morgen, Manolescus Memoiren* (as George Manolescu), *Sehnsucht, Der Gang in die Nacht, Der Graf von Cagliostro, Das Geheimnis von Bombay* 1920; *Lady Hamilton* (as Lord Nelson), *Das indische Grabmal/The Indian Tomb/Mysteries of India/Above All Law* 1921; *Lukrezia Borgia/Lucretia Borgia* (as Cesare Borgia), *König Richard III* (title role; also co-prod.), *Lord Byron* (also dir., sc., co-prod.) 1922; *Paganini* (title role; also prod.), *Wilhelm Tell/William Tell* (as Gessler) 1923; *Karlos und Elisabeth* (in dual role, as Carlos V and Don Carlos), *Das Wachsfigurenkabinett/Waxworks/The Three Wax Works/Three Wax Men* (as Ivan the Terrible), *Nju/Husbands or Lovers* 1924; *Orlacs Hände/The Hands of Orlac* (title role; Aus.) 1925; *To the Orient* (Sw.), *Henry IV* (It.), *Der Geiger von Florenz/Impetuous Youth/The Violinist of Florence, Die Brüder Schellenberg/The Two Brothers* (in dual title role), *Der Student von Prag/The Man Who Cheated Life/The Student of Prague* 1926. In the US—*The Beloved Rogue* (as Louis XI), *A Man's Past* 1927; *The Man Who Laughs* 1928; *The Last Performance* 1929. In Germany—*Das Land ohne Frauen/Bride 68* 1929; *Die letzte Kompagnie/Thirteen Men and a Girl/The Last Company, Menschen im Käfig* (German-language version of UK's *Cape Forlorn/Love Storm*) 1930; *Der Kongress tanzt/The Congress Dances* (as Count Metternich) 1931; *Rasputin* (title role), *Der schwarze Husar, F.P.1* (English-language version of *F.P.1 antwortet nicht*) 1932. In the UK—*Rome Express, Ich und die Kaiserin* (Ger.), *The Wandering Jew, I Was a Spy* 1933; *Jew Suss/Power, Wilhelm Tell/The Legend of William Tell* (remake; again as Gessler), *Bella Donna* 1934; *The Passing of the Third Floor Back* 1935; *King of the Damned* 1936; *Under the Red Robe, Dark Journey* 1937. In France—*Tempête sur l'Asie, Le Joueur d'Echecs/The Devil Is an Empress/The Chess Player* 1938. In the UK—*The Spy in Black/U-Boat 29* 1939; *Contraband/Blackout, The Thief of Baghdad/The Thief of Bagdad* 1940. In the US—*Escape* 1940; *A Woman's Face, Whistling in the Dark, The Men in Her Life* 1941; *Nazi Agent* (dual role); *All Through the Night* 1942; *Casablanca, Above Suspicion* 1943.

Veiller, Anthony. Screenwriter, producer. *b.* June 23, 1903, New York City. *d.* 1965. *ed.* Antioch Coll.; Union College (NYC). The son of the late screenwriter-director-producer Bayard Veiller (*b.* Jan. 2, 1869, Brooklyn, N.Y.), he was a reporter, a theater manager, and a publicist before entering films as a screenwriter in the early 30s. He wrote a number of distinguished screenplays, alone or in collaboration, as well as many routine ones. He was also the author of several plays. He produced a number of films beginning in 1940.

FILMS INCLUDE (as screenwriter): *Breach of Promise* (dial.) 1932; *The Notorious Sophie Lang* 1934; *Star of Midnight, Break of Hearts, Jalna, Seven Keys to Baldpate* 1935; *The Ex-Mrs. Bradford, A Woman Rebels, Winterset* 1936; *The Soldier and the Lady/Michael Strogoff, Stage Door* 1937; *Let Us Live, Disputed Passage* 1939; *Victory* (prod. only) 1940; *New York Town* (prod. only) 1941; *Her Cardboard Lover* 1942; *Assignment in Brittany, The Battle of Russia* (doc.) 1943; *Tunisian Victory* (doc.; also narrator) 1944; *Adventure, The Stranger, The Killers* 1946; *State of the Union* 1948; *Colorado Territory* (prod. only) 1949; *Chain Lightning* (prod. only) 1950; *Dallas* (prod. only), *Force of Arms* (prod. only) 1951; *Red Planet Mars* (also prod.) 1952; *Moulin Rouge* 1953; *Safari* 1956; *Monkey on My Back* 1957; *Solomon and Sheba* 1959; *The List of Adrian Messenger* 1963; *The Night of the Iguana* 1964.

Velez, Lupe. Actress. *b.* Maria Guadalupe Velez de Villalobos, July 18, 1908, San Luis Potosi, Mexico. *d.* 1944. Educated in a San Antonio, Tex., convent. She danced on the Mexican stage and in a Hollywood nightclub revue before breaking into films in 1926 in Hal Roach comedy shorts. She made her mark the following year as Douglas Fairbanks's fiery leading lady in *The Gaucho.* She subsequently played tempestuous, temperamental leads in many other features, notably in Griffith's *Lady of the Pavements* and De Mille's *The Squaw Man.* In the 40s she teamed up with Leon Errol in the "Mexican Spitfire" feature comedy series. She was as stormy and volatile in her personal life as she was on the screen. After being shunned by Gary Cooper at the end of a romantic affair, she married Johnny WEISSMULLER in 1933. Their quarrels in public got frequent space in the scandal press. They divorced in 1938. Following one of several subsequent unfortunate love affairs, Miss Velez committed suicide in grand theatrical style, swallowing a tubeful of pills in a room decorated with flowers after a carefully planned session with her hairdresser and makeup man.

FILMS INCLUDE: *Sailors Beware* (Laurel & Hardy short), *The Gaucho* 1927; *Stand and Deliver* 1928; *Wolf Song, Lady of the Pavements, Where East Is East, Tiger Rose* 1929; *Hell Harbor, The Storm, East Is West* 1930; *Resurrection, The Squaw Man, The Cuban Love Song* 1931; *The Broken Wing, Kongo* 1932; *Hot Pepper* 1933; *Palooka, Strictly Dynamite, Laughing Boy* 1934; *Gypsy Melody* (UK) 1936; *Mad About Money/He Loved an Actress* (UK) 1938; *The Girl from Mexico* 1939; *Mexican Spitfire* 1940; *Six Lessons from Madame La Zonga, Playmates, Honolulu Lu* 1941; *Ladies' Day, Redhead from Manhattan* 1943; *Nana* (Mex.) 1944.

velocilator. A large wheeled camera mount, bulkier and more complex than a regular dolly, but less so than a crane. It has seats for an operator and a focus puller and is designed to lift a camera to the height of six feet. Some velocilators are hand-pushed; others are powered.

Venable, Evelyn. Actress. *b.* Oct. 18, 1913, in Cincinnati. *d.* 1993. The daughter of a college professor, she began acting in high school. After briefly attending Vassar and the University of Cincinnati, she joined Walter Hampden's stock company. She was seen playing Ophelia in Los Angeles by a Paramount talent scout and was signed to a movie contract. A fragile beauty, she starred in several quality productions of the early 30s but later was cast in a succession of poor vehicles, although she did serve as the model for Columbia Pictures' torch-bearing logo. She retired from the screen in the early 40s to raise the children from her marriage to cameraman Hal MOHR. She subsequently returned to college and taught at UCLA.

FILMS INCLUDE: *Cradle Song* 1933; *Death Takes a Holiday, David Harum, Double Door, Mrs. Wiggs of the Cabbage Patch* 1934; *The Country Chairman, The Little Colonel, Vagabond Lady, Alice Adams* 1935; *Star for a Night, North of Nome* 1936; *Racketeers in Exile* 1937; *The Hollywood Stadium Mystery, Female Fugitive* 1938; *Heritage of the Desert* 1939; *Lucky Cisco Kid* 1940; *He Hired the Boss* 1943.

Venezuela. Film production in this country of 19 million people on the north coast of South America was negligible until the 1950s. It was then that Margot Benacerraf came on the scene with two documentaries, *Reverón* (1952) and *Araya* (1958), that won international acclaim. Independent documentary production flourished in the late 60s, with such filmmakers as Alfredo Anzola (*Santa Teresa*, 1969), Jesús Enrique Guedes (*The City Which Sees Us*, 1967), and Carlos Rebolledo (*Dead Well*, 1967). In the 70s, the Venezuelan government began to see the importance of supporting a national feature film industry. Following a 1973 resolution, the government introduced state funding of motion picture production and legislation to restrict competition from foreign films. Between 1975 and 1980, the state co-financed 29 feature films, many of which gained both critical praise and large audiences. These included satirical fiction films by the former documentarist Anzola, such as *Wanted: Good Looking Receptionist and Messenger with His Own Motorcycle* (1977) and *Manuel* (1979), along with Román Chalbaud's *The Fish That Smokes* (1977), Iván Feo's and Antonio Llerandi's *Portable Country* (1978), Carlos Rebolledo's *Alias the Joropo King* (1978), and Mauricio Wallerstein's *Sacred and Obscene* (1975).

A severe recession in the early 80s rocked Venezuela's nascent film industry. By the end of the decade, only a few independent films were being released each year, while the government debated whether and how to support a national cinema. In the early 90s, the state production agency Foncine developed a plan to restructure and finance the domestic film industry, in part by creating a National Film Center to coordinate and promote production. The government also joined other Latin American nations in working toward a common market in which Latin American films could be traded freely among signatories. The film department of the University of the Andes in Mérida, long active in film production and training, hosts a biennial national film festival. The National Cinémathèque promotes archival restoration and research.

Venezuelan directors of the 80s and 90s include Anzola (*Shrimp Cocktail*, 1983), Carlos Azpurúa (*Shoot to Kill*, 1992), Olegario Barrera (*Little Revenge*, 1985), Chalbaud (*Flaming Knives*, 1992), Leonardo Henriquez (*Tender Is the Night*, 1992), Oscar Lucién (*A Dream in the Abyss*, 1992), and Augusto Pradelli (*Hollywood*, 1991).

Ventura, Lino. Actor. *b.* Lino Borrini, July 14, 1919, in Parma, Italy. *d.* 1987. When he was eight his family settled in Paris. He promptly dropped out of school and worked as a mechanic's apprentice and at various other occupations, eventually turning to the ring as a prizefighter. He entered French films in 1953, and thanks to his husky physique, he was frequently employed in tough-guy roles, often as a gangster. Within several years he had developed from a minor character actor to a tough-guy lead with a vastly improved acting ability and quite a following among Continental audiences.

FILMS INCLUDE: *Touchez pas au Grisbi/Grisbi* 1954; *Razzia sur la Chnouf/Razzia* 1955; *Crime et Châtiment/Crime and Punishment* 1956; *Le Rouge est mis/Speaking of Murder* 1957; *Ascenseur pour l'Echafaud/Frantic, Le Gorille vous salue bien, Montparnasse 19/Modigliani of Montparnasse, Marie-Octobre* 1958; *Classe tous Risques/The Big Risk* 1960; *Un Taxi pour Tobrouk/Taxi for Tobruk* 1961; *Die Dreigroschenoper/The Threepenny Opera* (as Tiger Brown; Ger./Fr.), *Cent Mille Dollars au Soleil/Greed in the Sun* 1963; *Les Barbouzes/The Great Spy Chase* 1964; *La Metamorphose des Cloportes/Cloportes, L'Arme à Gauche* 1965; *Le Deuxième Souffle/Second Breath* 1966; *Les Aventuriers/The Last Adventure* 1967; *La Rapace* 1968; *Le Clan des Siciliens/The Sicilian Clan, L'Armée des Ombres/Army of Shadows* 1969; *Dernier Domicile connu* 1970; *Boulevard du Rhum* 1971; *Joe Valachi—i Segreti di Cosa Nostra/The Valachi Papers* (It./Fr.), *L'Aventure c'est l'Aventure/Money Money Money* 1972; *Les Silencieux/Escape to Nowhere, La Bonne Année/Happy New Year, L'Emmerdeur/A Pain in the A. . .* 1973; *La Gifle/The Slap* 1974; *La Cage, Adieu Poulet/The French Detective* 1975; *Cadaveri eccelenti/Illustrious Corpses/The Context* (It./Fr.) 1976; *The Medusa Touch* (UK), *Un Papillon sur l'Epaule* 1978; *L'Homme en Colère/Jigsaw/The Angry Man* (Fr./Can.), *Labyrinthe* (Can./Fr.) 1979; *Sunday Lovers* (UK) 1980; *Garde a Vue* (Fr.) 1981; *Le Ruffian* (Fr.) 1983; *Cento Giorni A Palermo, Le Septieme Cible* (Fr.) 1984; *La Rumba* (Fr.), *Sword of Gideon* (US) (TV) 1986.

Ventura, Ray. Producer. *b.* Raymond V. Ventura, April 16, 1908, Paris. *d.* 1979. A famous bandleader in the 30s and early 40s, he appeared in prewar French films, alone or with his band. Turning producer in the late 40s, he began with light musical films and subsequently tackled more ambitious productions. He also directed two dance shorts in 1951.

FILMS INCLUDE: As actor or orchestra leader—*L'Amour à l'Américaine* 1931; *Minuit Place Pigalle* 1934; *Feux de Joie* 1938; *Tourbillon de Paris* 1939; *Mademoiselle s'amuse* 1948. As producer or co-producer—*La Petite Chocolatière* 1949; *Nous irons à Paris* (also act.) 1950; *Memoire d'un Héros* (short; also dir.), *Méphisto-Valse* (short; also dir.), *Sans laisser d'Adresse, Nous irons à Monte Carlo/Monte Carlo Baby* 1951; *La Jeune Folle/Desperate Decision* 1952; *La Carosse d'Or/The Golden Coach, Femmes de Paris* (also co-sc.) 1953; *Les Amants du Tage/Lover's Net* 1955; *En Effeuillant la Marguerite/Please Mr. Balzac* 1956; *Sait-on jamais?/No Sun in Venice* 1957; *En Cas de Malheur/Love Is My Profession* 1958; *Le Bois des Amants* 1960; *Vive Henri IV—Vive l'Amour* 1961; *Le Train de Berlin est arrêté/Stop Train 349* 1964.

Vera-Ellen. Dancer, actress. *b.* Vera-Ellen Westmeyr Rohe, Feb. 16, 1926, Cincinnati. *d.* 1981, of cancer. Dancing from the age of ten, she was a Radio City Music Hall Rockette and appeared in nightclubs and in Broadway musicals before her film debut in the mid-40s. A petite, energetic blonde, she stood out as one of Hollywood's most accomplished and most versatile dancers, opposite such partners as Fred Astaire and Gene Kelly. She retired from the screen in the late 50s.

FILMS: *Wonder Man* 1945; *The Kid from Brooklyn, Three Little Girls in Blue* 1946; *Carnival in Costa Rica* 1947; *Words and Music* 1948; *On the Town* 1949; *Love Happy, Three Little*

Words 1950; *Happy Go Lucky* (UK) 1951; *The Belle of New York* 1952; *Call Me Madam, The Big Leaguer* 1953; *White Christmas* 1954; *Let's Be Happy* (UK) 1957.

Verdon, Gwen. Actress, dancer, singer. Born on Jan. 13, 1925, in Culver City, Calif. On the stage professionally from 1947, she became a top star of Broadway musicals in the 50s, winning two Donaldson awards and a Tony award for 'Can-Can' (1953) and additional Tony awards for 'Damn Yankees' (1955–56), 'New Girl in Town' (1957), and 'Redhead' (1959). She appeared in only a handful of films, memorably in *Damn Yankees* (1958), in which she repeated her stage role as Lola. In 1975 she returned to Broadway after a long absence in the role of Roxie Hart in the musical 'Chicago,' which, like several of her other plays, was directed by her former husband Bob FOSSE. She returned to films after a twenty-five-year absence in 1984.

FILMS: *On the Riviera, David and Bathsheba, Meet Me After the Show* 1951; *The Mississippi Gambler, The Farmer Takes a Wife* 1953; *Damn Yankees* 1958; *The Cotton Club* 1984; *Cocoon* 1985; *Nadine* 1987; *Cocoon: The Return* 1988; *Alice* 1990; *Marvin's Room* 1996.

Verdugo, Elena. Actress. Born in 1926, in Hollywood. Leading lady of Spanish descent. She played the feminine lead in B pictures and second leads in A productions of the 40s and 50s. She also starred in the TV series 'Meet Millie' and 'Marcus Welby, M.D.'

FILMS INCLUDE: *Down Argentine Way* (bit) 1940; *Belle Starr* 1941; *The Moon and Sixpence* 1942; *Rainbow Island* 1944; *House of Frankenstein, The Frozen Ghost* 1945; *Little Giant* 1946; *Song of Scheherazade* 1947; *Tuna Clipper, The Big Sombrero* 1949; *The Lost Volcano, Cyrano de Bergerac* 1950; *The Thief of Damascus, The Pathfinder* 1952; *Knights of the Round Table* 1954; *Panama Sal* 1957; *Day of the Nightmare* 1965; *How Sweet It Is!* 1968; *Angel in My Pocket* 1969.

Vergano, Aldo. Director. *b.* Aug. 27, 1894, Rome. *d.* 1957. A confirmed anti-Fascist, he quit journalism in 1922, when Mussolini came to power, and worked at a variety of odd jobs. In the early 30s he began collaborating on the screenplays of films, which were less severely censored than the press. In 1937 he turned director. His films, although not in themselves important, heralded the advent of neorealism. His best-known film is *Il Sole Sorge ancora/Outcry* (1947), a tribute to the Italian resistance movement.

FILMS: *Pietro Micca* 1937; *Quelli della Montagna* 1942; *Il Sole Sorge ancora/Outcry* (also co-sc.) 1947; *Czarny Zleb/The Devil's Power* (co-dir., co-sc.; Pol.) 1949; *I Fuorilegge* (also co-sc.) 1950; *Santa Lucia Luntana* (also co-sc.), *La Grande Rinuncia* 1951; *Amore Rosso* (also co-sc.), *Shicksal am Lenkard* (Aus.) 1953.

Verhoeven, Paul. Director. Born on July 18, 1938, in Amsterdam, the Netherlands. *ed.* U. of Leiden. Dutch director, in Hollywood from the mid-80s. Though he earned his Ph.D. in mathematics and physics, filmmaking interested him more, and he turned to creating documentaries for the Royal Dutch Navy and Dutch television. After success with the TV series 'Floris,' he made his feature debut with *Business Is Business* (1971), then gained wider recognition with the domestic and international box-office hit *Turkish Delight* (1973). The aggressively erotic satire about the unhappy marriage of a sculptor (played by Rutger Hauer) brought recognition not only to Verhoeven but to the emerging Dutch feature film industry. His next film, *Soldier of Orange* (1977), was also an art-house hit, a drama about six university students whose lives are irreversibly changed by World War II. In subsequent films, he returned to the themes of sexuality and obsession he had begun to develop in *Turkish Delight*. *Spetters* (1980) was a graphically sexual and violent look at the lives of gay and straight teenagers enamored of motorcycle racing. *The Fourth Man* (1983) was a stylish, hallucinatory, darkly comic thriller about a gay novelist on the trail of a blonde woman he suspects to be a husband-killer. Frequently working with cinematographers Jost Vacano and Jan De Bont and actors Hauer, Jeroen Krabbé, and Renée Soutendjik, Verhoeven established a characteristic visual style that was both haunting and kinetic.

Verhoeven's work caught the notice of Hollywood, resulting in his first English-language film, the American-Dutch co-production *Flesh + Blood* (1985). Grim, bloody, and sexually explicit, the 16th-century adventure starring Hauer narrowly escaped an X rating and did poorly at the box office. However, in his next films, Verhoeven transferred the commercial adroitness he had developed on the art-house circuit to the larger scale of Hollywood blockbusters. Beginning with *Robocop* (1987), his US films have been violent, action-oriented narratives that pack the theaters even as they arouse critical controversy. *Robocop* and *Total Recall* (1990) were science-fiction thrillers, laden with special effects, that managed to explore issues of urban decay, political repression, and the hunger for identity while spinning witty, suspenseful, and visually striking comic book tales. *Basic Instinct* (1992) added the graphic sex characteristic of Verhoeven's Dutch films to the violent thriller format he had perfected in Hollywood. This story of a police detective's affair with a seductive, bisexual murder suspect (Sharon Stone) angered gay activists for its depiction of lesbians, family groups for its sex and violence, and critics for its confusing screenplay, but made a great deal of money just the same. Verhoeven continued to be a critical anomaly, a gifted filmmaker whose knack for what is both shocking and commercial attracts equal parts admiration and outrage.

FILMS: *Wat Zien Ik/Business Is Business* 1971; *Turks Fruit/Turkish Delight* 1973; *Keetje Tippel/Cathy Tippel* 1975; *Soldier of Orange* (also sc.) 1979; *Spetters* 1980; *De Vierde Man/The Fourth Man* 1982; *Flesh + Blood/The Rose and the Sword* (also sc.) 1985; *Robocop* 1987; *Total Recall* 1990; *Basic Instinct* 1992; *Showgirls* 1995; *Starship Troopers* 1997.

Verneuil, Henri. Director. Born Achod Malakian, on Oct. 15, 1920, in Rodosto, Turkey, of Armenian descent. Long in France, he started out as a journalist and radio commentator. He began directing short films in 1946 and turned to features in the early 50s, largely thanks to FERNANDEL. He directed several of the comedian's films as well as other productions of box-office appeal, often thrillers starring Jean Gabin.

FEATURE FILMS: *La Table aux Crevés/The Village Feud* (also co-sc.), *Brelan d'As, Le Fruit défendu/Forbidden Fruit* (also co-sc.) 1952; *Le Boulanger de Valorgue/The Wild Oat, Carnaval, L'Ennemi Public No. 1/The Most Wanted Man* 1953; *Le Mouton à Cinq Pattes/The Sheep Has Five Legs* (also co-story) 1954; *Les Amants du Tage/Lovers' Net* 1955; *Des Gens sans Importance* (also co-sc.), *Paris-Palace-Hôtel/Paris Hotel* (also co-sc.) 1956; *Une Manche et la Belle/What Price Murder* (also co-sc.) 1957; *Maxime* (also co-sc.) 1958; *Le Grand Chef/The Big Chief* (also co-sc.), *La Vache et le Prisonnier/The Cow and I* (also co-sc.) 1959; *L'Affaire d'une Nuit/It Happened All Night, La Française et l'Amour/Love and the Frenchman* ("Adultery" episode) 1960; *Le Président* (also co-sc.), *Les Lions sont lâchés* 1961; *Un Singe en Hiver/A Monkey in Winter* 1962; *Mélodie en Sous-Sol/Any Number Can Win* (also co-sc.) 1963; *Cent Mille Dollars au Soleil/Greed in the Sun* (also co-adapt.), *Week-End à Zuydcoote/Weekend at Dunkirk* 1964; *La 25e Heure/The 25th Hour* (also co-sc.) 1967; *La Bataille de San Sebastián/Guns for San Sebastian* 1968; *Le Clan des Siciliens/The Sicilian Clan* (also co-sc.) *Le Casse/The Burglars* (also prod., co-sc.) 1971; *Le Serpent/The Serpent* (also prod., co-sc.) 1973; *Peur sur la Ville/Night Caller* (also prod., co-sc.) 1975; *Le Corps de mon Ennemi* (also co-sc.) 1976; *Mille Milliards de Dollars* 1981; *Les Morfalous* 1984; *Mayrig/Mother* 1991; *588 rue Paradis* 1992.

Vernon, Anne. Actress. Born Edith Antoinette Alexandrine Vignaud, on Jan. 24, 1925, in Saint-Denis, France. A graduate of the Paris Ecôle des Beaux Arts, she modeled and apprenticed in advertising design before turning stage and screen actress in the late 40s. She played light leads and supporting roles in French as well as in some British and American films.

FILMS INCLUDE: *Le Mannequin assassiné* 1947; *Warning to Wantons* (UK) 1948; *Patto col Diavolo* (It.), *Ainsi finit la Nuit/L'Affaire* 1949; *Shakedown* (US) 1950; *Edouard et Caroline/Edward and Caroline, A Tale of Five Cities/A Tale of Five Women* (UK/Fr./It./Ger.) 1951; *Massacre en Dentelles* 1952; *Rue de l'Estrapade, Jeunes Mariés, Terror on a Train/Time Bomb* (UK) 1953; *The Love Lottery* (UK) 1954; *Bel Ami* (Aus.), *L'Affaire des Poisons, La Donna più Bella del Mondo/Beautiful but Dangerous* (It.) 1955; *Le Long des Trottoirs/Diary of a Bad Girl* 1956; *Les Suspects, Police judiciaire* 1957; *Il Generale della Rovere/General Della Rovere* (It.) 1959; *Arsène Lupin contre Arsène Lupin* 1962; *Les Parapluies de Cherbourg/The Umbrellas of Cherbourg, Patate/Friend of the Family* 1964; *Le Démoniaque* 1967; *Therese and Isabelle* (US/Ger.) 1968.

Vernon, Bobby. *b.* Silvion de Jardins, Mar. 9, 1897, Chicago. *d.* 1939. The son of veteran stage and screen actress Dorothy Vernon, he began a stage career at age 11 and was only 16 when he made his film debut in Universal's Joker Comedies. In 1915 he joined Mack SENNETT's Keystone-Triangle, where he was paired with Gloria SWANSON in a series of romantic comedies. They were often joined by Teddy, a popular Great Dane. Early in his career Vernon was sometimes billed under his real name. In 1917 he went over to the Al CHRISTIE Comedies, continuing in the same romantic vein opposite an assortment of heroines. He remained a popular star of comedy shorts throughout the silent era, but his career ended with the switch to sound. In the 30s he was employed as a comedy supervisor at Paramount, in which capacity he worked on several W. C. Fields and Bing Crosby films. He died of a heart attack at 42.

FILMS INCLUDE: *Almost an Actress, Mike and Jake at the Beach* 1913; *The Mystery of a Taxi Cab, Love and Graft, Love and Electricity* 1914; *Fickle Fatty's Fall, His Father's Footsteps, The Hunt* 1915; *Hearts and Sparks, His Pride and Shame, A Social Cub, Love on Skates, The Danger Girl* 1916; *The Nick of Time Baby, Teddy at the Throttle, Dangers of a Bride, The Sultan's Wife* 1917; *Second Childhood* 1922; *Bright Lights, French Pastry* 1925; *Footloose Widows* 1926; *Cry Baby* 1928; *Stout Heart and Willing Hands* 1931; *Ship a-Hooey* 1932.

Vernon, John. Actor. Born on Feb. 24, 1932, in Montreal. He won a scholarship to the Royal Academy of Dramatic Art in London as a result of his success on the stage with Canadian amateur groups. While in England he appeared with various repertory companies and lent his voice to the film *1984* (1956), in which he was heard offscreen as the voice of Big Brother. Returning home, he appeared on Canadian TV, specializing in Shakespeare, and in the theater, and made his screen debut in 1964. After appearing on Broadway in 'Royal Hunt of the Sun,' he began to be featured regularly in Hollywood films, typically portraying crafty villains.

FILMS INCLUDE: *1984* (v/o, as Big Brother; UK) 1956; *Nobody Waved Goodbye* (Can.) 1964; *Point Blank* 1967; *Justine, Topaz, Tell Them Willie Boy Is Here* 1969; *One More Train to Rob, Dirty Harry* 1971; *Fear Is the Key, Charley Varrick* 1973; *The Black Windmill* (UK/US), *Sweet Movie* (Yug./Fr.), *Brannigan* (UK/US) 1975; *The Outlaw Josey Wales* 1976; *Una Giornata speciale/A Special Day* (It./Can.), *Golden Rendezvous* 1977; *Angela* (Can.), *National Lampoon's Animal House* 1978; *It Rained All Night the Day I Left* (Can./Isr./Fr.), *Crunch* 1979; *Herbie Goes Bananas* 1980; *Airplane II: The Sequel* 1982; *Curtains* (Can.), *Chained Heat, Savage Streets* 1983; *The Blood of Others* (TV; Fr.) 1984; *Fraternity Vacation, Doin' Time, Jungle Warriors* 1985; *Blue Monkey, Killer Klowns from Outer Space, Ernest Goes to Camp* 1987; *Dixie Lanes, Border Heat, Deadly Stranger* 1988; *War Bus Commando* (It.), *Terminal Exposure, I'm Gonna Git You Sucka* 1989; *Bail Out, Mob Story* 1990.

Versois, Odile. Actress. *b.* Katiana de Poliakoff-Baidaroff, June 14, 1930, Paris. *d.* 1980. The daughter of a noted painter and sister of actresses Hélène Vallier (*b.* Militza de Poliakoff-Baidaroff, 1932, Paris) and Marina VLADY, she was a child dancer in the Corps de Ballet of the Paris Opera before entering films at the age of 16. She portrayed gentle, pleasant leading ladies in French and other European films.

FILMS INCLUDE: *Dernières Vacances* 1948; *Fantômas contre Fantômas* 1949; *Orage d'Eté, Paolo e Francesca/Paolo and Francesca/Francesca di Rimini* (as Francesca; It.), *Les Anciens de Saint-Loup* 1950; *Into the Blue/Man in the Dinghy* (UK), *Mademoiselle Josette ma Femme, Bel Amour* 1951; *Domenica* 1952; *A Day to Remember* (UK) 1953; *The Young Lovers/Chance Meeting* (UK) 1954; *To Paris with Love* (UK) 1955; *Checkpoint* (UK) 1956; *Herrscher ohne Krone/King in Shadow* (Ger.) 1957; *Passport to Shame/Room 43* (UK), *Toi le Venin/Nude in a White Car* 1959; *Le Rendez-vous* 1961; *Cartouche* 1962; *Le Dernier Tiercé* 1964; *Benjamin* 1968; *Eglantine* 1972; *Le Crabe-Tambour* 1977.

Vertov, Dziga. Director, film theoretician. *b.* Denis Arkadievitch Kaufman, Jan. 2, 1896, Bialystok, Poland (at that time annexed to Czarist Russia). *d.* 1954. The son of a librarian and the elder brother of Mikhail and Boris KAUFMAN, he began writing poetry at the age of ten and at 16 enrolled at the Bialystok Music Conservatory. In 1915, just before the German invasion of Poland, the Kaufman family moved to Moscow. Young Denis became a medical student and at the same time wrote and published poems, satirical verses, science-fiction novels, and essays. It was around this time that he took the pseudonym Dziga Vertov, Dziga meaning a spinning top in Ukrainian, and Vertov, the act of turning in Russian.

In 1916, Vertov transferred to a medical school at St. Petersburg, where he set up an auditory laboratory for experimentation with the recording and editing of noises and the possibility of documenting natural sounds in writing. In style and approach he associated himself with the futurist movement. In technique he employed the principles of montage. It was only a short step from here to the cinema. Not long after the Revolution of October 1917, Vertov became an editor and writer for the newsreel section of the Moscow Cinema Committee. In the fall of 1918 he began working under Lev Kuleshov's supervision on *Kino-Nedelia (Cinema Weekly)*, a screen periodical that featured news clips from various areas of Soviet life. Montage techniques were used to manipulate the material for greater impact.

In July of 1919, Vertov quit *Kino-Nedelia* and began editing a feature-length compilation film, *Anniversary of the Revolution,* from various past issues of the screen magazine. He followed this with another compilation feature, *The Battle of Tsaritsyn,* a conflict between the Red and White armies which he had covered as a combat film correspondent. Also early in 1920 he accompanied Soviet Chairman Mikhail Kalinin on a propaganda train that toured Russia for several weeks. He made a filmed record of the trip, *Kalinin—The Elder Statesman of All Russians.*

During this period a heated controversy raged among Soviet intellectuals, filmmakers, and other artists over the role of the artist and the kind of art that would best serve the needs of the people of the newly emerging society. Vertov was one of the most outspoken of the debaters. In 1919 he published the Kinoks-Revolution manifesto, the first of several position papers in which he attacked the "impotence" and "backwardness" of fiction films and called for a new style of film reportage taken from real life. He expanded on these ideas in a 1922 magazine article, in which he introduced his theory of Kino-Glaz, or Kino-Oki (Cine-Eye or Kino-Eye). He spoke of the camera as an eye, more perfect than the human eye in its ability to move in time and space and perceive and record impressions: "I am eye. I am a mechanical eye. I, a machine, am showing you a world the likes of which only I can see. I free myself from today and forever from human immobility. . . . I apparatus, maneuvering in the chaos of movements, recording one movement after another in the most complex combinations. . . . My road is towards the creation of a fresh perception of the world. Thus I decipher in a new way the world unknown to you."

The pleas of Vertov and his followers resulted early in 1922 in a decree by Lenin that established a fixed ratio (known as the Lenin Proportion) between entertainment and documentary films in the Soviet cinema. Later that year Vertov started *Kino-Pravda* (literally: cinema truth), a screen magazine named after the Soviet daily newspaper *Pravda.* Released irregularly, each edition of *Kino-Pravda* ran about one reel in length and consisted of two or three news episodes. Although his declared purpose was to capture truth on film, excluding anything not emanating from life itself, Vertov resorted to montage and other manipulative editing techniques in the belief that, by enhancing the emotional impact of film, he was reaching into "the purest possible essence of truth," providing a systematic "research into the chaos of visual phenomena filling the universe."

Vertov turned out 23 editions of *Kino-Pravda* between 1922 and 1925. During the same period he also put together several compilation films. From 1924 he often collaborated with his wife, Elizoveta Svilova, who co-directed several of his films and worked on the script and the editing of many others. Vertov's brother, Mikhail Kaufman, was frequently their cameraman. Vertov's inventive experimentations with form and style resulted in 1924 in *Kino-Glaz/Cinema Eye/Life Unawares* (not to be confused with his theoretic proclamation of the same name), a feature-length film composed mainly of candid camera shots of people who were unaware they were being photographed. Much of the impact of the film was achieved in the cutting room through effective structural symmetry. Striving for a lyrical effect on film, Vertov subtitled his *Stride Soviet!* (1926) "A Symphony of Creative Work," and the film *A Sixth of the World* (also 1926), "A Lyrical Cine-Poem."

Vertov's best-known production is *Man with a Movie Camera* (also shown in the US as *Moscow Today* and *Living Russia or the Man with the Camera;* 1929), a dawn-to-dusk view of Moscow which is set apart from other CITY SYMPHONIES in that it is concerned less with capturing glimpses of city life than with commenting on the relation between cinema and reality. The city scenes are fleeting and seemingly filmed haphazardly. But the structure is original in conception. As we watch the film, we are constantly made aware of the cameraman who shoots it, and at one point we watch on the screen a group of people watching the same film we are watching. Vertov utilized a great many cinematic effects in this film, including split screens, multiple superimpositions, and variable speeds, in an evident attempt to give physical support to his theoretical claim of the power of the camera eye.

Having experimented with sound recording and editing, Vertov enthusiastically welcomed the arrival of sound to films. In 1929 he wrote that sounds could be edited as easily as film, "in harmony or not in harmony with the visuals." He proved his point in his first sound film, *Enthusiasm/Symphony of the Donbas* (1931), a tribute to miners of the Don Basin who fulfilled their five-year-plan quotas. The film was noted for its innovative use of sound, in synchronization as well as in counterpoint. Even more original and imaginative in its use of sound as well as visual technique and pictorial lyricism was Vertov's *Three Songs About Lenin* (1934), an emotionally stirring production composed from stock footage and newly shot material that glorified the memory of Lenin through the eyes and the songs of Soviet peasants. Vertov deviated markedly from his Kino-Eye theory to achieve the brilliant formal construction of this film, a concession he had made to a lesser degree with *Man with a Movie Camera.*

The early 30s witnessed an extreme change in Soviet artistic life. Following Stalin's consolidation of power, all artistic activity in the Soviet Union was brought under the control of the Central Committee, and an officially sanctioned style of socialist realism was imposed from above. Such directors as Kuleshov and Eisenstein were ostracized for "formalism," and Vertov, although not directly rebuked, was allowed to fade gradually away. He directed his last feature-length personal film, *Lullaby,* in 1937. Afterward he worked mainly on compilation films, documentaries, and newsreels. From 1947 until his death of cancer in 1954 he worked for the newsreel "Novosti Dnia" ("News of the day"). He left behind notes and partly finished manuscripts for memoirs, which have never been published.

A modernist of intellectual foresight and bold artistic vision, Vertov influenced in his ideas and films the works not only of his Soviet colleagues but also of many filmmakers on the international scene. Present-day practitioners of CINÉMA VÉRITÉ consider him the father of their movement. In his writing he forecast such modern communication phenomena as television and mixed media. During his lifetime he was considered by many an eccentric, but his single-minded obsession with cinematic expression has had a lingering impact on the development of the art and science of film.

FILMS INCLUDE: *Anniversary of the Revolution* 1919; *The Battle of Tsaritsyn, Kalinin—The Elder Statesman of All Russians, The Exhumation of the Remains of Sergei Radonezhsky, The Mironov Trial* 1920; *Train of the Central Committee/Agit-Train/The Train* 1921; *History of the Civil War, The Ezerov Trial/The Trial of the Social Revolutionaries, Univermag/Universal Department Store/Gum* 1922; *October Cinema Truth/Yesterday Today Tomorrow* (special three-reel edition of *Kino-Pravda*), *Five Years of Struggle and Victory* 1923; *Today* (animated cartoon), *Soviet Playthings* (animated cartoon), *Kino-Glaz/Cinema Eye/Life Unawares* 1924; *Stride Soviet!, A Sixth of the World* 1926; *The Eleventh Year/The Tenth October Anniversary* 1928; *Man with a Movie Camera/Moscow Today/Living Russia or the Man with the Camera* 1929; *Enthusiasm/Symphony of the Donbas* 1931; *Three Songs About Lenin* 1934; *Lullaby, Sergei Ordzhonikidze* 1937; *Three Heroines* 1938; *Elevation A, Blood for Blood—Life for Life, Camera Reporters on the Line of Fire* 1941; *On to the Front!/The Kazakhstan Front* 1943; *On the Mountains of Ala-Tau* 1944; *The Oath of Youth* 1947.

Vicas, Victor. *b.* Mar. 25, 1918, in Moscow. *d.* 1985. Educated in Paris, he entered films as assistant cameraman in the late 30s. He served in the French army during the German invasion and was taken prisoner. However, he managed to escape and in 1942 came to the US, where he directed documentary shorts. He continued with the production of shorts after returning to Paris in 1945. After switching to feature films in the early 50s, he worked mostly in Germany but also in other Western countries and on French television.

FILMS INCLUDE: *Weg ohne Umkehr/No Way Back* (Ger.) 1953; *Das zweite Leben/A Double Life* (Ger.) 1954; *Herr über Leben und Tod* (Ger.) 1955; *Je reviendrai à Kandara* (Fr.), *The Wayward Bus* (US) 1957; *Count Five and Die* (UK), *SOS Gletscherpilot* (Switz.) 1958; *Jons und Erdme* (Ger.) 1959; *Zwei unter Millionen* (Ger.) 1961; *La Train de Berlin est arrêté* (sc. only; Fr./Ger./It.) 1964.

Vickers, Martha. Actress. *b.* Martha MacVicar, May 28, 1925, Ann Arbor, Mich. *d.* 1971. A photographer's model, she made her first film appearance at the age of 18 in a nonspeaking role, as a murder victim in *Frankenstein Meets the Wolf Man* (1943). She had a promising role as Lauren Bacall's younger sister in *The Big Sleep* but subsequently played routine feminine leads. She was billed under her real name in 1943–44. She was married to Mickey ROONEY from 1949 until 1952.

FILMS: As Martha MacVicar—*Frankenstein Meets the Wolf Man, Captive Wild Woman, Top Man, Hi Ya Sailor* 1943; *This Is the Life, Marine Raiders, The Mummy's Ghost, The Falcon in Mexico* 1944. As Martha Vickers—*The Big Sleep, The Time the Place and the Girl* 1946; *The Man I Love, That Way with Women, Love and Learn* 1947; *Ruthless* 1948; *Bad Boy, Alimony, Daughter of the West* 1949; *The Big Bluff* 1955; *The Burglar* 1957; *Four Fast Guns* 1960.

Victor, Henry. Actor. *b.* Oct. 2, 1898, London. *d.* 1945. Tall leading man of British silent films. Raised in Germany, he had a noticeable accent that caused him to switch from leads to character roles with the advent of sound. He typically played villains, often Nazis, in both British and Hollywood talkies. Memorable as Hercules, the circus strongman in *Freaks* (1932).

FILMS INCLUDE: In the UK—*Revolution* 1915; *She, The Picture of Dorian Gray* 1916; *Call of the Sea* 1919; *The Old Wives' Tale* 1921; *A Bill of Divorcement, The Crimson Circle* 1922; *The Prodigal Son, Scandal* 1923; *Slaves of Destiny* 1924. In the US—*The White Monkey* 1925; *Crossed Signals* 1926; *The Beloved Rogue, Topsy and Eva, The Fourth Commandment* 1927. In the UK—*The Guns of Loos* 1928; *After the Verdict, The Hate Ship* 1929. In the US—*One Heavenly Night, The Seas Beneath, Suicide Fleet* 1931; *Freaks, The Mummy* 1932. In the UK—*I Spy, The Scotland Yard Mystery* 1933; *Conquest of the Air* (UK) 1936; *The Great Barrier/Silent Barriers* 1937. In the US—*Confessions of a Nazi Spy, Hotel Imperial, Pack Up Your Troubles* 1939; *Zanzibar* 1940; *King of the Zombies* 1941; *To Be or Not to Be, Desperate Journey* 1942; *That Nazty Nuisance* 1943.

Vidal, Gore. Novelist, playwright, screenwriter, essayist. Born on Oct. 3, 1925, in West Point, N.Y. He wrote his first novel at the end of WW II while still in US Army uniform. He has since authored many novels, plays, screenplays, detective stories (under the pseudonym Edgar Box), and essays, as well as numerous short stories, magazine articles, and literary and drama reviews. The grandson of Senator T. P. Gore of Oklahoma, he has long been active in liberal politics and in 1960 ran unsuccessfully for the US Congress as a Democratic-Liberal candidate in New York. In the late 60s he lived in Rome. He appeared as himself in *Fellini's Roma* (1972).

FILMS INCLUDE: *The Catered Affair* 1956; *The Left-Handed Gun* (teleplay basis only: 'The Death of Billy the Kid'), *I Accuse!* 1958; *The Scapegoat, Suddenly Last Summer* 1959; *Visit to a Small Planet* (teleplay and play basis only) 1960; *The Best Man* (from his own play) 1964; *Is Paris Burning?* 1966; *The Last of the Mobile Hotshots, Myra Breckinridge* (novel basis only) 1970; *Caligula* 1977; *Bob Roberts* (act. only) 1992; *With Honors* (act. only) 1994; *The Shadow Conspiracy* (act. only) 1997.

Vidal, Henri. Actor. *b.* Nov. 26, 1919, Clermont-Ferrand, France. *d.* 1959. Ruggedly handsome, athletic leading man of French films. He is best remembered, however, for his appearance in an Italian production, *Fabiola* (1948). He was the husband of Michèle MORGAN.

FILMS INCLUDE: *Montmartre-sur-Seine* 1941; *L'Ange de la Nuit* 1942; *Les Maudits/The Damned, L'Eventail/Naughty Martine* 1947; *Fabiola* (It.) 1948; *Le Paradis des Pilotes perdus* 1949; *La Belle que violà, Quai de Grenelle/The Strollers* 1950; *La Passante, L'Etrange Madame X* 1951; *Les Sept Péchés capitaux/The Seven Deadly Sins, La Jeune Folle/Desperate Decision* 1952; *Orient Express* (It./Fr./Ger.), *Attila* (It./Fr.), *Le Port du Désir/The House on the Waterfront* 1954; *Napoléon, Série noire* 1955; *Les Salauds vont en Enfer/The Wicked Go to Hell* 1956; *Porte de Lilas/Gates of Paris, Une Parisienne, Une Manche et la Belle/What Price Murder* 1957; *Charmants Garçons, Soi Belle et tais-toi/Be Beautiful and Shut Up* 1958; *Voulez-vous danser avec moi?/Come Dance with Me!* 1959.

video. 1. From the Latin for "I see," the visual content of a sound picture as opposed to its aural track. The term is usually applied to television images but is sometimes used with motion pictures. 2. A general term for television transmission, including both picture and sound elements. 3. A synonym for videotape, a magnetic tape on which sound and picture elements can be recorded, played back, and transmitted through television systems. 4. Performances or productions recorded on videotape, for example, music videos.

Videotape technology dates back to the 50s, when the first images were recorded on reels of two-inch magnetic tape. By the end of the 60s videotape was part of the basic equipment of television recording and transmission, though its picture quality, in terms of resolution, density, contrast, and color, was nowhere near that of the 35 mm film stock used in theatrical exhibition. Even so, as videotape improved in quality and the associated equipment became less bulky and more affordable, television producers found ever more uses for it. Many documentarists, avant-garde artists, and makers of educational and industrial films also found it more convenient to work in video than film. The introduction of home video "camcorders" in the mid-80s largely replaced the 8 mm and Super 8 mm film gauges formerly used for home movies.

By the 80s, the motion picture industry was using video to support film production. Because videotape can be played back immediately after recording, directors on a film set can instantly view the results of a take through VIDEO ASSIST systems, video cameras and monitors tied to the viewfinders of film cameras. Because videotape can be edited electronically and easily copied, VIDEO EDITING SYSTEMS allow a film editor to craft multiple video versions of a film before selecting a final sequence, which is then used as a guide in cutting and assembling the film negative. VIDEO COLOR ANALYZERS are used in TIMING, or balancing the density and tonal value of a film. Electronic manipulation of video images is used to plan and try out special effects shots that are then replicated on film through optical or digital means (see OPTICAL PRINTER, DIGITAL EFFECTS).

The piece of video technology with the greatest impact on the motion picture business has been the videocassette recorder (VCR). VCRs suitable for home use were introduced in the mid-70s in two formats, Betamax or Beta, pioneered by Sony, and VHS, pioneered by JVC. After years of fierce competition, during which both systems rapidly improved in quality and price, VHS drove Beta out of existence. In the process, videocassette recorders became nearly as commonplace as television sets, with 77 percent of American households owning VCRs by 1992.

Though Hollywood was at first wary of competition from the home video market, it soon became aware of the financial bonanza to be reaped. No longer did revenue from a film end with its worldwide theatrical release and sale to television. Videocassette copies of the film could now be sold to retailers, who resold them to consumers or rented them out for overnight viewing. Consumers enjoyed the freedom of selecting virtually any film they wanted to see without having to go out to a theater or wait for it to run on television. Studios, now with video distribution subsidiaries, were able to make more money off box-office hits and give a second chance to flops. Some low-budget producers began to specialize in films earmarked for release "straight to video," without any theatrical run at all.

Despite the fact that 35 mm film remains the standard for theatrical exhibition, high-definition video has developed to the point where it rivals the image quality of film, in addition to offering potential economies in production. However, the impracticality of replacing thousands of traditional theater projectors with high-definition television (HDTV) systems means that motion pictures will probably continue to be made on film for some time to come.

video analyzer. See VIDEO COLOR ANALYZER.

video assist. Also called a "video tap," a device attached to a motion picture camera that allows a shot to be viewed on a video monitor during filming and replayed on videotape immediately afterward. The video assist is usually connccted to the camera's reflex viewfinder, so that the video image is an accurate representation of the setup that will appear on film, thus providing instant DAILIES.

video color analyzer. Also called a "video analyzer," a device for assessing and altering the density and color of a film image during the process called TIMING. The system transmits the film negative in positive form to a video screen, where the timer can see and work with the image. The analyzer generates a coded control band, which is used in printing to make precise adjustments in density and tonal value. A commonly used video color analyzer is the Hazeltine, named for its manufacturer.

video editing system. An editing machine that transfers film frames to videotape and transmits them to one or more monitors, where the editor can examine and rearrange them electronically without the need for physical cutting and splicing of a WORK PRINT (see EDITING). Alternative sequences can be easily tested, compared, and altered before being recorded. A computer codes the frames, simplifying the process of NEGATIVE CUTTING. Faster and easier than traditional cutting and splicing, video systems have been adopted by many editors.

video tap. See VIDEO ASSIST.

videotape. See VIDEO.

Vidor, Charles. Director. *b.* July 27, 1900, Budapest. *d.* 1959. *ed.* U. of Budapest, U. of Berlin. An infantry lieutenant in WW I. He served his film apprenticeship at the UFA studios in Berlin. He came to the US in 1924, and after singing in Wagnerian opera, he spent several years in Hollywood as assistant director, film editor, and screenwriter before directing his first feature film in 1932. A solid craftsman, he treated the most mundane subjects with a certain technical flair. Along with many routine films, he directed a number of top-quality pictures, most notably the evergreen of American screen erotica, *Gilda.* He died during the production of *Song Without End* (1960). (The film was completed by George Cukor.)

FILMS: *The Bridge* (short) 1931; *The Mask of Fu Manchu* (uncredited; co-dir. with Charles Bralin) 1932; *Sensation Hunters* 1933; *Double Door* 1934; *Strangers All, The Arizonian, His Family Tree* 1935; *Muss 'Em Up* 1936; *A Doctor's Diary, The Great Gambini, She's No Lady* 1937; *Romance of the Redwoods, Blind Alley, Those High Grey Walls* 1939; *My Son My Son!, The Lady in Question* 1940; *Ladies in Retirement, New York Town* 1941; *The Tuttles of Tahiti* 1942; *The Desperadoes* 1943; *Cover Girl, Together Again* 1944; *A Song to Remember, Over 21* 1945; *Gilda* 1946; *The Loves of Carmen* (also prod.) 1948; *It's a Big Country* (co-dir. with six others), *Hans Christian Andersen* 1952; *Thunder in the East* 1953; *Rhapsody* 1954; *Love Me or Leave Me* 1955; *The Swan* 1956; *The Joker Is Wild* 1957; *A Farewell to Arms* 1958; *Song Without End* (completed by George Cukor) 1960.

Vidor, Florence. Actress. *b.* Florence Cobb, July 23, 1895, Houston, Tex. *d.* 1977. Popular star of Hollywood silents. Her name was changed to Arto when her mother remarried and to Vidor when she herself married a young film enthusiast, King VIDOR, in 1915. That same year they both headed for Hollywood, where she began acting in Vitagraph films and he started a slow ascent toward prominence as a director. Florence first drew attention in a secondary role in *A Tale of Two Cities* (1917) and graduated to leads that same year at Famous Players-Lasky, opposite Sessue HAYAKAWA. But she really came into her own in the 20s, when she starred in a string of successful dramas and comedies, doing particularly well in the sophisticated light films of Lubitsch and Mal St. Clair. She was separated from Vidor in 1923 and they later divorced. In 1928 she married violinist Jascha Heifetz and they divorced in 1945. Her career came to an end in 1929 after a disastrous single appearance in a talkie in which her voice proved unsuitable for sound pictures.

FILMS INCLUDE: *The Yellow Girl* 1916; *A Tale of Two Cities, Hashimura Togo* 1917; *The Honor of His House, Old Wives for New, Till I Come Back to You* 1918; *The Other Half, Poor Relations* 1919; *The Jack-Knife Man, The Family Honor* 1920; *Lying Lips, Beau Revel, Hail the Woman* 1921; *Skin Deep, The Real Adventure, Conquering the Woman, Dusk to Dawn* 1922; *Alice Adams* (title role), *Main Street* (as Carol Kennicott), *The Virginian* 1923; *The Marriage Circle, Welcome Stranger, Barbara Frietchie* (title role), *Borrowed Husbands, Christine of the Hungry Heart, Husbands and Lovers* 1924; *The Mirage, The Girl of Gold, Are Parents People?, Grounds for Divorce, Marry Me, The Trouble with Wives* 1925; *The Enchanted Hill, The Grand Duchess and the Waiter, Sea Horses, You Never Know Women, The Eagle of the Sea, The Popular Sin* 1926; *Afraid to Love, One Woman to Another, The World at Her Feet, Honeymoon Hate* 1927; *Doomsday, The Magnificent Flirt, The Patriot* 1928; *Chinatown Nights* 1929.

Vidor, King. Director. *b.* Feb. 8, 1894, Galveston, Tex. *d.* 1982. The son of a prosperous lumber manufacturer, he became infatuated with cinema as a child and while still a schoolboy he went to work at a local nickelodeon as a ticket taker and standby projectionist. He had the opportunity to study the same films numerous times and soon felt an urge to make pictures himself. He began by shooting local events and selling the footage to regional exchanges and newsreel companies. In 1915 he married Florence Arto, a pretty Houston girl, and they set out to Hollywood in their Model-T Ford. While his wife, as Florence VIDOR, rapidly rose in films from bit player to famous star, Vidor accepted any film work he could get. He worked as an extra and a studio clerk and tried unsuccessfully to sell the many scripts he wrote in his spare time. Eventually, he began directing two-reelers at Universal and finally made his debut as a feature director with *The Turn in the Road* (1919).

Vidor soon formed his own small studio, Vidor Village, in

which he made a number of modest productions, many of them starring his wife, then joined the MGM staff. His reputation increased steadily and he became firmly established in the front rank of Hollywood's directors with *The Big Parade* (1925), a large-scale antiwar film notable both as an impressive spectacle and as a sensitive, if sentimental, human document. Having divorced Florence Vidor in 1924, he married another of his stars, Eleanor BOARDMAN, in 1926 (the marriage lasted only several years and he later was married for a third time, to writer Elizabeth Hill). A second important milestone in Vidor's career, after *The Big Parade*, was *The Crowd* (1928), one of the most remarkable American silent films, a starkly realistic and deeply pessimistic drama about the predicament of an individual in the anonymity of a big city. The technical virtuosity and the humanistic quality that distinguished this film were further demonstrated in Vidor's subsequent important productions, notably *Hallelujah, Street Scene,* and *Our Daily Bread.*

In his sound films, Vidor's experimentations with the plastic force of the moving image extended into exploring the potential of the sound track and achieved some startling effects with the juxtaposition of sound and image. Certain sequences in Vidor's films stand out as among the most memorable in the annals of cinema: the "acrobatic" and very meaningful shot in *The Crowd* in which the camera scales the heights of a skyscraper and glides through a window into a large, crowded office, finally stopping at the hero's desk; the sexually charged sequences in *Hallelujah;* the virtuosic camera mobility in *Street Scene;* the famous climactic montage sequence celebrating the flow of water in the irrigation system in *Our Daily Bread;* and many, many others. But in their entirety, Vidor's films rarely matched the power of such remarkable individual scenes, and the naïve humanistic idealism of his early period often descended into maudlin sentimentality.

After *Our Daily Bread* (1934), in which Vidor exalted the merits of returning to nature and the value of cooperative farms, his films were motivated mostly by the commercial demands of the box office. The peak achievement of his commercial period was *Duel in the Sun* (1947), a sprawling epic Western that demonstrated the full maturity of his craftsmanship. Vidor retired from films in the late 50s following the critical and commercial failure of *Solomon and Sheba.* In the 60s he taught a graduate cinema class at UCLA. In 1964 he was awarded a special prize for the cumulative body of his work at the Edinburgh Film Festival. His autobiography, *A Tree Is a Tree,* was published in 1953. In 1979 he tried to raise capital for the production of *The Actor,* a film based on the tragic life of James MURRAY, who starred in Vidor's *The Crowd.* Also in that year he was awarded an honorary Oscar for "his incomparable achievements as a cinematic creator and innovator." He had been nominated in the best director category five times.

FEATURE FILMS: *The Turn in the Road* (also sc.), *Better Times* (also sc.), *The Other Half* (also sc.), *Poor Relations* (also sc., from his own play) 1919; *The Family Honor* (also prod.), *The Jack-Knife Man* (also prod., co-sc.) 1920; *The Sky Pilot, Love Never Dies* (also prod., sc.) 1921; *The Real Adventure, Dusk to Dawn* (also prod.), *Conquering the Woman* (also prod.), *Peg o' My Heart* 1922; *Alice Adams* (prod. only), *The Woman of Bronze, Three Wise Fools* (also co-sc.) 1923; *Wild Oranges* (also sc.), *Happiness, Wine of Youth* (also prod.), *His Hour, Wife of the Centaur* 1924; *Proud Flesh, The Big Parade* (also prod.; re-released in 1927) 1925; *La Boheme* (also prod.), *Bardelys the Magnificent* 1926; *The Crowd* (also story, co-sc.), *The Patsy, Show People* 1928; *Hallelujah* (also story) 1929; *Not So Dumb, Billy the Kid* 1930; *Street Scene, The Champ* (also prod.) 1931; *Bird of Paradise, Cynara* 1932; *The Stranger's Return* (also prod.) 1933; *Our Daily Bread* (also prod., co-sc.) 1934; *The Wedding Night, So Red the Rose* 1935; *The Texas Rangers* (also prod., co-story) 1936; *Stella Dallas* 1937; *The Citadel* 1938; *The Wizard of Oz* (directed some scenes only during Victor Fleming's absence) 1939; *Northwest Passage, Comrade X* 1940; *H. M. Pulham Esq.* (also prod., co-sc.) 1941; *An American Romance* (also prod., story) 1944; *Duel in the Sun* 1947; *On Our Merry Way/A Miracle Can Happen* (co-dir. with Leslie Fenton) 1948; *The Fountainhead, Beyond the Forest* 1949; *Lightning Strikes Twice* 1951; *Japanese War Bride, Ruby Gentry* (also co-prod.) 1952; *Man Without a Star* 1955; *War and Peace/Guerra e Pace* (also co-sc.; US/It.) 1956; *Solomon and Sheba* 1959.

Vierny, Sacha. Director of photography. Born on Aug. 10, 1919, in Bois-le-Roi, France. A graduate of IDHEC, he collaborated on many shorts from 1953 and graduated to features in 1958. He has since worked on the films of Alain RESNAIS and Chris MARKER, among others. His photography is noted for its meticulous lighting and its command of the deep-focus shot.

FILMS INCLUDE: *Le Chant du Styrène* (short) 1957; *Lettre de Sibérie/Letter from Siberia* (medium-length doc.), *Le Bel Age* 1958; *Hiroshima mon Amour* 1959; *La Morte-Saison des Amours/The Season for Love, L'Année dernière à Marienbad/Last Year at Marienbad* 1961; *Muriel ou le Temps d'un Retour/Muriel* 1963; *La Guerre est finie, La Musica* 1966; *Belle de Jour* 1967; *Le Tatoué* 1968; *La Nuit bulgare* 1970; *Stavisky* 1974; *Baxter—Vera Baxter* (US), *Le Diable dans la Boîte, La Vocation Suspendue* 1977; *La Bravade Legendaire, L'Hypothese du Tableau Vole* 1978; *Mon oncle d'Amerique* 1980; *Beau Pere* 1981; *Les Trois couronnes du metelot* 1983; *L'Amour a mort, Clash, La Femme Publique, Flugel unde Felleln* (Ger.) 1984; *A Zed and Two Noughts* (UK) 1985; *The Belly of an Architect* (UK) 1987; *The Cook the Thief His Wife and Her Lover* (UK) 1990; *Drowning By Numbers, Prospero's Books* (UK) 1991; *The Baby of Macon* 1993; *The Pillow Book* 1997.

Viertel, Berthold. Director. *b.* June 28, 1885, Vienna. *d.* 1953. *ed.* U. of Vienna. A poet, a novelist, a playwright, and an essayist, he started out as an actor and stage director and turned to German films in the early 20s. He directed in Hollywood from the late 20s and in England from 1933. In addition, he collaborated on the scripts of F. W. Murnau's American films *Four Devils* (1929) and *City Girl* (1930). He was married to Polish-born actress Salka Steuermann Viertel (1889–1978), who collaborated on the screenplays of several Greta Garbo Hollywood films in the 30s and early 40s (*Queen Christina, Anna Karenina, Conquest,* etc.). Their son is Peter Viertel, novelist, screenwriter (*Saboteur, We Were Strangers, The Sun Also Rises, The Old Man and the Sea,* etc.), and the husband of Deborah KERR.

FILMS: In Germany—*Ein Puppenheim* (also co-sc.) 1922; *Nora* (also co-sc.) 1923; *Die Perücke* (also sc.) 1924; *Die Abenteuer eines Zehnmarkscheines/Uneasy Money* 1926. In the US—*The One Woman Idea, Seven Faces* 1929; *Die heilige Flamme* (German version of *The Sacred Flame*), *Man Trouble* 1930; *The Spy, The Magnificent Lie* 1931; *The Wiser Sex, The Man from Yesterday* 1932. In the UK—*Little Friend* 1934; *The Passing of the Third Floor Back* 1935; *Rhodes of Africa/Rhodes* 1936.

viewer. A motorized or hand-operated device for rapid viewing of film. It is especially useful in running through great lengths of film in search of a particular shot.

viewfinder. A sighting device that enables a camera operator to compose a shot and view the action during filming. The viewfinder may be attached to the camera or built into its mechanism. The main drawback of a viewfinder attached near the camera lens has been the need to compensate for parallax error in framing. In the early days of motion pictures this could be avoided by a device that enabled the operator to view the action through the thickness of the film itself. But the advent of antihalation backing (see HALATION) made this impossible. One of the many solutions attempted was the rackover system, which allowed viewing through the lens by displacing film behind the lens with a viewing tube. This worked perfectly for the initial framing of a shot but did not permit viewing the action while the camera was actually running. A far more practical solution has been the reflex viewing system, in which the viewed image is reflected by the shutter and formed on a plate of ground glass.

vignette. 1. A photographed image that gradually fades out at the edges of the frame, leaving no sharply defined line at the border. The effect may be achieved by a matte process, either in the camera or in the optical printer. 2. A brief, carefully etched scene or performance.

Vignola, Robert G. Director. *b.* Aug. 5, 1882, Trivigno, Italy. *d.* 1953. In the US from an early age, he was raised in Albany, N.Y. He started his career on the stage as a Shakespearean actor, entered films as an actor with Kalem, and began directing around 1911. He turned out numerous silents of varying importance and quality but directed only a handful of low-budget films after the advent of sound.

FILMS INCLUDE: *Arizona Bill* (co-dir. with George Melford) 1911; *A Virginia Feud* 1913; *The Vampire's Trail* (co dir., co-sc. with T. Hayes Hunter), *Barefoot Boy* (also sc.) 1914; *The Scorpion's Sting, The Stolen Ruby, A Sister's Burden, Honor Thy Father, Don Caesar De Bazan* (also sc.), *The Vanderhoff Affair* (also act.), *The Pretenders, The Luring Lights* 1915; *The Black Crook, The Spider, Audrey, The Moment Before, The Evil Thereof, The Velvet Paw, The Reward of Patience, Seventeen* 1916; *Great Expectations, The Fortunes of Fifi, Her Better Self, Double Crossed, The Hungry Heart* 1917; *The Knife, Madame Jealousy, The Reason Why, His Official Fiancee, The Claw, The Girl Who Came Back, Woman's Weapons* 1918; *Experimental Marriage, You Never Saw Such a Girl, The Winning Girl, The Home Town Girl, Louisiana, The Third Kiss, The Heart of Youth, An Innocent Adventuress, More Deadly Than the Male* 1919; *The Thirteenth Commandment, The World and His Wife* 1920; *The Passionate Pilgrim, Straight Is the Way, The Woman God Changed, Enchantment* 1921; *Beauty's Worth, The Young Diana* (co-dir. with Albert Capellani), *When Knighthood Was in Flower* 1922; *Adam and Eva* 1923; *Yolanda, Married Flirts* 1924; *The Way of a Girl, Déclassée* 1925; *Fifth Avenue* 1926; *Cabaret* 1927; *Tropic Madness* 1928; *The Red Sword* 1929; *Broken Dreams* 1933; *The Scarlet Letter* 1934; *The Perfect Clue* 1935; *The Girl from Scotland Yard* 1937.

Vigo, Jean. Director. *b.* Apr. 26, 1905, Paris. *d.* 1934. The son of a famous militant French anarchist who was found dead in his prison cell in 1917, he spent an unhappy childhood at a number of boarding schools. Suffering from tuberculosis, he settled as a young adult in the warm climate of Nice, where he directed his first film, the satiric social documentary *A propos de Nice.* The film was influenced by the work of Dziga VERTOV, whose brother, Boris KAUFMAN, served as Vigo's cameraman. Kaufman also handled the photography on Vigo's two later feature films, *Zéro de Conduite* and *L'Atalante,* which he filmed after moving to Paris in the early 30s.

Both *Zéro de Conduite* and *L'Atalante* were experimental and innovative in style, blending lyricism with realism and surrealism and underlining the whole with a cynical anarchic approach to life. *Zéro,* an eloquent parable of freedom versus authority, is set at a boys' boarding school and undoubtedly echoes Vigo's own unhappy experiences as a child. Under the pressure of various civic groups the film was removed from screens several months after its release in 1933. It was branded "anti-French" by the censors and was not shown again in France until 1945. *L'Atalante,* considered Vigo's masterpiece, was severely mutilated by its producers, who feared that its slashing attack on the essence of French bourgeoisie would not be well accepted by the public.

Vigo fell ill during the production of *L'Atalante.* His death of leukemia at the age of 29 robbed French cinema of one of its most original talents. He left behind only three feature films and one short. A Jean Vigo Prize is awarded each year in France in memory of a filmmaker whose work is characterized by "independence of spirit and quality of directing."

FILMS: *A Propos de Nice* 1930; *Taris Champion de Natation* (short) 1931; *Zéro de Conduite/Zero for Conduct* 1933; *L'Atalante* 1934.

Vilar, Jean. Actor, stage director. *b.* Mar. 25, 1912, Sète, France. *d.* 1971. *ed.* U. of Montpellier; U. of Paris. Initially a jazz musician and later a distinguished actor of the Paris stage, he also directed many productions and was the director of the Théâtre National Populaire and manager of the Palais de Chaillot from 1951 till 1963. His film appearances were few but striking.

FILMS INCLUDE: *Les Portes de la Nuit/Gates of the Night* 1946; *Les Frères Bouquinquant* 1947; *Le Carrefour du Crime, Bagarres* 1948; *La Soif des Hommes/The Thirst of Men* 1950; *Casabianca, Jocelyn* 1951; *Till l'Espiègle* 1956; *Raphaël ou le débauché, Le Petit Matin* 1971.

Vincent, Jan-Michael. Actor. Born on July 15, 1944, in Denver. *ed.* Ventura (Calif.) City Coll. Youthful leading man of Hollywood films of the 70s. Discovered by an agent after completing his service with the National Guard, he made his screen debut in 1967 in a Mexican production and subsequently starred in many television programs, TV movies, and motion pictures, later of the low-budget variety. He used the name Michael Vincent until 1970.

FILMS INCLUDE: *Los Bandidos* (Mex.) 1967; *Journey to Shiloh* 1968; *The Undefeated* 1969; *Tribes* (orig. for TV) 1970; *Going Home* 1971; *The Mechanic* 1972; *The World's Greatest Athlete* 1973; *Buster and Billie* 1974; *Bite the Bullet, White Line Fever* 1975; *Vigilante Force, Baby Blue Marine, Shadow of the Hawk* (Can.) 1976; *Damnation Alley/Survival Run* 1977; *Big Wednesday, Hooper* 1978; *Defiance* 1979; *The Return, Hard Country* 1981; *Last Plane Out* 1983; *Born in East L.A., Enemy Territory* 1987; *Deadly Embrace* 1988; *Demonstone, Alienator, Hit List* 1989; *Hangfire* 1990; *In Gold We Trust, Haunting Fear, Raw Nerve, The Divine Enforcer* 1991; *Beyond the Call of Duty, Animal Instincts, Xtro II, Deadly Avenger* 1992; *Indecent Behavior* 1994.

Vinson, Helen. Actress. Born Helen Rulfs on Sept. 17, 1907, in Beaumont, Tex. *ed.* U. of Texas. Leading lady of Hollywood films of the 30s and early 40s, following stage experience on Broadway. The daughter of an oil company executive, she typically played sophisticated, aloof, sometimes kittenish heroines or second leads. Her second of three husbands was British tennis pro Fred Perry.

FILMS INCLUDE: *Jewel Robbery, Two Against the World, They Call It Sin, I Am a Fugitive from a Chain Gang, Lawyer Man* 1932; *Grand Slam, The Little Giant, Midnight Club, The Power and the Glory, The Kennel Murder Case, As Husbands Go* 1933; *The Life of Vergie Winters, Gift of Gab, The Captain Hates the Sea, Broadway Bill* 1934; *A Notorious Gentleman, The Wedding Night, The Age of Indiscretion, Private Worlds, Transatlantic Tunnel* (UK) 1935; *King of the Damned* (UK), *Love in Exile* (UK), *Reunion* 1936; *Vogues of 1938, Live Love and Learn* 1937; *In Name Only* 1939; *Enemy Agent, Torrid*

Zone, Beyond Tomorrow 1940; *Nothing but the Truth* 1941; *The Lady and the Monster, Are These Our Parents?* 1944; *The Thin Man Goes Home* 1945.

Visconti, Luchino. Director. *b.* Count Don Luchino Visconti di Modrone, on Nov. 2, 1906, in Milan, Italy. *d.* 1976. Born into Milan's highest ranking nobility and one of the leading aristocratic families in all of Italy. After completing his military service, he spent much of his youth cultivating his tastes for music and art and breeding horses. His only association with the performing arts during that period was as a set designer for a 1928 play. He was 30 years old when he began his career as a working artist, joining Jean RENOIR in Paris as costume designer and assistant director on such films as *A Day in the Country* and *The Lower Depths.* Away from the restrictive atmosphere of Fascist Italy, he came under the influence of communist ideology, to which he was to remain committed in the ensuing years, in sharp contrast to his aristocratic, almost feudal private lifestyle. In the late 30s he came briefly to the US but felt uncomfortable in the atmosphere of Hollywood and returned to Italy disappointed.

After working as an assistant on *La Tosca* (1940), Visconti set out to make his own first film. He wanted to adapt to the screen a work by Giovanni Verga, a Sicilian novelist idolized by the Italian leftist underground for his naturalistic style, or *verismo.* When Visconti's project met with strong opposition by Fascist censors, Visconti allayed their suspicions by submitting a script adapted from the American novelist James Cain's *The Postman Always Rings Twice.* The resultant film, *Ossessione* (1942), was ostensibly a drama about the destructive powers of sexual passion and betrayal, but its realistic depiction of proletariat life under fascism enraged the authorities, who mutilated the film. Although relatively polished, *Ossessione* heralded the Italian neorealist movement in its naturalistic setting and earthy texture.

With his second feature, *La Terra Trema/The Earth Trembles,* a sprawling drama of the Italian South, Visconti moved away from pure realism toward the elaborate decorative style that was to characterize his later films. It is a masterful work combining such documentary elements as local dialect in the sound track and a nonprofessional cast, with elaborately structured compositions and movements and stunning lighting effects. The transition from neorealism to a nearly operatic grand cinema style was even more evident in Visconti's *Senso,* a striking color production of flamboyant proportions and an acknowledged classic of postwar Italian cinema.

Visconti's international reputation was established early in his career and remained undiminished despite occasional misfires. His films were infrequent and each was awaited by his many admirers as a special event. He also gained much prestige as an innovative theater and opera director and was credited with the development of Maria Callas as an operatic superstar.

A recurrent theme in Visconti's films is the moral disintegration of a family, ranging from the tragic transplantation of southern proletariats to Milan in *Rocco and His Brothers* to the decadence of the wealthy Krupp family in *The Damned.* Visconti's *The Leopard* won the Palme d'Or at the Cannes Festival in 1963, and his *Vaghe Stelle dell'Orsa/Sandra* won the Golden Lion at the Venice Festival of 1965. In 1971 his very personal interpretation of Thomas Mann's *Death in Venice* lost in Cannes to Losey's *The Go-Between,* but he was compensated with a special "25th Anniversary Award" for his cumulative work.

FILMS: *Ossessione* (also co-sc.) 1942; *Giorni di Gloria* (medium-length doc.; co-dir.) 1945; *La Terra Trema/The Earth Trembles* (also sc.) 1948; *Appunti su un Fatto di Cronaca* (doc. short), *Bellissima* (also co-adapt., co-dial.) 1951; *Siamo Donne/We the Women* (Anna Magnani episode; in the US it was added to another film, *Questa è la Vita/Of Life and Love*) 1953; *Senso/The Wanton Contessa* (also co-sc.) 1954; *Le Notti bianche/White Nights* (also co-sc.) 1957; *Rocco e i suoi Fratelli/Rocco and His Brothers* (also co-sc.) 1960; *Boccaccio '70* ("The Job" episode; also co-sc.) 1962; *Il Gattopardo/The Leopard* (also co-sc.) 1963; *Vaghe Stelle dell'Orsa/Sandra* (also co-sc.) 1965; *Le Streghe/The Witches* ("The Witch Burned Alive" episode), *Lo Straniero/The Stranger* (also co-sc.) 1967; *La Caduta degli Dei/Götterdämmerung/The Damned* (also co-sc.) 1969; *Morte a Venezia/Death in Venice* (also prod., co-sc.) 1971; *Ludwig II* (also co-story, co-sc.) 1972; *Gruppo di Famiglia in uno Interno/Conversation Piece* (also co-sc.) 1975; *L'Innocente/The Innocent/The Intruder* (also co-sc.) 1976.

VistaVision. See WIDE-SCREEN PROCESSES.

visual effects. SPECIAL EFFECTS achieved by combining or altering film images. They are also called photographic or optical effects, though the latter term more precisely refers to effects done on an OPTICAL PRINTER. Visual effect techniques include MATTES, BACK PROJECTION, FRONT PROJECTION, and digital compositing (see DIGITAL EFFECTS). They are to be distinguished from MECHANICAL EFFECTS, which are achieved through physical means on the set.

Vita, Perlo. See DASSIN, Jules.

Vitagraph. A motion picture production company founded in New York City in 1896 by two immigrants from Britain, J. Stuart BLACKTON and Albert E. Smith. Encouraged by their success with projecting Edison films in a vaudeville act, they decided to enter the filmmaking business. Smith devised a motion picture camera and within days the pair had made their first film. In the beginning they shot mostly topical material with little regard to authenticity. To save the cost of travel fare, they shot a film about the Niagara Falls at the Passaic Falls in nearby New Jersey and passed it off as the real thing. During the Spanish-American War they faked the Battle of Santiago Bay in a water tank. Vitagraph presented its first fictional film, *The Burglar on the Roof,* in 1897. It was shot in the company's "studio" on top of the Morse building at 140 Nassau Street in New York.

Vitagraph's output was prolific and within several years the company had become established as a leader in motion picture production. In 1906 it opened a studio in Brooklyn's Flatbush section and in 1911 added another in California. Its films were the most popular among cinema audiences in the early silent era. Among the many stars who started out with Vitagraph were Florence Turner (the "Vitagraph Girl"), Maurice Costello, John Bunny, Norma Talmadge, Anita Stewart, Rudolph Valentino, Adolphe Menjou, and Clara Kimball Young. Vitagraph was the only member of the MOTION PICTURE PATENTS COMPANY group to survive the aftermath of the antitrust court decision that caused most member companies to be dissolved. Vitagraph continued to prosper into the 20s, until its sale in 1925 to the Warner brothers.

Vitaphone. A subsidiary of Warner Bros. formed in 1926 in association with Western Electric to exploit a sound-on-disc system for motion pictures. Following experimentation with short subjects, Warners made history in 1927 when it presented the feature-length film *The Jazz Singer* with synchronized song sequences and two brief passages of dialogue. The film heralded the coming of the sound era, but the Vitaphone system itself was short-lived. It was severely handicapped by the constant risk that film and disc might lose synchronization in the course of projection. It was finally abandoned in 1931, when sound-on-film systems proved their definite superiority.

Vitti, Monica. Actress. Born Maria Louisa Ceciarelli, on

Nov. 3, 1931, in Rome. Having appeared in amateur plays from the age of 15, she enrolled at Rome's National Academy of Dramatic Arts and graduated in 1953. She began her professional stage career in the same year and made her screen debut in 1955. A decisive event in her life was an encounter with director Michelangelo ANTONIONI, who cast her in several of his stage plays of the late 50s and made her the heroine of *L'Avventura* and three of his subsequent films. Vitti was an ideal Antonioni protagonist, impassioned, remote, and convincingly anguished. She has proved less effective under other directors, although she is still a delight to watch, both as a talented actress and a beautiful woman equally at home in drama and comedy. She co-wrote and directed herself in *Scandalo Segreto/Secret Scandal* in 1989.

FILMS INCLUDE: *Ridere Ridere Ridere* 1955; *L'Avventura* 1960; *La Notte/The Night* 1961; *L'Eclisse/Eclipse, Les Quatres Verités/Three Fables of Love* (Fr./It./Sp.) 1962; *Dragées au Poivre/Sweet and Sour* (Fr./It.), *Château en Suède/Nutty Naughty Chateau* (Fr./It.) 1963; *Alta Infidelità/High Infidelity, Il Deserto rosso/Red Desert* 1964; *Le Bambole/The Dolls* 1965; *Modesty Blaise* (UK), *Le Fate/The Queens* 1966; *Ti ho Sposato per Allegria/I Married You for Fun, La Cintura di Castità/The Chastity Belt/On My Way to the Crusades I Met a Girl Who. . .* 1967; *La Ragazza con la Pistola* 1968; *La Femme écarlate* (Fr.) 1969; *Drama della Gelosia/The Pizza Triangle* 1970; *La Pacifista* 1971; *Teresa la Ladra* 1972; *Tosca* 1973; *Le Fântome de la Liberté* (Fr.) 1974; *A Mezzanotte va la Ronda del Piacere/Midnight Pleasures* 1975; *L'Anitra all'Arancia, Mimi Bluette, La Goduria* 1976; *L'Altra Meta del Cielo* 1977; *La Raison d'Etat* (Fr./It.), *Amore Miei* 1978; *Take Two, Letti selvaggi, Per vivere meglio, An Almost Perfect Affair* (US) 1979; *Il Mistero di Oberwald/The Mystery of Oberwald* 1980; *Tango della Gelosia/Tigers in Lipstick* 1981; *Io So Chew Tu Sai Che Io So* 1982; *The Flirt* (also sc.), *Scusa se e poco, Trenta Minuti D'Amore, When Veronica Calls* 1983; *Scadalo Segreto/Secret Scandal* (also dir., co-sc.) 1989.

Vlady, Marina. Actress. Born Marina de Poliakoff-Baidaroff, on Mar. 10, 1938, Clichy, France. Exquisite blonde star of French and international films. The sister of actresses Hélène Vallier and Odile VERSOIS, she made her screen debut as a child of ten, after several years in ballet under the name Marina Versois. She developed into a graceful and intriguing leading lady. In 1963 she won the best actress award at the Cannes Festival for her performance in the Italian film *Una Storia Moderna/L'Ape Regina/The Conjugal Bed.* She is divorced from Robert HOSSEIN, her former director and co-star.

FILMS INCLUDE: *Orage d'Eté* 1950; *Le Infedeli* (It.), *Canzoni Canzoni Canzoni/Cavalcade of Song* 1953; *Avant le Deluge, Sie* (Ger.), *Le Avventure di Giacomo Casanova/Sins of Casanova* (It./Fr.), *Sinfonia d'Amore—Schubert* (It.) 1954; *Sophie et le Crime/The Girl on the Third Floor* 1955; *Les Salauds vont en Enfer/The Wicked Go to Hell, La Sorcière, Pardonnez nos Offenses, Crime et Châtiment/Crime and Punishment* 1956; *Toi le Venin/Nude in a White Car, La Sentence, La Nuit des Espions/Night Encounter* 1959; *Les Canailles, La Ragazza in Vetrina* (It./Fr.) 1960; *La Princesse de Clèves, Adorable Menteuse* 1961; *Les Sept Péchés capitaux/Seven Capital Sins* 1962; *Le Meutrier/Enough Rope, Les Bonnes Causes/Don't Tempt the Devil, La Steppa/The Steppe* (It./Fr.), *Una Storia Moderna/L'Ape Regina/The Conjugal Bed* (It.), *Dragées au Poivre/Sweet and Sour* 1963; *Una Moglie Americana/Run for Your Wife* (It./Fr.) 1965; *Falstaff/Chimes at Midnight* (as Kate Percy; Sp./Switz.) 1966; *Deux ou Trois Choses que Je Sais d'elle/Two or Three Things I Know About Her* 1967; *Theme for a Short Story/Lika le Grand Amour de Tchekov* (USSR/Fr.), *Sirokkò/Winter Wind* (Hung./Fr.) 1969; *Tout le Monde il est Beau tout le Monde il est Gentil* 1972; *Le Complot* 1973; *Que la Fête commence/Let Joy Reign Supreme* 1974; *Sept morts sur Ordonnance* 1975; *Ok Ketten/The Two of Them* (Hun.), *Il Triangolo delle Bermude/The Bermuda Triangle* (It.) 1977; *The Thief of Baghdad* (UK), *Duos sur Canape, Il Malato Immaginario, L'Oeil du Maitre* 1979; *Les Jeux de la Comtesse Dolingen de Gratz* 1980; *Bordello, Tangos—L'Exil de Gardel/Tangos: The Exile of Gardel* 1985; *Una Casa in Bilico* (Sp.), *Sapore del Grano* (Sp.), *Twist Again a Moscow* 1986; *Les Exploits d'un jeune Don Juan* 1987; *Migrations, Notes pour Debussy* 1988; *Follow Me, Splendor* 1989; *Kodayu* 1992; *Dreams of Russia* 1993; *Wind Over the City* 1996.

Vlasek, June. See LANG, June.

Vogel, Paul C. Director of photography. *b.* Aug. 22, 1899, New York City. *d.* 1975. In films from the mid-20s, he was given an opportunity to act as a lighting cameraman on two productions as early as 1927 but did not become a director of photography on a regular basis for another decade. His career picked up following his return from WW II service, when he executed the complex subjective-camera photography of Robert Montgomery's *Lady in the Lake* (1947). Two years later he won an Academy Award for the black-and-white cinematography of *Battleground.* He spent much of his career with MGM, shooting exclusively in black and white until the mid-50s, when he began to handle color assignments. His brother, Joseph R. Vogel, was for many years a vice president of Loew's, Inc., and later president of MGM.

FILMS INCLUDE: *The Potters, Running Wild* 1927; *Fit for a King* 1937; *Wide Open Faces* 1938; *Kid Glove Killer* 1942; *Lady in the Lake, High Wall* 1947; *Scene of the Crime, Battleground* 1949; *Black Hand, The Happy Years* 1950; *Go for Broke!, The Tall Target, Angels in the Outfield* 1951; *The Sellout* 1952; *Rogues' March, The Clown* 1953; *Rose Marie, The Student Prince* 1954; *Jupiter's Darling* (co-phot.), *Interrupted Melody, The Tender Trap* 1955; *The Rack, High Society* 1956; *The Wings of Eagles, Bernardine* 1957; *The Time Machine* 1960; *The Wonderful World of the Brothers Grimm* 1962; *The Gun Hawk* 1963; *Signpost to Murder, The Rounders* 1965; *The Money Trap, Return of the Seven* 1966; *Riot on Sunset Strip* 1967.

voice over (abbreviated **V.O.** or **v/o**). Narration or dialogue spoken by a person not seen on the screen at the time his voice is heard.

Voight, Jon. Actor. Born on Dec. 29, 1938, in Yonkers, N.Y. The son of a golf pro of Czech descent, he took part in dramatic productions at the Archbishop Stepinac High School in Yonkers and at Catholic University, from which he graduated in 1960. He then trained for the stage at New York's Neighborhood Playhouse and landed a part in the Broadway hit musical 'The Sound of Music.' He gained further experience off Broadway, in stock, and on TV before making his film debut in 1967. He was catapulted to sudden stardom by his subtle portrayal of Joe Buck, the pathetic hustler, in John Schlesinger's *Midnight Cowboy* (1969). Both he and co-star Dustin Hoffman were nominated for Oscars for their performances in that film and Voight was named best actor by the New York Film Critics. A handsome blond, Voight has shunned pretty-boy leads in films, opting instead for "relevant" character studies. He was less than fortunate in picking some of his subsequent roles but scored another success with *Deliverance,* in 1972. A committed pacifist, he was active during the Vietnam conflict on behalf of Jane Fonda's Entertainment People for Peace and Justice. In 1978 he was named best actor at the Cannes Festival for his performance in *Coming Home,* a film for which he also won the year's Oscar for best actor. In 1985, he was nominated for the same award for *Runaway Train.*

FILMS: *Hour of the Gun, Fearless Frank/Frank's Greatest*

Adventure 1967; *Out of It, Midnight Cowboy* 1969; *Catch-22, The Revolutionary* 1970; *Deliverance* 1972; *The All-American Boy* 1973; *Conrack, The Odessa File* (UK) 1974; *Der Richter und sein Henker/End of the Game* (Ger./It.) 1975; *Coming Home* 1978; *The Champ* 1979; *Lookin' to Get Out* (also prod., sc.) 1982; *Table for Five* (also prod.) 1983; *Desert Bloom, Runaway Train* 1985; *Eternity* (also sc.) 1990; *Heat* 1995; *Mission: Impossible* 1996; *Anaconda, Rosewood* 1997.

Volonté, Gian Maria. Actor. *b.* Apr. 9, 1933, in Milan. *d.* 1994. Serious-minded leading man of Italian films and European co-productions. A militant leftist, he has been visibly active in his country's political affairs.

FILMS INCLUDE: *Sotto Dieci Bandiere/Under Ten Flags* (It./US) 1960; *Ercole alla conquista di Atlantide/Hercules and the Captive Women, La Ragazza con la Valigia/Girl with a Suitcase* 1961; *Le Quattro Giornate di Napoli/The Four Days of Naples* (It./US), *A Cavallo della Tigre, Un Uomo da bruciare* 1962; *Il Terrorista* 1963; *Il Magnifico Cornuto/The Magnificent Cuckold, Per un Pugno di Dollari/A Fistful of Dollars* 1964; *L'Armata Brancaleone* 1965; *Per qualche Dollari in più/For a Few Dollars More, Svegliati e Uccidi/Wake Up and Die, La Strega in Amore/The Witch* 1966; *Quien Sabe?/A Bullet for the General, A ciascuno il suo/We Still Kill the Old Way* 1967; *Banditi a Milano/The Violent Four, Faccia a Faccia* 1968; *Sotto il Segno dello Scorpione, Le Vent d'Est/Wind from the East/East Wind* (Fr./It./Ger.) 1969; *Indagine su un Cittadino al di sopra di ogni Sospetto/Investigation of a Citizen Above Suspicion, Le Cercle rouge* (Fr./It.), *Uomini contro* 1970; *Sacco e Vanzetti, La Classe operaia va in Paradiso/Lulu the Tool* 1971; *Il Caso Mattei/The Mattei Affair, L'Attentat/The French Conspiracy* (Fr./It.), *Sbatti il Mostro in Prima Pagina* 1972; *A proposito Lucky Luciano/Re: Lucky Luciano* (title role) 1973; *Actas de Marusia* (Mex.), *Todo Modo* 1976; *Le Soupçon* (Fr./It.) 1977; *Cristo si e fermato a Eboli/Christ Stopped at Eboli, Operation Ogro, Tunnel* 1979; *The Secret Policeman's Other Ball* (UK), *Vera Storia Della Signora Delle Camelie, For Your Eyes Only* (US) 1981; *Bullshot* (UK), *La Mort de Mario Ricci, Scherzo del Destino in Agguato Dietro L'Angolo Come un Brigante di Strada* 1983; *Greystoke: The Legend of Tarzan, Lord of the Apes* (US) 1984; *Revolution* (US) 1985; *Il Caso Moro* 1986; *Croanaca di una Morte Annunciata/Chronicle of a Death Foretold* 1987; *Tre Colonne in Cronaca* 1989; *Porte Aperte/Open Doors* 1990; *Una Storia Semplice/A Simple Story* 1991; *Funes, un Gran Amor* (Arg.) 1993; *Tirano Banderas* 1994.

von Brandenstein, Patrizia. See BRANDENSTEIN, Patrizia von.

von Harbou, Thea. See HARBOU, Thea von.

von Nagy, Käthe. See NAGY, Käthe von.

von Seyffertitz, Gustav. See SEYFFERTITZ, Gustav von.

von Sternberg, Josef. See STERNBERG, Josef von.

von Stroheim, Erich. See STROHEIM, Erich von.

von Sydow, Max. See SYDOW, Max von.

von Trotta, Margarethe. See TROTTA, Margarethe von.

Vorhaus, Bernard. Director. Born in 1898(?), in Germany. He directed low- to medium-budget films competently in England, then in Hollywood. But his career ended in the early 50s, when he was identified as a Communist before the House Un-American Activities Committee (by Edward DMYTRYK and Frank TUTTLE, among others) and blacklisted by the industry.

FEATURE FILMS: In the UK—*On Thin Ice, Money for Speed* (also story), *Crime on the Hill* (also co-sc.), *The Ghost Camera* 1933; *Night Club Queen, The Broken Melody* 1934; *Street Song* (also co-story), *The Last Journey, Ten Minute Alibi, Dark World* 1935; *Dusty Ermine* 1936; *Cotton Queen* 1937. In the US—*King of the Newsboys, Tenth Avenue Kid* 1938; *Fisherman's Wharf, Way Down South, Meet Dr. Christian* 1939; *The Courageous Dr. Christian, Three Faces West* 1940; *Lady from Louisiana, Angels with Broken Wings, Hurricane Smith, Mr. District Attorney in the Carter Case* 1941; *The Affairs of Jimmy Valentine, Ice Capades Revue* 1942; *Bury Me Dead, Winter Wonderland* 1947; *The Spiritualist* 1948; *So Young So Bad* (also co-story, co-sc.) 1950; *Pardon My French* 1951. In Italy—*Fanciulle di Lusso* 1952.

Vorkapich, Slavko. Montage expert, art director, special effects artist. *b.* 1892, Yugoslavia. *d.* 1976. Educated in Belgrade and Budapest, he worked as a commercial artist in Paris and New York before coming to Hollywood in 1922. He served as an art director, special effects director, and producer of shorts, but earned his greatest reputation as a montage expert for several studios, including MGM and Columbia. He was also a film theoretician who directed the feature film *Hanka* (1955) to demonstrate principles of filmmaking.

FILMS INCLUDE (as montage expert or special effects director): *The Prisoner of Zenda* (art dir. only) 1922; *The Past of Mary Holmes* (co-dir. only) 1933; *Manhattan Melodrama, Viva Villa, Crime Without Passion* 1934; *David Copperfield* 1935; *San Francisco* 1936; *The Good Earth, The Last Gangster, They Gave Him a Gun, Broadway Melody of 1938, Maytime, The Firefly* 1937; *The Shopworn Angel, Test Pilot, Boys Town, The Girl of the Golden West, Sweethearts, Marie Antoinette, The Crowd Roars* 1938; *Mr. Smith Goes to Washington* 1939; *The Howards of Virginia* 1940; *Hanka* (dir. only, Yug.) 1955; *The Mask* (co-sc. only) 1961.

Vukotič, Dušan. Animator. Born in 1927, in Bileca, Montenegro (Yugoslavia). He studied architecture but instead became a cartoonist with a satirical magazine. A film animator since the early 50s, he has contributed much to the international reputation of Yugoslav animation. His cartoons have fetched dozens of awards in film festivals. One of these, *Ersatz,* was the first non-American cartoon to win an Academy Award in 1961. He has created a full-length animation feature, *The Seventh Continent,* a Yugoslav-Czech co-production.

FILMS INCLUDE: *How Kico Was Born* 1951; *The Disobedient Robot* 1956; *Cowboy Jimmy* 1957; *Abracadabra, Concerto for Sub-Machine Gun, The Cow on the Moon* 1959; *Piccolo* 1960; *Ersatz* 1961; *The Play* 1962; *The Seventh Continent* (feature; Yug./Czech.) 1966; *A Stain on the Conscience* 1969; *Opera Cordis* 1970; *Ars Gratia Artis* 1971; *Operation Stadium* 1977.

Vye, Murvyn. Actor. *b.* July 15, 1913, Quincy, Mass. *d.* 1976. *ed.* Yale. In Hollywood from the late 40s, following Broadway experience, he often played heavies. Occasionally he was given the opportunity to demonstrate his deep baritone singing voice. He also did much TV, including the 'Bob Cummings Show.'

FILMS INCLUDE: *Golden Earrings* 1947; *Whispering Smith, A Connecticut Yankee in King Arthur's Court* 1949; *Road to Bali, Pickup on South Street* 1953; *River of No Return, Green Fire, Black Horse Canyon* 1954; *Escape to Burma* 1955; *Voodoo Island* 1957; *Al Capone* 1959; *Andy* 1965.

Wademant, Annette. Screenwriter. Born on Dec. 19, 1928, in Brussels. A graduate of IDHEC in Paris, she made her mark in the early 50s with two films of Jacques BECKER. She later collaborated on screenplays for Max OPHÜLS and other noted French directors. In 1977 she appeared as an actress in *Une Sale Histoire.*

FILMS INCLUDE: *Edouard et Caroline* 1951; *Rue de l'Estrapade/Françoise Steps Out, Madame de. . . /The Earrings of Madame De* 1953; *Lola Montès/The Sins of Lola Montes* 1955; *Typhon sur Nagasaki, Une Parisienne, Une Manche et la Belle/What Price Murder* 1957; *Faibles Femmes/Women Are Weak* 1959; *Voulez-vous danser avec moi?/Come Dance with Me!, La Française et l'Amour/Love and the Frenchwoman ("Virginity" episode)* 1960; *Les Parisiennes/Tales of Paris* ("Tale of Antonia" episode) 1962; *La Leçon particulière/The Tender Moment* 1969; *Du Soleil plein les Yeux* 1970.

Wadsworth, Henry. Actor. *b.* 1897, Maysville, Ky. *d.* 1974. *ed.* U. of Kentucky; Carnegie Tech. Drama School. He entered films in the late 20s, following experience in vaudeville and stock and on Broadway, and despite chronological maturity kept playing juvenile roles through the 30s. After retiring from the screen, he briefly returned to the stage, then became active in union affairs and for a while served as president of the AFL's Film Council and administrator of the Motion Picture Health and Welfare Plan.

FILMS INCLUDE: *Applause* 1929; *Slightly Scarlet, Fast and Loose* 1930; *Luxury Liner* 1933; *This Side of Heaven, Operator 13, The Thin Man, Evelyn Prentice* 1934; *West Point of the Air, Mark of the Vampire, The Big Broadcast of 1936* 1935; *Ceiling Zero, The Voice of Bugle Ann* 1936; *Doctor Rhythm* 1938; *Silver Skates* 1943.

Waggner, George. Director, producer, screenwriter, actor. *b.* George Waggoner, Sept. 7, 1894, in New York City. *d.* 1984. A graduate of the Philadelphia College of Pharmacy. He went to Hollywood after completing his WW I military service and started in 1920 as an actor. During the switch to sound in the late 20s he became a songwriter, then worked as a screenwriter on numerous routine low-budget films of the 30s. In the early 40s he turned director and producer of horror films and other action potboilers.

FILMS INCLUDE: As actor—*The Sheik* 1921; *Branded Men* 1922; *Desert Driven* 1923; *The Iron Horse* (as Buffalo Bill), *His Hour* 1924; *Love's Blindness* 1926. As songwriter—*The Flying Fool* 1929; *Good News* 1930. As screenwriter (alone or in collaboration)—*The Sweetheart of Sigma Chi* 1933; *City Limits, The Line-Up, Among the Missing* 1934; *The Nut Farm, Dizzy Dames, The Keeper of the Bees, Spring Tonic* 1935; *Don't Get Personal, Sea Spoilers* 1936; *Three Legionnaires, I Cover the War, Idol of the Crowd* 1937; *The Spy Ring* 1938. As director (complete)—*Western Trails, Outlaw Express, Guilty Trails, Prairie Justice, Black Bandit, Ghost Town Riders* 1938; *Honor of the West, Mystery Plane, Wolf Call, Stunt Pilot, The Phantom Stage* 1939; *Drums of the Desert* 1940; *Man-Made Monster, Horror Island, South of Tahiti* (also assoc. prod.), *Sealed Lips, The Wolf Man* (also assoc. prod.) 1941; *The Climax* (also prod.) 1944; *Frisco Sal* (also prod.), *Shady Lady* (also prod.) 1945; *Tangier* 1946; *Gunfighters* 1947; *The Fighting Kentuckian* (also sc.) 1949; *Operation Pacific* (also sc.) 1951; *Pawnee* (also co-sc.), *Destination 60,000* (also sc.) 1957; *Fury River* (co-dir. with Jacques Tourneur, Alan Crosland, Jr., and Otto Lang), *Mission of Danger* (co-dir. with Tourneur) 1959. As producer—*The Ghost of Frankenstein, Sin Town* 1942; *Frankenstein Meets the Wolf Man, White Savage, The Phantom of the Opera* 1943; *Cobra Woman, Gypsy Wildcat* 1944.

Wagner, Fritz Arno. Director of photography. *b.* Dec. 5, 1889, Schmiedefeld am Rennsteig, Germany. *d.* 1958, in an auto crash. After commercial studies at the University of Leipzig, he went to Paris at age 20 and while attending the Academy of Fine Arts joined the Pathé film company as a clerk. He became interested in cinematography and was sent to New York as a newsreel cameraman. Returning to Berlin in 1919, he joined Decla-Bioscop as feature cameraman. He soon emerged as the most important cinematographer of the German silent cinema. Collaborating on the photography of films of MURNAU, LANG, and other directors, he contributed considerably to the expressionist movement with his mood-setting camera work, which emphasized deep shadows and strong black-and-white contrast. Wagner's importance declined along with the fortunes of German cinema after the Nazi takeover in 1933, although he continued working prolifically for decades.

FILMS INCLUDE: *Der Galeerensträfling* (co-phot. 1919; *Arme Violetta/The Red Peacock* 1920; *Der müde Tod/Between Two Worlds* (co-phot.), *Schloss Vogelöd/The Haunted Castle* (co-phot.) 1921; *Der brennende Acker/Burning Soil* (co-phot.), *Nosferatu/Nosferatu the Vampire* (co-phot.) 1922; *Schatten/Warning Shadows* 1923; *Zur Chronik von Grieshaus/At the Grey House* (co-phot.) 1925; *Eine Dubarry von Heute/A Modern Du Barry* 1926; *Der Liebe der Jeanne Ney/The Loves of Jeanne Ney* (co-phot.) 1927; *Spione/Spies* 1928; *Waterloo* (co-phot.) 1929; *Westfront 1918/Comrades of 1918* (co-phot.), *Skandal um Eva* 1930; *M, Die Dreigroschenoper/The Threepenny Opera/The Beggar's Opera, Kameradschaft/Comradeship* (co-phot.) 1931; *Das Testament des Dr. Mabuse/The Testament of Dr. Mabuse* (co-phot.) 1932; *Amphytrion* (co-phot.) 1935; *Der Mann der Sherlock Holmes war* 1937; *Robert Koch* 1939; *Friedrich Schiller* 1940; *Ohm Krüger* (co-phot.) 1941; *Die Brücke/The Bridge* 1949; *Ohne Mutter geht es nicht* 1958.

Wagner, Robert. Actor. Born on Feb. 10, 1930, in Detroit. The son of a wealthy steel executive, he intended to go into business, but his good looks and easygoing manner got him into films with 20th Century-Fox in the early 50s. He gradually matured from an awkward juvenile lead and bobby-sox idol into a smooth, assured leading man. Popular on TV in the 'It Takes a Thief,' 'Switch,' and 'Hart to Hart' series. He married, divorced, and remarried Natalie WOOD, to whom he was married at the time of her death in 1981. He later married actress Jill ST. JOHN, a close friend of the Wagners. In between his marriages to Wood he was married to actress Marion Marshall.

FILMS: *The Happy Years* 1950; *The Halls of Montezuma, The Frogmen, Let's Make It Legal* 1951; *With a Song in My Heart, What Price Glory, Stars and Stripes Forever* 1952; *Titanic, Beneath the 12-Mile Reef* 1953; *Prince Valiant* (title role), *Broken Lance* 1954; *White Feather* 1955; *A Kiss Before Dying, Between Heaven and Hell, The Mountain* 1956; *The True Story of Jesse James* (title role), *Stopover Tokyo* 1957; *The Hunters, In Love and War* 1958; *Say One for Me, All the Fine Young Cannibals* 1960; *Sail a Crooked Ship, The Longest Day, The War Lover* (UK), *I Sequestrati di Altona/The Condemned of Altona* (It./Fr.) 1962; *The Pink Panther* 1964; *Harper* 1966; *Banning* 1967; *The Biggest Bundle of Them All* (US/It.), *Don't Just Stand There!* 1968; *Winning* 1969; *The Towering Inferno* 1974; *Midway* 1976; *Airport '79 Concorde* 1979; *Trail of the Pink Panther* 1982; *Curse of the Pink Panther, I Am the Cheese* 1983; *Delirious, The Player* (cameo) 1992; *Austin Powers* 1997.

Waits, Tom. Actor, composer, singer, musician. Born on Dec. 7, 1949, in Pomona, Calif. Raspy-voiced singer-songwriter who has gained second career as a composer and actor. He released his first critically praised album, *Closing Time*, in 1973 and debuted on the screen in 1978. In the 80s, he had supporting roles in several movies, many by Francis Ford Coppola. His songs have appeared in films by directors ranging from Coppola to Jean-Luc Godard. Waits was the subject of *Big Time* (1988), a quasi-concert movie that attempted to combine concert footage with dramatic sequences inspired by his songs. In the 90s he continues to act in films by leading directors.

FILMS INCLUDE (as actor): *Paradise Alley*, *On the Yard* 1978; *On the Nickel* (songs only) 1979; *Bad Timing* (songs only), *Divine Madness* (songs only) 1980; *Den Tuchtigen Gehort Die Welt* (comp. only; Ger.), *Wolfen* (songs only) 1981; *One from the Heart* (songs only), *The Outsiders*, *Prenom Carmen/First Name: Carmen* (songs only; Fr.), *Rumble Fish* 1983; *The Cotton Club* 1984; *Streetwise* (songs only) 1985; *Down By Law* (also songs) 1986; *Candy Mountain* (also comp.), *Ironweed* (also comp.), *Wochin?* (comp. only) 1987; *Big Time* (also sc., comp., songs), *Let's Get Lost* (songs only) 1988; *Bearskin: An Urban Fairytale* (also songs), *Cold Feet, In una notte di chiaro di luna* (comp. only; It.), *Mystery Train*, *Sea of Love* (songs only), *Wait Until Spring, Bandini* (comp. only) 1989; *Queens Logic*, *The Fisher King*, *At Play in the Fields of the Lord* 1991; *Night on Earth* (comp. only), *Deadfall*, *Bram Stoker's Dracula, Léolo* (mus. only) 1992; *Short Cuts* 1993.

Wajda, Andrzej. Director. Born on Mar. 6, 1926, in Suwalki, Poland. Poland's leading filmmaker and one of the major figures in postwar East European cinema. The son of a cavalry officer who was killed in WW II, he became a Resistance fighter at the age of 16. After the Liberation, he studied painting at the Kraków Academy of Fine Arts, but in 1950 he decided on a film career and enrolled at the famous Lodz film school. After graduating, in 1952, he worked as Alexander Ford's assistant on *Five Boys from Barska Street.* He established himself as a key figure in the new Polish cinema with his very first feature film, *A Generation* (1954), a penetrating study of the effects of war on the psychology of a nation's disillusioned youth. This film and the subsequent *Kanal* (1957) and *Ashes and Diamonds* (1958) form a powerful trilogy in which Wajda examines with intense sensitivity the predicament of individuals caught in events beyond their control and bitterly questions the traditional glorification of heroism in battle. Although Wajda was to prove himself a most versatile director in future years, turning out romantic films, comedies, and epics, as well as dramas, he periodically returned to themes relating to his WW II memories. In *Lotna* (1959) he bemoans the futility of noble traditions by depicting a tilted battle between obsolete Polish cavalry and German tanks. *Ashes* (1965) and *Landscape After the Battle* (1970), although both deal with wars of the historic past, still echo Wajda's obsession with the futility of heroism and the bitter aftermath of war. *Everything for Sale* (1968), Wajda's most personal and possibly most poignant film, is an introspective tribute to Zbigniew CYBULSKI, the young star of Wajda's trilogy, who was killed in a tragic accident in 1967. In the late 70s his films became known for their reflection of his country's political unrest. *Man of Marble* and *Without Anesthesia* study Poland's turmoil from the viewpoint of individuals ruined by the country's widespread oppression, a bricklayer in *Man of Marble*, a journalist in *Without Anesthesia*. His 1981 film, *Man of Iron*, a sequel to *Man of Marble*, chronicled the development of the Solidarity movement. Released just as the Solidarity strikes were taking place, it became a timely marker of Solidarity for the world, generating through its international acclaim awareness of and support for the movement. Shortly after the strikes, the government forced Wajda out of his Studio X production studio and mandated his resignation from the head of the filmmaker's association. He moved to France, where his first filmmaking effort, *Danton*, was an allegory about Solidarity and revolution. By 1989 the political atmosphere in Poland had become more liberalized and he could return. He received an appointment as the artistic director of Teatr Powszechny, the official Warsaw Theater and was elected to political office as a senator.

FILMS: Shorts—*While You Sleep, The Bad Boy* 1950; *The Pottery of Ilza* 1951; *I Go to the Sun* 1955; *Roly-Poly* (for TV) 1968. Features—*A Generation* 1954; *Kanal* 1957; *Ashes and Diamonds* (also co-sc.) 1958; *Lotna* (also co-sc.) 1959; *Innocent Sorcerers* (also co-sc.) 1960; *Samson* (also co-sc.) 1961; *Siberian Lady Macbeth/Fury Is a Woman, L'Amour à vingt Ans/Love at Twenty* ("Warsaw, Poland" episode; Fr./It./Jap./Pol./Ger.) 1962; *Ashes* 1965; *Gates to Paradise* (UK) 1967; *Everything for Sale* (also sc.) 1968; *Hunting Flies* 1969; *Landscape After the Battle* (also co-sc.) 1970; *The Birch-Wood* (also sc.) 1971; *Pilatus und andere* (for W.Ger. TV), *The Wedding* 1972; *Promised Land* (also sc.) 1974; *Shadow Line* (also co-sc.) 1976; *Man of Marble* 1977; *Bez Znieczulenia/Without Anesthetic* (also sc.), *Panny z Wilka/The Girls from Wilko* (Pol./Fr.) 1979; *Dyrygent/The Orchestra Conductor* 1980; *Cziowiek z Zelaza/Man of Iron* 1981; *Danton* (also sc.; Pol./Fr.), *Przesluchanie/Interrogation* (exec. prod.) 1982; *Eine Liebe in Deutschland/A Love in Germany* (also sc.; Fr./Ger.), *Wajda's Danton* (act. only) 1983; *Visage de Chien* (tech. consult. only) 1985; *Kronika Wypadkow Milosnych/Chronicle of Love Affairs* (also sc.) 1986; *Les Possedes/The Possessed* (also sc.) 1987; *Korczak/Dr. Korczak* 1990; *The Ring with a Crowned Eagle* 1993; *Nastazjai* 1994.

Wakhévitch, Georges. Art director. *b.* Aug. 18, 1907, in Odessa, Russia. *d.* 1984. In Paris from early youth, he studied painting and the decorative arts before entering French films in the late 20s as assistant to Lazare MEERSON. He designed costumes and sets for many stage, opera, and ballet productions as well as many important films, for Renoir and other directors.

FILMS INCLUDE: *Baroud/Love in Morocco* (co-art dir.), *L'Homme à l'Hispano* 1933; *Madame Bovary* (co-art dir.) 1934; *La Grande Illusion/Grand Illusion* (asst. art dir.) 1937; *La Marseillaise* (co-art dir.), *Prison sans Barraux/Prison Without*

Bars 1938; *Les Visiteurs du Soir/The Devil's Envoys* (co-art dir.) 1942; *L'Eternel Retour/The Eternal Return* 1943; *La Vie de Bohème* 1945; *L'Homme au Châpeau rond* 1946; *Ruy Blas, Dedée d'Anvers/Dedee, L'Aigle à Deux Têtes/Eagle with Two Heads* (co-art dir.) 1948; *Miquette et sa Mère/Miquette* 1950; *The Medium* (US/It.), *Barbe-Bleue/Bluebeard* 1951; *The Beggar's Opera* (UK) 1953; *Ali Baba et les Quarante Voleurs* 1954; *Don Juan* 1956; *Tamango, Me and the Colonel* (co-art dir.; US) *La Femme et le Pantin, Marie-Octobre* 1959; *Un Deux Trois Quatre/Les Collants noirs/Black Tights* 1960; *King of Kings* (US), *Les Amours célèbres* 1961; *Le Crime ne paie pas/Crime Does Not Pay* 1962; *Le Journal d'une Femme de Chambre/Diary of a Chambermaid, Echappement libre/ Backfire, Peau de Banane/Banana Peel* 1964; *Les Fêtes galantes* 1965; *Tendre Voyou/Tender Scoundrel* 1966; *Carmen* (Switz.) 1967; *Giselle* (sets), *Mayerling* (UK/Fr.) 1968; *La Folie des grandeurs* (art dir.), *King Lear* (UK/Den.) 1971; *Meetings with Remarkable Men* (phot. dir.) 1979; *La Tragedie de Carmen* (art dir.) 1983.

Walas, Chris. Special effects and makeup artist, director. Born in Chicago. *ed.* William Peterson Coll., N.J.; Los Angeles City Coll. Expert in horrific makeup and creature effects. His makeup designs and grisly puppets have enhanced numerous films by director David Cronenberg and producer Steven Spielberg, among others. He shared an Academy Award for makeup for *The Fly* (1986), and branched out as a director with the sequel to that film, *The Fly II* (1989).

FILMS INCLUDE: *Galaxina* (makeup) 1980; *Scanners* (makeup), *Raiders of the Lost Ark* (makeup), *Caveman* (creature) 1981; *Return of the Jedi* (creature consult.) 1983; *Gremlins* (creatures) 1984; *Enemy Mine* (creature eff.) 1985; *The Fly* (spec. eff., makeup) 1986; *House II: The Second Story* (creature eff., makeup) 1987; *The Kiss* (creature eff., makeup) 1988; *The Fly II* (dir.) 1989; *Arachnophobia* (creatures) 1990; *Naked Lunch* (creatures) 1991; *The Vagrant* (dir.) 1992.

Walbrook, Anton. Actor. *b.* Adolf Anton Wilhelm Wohlbrück, Nov. 19, 1900, Vienna. *d.* 1967. A descendant of ten generations of circus clowns, he chose the legitimate stage and after a period of training he appeared in various Austrian and German theaters. He made his screen debut in the early 20s, but it wasn't until the early 30s that he began playing starring roles. Having made a name for himself in German films, as Adolf Wohlbrück he went to Hollywood for *The Soldier and the Lady* (1937), in which he repeated the success he had had in the German/French versions of *Michael Strogoff.* He then settled in Britain, where he rose to prominence on the stage and screen as an aristocratic Continental leading man of suave charm. He became a British citizen in 1947. In the 50s he figured importantly in two French films of Max OPHÜLS, *La Ronde,* as the master of ceremonies, and in *Lola Montès,* as the King of Bavaria.

FILMS INCLUDE: In Germany-Austria—*Mater Dolorosa* 1922; *Salto Mortale/Trapeze* 1931; *Melodie der Liebe* 1932; *Walzerkrieg/War of the Waltzes/Waltz Time in Vienna, Viktor und Viktoria* 1933; *Maskerade/Masquerade in Vienna* 1934; *Zigeunerbaron, Der Student von Prag* 1935; *Der Kurier des Zaren* (and French version, *Michel Strogoff;* title role), *Port Arthur/I Give My Life* (Ger./Fr.). In the US—*The Soldier and the Lady/Michael Strogoff* (title role) 1937. In the UK—*Victoria the Great* (as Prince Albert), *The Rat* 1937; *Sixty Glorious Years* (as Prince Albert) 1938; *Gaslight/Angel Street* 1940; *Dangerous Moonlight/Suicide Squadron, 49th Parallel/The Invaders* 1941; *The Life and Death of Colonel Blimp* 1943; *The Man from Morocco* 1944; *The Red Shoes* 1948; *The Queen of Spades* 1949; *La Ronde* (as the Master of Ceremonies; Fr.) 1950; *Wien tanzt/Vienna Waltzes* (as Johann Strauss; Aus.) 1951; *L'Affaire Maurizius/On Trial* (Fr.) 1954; *Oh Rosalinda/Fledermaus '55* (UK/Ger.), *Lola Montès/The Sins of Lola Montes* (as the King of Bavaria; Fr./Ger.) 1955; *Saint Joan* (as Cauchon) 1957; *I Accuse!* (as Major Esterhazy) 1958.

Wald, Jerry. Producer, screenwriter. *b.* Jerome Irving Wald, Sept. 16, 1911, Brooklyn, N.Y. *d.* 1962. The son of a dry goods salesman, he studied journalism for two years at NYU before starting a radio column in the New York *Graphic.* He used this as a springboard for a series of shorts featuring radio stars which he produced for Warners in 1933. He then joined Warners as a screenwriter and collaborated on numerous scripts through the early 40s, when he turned producer. A dynamic, indefatigable worker (he is said to have provided at least a part model for Budd SCHULBERG's *What Makes Sammy Run?*), he produced many of the most successful Warner pictures of the 40s. In 1950 he formed a production company with Norman Krasna. In 1953 he joined Columbia as vice president in charge of production. In 1956 he formed Jerry Wald Productions, releasing through Fox. He was the recipient of the Irving Thalberg Memorial Award at the 1948 Oscar ceremonies. He collaborated on many scripts without seeking screen credit.

FILMS INCLUDE: As screenwriter—*Huddle* (story basis only) 1932; *Gift of Gab* 1934; *In Caliente* 1935; *Brother Rat* 1938; *The Roaring Twenties* 1939; *Torrid Zone, They Drive by Night* 1940; *Out of the Fog, Manpower* 1941. As producer—*All Through the Night, Across the Pacific* 1942; *The Hard Way, Action in the North Atlantic* 1943; *Destination Tokyo* 1944; *Objective Burma, Pride of the Marines, Mildred Pierce* 1945; *Humoresque* 1946; *Possessed, Dark Passage* 1947; *Key Largo, Johnny Belinda, Adventures of Don Juan* 1948; *Flamingo Road, Task Force, The Inspector General* 1949; *Young Man with a Horn, Caged, The Glass Menagerie, The Braking Point* 1950; *The Blue Veil* 1951; *Clash by Night, The Lusty Men* 1952; *Miss Sadie Thompson* 1953; *The Eddy Duchin Story* 1956; *Peyton Place* 1957; *The Long Hot Summer* 1958; *The Best of Everything* 1959; *The Story on Page One, Sons and Lovers, Let's Make Love* 1960; *Wild in the Country* 1961; *Mr. Hobbs Takes a Vacation* 1962; *The Stripper* 1963.

Walken, Christopher. Actor. Born on Mar. 31, 1943, in Astoria, Queens, N.Y., a baker's son. *ed.* Hofstra. Sensitive, nervous-looking lead and supporting player of the American stage and screen. He won both a New York Film Critics Award and an Oscar as best supporting player for his performance in *The Deer Hunter* (1978). A character actor throughout the 80s and early 90s, effective in psychologically charged roles.

FILMS: *Me and My Brother* (bit) 1969; *The Anderson Tapes* 1971; *The Happiness Cage* 1972; *Next Stop Greenwich Village* 1976; *The Sentinel, Annie Hall, Roseland* 1977; *The Deer Hunter* 1978; *Last Embrace, Heaven's Gate* 1979; *The Dogs of War, Shoot the Sun Down, Pennies from Heaven* 1981; *Brainstorm, The Dead Zone* 1983; *A View to a Kill* 1985; *At Close Range* 1986; *Deadline* 1987; *Biloxi Blues, Homeboy, The Milagro Beanfield War* 1988; *Communion* 1989; *King of New York, The Comfort of Strangers* 1990; *McBain, All-American Murder* 1991; *Le Grand Pardon/Day of Atonement* (Fr.), *Mistress, Batman Returns* 1992; *True Romance, Wayne's World 2* 1993; *Pulp Fiction* 1994; *The Addiction, Nick of Time, Things To Do in Denver When You're Dead* 1995; *Basquiat, The Funeral, Last Man Standing* 1996; *Excess Baggage, Touch* 1997.

Walker, Clint. Actor. Born on May 30, 1927, in Hartford, Ill. Muscular leading man of American TV ('Cheyenne,' 'Kodiak' series) and films. A veteran of the merchant marine, he was a sheet metal worker, carpenter, deputy sheriff, and oil prospector before breaking into films in the mid-50s.

FILMS INCLUDE: *The Ten Commandments* 1956; *Fort Dobbs* 1958; *Yellowstone Kelly* 1959; *Gold of the Seven Saints* 1961; *Send Me No Flowers* 1964; *None but the Brave* 1965; *The Night of the Grizzly, Maya* 1966; *The Dirty Dozen* 1967; *More Dead Than Alive, Sam Whiskey, The Great Bank Robbery* 1969; *The Phynx* (cameo) 1970; *Pancho Villa* 1974; *Baker's Hawk* 1976; *The White Buffalo* 1977; *Hysterical* 1983; *Serpent Warriors* 1986.

Walker, Hal. Director. *b.* Mar. 20, 1896, Ottumwa, Iowa. *d.* 1972. A former actor, he came to Hollywood in the early 30s as assistant director at Paramount. Graduating to a director in the 40s, he specialized in light fare. In the early 50s he left films to direct the 'I Married Joan' TV series.

FILMS: *Out of This World, Duffy's Tavern, The Stork Club* 1945; *Road to Utopia* 1946; *My Friend Irma Goes West* 1950; *At War with the Army, That's My Boy* 1951; *Sailor Beware* 1952; *Road to Bali* 1953.

Walker, Helen. Actress. *b.* 1920, Worcester, Mass. *d.* 1968. Leading lady of Hollywood films of the 40s and early 50s, following brief experience on the stage. Her career deteriorated following a serious automobile accident in 1946, and nine years later she retired from the screen. She died of cancer at 47.

FILMS INCLUDE: *Lucky Jordan* 1942; *Abroad with Two Yanks, The Man in Half Moon Street* 1944; *Brewster's Millions, Murder He Says* 1945; *People Are Funny, Cluny Brown, Her Adventurous Night* 1946; *Nightmare Alley* 1947; *Call Northside 777* 1948; *Impact* 1949; *My True Story* 1951; *Problem Girls* 1953; *The Big Combo* 1955.

Walker, Johnnie (Johnny). Actor. *b.* 1894, New York City. *d.* 1949. *ed.* Fordham. Athletic leading man of Hollywood silents of the 20s following a brief career on the stage. Moderately popular, he starred in many productions, both romantic comedies and melodramas. He also produced a couple of Eddie Polo Westerns in 1923. In the early 30s, with his acting career in decline, he tried his hand at directing but gave up after only one film, *Mr. Broadway* (1933).

FILMS INCLUDE: *Over the Hill to the Poor House* 1920; *Live Wires, The Jolt* 1921; *Extra! Extra!, In the Name of the Law, Captain Fly-by-Night* 1922; *The Third Alarm, Broken Hearts of Broadway, The Fourth Musketeer, Children of Dust, Red Lights, Shattered Reputations* 1923; *The Spirit of the USA, Girls Men Forget, Wine of Youth, The Slanderers* 1924; *The Reckless Sex, The Mad Dancer, The Scarlet West, Children of the Whirlwind* 1925; *Transcontinental Limited, Lightning Reporter, Old Ironsides* 1926; *Wolves of the Air, The Snarl of Hate* (dual role), *Where Trails Begin, The Clown, Rose of the Bowery, Pretty Clothes, A Boy of the Streets* 1927; *Bare Knees, So This Is Love, The Matinee Idol* (dual role), *Vultures of the Sea* (serial) 1928; *The Melody Man, Ladies of Leisure, Ladies in Love, The Girl of the Golden West, Up the River* 1930; *Enemies of the Law* 1931; *Mr. Broadway* (dir. only) 1933.

Walker, Joseph (Joe). Director of photography. *b.* 1892, in Denver. *d.* 1985. In Hollywood from the late 1910s, he distinguished himself in the 30s and 40s as the lighting cameraman of many of Columbia's most important productions, including Frank Capra's films. An expert in optics, he was famous for his collection of lenses and for pioneering in the use of the zoom lens. In the early 50s he retired from film work to devote his time to optical research. He invented the Electra-Zoom, a lens used in television cameras.

FILMS INCLUDE: *The Girl from God's Country* 1921; *Danger, Richard the Lion-Hearted* 1923; *The Wise Virgin* 1924; *North Star, The Pleasure Buyers* 1925; *Tarzan and the Golden Lion, The Great Mail Robbery, The Tigress, Shanghaied* 1927; *Court-Martial, The Street of Illusion, Restless Youth, Submarine* 1928; *Flight* (co-phot.), *The Song of Love* 1929; *Ladies of Leisure, Midnight Mystery, Rain or Shine* 1930; *Dirigible, The Miracle Woman, Platinum Blonde* 1931; *Forbidden, American Madness* 1932; *The Bitter Tea of General Yen, Lady for a Day* 1933; *It Happened One Night, One Night of Love, Broadway Bill* 1934; *Let's Live Tonight, Love Me Forever* 1935; *Mr. Deeds Goes to Town, Theodora Goes Wild* 1936; *Lost Horizon, The Awful Truth* 1937; *You Can't Take It with You, Joy of Living* 1938; *Only Angels Have Wings* (co-phot.), *Mr. Smith Goes to Washington* 1939; *His Girl Friday, Too Many Husbands, Arizona* 1940; *Penny Serenade, Here Comes Mr. Jordan, You Belong To Me, Bedtime Story* 1941; *Tales of Manhattan, My Sister Eileen, A Night to Remember* 1942; *Together Again* 1944; *Roughly Speaking* 1945; *It's a Wonderful Life* (co-phot.), *The Jolson Story* 1946; *The Mating of Millie* 1948; *The Dark Past, Tell It to the Judge* 1949; *No Sad Songs for Me, Harriet Craig, Never a Dull Moment* 1950; *Born Yesterday, The Mob* 1951; *The Marrying Kind, Affair in Trinidad* 1952.

Walker, Lillian. American actress. *b.* 1887. *d.* 1975. Vivacious blonde star of early American silent films, widely known as "Dimples" Walker at the height of her popularity in the late 1910s. She entered films with Vitagraph in 1911 and starred in many productions, both comedies and dramas, often opposite John BUNNY. She left Vitagraph in 1918 to form her own company, Crest Productions, for which she starred in many films until the early 20s, when she retired. She later tried a comeback in vaudeville, appeared in three Broadway productions in 1927 and 1934, and made a couple of isolated screen appearances before retreating from public view in the mid-30s. She died at 88 in Trinidad, where she had been living in retirement for many years.

FILMS INCLUDE: *The New Stenographer* 1911; *Alma's Champion, The Troublesome Stepdaughters, The Reincarnation of Karma* 1912; *Stenographers' Troubles, The Artist's Great Madonna, The Carpenter, The Autocrat of Flapjack Junction* 1913; *Love Luck and Gasoline, The Accomplished Mrs. Thompson, The Persistent Mr. Prince* 1914; *A Model Wife* 1915; *The Blue Envelope Mystery* 1916; *Kitty Mackay, The Princess of Park Row, The Lust of the Ages* 1917; *The Grain of Dust, The Embarrassment of Riches* 1918; *The Better Wife, White Man's Chance, The Love Hunger, A Joyous Liar* 1919; *The Woman God Changed* 1921; *Love's Boomerang* 1922; *The Pusher-in-the-Face* (three-reeler) 1928; *Enlighten Thy Daughter* 1934.

Walker, Nella. Actress. *b.* 1880(?), in Chicago. *d.* 1971. A former salesgirl and vaudevillian, she played character roles in numerous Hollywood films of the 40s and 50s, typically as a charming upper-crust society matron. At one time she was married to actor Wilbur Mack, with whom she formed the Mack and Walker vaudeville team.

FILMS INCLUDE: *The Vagabond Lover, Seven Keys to Baldpate* 1929; *What a Widow!* 1930; *The Hot Heiress, Indiscreet* 1931; *They Call It Sin* 1932; *20,000 Years in Sing Sing, Humanity, Reunion in Vienna* 1933; *All of Me, Madame Du Barry* 1934; *McFadden's Flats, Captain January* 1936; *Three Smart Girls, Stella Dallas* 1937; *Young Dr. Kildare, Three Smart Girls Grow Up, When Tomorrow Comes* 1939; *I Love You Again* 1940; *Kitty Foyle, Back Street, Buck Privates, Hellzapoppin* 1941; *We Were Dancing* 1942; *Two Sisters from Boston* 1946; *The Locket, This Time for Keeps* 1947; *Nancy Goes to Rio* 1950; *Sabrina* 1954.

Walker, Norman. Director. *b.* Oct. 8, 1892, in Bolton, England. *d.* 1963. A stage director from 1912, he entered British films as assistant director in 1920 following WW I service as an army captain. He also appeared as an actor in several productions directed by others.

FILMS INCLUDE: *Tommy Atkins* 1928; *Hate Ship, The Middle Watch* 1930; *Uneasy Virtue* 1931; *Mr. Bill the Conqueror/The Man Who Won, Fires of Fate* 1942; *Lilies of the Field* 1934; *Turn of the Tide* 1935; *Sunset in Vienna/Suicide Legion, Our Fighting Navy* 1937; *The Man at the Gate* 1941; *The Great Mr. Handel* 1942; *The Promise* 1952; *Supreme Secret* 1957.

Walker, Robert. Actor. *b.* Oct. 13, 1918, Salt Lake City. *d.* 1951. He began showing acting promise in productions staged at his school, the San Diego Army and Naval Academy, and in 1938 enrolled at New York's Academy of Dramatic Arts. Early the following year he married a fellow student, Phyllis Isley, later to become better known as Jennifer JONES. On their honeymoon, they set out for Hollywood, hoping to break into films, but initially neither managed to secure more than bit roles in an occasional production. They returned East, where she gave birth to future actors Robert Walker, Jr. (*b.* April 15, 1940, NYC) and Michael Walker (*b.* Mar. 13, 1941, NYC), and Robert Senior soon landed a regular part in a network radio series. They were back in Hollywood in 1942, she under contract to Selznick and he with an MGM deal. While Jennifer scored immediately, winning an Academy Award for her performance in *The Song of Bernadette,* he staged a modest ascent of his own as an open-faced boy-next-door-type of leading man with an ingratiating smile in such productions as *See Here Private Hargrove* and *The Clock.*

Jennifer and Robert co-starred in Selznick's *Since You Went Away* (1944), although they were separated at the time and she was romantically linked to Selznick. They were divorced in 1945 and she married Selznick in 1949. Robert, who had been struggling with anxiety since his broken-home childhood, took to drinking and suffered a series of nervous breakdowns. In 1948 he married John Ford's daughter, Barbara, but the marriage lasted only six weeks. Several months later he was arrested for drunken driving and institutionalized with a nervous breakdown for nearly a year. He then returned to film work and did remarkably well in Hitchcock's *Strangers on a Train,* in which he was cast as a charming, perverted, murderous psychopath. He died suddenly in 1951, in the midst of filming *My Son John,* after doctors had given him sedatives to calm yet another of his frequent emotional outbursts.

FILMS: *Winter Carnival* (bit), *These Glamour Girls* (bit), *Dancing Co-Ed* (bit) 1939; *Pioneer Days* (bit) 1940; *Bataan, Madame Curie* 1943; *See Here Private Hargrove, Since You Went Away, Thirty Seconds Over Tokyo* 1944; *The Clock, Her Highness and the Bellboy, What Next Corporal Hargrove?* 1945; *Till the Clouds Roll By* (as Jerome Kern), *The Sailor Takes a Wife* 1946; *The Sea of Grass, The Beginning or the End, Song of Love* (as Johannes Brahms) 1947; *One Touch of Venus* 1948; *Please Believe Me, The Skipper Surprised His Wife* 1950; *Vengeance Valley, Strangers on a Train* 1951; *My Son John* 1952.

Walker, Stuart. Director. *b.* 1887, Augusta, Ky. *d.* 1941. *ed.* U. of Cincinnati. A former stage actor, director, producer, and playwright, he directed a handful of films for Paramount and Universal in the early 30s. Most of his assignments were routine, but he demonstrated some skill with the handling of the pacifist drama *The Eagle and the Hawk* (1933) and the thrillers *The Mystery of Edwin Drood* and *The Werewolf of London* (both 1935).

FILMS: *The Secret Call, The False Madonna* 1931; *The Misleading Lady, Evenings for Sale* 1932; *Tonight Is Ours, The Eagle and the Hawk, White Woman* 1933; *Romance in the Rain, Great Expectations* 1934; *The Mystery of Edwin Drood, The Werewolf of London, Manhattan Moon* 1935.

Walker, Vernon. Special effects expert. *b.* May 2, 1894, Detroit. *d.* 1948. A veteran cameraman, he was appointed head of the special effects department at RKO in the early 30s.

FILMS INCLUDE: *Flying Down to Rio* 1933; *Son of Kong* 1934; *She, The Last Days of Pompeii* 1935; *Sylvia Scarlett, Mary of Scotland, Winterset* 1936; *This Land Is Mine* 1943; *None but the Lonely Heart* 1944; *Notorious, The Spiral Staircase* 1946; *Sinbad the Sailor* 1947.

walk-on. A small part in a movie or a play; a bit. It is usually a nonspeaking part of limited duration or significance.

Wallace, Irving. Novelist, screenwriter. *b.* Mar. 19, 1916, in Chicago. *d.* 1990. A freelance foreign correspondent from the mid-30s, he wrote screenplays for routine Hollywood films of the 50s before achieving success as a best-selling novelist and the co-author of *The Book of Lists* and its sequels.

FILMS INCLUDE: As screenwriter—*The West Point Story* 1950; *Split Second, Bad for Each Other* 1953; *The Gambler from Natchez* 1954; *Sincerely Yours* 1955; *The Burning Hills* 1956; *Bombers B-52* 1957; *The Big Circus* 1959. Films based on his novels—*The Chapman Report* 1962; *The Prize* 1963; *The Seven Minutes* 1971; *The Man* 1972.

Wallace, Jean. Actress. *b.* Jean Wallasek, Oct. 12, 1923, in Chicago. *d.* 1990. Blonde leading lady of American films; in Hollywood from the early 40s. The former (1941–48) wife of Franchot TONE, she was married from 1951 until his death in 1989 to actor-director Cornel WILDE and starred in several of his independent productions.

FILMS INCLUDE: *Louisiana Purchase* 1941; *You Can't Ration Love* 1944; *It Shouldn't Happen to a Dog* 1946; *Blaze of Noon* 1947; *When My Baby Smiles at Me* 1948; *Jigsaw* 1949; *The Man on the Eiffel Tower, The Good Humor Man* 1950; *Native Son* 1951; *The Big Combo* 1955; *Storm Fear, Star of India* 1956; *The Devil's Hairpin* 1957; *Maracaibo* 1958; *Lancelot and Guinevere/Sword of Lancelot* (UK) 1963; *Beach Red* 1967; *No Blade of Grass* (UK) 1970.

Wallace, Richard. Director. *b.* Aug. 26, 1894, Sacramento, Calif. *d.* 1951. He attended Chicago's Rush Medical College, intending to become a surgeon, but was forced to leave school for lack of funds and joined a carnival company as the merry-go-round operator. His travels took him to Hollywood, where he entered films as assistant cutter with Mack Sennett. He was later employed in various other capacities at different studios, before turning director in the mid-20s. Many of his films were commercially successful.

FILMS: *Syncopating Sue* 1926; *McFadden's Flats, The Poor Nut, American Beauty, A Texas Steer* 1927; *Lady Be Good, The Butter and Egg Man* 1928; *The Shopworn Angel, Innocents of Paris, River of Romance* 1929; *Seven Days Leave, Anybody's War, The Right to Love* 1930; *Man of the World, Kick In, The Road to Reno* 1931; *Tomorrow and Tomorrow, Thunder Below* 1932; *The Masquerader* 1933; *Eight Girls in a Boat, The Little Minister* 1934; *Wedding Present* 1936; *John Meade's Woman, Blossoms on Broadway* 1937; *The Young in Heart* 1938; *The Under-Pup* 1939; *Captain Caution* 1940; *A Girl a Guy and a Gob, She Knew All the Answers, Obliging Young Lady* 1941; *The Wife Takes a Flyer* 1942; *A Night to Remember, Bombardier, The Fallen Sparrow, My Kingdom for a Cook* 1943; *Bride by Mistake* 1944; *It's in the Bag, Kiss and Tell* 1945; *Because of Him* 1946; *Sinbad the Sailor, Framed, Tycoon* 1947; *Let's Live a Little* 1948; *Adventure in Baltimore* 1949; *A Kiss for Corliss* 1950.

Wallach, Eli. Actor. Born Dec. 7, 1915, Brooklyn, N.Y. *ed.* U. of Texas (B.A.); CCNY (M.A. in education). Having made his first public appearance at 15, in a boy's club presentation, he trained for the stage at New York's Neighborhood Playhouse and after WW II military service made his Broadway debut in 1945. In the 50s he emerged as one of the American theater's most respected actors, a leading exponent of "the Method," a versatile performer of admirable range. He made his screen debut in the role of the unscrupulous seducer in Elia Kazan's *Baby Doll* (1956). He then appeared in many films, often playing mean heavies. Particularly active in TV and made-for-cable films in the 80s. He has frequently shared the limelight with his wife, Anne JACKSON. His son, Peter Wallach, is a special effects designer.

FILMS INCLUDE: *Baby Doll* 1956; *The Lineup* 1958; *Seven Thieves, The Magnificent Seven* 1960; *The Misfits* 1961; *How the West Was Won* 1962; *The Victors* (UK/US), *Act One* (1963); *The Moonspinners* 1964; *Lord Jim, Genghis Khan* 1965; *How to Steal a Million, Il Buono il Brutto il Cattivo/The Good the Bad and the Ugly* (It.) 1966; *The Tiger Makes Out* 1967; *Il Quattro dell'Ave Maria/Ace High* (It.), *How to Save a Marriage—And Ruin Your Life, A Lovely Way to Die* 1968; *Le Cerveau/The Brain* (Fr./It.), *Mackenna's Gold* 1969; *Zigzag, The Angel Levine, The People Next Door* 1970; *Romance of a Horse Thief* 1971; *Los Guerilleros/Don't Turn the Other Cheek* (Sp./It.) 1972; *Cinderella Liberty* 1973; *Crazy Joe* (It.) 1974; *Occhio del Gatto/Eye of the Cat* (It.) 1975; *Independence* (short; as Benjamin Franklin), *Nasty Habits* (UK), *Paura* (It.) 1976; *The Sentinel, The Domino Principle, The Deep* 1977; *Girlfriends, The Silent Flute, Movie Movie* 1978; *Winter Kills, Circle of Iron, Firepower* 1979; *The Salamander* 1980; *Acting: Lee Strasberg and the Actors Studio* (documentary), *The Hunter* 1981; *Sam's Son* 1984; *Tough Guys* 1986; *Hello Actors Studio* (documentary), *Nuts* 1987; *Funny* 1988; *Terezin Diary* 1989; *The Two Jakes, The Godfather Part 3* 1990; *Article 99, Mistress* 1992; *The Associate, Two Much* 1996.

Waller, Fred. Inventor, promoter. *b.* 1886, Brooklyn, N.Y. *d.* 1954. An engineer, he took an early interest in film techniques and in the late 20s headed Paramount's special-effects department. In 1939, at the New York World's Fair, he presented his Vitarama, an 11-projector wide-screen system he had developed in 1937. The invention was a sensational attraction at the Fair but proved impractical for regular commercial use in cinema theaters. During WW II he adapted the system for use in gunnery training, utilizing the multiple screens to simulate combat conditions. Undaunted by the commercial failure of the Vitarama, he continued his research and in 1952 launched an improved system, the three-projector CINERAMA, which has since been successfully exploited in theaters all over the world.

Wallis, Hal B. Producer. *b.* Harold Brent Wallis, Sept. 14, 1899, in Chicago. *d.* 1986. Forced to leave school at 14 to help support his family, he started out as an office boy and later became a road salesman for an electric heating company. In 1922 he moved to Los Angeles, where he was hired as the manager of a leading motion picture theater, the Garrick. His success there brought him to the attention of the Warner brothers, whom he joined the following year as assistant to the head of publicity. Three months later he took over the department's top position and in 1928 he was made studio manager and, shortly after, production executive. In 1931 he was replaced by Darryl ZANUCK, but when the latter left Warners to form 20th Century in 1933, Wallis regained his position as executive producer in charge of production. During his tenure with Warners he was responsible for many successful productions in a variety of genres, notably the company's crime and social cycle and its famous musicals of the 30s.

In 1944 he left Warners and formed his own Hal Wallis Productions, producing independently for release by Paramount. From the late 60s he released through Universal. He was one of Hollywood's most successful producers and production executives, both within and outside of the studio system. For 45 years he produced, co-produced, or supervised the production of more than 400 films, most of them commercially profitable and many critical successes as well. Many won Academy Awards. A retrospective of his most famous productions was held by the British Film Institute in 1969 and by New York's Museum of Modern Art in 1970. Divorced after many years of marriage from film star Louise FAZENDA, he married Martha HYER, to whom he was married at the time of his death.

FILMS INCLUDE: *The Dawn Patrol, Little Caesar* 1930; *Five Star Final* 1931; *I Am a Fugitive from a Chain Gang* 1932; *Mystery of the Wax Museum, Gold Diggers of 1933, Foot-light Parade* 1933; *G-Men, A Midsummer Night's Dream, Captain Blood* 1935; *The Story of Louis Pasteur, Anthony Adverse, The Charge of the Light Brigade, Green Pastures* 1936; *Marked Woman, Kid Galahad, The Life of Emile Zola* 1937; *A Slight Case of Murder, Jezebel, The Adventures of Robin Hood, Boy Meets Girl, Four Daughters, The Sisters, Brother Rat* 1938; *Dark Victory, Juarez, The Old Maid, The Private Lives of Elizabeth and Essex, The Roaring Twenties* 1939; *Dr. Ehrlich's Magic Bullet, Torrid Zone, They Drive by Night, The Sea Hawk, A Dispatch from Reuters, The Letter* 1940; *High Sierra, The Sea Wolf, The Great Lie, Sergeant York, The Maltese Falcon* 1941; *The Man Who Came to Dinner, Kings Row, Yankee Doodle Dandy, Now Voyager* 1942; *Casablanca, Air Force, Watch on the Rhine, Princess O'Rourke* 1943; *Passage to Marseille* 1944; *Love Letters* 1945; *The Strange Love of Martha Ivers* 1946; *I Walk Alone* 1947; *So Evil My Love, Sorry Wrong Number, The Accused* 1948; *Rope of Sand* 1949; *Paid in Full, The Furies, Dark City* 1950; *September Affair, That's My Boy* 1951; *Come Back Little Sheba* 1952; *About Mrs. Leslie* 1954; *The Rose Tattoo* 1955; *Artists and Models, The Rainmaker* 1956; *Gunfight at the O.K. Corral* 1957; *King Creole, Hot Spell* 1958; *Last Train from Gun Hill, Career* 1959; *G.I. Blues* 1960; *Summer and Smoke* 1961; *Becket* 1964; *The Sons of Katie Elder, Boeing Boeing* 1965; *Barefoot in the Park* 1967; *True Grit, Anne of the Thousand Days* 1969; *Norwood* 1970; *Red Sky at Morning, Shoot Out, Mary Queen of Scots* (UK) 1971; *Follow Me/The Public Eye* (UK) 1972; *A Bequest to the Nation/The Nelson Affair* (UK), *The Don Is Dead* 1973; *Rooster Cogburn* 1975.

Walls, Tom. Actor, director. *b.* Feb. 18, 1883, Kingsthorpe, England. *d.* 1949. A former policeman and jockey, he made his stage debut in 1905. He rose to popularity in the mid-20s as the star and producer of a string of successful farces at London's Aldwych Theatre. He adapted many of these to the screen in the 30s, in a series of comedies which he directed and in which he also starred. He remained in films through the 40s as a character actor.

FILMS INCLUDE: As actor-director—*Rookery Nook, On Approval* 1930; *Plunder* 1931; *A Night Like This* 1932; *The Blarney Stone/The Blarney Kiss, Just Smith, A Cuckoo in the Nest, Turkey Time* 1933; *A Cup of Kindness, Dirty Work* 1934; *Fighting Stock, Stormy Weather, Foreign Affairs* 1935; *Pot Luck* 1936; *For Valor* 1937; *Old Iron* 1938. As actor—*Crackerjack/Man with 100 Faces* 1938; *Undercover* 1943; *Halfway House, Love Story/A Lady Surrenders* 1944; *Johnny Frenchman* 1945; *This Man Is Mine* 1946; *Master of Bankdam* 1947; *Spring in Park Lane* 1948; *Maytime in Mayfair, The Interrupted Journey* 1949.

Walsh, Bill. Producer, screenwriter. *b.* Sept. 30, 1914, New York City. *d.* 1975. *ed.* U. of Cincinnati. A former newspaper reporter and magazine writer, he produced and co-scripted Walt Disney TV programs in the early 50s, then produced or wrote, or both, a string of commercially successful Disney feature films.

FILMS INCLUDE (as producer): *Davy Crockett—King of the Wild Frontier, The Littlest Outlaw* (sc. only) 1955; *Westward Ho the Wagons* 1956; *The Shaggy Dog* (also co-sc.) 1959; *Toby Tyler* (also co-sc.) 1960; *The Absent-Minded Professor* (also sc.) 1961; *Bon Voyage* (co-prod., co-sc.) 1962; *Son of Flubber* (co-prod., co-sc.) 1963; *Mary Poppins* (also co-sc.) 1964; *That Darn Cat* (co-prod., co-sc.) 1965; *Lt. Robinson Crusoe USN* (co-prod., co-sc.) 1966; *Blackbeard's Ghost* (also co-sc.) 1968; *The Love Bug* (also co-sc.) 1969; *Scandalous John* (also co-sc.), *Bedknobs and Broomsticks* (also co-sc.) 1971; *The World's Greatest Athlete* 1973; *Herbie Rides Again* (also sc.) 1974; *One of Our Dinosaurs Is Missing* (also sc.; US/UK) 1975.

Walsh, David M. American director of photography. He worked as camera assistant and camera operator on a number of expensive Hollywood productions of the 60s and graduated to lighting cameraman in 1970. He is noted for striking color cinematography.

FILMS INCLUDE: *I Walk the Line, Monte Walsh* 1970; *A Gunfight* 1971; *Everything You Always Wanted to Know About Sex* 1972; *Cleopatra Jones, Ace Eli and Rodger of the Skies, The Laughing Policeman, Sleeper* 1973; *The Crazy World of Julius Vrooder* 1974; *The Other Side of the Mountain, Whiffs, The Sunshine Boys* 1975; *W. C. Fields and Me, Murder by Death, Silver Streak* 1976; *Scott Joplin, Rollercoaster, The Goodbye Girl* 1977; *Foul Play, House Calls, California Suite* 1978; *The In-Laws* 1979; *Seems Like Old Times* 1980; *Only When I Laugh* 1981; *Max Dugan Returns, Romantic Comedy* 1983; *Unfaithfully Yours, Johnny Dangerously, Country, Teachers* 1984; *My Science Project* 1985; *Fatal Beauty, Outrageous Fortune, Summer School* 1987; *Second Sight* 1989; *Taking Care of Business* 1990.

Walsh, George. Actor. *b.* 1892, New York City. *d.* 1981. Younger brother of director Raoul WALSH, he studied law at Fordham and Georgetown universities before deciding to enter films in 1914. After playing supporting parts in *Intolerance* (the bridegroom in the "Marriage at Cana" sequence) and other films, he became a star at Fox. His success relied heavily on his muscular prowess and for a while he rivaled Douglas Fairbanks with his daring screen athletics. He was popular enough by the early 20s to be designated the star of the upcoming supercolossal Goldwyn production *Ben-Hur.* But production delays and the merger of Goldwyn into MGM caused the dismissal in midproduction of the film's director Charles Brabin and the star and their replacement by Fred Niblo and Ramon Novarro. Walsh continued appearing in films, but his starring days were over. From 1916 to 1924 he was married to actress Seena OWEN.

FILMS INCLUDE: *The Fencing Master, The Celestial Code, Don Quixote* 1915; *Intolerance, The Serpent* (also co-sc.), *The Beast, Blue Blood and Red* 1916; *Melting Millions, This Is the Life, The Yankee Way, The Honor System* 1917; *The Pride of New York, I'll Say So, On the Jump, Brave and Bold, The Kid Is Clever* 1918; *The Winning Stroke, Luck and Pluck, Never Say Quit* 1919; *The Shark, From Now On, The Dead Line, A Manhattan Knight* 1920; *Dynamite Allen, Serenade* 1921; *Stanley in Africa* (serial) 1922; *Vanity Fair, Rosita, Slave of Desire, The Miracle Makers, Reno* 1923; *Blue Blood, American Pluck* 1925; *The Count of Luxembourg, The Prince of Broadway, The Kick-Off, A Man of Quality* 1926; *His Rise to Fame, The Broadway Drifter, The Winning Oar, Combat* 1927; *Inspiration* 1928; *The Big Trail* 1930; *Me and My Gal* 1932; *The Bowery* 1933; *Belle of the Nineties* 1934; *Under Pressure* 1935; *Klondike Annie* 1936.

Walsh, J. T. Actor. Born James Patrick Walsh on September 28, 1943, in San Francisco. *ed.* University of Rhode Island. This veteran character actor spent his early years after graduation in a variety of jobs from social worker and journalist to teacher. At the age of 30, he turned to acting, appearing in a number of highly acclaimed dramas on the New York stage. His extensive film career illustrates his versatility.

FILMS: *Eddie Macon's Run* 1983; *Hannah and Her Sisters, Hard Choices, Power* 1986; *Good Morning Vietnam, House of Games, Tin Men* 1987; *Tequila Sunrise, Things Change* 1988; *The Big Picture, Dad, Wired* 1989; *Crazy People, The Grifters, Misery, Narrow Margin, The Russia House* 1990; *Backdraft, Defenseless, Iron Maze, True Identity* 1991; *A Few Good Men, Hoffa* 1992; *National Lampoon's Loaded Weapon I, Needful Things, Red Rock West, Sniper* 1993; *Blue Chips, Charlie's Ghost Story, The Client, The Last Seduction, Miracle on 34th Street, Silent Fall* 1994; *The Babysitter, Executive Decision, Nixon, Outbreak* 1995; *Sling Blade* 1996.

Walsh, Kay. Actress. Born in 1914, in London. A former dancer, she played leads in many British films from the mid-30s before easing into character parts in the early 60s.

FILMS INCLUDE: *How's Chances?* 1934; *The Luck of the Irish* 1935; *The Secret of Stamboul* 1936; *The Last Adventurers* 1937; *The Middle Watch* 1939; *The Chinese Bungalow/Chinese Den* 1940; *In Which We Serve* (also co-sc.), *This Happy Breed* 1944; *The October Man, Vice Versa* 1947; *Oliver Twist* (as Nancy) 1948; *Stage Fright, Last Holiday, The Magnet* 1950; *Encore, The Magic Box, Hunted/The Stranger in Between* 1951; *Young Bess* (US) 1953; *Lease of Life* 1954; *Cast a Dark Shadow* 1955; *The Horse's Mouth* 1958; *Tunes of Glory* 1960; *The L-Shaped Room, Reach for Glory* 1962; *Circus World* (US) 1964; *A Study in Terror* 1965; *The Witches/The Devil's Own* 1966; *The Virgin and the Gypsy* 1970; *Scrooge* 1971; *The Ruling Class* 1972; *Night Crossing* 1982.

Walsh, M. Emmet. Actor. Born Michael Emmet Walsh on March 22, 1935, in Ogdensburg, N.Y. *ed.* Clarkson Coll., N.Y.; AADA, New York. Stocky, versatile character actor, often in villainous roles. Active since appearing in an uncredited role in *Midnight Cowboy*.

FILMS INCLUDE: *Midnight Cowboy* (uncredited), *Alice's Restaurant, Stiletto* 1969; *Little Big Man, The Traveling Executioner* 1970; *They Might Be Giants* 1971; *Get to Know Your Rabbit, What's Up Doc?* 1972; *Serpico* 1973; *The Gambler* 1974; *At Long Last Love* 1975; *Mikey and Nicky, Nickelodeon* 1976; *Airport 77, Slap Shot* 1977; *Straight Time* 1978; *The Fish That Saved Pittsburgh, The Jerk* 1979; *Brubaker, Ordinary People, Raise the Titanic* 1980; *Back Roads, Reds* 1981; *Blade Runner, Cannery Row, The Escape Artist, Fast-Walking* 1982; *Silkwood* 1983; *Blood Simple, Courage, Missing in Action, The Pope of Greenwich Village, Scandalous* 1984; *Fletch* 1985; *Back to School, The Best of Times, Critters, Wildcats* 1986; *Harry and the Hendersons, No Man's Land, Raising Arizona* 1987; *Clean and Sober, The Milagro Beanfield War, Sunset* 1988; *War Party, Red Scorpion, The Mighty Quinn* 1989; *Chattahoochee, Narrow Margin* 1990; *Sundown, The Vampire in Retreat* 1991; *White Sands* 1992; *Equinox* 1993; *Camp Nowhere, Cops and Robbersons* 1994; *Panther* 1995; *Albino Alligator, Romeo & Juliet, A Time to Kill* 1996.

Walsh, Raoul. Director. *b.* Mar. 11, 1887, New York City. *d.* 1980. *ed.* Seton Hall. The son of a clothes designer, he ran away to sea as a boy and later broke horses in cattle drives in Mexico, Texas, and Montana. He did some stage acting from 1910 and entered films in 1912 as an actor and assistant director to D. W. Griffith at Biograph. It was Griffith who gave him his first directorial assignment, in collaboration with Christy Cabanne, *The Life of General Villa* (1914), a seven-reel mixture of staged scenes and authentic footage of Pancho Villa's military campaign starring the Mexican bandit himself. Walsh's most notable appearance as an actor was in the role of John Wilkes Booth in Griffith's *The Birth of a Nation* (1915). He subsequently appeared in occasional films but by and large devoted his career to directing. Over the next half-century he distinguished himself as one of the most durable, prolific, and proficient of Hollywood's directors.

A straightforward storyteller, he made many fine, unpretentious, smoothly paced films with the accent on entertainment and slick production values. He tackled a variety of genres but was at his best with virile outdoor action dramas, which he often mellowed with moments of genuine tenderness. Douglas Fairbanks, Sr., Errol Flynn, James Cagney, Humphrey Bogart, Gary Cooper, and Clark Gable were among the masculine symbols that typified his screen heroes. A dynamic, instinctive director, he is considered by many critics as one of the great primitive artists of the screen. Walsh lost an eye while shooting *In Old Arizona* (1929), Hollywood's first outdoor talkie, and was seen wearing an eye patch ever after. Nearing blindness in his other eye, he retired from film work in 1964. His brother, George WALSH, was a popular silent star. Raoul's first of three wives, Miriam COOPER, starred in many of his early films. Autobiography: *Each Man in His Time* (1974).

FILMS (as director): *The Life of General Villa* (co-dir. with Christy Cabanne; also sc., act.), *The Double Knot* (also prod., sc., act.), *The Mystery of the Hindu Image* (also prod., sc.), *The Gunman* (also prod., sc.; credit contested), *The Final Verdict* (also prod., sc., act.) 1914; *The Death Dice* (*Dies?;* also prod., sc.; credit contested), *His Return* (also prod.), *The Greaser* (also prod., sc., act.), *The Fencing Master* (also prod., sc.), *A Man for All That* (also prod., sc., act.), *Eleven-Thirty P.M.* (also prod., sc.), *The Buried Hand* (also prod., sc.), *The Celestial Code* (also prod., sc.), *A Bad Man and Others* (also prod., sc.), *The Regeneration* (also prod., co-sc.), *Carmen* (also prod., sc.) 1915; *Pillars of Society* (under Griffith's supervision), *The Serpent* (also prod., co-sc.), *Blue Blood and Red* (also prod., story, sc.) 1916; *The Honor System* (also prod., sc.), *The Conqueror* (also co-sc.), *Betrayed* (also prod., co-story, sc.), *This Is the Life* (also co-story, co-sc.), *The Pride of New York* (also story, sc.), *The Silent Lie, The Innocent Sinner* (also sc.) 1917; *The Woman and the Law* (also sc.), *The Prussian Cur* (also story, sc.), *On the Jump* (also story, sc.), *Every Mother's Son* (also story, sc.), *I'll Say So* 1918; *Evangeline* (also prod., sc.), *The Strongest* (also sc.), *Should a Husband Forgive?* (also sc.) 1919; *From Now On* (also sc.), *The Deep Purple* 1920; *The Oath* (also prod.), *Serenade* (also prod.) 1921; *Kindred of the Dust* (also prod.) 1922; *Lost and Found on a South Sea Island* (also prod.) 1923; *The Thief of Bagdad* 1924; *East of Suez, The Spaniard, The Wanderer* 1925; *The Lucky Lady* (also prod.), *The Lady of the Harem, What Price Glory* 1926; *The Money Talks* (also prod.), *The Loves of Carmen* 1927; *Sadie Thompson* (also sc., act.), *The Red Dance* (also prod.), *Me Gangster* (also co-sc.) 1928; *In Old Arizona* (co-dir. with Irving Cummings), *The Cock-eyed World* (also sc.), *Hot for Paris* (also story) 1929; *The Big Trail* 1930; *The Man Who Came Back, Women of All Nations, The Yellow Ticket* (also prod.) 1931; *Wild Girl, For Me and My Gal/Pier 13* 1932; *Sailor's Luck, The Bowery, Going Hollywood* 1933; *Under Pressure, Baby Face Harrington, Every Night at Eight* 1935; *Klondike Annie, Big Brown Eyes* (also co-sc.), *Spendthrift* (also co-sc.) 1936; *O.H.M.S./You're in the Army Now* (UK), *Jump for Glory/When Thief Meets Thief* (UK), *Artists and Models, Hitting a New High* 1937; *College Swing* 1938; *St. Louis Blues, The Roaring Twenties* 1939; *Dark Command* (also prod.), *They Drive by Night* 1940; *High Sierra, Strawberry Blonde, Manpower, They Died with Their Boots On* 1941; *Desperate Journey, Gentleman Jim* 1942; *Background to Danger, Northern Pursuit* 1943; *Uncertain Glory* 1944; *Objective Burma!, The Horn Blows at Midnight, San Antonio* (co-dir. with David Butler; uncredited), *Salty O'Rourke* 1945; *Stallion Road* (co-dir. with James V. Kern; uncredited), *The Man I Love, Pursued, Cheyenne/The Wyoming Kid* 1947; *Silver River, Fighter Squadron, One Sunday Afternoon* 1948; *Colorado Territory, White Heat* 1949; *Montana* (co-dir. with Ray Enright; uncredited) 1950; *The Enforcer* (co-dir. with Bretaigne Windust; uncredited), *Along the Great Divide, Captain Horatio Hornblower, Distant Drums* 1951; *Glory Alley, The World in His Arms, Blackbeard the Pirate* 1952; *The Lawless Breed, Sea Devils, A Lion Is in the Streets, Gun Fury* 1953; *Saskatchewan* 1954; *Battle Cry, The Tall Men* 1955; *The Revolt of Mamie Stover, The King and Four Queens* 1956; *Band of Angels* 1957; *The Naked and the Dead, The Sheriff of Fractured Jaw* (UK) 1958; *A Private's Affair* 1959; *Esther e il Re/Esther and the King* (also prod., co-sc.; It./US) 1960; *Marines Let's Go!* (also prod., story) 1961; *A Distant Trumpet* 1964.

Walston, Ray. Actor. Born on Nov. 22, 1918, in New Orleans. Veteran character comedian of the stage, TV, and films. Memorable as the Devil in both the Broadway (Tony Award) and Hollywood versions of the musical *Damn Yankees,* and as the Martian in the TV series 'My Favorite Martian.'

FILMS: *Kiss Them for Me* 1957; *South Pacific, Damn Yankees* 1958; *Say One for Me* 1959; *Tall Story, The Apartment, Portrait in Black* 1960; *Convicts 4* 1962; *Wives and Lovers, Who's Minding the Store?* 1963; *Kiss Me Stupid* 1964; *Caprice* 1967; *Paint Your Wagon* 1969; *The Sting* 1973; *Silver Streak* 1976; *The Happy Hooker Goes to Washington* 1977; *Popeye, Galaxy of Terror* 1981; *Fast Times at Ridgemont High, O'Hara's Wife* 1982; *Private School* 1983; *Johnny Dangerously, That's Singing!* (documentary) 1984; *RAD, From the Hip* 1986; *O. C. and Stiggs* 1987; *Blood Relations, Saturday the 14th Strikes Back, Paramedics, Man of Passion* 1988; *Ski Patrol* 1989; *Blood Salvage* 1990; *Popcorn* 1991; *Of Mice and Men, The Player* (cameo) 1992; *House Arrest* 1996.

Walt Disney Co. See DISNEY CO., The Walt.

Walter, Jessica. Actress. Born on Jan. 31, 1940, in Brooklyn, N.Y. Trained for the stage at Bucks County Playhouse and New York's Neighborhood Playhouse, she made her mark on Broadway in the early 60s and subsequently played leads on the stage, on TV ('The Defenders,' 'Ben Casey,' etc.), and in films, notably as the would-be love interest of Clint Eastwood in *Play Misty for Me.*

FILMS: *Lilith* 1964; *The Group, Grand Prix* 1966; *Bye Bye Braverman* 1968; *Number One* 1969; *Play Misty for Me* 1971; *Goldengirl* 1979; *Going Ape!* 1981; *Spring Fever* 1983; *The Flamingo Kid* 1984; *Tapeheads* 1988.

Walters, Charles. Director. *b.* Nov. 17, 1911, Brooklyn, N.Y. *d.* 1982. *ed.* USC. A former actor, dancer, and director, he entered films as a choreographer of MGM musicals of the early 40s (*Du Barry Was a Lady, Meet Me in St. Louis, Ziegfeld Follies,* etc.). Turning director in 1947, he reinforced the already powerful team of musical film directors (Vincente MINNELLI, Stanley DONEN) at MGM with his expert handling of palatable, sparkling light entertainment. He came out of retirement in the early 70s as director of two Lucille Ball TV specials.

FILMS: *Good News* 1947; *Easter Parade* 1948; *The Barkleys of Broadway* 1949; *Summer Stock* 1950; *Three Guys Named Mike, Texas Carnival* 1951; *The Belle of New York* 1952; *Lili* (also co-choreographed), *Dangerous When Wet, Torch Song* (also choreographed, danced, partnering with Joan Crawford), *Easy to Love* 1953; *The Glass Slipper, The Tender Trap* 1955; *High Society* 1956; *Don't Go Near the Water* 1957; *Ask Any Girl* 1959; *Please Don't Eat the Daisies* 1960; *Two Loves* 1961;

Jumbo 1962; *The Unsinkable Molly Brown* 1964; *Walk Don't Run!* 1966.

Walters, Julie. Actress. Born on Feb. 22, 1950, in Birmingham, England. *ed.* Manchester Polytechnic. Lively, straightforward, stage-trained screen and TV lead. Largely completed with nursing studies, she abandoned the profession for acting, and performed widely throughout England in plays and as a singer/dancer. Debuted in film with her Academy Award–nominated recreation of her stage role of the working-class student in *Educating Rita*; awarded a Tony for her stage performance.

FILMS INCLUDE: *Educating Rita* 1983; *DreamChild, Car Trouble* 1985; *Prick Up Your Ears, Personal Services* 1987; *Buster* 1988; *Mack the Knife* 1989; *Stepping Out* (US) 1991; *The Wedding Gift* 1993; *Just Like Woman* 1994.

Walthall, Henry B. Actor. *b.* Mar. 16, 1878, Shelby City, Ala. *d.* 1936. After law studies in the South, he came to New York and gained growing recognition as an actor on Broadway. In 1909 he joined D. W. Griffith's troupe at Biograph and subsequently played leads in many of the director's famous early films, often opposite Mary Pickford. His most memorable role was that of the Little Colonel in *The Birth of a Nation* (1915), one he played with great tenderness and admirable restraint. Unfortunately for his career, Walthall decided to leave Griffith at that point. Many of his subsequent film vehicles did not present him with the opportunity to develop his full potential; yet he often came up with interesting offbeat characterizations. He gradually shifted to character parts, in which he was quite effective. He died in the midst of production of *China Clipper* (1936).

FILMS INCLUDE: *A Convict's Sacrifice, A Strange Meeting, Pranks, The Sealed Room, In Old Kentucky, A Corner in Wheat, Choosing a Husband* 1909; *The Honor of His Family, In Old California, The Gold Seekers, Ramona, The Oath and the Man, The Sorrows of the Unfaithful, A Summer Idyl, The Armorer's Daughter* 1910; *A Little Child* 1911; *Home Folks, The Miser's Daughter, Friends, In the Aisles of the Wild, The Informer, My Hero, The God Within* 1912; *Oil and Water, Death's Marathon, Broken Ways, The Vengeance of Galora, Two Men of the Desert, The Wedding Gown* 1913; *The Battle of Elderbush Gulch, The Gangsters of New York, Ashes of the Past, Judith of Bethulia* (as Holofernes), *Lord Chumley, Strongheart, Home Sweet Home* (as composer John Howard Payne), *The Avenging Conscience, The Odalisque, The Mountain Rat* 1914; *The Birth of a Nation* (as the Little Colonel), *Ghosts, The Woman Hater, The Raven* (as Edgar A. Poe) 1915; *The Strange Case of Mary Page* (serial), *The Pillars of Society* 1916; *The Great Love, His Robe of Honor* 1918; *False Faces, The Confession, The Boomerang* 1919; *A Splendid Hazard* 1920; *Flower of the North* 1921; *One Clear Call, The Long Chance, The Marriage Chance* 1922; *The Face on the Barroom Floor, Boy of Mine, The Unknown Purple* 1923; *The Bowery Bishop, Single Wives* 1924; *The Golden Bed, Dollar Down, Kentucky Pride, Simon the Jester, The Plastic Age* 1925; *Three Faces East, The Barrier, The Unknown Soldier, The Road to Mandalay, The Scarlet Letter* (as Roger Prynne), *Everybody's Acting* 1926; *The Enchanted Island, A Light in the Window, Wings, London After Midnight* 1927; *Love Me and the World Is Mine, Freedom of the Press* 1928; *The Jazz Age, From Headquarters, Speakeasy, The Bridge of San Luis Rey* (as Father Juniper), *Black Magic, River of Romance, The Trespasser, In Old California* 1929; *Temple Tower, Abraham Lincoln, Tol'able David* 1930; *Police Court, Strange Interlude, Cabin in the Cotton, Chandu the Magician* 1932; *Whispering Shadows* (serial), *42nd Street* 1933; *Dark Hazard, Viva Villa!, The Lemon Drop Kid* 1934; *Helldorado, Dante's Inferno, A Tale of Two Cities* (as Dr. Manette) 1935; *The Garden Murder Case, China Clipper* 1936.

Walton, Sir William. Composer. *b.* Mar. 29, 1902, Oldham, England. *d.* 1983. One of England's most important concert-hall composers in the 20th century. In addition to composing symphonies, concertos, operas, oratorios, and other musical pieces, he created the scores for a number of important British films.

FILMS: *Escape Me Never* 1935; *As You Like It* 1936; *A Stolen Life* 1939; *Major Barbara* 1941; *The Foreman Went to France, Next of Kin, The First of the Few* 1942; *Henry V* 1945; *Hamlet* 1948; *Richard III* 1956; *Battle of Britain* ("Battle in the Air" music) 1969; *Three Sisters* 1970.

"Wampas Baby Star." A title bestowed annually on select Hollywood starlets by the Western Association of Motion Picture Advertisers in the years 1922–34. The winners, 13 each year, were deemed most likely to succeed as future stars. Some did; many others never made it. In the 20s the competition aroused public interest not unlike the attention given today to the Oscar ceremonies. Some of the more famous Wampas babies were (year of election in parentheses): Bessie Love (1922), Eleanor Boardman (1923), Clara Bow (1924), Mary Astor, Joan Crawford, Dolores Del Rio, Janet Gaynor, Fay Wray (all 1926), Lupe Velez (1928), Jean Arthur, Loretta Young (both 1929), Joan Blondell, Rochelle Hudson, Anita Louise (all 1931), Ginger Rogers (1932), and Jacqueline Wells (Julie Bishop) (1934).

Wanamaker, Sam. Actor, director. *b.* June 14, 1919, in Chicago. *ed.* Drake U. *d.* 1993. Trained for the stage at Chicago's Goodman Theater, he made his debut at the age of 17 and went on to appear in many plays in stock, on the road, and on Broadway. Returning from WW II military service, he made his screen debut in *My Girl Tisa* (1948), but because of his leftist political associations he thought it wise to transfer to England, although as it turned out his name was not mentioned in either the 1947 or 1951 investigations of the House Un-American Activities Committee. He played the lead in DMYTRYK'S socialist-themed film *Give Us This Day* (1949) and appeared in one other British film before being placed on Hollywood's long-reaching blacklist. Unable to work in films (except for one occasion), he turned to the stage and soon became very active in the British theater both as an actor and as a director and producer. He renewed his film activity in the 60s, working mostly in England at first. He directed five features and a telefilm.

FILMS: As actor—*My Girl Tisa* (US) 1948; *Give Us This Day* 1949; *Mr. Denning Drives North* 1951; *The Secret* 1955; *The Battle of the Sexes* (narr. only) 1959; *The Criminal/The Concrete Jungle* 1960; *Taras Bulba* (US) 1962; *Man in the Middle* (UK/US) 1964; *Those Magnificent Men in Their Flying Machines, The Spy Who Came in from the Cold* 1965; *Warning Shot* (US), *The Day the Fish Came Out* (UK/Gr.), *Danger Route* 1967; *Billy Jack Goes to Washington, The Sell Out, Voyage of the Damned* 1976; *Death on the Nile* (UK) 1978; *De l'enfer a la Victoire/From Hell to Victory* (Sp./Fr.) 1979; *Private Benjamin, The Competition* 1980; *Irreconcilable Differences* 1984; *The Aviator* 1985; *Raw Deal* 1986; *Superman 4: The Quest for Peace, Baby Boom* 1987; *Judgment in Berlin* 1988; *Cognac* 1990; *Guilty by Suspicion, Pure Luck* 1991. As director—*The File of the Golden Goose* 1969; *The Executioner* 1970; *Catlow* 1971; *Sinbad and the Eye of the Tiger* (US) 1977; *Charlie Muffin* 1979.

Wang, Wayne. Director. Born in 1949, in Hong Kong. *ed.* College of Arts and Crafts, Calif. Director of wry, incisive portraits of Chinese and Chinese-American life. Named for John

Wayne after his parents saw *Red River*. Returning to Hong Kong following his schooling, he worked on a TV comedy show but gained his first directorial experience in film, directing the Chinese scenes in the 70s thriller *Golden Needles*. Back in the US, he co-directed his first feature, the atmospheric San Francisco–based drama *A Man, a Woman and a Killer*. With grants from AFI and the National Endowment of the Arts, he made his first solo film, the quirky comedy *Chan Is Missing*. Set in San Francisco's Chinatown, it revealed a previously unexpressed insider's view of modern Chinese-American culture. A word-of-mouth success, the $22,000 film led to a number of independent entries about Chinese-American culture, including *Eat a Bowl of Tea*, *Life is Cheap... But Toilet Paper is Expensive*, and *Dim Sum: A Little Bit of Heart*, which explored mother-daughter relationships. He would undertake another view of the same subject in his adaptation of the novel *The Joy Luck Club*, his first engagement with a major studio, Touchstone. The film, like several of his previous efforts, was praised for its evocativeness and universality. An effort into standard genres, *Slam Dance*, was a disappointment. Married actress Cora Miao.

FILMS INCLUDE: *A Man a Woman and a Killer* (co-dir.) 1975; *Chan Is Missing* (also sc.) 1981; *Dim Sum: A Little Bit of Heart* 1985; *Slam Dance* 1987; *Eat a Bowl of Tea* 1989; *Life is Cheap... But Toilet Paper Is Expensive* 1989; *The Joy Luck Club* (also co-pr.) 1993; *Smoke* 1994; *Blue in the Face* (also sc.) 1995.

Wanger, Walter. Producer. *b.* Walter Feuchtwanger, July 11, 1894, San Francisco. *d.* 1968. *ed.* Dartmouth. After producing one play on Broadway in 1917, he served as an officer with Army Intelligence in WW I and was on President Wilson's staff at the Paris Peace Conference. Returning to civilian life, he joined Paramount as producer, later becoming the company's production chief. He subsequently served in similar capacities with Columbia and MGM and produced independently, releasing through United Artists and other companies. His productions ranged from ambitious undertakings to routine potboilers. Wanger received unwanted publicity in the early 50s when he was convicted of shooting and injuring the agent of his second wife (from 1940), actress Joan BENNETT, in a jealous rage. He served a brief jail sentence, after which he returned to Miss Bennett. They divorced in 1962.

FILMS INCLUDE: *The Cocoanuts* 1929; *Gabriel Over the White House, Going Hollywood* 1933; *Queen Christina, The President Vanishes* 1934; *Private Worlds, Shanghai* 1935; *The Trail of the Lonesome Pine, Big Brown Eyes, The Moon's Our Home* 1936; *You Only Live Once, History Is Made at Night, 52nd Street* 1937; *Blockade, Algiers, Trade Winds* 1938; *Stagecoach* (exec. prod.) 1939; *The Long Voyage Home, Foreign Correspondent* 1940; *Sundown* 1941; *Arabian Nights* 1942; *Gung Ho!* 1943; *Scarlet Street* (exec. prod.), *Salome—Where She Danced* 1945; *Canyon Passage* 1946; *Smash-Up, The Lost Moment* 1947; *Joan of Arc* 1948; *The Reckless Moment* 1949; *Riot in Cell Block 11* 1954; *Invasion of the Body Snatchers* 1956; *I Want to Live!* 1958; *Cleopatra* (replaced by Darryl Zanuck) 1963.

Ward, Fred. Actor, producer. Born in 1943 in San Diego, Calif. *ed.* Herbert Berghof Studio, New York. Screen lead often cast in hard-edged, offbeat roles. Born of Irish, Scots, and Cherokee Indian descent, he grew up in Texas and in the French Quarter of New Orleans with his aunt after the death of his mother when he was 13. After serving in the Air Force, he studied acting in New York, which he financed by working as a janitor and demolition man in Hell's Kitchen. After a stint as a lumberjack in Alaska, he settled in Europe and appeared in two TV movies directed by Roberto Rossellini. He also dubbed films into English for Italian and Spanish spaghetti Westerns. Back in the US in late 1975, he worked with theater groups across the country before gaining widespread recognition as astronaut Gus Grissom in *The Right Stuff* (1983). Following his role in *Reno Williams: The Adventure Begins*, he was billed the "Blue Collar James Bond." He has since taken more challenging roles, notably portraying Henry Miller in *Henry & June* (1990).

FILMS INCLUDE: *Escape from Alcatraz, Tilt* 1979; *Carny, UFOria* 1980; *Southern Comfort* 1981; *Timerider: The Adventure of Lyle Swann* 1982; *The Right Stuff, Silkwood, Uncommon Valor* 1983; *Swing Shift* 1984; *Remo Williams: The Adventure Begins...*, *Secret Admirer* 1985; *Big Business, Off Limits, The Price of Life, The Prince of Pennsylvania* 1988; *Backtrack, Henry & June, Miami Blues* (also co-exec. prod.), *Tremors* 1990; *The Dark Wind* 1991; *The Player, Thunderheart, Equinox, Bob Roberts* 1992; *Short Cuts* 1993; *Naked Gun 33⅓: The Final Insult* 1994; *The Blue Villa* 1995; *Chain Reaction* 1996.

Ward, Simon. Actor. Born on Oct. 19, 1941, in Beckenham, England. Suave, blond British lead of stage and screen. Active since the 60s, he has often been cast as aristocratic types in films such as *Young Winston* (1972), *The Three Musketeers* (1973), and *Zulu Dawn* (1979).

FILMS INCLUDE: *If...* 1968; *Frankenstein Must Be Destroyed, I Start Counting* 1969; *Quest for Love* 1970; *Young Winston* 1972; *Hitler: The Last Ten Days, The Three Musketeers* 1973; *Butley* (sc. only, from play), *Children of Rage* 1974; *All Creatures Great and Small, The Four Musketeers* 1975; *Aces High* 1976; *Dominique, Holocaust 2000, Die Standarte/The Battle Flag* (Ger.) 1977; *The Chosen* 1978; *La Sabina, Zulu Dawn* 1979; *The Monster Club* 1981; *L'Etincelle* (Fr.) 1983; *Supergirl* 1984; *Leave All Fair* 1985; *Double X* 1992.

Warden, Jack. Actor. Born on Sept. 18, 1920, in Newark, N.J. A former prizefighter, he turned to the stage after returning from WW II service as a paratrooper. Starting out in Dallas repertory, he has since appeared on Broadway and in much TV. In films since the early 50s, he has typically played tough characters, often military men. He was nominated for an Oscar as best supporting actor for *Shampoo* (1975) and for *Heaven Can Wait* (1978).

FILMS INCLUDE: *You're in the Navy Now, USS Teakettle, The Frogmen* 1951; *Red Ball Express* 1952; *From Here to Eternity* 1953; *Edge of the City, The Bachelor Party, 12 Angry Men* 1957; *Darby's Rangers, Run Silent Run Deep* 1958; *That Kind of Woman* 1959; *Wake Me When It's Over* 1960; *Escape from Zahrain* 1962; *Donovan's Reef* 1963; *The Thin Red Line* 1964; *Blindfold* 1966; *Bye Bye Braverman* 1968; *Summertree, Who Is Harry Kellerman and Why Is He Saying Those Terrible Things About Me?* 1971; *The Man Who Loved Cat Dancing* 1973; *The Apprenticeship of Duddy Kravitz* (Can.) 1974; *Shampoo* 1975; *All the President's Men* 1976; *The White Buffalo* 1977; *Heaven Can Wait, Death on the Nile* 1978; *The Champ, Dreamer, Beyond the Poseidon Adventure, And Justice for All, Being There* 1979; *Used Cars* 1980; *Carbon Copy, Chu Chu and the Philly Flash, The Great Muppet Caper* (cameo), *So Fine* 1981; *The Verdict* 1982; *Crackers* 1984; *The Aviator* 1985; *September* 1987; *The Presidio* 1988; *Everybody Wins, Problem Child* 1990; *Problem Child 2* 1991; *Passed Away, Night and the City* 1992; *Guilty as Sin* 1993; *Bullets Over Broadway* 1994; *Mighty Aphrodite, Things To Do in Denver When You're Dead, While You Were Sleeping* 1995; *Ed* 1996.

wardrobe master/mistress. See COSTUMER.

Warhol, Andy. Pop artist, filmmaker. *b.* Andrew Warhola, Aug. 8, 1927, in Cleveland. *d.* 1987. The son of Czech immigrants, he studied art at the Carnegie Institute of Technology and designed ads for women's shoes before bursting upon the American cultural scene in the early 60s as the high priest of pop art. After gaining fame and fortune with reproductions of such curious items as Campbell soup cans and silk screenings of Marilyn Monroe, he went into filmmaking in 1963. His early films were interminable exercises in camera passivity. Typical of these were *Sleep,* in which the camera remained fixed on a man sleeping for the duration of eight hours, and *Empire,* which consisted of a seemingly endless shot of the Empire State Building. Avant-gardists saw in these films important experimentations in the exploration of cinema time and space, but to the public and most critics they amounted to little more than primitive exercises in nontechnique which pushed back the boundaries of boredom and set new limits to audience endurance. After turning out a good number of these silent, plotless, single-action films, Warhol's "factory" advanced to pictures with a crude sound track and a semblance of script. Gradually, the sound track improved and the camera work became less haphazard. But the scripts remained tenuous and much of the dialogue was improvised by the freaky-looking characters who typically inhabited Warhol's films. His performers were usually disciples and hangers-on, a strange assortment of exhibitionists, transvestites, groupies, and ordinary "beautiful people," several of whom emerged as "superstars" of the underground, under such colorful pseudonyms as Viva, Ultra Violet, Mario Montez, Candy Darling, and Ingrid Superstar.

Warhol's performers did not act in the ordinary sense of the word, just as his films do not reflect reality in the accepted sense. For better or for worse, they represent themselves and private worlds that hover in the twilight zone between reality and fantasy. The films, typically loosely structured affairs, cannot be categorized as either fiction or documentary. The camera captures the reality before it, but that reality is subjective and personal, a reflection of the semihallucinatory world of characters who often superimpose assumed identities of famous Hollywood personalities on top of their own. The director, if there is one, plays the part of an observer with no opinion about what goes on in front of the camera and little or no concern about how it is framed, cut, and shown on the screen. Death and sex are recurrent themes in Warhol's films. Sexuality is explicit, spanning the gamut of human experience, with no visible boundaries between heterosexual, homosexual, bisexual, transsexual, and androgynous identities and activities. The exhibition of these films in art theaters helped accelerate the trend toward legitimizing explicit sex on the American screen.

Warhol's gradual withdrawal from direct involvement with the production of his films coincided with his near-fatal shooting in 1968 by a female "factory" reject affiliated with an anti-male hate group. During his long period of recovery, the actual directorial duties of Warhol's films passed into the hands of his one-time assistant and cameraman Paul MORRISSEY. Under the aegis of Morrissey, the Warhol product became more structured and more commercial, with a growing emphasis on conventional film techniques. This trend culminated in the 70s with offbeat but marketable versions of *Frankenstein* and *Dracula,* both of which were shot by Morrissey in Rome in 1974, the former in 3-D.

Warhol founded *Interview* magazine in the early 70s. He remained a powerful pop culture figure into the 80s, appearing in music videos and revamping his artistic style, thanks in part to associations with younger artists. He died suddenly in 1987, following a routine gallbladder operation. Two years later, *The Andy Warhol Diaries* (Pat Hackett, ed.) hit the bestseller lists. The enormous book contained gossip on nearly every star, culled from Warhol's years as a party fixture.

FILMS INCLUDE: As director-producer—*Kiss, Eat, Sleep, Haircut* 1963; *Tarzan and Jane Regained. . . Sort Of, Dance Movie/Roller Skate, Blow Job, Batman Dracula, Salome and Delilah, Soap Opera* (co-dir.), *Couch, 13 Most Beautiful Women, Harlot* 1964; *The Life of Juanita Castro, Empire, Poor Little Rich Girl, Screen Test, Vinyl, Beauty #2, Horse, My Hustler, Camp, Afternoon, Suicide, Drunk, Bitch, Prison, Space, The Closet, Henry Geldzahler, Taylor Mead's Ass* 1965; *Face, Outer and Inner Space, The 14-Year-Old Girl/Hedy/Hedy the Shoplifter, More Milk Yvette/Lana Turner, The Velvet Underground and Nico, Kitchen, Lupe, The Chelsea Girls* 1966; *I'm a Man, Bike Boy, Nude Restaurant, ****/Four Stars/24-Hour Movie* 1967; *The Loves of Ondine, Lonesome Cowboys* 1968; *Blue Movie/Fuck* 1969; *Women in Revolt* (co-dir. with Paul Morrissey) 1972; *L'Amour* (co-dir., co-sc. with Morrissey) 1973. As producer—*Flesh* 1968; *Trash* 1970; *Heat* 1972; *Andy Warhol's Frankenstein, Andy Warhol's Dracula* 1974; *Underground and Emigrants* (documentary; act. only) 1976; *Andy Warhol's Bad* 1977; *An Unmarried Woman* (art collab.) 1978; *Cocaine Cowboys* (act. only) 1979; *The Look* (act. only) 1985; *Vamp* (contrib. art.) 1986; *Superstar: The Life and Times of Andy Warhol* (documentary) 1991.

Warm, Hermann. Art director. Born in 1889, in Berlin. In German films from 1912, following some work for the stage, he stood out as one of the most prominent set designers in the expressionist movement. He also worked elsewhere in Europe, notably in France on Dreyer's *The Passion of Joan of Arc* and *Vampyr.* He spent the WW II years in Switzerland, then returned to Germany, where he resumed his work in 1947 and retired in 1960.

FILMS INCLUDE (art dir. alone or in collaboration): *Der Andere* 1913; *Der Hund von Baskerville* 1914; *Das Kabinett des Dr. Caligari/The Cabinet of Dr. Caligari, Die Pest in Florenz* 1919; *Die Spinen/The Spiders* (Pt. I, II) 1919–20; *Der Müde Tod/Between Two Worlds/Between Worlds, Schloss Vogelöd* 1921; *Phantom* 1922; *Gräfin Donelli* 1924; *Liebe, Der Student von Prag/The Student of Prague* 1926; *Die Liebe der Jeanne Ney/The Love of Jeanne Ney* 1927; *La Passion de Jeanne d'Arc/The Passion of Joan of Arc* (Fr.) 1928; *Dreyfus* 1930; *Vampyr* (Fr.) 1931; *Peer Gynt* 1934; *Der Student von Prag/The Student of Prague* 1935; *Jugend* 1938; *Wozzeck* 1947; *Hokuspokus* 1953; *Helden/Arms and the Man* 1959; *Die Botschafterin* 1960.

Warner, David. Actor. Born on July 29, 1941, in Manchester, England. Gawky leading man of British stage and films. A former book salesman, he trained for the stage at the Royal Academy of Dramatic Art and made his mark on the screen playing the offbeat title role in *Morgan!* (1966). He is a member of the Royal Shakespeare Company.

FILMS INCLUDE: *Tom Jones* (as Master Blifil) 1963; *Morgan—A Suitable Case for Treatment/Morgan!* 1966; *The Deadly Affair* 1967; *Work Is a Four-Letter Word, The Bofors Gun, The Fixer, The Sea Gull* (as Konstantin) 1968; *The Ballad of Cable Hogue* (US), *Perfect Friday* 1970; *A Doll's House* (as Torvald) 1973; *From Beyond the Grave, Mr. Quilp* 1975; *The Omen* (US) 1976; *Providence* (Fr.), *Cross of Iron* (UK/Ger.), *Silver Bears* (US) 1977; *The Disappearance* (Can.) 1978; *Nightwing* (US), *Airport '79 Concorde* (US), *The 39 Steps, Time After Time* (US) 1979; *The Islands* 1980; *The French Lieutenant's Woman* (US), *Disappearance* (Can.), *Time Bandits* 1981; *Tron* (US) 1982; *The Man with Two Brains* (US) 1983; *The Company of Wolves* (US) 1984; *Hansel and Gretel* 1987; *Mr. North* (US), *My Best Friend is a Vampire* (US), *Waxwork* (US), *Silent Night, Pulse Pounders, Key to Freedom, Hostile Takeover* (US), *Magdalene* (US), *Hanna's War* (US) 1988; *Mortal Passions* (US), *Star Trek 5: The Final Frontier* (US),

Office Party, S.P.O.O.K.S. 1989; *Grave Secrets* (US), *Tripwire* (US), *Blue Tornado* (US) 1990; *Teenage Mutant Ninja Turtles 2: The Secret of the Ooze* (US), *Star Trek 6: The Undiscovered Country* (US), *Drive* 1991; *La Terreur de Midi/Dark at Noon* (Fr.), *The Unnameable Returns* 1992; *In the Mouth of Madness* 1995; *Seven Servants* 1996; *Money Talks* 1997.

Warner, H. B. Actor. *b.* Henry Byron Warner, Oct. 26, 1876, London. *d.* 1958. The son of Charles Warner, a famous 19th-century actor of the British stage, he made his debut at the age of seven at his father's theater. He later studied medicine at London's University College but finally chose acting and had a distinguished career on the British and American stage. In American films from 1914, he played character leads in numerous silents and talkies, notably as Christ in De Mille's *The King of Kings* (1927). He was nominated for an Oscar as best supporting actor for his performance as Chang in *Lost Horizon* (1937).

FILMS INCLUDE: *The Lost Paradise, The Ghost Breaker* 1914; *The Raiders, The Beggar of Cawnpore, The Market of Vain Desire, The Vagabond Prince* 1916; *Wrath, God's Man* 1917; *The Man Who Turned White, The Pagan God* 1919; *One Hour Before Dawn, The White Dove* 1920; *Below the Dead Line* 1921; *Zaza* 1923; *Is Love Everything?* 1924; *Whispering Smith, Silence* 1926; *The King of Kings* (as Jesus Christ), *Sorrell and Son, French Dressing* 1927; *Romance of a Rogue, Man-Made Women, The Naughty Duchess* 1928; *Conquest, The Doctor's Secret, The Divine Lady* (as Sir William Hamilton), *Stark Mad, The Trial of Mary Dugan, The Gamblers, The Show of Shows, Tiger Rose* 1929; *The Green Goddess, The Furies, Wild Company, Liliom* 1930; *The Reckless Hour, Five Star Final* 1931; *Charlie Chan's Chance, A Woman Commands, The Menace, Cross Examination, Tom Brown of Culver, The Crusader* 1932; *Supernatural, Jennie Gerhardt* (as William Gerhardt), *Christopher Bean* 1933; *Sorrell and Son* (remake) 1934; *Behold My Wife, A Tale of Two Cities* 1935; *The Garden Murder Case, Mr. Deeds Goes to Town* 1936; *Lost Horizon* (as Chang), *Victoria the Great* (as Lord Melbourne; UK) 1937; *The Girl of the Golden West, Kidnapped* (as Mr. Rankeillor), *The Toy Wife, Bulldog Drummond in Africa* (and several other films in the series, as Colonel Nielson), *You Can't Take It with You* 1938; *Let Freedom Ring, The Gracie Allen Murder Case, The Rains Came* (as the Maharajah), *Nurse Edith Cavell, Mr. Smith Goes to Washington* 1939; *New Moon* 1940; *All That Money Can Buy, The Corsican Brothers* 1941; *Crossroads* 1942; *Hitler's Children* 1943; *Action in Arabia* 1944; *It's a Wonderful Life* 1946; *High Wall* 1947; *The Judge Steps Out* 1949; *Sunset Boulevard* (as himself) 1950; *The First Legion, Here Comes the Groom, Journey Into Light* 1951; *The Ten Commandments* (as Amminadab) 1956.

Warner, Jack. Actor. *b.* Jack Waters, Oct. 24, 1894, in Bromley-by-Bow, England. *d.* 1981. A former variety comedian, he played some leads and many sympathetic key character parts in British films from the early 40s.

FILMS INCLUDE: *The Dummy Talks* 1943; *The Captive Heart* 1946; *Hue and Cry, It Always Rains on Sunday, Dear Murderer, Holiday Camp* 1947; *Easy Money, Against the Wind, My Brother's Keeper, Here Come the Huggetts* 1948; *The Blue Lamp* 1950; *Talk of a Million/You Can't Beat the Irish, Scrooge/A Christmas Carol* (as Mr. Jorkins), *Valley of the Eagles* 1951; *Emergency Call/Hundred Hour Hunt, Meet Me Tonight/Tonight at 8:30* 1952; *The Final Test* 1953; *Forbidden Cargo* 1954; *The Ladykillers* 1955; *Carve Her Name with Pride* 1958; *Jigsaw* 1962.

Warner, Jack L. Executive. *b.* Aug. 2, 1892, London, Ontario, Canada, thc youngest of 12 children of Jewish immigrants from Poland. *d.* 1978. Having arrived in Baltimore in 1883, the family moved about the US and Canada until its head, a pedlar, decided to settle finally in Youngstown, Ohio, where he opened a cobbler's shop, a butchery, and then a bicycle shop. The children all took part in the operation of the expanding family business. In 1903 the family gambled its meager resources on the acquisition of a nickelodeon in Newcastle, Pa. Jack, who had a fine voice, entertained the audience during intermission. Two years later, aware of the growing potential of the film business, four of the Warner brothers—Harry (1881–1958), Albert (1884–1967), Sam (1888–1927), and Jack—ventured into film distribution, but they were soon forced to sell out to the Patents Company. They returned briefly to exhibition and in 1912 took their first stab at production with a series of not-too-successful shorts.

They had their first success in 1917 with *My Four Years in Germany* and went on to establish one of Hollywood's major studios, at Burbank, near Hollywood, which they named simply Warner Bros. Harry, the business brains of the family, became the company's president, Sam the chief executive, Albert the treasurer, and Jack the production chief. In 1925 they acquired Vitagraph and its network of exchanges and First National Pictures, and began a systematic acquisition of motion picture theaters. Their biggest coup came in 1927, when they launched the sound era with *The Jazz Singer.* Jack Warner ran the studio with a firm and frugal hand and often clashed with his producers, writers, and stars, most famously with Bette Davis, Olivia de Havilland, Humphrey Bogart, and James Cagney. A frustrated vaudevillian, he spiced his quarrels with a robust sense of humor and practical jokes. He has also been famous for his hawkish political views and occasional tactless cracks. (Once, when he was introduced to Mme. Chiang Kai-chek, he muttered that he had forgotten his laundry.) During WW II he was commissioned a major with the Army Signal Corps and later was elevated in rank to colonel.

In 1956, Harry and Albert Warner sold most of their shares in the company, but Jack stayed on as studio boss and largest single stockholder. In 1967 he sold his interest in Warner Bros. to Seven Arts and became an independent producer, releasing through the company, which still bears his name. In 1965 he published his autobiography, *My First Hundred Years in Hollywood.*

FILMS INCLUDE (personally produced): *A Dangerous Adventure* (feature and serial versions; also co-dir. with Sam Warner) 1922; *This Is the Army* 1943; *My Fair Lady* 1964; *Camelot* 1967; *1776, Dirty Little Billy* 1972.

Warner Bros. An American motion picture company incorporated in 1923 by the brothers Harry, Albert, Sam, and Jack L. WARNER, who had started in the film business in 1903 with a small nickelodeon in Newcastle, Pa. They gradually expanded into distribution and production and in 1925 absorbed Vitagraph and First National Pictures. In 1926 the company formed a subsidiary, Vitaphone, in association with Western Electric to develop a sound-on-disc system for motion pictures. After some experimentation with short subjects and with such features as *Don Juan,* Warner Bros. made motion picture history in 1927 when it released *The Jazz Singer,* the first film with synchronized songs and lines of dialogue. Almost overnight, Warners forged ahead from a minor company to one of Hollywood's major studios.

During the 30s the company led the way in the production of films inspired by the stresses and strains of the Depression era. Under the guidance of Jack Warner, Darryl ZANUCK, and Hal WALLIS, the company produced a memorable cycle of gangster pictures, many of them starring James Cagney, Edward G. Robinson, and Humphrey Bogart, as well as social dramas that reflected the mood of the period. Even the plots of the company's successful cycle of musicals typically dealt with struggling chorus girls and boys working hard to get out of their rut. Also prominent during that period was a string of film biographies of such personalities as Pasteur, Zola, Juárez, Dr. Ehrlich, and Reuter. The company's production policy was largely dictated by a necessity to economize. Its directors (Michael Curtiz, Mervyn LeRoy, etc.) and its impressive roster of stars (including Bette Davis, Paul Muni, Errol Flynn, and Olivia de Havilland, as well as Bogart, Cagney, and Robinson) worked at a pace more frantic than in any other Hollywood studio, usually at lower salaries. This often led to stormy clashes between management and employees. The company's films too reflected the tight-purse policy; they were often tight, compact, unadorned.

In the 40s, Warners solidified its position as a leading Hollywood studio with a long list of successful films, including the adventure pictures of Errol Flynn, the melodramas of Joan Crawford, and a series of mystery dramas starring Humphrey Bogart and often featuring Peter Lorre and Sydney Greenstreet. In the 50s the company struggled along with the other Hollywood studios in face of the competition from TV; it had also suffered the loss of its theater chain as a result of government antitrust action. A sign of its declining fortunes was the sale in 1956 of its library of pre-1950 features, shorts, and cartoons to Associated Artists, which promptly resold the rights to UNITED ARTISTS. Thirty years later, the priceless collection passed to cable magnate Ted TURNER when he acquired MGM/UA Entertainment in 1986 (see METRO-GOLDWYN-MAYER).

In 1967 Warner Bros. was acquired by Seven Arts Productions, a Canadian-based corporation, and the name was briefly changed to Warner Bros.-Seven Arts. In 1969 the company passed into the hands of Kinney National Service, a conglomerate headed by Steven J. Ross (*b.* Steven Jay Rechnitz, April 5, 1927, Brooklyn, N.Y.; *d.* 1992). Originally a parking garage, car rental agency, and funeral parlor business, Kinney was renamed Warner Communications two years later as Ross presided over its diversification into many areas of entertainment, including TV production, music recording, publishing, merchandising, cable systems, and theme parks. Ross's management style was to let talented executives do their work without interference, encouraged by generous incentives and loyal support. The policy paid off at Warner Bros. in the ensuing decades as the studio re-emerged as one of the most successful Hollywood companies.

Former talent agent Ted Ashley, who served as chairman and CEO of Warner Bros. from 1969 to 1980, helped to restore the studio's fortunes with box-office hits like *The Exorcist* (1973), *The Towering Inferno* (co-produced with 20TH CENTURY-FOX in 1974), *All the President's Men* (1976), and *Superman* (1978). In 1980 Robert A. Daly was named chairman and CEO and Terry Semel president and COO. Famed for the stability of their partnership and their gift for maintaining talent relations, Daly and Semel presided over an even more impressive string of successes in the 80s and 90s, including the films of Clint Eastwood, the *Lethal Weapon* and *Police Academy* series, *Risky Business* (1983), *Gremlins* (1984), *Batman* (1989), *Robin Hood: Prince of Thieves* (1991), *The Bodyguard* (1992), and *The Fugitive* (1993).

In 1989 the publishing giant Time Inc. acquired Warner Communications to create one of the largest communications empires in the world, Time Warner. In trying to swallow pieces of the combined Time Warner empire, turbulence occurred, but when the dust settled, Robert Daly and Terry Semel had solidified their power within the conglomerate. The newly acquired Ted Turner companies were accommodated, with Turner gaining a board position. Music company executives went through a revolving door before settling down, yet the company is still the most stable film studio today, though Disney's Buena Vista tops it in box-office percentages.

Warren, Charles Marquis. Screenwriter, director, producer, novelist. *b.* 1912, in Baltimore. *d.* 1990. *ed.* Baltimore City Coll. A specialist in the lore of the American West, he turned to screenwriting and directing following WW II service as a commander in the Navy. In addition to working in films, he was also much involved in TV, for which he created and produced, and sometimes also directed, popular Western series like 'Gunsmoke,' 'Rawhide,' and 'The Virginian.'

FILMS INCLUDE: As screenwriter—*Beyond Glory* 1948; *Streets of Laredo* 1949; *Only the Valiant* (novel basis only), *Oh! Susanna* (novel basis only) 1951; *Springfield Rifle* 1952; *Pony Express* 1953; *Day of the Evil Gun* 1968. As director (complete)—*Little Big Horn* (also sc.) 1951; *Hellgate* (also sc.) 1952; *Arrowhead* (also sc.), *Flight to Tangier* (also sc.) 1953; *Seven Angry Men* 1955; *Tension at Table Rock* 1956; *The Black Whip, Trooper Hook* (also co-sc.), *Back from the Dead, The Unknown Terror, Copper Sky* (also exec. prod.), *Ride a Violent Mile* (also exec. prod., story) 1957; *Desert Hell* (also exec. prod., story), *Cattle Empire* (also exec. prod.), *Blood Arrow* (also exec. prod.) 1958; *Charro!* (also prod., sc.) 1969.

Warren, Harry. Composer, songwriter. *b.* Dec. 24, 1893, Brooklyn, N.Y. *d.* 1981. After starting out as a drummer in a carnival band, he joined the Vitagraph studios as a combination prop man, stagehand, assistant director, and extra. All the while, he kept composing, and scored his first hit song in the early 20s. From the early 30s, he composed many hit songs for Hollywood films (Warners, then Fox, MGM, and Paramount) and some Broadway musicals. He won Academy Awards for the songs 'Lullaby of Broadway' from *Gold Diggers of Broadway* (1935), 'You'll Never Know' from *Hello Frisco Hello* (1943), and 'The Atchison, Topeka and the Santa Fe' from *The Harvey Girls* (1946).

FILMS INCLUDE: *Spring Is Here* 1930; *Roman Scandals, 42nd Street* (title song, 'Shuffle Off to Buffalo,' etc.), *Gold Diggers of 1933, Footlight Parade* 1933; *Dames* ('I Only Have Eyes for You,' etc.), *Wonder Bar* 1934; *Go Into Your Dance, In Caliente, Gold Diggers of Broadway, Broadway Gondolier* ('Lulu's Back in Town,' etc.), *Stars Over Broadway* ('September in the Rain,' etc.) 1935; *Gold Diggers of 1937* 1936; *Hard to Get* ('You Must Have Been a Beautiful Baby,' etc.), *Going Places* ('Jeepers Creepers,' etc.) 1938; *Down Argentine Way, Tin Pan Alley* 1940; *The Great American Broadcast, That Night in Rio, Weekend in Havana, Sun Valley Serenade* ('Chattanooga Choo Choo,' etc.) 1941; *Orchestra Wives, Song of the Islands, Iceland* 1942; *Hello Frisco Hello, Sweet Rosie O'Grady* 1943; *Diamond Horseshoe* ('The More I See You,' etc.), *Yolanda and the Thief* 1945; *The Harvey Girls, Ziegfeld Follies* 1946; *Summer Holiday* 1948; *The Barkleys of Broadway, My Dream Is Yours* 1949; *Summer Stock* ('You Wonderful You,' etc.) 1950; *Belle of New York, Skirts Ahoy!* 1952; *The Caddy* ('That's Amore,' etc.) 1953; *Artists and Models* 1956; *Ladies' Man* 1961; *Satan Never Sleeps* (co-title song) 1962; *Fate Is the Hunter* ('No Love No Nothin'') 1964; *Rosie* (title song) 1967.

Warren, Lesley Ann. Actress. Born on August 16, 1947, in New York, N.Y. *ed.* Lee Strasberg Studio. Slender, dark-haired supporting player with comedic bent. After making her Broadway debut in 1963, she became a TV heroine for years afterward as the lead in the small-screen production of Rogers and Hammerstein's 'Cinderella.' Spotted by a Disney scout, she appeared in family films until the 1970s, when she graduated to adult dramas. Although she has been consistently active in films since the 1970s, the vehicles in which she has appeared largely fail to highlight her talents. Nominated for an Academy Award for her earthy performance as a low-voltage singer and girlfriend in *Victor/Victoria*. Regular on TV series 'Mission: Impossible'; appeared in TV movies of 70s and 80s.

FILMS INCLUDE: *The Happiest Millionaire* 1967; *The One and Only Genuine Original Family Band* 1968; *Pickup on 101* 1972; *Harry and Walter Go to New York* 1976; *Race to the Yankee Zephyr* (Austral./NZ) 1981; *Victor/Victoria* 1982; *A Night in Heaven* 1983; *Choose Me, Songwriter* 1984; *Clue* 1985; *Burglar* 1987; *Cop* 1988; *Worth Winning* 1989; *Life Stinks* 1991; *Pure Country* 1992; *Color of Night* 1994; *The Birdcage* 1996.

Warrick, Ruth. Actress. Born on June 29, 1915, in St. Louis, Mo. *ed.* U. of Missouri. Brunette leading lady of Hollywood films of the 40s. A former radio singer, she made her screen debut in *Citizen Kane*, playing Kane's first wife. After a long absence, she returned to the screen in the late 60s in character roles. She is still active on the stage and in nightclubs and has been the star of the TV soap opera 'All My Children' for over two decades. Autobiography: *The Confessions of Phoebe Tyler* (1980).

FILMS INCLUDE: *Citizen Kane, The Corsican Brothers* 1941; *Journey Into Fear* 1942; *Forever and a Day, The Iron Major* 1943; *Secret Command, Mr. Winkle Goes to War* 1944; *China Sky* 1945; *Perilous Holiday, Song of the South* 1946; *Daisy Kenyon* 1947; *The Great Dan Patch* 1949; *Let's Dance, Three Husbands* 1950; *Ride Beyond Vengeance* 1966; *The Great Bank Robbery* 1969; *The Returning* 1983; *Deathmask* 1984.

Warwick, Robert. Actor. *b.* Robert Taylor Bien, Oct. 9, 1878, Sacramento, Calif. *d.* 1964. He sang in a church choir from boyhood and prepared himself in Paris for an operatic career but instead became a matinee idol on Broadway early in the century. He entered films in 1914 and was the romantic star of many productions through the early 20s, with an interval in 1917 in Army captain's uniform. He returned to the stage in the 20s but was back in films as a character actor with the switch to sound, usually playing stern but benevolent leading citizens or dignified military officers.

FILMS INCLUDE: *The Man of the Hour, The Dollar Mark, Across the Pacific* 1914; *Alias Jimmy Valentine, The Face in the Moonlight* 1915; *Human Driftwood* 1916; *The Argyle Case, The Silent Master, The Mad Lover* 1917; *Secret Service, In Mizzoura* 1919; *The City of Masks* 1920; *The Spitfire* 1924; *Unmasked* 1929; *The Royal Bed* 1931; *The Woman from Monte Carlo, So Big, The Dark Horse, Doctor X, I Am a Fugitive from a Chain Gang* 1932; *Whispering Shadows* (serial), *Pilgrimage* 1933; *Cleopatra, The Dragon Murder Case* 1934; *Night Life of the Gods* (as Neptune), *A Shot in the Dark, A Tale of Two Cities* 1935; *Whipsaw, Ace Drummond* (serial), *Sutter's Gold, Mary of Scotland* (as Sir Francis Knollys), *Romeo and Juliet* (as Lord Montague) 1936; *The Prince and the Pauper* (as Lord Warwick), *The Road Back, The Life of Emile Zola, Conquest, The Awful Truth* 1937; *The Adventures of Robin Hood* (as Sir Geoffrey), *Blockade, Gangster's Boy* 1938; *Juarez, The Magnificent Fraud, The Private Lives of Elizabeth and Essex* 1939; *The Sea Hawk* 1940; *A Woman's Face, Sullivan's Travels* 1941; *I Married a Witch, The Palm Beach Story, Tennessee Johnson* 1942; *The Princess and the Pirate* 1944; *Sudan* 1945; *Gentleman's Agreement* 1947; *Adventures of Don Juan* 1949; *Francis, In a Lonely Place* 1950; *Salome* 1953; *Lady Godiva* 1955; *While the City Sleeps* 1956; *The Buccaneer, It Started with a Kiss* 1959.

Washbourne, Mona. Actress. *b.* Nov. 27, 1903, in Birmingham, England. *d.* 1988. Trained as a pianist at the Birmingham School of Music, she gave recitals in concert halls and on radio before making her stage debut in 1924. She later appeared in numerous plays on both sides of the Atlantic. From the late 40s she played character roles in many films in between stage engagements. She also appeared in the PBS miniseries *Brideshead Revisited* (1982).

FILMS INCLUDE: *The Winslow Boy* 1948; *Maytime in Mayfair* 1949; *Child's Play* 1953; *Doctor in the House, To Dorothy a Son/Cash on Delivery* 1954; *Cast a Dark Shadow* 1955; *The Good Companions* 1957; *A Cry from the Streets* 1958; *Count Your Blessings* (US) 1959; *The Brides of Dracula* 1960; *Billy Liar* 1963; *My Fair Lady* (US), *Night Must Fall* 1964; *The Collector* (UK/US), *The Third Day* (US), *One-Way Pendulum* 1965; *Mrs. Brown You've Got a Lovely Daughter* (as Mrs. Brown) 1968; *If. . . , The Bed Sitting Room* 1969; *The Games, Fragment of Fear* 1970; *Romeo and Juliet '71/What Became of Jack and Jill?* 1971; *Oh Lucky Man!* 1973; *Identikit/The Driver's Seat* (It.) 1974; *Mr. Quilp* 1975; *The Blue Bird* (US/USSR) 1976; *Stevie* 1978; *The London Affair* (orig. made for TV) 1979.

Washburn, Bryant. Actor. *b.* Apr. 28, 1889, Chicago. *d.* 1963. Following some stage experience, he joined Essanay in 1910 and developed into a popular star of silent films, in both dramas and comedies. He continued in character roles through the late 40s, often as a villain.

FILMS INCLUDE: *The New Manager* 1911; *Out of the Depths, Chains, The Virtue of Rags, The Eye That Never Sleeps, The Voice of Conscience* 1912; *The Lost Chord* 1913; *At the End of a Perfect Day, The Elder Brother, Sparks of Fate, A Splendid Dishonor, The Chasm, One Wonderful Night, Any Woman's Choice* 1914; *The Misjudged Mr. Hartley, The Great Silence, Graustark, The Little Straw Wife, The Blindness of Virtue, The Woman Hater* 1915; *The Havoc* 1916; *Skinner's Dress Suit, Skinner's Baby, The Fibbers* 1917; *Till I Come Back to You, The Gypsy Trail* 1918; *The Way of a Man with a Maid, It Pays to Advertise, Why Smith Left Home* 1919; *What Happened to Jones* 1920; *An Amateur Devil, The Road to London* 1921; *June Madness, Hungry Hearts* 1922; *Rupert of Hentzau* (as Count Fritz), *Temptation, Mine to Keep, The Love Trap, The Common Law* 1923; *Try and Get It, My Husband's Wives, Star Dust Trail* 1924; *The Parasite, Passionate Youth, The Wizard of Oz* 1925; *Wet Paint, Flames, Young April, The Sky Pirate* 1926; *The Love Thrill, Beware of Widows, The King of Kings, Breakfast at Sunrise* 1927; *A Bit of Heaven, Skinner's Big Idea, Nothing to Wear, Jazzland* 1928; *Swing High* 1930; *Kept Husbands* 1931; *Night of Terror, Devil's Mate* 1933; *The Return of Chandu* (serial) 1934; *The World Accuses* 1935; *The Clutching Hand* (serial), *The Preview Murder Mystery, Sutter's Gold* 1936; *Conflict, Jungle Jim* (serial) 1937; *Stagecoach* 1939; *King of the Royal Mounted* (serial) 1940; *The Adventures of Captain Marvel* (serial), *The Spider Returns* (serial) 1941; *Sin Town* 1942; *The Falcon in Mexico* 1944; *Two O' Clock Courage* 1945; *Sweet Genevieve* 1947.

washing. A stage in film development procedure in which developing and fixing chemicals are removed from the film, usually by ordinary running water.

Washington, Denzel. Actor. Born on Dec. 28, 1954, in Mt. Vernon, N.Y. *ed.* Fordham Univ.; American Conservatory Theatre, San Francisco. Commanding, fine-featured screen lead. Originally interested in becoming a doctor or journalist, he decided on acting and spent several years on the stage, appearing in both Shakespearean and modern theater productions. He debuted in film in 1981; his strong screen presence was established shortly thereafter in *A Soldier's Story*. This led to a starring role as South African activist Steven Biko in *Cry Freedom* and an Academy Award for his fiery supporting performance in *Glory*. By the early 90s he had become a critically acclaimed screen actor and major box-office draw. Praised for his multi-layered incarnation of Malcolm X in the film of that name. His production company is Mundy Lane Entertainment. Regular on the TV drama series 'St. Elsewhere.'

FILMS: *Carbon Copy* 1981; *License to Kill* 1984; *Power* 1986; *Cry Freedom* 1987; *The Mighty Quinn* (also song); *Reunion, For Queen and Country, Glory* 1989; *Heart Condition, Mo' Better Blues* 1990; *Mississippi Masala, Ricochet* 1991; *Malcolm X* 1992; *Much Ado About Nothing, The Pelican Brief* 1993; *Crimson Tide, Devil in a Blue Dress, Virtuosity* 1995; *Courage Under Fire, The Preacher's Wife* 1996.

Waters, Ethel. Singer, actress. *b.* Oct. 31, 1896, Chester, Pa. *d.* 1977. Raised in utter poverty, she married her first husband (of three) at the age of 12 and worked as a scrubwoman, laundress, and chambermaid before beginning her road to success in nightclubs and vaudeville at 17 as Sweet Mama Stringbean. A soulful interpreter of the blues, she popularized such hits as 'Dinah,' 'Stormy Weather,' and 'Heat Wave' and was the first black woman to receive star billing on the American stage and screen. Beginning in 1927 she made her mark on Broadway, both as a singer and a dramatic player in such musicals as 'Africana,' 'As Thousands Cheer,' and 'Cabin in the Sky' and such straight plays as 'Mamba's Daughters' and 'The Member of the Wedding.' She was equally successful in films and was nominated for an Academy Award for her performance in *Pinky* (1949). She gave another memorable performance in *The Member of the Wedding* (1952). Her 1951 autobiography, *His Eye Is on the Sparrow,* takes its title from the song she sang in the latter production. She published a sequel memoir, *To Me It's Wonderful,* in 1972. She also starred in the TV series 'Beulah.'

FILMS: *On with the Show* 1929; *Gift of Gab* 1934; *Tales of Manhattan, Cairo* 1942; *Cabin in the Sky, Stage Door Canteen* 1943; *Pinky* 1949; *The Member of the Wedding* 1952; *The Heart Is a Rebel* 1956; *The Sound and the Fury* 1959.

Waters, John. Director, screenwriter, producer, cinematographer. Born on April 22, 1946 in Baltimore, Md. Audacious director of generally shocking modern satires. Raised in Baltimore to a comfortable Catholic family, he schooled himself in marginal cinema at the local XXX houses and eventually by making his own 8 mm exploitation shorts (*Hag in a Black Leather Jacket, Eat Your Makeup*). Over the course of making these early films, some of which were screened in the city, he came to form an acting ensemble that included Mink Stole and a 300-pound high school friend named Harris Glenn Milstead, or Divine. His first features, *Mondo Trasho* and *Multiple Maniacs* introduced the high satire depicted through offensiveness that would come to permeate (in all senses of the word) his films. His $10,000 third effort about "the filthiest person alive," *Pink Flamingos*, gained national distribution and a following on the cult art-house circuit; it also included what may be the best-known scene of all his films, the act of Divine eating dog excrement. In his next features *Female Trouble, Desperate Living*, and *Polyester* he refrained from a wholly nauseating act to complete his satiric skewering of middle-class values. However, in none of the films does the suburban status quo remain intact. *Polyester* is also notable for the reintroduction of the theater gimmick, in this case a set of scratch-and-sniff cards called Odorama cards, as well as for the use of faded but familiar movie stars like Tab Hunter to lend an odd historical perspective to the film. His cult following secure, Waters entered mainstream filmmaking in the late 80s with the musical comedy *Hairspray*, which views the coming of racial integration to Baltimore in the early 1960s through changes at a local dance program called "The Corny Collins Show." The film is based in part on an essay about an actual Baltimore dance show that appears in one of his books, *Crackpot*. His subsequent foray into popular filmmaking, *Cry-Baby*, yielded less satisfactory results. Although lacking the mainstream success of its other Baltimore native Barry Levinson, Waters is so appreciated as a hometown son that the mayor of Baltimore proclaimed February 7, 1985, as "John Waters Day." Autobiography: *Shock Value*. He lives in Baltimore.

FILMS INCLUDE (as director): *Mondo Trasho* (also prod., sc., cinematog., ed.) 1970; *Multiple Maniacs* 1971; *Pink Flamingos* (also prod., sc., cinematog., ed.) 1972; *Female Trouble* (also prod. sc., cinematog., song) 1975; *Desperate Living* (also prod., sc., cinematog.) 1977; *Polyester* (also prod., sc.) 1981; *Something Wild* (act. only) 1986; *Hairspray* (also prod., sc., act.) 1988; *Homer and Eddie* (act. only), *Cry-Baby* (also sc., lyric adaptation) 1990; *Serial Mom* 1994.

Waterston, Sam. Actor. Born on Nov. 15, 1940, in Cambridge, Mass. *ed.* Yale. Intelligent, introspective leading man of the American stage and screen. He won the Drama Desk Award as best actor for his role in Joseph Papp's Broadway production of 'Much Ado About Nothing' (1972–73). On the screen since 1967, he established his reputation in the early 70s with sensitive performances in such films as *The Great Gatsby* (1974) and *Rancho DeLuxe* (1975). He was nominated for an Academy Award as best actor for *The Killing Fields* (1984). Appeared regularly in the 90s TV series 'I'll Fly Away' and 'Law and Order.'

FILMS: *Fitzwilly* 1967; *Generation, Three* 1969; *The Plastic Dome of Norma Jean, Cover Me Babe* 1970; *Who Killed Mary Wat's'ername?* 1971; *Savages* 1972; *The Great Gatsby* (as Nick Carraway) 1974; *Rancho DeLuxe, Journey Into Fear* 1975; *Sweet Revenge/Dandy—the All-American Girl* 1976; *Coup de Foudre* (Fr.) 1977; *Capricorn One, Interiors* 1978; *Sweet William* (UK), *Eagle's Wing* (UK), *Heaven's Gate* 1979; *Hopscotch* 1980; *The Killing Fields* 1984; *Warning Sign* 1985; *Flagrant Desir* (Fr.), *Hannah and Her Sisters, Just Between Friends* 1986; *Devil's Paradise, September* 1987; *Crimes and Misdemeanors, Welcome Home* 1989; *Mindwalk, The Man in the Moon* 1991; *Serial Mom* 1994; *The Journey of August King* (also co-prod.) 1995; *The Proprietor* 1996; *The Shadow Conspiracy* 1997.

Watkin, David. Director of photography. Born in 1925, in England. He entered the industry as a messenger boy with a documentary unit and in 1955 became a documentary cameraman. He has been working on feature films since the mid-60s, at first in England, then also in the US, with growing international repute. He worked mainly in the US through the 80s and 90s, winning the Oscar for best cinematography for *Out of Africa* (1985).

FILMS INCLUDE: *The Knack and How to Get It, Help!* 1965; *Mademoiselle* (English version only; UK/Fr.) 1966; *The Marat/Sade, How I Won the War* 1967; *The Charge of the Light Brigade* 1968; *The Bed Sitting Room* 1969; *Catch-22* (US) 1970; *The Devils, The Boy Friend* 1971; *The Homecoming* (US), *A Delicate Balance* (US) 1973; *The Three Musketeers* 1974; *The Four Musketeers, Mahogany* (US) 1975; *To the Devil a Daughter* (UK/Ger.), *Robin and Marian* 1976; *Joseph Andrews* 1977; All following are US unless noted: *Cuba, Hanover Street, That Summer* (UK) 1979; *Endless Love, Chariots of Fire* (UK) 1981; *Yentl* 1983; *The Hotel New Hampshire* 1984; *Return to Oz, White Nights, Out of Africa* 1985; *Sky Bandits* 1986; *Moonstruck* 1987; *Masquerade, The Good Mother, Last Rites* 1988; *Memphis Belle, Hamlet* 1990; *The Object of Beauty* 1991;

This Boy's Life 1993; *Milk Money, Bopha!* 1994; *Jane Eyre* 1996; *Night Falls on Manhattan* 1997.

Watkins, Linda. Actress. *b.* May 23, 1908, Boston. *d.* 1976. A product of the Theatre Guild's school for young actors, she made her Broadway debut at 16 and then played ingenue and leading-lady roles in a score of New York stage productions. Famous for her blonde beauty as well as her acting ability, she also starred in a number of Hollywood films of the early 30s but enjoyed only modest success and returned to the stage. She reappeared on the screen in the late 50s, in character roles. She was also seen in many TV dramas.

FILMS INCLUDE: *Sob Sister, Good Sport* 1931; *Charlie Chan's Chance, Cheaters at Play, The Gay Caballero* 1932; *From Hell It Came* 1957; *Ten North Frederick* 1958; *The Parent Trap* 1959; *Good Neighbor Sam* 1964; *Huckleberry Finn* (as Mrs. Grangerford) 1974.

Watkins, Peter. Director. Born on Oct. 29, 1935, Norbiton, England. *ed.* Christ Coll., Cambridge; RADA. He started out as an assistant producer on commercials and in the late 50s began making amateur films, including *The Diary of an Unknown Soldier* (1959) and *The Forgotten Faces* (1961). Two feature-length semidocumentaries he made for BBC-TV in 1964–65, *Culloden* and *The War Game,* revealed him as an anti-Establishment man who uses an unadorned newsreel style and nonprofessional actors to express his ideas. The second of these depicted the horrors of a nuclear war in vivid terms and did not get on the air. Instead, it was exhibited successfully in theaters and won an Oscar as best documentary in 1966. He was far less successful with his first commercial feature enterprise, *Privilege* (1977), and subsequently directed in Sweden and the US.

FEATURE FILMS: *Culloden* (made for TV; also sc.) 1964; *The War Game* (made for but not shown on TV; also prod., sc.) 1966; *Privilege* (also addnl. dial.) 1967; *Gladiators/The Peace Game* (Sw.) 1969; *Punishment Park* (also co-sc.) 1971; *Edvard Munch* (also sc., narr.; Sw./Nor.) 1976; *Aftenlandet/Evening Land* (also co-story, co-sc., ed.; Den.) 1977; *The Journey* (also prod., sc., ed., sound ed.; TV) 1987.

Watson, Bobby (Robert). Actor *b.* Robert Watson Knucher, 1888, Springfield, Ill. *d.* 1965. Mild-mannered general-purpose character player of Hollywood films, mainly light musicals, following vaudeville and legitimate stage experience, who benefited during WW II from his resemblance to Adolf Hitler and made a virtual career of portraying the Führer on the screen. Hitler's fall precipitated a rapid decline in Watson's career.

FILMS INCLUDE: *That Royle Girl* 1925; *The Song and Dance Man* 1926; *Syncopation* 1929; *Follow the Leader* 1930; *Manhattan Parade* 1931; *High Pressure* 1932; *Moonlight and Pretzels, Going Hollywood* 1933; *The Countess of Monte Cristo* 1934; *Society Doctor* 1935; *Mary of Scotland* 1936; *The Adventurous Blonde* 1937; *Everything's on Ice* 1939; *The Devil with Hitler* (as Hitler) 1942; *Hitler—Dead or Alive* (as Hitler), *That Nazty Nuisance* (as Hitler), *The Miracle of Morgan's Creek* 1943; *The Hitler Gang* (as Hitler), *Practically Yours* 1944; *Hold That Blonde* 1945; *The Paleface* 1948; *Copper Canyon* 1950; *The Story of Mankind* (back as Hitler) 1957.

Watson, Bobs. Actor. Born in 1930, in Hollywood, Calif. The son of show people, he appeared in short subjects while still in diapers and became quite popular as a tear-shedding child star in Fox and MGM films of the 30s, memorably as little Pee Wee in *Boys Town* (1938) and as Pud in *On Borrowed Time* (1939). He retired from films in the early 40s and later returned in occasional character parts. He played his last movie role in 1967 and in the following year was ordained a minister of the United Methodist Church. He has often been confused with veteran character actor Bobby WATSON, the Hitler specialist. Bobs's brothers, Billy and Delmar, as well as three other siblings, were also child actors on the screen.

FILMS INCLUDE: *In Old Chicago, Boys Town, Kentucky* 1938; *The Story of Alexander Graham Bell, Dodge City, On Borrowed Time, Blackmail* 1939; *Wyoming, Dr. Kildare's Crisis* 1940; *Men of Boys Town* 1941; *Hi Buddy!* 1943; *The Bold and the Brave* 1956; *Saintly Sinners, What Ever Happened to Baby Jane?* 1962; *First to Fight* 1967.

Watson, Lucile. Actress. *b.* May 27, 1879, Quebec, Canada. *d.* 1962. Convent-educated. She trained for the stage at the American Academy of Dramatic Arts and played leads on Broadway from the turn of the century. She went to Hollywood in 1934 and soon established herself as a leading character actress, typically playing well-bred haughty matrons. She was nominated for an Oscar for her role as Bette Davis's mother in *Watch on the Rhine* (1943). She was the widow of playwright Louis Shipman, who died in 1934.

FILMS INCLUDE: *What Every Woman Knows* 1934; *A Woman Rebels, The Garden of Allah, Three Smart Girls* 1936; *The Young in Heart, Sweethearts* 1938; *Made for Each Other, The Women* 1939; *Waterloo Bridge* 1940; *Mr. and Mrs. Smith, Rage in Heaven, The Great Lie* 1941; *Watch on the Rhine* 1943; *Uncertain Glory, Till We Meet Again* 1944; *The Thin Man Goes Home* 1945; *My Reputation, Tomorrow Is Forever, The Razor's Edge, Song of the South* 1946; *Ivy* 1947; *The Emperor Waltz, That Wonderful Urge* 1948; *Little Women* (as Aunt March) 1949; *Harriet Craig* 1950; *My Forbidden Past* 1951.

Watt, Harry. Director. *b.* Oct. 18, 1906, in Edinburgh, Scotland. *d.* 1987. *ed.* Edinburgh U. He joined the Empire Marketing Board's film unit in 1931 and developed under the guidance of John GRIERSON into one of England's foremost documentary filmmakers. After assisting Flaherty on the famous *Man of Aran* (1934), he gained increasing respect for his own documentaries and, eventually, his feature-length films. Autobiography: *Don't Look at the Camera* (1974).

FILMS: Documentaries—*Night Mail* (co-dir. with Basil Wright), *6:30 Collection* 1936; *Big Money* (co-dir. with Pat Jackson), *The Savings of Bill Blewitt* 1937; *North Sea, Health in Industry* 1938; *The First Days* (co-dir. with Humphrey Jennings and Pat Jackson) 1939; *Squadron 992, London Can Take It* (co-dir. with Jennings), *The Front Line, Britain at Bay* 1940; *Target for Tonight* (also sc.), *Christmas Under Fire* 1941; *Dover Revisited, 21 Miles* 1942. Features—*Nine Men* (also sc.) 1943; *Fiddlers Three* (also sc.) 1944; *The Overlanders* (also sc.) 1946; *Eureka Stockade/Massacre Hill* (also sc.) 1949; *Where No Vultures Fly/Ivory Hunter* 1951; *West of Zanzibar* (also story) 1954; *People Like Maria* 1958; *The Siege of Pinchgut* (also co-sc.) 1959.

waxing. The process of applying wax to the edges of projection prints in order to ensure their smooth running while in use.

Waxman, Franz. Composer. *b.* Franz Wachsmann, Dec. 24, 1906, Königshütte, Germany (now Chorzow, Poland). *d.* 1967. A piano player from early childhood, he quit a job as a bank clerk at 17 to enroll at the Dresden Music Academy and later the Berlin Music Conservatory. He worked his way through school playing the piano in cafés and nightclubs. He joined UFA in 1930 and orchestrated and later scored a number of German films. In 1934, after being beaten up on a Berlin street by a gang of anti-Semitic hooligans, he moved to Paris, and the following year he emigrated to the US. He immediately found work in Hollywood and rapidly gained recognition as one of the most gifted composers of American film music. At his most effective with suspenseful and psychological motifs, he scored several of

Hitchcock's films. He won Academy Awards for the music of *Sunset Boulevard* (1950) and *A Place in the Sun* (1951) and was nominated for several other Oscars. In 1947 he founded the Los Angeles Music Festival, to which he devoted much of his energy over the years.

FILMS INCLUDE: *Der blaue Engel/The Blue Angel* (arranger only; Ger.) 1930; *Liliom* (Ger.) 1933; *The Bride of Frankenstein* 1935; *Magnificent Obsession, Sutter's Gold, Fury* 1936; *Captains Courageous, A Day at the Races* 1937; *Three Comrades, A Christmas Carol* 1938; *At the Circus* 1939; *Strange Cargo, Rebecca, Boom Town* 1940; *The Philadelphia Story, Dr. Jekyll and Mr. Hyde, Suspicion* 1941; *Woman of the Year, Tortilla Flat* 1942; *Air Force, Edge of Darkness, Old Acquaintance* 1943; *Destination Tokyo* 1944; *Objective Burma, Pride of the Marines* 1945; *Humoresque, Nora Prentiss, The Two Mrs. Carrolls, Possessed, Dark Passage, The Unsuspected* 1947; *The Paradine Case, Sorry Wrong Number* 1948; *Night and the City, Sunset Boulevard* 1950; *He Ran All the Way, A Place in the Sun, The Blue Veil* 1951; *My Cousin Rachel, Come Back Little Sheba, Stalag 17* 1953; *Rear Window, Prince Valiant, The Silver Chalice* 1954; *Mister Roberts* 1955; *Crime in the Streets* 1956; *The Spirit of St. Louis, Love in the Afternoon, Sayonara, Peyton Place* 1957; *The Nun's Story* 1959; *The Story of Ruth, Cimarron* 1960; *King of the Roaring 20s* 1961; *Taras Bulba* 1962; *Lost Command* 1966.

Waxman, Harry. Director of photography. *b.* Apr. 3, 1912, in London. *d.* 1984. He entered films at 14 as a darkroom assistant and three years later became an assistant cameraman. Returning from WW II service with the Film Production Unit of the RAF, he graduated to lighting cameraman in 1945 and subsequently received cinematographer's credit on many British productions.

FILMS INCLUDE: *Journey Together* 1945; *Brighton Rock/Young Scarface* 1947; *Trottie True/The Gay Lady* 1949; *Valley of the Eagles* 1951; *The Gift Horse/Glory at Sea, The Long Memory* 1953; *Father Brown/The Detective, The Sleeping Tiger* 1954; *Diane* (US), *Lost* 1956; *Sapphire* 1959; *Swiss Family Robinson* (UK/US), *Man in the Moon* 1960; *The Roman Spring of Mrs. Stone* (UK/US), *The Day the Earth Caught Fire* 1961; *Stolen Hours* (US), *Sword of Lancelot* 1963; *She, The Nanny* 1965; *Khartoum* (2nd-unit phot.), *The Family Way* 1966; *Danger Route, The Trygon Factor* 1967; *The Anniversary, Twisted Nerve* 1968; *There's a Girl in My Soup* 1970; *The Beast in the Cellar, Forbush and the Penguins/Cry of the Penguins* (co-phot.) 1971; *Alf 'n' Family* 1972; *Vampyres* (US), *Journey Into Fear* 1975; *The Pink Panther Strikes Again* 1976.

Wayans, Damon. Actor, comedian. Born in 1960, in New York, N.Y. After working as a stand-up comic, he appeared for a season as a regular on the TV comedy show 'Saturday Night Live' and later on 'In Living Color.' Acting in films, primarily comedies, since the mid-80s; he directed his first film in 1992. His brother Keenen Ivory WAYANS is a screenwriter and director.

FILMS INCLUDE: *Beverly Hills Cop* 1984; *Roxanne, Hollywood Shuffle* 1987; *Punchline, I'm Gonna Git You Sucka, Colors* 1988; *Earth Girls Are Easy* 1989; *Look Who's Talking Too* (v/o) 1990; *The Last Boy Scout* 1991; *Mo' Money* (also sc., co-exec. prod.) 1992; *Last Action Hero* 1993; *Blankman* 1994; *Don't Be a Menace to South Central While Drinking Your Juice in the Hood, Major Payne* 1995; *Bulletproof, The Great White Hype* 1996.

Wayans, Keenen [also Keenan] Ivory. Screenwriter, director, actor. Born on June 8, 1958, in New York, N.Y. *ed.* Tuskegee Institute. Innovative force best known for helping to redefine African-American humor on TV's 'In Living Color.' Trained as a comic, he debuted as a film director in the 80s with the send-up of blaxploitation movies, *I'm Gonna Git You Sucka*. His brother Damon WAYANS is also an actor.

FILMS INCLUDE (as screenwriter): *Hollywood Shuffle* (co-sc., also act.), *Eddie Murphy Raw* (co-sc.) 1987; *I'm Gonna Git You Sucka* (also dir., act.) 1988; *The Five Heartbeats* (co-sc.) 1991; *A Low Down Dirty Shame* (also dir., act.) 1994; *Don't Be a Menace to South Central While Drinking Your Juice in the Hood* (prod.) 1995; *Glimmer Man* (act. only) 1996.

Waycoff, Leon. See AMES, Leon.

Wayne, David. Actor. Born Wayne McMeekan, on Jan. 30, 1914, in Traverse City, Mich. *ed.* Western Michigan Coll. He worked briefly as a statistician before making his stage debut in 1936. On Broadway from 1938, he achieved stardom in the late 40s in such plays as 'Finian's Rainbow' and 'Mister Roberts' and won more acclaim in the early 50s as the original Sakini in 'The Teahouse of the August Moon.' A versatile actor, he has played a wide variety of lead and character roles in films since the late 40s, excelling in both comedy and drama. In the 60s he was a regular member of the Lincoln Center Repertory Theater. In the early 80s, he was a regular on TV's 'House Calls.'

FILMS: *Portrait of Jennie, Adam's Rib* 1949; *The Reformer and the Redhead, Stella, My Blue Heaven* 1950; *Up Front, M, As Young As You Feel* 1951; *With a Song in My Heart, Wait Till the Sun Shines Nellie, We're Not Married, O. Henry's Full House* 1952; *Tonight We Sing* (as impresario Sol Hurok), *Down Among the Sheltering Palms, How to Marry a Millionaire* 1953; *Hell and High Water* 1954; *The Tender Trap* 1955; *The Naked Hills* 1956; *The Three Faces of Eve, The Sad Sack* 1957; *The Last Angry Man* 1959; *The Big Gamble* 1961; *The Andromeda Strain* 1971; *Huckleberry Finn* (as Duke), *The Front Page* 1974; *The Apple Dumpling Gang* 1975; *Lassie: The New Beginning* 1979; *Finders Keepers* 1984; *The Survivalist* 1987.

Wayne, John ("Duke"). Actor. *b.* Marion Michael Morrison, May 26, 1907, Winterset, Iowa. *d.* 1979. Raised in California, he went to USC on a football scholarship. During summer vacations he was employed as a laborer and third-string prop man on the Fox lot and soon developed a warm personal relationship with director John FORD, who was to play a decisive role in Wayne's future as a superstar. In 1928, Wayne began playing bit roles in the films of Ford and others, initially unbilled or billed as Duke Morrison, and in 1930 he was given his first real break when Ford recommended him to director Raoul Walsh for the lead part in the Western epic *The Big Trail.* A tall (6' 4"), strong, and silent type, he subsequently rode tall in the saddle in innumerable other low-budget Westerns, serials, and sundry forgettable films after *The Big Trail* failed to click with audiences. For eight years he languished as the hero of some 80 films and seemed firmly entrenched in the position of a low-paid lowly star when Ford, who had remained a close friend, cast Wayne in the role of the Ringo Kid in his Western classic, *Stagecoach* (1939).

The success of the film provided the turning point in Wayne's career and the impetus for a hero's image that over the years has assumed mythical proportions. Year by year, often in films directed by Ford, Wayne developed into one of the biggest box-office attractions the screen has ever known. As he matured and his features began to crack, Wayne's image came even more to embody the American spirit. Usually garbed in a cowboy's outfit or an officer's uniform, he came to project the essence of strength and confidence in his many bigger-than-life roles as a crusader for just causes and a leader of men. Compared to many actors, he spoke little, but as Ford once observed, "what he said *meant* something."

In addition to cementing his stardom, Ford Westerns of the 40s and 50s also gave Wayne an opportunity to display depth and poignancy, particularly in the role of Captain Nathan Brittles, the aging cavalry officer reluctant to end a way of life in *She Wore a Yellow Ribbon*. Equally defining was his role as the harsh, uncompromising Tom Dunson leading a cattle drive in Howard Hawks's *Red River*. Less sympathetic than any of his previous performances, Wayne's new take on his trademark stoicism prompted Ford to remark, "I never knew the big son of a bitch could act." In his 1956 film *The Searchers*, he offered what may be his most complete role, that of obsessed Indian hunter Ethan Edwards. Both frightening in his determination and moving in his inability to become part of society, he embodies both sides of the myth of the western frontier.

As his screen persona projected American values, so too did Wayne the public figure project the image of the ultra-American, a superpatriot in the most rigid Old Guard style. During the McCarthy era he helped form the Motion Picture Alliance for the Preservation of American Ideals and eventually became the group's president. A fundamentalist and a superhawk, he made the Vietnam War a personal crusade and paid it a Technicolor tribute as the co-director and star of *The Green Berets* (1968). It was his second film as director. In 1960 he had produced, directed, and starred in *The Alamo,* the gallant saga of the historical event he saw as a metaphor for America.

Wayne was the father of seven and the grandfather of 16 from his three marriages, all to women of Latin extraction. His son Michael (*b.* Nov. 23, 1934, Los Angeles) was in charge of Wayne's own production company, Batjac Productions, and produced his father's later films. The younger Patrick WAYNE is a screen actor.

At the end of 40 years as a screen star during which he appeared in some 250 films, Hollywood paid its highest tribute to John Wayne when it awarded him the best actor Oscar for his performance as a hard-drinking Western marshal with an eye patch in *True Grit* (1969). However, it is his final film, *The Shootist*, which provides the more genuine coda to his career. As longtime killer John Bernard Books attempting to live his last days dying of cancer in peace, he more accurately reflected the decline of the Western and the personal fight he had been waging for years. Offscreen, Wayne had recovered from three major operations. In 1963 he had a cancerous lung removed, in 1978 he underwent open-heart surgery, and in 1979 he had his stomach removed. Until his death he showed remarkable courage. A Congressional Medal was struck in his honor, a tribute to the man who, as Joan Didion said in her essay on Wayne, "determined forever the shape of certain of our dreams."

FILMS (as actor): *The Drop Kick* (unbilled bit as member of USC's football team) 1927; *Hangman's House* (unbilled bit) 1928; *Words and Music* (billed as Duke Morrison), *Salute* (bit as football player) 1929; *Men Without Women* (bit), *Rough Romance* (bit), *Cheer Up and Smile* (bit), *The Big Trail* 1930; *Girls Demand Excitement, Three Girls Lost, Men Are Like That/Arizona, The Deceiver* (bit as a corpse), *Range Feud, Maker of Men* 1931; *The Voice of Hollywood No. 13* (short), *Shadow of the Eagle* (serial), *Texas Cyclone, Two-Fisted Law, Lady and Gent/The Challenger, The Hurricane Express* (serial), *The Hollywood Handicap* (short), *Ride Him Cowboy, The Big Stampede, Haunted Gold* 1932; *The Telegraph Trail, The Three Musketeers* (serial), *Central Airport* (bit), *Somewhere in Sonora, His Private Secretary, The Life of Jimmy Dolan* (bit), *Baby Face, The Man from Monterey, Riders of Destiny, College Coach* (bit), *Sagebrush Trail* 1933; *The Lucky Texan, West of the Divide, Blue Steel, The Man from Utah, Randy Rides Alone, The Star Packer, The Trail Beyond, The Lawless Frontier, 'Neath Arizona Skies* 1934; *Texas Terror, Rainbow Valley, The Desert Trail, The Dawn Rider, Paradise Canyon, Westward Ho, The New Frontier, The Lawless Range* 1935; *The Oregon Trail, The Lawless Nineties, King of the Pecos, The Lonely Trail, Winds of the Wasteland, The Sea Spoilers, Conflict* 1936; *California Straight Ahead, I Cover the War, Idol of the Crowds, Adventure's End, Born to the West/Hell Town* 1937; *Pals of the Saddle, Overland Stage Raiders, Santa Fe Stampede, Red River Range* 1938; *Stagecoach, The Night Riders, Three Texas Steers, Wyoming Outlaw, New Frontier/Frontier Horizon, Allegheny Uprising* 1939; *The Dark Command, Three Faces West/The Refugee, The Long Voyage Home, Seven Sinners, Melody Ranch* (stunt work only; participation unconfirmed) 1940; *A Man Betrayed/Wheel of Fortune, Lady from Louisiana, The Shepherd of the Hills* 1941; *Lady for a Night, Reap the Wild Wind, The Spoilers, In Old California, Flying Tigers, Reunion in France, Pittsburgh* 1942; *A Lady Takes a Chance/The Cowboy and the Girl, In Old Oklahoma/War of the Wildcats* 1943; *The Fighting Seabees, Tall in the Saddle* 1944; *Flame of the Barbary Coast, Back to Bataan, They Were Expendable, Dakota* 1945; *Without Reservations* 1946; *Angel and the Badman* (also prod.), *Tycoon* 1947; *Fort Apache, Red River, Wake of the Red Witch* 1948; *Three Godfathers, The Fighting Kentuckian* (also prod.), *She Wore a Yellow Ribbon* 1949; *Sands of Iwo Jima, Rio Grande* 1950; *Operation Pacific, The Bullfighter and the Lady* (prod. only), *Flying Leathernecks* 1951; *The Quiet Man, Big Jim McLain* (also co-exec. prod.) 1952; *Trouble Along the Way, Island in the Sky* (also co-exec. prod.), *Hondo* (also co-exec. prod.) 1953; *The High and the Mighty* (also co-exec. prod.) 1954; *The Sea Chase, Blood Alley* (also exec. prod.) 1955; *The Conqueror, The Searchers* 1956; *The Wings of Eagles* (as Lt. Comdr. Frank WEAD), *Jet Pilot, Legend of the Lost* (also co-exec. prod.) 1957; *I Married a Woman* (cameo), *The Barbarian and the Geisha* (as merchant-diplomat Townsend Harris) 1958; *Rio Bravo, The Horse Soldiers* 1959; *The Alamo* (as Davy Crockett; also prod., dir.), *North to Alaska* 1960; *The Comancheros* (also dir. some scenes; uncredited) 1961; *The Man Who Shot Liberty Valance, Hatari!, The Longest Day, How the West Was Won* (as General William T. Sherman) 1962; *Donovan's Reef, McLintock!* (also exec. prod.) 1963; *Circus World* 1964; *The Greatest Story Ever Told, In Harm's Way, The Sons of Katie Elder* 1965; *Cast a Giant Shadow* (also co-exec. prod.) 1966; *The War Wagon* (also co-exec. prod.), *El Dorado* 1967; *The Green Berets* (also exec. prod., co-dir. with Ray Kellogg and uncredited Mervyn LeRoy) 1968; *Hellfighters, True Grit, The Undefeated* 1969; *Chisum, Rio Lobo* 1970; *Big Jake* (also exec. prod.) 1971; *The Cowboys, Cancel My Reservation* (cameo) 1972; *The Train Robbers* (also exec. prod.), *Cahill—United States Marshal* (also exec. prod.) 1973; *McQ* 1974; *Brannigan* (UK/US), *Rooster Cogburn* 1975; *The Shootist* 1976.

Wayne, Patrick. Actor. Born on July 15, 1939, in Los Angeles. *ed.* Loyola. The son of John WAYNE, he began his screen career at 16, playing juvenile roles in John Ford films. In the late 50s and during the 60s he supported his father in a number of productions and from the early 70s developed into a leading man in his own right.

FILMS INCLUDE: *The Long Gray Line, Mister Roberts* 1955; *The Searchers* 1956; *The Alamo* 1960; *The Comancheros* 1961; *Donovan's Reef, McLintock!* 1963; *Cheyenne Autumn* 1964; *Shenandoah* 1965; *An Eye for an Eye* 1966; *The Green Berets* 1968; *La Spina Dorsale del Diavolo/The Deserter* (It./Yug.), *Big Jake* 1971; *The Gatling Gun, Beyond Atlantis* 1973; *The Bears and I* 1974; *Mustang Country* 1976; *Sinbad and the Eye of the Tiger, The People That Time Forgot* 1977; *Rustler's Rhapsody* 1985; *Revenge* 1986; *Young Guns* 1988; *Her Alibi* 1989; *Blind Vengeance, Chill Factor* 1990.

Wead, Lt. Comdr. Frank ("Spig"). Screenwriter. *b.*

1895(?). *d.* 1947. An ace pilot in the US Navy during WW I, he devised the "baby carrier" and did much to vitalize the Navy's air wing between the wars. Paralyzed as a result of an accident, he turned to writing novels, stories, and screenplays, usually concerning war and the men of the armed forces. John Ford's *The Wings of Eagles* (1957) is a tribute to "Spig" Wead's courage. The film's script was based on Wead's writings, mainly his biographical history *Wings for Men.* He was portrayed in the film by John Wayne.

FILMS INCLUDE: *The Flying Fleet* 1929; *Dirigible, Hell Divers* (both story only) 1931; *Air Mail* 1932; *Midshipman Jack* 1933; *West Point of the Air, Murder in the Fleet* 1935; *Ceiling Zero, China Clipper* 1936; *Sea Devils, Submarine D-1* 1937; *Test Pilot* (story only), *The Citadel* 1938; *Tail Spin* 1939; *Moon Over Burma* 1940; *Dive Bomber* 1941; *Destroyer* 1943; *They Were Expendable* 1945; *The Hoodlum Saint* 1946; *The Beginning or the End, Blaze of Noon* 1947.

Weathers, Carl. Actor. Born on Jan. 14, 1948, in New Orleans, La. *ed.* San Diego State Univ. (dramatic arts). Brawny actor often featured in action films. After college, he played pro football with the Oakland Raiders and British Columbia Lions in the Canadian League. In off-seasons, however, he performed with San Francisco theater companies, and after retiring pro football in 1974, he pursued a film career. He established himself in the role of heavyweight champion Apollo Creed in *Rocky.* With the exception of a starring role in *Action Jackson,* he has since concentrated on supporting roles. Also works with Big Brothers and the US Olympic Committee, among other charities.

FILMS INCLUDE: *Bucktown, Friday Foster* 1975; *Rocky* 1976; *Close Encounters of the Third Kind, Semi-Tough* 1977; *The Bermuda Depths, Force 10 from Navarone* 1978; *Rocky II* 1979; *Death Hunt* 1981; *Rocky III* 1982; *Rocky IV* 1985; *Predator* 1987; *Action Jackson* 1988; *Hurricane Smith* 1992; *Happy Gilmore* 1996.

weave. A lateral shift of projected film as a result of improper threading or a faulty projector mechanism.

Weaver, Fritz. Actor. Born on Jan. 19, 1926, in Pittsburgh. Leading man and character player of the American stage, he has appeared infrequently but convincingly in Hollywood films, usually in supporting roles. Portrayed Sherlock Holmes in the Broadway musical 'Baker Street' and has appeared in numerous TV dramas.

FILMS INCLUDE: *Fail Safe, The Guns of August* (narr.) 1964; *To Trap a Spy* 1966; *The Maltese Bippy* 1969; *A Walk in the Spring Rain, Company of Killers* 1970; *The Day of the Dolphin* 1973; *Marathon Man* 1976; *Demon Seed, Black Sunday* 1977; *The Big Fix* 1978; *The Martian Chronicles* (TV), *Jaws of Satan* 1979; *Creepshow* 1982; *Power* 1985.

Weaver, Marjorie. Actress. Born on Mar. 2, 1913, in Grossville, Tenn. *ed.* U. of Kentucky; U. of Indiana. Vivacious brunette leading lady of Hollywood films of the late 30s to late 40s, following some experience as a band vocalist, model, and actress in stock. Usually played wholesome types, often in B mysteries at Fox.

FILMS INCLUDE: *Transatlantic Merry-Go-Round* 1934; *China Clipper* 1936; *The Californian, This Is My Affair, Second Honeymoon* 1937; *Sally Irene and Mary, Kentucky Moonshine, Three Blind Mice, I'll Give a Million, Hold That Co-Ed* 1938; *Young Mr. Lincoln* (as Mary Todd), *The Honeymoon's Over, The Cisco Kid and the Lady* 1939; *Shooting High, Charlie Chan's Murder Cruise, Maryland, Michael Shayne Private Detective* 1940; *Murder Among Friends, Man at Large* 1941; *The Man Who Wouldn't Die, Just Off Broadway* 1942; *Let's Face It* 1943; *The Great Alaskan Mystery* (serial), *Shadows of Suspicion* 1944; *Fashion Model* 1945; *We're Not Married* 1952.

Weaver, Sigourney. Actress. Born Susan Alexandra Weaver on October 8, 1949, in New York, N.Y. *ed.* Stanford, Yale School of Drama. Cool, patrician screen lead. Daughter of NBC president Sylvester "Pat" Weaver and actress Elizabeth Inglis, and niece of comedian Doodles Weaver. After appearing widely off Broadway, she rose to prominence in film as the resourceful (and only surviving) crew member Ripley in *Alien,* whom she extended in the film's two sequels to become a protective Ur-Mother figure. As a major box-office draw of the 80s, she played a variety of roles, from supporting comedic parts (*Ghostbusters*) to romantic leads (*The Year of Living Dangerously*) to dramatic starring roles (*Gorillas in the Mist*). Most of her characters are independent women who come to care passionately about another being—whether a man, a child, or an animal. Her first name was borrowed from a character in F. Scott Fitzgerald's novel 'The Great Gatsby.'

FILMS: *Annie Hall* 1977; *Madman* (Isr.) 1978; *Alien* (US/UK) 1979; *Eyewitness* 1981; *The Year of Living Dangerously* (Austral.), *Deal of the Century* 1983; *Ghostbusters* 1984; *One Woman or Two* (Fr.) 1985; *Half Moon Street, Aliens* 1986; *Gorillas in the Mist, Working Girl* 1988; *Ghostbusters II* 1989; *Alien 3* (also co-prod.), *1492* 1992; *Dave* 1993; *Death and the Maiden* 1994; *Beyond Rangoon, Copycat, Jeffrey* 1995; *Alien 4: The Resurrection, Ice Storm* 1997.

Webb, Clifton. Actor. *b.* Webb Parmallee Hollenbeck, Nov. 19, 1891, Indianapolis. *d.* 1966. Trained as a dancer and an actor from early childhood, he was a seasoned performer by the age of ten. At 13 he quit grade school to study painting and music and at 17 he sang with the Boston Opera Company. At 19 he turned to dancing in earnest and soon became a leading ballroom dancer in New York night spots, often partnering with Bonnie Glass. From 1917 he appeared in musical comedies and in the 20s he began playing straight dramatic parts on the London stage, on Broadway, and in occasional silent films. He returned to the screen in 1944, after some 20 years of absence, as the fastidious and elegant villain in *Laura* (1944). He was cast in the picture by Otto Preminger over the objections of producer Darryl Zanuck and was nominated for an Academy Award for his performance. He was nominated again for an Oscar as best supporting player for *The Razor's Edge* (1946). He was subsequently typecast as a waspish, acidulous, pedantic bachelor and gained great popularity as the pompous babysitter Mr. Belvedere in the hilarious comedy *Sitting Pretty* and its several sequels.

FILMS: *Polly with a Past* 1920; *Let Not Man Put Asunder* (participation unconfirmed) 1924; *New Toys, The Heart of a Siren* 1925; *Laura* 1944; *The Dark Corner, The Razor's Edge* 1946; *Sitting Pretty* 1948; *Mr. Belvedere Goes to College* 1949; *Cheaper by the Dozen, For Heaven's Sake* 1950; *Mr. Belvedere Rings the Bell, Elopement* 1951; *Dreamboat, Stars and Stripes Forever* (as John Philip Sousa) 1952; *Titanic, Mister Scoutmaster* 1953; *Three Coins in the Fountain, Woman's World* 1954; *The Man Who Never Was* 1956; *Boy on a Dolphin* 1957; *The Remarkable Mr. Pennypacker, Holiday for Lovers* 1959; *Satan Never Sleeps* 1962.

Webb, Jack. Actor, director, producer. *b.* Apr. 2, 1920, Santa Monica, Calif. *d.* 1982. Following WW II service with the Army Air Force, he began his career as a radio announcer in San Francisco. By 1946 he was starring in his own radio series and in 1949 he conceived and launched the radio police-drama series 'Dragnet,' which he later turned into a gold mine on TV. He became closely identified with the clipped, factual delivery of the series' main character, Detective Joe Friday. In the 50s he incorporated the 'Dragnet' staccato style into a number of feature films he directed and produced with less satisfying results.

He returned to TV as a Warner executive, then produced a number of new series, including 'Adam-12' and 'Emergency.' His first wife was actress-singer Julie LONDON; his third, Miss USA of 1952, Jackie Loughery.

FILMS (as actor): *He Walked by Night* 1948; *The Men, Sunset Boulevard, Dark City* 1950; *The Halls of Montezuma, You're in the Navy Now/USS Teakettle, Appointment with Danger* 1951; *Dragnet* (also dir.) 1954; *Pete Kelly's Blues* (also dir.) 1955; *The D.I.* (also dir., prod.) 1957; *-30-* (also dir., prod.) 1959; *The Last Time I Saw Archie* (also dir., prod.) 1961; *The Man from Galveston* (exec. prod. only) 1963; *Little Mo* (orig. made for TV; exec. prod. only) 1978.

Webb, James R. Screenwriter. *b.* Oct. 4, 1909, Denver, Colo. *d.* 1974. *ed.* Stanford U. A short-story writer for various magazines, he went to Hollywood in the late 30s and was assigned to scripting mainly low-budget Westerns starring Roy Rogers. After distinguished WW II service as a major, he returned to films in the late 40s. He then wrote screenplays, alone or in collaboration, for major Westerns and other pictures emphasizing action. He won an Academy Award for the original screenplay of *How the West Was Won* (1962).

FILMS INCLUDE: *S.O.S. Tidal Wave* (story only) 1939; *Nevada City* 1941; *South of Santa Fe* 1942; *South of St. Louis* 1949; *Woman in Hiding* (story only), *Montana* 1950; *The Big Trees, The Iron Mistress* 1952; *Phantom of the Rue Morgue, Apache, Vera Cruz* 1954; *Illegal* 1955; *Trapeze* 1956; *The Big Country* 1958; *Pork Chop Hill* 1959; *Cape Fear, How the West Was Won* 1962; *Cheyenne Autumn* 1964; *La Bataille de San Sebastian/Guns for San Sebastian* (Fr./US/It./Mex.; English version only) 1968; *Alfred the Great* (UK), *Sinful Davey* (UK) 1969; *The Hawaiians, They Call Me Mr. Tibbs* 1970; *The Organization* 1971.

Webb, Millard. Director. *b.* Dec. 6, 1893, Clay City, Ky. *d.* 1935. *ed.* Nevada School of Mining and Engineering. A civil engineer, he turned to stage acting after an on-the-job injury. After brief experience in stock, he was hired as an extra by D. W. Griffith in 1915. He appeared in a number of films but graduating switched to screenwriting and eventually to directing. He piloted a number of prestige films in the 20s, notably *The Sea Beast,* an adaptation of Melville's *Moby Dick,* starring John Barrymore.

FILMS (as director): *Oliver Twist Jr.* (also sc.), *Hearts of Youth* (co-dir. with Tom Miranda; also sc.) 1921; *Where is My Wandering Boy Tonight?* (co-dir. with James P. Hogan) 1922; *Her Marriage Vow* (also sc.), *The Dark Swan/The Black Swan* (also co-phot.) 1924; *My Wife and I* (also co-sc.) 1925; *The Golden Cocoon, The Sea Beast* 1926; *An Affair of the Follies, The Love Thrill* (also co-story), *Naughty but Nice, The Drop Kick* 1927; *Honeymoon Flats* 1928; *Gentlemen of the Press, The Painted Angel, Glorifying the American Girl* (also story, sc.) 1929; *The Golden Calf* 1930; *Happy Ending* (UK) 1931.

Webb, Robert D. American director. *b.* Jan. 3, 1903. *d.* 1990. He entered films at 16 as camera assistant, and after many years in various capacities, including assistant director and associate producer, he began directing action-oriented films in the mid-40s. From time to time he served as second-unit director on large-scale productions requiring action expertise, including *Captain from Castile* (1947), *Prince of Foxes* (1949), *Captain Newman, M.D., A Gathering of Eagles* (both 1963), *The Agony and the Ecstasy* (1965), and *Assault on a Queen* (1966).

FILMS: *The Caribbean Mystery, The Spider* 1945; *The Glory Brigade, Beneath the 12-Mile Reef* 1953; *White Feather, Seven Cities of Gold* 1955; *On the Threshold of Space, The Proud Ones, Love Me Tender* 1956; *The Way to the Gold* (also sc.) 1957; *Guns of the Timberland* 1960; *Pirates of Tortuga, Seven Women from Hell* 1961; *The Capetown Affair* (So. Afr.) 1967.

Webber, Robert. Actor. *b.* Oct. 14, 1924, in Santa Ana, Calif. *d.* 1989. On the stage from the early 40s, he reached Broadway in the late 40s, after returning from WW II service with the Marines. He appeared in films and on innumerable TV shows from the early 50s, often playing a villain or a heel with deceiving Madison Avenue junior-executive looks and manners.

FILMS INCLUDE: *Highway 301* 1951; *12 Angry Men* 1957; *The Stripper* 1963; *The Sandpiper, The Third Day, Hysteria* (UK) 1965; *The Silencers, Tecnica di un Omicidio/The Hired Killer* (It./Fr.), *Harper, Dead Heat on a Merry-Go-Round* 1966; *Don't Make Waves, The Dirty Dozen* 1967; *The Big Bounce* 1969; *The Great White Hope* 1970; *$* 1971; *Bring Me the Head of Alfredo Garcia* 1974; *Midway* (as Rear-Admiral Frank Fletcher), *Passi di Morte Perduti nel Buio* (It.) 1976; *Madame Claude* (Fr.), *L'Imprecateur* (Fr.), *The Choirboys* 1977; *Casey's Shadow, Revenge of the Pink Panther* 1978; *Gardenia* (It.), *10, Courage Fuyons* (Fr.) 1979; *Private Benjamin, Tous Vedettes* (Fr.) 1980; *S.O.B.* 1981; *Wrong is Right, The Final Option/Who Dares Wins* (UK) 1982; *Starflight One/Starflight: The Plane that Couldn't Land* 1983; *Wild Geese 2* 1984; *Nuts* 1987.

Weber, Joe. Comic actor. *b.* Morris Weber, 1867, New York City. *d.* 1942. Vaudeville, burlesque, stage, and screen comedian. Partner in the popular comedy team Weber and Fields. For screen credits, see FIELDS, Lew.

Weber, Lois. Director. *b.* 1882, Allegheny, Pa. *d.* 1939. A former concert pianist, she entered films as an actress during the infancy of the industry and co-starred with her husband, actor Phillips SMALLEY, in many of the early dramatic productions of the American screen. She turned to directing in 1913, joining Universal, and before long became known as the highest salaried woman director in the world. She specialized in social topics and caused a controversy when she dealt openly and clinically with the subject of birth control in *Where Are My Children?* (1916). She also dealt frequently and compassionately with the concerns of women in contemporary society.

FILMS INCLUDE: As actress—*The Heiress, On the Brink* 1911. As director—*The Troubadour's Triumph* 1912; *The Jew's Christmas* (co-dir. with Phillips Smalley; also sc., act.), *The Female of the Species* (also act.) 1913; *The Merchant of Venice* (co-dir. with Smalley; also sc., act. as Portia), *A Fool and His Money* (also act.), *Behind the Veil* (co-dir. with Smalley; also sc., act.), *False Colors* (co-dir., co-sc. with Smalley; also act.) 1914; *Sunshine Molly* (co-dir. with Smalley; also sc., act.), *A Cigarette—That's All* (sc. only), *Scandal* (co-dir. with Smalley; also sc., act.) *Hypocrites* (also sc.), *It's No Laughing Matter* (also sc.) 1915; *The Dumb Girl of Portici* (co-dir. with Smalley), *Saving the Family Name* (also act.), *Hop—The Devil's Brew* (co-dir. with Smalley; also sc., act.), *The People vs. John Doe* (also act.), *Idle Wives, Where Are My Children?* (co-dir. with Smalley; also sc.), *The Flirt* (co-dir. with Smalley) 1916; *The Hand That Rocks the Cradle* (also prod., act.), *Even as You and I, The Price of a Good Time, The Mysterious Mrs. M.* 1917; *For Husbands Only* (also prod.), *The Doctor and the Woman, Borrowed Clothes* 1918; *Mary Regan, A Midnight Romance* (also sc.), *When a Girl Loves, Home* 1919; *Forbidden, To Please One Woman* (also co-story, sc.) 1920; *What's Worth While?* (also prod.), *Too Wise Wives* (also prod., sc.), *The Blot* (also prod., sc.), *What Do Men Want?* (also prod., sc.) 1921; *A Chapter in Her Life* (also co-sc.) 1923; *The Marriage Clause* (also sc.) 1926; *Sensation Seekers* (also sc.), *The Angel of Broadway* 1927; *White Heat* 1934.

Webster, Paul Francis. Lyricist. *b.* Dec. 20, 1907, New York City. *d.* 1984. *ed.* NYU; Cornell. He was a seaman on a China-bound freighter and a dance instructor at Arthur Murray's before beginning a long and successful career as a songwriter for films and recordings. Many of his songs were nominated for Academy Awards and three—'Secret Love' from *Calamity Jane,* the title song from *Love Is a Many Splendored Thing,* and 'The Shadow of Your Smile' from *The Sandpiper*—won the coveted Oscars. He also co-wrote the story that provided the basis for the script of *Nora Prentiss.*

FILMS INCLUDE: *Under the Pampas Moon* 1935; *Rainbow on the River* 1936; *You Only Live Once* 1937; *Presenting Lily Mars, Thousands Cheer* 1943; *The Stork Club* 1945; *The Great Caruso* ('The Loveliest Night of the Year,' etc.) 1951; *The Merry Widow* 1952; *Calamity Jane* 1953; *Love Is A Many Splendored Thing* 1955; *Giant, Anastasia, Friendly Persuasion* 1956; *A Farewell to Arms, April Love* 1957; *Raintree County, A Certain Smile, Marjorie Morningstar* 1958; *Rio Bravo* 1959; *The Alamo* ('The Green Leaves of Summer,' etc.) 1960; *El Cid, The Guns of Navarone* 1961; *Mutiny on the Bounty, Tender Is the Night* 1962; *55 Days at Peking* 1963; *The Sandpiper* 1965; *An American Dream, Who's Afraid of Virginia Woolf?* 1966; *Far from the Madding Crowd* 1967; *The Shoes of the Fisherman* 1968; *Topaz* 1969; *Airport* ('The Winds of Chance') 1970; *The Stepmother* 1973; *The Teacher* 1974; *The Specialist, Mr. Sycamore* 1975.

Wechsler, Lazar. Producer. Born on July 28, 1896, in Petrikau, Poland. In Switzerland since 1914, he pioneered in the production of Swiss feature films. His pictures of the 40s and 50s gave the Swiss industry an international reputation and many awards.

FILMS INCLUDE: *Jä-soo* 1935; *Fuslier Wipf* 1938; *Wilder Urlaub* 1943; *Marie Louise* 1944; *Die lezte Chance/The Last Chance* 1945; *The Search* (US/Switz.) 1948; *Swiss Tour/Four Days' Leave* 1949; *Die Vier im Jeep/Four in a Jeep* 1951; *Heidi* 1952; *Unser Dorf/The Village* 1953; *Heidi und Peter/Heidi and Peter* 1954; *Zwischen uns die Berge* 1956; *Es geschah am lichten Tage/It Happened in Broad Daylight* (co-prod.; Ger./Switz.) 1957; *Die Schatten werden länger/The Shadows Grow Longer* (co-prod.; Switz./Ger.) 1961; *Die Sittlichkeitsverbrecher/The Molesters* 1963; *Der Arzt stellt fest/Angelklagt nach Paragraph 218/The Doctor Says* (Switz./Ger.) 1966.

Wegener, Paul. Actor, director. *b.* Dec. 11, 1874, Bischdorf, East Prussia. *d.* 1948. A stage actor from 1895, following law studies, he joined Max REINHARDT's Deutsches Theater in Berlin in 1906 and developed into one of the giants of German drama. A massive man, with an enormous stage presence, he played many classical roles, from Oedipus Rex to Macbeth. He made an impressive screen debut in the first version of *Der Student von Prag/The Student of Prague* (1913), in which he played a dual role with a restraint uncommon in the German cinema of the period. The following year he co-directed and played the title role in *Der Golem/The Golem,* the first of three versions he was to make from the ancient mystical Jewish legend. He subsequently directed a number of other films, notably *Der Rattenfänger von Hamelin/The Pied Piper of Hamelin,* and appeared in scores of others. During the Nazi era he made several propaganda films and was named Actor of the State. His five marriages included Lyda Salmonova (*b.* 1889, Prague; *d.* 1968), who appeared in many of his films.

FILMS INCLUDE (as actor): *Der Student von Prag/The Student of Prague* (also co-sc.) 1913; *Die Augen des Ole Brandis* (also co-dir.), *Der Golem/The Golem* (also co-dir.) 1914; *Peter Schlemihl* (also co-sc.) 1915; *Rubezahls Hochzeit* (also co-dir., act.), *Der Rattenfänger von Hamelin/The Pied Piper of Hamelin* (also co-dir.), *Der Yoghi/The Yogi* (also co-dir.) 1916; *Hans Trutz in Schlaraffenland* (also dir.), *Der Golem und die Tänzerin* (also co-dir.) 1917; *Der fremde Fürst* (also co-dir., sc.), *Welt ohne Waffen* (doc.; dir. only) 1918; *Der Golem—wie er in die Welt Kam/The Golem* (also co-dir., sc.), *Medea, Sumurun/One Arabian Night* 1920; *Der verlorene Schatten/The Lost Shadow* (also co-dir., sc.), *Das Weib des Pharao/Loves of Pharaoh* 1921; *Herzog Ferrantes Ende* (also co-dir.), *Lukrezia Borgia, Monna Vanna, Vanina* 1922; *Lebende Buddhas* (also prod., dir., co-sc.) 1924; *The Magician* (US; shot in France) 1926; *Alraune/Unholy Love, Ramper der Tiermensch/The Strange Case of Captain Ramper, Svengali, Die Weber/The Weavers* 1927; *Unheimliche Geschichten/The Living Dead* 1932; *Inge und die Millionen, Horst Wessel* 1933; *Ein Mann will nach Deutschland* (dir. only), *Die Freundin eines grossen Mannes* (dir. only) 1934; *August der Starke* (dir. only), *Moskau-Shanghai* (dir. only), *Die Stunde der Versuchung* (dir. only) 1936; *Unter Ausschluss der Oeffentlichkeit* (dir. only), *Krach und Gluck um Künnemann* (dir. only) 1937; *Stärker als die Liebe/Stronger Than Love* 1938; *Das unsterbliche Herz, Das Recht auf Liebe* 1939; *Der grosse König* 1942; *Der grosse Mandarin* 1949.

Weidler, Virginia. Actress. *b.* Mar. 21, 1927, Eagle Rock, Calif. *d.* 1968. Child star of Hollywood films of the 30s and early 40s. The daughter of an architect and a former German opera singer known professionally as Margaret Theresa Louise, she began her film career at age three and developed at Paramount and later at MGM into a competent performer specializing in mischievous but lovable little imps. She was memorable as the child who threatens to hold her breath until she turns blue in *Mrs. Wiggs of the Cabbage Patch* (1934) and as John Barrymore's precocious daughter in *The Great Man Votes* (1939). Unable to find film roles after adolescence, she tried unsuccessfully for stage and nightclub careers, then retired from show business in 1945. She died at 40 of a heart attack.

FILMS INCLUDE: *Surrender* 1931; *After Tonight* 1933; *Mrs. Wiggs of the Cabbage Patch* 1934; *Laddie, Freckles, Peter Ibbetson* 1935; *Timothy's Quest, The Girl of the Ozarks, The Big Broadcast of 1937, Trouble for Two* 1936; *Maid of Salem, The Outcasts of Poker Flat, Souls at Sea* 1937; *Scandal Street, Mother Carey's Chickens, Too Hot to Handle, Men with Wings, Out West with the Hardys* 1938; *The Great Man Votes, Fixer Dugan, The Under-Pup, The Women, Bad Little Angel* 1939; *Young Tom Edison, All This and Heaven Too, Gold Rush Maisie, The Philadelphia Story* 1940; *Barnacle Bill* 1941; *Babes on Broadway, Born to Sing* 1942; *The Youngest Profession, Best Foot Forward* 1943.

Weill, Claudia. Director. Born in 1947, in New York City, a distant cousin of composer Kurt Weill. She began making amateur films while still a student at Radcliffe College, from which she was graduated *cum laude* in 1969. She later studied painting with Oskar Kokoschka in Salzburg and still photography with Walker Evans at Yale. Alone or in collaboration, she made a variety of experimental and documentary shorts, including such titles as *This Is the Home of Mrs. Levant Grahame, Lost and Found, Roaches' Serenade,* and *Joyce at 34.* She also directed segments of 'Sesame Street' and other programs for public television. She shared with Shirley MacLaine an Academy Award nomination as co-director of the feature-length documentary *The Other Half of the Sky: A China Memoir* (1975), a film she also photographed and co-edited. Her first feature film, *Girlfriends* (1978), which she also produced and co-wrote, was made on a shoestring budget, partly with funds from institutional grants, but was eventually picked up for world distribution by a major studio, Warner Bros. She later worked mainly in television, directing the late 80s series 'thirtysomething.'

FILMS INCLUDE: *This is the Home of Mrs. Levant Grahame* (short), *Roaches' Serenade* (short) 1971; *Joyce at 34* (short) 1972; *The Year of the Woman* (cin.) 1973; *The Other Half of the Sky: A China Memoir* (also cin., ed.) 1975; *The Scenic Route* (act. only), *Girlfriends* (also prod., story) 1978; *It's My Turn* 1980; *Calling the Shots* (act. only) 1988.

Weingarten, Lawrence. Producer. *b.* 1898, Chicago. *d.* 1975. He entered films as a publicist after WW I. In the late 20s he joined MGM, where he worked his way up from assistant to associate producer under Irving Thalberg. He married Thalberg's sister, Sylvia, and was later appointed production supervisor of the company's light films. He produced many films since the late 20s, dramas as well as comedies.

FILMS INCLUDE: *Broadway Melody, Spite Marriage* 1929; *The Nuisance* 1933; *Sadie McKee* 1934; *Rendezvous* 1935; *Libeled Lady* 1936; *The Last of Mrs. Cheyney* 1937; *Too Hot to Handle* 1938; *Balalaika* 1939; *Escape* 1940; *Without Love* 1945; *Adam's Rib* 1949; *Pat and Mike* 1952; *The Actress* 1953; *Rhapsody* 1954; *The Tender Trap, I'll Cry Tomorrow* 1955; *Cat on a Hot Tin Roof* 1958; *The Gazebo* 1960; *Ada, The Honeymoon Machine* 1961; *Period of Adjustment* 1962; *The Unsinkable Molly Brown* 1964; *Signpost to Murder* 1965; *The Impossible Years* 1968.

Weinstein, Bob and Harvey. See MIRAMAX FILMS.

Weintraub, Jerry. Producer, agent, promoter. Born on September 26, 1937, in Brooklyn, N.Y. Producer of often substantive dramas and comedy-dramas since the 1970s. Son of a gem salesman, he entered the entertainment business in the 1950s as a talent agent for MCA, representing such clients as Jack Paar and singer Jane Morgan, who would become his second wife. In the 70s, he produced his first film, *Nashville*, to critical success. At that time, he also began to produce TV specials, including 'Sinatra—the Main Event' and 'An Evening with John Denver,' which won an Emmy. He has been the agent and promoter for several major recording acts, including Elvis Presley and Frank Sinatra. His production company is Jerry Weintraub Productions.

FILMS INCLUDE: *Nashville* (exec. prod.) 1975; *Oh God!, 9/30/55* 1977; *Cruising* (co-prod.) 1980; *All Night Long* 1981; *Diner* 1982; *The Karate Kid* 1984; *The Karate Kid Part II* 1986; *Happy New Year* 1987; *The Karate Kid Part III* 1989; *Pure Country* 1992; *The Next Karate Kid, The Specialist* 1994; *Vegas Vacation* 1997.

Weir, Peter. Director. Born Peter Lindsay Weir on August 8, 1944, in Sydney, Australia. *ed.* Univ. of Sydney. Haunting, atmospheric director of the Australian film renewal. Son of a real estate broker, he abandoned school and a stint at his father's business to travel Europe and eventually work with the Commonwealth Film Unit in Australia. Through his work there behind the camera and in production, he came to direct. His early efforts, the horror tale *The Cars That Ate Paris* and disturbing dramas *Picnic at Hanging Rock* and *The Last Wave* introduced the wonder and respect for the power of nature that would infuse many of his later films. His next film, *Gallipoli*, the World War I drama about Australian soldiers serving for the British empire, highlighted another recurring element of his work: the clash of cultures that promotes one society's isolation. Similar culture clashes arise in his next two films, *The Year of Living Dangerously* and his first film in Hollywood, *Witness*. Both also interweave a strong sense of place with an equally strong love story featuring burgeoning mainstream players like Mel Gibson and Sigourney Weaver. The commercial success generated by both films established him as an important Hollywood director who can command large budgets and major actors. In large part his recent films, *The Mosquito Coast, Dead Poets Society*, and *Fearless*, reflect that status, though they continue to contain elements of isolation, natural wonder, and cultures set apart.

FILMS INCLUDE: *Three to Go* (also sc., "Michael") 1970; *The Cars That Ate Paris* (also sc., story) 1975; *Picnic at Hanging Rock* 1975; *The Last Wave* (also sc.) 1977; *The Plumber* (also sc., made for Australian TV, released theatrically elsewhere) 1980; *Gallipoli* (also story) 1981; *The Year of Living Dangerously* (also co-sc.) 1982; *Witness* 1985; *The Mosquito Coast* 1986; *Dead Poets Society* 1989; *Green Card* 1990; *Fearless* 1993.

Weis, Don. Director. Born on May 13, 1922, in Milwaukee. He entered the industry as a messenger at Warners, after studying film at USC. Returning from WW II service he became a script supervisor and dialogue director and was elevated to director in the early 50s. He acquired a following among some European film cultists for his stylish handling of simple-minded films like *I Love Melvin, The Affairs of Dobie Gillis,* and *The Adventures of Haji Baba.* But most of his subsequent films hardly justified his fans' enthusiasm.

FILMS: *Bannerline* 1951; *It's a Big Country* (co-dir.), *Just This Once, You for Me* 1952; *I Love Melvin, Remains to Be Seen, A Slight Case of Larceny, The Affairs of Dobie Gillis, Half a Hero* 1953; *The Adventures of Haji Baba* 1954; *Ride the High Iron, Deadlock* (originally made for TV) 1957; *Mr. Pharaoh and His Cleopatra* (made in Cuba; never released), *The Gene Krupa Story* 1959; *Critic's Choice* 1963; *Looking for Love, Pajama Party* 1964; *Billie* (also prod.) 1965; *The Ghost in the Invisible Bikini* 1966; *The King's Pirate* 1967; *Did You Hear the One About the Traveling Saleslady?* 1968; *Zero to Sixty* 1978.

Weisbart, David. Producer. *b.* Jan. 21, 1915, Los Angeles. *d.* 1967. *ed.* USC. He entered films as a cutter in 1935, straight out of college, and had worked his way up to producer by the early 50s. *Rebel Without a Cause* stands out as his one important project among mostly routine productions.

FILMS INCLUDE: *Mara Maru* 1952; *The Charge at Feather River* 1953; *The Command, Them* 1954; *Rebel Without a Cause* 1955; *Between Heaven and Hell, Love Me Tender* 1956; *April Love* 1957; *A Private's Affair* 1959; *Flaming Star* 1960; *Follow That Dream* 1962; *Kid Galahad* 1963; *Rio Conchos, The Pleasure Seekers* 1964; *Valley of the Dolls* 1967.

Weiss, Jiùri. Born in 1913, in Prague. He abandoned his law studies at Charles University for journalism. After gaining a Venice Award for his 16 mm amateur documentary *People in the Sun,* he considered turning professional filmmaker but was forced to leave his country in 1938 following the German takeover. He went to Paris, then to London, where he made such documentaries as *The Rape of Czechoslovakia* (1939), *Eternal Prague* (1941), and *Before the Raid* (1943). He returned to Czechoslovakia in 1947 and immediately turned to feature films. He soon became established as the foremost director of the intermediate generation of Czech filmmakers. However, his position declined somewhat in the 60s with the advent of a new wave in the Czech cinema.

FEATURE FILMS: *The Stolen Frontier* 1947; *Wild Beasts* 1948; *The Last Shot* 1950; *New Warriors Shall Arise* 1951; *My Friend the Gypsy* 1954; *Doggy and the Four* 1955; *Life Was the Stake* 1956; *Wolf Trap* 1957; *Appassionata* 1959; *Romeo Juliet and Darkness/Sweet Light in a Dark Room* 1960; *The Coward* 1961; *The Golden Fern* 1963; *90 Degrees in the Shade* 1964; *Murder Czech Style* 1967.

Weiss, Peter. Playwright, filmmaker. *b.* Nov. 8, 1916, Berlin. *d.* 1982. The celebrated author of such controversial plays as 'The Persecution and Assassination of Jean-Paul Marat as Performed by the Inmates of the Asylum of Charenton Under the Direction of the Marquis de Sade' ('Marat/Sade') and 'The Investigation' began his career as a filmmaker in Sweden. His Swiss-Czech family took refuge from Nazi persecution in neutral Sweden, and Weiss, a former student of Prague's Academy of Arts, began making experimental avant-garde films in the early 50s. The culmination of his film work was the feature *Mirage* (1959).

FILMS: Shorts—*Study I, Study II/Hallucinations* 1952; *Study III* 1953; *Study IV* 1954; *Study V* 1955; *The Studio of Dr. Faust, Faces in the Shadows* (co-dir. with Christer Stromholm) 1956; *Nothing Unusual, According to the Law* 1957; *What Shall We Do Now?* 1958; *Behind Uniform Façades* 1961. Feature—*The Mirage* (also sc.) 1959.

Weissmuller, Johnny. Actor. *b.* Peter John Weissmuller, June 2, 1904, Windber, Pa. *d.* 1984. *ed.* U. of Chicago. A champion swimmer, he won five gold medals at the 1924 and 1928 Olympics and set many US and world freestyle records. After appearing in swimming extravaganzas and several sports shorts, he was approached by MGM to play Tarzan in a contemplated series of films. His powerful physique made him an ideal king of the jungle and he swung, swam, and grunted his way through a dozen commercially successful "Tarzan" adventures opposite such Janes as Maureen O'Sullivan and Brenda Joyce. In the late 40s, when the series lost much of its appeal, he moved to Columbia, where he starred in the lower-budget Jungle Jim series, substituting a hunter's outfit for the loincloth. The series moved to television in 1958, and Weissmuller did not return to the screen until 1970, when he played a cameo in *The Phynx*. He was vice president of the Johnny Weissmuller Pool Company and was associated with other business enterprises exploiting his name. He was married six times and divorced five times. His public quarrels with his third wife, (1933–38) actress Lupe Velez, were given frequent coverage in the press. Autobiography: *Water, World and Weissmuller* (1967).

FILMS: *Glorifying the American Girl* (cameo as himself) 1929; *Tarzan the Ape Man* 1932; *Tarzan and His Mate* 1934; *Tarzan Escapes* 1936; *Tarzan Finds a Son* 1939; *Tarzan's Secret Treasure* 1941; *Tarzan's New York Adventure* 1942; *Tarzan Triumphs, Stage Door Canteen* (cameo), *Tarzan's Desert Mystery* 1943; *Tarzan and the Amazons* 1945; *Tarzan and the Leopard Woman, Swamp Fire* 1946; *Tarzan and the Huntress* 1947; *Tarzan and the Mermaids, Jungle Jim* 1948; *The Lost Tribe* 1949; *Captive Girl, Mark of the Gorilla, Pygmy Island* 1950; *Fury of the Congo, Jungle Manhunt* 1951; *Jungle Jim in the Forbidden Land, Voodoo Tiger* 1952; *Savage Mutiny, Valley of the Headhunters, The Killer Ape* 1953; *Jungle Man-Eaters, Cannibal Attack* 1954; *Jungle Moon Men, Devil Goddess* 1955; *The Phynx* (cameo) 1970.

Welch, Raquel. Actress. Born Raquel Tejada, on Sept. 5, 1940, in Chicago, to a Bolivian-born engineer and a mother of English stock. Raised in California, she took ballet lessons as a child and began entering and winning beauty contests at 14. At 18 she married high school classmate James Welch, hence her professional name. She bore him two children before their separation in 1961. Driven by an ambition to become a movie star, she attended the drama department of San Diego State College and did some repertory work with local groups. After her divorce, she headed for Dallas, Tex., where she modeled and hustled cocktails to have her nose fixed before launching her assault on Hollywood in 1963. Raquel's early steps in movieland were not too encouraging. She landed bit parts in two films and had difficulty paying her small rent. But then Raquel met Patrick Curtis (née Smith), an enterprising former child actor (he played Olivia de Havilland's baby in *Gone With the Wind*) and press agent. They formed Curtwell Enterprises and set out to merchandise Raquel's main assets—her voluptuous figure and sensuous face. He got her a 20th Century-Fox contract and a couple of TV appearances, then married her and took her on a blazing publicity tour of Europe. The results were phenomenal. Without having appeared in a single important film, Miss Welch became a major international star, the undisputed sex goddess of the 60s and one of the highest paid women in the business. In 1971, Curtis left Welch and dissolved their partnership. But by then she was firmly entrenched in the Wonder Woman image he had created for her, a living symbol of the idealized mid–20th century female. Her career faltered in the 70s as film roles dried up, and she was forced to sue over a lost role in *Cannery Row* (1982), which was given to Welch then denied her in favor of the younger Debra Winger. Welch won the suit, and went on to shake her glamour image for a serious dramatic role in the telefilm *Right to Die*. In the 90s, the ever-youthful Welch endorsed fitness products including her own successful exercise video, and also appeared in an infomercial. Her daughter, Tahnee Welch, is also an actress.

FILMS: *A House is Not a Home* (bit), *Roustabout* (bit) 1964; *A Swingin' Summer* 1965; *Spara Forte... più Forte... non capisco/Shoot Loud... Louder... I Don't Understand* (It.), *Le Fate/The Queens* (It./Fr.), *Fantastic Voyage, One Million Years B.C.* (UK) 1966; *Le plus Vieux Métier du Monde/The Oldest Profession* (Fr./It./Ger.), *Fathom* (UK), *Bedazzled* (UK) 1967; *The Biggest Bundle of Them All* (US/It.), *Bandolero!, Lady in Cement* 1968; *Flareup, 100 Rifles, The Magic Christian* (UK) 1969; *Myra Breckinridge* 1970; *Hannie Caulder* (UK) 1971; *The Beloved* (Gr.), *Bluebeard* (Hung.), *Fuzz, Kansas City Bomber* 1972; *The Last of Sheila* 1973; *The Three Musketeers* (as Constance; UK) 1974; *The Four Musketeers* (again as Constance; UK), *The Wild Party* 1975; *Mother Jugs and Speed, The Prince and the Pauper/Crossed Swords* (UK), *L'Animal/Stuntwoman* (Fr.) 1977; *Naked Gun 33⅓: The Final Insult* 1994.

Weld, Tuesday. Actress. Born Susan Ker Weld, on Aug. 27, 1943, in New York City. At the age of three she became the sole support of her widowed mother and two siblings, working as a child model and later also as a TV performer. She had her first nervous breakdown at the age of nine, began drinking heavily at ten, and attempted suicide at 12. Making her screen debut at 13, she specialized in portraying unpredictable, cherubic-faced often predatory nymphets and sex kittens. She was often cast in low-grade exploitation films and soap operas and was largely ignored by serious critics. She drew more attention from the gossip columnists who saw in her freewheeling style of life a "menace" to the reputation of the industry. She went through a long period of depression and seclusion, during which she married, had a child, divorced, and saw her house burn down. Her film career seemed all but finished when fans began to notice that she had been a first-rate actress all along but had had the misfortune and bad judgment of being cast in bad films. In the mid-60s she became the center of a growing cult. Special Tuesday Weld film festivals have since been held in Manhattan and elsewhere. Her dramatic roles from the late 60s through the 90s, both in film and on television, were meatier and more varied. Miss Weld was married to Dudley Moore, then married violinst Pinchas Zuckerman.

FILMS: *Rock Rock Rock* 1956; *Rally Round the Flag Boys!* 1958; *The Five Pennies* 1959; *Because They're Young, Sex Kittens Go to College, High Time, The Private Lives of Adam and Eve* 1960; *Return to Peyton Place, Wild in the Country* 1961; *Bachelor Flat* 1962; *Soldier in the Rain* 1963; *The Cincinnati Kid, I'll Take Sweden* 1965; *Lord Love a Duck* 1966; *Pretty Poison* 1968; *I Walk the Line* 1970; *A Safe Place*

1971; *Play It as It Lays* 1972; *Looking for Mr. Goodbar* 1977; *Who'll Stop the Rain?* 1978; *The Serial* 1979; *Thief* 1981; *Author! Author!* 1982; *Once Upon a Time in America* 1984; *Heartbreak Hotel* 1988; *Falling Down* 1993; *Feeling Minnesota* 1996.

Weller, Peter. Actor. Born on June 24, 1947, in Stevens Point, Wisc. *ed.* North Texas State U.; AADA, New York. Lean, unfettered lead of screen and stage. An effective stage actor of contemporary drama (David Mamet and David Rabe), he established his dramatic and comedic capabilities on the screen before combining the two in his wry, deadpan performance in the title role in *Robocop* and *Robocop 2*.

FILMS INCLUDE: *Butch and Sundance: The Early Days* 1979; *Just Tell Me What You Want* 1980; *Shoot the Moon* 1981; *Of Unknown Origin* 1983; *The Adventures of Buckaroo Banzai Across the Eighth Dimension, Firstborn* 1984; *A Killing Affair* 1985; *Robocop* 1987; *Shakedown* 1988; *Cat Chaser, Leviathan* 1989; *Robocop 2* 1990; *Naked Lunch* 1991; *The New Age* 1994; *Mighty Aphrodite, Screamers* 1995; *Beyond the Clouds* 1996; *End of Summer* 1997.

Welles, Orson. Director, producer, screenwriter, actor. *b.* George Orson Welles, May 6, 1915, in Kenosha, Wisc. *d.* 1985. The second son of a wealthy inventor and a beautiful concert pianist, he showed remarkable gifts as a child, excelling at poetry, painting, cartooning, acting, the piano, and magic. At the age when most children first learn to read, he was versed in Shakespeare, staging his own little productions of the Bard's plays in his playroom. Raised in Chicago, he was educated informally in his early years. When his mother died in 1923, he embarked upon a world tour with his father, spending a good part of the trip in Shanghai. In 1926 he entered the private Todd School in Woodstock, Ill., where he enlivened the drama program with his performances and directorial interpretations of Shakespeare, Marlowe, and Ben Jonson as well as modern playwrights. After his father's death in 1927, the 12-year-old Welles became the ward of Dr. Maurice Bernstein, a Chicago physician. The name Bernstein would later figure prominently as that of the manager of Kane's newspapers in Welles's screen masterpiece *Citizen Kane,* as would incidents from the director's early life.

Graduating from Todd in 1931, Welles eschewed college, turning down several scholarships, and instead set forth on a sketching tour of Ireland. At Dublin he misrepresented himself to the director of the famous Gate Theatre as a star of New York's Theatre Guild and despite an erratic audition won a leading role in a production of 'Jew Suss' and later appeared in and directed several other plays. Encouraged by his success, he tried crashing the London stage but was unable to work there because of labor restrictions on foreigners. Snubbed by Broadway upon returning to the US in 1932, Welles resumed his travels, going to Morocco, then to Spain, where he fought in the bullring. Back in the US, he was finally able to secure a role with Katharine Cornell's road company, thanks to recommendations by Thornton Wilder and Alexander Woollcott. In 1934 he made his Broadway debut with Cornell's company as Tybalt in 'Romeo and Juliet' and married Virginia Nicholson, a Chicago socialite and actress. Also in that year he co-directed a four-minute short, *The Hearts of Age,* in which both he and his wife appeared, and gave his first performance on radio.

At about this time, Welles met John HOUSEMAN, with whom he began collaborating on productions for the latter's Phoenix Theatre Group. The two men later produced and directed for the Federal Theater Project, then, in 1937, formed the Mercury Theatre, which soon became famous for its original, bold productions. In the following year they branched into radio broadcasting with 'The Mercury Theatre on the Air,' an anthology program of quality drama that became noted for its experimental inventiveness. The program remains famous for its dramatization of H. G. Wells's 'The War of the Worlds' on Sunday evening, Oct. 30, 1938. Intended as a Halloween prank, the show's vivid description of an invasion by space creatures of Grovers Mills, N.J., was so realistic that thousands of listeners became panic-stricken, many evacuating their homes despite clear disclaimers that the broadcast was fictional. Welles played the lead and directed the broadcast from a script by Howard Koch.

During the spring of 1938, Welles made a 40-minute film, an adaptation of William Gillette's farce 'Too Much Johnson,' which he intended to use in conjunction with a Mercury Theatre stage production. The cast included Joseph Cotten, Virginia Nicholson, Edgar Barrier, Arlene Francis, Ruth Ford, Mary Wickes, John Berry, and composer Marc Blitzstein. The play never reached Broadway, and as a result the film was never shown publicly. The only known print of this reputedly fast-paced, hilarious spoof was destroyed in a 1970 fire at Welles's villa in Madrid. However, the experience was to prove useful when Welles ventured into a brilliant and erratic commercial film career in 1939.

Welles's entry into movies came about partly as a result of the Mercury Theatre's need for an infusion of cash to bring to Broadway 'Five Kings,' an ambitious anthology of scenes from Shakespeare plays. On the other hand, RKO, the studio that had lured Welles to Hollywood, was undergoing a severe financial crisis at the time and hoped to parlay Welles's growing reputation into success at the box office. Welles's initial assignment when he arrived in Hollywood was a screen adaptation of Joseph Conrad's *Heart of Darkness.* But the project proved too costly and technically complex and was soon abandoned. Welles then wrote scripts for two other films, *The Smiler with the Knife* and *Mexican Melodrama,* neither of which got past the preproduction stage. Meanwhile, Welles earned his keep at RKO as the offscreen narrator of the film *The Swiss Family Robinson* (1940).

Perhaps no other director's first publicly shown film has caused as great a stir or created a greater impact than Welles's *Citizen Kane* (1941). Even while it was being shot and edited, rumor and speculation abounded about the subject and content of the impending work of the "boy wonder" from the East. Welles's contract with RKO gave the tyro director total artistic control over production within the boundaries of a rather thrifty budget. He used this freedom to create a film of cataclysmic power, a screen work whose inventive construction and innovative cinematographic and sound techniques have greatly influenced filmmakers in America and elsewhere. *Citizen Kane* remains memorable for its creative use of the sound track, deep-focus camerawork (by Gregg TOLAND), and low-angle compositions. But the film's most striking achievement was the original structure of its story, capped by the clever imitation of narrative style of a "March of Time" newsreel.

The authorship of the excellent script of *Citizen Kane* has been a source of controversy from the start. Welles claimed sole credit for himself, and it took the intervention of the Writers Guild to secure co-screenplay credit for Welles's collaborator, Herman J. MANKIEWICZ. The screenplay went on to win an Academy Award. The controversy over the authorship flared up anew in the early 70s, when critic Pauline Kael, in *The New Yorker* magazine and later in *The Citizen Kane Book* (1971), set out to prove that Mankiewicz rather than Welles was the man most responsible for the film's screenplay, from the inception of the idea through the shooting script. Whatever the merits of the argument, *Citizen Kane* is above all a work of bold and inspired direction, and at least in that all-important respect it unquestionably belongs to Welles alone.

The release of *Citizen Kane,* initially scheduled for February of 1941, was delayed for several months as newspaper magnate William Randolph Hearst, on whom the character of Kane was largely modeled, exercised his considerable powers in an all-out effort to suppress the film. Hearst banned any mention of the film in his newspapers and offered to compensate RKO for all its expenses provided the studio destroy the negative and all existing prints. The ban on mentioning *Citizen Kane* was later lifted, and instead the Hearst newspapers began a systematic attack on the film. However, RKO withstood the pressure, and *Citizen Kane* opened in May to rave reviews, many of the critics hailing it as a masterpiece. (In 1958 it was included among the 12 best films ever made in a poll of international critics conducted in Brussels.) It was also well received by audiences in New York and other big cities but failed to sustain a box office in provincial theaters. The commercial failure of the initial release moved the disappointed RKO officials to strip Welles of creative freedom on the director's subsequent projects.

The effect of the restrictions became evident in Welles's next film, *The Magnificent Ambersons* (1942). This leisurely paced, pictorially graceful evocation of the American past was made under much closer studio supervision. Shortly after the completion of filming, in January of 1942, Welles left for South America to start shooting another film as part of his commitment to RKO. Entitled *It's All True,* the project was envisioned as a three-episode semidocumentary and was aimed at fostering Pan-American relations and countering Nazi propaganda in Latin America. Welles took along a rough cut of *The Magnificent Ambersons* and tried to co-ordinate the cutting long-distance with editor Robert Wise in Hollywood. The result was a 148-minute film that the studio, after disappointing sneak previews, insisted must be cut down to 88 minutes so that it could be presented as part of a double bill. Several key scenes were eliminated and two or three reels completely reshuffled in Welles's absence before the film was finally released in August of 1942 as part of a double bill with a Lupe Velez lowbrow comedy, *Mexican Spitfire Sees a Ghost.* It was ignored by large sections of the movie-going public and less than enthusiastically received by most of the critics. Only years later was it reappraised as a superior achievement of the American screen, even in its mutilated form.

Meanwhile, the corporate power struggle raging at RKO ended in defeat for Welles's main supporter there, Nelson Rockefeller, and victory for those executives who saw the company's future in the production of efficiently made little double features rather than prestigious quality films. *It's All True* was one of the first casualties of the new policy. Welles was recalled from Rio, and the staff of his Mercury Productions was ordered to vacate the RKO lot to make room for the production crew of a Tarzan movie. They were all promptly taken off the payroll. Adding insult to injury, Welles was dismayed to discover on returning from Brazil that another of his films, the espionage thriller *Journey Into Fear* (1943), had been edited in his absence without his final approval and previewed to the public with an unsatisfactory ending. Welles had produced the film, had co-written the script with Joseph Cotten, and appeared in it in a key featured role, but pressed for time, he had turned the directing duties over to Norman Foster, his collaborator on *It's All True.* Welles threatened to sue RKO, but the issue was finally settled when the studio permitted Welles to re-shoot and re-edit the final scenes. On a happier note, Welles, who had been divorced from his first wife since 1939, married Rita HAYWORTH, one of Hollywood's most glamorous stars, in 1943. The following year, Welles enhanced his own position as a screen star with an overpowering performance as Rochester in *Jane Eyre,* a film whose direction he probably influenced.

Hampered by a poor track record as a commercially viable director, Welles spent a couple of idle years before he was given another opportunity to direct by producer Sam Spiegel (then known as S. P. Eagle). To secure the assignment on *The Stranger* (1946), the director agreed to adhere closely to the completed script and to a preplanned scheme of editing. The result was a solidly workmanlike but uninspired and unremarkable suspense melodrama that Welles the actor dominated more than Welles the director. Commercially, it was the most profitable of Welles's films, but one that the director himself has called "the worst of my films," one that he clearly made to prove that he could turn out a conventional production without exceeding the schedule or the budget.

Welles's businesslike attitude in the making of *The Stranger* helped pave the way for his employment by Columbia's Harry Cohn as the director and co-star, with Rita Hayworth, of *The Lady from Shanghai* (1948). It was a surprising assignment, considering Cohn's earlier anger at Welles for having impaired the box-office value of Columbia's reigning sex siren by marrying Miss Hayworth. Shooting began in the fall of 1946 and proceeded under near-chaotic circumstances on locations in New York City and Mexico and on Errol Flynn's yacht off the shores of Acapulco. Welles rewrote many lines of the script as the shooting progressed, putting great stress on the actors, who responded with high-strung performances that suited the director's scheme.

The Lady from Shanghai is a bizarre morality thriller with a plot that is often confusing and a visual style that is free and spontaneous throughout and brilliant in a number of memorable scenes, most notably the climactic "hall of mirrors" sequence. In that sequence, a cold, calculating Hayworth and her long-suffering, crippled, scheming screen husband, played by Everett Sloane, repeatedly shoot at each other's multiple mirror images until they both die amid a symbolic heap of shattered glass. Also shattered during the filming of *The Lady from Shanghai* was the Welles-Hayworth marriage. As soon as the shooting ended in 1947, Miss Hayworth filed for divorce. Meanwhile, the film's release was held up as it went through several editorial revisions. Cohn and others at Columbia found the film's plot incomprehensible and were also seemingly alarmed by the damage to the stellar image of Miss Hayworth which might result from her screen portrayal of a monstrous character. *The Lady from Shanghai* was finally released in mid-1948, without much publicity or fanfare. It was a resounding commercial flop.

Labeled box-office poison by the major Hollywood studios, Welles reached out for his next project—a screen adaptation of 'Macbeth'—to an unlikely sponsor: Republic studios, home of the quickie serial and the B Western. Welles's lifelong love affair with Shakespearean drama is legendary. Ever since he first went to Hollywood he had tried to interest producers in a low-cost screen adaptation of 'Macbeth,' which he considered the most filmic of the Bard's plays. He finally persuaded Herbert Yates, president of Republic, to undertake the project in the hope of gaining a prestige production for his humble studio at a low risk. Welles stayed well within the boundaries of the brief shooting schedule and minuscule budget, but the technical deficiencies of the film, especially the poor sound track, and several mediocre performances combined to undermine the director's bold, unconventional concept of the play, and *Macbeth* (1948) was generally dismissed by critics as a failure.

Disenchanted with the ways of Hollywood and with the pariah status he had acquired at the major studios, Welles headed for a prolonged self-exile in Europe. Originally, he went to the Continent as an actor, to play on location the role of Cagliostro, the legendary charlatan, in Gregory Ratoff's *Black Magic* and that of Cesare Borgia in Henry King's *Prince of Foxes* (both released in 1949). He stayed on to play one of his most memorable screen roles, as black marketeer Harry Lime in Carol Reed's British classic *The Third Man* (1949) and later appeared in a number of other European productions, all the while saving his earnings and scraping together fragments of investment for his next project as director, a screen adaptation of Shakespeare's 'Othello.'

Othello (1952) was shot in spurts between acting assignments and fund-raising trips across the Continent. Without the organizational machine of Hollywood to support him, Welles handled the production of *Othello* and his subsequent European films in a haphazard, near-chaotic manner. Generally, the director's European productions lacked the technical polish of his Hollywood period. But in forfeiting the structure and discipline of the American movie capital, Welles seems to have gained greater creative freedom while at the same time achieving in his films a new level of artistic maturity. *Othello* was filmed at a Rome studio and on locations in Italy and in Morocco. Shooting began in 1949 in Morocco, where Welles happened to be working as the co-star of Henry Hathaway's *The Black Rose* (1950), but *Othello* was not completed until 1952. It was shown that year at Cannes but it wasn't released in the US until 1955. Despite the considerable liberties Welles took with the substance of Shakespeare's play, his *Othello* emerged as a daring and visually exciting screen production.

Welles's next undertaking, *Mr. Arkadin/Confidential Report,* was similarly made under difficult circumstances. The director began planning the film in 1951 but could not begin actual filming until 1954, when he finally got the necessary financial backing from Spanish and Swiss investors. The film was shown in Europe in 1955 but did not reach American shores until 1962. In *Mr. Arkadin,* a study of the shady background of a powerful mystery man, Welles hoped to recapture some of the ingredients that had made *Citizen Kane* a success. But at best he succeeded in parodying his own earlier work. The film has its impressive moments and an abundance of visual thrills, but on the whole it seems like an aimless exercise in self-indulgence.

In 1955, Welles started production on a film he never finished, a humorous screen adaptation of Cervantes' *Don Quixote.* Filming took place in Paris and in various Mexican cities with Mexican actor Francisco Reiguera in the title role and Akim Tamiroff as Sancho Panza. It was but one of several projects that Welles had started but could not—some say dared not—bring to a finish.

Welles married actress Paola Mori in 1956. During the same year, he interrupted his long absence from the US to appear in his own Broadway production of 'King Lear.' While in the country, he was offered the leading character role of a police chief in an upcoming screen melodrama that producer Albert Zugsmith was preparing for Universal. For some reason, the film's star, Charlton Heston, assumed that Welles would also direct the production. To keep his star happy, Zugsmith acquiesced, although the producer had had no such intention. Thus, acquiring the assignment through what was basically a misunderstanding, Welles proceeded to toss away the intended script, writing his own screenplay as a free adaptation of the Whit Masterson novel *Badge of Evil.* Renamed *Touch of Evil,* the film was shot at Universal's Hollywood studios and at Venice, Calif., and released in 1958. This nightmarish thriller of corruption was rather well received by American critics for its imaginative style if not for its simplistic good-versus-evil theme, but its US distribution was scant and unprofitable, dooming any hope Welles might have had of a Hollywood comeback. However, in Europe, and especially France, the film was welcomed as a masterpiece, and it won a prize at the 1958 Brussels World's Fair.

Returning to Europe, Welles resumed the pattern of appearing as an actor in other directors' films while raising funds for and preparing and shooting his own productions. His next film as director, a screen adaptation of Kafka's *The Trial* (1962), turned out to be one of his least satisfactory undertakings. The production was beset by budgetary and technical problems, inhibiting Welles from realizing some of his original intentions. At any rate, the outcome disappointed even the director's most loyal admirers.

Welles then tackled *Chimes at Midnight/Falstaff* (1966), an ambitious and intermittently inspired Shakespearean adaptation culled from scenes from the plays 'Richard II,' 'Henry IV' (Parts I and II), 'Henry V,' and 'The Merry Wives of Windsor.' The film had divided critical opinion. Some considered this to be Welles's most mature production, perhaps his greatest all-round accomplishment since *Citizen Kane,* while others, more cognizant of the film's technical imperfections, especially the poor sound track, dismissed it as clumsy and confusing. As portrayed by Welles, Falstaff, used by Shakespeare basically as comic relief, emerges here as a tragic universal symbol of humanity's innocence doomed by its own failure to come to grips with reality.

Welles's next film, *Une Histoire immortelle/The Immortal Story* (1968), was an hour-long intimate production, originally made for French TV. Pictorially lovely, it is a slow-moving, meditative miniature of a film, marred in its English-language dubbed version by an atrocious sound track. The director's lifelong fascination with magic and trickery found a most delightful expression in his next and last completed film, *F for Fake* (1975), which was based in part on documentary material shot by Frenchman François Reichenbach on the island of Ibiza. It is a witty, mischievous, wholly delectable essay on the essence of art and reality as reflected in the infamous exploits of art forger Elmyr de Hory and his neighbor-biographer Clifford Irving, who himself won notoriety as author of a fake biography of Howard Hughes. *The Other Side of the Wind*, an autobiographical film that was to star his friend actor-director John Huston as a struggling filmmaker, was never completed.

Back in America after nearly three decades of voluntary exile, Welles was honored in 1975 as a recipient of the American Film Institute's Life Achievement Award. No longer active as a director, he appeared frequently on television shows and in TV commercials, as well as in films, seemingly feeling no bitterness over the long separation and enjoying his newly acquired status as a widely admired prodigal son. In 1984 the Directors Guild of America bestowed on him its highest honor, the D. W. Griffith Award. Obesity had long been a problem for Welles, and it contributed to his death of a heart attack in 1985. Several films containing footage of Welles's performances were released posthumously. His reputation as a master filmmaker, albeit a frustrated one, has grown even stronger since his death, with retrospectives and with the regular appearance of his films on 'best of all time' lists. In 1993, the surviving body of *It's All True*, along with related footage, was released as a documentary by Richard Wilson, Myron Meisel, and Bill Krohn, entitled *It's All True: Based on an Unfinished Film by Orson Welles*.

FILMS: As director—*The Hearts of Age* (4-min. 16 mm short; co-dir. with William Vance; also act.) 1934; *Too Much Johnson* (40-min. 16 mm film intended as insert in stage play;

also co-prod., sc.; never shown publicly) 1938; *Citizen Kane* (also prod., co-sc., act. in title role) 1941; *It's All True* (semidoc.; partly dir. by Norman Foster; also prod., co-sc.; unfinished—released in 1993 with added footage), *The Magnificent Ambersons* (also prod., sc., offscreen narrator) 1942; *Journey Into Fear* (uncredited as co-dir. with Foster; also prod., co-sc., act.) 1943; *The Stranger* (also co-sc., uncredited; act.) 1946; *The Lady from Shanghai* (also sc., act.), *Macbeth* (also prod., sc., act. in title role) 1948; *Othello* (also prod., sc., act. in title role; filmed in Italy and Morocco) 1952; *Mr. Arkadin/Confidential Report* (also story, sc., art dir., cost., act. in title role; Sp./Switz.), *Don Quixote* (also co-prod., sc., act. as himself; unfinished) 1955; *Touch of Evil* (also sc., act.) 1958; *Le Procès/The Trial* (also sc., act.; Fr./It./Ger.) 1962; *Campanadas a Medianoche/Chimes at Midnight/Falstaff* (also sc., cost., act. as Sir John Falstaff; Sp./Switz.) 1966; *Une Histoire immortelle/The Immortal Story* (also sc., act.; orig. made for French TV) 1968; *The Deep* (also sc., act.; unfinished) 1969; *The Other Side of the Wind* (also sc.; unfinished) 1970; *F for Fake* (addnl. footage by François Reichenbach; also sc., act.; Fr.) 1975. As actor only—*The Swiss Family Robinson* (narr. only) 1940; *Jane Eyre* (as Edward Rochester), *Follow the Boys* (as himself) 1944; *Tomorrow Is Forever* 1946; *Duel in the Sun* (narr. only) 1947; *Black Magic* (as Cagliostro), *Prince of Foxes* (as Cesare Borgia), *The Third Man* (as Harry Lime; UK) 1949; *The Black Rose* 1950; *Return to Glennascaul* (medium-length) 1951; *Trent's Last Case* (UK), *L'Uomo la Bestia e la Virtù* (as The Beast; It.) 1953; *Si Versailles m'était conté/Royal Affairs in Versailles* (as Benjamin Franklin; Fr.), *Trouble in the Glen* (UK) 1954; *Three Cases of Murder* (UK), *Out of Darkness* (doc.; narr. only), *Napoleon* (as Gen. Hudson Lowe; Fr.) 1955; *Moby Dick* (as Father Mapple; UK/US) 1956; *Man with a Shadow/Pay the Devil* 1957; *The Long Hot Summer, The Roots of Heaven, Cinerama's South Seas Adventure* (narr. only), *The Vikings* (narr. only), *Les Seigneurs de la Forêt/Masters of the Congo Jungle* (doc.; co-narr. only; Belg.) 1958; *High Journey* (medium-length doc. made in France for NATO; narr. only), *Compulsion, Ferry to Hong Kong* (UK) 1959; *David e Golia/David and Goliath* (as King Saul; It.), *Crack in the Mirror, Austerlitz/Battle of Austerlitz* (as Fulton; Fr./It.) 1960; *I Tartari/The Tartars* (It./Yug.), *King of Kings* (narr. only), *Désordre* (short; Fr.) 1961; *Lafayette* (as Benjamin Franklin; Fr./It.), *Der grosse Atlantik* (doc.; narr. only; Ger.), *Rogopag/Laviamoci il Cervello* (It./Fr.) 1962; *The V.I.P.s* (UK) 1963; *The Finest Hours* (doc.; narr. only; UK) 1964; *La Fabuleuse Aventure de Marco Polo/Marco the Magnificent* (Fr./It./Afg./Eg.), *A King's Story* (doc.; narr. only; UK) 1965; *Paris brûle-t-il?/Is Paris Burning?* (Fr./US), *A Man for All Seasons* (as Cardinal Wolsey; UK) 1966; *Casino Royale* (UK), *The Sailor from Gibraltar* (UK), *I'll Never Forget What's 'Is Name* (UK) 1967; *Oedipus the King* (as Tiresias; UK), *Kampf um Rom* (as Emperor Justinian; Ger./It./Rum.) 1968; *L'Etoile du Sud/The Southern Star* (Fr./UK), *Tepepa* (It./Sp.), *Barbed Water* (doc.; narr. only), *Una su 13* (It./Fr.), *Michael the Brave* (Rum.), *House of Cards* 1969; *Battle of Neretva* (Yug./It./Fr.), *Start the Revolution Without Me* (narr. only), *The Kremlin Letter, Catch-22* (as General Dreedle), *Waterloo* (as King Louis XVIII; It./USSR) 1970; *Directed by John Ford* (doc.; narr. only), *Sentinels of Silence* (doc.; narr. only), *A Safe Place* 1971; *La Decade prodigieuse/Ten Days' Wonder* (Fr./It.), *Malpertuis* (Belg./Fr.), *I Racconti di Canterbury/The Canterbury Tales* (It.), *Treasure Island* (as Long John Silver; also co-sc.; UK/Fr./Ger./Sp.), *Get to Know Your Rabbit, Necromancy* 1972; *Bugs Bunny Superstar* (narr. only) 1975; *Challenge of Greatness/The Challenge* (doc.; narr. only), *Voyage of the Damned* (UK/US) 1976; *The Filming of Othello* (doc. about Welles at work, orig. made for German TV) 1978; *The Late Great Planet Earth* (on-camera co-narr. only), *The Muppet Movie* (cameo), *Tesla* (as J. P. Morgan; Yug.) 1979; *The Man Who Saw Tomorrow* (narr.), *Genocide* 1981; *History of the World Part I, Butterfly, Orson Welles a la Cinematheque* (doc.; Fr.) 1982; *Almonds and Raisins, In Our Hands* 1983; *Slapstick of Another Kind, Where is Parsifal?* 1984; *Transformers: The Movie* (v/o) 1986; *Someone to Love* 1987; *Hollywood Mavericks* (doc.) 1990.

Wellman, William A(ugustus). Director. *b.* Feb. 29, 1896, Brookline, Mass. *d.* 1975. A restless, vigorous youth, he was put on probation for car theft and dropped out of high school to join a professional minor-league hockey team. During WW I he joined the French army's Foreign Legion as an ambulance driver, and when America entered the war he became an ace pilot with the famed Lafayette Escadrille. He was invalided out of the service with a broken back after his plane was shot down and he was awarded the Croix de Guerre with four gold palm leaves and five US citations. Returning to civilian life, he quickly became bored with a succession of salesman's jobs and became a wing-walking stunt pilot in a barnstorming air show. A forced landing on the polo grounds on Douglas Fairbanks's estate led to the beginning of his film career. In 1919 he supported Fairbanks as a featured actor in the film *Knickerbocker Buckaroo* but found the experience petrifying and decided he was more interested in the production end of the business.

In three years Wellman worked his way up from messenger boy and property man to assistant director and in 1923 made his debut as director at Fox. He gradually progressed from low-budget Buck Jones Westerns to major productions. By 1927 he was sufficiently established to land a plum assignment at Paramount, the now-classic aviation film *Wings.* Drawing on his wartime experience, he created thrilling air sequences that remain impressive today. The film won Hollywood's very first best picture Academy Award.

Wellman's reputation was augmented in the 30s with such diverse productions as the gangster melodrama *The Public Enemy* (1931), which catapulted James Cagney to stardom, the highly romantic initial version of *A Star Is Born* (1937), the satiric comedy *Nothing Sacred* (also 1937), and the rousing Foreign Legion action adventure *Beau Geste* (1939). His reputation was further enhanced in the 40s with *The Ox-Bow Incident* (1943), a superb anti-lynching drama despite its technical and logical flaws, and two superior war films, *The Story of G.I. Joe* (1945) and *Battleground* (1949). But these and other films, often marked by a commitment to humanism, were all to frequently interspersed with routine productions of the Hollywood-factory mold.

Among Hollywood insiders, Wellman was known as "Wild Bill," because of his maverick personality and his frequent clashes with studio bosses. A hard-drinking, rough-talking man, he was a tough taskmaster on the set. On one occasion he got into a fist fight with Spencer Tracy and on another nearly came to blows with John Wayne. He was among the most colorful characters in the film colony and for many years enjoyed a hero's status because of his roisterous personality and the memory of his WW I exploits. After four unsuccessful marriages, he enjoyed a lasting union with Dorothy Coonan, who starred in his film *Wild Boys of the Road* (1933). He died at 79 of leukemia. According to his wishes, his body was cremated and the ashes scattered over the countryside from a plane. He had published a book of memoirs, *A Short Time for Insanity,* in 1974, and completed another, *Growing Old Disgracefully,* just before his death. His son, William Wellman, Jr., appeared in films in a variety of roles from the late 50s.

FILMS: *The Man Who Won, Second Hand Love, Big Dan, Cupid's Fireman* 1923; *The Vagabond Trail, Not a Drum Was Heard, The Circus Cowboy* 1924; *When Husbands Flirt* 1925; *The Boob, The Cat's Pajamas, You Never Know Women* 1926; *Wings* 1927; *The Legion of the Condemned, Ladies of the Mob, Beggars of Life* 1928; *Wings* (re-released with sound), *Chinatown Nights, The Man I Love, Woman Trap* 1929; *Dangerous Paradise, Young Eagles, Maybe It's Love* 1930; *Other Men's Women/The Steel Highway, The Public Enemy, Night Nurse, The Star Witness, Safe in Hell* 1931; *The Hatchet Man, So Big, Love Is a Racket, The Purchase Price, The Conquerors* 1932; *Frisco Jenny, Central Airport, Lilly Turner, Midnight Mary, Heroes for Sale, Wild Boys of the Road, College Coach* 1933; *Looking for Trouble, Stingaree, The President Vanishes* 1934; *Call of the Wild* 1935; *The Robin Hood of El Dorado* (also co-sc.), *Small Town Girl* 1936; *A Star Is Born* (also co-story), *Nothing Sacred* 1937; *Men with Wings* (also prod.) 1938; *Beau Geste* (also prod.), *The Light That Failed* (also prod.) 1939; *Reaching for the Sun* (also prod.) 1941; *Roxie Hart, The Great Man's Lady* (also prod.), *Thunder Birds* 1942; *The Ox-Bow Incident, Lady of Burlesque* 1943; *Buffalo Bill* 1944; *This Man's Navy, The Story of G.I. Joe* 1945; *Gallant Journey* (also prod., co-sc.) 1946; *Magic Town* 1947; *The Iron Curtain, Yellow Sky* 1948; *Battleground* 1949; *The Happy Years, The Next Voice You Hear* 1950; *Across the Wide Missouri* 1951; *It's a Big Country* (co-dir.), *Westward the Women, My Man and I* 1952; *Island in the Sky* 1953; *The High and the Mighty, Track of the Cat* 1954; *Blood Alley* 1955; *Goodbye My Lady* 1956; *Darby's Rangers, Lafayette Escadrille* (also story) 1958.

Wells, George. Screenwriter. Born on Nov. 8, 1909, in New York City. *ed.* NYU. The son of a vaudeville performer-writer, he began his career as a radio writer. He joined MGM in the mid-40s and has written screenplays, alone or in collaboration, for many films, mostly on the light side. In the early 50s he also produced a number of films. He won an Academy Award for the script of *Designing Woman.*

FILMS INCLUDE: *Till the Clouds Roll By* 1946; *The Hucksters, Merton of the Movies* 1947; *Take Me Out to the Ball Game* 1949; *Three Little Words, Summer Stock, The Toast of New Orleans* 1950; *Angels in the Outfield* 1951; *It's a Big Country, Everything I Have Is Yours* (also prod.) 1952; *I Love Melvin* (also prod.), *Dangerous When Wet* (prod. only) 1953; *Jupiter's Darling* (prod. only) 1955; *Don't Go Near the Water, Designing Woman* 1957; *Ask Any Girl* 1959; *The Gazebo, Where the Boys Are* 1960; *The Honeymoon Machine* 1961; *The Horizontal Lieutenant* 1962; *Penelope* 1966; *The Impossible Years* 1968; *Cover Me Babe* 1970.

Wells, Jacqueline. See BISHOP, Julie.

Wenders, Wim. Director. Born 1945. Leading representative of the young German cinema of the 70s, later a highly respected and influential filmmaker of the 80s and 90s. Anxiety and alienation and male wanderlust are frequent themes in his work. His first American effort was *Hammett*, under the auspices of Francis Ford Coppola's Zoetrope Studios. The experience was a disaster, resulting in the film's delay from 1980 to 1983, when it was released in a much-altered form. But Wenders's next outing, *Paris, Texas* (1984), won the Palme d'Or at Cannes and catapulted him to international critical acclaim. He won the best director award at Cannes in 1987 for the wistful, haunting *Der Himmel uber Berlin/Wings of Desire.*

FILMS: *Summer in the City (Dedicated to the Kinks)* (also act., prod., sc.) 1970; *Die Angst des Tormanns beim Elfmeter/The Anxiety of the Goalie at the Penalty Kick* (also sc.) 1972; *Der Scharlachrote Buchstabe/The Scarlet Letter* (also sc.) 1973; *Alice in den Stadten/Alice in the Cities* (also sc.) 1974; *Falsche Bewegung/Wrong Move* 1975; *Im Lauf der Zeit/Kings of the Road* (also prod., sc.) 1976; *Der amerikanische Freund/The American Friend* (also sc.), *Die Linkshandige Frau/The Left-Handed Woman* (prod. only) 1977; *Long Shot* (act. only) 1978; *Radio On* (assoc. prod.) 1979; *Lightning Over Water* (also act., sc.) 1980; *Als Diesel Geboren* (exec. prod. only), *Chambre 666* (also act.), *Der Stand der Dinge/The State of Things* (also sc.; film account of the troubled making of *Hammett*) 1982; *Hammett* (partially re-shot by Francis Ford Coppola; US) 1980–1983; *Aus Fer Familie der Panzereschen* (short), *Paris Texas* (US) 1984; *I Played It for You* (also act., addnl. cin.), *King Kong's Faust* (act. only), *Tokyo-Ga* (also sc., ed.) 1985; *Der Himmel uber Berlin/Wings of Desire* (also prod., sc.), *Yer demir, gok bakir* (prod. only) 1987; *Helsinki Napoli All Night Long* (act. only) 1988; *Aufzeichnungen zu Kleidern und Stadten/A Notebook on Clothes and Cities* (also act., sc., phot.) 1989; *Motion and Emotion* (act. only) 1990; *Bis ans Ende der Welt/Jusqu'au bout du monde/Until the End of the World* (also sc., story; Fr./Ger.) 1991; *In Weiter Ferne So Nah/Faraway, So Close!* 1993; *Beyond the Clouds* (co-dir. with Michelangelo Antonioni) 1996; *Lisbon Story* (also scr.) 1995; *The End of Violence* (also prod. story) 1997.

Wendkos, Paul. Director. Born on Sept. 20, 1922, in Philadelphia. *ed.* Columbia. He worked in the theater of the avant-garde and made numerous documentaries before embarking on a career as a feature director in the late 50s. He impressed visually aware critics with his stylish handling of low-budget melodramas but disappointed them when he was given bigger budgets to work with. On the whole, his work has been too inconsistent for a clear evaluation. He has also directed for TV, including episodes for 'Naked City' and 'Mr. Novak,' and TV movies that have been released theatrically abroad, notably 'Honor Thy Father' (1973).

FILMS: *The Burglar* 1957; *The Case Against Brooklyn, Tarawa Beachhead* 1958; *Gidget, Face of a Fugitive, Battle of the Coral Sea* 1959; *Because They're Young* 1960; *Gidget Goes Hawaiian, Angel Baby* 1961; *Gidget Goes to Rome* 1963; *Johnny Tiger* 1966; *Attack on the Iron Coast* (US/UK) 1968; *Guns of the Magnificent Seven* 1969; *Cannon for Cordoba* 1970; *The Mephisto Waltz* 1971; *Special Delivery* 1976.

Werker, Alfred L(ouis). Director. Born on Dec. 2, 1896, in Deadwood, S.Dak. In Hollywood from 1917, he worked in various production capacities before turning director in the mid-20s. His career began and ended (in the late 50s) with minor Westerns. However, in the intervening years he directed, for Fox and other studios, many medium-budget productions in a variety of genres. Most were routine, but several suggested the work of an unfulfilled talent, notably *The House of Rothschild* (1934), *The Adventures of Sherlock Holmes* (1939), *He Walked by Night* (1948), and *Lost Boundaries* (1949).

FILMS: *Ridin' the Wind* (co-dir. with Del Andrews) 1925; *Jesse James* (prod. only) 1927; *The Pioneer Scout* (co-dir. with Lloyd Ingraham), *The Sunset Legion* (co-dir. with Ingraham), *Kit Carson* 1928; *Blue Skies, Chasing Through Europe* (co-dir. with David Butler) 1929; *Double Cross Roads, Last of the Duanes* 1930; *Fair Warning, Annabelle's Affairs, Heartbreak* 1931; *The Gay Caballero, Bachelor's Affairs, Rackety Rax* 1932; *It's Great to Be Alive, Hello Sister!* (reworked version of Erich von Stroheim's unreleased film *Walking Down Broadway*), *Advice to the Forlorn* 1933; *The House of Rothschild, You Belong to Me* 1934; *Stolen Harmony* 1935; *Love in Exile* (UK) 1936; *We Have Our Moments, Wild and Woolly, Big Town Girl* 1937; *City Girl, Kidnapped, Up the River* 1938; *It Could Happen to You, News Is Made at Night, The Adventures of Sherlock Holmes* 1939; *The Reluctant Dragon* (Disney cartoon feature), *Moon Over Her Shoulder* 1941; *Whispering Ghosts, A-Hunting We Will Go, The Mad Martindales* 1942; *My Pal Wolf* 1944; *Shock* 1946; *Repeat Performance, Pirates of Monterey* 1947; *He Walked by Night* 1948; *Lost Boundaries* 1949; *Sealed Cargo* 1951; *Walk East on Beacon* 1952; *The Last Posse, Devil's Canyon* 1953; *Three Hours to Kill* 1954; *Canyon Crossroads, At Gunpoint* 1955; *Rebel in Town* 1956; *The Young Don't Cry* 1957.

Werner, Gosta. Director. Born on May 15, 1908, in Ostra Vemmenhog, Sweden. *ed.* Lund U. A former journalist, he entered films in the mid-40s and immediately established himself as one of Europe's most imaginative and eloquent directors of short subjects. The most famous among the many he has directed are the lyrical and rhythmically cut *Midwinter Sacrifice* and *The Train.* He has also piloted several somber features with less notable success and has also written several books and many articles on cinema.

FILMS INCLUDE (shorts unless otherwise noted): *Early Morning* 1945; *Midwinter Sacrifice* 1946; *Spring at Skansen* 1947; *Loffe the Vagabond, Miss Sun-Beam* (both features), *The Train* 1948; *The Street* (feature), *The Tale of Light* 1949; *Backyard* (feature) 1950; *Meeting Life* (feature), *Spring, To Kill a Child* 1952; *The Butterfly and the Flame* 1954; *Matrimonial Announcement* (feature), *City Twilight* 1955; *The Forgotten Melody* 1957; *Land of Liberty* 1958; *A Glass of Wine* 1960; *Living Color* 1962; *Human Landscape* 1965; *When People Meet* 1966.

Werner, Oskar. Actor. *b.* Oskar Josef Bschliessmayer, Nov. 13, 1922, in Vienna. *d.* 1984. He began playing bit roles in films while still attending high school. At the same time, he attended acting classes and in the early 40s he joined Vienna's famous Burgtheater. Although in uniform during WW II, he was kept from action by injuries he had received in a bombardment and was able to continue his acting career. He re-entered films as a leading man in 1948, but for several years he remained basically a stage actor and scored a personal triumph in Frankfurt with his portrayal of Hamlet. Meanwhile, on the screen he drew some international attention in Ophüls's *Lola Montès* (1955), but his film career really picked up only in the 60s, following his thoroughly convincing performance as Jules in Truffaut's *Jules et Jim/Jules and Jim.* An intelligent, sensitive actor with an admirable range, he later played lead roles in films of several nations and was nominated for an Oscar as best actor in the US production *Ship of Fools* (1965).

FILMS INCLUDE: *Der Engel mit der Posaune/Angel with the Trumpet* (Aus./UK) 1948; *Eroica* (Aus.) 1949; *Decision Before Dawn* (US), *Wonder Boy* (UK) 1951; *Lola Montès/The Sins of Lola Montes* (Fr./Ger.), *Der letzte Akt/The Last Ten Days* (Aus.), *Mozart/The Life and Loves of Mozart* (Aus.) 1955; *Jules et Jim/Jules and Jim* (Fr.) 1961; *Ship of Fools* (US), *The Spy Who Came in from the Cold* (UK) 1965; *Fahrenheit 451* (UK) 1966; *Interlude* (UK), *The Shoes of the Fisherman* (US) 1968; *Voyage of the Damned* (UK) 1976.

Wertmuller, Lina. Director. Born Arcangela Felice Assunta Wertmuller von Elgg, on Aug. 14, 1928, in Rome. The daughter of a Roman lawyer of aristocratic Swiss ancestry, she was by her own admission a rebellious and difficult child and was thrown out of more than a dozen Catholic schools but eventually started her own working life as a schoolteacher. Her father wanted her to become a lawyer, but she was drawn to the theater through the influence of Flora, a schoolmate who later married Marcello Mastroianni. She enrolled at Rome's Theatre Academy and, after graduating, toured Europe with a puppet show. She later worked for ten years in the legitimate theater as actress, director, and playwright. It was there that she first directed Giancarlo GIANNINI, who would one day become the favorite star of her films. It was through her friendship with the Mastroiannis that Miss Wertmuller got her first job in films, as an assistant of director Federico Fellini on *8½* (1963). During that same year she wrote and directed her own first film, *I Basilischi/The Lizards.* The film was favorably received by Italian critics but hardly exhibited abroad. Wertmuller's second film, the multi-episode *Questa Volta parliamo di Uomini/Let's Talk About Men* (1965), was made on a very tight budget and looked it. After that, she began her long and fruitful association with Giannini, who starred in most of her subsequent films and became a partner in her production company, Liberty Films. It wasn't until her fifth picture, *Mimi Metallurgio Ferito nell'Onore/The Seduction of Mimi* (1972), that Wertmuller began asserting herself on the international scene, winning the best director award at Cannes. Characteristically, the film dealt seriocomically with sex, politics, and social mores, pitting a Chaplinesque little guy against a system he cannot fully comprehend, elements Wertmuller further developed in her subsequent product, *Film d'Amore e d'Anarchia/Love and Anarchy* (1973) and *Tutto a Posto e Niente in Ordine/All Screwed Up* (1974). She reached a new level of maturity and complexity with *Travolti da un Insolito Destino nell'Azzurro Mare d'Agosto/Swept Away* (1974), a sociopolitical allegory masqueraded as a battle-of-the-sexes tragicomedy, and achieved her first true masterpiece with *Pasqualino Settebellezze/Seven Beauties* (1976). American critics vied for superlatives in lavishing praise on *Seven Beauties,* a terrifying vision of life and death, pride and degradation, honor and survival in a Nazi concentration camp, intensified by Wertmuller's sense of the comic and the absurd and deepened by her humanity and taste for paradox. For her work on the film, she became the first woman to be nominated for an Academy Award for directing.

After *Seven Beauties,* Wertmuller became a virtual cult figure in the United States and other countries outside Italy. Following the film's huge success, she was signed by Warner Bros. on an exclusive contract to direct four films in the English language, at least two in the US. In 1977 she completed the first film under the agreement, *The End of the World in Our Usual Bed in a Night Full of Rain,* starring Giannini and Candice Bergen. The film opened in January of 1978 to generally negative reviews from disappointed critics. Later in that year, Miss Wertmuller and Warner Bros. mutually canceled their agreement and she returned to independent work.

An energetic, inexhaustible worker, Miss Wertmuller has the reputation of a slave driver on the set, a temperamental tyrant who bullies her actors into submission. She is also famous for her spontaneous invention and has been known to change many a scene on the spur of the moment, overhauling a minutely detailed script and rendering useless many weeks of preparation. Her ratio of shooting (total footage filmed versus the length of the actual film screened) on *Seven Beauties* was a wasteful 50:1. She works closely with her husband, Enrico Job, a sculptor and conceptual artist, who is her business partner and regular set designer. She has written the scripts for all her own films and has contributed screenplays, alone or in collaboration, for several films of other directors.

FILMS (as director-screenwriter): *I Basilischi/The Lizards* 1963; *Questa Volta parliamo di Uomini/Let's Talk About Men* 1965; *Rita la zanzara/Rita the Mosquito* (directed musical numbers only) 1966; *Non stuzzicate la zanzara/Don't Sting the Mosquito* 1967; *Mimi Metallurgio Ferito nell'Onore/The Seduction of Mimi* 1972; *Film d'Amore e d'Anarchia/Love and Anarchy* 1973; *Tutto a Posto e Niente in Ordine/All Screwed Up, Travolti da un Insolito Destino nell'Azzurro Mare d'Agosto/Swept Away* 1974; *Pasqualino Settebellezze/Seven Beauties* 1976;

The End of the World in Our Usual Bed in a Night Full of Rain (US), *Shimmy Lagano Tarantelle e Vino* 1978; *Si sospettano moventi politici/Blood Feud* 1979; *Scherzo del Destino in Agguato Dietro L'Angolo Come un Brigante di Strada/A Joke of Destiny Lying in Wait Around the Corner Like a Robber* 1983; *Un Complicato Intrigo di Donne, Vicoli e Delitti/A Complex Plot About Women Alleys and Crimes, Sotto Sotto/Softly Softly* 1985; *Notte d'Estate con Profilo Greco Occhi a Mandorla e Odore di Basilico/Summer Night with Greek Profile Almond Eyes and Scent of Basil* 1986; *Il Decimo Clandestino/The Tenth One in Hiding, In una Notte di Chiaro di Luna o Di Cristallo o ol Genere ol Fuoco o di Vento Purche sia Amore/Of Crystal or Cinders Fire or Wind as Long as It's Love* 1989; *Sabato Domenica e Lunedi/Saturday Sunday and Monday* 1990; *Me Let's Hope I Make It* 1993; *Ciao Professore* (also co-sc.) 1994; *The Nymph* 1996; *The Worker and the Hairdresser* 1997.

West, Adam. Actor. Born William Anderson, on Sept. 19, 1928, in Walla Walla, Wash. *ed.* Whitman Coll. Leading man of American TV and films. His big-screen career has been minor, but on the small tube he enjoyed long stretches of popularity, first as Robert Taylor's co-star in 'The Detectives,' then in the title role of the 'Batman' series.

FILMS INCLUDE: *The Young Philadelphians* 1959; *Geronimo* 1962; *Tammy and the Doctor, Soldier in the Rain* 1963; *Robinson Crusoe on Mars* 1964; *Mara of the Wilderness* 1965; *Batman* (title role) 1966; *The Girl Who Knew Too Much* 1969; *The Marriage of a Young Stockbroker* 1971; *Partisani/ Hell River* (Yug./US) 1974; *The Specialist* 1975; *Hooper* 1978; *The Happy Hooker Goes to Hollywood* 1980; *Swamp Thing, One Dark Night* 1982; *Hellriders* 1984; *Young Lady Chatterly 2* 1985; *Zombie Nightmare* 1986; *Doin' Time on Planet Earth* 1988; *Omega Cop, Mad About You* 1990; *Return Fire, Maximum Xul* 1991; *Night Raiders* 1992; *The New Age* 1994.

West, Billy. Actor. *b.* Roy B. Weissberg, in 1893, in Russia. *d.* 1975. In the US with his Jewish immigrant parents from the age of two, he was raised in Chicago, where his father supported the family as a peddler. Billy quit school at 14 and began performing in vaudeville as William B. West. In 1915 he developed an act, imitating Charlie Chaplin, on the strength of which he was offered a film role in 1916. For the next few years West starred in many comedy shorts for a succession of small production companies and enjoyed moderate success as the best of several Chaplin imitators. He later developed his own comic character. His supporting casts included such future stars as Oliver Hardy and Leatrice Joy. His films were made in Chicago, Florida, New York, and finally California. He appeared in several features as well as in many shorts.

FILMS INCLUDE: *His Waiting Career* 1916; *His Day Out, Cupid's Rival, The Straight and the Narrow* 1917; *The Slave, The Rogue, Playmates, He's In Again* 1918; *A Wild Woman* 1919; *Sweethearts* 1921; *Don't Be Foolish* 1923(?); *Thrilling Youth* (feature; also prod.) 1926; *Lucky Fool* (feature) 1927; *The Diamond Trail* (feature) 1933; *Motive for Revenge* (feature) 1935.

West, Mae. Actress. *b.* Aug. 17, 1892, Brooklyn, N.Y. *d.* 1980. The daughter of a heavyweight boxer, she became an entertainer at the age of five. After several years in stock, she moved into burlesque, where she was billed as "The Baby Vamp." At 14 she began appearing in vaudeville and Broadway revues and was the first to introduce the shimmy to the stage. During that period (1907–18) she frequently rewrote her material and soon felt confident that she could write a play. In 1926 she caused a sensation with her first play, 'Sex,' which she wrote, produced, and directed on Broadway. The law stepped in to stop the show, and Miss West was brought to court on charges of obscenity and jailed for ten days on Welfare Island. She directed, but did not appear in, her next play 'Drag' (1927), about homosexuals. It was a smash hit in Paterson, N.J., but she was warned not to bring it to Broadway. She scored a triumph on Broadway and later on the road with her 1928 play 'Diamond Lil' and after two additional stage successes she accepted a Paramount offer to star in films.

Preceded by her reputation, she inevitably clashed head-on with the Hollywood censors, but with typical shrewdness she managed to bring across in her films her message of sex by innuendo and double entendre. She wrote her own lines and collaborated on the script and dialogue for most of her films. Her witticisms soon became part of the national folklore. Phrases like "It's better to be looked over than overlooked" and "It's not the men in my life that count; it's the life in my men" found their way into the public domain, and lines like "Come up and see me sometime" and "Beulah, peel me a grape" were among the most frequently imitated and parodied in show business.

Blowsy and buxom, Miss West owed much of her popularity as a star to her ability to be both a sex symbol and a parody of her own image as a sex symbol at one and the same time. In 1935 she was the highest paid woman in the United States. At the height of her popularity, pilots and sailors named their inflatable emergency life jackets after her. Throughout the 30s, each of her films was anticipated by fans as an event. Her co-stars ranged from Cary Grant to W. C. Fields. But by the end of the decade she seemed to be running out of steam. She made what she thought would be her last film in 1943, and it was not a success. She returned to Broadway with a revue, 'Catherine Was Great,' based on material for a film about Catherine the Great that she had proposed as a project to Paramount in the late 30s. In 1947 she took 'Diamond Lil' on a tour of England and the US which lasted several years. In 1954, at the age of 62, she started a nightclub act in which she was surrounded by musclemen. It enjoyed an enormous success for three years.

By now a show business legend, Miss West disappeared from the public eye for more than a decade, except for a single guest spot on TV. In 1959 she published an autobiography, *Goodness Had Nothing to Do with It.* In 1970, at the age of 78, she made a comeback in *Myra Breckinridge* which wasn't spoiled by the failure of the film. She wrote her own dialogue. She stole the show during the film's New York premiere and announced that her next project would be a new screen adaptation of her play 'Diamond Lil.' In 1978, at the age of 85, she lasciviously returned to the screen as the star of *Sextette.*

FILMS: *Night After Night* 1932; *She Done Him Wrong* (also play basis, 'Diamond Lil'), *I'm No Angel* (also story, sc.) 1933; *Belle of the Nineties* (also story, sc.) 1934; *Goin' to Town* (also sc.) 1935; *Klondike Annie* (also co-story, co-sc.), *Go West Young Man* (also sc.) 1936; *Every Day's a Holiday* (also story, sc.) 1938; *My Little Chickadee* (also co-sc.) 1940; *The Heat's On* 1943; *Myra Breckinridge* (also co-dial.) 1970; *Sextette* (also play basis) 1978.

West, Raymond B. Director. *b.* 1886, Chicago. *d.* 1918. A former gas bill collector, he entered films in 1909 as an apprentice and in 1912 joined the Thomas Ince company as a special-effects expert. He soon began directing but for a while continued as an effects specialist and scored a technical coup staging a volcanic eruption for Reginald Barker's *The Wrath of the Gods* (1914). In addition to directing many films himself during his few remaining years, he collaborated with Ince and Reginald Barker on the direction of the company's most ambitious film, *Civilization* (1916).

FILMS INCLUDE: *The Altar of Death* 1912; *The Witch of*

Salem 1913; *Civilization* (co-dir. with Thomas Ince and Reginald Barker), *The Moral Fabric, The Payment, The Wolf Woman, The Female of the Species* 1916; *Madcap Madge, Paddy O'Hara, Redemption* 1917; *Those Who Pay, Within the Cup* 1918.

West, Roland. Director. *b.* 1887, Cleveland. *d.* 1952. A stage actor from his teens, he played juvenile leads in stock and in vaudeville before turning director and producer of Hollywood silents and early talkies. His film work was sparse but quite highly regarded for its creation of atmosphere. His wife, Jewel Carmen, starred in several of his films.

FILMS: *De Luxe Annie* 1918; *The Silver Lining* (also prod., story), *Nobody* (also prod., story, co-sc.) 1921; *The Unknown Purple* (also co-play basis, co-sc.) 1923; *The Monster* 1925; *The Bat* (also prod., adapt.) 1926; *The Dove* (also co-adapt.) 1928; *Alibi* (also prod., sc.) 1929; *The Bat Whispers* (also sc.), *Corsair* 1931.

Westcott, Helen. Actress. Born Myrthas Helen Hickman, in 1928, in Hollywood, Calif. A stage actress from childhood, she made a single screen appearance as a child in Reinhardt's *A Midsummer Night's Dream* (1935). She returned to films as an adult in the late 40s and for a decade played standard feminine leads and second leads in mainly routine productions.

FILMS INCLUDE: *A Midsummer Night's Dream* 1935; *Adventures of Don Juan* 1948; *Flaxy Martin, Homicide, The Girl from Jones Beach* 1949; *Three Came Home, The Gunfighter* 1950; *Take Care of My Little Girl, The Secret of Convict Lake* 1951; *Phone Call from a Stranger, The Return of the Texan, With a Song in My Heart* 1952; *The Charge at Feather River, Cow Country, Abbott and Costello Meet Dr. Jekyll and Mr. Hyde* 1953; *Hot Blood* 1956; *God's Little Acre, The Last Hurrah, Invisible Avenger* 1958; *Studs Lonigan* 1960; *Bourbon Street Shadows* 1962; *Pieces of Dreams, I Love My Wife* 1970.

Westley, Helen. Actress. *b.* Henrietta Meserole Manney, Mar. 28, 1875, Brooklyn, N.Y. *d.* 1942. A graduate of the American Academy of Dramatic Arts, she appeared on Broadway at the turn of the century, then worked in vaudeville and stock and was among the founders of the Greenwich Square Players in 1915 and the Theatre Guild in 1918. She appeared in many of the Guild's productions through 1934, when she settled in Hollywood as a character actress. She played crusty, often domineering, old matrons in many films of the 30s, mainly for Fox.

FILMS INCLUDE: *Moulin Rouge, Death Takes a Holiday, The House of Rothschild, Anne of Green Gables* 1934; *Roberta, Splendor* 1935; *Show Boat, Dimples, Banjo on My Knee, Stowaway* 1936; *Cafe Metropole, Heidi, I'll Take Romance* 1937; *The Baroness and the Butler, Rebecca of Sunnybrook Farm, Alexander's Ragtime Band* 1938; *Zaza, Wife Husband and Friend* 1939; *Lillian Russell, All This and Heaven Too* 1940; *Adam Had Four Sons, Sunny* 1941; *Bedtime Story, My Favorite Spy* 1942.

Westman, Nydia. Actress. *b.* Feb. 19, 1902, New York City. *d.* 1970. The daughter of actor-composer Theodore Westman and actress-playwright Lily Wren Westman, she began her stage career as a child, appearing in her family's act. From the age of 16, she appeared in many Broadway and stock productions and from 1932 appeared regularly in films. A pudgy little woman, she played supporting roles, mainly comic, in many Hollywood productions, often as a nervous old maid.

FILMS INCLUDE: *Strange Justice* 1932; *King of the Jungle, Bondage, The Way to Love, Little Women* 1933; *The Trumpet Blows, One Night of Love* 1934; *Sweet Adeline, A Feather in Her Hat* 1935; *The Invisible Ray, The Gorgeous Hussy, Craig's Wife* 1936; *Bulldog Drummond's Revenge* 1937; *The Goldwyn Follies* 1938; *When Tomorrow Comes, The Cat and the Canary* 1939; *Forty Little Mothers* 1940; *The Bad Man, The Chocolate Soldier* 1941; *They All Kissed the Bride* 1942; *Princess O'Rourke* 1943; *The Late George Apley* 1947; *The Velvet Touch* 1948; *The Chase, The Swinger* 1966; *The Horse in the Gray Flannel Suit* 1968; *Rabbit Run* 1970.

Westmores. Family of Hollywood makeup artists who dominated the profession for more than half a century and whose descendants continue to work in films. The dynasty was founded by George Westmore (1879–1931), a British wigmaker and "tonsorial saloon" operator who, after emigrating to the US, began his career as a movie makeup artist at the Metro studios in Hollywood in 1917. At a time when many actors still applied their own makeup, Westmore experimented with diverse techniques and established standards that are still in use. Westmore taught the craft to his six American-born sons, Montague or Monte (1902–40), Perc (1904–70), Ernest or Ern (1904–68), Wally (1906–73), Bud (1918–73), and Frank (1923–85). After George's death in 1931, the sons went on to illustrious film careers of their own in addition to founding the House of Westmore, a Hollywood beauty salon in business from 1936 to 1965, and the House of Westmore cosmetics company. Monte or Mont, the eldest, signed with Selznick International and supervised the makeup for *Gone With the Wind* (1939) just before his untimely death. Perc, who worked on such Warner Bros. films as *Casablanca* (1943), became an authority on feminine beauty. Ern did makeup for 20th Century-Fox and low-budget Eagle-Lion. Wally, whose credits included *Dr. Jekyll and Mr. Hyde* (1932), headed Paramount's makeup department for 43 years. Bud, who was christened Hamilton Adolph but changed his name to George Hamilton after World War II started, headed Universal's makeup department, with a specialty in monsters, for 24 years. Frank, the youngest, did the makeup for De Mille's remake of *The Ten Commandments* (1956) and worked regularly in TV and films until his death in 1985. As the last surviving brother, Frank wrote a book about the clan, *The Westmores of Hollywood* (1976).

Scions of the Westmore dynasty continue to pursue the family business, including Mike or Michael George (*b.* 1938), a son of Monte, who is skilled in special makeup effects and whose credits include *Rocky* (1976), *Raging Bull* (1980), *Blade Runner* (1982), *2010* (1984), *Mask* (co-makeup, 1985), *The Clan of the Cave Bear* (1986), *Roxanne* (1987), and *Revenge* (1990). Also working in films are Kevin (*Predator 2*, co-makeup, 1990), Marvin (*The Buddy Holly Story*, 1978), Monty Jr. (*Blaze*, 1989), and Pamela S. (*Dominick and Eugene*, 1988).

FILMS INCLUDE: Bud—*Detour* 1945; *The Wistful Widow of Wagon Gap, Ride the Pink Horse, A Double Life* 1947; *Abbott and Costello Meet Frankenstein, Letter from an Unknown Woman, The Naked City* 1948; *Johnny Stool Pigeon, Abbott and Costello Meet the Killer Boris Karloff* 1949; *Spy Hunt* 1950; *The Strange Door* 1951; *It Came from Outer Space* 1953; *Abbott and Costello Meet Dr. Jekyll and Mr. Hyde, The Creature from the Black Lagoon* 1954; *The Mole People* 1956; *Man of a Thousand Faces* 1957; *Operation Petticoat, Pillow Talk* 1959; *Spartacus, The Great Impostor* 1960; *Tammy Tell Me True* 1961; *That Touch of Mink, To Kill a Mockingbird* 1962; *The List of Adrian Messenger* 1963; *Island of the Blue Dolphins, McHale's Navy, Send Me No Flowers* 1964; *The War Lord* 1965; *Munster Go Home* 1966; *Thoroughly Modern Millie* 1967; *Madigan, The Secret War of Harry Frigg* 1968; *Tell Them Willie Boy Is Here* 1969; *Skullduggery* 1970; *Soylent Green* 1973.

Ern—*Under the Pampas Moon, Dante's Inferno* 1935; *Human Cargo* 1936; *The Gangster, Railroaded* 1947; *He Walked by Night, The Noose Hangs High* 1948; *Port of New York, Red Stallion in the Rockies* 1949; *One Too Many* 1950.

Frank—*Canon City* 1948; *Storm Warning* 1950; *Rancho Notorious* 1952; *The Ten Commandments* 1956; *My Geisha* 1962; *Irma La Douce* 1963; *Who's Been Sleeping in My Bed?* 1963; *What a Way to Go* 1964; *Two Mules for Sister Sara* 1970; *Farewell My Lovely* 1975; *Being There* 1979; *Just One of the Guys* 1985.

Monte—*Forbidden* 1932.

Perc—*Doorway to Hell* 1930; *The Millionaire* 1931; *Footlight Parade* 1933; *Here Comes the Navy, Jimmy the Gent* 1934; *A Midsummer Night's Dream* 1935; *The Life of Emile Zola* 1937; *Each Dawn I Die, The Oklahoma Kid, The Private Lives of Elizabeth and Essex, The Roaring Twenties* 1939; *The Fighting 69th, Santa Fe Trail, They Drive by Night, Virginia City* 1940; *City for Conquest, High Sierra, The Maltese Falcon, Manpower* 1941; *Gentleman Jim, They Died with Their Boots On, Yankee Doodle Dandy* 1942; *Casablanca, Action in the North Atlantic* 1943; *The Mask of Dimitrios, Mr. Skeffington* 1944; *Mildred Pierce, Objective Burma!* 1945; *Cloak and Dagger, Night and Day* 1946; *Life with Father, The Two Mrs. Carrolls* 1947; *Key Largo, June Bride, Rope, The Treasure of the Sierra Madre* 1948; *Flamingo Road, The Great Gatsby, The Fountainhead, White Heat* 1949; *Caged, The Glass Menagerie, Young Man with a Horn* 1950; *The Good Guys and the Bad Guys* 1969; *There Was a Crooked Man* 1970.

Wally—*Dr. Jekyll and Mr. Hyde* 1932; *Alice in Wonderland, Island of Lost Souls* 1933; *Make Way for Tomorrow* 1937; *If I Were King* 1938; *The Great McGinty* 1940; *The Lady Eve, Sullivan's Travels* 1941; *The Major and the Minor, I Married a Witch, The Palm Beach Story, Star Spangled Rhythm* 1942; *For Whom the Bell Tolls* 1943; *Double Indemnity, Hail the Conquering Hero, The Miracle of Morgan's Creek* 1944; *The Lost Weekend, The Strange Love of Martha Ivers* 1946; *Road to Rio, Unconquered* 1947; *A Connecticut Yankee in King Arthur's Court, The Heiress, Samson and Delilah* 1949; *Sunset Boulevard, Union Station* 1950; *The Big Carnival, Detective Story, A Place in the Sun* 1951; *The Greatest Show on Earth, The Turning Point* 1952; *Stalag 17, The War of the Worlds* 1953; *The Bridges at Toko-Ri, Sabrina* 1954; *The Desperate Hours, We're No Angels* 1955; *The Ten Commandments, The Rainmaker* 1956; *Funny Face* 1957; *King Creole, Vertigo* 1958; *One-Eyed Jacks, Pocketful of Miracles* 1961; *The Man Who Shot Liberty Valance* 1962; *Come Blow Your Horn, Hud, The Nutty Professor* 1963; *The Patsy, Robinson Crusoe on Mars* 1964; *Sylvia, Village of the Giants* 1965; *Johnny Reno, The Oscar* 1966; *The President's Analyst* 1967; *The Odd Couple* 1968; *The Molly Maguires* 1970.

Weston, Jack. Actor. Born Jack Weinstein, in 1925, in Cleveland, the son of a shoe repairman. He began his training for the stage at the age of ten at the Cleveland Playhouse. He dropped out of school at 15, after his father died in an accident, and began a dual career as a movie theater usher and stage actor. After WW II service as a machine gunner and USO performer, he came to New York to study at the American Theatre Wing, supporting himself and his wife, actress Marge Redmond, as a dishwasher, elevator operator, and postal clerk, among other things. He began playing featured roles on Broadway and in television in 1950 and made his film debut in 1958. Rotund and balding, he has been used effectively in both comic and heavy character roles, typically as a clumsy ne'er-do-well. His career gained sudden momentum in the mid-70s when he starred on the stage in Neil Simon's 'California Suite' and on the screen in the film version of *The Ritz* (1976).

FILMS: *Stage Struck* 1958; *Please Don't Eat the Daisies* 1960; *All in a Night's Work, The Honeymoon Machine* 1961; *It's Only Money* 1962; *Palm Springs Weekend* 1963; *The Incredible Mr. Limpet* 1964; *Mirage, The Cincinnati Kid* 1965; *Wait Until Dark* 1967; *The Counterfeit Killer, The Thomas Crown Affair* 1968; *The April Fools, Cactus Flower* 1969; *A New Leaf* 1971; *Fuzz* 1972; *Marco* 1973; *Gator, The Ritz* 1976; *Cuba* 1979; *Can't Stop the Music* 1980; *The Four Seasons* 1981; *High Road to China* 1983; *The Longshot, RAD* 1985; *Dirty Dancing, Ishtar* 1987; *Short Circuit 2* 1988.

Wexler, Haskell. Director of photography, director, producer. Born in 1926, in Chicago. *ed.* U. of California. An amateur filmmaker since his teens, he made educational and industrial films for ten years before breaking into the feature film field as the cameraman of the celebrated semidocumentary *The Savage Eye* (1959). His later camera work gained increasing recognition in the industry, and in 1966 he won an Academy Award for the black-and-white cinematography of *Who's Afraid of Virginia Woolf?* At the same time, he sought other avenues of expression. In 1965 he co-produced *The Loved One*, which he also photographed; and produced, directed, wrote, and photographed a documentary, *The Bus*, about a trip by San Franciscans to join a civil rights march on Washington. His achievements in the 60s culminated in *Medium Cool* (1969), a poignant visual statement on violence in America, setting a small personal drama against the real turbulence of the 1968 Democratic convention in Chicago. Wexler directed, wrote, photographed, and co-produced this striking film, which made quite an impact on critics and the public. He later directed in collaboration several politically motivated documentaries while continuing to work on major feature productions as a cinematographer. His work on the visually breathtaking *Days of Heaven* has been widely praised. He has remained active in the 80s and 90s, lending his distinctive talents to many period or socially aware films, including *Matewan*. He won an Oscar for the cinematography of *Bound for Glory* (1976).

FILMS INCLUDE (as director of photography): *The Savage Eye* 1959; *The Hoodlum Priest, Angel Baby* 1961; *A Face in the Rain* 1963; *America America, The Best Man* 1964; *The Loved One* (also co-prod.), *The Bus* (doc.; also prod., dir., sc.) 1965; *Who's Afraid of Virginia Woolf?* 1966; *In the Heat of the Night* 1967; *The Thomas Crown Affair* 1968; *Medium Cool* (also co-prod., dir., sc.) 1969; *Gimme Shelter* (co-phot. with many others) 1970; *Brazil: A Report on Torture* (doc.; also co-prod., co-dir. with Saul Landau) 1971; *The Trial of the Catonsville Nine* 1972; *Introduction to the Enemy* (doc.; also co-prod., co-dir., co-sc. with Jane Fonda and others) 1974; *One Flew Over the Cuckoo's Nest* (co-phot.) 1975; *Underground* (doc.; also co-prod., co-dir., co-sc. with Emil De Antonio and Mary Lampson), *Bound for Glory* 1976; *Coming Home, Days of Heaven* (co-phot.) 1978; *No Nukes* (also co-dir.), *Second-Hand Hearts* 1980; *Richard Pryor: Live on the Sunset Strip, Lookin' to Get Out* 1982; *The Man Who Loved Women* 1983; *Latino* (dir., sc. only) 1986; *Matewan* 1987; *Colors* 1988; *Three Fugitives, Blaze* 1989; *Through the Wire* 1990; *Other People's Money* 1991; *The Babe, Through the Wire, The Rolling Stones at the MAX* 1992; *The Secret of Roan Inish* 1994; *Canadian Bacon* 1995; *Rich Man's Wife* 1996.

Whale, James. Director. *b.* July 22, 1896, Dudley, England. *d.* 1957. A former newspaper cartoonist, he began acting during WW I in a prisoner-of-war camp while in lieutenant's uniform. After the armistice, he made the stage his career, at first as an actor, then as a set designer and a director. He was imported to Hollywood in 1930 to direct the screen version of his stage success *Journey's End* and stayed to direct many other films. He is best remembered for his four stylish horror films—*Frankenstein, The Old Dark House, The Invisible Man,* and *The Bride of Frankenstein*—excellent examples of the genre, noted for their semi-expressionist mood and understated black humor.

But he also directed refined and intelligent films in other genres, usually adaptations from literature or the stage, marked by the same fluid camera movement, leisurely pace, emphasis on detail, and discriminating restraint that characterized his more famous horror pictures. He retired from films in the early 40s to pursue another passion, painting, but was lured back in 1949 for a project that was abandoned before completion. He drowned in his swimming pool under mysterious circumstances.

FILMS: *Hell's Angels* (dial. dir. only), *Journey's End* 1930; *Waterloo Bridge, Frankenstein* 1931; *The Impatient Maiden, The Old Dark House* 1932; *The Kiss Before the Mirror, The Invisible Man, By Candlelight* 1933; *One More River* 1934; *The Bride of Frankenstein, Remember Last Night?* 1935; *Show Boat* 1936; *The Road Back* (also prod.), *The Great Garrick* (also prod.) 1937; *Sinners in Paradise, Wives Under Suspicion, Port of Seven Seas* 1938; *The Man in the Iron Mask* 1939; *Green Hell* 1940; *They Dare Not Love* 1941; *Hello Out There* (episode for planned multipart film; made in 1949; never released).

Whalley-Kilmer, Joanne. Actress. Born Joanne Whalley on Aug. 25, 1964, in Manchester, England. Striking brunette stage and screen player. Before age 20, she began appearing at the Royal Court Theatre in England and later acted in New York. Active in film since the 80s, she was memorable in her arresting performance in *Scandal*, as Christine Keeler, linchpin of the Profumo scandal. Appeared in the TV miniseries *The Singing Detective*. Divorced from actor Val KILMER, with whom she has appeared in films.

FILMS INCLUDE: *Pink Floyd—The Wall* (UK) 1982; *Dance with a Stranger* (UK) 1985; *The Good Father, No Surrender* 1986; *To Kill a Priest* (US/Fr.), *Willow* 1988; *Kill Me Again, Scandal* 1989; *Navy SEALS* 1990; *Crossing the Line* (UK: Eng./Scot.), *Shattered* 1991; *Storyville* 1992; *The Secret Rapture* 1993; *A Good Man in Africa, Trial by Jury* 1994; *Some Mother's Son* 1996.

Wheeler, Bert. Actor. *b.* Albert Jerome Wheeler, 1895, Paterson, N.J. *d.* 1968. On the stage from boyhood, he became a vaudeville comedy headliner in his early 20s, in an act with his first wife, Betty. They achieved Broadway stardom in 'The Ziegfeld Follies' of 1923. In 1927, Ziegfeld teamed Wheeler with Robert WOOLSEY in the Broadway musical 'Rio Rita.' After repeating their stage roles in the screen version in 1929, they remained a highly successful comedy team until Woolsey's death in 1938, starring in many wacky comedy films, both features and shorts, which were largely ignored by the critics but were highly profitable at the box office. After Woolsey's death Wheeler appeared in various shows on Broadway and on the road and in occasional films. In the mid-50s he was a regular on the TV series 'Brave Eagle.' In the 60s he played nightclub engagements in Las Vegas and New York.

FILMS INCLUDE (with Woolsey unless otherwise noted): *Captain Fly-by-Night* (alone) 1922; *The Brown Derby* (sc. only) 1926; *Rio Rita* 1929; *The Cuckoos, Dixiana, Half Shot at Sunrise, Hook Line and Sinker* 1930; *Too Many Cooks* (alone), *Cracked Nuts, Caught Plastered, Peach O'Reno* 1931; *Girl Crazy, Hold 'Em Jail* 1932; *So This Is Africa, Diplomaniacs* 1933; *Hips Hips Hooray, Cockeyed Cavaliers, Kentucky Kernels* 1934; *The Nitwits* 1935; *Mummy's Boys* 1936; *On Again Off Again, High Flyers* 1937; *Cowboy Quarterback* (alone) 1939; *Las Vegas Nights* (alone) 1941; *The Awful Sleuth* (short; alone) 1951.

Wheeler, Lyle. Art director. *b.* Feb. 2, 1905, Woburn, Mass. *d.* 1990. *ed.* USC. A former magazine illustrator and industrial designer, he entered films in the mid-30s. In 1944 he was appointed supervising art director at 20th Century-Fox and in 1947 head of the art department. He designed many impressive sets for major films, alone or in collaboration, winning Academy Awards for *Gone With the Wind* (1939), *Anna and the King of Siam* (1946), *The Robe* (1953), and *The Diary of Anne Frank* (1959).

FILMS INCLUDE: *Garden of Allah* 1936; *A Star Is Born, The Prisoner of Zenda* 1937; *Nothing Sacred, The Adventures of Tom Sawyer* 1938; *Gone With the Wind, Intermezzo* 1939; *Rebecca* 1940; *Laura* 1944; *Hangover Square, A Tree Grows in Brooklyn* 1945; *Anna and the King of Siam, My Darling Clementine* 1946; *Forever Amber, Gentlemen's Agreement, Nightmare Alley* 1947; *Call Northside 777* 1948; *Thieves' Highway, Pinky, Twelve O' Clock High* 1949; *Panic in the Streets, All About Eve* 1950; *14 Hours* 1951; *Deadline USA, Viva Zapata!, The Snows of Kilimanjaro* 1952; *The Robe, Call Me Madam, Gentlemen Prefer Blondes* 1953; *River of No Return, Garden of Evil, Desiree* 1954; *Love Is a Many Splendored Thing, Daddy Long Legs, The Seven Year Itch* 1955; *Bus Stop, The King and I* 1956; *The Sun Also Rises, Peyton Place* 1957; *South Pacific, The Young Lions, Ten North Frederick, The Long Hot Summer* 1958; *Compulsion, Blue Denim, The Diary of Anne Frank* 1959; *From the Terrace, Wild River* 1960; *Advise and Consent* 1962; *The Cardinal* 1963; *The Best Man* 1964; *In Harm's Way* 1965; *Marooned* 1969; *Tell Me That You Love Me Junie Moon* 1970; *The Love Machine* 1971; *Posse* 1975.

Wheeler, René. Screenwriter, director. Born on Feb. 8, 1912, in Paris. He collaborated on screenplays and dialogue for a number of important French films and directed three flawed but intimately personal films of his own.

FILMS INCLUDE (as screenwriter): *L'Innocent/Bouquets from Nicholas* 1938; *La Cage aux Rossignols/A Cage of Nightingales* 1945; *La Vie en Rose* 1948; *Jour de Fête* 1949; *Premières Armes/The Winner's Circle* (also dir.) 1950; *Fanfan la Tulipe/Fanfan the Tulip* 1952; *L'Amour d'une Femme, Châteaux en Espagne* (also dir.), *Teodora Imperatrice di Bisanzio/Theodora Slave Empress* (It./Fr.) 1954; *Du Rififi chez les Hommes/Rififi* 1955; *Till l'Espiègle* 1956; *Méfiez-vous Fillettes/Young Girls Beware* 1957; *Vers l'Extase* (also dir.) 1960; *Le Crime ne paie pas/Crime Does Not Pay* 1962; *Le Journal d'une Femme en Blanc* 1965.

Whelan, Arleen. Actress. Born on Sept. 16, 1916, in Salt Lake City. Pretty redheaded leading lady of Hollywood films from the late 30s, a former beauty salon manicurist. She retired from the screen in the mid-50s following a sharp decline in roles. Her first of three husbands (all divorced) was actor Alex D'Arcy.

FILMS INCLUDE: *Kidnapped, Gateway, Thanks for Everything* 1938; *Young Mr. Lincoln, Sabotage* 1939; *Young People* 1940; *Charley's Aunt* 1941; *Castle in the Desert* 1942; *Ramrod, The Senator Was Indiscreet* 1947; *That Wonderful Urge* 1948; *Dear Wife* 1950; *Passage West, Flaming Feather* 1951; *The Sun Shines Bright* 1953; *Raiders of Old California* 1957.

Whelan, Tim. Director, screenwriter. *b.* Nov. 2, 1893, Indiana. *d.* 1957. A former stage actor and director, he entered films in 1920 as a screenwriter. He wrote gags and collaborated on the scripts of several Harold Lloyd silents, including *Safety Last* (1923), *Girl Shy, Hot Water* (both 1924), *The Freshman* (1925), and *Tramp Tramp Tramp* (1926). Turning director in the late 20s, he worked both in England and the USA. On the whole, his British films were better than the Hollywood ones. He often collaborated on his own screenplays.

FILMS (as director): In the UK—*Adam's Apple* 1928; *When Knights Were Bold* 1929; *It's a Boy, Aunt Sally/Along Came Sally* (also sc.) 1933; *The Camels Are Coming* 1934; *The*

Murder Man (also co-story, co-sc.; US), *The Perfect Gentleman* (US) 1935; *Two's Company* 1936; *Smash and Grab/Larceny Street* (also story), *The Mill on the Floss* (also co-sc.), *Farewell Again/Troopship, Action for Slander* 1937; *The Divorce of Lady X, St. Martin's Lane/Sidewalks of London* 1938; *Q Planes/Clouds Over Europe, Ten Days in Paris/Missing Ten Days* 1939; *The Thief of Baghdad/The Thief of Bagdad* (co-dir. with Ludwig Berger and Michael Powell) 1940. In the US—*The Mad Doctor, International Lady* 1941; *Twin Beds, Nightmare, Seven Days' Leave* (also prod.) 1942; *Higher and Higher* (also prod.) 1943; *Swing Fever, Step Lively* 1944; *Badman's Territory* 1946; *This Was a Woman* (UK) 1948; *Rage at Dawn, Texas Lady* 1955.

whip shot. See SWISH PAN.

whirly. See CRANE.

Whitaker, Forest. Actor. Born on July 15, 1961, in Longview, Tex. ed. Pomona Coll., USC (music). Solid, towering stage-trained character player. A former all-league defensive tackle in college, he concentrated on acting by appearing widely on the stage in the US and London. Debuting in film in 1982, he has demonstrated an impressive dramatic range in complex roles including the title role of jazz great Charlie Parker in *Bird* and the British soldier in *The Crying Game*. Gained best actor award at Cannes for *Bird*.

FILMS INCLUDE: *Fast Times at Ridgemont High* 1982; *Vision Quest* 1985; *The Color of Money, Platoon* 1986; *Good Morning Vietnam, Stakeout* 1987; *Bird, Bloodsport* 1988; *Johnny Handsome* 1989; *Downtown* 1990; *A Rage in Harlem* (US/UK, also prod.) 1991; *Article 99, The Crying Game, Diary of a Hitman, Consenting Adults* 1992; *Bank Robber* 1993; *Blown Away, Body Snatchers, Jason's Lyric, Lush Life, Ready to Wear, Smoke* 1994; *Species* 1995; *Waiting to Exhale* (dir. only) 1995.

White, Alice. Actress. *b.* Alva White, Aug. 28, 1907, Paterson, N.J. *d.* 1983. *ed.* Roanoke Coll. Pert, vivacious leading lady of late silent and early sound Hollywood films. A former secretary, she sneaked into films through the back door as a script girl for Josef von Sternberg and was given her first chance as an actress in John Francis Dillon's *The Sea Tiger* (1927). She was compared with Clara Bow and rose quickly to stardom, but her decline was nearly as swift, and by the mid-30s she was relegated to supporting parts. Her film career had ended by the late 40s and she later returned to secretarial work. At one time she was married to screenwriter-producer Sy BARTLETT.

FILMS INCLUDE: *The Sea Tiger, The Satin Woman, American Beauty, Breakfast at Sunrise, The Private Life of Helen of Troy* 1927; *The Big Noise, Gentlemen Prefer Blondes, The Mad Hour, Lingerie, Harold Teen, Show Girl* 1928; *Naughty Baby, Hot Stuff, Broadway Babies, The Girl from Woolworth's* 1929; *Playing Around, Show Girl in Hollywood, Sweet Mama, The Widow from Chicago, Sweethearts on Parade* 1930; *The Naughty Flirt, Murder at Midnight* 1931; *Employees' Entrance, Luxury Liner, Picture Snatcher, King for a Night* 1933; *Cross Country Cruise, Jimmy the Gent, Gift of Gab* 1934; *Sweet Music, Coronado* 1935; *Big City* 1937; *King of the Newsboys* 1938; *The Night of January 16th* 1941; *Flamingo Road* 1949.

White, Carol. Actress. *b.* Apr. 1, 1942, in London. *d.* 1991. Leading lady of British films. She began appearing on TV as a child and was seen in films from her teens. But it was in the late 60s that she established herself in a number of offbeat productions. Later troubles with drink and drugs led to her death of an overdose.

FILMS INCLUDE: *Circus Friends* 1956; *Carry on Teacher* 1959; *Beat Girl, Never Let Go, Linda* 1960; *A Matter of WHO* 1961; *Bon Voyage!* (US), *The Boys* 1962; *Slave Girls/Prehistoric Women, Poor Cow, I'll Never Forget What's 'Is Name* 1967; *The Fixer* (US) 1968; *Daddy's Gone A-Hunting* (US) 1969; *The Man Who Had Power Over Women* 1970; *Something Big* (US), *Dulcima* 1971; *Made* 1972; *Some Call It Loving* (US) 1973; *The Squeeze* 1977; *The Spaceman and King Arthur* 1978; *Nutcracker* 1982.

White, Chrissie. Actress. *b.* May 23, 1894, in London. *d.* 1989. A child star of early British silents, she matured into a highly popular leading lady. She married her frequent co-star and director, Henry EDWARDS.

FILMS INCLUDE: *For the Little Lady's Sake* 1908; *Tilly the Tomboy Goes Boating* 1910; *The Mermaid* 1912; *The Cloister and the Hearth* 1913; *David Garrick* 1914; *Barnaby Rudge, Sweet Lavender* 1915; *The Eternal Triangle, Broken Threads* 1917; *The City of Beautiful Nonsense* 1919; *The Amazing Quest of Mr. Ernest Bliss* 1920; *The Bargain* 1921; *Lily of the Alley* 1923; *The World of Wonderful Reality* 1924; *Call of the Sea* 1930; *General John Regan* 1933.

White, Jesse. Actor. Born on Jan. 3, 1919, Buffalo, N.Y. *d.* 1997. Raised in Akron, Ohio, he made his first amateur appearance on the local stage at the age of 15. But before breaking into the professional theater in the early 40s, he tried his hand at a variety of odd businesses, including selling beauty supplies and lingerie. He reached Broadway in 1943 via the vaudeville, burlesque, and stock company route. A Hollywood character actor since the early 50s, he has often played heels and small-time gangsters on the comic rather than the sinister side. He has also been featured in a number of TV series. In the late 60s he repeated in a Broadway revival his first, and probably most memorable, screen role, supporting James Stewart in *Harvey.* For 22 years, he played the repairman in a Maytag TV commercial.

FILMS INCLUDE: *Harvey* 1950; *Bedtime for Bonzo, Death of a Salesman* 1951; *Million Dollar Mermaid* 1952; *Gunsmoke* 1953; *Witness to Murder* 1954; *Not as a Stranger* 1955; *The Bad Seed* 1956; *Designing Woman* 1957; *Marjorie Morningstar* 1958; *The Rise and Fall of Legs Diamond* 1960; *On the Double* 1961; *It's Only Money* 1962; *It's a Mad Mad Mad Mad World* 1963; *A House Is Not a Home* 1964; *The Ghost in the Invisible Bikini* 1966; *The Reluctant Astronaut* 1967; *Bless the Beasts and Children* 1971; *The Brothers O'Toole* 1973; *Return to Campus* 1975; *Las Vegas Lady, Nashville Girl* 1976; *New Girl in Town* 1977; *The Cat from Outer Space* 1978; *Monster in the Closet* 1986; *Matinee* 1993.

White, Pearl. Actress. *b.* Mar. 4, 1889, Green Ridge, Mo. *d.* 1938. A farmer's daughter, she made her amateur stage debut at the age of six, playing Eva in a production of 'Uncle Tom's Cabin.' She then played child leads in many other plays. She bought a horse with part of her earnings and by the age of 13 was proficient enough a rider to join a circus as an equestrienne, but she suffered a spinal injury falling from a horse and was forced to leave the circus. She then performed in stock and traveling companies, but, failing to crash Broadway, she found a job as a secretary with the small Powers film company. An attractive, personable girl, she caught the eye of director Joseph A. Golden, who needed an urgent replacement for the ailing female lead of his forthcoming three-reel Western *The Life of Buffalo Bill.* Her success led to starring roles in more than 100 comedies, adventure dramas, and Westerns of several companies, mostly one or two reels long. Her frequent co-stars were Paul PANZER and Henry B. WALTHALL.

White's big break came when she was recruited by Louis Gasnier as the star of his serial for Pathé, *The Perils of Pauline* (1914). The serial enjoyed an enormous success and remains the best-known chapter play ever filmed. This and subsequent serials made Pearl the most popular star of her day, surpassing for several years the popularity of Mary Pickford and other leading stars of feature films. Her serials emphasized mystery and suspense more than action. She usually performed her own stunts, but because of her spinal injury required doubles (slightly built men) for the more demanding acrobatics. However, dissatisfied with her limited image as a serial heroine, she signed with Fox in 1920 as a leading lady in feature dramas. She wasn't too successful in her new role and returned to Pathé to do a serial in 1923. She made her last film in France the following year, then retired. She remained in France until her death. Betty Hutton and Pamela Austin portrayed her in loose screen biographies of 1947 and 1967 respectively. Both productions were titled *The Perils of Pauline.* Both of Miss White's husbands were actors, Victor C. Sutherland (1907–14) and Wallace McCutcheon (1919–21). Autobiography: *Just Me* (1919).

FILMS INCLUDE (serials are designated "S"): *The Life of Buffalo Bill, The Girl from Arizona, The Hoodoo, A Summer Flirtation, The New Magdalene, The Maid of Niagara, The Woman Hater* 1910; *Home Sweet Home, The Angel of the Slums, For the Honor of the Name, The Lost Necklace* 1911; *Pals, Bella's Beau, The Girl in the Next Room, Oh Such a Night!, The Chorus Girl* 1912; *Heroic Harold, Pearl as a Detective, Accident Insurance, The Girl Reporter* 1913; *Shadowed, The Ring, The Perils of Pauline* (S), *Lizzie and the Iceman, Willie's Disguise* 1914; *The Exploits of Elaine* (S), *The New Exploits of Elaine* (S), *The Romance of Elaine* (S) 1915; *The Iron Claw* (S), *Pearl of the Army* (S), *The King's Game* 1916; *The Fatal Ring* (S) 1917; *The House of Hate* (S), *The Lightning Raider* (S) 1918; *Black Secret* (S) 1919; *The White Moll, Black Is White, The Dark Mirror, The Thief* 1920; *A Virgin Paradise, The Mountain Woman, Know Your Men, Beyond Price* 1921; *Any Wife, Without Fear, Broadway Peacock* 1922; *Plunder* (S) 1923; *Terreur/Perils of Paris* (S; Fr.) 1924.

White, Ruth. Actress. *b.* Apr. 24, 1914, Perth Amboy, N.J. *d.* 1969. *ed.* Douglass College. Trained for the stage by Maria OUSPENSKAYA, she made her debut early in the 40s in stock. She reached Broadway in 1949 and subsequently gained much praise and a number of awards for her frequently offbeat characterizations, the last of which was the role of the landlady in Pinter's 'The Birthday Party.' In and out of films since the late 50s, she played some memorable character parts until her death of cancer. Miss White, who often played spinsters, never married.

FILMS: *Edge of the City* 1957; *The Nun's Story* 1959; *A Rage to Live, To Kill a Mockingbird* 1963; *Baby the Rain Must Fall* 1965; *Cast a Giant Shadow* 1966; *Up the Down Staircase, The Tiger Makes Out* 1967; *No Way to Treat a Lady, Hang 'em High, A Lovely Way to Die, Charly* 1968; *Midnight Cowboy, The Reivers* 1969; *The Pursuit of Happiness* 1971.

White, Wilfrid Hyde. See HYDE-WHITE, Wilfrid.

Whitelaw, Billie. Actress. Born June 6, 1932, Coventry, England. On the British stage since 1950, after some experience as an assistant stage manager, she rose to prominence in the 60s as a leading lady of the theater, television, and films. She won the British Film Academy (BFA) Award for *Charlie Bubbles.*

FILMS INCLUDE: *Bobbikins* 1959; *Hell Is a City, Mr. Topaze/I Love Money, Make Mine Mink* 1960; *No Love for Johnnie* 1961; *Charlie Bubbles, Twisted Nerve* 1968; *The Adding Machine* 1969; *Start the Revolution Without Me* (US), *Leo the Last* 1970; *Eagle in a Cage* 1971; *Gumshoe, Frenzy* 1972; *Night Watch* 1973; *The Omen* (US) 1976; *The Water Babies* 1979; *The Dark Crystal* (v/o; US), *An Unsuitable Job for a Woman* 1982; *Slayground* 1984; *The Chain, Shadey* 1986; *The Secret Garden* (US), *Maurice* (US) 1987; *The Dressmaker* 1988; *Joyriders* 1989; *The Krays* 1990; *Freddie as F.R.O.7.* (v/o) 1992; *Deadly Advice* 1994.

Whiteley, Jon. Child actor. Born Feb. 19, 1945, Monymusk, Scotland. Winner of a special Oscar for his performance in the 1953 British film *The Kidnappers* (released in the US in 1954 as *The Little Kidnappers*), he later appeared in only a handful of productions.

FILMS INCLUDE: *Hunted/The Stranger in Between* 1951; *The Kidnappers/The Little Kidnappers* 1953; *Moonfleet* 1955; *The Weapon, The Spanish Gardener* 1956; *The Capetown Affair* 1967.

"white telephone." A caustic appellation for a type of motion picture characterized by luxurious backgrounds and peopled with characters of social position, independent means, and a great deal of leisure. Hollywood produced scores of "white telephone" films in the 30s, at the height of the Depression era, when audiences seemed to prefer escapist fare to realistic social dramas. See also ITALY.

Whitlock, Albert J. Special effects artist. Born in 1915, in London. Technician and designer of special effects in numerous movies. Famed for his realistic matte paintings, he first gained recognition for designing the frightening special effects in Alfred Hitchcock's *The Birds* (1963), the same year he began a long association with Universal. He played a bit part in Mel Brooks's *High Anxiety* (1977), which fondly parodied the films of Hitchcock, with whom Whitlock had often worked. Whitlock shared Academy Awards for the visual effects in *Earthquake* (1974) and *The Hindenburg* (1975) and an Emmy for the effects in the miniseries *A.D.* (1985).

FILMS INCLUDE (alone or in collaboration): *The Man Who Knew Too Much* 1956; *Greyfriars Bobby* 1961; *The Birds, Captain Newman M.D.* 1963; *The Island of the Blue Dolphins, Marnie* 1964; *Mirage, The War Lord* 1965; *Ship of Fools* 1965; *Beau Geste, Munster Go Home, Tobruk, Torn Curtain* 1966; *The Reluctant Astronaut, Thoroughly Modern Millie, The War Wagon* 1967; *Hellfighters, The Shakiest Gun in the West* 1968; *Colossus: The Forbin Project, Topaz* 1969; *Skullduggery, Catch-22* 1970; *Diamonds Are Forever, The Andromeda Strain* (mattes only) 1971; *Slaughterhouse-Five* (matte superv.), *Frenzy* 1972; *The Day of the Dolphin, The Sting* 1973; *Earthquake* (1974); *The Hindenburg, Funny Lady, The Man Who Would Be King* (mattes only), *Day of the Locust* 1975; *Two-Minute Warning, Family Plot, W. C. Fields and Me, Bound for Glory* 1976; *Exorcist II: The Heretic, Rollercoaster, Airport '77, The Last Remake of Beau Geste, The Sentinel, The Car, High Anxiety* (also act.) 1977; *The Wiz, I Wanna Hold Your Hand* 1978; *The Prisoner of Zenda, Dracula* 1979; *Cheech and Chong's Next Movie, The Blues Brothers, The Island, In God We Trust* 1980; *Heartbeeps, Ghost Story, History of the World Part I* 1981; *Cat People, Missing, The Thing, The Best Little Whorehouse in Texas* 1982; *Psycho II, The Sting II, The Wicked Lady* 1983; *Greystoke: The Legend of Tarzan Lord of the Apes, The Lonely Guy* 1984; *Clue* (matte consultant), *Red Sonja, Dune* 1985; *Coming to America* 1988; *Millennium* 1989; *Neverending Story II: The Next Chapter, Stephen King's Graveyard Shift* 1990.

Whitman, Stuart. Actor. Born Feb. 1, 1926, San Francisco. After a three-year stint (1945–48) with the Army Corps of Engineers, during which he competed as a light heavyweight boxer, he studied drama at the Los Angeles City College and became a member of the Chekhov stage group. He entered films in the early 50s and gradually advanced from bits and supporting parts to lead roles. Combining a rugged physique with a sensitive, intelligent face, he gained steady screen employment and, while never becoming an important star, he quietly amassed a fortune estimated at nearly $100 million through investments in securities, real estate, cattle, and Thoroughbred horses. He was nominated for an Oscar for his sensitive portrayal of a former sex criminal trying to turn a new leaf in the British film *The Mark* (1961). He has also appeared much on TV, including in the series 'Cimarron Strip.'

FILMS INCLUDE: *When Worlds Collide, The Day the Earth Stood Still* 1951; *Rhapsody* 1954; *Seven Men from Now* 1956; *War Drums, Johnny Trouble* 1957; *Darby's Rangers, Ten North Frederick, The Decks Ran Red, China Doll* 1958; *The Sound and the Fury, These Thousand Hills* 1959; *Hound-Dog Man, The Story of Ruth* (as Boaz), *Murder Inc.* 1960; *The Mark* (UK), *Francis of Assisi, The Fiercest Heart, The Comancheros* 1961; *Convicts 4, The Longest Day* 1962; *Le Jour et l'Heure/ The Day and the Hour* (Fr./It.) 1963; *Shock Treatment, Rio Conchos* 1964; *Those Magnificent Men in Their Flying Machines* (UK), *Sands of the Kalahari* (UK), *Signpost to Murder* 1965; *An American Dream* 1966; *The Last Escape, The Invincible Six, The Only Way Out Is Dead* (Can.) 1970; *Captain Apache* (US/Sp.) 1971; *Night of the Lepus* 1972; *Welcome to Arrow Beach/Tender Flesh* 1974; *Call Him Mr. Shatter* (UK), *Crazy Mama* 1975; *Las Vegas Lady, Tony Saitta/Tough Tony* (It.) 1976; *Strange Shadows in an Empty Room* (It.), *Ruby, The White Buffalo, Death Trap/Eaten Alive, Maniac/Ransom/Assault on Paradise, Oil* (It.) 1977; *La Mujer de la Tierra Caliente* (Sp./It.), *Thoroughbred/The Thoroughbreds/Run for the Roses* 1978; *Delta Fox, Guyana—Crime of the Century* (as Rev. Jim Jones; Mex.), *Key West Crossing/Kill Castro/Assignment: Kill Castro/Cuba Crossing/The Mercenaries, Treasure of the Amazon/The Treasure Seekers* 1979; *Guyana: Cult of the Damned* 1980; *Demonoid: Messenger of Death* 1981; *Butterfly* 1982; *The Vultures* 1984; *The Monster Club* 1985; *John Travis: Solar Survivor, Deadly Reactor, Moving Target* 1989; *Mob Boss, Omega Cop* 1990; *The Color of Evening, Smooth Talker* 1991; *Trial by Jury* 1994.

Whitmore, James. Actor. Born on Oct. 1, 1921, in White Plains, N.Y. *ed.* Yale, where he joined the Yale Drama School Players and was among the founders of the Yale radio station. After WW II service with the Marines, he appeared in stock and made his Broadway debut in 1947 as a wisecracking sergeant in 'Command Decision.' In films from 1949, he played key supporting character roles for the most part, typically as a tough but humane individual and was nominated for an Oscar as best supporting actor for his performance in *Battleground* (1949), only his second film. He also played occasional leads, as in *The Next Voice You Hear, Them,* and *Black Like Me.* In the early 60s he starred in the TV series 'The Law and Mr. Jones.' He received accolades and a nomination for a best actor Oscar for his *tour de force* performance as President Truman in the one-man film *Give 'Em Hell Harry!* (1975). He gave another strong portrayal of a President in *Bully* (1978), as Theodore Roosevelt. His son, James Whitmore, Jr., is also an actor.

FILMS INCLUDE: *The Undercover Man, Battleground* 1949; *The Asphalt Jungle, Please Believe Me, The Next Voice You Hear, Mrs. O'Malley and Mr. Malone* 1950; *It's a Big Country, Because You're Mine* 1952; *Above and Beyond, Kiss Me Kate* 1953; *Them* 1954; *Battle Cry, The McConnell Story, Oklahoma!* 1955; *Crime in the Streets, The Eddy Duchin Story* 1956; *The Deep Six* 1958; *Who Was That Lady?* 1960; *Black Like Me* 1964; *Chuka* 1967; *Planet of the Apes, Madigan* 1968; *Guns of the Magnificent Seven* 1969; *Tora! Tora! Tora!* 1970; *Chato's Land* 1972; *The Harrad Experiment* 1973; *Where the Red Fern Grows* 1974; *Give 'Em Hell Harry!* (as Harry Truman) 1975; *The Serpent's Egg* (Ger./US) 1977; *Bully* (as Theodore Roosevelt) 1978; *The First Deadly Sin* 1980; *The Adventures of Mark Twain* (v/o) 1985; *Nuts* 1987; *Old Explorers* 1990; *The Shawshank Redemption* 1994; *The Relic* 1996.

Whitty, Dame May. Actress. *b.* June 19, 1865, Liverpool, England. *d.* 1948. The daughter of a newspaper (the Liverpool *Post*) editor, she made her debut in ballet at 16 and on the London stage at 17 and by the turn of the century was a highly respected actress in theaters on both sides of the Atlantic. In 1918 she was created Dame Commander of the British Empire for her services to Britain during WW I. In addition to making numerous stage appearances, she appeared occasionally in silent films, including a supporting role in Christy Cabanne's *Enoch Arden* (1915). After a string of Broadway successes in the early 30s, she settled in Hollywood, where she became a symbol of British dignity in a series of distinguished character roles for MGM and other studios. She was nominated for an Oscar for her outstanding performance in the role of a terrified old lady in her very first sound film, *Night Must Fall* (1937), and again for *Mrs. Miniver* (1942). Among her other memorable parts was the title role in Hitchcock's British-made suspense film *The Lady Vanishes* (1938). She was the wife of stage actor Ben Webster and mother of the late stage-actress-director-producer-playwright Margaret Webster.

FILMS (talkies complete): *Enoch Arden* 1915; *Night Must Fall, The 13th Chair, Conquest* 1937; *I Met My Love Again, The Lady Vanishes* (UK) 1938; *Raffles, A Bill of Divorcement* 1940; *One Night in Lisbon, Suspicion* 1941; *Mrs. Miniver, Thunder Birds* 1942; *Forever and a Day, Slightly Dangerous, Crash Dive, Stage Door Canteen, The Constant Nymph, Lassie Come Home, Flesh and Fantasy, Madame Curie* 1943; *The White Cliffs of Dover, Gaslight* 1944; *My Name is Julia Ross* 1945; *Devotion* 1946; *Green Dolphin Street, This Time for Keeps* 1947; *If Winter Comes, The Sign of the Ram, The Return of October* 1948.

Whorf, Richard. Actor, director, producer. *b.* June 4, 1906, Winthrop, Mass. *d.* 1966. He quit school at 15 to join a stage company in Boston and remained on the stage for many years as actor and later also director and set designer. He made his Broadway debut in 1927 and gained recognition for his association with the Lunts in Theatre Guild productions of the late 30s. He made an isolated film appearance in *Midnight* (1934), then settled in Hollywood in 1940 as a contract player at Warners and later MGM. He turned director in 1944, specializing in light films. With the exception of *Champagne for Caesar,* a delightful spoof of TV quiz shows starring Ronald Colman, his productions were rather bland. He returned to Broadway in 1949 to play Richard III in a production he also designed. He returned briefly to films in the late 50s as a producer. He then switched to TV, for which he directed numerous segments for such popular series as 'Gunsmoke,' 'Wagon Train,' 'Alfred Hitchcock Presents,' 'The Beverly Hillbillies,' and 'Petticoat Junction.'

FILMS: As actor—*Midnight* 1934; *Blues in the Night* 1941; *Yankee Doodle Dandy, Juke Girl, Keeper of the Flame* 1942; *Assignment in Brittany, The Cross of Lorraine* 1943; *The Impostor, Christmas Holiday* 1944; *Chain Lightning* 1950. As director (complete)—*Blonde Fever* 1944; *The Hidden Eye* 1945; *The Sailor Takes a Wife, Till the Clouds Roll By* 1946; *It Happened in Brooklyn, Love from a Stranger* 1947; *Luxury Liner* 1948; *Champagne for Caesar* 1950; *The Groom Wore Spurs* 1951. As producer—*The Burning Hills* 1956; *Shoot-Out at Medicine Bend, Bombers B-52* 1957.

"Why We Fight." See COMPILATION FILMS; DOCUMENTARY.

Wickes, Dame Mary. Actress. Born Mary Isabelle Wickenhauser, in 1916, in St. Louis, Mo. *ed.* Washington U. (St. Louis); UCLA. Lanky, gawky character comedienne. Following experience in stock and on Broadway, she began her film career, typically playing wisecracking busybodies. Following a long hiatus, she made a comeback in the 1990s as a nun in the *Sister Act* films. She has also appeared on numerous TV shows, including the series 'Doc.'

FILMS INCLUDE: *The Man Who Came to Dinner, Private Buckaroo, Now Voyager, Who Done It?* 1942; *Happy Land, Higher and Higher* 1943; *June Bride* 1948; *Anna Lucasta* 1949; *The Petty Girl* 1950; *On Moonlight Bay, I'll See You in My Dreams* 1951; *Young Man with Ideas* 1952; *The Actress* 1953; *White Christmas* 1954; *Good Morning Miss Dove* 1955; *Don't Go Near the Water* 1957; *It Happened to Jane* 1959; *Cimarron* 1960; *The Music Man* 1962; *Dear Heart* 1964; *How to Murder Your Wife* 1965; *The Trouble with Angels* 1966; *Where Angels Go Trouble Follows* 1968; *Napoleon and Samantha, Snowball Express* 1972; *Touched by Love/To Elvis with Love* 1980; *Postcards from the Edge* 1990; *Sister Act* 1992; *Sister Act 2: Back in the Habit* 1993; *Little Women* 1994.

Wicki, Bernhard. Actor, director. Born on Oct. 28, 1919, in St. Polten, Austria, to Swiss-Hungarian parents. Trained at actors' academies in Berlin and Vienna, he played a variety of roles on the German, Austrian, and Swiss stage and made his screen acting debut in 1950. He turned to directing in the late 50s. Following a good feature-length documentary, he made one of Germany's best postwar films, *Die Brücke/The Bridge,* a grim account of German schoolboys drafted into service toward the end of WW II. He received the best director award at the Berlin Film Festival for his next production, *Das Wunder des Malachias,* and later became involved in international productions.

FILMS INCLUDE: As actor—*Der fallende Stern* 1950; *Rummelplatz der Liebe/Circus of Love, Die letzte Brücke/The Last Bridge* (Aus./Yug.), *Die Mücke* 1954; *Ewiger Walzer/The Eternal Waltz* (as Johann Strauss), *Kinder Mütter und eine General, Es geschah am 20. Juli, Rosen im Herbst/Effi Briest* 1955; *Frucht ohne Liebe* 1956; *Königin Luise, Die Zürcher Verlobung/The Affairs of Julie* 1957; *Unruhige Nacht/Restless Night, La Chatte/The Cat* (Fr.) 1958; *La Notte/The Night* (It./Fr.) 1961; *L'Amore Difficile/Erotica/Of Wayward Love* (It./Ger.) 1962; *Crime and Passion* (US/Ger.) 1976; *Die linkshändige Frau/The Left-Handed Woman* 1977; *Despair, Die gläserne Zelle* 1978; *La Mort en Direct/Deathwatch* 1979; *Domino* 1982; *Eine Liebe in Deutchland/A Love in Germany* 1983; *La Diagonale du Fou/Dangerous Moves, Fruhlingssinfonie/Spring Symphony, Paris Texas* (US) 1984; *Killing Cars, Marie Ward* 1985. As director—*Warum sind sie gegen uns?* (feature-length doc.; also sc.) 1958; *Die Brücke/The Bridge* 1959; *Das Wunder des Malachias* (also co-sc.) 1961; *The Longest Day* (German sequences only; US) 1962; *Der Besuch/The Visit* (Ger./It./Fr./US) 1964; *Morituri/The Saboteur—Code Name Morituri* (US) 1965; *Das falsche Gewicht* (also co-sc.) 1971; *Die Eroberung der Zitadelle* (also co-sc.) 1977; *Die Grunstein-Variante* 1985; *Das Spinnennetz/The Spider's Web* (also sc.) 1989; *Erfolg/Success* 1990.

wide-angle lens. A lens of shorter-than-normal focal length and magnification power which covers a large field of view (in excess of 60 degrees) and tends to exaggerate perspective, making an area appear larger than it actually is, particularly useful in obtaining ESTABLISHING SHOTS and other LONG SHOTS and for shooting action in confined areas. Shots taken with a wide-angle lens are often merely called "wide-angle shots."

Widerberg, Bo. Director. *b.* June 8, 1930, in Malmö, Sweden. *d.* 1997. After completing high school he found his first employment at a mental hospital but soon switched to a small-town newspaper as a night editor. He began writing short stories at the age of 20 and in 1951 published a collection of these titled *Kissing* and a novel, *Autumn Term.* He took a growing interest in cinema as a mode of expression and in 1960 became film critic for Sweden's largest newspaper. The following year he co-directed a short for Swedish TV and in 1962 he caused a storm of controversy with his book *The Vision of Swedish Cinema,* a scathing attack on his country's film industry and its tastemakers, and particularly on its monopolization by Ingmar BERGMAN and his followers. He then set out to demonstrate his own filmic vision with a number of productions that brought him international acclaim.

His most famous film outside Sweden is *Elvira Madigan,* a visually exquisite pastoral film stroked with color evocative of Renoir and the impressionist painters. In this as in his *Raven's End* and *Adalen 31/The Adalen Riots* he commented on current manifestations of contemporary Swedish society in terms of the past. In 1970 he came to the US to direct *Joe Hill.* Widerberg writes all his own scripts and has been known to improvise not only lines but whole sequences just moments before the shooting of a scene. He likes to work with nonprofessional actors and edit his own films. A meticulous craftsman, he personally supervises the lab processing of his color films.

FILMS: *The Boy and the Kite* (short; co-dir. with Jan Troell) 1961; *The Baby Carriage/The Pram, Raven's End* 1963; *Love 65* 1965; *Thirty Times Your Money* 1966; *Elvira Madigan* 1967; *The White Game* (doc.; co-dir.) 1968; *The Adalen Riots* 1969; *Joe Hill* (also prod.; Sw./US) 1971; *Fimpen/Stubby* 1974; *Man on the Roof* (also sc., co-edit.) 1977; *Victoria* (also sc., ed.; Sw./Ger.) 1979; *Mannen Fran Mallorca/The Man from Majorca* (also sc., ed.) 1984; *Ormen's vag pa halleberget/The Serpent's Way* (also sc., ed.) 1986; *Up the Naked Rock* 1988; *End All Things Fair* 1995.

wide-screen processes. Projection systems utilizing screen proportions larger than the standard aspect ratio (width to height) of 1.33:1 (4:3). The standard ratio was established early in the history of cinema in accordance with the specifications set by Thomas A. Edison, who introduced 35 mm film with four perforations on each side of every frame. Projection systems with wider aspect ratios had existed before the standard was set, but most were abandoned in the first decade of the 20th century. However, experimentation with a variety of screen sizes continued and new filming and projection systems were announced and tried periodically. They fell into four broad categories: 1. systems using film wider than the standard 35 mm; 2. systems using a special anamorphic lens that "squeezes" the image in filming and "unsqueezes" it in projection; 3. systems using more than one camera and more than one projector; and 4. simply, the masking of the top and bottom of conventional film during projection to produce the effect of width.

Among the more successful early systems utilizing wider film were Natural Vision, Grandeur, Magnifilm, Realife, and the German Tri-Ergon. Systems utilizing multiple cameras have included Widescope, Vitarama, and the French triptych processes—Abel Gance's Polyvision, which he used in his *Napoléon,* and Claude Autant-Lara's Hypergonar, which he introduced in his *Pour Construire un Feu.* Both films were released in 1927. The most durable of the early wide-screen processes was Magnascope, which was introduced in the 20s and used intermittently by Hollywood until the early 50s. The system utilized a special projection lens to magnify normal images onto a huge screen.

In the early 50s the wide screen was suddenly transformed from a sometime novelty into a permanent fixture in motion picture theaters the world over. The impetus for the change was provided by the crisis that Hollywood faced during that period as a result of increasing competition from TV and the resultant dwindling of cinema audiences. The advent of the modern wide-screen era was signaled in 1952 by Cinerama, a three-panel process utilizing three cameras and three projectors and a mammoth curved screen to create the effect of huge space. The following year saw the premiere of CinemaScope, an anamorphic lens system based on a 25-year-old invention by Professor Henri Chrétien.

Other wide-screen systems with aspect ratios of up to 2.55:1 followed in rapid succession in Europe as well as in the US. Among the more successful have been Panavision, Vista Vision, and Todd-AO. See also ASPECT RATIO; CINEMASCOPE; CINERAMA; SCREEN.

Widmark, Richard. Actor. Born on Dec. 26, 1914, in Sunrise, Minn. Raised in South Dakota, Missouri, and Illinois, he enrolled at Lake Forrest College, with the intention of going into law, but found himself sidetracked by football and drama. Graduating in 1936, he remained at the college for two years as a drama instructor. In 1938 he went to New York, where he became regularly employed in radio dramas. In the early 40s he appeared in several Broadway plays. In 1947 he made a memorable screen debut, playing a psychopathic killer with a tittering, chilling laugh in *Kiss of Death,* a performance that earned him a nomination for an Oscar as best supporting player. For a brief spell he was typed in similar roles, but he soon broadened his range to include sympathetic heroes as well as occasional villains. In either category, he has typically played tough, purposeful, hard-to-bend loners.

Except for an occasional miscasting, as in the role of the infantile Dauphin in Preminger's *Saint Joan,* Widmark's performances have been consistently convincing and he remains one of Hollywood's most durable stars. He has also produced two films through his company, Heath Productions. In 1971 he reluctantly broke a long-time boycott of television by starring in a two-part, four-hour, $2 million NBC special, 'Vanished,' in which he portrayed a President of the United States. He later starred in the TV series 'Madigan.' Widmark, who has kept his private life sheltered from publicity, has been married for 50 years to former actress and sometime screenwriter Jean Hazlewood. He is the father-in-law of baseball's former star pitcher Sandy Koufax.

FILMS: *Kiss of Death* 1947; *The Street with No Name, Road House, Yellow Sky* 1948; *Down to the Sea in Ships, Slattery's Hurricane* 1949; *Night and the City, Panic in the Streets, No Way Out* 1950; *The Halls of Montezuma, The Frogmen* 1951; *Red Skies of Montana, Smoke Jumpers, Don't Bother to Knock, O. Henry's Full House, My Pal Gus* 1952; *Destination Gobi, Pickup on South Street, Take the High Ground* 1953; *Hell and High Water, Garden of Evil, Broken Lance* 1954; *A Prize of Gold* (UK), *The Cobweb* 1955; *Backlash, Run for the Sun, The Last Wagon* 1956; *Saint Joan* (as the Dauphin; UK), *Time Limit* (also co-prod.) 1957; *The Law and Jake Wade, Tunnel of Love* 1958; *The Trap, Warlock* 1959; *The Alamo* (as Jim Bowie) 1960; *The Secret Ways* (also prod.), *Two Rode Together, Judgment at Nuremberg* 1961; *How the West Was Won* 1963; *Flight from Ashiya, The Long Ships, Cheyenne Autumn* 1964; *The Bedford Incident* 1965; *Alvarez Kelly* 1966; *The Way West* 1967; *Madigan, A Talent for Loving* (made in 1968; not yet released) 1968; *Death of a Gunfighter* 1969; *The Moonshine War* 1970; *When the Legends Die* 1972; *Murder on the Orient Express* (UK) 1974; *Midas Run* (Ger.) 1975; *The Sell Out* (UK), *To the Devil a Daughter* (UK/Ger.) 1976; *Twilight's Last Gleaming, The Domino Principle, Rollercoaster, The Perfect Killer* (Sp.) 1977; *Coma, The Swarm, Dinero Maldito* (release delayed from 1971) 1978; *Bear Island* (UK/Can.) 1979; *Who Dares Wins, Hanky Panky, National Lampoon's Movie Madness\National Lampoon Goes to the Movies, The Final Option* 1982; *Against All Odds* 1983; *Blackout* 1985; *Texas Guns* 1990; *True Colors* 1991.

Wieck, Dorothea. Actress. *b.* Jan. 3, 1908, in Davos, Switzerland. *d.* 1986. Trained for the stage by Max Reinhardt, she rose to become a leading star of the German theater and cinema in the late 20s and early 30s. After her great success in *Maädchen in Uniform* (1931), she starred in two Hollywood films but failed to click and returned to Germany. A baroness by marriage, she played character parts after WW II.

FILMS INCLUDE: *Heimlich Sünder* 1926; *Klettermaxe* 1927; *Mädchen in Uniform* 1931; *Gräfin Maritza, Theodor Körner, Trenck, Teilnehmer antwortet nicht, Ein toller Einfall* 1932; *Anna und Elisabeth, Cradle Song* (US) 1933; *Miss Fane's Baby Is Stolen* (US) 1934; *Lisolette von der Pfalz/The Private Life of Louis XIV, Der Student von Prag* 1935; *Die unmögliche Frau* 1936; *Liebe kann lügen* 1937; *Dein Leben gehört mir* 1939; *Panik* 1943; *Der grüne Salon* 1944; *Herz der Welt* 1952; *Man on a Tightrope* (US) 1953; *Anastasia—Die letzte Zarentochter* 1956; *A Time to Love and a Time to Die* (US) 1958; *Menschen im Hotel* 1959; *Schachnovelle/ Brainwashed/ The Royal Game* 1960.

Wiene, Robert. Director. *b.* 1881, Sasku, Germany. *d.* 1938. A former stage actor and director, he entered German cinema in 1914 as a screenwriter and within months began getting directing assignments. He rose to prominence and international fame in 1919 as the director of *The Cabinet of Dr. Caligari,* a film that marked the apogee of the expressionist style in German cinema. But the mediocrity of many of Wiene's subsequent films led historians to re-evaluate his importance and to speculate that it was the contribution of the screenwriters, set designers, and actors, and not his direction, that made the film unique. After the Nazi takeover, he emigrated to Paris, where he died in 1938 in the midst of shooting his last film, *Ultimatum,* which was completed by Robert SIODMAK. His brother, Conrad Wiene, also a director, is best known for *Die Macht der Finsternis/The Power of Darkness* (1923), a Leo Tolstoy adaptation scripted by Robert and featuring players of the Moscow Art Theater.

FILMS INCLUDE: *Arme Eva* (co-dir. with A. Berger) 1914; *Die Konservenbraut* 1915; *Die Liebesbrief der Königin, Der Mann im Spiegel, Die Räuberbraut, Das wandernde Licht* 1916; *Ein gefährliches Spiel* (also sc.), *Das Kabinett des Dr. Caligari/The Cabinet of Dr. Caligari* 1919; *Die drei Tänze der Mary Wilford, Genuine, Die Nacht der Königin Isabeau* (also sc.), *Die Rache einer Frau* 1920; *Höllische Nacht, Das Spiel mit dem Feuer* (co-dir. with Georg Kroll) 1921; *Salome, Tragikomödie* (also co-prod.) 1922; *I.N.R.I./Crown of Thorns* (also sc.), *Der Puppenmacher von Kiang-Ning, Raskolnikow/ Schuld und Sühne/Crime and Punishment* (also sc.) 1923; *Orlacs Hände/The Hands of Orlac* (Aus.), *Pension Groonen* 1925; *Der Gardeoffizier/The Guardsman, Die Königin vom Moulin-Rouge, Der Rosenkavalier* (also co-sc.) 1926; *Die berühmte Frau/The Dancer of Barcelona, Die Geliebte* 1927; *Die Frau auf der Folter/A Scandal in Paris, Die grosse Abenteurerin, Leontines Ehemänner, Unfug der Liebe* 1928; *Der Andere* 1930; *Panik in Chikago, Der Liebes-express/Acht Tage Glück* 1931; *Polizeiakte 909* (also sc.), *Eine Nacht in Venedig* (also sc.) 1934; *Ultimatum* (completed by Robert Siodmak after Wiene's death; Fr.) 1938.

Wiener, Jean. Composer. *b.* Mar. 19, 1896, Paris. *d.* 1982. He wrote numerous scores and popular tunes for the French theater, music hall, and cinema, and several orchestral works, including a *Franco-American Piano Concerto* and a *Concerto for Accordion and Orchestra.* He composed for Renoir, Duvivier, Becker, Daquin, and Bresson, among other directors. His daughter, Elisabeth Wiener (*b.* 1946, Paris), is an actress in French films (*Marry Me! Marry Me!, La Prisonnière,* etc.).

FILMS INCLUDE: *L'Homme à l'Hispano* 1933; *Les*

Affaires publiques, Maria Chapdelaine/The Naked Heart 1934; *La Bandera/Escape from Yesterday* (co-composer) 1935; *Le Crime de M. Lange/The Crime of Monsieur Lange, L'Homme du Jour/The Man of the Hour, Les BasFonds/The Lower Depths* 1936; *Untel Père et Fils/Heart of a Nation* 1943; *Le Père Goriot* 1944; *Patrie* 1946; *Les Frères Bouquinquant* 1947; *Le Point du Jour, Rendez-vous de Juillet* 1949; *Sous le Ciel de Paris/Under the Paris Sky, Maître apres Dieu* 1951; *Touchez pas au Grisbi/Grisbi* 1954; *PotBouille* 1957; *La Femme et le Pantin/The Female* 1959; *Lady L* (act. only; US/Fr./It.) 1965; *Au Hasard Balthazar* 1966; *Mouchette* 1967; *Benjamin* 1968; *Une Femme douce* 1969; *La Faute d'Abbé Mouret/The Demise of Father Mouret* 1970.

Wiest, Dianne. Actress. Born on March 28, 1948, in Kansas City, Mo. *ed.* Univ. of Md. Intelligent, excitable stage and screen lead and supporting player. After switching from ballet to theater studies in college, she worked with top theater companies, including Yale Repertory and the New York Shakespeare Festival. Beginning in the 80s, she became known in film for her finely detailed performances of contemporary, often urban, women. She received supporting actress Academy Awards for performances as the flighty sister in *Hannah and Her Sisters* (1986) and the over-the-top drama queen in *Bullets Over Broadway* (1994).

FILMS INCLUDE: *It's My Turn* 1980, *I'm Dancing as Fast as I Can* 1982; *Independence Day* 1983; *Footloose, Falling in Love* 1984; *The Purple Rose of Cairo* 1985; *Hannah and Her Sisters* 1986; *The Lost Boys, Radio Days, September* 1987; *Bright Lights Big City* 1988; *Parenthood, Cookie* 1989; *Edward Scissorhands* 1990; *Little Man Tate* 1991; *Bullets Over Broadway, Cops and Robbersons, The Scout* 1994; *The Associate, The Birdcage, Drunks* 1996.

wigwag. A red warning light that is flashed automatically outside the doors of a studio's sound stage whenever a sound scene is being shot. No one is allowed to enter the sound stage while the warning signal is on.

Wilbur, Crane. Actor, screenwriter, director. *b.* Erwin Crane Wilbur, Nov. 17, 1889, Athens, N.Y. *d.* 1973. On the stage from 1904, he played in much stock and repertory before entering films in 1910. He co-starred in many of Pearl White's early silents and was her leading man in the famous serial *The Perils of Pauline.* He was considered one of the handsomest screen personalities of that period. Later in the silent period, he divided his time between Broadway and Hollywood and began writing plays and screenplays. He wrote many scripts, mainly for action films. From the mid-30s he also directed a number of pictures, mostly in the same vein.

FILMS INCLUDE: As actor—*A Summer Flirtation* 1910; *For Massa's Sake* 1911; *The Compact, A Nation's Peril* 1912; *The Artist's Trick* 1913; *The Ghost, The Corsair, All Love Excelling, The Perils of Pauline* (serial) 1914; *Road o' Strife* (serial) 1915; *The Painted Lie, The Eye of Envy, The Blood of His Fathers* 1917; *Breezy Jim, Unto the End, Finger of Justice* 1919; *The Heart of Maryland* 1921; *Public Opinion* 1935. As screenwriter (alone or in collaboration)—*The Monster* 1925; *Lord Byron of Broadway* 1930; *Alcatraz Island, West of Shanghai* 1937; *The Invisible Menace, Over the Wall, Crime School* 1938; *Blackwell's Island, Hell's Kitchen* 1939; *Roger Touhy—Gangster* 1944; *Red Stallion* 1947; *Adventures of Casanova, He Walked by Night* 1948; *I Was a Communist for the FBI* 1951; *The Lion and the Horse, The Miracle of Our Lady of Fatima* 1952; *House of Wax* 1953; *Crime Wave, The Mad Magician* 1954; *Women's Prison, The Phenix City Story* 1955; *Solomon and Sheba* (story only) 1959; *Mysterious Island* (US/UK) 1961; *The George Raft Story* 1962. As director (complete)—*Tomorrow's Children* (also sc., act.) 1934; *High School Girl* (also act.), *The People's Enemy* 1935; *The Devil on Horseback* (also sc.), *Yellow Cargo* (also sc., act.), *We're in the Legion Now* 1936; *Navy Spy* (also sc.) 1937; *The Patient in Room 18* (co-dir. with Bobby Connolly) 1938; *I Am Not Afraid* 1939; *The Devil on Wheels* 1947; *Canon City* (also sc.) 1948; *The Story of Molly X* (also sc.) 1949; *Outside the Wall* (also sc.) 1950; *Inside the Walls of Folsom Prison* (also sc.) 1951; *The Bat* (also sc.) 1959; *House of Women* (co-dir. with Walter Doniger, uncredited; also sc.) 1962.

Wilcox, Fred M. Director. *b.* 1905, Tazewell, Va. *d.* 1964. *ed.* U. of Kentucky. He joined MGM in 1926 as publicist. After a long apprenticeship as a script clerk (to King Vidor), assistant director, and second-unit director, he made his bow as a director in 1943 with a highly successful family entertainment film, *Lassie Come Home.* He later directed two routine sequels to that film and a fine children's fantasy picture, *The Secret Garden.* But for some reason he obtained few assignments and amassed only a handful of screen credits.

FILMS: *Lassie Come Home* 1943; *The Courage of Lassie* 1946; *Three Daring Daughters, Hills of Home* 1948; *The Secret Garden* 1949; *Shadow in the Sky* 1952; *Code Two* 1953; *Tennessee Champ* 1954; *Forbidden Planet* 1956; *I Passed for White* (also prod., sc.) 1960.

Wilcox, Herbert. Producer-director. *b.* Apr. 19, 1892, Cork, Ireland. *d.* 1977. A young journalist at the outbreak of WW I, he served as a pilot with the Royal Flying Corps. In 1919 he entered the British film business handling film rentals. In 1922 he moved into production and immediately proved himself a born showman with a finger on the pulse of the public taste and a flair for extravagance. He employed Hollywood methods of production and publicity and occasionally imported Hollywood stars for his lavish films (e.g., Dorothy Gish for *Nell Gwyn* and several other productions). In 1926 he founded the Elstree studios and by the end of the silent period he was a dominant figure in the British film industry, although his ability as a director seldom matched his flair as a producer. In the early 30s he discovered Anna NEAGLE, developed her into the biggest star in the history of British films, and eventually (in 1943) married her. He directed all but two of her films.

In 1939 Wilcox and Neagle came to Hollywood in the wake of their success with *Sixty Glorious Years* and made several films, mostly old-fashioned musicals, under an arrangement with RKO. But their success was modest and they returned to England, where their style was much better appreciated. The Wilcox formula worked successfully through the early 50s, when he suddenly seemed to have lost his touch. He had always been a mediocre director whose talents as producer and promoter enabled him to turn out many box-office hits. Now several errors of judgment and unfortunate investments caused a rapid reversal in his fortunes. In 1964 he went into bankruptcy and his film career ended. In 1967 he published an autobiography, *Twenty-Five Thousand Sunsets.*

FILMS (as director-producer unless otherwise noted): *The Wonderful Story* (prod. only), *Flames of Passion* (prod. only) 1922; *Paddy the Next Best Thing* (prod. only), *Chu Chin Chow* 1923; *Southern Love, Decameron Nights* (and German-language version, *Dekameron-Nächte*) 1924; *The Only Way* 1925; *Nell Gwyn* (also sc.), *London/Limehouse* (also sc.) 1926; *Tiptoes/Tip Toes* (also sc.), *Madame Pompadour, Mumsie, The Luck of the Navy* (co-prod. only) 1927; *Dawn, The Bondman* 1928; *The Woman in White* 1929; *Rookery Nook* (prod. only), *The Loves of Robert Burns, Wolves/Wanted Men* (prod. only) 1930; *The Rosary* (prod. only), *Chance of a Night-Time* (co-dir. with Ralph Lynn), *Carnival* 1931; *Thark* (prod. only), *The Flag Lieutenant* (prod. only), *Say It with Music* (prod. only), *The Love Contract* (prod. only), *The Blue Danube, Goodnight Vienna/Magic Night* 1932; *Yes Mr. Brown, The King's Cup, Bitter Sweet, Sorrell and Son* (prod. only), *The Little Damozel* 1933; *The Queen's Affair, Nell Gwyn* (remake starring Anna Neagle) 1934; *Brewster's Millions* (prod. only), *Escape Me Never* (prod. only), *Peg of Old Drury* 1935; *Limelight, The Three Maxims, This'll Make You Whistle* 1936; *The Gang Show* (prod. only), *The Frog* (prod. only), *The Rat* (prod. only), *Sunset in Vienna/Suicide Legion* (prod. only), *London Melody/Girl in the Street, Our Fighting Navy/Torpedoed, Victoria the Great* 1937; *Blondes for Danger* (prod. only), *Sixty Glorious Years* 1938; *Nurse Edith Cavell* (US) 1939; *Irene* (US), *No No Nanette* (US) 1940; *Sunny* (US) 1941; *They Flew Alone/Wings and the Woman* 1942; *Forever and a Day* (co-dir., co-prod. with several others; US), *The Yellow Canary* 1943; *I Live in Grosvenor Square/A Yank in London* 1945; *Piccadilly Incident* 1946; *The Courtneys of Curzon Street/The Courtney Affair/Kathy's Love Affair* 1947; *Spring in Park Lane, Elizabeth of Ladymead* 1948; *Maytime in Mayfair* 1949; *Odette* 1950; *Into the Blue/Man in the Dinghy* (dir. only), *The Lady with the Lamp* 1951; *Derby Day* 1952; *Trent's Last Case, The Beggar's Opera* (co-prod. only), *Laughing Anne* 1953; *Trouble in the Glen, Lilacs in the Spring/Let's Make Up* 1954; *King's Rhapsody* 1955; *My Teenage Daughter* 1956; *These Dangerous Years* (dir. only) 1957; *The Man Who Wouldn't Talk, Wonderful Things* (dir. only) 1958; *The Lady Is a Square, The Heart of a Man* (dir. only) 1959.

Wilcoxon, Henry. Actor. *b.* Harry Wilcoxon, Sept. 8, 1905, Dominica, West Indies, to British parents. *d.* 1984. After seven years on the London stage, he made his debut in British films in the early 30s. A tall and rugged leading man, he achieved stardom in Hollywood when he was imported by Cecil B. DE MILLE in 1934 to play Marc Antony to Claudette Colbert's Cleopatra. He played another important part, Richard the Lion-Hearted, in De Mille's *The Crusades,* but then slipped into supporting roles in major pictures and played leads in B productions only. He remained a close friend of De Mille, acted as his associate producer on *The Ten Commandments* and *The Greatest Show on Earth,* and produced *The Buccaneer* for him. Formerly married to actresses Heather ANGEL and Joan WOODBURY.

FILMS INCLUDE: In the UK—*The Perfect Lady* 1931; *The Flying Squad* 1932; *Lord of the Manor* 1933; *Princess Charming* 1934. In the US—*Cleopatra* (as Marc Antony) 1934; *The Crusades* (as King Richard the Lion-Hearted) 1935; *The Last of the Mohicans* (as Major Duncan Heyward), *The President's Mystery, A Woman Alone/Two Who Dared* (UK) 1936; *Jericho/Dark Sands* (UK), *Souls at Sea* 1937; *Prison Nurse, Keep Smiling, Mysterious Mr. Moto, If I Were King* 1938; *Woman Doctor, Tarzan Finds a Son* 1939; *Free Blonde and 21, Earthbound, Mystery Sea Raider* 1940; *That Hamilton Woman, The Lone Wolf Takes a Chance, Scotland Yard, The Corsican Brothers* 1941; *Mrs. Miniver* 1942; *Johnny Doughboy* 1943; *Unconquered, The Dragnet* 1947; *A Connecticut Yankee in King Arthur's Court* (as Sir Lancelot), *Samson and Delilah* 1949; *The Miniver Story* 1950; *The Greatest Show on Earth* (also assoc. prod.), *Scaramouche* 1952; *The Ten Commandments* (also assoc. prod.) 1956; *The Buccaneer* (prod. only) 1959; *The War Lord* 1965; *The Private Navy of Sgt. O'Farrell* 1968; *Man in the Wilderness* 1971; *Against a Crooked Sky* 1975; *Pony Express Rider* 1976; *F.I.S.T.* 1978.

Wild, Harry J. American cinematographer. *b.* ca. 1900. *d.* 1961. Director of photography who worked steadily at RKO and occasionally for other studios from the 30s to the 50s. Among his credits are *The Magnificent Ambersons* (1942; co-photographed with Stanley Cortez and Russell Metty) and numerous films starring Jane Russell, including *Gentlemen Prefer Blondes* (1953).

FILMS INCLUDE: *The Big Game* 1936; *Don't Tell the Wife* (co-phot.) 1937; *Lady Behave, Portia on Trial, Racing Lady* 1938; *Army Girl, Lawless Valley, The Painted Desert* 1938; *Arizona Legion, The Fighting Gringo, The Rookie Cop, Trouble in Sundown* 1939; *Bullet Code, Laddie, Millionaires in Prison, Wagon Train* 1940; *The Bandit Trail, Dude Cowboy, The Fargo Kid, Robbers of the Range, The Saint in Palm Springs, Six Gun Gold* 1941; *The Magnificent Ambersons* (co-phot.), *Come on Danger, Riding the Wind, Valley of the Sun* 1942; *So This Is Washington, Stage Door Canteen, Tarzan Triumphs, Tarzan's Desert Mystery* (co-phot.), *Rookies in Burma* 1943; *The Falcon Out West, Mademoiselle Fifi, Nevada* 1944; *Cornered, First Yank Into Tokyo, Johnny Angel, Murder My Sweet, West of the Pecos* 1945; *Nocturne, Till the End of Time, The Falcon's Adventure* (co-phot.) 1946; *Tycoon* (co-phot.), *The Woman on the Beach* (co-phot.), *They Won't Believe Me* 1947; *Pitfall, Station West* 1948; *The Big Steal, Easy Living, The Threat* 1949; *Gambling House, Walk Softly Stranger* 1950; *My Forbidden Past, Two Tickets to Broadway* (co-phot.) 1951; *The Las Vegas Story, Macao, Son of Paleface* 1953; *Gentlemen Prefer Blondes, Affair with a Stranger* 1953; *The French Line, She Couldn't Say No* 1954; *Underwater!, Top of the World* (co-phot.) 1955; *The Conqueror* (co-phot.) 1956.

Wilde, Cornel. Actor, director, producer. *b.* Cornelius Louis Wilde, Oct. 13, 1915, in New York City, to Hungarian-Czech parents. *d.* 1989. He spent a good part of his childhood and adolescence in Europe, accompanying his father, a Hungarian citizen representing a cosmetics firm in New York, on his travels and acquiring fluency in several languages. The family finally settled permanently in the US in 1932. The following year he enrolled at New York's City College as a premed student, earning his tuition as a Macy's toy salesman, commercial artist, and advertising salesman for a French-language newspaper, among other odd jobs. In 1935 he won a scholarship to Columbia University's College of Physicians and Surgeons but his plans to become a surgeon were soon abandoned because of his growing interest in the theater. After some appearances in stock he landed a lead on Broadway and dropped out of school. He also quit the US fencing team to the 1936 Berlin Olympics, of which he was a leading member, to devote his full energies to acting. He appeared in a number of stage productions in New York and on the road, in roles ranging from bits to leads, but enjoyed only a modest success. A turning point that would lead to his film career came when he was hired as a fencing instructor and a featured player (as Tybalt) for the 1940 Laurence Olivier–Vivien Leigh Broadway production of 'Romeo and Juliet.' Some of the rehearsals were held in Hollywood, where Wilde accepted a contract with Warner Bros. After several disappointing small roles as a heavy, he switched to 20th Century-Fox, where he rapidly moved into lead roles in B pictures. Tall, dark, and handsome, with romantic eyes and a powerful physique, he zipped into the big time in 1945, on loan to Columbia, portraying a sickly Chopin in *A Song to Remember.* Many thought the casting odd, but he was nominated for an Oscar as best actor and went on to star in several other A pictures, including the expensive but dull *Forever Amber* (1947). But by the early 50s he was back on the B trail in action pictures, in which he often appeared as a dueling swashbuckler, banking on his athletic physique and fencing expertise. In 1955 he formed his own company, Theodora Productions, and set out to produce and direct his own pictures, mostly shot abroad with limited budgets. Several of these turned out to be quite good—especially the picturesque and action-filled *The Naked Prey*

(1966)—despite the simplistic naïveté that is characteristic of some of the scripts. Divorced from actress Patricia Knight, Wilde married Jean WALLACE, who was his business partner and frequent co-star.

FILMS: As actor—*The Lady with Red Hair* 1940; *High Sierra, Knockout, Kisses for Breakfast, The Perfect Snob* 1941; *Right to the Heart, Manila Calling, Life Begins at Eight-Thirty* 1942; *Wintertime* 1943; *A Song to Remember* (as Frederic Chopin), *A Thousand and One Nights* (as Aladdin), *Leave Her to Heaven* 1945; *The Bandit of Sherwood Forest* (as Robert of Nottingham, son of Robin Hood), *Centennial Summer* 1946; *Stairway for a Star, The Homestretch, Forever Amber, It Had to Be You* 1947; *The Walls of Jericho, Road House* 1948; *Shockproof, Swiss Tour/Four Days Leave* (Switz./US) 1949; *Two Flags West* 1950; *The Greatest Show on Earth, At Sword's Point* (as D'Artagnan), *California Conquest, Operation Secret* 1952; *Treasure of the Golden Condor, Main Street to Broadway* (cameo) 1953; *Saadia, Woman's World, Passion* 1954; *The Big Combo, The Scarlet Coat* 1955; *Star of India, Hot Blood* 1956; *Beyond Mombasa, Omar Khayyam* (title role) 1957; *Edge of Eternity* 1959; *Constantino il Grande/Constantine and the Cross* (title role; It.) 1961; *The Comic* 1969; *The Horseman* 1978. As director-producer-actor—*Storm Fear* 1956; *The Devil's Hairpin* (also co-sc.) 1957; *Maracaibo* 1958; *Lancelot and Guinevere/Sword of Lancelot* (as Lancelot; UK) 1963; *The Naked Prey* (US/S. Afr.) 1966; *Beach Red* 1967; *No Blade of Grass* (dir., prod. only; UK) 1970; *Shark's Treasure* (also sc.) 1975; *The Norseman, The 5th Musketeer* (as D'Artagnan; Aus.) 1979; *Flesh and Bullets* 1985.

Wilder, Billy. Director, screenwriter, producer. Born Samuel Wilder, on June 22, 1906, in Vienna. The son of a hotelier-businessman, he enrolled at the University of Vienna, intending to study law. But he gave up academic life after one year to become a reporter for a leading newspaper in the Austrian capital. After gaining some experience, he went to Berlin, where he joined the staff of the city's largest tabloid. In an interview, he has volunteered that during that period he supplemented his income as a taxi dancer in a hotel. "I was a gigolo," he said in his typical forthright, cynical way. At the same time, he tried to break into films as a screenwriter. He got his first break collaborating on Robert Siodmak's semidocumentary *Menschen am Sonntag/People on Sunday* (1929). He later collaborated on the scripts of many other German films, but in 1933, when Hitler came to power, the Jewish Wilder was forced to flee to Paris, where he co-directed a film starring Danielle Darrieux. The following year he went to the US via Mexico. His mother and other members of the family he left behind died in concentration camps.

Wilder arrived in Hollywood with little money and no knowledge of the English language. He moved in with actor Peter Lorre and for several years led a penurious existence on income derived from occasional script collaborations. A turning point in his career came in 1938 when he began a long and fruitful collaboration with screenwriter Charles BRACKETT. Their collaboration, which lasted until 1950, produced a long succession of box-office hits and some of the brightest scripts in the American cinema of the late 30s and 40s. After scoring successfully as a writing team with such sophisticated comedies as Leisen's *Midnight,* Lubitsch's *Ninotchka,* and Hawks's *Ball of Fire,* Wilder and Brackett further extended their partnership into a producer-director-writer relationship, in which, starting in 1942, Wilder assumed the role of director and Brackett that of producer while both continued collaborating on the screenplays.

Except for the duration of 1945, which Colonel Wilder spent in Germany as head of the US Army's Psychological Warfare Division, the Wilder-Brackett partnership continued successfully until 1950, when it culminated in the powerful *Sunset Boulevard.* It had produced such fine films as the WW II thriller *Five Graves to Cairo* and the suspenseful crime melodrama *Double Indemnity.* Wilder had won the best director Academy Award for *The Lost Weekend* (1945), a harsh, unrelenting drama of alcoholism, and shared an Oscar with Brackett for the screenplay. The film was cited as best picture of the year. They shared another Oscar for the screenplay of *Sunset Boulevard* (1950), a poignant drama about a fading silent movie star.

Since he broke up with the refined and cultivated Brackett, Wilder's own bitter cynicism and occasional penchant for vulgarity have become more evident in some of his films. *Ace in the Hole* (or as it was later re-titled, *The Big Carnival*) was a grim, hard-hitting, relentlessly cynical drama about a reporter who capitalizes on a tragedy to advance his career. It was Wilder's most disastrous commercial flop, but a solid critical success. *Stalag 17,* a suspenseful prisoner-of-war-camp thriller-comedy; *Love in the Afternoon,* a romantic comedy à la Lubitsch; *Witness for the Prosecution,* a gripping courtroom suspense drama; and *Some Like It Hot,* a howlingly funny Roaring 20s sex comedy, all did spectacularly well both with the critics and with ticket-buying audiences. In 1960, Wilder won an Academy Award for directing the comedy-drama *The Apartment,* which was also named best picture of the year. He also shared the Oscar for the film's script with his regular collaborator from the late 50s, the late I. A. L. DIAMOND. After splitting with Brackett, Wilder was his own producer. His films were consistent moneymakers, grossing a total of nearly $100 million over the span of his Hollywood career. In the 90s, a stage musical based on his *Sunset Boulevard* opened in London and the US. He has long been an avid art collector.

FILMS: As co-screenwriter—In Germany: *Menschen am Sonntag/People on Sunday, Der Teufelsreporter* 1929; *Seitensprünge* (story only) 1930; *Der falsche Ehemann, Emil und die Detektive/Emil and the Detectives* (scripted alone), *Der Mann der seinen Mörder sucht, Ihre Hoheit befiehlt* 1931; *Das Blaue vom Himmel, Ein blonder Traum, Es war einmal ein Walzer, Scampolo—ein Kind der Strasse* 1932; *Was Frauen träumen, Madame wünscht keine Kinder* 1933. In the US: *Adorable* (co-story only; based on his co-script for *Ihre Hoheit befiehlt*) 1933; *One Exciting Adventure* (co-story only), *Music in the Air* 1934; *Lottery Lover* 1935; *Champagne Waltz* (co-story only) 1937; *Bluebeard's Eighth Wife* 1938; *Midnight, What a Life, Ninotchka* 1939; *Rhythm on the River* (co-story only), *Arise My Love* 1940; *Hold Back the Dawn* 1941; *Ball of Fire* 1942; *A Song Is Born* (based on his co-sc. for *Ball of Fire*) 1948; *Casino Royale* (addnl. writing, uncredited; UK) 1967. As director and co-screenwriter—In France: *Mauvaise Graine* (co-dir. with Alexander Esway, story) 1933. In the US: *The Major and the Minor* 1942; *Five Graves to Cairo* 1943; *Double Indemnity* 1944; *The Lost Weekend* 1945; *The Emperor Waltz, A Foreign Affair* 1948; *Sunset Boulevard* 1950. As producer-director and co-screenwriter—*Ace in the Hole/The Big Carnival* 1951; *Stalag 17* 1953; *Sabrina* 1954; *The Seven Year Itch* 1955; *The Spirit of St. Louis* (dir., co-sc. only), *Love in the Afternoon* 1957; *Witness for the Prosecution* (dir., co-sc. only) 1958; *Some Like It Hot* 1959; *The Apartment* 1960; *One Two Three* 1961; *Irma la Douce* 1963; *Kiss Me Stupid* 1964; *The Fortune Cookie* 1966; *The Private Life of Sherlock Holmes* (US/UK) 1970; *Avanti!* 1972; *The Front Page* (dir., co-sc. only) 1974; *Fedora* (Ger./Fr.) 1978; *Buddy Buddy* 1981; *Directed by William Wyler* (act. only) 1986; *The Exiles* (act. only) 1989.

Wilder, Gene. Actor. Born Jerry Silberman, on June 11, 1935, in Milwaukee. *ed.* U. of Iowa. The son of an immigrant from Russia who prospered as the manufacturer of miniature beer and whiskey bottles, he began taking drama classes while at college and played some summer stock in the East. Upon graduation, he went to England, where he enrolled at the Old Vic Theatre School in Bristol. He won the fencing championship of the school and after returning to the US taught fencing for a living. He also worked as a chauffeur and a toy salesman before making his off-Broadway debut in 1961. He joined the Actors Studio and soon began playing important parts on Broadway. He drew much favorable comment with his first screen exposure, a small but memorable role as a frightened young undertaker abducted for a joy ride in *Bonnie and Clyde.* He was nominated for an Oscar for his second film role as a neurotic misfit in Mel Brooks's *The Producers* (1968). A protégé of Brooks, he later developed into one of the prime comedians of the American screen of the 70s, finding his niche in the portrayal of jittery, vulnerable, often embarrassed or disgraced comic characters, notably Dr. Frederick Frankenstein (that's FRONK-en-steen) in *Young Frankenstein.* He made his debut as a director in 1975, directing himself from his own script in *The Adventure of Sherlock Holmes' Smarter Brother.* He was married to comedienne Gilda RADNER from 1984 until her death from cancer in 1989. Since her death, he has been a vocal supporter of various cancer causes and the founder of a safehouse (named for Radner) for patients.

FILMS: *Bonnie and Clyde* 1967; *The Producers* 1968; *Start the Revolution Without Me, Quackser Fortune Has a Cousin in the Bronx* 1970; *Willy Wonka and the Chocolate Factory* 1971; *Everything You Always Wanted to Know About Sex* 1972; *Rhinoceros, Blazing Saddles, Young Frankenstein* (title role; also co-sc.), *The Little Prince* (as The Fox) 1974; *The Adventure of Sherlock Holmes' Smarter Brother* (title role; also dir., sc.) 1975; *Silver Streak* 1976; *The World's Greatest Lover* (also prod., dir., sc.) 1977; *The Frisco Kid* 1979; *Stir Crazy, Sunday Lovers* (also dir., sc. one segment) 1980; *Hanky Panky* 1982; *The Woman in Red* (also dir.) 1984; *Haunted Honeymoon* (also dir.) 1986; *See No Evil, Hear No Evil* 1989; *Funny About Love* 1990; *Another You* 1991.

Wilder, Thornton. Playwright, novelist, screenwriter. *b.* Apr. 17, 1897, Madison, Wis. *d.* 1975. *ed.* Berkeley; Yale; Princeton. The celebrated author, winner of three Pulitzer Prizes (for the plays 'Our Town' and 'The Skin of Our Teeth' and the novel *The Bridge of San Luis Rey*), also collaborated on the screenplay of his 'Our Town' (1940) and that of the Hitchcock thriller *Shadow of a Doubt* (1943). Other writers adapted to the screen the novel *The Bridge of San Luis Rey* (1929, 1944) and his play 'The Matchmaker' (1958), which also provided the story basis for the musical 'Hello Dolly!' (filmed 1969).

Wilding, Michael. Actor. *b.* July 23, 1912, Westcliff-on-Sea, England. *d.* 1979. Polished, charming leading man of the British (and occasionally American) screen, the son of a career army officer and an actress. He started out a portraitist and commercial artist and in 1933 joined the art department of a British film studio. He soon switched to acting on the London stage and in films and by the late 40s had developed into a popular star, specializing in patrician roles. However, he was best known in the US as the second husband (1952–57) of Elizabeth TAYLOR and the father of two of her children. She was his second wife. He married his fourth, actress Margaret LEIGHTON, in 1964.

FILMS INCLUDE: *Pastorale* (Aus.) 1933; *Wedding Group* 1935; *Tilly of Bloomsbury, Convoy* 1940; *Kipps* (as Ronnie Walshingham), *Ships with Wings* 1941; *In Which We Serve* 1942; *Dear Octopus/The Randolph Family* 1943; *English Without Tears/Her Man Gilbey* 1944; *Piccadilly Incident, Carnival* 1946; *The Courtneys of Curzon Street/The Courtney Affair/Kathy's Love Affair, An Ideal Husband* (as Lord Goring) 1947; *Spring in Park Lane* 1948; *Under Capricorn, Maytime in Mayfair* 1949; *Stage Fright* 1950; *Into the Blue/Man in the Dinghy* (also prod.), *The Law and the Lady* (US), *The Lady with the Lamp* 1951; *Derby Day* 1952; *Trent's Last Case, Torch Song* (US) 1953; *The Egyptian* (US) 1954; *The Glass Slipper* (as Prince Charming; US), *The Scarlet Coat* (US) 1955; *Zarak* 1956; *Danger Within/Breakout* 1959; *The World of Suzie Wong* (US/UK) 1960; *The Naked Edge* (US/UK), *I Due Nemici/The Best of Enemies* (It./UK) 1961; *A Girl Named Tamiko* (US) 1963; *The Sweet Ride* (US) 1968; *Waterloo* (as Sir William Ponsonby; USSR/It.) 1970; *Lady Caroline Lamb* 1972.

wild motor. See VARIABLE-SPEED MOTOR.

wild picture. See M.O.S.

wild sound. Motion picture industry colloquial term for sound recorded without an accompanying picture or along with filming but not in synchronization with the footage being shot. Wild sound is often recorded on location by the sound engineer to capture available natural sounds and sound effects. These are later synchronized with the picture in the cutting room. See also M.O.S.; SOUND EFFECTS; WILD TRACK.

wild track (also **"wild sound," "wild recording"**). A sound recording not intended to synchronize precisely with the corresponding picture. It may be recorded while the film is being shot or separately and usually consists of such sound items as crowd noises, random voices, or the humming of birds. A wild track may also be used as a guide to a film editor in editing a sound scene that includes a number of CUTAWAYS.

Willat, Irvin. Director. *b.* 1892, Stamford, Conn. *d.* 1976. He entered films as an actor with IMP in 1910 and appeared in a number of Mary Pickford vehicles. He later developed an interest in the technical side of films and worked in a processing lab and in the manufacture of cameras and lenses. In 1916 he was the director of photography on Thomas Ince's ambitious production *Civilization.* After turning director the following year, he made a good number of quality films, typically emphasizing action and adventure. His career virtually ended with the switch to sound. He was at one time married to silent star Billie DOVE.

FILMS INCLUDE: *The Zeppelin's Last Raid* 1917; *The Claws of the Hun* 1918; *The False Faces, Behind the Door* 1919; *Partners of the Tide, Face of the World, Fifty Candles* 1921; *Yellow Men and Gold, The Siren Call, Pawned, On the High Seas* 1922; *All the Brothers Were Valiant, Fog Bound* 1923; *Three Miles Out, The Heritage of the Desert, The Wanderer of the Wasteland, North of 36, The Story Without a Name* 1924; *The Air Mail, Rugged Water, The Ancient Highway* 1925; *The Enchanted Hill, Paradise* 1926; *Back to God's Country* 1927; *Submarine, The Michigan Kid, The Cavalier* 1928; *The Isle of Lost Ships* 1929; *Damaged Love* 1931; *Old Louisiana* 1937.

William, Warren. Actor. *b.* Warren Krech, Dec. 2, 1895, Aitkin, Minn. *d.* 1948. The son of a newspaper publisher, he started out as a reporter, but after returning from WW I service in Europe he decided on a stage career. After training at the American Academy of Dramatic Arts, he played in stock and under his real name appeared in occasional silent films, including the serial *Plunder,* opposite Pearl White. By the mid-20s he was a leading man on Broadway. Settling in Hollywood in the early 30s, he played suave, intelligent leading men but was restricted for the most part to B pictures. A notable exception was De Mille's *Cleopatra,* in which he portrayed Julius Caesar, but more typically he played smart detectives, reporters, and adventurers in slick low-budget thrillers, including the title role in "The Lone Wolf" series and such mystery heroes as Philo Vance and Perry Mason. He often co-starred with Bette Davis in her early pictures.

FILMS INCLUDE: As Warren Krech—*The Town That Forgot God* 1922; *Plunder* (serial) 1923. As Warren William—*Honor of the Family, Expensive Women* 1931; *The Woman from Monte Carlo, Beauty and the Boss, The Mouthpiece, The Dark Horse, Skyscraper Souls, Three on a Match, The Match King* 1932; *Employees' Entrance, The Mind Reader, Gold Diggers of 1933, Goodbye Again, Lady for a Day* 1933; *Bedside, Upper World, Dr. Monica, Cleopatra* (as Julius Caesar), *The Dragon Murder Case* (as Detective Philo Vance), *The Case of the Howling Dog* (as Perry Mason), *Imitation of Life* 1934; *The Secret Bride, Living on Velvet, The Case of the Curious Bride* (as Perry Mason), *Don't Bet on Blondes, The Case of the Lucky Legs* (as Perry Mason) 1935; *Times Square Playboy, Satan Met a Lady, The Case of the Velvet Claws* (as Perry Mason), *Stage Struck, Go West Young Man* 1936; *Outcast, Midnight Madonna, The Firefly, Madame X* 1937; *Arsene Lupin Returns, The First 100 Years, Wives Under Suspicion* 1938; *The Lone Wolf Spy Hunt* (title role), *The Gracie Allen Murder Case* (as Philo Vance), *The Man in the Iron Mask* (as D'Artagnan), *Day-Time Wife* 1939; *The Lone Wolf Strikes* (title role), *Lillian Russell, Trail of the Vigilantes, Arizona* 1940; *The Lone Wolf Takes a Chance* (title role), *Wild Geese Calling, The Wolf Man* 1941; *Counter-Espionage* 1942; *One Dangerous Night, Passport to Suez* 1943; *Fear* 1946; *The Private Affairs of Bel Ami* 1947.

William Morris Agency. The world's oldest talent agency, founded in 1898 in New York City by William Morris, Sr. His son, William, Jr., took over upon the founder's death in 1932 and remained president until 1952. The agency's clients during the first fifty years of motion pictures included James Cagney, Eddie Cantor, Katharine Hepburn, Al Jolson, Marilyn Monroe, Will Rogers, and Frank Sinatra. Its role as one of Hollywood's most powerful arbiters was somewhat eclipsed throughout the 80s by such agencies as CREATIVE ARTISTS AGENCY and INTERNATIONAL CREATIVE MANAGEMENT, but by the 90s this stalwart re-emerged once again as a powerhouse. See AGENT.

Williams, Bill. Actor. *b.* Herman Katt, in 1916, in Brooklyn, N.Y. *d.* 1992. *ed.* Pratt Institute (Brooklyn). A former swimming pro, he began his acting career in stock and vaudeville. He entered films in 1944, following WW II military service. Blond, rugged, and honest-faced, he played nice-guy leads and second leads in many films, mostly in low-budget productions, often opposite Barbara HALE, who became his wife. Their son, William KATT, is a film and TV actor.

FILMS INCLUDE: *Murder in the Blue Room, Thirty Seconds Over Tokyo* 1944; *West of the Pecos* 1945; *Deadline at Dawn, Till the End of Time* 1946; *A Likely Story* 1947; *The Clay Pigeon, A Woman's Secret, The Stratton Story* 1949; *Blue Grass of Kentucky, The Cariboo Trail* 1950; *The Last Outpost* 1951; *Son of Paleface* 1952; *Apache Ambush* 1955; *The Halliday Brand* 1957; *Space Master X-7, Legion of the Doomed* 1958; *Alaska Passage* 1959; *Oklahoma Territory* 1960; *The Scarface Mob* 1962; *Law of the Lawless* 1964; *The Hallelujah Trail* 1965; *Buckskin* 1968; *Rio Lobo* 1970; *Scandalous John* 1971; *The Giant Spider Invasion* 1975; *69 Minutes* 1977.

Williams, Billy. British director of photography. Born in 1929. Elevated to lighting cameraman late in the 60s, he rapidly established a reputation as a highly gifted color cinematographer and has since worked on a number of major productions on both sides of the Atlantic. He was nominated for an Academy Award for best cinematography for *On Golden Pond* (1981) and won the following year in the same category for *Gandhi* (1982).

FILMS INCLUDE: *Just Like a Woman* 1966; *Billion Dollar Brain* 1967; *The Magus* 1968; *Women in Love* 1969; *Sunday Bloody Sunday* 1971; *Zee & Co./X Y & Z, Pope Joan* 1972; *Kid Blue* (US), *Night Watch, The Exorcist* (co-phot.; US) 1973; *The Wind and the Lion* (US) 1975; *Voyage of the Damned* 1976; *Eagle's Wing, The Silent Partner* (Can.), *Saturn 3* (US) 1979; *On Golden Pond* (US) 1981; *Gandhi, Monsignor* (US) 1982; *Survivors* (US) 1983; *Dreamchild, Eleni* (US), *Ordeal by Innocence* (US) 1985; *The Manhattan Project* (US) 1986; *Suspect* (US) 1987; *Just Ask for a Diamond/Diamond's Edge* (US) 1988; *The Rainbow* 1989; *Stella* (US) 1990; *Shadow of the Wolf* 1993.

Williams, Billy Dee. Actor. Born on Apr. 6, 1937, in New York City. Poised, suave, athletic leading man of the American stage, TV, and films. Raised in Harlem, he made his stage debut at age seven and after a varied career as an entertainer, and training at Sidney Poitier's acting workshop, returned to the Broadway stage as an adult in 1961. He appeared sporadically in films from the late 50s and shot to stardom in the early 70s as Diana Ross's leading man in *Lady Sings the Blues* and *Mahogany.* In *The Empire Strikes Back* and *Return of the Jedi* he was the scoundrel-turned rebel Lando Calrissian. He has also appeared in many TV series episodes and co-starred in the highly acclaimed teleplay 'Brian's Song.'

FILMS INCLUDE: *The Last Angry Man* 1959; *The Out-of-Towners, Lost Flight* 1970; *Lady Sings the Blues, The Final Comedown* 1972; *Hit!* 1973; *The Take* 1974; *Mahogany* 1975; *The Bingo Long Traveling All-Stars and Motor Kings, Blast* 1976; *Scott Joplin* 1977; *The Empire Strikes Back* 1980; *Nighthawks* 1981; *Return of the Jedi, Marvin and Tige* 1983; *Fear City* 1985; *Number One with a Bullet, Deadly Illusion* 1987; *The Impostor* 1988; *Batman* 1989; *The Pit and the Pendulum, Driving Me Crazy* 1992.

Williams, Cara. Actress. Born Bernice Kamiat, on June 29, 1925, in Brooklyn, N.Y. An actress since childhood, she came to Hollywood in her teens and for a while lent her voice to the dubbing of animated cartoons. She was signed by Fox in 1942 and subsequently played supporting parts, both dramatic and comic, and an occasional lead. She was featured prominently in such diverse films as *Boomerang* and *The Girl Next Door* and was nominated for an Oscar for her performance in *The Defiant Ones.* She has also appeared much on TV, including in her own comedy series, 'The Cara Williams Show.' She was married to John BARRYMORE, JR., from 1952 until 1959.

FILMS INCLUDE: *Happy Land* 1943; *Something for the Boys, In the Meantime Darling* 1944; *Don Juan Quilligan* 1945; *Boomerang* 1947; *Sitting Pretty, The Saxon Charm* 1948; *Knock on Any Door* 1949; *The Girl Next Door* 1953; *Monte Carlo Baby, The Great Diamond Robbery* 1954; *Meet Me in Las Vegas* 1956; *The Helen Morgan Story* 1957; *The Defiant Ones* 1958; *Never Steal Anything Small* 1959; *The Man from the Diners' Club* 1963; *Doctors' Wives* 1971; *The White Buffalo* 1977.

Williams, Cindy. Actress. Born on Aug. 22, 1947, in Van Nuys, Calif. *ed.* Los Angeles City Coll. A drama major, she went to Hollywood directly from college and served tables in a local restaurant for months before she began landing small roles on TV and in films. She first gained attention on the big screen in *American Graffiti* (1973), but it was on TV that she became a popular star as Shirley in the successful late 70s TV comedy series 'Laverne and Shirley.' She also appeared on TV in the 80s and 90s.

FILMS: *Gas-s-s-s* 1970; *Drive He Said* 1971; *Travels with My Aunt* 1972; *American Graffiti, The Killing Kind* 1973; *The Conversation* 1974; *Mr. Ricco* 1975; *The First Nudie Musical* 1976; *More American Graffiti* 1979; *Uforia, Spaceship/The*

Creature Wasn't Nice 1981; *Big Man on Campus, Rude Awakening* 1989; *Bingo!* 1991; *Father of the Bride* (co-prod. only), *The Leftovers* 1992; *Meet Wally Sparks* 1997.

Williams, Earle. Actor. *b.* Feb. 28, 1880, Sacramento, Calif. *d.* 1927. For many years the top male star of Vitagraph and one of the leading personalities of the early silent screen. Coming from the stage in 1908, he starred in scores of films of a wide variety, often opposite Edith STOREY, Anita STEWART, and Clara Kimball YOUNG.

FILMS INCLUDE: *Antony and Cleopatra, Barbara Fritchie* 1908; *The Life of Moses* 1909–10; *Uncle Tom's Cabin, Capital vs. Labor* 1910; *The Wager, A Tale of Two Cities, The Prince and the Pumps, An Aeroplane Elopement* 1911; *The Lady of the Lake, The Seventh Son, Saving an Audience, Two Women and Two Men* 1912; *The Delayed Letter, The Ambassador's Disappearance, The Tiger Lily, The Artist's Great Madonna, Soul in Bondage, The Carpenter, A Modern Psyche, Love's Sunset, My Lady of Idleness* 1913; *Happy-Go-Lucky, My Official Wife, The Christian, Memories That Haunt, Lily of the Valley* 1914; *Two Women, The Goddess* (serial), *The Juggernaut, The Awakening, Sins of the Mothers, From Headquarters* 1915; *My Lady's Slipper, The Scarlet Runner* (serial) 1916; *Arsene Lupin, The Love Doctor, The Soul Master, The Hawk* 1917; *The Seal of Silence, A Diplomatic Mission* 1918; *Rogues of Romance, A Gentleman of Quality* 1919; *The Fortune Hunter, Captain Swift* 1920; *Lucky Carson, Diamonds Adrift, The Silver Car* 1921; *The Man from Downing Street, Restless Souls, You Never Know* 1922; *Masters of Men, The Eternal Struggle, Jealous Husbands* 1923; *Borrowed Husbands* 1924; *Lena Rivers, The Adventurous Sex, The Ancient Mariner* 1925; *Skyrocket, Diplomacy* 1926; *Red Signals, Say It with Diamonds* 1927.

Williams, Elmo. Director, producer, film editor. Born on Apr. 30, 1913, in Oklahoma City, Okla. He began his film career in England as a cutter in 1933. Returning to the US in 1939, he joined RKO, for which he edited many films through the late 40s. In 1952 he shared the Academy Award for the editing of *High Noon.* The following year he directed his first film, *The Tall Texan,* a taut, offbeat Western. In 1954 he surpassed this first achievement with an excellent feature documentary of the real American West, *The Cowboy,* which he also produced. He subsequently worked as second-unit director on several films and was associate producer and coordinator of battle episodes on *The Longest Day* (1962). He was then put in charge of Fox's operations in Britain. In 1970 he produced *Tora! Tora! Tora!* and the following year was appointed head of worldwide production at Fox.

FILMS: As director—*The Tall Texan* 1952; *The Cowboy* (also prod.) 1954; *Apache Warrior, Hell Ship Mutiny* (co-dir. with Lee Sholem) 1957; *The Vikings* (2nd-unit dir. only) 1958; *The Big Gamble* (African action sequences only) 1961. As producer—*The Longest Day* (assoc. prod. and action coordinator) 1962; *Zorba the Greek* 1964; *The Blue Max* (exec. prod.) 1966; *Tora! Tora! Tora!* 1970; *Sidewinder One* 1977; *Man Woman and Child* 1983.

Williams, Emlyn. Actor, playwright, screenwriter, director. *b.* George Emlyn Williams, Nov. 26, 1905, in Mostyn, Wales. *d.* 1987. Raised in a poor mining community, he was spared the lot of a coal miner, thanks to the interest of an understanding teacher. He received an excellent education on scholarships in Switzerland and in Oxford and rose to eminence on the English and American stage. He made both his London and New York debuts in 1927 and by the mid-30s was an established actor, playwright, and stage director. The best known of his many plays is 'The Corn Is Green' (1938), a dramatization of his own boyhood, which received the New York Drama Critics Award as the best foreign play in 1941. He also wrote two volumes of autobiography, *George* (1961) and *Emlyn* (1973), and *Beyond Belief* (1967), a study of murder, as well as a number of screenplays. He appeared prominently in many British and some Hollywood films from 1932 until his retirement in 1970.

FILMS (as actor): *The Frightened Lady/Criminal at Large, Men of Tomorrow, Sally Bishop* 1932; *Friday the 13th* (also sc.) 1933; *The Man Who Knew Too Much* (addnl. dial. only), *Evergreen* (co-sc. only), *My Song for You, Evensong, Roadhouse* 1934; *The Iron Duke, The Dictator/The Love Affair of the Dictator/Loves of a Dictator* (as King Christian VII of Denmark), *City of Beautiful Nonsense, The Divine Spark* (co-sc. only) 1935; *Broken Blossoms* (also sc.) 1936; *Night Must Fall* (play basis only; US), *I Claudius* (as Caligula; unfinished) 1937; *Dead Men Tell No Tales* (also addnl. dial.), *A Night Alone, The Citadel* (also addnl. dial.) 1938; *They Drive by Night, Jamaica Inn, The Stars Look Down* 1939; *The Girl in the News, You Will Remember* 1940; *This England* (also sc.), *Major Barbara* (as Snobby Price), *Hatter's Castle* 1941; *Life Begins at Eight-Thirty* (play basis only; US) 1942; *The Corn Is Green* (play basis only; US) 1945; *The Last Days of Dolwyn/Dolwyn* (also dir., sc.) 1949; *Three Husbands* (US) 1950; *The Scarf* (US), *The Magic Box, Another Man's Poison* 1951; *Ivanhoe* (as Wamba the Jester; US/UK) 1952; *The Deep Blue Sea* 1955; *I Accuse!* (as Emile Zola) 1958; *Beyond This Place, The Wreck of the Mary Deare* (US) 1959; *The L-Shaped Room* 1962; *Night Must Fall* (play basis only) 1964; *Eye of the Devil* 1967; *The Walking Stick, David Copperfield* (as Mr. Dick) 1970.

Williams, Esther. Actress. Born on Aug. 8, 1923, in Los Angeles. A champion swimmer at 15 and later a part-time model at a department store, she interrupted her studies at the L.A. City College to join Billy Rose's Aquacade, where she was spotted by an MGM scout. Like many other starlets of the company in the 40s, she was introduced to the public modestly in an "Andy Hardy" film in 1942. Her career was really launched two years later in *Bathing Beauty,* the first of a long string of escapist musical comedies in luscious color featuring lavish song and dance numbers and highlighted by spectacular underwater scenes. Miss Williams, billed by publicity as "Hollywood's Mermaid" or "The Queen of the Surf," looked delicious in bathing suits and peachy in Technicolor and most of her films were top box-office hits. But in the late 50s, when she tried to emerge from the water into dramatic roles, her film career came to a quick end. She retired from the screen in the early 60s and invested in various business ventures, including Esther Williams Swimming Pools. Her third husband until the time of his death was actor Fernando LAMAS.

FILMS: *Andy Hardy's Double Life* 1942; *A Guy Named Joe* 1943; *Bathing Beauty* 1944; *Thrill of a Romance* 1945; *Ziegfeld Follies, The Hoodlum Saint, Easy to Wed* 1946; *Till the Clouds Roll By* (cameo), *Fiesta, This Time for Keeps* 1947; *On an Island with You* 1948; *Take Me Out to the Ball Game, Neptune's Daughter* 1949; *Duchess of Idaho, Pagan Love Song* 1950; *Callaway Went Thataway* (unbilled cameo), *Texas Carnival* 1951; *Skirts Ahoy!, Million Dollar Mermaid* (as swimmer-actress Annette Kellerman) 1952; *Dangerous When Wet, Easy to Love* 1953; *Jupiter's Darling* 1955; *The Unguarded Moment* 1956; *Raw Wind in Eden* 1958; *The Big Show, The Magic Fountain* (made in Spain; never released in the US) 1961.

Williams, Guinn ("Big Boy"). Actor. *b.* Apr. 26, 1899, Decatur, Tex. *d.* 1962. The son of a US congressman, he played some professional baseball before arriving in Hollywood in 1919. Following a number of bit parts in Goldwyn films, he starred in many Westerns for various independent companies in the early 20s. He gradually shifted to character parts, often in support of Will Rogers. It was Rogers who nicknamed him "Big Boy" for his size, and he was known as Big Boy Williams for most of his career. Williams was briefly back in the saddle as a cowboy star in the 30s, but he soon reverted to character parts again, mostly playing comedy relief, often as a slow-witted cowhand but sometimes also as a tough heavy.

FILMS INCLUDE: *Almost a Husband* 1919; *The Jack Rider, The Vengeance Trail, Western Firebrands* 1921; *Across the Border, The Cowboy King, Blaze Away, Trail of Hate, The Freshie* 1922; *Cyclone Jones, Riders at Night* 1923; *The Avenger, The Eagle's Claw* 1924; *Red Blood and Blue, Fangs of Wolfheart, Sporting West, Whistling Jim, Big Stunt* 1925; *Brown of Harvard* 1926; *Slide Kelly Slide, Backstage, Babe Comes Home, Lightning, The College Widow* 1927; *My Man, Burning Daylight, Ladies' Night in a Turkish Bath, Vamping Venus* 1928; *Noah's Ark, From Headquarters, Lucky Star, The Forward Pass* 1929; *The Big Fight, Liliom* 1930; *The Bachelor Father* 1931; *You Said a Mouthful* 1932; *Mystery Squadron* (serial), *Phantom Broadcast, College Coach* 1933; *Palooka, Half a Sinner, Here Comes the Navy, Flirtation Walk* 1934; *Private Worlds, The Glass Key, The Littlest Rebel* 1935; *The Vigilantes Are Coming* (serial), *Muss 'Em Up, Powdersmoke Range, Kelly the Second, You Only Live Once, A Star Is Born, The Singing Marine, Big City* 1937; *The Bad Man of Brimstone, You and Me, Professor Beware, Hold That Co-Ed* 1938; *Dodge City, 6000 Enemies, Mutiny on the Blackhawk, Bad Lands, Blackmail* 1939; *The Fighting 69th, Castle on the Hudson, Wagons Westward, Dulcy, Santa Fe Trail* 1940; *Billy the Kid, You'll Never Get Rich, Swamp Water* 1941; *The Bugle Sounds* 1942; *The Desperadoes* 1943; *Belle of the Yukon* 1945; *Brimstone* 1949; *Rocky Mountain* 1950; *Springfield Rifle, Hangman's Knot* 1952; *Southwest Passage* 1954; *The Alamo* 1960; *The Comancheros* 1962.

Williams, Hugh. Actor, playwright. *b.* Brian Williams, Mar. 6, 1904, Bexhill, England. *d.* 1969. He trained for the stage at the Royal Academy of Dramatic Art, appeared in many plays from the age of 17, and within several years developed into a popular leading man with the Liverpool Repertory and on London's West End. He came to the US to appear on Broadway in 1929 and the following year made his screen debut in the Hollywood production of *Charley's Aunt,* in which he co-starred with Charlie Ruggles. He then played leads and supporting parts in many British and some American films. He was the author of several plays, some in collaboration with his wife, Margaret Vyner. He also collaborated on the screenplay for the Hollywood screen adaptation of his play *The Grass Is Greener* (1960).

FILMS INCLUDE: *Charley's Aunt* (US) 1930; *A Night in Montmartre* 1931; *In a Monastery Garden, White Face, Rome Express* 1932; *Bitter Sweet, Sorrell and Son* 1933; *Outcast Lady* (US) 1934; *David Copperfield* (as Steerforth; US), *Let's Live Tonight* (US), *The Last Journey* 1935; *The Amateur Gentleman* 1936; *Dead Men Tell No Tales, Bank Holiday* 1938; *Wuthering Heights* (as Hindley; US), *Dark Eyes of London/The Human Monster, Inspector Hornleigh* 1939; *Ships with Wings* 1941; *One of Our Aircraft Is Missing, The Day Will Dawn/The Avengers* 1942; *A Girl in a Million* 1946; *An Ideal Husband* (as Sir Robert Chiltney), *Take My Life* 1947; *The Blind Goddess* 1948; *The Gift Horse/Glory at Sea, The Holly and the Ivy* 1952; *The Intruder* 1953; *Khartoum* 1966; *Doctor Faustus* 1967.

Williams, JoBeth. Actress. Born in 1953 in Houston, Tex. *ed.* Brown U. Handsome, charming screen lead. After being named one of the top ten college girls of 1969–70 by *Glamour* Magazine, she acted with regional theater companies along the eastern corridor and spent two years working in daytime serials. She debuted in film in 1979 and established her appeal as the longing suburban matron in *The Big Chill.* Film appearances since the early 80s, however, have been limited and mixed in quality. Active in TV movies. Married TV director John Pasquin.

FILMS INCLUDE: *Kramer vs. Kramer* 1979; *The Dogs of War, Stir Crazy* 1980; *Endangered Species, Poltergeist* 1982; *The Big Chill* 1983; *American Dreamer, Teachers* 1984; *Desert Bloom, Poltergeist II: The Other Side* 1986; *Memories of Me* 1988; *Welcome Home* 1989; *Switch, Dutch* 1991; *Stop! or My Mom Will Shoot, Me Myself and I* 1992; *Wyatt Earp* 1994; *Jungle 2 Jungle* 1997.

Williams, John. Actor. *b.* Apr. 15, 1903, Chalfont St. Giles, England. *d.* 1983. *ed.* Lancing Coll. On the British stage at 13 and frequently also on Broadway from the age of 21, he played leads, then suave character parts, in many plays. He appeared in British films from the mid-30s and in Hollywood productions from the late 40s. Memorable as Inspector Hubbard in the stage, screen, and TV versions of *Dial M for Murder.*

FILMS INCLUDE: In the UK—*Emil and the Detectives/Emil* 1935; *The Foreman Went to France/Somewhere in France, Next of Kin* 1942. In the US—*A Woman's Vengeance* 1948; *Kind Lady* 1951; *Thunder in the East* 1953; *Dial M For Murder, The Student Prince, Sabrina* 1954; *To Catch a Thief* 1955; *D-Day the Sixth of June, The Solid Gold Cadillac* 1956; *Will Success Spoil Rock Hunter?* 1957; *Witness for the Prosecution* 1958; *The Young Philadelphians* 1959; *Visit to a Small Planet, Midnight Lace* 1960: *Dear Brigitte, Harlow* (Carol Lynley version) 1965; *The Last of the Secret Agents?* 1966; *Double Trouble* 1967; *The Secret War of Harry Frigg, A Flea in Her Ear* (US/Fr.) 1968; *Lost in the Stars* 1974; *No Deposit No Return* 1976; *Hot Lead and Cold Feet* 1978.

Williams, John (Johnny). Composer. Born in 1932, in Floral Park, N.Y. *ed.* UCLA; Juilliard School of Music. A former jazz pianist and recording artist, he began composing for TV in the late 50s and for films in the early 60s. An original and versatile artist, he composed scores for numerous films in a wide range of styles. In 1971 he won an Oscar for the orchestration of *Fiddler on the Roof.* He received another Academy Award for the score of Steven Spielberg's *Jaws* (1975) and a third for George Lucas's *Star Wars* (1977). These scores marked the beginning of his status as the premier contemporary composer of lush epic themes, particularly for the films of Spielberg, with whom he has worked since the director's first feature, *The Sugarland Express* (1974). In all, Williams has received over a dozen Oscar nominations. He has also composed for the concert hall.

FILMS INCLUDE: *I Passed for White* 1960; *Bachelor Flat* 1962; *Diamond Head* 1963; *The Killers* 1964; *None but the Brave* 1965; *The Rare Breed, How to Steal a Million, The Plainsman, Penelope* 1966; *A Guide for the Married Man, Fitzwilly, Valley of the Dolls* 1967; *Sergeant Ryker* 1968; *Daddy's Gone A-Hunting, Goodbye Mr. Chips* (cond. and mus. superv. only) 1970; *Jane Eyre, Fiddler on the Roof* (scoring only) 1971; *The Cowboys, Images, The Poseidon Adventure, Pete 'n' Tillie* 1972; *The Long Goodbye, The Man Who Loved Cat Dancing, Cinderella Liberty* 1973; *The Sugarland Express, Conrack, Earthquake, The Towering Inferno* 1974; *The Eiger Sanction, Jaws* 1975; *Family Plot, The Missouri Breaks, Midway* 1976; *Star Wars, Close Encounters of the Third Kind* 1977; *Jaws 2, The Fury, Superman, The Stud* 1978; *Dracula* 1979; *Airplane!, Superman 2, The Empire Strikes Back* 1980; *Raiders of the Lost Ark, Heartbeeps* 1981; *E.T.—The Extra-Terrestrial, Yes, Giorgio* 1982; *Beyond the Limit, The Big Chill,*

Jaws 3: 3-D, Return of the Jedi, Monsignor, Superman 3 1983; *Indiana Jones and the Temple of Doom, Best Defense, The River* 1984; *Terror in the Aisles, Top Secret!, Emma's War, Spacecamp* 1985; *Ferris Bueller's Day Off* 1986; *The Witches of Eastwick, Empire of the Sun, Jaws: The Revenge, Superman 4: The Quest for Peace* 1987; *The Accidental Tourist* 1988; *Always, Born on the Fourth of July, Indiana Jones and the Last Crusade* 1989; *Home Alone, Presumed Innocent, Stanley and Iris* 1990; *JFK, Hook* 1991; *Far and Away* 1992; *Jurassic Park, Schindler's List* 1993; *Nixon, Sabrina* 1995; *Sleepers* 1996; *Devil's Advocate, The Lost World, Rosewood* 1997.

Williams, Kathlyn. Actress. *b.* 1888, Butte, Mont. *d.* 1960. *ed.* Wesleyan. She entered films in 1910 following some stage experience, and soon became the most popular star on the Selig lot, at first anonymously as "the Selig Girl," then by her own name. She starred in a variety of productions, often opposite Tom MIX, specializing in melodrama and jungle adventure films. In 1913 she made film history as the star of America's first screen serial, *The Adventures of Kathlyn.* The following year she played the feminine lead in the first of several screen adaptations of Rex Beach's novel *The Spoilers,* an ambitious nine-reel production. She remained a top star at Selig until the company's demise, then joined Paramount, where she continued as a star through the mid-20s. She gradually shifted to supporting roles in the latter part of the decade and remained active through the mid-30s. She tried a comeback as a character actress in the late 40s, but a car accident in which she lost a leg ended her career. She died ten years later of a heart attack. Her second husband (from 1916) was film producer Charles Eyton.

FILMS INCLUDE: *The Fire Chief's Daughter, Mazeppa* 1910; *Captain Kate, The Two Orphans, Lost in the Jungle, Back to the Primitive, Maud Muller* 1911; *The Brotherhood of Man, The Adopted Son, The Last Dance* (also sc.), *Harbor Island* 1912; *A Little Child Shall Lead Them, The Governor's Daughter, A Mansion of Misery, The Artist and the Brute, A Wise Old Elephant, The Adventures of Kathlyn* (serial), *The Child of the Sea, Thor—Lord of the Jungle, When May Weds December, The Love of Penelope* 1913; *The Leopard's Foundling, Caryl of the Mountains, Chip of the Flying U, The Spoilers, Her Sacrifice, Hearts and Masks* 1914; *The Vision of the Shepherd, A Carpet of Bagdad, The Rosary, A Sultan of the Desert* (also sc.) 1915; *The Ne'er-Do-Well* 1916; *Redeeming Love, Big Timber* 1917; *We Can't Have Everything, The Highway of Hope* 1918; *Just a Wife, Conrad in Quest of His Youth* 1920; *Hush, Morals, Forbidden Fruit, A Private Scandal, A Man's Home* 1921; *Clarence* 1922; *The World's Applause, Trimmed in Scarlet, Broadway Gold, The Spanish Dancer* 1923; *Wanderer of the Wasteland, Single Wives, The Enemy Sex, The City that Never Sleeps* 1924; *The Best People, The Wanderer, Locked Doors* 1925; *Sally in Our Alley* 1927; *We Americans, Our Dancing Daughters, Honeymoon Flats* 1928; *The Single Standard* 1929; *Road to Paradise* 1930; *Daddy Long Legs* 1931; *Unholy Love* 1932; *Blood Money* 1933; *Rendezvous at Midnight* 1935; *The Other Love* 1947.

Williams, Paul. Singer, composer, songwriter, actor. Born on Sept. 19, 1940, in Omaha, Nebr. Versatile, blond, diminutive (5' 2") performer-composer of American TV, recordings, and films. An apprentice jockey at 13, he later worked for an insurance company, joined a skydiving show, and appeared on the stage in summer stock. He began playing bit roles in films in the mid-60s and gained popularity in the 70s as a singer, songwriter ('We've Only Just Begun,' 'You and Me Against the World,' etc.) and frequent guest and host on TV series and variety and talk shows. He composed the music for and starred in *Phantom of the Paradise* (1974), a rock screen version of *The Phantom of the Opera.* He shared an Academy Award with Barbra Streisand for the song 'Evergreen' from *A Star Is Born* (1976).

FILMS INCLUDE: *The Loved One* (act.) 1965; *The Chase* (act.) 1966; *Watermelon Man* (act.) 1970; *Battle for the Planet of the Apes* (act.), *Cinderella Liberty* (songs, vocals only) 1973; *Phantom of the Paradise* (music, songs, act.) 1974; *Lifeguard* (co-songs), *Bugsy Malone* (music, songs, vocals), *A Star Is Born* (co-songs with Barbra Streisand) 1976; *One on One* (co-songs), *Smokey and the Bandit* (act.) 1977; *The End* (music), *The Cheap Detective* (act.) 1978; *Agatha* (song), *The Muppet Movie* (songs, cameo) 1979; *Smokey and the Bandit 2* (act.), *Stone Cold Dead* (act.) 1980; *Smokey and the Bandit 3* (act.) 1983; *Best Enemies* (act.; UK) 1985; *Ishtar* (music), *Zombie High* (act.) 1987; *The Chill Factor* (act.) 1990; *The Doors* (act.) 1991.

Williams, Paul. Director. Born in 1944, in New York City. Turned to feature films in the late 60s, after directing a prize-winning short, *Gold.* Showed promise with his two initial features, *Out of It* (made in 1967 but released in 1969), a sincere if awkward seriocomic exploration of the dreams and frustrations of youth, and *The Revolutionary* (1970), an equally sincere and quite effective low-budget drama about young anarchists in a fantasy world not defined geographically. Both films starred Jon VOIGHT. Williams's activity since has been sporadic.

FEATURE FILMS: *Out of It* (also sc.) 1969; *The Revolutionary* 1970; *Dealing: Or the Berkeley-to-Boston Forty-Brick Lost-Bag Blues* (also co-sc.) 1972; *Nunzio* 1978; *Miss Right* (also story) 1981; *The Black Planet* (Austral.) 1982; *Breaking Up with Paul* (act. only) 1991; *Crosspoint* (also act.) 1992; *November Men* 1993; *A Million to Juan* 1994.

Williams, Rhys. Actor. *b.* 1897, Wales. *d.* 1969. He was brought to Hollywood as a technical advisor and dialect coach on *How Green Was My Valley* and was assigned an important supporting part by the film's director, John FORD. He later played intense character parts in numerous productions.

FILMS INCLUDE: *How Green Was My Valley* 1941; *This Above All, Mrs. Miniver, Cairo, Gentleman Jim, Random Harvest* 1942; *No Time for Love* 1943; *The Corn Is Green, Blood on the Sun, The Bells of St. Mary's* 1945; *The Spiral Staircase* 1946; *The Farmer's Daughter, Moss Rose* 1947; *If Winter Comes, The Black Arrow, Hills of Home* 1948; *Tokyo Joe, The Inspector General* 1949; *Kiss Tomorrow Goodbye* 1950; *Lightning Strikes Twice* 1951; *Les Miserables* 1952; *Scandal at Scourie* 1953; *Johnny Guitar* 1954; *The Kentuckian* 1955; *Raintree County* 1957; *Merry Andrew* 1958; *Midnight Lace* 1960; *The Sons of Katie Elder* 1965; *Our Man Flint* 1966; *Skullduggery* 1970.

Williams, Richard. Animator. Born in 1933, in Canada. Dabbling in film animation from the age of 12, he worked briefly for Disney and UPA in the late 40s, then went to England in 1955. There he took his place among that country's leading animators with his very first film, the 30-minute cartoon *The Little Island.* He has since built his own studio and made other successful animation films as well as TV commercials. He also designed the title sequences for feature films of others—*What's New Pussycat?, A Funny Thing Happened on the Way to the Forum,* and *The Charge of the Light Brigade,* for example. He won his first Oscar for his feature-length *A Christmas Carol* (1971), originally made for TV. He won another Oscar and a host of other awards for his work on *Who Framed Roger Rabbit* (1988).

FILMS INCLUDE: *The Little Island* 1958; *A Lecture on Man, Love Me Love Me Love Me* 1962; *Circus Drawings* 1964; *Diary of a Madman* 1965; *The Dermis Probe* 1966; *A Christmas Carol* 1971; *Nasrudin* 1972; *Raggedy Ann & Andy* 1977; *Who Framed Roger Rabbit* (anim. dir.) 1988; *Arabian Knight* 1995.

Williams, Robin. Actor, comedian. Born on July 21, 1952, in Chicago, Ill. *ed.* Claremont Men's College, Calif.; College of Marin, Calif.; Juilliard (drama). Whimsical, highly charged screen lead. Son of a Ford Motor Company executive in Detroit, he trained on the West coast as a stand-up comic and in New York under John Houseman, gaining early fame as the innocent, wisecracking extraterrestrial Mork from Ork on the TV sitcom 'Happy Days.' His role was parlayed into a popular spin-off, 'Mork and Mindy,' exposure from which led to a film career. However, his uncanny improvisational skills did not find an adequate film showcase until the mid-80s, when he portrayed the iconoclastic disk jockey Adrian Cronauer in *Good Morning, Vietnam*. Later films, notably *Dead Poets Society* and *The Fisher King*, have allowed him to further extend his dramatic range, imbuing his guileless expressionism with a search for larger meaning. Nominated for an Academy Award for *Good Morning, Vietnam* and *Dead Poets Society*. Divorced from his first wife, he is married to his child's former nanny, Marsha Garces, with whom he formed a production company in the 90s. Since the 80s, he, Billy Crystal, and Whoopi Goldberg have teamed to offer the 'Comic Relief' fundraising events for the homeless.

FILMS: *Can I Do It. . . Til I Need Glasses* 1977; *Popeye* 1980; *The World According to Garp* 1982; *The Survivors* 1983; *Moscow on the Hudson* 1984; *Club Paradise, The Best of Times* 1986; *Good Morning Vietnam* 1987; *Dear America: Letters Home from Vietnam* (narr.) 1988; *The Adventures of Baron Munchausen* (uncredited; UK), *Dead Poets Society* 1989; *Cadillac Man* 1990; *Dead Again* (uncredited), *Shakes the Clown* (uncredited), *The Fisher King, Hook* 1991; *Aladdin* (v/o), *FernGully. . . The Last Rainforest* (v/o), *Toys* 1992; *Mrs. Doubtfire* (also co-prod.) 1993; *Being Human* 1994; *Jumanji, To Wong Foo Thanks for Everything Julie Newmar* (unbilled) 1995; *The Birdcage, Hamlet, Jack, The Secret Agent* 1996; *Father's Day* 1997.

Williams, Tennessee. Playwright, screenwriter. *b.* Thomas Lanier Williams, Mar. 26, 1914, Columbus, Miss. *d.* 1983. *ed.* U. of Missouri; Washington U. (St. Louis); U. of Iowa. Many of the successful plays of this Pulitzer Prize–winning author have been adapted to the screen, some by Williams himself, alone or in collaboration. In most cases, the recurrent themes of sexual depravity and moral decadence had to be mitigated to meet with the requirements of Hollywood's production code. An unexpurgated version of the 1951 *A Streetcar Named Desire* saw limited theatrical release in the 90s.

FILMS: *The Glass Menagerie* 1950; *A Streetcar Named Desire* 1951; *The Rose Tattoo* 1955; *Baby Doll* 1956; *Cat on a Hot Tin Roof* (play basis only) 1958; *Suddenly Last Summer* 1959; *The Fugitive Kind* 1960; *Summer and Smoke* (play basis only), *The Roman Spring of Mrs. Stone* (novel basis only) 1961; *Sweet Bird of Youth, Period of Adjustment* (both play basis only) 1962; *The Night of the Iguana* (play basis only) 1964; *This Property Is Condemned* (one-act-play basis only) 1966; *Boom!* (from his play 'The Milktrain. . . ') 1968; *Last of the Mobile Hot-Shots* (play basis only) 1970.

Williams, Treat. Actor. Born Richard Williams, on Dec. 1, 1952, in Rowayton, Conn. *ed.* Franklin and Marshall College, Lancaster, Pa. Handsome leading actor of commanding presence. The son of a business executive, he gained his nickname from an ancestor on his mother's side, Robert Treat Payne, a signer of the Declaration of Independence. After acting in repertory theater in Pennsylvania, he served as John Travolta's understudy and eventual lead in the Broadway musical 'Grease.' A role in the Broadway musical 'Over There' led to his entry in films. Best known for performance as a New York police detective turned Justice Department informant in *Prince of the City* (1981). In the late 1980s, Williams formed the rock 'n' roll band Crime and Punishment with fellow actors Kevin Kline, Rex Smith, Mary Elizabeth Mastrantonio, and Peter Riegert. Appeared as Stanley Kowalski in TV version of *A Streetcar Named Desire* (1984).

FILMS INCLUDE: *The Ritz, Deadly Hero, The Eagle Has Landed* 1976; *1941, Hair* 1979; *Why Would I Lie?* 1980; *Prince of the City, The Pursuit of D. B. Cooper* 1981; *Stangata napoletana-La trastola* (It.) 1983; *Flashpoint, Once Upon a Time in America* 1984; *Smooth Talk* 1985; *The Men's Club* 1986; *La Notte degli Squali* (It.)1987; *Dead Heat* 1988; *Burro, Heart of Dixie, Russicum, Sweet Lies* 1989; *Beyond the Ocean* (also co-sc.) 1990; *Things To Do in Denver When You're Dead* 1995; *Mulholland Falls, The Phantom* 1996; *The Devil's Own* 1997.

Williamson, Fred. Actor, director, producer, screenwriter. Born on Mar. 5, 1938, in Gary, Ind. *ed.* Northwestern. A professional football player for ten years, he broke into films as an actor in 1970 and soon became established as one of the American screen's leading black stars. Tall, slick, and personable, he has since played affable "macho" roles in many films as well as the role of Diahann Carroll's boyfriend in the TV series 'Julia.' He began directing, producing, and writing some of his own films in the mid-70s.

FILMS (as actor): *M*A*S*H, Tell Me That You Love Me Junie Moon* 1970; *The Legend of Nigger Charley, Hammer* 1972; *Black Caesar, The Soul of Nigger Charley, That Man Bolt, Hell Up in Harlem, Three Tough Guys* (It.), *Crazy Joe* (It.) 1973; *Black Eye, Three the Hard Way* 1974; *Boss Nigger* (also sc., co-prod.), *Bucktown, Take a Hard Ride* 1975; *Adios Amigo* (also prod., dir., sc.), *Mean Johnny Barrows/Johnny Barrows, El Malo* (also dir.), *Death Journey* (also dir.), *No Way Back* (also prod., dir., sc.), *Joshua* (also story, sc.) 1976; *Destinazione Roma/Mr. Mean* (also dir., prod.; It./US) 1977; *Deadly Mission, Blind Rage* (Phil.) 1978; *Due nelle Stelle* (It.) 1979; *Fist of Fear, Touch of Death* 1980; *Fear in the City* (It.) 1981; *New York Ripper* (It.), *One Down, Two to Go!* (also dir.), *The Last Fight* (also dir.) 1982; *Vigilante, 1990: The Bronx Warriors* (It.), *Warriors of the Wasteland/The New Barbarians* (It.), *White Fire, The Big Score* (also dir.) 1983; *Deadly Impact* (It.) 1984; *Jornada de Muerte* (Sp.) ca. 1985; *Foxtrap* (also dir.) 1986; *Delta Force Commando, The Black Cobra* (It.), *The New Gladiators* (It.), *The Messenger* (also dir.) 1987; *Deadly Intent* 1988; *The Kill Reflex* (also dir.), *Black Cobra 2, The Soda Cracker* (also prod., dir.) 1989; *Black Cobra 3: The Manila Connection* 1990; *Delta Force Commando 2* (It.) 1991; *Steele's Law* (also prod., dir.) 1992; *From Dusk Till Dawn* 1995.

Williamson, James. Director, pioneer producer of British films. *b.* 1855, Scotland. *d.* 1933. A photography enthusiast, he bought a projector in 1896 and converted it into a motion picture camera, with which he filmed various events and scenes he had staged in his backyard. As early as 1900 he employed parallel action and cross-cutting techniques in such films as *Attack on a China Mission Station.* In 1902 he founded a studio at Brighton and in 1904 established the Williamson Kinematographic Company for the manufacture of film stock and motion picture equipment. He bowed out of actual film production in 1909.

FILMS INCLUDE: *Two Naughty Boys Upsetting the Spoons* 1898; *The Jovial Monks* 1899; *Attack on a China Mission Station* 1900; *The Big Swallow, Stop Thief!, Fire* 1901; *A Reservist Before the War and After the War* 1902; *The Deserter* 1903; *Two Little Waifs* 1905; *Our New Errand Boy* 1906; *The Brigand's Daughter* 1907; *Tower of London* 1909.

Williamson, Nicol. Actor. Born on Sept. 14, 1938, in Hamilton, Scotland. Imposing leading man of British stage and screen. He was nominated for a Tony Award for his performance in 'Inadmissible Evidence' on Broadway in 1966. Later played *Hamlet* and was invited to give a one-man show at the White House. He received enthusiastic notices for his portrayal of a cocaine-sniffing Sherlock Holmes in the film *The Seven-Per-Cent Solution* (1976). Formerly married to actress Jill Townsend.

FILMS: *Inadmissible Evidence, The Bofors Gun* 1968; *Laughter in the Dark, The Reckoning, Hamlet* (title role) 1969; *The Jerusalem File* (Isr./UK) 1972; *The Wilby Conspiracy* 1975; *Robin and Marian* (as Little John), *The Seven-Per-Cent Solution* (as Sherlock Holmes) 1976; *The Goodbye Girl* (cameo; US) 1977; *The Cheap Detective* (US) 1978; *The Human Factor* (UK/It.) 1979; *Venom, Excalibur* (US) 1981; *I'm Dancing as Fast as I Can* (US) 1982; *Return to Oz* (US) 1985; *Black Widow* (US) 1987; *William Peter Blatty's The Exorcist 3* (US) 1990; *Apt Pupil* 1992; *Hour of the Pig* 1993; *The Advocate* 1994; *Spawn* 1997.

Willis, Bruce. Actor, singer. Born on March 19, 1955, in West Germany. *ed.* Montclair State Coll., N.J. Amiable, sometimes tough screen lead. Raised in New Jersey, he spent his first post–high school years working at a chemical factory and began acting in college. Afterward he moved to New York, where he appeared on the stage and in jeans commercials, and supplemented his income through work as a nightclub bartender. A relative unknown when selected to appear in the TV romantic drama series 'Moonlighting,' he gained immediate celebrity through his incarnation of suave, wisecracking detective David Addison. Following equally successful performances as a tough-guy cop in *Die Hard* and *Die Hard 2*, he has appeared in a number of roles, but has not regenerated the box-office appeal he enjoyed in the 80s. He was awarded an Emmy in 1987 for 'Moonlighting.' Married to actress Demi MOORE.

FILMS: *Blind Date* 1987; *Sunset* (also co-exec. prod.), *Die Hard* 1988; *In Country, Look Who's Talking* (v/o) 1989; *Die Hard 2, The Bonfire of the Vanities, Look Who's Talking Too* (v/o, also song) 1990; *Mortal Thoughts, Hudson Hawk* (also co-story), *Billy Bathgate, The Last Boy Scout* 1991; *Death Becomes Her, The Player* 1992; *Striking Distance* 1993; *Color of Night, Nobody's Fool, North, Pulp Fiction* 1994; *12 Monkeys, Die Hard with a Vengeance, Four Rooms* (unbilled) 1995; *Beavis and Butt-head Do America* (unbilled cameo), *Last Man Standing* 1996; *The Fifth Element, The Jackal* 1997.

Willis, Gordon. American director of photography. A cinematographer since 1970, he rapidly gained a reputation for top-quality work and has since worked on several major Hollywood and New York productions. He directed a first film, *Windows*, in 1980. He was nominated for Oscars for his photography of *Zelig* (1983) and *The Godfather, Part 3* (1990).

FILMS INCLUDE: *End of the Road, Loving, The Landlord, The People Next Door* 1970; *Little Murders, Klute* 1971; *The Godfather, Bad Company, Up the Sandbox* 1972; *Paper Chase* 1973; *The Parallax View, The Godfather Part II* 1974; *The Drowning Pool* 1975; *All the President's Men* 1976; *Annie Hall* 1977; *Interiors, Comes a Horseman* 1978; *Corky, Manhattan* 1979; *Stardust Memories, Windows* (also dir.) 1980; *Pennies from Heaven* 1981; *A Midsummer Night's Sex Comedy* 1982; *Zelig* 1983; *Broadway Danny Rose* 1984; *The Purple Rose of Cairo, Perfect* 1985; *The Money Pit* 1986; *The Pick-Up Artist* 1987; *Bright Lights Big City* 1988; *Presumed Innocent, The Godfather Part 3* 1990; *Malice* 1993; *The Devil's Own* 1997.

Wills, Chill. Actor. *b.* July 18, 1903, Seagoville, Tex. *d.* 1978. A performer since early childhood, he appeared in tent shows, vaudeville, and stock throughout the Southwest. In the 30s he formed a singing group, Chill Wills and the Avalon Boys, with which he appeared in several Westerns from 1935. In 1938 he disbanded the group, of which he was leader and bass vocalist, and began a long career as a character player, appearing in numerous Westerns and many films of other genres. He also provided the offscreen voice of Francis, the Talking Mule, in films of the comedy series. He was nominated for an Oscar as best supporting actor for his performance in *The Alamo* (1960). In 1975 he released a first singing album.

FILMS INCLUDE: *Bar 20 Rides Again* 1935; *The Call of the Prairie* 1936; *Way Out West* 1937; *Arizona Legion, Allegheny Uprising* 1939; *Boom Town, The Westerner* 1940; *Western Union, Honky Tonk, Belle Starr* 1941; *Tarzan's New York Adventure* 1942; *Best Foot Forward* 1943; *Meet Me in St. Louis* 1944; *Leave Her to Heaven* 1945; *The Harvey Girls, The Yearling* 1946; *The Saxon Charm* 1948; *Red Canyon* 1949; *Rio Grande* 1950; *Oh! Susanna* 1951; *The Man from the Alamo* 1953; *Giant* 1956; *The Alamo* 1960; *The Deadly Companions* 1961; *McLintock!, The Wheeler Dealers, The Cardinal* 1963; *The Rounders* 1965; *The Liberation of L. B. Jones* 1970; *Pat Garrett and Billy the Kid* 1973; *Mr. Billion* 1977.

Wilson, Carey. Screenwriter, producer. Born on May 19, 1889, in Philadelphia. A veteran of the Goldwyn company, he became an employee of MGM when his old studio merged with Metro, where he became a favorite of Irving THALBERG. He wrote numerous stories and scripts, mostly alone, some in collaboration, for MGM and other studios, occasionally also producing. He became a full-time producer in the 40s and was the executive producer of the "Andy Hardy" and "Dr. Kildare" series.

FILMS INCLUDE: As screenwriter—*The Cup of Life* (story only) 1921; *Broken Chains* 1922; *The Eternal Three, Red Lights* (co-sc.) 1923; *Three Weeks* (adapt. only), *Wine of Youth, Sinners in Silk, He Who Gets Slapped* (co-sc.) 1924; *Lights of Old Broadway, The Masked Bride, Soul Mates* 1925; *Monte Carlo* (story only), *Midnight Lovers, The Silent Lover, Ben-Hur* (co-sc.) 1926; *The Sea Tiger* (also prod.), *Orchids and Ermine* (also story), *Naughty but Nice, The Stolen Bride* (also prod.), *American Beauty* (also prod.) 1927; *The Private Life of Helen of Troy* (also prod.), *Oh Kay!, Lilac Time, The Awakening* 1928; *Why Be Good?, His Captive Woman* 1929; *Peacock Alley* (story, co-dial. only), *The Bad One* (co-sc.) 1930; *The Flying Fool* 1931; *Arsene Lupin* 1932; *Gabriel Over the White House* 1933; *Bolero* (co-story only) 1934; *Sequoia, Mutiny on the Bounty* (co-sc.) 1935; *Dangerous Number* 1937; *Judge Hardy and Son* 1939. As producer—*The Postman Always Rings Twice* 1946; *Dark Delusion, Green Dolphin Street* 1947; *The Red Danube* 1949; *Scaramouche* 1952; *This Is Russia* (feature doc.; also narr.) 1957.

Wilson, Dooley. Actor, musician. *b.* Arthur Wilson, Apr. 3, 1894, Tyler, Tex. *d.* 1953. A minstrel performer at 12, he later performed in vaudeville and acted in stock and in the 20s led his own band in Paris and London nightclubs, performing as a singing drummer. Returning to the US in 1930, he appeared in Federal Theater productions of Orson Welles and John Houseman and in the Broadway musical 'Cabin in the Sky' before making his film debut in 1942. His screen career consisted mainly of minor supporting roles, but he became a memorable part of film nostalgia thanks to his role as the pianist-singer who reluctantly responds to Ingrid Bergman's request in *Casablanca* (1943): "Play it, Sam. . . play 'As Time Goes By.'" Reputedly, he couldn't play a note and the piano accompaniment was dubbed.

FILMS: *My Favorite Blonde, Night in New Orleans, Take a Letter Darling, Cairo,* 1942; *Casablanca, Two Tickets to London, Stormy Weather, Higher and Higher* 1943; *Seven Days Ashore* 1944; *Triple Threat, Racing Luck* 1948; *Free for All, Come to the Stable* 1949; *Passage West* 1951.

Wilson, Lester. Choreographer. *b.* ca. 1942, New York

City. *d.* 1993. *ed.* Juilliard School of Music. Born in Jamaica, Queens, he was a dancer in the African Room in Harlem when Bob Fosse discovered him and cast him in a revival of the stage musical 'Pal Joey' (1963). He later performed in London with Sammy Davis, Jr., and became friends with Josephine Baker. He became a choreographer of Broadway musicals, including 'Me and Bessie' (1975) and 'Grind' (1985). But he was best known to movie audiences for arranging the dance numbers in *Saturday Night Fever* (1977).

FILMS INCLUDE: *Sparkle* 1976; *Saturday Night Fever* 1977; *Beat Street* 1984; *Mr. Saturday Night, Sister Act* 1992.

Wilson, Lois. Actress. *b.* June 28, 1896, Pittsburgh. *d.* 1983. A former schoolteacher and briefly a stage actress, she entered films in 1916 and starred in an impressively large number of important Paramount silent productions, most notably James Cruze's Western classic *The Covered Wagon* (1923). She continued playing leads well into the sound era, usually in unglamorous roles. She retired from the screen in 1941 but went on appearing on the stage and on TV. She returned to films in 1949 for a single character role. She never married. Two of her sisters, Diana Kane and Connie Lewis, were also actresses.

FILMS INCLUDE: *The Dumb Girl of Portici* 1916; *A Man's Man* 1917; *The Bells, His Robe of Honor* 1918; *It Pays to Advertise, End of the Game* 1919; *Midsummer Madness* 1920; *What Every Woman Knows, The City of Silent Men, The Lost Romance, Miss Lulu Bett* 1921; *The World's Champion, Is Matrimony a Failure?, Broad Daylight, Our Leading Citizen, Manslaughter* 1922; *Bella Donna, A Man's Man, Only 38, Ruggles of Red Gap, The Covered Wagon, To The Last Man, Call of the Canyon* 1923; *Icebound, Another Scandal, Monsieur Beaucaire, North of 36* 1924; *Contraband, Welcome Home, The Vanishing American, Irish Luck* 1925; *Bluebeard's Seven Wives, Let's Get Married, The Show-Off, The Great Gatsby* (as Daisy Buchanan) 1926; *New York, Broadway Nights, Alias the Lone Wolf, French Dressing* 1927; *Coney Island, On Trial, Ransom, Object—Alimony* 1928; *Conquest, Kid Gloves, The Gamblers, Wedding Rings* 1929; *Lovin' the Ladies, The Furies, Once a Gentleman* 1930; *The Age for Love* 1931; *Law and Order, The Expert, Rider of Death Valley, Divorce in the Family* 1932; *Obey the Law, The Deluge, Female* 1933; *The Show-Off* (remake), *No Greater Glory, There's Always Tomorrow, Bright Eyes* 1934; *Public Opinion* 1935; *Wedding Present* 1936; *Nobody's Children* 1940; *The Girl from Jones Beach* 1949.

Wilson, Marie. Actress. *b.* Katherine Elizabeth Wilson, Dec. 30, 1916, Anaheim, Calif. *d.* 1972. Lovable "dumb blonde" of many Hollywood films, both in leads and supporting parts. She excelled as the wide-eyed expectant mother in *Boy Meets Girl* and in the featherbrained title role of the radio, TV, and screen versions of *My Friend Irma.* From the late 50s she was mostly seen in road stage productions and in nightclubs. The first of her three husbands was director Nick GRINDE. The others were actor Alan Nixon and TV producer Robert Fallon. She died of cancer.

FILMS INCLUDE: *Babes in Toyland* 1934; *Stars Over Broadway* 1935; *Colleen, Satan Met a Lady, China Clipper* 1936; *The Great Garrick* 1937; *The Invisible Menace, Fools for Scandal, Boy Meets Girl, Broadway Musketeers* 1938; *The Sweepstakes Winner* 1939; *Virginia* 1941; *Broadway* 1942; *Shine on Harvest Moon, Music for Millions, You Can't Ration Love* 1944; *Young Widow, No Leave No Love* 1946; *The Fabulous Joe, The Private Affairs of Bel Ami* 1947; *My Friend Irma* 1949; *My Friend Irma Goes West* 1950; *A Girl in Every Port* 1952; *Never Wave at a Wac, Marry Me Again* 1953; *The Story of Mankind* (as Marie Antoinette) 1957; *Mr. Hobbs Takes a Vacation* 1962.

Wilson, Michael. Screenwriter. *b.* July 1, 1914, McAlester, Okla. *d.* 1978. *ed.* U. of California. He taught and wrote short stories before going to Hollywood in 1940. His early work consisted mainly of William Boyd Westerns. But after returning from WW II service as a lieutenant with the Marines, he was assigned to important productions and in 1951 he shared an Academy Award for the script of *A Place in the Sun.* But his refusal to affirm or deny past membership in the Communist Party in testimony before the House Un-American Activities Committee in 1951 led to his blacklisting by the industry. The only work he could obtain was on Herbert Biberman's independently produced semidocumentary *Salt of the Earth* (1954) and several "underground" assignments allowing him to collaborate on major films without receiving screen credit. He finally resurfaced in the late 60s.

FILMS: *The Men in Her Life* 1941; *Border Patrol, Colt Comrades, Bar 20* 1943; *Forty Thieves* 1944; *A Place in the Sun* 1951; *Five Fingers* 1952; *Salt of the Earth* 1954; *Friendly Persuasion* (uncredited) 1956; *The Bridge on the River Kwai* (uncredited) 1957; *Lawrence of Arabia* (uncredited) 1962; *The Sandpiper* 1965; *Planet of the Apes* 1968; *Che!* 1969.

Wilson, Richard. Director, producer, screenwriter, actor. *b.* Dec. 25, 1915, in McKeesport, Pa. *d.* 1991. *ed.* U. of Denver. A former radio actor, he joined Orson Welles's Mercury Theater in 1937 and became involved in many of Welles's stage, radio, and film enterprises through 1951 as an actor, stage manager, associate producer, and trusted aide. He played bits in *Citizen Kane* (1941) and *The Lady from Shanghai* (1948) and was associate producer on the latter and on *Macbeth* (1948). On his own from the early 50s, he produced such non-entities as *The Golden Blade* (1953) and *Ma and Pa Kettle at Home* (1954), then turned director of mostly Westerns and gangster pictures, several of which are noted for their exacting realism.

FILMS (as director): *Man with the Gun* (also co-sc.) 1955; *The Big Boodle* 1957; *Raw Wind in Eden* (also co-sc.) 1958; *Al Capone* 1959; *Pay or Die* (also prod.) 1960; *Wall of Noise* 1963; *Invitation to a Gunfighter* (also prod., co-sc.) 1964; *Three in the Attic* (also prod.) 1968; *How to Get Ahead in Business* (UK) (act. only) 1989.

Wilson, Whip. Actor. *b.* Charles Meyer, June 16, 1919, Pecos, Tex. *d.* 1964. Cowboy star of low-budget Monogram Westerns of the late 40s and early 50s. His horse was Silver Bullet, his sidekick Andy CLYDE, and his weapon the whip, which he lashed skillfully at his enemies.

FILMS INCLUDE: *Silver Trails* 1948; *Shadows of the West* 1949; *Cherokee Uprising, Arizona Territory, Gunslingers* 1950; *Abilene Trail, Canyon Raiders, Nevada Badmen* 1951; *The Gunman* 1952.

Wimperis, Arthur. Screenwriter. *b.* Dec. 3, 1874, London. *d.* 1953. *ed.* University College (London). A veteran of the Boer War and WW I, a newspaper artist and a librettist, he collaborated on the screenplays of many British, then Hollywood films. He shared the Academy Award with three others for the script of *Mrs. Miniver.*

FILMS INCLUDE (alone or in collaboration): In the UK—*The Private Life of Henry VIII* 1933; *Catherine the Great* 1934; *Sanders of the River, The Scarlet Pimpernel* 1935; *Rembrandt, The Beloved Vagabond* 1936; *Dark Journey* 1937; *The Drum/Drums* 1938; *The Four Feathers* 1939. In the US—*Mrs. Miniver, Random Harvest* 1942; *If Winter Comes* 1948; *The Red Danube* 1949; *Calling Bulldog Drummond* 1951; *Young Bess* 1953.

Wincer, Simon. Director. Born 1943 in Sydney, Australia. A prolific director, he helmed hundreds of hours of TV fare in the 70s, becoming one of the Australian "New Wave" in the late

70s and 80s. Hollywood beckoned and he continues to make his direcorial mark on current films.

FILMS: *Harlequin* 1980; *The Man From Snowy River* 1982; *Phar Lap* 1983; *D.A.R.Y.L.* 1985; *The Last Frontier* 1986; *The Lighthorseman* 1987; *Bluegrass* 1988; *Quigley Down Under* 1990; *Harley Davidson & the Marlboro Man* 1991; *Free Willy* 1993; *Lighning Jack* (also prod.) 1994; *Operation Dumbo Drop* 1995; *Eraser, The Phantom* 1996; *Hoodlum* 1997.

winding. The process of transferring film from one reel to another, usually by means of a pair of REWINDS. Care must be taken during winding to avoid damage to film through uneven or excessive tension or by friction.

wind machine. A large fan designed to create wind effects in the production of a motion picture. It is often used in conjunction with a wind howler, a device producing the sound effect of a howling wind.

Windsor, Claire. Actress. *b.* Clara Viola Cronk, 1897, Cawker City, Kans. *d.* 1972. Blonde, blue-eyed star of Hollywood silents of the 20s. She had worked as an extra for a couple of years before getting her break as the heroine of a string of Lois Weber films of 1920–21. She was briefly (1925–27) married to co-star Bert LYTELL and was a frequent Chaplin date. She retired shortly after the advent of sound but later returned to the screen for isolated appearances in character roles.

FILMS INCLUDE: *To Please One Woman* 1920; *What's Worth While?, Too Wise Wives, The Raiders, The Blot, What Do Men Want?* 1921; *Broken Chains, Grand Larceny, Fools First, One Clear Call, Rich Men's Wives, Brothers Under the Skin* 1922; *The Stranger's Banquet, The Little Church Around the Corner, Rupert of Hentzau, The Eternal Three, The Acquittal* 1923; *Nellie the Beautiful Cloak Model, Born Rich, A Son of the Sahara, For Sale* 1924; *The Dixie Handicap, The Denial, Just a Woman, The White Desert, Souls for Sables* 1925; *Dance Madness, Money Talks, Tin Hats* 1926; *Blondes by Choice, The Frontiersman, A Little Journey, The Claw, The Bugle Call, Foreign Devils* 1927; *Satan and the Woman, Nameless Men, Fashion Madness* 1928; *Captain Lash, Midstream* 1929; *Sister to Judas* 1933; *Cross Streets* 1934; *Barefoot Boy* 1938; *How Do You Do?* 1945.

Windsor, Marie. Actress. Born Emily Marie Bertelson, on Dec. 11, 1922, in Marysvale, Utah. *ed.* Brigham Young. A former Miss Utah, she trained for the stage under Maria OUSPENSKAYA. After several years as a telephone operator, a stage and radio actress, and a bit and extra player in films, she began playing featured and lead parts in 1947. She often portrayed aggressive types, vulgar, domineering, and sometimes downright nasty and vicious, but sometimes also conventional leading ladies, frequently in crime melodramas and in Westerns in which she demonstrated her uncommon skill as a rider. Also seen much on TV.

FILMS INCLUDE: *All American Co-Ed* 1941; *Song of the Thin Man* 1947; *Force of Evil* 1948; *Outpost in Morocco, The Fighting Kentuckian* 1949; *Dakota Lil* 1950; *Little Big Horn, Hurricane Island* 1951; *The Narrow Margin, Outlaw Woman, The Sniper, The Jungle* 1952; *The Tall Texan, Trouble Along the Way* 1953; *The Bounty Hunter* 1954; *Abbott and Costello Meet the Mummy, No Man's Woman* 1955; *The Killing* 1956; *The Story of Mankind* (as Napoleon's Josephine), *The Unholy Wife* 1957; *Day of the Bad Man, Island Women* 1958; *Paradise Alley* 1962; *Critic's Choice, The Day Mars Invaded the Earth* 1963; *Bedtime Story* 1964; *Chamber of Horrors* 1966; *The Good Guys and the Bad Guys* 1969; *One More Train to Rob, Support Your Local Gunfighter* 1971; *Cahill—US Marshall* 1973; *The Outfit* 1974; *Hearts of the West* 1975; *Freaky Friday* 1977; *Lovely. . . But Deadly* 1982; *Commando Squad* 1987.

Windust, Bretaigne. Director. *b.* Jan. 20, 1906, Paris, to American parents. *d.* 1960. *ed.* Princeton. The son of a violinist and a concert soprano, he was among the founders of the University Players in Falmouth, Mass., along with Joshua LOGAN, Henry FONDA, and James STEWART, among others. He later acted and directed on Broadway and in the late 40s went to Hollywood, where he directed a number of films, notably the taut Bogart crime drama *The Enforcer,* which he made with the uncredited collaboration of Raoul Walsh.

FILMS: *Winter Meeting, June Bride* 1948; *Perfect Strangers, Pretty Baby* 1950; *The Enforcer* 1951; *Face to Face* ("The Bride Comes to Yellow Sky" episode) 1952; *The Pied Piper of Hamelin* (originally made for TV) 1957.

Winfield, Paul. Actor. Born on May 22, 1940, in Los Angeles, Calif. *ed.* Univ. of Portland; Stanford U.; L.A. City College; UCLA. Stage-trained screen character player and lead, usually in empathetic dramatic roles or in action films. Raised in Watts, he established himself as a serious film actor in *Sounder*, for which he was nominated for an Academy Award. Later films have seen him relegated to supporting, less complex roles. Active in TV since the 60s, appearing regularly on the comedy 'Julia' and as Martin Luther King, Jr., in the miniseries 'King.'

FILMS INCLUDE: *The Lost Man* 1969; *R.P.M.* 1970; *Brother John, Sounder, Trouble Man* 1972; *Gordon's War* 1973; *Conrack, Huckleberry Finn* 1974; *Hustle* 1975; *Damnation Alley, A Hero Ain't Nothin' But a Sandwich, High Velocity, Twilight's Last Gleaming, The Greatest* 1977; *Carbon Copy* 1981; *Star Trek II: The Wrath of Khan, White Dog, On The Run* 1982; *Mike's Murder, The Terminator* 1984; *Blue City* 1985; *Death Before Dishonor, Big Shots* 1987; *The Serpent and the Rainbow* 1988; *Presumed Innocent* 1990; *Dennis the Menace* 1993; *Mars Attacks!* 1996.

Winfrey, Oprah. Host, actress, producer. Born on Jan. 29, 1954, in Kosciusko, Miss. *ed.* Tenn. State U. Highly popular TV talk-show host and occasional screen supporting player or lead. After a stint as a radio journalist, she worked as a TV reporter and anchor in Nashville and Baltimore. In Baltimore, she hosted her first TV talk show, then hosted 'AM Chicago,' which would become the top-rated morning show in Chicago. Syndicated in 1986, within two years it became known as 'The Oprah Winfrey Show.' Nominated for an Academy Award for her film debut in *The Color Purple* and praised for her performance in the TV film 'The Women of Brewster Place.' Her production company is Harpo Productions, Inc.; her film and TV production facility is Harpo Studios.

FILMS: *The Color Purple* 1985; *Native Son* 1986; *Throw Momma from The Train* 1987.

Winger, Debra. Actress. Born on May 17, 1955, in Cleveland, Ohio. *ed.* Calif. State U. (sociology). Forceful, unadorned screen lead. After spending part of her youth in Israel and serving three months in the Israeli army, she moved to California, where she decided to pursue a serious acting career following a severe accident at a local amusement park at which she was performing. Her performances as fiery, independent women in *Urban Cowboy*, *An Officer and a Gentlemen*, and *Terms of Endearment* established her presence in Hollywood. Subsequent performances throughout the next several years have often been praised but did not generate huge box-office success, making her a respected actress but uncertain star draw. Nominated for Academy Awards for *An Officer and a Gentleman* and *Terms of Endearment*. Once married to actor Timothy HUTTON; they have one son.

FILMS INCLUDE: *Slumber Party '57* 1977; *Thank God It's Friday* 1978; *French Postcards* 1979; *Urban Cowboy* 1980; *Mike's Murder, An Officer and a Gentleman, E.T The Extra-*

Terrestrial (v/o, uncredited) 1982; *Terms of Endearment* 1983; *Legal Eagles* 1986; *Black Widow, Made in Heaven* 1987; *Betrayed* 1988; *Everybody Wins, The Sheltering Sky* 1990; *Leap of Faith* 1992; *Wilder Napalm, A Dangerous Woman, Shadowlands* 1993; *Forget Paris* 1995.

Winkler, Irwin. Producer. Born 1931 in New York City. *ed.* NYU. In the late 60s he formed a partnership with Robert Chartoff which has resulted in several successful Hollywood films as well as a number of box-office duds. For list of credits, see CHARTOFF, Robert.

Winner, Michael. Director. Born in 1935, in London. *ed.* Cambridge (law). A film critic and entertainment columnist at 16, he began making TV films for the BBC in the mid-50s and motion pictures in the early 60s. His films are typically well paced and visually appealing, if at times overly gimmicky in style and cynical in content. On the set, he likes to use an unusually large number of setups but shoots relatively few takes. Since the early 70s he has been working mainly in Hollywood, most effectively on Charles Bronson adventures.

FEATURE FILMS: In the UK—*Climb Up the Wall* (also sc.), *Shoot to Kill* (also sc.) 1960; *Old Mac, Some Like It Cool* (also assoc. prod., sc.), *Out of the Shadow/Murder on the Campus* (also assoc. prod., sc.) 1961; *Play It Cool* 1962; *The Cool Mikado* (also sc.), *West II* 1963; *The System/The Girl Getters* 1964; *You Must Be Joking!* (also co-story) 1965; *The Jokers* (also sc.) 1966; *I'll Never Forget What's 'is Name* (also prod.) 1967; *Hannibal Brooks* (also prod., co-story) 1969; *The Games* (also co-exec. prod.) 1970. In the US—*Lawman* (also prod.) 1971; *Chato's Land* (also prod.), *The Nightcomers* (also prod.; UK), *The Mechanic* 1972; *Scorpio, The Stone Killer* (also prod.; US/UK) 1973; *Death Wish* (also co-prod.) 1974; *Won Ton Ton—The Dog Who Saved Hollywood* (also co-prod.) 1976; *The Sentinel* (also co-prod., sc.) 1977; *The Big Sleep* (also co-prod., sc.; UK) 1978; *Firepower* (also prod., co-sc.; UK) 1979; *Death Wish 2* (also ed.) 1981; *The Wicked Lady* (also sc., ed.) 1983; *Scream for Help* (also prod.) 1984; *Death Wish 3* (also prod., ed.) 1985; *Appointment with Death* (also prod., sc., ed.) 1988; *A Chorus of Disapproval* (also prod., sc.; UK) 1989; *Bullseye!* (also prod., story, ed.) 1990; *Dirty Weekend* (also sc.) 1991; *Decadence* 1994.

Winninger, Charles. Actor. *b.* May 26, 1884, Athens, Wis. *d.* 1969. The son of show people, he quit school at age nine to join the family act on the vaudeville circuit. As an adult, he played in stock and repertory and made his first Broadway appearance in 1912. He appeared in L-KO comedy shorts from 1915 and in a number of feature films in the 20s. He was also featured in a number of the Ziegfeld Follies stage spectacles and played the original Cap'n Andy in the 1927 Broadway production of 'Show Boat.' He remained with the show for three years, then settled in Hollywood, where he played key character parts in many films, typically as a genial and cunningly charming senior citizen.

FILMS INCLUDE: *Pied Piper Malone* 1924; *The Canadian, Summer Bachelors* 1926; *Soup to Nuts* 1930; *Bad Sister, The Sin of Madelon Claudet* 1931; *Show Boat, White Fang, Three Smart Girls* 1936; *Cafe Metropole, Nothing Sacred, You Can't Have Everything* 1937; *Goodbye Broadway* 1938; *Babes in Arms, Destry Rides Again, Barricade* 1939; *If I Had My Way, Little Nellie Kelly* 1940; *Ziegfeld Girl* 1941; *Friendly Enemies* 1942; *Coney Island, A Lady Takes a Chance, Flesh and Fantasy* 1943; *Sunday Dinner for a Soldier* 1944; *State Fair* 1945; *Something in the Wind* 1947; *Give My Regards to Broadway* 1948; *Father Is a Bachelor* 1950; *The Sun Shines Bright* 1953; *Las Vegas Shakedown* 1955; *Raymie* 1960; *The Miracle of Santa's White Reindeer* 1963.

Winningham, Mare. Actress/Singer. Born Mary Winningham May 16, 1959, in Phoenix, Ariz. *ed.* Teenage Drama Workshop of California State University at Northridge. This versatile actress began her career as a teen singing on 'The Gong Show' and starring in her school's production of 'The Sound of Music.' After a number of fine roles on TV including her Emmy-winning performance in ABC's 'Amber Waves,' she moved into films, winning an Oscar nomination for her role in *Georgia*.

FILMS: *Off the Minnesota Strip, One-Trick Pony* 1980; *Threshold* 1981; *St. Elmo's Fire* 1985; *Nobody's Fool* 1986; *Made in Heaven, Shy People* 1987; *Miracle Mile, Turner & Hooch* 1989; *Fatal Exposure, Hard Promises* 1991; *Better Off Dead* 1993; *The War, Wyatt Earp* 1994; *Georgia* 1995.

Winslet, Kate. Actress. Born 1975 in Reading, England. Coming from three generations of theater performers, it was only natural that this winsome beauty would take to the stage. She began with a cereal commercial which led to theater and television. *Heavenly Creatures* (1994) was the film that thrust Winslet onto the international cinematic scene. She is an actress in high demand at present.

FILMS: *Heavenly Creatures* 1994; *A Kid in King Arthur's Court, Sense and Sensibility* 1995; *Hamlet, Jude* 1996.

Winslow, George "Foghorn." Child actor. Born George Wentzlaff, on May 3, 1946, in Los Angeles. Popular boy performer of the 50s whose main appeal was a thundering bullfrog basso. First introduced on Art Linkletter's TV show 'People Are Funny,' he contributed amusing moments to several Hollywood films but retired from show business at the age of 12, when the little-boy-with-a-big-voice gimmick had outlived its effectiveness.

FILMS: *Room for One More, My Pal Gus, Monkey Business* 1952; *Gentlemen Prefer Blondes, Mister Scoutmaster* 1953; *The Rocket Man* 1954; *Artists and Models, Rock Pretty Baby* 1956; *An Affair to Remember* 1957; *Summer Love, Wild Heritage* 1958.

Winston, Stan. Makeup and special effects artist. Born ca. 1946. *ed.* U. of Virginia (painting and sculpture). He originally planned to be an actor, but after beginning an apprenticeship in the makeup department at Walt Disney Studios in 1969, he learned he could create characters more effectively through makeup. With Rick Baker, he won an Emmy for the prosthetics used to age Cicely Tyson in the TV movie *The Autobiography of Miss Jane Pittman* (1974). He came to specialize in fantasy makeup and creature effects. His makeup designs have transformed actors into such bizarre, expressive characters as the Penguin in *Batman Returns*. His puppeteered creatures, notably the alien queen in *Aliens* and the dinosaurs in *Jurassic Park*, are realized through an array of live-action techniques, from hand and rod manipulation to high-tech animatronics. Winston shared Academy Awards for best visual effects for *Aliens* and best makeup and best visual effects for *Terminator 2*. He made his directorial debut with *Pumpkinhead* (1988). His Stan Winston Studio is in Van Nuys, Calif.

FILMS INCLUDE: *The Man in the Glass Booth* 1975; *W. C. Fields and Me* 1976; *The Wiz* 1978; *Dead and Buried, Heartbeeps* 1981; *Parasite* 1982; *The Terminator* 1984; *Aliens* 1986; *Pumpkinhead* (also dir.) 1988; *Leviathan* 1989; *Edward Scissorhands, Predator 2* 1990; *Terminator 2: Judgment Day* 1991; *Batman Returns* 1992; *Jurassic Park* 1993; *Congo, Tank Girl* 1994; *The Ghost and the Darkness, The Island of Dr. Moreau* 1996; *The Lost World, The Relic* 1997.

Winter, Vincent. Child actor. Born on Dec. 29, 1947, in Aberdeen, Scotland. He received a special Oscar for his very first role, in the British film *The Kidnappers* (titled *The Little*

Kidnappers in the US), and later appeared in several other films, then settled in Australia, where he remains active on the stage.

FILMS INCLUDE: *The Kidnappers/The Little Kidnappers* 1953; *The Warriors/The Dark Avenger* (US/UK) 1955; *Time Lock* 1956; *The Bridal Path* 1959; *Gorgo* 1960; *Almost Angels* (US/UK) 1962; *The Three Lives of Thomasina* (US/UK) 1963; *The Horse Without a Head* 1964.

Winters, Jonathan. Actor. Born on Nov. 11, 1925, in Dayton, Ohio. *ed.* Kenyon Coll. Rotund, moon-faced comedian, superbly adept at mimicry, characterizations, and madcap impersonations. He started out on local radio, and, beginning with 'The Garry Moore Show,' gained popularity in guest spots on TV variety and talk shows. Portrayed the son of Mork (Robin Williams) on TV's 'Mork and Mindy' in the early 80s and starred in his own comedy-variety program. In films since the early 60s.

FILMS: *It's a Mad Mad Mad Mad World* 1963; *The Loved One* 1965; *The Russians Are Coming the Russians Are Coming, Penelope* 1966; *Oh Dad Poor Dad—Mama's Hung You in the Closet and I'm Feeling So Sad, Eight on the Lam* 1967; *Viva Max!* 1969; *The Fish That Saved Pittsburgh* 1979; *The Longshot, Say Yes!* 1986; *Moon Over Parador* 1988; *The Flintstones, The Shadow* 1994; *Arabian Night* (v/o) 1995.

Winters, Linda. See COMINGORE, Dorothy.

Winters, Roland. Actor. *b.* Nov. 22, 1904, in Boston. *d.* 1989. A veteran of the stage and radio, he was brought to Hollywood by Monogram in the late 40s, as the third, last, and least effective screen interpreter of Charlie Chan, the wise Chinese detective. He also played character parts in a variety of other films.

FILMS INCLUDE: *The Chinese Ring* 1947; *Cry of the City, The Golden Eye* 1948; *Abbott and Costello Meet the Killer Boris Karloff, The Feathered Serpent* 1949; *Malaya, Captain Carey USA, Convicted* 1950; *So Big* 1953; *Bigger Than Life* 1956; *Top Secret Affair* 1957; *Never Steal Anything Small* 1959; *Cash McCall* 1960; *Blue Hawaii* 1961; *Loving* 1970.

Winters, Shelley. Actress. Born Shirley Schrift, on Aug. 18, 1922, in St. Louis; raised in Brooklyn, N.Y. She appeared in plays staged by her high school and worked as a store clerk and a model to finance dramatic studies. In her senior year she played in summer stock and worked as a chorus girl in a nightclub while aggressively seeking to break into the legitimate theater. She made her Broadway debut in 1941, and following a number of supporting roles she was brought out to Hollywood by Columbia in 1943. Her film career amounted to little before 1948, when she captured attention in the role of a waitress strangled by Ronald Colman in *A Double Life.* She quickly rose to lead roles in films that, typically, emphasized her earthy sexuality. The film that established her reputation as a fine actress was George Stevens's *A Place in the Sun* (1951). She was nominated for an Academy Award for her portrayal of a pregnant factory girl drowned by her seducer (Montgomery Clift).

But few of her subsequent roles were nearly as rewarding and in 1955 she returned to Broadway. She came back to the screen in 1959, now plumper and more mature, and in the 60s began displaying a unique talent for portraying suffering mothers, blowsy, promiscuous matrons, and veteran whores. She won Oscars in the "supporting" category for her mother roles in *The Diary of Anne Frank* (1959) and *A Patch of Blue* (1965), and was nominated in the same category for *The Poseidon Adventure* (1972). In the early 70s she scored a success on Broadway, playing the mother of the Marx Brothers in 'Minnie's Boys,' but was clobbered by the critics in her debut as a playwright for 'One Night Stands of a Noisy Passenger,' a bill of three short semi-autobiographical plays which closed shortly after its off-Broadway premiere. She later had a recurring role on TV's 'Roseanne' in the early 90s. The candid, mercurial, tempestuous, and politically active Miss Winters is the author of two kiss-and-tell autobiographies, *Shelley, Also Known as Shirley* (1981) and *Shelley II: The Middle of My Century (The Best of Times, the Worst of Times)* (1989). She has been married three times. Her second marriage, to Italian actor Vittorio GASSMAN, lasted but two years (1952–54); her third, to Anthony FRANCIOSA, three years (1957–60).

FILMS: *What a Woman!* 1943; *The Racket Man, Nine Girls, Two-Man Submarine, Knickerbocker Holiday, She's a Soldier Too, Sailor's Holiday, Cover Girl* 1944; *Tonight and Every Night, A Thousand and One Nights* 1945; *Living in a Big Way, The Gangster* 1947; *A Double Life, Larceny, Red River, Cry of the City* 1948; *Take One False Step, The Great Gatsby, Johnny Stool Pigeon* 1949; *South Sea Sinner, Winchester '73* 1950; *Frenchie, He Ran All the Way, A Place in the Sun, Behave Yourself, The Raging Tide* 1951; *Phone Call from a Stranger, Meet Danny Wilson, Untamed Frontier, My Man and I* 1952; *Saskatchewan, Executive Suite, Tennessee Champ, Playgirl, To Dorothy a Son/Cash on Delivery* (UK) 1954; *Mambo* (It./US), *I Am a Camera* (UK), *The Night of the Hunter, The Big Knife, I Died a Thousand Times, The Treasure of Pancho Villa* 1955; *The Diary of Anne Frank, Odds Against Tomorrow* 1959; *Let No Man Write My Epitaph* 1960; *The Young Savages* 1961; *Lolita, The Chapman Report* 1962; *The Balcony, Wives and Lovers* 1963; *Gli Indifferenti/Time of Indifference* (It./Fr.), *A House Is Not a Home* (as Madam Polly Adler) 1964; *The Greatest Story Ever Told, A Patch of Blue* 1965; *Alfie* (UK), *Harper* 1966; *Enter Laughing* 1967; *The Scalphunters, Wild in the Streets* 1968; *Buona Sera Mrs. Campbell, The Mad Room* 1969; *Bloody Mama, How Do I Love Thee?, Flap* 1970; *What's the Matter with Helen?, Who Slew Auntie Roo?* (UK) 1971; *Something to Hide* (UK), *The Poseidon Adventure* 1972; *Blume in Love, Cleopatra Jones* 1973; *Poor Pretty Eddie, Diamonds* (Isr./US/Switz.), *That Lucky Touch* (UK/It./Fr.), *Journey Into Fear* (UK) 1975; *Next Stop Greenwich Village, Le Locataire/The Tenant* (Fr.), *La Dahlia Scarlatta* (It.), *Mimi Bluette* (It.) 1976; *Un Borghese Piccolo Piccolo* (It.), *Tentacoli/Tentacles* (It.), *Pete's Dragon, Gran Bollito* (It.), *The Three Sisters* 1977; *The Magician of Lublin* (Isr./Ger.), *City on Fire* (Can.), *King of the Gypsies, Redneck County Rape, The Visitor* 1979; *Looping, My Mother My Daughter, S.O.B.* 1981; *Fanny Hill* (UK), *Over the Brooklyn Bridge* 1983; *Very Close Quarters, Ellie* 1984; *Deja Vu* (UK) 1984; *George Stevens: A Filmmaker's Journey* (documentary interviewee) 1985; *Witchfire* (also assoc. prod.), *The Delta Force* 1986; *Hello Actors Studio* (documentary interviewee) 1987; *The Order of Things, Rudolph and Frosty's Christmas in July* (v/o), *Purple People Eater* 1988; *An Unremarkable Life* 1989; *Superstar: The Life and Times of Andy Warhol* (documentary interviewee), *Touch of a Stranger* 1990; *Stepping Out* 1991; *The Pickle* 1993; *Heavy, The Portrait of a Lady* 1996.

Winwood, Estelle. Actress. *b.* Estelle Goodwin, Jan. 24, 1883, in Lee, England. *d.* 1984. For many decades a veteran of the stage, admired on both sides of the Atlantic for her wide array of character portrayals, she contributed only sporadic, but highly memorable, characterizations to the British and American screen, often in eccentric roles.

FILMS INCLUDE: *The House of Trent* (UK) 1933; *Quality Street* 1937; *The Glass Slipper* 1955; *The Swan, 23 Paces to Baker Street* 1956; *This Happy Feeling* 1958; *Alive and Kicking* (UK) 1959; *The Misfits* 1961; *The Cabinet of Caligari, The Notorious Landlady* 1962; *Dead Ringer* 1964; *Games, Camelot* 1967; *The Producers* 1968; *Jenny* 1970; *Murder by Death* 1976.

wipe. A transitional effect in which one scene gradually erases and replaces another as if it were wiping it off the screen. Wipes are achieved optically and may appear in a variety of forms. The edge line may be straight or jagged, sharp or soft, and may proceed horizontally, vertically, or diagonally. A wipe of an irregular geometric shape is known as an "explosion wipe" or "burst wipe." Wipes were used abundantly in silent films, but because of their overly dramatic impact they lost much of their attraction as film audiences became more sophisticated. During the sound era they were used mostly in serials, low-budget thrillers, and promotion trailers. Since the 70s they have been used in comedies such as *The Sting* and tongue-in-cheek adventures such as the Indiana Jones films to create a period feeling or for arch comic effect.

Wisdom, Norman. Actor. Born on Feb. 4, 1920, in London. Pint-sized cockney comedian of British music halls since 1946, following WW II military service. He has enjoyed enormous success in England as the star of slapstick screen comedies of the 50s and 60s, but his popularity has remained confined to British shores. He had some success on Broadway in 1967 with 'Walking Happy,' for which he was nominated for a Tony Award. He has since appeared occasionally on American TV.

FILMS INCLUDE: *Trouble in Store* 1953; *One Good Turn* 1954; *Man of the Moment* 1955; *Up in the World* 1956; *Just My Luck* 1957; *The Square Peg* 1958; *Follow a Star* 1959; *There Was a Crooked Man* 1960; *On the Beat* 1962; *A Stitch in Time* 1963; *The Early Bird* 1965; *The Sandwich Man* 1966; *The Night They Raided Minsky's* (US) 1968; *What's Good for the Goose* 1969; *Double X* 1992.

Wise, Robert. Director, producer. Born on Sept. 10, 1914, in Winchester, Ind. Forced to quit Franklin College in the thick of the Depression, he entered films in 1933 as an assistant cutter at RKO, thanks to his older brother David, who worked in the accounting department of the company. Slowly working his way up to the position of film editor, Robert shared editing credits in 1939 with William Hamilton on such films as *The Story of Vernon and Irene Castle* and *The Hunchback of Notre Dame.* On his own, he gained prominence in the early 40s as the editor of Orson Welles's masterpieces *Citizen Kane* and *The Magnificent Ambersons* and of such other films as *All That Money Can Buy* and *The Fallen Sparrow.* Wise became a director by default when Gunther von Fritsch failed to meet the production schedule of the horror film *The Curse of the Cat People* (1944). Wise took over and completed the film in ten days. It turned out to be a high-quality psychological thriller, one of the best in the Val LEWTON cycle of horror films. The following year, Wise directed for Lewton a classic of the horror genre, *The Body Snatcher,* notable for its period atmosphere and intelligent exploitation of the macabre.

After directing a number of routine B pictures in the late 40s, Wise made what many consider the best boxing drama ever filmed, *The Set-Up* (1949), a mercilessly candid portrait of the seedy world of the professional ring. It won the Critics Prize at the Cannes Festival. Wise followed this in the 50s with such high-quality films as *The Day the Earth Stood Still, Executive Suite, Somebody Up There Likes Me, I Want to Live,* and *Odds Against Tomorrow,* as well as several less interesting productions. In the 60s his name was associated with large-scale expensive productions. He won Academy Awards for the direction of *West Side Story* (in collaboration with choreographer Jerome Robbins) and *The Sound of Music.* His post–60s efforts have been tepidly received.

FILMS (as director): *The Curse of the Cat People* (co-dir. with Gunther von Fritsch), *Mademoiselle Fifi* 1944; *The Body Snatcher, A Game of Death* 1945; *Criminal Court* 1946; *Born to Kill* 1947; *Mystery in Mexico, Blood on the Moon* 1948; *The Set-Up* 1949; *Two Flags West, Three Secrets* 1950; *The House on Telegraph Hill, The Day the Earth Stood Still* 1951; *The Captive City, Something for the Birds* 1952; *The Desert Rats, Destination Gobi, So Big* 1953; *Executive Suite* 1954; *Helen of Troy* 1955; *Tribute to a Bad Man, Somebody Up There Likes Me* 1956; *This Could Be the Night, Until They Sail* 1957; *Run Silent Run Deep, I Want to Live* 1958; *Odds Against Tomorrow* (also prod.) 1959; *West Side Story* (co-dir., with Jerome Robbins, prod.) 1961; *Two for the Seesaw* 1962; *The Haunting* (also prod.; US/UK) 1963; *The Sound of Music* (also prod.) 1965; *The Sand Pebbles* (also prod.) 1966; *Star!* 1968; *The Andromeda Strain* (also prod.) 1971; *Two People* (also prod.) 1973; *The Hindenburg* 1975; *Audrey Rose* 1977; *Star Trek—The Motion Picture* 1979; *50 Years of Action!* (documentary interviewee), *The Fantasy Film World of George Pal* (documentary interviewee) 1986; *Wisdom* (exec. prod. only) 1987; *Rooftops* 1989.

Wiseman, Joseph. Actor. Born on May 15, 1918, in Montreal. On the American stage from 1936, he has played imposing character parts in films since the early 50s. Gaunt and sharp-eyed, he has often played villains of the cerebral-sinister type, memorably in the title role of the first James Bond film, *Dr. No.* He spent much of the 60s with the Lincoln Center Repertory Theater.

FILMS INCLUDE: *With These Hands* 1950; *Detective Story* 1951; *Viva Zapata!, Les Miserables* 1952; *The Silver Chalice* 1954; *The Prodigal* 1955; *The Garment Jungle* 1957; *The Unforgiven* 1960; *The Happy Thieves, Dr. No* (UK) 1962; *Bye Bye Braverman, The Night They Raided Minsky's, The Counterfeit Killer* 1968; *Stiletto* 1969; *Lawman* 1971; *Joe Valachi: I Segreti di Cosa Nostra/The Valachi Papers* (It./Fr.) 1972; *The Apprenticeship of Duddy Kravitz* (Can.) 1974; *Journey Into Fear* (UK) 1975; *The Betsy* 1978; *Buck Rogers in the 25th Century, Jaguar Lives* 1979; *The Ghost Writer* 1984.

Withers, Googie. Actress. Born Georgette Lizette Withers, on Mar. 12, 1917, in Karachi, India (now West Pakistan), to a British captain and his Dutch wife, and convent-educated in London. She made her stage debut in 1929 and subsequently played leads in many plays. From the mid-30s she appeared in numerous British films, playing leading ladies in both drama and comedy, sometimes on the bitchy side. Since the late 50s she has been living in Australia with her husband, actor John MCCALLUM.

FILMS INCLUDE: *The Love Test* 1934; *Accused, Crime Over London* 1936; *Paradise for Two/The Gaiety Girls* 1937; *The Lady Vanishes* 1938; *Busman's Honeymoon/Haunted Honeymoon, Bulldog Sees It Through* 1940; *Jeannie* 1941; *The Silver Fleet, One of Our Aircraft Is Missing* 1942; *On Approval, They Came to a City* 1944; *Dead of Night, Pink String and Sealing Wax* 1945; *It Always Rains on Sunday* 1947; *Miranda* 1948; *Once Upon a Dream* 1949; *Night and the City* 1950; *White Corridors* 1951; *Derby Day* 1952; *Devil on Horseback* 1954; *Port of Escape* 1956; *The Nickel Queen* 1970; *Time After Time* 1985; *The Country Life* 1995; *Shine* 1996.

Withers, Grant. Actor. *b.* Granville G. Withers, Jan. 17, 1904, Pueblo, Colo. *d.* 1959. Tall, rugged leading man and supporting player of some 200 Hollywood films from the late 20s. A former salesman and newspaper reporter, he started out as the star of some A productions but soon found his niche in low-budget action pictures and serials. By the early 40s he was relegated mostly to supporting parts. He made headlines in 1930, when he eloped to Yuma, Ariz., with 17-year-old Loretta YOUNG. Their marriage was annulled in 1931. He died of an overdose of sleeping pills, leaving a suicide note behind.

FILMS INCLUDE: *The Gentle Cyclone* 1926; *Upstream, The Final Extra, College* 1927; *Bringing Up Father, Tillie's Punctured Romance* 1928; *Saturday's Children, The Time the Place and the Girl, Madonna of Avenue A, Hearts in Exile, Tiger Rose* 1929; *The Second Floor Mystery/The Second Story Murder, Soldiers and Women, Back Pay, Dancing Sweeties, Sinners' Holiday, Scarlet Pages* 1930; *Other Men's Women, Too Young to Marry, Swanee River* 1931; *Gambling Sex, Red-Haired Alibi* 1932; *Secrets of Wu Sin* 1933; *The Red Rider* (serial) 1934; *Fighting Marines* (serial), *Hold 'Em Yale, Goin' to Town* 1935; *Border Flight* 1936; *Jungle Jim, Radio Patrol* (both serials), *Paradise Express* 1937; *Held for Ransom, Mr. Wong—Detective* 1938; *Navy Secrets* 1939; *Doomed to Die, Phantom of Chinatown* 1940; *Billy the Kid* 1941; *Tennessee Johnson* 1942; *A Lady Takes a Chance, No Time for Love, In Old Oklahoma* 1943; *The Fighting Seabees* 1944; *Dakota* 1945; *My Darling Clementine* 1946; *The Gunfighters, Blackmail, Tycoon* 1947; *Fort Apache* 1948; *Rio Grande* 1950; *Hoodlum Empire* 1952; *The Sun Shines Bright* 1954; *Run for Cover* 1955; *I Mobster* 1958.

Withers, Jane. Actress. Born on Apr. 12, 1926, in Atlanta. Performing in vaudeville and on radio from the age of four, she made her screen debut at six and soon ranked among Hollywood's top child stars of the 30s. She was a pudgy little thing and not very pretty, but made up for the lack of Shirley Temple glamour with mischievous charm and boundless vitality. She enjoyed less popularity in teenage ingenue roles in films of the 40s, retired in 1947, and has since returned in rare character parts. She has made a fortune from her portrayal of Josephine the Plumber in a long-running series of TV commercials for a leading cleanser.

FILMS INCLUDE: *Handle with Care* 1932; *Bright Eyes* 1934; *Ginger, The Farmer Takes a Wife* 1935; *Paddy O'Day, Gentle Julia, Little Miss Nobody, Pepper* 1936; *The Holy Terror, Angel's Holiday, Wild and Woolly, 45 Fathers* 1937; *Checkers, Rascals, Keep Smiling, Always in Trouble* 1938; *The Arizona Wildcat, Pack Up Your Troubles, Boy Friend* 1939; *High School, Shooting High, Youth Will be Served, The Girl from Avenue A* 1940; *A Very Young Lady, Her First Beau* 1941; *Young America, The Mad Martindales* 1942; *Johnny Doughboy, The North Star* 1943; *My Best Gal* 1944; *The Affairs of Geraldine* 1946; *Danger Street* 1947; *Giant* 1956; *The Right Approach* 1961; *Captain Newman M.D.* 1964.

Witherspoon, Cora. Actress. *b.* Jan. 5, 1890, New Orleans. *d.* 1957. A veteran of the stage, she played character parts in Hollywood films of the 30s and 40s, typically as a haughty matron or domineering wife. She was memorable as W. C. Fields's mate in *The Bank Dick.*

FILMS INCLUDE: *Night Angel* 1931; *Ladies of the Jury* 1932; *Midnight* 1934; *Piccadilly Jim, Libeled Lady* 1936; *On the Avenue, Quality Street, Personal Property, Madame X* 1937; *Professor Beware, Port of Seven Seas, Marie Antoinette* (as the Countess de Noailles) 1938; *Dodge City, Dark Victory, The Women* 1939; *The Bank Dick* 1940; *Over 21* 1945; *I've Always Loved You* 1946; *The Mating Season* 1951; *Just for You* 1952.

Witherspoon, Reese. Actress. Born 1976 Nashville, Tenn. *ed.* Stanford University. This lovely young actress began her career as a child model, but it was her appearance in a TV movie 'Wildflower' directed by Diane Keaton that led to other parts in major TV films and then Hollywood.

FILMS: *The Man in the Moon* 1991; *A Far Off Place, Jack the Bear* 1993; *S.F.W.* 1995; *Fear, Freeway* 1996.

Witney, William. Director. Born on May 15, 1910, in Lawton, Okla. Entering films as a messenger boy, he worked his way up to the position of script supervisor at Republic and in 1937 he was assigned to direct serials for the company. He turned out many chapter plays, mostly in collaboration, before joining the Marines in 1943. Returning to Republic in 1946, he was assigned to direct the low-budget Westerns of Roy Rogers. In the mid-50s he extended his range somewhat to include action pictures of other genres. His most effective film has been the science-fiction thriller *Master of the World* (1961).

FILMS INCLUDE: Serials (mostly co-dir.)—*SOS Coast Guard, Zorro Rides Again* 1937; *Dick Tracy Returns, The Lone Ranger* 1938; *Dick Tracy's G-Men* 1939; *Adventures of Red Ryder, Drums of Fu Manchu, King of the Royal Mounted, Mysterious Dr. Satan* 1940; *Adventures of Captain Marvel, Jungle Girl* 1941; *King of the Mounties, Spy Smasher* 1942; *G-Men vs. the Black Dragon* 1943. Features—*The Trigger Trio* 1937; *Hi-Yo Silver* (co-dir. with John English) 1940; *Outlaws of Pine Ridge* 1942; *Helldorado* 1946; *Apache Rose* 1947; *The Far Frontier* 1949; *The Last Musketeer* 1952; *The Outcast* 1954; *Headline Hunters, City of Shadows* 1955; *A Strange Adventure* 1956; *Panama Sal* 1957; *Young and Wild, Juvenile Jungle, The Cool and the Crazy, The Bonnie Parker Story* 1958; *Paratroop Command* 1959; *Secret of the Purple Reef* 1960; *Master of the World, The Long Rope* 1961; *Apache Rifles* 1964; *The Girls on the Beach* 1965; *Arizona Raiders, Forty Guns to Apache Pass* 1966; *I Escaped from Devil's Island* 1973; *Darktown Strutters* 1975.

Wohlbrück, Adolf. See WALBROOK, Anton.

Wolf, Konrad. Director. *b.* Oct. 20, 1925, Hechingen, Germany. *d.* 1982. The son of physician, playwright, and screenwriter Friedrich Wolf (*b.* Dec. 23, 1888, Berlin; *d.* 1953), he emigrated with his parents to Russia after the Nazi takeover of 1933. Released from WW II service with the Red Army, he studied filmmaking in Moscow under Sergei Gerasimov. He settled in East Germany in 1954 and developed into one of that country's most distinguished directors. His best-known film in the West, *Sterne/Stars,* an East German–Bulgarian co-production, was enthusiastically received in Cannes, winning a special Jury Prize. For many years, beginning in 1965, he was president of the Academy of Arts of the German Democratic Republic.

FILMS INCLUDE: *Einmal ist keinmal* 1955; *Genesung* 1956; *Lissy* (also co-sc.) 1957; *Sterne/Stars, Die Sonnesucher* 1958; *Leute mit Flügeln* 1960; *Professor Mamlock* (also co-sc. from his father's original script for the 1938 Soviet version) 1961; *Der geteilte Himmel* (also co-sc.) 1964; *Ich war neunzehn/I Was 19* (also co-sc.) 1968; *Goya oder der arge Weg zur Erkenntnis* (also co-sc.) 1971; *The Naked Man on the Athletic Field, Mama ich lebe* 1977.

Wolfe, Ian. Actor. *b.* 1896, in Canton, Ill. *d.* 1992. A veteran of the stage, he played character parts in numerous Hollywood films beginning in the mid-30s, often as a cowardly, shady, or treacherous type.

FILMS INCLUDE: *The Fountain, The Barretts of Wimpole Street* 1934; *Clive of India, The Raven, Mad Love, Mutiny on the Bounty* 1935; *The League of Frightened Men* 1937; *Arsene Lupin Returns* 1938; *On Borrowed Time* 1939; *Earthbound, The Son of Monte Cristo* 1940; *Saboteur* 1942; *The Moon Is Down* 1943; *The Invisible Man's Revenge, The Scarlet Claw* 1944; *Confidential Agent* 1945; *Bedlam* 1946; *Johnny Belinda, Julia Misbehaves* 1948; *A Place in the Sun* 1951; *Julius Caesar* (as Ligarius) 1953; *Seven Brides for Seven Brothers* 1954; *Rebel Without a Cause, The Court-Martial of Billy Mitchell* 1955; *Witness for the Prosecution* 1958; *The Lost World* 1960; *The Wonderful World of the Brothers Grimm* 1962; *Diary of a Madman* 1963; *Games* 1967; *The Terminal Man, Homebodies* 1974; *The Fortune, Mr. Sycamore* 1975; *Seniors* 1978; *Jinxed* 1982.

Wolfit, Sir Donald. Actor. *b.* Apr. 20, 1902, Newark-on-

Trent, England. *d.* 1968. A distinguished actor of the British stage (from 1920), he was knighted in 1957 for his achievements in presenting, with his own company, Shakespearean plays and other works of the classical repertoire on innumerable tours of the English provinces and international cities. An actor of commanding presence, he appeared in hundreds of plays but in only a score of films, notably in the title role of *Svengali* (1954). Autobiography: *First Interval* (1955).

FILMS INCLUDE: *Death at Broadcasting House* 1934; *Drake of England* 1935; *Ringer* 1952; *The Pickwick Papers* (as Sergeant Buzfuz) 1953; *Svengali* (title role) 1954; *A Prize of Gold* 1955; *Guilty, Satellite in the Sky* 1956; *I Accuse!, Blood of the Vampire* 1958; *Room at the Top, The House of Seven Hawks* 1959; *The Hands of Orlac* 1960; *The Mark* 1961; *Lawrence of Arabia* 1962; *Dr. Crippen* 1963; *Becket* 1964; *90 Degrees in the Shade* (Czech./UK), *Life at the Top* 1965; *Decline and Fall, The Charge of the Light Brigade* 1968.

Wolheim, Louis. Actor. *b.* Mar. 28, 1880, New York City. *d.* 1931. The holder of an engineering degree from Cornell, he remained at the university for six years as a mathematics instructor before beginning an acting career on the stage. He entered films in 1920. His squat, rugged physique and crude, ugly face, marked by a broken nose he had received as a Cornell halfback, led to his typecasting as a brute and a thug. On Broadway, he was the original Captain Flagg in 'What Price Glory' and the first interpreter of 'The Hairy Ape.' On the screen, he played brutish villains in such silent films as *Dr. Jekyll and Mr. Hyde* (the John Barrymore version, 1920) and D. W. Griffith's *America* (1924), but he is best remembered for his excellent portrayal of a sympathetic part in *All Quiet on the Western Front* (1930). He died of cancer.

FILMS INCLUDE: *The Carter Case* (serial) 1917; *The House of Hate* (serial) 1918; *Dr. Jekyll and Mr. Hyde* 1920; *Orphans of The Storm, Experience* 1921; *Sherlock Holmes, The Face in the Fog* 1922; *Little Old New York, The Last Moment, Unseeing Eyes* 1923; *America, The Story Without a Name* 1924; *Lover's Island* 1925; *Two Arabian Knights, Sorrell and Son* 1927; *Tempest, The Racket, The Awakening* 1928; *Wolf Song, The Shady Lady, Frozen Justice, Condemned* 1929; *The Ship from Shanghai, All Quiet on the Western Front* (as Katczinsky), *The Silver Horde, Danger Lights* 1930; *The Sin Ship, Gentleman's Fate* 1931.

Wollen, Peter. Theorist, filmmaker. Born in 1938 in London. Author of the influential book, *Signs and Meaning in the Cinema* (1969, revised 1972). In it, he draws on structuralism and semiotics to attempt to release film study from the "closed and idiosyncratic universe of discourse" it had inhabited and offer ideas of how film aesthetics can "keep pace with and be responsive to changes and developments in the study of other media, other arts, other modes of communication and expression." With his wife Laura MULVEY, he made several experimental films meant to unite the two reigning schools of avant-garde filmmaking and critique mainstream commercial filmmaking, notably *Riddles of the Sphinx*. Other books include *Readings and Writings: Semiotic Counter-Strategies* (1982) and *Singin' in the Rain* (1992), a critical and historical study of the movie. Co-screenwriter (with Michelangelo Antonioni) of *The Passenger*. He teaches film at UCLA.

FILMS INCLUDE: *The Passenger* (co-sc.) 1975; *Penthesilea* (co-dir.) 1974; *Riddles of the Sphinx* (co-dir., co-prod., co-sc.) 1977; *Amy!* (act., dir., sc.) 1980; *Crystal Gazing* (co-dir., co-sc.) 1982; *The Man Who Envied Women* 1985; *Friendship's Death* (dir., sc.) 1987.

Wolper, David L. Producer, executive. Born on Jan. 11, 1928, in New York City. *ed.* Drake U.; USC. In the film business since his student days, he gained esteem for his many TV documentaries and compilation films. In the late 60s his company, Wolper Productions, ventured into feature films and was absorbed by Metromedia. Wolper produced some of the films himself and was executive producer on others. He produced the 1977 TV miniseries 'Alex Haley's: Roots.' He received the Jean Hersholt Humanitarian Award in 1985.

FILMS INCLUDE: *Four Days in November* (doc.; exec. prod.) 1964; *The Devil's Brigade* 1968; *If It's Tuesday It Must Be Belgium* (exec. prod.), *The Bridge at Remagen* 1969; *I Love My Wife* (exec. prod.) 1970; *Willy Wonka and the Chocolate Factory* (co-prod.) 1971; *One Is a Lonely Number* (exec. prod.), *Herzbube/King Queen Knave* (Ger./US) 1972; *Visions of Eight* (Munich Olympics doc.; exec. prod.) 1973; *The Man Who Saw Tomorrow* (exec. prod.) 1980; *This is Elvis* 1981; *Imagine: John Lennon* 1988.

Wong, Anna May. Actress. *b.* Wong Liu Tsong, Jan. 3, 1907, Chinatown, Los Angeles. *d.* 1961. She entered films as an extra at the age of 12 and after playing a number of featured parts, she attracted attention at 16 in the plum role of a slave girl in Douglas Fairbanks's *The Thief of Bagdad.* A vogue for Oriental mysteries elevated her to stardom in the late 20s. Her fame was international and in 1929 she went to Europe, where she lectured and starred in British and German films. She also appeared on the stage, co-starring with Laurence Olivier in 'Circle of Chalk.' On the screen, she figured prominently in Josef von Sternberg's *Shanghai Express* (1932), but her Hollywood films of the late 30s and early 40s were mostly cheap crime melodramas in which she often played mysterious villainesses. She retired from the screen in 1942 and later appeared in only two films. Miss Wong, who never married, died in her sleep of a heart attack.

FILMS INCLUDE: *Red Lantern* 1919; *Bits of Life, Shame* 1921; *The Toll of the Sea* 1922; *Drifting, Thundering Dawn* 1923; *The Thief of Bagdad, The Alaskan, Peter Pan, The 40th Door* 1924; *Forty Winks* 1925; *Fifth Avenue, The Desert's Toll, A Trip to Chinatown* 1926; *Mr. Wu, Old San Francisco, The Devil Dancer, Streets of Shanghai, The Chinese Parrot* 1927; *Across to Singapore, Chinatown Charlie, Song/Wasted Love* (Ger./UK), *The Crimson City* 1928; *Piccadilly* (UK) 1929; *The Flame of Love* (UK) 1930; *Daughter of the Dragon* 1931; *Shanghai Express* 1932; *A Study in Scarlet, Tiger Bay* (UK) 1933; *Chu Chin Chow* (UK), *Java Head* (UK), *Limehouse Blues* 1934; *Daughter of Shanghai* 1937; *Dangerous to Know* 1938; *King of Chinatown, Island of Lost Men* 1939; *Ellery Queen's Penthouse Mystery* 1941; *Bombs Over Burma, Lady from Chungking* 1942; *Impact* 1949; *Ombre bianche/The Savage Innocents* (It./Fr./UK), *Portrait in Black* 1960.

Wontner, Arthur. Actor. *b.* Jan. 21, 1875, London. *d.* 1960. A veteran of the English stage (from 1897), he starred in silent British films and stretched his popularity into the 30s playing Sherlock Holmes in a number of thrillers. He was later seen in character roles.

FILMS INCLUDE: *The Bigamist* 1915; *Lady Windermere's Fan* 1916; *Bonnie Prince Charlie* 1923; *The Diamond Man* 1924; *The Infamous Lady* 1928; *The Sleeping Cardinal/Sherlock Holmes's Fatal Hour* (title role) 1931; *The Missing Rembrandt* (as Sherlock Holmes), *Condemned to Death, The Sign of Four* (as Sherlock Holmes) 1932; *The Triumph of Sherlock Holmes* (title role) 1935; *Thunder in the City, Storm in a Teacup, Silver Blaze/Murder at the Baskervilles* (as Sherlock Holmes) 1937; *The Terror* 1938; *The Life and Death of Colonel Blimp* 1943; *Blanche Fury* 1947; *The Elusive Pimpernel/The Fighting Pimpernel* 1950; *Brandy for the Parson* 1952; *Genevieve* 1953; *Three Cases of Murder* 1955.

Woo, John. Director. Born in 1946 in Guangzhou, Canton Province, China. *ed.* Matteo Ricci College, Hong Kong. Feature director in Hong Kong and the US, best known for a series of crime and action dramas from the salad days of the Hong Kong cinema in the 80s. His family emigrated to Hong Kong in 1950. After college there, he began his film career in 1969, apprenticing at the Cathay and Shaw Brothers studios. At Shaw Brothers, he directed his first feature, *The Young Dragons*, a martial arts film. That same year, he secured a long-term contract with the Golden Harvest studio, where he worked for two decades.

While he worked consistently through the 70s making action films and comedies, he made his mark with the elemental gangster film *A Better Tomorrow* (1986). This film provided the model for his subsequent features: anguished and sometimes brutal central characters (often portrayed by actor Chow Yun-Fat); a serious-minded story about loyalty and betrayal; and graphic, cathartic violence. His films gathered an American cult of critics and fans, who (often condescendingly) viewed the films as camp; *The Killer* (1989), starring Chow, became the highest grossing Hong Kong film in America since Bruce Lee's *Enter the Dragon* (1973). His pictures after *A Better Tomorrow* fed Woo's reputation for technical proficiency and visual imagination. They included a sequel (*A Better Tomorrow II*, 1987); an epic film set during the Vietnam War (*A Bullet in the Head,* 1990); and a heist comedy (*Once A Thief,* 1991). In 1992 he relocated to the US; his first American feature, *Hard Target*, was released in 1993.

FILMS INCLUDE (as director): *The Young Dragons* (co-director) 1973; *The Dragon Tamers* 1974; *Countdown to Kung Fu, Princess Chang Ping* 1975; *Money Crazy, Follow the Star* 1977; *Last Hurrah for Chivalry* 1978; *From Rags to Riches* 1979; *To Hell with the Devil* 1981; *Laughing Times* 1981; *Plain Jane to the Rescue* 1982; *The Sunset Warrior* 1983; *The Time You Need a Friend* 1984; *Run Tiger Run* 1985; *A Better Tomorrow,* 1986; *A Better Tomorrow II* 1987; *The Killer* 1989; *Bullet in the Head* 1990; *Once A Thief* 1991; *Hard-Boiled* 1992; *Hard Target* (US) 1993; *The Madness of King George* 1994; *Broken Arrow; Face/Off* 1996.

Wood, Edward D., Jr. American director, producer, screenwriter. *b.* 1922. *d.* 1978. Independent filmmaker of the 50s widely regarded as the worst director of all time. Producing, writing, and directing films with abysmal casts and ludicrously cheap production values, he has paradoxically gained a loyal cult following. A reputed transvestite, he dealt with transvestitism in *Glen or Glenda?* (1952), but is best known for *Plan 9 from Outer Space* (1959), often cited as the worst film of all time. It includes the last performance of Bela Lugosi, whose role in the film, following his death, was completed by Wood's wife's chiropractor.

FILMS: *Glen or Glenda?/I Changed My Sex* 1952; *Bride of the Monster* 1953; *Jail Bait* 1954; *Plan 9 from Outer Space* 1959; *Night of the Ghouls* 1960; *Necromancy* 1972.

Wood, Natalie. Actress. *b.* Natasha Gurdin, July 20, 1938, San Francisco, Calif. *d.* 1981. The daughter of an architect of Russian descent and a ballet dancer of French extraction, she began taking dancing lessons before she could walk properly. When she was five she appeared in a bit part in *Happy Land* (1943), a film in which many of the residents of her hometown, Santa Rosa, Calif., were used as extras. She left an impression on the film's director, Irving Pichel, who three years later signed her to play a featured role, in support of Orson Welles and Claudette Colbert, in *Tomorrow Is Forever* (1946). She continued as a child star in many other films, notably as the skeptical friend of Kris Kringle (Edmund Gwenn) in *Miracle on 34th Street.* Unlike most child performers she subsequently made a smooth transition to teenage and ingenue roles, and bloomed into a beautiful and popular leading lady. She was nominated for an Academy Award for *Rebel Without a Cause* (1955), *Splendor in the Grass* (1961), and *Love with the Proper Stranger* (1963), but her range of emotional expression left some critics unmoved, and the *Harvard Lampoon* initiated the annual "Natalie Wood Award" for the worst performance by an actress. She drowned in a yachting accident in 1981. Miss Wood married (1957), divorced (1963), and remarried (1972) Robert WAGNER. She was the sister of actress Lana Wood and the mother, by producer Richard Gregson, of actress Natasha Wagner.

FILMS: *Happy Land* 1943; *Tomorrow Is Forever, The Bride Wore Boots* 1946; *Miracle on 34th Street, The Ghost and Mrs. Muir, Driftwood* 1947; *Scudda-Hoo Scudda-Hay!, Chicken Every Sunday, The Green Promise, Father Was a Fullback* 1949; *No Sad Songs for Me, Our Very Own, Never a Dull Moment, The Jackpot* 1950; *Dear Brat, The Blue Veil* 1951; *Just for You, The Rose Bowl Story* 1952; *The Star* 1953; *The Silver Chalice* 1954; *One Desire, Rebel Without a Cause* 1955; *The Searchers, The Burning Hills, A Cry in the Night, The Girl He Left Behind* 1956; *Bombers B-52* 1957; *Marjorie Morningstar, Kings Go Forth* 1958; *Cash McCall, All the Fine Young Cannibals* 1960; *Splendor in the Grass, West Side Story* 1961; *Gypsy* (as Gypsy Rose Lee) 1962; *Love with the Proper Stranger* 1963; *Sex and the Single Girl* 1964; *The Great Race* 1965; *Inside Daisy Clover, This Property Is Condemned, Penelope* 1966; *Bob & Carol & Ted & Alice* 1969; *The Candidate* (unbilled cameo) 1972; *Peeper* 1976; *Meteor* 1978; *The Last Married Couple in America* 1979; *Willie and Phil* 1980; *Brainstorm* (died during filming; released re-edited posthumously) 1983.

Wood, Peggy. Actress. *b.* Margaret Wood, Feb. 9, 1892, Brooklyn, N.Y. *d.* 1978. The daughter of a newspaperman-humorist, she began taking singing lessons at the age of eight and made her professional debut at 18 in the chorus line of 'Naughty Marietta' on Broadway. She developed into a superb performer, a versatile actress whose stage repertoire ranged from musicals to Shakespeare. However, her screen appearances have been sporadic. She was nominated for an Oscar as best supporting actress for her performance as the Mother Abbess in *The Sound of Music* (1965). She starred in the long-running (1949–57) TV series 'Mama.'

FILMS: *Almost a Husband* 1919; *Wonder of Women* 1929; *Handy Andy* 1934; *The Right to Live, Jalna* (as Meg) 1935; *A Star Is Born, Call It a Day* 1937; *The Housekeeper's Daughter* 1939; *The Bride Wore Boots, The Magnificent Doll* 1946; *Dream Girl* 1948; *The Story of Ruth* (as Naomi) 1960; *The Sound of Music* 1965.

Wood, Sam. Director. *b.* Samuel Grosvenor Wood, July 18, 1883, Philadelphia. *d.* 1949. A former real estate broker, he appeared as an actor in a few two-reelers around 1908, under the name Chad Applegate, and in 1915 became an assistant director to C. B. DE MILLE. Late in 1919 he was graduated to director at Paramount. In the 20s he handled many of the films of Gloria SWANSON and Wallace REID, developing a reputation as a reliable craftsman who could turn mediocre material into acceptable entertainment. He solidified his position in the 30s when, at MGM, he effectively directed, along with a large number of routine productions, such diverse films as the superb Marx Brothers comedy *A Night at the Opera* and the maudlin schooldays drama *Goodbye Mr. Chips.* He reached the peak of his craft toward the end of his career, in the 40s, when he turned out with sure-handed skill such films as *Our Town, Kitty Foyle, For Whom the Bell Tolls, The Pride of the Yankees, Command Decision,* and the excellent drama *Kings Row.* Despite these achievements, Wood's contribution to American cinema has been largely ignored by film historians, perhaps because of his dedication to conservative-hawkish politics. He was president of the Motion Picture Alliance for the Preservation of American Ideals and his testimony before the House Un-American Activities Committee in 1947 helped fan the notion of Communist infiltration in the film industry. His daughter is actress K. T. Stevens.

FILMS: *Double Speed, Excuse My Dust, The Dancin' Fool, Sick Abed, What's Your Hurry?, A City Sparrow, Her Beloved Villain, Her First Elopement* 1920; *The Snob, Peck's Bad Boy* (also sc.), *The Great Moment, Under the Lash, Don't Tell Everything* 1921; *Her Husband's Trademark, Beyond the Rocks, Her Gilded Cage, The Impossible Mrs. Bellew* 1922; *My American Wife, Prodigal Daughters, Bluebeard's Eighth Wife, His Children's Children* 1923; *The Next Corner, Bluff, The Female, The Mine with the Iron Door* 1924; *The Re-Creation of Brian Kent* 1925; *Fascinating Youth, One Minute to Play* 1926; *Rookies, A Racing Romeo, The Fair Co-Ed* 1927; *The Latest from Paris, Telling the World* 1928; *So This Is College, It's a Great Life* 1929; *They Learned About Women* (co-dir. with Jack Conway), *The Girl Said No, Sins of the Children, Way for a Sailor, Paid* 1930; *A Tailor-Made Man, The Man in Possession, Get-Rich-Quick Wallingford/New Adventures of Get-Rich-Quick Wallingford* 1931; *Huddle, Prosperity* 1932; *The Barbarian, Hold Your Man* (also prod.), *Christopher Bean* 1933; *Stamboul Quest* 1934; *Let 'Em Have It, A Night at the Opera* 1935; *Whipsaw, The Unguarded Hour* 1936; *A Day at the Races* (also co-prod.), *Navy Blue and Gold, Madame X* 1937; *Lord Jeff* (also co-prod.), *Stablemates* 1938; *Gone With the Wind* (some scenes only, uncredited), *Goodbye Mr. Chips, Raffles* 1939; *Our Town, Rangers of Fortune, Kitty Foyle* 1940; *The Devil and Miss Jones* 1941; *Kings Row, The Pride of the Yankees* 1942; *The Land Is Bright* (doc.; superv. only), *For Whom the Bell Tolls* (also prod.) 1943; *Address Unknown* (prod. only), *Casanova Brown* 1944; *Saratoga Trunk, Guest Wife* 1945; *Heartbeat* 1946; *Ivy* (also co-prod.) 1947; *Command Decision, The Stratton Story* 1949; *Ambush* 1950.

Woodard, Alfre. Actress. Born on Nov. 8, 1953, in Tulsa, Okla. *ed.* Boston U. Controlled, stage-trained supporting and lead player, adept at both drama and comedy. After college, she worked in Washington D.C.'s Arena Stage and made her film debut in 1978. In the 80s and 90s she played a variety of screen and TV roles, winning an Academy Award nomination for her performance in *Cross Creek* and Emmys for appearances on *Hill Street Blues* and *L.A. Law*. Series regular on TV drama 'St. Elsewhere.'

FILMS INCLUDE: *Remember My Name* 1978; *Health* 1980; *Cross Creek* 1983; *Extremities* 1986; *Scrooged* 1988; *Miss Firecracker* 1989; *Grand Canyon* 1991; *Rich in Love, Passion Fish, The Gun in Betty Lou's Handbag* 1992; *Heart and Souls, Bopha!* 1993; *Blue Chips, Crooklyn* 1994; *How To Make an American Quilt* 1995; *Primal Fear, Star Trek: First Contact* 1996; *Follow Me Home* 1997.

Woodbury, Joan. Actress. *b.* Dec. 17, 1915, in Los Angeles. *d.* 1989. Convent-educated. She was a dancer before entering films in the mid-30s. She played leads and second leads in numerous productions, mostly low-budget action pictures. Later produced and directed stage plays and light operas in California. Once married to Henry WILCOXON.

FILMS INCLUDE: *Eagle's Brood* 1935; *Anthony Adverse, The Lion's Den* 1936; *Super Sleuth, Charlie Chan on Broadway* 1937; *Crashing Hollywood, Algiers, Night Spot* 1938; *While New York Sleeps* 1939; *King of the Zombies, I Killed That Man, Paper Bullets/Gangs Incorporated, Confessions of Boston Blackie* 1941; *Man from Headquarters, Phantom Killer,* 1942; *The Hard Way, The Desperadoes* 1943; *The Whistler, The Chinese Cat* 1944; *Brenda Starr—Reporter* (serial), *Flame of the West* 1945; *The Arnelo Affair* 1947; *Boston Blackie's Chinese Venture* 1949; *The Ten Commandments* 1956; *The Time Travelers* 1964.

Woods, Arthur. Director. *b.* Aug. 17, 1904, Liverpool, England. *d.* 1942. The son of a shipping magnate, he gave up his medical studies at Cambridge to join a repertory company as an actor. He entered films in 1926 as a cutter of a documentary series. He became assistant director in 1930 and after collaborating on a number of screenplays, he began directing in 1933. He was killed in action during WW II.

FILMS INCLUDE: *On Secret Service/Spy 77* 1933; *Drake of England* 1935; *One in a Million* 1936; *Mayfair Melody, The Windmill* 1937; *The Dark Stairway, Mr. Satan, The Return of Carol Deane* 1938; *Q Planes/Clouds Over Europe* (co-dir. with Tim Whelan), *They Drive By Night, Confidential Lady* 1939; *Busman's Honeymoon/Haunted Honeymoon* 1940.

Woods, Donald. American actor. Born Ralph L. Zink, 1904, Brandon, Canada. In Hollywood after some stage experience, he played leads in numerous B pictures, often crime dramas, and second leads in occasional major productions. From the 50s he has worked mainly on the stage and in TV. He has also been a real estate broker.

FILMS INCLUDE: *As the Earth Turns, Fog Over Frisco, She Was a Lady* 1934; *Sweet Adeline, The Case of the Curious Bride, The Florentine Dagger, Stranded, Frisco Kid, A Tale of Two Cities* (as Charles Darnay) 1935; *The Story of Louis Pasteur, Road Gang, The White Angel, Anthony Adverse* (as Vincent Nolte), *A Son Comes Home* 1936; *Talent Scout, Charlie Chan on Broadway, The Case of the Stuttering Bishop, Big Town Girl* 1937; *The Black Doll, Danger on the Air* 1938; *Beauty for the Asking, Heritage of the Desert* 1939; *Mexican Spitfire, City of Chance* 1940; *Sky Raiders* (serial), *I Was a Prisoner on Devil's Island* 1941; *Thru Different Eyes* 1942; *Corregidor, Watch on the Rhine* 1943; *The Bridge of San Luis Rey* (as Brother Juniper), *Enemy of Women* 1944; *Roughly Speaking, Wonder Man* 1945; *Night and Day, Never Say Goodbye* 1946; *The Return of Rin Tin Tin* 1947; *Scene of the Crime, Barbary Pirate* 1949; *Mr. Music* 1950; *The Beast from 20,000 Fathoms* 1953; *13 Ghosts* 1960; *Kissin' Cousins* 1964; *Moment-to-Moment* 1966; *True Grit* 1969.

Woods, Harry. American actor. *b.* 1889. *d.* 1968. One of the meanest heavies in the annals of Hollywood films. A former millinery salesman and stage actor, he played minor but vicious villains in scores of films and met violent death in most.

FILMS INCLUDE: *The Perils of Pauline* (serial) 1914; *The Romance of Elaine* (serial) 1915; *The Iron Claw* (serial) 1916; *Don Quickshot of the Rio Grande* 1923; *A Cafe in Cairo* 1925; *Jesse James* 1927; *The Sunset Legion* 1928; *The Viking* 1929; *The Lone Rider* 1930; *Palmy Days, Monkey Business* 1931; *I Am a Fugitive from a Chain Gang* 1932; *Belle of the Nineties, The Scarlet Empress* 1934; *The Phantom Rider* (serial) 1936; *The Plainsman* 1937; *Blockheads* 1938; *The Man in the Iron Mask, Union Pacific, Beau Geste* 1939; *Winners of the West* (serial) 1940; *The Forest Rangers, Reap the Wild Wind* 1942; *Tall in the Saddle* 1944; *My Darling Clementine* 1946; *She Wore a Yellow Ribbon* 1949; *Lone Star* 1952; *Hell's Outpost* 1954; *The Ten Commandments* 1956.

Woods, James. Actor. Born on April 18, 1947, in Vernal, Utah. *ed.* MIT. Wiry stage-trained screen lead, usually as foreboding types. After appearing widely on the stage in Boston during his college years, he moved to New York and established himself in several off- and on-Broadway dramas, including 'Conduct Unbecoming,' for which he won an Obie. Debuted in film in the 70s and has since distinguished himself as an original, highly charged presence, equally able to project villainousness or moral ambiguity. Nominated for Academy Awards for his performances as an opportunistic journalist in *Salvador* and as the self-confessed racist and murderer of civil rights leader Medgar Evers in *Ghosts of Mississippi* (1996) Won an Emmy for his performance as disturbed brother in TV movie *Promise*.

FILMS INCLUDE: *The Visitor, Hickey and Boggs* 1972; *The Way We Were* 1973; *The Gambler* 1974; *Distance, Night Moves* 1975; *Alex and the Gypsy* 1976; *The Choirboys* 1977; *The Onion Field* 1979; *The Black Marble* 1980; *Eyewitness* 1981; *Fast-Walking, Split Image* 1982; *Videodrome* 1983; *Against All Odds, Once Upon a Time in America* (US/It./Can.) 1984; *Cat's Eye, Joshua Then and Now* (Can.) 1985; *Salvador* 1986; *Best Seller* 1987; *Cop* (also co-prod.), *The Boost* 1988; *True Believer, Immediate Family* 1989; *The Hard Way* 1991; *Straight Talk, Diggstown* 1992; *Curse of the Starving Class, The Getaway, The Specialist* 1994; *Casino, Nixon* 1995; *For Better or For Worse, Ghosts of Mississippi* 1996; *Contact, Hercules* (v/o), *Kicked in the Head* 1997.

Woodward, Edward. Actor, singer. Born on June 1, 1930, in Croydon, England. *ed.* Kingston College; Royal Academy of Dramatic Art, London. Son of a chicken farmer. Following dramatic studies, he established himself as a critically acclaimed British stage performer as well as a top-selling recording artist with eleven albums to his credit. Gained international recognition for his complex portrayal in the title role of *Breaker Morant* (1979). In 1986 married Michelle Dotrice, actress daughter of actor Roy Dotrice. Best known in the US for his starring role in the television series 'The Equalizer' (1986–89).

FILMS INCLUDE: *Becket* 1964; *The File of the Golden Goose* 1969; *Sitting Target, Young Winston* 1972; *The Wicker Man* 1973; *Stand Up Virgin Soldiers* 1977; *Breaker Morant* (also song composer) 1979; *Comeback, Who Dare Wins* 1982; *Champions* 1983; *King David* 1985; *Mister Johnson* 1991; *The Assassin, Richard III* 1995.

Woodward, Joanne. Actress. Born on Feb. 27, 1930, in Thomasville, Ga., the daughter of a publishing executive. She began acting in high school plays and gained additional stage experience at Louisiana State University. After some professional engagements at the Greenville, S.C., community theater, she enrolled as a student at New York's Neighborhood Playhouse. While still a student, she understudied on Broadway in 'Picnic' and appeared in a number of TV dramas. She made her screen debut in 1955. Two years later she was the winner of the best actress Academy Award for her multifaceted performance in *The Three Faces of Eve.* Combining the qualities of an accomplished actress and a radiant personality, she has since remained one of the most highly regarded performers of the American stage and screen. She has often co-starred with her husband since 1958, Paul NEWMAN, who directed her in one of her best screen appearances, *Rachel, Rachel* (Oscar nomination, 1968). She was named best actress at Cannes for *The Effect of Gamma Rays on Man-in-the-Moon Marigolds* (1972), also directed by Newman. She won Emmys as best actress for her performances in the TV movies 'See How She Runs' (1978) and 'Do You Remember Love?' (1985). She is among the most intense of the political and social activists in show business and has campaigned vigorously for various liberal causes.

FILMS: *Count Three and Pray* 1955; *A Kiss Before Dying* 1956; *The Three Faces of Eve, No Down Payment* 1957; *The Long Hot Summer, Rally Round the Flag Boys!* 1958; *The Sound and the Fury* 1959; *The Fugitive Kind, From the Terrace* 1960; *Paris Blues* 1961; *The Stripper, A New Kind of Love* 1963; *Signpost to Murder* 1965; *A Big Hand for the Little Lady, A Fine Madness* 1966; *Rachel Rachel* 1968; *Winning* 1969; *King* (doc.), *WUSA* 1970; *They Might Be Giants* 1971; *The Effect of Gamma Rays on Man-in-the-Moon Marigolds* 1972; *Summer Wishes Winter Dreams* 1973; *The Drowning Pool* 1975; *The End* 1978; *Harry and Son* 1984; *The Glass Menagerie* 1987; *Mr. and Mrs. Bridge* 1990; *Philadelphia* 1993.

Woolf, James (*b.* 1919, London; *d.* 1966) and **John** (*b.* 1913, London). Producers. The sons of veteran British producer C. M. Woolf, they founded in 1949 the London-based Romulus Films, which produced such Anglo-American productions as *Pandora and the Flying Dutchman* (1951), *The African Queen* (1951), and *Moulin Rouge* (1953). Later they personally produced a number of first-rate British films.

FILMS INCLUDE: Produced by both James and John—*Three Men in a Boat* 1956; *Room at the Top* 1959. By James alone—*The L-Shaped Room, Term of Trial* 1962; *Of Human Bondage, The Pumpkin Eater* 1964; *King Rat, Life at the Top* 1965. By John alone—*Oliver!* 1968; *The Day of the Jackal* 1973; *The Odessa File* 1974.

Woolley, Monty. Actor. *b.* Edgar Montillion Woolley, Aug. 17, 1888, New York City. *d.* 1963. The son of a Saratoga Springs hotel proprietor, he studied at both Yale and Harvard and returned to the former as an English instructor and coach of graduate dramatics. Among his students were Thornton WILDER and Stephen Vincent Benèt. He gave up the academic life in 1936 when he made his debut on the Broadway stage. The following year he appeared in the first of many films in which he typically played shrewd, gregarious character leads and supporting parts. Nicknamed "The Beard" for his neat whiskers by Yale classmate Cole PORTER, Woolley remains most memorable for his stage and screen interpretation of the title role in *The Man Who Came to Dinner.* He was nominated for an Oscar as best actor for *The Pied Piper* (1942) and as best supporting actor for *Since You Went Away* (1944). He portrayed himself in the film biography of Cole Porter, *Night and Day* (1946).

FILMS: *Live Love and Learn, Nothing Sacred* 1937; *Arsene Lupin Returns, Everybody Sing, The Girl of the Golden West, Three Comrades, Lord Jeff, Young Dr. Kildare, Artists and Models Abroad* 1938; *Midnight, Man About Town, Dancing Co-Ed, Never Say Die* 1939; *The Man Who Came to Dinner, The Pied Piper, Life Begins at Eight-Thirty* 1942; *Holy Matrimony* 1943; *Since You Went Away, Irish Eyes Are Smiling* 1944; *Molly and Me* 1945; *Night and Day* 1946; *The Bishop's Wife* 1947; *Miss Tatlock's Millions* 1948; *As Young As You Feel* 1951; *Kismet* 1955.

Woolsey, Robert. Actor. *b.* Aug. 14, 1889, Oakland, Calif. *d.* 1938. A jockey, he was forced to give up racing after being thrown off a horse. After a variety of odd jobs, he turned to the stage and eventually reached Broadway. In 1927 he was teamed up with Bert WHEELER in Ziegfeld's Broadway musical 'Rio Rita.' They appeared together in the 1929 screen version of the play and went on to star as a team in vaudeville and in many film comedies of the 30s. Woolsey and his perennial cigar appeared alone in a couple of shorts and in the feature *Everything's Rosie* (1931). For their joint screen credits see WHEELER, Bert.

Worden, Hank. Actor. *b.* 1901 in Rolfe, Iowa. *d.* 1992. *ed.* Stanford; Univ. of Nevada. Slim, expressive character player of screen and TV, often in Westerns. Trained as a bronco rider, he made his film debut in 1936 in *The Plainsman*. In his more than 50 years on the screen he made over 100 films, many with major stars of Westerns, including Kirk Douglas, Clint Eastwood, and John Wayne, with whom he made 15 films. He appeared often on TV, in series ranging from 'The Lone Ranger' to 'Twin Peaks.' Notable as the addled but crafty Mose in *The Searchers*. A member of John Ford's acting ensemble.

FILMS INCLUDE: *The Plainsman* 1936; *The Stranger*

from Arizona, Where the Buffalo Roam, Rollin' Plains 1938; *Oklahoma Frontier* 1939; *Gaucho Serenade, Northwest Passage* 1940; *Code of the Outlaw* 1942; *Undercurrent, Duel in the Sun, The Lawless Breed* 1946; *Angel and the Badman, The Sea of Grass, The Secret Life of Walter Mitty* 1947; *Red River, Fort Apache, Yellow Sky* 1948; *The Fighting Kentuckian, Three Godfathers, Hellfire* 1949; *Father Is a Bachelor, When Willie Comes Marching Home, Wagonmaster* 1950; *Sugarfoot, Joe Palooka in Triple Cross* 1951; *The Quiet Man, Boots Malone, The Big Sky* 1952; *Ma and Pa Kettle at Home, Crime Wave* 1954; *The Searchers* 1956; *Forty Guns, The Buckskin Lady* 1957; *The Horse Soldiers* 1959; *Sergeant Rutledge, The Alamo* 1960; *One-Eyed Jacks* 1961; *The Music Man* 1962; *McLintock!* 1963; *True Grit* 1969; *Chisum, Rio Lobo* 1970; *Big Jake* 1971; *Cahill—United States Marshall* 1973; *Which Way Is Up?* 1977; *Sgt. Pepper's Lonely Hearts Club Band, Every Which Way But Loose* 1978; *Bronco Billy* 1980; *The Ice Pirates* 1984; *Almost an Angel* 1990.

working title. A temporary title assigned to a film during production and editing, pending a decision on a permanent one that must be reached before the film is promoted and released.

work print (also **workprint** or **cutting copy).** The print of a film with which the editor works in the process of shaping a motion picture. It is composed of selected takes from the DAILIES and is gradually trimmed from a ROUGH CUT to a FINE CUT stage. In its final form it serves as the model for the cutting of the negative from which the eventual release print is made.

Woronov, Mary. Actress. Born ca. 1943. *ed.* Cornell U. American comic performer in independent films, particularly those of Andy Warhol, Paul Bartel, and Roger Corman. A cult favorite as an actress, she is also an artist who has exhibited her work in New York and London.

FILMS INCLUDE: *Hedy* 1965; *The Chelsea Girls* 1966; *Kemek* 1970; *Sugar Cookies* 1973; *Seizure* 1974; *Cover Girl Models, Death Race 2000* 1975; *Cannonball, Death Threat, Hollywood Boulevard, Jackson County Jail* 1976; *Bad Georgia Road, Mr. Billion* 1977; *The One and Only* 1978; *The Lady in Red, Rock 'n' Roll High School* 1979; *Angel of H.E.A.T.* 1981; *Eating Raoul, National Lampoon Goes to the Movies* 1982; *Get Crazy* 1983; *Hellhole, Movie House Massacre, Night of the Comet* 1984; *My Man Adam, Nomads* 1985; *Chopping Mall, TerrorVision* 1986; *Black Widow* 1987; *Mortuary Academy, Scenes from the Class Struggle in Beverly Hills* 1988; *Let It Ride, Warlock* 1989; *Dick Tracy, Watchers II* 1990; *Club Fed, Rock 'n' Roll High School Forever* 1991; *Hellroller, The Living End* 1992.

Wray, Fay. Actress. Born on Sept. 15, 1907, in Alberta, Canada. Raised in Los Angeles, she began haunting studio casting offices in her early teens and landed occasional parts in films from 1919. She soared to sudden stardom in 1928 as a result of her casting in the lead feminine role in Erich von Stroheim's *The Wedding March.* She subsequently starred in many other productions, opposite such leading men as Gary Cooper, Ronald Colman, Fredric March, William Powell, and Richard Arlen. But she remains most closely identified with her role in *King Kong* (1933), as the frightened girl carried by an infatuated gorilla to the top of the Empire State Building. It is largely because of that role that she became a cult figure among cinema and nostalgia buffs in the 60s and 70s. She also screamed effectively in several other horror films of the period. From the mid-30s, Miss Wray was primarily cast in low-budget action pictures. She retired from the screen in 1942 after her marriage to screenwriter Robert RISKIN (her second husband; her first—from 1928 to 1939—was playwright-screenwriter John Monk SAUNDERS). She made a comeback in the 50s in character parts after Riskin's death, but finally retired in 1958. She made one television appearance after her retirement, in 'Gideon's Trumpet' (1980). Miss Wray has written a number of plays and stories, none too successful. Autobiography: *On the Other Hand* (1989).

FILMS: *Blind Husbands* 1919; *Gasoline Love* 1923; *The Coast Patrol* 1925; *The Man in the Saddle, The Wild Horse Stampede, Lazy Lightning* 1926; *Loco Luck, A One Man Game, Spurs and Saddles* 1927; *Legion of the Condemned, The Street of Sin, The First Kiss, The Wedding March* 1928; *The Four Feathers, Thunderbolt, Pointed Heels* 1929; *Behind the Makeup, Paramount on Parade, The Border Legion, The Sea God, Captain Thunder* 1930; *The Finger Points, The Conquering Horde, Not Exactly Gentlemen/Three Rogues, Dirigible, The Lawyer's Secret, The Unholy Garden* 1931; *Stowaway, Doctor X, The Most Dangerous Game/Hounds of Zaroff* 1932; *The Vampire Bat, The Mystery of the Wax Museum, King Kong, Below the Sea, Ann Carver's Profession, The Woman I Stole, The Big Brain, One Sunday Afternoon, Shanghai Madness, The Bowery, Master of Men* 1933; *Madame Spy, Once to Every Woman, The Countess of Monte Cristo, Viva Villa!, Black Moon, The Affairs of Cellini, The Richest Girl in the World, The Captain Hates the Sea, Cheating Cheaters, Woman in the Dark, White Lies* 1934; *Bulldog Jack/Alias Bulldog Drummond* (UK), *The Clairvoyant* (UK), *Come Out of the Pantry, Mills of the Gods* 1935; *Roaming Lady, When Knights Were Bold, They Met in a Taxi* 1936; *It Happened in Hollywood, Once a Hero, Murder in Greenwich Village* 1937; *The Jury's Secret, Smashing the Spy Ring* 1938; *Navy Secrets* 1939; *Wildcat Bus* 1940; *Adam Had Four Sons, Melody for Three* 1941; *Not a Ladies' Man* 1942; *Treasure of the Golden Condor, Small Town Girl* 1953; *The Cobweb, Queen Bee* 1955; *Hell on Frisco Bay* 1956; *Rock Pretty Baby, Crime of Passion, Tammy and the Bachelor* 1957; *Summer Love, Dragstrip Riot* 1958.

Wray, John Griffith. Director, actor. *b.* John Griffith Malloy, Feb. 13, 1888, Philadelphia. *d.* 1940. In the early 20s, he was among the leading directors of the Thomas Ince stable. Among his notable dramas was *Human Wreckage,* a probe into drug addiction based on material by Dorothy Davenport, the widow of Wallace Reid, who was a victim of heroin. He also directed the first screen version of O'Neill's *Anna Christie* (1923), starring Blanche Sweet. He directed other fine productions for the duration of the silent period, then inexplicably turned to acting and, as John Wray, played character parts in many films until 1940.

FILMS INCLUDE: As director (complete)—*Home Spun Folks* 1920; *Lying Lips, Beau Revel, Hail the Woman* 1921; *What a Wife Learned, The Soul of a Beast, Human Wreckage, Anna Christie* 1923; *The Marriage Cheat* 1924; *The Winding Stair* 1925; *Hell's 400, The Gilded Butterfly* 1926; *Singed* 1927; *The Gateway of the Moon* 1928; *The Careless Age, A Most Immoral Lady* 1929. As actor—*New York Nights* 1929; *All Quiet on the Western Front* (as Himmelstoss), *The Czar of Broadway* (lead role) 1930; *Quick Millions, Silence* 1931; *The Woman from Monte Carlo, High Pressure, The Miracle Man, The Mouthpiece, Doctor X, I Am a Fugitive from a Chain Gang, The Death Kiss* 1932; *After Tonight* 1933; *The Big Shakedown, The Captain Hates the Sea* 1934; *The Whole Town's Talking, Men Without Names, Frisco Kid* 1935; *Mr. Deeds Goes to Town, The Poor Little Rich Girl, Valiant Is the World for Carrie* 1936; *You Only Live Once, Outcast* 1937; *Gangs of New York, Spawn of the North, Crime Takes a Holiday* 1938; *Pacific Liner, Each Dawn I Die, Blackmail* 1939; *Remember the Night, The Swiss Family Robinson, The Man from Dakota* 1940.

Wright, Basil. Documentary director-producer. *b.* June 12, 1907, in London. *d.* 1987. He became interested in films while studying classics and economics at Cambridge and made an amateur short, *Strandfest,* which caught the eye of John GRIERSON of the Empire Marketing Board Film Unit. After graduation, Wright joined Grierson in 1929, and following an editing assignment began directing in 1931. He stayed with Grierson during the switch to the GPO Film Unit in 1934, then left the unit three years later and founded Realist Films with John Taylor and Alberto CAVALCANTI. In 1939 he joined Film Centre and produced numerous WW II propaganda films. Wright was among the leading figures during the formative years of the British documentary school. He directed or produced some of the most notable fact films of the 30s and early 40s, including the celebrated *Song of Ceylon* (1934) and *Night Mail* (1936). In 1947 he formed a production company, International Realist, Ltd., and then made films for UNESCO and lectured on filmmaking at the University of California and in various underdeveloped nations. Author: *The Use of Film* (1948); *The Long View* (a critical history of film, 1974).

FILMS (as director); *The Country Comes to Town* (also sc.) 1931; *O'er Hill and Dale* (also sc., phot.), *Gibraltar* (also sc., phot.) 1932; *Windmill in Barbados* (also sc., phot.), *Cargo from Jamaica* (also phot.), *Liner Cruising South* (also sc., phot.); *Song of Ceylon* (also sc., phot.) 1934; *Night Mail* (co-dir. with Harry Watt) 1936; *Children at School* (also sc.) 1937; *The Face of Scotland* (also sc.) 1938; *Harvest Help* 1940; *This Was Japan* 1945; *Bernard Miles on Gun Dogs* (also prod., sc.) 1948; *Waters of Time* (co-dir. with Bill Launder, prod., sc.) 1950; *World Without End* (co-dir. with Paul Rotha, prod.) 1953; *The Stained Glass at Fairford* (also prod.) 1955; *The Immortal Land* (also co-prod.) 1958; *Greek Sculpture* (co-dir. with Michael Ayrton, co-prod.) 1959; *A Place for Gold* (also prod.) 1960.

Wright Penn, Robin. Actress. Born April 8, 1966, Dallas, Tex. A statuesque blonde, she began her career as a model, became a regular on NBC's daytime soap 'Santa Barbara.' This won her two Daytime Emmy nominations and Hollywood offers followed. Her appearance in 'Forrest Gump' (1994) was the open sesame to a succession of leading roles. She is married to actor-director Sean Penn.

FILMS: *Hollywood Vice Squad* 1986; *The Princess Bride* 1987; *State of Grace* 1990; *Denial* 1991; *The Playboys, Toys* 1992; *Forrest Gump* 1994; *The Crossing Guard* 1995; *Moll Flanders* 1996; *Loved, She's So Lovely* 1997.

Wright, Teresa. Actress. Born Muriel Teresa Wright, on Oct. 27, 1918, in New York City. Apprenticed at the Wharf Theater, in Provincetown, Mass., she made her Broadway debut in 1938 as Martha Scott's understudy in 'Our Town.' Her performance in the ingenue part in 'Life with Father,' the following year, was seen by Samuel Goldwyn, who signed her on a long-term screen contract. A sensitive and conscientious actress, she shied away from Hollywood glamour and publicity and concentrated on her profession. She was nominated for an Academy Award, in the supporting actress category, for her first screen performance, in *The Little Foxes* (1941). The following year she received two nominations: in the best actress category for *The Pride of the Yankees* and in the best supporting actress category for *Mrs. Miniver.* She won the latter Oscar. She played other memorable roles in *Shadow of a Doubt* and *The Best Years of Our Lives,* but many of her subsequent vehicles were routine. Divorced from novelist-screenwriter Niven BUSCH (1942–52), she retired from the screen in 1959 when she married playwright Robert ANDERSON (they later divorced and remarried). She returned to the New York stage in 'Mary Mary,' in 1962, and to films in character parts in 1969. In the 70s she appeared in TV dramas and scored a success in the 1975 Broadway revival of 'Death of a Salesman.'

FILMS: *The Little Foxes* (as Alexandra Giddens) 1941; *Mrs. Miniver, The Pride of the Yankees* (as Eleanor Gehrig) 1942; *Shadow of a Doubt* 1943; *Casanova Brown* 1944; *The Best Years of Our Lives* 1946; *Pursued* 1947; *Enchantment* 1948; *The Capture, The Men* 1950; *Something to Live For, California Conquest, The Steel Trap* 1952; *The Actress, Count the Hours* 1953; *Track of the Cat* 1954; *The Search for Bridey Murphy* 1956; *Escapade in Japan* 1957; *The Restless Years* 1958; *Hail Hero!, The Happy Ending* 1969; *Roseland* 1977; *Somewhere in Time* 1979; *The Good Mother* 1988.

Writers Guild of America. The union of film and television writers, formerly known as the Screen Writers Guild. It is organized into two branches, Writers Guild of America East and Writers Guild of America West.

Wuhl, Robert. Actor. Born October 9, 1951 in Union, N.J. *ed.* University of Houston. This high-energy peformer was a classmate of Dennis Quaid at the University of Houston but chose to pursue a career as a standup comedian. After a number of years on the circuit, he moved to L.A. to begin his film career. He even doubled as a writer when he couldn't get acting jobs. His association with Billy Crystal on some of his Grammy TV appearances brough Wuhl to studio attention.

FILMS: *The Hollywood Knights* 1980; *Flashdance* 1983; *Good Morning, Vietnam* 1987; *Bull Durham* 1988; *Batman, Blaze* 1989; *The Bodyguard, Mistress* 1992; *Percy and Thunder* 1993; *Blue Chips, Cobb* 1994; *Dr. Jekyll and Ms. Hyde* 1995; *Open Season* (also dir., scr.) 1996.

Wurtzel, Sol M. Producer. *b.* Sept. 12, 1881, New York City. *d.* 1958. He joined Fox in 1914 as a stenographer and became private secretary to movie mogul William Fox in 1917. Appointed producer in the early 30s, Wurtzel turned out numerous films for the company. Few of these were major productions; most were minor B action pictures, such as the "Mr. Moto" series, as well as four of the weakest of the Laurel and Hardy comedies. For a number of years he served as executive producer of the company's low-budget output.

FILMS INCLUDE: *Smoky* 1933; *Handy Andy, Bright Eyes* 1934; *Life Begins at 40, Dante's Inferno, Steamboat Round the Bend* 1935; *Thank You Jeeves!, Ramona* 1936; *Think Fast Mr. Moto* 1937; *While New York Sleeps* 1938; *Frontier Marshal* 1939; *Charlie Chan in Panama, Earthbound* 1940; *Great Guns* 1941; *A-Haunting We Will Go* 1942; *Chetniks, Jitterbugs* 1943; *The Big Noise* 1944; *Tucson* 1949.

Wyatt, Jane. Actress. Born on Aug. 12, 1911, in Campgaw, N.J. *ed.* Barnard Coll. Born into one of America's oldest families, the daughter of an investment banker and of a drama critic, she showed an early interest in the theater and made her Broadway debut as an understudy at 19. After that she played ingenues and leading ladies in a number of successful plays. Brought to Hollywood by Universal in 1934, she appeared in 30 films over a period of 30 years, during which she alternated between the stage and the screen. She was often cast as an understanding wife. Among her more memorable film roles were those in *Lost Horizon, None but the Lonely Heart,* and *Boomerang,* but most of her films were routine and she never reached top stardom. She was much more successful on TV as co-star (with Robert Young) of the long-running comedy series 'Father Knows Best,' for which she won an Emmy Award three successive years, 1958–60. She remained active on TV in guest roles and in telefilms into her eighties. She returned to the big screen in 1976 after an 11-year absence.

FILMS INCLUDE: *One More River* 1934; *Great Expectations* 1935; *We're Only Human, The Luckiest Girl in the World* 1936; *Lost Horizon* 1937; *The Girl from God's Country* 1940; *Weekend for Three* 1941; *Army Surgeon, The Navy Comes*

Through 1942; *Buckskin Frontier* 1943; *None but the Lonely Heart* 1944; *The Bachelor's Daughters* 1946; *Boomerang, Gentleman's Agreement* 1947; *Pitfall, No Minor Vices* 1948; *Canadian Pacific, Task Force* 1949; *House by the River, Our Very Own, My Blue Heaven* 1950; *The Man Who Cheated Himself, Criminal Lawyer* 1951; *Interlude* 1957; *Never Too Late* 1965; *Treasure of Matecumbe* 1976; *Star Trek 4: The Journey Home* 1986.

Wycherly, Margaret. Actress. *b.* 1881, London. *d.* 1956. Raised and educated in the US, she played leads on Broadway from her teens and gradually moved into character roles, notably in 'Tobacco Road' (1933). From 1929 she also played character parts in many films, often portraying devoted mothers. She was nominated for an Oscar as best supporting actress for *Sergeant York* (1941).

FILMS INCLUDE: *The 13th Chair* 1929; *Midnight* 1934; *Victory* 1940; *Sergeant York* 1941; *Crossroads, Random Harvest, Keeper of the Flame* 1942; *The Moon Is Down, Hangmen Also Die* 1943; *The Yearling* 1946; *Forever Amber* 1947; *White Heat* 1949; *The Man with a Cloak* 1951; *The President's Lady* 1953.

Wyler, William. Director. *b.* July 1, 1902, Mulhouse, Alsace, then part of Germany. *d.* 1981. The son of a Swiss-born dry-goods merchant, he received a business education in Lausanne, Switzerland, then studied the violin at the National Music Conservatory in Paris. It was there in 1922 that he met Carl LAEMMLE, who was the head of Universal Pictures and a distant cousin of Wyler's mother, and offered him a job with his company. Wyler began his film career at Universal's New York headquarters, writing publicity for foreign publications. He was then transferred to Hollywood, where he apprenticed as prop man, grip, script clerk, cutter, casting director, and assistant director (on the Lon Chaney version of *The Hunchback of Notre Dame,* 1923) before making his debut as director in 1925, at the age of 23. He was production assistant on the silent version of *Ben-Hur,* made in 1925 but not released until 1926. During his first two years as director, he turned out more than 40 two-reel Westerns packed with action. Gradually he moved up to feature-length films and away from Westerns and in the early 30s he began acquiring a modest reputation with such films as *Hell's Heroes, A House Divided, Counsellor at Law,* and *The Gay Deception.* In 1934 he married one of his stars, Margaret SULLAVAN. They divorced in 1936.

The same year, Wyler left Universal and began a long and fruitful association with producer Sam GOLDWYN. Their first production, *These Three,* an adaptation of Lillian Hellman's controversial play 'The Children's Hour,' also marked Wyler's first collaboration with cameraman Gregg TOLAND, whose excellent work was to figure prominently in many of Wyler's future films. Toland's technical ingenuity and Wyler's meticulous craftsmanship combined to create a succession of superior films in the 30s and 40s. The revolutionary deep-focus shot perfected by Toland enabled Wyler to develop his favorite technique of filming long takes in which characters appear in the same frame for the duration of entire scenes, rather than cutting from one to another and thus disrupting intercharacter relationships.

This technique required a great deal of discipline on the part of screen actors, who were used to acting in bits and pieces, and sometimes caused tension between director and star, as was the case with Bette Davis, who played some of her best roles under Wyler's direction but clashed with him incessantly. A perfectionist and a taskmaster, he was nicknamed "90-take Wyler" for the many takes he filmed of every shot until he was satisfied that he had achieved a desired effect or nuance. Many performers who resented his tyranny on the set later found themselves grateful for the Oscars they won for their performances in his films. Wyler himself won the best director Academy Award for *Mrs. Miniver* (1942), *The Best Years of Our Lives* (1946), and *Ben-Hur* (1959). All three productions also won best film Oscars.

After completing *Mrs. Miniver,* a tribute to England's courage under the Blitz, Wyler enlisted in the US Air Force and was attached to a bomber group stationed in England. During the war, he made two feature-length documentaries about bombing missions over Germany, *The Memphis Belle* and *Thunderbolt.* Returning to civilian life with the rank of lieutenant colonel, an Air Medal, and loss of hearing in one ear (the result of high-altitude flying), Wyler directed what is probably still his most important film, *The Best Years of Our Lives,* a sincere, compelling drama about the painful readjustment of three returning servicemen to civilian life. The film boasts several excellent performances and some of the most intricate compositions ever seen on celluloid.

Wyler was a superb craftsman and one of the most inventive stylists of the American screen. But his reputation declined in the 60s as a result of what some critics saw as a "meandering attitude in choice of subject matter and a growing tendency for pomposity and pretense." In addition to his three best director Oscars, Wyler received the Irving G. Thalberg Memorial Award for his cumulative work in 1965. He was presented with the Life Achievement Award by the American Film Institute in 1976.

FEATURE FILMS: *Crook Busters* 1925; *Lazy Lightning, Stolen Ranch* 1926; *Blazing Days, Hard Fists, Straight Shootin'/Shooting Straight/Range Riders, The Border Cavalier, Desert Dust* 1927; *Thunder Riders, Anybody Here Seen Kelly?* 1928; *The Shakedown, The Love Trap* 1929; *Hell's Heroes, The Storm* 1930; *A House Divided, Tom Brown of Culver* 1932; *Her First Mate, Counsellor-at-Law* 1933; *Glamour* 1934; *The Good Fairy, The Gay Deception* 1935; *These Three, Dodsworth, Come and Get It* (co-dir. with Howard Hawks) 1936; *Dead End* 1937; *Jezebel* 1938; *Wuthering Heights* 1939; *The Westerner, The Letter* 1940; *The Little Foxes* 1941; *Mrs. Miniver* 1942; *The Memphis Belle* (doc.; also prod., sc., co-phot.) 1944; *Thunderbolt* (doc.; co-dir. with John Sturges) 1945; *The Best Years of Our Lives* 1946; *The Heiress* (also prod.) 1949; *Detective Story* (also prod.) 1951; *Carrie* (also prod.) 1952; *Roman Holiday* (also prod.) 1953; *The Desperate Hours* (also prod.) 1955; *Friendly Persuasion* (also prod.) 1956; *The Big Country* (also prod.) 1958; *Ben-Hur* 1959; *The Children's Hour* (also prod.) 1962; *The Collector* (US/UK) 1965; *How to Steal a Million* 1966; *Funny Girl* 1968; *The Liberation of L. B. Jones* 1970.

Wyman, Jane. Actress. Born Sarah Jane Fulks, on Jan. 4, 1914, in St. Joseph, Mo. The daughter of the town's sometime mayor, she was encouraged by her mother to try her luck in films as a child actress. They spent several fruitless months in Hollywood before giving up on the idea. Sarah Jane returned to school, attended the University of Missouri, and worked variously as a manicurist and switchboard operator. She finally broke into show business as a radio singer, using the name Jane Durrell, and in the mid-30s began a modest Hollywood career as a chorus girl and bit player. For ten years she played snub-nosed brassy blondes, getting some leads, but for the most part providing comedy relief in secondary roles. Then suddenly she blossomed into a major star. The turning point was the film *The Lost Weekend* (1945), which enabled her to demonstrate for the first time her ability as a serious actress. She was nominated for an Academy Award for her performance in *The Yearling* (1946). She won the Oscar for her superb portrayal of a deaf-mute rape victim in *Johnny Belinda* (1948). She subsequently starred in many other films, proving her versatility by moving with ease from tearful melodramas to lighthearted comedies. She received two additional Oscar nominations, for the tearjerkers *The Blue Veil* (1951) and *Magnificent Obsession* (1954). She was highly visible on TV throughout the 80s as the black-hearted matriarch of 'Falcon Crest.' Her second (of four) husbands was actor-turned-President of the United States Ronald REAGAN, whom she married in 1940 and divorced in 1948. Their daughter Maureen Reagan was a singer-actress, mainly on TV, before becoming involved in political activism.

FILMS: *Gold Diggers of 1937, My Man Godfrey, King of Burlesque* 1936; *Smart Blonde, Stage Struck, The King and the Chorus Girl, Ready Willing and Able, Slim, The Singing Marine, Public Wedding, Mr. Dodd Takes the Air* 1937; *The Spy Ring, He Couldn't Say No, Wide Open Faces, Fools for Scandal, The Crowd Roars, Brother Rat* 1938; *Tail Spin, Private Detective, The Kid from Kokomo, Torchy Plays with Dynamite, Kid Nightingale* 1939; *Brother Rat and a Baby, An Angel from Texas, Flight Angels, My Love Came Back, Tugboat Annie Sails Again, Gambling on the High Seas* 1940; *Honeymoon for Three, Bad Men of Missouri, You're in the Army Now, The Body Disappears* 1941; *Larceny Inc., My Favorite Spy, Footlight Serenade* 1942; *Princess O'Rourke* 1943; *Make Your Own Bed, Crime by Night, The Doughgirls, Hollywood Canteen* 1944; *The Lost Weekend* 1945; *One More Tomorrow, Night and Day* 1946; *The Yearling, Cheyenne, Magic Town* 1947; *Johnny Belinda* 1948; *A Kiss in the Dark, It's a Great Feeling* (cameo), *The Lady Takes a Sailor* 1949; *Stage Fright, The Glass Menagerie* 1950; *Three Guys Named Mike, Here Comes the Groom, The Blue Veil, Starlift* 1951; *The Story of Will Rogers, Just for You* 1952; *Let's Do It Again, So Big* 1953; *Magnificent Obsession* 1954; *Lucy Gallant* 1955; *All That Heaven Allows, Miracle in the Rain* 1956; *Holiday for Lovers* 1959; *Pollyanna* 1960; *Bon Voyage!* 1962; *How to Commit Marriage* 1969.

Wymore, Patrice. Actress. Born on Dec. 17, 1926, in Miltonvale, Kans. Leading lady of Hollywood films of the 50s. The daughter of a film exhibitor, she began her career as a child performer and appeared in tent shows, county fairs, and vaudeville in a song-and-dance act. As a young adult, she modeled, sang in nightclubs, and appeared in stock and on the New York stage before making her film debut in 1950. The same year she married Errol FLYNN. She retired in 1953 to give birth to Flynn's daughter and stayed out of films to help her husband through the most difficult period of his career. She returned briefly to the screen after Flynn's death in 1959.

FILMS INCLUDE: *Tea for Two, Rocky Mountain* 1950; *I'll See You in My Dreams* 1951; *The Big Trees, The Man Behind the Gun* 1952; *She's Back on Broadway* 1953; *The Sad Horse* 1959; *Ocean's Eleven* 1960; *Chamber of Horrors* 1966.

Wynn, Ed. Actor. *b.* Isaiah Edwin Leopold, Nov. 9, 1886, Philadelphia. *d.* 1966. The son of European immigrants, he ran away from home at 15 to join a traveling stage company as a utility boy and eventually an actor. He returned home after the company's failure and sold hats for a living until his next adventure. This time he went to New York, where he became a successful vaudeville comic headliner before reaching 18. He appeared in several Ziegfeld Follies editions from 1914, billed as The Perfect Fool, and got into a widely publicized feud with another headliner in the musical extravaganza, W. C. FIELDS. In 1919, at the height of his popularity as a Broadway comedy star, Wynn was boycotted by the Shuberts because of his part in organizing an actors' strike. Undaunted, he wrote and produced his own shows, which enjoyed an enormous success in the 20s at the box office and with the critics. He also appeared in occasional films.

In the 30s, Wynn gained additional fans on radio, as the Texaco Fire Chief, but he fell on bad times toward the end of the decade, when several of his business ventures, including a radio chain, failed. He suffered a nervous collapse and his career seemed all but washed up. But in the 40s he returned to Broadway and in 1949 won the first TV Emmy Award as best actor in a series. He was out of work again in the early 50s, when his traditional baggy pants comedy style was a thing of the past, but thanks to the encouragement and help of his son, Keenan WYNN, he entered films in the latter part of the decade as a dramatic character actor, and was nominated for an Oscar as best supporting actor for his performance in *The Diary of Anne Frank* (1959). He appeared successfully in both serious and light films and in TV dramas until his death at the age of 80.

FILMS: *Rubber Heels* 1927; *Follow the Leader* 1930; *The Chief* 1933; *Stage Door Canteen* 1943; *The Great Man* 1957; *Marjorie Morningstar* 1958; *The Diary of Anne Frank* 1959; *Cinderfella* 1960; *The Absent-Minded Professor, Babes in Toyland* 1961; *Son of Flubber* 1963; *The Patsy* (cameo), *Mary Poppins, Those Calloways* 1964; *Dear Brigitte, The Greatest Story Ever Told, That Darn Cat* 1965; *The GnomeMobile* 1967.

Wynn, Keenan. Actor. *b.* Francis Xavier Aloysius Wynn, July 27, 1916, in New York City. *d.* 1986. *ed.* St. John's Military Acad. The son of Ed WYNN and the grandson of silent film actor Frank Keenan on his mother's side, he appeared on radio, in stock, and on Broadway before making his screen debut in 1942. He later played key character parts and occasional leads in numerous films of various genres, mostly for MGM, stretching his range from genial, fast-talking sharpies in comedy to gutsy types, often heels and repulsive villains, in drama. For three decades he was among Hollywood's most dependable, versatile, and prolific supporting actors. His son is screenwriter Tracy Keenan Wynn.

FILMS INCLUDE: *For Me and My Gal* 1942; *See Here Private Hargrove, Lost Angel, Since You Went Away* 1944; *Without Love, The Clock, Weedend at the Waldorf* 1945; *Ziegfeld Follies, Easy to Wed, The Thrill of Brazil, No Leave No Love* 1946; *The Hucksters, Song of the Thin Man* 1947; *The Three Musketeers* (as Planchet), *My Dear Secretary* 1948; *Neptune's Daughter, That Midnight Kiss* 1949; *Annie Get Your Gun, Three Little Words* 1950; *Royal Wedding, Kind Lady, Texas Carnival, Angels in the Outfield* 1951; *It's a Big Country, Phone Call from a Stranger, The Belle of New York* 1952; *Kiss Me Kate, All the Brothers Were Valiant* 1953; *Men of the Fighting Lady, Tennessee Champ* 1954; *The Glass Slipper, Running Wild* 1955; *The Man in the Gray Flannel Suit, Johnny Concho* 1956; *The Great Man* 1957; *The Deep Six* 1958; *The Perfect Furlough* 1959; *The Absent-Minded Professor, King of the Roaring 20s* 1961; *The Scarface Mob* 1962; *Dr. Strangelove, The Patsy, The Americanization of Emily* 1964; *The Great Race* 1965; *Stagecoach, The Night of the Grizzly* 1966; *Warning Shot, Welcome to Hard Times, The War Wagon, Point Blank* 1967; *Finian's Rainbow, C'era una Volta il West/Once Upon a Time in the West* (It.) 1968; *Smith!, McKenna's Gold, Viva Max!* 1969; *Loving* 1970; *Pretty Maids All in a Row* 1971; *Cancel My Reservation, The Mechanic, Snowball Express* 1972; *The Internecine Project* (UK), *Herbie Rides Again* 1974; *Nashville, The Man Who Would Not Die, The Devil's Rain, A Woman for All Men* 1975; *The Killer Inside Me, The Shaggy D.A.* 1976; *Kino, the Padre on Horseback/The Father Kino Story/Mission to Glory, Orca. . . Killer Whale, High Velocity* 1977; *Coach, Laserblast, Piranha* 1978; *Parts: The Clonus Horror, The Bushido Blade* (Jap.), *The Dark, Just Tell Me What You Want, Sunburn* 1979; *The Glove* 1981; *Best Friends, The Last Unicorn* (v/o) 1982; *Hysterical, Wavelength* 1983; *Prime Risk* 1985;

Black Moon Rising, Hyper Sapien: People from Another Star 1986.

Wynter, Dana. Actress. Born Dagmar Spencer-Marcus, on June 8, 1930, in London. The daughter of a noted surgeon, she moved with her family to Southern Rhodesia, where she became a premed student at Rhodes University. Sidetracked by amateur theatrics, she continued appearing on the stage and in occasional films after returning to England in the early 50s. In Hollywood since the mid-50s, she has played elegant, reserved leading ladies in many films and appeared in many TV dramas, including the series 'The Man Who Never Was.'

FILMS INCLUDE: *White Corridors* (UK) 1951; *The View from Pompey's Head* 1955; *Invasion of the Body Snatchers, D-Day the Sixth of June* 1956; *Something of Value* 1957; *Fraulein, In Love and War* 1958; *Shake Hands with the Devil* (Ire.) 1959; *Sink the Bismarck!* (UK) 1960; *On the Double* 1961; *The List of Adrian Messenger* 1963; *If He Hollers Let Him Go!* 1968; *Airport* 1970; *Santee* 1973; *Le Sauvage/The Savage/Lovers Like Us* (Fr.) 1975; *Hyper Sapien: People from Another Star* 1986; *Dead Right* 1988.

Wynyard, Diana. Actress. *b.* Dorothy Isobel Cox, Jan. 16, 1906, London. *d.* 1964. A distinguished leading lady of the British stage, she was signed by Hollywood in 1932 following a triumphant Broadway appearance opposite Basil Rathbone in 'The Devil Passes.' She brought charm, grace, and reserved good looks to several American films of the early 30s, notably *Cavalcade* (1933), for which she was nominated for an Oscar, then returned to England and to her stage career, subsequently appearing only occasionally in films. Her second husband (1943–47) was director Carol REED.

FILMS: In the US—*Rasputin and the Empress* (as Princess Natasha), *Cavalcade, Men Must Fight, Reunion in Vienna* 1933; *Where Sinners Meet, Let's Try Again, One More River* 1934. In the UK—*On the Night of the Fire/The Fugitive* 1939; *Freedom Radio/The Voice in the Night, The Prime Minister* (as Mrs. Disraeli), *Gaslight/Angel Street* 1940; *Kipps* (as Helen Walsingham) 1941; *An Ideal Husband* (as Lady Chiltren) 1947; *Tom Brown's School Days* (as Mrs. Arnold) 1951; *The Feminine Touch* 1956; *Island in the Sun* 1957.

X, Y, Z

X. 1. An abbreviation for a single "exposure." 2. See RATING.

X-dissolve. An abbreviation for "cross-dissolve."

Xie Jin. Director. Born in 1923 in Shaoxing, China. *ed.* Jiang'an School of Dramatic Arts, Szechuan. Prime figure in post-1949 Chinese cinema. He began his career after the revolution, but avoided the socialist realist style of his contemporaries. Throughout his career, he has opted for stories that portrayed heroic (or tragic) individuals within a group (*The Red Detachment of Women, Woman Basketball Player No. 5*) or a nation (*Qiou Jin*). Also regarded as a "women's director," his films have often featured professional women (a doctor in *Youth*, actresses in *Two Stage Sisters*, a sergeant in *Ah, Cradle*). Through his films he has debuted and promoted the careers of many Chinese actresses. During the Cultural Revolution he suffered public denouncement (including imprisonment and the separation of his family), but was able to resume his work in the 70s with no diminution in energy or spirit.

FILMS INCLUDE: *A Crisis, A Wave of Unrest, Rendezvous at Orchard Bridge* 1954; *Woman Basketball Player No. 5* 1957; *The Red Detachment of Women* 1960; *Big Li Young Li and Old Li* 1962; *Two Stage Sisters* 1964; *Youth* 1977; *Ah Cradle* 1980; *The Legend of Tianyuan Mountain* 1981; *The Herdsman* 1983; *Qiu Jin* 1983; *Reeds at the Foot of the Mountain* 1984; *Hibiscus Town* 1990.

Yamada, Isuzu. Actress. Born on Feb. 5, 1917, in Osaka, Japan. An actor's daughter, she trained for the stage from early childhood, entering films at 14. She gained prominence in the 30s in films directed by Kenji MIZOGUCHI and later worked frequently for director Teinosuke KINUGASA, who was one of her six husbands. She played leads and later character roles in numerous Japanese productions and is best known in the Western world for her performances in such films as *Hiroshima* (1953), *Throne of Blood, The Lower Depths* (both 1957), and *Yojimbo* (1961). She has also been prominent on the Japanese stage. Her daughter, Michiko Saga (*b.* Mar. 3, 1935), is also a film actress.

FILMS INCLUDE: *The Revenge Champion* 1931; *The Pass of Love and Hate, Paper Cranes of Osen* 1934; *The Virgin from Oyuki* 1935; *Osaka Elegy, Sisters of the Gion* 1936; *Yoshida Palace* 1937; *Miss Snake Princess* 1940; *Song of a Lantern* 1943; *Bijomaru Sword* 1945; *Actress* 1947; *Fencing Master* 1950; *Postwar Japan* 1952; *Hiroshima* 1953; *The Loyal 47 Ronin* 1954; *Christ in Bronze, Because I Love* 1955; *Flowing* 1956; *The Throne of Blood, Tokyo Twilight, Black River, The Lower Depths* 1957; *Four Seasons of Love, Days of Evil Women* 1958; *Wandering, Flowing Night, Goodbye to Glory* 1960; *The Shrikes, Daredevil in the Castle, Yojimbo* 1961; *The Body, The Great Wall* 1962; *Buddha* 1963; *The Shogun and His Mistress* 1967.

Yamamoto, Kajiro. Director. *b.* Mar. 15, 1902, Tokyo. *d.* 1974. He entered Japanese films at 18 as an actor and gradually rose through screenwriter and assistant director to director in 1924. During the early part of his career he helmed mostly light comedies of popular appeal. In the 40s he broadened his range to include films of all genres, notably *Horse* (1941), which strongly influenced the Japanese documentary movement. But his most important contribution to Japanese cinema was as the teacher and mentor of Akira KUROSAWA.

FILMS INCLUDE: *Danun* 1924; *Bomb Hour* 1925; *Ordeal* 1932; *Love Crisis* 1933; *I Am a Cat* 1936; *A Husband's Chastity* 1937; *The Loves of a Kabuki Actor* 1938; *Easy Alley, The Loyal 47 Ronin* 1939; *Horse* 1941; *The Hope of Youth* 1942; *Misfortunes of Love* 1945; *Those Who Make Tomorrow* (co-dir.) 1946; *Wind of Honor, Spring Flirtation* 1949; *Elegy* 1951; *Girls Among the Flowers* 1953; *Mr. Valiant, Saturday Angel* 1954; *A Man Among Men, The History of Love* 1955; *The Underworld* 1956; *An Elephant* 1957; *The Rise and Fall of a Jazz Girl, Holiday in Tokyo* 1958; *Ginza Tomboy* 1960; *Samurai Joker, Thief on the Run* 1965; *Swindler Meets Swindler* 1967.

Yamamoto, Satsuo. Director. *b.* July 15, 1910, Japan. *d.* 1983. A former stage actor, he entered Japanese films in 1933 as an assistant director. Becoming a director in 1937, he gained recognition in the Western world the following year with the first screen version of André Gide's *La Symphonie pastorale.* He subsequently directed other successful films, many of them literary adaptations. But it wasn't until the early 50s that he emerged as a major director with a strong, almost violent personal style, which he applied to a string of independently made films, marked by an unwavering commitment to left-wing politics. The most notable of these have been *Storm Clouds Over Mount Hakone, Vacuum Zone,* and *The Street Without Sun.*

FILMS INCLUDE: *Young Miss* 1937; *La Symphonie pastorale, Family Diary* 1938; *The Street* 1939; *End of Engagement* 1940; *Hot Wind* 1943; *War and Peace* (co-dir.) 1945; *The Street of Violence* 1950; *Storm Clouds Over Mount Hakone* 1951; *Vacuum Zone* 1952; *The Street Without Sun* 1954; *Avalanche, Typhoon* 1956; *The Song of the Cart, The Human Wall* 1959; *Battle Without Arms* 1960; *A Band of Assassins* 1962; *Red Water* 1963; *Tycoon* 1964; *The Burglar Story, The Spy* 1965; *Freezing Point, The Great White Tower* 1966; *The Bride from Hades* 1968; *The Family* 1974; *Annular Eclipse* 1975; *The Story of Yugaku Ohara* 1976; *The Barren Ground* 1977; *August Without the Emperor* 1978.

Yamamura, So. Director, actor. Born on Feb. 29, 1910, in Naka, Japan. A veteran character actor of many Japanese films, he turned director in the early 50s. He asserted himself with two excellent first productions, *The Crab-Canning Ship,* influenced by Eisenstein's *Potemkin,* and *Black Tide.* But his subsequent films were rather routine and he gave up directing in the early 60s to concentrate on acting.

FILMS INCLUDE: As director (complete)—*The Crab-Canning Ship* 1953; *Black Tide* (also act.) 1954; *A Mother and Her Children* (also act.), *The Maidens of Kashima Sea* 1959; *The Song of Fukagawa* 1960. As actor—*For Life* 1946; *The Love of Sumako the Actress* 1947; *Muddy Waters, Tokyo Story* 1953; *Yang Kwei Fei* 1955; *The Barbarian and the Geisha* (US) 1958; *The Human Condition/No Greater Love* 1959; *Life of a Country Doctor* 1960; *My Daughter and I* 1962; *Diary of a Mad Old Man* 1963; *School of Love* 1965; *The Emperor and the General* 1967; *Tora! Tora! Tora!* (as Admiral Yamamoto; US/Jap.) 1970; *The Militarist* 1973.

Yang, Edward. Born in 1947 in Shanghai, China. *ed.* Univ. of Florida (engineering and computer science); USC (film). Leading contributor to Taiwan new wave of the 80s. His family moved to Taiwan in 1949 at the time of the mainland revolution. Following college, he studied for one semester at the USC film school, then relocated to Seattle to work on computer design at the University of Washington.

His film career began in 1981 when he returned to Taiwan to write and help produce *The Winter of 1905* (1981), directed by his former student Yu Weizheng. From this experience, he moved into television production (*Floating Weeds*, 1981) and was commissioned to direct an episode of a government-sponsored feature, *In Our Time* (1981). His early successes afforded him the liberty to direct (and later produce) his feature films at a slower pace than his commercial compatriots. Like others in the new wave, he pursued provocative subject matter (critiquing the island's rapid industrialization), hired nonprofessional actors (an aesthetic choice, as well as a fiscal necessity), and employed new film technology (eschewed by the domestic film studios). His films, especially *A Brighter Summer Day* (1991), have enjoyed wide acclaim in Taiwan (where he has won national critics' awards) and at international film festivals.

FILMS INCLUDE (as director and co-screenwriter): *That Day, On the Beach* 1983; *Taipei Story* 1985; *The Terroriser* 1986; *A Brighter Summer Day* 1991. As screenwriter/first assistant: *The Winter of 1905* 1981; *A Brighter Summer Day* 1991; *A Confucian Confusion* 1994; *Mahjong* 1996.

Yanne, Jean. Actor, director, producer, screenwriter. Born Jean Gouyé, in 1933, in France. He started out as a stand-up satirical comic but made his debut in French films in 1963 as a dramatic actor. In the late 60s he figured prominently in such films as Godard's *Weekend* (1967) and Chabrol's *Que la Bête meure/This Man Must Die* (1969) and *Le Boucher* (1970). In 1972 he won the best actor award at Cannes for his role in Maurice Pialat's *Nous ne viellirons pas ensemble.* That same year he took Paris by storm with his first film as a producer-director-writer-actor, *Tout le Monde il est Beau—Tout le Monde il est Gentil,* an anarchic, irreverent, self-indulgent satire on the French social scene, which became the top box-office attraction in France that year, grossing over $2 million in the Paris first-run alone. He followed this film with other hits, the success of which having been limited to the French market because of their local humor and appeal.

FILMS INCLUDE (as actor): *La Vie à l'Envers/Life Upside Down/Inside Out* 1964; *L'Amour à la Chaîne/Tight Skirts Loose Pleasures* 1965; *La Ligne de Démarcation/The Line of Demarcation* 1966; *Weekend* 1967; *Ces Messieurs de la Famille* 1968; *Erotissimo* (It./Fr.), *Que la Bête meure/This Man Must Die* 1969; *Le Boucher* 1970; *Nous ne viellirons pas ensemble, Tout le Monde il est Beau—Tout le Monde il est Gentil* (also dir., prod., sc.) 1972; *Moi y en avoir des Sous* (also dir., prod., sc.) 1973; *Les Chinois à Paris* (also dir., prod., co-sc.) 1974; *Armaguedon, L'Imprecateur, Moi Fleur bleue* 1977; *La Raison d'Etat* 1978; *Je te tiens, tu me tiens par la Barbichette/I've Got You, You've Got Me by the Chin Hairs* (also dir., exec. prod., sc.) 1979; *Asphalte* 1981; *Deux heures moins le quart avant Jesus Christ* (also dir., sc., music), *Une Journee en Taxi* 1982; *Hanna K., Papy Fait de la Resistance* 1983; *Le Telephone sonne toujours deux fois!!* 1984; *Liberte, Egalite, Choucroute* (also dir., sc., music) 1985; *Le Paltoquet, The Wolf at the Door* (Den./Fr.) 1986; *Attention Bandits, Cayenne-Palace, Fucking Fernand* 1987; *Quicker Than the Eye* (US) 1988; *Madame Bovary* 1991.

Yarbrough, Jean. Director. Born on Aug. 22, 1900, in Marianna, Ark. *ed.* U. of the South. He entered films in 1922 as prop man with Hal Roach. After several years as assistant director, he graduated to director in the late 30s. Most of his films were low-budget fare, including a number of routine horror stories and several Abbott and Costello comedies. He worked mainly for Monogram and Universal.

FILMS: *Rebellious Daughters* 1938; *The Devil Bat* 1940; *Caught in the Act, South of Panama, King of the Zombies, The Gang's All Here, Father Steps Out, Let's Go Collegiate, To Sergeant Mulligan* 1941; *Freckles Comes Home, Man from Headquarters, Law of the Jungle, So's Your Aunt Emma!/Meet the Mob, She's in the Army, Police Bullets, Criminal Investigator, Lure of the Islands, Silent Witness* 1942; *Follow the Band, Good Morning Judge, Get Going, Hi' Ya Sailor* (also prod.), *So's Your Uncle* (also prod.) 1943; *Weekend Pass, Moon Over Las Vegas* (also prod.), *South of Dixie, In Society, Twilight on the Prairie* 1944; *Under Western Skies, Here Come the Co-Eds, The Naughty Nineties, On Stage Everybody* 1945; *House of Horrors, She-Wolf of London, Inside Job* (also prod.), *Cuban Pete* 1946; *The Brute Man* 1947; *The Challenge, Shed No Tears, The Creeper, Triple Threat* 1948; *Henry the Rainmaker, The Mutineers, Leave It to Henry, Angels in Disguise, Holiday in Havana, Master Minds* 1949; *Joe Palooka Meets Humphrey, Square Dance Katy, Father Makes Good, Joe Palooka in*

Humphrey Takes a Chance, Sideshow, Triple Trouble, Big Timber 1950; *Casa Mañana, According to Mrs. Hoyle* 1951; *Jack and the Beanstalk, Lost in Alaska* 1952; *Night Freight* 1955; *Crashing Las Vegas, Yaqui Drums, The Women of Pitcairn Island, Hot Shots* 1956; *Footsteps in the Night* 1957; *Saintly Sinners* 1962; *Hillbillies in a Haunted House* 1967.

Yates, Herbert J. Executive. *b.* Aug. 24, 1880, Brooklyn, N.Y. *d.* 1966. *ed.* Columbia. A tobacco sales executive at the age of 19, he entered the film business in 1910 by financing several Roscoe "Fatty" Arbuckle productions. In 1912 he set up a processing laboratory that eventually grew through consolidations and mergers into Republic Pictures Corporation, of which he became president and chairman of the board. In 1952 he married Vera Hruba RALSTON, whom he had made into Republic's top star. He retired from the business in 1959.

Yates, Peter. Director. Born on July 24, 1929, in Aldershot, England. *ed.* RADA. He was only 19 when he began directing plays in the British provinces. He entered films in 1953 as a dubbing assistant and eventually moved up to assistant director on such films as *The Guns of Navarone* and *A Taste of Honey* (both 1961). A film and TV director since 1963, he has shown a flair for choreographing action and fast chases, which led to his importation by Hollywood. He scored a commercial hit in 1977 with *The Deep.* He was nominated for Oscars for his direction of *Breaking Away* (1979) and *The Dresser* (1983), both of which also earned him nominations for best picture as their producer. His output has varied widely from genre flops (*Krull*, 1983) to well-regarded dramatic pieces (*Eleni*, 1985). For TV he directed episodes for 'Danger Man,' 'The Saint,' and other series.

FILMS: In the UK—*Summer Holiday* 1963; *One Way Pendulum* 1964; *Robbery* (also co-sc.) 1967. In the US—*Bullitt* 1968; *John and Mary* 1969; *Murphy's War* (UK) 1971; *The Hot Rock* 1972; *The Friends of Eddie Coyle* 1973; *For Pete's Sake* 1974; *Mother Jugs and Speed* (also co-prod.) 1976; *The Deep* 1977; *Breaking Away* (also prod.) 1979; *Eyewitness* 1981; *Krull, The Dresser* (also prod.) 1983; *Eleni* 1985; *Suspect* 1987; *The House on Carroll Street* (also prod.) 1988; *Hard Rain/An Innocent Man* 1989; *Year of the Comet* 1992; *Roommates, The Run of the Country* 1995.

Yim Ho. Director. Born in 1952 in Hong Kong. Independent director of fine dramas. His career began in Hong Kong television during the mid-70s, where he worked as director, producer and writer. He launched a second career as filmmaker with the widely acclaimed *The Happenings* (1979). His films invariably are set and concern events in China. *Red Dust* (1990) follows four characters through the turbulent history of 20th century China. *The King of Chess* (1991), co-directed with Tsui Hark, involves parallel stories set in China during the Cultural Revolution (the segments directed by Yim Ho) and in contemporary Taipei. His films are marked by an epic visual style and a contrasting restraint with his actors.

FILMS INCLUDE: *The Extras* 1978; *The Happenings* 1979; *Wedding Bells, Wedding Belles* 1980; *The Homecoming* 1984; *Buddah's Lock* 1987; *Red Dust* 1990; *The King of Chess* 1991 (co-dir.).

Yordan, Philip. Screenwriter, producer, playwright, novelist. Born in 1913, in Chicago, *ed.* U. of Illinois (B.A.), Kent Col. (law). Since the early 40s, he has written three Broadway plays and many gutsy screenplays, alone or in collaboration, for films ranging in quality from excellent to poor, some of which he also produced. It has been alleged that he allowed his name to be used on a couple of scripts written by blacklisted Hollywood writers. He won an Oscar for the story of *Broken Lance* (1954).

FILMS INCLUDE (as screenwriter): *Syncopation* 1942; *The Unknown Guest* 1943; *Dillinger* 1945; *Whistle Stop, Suspense* 1946; *House of Strangers, Anna Lucasta* (from his own play; also prod.), *The Black Book/Reign of Terror* 1949; *Edge of Doom* 1950; *Detective Story* 1951; *Mara Maru* (co-story only), *Mutiny* 1952; *Houdini, Blowing Wild* (also story) 1953; *The Naked Jungle, Johnny Guitar, Broken Lance* (story only) 1954; *The Big Combo, Conquest of Space, The Man from Laramie, The Last Frontier* 1955; *Joe Macbeth, The Harder They Fall* (also prod.) 1956; *Men in War, Gun Glory* (novel basis only, *Man of the West*), *No Down Payment* 1957; *The Bravados, God's Little Acre, The Fiend Who Walked the West* 1958; *Anna Lucasta* (from own play), *Day of the Outlaw* 1959; *The Bramble Bush, Studs Lonigan* (also prod.) 1960; *King of Kings, El Cid* 1961; *The Day of the Triffids* (also exec. prod.), *55 Days at Peking* 1963; *The Fall of the Roman Empire* 1964; *Crack in the World* (exec. prod. only), *Battle of the Bulge* (also co-prod.) 1965; *The Royal Hunt of the Sun* (also co-prod.; UK/US) 1969; *Captain Apache* (also co-prod.) 1971; *Cataclysm/Satan's Supper* 1981; *Savage Journey* (also prod.) 1983; *Night Train to Terror* 1985; *Bloody Wednesday* (also prod.), *Cry Wilderness* (also prod.) 1987; *The Unholy* (co-sc.) 1988.

York, Michael. Actor. Born on Mar. 27, 1942, in Fulmer, England. *ed.* Oxford. Assertive blond leading man of British and international cinema. He entered films in the late 60s, following stage experience with the Oxford University Dramatic Society and the Dundee Repertory, and was quickly much in demand as a leading man in major productions, on television, and in made-for-cable films. He has also been seen in the TV series 'The Forsyte Saga.' Autobiography: *Travelling Player* (1991).

FILMS: *The Taming of the Shrew* (as Lucentio; US/It.), *Accident, Smashing Time* 1967; *The Strange Affair, Romeo and Juliet* (as Tybalt; UK/It.) 1968; *The Guru* (US/Ind.), *Justine* (US), *Alfred the Great* (as King Guthrum) 1969; *Something for Everyone* (US) 1970; *La Poudre d'Escampette/Touch and Go* (Fr.), *Zeppelin* 1971; *Cabaret* (US) 1972; *Brother Sun Sister Moon* (cameo; UK/It.), *Lost Horizon* (US), *England Made Me* 1973; *The Three Musketeers* (as d'Artagnan), *Murder on the Orient Express* 1974; *The Four Musketeers* (as d'Artagnan), *Conduct Unbecoming* 1975; *Logan's Run* (US), *Seven Nights in Japan* (UK/Fr.) 1976; *The Last Remake of Beau Geste* (as Beau Geste; US), *The Island of Dr. Moreau* (US) 1977; *Fedora* (cameo as himself; Ger./Fr.) 1978; *The Riddle of the Sands* (also assoc. prod.), *A Man Called Intrepid* (UK/Can.), *The White Lions* (US) 1979; *Final Assignment* (Can.) 1980; *Au nom de tous les Miens* (Fr.), *The Weather in the Streets* (US) 1983; *Success Is the Best Revenge* (UK) 1984; *L'Aube/The Dawn* (Fr.) 1986; *Der Joker/Lethal Obsession* (Ger.) 1987; *Midnight Cop* (Ger.), *Phantom of Death* (It.) 1988; *The Return of the Musketeers* (UK/Fr./Sp.) 1989; *Come and See the Paradise* (US) 1990; *Eline Vere* (It.) 1991; *The Wide Sargasso Sea* (US/Austral.) 1993; *Our Lady* 1994; *Austin Powers* 1997.

York, Susannah. Actress. Born Susannah Yolande Fletcher, on Jan. 9, 1941, in London; raised in a remote Scottish village. Intriguing blonde, blue-eyed leading lady of British and occasionally American films, she graduated from London's Royal Academy of Dramatic Art and began her career on the provincial stage, in rep and pantomime, making her screen debut in 1960. After several engaging but ordinary ingenue roles, she began emerging as a capable actress in John Huston's *Freud* (1962) and as a star exuding sexuality in *Tom Jones* (1963). In one of her best-known roles, she participated in a controversial nude lesbian love scene in Robert Aldrich's *The Killing of Sister George* (1968) and was then thrown into a similar situation with Elizabeth Taylor in *Zee & Co./X Y & Z* (1972). She was nominated for an Oscar for her role in *They Shoot Horses Don't*

They? (1969) and won the best actress prize at Cannes for her performance in Robert Altman's *Images* (1972). She co-wrote the screenplay for her vehicle *Falling in Love Again* (1980). In the 80s, she found steady employment in the *Superman* films, as Superman's Kryptonian mother. She lives on a Sussex farm with her husband, actor-writer Michael Wells, and two children. In the early 70s she had success with her first effort as an author, the children's fantasy book *In Search of Unicorns.* She is also the author of *Lark's Castle.*

FILMS: *Tunes of Glory, There Was a Crooked Man* 1960; *The Greengage Summer/Loss of Innocence* 1961; *Freud* (US; filmed in UK) 1962; *Tom Jones* (as Sophia Western) 1963; *The 7th Dawn* (US/UK) 1964; *Sands of the Kalahari* 1965; *Kaleidoscope, A Game Called Scruggs, A Man for All Seasons* (as Margaret More) 1966; *Sebastian, Duffy, The Killing of Sister George* (US) 1968; *Lock Up Your Daughters, Oh! What a Lovely War, Battle of Britain, They Shoot Horses Don't They?* (US) 1969; *Country Dance/Brotherly Love* 1970; *Jane Eyre* (title role), *Happy Birthday Wanda June* (US) 1971; *Zee & Co./X Y & Z, Images* 1972; *Gold* 1974; *The Maids, Conduct Unbecoming, That Lucky Touch* 1975; *Sky Riders* (US/Gr.), *Eliza Fraser* (Austral.) 1976; *The Shout, Superman* (US) 1978; *The Riddle of the Sands, The Silent Partner* (Can.), *Long Shot* 1979; *The Awakening* (US), *Falling in Love Again/In Love* (also co-sc.; US), *Superman 2* (US) 1980; *Loophole* 1981; *Montgomery Clift* (documentary interviewee) 1982; *Nelly's Version, Yellowbeard* 1983; *Alice, Daemon* 1986; *Barbablu Barbablu/Bluebeard Bluebeard, Mio min Mio, Prettykill* (US), *The Land of Faraway* (Sw.), *Superman 4: The Quest for Peace* (v/o; US) 1987; *American Roulette, Diamond's Edge/Just Ask for a Diamond* (US), *A Summer Story* 1988; *En Handfull Tid/A Handful of Time* (Ger.), *Melancholia* 1989; *Fate* 1991 (US); *Pretty Princess* 1993.

Yorkin, Bud. Director. Born Alan David Yorkin, on Feb. 22, 1926, in Washington, Pa. *ed.* Carnegie Tech; Columbia. He was in the Navy at 16 and after completing his WW II military service and his university studies, joined the NBC-TV engineering staff in 1949. In the 50s he became producer-director of comedy-variety shows. Among the stars whose shows he directed were Martin and Lewis, Abbott and Costello, The Ritz Brothers, Tony Martin, George Gobel, and Tennessee Ernie Ford. In 1959 he formed Tandem Productions with Norman LEAR, a partnership that resulted in several brisk, glossy comedy feature films that Yorkin usually directed and Lear produced and wrote, and a number of highly successful TV series of which Yorkin became the executive producer.

FILMS: *Come Blow Your Horn* (also co-prod.) 1963; *Never Too Late* 1965; *Divorce American Style* 1967; *The Night They Raided Minsky's* (co-exec. prod. only), *Inspector Clouseau* 1968; *Start the Revolution Without Me* (also prod.) 1970; *Cold Turkey* (exec. prod. only) 1971; *The Thief Who Came to Dinner* (also prod.) 1973; *Deal of the Century* (prod. only) 1983; *Twice in a Lifetime* (also prod.) 1985; *Arthur 2: On the Rocks* 1988; *Love Hurts* (also prod.) 1990; *For the Boys* (act. only) 1991; *Intersection* (co-prod. only) 1994.

Yoshida, Yoshishige. Director. Born in 1933, in Fukui, Japan. *ed.* U. of Tokyo. In Japanese films since the mid-50s, he turned director in 1960 and has emerged as a leading figure in the new Japanese cinema. He spent much of the early 70s in Europe making TV documentaries on the fine arts.

FILMS INCLUDE: *Good-for-Nothing/Dry Earth* 1960; *An Affair at Akitsu* 1962; *Nippon Escape* 1964; *Forbidden Love* 1965; *Woman of the Lake/The Lake* 1966; *Juhyo no Yorumeki/Affair in the Snow, Impasse* 1967; *Farewell to Summer Light* 1968; *Eros Purasu Gyakusatsu/Eros and Massacre* 1969; *Rengoku Eroica* 1970; *Kaigenre/Coup d'Etat* 1973; *Arashi ga Oka/Wuthering Heights* 1989.

Yoshimura, Kozaburo (Kimisaburo). Director. Born on Sept. 9, 1911, in Hiroshima. He entered Japanese cinema at 18 as an apprentice and assistant to director Yasujiro Shimazu and directed his first film, a silent production, in 1934. He subsequently made many other films, emerging as an important director after his return from WW II military service. In 1950 he formed an independent production company with Kaneto SHINDO, who has written the screenplays for some of Yoshimura's best films. Strongly influenced by MIZOGUCHI, Yoshimura is a highly versatile director who has successfully worked in both comedy and drama against modern as well as period backgrounds.

FILMS INCLUDE: *Nukiashi Sashiashi* 1934; *Tomorrow's Dancers* 1939; *The Story of Tank Commander Nishizumi* 1940; *Blossom* 1941; *South Wind* 1942; *On the Eve of War* 1943; *The Fellows Who Ate the Elephant* 1947; *Temptation* 1948; *Jealousy, Waltz at Noon* 1949; *Spring Snow* 1950; *A Tale of Genji* 1951; *The Sisters of Nishijin, Violence* 1952; *Before Dawn* 1953; *Cape Ashizuri* 1954; *Because I Love* (one episode), *Women of the Ginza, Beauty and the Dragon* 1955; *Undercurrent* 1956; *An Osaka Story* (begun by Mizoguchi), *Night Butterflies* 1957; *A Grain of Wheat* 1958; *A Woman's Testament* (one episode), *Women of Kyoto* 1960; *Design for Dying* 1961; *Their Legacy, A Night to Remember* 1962; *The Bamboo Doll* 1963; *A Fallen Woman* 1967; *The House of the Sleeping Virgins, A Hot Night* 1968; *A Ragged Flag* 1974.

Young, Alan. Actor. Born Angus Young, on Nov. 19, 1919, in North Shields, England; raised in Canada. Made his debut as a comedy monologuist at 13. He later worked as a commercial artist and cartoonist, appeared on Canadian and American radio and served in the Canadian navy before entering films in 1946. His bid to become a top comedy star in films was largely unsuccessful, despite such good opportunities as the title role in *Androcles and the Lion* (1953). But he subsequently achieved a measure of popularity on TV as the star of 'The Alan Young Show' and the 'Mr. Ed' comedy series. He returned to the big screen for a time in the mid-70s after several years of absence, during which he headed the film and broadcasting department of the Christian Science Church. He later retired to cartoon voiceovers.

FILMS: *Margie* 1946; *Chicken Every Sunday, Mr. Belvedere Goes to College* 1949; *Aaron Slick from Punkin Crick* 1952; *Androcles and the Lion* 1953; *Gentlemen Marry Brunettes* 1955; *Tom Thumb* 1958; *The Time Machine* 1960; *Baker's Hawk* 1976; *The Cat from Outer Space* 1978; *The Great Mouse Detective* (v/o) 1986; *Duck Tales: The Movie* (v/o) 1990; *Beverly Hills Cop III* 1994.

Young, Burt. Actor, writer. Born on Apr. 30, 1940, in New York, N.Y. Stocky, stage-trained character actor, usually typecast as a thug. Born to Italian immigrants in Queens, he worked at a variety of jobs before studying drama with Lee Strasberg at the Actor's Studio. After a series of off-Broadway plays, he made his screen debut in *The Gang That Couldn't Shoot Straight* (1971). For his role as the tender, frustrated brother-in-law Paulie in the original *Rocky*, he won an Academy Award nomination. Work on the *Rocky* cycle allowed him time to write, direct, and appear in plays.

FILMS INCLUDE: *The Gang That Couldn't Shoot Straight* 1971; *Cinderella Liberty* 1973; *Chinatown, The Gambler, Live a Little Steal a Lot* 1974; *The Killer Elite* 1975; *Harry and Walter Go to New York, Rocky* 1976; *The Choirboys, Twilight's Last Gleaming* 1977; *Convoy, Uncle Joe Shannon* (also sc.) 1978; *Rocky II* 1979; *Blood Beach* 1980; *All the*

Marbles 1981; *Amityville II: The Possession, Lookin' to Get Out, Rocky III* 1982; *Over the Brooklyn Bridge* 1983; *Once Upon a Time in America, The Pope of Greenwich Village* 1984; *Rocky IV* 1985; *Back to School* 1986; *Beverly Hills Brats, Blood Red, Last Exit to Brooklyn, Medium Rare, Wait Until Spring, Bandini* 1989; *Backstreet Dreams, Betsy's Wedding, Bright Angel, Diving In, Rocky V* 1990; *Red American, Club Fed* 1991; *Excessive Force* 1993; *North Star* 1997.

Young, Carleton. American actor. *b.* 1907. *d.* 1971. Suave character player of numerous Hollywood productions, often in tough supporting roles, occasionally in leads. He was better known as a radio performer and played the title roles in the "Ellery Queen" and "Count of Monte Cristo" series. Later in his career, he appeared regularly in the "Wyatt Earp" and other TV series. He was the father of film and TV actor Tony Young.

FILMS INCLUDE: *Happy Go Lucky* 1936; *Join the Marines, Dick Tracy* (serial) 1937; *Buck Rogers* (serial) 1939; *Adventures of Red Ryder* (serial), *Pride of the Bowery* 1940; *Adventures of Captain Marvel* (serial), *Buck Privates* 1941; *Take It or Leave It* 1944; *Thrill of a Romance* 1945; *Smash-Up* 1947; *The Kissing Bandit* 1958; *The Mob, People Will Talk, The Day the Earth Stood Still* 1951; *Deadline USA, My Six Convicts, Red Mountain* 1952; *Niagara* 1953; *Riot in Cell Block 11, 20,000 Leagues Under the Sea* 1954; *Cry Terror, The Last Hurrah* 1958; *The Horse Soldiers* 1959; *Sergeant Rutledge* 1960; *Army Command* 1961; *The Man Who Shot Liberty Valance* 1962; *Cheyenne Autumn* 1964.

Young, Clara Kimball. Actress. *b.* Clara Kimball, 1890, Chicago. *d.* 1960. The daughter of a stage actor and actress, she made her debut at age three and was an accomplished performer in vaudeville and stock when she entered films with Vitagraph in 1909. She rose quickly to prominence under the guidance of her husband, director-actor James YOUNG, whom she had met in Salt Lake City stock. A raven-haired beauty, she was voted the most popular screen actress by a fan magazine in 1914. She played some comedy roles, but more typically she was cast, even in her early films, in mature, worldly roles in serious drama. In 1915 she left Vitagraph to become the prize star of the World Film Corporation, newly formed by Lewis J. SELZNICK. The following year, when Selznick was edged out of the company by his partners, she went along and he rewarded her by forming the Clara Kimball Young Film Corporation, solely devoted to producing her films. Her popularity continued to soar for a while, but her career took a sudden dip in the early 20s when she allowed her former agent and new husband, Harry Garson (she had divorced Young in 1916), to take charge of her films as producer and director. The quality of her productions deteriorated rapidly and she was forced to retire from the screen to seek her living in vaudeville. She returned to films in the early 30s playing character parts, mostly in low-budget productions, then retired altogether in 1941, all but forgotten.

FILMS INCLUDE: *Washington Under the American Flag, A Midsummer Night's Dream* 1909; *Uncle Tom's Cabin* 1910; *Cardinal Wolsey* (as Anne Boleyn), *Lincoln's Gettysburg Address, Lord Browning and Cinderella* 1912; *Beau Brummel, The Little Minister, Cupid Versus Women's Rights, Delayed Proposals, Fellow Voyagers, Love's Sunset, Beauty Unadorned* 1913; *The Violin of M'sieur, Happy-Go-Lucky, My Official Wife, Lola/Without a Soul* 1914; *The Fates and Flora Fourflush* (serial), *Camille* (title role), *Trilby* (title role), *The Deep Purple, Hearts in Exile* 1915; *The Yellow Passport, The Feast of Life* 1916; *The Easiest Way, Magda, The Price She Paid* 1917; *The Savage Woman, The Marionettes, The Claw* 1918; *Cheating Cheaters, Eyes of Youth* 1919; *The Forbidden Woman, Mid-Channel* 1920; *Straight from Paris, What No Man Knows, Hush, Charge It* 1921; *Enter Madame, The Hands of Nara, The Worldly Madonna* 1922; *Cordelia the Magnificent, A Wife's Romance, The Woman of Bronze* 1923; *Lying Wives* 1925; *Kept Husbands, Mother and Son, Women Go on Forever* 1931; *File No. 113, Probation* 1932; *The Return of Chandu* (feature and serial versions) 1934; *She Married Her Boss, His Night Out* 1935; *The Black Coin* (serial), *Three on the Trail* 1936; *The Frontiersman* 1938; *The Roundup* 1941.

Young, Frederick A. (Freddie). Director of photography. Born in 1902, in England. He entered British films at the age of 15 and worked in various capacities before becoming a lighting cameraman in the late 20s. He has worked on many major British and Anglo-American films, excelling in black-and-white cinematography and since the early 50s in color photography of remarkable beauty and lushness. His most famous collaboration has been with director David LEAN, for whom he photographed a number of sumptuous productions, winning Academy Awards for the cinematography of *Lawrence of Arabia* (1962), *Doctor Zhivago* (1965), and *Ryan's Daughter* (1970). He made his directorial debut at age 82 with *Arthur's Hallowed Ground* (TV) (1985).

FILMS INCLUDE: *The Flag Lieutenant* (co-phot.) 1926; *The W Plan* (co-phot.) 1930; *The Blue Danube* 1932; *Bitter Sweet* 1933; *Nell Gwyn* 1934; *When Knights Were Bold* 1936; *Victoria the Great* (co-phot.) 1937; *Sixty Glorious Years* 1938; *Goodbye Mr. Chips* 1939; *49th Parallel/The Invaders* 1941; *The Young Mr. Pitt* 1942; *Caesar and Cleopatra* (co-phot.), *Bedelia* 1946; *The Winslow Boy* 1948; *Edward My Son* 1949; *Treasure Island* 1950; *Ivanhoe* 1952; *Mogambo* (co-phot.) 1953; *Knights of the Round Table* 1954; *Lust for Life* (co-phot.), *Bhowani Junction* 1956; *Island in the Sun* 1957; *The Inn of the Sixth Happiness* 1958; *Solomon and Sheba* 1959; *Lawrence of Arabia* 1962; *The 7th Dawn* 1964; *Lord Jim, Doctor Zhivago* 1965; *The Deadly Affair, You Only Live Twice* 1967; *Battle of Britain* 1969; *Ryan's Daughter* 1970; *Nicholas and Alexandra* 1971; *Luther, The Tamarind Seed* 1974; *Permission to Kill* 1975; *The Blue Bird* (co-phot.; US/USSR) 1976; *Stevie* 1978; *Sidney Sheldon's Bloodline* 1979; *Rough Cut* (US) 1980; *Richard's Things* 1981; *Sword of the Valiant: The Legend of Gawain and the Green Knight, Invitation to the Wedding* (US) 1984; *Arthur's Hallowed Ground* (TV; dir. only) 1985.

Young, Gig. Actor. *b.* Byron Elsworth Barr, Nov. 4, 1913, St. Cloud, Minn. *d.* 1978. Raised in Washington, D.C., he began acting in high school plays and after graduation appeared nights with an amateur group and worked days in a local automobile agency. He gained a scholarship to the Pasadena Playhouse, and his work there led to a contract with Warners. He played several bits under the billing Byron Barr before landing his first featured role as Gig Young in *The Gay Sisters* (1942). The character he portrayed was named Gig Young, and Barr adopted this as his professional pseudonym to avoid confusion with another Hollywood actor called Byron Barr (whose credits are still often erroneously assigned to Young). Young also used the name Bryant Fleming in some of his early films. After returning from WW II service with the Coast Guard, Young freelanced at various studios and became typecast as a second leading man, often playing bons vivants or unsuccessful suitors in sophisticated comedies. Only occasionally was he assigned the lead, usually in a B picture.

A capable and versatile actor who projected lighthearted amiability and earnestness with equal ease, Young was nominated for Academy Awards in the supporting category for the drama *Come Fill the Cup* (1951) and the comedy *Teacher's Pet* (1958) and finally won the Oscar for his performance in *They Shoot Horses, Don't They?* (1969). He also appeared much on the stage and on TV, including in the series 'The Rogues.' His third wife (1956–63) was actress Elizabeth Montgomery. Young died in tragic circumstances. His body was found by police in a Manhattan apartment next to the body of his bride of three weeks, a 31-year-old German-born actress. His hand was clutching a gun. Police theorized he had shot his wife, then turned the gun on himself. Ironically, his last film was titled *The Game of Death.*

FILMS INCLUDE: *Misbehaving Husbands* 1940; *Dive Bomber* (bit), *Sergeant York* (bit) 1941; *The Male Animal, The Gay Sisters* 1942; *Air Force, Old Acquaintance* 1943; *Escape Me Never* 1947; *The Woman in White, The Three Musketeers* (as Porthos), *Wake of the Red Witch* 1948; *Lust for Gold* 1949; *Hunt the Man Down* 1950; *Only the Valiant, Come Fill the Cup* 1951; *Holiday for Sinners* 1952; *The City That Never Sleeps, Arena, Torch Song* 1953; *Young at Heart, The Desperate Hours* 1955; *Desk Set* 1957; *Teacher's Pet, The Tunnel of Love* 1958; *Ask Any Girl* 1959; *The Story on Page One* 1960; *That Touch of Mink* 1962; *Five Miles to Midnight, A Ticklish Affair* 1963; *Strange Bedfellows* 1965; *The Shuttered Room* 1968; *They Shoot Horses Don't They?* 1969; *Lovers and Other Strangers* 1970; *Bring Me the Head of Alfredo Garcia* 1974; *The Killer Elite, The Hindenburg* 1975; *The Game of Death* 1979.

Young, Harold. Director. *b.* Nov. 13, 1897, in Portland, Ore. *d.* 1970. *ed.* Columbia. He entered films as a cutter in 1920 and in the early 20s was sent to Paris and London as supervising editor of Paramount's European productions. He later worked in a similar capacity for Alexander KORDA, for whom he edited *Catherine the Great,* among other films. He made an auspicious start as director with the excellent Korda costume thriller *The Scarlet Pimpernel* (1934), then returned to Hollywood, where he was assigned routine films by Paramount, Universal, and other studios. In the 40s he formed his own Harold Young Productions and gradually drifted into obscurity.

FILMS: *The Scarlet Pimpernel* (UK), *Too Many Millions* (UK) 1934; *Without Regret* 1935; *Woman Trap, My American Wife* 1936; *Let Them Live, 52nd Street* 1937; *Little Tough Guy, The Storm* 1938; *Newsboys' Home, Code of the Streets, The Forgotten Woman, Sabotage, Hero for a Day* 1939; *Dreaming Out Loud* 1940; *Bachelor Daddy* 1941; *Juke Box Jenny, Rubber Racketeers, The Mummy's Tomb, There's One Born Every Minute* 1942; *Hi Buddy, Hi' Ya Chum, I Escaped from the Gestapo, Spy Train* 1943; *Machine Gun Mama* 1944; *The Three Caballeros* (Disney cartoon-live action feature), *Jungle Captive, The Frozen Ghost, I Remember April, Song of the Sarong* 1945; *Citizen Saint* 1947; *Roogie's Bump* 1954.

Young, James. Director, actor. *b.* 1878, Baltimore. Deceased. A former stage actor, he joined Vitagraph in 1910 as co-director of the series "Scenes of True Life" and later directed many of the studio's more ambitious productions, occasionally acting in his own films. His wife, Clara Kimball YOUNG, his former co-star in a Salt Lake City stock company, played the lead in many of his films through 1916, when they divorced. Exile Leon Trotsky acted as a technical advisor and played a small role in one of Young's successful films, *My Official Wife* (1914).

FILMS INCLUDE (as director): *Lincoln's Gettysburg Address* (co-dir. with J. Stuart Blackton; also act.), *As You Like It* (co-dir. with Blackton; also act.) 1912; *When Mary Grew Up, The Little Minister* (also sc., act.), *Beau Brummel* (also act. in title role), *The Dog House Builders, And His Wife Came Back* (also sc.), *Delayed Proposals, When Women Go on the Warpath* (co-dir. with W. North), *Beauty Unadorned* (co-dir. with L. Rogers Lytton; also act.) 1913; *Hamlet* (unfinished), *A Model Young Man* (also sc.), *Goodness Gracious or Movies as They Shouldn't Be* (also sc., act.), *Happy-Go-Lucky, The Violin of M'sieur* (also act.), *My Official Wife, Lola/Without a Soul* (also sc., act.) 1914; *Deep Purple* (also sc.), *Hearts in Exile* (also sc.), *The Little Miss Brown, The Heart of the Blue Ridge* 1915; *Forbidden Paths* 1917; *Temple of Dusk, White Man's Law, Rose o' Paradise, Missing, Dawn of Understanding, The Man Who Wouldn't Tell* 1918; *Gentleman of Quality, Hornet's Nest, The Usurper, The Wolf, A Regular Girl* 1919; *Daughter of Two Worlds* 1920; *The Devil, Without Benefit of Clergy* 1921; *The Infidel* (also sc.), *The Masquerader, Omar the Tentmaker* 1922; *Trilby, Wandering Daughters* (also sc.) 1923; *Welcome Stranger* (also co-sc.) 1924; *The Unchastened Woman* 1925; *The Bells* 1926; *Driven from Home* 1927; *Midnight Rose* 1928.

Young, Loretta. Actress. Born Gretchen Michaela Young, on Jan. 6, 1913, in Salt Lake City. When she was three, her parents separated and her mother moved with the children to Hollywood, where she opened a boardinghouse. Miss Young was only four when she began appearing as a child extra in movies. So did her sisters, Polly Ann Young (*b.* Oct. 25, 1908, Denver) and Elizabeth Jane, later better known as Sally Blane. She stopped appearing in films while attending a convent school but returned to the screen at the age of 14, playing a supporting part in a Colleen Moore vehicle, *Naughty but Nice* (1927). She had gotten the part by default. Director Mervyn LeRoy telephoned her home, asking for her older sister Polly Ann. The latter was not available for work and Gretchen asked if she might do. It was only a bit role, but it resulted in a contract with First National, and Gretchen, whose name was changed to Loretta, was on her way to a successful starring career.

Rapidly advancing from teenage to ingenue and leading lady roles, she appeared in films with increasing frequency and made a smooth transition to talkies. Most of her vehicles were routine programmers, but there were enough of them to establish her as an important star by the mid-30s, when she switched to Fox. For most of her roles she relied on her elegant beauty—rosy complexion, full lips, and prominent cheekbones—but on occasion she was also called upon to act and she did so convincingly in such films as *The Farmer's Daughter* (1947), for which she won the Academy Award, *Rachel and the Stranger* (1948), *Come to the Stable* (Oscar nomination, 1949), and *Cause for Alarm* (1951).

Miss Young retired from the screen in 1953 to begin a second, and highly successful, career as the star of TV's 'The Loretta Young Show.' For eight years she made a glamorous entrance at the start of each weekly show to announce the half-hour drama that followed. She also played the leads in about half of the drama series, winning three Emmy Awards. Miss Young, who since the early 60s has been devoting most of her energies to Catholic charities, has been married twice. Her 1930 elopement marriage to actor Grant WITHERS was annulled the following year. She is separated from her second husband, producer-writer Thomas Lewis. In 1961 she published a book of memoirs, *The Things I Had to Learn.* In 1972 she won $600,000 in a suit against NBC for unlawfully exhibiting her TV shows abroad. She returned to TV drama with *Christmas Eve* (1986).

FILMS: *Naughty but Nice* 1927; *The Whip Woman, Laugh Clown Laugh, The Magnificent Flirt, The Head Man, Scarlet Seas* 1928; *The Squall, The Girl in the Glass Cage, The Fast Life, The Careless Age, The Show of Shows, The Forward Pass* 1929; *The Man from Blankley's, The Second Floor Mystery, Loose Ankles, Road to Paradise, Kismet, The Truth About Youth, The Devil to Pay* 1930; *Beau Ideal, The Right of Way, Three Girls Lost, Too Young to Marry, Big Business Girl, I Like Your Nerve, Platinum Blonde, The Ruling Voice* 1931; *Taxi, The Hatchet Man, Play Girl, Weekend Marriage, Life Begins, They Call It Sin* 1932; *Employees' Entrance, Grand Slam, Zoo in Budapest, The*

Life of Jimmy Dolan, Midnight Mary, Heroes for Sale, The Devil's in Love, She Had to Say Yes, A Man's Castle 1933; *The House of Rothschild, Born to Be Bad, Bulldog Drummond Strikes Back, Caravan, The White Parade* 1934; *Clive of India, Shanghai, Call of the Wild, The Crusades* 1935; *The Unguarded Hour, Private Number, Ramona, Ladies in Love* 1936; *Love Is News, Cafe Metropole, Love Under Fire, Wife Doctor and Nurse, Second Honeymoon* 1937; *Four Men and a Prayer, Three Blind Mice, Suez, Kentucky* 1938; *The Story of Alexander Graham Bell* (as Mrs. Bell), *Wife Husband and Friend, Eternally Yours* 1939; *The Doctor Takes a Wife, He Stayed for Breakfast* 1940; *The Lady from Cheyenne, The Men in Her Life* 1941; *Bedtime Story, A Night to Remember* 1942; *China* 1943; *Ladies Courageous, And Now Tomorrow* 1944; *Along Came Jones* 1945; *The Stranger, The Perfect Game* 1946; *The Farmer's Daughter, The Bishop's Wife* 1947; *Rachel and the Stranger* 1948; *The Accused, Mother Is a Freshman, Come to the Stable* 1949; *Key to the City* 1950; *Cause for Alarm, Half Angel* 1951; *Paula, Because of You* 1952; *It Happens Every Thursday* 1953; *Going Hollywood: The War Years* (archival footage) 1988.

Young, Robert. Actor. Born on Feb. 22, 1907, in Chicago. Raised in California, he worked at a variety of odd jobs while gaining acting experience at the Pasadena Playhouse and playing extra parts in films. In 1931 he was signed by MGM and began a long and prolific career that saw him star in some 100 productions, typically as a wholesome, amiable leading man. In a motion picture career that spanned more than 20 years and included many routine productions, he gradually progressed from carefree, debonair romantic leads to charming husbands and eventually benevolent fathers. In the mid-50s, when films no longer offered him suitable roles, he switched to TV and enjoyed rejuvenated popularity in the long-running series 'Father Knows Best.' In the late 60s he launched another highly popular TV series, 'Marcus Welby M.D.' He has been married to the same woman since 1933, a rarity among Hollywood residents.

FILMS: *The Black Camel, The Sin of Madelon Claudet, The Guilty Generation* 1931; *Hell Divers, The Wet Parade, New Morals for Old, Unashamed, Strange Interlude* (as Gordon), *The Kid from Spain* 1932; *Men Must Fight, Today We Live, Hell Below, Tugboat Annie, Saturday's Millions, The Right to Romance* 1933; *Carolina, Spitfire, The House of Rothschild, Whom the Gods Destroy, Paris Interlude, Death on the Diamond, The Band Plays On* 1934; *West Point of the Air, Vagabond Lady, Calm Yourself, Red Salute, Remember Last Night?, The Bride Comes Home 1935; Secret Agent* (UK), *It's Love Again* (UK), *The Three Wise Guys, Sworn Enemy, The Bride Walks Out, The Longest Night, Stowaway* 1936; *Dangerous Number, I Met Him in Paris, The Emperor's Candlesticks, Married Before Breakfast, The Bride Wore Red, Navy Blue and Gold* 1937; *Paradise for Three, Three Comrades, Josette, The Toy Wife, Rich Man Poor Girl, The Shining Hour* 1938; *Honolulu, Bridal Suite, Maisie, Miracles for Sale* 1939; *Northwest Passage, Florian, The Mortal Storm, Sporting Blood, Dr. Kildare's Crisis* 1940; *Western Union, The Trial of Mary Dugan, Lady Be Good, Married Bachelor, H. M. Pulham Esq.* 1941; *Joe Smith American, Cairo, Journey for Margaret* 1942; *Slightly Dangerous, Sweet Rosie O'Grady, Claudia* 1943; *The Canterville Ghost* 1944; *The Enchanted Cottage, Those Endearing Young Charms* 1945; *The Searching Wind, Claudia and David, Lady Luck* 1946; *They Won't Believe Me, Crossfire* 1947; *Relentless, Sitting Pretty* 1948; *Adventure in Baltimore, That Forsyte Woman* (as Philip Bosinney), *Bride for Sale, And Baby Makes Three, The Second Woman, Goodbye My Fancy* 1951; *The Half-Breed* 1952; *Secret of the Incas* 1954.

Young, Roland. Actor. *b.* Nov. 11, 1887, London. *d.* 1953. The son of an architect, he was educated at Sherborne College and London University and trained for the stage at the Royal Academy of Dramatic Art. He made his London debut in 1908 and his first New York appearance in 1912. He remained in this country and served with the US Army in WW I. In the early 20s he appeared in two silent films, in one of which he played Dr. Watson to John Barrymore's Sherlock Holmes. But it was in the 30s and 40s that he became established as a screen personality, playing character comedy parts in numerous Hollywood films, typically portraying whimsical, bemused, quizzical characters, most memorably in the title role of *Topper* (Oscar nomination, 1937) and its sequels.

FILMS INCLUDE: *Sherlock Holmes/Moriarty* (as Dr. Watson) 1922; *Grit* 1924; *The Unholy Night* 1929; *The Bishop Murder Case, Madame Satan* 1930; *New Moon, The Prodigal, The Squaw Man, The Guardsman* 1931; *A Woman Commands, One Hour with You, This Is the Night, Wedding Rehearsal* (UK) 1932; *A Lady's Profession, Pleasure Cruise* 1933; *His Double Life, Here Is My Heart* 1934; *David Copperfield* (as Uriah Heep), *Ruggles of Red Gap* 1935; *The Unguarded Hour, The Man Who Could Work Miracles* (UK) 1936; *King Solomon's Mines* (as Captain Good; UK), *Topper* (title role), *Ali Baba Goes to Town* 1937; *Sailing Along* (UK), *The Young in Heart, Topper Takes a Trip* (title role) 1938; *Yes My Darling Daughter* 1939; *Star Dust, Irene, Private Affairs, Dulcy, No No Nanette, The Philadelphia Story* 1940; *Topper Returns* (title role), *The Flame of New Orleans, Two-Faced Woman* 1941; *The Lady Has Plans, They All Kissed the Bride, Tales of Manhattan* 1942; *Forever and a Day* 1943; *Standing Room Only* 1944; *And Then There Were None* 1945; *Bond Street* (UK) 1947; *You Gotta Stay Happy* 1948; *The Great Lover* 1949; *Let's Dance* 1950; *That Man from Tangier* 1953.

Young, Sean. Actress. Born on Nov. 20, 1959, in Louisville, Ky. *ed.* Interlochen Arts Academy, Mich. Tempestuous screen beauty, often in supporting roles. Following her arts study, which included dance, flute, voice, and writing, she moved to New York, where she worked briefly as a receptionist. Debuted in film in 1980s; gained notice as a potential lead in *No Way Out*, largely through a sizzling backseat *contretemps* scene with Kevin Costner. Due to tepid film choices and unfavorable press for her highly expressive actions, she has not lived up to her early promise.

FILMS INCLUDE: *Jane Austen in Manhattan* 1980; *Stripes* 1981; *Blade Runner, Young Doctors in Love* 1982; *Baby. . . Secret of the Lost Legend, Dune* 1985; *No Way Out, Wall Street* 1987; *The Boost* 1988; *Cousins* 1989; *Fire Birds* 1990; *A Kiss Before Dying* 1991; *Blue Ice, Once Upon a Crime, Love Crimes* 1992; *Hold Me Thrill Me Kiss Me, Fatal Instinct* 1993; *Ace Ventura Pet Detective, Even Cowgirls Get the Blues* 1994; *Dr. Jekyll and Ms. Hyde* 1995; *The Proprietor* 1996.

Young, Terence. Director. *b.* June 20, 1915, in Shanghai, to British parents. *d.* 1994. *ed.* Cambridge. He entered British films in 1936 and collaborated on several screenplays before going into WW II military service. Returning to civilian life, he made his directorial debut in 1948, but it wasn't until the 60s that his work could be much distinguished from that of the average British director. He asserted himself with Dr. No and a couple of other James Bond adventure spectaculars as a masterful technician in the best Hollywood tradition, capable of attaining dazzling visual effects and sustaining a dynamic pace throughout an entire production. He has since worked with varying degrees of success on international productions, often distinguished by surface gloss and an accent on violent action.

FILMS: *Men of Arnhem* (WW II doc.; co-dir. with Brian

Desmond Hurst) 1944; *Corridor of Mirrors, One Night with You, Woman Hater* 1948; *They Were Not Divided* (also prod., sc.) 1950; *Valley of the Eagles* (also prod., sc.) 1951; *The Tall Headlines/The Frightened Bride* 1952; *The Red Beret/ Paratrooper* 1953; *That Lady* 1954; *Storm Over the Nile* (co-dir. with Zoltan Korda) 1955; *Safari, Zarak* 1956; *Action of the Tiger, No Time to Die/Tank Force* (also co-sc.) 1957; *Serious Charge* 1959; *Un Deux Trois Quatre/Les Collants noirs/Black Tights* (Fr.), *Too Hot to Handle* 1960; *Orazi e Curiazi/Duel of Champions* (co-dir. with Ferdinando Baldi; It.) 1961; *Dr. No* 1962; *From Russia with Love* 1963; *The Amorous Adventures of Moll Flanders, Thunderball, La Guerre secrète/The Dirty Game* (co-dir. with Carlo Lizzani, Christian-Jaque, and Werner Klinger; It./Fr./Ger.) 1965; *Triple Cross* (UK/Fr.), *The Poppy Is Also a Flower* (an International United Nations production) 1966; *Wait Until Dark* (US), *L'Avventuriero/The Rover* (It.) 1967; *Mayerling* (also sc.; UK/Fr.) 1968; *L'Arbre de Noël/The Christmas Tree* (Fr./It.) 1969; *De la Part des Copains/Cold Sweat* (Fr.) 1970; *Soleil rouge/Red Sun* (Fr.) 1971; *Joe Valachi: I Segreti di Cosa Nostra/The Valachi Papers* (It./Fr.) 1972; *Le Guerriere del Sno Nuda/War Goddess/The Amazons* (It.) 1973; *The Klansmen* (US) 1974; *Jackpot* 1975; *Sidney Sheldon's Bloodline* (US) 1979; *Inchon* 1982; *The Jigsaw Man, Where is Parsifal?* (exec. prod. only) 1984.

Young, Victor. Composer, music director. *b.* Aug. 8, 1900, Chicago. *d.* 1956. A child prodigy and a graduate of the Warsaw (Poland) Conservatory, he was a concert violinist before coming to Hollywood early in the sound era. He composed and arranged scores and wrote songs for numerous productions, most at Paramount.

FILMS INCLUDE: *Anything Goes, Klondike Annie, Big Broadcast of 1937* 1936; *Maid of Salem, Make Way for Tomorrow, Artists and Models* 1937; *The Light That Failed, Golden Boy* 1939; *North West Mounted Police* 1940; *I Wanted Wings* 1941; *The Palm Beach Story, Reap the Wild Wind* 1942; *For Whom the Bell Tolls* 1943; *Ministry of Fear, Frenchman's Creek* 1944; *Love Letters* 1945; *The Searching Wind, Kitty, Two Years Before the Mast* 1946; *Golden Earrings, I Walk Alone* 1947; *State of the Union, The Big Clock, The Paleface, The Emperor Waltz* 1948; *Samson and Delilah, My Foolish Heart* 1949; *Rio Grande* 1950; *Scaramouche, The Quiet Man, The Greatest Show on Earth* 1952; *Shane* 1953; *Johnny Guitar, Three Coins in the Fountain* 1954; *Strategic Air Command* 1955; *Around the World in 80 Days* (Academy Award) 1956; *Run of the Arrow* 1957.

Young, Waldemar. Screenwriter. *b.* 1890(?), Salt Lake City. *d.* 1938. *ed.* Stanford U. He entered films in 1917 and subsequently wrote a great many screenplays, alone or in collaboration, for various studios, often for major productions. In the 20s he frequently worked with director Tod BROWNING and in the 30s with C. B. DE MILLE.

FILMS INCLUDE: *The Fire Flingers, Unpainted Woman* 1919; *Suds* 1920; *Experience, A Prince There Was* 1921; *Our Leading Citizen, Ebb Tide* 1922; *You Can't Fool Your Wife, Java Head, Salomy Jane* 1923; *Poisoned Paradise, Dorothy Vernon of Haddon Hall* 1924; *The Great Divide, The Unholy Three, The Mystic* 1925; *The Black Bird* 1926; *The Show, The Unknown, London After Midnight, Women Love Diamonds* 1927; *The Big City, West of Zanzibar* 1928; *Trail of '98, Tide of Empire, Where East Is East, Sally* 1929; *Girl of the Golden West* 1930; *Chances, Penrod and Sam* 1931; *The Miracle Man, Love Me Tonight, Island of Lost Souls* 1932; *Sign of the Cross* 1933; *Men in White, Cleopatra* 1934; *Lives of a Bengal Lancer, The Crusades, Peter Ibbetson* 1935; *Desire, Poppy, The Plainsman* 1936; *Man-Proof, Test Pilot* 1938.

Youngson, Robert. Producer. *b.* Nov. 27, 1917, Brooklyn, N.Y. *d.* 1974. *ed.* NYU; Harvard. He joined Pathé News in 1941 and after WW II service returned to Pathé, which was taken over by Warner Bros. in 1948, as producer-writer-director of short subjects. Two of his shorts won Academy Awards, *World of Kids* (1951) and *This Mechanical Age* (1954). In the 50s and 60s, he produced a number of feature-length compilation films comprising highlight clips of silent and early sound screen comedies, which enjoyed considerable success in motion picture theaters.

FILMS INCLUDE: *Fifty Years Before Your Eyes* 1950; *The Golden Age of Comedy* 1957; *Noah's Ark* 1958; *When Comedy Was King* 1960; *Days of Thrills and Laughter* 1961; *30 Years of Fun* 1963; *M-G-M's Big Parade of Comedy* 1964; *Laurel and Hardy's Laughing 20s* 1965; *The Further Perils of Laurel and Hardy* 1968; *Four Clowns* 1970.

Yugoslavia. Limited film production in this multinational Balkan land had started long before its patchwork of states and territories emerged in 1918 as the unified Kingdom of Serbs, Croats, and Slovenes. But it wasn't until after WW II that the foundations of a true film industry were laid. The first films, a program of Lumière shorts, were shown in Belgrade in June of 1896, and some shooting of local footage took place the following year. The first domestic filmmaker of note was Milton Manaki (1880–1964), who began turning out reportage films in 1905. The first domestically produced feature, *Karageorge* (1910), a biography of the Serbian national hero, was a co-production with France's Pathé company, directed by a Frenchman, Jules Barry. There was some interesting cinematographic coverage of the Balkan Wars by war correspondent Josip Halla of Zagreb, but that conflict and WW I, which immediately followed it, halted the little production activity that had taken place in the early 1910s.

Feature production on a small scale resumed in the early 20s and accelerated in the 30s with no significant results. A leading filmmaker of the period was Mihailo-Mika Popovič, whose *With Faith in God* (1934) is considered the country's most important feature before WW II. Production came to a standstill at the outbreak of World War II, but in 1942 a group of partisans began recording combat footage with camera equipment captured from the Germans, and a circus strongman by the name of Dragoljub clandestinely made a patriotic feature, *Innocence Unprotected.*

Immediately after the liberation of Belgrade, in October of 1944, the provisional revolutionary government set up a film section as a foundation for a state-controlled industry. The organization's first undertaking was a series of war compilation films titled "Kinokronika." In 1945, soon after the war ended, the State Film Enterprise was founded, and well-equipped studios were established in all six republics. Progress was hampered, however, by the lack of experienced personnel, and only ten features were turned out through 1950, the first of which was Vjekoslav Afric's *Slavica* (1947). Many of the early films, features as well as documentaries, dealt with the experiences of the war, mainly with the heroics of the partisans, and it wasn't until the late 50s that contemporary themes were first attempted. Generally, the early postwar films were naïve and rather crudely made, but several stood out for their sincere compassion.

In contrast with the slow development of the quality feature film, the rise of the animated film in Yugoslavia was phenomenal. Long before Yugoslav features began making an impression abroad, the animated shorts of the "Zagreb school" were winning admiration at international festivals. The founder of the movement was Dušan VUKOTIČ, whose *How Kico Was Born* (1951) signaled a departure from the traditional "Disney style" and set the pattern for the inventive, freewheeling form for which the Yugoslav cartoon became famous. He won an Oscar for *Ersatz/The Substitute* (1961). Other noted members of the movement have included Nedeljko Dragic, Vladimir Jutriša, Vladimir Kristl, and Vatroslav Mimica. The latter also directed many "live" feature films.

The documentary movement, too, developed more rapidly than the feature industry and has been noted mainly for the output of the "Belgrade school." Leading fact-film directors have included Ante Babaja, Puriša Djordjević, Aleksander PETROVIĆ, Krsto Skanata, Stejpan Zaninović, and Zelimir Zilnik.

Feature film production gained significance both in quality and quantity in the early 60s. Fifteen or more features were being produced annually, increasingly becoming a factor at international film festivals. Several of the documentary directors moved on to features, among them Djordjević (the "War Trilogy," comprising *The Girl, The Dream, and Morning,* 1965–67; *Noon,* 1968; *Cross Country Runner,* 1969); Mimica (*Prometheus from the Island of Visevica,* 1965; *Kaya I'll Kill You,* 1967; *An Event,* 1969); Petrović (*Three,* 1965; *I Even Met Happy Gypsies,* 1967; *It Rains in My Village,* 1969); and Zilnik (*Early Works,* 1969). Other feature directors of note active during the 60s included Znovimir Berković (*Rondo,* 1966); Fadil Hadzić (*Alphabet of Fear,* 1961; *The Other Side of the Medal,* 1965; *Protest,* 1967; *Three Hours for Love,* 1968); Boštjan Hladnik (*Dance in the Rain,* 1961; *Sandcastle,* 1962; *Erotikon,* 1963); Zilka Mitrović (*Bitter Grass,* 1965; *The Knife,* 1966; *Operation Belgrade,* 1968); Zivojin Pavlović (*The Enemy,* 1965; *The Return,* 1966; *The Rats Wake Up,* 1967; *When I'm Dead and White,* 1968); Kokan Rakonjac (*Raindrops,* 1962; *The Traitor,* 1963; *The Restless Ones,* 1967; *Wild Shadows,* 1968); Vladan Slijepcevic (*The Protégé,* 1966); and veteran France Stiglić (*The Ninth Circle,* 1960; *That Fine Day,* 1963).

The Yugoslav director best known abroad was Dušan MAKAVEJEV, a controversial figure at home, whose films of the 60s were *A Man Is Not a Bird* (1966), *The Switchboard Operator/Love Affair* (1967), and *Innocence Unprotected* (1968). His *WR—Mysteries of the Organism* (1971) was banned from the Pula Festival of Yugoslav films but was well received abroad. Another Yugoslav director who gained international repute was Veljko BULAJIĆ, who directed the spectacular *The Battle of Neretva* (1969) and other expensive co-productions.

International co-production became an important business factor for the Yugoslav film industry in the 70s. Many foreign producers were attracted by the country's dependable climate, the relative cheapness of labor, and various government inducements. Parallel to this development, the Yugoslav cinema experienced in the 70s a gradual decline from the artistic peak it had achieved in the late 60s. Leading directors like Makavejev, Petrović, and Zilnik worked mainly abroad, and others who stayed found work hard to get unless they agreed to compromise their personal integrity by adhering to themes and styles approved by the state. The irreverent black humor that characterized some of the best films of the peak period was now sadly missing from the screen.

In the late 70s and early 80s, Yugoslav cinema began to revive amid a more relaxed political atmosphere. Self-exiled filmmakers returned home and a new generation of directors, screenwriters, and cinematographers began to assert itself. Known as the "Prague school" because of their training in Czechoslovakia, these filmmakers began their careers in television and frequently collaborated on each other's projects, which ranged from realistic social satires to genre films inspired by Hollywood blockbusters. Many of the new Yugoslav films were commercial and critical successes at home as well as abroad, countering the tendency seen in many European countries toward foreign (particularly American) domination at the box office. The Prague school included such directors as Rajko Grlić (*Bravo Maestro*, 1978; *The Melody Haunts My Memory*, 1981), Srdjan Karanović (*Social Game*, 1972; *The Fragrance of Wild Flowers*, 1977; *Petria's Wreath*, 1980; *Something in Between*, 1983), Goran Marković (*Special Education*, 1977; *National Class*, 1979; *Variola Vera*, 1982; *Tito and Me*, 1991), Goran Paskaljević (*The Beach Guard in Winter*, 1976; *The Dog Who Loved Trains*, 1977; *Tango Argentina*, 1992), and Lordan Zafranović (*The Occupation in 26 Pictures*, 1978). Another member was Emir KUSTURICA, whose *Do You Remember Dolly Bell?* (1981) was screened at Venice and whose *When Father Was Away on Business* (1985) won the Palme d'Or at Cannes and an Oscar nomination for best foreign film. Other directors of the 80s and 90s have included Soja Jovanović, Nića Milosević , Slobodan Sijan, and Stojan Stojccić. The period also saw new films by veteran directors such as Makavejev (*Gorilla Bathes at Noon*, 1993) and Pavlović (*The Deserter*, 1991).

The Yugoslavian film industry received a crippling, if not fatal, blow with the disintegration of the country into warring republics beginning in 1991. Filmmakers who had once cooperated in producing and distributing their releases across regional lines were now isolated within the boundaries of Serbia and Montenegro (sole inheritors of the name Yugoslavia), Croatia, or Bosnia and Herzegovina. Ethnic warfare between Serbs and Muslims in the latter republic, together with United Nations economic sanctions against Serb-led Yugoslavia for its support of the Bosnian Serb rebels, all but shut down a respected and thriving cinematic tradition.

Yurka, Blanche. Actress. *b.* Blanche Jurka, June 18, 1887, Czechoslovakia. *d.* 1974. Brought to the US as an infant by her Bohemian parents, she was initially raised in St. Paul, Minn. When she was 11 the family moved to New York, and at 15 she was awarded a scholarship to the Metropolitan Opera's school. She sang with the Met in a production of *Parsifal* but was drawn to the legitimate stage and made her Broadway debut in 1907 as a protégée of David Belasco. She rose to prominence in the 20s after playing Gertrude to John BARRYMORE's Hamlet (1922) and Gina in Ibsen's 'The Wild Duck' (1925). Specializing in the portrayal of strong-willed women, she starred in numerous stage productions, both classic and modern, and was considered among the top tragediennes of her time. She was nearing 50 when she made her screen debut in 1935 and was limited in films to character parts, usually dominant, often somber or sinister. During the 20s she was married to actor Ian KEITH. Autobiography: *Bohemian Girl* (1970).

FILMS: *A Tale of Two Cities* (as Madame Defarge) 1935; *Queen of the Mob* (title role), *City for Conquest, Escape* 1940; *Ellery Queen and the Murder Ring* 1941; *Lady for a Night, Pacific Rendezvous, A Night to Remember, Keeper of the Flame* 1942; *Tonight We Raid Calais, Hitler's Madman, The Song of Bernadette* 1943; *The Bridge of San Luis Rey* (as the Abbess), *The Cry of the Werewolf, One Body Too Many* 1944; *The Southerner* 1945; *13 Rue Madeleine, The Flame* 1947; *The Furies* 1950; *At Sword's Point* 1952; *Taxi!* 1953; *Thunder in the Sun* 1959.

Yutkevich, Sergei. Director. *b.* Sept. 15, 1904, in St. Petersburg, Russia. *d.* 1985. He became immersed in the cultural activities of the Soviet avant-garde while still in his teens and in 1922 was among the founders of the experimental Factory of the Eccentric Actor (FEX). After art studies in Kiev and Moscow and a course in film directing, he worked as a set designer in Moscow theaters and on a number of films and was Abram ROOM's assistant on *Traitor* (1926) and *Bed and Sofa*

(1927). The following year he made his debut as director. He remained one of the most highly regarded of the Soviet filmmakers throughout his career, a versatile director who had a broad range of themes, both historic and contemporary. His *Skanderbeg* was awarded a special jury prize at the Cannes Festival in 1954. In 1956 he won the best director award at Cannes for *Othello*. Yutkevich, who held a doctoral degree in the theory of art, was also a noted film historian and was a professor at Moscow's State Institute of Cinematography for over forty years.

FILMS: *Give Us Radio!* (co-dir. with S. Greenberg) 1925; *Lace* (also co-sc.) 1928; *The Black Sail* 1929; *Golden Mountains* (also co-sc.) 1931; *Counterplan/Pozor/Shame* (co-dir. with Friedrich Ermler, co-sc.) 1932; *Ankara—Heart of Turkey* (doc.; co-dir. with Lev Arnshtam) 1934; *The Miners* 1937; *The Man with the Gun* 1938; *Yakov Sverdlov* (also co-sc.) 1940; *The New Adventures of Schweik* 1943; *Dimitri Donskoi* (doc.) 1944; *France Liberated* (doc.), *Hello Moscow!* (doc.), *Our Country's Youth* (doc.) 1946; *Light Over Russia* (never released) 1947; *Three Encounters* (co-dir., with Vsevolod Pudovkin and Alexander Ptushko) 1948; *Przhevalsky* 1951; *Skanderbeg* (USSR/Alb.) 1954; *Othello* (also sc.) 1956; *Stories About Lenin* 1958; *Encounter with France* (doc.) 1960; *The Bath House* (animation—live action film; co-dir. with Anatoly Karanovich) 1962; *Lenin in Poland/Portrait of Lenin* (USSR/Pol.) 1966; *Theme for a Short Story/Lika le Grand Amour de Tchekov* (USSR/Fr.) 1969; *Mayakovsky Laughs* (co-dir., co-sc. with Anatoli Karanovich) 1976.

Zaentz, Saul. Producer. Born in 1911 in Passaic, N.J. Zaentz achieved his first success as a music producer with Fantasy Records, carrying such artists as Creedence Clearwater Revival. He became a feature film producer with *One Flew Over the Cuckoo's Nest,* a surprise hit that earned the 1975 best picture Oscar, an honor Zaentz shared with co-producer Michael Douglas. Zaentz has specialized since in literary adaptations, notably with the tremendously successful *Amadeus* (1984), an adaptation of the Peter Shaffer play, as well as the epic romance *The English Patient* (1996), both honored with numerous Academy Awards including best picture. In the early 1980s, he opened a postproduction facility, the Saul Zaentz Company Film Center. In 1997, Zaentz was singled out by the Academy of Motion Picture Arts and Sciences for his lifetime achievement in the film industry with a special Oscar.

FILMS INCLUDE: *One Flew Over the Cuckoo's Nest* 1975; *Three Warriors* 1977; *The Lord of the Rings* 1978; *Amadeus* 1984; *The Mosquito Coast* (exec. prod.) 1986; *The Unbearable Lightness of Being* 1988; *At Play in the Fields of the Lord* 1991; *The English Patient* 1996.

Zaillian, Steven. Screenwriter, director, editor. Born 1953 in Fresno, Calif. A screenwriter turned director, Zaillian is associated with serious, dramatic scripts, often drawn upon actual events. His first screenplay for *The Falcon and the Snowman* (1986) served as a catalyst for a number of top scripting assignments culminating in his Oscar-winning screenplay adaptation for Steven SPIELBERG's overwhelming holocaust drama *Schindler's List* (1993). He made his directorial debut that same year with the well-received *Searching for Bobby Fischer.*

FILMS: *Kingdom of the Spiders* (ed.) 1977; *Starhops* (ed.) 1978; *Below the Belt* (ed.) 1980; *The Falcon and the Snowman* (sc.) 1986; *Awakenings* 1990; *Jack the Bear, Schindler's List, Searching for Bobby Fischer* (also dir.) 1993; *Clear and Present Danger* 1994; *Primal Fear* 1996; *Amistad* (co-scr. only) 1997.

Zampa, Luigi. Director. *b.* Jan. 2, 1905, in Rome. *d.* 1991. Trained as an engineer, he abandoned his studies in 1928 to begin a career on the stage as actor and playwright. In 1935 he enrolled at Rome's Centro Sperimentale film school and in 1938 entered Italian films as a screenwriter. A director from the early 40s, he became part of the postwar neorealist movement and in 1946 made his first important film, *Vivere in Pace/To Live in Peace,* in which he tried to demonstrate that the average Italian had really wanted no part of WW II. He later directed other films in the neorealist vein, notably *Anni difficili/Difficult Years.* His position in Italian cinema declined during the 50s, when he proved unable to adapt successfully to the changing styles. He collaborated on most of his scripts.

FILMS INCLUDE (as director and co-screenwriter): *L'Attore Scomparso, Fra Diavolo* 1941; *Signorinette* 1942; *Un Americano in Vacanza/A Yank in Rome, Vivere in Pace/To Live in Peace* 1946; *L'Onorevole Angelina/Angelina* 1947; *Anni difficili/Difficult Years* 1948; *Campane a Martello/Children of Change* 1949; *E più facile che un Cammello/His Last Twelve Hours, Cuori senza Frontière/The White Line* 1950; *Processo alla Città/City on Trial* 1952; *Anni facili/Easy Years, Siamo Donne/We the Women* (one episode) 1953; *La Romana/Woman of Rome* 1954; *Ragazze d'Oggi* 1956; *La Ragazza del Palio/The Love Specialist* 1957; *Il Magistrato/The Magistrate* 1959; *Il Vigile* 1960; *Gli Anni ruggenti/Roaring Years* 1962; *Frenesi de l'Estate* 1963; *Una Questione d'Onore/A Question of Honor* 1965; *I Nostri Mariti* ("Il Marito di Olga" episode) 1966; *Le Dolci Signore/Anyone Can Play* 1967; *Il Medico della Mutua* 1968; *Bello Onesto Emigrato Australia Sposerebbe Compaesana Illibata/A Girl in Australia* 1971; *Bisturi: Mafia bianca* 1973; *Gente di Rispetto* 1975; *Il Mostro* 1977; *Letti selvaggi/Tigers in Lipstick/Wild Beds* 1979.

Zampi, Mario. Director. *b.* Nov. 1, 1903, Rome. *d.* 1963. A juvenile lead in Italian films, he came to England at the age of 19 and joined the London branch of Warner Bros. as a film editor. In 1937 he co-founded Two Cities Films, for which he produced, wrote, and directed a number of productions. The best of these were his hilarious comedies of the 50s, most memorably *Laughter in Paradise* (1951).

FILMS: *Thirteen Men and a Gun* 1938; *French Without Tears* (prod. only), *Spy for a Day* 1940; *The Phantom Shot* 1947; *The Fatal Night* 1948; *Shadow of the Past, Come Dance with Me* 1950; *Laughter in Paradise* 1951; *Top Secret/Mr. Potts Goes to Moscow* 1952; *Ho scelto l'Amore* (It.) 1953; *Happy Ever After/Tonight's the Night* 1954; *Now and Forever* 1956; *The Naked Truth/Your Past Is Showing* 1957; *Too Many Crooks* 1959; *Bottoms Up* 1960; *Five Golden Hours* 1961.

Zane, Billy. Actor. Born February 14, 1966, in Chicago, Ill. Darkly handsome, imposing young leading actor of Hollywood films from the 80s. His menacing turn in *Dead Calm* (1989) placed him on the Hollywood roster of screen villains, but this versatile actor has become known for his ability to play in a wide range of roles, including donning a cape for the action/adventure film *The Phantom* (1996).

FILMS: *Back to the Future* 1985; *Critters* 1986; *Back to the Future Part II, Dead Calm* 1989; *Femme Fatale* 1991; *Orlando, Poetic Justice, Posse, Sniper, Tombstone* 1993; *Only You, Silence of the Hams* 1994; *Tales from the Crypt Presents Demon Knights* 1995; *The Phantom* 1996; *This World Then the Fireworks* 1997.

Zanuck, Darryl F. Studio executive, producer, screenwriter. *b.* Sept. 5, 1902, Wahoo, Nebr. *d.* 1979. He had his first brush with the film world at the age of eight, when he played a little Indian in a silent Western. At 15 he joined the Nebraska National Guard, lying about his age, and saw WW I action in France. He also saw action in the ring as a bantamweight in intramilitary competition. When several of his letters home were published in *Stars and Stripes* he decided to become a writer.

But before he could realize this goal he toiled at a wide assortment of odd jobs, from laboring on the waterfront to drugstore clerking. All the while, he kept sending stories to magazines, and after many rejections he saw some in print. Encouraged, he began submitting stories to motion picture studios and in 1923 he joined Warner Bros. as a staff screenwriter.

A dynamic, restless man, he turned out numerous scripts, which characteristically were noted more for their inventive plots than for their literary merit. Typical of these were his screenplays for a series of adventure films featuring the dog star Rin Tin Tin. But his enthusiasm and administrative ability gained him the confidence of the brothers Warner and he was appointed studio manager in 1928. The following year, he was put in charge of production. As Jack Warner's right hand, he helped guide the studio during the transition to sound and was responsible for the successful cycles of gangster and social dramas and the popular musicals the studio produced in the early 30s.

Following a rift with the Warners over studio policy, Zanuck resigned in 1933 and formed a new company, 20th Century Pictures, in association with Joseph SCHENCK. The following year the company merged with Fox to form 20th Century-Fox, and Zanuck, as chief of production, quickly elevated the new concern to a leading position among Hollywood's studios. With the exception of the WW II years, during which he served as a lieutenant colonel in charge of a documentary film unit, Zanuck remained at the production helm at 20th until 1956, when he became an independent producer in a special releasing arrangement with the company. During his long stint as chief of production, he was known as a firm but volatile taskmaster whose attitude as boss was perhaps best summed up by his now-famous snarl at a retinue of underlings: "For God's sake, don't say yes until I finish talking!" He took an active part in story conferences and contributed valuable ideas to many films. As an independent producer, he operated from France.

After several commercial misfires, Zanuck hit the box-office jackpot with *The Longest Day* in 1962. That same year he responded to an appeal by members of the Board of 20th Century-Fox to try to salvage the company from the financial hole in which it found itself as a consequence of the *Cleopatra* debacle. He wrested control of the company from Spyros Skouras and was elected president of 20th Century-Fox. He appointed his son, Richard ZANUCK, vice president in charge of production. In 1969, Darryl became chairman and chief executive of the company and Richard president. But in December of 1970, in the midst of a bitter proxy fight in which he found himself under fire for the company's failing business affairs, Darryl Zanuck fired his son from the presidency and managed to retain his own position in the company but for only several more months. In May of 1971 he resigned as chief executive, retaining the empty title of chairman emeritus.

FILMS INCLUDE (as producer): *Noah's Ark* 1929; *The Bowery* 1933; *The House of Rothschild* 1934; *Les Misérables* 1935; *Lloyds of London* 1936; *In Old Chicago, Alexander's Ragtime Band* 1938; *Jesse James, Young Mr. Lincoln, Drums Along the Mohawk* 1939; *The Grapes of Wrath* 1940; *Tobacco Road, Blood and Sand, How Green Was My Valley* 1941; *Wilson* 1944; *The Razor's Edge* 1946; *Gentleman's Agreement* 1947; *Pinky* 1949; *All About Eve* 1950; *Viva Zapata!* 1952; *The Man in the Gray Flannel Suit* 1956; *The Sun Also Rises* 1957; *The Roots of Heaven* 1958; *The Longest Day* 1962.

Zanuck, Richard Darryl. Producer, production executive. Born on Dec. 13, 1934, in Los Angeles. *ed.* Stanford U. The son of Darryl ZANUCK, he began his film career in the story department of 20th Century-Fox while still attending college. When his father became an independent producer in 1956, working out of Paris, Richard became vice president of Darryl F. Zanuck productions, in charge of the company's operations in the US. In 1962, when Zanuck senior regained effective control of 20th Century-Fox, Richard was made vice president in charge of production of the studio. In 1969 he became the company's president but was removed from the position the following year following a bitter proxy fight. He served briefly in 1971–72 as senior executive vice president but resigned to form his own production company in partnership with David BROWN, releasing through Universal. The Zanuck-Brown company was responsible for two of the biggest moneymaking films of all time, *The Sting* (1973) and *Jaws* (1975). In 1988, he left the partnership to form The Zanuck Company with his wife, producer/director Lili Fini Zanuck. They soon struck gold, winning Academy Awards for their production of *Driving Miss Daisy* (1989). Lili Fini Zanuck directed her first feature in 1991.

FILMS INCLUDE (as producer): Alone—*Compulsion* 1959; *Sanctuary* 1961; *The Chapman Report* 1962. In collaboration with David Brown—*The Sting* 1973; *Willie Dynamite, The Sugarland Express, The Black Windmill* (exec. prod.; UK), *The Girl from Petrovka* 1974; *The Eiger Sanction* (exec. prod.), *Jaws* 1975; *MacArthur the Rebel General* (exec. prod.) 1977; *Jaws 2* 1978; *The Island* 1980; *Neighbors* 1981; *The Verdict* 1982; *Cocoon, Target* 1984; *Cocoon: The Return* 1988; *Driving Miss Daisy* 1989; *Rush* 1991; *Rich in Love* 1993; *Clean Slate* 1994; *Wild Bill* 1995; *Chain Reaction* 1996.

Zanussi, Krzysztof. Director. Born on July 17, 1939, in Warsaw. A graduate of the physics department of the University of Warsaw, he began making amateur films in the late 50s, after completing a film course as part of his elective curriculum. In 1960 he enrolled at the Lodz film school and remained there for six years. His graduation film, the half-hour-long *Death of a Provincial* (1966), won awards at several festivals, including Venice. This and his next short, *Face to Face* (1967), which he made for Polish TV, contained some of the elements of style and content that would characterize his future feature films, namely the ascetic use of camera technique, a concern with ideas rather than passions, and characters that are more intellectually than emotionally motivated. A strong partisan of the Solidarity movement, he was compelled to work abroad after its temporary defeat in the 1980s. One of his films, *The Catamount Killing* (1974), was shot in English in the US. He writes his own scripts.

FEATURE FILMS (as director-screenwriter): *The Structure of Crystals* 1969; *Family Life, Behind the Wall* 1971; *Illumination* 1973; *The Catamount Killing* (shot in English in the US) 1974; *Quarterly Balance/A Woman's Decision* 1975; *Barwy Orchronne/Camouflage* 1977; *Spirale/The Spiral* 1978; *Amator/Camera Buff* (act. only), *Wege in der nacht/Ways in the Night* 1979; *The Constant Factor* (dir. only), *Contract* (dir. only), *From a Far Country* (dir. only) 1980; *Imperativ/Imperative, Die Unerreichbare* 1982; *Blaubart/Bluebeard, Rok Spokonjnego Slonca/The Year of the Quiet Sun* 1984; *Le Pouvoir du Mal/The Power of Evil* 1985; *Le Jeune Magicien* (prod. only) 1987; *Gdzieskolwiek jest, jeslis jest, The Road Home* (art. dir. only) 1988; *And the Violins Stopped Playing* (exec. prod. only), *Stan Posiadania* 1989; *Life for a Life: Maximilian Kolbe* 1990; *Dotkniecie/The Touch* 1992.

Zanville, Bernard. See CLARK, Dane.

Zarkhi, Alexander. Director. Born in 1908, in St. Petersburg, Russia. A graduate of the Leningrad School of Screen Art, he directed many films from 1928 till 1950 in collaboration with fellow-student Josef HEIFITZ. Their most notable collaboration was on *Baltic Deputy* (1937), a forerunner of the "historic realism" style in Soviet films. Working alone since the early 50s, Zarkhi has directed a number of films that have been marked by a straightforward narrative style.

FILMS (directed alone; for films 1928–50 see HEIFITZ, Josef): *Pavlinka* 1952; *Nesterka* 1955; *The Heights* 1957; *Men on the Bridge* 1960; *My Younger Brother* 1962; *Anna Karenina* (also co-sc.) 1967; *Towns and Years* 1973.

Zavattini, Cesare. Screenwriter, film theoretician, novelist. *b.* Sept. 29, 1902, in Luzzara, Italy. *d.* 1989. A former journalist, he began publishing short stories and novels in the early 30s and wrote his first screenplay in 1935. In the 40s he emerged as a key figure of Italian neorealism with his theoretical writings and screenplays for some of the most important productions of the movement, notably the films of Vittorio DE SICA. A highly prolific writer, he collaborated on scores of scripts for major Italian films, and his influence is still felt in the Italian cinema.

FILMS INCLUDE (as screenwriter in collaboration): *Darò un Milione* 1935; *I'll Give a Million* (based on his co-script for latter film; US) 1938; *Quattro Passi fra le Nuvole/Four Steps in the Clouds* 1942; *I Bambini ci guardano/The Children Are Watching Us* 1943; *La Porta del Cielo* 1945; *Un Giorno nella Vita, Sciuscià/Shoe-Shine* 1946; *Ladri di Bicicletta/The Bicycle Thief, Caccia tragica/Tragic Hunt* 1948; *Au-delà des Grilles/La Mura di Malapaga/Walls of Malapaga* (Fr./It.) 1949; *E Primavera/It's Forever Springtime, Domenica d'Agosto/Sunday in August, Prima Communione/Father's Dilemma, Il Cielo è Rosso/The Sky Is Red* 1950; *Miracolo a Milano/Miracle in Milan* 1951; *Bellissima* (story only), *Il Cappotto/The Overcoat, Umberto D, Roma Ore 11/Rome 11 O'Clock* 1952; *Amore in Città/Love in the City, Siamo Donne/We the Women, Un Marito per Anna Zaccheo/A Husband for Anna, Stazione Termini/ Indiscretion of an American Wife* 1953; *L'Oro di Napoli/Gold of Naples* 1954; *Il Segno di Venere/Sign of Venus* 1955; *Il Tetto/The Roof* (story, sc. alone), *Suor Letizia/The Awakening* 1956; *La Donna del Giorno/The Doll That Took the Town, Era di Venerdì 17/The Virtuous Bigamist* 1957; *La Ciociara/Two Women* 1960; *Il Giudizio universale* (story, sc. alone) 1961; *Boccaccio '70, La Isola di Arturo/Arturo's Island, I Sequestrati di Altona/The Condemned of Altona* 1962; *Ieri Oggi e Domani/Yesterday Today and Tomorrow, Il Boom* (alone) 1963; *Un Mondo Nuovo/A Young World* (story, sc. alone), *Caccia alla Volpe/After the Fox* (US/UK/It.) 1966; *Le Streghe/The Witches, Sept fois Femme/ Woman Times Seven* (sc. alone; US/Fr./It.) 1967; *Amanti/A Place for Lovers* 1968; *I Girasoli/Sunflower* 1969; *Il Giardino dei Finzi-Contini/The Garden of the Finzi-Continis* 1971; *Una Breve Vacanza/A Brief Vacation* (sc. alone) 1973; *The Children of Sanchez* (co-sc. only; US/Mex.), *Un Cuore Semplice* (sc. only), *Ligabue* 1978; *La Verità-a-a-a-a-a/The Truth* (orig. made for TV) 1979; *Strand—Under the Dark Cloth* (act. only) 1989.

Zecca, Ferdinand. Director, producer. *b.* 1864, Paris. *d.* 1947. A former café entertainer, he entered the infant French film industry as an actor in 1899 and began directing for Pathé in 1901. He was primarily business-oriented, and unlike his rival of this pioneering period, Georges MÉLIÈS, whose ideas he often plagiarized, he sought to exploit the commercial potential of the new medium rather than innovate themes and techniques. But in his quest for sensational material, he did introduce to the screen the genre of lowlife and crime melodrama through such films as *Histoire d'un Crime* (1901) and *Les Victimes de l'Alcoolisme* (1902). He directed and produced numerous short films until 1910 when he was appointed general manager of the Pathé organization. In 1913 he was dispatched to the US to supervise the activities of the Pathé Exchange in New Jersey. On returning to France, in 1920, he assumed the leadership of Pathé Baby, the skeleton organization that survived the Pathé corporate reorganization. He retired from the business in 1939.

FILMS INCLUDE: *Histoire d'un Crime, La Conquête de l'Air, L'Illusioniste mondain* (also act.), *Quo Vadis?* 1901; *Les Victimes de l'Alcoolisme, Ali Baba et les 40 Voleurs, L'Assassinat de McKinley* 1902; *Puss 'n' Boots, Samson et Delilah, La Passion* 1903; *La Grève* 1904; *Au Pays noir, Rêve à la Lune, Vendetta* 1905; *L'Affaire Dreyfus* 1908; *Messalina* 1910; *La Comtesse noire* (co-dir.) 1912; *Le Roi de l'Air* (co-dir.) 1913.

Zeffirelli, Franco. Director. Born on Feb. 12, 1923, in Florence, Italy. He began his career as an actor, appearing in several of Luchino VISCONTI's stage plays. Later, he was Visconti's assistant on such films as *La Terra trema* (1948), *Bellissima* (1951), and *Senso* (1954). In 1945 he began a successful career as set and costume designer for operas and stage plays. Since the early 50s he has directed numerous operas and plays in Milan, London, New York, and other cities and has gained a reputation for the opulence of his productions, many of which he still designs. He made his debut as a film director in the late 60s. His films, like his stage productions, are distinguished by their opulence. His 1977 TV drama *Jesus of Nazareth* has been aired for years during the Easter season.

FILMS: *La Bohème* (filmed opera; also asst. dir.; Switz.) 1965; *Florence—Days of Destruction* (doc.) 1966; *The Taming of the Shrew* (also co-prod. co-sc.; US/It.) 1967; *Romeo and Juliet* (also exec. prod., co-sc.; UK/It.) 1968; *Fratello Sole Sorella Luna/Brother Sun Sister Moon* (also co-sc.; It./UK) 1973; *Jesus of Nazareth* (orig. made for TV) 1978; *The Champ* (US) 1979; *Endless Love* (US) 1981; *La Traviata* (also sc., prod.) 1983; *Otello* (also sc.) 1986; *Il Giovane Toscanini/Young Toscanini* (also story) 1988; *Hamlet* (also sc.; US) 1990; *Sparrow* 1993; *Jane Eyre* 1996.

Zeman, Karel. Director, animator. *b.* November 1910, in Moravia, Czechoslovakia. *d.* 1989. A former window dresser and poster artist, he made a number of advertising films before entering the Czech film industry in the mid-40s. An original and inventive artist, he created a popular cartoon character, the stoical Mr. Prokouk, and made many short films combining cartoon and puppet figures as well as other forms of animation. From the early 50s to the late 60s, he directed highly imaginative feature-length films that combine animation and live action and are marked by their fantastic trick effects.

FILMS INCLUDE: Shorts—*Christmas Dream* 1946; *Prokouk the Bureaucrat* 1947 (and other Prokouk films through 1958); *Inspiration* 1949; *King Lavra* 1950. Features—*The Treasure of Bird Island* 1952; *Journey to the Beginning of Time* 1955; *An Invention for Destruction/The Fabulous World of Jules Verne* 1957; *Baron Prasil/Baron Munchhausen* 1962; *The Jester's Tale* 1964; *The Stolen Airship* 1966; *Mr. Sverdac's Ark* 1968.

Zemeckis, Robert. Director. Born in 1952 in Chicago, Ill. *ed.* Northern Illinois University; USC (film). Immensely creative force behind a pair of the most inventive films of the 80s. He gained early experience in film working as a film cutter for NBC News in Chicago during a summer break from school and also edited commercials in his home state. While at school in California, he paired with Bob GALE, with whom he would collaborate on the screenplays for a number of films, including Steven Spielberg's *1941*. This early work, though not generating box-office success, led to his first directing job, the comedy/adventure film, *Romancing the Stone*. He topped this commercial success with an even greater one: the witty time-travel comedy *Back to the Future*. His follow-up film, the merry paean to classic cartoons and film *noir*, *Who Framed Roger Rabbit*, employed an unparalleled mix of live-action and animation and helped to stimulate the boom in animation that was to come. Reaching a peak in 1994, Zemeckis helmed one of the top-grossing films of all time, *Forrest Gump*, earning an Academy Award as best director while the film took home the statue for best picture.

FILMS (as director): *I Wanna Hold Your Hand* (also sc.) 1978; *Used Cars* (also sc.) 1980; *Romancing the Stone* (also sc.) 1984; *Back to the Future* (also sc.) 1985; *Who Framed Roger Rabbit* 1988; *Back to the Future II* (also story) 1989; *Back to the Future III* (also story) 1990; *Death Becomes Her, The Public Eye* (exec. prod. only) 1992. As screenwriter: *1941* (story) 1979; *Trespass* 1992; *Forrest Gump* 1994; *The Frighteners* (prod. only), *Tales from the Crypt: Bordello of Blood* (prod. only) 1996; *Contact* 1997.

Zetterling, Mai. Actress, director. *b.* May 24, 1925, Vasteras, Sweden. *d.* 1994. Trained at Stockholm's Royal Dramatic Theater School, she made both her stage and screen debuts at 16 and subsequently pursued successful careers in both dramatic forms. On the screen, she attracted attention in 1944 in Alf Sjöberg's *Hets* (known as *Torment* in the US and *Frenzy* in the UK), a landmark film of Swedish cinema, made from a script by Ingmar Bergman. Her sensitive portrayal of a simple girl victimized by a sadistic professor brought her international fame and in 1946 she was invited to Britain to star in the film *Frieda.* A beautiful blonde, she subsequently appeared in many other British films as well as in several American productions.

In the early 60s she decided to switch to the other side of the camera. Her first effort as a director, the documentary short *The War Game,* which she co-wrote with her second husband, David Hughes, won a first prize at Venice in 1963. She then directed several feature films in Sweden, the themes of which often dealt with the position of women in modern society and which have been noted for their intense dramatic sense, fluid visual style, and explicit sexuality. She has also written a number of novels, one of which, *Night Games,* provided the basis for her second feature film.

FILMS INCLUDE: As actress—In Sweden: *Lasse-Maja* 1941; *Hets/Torment/Frenzy* 1944; *Iris and the Lieutenant, Sunshine Follows Rain* 1946; *Night Is My Future* 1948. In the UK: *Frieda* 1947; *Quartet, A Portrait from Life/The Girl in the Painting* 1948; *The Lost People, The Bad Lord Byron* 1949; *The Tall Headlines/The Frightened Bride* 1952; *Desperate Moment* 1953; *Knock on Wood* (US) 1954; *A Prize of Gold* 1955; *Seven Waves Away/Abandon Ship!, Giftas/Married Life/Of Love and Lust* ("A Doll's House" episode; Sw.) 1957; *The Truth About Women* 1958; *Jet Storm* 1959; *Offbeat* 1961; *Only Two Can Play* 1961; *The Main Attraction* 1963; *The Vine Bridge* (Sw.) 1965; *Hidden Agenda, The Witches* 1990. As director—*The War Game* (short; UK) 1963; *Loving Couples* (also co-sc.; Sw.) 1964; *Night Games* (also co-sc., from own novel; Sw.) 1966; *Doctor Glas* (also co-sc.; Den.) 1968; *The Girls* (also co-sc.) 1969; *Vincent the Dutchman* (doc.; also co-sc.) 1972; *Visions of Eight* (Munich Olympics doc.; "The Strongest" episode) 1973; *We Have Many Faces* (also sc.) 1975; *Of Seals and Man* 1980; *Love* (also sc.) 1981; *Scrubbers* (also sc.) 1982; *Amarosa* (also sc., story, ed.) 1986.

Zhang Yimou. Director. Born in 1950, in Xi'an, China. Internationally successful Chinese Fifth Generation director. Following the Cultural Revolution from 1968 to 1978 he toiled as a farm hand and unskilled laborer. As a hobby, he honed his skills as a photographer. When the Beijing Film Academy was re-opened in 1978, he enrolled and was admitted, despite his relatively advanced age of 27. He began his film career as a cinematographer on *One and the Eight* (1982) and two films directed by another key Fifth Generation figure, Chen Kaige (*Yellow Earth*, 1983, and *The Big Parade*, 1985).

As a director, he began auspiciously with *Red Sorghum* (1988), the story of a young woman (Gong Li) sold into a loveless marriage with a prosperous winemaker. He continued to feature Gong Li in his subsequent features (*Ju Dou, Raise the Red Lantern, The Story of Qiuju*). His great strength is his mastery of filmmaking technique: photography, set design, use of sound and color are always vivid and impeccable. As a narrator, he favors complex, tragic melodramas that plot the shifting center of power and control in human relations. His films have often been deemed unflattering political allegories. As a result, despite drawing considerable critical acclaim overseas, they have been banned or greatly restricted by the Chinese government.

A Renaissance man of the cinema, Zhang not only directs but acts, notably in the action-comedy *The Terra-Cotta Warrior* and the drama *Old Well*. *Ju Dou* was nominated for an Academy Award in the US.

FILMS INCLUDE (as director): *Red Sorghum* 1988; *Operation Cougar* 1989; *Ju Dou* 1990; *Raise the Red Lantern* 1991; *The Story of Qiuju* 1992; *The Great Conqueror's Concubine* (exec. prod. only), *To Live* 1994; *Shanghai Triad* 1995; *Keep Cool* 1997.

Zidi, Claude. Director. Born on July 25, 1934, in Paris. A former camera operator, then director of photography, he began directing in the early 70s and has since turned out a number of entertaining comedy-burlesque films. He won the French Cesar for best director with *My New Partner* (1984). He collaborates on his own screenplays.

FILMS: *Les Bidasses en Folie, Les Fous du Stade* 1972; *Le Grand Bazar* 1973; *La Moutarde me monte au Nez/Lucky Pierre, Les Bissades s'en vont en Guerre* 1974; *La Course a l'Echalotte/The Wild Goose Chase* 1975; *L'Aile ou la Cuisse* 1976; *L'Animal/Stuntwoman* 1977; *La Zizanie* 1978; *Dumb but Disciplined* 1979; *My New Partner* 1984.

Zieff, Howard. Director. Born in 1943 in Chicago, Ill. *ed.* Los Angeles Art Center. Trained in commercials, he turned, with moderate success, to directing low-key comedic fare in the 70s, notably the wry *Hearts of the West*.

FILMS INCLUDE: *Hearts of the West* 1975; *Slither* 1976; *House Calls* 1978; *The Main Event* 1979; *Private Benjamin* 1980; *Unfaithfully Yours* 1983; *The Dream Team* 1989; *My Girl* 1991; *My Girl 2* 1994.

Zimbalist, Efrem, Jr. Actor. Born on Nov. 30, 1923, in New York City. *ed.* Yale. The son of concert violinist Efrem Zimbalist and opera singer Alma Gluck, he showed an early interest in the theater and trained for the stage at New York's Neighborhood Playhouse. After returning from WW II service with a Purple Heart, he appeared in many plays and made his film debut in 1949. But following the sudden death of his first wife, he gave up acting and for several years devoted his time to music research. He returned to acting in the late 50s and emerged a star on TV, in the '77 Sunset Strip' and 'The FBI' series and in a succession of films in which he has typically played dependable, trustworthy leading men. He is the father of TV actress Stephanie Zimbalist.

FILMS INCLUDE: *House of Strangers* 1949; *Band of Angels, Bombers B-52* 1957; *The Deep Six, Too Much Too Soon, Home Before Dark* 1958; *The Crowded Sky* 1960; *A Fever in the Blood, By Love Possessed* 1961; *The Chapman Report* 1962; *Harlow* (Magna version), *The Reward* 1965; *Wait Until Dark* 1967; *Airport 1975* 1974; *Terror Out of the Sky* 1979; *Hot Shots!* 1991.

Zimbalist, Sam. Producer. *b.* Mar. 31, 1904, New York City. *d.* 1958. He entered films at 16 as a cutter at Metro and after editing many silent MGM productions moved up in 1929 to the position of assistant to producer Hunt STROMBERG. A producer from 1936, he gradually progressed from modest-budget pictures to major productions. He died during the preparation of *Ben-Hur,* his most ambitious film.

FILMS INCLUDE: *Tarzan Escapes* 1936; *London by Night* 1937; *The Crowd Roars* 1938; *Boom Town* 1940; *Tortilla Flat* 1942; *Thirty Seconds Over Tokyo* 1944; *Adventure* 1946; *Killer McCoy* 1947; *Side Street, King Solomon's Mines* 1950; *Quo Vadis* 1951; *Mogambo* 1953; *Beau Brummell* 1954; *Tribute to a Bad Man, The Catered Affair* 1956; *The Barretts of Wimpole Street* 1957; *I Accuse!* 1958; *Ben-Hur* 1959.

Zimmer, Hans. Composer. Born 1958. Early on in his career, he was associated with Stanley Myers on a number of film scores. He is one of the first composers to experiment with computer-generated music and his style for matching music with mood has made him one of the most respected composers in Hollywood.

FILMS INCLUDE: *Moonlighting* 1982; *My Beautiful Launderette* 1985; *The Wind* 1987; *Rain Man, A World Apart* 1988; *Black Rain, Driving Miss Daisy* 1989; *Bird on the Wire, Days of Thunder, Green Card, Pacific Heights* 1990; *Backdraft, Regarding Henry, Thelma & Louise* 1991; *A League of Their Own, Memoirs of an Invisible Man, The Power of One, Radio Flyer, Toys* 1992; *Cool Runnings, The House of the Spirits, Point of No Return, True Romance* 1993; *Drop Zone, I'll Do Anything, The Lion King* (mus., song perf., mus. superv.), *Renaissance Man* 1994; *Something To Talk About* 1995; *Two Deaths* 1996; *Smilla's Sense of Snow* 1997.

Zinnemann, Fred. Director. *b.* on Apr. 29, 1907, in Vienna. *d.* 1997. As a child, he studied the violin, hoping to become a musician. Later, inspired by the films of von STROHEIM and King VIDOR, he abandoned plans for a legal career, after receiving a master's degree in law from the University of Vienna, to become an assistant cameraman in Paris and Berlin. Among the films on which he worked was Robert Siodmak's famous documentary *Menschen am Sonntag/People on Sunday* (1929). In 1929 he emigrated to the US and headed directly for Hollywood, where all he could land was an extra part in *All Quiet on the Western Front* (1930). He eventually obtained some work as a cutter and became an assistant to director Berthold Viertel, and in 1931 to Robert Flaherty on an aborted documentary project in Russia. Zinnemann also assisted Busby Berkeley on the dance numbers of *The Kid from Spain* (1932). In 1934–35 he made his debut as co-director on producer-screenwriter Paul Strand's documentary feature *Redes/Pescados/The Wave,* which he shot on location in Mexico. In 1937 he was signed by MGM as a director of shorts, including "Pete Smith Specialties" and the "Crime Does Not Pay" series. He won an Oscar for *That Mothers Might Live* (1938), part of the "Historical Mysteries" series. He was elevated to a feature director in 1941 but was given little opportunity to exercise his craft until 1948, when he was assigned to direct *The Search,* a moving drama of the WW II aftermath, in Europe. He subsequently directed several other productions noted for their realism and meticulous handling but not for their box-office appeal.

In 1952–53 he directed two commercial blockbusters, *High Noon,* an uncommon Western, and *From Here to Eternity,* a sizzling drama of the military, for which he won his second Academy Award. He won his third Academy Award for *A Man for All Seasons* (1966). Zinnemann's work has been criticized as often being plodding, uninspired, humorless, and emotionally distant. He is acknowledged, however, as a sincere and conscientious director who has mastered his craft and has worked hard at maintaining high professional standards. He has indisputably enriched the American screen with several important productions. Autobiography: *A Life in the Movies* (1992).

FILMS: Shorts—*A Friend Indeed, The Story of Dr. Carver, That Mothers Might Live, Tracking the Sleeping Death, They Live Again* 1938; *Weather Wizards, While America Sleeps, Help Wanted, One Against the World, The Ash-Can Fleet, Forgotten Victory* 1939; *The Old South, Stuffie, A Way in the Wilderness, The Great Meddler* 1940; *Forbidden Passage, Your Last Act, The Lady or the Tiger?* 1941; *Benjy* (doc. for Orthopedic Foundation) 1951. Features—*Redes/Pescados/The Wave* (doc.; co-dir. with Gomez Muriel; Mex.) 1935; *Kid Glove Killer, Eyes in the Night* 1942; *The Seventh Cross* 1944; *Little Mister Jim/Army Brat* 1946; *My Brother Talks to Horses* 1947; *Die Gezeichneten/The Search* (Switz./US) 1948; *Act of Violence* 1949; *The Men* 1950; *Teresa* 1951; *High Noon* 1952; *The Member of the Wedding, From Here to Eternity* 1953; *Oklahoma!* 1955; *A Hatful of Rain* 1957; *The Old Man and the Sea* (production taken over by John Sturges, who received director's credit) 1958; *The Nun's Story* 1959; *The Sundowners* 1960; *Behold a Pale Horse* (also prod.) 1964; *A Man for All Seasons* (also prod.; UK) 1966; *The Day of the Jackal* (UK/Fr.) 1973; *Julia* 1977; *Five Days One Summer* (also prod.) 1982; *George Stevens: A Filmmaker's Journey* (documentary interviewee) 1985.

zip pan. See SWISH PAN.

Zoetrope. Device, also called a Daedaleum, invented by William George HORNER in Britain in 1834 to create the illusion of movement. Sequential drawings were wrapped around the inside of a rotating drum; when the viewer peered through slits in the drum, the drawings appeared to move. A precursor to motion picture technology, the device provided a name for Francis Ford COPPOLA's independent production company, American Zoetrope, in 1969, later renamed Zoetrope Studios.

Zoetrope Studios. See COPPOLA, Francis Ford.

zone focusing. Focusing on a general area of a scene rather than on a specific object. It is usually done by merely selecting a lens setting whose depth of field is sufficient to cover the general area in which the action evolves.

zoom. The real or apparent effect of camera movement toward or away from a subject during a single continuous shot. In animation, the effect is achieved by moving the camera in relation to the animation stand. In live-action cinematography, however, it is usually achieved by means of the ZOOM LENS, with the camera remaining stationary. The camera operator is said to be *zooming in* when he brings the subject closer to view and to be *zooming out* or *zooming back* when he withdraws farther from the image. In its broadest sense, the term "zoom shot" is used interchangeably with a TRACKING SHOT or DOLLY SHOT.

zoom lens. A variable-focus lens that is designed to provide various degrees of magnification during a continuous shot with no loss of focus. Using this type of lens, a cameraman can move rapidly from a long shot to a close-up of the same subject without moving the camera and without having to adjust focus or aperture. Conversely, he may start with a close-up of the subject, then zoom out to reveal the background location for the action. Zoom lenses may be operated manually or by an electric motor. The first method offers the operator greater control over the duration of the zoom shot; the latter ensures him a smoother movement at a constant rate of speed. The zoom lens can, of course, be used as a normal lens for non-zoom shots when it is set at any focal length along its range of magnification and not pulled back and forth.

Zorina, Vera. Dancer, actress. Born Eva Brigitta Hartwig, on Jan. 2, 1917, in Berlin, to Norwegian parents. Dancing professionally from the age of seven, she first attracted attention at the age of 12 as the first elf in the 1929 Berlin stage production of Max Reinhardt's 'A Midsummer Night's Dream.' In 1933 she joined the famed Ballet Russe, with which she appeared at New York's Metropolitan Opera and London's Covent Garden. In 1937 she was seen performing in the London version of the musical 'On Your Toes' by producer Sam Goldwyn, who signed her to appear in his forthcoming film *The Goldwyn Follies* (1938). In that same year she made her Broadway debut in 'I Married an Angel' and married choreographer George Balanchine. After their 1946 divorce, she married Goddard Lieberson, president of Columbia Records. Zorina's brief film career, which was highlighted by some fine dance sequences but was unmemorable for acting, fizzled in the late 40s and she subsequently limited her professional appearances to occasional dramatic stage roles and the concert hall narration of musical works by modern composers like Stravinsky, Hindemith, Honegger, and William Walton. She has also directed several opera seasons in Santa Fe, New Mexico, and was named managing director of the Norwegian Opera in 1976. In 1978, as Brigitta Lieberson, she was appointed music consultant and album producer at CBS (Columbia) Records.

FILMS: *The Goldwyn Follies* 1938; *On Your Toes* 1939; *I Was an Adventuress* 1940; *Louisiana Purchase* 1941; *Star Spangled Rhythm* 1942; *Follow the Boys* 1944; *Lover Come Back* 1946.

Zsigmond, Vilmos (William). Director of photography. Born on June 16, 1930, in Hungary. A graduate of the Budapest Film School, he fled to the US during the 1956 uprising with a fellow student, Laszlo KOVACS. In Hollywood, he worked as still photographer, lab technician, cameraman on educational shorts, and camera assistant, before making his debut as cinematographer in 1963. He worked on many bottom-budget productions but gained prominence in the early 70s when he worked on such films as Robert ALTMAN's *McCabe and Mrs. Miller* (1971) and John BOORMAN's *Deliverance* (1972). He shared an Academy Award with several others for the cinematography of *Close Encounters of the Third Kind* (1977). In 1992, he made a directorial debut with *The Long Shadow*.

FILMS INCLUDE: *The Sadist* 1963; *The Time Travelers* 1964; *Rat Fink* 1965; *Mondo Mod* (doc., co-phot.) 1967; *The Name of the Game Is Kill!* 1968; *The Monitors, Five Bloody Graves* 1969; *Horror of the Blood Monster* (co-phot.) 1970; *Red Sky at Morning, McCabe and Mrs. Miller, The Hired Hand* 1971; *Images, Deliverance* 1972; *The Long Goodbye, Scarecrow, Cinderella Liberty* 1973; *The Sugarland Express, The Girl from Petrovka* 1974; *Sweet Revenge, Obsession* 1976; *Close Encounters of the Third Kind* (co-phot.) 1977; *The Last Waltz* (co-phot.), *The Rose, The Deer Hunter* 1978; *Winter Kills* 1979; *Heaven's Gate* 1980; *Blow-Out, The Border* (addnl. phot.) 1981; *Jinxed!* 1982; *Table for Five* 1983; *No Small Affair, The River* 1984; *Real Genius* 1985; *The Witches of Eastwick* 1987; *Journey to Spirit Island* 1988; *Fat Man and Little Boy* 1989; *The Bonfire of the Vanities, The Two Jakes* 1990; *The Long Shadow* (dir.) 1992; *Intersection, Maverick* (also act.) 1994; *Assassins, The Crossing Guard* 1995; *The Ghost and the Darkness* 1996.

Zucco, George. Actor. *b.* Jan. 11, 1886, Manchester, England. *d.* 1960. Made his acting debut in Canada, in 1908, and subsequently appeared in American vaudeville, in stock, and on the London and Broadway stage. In films from the early 30s, he appeared in numerous productions, typically portraying master criminals (Professor Moriarty, etc.), mad scientists, and an assortment of other arch villains.

FILMS INCLUDE: In the UK—*The Dreyfus Case* 1931; *The Good Companions* 1933; *Autumn Crocus* 1934; *The Man Who Could Work Miracles* 1936. In the US—*After the Thin Man* 1936; *Parnell, Saratoga, Souls at Sea, London by Night, The Firefly, Conquest, Rosalie* 1937; *Arsene Lupin Returns, Suez, Marie Antoinette* 1938; *Captain Fury, The Adventures of Sherlock Holmes* (as Moriarty), *The Cat and the Canary, The Hunchback of Notre Dame* 1939; *New Moon, The Mummy's Hand, Arise My Love* 1940; *The Monster and the Girl, A Woman's Face, Ellery Queen and the Murder Ring* 1941; *My Favorite Blonde, The Mummy's Tomb, The Black Swan* 1942; *The Black Raven, Dead Men Walk, The Mad Ghoul* 1943; *The Mummy's Ghost, The Seventh Cross, The Voodoo Man* 1944; *House of Frankenstein, Having a Wonderful Crime, Sudan, Confidential Agent, Fog Island* 1945; *Moss Rose, Lured, Captain from Castile* 1947; *The Pirate, Joan of Arc* 1948; *Madame Bovary* 1949; *The First Legion, David and Bathsheba* 1951.

Zucker, David. Director, producer, screenwriter, actor. Born on October 16, 1947, in Milwaukee, Wis. *ed.* Univ. of Wis. Producer of hugely successful comedies of 80s and 90s. See Jerry ZUCKER.

FILMS INCLUDE: *The Kentucky Fried Movie* (act., co-sc. only) 1977; *Airplane!* (act., co-dir., co-sc.) 1980; *Top Secret!* (co-dir., co-exec. prod., co-sc.) 1984; *Ruthless People* (co-dir. only) 1986; *The Naked Gun: From the Files of Police Squad!* (dir., co-exec. prod., co-sc.) 1988; *The Naked Gun 2½: The Smell of Fear* (act., dir., co-exec. prod., co-sc.) 1991; *Brain Donors* (co-exec. prod.) 1992; *Naked Gun 33⅓: The Final Insult* 1994; *First Knight, A Walk in the Clouds* 1995; *High School High* 1996.

Zucker, Jerry. Director, producer, screenwriter. Born on March 11, 1950, in Milwaukee, Wis. *ed.* Univ. of Wis. With the founding of the Kentucky Fried Theatre in Madison, Wis., in 1970, he formed a partnership with brother David ZUCKER and Jim ABRAHAMS that was to result in some of the daffiest, most commercially successful comedies of the 1980s. Their spoofs of disaster and cop genres (*Airplane!*, *The Naked Gun*) provided a successor to Mel Brooks's fast-paced parodies of the 70s and regenerated industry and audience interest in the genre. His later direction of the successful romantic drama *Ghost* signaled a move to more serious fare. Co-executive producer of TV series 'Police Squad.'

FILMS INCLUDE: *The Kentucky Fried Movie* (act., co-sc. only) 1977; *Rock 'n' Roll High School* (second unit dir. only) 1979; *Airplane!* (act., co-dir., exec. prod., co-sc.) 1980; *Top Secret!* (co-exec. prod., co-dir., co-sc., lyrics) 1984; *Ruthless People* (co-dir. only) 1986; *The Naked Gun: From the Files of Police Squad!* (co-exec. prod., co-sc.) 1988; *Ghost* (dir. only) 1990; *The Naked Gun 2½: The Smell of Fear* (co-exec. prod.) 1991; *Brain Donors* (co-exec. prod.) 1992; *My Life* 1993; *Naked Gun 33⅓: The Final Insult* 1994; *First Knight, A Walk in the Clouds* 1995; *High School High* 1996; *My Best Friend's Wedding* (prod. only) 1997.

Zuckmayer, Carl. Playwright, poet, screenwriter. *b.* Dec. 27, 1896, Nackenheim, Germany. *d.* 1977. The son of a cork manufacturer, he volunteered for WW I service with the German army directly out of high school and received several decorations for valor in battle. He then studied at the universities of Frankfurt and Heidelberg and, after achieving some success as a lyrical poet, turned to playwriting. In the 20s he gained a reputation as Gerhart Hauptmann's successor in German drama. He received international acclaim in 1930 for his masterpiece, *Der Hauptmann von Köpenick/The Captain of Koepenick,* which he also co-adapted to the screen in 1931 and again in 1956. He also collaborated on the script of Josef von STERNBERG's famous *Der blaue Engel/The Blue Angel* (1930), the film that launched the international career of Marlene DIETRICH.

After the Nazi takeover of 1933, the liberal Zuckmayer,

whose mother was a convert from Judaism, found himself in disfavor with the regime and his plays were banned by Hitler. He wrote screenplays for a couple of British films, including Korda's *Rembrandt* (1936), and lived in Austria until the 1938 Anschluss, when he emigrated to the US via France. He lived in Vermont, taught playwriting at New York's New School for Social Research, and worked in Hollywood. It was here that he wrote his second-best-known play, 'Des Teufels General/The Devil's General' (1946), which provided the basis for a successful German film in 1955. In 1946 he returned to Europe and became a resident and citizen of Switzerland. Autobiographies: *Second Wind* (1940), originally published in English, and *Als wär's ein Stück von mir* (1966), published in English in 1970 as *A Part of Myself.*

FILMS INCLUDE: *Qualen der Nacht* (co-sc. from own play; Ger.) 1926; *Schinderhannes* (play basis only; Ger.) 1928; *Der blaue Engel/The Blue Angel* (co-sc.; Ger.) 1930; *Der Hauptmann von Köpenick/The Captain of Koepenick* (co-sc. from own play; Ger.) 1931; *Escape Me Never* (sc.; UK) 1935; *Rembrandt* (sc.; UK) 1936; *De Mayerling à Sarajevo/Mayerling to Sarajevo* (story, co-sc.; Fr.) 1940; *I Was a Criminal* (American version of *Der Hauptmann von Köpenick;* co-sc. from own play; US) 1941; *Des Teufels General/The Devil's General* (play basis only; Ger.) 1955; *Der Hauptmann von Köpenick/The Captain of Koepenick* (co-sc. from own play; Ger.) 1956; *The Blue Angel* (based on his 1930 co-script for *Der blaue Engel;* US) 1959.

Zugsmith, Albert. Producer, director, screenwriter. Born on Apr. 24, 1910, in Atlantic City, N.J. *ed.* U. of Virginia. The publisher-editor of the Atlantic City *Daily News* and a prominent broadcasting executive, he entered the film business in the early 50s and for a while produced some interesting dramas for Universal. But he soon moved into the more lucrative field of cheap exploitation films and has produced, and sometimes directed or written, many shrill melodramas with sensational sex overtones.

FILMS INCLUDE: As producer—*Invasion USA* 1952; *Top Banana* 1954; *Female on the Beach* 1955; *Raw Edge* 1956; *Written on the Wind, The Incredible Shrinking Man, The Tattered Dress, Slaughter on Tenth Avenue* 1957; *Man in the Shadow, Touch of Evil, The Tarnished Angels, The Female Animal* (also story), *High School Confidential* 1958; *Night of the Quarter Moon, The Beat Generation* (also story) 1959; *Fanny Hill: Memoirs of a Woman of Pleasure* (US/Ger.) 1965. As director-producer—*College Confidential, Sex Kittens Go to College* (also story), *The Private Lives of Adam and Eve* (co-dir. with Mickey Rooney) 1960; *Dondi* (also sc.) 1961; *Confessions of an Opium Eater* 1962; *The Incredible Sex Revolution* (sex instruction feature; also sc.) 1965; *Movie Star American Style or LSD—I Hate You* (dir., story, co-sc. only), *On Her Bed of Roses* (dir., sc. only) 1966; *Sappho Darling* (sc. only; Sw.) 1968; *The Very Friendly Neighbors* (dir., sc. only), *Two Roses and a Golden-Rod* (dir., sc. only) 1969.

Zukor, Adolph. Executive. *b.* Jan. 7, 1873, Risce, Hungary. *d.* 1976. Immigrating to the US at the age of 15, he worked his way up from a sweeper's job at a New York fur store to ownership of a prosperous fur business in Chicago. In 1903 he ventured into the novel penny-arcade business, in which he was joined two years later by Marcus LOEW and eventually became the treasurer of the vast Loew's chain of motion picture theaters. In 1912 he made a small fortune as the American distributor of the four-reel European production *Queen Elizabeth* and invested the proceeds in the formation of his own production company, FAMOUS PLAYERS. Under the slogan "Famous Players in Famous Plays," he sought to duplicate the success of the French FILM D'ART company by bringing to the screen popular plays from the stage repertoire starring famous Broadway personalities. The resulting feature-length films were mostly static and stagy, but they introduced wide audiences to literary and dramatic works to which they had had no access. The gamble paid off handsomely in box-office receipts.

In addition, the diminutive, dynamic Zukor scored a financial coup by signing up Mary PICKFORD, "America's Sweetheart," who became a virtual gold mine for his company in its formative years. In 1916, Famous Players merged with the Jesse L. LASKY Feature Play Company to form the Famous Players—Lasky Corporation, of which Zukor became president. The company absorbed a small firm, Paramount, as a distributing arm and eventually changed its corporate name to PARAMOUNT. Paramount acquired a chain of motion picture theaters and grew into one of Hollywood's major studios. As its president, Zukor was one of the most influential men in the industry. During the company's financial crisis in the early 30s he survived attempts to remove him from his position, but in 1936 he was replaced as president by Barney Balaban, moving up to the figurehead position of chairman of the board. In 1949, Zukor was honored with a special Academy Award for his "contribution to the industry." In 1953 he published an autobiography, *The Public Is Never Wrong.* At the time of his death in 1976, at the impressive age of 103, his name still appeared on the Paramount roster as chairman of the board emeritus.

Zurlini, Valerio. Director, screenwriter. *b.* Mar. 19, 1926, Bologna, Italy. *d.* 1982. While studying toward his law degree, he became involved in university dramatics. He began directing documentary shorts in 1948 and moved into the feature film field in 1955. He later acquired a reputation as one of the most literate and inspired Italian directors of his time, a filmmaker of sensitivity and sensibility with a concern for human values and an eye for visual beauty.

FEATURE FILMS: *Le Ragazze di San Frediano* 1954; *Estate Violenta/Violent Summer* (also co-sc.) 1959; *La Ragazza con la Valigia/Girl with a Suitcase* (also story, co-sc.) 1961; *Cronaca Familiare/Family Diary* (also co-sc.) 1962; *Le Soldatesse/The Camp Followers* 1965; *Seduto alla sua Destra/Black Jesus* (also co-sc.) 1968; *La Prima Notte di Queiete* (also story, co-sc.) 1972; *Il Deserto dei Tartari/Le Désert des Tartares* (It./Fr./Iran) 1976.

Zwick, Edward. Director, producer, screenwriter. Born on October 8, 1952, in Winnetka, Ill. *ed.* Harvard; AFI, Los Angeles. A widely published journalist, he became involved in TV as a writer, producer, and director on the drama 'Family' and later as the creator and executive producer of 'thirtysomething.' Directing films since the mid-80s, his *Glory*, about a black regiment in the Civil War, was nominated for several Academy Awards.

FILMS: *About Last Night. . .* 1986; *Glory* 1989; *Leaving Normal* 1992; *Legends of the Fall* (also co-prod.) 1994; *Courage Under Fire 1996.*